준 시간대

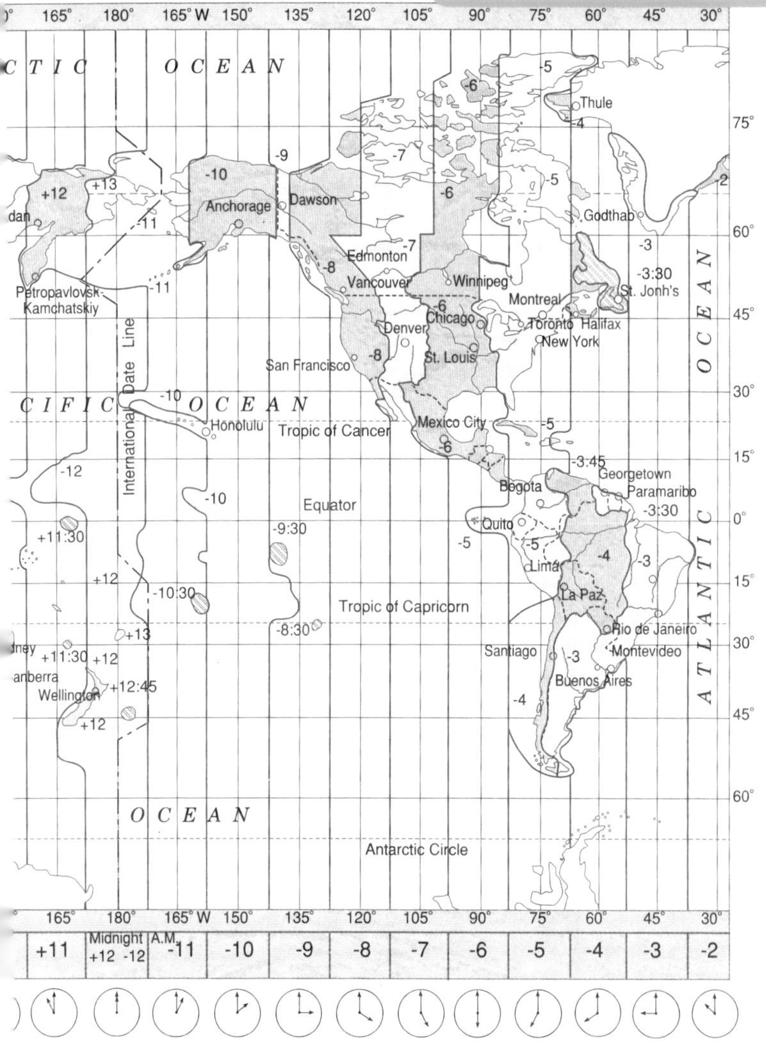

1	스페인	07	34	이란	00	98	터키	99	90
3	싱가포르	005	65	이스라엘	00	972	프랑스	19	33
2	아일랜드	16	353	이탈리아	00	39	하와이	011	1
5	알제리	00	213	일본	001	81	한국	001	82
6	영국	010	44	캐나다	011	1	홍콩	001	852
6	오스트레일리아	0011	61	쿠웨이트	00	965			
1	이라크	00	964	타이완	001	886			

DONG -A' S

PRIME

KOREAN-ENGLISH DICTIONARY

프라임 韓英辭典

제2판

교열 · 감수
서강대학교 영어 영문학과 교수
김용권(문학박사), William Burns

두산동아

머 리 말

오늘날 우리는 첨단 미디어의 시대, 상반된 이미지·상징 및 사실들의 홍수 속에서 살아가고 있습니다. 21세기에 다가올 고도 변화의 경쟁에 대응할 능력이 없는 국가나 사회는 자연 도태되거나 뒷전으로 밀려날 것이며, 이러한 점에서 본다면 국제간의 경제·산업·정치적 이해 관계를 축(軸)으로 자국의 이익을 위해 전개되는 국제 경쟁 속에서 커뮤니케이션의 활동과 역할의 중요성은 어느때보다도 강조되고 있습니다.

따라서 이번 제2판은 과거의 한영사전이 단순한 어휘의 대역(對譯) 및 문장어(文章語)에 치중하여 온 것에 반해 국제적 커뮤니케이션의 실무적 도구(道具)로 활용할 수 있도록 산업·경제·외교·정치·문화·과학·군사·환경문제 등 각 분야에 걸쳐 필요한 정보와 자료의 제공을 최대의 목표로 삼아 새롭게 꾸몄습니다.

이러한 편집 방침에 따라 지금까지 학교에서 배운 영어라 할지라도 오늘날 상황에 맞지 않을 때는 과감히 수정하였고, '90년대의 최신 자료 및 외국 유명 잡지·신문 등을 분석하여 신어(新語) 및 신어의(新語義)를 선정, 각각의 어휘에 대한 역어(譯語) 및 역문(譯文)을 대입함에 있어서도 가능한한 우리 말의 뜻을 정확히 정의하면서도 현대 영어에 가장 잘 대응할 수 있도록 각 항(項)마다 방대한 양의 자료를 분류, 카드화하여 살아 있는 표현을 싣기에 최선을 다하였습니다. 더욱이 표제어에 대한 우리말 말갈래의 분류에 있어서도 국어사전적 정의(定義)에 의존하기보다는 영어 표현을 위주로 하여 그 표현과 용례의 실용성을 최대로 하였습니다. 또한 ㄱ에서 ㅎ항까지 서강대 김용권 교수와 한국어에 정통한 William Burns 교수의 교열로 우리말과 영어의 어휘 하나하나마다 그 상위점(相違點)에 대해 면밀히 체크하여 최종 검증을 하였습니다.

이러한 일련의 사전 편집 과정에서 특히 열거할 만한 제2판의 몇 가지 특징을 든다면

(1) 현대 생활에서의 일상적인 어휘뿐만 아니라 관용적으로 쓰이는 외래어, 경제·문화·과학·의학·예술·사회·국제 정치·군사·환경 등 각 분야에 자주 등장하는 시사어, 전문어 등 신어 약 3,000여 어를 비롯, 현재는 잘 쓰이지 않는 옛 어구도 우리말의 실용화에 뜻을 두어 가급적 폭 넓게 수용, 총 10만여 어로 중사전에 버금가는 어휘를 수록하였다.

(2) 비교적 사용 빈도가 높은 일상어 중 8,000여 어를 선별, 사용 빈도에 따라 별표로 3단계 구분하였고, 이에 대해 현장에서 통용되는 표현의 실용적 용례를 최대한 수록, 어떠한 상황에서도 유용하게 활용할 수 있도록 하였다. 또한 영·미에서 일상적으로 쓰이는 구어(口語)·속어(俗語)·비어

(卑語)도 최대한 수록하였다.

(3) 보다 깊은 지식과 이해를 필요로 하는 문법·작문 관계 및 회화·문화정보 등 각 분야별 60여 항목을 선정, 별면으로 box 처리함으로써 한 눈에 알아보기 쉽게 하였고, 우리말 중 유사 표현에 대한 한·영 비교의 **참고**란을 두어 상황에 알맞는 영어 표현을 사용할 수 있도록 하였다. 또한 우리말의 관용표현이나 속담을 고딕체로 별행 처리하여 영문 작성에 활용할 수 있게 하였다.

(4) 인체·축구 등 부분 명칭이 필요한 33여 항목은 별도의 컷이나 도판(圖版)으로 처리, 도해(圖解) 사전식 자료를 제공함으로써 백과 사전적 편집을 시도하였다.

(5) 또한 부록으로 해외 여행을 위한 시추에이션 생활영어·회의·국제 비즈니스에 관련된 사항 등, reference book로서도 활용할 수 있도록 배려하였다.

'1981년 증보 신판 후 실로 14년만에 프라임한영사전의 제2판을 발간하면서, 이미 3판의 개정판을 거듭하고 있는 자매 상품인 프라임영한사전에 보내온 독자 제현의 한결같은 성원에 보답하고자, 기획 단계에서부터 여러번에 걸친 편집 회의와 1년여 동안의 자료 수집·분석, 그리고 3년여에 걸친 원고집필에서의 보완, 수정을 거듭하여 선진 외국의 사전에 조금도 뒤지지 않는 사전을 만들고자 최선을 다했습니다. 저희 동아출판사는 본 제2판이 개정을 거듭할수록 더 알찬 내용과 구성으로 학생을 위한 학습용의 사전에 그치지 않고 각 계층의 일반 독자의 반려자로서 다가올 21세기의 국제화, 정보화 시대를 선도하는 사전이 될 수 있도록 배전의 노력을 기울일 것을 다짐합니다.

끝으로 바쁘신 중에도 어휘 하나하나를 체크하며 교열과 감수를 맡아주신 서강대 김용권, Burns 교수님 두 분께 진심으로 감사드리는 바입니다.

1995년 8월

동아출판사
사전편찬실

일 러 두 기

Ⅰ 표제어(表題語)

(1) 표제어의 배열은 가나다 순(順)을 원칙으로 하여, 우리말→한자어→외래어→접두사→접미사의 순으로 순서를 정했으며, 된소리는 예사소리가 끝난 다음에 몰아서 넣었다.

(2) 우리말 중 글자와 음은 같으나 어원의 뜻이 다른 말은 그 말 오른편 어깨에 각각 1, 2, 3 등의 번호를 매겨 구별하였다.

길[1], **길**[2], **놓다**[1], **놓다**[2]

(3) 한자어(漢字語) 표제어에는 그 한자를 달아 주었으며, 한자가 두 가지 이상으로 표기할 수 있는 경우에는 그 한자들을 가능한 한 모두 표기했다.

박람회 博覽會 **반지 班指, 半指**

(4) 모든 한글 표기는 1988년 1월 19일에 교육부에서 고시한 '한글 맞춤법'에 따랐으며, 외래어 표기는 1986년 1월 7일에 교육부에서 고시한 '외래어 표기법'에 따랐다.

(5) 센말·거센말은 원칙적으로 따로 표제어로 삼지 않고 예사말과 병기해 놓았다.

보로통하다, 뽀로통하다 **졸깃졸깃, 쫄깃쫄깃**

(6) 접두어·접미어로 구성된 표제어에는 그 앞뒤에 하이픈(-)을 달았다.

늦- late ; belated ¶ 늦곡식 late crop

-공 工 [직공] a worker ; a mechanic ; a workman

(7) 표제어 중에서 명사에 접미어 「—하다」가 붙어 동사·형용사가 되는 말은 별도 표제어로 하지 않고 「**—하다**」로 표시하였다.

전형 銓衡 screening ; selection ; choice **—하다** select ; make choice of ; screen...

정결 貞潔 chastity ; faithfulness **—하다** (be) chaste and pure ; faithful ¶ 정결한 부인 a chaste〔faithful〕 wife

(8) 표제어 중에서 부사에 접미어 「—하다」가 붙어 동사·형용사가 되는 말은 원칙적으로 별도 표제어로 삼지 않고 「**—하다**」로 표시하였다.

반들반들, 빤들빤들 ① [윤나게] smoothly ; glossily ; lustrously ; shiningly **—하다** (be) smooth ; glossy ; lustrous ; shiny...

잘록잘록, 짤록짤록 pinched〔sloped〕 in (in many places) **—하다** (be) pinched〔sloped〕 in (in many places)

Ⅱ 용례(用例)

(1) 용례는 역어 다음의 (¶) 기호 다음에 수록하였고 국문 표기에는 마침표(.) 물음표(?) 따위를 일체 찍지 않았다.

(2) 용례의 예문을 두 가지 이상으로 표현할 때는 (/) 표시로 구분하고, 별도의 예문은 (//)로 구분하였다.

(3) 용례의 배열은 불가분의 관계에 있는 경우를 제외하고는 명사구 → 형용사구·절 → 부사구·절 → 문장의 순서로 배열함을 원칙으로 하였다.

(4) 용례의 단어 중 다른 말과 대체하여 쓸 수 있거나 중복 해설을 피하고자 할 때는 〔 〕를

사용하여 표시하였다.

Ⅲ 복합어(複合語)

복합어는 표제어 갈래에 구애됨이 없이 해당 표제어의 본문이 끝난 다음에 한데 실었으며, 「표제어+명사」 → 「명사+표제어」 → 「명사+표제어+명사」의 유형으로 가나다 순으로 배열하였다.

국교 國敎 a state religion〔church〕 ¶ 국교로 정하다 establish《a church》
— 신봉자 an establishmentarian **영국 —회** the Church of England ; the Anglican Church ; the (Church) Establishment **비—도** a nonconformist ; a dissenter

Ⅳ 어의(語義)

(1) 표제어가 몇 가지 다른 뜻을 지니고 있을 경우에는 ①, ②, ③ 등의 번호로 그 뜻을 분류하였다.

쏘이다 ① [벌레에] be stung ¶ 벌에 쏘이다 get stung by a bee ... ② [볕에] expose to sun ⇨ 쐬다

(2) 표제어의 뜻이 ①, ②, ③ 등으로 분류되는 경우에 **—하다**는 ①, ②, ③마다 각각 따로 넣어 주었고, 역어의 분량이 적은 경우에는 ①, ②, ③...의 뜻을 종합하여 맨 뒤에만 **—하다**를 넣었다. 그리고, 한 표제어의 분류 내용이 길 경우에는 번호별로 별행 처리하였다.

연발 連發 ① [사격] firing in succession ; running fire ; a volley **—하다** fire in rapid succession ; fire in volleys

② [발생] occurrence in succession ; successive occurrence **—하다** occur〔happen〕 one after another ; take place in succession....

자기 自記 ① [자기가 씀] writing by oneself ② [자동 작용] self-register **—하다** write by oneself ; register (automatically)...

(3) 표제어의 뜻을 명확하게 하기 위해서 보충 설명이나 동의어 등을 역어 앞 [ ] 안에 두었다.

서이 [세 사람] three persons ; [셋] three ¶ 아이가 서이 있는 아버지 a father of three children

(4) 표제어 및 용례의 뜻을 보충하고, 역어를 올바르게 사용하는 데 필요한 사항이나 어법에서 주의할 사항 및 역어의 뉘앙스 차이는 역어 뒤의 ( )에 기입하였다.

도약 跳躍 a jump ; a spring ; a leap ; a skip ; jumping (경기) ; a curvet (말의)...

Ⅴ 역어(譯語)

(1) 역어는 현대의 영·미인들이 사용하는 표준영어를 원칙으로 가장 일반적인 표현에서부터 어려운 표현 및 특수한 표현에 이르도록 배열하였으며, 영국과 미국에서 달리 쓰이는 표현은 《영》·《미》 표시를 하였다. 또한 필요에 따라 구어, 속어, 비어 등을 《 》 안에 표시하여 쓰임새를 구분하였다.

찬부 贊否 approval or disapproval ; yes or no ; ayes or noes ; for and against ; pros and cons...

볼멘소리 sullen〔sulky〕 words ; grouchy words 《미·구》 ...

전철 轉轍 **— 하다** switch ; shunt
— 기 points 《영》 ; a switch 《미》...

(2) 표제어 또는 용례의 역어가 둘 이상 있을 때에는 (;)으로 구분하였고 역어가 둘 이상의 문장일 경우에는 (/)를 써서 구분하였다.

만심 慢心 pride ; self-conceit ; a vanity-swelled head **— 하다** be proud ; be self-conceited ; be puffed up 《with》 ; have a swelled head ¶ 그는 성공하여 만심하고 있다 He is puffed up〔swollen〕 with his success. /Success has gone to his head.

(3) 표제어 가운데 동의어나 어형이 변한 말 따위는 역어를 삭제하거나 역어를 하나 또는 둘만 실어 주고 (⇨)를 사용하여 해당 표제어를 참조토록 하였다.

어두움 darkness ⇨ 어둠

(4) 전문어에는 그 표시를 하였다. 단, 전문어 중에서 기본 어휘에 속하는 말에는 그 표시를 하지 않았다.

곽란 霍亂 〖의학〗 cholera morbus〔nostras〕 ; an intestinal convulsion
구축함 驅逐艦 a (torpedo) destroyer ¶ 구축함대 a destroyer-flotilla

(5) 역어가 영어의 입장에서 외래어인 경우에는 외래어임을 표시하였다.

안마 按摩 massage ; shampoo (ing) ; [운동 중 또는 운동 후의] rubdown...
— 사 a massagist ; a masseur (남) 《프》 ; a masseuse (여) 《프》...
임시 臨時 ¶ 임시의 temporary ; special ; extra ; extraordinary ; pro tempore〔pro tem〕 《라》...

(6) 역어의 생략형이나 원형 및 그 밖의 기호 등은 《 》에 기입하였다.

공군 空軍 the air force ; a flying corps...
...**한국** — the Republic of Korea Air Force 《R. O. K. A. F.》
상환 相換 interchange ; exchange 《for》 **— 하다** interchange ; exchange
...**대금** — collect (on delivery) 《미》 ; cash on delivery 《C. O. D.》

(7) 형용사 표제어인 경우에는 한정·서술 양쪽으로 쓰이면 역어 앞에 (be)를 달아주고, 역어가 둘 이상이면 맨 앞의 형용사에만 (be)를 달아 주었다. 그러나, 서술적으로만 쓰이는 형용사에는 be를 낱낱이 달아 주었다.

아름답다 (be) beautiful ; pretty ; lovely ; fine...
안태우다 be worried〔annoyed〕 ; be anxious 《about》...

(8) 가산 명사에는 복수형을 제외하고는 관사 a를 달았다. 가산·불가산 어느 쪽으로도 사용되는 명사에는 (a)를 달았으며, 정관사를 늘 동반하는 말에는 the를 붙였다.

국어 國語 [언어] a language ; [자국어] one's mother tongue ; the national〔native〕 language ; [한국어] the Korean language ; Korean...
소리 ① [음향] (a) sound ; (a) noise... ② [음성] a voice ; a call... ③ [노래] a folk song ; a ballad...

(9) 복수형이 불규칙적인 변화를 하거나 규칙적인 변화에 속하더라도 틀리기 쉬운 역어 따위는 《*pl.*》 안에 변화형을 표시하였고, 단수형은 《*sg.*》 안에 표시하였다.

동면 冬眠 winter sleep ; hibernation...
— 장소 winter quarters ; a hibernaculum 《*pl.* -la》...
반경 半徑 〖수학〗 a radius 《*pl.* ～es, -dii》 ; a semidiameter...

자료 資料 material ; data ⟪*sg.* datum⟫...

(10) 역어가 취하는 전치사·목적어는 ⟪ ⟫ 안에 기입하였다. 단, 역어가 숙어인 경우에는 전치사에 ⟪ ⟫를 두르지 않았다.

노대가 老大家 an old master ; a veteran authority ⟪on⟫...

대주다 supply〔provide, furnish, find〕 ⟪a person with a thing⟫...

뭉뚱그리다 bundle up crudely ; wrap up in a slipshod way...

(11) 역어 가운데 사람을 표시하는 명사·대명사의 일반적인 형으로 one과 a person을 사용했다. 목적어가 주어와 일치할 때는 one을, 다른 사람을 표시할 때는 a person을 사용하였다. 또한, 사물 따위를 표시하는 일반적인 형으로는 각각 a thing, a matter, a place를 사용했다.

어느덧 before one knows〔is aware〕 ; while one is not aware of it...

엎발치 at〔close to〕 the feet of ⟪a person⟫ lying down

맡기다 ① [물건을] give ⟪a thing⟫ into ⟪a person's⟫ keeping〔custody〕...

떠맡기다 leave ⟪a matter⟫ to others ; saddle ⟪a thing⟫ upon ⟪a person⟫...

(12) 사람을 표시하는 명사·대명사의 소유격을 나타내는 일반적인 형으로, 주어와 일치하는 사람의 경우에는 one's를, 주어와 일치하지 않는 경우에는 a person's를 사용했다.

봉사 奉祀 ―하다 offer sacrifice to one's ancestors...

입맞추다 kiss ; give ⟪a person⟫ a kiss ; press one's lips against ; osculate ; smack ¶ 사람의 손에 입맞추다 kiss ⟪a person's⟫ hand...

(13) 재귀 대명사의 일반적인 형으로는 oneself를 사용하였다.

애태우다 ① [자기] worry oneself ⟪about⟫ ; feel anxiety ; concern oneself ⟪about⟫...

(14) 동사의 일반적인 형은 do, doing을 사용하여 ⟪ ⟫ 안에 넣었다.

시들하다 ① be disinclined〔indisposed〕 to ⟪do⟫ ; be reluctant to ⟪do⟫...

(15) 일부 철자, 어구 등을 생략할 수 있을 경우에는 생략되는 부분을 ( ) 안에 넣었다.

내주 來週 next week ; the coming week ¶ 내주의 오늘 this day (next) week...

사단 師團 a (an army) division...

(16) 일부 철자 및 어구 등을 다른 것과 대체할 수 있을 경우에는 대체되는 어구를 〔 〕 안에 넣었다.

막아내다 ward off ; keep away〔out, off, back〕 ; ...

Ⅵ 철자(綴字)

역어·역문의 철자는 미식 철자를 채용하되, 국문의 영자 표기는 이탤릭체로 표시하였다.

바둑 *paduk* (game) ; Korean checkers ¶ 바둑을 두다 play (a game of) *paduk*...

서울 *Seoul*〔the capital of Korea〕 ; [수도] a capital ¶ 영국의 서울 런던 London, the capital of England...

Ⅶ 관용어·속담

속담·관용은 해당 표제어의 복합어 다음의 맨 끝에 두어 따로 익힐 수 있도록 하였다.

구렁이 〚동물〛 a big snake ; a huge serpent ; a boa (열대산)...

구렁이 담 넘어가듯 하다 속담 play tricks cautiously without arousing suspicion

예술 藝術 art ; an art (특정의) ; fine arts (미술)...

예술은 길고 인생은 짧다 관용 Art is long, life is short.

Ⅷ 참고

표제어의 역어 중 표현에 따라 달리 쓸 수 있는 유사 표현은 따로 box로 묶어 정리하였다.

국내 國內 the interior of a country ; (within) the country...

> 참고 《미》에서는 **domestic**을, 《영》에서는 **home**을 쓰는 일이 많다

Ⅸ 학습 기본 어휘의 표시

표제어 가운데 일상 생활에서 흔히 쓰이는 어휘를 기준으로 약 8,000여 어를 채록, 빈도수에 따라 3단계(† ⁑ *)의 별표로 구분하였다.

†야구 野球 baseball ; ball (game)...

⁑정교 精巧 elaborateness ; exquisiteness ; ingenuity ; delicacy...

***동맥 動脈** 〖해부〗 an artery...

Ⅹ 괄호·기호의 사용법

(1) ¶ : 표제어 및 복합어의 용례 기호로 사용하였다.

도거리 ... ¶ 도거리로 in a lump ; in one lot ; in the gross...

(2) — : 표제어를 대신하는 기호로서 다른 명사와 더불어 복합어를 이룬다.

사관 史觀 a historical view

유물 — the materialistic view of history **유심** — the idealistic view of history

(3) [ ] : 표제어의 분류 및 복합어와 용례의 뜻을 부연하거나, 바꾸어 말하거나, 동의어 따위를 기입하는 데 사용하였다. 그 밖에도 역어·역문의 문법·어법 사항, 용법상의 주의·보족 사항 따위를 기입하였다.

내치 內治 ① [내과 치료] cure by internal treatment〔medicine〕 ② [내정] home administration〔policy〕 ; internal〔domestic〕 affairs...

서운하다 [주로 1인칭 주어] (be) sorry ; regrettable ; unsatisfied ; feel somewhat unsatisfied ; miss...

(4) 《 》: ① 용법상의 참고 사항을 기입하였다.

멋쟁이 a dude 《미》 ; a dandy ; a fop ; a swell 《구》 ; a classy dresser ; a cockscomb

— **양복** a stylish suit — **아가씨** a body soxer 《미·속》...

② 외래어의 원말을 표시하였다.

사후 事後 ¶ 사후의 after the fact〔matter〕 ; ex post facto 《라》 // 사후에 after the fact ; post factum...

(5) 《 》: ① 전치사·목적어·주어 그리고 명사·대명사의 일반형 및 동사의 일반형 따위를 기입하였다.

달리다[4] ① [걸리다] hang 《on, from》 ; be suspended 《from》...

목매다 ① [남을] strangle 《a person to death》 ② [스스로] strangle oneself 《with a cord》

능사 . . . ¶ 능사로 삼다 consider 《something》 as one's work ; make it one's business 《to do》. . .

② 복수형과 때로는 단수형을 표시하였다.

번데기 a chrysalis 《*pl.* ～es, -lides》 ; a pupa 《*pl.* ～s, -pae》

③ 약어를 기입하였다.

신학 神學 theology

—교 a theological school〔seminary〕 **— 박사** a Doctor of Divinity 《D. D. 》. . .

(6) ( ) : ① 생략할 수 있는 철자·어구를 기입하였다.

개력하다 《nature》 undergo a (complete) change ; have a convulsion of nature

초안 草案 a (rough) draft. . .

② 역어의 차이 및 기타 주의·참고 사항을 기입하였다.

구대륙 舊大陸 the Old World (유럽·아시아) ; the Old Continent ; the European Continent (유럽)

비매품 非賣品 an article not for sale ; Not for sale. (게시)

③ 학명임을 표시하였다.

뜸부기 〖새〗 a crake ; water rail ; Porzana (학명)

(7) 〔 〕: 서로 대체할 수 있는 어구를 기입하였다.

시정 市政 municipal〔city〕 government〔administration〕 ; civic affairs. . .

돌결 the grain of a stone ¶ 돌결이 곱다〔거칠다〕 The stone has a fine〔coarse〕 grain.

(8) ⇨: 서로 관련이 있는 표제어를 참조하도록 지시하는 기호로 사용하였다.

숭숭 minced ; perforated ⇨ 송송

(9) //: 용례가 둘 이상일 때는 그 사이를 구분하였다.

역병 疫病 an epidemic ; a plague ; a pestilence ¶ 역병이 유행하다 the plague is prevalent // 역병이 발생하다 an epidemic breaks out

(10) ; : 표제어 및 복합어, 용례의 역어가 둘 이상일 때는 그 사이를 구분하였다.

잔술 盞— liquor by the cup ; draft liquor. . .

(11) / : 표제어 및 복합어, 용례의 역어가 둘 이상의 문장일 경우, 그 사이를 구분하였다.

살내리다 get〔become〕 thin ; lose weight ; 《flesh》 fall away ¶ 살 내리는 약 a fat-reducer ; a flesh-reducer ; an antifat remedy // 너는 그전보다 살이 내린 것 같다 You have got much thinner than you were. /You appear to have lost weight.

에비 Look out ! /Mustn't touch ! /Naughty-naughty !

(12) 〖 〗: 전문어임을 표시하였다.

변류기 變流器 〖기계〗 a converter ; a current transformer

(13) ～ : 명사·대명사의 복수형을 표시하는 데 표제어 전체를 대표하는 기호로 사용하였다.

분광 分光 spectrum 《*pl.* ～s, -ra》. . .

약 어 표

◆ 외래어에 관한 것

(프) French (프랑스어)	(포) Portuguese (포르투갈어)
(도) German (도이치어)	(범) Sanskrit (梵語)
(이) Italian (이탈리아어)	(그) Greek (그리스어)
(스) Spanish (스페인어)	(라) Latin (라틴어)
(러) Russian (러시아어)	(중) Chinese (중국어)

◆ 용법에 관한 것

(영) 영어	(영·속) 영·속어	(속) 속어	(비) 비어
(미) 미어	(미·구) 미·구어	(문) 문어	(아) 소아어
(구) 구어	(미·속) 미·속어	(시) 시어	(영·구) 영·구어

◆ 전문어에 관한 것

【건축】	建築	【민속】	民俗	【음악】	音樂
【경기】	競技	【 법 】	法律(學)	【의학】	醫學
【경영】	經營	【병리】	病理學	【인쇄】	印刷
【경제】	經濟學	【부기】	簿記學	【전기】	電氣
【고고】	考古學	【불교】	佛敎	【정구】	庭球
【고생물】	古生物	【사진】	寫眞術	【정치】	政治
【곤충】	昆蟲(學)	【사회】	社會學	【조각】	彫刻
【광물】	鑛物(學)	【상업】	商業	【조개】	貝類
【광산】	鑛山(學)	【 새 】	鳥類(學)	【종교】	宗敎
【교육】	敎育學	【생리】	生理學	【주식】	株式·去來
【군사】	軍事	【생물】	生物學	【증권】	證券
【기계】	機械工學	【성경】	聖經	【지리】	地理學
【기독교】	基督敎	【수사】	修辭學	【지질】	地質學
【기상】	氣象學	【수학】	數學	【천문】	天文學
【기하】	幾何	【 시 】	詩學	【철학】	哲學
【논리】	論理學	【식물】	植物(學)	【체조】	體操
【농업】	農業	【심리】	心理學	【크리켓】	크리켓
【당구】	撞球	【야구】	野球	【토목】	土木工學
【대수】	代數	【야금】	冶金	【한의】	漢醫學
【동물】	動物(學)	【 약 】	藥學·藥品	【항공】	航空術
【문법】	文法	【언어】	言語學	【항해】	航海術
【문예】	文藝	【역사】	歷史	【해부】	解剖學
【물고기】	魚類(學)	【연극】	演劇	【화학】	化學
【물리】	物理學	【영화】	映畫	【회화】	繪畫
【미학】	美學	【우주항공】	宇宙航空		

박스 항목 색인

ㄱ

ㄱ (기역) the first letter of the Korean alphabet ¶ ㄱ자 집 an L-shaped house 낫 놓고 ㄱ자도 모른다 속담 He cannot say B to a battledore.

ㄱㄴ순 —順 alphabetical order ¶ 이름을 ㄱㄴ순으로 적다 list names alphabetically

가¹ 〖음악〗 la (음계의 제6음)
—음(音) la —조(調) the tone A 내림 — A flat 《기호 : A♭》 올림 — A sharp 《기호 : A#》

가² ① [가장자리] the edge ; the verge ; the brink ; the rim ; the fringe ; [둘레] by ; near ¶ 물가 the water's edge ; the edge〔verge, brink〕 of the water ; the waterside ; a beach // 강가 the riverside // 길가 the roadside ; the wayside // 마을가 the outskirts of a town // 호숫가 the lakefront // 창가의 책상 the desk near the window // 연못가를 둘러싼 나무들 a fringe of trees on a pond // 난롯가에 by the fire // 입가에 미소를 띄우다 have a smile playing about one's lips
② [공간의 끝] the end ; the limit ; (the) bounds ¶ 가없는 바다 the endless sea ; the boundless ocean
③ [그릇의 아가리 쪽 언저리] the brim ¶ 컵가로 넘치는 와인 wine flowing 〔running〕 over the brim of the cup

가 加 [덧붙임] addition ; plus —하다 ⇨ 가하다 ¶ 보충 설명을 가하다 give a supplementary explanation // 열을 가하다 apply heat // 압력을 가하다 put pressure (up) on

가 可 ① [옳음] (fairly) good ; [찬성] approval ; yes ; yea ; aye ; OK —하다 (be) right ; good ¶ 가 20 부 5 ayes 20 and noes 5/There were twenty ayes against five noes. // 미성년자 관람 가 viewing open to minors // 분할 구입 가 buyable on the installment plan // 이 시험에서는 사전 사용이 가하다 You can use a dictionary for this exam.
② [등급] passable ; [성적의] D (수·우·미·양·가의) ¶ 이번 시험에서 가를 받은 과목은 영어와 수학이다 I got two D's in the English and mathematics examinations.

가- 假 [임시의] temporary ; provisional ; makeshift ; stopgap ; interim ; [가짜의] assumed ; false ; pretended
—건물 a temporary〔makeshift〕 building —계정 a suspense〔temporary〕 account —석방 parole ; release on parole —수요(需要) imaginary〔fictitious, disguised〕 demand —영수증 an interim receipt —정관 provisional articles —협정〔약정〕 a provisional agreement

-가 哥 [성] the family name ; the surname
¶ 네 성이 김가냐 Is your family name *Kim* ? // 한국에는 이가가 많다 There are many *Lees* in Korea.

-가 街 [거리] a street ; an avenue ; [구역] a district ; a center ; a quarter ¶ 번화가 business〔shopping〕 quarters // 상점가 a shopping center // 5번가 the Fifth Avenue // 종로 3가 the 3rd block of *Chongno* // 주택가 a residential area // 지하 상가 an underground shopping center // 유태인가 a ghetto 《*pl.* ～(e)s》 ; Jewish quarter

-가 歌 song
농부(農夫)— a farmer's song 애국(愛國)— the national anthem 응원— a cheering〔rooter's〕 song 진군— a marching song 찬불— a Buddhist hymn

†-가 價 ① [값] a price
공정(公定)— an official price 기준— a standard price 도매— a wholesale price 생산— the producer price 원— the prime〔first〕 cost 최저(最低)— the lowest price 판매— a selling price 현찰— a cash price
② [원자가] valence

-가 家 [전문인] a specialist ; a professional ; an authority ; [집안] the 《Kennedy》 family ¶ 낙천가 an optimist // 정력가 a man of energy // 소설가 a novelist // 전략가 a strategist // 애연가 a heavy〔habitual〕 smoker

가가호호 家家戶戶 every〔each〕 house ; all the houses ¶ 가가호호마다 at every door ; from door to door ; from house to house ; house by house

가감 加減 〖수학〗 addition and subtraction ; [증감] increase and decrease ; [조절] modulation ; adjustment —하다 add and subtract ; increase and decrease ; moderate ; adjust ¶ 수요에 따라 공급량을 가감하다 balance the supply and the demand // 음식은 간을 잘 가감하여야 제 맛이 난다 A well seasoned dish tastes good. // 약간의 가감이 필요하다 It needs light adjustment.
— 계산기 an arithmometer —법 the method of addition and subtraction — 저항 adjustable resistance — 콘덴서 〖전기〗 an adjustable condenser —판

ㄱ

(瓣) an adjustable〔adjusting〕 valve ; [디젤 기관의] a spill valve 저항 —기 a regulator ; an adjusting device

가감승제 加減乘除 the four rules of arithmetic ; addition, subtraction, multiplication and division

†가게 [상점] a shop 《영》; a store 《미》 [시장 따위의 매점] a booth ; [노점 따위] a stall ; a stand ; a booth ; a kiosk ; [상회] a firm ; a house ¶ 잘되는 가게 a popular〔prosperous〕 store〔shop〕// 가게 보는 사람 a shopkeeper ; a storekeeper ; a shop assistant 《영》; a clerk 《미》; [판매원] a salesman ; [여자 판매원] a saleslady 《영》; a salesgirl 《미》// 가게를 내다 open〔start, set up〕 a store ; open〔start〕 business ; set up in business // 가게를 닫다 close the store ; shut〔close〕 doors // 가게를 보다 tend〔mind〕 the shop ; keep a shop〔store〕// 가게를 그만두다 close〔shut〕 up one's shop〔doors〕; give up one's business // 길가에 구멍가게를 벌이다 keep a small shop by the roadside // 가게를 팔다 sell one's business

—채 a house with a shop in it ; the shop part of a house 가겟방 a store ; a house used as a store 구멍— a penny candy store ; a small store 반찬— a grocery store

†가격 價格 price ; cost ; figure ; [가치] value ; worth ¶ 도매 가격으로 주다 offer goods for a wholesale price // 생각보다 가격이 너무 비싸다 The price is far higher than anticipated. // 만일 더 싼 가격을 발견하신다면 그것과 똑같은 가격에, 아니 그보다 더 싸게 드리겠습니다 If you should find a lower price, we'll match it, no, we'll beat it. // 대형 TV의 가격 좀 알아보려고 전화했습니다 I just called to price big-screen TV sets. // 당신 집을 최고의 가격으로 팔아 드리겠습니다 I'll sell your house for top dollar.

— 변동 fluctuation of price — 변동 조항 an escalator clause — 분석 price analysis — 설정 price-setting — 설정자 a price maker — 인상 a price advance — 자유화 free pricing — 조작 price manipulation — 주도 기업 price leader — 지수 price index —차 a price margin — 체계 a price structure〔system〕 — 카르텔 a price cartel —표 a price list — 표기 declaration of value — 표기 우편 mail matter with value declaration — 협정 an agreement on prices 고시 — an official price 소비자 — the consumer price 수입 — an import price 수출 — an export price 시장 — the market price 허가〔신고〕 — the approved〔reported〕 price

가격 加擊 ① [때림] ¶ 힘껏 가격하다 strike 《a person》 hard ② [공격] ¶ 적의 진지를 미사일로 가격하다 strike the enemy's fort with missiles

*가결 可決 passage ; adoption ; approval ; O.K. 《미·속》 —하다 pass 《a bill》; carry 《a motion》; vote (투표로) ; adopt ; approve of ¶ 가결되다 be passed〔carried〕; pass // 의안을 가결하다 pass a bill // 48표 대 5표로 가결되다 be passed by 48 votes against〔to〕 5 // 동의(動議)는 가결되었다 The motion was carried. // 원안대로 가결되었다 The bill passed as drafted. // 만장 일치로 가결되었다 The bill was passed unanimously.

가경 佳景 fine scenery ; a picturesque〔charming, lovely〕 scene ; a fine view ; a superb landscape

가경 佳境 ① [고비] a delightful〔thrilling, exciting, interesting〕 part 《of a story, of a narrative》; the climax 《of a story》 ¶ 점입가경이다 approach the climax ; get to the best part // 이야기는 가경으로 들어간다 The plot thickens. /[소설 따위에서] We are now in the most interesting part of the story.

② [경치] a beautiful spot ⇨ 가경(佳景)

*가계 家系 a family line ; lineage ; genealogy ; a pedigree ; ancestry ; stock

—도 a family tree ; a genealogical chart ; pedigree (chart)

가계 家計 [집안의 경제] household economy ; family budget ; family circumstances ; family finances ; housekeeping expenses ; [생계] living ; livelihood ¶ 가계가 풍족〔곤란〕하다 be in easy〔straitened, narrow〕 circumstances ; be well〔badly〕 off // 가계를 돕다 help support a family // 가계를 줄이다 keep one's family expenses down

—부(簿) a housekeeping book ; a housekeeping〔domestic〕 accounts book —비(費) household〔housekeeping〕 expenses ; a family budget — 수표 a personal check

가계약 假契約 a provisional〔temporary, an interim〕 contract

가곡 歌曲 a song ; a lied 《*pl.* lieder》《도》; [곡조] a melody ; an air ; a tune ; an aria

— 작곡가 a song composer —집 a collection of songs — 형식 the song form 소— an arietta

†가공 加工 processing ; industrial process ; manufacturing ; treatment ; working ; [보석 따위의] cutting —하다 process ; manufacture ; treat ; improve ; work 《upon》 ¶ 야채를 가공하다 process vegetables

— 공장 a processing plant — 무명 processed cotton cloth ; finished cotton textiles — 무역 processing trade —비 processing cost — 산업 processing industry —세 a processing tax — 시설

processing facilities — 식품 processed 〔process〕 foodstuffs —업 processing industries —업자 a processor ; a process manufacturer — 원료 worked material —지 processed paper ; coated paper —품 processed〔wrought〕 goods ; finished goods〔articles〕 식품 —기계 food processing machinery

가공 架空 ① [공상] fiction ¶ 가공의 fanciful ; visionary ; imaginary ; air-built ; dreamy ; fictitious ; Utopian // 가공의 인물 a fictitious character ; a man of straw // 가공의 이야기 a fanciful story ; a pure fabrication

② [공중 가설] ¶ 가공의 overhead ; aerial ; trolley 《미》

—선 [전신·전화의] an overhead line 〔wire〕 ; an aerial cable ; [전차의] a trolley line 《미》 —식 a trolley〔an aerial〕 system —식 옥외선 the aerial system of external wiring — 장치 overhead equipment — 전력선 an overhead electric power line — 지선(地線) an overhead earth〔ground〕 wire — 철도 an aerial railway — 컨베이어 an aerial conveyor

가공 可恐 —하다 ¶ 가공할 fearful ; fearsome ; terrible ; formidable ; awesome // 핵무기의 가공할 파괴력 the horrible destructive power〔annihilating power〕 of nuclear weapons

가공 삭도 架空索道 an aerial cableway 〔ropeway〕

가과 假果 〖식물〗 a pseudocarp ; an imitation fruit

가관 可觀 ① [볼 만함] a spectacle ; an attraction ; a (spectacular) feature ; a highlight 《미》 ¶ 그 박람회에서는 실물 크기의 우주선 모형이 가관이었다 The exhibition was highlighted〔featured〕 by life-size models of spaceships. // 설악산의 눈꽃이 가관이었다 The snow-capped 〔-covered〕 Mt. *Sŏrak* was a magnificent spectacle. // 그것 참 가관이다 It really is something to see.

② [꼴불견] a sight ; unbecoming ¶ 그의 꼴이 가관이다 He looks a fright 〔sight〕. // 그들의 옷차림이 가관이었다 Their clothes were a sight. // 그의 젠체하는 꼴이 정말 가관이었다 His affected airs were a sight.

가교 假橋 a temporary〔makeshift, flying〕 bridge ¶ 계곡 사이에 놓인 철제 가교 an iron bridge spanning the valley

가구 家口 a family (식구) ; a household ; a house (집) ¶ 이 집안에는 두 가구가 산다 Two families are living in this house.

—수 the number of households〔families〕

⁑**가구 家具** (household) furniture〔furnishings〕 ; household goods〔utensils, articles〕 ¶ 가구 10점 ten pieces of furniture // 가구 한 벌 a set〔suite〕 of furniture // 많은〔얼마 안되는〕 가구 much 〔little〕 furniture // 가구를 비치한 셋집 a furnished house to let // 응접실은 화려한 가구로 꾸며져 있었다 The reception room was luxuriously furnished. // 가구가 딸린 방을 찾고 있다 I'm looking for a furnished room.

— 배치도 a plan of furniture arrangement —장이 a furniture maker ; a maker of furniture ; a cabinetmaker

가구상 家具商 a furniture dealer ; a dealer in furniture

가구점 家具店 a furniture〔furnishing goods〕 store〔shop〕

가구주 家口主 a householder

가권 家眷 one's family ⇨ 권속(眷屬)

가규 家規 family rules〔constitution〕

가극 歌劇 an opera ; a lyric drama ; [소가극] an operetta

— 가수(歌手) an opera singer —계 the operatic stage —단 an opera company〔troupe〕 — 대본 the words〔text〕 of an opera ; a libretto — 작곡가 an operatic composer —장(場) an opera house〔theater〕

⁑**가금 家禽** domestic fowls ; poultry 《총칭》

— 상인 a poulterer ; poultryman 《영》

가급 加給 [정해진 액수보다 더 줌] pay more than a (set) price

가급적 可及的 as...as possible ; as...as one can ¶ 가급적 주의하다 take the greatest possible care ; be as careful as possible ; act with utmost caution // 가급적 회의에 참석해 주십시오 Please do your best to attend the meeting. // 가급적 속히 이리로 와 주세요 Come here as soon〔quickly〕 as possible.

가긍하다 可矜— (be) poor ; pitiful ; touching ; miserable ¶ 가긍히 pitifully // 참으로 가긍한 장면이었다 The scene was really touching.

가기 佳期 [좋은 철] a good〔favorable〕 season ; [혼기] marriageable age 《of girls》

가까스로 just ; barely ; narrowly ; with difficulty ; laboriously ; in some fashion ¶ 가까스로 …하다 barely manage 《to》 // 가까스로 합격하다 just pass the examination ; scrape through the examination // 가까스로 모면하다 escape barely ; have a narrow escape // 그는 가까스로 당선됐다 He was elected by a narrow majority. // 가구를 혼자서 가까스로 옮겨 놓았다 I had a hard time arranging the furniture alone. // 가까스로 제 시각에 가 닿았다 I managed to get there in time. // 가까스로 원하는 대학에 들어갔다 I was just admitted to the college of my choice.

가까워지다 [거리] get near to 《a place》 ; come up to ; come near ;

ㄱ

approach ; draw near 《to》; [시간] approach ; be at hand ; draw〔come〕 near ; [사이가] become intimate ; be acquainted with 《a person》; know 《a person》 better ; get in with ; get thick with ¶ 겨울이 가까워지면 with the approach of winter // 완성에 가까워지다 be near〔nearing〕 completion // 종말에 가까워지다 draw to a close〔end〕// 목적지가 가까워지다 get near to the destination // (배가) 육지에 가까워지다 approach land ; close with the land ; draw toward the shore // 서로 곧 가까워지다 soon become intimate with each other // 서먹하던 사이가 다시 가까워졌다 The estranged friends became intimate again. // 시험이 가까워지고 있다 The examination is drawing near〔near at hand〕. // 이제 겨울이 가까워졌다 Winter's not far off now.

†**가까이** [거리] near ; close to ; in the neighborhood ; [시간] shortly ; before long ; close〔near〕 at hand ; [거의] nearly ; almost ; about ; approximately ¶ 우리 집 가까이에 in my neighborhood // 가까이 오다 come up close 《to》 // 100명 가까이 nearly one hundred persons // 시험이 가까이 다가왔다 The examination is near〔close〕 at hand. // 벌써 3년 가까이 된다 It is almost〔nearly〕 three years.

가까이하다 [사귀다] associate with ; make friends with ; get〔become〕 acquainted with ; keep company with ; [즐기다] love ; indulge in ; be interested in ¶ 가까이하기 쉬운 accessible ; approachable ; easy of access // 가까이하기 어려운 inaccessible ; unapproachable ; difficult〔hard〕 of access // 가까이하기 어려운〔쉬운〕 사람 a man of difficult〔easy〕 access // 책을 가까이하다 devote oneself to (reading) one's books ; spend a lot of time reading books // 그는 여러 층의 사람들과 곧잘 가까이할 수 있었다 He could easily get acquainted with people in every walk of life. // 그런 사람 가까이하지 마라 Keep away from such company. /Don't mix with such people. // 그는 술을 가까이한다 He loves〔indulges in〕 drinking. // 그는 사람을 가까이하지 않는다 He is not a sociable man. /He associates with nobody.

†**가깝다** ① [거리] (be) near ; be close〔near〕 by ; be not far off ; be (close) at hand ¶ 강에 가깝다 It is near the river. // 우리 집은 여기에서 가깝다 My house is only a little way from here. // 그는 버스 정류소에서 가까운 곳에 산다 He lives close to a bus stop. // 자네가 문에서 더 가까운 침대를 쓰게나 You take the bunk nearer the door. // 그녀의 직장은 가까운 곳에 있다 The company she works for is at a stone's throw.

② [시간] (be) near ; early ; immediate ; soon ; be close in time ¶ 가까운 장래에 in the near〔immediate〕 future ; at an early date // 가까운 날에 someday soon // 12시에 가깝다 It is getting on for twelve. // 크리스마스가 가깝다 Christmas is near at hand.

③ [관계] be close to ; be intimate with ; be friendly with ; be related to ¶ 가까운〔먼〕 일가 a near〔distant〕 relative // 가까운 친구 a close friend // 그 사람은 나의 가까운 친척은 아니다 I am not very closely related to him. // 그녀는 그와 아주 가까운 사이인 것 같다 (성적 관계가 있다) She must be intimate with him, I guess.

④ [거의] be nearly ; be almost ; be next to ; be close upon ¶ 10만에 가까운 군중 a crowd of nearly one hundred thousand // 완벽에 가깝다 It is nearly perfect. /It approaches perfection. // 나이가 60에 가깝다 He is nearly〔close upon〕 sixty. // 수가 500 가까이 된다 The number approaches five hundred. // 그는 스무 살에 가깝다 He is nearing〔pushing〕 twenty.

⑤ [성질·모양·상태·내용 등이 유사] be akin to ; resemble ; be allied to ; verge on ; close to ¶ 무모에 가까운 용기 courage verging on foolhardiness // 원숭이는 사람에 가깝다 The ape is closely allied to man. // 동정은 사랑에 가깝다 Pity is akin to love. // 그의 무모한 처사는 정치적 자살에 가까운 것이다 His reckless conduct is, so to speak, a kind of political suicide. // 나의 의견도 너의 것과 가깝다 My opinion is very close to yours. // 하는 짓이 미치광이에 가깝다 His behavior verges on madness. // 프랑스어보다 이탈리아어가 라틴어에 가깝습니까 Is Italian closer to Latin than French is? // 추측이 대충 사실에 가깝다 Your guess is in the ball park.

가까운 무당보다 먼 데 무당이 영하다 〔속담〕 Intimacy lessens fame. /A maid oft seen, and a gown oft worn, are disesteemed in scorn. /Respect is greater from a distance.

가까운 이웃이 먼 일가보다 낫다 〔속담〕 A good neighbor is better than a brother far off.

***가꾸다** ① [자라게 하다] grow ; cultivate ; rear ; take care of 《plants》 ¶ 야채를 가꾸다 grow vegetables

② [치장하다] decorate ¶ 외양을 가꾸다 dress up ; deck out ; adorn oneself // 얼굴을 가꾸다 make oneself up ; make up 《one's face》 // 꽃으로 집안을 아름답게 가꾸다 decorate〔embellish〕 one's living quarters with flowers

가꾸러뜨리다 throw down
가꾸러지다 fall head first ; fall headlong
가꾸로 upside down
*__가끔__ sometimes ; at times ; (every) now and then ; occasionally ; once in a while ¶ 가끔 들르다 drop in from time to time ; make frequent calls 《at》; frequent 《a place》// 가끔 만나는 친구 a remote friend // 가끔 네 생각을 한다 I think of you every now and then.
가나 (the Republic of) Ghana ¶ 가나의 Ghanaian
— **사람** a Ghanaian
가나다(라) [한글] the Korean syllabary 〔alphabet〕; [초보] the ABC 《of》; the rudiments〔elements〕 《of》; the first step ¶ 가나다부터 배우는 사람〔초보자〕 an abecedarian // 가나다순으로 배열하다 arrange alphabetically〔in alphabetical order〕; alphabetize // 무식해서 가나다도 모른다 He is so ignorant that he does not know his ABC. // 정치 경제학의 가나다부터 배우기 시작했다 He has begun to study political economy at the foot of the ladder.
가나다순 —順 alphabetical order
가나오나 wherever〔no matter where〕 one may go ; everywhere you turn ; [언제나] always ; all the time ; constantly ¶ 가나오나 그는 말썽을 일으킨다 He makes trouble wherever he may be.
†**가난** poverty ; want ; indigence ; [궁핍] destitution ; penury ; poorness

> 참고 **poverty** 일반 생활 필수품이 부족한 상태 **want** 생활 물자가 결핍되어 몹시 곤궁한 상태 **destitution** 의식주에 몹시 곤란한 상태 특히 영락한 빈궁 상태 **indigence** 영락 **penury** 비굴감을 느낄 정도의 극도의 빈곤 **poorness** 「가난」의 뜻보다는 「결핍」「부족」 따위의 비유적 뜻으로 많이 사용된다

— **하다** (be) poor ; needy ; indigent ; destitute ; penurious ; poverty-stricken ; be in poverty〔need, want〕; be in needy〔straitened〕 circumstances ; be badly off ¶ 가난한 사람들 the poor ; poor people〔folks〕; the indigent // 가난한 집에 태어나다 be born poor〔to poverty〕// 가난한 살림을 꾸려 나가다 eke out a scanty livelihood // 찢어지게 가난하다 be extremely poor ; be as poor as a church mouse // 근면과 절약으로 가난에서 벗어나다 overcome one's poverty〔difficulties〕 through industry and thrift // 집이 가난해서 학교를 못 다녔다 Want kept him from school. // 나도 가난의 맛을 알고 있다 I am no stranger to poverty. // 그가 가난해진 것은 자업자득이다 He has brought himself to poverty. // 가난한 사람은 쉴 겨를이 없다 Poor men have no leisure. // 뭐니뭐니 해도 가난만큼 견디기 힘든 것은 없다 There is nothing so hard to bear as poverty.
가난 구제는 나라도 못한다 속담 His 〔The〕 poverty is incurable〔beyond cure〕.
가난이 싸움이라 속담 Poverty breeds strife. /When poverty comes in at the door, love flies out of the window. / Want makes strife 'twixt man and wife.
가난이 죄다 속담 Poverty is the mother of crime.
가난할수록 기와집 짓는다 속담 He that has not silver in his purse, should have silver on his tongue.
가난 들다 ① [살림이] become poor ; be in need ; be in reduced circumstances ② [부족·결핍] run short〔low〕 《of》; be deficient〔lacking〕 《of》; get 〔become〕 scarce ¶ 인재가 가난 들다 suffer from a dearth〔shortage, scarcity, need〕 of talent
가난뱅이 a poor man ; a pauper ; [총칭] the poor ; the indigent
가납 假納 a deposit
— **금** a deposit ; a cover
가납 嘉納 [물건의] acceptance ; [충고의] approval ; appreciation — **하다** accept 《a thing》 with pleasure ; approve ; appreciate ¶ 왕은 대신의 진언을 가납하셨다 The king appreciated the minister's counsel.
가납사니 a talkative person ; a prattler ; a tattler ; a chatterbox ; a gasbag 《속》
가내 家內 a family ; a household ; one's people〔folks〕 ¶ 가내 일동 the whole family ; all one's family // 가내 평안하신지요 Are your family all well?
— **공장** a domestic factory — **노동** home work — **문제** a family〔household〕 affair
가내 공업 家內工業 a home〔domestic, cottage, household〕 industry ; homecraft
*__가냘프다__ (be) slender ; delicate ; slim ; fragile ; faint ; feeble ¶ 가냘픈 허리 a slim waist // 가냘픈 여자의 몸 a frail woman // 맥이 가냘프게 뛰고 있다 The pulse is beating faintly.
가녀리다 ⇨ 가냘프다
가년스럽다 (be) shabby ; threadbare
가노 家奴 ⇨ 가복(家僕)
가누다 keep steady ; keep the balance of one's body ; control ; keep under control ; handle ; hold up ¶ 한 발로 몸을 가누다 balance oneself on one leg // 정신을 가누다 collect one's senses // 그는 몹시 취해서 몸을 가누지 못한다 He is so drunk (that) he can't keep himself steady. // 가쁜 숨결을 가까스로 가누었다 He could barely contain his

breath.

가느다랗다 (be) very thin〔fine, slender〕 ¶ 가느다란 목 a very slender neck // 가느다란 목소리 a thin〔faint〕 voice

가느스름하다 (be) rather slender〔thin, fine〕

가는귀먹다 be hard of hearing ; be a little deaf ; become somewhat hard of hearing

***가늘다** ① [길다랗고 둘레가 좁다] (be) thin ; fine ; slender ; slim ; narrow ¶ 가는 눈 half-closed eyes // 가는 목 a slender neck // 팔이 가늘다 have slender arms // 가는 실 a fine thread // 가는 허리 a slim waist // 가는 비 fine〔misty〕 rain // 눈을 가늘게 뜨다 narrow one's eyes ; look with half-closed eyes // 가늘어지다 become thin〔thinner, more slender〕
② [촘촘하다] fine ; close ; delicate ¶ 가는 체 a fine sieve // 가는 모시 fine textured ramie cloth
③ [낟알이 작다] fine ; small ¶ 가는 소금 refined salt // 가는 고춧가루 finely powdered red pepper
④ [약하다] weak ; faint ; small ¶ 가는 목소리로 in a small〔faint〕 voice // 소리가 점점 가늘어지다 one's voice grows fainter

가늠 ① [겨냥] aim ; sight **—하다** take aim 《at》 ; aim 《at》 ; sight 《a target》 ; level〔point〕 a gun 《at》
② [판단·어림] judgement ; discernment ; estimation ; sense of proportion **—하다** use one's sense of proportion 《on》 ; watch ; study ; weigh 《one plan against another》 ¶ 정세를 가늠하다 watch the development of a situation ; see how the wind lies〔is blowing〕 ; see how the land lies // 물가 변동을 가늠할 수가 없다 The price fluctuations are difficult to forecast〔predict〕.
—각 an elevation 《of a gun》

가늠쇠 the bead ; the front sight ; the foresight

가늠자 the backsight

⁑가능 可能 possibility **—하다** (be) possible ; feasible ; practicable ; be within the range〔bounds〕 of possibility ¶ 실행이 가능한 practicable ; feasible // 가능한 범위에서 as much〔far〕 as possible ; within the limits of the possible〔possibility〕 // 불가능을 가능케 하다 turn an impossibility into a possibility ; make the impossible possible // 그렇게 하기는 가능하다 It is possible for us to do. /We can do so. // 가능한 한 포기를 하는 것이 좋겠군요 If at all possible, you should give it up.

⁑가능성 可能性 possibility ; likelihood ; chance ¶ 가능성이 있다 be possible ; be feasible (실행할) // 가능성이 없다 be impossible ; be not possible // 인간의 무한한 가능성 the infinite possibilities of man // 전혀 가능성이 없다 be out of the bounds of possibility ; be absolutely impossible // 가능성은 별로 없는 것 같다 I don't see much chance of it. // 성공할 가능성이 없다〔많다〕 There is little〔an ample〕 hope for success. // 그건 네가 벼락에 맞을 가능성보다 더 희박해 That's even slimmer than your chance of being struck by a lightning. // 내가 승진할 가능성은 별로 없다 My chances for promotion aren't good.

†가다¹ ① [일반적] go ; proceed ; travel ; frequent 《a place》 ; attend 《school》 ; 《a road》 lead to 《the station》 ; leave for 《*Seoul*》 ; 《I will》 come 《to see you》 ¶ 목포로 가는 기차 a train (bound) for *Mokp'o* // 가는 도중에 on one's〔the〕 way to ; en route to // 대문 쪽으로 가다 make for the gate // 오른쪽으로 가다 turn to the right // 하루 30마일을 가다 make〔measure, do〕 thirty miles a day // 밤길을 혼자 가다 go〔travel〕 by night alone // 그 거리를 다섯 시간에 가다 cover〔do, travel〕 the distance in five hours // 혼자 갈 수 있다 I can find my way 《to》. // 그 친구 집에 다시는 안 가겠다 I shall never darken his door〔visit him〕. // 저리 가 Get〔Go〕 away ! /Away〔Be off, Get along〕 with you ! /Be gone ! // 걸어서 20분이면 갈 수 있다 It's only 20 minutes' walk. // 내 책이 어디 갔나 Where is my book, I wonder ? // 어둡기 전에 갔다 오긴 어려울 걸 It will be difficult for us to be back before evening. // 미국에 가 본 적이 있는가 Have you ever been in〔to〕 America ? /Did you ever go to America ? // 어디 갔다 왔니—극장에 갔다 왔지 Where have you been ? I have been to the theater. // 일본에는 몇 번이나 다녀오셨습니까 How often have you been to Japan ? // 그녀는 미국으로 가버렸다 She has gone to America. // 이 길을 따라 가시다가 두번째 신호등에서 왼쪽으로 도십시오 Go down this street and make a left at the second signal. // 가는 데만 한 시간이 걸린다 An hour one way. // 제가 화장실에 가 있는 동안 우리 아기 좀 잠깐 봐주시겠습니까 Could you please keep an eye on my baby while I'm gone to the rest room ? // 여기서 쓰실 겁니까 가지고 가실 겁니까 Here or to go ? // 어디를 가나 서로 부딪칠 정도로 차가 많고 조금 가다가 서고 조금 가다가 서고 한다 It's bumper-to-bumper and stop-and-go every where. // 얼마나 오래 가 있으실 겁니까 How long will you be gone ? // 오늘 너희 집에 가도 되니 Can I come over to your house today. // 이제 슬슬 가는 게 좋겠다 I'd better be on my way.

② [꺼지다] be out ; go out ¶ 전깃불이 갔다 The electric lights are out〔have gone out〕. /The electric light has failed.
③ [죽다] die ; pass away ; depart (from) this life ¶ 그는 가고 없다 He is dead and gone. /He is no more.
④ [시간이 흐르다] pass ; elapse ; go by ; roll on ¶ 시간이 감에 따라서 as time passes
⑤ [맛 등이 없어지다] 《a food》 spoil ¶ 맥주 맛이 갔다 The beer tastes flat.
⑥ [맛 등이 상하다] ¶ 김치 맛이 갔다 This *kimchi* has gone bad〔turned sour〕.
⑦ [보존되다] wear ; last long ; keep (good) ; hold ; endure ; be durable ; [목숨이] live out ; survive ¶ 오래가다 last〔keep〕 long ; wear well ; be durable ; give excellent wear // 두 배나 오래가다 give double wear // 이 물건은 오래 못 가겠는데요 I am afraid this stuff won't wear well. // 그 환자는 앞으로 1년도 못 갈 것 같다 The patient will not last another year. // 이 상태로는 앞으로 한 시간도 채 못 가겠습니다 I fear from his condition that he will not have an hour to live. // 이 수프가 내일까지 갈지 모르겠군요 I wonder if this soup will keep till tomorrow.
⑧ [금·주름이 생기다] get creased ; be wrinkled ; be cracked ¶ 주름이 간 얼굴 a wrinkled face // 접시에 금이 갔다 There is a crack in the plate. // 벽에 금이 갔다 There is a crack in the wall. // 그 때문에 그들의 우정에 금이 갔다 That has impaired〔caused a crack in〕 their friendship.
⑨ [소요되다] be required〔needed〕 ¶ 그것은 손이 많이 가야 한다 It requires a great deal of care.
⑩ [값] cost ; be worth ¶ 쌀이 한 가마에 120,000원 간다 The price of rice is 120,000 *won* a bag. // 양복 한 벌에 20만원 정도 간다 A suit costs about 200,000 *won*. // 그것은 600만원 이상 가는 땅이다 It is a piece of land worth more than six million *won*.
⑪ [통하다] ¶ 종로로 가려면 어느 길로 가야 합니까 Which road shall I take to *Chongno*? // 이 길로 가면 종로가 나옵니다 This street leads〔goes〕 to *Chongno*. // 서울로 가는 길 a way to *Seoul* ; a road leading to *Seoul* // 시장으로 가는 길 a way to the market
⑫ [몸 담을 곳으로] ¶ 군대를 가다 enlist in the army ; enter the service // 교도소에 가다 be imprisoned // 시집을 가다 get married
⑬ [마음이 끌리다] ¶ 호감이 가다 become fond

가는 말에 채찍질 속담 as unnecessary as whipping a galloping horse

가는 말이 고와야 오는 말이 곱다 속담 Nice words for nice words.

가는 방망이 오는 홍두깨 속담 Sow the wind and reap a whirlwind.

갈수록 수미산〔태산〕이라 속담 Hills peep o'er hills, and Alps on Alps arise!

가다² [진행] ¶ 사과가 붉게 익어 간다 The apples are turning red. // 날이 어두워 간다 It is darkening〔getting dark〕. // 배를 저어 가다 go rowing a boat // 만사가 잘되어 간다 Everything is going well〔all right〕 with me.

가다가 sometimes ; occasionally ; at times ; now and then ¶ 가다가 실수하다 sometimes make a mistake ; make an occasional slip // 가다가 한 번씩 심술을 부린다 He grows nasty now and then. /He behaves perversely once in a while.

가다귀 [땔나무] brushwood ; oak-brush firewood

가다듬다 ① [정신을 차리다] brace〔collect, gather〕 oneself (up) ; [마음을 안정시키다] calm〔compose〕 oneself ; keep cool
② [조절하다] put 《things》 in order 〔trim〕 ; set in good order ; tidy up ¶ 매무새를 가다듬다 adjust oneself〔one's dress〕 ; straighten one's dress 〔clothes〕 ; tidy oneself // 목소리〔목청〕를 가다듬다 clear one's throat

가다랭이 〖물고기〗 a bonito ; a shipjack

가다리 〖농업〗 tilling〔plowing〕 a rice field at piecework ¶ 가다리맡다 contract to plow at piecework

가다오다 ¶ 가다오다 만난 사람 a chance acquaintance

가닥 a piece ; a strip ; a strand ; a fork 《of a road》 ¶ 실 한 가닥 a piece of string // 한 가닥의 천 a strip of cloth // 한 가닥 길 one fork of the road // 세 가닥으로 꼰 밧줄 a rope of three strands // 한 가닥의 희망을 걸다 have (a) faint hope
—수 the number of strips

가단조 —短調 A minor ⇨ 가¹

가단성 可鍛性 malleability

가담 加擔 ① [편듦] siding with ; [관여] participation ; [공모] conspiracy
② [원조] support ; help **—하다** side with ; stand by ; take part in ; participate in ; conspire with ; [연좌하다] be implicated〔involved〕 in ¶ 그는 음모에 가담했다 He was privy to the plot. // 그는 폭동에 가담했다는 이유로 구속되었다 He was taken up on a charge of complicity in the riot. // 그러한 계획에는 가담할 수 없다 I cannot lend myself to such a project. // 그는 어느 편에도 가담하지 않는다 He is (sitting) on the fence. /He is neutral. // 그는 반핵 운동에 가담하고 있다 He is engaged in an

ㄱ

antinuclear campaign〔movement〕.
—자 a confederate ; an accomplice ; a conspirator

가당 可當 —하다 [타당] (be) just ; right ; proper ; fair ; appropriate ; adequate ; fit ; [감당] be able to cope with ; be equal to 《a task》 ¶ 가당한 말이다 He is right in what he says./He is right when he says that./He speaks the truth.// 그 놈은 죽어(도) 가당하다 He deserves death.// 그가 의장에 뽑힌 것은 가당하다 It is proper that he (should) be chosen chairman.

가당찮다 可當— (be) unjust ; unfair ; unreasonable ; [지나치다] undue ; excessive ; outrageous ; [대단하다] awful ; unbearable ¶ 가당찮은 요구 an excessive〔unreasonable〕 demand// 가당찮게 비싼 값 a ridiculously high price ; an exorbitant〔outrageous〕 price // 날씨가 가당찮게 춥다 It's awfully cold.

가대 架臺 a holder ; a stand ; a frame

가댁질 a (game of) tag **—하다** play tag

가도 街道 a highway ; a highroad ; a road ; a thoroughfare
경인 — the *Kyŏng-In*〔*Seoul-Inch'ŏn*〕 Highway

가도 家道 ① [가풍] family customs ; family traditions ② [생계] livelihood

가돈 家豚 [편지에서] my son ; he

가동 可動 ¶ 가동의 movable ; mobile
— 기중기 a movable crane **—댐** a movable dam **— 레일〔궤조(軌條)〕** 〖토목〗 a movable〔slide〕 rail **—부** a moving part ; a moving element **—성** movability ; mobility **— 코일** 〖전기〗 a moving〔movable〕 coil

가동 稼動 operation ; work **—하다** operate ; run ; put into operation ¶ 가동 중이다 be in 《full》 operation ; be at work ; be operated
— 시간 hours of operation **— 시설** available〔working, operative〕 equipment **— 인구** the manpower **— 일수** the number of workdays〔days worked, working days〕 **완전 —** full〔full-scale〕 operation **추정 — 인구** the potential manpower ; the potential working〔labor〕 force

가동거리다 [어린애를] dandle (a baby)

가동관절 可動關節 a movable joint

가동교 可動橋 a movable bridge

가동력 稼動力 manpower

가동률 稼動率 the rate of operation ; the working ratio

가동이치다, 가동질하다 ⇨ 가동거리다

가두 街頭 a street ¶ 가두에서 in〔on〕 the street// 서재에서 가두로 from the library to the street// 가두로 몰려 나온 환영 인파 the welcoming crowd who took to the street
— 검색 an on-the-street search (of suspects) **— 사진** pavement〔street〕 snapshot **— 자유 토의** free discussion with men on the street **— 풍경** a street scene **— 화가** a pavement artist

가두 녹음 街頭錄音 [라디오 프로] "a man-in-the-street interview"

***가두다** shut in〔up〕 ; lock in〔up〕 ; coop in〔up〕 ; pen up ; bottle up ; confine ; trap ¶ 방에 가두다 confine 《a person》 to a room ; shut〔lock, coop〕 《a person》 up in a room ; keep 《a person》 indoors// 감방에 가두다 throw 《a person》 into prison ; put 《a person》 behind ; lock 《a person》 in ; straitjacket (미친 사람을)

***가두리** a brim (모자·그릇 따위의) ; a rim (모자·안경 따위의) ; a hem (수건 따위의) ; a frill (장식된) ¶ 접시의 가두리 the edge〔rim〕 of a tray

가두 모금 街頭募金 street fund raising ; a collection of subscriptions in the street ¶ 가두 모금 운동을 시작하다 launch〔start〕 an on-the-street campaign for raising funds 《for》

가두 선전 街頭宣傳 street〔wayside〕 propaganda〔advertising〕 ¶ 가두 선전을 하다 propagandize〔make propaganda〕 in〔on〕 the street

가두 연설 街頭演說 a wayside speech ; soapbox oratory ¶ 가두 연설을 하다 make a speech in the street

가두 판매 街頭販賣 street peddling

가둥거리다 sway one's hips ¶ 가둥가둥 swaying one's hips

가드락거리다 behave flippantly and rudely ; strut ⇨ 거드럭거리다

가드레일 a guardrail

***가득** full ; to capacity ; filled (with) ¶ 포도주가 가득 부어진 컵 a cup brimful of wine// 가득 차다 be chock-full ; be full to the brim// 광장을 가득 메운 군중 the people packing〔crowding〕 a square // 한잔 가득 붓다 fill a glass full ; fill the glass to the brim// 광에 곡식이 가득 쌓여 있다 The barns are bursting with grain. // 가방에다 가득 채우시오 Pack the trunk tight. // 이 방은 가득 채우면 300명은 들어간다 We could pack 300 men in this hall.

가득 稼得 earnings

가득가득, 가뜩가뜩 all filled ; each one filled **—하다** 《pots》 be all filled ; 《each one》 be full

***가득하다** (be) full ; be filled to the brim ; be chock-full ; be full up ¶ 눈에 눈물이 가득했다 Her eyes were filled〔brimming〕 with tears. // 그 방은 사람들로 가득했다 The room was crowded〔packed, crammed〕 with people. // 관람석은 관객으로 가득했다 The stands were filled〔filled solidly〕 with the audience. // 그녀의 마음은 남편의 행복을 비는 생각으로 가득했다 All her thoughts were occupied with the happiness of her husband.

가든그리다 ⇨ 거든그리다

가든하다, 가뜬하다 [옷 따위] (be) light ; [마음이] feel light ; feel good ¶ 가뜬한 여름옷 a light summer suit // 가뜬히 lightly ; without difficulty〔trouble〕; lightheartedly // 마음이 가뜬하다 feel lighthearted ; feel good // 가뜬하게 차리다 be lightly dressed ; wear a light suit // 짐을 더니 가뜬하군 I'm relieved〔lightened〕 of my baggage〔burden〕. // 잠을 푹 잤더니 몸이 아주 가뜬하다 After a sound sleep I feel refreshed.

가들거리다 ⇨ 가드락거리다

가들막거리다 swagger ; strut about ; stalk about ; bear oneself haughtily ; act in a lordly manner ; put on airs

가들막하다 ⇨ 그들먹하다

가등 街燈 ⇨ 가로등(街路燈)

가등기 假登記 provisional registration

가뜩 [가득] full ; [가뜩이나] on top of everything else ⇨ 가뜩이나

가뜩이나 in addition to〔that〕; what is worse ; to make matters worse ; on top of 《it》 ¶ 가뜩이나 요즈음은 술까지 시작했다 And, to make matters worse, he has taken to drinking. // 가뜩이나 피로한데 또 일을 하란다 I am dog-tired and still they want me to work.

가라말 an all-black horse

가라사대 say ; as 《a saint, a wiseman》 says… ¶ 예수 가라사대 As Jesus says… // 공자 가라사대 Confucius says… // 성경에 가라사대 The Bible says…

†가라앉다 ① [바닥으로] sink ; go down ; settle down ; go to the bottom ¶ 배는 이물부터 가라앉았다 The ship settled down by the bow. // 밑바닥에 가라앉아 있다 It lies in the bottom.

② [마음이] get〔become〕 calm〔quiet〕; cool〔calm〕 down ; recover one's composure ; become composed〔collected〕 ¶ 그 그림을 보면 마음이 가라앉는다 The picture has a calming effect upon my soul. // 이 방에서는 마음이 가라앉지 않는다 I don't feel at home in this room. // 노여움이 가라앉았다 His anger subsided.

③ [조용해지다] become quiet〔calm, still〕; quiet down ; [풍파 따위가] go down ; die down ; subside ; abate ; [먼지 따위가] settle ¶ 바람이 가라앉는다 The wind dies down. /The wind abates〔blows itself out〕. // 폭풍이 가라앉는다 The storm subsides〔abates〕. // 소란이 가라앉았다 The row quieted down.

④ [고통 따위가] abate ; go down ¶ 열이 가라앉았다 The fever has left him. // 열이 가라앉지 않는다 I can't get rid of the fever. // 부은 데가 가라앉았다 The swelling has gone down. // 이 약을 드시면 통증이 곧 가라앉습니다 If you take this medicine, your pain will soon be over.

†가라앉히다 ① [뜬 것을] sink ; send to the bottom ; make 《dregs》 settle ¶ 바닷속에 가라앉히다 submerge 《a thing》 in the sea // 배를 가라앉히다 sink a ship ; send a ship to the bottom

② [마음을] calm〔compose〕 oneself ; keep cool ; gather one's wits ¶ 신경〔흥분〕을 가라앉히다 soothe〔quiet〕 one's nerves〔mental excitement〕// 성을 가라앉히다 control one's anger ; [남의] soften〔appease, pacify〕《a person's》 anger

③ [조용해지게] calm ; quiet (down) ; still ; cool off ; pacify ; [먼지를] settle 《the dust》 ¶ 여론을 가라앉히다 quiet down public sentiments

④ [부기·고통 따위를] allay ; alleviate ; lessen ; lighten ; mitigate ; relieve ¶ 통증을 가라앉히다 ease the pain // 아스피린이 고통을 가라앉혀 주었다 Aspirin relieved the pain.

가라지 ⇨ 강아지풀

가락[1] ① [음조] a key ; a pitch ; a tune ; a tone ; strain ; [박자] time ; rhythm ; pace ; tempo ¶ 가락이 고운 melodious ; harmonious // 가락이 안 맞는 노래 a song out of tune // 높은〔낮은〕 가락으로 in a high〔low〕 key // 가락을 맞추다 [음조를] tune 《a piano》; [장단을] keep time 《with》// 가락을 올리다〔낮추다〕 raise〔lower〕 the pitch〔voice〕

② [솜씨] dexterity ; skill ; efficiency ¶ 일에 가락이 나다 warm up 《into work》; go with a swing // 원래의 가락이 나다 hit〔get into, strike〕 one's stride

가락[2] ① [물렛가락] a spindle

② [낱개] a stick ; a long slender object ¶ 젓가락 chopsticks // 엿 한 가락 a stick of rice candy // 손가락 a finger

가락국수 Korean noodle〔vermicelli〕

가락지 a set of twin rings ; a (finger) ring ¶ 가락지를 낀 손가락 a ringed finger // 가락지를 끼다 put〔slip〕 a ring on one's finger // 가락지를 빼다 slip a ring off one's finger // 가락지를 끼고 있다 have〔wear〕 a ring on one's finger

가람 伽藍 a Buddhist temple

가랑가랑[1] [되풀이] ding ; clink ; tinkle ; [숨결] 약한 숨결을 가랑가랑 이어 갔다 He kept on breathing feebly.

가랑가랑[2] [눈물·액체가] 그릇에 가랑가랑 담긴 물 the water filling the glass to the brim ; a glass brimful of water // 눈에 눈물이 가랑가랑하며 목이 메었다 I was choked with tears.

가랑눈 fine〔powdery〕 snow

가랑니 a baby louse ; a nit

가랑머리 hair braided in two plaits (down the back) ; a hairdo with two

pigtails
가랑무 a forked radish
***가랑비** a drizzle ; a drizzling〔misty, light〕 rain ; a fine rain ; a sprinkle ¶ 가랑비가 내리고 있었다 It was drizzling.
가랑비에 옷 젖는 줄 모른다 관용 Many a little makes a mickle. /Many drops make a flood.
가랑이 [끝이 갈라진 부분] a fork ; a crotch ; [다리] the crotch ; legs ¶ 나무 가랑이에 걸터앉다 sit in the crotch of a tree // 가랑이를 벌리다 set one's legs apart // 가랑이 찢어지다〔째어지다〕 suffer from the hardships of life
가랑이가 찢어지게 가난하다 속담 As poor as a church mouse. /As poor as Job.
가랑이지다 be forked ¶ 길이 가랑이지다 The road forks.
가랑잎 dead〔withered〕 leaves ; [떡갈잎] an oak leaf
가랑잎으로 눈 가리고 아웅한다 속담 Cheat a person with a transparent lie.
가랑잎이 솔잎더러 바스락거린다고 한다 속담 The pot calls the kettle black. /Ill may kiln call the oven burnt-tail. /The frying-pan said to the kettle, 'Avaunt, black brows.'/The kettle calls the pot burnt-arse.
⁑**가래**[1] [농기구] a shovel (with a rope attached to each side of the blade) ; a spade // 가래로 파다 spade〔shovel〕 《a trench》 ; dig with a spade
가래[2] [담] phlegm ; sputum 《*pl* ~s, -ta》 ¶ 가래를 뱉다 bring〔cough〕 up phlegm ; expectorate // 피가 섞인 가래 bloody phlegm ; a little blood in the sputum // 기침이 심하고 가래가 계속 올라옵니다 I have this severe cough and keep spitting up phlegm.
가래[3] 〖식물〗 a wild walnut
가래[4] ① [낱개] a piece ; a stick〔bar, rod〕 ¶ 엿〔떡〕 한 가래 a piece of rice-candy〔-cake〕 ② [떡가래] a strip of rice cake
가 래 다 discriminate ; distinguish 《between》 ; tell 《A》 from 《B》 ¶ 선악을 가래다 distinguish between good and evil ; tell good from evil
가래떡 a stick of rounded rice cake
가래엿 a stick of rounded taffy
가래질 〖농업〗 spadework ; spading ; shoveling **—하다** spade ; shovel ; do spadework ; turn over 《soil》 with a spade
가래침 spit ; spittle ¶ 가래침을 뱉다 spit ; expectorate // 사람에게 가래침을 뱉다 spit at 《a person》 // 가래침을 함부로 뱉지 마라 No spitting on the floor.
가래톳 the swelling of the lymphatic gland in the groin
가래톳이 서다 관용 have a bubo

***가량 假量** ① [쯤] about ; almost ; some ; more or less ; something like ; or so ¶ 10마일 가량 about〔some〕 ten miles ; ten miles or so ; ten miles or thereabouts ; around ten miles 《미》 ; round about ten miles // 연 1할 2푼 가량 about〔something like〕 ten to two percent a year // 여기서 얼마 가량이나 되겠습니까 About how far is it from here ? // 회원이 스무 사람 가량 된다 The membership numbers about 20. // 거기에는 50명 가량 있었다 There were some〔approximately〕 fifty people over there.
② [어림짐작] estimate ; guess ¶ 가량없는 사람 a man of very poor judgment // 가량없는 짓 outrageous conduct
가량가량하다 be thin but look healthy
가량스럽다 (be) unbecoming ; unstylish
가량없다 假量— [어림없다] be poor at guessing ; have poor judgment ; [당치 않다] be wide of the mark ; be outrageous ; absurd〔preposterous〕 ; [어림할 수 없다] immeasurable ; inestimable ¶ 가량없게 높은 하늘 the infinitely deep 〔high〕 sky
가려내다 ① [추려내다, 골라내다] sort out ; classify ; pick out ; single out ; separate ; winnow
② [잘잘못을 밝혀내다] ¶ 시비를 가려내다 decide between right and wrong
가려먹다 be particular about food
가려잡다 choose ; select ; pick out ; single 《someone》 out

> 참고 **choose** 주어진 2개 이상의 것에서 자기 판단에 의해 고르다 **select** 넓은 범위 중에 잘 생각하여 고르다

가려하다 佳麗— (be) beautiful ; pretty ; lovely ; fine ; graceful ; elegant
***가련하다 可憐—** (be) poor ; pitiful ; wretched ; miserable ; sad ; touching ; pathetic
가렴주구 苛斂誅求 extortion ; exaction
***가렵다** [피부가] (be) itchy ; itching ; feel itchy ; itch ¶ 가려워하다 complain of itching // 가려운 데를 긁다 scratch an itchy place // 등이 가렵다 My back itches. /I feel itchy in my back.
가령 假令 if ; suppose 《that》 ; supposing 《that》 ; (even) if ; granting〔granted, admitting〕 《that》 ; let us suppose 《that》 ¶ 가령 네 말이 사실이라 치더라도 변명이 되지 않는다 Granted that 〔Even if〕 your statement is true, that is no answer to the charge. // 가령 이렇게 한다면 어떨까 What if we did it this way ?
가례 家禮 the customary formalities 〔proprieties〕 of a family
가례 嘉禮 an auspicious ceremony at court (such as a state wedding or

enthronement)

⁑가로 the width ; the breadth ; [부사적] across ; crosswise ; sideways ; horizontally ¶ 가로 2피트 two feet in width ; two feet wide // 가로 선을 긋다 draw a horizontal line // 머리를 가로 젓다 shake one's head sideways ; shake one's head negatively ; say no ; refuse

—축 the horizontal axis

가로 街路 a street ; a road ; [대로] an avenue 《미》

—망 street network — 청소부 a street sweeper〔cleaner〕; a scavenger ; whitewing 《미》

가로놓이다 lie ; lie across ; lie sideways ; stand in the〔one's〕 way

가로누이다 lay down ; place〔put, lay〕 across

가로닫이 a sliding window〔door〕

가로등 街路燈 a street light〔lamp〕

가로되 say ⇨ 가라사대

⁑가로막다 interrupt ; obstruct ; hinder ; bar ; cut off ¶ 길을 가로막다 bar 《a person's》 way〔passage〕; stand in 《a person's》 way // 남의 이야기를 가로막다 cut 《a person》 short ; interrupt 《a person》 // 입구가 좁으니 가로막지 마십시오 The entrance is narrow, so don't block it, please.

가로막히다 be obstructed ; be blocked (up) ; be intercepted ; be interrupted ¶ 댐에 가로막혀 보이지 않는다 The dam blocks the scenery.

가로맡다 take over 《another's business》; take upon oneself ; assume 《another's responsibility》 ¶ 싸움을 가로맡아서 했다 He made the fight his own. // 누가 이 일을 가로맡아 주었으면 좋겠는데 I wish someone would take the work off my hands. // 나머지는 그가 가로맡았다 He handled the rest.

가로변 街路邊 the roadside

가로새다 steal out of ; slip out of 《a room, house》; sneak away from 《company》 ¶ 수업 중 가로새다 cut a class and beat it 《미·속》 // 그는 어느새 가로새 버리고 말았다 He got away unnoticed.

가로서다 stand sideways ; stand aside ; stand looking aside〔the other way〕

가로세로 ① [가로와 세로] length and breadth〔width〕

② [부사적] vertically and horizontally ; lengthwise and crosswise ; from point to point ¶ 가로세로 선을 긋다 draw lines vertically and horizontally

③ [사방으로] in all directions ; in every direction ; to all points ¶ 가로세로 달리는 철도망 a network of railways // 적을 가로세로 무찌르다 slash about the enemy right and left // 하수도가 시내를 가로세로 관통하고 있다 The sewer system runs in all directions through the city.

가로쓰기 writing laterally ; writing from left to right ; horizontal writing

†가로지르다 cross ; traverse ; go〔cut〕 across ; intersect ¶ 평원을 가로질러서 뻗어 있는 철로 a railway traversing a plain // 가로질러 건너다 go across ; traverse ; cut across // 행렬을 가로지르다 break through a procession // 앞길을 가로지르다 cross the path of 《a person》

가로차다 snatch ⇨ 가로채다

*가로채다 ① seize (on the way) ; snatch ; usurp ; intercept ; steal ¶ 왕위를 가로채다 usurp a throne // 핸드백을 가로채다 snatch a handbag from her hand // 편지를 가로채다 intercept a letter // 남의 아내를 가로채다 steal a woman from her husband ; win away another's wife // 남의 말을 가로채다 interrupt 《a person》 in his speech

② [가로채이다] get seized (on the way) ; be snatched〔intercepted, usurped〕 ¶ 상대 선수에게 공을 가로채였다 The opponent made a snatch at the ball.

가로퍼지다 spread out ; grow broad ; get pudgy〔stocky〕 ¶ 가로퍼진 남자 a stocky〔pudgy, dumpy, thickset〕 man ; a humpty-dumpty

가뢰 〖곤충〗 a blister beetle ; a meloid

가료 加療 medical treatment〔care〕 —하다 treat 《a patient》 ¶ 가료 중이다 be under the doctor's〔medical〕 treatment

†가루 [곡식의] flour ; meal ; [분말] powder ; dust ¶ 가루를 만들다 powder ; pulverize

—눈 powdery snow —받이 a duster —분 cosmetic〔face〕 powder — 비누 soap powder —약 medicinal powder ; powdered medicine — 우유 powdered milk —차(茶) dust〔pulverized, broken〕 tea —체 a flour bolter — 치약 tooth powder 석탄 — coal dust

가류 加硫 ⇨ 가황(加黃)

†가르다 ① [분할하다] divide 《into》; [분배하다] share 《a thing》 with 《a person》; distribute 《things》 among 《the three》; deal out ; [분류하다] classify 《into》; sort ; [분리하다] separate ¶ 가를 수 없는 indivisible ; inseparable // 다섯 몫으로 가르다 divide into five shares // 한 학급을 둘로 가르다 divide a class into two // 사과를 둘로 가르다 slice an apple into two // 이익을 공평하게 가르다 divide profits equally

② [구별하다] discriminate between good and bad ; tell good〔right〕 from bad〔wrong〕

③ [물·공기 등을 헤치며 나아가다] ¶ 새벽공기를 가르며 날아가는 비행기 an airplane cutting through (waves of) morning air

가르랑거리다 wheeze ¶ 가르랑가르랑 wheezing(ly)
†가르치다 [지식·기술을] teach ; instruct《in》; give lessons《in》; [교육] educate ; school ; [지시] show ; direct ¶ 영어를 가르치다 teach English ; give lessons in English // 장사의 비결을 가르치다 initiate《a person》in〔into〕the tricks of the trade // 꽃꽂이를 가르치다 give lessons in flower arrangement // 아이들의 버릇을 가르치다 teach children manners // 어떻게 만드는지 가르쳐 주시오 Show me how to make it. // 젊은 사람들을 가르치는 것은 매우 의미있는 일이다 It is a task of great significance to educate young people.
가르친사위 a stupid person who is unable to do anything by himself
가르침 [교훈] teachings ; a lesson ; an instruction ; [계율] a precept ; [교의] a doctrine ; a dogma ¶ 공자의 가르침 the teachings〔doctrines〕of Confucius // 어머니의 가르침에 따르다 follow one's mother's instructions // 가르침을 받다 receive instruction ; study under《a master》
가름 [분할] cutting ; dividing ; [분류] classifying ; [구별] distinguishing ; judging ; [분배] distributing ; [분리] separating **—하다** ⇨ 가르다
가름대 the crossbar dividing the upper and lower sections of an abacus
가리[1] [물고기 잡는] a weir ; a fish trap ; a fish pound
가리[2] 〖방언〗 an ox rib ; a cut of beef containing a rib ⇨ 갈비
가리[3] [더미] a heap ; a pile ; a stack ; a rick ; accumulation ¶ 땔나무가리 a stack of wood // 건초가리 a haystack ; a hayrack // 노적가리 a pile of harvested rice plants in the open air
가리[4] the drift of an affair ⇨ 가리새[1]
가리가리 to pieces ; to〔into〕shreds ¶ 가리가리 찢다 tear〔rend〕to pieces〔ribbons, shreds, threads〕; tear into strips ; tear piecemeal
가리개 a twofold screen
가리나무 fallen pine needles gathered for fuel
*가리다[1] ① [선택] single〔pick〕out ; sort out ; select ; choose ; make choice of ; prefer ; [구별] discriminate《between》; tell《one thing》from《another》; [음식을] be particular〔fussy〕《about food》¶ 수단을 가리지 않고 by fair means or foul ; by hook or by crook // 선악을 가리다 tell good from bad // 음식을 가리다 be fastidious〔particular〕about food // 모래에서 황금을 가려내다 separate gold from sand // 물불을 가리지 않다 go through fire and water ; be willing to take any risk // 아이가 오줌을 가리다 be grown up enough to go to the toilet by oneself // 목적을 위해서 수단을 가리지 않다 stop at nothing to gain one's end // 친구는 잘 가려서 사귀어야 한다 You must be careful in choosing your friends. // 왜 그렇게 가리는 것이 많은가 Why do you have so many likes and dislikes? // 그 개 대소변은 가립니까 Is the dog housebroken?
② [머리 빗다] comb〔tidy〕one's hair ; give《one's hair》a rough combing ¶ 헝클어진 머리를 가리고 뛰어나갔다 Roughly combing her hair, she rushed out.
③ [아이가 낯을] be shy of strangers ¶ 우리 아이는 매우 낯을 가린다 My baby is very shy of strangers.
④ [셈을] settle〔square〕accounts《with a person》; settle one's accounts ; pay〔settle up〕a《hotel》bill ¶ 그와 셈을 가리다 square accounts with him // 빚을 가리다 settle a debt ; clear off〔up〕one's debts // 손익을 가리다 make a calculation of profit and loss
가리다[2] [쌓다] heap (up) ; pile up ; stack ¶ 산더미처럼 가려 놓다 pile up mountain-high
‡가리다[3] [보이지 않게] hide ; conceal ; shield ; shelter ; screen ; cover ; obstruct ; bury ; cloak ; veil ¶ 우산으로 얼굴을 가리다 screen one's face with one's umbrella // 손수건으로 얼굴을 가리다 bury one's face in one's handkerchief ; cover one's face with a handkerchief // 두 손으로 얼굴을 가리다 cover〔hide〕one's face with one's hands ; sink one's face into one's hands // 손으로 입을 가리다 put a hand over one's mouth // 결점을 가리다 draw a veil over one's fault ; smooth over a fault // 사람의 눈을 가리다 cover up《a person's》eyes ; hoodwink ; deceive // 신문 기자들에게 얼굴을 안 보이려고 모자로 얼굴을 가렸다 He shielded his face from several newspapermen with his hat. // 나무가 해를 가리고 있다 A tree keeps the sun off. // 구름이 태양을 가리고 말았다 The clouds blotted out the sun. // 자욱한 안개에 시계가 가렸다 The dense fog hid my view. // 블라인드로 햇빛을 가렸다 She drew the blind to shade off the sunlight.
가리마 a part (in one's hair) ¶ 한가운데에〔왼쪽에〕가리마를 타다 part one's hair in the middle〔at the left〕
가리맛 〖조개〗 a kind of razor clam ; Sinonovacula constricta (학명)
—살 razor-clam meat
가리비 〖조개〗 a scallop
가리사니 ① [분별] discretion ; prudence ; sense ② [지각] knowledge ; wisdom ③ [실마리] a clue ; the drift of an affair ¶ 가리사니 없는 여자 a senseless〔foolish〕woman // 가리사니를

잡을 수 없다 have no idea ; be unable to figure it out

가리새[1] the drift〔thread〕 of an affair ¶ 어찌된 영문인지 가리새를 모르겠다 I can't make out what it's all about. /I can make nothing of it.

가리새[2] 〖새〗 a spoonbill

가리어지다 become hidden〔concealed〕; get covered〔buried〕; be cloaked〔veiled〕; be screened〔shielded, sheltered〕 ¶ 안개 속에 가리어졌다 The view was hidden by the fog. // 햇빛이 구름에 가리어졌다 The sun was covered by the clouds. // 이 일은 어둠에 가리어져 있다 This matter is enveloped in darkness.

가리온 a white horse with a black mane

가리우다 screen ; obstruct ⇨ 가리다[3]

가리이다 be screened ; be obstructed ¶ 달이 구름에 가리어서 보이지 않았다 The moon was covered by the clouds. // 저 건너 경치가 숲에 가리어서 보이지 않는다 The view is obstructed by a cluster of trees.

†**가리키다** point to〔at〕; indicate ; point out ; show ; denote ; tell ; mean ¶ 손가락으로 사람을 가리키다 point at 《a person》 with one's finger // 자침은 북을 가리킨다 The magnetic needle points to the north. // 온도계는 50도를 가리키고 있다 The thermometer registers〔shows〕 50 degrees. // 표지판의 화살표가 옳은 진로를 가리킨다 The arrow on the sign indicates the right way to go. // 시계 바늘이 정각 12시를 가리킨다 The hands of the clock stands〔indicates〕 at twelve. // 저런 사람을 가리켜 구두쇠라고 한다 We call a man like him a miser. // 나는 특별히 누구를 가리켜 말한 것은 아니었다 I did not mean anyone in particular.

가리틀다 ① [훼방하다] thwart ; hinder ; interrupt ; interfere with 《a plan》; stand in another's way ; work against ② [부당한 요구] demand a share in 《a person's》 windfall〔unexpected gain〕

가린스럽다 (be) miserly ; stingy ; niggardly

가마[1] [머리의] the whirl〔whorl〕 of hair on the crown of the head ; a hair whirl〔whorl〕

가마[2] [가마솥] an iron pot ; a kettle ; a caldron ; [빵 굽는] an oven ; [기와 굽는] a kiln ; a furnace ¶ 기와 굽는 가마 a tile-kiln // 질그릇 굽는 가마 a pottery〔porcelain〕 kiln // 빵 굽는 가마 a baker's oven

가마[3] [탈것] a palanquin ; a sedan chair ¶ 가마를 타다 ride in a sedan chair
가마타고 시집가기는 다 틀렸다 [속담] It is impossible to stand on ceremony.

가마[4] ① [가마니] a bag ; a bale ; a sack ¶ 쌀〔솜〕 열 가마 ten bags of rice〔bales of cotton〕 ② [단위] a group of 100, specially used to count tobacco pouches and tarpaulin bags

가마꾼 a palanquin〔sedan chair〕 bearer

가마노르께하다 (be) dark yellowish

***가마니** a straw bag ; a bale ; a sack ¶ 쌀가마니 a straw rice-bag // 모래를 가마니에 담다 shovel the sand into a straw bag

가마리 a person who is the butt〔the target, the mark, the object〕 of ridicule〔beating, criticism, scolding〕 ¶ 욕가마리 the butt of abuse // 조소가마리 the laughingstock ; the object of ridicule〔derision〕 // 비난가마리 the focus of (public) censure

가마솥 a caldron ; an iron pot ; a large kettle ; [증기] a boiler
가마솥에 콩도 삶아야 먹는다 [속담] No pains, no gains.
가마솥이 노구솥 밑 검다 한다 [속담] The kettle calls the pot black-brows.

가마아득하다 be far-off ; faraway ; distant ¶ 도서관은 여기서 가마아득히 멀다 The library is far away from here. // 봄은 아직도 가마아득히 멀다 The spring is still a long way off. // 전화가 가마아득히 멀다 We have a bad connection. // 저 멀리 가마아득한 수평선 the far-off horizon // 가마아득한 청춘 the far-off days of my youth

가마우지 〖새〗 a cormorant ; Phalacrocorax carbo (학명)

가마채 the shafts of a palanquin

가마호수 一戶首 a fireman〔stoker〕 at a kiln

가막사리 〖식물〗 a kind of cosmos plant ; Bidens tripartita (학명)

가막소 a prison

가막쇠 a door〔window〕 latch

가막조개 a corbicula ; a kind of small shell

가만 ① ⇨ 가만히 ② [조용히] Be silent ! ; Hush ! ; Keep quiet ! ¶ 가만, 누가 온다 Soft ! Someone comes. // 가만, 무슨 소리가 났어 Sh ! I heard a noise (sound). // 가만, 그리 서두를 것 없어 Wait, there is no hurry. ③ [그대로] just as it is ; with no interference ¶ 그녀를 가만히 내버려 두어라 Leave〔Let〕 her alone. // 있는 그대로 가만 두어라 Leave it as it is now.

가만가만 quietly ⇨ 가만히 ¶ 가만가만 걷다 walk softly ; go with soft〔stealthy〕 step

가만두다 leave〔let〕 alone ; leave as it is ; leave undisturbed ; leave intact

가만있다 ① remain still〔quiet〕; keep silent ; stay motionless ; sit still ; stand idle ¶ 한시도 가만있지 않다 do not keep still for a minute // 떠들지 말고 가만있어 Don't make a noise, keep quiet.

ㄱ

ㄱ

② [감탄사로] well ; let me see ; just a minute ¶ 가만있자, 그걸 내가 어디 두었더라 Let me see, where did I put it? // 가만있거라, 이게 누구더라 Well, well, who is this?

가만하다 (be) quiet ¶ 입가에 가만한 미소가 번지다 smile quietly

가만히 [조용히] still ; quietly ; silently ; [살짝·몰래] quietly ; softly ; stealthily ; on the sly ; secretly ; [곰곰이] seriously ; deliberately ; inevitably ¶ 가만히 있다 keep〔stand, sit〕 still ; be〔remain〕 motionless〔quiet〕 ; [방관] look on ; stand by idly // 가만히 기다리다 sit and wait ; wait calmly 《for》 // 가만히 두다 leave 《a thing》 as it is〔alone〕 ; let 《a person》 alone // 가만히 걷다 walk softly 〔stealthily〕 ; walk on tiptoe // 가만히 집을 나가다 steal〔slip〕 out of the house // …을 가만히 보다 steal a glance at 《a person, a thing》 ; look furtively 《at》 // 가만히 방안을 들여다 보다 peek into a room // 가만히 물어보다 ask 《a person》 a question in secret〔privately〕 // 가만히 남의 속을 떠보다 sound (out) 《a person》〔another's views〕 ; fathom another's thoughts ; beat about the bush // 가만히 앉아서 헛되이 세월만 보내다 waste time doing nothing // 가만히 그 일을 생각해 보다 turn the matter over in one's mind // (사진기를 대고) 그대로 가만히 Hold on, please! // 사진을 찍을 동안 가만히 있어라 Don't move while I take your picture. // 더 이상 가만히 못 있겠다 I can't bear〔stand〕 this any longer. // 그 사건에 대해서는 가만히 있는 게 좋겠다 You had better keep the matter in the dark. /You had better keep quiet about it. // 왜 말하지 않고 가만히 있었느냐 Why haven't you told it to me? // 가만히 있어도 책이 잘 팔린다 The book sells well〔steadily〕. // 지난 10년을 가만히 되새겨 본다 I reflect on the past ten years of my life. // 이대로 가만히 당하고만 있을 것인가 How can you suffer the abuse〔disgrace〕 helplessly? // 그는 오늘 데이트가 있어서 흥분하여 가만히 앉아 있을 수가 없다 He's got a date today, so he's so excited he can't sit still. // 아이들이란 가만히 있으려 들지 않는다 Kids simply won't stay put.

가말다 manage ; conduct ; dispose of ; deal with ; take care of 《a matter》

†**가망 可望** hope ; promise ; [전망] prospect ; [가능성] likelihood ; probability ; possibility ; chance(s) ; odds ¶ 가망이 있다 be promising〔hopeful〕 ; have a bright prospect〔future〕 ; bid fair 《to succeed》 // 가망이 없다 be hopeless ; be unpromising // …할 가망이 꽤 있다 there is a fair chance 《that》 ; the odds are pretty fair 《that》 // 시험에 합격할 가망이 없다 He is not likely to pass the examination. // 이길 가망이 없다 The chances〔odds〕 are against me. // 그녀는 회복할 가망이 없다고 의사가 말한다 The doctor gives no hope for her recovery. // 오늘 돌아올 가망은 거의 없다 There is little〔small〕 likelihood of his returning〔that he will return〕 today. /He is not likely to return today. // 열전이 금방 일어날 가망은 없다 Fierce warfare 〔fighting〕 is not an immediate prospect. // 군축 협상의 실질적 진전은 가망이 희박하다 The chances of substantial progress in the disarmament talks appear slim. // 네가 이길 가망은 십중팔구 없다 The odds are ten to one against your winning. // 너는 가망이 전혀 없다 You don't have a chance. /Not a chance. /You don't have a prayer. /Not a prayer. // 나같은 사람은 가망성이 없다 Someone like me doesn't stand a chance.

가맣다, 까맣다 ① [검다] (be) black ; dark

② [아득하다] (be) far ; far off〔away〕 ; be in the distance ; be beyond one's reach ; be long way off 《perfection》 ¶ 북한산이 가맣게 보인다 We see *Puk'ansan* far away. // 서울까지는 아직도 가맣다 It is a long way yet to *Seoul*. // 먼 바다에 가맣게 흰 돛단배가 보인다 A white sail is seen far out at sea. // 완벽한 영어를 하기에는 아직도 가맣다 His English is still far from perfection.

③ [전혀 모르다] (be) utterly ignorant ; forgotten ¶ 가맣게 모르다 know nothing about // 가맣게 잊다 have long 〔clean, completely〕 forgotten // 그렇게 신신당부하였는데도 가맣게 잊고 있다니 How could you have completely forgotten what I have asked you over and again? // 그 사람은 법률에 대해서는 아주 가맣다 He is utterly ignorant of law.

가매 假寐 [졸음] a nap ; a doze ; [거짓 졸음] sham〔feigned〕 sleep

가매장 假埋葬 temporary burial **—하다** bury 《a person》 temporarily ¶ 행려병사자를 가매장하다 bury the body of a charity patient temporarily

가매지다 ⇨ 까매지다

가맹 加盟 joining ; affiliation ; participation **—하다** join ; be affiliated 《with》 ; become a member 《of》 ; participate 《in》 ¶ 조합에 가맹하다 join an association // 국제 연맹에 가맹하다 join the United Nations

— 단체 a member organization **—자 (者)** a participant ; a member **— 조합** 〖노동〗 an affiliated union

가맹국 加盟國 a member nation 《of the United Nations》

***가면 假面** ① [탈] a mask ; a dis-

guise ; a cloak ¶ 가면을 쓰다 wear a mask ; mask one's face ; put on a mask // 가면을 벗다 unmask ; throw off 〔put off, take off〕 the mask 《of》; show one's true colors (정체) // 가면을 벗기다 unmask〔take off the mask of〕《a villain》 ② [위선] play the hypocrite ¶ 자선이란 가면을 쓰고 under the mask〔cloak, color〕 of charity
—극 a masque — 무도회 a masked ball ; a masquerade

가면허 假免許 a temporary〔provisional〕 license

가명 假名 an assumed name ; an alias ; [필명] a pen name ; a pseudonym ¶ 가명으로 under an assumed name ; under a pseudonym // 존슨이란 가명으로 통하다 go by the alias of Johnson

가모 家母 ① [자기 어머니] my mother ; Mother ② a housewife (주부)

가묘 家廟 a family shrine

가무 歌舞 singing and dancing ; all musical and other entertainments ¶ 가무를 즐기다 indulge in merriment // 가무곡 일체가 금지되었다 The government ordered a suspension of all public performances of music and dancing.

가무러지다, 까무러지다 faint (away) ; become faint 《with》; swoon ¶ 공복으로〔더위로〕 까무러지다 faint with hunger〔from the heat〕

가무러치다, 까무러치다 faint (away) ; swoon ; suffer a fainting fit ; fall senseless〔unconscious〕 ¶ 얻어맞고 까무러치다 be stunned ; be knocked unconscious // 까무러칠 듯이 놀라다 be frightened out of one's senses〔wits〕 // 그녀는 그 소식을 듣고 까무러쳤다 She fainted 〔swooned〕 at the news.

가무리다 make away with surreptitiously ; steal 《a thing》 unnoticed

가무스름하다 blackish

⁑**가문 家門** one's family〔clan〕 ¶ 가문의 명예 a credit〔an honor〕 to one's family // 가문을 더럽히다 bring disgrace on one's family ; disgrace one's family // 좋은 가문에 태어나다 come of (a) good stock〔a good family〕 // 가문을 흐리게 하다 disgrace one's family

***가문비나무** 〖식물〗 a spruce ; a silver fir ; Picea jezoensis (학명)

가문서 假文書 a forged〔false〕 document

***가물** dry weather ; a drought ; a drouth ; a dry spell ; want of rain ¶ 오랜 가물 a long drought ; a (long) spell of dry weather // 가물철 the dry season // 한 달 이상이나 가물이 들다 have a drought for over one month // 올해는 가물어서 흉작이었다 Owing to the drought, the crops have failed this year. /Due to the long drought, the farmers have had poor crops this year. // 벼는 가물을 잘 탄다 The rice crop is easily damaged by droughts. // 전역에 걸쳐 가물이 격심하다 Over the area droughty conditions prevail.
가물에 콩 나듯하다 속담 be very rare ; be few and far between

가물가물 ① [불·빛·물체가] flickeringly ; blinkingly ; dimly ; hazily ¶ 먼 수평선 위에 가물가물 움직이는 고깃배들 fishing boats flickering on the distant horizon // 등불이 가물가물하다가 꺼졌다 The light flickered out. ② [정신이] ¶ 기억이 가물가물하다 have a dim〔faint〕 memory

가물거리다 ① [불빛이] flicker ; gleam ; glimmer ¶ 가물거리는 불빛 a flickering light // 촛불이 바람에 가물거렸다 The candle flickered in the breeze.
② [먼 곳의 물건이나 정신이] be dim ; be misty ; grow hazy ; be blurred ; blink ; loom ¶ 멀리서 가물거리는 섬 an island dim in the distance // 가물거리는 기억 a faint〔dreamy〕 memory // 가물거리는 과거의 추억 misty recollections of the past // 그는 가물거리는 기억을 더듬어 가며 당시의 감격을 말했다 Tracing back his vague memory, he explained how deeply he was impressed. // 수면 부족으로 정신이 가물거린다 I feel my brain muddled owing to want of sleep.

***가물다** 《the weather》 (be) droughty ; dry ; rainless ; arid ¶ 계절치고는 날씨가 가물다 It is very dry for this season of the year. // 가뭄이 계속되어 저수지 바닥이 갈라졌다 The long drought exposed the cracked floor of the reservoir.

가물들다 ① [날씨가] become droughty ; enter a period of drought ¶ 날씨가 가물들다 a drought sets in ; have a spell of dry weather
② [피해·부족] suffer from a drought ¶ 인재에 가물들다 suffer from a shortage of talented people

가물음 drought ⇨ 가물

가물치 〖물고기〗 a snake fish ; a snakehead ; a mullet ; Channa argus (학명)

가뭄 ⇨ 가물

가뭇가뭇 dotted〔spotted〕 with black — **하다** be dotted〔speckled〕 with black

가뭇없다 [보이던 것이] be nowhere to be seen ; leave no trace〔clue〕 behind ; [소식이] hear nothing of 《a person》 ¶ 그의 소식은 가뭇없다 His whereabouts are utterly unknown. // 수평선에 아른거리던 배들이 가뭇없게 사라졌다 The boats dim on the distant horizon have just disappeared.

가뭇하다 (be) blackish ⇨ 가무스름하다

가미 加味 — **하다** [맛을 더하다] season〔flavor〕 《a thing》 with ; [부가하다] add ; introduce ; [다른 약제를] add 《something》 to a regular medical prescription ¶ 교육 제도에 종교를 가미하

다 introduce religion into the educational system // 법에 인정을 가미하다 temper justice with mercy

가발 假髮 a wig ; false hair ; toupee (대머리용) ¶ 가발을 쓰다 wear a wig // 가발이 벗겨졌다 His wig slipped off〔fell off〕.

†가방 a bag ; [소형] a handbag ; a valise ; a suitcase ; a briefcase ; [대형] a trunk ¶ 가방에 넣다 put into a bag // 가방에서 꺼내다 take〔get〕 out of a bag

가배 嘉俳 a game played in *Silla* times on midautumn day ; the midautumn festival day (가윗날)

가법 家法 family rules ; a family tradition ; household etiquette

가법 加法 〖수학〗 addition

가변 可變 variableness ; changeableness ; [형용사적] variable ; changeable — 발동기 a variable engine —익(翼) variable wings — 전압 발전기 a variable voltage generator — 행정(行程) 펌프 a variable stroke pump

가변 비용 可變費用 variable expenses

가변 자본 可變資本 variable capital

가변 저항기 可變抵抗器 a variable resistor ; a rheostat

가변 콘덴서〔축전기〕 可變—〔蓄電器〕 〖전기〗 a variable condenser

*가볍다 ① [무게] (be) light ¶ 가벼운 짐 a light load〔baggage〕 // 짐을 가볍게 하다 lighten a burden // 체중이 가볍다 be light in weight ; one's weight is light

② [경미] (be) slight ; mild ¶ 가벼운 병 a slight illness // 가벼운 범죄 minor offense // 가벼운 위궤양 a mild stomach ulcer // 가벼운 일사병 a touch of the sun // 가벼운 상처 a slight wound 〔injury〕 // 가벼운 농담 a slight jest 〔joke〕

③ [경솔] (be) careless ; imprudent ; thoughtless ; undignified ; rash ; frivolous ; flippant ¶ 가볍게 굴다 act imprudently // 입이 가볍다 He cannot keep a secret. / He is talkative. /He has a loose tongue. / He is indiscreet in his speech.

④ [비중·가치] (be) insignificant ; unimportant ; trivial ¶ 책임이 가볍다 be not in a very responsible position // 가볍게 여기다 take 《a thing》 lightly ; make light of 《a thing》 ; despise ; look down upon // 목숨을 가벼이 여기다 make〔think〕 nothing of one's life ; hold one's life as of no account

⑤ [감정·기분·옷차림 따위가] (be) easy ; simple ; plain ; light ¶ 가벼운 식사 a light meal〔snack〕 // 가벼운 걸음으로 with a springy step ; lightly ; buoyantly // 가벼운 기분으로 with a light heart // 가벼운 읽을거리 light〔easy〕 reading // 가벼운 감기 a slight cold // 부드러운 바람이 가볍게 불어온다 There is a gentle breeze.

⑥ [다루기가 쉽다] easy ; light ¶ 상대 선수를 가볍게 물리치다 beat the rival champion with ease

가보 nine-point hand 《화투의 아홉 끗》

가보 家寶 a family treasure ; an heirloom ¶ 역대의 가보 an heirloom of the family handed down for generations // 그 그림은 가보로 소중히 간수되고 있다 The picture is treasured as an heirloom in the family.

가보 家譜 a family tree ; genealogy ; lineage ; pedigree ; a genealogical table 〔chart〕

가복 家僕 a (man) servant ; a domestic

가본 假本 a counterfeit copy 《of books, calligraphy, pictures》 ; a spurious edition

가봉 假縫 basting ; tacking ; the first fitting —하다 baste ; tack ; [양복 따위를] fit on ; try on ¶ 가봉이 다 되었습니다 Your suit is ready for trying on. / We are ready to fit you.

가부 可否 [옳고 그름] right or wrong ; good or bad ; [찬부] aye〔yes〕 and no ; pro and con ; for and against ; [적부] advisability ; propriety ; proper or improper ¶ 가부간 right or wrong ; anyhow ; in any case // 가부를 논하다 argue for and against 《a matter》 ; argue pro and con // 법안의 가부를 투표에 붙이다 have a vote on a bill // 상정된 의안의 가부를 묻다 take a vote on the proposed bill // 이 문제에 관해서는 가부 양론이 있었다 There were pros and cons on this question. // 남녀 공학의 가부를 논했다 They argued about the advisability of coeducation. // 가부가 상반되었다 The votes were equally divided. // 가부 동수인 경우에는 의장이 이를 결정한다 In case of a tie, the presiding officer shall decide the issue. // 가부간 빨리 알려주세요 At any rate, please let me know the result.

가부 家父 my father ; Father

가부 家夫 my husband ; [아내에게] I, your husband

가부장 家父長 〖법〗 a paterfamilias ; a patriarch (남자) ; a matriarch (여자) ⇨ 가장(家長)

가분가분 lightly ; nimbly ; easily ; airily ; gently —하다 (be) light ; nimble ¶ 날 듯이 가분가분 언덕을 내려가다 go down a hill nimbly // 손에 든 짐들이 모두 가분가분하다 All the package in his hands are light.

가분수 假分數 an improper fraction

가분하다 (be) light ; be not heavy ; (be) nimble (민첩하다) ¶ 가뿐히 lightly ; easily ; without effort ; [동작·마음 따위] gently ; nimbly ; easily // 잘못을 털어놓고 나니 마음이 가뿐하다 one's mind is relieved of one's burden〔anxiety〕

가불 假拂 [미리 주는] an advance ; advance payment ; [임시로 주는] suspense payment ; a temporary advance **— 하다** pay in advance ; advance ; draw 《a part of one's salary》 in advance ¶ 고용주에게 1개월 분의 봉급을 가불해 달라고 신청했다 He asked his employer to advance him a month's salary. // 그는 가불받은 돈으로 집세를 냈다 He used the advance to pay the rent. // 나는 매달 월급을 가불한다 I draw my salary in advance every month. // 내 봉급에서 가불 좀 해주실 수 없겠습니까 Can't you give me an advance on my salary?

가불가 可不可 ⇨ 가부(可否)

가붓가붓 — 하다 (be) light ; very light

가빈 家貧 domestic poverty **— 하다** be of a poor family

가뿐하다 ⇨ 가분하다

가뿟가뿟 ⇨ 가붓가붓

가뿟하다 (be) rather light

***가쁘다** ① [숨이] be out of breath ; gasp for breath ; pant ② [힘겹다] (be) hard ; trying ¶ 가쁜 일 hard work // 숨이 가쁘다 be short of breath

가사 假死 syncope ; suspended animation ; apparent death ¶ 그는 가사 상태에 빠져 있다 He is in a state of suspended animation.

가사 家事 household〔domestic〕 duties ; household affairs ; family matters ; housekeeping ; housework ¶ 가사를 처리하다 manage household duties ; take care of household affairs // 가사 형편으로 for family reasons // 그 여자가 가사를 돌봐 주고 있다 She keeps house for me. // 그녀는 가사에 얽매였다 She is tied up with household chores. // 그녀는 가사에 쫓긴다 She is busy with her housework.

—비 household expenses

가사 歌詞 the words of a song ; words ; the text ; the libretto (오페라의) ¶ 하이네 작의 가사 words by Heine // 곡이 가사에 꼭 들어맞는다 The tune exactly fits the words.

—집 a wordbook

가사 歌辭 an old form of Korean verse

가사 袈裟 a surplice ; a stole ; a cope ; a monk's robe

가산 加算 addition ; inclusion **— 하다** add ; include (산입하다) ¶ 이자를 가산하다 include interest to 《principal》

—액 [원가에 대한] markup

가산 家産 family property〔estate〕 ¶ 가산을 모으다〔탕진하다〕 make〔squander〕 one's fortune // 가산이 기울었다 His fortune began to ebb.

가산금 加算金 additional charges ; a fine for default (세금 체납시의)

가산 · 불가산 명사 可算 · 不可算名詞 countable and uncountable nouns

가산세 加算稅 an additional tax

가살 a hateful stuck-up attitude

가살(을) 떨다 [관용] behave detestably

가살(을) 부리다 [관용] behave in a hateful stuck-up way ; display nasty behavior

가살(을) 빼다 [관용] behave provocatively

가살스럽다 be stuck-up and hateful

가살쟁이 a hateful stuck-up〔arrogant〕 person

가삼 家蔘 cultivated〔farmed〕 ginseng ⇔ 산삼

가상 假象 a semblance ; an appearance

가상 假像 a ghost ; a secondary〔false〕 image ; [광물에서의] a pseudomorph

가상 假想 imagination ; supposition **— 하다** imagine ; assume ; suppose ¶ 가상적인 imaginary ; assumed ; hypothetical // 가상적인 상황 a hypothetical condition

— 변위(變位) 〖기계〗 virtual displacement **— 원자전** a simulated atomic war **— 적(국)** a hypothetical〔an imaginary, a potential, a supposed〕 enemy **— 질량** virtual mass

가상하다 嘉尙— approve 《of》 ; commend ; praise ¶ 선행을 가상히 여기다 commend 《a person》 for his good act

가새지르다 cross 《each other》 ; intersect 《each other》 ; join crosswise ; cut across ¶ 두 선이 가새지르는 점 the junction of two lines // 총을 가새지르다 stack arms // 깃대를 가새지르다 The flag poles are crossed.

가서 家書 a letter from〔to〕 one's home

가석 可惜 — 하다 (be) regrettable ; deplorable ; lamentable ; unfortunate ¶ 가석하게도 to one's regret // 가석한 일이다 It is to be regretted 《that》 ; It is a matter for regret 《that》 ; It is a pity 《that》 ; I am sorry 《that》 ; It is too bad 《that》 // 그의 죽음은 참으로 가석한 일이다 His death cannot be too much deplored.

가석방 假釋放 parole ; [가출옥] (a) release on parole **— 하다** release 《a person》 on parole ¶ 가석방되다 be paroled

—자 a criminal on parole ; a parolee 《미》

가선 —線 ① [옷의] the hem ; the border ② [눈의] the wrinkles of a double eyelid fold ¶ 가선이 졌다 Wrinkles started around his eyes.

가선을 두르다 [관용] hem 《a handkerchief》 ; put a border on 《an apron》 ; edge ; rim

가선 架線 wiring (공사) ; a wire (선)

—공 a lineman **— 공사** wiring work **— 교** [신호 장치의] 〖철도〗 a gantry

ㄱ

*가설 架設 construction ; installation — 하다 build ; construct ; [전화 따위를] install ; [전선 따위를] lay ¶ 전화를 가설하다 install a telephone // 강에 다리를 가설하다 build a bridge over a river ; span a river with a bridge // 가설 중이다 be under construction ; be in process of being installed
— 공사 building〔construction〕 work —도 an erection diagram〔drawing〕 —비 the building〔installation〕 cost —응력(應力) erection stress

*가설 假設 ① [일시적] temporary installation ② [상정] hypothesis ; supposition ; 〖법〗 fiction — 하다 install temporarily ; suppose ; assume ¶ 가설의 temporary ; provisional ; hypothetic(al) // 가설 사무소를 열다 open a temporary office
—각 a hypothetical〔given〕 angle — 건축물 a temporary construction〔building〕 —교 a temporary bridge — 극장 a temporary theater — 무대 makeshift stage —인 〖법〗 a fictitious person — 정거장 a temporary station — 주택 a temporary dwelling —철도 [건설 공사를 위한] a construction railway

가설 假說 〖논리〗 a hypothesis ; [가정] an assumption ; a supposition ¶ 가설적 hypothetical // 가설을 세우다 hypothesize ; assume
— 추리 hypothetic inference

가성 家聲 the family honor ⇨ 가명(家名)

가성 苛性 〖화학〗 causticity ¶ 가성의 caustic // 가성 칼리〔소다〕 caustic potash〔soda〕 // 가성 알칼리 caustic alkali // 가성 알코올 caustic alcohol

가성 假聲 a feigned〔an assumed〕 voice ; falsetto (음악) ¶ 가성을 내다 disguise one's voice ; make up the voice

가성 근시 假性近視 false nearsightedness

가성대 假聲帶 〖해부〗 a false vocal cord

가세 加勢 help ; assistance ; aid ; support ; backing ; [원병] reinforcements — 하다 help ; aid ; assist ; back ; give support to ; line up with ; stand by ; take the side of ; take sides〔a side〕 with ; side with ; [변론에서] plead〔speak〕 for another ; reinforce (원병) ¶ 약한 편에 가세하다 take side with〔stand by〕 the weaker // 적에게 가세하다 line up with the enemy

가세 家勢 a family's financial condition〔economic circumstances〕 ¶ 가세가 넉넉하다〔넉넉하지 못하다〕 be well〔badly〕 off // 가세가 기운 집안 a family fortune on the wane

가소 可塑 ¶ 가소의 plastic // 가소성 물질 plastics

가소롭다 可笑— (be) laughable ; ridiculous ; silly ; absurd ¶ 하찮은 상대가 겨루겠다니 가소롭다 It is ridiculous that a little squirt like him should challenge me to a game.

가소물 可塑物 plastics

가소성 可塑性 plasticity

가속 家屬 (the members of) a family〔household〕 ; one's people

가속 加速 〖물리〗 acceleration ⇔ 감속(deceleration) ¶ 가속적 accelerative // 가속적으로 with increasing speed — 하다 accelerate ; speed up ; soup up 《미·속》
—기(器) an accelerator —력 accelerating〔acceleration〕 force — 로켓 a booster (rocket) — 보행 〖의학〗 festination — 온수 난방 accelerated hot water heating — 운동 an accelerated motion ; quickened movement — 장치 an accelerator — 전극(電極) an accelerating〔acceleration〕 electrode — 전압 acceleration voltage — 펌프 an accelerator pump — 페달 an accelerator pedal 등(等) — 운동 a uniformly accelerated motion 입자(粒子) — 장치 a particle accelerator

가속도 加速度 (degree of) acceleration
—계(計) an accelerometer ; 〖항공〗 a G-meter — 계수(係數) 〖경제〗 an acceleration coefficient — 곡선 an accelerating curve —병(病) 〖의학〗 kinetosis — 운동 an accelerated motion — 원리 〖경제〗 the acceleration principle — 지진계 an accelerograph 정(正)〔등(等), 부등, 발동〕— normal〔uniform, variable, starting〕 acceleration 중력 — acceleration of gravity 내(耐)—복(服) 〖항공〗 an anti-G suit ; a G suit

가솔 家率 one's family ; members of one's family

*가솔린 gasoline ; gas 《미》 ; petrol 《영》 ; juice 《속》
— 보급 a fill-up 《미》 — 엔진 a gasoline engine —차 a gasoline car

‡가수 歌手 a singer ; a vocalist ; a vocal performer
여자 — a woman singer ; a songstress
오페라 — an opera(tic) singer 유행가 — singer of popular songs ; a pop singer ; a crooner 《미·속》

가수 假數 〖수학〗 a mantissa

가수 假睡 a feigned sleep

가수금 假受金 a suspense receipt

가수 분해 加水分解 〖화학〗 hydrolysis — 하다 hydrolyze ; decompose in water

가수요 假需要 imaginary demand ; fictitious use ; [투기] speculative demand

†가스 gas ; natural gas ; coal gas ¶ 가스를 켜다〔끄다〕 turn on〔off〕 the gas // 가스불을 크게〔작게〕 하다 turn up〔down〕 the gas // 가스를 쓰다 burn〔use〕 the

gas // 가스를 끌다 lay on gas // 가스불로 요리하다 cook food by gas // 가스가 새다 the gas escapes // 뱃속에 가스가 괴다 have gas〔wind〕 in the bowels // 가스가 나오고〔나오지 않고〕 있다 The gas is on〔off〕. // 배에 가스가 차다 have gas 〔wind〕 in the bowels // 그는 가스 중독이 었다 He was gassed.

— 계량기(計量器) a gas meter ; a gasometer ; an aerometer — 공사 gas fitting work — 관〔파이프〕 a gas pipe ; a gas main — 기관〔엔진〕 a gas engine — 난로 a gas stove ; a gas heater — 난방 gas heating — 라이터 a gas lighter — 발동기 a gas motor — 버너 a gas burner — 원심 분리기 gas centrifuge — 오븐 a gas oven — 온도계 a gas thermometer — 요금(料金) gas rate — 요금 징수인 a gasman — 용접 gas〔autogenous〕 welding — 전지 a gas battery〔cell〕 — 조절기 a gas regulator — 중독 gas poisoning —탄(彈) a gas shell — 탱크 a gas tank ; a gasometer — 폭발 a gas explosion — 화학 gas chemistry — 회사 a gas company 가정용 — household gas 도시 — city gas 독(毒)— poison gas 등화용 — illuminating gas 천연 — natural gas

가스등 —燈 a gas lamp

가스 레인지 a gas range ; gas cooker 《영》 ; gas stove

가스러지다 [성질이] become intractable ; [잔털이] bristle

가스 마스크 a gas mask

가스 성운 —星雲 a gaseous nebula

가스실 —室 a gas chamber ; a gas oven

가스 연료 —燃料 gas fuel

가슬가슬 **—하다** [성질이] (be) intractable ; [살결이] (be) rough ⇨ 거슬거슬

†**가슴** [흉부] the breast ; the chest ; the bosom ; the bust (여자의) ; [마음] the heart ; the bosom ; the mind ; [의복의] the breast

> 참고 **breast**는 가슴의 앞쪽 특히 유방을 가리키며 부인 앞에서는 대신 **bosom**을 사용하는 편이 좋겠다 **chest**는 「가슴 전체」 **heart**는 추상적으로 「가슴」을 말한다

¶ 가슴을 드러낸 bare-bosomed // 가슴이 풍만한 full-bosomed ; busty // (여자가) 가슴이 납작하다 be (flat-)chested ; saggy 가슴이 아프다 have a pain in the chest // 그의 이야기를 듣고 가슴이 아팠다 It pained my heart to hear his story. // 가슴이 답답하다 feel oppressed in the breast〔chest〕 ; one's heart is choked 《with》 // 가슴이 뭉클해지다 feel very sad ; one's heart is choked with emotion ; feel a lump (rise) in one's throat // 가슴이 터지도록 울다 cry〔sob〕 one's heart out // 슬픔으로 가슴이 찢어질 듯하다 one's heart almost bursts with grief // 가슴이 뛰다〔두근거리다〕 one's heart throbs〔beats fast, leaps〕 ; one's heart leaps〔jumps〕 up // 가슴이 후련하다 feel much relieved // 기대로 가슴이 부풀다 be buoyant with expectations // 가슴에 사무치다 pierce〔come home to〕 one's heart ; cut〔sting〕 to the heart // 가슴에 품다 embrace ; hold in one's arms ; hug ; [희망·원한 따위를] bear ; hold ; entertain ; cherish ; harbor // 가슴을 쓰다듬다 pass one's hand over one's chest ; [안심] feel relieved ; have a sigh of relief // 가슴을 펴다 throw out one's breast // 아버님의 훈계는 가슴을 찌르는 듯했다 My father's reproof went home to my heart // 가슴에 훈장을 달다 wear a decoration on one's breast // 가슴을 태우다 pine〔sigh〕 for ; burn with passion 《for a person》 // 그 여자는 미끈한 다리 풍만한 가슴 멋있는 곡선미하며 다 갖췄군 She is leggy, bosomy, curvacious, everything.

가슴을 앓다 관용 have a chest trouble ; fret oneself

가슴걸이 a martingal(e) ¶ 가슴걸이식 마구 breast harness

가슴둘레 the girth ; the bust (양장의)

가슴속 one's mind ; one's intention ; one's inmost thoughts ¶ 가슴속을 털어놓다 unbosom oneself ; open one's mind〔heart〕 ; make a clean breast of // 가슴속 깊이 간직했다 She kept it 〔locked it up〕 in her heart.

가슴앓이 heartburn ; a sour stomach ; pyrosis ; cardialgia ¶ 가슴앓이를 앓다 have (a) heartburn

가슴지느러미 a pectoral (fin)

가슴츠레하다 (be) sleepy-〔drowsy-〕 eyed ; sleepy-looking ¶ 잠이 와서 눈이 가슴츠레하구나 Your eyes look heavy. / You are heavy-eyed.

가슴털 hair on the chest ; [새의] breast down ¶ 가슴털이 난 남자 a man with a hairy chest ; a hairy-chested man

가슴통 the chest ; [너비] the breadth of the chest

가슴패기 the chest 《속》 ⇨ 가슴통

가습 加濕 〖건축〗 [공기의] humidification **—하다** humidify

가습기 a humidifier

*****가시**¹ [장미 등의] a thorn ; [풀잎의] a prickle ; [밤송이의] a bur ; [생선의] a spine ; a fish bone ; [살에 박힌] a splinter ; [눈의 가시] an eyesore ; an encumbrance ¶ 가시가 있는 thorny ; prickly ; spined // 손가락에 가시가 박히다 run a thorn〔splinter〕 into one's finger // 가시를 빼다 pull〔draw〕 out a thorn ; extract a thorn // 가시 돋친 말 harsh language ; stinging words // 그의 말에는

ㄱ

가시가 있다 He has a biting tongue./His words carry a sting. //가시 많은 나무 a thorny plant//목소리엔 가시가 돋쳐 있었다 There was an edge to his voice. //그는 나를 눈엣가시로 여긴다 He thinks I am a pain in the neck. //손을 장미 가시에 찔리다 get a hand pricked by a thorn
— 면류관 a crown of thorns —섶 thorny firewood
가시 세다 관용 (be) stubborn; obstinate; stiff-necked; unyielding

가시 거리 可視距離 visibility range

가시 (광)선 可視(光)線 a visible ray

가시나무 ① [가시 있는 나무] a bramble; a thorn
② 〖식물〗 [가시목] the white oak
가시나무에 가시 난다 속담 One cannot gather grapes of thorns or figs of thistles.

*가시다 ① [씻다] wash (out); rinse (off) ¶ 입을 가시다 rinse〔wash out〕 the mouth 《with water》; take away the aftertaste from one's mouth//병을 가시다 rinse out a bottle//물로 가시다 rinse in clear water
② [없어지다] leave; abate; be gone; disappear; vanish; get out of sight ¶ 상처가 가시다 the scar dies away〔disappears〕//애티가 가시다 grow up; outgrow one's childish habits//고통이 가셨다 The pain is gone〔has left me〕./The pain is eased. //취기가 가실 때까지 그냥 쉬고 있을 생각이다 I think I'll relax here a little until the alcohol wears off.

가시덤불 a thornbush; a thorn thicket; a bramble ¶ 가시덤불길 a thorny path

가시랭이 a scrap of a thorn〔prickle〕

가시밭 a thornbush; a thorn thicket; brambles ¶ 가시밭길을 걷다 follow a thorny path〔road〕//가시밭을 헤쳐 나가다 make one's way through thornbushes

가시버시 man and wife; a couple

가시철 —鐵 barbed wire
—망 (barbed) wire entanglements

가식 假飾 affectation; pretense; hypocrisy; ostentation —하다 make an outward show; keep up appearances; put a good face on 《a matter》; play the hypocrite; pretend; affect ¶ 가식의 false; affected; hypocritical//가식적인 ostentatious; showy

가신 家信 a message〔letter〕 from one's home ⇨ 가서

가신 家臣 a retainer; a vassal

가신 家神 a guardian; deity of one's family

가심 washing; rinsing; [뒷맛을] taking away the aftertaste from one's mouth —하다 wash; rinse

*가십 gossip

가압 加壓 pressurization —하다 pressurize; apply〔give〕 pressure 《to》

가압류 假押留 〖법〗 provisional seizure〔attachment〕 —하다 put under provisional attachment; attach〔seize〕 《another's》 property provisionally//그들의 동산이 가압류되었다 Their goods were seized provisionally.
— 결정 a ruling of provisional attachment — 영장 a writ of attachment

가야금 伽倻琴 a *kayakum*; a Korean musical instrument with twelve strings

가약 佳約 ① [연인의] a lover's rendezvous ② the pledge of eternal love; a marriage vow ¶ 백년 가약을 맺다 pledge one's eternal love; get married; become man and wife

가얏고 ⇨ 가야금

가양(주) 家釀(酒) home-brewed liquor

가언 假言 〖논리〗 a hypothesis ⇨ 가설(假說)
—적 명제 a hypothetical proposition —적 판단 hypothetical judgment

가업 家業 [직업] one's trade〔occupation, business, calling, vocation, profession〕; a family occupation; the traditional occupation of a family (세업) ¶ 가업은 목수다 be a carpenter by trade//가업을 잇다 succeed to one's father's occupation//가업에 힘쓰다 attend closely to one's trade; be diligent in one's trade; pursue one's business in earnest〔with diligence〕//가업을 게을리하다 neglect one's business //그는 가업이 무엇인가 What trade is he in?/What is his trade?/What is he by trade? //그는 가업을 물려받기 위해 귀국했다 He went home to take over the family business.

가없다 (be) endless; boundless ¶ 가없이 endlessly; eternally//가없이 넓은 바다 a boundless ocean

가역 可逆 ¶ 가역의 reversible
— 기관 a reversible engine — 레벨 a reversible level — 승압기(昇壓器) a reversible booster — 압연기(壓延機) a reversing rolling mill — 전동기 a reversible motor — 전지 a reversible cell — 진자(振子) a reversible pendulum

가역 반응 可逆反應 〖화학〗 reversible reaction

가역 변화 可逆變化 〖화학〗 reversible change

가연 佳宴 a pleasant party

가연 佳緣 a good〔desirable〕 match

가연물 可燃物 combustibles; inflammables

가연성 可燃性 combustibility; inflammability ¶ 가연성의 combustible; flammable; inflammable

*가열 加熱 heating —하다 heat; apply

heat to ¶ 가열하여 살균하다 sterilize by heating ; heat-treat 《milk》// 가열하여 압착하다 hot-press 《a thing》
— 곡선 a heating curve —기 a heater ; a heating device —대(帶) a heating zone — 면적 a heating area — 분해 decomposition by heating — 시험 a heating〔heat〕 test — 압착기〔프레스〕 a hot-press — 야금법(冶金法) pyrometallurgy — 열화(劣化) heat deterioration —염(炎) a heating flame —선 a hot wire — 착색(着色) heat tinting

*가엾다 (be) poor ; pitiable ; pitiful ; sad ; pathetic ; touching ¶ 가엾은 고아 a poor orphan // 가엾은 이야기 a sad 〔pitiful〕 story // 가엾게 여기다 pity 《a person》 ; take pity on 《a person》 ; have compassion for 《a person》 // 가엾게 여겨 out of pity〔sympathy〕 // 가엾어라 What a pity ! /Poor thing〔girl, child〕! // 가엾게 생각하여 살려 주시오 For pity's sake, save the poor fellow. /Spare him out of pity. // 그녀는 매우 가엾다 She deserves our pity. /She is very much to be pitied.

가오리 〚물고기〛 a stingray ; a stingaree

가옥 家屋 a house ; a building ; 〚법〛 messuage ¶ 가옥 토지 매매에 종사하다 deal in real estate // 가옥을 수리하다 repair a house
— 감가 상각비(減價償却費) the depreciation expense of a house — 내용 연한(耐用年限) the life time of a house — 대장 a house register〔ledger〕 — 배수관 a house drain — 번호 a house number — 세법 the House Tax Law —세 부과 대장 a house-tax ledger — 유지〔관리, 수선〕비 the upkeep〔managing, repairing〕 expense of a house — 하수관 a house sewer

가옥 假屋 a temporary shed ; a shanty

가옥세 家屋稅 a house tax

가외 加外 extra ; excess ; surplus ¶ 가외의 extra ; excessive ; spare ; superfluous // 가욋일을 하다 do extra work ; work overtime // 가욋돈을 가지다 carry some extra money ; have some money to spare
— 비용 extra expense — 수입 extra income — 시간 time to spare 가욋돈 extra money ; money to spare 가욋일꾼 extra workers (or hands)

가외로 加外— extra ; additionally ¶ 가외로 하나 더 얹어 주다 give an extra

가욋일 加外— extra work

가요 歌謠 a song ; a ballad ; an air ; a lied
— 작가 a songwriter 대중 — a popular song 한국 —사 a history of Korean songs and ballads

가요계 歌謠界 the world of singers ¶ 1995년 가요계에는 수많은 반짝 가수들이 나타났다 사라졌지 1995 saw a bunch of flashes in the pan in the pop music industry.

가요곡 歌謠曲 [민요] a folksong ; [대중가요] a popular song

가요제 歌謠祭 a song festival

가용 家用 ① [집안의 씀씀이] household expenses ; living expenses ; the cost of living ¶ 시골 살림은 도회지 살림보다 가용이 덜 든다 Living in the country is less expensive〔costs less〕 than in the city.
② [집에서 쓸] domestic use ; home consumption ; private use

가용 可溶 soluble
—물 a soluble (body) —성 전분 soluble starch — 양극(陽極) a soluble anode —화(化) solubilization

가용 可鎔 fusible
—금 a fusible metal —물 a fusible (body) —성 fusibility — 합금 a fusible alloy

가용성 可溶性 solubility

가용 인구 可容人口 supportable population

가우스 〚전기〛 a gauss 《전자(電磁)의 단위로 기호는 G》

*가운 a gown ; [법복] robe ; [야회복] evening gown

가운 家運 the fortunes of a family ¶ 가운을 만회하다 retrieve one's fortunes // 가운이 기울어진다 The family fortunes are on the wane〔decline〕. // 가운을 만회시킬 방법을 강구했다 He thought of some way of patching up〔repairing〕 his shattered fortunes. // 가운이 걸린 일이다 It is a matter of one's fortunes at stake.

*가운데 ① [복판] the middle ; the center ; the heart ; the midst ¶ 가운데 형 the middle brother // 머리를 가운데서 가르다 part one's hair in the middle // 가운데를 자르다 cut in two in the middle
② [안쪽] the interior ; the inside ; within ¶ 가운데로 들어가다 step inside // 깊은 물 가운데로 가라앉았다 It sunk into the deep water〔the depths〕. // 호수 가운데로 노저어 가다 row a boat to the middle of a lake // 가방은 상자 가운데에 있다 The bag is inside〔in〕 the box.
③ [중간·사이] the middle ; midway ¶ 가운데에 있다 lie (midway) between // 두 사람 가운데에 들다 mediate between two persons ; act as intermediary // 두 사람 가운데로 파고 들어가 싸움을 말리다 He got between the two and stopped the fight.
④ [둘의] between ; [셋 이상의] among ; of ; out of ¶ 여럿 가운데서 고르다 select out of〔from, among〕 the many // 영국 근대 작가 가운데서는 하디가 제일 좋다 I like Hardy best of all the modern novelists of England. // 너

ㄱ

회들 가운데 누가 범인이지 Which of you is the criminal? // 학과 가운데 영어가 가장 좋다 I like English best of all my subjects.
⑤ [과정] as; in the course of; while; at the same time 《that》 ¶ 가난한 생활 가운데서 while living in poverty // 바쁘신 가운데 와 주셔서 고맙습니다 Thank you for coming when you are busy.

*가운뎃손가락 the middle finger

가운뎃점 —點 ⇨ 중점

가웃 (and) a half 《되·말·자 등으로 잴 때의》 ¶ 다섯 말 가웃 five *mal* and a half

*가위¹ scissors; [큰] shears; [양털 따위를 베는] clippers ¶ 가위 한 자루 a pair of scissors // 가위로 베다 cut 《a thing》 with scissors〔shears〕; scissor〔shear〕// 신문 기사를 가위로 오려 내다 scissor out a paragraph from a newspaper // 누가 가느냐를 가위바위보로 결정하다 toss a coin to decide who to go // 가위로 다듬다 trim〔prune〕// 가위가 잘 든다 scissors cut well〔are sharp〕// 가위가 잘 들지 않는다 scissors don't cut well〔aren't sharp〕
—질 scissoring ¶ 가위질하다 scissor; cut with scissors

가위² a nightmare; an incubus

가위³ ⇨ 가윗날

가위 可謂 literally; truly; practically; in a sense; so to speak; as can be said; what is well named ¶ 그는 가위 군자이다 He can truly be called a gentleman. // 가위 천하의 절색이다 She is truly a woman of peerless beauty.

가위눌리다 have a nightmare〔an incubus〕; suffer from a nightmare; be troubled by a nightmare; have a horrible dream ¶ 자주 가위눌린다 She has habitual nightmares.

가위바위보 *kawibawibo* ¶ 가위바위보로 정하다 divide by *kawibawibo* // 가위바위보에서 이기다〔지다〕 win〔lose〕 the toss

가위춤 working a pair of scissors in the air; fooling with scissors ¶ 가위춤 추다 play with one's scissors

가위표 —標 a cross; an × ¶ 가위표를 하다 mark with a cross; mark an × 《on》 // 가위표로 지우다 cross〔×〕 out 《what one has written》

가윗날 the midautumn festival day 《the fifteenth of August by the lunar calendar》

가윗밥 waste scraps from cutting; scraps of cloth

가으내 the whole autumn; all through the fall ¶ 가으내 시골에서 농사일을 거들었다 I stayed in the country helping with the farming all through the fall.

†가을 autumn; fall 《미》; the fall season ¶ 가을의 autumn; autumnal; fall 《미》 // 초가을 early autumn〔fall〕// 가을 경치 autumn scenery // 맑은 가을 날씨 a clear autumn day; fine autumn weather // 가을에 피는 꽃 an autumn〔a fall-blooming〕 flower
—달 the autumn moon —바람 an autumn wind〔breeze〕 —볕 autumn sunshine; the autumn sun —비 an autumn(al) rain; a drizzling autumn rain —작물 [가을에 재배하는] autumn-sown crops; [가을에 익는] autumn crops —장마 the rainy spell in autumn

가을에는 부지깽이도 덤벙인다 속담 In autumn, even a kitchen poker becomes busy.

가을갈이 autumn plowing —하다 plow in autumn

가을걷이 autumn reaping〔harvesting〕

가을날 autumn weather

가을보리 autumn barley

가을일 a harvest; harvesting; gathering 《in》; reaping —하다 harvest; reap a harvest; reap in; crop

가을카리 ⇨ 가을갈이

가이거 계수관 —計數管 〖물리〗 a Geiger counter

가이거뮐러 계수관 —計數管 a Geiger-Müller counter

가이던스 〖교육〗 guidance; an orientation lecture

가이드 a (tour) guide; guiding; a guidebook
—시험 the examination for a guide's license 1급 — a competent guide

가이드라인 a guideline

⁑가이드북 a guidebook

가인 佳人 a beauty; a beautiful woman ¶ 가인은 박명하다 Beauties die young. / Beauty and luck seldom go together. / Whom the gods love die young.
—재자(才子) wit and beauty; a beautiful woman and a man of talent

가인 家人 [식구] the family; a member of one's family; family members; one's people〔folks〕; [자기 아내] my wife

가일 佳〔嘉〕日 a lucky〔an auspicious〕 day

가일층 加一層 more (and more); still more; all the more ¶ 가일층 공부하다 work harder // 가일층 노력하다 make a greater effort // 내가 외국인이라 가일층 친절했다 They were (all) the kinder to me because I was a foreigner. // 가일층 분발해 주시기 바랍니다 I like to urge you to make greater efforts.

*가입 加入 ① [참가] joining; [가맹] affiliation; [전화 따위의] subscription —하다 join; become a member 《of》; affiliate oneself 《with》; subscribe 《for》 ¶ 조합에 가입하다 join in association // 가입 신청을 하다 apply for

가족 관계 家族關係 family relations
가족법 家族法 the Family Rights Law
가족 수당 家族手當 a family allowance
가족 요법 家族療法 family therapy
가족 제도 家族制度 the family system
가주소 假住所 one's temporary address
†가죽 skin ; [소·말 따위] hide ; [무두질한] leather ; [사슴가죽] chamois leather ; [모피] a fur ; [날가죽] a pelt ¶ 호랑이 가죽 a tiger's skin // 가죽을 벗기다 skin 《a tiger》 // 가죽을 무두질하다 tan〔taw, dress〕 a hide // 뼈와 가죽만 남았다 The poor man was all skin and bone. // 가죽같이 질긴 쇠고기 tough beef
— 가방 a leather bag ; a briefcase — 공장 a tannery —끈 a (leather) strap ; a thong ; a leash (개끈) —띠 a leather belt — 무두질 tanning ; tannage — 부대 a leather bag ; [물을 나르는] a waterskin ; [술을 넣는] a wineskin — 세공(細工) leatherwork ; leathercraft — 숫돌 a razor strap ; a strop — 장갑 leather gloves — 제본(製本) leather binding — 제품 leather products 〔goods〕 — 직공 a leather dresser — 표지 a leather cover — 표지책 a leather-bound book ; a book bound in leather — 혁대 a leather belt 모조 — imitation leather ; leatherette
가죽나무 假— 〖식물〗 a tree-of-heaven ; an ailanthus ; Ailanthus altissima (학명)
가중 加重 weighting ; adding an extra weight ; 〖법〗 aggravation —하다 weight ; add an extra weight 《on》 ; aggravate ; make severe ; worsen ¶ 부담이 가중된다 The burden grows heavier.
— 과세(課稅) surcharge — 절도죄 aggravated larceny — 폭행 an aggravated assault
가중 苛重 —하다 (be) heavy ; excessive ; burdensome ; exorbitant ¶ 가중한 과세에 시달리다 groan under〔suffer from〕 the heavy burden of taxation
가중 (산술) 평균 加重(算術)平均 a weighted average〔mean〕
가중치 加重值 〖통계〗 weight
가즈런하다 ⇨ 가지런하다
가즈럽다 [허세부리다] (be) conceited ; smug ; complacent ; blustery 《words》 ; [서술적] make a bluff
가증 可憎 abomination —하다 (be) hateful ; detestable ; abominable ; disgusting ; offensive ¶ 가증한 처사 spiteful conduct // 가증스레 detestably
†가지[1] a branch ; [큰가지] a bough ; a limb ; [잔가지] a twig ; a sprig ; a spray ; shoot ¶ 가지를 뻗다 put out branches ; spread into branches ; branch out // 가지를 꺾다 break off a branch // 가지가 잘 뻗은 소나무 a shapely pine // 가지가 긴 붉은 장미 12송이만 보내 주세요 Send a dozen long-stemmed red roses, please.
가지 많은 나무에 바람 잘 날이 없다 속담 A mother with a large brood never has a peaceful day.
가지를 치다 관용 take branches off a tree〔plant〕 ; prune 《a tree》
가지[2] 〖식물〗 an eggplant ; an egg apple
가지[3] a kind ; a sort ; a class ; a variety ¶ 여러 가지 이유로 for variety of reasons // 그것에는 여러 가지가 있다 There are several kinds of it. // 그것을 하는 데는 두 가지 방법이 있다 There are two ways of doing it. // 그의 결점은 한두 가지가 아니다 He has a good many〔more than one or two〕 faults. // 한 가지 청이 있습니다 I have a favor to ask of you.
*가지가지 various kinds of ; a variety of ; all sorts of ; of every kind〔sort〕 ; all manner of ¶ 가지가지 이유로 for various reasons // 가지가지 경험 a varied experience // 가지가지의 변명 variant excuses // 가지가지 물건 many different things // 가지가지로 극진히 대접하다 treat 《a person》 to all kinds of delicacies // 가지가지 생각이 난다 Many things come to mind. // 취미도 가지가지다 There are various kind of hobbies.
†가지각색 —各色 (of) every kind and description ¶ 가지각색의 various ; diverse ; motley ; of all kinds〔sorts〕 // 가지각색의 사람들 all sorts and conditions of people ; a motley population // 사람의 마음은 가지각색이다 So many men, so many minds. /Every man has his humor. // 세상에는 인종도 가지가지요, 풍습도 가지각색이다 So many races, so many customs.
가지고 [상태·동작·방법·도구·이유·원인] from ; with ; by means of ¶ 그의 세력을 가지고도 with all his influence // 안색을 가지고 알아차리다 know 《something》 from 《a person's》 looks // 연금을 가지고 살다 live on an annuity // 행실을 가지고 사람을 판단하다 judge (of) a person by his conduct // 연필을 가지고 쓰다 write with a pencil〔in pencil〕 // 이것을 가지고 보면 from what has been said ; in view of this fact // 공을 가지고 놀다 play with a ball // 테이블은 나무를 가지고 만든다 The table is made of wood. // 그쯤 일 가지고 화내지 말게 Don't get offended at such trifles. // 그의 설명을 가지고는 만족할 수 없다 His explanation does not give us entire satisfaction. // 이 사실만을 가지고도 그가 정직하다는 것을 알 수 있다 This fact alone is enough to show how honest he is. // 그는 히트송 하나를 가지고 유명해졌다 He became a celebrity on the strength of one hit song. // 책을 사 가지고 왔다 I bought a book and came home. // 무얼

ㄱ

가지고 그리 싸우느냐 What are you quarreling about? // 가뜩이나 화난 사람 가지고 왜 그래 Why do you provoke an already angry man?

가지고야 only with; alone ¶ 이 돈 가지고야 살 수 없지 You certainly can't live with this amount of money. // 이래 가지고야 제 시간에 댈 수 있겠어 Can we make〔get〕 it there in time driving like this?

가지급 假支給 provisional payment; prepayment; an advance

가지기 a widow who cohabits with a man

†**가지다** ① [손에] have; hold 《in one's hand》; [휴대] carry; have 《a thing》 with〔about〕 one ¶ 이 꾸러미를 가지고 계십시오 Hold this bundle for me, please. // 돈을 좀 가지고 있다 I have some money with me. // 돈은 절대로 많이 가지고 다니지 않는다 I never carry much money. // 강도는 권총을 가지고 있었다 The burglar was armed with a pistol.

② [소유] have; possess; be possessed 《of》; own; hold; [경영] keep; run; [품다] have; cherish; entertain 《hopes》

> 참고 **have** 「소유하다」의 뜻의 일반어 **hold** 「마음대로 할 수 있다」 「계속 가지다」의 뜻이 포함되어 있다 **own** 법률상의 소유권을 가지다 **possess** own과 뜻이 같고 광의로는 「성질을 가지는」 뜻으로도 쓰인다

¶ 양서를 많이 가지고 있다 have many foreign books // 가게를 가지고 있다 keep a shop // 개를 가지고 있다 have a dog; keep a dog // 큰 뜻을 가지고 있다 have〔cherish〕 a great ambition // 그는 법률을 만들 권한을 가지고 있지 않았다 He had no authority to make laws. // 그 나라 여성은 투표권을 가지고 있지 않다 In that country women do not have the right to vote. // 그녀는 아름다운 목소리를 가지고 있다 She has a lovely voice.

③ [아이·새끼를] be pregnant; be expecting; be in the family way; [동물이] be with young

④ [관계] ¶ 깊은 유대를 가지고 있는 두 나라 사이 the two countries with close ties

⑤ [마음에 지니다] have; cherish; harbor ¶ 용기를 가지다 have courage // 희망을 가지다 cherish the hope // 의심을 가지다 harbor suspicion against // 그는 비행기에 흥미를 가지고 있다 He is interested in airplanes.

***가지런하다** be in order; be arranged neatly; [높이가] be of equal〔uniform〕 size ¶ 가지런히 evenly; uniformly; neatly; in order // 신을 가지런히 놓다 arrange shoes in order // 높이가 가지런하다 be of uniform height

가지치다 ① [돋아나다] spread〔put out〕 branches ② [자르다] cut off branches; trim a tree

가직하다 be near〔close〕 by; be rather near; be a little way off

가집 歌集 a collection of poems; an anthology

가집행 假執行 〖법〗 provisional execution; a temporary injunction **—하다** execute provisionally; place under a temporary injunction

가짜 假— ① [모조품] an imitation; a sham; bogus; a spurious article; a fake; a pinchbeck; a duffer; a phony 《미·속》; [위조품] a counterfeit; a forgery ¶ 이 보석은 진짜냐 가짜냐 Is this a real jewel or just an imitation? // 가짜에 조심하시오 Beware of imitations. // 이 서명은 가짜다 This signature is a forgery. // 가짜를 속아 샀다 He was cheated into buying a fake.

— 골동품(骨董品) fake antiques **— 도장** a forged seal **—돈** counterfeit〔bogus, fake〕 money; [경화] a counterfeit〔false, bad〕 coin; [지폐] a forged〔false〕 bank note **— 문서** a forgery **— 보석** sham〔flash〕 jewelry **— 수표** a forged check〔cheque 《영》〕 **— 증서(證書)** a counterfeit〔forged〕 bond

② [사람] a charlatan; a pretender; an imposter; a fraud

— 의사 a quack (doctor); a (medical) charlatan; a quacksalver **— 학생** a bogus student

가차압 假差押 ⇨ 가압류

가차없다 假借— (be) ruthless; unsparing; relentless; merciless; severe ¶ 가차없이 relentlessly; ruthlessly; without mercy〔remorse〕 // 가차없이 벌을 주다 punish ruthlessly〔without mercy〕; show 《them》 no mercy // 가차없이 처분하다 handle 《a culprit》 without gloves〔reserve〕 // 가차없이 나무라다 give a good scolding

가창 歌唱 [노래부름] singing; [노래] a song ¶ 그 신인 가수는 가창력이 있다 The new singer has singing ability〔talent〕.

가창오리 〖새〗 a spectacled teal; Anas formosa (학명)

가책 呵責 [꾸짖음] scolding; [책망] blame; censure; [양심의] compunction ¶ 양심의 가책을 받다 feel qualms〔pricks〕 of conscience; be conscience-stricken; feel pangs of remorse; be tormented by a guilty conscience // 그는 그 돈을 받은 일에 약간의 가책을 느꼈다 He felt some qualms at receiving the money. // 그 녀석은 거짓말하는 데에 대해서 양심의 가책을 느끼지 않는다 That guy has no qualms about lying.

가책 苛責 a sharp〔severe〕 scolding
가처분 假處分 〖법〗 provisional disposition ━하다 make provisional disposition
가처분 소득 可處分所得 〖법〗 a disposable income
가철 假綴 temporary〔paper〕 binding ━하다 bind temporarily〔in paper〕
━본 a paper-bound book ; a temporarily bound book
가첨 加添 an addition ; a supplement ━하다 supplement ; add〔append〕 《something》 to ; tack〔fix, stick〕 《it》 to
가청 可聽 audible ; audio
━ 거리 earshot ━도(度) audibility ━ 범위 the range of hearing ; the audible range ━ 신호(信號) an audible signal ; baudio signals ━역(閾) 〖심리〗 the threshold of audibility ━ 주파수(周波數) audio frequency 《A. F.》 ━ 주파 증폭기 an audio frequency amplifier ━ 한계 〖물리〗 the audible limit
가청음 可聽音 audible sounds
가축 good keeping ; taking good care 《of a thing》 ¶ 겨울 옷을 잘 가축해 두다 take good care of winter clothing
*가축 家畜 domestic cattle〔animals〕 ; cattle ; livestock ¶ 가축의 떼 a herd of cattle ; a drove of cattle 《미》 // 가축을 치다 raise domestic cattle ; raise livestock
━ 개량 improvement of livestock ━ 병원 a veterinary hospital ; [애완 동물의] a pet hospital ━사(舍) a cattle stall ━ 사료 feed-stuff ; stock feed ━ 사육 livestock husbandry ; livestock farming ━ 상인 a drover ; a cattle dealer ━선(船) a cattle carrier ━ 시장 a livestock market ━ 우리 cattle pen ━차(車) a stock car ; cattle truck 《영》
가출 家出 disappearance from home ━하다 run〔go, drift〕 away from home ; leave home〔one's house〕 ; disappear〔fly〕 from home ¶ 요즈음 가출 청소년이 늘고 있다 The number of runaway teenagers is increasing these days.
━ 소녀 a runaway girl
가출옥 假出獄 〖법〗 release on parole ; provisional release ━하다 be paroled from prison ; be released on parole
━자(者) a paroled man ; a man on parole ; a parolee (from a prison) ; a ticket-of-leave man
가치 假齒 ⇨ 의치
†가치 價値 value ; worth ; merit

> 참고 **worth**는 실체 그 자체가 가진 절대적 가치 **value**는 그 물건에 대하여 사람들이 인정하는 상대적 가치를 말한다

¶ 가치 있는 valuable ; worthy ; of value // 매우 가치 있는 invaluable ; priceless // 가치없는 worthless ; valueless ; of no value // 교육의 가치 the value of education // 인간의 가치 human worth ; a man's worth // 책의 가치 the merit of a book // 종교적〔예술적〕 가치 religious〔artistic〕 value // 가치가 크다〔작다, 없다〕 be of great〔little, no〕 value // 건강에 대한 운동의 가치 the value of exercise for health // 5천원의 가치가 있는 물품 an article worth 5,000 *won* // 볼〔읽을, 들을〕 만한 가치가 있다 It is worth seeing〔reading, listening to〕. // 이 사실은 주목할 만한 가치가 있다〔없다〕 This fact is worthy of〔beneath our〕 notice. /This fact merits attention〔no attention〕. // 달러의 가치는 많이 변동됐다 The value of the dollar has varied greatly. // 그의 행위는 극구 칭찬할 만한 가치가 있다 His conduct deserves〔is worthy of〕 the highest praise. // 그 증거의 가치에 대해서는 의견이 구구하다 Opinions differ as to the value of the evidence.
━ 척도 a measure of value 경제 ━ commercial〔economic〕 value 교환 ━ exchange value ; value in exchange 사용 ━ value in use 실용 ━ practical〔actual〕 value 영양 ━ nutritive value 이용 ━ utility value 잉여 ━ surplus value ━ 희소 ━ scarcity value
가치관 價值觀 one's values
가치론 價值論 the theory of value ; axiology
가치 판단 價值判斷 valuation ; evaluation ¶ 사물의 가치 판단을 못하는 사람 a poor judge of values
가친 家親 my father
가칠 加漆 additional coating with lacquer ; recoating ; repainting ━하다 give an added coat of lacquer ; recoat ; repaint
가칠하다 (be) haggard ; emaciated ; gaunt ; thin ; careworn ; look worn-out ¶ 가칠한 얼굴 a haggard face ; a worn-out look ; a worn and drawn look // 그녀는 병으로 얼굴이 가칠해졌다 She became thin because of her illness. / She looked gaunt after the illness.
가칭 假稱 [임시의] a tentative〔provisional〕 name ; [가짜] false representation ; misrepresentation ━하다 call tentatively ; represent oneself (falsely) ; assume ¶ 가칭 「동아 재단」 tentatively named "*Dong-A* Foundation"
가타부타 可━否━ ¶ 가타부타 말이 없다 say neither yes nor no ; make no response whatever ; remain silent
가탁 假託 pretext ; pretense ; excuse ; plea ━하다 make an excuse〔a pretext〕 《of》 ; pretend ¶ …에 가탁하여 on〔under〕 the plea〔pretense〕 《of》 ; under the cloak〔color〕 《of》
가탄 可歎 ━하다 (be) lamentable ;

ㄱ

deplorable ; regrettable ; sad ; mournful ¶ 가탄지사 a lamentable〔deplorable〕 thing ; a matter for regret // 사회 풍기가 이렇게 문란한 것은 실로 가탄할 일이다 It is deplorable〔a matter for regret〕 that the public morals should be so corrupt.

가탈¹ [방해·트집] an obstacle ; a hitch ; a hindrance ; an impediment ¶ 가탈부리다 pick on ; pick a hole ; complicate matters // 처음 시작한 사업이라 가탈도 많다 There are a lot of impediments to my new business. **—스럽다** be troublesome ; be intricate ; be complicated ¶ 그는 성질이 가탈스럽다 He is hard to please. /He is particular〔fastidious, fussy, choosy〕.

가탈² [말의] unsteady〔tottering〕 gait ¶ 가탈 걸음 a tottering〔staggering〕 pace // 가탈거리다 《a horse》 walk unsteadily ; totter ; stagger

가택 家宅 a house ; a residence ; 〖법〗 a domicile

가택 수색 家宅搜索 〖법〗 domiciliary search〔visit〕 ; the search of a house 《by the police》 ; a house search **—하다** search a house ; undertake a house search ¶ 가택 수색을 당했다 I had my house searched. // 경찰이 가택 수색을 했다 The policemen searched the house.

— 영장 a search warrant ; a warrant for the search of a house

가택 침입 家宅侵入 housebreaking ; trespassing on another's house ; unlawful entry ; intrusion **—하다** trespass on another's premises ; break and enter

—자(者) a trespasser ; a housebreaker

—죄(罪) trespass ; housebreaking

가토 加土 —하다 [뿌리에] earth up ; put on (fresh) earth ; [무덤에] recover a grave with earth

가톨 [밤의] side nuts in a chestnut-burr

가톨릭 Catholic ⇨ 카톨릭

가통 家統 family lineage ¶ 가통을 잇다 carry on a family lineage

가트 GATT 《the General Agreement on Tariffs and Trade ; 관세와 무역에 관한 일반 협정》

†**가파르다** (be) steep ; precipitous ; sheer ; sharp ¶ 가파른 산길 a steep mountain pass // 언덕이 아주 가파르다 The hills are very steep.

가판 街販 ⇨ 가두 판매

가편 可便 the ayes ; the consenting party ; [토론의] the affirmative side ¶ 가편과 부편 ayes and noes ; pros and cons ; for and against

가편 加鞭 whipping **—하다** whip ; apply the whip ; whip up ¶ 주마 가편하다〔더욱 독려하다〕 spur〔urge〕 on ; encourage ; urge a horse on (말을) ; whip a galloping horse

가표 加票 plus sign 《+》

가표 可票 an affirmative vote

가풀막 a steep slope ; a steep ascent 〔acclivity〕 ; a steep descent〔declivity〕 ¶ 가풀막지다 slope up〔down〕 sharply ; be precipitous

가품 家品 the character〔disposition〕 of a family ; refinement (품성)

가풍 家風 a family tradition〔custom〕 ; domestic habits ¶ 가풍에 안 맞다 be not in harmony with the family tradition ; fail to conform to the family's traditions ; be not fit into one's family tradition

가필 加筆 (a) correction ; (a) revision ; retouch **—하다** touch up ; correct ; retouch ; revise ; add some touches to

가하다 可— [옳다] (be) right ; reasonable ; [좋다] passable ; fairly good ¶ 네 말이 가하다 What you say is right. // 둘 중에 어느 것을 택해도 가하다 You may choose either of the two. /Either will do. // 학생의 관람도 가하다 The viewing is open to students.

†**가하다 加—** ① [가산] add 《up》 ; sum up ; [부가] add ; [증가] increase ¶ 원금에 이자를 가하다 add interest to the principal // 속력을 가하다 gain in velocity ; gather speed // 하나에 둘을 가하면 셋이다 One and two are〔make〕 three. ② [주다] give ; inflict 《on》 ; subject 《a person》 to ¶ 비판을 가하다 criticize ; pass judgment 《upon》 // 압력을 가하다 give〔apply〕 pressure 《to》 ; press 《on》 // 타격을 가하다 deal 《a person》 a blow ; affect adversely // 적에게 손해를 가하다 inflict losses on the enemy // 무역 압박을 가하다 impose trade pressure

가학 苛虐 cruel treatment ; maltreatment ; cruelty **—하다** treat 《a person》 with cruelty ; be cruel to 《a person》 ¶ 가학애 sadism // 가학성 성욕 이상자 a sadist

가합 可合 —하다 (be) reasonable ; rational ; proper ¶ 가합한 의견 a reasonable opinion

가해 加害 assault ; violence ; wrong ; wrongdoing **—하다** do harm〔injury〕 《to》 ; inflict injury 《on》 ; commit violence 《on》 ¶ 가해 행위를 한 자 〖법〗 a person who has committed violence on〔has assaulted〕 another person

가해자 加害者 an assaulter ; an injurer ; an assailant ; a person who has caused damage ; a murderer ; a killer (살해자) ; a hit man (살인 청부자)

— 행위 a harmful act ; violence

가향 家鄕 ⇨ 고향

가형 家兄 my elder brother

가호 加護 divine protection ; special providence ; blessing ¶ 하느님의 가호를 빌다 pray to God for help

***가혹 苛酷** severity ; harshness ; cruelty ; rigor **—하다** (be) severe ; harsh ; cruel ; brutal ; merciless ; relentless ¶ 가혹한 벌 a severe punishment // 가혹한 법률 a rigorous law // 가혹한 처사 harsh treatment // 머슴을 가혹하게 부려먹다 drive servants too hard ; sweat one's servants // 그 죄수는 가혹한 대우를 받았다 The criminal was treated brutally 〔mercilessly〕. // 운명의 가혹함 the cruelty of fate

가환 家患 [병] sickness〔disease〕 in one's family ; [걱정] family troubles 〔misfortunes〕 ; domestic cares〔worries〕

가황 加黃 〖화학〗 vulcanization **—하다** vulcanize

— 고무 vulcanized rubber **—유(油)** vulcanized oil

가효 佳肴 a tasty side dish to go with wine ; delicacies to be eaten with wine ; a relish taken with wine ; hors d'oeuvre (전채)

가훈 家訓 family precepts ; the family code of conduct

가히 可— fully ; 《may》 well ; easily ; most likely ¶ 네 심정을 가히 짐작할 수 있다 I can easily figure out how you feel. // 가히 그렇게 말할 만하다 You may well say that. /It is natural for you to say so. // 한글의 우수성은 가히 세계에 자랑할 만하다 You can rightly take pride in the worldwide recognition of *Han-gŭl*.

각 各 each ; every ¶ 각 개인 each individual

***각 角** [모] a corner ; [네모] a square ; [각도] an angle ; [뿔] a horn ; [사슴의] an antler

—가속도 angular acceleration **—계수(係數)** an angularity coefficient **—대(臺)** 〖수학〗 the frustum of a pyramid ; a prismoid **—배율(倍率)** angular magnification **—변수(變數)** an angle variable **—운동** angular motion

각 刻 [새김] engraving ; carving ; [시간] a quarter-hour ; a period of 15 minutes

각 脚 one of the four or five parts into which a slaughtered animal is cut

각을 뜨다 관용 cut up 《a slaughtered animal》 in parts

각가지 各— various kinds ; all sorts ; all and sundry ; every kind ; a variety ¶ 각가지의 varieties of ; all sorts of ; diverse // 각가지 물건 all sorts of things

각거리 角距離 〖물리〗 an angular distance

***각각 各各** each ; every ; all ; separately ; individually ; respectively ; apart ; severally ¶ 각각 따로 자다 sleep in separate rooms // 물건을 각각 따로 두다 keep things apart // 죄수는 각각 따로따로 수용된다 The prisoners are kept separate one from another. // 각각 자기 방이 있다 Each one of us has a room to himself. /We each have our own room. // 학생들은 각각의 방으로 돌아갔다 The students went back to their respective rooms.

각각으로 刻刻— hourly ; from hour to hour ; hour by hour ; momentarily ; every moment ; moment by moment ¶ 각각으로 변하다 change every moment // 각각으로 불안은 더해 가기만 했다 Fears were mounting every moment.

각개 各個 each ; each one ; every one

— 격파 "divide and rule" ; divide et impera 《라》 ; defeating one by one ¶ 각개 격파하다 defeat 《the opposing members》 one by one ; smash 《the enemy》 one by one ; argue down one after another (토론 따위에서) **— 교련** individual drill **— 약진** individual rushes ; advance of individuals **— 전투** individual combat **— 점호** individual roll call **— 훈련** individual training

각개인 各個人 each one〔individual〕 ; each ; each person ¶ 각개인의 문제 a matter of private concern for each individual

각거 各居 —하다 live apart〔separately〕 ; live in separate houses (가족이)

각계 各界 all walks of life ; every field 〔sphere〕 of life ; various circles〔quarters〕

각계 각층 各界各層 ¶ 각계 각층의 명사 notable men and women in every walk of life ; notables representing various social circles

각고 刻苦 hard work ; tireless effort ; arduous labor **—하다** work hard ; spare no effort ¶ 각고 10년에 초지를 관철하다 accomplish〔carry out〕 one's original intention after ten years of arduous labor // 각고의 노력 끝에 성공하다 He achieved success after years of hard work.

각골 刻骨 —하다 engrave in one's mind〔memory〕 ; impress on one's mind ; be deeply impressed on one's mind

각골난망 刻骨難忘 remembering forever ; cherishing the memory of **—하다** be deeply impressed 《with, by》 ; grave 《the words》 in the heart ; be brought home to 《one》 ; be deeply impressed on〔engraved in〕 one's mind

각골명심 刻骨銘心 —하다 bear〔have, keep〕 in mind ; strongly impress on one's memory

각골 통한 刻骨痛恨 bitter regret **—하다** take to heart ; feel regret for

각괄호 角括弧 bracket(s)

***각광 脚光** footlights ; float(s) ; highlights ; spotlight ¶ 세계 외교 무대에서 각광을 받았다 He stood in the spotlight of world diplomacy. // 그녀는 연극인으로

각광을 받고 있다 As a player, she is in the spotlight〔limelight〕.
각광을 받다 [관용] [극작품이] be staged ; be performed before the footlights ; [예술인이] make an appearance before the footlights ; be limelighted ; [인기] be highlighted ; be spotlighted
*각국 各國 every country ; each nation ; various countries〔nations〕 ¶ 세계 각국 all countries of the world // 유럽 각국을 시찰하다 make a tour of inspection in various European countries
각근 恪勤 faithful service ; hard working ; attending faithfully to one's duties
각기 各其 each ; respectively ; severally ¶ 각기 의견을 말하다 give one's individual opinions // 그들에게 사과를 각기 두 개씩 주어라 Give them two apples each. // 각기 제 할 일을 해라 Go to your respective jobs.
각기 脚氣 〖의학〗 beriberi ¶ 각기를 앓다 suffer from beriberi
각기둥 角― 〖수학〗 a prism
각다귀 ① [모기의 일종] a striped mosquito ; an aëdes ② [착취자] an exploiter ; an extortioner ; a bloodsucker ; a vampire ; a sponge
각다귀판 a dog-eat-dog situation ; a state of mutual parasitism
각다분하다 《a job》 prove difficult ; be hard and tedious
각단 the drift and shape of an affair ; the first step of an affair〔a matter〕
†각도 角度 an angle ; angular measure ; degrees of an angle ¶ 40도의 각도로 at an angle of 40 degrees // 모든 각도에서 문제를 검토하다 look at a question from all angles〔viewpoints, standpoints〕
각도계 角度計 an angle meter ; a goniometer
각도기 角度器 a (graduated) protractor ; a graduator
반원(半圓) ― a semicircular protractor
전원(全員) ― a circular protractor
각띠 角― a sash (worn by officials in former days)
각력 脚力 the strength of one's legs ; [보행력] one's distance walking ability ; [주력] one's running ability
각령 閣令 a Cabinet order〔decree〕
각론 各論 a discussion of details ; a special treatise ; detailed exposition ¶ 각론에 들어가다 go into details // 총론에서 각론으로 들어가다 descend from generalities to particulars
각료 閣僚 ministers of state ; Cabinet members〔ministers〕 ; the Ministerial〔Cabinet〕 colleagues 《총칭》 ¶ 경제 담당 각료 회의를 소집하다 call a meeting of cabinet ministers in charge of economic affairs
―급 회담 a conference at〔on〕 ministerial level ; a minister-level conference ― 회의 a Cabinet meeting 한일 ― 회담 the Korea-Japan Ministerial Meeting
각루 刻漏 a water clock ⇨ 물시계
각막 角膜 〖해부〗 the cornea (of the eye)
―계(計) a keratometer ; a keratoscope ― 렌즈〔정체(晶體)〕 a corneal lens ― 백반(白斑) keratoleucoma ― 절개(切開) corneal section
각막염 角膜炎 inflammation of the cornea ; corneitis ; keratitis
각막이식 角膜移植 corneal transplant(ation)〔grafting〕 ; keratoplasty
각목 角木 a square bar ; scantling ; 〖건축〗 a balk ; baulk
각박 刻薄 ―하다 (be) stony〔hard〕-hearted ; harsh ; insusceptible to pity ¶ 그는 각박한 사람이다 He has a heart of stone. // 요즘 물가가 올라 인심이 각박해져 가고 있다 People are getting hard-hearted in these days of high prices. // 각박한 세상이다 These are hard times. /Things are tough nowadays.
*각반 脚絆 gaiters ; leggings ; [짧은] spats ; [감는] puttees ¶ 각반을 치고 with gaitered legs
각반병 角斑病 angular leaf spot
각방 各方 ⇨ 각방면
각방 各房 each〔every〕 room ; all rooms ¶ 각방 거처하다 have each a room to himself
각방면 各方面 every direction〔quarter, sector〕 ; various spheres〔fields〕 ¶ 각방면으로 in every direction〔quarter〕 ; in all quarters〔directions〕 각방면으로부터 from all quarters ; from many sources // 사회의 각방면 all strata of society // 각방면으로부터의 정보가 모두 일치하고 있다 All accounts agree〔tally〕 with one another. // 그는 각방면에 아는 사람이 많다 He is acquainted with all classes.
각배 各― ① [짐승] different litters from the same mother ② [사람] having different mothers
각별 恪別 ―하다 ① [특별] (be) particular ; special ; especial ; [현저] marked ; noticeable ; [예외] exceptional ¶ 각별히 particularly ; especially ; in particular ; exceptionally // 각별한 일도 없이 uneventfully // 건강에 각별히 주의하다 take good care of oneself // 각별한 용무가 있는 것은 아니다 I have nothing particular to do. /I am not particularly engaged. // 오늘 더위는 각별하다 This is an awfully hot day. // 그는 우리 학급에서도 각별히 뛰어났다 In my class he was head and shoulders above everyone else.
② [깍듯하다] (be) courteous ; polite ; civil ¶ 각별히 courteously ; civilly ;

politely∥각별한 대우를 받다 be received with much courtesy
각본 脚本 a play ; a drama ; a playbook ; a scenario ; a script ; [비유적] plan ; intention ; design ; program ¶ 각본을 쓰다 write a play∥각본을 상연하다 stage〔represent〕 a play〔drama〕∥각본화하다 dramatize 《a novel》 ; [영화] cinematize∥일이 각본대로 진행되고 있다 Everything is going according to plan.
—가〔작가〕 a dramatist ; a playwright ; a scenario〔screenplay〕 writer ; a scriptwriter — 낭독 cold reading (of a play)
각봉 各封 —하다 seal 《a letter》 in separate cover ¶ 각봉하여 우송하다 send a letter in separate cover
각부 各部 [부분] each〔every〕 part ; [부서] each〔every〕 department〔section〕 ; [정부의] every ministry〔department〕 ¶ 각부 장관 the minister of each department
각부분 各部分 each〔every〕 part ; various parts
각분산 角分散 angular displacement
각빙 角氷 an ice cube
각뿔 各— 『수학』 a pyramid
각사탕 角砂糖 cube〔lump〕 sugar ; sugar cubes
각살림 各— living separately (가족의) —하다 live separately ; establish〔set up〕 a separate family
각상 各床 separate tables ; dinner laid separately for each person —하다 set individual tables ; dine at individual tables (먹다)
각색 各色 ① [색채] each〔every〕 color ② [종류] all sorts〔kinds〕 ; various kinds ¶ 각색 인종 all races ; people of various races∥각양각색의 various ; diverse ; manifold ; multifarious ; of every kind ; of all sorts
*각색 脚色 dramatization ; stage version ; picturization ; cinematization ; filmization ; [소설 따위의] adaptation —하다 dramatize 《a play》 ; adapt 《a novel》 for a play ; picturize ; scenarize ; script 《미》 ; cinematize ¶ 잡지 소설을 각색하다 dramatize a magazine story∥김씨 각색 adapted by *Kim*∥그 소설은 영화〔연극〕로 각색되었다 The novel was adapted for the screen〔stage〕.
—자(者) a dramatizer ; an adapter ; a scriptwriter (영화의)
†각서 覺書 a memorandum 《*pl.* ~s, -da》 ; [외교상의] a note ; a protocol (의정서) ; 『법』 factum 《*pl.* -ta》 《라》 ¶ 각서의 교환 an exchange of notes〔memoranda〕∥이 문제에 관한 미국 정부의 각서 the American note on this subject
공동 — a collective note
각석 角石 a square stone
각선미 脚線美 the beauty of leg lines ¶ 각선미를 가진 여자 a woman with shapely legs∥각선미를 강조한 사진 a cheesecake 《미·속》∥그 여자 각선미가 좋은데… She has beautiful legs./Her legs are shapely.
각설 却說 —하다 return to the topic〔main subject〕 ; resume one's story ¶ 각설하고 to resume our story ; now let us proceed∥각설(하면) 그때 큰 가뭄이 들었다 To resume our story, they had a bad drought at that time.
각설이 却說— a singing beggar
각설탕 角雪糖 ⇨ 각사탕
각섬석 角閃石 『광물』 amphibole
각성 覺醒 awakening ; disillusion ; disenchantment —하다 awake ; wake up ; be aroused ; come to one's senses ; be disillusioned ¶ 각성시키다 awaken ; arouse ; disillusion∥국민은 아직 각성하지 못하고 있다 The nation is not yet awakened.∥당국의 각성을 촉구한다 The anthorities need to be awakened urgently.∥패전은 국민을 크게 각성시켰다 The defeat was a great eye-opener for the people.∥지금이야말로 민족적 각성이 요구되는 때다 This is the right time for (a) national awakening.
각성 各姓 different surnames ; people with different surnames
—바지 men〔half brothers〕 of different surnames
각성제 覺醒劑 an antihypnotic〔a stimulant〕 (drug) ; a pep pill
각세공 角細工 hornwork ; hornware ; horn manufactures
각소금 角— salt tablet
각속도 角速度 『물리』 angular velocity
각수 刻手 an engraver ; a carver ; a sculptor
각시 ① [인형] a maiden doll ② [새색시] a bride ; a newly married woman
각시놀음 —하다 play with dolls
각아비자식 各—子息 sons of different fathers ; uterine brothers ; half brothers
각양각색 各樣各色 diversity ; variety ; multifariousness ; manifoldness ; all sorts ¶ 각양각색의 물건 things of all sorts∥각양각색의 문체 various styles of writing
각연초 刻煙草 ⇨ 살담배
*각오 覺悟 ① [마음의 준비] preparedness ; readiness ; [결심] resolution —하다 prepare oneself for ; make up one's mind 《to do》 ¶ 각오하고 있다 be prepared〔ready〕 for ; be resolved〔determined〕 to 《do》∥그는 죽음을 각오하고 있다 He is prepared for death.∥그것을 단행할 각오이다 I am resolved to carry it out.∥나는 그것에 대해 이미 각오를 했다 I've already braced myself for it.
② [깨달음] perception —하다 per-

ㄱ

ceive 《the truth》; understand
각운 脚韻 a rhyme ¶ 각운을 맞추다 rhyme lines ↔ 두운
각운동 角運動 〖물리〗 angular motion
각위 各位 all; every one; [편지에서] Sirs; Gentlemen ¶ 회원 각위에게 to the members // 관계자 각위 to whom it may concern // 내빈 각위의 건강을 축하합니다 I drink to the health of all the guests present. (건배)
각의 閣議 a Cabinet council〔meeting, conference〕 ¶ 임시 각의를 소집하다 call〔summon〕 an extraordinary Cabinet meeting // 각의에 상정하다 submit to〔lay before〕 a Cabinet council
— 결정 사항 matters decided upon by the Cabinet 정례〔임시〕 — a regular〔an extraordinary〕 session of the Cabinet council
각인 刻印 —하다 carve a seal
각인 各人 everybody; everyone; each one; all men ¶ 각인 각색 So many men, so many minds. /Everyone has his taste. /Every man has his humors. // 각인 각색의 의견 various opinions // 각인 각색으로 in all their respective ways
각일각 刻一刻 ⇨ 시시각각
*각자 各自 each one; every one; [부사적] each; individually; respectively; severally ¶ 각자의 each; several; respective // 각자 갈 길을 갔다 They went their several ways. // 각자 집으로 돌아갔다 They returned to their several homes. // 도구는 각자 준비할 것 Being your (own) tools. // 각자 내지 그래 why don't we go Dutch? // 신청은 각자가 하십시오 We would appreciate your making your applications on an individual basis.
각자 刻字 —하다 carve〔engrave, sculpture〕 letters 《on a surface》
각장 各葬 a separate burial
각재 角材 square timber; a square lumber《미》; squares; [작은 것] a scantling; baby squares
각종 各種 every kind〔description〕; various kinds; varieties; all kinds 《of》 ¶ 각종의 of every kind; of all sorts; all sorts〔kinds〕 of; varieties of; various
— 경기 all sorts of sports〔games〕 — 사물 all sorts of things; things of every sort and variety — 직업 occupations of various kinds — 학교 (one of the) miscellaneous schools
각주 角柱 a square pillar; 〖수학〗 a prism
*각주 脚註 a footnote ¶ 풍부한 각주 copious footnotes // 각주를 달다 put in〔add, append〕 a footnote
각지 各地 [모든 지방] every part〔section〕; all parts; [여러 지방] various parts; all districts ¶ 그 대회에는 세계 각지에서 많은 사람들이 참가했다 Many people from various countries attended the conference. // 태풍이 전국 각지에 큰 피해를 주었다 The typhoon caused much damage to all parts of the country.
각질 脚疾 〖의학〗 leg ailments
각질 角質 horny substance; chitin 《곤충의 껍질 따위》; 〖화학〗 keratin (각소) ¶ 각질의 horny; corneous
— 조직 corneous〔horny〕 tissue —층 a horny layer; a stratum corneum
각처 各處 each〔every〕 place; all places; various places ¶ 각처에 [모든 곳] everywhere; [여러 곳] in several places; in various parts; [여기저기] here and there // 시내 각처에 물난리가 났다 The city was flooded in several places. /There were floods in various parts of the city. // 전국 각처에서 항의 시위가 잇달았다 There were demonstrations throughout the nation (nationwide).
각추 角錐 〖기하〗 a pyramid.
각추렴 —하다 defray by proportional shares; collect from each; club together; chip in; split 《the expenses》 ⇨ 추렴
각축 角逐 competition; rivalry; contest; struggle —하다 compete〔vie〕 《with》; contend 《with, against》; emulate 《with》 ¶ 우승을 놓고 서로 각축을 벌이다 vie with each other for victory〔championship〕
—장(場) the arena of competition ¶ 세계 열강의 각축장 the arena of the struggle among the world powers
각층 各層 [사회의] each class (of society); each stratum of society; [건물의] each〔every〕 floor〔story〕 ¶ 각계각층의 《people》 of all social standings; all levels of society // 각층에 서는 승강기 an elevator that stops at every floor
각치다 ① scratch ⇨ 할퀴다 ② [부아를 돋움] needle 《a person》; make 《a person》 mad
각통질 bloating an ox with fodder and water before selling it —하다 force fodder and water down 《an ox》
각파 各派 [정당] each party; all political parties〔groups〕; each faction (파벌); [예술계 따위의] all schools; [종파] all denominations〔sects〕
— 교섭회 [정당간의] an interparty liaison meeting; [당내의] an interparty liaison meeting
각판 刻版 ① [널판] a block of wood to be engraved for printing; a wood block; a woodcut; wood engraving
② [각판본] ⇨ 각판본(刻版本)
각판본 刻版本 a book printed from a block〔plate〕
각피 角皮 〖해부〗 cuticle
—소(素) cuticula

각하 却下 dismissal ; rejection **—하다** dismiss ; reject ; turn down ¶ 상고를 각하하다 dismiss 《a person's》 appeal // 원서를 각하하다 reject an application // 이의 신청이 각하되었다 His objection was overruled.

각하 閣下 [2인칭] Your Excellency ; [3인칭] His〔Her〕 Excellency 《*pl.* Their Excellencies》 ¶ 각하 그리고 신사 숙녀 여러분 Your Excellencies, ladies and gentlemen !
대통령 — Your〔His〕 Excellency the President

각항 各項 each〔every〕 item〔paragraph, clause, provision〕

각화 角化 〖의학〗 cornification ; keratinization

각화증 角化症 keratodermia ; hyperkeratosis

간 ① [염분의 정도] saltiness ; a salt taste ② [염분으로 맛을 들임] salting ; applying salt for seasoning **—하다** salt ; apply salt for seasoning ¶ 간이 짜다〔싱겁다〕 be too salty〔be not salty enough〕 // 생선에 간을 하다 salt fish // 국간이 꼭 맞다 The soup is just salty enough.
간을 보다 관용 taste (to see whether a thing is salty enough)

간 肝 [간장] the liver ; [담력] courage ; spirit ; pluck ; nerve ¶ 간이 큰 daring ; bold ; plucky // 간이 작은 timid ; faint-hearted ; hare-hearted ; lily-livered ; chicken-hearted // 간이 타다 be anxious // 간이라도 빼어 먹이겠다 I'll pluck out my liver for you. / I'll go to any lengths for you.
—농양(膿瘍) hepatic abscess **— 소시지** liver sausage
간이 콩알만해지다 관용 be frightened out of one's wits ; be scared stiff ; be amazed ; be thunderstruck
간에 기별도 안가다 관용 be hardly enough to be worth eating ; barely begin to satisfy one's stomach〔hunger〕
간 빼먹고 등쳐 먹다 관용 frighten 《a person》 into giving away their possessions
간에도 차지 않다 관용 be hardly enough to be worth eating
간(을) 녹이다 관용 fascinate ; ravish ; enthrall // 간이라도 빼어 먹이겠다 I'll pluck out my liver for you. / I'll go to any lengths for you.
간이 붓다 관용 be bold ; daring ; plucky
간이 오그라들다 관용 be frightened out of one's wits
간에 붙었다 쓸개에 붙었다 하다 관용 change one's front〔side〕 readily ; turn one's coat readily

간 間 ① [가옥의] a room ② [길이의 단위] a *kan* 《about six feet》 ③ [동안] duration ; for ; [장소] between ¶ 1개월간 for a month // 서울 부산간의 거리 the distance between *Seoul* and *Pusan*
④ [관계] relationship ; between ; among ¶ 숙질간 the relationship of uncle and nephew // 3국간의 협정 an agreement among〔between(2국씩)〕 three powers

간간이[1] 間間— ⇨ 칸칸이

간간이[2] 間間— ① [시간적] occasionally ; now and then ; from time to time ; once in a while ¶ 간간이 온다 He comes occasionally〔now and then〕.
② [공간적] at intervals ; here and there ¶ 반바지 차림의 사람들이 간간이 눈에 띈다 People wearing shorts are seen here and there.

간간짭잘하다 be pleasantly salty〔good and salty〕

간간하다[1] (be) saltish ; a bit salty ; have a briny flavor ¶ 간간하니 맛나다 be nicely salted

간간하다[2] [재미있다] (be) tickling ; interesting ; exciting ; [위태롭다] thrilling ; breath-taking ¶ 이야기의 간간한 대목 the thrilling climax of a story

간거르다 間— leave an interval 《between》 ; be alternate ; skip 《a thing》 every other line

⁑**간격 間隔** ① [시간·공간·거리] a space ; an interval ; spacing ; a gap ¶ 2피트 간격으로 at intervals of two feet ; two feet apart // 일정한 간격을 두고 at regular〔stated〕 intervals // 간격을 두다 leave a space // 전차는 5분 간격으로 떠난다 The streetcars leave at five-minute intervals.
② [소원함] friction ; alienation ; estrangement ; coolness ¶ 두 사람 사이에 간격이 생겼다 They have become estranged (from each other). / They have lost their former intimacy. // 노사간에 약간의 간격이 있었다 There has been some friction between labor and management.
— 부호(符號) a spacing signal **— 전류** a spacing current **—파(波)** a spacing wave **운전 —** a headway

†**간결 簡潔** conciseness ; terseness ; laconism ; compactness ; pithiness ; brevity ; neatness 《of expression》 ¶ 말은 간결이 생명이다 Brevity is the soul of wit. (*Hamlet* 중에서) **—하다** (be) concise ; terse ; brief ; laconical ; succinct ; pithy ; short and sweet ¶ 간결하게 concisely ; with concision ; briefly ; tersely ; compactly // 설명을 간결하게 하다 make one's explanation short and clear ; explain the issue briefly and to the point〔concisely〕 ; give a concise account of the issue // 간결한 문체로 쓰

다 write in laconical style // 간결한 진술 a concise statement

간경변 肝硬變 〚의학〛 cirrhosis of the liver ; hepatocirrhosis

간계 奸計 a dark〔crafty, evil〕 design ; wiles ; a trick ; an artifice ; a cheat ; a nasty〔evil〕 scheme ¶ 간계를 꾸미다 form dark designs ; resort to (ruses and) wiles // 적의 간계에 빠지다 play into the enemy's hands ; play into the hands of the enemy

간고 艱苦 [고생] hardships ; privations ; trials ; suffering ; [곤궁] poverty ; need ; destitution **—하다** (be) poor ; destitute ; afflicted ; distressed ¶ 간고를 겪다 undergo〔go through〕 many hardships // 간고를 견디어내다 endure 〔overcome, bear, suffer〕 hardships ; bear〔endure〕 tribulation

간곡 懇曲 kindness ; cordiality ; warmth **—하다** (be) kind ; cordial ; earnest ; painstaking ¶ 간곡한 부탁 an earnest desire〔request〕 ; entreaty // 간곡히 설명하다 take pains to explain ; explain earnestly // 간곡히 타이르다 give 《a person》 a good talking // 그는 간곡한 사연이 있었다 He had serious reasons.

간과 干戈 [무기] arms ; weapons ; shields and spears ; [전쟁] warfare ¶ 서로 간과를 들다 open hostilities ; take up arms against each other ; take up the hatchet // 간과를 거두다 lay down arms ; sheathe the sword ; bury the hatchet

*__간과 看過__ [못보고 빠뜨림] passing over ; failure to notice ; miss ; [묵인함] connivance ; overlooking **—하다** pass over ; overlook ; fail to notice ; connive at ; wink at 《a fault》 (묵인) ¶ 그는 이 사실을 결코 간과하지 않을 것이다 He would be the last to overlook this fact.

간교 奸巧 craft ; wiliness ; cunning ; artfulness ¶ 간교한 artful ; cunning ; sly // 간교한 사람 a sly dog // 간교하게 slyly ; cunningly **—하다** (be) crafty ; cunning ; sly ; wily

간구 懇求 an earnest desire〔request〕 ; entreaty ; solicitation **—하다** beg ; ask ; request earnestly ; entreat ; solicit

간국 salty liquids ; brine

간균 桿菌 〚식물〛 a bacillus 《*pl.* -lli》 ; a bacterium 《*pl.* -ria》 ¶ 간균의 bacterial

간극 間隙 [틈] a gap ; an opening ; aperture ; a chink ; [불화] an estrangement ; a difference ; a cleavage ; a rift ; a split ¶ 간극을 메우다 stop〔fill up, bridge〕 a gap // 간극이 생기다 fall out with each other

간기 刊記 a colophon ; an imprint ; a postscript 《to a book》

간기 —氣 a salty taste

간나위 a cunning〔sly〕 person

간난 艱難 hardships ; privations ; ordeal ; trouble ; tribulation(s) ; trials ; difficulties ; afflictions ; adversity ¶ 간난을 이겨내다 overcome difficulties 〔tribulations, adversity〕 // 간난을 겪다 undergo〔go through〕 hardships ; have a rough time ; suffer privations // 간난에 견디다 endure hardships ; stand adversity

간난 신고 艱難辛苦 hardships ¶ 간난 신고하여 자식을 기르다 manage to bring up one's child under difficulties // 간난 신고 끝에 드디어 합격하다 finally succeed in passing with much difficulty

간닥거리다, 깐닥거리다 budge ; tremble ; be shaky ; be loose ¶ 몸을 깐닥거리다 shake oneself // 이가 깐닥거린다 A tooth is loose.

간단 間斷 interruption ; intermission ; a break ; a pause ¶ 간단없는 incessant ; ceaseless ; continual ; continuous ; unremitting 《industry》 // 간단없이 incessantly ; ceaselessly ; uninterruptedly ; continuously ; without interruption〔stopping, let-up〕 ; without a break 〔pause〕 ; straight through // 간단없이 계속되다 go on〔continue〕 without a break

⁑__간단 簡單__ simplicity ; conciseness ; brevity ; shortness ; plainness ; laconism **—하다** (be) simple ; brief ; short ; plain ; [간편] light ; easy (용이) ¶ 간단한 문제 a simple〔an easy〕 question 〔problem〕 // 간단한 식사 a light meal ; a snack // 간단한 일 a simple task // 간단히 말하자면 in short〔brief〕 ; to be brief ; in a word ; to make a long story short ; to put it simply // 간단하게 하다 simplify ; make simple〔brief〕 // 좀 간단히 설명하여 주시오 Explain the situation briefly. /Explain simply. /Please give us a short account of it. // 간단한 복장으로 오십시오 Please come in simple clothes. // 그를 속이는 것은 간단하다 It's easy to take him in. // 이 문제는 네가 생각하듯이 간단하지 않다 This problem is not as simple as you think. // 요즈음 젊은이들은 회사를 간단하게 그만두는 것 같다 It seems that young people today feel no compunction at all about quitting their jobs.

간단 명료 簡單明瞭 simplicity and clarity ; conciseness **—하다** (be) plain and simple ; clear and concise ; be short〔brief〕 and to the point ; (be) concise ; terse ; laconic ¶ 글은 간단 명료함이 생명이다 Brevity is the soul of writing. // 간단 명료하게 답변하다 answer briefly〔concisely and clearly〕

⁑__간담 肝膽__ ① [간과 쓸개] liver and gall ② [마음·심중] one's innermost heart ¶ 간담을 서늘케 하는 광경 an appalling

〔a dreadful〕 sight // 간담 상조(相照)하다 be great friends ; exchange confidences // 간담을 서늘케 하다 strike terror into 《a person's》 heart ; make 《a person》 shiver ; chill 《a person's》 heart ; curdle 〔chill, freeze〕 《a person's》 blood ; make 《a person's》 blood run cold // 그녀는 그 소식을 듣고 간담이 내려 앉았다 She was astonished at the news.

간담이 내려 앉다 관용 be astonished 〔surprised〕

간담이 떨어지다 관용 one's blood runs cold

간담 懇談 a familiar〔friendly〕 talk ; a chat ; a confabulation ; a confab 《구》 ; consultation **—하다** confabulate 《with》 ; have a (friendly) talk 《with》 ; chat 《with》 ¶ 간담식으로 이야기하다 have an informal talk 《with》 ; talk in a friendly way // 김 박사를 모시고 간담하다 have a talk with Dr. *Kim* as its center 〔central figure〕

—회 a social gathering〔meeting〕 ; a gathering for familiar talk ; a bull session ; a (coffee) klatch

간댕거리다 shake ; tremble ; dangle ; swing ; sway (to and fro) ¶ 마른 나뭇잎이 바람에 간댕거리다 a withered leaf trembles in the wind

간덩이 肝— 《속》 liver

간덩이가 붓다 관용 (be) fearless (of) ; have the guts (to)

간덩이가 크다 관용 (be) shameless ; impudent ; plucky

간데없다 disappear (like a puff of smoke) ; suddenly go away ; vanish ; fade (away) ; vanish into thin air

간도 奸徒 a group of wily characters ; villains

간독 懇篤 kindness ; cordiality **—하다** (be) kind ; cordial ; warm ; genial ¶ 간독히 대접하다 receive 《a person》 cordially〔warmly〕 ; entertain 《a person》 hospitably

간동간동 bundling up neatly

간동그리다 bundle up neatly ; arrange neatly

간동하다 be neatly bundled〔arranged〕

간두 竿頭 the greatest extreme ; the top of a pole ¶ 간두지세(之勢) the most critical situation // 백척간두에서 한 걸음 나아가다 go a step farther ; make one more effort

간드랑간드랑 dingle-dangle ; swaying

간드랑거리다 swing gently ; dangle ; waver ¶ 초롱이 바람에 간드랑거린다 A lantern dangles in the breeze.

간드러지다 (be) coquettish ; (be) willowy ; (be) coy ; charming ; fascinating ; bewitching ; captivating ; haunting ¶ 노래를 간드러지게 부르다 sing a song with a charming lilt // 간드러진 웃음을 보내다 give 《a person》 a coy smile

간드작간드작 swaying slightly

간드작거리다 sway slightly

간들간들 [바람이] gently ; softly ; [태도가] coquettishly ; flirtingly

간들거리다 ① [바람이] blow gently 〔softly〕 ② [물체가] shake ; sway ; dangle ; tremble ¶ 나뭇잎이 바람에 간들거리고 있다 The leaves are trembling in the breeze. ③ [태도가] play the flirt ; act in a charming〔flirtatious〕 manner ; act coquettishly

간디스토마 肝— a liver fluke ; a flukeworm ; trematode

간략 簡略 simplicity ; conciseness ; brevity ; informality ; terseness **—하다** (be) simple ; concise ; brief ; terse ; casual ; informal ¶ 간략히 shortly ; in short ; briefly ; in brief // 간략하게 하다 simplify ; shorten ; make brief // 요점만 간략하게 말하다 talk briefly and to the point // 요점만 간략히 말하라 Will you get〔come〕 to the point briefly ? // 수속이 간략하게 되었다 The formalities have been simplified.

간릉 幹能 being sly〔clever, wily〕 ; subtleness ; cunning **—하다** (be) sly ; clever ; wily ; insidious ¶ 간릉스러운 웃음 a sly smile

간릉부리다 幹能— act craftily

간막이 間— ⇨ 칸막이

간만 干滿 ebb and flow ; flux and reflux ; tide ; rise and fall ¶ 간만의 차 the difference between the rise and fall of the tide // 바닷물에는 간만이 있다 The tide rises and falls in the sea. /The tide ebbs and flows in the sea.

간망 懇望 entreaty ; solicitation ; an earnest request **—하다** entreat ; earnestly request ; implore ; solicit 《a person for》 ; earnestly request〔ask〕 for ¶ 간망을 받아들이다 listen to 《a person's》 entreaty ; comply with 《a person's》 earnest request

간맞다 be well salted〔seasoned〕 ; be salted〔seasoned〕 properly

간맞추다 salt properly ; season well

간명 簡明 conciseness ⇨ 간단 명료

간물 salty water ; brine

간물 奸物 a crafty〔wily〕 fellow ; a wicked man ; a sly guy

간물 乾物 dry foods ; dried provisions 〔fish or meat〕

간물상 乾物商 a drysaltery (상점) ; a drysalter (상인)

간밤 last night〔evening〕 ¶ 간밤에 도둑이 들었다 A burglar broke into my house last night. // 간밤에 내린 비 last night's rain

간방 艮方 the northeast ; the northeastern quarter

간벌 間伐 thinning **—하다** thin out

ㄱ

《forest》
ㅡ재(材) lumber〔timber〕 from thinning
간병 看病 nursing ; attendance **ㅡ하다** nurse ; tend〔wait on〕 《a sick person》 ; take care of ; care for ; look after ; attend on ¶ 정성어린 간병 careful nursing // 자지 않고 간병하다 sit up with a sick person
ㅡ인(人) a (sick) nurse
간보다 taste ; see how the food is salted〔seasoned〕
간부 姦夫 an adulterer
간부 姦婦 an adulteress
간부 奸婦 a wicked woman
간부 幹部 members of the executive ; the executive members ; the management ; the managing staff ; the managing〔governing〕 body ; the leaders ; the leading member ; the executive (회사·조합의) ¶ 민주당의 간부 the executive members of the Democratic party // 간부급에 있는 사람 a person in an executive position〔on the executive board〕 《미》 ; an executive ; a person in the administrative post 《영》 // (군대의) 최고 간부 the top brass // 간부가 되다 become a leader
ㅡ 요원 an official in a responsible post ㅡ임원(任員) executive〔staff〕 officials ; executives 《미》 ㅡ 직원 officials in responsible posts ㅡ회 a meeting of the managing staff ; a directorial meeting ㅡ 회의 an executive session〔council〕 ㅡ 후보생 a military cadet (육군의) ; a candidate-executive (회사 등의)
간빙기 間氷期 〖지질〗 an interglacial period〔interval, phase〕
간사 奸詐 cunning(ness) ; slyness ; craft **ㅡ하다** (be) cunning ; sly ; foxy ; deceitful ; crafty ; wily
간사 부리다〔떨다〕 관용 play a sly game
간사 幹事 [직무] administering affairs ; management ; [처리자] an executive secretary ; a manager
ㅡ장 a chief secretary ; secretary-general 동창회 ㅡ the secretary of an alumni association 클럽 ㅡ a club secretary 클럽 ㅡ회 the board of governors of a club 《영》
간사위 resourcefulness ; versatility ; flexibility
간살 sycophancy ; toadyism ; flattery ; coquetry ; flattering
간살부리다 flatter 《a person》 ; fawn upon 《a person》 ; play up to 《a person ; curry favor with 《a person》 ; coquet ; toady ; adulate ; oil one's〔the〕 tongue
간살쟁이 a flatterer〔sycophant〕 ; a bootlicker
간상 奸商 a dishonest merchant ; a crooked dealer ; a profiteer
ㅡ배 (a group of) racketeers
간상균 桿狀菌 ⇨ 간균
간색 看色 [견본] a sample ; [판단] sampling **ㅡ하다** sample ; take a sample of ; test〔judge〕 by a sample
ㅡ대 a sharp-edged bamboo〔metal〕 scoop
간색 間色 a compound〔secondary〕 color ; half tone ; an intermediate〔in-between〕 shade
간서리목 肝ㅡ liver shish kebab
간석지 干潟地 a tideland ; a beach at ebb tide ; a dry beach ; a tidal〔mud〕 flat ; a muddy riverside
간선 幹線 a trunk〔main〕 line ; an artery of railroad traffic
ㅡ거(渠) a trunk〔main〕 sewer ㅡ 배수(排水) arterial drainage
간선 間選 [간접 선거] indirect election ; voting for the presidential electors (대통령) 《미》 **ㅡ하다** elect indirectly ; have an indirect election ; vote for the presidential electors (대통령의) 《미》
ㅡ제 indirect election system
***간선 도로** a principal〔trunk〕 road ; a main road ; an arterial road〔street〕 《영》 ; a boulevard 《미》
***간섭 干涉** [참견] interference ; meddling ; [타국의 내정에] intervention **ㅡ하다** interfere 《in a matter, with a person》 ; intervene 《in》 ; meddle 《in, with》 ; step in ; butt in ; poke〔stick, put〕 one's nose into ; [전파·음파·광파 등의] interference ¶ 주제넘는 간섭 officious interference // 외부의 간섭 outside intervention // 타국의 내정을 간섭하다 interfere in the internal〔domestic〕 affairs 《of another country》 // 타국의 내전에 간섭하다 intervene in the civil war of another country // 간섭을 받다 be interfered 《with》 // 사생활을 간섭하다 step into one's private life // 타국의 간섭을 초래하다 invite〔lead to〕 foreign intervention // 내 일에 간섭 말아 주게 Leave me alone. // 남의 일에 간섭하다 interfere in another's business ; put〔poke, thrust〕 one's nose into another's business // 일일이 간섭하다 meddle in everything // 쓸데없이 간섭하다 intrude where one is not wanted // 간섭을 받지 않다 be free from intervention
ㅡ자 an intervener ㅡ주의 interventionism ; an interference policy ㅡ 현상 〖의학〗 an interference phenomenon 공동 ㅡ collective〔joint〕 intervention 무력(武力) ㅡ armed intervention 선거 ㅡ government interference in the election 학원 ㅡ government interference in campus activities
간섭계 干涉計 〖물리〗 an interferometer
간섭 굴절계 干涉屈折計 an interference refractometer

간섭 분광법 干涉分光法 interference spectroscopy
간섭색 interference colors
간섭상 干涉像 〖물리〗 an interference figure
간성 干城 a bulwark ; a citadel ; a defender ; a safeguard ; a stronghold ¶ 국가의 간성 the bulwark of the state // 자유의 간성 a bulwark of liberty
간세 間稅 an indirect tax ⇨ 간접세
†간소 簡素 simplicity ; plainness ; frugality (검약) ; thrift ; economy ━하다 (be) simple ; plain ¶ 간소한 식사 a frugal 〔homely〕 meal // 간소한 생활 a simple life ; a frugal way of life // 간소한 차림새 simple dress〔attire〕 // 차림새가 간소하다 be simply attired
간소화 簡素化 simplification ¶ 생활의 간소화 simplification of one's way of life // 사무 절차를 간소화하다 simplify office procedure // 관청〔행정〕 기구를 간소화하다 simplify the government〔administration〕 setup〔structure〕
간솔 簡率 being honest and direct ; outspokenness ; candidness ; straightforwardness ━하다 (be) simple and honest ; outspoken ; candid ; straightforward ; direct
*간수 keeping ; safekeeping ; custody ; charge ; storage ; preserving ; treasuring ━하다 keep ; preserve ; put aside for future use ; treasure (단단히) ¶ 가구를 창고 속에 간수하다 store the furniture in a warehouse // 그것을 단단히 간수해 둬라 Keep it in a safe place. // 앞날을 대비해 이것을 간수하겠다 I'll keep this for future use. // 이 책을 간수해 주시겠습니까 Will you keep this book for me?
간수 ━水 bittern ; brine ; salt water
간수 間數 ⇨ 칸수
간수 看守 a (prison) guard ; a warder ; a jailer〔jailor〕 《미》 ; a gaoler 《영》 ⇨ 교도관
━장 a chief guard 건널목 ━ a (railroad) crossing gateman 여자 ━ a wardress ; a gaoleress 《영》
간식 間食 food eaten between regular meals ; eating between meals ; a light meal ; a snack ; a between-meal snack ━하다 eat between meals ; have〔eat〕 a snack ; snack
간신 奸臣, 姦臣 a villainous retainer ; a treacherous subject
간신 諫臣 a councilor〔an adviser〕 to the king ; a remonstrant to the king ; a devoted〔plain-spoken〕 retainer
간신 艱辛 hardships ⇨ 간난
†간신히 艱辛━ [곤란을 겪고] with difficulty ; with much effort ; [가까스로] barely ; narrowly ; as best one can ; with one's bare life ; just ; only ¶ 간신히 도망가다 have a narrow escape 〔shave, squeak 《구》〕 ; barely escape // 간신히 잠들다 finally doze off // 간신히 기차 시간에 댔다 I was barely in time for the train. / I just caught the train. // 간신히 해치웠다 I just managed it. / I was just able to manage it. // 간신히 이기다 win 《a game》 by a shave〔narrow margin〕
간실간실, 깐실깐실 flatteringly ; fawningly ; in a fawning manner ; ingratiatingly ━하다 cringe 《to》 ; ko(w)tow ; crouch ; fawn 《upon, on》 ; be servile
간악 奸惡 wickedness ; treacherousness ¶ 간악한 신하 a treacherous retainer ━하다 (be) wicked ; treacherous
간암 肝癌 cancer of the liver ; liver cancer ¶ 간암에 걸리다 get a cancer in his liver // 간암으로 죽다 die of liver cancer
간언 間言 mischief-making remarks ; sowing discord ; mischievous gossip ; estranging〔alienating〕 words
간언 諫言 remonstrance ; expostulation ; admonition ━하다 remonstrate 〔expostulate〕 with 《a person》 ; admonish ; advice ; counsel (충고) ¶ 간언에 귀를 기울이지 않다 give no ear to 《a person's》 expostulation // 간언을 듣다 listen〔yield〕 to 《a person's》 remonstrance // 간언에 따르다〔따르지 않다〕 follow〔reject〕 《a person's》 advice // 간언은 귀에 거슬리는 법이다 Good advice is 〔sounds〕 harsh to the ear.
간여 干與 ⇨ 관여(關與)
간염 肝炎 〖의학〗 inflammation of the liver ; hepatitis
A형〔전염성〕 ━ hepatitis A ; infectious hepatitis B형〔혈청(血淸)〕 ━ hepatitis B ; serum hepatitis
간엽 肝葉 〖해부〗 the lobe of the liver
간원 懇願 entreaty ; solicitation ; an earnest appeal ━하다 beg ; entreat for, of》 ; implore ; appeal 《to》 ; beseech ; solicit ¶ 간원하듯 entreatingly ; imploringly // 간원을 받아들이다 listen〔accede〕 to 《a person's》 entreaties // 간원에 귀기울이지 않다 be deaf to 《a person's》 entreaties // 귀하의 허락을 간원합니다 I entreat your pardon. // 도와줄 것을 간원하다 entreat 《a person》 to show mercy ; solicit 《a person》 for his help
━자 a solicitor ; a supplicant
간유 肝油 (cod-)liver oil
간음 姦淫 adultery ; illicit intercourse ; (sexual) misconduct ; fornication (미혼자의) ; 〖법〗 criminal conversation 《미》 ━하다 commit adultery ; misconduct oneself ; have illicit intercourse 《with》 ; fornicate ; commit fornication 《with》 ¶ 폭행 또는 협박에 의해서 부녀자를 간음한 자 a person who, by violence or threat, has obtained carnal

knowledge of a woman
—자 a fornicator ; an adulterer ; an adulteress (여자) —죄 adultery

간이 簡易 simplicity ; ease ; easiness ; handiness —하다 (be) simple ; simplified ; easy ; plain ; handy
— 도서관 a handy public library ; a reference library 《미》 — 보험 postal life insurance — 보험 증서 a post-office life insurance policy — 수도 a small water-supply system — 숙박소 day-laborers' lodgings ; a common〔public〕laborer's lodgings ; a common〔public〕lodging house ; a doss house 《영》 ; a flophouse 《미·속》 — 재판소 a summary court ; a police court — 주택 a simple frame house ; a Quonset hut (조립식의) ; a prefabricated house — 차고 a carport —화(化) simplification

간이식 簡易食 a plain diet

간이 식당 簡易食堂 a quick-lunch room ; a snack bar 《미》 ; a cafeteria (자급식의) 《미》

간인 奸人 a knave ; a villain ; a crook ; a crafty〔wily〕fellow ; a villainous〔wicked, vicious〕person

간자 a spoon ⇨ 숟가락

간자미 〖물고기〗 a young stingray

간작 間作 catch cropping ; intercropping ; [작물] a catch crop —하다 intercrop ; grow 《some vegetables》 between the rows of another crop ¶ 무를 간작으로 가꾸다 grow radishes as a catch crop with other vegetables

간잔지런하다 [눈이] have sleepy eyes 〔be drowsy〕 with lack of sleep〔drunkenness〕; one's eyelids are heavy ; [물건·모양이] be arranged neatly〔qually, evenly〕

간장 —醬 soy ; soy sauce
—통 a soy keg

간장 肝腸 bowels and intestines ¶ 그녀의 미모는 뭇 남성의 간장을 녹여버렸다 Her beauty captivated every man.
간장을 태우다 관용 worry (oneself) ; be anxious〔nervous〕 《about》 ; bother (oneself) 《about》 ; fidget〔fitter〕 about ; be fidgety ; burn with love〔passion〕 《for》 ; be dying for
간장을 끊다 관용 devour one's heart ; feel one's heart torn to pieces
간장을 녹이다 관용 captivate ; bewitch ; enslave

***간장 肝臟** 〖해부〗 the liver
— 기능 부전(機能不全) hepatic insufficiency — 디스토마 distoma hepaticum ; distomatosis ⇨ 간디스토마 — 병 the liver trouble〔complaint〕 — 비대(肥大) hypertrophy of the liver — 엑스 a liver extract —염 ⇨ 간염 — 절개(切開) hepatotomy — 종창(腫脹) swelling〔enlargement〕 of the liver

간적 奸賊 a robber ; a bandit ; an outlaw ; a traitor ; a rebel

***간절 懇切** earnest ; eagerness ; ardentness ; sincerity —하다 (be) earnest ; eager ; sincere ; ardent ¶ 간절한 부탁〔소원〕 an earnest request〔desire〕 // 간절한 충고 sincere advice // 간절한 호소 an ardent〔emotional〕 appeal // 외국 유학할 생각이 간절하다 be keen on studying abroad // 술 생각이 간절하다 be thirsty for a drink // 간절히 타이르다 give 《a person》 a good talking to // 고향 생각이 간절하다 I feel homesick. /I yearn〔long〕 for my home〔hometown〕. // 하고 싶은 생각이 간절하다 be anxious〔solicitous, dying, impatient, eager〕 to 《do》 ; long to 《do》

간절히 懇切— earnestly ; sincerely ; seriously ; honestly ; soberly ; eagerly ; ardently ; heartily ¶ 간절히 바라다 sincerely hope ; desire earnestly ; wish eagerly ; long for // 간절히 타이르다 give 《a person》 a good talking to // 간절히 부탁하다 entreat 《a person》 to do // 간절히 …을 하고 싶다 long to 《do》

***간접 間接** indirectness ; indirection ¶ 간접적인 indirect ; roundabout ; circuitous // 간접적으로 indirectly ; at secondhand ; in a roundabout way // 간접적인 원인 an indirect cause // 그것을 간접적으로 알다〔듣다〕 learn of〔hear about〕 it indirectly〔at secondhand〕 // 적의 간접 침략을 분쇄하다 halt the enemy's subversive infiltration〔indirect aggression〕
— 가열기 an indirect heater — 감독 indirect supervision — 공임 indirect labor cost —광(光) borrowed light — 난방 indirect heating — 무역 indirect commerce〔trade〕 —법(法) an indirect method — 비료 〖농업〗 indirect manure 〔fertilizer〕 —세 indirect tax〔taxation〕 — 손해 consequential damage — 전동 indirect transmission — 조속기(調速機) a relay governor — 증거 indirect evidence — 측정 indirect measurement — 침략 an indirect invasion〔aggression〕 — 통제 indirect control — 핵분열(核分裂) 〖생물〗 karyokinesis — 화법 indirect narration〔discourse, speech〕 — 흡연 passive〔second-hand〕 smoking ¶ 간접 흡연은 건강에 매우 해롭다 Second-hand smoking is a big health hazard.

간접 목적어 間接目的語 〖문법〗 an indirect object

간접비 間接費 〖회계〗 overhead (cost) ; indirect cost

간접 선거 間接選擧 indirect election ; voting for the presidential electors (대통령의) 《미》

간접 전염 間接傳染 infection

간접 조명 間接照明 indirect lighting

간접 촬영 間接撮影 fluoroscopy (X선의)

간접 추리 間接推理 mediate inference

간정되다 become quiet〔still〕; calm〔quiet〕 down; grow still
간조 干潮 ebb tide; low water
—면(面)〔선(線)〕 a low-water level〔line〕 —표(標) a low-water mark
간종간종 in good order; neat and tidy; evening up 《things》
간종그리다 even up; tidy up
†간주 看做 —하다 regard〔consider, think of〕 《as》; look upon〔on〕 《as》; treat 《as》; take 《for》; deem; reckon; count 《as, for》 ¶ 농담으로 간주하다 treat〔look upon〕 it as a joke // 돈이 없어진 것으로 간주하다 regard the money as gone // 다 해결된 것으로 간주하다 look upon 《a matter》 as all squared up // 웃음을 승낙으로 간주하다 regard a smile as consent // 요주의 인물로 간주하다 regard 《a person》 as a dangerous〔questionable〕 character // 그 계약은 파기된 것으로 간주한다 We consider the contract canceled.
간주곡 間奏曲 〖음악〗 an interlude; an intermezzo
간증 干證 [증인] an eyewitness; 〖기독교〗 a confession —하다 witness; make a confession; confess
간지 奸智 craft; cunning; guile; wiles
간지 簡紙 letter-paper; stationery
간지 諫止 dissuasion —하다 dissuade 《a person from doing》
간지다 ① [떨어질 듯함] (be) ready to fall〔drop〕; be likely to fall ¶ 간지게 매달려 있는 호박 pumpkin ready to fall ② [간드러짐] (be) coquettish; charming; bewitching; captivating ¶ 노래를 간지게 부르다 sing a song with a charming lilt
*간지럼 tickle; ticklish〔tickling〕 sensation〔feeling〕 ¶ 간지럼을 타다 be keenly sensitive to tickling; be promptly react to tickling; be easily tickled // 간지럼 치다 tickle 《a person》
간지럽다 (be) ticklish; feel ticklish; feel a tickle ¶ 간지러운 수작 an obvious flattery // 코가〔목이〕 간지럽다 one's nose〔throat〕 tickles // 아이 간지러워 그만 둬 Stop! Don't tickle me. // 칭찬받으니 간지럽다 I am flattered〔tickled〕.
*간직하다 ① [물건을] keep; have 《a thing》 in one's keeping; save; store; treasure (up); hoard (up) 《money》 ¶ 자물쇠를 채워 물건을 간직하다 keep goods under lock and key // 훗날 쓰게 잘 간직해 두어라 Store it away for future use. ② [마음에] hold in mind; cherish; entertain ¶ 추억을 간직하다 cherish one's memory; store up something in one's memory // 가엾은 소녀는 그 일을 홀로 가슴 속에 간직하고 있었다 The poor girl kept it all to herself. // 그의 말은 내 기억 속에 간직되어 있다 His words are graven on my memory.

간질 癎疾 epilepsy ¶ 간질병의 epileptic // 간질 발작 grand mal
— 환자 an epileptic 경증(輕症) — minor〔masked〕 epilepsy 중증(重症) — major epilepsy
간질간질 with a tickling sensation —하다 [몸이] tickle; (be) tickling; ticklish; [마음이] impatient 《for》; anxious〔eager〕 《for, to do》; irritated; nervous; spoiling 《for》; itchy 《for action》 ¶ 등이 간질간질하다 feel one's back itchy〔creepy〕; one's back itches // …하고 싶어 간질간질하다 have an itch 《for, to do》
간질거리다 ① [간지럽다] feel a tickle; be ticklish; be sensitive to tickling; itch ② [간질이다] tickle; titillate
간질 세포 間質細胞 interstitial cells
*간질이다 tickle; titillate ¶ 발바닥을 간질이다 tickle the soles of 《a person's》 feet // 못살게 간질이다 tickle to death // 털로 간질이다 tickle 《a person》 with a feather // 겨드랑이를 간질이다 tickle 《a person》 under his arms〔at his armpits〕 // 간질여서 웃기다 tickle a laugh out of 《a person》
간짓대 a (long) bamboo pole
간책 奸策 wiles; a trick; a sinister〔an evil〕 scheme ¶ 간책을 쓰다 resort to tricks; indulge in trickery // 간책에 걸려들다 fall victim to a scheme; fall into another's snare; fall into the trap
간척 干拓 land reclamation by drainage —하다 reclaim 《land》 by drainage
— 계획 a (land) reclamation program — 공사 reclamation works — 사업 a (land) reclamation project —지 reclaimed land ¶ 바다를 막아 만든 얕은 간척지 a tract of low land reclaimed from the sea
*간첩 間諜 a spy; a secret agent; an (espionage) agent; an informer; an emissary; an intelligence agent; a double agent (이중 간첩); a mole (조직 속에 숨어서 이적 행위를 하는 사람) ¶ 간첩단의 우두머리 a spymaster // 간첩 행위를 하다 be a spy 《for》; play the spy; be engaged in espionage // 간첩을 보내다 send out a spy // 간첩을 색출하다 hunt〔seek〕 out spies; dig up spies; discover a mole // 적의 간첩 노릇을 하다 spy for the enemy
—망(網) a spy network —선 spy ship —자수 기간 a surrender period set for (Communist) espionage agents —죄 (the crime of) espionage — 행위(行爲) (an act of) espionage — 활동 《have》 espionage activities; 《do》 espionage work 경제 — industrial espionage; an industrial spy (사람); economic espionage (일) 대— 대책 본부 the Counter Espionage Operations Headquarters 《CEOH》 대— 작전

counter espionage operations **무장** — an armed espionage agent **이중** — a double agent ; a mole

‡간청 懇請 entreaty ; supplication ; solicitation ; an earnest request〔appeal〕 —**하다** make request(s) for ; request《a person》 to do《a thing》; entreat ; beg ; make supplication to《a person》; beseech ; implore ¶ 간청에 의하여 at the request of《a person》; at《a person's》 earnest request ; at one's solicitation ; by request // 간청을 들어주다 listen to《a person's》 entreaty ; comply with《a person's》 request // 간청대로 as requested // 학교장 간청에 못이겨 연설하다 make a speech at the principal's earnest request // 구명을 간청하다 supplicate《a person》 to spare one's life // 그는 내가 그 곳에 있어줄 것을 간청했다 He requested that I should be there. // 부디 참석해 주시기를 간청합니다 We request the honor〔pleasure〕 of your company.

간초 艱楚 hardships ; suffering ; privation(s) ¶ 간초를 극복하다 overcome hardships

간촉 懇囑 an earnest request ⇨ 간청

‡간추리다 sum up ; summarize ; digest ; abridge ; brief《미》; hit the high spots《미·구》

간취 看取 —**하다** notice ; perceive ; grasp ; detect ; see through《a plot》; get wind of《a plot》

간치다 salt ; season

간친 懇親 friendliness ; sociability —**하다** be intimate《with》; be on good terms with《a person》; have friendly relations with《a person》

—**회** a social meeting〔gathering〕; a sociable《미》; a get-together (meeting)

***간통 姦通** adultery ; illicit intercourse〔intimacy〕; liaison ;〖법〗 criminal conversation ; misconduct ; criminal connection《영》 —**하다** commit adultery〔misconduct〕《with》; have illicit intercourse《with》; have a liaison with ¶ 기혼자와 독신자의 간통 single adultery // 기혼자간의 간통 double adultery

—**자(者)** an adulterer (남자) ; an adulteress (여자) —**죄** criminal conversation ; adultery **혈족** — incest

간투사 間投詞〖문법〗 an interjection

간특 奸慝 cunning ; craftiness ; craft ; artfulness —**하다** (be) cunning ; sly ; artful ; crafty ; tricky ¶ 간특한 인간 a crafty〔tricky〕 person ; an old fox ; a sly dog

간파 看破 —**하다** see through《a fraud》; read《a person's thought》; penetrate《a person's motive》

‡간판 看板 ① a sign ; a signboard ; [그림 간판] a billboard ; [사무소의] a door plate ; a shingle《미》 ¶ 상점의 간판 a store sign // 세워 놓은 간판 a standing signboard // 간판을 내다 set〔hang〕 out one's sign // 간판을 내걸다 put〔set〕 up a sign〔signboard〕; hang out a signboard〔shingle〕 // 간판을 내릴 시간이다 It's closing time.

② [인물] a big draw ; drawing card ; appearance ; look ; feature ; front (man) ; figure head ; show ¶ 자선이란 간판을 내걸고 under the cloak of charity // 간판은 근사하지만 실속이 없다 It looks interesting, but in fact it is quite dull. // 간판은 그럴듯 하다 make a good show // 간판 뿐이다 be big to look at but small at heart ; be not as〔so〕 good as one looks // 우리 사장은 회사 간판에 불과하다 Our president is just a figurehead. // 그녀는 이 흥행단의 유일한 간판이다 She is the only star〔big draw〕 of this troupe. // 간판 노릇을 하다 serve as a front man // 그 식당은 도박 행위를 숨기기 위한 간판에 불과하다 The restaurant is just a front for a gambling operation.

③ [학벌] a school career ; an academic background〔career〕; an academic clique ; academical cliquism ¶ 간판이 좋다 have a good academic career〔background〕

— **그림** a billboard picture —**집** a sign-maker's shop **가게** — a store sign **광고** — an advertizing sign **여인숙** — an inn sign **이발소** — a hairdresser's sign **전광(電光)〔전기(電氣)〕** — an electric sign《of a store》 **지붕** — a roof sign ; a sky sign《미》

간판을 떼다 관용 take away〔off〕 a sign ; remove a signboard

간판을 내리다 관용 pull down one's signboard ; close a door〔shop〕

간판장이 看板— a sign painter〔maker〕

간편 簡便 convenience ; handiness —**하다** (be) convenient ; simple ; easy ; handy ; portable (들고 다니기에) ¶ 간편한 물건 a simple and convenient article // 간편한 방법 a simple and easy way ; a simple method // 간편한 옷 casual wear〔clothes, attire〕 // 입국 절차가 간편해졌다 Entry formalities have been simplified. // 짐을 간편하게 꾸리다 pack things conveniently (so that they will be handy)

간품 看品 sampling ; inspection —**하다** sample ; check quality ; inspect

간핍 艱乏 utter destitution —**하다** (be) utterly destitute

간하다 salt ⇨ 간

간하다 諫— remonstrate with《a person》 on《a matter》; expostulate with《a person》; admonish ; advise《a king, one's superior》 ¶ 순수한 충성심에서 왕을 간하다 expostulate with the king in all loyalty // 간하는 말을 듣지 않다 give no ear to one's expostulation ; turn a deaf ear to one's remonstration

간해 last year

간행 刊行 publication ; issue **— 하다** publish ; bring out ; issue ¶ 그 출판사는 그 사전을 5만부 간행하였다 The publisher printed 50,000 copies of the dictionary. // 그 시집은 5천부 간행되었다 Five thousand volumes of this collection of poems were printed. // 간행 연월일 the date of publication // 정기 간행물 a periodical

— 날짜 the publication date〔day〕; the date of publication **—물** a publication **—본** a (published) book **—지(地)** the place of publication

간헐 間歇 intermittence **— 하다** intermit ¶ 간헐적인 intermittent ; occasional // 간헐적으로 intermittently ; by fits and starts ; at intervals ; not continuous ; occasionally // 간헐적으로 내리는 비 an intermittent rain

— 기록 계기(記錄計器) an intermittent recorder **— 난방** intermittent heating **— 동작** a sampling action〔working〕 **— 방전(放電)** an intermittent discharge **— 사여과기(砂濾過器)** an intermittent sand filter **—성(性) 말라리아열(熱)** malarial fever **—성 파행증(性跛行症)** intermittent claudication **—열** intermittent fever **— 운동** intermittent movement **— 전류** an intermittent current **—천〔온천〕** a geyser ; an intermittent fountain〔spring〕

†**간호 看護** nursing ; tending 《a sick person》; care (of the sick) **— 하다** nurse ; tend ; care for ; attend ¶ 정성어린 간호 careful nursing // 간호하여 완쾌시키다 nurse 《a person》 back to health // 자지 않고 간호하다 sit up with 《a sick person》

— 과장 a director of nursing service **— 보조원** a nurse's aide **—학** the science of nursing **—학과** the department of nursing science **— 학교** a nurses' training school

간호법 看護法 the art of nursing

간호병 看護兵 a nurse ; a hospital orderly ; a medical-corps man ; a corpsman 《미·해군》

†**간호사 看護師** a (sick) nurse ; a hospital nurse ; a sister 《영》; a trained nurse 《미》; a male nurse (남자)

병원 — a hospital nurse **수(首)—** a head nurse ; a matron **수습 —** a practical nurse 《미》 **야근 —** a night nurse〔sister〕 **유자격 —** a trained〔graduate 《미》, registered〕 nurse

간호원 看護員 ⇨ 간호사

***간혹 間或** [시간적] sometimes ; occasionally ; on occasion ; now and then ; once in a while ; between whiles ; at intervals ; from time to time ; [공간적] in places ; few and far between ; sparsely ; thinly ¶ 간혹 오는 손님 a casual visitor ; a stray customer (상점에) // 간혹 들르다 drop once in a while // 간혹 있는 사건 a rare occurrence // 거기에는 인가가 간혹 가다 하나 둘 있다 The place is sparsely dotted with cottages.

간활 奸猾 cunning ; craftiness ; wiles ; slyness **— 하다** (be) sly ; crafty ; cunning

간흉 奸凶 viciousness ; utter wickedness **— 하다** (be) vicious ; utterly wicked

간힘쓰다 hold one's breath to withstand pain ; withstand pain with one's teeth clenched〔set〕

간힘주다 ⇨ 간힘쓰다

***갇히다** be confined ; be shut in〔up〕; be kept indoors ; be locked in ; [감옥에] be imprisoned ; be behind bars ; be put in prison ; be〔lie〕 in prison ¶ 방에 갇히다 be locked in a room ; be kept in a room under lock and key // 눈에 갇히다 be housebound by the snow ; be snowbound ; be kept in one's room by the snow // 감기로 방에 갇혀 있다 He is confined to his bed with a cold. // 가택 연금하에 있다 be placed under house arrest

갈[1] [갈대] a reed

갈[2] 〖건축〗 [사개·인방의] a fork of a forked tenon

갈[3] [가을] autumn ; fall 《미》 ⇨ 가을

갈[4] [학(學)] science of ; study of ; -ology

소리— phonology **월—** syntax **한글—** the study of the Korean language

갈 碣 [작은 비석] a small monument〔tombstone〕 with rounded top

갈가리 in pieces ⇨ 가리가리

갈가마귀 〖새〗 a jackdaw

갈가위 a screw ; a grasping person ; a miser ¶ 그는 갈가위 같다 He is grasping.

갈갈 avidly ; greedily ¶ 갈갈거리다 (be) greedy ; ravenous 《for》

갈갈이 fall plowing

갈강갈강 wheez ; wheezing

갈개 a ditch ; a gutter ; a drain

갈개꾼 a laborer who strips off the bark of mulberry trees ; [훼방꾼] a hinderer ; an interrupter ; a meddler

갈개발 [연의] a pair of tails hanging from a kite ; [사람] an ass in lion's skin ; a hanger-on

갈걍갈걍하다 (be) thin but sturdy ; look slender but stout

갈거미 〖동물〗 a long-legged spider

갈건 葛巾 a hood made of kudzu fiber ; a ko-hemp hood

갈건야복 葛巾野服 a ko-hemp hood

and cotton clothes ; a plain dress of a hermit

갈겨먹다 snatch away 《food, a thing》 from 《a person》; seize ; wrench ; extort

‡**갈겨쓰다** scrawl ; scribble ; dash off ; write hurriedly〔carelessly〕 ¶ 편지를 갈겨쓰다 scribble a letter

갈고랑 막대기 a hook-shaped stick

갈고랑쇠 a hook ; a crook ; a gaff ; [사람] an eccentric (person) ; a fastidious person ; [구어] screwball ; crank ; faddist

‡**갈고랑이** a hook ; a crook ; a gaff ¶ 갈고랑이 모양의 hooked // 갈고랑이에 걸다 hook

갈고리 a hook ⇨ 갈고랑이

갈고리눈 a crescent-shaped eye ; a hook-shaped eye

갈고리달 a new〔young〕 moon ; a crescent ; the sickle〔horned〕 moon

갈고리촌충 [동물] a hooked tapeworm

갈고쟁이 a wooden hook

갈구 渴求 thirst 《for》; lust 《for》; craving 《for》; a longing 《for》; earnest desire 《for》; an ardent wish 《for》 ⇨ 갈망(渴望) **―하다** crave〔yearn, thirst〕 for ; have a craving for ; long for ; hunger for〔after〕; desire eagerly

갈그랑거리다 wheeze ⇨ 가르랑거리다

갈근 葛根 the root of an arrowroot ; the root of Pueraria

갈근거리다 ① [목이] have an itch in throat ; be tickled with phlegm
② [탐내다] covet ; desire eagerly

*__갈기__ a mane ¶ 갈기가 있는 maned

갈기갈기 to〔in〕 pieces ; to〔into〕 shreds ¶ 갈기갈기 찢다 tear 《paper》 to pieces 〔shreds, ribbons〕; shred into〔in〕 // 편지를 갈기갈기 찢다 tear a letter in〔to〕 pieces // 갈기갈기 찢기다 be torn to pieces〔tatters, shreds〕

*__갈기다__ ① [치다] strike ; beat ; cuff ; knock ; hit ¶ 몽둥이로 머리를 갈기다 strike〔club〕 《a person》 on the head with a stick // 빰을 갈기다 slap 《a person's》 cheek〔face〕; box〔slap〕 《a person》 on the ear(s) ; give 《a person》 a box on the ear(s) // 채찍으로 갈기다 flog ; lash ; whip // 콧등을 갈기다 punch 《a person's》 nose // 녹초가 되게 갈기다 pommel ; beat to a jelly ; batter // 호되게 갈기다 give a sound thrashing to ; give 《a person》 a good licking
② [발로 지르다] kick ; give a kick
③ [연장으로 베다] cut ; strike a blow 《with a sharp instrument》; slash
④ [글씨를] scrawl ; scribble ; dash off
⑤ [쏘다] fire ; shoot ; hit ; loose (off) 《a pistol》; fire 《guns》 by volleys
⑥ [오줌을] urinate ; make〔pass〕 water

*__갈다__[1] [바꾸다] change ; replace ; substitute ; [갈아타다] transfer ¶ A를 B로 갈다 replace A with B ; substitute B for A // 사람을 갈다 replace 《a person》 by 〔with〕 《another》 // 의사를 갈다 consult another doctor // 구두를 갈아 신다 change one's shoes // 낡은 타이어를 새 것으로 갈다 replace〔change〕 a worn tire by〔with〕 a new one // 욕조의 물을 갈다 refill a bathtub // 버스에서 지하철로 갈아타다 transfer from bus to subway train // 서울행 지하철로 갈아타다 change subway trains for Seoul // 갈아탈 차편 〔비행기편〕 connection ; connecting flight // 갈아타는 지점 transfer // 투수를 다른 선수로 갈다 change off with another pitcher // 더러운 셔츠를 깨끗한 것으로 갈아입다 change a dirty shirt for a clean one

†**갈다**[2] ① [칼을] sharpen 《a knife》; grind 《edged tools》; hone 《a razor》; strop 《a razor》 ¶ 낫을 숫돌에 갈다 whet a scythe on the stone
② [맷돌로] grind ¶ 밀을 갈다 grind wheat into flour // 가루가 되게 갈다 rub into fine powder
③ [윤나게] polish ; cut 《a diamond》; [먹을] rub 《an ink stick》
④ [이를] gnash〔grind〕 one's teeth ; grit〔grate〕 the teeth ¶ 이를 갈며 맹세하다 grind out an oath // 생각만 해도 이가 갈리다 gnash one's teeth at the thought // 분해서 이를 갈았다 That made them grit their teeth
⑤ [연마하다] drill ; practice ; train ; cultivate ; exercise ; whet ¶ 무예를 갈고 닦다 train〔soldier〕 in martial arts

‡**갈다**[3] [밭을] till ; cultivate ; plow ¶ 밭을 갈다 plow a field ; till〔cultivate〕 the soil // 밀을 갈다 sow wheat ; plant 《a field》 with wheat

‡**갈대** a reed ¶ 여자의 마음은 갈대와 같다 Woman is as fickle as a reed. // 사람은 갈대에 지나지 않는다 그러나 생각하는 갈대다 Man is but a reed, but he is a thinking reed.
―꽃 reed flowers ; the ears of a reed
―밭 a field of reeds **― 피리** a reed flute〔pipe〕

갈대발 a hanging screen made of reeds ; a reed blind

갈등 葛藤 complications ; trouble ; difficulties ; discord ; tangle ; dissension ; conflict ; [반목] a feud ¶ 당 내부의 갈등 a party feud // 심리적 갈등 a mental conflict // 갈등이 나다 have a feud 《with》; be at enmity 《with》 // 갈등을 일으키다 cause〔give rise to〕 complications 《between the two》 // 갈등을 해소하다 disentangle〔unravel〕 a complicated matter ; settle 《a problem》

갈라내다 sort out ; assort

갈라놓다 ① [떼어놓다] estrange 《people》; alienate 《a person》 from 《another》; sever ; separate ¶ 싸우고

있는 두 소년을 갈라놓다 separate the two boys who are fighting // 부부 사이를 갈라놓다 separate husband and wife // 팀을 두 편으로 갈라놓다 divide a team into two parts
② [구분하다] part ; divide ; classify ; sort 《A》 from 《B》 ¶ 카드를 색깔별로 갈라놓다 sort cards according to their colors // 이 제안으로 학급이 둘로 갈라졌다 The proposal split our class into two.

갈라붙이다 divide and assign〔allocate〕; divide ; part ; split up

갈라서다 ① [줄을] line up separately ; stand apart ¶ 세 줄로 갈라서다 line up in three files
② [이혼·절연] divorce 《oneself》 from ; get a divorce ; separate ; be divorced 《from》; break with 《a person》; break off relations 《with》; be through with 《미》 ¶ 그들은 갈라선 지 오래다 They have long divorced. // 친구하고 갈라서다 finish〔break〕 with a friend ; break off relations with a friend // 왜 너희들은 갈라서게 되었니 Why did you two split up?

†**갈라지다** ① [쪼개지다] be divided ; cleave ; fissure ; crack ; gape (땅이) ; break up ; split ; part ; [구분되다] be divided 《into》; [분기하다] be divided ; branch off ; fork ¶ 길이 두 갈래로 갈라지다 a road forks // 당은 여러 분파로 갈라졌다 The party split into several fractions. // 지진으로 땅이 갈라졌다 The ground was cracked by the earthquake. // 가뭄으로 갈라진 논 a rice paddy cracked from a drought // 세 부분으로 갈라지다 be divided into three parts // 이 나무는 쉽게 갈라진다 This wood splits〔cleaves〕 easily. // 그 문제로 당은 두 파로 갈라졌다 The party split〔divided〕 into two parts on the issue. // 레코드가 떨어져 두 조각으로 갈라졌다 The record fell to the floor and broke into two.
② [사이가] part 《from, with》; be estranged 《from》; split with ; separate from ; part company〔ways〕 《with》 ¶ 처와 갈라지다 separate from one's wife ; leave one's wife 《at a place》 // 사이가 갈라지다 split with 《a person》 // 그들은 갈라졌다 Their marriage broke up.

갈래 [분파] a branch ; an offshoot 《from》; [분기] a fork ; [구분] a division ; a section ¶ 여러 갈래의 의견 various opinions // 여러 갈래로 나누다 divide into several parts〔sections〕 // 모퉁이를 돌면 길은 세 갈래로 갈라진다 Turning the corner, the road breaks 〔forks, branches, divides〕 into three. // 갈래를 잡을 수 없다 cannot understand ; cannot make anything of

갈래다 ① [정신이] become〔get〕 confused ; lose one's wits〔head〕 ¶ 정신이 갈래다 feel one's mind wander〔roam〕; be distracted ② [동물이] go astray ; roam ; wander ; run about aimlessly

갈륨 〖화학〗 gallium 《Ga》

갈리다[1] [분열되다] be divided 《into》; split ; be split ; [분기되다] branch off ; diverge 《from》; ramify ; be forked ¶ 여러 파로 갈리다 be divided into several groups // 길은 여기서 갈린다 Here the road branches off. // 의견이 서로 갈렸다 Their opinions are divided.

갈리다[2] [교대] be replaced 《by》; be superseded 《by》; give place to ¶ 담임 선생님이 갈렸다 A new teacher has taken over our class. // 도지사가 대폭 갈렸다 A sweeping change of provincial governors has taken place.

갈리다[3] ① [갈려지다] be whetted ; be ground ; be sharpened ; be rubbed ¶ 이 밀은 잘 갈린다 This wheat grinds〔is ground〕 well〔fine〕. // 강철은 갈려서 날카로운 날이 된다 Steel grinds to a fine edge.
② [갈게 하다] make 《a person》 whet 〔grind〕; have 《a person》 sharpen 《a knife》; have 《a person》 rub〔polish〕

갈리다[4] ① [논을] make〔let〕 《a person》 plow〔plough 《영》〕; have 《a person》 cultivate ; make 《a person》 till ¶ 아들에게 논을 갈리다 have one's son plow the paddy field // 이 밭은 잘 갈린다 This field plows easily.
② [땅이] be plowed〔tilled, cultivated〕

갈림길 [갈라진 길] a branch〔side〕 road ; a forked road ¶ 갈림길에 이르다 come to the fork of a road // 왼쪽 갈림길로 접어들다 take the left-hand fork ; [선택한 처지] turning point ; a crossroad ¶ 인생 항로의 갈림길에 서 있다 He is standing at the turning point〔crossroads〕 of his life.

갈림목 a fork of the road ; a corner at a juncture of streets ; a junction ; a juncture

갈마들다 take turns ; alternate ; come on by turns ; be employed by turns ¶ 가뭄과 장마가 갈마들다 The dry spell and the rainy spell alternate with each other. // 기쁨과 슬픔이 갈마들다 alternate between joy and grief

갈마들이다 change turns ; employ by turns

갈마쥐다 ① [옮겨 쥐다] shift 《a thing》 from hand to hand ② [이것저것을] grasp one thing after another

갈망 control ; management ; conduct ; setting 《matters》 right ; winding-up
— 하다 cope with 《a problem》; answer 《a question》; set 《matters》 right ; dispose of 《matters》 ¶ 빚을 갈망하다 pay off〔settle〕 debts // 뒷갈망을

하다 wind up ; square away ; settle // 그 일은 내가 갈망할 수 없다 I am not equal to the task.

‡**갈망 渴望** a longing〔yearning, craving〕《for》; thirst 《for》; an eager〔earnest〕desire 《for》; lust《for, of》; an aspiration

> 참고 **eager** 아주 열심히 어떤 일을 하기를 희망하고 있는 **anxious** 강한 희망을 갖고 있지만 그것의 달성 여부에 대해 불안한 마음을 품고 있는

— 하다 long〔crave, yearn〕《for》; thirst 《after, for》; be eager〔anxious〕《for》; desire eagerly ; crave 《fame》¶ 미국 유학을 갈망하고 있다. He is anxious to continue his study in the United States. // 남북〔민족〕 통일을 갈망하다 have intense aspirations for unification of North and South (Korea)〔the nation〕// 그는 학자가 되기를 갈망하고 있다 He has an aspiration to become a scholar. // 그들은 평화와 자유를 갈망하고 있다 They long〔are longing〕 for peace and liberty. // 지식에 대한 갈망을 만족시키다 satisfy one's hunger〔thirst, craving〕 for knowledge

갈매 ① [색] deep green ② [열매] fruit of the buckthorn
—나무〖식물〗the Dahurian buckthorn

***갈매기** 〖새〗 a (sea) gull ; a mew gull ; a (sea) mew

갈모 a rain cover for a hat

갈목 a spike of reed
—비 a rush broom ; a broom made of reed spikes

갈무리 [챙기어 간수함] putting 《things》 in order ; setting 《things》 in order ; tidying up ; management ; conduct ; dealing ; disposition **— 하다** put away in order ; [마무리] finish up ; put the finishing touch on ¶ 제 앞 갈무리도 못 하면서 남의 일에 참견한다 Unable to handle his own business, he pokes his nose into another's.

갈묻이 turning over 《the soil of a field》; tilling **— 하다** turn over〔up〕《the soil of a field》; break up 《land》; till

갈바람 〖항해〗 [서풍] a west wind ; [남서풍] a southwest wind

갈바래다 turn over 《the soil》 and expose it to the sun and wind

갈밭 a field of reeds

갈범 a tiger (in comparison with a leopard)

갈보 a prostitute ; a harlot ; a whore ; a streetwalker ; hooker 《미·속》 ¶ 갈보 노릇을 하다 walk the streets ; go on the streets ; prostitute *oneself* ; practice prostitution ; enter into prostitution
—집 a brothel ; a whorehouse

갈분 葛粉 arrowroot (starch)

갈붙이다 alienate 《a person from another》; separate 《a person from》; play 《a person》 against 《another》; play off 《a person against another》; estrange 《a person from another》

갈비[1] the ribs ; a skinny〔lean, weedy, scrawny〕 person (말라깽이) ¶ 갈비가 휘다 be overburdened with painstaking work // 돼지〔쇠〕 갈비를 굽다 roast〔broil, grill〕 the ribs of pork〔beef〕
— 새김 rib meat **—찜** steamed short ribs **—탕** beef-rib soup **돼지 —** ribs of pork **쇠—** ribs of beef

갈비[2] 〖건축〗 the width of a roof〔housetop〕

갈비[3] a rush broom ⇨ 갈목(-비)

갈비뼈 ⇨ 갈빗대

갈빗대 the ribs ; a rib-bone ; the ribcage ¶ 갈빗대를 부러뜨리다 break〔fracture〕 a rib
갈빗대가 휘다 관용 be laborious〔arduous〕; strenuous ; toilsome ; troublesome ; painful ; beyond one's ability

갈새 〖새〗 the reed warbler

†**갈색 褐色** brown ; brownness ¶ 짙은 갈색 dark brown ; olive brown ; dun ; umber // 연한 갈색 light brown // 갈색이 도는 brownish〔browny〕// 갈색눈 a brown eye // 갈색 피부 brown skin
— 인종 the brown races **— 착색제** browning (음식에 치는) **—토** brown soil (토양) **—화약** brown powder (총포용)

갈서다 stand abreast

갈수 渴水 the shortage of water supply ; water famine
—기(期) the dry〔low water〕 season **—년(年)** a dry year **—량** minimum flow **—위(位)** the droughty water level **—유량(流量)** droughty water discharge

갈수록 as time goes by ; as one goes along ; in the process of time ; the more(-er) ... the more(-er) ; the more... the less... ¶ 날이 갈수록 as days go by ; as the days roll by〔on〕// 갈수록 해가 길어진다 The days are becoming longer. // 갈수록 더위가 심해진다 It's growing warmer and warmer. // 갈수록 낮이 짧아진다 The days are growing shorter. // 갈수록 애정을 느끼게 되다 grow more and more in love with 《a person》// 나이가 들어갈수록 더 많은 경험과 지식을 얻게 된다 The older one grows the more knowledge and experience one acquires. // 높이 올라갈수록 추워진다 The higher up we go, the colder it becomes.
갈수록 태산이라 관용 things get worse and worse〔go from bad to worse〕

갈씬거리다 barely reach〔touch〕; graze 《along, by》

갈씬하다 《a skirt》 almost touch 《the

floor》; drags
갈아내다 replace ; supplant ; take out an old one (with intent to replace) ; substitute 《one thing for another》 ¶ 충치를 갈아내다 pull out a decayed tooth
갈아대다 (ex)change ; replace 《a thing with another》; renew ; substitute ; put in a new one (as a replacement) ¶ 구두창을 갈아대다 resole shoes // 사람을 갈아대다 replace 《a person》 with〔by〕 another ; change people〔personnel〕
갈아들다 move in (as a replacement) ; take another's place ; serve as a replacement〔substitute, relief〕 ¶ 새 집에 갈아들다 move into a new house // 새 식모가 갈아들었다 A new maidservant has replaced the old one.
갈아들이다 change 《a person》; replace 《a person》 with 《another》; substitute 《a person》 ¶ 매달 하인을 갈아들이다 change one's servant every month // 가정부를 새로 갈아들이다 take a new housemaid
갈아붙이다 [이를] grind one's teeth with vexation ; grind one's teeth spitefully [벽보 등을] attach anew ; paste anew ¶ 벽에 포스터를 갈아붙이다 change the poster (pasted) on the wall
†갈아입다 change 《one's clothes》 ¶ 젖은 옷을 마른 옷으로 갈아입다 change wet clothes for dry ones // 여름옷으로 갈아입다 change into a light summer suit
갈아주다 [물건을 사다] buy ; purchase ; get ; take ; [새것으로] change ; renew ¶ 욕조에 물을 갈아주다 refill a bathtub
†갈아타다 change 《for another train, to another line》; change cars〔trains〕; transfer 《to another car》; [배를] change to 《another ship》; transship ¶ 갈아타지 않고 without changing // 갈아타는 역 a station for changing 《cars》; a junction // 말을 갈아타다 change horses // 다른 버스로 갈아타다 change〔switch〕 to another bus // 지하철로 가면 갈아타야 한다 we have to change trains if we went by subway.
갈음 [바꿈] substituting ; replacing ; changing ; switching —하다 substitute ; replace ; change ; renew
갈음질 sharpening ; whetting ; grinding
갈이[1] [경작] plowing ; tillage ; cultivation ; [넓이] the acreage to be covered by a day's plowing ¶ 열흘 갈이 the acreage that can be plowed by one person in ten days
갈이[2] [대체] replacement ; change ; substitution
갈이질 [경작] plowing with plow ; [갈이틀로] turning on〔operating〕 a lathe —하다 work with a three-man Korean plow ; operate a lathe
갈잎 [가랑잎] fallen〔dead〕 leaves ; [떡갈잎] leaves of the overcup oak
갈증 渴症 thirst ¶ 갈증이 나다 feel thirsty ; be very thirsty // 갈증을 풀다 quench〔slake〕 one's thirst ; appease 〔slake〕 one's thirst ; relieve one's thirst
갈지자걸음 —之字— staggering gait ; reeling gait ¶ 술에 취해 갈지자걸음으로 걷다 walk zigzag under the influence of drink // 갈지자걸음으로 길을 건너다 lurch〔stagger〕 across the road
갈지자형 —之字形 a zigzag ¶ 길이 갈지자형으로 구불구불하다 The road zigzags.
갈진 竭盡 running out ; exhaustion ; complete consumption —하다 run out ; be〔get〕 exhausted
갈쭉하다 (be) thick ; stiff ; tough ; heavy ¶ 갈쭉한 국 thick soup
갈참나무 〖식물〗 a white oak
†갈채 喝采 cheers ; applause ; an ovation ; plaudits —하다 applaud ; cheer ; give cheers〔an ovation〕 ¶ 갈채 속에 amid cheers ; amid acclamation 우레와 같은 박수 갈채 a storm of applause // 열광적인 박수 갈채를 받다 draw enthusiastic applause // 갈채를 받다 win applause // 만장의 갈채를 받다 bring down the house ; receive a standing ovation // 박수 갈채 속에 amidst loud acclamations // 박수 갈채로 맞이하다 greet 《a person》 with loud applause ; welcome with cheers ; hail with acclamation(s) // 청중은 열광적으로 박수 갈채하였다 The audience applauded frantically.
갈철광 褐鐵鑛 〖광물〗 limonite
갈청 the thin white membrane inside a reed ; the pith of a reed
갈초 —草 winter hay
갈치 〖물고기〗 a hairtail ; a kind of scabbard fish ; cutlass fish ; Trichiurus japonicus (학명)
*갈퀴 a (leaf) rake ¶ 갈퀴로 낙엽을 긁어모으다 rake fallen leaves ; rake together the dead leaves
—나무 dead leaves〔dry herbs〕 for fuel
갈퀴다 rake (up)
갈퀴질 raking —하다 rake (together, up)
갈퀫발 tines of a rake
갈탄 褐炭 brown coal ; lignite ; subbituminous coal
갈파 喝破 proclamation ; pronouncement 《of truth》 —하다 proclaim ; declare ; expound 《a truth》; affirm
갈팡질팡 —하다 go this way and that ; run about in a hubbub ; be confused ; be at a loss ; run about in confusion ; cannot catch the point ; be embarrassed〔confused〕 ¶ 갈팡질팡하지 말고 나 하라는 대로 해 Don't be flustered, do just as I tell you. // 그녀 앞에서 갈팡질팡하고 말았다 I felt embar-

rassed〔nervous〕 in her presence.

갈포 葛布 arrowroot cloth ; cloth woven of arrowroot
— 벽지 arrowroot wallpaper

갈품 reed blossoms which have not fully come out ; the flower bud of a reed

갈피 ① [한 겹의] a space between folds 〔layers, pages〕 ¶ 책갈피에 끼워 두다 put 《a thing》 between the leaves of a book ② [사물의 어름] the point ; the sense ; the drift ¶ …의 갈피를 잡을 수 없다 cannot make head or tail 《of》 ; cannot grasp the meaning 《of》 ; can make neither head nor tail 《of》∥그가 하는 말은 전혀 갈피를 잡을 수 없다 I cannot get the point of his argument at all.∥저 사람 설명이 서툴러서 더욱 갈피를 잡을 수 없을 거야 He's so bad at explaining things you're just going to get even more mixed up.

갈피갈피 (between) leaf after leaf ; page after page ; layer after layer ; fold after fold ¶ 옷을 갈피갈피 뒤져 보다 search through the clothes one by one∥책을 갈피갈피 넘기다 turn over〔go through〕 the pages〔leaves〕

갈화 葛花 flowers of an arrowroot

*__갉다__ [앞니·칼 끝으로] scratch ; gnaw 《in, into, through》; [갈퀴로] rake 《together, up》; [트집잡다] carp〔nag〕 《at a person's fault》; peck 《at》; cavil 《at, about》; [재물을] squeeze ; extort ; exploit ¶ 쥐가 판자를 갉아 구멍을 냈다 Rats gnawed a hole in〔into, through〕 a board.∥갉아서 벽에 구멍을 내다 gnaw into a wall∥뒤에서 남을 갉구다 backbite ; speak ill of 《a person》 behind his back

갉아먹다 nibble 《at》; gnaw 《upon》; bite 《at》; [재물을] squeeze ; extort ; exploit ⇨ 긁어 먹다 ¶ 뼈에 붙은 고기를 갉아먹다 gnaw the meat out of a bone∥재산을 갉아먹다 nibble away one's fortune∥잎을 갉아먹다 nibble away the leaves

갉이 an iron piece used for polishing silverwork

갉작거리다 scratch and scratch ¶ 갉작갉작하다 be scratching and scratching

갉죽거리다 ⇨ 갉작거리다

갉히다 be scratched ⇨ 긁히다

*__감__[1] 〖식물〗 a persimmon
—나무 a persimmon (tree)
감나무 밑에 누워서 연시 입에 떨어지기 기다린다 속담 You may gape long enough ere a bird fall in your mouth. /To lie in bed till meat falls in one's mouth.

감[2] [재료] material ; stuff ; matter ; [수량을 세는 단위] a pattern 《미》; [인재] a suitable person 《for》 ¶ 저고리 한 감 a pattern of a *chŏgori*〔a Korean-style jacket〕∥신랑〔신부〕감으로 적절한 사람 a suitable marriage partner
사윗— a likely son-in-law ; a man who would make a good son-in-law **옷—** (dress) material ; cloth **장군—** a man who would make a good general

감 感 [느낌] feeling ; sensation ; sense ; sentiment ; [인상] impression ; effect ¶ …한 감을 주다 feel ; be moved 〔impressed〕; it feels like ; impress 〔strike〕 《a person as》; give 《a person》 an impression of∥이상한 감을 주었다 It struck me as strange.∥뭔가 무서운 일이 일어날 것 같은 감이 든다 I have a feeling that something dreadful is going to happen.∥그는 정직한 사람이라는 감이 든다 He impressed me as honest〔an honest person〕.∥그는 책임감이 강하다 He has a strong sense of responsibility.∥이미 때 늦은 감이 있다 I have the feeling that it is rather too late.∥그녀는 진실을 말하고 있지 않는 것 같은 감이 든다 It strikes me (that) she is not telling the truth.∥이 그림은 전체적인 감이 좋다 The general effect of this picture appeals to me.
공복— a sense of hunger **공포—** a sensation of fear **도덕—** the moral sense **만족〔행복〕—** a feeling of satisfaction〔happiness〕 **안도—** a feeling of relief **적막—** a feeling of loneliness **정의—** a sense of justice **제육—(第六感)** the sixth sense **죄책—** a sense of guilt

감 減 decrease ; deduction ; reduction ; [감산] subtraction **—하다** decrease ; deduct ; reduce ; subtract ¶ 세금을 감하다 reduce taxes∥1할을 감하다 make 〔allow〕 a 10 percent discount∥형을 감하다 reduce〔commute〕 the sentence∥월급이 2할 감해졌다 My salary has been reduced by 20 percent.

감가 減價 (a price) reduction ; reduction of〔in〕 price ; discount ; depreciation **—하다** reduce the price 《of》; discount ; depreciate ¶ 3할 감가하여 팔다 sell at a discount〔reduction〕 of 30 percent
— 판매 a discount sale

감가 상각 減價償却 〖경제〗 depreciation
—비 depreciation cost **—액** depreciation amount **— 자산** depreciable assets

†__감각 感覺__ sense ; sensation ; feeling ; sensibility

> 참고 **sense** 외계의 자극 영향에 응할 수 있는 감각적 정신적 힘 **sensation** 외계의 자극에 대한 감각적 특히 시각적 신경적 반응 **sensibility** 감각적 또는 정서적으로 감응하는 힘

¶ 감각적인 sensuous ; sensual ; sensible∥감각적 표현 sensuous description∥감각이 예민하다 have keen〔fine〕 senses ; be sharp 《at》; be sensitive∥미적

감각 a sense of beauty // 음악적〔예술적〕 감각 one's musical〔artistic〕 sense // 시간〔거리〕 감각 one's sense of time〔distance〕 // 감각이 둔하다 have dull senses ; be dull ; be thick-skinned // 다리에 감각이 없어졌다 I have no feeling in the legs. /My legs have got numb 《with cold》. /My legs have gone to sleep. // 음악〔색채〕에 대한 뛰어난 감각을 가지고 있다 He has a good ear for music〔an eye for color〕. // 그는 유머 감각이 뛰어나다〔둔하다〕 He has a keen〔dull〕 sense of humor. // 나는 방향감각이 없다 I have a poor sense of direction. // 감각이 없다 insensible ; senseless ; devoid of sense
— 감퇴 hyp(a)esthesia — 과민 hyper(a)esthesia ; hypersensitivity —권 a sensory circle — 기관 a sense organ ; sensory organ ; the sensorium — 기관학 aesthophysiology — 기능 a sense ; a faculty of sensation —력 sensibility —론(論) sensationalism ; sensualism — 마비 〖의학〗 sensory paralysis —모(毛) 〖동물〗 a sensory hair ; 〖식물〗 a sensitive hair — 묘사 〖예술〗 sensual description —미 sensuous beauty — 생리학 aestho-physiology ; (a)esthesiophysiology — 세포 a sensory cell — 식물 a sensitive plant — 신경 a sensory nerve — 이상 par(a)esthesia — 자료 〖심리〗 a sense datum —주의 sensualism —주의자 a sensualist — 중추 the sense center ; the sensorium ; the seat of sensation — 착오 errors of sense —파 〖예술〗 the sensualists

감감 **—하다** ① [소식이] hear nothing 〔have no news, receive no word〕 from 《a person》 ¶ 며칠이 지나도 소식이 감감하다〔감감무소식이다〕 Days passed without a line from him. /Nothing has been heard from him since he left.
② [아득하다] be far off〔away〕 ; be a good way off ; (be) remote ; distant ¶ 감감하게 먼 바다 위에 흰 돛이 보인다 A white sail is seen far out on the sea.
③ [전도 요원] be far from ; be long 《before》 ¶ 밀린 일을 다하려면 아직 감감하다 It will be long before I can clear up belated business. // 제트기 완성은 아직 감감하다 A jet plane was still way a long off.

감감무소식 no news for a long time ¶ 그는 그 후 감감무소식이다 I have no news from him at all since then.

감개 **感慨** deep emotion ¶ 조국에 돌아오니 감개가 새롭다 Returning home, I have an indescribable sentiment. // 감개무량하다 My heart is full of deep emotion. // 지난날을 회상하니 참으로 감개 무량하다 A thousand emotions crowd on〔well in〕 my mind, looking back upon the past.

⁑**감격** **感激** deep emotion ; impression ; strong feeling ; inspiration **—하다** be deeply moved〔touched, impressed, inspired〕 by ; be deeply stirred ; be carried away with emotion ¶ 감격적인 inspiring ; impressive ; touching // 감격적인 장면 a dramatic〔moving, touching〕 scene // 감격시키다 move〔touch, affect, impress, inspire〕 《a person》 deeply // 감격의 눈물을 흘리다 be moved to tears // …의 친절에 감격하다 be deeply moved〔touched〕 by 《a person's》 kindness // 그들의 깊은 우정에 우리는 감격했다 Their deep friendship moved us deeply. // 그녀는 그의 말에 감격했다 She was moved by his speech.

감경 **減輕** reduction〔mitigation〕 of penalty ; commutation ; remission **—하다** reduce ; mitigate ; commute ; remit

감고 **甘苦** sweets and bitters ; pleasures and pains ; joys and sorrows ; the ups and downs of life ¶ 감고를 함께하다 share (in) another's joys and sorrows // 인생의 감고를 맛보다 taste the sweets and bitters of life // 감고의 노력 an arduous〔tireless, laborious〕 effort ; a blood-and-tears endeavour

감관 **感官** a sense〔sensory〕 organ

감광 **感光** exposure (to light) ; sensitization **—하다** be exposed to light ¶ 감광시키다 expose (to light) ; sensitize // 감광도가 강하다 be highly sensitive to light
—기(期) 〖식물〗 the photostage — 기관 〖동물〗 an eyespot — 기록 계기 a photographic recorder —면 a photosensitive surface —성 (photo)sensitivity — 재료 (photo)sensitive〔sensitized〕 materials ; sensitized goods —체 a visual receptor (눈의) — 측정 sensitometry

감광 **減光** 〖천문〗 extinction **—하다** dim〔lower〕 the lights ; dim out

감광계 **感光計** a sensitometer (사진의) ; an actinometer (화학선의)

감광도 (photo)sensitivity 《of a film》 ¶ 감광도가 높은 필름 highly sensitive film // 감광도를 낮추다〔줄이다〕 desensitize

감광제〔약〕 **感光劑〔藥〕** a sensitizer

감광지 **感光紙** (photo)sensitive〔sensitized〕 paper

감광판 **感光板** a sensitive〔dry〕 plate

감광 필름 **感光—** a sensitive film

감국 **甘菊** 〖식물〗 a mother chrysanthemum ; Chrysanthemum indicum (학명)

감군 **減軍** a cut in the armed forces ; a military manpower reduction ; arms 〔armament〕 reduction

감궂다 (be) wicked ; ferocious ; atrocious ; devilish

감귤 **柑橘** a tangerine ; a mandarin (orange) ; Citrus tangerina (학명)
— 농장 a tangerine orchard〔plantation〕 —류 citrus fruits ; oranges

감금 監禁 confinement ; detention ; imprisonment **— 하다** confine ; detain ; imprison ; keep〔hold〕《a person》 in custody〔a room〕 ¶ 불법 감금 illegal confinement〔detention〕 ; false imprisonment // 독방에 감금하다 keep 《a person》 in solitary confinement

***감기 感氣** a cold ; [유행성] an influenza ; a flu 《구》 ¶ 가벼운 감기 a slight cold // 심한 감기 a bad〔severe〕 cold // 감기 기운이 있다 have a slight〔a touch of〕 cold // 감기 걸리다 catch〔take, get〕 (a) cold // 감기에 걸려 있다 have a cold // 감기로 누워 있다 be in bed with a cold ; be down〔laid up〕 with a cold // 그는 감기에 잘 걸린다 He easily catches colds. // 감기가 유행하고 있다 There's a lot of flu about. /Everybody's catching colds. // 감기는 만병의 근원이다 A cold may develop into all kinds of illness. // 감기가 떨어지지 않는다 can't throw〔shake〕 off one's cold ; can't get rid of one's cold // 감기가 오는 것 같다 I feel a cold coming on.
—약 a remedy〔medicine〕 for cold ; cold tablets ; a cold remedy **코—** a cold in the head〔nose〕

감기다[1] ① [실 따위가] be wound (up) ; be rolled (up) ; [거치적거리다] cling to ; keep close to ; [걸리다] be 〔get〕 caught in 《the wire》 ¶ 실이 실패에 감기다 thread is wound on a reel // 젖은 옷이 몸에 감기다 wet clothes cling to one's body // 치맛자락이 발에 감겨 걷기가 힘들다 I have trouble in walking with my skirt clinging to my legs.
② [실 따위를 감게 하다] make〔let〕 《a person》 wind〔roll, coil〕 《something》 ¶ 아들에게 시계 태엽을 감기다 have one's son wind the clock

감기다[2] [눈이 스스로] 《one's eyes》 be shut〔closed〕 of their own accord〔of themselves〕 ; [감게 하다] let 《a person's》 eyes fall shut ¶ 졸려서 눈이 감기다 be so sleepy (that) one's eyes are falling shut

감기다[3] [멱을] give 《a person》 a wash 〔bath〕 ; wash 《a person》 ; bathe 《a baby》 ¶ 어린애 머리를 감기다 wash a baby's hair

감내 堪耐 perseverance ; patience ; endurance ; fortitude **— 하다** bear 〔endure〕 patiently ; put up with 《an insult》 ; persevere 《in》 ; endure ¶ 감내하기 어려운 unbearable ; intolerable // 나는 그것을 더 이상 감내할 수 없다 I cannot endure〔stand〕 it any longer.

†감다[1] [실 따위를] wind ; roll (up) ; [사리다] coil ; [두르다] tie round (둘레에) ; bandage (붕대를) ; [입다] wear ; put on ¶ 실을 실패에 감다 wind thread on a reel ; wind a reel with thread // 시계 태엽을 감다 wind a clock〔watch〕 ; wind up one's watch // 목도리를 목에 감다 wind a scarf around one's neck ; tie a neckerchief round one's neck // 밧줄을 똘똘 감다 coil a rope // 뱀이 동굴 속에서 몸을 감고 있었다 The snake coiled up in the cave. // 나팔꽃이 대나무 장대에 감겨 있다 The morning glory winds around a bamboo pole. // 감은 것을 풀다 unwind ; unroll ; uncoil ; wind off // 다리를 감아 넘어뜨리다 trip 《a person》 (up) // 그녀는 녹색 스카프를 목에 감고 있다 She has a green scarf around her neck. // 그 남자는 누더기를 감고 있다 He is wearing in rags.

감다[2] [씻다] wash ; bathe ; have〔take〕 a bath ¶ 머리를 감다 wash one's hair // 미역감다 wash oneself ; have a swim

감다[3] [눈을] close〔shut〕 one's eyes ; [죽다] breathe one's last ¶ 눈을 감고 생각에 잠기다 be lost in thought with one's eyes shut

감다[4], **깜다** (be) black ; dark ⇨ 검다

†감당 堪當 — 하다 be equal to ; be capable of carrying out〔discharging〕 ; be up to doing ; cope with ; manage ; deal well with ¶ 일을 감당할 수 있다〔없다〕 be equal〔unequal〕 to the task // 난국을 잘 감당해 내다 cope with a difficulty // 그들은 적을 감당해 내지 못했다 They could not cope with the enemy. // 이 일은 감당하기가 어렵다 I find myself unequal to the task. /I cannot manage it alone. // 그는 무엇을 맡겨도 능히 감당해 낼 것이다 He will rise〔be equal〕 to any occasion. // 직무를 훌륭히 감당해 내다 fill one's office satisfactorily // 그는 그 일을 충분히 감당할 수 있는 사람이다 He is quite capable of filling the post.

감도 感度 [라디오·TV의] sensitivity ; sensitiveness ; (radio) reception ¶ 감도가 좋은 hypersensitive ; sensitive ; of high sensitivity // 감도가 뛰어난〔낮은〕 필름 a fast〔low〕 film
— 시험 a sensitivity test **— 측정** sensitometry

†감독 監督 [단속] superintendence ; supervision ; direction ; [감독자] a supervisor ; an overseer ; an inspector ; a director ; a bishop (교회의) ; a foreman (직공의) ; a manager (운동부의) ; an impresario (무대의) ; a director (영화의) **— 하다** supervise ; superintend ; oversee ; take〔have〕 charge of ; direct ; control ; look after ¶ …의 감독하에 under the supervision of. . . // 근로자를 감독하다 supervise workers // 직공을 감독하다 oversee workmen // 시험을 감독하다 proctor 〔invigilate〕 an examination // 학생을 감독하다 look after〔take charge of〕 the students // 김씨의 감독하에 under the supervision〔direction〕 of Mr. *Kim* // 정

부의 감독하에 두다 place 《a thing》 under government control〔supervision〕 ∥감독 불충분으로 견책당하다 be reprimanded for lack of supervision∥감독을 한층 강화하다 exercise closer supervision ; tighten supervision∥감독을 완화하다 ; ease up on supervision ; relax supervision∥감독을 게을리 하다 slack supervision
—관 a superintendent ; an inspector —관청 the supervisory office ; the competent〔proper〕 authorities — 기관 the competent institutions — 기사 a superintendent engineer — 대리 〖종교〗 a commissary —생 a monitor — 제도 [교회의] episcopacy ; the episcopalian system ; prelatism — 행정 supervisory administration 공사 — a taskmaster 공장 — a factory inspector 농사 — a bailiff in husbandry 대리 — 〖야구〗 an acting manager 무대 — a stage manager 시험 — the supervisor of an examination ; a proctor 《미》 ; an invigilator 《영》 영화 — the director of a film ; a film director 총— 〖야구〗 a general manager 판매장 — a floor supervisor ; a shopwalker ; a floorwalker 《미》 현장 — a field overseer ; an overseer 《at a construction site》
감독 교회 監督敎會 the Episcopal 〔Anglican 《영》〕 Church
—원(員) an Episcopalian ; an Anglican 《영》
감돌다 turn〔go〕 round ; turn and turn about ; circle around ; turn〔take〕 a curve ; [빙빙 돌다] 《a river》 make a curve around ; follow a bend ; meander ; curve ; go round a curve [머무르다] 《a thought》 linger (in one's mind) ¶ 강이 산모퉁이를 감돌며 흐른다 The river curves around the bend of the mountain. /The river winds along the side of the mountain. ∥전운(戰雲)이 감돌다 War clouds hang over. ∥생각이 머리〔마음〕에서 감돌다 The idea hangs in one's head〔mind〕.
감돌아들다 《a river》 make a curve around
감돌이 a person of mercenary spirit ; a calculating man ¶ 그 치는 감돌이야 He is coldly utilitarian. /He is always thinking of his own interest.
†**감동** 感動 impression ; deep emotion ; excitement ; sensation 《among the audience》 —하다 be moved〔touched, affected〕 《by》 ; be impressed ; feel emotion 《at》¶감동적인 연설〔장면〕 a touching〔moving〕 speech〔scene〕∥감동시키다 move ; impress ; inspire ; make an impression 《on》 ; appeal to 《a person》∥감동의 눈물을 흘리다 be moved to tears∥그녀의 노래는 우리들을 크게 감동시켰다 Her singing moved us deeply. ∥청중에게 깊은 감동을 주었다 He made a deep impression on the audience. ∥그의 연설은 청중에게 큰 감동을 주었다 His speech created a sensation among the audience. ∥그녀의 말에 감동했다 I was moved by her words. ∥이 책에서 큰 감동을 받았다 I am extremely impressed by this book. ∥그 말은 아무런 감동도 주지 못했다 It called forth no response in my heart.
감득 感得 —하다 [느끼어] become conscious 《of》 ; take hint 《of》 ; get wise 《to》 ; become aware 《of》 ; realize ; perceive ; [영감으로] be inspired
감등 減等 lowering the grade ; demotion ; [감형] commutation ; mitigation —하다 demote ; lower the grade ; commute ; mitigate
감때사납다 (be) very rough〔tough〕 ; unbending ; coarse ; rude ; ferocious ¶ 감때사나운 태도 rough manners
감떡 a cake made from rice flour and persimmons
감또개 young persimmons fallen off trees
감람 橄欖 〖식물〗 an olive (tree)
—나무 〖식물〗 a kanari ; a canari ; a Java almond —색 olive color〔green〕 —암(岩) peridotite
감람산 橄欖山 the Mount of Olives
감람석 —石 olivine ; peridot
감람유 —油 olive oil
감량 減量 a loss in quantity〔weight〕 ; [운반 중에 생긴 상품의] outage ; ullage ; [운동 선수의] reduction of one's weight —하다 reduce the quantity 《of》 ; [체중을] reduce one's weight
감량 경영 減量經營 retrenchment〔austerity〕 of management
감로 甘露 [이슬] sweet dew ; [달콤한 즙] nectar ; manna ; honeydew ; [불교] amrta ¶ 감로 같은 맛이 나다 taste like nectar∥감로로다 Delicious !
—수 sugared water ; sweet water —주 sweet liquor
감루 感淚 tears of gratitude ; tears from deep emotion ¶ 감루를 흘리다 be moved to tears ; shed tears of gratitude
감률 甘栗 a sweet chestnut ; [군밤] a fired〔grilled〕 chestnut
감리 監理 supervision ; superintendence ; control ; management
감리사 監理師 a Methodist District Superintendent (감리교의)
*__감리교__ 監理敎 the Methodist Church
감리교회 監理敎會 a Methodist church
감마선 —線 〖물리〗 gamma rays
감마제 減摩劑 a lubricant
감면 減免 reduction and exemption ; [형벌의] mitigation and remission —하다 [세금 따위] reduce and exempt ; [형벌

을] mitigate and remit
— 소득 reduction and exemption from income — 조건 the condition of reduction and exemption 세금 — tax cut

⁑**감명 感銘** deep impression ; an impression **—받다** be deeply impressed 《with》 ; be deeply moved〔touched〕 《by》 ; be engraved on one's mind ¶ 감명적인 설교 an impressive sermon // 감명을 주다 impress 《a person》 ; make a great impression on 《a person, a person's mind》 // 그의 연설은 깊은 감명을 주었다 His speech created〔made〕 a great〔deep〕 impression (on the audience).

†**감미 甘味** sweetness ; a sweet taste ¶ 감미로운 추억 sweet memories // 감미로운 목소리 a gentle〔soft〕 voice ; a mellifluous voice // 감미로운 음악 a melodious music // 감미롭다 be sweet ; be sweet-flavored // 감미가 돌다 taste sweet ; have a sweet taste

감미료 甘味料 a sweetening (agent) ; a sweetener ; sweetenings

감바리 ⇨ 감발저뀌

감발 [발감개] a cotton bandage〔a strip of cloth〕 for wrapping the feet (in place of socks) **—하다** wrap one's feet with bandages

감발저뀌 a person who has a quick eye for gain ; a shrewd man of business

감방 監房 a cell (prison) ; a ward ¶ 사형수 감방 a condemned ward // 감방에 처넣다 throw〔cast〕 《a person》 into a cell ; land〔run〕 《a person》 in a ward

감배 減配 [배당의] (a) reduction in a dividend ; [배급의] reduction in ration 〔of distribution quota〕 **—하다** reduce a dividend ; reduce〔cut〕 the ration

감법 減法 〖수학〗 subtraction

감별 鑑別 discrimination ; judgment ; discernment **—하다** discriminate ; distinguish 《between A and B》 ; judge ¶ 병아리를 감별하다 sex chicks
—법 differentiation ; discrimination (병아리) —사 (a chicken) sexer — 진단 〖의학〗 a differential diagnosis

감복 感服 admiration ; wonder **—하다** admire ; be impressed 《with, by》 ; be struck with admiration 《at, for》 ; wonder 《at》 ¶ 용기에 감복하다 admire 《a person》 for his courage // 그의 새 작품에 깊이 감복하였다 His new work did appeal to me very much. // 그의 정성에 감복하였다 I admired him for his devotion.

감복숭아 〖식물〗 an almond ; Prunus amygdulus

감봉 減俸 a salary reduction ; a wage cut ; a punitive wage cut **—하다** reduce 《a person's》 salary 《from 600,000 to 550,000 *won*》 ; dock 《a person's》 pay ¶ 10,000원 감봉당하다 have one's pay cut by 10,000 *won* // 1만원을 감봉하다 dock ten thousand *won* from 《a person's》 wages

감빨다 [입맛] lick up with a good appetite ; enjoy licking up 《a taffy》 ; [욕심] be greedy 《for》 ; be bent upon gain ; seek personal interest ; covet 《another's》 possessions

감빨리다 [입맛] have a sharp appetite ; [욕심] be tempted by gain ; become covetous

감사 監査 inspection ; superintendence **—하다** inspect ; superintend ; make an inspection ¶ 회계를 감사하다 audit 〔examine〕 accounts // 엄중한 감사를 하다 conduct〔carry out〕 a strict inspection
—과 the inspection department — 보고 an audit report —부 the Division of Appraisement (세관의) —역(役) an auditor ; an inspector ; a comptroller — 위원 a committee of inspection ; an inspection commissioner — 제도 an audit system 국정 — (국회의) parliamentary inspection of the administration 상임 —역 a standing auditor

감사 監事 [회계] an auditor ; [법인체의] a corporation supervisor ; [절의] a monk in charge of the property of a Buddhist temple

감사 監司 a governor ; the ruler of the province
평양 감사도 제 싫다면 그만이다 〔속담〕 You can lead a horse to water, but you cannot make him〔it〕 drink.

†**감사 感謝** thanks ; gratitude ; acknowledgement ; appreciation ; thanksgiving (특히 신에게) **—하다** thank 《a person》 《for》 ; be thankful〔grateful〕 《to a person for》 ; express one's gratitude〔appreciation〕 ; appreciate ¶ 감사의 말 appreciative words ; words〔a speech〕 of thanks〔gratitude〕 // 감사의 눈물을 흘리다 shed tears of gratitude ; weep for gratitude // 감사 기도를 드리다 say 《your》 prayers〔grace〕 // 신에게 감사하다 thank God ; bless God 《for》 ; give thanks to God // 감사의 표시로 in〔as a〕 token of one's gratitude // 감사를 표하다 express one's (sense of) gratitude 《to a person》 // …에 감사하며 in appreciation of // 진심으로 감사합니다 I'd like to express my heartfelt thanks to you. /I thank you from the bottom of my heart. /I am deeply grateful to you. // 뭐라고 감사의 말씀을 드려야 할지 모르겠습니다 I can never thank you enough. / I have no words to express my gratitude. // 와주셔서 대단히 감사합니다 Thank you very much for coming. // 호의에 깊이 감사드립니다 I offer you my heartfelt thanks for your favor.

— 만찬회 a testimonial dinner —절 Thanksgiving Day —패 a plaque of thanks ; an appreciation plaque — 편지 a letter of thanks ; an appreciative letter ☞ ◖p. 62◗

감사납다 [생김새, 성질이] (be) tough ; rough ; coarse ; intractable ; unmanageable ¶ 감사납게 생긴 사나이 a tough-looking guy

감사장 感謝狀 a letter of appreciation 〔thanks〕 ¶ 귀하의 탁월한 공적을 인정함과 아울러 감사의 뜻을 표하며 이에 감사장을 드립니다 In recognition of and with gratitude for your outstanding service, I present you this letter of appreciation.

감산 甘酸 [맛] the sweet and the sour ; [고락] the sweet and the bitter ; pleasures and pains ; joys and sorrows ¶ 삶의 감산을 맛보다 taste the sweets and bitters of life

감산 減算 〖수학〗 subtraction —하다 subtract

감산 減産 [인위적인] curtailment 〔restriction〕 of production〔output〕 ; a crop reduction (농산물의) ; [자연적인] a decrease in production —하다 curtail production〔output〕 ¶ 2할 감산하다 curtail production by 20 percent

감상 鑑賞 appreciation —하다 appreciate ; enjoy ; relish ¶ 문학을 감상하다 appreciate literature // 취미는 음악 감상이다 My hobby is listening to music.
—가 an appreciator 《of art》 —력 an appreciative power ¶ 예리한 감상력이 있다 have a keen appreciation 《of art》
— 비평 appreciative criticism 명화 —회 a special show of noted films

감상 感傷 sentimentality ; sentiment ¶ 감상적 sentimental ; emotional ; melodramatic // 감상적인 소설 a sentimental 〔anemotional〕 story ; a sob story 《미》 ; melodrama // 감상적으로 되다 grow〔get〕 sentimental over 《a matter》 // 나이를 먹어감에 따라 감상적이 되다 She is getting sentimental in her old age. // 감상에 젖다 sentimentalize over 〔about〕 // 그녀는 그 책을 읽고 감상적인 기분이 되었다 She became sentimental reading the book.

***감상 感想** [인상] impressions ; feelings ; thoughts ; [추상] memories ; [소감] sentiments ¶ 감상을 말하다 give one's impressions 《of》 ; describe one's feelings // 감상을 묻다 ask for 《a person's》 opinion〔impressions〕 《of》 // 서울에 오신 감상이 어떻습니까 How does *Seoul* strike you? /How do you like *Seoul*? // 감상이 어떻습니까—없습니다 What do you think of it? No comment.
—담(談) observations —록(錄) a record of impressions —문(文) a (written) description of one's impressions

감상주의 感傷主義 sentimentalism

감색 紺色 dark〔deep, navy〕 blue

감성 感性 [감각력] sensitivity ; sensibility ; sensitive faculty ; the sense ; [감수성] susceptibility

> 참고 **sensitive** 외부의 영향에 반응하거나 느끼거나 하기 쉬운 **susceptible** 외부로부터의 영향에 흔들리기 쉬운

¶ 미에 대한 감성이 빠르다 be sensitive to beauty // 감성이 예민하다 be sensitive 〔susceptible〕 to nature ; respond sensitively to nature // 감성이 풍부한 작가 a sensitive writer
—계(界) 〖철학〗 the material world ; the world of sense —론 〖철학〗 (a) esthetics

감세 減稅 tax reduction〔cut〕 —하다 reduce〔cut, lower〕 taxes
—안 a tax reduction bill

†**감소 減少** diminution ; decrease ; decline ; drop ; reduction —하다 diminish ; decrease ; dwindle ; fall (off) ; shrink ; lessen ; drop ; bring down ; go down

> 참고 **decrease** 서서히 자꾸 감퇴하다 **diminish** 타율의 힘에 의하여 감소해 가다 **dwindle** 소모되어 마침내 없어지다 **lessen** 감소하다

¶ 다소 감소를 나타내다 show a slight decline // 수요가 감소하다 the demand falls off // 전년보다 5%의 감소 a decrease of 5% compared with the previous year // 오염을 감소시키다 reduce pollution // 인구의 급격한 감소 a rapid decrease in population // 감소하고 있다 be on the decrease // 그의 영향력은 점차 감소하고 있다 His influence is on the ebb. // 자동차 사고의 5% 감소 a 5% reduction in auto accidents

***감속 減速** 〖물리〗 reduction〔dropping〕 of speed ; retardation ; [감속 운동] negative acceleration ; deceleration ¶ 눈·비올 때 감속 운행 Low gear when wet. (게시) —하다 reduce speed ; slow down ; decelerate ¶ 차의 속도를 감속하다 slow down the car // 열차는 시속 30 마일로 감속했다 The train slowed (down) to thirty miles an hour.

감속 장치 減速裝置 a reduction gear ; a speed reducer

감속재 減速材 〖물리〗 a moderator

감손 減損 [줄어짐] decrease ; diminution ; [손해] loss ; [마손] wear —하다 diminish ; decrease ; lessen ; be impaired ; wear out (닳다)
—액 depreciation

감쇄 減殺 diminution ; decrease ; reduction ; attenuation ; detraction —하다

감사에 대한 표현

① 일반적인 표현

감사합니다. Thanks. / Thank you. / Great. (★ 허물없는 사이에) // 매우 감사합니다. Thanks a million (*for*...). / Thanks [Thank you] very much (indeed). (★ 강한 표현) / Thanks a lot. / Thanks [Thank you] ever so much. // …에 대해 감사합니다. Many thanks (*for* ...). // 감사합니다. Much appreciated. / (I'm) Much obliged. (★ 부탁 등을 했을 때, 격식 차린 표현) // (…에 대해) 무어라 감사를 드려야 할지 모르겠습니다. I really can't thank you enough (*for* ...). / I should like to express my gratitude [appreciation] (*for* ...). / I should like to say how (very, deeply, etc.) grateful I am. (★ 격식 차린 표현) // 편지 보내주셔서 감사합니다. Thank you for your letter. // 여러모로 감사합니다. Thanks for everything. // 도와주셔서 감사합니다. Thank you for your help. / Thank you for helping me. / I appreciate your help. // 이렇게 먼 길을 와주셔서 감사합니다. Thank you very much for coming all this way [all the way here, such a long way]. // 그렇게 말씀해주시니 정말 감사합니다. It's very nice [kind, thoughtful] of you to say so [that].

② 응답

천만에요. You're (quite [very]) welcome. (★ quite 또는 very를 넣으면 정중한 표현) / That's OK. / That's all right. / My pleasure. / The pleasure is mine. // 별말씀을. Not at all. (★ 별것 아니라는 뜻) // 천만의 말씀. Don't mention it. / It's no trouble at all. (★ 약간 딱딱한 표현) // 언제든지요. Any time. (★ 허물없는 사이에) // 들어주셔서 고맙습니다. — 천만의 말씀입니다. Thank you very much for the lift. — I'm glad to have been of (some) service. / Delighted I was able to help. (★ 공항·호텔 등에서 처음 만나는 고객 등에)

---

lessen ; diminish ; reduce ; [약화] attenuate ; deaden ⟪force⟫ ; impair ⟪the beauty⟫ ; detract ⟪from one's merits⟫ ¶ 활동력을 감쇄하다 diminish the (vigor of) activity

감쇠 減衰 decrement ; decrease ; attenuation ; damping **— 하다** damp ; be attenuated ¶ 감쇠하지 않은 undamped
—기(器) 〚전기〛 an attenuator

감수 甘受 willing submission ; resignation **— 하다** willingly submit to ; be ready to suffer ; resign ⟪oneself⟫ ¶ 모욕을 감수하다 submit tamely to an insult ; swallow〔put up with〕 an insult // 운명을 감수하다 meet〔accept〕 one's fate with resignation ; be resigned to one's fate // 그는 일이 힘든 것을 감수하고 있는 듯하다 He seemed (to be) resigned to the hard work.

감수 甘水 fresh〔sweet〕 water ; (drinking) water ; potable water ; tap water

감수 減水 the receding〔subsiding〕 of water **— 하다** ⟪water⟫ decrease ; recede ; go down ; fall ; subside ¶ 강물이 2피트 감수됐다 The river subsided〔fell, went down〕 2 feet. // 우물이 꽤 감수되었다 The well has sunk considerably.

감수 減收 [수입의] a decrease in income ; [세입의] decreased revenue ; [수확의] a decrease in production〔crop〕 ¶ 금년 미작은 약 100만톤이 감수됐다 The rice crop this year shows a decrease of about a million tons. // 매상고가 감수하다 the receipts are on the decrease // 태풍으로 인한 농작물의 감수 a decrease in farm products by a typhoon
—율(率) the rate of decrease in income

감수 減壽 shortening one's life **— 하다** ⟪one's life⟫ be shortened ¶ 감수하는 느낌이다 feel as if one's life were shortened // 술을 한 잔씩 마실 때마다 그만큼 감수하고 있는 셈이야 Every glass of spirits you take is a nail in your coffin. // 십년감수하다 feel as if one's life were shortened by ten years ; be frightened out of one's wits // 그 사고로 십년감수 했다 The accident scared me out of my wits.

감수 感受 impression ; reception **— 하다** receive an impression ; be impressed with ; [무전] pick up
—기(器) 〚생리〛 a (sensory) receptor
—율(率) ⟪electric⟫ susceptibility

감수 監修 editorial supervision **— 하다** supervise ⟪the compilation of⟫ ; be chief editor of the compilation ¶ 김 박사 감수하에 편찬되다 be compiled under the supervision〔editorship〕 of Dr. *Kim*

감수 減數 〚수학〛 a subtrahend

감수 분열 減數分裂 〚생물〛 reduction

division ; reducing division ; meiosis

*감수성 感受性 sensibility ; susceptibility ; receptivity ¶ 감수성이 예민하다 be sensitive by nature ; be of a sensitive nature // 감수성이 풍부한 음악가 a sensitive musician

집단 — 훈련 sensitivity training

감수자 監修者 an editor ; a supervisor ; a chief editor

감숭하다 (be) dark ; blackish ; be dark here and there〔scatteringly〕 (털 따위가) ¶ 감숭감숭 《sprouting》 darkly here and there ; dotted sparsely // 감숭감숭한 턱수염 a sparse beard

⁑감시 監視 watch ; observation ; vigil ; lookout ; picketing ; [감독] supervision ; [형법상의] surveillance —하다 watch ; keep watch 《over》 ; keep an eye 《on》 ; put〔keep〕 《a person》 under surveillance ; observe ; superintend ; oversee ; conduct〔keep〕 surveillance ¶ 엄중히 감시하다 watch closely ; keep (a) close〔careful〕 watch on 《the suspect》 // 감시를 게을리하다 neglect〔fail〕 to watch // 감시를 게을리하지 않다 keep watch and ward // …의 감시하에 under the supervision of ; under surveillance // 엄중한 감시를 받다 be placed under strict surveillance // 24시간 감시 around-the-clock surveillance // 용의자의 행동을 감시하다 keep an eye on the movements of a suspect // 경찰의 감시를 받고 있다 be under police surveillance // 정전의 준수를 감시하다 police a cease-fire // 군축 협정의 실시를 감시하다 monitor a disarmament agreement

— 계전기(繼電器) a supervisory relay —국 a monitor station — 근무 guard (duty) — 기관 a supervisory organization —등(燈) a monitoring lamp — 비행기 [총칭] watch-dog aircraft —선(船) a guard boat ; a cutter 《미》 —선(線) a picket line — 신호 a supervisory signal — 장치 〖통신〗 a monitor — 전류 a pilot current — 전자 회로 a monitoring circuit — 제어 supervisory control —탑 a watch tower —함〔정〕 a guardship

감시소 監視所 a guard box ; a watch-house ; a lookout 《미》 ; 〖군사〗 an observation post〔point〕 ; a spotting station ; a spotter ; 〖항해〗 a crow's nest

감시원 監視員 a watchman ; a watch-dog ; a guard ; a surveillant ; a guardian ; a custodian ; a keeper ; a picket (쟁의의)

*감식 鑑識 [감정] judgment ; discernment ; [식별] discrimination ; [범죄의] identification 《through fingerprints》 —하다 judge ; discern ; discriminate ; identify ¶ 미술품의 감식에 조예가 있다 He has an eye for works of art.

—력 a discerning eye ; discernment —안(眼) a discerning eye ; a critical talent 범죄 — criminal identification 지문 — fingerprint identification

감식 減食 reduction of one's diet〔food, intake〕 ; dieting —하다 reduce one's diet ; cut down one's food ; diet ; underfeed oneself

감식가 鑑識家 a judge ; a discerner ; [미술품] a connoisseur

감식과 鑑識課 [경찰국의] the Section of (Criminal) Identification ; the Identification Section

감식 요법 減食療法 cure by reduction of diet ; a reduced diet cure ¶ 감식 요법을 하다 go on a diet

감식주의 減食主義 dieting ; underfeeding oneself

감실감실 ① [털이] 《sprout out》 in sparse short black curls ; [감숭감숭] darkly here and there —하다 be short〔dark, curled〕 and sparse ; be dark here and there ¶ 털이 감실감실 나다 short black curls sprout out ② [가물거림] gleaming faintly

감실거리다 glimmer ; gleam faintly ; be seen moving at a dim distance ¶ 감실거리는 불빛〔희망〕 a glimmer of light 〔hope〕

감심 感心 admiration ; wonder —하다 admire ; be impressed 《with, by》 ; be struck with admiration 《at》 ; wonder 《at》

*감싸다 protect ; shield ; shelter ; cover 《a person from》 ; plead for 《another》 (보호) ; plead in 《a person's》 favor ; take 《a person》 under one's wing ¶ 죄인을 감싸다 shelter a culprit // 아무도 그를 감싸 주지 않았다 No one took care of him. // 김씨는 항상 그를 감싸 주고 있다 He is always under Mr. *Kim's* patronage.

감아 올리다 roll up ; wind up ; hoist ; heave 《the anchor》 ¶ 발을 감아 올리다 roll up the screen // 돛을 감아 올리다 hoist a sail // 선원들은 닻을 감아 올렸다 The sailors heaved the anchor.

감안 勘案 [참작] allowance(s) ; [생각] consideration —하다 take 《a matter》 into account〔consideration〕 ; give consideration 《to》 ; allow for ; make allowance(s) for ¶ 실정을 감안하다 take the circumstances into consideration // 감안해야 할 여러 가지 점 points to be duly considered // 그들의 형편을 충분히 감안하다 pay due regard to their convenience

감압 減壓 decompression —하다 reduce pressure ; decompress

— 밸브 a reducing valve — 장치 a decompression device

감압지 減壓紙 pressure sensitive paper

감액 減額 a reduction ; a curtailment ; a cut ; a cutback —하다 reduce ; make a reduction ; curtail ; cut back〔down〕

감언 甘言 sweet talk ; honeyed words

감언이설 甘言利說 flattery ; cajolery ; blarney ; soft and seductive language ¶ 감언이설에 속다 be taken in by honeyed words // 감언이설로 물건을 빼앗다 wheedle〔coax〕 a thing out of 《a person》 // 감언이설로 꾀어 결혼시키다 cajole〔wheedle〕 《her》 into a marriage // 감언이설로 처녀를 꾀다 entice〔allure, seduce〕 a girl with fair words // 그의 감언이설에 속아서 저금한 걸 전부 건네줬니 You fell for his sweet talk and handed over all your savings?

감연하다 敢然— (be) daring ; bold ; brave ; fearless ; resolute ; defiant ; dauntless ¶ 감연히 boldly ; daringly ; fearlessly ; resolutely ; dauntlessly // 감연히 난국에 대처하다 meet the difficult situation bravely ; take the bull by the horns // 감연히 일어서다 bravely stand up 《against the enemy》

*__감염 感染__ [공기나 물에 의한] infection ; [접촉에 의한] contagion ; contamination ¶ 재감염 reinfection // 공기 감염 aerial〔airborne〕 infection **—하다** [병에] be〔become〕 infected with ; contract ; catch ; develop ; be contaminated ; be influenced ; [병이] be contagious ¶ 감염성의 infectious ; contagious ; catching // 장티푸스에 감염됐다 He caught typhus. /He was infected with typhus. // 아이들은 한층 더 감염되기 쉽다 Children are more liable to infection.
— 경로 an infection way〔route〕 ; the route of infection **—력(力)** infectivity **—세균** infectious bacteria **—소(巢)** the focus of infection **—원(源)** the source of infection

감옥 監獄 a prison ; a jail 《미》 ; a gaol 《영》 ¶ 감옥살이 prison life ; serving one's term // 감옥에 넣다 put〔clap〕 《a person》 in prison ; imprison 《a person》 // 감옥에서 나오다 come out of prison ; be released from prison

감우 甘雨 a welcome〔seasonable, timely〕 rain ; a refreshing〔long-awaited〕 rain

감원 減員 a personnel cut ; a reduction of staff ; a cutting down of the personnel ; a layoff (일시적) **—하다** reduce the personnel 《of an office》 ; lay off ¶ 대폭 감원하다 make a drastic cut in the staff
— 반대 투쟁 a struggle against personnel reduction **— 선풍** a sweeping reduction of the personnel

감은 感恩 gratitude 《for a favor, kindness》 ; gratefulness **—하다** feel gratitude ; be grateful 《to a person ; for a person's kindness》

감음정 減音程 〖음악〗 diminished interval

감읍 感泣 —하다 be moved to tears ; shed tears of gratitude

감응 感應 [기원의] (divine) response ; answer ; [영감] inspiration ; [공감] sympathy ; [약의] efficacy ; effect ; [전기의] induction ; influence **—하다** [신명이] respond to ; sympathize with ; [약이] take effect ; [전기에] induce〔conduct〕 electricity ¶ 그의 기원에는 신명도 감응할 것이다 God will answer〔respond to, hear〕 his prayers.
— 기뢰 an influence mine **— 기전기(起電機)** an induction machine **— 기전력(起電力)** induced power **— 도체(導體)** an induction conductor **— 방사선** induced electricity **—성(性)** sympathy **— 시간** sensitive time **— 어뢰(魚雷)** a homing torpedo **— 유전** 〖생물〗 telegony **— 작용** induction ; inductility ; a responsive effect **— 전기** induced electricity **— 전동력** induced electromotive force **— 전류** induced current **— 코일** an induction coil

감응도 感應度 sensitivity

감응력 感應力 influence

감응 반응 感應反應 (an) induced reaction

감익 profit decrease

†**감자** a potato ; a white〔an Irish〕 potato (고구마와 구별하여)
—밭 a potato field〔patch, plot〕 **씨—** a seed potato **햇—** a new potato

감자 減資 reduction〔curtailment〕 of capital ; a capital decrease **—하다** reduce〔curtail〕 capital
— 잉여금 a reduction surplus **— 차익** gains from stock retirement

감작 減作 a short〔reduced, curtailed〕 crop ⇨ 감수

감잡이 ① [거멀쇠] a splice plate〔a joint bar〕 (of a pillar) ; a large metal staple ② [수건] a towel used after sexual intercourse

감잡히다 be taken advantage of one's weakness ; get caught up on a weak argument ; give a handle 《to the enemy》

감장¹ self-help ; doing by oneself ; getting along without depending on others **—하다** help oneself ; do by oneself ; manage one's own concerns〔affairs〕

감장², 깜장 black ⇨ 검정

*__감전 感電__ (receiving) an electric shock ¶ 감전되다 receive an electric shock ; be struck〔affected〕 by electricity // 감전으로 죽다 be killed by an electric shock ; be electrocuted

감전사 感電死 (a) death from electric shock

감점 減點 a demerit mark **—하다** give 《a person》 a demerit mark ; make a cut in marks ¶ 감점당하다 receive a

cut in marks
—법(法) 〖경기〗 a bad mark system ; a penalty count system
감접이 hems at the ends of a bolt of cloth
감정 鑑定 [판정] judgment ; an expert opinion ; [평가] appraisal ; estimation ; criticism —하다 judge ; give an (expert) opinion 《on》; [가격을] appraise ; estimate ; criticize ¶ 감정해 달라고 하다 have 《a thing》 judged 《by》; seek an expert opinion // 감정을 잘〔잘못〕하다 be a good〔poor〕 judge 《of》 // 가격을 감정하다 appraise the value
—관 [세금의] an appraiser ; [세관의] a (customs) appraiser ; a supervisor 《미》 —인 증언 〖법〗 expert evidence〔testimony〕; technical evidence 한국 —원 the Korea Appraisal Board
감정 戡定 suppression —하다 suppress 《a revolt》; clean up ; mop up
†감정 感情 feeling ; [정서] emotion ; sentiment ; [격정] passion ; [충동] impulse ¶ 감정이 메마른 사람 a prosaic person // 감정적 emotional ; sentimental ; impulsive // 감정적으로 되기 쉽다 apt to be emotional // 감정을 나타내다〔숨기다〕 show〔conceal〕 one's feelings ; display〔hide〕 one's emotions // 감정을 상하다 [남의] hurt〔do violence to〕 《a person's》 feelings ; give 《a person》 offense ; [자기의] be offended 《at》 // 감정에 지배되다 be swayed〔influenced〕 by sentiment // 감정에 치우치기 쉽다 tend to become emotional // 그는 좀처럼 감정을 드러내지 않는다 He seldom betrays〔shows〕 his feelings. // 감정을 억누르다 control one's feelings // 나는 네게 아무 감정도 없다 I owe you no grudge. // 인간은 감정의 동물이다 Man is a creature of feelings〔impulse〕. // 그는 감정대로 행동한다 He is a thrall to his passions.
— 감각 feeling sensation — 교육 sentimental education —극(劇) an emotional play —론 an argument charged with emotion —선(線) [손금의] the line of the heart ; the heart line —성 범죄인 an emotional criminal — 이입(移入) empathy — 이입설 the empathy theory — 전위(轉位) 〖정신 분석〗 displacement
감정 憾情 ill feeling ; a grudge ; resentment ; indignation ; ill〔bad〕 blood ¶ 감정이 있다 bear 《a person》 a grudge ; bear〔nurse〕 a grudge against 《a person》; have it in for 《a person》 // 감정을 내다 get angry ; be offended // 감정을 사다 court displeasure ; earn 《a person's》 resentment ; incur 《a person's》 grudge
감정가 鑑定家 [미술품의] a connoisseur ; a virtuoso ; an expert witness
감정 가격 鑑定價格 appraised〔estimated〕 value ; an appraisement
감정료 鑑定料 [미술품의] a fee for an expert opinion ; 〖법〗 a fee for legal advice ; [상품의] a surveying fee
감정서 鑑定書 [미술품의] a written statement of an expert opinion ; [상품의] a surveyor's〔surveying〕 report ; 〖법〗 an expert opinion in writing
감제풀 〖식물〗 the giant knotweed
감죄 減罪 commutation ; mitigation ; remission —하다 commute a sentence ; mitigate a punishment ; remit
감주 甘酒 a sweet drink made from rice
†감지 感知 perception ; sensing —하다 perceive ; sense 《danger》; become aware of
감지덕지 感之德之 very thankfully ; with deep gratitude ; with many〔grateful, hearty, heartfelt〕 thanks ¶ 내가 준 얼마 안 되는 돈을 그는 감지덕지 고마워했다 He was very grateful to me for the little money I offered him.
감지 장치 感知裝置 〖전자공학〗 a sensor
감질 疳疾 an insatiable〔a never satisfied〕 appetite (식욕) ; a perpetually unsatisfied desire ¶ 감질나다 feel insatiable ; never feel satisfied ; have an unsatisfied feeling ; feel something lacking ; feel tantalized ; feel eager to eat more〔have more〕
감쪼으다 鑑— show 《a thing》 to one's superior ; submit 《a thing》 to one's superior's inspection
*감쪽같다 ① [원상대로] be perfect in 《mending》; be just as it was ; be just as before ; be restored to the former state ; be as good as new ¶ 감쪽같이 고쳐 놓다 mend 《it》 just as it was // 세탁을 하니 감쪽같았다 When washed, it was as good as before.
② [완전] (be) complete ; perfect ¶ 감쪽같이 perfectly ; completely // 감쪽같이 속다 be completely deceived〔taken in〕 // 감쪽같이 도망치다 succeed in escaping〔getting away〕 // 감쪽같이 사라지다 vanish completely
감찰 鑑札 a license plate ; a license ; a permit ¶ 무감찰의〔로〕 without a license ; unlicensed // 감찰을 교부하다 give 《a person》 a license // 감찰을 받다 take (out) a license // 감찰을 몰수하다 revoke 《a person's》 license // 감찰을 갱신하다 renew a license
—료 a license fee 수렵 — shooting license 영업 — a business〔trade〕 license
감찰 監察 inspection —하다 inspect ; supervise
감찰감 監察監 〖군사〗 the Inspector General
감찰관 監察官 an inspector ; a supervi-

sor

감채 減債 partial payment of a debt ; reducing one's debt
— **기금** a sinking fund ; an amortization fund ¶ 감채 기금으로 상각하다 amortize ; sink — **적립금** a sinking-fund reserve

감천 甘泉 a spring of sweet〔fresh〕 water ; a sweet spring

감천 感天
지성이면 감천이라 속담 Sincerity moves Heaven./Faith will move a mountain.

감청 紺靑 deep blue ; navy blue ; ultramarine ; Prussian blue

감초 甘草 licorice root ¶ 약방의 감초 an indispensable man ; a key man ; a person active in all sorts of affairs ; Jack-of-all-trades
— **분말** powdered licorice ; licorice powder — **엑스** an extract of licorice ; Spanish licorice

감촉 感觸 (the sense of) touch ; feeling **—하다** feel ; perceive through the senses ; sense ¶ 감촉이 부드럽다 It feels soft (to the touch).//감촉이 좋다 be agreeable to the touch

*__감추다__ [숨기다] hide 《away》; conceal ; [비호] harbor ; shelter ; [덮어서] cover ; [가려서] veil ; screen ; [비밀로 하다] keep〔hide, conceal〕《a matter》 from 《a person》; keep secret ; keep back ¶ 감추지 않고 without concealing ; frankly ; candidly//몸을 감추다 hide oneself ; be in hiding//나이를 감추다 conceal one's age//종적〔행방〕을 감추다 disappear ; go into hiding ; cover one's trail ; abscond//범죄를 감추다 cover a crime//감정을 감추다 conceal one's feelings//호주머니에 감추다 hide 《a thing》 in one's pocket//서랍 속에 감추다 put away 《a thing》 in a cabinet drawer//마음의 동요를 감추다 cover one's confusion//기쁨을 감추지 못하다 cannot conceal one's joy//어둠이 산을 감추어 버렸다 Darkness has covered the hills.

감축 感祝 —하다 [감사] be thankful 〔grateful〕; [경하] congratulate enthusiastically ; offer one's congratulations

감축 減縮 reduction ; diminution ; retrenchment ; curtailment **—하다** reduce ; diminish ; retrench ; curtail ; cut down ¶ 경비를 감축하다 cut (down)〔curtail〕 the expenses ; curtail 〔retrench〕 expenditures//주한 미군의 감축 the reduction of the US Forces in Korea//대통령은 적자 감축을 위해 모든 것을 걸고 있다 The president sticks his neck out for deficit reduction.

감치다[1] [마음에] be always on one's mind ; linger in one's mind

감치다[2] [가장자리를] hem ; hemstitch ; sew 《up》; seam ¶ 옷단을 감치다 hem the edge of a garment

감칠맛 [맛] flavor ; taste ; savor ; savory taste ; relish ; [매력] charm ; magnetic power 《속》 ¶ 감칠맛 나는 요리 a tasty dish//감칠맛이 없다 be flat〔tasteless, vapid, insipid〕

감침질 hemming ; darning ; putting in hems **—하다** ⇨ 감치다[2]

†**감탄 感歎, 感嘆** admiration ; wonder ; exclamation **—하다** admire ; marvel 《at》; wonder 《at》; be struck with admiration ¶ 감탄할 만한 admirable ; wonderful ; marvelous//감탄해 마지않다 be full of〔filled with〕 admiration ; be lost in admiration//그의 아량에 감탄했다 I was moved to admiration by his generosity. ☞ ◖p. 67◗

감탄문 感歎文 〖문법〗 an exclamatory sentence

감탄 부호 感歎符號 〖문법〗 an exclamation mark〔point〕

‡**감탄사 感歎詞** an exclamation ; an interjection

감탕 slime ; liquid mud ; [진창] a mire ; a quagmire

감탕밭 a bog-land ; a marsh land ; a marshy〔swampy〕 place

감퇴 減退 decrease ; decline ; loss ; recession **—하다** decrease ; fall off ; [홍수가] recede ¶ 시력〔기억〕의 감퇴 failing of eyesight〔memory〕//식욕의 감퇴 loss of appetite//정력의 감퇴 a decline in energy//본래 시원찮았던 그녀의 식욕이 눈에 띄게 감퇴하였다 Her appetite, little as it was, fell off appreciably.

감투 ① [모자] a horsehair cap formerly worn by gentry or officials ② [벼슬] a government post ¶ 감투를 쓰다 be appointed an high government official ; become a government official ; assume office//감투를 벗다 resign a government〔prominent〕 post ; leave one's post

감투 敢鬪 —하다 fight courageously

감투거리 sexual intercourse with the woman on top

감투상 敢鬪賞 the fighting spirit prize

감투싸움 a struggle for getting an influential post

감투 정신 敢鬪精神 fighting spirit ; a game spirit ¶ 감투 정신이 왕성하다 have plenty of fight in one

감파르다 (be) dark-blue ; blueblack

감파르족족하다 (be) tawny with a blue tint

감표 減票 a minus〔subtraction〕 sign ; a minus

감표 監票 supervision〔superintendence〕 of the poll **—하다** supervise〔superintend〕 the poll
—인 the superintendent of the poll

감 탄

① 감탄사

기쁨·슬픔·놀람 등의 감정을 나타내는 말로 문장 중에 다른 부분과 문법적 관계를 갖지 않고 독립적 성질을 갖는 것을 감탄사라 한다.

¶ 어!, 아! *Ah!* 《슬픔·걱정·놀람 등》 // 만세! (우리가 이겼다) *Hurrah!* (We won.) // 아아, 슬프도다! *Alas* (the day)! // 아! 놀래라! *Oh!* What a surprise! // 아얏! *Ouch!* // 잘한다, 좋아! *Bravo!* // 원, 저런! *Dear* (*me*)! 《놀람·곤혹 등》 // 어머나, 야단났네! (버스가 떠났네) *Good heavens!* (The bus has left.) 《놀람·연민 등》 // 뭣!, 저런!, 어머나! *My goodness!* / *Goodness me!* 《놀람·분노의 소리》 // 야, 와! *Wow!* 《놀람·기쁨, 고통 등》 // 여보게, 잠깐! *Yoo-hoo!* 《주의·환기 등》

② 감탄문

감탄문의 형식은 보통 what이나 how를 써서 표현한다.

¶ 참으로 많이 자랐구나! How tall you've grown. // 참으로 용감한 소년이로군! What a brave boy (he is)! / How brave a boy (he is)! (★ he is는 보통 생략)

이러한 감탄문은 He is a very brave boy. / The boy is very brave.의 very를 what이나 how로 바꾸어서 문장 앞에 보낸 것이다. 주의할 것은 what은 형용사, how는 부사이기 때문에 what 뒤에는 명사가, how 뒤에는 형용사나 부사가 뒤따른다. 또한 감탄문과 what이나 how를 사용하는 의문문의 차이는 감탄문에서는 주어와 술어의 어순이 평서문과 같다는 것이다.

How tall is that building? (의문문)
How tall that building is! (감탄문)

what으로 시작하는 감탄문에서는 단수의 경우 「관사＋형용사＋명사」의 순이 된다.

¶ 참 예쁜 아기로군! What a cute baby! // 참 재미있는 이야기로구나 What a funny story (it is)! (★ 이 경우 How cute! / How funny (that story is)! 처럼 주어와 술어를 생략할 수도 있다.) // 참으로 대단한 소녀로군! What a girl! // 고약한 날씨로군! What nasty weather!

감풀 [모래톱] a low-tide sandbar〔sandpit〕

***감하다 減—** subtract ; reduce ⇨ 감(減)

감행 敢行 decisive〔daring, resolute〕 action **—하다** venture ; take decisive action ; carry out resolutely ; dare

감형 減刑 commutation ; mitigation ; remission **—하다** commute ; remit ; reduce ; mitigate ¶ 사형이 종신형으로 감형되다 The (death) sentence is commuted〔reduced〕 to life imprisonment.

감호 監護 『법』 care and custody ; superintendence **—하다** [감독하다] superintend ; supervise ; [보호하다] take care of ; look after ¶ 감호 조치를 취하다 take a measure for care and custody

감홍 甘汞 『화학』 calomel ; mercurous chloride

†감화 感化 influence ; conversion ; [교정] (moral) reform **—하다** influence ; exert influence upon 《a person》 ; inspire ; [바로잡다] reform ; correct ¶ 감화를 받다 be influenced by ; fall〔come〕 under 《a person's》 influence ; be under the influence 《of》 ; feel another's influence // 감화를 미치다 exert influence upon 《a person》 // 감화 받기 쉽다 be easily influenced ; be susceptible to influence // 내가 공부를 좋아하게 된 것은 할아버지의 감화 때문이다 My grandfather inspired me with a love of learning. // 선생님은 학생들에게 상당한 감화를 주었다 The teacher had a good influence over his students.

감화 교육 感化教育 reformatory instruction〔training〕 ; correctional education

감화력 感化力 influence ; power to influence

감화 사업 感化事業 reformatory work

감화원 感化院 a (juvenile) reformatory ; a reform school

감회 感懷 [회포] sentiments ; feelings ; [회상] memories ; reminiscences ; retrospection ¶ 감회가 깊다 be deeply moved 《by》 // 감회를 말하다 give 〔express〕 one's sentiment(s)〔feelings〕 《about》 // 감회에 젖다 give oneself up to deep emotion〔recollection〕 // 감회로 벅차다 be filled with emotion

감흥 感興 interest ; fun ; [영감] inspiration ¶ 감흥을 깨뜨리다 spoil the fun 〔interest〕 《of》 ; throw a wet blanket 《on》 ; break the spell // 감흥이 일다 be inspired 《by》 ; feel a sensation of pleasure // 그런 것으로는 아무런 감흥도 일지 않았다 That left me cold. // 문득 시적 감흥이 일어났다 I had a sudden poetic inspiration.

†감히 敢— boldly ; fearlessly ; daringly ; without hesitation ; [주제넘게] affectedly ; impudently ¶ 감히 …하다 dare 《to do》 ; venture 《to do》 ; [주제넘게] have the cheek〔face〕 to 《do》 ; be impudent enough to 《do》 // 그들은 감히 오지 못했다 They did not dare to come. // 감히 죽음을 무릅쓰다 dare to risk one's life // 그는 감히 반대하려고 하지 않았다 He dared not oppose me. /He did not dare to oppose me. /감히 일독을 권합니다 Allow me to recommend the book to the public. // 나한테 어떻게 감히 그런 말을 하느냐 How dare you say such a thing to me?

갑 甲 [십간(十干)의] the first of the ten celestial stems ; [차례의] A ; the former ; the one ; [성적의] class〔grade〕 "A"/"Excellent" ; [갑옷] a piece of armor ; [갑각] a shell ¶ 갑과 을 A and B ; the former and the latter ; the one and the other

갑 匣 a casket ; a tiny case ; [담배 따위의] a pack ¶ 담배 한 갑 a packet 〔pack〕 of cigarettes // 하루에 담배를 몇 갑이나 피느냐 How many packs of cigarettes do you smoke every day?

갑 岬 a cape ; a promontory ; a headland

갑각 甲殼 a shell ; a carapace ; a crust

갑각류 甲殼類 Crustacea (학명)
— 동물(動物) a crustacean **—학(學)** crustaceology **— 학자(學者)** crustaceologist

갑갑증 —症 ennui ; irksomeness ; boredom ; tedium

***갑갑하다** (be) boring ; tedious ; dull ; feel bored ; have a dull time ; [답답하다] (be) stuffy ; suffocating ; stifling ; [좁아서] stiff ; pinched ; confined ; cramped ¶ 갑갑해 죽겠다 be bored to death ; be oppressed with tedium // 문체가 갑갑하다 the style is stodgy // 견해가 갑갑하다 have a narrow view of things // 배가 갑갑하다 feel heavy in the stomach // 방이 갑갑해 못 견디겠다 — 문 좀 열어라 Please open the window. I feel stifled in this room.

갑골 문자 甲骨文字 〖역사〗 inscriptions on bones and tortoise carapace

갑근세 甲勤稅 the Grade A earned income tax ¶ 갑근세를 봉급에서 공제하다 deduct the earned income tax of Grade A from one's salary

갑년 甲年 the year of one's sixty-first birthday

갑론을박 甲論乙駁 an argument pro and con ; pros and cons
—하다 argue pro and con ; argue for and against 《a matter》 ; divide in opinion

갑문 閘門 [물문] a floodgate ; a penstock ; a sluice (gate) ; [운하의] a lock gate ¶ 갑문식 운하 a lock canal

갑방 甲方 east-by-northeast

갑번 甲番 the first turn〔work-shift〕

갑부 甲富 the richest man (in a community) ; a millionaire ; a magnate

갑사 甲紗 fine gauze

갑상선 甲狀腺 〖해부〗 the thyroid gland **— 기능 부전** hypothyroidism **— 기능 항진** hyperthyroidism **— 동맥〔정맥〕** the thyroid artery〔vein〕 **—염** thyroiditis **— 자극 호르몬** thyroid stimulating hormone **— 절제술** thyroidectomy

갑상선종 甲狀腺腫 〖의학〗 a goiter ; a struma 《*pl.* -mae》

갑상선 호르몬 thyroid hormone ; thyroxine

갑상 연골 甲狀軟骨 〖의학〗 the thyroid cartilage ; the thyroid

갑석 —石 a flat stone laid on another stone

갑시 甲時 the 6th of the 24 periods of the day (according to Oriental tradition)《4 : 30—5 : 30 a. m.》

갑시다 be choked 《with》 ; be stifled 《by》 ; be suffocated〔smothered〕 《with》 ; get choked 《on water》 ¶ 연기로 갑시다 be choked with〔stifled by〕 smoke

갑신 甲申 the 21st year of the sexagenary cycle ; the Year of the monkey Ape

갑오 甲午 the 31st binary term of the sexagenary cycle

갑오 경장 甲午更張 the *Kap-o* Reform of 1894

*__갑옷 甲—__ a suit〔piece〕 of armor ; a suit〔coat〕 of mail ¶ 갑옷을 입다 put〔buckle〕 on 《one's》 armor // 갑옷을 입고 있다 be (clad) in armor ; be steel-clad // 갑옷과 투구 armor and helmet
— 미늘 the metal scales on a coat of armor

갑의 甲衣 a suit of armor ⇨ 갑옷

갑일 甲日 one's 61st birthday

†**갑자기** [별안간] suddenly ; all of a sudden ; on a sudden ; all at once ; [뜻밖에] unexpectedly ; without warning 〔notice〕 ¶ 갑자기 나빠지다 take a sudden turn for a worse // 갑자기 도착하다 arrive unexpectedly // 갑자기 돌아서다 turn back abruptly // 갑자기 죽다 drop dead // 갑자기 사직하다 resign without notice // 갑자기 해고하다 dismiss 《a person》 without notice // 갑자기 들이닥치다 drop in〔assault〕 without warning // 갑자기 달려들다 spring at 《a person》 without any warning // 갑자기 울음을 터뜨렸다 She burst into tears. /She burst out crying. // 갑자기 물어서 죄송합니다만… Excuse my abrupt question, but...

†**갑작스럽다** (be) sudden ; abrupt ; unexpected ; unlooked-for ; unannounced ¶ 갑작스러운 손님 the unexpected caller //

갑작스러운 초대 a surprise invitation // 사태의 갑작스러운 변화 an unexpected turn of affairs // 갑작스러운 질문을 받고 어리둥절했다 I was at a loss for a reply to his unexpected question.

갑작스레 suddenly ⇨ 갑자기

***갑절** ① [두배] double ; two times ; twice ; twofold **—하다** double ; redouble ¶ 갑절의 double ; twice as much 〔many, large, long〕 again // 거리를 갑절로 하다 double the distance ; make the distance double ; make double the distance // 무게가 갑절로 된다 The weight doubles. /The weight becomes 〔gets〕 doubled. // 인구가 갑절로 되었다 The population has (been) doubled. // 그의 재산은 나의 갑절이나 된다 His fortune doubles mine. // 남의 갑절(이나) 일을 한다 He works twice as hard as others. // 이것은 갑절이나 좋다 This is twice as good as that. // 갑절 비싸다 cost twice as much

② [-배] -times ; -for ⇨ 배 ¶ 세 갑절 three times ; treble ; thrice // 반갑절 half // 갑절 반 half again as much

갑종 甲種 grade A ; first〔top〕 grade

갑종 근로 소득세 甲種勤勞所得税 ⇨ 갑근세

갑주 甲冑 armor ; armor and helmet ; panoply ¶ 갑주를 입다 put〔buckle〕 on armor // 갑주로 몸을 싸다 be armed to the teeth ; be encased〔clad〕 in armor.

갑철판 甲鐵板 an armor-plate ; armor plating 《총칭》

‡**갑충 甲蟲** 〖곤충〗 a beetle

†**갑판 甲板** a deck ¶ 갑판에 나가다 go 〔come〕 on deck // 갑판에서 바다로 뛰어들다 jump overboard // 갑판을 깔다 deck // 전원 갑판으로 All hands on deck!

— 사관 a deck officer **— 선실** a deck cabin **— 승강구** a hatchway **— 여객** a deck passenger **— 일지** a deck log **— 적하** deck cargo **— 차장** a boatswain's mate **앞—** the forward deck ; the foredeck **유보(游步) —** the promenade deck **정(正)〔상, 중, 하〕—** the main〔upper, middle, lower〕 deck **평—** a flat ; a flush deck **후—** the quarter deck ; the afterdeck

갑판원 甲板員 a deck hand

갑판장 甲板長 a boatswain ; a bosun

갑피 甲皮 the uppers of leather (shoes) ; shoes without soles

갑화 —火 [도깨비불] an elf fire ; a will-o'-the-wisp ; a jack-o'-lantern

†**값** ① [가치] value ; worth ; merit (장점) ¶ 값이 있다 be worth ; be valuable ; be of value ; be worthy // 밥먹은 값을 하다 sing for one's supper ; earn one's bread〔board〕 ; render a service for what one has eaten

② [가격] price ; cost ; charge

> 참고 **price** 특히 파는 값 **charge** 노동봉사에 대해서 구하는 대가 **cost** 물건 노동 기타의 획득에 대해 지불하는 값

¶ 값(이) 닿으면 if the price is reasonable〔satisfactory, moderate〕 // 값이 싸다〔비싸다〕 be cheap〔expensive〕 ; be low〔high〕 in price ; be low-〔high-〕priced // 값을 치르다 pay for 《an article》 // 값을 정하다 fix a price ; set the price 《of》 // 값이 오르다〔내리다〕 go up〔down〕 in price ; rise〔fall〕 in price ; the price goes up〔down〕 // 값을 올리다〔내리다〕 raise〔lower〕 the price ; put up〔down〕 the price // 값을 깎다 haggle over (the price) ; beat down the price // 값이 얼마요 What is the price (of this)? /How much is this〔does this cost〕? /What do you charge for this? // 값을 좀 싸게 할 수 없습니까 Can't you come down a little? // 값을 500원만 깎아주신다면 모르겠소만 I might consider it if you reduced the price by 500 *won*. // 값(을) 보다 estimate ; offer a price ; appraise // 값놓다〔부르다〕 [손님이] name a price ; make a bid ; offer 《ten dollars for a book》 ; make an offer ; [장수가] demand〔ask〕 a price // 값을 치다 fix the price of 《a thing》 // 값이 닿다 《the bid》 reach a price one has in mind ; 《the price》 be reasonable〔satisfactory〕 // 값치다 put〔charge〕 《a price on an article》 ; fix the price of 《an article》 ; value 《something》 at // 값치르다 pay for 《an article》 ; defray ; fork out 《구》

값나가다 be of value ; be costly ; be valuable ; be expensive ¶ 값나가는 물건 a valuable article ; an expensive article ; valuables ; a golden-egg hen ; the hen that lays the golden egg 《속》

값싸다 (be) cheap ; inexpensive ; low-priced ; low in price ¶ 값싼 물건 a cheap〔an inferior〕 article ; a (good) bargain

값어치 value ; worth ¶ 한 푼의 값어치도 없다 be not worth a farthing〔hair, straw〕 // 보기보다 값어치가 없다 It is showy but worthless. /It is not so good as it looks. // 한번 읽어볼 값어치가 있다 be worth reading // 그만한 값어치가 있다고 생각합니다 I think you got your money's worth.

값없다 ① [무한 가치] (be) priceless ; invaluable ¶ 값없는 보배 priceless treasures ② [무가치] (be) valueless ; worthless ; unworthy ; be of no merit (장점이 없다)

값지다 (be) costly ; expensive ; valuable ¶ 값진 물건 a costly〔high-priced〕 article ; a precious object // 그것은 너무나 값진 물건이어서 값을 매길 수가 없다 It is of too high a value to be given a price.

갓¹ [쓰는] a traditional cylindrical Korean hat (made of bamboo or horsehair, formerly worn by a married gentleman)

갓² ① [금방·처음] fresh ; brand-new ; spick-and-span ; just now ¶ 갓 구운 빵 bread fresh from the oven // 대학을 갓 나온 젊은 기사 a young engineer fresh from college // 갓 만든 음식 a steaming dish // 갓 핀 꽃 fresh-blown flowers // 갓 사온 시계 a brand-new watch // 갓난 고양이 새끼 a newly-born kitten // 시골에서 갓 나온 아가씨 a girl new〔fresh〕 from the country 〔provinces〕 // 갓 결혼한 부부 a couple who have just married ; the newlyweds 《미·구》 // 그는 대학을 갓 졸업한 것 같다 It seems that he's just fresh out of college.

② [겨우·바로] just ; exactly ¶ 나이가 갓 스물이다 be barely twenty years of age ; be just twenty years old

갓³ 〖식물〗 leaf mustard

갓⁴ [말림갓] a preserve

갓⁵ [굴비 따위의] a bundle〔bunch〕 of ten (flat dried fish) tied together ¶ 굴비 두 갓 two bunches of dried fish

갓김치 pickled mustard leaves and stems ; mustard pickles

갓끈 a hat string (tied under the chin)

갓나다 be just born ; be newly born ; have seen the light ; have just started to sprout (싹이)

†**갓난아이** a newborn baby ; a suckling ; a baby ; an infant ; a babe ¶ 갓난아이 같은 babylike ; babyish // 갓난아이 취급을 하다 treat 《a person》 like a baby ; baby 《a person》

갓방 —房 a hat-maker's shop

갓양(태) the brim of a Korean hat

강- severe ; harsh ; forced ; rough ; trying ; unreasonable ; straight ; pure ; unadulterated ; unmitigated ; dry ; pretended ¶ 강추위 a spell of dry cold weather // 강샘 unreasonable jealousy ; intense〔burning〕 jealousy // 강더위 a spell of intense heat with no rain at all

†**강** 江 a river ¶ 강바닥 a river-bed ; the bottom of a river // 강을 끼고 along a river // 강 건너편 the opposite〔other〕 side of the river ; across the river // 강 건너에 on the opposite bank (shore) // 강을 거슬러 올라가다〔내려가다〕 go up〔down〕 a river // 강을 건너다 cross a river ; [걸어서] wade (across) a brook // 강에 다리를 놓다 build〔throw〕 a bridge across a river // 비가 와서 강의 수위가 5미터로 올라갔다 Rain caused the river to rise to the height of five meters.

강 건너 불 보듯하다 관용 look on 《a person's trouble》 unconcernedly (with indifference)

강 綱 a class

강 講 recitation (외는 일) ; a lecture (강의) **—하다** recite ; give a lecture

-강 强 strong ; a little over ; and a fraction ¶ 3할강 a little over 30 percent // 1,000명강 one thousand strong ; a little over one thousand // 2피트강의 길이 be a shade longer than two feet

강가 江— a river-bank ; a riverside ¶ 강가의 호텔 a hotel by the riverside ; a riverside hotel // 강가에 살다 live on the banks of a river // 강가를 거닐다 walk 〔stroll〕 along the river

강가 降嫁 the marriage of a princess to a subject〔commoner〕 **—하다** 《a princess》 marry a commoner

강간 强姦 rape ; violation ; outrage ; acquaintance rape (아는 남자에 의한) ; a date rape (데이트 상대의 남자에 의한) ; a statutory rape (미성년자 강간) **—하다** violate ; rape ; outrage ; force ; assault ¶ 습격하여 강간하다 assault and rape 《a woman》 // 강간당하다 be violated ; be outraged ; be raped **— 미수** an attempted rape〔criminal assault〕 **—범** a rapist ; a violator **—죄** rape ; criminal assault

강강술래 a Korean circle〔round〕 dance ; a group dance in a ring ; the song that goes with the dance

강강하다 剛剛— [마음·기력이] (be) adamant ; sturdy ; hardy ; stout-hearted ; unyielding ; [날씨가] chilly ; severely cold ¶ 강강한 날씨 chilly weather // 성미가 강강하다 be of stout nature

강개 慷慨 righteous wrath〔indignation〕 **—하다** be indignant 《at》 ; deplore

***강건** 强健 robustness ; healthiness ; sturdiness **—하다** (be) strong ; robust ; hardy ; healthy ¶ 강건한 청년 a robust youngster // 강건한 몸을 기르다 build a strong body ; strengthen one's body

강건 剛健 virility ; potency ; vigor ; sturdiness **—하다** (be) virile ; vigorous ; sturdy ¶ 강건한 정신 a virile spirit // 강건한 문체 a virile style

강견 强肩 〖야구〗 a strong arm **— 외야수** strong-armed out-fielder **— 투수** a strong-armed pitcher **— 포수** a hot-corner catcher

강경 强硬 firmness ; resoluteness ; stubbornness ; toughness ; vigor **—하다** (be) strong ; firm ; vigorous ; tough ; unyielding ; uncompromising ¶ 강경한 결의문 a strongly worded resolution // 강경한 태도를 취하다 take a firm attitude〔stand〕 ; stand firm 《against》 // 강경한 조치를 하다 take a strong measure // 강경히 strongly ; firmly ; stoutly ; resolutely // 강경히 반대하다 oppose 《it》 strongly〔vigorously〕; offer strong opposition // 강경히 주장하다 strenuously insist 《on》// 강경히 항의하다 file a vigorous protest 《against》// 강경히 요구하다 strongly demand

강경 노선 强硬路線 a hard line

강경론자 强硬論者 [대외 정책에 대한] a hard-liner

강경 수단 强硬手段 a drastic〔strong〕 measure ; a decisive step

강경 정책 强硬政策 a hard-line policy

강경파 强硬派 the tough elements ; the hard-liners ; the hawks

강계 疆界 the frontier ; the boundary 〔border〕 of a country

강고 强固 —하다 (be) strong and firm ; stable ; solid ; sound ; steady ; constant

강골 强骨 a (person of) sturdy constitution

강관 鋼管 a steel pipe〔tube〕

강괴 鋼塊 a steel ingot

강교 江郊 the suburbs near the river ; the river neighborhood

강구 江口 the mouth of a river ; an estuary
—항(港) an estuary harbor

강구 强求 a strong〔insistent〕 demand ; insistence —하다 demand strongly ; insist on ; force

강구 講究 study ; consideration ; deliberation —하다 [안출] find〔think〕 out ; devise ; consider ; [수단을] take 《measures, steps》; provide 《a means》; conceive 《a plan》 ¶ 안〔방법〕을 강구하다 devise a scheme〔means〕// 아무런 수단도 강구하지 않다 take no steps to 《do》// 대책을 강구하다 consider a countermeasure ; consider how to cope with the situation

강국 强國 a strong power〔country〕; a great power ; a powerful state ¶ 세계의 강국 a world power

강군 强軍 [군대] a powerful〔strong〕 army ; a powerful force ; [경기 단체] a strong team

강굽이 江— a river bend ; the crooks of a river

강권 强權 (the power of) authority ; influence ¶ 법의 강권 the strong arm of the law ; legal authority // 강권을 발동하다 take strong measures ; enforce authority ; invoke legal authority

강권 强勸 a persistent〔insistent〕 recommendation —하다 press 《upon a person》; force 《upon》; compel〔impel〕 《a person》 to 《do》; urge ; recommend against 《a person's》 will ¶ 술을 강권하다 press a drink on〔upon〕 《a person》
— 발동 invocation of the legal power
— 정치 power〔a high-handed〕 politics
—주의 authoritarianism

강기 剛氣 fortitude ; sturdiness ; manliness ; hardihood ; firmness of character

강기 强記 a good〔retentive, powerful, strong, tenacious〕 memory ; tenacity (of memory) ; retentiveness —하다 be retentive of ; be tenacious of memory ; have a good〔prodigious〕 memory ¶ 박람(博覽) 강기의 선비 a scholar well-informed and retentive in memory ; a man of erudition and strong memory

강기 綱紀 [기율] official〔governmental〕 discipline ; [질서] public order ; law and order ; the laws

강기 문란 綱紀紊亂 (gross) breach〔the degradation〕 of (official) discipline

강기 숙정 綱紀肅正 enforcement of official discipline ¶ 강기 숙정을 단행하다 enforce strict official discipline

강기슭 江— a riverside ; the banks 〔shores〕 of a river

강기 이완 綱紀弛緩 relaxation of law and order ; slack discipline

강낭콩 江南— 『식물』 a kidney bean 《미》; a French bean 《영》; a haricot ; a bean

강다리 crosswise support sticks ; [장작 100개비] a hundred pieces of firewood

강다짐 —하다 ① [밥을] eat rice without soup or other liquid ② [강요] force 《a person》 to work without pay ③ [나무라다] scold〔reprove〕 《a person》 without listening to his side of the story

강단 剛斷 decisiveness ; determination ; resolution

강단 講壇 a (lecture) platform ; a rostrum ; [설교단] a pulpit ¶ 강단에 서다 stand〔appear〕 on the (speaker's) platform ; occupy the platform ; take the platform

강담 a stone wall made without mud

강담 講談 a discourse ; storytelling ; a speech (강연) ; a sermon (설교) ; a presentation (발표)

***강당 講堂** a (lecture) hall ; [학교의] an assembly hall 《영》; an auditorium 《미》

강대 强大 —하다 (be) big and strong ; mighty ; powerful ¶ 강대한 해군 a powerful navy // 강대한 군비 heavy armament ; powerful armed forces

***강대국 强大國** a powerful〔big〕 country

****강도 强度** intensity ; powerfulness ; degree of strength ; [경도] solidity ¶ 강도의 strong ; thick 《glasses》; powerful 《lens》; intense 《light》// 강도의 근시 안경 thick-lensed glasses // 지진의 강도 seismic intensity
— 현미경 a powerful〔highpower〕 microscope

강도 講道 expounding and teaching 《doctrines》; preaching (설교) —하다 expound 《a text of Scripture》; preach ; lecture on

*강도 强盜 [사람] a burglar ; a robber ; a housebreaker ; [소행] burglary ; robbery ¶ 흉기를 가진〔복면〕 강도 an armed〔a masked〕 robber // 삼인조 강도 a trio of burglars // 강도질하다 commit robbery〔burglary〕 // 강도가 들다 have one's house broken into ; be robbed by a burglar // 어느 날 밤 그 집에 강도가 들었다 One evening the family were robbed. /One night there was a robbery in that house. // 나는 노상 강도를 당했다 I was mugged.

—질 burglary ; robbery — 용의자 a robber-suspect 권총 — [사람] a holdup man ; a gunman 《미·속》; [행위] a holdup 노상 — [사람] a mugger ; a highwayman ; a gentleman〔knight, squire〕 of the road ; [행위] highway robbery 무장〔복면〕 — an armed〔a masked〕 robber 살인 —죄 burglary and murder 은행 — [사람] a bank burglar ; [행위] bank robbery 택시 — [사람] a taxi robber ; [행위] taxi robbery

강독 講讀 reading with comments ; textual exposition ; translation

강동거리다, 깡뚱거리다 jump up and down lightly ; hop ; skip ; romp ; gambol ¶ 강동강동〔깡뚱깡뚱〕 skipping ; hopping ; briskly ; playfully

강동하다, 깡뚱하다 [옷이] (be) too short ; very short ; unbecomingly short ; be in〔wear〕 a very short garment

강두 江頭 a landing place ; a wharf ; a quay ; a (landing) stage ; a pier ; moorings

강둑 a river embankment ; a levee

강등 降等 degradation ; demotion —하다 degrade ; demote ¶ 강등시키다 degrade a person to a lower grade〔rank〕

강똥 hard stools ; turds

*강력 强力 great strength〔power〕 ; being strong〔powerful, mighty〕 —하다 (be) strong ; powerful ; mighty ¶ 강력한 내각 a strong cabinet // 강력한 망원경 a powerful telescope // 강력한 후원자 a powerful supporter // 강력히 요구하다 make a pressing demand // 강력히 항의하다 make a strong protest 《against》

강력계 强力係 [사람] an officer〔official〕 in charge of crimes of violence ; [부서] a section in charge of crimes of violence

강력범 强力犯 [범인] a felonious〔major〕 criminal ; a violent criminal ; [행위] a crime of violence ; a major crime ; a felony

강렬 强烈 —하다 (be) strong ; intense ; severe ¶ 강렬한 의지 a strong will // 강렬한 색채 a loud〔gaudy〕 color // 강렬 자극 a strong stimulus

강령 綱領 main principles ; a general plan ; essential points ; general principles ¶ 정당의 강령 a party platform 《미》; a party programme 《영》; [항목] a plank // 공화당의 주요 강령의 하나 one of the chief planks of the Republican platform

10대 — a 10-point program

강론 講論 [토론] exposition ; discussion ; [강의] preaching ; teaching ; a sermon —하다 expound ; discuss ; preach ; teach

강린 强隣 a formidable neighboring country ; a formidable rival

강림 降臨 advent ; descent ; epiphany ; coming down ; arrival —하다 descend on to the earth ; 《God》 come down

강림절 降臨節 Advent

강마르다 [땅이] (be) dried up ; parched

강매 强買 exacting〔forcing〕 a purchase —하다 force 《a person》 to sell

강매 强賣 forcing a sale ; high-pressure salesmanship 《미》; forced sale (auction) (공매) —하다 force a sale 《on》; importune a sale 《on》; force〔thrust〕 an article 《upon》; push wares 《on》

강멱 降冪 〖수학〗 descending powers〔series〕

강명 剛明 —하다 (be) intrepid and bright

강모 young rice plants planted in a dry paddy

강모 剛毛 a bristle ; a seta 《*pl.* -tae》 ¶ 강모가 난 setaceous ; setose

강목 〖광산〗 waste〔unproductive, fruitless〕 mining operations ¶ 강목치다 make vain〔fruitless〕 efforts ; beat the air

강목 綱目 an outline and details ; divisions and subdivisions ; [요점] the main points ¶ 강목을 나누다 classify (and itemize)

강무 講武 military training ; training in the art of war —하다 get military training ; train oneself in the art of war

강물 江— river water ; the river ¶ 강물이 불었다 The river is swollen〔risen〕. // 강물이 넘치다 The river overflows. // 강물이 준다 The river sinks.

‡강바닥 江— the river bed ; the river bottom

강바람 [건조한 바람] a strong wind bringing no rain ; a dry wind

강바람 江— [강에서 불어오는] a breeze from the river

강박 强迫 compulsion ; coercion ; duress ; constraint —하다 compel ; coerce

— 신경증 〖의학〗 obsessional〔obsessive-compulsive〕 neurosis

강박 관념 强迫觀念 an imperative idea〔conception〕 ; an obsession ¶ 강박 관

념에 사로잡히다 suffer from an obsession
강반 江畔 a riverside ; the bank (edge) of a river ; bottomlands ; bottoms
강밥 a snack of rice taken without soup ; rice eaten without accompanying soup
강밭다 (be) very stingy〔mean〕
강배 江— a river boat ; a river craft ; a barge ; a ferryboat
*강변 强辯 a sophism ; sophistry ; quibbles ; quips ; an objection for objection's sake —하다 sophisticate ; chop logic ; quibble ; argue for argument's sake ; give a strained meaning ¶ 그런 강변은 통하지 않는다 Such a farfetched argument won't work.
강변 江邊 the riverside
강변 도로 江邊道路 a riverside road 〔drive〕
강변화 强變化 〖문법〗 [동사의] strong conjugation
— 동사(動詞) strong verbs
강병 —病 pretended〔feigned〕 illness ; counterfeit sickness〔illness〕; fake sickness 《미》; malingering
강병 强兵 a powerful army ; a strong soldier ; military buildup
부국(富國)— wealth and military strength〔power〕 of a nation ; national prosperity and defense 부국 —책 a measure to enrich and strengthen a country
강보 襁褓 swaddling clothes ; a diaper ; a baby's quilt ¶ 아이를 강보에 싸다 wrap an infant in swaddling clothes
— 유아 an infant ; a baby ; a newborn child
강보합 强保合 〖증권〗 ¶ 강보합의 firm 〔steady〕 with an upward tendency
강복 降福 God's blessing ; 〖카톨릭〗 benediction —하다 bless
강북 江北 the north of a river〔the *Han* river〕
†강사 講士 a speaker ; a lecturer
강사 講師 a lecturer 《영》; an instructor 《미》; [직분] lectureship ¶ 서울 대학교 강사 a lecturer at *Seoul* University // 강사로 임명되다 be appointed (a) lecturer ; be appointed to lectureship 《at》
시간 — a part-time lecturer ; [중고교의] a part-time teacher 전임 — an (a full-time) instructor 철학 — a lecturer on〔in〕 philosophy
강사직 講師職 lectureship
강삭 鋼索 a (steel) wire rope ; a cable ; a hawser
— 철도 a cable railway ; a rope railway
강산 江山 rivers and hills ; [경치] landscape ; scenery ; [강토] a country ; a land ; a realm ; a domain
금수— a beautiful land ; a country noted for the beauty of its landscape
삼천리 금수— the beautiful land of Korea
강상 江上 [물가] (on) the riverbank ; [물위] (on) the surface of the river 〔water〕
강상 綱常 moral principles ; a code of morals ; morality
강샘 unreasonable〔burning, intense〕 jealousy —하다 feel a surge of unreasonable jealousy ; become intensely jealous ; burn with jealousy ; be green with envy
강생 降生 incarnation —하다 become incarnate
강서 講書 expounding ; exposition of 《ancient writings》 —하다 expound ancient writings
강서리 heavy frost
강석 講席 a lecture hall ; a lecturing place〔seat, chair〕
강석 講釋 an exposition ; an explanation ; a lecture —하다 expound ; give an exposition 《of》; explain ; lecture 《on》
강설 講說 a lecture ; a talk —하다 expound ; lecture〔talk〕 on 《a subject》
*강설 降雪 snowing ; a snowfall ¶ 강설이 30센티 가량 쌓였다 Snow fell thirty centimeters deep. // 5내지 15인치의 강설이 있었다 There was a snowfall of from 5 to 15 inches.
강설량 降雪量 (the amount of) snowfall ¶ 이번 겨울은 강설량이 적었다 We have had little snow during the winter.
강성 强盛 —하다 [몸이] (be) vigorous ; energetic ; [번영] powerful ; thriving ; flourishing
‡강세 强勢 〖음성〗 stress ; emphasis ; accent ; a strong〔firm〕 tone ; [시세] a bullish tendency ¶ 강세가 있는 음절 an emphatic〔a stressed, an accented〕 syllable // 강세를 두다 accent a word 《on the first syllable》; put emphasis 《on》// 시장은 강세를 보이고 있다 The tone of the market is strong.
— 시장 (a) bull〔strong〕 market — 요인 a bullish factor —주 bull shares
강세 降世 incarnation ⇨ 강생(降生)
강속구 强速球 〖야구〗 a fast〔speed〕 ball ; a fireball ; a smoke ball ¶ 강속구를 던지다 throw a fast〔speed〕 ball
— 투수 a strong-armed pitcher ; a smoke-ball hurler ; a speedballer 《미·속》
강송 强送 enforced sending ; enforced repatriation —하다 send by force ; repatriate by force
강송 講誦 recitation —하다 recite
강쇠 降衰 decline ; wane ; decadence —하다 decline ; wane ; be on the decline〔wane〕; decay
강쇠바람 the east〔easterly〕 wind which

blows in early autumn〔fall〕

강수 降水 precipitation
— 시간 rainfall duration — 밀도 rainfall density

강수량 降水量 rainfall ; precipitation

강술 a drink without any food ; just liquor ¶ 강술을 마시다 have a drink without eatables

강술 講述 lecturing ; expounding —하다 lecture 《on》; expound

강습 强襲 [공격] a storm ; an assault —하다 storm ; assault ¶ 강습 점령하다 take 《a fort》 by storm ; carry 《a fort》 by assault

강습 講習 a short〔brief〕 training course ; learning ; studying ¶ 강습을 받다 attend a class ; take a short training course 《in》; take lessons 《in swimming》

강습생 講習生 a student ; a trainee

강습소 講習所 a training school

강습회 講習會 an institute ; a short course (of study) ; a (lecture) class
교원 — a teacher's institute 《미》 하계 — a summer school〔seminar〕

강신술 降神術 spiritualism ; mediumism
—자 a spiritualist

강심 江心 the very middle of a river

강심제 强心劑 a heart stimulant ; a cordial

***강아지** 〖동물〗 a pup ; a puppy ; a little dog

강아지풀 〖식물〗 a foxtail

강안 江岸 a riverside

강압 强壓 oppression ; repression ; coercion ; compulsion ; pressure ; duress ; high-handedness —하다 bring pressure to bear upon ; oppress ; repress 《a volt》; overbear 《a person's objections》 ¶ 강압적(인) oppressive ; overbearing ; high-handed ; compulsive // 그의 태도는 매우 강압적이다 His attitude is very heavy-handed〔coercive〕. // 강압 수단으로 유권자를 누르다 coerce voters with a high hand // 강압하여 복종시키다 coerce 《a person》 into submission // 노총 간부진에 강압을 가하여 조합을 해산시켰다 He high-pressured the Union leaders into disbanding the organization.
— 통풍(通風) forced draft〔draught〕

강압 수단 强壓手段 a coercive〔high-handed〕 measure ; a repressive measure

강압 정책 强壓政策 a high-handed policy ; a big-stick policy 《미》

강약 强弱 strength and〔or〕 weakness ; the strong and the weak ; strength ; power ¶ 일국의 강약 the strength of a nation // 강약을 겨루다 contend for mastery

강약법 强弱法 〖음악〗 dynamics

강어귀 江— ⇨ 강구(江口)

강역 疆域 a territory ; a domain

강연 講演 a lecture ; an address ; a talk ; a discourse —하다 lecture 《on》; give a lecture 《on》; address 《students, a club》 《on》; talk〔speak〕 《on》; make a speech ¶ 그 문제에 대해 강연하다 give a lecture〔talk〕 on the subject // 강연을 의뢰하다 ask 《a person》 to give a lecture ; ask 《a person》 to address〔speak to〕 《students》 // 라디오를 통해서 강연하다 make a lecture over the radio〔on the air〕
—대 a lecture table —료 a lecturer's fee —자 a lecturer ; a speaker 공개 — a public lecture 연속 — a series of lectures ; a lecture in a series

강연회 講演會 a lecture meeting

강옥 鋼玉 corundum ⇨ 강옥석

강옥석 鋼玉石 〖광물〗 corundum ; ruby (붉은 것) ; sapphire (푸른 것)

강온 强穩 resoluteness and moderation ; toughness and moderateness ; carrot and stick
— 양면 정책 a carrot-and-stick policy
—양파 the tough elements〔hard-liner〕 and the moderates ; [매파와 비둘기파] the hawks and the doves

강요 綱要 [골자] elements ; essentials ; [개요] an outline ; a summary ; a synopsis
물리학 — the Elements of Physics (책 이름)

***강요 强要** enforcement ; exaction ; extortion ; compulsion —하다 exact ; demand ; force ; compel ¶ …에게 …하도록 강요하다 force〔compel〕 《a person》 to 《do》 // 복종을 강요하다 exact obedience from 《a person》 // 기부를 강요하다 solicit tenaciously for contributions // 자백을 강요하다 extort a confession from // 사직을 강요당한 끝에 그만두었다 He has been forced out of office. / He was compulsorily relieved of his post. // 나에게 술을 강요하지 말아라 Don't press a drink on me. // 그는 강요당하여 굴복했다 He was forced to submit.

강용 剛勇 valor ; intrepidity ; doughtiness ; prowess —하다 (be) intrepid ; daring ; valiant

***강우 降雨** rain ; rainfall ; 〖기상〗 precipitation ¶ 30밀리의 강우 30 millimeters of rain // 심한 강우 a heavy rain ; a downpour 《미》 // 많은 강우 a copious〔an abundant〕 rain // 강우가 계속되다 have a long spell of rainy weather // 다량의 강우가 있었다 We have had much rain. / There has been much rain.
— 강도 rainfall intensity —계 a rain gauge — 계속 시간 duration of rainfall —대(帶) a rain belt —림(林) a rain forest — 분포 rainfall distribution

강우기 降雨期 the rainy season

강우도 降雨圖 a rain chart〔map〕

*강우량 降雨量 (the amount of) rainfall ; (the record of) precipitation ¶ 부산의 연강우량 the annual rainfall in Pusan
강우 전선 降雨前線 a rain front
강울음 sham〔make-believe〕 crying ; forced〔pretended〕 weeping ¶ 강울음 울다 shed crocodile〔sham〕 tears ; shed feigned tears
강유 剛柔 sturdiness and gentleness of a man's character ; hardness and softness ¶ 강유겸전하다 combine hardness and softness ; join strength with elasticity
강음 强音 accent ; stress ; emphasis ¶ 강음의 forte 《이》 // 강음 부호를 붙이다 accentuate ; accent 《a syllable》 ; put stress on 《the first syllable》
강음 强飮 ─하다 drink against one's will ; drink reluctantly
강의 强意 ¶ 강의의 intensive // 강의적으로 as (an) intensive〔intensifier〕
─어 〖문법〗 an intensive (word) ; an intensifier
강의 剛毅 sturdiness ; manliness ; hardihood ─하다 (be) sturdy ; hardy ; manly ; stout-hearted
*강의 講義 a lecture ; a discourse ; [해설] exposition ; [설명] explanation ─하다 lecture 《on》 ; give a lecture 《on》 ; [연속적으로] give a course 《in》 ¶ 영국사 강의 lectures on English history // 강의에 출석하다 attend〔be present at〕 a lecture // 강의 내용을 노트에 적다 take notes on〔of〕 a lecture // 강의 시간을 빼먹다 cut a lecture ; play truant 《영》 ; play hooky 《미》 // 영어로 강의하다 give a lecture in English // 김 교수는 다음 학기부터 「햄릿」을 강의한다 Professor *Kim* will read Hamlet with us for the new term.
─ 방법 the manner of lecturing ─실 a lecture room 과외 ─ an extracurriculum lecture 집중 ─ an intensive course of lectures
강의록 講義錄 a transcript of lecture ; a correspondence course ¶ 강의록을 발행하다 offer〔give〕 a correspondence course // 강의록으로 영어를 공부하다 study English by〔through〕 correspondence
*강인 强靭 toughness ; tenacity ; perseverance ─하다 (be) strong ; persevering ; tough ; tenacious ¶ 강인한 의지 a tough spirit ; an iron will // 강인하게 with tenacity ; steadfastly
─성 tenacity ; toughness ; solidarity
강잉히 强仍─ reluctantly ; unwillingly ; against one's will ; with a bad grace
*강자 强者 a strong man ; [총칭] the strong ; the powerful ¶ 강자와 약자 the strong and the weak
강자성 强磁性 ferromagnetism ¶ 강자성의 ferromagnetic
─체 a ferromagnetic body〔substance〕 반─체 an antiferromagnetic body〔substance〕
강장 强壯 robustness ; healthiness ─하다 (be) strong ; robust ; sturdy ; stout ; husky 《미·구》 ¶ 강장한 체격 a strong〔hard〕 constitution ; a stout physique // 강장한 사나이 a man of sturdy build ; 《미》 a husky fellow // 강장하게 하다 strengthen ; make strong // 강장해지다 grow strong // 그는 몸이 강장하다 He is in robust health. /He is going strong.
강장거리다, 깡짱거리다 trot ; walk with short〔mincing〕 steps ¶ 강장강장〔깡짱깡짱〕 at a trot ; with short〔mincing〕 steps
강장동물 腔腸動物 a coelenterate
강장 음료 强壯飮料 a tonic drink
*강장제 强壯劑 a tonic (medicine) ; a cordial ; a restorative ¶ 강장제 주사를 맞다 have a tonic shot 《in the arm》
강재 鋼材 steel materials ; [건축용] structural steel ; [압연강] rolled steel
재생 ─ rerolled steel
강적 强敵 a formidable foe〔rival〕 ; a great〔powerful〕 enemy〔adversary〕 ¶ 단결하여 강적에 대항하다 unite themselves against a powerful enemy // 강적이 나타났다 A powerful rival has come to the front. // 강적과 싸우다 fight against a powerful enemy ; contend against heavy odds // 그는 강적이었다 I found a formidable rival in him.
†강점 强點 one's strength〔power〕 ; a strong point ; one's forte ; an element of strength ¶ 강점이 있다 have the advantage of // (상대방에 대하여) 강점을 가지고 있다 have an advantage over〔an edge on〕 《a person》 // 그의 강점은 …이다 His strength lies in… // 그의 최대의 강점은 …이다 His strongest asset is…
강점 强占 occupation〔possession〕 by force ─하다 occupy〔possess〕 《a person's house》 by force
강정 [찹쌀 가루로 만든] a glutinous rice cracker frizzled in oil ; [엿] a kind of cake made from rice〔sesame, bean〕 mixed with glutinous rice-jelly
강제 强制 compulsion ; constraint ; coercion ─하다 force ; compel ; coerce ¶ 강제적 compulsory ; forced ; coercive // 강제적으로 by force ; forcibly ; by compulsion // 강제당하여 under〔upon〕 compulsion // 강제 결혼시키다 force 《a person》 into a marriage // 강제 수용하다 put into custody // 법적으로 강제당하다 be compelled by law 《to do》 // 강제 수단을 쓰다 resort to coercive measures
─ 결혼 a forced marriage ; a marriage by force ─ 경매 forced〔compulsory〕 sale by auction ─ 공제(控除) [조합비

따위] a compulsory checkoff — 공채(公債) forced loan — 관리(管理) compulsory administration — 보험 compulsory insurance — 소개(疏開) forced〔compulsory〕 evacuation〔removal〕 — 수색권 the official right to search — 예금 a compulsory deposit — 이주 deportation — 이행 compulsory performance — 접종(接種) compulsory vaccination — 조정 compulsory mediation — 중재 〖노동〗 compulsory arbitration ; legal intervention — 착륙 forced landing — 통화 compulsory currency ; legal tender (법화) — 파산 involuntary bankruptcy

강제 가격 强制價格 a forced price

강제 격리 强制隔離 forced segregation

강제 노동 强制勞動 compulsory〔forced〕 labor ¶ 강제 노동을 과하다 impose forced labor

강제 노동자 수용소 强制勞動者收容所 a labor camp ; a slave pen

강제력 强制力 compelling power〔force〕 ; legal force

강제 명령 强制命令 〖법〗 a mandatory injunction

강제 송환 强制送還 enforced〔forced〕 repatriation ; extradition

강제 수단 强制手段 a compulsory measure ; [수송 따위] a legal step

강제 수사 强制搜査 a mandatory search

강제 수용 强制收容 detention by legal force
—소 a (concentration) camp

강제 집행 强制執行 (compulsory) execution ; 〖법〗 distrain
— 영장 an〔a writ of〕 execution ; the final process — 정지 a stay of execution

강제 징수 强制徵收 a mandatory levy

강제 처분 强制處分 legal disposition ; disposition by legal force

강제 철거 强制撤去 [건물의] forced demolition

†강조 强調 stress ; emphasis ; accentuation ¶ 불조심 강조 주간 Fire Prevention Week —하다 stress ; emphasize ; accentuate ; lay stress〔emphasis〕 on ; give prominence to ; highlight ¶ 별로 강조되지 않다 be〔get〕 de-emphasized // 국방의 필요성을 강조하다 stress the need〔necessity〕 of national defense // 특히 강조할 가치가 있다 deserves special emphasis ☞ ◀ p. 77 ▶

강조밥 millet boiled without mixing rice〔with no rice in it〕

강좌 講座 [대학의] a chair ; a lectureship ; a professorship ; a lecture ; [강습의] a course ¶ 강좌를 개설하다 establish〔create, found〕 a chair // 경제학 강좌를 담당하다 hold〔occupy〕 a chair of economics
공개 — an〔a university〕 extension course ; an open lecture ; an extramural course 《영》 라디오 영어 — a radio English course ; radio English lessons 영문학 — a course in English literature 음악 — lectures on music 특별 — a special〔temporary〕 course 《of English literature》 자유 — a free chair

강주정 —酒酊 an affected drunkenness ; a feigned intoxication —하다 pretend to be drunk

강줄기 江— a river course ; the course of a river ¶ 강줄기를 따라 along a river

강즙 薑汁 ginger juice

강직 剛直 sturdiness ; staunchness ; uprightness ; probity ; rectitude ; integrity —하다 (be) upright ; staunch ¶ 강직한 사람 a man of integrity

강직 强直 [사후의] rigidity ; stiffness —하다 (be) rigid ; stiff
— 경련 [근육의] tetanus 관절 — ankylosis ; anchylosis

강진 强震 a severe〔violent〕 earthquake ; a severe shock (of earthquake)

강진계 强震計 a strong-motion seismograph

강짜 unreasonable jealousy
강짜(가) 나다 관용 feel〔become〕 jealous ; get terribly jealous
강짜(를) 부리다 관용 show unreasonable jealousy

강참숯 pure charcoal

†강철 鋼鐵 steel ¶ 강철 같은〔의〕 steely // 강철제의 steel(-made, -built) // 강철 같은 의지 an iron will
— 공장 a steel mill ; a steel works — 벨트 a steel band〔belt〕 —선(線) a steel wire — 세공 steelwork —자 a steel tape measure —차 a steel car〔coach, wagon〕 —함(艦) a steel-clad warship

강철관 鋼鐵管 a steel pipe〔tube〕

강철판 鋼鐵板 steel plate〔plank〕

강청 强請 [강요] exaction ; importunity ; persistent demand ; [공갈로] blackmail extortion —하다 demand persistently ; force 《a person to do》 ; importune 《a person to do》 ; exact payment》 ; blackmail ; extort ; wring

강체 剛體 a rigid body
— 역학 geostatic

강촌 江村 a riverside village

*강추위 a spell of cold dry weather ; intense〔bitter〕 cold

강치 〖동물〗 a sea lion

†강타 强打 ① [세게 침] a heavy〔hard, hefty〕 blow ; a wallop (권투) 《구》 —하다 deal 《a person》 a heavy blow ; hit hard ; slug 《미·구》 ; swat〔wallop〕 《a ball》 《구》 ¶ 가슴을 강타당하다 be hit hard〔receive a hard blow〕 on one's chest
② [충격] a fatal blow〔shock〕 ¶ 계속

강조의 표현

문장 중의 특정 어구를 특히 강조해서 표현하는 것을 강조라고 한다. 대화의 경우에는 강세·음조·몸짓 등에 의해서 강조를 표현할 수 있지만 문장에서는 몇 가지 문어적 방법에 의해 나타낸다.

1 강조구문 It is ... that [who, which, etc.] ....

¶ 존이 이 문제를 풀었다. It was John that solved this problem. // 내가 여기 온 것은 카메라를 사기 위해서다. It was to buy a camera that I came here. // 그의 물건이 팔리는 것은 값이 싸서가 아니라 품질 때문이다. It is not the low prices but the quality which sells his goods.

2 조동사 do에 의한 강조

동사를 강조하기 위해 do를 쓰며 시제·인칭·수 등의 일치를 do에 맡기고 본래 동사를 원형으로 한다. 이때 발음은 본동사에 두지 않고 do에 둔다.

¶ 진정으로 네가 가야 한다고 생각한다. I do think you ought to go. // 예, 아주 잘 기억하고 있고 말고요. Yes, I do remember it quite well. // 누가 창을 부쉈지? Who did break the window? // 꼭 다시 한번 들러 주십시오. Do come to see me again.

3 어순도치에 의한 강조

¶ 나는 그녀를 뚜렷이 기억하고 있다. Well do I remember her. // 거기서 그를 만나리라고는 꿈에도 생각하지 못했다. Never did I dream that I should see him there.

4 반복어구에 의한 강조

¶ 나는 몇 시간이고 기다렸다. I waited for hours and hours. // 생각하고 또 생각해 봤지만 어떻게 해야 좋을지 모르겠다. I've thought and thought, and I can't see what to do. // 오직 이것만이 그녀의 생명을 구할 수 있다. This, this alone, can save her life.

5 강의(强意)어구에 의한 강조

① 부정의 강조

not a ..., at all, in the least, by any means, on earth, whatever 등

¶ 전혀 의심의 여지가 없다. There is no doubt whatever. // 그는 전혀 취하지 않았다. He doesn't drink at all. // 그는 선악에 대한 판단력을 전혀 갖추지 못한 사람이다. He hasn't the least knowledge of good and evil. // 모든 사람을 만족시키기란 결코 쉬운 일이 아니다. It is by no means easy to satisfy everyone.

② 의문의 강조

ever, on earth, in the world 등

¶ 도대체 그런 일을 들어본 적이 있습니까? Did you ever hear of such a thing? // 도대체 무슨 짓을 저지른 것이냐? What on earth did you do?

③ 재귀대명사에 의한 강조

¶ 네 자신이 하는 것이 당연하다. You ought to do that yourself. // 그녀는 참을성이 많다. She is patience itself.

④ all, every의 강조

「가능한, 생각[상상]할 수 있는」의 뜻의 possible, conceivable, imaginable 등을 붙여 쓴다.

¶ 우리는 상상할 수 있는 [가능한] 모든 수단을 동원하게 될 것이다. We shall employ every means conceivable [possible].

⑤ 비교급·최상급의 강조

「much+비교급」; 「far, by far+비교급」; 「by far, very, much+최상급」

¶ 그것이 훨씬 좋다. That's much better. // 이 책이 저것보다 훨씬 어렵다. This book is far more difficult than that. // 그는 반에서 단연 키가 크다. He is by far the tallest in the class. // 모든 것 중에서도 이것이 가장 좋다. This is much the best of all. / This is the very best of all. (★ much와 very의 어순에 주의).

⑥ 부사(구)의 강조

very, quite, so, too, really, truly exceedingly, extremely, unusually, uncommonly, considerably, terribly, awfully, dreadfully 등

¶ 당신을 만나서 매우 기쁩니다. I'm very pleased to meet you. // 오늘 아침은 유별나게 춥다. It is unusually cold this morning. // 나는 그 소식을 듣고 무척 놀랐다. I was very surprised at the news. // 그는 몹시 충격을 받았다. He was terribly shocked. // 너는 내가 농담하는 줄 알지만 나는 정말 심각하다. You think I'm joking, but I'm dead serious.

해서 강타하다 rain hard blows 《on》 ③ [야구] a heavy〔terrific〕 hit ; a slug〔slog〕 **—하다** slug〔slog〕

강타자 强打者 a heavy hitter ; a slugger 《구》 ; a swatter ; slogger ; a power 〔long-ball〕 hitter

강탄 降誕 [탄생] birth ; nativity ; [강림] advent ; incarnation **—하다** be born ; see the light ; be incarnated ¶ 예수의 강탄 the Nativity // 예수 강탄절 Christmas

⁑강탈 强奪 depredation ; robbery ; seizure ; extortion ; despoilment ; plunder ; pillage ; looting **—하다** rob 〔despoil, plunder, loot〕 《a person》 of 《a thing》 ; snatch 《a thing》 from 《a person》 ; hijack ; stick up 《a person, a store, a bank》 ¶ 강탈당하다 be robbed of 《a thing》 ; have 《a thing》 taken〔snatched〕 away

—물 plunder ; loot ; booty **—자** a plunderer ; a looter

강태공 姜太公 an angler ; a rodster ; a Waltonian

강토 疆土 a territory ; a realm ; a domain

강파르다 ① [됨됨이가] (be) thin and touchy ; lean and impetuous〔fiery〕 ② [가파르다] (be) steep

강파리하다 look (a bit) thin and eager

강판 降板 〖야구〗 **—하다** be driven from the hill ; be chased off the mound ; be belted from the box ¶ 강판시키다 knock 《a pitcher》 out (of the box) ; drive 《a pitcher》 from the mound

강판 鋼板 a steel sheet ; sheet steel ; [두꺼운] a steel plate

강판 薑板 a grater

강팔지다 (be) narrow-minded ; small-minded ; ungenerous ; intolerant ; fault-finding ; critical

강퍅 剛愎 —하다 (be) stubborn ; obstinate ; stiff-necked ; peevish ; perverse ; impetuous ; petulant ; cantankerous

강평 講評 comment ; criticism ; review **—하다** comment 《on》 ; review ; criticize

강포 强暴 outrage ; ferocity ; brutality ; wildness **—하다** (be) outrageous ; atrocious ; brutal ; wild ¶ 그는 성격이 강포하다 He is wild by nature.

강풀 thick paste〔starch〕 not tempered with water

강풀치다 overlay〔coat〕 with thick paste

강풍 江風 a river-breeze〔-wind〕

강풍 强風 a strong〔high〕 wind ; a gale ; 〖기상〗 a moderate gale ¶ 강풍에 견디다 stand a strong wind

강풍 주의보 强風注意報 a strong-wind warning

강하 江河 rivers ; rivers and streams

⁑강하 降下 falling ; dropping ; a fall ; a drop ; descent ; [기압의] depression **—하다** fall ; drop ; descend ; glide down 《to》 ¶ 기온의 강하 a drop in temperature // 핵실험에 따른 방사성 강하물 radioactive fallout from a nuclear test // 고도 1천 피트까지 강하하다 descend〔glide down〕 to a height of 1,000 feet // 기온이 급강하하였다 The temperature has shown a sharp fall.

—각 an angle of descent **—물** fallout **— 지대** [낙하산 부대의] a drop zone **급—** nose diving ; a nose dive **방사성 —물** radioactive fallout

†강하다 强— [강력] (be) strong ; powerful ; mighty ; [강건] robust ; [강렬] severe ; intense ; hard [바람·빛 등이] strong ; severe ; intense ¶ 강하게 hard ; severely ; strongly ; powerfully // 강한 나라 a strong power〔country〕 ; a great power // 초강국 a superpower // 강한 상상력 a lively imagination // 강한 어조 an emphatic tone // 강한 색채 a strong〔intense〕 color // 강한 의지 a strong will // 강한 바람 a strong〔severe, sharp〕 wind // 강한 술 a strong wine ; a hard liquor // 강하게 하다 make strong ; strengthen // 강하게 나오다 show a firm〔an unyielding〕 front ; put one's foot down // 강해지다 grow strong 〔powerful〕 // 돈의 힘은 강하다 Money is mighty // 나는 이 계약을 취소하고 싶은 생각이 강하게 든다 I have a good mind to cancel this contract.

***강하다 剛—** (be) hard ; adamant ; resistant ; tough

강한 强悍, 剛悍 —하다 (be) fierce ; ferocious ; rude ; harsh

강해 講解 explanation ; explication **—하다** explain ; elucidate ; explicate ; expound

강행 强行 enforcement ; forcing **—하다** force ¶ 고물가 정책을 강행하다 enforce a high-price policy // 억수 속에서 시합을 강행하다 keep playing a game in the downpour

강행군 强行軍 a forced march ¶ 강행군하다 go on a forced march

강호 强豪 a veteran (player) ¶ 강호 팀간의 대결 a match〔game〕 between powerful teams

강호 江湖 ① [강과 호수] rivers and lakes ; [자연] nature ② [은거처] a place〔country〕 of seclusion ; a retreat ③ [세상] the (general) public ; the world ¶ 강호 제언(諸彦)에 호소하다 appeal to the public ; call the attention of the general public to 《a fact》 // 강호 제언에게 권하다 commend〔recommend〕 《a book》 to the public

강화 講和 peace ; peace negotiations ; an amicable settlement ; reconciliation **—하다** make〔conclude〕 peace 《with》 ;

lay down one's arms ¶ 굴욕적 강화 a humiliating peace // 전면 강화 an overall peace (settlement) // 강화를 제의하다 sue for peace ; make overtures of peace hold out an olive branch
— 담판 peace negotiations ¶ 강화 담판을 하다 negotiate peace — 성립 conclusion of peace negotiation — 제의 overtures for peace — 조건 terms〔conditions〕 of peace — 회의 a peace conference 다면 — a multiple peace 다수 — a majority peace 단독 — a separate peace 전면 — an overall peace (settlement)

*강화 強化 strengthening ; intensification ; solidification ; consolidating ; reinforcement ; firming up ; fortification
— 하다 strengthen ; intensify ; increase ; consolidate ; reinforce ; firm up ¶ 내각을 강화하다 strengthen the Cabinet // 군사력을 강화하다 build〔beef〕 up the military strength // 지위를 강화하다 consolidate one's footing〔position〕 《in》 // 통제를 강화하다 clamp〔tighten〕 control 《of, over》 // 신인으로 팀을 강화하다 reinforce a team with new players
—물 a 《milk》 fortifier — 유리 tempered glass —제(劑) 〖화학〗 a reinforcing agent 비타민〔미네랄〕 —식품 vitamin-〔mineral-〕enriched food

*강화 講話 a lecture ; an address ; a talk
— 하다 lecture 《on a subject》 ; give a lecture 《on》 ; address 《a meeting》 ¶ 학생들에게 문학 강화를 하다 give the students a lecture on literature ; address the students on literature

강화 사절 講和使節 a peace envoy〔delegate〕

강화 사절단 講和使節團 a peace mission〔delegation〕

강화 조약 講和條約 a peace treaty〔pact〕 ; a treaty of peace

강화 훈련 強化訓練 intensified training

강황 薑黃 〖식물〗 turmeric ; Curcuma aromatica (학명)

강황지 薑黃紙 turmeric paper

강회 —膾 a small roll of boiled celery or scallion (eaten with drinks)

강회 剛灰 limestone ; quicklime

강훈 強訓 ⇨ 강화 훈련

갗— [털가죽] fur ; leather ; (ox-) hide ¶ 갗두루마기 a Korean robe lined with fur

†갗가지 ⇨ 가지가지

갖다¹ [구비] (be) well furnished〔equipped, provided〕 《with》 ; have all sorts ; have everything

갖다² have ; hold ⇨ 가지다

갖다 주다 bring (over) ¶ 물 한 잔 갖다 주시오 Get me a glass of water. // 그걸 갖다 주시오 Bring it (to) me.

갖두루마기 a Korean fur-lined robe

갖바치 a maker of leather shoes

갖바치 내일 모레 속담 Don't count on the date that was promised.

갖신 leather shoes

갖옷 fur-lined clothing

*갖은 all ; all sorts of ; every ; each and every ; every possible ; all. . . whatever ; complete ; well-made ; perfect ; various ; assorted ¶ 갖은 소리 unreasonable 〔unrealistic〕 words ; (self-) conceited words // 갖은 양념 all sorts of spices ; proper seasoning // 갖은 종류의 사람 all sorts〔manner〕 of men // 갖은 수단을 쓰다 try every means available 〔conceivable〕 ; try every possible means // 갖은 수고를 하다 take all the trouble imaginable // 갖은 고생을 하다 go through all kinds of hardships // 갖은 죄를 범하다 go through the catalogue of crimes ; have a long list of criminal acts // 갖은 욕을 다 보다 suffer all sorts of humiliation

갖은것 all sorts of things ; everything

갖저고리 a Korean fur-lined short coat

갖추 exhaustively ; thoroughly ; all ; inclusively ; completely ; fully ; thoroughly ¶ 세간살이를 갖추 차리다 get an assortment of household goods // 모든 예문을 갖추 들다 give complete examples // 음식을 갖추 차리다 prepare a full-course dinner

‡갖추다 [준비] get ready ; prepare ; stock 《a shop with goods》 ; [설비] furnish ; equip ; provide ; [서류를] fill in ; [조건을] meet ; satisfy ; [형식·격식을] observe ; go through ; [구비하다] possess ; have 《common sense》 ; be endowed with 《talent》 ; be armed with 《a weapon》 ¶ 형식을 갖추어 in accordance with formalities // 조건을 갖추다 meet〔satisfy〕 require- ments〔conditions〕 // 떠날 준비를 갖추다 get ready to leave // 근대적 설비를 갖추다 be equipped with modern conveniences // 필요한 서류를 갖추다 get all the necessary papers filled in // 상품을 갖추다 keep articles (in stock) // 풍부한 지식을 갖추다 have a good knowledge 《of》 ; be equipped with sufficient knowledge // 위엄을 갖추다 have dignity // 교과서를 빠짐없이 갖추다 get all the necessary textbooks // 살림을 갖추다 furnish a house 《with everything needed》 // 그는 교사로서 충분한 자격을 갖추고 있다 He is well qualified as a teacher. // 무기를 갖추다 be armed with a weapon // 파티준비를 갖추다 get ready for the party

갖추 쓰다 write 《a Chinese character》 without omitting any stroke

갖풀 glue (made from oxhide) ¶ 갖풀로 붙이다 glue (one thing to another)

†같다 ① [흡사] (be) like ; similar ; be

alike ¶ (꼭) 거지 같다 look like a beggar ; be no better than a beggar // 아주 같다 be very much alike // 새 것 같다 be as good as new // 죽은 거나 같다 be practically dead // 그는 갓난 애와 같다 He is no better than a baby. // 연구는 이제 끝난 것과 같다 Our research is now practically over.
② [동일] (be) the same ; identical 《with》; the selfsame [균일] equal 《to》; equivalent 《of》

> 참고 **identical**은 가장 엄밀한 의미에서 사용되고 **same**은 identical보다 자유스럽게 사용된다 또한 **same**은 as, that, who, which와 상관적으로 사용된다 **equal**은 주로 수 양 크기 가치 따위가 동일한 것 **equivalent**는 주로 가치 힘 뜻 따위가 동일한 것을 말한다

¶ 이것과 같은 원리로 on the same principle // 똑 같다 be the very same ; be just the same ; be all one // 같은 말을 되씹다 harp on the same string // 네 것과 똑같은 사전을 갖고 있다 I have the same dictionary as yours. // 우리는 서로 같은 인간이다 We are fellow human beings. // 오늘 가나 내일 가나 똑같다 It makes little〔no〕 difference whether I go today or tomorrow. // 다른 비평가들도 같은 말을 했다 Other critics traveled on the same road. // 나도 너와 똑같은 생각이다 Your thoughts echo mine. // 결국은 같다 It really makes no difference.
③ [동등] (be) equal 《to》; equivalent 《to》 ¶ 같은 자격으로 담판하다 negotiate on equal terms // 그는 나와 키가 같다 He is about as tall as I. // 두 책상의 높이는 같다 The two tables are of even height. // 같은 입장에서 on an equal〔the same〕 footing // 같은 조건으로 교섭하다 negotiate on equal terms
④ [종류] (be) a sort of ; like ¶ 떡 같은 것 something like a rice cake // 헛간 같은 것 a crude sort of barn // 그는 네가 생각하고 있는 것 같은 대학자가 아니다 He is not such a great scholar as you think. // 나는 그와 같은 말을 할 사람이 아니다 I am not the man to say such a thing.
⑤ [추측] appear ; seem ; look ; be likely 《to》 ¶ 비가 올 것 같다 It looks like rain. // 좀처럼 떠날 것 같지 않다 He doesn't seem to be leaving soon. // 재미있을 것 같다 It sounds like fun. // 그는 기뻐하는〔피곤한〕 것 같다 He looks pleased〔tired〕.
⑥ […라면] if ; in case ¶ 옛날 같으면 if these were the old days // 나 같으면 그런 짓은 않겠다 (If I were you,) I would not do so.
⑦ [답다] be worthy of ¶ 집 같은 집이 없다 There is no house to speak of 〔worth mentioning〕.
⑧ [비유] like ; alike ; as ¶ 천사 같은 소녀 an angel of a girl // 샛별 같은 눈 eyes like stars // 산더미 같은 파도 a mountain of waves
⑨ [공통] common ¶ 같은 동네 사람 a fellow townsman // 나 같은 일을 하고 있는 사람 a fellow worker

같은 값이면 if... at all ; if it is all the same 《to》; other things being equal ¶ 같은 값이면 잘해라 If you do it at all, do it well. // 같은 값이면 큰 것이 좋다 I will take the larger one, if I must take something.
같은 값이면 다홍치마 속담 Better a castle of bones than of stones.

†**같이** ① [흡사하게] like ¶ A는 B와 똑같이 만들어졌다 A is made exactly like B. // 쌍둥이는 똑같이 닮았다 The twins are as like as two peas (in a pod).
② [바로·그대로] as ; like ; in the way 〔manner〕 of ¶ 보통 때와 같이 just as ever ; as usual // 아시는 바와 같이 as you know〔see〕 // 약속한 바와 같이 as promised // 위에서 말한 바와 같이 as (stated) above
③ [함께] together ; with ; in company 《with》 ¶ 같이 살다 live together ; live in the same house with 《another》 // 같이 자다 share the bed // 같이 식사하다 eat together // 같이 일하다 do a job together ; share the task 《with another》 // 같이 사업하다 do business in partnership with... // 같이 기뻐〔슬퍼〕하다 share joys〔sorrows〕 with 《a person》 // 같이 웃다 join in the laughter // 같이 책임지다 share a common responsibility // 다 같이 소리치다 cry out with one accord // 같이 가시지 않겠어요 Will you〔Won't you〕 join us〔our company〕? // 같이 일하게 돼서 반갑습니다 Nice to have you with us. // 우리가 매주 적어도 하루나 이틀만이라도 차를 같이 타고 다니면 교통 체증이 훨씬 덜할 것이다 If we carpool at least one or two days a week, we would have far less traffic congestion. // 차를 같이 타고 다니는 것을 심각하게 생각할 때가 됐다 It's about time we gave serious thought to ridesharing. // 자리가 모두 찼다 같이 앉을 수 없을까 All the seats are taken, maybe we'll have to share a seat.
④ [처럼] as if ; so to speak ; as it were ¶ 어린애같이 취급하다 treat 《a person》 as a child // 친딸같이 키우다 bring her up as if she were his own daughter // 그는 모든 것을 아는 것 같이 떠벌린다 He talks as if he knew everything. // 대낮같이 밝다 be as bright as day
⑤ [동등하게] equally ; impartially ;

alike ; indiscriminately ¶ 같이 나누다 divide 《apples》 equally 《among themselves》 // 모든 사람을 같이 대우하다 treat all men alike // 같이 취급하다 treat 《men》 without discrimination ; treat 《all men》 alike
⑥ [동시에] at the same time ¶ 두 가지 일을 같이 해서는 안된다 You must not do two things at a time.
⑦ [때] ¶ 매일같이 almost every day ; day after day // 새벽같이 떠나다 leave at dawn〔daybreak, peep of day〕 // 그는 매일같이 바쁜 사람이다 His days are full.

같이하다 share 《something》 with ; take part〔participate〕 in ; partake of ¶ 고락을 같이하다 share joys and sorrows 〔one's fortunes〕 with ; be partner of 《a person's》 joys and sorrows // 때를 같이하여 at the same time〔hour〕 ; in the same instant ; simultaneously 《with》 // 운명을 같이하다 cast〔throw〕 in one's lot with〔among〕 ; share one's fate ; share each other's fortune ; face the same fate // 의견을 같이하다 have〔be of〕 the same views〔opinion〕 ; concur with // 이해(利害)를 같이하다 have common interests 《in a matter with a person》 // 일생을 같이하다 share one's life ; be one's life partner ; take each other for better or for worse // 마음을 같이하다 be of one mind 〔of the same mind〕

같잖다 [하찮다] (be) trivial ; insignificant ; be of no account ; (be) worthless ; useless ; [눈꼴사납다] foolish ; silly ; absurd ; nonsensical ; unseemly ; improper ; bothersome ; saucy ; impertinent ¶ 같잖은 물건 a no-good thing ; a worthless object ; wretched stuff ; rubbish ; trash ; a white elephant // 같잖은 인간 a worthless〔good-for-nothing〕 fellow ; an impertinent fellow // 같잖은 소리를 하다 talk impudently 《to》 ; give 《a person》 cheek〔some lip〕 ; get a mouth 《속》 // 같잖은 짓 마라 Don't get fresh !

⁑갚다 ① [빚을] pay back ; repay ; refund ; settle one's account ¶ 빚을 갚다 pay (back) one's debts ; pay off debts // 대미 차관으로 부채를 갚다 refund the debt by means of an American loan // 자 500원 갚겠습니다 Here's your five hundred *won* back.
② [보답] repay 《another's kindness》 ; return ; give (a thing) in return ; reward ; requite 《favors》 ; recompense 《a person》 for ; compensate for ¶ 은혜를 갚다 repay 《a person》 for his kindness ; repay〔return〕 another's kindness // 은혜를 원수로 갚다 return good with evil〔evil for good〕 // 나중에 신세 갚겠다 I'll make it up to you.
③ [원수를] retaliate ; revenge ; avenge ¶ 원수를 갚다 revenge 《oneself》 on ; be revenged〔avenged〕 《on》 ; take vengeance 《upon》 ¶ 아버지의 원수를 갚다 avenge one's father's murder

갚음 ―하다 pay ⇨ 갚다

개[1] [포구] the mouth of a river ; an inlet ; an estuary ; a cove ; an embayment

†개[2] 〖동물〗 a dog ; a hound ; a hunting 〔sporting〕 dog (사냥개) ; [수캐] a male dog ; [암캐] a she-dog ; a bitch ; [들개] a cur ; a stray dog ; a canine ; [잡종개] a mongrel (dog) ; a cur ; a mutt 《속》 ¶ 개 같은 doggish ; doglike // 개자식 a son-of-a-bitch ; a bitch // 개를 매다 chain up a dog // 개를 풀어주다 let a dog loose // 개조심 Beware of the Dog ! (게시) // 개를 기르다 keep a dog // 개가 짖다 a dog barks // 개수작을 하다 talk nonsense ; say silly things // 개만도 못한 놈이다 He is worse than a beast. // 그런 것은 개도 안 먹는다 Even a dog will turn up its nose at it. // 그는 나를 개 취급하듯 했다 He treated me like a dog.
― 감찰 a dog tag〔license〕 **―돼지** a brute **―목걸이** a dog collar **―싸움** a dogfight **―썰매** a dogsled **―장수** a dog fancier ; a kennel man ; a dogman **― 전시회** a dog〔bench〕 show **―줄** a dog lead ; a leash **―집** a kennel
개가 개를 낳지 [속담] We may not expect a good whelp from an ill dog. /Of an evil crow, an evil egg.
개같이 벌어서 정승같이 산다 [속담] Narrew gathered, widely spent.
개 꼬리 삼년 두어도 황모 못 된다 [속담] You can't make a silk purse out of a sow's ear. /A crow is never the white for washing herself.
개를 따라가면 측간으로 간다 [속담] If you lie down with dogs, you will get up with fleas. /Evil communications corrupts good manners.
개발에 주석 편자 [속담] To cast pearls before swine. /Be like the fox's skin sewed to the lion's.
개 팔자가 상팔자라 [속담] A dogs lot in the happiest gall.

개 個, 箇, 介 a piece ; a unit ; an item ¶ 사과 세 개 three apples // 비누 두 개 two cakes〔pieces〕 of soap // 각사탕 두 개 two lumps of sugar

개 蓋 a lid ; a cap ; a top ; a cover

개가 凱歌 a triumphal song ; a victory song ; a paean ¶ 현대 과학의 개가 a triumph of modern science
개가를 올리다 [관용] sing in triumph ; win a victory〔game〕 《over》 ; be victorious // 개가를 올리며 with colors flying ; in triumph

개가 改嫁 remarriage〔a second marriage, deuterogamy, digamy〕 《of a woman》 ―하다 《a woman》 marry again ; remarry ¶ 개가한 여자 a woman married again〔the second time〕

개각 介殼 a shell ; shells
―류 the shellfish ; the crustacea ―충 〚곤충〛 a scale (insect) ; a coccid (ium) 《*pl.* -ia》

개각 改閣 a reshuffle of the Cabinet ; a cabinet reshuffle ; a cabinet shake-up ¶ 개각을 단행하다 effect a cabinet reshuffle ―하다 reshuffle the cabinet

개각 도약 開脚跳躍 〚체조〛 [뜀틀넘기의] the astride〔straddle, vertical stride〕 vault

개각 등행 開脚登行 〚스키〛 herring-boning ―하다 herringbone

개간 改刊 reprinting ; a reprint ; a revised edition〔printing〕 ―하다 reprint ; print a revised edition

*개간 開墾 land clearing ; reclamation ; bringing 《wasteland》 under cultivation ―하다 clear 《a forest》 ; bring 《virginland》 under cultivation ; [늪 따위] reclaim ¶ 개간되다 be under cultivation
― 계획 development〔reclamation〕 program ― 보조금 a reclamation subsidy ― 사업 reclamation (work) ; land clearing 미(未)―지 virgin soil ; wild〔waste〕 land 산림 ― forest clearing

개간지 開墾地 developed land ; a cultivated area ; reclaimed land ; new broke ground ; a clearing

개감스럽다 (be) ravenous ; greedy ; voracious ¶ 개감스럽게 먹다 devour ; wolf one's food ; gormandize ; stodge 《속》

개갑 介甲 [딱지] a carapace ; a shell ; [갑옷] a coat of armor

개값 ¶ 개값으로 for a mere song ; at a sacrifice // 개값으로 팔다 sell dirt cheap 〔for a mere song〕

개강 開講 beginning a series of one's lectures ; the opening of a course (of study) ―하다 give one's first lecture ; begin a series of lectures ; [대학에서] open a course ; begin school ¶ 3월 2일 개강 (게시문) Lectures (will) begin on March 2.

†개개 個個, 箇箇 [낱낱] an individual ; an item ; [낱낱이] one by one ; piece by piece ; individually ; [모두] all ; everyone ¶ 개개의 individual ; separate ; several // 개개 다 시험해 보다 try everyone of 《the light bulbs》

개개다 abrade ; rub (off) ; wear (off)

개개비 〚새〛 the reedwarbler

개개인 個個人 each single person ; individuals

개개풀어지다 [국수 따위가] lose its stickiness ; come unstuck〔loose〕 ; [눈이] get bleary ; come fishy〔dull〕 ¶ 개개풀어진 눈 sleepy eyes

개갱 [강아지의 소리] whinning ; yelp ; yip ; yap ―하다 whine ; yap ; yelp ; yip

개거 開渠 an open sewer〔conduit, channel〕

개결 介潔 purity ; integrity ; incorruptibility ; honesty ―하다 (be) pure ; cleanhanded ; incorruptible

개고기 dog meat ; [사람] a bad child ; a wicked〔a cruel, an ill-tempered〕 person ; a devil ; a pest ; a nuisance

개골 《another's》 temper 〔anger, rage〕 ; hot temper ¶ 개골내다 《a person》 be out of temper ; get angry ; get into rage

*개골개골 croak ¶ 개골개골 울다 croak

개골창 a ditch ; a drain ; a gutter ; [하수] a sewer ¶ 개골창을 치다 clear a ditch

개과 改過 reformation ; repentance ; contrition ; penitence ; correction of erroneous ways ―하다 repent 《of》 ; be repentant〔penitent〕 ; correct one's ways ; turn over a new leaf ; reclaim 《a criminal》 ¶ 개과천선하면 죄는 용서된다 Repentance wipes out sin.

개관 開館 the opening of a hall〔theater〕 ―하다 open 《a building》 ¶ 개관식을 거행하다 perform the opening ceremony of a hall〔building〕 // 오전 8시에서 오후 5시까지 개관 Open from 8 a.m. to 5 p.m. (게시) // 8시 개관이다 The doors open at 8 o'clock.
―식 an inaugural meeting ; the opening ceremony

개관 概觀 a general survey〔view〕 ; an outline ; a general perspective〔outlook〕 ; a conspectus ―하다 survey ; take a bird's-eye〔general〕 view 《of》 ; make a general survey 《of》 ; give a conspectus 《of》
근대사 ― a bird's-eye view of modern history 역사적 ― a historical survey

*개괄 概括 a summary ; generalization ―하다 summarize ; sum up ; [일반적 결론으로 인도하다] generalize ¶ 개괄적 general ; sweeping // 개괄하여 말하면 to sum up ; generally speaking ; on the whole ; by and large // 너무 개괄적으로 표현되다 be expressed in too great a latitude

*개교 開校 the opening of a school ―하다 open a school ; found a school ¶ 개교식을 거행하다 hold the opening ceremony of a school ; open a school formally // 그 학교는 4월에 개교된다 The school will be opened in April.
― 기념일 an anniversary of the opening of a school ; Foundation Day ―식 the opening〔inauguration〕 ceremony of a school

개교식 開橋式 an opening ceremony of a new bridge
개구 開口 ―하다 open one's mouth ; begin to speak ; open one's case ¶ 그는 정부의 무능을 공박하는 것으로 개구했다 He opened〔began〕 his speech with an attack against〔by attacking〕 the incompetency of the Government.
―각 〖기계〗 an angular aperture ―계 an apertometer ―비(比) an opening 〔open area〕 ratio ―수 numerical aperture ―음 〖음성〗 a broad (vowel) ―장치 shedding mechanism ―효율 [공중선의] an aperture efficiency
개구기 開口器 〖의학〗 a (mouth) gag (외과의)
*개구리 a frog ; [식용의] a bull frog ¶ 개구리가 운다 Frogs croak. // 개구리가 뛴다 The frog hops.
―알 frog spawn 식용 ― an edible frog 우물 안 개구리 (속담) a frog in a well ; a man of narrow views〔limited outlook〕 ; a man of limited scope
개구리 올챙이 적 생각을 못 한다 (속담) Danger past, God forgotten〔the Saint is mocked〕./The parish priest forgets that ever he has been holy water (parish) clerk.
개구리매 〖새〗 a marsh harrier
개구리밥 〖식물〗 a great duckweed
개구리참외 〖식물〗 a spotted cantaloupe ; Cucumis microsperma (학명)
개구리헤엄 the breast stroke
개구멍 a doghole
개구멍바지 baby trousers with a slit in the bottom
개구멍받이 a foundling ; a baby left 〔abandoned〕 on the doorstep
개구쟁이 a naughty〔mischievous〕 boy ; an urchin ; an imp ; a bully ; a brat ¶ 개구쟁이의 naughty ; mischievous ; impish // 개구쟁이 짓 naughtiness ; brattiness // 우리집 개구쟁이 my dear little devil〔monkey〕 // 개구쟁이 짓을 하다 play pranks 《on a person》
개국 開國 [건국] the foundation of the state〔country〕 ; [통상 개시] the opening up of the country 《to foreign intercourse》 ―하다 found the state ; open the country 《to foreign intercourse》
―주의 the principle of opening the country to foreign intercourse ; the open-door policy
개국 공신 開國功臣 a meritorious retainer at the founding of a dynasty
개그 a gag ¶ 개그를 넣다 (put a) gag ; toss off a gag
―맨 a gagman ; a gagster
개근 皆勤 regular〔perfect〕 attendance ; non-absence ―하다 attend regularly 〔every day〕 ¶ 나는 개근했다 I have not missed a day.
개근상 皆勤賞 a reward for perfect attendance
개근 상장 皆勤賞狀 a certificate for a person who hasn't missed a day
개근 수당 皆勤手當 allowance for non-absence service
개근자 皆勤者 a person who has not missed a day 《at office, school》
개금 開襟 [흉금] unbosoming oneself to ; [옷깃] an open collar ―하다 unbosom oneself to ; open〔lay bare〕 one's heart ; admit 《a person》 into one's confidence
― 셔츠 an open-collared shirt ; a sport shirt
개기 開基 [터를 닦음] ground breaking ; laying a foundation ; [사찰의] founding of a temple ; [개기승] the founder (of a Buddhistic sect) ¶ 이 절의 개기는 원효대사라고 한다 This temple is said to have been founded by *Wonhyo*. ―하다 level〔smooth〕 the ground ; lay a foundation
개기 皆旣 [개기식] 〖천문〗 a total eclipse 《of the sun》
―기(期) totality ―월식〔일식〕 a total eclipse of the moon〔sun〕
개기름 grease on one's face ; skin oiliness ¶ 개기름 낀 얼굴 an oily〔a greasy〕 complexion〔face〕
개꼴 [체면] disgrace ; shame ; humiliation ; dishonor ; wretched〔miserable〕 condition ; discredit ; infamy ¶ 개꼴이 되다 be put to shame ; bring disgrace upon oneself ; lose face ; disgrace oneself ; humiliate oneself ; be clothed with shame
개꽃 〖식물〗 the scentless false-camomile
개꿀 comb honey
개꿈 a wild〔silly, an empty〕 dream
개나리 〖식물〗 ① [목서과의] a forsythia ; the golden-bell tree ② [들나리] a wild lily ¶ 개나리는 봄의 상징이다 The forsythia is the symbol of the spring.
―꽃 (the blossom of) a golden bell
*개념 概念 a general idea ; a concept ; a notion ; an idea ¶ 개념적인 conceptual ; general ; notional // 「사람」이라는 개념 a concept of man // 미의 개념 notions of beauty // 과학의 개념 a general idea of science // 행복의 개념 idea of happiness // 개념화된 지식 a generalized knowledge // …에 대한 개념을 얻다 get〔have〕 a general idea 《of》
―시(詩) a conceptional poem ―실재론 realism ―작용 conception 기본 ― fundamental notions 동일(同一) ― an identical conception
개념론 概念論 conceptualism
†개다¹ [날씨가] clear up ; become clear ; [비가] hold up ; stop raining ; cease to rain ; rain is over ; [안개가] lift ; clear

off〔away〕; break away ¶ 날씨가 활짝 개었다 The sky is bright and clear. // 비가 개었다 The rain is over. // 안개가 갰다 The fog lifted. /The mist cleared away. // 날씨가 갤 것 같다 The weather shows signs of clearing. /It's likely to clear up.

개다² [으깨다] knead ; mix up ; temper ; pug ; soften with water ¶ 가루 반죽을 개다 knead dough // 풀을 개다 temper paste 《with water》// 진흙을 개다 temper〔pug〕 clay // 퍼티는 잘 개어진다 Putty works easily. // 모르타르를 개다 work mortar

개다³ fold (up) 《quilts》 ¶ 옷을 개다 fold one's clothes ; lay the clothes away // 이불을 개다 fold up the beddings ; put away a bed // 천막을 개다 fold up a tent ; strike a tent

개다래 fruit of the silvervine

개다래나무 〖식물〗 a silvervine

개다리 a dog's leg

— **밥상〔소반(小盤)〕** a small dining table with cabrioles — **상제** an ill-mannered〔unmannerly〕 mourner —**질** mean and nasty conduct

개도국 開途國 ⇨ 개발 도상국

개두릅 fresh shoots〔sprouts〕 of thorny ash (tree)

개떡 a bran cake ; a pie-shaped cake made of coarse barley flour

개떡같다 be trivial〔trifling〕; be beneath notice ; be unimportant ; be rubbish ; be good-for-nothing ; be nonsense ¶ 개떡같은 수작 nonsense ; rubbish // 개떡같은 녀석 a punk 《미》; a worthless fellow // 개떡같은 소리를 하다 talk nonsense〔rot, rubbish〕; talk idly ; say useless things ; tattle

개똥 ① [개의 똥] dog dung〔droppings〕; a dog turd ; merde 《프》 ② [천한 것] a rubbish〔trash〕; garbage ¶ 개똥같다 be trash ; be not worth a damn

개똥밭 a filthy place〔land〕 covered with dog droppings here and there

개똥 참외도 먼저 맡는 이가 임자다 속담 Finding's keeping.

*__개똥벌레__ 〖곤충〗 a glowworm ; a firefly

개똥 상놈 —常— a low〔mean, vulgar〕 fellow ; a churl ; a cad ; a ribald ; a yahoo ¶ 이 개똥 상놈아 You swine 〔skunk〕! /You dirty〔lousy〕 guy ! / You bloody villain !

개똥지빠귀 〖새〗 a thrush ; a dusky ouzel

개똥참외 a wild melon

개똥 철학 a mockery of philosophy

개략 概略 an outline ; a summary ; the gist ; a résumé 《프》; the epitome ; a compendium ¶ 개략을 말하자면 roughly speaking

*__개량 改良__ improvement ; betterment ; amelioration ; reform —**하다** improve ; make 《a thing》 better ; better ; ameliorate ; reform ¶ 개량의 여지가 있다〔없다〕 There is (no) room for improvement.

— **농지(農地)** improved〔reclaimed〕 farmland —**종(種)** a select breed ; an improved variety —**주의** reformism —**형(型)** an improved model **사회** — a social reform

*__개런티__ [출연 계약금] a guarantee ; a guaranteed minimum amount of payment 《to an entertainer》

개력하다 《nature》 undergo a (complete) change ; have a convulsion of nature

개론 槪論 a survey ; an introduction ; an outline ; general remarks —**하다** give a survey ; give the outline 《of》; outline ; summarize ¶ 개론에서 각론으로 들어가다 descend〔proceed〕 from generals to particulars

철학 — an introduction to philosophy

개리 〖새〗 the Chinese goose〔swan〕

개막 開幕 raising the curtain ; the commencement of a performance ; the opening —**하다** raise the curtain ; commence〔begin〕 the performance ¶ 오후 6시 개막이다 The curtain rises〔goes up〕 at 6 p.m. // 스키 시즌의 개막 the opening of the ski season

—**극(劇)** a curtain raiser — **시간(時間)** the time of the rising of the curtain —**식** the opening ceremony〔pageant〕 —**예행연습** an opening ceremony rehearsal —**일** the opening day —**전〔경기〕** an opening game〔match〕; an opener

개망나니 a tough 《구》; a rowdy ; a roughneck 《미·구》

개망신 —亡身 a deep disgrace ; a sore indignity ; a burning〔crying〕 shame —**하다** disgrace oneself in public ; bring burning shame on oneself ¶ 너의 나쁜 행동은 학교 전체의 개망신이다 Your bad behavior brings shame on the whole school.

개맹이 spirit ; pep ; vigo(u)r ; liveliness ; sprightliness

개머루 〖식물〗 wild grapes

개머리 the stock of a rifle ; a gunstock ¶ 개머리판 a butt plate (of a rifle)

개먹다 get worn down ; get rubbed off ; abrade

개명 改名 —**하다** change one's name 《to》; rechristen ; rename 《the shop》 ¶ A를 B로 개명하다 change one's name from A to B // 개명계를 내다 send in a report of one's changed name

개명 開明 civilization ; enlightenment ; (a) flowering of culture —**하다** become civilized ; be enlightened ; open up new knowledge

—국 a civilized country — 시대 an enlightened age ; the age of civilization

개문 開門 opening the gate —하다 open the gate ¶ 오후 8시 개문 예정 The gate is to open at 8 p.m..

— 발차(發車) starting with doors open

개미¹ [연줄에 먹이는] powdered glass 〔porcelain〕 mixed with glue ¶ 개미먹이다 coat 《kite strings》 with powdered glass〔porcelain〕

*개미² 〖곤충〗 an ant ¶ 개미의 formic // 개미 새끼 하나 얼씬 못 하다 Even no ant is let loose.

— 구멍 an ant hole ; an ant's nest — 굴 an ant tunnel —귀신 an ant lion ; a doodlebug —떼 a swarm〔colony〕 of ants — 마을 a colony of ragpickers — 지옥 an ant lion's pit — 행렬 a column〔line〕 of ants 여왕 — a queen ant

개미 구멍으로 공든 탑 무너진다 (속담) A small leak will sink a great ship. /A little fire burns up a great deal of corn. /Of a small spark, a great fire.

개미 금탑 모으듯 한다 (속담) save up little by little/Little and often fills the purse. /Penny and penny laid up will be many. /A pin a day is a groat a year. /Many a little makes a mickle.

개미 쳇바퀴 돌듯 (속담) going round and round (as an ant goes round the frame of a sieve)

개미벌 〖동물〗 a velvet ant ; a solitary ant

개미산 —酸 〖화학〗 formic acid

개미자리 〖식물〗 a pearlwort ; (a) white 〔Dutch〕 clover ; (a) clover

개미집 a formicary ; an ant's nest ; a formicarium 《*pl.* -caria》

개미탑 ⇨ 개밋둑

개미핥기 〖동물〗 an anteater

개미허리 a slender〔wasp〕 waist ¶ 개미허리 미인 a beauty with a slender figure

개밋둑 an ant hill ; an ant heap ; a formicary

†개발 開發 [개척] reclamation ; clearing ; exploitation ; development ; colonization ; [계발(啓發)] improvement ; enlightenment —하다 develop ; exploit ; open up ; improve ; enlighten ¶ 개발적 교수법 the inductive method of teaching // 경제 개발 5개년 계획 a 5-year economic development plan // 우주 개발 계획 a space development program // 제주도를 개발하다 develop 〔exploit〕 *Cheju-do* // 지능을 개발하다 improve the mind ; develop the intellectual faculties // 소택지를 개발하다 reclaim a swamp // 자원이 아직 개발되지 않았다 These resources are as yet undeveloped. // 신제품을 개발하다 develop new products // 황무지를 개발하다 reclaim wasteland

— 계획 a development project〔program, plan〕 — 교육 developmental education — 사업 development work — 원조 그룹 the Development Assistance Group 《약어 D. A. G.》 — 융자 development loan —자 a developer — 자금 a development fund — 제한 지역 limited development district — 차관 기금(借款基金) Development Loan Fund 《D. L. F》 — 촉진 지역 development promoted district 경제 — economic development〔exploitation〕 미개 지역(未開地域)— the development of backward regions 한국 — 연구원 the Korea Development Institute 《K. D. I》 한국 해외 — 공사 the Korean Overseas Development Corporation 《 K. O. D. C》

개발 도상국 開發途上國 a developing country

개발비 開發費 development costs 〔expense〕

개발주의 開發主義 〖교육〗 inductive method of teaching

개발코 a snub nose ; a pug nose

개밥 feed for dogs ; dog food

개밥에 도토리 (속담) an outcast ; an ostracized person

개밥바라기 the evening star ; 〖천문〗 Venus ; Hesper(us)

개방 開方 〖수학〗 evolution ; extraction of a 《square》 root —하다 extract the square root of

†개방 開放 [열어 놓음] opening ; throwing open ; leaving 《a door》 open ; [허용] lifting the ban ¶ 개방적인 frank ; candid ; open-hearted // 나라를 개방하다 open a country to foreign intercourse // 정원을 개방하다 throw open a garden to the public // 문호 개방 정책 the open-door policy

— 도시 an open city — 장치 a releasing device — 전류(電流) a released current —주의 laissez-faire 《프》 ; unrestraint

개방성 開放性 openness ; 〖의학〗 patency ; persistence

— 결핵 open tuberculosis

개방 요법 開放療法 open-air treatment

개방 정책 開放政策 an open-door policy

개백장 a dog killer ; a dog catcher

개버딘 〖직물〗 gabardine

개벽 開闢 the beginning of the world ; the Creation ; [새시대, 새로운 사상, 첫 출현 등] the dawn of civilization〔of history, of hope, of the new technology〕 ¶ 개벽 이래 since the world began ; since the creation of the world ; since the dawn of history // 개벽 이전의 antemundane // 개벽 이래 처음 보는 사건 an unprecedented event // 천지 개벽이 일어나도 though the heavens fall

개변 改變 change ; alteration ; innovation ; renovation ; reformation —하다 change ; alter ; innovate ; renovate

개별 個別 an individual〔a particular〕case ; individualization ¶ 개별적으로 individually ; separately ; severally ; one by one ; singly

— 개념 〖철학〗 distributive concept — 선택 〖보험〗 individual selection — 심사(審査) individual screening —화(化) individualization

개별 지도 個別指導 individual guidance

개병 皆兵 universal conscription

국민 — 제도 a universal conscription system

개복 開腹 —하다 cut the abdomen open

개복 수술 開腹手術 〖의학〗 ventrotomy ; laparotomy ; an abdominal operation ¶ 개복 수술을 하다〔받다〕 perform〔undergo〕 laparotomy

개봉 開封 [편지 따위] unsealing ; opening 《a letter, a seal》 ; [영화] release ; a first run ; a premiere —하다 break〔take off〕 the seal ; open〔unseal〕 《a letter》 ; tear 《a letter》 open ; release〔premiere〕 《a film》 ¶ 편지를 개봉하지 않고 돌려보내다 return 《a letter》 unopened // 편지를 개봉하여 보내다 send a letter unsealed // 최근에 개봉된 영화 a recently released film // 개봉되고 있다 be in release

— 상연 the first showing〔run〕 ; a first-run showing — 영화 시사회 a trade show

개봉관 開封館 a first-run theater ; a first-runner ; a cinema that shows newly-released films 《영》

개봉 영화 開封映畫 a newly-released film ; a first-run film

개불알꽃 〖식물〗 a lady('s) slipper ; a moccasin flower

개비 a piece of split wood〔timber〕 ¶ 성냥 개비 a matchstick ; a match // 장작 개비 a piece of split firewood

개비 改備 [새것으로] (a) renewal ; replacing —하다 renew ; replace 《one thing by〔with〕 another》 ; refurnish ; refixture

개산 開山 〖불교〗 founding a Buddhist temple —하다 found〔establish〕 a temple

—일〔날〕 the dedication day of a Buddhist temple — 조사(祖師)〔시조(始祖)〕 the founder〔founding father, dedicator〕 of a Buddhist temple〔sect〕 — 탑(塔) a pagoda under which the remains of the founder of a temple is buried

개산 概算 a rough estimate〔calculation〕 ; approximate figures ; approximation —하다 estimate〔calculate〕 roughly ; make a rough estimate ¶ 나의 개산으로는 in my (rough) estimation // 개산으로 100만 approximately a million ; a million in round figures // 서울의 개산 인구 the estimated population of *Seoul*

— 가격 approximate value〔price〕 — 견적 an approximate estimate —불(拂) payment by rough estimate —서(書) a written rough estimate — 수량 approximate quantity —액 a rough amount

개살구 〖식물〗 a wild apricot

빛좋은 개살구 (속담) Never judge from appearance.

개상 —床 a wooden thrasher with four legs ; a log threshing-stand

개상어 〖물고기〗 a dog shark

개새끼 ① [개의] a pup (of a dog) ; a puppy ② [개자식] a "son-of-a-bitch〔gun〕" (S. O. B/SOB) ; a bitch ¶ 이 개새끼야 Damn you ! /You rascal ! /You son of a bitch ! /You dog !

개서 改書 ① [다시 씀] rewriting ; [다시 쓴 것] a rewrite —하다 rewrite ; write over (again) ; [정서하다] copy clearly ¶ 원고를 두 차례 개서하다 write over manuscripts twice ② [어음·증서 따위의] (a) renewal —하다 renew 《a bill, a bond》

— 어음 a renewed bill

†개선 改善 improvement ; betterment ; amelioration ; reformation ; reform ¶ 체질의 개선 improvement of habitude ; constitutional improvement —하다 improve ; better ; make 《a thing》 better ; change for the better ; reform ¶ 처우를 개선하다 improve treatments ; give better treatment to 《workers》 // 생활을 개선하다 improve one's way of life // 사태를 개선하다 remedy the state of things // 도로를 개선하다 improve〔mend〕 the roads // 개선을 가하다 improve on 《the old model》 // 개선되다 be improved ; undergo improvements // 개선 중이다 It is being improved. /It is on the mend. // 개선의 여지가 다분히 있다 It leaves much room for improvement. /There is much to be desired.

대우 — betterment〔amelioration〕 of working conditions 생활 — the betterment of living ; the reformation〔improvement〕 of the mode of living 설비 — improvement in accommodation

개선 改選 re-election —하다 re-elect 《members》 ¶ 3년 만에 의원의 반수를 개선키로 한다 Election for half the members shall take place every three years.

개선 凱旋 a triumphal return〔entry〕 —하다 return in triumph ; return triumphantly ; return from a victorious campaign ¶ 서울로 개선하다 return in triumph to *Seoul* // 장군은 유럽으로부터

개선했다 The general returned from his victories in Europe.
—군 victorious returning troops —식 a triumphal celebration — 행렬 a triumphal procession〔parade〕
개선 疥癬 the itch ; scabies ; 〚의학〛 ascariasis ; psora ; scotch fiddle 《속》; mange (말, 개의)
개선가 凱旋歌 a triumphal song ; paean
개선문 凱旋門 a triumphal〔victory〕 arch ; an arch of triumph ; the Arc de Triomphe (파리의)
개선장군 凱旋將軍 a triumphant general
개선책 改善策 a remedy ; a reform measure
개선충 疥癬蟲 a scab mite ; an itch mite ; a scabies worm
개설 開設 establishment ; opening ; inauguration ; installation 《of a telephone》 —하다 establish ; set up ; open ; inaugurate ¶ 병원을〔학교를〕 개설하다 establish a hospital〔school〕// 전화를 개설하다 have a telephone installed 《in one's house》// 영어 강좌를 개설하다 open an English language course // 특약점을 개설하다 set up a special agency // 예금계좌를 개설하다 open a deposit〔savings〕 account
*개설 概說 an introduction ; a summary ; a general statement ; an outline —하다 give an outline 《of》; treat 《a subject》 in outline ; make an introduction 《to》; make a summary 《of》
개성 改姓 a change of one's family name〔surname〕 —하다 change one's family name〔surname〕
*개성 個性 individuality ; idiosyncrasy ; personality ; individual traits ; individual character ¶ 뚜렷한 개성 a marked individuality // 개성을 존중〔무시〕하다 respect〔disregard, ignore〕 《a person's》 individuality // 개성을 발달시키다 develop one's personality // 개성을 발휘하다 show〔display〕 one's originality // 개성을 억제하다 stifle 《a person's》 individuality // 그의 작품에는 개성이 뚜렷하게 나타나 있다 His writings are marked by his strong individuality // 옷은 그 사람의 개성을 나타낸다 Dress expresses the wearer's individuality. // 그녀는 개성이 매우 강하다 She has a very strong 〔clear-cut〕 personality.
— 검사 a personality test — 교육 individual upbringing〔education〕 — 심리학 individual psychology
개세 蓋世 —하다 surpass all ; stand unchallenged ; hold sway over ; reign supreme ¶ 개세의 영웅 a most prominent hero of the day
개소 個所 [장소] a place ; a site ; a spot ; a section (구간) ; a point (지점) ; [부분] a part ; a portion ; a passage (문장의) ¶ 3개소에서 강도질을 하다 commit burglary at three houses // 수개소가 침수하다 be flooded in several places
개소리 nonsense ; stupid talk ; rubbish ¶ 개소리 마라 Nonsense ! /Stuff and nonsense ! /Don't talk rubbish ! // 개소리 하는군 You talk nonsense.
개수 ⇨ 개숫물
개수 改修 repair ; mending ; improvement ; conservancy —하다 repair ; mend ; improve 《a road》 ¶ 도로의 개수 the improvement of roads // 대대적으로 개수하다 carry out large repairs
— 공사 repair works
개수 概數 round figures〔numbers〕; an approximate number
개수 個數, 箇數 the number 《of articles, items》 ¶ 개수를 확인하다 ascertain〔check〕 the number ; count // 개수는 얼마나 됩니까 How many (pieces) are there ?
—불 임금(拂賃金) piecework wages ; piece rate
개수작 —酬酌 a foolish remark ; silly words ; nonsense ; rubbish ; rot ¶ 개수작 마라 Nonsense ! /Stuff ! /How absurd ! /Stuff and nonsense ! /Humbug !
개수통 a dishwater bucket ; a dishpan ; a slop-basin
개술 概述 summarizing ; giving an outline〔a summary〕 —하다 summarize ; give an outline
개숫물 —水— dishwater ; slops ; liquid refuse ; swill ¶ 개숫물을 버리다 empty the slops ; carry off dirty water
*개시 開市 ① [시장을 열다] opening up a market ② [마수걸이] the first sale (of the day) ; an opening sale —하다 open up a market ; begin to sell ; make the first sale ¶ 아직 개시도 못했다 I haven't made a sale yet today.
†개시 開始 opening ; commencement ; inauguration ; beginning ; start —하다 begin ; commence ; open 《an account, a game》; enter into〔upon〕 《negotiations》; start 《business》; inaugurate 《bus service》; be opened ; get started ¶ 시판을 개시하다 begin to sell // 방송 개시는 오전 6시다 The broadcast begins at 6 a. m. // 북한은 핵실험을 개시했다 North Korea started nuclear bomb tests.
개시 皆是 all ; every ⇨ 모두
개시 손님 開市— the first customer 〔buyer〕 of the day
개식 開式 the opening of a ceremony —하다 open a ceremony
개식사 開式辭 an opening speech 〔address〕 《of a ceremony》
개신 改新 renewing ; renovation ; innovation ; reformation —하다 renew ;

renovate ; innovate ; reform
개신거리다 stir languidly ⇨ 기신거리다
‡개심 改心 reform ; amendment ; reclamation ; repentance (종교적) ; contrition —하다 mend one's ways〔life〕 ; turn from one's evil ways ; turn over a new leaf ; reform 《oneself》 ; start one's life all over again ¶ 개심시키다 reform 《a person》 ; reclaim 《a criminal》 // 청년을 개심시키다 lead a young man into better ways // 그는 이미 개심했다 Now he is a reformed man. /He is quite penitent now. // 그 문제아는 개심할 가망이 〔여지가〕 없는 것 같았다 The problem child seemed to be past〔beyond〕 reclaim. // 그는 개심하여 좋은 사람이 되기로 맹세했다 He swore to turn over a new leaf.
—자(者) a reformed man ; a penitent
개악 改惡 a change for the worse ; a bad change ; undesirable amendment ; deterioration —하다 change 《a matter》 for the worse ; make 《things》 worse for the change ; deteriorate ¶ 노동법의 개악 the retrogressive revision of the Labor Law // 헌법을 개악하다 change〔revise〕 the constitution for the worse
개안 開眼 ① [눈을 뜸] opening one's eyes ; [눈이 보이게 됨] gaining eyesight ② [悟道] spiritual awakening ; enlightenment ; open one's eyes to 《the beauty of...》 —하다 open one's eyes ; gain eyesight ; be awakened 《to a fact》 ; be (spiritually) enlightened
— 수술 an eyesight recovery operation
개암[1] [매의 먹이] a small wad of cotton put in a falcon's feed ¶ (매가) 개암도르다 (a falcon) throw up〔vomit〕 the cotton wad after digesting the meat
개암[2] [개암나무의 열매] a hazel ; a hazelnut ; a filbert
— 사탕 hazelnut candy —장(醬) hazelnut sauce —죽 rice gruel boiled in hazelnut juice
개암나무 〖식물〗 a hazel (tree)
개암들다 have complications〔suffer sequelae〕 after childbirth
개어귀 an estuary ; the mouth of a river ; an entry to a river
†개업 開業 opening〔commencement〕 of (a) business〔trade〕 ; establishment in business —하다 open (for business) ; begin business ; establish oneself in business ; set oneself up in business ; enter upon business [의사·변호사가] start practice ¶ 식료품 가게를 개업했다 He set up as a grocer. /He established himself as a grocer. // 그 은행은 금일부터 개업한다 The bank begins〔opens for〕 business today. // 내과의를 개업하고 있다 He is in practice as a physician. // 식당 개업을 하신다고 들었습니다 I hear that you're going to open a restaurant.
—비 the initial cost of business — 안내 the announcement of opening a business
개업식 開業式 the opening〔inauguration〕 ceremony
*개업의 開業醫 a medical practitioner ; a practicing doctor〔physician〕
개역 改易 change ; alteration ; replacement —하다 change ; alter ; replace
개역 改譯 retranslation —하다 retranslate ; revise a translation
—자 a retranslator —판 a revised version
개역 성경 改譯聖經 the Revised Version of the Bible
개연 開演 the raising of the curtain ; the commencement of a performance ; [상연] staging —하다 raise the curtain ; commence〔open〕 a performance ; stage 《a play》 ¶ 개연중에 while the curtain is up // 그 연극은 시민회관에서 개연 예정이다 The play is to be on at the City Hall. // 오후 7시 개연 The curtain rises〔is raised〕 at 7 p. m.
개연 慨然 —하다 (be) indignant ; lamenting ; deploring ¶ 개연히 indignantly ; in indignation ; lamentingly ; deploringly // 개연히 자리를 떠남이 마땅하다 It is natural that he should quit his post in indignation.
개연론 蓋然論 〖철학〗 probabilism
개연성 蓋然性 〖철학〗 probability
개염 covetousness ⇨ 게염
개오 開悟 〖불교〗 spiritual awakening 〔enlightenment〕 —하다 become enlightened ; have spiritual awakening ; attain enlightenment
개오 改悟 repentance ⇨ 개전(改悛)
개와 蓋瓦 ① ⇨ 기와 ② [지붕 이기] roofing ; tiling —하다 roof with tiles ; tile over ; tile a house〔roof〕
—장(匠) a roofer ; a tiler ⇨ 기와장이
†개요 槪要 an outline ; a summary ; a résumé 《프》 ; an epitome ; a synopsis ; an abstract ¶ 개요를 말하다 give an outline 《of》 ; outline
개운 開運 the beginning〔opening〕 of good fortune ; the coming〔arrival〕 of a lucky〔good〕 break —하다 《one's fortune》 change for the better ; 《fortune》 turn in one's favor ; be favored by fortune ; be in luck's way ; have fortune open up for one ¶ 개운을 빕니다 May fortune smile on you.
개운하다 ① [기분이나 몸이] (be) refreshed ; feel refreshed〔fine, well, all right, relieved〕 ¶ 개운한 기분 a refreshed〔carefree〕 frame of mind // 이제 몸이 개운하다 I feel quite well now. /Now I feel refreshed ! /I feel myself another man. // 푹 잤더니 몸이 개운하다

After a sound sleep I feel refreshed. ② [음식 따위에서 느끼는] plain ; simple ; refreshing ¶ 조개탕 맛이 개운하다 Thin clam soup tastes refreshing.

*개울 a brook ; a little stream ; a rivulet ¶ 개울에서 가재를 잡다 catch lobsters in a little stream

개울가 by the brook

개울물 the stream water

개원 改元 a change of era **—하다** change the name of the era

개원 開院 the opening of 《the National Assembly, a hospital》 **—하다** open 《the National Assembly, a hospital》

—식 the opening ceremony of the House〔National Assembly〕

개월 個月 months ¶ 그 건축물은 3년 10개월 만에 준공되었다 It took three years and 10 months for the completion of the building.

개으르다 (be) lazy ⇨ 게으르다

개으름 laziness ⇨ 게으름

개의 介意 **—하다** mind ; be concerned 《about》; take 《something》 to one's heart ; care 《about》; trouble〔concern〕 oneself 《about》 ¶ 조금도 개의치 않다 do not care a bit〔pin, straw, button〕; be quite indifferent to // 남의 말에는 개의치 말게 Don't mind what others say. // 그런 일에 너무 개의치 마십시오 Don't trouble yourself〔Never mind〕 about that. // 그 사람은 남의 이해 따위는 개의치 않는다 He has no regard for〔is indifferent to〕 another's〔others'〕 interests. // 당신과는 상관없는 일이니 개의치 마시오 Don't trouble yourself about the matter that is not your concern. // 그녀는 남의 사정 따위는 조금도 개의치 않는다 She was totally indifferent to others' circumstances. // 그는 이 회사에서 아무것도 개의치 않는 것 같다 He gives the impression that nothing in this office fazes him.

개의 改議 ① [다시 의논함] rediscussion ; reconsideration **—하다** discuss 《a matter》 over again ; reconsider ② [동의에 대한] moving an amendment ; a motion for amendment **—하다** move an amendment 《to》 ¶ 의안을 개의하다 amend the bill

개의 開議 start the deliberation of the bill(s) introduced.

개의 概意 a summary : a synopsis

개인 改印 **—하다** change one's name seal

†개인 個人 an individual ; [사인(私人)] a private person〔individual, citizen〕 ¶ 개인적 individual ; private ; personal // 개인적으로 individually ; privately ; personally // 개인으로서(는) personally ; as an individual // 개인으로서의 의견 one's personal〔private〕 opinion // 개인 또는 법인 a natural or juridical person // 개인용 의자 chairs for individual use // 개인 플레이하다 demonstrate one's personal skill (단체 경기에서) // 개인 자격으로 in one's private capacity ; in the capacity of a private person // 개인의 자유 the freedom of the individual // 개인의 권리 the rights of the individual // 개인적으로는 그분과 관계가 없다 I have no personal relations with him. // 개인적인 교제였었다 We knew each other on a personal basis. // 개인의 권리는 자유 사회에서 가장 중요한 권리이다 The rights of the individual are the most important rights in a free society. // 개인적인 용무입니다 It's kind of personal. // 톰을 개인적으로 압니까 Do you know Tom personally? // 무슨 개인적인 유감이 있었던 것은 아니다 I didn't mean anything personal. // 개인적인 질문을 하지 마라 Don't ask personal questions.

— 감정 personal feeling **— 경영(經營)** private management **— 경영 상점** a private concern **— 공격** personal criticism **— 관계** personal relations **— 교섭** individual bargaining **— 문제** a private〔personal〕 matter **— 상점** a private concern ; a one-man business firm **— 소비** personal〔private〕 consumption **— 소비 지출** expenditure on personal consumption **— 숭배** the cult of personality **— 식별(識別)** identification **— 심리학** individual psychology **— 전용선(專用線)** a private wire **— 제도** an individual system **— 종목** an individual event **— 종합 경기** individual combined exercises **— 주택** an individual home ; a private residence **— 지도** personal guidance in the course of 《a person's》 studies ¶ 개인 지도를 하다 give personal guidance to ; coach ; tutor

개인 경기 個人競技 an individual sport〔event〕

개인계 改印屆 a notice of the change of one's seal

개인 교수 個人教授 private lessons〔instruction〕; individual instruction **—하다** give private lessons 《to》; coach ; tutor ¶ 개인 교수를 받다 study exclusively〔individually〕 under a tutor

—료 a fee for separate lessons

개인기 個人技 individual skill ¶ 개인기가 뛰어나다 be excellent〔excel others〕 in individual skill

개인 기업 個人企業 an individual enterprise ; a one-man business

개인성 個人性 individual character ; individuality ; personality

개인 소득 個人所得 an individual income ; a personal income

개인 어음 個人 — a personal bill

개인 영업 個人營業 a private business〔enterprise〕

개인용 컴퓨터 a personal computer

개인 위생 **個人衛生** personal hygiene
개인 윤리 **個人倫理** personal ethics
*개인적 **個人的** individual ; private ; personal
개인전 **個人展** a one-man show ; a picture show by a single artist ; a private exhibition ; a one-man exhibition (of his works)
*개인주의 **個人主義** individualism ¶ 개인주의적 individualistic ; [이기적] egoistic ; egotistic ; selfish
—자 an individualist ¶ 철저한 개인주의자 a rugged individualist
개인차 **個人差** difference among individuals ; individual variations ; personal equation (개인 오차) ¶ 늘 개인차는 있기 마련이다 There's always a difference between individuals.
개인 택시 **個人—** an owner-driver taxi
— 운전사 an owner-driver cabby ; an owner-cabdriver
개인 플레이 a personal action ¶ 단체 경기에서 개인 플레이는 절대 금물이다 Egotistic play by individual players in a group game is absolutely discouraged.
개인 회사 **個人會社** a private firm〔company〕
개입 **介入** intervention ; meddling **—하다** intervene in ; meddle in ¶ 군사〔무력〕 개입 military〔armed〕 intervention // 분쟁에 개입하다 intervene in a dispute // 한국은행은 외환 시장에 적극 개입하고 있다 The Bank of Korea is aggressively intervening in the foreign exchange markets. // 폭동이 일어났을 때 경찰은 개입하지 않을 수 없었다 When rioting broke out, the police were obliged to intervene. // 노동 쟁의에 대한 정부의 개입은 도움이 되지 않을 것이다 The government's intervention in the labor dispute will not help.
개자 **芥子** mustard
개자리¹ 〖식물〗 medick ; trefoil ; snail clover ; alfalfa ; Medicago minama (학명)
개자리² [과녁 앞의] an archery marker's pit in front of the wand
개자식 a son-of-a-bitch ; a bastard
*개작 **改作** an adaptation 《from》 ; remaking **—하다** adapt ¶ 소설을 무대용으로 개작하다 adapt a novel for the stage // 프랑스 광대극을 개작한 연극 a play adapted from a French farce // 소설을 연극으로 개작하다 dramatize a novel ; adapt a novel for a play // 이것은 춘원의 작품을 개작한 것이다 This is an adaptation from one of *Chunwon*'s works.
—자 an adapter
개잘량 a dog-skin rug
개잠 sleeping curled up (like a dog) ¶ 개잠자다 lie huddled up in bed ; curl (oneself) up
개잠 **改—** a sleep after waking up once in the morning
개잠들다 **改—** fall asleep〔drop off to sleep〕 again after waking up once in the morning
개잡년 **—雜—** a bitch of a woman ; a wanton ; a slut ; a woman of loose morals
개잡놈 **—雜—** [잡스러운] a licentious sloven ; a philanderer ; a lounge lizard ; a sofa pup ; [쓸모없는] a dog of a man ; a low fellow ; a cad
개장 **改葬** reinterment ; reburial **—하다** reinter ; rebury
개장 **開場** opening 《a place》 **—하다** open 《a place》 ; open the doors ¶ 오후 3시 개장 The doors open at 3 p. m. // 개장과 동시에 사람들이 백화점에 몰려들었다 People surged into the department store as soon as the doors were opened. // 개장 시간 9시 정각 The opening hour at nine (o'clock sharp)
— 시간 the opening hour **—식** the opening〔inauguration〕 ceremony ¶ 개장식을 행하다 hold the opening〔inauguration〕 ceremony
개장 **改裝** remodeling ; conversion ; modernization (현대식으로) **—하다** remodel ; refit ; reequip ; convert ¶ 건물의 개장 공사 the remodeling work to the building // 점포를 개장하다 remodel a shop // 순양함으로 개장하다 convert a ship into a cruiser // 관내 개장중 휴관함 Closed for renovation. (게시)
개장국 dog-meat soup
*개재 **介在** interposition ; intervention (개입) **—하다** lie〔stand〕 between ; interpose 《between》 ; intervene 《between》 ¶ 제3국의 개재를 불허하다 permit no third power intervention // 공적인 인사에 정실이 개재되면 안 된다 Personal favors must not be allowed in personnel management.
개전 **開戰** declaring war ; the outbreak〔beginning〕 of war ; the commencement of hostilities **—하다** open〔begin〕 war〔hostilities〕 《against》 ; make war 《on》 ; wage war 《against》 ¶ 개전 전〔후〕 before〔after〕 hostilities begin // 개전을 선포하다 declare war 《against, on》
개전 **改悛** repentance ; penitence **—하다** repent 《of one's sins, of one's errors》 ; be penitent 《of》 ; mend one's way ¶ 개전의 정이 보였다 He showed sincere repentance.
개점 **開店** **—하다** [처음으로] open a shop〔store〕 ; establish a shop ; open 《for business》 ; [휴업중이던 것이] open its doors ; [그날 그날] open the store (for the day) ¶ 개점 인사 the announcement of opening a store // 이번에 개점한 가게 a newly opened shop // 개점 축하로 in celebration of the open-

ing of a shop // 철물점을 개점하다 establish a hardware store // 개점 휴업 상태다 The door is open, but practically no business is done within. // 은행은 오전 9시 30분에 개점한다 The bank opens at 9 : 30 a. m. // 개점을 알리다 announce〔advertize〕 the opening of a store
— 시간 the opening hour of a store — 안내 the announcement of the opening of a shop

*개정 改正 [수정] revision ; amendment ; [변경] change ; alteration ; [개량] improvement —하다 revise ; amend ; change ; alter ; improve ¶ 시구(市區)를 개정하다 improve the streets ; remodel city blocks // 이달 5일부터 시간표가 개정된다 The revised timetable will be put into force beginning on the 5th of this month. // 국회 의원들은 악법의 개정에 힘썼다 The members of the National Assembly made an effort to amend the evil laws.
—가 the revised price — 세율(稅率) revised duties〔rates〕 — 시간표 a revised〔new〕 timetable 조약(條約) — treaty revision 헌법 — the amendments of the National Constitution

개정 改定 a reform ; fixing anew —하다 reform ; fix 《a date》 anew ¶ 규칙의 개정 a revision of rules
— 요금 the readjusted note

*개정 改訂 revision —하다 revise ¶ 전면 개정 total revision // 전면 개정판 a completely revised version〔edition〕 // 전면 증보 revision and enlargement // 전면 증보판 a revised and enlarged edition // 사전을 전면 개정하다 revise a dictionary completely

†개정 開廷 the opening〔holding, sitting〕 of a court ; [공판] a hearing ; a trial —하다 open〔hold〕 a court ; give a hearing ; sit 《on a case》 ¶ 6시에 개정한다 The court opens at 6. // 개정중이다 The court is now sitting.
—일(日) a juridical day ; a court day

개정안 改正案 a revised bill

개정판 改訂版 a revised edition

개제 改題 a change of the title ; retitling —하다 change the title 《of a book》 ; retitle ¶ 그 잡지는 "시사영어"로 개제되어 다시 간행되었다 The magazine was reissued under the new title of "Current English."

개조 開祖 ① [종파의] the founder 《of a sect, of a temple》 ; the apostle 《of Ireland》 ② [창시자] the originator ; the author ; the inventor

개조 個條 an item ; an article ; a clause ¶ 열두 개조로 된 법조문 a statute consisting of 12 provisions
신앙 — articles of faith

개조 改造 remodeling ; reconstruction ; rebuilding ; conversion —하다 remodel ; reconstruct ; rebuild ; reorganize ; convert 《into》 ¶ 군함을 정기선으로 개조하다 convert a warship into a liner // 의식의 개조 reconstruction of consciousness // 방을 개조하다 have a room made over // 집을 개조하여 상점을 만들다 remodel a house into a store // 군함을 상선으로 개조하다 convert a warship into a merchant ship

개조 改組 reorganization —하다 reorganize 《a company》 ; reshuffle 《a cabinet》 ¶ 내각 개조 a cabinet reshuffle // 내각을 개조하다 reshuffle〔reorganize〕 the Cabinet ; revamp the Cabinet 《미》

개종 改宗 conversion —하다 be〔become〕 converted 《to》 ; change one's religion ¶ 기독교로 개종시키다 convert 《a person》 to Christianity

개종 開宗 founding a Buddhist sect —하다 found a sect

개종자 改宗者 a convert 《to Buddhism》 ; a proselyte ; a neophyte

개종조 開宗祖 the founder 《of a sect》

개주 改鑄 [화폐의] recoinage ; [종 따위의] recasting —하다 recoin ; remint ; recast

개죽음 throwing away one's life ; an ignominious death ¶ 개죽음을 당하다 die in vain ; die to no purpose ; throw away one's life

개중 個中 among 《them》 ; some 《of them》 ¶ 개중에는 좋은 것도 있고 나쁜 것도 있다 Some are good, but some bad. // 개중에는 쓸 만한 물건이 더러 있다 Some of them can be saved for use.

개지랄 ¶ 개지랄 마라 Don't be such a pig!

개진 開陳 statement —하다 express ; set forth 《one's view》 ; state ; make a statement ¶ 여러 사람 앞에서 자기의 소신을 개진하다 He stated his views to the audience.

개짐 a sanitary napkin〔shield, belt〕 ; a menstrual cloth

개집 a doghouse ; a kennel

개차반 a man of ill-conduct ; a scamp ; an outlaw ¶ 행실이 개차반이다 be mean in one's conduct ; behave badly

개착 開鑿 excavation —하다 excavate 《a tunnel》 ; cut 《a road, a canal》 ; dig〔sink〕 《a well》
— 펌프 a sinking pump 운하 —자 a canal builder〔constructor〕

개착 공사 開鑿工事 excavation works

개착기 開鑿機 an excavator ; a steam shovel

개찬 改竄 correction ; revision —하다 correct 《errors, wrong spellings》 ; revise ; alter 《the text》 dishonestly ; falsify 《a receipt》 ; cook 《the books》 《속》 ; juggle 《figures》

개찰 開札 opening of the bids〔tenders〕 ━하다 open (the bids)

개찰 改札 the examination of tickets ; [철도에서] punching ━하다 examine 〔punch〕 tickets

─ 가위 a ticket punch ; (a pair of) cancels ─원(員) a ticket examiner 〔clipper, puncher〕

개찰구 改札口 a (platform) wicket ; a ticket gate ; a gate

개창 疥瘡 the itch ⇨ 옴

†개척 開拓 [개간] cultivation ; clearing ; [자원의] exploitation ; development ; colonization ━하다 bring under cultivation ; reclaim 《wasteland》 ; clear ; develop ; exploit ; colonize ¶ 진로를 개척하다 carve out a future // 새로운 시장을 개척하다 open up〔find〕 a new market // 운명을 개척하다 improve one's lot ; carve out a fortune // 황무지를 개척하다 reclaim wasteland // 사업의 새로운 분야를 개척하다 open a new field of enterprise

개척민 開拓民 a colonist ; a settler ; a frontiersman

개척사 開拓史 a history of settlement 〔colonization〕

개척 사업 開拓事業 reclamation 〔exploitation〕 work

개척자 開拓者 [이주자] a colonist ; a settler ; [새로운 분야의] a pioneer ; a trail blazer ; a pathfinder

─ 정신 the pioneer〔frontier〕 spirit

개척지 開拓地 reclaimed land ; a settlement area ; a clearing

개천 開川 a creek ; a rivulet ; a small stream ; a streamlet ; an open sewer 〔ditch〕

개천에서 용 난다 속담 It is a case of a black hen laying white eggs.

개천가 開川─ by a brook

*개천절 開天節 the Foundation Day of Korea

개청 開廳 inauguration ; opening (of an office) ━하다 inaugurate ; open (a government) office

‡개체 個體, 箇體 an individual

─ 관념 〖논리〗 an individual concept ─군(群) 〖동물〗 population ─ 발생(發生) 〖생물〗 ontogeny ─ 변이(變異) individual variation ─성(性) individuality 전(全)─ 수(數) population

개체 改替 [바꿈] (a) change ; (an) exchange ; swapping ; [새것과] (a) renewal ; replacing ━하다 exchange 〔change, swap, barter〕 《one thing for another》 ; [새것과] renew ; replace 《one thing by〔with〕 another》 ; substitute 《one thing for another》

개초 蓋草 [이엉] thatch ; [이기] thatching ; roofing with thatch ━하다 thatch 《a roof》 ; roof with thatch

†개최 開催 ━하다 hold〔have〕 《a meeting》 ; open 《an exhibition》 ¶ 개최중이다 be open ; be in session (회의) // 회의는 워싱턴에서 개최중이다 The conference is now meeting〔in session〕 in Washington. // 월드컵은 4년에 한 번씩 다른 나라에서 개최된다 The World Cup is held every four years in a different country.

─국(國) the host country ─ 기간 [박람회·견본 등의] the period in which 《an exhibition, a trade fair》 is held ; [기간] a term ; a period ─일(日) the day fixed for a meeting ; a fixture (경기·경마의) ─지(地) the site 《of an exposition》 ; the location 《of a conference》 ; a venue 《of an exposition, for a conference》

개축 改築 rebuilding ; reconstruction ; remodeling ━하다 rebuild ; remodel ; reconstruct ¶ 개축중이다 be under reconstruction // 낡은 건물을 개축하다 remodel an old building

─ 공사 rebuilding〔reconstruction〕 works ─비 the expenses of rebuilding〔reconstruction〕

개칠 改漆 ① [글씨 획을] correction ; retouch ② [칠을] repainting ; recoating

개칭 改稱 the change of a title〔name, designation〕 ━하다 change the name 〔title〕 ; rename ; retitle ¶ …으로 개칭되다 the name〔title, designation〕 is changed 《to》

개키다 fold (up) ¶ 옷을 개키다 fold one's clothes // 이부자리를 개키다 fold up the bedding

개탄 慨歎 deploring ; lamentation ; regret ━하다 deplore ; lament ; grieve ; regret ¶ 개탄할 deplorable ; lamentable ; regrettable // 개탄할 행위 deplorable〔lamentable〕 conduct // 시대의 병폐를 개탄하다 deplore the evils of the time // 개탄을 금할 수 없다 It is most deplorable 《that》 ; It is really a matter for regret 《that》

개탕 a groove ; a quirk ¶ 개탕치다 groove ; make a groove in

─ 대패 a groover ; a grooving plane ─ 톱 a grooving saw

*개통 開通 opening to traffic ━하다 [도로가] be opened to〔for〕 traffic ; [불통선이] be reopened for service〔communication〕 ¶ 불통 구간은 5시간 후 개통됐다 The damaged section was restored〔reopened to traffic〕 five hours later. // 두 나라 사이에 국제 전화가 개통되었다 International telephone service between the two countries has been started.

─ 구간 a section open to〔for〕 traffic 〔in operation〕

개통식 開通式 an opening ceremony 《of a railroad》

개판 utter confusion or disorder ; a

mess ; a jumble ¶ 개판이 되다 fall into utter confusion // 회의라는 게 질서도 없이 온통 개판이다 The meeting fell into disorder and a complete mess.

개판 改— [씨름에서] a run-off bout ; a deciding〔the final〕 bout〔round〕 in wrestling

개판 改版 revision ; [개판본] a revised edition **—하다** revise 《the old edition》 ; issue a revised〔new〕 edition

개판 蓋板 a shingle

개펄 slime along the bank of an inlet ; silt at an estuary

개편 改編 reorganization ; reform ; modification **—하다** reorganize ; [책을] reedit ¶ 교과서를 개편하다 re-edit a textbook // 당직 개편 reorganization of a party's hierarchy // 인사 개편 a reshuffle of offices // 기구를 개편하다 reorganize a structure // 정부 기구의 개편 reorganization of government setups
내각 — a Cabinet reshuffle

개평 a winner's tip to losers or onlookers in gambling ; a free share of the winnings ¶ 개평주다 give away a share of one's winnings ; give a cut // 개평을 얻다 get the winner's tip
개평 떼다 관용 take away the winner's tip

개평 概評 a general review〔comment〕 ; an overall criticism **—하다** give a general comment on ; give an overall criticism 《of》

개평 開平 evolution

개평 개립 開平開立 evolution and involution

개평근 開平根 the square root

개평꾼 onlookers expecting some of the money given away by the gamblers

개평방 開平方 〖수학〗 evolution

개폐 開閉 opening and shutting〔closing〕 **—하다** open and shut〔close〕
—소(所) a switching station **— 신호기** a switch signal **—실(室)** a switchgear room **— 운동** opening and closing movement **— 장치** switchgear **— 회로** a keying circuit **자동 —기** an automatic switch **자동 — 장치** an automatic switchgear

개폐 改廢 alteration(s) and abolition(s) ; reorganization ; a change **—하다** reorganize ; make a change on ¶ 부내 기구의 개폐를 단행하다 reorganize 《a Ministry》 ; carry out the reorganization of 《a Ministry》

개폐교 開閉橋 [가동교] a drawbridge ; [도개교] a balance〔bascule〕 bridge ; [선회교] a swing bridge

개폐기 開閉器 〖전기〗 a switch

개폐 운동 開閉運動 〖식물〗 opening and closing movement

개표 開票 the official counting of votes ; ballot counting ; official canvass of the votes 《미》 **—하다** count the ballots〔votes〕 ; open the ballot boxes ; make a canvass 《of the votes》 《미》 ¶ 개표의 결과 on the votes counted // 감시인 입회하에 개표하다 count the votes with witnesses attending
— 감시인 a supervisor of ballot counting **— 결과** election returns

개표소 開票所 a ballot-counting place

개표 참관인 開票參觀人 a ballot-counting witness

개풀 plants growing on the tidal flat

개피떡 a rice-cake stuffed with bean jam

개학 開學 starting school (after a vacation) ; the beginning of school **—하다** begin school ; 《school》 begin
—식 the opening ceremony of the school year〔term〕 **—일** the opening day of the school year〔term〕

개항 開港 the opening of a port **—하다** open a port 《to foreign trade》

개항장 開港場 an open port ; a treaty port

개헌 改憲 an amendment to the constitution ; a constitutional amendment〔revision, reform〕 **—하다** amend〔revise, reform〕 the constitution
— 운동 a movement for constitutional amendment **— 저지 투쟁(沮止鬪爭)** fight against the constitutional amendment〔revision〕

개헌안 改憲案 a bill for amending the constitution

개헤엄 the dog paddle ¶ 개헤엄치다 dog paddle ; swim with the dog paddle

⁑**개혁 改革** reform ; reformation **—하다** reform ; carry out a reform ¶ 낡은 제도를 개혁하다 reform the obsolete system // 종교 개혁 religious reformation ; 〖역사〗 the Reformation // 근본적인 개혁을 단행하다 make a radical〔drastic〕 reform ; reform from top to bottom
대(大)— a large reform ; a shakeup 《미》 **사회 —** social reform **행정 —** administrative reform

개혁안 改革案 a reform bill

개혁자 改革者 a reformer

개호 改號 changing one's pen name〔nom de plume 《프》〕

개호주 〖동물〗 a tiger cub

⁑**개화 開化** enlightenment ; civilization **—하다** become civilized〔enlightened〕 ¶ 개화한 civilized ; enlightened // 개화된 나라 a civilized country // 개화된 국민 civilized people // 문명 개화의 시대 a civilized age

개화 開花 blooming ; efflorescence **—하다** come〔burst〕 into bloom ; bloom ; flower ¶ 문명의 개화 the flowering〔efflorescence〕 of civilization
— 촉진 호르몬 florigen

개화기 開花期 the time of flowering ; the flowering time〔season〕
개화 사상 開化思想 The Enlightenment Thought
개화인 開化人 a civilized person
개활 開豁 —하다 [트임] (be) wide open ; [마음이] broad-minded ; open-hearted ; liberal ¶ 개활한 평야 a vastly open land
개황 概況 an overall condition ; a general situation ; an outlook ¶ 일기 개황 a general weather outlook
개회 開會 the opening of a meeting ; opening a session —하다 open the meeting〔session〕; go into session ¶ 개회를 선언하다 call the meeting to order ; declare the meeting open // 개회 중이다 be in session ; be sitting (의회)
—일 the opening day
개회사 開會辭 an opening address
개회식 開會式 the opening ceremony
개흘레 〖건축〗 an alcove ; [교미] the copulation of dogs
개흙 mud〔slime〕 on the bank of an inlet ; silt at an estuary
객 客 ① [손님] a guest ⇨ 손 ② [덧붙음] extra ; superfluous ; uncalled for
—어(語) 〖논리〗 the predicate (빈사) ; 〖문법〗 an object (목적어) 일등 선— a first-class〔cabin〕 passenger 일반— 《총칭》 [백화점·상점의] the ordinary buying public
객 客 extra ; additional ; needless ; useless ¶ 객식구 a hanger-on // 객소리 idle talk
객 客 a certain person ¶ 불청객 an uninvited guest // 환영객 an invited guest
객거 客居 staying away from home ; living in a strange place —하다 stay〔live〕 away from home
객고 客苦 discomforts of a person who is away from home ¶ 객고에 시달리다 be travel-worn ; be wayworn
객공 客工 ① [임시 직공] a temporary worker ② [객공잡이] a timeworker ; a pieceworker
객관 客觀 [객관성] objectivity ; [대상] the object
—법(法) an objective method —식 시험 ⇨ 객관적 테스트 — 정세 the objective situation〔circumstances〕
객관 가치설 客觀價値說 theory of objective values
객관 묘사 客觀描寫 objective description
객관성 客觀性 objectivity
객관적 客觀的 objective ¶ 객관적으로 objectively // 비객관적인 nonobjective // 객관적으로 보다 view〔look at〕 《a matter》 objectively ; take an objective view 《of》 // 객관적으로 관찰하다 make an objective observation // 객관적으로 자신을 보기는 어렵다 It is not easy for us to see ourselves as others see us.
객관적 가치 客觀的價値 objective validity
개관적 관념론 客觀的觀念論 objective idealism
객관적 도덕 客觀的道德 objective morality
객관적 비평 客觀的批評 objective criticism
객관적 타당성 客觀的妥當性 objective validity
객관적 테스트 客觀的— an objective test
객관주의 客觀主義 objectivism
—자 an objectivist
객관화 客觀化 objectification
객귀 客鬼 the ghost of a man who died while staying abroad
객기 客氣 ill-advised bravery ; rashness ; blind daring
객기를 부리다 관용 be carried away by ill-advised bravery
객년 客年 last year
객담 客談 idle talk ; bosh 《구》 ; an uncalled-for remark —하다 waste words ; make an uncalled-for remark ¶ 객담이나 하며 시간을 보내다 idle away one's time gossiping
객담 客痰 expectoration ; phlegm ; sputum —하다 expectorate 《phlegm》 ; cough up phlegm
객담 검사 喀痰檢査 the examination of one's sputum
객동 客冬 last winter
객랍 客臘 last December
객반위주 客反爲主 putting the last before the first ; putting the cart before the horse
객비 客費 [객쩍은] wasteful expenses ; [객지의] expenses (of a traveler) ; travel expenses
객사 客死 —하다 die while staying away from home〔sojourning abroad〕; die in a foreign land ¶ 그는 로마에서 객사했다 He passed away during his stay in Rome.
객사 客舍 a hotel ; an inn
객상 客商 a (travelling) merchant
객상 客床 an extra meal prepared for a guest ; a guest (dining-)table
객석 客席 a seat for a guest ¶ 회관에 2,000개의 객석이 있다 The hall seats〔has seats for〕 2,000. // 객석을 꽉 메운 청중 a full house
객선 客船 a passenger boat〔steamer〕
객설 客說 useless talk ⇨ 객소리
객소리 客— an uncalled-for〔unnecessary〕 remark ; idle〔useless〕 talk ; bosh ; prattle ; tattle ¶ 객소리마라 Quit your idle talk ! /Don't talk bosh ! / Humbug !
객수 客水 ① [바라지도 않는 때에 내리는 비] unwanted〔unwelcome〕 rain

② [다른 데서 들어온 겉물] unwanted water
③ [끼니때 이외에 마시는 물] water drunk at times other than meal times
객수 客愁 homesickness ; nostalgia ¶ 객수를 달래다 console the weary heart of a traveler
객스럽다 客— (be) unnecessary ; useless ; be〔seem〕 out of place ; uncalled-for
객승 客僧 a traveling priest (monk)
객식구 客食口 a temporary addition to a family ; a hanger-on 《구》
*객실 客室 [배의] a stateroom ; passenger quarters ; [여관의] a guest room ; [가정의] a drawing room ; a parlor 《미》
— 담당자〔주임, 계원〕 (호텔의) a room clerk — 승무원 a cabin steward, stewardess
객연 客演 guest appearance
객원 客員 a guest〔an honorary〕 member ; a non-regular member ¶ 객원 지휘자 a guest conductor // 객원으로 초빙되어 온 학자 a guest scholar (visiting)
객원 강사 客員講師 a visiting lecturer
객원 교수 客員教授 a guest〔visiting〕 professor
객월 客月 last month
객인 客人 [손님] a guest ; [객쩍은 사람] a person of no importance ; a nobody ; an insignificant person
객정 客情 a traveler's lonely feelings
객주 客主 [거간] a commission agency ; [객줏집 (주인)] a peddler's inn ; (the keeper of) an inn for merchants〔traveling salesmen〕
객줏집 客主— a peddlers' inn ; a commission agency home
객중 客中 while one is away from home on a trip ; on one's journey ; en route 《프》 ; in transit
객지 客地 a strange land where one is staying on a trip ; one's stopping place on a journey ; a foreign land ¶ 객지에서 away from home ; in a strange land // 나는 5년 동안 객지 생활을 했다 I have lived for five years in a foreign land. // 객지 생활도 벌써 10년째 접어들었다 It's already 10 years since I took up residence in the foreign land. // 객지에서 병들었다 I was taken ill while travelling.
객쩍다 (be) uncalled-for ; be out of place ; (be) useless ; officious ; pert ¶ 객쩍은 소리를 하다 make uncalled-for 〔impertinent, uninvited〕 remarks // 객쩍은 소리 그만하고 속마음을 털어놓아라 Stop talking nonsense and come to the point.
객차 客車 a (railway) passenger coach ; a (railroad) passenger coach 《미》 ¶ 객차 편으로 보내다 send 《a package》 by passenger train
— 수입 passenger traffic receipts 특별 — a family saloon ; a parlor car (고급)
객체 客體 ① 〖법·철학〗 the object ¶ 범죄의 객체 the object of a crime // 영토와 국민은 국가의 객체이다 The territory and people are the objects of the state. ② a person who is away on a journey〔(far) away from home〕
객체계 客體界 the phenomenal world
객초 客草 tobacco〔cigarettes〕 for guests
객추 客秋 last autumn
객춘 客春 last spring
객토 客土 the soil brought from another place (to improve the soil)
객향 客鄕 a strange land ; a place 〔town, city〕 where one stays as a stranger ; a foreign land ¶ 객향에서 away from home ; in a strange land
객혈 喀血 hemoptysis ; a hemorrhage of the lungs —하다 spit〔cough up〕 blood ; have a hemorrhage of the lungs
객회 客懷 homesickness ; nostalgia ; a traveler's lonely feelings ; one's feelings while away from home〔in a strange place〕
갠지스 강 —江 the Ganges
갤러리 a picture〔an art〕 gallery
*갤런 a gallon ¶ 1갤런으로 10마일을 달리다 do ten miles to the gallon
갬대 a wooden weeding knife
*갭 a gap ¶ 갭을 메우다 bridge the gap ; supply〔fill, stop〕 a gap // 갭을 줄이다 close a gap // 갭이 생기게 하다 make〔leave〕 a gap // 두 사람의 관점에는 큰 갭이 있다 There is a wide gap between the viewpoints of the two.
갭직하다 (be) a bit light (in weight)
갯가 the shore of an estuary〔inlet〕
갯가재 〖동물〗 a squilla ; a mantis crab
갯값 a dirt-cheap〔dog-cheap〕 price ; a ridiculously〔absurdly〕 cheap price ¶ 갯값으로 at a sacrifice ; for a mere song // 갯값으로 팔다 sell at a loss〔sacrifice, cut-rate price〕 ; sacrifice ; dump // 갯값이다 be absurdly low (in price) // 배추 값이 갯값으로 폭락하다 The price of cabbage dropped sharply.
갯고랑 a small channel of tidewater on the shore of an inlet
갯골 ⇨ 갯고랑
갯마을 sea-side (fishing) villages
갯물 [해수] the salt water of an estuary 〔inlet〕 ; [개] an estuary ; an inlet
갯바람 a wind blowing from the sea ; a sea breeze
갯밭 a field along the shore of an estuary
갯버들 〖식물〗 a pussy willow
갯장어 —長魚 〖생물〗 a pike conger ; a pike eel
갯지렁이 〖동물〗 a lugworm ; a lob-

worm ; a clam worm ; a nereid
갱 a gangster 《미》 ; a gunman ; a gang 《of robbers》 《총칭》 ¶ 갱 영화 a gangster film
갱 坑 [수직으로 된] a pit ; a shaft ; [갱도] a drift ; a gallery ; [사금광의] a drain
갱구 坑口 a pithead ; a minehead ; a pit mouth ; a bank
갱내 坑內 (inside) a mining pit〔shaft〕 ¶ 갱내로 들어가다 go down a pit // 갱내를 순시하다 inspect a mine
— **가스** mine gas — **감독** a mine foreman — **권양기〔윈치〕** a mine hoist — **궤도(軌道)** a pit line ; a mine track — **사고** a mine accident —**수(水)** mine water — **화재** a pit〔an underground〕 fire
갱내 노무자 坑內勞務者 a pit worker ; an underground worker
갱내 작업 坑內作業 pit〔inside〕 labor ; underground work
갱내 채굴 坑內採掘 pit〔underground〕 digging
갱년기 更年期 the turn〔change〕 of life ; climacteric ; [여성의] the menopause ¶ 갱년기의 변화 climacteric changes
갱년기 장애 更年期障碍 a menopausal disorder
갱도 坑道 [가로로 된] a gallery ; a drift ; a level ; [세로로 된] a shaft 〔pit〕 ; [굴] a tunnel ; 〖군사〗 a mine ¶ 갱도를 파다 mine〔drive〕 《into rock》 // 갱도가 무너져 광부들이 갇혔다 The miners were trapped by the collapse of the tunnel roof.
— **작업** drift work — **지주(支柱)** timbering **주(主)**— a gangway
갱독 更讀 rereading
갱목 坑木 a mine post〔pillar〕 ; pit wood ; mine timber ; a (mine〔pit〕) prop
갱미 粳米 nonglutinous rice
갱부 坑夫 a miner ; a mine worker ¶ 갱부로서 일하다 work in a mine
—**병** miner's disease — **십장** a foreman ; a reeve 《영·방》
갱생 更生 revival ; regeneration ; rebirth ; resuscitation ; renaissance ; [고풍의] rejuvenation —**하다** revive ; be born again ; start life anew ; be regenerated ; rejuvenate ¶ 범죄자의 갱생 the rehabilitation of an offender // 갱생시키다 regenerate 《a person》 // 갱생의 길을 걷다 start a new life
— **보호 시설** relief and rehabilitation facilities ; facilities for the relief and rehabilitation 《of criminal offenders》 — **운동** a movement for regeneration ; [개인의] a career renovation movement — **원(院)** a rehabilitation center ; a juvenile guidance center **자력** — rehabilitation by one's own efforts ; self-rehabilitation
갱생 고무 更生— reclaimed rubber
갱생 보호 更生保護 relief and rehabilitation
갱생 사위 更生— an opportunity for a narrow escape〔for revival〕
갱생 지도 更生指導 rehabilitation guidance
갱소년 更少年 growing younger ; rejuvenation —**하다** grow younger ; be rejuvenated
갱스터 gangster
갱신 更新 renewal ; renovation ; innovation —**하다** renew ; renovate ¶ 기록을 갱신하다 make a new record // 생산 실적이 날로 갱신되다 The production rate〔productivity〕 is breaking the record each day.
갱신못하다 be too tired to stir ; be too exhausted to move about ; cannot stir 〔move〕 a muscle 《from exhaustion》
갱엿 black taffy
갱외 坑外 ¶ 갱외에(서)〔의〕 out of the pit
— **노무자** an out-of-pit〔a grass, a surface 《미》〕 worker — **설비** surface equipment — **작업** mine work done at the surface ; surface work 《미》
갱외부 坑外夫 an out-of-pit〔a grass, a surface 《미》〕 worker
갱지 更紙 pulp paper ; rough (printing) paper
갱지미 a brass soup-bowl (for children)
갱충쩍다 (be) careless and stupid ; negligent ; rash ; indiscreet ; imprudent ; sloppy ; slovenly
갸기 pride ; arrogance ; haughtiness
갸기부리다 be proud〔arrogant, haughty〕 ; swagger
갸륵하다 (be) admirable ; exemplary ; laudable ; commendable ; praiseworthy ; glorious ; gallant ; to be commended ¶ 갸륵히 laudably ; commendably // 갸륵한 일 nice work ; a fine job ; a good deed // 갸륵한 행실 exemplary behavior ; good conduct // 갸륵한 마음씨 a commendable purpose // 갸륵한 젊은이 an admirable youth // 갸륵한 일을 하다 do a good deed
갸름하다 (be) small and longish ; pleasantly oval ; nicely slender ¶ 갸름한 얼굴 an oval face
갸우듬하다 (be) somewhat slanted ⇨ 기우듬하다
갸우뚱 moving slantwise ¶ 갸우뚱거리다 (-대다) move slantwise again and again // 고개를 갸우뚱하다 nod the head slantwise
갸울다 (be) slanted ; sinking〔drooping〕 ; declining ⇨ 기울다
갸울어뜨리다 tip over on one side
갸울이다 bend ; tip 《the bottle》

갸웃 ¶ 갸웃거리다 peek 《into》; snoop around
갸자 a large food-box with bearers' side poles
갹금 醵金 collection of funds; raising of money; [기부금] a contribution; a subscription **—하다** raise money; collect funds; collect contributions〔subscriptions〕; raise a subscription; pass round the hat; make up a purse; [기부하다] contribute; subscribe; donate 〔give〕 《money, a thing, service》 toward 《relieving the needy》 ¶ 사원 일동이 갹금하여 고인의 유족에게 증정했다 Contributions were collected from the staff for the bereaved family.
갹출 醵出 (a) donation; offering a share of money; chipping in; (a) contribution **—하다** donate; chip in; contribute ¶ 야유회 비용을 갹출하다 chip in for a picnic
갸쭉하다 (be) longish; somewhat 〔rather〕 long ¶ 얼굴이 갸쭉하다 have an oval face
갸쯔막하다 (be) rather long and slender
갸쯤하다 (be) quite longish
갸찍하다 (be) rather long
거[1] [그것] Well! ; Why! ; There! ¶ 거 참 안됐다 Oh, that's too bad! // 거 참 아름답다 Why, that's beautiful. // 거 참 기가 막히게 좋구나 Why, that's awfully nice!
거[2] [거기] 문 밖에 거 뉘시오 Who is there outside? /Is there somebody outside?
거 車 vehicle; carriage; chariot
거가 車駕 [수레] the royal carriage 〔coach〕; [행차] a royal trip
거가 擧家 the whole family
거가 대족 巨家大族 a distinguished and powerful〔influential〕 family; a mighty clan
거각 소권 拒却訴權 〖법〗 the right to refuse another's demand and to raise a lawsuit
거간 居間 [일] brokerage; [사람] a broker; a middleman; an agent **—하다** act as a broker; do (the) brokerage
거간꾼 居間— a broker; a middleman; an agent
집〔토지〕 — a house〔land〕 agent〔broker〕; a real-estate agent
거개 擧皆 ① [거의 모두, 대부분] the greater〔most〕 part; the majority〔bulk〕 ¶ 승무원은 거개가 중노동과 굶주림으로 죽었다 Most of the crew died from hard work and hunger. // 이 동네 사람들은 거개가 농민이다 Most of the people of this village are farmers.
② [부사적 용법] for the most part; in the main; most; almost all; mostly ¶ 큰불이 나서 거개 불타 버렸다 Most of the houses were burnt down in a big fire.
거거년 去去年 the year before last
거거 익심 去去益甚 —하다 go from bad to worse; be worse than ever; be worse and worse (as time goes on)
거경 巨鯨 a big whale
거골 距骨 the ankle; the anklebone; the astragalus
거괴 巨魁 a ringleader; a chief; a boss ¶ 폭도의 거괴 the ringleader of the rioters
거구 巨軀 a massive figure; a big frame ¶ 6척 40관의 거구 a massive figure of 6 ft. in stature and 360 pounds in weight
거국 擧國 the whole country〔nation〕
거국 일치 擧國一致 national unity; a united front; the whole nation in a body ¶ 거국 일치하여 일어섰다 The nation rose〔stood up〕 as one man. // 거국일치하여 정부의 정책을 지지했다 The whole nation supported the government policy.
거국 일치 내각 擧國一致內閣 a cabinet supported by the whole nation; a pan-national cabinet; a broadly based cabinet
거국적 擧國的 nationwide ¶ 거국적으로 on a nationwide scale; throughout〔all over〕 the country // 거국적으로 정부의 정책을 지지했다 The whole nation supported〔The people gave solid support to〕 the government policy. // 그들은 거국적으로 대통령을 환영했다 The whole nation welcomed the president.
거금 巨金 a large〔big〕 sum (of money); a pile of money ¶ 거금 천만 원 as much as〔no less than〕 ten million won; a cool ten million won 《구》 // 거금을 들여 학교를 세우다 use a huge sum of money to found a school
거금 距今 ago; back from today ¶ 거금 1,000년 전 one thousand years ago
거금 醵金 collection of funds ⇨ 갹금(醵金)
***거기** ① [장소] that place; there; [거기에] there; to that place; thither ¶ 거기서부터 from there; (from) thence; whence // 어이 거기 가는 친구 Hi! You there! // 거기서 기다려라 Wait there. // 거기까지 한 시간에 걸어갈 수 있다 I can walk there〔to that place〕 in an hour. // 거기에는 누군가가 있었다 There was someone there.
② [그 일·그 정도] that; so far〔to that extent〕; then; thereupon ¶ 거기가 문제야 That is the question〔trouble〕. // 거기까지는 생각 못했는걸 I never thought of that. // 거기까지는 좋았지만… So far so good, 《but》 // 거기까지는 인정한다 I admit so much. // 길을 잃었는데 거기에

다 비마저 오기 시작했다 I lost my way and, what was worse, it began to rain.

*거꾸러뜨리다 ① [넘어뜨리다] make fall head first〔foremost〕; make fall flat 〔headlong〕; throw〔bring〕 down ; knock down (때려서) ¶ 다리를 걸어서 거꾸러뜨리다 trip《a person》 up // 너쯤 거꾸러뜨리기는 쉬운 일이야 It's a cinch to get you down. /It's an easy job to throw you to the ground.
② [지우다] beat ; defeat ; [망치다] overthrow ; ruin ; upset ; destroy ¶ 내각을 거꾸러뜨리다 overthrow〔unseat〕 the Cabinet // 선수권자를 거꾸러뜨리다 beat〔topple〕 a champion // 독재자를 거꾸러뜨려라 Down with the dictator !
③ [죽이다] kill ; do away with ; put《a person》 to death

*거꾸러지다 ① [엎어지다] fall head first 〔foremost〕; fall flat〔headlong〕; fall (down) ; tumble down ¶ 땅에 거꾸러지다 fall to the ground ; fall down on the ground // 술에 취하여 거꾸러지다 collapse〔fall down〕 dead-drunk // 앞으로 거꾸러지다 fall forward // 지쳐서 거꾸러지다 break down from exhaustion ; break down from〔through〕 overwork // 큰 대자로 거꾸러지다 fall flat ; fall full length ; measure one's length on the ground // 그는 실신하여 한길에 거꾸러져 있었다 He was found lying unconscious on the road.
② [지다] be defeated〔beaten〕; lose《a battle》; [망하다] be overthrown 〔upset〕; be ruined ; go to ruin ; perish ¶ 거꾸러져 가는 회사 a company on the verge of bankruptcy // 은행이 거꾸러졌다 The bank failed. // 적은 드디어 거꾸러졌다 The enemy fell〔collapsed〕 at last.
③ [죽다] die ; succumb《to a disease》 ¶ 암으로 거꾸러지다 die of〔from〕 cancer ; succumb〔fall a victim〕 to cancer // 거꾸러져라 Drop dead ! /Go to hell〔the devil〕!

‡거꾸로 topsy-turvy ; inside〔the wrong side〕 out ; headlong ; head over heels ; (in) the wrong way ; the other way (about) ; reversely ; inversely ; [위아래를] upside down ; bottom(-side) up ; [좌우를] the right side to the left ; [오히려] instead ; on the contrary ¶ 총을 거꾸로 들고 with reversed arms // 우표를 거꾸로 붙이다 attach a stamp the wrong side up // 연필을 거꾸로 쥐다 hold a pencil by the wrong end // 젓가락을 거꾸로 들다 hold one's chopsticks upside down // ABC를 거꾸로 말하다 say the alphabet backward // 이 어구는 거꾸로 읽으면 알 수 있다 This phrase may be understood when it is read bottom up. // 자네는 일을 거꾸로 하고 있네 You are putting the cart before the horse there. // 주인이 하인의 비위를 맞추는 것은 거꾸로 된 일이다 It's topsy-turvy for a master to humor his maid. // 그의 말을 거꾸로 받아들이게 Interpret his remarks by contraries.
거꾸로 박히다 [관용] fall on one's head ; fall head foremost〔headlong〕

거나 whether...or ; [양보] whatever ; however ; whenever ¶ (너야) 좋아하거나 말거나 Whether you like it or not. // 비가 오거나 말거나 모임에 참석하겠다 I will attend the meeting whether〔if〕 it rains or not. // 네가 누구를 좋아하거나 난 상관없다 I don't mind whomever you like. // 손뼉을 치거나 큰 소리로 웃거나 하지 마시오 Don't slap your hands or laugh loudly.

거나하다 (be) tipsy ; mellow ; hazy ; happy ; slightly〔partly〕 intoxicated 〔drunk〕; look gay with drink ; have a drop in one's eye ¶ 거나하게 취하다 be pleasantly drunk // 자리를 뜰 때 이미 그는 거나해 있었다 He was already warm with wine when he rose from the seat.

거냉 去冷 ─하다 warm〔heat〕 up 《liquor》; take the chill off ¶ 거냉만 하시오 Just warm it up a little.

거년 去年 last year

거년스럽다 (be) shabby

*거느리다 head ; lead ; command ; have 《a subordinate, a person》 with one ; be with〔accompanied by〕 one's subordinates ¶ 처자를 거느리다 have a wife and children ; head a family // 백만 대군을 거느리다 command a large army // 암탉이 병아리들을 거느리다 a hen leads a brood of chickens // 부하 다섯을 거느리고 with〔accompanied by〕 five subordinates // 많은 동조자를 거느리고 있는 정치 지도자 a political leader with a large following // 많은 식구를 거느리고 있다 He has a large family to support〔provide for〕. // 이순신 장군은 작은 함대를 거느리고 왜군의 침략을 저지했다 Admiral *Yi Sun-shin*, commanding his small fleet, succeeded in checking the Japanese aggression.

거느림채 an outhouse ; an outbuilding ; an annex ; a detached house

거늑하다 (be) sufficient ; ample ; abundant ; enough

거늘 ① [이미 …한데] now that ; since ; as ; on〔upon〕 ¶ 이제 그의 심중을 알았거늘 어찌하려는가 Now that you know his mind, what do you plan to do ?
② […지만] although ; while ¶ 형제들이 다 상당한 재산을 가졌거늘 그만이 가난하다 He has remained poor, while all his brothers are quite rich.

거니 ① […한데, …인데] ¶ 돈이 없거니 그것을 어찌 사랴 Since we have no

money, we can't buy it. ② [기대·예상] ¶ 저녁은 잘 먹겠거니 생각하고 점심은 간단히 먹었다 He ate a light lunch in expectation of a good dinner.

거니와 as well as ; not only... but also... ; besides ; admitting that ; but ¶ 그 문제는 그렇거니와 apart from this question ; setting〔leaving〕 aside this question // 얼굴도 곱거니와 마음씨도 곱다 She has a lovely disposition as well as a pretty face. /She has not only a pretty face but also a lovely disposition.

거니채다 sense ; perceive ; become aware of ; suspect

‡거닐다 walk〔stroll〕 (aimlessly) ; saunter (leisurely) ; wander about ; loiter ; ramble ¶ 거리를 거닐다 stroll through the streets // 토요일 오후에 그녀와 명동을 거닐었다 I took a stroll along the *Myŏngdong* (street) with her saturday afternoon.

거담 祛痰 the discharge of phlegm **—하다** loosen〔discharge〕 phlegm

거담약 祛痰藥 an expectorant

거담제 祛痰劑 ⇨ 거담약

거당 擧黨 the whole party

거당적 擧黨的 of the whole party

†거대 巨大 —하다 (be) huge ; gigantic ; enormous ; immense ; mammoth ; massive ; colossal ; monstrous ; Titanic ; stupendous ¶ 거대한 건물 a massive〔colossal〕 building // 거대한 바다의 괴물 a monster of the deep

거대 도시 巨大都市 a megalopolis

거대증 巨大症 〖의학〗 gigantism ; giantism

거덕거덕, 꺼덕꺼덕 being damp-dried **—하다** (be) damp-dried

거덕치다, 꺼떡치다 (be) awkward ; be out of place ; (be) unbecoming ; unseemly ; indecent

거덜거덜하다 (be) unsteady ; tottering ; shaky ; be about to fall ; (be) broken ; limping ¶ 거덜거덜하는 건물 a tottering building

거덜나다 collapse ; crumble ; break down ; go to pieces ; [결딴나다] be ruined ; fail ; burst 《속》 ; [파산하다] go bankrupt〔into bankruptcy〕 ; go broke 《속》 ¶ 사업이 거덜나다 His business went broke. // 살림이 거덜나다 His livelihood failed. // 최근의 불경기로 그 은행은 거덜나고 말았다 The bank has failed owing to the recent business depression. // 한푼도 남김없이 거덜났다 I'm down to my last penny.

거도 巨盜 a great robber ; a robber baron

거독 去毒 removal〔neutralization〕 of poison in medical herbs ; detoxication **—하다** detoxicate 《medical herbs》

거동 去冬 last winter

***거동 擧動** [처신] conduct ; behavior ; manner ; carriage ; demeanor ; deportment ; [행동] action ; movements ; doings ¶ 거동을 주시하다 watch 《a person's》 movements ; keep an eye on 《a person》 // 거동이 신사답다 behave〔bear〕 oneself like a gentleman // 거동이 수상해서 경찰서에 연행되었다 He was taken to the police station on account of his suspicious behavior.

거두 巨頭 a prominent leader ; a magnate ; a prominent figure ; a big shot〔bug, whale, name〕 《미·속》 ; a tycoon ; a V. I. P. ¶ 재계의 거두 a leading financier // 정계의 거두 a political leader

— 회담 a top level conference **삼(三) — 회담** "Big Three" talks〔conference〕

***거두다** ① [모아들이다] gather ; collect ; get〔bring, put〕 together ; get in ; make a collection of ; harvest ; reap ¶ 기부금을 거두다 get in donations // 농작물을 거두다 harvest (a crop) ; reap〔gather in〕 a crop // 세금을 거두다 collect taxes ; levy

② [얻다] gain ; obtain ; earn ; achieve ¶ 훌륭한 성과를 거두다 obtain excellent results // 인내력이 있는 자가 최후의 승리를 거두는 법이다 Perseverance will prevail in the long run. // 회사는 투자에 대해서 겨우 1%의 이윤을 거두고 있다 The company is earning a bare one percent on its investment.

③ [돌보다] look after ; take care〔charge〕 of ; care for ; attend on ; see to ; mind ; tend ¶ 그 아이는 거두는 데 힘이 안 든다 The child is easy to look after. /The child gives little trouble. // 조부모님이 그 고아를 거두게 되었다 The orphan was left in the care of his grandparents. // 집안일을 알뜰히 거두다 tend a home ; take good care of a home

④ [모양내다] tidy up one's appearance ¶ 회의에 참석하기 전에 몸을 거두다 tidy up oneself before attending a conference

⑤ [그치다] stop ; end ; quit ; break〔leave〕 off ¶ 눈물을 거두다 stop crying ; dry one's tears // 숨을 거두다 die ; breathe one's last

‡거두어들이다 ¶ 곡식을 거두어들이다 gather〔get〕 in crops ; harvest crops

거두 절미 去頭截尾 ① [자름] cutting off the head and tail **—하다** cut off the head and tail 《of it》

② [요약] leaving out the introduction and the conclusion **—하다** leave out the introduction and the conclusion 《of》 ; make a short story 《of》 ; summarize

거둠질 harvesting ; reaping ; gathering ; collecting **—하다** harvest〔collect〕 ; do the harvesting

거둥 a royal visit ; a royal procession **—하다** pay a (royal) visit《to》;《the king》proceed outside the palace

거드럭거드럭, 꺼드럭꺼드럭 swaggeringly ; arrogantly ; with a dignified air

거드럭거리다, 꺼드럭거리다 swagger ; show off ; give oneself airs〔consequence〕; assume〔put on〕airs (of importance) ; stand on one's dignity ; put on (the) dog《미》¶ 거드럭거리면서 말하다 speak with an air of importance〔in a lordly manner〕// 거드럭거리면서 걷다 strut about ; walk with a dignified air ; swagger ; stalk about

거드름 a haughty attitude〔air, demeanor〕¶ 거드름스럽다 be arrogant ; be haughty ; be proud ; be overbearing ; be insolent ; be uppish《구》; be toplofty《미》// 거드름스럽게 걷다 strut〔swagger〕《about, along》

†**거드름부리다** assume a haughty attitude ; hold one's head high ; ride〔mount〕one's high horse

-거든 ① [가정] if ; when ; provided (that) ¶ 그를 만나거든 들러 달라고 전해다오 If〔Provided〕you meet him, tell him to call on me. // 다 썼거든 돌려주게나 Return it to me when you have done with it. // 작거든 큰 것으로 바꾸어라 If it is too small, change it with a bigger one. // 오시거든 방으로 모셔라 When he comes, bring him into the parlor. // 청소를 다하였거든 돌아가라 You may leave when you have done with cleaning.
② [하물며] still more ; how much more ¶ 개도 주인의 공을 알거든 하물며 사람에 있어서랴 If a dog is so faithful to its master, how much more should we human beings be ! // 어린 학생이 해내거든 큰 학생이 못 해낼까 If a little boy does it, how couldn't a big boy do it ?
③ [느낌꼴] surely ; indeed ¶ 참 좋거든 Yes, it surely is wonderful ! // 비가 참 많이 왔거든 It certainly did rain !

거든하다, 거뜬하다 (be) light ; nimble ; agile ; feel light ; feel good (몸이) ⇨ 가뜬하다

거들 a girdle

거들거리다 give oneself airs ⇨ 거드럭거리다

†**거들다** ① [도와주다] give《a person》a hand ; help ; aid ; assist ; support ; second ; stand by ¶ 일을 거들다 help《a person》in〔with〕his work // 남의 말을 거들다 second another's words // 아무도 거들어 줄 사람이 없다 I have not got anyone to help me. ② [남의 일에 참견하다] ¶ 자네가 거들고 나설 일이 아닐세 It's none of your business.

거들떠보다 lift one's eyes and look at《a person》; turn one's face ; glance up at ; notice ; pay attention to ; look toward《us》¶ 거들떠보지도 않고 without even〔so much as〕casting a look // 너 따위는 거들떠보지도 않을 거다 She will not even look〔glance up〕at you. // 책을 거들떠볼 사이가 없었다 I hadn't time to glance over the book.

***거들먹거리다** act rashly〔behave imprudently〕; being elated《by success》; let oneself go ¶ 거들먹거리면서 말하다 talk without reserve〔restraint〕// 거들먹거리면서 걷다 strut ; swagger

거듬거듬 desultorily ; roughly ; in a cursory〔desultory, slovenly〕way〔manner〕; skipping over ; without order ¶ 거듬거듬 다루다 handle roughly // 거듬거듬 싸다 wrap loosely // 거듬거듬 읽다 glance over《a letter》; run over《papers》; skim through《a letter》; take a cursory view of ; give《a thing》the once-over《미·구》

***거듭** (over) again ; once (and) again ; repeatedly ; anew **—하다** repeat ; do again ¶ 거듭 말씀드릴 것도 없이 needless to say again // 거듭 경고했음에도 in spite of repeated warnings // 손해를 거듭하다 suffer loss after loss ; sustain loss upon loss ; incur several losses // 판(版)을 거듭하다 go through several editions // 회의를 거듭하다 sit〔meet〕in conference several times // 거듭 말하거니와 다시는 그런 일이 없도록 해라 I repeat that you try not to do such a thing again. // 해를 거듭할수록 두고 온 고향 생각이 간절하다 As years go by, I feel more homesick.

거듭거듭 repeatedly ; over and over again ¶ 그는 같은 말을 거듭거듭 되뇌었다 He repeated the same words over and over again. // 거듭거듭 사과하다 I apologize to you once and again.

거듭나다 〖기독교〗 be born again ; be reborn ; come to life again ; resuscitate

거듭되다 repeat ¶ 실수가 거듭되다 repeat mistakes // 거듭된 실패를 극복하다 overcome repeated failures

거듭제곱 〖수학〗 (raising《a term》to a higher) power ; involution

거듭제곱근 一根 〖수학〗 a radical root

거란 契丹 〖역사〗 the Kitan〔Ch'itan, Khithai〕; a Tungustic people in Manchuria

거란지(뼈) the tailbone〔coccyx〕of an ox〔a cow〕

†**거래** 去來 business ; transaction ; dealings ; trade ; a deal《속》**—하다** do〔transact〕business with《a person》; trade in《an article》with《a person》; have an account with《a person》¶ 거래가 있다 have business relations《with》; have an account《with》; be connected in business dealings《with》

//거래를 트다 open an account with ((a person, a firm))//거래를 끊다 break off business relations ; close an account//사업상의 거래 business transactions ; the transaction of business//큰 거래를 하다 do a large (volume of) business //어제의 거래액은 약 150만원이었다 The turnover was about one and a half million *won* yesterday. //저희 회사와 거래해 주셔서 감사합니다 Thank you for your business. //우리와 거래를 해 주시면 절대로 실망하시지 않을 겁니다 Give us your business and you will never be let down. //당신하고 거래는 이것으로 마지막이다 This is the last time I'll ever do business with you.
— 가격 the market price ; the price agreed on — 건수 [주식] markings — 관계 business relations[connections] — 방법 the mode of dealing[transaction] — 안내 a store bulletin —일(日) a business day — 제한 restraint of trade — 조건 terms and conditions of business 공정 — fair trade[transactions] ; straight dealings ; a square deal 국내[지방, 외국] — home[local, foreign] trade 금전 — lending and borrowing money ; [매수] bribery ; payola ; a payoff scandal ; [이권 관련의] graft 무역[무역 외] — visible[invisible] trade 보통 — [주식] ordinary contracts 부정[불법] — illicit[shady, illegal, unlawful] traffic[transactions] 선물(先物) — forward transactions 신규(新規) — new business 신용 — credit transactions 증권 — transactions on the Stock Exchange 현금 — cash transactions

거래법 去來法 transaction regulations

거래소 去來所 an exchange ; [주식] a stock exchange[market]

거래소 세법 去來所稅法 the Exchange Tax Act

거래액 去來額 the volume of business ; the turnover

거래 은행 去來銀行 one's bank ; a bank with which one has an account

거래처 去來處 [고객] a customer ; a client ; [거래 관계자] a business acquaintance ; [전체] a (business) connection ; [지방에 있는] a correspondent

거량 擧揚 [불교] invocation of the spirit (of a dead person)

거레 loafing ; lingering ; dawdling **—하다** loaf ; linger ; ramble ; dawdle ; loiter ; dally

거론 擧論 —하다 make ((it)) a subject of discussion ; make ((it)) an object of criticism ¶ 행락철을 맞아 자연 보호 문제를 거론하다 raise an issue of environmental protection in the holiday season

거룡 巨龍 [고생물] a megalosaur

거루 a single-oar rowboat

***거룩하다** (be) divine ; sacred ; holy ; sublime ; solemn ; venerable ; [위대] great ; grand ; glorious ¶ 거룩하신 은혜 divine grace//거룩하신 가르침 holy teachings ; a sacred discourse//거룩한 정신 lofty[noble] spirit ; lofty sentiments//거룩한 자기 희생 sublime self-sacrifice//높고 거룩하신 분 the high and lofty One

거룻배 a single-oar boat

거류 去留 leaving and staying ; life and death ; things done and undone

거류 居留 residence ; residing **—하다** live ; reside ; dwell
— 외국인 a resident foreigner ; a foreign resident ; foreign community ((총칭))

거류민 居留民 residents

거류민단 居留民團 a settlement corporation

거류지 居留地 a foreign concession ; an international settlement ¶ 공동 거류지를 만들다 establish a common settlement

거르다¹ [여과] filter ; leach ; strain ; percolate ¶ 모래로 물을 거르다 filter water through sand//불순물을 거르다 filter out impurities//간장을 체로 거르다 strain soy sauce through a sieve//술을 체에 거르다 strain liquor through a sieve

거르다² [차례를] skip (over) ; omit ¶ 하루[이틀] 걸러 every other[third] day //한 줄씩 걸러 쓰다 write on every other line//책 한 부분을 거르다 skip over some parts of a book//오늘 점심은 거를 참이다 I am going to skip lunch today. //한 집 걸러 다음 집 the next door but one

***거름** manure ; muck ; dressing ; [화학 비료] fertilizer ; [인분] night soil ; [마분 따위] dung **—하다** manure ; fertilize ; dress ; muck ¶ 밭에 거름을 주다 manure a field ; fertilize the soil//나라의 거름이 되다 lay down[sacrifice] one's life for one's country

거름더미 a heap of manure

거름종이 filter paper

거름통¹ —桶 a night-soil bucket[pail] ; a honey bucket ((미·속)) ; a manure tub

거름통² —桶 a filter box

거름하다 manure ; fertilize ; dress ; muck

†**거리¹** a street ; a road ; a thoroughfare ; a town ; a quarter ¶ 거리의 천사 a homeless child ; a street urchin//거리의 불량배 street roughs[hooligans, hoodlums]//거리의 여인 a woman of the streets ; a streetwalker//거리의 도락사 a man of the town//거리의 소문 the talk of the town//샌프란시스코의 중국인 거리에 가 본 적이 있습니까 Have you ever been to the Chinese quarter in San Francisco ?

뒷— a back street〔lane〕

거리² ① [재료] material ; stuff ; makings ; substance ¶ 국거리 soup stock ; soup makings // 반찬거리 side dish makings

② [대상] the cause ; the source ; the origin ; the subject (주제) ¶ 걱정거리 a cause of worry // 웃음거리 a laughing stock ; a butt of ridicule // 일거리 a piece of work ; a job ; a task // 사람을 웃음거리로 만들다 make 《a person》 the butt of ridicule // 곧 이야깃거리가 끊어졌다 We soon ran short of〔exhausted〕 topics of conversation. // 그는 이야깃거리가 딸리는 법이 없다 He has no end of things to talk about. // 재론할 거리조차 안되는 안건이다 The topic is not worth reviewing.

거리³ [단위] a group of 50 《cucumbers, eggplants》 ¶ 오이 두 거리 100 cucumbers

거리 巨利 a big〔an enormous〕 profit ¶ 거리를 얻다 make〔reap〕 a big profit // 그는 이 거래로 거리를 얻었다 He gained an enormous profit in this transaction.

†**거리 距離** distance ; [사정 거리] range ; [간격] an interval ; [차이] a difference ; a gap ¶ 거리에 따라 다르다 (요금 따위가) vary with the distance // 100미터 거리를 두고 at intervals of a hundred meters // 조금 거리를 두고 at a short distance ; a little way off // 거리가 10마일이다 It is 10 miles distant. // 그곳은 한 시간의 거리다 The place is one hour distant. // 여기서 부산까지의 거리는 얼마인가 How far is it from here to *Pusan* ? /What is the distance from here to *Pusan* ? // 우리들의 의견에는 서로 큰 거리가 있다 We are very different in our opinions. // 요즘 그들 부부는 서로 어떤 거리를 느끼는 것 같았다 It looks that the couple feel estranged from each other these days. // 이것은 진짜 프랑스 요리 맛과는 거리가 멀다 This is nowhere near the taste of real French cuisine.

비행 — fly ; a flight 순항 — a cruising distance 직선 — distance in a straight line 활주 — (항공기의) a taxing distance

거리감 距離感 the sense of distance(s)

거리 감각 距離感覺 one's sense of distance

거리 경주 距離競走 〖스키〗 a distance race

거리계 距離計 a range finder ; a telemeter

거리끼다 [사물에] stand〔be〕 in the way 《of》 ; become a drag 《on》 ; become a bar 《to》 ; be restrained〔prevented, hindered〕 by ; [마음에] weigh on one's mind ; lie at one's heart ; get on one's nerves ¶ 그 일이 마음에 거리낀다 That matter weighs heavy on my mind. // 아무래도 마음에 거리낀다 It haunts me. // 전처 자식이 거리끼어 재혼이 어렵게 되었다 The child by his former wife became an obstacle to his second marriage. // 양심에 거리끼는 일은 하지 말아야 한다 One should not do what troubles one's conscience.

거리낌없이 openly ; without reserve〔hesitation〕

거리 측정기 距離測定器 a range finder ; a range-finding device ; a telemeter

거리표 距離標 a distant mark〔post〕 ; milepost ; milestone

거마 車馬 horses and vehicles ; traffic ; transportation ¶ 거마의 교통 vehicle〔vehicular〕 traffic // 거마 통행 금지 No thoroughfare for horses and vehicles. (게시)

거마비 車馬費 traffic expenses ; carfare

거만 巨萬 millions ; a vast〔fabulous〕 fortune ¶ 거만의 갑부이다 have millions in wealth ; be a millionaire // 거만의 부를 쌓다 amass a vast fortune ; make〔coin〕 a mint of money 《미》 ; make a big pile ; become a millionaire // 거만의 재산을 써 버리다 spend millions 《on a thing》

†**거만 倨慢** arrogance ; insolence ; haughtiness ; self-importance ; self-conceit ; pomposity ; pride ; toploftiness 《미·속》 **—하다** be arrogant ; haughty ; pompous ; proud ; puffed up ; stuck up ; toplofty ; have one's nose in the air ¶ 거만한 태도 a haughty air〔attitude〕 // 거만을 빼다 give oneself airs ; ride〔get on〕 one's high horse // 그는 출세하더니 거만해졌어 He is stuck up by his success. // 그는 신입 사원치고는 거만하다 For a new employee, he sure acts big.

거머들이다 drive 《it》 in greedily ; rake 《them》 in greedily

***거머리** 〖동물〗 a leech ¶ 거머리 같은 사람 a nuisance ; a pest // 거머리처럼 달라붙다 stick like a leech〔bur〕

거머먹다 devour〔eat〕 greedily〔ravenously〕 ; wolf 《속》

거머무트름하다, 꺼머무트름하다 (be) dark and chubby

거머삼키다 swallow (up) greedily ; gulp (down) voraciously

거머안다 clutch eagerly to one's bosom ; hug

거머잡다 grab〔clutch〕 greedily

거머쥐다 grasp ; grip ; grab 《up》 (greedily) ; clutch〔take hold of〕 greedily ¶ 잔뜩 거머쥐다 take all that one's fist can hold

거머채다 grab

거멀못 a clamp ; a cramp ; a rivet ; a clincher

거멀쇠 an iron clamp
거멀장 a clamp ; a cramp ; a rivet ; a metal reinforcement for a joint ¶ 거멀장을 대다 fasten〔hold〕 things with cramps
거멀 장식 an ornamental stud ; an ornamental metal reinforcing piece
거멓다, 꺼멓다 (be) deep-〔jet-〕black ; coal-black ; sooty ; be as black as coal ¶ 햇볕에 꺼멓게 타다 be tanned almost black
거메지다, 꺼메지다 get dark ; darken ; turn black ; blacken ; tan (in the sun)
거목 巨木 ① [매우 큰 나무] a big 〔great, large〕 tree ; a gigantic〔towering〕 tree
② [큰 인물] a great man ¶ 그분이야 말로 한국 경제계의 거목이시다 He is indeed a great leader of Korean economy.
거무데데하다, 꺼무데데하다 (be) darkish ; dusky ; murky ; swarthy ; dark sallow (얼굴빛 따위가)
†**거무스름하다** (be) dark ; darkish ; dusky ; swarthy ; dark-colored ¶ 얼굴이 거무스름하다 have a dark complexion ; be dark-skinned ; be dark-complexioned // 피부색이 거무스름한 여자 a brunette
*__거무죽죽하다__ (be) blackish ; dark ; fuscous ; somber ¶ 눈 가장자리가 거무죽죽하다 have dark rings around one's eyes // 거무죽죽한 타박상 livid marks of blows // 거무죽죽한 벽지 dingy wallpaper
거무칙칙하다 (be) dusky ; dark-colored ; murky ; dark
거문고 a Korean harp (with six strings) ¶ 거문고를 뜯다 play a Korean harp
거물 巨物 a leading figure ; a prominent 〔great, big〕 figure ; a captain ; a big-timer ; a big wig 《속》 ; a big shot 《미·속》 ; [높은 사람] a big〔great〕 gun ; a V. I. P. ¶ 당대의 거물 the lion of the day // 정계의 거물 a leading figure in politics ; a conspicuous figure in the political world // 재계의 거물 a financial magnate // 문단의 거물 a great figure 〔lion〕 of the literary world ; a literary star // 산업계의 거물 a captain of industry ; an industrial magnate ; a tycoon 《미》
— **정치가** a politician of great caliber
거물거리다, 꺼물거리다 flicker ⇨ 가물거리다
거뭇거뭇, 꺼뭇꺼뭇 —하다 (be) blackish ; be dotted with black (spots)
거뭇하다, 꺼뭇하다 (be) darkish ⇨ 거무스름하다
⁑**거미** 〖동물〗 a spider ¶ 거미가 집을 짓다 A spider weaves〔spins〕 its web.
거미줄 spider's thread ; cobweb ¶ 거미줄을 친 cobwebbed // 거미줄에 걸리다 be caught in a spider's web // 그 창고에는 거미줄이 많아서 내가 없앴다 The storage shed was filled with cobwebs, so I cleared them away.
거미줄(을) 늘이다 관용 cast a dragnet 《around the district》 ; draw〔post, place〕 a (police) cordon
거미줄(을) 치다 관용 ① [거미가] spin 〔weave〕 a web ② [굶다] starve ; famish ; be starved〔famished〕 ; be〔go〕 hungry ; be〔run〕 out of livelihood ③ [경계망을] cast a dragnet ⇨ 거미줄 늘이다
⁑**거미집** a spider's web ; cobweb ¶ 거미집을 걷다 clear 《the ceiling》 of cobwebs
거미치밀다 be overwhelmed with envy 〔greed〕 ; become covetous
거반 居半 over half ; nearly all
거방지다 have dignified〔commanding, fine, imposing〕 presence ; be stately in mien
거번 去番 [저번] the last time ; the other day
거베 thick hemp ; gunny
거벽 巨擘 ① [대학자] a leading scholar ; a great authority ¶ 문단의 거벽 a star of the literary world ② [엄지손가락] a thumb
거볍다 (be) light (in weight) ⇨ 가볍다
거병 擧兵 raising〔mustering〕 an army ; rising in arms **—하다** raise〔muster〕 an army ; rise in arms ; take up arms
거보 巨步 a giant step ; a mammoth stride ¶ 거보를 내디디다 make long strides 《in》
거봐라 Look ! ; You see ! ; I told you so ! ¶ 거봐라 내가 뭐라든 There, I told you (so) ! /Didn't I tell you ?
거부 巨富 a man of (great) wealth ; a millionaire ; a multimillionaire ; a billionaire ; a person as rich as Croesus ; a Croesus
†**거부 拒否** refusal ; rejection ; disapproval ; denial ; veto ; disallowance ; traverse (법적) **—하다** refuse ; deny ; veto ; reject ; turn down ; disapprove of ; put a veto on ; make a denial of ; give a denial to ¶ 거부할 수 있는 deniable // 요구를 거부하다 reject〔turn down〕 a request // 의안을 거부하다 veto a legislative bill // 초대를 거부하다 decline an invitation // 거부하지 못하게 하다 take no denial // 그는 그의 신분을 밝히기를 거부했다 He refused to reveal his identity. // 대통령은 거부 교서 〔통고서〕를 의회에 제출했다 The president delivered his veto to Congress.
—자 〖법〗 a traverser
*__거부권 拒否權__ a veto ; the veto right ¶ 대국(大國)의 거부권 the veto right of the big powers // 거부권을 행사하다 exercise one's veto power ; veto ; exercise the veto 《over》 // 이 결의안은 러시

아의 거부권 행사로 부결될 것이다 The resolution will die on a Russian veto.

거부 반응 拒否反應 〖의학〗 rejection (symptoms) ¶ 이식 피부가 거부 반응을 일으켰다 The skin graft was rejected.

거북 〖동물〗 a tortoise ; a terrapin ; a (sea) turtle

— 양식(養殖) turtle farming

거북이 잔등의 털을 긁는다 속담 It is very hard to shave an egg.

거북딱지 a shell of bony dermal plates of a turtle

거북선 —船 the "Turtle Ship" ; an iron-clad warship shaped like a turtle (invented by Admiral *Yi Sun-shin* in 1592 or so, during the reign of King *Sonjo* of the *Choson Dynasty*)

거북점 —占 divination by burning tortoise shells ; [골패로] divination by using a set of dominoes of tortoise shapes ¶ 거북점을 치다 tell fortunes by burning tortoise shells

⁑**거북하다** feel awkward〔embarrassed〕; feel shy〔bashful〕; feel ill at ease ; feel unwell ; feel uncomfortable ; feel like a cat in a strange attic ; [사물이 주어] (be) embarrassing ; not convenient ; inconvenient ; unhandy ¶ 입장이 거북한 feel awkward // 거북한 자리 an uncomfortable seat ; an awkward meeting // 수영복 차림으로 남의 앞에 나가기는 좀 거북했다 I felt kind of shy to be seen in public in a bathing suit. // 선생님 앞이라 참 거북했다 I felt quite awkward〔ill at ease〕 before my teacher. // 지나친 칭찬은 거북한 법이다 Too high a compliment〔Extreme praise〕 is sometimes embarrassing. // 그 사람이 이 자리에 나오면 거북해 It will be inconvenient for us to have him here. // 너무 먹었나 봐 속이 거북해 It seems I ate too much, I feel quite unwell〔I got my stomach out of order〕. // 그 소녀는 낯선 사람들 앞에서 거북함을 느꼈다 The girl felt awkward with strangers.

거분하다, 거뿐하다 (be) light ; nimble

거불거리다, 꺼불거리다 behave frivolously

거붓하다, 거뿟하다 (be) rather light

거비 巨費 enormous expenditures ; a great cost ¶ 거비를 들여 at a great cost

거사 居士 [불교도] a Buddhist devotee ; [처사] a scholar out of government service ; a hermit

거사 擧事 —하다 launch an undertaking ; take〔initiate〕 an action ; undertake 《a riot》; set 《a plan, a movement》 on foot〔afoot, agoing〕; start 《a rising, a revolt, an insurrection》; rise 《in rebellion》; raise〔foment, create〕 《a rebellion, a commotion》 ¶ 혁명을 거사한 사람들 those who started a revolution // 거사를 모의하다 plot a rebellion〔revolt〕

거상 巨商 a wealthy〔rich〕 merchant ; a merchant prince ; a business magnate ; a taipan .

거상 居喪 mourning ; [상복] mourning attire

거상 巨像 a gigantic〔colossal〕 statue ; a colossus 《*pl.* -si, ~es》

거석 巨石 a huge stone ; a megalith (유사 이전의)

— 건축물 a megalithic structure **— 기념물** a megalithic monument **—묘(墓)** a megalithic tomb

거석 문화 巨石文化 megalithic culture

거선 巨船 a big〔huge, mighty〕 ship ; an ocean liner ; a superliner ; a leviathan

거성 巨星 a giant star ; [위인] a great man ; a prominent man ; a leading figure ; a big shot 《속》 ¶ 악단의 거성 a great musician // 문단의 거성 a literary genius // 그는 음악계의 거성이다 He is a musical superstar.

거세 去勢 ① [가축 따위의] castration ; sterilization ; [정신적으로] emasculation ¶ 고양이를 거세시키려고 합니다 I want my cat neutered
② [세력의] exclusion ; weakening ; eradication **—하다** emasculate ; geld ; castrate ; sterilize ; exclude ; weaken ; e radicate ¶ 신헌법에 의하여 그 나라의 반민주 세력은 거세되었다 The antidemocratic forces in the country were eradicated in accordance with the new Constitution.

—계(鷄) a capon **—돈(豚)** a castrated pig **—마(馬)** a gelding ; a castrated 〔cut〕 horse **—술(術)** castration ; gelding **—양** a wether **—우(牛)** a bullock ; a steer

거세다 (be) rough ; wild ; violent ; fierce ; raging ; outrageous ; heavy ; tough ; strong ; unruly ; unbridled ; ungovernable ; uncontrollable ¶ 거센 파도 wild〔heavy〕 sea〔waves, waters〕; stormy〔wild, furious, raging〕 seas // 거센 바람 fierce〔strong, heavy〕 wind // 거센 여자 an unruly woman ; a woman of spirit ; a vixen ; a termagant // 거센 성격 wild nature ; unruly〔ungovernable, uncontrollable〕 temper ; savage disposition // 거센 입심 unbridled tongue ; violent language // 거센 목소리 gruff 〔coarse〕 voice ; harsh tone // 평결에 거세게 항의하다 enter〔make, lodge〕 a strong protest against the verdict

거소 居所 one's address ; one's place of residence ; one's whereabouts ¶ 확정된 거소 a permanent address

거수 擧手 raising one's hand ; [가부의] a show of hands **—하다** raise〔show〕 one's hand ¶ 거수 가결로 하다 take a show of hands ; decide 《on a thing》 by show of hands // 거수 경례를 하다 raise one's hand in salute ; make a military salute // 찬성하시는 분은 거수하시기 바랍니다 Let those in favor show their hands.

거수 경례 擧手敬禮 a hand salute ; a military salute **—하다** raise one's hand in salute ; make a military salute

거수기 擧手機 [국회 의원 따위] a rubber stamp 《구》 ¶ 거수기 노릇을 하다 rubber-stamp // 행정부 정책의 거수기 노릇을 하다 rubber-stamp〔be an amenable rubber stamp〕 for an administration policy

거수 투표 擧手投票 voting by show of hands

거스러미 [손톱의] an agnail ; a hangnail ; [나무의] a splinter ; a sticker ¶ 손거스러미가 생기다 have a hangnail // 나무거스러미가 손가락에 박혔다 I've run a splinter into my finger.

거스러지다 ① [성질이] become〔grow〕 unmanageable〔uncontrollable, incorrigible, refractory, rebellious, disobedient, intractable, beyond one's control〕 ; get out of hand ; grow stubborn〔unruly, wild〕 ¶ 아이가 거스러졌다 The child has become intractably wild.
② [잔털이] 《its feathers》 get ruffled up ; bristle up ; stand on end ¶ 털이 거스러진 참새 a sparrow all ruffled up

***거스르다**[1] [반대하다] oppose ; go〔act〕 against ; act contrary to ; run counter to ; cross ; offend ¶ …에 거슬러 against ; contrary to ; in defiance of ; in the face〔teeth〕 of // 어버이의 말을 거스르다 contradict〔disobey〕 one's parents // 뜻을 거스르다 cross another's will ; act against another's wishes // 천의(天意)를 거스르다 fly in the face of Providence ; give offense to the will of God // 중론을 거스르다 stem the tide of public opinion // 시대의 흐름을 거스르다 go against the stream〔current〕 of the times // 운명을 거스르다 strive against fate

거스르다[2] [돈을] give change ¶ 거슬러 주다 give (back) the change // 거슬러 받다 get the change

***거스름돈** (one's) change ¶ 거스름돈을 주다〔받다〕 give〔get〕 the change // 거스름돈을 주지 않다 refuse change // 거스름돈으로 400원을 주다 give four hundred *won* in change 《to》 // 거스름돈 받으십시오 Here is your change. // 거스름돈은 100원이 됩니다 That makes a hundred *won* change. // 거스름돈은 그만둬요 You may keep the (small) change. /Keep the rest for yourself. // 거스름돈은 동전으로 주시오 Give me my change in pennies (coins). // 그들이 거스름돈을 속인 것 같다 I think they short-changed me.

거슬거슬 —하다 ① [성질] (be) stubborn ; unruly ; wild ; disobedient ; intractable ; refractory ¶ 거슬거슬한 성질 a refractory〔rebellious, obstinate〕 disposition ; a wild nature ② [피부] (be) rough

***거슬러 올라가다** ① [상류로] go upstream ; go up〔ascend〕 《a river》 ¶ 배를 타고 강을 거슬러 올라가다 scull〔row〕 upstream ; brave the current // 헤엄쳐서 강을 거슬러 올라가다 swim upstream
② [과거로] go back 《to the past》 ; retroact 《to》 ; retrospect 《to》 ¶ 태고로 거슬러 올라가다 trace back to remote antiquity // 과거로 거슬러 올라가서 적용시키다 apply 《a law》 retroactively 《to》 // 이야기는 1890년대로 거슬러 올라간다 The story goes way back to the eighteen nineties.

⁑**거슬리다** ① [거스른 상태] be opposed ; be disobeyed ; be contradicted ② [비위에] be against one's taste ; be unpleasant ; rub 《a person》 the wrong way ; be not congenial ¶ 귀에 거슬리다 be harsh to the ear // 눈에 거슬리다 be unpleasant to the eye ; be repellent ; be out of one's favor // 그것은 내 성미에 거슬린다 It goes against the grain with me.

거슴츠레하다 《one's eyes》 (be) heavy ; drowsy ; dull ; sleepy ¶ 잠이 와서 눈이 거슴츠레하군 Your eyes look heavy. /You are heavy-eyed. /You have heavy eyes.

거시기 ① well ; let me see ; er- ; what-do-you-call-it ; what-do-you-call-it ; what-is-it ; what-not ; so-and-so ; what's-his-name ¶ 거시기 어디 갔지 Where is Mr. So-and-so〔What's-his-name〕? // 거시기 어디 갔나 Where is my what- do-you-call-it? ② [감탄사적] ¶ 거시기 그게 뭐라더라 That—what was it called?

거시적 巨視的 『물리』 macroscopic ; [관점이] comprehensive ; all-inclusive ¶ 거시적으로 보다 take a broad view 《of》
— 경제학 macroeconomics **— 물리학** macrophysics **— 분석** 『경제』 macroscopic analysis ; macroanalysis

거식 擧式 —하다 hold a ceremony ; [결혼] celebrate〔solemnize〕 a wedding

거식하다 ① [동사로서] do something or other 《with》 ; fiddle around 《with》 ¶ 어떻게 거식해 봐 Try and do it somehow or other. ② [형용사로서] be some sort of ; be somehow—I don't know— ; be hard to describe ; [거북함] be reluctant 《to say》 ; be uncertain whether one should 《say》 ¶ 어쩐지 마음이 거식하다 Somehow I feel uneasy

거실

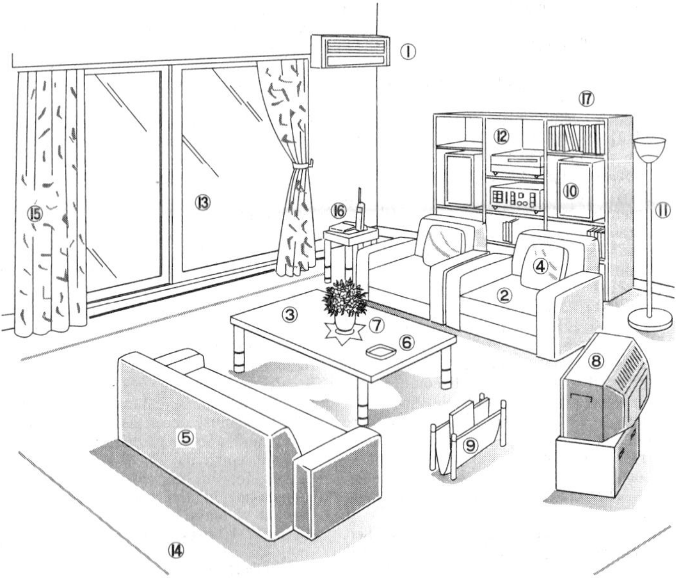

① 에어컨 air conditioner
② 안락 의자 easy chair
③ 테이블 table
④ 쿠션 cushion
⑤ 소파 sofa
⑥ 재떨이 ashtray
⑦ 화병 vase
⑧ 텔레비전 television (set)
⑨ 잡지꽂이 magazine rack
⑩ 스피커 speaker
⑪ 전기 스탠드 floor lamp
⑫ 전축 stereo
⑬ 미닫이문 sliding door
⑭ 카펫 carpet
⑮ 커튼 curtain
⑯ 전화 telephone
⑰ 책장 bookcase

(about) it. /I feel kind〔sort〕 of shy.

⁑거실 居室 [자기의] one's own〔private〕 room ; [가족의] a sitting room ; a parlor ; a living room 《미》

거액 巨額 a big〔great, huge, vast, colossal〕 sum ; an enormous amount of money ¶ 거액의 돈 a large amount of money // 거액에 달하다 amount to a huge sum // 거액을 기부하다 make a big donation

거여목 〖식물〗 a clover ; a snail clover ; a trefoil ; a medic

거역 巨役 a big job ; a colossal〔large〕 undertaking

거역 拒逆 disobedience ; insubordination ; opposition ; objection **—하다** disobey ; protest against ; object to ; oppose ; act against ¶ 부모를 거역하다 disobey〔contradict〕 one's parents // 상관의 명을 거역하다 object to〔protest against〕 the order of one's superior ; disobey〔run counter to〕 commands of one's superior // 명령은 절대 거역하지 않겠습니다 I will be all obedience to your commands. // 그에게 거역하지 않는 편이 좋다 You'd better not go against him.

거우다 provoke 《a person to anger》 ; irritate〔fret, nettle, tease, vex〕 《a person》 ; make 《a person》 feel impatient

거우듬하다 (be) somewhat slanted

거우르다 tilt ; slant ; skew ; tip

⁑거울 ① a mirror ; a looking glass ¶ 거울을 보다 look into a mirror〔glass〕 ; look at oneself in a mirror // 거울에 비치다 be reflected in a mirror // 거울 같은 바다 a glassy sea
② [모범] a model ; a pattern ; an example ; a paragon ¶ 부덕의 거울 the model of womanhood〔chastity〕 // 남의 거울이 되다 become a model for oth-

ers ; set an example to the world // 거울로 삼다 pattern〔model〕 after ; follow the example of ; take a lesson from
— 전류계(電流計) 〖물리〗 a mirror-galvanometer 화장 — a toilet mirror

거울삼다 model after〔on〕 ; take 《someone》 for model〔pattern〕 ; make 《someone》 an example ; model oneself on 〔upon〕 another ; learn 《from》 ; imitate ; get〔draw, glean〕 a lesson from》 ; follow the example of ; take one's cue from ; draw one's model from ¶ …을 거울삼아 on〔after〕 the model of // 부모를 거울삼다 follow the pattern of one's parents // 잘못〔실패〕을 거울삼다 take a lesson from one's mistakes〔failures〕 // 그를 거울삼다 pattern oneself on him // 당신을 거울삼겠습니다 I will take a leaf out of your book. // 그를 거울삼아 힘을 내어 다시 일에 착수했다 I set to work again encouraged by his example.

거웃[1] pubic hair ; pubes

거웃[2] [두둑] a plowed furrow in a field (paddy)

거월 去月 last month ; ultimo 《ult.》 ¶ 거월 3일에 on the 3rd (of) last month ; on the 3rd ult.

⁑**거위**[1] 〖새〗 a goose 《*pl.* geese》 ¶ 거위 같은 goosey
— 고기 goose flesh — 새끼 a gosling —알 a goose egg 숫— a gander 집— a domestic goose

거위[2] a roundworm ; an intestinal worm ; an ascarid ; Ascaris lumbricoides (학명)

거위배 stomach trouble caused by worms

거유 巨儒 a great〔learned〕 Confucianist ; a great scholar of Confucianism

†**거의** [대체로] almost ; nearly ; practically ; all but ; as good as ; no more than ; little short of ; near〔nigh〕 upon ; well-nigh ; close up on ; next to ; within an breath〔inch〕 of ; on the brink〔point, verge, threshold〕 of ; about ; about to ; [부정적] scarcely ; hardly ; little ; few ; [약] about ; some ; [대부분] for the most part ; mostly

> 참고 **almost**와 **nearly**는 대개의 경우 어느 편을 사용해도 되거니와 almost는 순전히 정도를 나타내는 부사이지만 nearly는 almost보다 강조하는 의미가 강하기 때문에 무엇인가 특별히 함축성이 있을 경우에는 nearly를 사용하는 경향이 있다 가령 마음의 상태를 나타내는 동사나 형용사를 수식하는 것은 almost이고 nearly가 아니다 I am almost glad he has failed. (그가 실패해서 잘됐다고 생각할 지경이다)

¶ 거의 전부 almost〔nearly〕 all // 거의 언제나 almost always // 거의 … 않다 almost never〔no, nothing〕 // 그가 죽었다는 것을 믿는 사람이 거의 없었다 Almost no one believed that he was dead. // 이곳은 거의 눈이 내리지 않는다 It almost never snows here. // 건축은 거의 완성되었다 The building is almost〔nearly, practically〕 finished. // 저녁 준비가 거의 다되었다 Dinner is almost ready. // 거의 익사할 뻔했다 I nearly drowned. // 적군은 거의 전멸됐다 The enemies were all but annihilated. // 거의 의미가 없다 There is little point in it. // 거의 의심할 바 없다 You can hardly doubt it. // 거의 아무것도 얻지 못하였다 I scarcely gained anything. // 거의 무일푼이다 I am little short of〔as good as〕 broke. // 거의 죽은 사람이나 다름없다 He is as good as dead. // 거의 거지나 다름없다 He is no more than a beggar. // 완쾌한 것은 거의 기적에 가깝다 His recovery is little short of a miracle. // 이 문제의 해결은 거의 불가능하다 It is next to impossible for me to solve this problem. // 영화는 거의 끝나가고 있다 The movie has almost reached the end. // 거의 모든 사람들이 밖으로 나왔다 Almost all the people came out. // 성공할 가망은 거의 없다 There is not the remotest chance of success. // 득실은 거의 반반이다 The gains and losses are about on a par. // 거의 떠날 참이었다 We were just about to start. // 그의 힘에 당할 사람은 거의 없다 Very few can equal him. // 네가 먹는 꼴을 보니까 체중이 줄 가능성은 거의 없겠다 The way you eat, you have a fat〔slim, little〕 chance to lose any weight.

거의거의 almost ; nearly ⇨ 거의

†**거인 巨人** a giant ; a colossus 《*pl.* -si》 ; a Titan ; [위인] a great man ¶ 재계의 거인 a leading figure in financial circles ; a financial magnate

거인국 巨人國 a land of giants ; [걸리버 여행기의] Brobdingnag

거일 去日 bygone days ; days past

거장 巨匠 a great master ; a great artist ¶ 악단의 거장 a celebrated musician ; a master musician ; a maestro 《*pl.* ∼s, -ri》 (이)

*__거저__ without paying anything ; free (of charge) ; without cost ; gratis ; gratuitously ; for nothing ; as a gift ; without doing anything ; with nothing (in hand) ; for a song ¶ 거저 얻다 get 《a thing》 for nothing // 거저 얻을 수 있다 can be had for the asking〔taking〕 ; can be got for nothing // 거저라도 필요 없다 I would not have〔take〕 it (even) as a gift. // 이거 거저나 마찬가지구나 It's a steal. // 거저 수고시키지는 않겠다

I will pay you for your trouble. // 거저 들어갈 수 있습니까 Is admission free?/Can we get in free? // 거저 해 드리지요 I will make no charge for the work. // 100원입니다 거저나 다름없지요 It is one hundred *won* and a present at that. // 거저나 다름없는 값입니다 It's merely a nominal price./It is quite a bargain. // 오늘이 개점 1주년이기 때문에 술값은 거저 입니다 Today's the first anniversary of our opening, so it's on the house.

거저먹기 an easy job〔task, thing〕 to do ; soft job ; a cinch〔snap, child's play〕 ¶ 그것은 거저먹기다 It's quite an easy job./That's a very easy matter for me./ That's a soft job./That's nothing./That's a cinch〔soft snap〕. // 그 사람에게 이기는 것은 거저 먹기다 It's child's play to beat him.

거적 a (straw) mat ; matting ¶ 거적을 깔다 spread a mat // 거적을 만들다 weave〔make, plait〕 a straw mat // 거적을 덮다 cover with matting

—때기 a piece〔fragment〕 of a straw mat **—문(門)** a door made of matting **— 송장** a corpse wrapped in straw matting **— 자리** a straw mat ; a mat (for a seat)

거적문에 돌쩌귀 속담 Don't use a nail when string will do./Throw〔Cast〕 pearls before swine.

거적눈 eyes with drooping eyelids

†**거절 拒絶** refusal ; rejection ; rebuff ; turning down **—하다** refuse ; decline ; reject ; rebuff ; turn down 《on》 ; deny

> 참고 **refuse**는 단호하게 거절하는 것 **decline**은 refuse보다는 강하지 않은 거절 **reject**는 refuse보다 더욱 강한 태도로 거절하는 것

¶ 단호한 거절 flat〔complete, outright, total〕 rejection // 딱 잘라 거절하다 give an outright denial // 요구를 거절하다 reject 《a person's》 demands // 면회를 거절하다 refuse to see ; deny oneself to 《a caller》 // 신청을 거절하다 turn down 《a person's》 application // 입장을 거절하다 deny 《a person》 admission // 그는 나의 도움을 거절했다 He rebuffed my attempts to help. // 노동자들은 임금 인상 요구를 거절당하자 파업에 들어갔다 The workers went on strike, their demands for higher wages being rejected. // 역시 이 일은 거절하는 것이 좋겠다 I guess we'd better turn down this job after all. // 그런 수지가 안 맞는 일은 거절하겠다 There's no way I'll work for such low pay.

— 증서(證書) 〖법〗 a protest **인수(引受) — 증서** a protest for nonacceptance **지불 — 증서** a protest for nonpayment

거점 據點 a position ; a point ; a stronghold ¶ 중요한 군사 거점 a strategic position〔stronghold〕 ; a key position // 불량배들의 거점을 기습하다 surprise the den of hooligans〔hoodlums〕

공격(攻擊) — a strongpoint for one's attacks 《on the enemy》 **군사 —** a military〔naval〕 base ; a strategic point 〔position〕 **중요 —** a key point〔position〕

거조 擧措 behavior ; manner ; conduct ; demeanor ; bearing ; carriage

거족 巨族 a distinguished〔powerful, influential〕 family ; a mighty clan

거족 擧族 the whole nation ¶ 거족적 nationwide

거좌 踞坐 —하다 get〔sit, ride, seat oneself〕 astride

*****거주 居住** dwelling ; residence ; abode ; habitation

—하다 live ; reside ; dwell ; inhabit ; make one's home ; take (up) residence ¶ 거주의 자유 the freedom of residence // 거주가 일정치 않다 have no fixed abode〔habitation〕 ; be homeless ; be vagrant

— 불명(不明) Addressed wrong./Wrong address. **— 인구** the resident population 《of a city》 **— 자격** the residential qualification 《for a voter》 **— 증명서** a certificate of residence **— 지역(地域)** a residential district〔quarter〕 **불법 —자** [공유지의] a squatter **외인(外人) —자** a foreign resident

거주권 居住權 the right of residence ¶ 거주권을 침해하다 violate〔infringe on〕 《a person's》 right of residence

*****거주민 居住民** an inhabitant ; a resident ; a dweller ; [시민] a citizen ; [토착민] a native ; an indigenous inhabitant ; [원주민] an original inhabitant

거주자 居住者 a resident ; an inhabitant ; a dweller

거주지 居住地 a place of residence ; domicile

거죽 [표면] the surface ; the face ; [옷의] the right-side ; [외면부] the exterior ; outside ; outer side ; [외견] the (outward) appearance ; the outward show ¶ 거죽만 outwardly ; in appearance ¶ 너는 사물의 거죽만 본다 You look only at the surface of things. // 거죽만 봐서는 진상을 모른다 The true condition of affairs is not to be known by external appearance.

거중 조정 居中調停 mediation ; intermediation ; intervention ; arbitration **—하다** intermediate ; intervene ; arbitrate ; mediate 《between two countries》 ; use one's good offices

거증 擧證 giving evidence ; the establishment of a fact (by evidence)
— **책임** the burden of proof ; the onus probandi 《라》

*⁑***거지** a beggar ; a mendicant ; a tramp ¶ 거지꼴 shabby look ; beggarly〔miserable〕 appearance // 거지 근성 a mean spirit ; the beggar // 거지 같은 놈 a good-for-nothing (fellow) // 거지 같은 물건 rubbish ; trash // 거지 생활을 하다 go (about) begging ; beg one's bread ; live as a beggar // 거지가 되다 be reduced to beggary ; be brought to begging // 거지로 죽다 die a beggar ; die in a ditch // 거지같다 [일·상황이] (be) unsatisfactory ; disagreeable ; offensive ; poor ; humble ; worthless ; of little value
거지도 부지런하면 더운 밥을 얻어 먹는다 속담 The early bird catches the worm.

거지반 居之半 [반수 이상] the (great) majority ; the bulk ; [태반] the greater〔best, most〕 part ; the great〔large〕 portion ; [대개] mostly ; for the most part ; nearly all ; very nearly ; generally ¶ 직공들의 거지반 the majority of the workmen ; most workmen // 교사의 거지반 the greater part of the school building // 참석자는 거지반이 대학생이었다 Those who were present were almost all college students. // 전 시가의 거지반이 파괴되었다 The bulk of the whole city was wiped out. // 그는 생애의 거지반을 동양에서 보냈다 He lived in the Orient for a great portion of his life.

†**거짓** ① [거짓말] a lie ; falsehood ; falsity ; fraud ; a fabrication ; fiction ; untruth ; humbug ¶ 거짓이 있다 be false ; be untrue ; be dishonest ; be deceitful // 그의 말에는 거짓이 없다 All he said is true.
② [부사적] falsely ; fictitiously ; deceitfully ; dishonestly ¶ 거짓 패하고 달아나다 pretend to be defeated and run away // 거짓 친절한 체하다 feign kindness ; pretend to be kind

†**거짓말** a lie ; a falsehood ; a fiction ; an invention ; a fabrication ; a fake ; a fib (사소한) ; an untruth ; falsity **—하다** tell a lie ; lie ; tell an untruth〔a falsehood〕

> 참고 **lie**는 강한 비난의 감정이 포함된 말 **fib**는 해가 되지 않는 가벼운 거짓말 **falsehood**는 일부러 하는 거짓말로 부득이한 경우에 쓴다

¶ 거짓말투성이 a pack〔web, tissue〕 of lies // 뻔뻔스러운 거짓말 a bold-faced lie ; a direct lie // 속보이는 거짓말 a blatant〔brazen〕 lie // 허물없는 거짓말 a white lie ; a fib // 터무니없는〔멀쩡한, 새빨간〕 거짓말 a lie (made) out of (the) whole cloth ; a whopping lie ; a downright〔an arrant, a barefaced〕 lie ; a pure fabrication ; a monstrous〔outright〕 lie // 악의 없는〔죄가 되지 않는〕 거짓말 a white lie // 뻔히 들여다 보이는 거짓말 a transparent〔hollow〕 falsehood〔lie〕 // 그럴듯한 거짓말 a plausible〔specious〕 lie // 앞뒤를 잰 거짓말 a deliberate lie // 믿을 수 없는 거짓말 an incredible story // 거짓말 같은 정말 a case of fact // 천연덕스럽게 거짓말하다 make no bones of〔about〕 telling a lie // 그럴듯하게 거짓말하다 lie like the truth // 거짓말했다고 욕하다 give 《a person》 the lie ; call a man a liar to his face // 너는 거짓말을 하고 있다 You're lying to me. // …을 거짓말쟁이라고 책망하다 give the direct lie to // 거짓말을 하여 남의 명성을 떨어뜨리다 lie a person's reputation away // 거짓말을 하여 남의 돈을 빼앗다 lie 《a person》 out of his money // 새빨간 거짓말을 하다 lie in one's teeth〔throat〕 // 그는 거짓말을 하여 겨우 곤경에서 벗어났다 He managed to lie himself out of difficulties. // 거짓말 마라 You're a liar ! /What a story ! / You're just kidding me. /Says you ! 《미·속》 // 절대로 거짓말이 아니야 I mean everything I say. // 병이라던 것은 멀쩡한 거짓말이었다 His illness was a perfect fake. // 거짓말할 사람이 아니다 He is not a man to tell a lie. /He is incapable of〔above〕 telling a lie.

*⁑***거짓말쟁이** a liar ; a fibber ; an Ananias ; a storyteller (완곡한 표현)

거짓말 탐지기 —探知器 a lie〔counterfeit〕 detector ¶ 거짓말 탐지기로 조사하다 give a lie detector test to 《a person》 // 거짓말 탐지기 테스트를 받다 take a lie detector test

거짓부렁 a lie ⇨ 거짓말

거짓 이름 a false〔an assumed〕 name ¶ 거짓 이름으로 under a false name 《of》 // 거짓 이름을 칭하다 assume a false name

거찰 巨刹 a grand (big) Buddhist temple ; a cathedral

***거창** large〔huge〕 scale **—하다** (be) large〔grand〕 scale(d) ; enormous ; gigantic ¶ 거창하게 on a large〔an extensive, a gigantic〕 scale ; in a big way

거처 居處 dwelling 《in》 ; living 《in》 ; [거소] a dwelling place〔house〕 ; a (place of) residence ; an abode ; [행방] whereabouts ; [주소] an address **—하다** dwell in ; live in ¶ 거처를 정하다 make one's home ; take up one's abode〔residence〕 《at, in》 ; settle down // 거처를 옮기다 move〔remove〕 to ; change one's address // 그는 거처를 밝

히지 않는다 He doesn't give me his address. // 아직 그의 거처는 불명이다 His whereabouts is〔are〕 still unknown. // 그의 아버지의 거처를 모른다 The whereabouts of his father is〔are〕 unknown.

거청숫돌 a rough grindstone

거체 巨體 a huge form〔body〕; a gigantic figure; a giant

거촉 炬燭 torches and candles

거추 去秋 last autumn

거추없다 (be) nonsensical; silly; absurd; insipid; flat; stale

거추장스럽다 (be) burdensome; cumbersome; cumbrous; troublesome; vex atious; bothersome; plaguy 《구》 ¶ 거추장스러운 것 a burden; a drag 《on》// 거추장스러운 사람 a nuisance // 거추장스럽게 여기다 find〔regard, consider〕 《a thing》 troublesome // 그 따위 것을 가지고 있어 봤자 거추장스럽기만 하다 It's a white elephant to me. // 우산 따위를 가지고 다니면 거추장스럽다 I don't like carrying an umbrella. /It is burdensome to carry an umbrella. // 그는 자기 자식들을 거추장스럽게 여기고 있다 He regards〔looks upon〕 his children as so many encumbrances.

거추하다 take care of; look after; keep an eye on〔stand by〕 to help

거춘 去春 last spring

거춤거춤 roughly; cursorily; in a cursory way〔fashion〕 ¶ 방을 거춤거춤 치우다 clean a room roughly // 일을 거춤거춤 하다 make a hasty job of; scamp 《over》// 책을 거춤거춤 읽다 skim over〔through〕 a book

거취 去就 [행동] one's course of action; [태도] one's attitude; manner; behavior ¶ 거취를 결정하다 decide (on) one's course of action; decide one's attitude // 거취가 수상하다 exhibit strange behavior // 거취를 분명히 하다 define one's attitude // 거취를 결정치 못하고 망설이다 be at a loss (about) how to act; do not know which course to take // 의회의 대세는 중립 의원의 거취 여하에 따라 결정된다 The situation in the House hinges upon the attitude of the Independents.

거치 据置 leaving 《a loan unredeemed》; deferment **—하다** [부채 따위를] leave 《a loan》 unredeemed; [지불 따위를] defer〔delay, put off〕 《the payment of a loan》 ¶ 거치의 unredeemed; unredeemable; deferred // 3년 거치의 보험 insurance deferred for three years // 10년 거치의 차관 a loan unredeemable for ten years // 3년 거치 5년 상환 repayment in five years with a three-year grace period // 5년 거치이다 be uncallable for five years

— 기간 the term unredeemed; the term of a loan **— 연금〔배당금, 공채〕** a deferred annuity〔dividend, bond〕 **— 자산〔부채〕** 〖부기〗 deferred assets〔liabilities〕 **— 저금** deferred savings; a fixed deposit

거치다 pass by〔through〕; go〔get〕 through; go via〔by way of〕; undergo; suffer; endure; experience ¶ 세관을 거치다 pass a customhouse // 시험을 거치다 pass an examination // 시험을 거쳐〔거치지 않고〕 on〔without〕 examination // 수많은 고난을 거치다 go through hardships and privations; undergo many hardships // 그는 많은 고난을 거쳐 마침내 성공했다 After going through〔experiencing〕 many difficulties, he finally succeeded. // 서류 심사를 거치다 pass through the documentation // 런던을 거쳐 뉴욕으로 갔다 He went to New York via London. // 그는 내 집을 거쳐 갔다 He dropped into my house on his way.

거치적거리다, 꺼치적거리다 stand〔be〕 in one's way; block (up); be an encumbrance to; hamper; obstruct; encumber ¶ 소용없는 상자들이 거치적거리는 통로 a passage obstructed with useless boxes // 긴 외투가 거치적거려서 걷기 힘들었다 She was hampered by her long cloak.

†거칠다 ① [가루·모래 따위가] (be) coarse; rough ¶ 거친 모래 coarse sand // 거친 천 coarse cloth
② [살결 따위가] (be) coarse; scabrous; rough; harsh ¶ 거친 살결 a rough skin // (피부가) 거칠어지다 roughen; become rough; get chappy; be chapped 《by, with》// 겨울에 거칠어진 손 hands chapped in winter // 나는 피부가 이렇게 거친 것이 정말 싫다 I really hate having such coarse skin.
③ [성질·말·글 따위가] (be) rude; wild; harsh; violent; crude; coarse; rugged; indelicate; uncouth; unfinished ¶ 거친 말 coarse language // 거친 문체 a rude style // 거칠게 들리는 harsh to ear // 그는 태도는 거칠지만 천성은 착하다 He has a rough manner, but deep down he's quite nice.
④ [산야·농토 따위가] (be) rough; rugged; waste; wild; desolate; coarse
⑤ [바람·날씨 따위가] (be) turbulent; rough; wild; raging; tempestuous; viol ent; furious
⑥ [손버릇이] (be) light-fingered

거칠하다, 꺼칠하다 look emaciated; (be) haggard; look worn-out; (be) thin; skinny; tired ¶ 꺼칠해지다 become haggard〔emaciated, worn-out〕 // 꺼칠한 얼굴〔모습〕 a haggard〔worn〕 face〔figure〕 // 병을 앓아 꺼칠해지다 become worn-out from illness; be pulled down by one's illness

거침 [지장] a hitch ; an obstacle ; an impediment ; hindrance ; a snag ; [주저] hesitation ; reserve ; shyness
거침새 an obstacle ; an obstruction ; an impediment ; a hindrance ; a snag ¶ 거침새가 많다 be full of snags
거침없다 [막힘이 없다] (be) trouble-free ; [거리낌없다] (be) unhindered ; be free from an impediment〔hindrance, difficulty〕; be without hesitation〔a hitch, reserve, shyness, being ashamed, blushing〕 ¶ 거침없이 풀다 solve a problem easily〔without an effort〕 // 거침없이 말하다 say without reserve // 거침없이 진척되었다 The matter went on swimmingly. // 거침없이 거짓말할 사람이다 He is a cool hand at lying. // 남의 앞에서 거침없이 그런 소리를 했다 He had the cheek〔face, nerve, so little reserve as〕 to say such a thing in public. // 그는 생각하는 바를 거침없이 말하는 사람이다 He is the man who says straight out whatever is on his mind.
거칫거리다, 꺼칫거리다 keep feeling rough ; keep getting〔standing〕 in the way ; catch ⟪on, in⟫ ; be caught ⟪in, on⟫ ; tug〔pull〕 at ¶ 처진 바짓자락이 발에 거칫거리다 the trailing ends of one's trousers keep pulling at one's legs
거칫거칫, 꺼칫꺼칫 feeling rough〔uneven〕 all the time ; nagging away ⟪at one's attention⟫
거칫하다, 꺼칫하다 ① [수척하다] (be) emaciated ; haggard ; gaunt ② [거칠다] (be) rough ; coarse
거쿨지다 (be) manly ; valiant ; commanding ; stately ; imposing ; masterful
거탈 the outward appearance ; the surface
거통 ① [생김새] a grand appearance ; a dignified attitude ② [실속 없는 지위] a nominal position ; a figurehead
거포 巨砲 a big〔great, huge, mammoth, monster〕 gun〔cannon〕
거푸 over again ; again and again ; repeatedly ¶ 거푸거푸 over and over again ; repeatedly ; in rapid succession // 맥주를 (연)거푸 석 잔을 마시다 take〔drink〕 three glasses of beer in quick succession // 담배 두 대를 (연)거푸 피우다 smoke two cigarettes on end
⁑거푸집 ① [주형] a mold〔mould〕 ; a cast ; a pig ; a matrix ; a die
② [겉모양] one's figure ; the outer appearance of one's body
③ [뜬 곳] a blister ; a raised spot of wallpaper caused by incomplete pasting
거푼거리다 flutter ; flap ; wave ; waver ¶ 거푼거푼 flutteringly ; waveringly // 깃발이 바람에 거푼거리다 a flag flaps in the wind
거풀거리다 flutter ; flap ⇨ 거푼거리다
⁑거품 a bubble ; foam ; froth ; [맥주의] froth ⟪of beer⟫ ; [비누의] lather ; soap suds ; [벌레의] spit ; spittle ; [유리 속의] an air-bubble ; a seed ¶ 거품이 이는 foamy ; frothy ; bubbly ; spumous ; barmy // 거품이 꺼지다 a bubble breaks〔bursts〕 // 거품처럼 사라지다 come to nothing〔naught〕 ; end in smoke〔a failure〕 // 인생은 물거품 Life is but a span.
— 경제 bubble economy **— 상자** 〖물리〗 a bubble chamber
거피 去皮 —하다 skin ; rind ⟪melons, cheese⟫ ; peel ⟪an orange, a potato⟫ ; pare ⟪an apple⟫ ; shell ⟪peas, an egg⟫ ; hull ⟪rice, beans⟫ ; husk ⟪corn⟫ ; bark ⟪a tree⟫ ; strip off ⟪the bark of a tree⟫
거하 去夏 last summer
거한 巨漢 a giant ; a Titan ; a big man〔fellow〕 ; a colossus ⟪*pl.* -si, ~es⟫
거함 巨艦 a big〔monster, mighty〕 warship ; a leviathan
거행 擧行 performance ; celebration ; solemnization **—하다** have〔hold, give〕 ⟪a reception⟫ ; perform〔conduct, carry out〕 ⟪a ceremony⟫ ; celebrate ⟪one's birthday⟫ ; solemnize ⟪a wedding⟫ ¶ 거행되다 be held ; take place // 결혼식을 거행하다 perform a wedding〔marriage〕 // 장례식을 거행하다 hold〔conduct〕 a funeral service // 명령대로 거행하다 act upon ⟪a person's⟫ order // 내일 졸업식이 거행된다 The graduation will be held tomorrow.
거화 炬火 torch ; torchlight
걱실거리다 behave agreeably ; bear oneself cheerfully ; move about in a cheerful spirit ; carry oneself sprightly ; behave buoyantly
걱실걱실 behaving buoyantly ; in a generous and cheerful manner〔attitude〕
†걱정 ① [근심] anxiety ; concern ; apprehension ; worry ; suspense ; trouble ; care ; fear ; uneasiness ; misgivings ; solicitude

> 참고 **anxiety**는 재앙 따위를 두려워하는 불안 **uneasiness**는 불안한 마음 **fear**는 공포 **suspense**는 까닭 없이 마음을 졸이는 것 **apprehension**은 미래에 대한 불안감 **care**는 비교적 조그마한 걱정거리 **concern**은 anxiety보다 다소 부드러운 걱정 **worry**는 지나친 애태움을 의미한다

—하다 feel anxiety ; be anxious ⟪about⟫ ; be concerned ⟪about⟫ ; feel concern⟪for⟫ ; worry (oneself) about ; be worried ⟪about⟫ ; trouble oneself about⟫ ; be troubled ⟪about⟫ ; feel misgiving ; feel uneasy ; be ill at ease ; fear ; be in fear ¶ 걱정하여 with anxiety // 걱정스러운 얼굴 표정 an anxious look // 돈 걱정 money troubles // 집안 걱정 family cares // 안부를 걱정하다 be apprehensive for 《a person's safety》 // 그녀는 돈 걱정을 안한다 She is carefree with money. // 자식의 건강에 대한 걱정 her anxiety about her child's wealth // 매우 걱정하고 있다 be in great anxiety // …에게 걱정을 끼치다 give anxiety to // 그의 건강이 걱정스럽다 I'm anxious about his health. // 그가 실패하지 않을까 걱정이다 I am anxious lest he (should) fail. /I am anxious that he may〔might〕 fail. // 그 일로 걱정하지 마라 Don't worry yourself about that. // 그녀가 늦어서 걱정이다 I am worried by her lateness. // 그는 실수를 하지는 않았나 하고 걱정하고 있다 He's worrying that he may have made a mistake. // 걱정 말게 Never mind ! /Don't worry ! // 걱정할 것까지는 없어 It's nothing to worry about. /That's nothing serious. // 그는 언제나 쓸데없는 걱정을 하고 있어 He always over-worries himself. /He's a worrywart. // 돈이 있으면 걱정이 생긴다 Much coin, much care. // 당신 일이나 걱정하시오 Mind your own business.

② [나무람] scolding ; lecture ; reproach ; reprimand ; reproof ; admonition **—하다** scold ; reprove ; reprimand ¶ 걱정 듣다 be reproved〔reprimanded〕; draw〔receive〕 a reproof 《from》 // 아들을 앞에 놓고 늘 걱정하시었다 He used to give lectures to his son.

걱정거리 worriment ; a worry ; a source 〔matter〕 of anxiety ; a cause of〔for〕 anxiety ¶ 걱정거리가 또 하나 생겼다 I have another weight on my mind.

걱정꾸러기 ① [나무람 듣는] a troublesome〔worrisome〕 child ; a troublemaker ; a worry ; a black sheep ¶ 저 애는 참 걱정꾸러기야 What a little worry that child is ! /He is a constant trouble. // 어느 집이나 걱정꾸러기는 있는 법이다 There is a black sheep in every flock.

② [걱정 많은] a person given to worries ; a person loaded with cares ; one who always borrows trouble ; a person with the worry habit ; a person of nervous temperament ; a pessimist

***걱정스럽다** feel uneasy〔concerned〕; (be) anxious 《over》 ; worried 《about》 ; troubled ; concerned ; apprehensive 《of, for, about》 ¶ 걱정스러운 태도 a concerned air // 걱정스러운 얼굴을 하다 look worried〔concerned〕 // 그의 아들이 시험에 실패하지 않을까 걱정스럽다 We are apprehensive that his son may fail in the examination.

건 巾 a head-cover made of cloth ; [두건] a hemp cap worn by a mourner ; [천] napkin ; kerchief ; towel ; cap

건 鍵 [열쇠] a key (to a lock) ; 〖음악〗 a key 《of a piano》 ¶ 88건의 피아노 a piano with 88 keys

백— a white〔natural〕 key **흑—** a black 〔chromatic〕 key

건 件 [일·사건·문제] a case ; a subject ; a matter ; an affair ; [항목] an item ¶ 예의 건 the matter you have been talking about // 사고 건수 the (number of) cases of accidents // 그 건은 어떻게 되었나 What has become of that matter ? /How does the matter stand now ?

건 腱 〖해부〗 a tendon ¶ 아킬레스건 the Achilles' tendon

건 乾 [마른] dry ; dried ; [건괘] the trigram

—량(糧) (sun-) dried food

건각 健脚 iron legs ; strong〔powerful〕 legs ; being a good walker ¶ 건각의 iron-legged ; strong in walking // 건각의 소유자다 He is really a good walker 〔pedestrian〕. // 수십명의 건각의 젊은이들이 경기에 참가했다 Scores of iron-legged youths participated in the race.

†**건강 健康** health **—하다** (be) healthy ; well ; sound ; wholesome ; healthful

> 참고 **healthy**는 장기간에 걸친 건강을 의미하고 일시적인 건강에는 **well**을 사용한다 **healthful**은 보통 건강에 좋다는 뜻

¶ 건강하게 보이는 healthy-looking // 허약한 건강 상태 feeble〔fragile, bad, broken, frail, ill, poor〕 health // 강건한 건강 상태 robust〔good〕 health // 건강이 좋지 않다 be in poor〔ill, delicate〕 health ; be out of health〔condition〕 // 건강에 좋다 be good for (the) health ; be healthful ; be beneficial to (the) health ; do 《a person》 good // 건강에 해롭다 be bad for (the) health ; be injurious to (the) health // 건강을 해치다 injure〔ruin, lose〕 one's health ; one's health gives way〔breaks down〕 // 흡연은 건강에 해롭다 Smoking is bad for your health. /It's bad for you to smoke. // 건강이 나빠지다 one's health fails ; one is in failing health // 건강을 유지하다 keep〔preserve〕 one's health // 건강을 회복하다 be restored to health ; regain 〔recover〕 one's health ; one's health improves // 건강을 증진하다 promote health ; be conducive to health // (건배하여) 건강을 축하하다 drink to 《a person's》 health ; toast // 건강에 주의하다 take good care of oneself〔one's health〕 // 그는 건강하다 He is fine. /He is very〔quite〕 well. /He is enjoying good health. // 참 건강하십니다 You are in

very good shape. //그의 건강은 술로 손상되었다 His health was undermined by drink. //건강을 유지하기 위해 무엇을 하세요 what do you do to keep in shape? //그것이 나의 건강 유지 비결입니다 That's how I keep in the pink.
— 보험 health insurance — 상담 a health consultation — 상담소 a health clinic — 상태 the condition of one's health ¶ 건강 상태가 좋다〔나쁘다〕 be in a good〔bad〕 state of health — 증진(增進) promotion of health —체(體) healthy condition ; a healthy body 육체적 — physical health 정신적 — mental health

건강 관리 健康管理 health care 《for the aged》 ¶ 환절기의 건강 관리 health care at the change of season

건강미 健康美 healthy beauty

건강법 健康法 how to maintain one's health ; how to keep fit〔health〕; hygiene ¶ 이것이 나의 건강법이다 This is what I'm doing to maintain my health.

건강 식품 健康食品 health foods ; natural foods

건강아 健康兒 a healthy child

건강 증명서 健康證明書 a certificate of health ; a bill of health (검역 때)

건강 진단 健康診斷 a health〔medical〕 examination ; physical examination ; a checkup 《미》 ¶ 건강 진단을 받다 take a physical examination

건건사사 件件事事 each and every event〔matter, case, affair〕

건건이 salted side dishes ; salty tidbits

건건찝질하다 (be) a bit salty ; quite brackish

건건하다 (be) salty ; brackish

건경 健勁 sturdiness ; robustness —하다 (be) strong and valiant ; sturdy ; robust ; stout

건곡 乾穀 dried grain(s)

건곤 乾坤 [하늘과 땅] heaven and earth ; the universe ; [음양] Yin and Yang ; [남성과 여성] male and female

건곤 일척 乾坤一擲 staking all 《on》; playing a game of 'all or nothing' ; crossing the Rubicon ¶ 건곤 일척의 기회다 It is neck or nothing for us. /It is time to take our chance.

건과 乾果 ① nuts ② dry〔dried〕 fruits

건교자 乾交子 a table full of snacks to go with drinks

건국 建國 establishment〔founding〕 of a country —하다 found〔establish〕 a country
— 공로 훈장 the Order of Merit for National Foundation — 대본(大本) the principles upon which the state is established — 기념일 National Foundation〔Founding〕 Day — 포장(褒章) the National Foundation Medal

건군 建軍 the founding of the armed forces —하다 found the armed forces

건기 乾期 the dry season

건깡깡이 ① [매나니로 하는] slapdash ; perfunctory workmanship ; carelessness ; negligence ② [사람] a slapdash worker ; a careless worker

건너 the opposite〔other〕 side of ¶ 건넛마을 a village on the other side ; a village at the opposite side //길 건너에 over the road ; across the street

건너가다 go〔pass〕 over ; go across ; cross (over) ¶ 철길을 건너가다 cross the (railroad) track //바다를 건너가다 sail〔go〕 across the sea //미국으로 건너가다 go over to America

건너긋다 draw 《a line》 across〔over〕 《it》; write a horizontal stroke

†건너다 [지나다] go〔pass〕 over ; go〔walk, run〕 across ; cross (over) ; [나루를] ferry ; [소문 따위가] be carried ; spread ; circulate ¶ 다리를 건너다 cross a bridge //냇물을 건너다 cross〔wade across〕 a stream //배로 강을 건너다 get across a river by boat //입과 입을 건너 퍼진 소문 a rumor circulated from mouth to mouth //한해 건너 한번씩 방문하다 visit at intervals of one year

건너다보다 ① [저쪽을] look out over〔across〕 《at》 ② [남의 것을] covet ; envy ¶ 남의 재산을 건너다보다 covet another's possessions〔property〕

건너뛰다 jump across〔over〕; leap over ; clear ; [생략] skip (over) ; omit ; leave out ¶ 개울〔도랑〕을 건너뛰다 jump across a stream〔ditch〕 //6피트를 건너뛰다 clear six feet //3페이지를 건너뛰다 skip over three pages

건너오다 [사람이] come over〔across〕 《the sea》; cross over 《to Korea》; [사물이] be imported ; be brought over 〔from〕; be introduced ¶ 이리로 건너오시오 Come over here. //김군을 건너오라고 했어요 I asked Mr. *Kim* (to come) over to my seat. //기독교는 16세기에 벌써 한국에 건너왔다 Christianity found its way to Korea as early as the 16th century.

건너지르다 lay〔put〕 it across

건너짚다 guess ; anticipate ¶ 사람의 뜻을 건너짚다 read 《a person's》 mind ; guess what 《a person》 is thinking

***건너편 —便** the opposite side ; the other side ¶ 건너편에 opposite ; on the opposite side //건너편 집 the house opposite〔over the way, across the street〕 //이발소 건너편이 우리 집이다 My house is〔stands〕 opposite the barbershop. /My house is across the street from the barbershop.

건넌방 —房 a room across from the main living room

건널목 [도로의] a road crossing ; [철도

의] a railway〔highway, railroad〕 crossing ; a level〔grade〕 crossing
— 경보기 a crossing signal — 경보벨 a crossing bell — 사고 a crossing accident —지기 a gateman ; a watchman (at a crossing) ; a flagman 《미》 — 차단기 a crossing barrier〔gate〕
건넛집 an opposite house ; the house on the opposite〔other〕 side
†건네다 ① [건너게 하다] carry across ; take over (배로) ; lay〔place〕 over (건네어 놓다) ¶ 나룻배로 사람을 건네다 ferry 《a person》 across a river // 도랑 위로 판자를 건네다 lay a plank across a ditch
② [지불] hand over ; deliver ; pay ; make〔render〕 payment ; transfer ; transmit ; make over ; turn over ¶ 중도금을 건네다 hand over〔pay〕 the part payment // 현품을 건네다 give〔deliver〕 an article // 소유권을 건네다 convey 〔transfer〕 one's ownership to 《a person》
건네주다 pass〔put〕 《a person》 over 《a river》 ; carry across ; ferry 《a person》 over〔across〕 ¶ 저쪽으로 좀 건네줄 수 없습니까 Could you take us over to the other side ?
건달 乾達 a penniless rake ; a libertine ; a debauchee ; a dissipated character ; [불량배] a scamp ; a good-for-nothing ¶ 건달부리다 lead a dissolute life
—패(牌) a crowd〔group〕 of scamps
건답 乾畓 a dry rice paddy ; a rice field that dries easily
-건대 when ; if ; according to ; judging from ; in view of ; in the light of ; in respect of ¶ 내가 보건대 as I see ; according to my observation // 듣건대 as I hear ; according to the rumor ; as the rumor goes // 이 사실로 보건대 in the light of these facts // 내 경험으로 보건대 judging from my experience // 바라건대 I pray〔hope〕 《that》 ; my prayer is 《that》 // 결론을 말하건대 to conclude ; in conclusion ; the conclusion is 《that》 // 대체로 말하건대 as a whole ; in general ; generally speaking
건대 巾帶 a mourner's cowl and belt
건대구 乾大口 a dried cod
건더기 ① [국 속의] solid ingredients in a mixture of liquid and solids ; pieces of meat and vegetables in soup ¶ 국 건더기 solid food like meat or vegetables in soup
② [내용] a basis ; a ground ; a foundation ; substance ¶ 건더기 없는 이야기 an empty story ; a groundless story ; a story of little substance // 말할 건더기가 없다 There is no excuse whatever.
건둥하다, 껀둥하다 (be) neat ; tidy ; be in good order
건드러지다 《a voice, a song》 be modulated in a charming〔bewitching〕 way
건드렁거리다 wobble ; sway ; waver ¶ 나뭇가지가 건드렁거리다 branches sway on a tree
건드렁건드렁 with wobbling〔wavering, swaying〕 motion
건드레하다 (be) half tipsy ; slightly intoxicated ; be a bit high ; (be) happy ¶ 건드레한 기분이다 be slightly intoxicated ; have a drop in one's eye ; be tipsy // 그는 건드레하다 He looks gay (with drink). / He is a happy man.
건드리다 [손·발로] touch ; meddle with ; give 《a thing》 a jog ; [비위·마음을] provoke ; vex ; irritate ; offend ; [여자를] make sport〔fun〕 of ; play〔sport〕 with ; have sexual relations〔intercourse〕 with 《a woman》 ¶ 이 물건을 건드리지 마라 Don't touch this article. /Hands off ! // 제발 남의 신경을 건드리지 말아요 Don't get on my nerves, please. /Don't irritate me, please. // 그의 신경을 건드리지 않도록 조심하라 Be careful not to get on his nerves. /Give him lots of room.
건들거리다 ① [움직이다] sway ; swing ; shake ; dangle ¶ 바위가 건들거린다 The rocks shake. ② [바람이] 《the wind》 blow a bit strong ③ [놀아대다] put on extravagant airs ; strut
건들건들 [바람] gently ; [사람] lithely
건들바람 a cool〔refreshing〕 breeze (in early autumn) ¶ 건들 바람이 불어왔다 A refreshing breeze came blowing pleasantly.
건들장마 a capricious rainy season in early autumn
건듯, 건뜻 quickly ; hastily ; hurriedly ¶ 일을 건듯 해치우다 make a quick job of it
건듯건듯 briefly ; cursorily ¶ 건듯건듯 설명하다 explain briefly // 건듯건듯 읽다 glance over〔through〕 《a letter》
건등 『광산』 the surface part of an ore vein
건땅 rich〔fertile〕 soil
건락 乾酪 cheese
— 제품 cheese products
건락소 乾酪素 casein
건량 乾糧 food made for (carrying on) a long way〔journey〕
건류 乾溜 dry〔destructive〕 distillation ; [석탄의] carbonization ¶ 저온 건류법 low-temperature carbonization —하다 dry (up) by distillation ; carbonize (석탄을)
건립 建立 erection ; building ; construction —하다 build ; erect ; construct ¶ 건립중이다 be in the course of erection ; be under construction // 절을 건립하다 build〔set up, raise〕 a (Buddhist)

temple // 기념비를 건립하다 erect a monument

-건마는 though ; in spite of ; despite ; for all ; with〔after〕 all ; notwithstanding ; however ; still ; nevertheless ; none the less ¶ 노력은 했건마는 실패했다 In spite of hard efforts, he failed. // 공부는 열심히 했건마는 낙제했다 He was plucked notwithstanding his great diligence. // 물건은 좋건마는 값이 비싸다 I admit its quality. Still, it is too dear. // 돈은 많건마는 행복하지는 못하다 He is none the happier for his wealth.

건망증 健忘症 forgetfulness ; oblivion ; amnesia ¶ 그는 건망증이 심하다 He is forgetful. /He has a short memory. // 건망증이 생기는 것 같아 I'm afraid I'm getting absent-minded.

건목 [일·물건] a rough job〔thing〕; a rough-finished article ; rough workmanship

건목치다 do a rough job of 《it》; rough-finish 《it》

건몸달다 make vain〔fruitless〕 efforts ; struggle〔sweat〕 in vain ; exert oneself to no purpose ; waste one's time and labor ; get all heated up to no avail ¶ 건몸달다가 병나다 fret〔worry〕 oneself ill

건물 乾— involuntarily emitted〔ejaculated〕 semen ; seminal fluid (ejaculated during a sexual dream)

*건물 建物 a building ; a structure ; an edifice

> 참고 **building** 일반적으로 많이 쓰이는 말 **edifice** 다소 딱딱한 말이며 웅장한 건물을 말한다 **structure** 건물이라도 특히 그 구조에 중점을 둔다

¶ 건물을 세우다 build〔erect, put up〕 a building // 건물을 개축하다 renovate a building // 건물을 파괴하다 demolish〔raze, tear down〕 a building // 건물 내부를 부수다 gut a building // 황폐한 건물 dilapidated〔gutted, ramshackle, tumbledown〕 building // 근대식 건물이다 It is of modern construction. // 정거장은 르네상스식의 훌륭한 건물이다 The station is a fine specimen of Renaissance structure. // 새로 지은 고층 건물이 관광 명소가 되었다고 들었습니다 I heard a newly-built high-rise building has become a tourist attraction.

목조 — a wooden building 석조 — a stone building 철근 콘크리트 — a ferroconcrete〔concrete steel〕 building ; a reinforced concrete building

건물로 乾— ① [공연히] blindly ; uselessly ; without knowing why ② [힘을 안 들이고] ¶ 남의 재산을 건물로 가로채다 take possession of another's property by force ; seize another's property

*건반 鍵盤 [피아노 따위의] a keyboard ; [바이올린 따위의] a fingerboard ; a clavier

— 음악 keyboard music

건반 악기 鍵盤樂器 keyboard instruments ; a clavier

건밤 a sleepless night ¶ 건밤을 새우다 sit〔stay〕 up all night ; spend a sleepless night

건방지다 (be) impertinent ; forward ; impudent ; pert ; perky ; insolent ; arrogant ; officious ; intrusive ; obtrusive ; contemptuous ; saucy ; overbearing ; affected ; snobbish ; (self-)conceited ; cocky ; fresh

> 참고 **impertinent**는 뻔뻔스럽고 주제넘은의 뜻으로서 무례함을 나타낸다 **impudent**는 impertinent에 비해 염치없고 뻔뻔스러운의 뜻을 더 지닌 무례함의 정도가 더 심한 말, **insolent**는 무례한의 뜻 **officious**는 주제넘게 나서는의 뜻

¶ 건방진 녀석 an impertinent〔a saucy〕 fellow ; a conceited pup ; a snob // 건방진 여자 a saucy girl ; a flapper // 건방진 대답 a pert answer ; a saucy reply // 건방진 소리하다 talk saucy〔fresh〕; have a saucy tongue ; give cheek // 건방지게 …하다 have the cheek〔impertinence〕 to 《do》; dare to 《do》 // 건방진 소리 마라 Don't say such cheeky things. / None of your cheek〔impertinence, lip〕! // 제가 건방진 말을 한 것 같습니다 I guess I spoke out of turn.

건배 乾杯 a toast

— 하다 drink the toast 《of》; drink〔give, make〕 a toast 《to》; toast 《a person》; drink to 《a person's health》 ¶ 아무의 건강을 위해 건배하다 drink (to) a person's health 〔(to) the health of a person〕; toast a person's health // 맥주로 건배하다 toast 《a person》 with beer〔with a glass of beer〕 // 잔을 마주쳐서 건배하다 clink glasses 《with》 // 당신의 건강을 위하여 건배 To your health! /Your health! / Prosit! /Cheers! // 당신을 위하여 건배합니다 Here's to you! /Here's luck to you! /Here's to your health!

건보 健步 a strong pace ; strong legs ; a good walker (사람)

건빵 乾— a biscuit ; hardtack

건사하다 ① [간수하다] keep ; take care of ; put carefully ; put aside (for future use) ¶ 김군 이 돈은 자네가 건사하게 You take care of this money, *Kim.* ② [보살피다] support ; take care of ; look after ; prepare for ; attend to ¶ 그 애는 아직 어려서 자기 몸도 건사할 줄 모른다 She is too young to take care

of herself. // 일곱 식구를 건사하려니 힘이 든다 It's a hard job for me to support a family of seven.
③ [일을] supervise ; direct 《a funeral service》; look after

건삼 乾蔘 skinned and dried ginseng with its fibrils cut off

건선거 乾船渠 a dry dock

†**건설** 建設 construction ; building ; [설립] establishment **—하다** construct ; build ; erect ; establish ; [창설] found ¶ 건설적인 constructive // 건설중이다 be under〔in the course of〕 construction // 완전한 민주 국가를 건설하다 build up〔establish〕 a thoroughly democratized country // 그것은 건설이 아니고 파괴다 It is an act of destruction, not of construction. // 관계 당국이 건설적 조치를 취하기로 결정하였음은 반가운 일이다 We are glad to note that the authorities concerned have at last decided to take a constructive step.
— 공사 construction〔building〕 work — 공채(公債) a construction bond —국(局) the Construction Bureau — 기계 construction machinery〔equipment〕 — 비(費) construction costs ; the cost of construction ; building expenses — 사무소 a building office — 사업(事業) the construction industry — 용지(用地) a building site〔plot, lot〕 —자(者) a builder ; a founder

건설방 a loafer (chasing women) ; an idling libertine ; a debauchee

건설부 建設部 the Ministry of Construction〔Works 《영》〕
— 장관 the Minister of Construction ; the Construction Minister

건설분과 위원회 建設分科委員會 [국회의] the Construction Committee

건성 inattention ; lack of attention ; abstraction ; absent-mindedness ¶ 건성으로 absent-mindedly ; abstractedly ; vacantly ; half-heartedly ; inattentively ; with inattention // 건성으로 듣다 listen to 《a person》 in an absent sort of way ; pay little attention to // 건성으로 읽다 read 《a thing》 inattentively // 건성으로 덤벼들다 try to do a thing without knowing anything about it // 그의 마음은 건성이다 His mind is faraway. // 건성으로 듣고 있으니까 알지 못한다 You cannot understand it, because you do not pay due attention (to it).
—꾼 a rash person ; a man who never looks before he leaps

건성 乾性 ¶ 건성의 dry
— 가스 a dry gas — 동물 a xeric animal — 수지(樹脂) element-convertible resin — 식물 a xerophyte

건성건성 in a casual〔superficial, desultory〕 way ; halfway ; in a half measure ; halfheartedly ¶ 일을 건성건성 해치우다 get one's work done in a casual〔hit-or-miss〕 way // 일을 건성건성하다 scamp〔fudge, slur over, fudge over〕 one's work〔duty〕

건성 늑막염 乾性肋膜炎 〖의학〗 dry pleurisy

건성울음 a sham cry ; shedding unfelt tears ; make-believe crying

건성울음 울다 shed feigned〔crocodile, false, perfunctory〕 tears ; feign〔sham〕 weeping

건성유 乾性油 drying oil

건수 乾嗽 a dry cough ; a hack

건수 件數 the number of cases〔items〕 ¶ 취급〔도난〕 건수 the number of cases handled〔of theft〕

건습 乾濕 dryness and wetness ; humidity
— 운동 〖식물〗 hygroscopic movement

건습구 온도계 乾濕球溫度計 a wet and dry bulb thermometer

건승 健勝 being in good health ¶ 건승을 빌다 pray for 《a person's》 good health

건시 乾柹 dried persimmons

건식 乾式 the dry process

건실 健實 steadiness ; soundness ; reliableness **—하다** (be) steady ; sound ; reliable ¶ 건실하게 steadily ; solidly ; soundly // 건실한 사상 sound ideas // 건실한 사람 a steady〔reliable〕 person // 건실한 사업〔투자〕 a sound enterprise〔investment〕 // 영업 방법이 건실하다 His method of business is sound.

건아 健兒 a stalwart youth ; a vigorous boy〔youth〕 ¶ 대한의 건아 a virile son of Korea

건어 乾魚 dried〔kippered〕 fish ; stockfish ¶ 건어로 만들다 dry〔cure, kipper〕 fish

건위 健胃 making one's stomach strong **—하다** strengthen one's stomach
—정(錠) a peptic tablet —제(劑) a peptic ; a stomachic ; a stomachal ; a digestive

건육 乾肉 dried meat ; pemmican (쇠고기의) ; jerky

건으로 乾— without reason〔purpose, cause〕 ; blindly

건의 建議 [제의] a proposal ; a recommendation ; a motion ; a suggestion ; [건언] a memorial **—하다** propose ; recommend ; [건언] memorialize ¶ 김씨의 건의로 at the instance of Mr. *Kim* // 정부에 건의하다 make a recommendation to the Government ; memorialize the Government

건의서 建議書 a memorial ; a petition ; a representation ; a recommendation ¶ 정부에 건의서를 제출하다 submit a recommendation to the government

건의안 建議案 a proposition ; a motion

¶ 건의안을 채택하다 adopt a proposition // 건의안을 가결〔부결〕하다 carry 〔reject〕 a motion

건의자 建議者 a proposer ; a sponsor

건의함 建議函 a suggestion box

건잠머리 general instructions for doing a job ━하다 provide the means to do the jobs

*건장 健壯 good〔robust〕 health ; healthiness ; healthfulness ━하다 (be) healthy ; healthful ; robust ; sound ; be in good health ; [특히 노인이] hale and hearty ¶ 건장한 체격 a robust〔strong〕 physique〔frame〕 // 아주 건장하다 be in excellent〔robust, perfect〕 health ; be in the best of health ; be in great shape // 나는 아직 건장하다 I still enjoy perfect health. /I am as fit as a fiddle.

건재 乾材 dried medicinal herbs

— 약국(藥局) a wholesale medicinal herb store ; an oriental medicinal herb drugstore.

건재 建材 building〔construction〕 materials

—상 a building materials dealer〔trader〕

건재 健在 ━하다 be (alive and) well ; be in good〔excellent〕 health ; (be) up and coming ; be as prosperous as usual (사업 따위가) ¶ 건재를 빕니다 I wish you good health. // 부모님은 건재하십니까 Are your parents well〔living〕? /How are your parents getting along〔on〕? // 그의 사업은 아직 건재하다 His business is still thriving.

†건전 健全 sound ; health ; healthiness ━하다 (be) healthy ; sound ; wholesome ¶ 건전한 문학 healthy literature // 건전한 사고 a healthy idea // 건전한 도서 wholesome books // 건전한 환경 wholesome environment // 건전한 재정〔투자, 발달, 판단〕 sound finance 〔investment, development, judgment〕 // 건전한 발달을 이룩하다 have a healthy growth〔development〕 // 건전한 정신을 갖고 있다 be sound-minded // 건전하지 못한 행동 unsound〔unwholesome〕 behavior // 모자가 다 건전하다 Both mother and baby are doing well. // 건전한 정신은 건전한 신체에 깃든다 A sound mind (dwells) in a sound body.

건전지 乾電池 a dry cell〔battery〕

‡건조 乾燥 dryness ; drying ; [정신·환경 등이] aridity ━하다 (be) dry ; arid ; dry (up) ; become dry ; season (목재를) ¶ 건조한 dry ; dried ; parched // 건조한 작품 a jejune piece of work // 건조한 목재 dry wood // 목재를 옥외에서 건조시키다 season wood in the open air // 건조한 생활을 하다 live a simple〔dull〕 life // 공기가 매우 건조하다 The air is exceedingly dry.

— 공기 dry air — 냉동법 dehydro-freezing ; freeze-drying — 밀도(密度) dry density — 비료 dried manure —솥 a drying kiln — 수축 drying shrinkage — 시험 a drying test — 식품 dehydrated food — 야채 dehydrated vegetables — 온도 drying temperature —율 a dryness factor — 인쇄 xerography — 중량 dry weight 공동(空洞) —기(器) a cavity drier 열풍(熱風) —기(器) a hot-air drier 이상 — abnormally dry weather 이상 — 주의보 a dry weather alert

건조 建造 construction ; building ━하다 construct ; build ¶ 건조 중이다 be under construction ; be in course of construction ; be being built ; be on the stocks ¶ 그 유조선은 지금 건조 중이다 The oil tanker is〔has been〕 under construction.

—독 a building dock —물(物) a building ; a structure ; a construction — 보험 builder's risk insurance — 보험 증권 a shipbuilder's risk policy —자 a builder

건조기 乾燥期 the dry season

건조기 乾燥器 a drier〔dryer〕 ; a drying machine ; [알·야채의] a desiccator

건조 기후 乾燥氣候 an arid climate

건조란 乾燥卵 desiccated eggs

건조무미 乾燥無味 dryness

건조 세탁 乾燥洗濯 dry cleaning

건조실 乾燥室 a drying room

건조 장치 乾燥裝置 a drier〔dryer〕

건조제 乾燥劑 a drier〔dryer〕 ; a drying agent

건조증 乾燥症 xeransis ; xerosis

건조지 乾燥地 dry ground〔land〕

건조 혈장 乾燥血漿 dried human (blood) plasma

건주정 乾酒酊 feigned drunkenness ; pretending to be drunk ; giving an outward show of drunkenness ━하다 feign drunkenness ; pretend to be drunk ; give a show of intoxication

건중건중 roughly ; cursorily

건중그리다 order〔arrange〕 《disorderly things》 roughly ; even up ⇨ 간종그리다

건지 a sounding-〔plumb-〕line (to test the depth of water)

*건지다 ① [액체 속의 것을] take〔bring〕 out of water ; pull〔draw〕 up ; refloat (배를) ; pick up 《a shipwrecked person》 ¶ 물 속에 빠뜨린 동전을 건지다 pick〔take〕 up a coin sunk in the water

② [위험·곤란 따위에서] help 《a person》 out of ; rescue 《a person》 from ; relieve 《a person》 from ; release 《a person》 from ; redeem 〔reclaim〕 《a person》 from (죄에서) ; deliver ¶ 조난한 선원들을 건지다 pick up shipwrecked crew // 물에 빠진 사람을 건지다 rescue 《a person》 from drowning // 곤경에서 건져내다 deliver 《a

person》 out of difficulties
③ [손해·투자한 것을] take〔get〕 back ; regain ; save ; retrieve ; recover ; cover up ¶ 손해를 좀 건졌나 Have you retrieved some of your loss? // 이번 화재에 건진 가구라곤 얼마 없다 Very little of the furniture was saved in the recent fire. // 사업의 실패로 본전도 못 건졌다 Even the principal was lost in the business failure.

건착망 巾着網 a purse net〔seine〕

건책 建策 making a plan **— 하다** plan ; make〔form, lay〕 a plan ; devise ; contrive

건천 乾川 a stream that dries up during spells of dry weather ; a dry stream

‡**건초 乾草** hay ; dried grass ; dried herb ¶ 건초 베는 칼 hay knife // 건초를 만들다 make hay
— 공수(空輸) haylift **— 더미** hay ; mow ; haystack (지붕을 씌운)
별 났을 때 건초를 만들어라 속담 Make hay while the sun shines.

건초열 乾草熱 〖의학〗 hay fever

†**건축 建築** building ; construction ; erection ; [건축물] a building ; structure ; architecture 《총칭》 **— 하다** build ; construct ; erect ¶ 석조 건물 a stone building〔structure〕 // 근대식 건축 modern architecture // 대 건축물 a large building ; an edifice ; a pile // 한국식 건축 Korean-style building // 건축상의 architectural // 건축 중이다 be building ; be under〔in course of〕 construction // 돌로 건축되어 있다 be built up of stones // 집을 건축하다 build a house // 건축에 부정이 있다 There is something scandalous in connection with the building. // 이 교사는 근년에 건축한 것이다 The schoolhouse is of recent construction.
— 기준법(基準法) 〖법〗 the Building Standards Act **— 노동자** a construction worker **— 부지** a building site **— 붐** building〔construction〕 boom **—세** the tax on construction ; the building tax **—술** building ; architecture **—용 철재〔강철재〕** structural iron〔steel〕 **— 음향학(音響學)** architectural acoustics **— 화가** an architectural painter **— 회사** a building company ; an architectural〔a construction〕 firm **서양식 벽돌 —** a brick structure in foreign〔western〕 style **주택 —** domestic architecture

‡**건축가 建築家** an architect ; a builder ; a building contractor (청부업자)

건축 공사 建築工事 construction work

건축 공학 建築工學 architectural engineering

건축 구조 建築構造 building construction
— 역학 structural mechanics

건축 기사 建築技師 a building engineer ; an architect

건축 기술 建築技術 building〔construction〕 techniques
—자 an architect and engineer

건축 면적 建築面積 building area

†**건축물 建築物** a building ; a structure ; an edifice (거대한)

건축 미술 建築美術 the fine art of architecture

건축 법규 建築法規 the building law ; the building code

건축 부지 建築敷地 a building site

건축비 建築費 the cost of building〔construction〕 ; building cost

건축 사무소 建築事務所 an architectural firm

건축 사업 建築事業 the building industry

건축 설계 建築設計 architectural design

건축 설비 建築設備 building equipment

건축 양식 建築樣式 a style of architecture ; architectural style ; construction structure (구조)

건축업 建築業 the building〔construction〕 industry ; construction
—자 a builder ; a constructor

건축 용지 建築用地 a building〔housing〕 lot

건축 용재 建築用材 ⇨ 건축재

건축재 建築材 building〔construction〕 materials

건축 조합 建築組合 a building society 《영》

건축 제한선 建築制限線 building line

건축 청부 建築請負 a building contract
—업자 a (building) contractor

건축 통제 建築統制 building control

건축학 建築學 architecture ; architectonics ; the science〔art〕 of construction

건축 허가 建築許可 a building permit

건투 健鬪 a good fight ; [노력] strenuous efforts **— 하다** put up a good fight ; fight bravely〔well〕 ; make strenuous efforts ¶ 건투를 빈다 I expect you to do your best. / Good luck to you!

건판 乾板 〖사진〗 a dry plate ; a plate ; 〖인쇄〗 a dryer ¶ 건판을 현상하다 develop a dry plate
—법(法) the dry-plate process

건평 建坪 a building area ; floor space ; floorage ¶ 건평 30평의 아파트 an apartment with a floor space of 30 *pyŏng* // 건평은 30평이다 The house covers an area of 30 *pyŏng*.

건폐율 建蔽率 the building-to-land ratio

건포 乾脯 dried meat〔fish〕 ; jerked meat
— 마찰(摩擦) a rubdown with a dry towel

건포도 乾葡萄 raisins ; dry grapes

건풍떨다 乾風— boast ; brag ; talk boastfully ; talk big

건필 健筆 a facile〔ready, prolific〕 pen ;

vigorous writing ¶ 건필을 휘두르다 wield a facile〔powerful〕 pen // 당신의 건필에는 젊은 학생들이 경탄하고 있소 Your facile pen commands the admiration of the young students.

건하다 ① [넉넉하다] (be) abundant ; ample ; plentiful ② [흥건하다] (be) brimful ③ [거나하다] (be) tipsy ; mellow

건하다 乾— (be) dry ; arid ; thirsty (목이)

건혼나다 startle〔be frightened〕 at nothing ; be startled for no reason

*__걷다[1]__ ① [말다] roll〔turn, pull〕 up 《one's sleeves》 ; tuck up ; bare〔strip〕 《one's arm》 ; gather up ; fold up ¶ 바지를 무릎까지 걷고 with one's trousers pulled 〔turned, rolled〕 up to the knees // 소매를 걷고 with bare arms ; with one's sleeves turned over one's elbows // 치맛자락을 걷다 gird〔tuck〕 up the skirt of the dress // 소매를 걷어 올리다 tuck〔roll〕 up one's sleeves // 걷은 것을 도로 내리다 undo〔let out〕 the tuck // 자리를 걷어라 Roll up the mat.
② [치우다] remove ; take away ; take off ; [내리다] take down ; strike ; lower ; bring down ; pull down ¶ 커튼을 걷다 gather up a curtain ; draw aside a curtain // 그물을 걷다 haul 〔draw〕 in〔up〕 a net // 기를 걷다 take 〔pull〕 down a flag ; strike a flag // 돛을 걷다 take in sails // 천막을 걷다 strike 〔pull down〕 a camp〔tent〕 ; break camp // 빨래를 걷다 remove the laundry from a clothesline ; gather up the laundry 〔washing〕
③ [거두다] collect ; gather ; get ¶ 걷은 돈 the collected money ; the money collected ; the collection of money // 외상을 걷다 collect bills // 기부금〔회비〕을 걷다 collect subscriptions〔membership fees〕 // 새로운 사업에 쓸 돈을 걷다 raise money for a new undertaking // 기부금〔회비〕은 전부 걷혔다 All the subscriptions have been collected.
④ [그만두다] settle 《a matter》 ; bring 《a matter》 to a conclusion ¶ 일을 걷다 settle one's affairs // 사업을 걷어 버리다 go out of business // 그는 일을 걷고 담배 한 대를 피웠다 He put aside his work to have a smoke.

†**걷다[2]** walk ; go on foot ; tramp ; step ; hike 《미·속》 ¶ 걸어가면서 as one goes ; on the way // 걸어가다 go on foot ; foot it 《속》 // 거리를 걷다 walk the street // 서울 시내를 걸어다니다 walk through the streets of *Seoul* // 학교를 걸어서 가다 go to school on foot ; walk to school // 걸어서 귀가하다 walk home // (환자, 갓난아기가) 걷게 되다 find 〔feel, get on〕 one's legs // (갓난아기가) 아장아장 걷다 toddle ; waddle // 성큼성큼 걷다 walk with big strides // 사뿐사뿐 걷다 walk lightly ; walk with light steps // 살금살금 걷다 walk with stealthy steps ; walk on tiptoe // 뚜벅뚜벅 걷다 walk〔tread〕 heavily ; tramp // 가벼운 걸음으로 걷다 tread lightly // 가만가만 걷다 walk softly // 천천히 걷다 walk slowly 〔leisurely〕 ; walk at a leisurely pace // 빠른 걸음으로 걷다 walk quickly 〔briskly〕 // 한가로이 걷다 stroll ; saunter // 터벅터벅 걷다 plod along ; trudge 《along》 ; shuffle 《along》 // 비칠비칠 걷다 walk unsteadily ; totter ; stagger // 뒤뚱뒤뚱 걷다 waddle 《along》 ; totter ; walk falteringly // 절룩거리며 걷다 walk lamely ; limp // 꺼덕꺼덕 걷다 swagger〔stalk〕 along // 마음내키는 대로 걷다 go wherever one's humor dictates // 지치도록 걸리다 walk 《a person》 off his legs // 하루에 10마일을 걷다 do 10 miles a day on foot // 역까지는 걸어서 15분이면 간다 It is an only fifteen minute walk to the station. // 버스 타는 곳은 집에서 걸어서 5분도 안 걸린다 The bus-stop is within five minutes' walk of my house. // 자네는 잘도 걷는군 You are a good walker〔pedestrian〕. // 어지간히 걸었군 We have done much walking. // 한국 경제는 이제 향상 일로를 걷고 있다 The Korean economy is now on the road to progress. / The Korean economy is now on the upswing.
걷기도 전에 뛰려고 한다 속담 Children learn to creep ere they can go.

걷다[3] [개다] lift ; clear off ; break away ¶ 안개가 걷다 a fog lifts〔clears off〕

걷몰다 drive 《cattle》 hurriedly ; drive hard ; spur〔urge〕 《a horse》 on ¶ 말을 걷몰다 press a horse // 일을 걷몰다 press one's work hard // 공명심에 걷몰리다 be urged〔driven〕 by ambition

걷어들다 take up ; tuck up ¶ 치맛자락을 걷어들다 tuck up one's skirt // 그물을 걷어들다 draw in a net

걷어붙이다 roll〔tuck, turn〕 up ¶ 팔을 걷어붙이다 roll up one's sleeves ; bare 〔strip〕 one's arm // 바지를 무릎까지 걷어붙이다 turn up one's trousers to the knees // 팔을 걷어붙이고 with bare arms ; with one's sleeves tucked up

걷어잡다 hold up ¶ 치맛자락을 걷어잡다 hold up (the ends of) one's skirt

걷어지르다 tuck 《into, on, behind》 ¶ 커튼 자락을 나무못에 걷어지르다 tuck the ends of a curtain behind a peg

걷어질리다 《one's eyes》 become hollow ; be sunken ; fall in ¶ 그는 오래 앓고 난 후라 눈이 걷어질렸다 His eyes were sunken after a long illness.

걷어차다 [저버리다] break off 《relations with a person》 ; break with 《a person》 ; kick hard ; give 《a person》 a hard kick ¶ 정강이를 걷어차다 give a hard kick on the shin//문을 걷어차서 열다 kick the door open//말이 사람의 머리를 걷어찼다 A horse kicked a person hard on the head.

걷어차이다 be kicked (hard); get a (hard) kick ¶ 옆구리를 걷어차이다 get a kick in the side

***걷어치우다** ① [물건 따위를] gather up and remove; clear away; put away; put in order ¶ 흩어진 물건을 걷어치우다 clear away scattered things
② [하던 일을] leave off; stop; quit; give up; shut up 《one's shop》; wind up 《one's affairs》 ¶ 하던 일을 걷어치우다 leave off one's work; stop doing one's job//가게를 걷어치우다 close down a shop; go out of business

-걷이 a gathering-up; a collection ¶ 가을걷이 harvest; gathering

걷잡다 hold; stop; keep; [막다] check 《the enemy's advance》; keep 《a danger, a disease》 at bay; control ¶ 걷잡을 새 없이 swiftly; quickly; speedily//달아나는 말을 걷잡다 stop a runaway horse//걷잡을 수 없는 혼란에 빠지다 get into uncontrollable confusion//눈물이 걷잡을 수 없이 흐른다 I cannot keep back my tears.//저 은행은 걷잡을 수 없게 되었다 The bank cannot hold out any longer.//소방원들은 용케 불기운을 걷잡았다 The firemen managed to keep the fire under (control).//정부는 인플레를 걷잡기 위하여 대책을 강구했다 The government has taken measures to hold back inflation.

걷히다 ① [구름 따위가] clear (up); vanish; lift; clear off; break away; be lifted; be cleared off; be broken away; be dispelled ¶ 안개가 걷혀간다 The fog is lifting〔breaking〕.//구름이 걷혔다 The clouds have cleared away.//너의 얘기로 나의 의심이 완전히 걷혔다 Your statement has dispelled all my doubts.//만일 한 시간쯤 안에 안개가 걷히지 않으면 012편은 다른 공항으로 가서 착륙할 것입니다 If the fog does not lift within an hour or so, flight 012 will be diverted to a different airport.
② [돈 따위가] be collected; be gathered ¶ 세금이 잘 걷힌다 The tax has a good yield.//기부금이 잘 걷히지 않았다 The collection of the subscriptions was unsuccessful〔far from satisfactory〕.

걸개 그림 a hanging picture

걸객 乞客 a beggar; a mendicant; a tramp

걸걸 hungrily; greedily; voraciously —**하다** ⇨ 걸걸거리다

걸걸거리다 be greedy; be gluttonous; behave greedily

걸걸하다 傑傑— [외양·성격이] (be) candid; open; openhearted; freehearted and cheerful; vivacious; bright(-spirited); [목소리가] guttural; husky ¶ 걸걸한 음성 a husky and resonant voice//그는 위인이 걸걸하다 He is a nonchalant 〔cheerful, freehearted, vivacious〕 fellow.

걸귀 [암퇘지] a mother sow; a sow that has dropped its young ones; [사람] a glutton; a gormandizer; a cormorant; a pig〔hog〕 《구》 ¶ 걸귀들린 gluttonous; voracious; ravenous; swinish; (as) greedy〔hungry〕 as a wolf//걸귀들리다 have a wolf in one's stomach; wolf down//걸귀들린 듯이 먹다 eat ravenously 〔greedily, voraciously〕

걸근거리다 ① [욕심내다] covet ② [목이] 《one's throat》 be tickled with phlegm

걸근걸근 [먹고 싶어] greedily; covetously; hankeringly; [목구멍이] ticklishly; scratchily

걸기대 乞期待 [게시] Please wait!/Coming soon!/[영화] Coming attractions!

걸기질 leveling〔smoothing〕 of the rice paddy —**하다** level〔smooth〕 the rice paddy

걸까리지다 (be) big and stout; of large build; large-〔big-〕built; of great stature

걸낭 —囊 ① [걸어 두는] a bag〔tobacco pouch〕 ② [바랑] a knapsack; a pack

:걸다¹ ① [매달다] hang 《a thing on a peg》; hook; suspend; put up; set up ¶ 간판을 걸다 hang〔put〕 up a signboard; hang out a sign//벽에 그림을 걸다 hang a picture on the wall//모자를 모자걸이에 걸다 hang one's hat on a hook〔peg〕//조기(弔旗)를 내걸다 hang a flag at halfmast//달력을 벽에 걸다 hang a calendar on the wall//현관 앞에 깃발이 걸려 있다 The front of the house is hung with a flag.//그림이 벽에 걸려 있다 There is a picture hanging on the wall.
② [말을] speak to 《a person》; address 《a person》; talk to 《a person》 ¶ 농을 걸다 play a joke on 《a person》//정중히 말을 걸다 speak seriously to 《a person》//낯선 사람이 말을 걸어 왔다 A stranger spoke〔called〕 to me.//말을 걸을 수 있을 정도의 영어 실력을 갖추다 have a speaking knowledge of English
③ [싸움·시비를] pick; provoke ¶ 싸움을 걸다 pick a quarrel with 《a person》; provoke 《a person》
④ [전화를] dial the number; telephone (to) 《a person》; call up; make a (telephone) call to 《a person》; ring 《a person》 up (on the telephone) 《영》; call 《a person》 (on the telephone) 《미》; phone 《a person》 ¶ 나에게 전화

가 걸려 왔다 I was called up. //112번으로 전화를 걸었다 I dialed 112. //경찰에 전화를 걸어라 Dial the police station. //나중에 다시 전화걸다 call back//그곳에 도착 즉시 전화를 걸어 주십시오 Phone me〔Give me a ring〕 as soon as you get there. //내일 아침 사무실로 전화 걸어 주십시오 Phone〔Call〕 me at my office tomorrow morning. //그 번호로 지금 한 번 걸어 보세요 Try the number now. //크라운 호텔에 전화 좀 걸어 주세요 Get Crown Hotel on the phone.
⑤ [기계의 작동을] start 《an engine》 going ¶ 자동차에 브레이크를 걸다 brake an automobile ; apply〔put on〕 the brake
⑥ [자물쇠 따위를] lock ; fasten ; turn a key ¶ 문에 자물쇠를 걸다 lock the door//금고에 자물쇠를 걸다 lock the safe
⑦ [선금을] pay ; advance ; deposit ¶ 선금〔약조금〕을 걸다 pay〔advance〕 money 《on a contract》//보증금을 걸다 place deposit money 《on》 ; have〔place〕 money on deposit//집〔새차〕에 계약금을 걸다 make a deposit on a house〔new car〕
⑧ [올가미를] set〔lay, place〕 a trap 《for mice》
⑨ [재판을] institute court proceedings 《against a person》 ; lodge 《a lawsuit against a person》
⑩ [돈·목숨 따위를] stake ; bet 《money on》 ; wager ; lay a wager 《on》 ; risk (무릅쓰다) ¶ 목숨을 걸다 risk〔stake〕 one's life ; take a risk of one's life//경마에 걸다 stake a horse ; stake〔bet〕 money on a horse race ; bet on a horse race//돈을 걸고 포커를 하다 play poker for money//내기에 걸다 lay〔make〕 a wager//10달러 걸다 wager ten dollars on it//말〔권투〕에 20달러 걸다 bet twenty dollars on a horse〔boxing match〕//가진 것을 몽땅 걸다 bet one's boots〔life, bottom dollar〕 《on》//직업에 일생을 걸다 stake one's life on the job//나의 명예를 걸고 그의 정직함을 보증한다 I stake my reputation on his honesty. //간첩은 목숨을 걸고 있다 A spy carries his life in his hands. //그는 목숨을 걸고 바다 속으로 뛰어들었다 He dived to the bottom of the sea at (the) risk〔at the peril, on peril〕 of his life. //그는 사업에 전재산을 걸었다 He staked all his fortune on business.
⑪ [희망·기대를] pin〔place, put〕 one's hopes 《on》 ¶ 그의 당선은 한 표에 걸려 있다 His victory hangs on〔upon〕 one vote. //그 미망인은 외아들에 희망을 걸고 있다 The widow puts her hopes on her only son. //그 부모는 아들의 장래에 큰 기대를 걸고 있다 The parents have great expectations for the future of their son.
⑫ [의안 따위를] refer 《a bill》 to ¶ 의안을 위원회에 걸다 refer a bill to a committee

걸다² ① [흙·비료 따위가] (be) rich ; fertile ¶ 땅이 걸다 The soil is rich〔fertile〕.
② [먹을 것이] (be) heavy ; rich ; sumptuous ¶ 잔치가 걸다 It is a sumptuous〔rich〕 feast.
③ [액체가] (be) thick ; heavy ; rich ¶ 건죽 thick gruel
④ [식성이] (be) gluttonous ; omnivorous ; be not particular〔fastidious〕 《about one's food》 ¶ 그는 입이 걸어서 무엇이든 잘 먹는다 He is not particular〔fastidious〕 about what he eats. /He is an omnivorous glutton.
⑤ [입이] (be) foul-mouthed ; abusive ; violent-tongued ; slanderous ¶ 입이 건 사람 a foul-mouthed fellow//입이 걸다 be rough of〔in〕 speech ; have a spiteful〔bitter〕 tongue ; have a nasty〔foul〕 tongue//그는 입이 걸어 남의 욕을 잘한다 His mouth breeds ready slander.
⑥ [손이] be good〔lucky〕 at ; be dexterous 《in, at》 ; have a good hand with ¶ 그는 손이 걸어 도박해서 잃는 일이 없다 With his luck〔lucky hand〕, he never loses a gamble.

걸대 a reaching pole to help hang things up high

걸때 the body ; the size of the body ¶ 걸때가 크다 have a huge body

걸러 skipping ; at intervals 《of》 ; apart ¶ 하루 걸러 every other〔second〕 day //이틀 걸러 every third day//30분 걸러 at intervals of 30 minutes ; every 30 minutes//보름 걸러 하루씩 every 15 days//한줄 걸러 쓰다 write on every other line//5미터 걸러 심다 plant trees 5 meters apart//5분 걸러 운행하다 operate on a 5-minute schedule//도로에는 3미터 걸러 나무가 심어져 있다 The road is planted with trees at intervals of 3 meters.

걸러뛰다 skip ; pass over ; bypass ; omit ¶ 5페이지를 걸러뛰다 skip five pages//A의 차례를 걸러뛰어 B가 하다 B takes his turn bypassing A. //걸러뛰고 읽다 skip a few lines in reading//이 근방은 번지수가 걸러뛰어 있다 The house numbers are not in regular order in this neighborhood.

***걸레** a floorcloth ; a dustcloth ; a duster ; a mop (긴 자루가 달린) ; a swab (갑판 소제용) ; [비유적] ⇨ 걸레부정 ¶ 마른〔물〕 걸레로 닦다 wipe 《a pane》 with a dry〔wet〕 duster//복도를 걸레로 훔치다 wipe the corridor〔hallway〕 with a mop//마룻바닥을 걸레로 닦다 mop the floor//갑판을 걸레로 닦다

swab (down) the decks

걸레부정 [물건] rubbish ; shabby〔worthless〕 stuff ; [사람] a good-for-nothing ; human debris ; the dregs of humanity

걸레질 wiping with a damp cloth 〔duster〕 ; mopping ; scrubbing ; swabbing (갑판의) **—하다** wipe with a (damp) cloth ; scrub ; mop ; swab ¶ 마른 걸레질 wiping with a dry cloth // 마루를 걸레질하여 깨끗이 하다 scrub the floor clean // 이 마룻바닥은 걸레질이 필요하다 This floor needs a good scrub. // 엎지른 물을 걸레질로 닦다 wipe up the spilt water // 카펫에 묻은 우유를 걸레질하다 wipe up milk from the carpet

†**걸리다**[1] ① [매달리다] hang 《from, on》 ; be suspended 《from》 ¶ 걸이못에 걸려 있는 모자 a hat hanging on〔from〕 a peg // 코트가 갈고리 못에 걸려 있다 The coat is hanging on the hook. // 그의 그림이 미술관에 걸려 있다 His picture is hung in the Museum of Art. // 벽에는 풍경화가 걸려 있었다 A landscape hung〔was hung〕 on the wall. // 그림이 벽에 걸려 있다 The picture is hanging on the wall. // 달이 중천에 걸려 있다 The moon is riding high. // 구름이 산꼭대기에 걸려 있다 Clouds are resting upon the mountaintop. /The top of the mountain is covered with〔hidden under〕 cloud. // 달이 서쪽 하늘에 걸려 있다 The moon hangs in the western sky. // 창문에는 커튼이 걸려 있었다 There were curtains hanging over the window.

② [법률 따위에] be against 《a law》 ; trespass〔violate〕 《a law》 ; be contrary 〔contradictory〕 to ¶ 법에 걸리다 be contrary to laws and regulations // 법망에 걸리다 fall into the meshes〔clutches〕 of the law ; be picked up by the law ; be brought to justice ; come within the grip of the law // 음주운전 일제 단속에 걸리다 be caught in a general crackdown on drunk drivers 〔drunken driving〕 // 교통순경에게 걸리다 be pinched by a traffic cop // 검열에 걸리다 fail to pass a censorship // 속도위반에 걸리다 get pinched for speeding // 그는 법망에 걸렸다 He was caught by the law.

③ [잡히다] be caught ; be hooked (낚시에) ; be entangled ¶ 고기가 그물에 걸리다 a fish is caught in a net // 나비가 거미줄에 걸렸다 A butterfly was 〔got〕 entangled in a spider's web.

④ [말려들다] be involved〔implicated〕 in ; be entangled 《with》 ¶ 사건에 걸리다 be implicated in an affair // 나쁜 여자에게 걸리다 get entangled with a bad woman // 사기꾼에 걸리다 be〔become〕 entangled with a swindler // 장관이 의혹사건에 걸렸다 A minister was involved in the scandal.

⑤ [차리다] put 《a thing》 over ¶ 냄비를 불에 걸다 put a pot over the fire

⑥ [함정 따위에] fall〔get〕 into ; run into ¶ 모략에 걸리다 fall into a trap ; be tricked // 계략에 걸리다 be entrapped ; fall into 《another's》 snare // 아첨하는 말에 걸려들기 쉽다 be easily entangled by insincere praise // 깡패에 걸리다 be tied up with a gangster // 쥐가 덫에 걸렸다 A rat is trapped.

⑦ [방해되다] catch ; be caught 《in, on》 ; hitch 《on a nail》 ; snag ; [목구멍에] be stuck ¶ 먹은 것이 가슴에 걸리다 food sits heavy on one's stomach // 옷자락이 못에 걸렸다 catch one's coat on a nail // 나의 옷자락이 못에 걸렸다 My coat was caught on a nail. // 의자의 깔쭉한 부분에 걸리어 스커트가 찢어지다 snag one's skirt on the rough edge of the chair // 덤불에 낚싯줄이 걸렸다 The fishing line got entangled in bushes. // 연이 나무에 걸렸다 The kite caught in a tree. // 가시가 목에 걸리다 have a bone stuck in one's〔the〕 throat ; have a bone in the throat // 돌부리에 걸려 넘어지다 fall〔tumble〕 over a stone ; trip on a stone // 도중에 걸려서 피아노를 들어가게 하는 데 꽤 힘들었다 We got stuck halfway through, so it was a real struggle getting the piano in.

⑧ [병에] suffer from ; be attacked ; catch ; be taken ill 《with》 ¶ 병에 걸리다 fall〔be taken〕 ill ; contract a disease // 감기에 걸리다 catch (a) cold // 이질에 걸리다 fall victim to dysentery // 암에 걸리다 get cancer

⑨ [소요되다] take ; need ; require (시간이) ¶ 사고의 원인을 알아내는 데에는 시간이 걸린다 To find out the cause of the accident will take〔cost〕 much time. // 이 일을 끝내는 데 7일 걸렸다 It took me a week to finish this.

⑩ [마음에] [사물이 주어] weigh on one's mind ; lie at one's heart ; [사람이 주어] feel uneasy about ; be anxious about ¶ 시험이 언제나 마음에 걸린다 Examinations weigh on my mind at all time. // 그 일이 몹시 마음에 걸린다 The matter weighs heavy on my mind. /It haunts me. // 그의 건강이 마음에 걸린다 I'm anxious about his health. // 무언가 마음에 걸리는 것이 있다 There is something that weighs on my mind.

⑪ [전화 따위가] 《a call》 be put through ; get connected 《with》 ; be on 《the line》 ¶ 전화가 잘 걸리지 않다 My call won't go through. /I can't get through on the phone. // 전화가 걸리지 않다 The phone〔wire〕 is dead. // 900-1234에 전화를 걸려고 하는데 전화

가 걸리지 않았습니다 I'm trying to reach 900－1234 but I couldn't get through.

⑫ [관계되다] be connected with ; concern 《oneself》 in ; have to do with ¶ 사활이 걸린 문제 a matter〔question〕 of life and death ; a vital question

걸리다² [걷게 하다] make 《a person》 walk ; walk 《a person》 ¶ 어린애를 걸리다 walk a child

걸망 —網 a Buddhist monk's knapsack

걸맞다 (be) well-matched〔-mated〕; well balanced ; nicely paired ; well-assorted ; suitable ; becoming ; befitting ¶ 걸맞지 않은 ill-matched ; ill-advised // 걸맞는 적수 a good match〔opponent〕 // 걸맞는〔걸맞지 않는〕 부부 a well-matched〔an ill-matched〕couple // 걸맞지 않는 결혼 an ill-assorted marriage // 신분에 걸맞지 않는 생활을 하다 live above oneself ; live beyond one's social standing // 그들은 서로 걸맞다 They are both of a sort. / There is little difference between them.

걸머맡다 assume ; undertake ; take over 《another's business》 ; take 《a job》 upon oneself ; be charged with (보호·관리를) ¶동생의 빚을 걸머맡다 shoulder one's brother's debts

걸머메다 shoulder 《a burden》 ; carry 《a burden》 on one's shoulder

걸머잡다 seize ; catch hold of ; grab ; grasp ; grip ; clutch at ¶ 여자의 머리채를 걸머잡다 seize a woman by the hair

걸머지다 ① [등에 지다] shoulder 《a burden》 ; carry〔take〕 on one's shoulder〔back〕 ; bear ¶ 배낭을 걸머지다 strap on a knapsack ; carry a knapsack on one's back // 한국의 앞날을 걸머진 사람들 those on whose shoulders rests the destiny of Korea // 중책을 걸머지다 shoulder〔assume〕 the important respon sibility ; saddle oneself with heavy responsibility

② [빚을] contract a debt ; fall〔run, get〕 into debt ; be saddled with a debt ¶ 남의 빚을 걸머지다 shoulder another's debt // 많은 빚을 걸머지다 make〔take on〕 a lot of debts

걸물 傑物 a great man〔character〕 ; a remarkable fellow ; an extraordinary person〔thing〕 ¶ 그는 조선계의 걸물이다 He is a czar〔baron〕 in the shipbuilding world.

‡**걸상** —床 a seat ; a bench ; a stool ; a couch ; a chair (의자)

‡**걸쇠** a latch ; a hasp ¶ 문의 걸쇠를 채우다 latch the door // 걸쇠를 열다 unlatch the door

문(門)— a door latch

걸식 乞食 begging ; mendicancy **—하다** beg 《one's bread》 ; go begging ¶ 문전 걸식하다 go begging from door to door // 걸식하며 가다 beg one's way 《to a place》

걸신 乞神 voracity ; ravenousness ; a pig 《속》 ¶ 걸신들리다 be greedy ; be voracious ; have a wolf in one's stomach ; have a voracious appetite // 걸신들린 듯이 먹다 eat greedily ; eat like a hog

—쟁이 a voracious〔greedy〕 person ; a person greedy for food ; a glutton

걸싸다 (be) quick ; prompt ; brisk ; nimble ¶ 걸음이 걸싸다 walk quickly ; have a brisk pace // 걸싸게 해치우다 make a smart work of 《it》

걸쌍스럽다 (be) charming〔attractive〕 《in working, in eating》

걸씬거리다 be almost reaching ; be close 《to》

걸씬하다 appear briefly

걸어가다 walk ; go on foot ; pace one's way 《to》 ¶ 집〔버스정류장〕까지 걸어가다 walk home〔to the bus stop〕 // 역까지 얼마나 멉니까—걸어서 갈 수 있습니까 How far is the station? Can I walk it?

걸어앉다 sit (down) ; take a seat ; seat oneself ¶ 의자에 걸어앉다 sit on a chair

걸어오다 come on foot ¶ 우리가 걸어온 길 the path we have followed

걸어총 —銃 〖군사〗 pile〔stack〕 of arms **—하다** stack arms ¶ 걸어총하고 쉬다 stack arms and take a rest // 걸어총 [구령] Pile〔stack〕 arms!

걸우다 fertilize ; enrich ; manure ¶ 밭을 걸우다 fertilize〔manure〕 a field

†**걸음** walking ; stepping ; a step ; pace ¶ 첫걸음 the first step // 한걸음 한걸음 step by step ; by degrees // 소걸음으로 at a snail's pace // 빠른 걸음으로 at a rapid〔quick, brisk〕 pace ; with a rapid step ; briskly // 걸음이 빠르다〔느리다〕 be quick 〔slow〕 of foot // 걸음을 재촉하다〔늦추다〕 quicken〔slacken〕 one's pace // 갑자기 걸음을 멈추다 come to a sudden stop // 한 걸음 앞서다〔뒤떨어지다〕 be a step ahead〔behind〕 // 한 걸음도 움직이지 마라 Do not stir a step. /Do not budge an inch. // 김선생님은 걸음이 빠르다〔느리다〕 Mr. *Kim* is a quick 〔slow〕 walker.

황소— a snail's pace〔gallop〕

천리길도 한 걸음부터 〔속담〕 Step after step the ladder is ascended.

†**걸음걸이** one's manner of walking ; gait ; a step ; walk ¶ 피로한 걸음걸이 a weary walk // 어색한 걸음걸이 a clumsy gait ; an awkward walk // 무거운〔가벼운〕 걸음걸이로 with heavy〔light〕 steps // 비틀거리는 걸음걸이 an unsteady gait ; totter ; wobble // 걸음걸이가 이상하다 He has a queer〔an odd〕 gait. /He walks with an odd gait. // 걸음걸이로 그

사람임을 알았다 I recognized him by his walk. // 한 어린 소녀가 걸음걸이도 가볍게 걸어왔다 A little girl came tripping along.

걸음마 toddling ; [아기에게] Let's walk now ! /Step firm. ¶ 걸음마를 하다 toddle ; find its way

걸음발타다 [어린애가] find one's way ; toddle one's way ; try one's feet ; start to toddle

걸음쇠 a pair of compasses

걸음짐작 pacing 《out》 ; measuring 《a distance》 by pacing〔in paces〕 ¶ 걸음짐작으로 거리를 재다 pace out a distance ; measure by pacing

⁑-걸이 a hanger ; a peg ; a rack ¶ 옷걸이 a clothes-hanger // 모자걸이 a hat-rack

걸인 乞人 a beggar ⇨ 거지

⁑걸작 傑作 a masterpiece ; a great work ; a fine piece of work〔literature〕 ; [우스꽝스러운] ridiculous talk〔behavior〕 ; a buffoon ; a ludicrous figure ¶ 불후의 걸작 an immortal〔enduring〕 masterpiece // 이 그림은 피카소의 걸작이다 This is Picasso at his best. // 이것은 그의 필생의 걸작이다 This is the crown of his life's work. // 그것 참으로 걸작이다 That's hilarious. // 그는 참 걸작이다 He is a jovial〔splendid〕 fellow.

걸작집 傑作集 a collection of masterpieces〔great novels〕

걸쩍거리다 be active ; be free-hearted and lively ; be always on the jump〔go〕

걸쩍걸쩍 actively ; animatedly ; free-heartedly

걸쩍지근하다 [식성이] (be) gluttonous ; [말씨가] foul-mouthed ⇨ 걸다[1]

걸쭉하다 [액체가] (be) thick ; heavy ; rich ¶ 걸쭉한 국 thick soup

걸차다 [땅이] (be) very fertile〔rich, productive〕 ¶ 걸찬 땅 rich〔productive〕 soil ; fertile land

걸채 a packsaddle ; a pannier〔dosser, loading〕 rack

걸쳐두다 leave 《an affair》 unsettled ; leave〔hold〕 《a matter》 in abeyance〔suspense〕 ; suspend ; hang up ¶ 교섭을 걸쳐두다 leave a negotiation in suspension

걸출 傑出 prominence ; eminence ; [사람] an outstanding person ; a master spirit ── 하다 stand out 《from》 ; stand preeminent ; (be) distinguished ; prominent ; marked ¶ 걸출한 작품 a work of outstanding merit // 학자로서 걸출한 인물이다 He stands out from〔towers above〕 others as a scholar.

*걸치다 ① [시간·공간적] extend 《over》 ; spread 《over》 ; range 《from A to B》 ; cover ; reach ; [계속하다] last ¶ 6개월에 걸쳐서 covering a six-month period〔a period of six months〕 // 몇 시간에 걸친 연설〔회의〕 a speech〔meeting〕 lasting several hours // 몇 세기〔마일〕에 걸치다 extend over several centuries〔miles〕 // 여러 차례에 걸쳐서 강연하다 deliver a series of lectures

② [해·달·구름이] ¶ 달이 산마루에 걸치어 있다 The moon is hanging on the ridge of a mountain.

③ [양끝에] stretch over ; span ; be laid across ¶ 강 위에 다리를 걸치다 throw〔build〕 a bridge across the river ; a bridge is laid across the river // 책상에 다리를 걸치다 rest one's feet on a table top // 빨랫줄에 옷을 걸쳐 널다 hang out clothes on a clothesline

④ [의복을] slip on ; throw on ¶ 급히 잠옷을 걸쳐 입다 slip on one's pajamas hurriedly // 외투를 걸쳐 입다 throw on one's overcoat // 누더기를 걸치다 be in tatters〔rags〕

⑤ [술을] drink ; have ; take ¶ 한 잔 걸치다 drink a glass of wine〔liquor〕 // 한 잔 걸치자 Let's have a drink.

걸태질 ── 하다 rake in money〔property〕 shamelessly ; exploit ; squeeze money 《out of a person》 ; grab the property 《from a person》

걸터듬다 grope for ; fumble for ; feel after〔for〕

걸터먹다 gobble up everything ; take eagerly

걸터앉다 sit astraddle〔astride〕 ; bestride ; straddle 《a fence》 ¶ 말 위에 걸터앉다 ride on horseback ; straddle a horse ; sit astride a horse

걸터타다 mount〔get up on〕 《a horse, an animal》 ; ride 《a horse》 ; straddle 《a horse》 ¶ 말 등에 걸터타고 있다 get up on horseback ; be mounted on horseback // 그녀는 안장도 없는 말을 걸터타고 달렸다 She mounted the horse and rode off even without the saddle.

걸핏하면 too often ; unduly often ; readily ¶ 걸핏하면 …하다 be apt〔liable, prone〕 to 《do》 // 걸핏하면 싸우다 pick a fight〔quarrel〕 at the slightest provocation // 그녀는 걸핏하면 운다 She is apt to cry blindly. /She weeps just too often. /She will cry over nothing. // 그는 걸핏하면 화를 낸다 He is quick to take offense〔at taking offense〕. // 그는 걸핏하면 설교하려 든다 He is always ready with a lecture. // 걸핏하면 내 흉을 본다 Whenever he gets a chance, he would find fault with me.

†검 劍 a sword ; [군도] a saber ; [총검] a bayonet ; [단검] a dagger ¶ 예복에 착용하는 검 a court〔dress〕 sword // 검으로 등을 찌르다 stab 《a person》 in the back with a dagger // 검으로 베어 죽이다 put 《a person》 to the sword // 검을 뽑다 draw the sword

—대 sword belt —무 sword dance

검객 劍客 a swordsman ; a fencer

검거 檢擧 an arrest ; a roundup —하다 arrest ; apprehend ; round up ; take 《a person》 in custody ¶ 용의자 일제 검거 a roundup of all suspects // 전원 검거하다 make a general roundup〔wholesale arrest〕《of》// 선거법 위반으로 검거되다 be arrested for violation of the election law // 거리의 불량배를 일제히 검거하다 round up a gang of hooligans〔street rogues, hoodlums〕// 범인이 아직 검거되지 않다 The criminal is still at large. // 수상이 검거되었다 They've put the prime minister under arrest.

검경판 檢鏡板 [현미경의] an object plate ; a slide

검극 劍戟 [칼과 창] swords and spears ; [무기] weapons ; arms

—물 a sword swinger

검기다 blacken ; soil ; stain

검기울다 turn dark ; become dark ; 《the sky》 darken up

검뇨 檢尿 urine examination —하다 examine one's urine ; have one's urine examined

검뇨기 檢尿器 a urinometer

검누렇다 (be) blackish yellow ; dark yellow

검누르다 be dark yellow

†**검다**[1], **껌다** ① [빛깔이] (be) black ; dark ¶ 검게 탄 얼굴 a sunburnt〔suntanned〕 face // 피부가 검은 여자 a dark-skinned woman // 검은 머리 black hair // 검게 염색하다 dye 《a thing》 (in) black ; get 《a thing》 dyed black // (볕에) 검게 타다 be〔get〕 tanned〔sunburnt〕; be swarthy // 검게 하다 blacken ; black ; make 《a thing》 black // 검어지다 black ; become black // 얼굴이 검다 be dark-complexioned ; have a dark complexion // 검은 옷을 입고 있다 She is dressed in black. /She is wearing a dark suit.

② [마음이] (be) blackhearted ; wicked ; evil-hearted ; evil-minded ¶ 속 검은 사람 a blackhearted person // 그는 뱃속이 검다 He is wicked at heart〔blackhearted〕.

검다[2] rake up ; scrape up ; gather up ¶ 낙엽을 검다 rake up fallen leaves

검대 劍帶 a sword belt

검댕 soot ; sootiness ¶ 검댕투성이의 sooty ; sooted // 검댕이 끼다〔앉다〕 become sooty〔sooted〕// 검댕을 털다 sweep away〔wipe off〕 the soot // 검댕이 묻다 be smeared with soot

검덕귀신 —鬼神 a person with a dirty face〔in filthy clothes〕

검도 劍道 [검술] the art of fencing ; [정신] swordsmanship ¶ 검도 5단 a fencer of the 5th grade // 검도를 하다 practice fencing // 그는 검도가 3단이다 He holds a third grade in fencing.

— 도구 fencing equipment — 도장 a fencing school — 사범 a fencing master — 시합 a fencing match〔bout〕

검둥개 a black dog

검둥개 목욕 감기듯 (속담) A crow is never the white for washing herself.

검둥이 [피부가 검은] a dark-skinned person ; [흑인] a Negro ; a black ; a colored man〔woman〕; a nigger〔darky〕(경멸적으로) ; [검둥개] a blacky ; a black dog

검디검다 (be) deep-black ; jet-〔coal-〕black ; inky(-black)

검뜯다 pester ; importune ; badger

검량 檢量 measuring ; weighing ; [공공기관에 의한 하물의] metage —하다 [양] measure ; take measure of ; [무게] weigh

—기(器) a gauging rod ; a gauger —료〔세(稅)〕 a weighing〔measuring〕 charge ; metage —인(人) a weigher

검류계 檢流計 [조류의] a current indicator ; [전류의] a galvanometer

검무 劍舞 a sword dance ¶ 검무를 하다 perform a sword dance

검문 檢問 inspection ; examination ; a check-up 《미》 —하다 inspect ; examine ; check up ¶ 불심 검문 questioning (of a suspicious person by a patrolman) // 통행인을 검문하다 check (up on) passers-by

검문소 檢問所 a checkpoint

검박 儉朴 plainness ; frugality ; thrift ; simplicity —하다 (be) plain ; simple ; frugal ; thrifty ¶ 검박한 생활 plain living // 검박하게 살아가다 lead a simple and plain life

검버섯 dark spots on an aged person's skin

검법 劍法 the art of fencing ; swordsmanship

검변 檢便 an examination of feces —하다 examine feces ; examine one's stools

검부나무 dried grass or leaves used for fuel

검부러기 remnants〔bits〕 of dry grass or leaves ¶ 짚 검부러기 bits of straw // 새끼 검부러기 bits of straw rope

검불 dry grass or leaves

검불덤불 pell-mell ; all a-jumble

검붉다 (be) dark red ; blackish red

†**검사** 檢査 inspection ; examination ; test ; [선박 따위의] overhaul ; [회계 따위의] auditing ; [수출품의] conditioning —하다 inspect ; examine ; overhaul ; audit 《accounts》; condition 《merchandise》 ¶ 검사를 받다 go through an examination ; be inspected ; submit 《a thing》 to inspection 검사중 under examination ; in review // 검사에 불합격

이 되다 fail to pass the inspection ; be rejected // 올해는 거의 전사원이 신체 검사를 받은 것 같다 It seems that almost all the staff took their physicals this year.
— 게이지 an inspection gauge — 보고서 a survey report —원 an inspector ; a checkup man ; a surveyor

검사 檢事 a public prosecutor ; a prosecuting attorney ; a district attorney 《미》; the prosecution 《총칭》 ¶ 검사로 있다 act as prosecutor
— 직무 대리 a probational prosecutor 지방 — a district public prosecutor ; a district attorney 《미》

검사관 檢査官 an inspector ; [세관의] an examining officer ; an〔a customs〕 examiner ; [회계의] an auditor

검사소 檢査所 an inspecting office ; [생사 따위의] a (silk) conditioning-house
국립 농산물 — the National Agricultural Products Inspection Center 국립 생사 — the National Raw Silk Inspection Center

검사장 檢事長 a chief public prosecutor

검사증 檢査證 a test certificate

검산 檢算 verification of accounts ; checking figures —하다 verify〔check〕 accounts ; prove 《a calculation》; check one's figures

검색 檢索 reference ; check ; [수색] a search —하다 refer to 《a dictionary》; look up 《a word》 in ; search a house》; check up ; look into〔over〕 thoroughly ; examine ¶ 검색에 편리하다 It is easy of reference.
—표(表) a key

검세다 (be) tough ; unyielding ; stubborn ; dogged

†**검소** 儉素 simplicity ; plainness ; [절약] frugality ; thrift ; economy —하다 (be) simple ; plain ; frugal ; thrift ; economical ¶ 검소하게 살다 live simply〔plainly, frugally〕; live in a small way // 그는 검소한 사람이다 He is of simple tastes. // 옷차림이 검소하다 He is dressed simply〔plainly〕. /He is simply dressed.

검속 檢束 [구인(拘引)] arrest ; apprehension ; custody ; [구속] restraint ; restriction —하다 take 《a person》 into custody ; place 《a person》 under arrest ; detain ; put restraint 《upon》; round up ¶ 보호 검속하다 detain 《a person》 for protection
보호 — protective custody

검술 劍術 fencing ; swordsmanship ¶ 검술의 대가 a master fencer〔swordsman〕
—가 a fencer ; a swordsman — 도장 a fencing hall — 사범 a fencing master — 시합 a fencing bout〔match〕

검숭검숭 —하다 (be) blackish ; sparsely black

검시 檢屍 an inquest ; a coroner's inquest ; an autopsy ; a postmortem examination —하다 hold an inquest on〔over〕 《a corpse》; make an autopsy 《over》; examine〔view〕 《a corpse》 ¶ 검시 결과 타살 혐의가 있는 것으로 인정됐다 The mortem examination raised a suspicion of foul play.
—실(室) a postmortem room

검시관 檢屍官 a coroner

검실거리다 gleam faintly

검실검실 —하다 be dark here and there

검쓰다 (be) very bitter ; be as bitter as gall

검안 檢眼 an eye examination〔test, check〕; optometry —하다 examine〔check〕 one's eyes ; test one's vision〔eyesight〕; have one's eyes examined〔checked, tested〕
—법 optometry —의(醫) an optometrist

검안 檢案 〖법〗 examination —하다 examine ¶ 시체를 검안하다 carry out〔conduct〕 a postmortem examination ; make an autopsy
—서 a death certificate ; a certificate of death

검안경 檢眼鏡 an ophthalmoscope ; an eye speculum

검압계 檢壓計 a pressure gauge

***검약** 儉約 economy ; thrift ; frugality —하다 economize 《in》; (be) thrifty ; frugal ; economical ; save ; pinch oneself》
—가(家) a thrifty〔frugal, saving〕 person ; an economist ; a man of economy

검역 檢疫 quarantine ; medical inspection —하다 quarantine ; inspect ¶ 검역을 받다 be quarantined // 검역을 위하여 입항〔상륙〕을 금지당하다 be held in quarantine // 검역 중이다 be in quarantine // 검역을 개시하다 institute〔start〕 quarantine 《on a vessel》
— 규칙 quarantine regulations — 기간 quarantine —법 〖법〗 the Quarantine Act — 신호 a quarantine signal —항(港) a quarantine port 해상〔육지〕 — maritime〔land〕 inspection

검역관 檢疫官 a quarantine officer

검역기 檢疫旗 a quarantine flag

검역선 檢疫船 a quarantine ship

검역소 檢疫所 a quarantine station

검역 의사 檢疫醫師 a quarantine doctor

검역필 檢疫畢 Passed Medical Inspection (게시)

***검열** 檢閱 inspection ; [출판·영화의] censorship ; [군대의] a review —하다 inspect ; make〔conduct〕 an inspection 《of》; carry out an inspection ; censor ; review ¶ 철저한 검열 a close〔thorough〕 inspection // 형식적인 검열 a cursory〔perfunctory〕 inspection // 검열필의 censored ; released by censorship // 신문

의 검열 press censorship // 검열을 받다 be inspected ; be censored ; be reviewed // 검열을 통과하다 pass censorship // 인쇄물〔영화〕의 엄밀한 검열을 행하다 exercise rigid censorship on printed matter〔films〕// 검열을 폐지하다 remove the censorship 《on cablegrams》// 사령관은 부대를 검열했다 The commander inspected the troops.
—과(課) the censorship section ; [신문·잡지·간행물의] the Press and Publication Censorship Section —국(局) [영화 따위의] the Board of Review — 규정 the code of censorship — 제도 the censorship system 사전(事前)〔사후(事後)〕 — pre-〔post-〕censorship 영화(映畫) —관(官) a film censor

검열관 檢閱官 a censor ; [군대의] an inspector

검열필 檢閱畢 censored ; passed inspection ; released by censorship

검은그루 a fallow land

검은깨 black sesame

검은방울새 〖새〗 a siskin

검은빛 a black color ; black ; an ink(y) black

검은엿 black taffy

검은자위 the colored part of the eye ; the iris

검은콩 a black soybean

검은팥 a black Indian bean

검이경 檢耳鏡 an auriscope ; an otoscope

검인 檢印 a seal〔stamp〕 of approval ¶ 검인을 찍다 seal ; stamp ; visa (여권의) // 책에 저자의 검인이 없다 This book bears no seal of the author. // 여권에는 영사의 검인이 있어야 한다 The passport must be duly visaed by the consul.
—증(證) an approval certificate —필(畢) approved and sealed

검인정 檢認定 ⇨ 검정(檢定) ¶ 교육부 검인정필 Approved by the Ministry of Education

검인정 교과서 檢認定敎科書 an authorized textbook

검자 檢字 an index of Chinese characters arranged by total stroke count

검적검적 —하다 be dotted with black spots

검전기 檢電器 a galvanoscope ; an electroscope ; a rheoscope ; a detector (누전용)
금박(金箔) — a gold-leaf electroscope

검접하다 [검질기게 붙잡다] grasp ; grip ; clinch ; hold fast ; keep hold of ; [달라붙다] stick 《to》; adhere 《to》; cling 《to》

†검정, 껌정 black ; black color ¶ 검정 물감 black dye // 검정 머리 black hair

*검정 檢定 official approval〔sanction, certification〕; authorization ; probation ; [검사] examination ; inspection —하다 give official approval 《to》; approve ; authorize ; examine ; inspect
— 게이지 a check〔checking, reference〕 gauge —기(器) a verifier ; a standardizing box —료(料) an authorization fee ; an examination fee 시험〔무시험〕 — license with〔without〕 examination ¶ 무시험 검정으로 교사의 자격을 얻다 get a teacher's license without examination

검정 고시 檢定考試 a qualification examination ; the examination for the license 《of teacher》 ¶ 대학 입학 자격 검정 고시에 합격하다 pass the qualification examination for college entrance
교원 자격(敎員資格) — the examination for the license of school teachers

검정 교과서 檢定敎科書 an authorized textbook

검정 시험 檢定試驗 an examination for a license

검증 檢證 verification ; evidence by inspection ; inspection 《of a locality》; probate (유언의) —하다 effect an inspection of evidence ; verify ; inspect ; probate ¶ 유언을 검증하다 probate a will
—물 data for verification 현장 — 조서 a protocol of on-the-spot inspection

검진 檢診 medical examination〔checkup〕; [성병의] (medical) examination of venereal diseases ; a V. D. check —하다 give〔conduct, administer〕 a medical examination ; examine 《a person》 medically ; check up 《on prostitutes' health》 ¶ 검진을 받다 take a medical examination ; have a medical checkup // 의사는 그 환자에게 정밀한 검진을 했다 The doctor did a thorough physical examination on the patient.
—일(日) a medical examination day 정기 — a periodic (medical) checkup 종합 — a comprehensive medical testing 집단 — collective medical examination

검질기다 (be) relentless ; persistent ; tenacious ; indefatigable ; untiring ; dogged

검차 檢車 inspection〔checkup〕 of a car 〔motor vehicles〕 —하다 inspect 〔check (up on)〕 a car
—원 a car inspector ; a motor vehicle checkup man

검차다 (be) tenacious〔persistent〕 and fierce〔violent, wild〕

검찰 檢札 examination of tickets —하다 examine〔clip〕 tickets ; check tickets 《미》
—계(係) a ticket inspector

검찰 檢察 examination ; investigation and prosecution —하다 examine ; investigate and prosecute
— 당국 the prosecutory authorities ; the prosecution — 사무 procuration

affairs — 서기 a secretary of the public prosecutor's office —청법(廳法) 〖법〗 the Public Prosecutor's Office Act

검찰측 檢察側 the prosecution ¶ 검찰측과 변호인측 the prosecution and the defense

—측 증인 a witness for the prosecution

검찰관 檢察官 a public procurator〔prosecutor〕; a prosecuting attorney 《미》

검찰청 檢察廳 the Public Prosecutor's Office

고등 — the 《*Seoul*》 High Public Prosecutor's office 대— the Supreme Public Prosecutor's Office 지방 — a district public prosecutor's office

검찰 총장 檢察總長 the Public Prosecutor-General ; the Attorney General 《영》; the Director of Public Prosecutions 《미》

검출 檢出 〖화학〗 (chemical) detection ; analyzing out —하다 detect 《a chemical substance》; analyze out

—기(器)〔장치〕 a detector —력(力) testing power

검측스럽다 (be) black-hearted ; treacherous ; deceitful ; crafty ; double-dealing ; covetous ; greedy

검측측하다 (be) very dark 《in color》; [마음이] black-hearted ; wicked ; crafty ; greedy

검측하다 (be) tricky ; sneaky ⇨ 검측스럽다

검치다 attach around a corner ; cap a corner with

검침 檢針 inspection of a meter —하다 check〔read〕 a meter

—원(員) a 《gas》 meterman

검침하다 黔沈— (be) evil-disposed ; blackhearted ; insidious ; treacherous ¶ 검침한 수단〔꾀〕 an insidious trick // 검침한 사람 an evil-disposed〔a black-hearted〕 person ; an insidious man

검토 檢討 examination ; investigation ; scrutiny ; study —하다 examine ; investigate ; scrutinize ; study ; weigh 《facts》 ¶ 검토한 결과 on〔upon〕 investigation // 검토 중 under investigation 〔examination〕 // 검토 중인 법안 the bill under consideration // 문제를 신중히 검토하다 give a problem one's careful consideration ; give careful consideration to a problem // 면밀히 검토하다 examine thoroughly〔closely〕 // 그 계획은 현재 정부에서 검토 중이다 The plan is now under consideration by the government. // 재검토하다 reexamine 《a problem》; reconsider 《a plan》; renew one's investigation // 재검토를 요하다 require further examination // 이 모든 서류들을 검토했다 I checked over all of these documents. // 우리에게 주신 자료를 검토해 보고 싶습니다 We'd like to go over the materials you gave us.

검특하다 黔慝— (be) black-hearted ; sneaky ; crafty ; treacherous ; insidious

검파 檢波 detection —하다 detect (waves)

— 계수(係數) a coefficient of detection ; a detection coefficient —관(管) a detector tube 광석〔진공관〕 —기(器) a crystal〔tube〕 detector 마르코니식 —기 a Marconi detector 열전(熱電) —기 a thermoelectric detector 자기(磁氣) —기 a magnetic detector 전해(電解) —기 an electrolytic detector

검파기 檢波器 a detector

—기 회로 a detector circuit

검표 檢票 examination of tickets —하다 clip〔examine〕 tickets ; check 《a person's》 ticket

—원(員) ticket examiner

검표 劍票 〖인쇄〗 [칼표] a dagger (mark) ; an obelisk

이중 — a double dagger

검푸르다 (be) dark blue ; blue-black

검호 劍豪 a great swordsman ; a master fencer ; a sword wizard

검화 〖식물〗 a dittany ; a fraxinella ; a gasplant ; Dictamnus albus (학명)

검흐르다 overflow a dish ; flow〔run, spill〕 over

*****겁** 怯 fear ; fright ; dread ; cowardice ¶ 매우 겁이 많은 (as) timid as a rabbit // 겁이 많다 be cowardly ; be timid ; be faint-hearted // 겁이 없다 be fearless ; be bold ; be intrepid ; be brave ; be daring // 겁을 주어 자백시키다 scare 《a person》 into confession // 겁을 집어먹다 be seized with fear ; be panic-stricken ; be overcome with fright // 불량배를 겁주어 쫓아 버리다 scare the ruffian away〔off〕 // 여자들은 겁을 먹고 외출을 하지 못한다 The women are too much frightened to go outside. // 겁주지마 You scared me ! // 그는 겁을 먹고 같이 투자하기로 한 사업 계획에서 빠지려고 했다 He got cold feet and wanted out of our joint investment project. // 모두 줄을 서 있는데 그 여자는 겁도 없이 끼어 들었다 Even though everyone was standing in line, she cut right in without batting an eye.

겁 劫 〖불교〗 a Kalpa ; an (a)eon

겁간 劫姦 rape

겁겁하다 劫劫— ① [성미가] (be) quick-tempered ; impatient ; impetuous ; petulant ; have a hot〔short〕 temper ② [급급하다] be engrossed in ; be absorbed in ; think only of ; be bent 〔intent〕 on

겁결 怯— the impetus of fear ¶ 겁결에 driven by fear ; in one's horror

겁기 劫氣 ① [험한 산의 기운] a horrible appearance of a steep mountain ② [궁

한 기색] an embarrassed look

⁑겁나다 怯— be seized with fear ; get scared〔frightened〕《at》; be panic-stricken ; be afraid of ; be thrown into a funk ¶ 겁나서 소리지르다 cry out for fear∥말할 수 없이 겁났다 I was scared to death.∥죽는 것은 조금도 겁나지 않는다 I am not afraid of death in the least.∥겁이 나기 시작했다 Fear came〔crept〕over me.∥그 끔찍한 장면을 보고 겁이 나서 몸이 굳어 버렸다 The horrible sight scared me stiff.∥개가 겁나서 들어가지 못했다 I could not enter for fear of the dog.

***겁내다 怯—** fear ; be scared of ; dread ; be afraid of ; be fearful of ; have a dread of ; be timid〔in fear, in funk〕《of》; show one's cowardice ¶ 아무것도 겁낼 것 없다 You have nothing to fear.

⁑겁쟁이 怯— a coward ; a pudding heart ; a chicken ; a poltroon ; a craven ; a faintheart ; a funk ; a dastard ; a pussyfoot〔yellowbelly〕《미·속》 ¶ 비열한 겁쟁이 an abject coward ; a dastardly coward ; a dirty coward∥너 겁쟁이는 아니겠지 You are not yellow, are you?

겁탈 劫奪 [약탈] plunder ; robbery ; [강간] rape ; violation **—하다** plunder ; rob ; take by force ; rape ; violate ; commit rape
—자 [약탈] a plunderer ; a burglar ; a looter ; [강간] a violator ; a rapist

겁화 劫火 〖불교〗 the cosmos-destroying conflagration at the close of a Kalpa ; a world-ending cataclysm ; an Armageddon ; a disastrous conflagration ; devouring flames

†것 ① [사물·현상·존재] one ; the one ; a thing ; an object ; a matter ; an affair ¶ 이것 this one〔thing, matter〕∥저것 that one〔thing, matter〕∥새것과 묵은 것 The new one and the old one∥모든 것은 하늘에 달렸다 Everything depends on God's will.∥먹을 것을 찾다 look for something to eat
② [사람·동물] a man ; a person ; [대명사적] one ; the one ¶ 어린 것 a young one∥너 같은 것 such a man like you∥너 같은 것이 참견할 일이 아니야 It's none of your business./Don't poke your nose into others' affairs.
③ [소유물] possession ; ownership ¶ 내 것 mine∥네 것 yours∥이 차는 누구 것이냐 Who owns this car?∥그것은 내 것이다 It belongs to me.
④ [내용·수준] contents ; substance ¶ 생각한 것이 고작 그 정도냐 Is that all that you have thought?∥나는 이것밖에 할 수 없다 This is the utmost I can do.
⑤ [사실·확인] a fact ; a thing ; conclusion ¶ 그가 겸손한 것은 사실이다 It's true that he is modest.∥부지런히 일하라 성공은 네 것이다 Work hard, and success will be yours.∥별로 염려할 것 없다 There is nothing to worry about.
⑥ [추측·예상] presumption ; a guess ; an estimation ; (an) inference ¶ 내일 비가 안 올 것이라 생각한다 I don't think it will rain tomorrow.
⑦ [필요] need ; necessity ¶ 서두를 것 없다 There is no need for haste./You need not hurry.∥그곳에 갈 것까지는 없다 It is unnecessary to go there.
⑧ [금지·의무] ¶ 이곳에서 담배를 피우지 말 것 No smoking in this area./Smoking is prohibited here.∥잔디밭에 들어가지 말 것 Keep off the grass.

-것다 ① [다짐·추측] I think〔suppose, presume, guess〕; I dare say ¶ 그 여자는 30세 이전이것다 She is under thirty, I should think.∥너는 나를 알것다 You must know me.
② [재확인] ¶ 너 말 다 했것다 How dare you say such a thing to me?/You are a fine one to talk to me like that!
③ [원인·조건의 구비] ¶ 젊것다 예쁘것다 무슨 걱정이야 You are young, you are pretty, so what's your worry?

겅그레 a support put at the bottom of an oven

겅더리되다 get thin〔lean, haggard, skinny, gaunt, emaciated〕《after an illness》

겅둥거리다, 껑뚱거리다 jump up and down lightly ; hop ; skip

겅둥하다, 껑뚱하다 (be) very〔too〕short

겅성드뭇하다 be all scattered around

겅정거리다, 껑쩡거리다 walk with large and bouncing strides ; stride along ¶ 껑쩡껑쩡 with a large stride

***겉** ① [표면] the surface ; the face ; [옷의] the right side ; the face (of a garment) ② [외면] the outside ; (outward) appearance ¶ 겉으로(는) outwardly ; ostensibly ; externally ; to all appearances∥겉으로는 아무렇지도 않다 keep calm outwardly ; keep an outward calm∥겉으로 나타나다 appear above the surface ; come to the surface∥(감정이) 겉에 나타나다 be seen in one's face ; betray an emotion∥겉에 (두드러지게) 드러나다 come to the fore〔front〕∥겉만 보고 판단하다 judge by appearance∥겉치레하다 make an outward show∥겉 다르고 속 다르다 Appearances are deceptive.
— 표지 a front〔an upper, an obverse〕cover

겉가량 —假量 a rough estimate ; measurement by eye
—하다 make a rough estimate〔calcu-

lation〕; estimate roughly
겉가루 the flour ground in the first grinding
겉가죽 the outer skin
겉감 the right side 《of texture》
겉겨 chaff ; bran ; outer husks〔hulls〕 of grain
겉곡식 —穀— unhulled grain
겉깃 outer lapels〔collar〕
겉꺼풀 the surface〔outer〕 coating ; scum
겉껍데기 a hard outer covering ; a crust ; a shell ; an incrustation
겉껍질 the outer covering〔skin, bark〕; [과일·옥수수 따위의] a husk ; a shuck ; [곡물의] a hull ; [싹 따위의] an envelope ; [외각] a crust ; a shell ; a case ; an integument ; 〖동·식물〗 a mantle ; 〖생물〗 an investment ; [피부의] the outer (most) layer of the skin ; the cuticle ; 〖해부〗 cortex ; 〖동·식물·해부〗 the epidermis
겉꾸리다 keep up appearances ; spruce up the appearance ; improve the looks ; put a good face on 《a matter》; make outward show ; gloss 〔smooth〕 over 《a fault》
겉꾸림 sprucing up the appearance ; keeping up appearances
겉나깨 bran
겉날리다 scamp 《one's work》; do 《one's work》 in a careless manner
겉놀다 [못·나사 따위가] slip ; do not fit ; [겉돌다] skid ; race ; do not get along well
겉눈감다 pretend to close one's eyes
겉눈썹 an eyebrow
겉늙다 look older than one's age ; look old for one's age ; be prematurely gray
겉대¹ [푸성귀의] an outer stalk of vegetables
겉대² [대의] the outer hard part of bamboo
겉대중 a rough estimate based on outward appearances
겉더껑이 the film ; the scum ¶ 우유의 겉더껑이를 걷어내다 skim milk
겉더께 surface scum
겉돌다 《a wheel》 spin free〔unengaged〕; do not mix freely ; [사이가] do not get along well ; be out of keeping with ¶ 그들은 겉도는 사이이다 They mix like oil and water.
겉똑똑이 a superficially bright〔clever〕 person
겉마르다 get dry on the surface ; [곡식이] dry out before ripening
겉말 mere words ; lip service ; lip homage ; shallow compliments ; honeyed words ¶ 겉말로만 좋게 이야기하다 just mouth fair words
겉맞추다 flatter ; show a surface friendliness to
겉면 —面 the surface ; the exterior
겉모습 outward appearance ; external features ¶ 사람을 겉모습을 보고 판단해서는 안된다 You should not judge people by the way they look.
겉모양 —貌樣 outward appearance ; show ; outlook ; look ; front ¶ 겉모양으로 사람을 판단하다 judge 《a person》 by his appearance // 겉모양에 속지 마라 Never be deceived by outward appearance. // 사물은 반드시 겉모양과 같지는 않다 Things are not always what they seem.
겉모양(을) 내다 관용 dress up ; put a good face on
겉물 ① [따로 도는 물] a liquid floating on another liquid and not mixing with it ② [건물] sperm ejaculated involuntarily ¶ 겉물돌다 《a liquid》 float on the surface without mixing
겉발림 insincere flattery
겉밤 chestnuts with their shells on ; an unhulled chestnut
겉보기 outward appearance〔show〕; look ¶ 겉보기엔 outwardly ; on the surface ; in appearance ; apparently ; seemingly ; on the face of it // 사람은 겉보기만으로는 알 수 없다 Appearances are deceptive.
겉보리 unhulled barley
†겉봉 —封 an envelope ; an outer envelope〔wrapper〕 ¶ 겉봉을 쓰다 address an envelope
겉살 bare skin
겉수수 unhulled millet〔sorghum〕
겉싸개 a cover〔wrapper〕; an outer covering〔wrapper〕
겉씨 식물 —植物 gymnosperm
겉약다 be clever in a superficial way ; be sharp merely in show
겉어림 a rough estimate〔guess〕
겉여물다 be ripe only to outer appearances
겉열매껍질 ⇨ 외과피(外果皮)
*겉옷 an outer garment
겉잎 the outer leaves
겉잠 a nap ; a doze ; a catnap ; a dognap ; a light〔surface〕 sleep ; a snooze 《구》 ¶ 겉잠들다 doze ; take a nap ; catnap
겉잡다 make a rough estimate ; make a guess ; guess ; get a rough idea of ¶ 겉잡을 수 없는 말을 하다 tell an incoherent story ; talk in a rambling way // 그 여자의 진의가 무엇이었는지 겉잡을 수가 없다 I am unable to make any guess about what she really meant. // 그의 말은 전혀 겉잡을 수가 없다 I can't make head or tail of what he is saying. // 겉잡아 이틀이면 족하다 In my estimation two days will be enough.
겉잣 pine-nuts with their shells on
겉장 the first〔front〕 page ; the cover of a book (표지)

겉저고리 a woman's outer jacket
겉절이 vegetables pickled〔salted〕 not long before eating
겉절이다 salt 《vegetables》 before seasoning elaborately ; salt 《vegetables》 not long before eating
겉조 unhulled millet
겉짐작 a rough guess〔estimate〕 (based on appearances) ; a random guess ; a reckless judgment ¶ 겉짐작을 하다 make a rough guess ; make a random estimate
겉창 —窓 an outer window ; a shutter
*겉치레 ostensible decoration ; ostentation ; outward show ; ostensible display **—하다** dress up ; keep up appearance ; show off ; cut a dashing figure ; put on a fair show ; make outward show ¶ 겉치레를 좋아하다 love grandstand play ; be fond of demonstration〔display〕 // 그 나라에서 의회는 겉치레에 지나지 않는다 The parliament is nothing more than an accessory in that country.
겉치마 an outer skirt
겉치장 —治粧 dressing up the outside ; making outward show ; improving one's appearance **—하다** dress up the outside ; make outward show ; keep up appearance ; put a good face on 《a matter》 ; gloss〔smooth〕 over 《a fault》
겉포장 —包裝 a cover ; a wrapper ; an envelope ; outer covering **—하다** cover ; wrap
겉표지 —表紙 the (outer) cover ; a cover ; a wrapper 《영》 ; a jacket
겉피 unhusked barnyard millet
겉핥기 a smattering ; (a) superficial knowledge ; dilettantism ; sciolism ¶ 겉핥기식의 half-learned〔-read〕 ; superficial ; shallow ; sciolistic ; half-baked
겉핥다 just scratch the surface 《of a situation》 ; have a superficial knowledge 《of》 ; have a smattering 《of》
게[1] [거기] there ; [너] you ; you there ¶ 게 누구 있느냐 Is anybody there ? // 게 섰거라 Stop ! You there. // 게 앉아라 Sit down, there.
게[2] [에게] for ; to ¶ 내게 온 편지 a letter for me // 나에게 차가 있다면 If I had a car, . . .
*게[3] 〖동물〗 a crab ¶ 게 통조림 canned 〔tinned〕 crab // 게의 살 crab meat // 게의 집게발 claws // 게에게 물리다 be nipped by a crab
게도 구럭도 다 잃었다 [속담] If you run after two hares, you will catch neither.
게를 똑바로 걸어가게 할 수는 없다 [속담] You cannot make crab walk straight. / What can you expect from a pig but a grunt ?
게[4] [것이] ¶ 그까짓게 that sort of thing ; a man like him // 그게 누구 것이냐 Whose is that ? // 너까짓게 할 수 있을까 You never could do it.
게[5] [고장·집] 《my, your, his》 place 〔house, address〕 ; one's home ; part of one's country ¶ 우리 게는 대풍이다 This is a year of abundance in our part of the country. // 자네는 내게서 자게 You sleep at my house !
-게 ① […하게] ¶ 쉽게 easily ; simply // 짧게 briefly ; in short // 아름답게 beautifully // 좋게 well ; nicely
② [하게 하다〔되다〕] ¶ 못 가게 하다 do not let 《a person》 go // 들어오게 하다 let in // 생활을 넉넉하게 하다 enrich one's life // 책을 좋아하게 되다 come to be fond of reading〔books〕
③ [반어적 가정] ¶ 그럼 좋게 Quite the contrary.
④ [반말의 명령] ¶ 이것을 먹게 Eat this. // 이리 좀 오게 Keep near to me.
⑤ [동작의 이유·조건] ¶ 첫차에 늦지 않게 일찍 일어나라 Get up early so as to be in time for the first train.
게거품 foam at the mouth of a crab ¶ 말의 아가리는 게거품투성이였다 The horse was foam-flecked. // 그는 말할 때 입에서 게거품을 낸다 He foams〔froths〕 at the mouth when talking.
게걸 greed for food ; voraciousness
게걸 들다 [관용] get greedy for food ; become voracious ; get an insatiable appetite
게걸거리다 grumble ; mutter ; murmur ; growl ; nag ¶ 게걸게걸 grumbling ; growling
게걸들리다 become greedy for food
*게걸스럽다 (be) ravenous ; voracious ; gluttonous ; greedy ¶ 게걸스럽게 먹다 devour ; wolf one's food 《down》 ; eat ravenously〔voraciously, greedily〕
게걸음 the side-crawl (of a crab) ; walking sideways
게검스럽다 (be) voracious ; greedy ; gluttonous ¶ 게검스럽게 먹다 devour ; eat voraciously
-게까지 to such an extent ; so〔thus〕 far ; that much ; even so that. . . ; until (the point that) it is〔one does〕 ¶ 늦게까지 till (it gets) late // 그렇게까지 서두를 것은 없다 Don't be in such a hurry.
게꽁지 a dull〔stupid〕 fellow ; a dull clod ; a dullard ; a blockhead ; a saphead 《구》 ¶ 게꽁지만한 학문 two-bits' worth of education ; a dunce
게꽁지만하다 [관용] (be) shallow ; superficial ; short
-게끔 […하도록] ¶ 그들이 알아듣게끔 분명히 말하시오 Speak clearly, so that they understand you.
게눈 ① a crab's eye(s) ② 〖건축〗 a swirl decoration on the end of a roof

beam
게 눈 감추듯 한다 속담 eat 《food》 up in no time at all ; eat 《food》 greedily〔quickly〕
†게다가 ① [거기에] there ; over there ; in that place ¶ 책을 게다가 놓아라 Put the books there.
② [거기에 더하여] besides ; moreover ; what is more ; in addition (to that) ; into the bargain ; on〔the〕 top of ; [설상가상으로] to make matters worse ; what is worse ¶ 게다가 몸까지 버렸다 What is worse〔more〕, he lost his health. // 게다가 병까지 걸렸다 To make matters more miserable, he fell ill. // 나는 피로하다 게다가 졸린다 I'm tired, besides, I am sleepy. // 그건 유용한 책이고 게다가 값도 싸다 It's a useful book and, what is more, not an expensive one. // 게다가 그는 많은 돈을 받았다 He received a large sum of money, besides. // 게다가 비까지 내리기 시작했다 Moreover〔Besides〕, it began to rain. // 게다가 미인이야 A beauty at that.
게두덜거리다 grumble 《about》 ; rumble ; growl ; complain ; [중얼거리다] mumble ; mutter
게딱지 the shell〔crust〕 of a crab ; a carapace ¶ 게딱지만한 집에 살다 live in a tiny house
게딱지만하다 관용 be small as a crab shell ; (be) tiny
게뚜더기 an eyebrow that has a stitched-up look owing to the scars of a boil ; a person with such an eyebrow
게라 『인쇄』 a printing galley ; galley proof 〔sheet〕
게르마늄 『화학』 germanium 《Ge》
게르만 the German (people) ¶ 게르만의 Germanic
—(민)족(民族) the Germanic race —주의자 a Pan-German ; a Pan-Germanist 범—주의 Pan-Germanism
게르치 『물고기』 Scombrops boops (학명)
*게릴라 a guer(r)illa
— 대원〔병〕 a guerilla ; a bush fighter ; a bushwhacker 《미》 ; a partisan —부대 a guerilla band ; a partisan unit —전 guerilla war(fare) ; guerilla fighting ; bush fighting ; a bushwhacking 《미》 ; a hit-and-run raid ; a kill-and-run war 《속》 ¶ 게릴라전을 펴다 launch guerilla warfare — 전술 《use》 guerilla tactics — 행동 guerilla actions ; bushwhacking activities 대(對)— 작전 counter-guerilla operations 대(對)—전 counter-guerilla warfare 도시 — guerillas fighting in the city streets
게스트 a guest
— 멤버 a guest member — 싱어 a guest singer
게슈타포 (the) Gestapo 《나치 독일의 비밀 국가 경찰》
*게시 揭示 a notice ; a bulletin —하다 post〔put up〕 a notice ; notify ; placard ¶ 게시를 붙이다 pin up a notice 《on the wall》 ; stick a sign 《on the wall》 // …라는 게시가 붙어 있다 There is a notice up saying 《that》 // 「입장 사절」의 게시 a "No Admission" sign ; an "Off Limits" notice 《미》 ; an "Out of Bounds" notice 《영》 ☞ 《p. 133》
-게시리 ⇨ -게끔
*게시판 揭示板 a bulletin〔notice〕 board
열차 발착 — [철도의] a railway station schedule
게양 揭揚 —하다 hoist ; fly ; raise ; display 《a flag》 ¶ 국기를 게양하다 hoist 〔raise〕 a national flag // (배가) 태극기를 게양하고 있다 have a Korean flag flying
게염 covetousness ¶ 게염나다 become covetous 《of》 // 게염스럽다 be covetous // 게염부리다 behave covetously ; covet
게우다 ① [먹은 것을] vomit ; throw up ; bring up ¶ 배멀미가 나서 게우고 싶다 Being seasick I have a desire to vomit. /I feel nausea.
② [부정 이익을] disgorge ; repay 〔refund, give up〕 ill-gotten money ¶ 도둑은 훔친 것을 게워냈다 The thief disgorged his ill-gotten gains.
‡게으르다 (be) idle ; lazy ; indolent ; slothful ; sluggish

> 참고 **idle** 때때로 일을 하지 않는다는 뜻으로 꼭 비난의 뜻이 포함되어 있지는 않다 **lazy** 일하는 것을 싫어하고 일을 해도 힘을 내서 하지 않음을 뜻하며 보통 비난의 뜻이 포함되어 있다 **indolent** 천성적 또는 습관적으로 일을 싫어함 **slothful** 「느리고 게으른」의 뜻

¶ 게으른 성품 an indolent disposition // 게으른 탓으로 그이한테 편지도 못하고 있다 I have been remiss in writing to him.
게으른 놈이 짐 많이 진다 속담 Idle folks have the most labour.
게으른 말 짐 탓한다 속담 Idle folks have the most labour.
게으른 선비 책장 세듯 속담 Idle folks lack no excuses.
게으름 laziness ; idleness ; indolence ; sluggishness ; [태만] neglect ; slight ¶ 게으름부리다〔피우다〕 be〔get〕 lazy ; be idle ; loaf ; slacken one's effort // 지금은 국민의 어느 누구도 게으름피우고 있을 때가 아니다 Now is the time for none of the whole nation to sit and idle away the time. // 그렇지만 나는 늘 게으름을 피우게 된다 But my lazy streak always gets the better of me.
*게으름뱅이 an idler ; a lazybones ; an

게 시

게시·광고는 필요한 정보를 단적으로 전하는 것이 목적이기 때문에 필요한 용어를 최소한으로 줄이고 관사와 동사 등도 생략하는 것이 보통이다. 때로는 마침표도 찍지 않고 전부를 대문자로 표기하는 경우도 많다.

1 장소

교환전화 Housephone《호텔·아파트 등의》/ 남성용 화장실 Gentlemen / 여성용 화장실 Ladies / 매표소 Ticket [Booking《영》] Office / 비상구 Emergency Exit / 안내소 Information / 입구 Entrance / 출구 Exit [Way Out《영》] / 일반인 출입금지 Private / 택시 승차장 Taxi / 화장실 Rest Room; Comfort Station [Toilet, Lavatory《영》]《공원·동물원 등의》

2 알림

① 명사를 사용하여

가옥 임대, 방 임대 House [Home《미》, Rooms] for rent. / 금일 휴진 No consultations today. / 무료 입장 Admission free. / 연말 대매출 Year-end sale. / 재고처리 세일 Clearance sale. / 전점포 대매출 Storewide sale. / 특판일, 염가 대매출 Bargain (sale) day.

② 명사+과거분사

구인 Staff wanted. / 금일 매진 All sold out today. / 꽃꽂이 강습 Instruction given in flower arrangement. / 영어 강습 Instruction given in English. / 카탈로그 무료 증정 Catalogue offered free. / 피아노 교습 Piano lessons given.

③ 과거분사만으로 상태를 표시

금일 개점 Opened. (★ "영업중"이란 뜻도 된다.) / 금일 휴업, 영업 끝 Closed. / 매진 Sold. / 사용중 Occupied.《비행기의 좌석이나 화장실 등》/ 예약 완료 Reserved.

④ 전치사+명사 (일이 진행중임을 나타냄)

수선중 Under repairs. / 공사중 Under construction. / 고장 Out of order. / 기중(忌中) In mourning. / 운행중 In operation. / 회의중 Now in session.

⑤ 형용사를 중심으로 한 것

음료수 Good for drinking. / 일반 공개 Open to the public. / 초보자 환영 Welcome to beginners.

3 주의를 촉구하는 것

① 명사

경고 Warning. / 바닥주의 Wet floor. / 위험 Danger. / 제한구역 Restricted area. / 칠주의 Wet [Fresh] paint. / 파손주의 Perishables. / 화기엄금 Inflammables.

② 형용사

정숙 Quiet. / 파손주의 Fragile.

③ 명령형

날치기 주의 Beware of pickpockets. / 누르시오 Push. / 맹견주의 Beware of savage dogs. / 발걸음 주의 Watch your step. / 습기주의 Guard against damp.; Keep dry. / 창밖 팔주의 Keep arm in. / 취급주의 Handle with care. / 화기주의 Beware of fire.

4 금지

① 동사+no+명사

벽보 부착금지 Post no bills. / 갈고리 사용금지 Use no hooks. / 소변금지 Commit no nuisance.

② No+...ing

금연 No smoking. / 낚시금지 구역 No fishing here. / 배회 금지 No loitering. / 출입금지 No trespassing.; No admission. / 쓰레기 버리지 마시오. No dumping. / 침을 뱉지 마시오. No spitting. / 휴지를 버리지 마시오. No littering.

③ Do not+동사

출입금지 Don't disturb.《호텔 등의 문고리에 거는》/ 동물에게 먹이를 주지 마시오. Don't feed the animals. / 전시품에 손 대지 마시오. Don't touch the exhibits. / 쓰레기 버리지 마시오. Don't leave litter. / 화물을 뒤집지 마시오. Do not turn over.

④ 기타

손 대지 마시오. Hands off. / 접근금지 Keep off. / 잔디밭에 들어가지 마시오. (Please) Keep off the grass.; Don't step on the grass. / 출입금지. Keep out.; Off limits. / 신발을 벗으시오. Shoes off. / 문을 닫아 주시오. (Please) Shut [Close] the door after you.

5 사절

No+명사+(allowed)

잡상인 금지 No peddlers or salesmen. / 건물내 강매금지 No solicitors allowed in this building. / 어린이 입장금지 No entrance to children. / 개 출입금지 No dogs allowed. / 면회 사절 No visitors allowed. / 공놀이금지 No ball playing allowed. / 관계자외 출입금지 No admission except on business. / 라디오 소음금지 No radios to be played.

⑥ **제한**

명사＋only

성인전용 Adults only. / 입석실 Room for standing only. / 직원전용 Employees [Staff] only. / 출구전용 Exit only. / 헌옷전문 Used clothing only. / 회원전용 Members only.

⑦ **교통표지판**

① **규제표지**

속도제한 Speed limit. / 우측통행 Keep right. / 우회전금지 No right turn (ahead). / 일방통행 One Way. / 일시정지 Stop.; Halt. / 주차금지 No Parking. / 중량제한 Load limit. / 진입금지 Do not enter. / 추월금지 No passing. / 회전금지 No U-turn. / 횡단금지 Do not cross here.

② **경계표지**

급커브 Sharp turn. / 낙석주의 Fallen rock ahead. / 막다른 길 Dead end road. / 비포장 갓길 Soft shoulder. / 철도건널목 Railroad crossing. / 커브길 Winding road. / 학교구역 School. / 합류교통구역 Merging traffic.

③ **안내표지**

우회로 Detour. / 톨 게이트 Toll gate.

idle〔a lazy〕 fellow ; a sluggard ; a do-nothing ¶ 그는 천성이 게으름뱅이다 He is a born idler.

게을러빠지다 (be) very lazy ; quite indolent

***게을리** **—하다** neglect ; be neglectful〔negligent〕 of ; slight ; fail to attend 《to》 ¶ 직무에 게을리하다 neglect one's duties // 공부를 게을리하다 neglect one's lessons ; fail to attend to one's studies // 답장을 게을리하다 be tardy in answering a letter ; fail to answer a letter // 그는 직무를 게을리하여 해고당했다 He was dismissed for neglecting his duties.

게이지 a gauge ; a gage
—강(鋼) gauge steel **궤간 —** 〚철도〛 a track gauge **표준 —** the standard gauge

게임 a game ¶ 게임을 하다 play a game 《of tennis》
— 세트 [심판의 말] 〚정구〛 Game and set. / [일반 경기] Game. / Game (is) over. / The game is over. **—차(差)** 〚야구〛 games behind **— 포인트** game point

게자리 〚천문〛 the Crab ; the Cancer

게장 —醬 ① [장] soy sauce in which crabs are preserved ; crab preserved in soy sauce ② [젓] pickled crabs

게재 **揭載** publication ; insertion ; printing **—하다** publish ; print ; insert ; report 《in a paper》 ¶ 연일 게재되는 appearing daily // 그 논문이 게재된 잡지 the magazine which carries the article // 신문에 게재되다 appear in the press〔newspapers〕 ; get into the press // 신문에 광고를 게재하다 insert an advertisement in a newspaper

게재 금지 **揭載禁止** a press ban ; prohibition〔suppression〕 of publication

게저분하다 (be) dirty ; unclean ; soiled ; be laden with superfluous〔dirty〕 things

게적지근하다 feel uneasy〔uncomfortable〕 about ; be not quite happy about ; feel restless

게접스럽다 (be) filthy ; dirty ; squalid

게젓 pickled crabs

게정 grumbling ; a complaint ; a murmur
—꾼 a grumbler ; a crab ; a crabber 《미·구》

게정내다 grumble

게정스럽다 be grumbly ; be malcontent

게줄 side ropes attached to the bulky tug-of-war

게줄다리기 tug-of-war with side ropes

게트림 an arrogant〔haughty〕 belch ; belching in a haughty manner **—하다** belch arrogantly〔haughtily〕 ; belch in a haughty manner

-겠구먼, -겠군 I realize it will be〔do〕 ; probably is〔does〕 ¶ 그럼 꽤 춥겠구먼요 I realize you must be quite cold. // 인제 출발해야겠군 But now we've got to leave.

-겠다 ① [결심·필연성] will do〔be〕 ¶ 나는 내일 가겠다 I will go tomorrow. // 그만 먹겠다 That's all I'll eat. ② [추측·판단] probably do〔be〕 ¶ 얼굴을 보니 착하겠다 To judge from his appearance, he must be gentle. // 재미있겠다 I bet it's fun. ③ [상대에게] ¶ 모르겠다 I wouldn't know. / I don't know. ④ [뜻밖] ¶ 별소리 다 듣겠다 Now I've heard everything.

겨 chaff ; hulls〔husks〕 of grain ; bran
겨 묻은 개가 똥 묻은 개를 흉본다〔나무란다〕 속담 The pot calls the kettle black.

겨끔내기 doing 《a thing》 on a two-shift basis ; alternating ¶ 겨끔내기로 in turns ; by shifts

†겨냥 ① aim ; mark ; [조준] sight ―하다 aim 《at》; take aim 《at》; level 《a gun at》 ¶ 겨냥이 틀리다 be wide of the mark ; aim wrongly // 겨냥이 빗나가다 miss the mark ; miss one's aim ; aim wrong // 겨냥이 틀리지 않다 aim true // 총을 겨냥하다 take aim with one's gun // 잘 겨냥하여 쏘다 take a careful〔good〕 aim and fire // 그는 새를 겨냥했다 He aimed at the bird. // 나는 권총으로 그를 겨냥했다 I aimed a revolver at him.
② [치수] measure ; size ; dimension ―하다 measure 《a person》; take the dimension of ; take 《a person's》 measurements ¶ 자로 겨냥하다 take measurements with a rule
―대 a measuring rod ; a yardstick ―도(圖) a (rough) sketch ; a sketch map〔drawing〕

겨냥내다 measure ; take measurements 〔the dimensions〕 of 《a room》; size

겨냥대다 take aim at ; bring into aim

겨냥보다 aim ; take aim at

†겨누다 ① [겨냥하다] (take) aim 《at》; level 《a gun at》 ¶ 과녁을 겨누다 aim at a mark // 정확히 겨누다 take accurate 〔sure〕 aim // 총으로 겨누다 point〔level〕 a gun 《at a person》// 잘 겨누고 쏘다 take good〔careful〕 aim and fire // 꿩을 겨누고 한 방 놓다 get a shot at a pheasant // 겨누지 않고 쏘다 shoot at random ② [대보다] measure ; take the measure of

겨눠보다 ① [겨냥] take tentative aim 《at》; try aiming 《at》 ② [대강 치수] take rough measurements

*겨드랑이 the armpit ; the axilla 《*pl.* axillae》; [옷의] the armhole ¶ 겨드랑이에 끼다 take〔hold, carry〕 《a thing》 under one's arm // 겨드랑이에서 땀이 나다 sweat under the arms // 겨드랑이가 터져 있다 There is a rip at the armhole.

겨레 offspring of the same forefather ; [형제] brothers ; brethren ; [민족] a people ; a nation ; one's countrymen ; compatriots
한― one and the same people

겨레말 a language ; one's mother tongue ; the national language

겨레붙이 members of a people〔nation〕

겨루기 ⇨ 겨룸
지혜― a duel of wits 힘― a contest of physical strength

‡겨루다 pit 《one's skill》 against ; vie 《with》; rival 《another in something》; compete ; contend ; struggle ; strive 《with another for》 ¶ 기량을 겨루다 match one's skill 《against》// 힘을 겨루다 measure oneself against another in strength // 1위를 겨루다 contend for the first place // 권력을 겨루다 contend with another for supremacy ; struggle〔fight〕 with one another for power // 그는 나와 한번 겨루어 볼 만한 상대이다 He is one of my matching rivals. // 어느 운동이건 너와는 겨룰 수 있다 I will match you in any sports. // 두 권투 선수가 세계 선수권을 걸고 링에서 겨루었다 The two boxers pitted their strength against one another at the ring contending the world championship. // 포도주에 있어서 프랑스와 겨룰 나라는 없다 For wine, no country can match France.

겨룸 contest ; competition ; rivalry ; contention ; measuring〔pitting〕 one's strength 〔talent〕 《with, against》

*겨를 leisure ; leisure time〔hours〕; free 〔spare〕 time ; time to spare ; free time ¶ 겨를이 없다 have no leisure (time to spare) ; be busy〔occupied〕 《with one's work》// 눈코 뜰 겨를이 없다 be so busily engaged 《in a matter》// 좀처럼 겨를이 없다 I am seldom at leisure. // 겨를이 있으면 와 주십시오 Come and see me, if you are free〔not doing anything, not busy, not engaged〕. // 아무리 바쁘다지만 부모님에게 편지 쓸 겨를도 없단 말인가 I know you are very busy, but you can spare time to write to your parents.

겨리 a plow drawn by a yoke of (two) oxen
―질 plowing with a two-ox plow 겨릿소 one of the oxen tethered to a two-ox plow

겨반지기 rice with much bran or chaff

†겨우 [가까스로] barely ; narrowly ; with difficulty ; [고작] only ; just ; at (the) most ; no more than ; merely ; at (the) best ¶ 겨우 입에 풀칠하다 live barely ; keep body and soul together ; have great difficulty making ends meet // 겨우 달아나다 escape barely ; have a narrow escape〔close shave〕// 일행 중 겨우 두 사람이 살아 남았다 Only two of the party survived. // 겨우 5만원을 모았다 We barely managed to collect 50,000 *won*. // 겨우 시험에 합격했다 He just managed to pass the examination. // 겨우 기차 시간에 대어갔다 I was barely in time for the train. // 하루에 겨우 만원밖에 벌지 못한다 earn at most 10,000 *won* a day // 겨우 5명만 합격했다 Only about〔No more than〕 five of them have passed.

겨우내 throughout the winter ; all through the winter ; all winter long ¶ 겨우내 눈이 온다 It snows all winter through.

*겨우살이¹ [옷] winter clothes〔wear〕; a winter suit ; [과동(過冬)] passing the winter

겨우살이² 〖식물〗 a mistletoe ; a parasite

†**겨울** winter ; the winter season ¶ 겨울의 wintry // 한겨울에 in midwinter ; in the depth of winter // 겨울다운 wintry // 겨울 준비를 하다 prepare for the winter —나기 wintering — 채비 preparations for the winter ; [겨울옷] a winter suit ; winter wear —철 winter ; the winter season — 파종 winter sowing

겨울날 winter days ; the winter weather

겨울 방학 —放學 a winter vacation〔holidays〕

겨울새 a winter bird〔resident, visitant〕

겨울옷 winter clothes ; (clothes for) winter wear ; a winter dress (여자의) ; a winter jacket (학생의)

겨울잠 winter sleep ; hibernation ¶ 겨울잠을 자다 hibernate

겨워하다 feel《it》difficult to《do ; think of《a task》to be beyond one's power〔ability, capacity〕; find《it》unmanageable〔uncontrollable〕; feel something to be much for one ¶ 그 젊은 과부는 혼자서 세 자녀를 기르는 것을 힘에 겨워하고 있다 The young widow feels it beyond her ability to take care of her three children by herself.

*__겨자__ [양념] mustard ; [풀] a mustard (plant)

겨자씨 mustard seed

겨죽 rice-bran gruel

격 格 ① [지위] standing ; status ; rank ; [등급] a class ; a grade ; [자격] capacity ; [인격] character ; [격식] formality ; social rules ; an established form ¶ 격을 갖추다 be formal ; complete the formalities ; go through the formalities // 격이 올라가다 be promoted to a higher rank〔grade〕; rise in rank // 격이 떨어지다 be reduced to a lower rank〔grade〕; fall in rank // 격이 다르다 not to be on the same level // 격에 안 맞는 짓을 하다 go against one's character ; do something unbecoming to one's standing ② 〖문법〗 the case
목적— the objective case 주— the nominative case

격감 激減 a sharp decrease ; a marked decline —하다 decrease〔decline, fall off〕sharply〔remarkably〕 ¶ 수출이 격감하다 exports fall off sharply // 수입이 격감한다 There is a big drop〔a marked falling off〕in imports.

격검 擊劍 (the art of) fencing —하다 do〔practice〕fencing ; fence ¶ 격검 시합을 하다 have a fencing match《with》

격구 擊毬 a kind of polo played by the military in former days

격나다 隔— become estranged〔alienated〕《from a person》; drift apart from each other ; break relations《with》; split with ¶ 그 일 이후로 두 사람은 자연히 격났다 Since that event the two have become estranged.

격납고 格納庫 a hangar ; an airplane〔aviation〕shed
— 갑판 [항공 모함의] a hangar deck — 담당자 a hangar-man 이동 — a portable hangar

격년 隔年 every other year —하다 have not seen each other for more than a year ¶ 격년 간행의 biennial

⁑**격노** 激怒 rage ; fury ; violent〔raving〕anger ; wrath ; exasperation —하다 get enraged〔infuriated〕; grow〔be〕furious ; fly into a passion ; be exasperated ; blow one's top ; have a fit ¶ 격노하여 in a rage ; with anger〔rage〕; in the fury of one's passion // 격노시키다 enrage ; infuriate ; rouse〔stir〕《a person's》wrath

격돌 激突 a violent collision ; a shock ; a crash —하다 crash into〔against〕《another train》 ¶ 열차의 격돌 a train crash // 적군과 격돌하다 encounter an enemy force

*__격동__ 激動 violent shaking ; concussion ; a severe〔violent〕shock ; [동요] excitement ; agitation ; convulsion ; upheaval —하다 shake violently ; convulse ; stir up ; excite ; agitate ; [동요하다] be stirred up ; be excited ; be agitated ¶ 격동하는 세계 정세 a turbulent world situation // 자연계의 격동 a convulsion of nature // 학계를 격동시키다 stir up academic circles // (지진으로) 가옥이 격동한다 Houses shake violently. // 전국적으로 민심이 격동하고 있다 Excitement prevails throughout〔across〕the country.

격랑 激浪 heavy〔great〕seas ; mountainous〔huge〕waves ; raging waves ¶ 격랑에 휩쓸리다 be swept away〔gulped down〕by the angry waves // 격랑은 산더미같이 높았다 Angry seas and frantic waves were mountain high.

†**격려** 激勵 urging ; encouragement ; incitement —하다 encourage ; spur《a person》on ; cheer up ¶ 격려의 말 words of encouragement // …의 말에 격려되어 encouraged〔spurred〕by《a person's》words // 격려의 연설을 하다 peptalk〔give a pep talk〕(미·속) // …하도록 격려하다 encourage《a person》to《do》// 더욱 노력하도록 격려하다 inspire《a person》to further efforts // 야구 선수들을 격려하다 cheer baseball players《on》
— 연설 a speech of encouragement《for a person》—자 an encourager

⁑**격렬** 激烈 fierceness ; intensity ; impetuosity ; severity ; violence —하다 (be) fierce ; violent ; furious ; severe ; vehement ; impetuous ; intense ¶ 격렬한 경쟁 fierce〔keen, cutthroat〕competition // 격렬한 포화 a heavy fire // 더욱 격

렬해지다 grow in intensity ; grow more and more furious//격렬한 논쟁을 벌이다 stir up a dispute 《about》; have an acrimonious〔a bitter, heated, sharp〕 dispute

격론 激論 a heated〔sharp, bitter〕 argument〔discussion〕; high words ; a hot 〔violent〕 controversy **—하다** have a bitter〔heated〕discussion ; argue hotly ; have high words ¶ 격론이 벌어지다 heated argument arises 《as to》// 격론을 벌이다 provoke〔arouse〕 a heated〔an animated〕 discussion//그와 격론하였다 I had a stormy discussion〔heated argument〕 with him.

격류 激流 a torrent ; a swift〔violent〕 current〔stream〕; rapids ; a rapid river ¶ 바위에 부딪치는 격류 a torrent dashing against rocks//격류에 휩쓸려 내려가다 be swept away by a torrent

*__격리 隔離__ [고립] isolation ; [흑인에 대한] segregation 《미》; [전염병 환자의] quarantine **—하다** isolate ; segregate ; quarantine ¶ 환자를 격리하다 isolate a patient ; keep a patient in isolation//천연두 환자는 격리되었다 People with smallpox were quarantined.

— 병실 an isolation〔a segregation〕 room **—실(室)** a quarantine room ; [우주 비행사의] a mobile quarantine facility **— 유리관** a glass tube separator **—판(板)** a separator

격리 병원 隔離病院 an isolation〔a segregation〕 hospital ; a detention hospital

격리 환자 隔離患者 a patient segregated from the others ; an isolated patient

격막 膈膜 〖해부〗 the diaphragm ; 〖생물〗 the septum

—사(絲) a mesenterial filament **— 섬유** septate fibre **— 형성체** 〖식물〗 a phragmoplast

격막염 膈膜炎 inflammation of the diaphragm ; diaphragmatitis

격멸 擊滅 destruction ; extermination ; annihilation **—하다** destroy ; exterminate ; annihilate ; wipe out ; rout

격무 激務 a busy office ; a severe〔toilsome〕 duty ; an arduous task〔duty〕; hard work ; [일의 번잡] pressure of business〔work〕 ¶ 격무에 시달리다 be worn to a frazzle by hard work//격무에 쓰러지다 succumb to the strain of overwork//격무를 감당 못하다 be unfit for a busy office

격문 檄文 a manifesto ; a written appeal ; a declaration ; a pronunciamento ¶ 격문을 내다 issue a manifesto ; appeal 《to》//전국에 격문을 띄우다 make a nationwide appeal in writing

격물 格物 the study of things and nature

격물치지 格物致知 gaining knowledge by the study of things

격발 擊發 percussion ¶ 권총에 격발 장치를 하다 make a revolver ready for firing

— 신관(信管) a percussion fuse **— 장치** percussion lock

격발 激發 an outburst ; a flush ; a fit ; explosion ; an attack 《of a disease》 **—하다** burst 《out》; explode ¶ 격발시키다 provoke ; incite ; bring on 《a fit》; awake//감정의 격발 an outburst of emotion//적대 의식을 격발시키다 provoke antagonism//계급 의식을 격발시키다 awake 《a person》 to class consciousness

격벽 隔壁 a partition ; 〖해부〗 a septum ; 〖식물〗 a dissepiment ; 〖화학〗 a diaphragm ; 〖선박·광산〗 a bulkhead ; 〖건축〗 a curtain ¶ 방수〔구면, 선수(船首)〕 격벽 watertight〔spherical, collision〕 bulkhead

격변 激變 a sudden〔rapid〕 change ; a convulsion ; a violent upheaval ; 〖지질〗 a cataclysm **—하다** change rapidly 〔suddenly〕; undergo a rapid〔marked〕 change ¶ 사회의 격변 rapid changes 〔an upheaval〕 of society//격변하는 사회〔정치〕 정세 a convulsion of the social 〔political〕 situation//물가의 격변 a wild〔sharp〕 fluctuation in price//기후의 격변으로 병이 나다 be affected by a sudden change of climate

지질 —론 the cataclysm theory

‡__격분 激奮__ vehement indignation〔resentment〕; enragement **—하다** become vehemently angry ; burn with indignation ; flare〔blow〕 up ; be enraged 《at, with》

격분 激忿 [격노] wild rage ; violent anger ; fury **—하다** rage ; be enraged ; fly into a violent tantrum

격세 隔世 a distant age ; another age ; a different world ; [시대를 거름] every second generation ¶ 당시를 생각하면 격세지감이 있다 As I recall those days, it seems as if we were separated by an age. //전후에 한국에 와보니 격세지감이 있다 I've found myself quite a Rip Van Winkle back here in postwar Korea.

격세 유전 隔世遺傳 〖생물〗 atavism ; (a) reversion ; (a) throwback ¶ 격세 유전의 atavistic

격식 格式 an established form ; social rules ; a form ; a formality ¶ 격식을 차리다 stick to〔stand on〕 formality//젊은 사람들은 격식을 싫어한다 Young people dislike all formalities.

격실 隔室 a compartment ; a bay

방수 — a watertight〔waterproof〕 compartment

격심 激甚 severity ; vehemence ; intensity ; keenness **—하다** (be) extreme ; keen ; vehement ; acute ; severe ; intense ¶ 격심한 경쟁 keen competition ; cutthroat competition // 격심한 고통 an acute pain // 격심한 물가고 an acute price increase // 격심한 물자 부족 acute shortage of the commodities // 격심한 추위 severe cold // 격심한 피해 extensive 〔irreparable, serious, severe〕 damage

격앙 激昂 [흥분] excitement ; [분격] resentment ; indignation **—하다** be excited 《about》 ; flare up ; lose one's temper〔head〕 ; be indignant 《about, at》 ; be incensed 《at》 ; take on 《구》 ¶ 격앙한 군중 an excited〔enraged, agitated〕 crowd // 격앙하기 쉬운 excitable ; choleric ; hotheaded // 격앙하여 excitedly ; in excitement ; in hot blood ; in a fit of passion〔temper〕 ; in a rage // 격앙시키다 excite 《a person》 ; enrage ; incense

***격언 格言** a maxim ; an adage ; a proverb ; a saying ; a saw ; an apothegm (경구) ¶ 격언에 가로되 A〔The〕 proverb says 《that》 ; As the saying goes〔is〕 ; As the proverb has it

격외 格外 exception ; speciality ¶ 격외의 extraordinary ; special ; exceptional **—품** a nonstandardized article

격원 隔遠 —하다 be a long way off ; be far away from ; (be) distant ; remote ; far-off

격월 隔月 every other〔second〕 month ; 《in》 alternate months ; a month's interval ¶ 격월의 bimonthly

격월간 隔月刊 a bimonthly (publication)

격의 隔意 reserve ; estrangement ¶ 격의 없는 친구 an inseparable friend ; a bosom friend // 격의 없는 unreserved ; confidential ; unconstrained ; free ; open (-minded) ; candid ; frank // 격의 없이 얘기하다 talk frankly with ; have a frank talk with // 격의 없이 의견을 교환하다 have a frank exchange of views

격일 隔日 a day's interval **—하다** have a day's interval ¶ 격일하여 every other 〔second〕 day ; on alternate days // 격일제로 근무하다 shift once in two days

격일열 隔日熱 〖의학〗 tertian fever

***격자 格子** ① [문의] a lattice ; [창문의] a latticework ; [천장의] a coffer ② [대갓끈의] beads attached to the strings of a Korean hat ¶ 격자로 된 latticed

격자 무늬 格子 — cross stripes ; check

격자문 格子門 a lattice door

격자 세공 格子細工 latticework ; latticing

격자창 格子窓 a lattice window

격전 激戰 a hot fight ; a severe〔fierce〕 battle ; a pitched battle ; [맹렬한 경쟁] a hot〔sharp〕 contest **—하다** fight hard ; have a fierce battle ; engage in hot combat ¶ 격전의 용사 a seasoned soldier // 격전이 벌어지고 있다 A fierce battle〔violent fighting〕 is raging〔going on〕. // 옛날 여기서 격전이 있었다 A fierce battle was once fought here.

격전지 激戰地 a hard-fought field ; [선거의] a closely contested constituency ; a close district 《미》

격절 隔絶 [고립] isolation ; [차단] blockade ; [분리] separation **—하다** be separated 《from》 ; be isolated 《from》 ; be far〔remote〕 《from》 ; be blockaded

격정 激情 strong〔violent〕 emotion ; passion ; fury ¶ 격정의 발작 a fit of passion 〔temper〕 // 격정을 못 이겨 carried away by a stroke of passion ; in a fit of passion ; out of temper

격조 隔阻 —하다 hear nothing ; have no news 《from a person》 ; live apart in a distant place ¶ 오랫동안 격조하였습니다 It's been a long time since I saw you last. // 오랫동안 격조하여 면목없습니다 I'm sorry I haven't kept in touch with you.

격조 格調 ① 〖문예〗 rhythm ; swing ② [사람의] personality ; character ¶ 격조 높은 noble ; refined ; high-toned

격주 隔週 a weekly interval ¶ 격주의 fortnightly ; biweekly // 격주로 every other〔second〕 week // 격주 월요일에 every alternate Monday

격증 激增 a sudden〔rapid, marked〕 increase ; a sharp gain ; [수량의] a heavy swell **—하다** increase rapidly〔sharply〕 ; [수량이] rise〔swell〕 rapidly ¶ 주문의 격증 a rush of orders // 그 수는 3,000으로 격증하였다 The number leaped〔jumped〕 to 3,000. // 해마다 인구가 격증하고 있다 There is a considerable increase in population year after year.

격지 [켜] (many) layers ; manifold ¶ 격지격지 in layers ; manifoldly

격지 隔紙 a sheet of paper inserted between two layers

격지 隔地 a distant〔remote〕 place〔area〕

격지다 隔— be broken up ; be at odds 《with》 ; get estranged

격진 激震 a destructive〔severe〕 earthquake〔shock〕 ¶ 오늘 아침 격진이 있었다 There was a severe earthquake〔A severe earthquake was felt〕 this morning. // 격진이 (지역을) 강타하다 A severe earthquake strikes 《the area》.

— 구역 a ruinous earthquake area

격차 格差, 隔差 difference in quality ¶ 소득의 격차를 없애다 smooth out earning differentials // 격차가 생기다〔안 생기다〕 make a〔no〕 difference // 격차를 좁히다 narrow the gap 《between》

기술 — a technological gap **세대간 —** a generation gap〔difference〕

***격찬 激讚** high praise ; a high tribute **—하다** praise highly ; speak highly of ; pay a high tribute 《to》 ; praise

〔extol〕《a person》 to the skies ¶ 근면을 격찬하다 praise 《a person》 highly for his industry // 미모를 격찬하다 rave over〔about〕 《a person's》 good looks // 용감한 행위를 격찬하다 speak highly of 《a person's》 heroic act ; praise 《a person》 highly for his heroic act

격추 擊墜 shooting down ; bringing down (지상에서) **—하다** shoot 《airplanes》 down ; bring down ; down 《a plane》

격침 擊沈 sinking ; sending 《a ship》 to the bottom **—하다** sink ; send 《a ship》 to the bottom ¶ 수뢰로 격침하다 torpedo (and sink) 《a ship》 // 잠수함에 의해서 격침되다 be torpedoed and sunk by a submarine

***격통 激痛** an acute〔intense, excruciating〕 pain ; a severe〔sharp, keen〕 pain ; a pang ¶ 복부에 격통을 느끼다 feel an acute pain in one's stomach

***격퇴 擊退** a repulse ; dislodgement ; [거절] rejection **—하다** repulse ; drive 〔beat〕 back ; repel ; [진지에서] dislodge 《them》 from 《their position》 ; reject ; refuse ¶ 적을 격퇴하다 drive the enemy back ; repulse〔fight off〕 the enemy ; clear out the enemy // 격퇴당하다 meet with〔suffer〕 a repulse

***격투 激鬪** furious〔severe〕 fisticuffs ; a hand-to-hand fight ; [난투] a scuffle **—하다** grapple〔fight〕 with ; come to blows ; fight hand-to-hand 《with a person》 ; scuffle ¶ 맹렬한 격투 a dogfight ; a free-for-all 《영》 // 격투 끝에 강도를 잡았다 He grappled with the robber and seized him.
— 장면 a fighting scene

격파 擊破 defeating ; destruction ; beating out **—하다** defeat ; beat out ; (put to) rout ; crush ; overthrow ; [논파하다] refute ; [쳐부수다] destroy ; smash up

격하 格下 degradation ; downgrading ; demotion 《미》 **—하다** lower 《a person》 in rank ; demean (oneself) ; downgrade
—품 degraded goods

격하다 隔— [거리를] separate ; set apart ; leave a space 《between》 ; [막다] screen ; shield ; [사이에 두다] interpose ; [시간을] leave an interval 《between》 ¶ 담장을 격한 이웃 a next-door neighbor // 강을 격하여 across a river // 10년을 격하여 after〔at intervals of〕 ten years // 5미터씩 격하여 at intervals of five meters // 2년 격하여 한번씩 once every two years

격하다 激— (be) strong ; violent ; intense ; vehement ; furious ; passionate ; [화내다] be infuriated ; be wrought up ¶ 격한 감정 a strong feeling ; a violent passion // 격한 성미 a violent〔fiery〕 temper // 격한 말 violent language ; passionate words ; fiery speech // 격한 의론 heated〔fiery〕 discussion // 사소한 일에 격하다 get excited over trifles // 논쟁이 격해졌다 The dispute grew hot〔heated up〕. // 말이 격해졌다 Words ran high.

격화 激化 intensification ; aggravation **—하다** be intensified ; be aggravated ; become violent〔intense〕 ¶ 정당간의 싸움의 격화 intensification of the party strife

격화소양 隔靴搔癢 having an itch that one cannot scratch ; leaving much to be desired ; being unsatisfactory ¶ 격화소양의 감이 있다 feel slightly annoyed that something cannot be done quite as hoped ; feel impatient 〔unsatisfied〕

***겪다** ① [경험하다] undergo ; suffer ; endure ; experience ; go〔pass〕 through ¶ 겪어 보지 않으면 모를 일 a matter beyond the imagination of those who have not experienced it // 겪어 본 적이 있다 have experience in // 갖은 고초를 겪다 undergo all sorts of hardships // 심한 고통을 겪다 suffer〔endure〕 a severe pain
② [치르다] receive ; entertain ; have a guest ¶ 손님을 겪다 entertain a guest ; give a reception

견 絹 silk ; [견본] a sheet of silk (used for painting or writing)
본— pure silk

견갑 肩胛 〖해부〗 the shoulder
— 관절 the shoulder joint **—부** the shoulder **— 탈구** dislocation of the shoulder joint **— 하동맥** the subscapular artery

견갑골 肩胛骨 the shoulder blade ; the scapula

견강 堅强 sturdiness ; solidity ; stoutness **—하다** (be) sturdy ; stout ; solid

견강부회 牽强附會 a farfetched view 〔interpretation, argument〕 ; distortion ; sophistry **—하다** strain 《the interpretation》 ; force 〔wrench〕 《the meaning》 ; distort 《the fact》 ; twist ; give a farfetched interpretation ¶ 견강부회의 forced ; overstrained ; farfetched ; distorted // 견강부회의 설 a farfetched argument〔version, theory〕

*‡**견고 堅固** **—하다** (be) strong ; solid ; firm ; secure ¶ 견고히 solidly ; strongly ; firmly ; securely // 견고한 진지 a strong position // 도덕심이 견고한 사람 a man of strict morality // 견고히 만든 solidly made〔built〕 // 방비가 견고하다 be strongly fortified // 견고히 하다 strengthen ; make solid〔firm〕 // 견고히 포장하다 pack securely

†**견과 堅果** a nut

†**견디다** ① [참다] bear (up) ; endure ; stand ; put up with ; tolerate ; suffer ¶

견딜 수 없는 더위 unbearable〔intolerable〕 heat // 견딜 수 없는 모욕 an intolerable〔unpardonable〕 insult // 고난을 견디다 bear〔endure〕 hardships // 견딜 수 있다 be bearable ; be endurable // 견딜 수 없다 be unbearable ; be unendurable ; be past bearing // 더 이상 견딜 수 없다 This is more than I can bear. /This is too much. /I can't stand this any more. // 올 여름의 더위는 견딜 수가 없다 I simply can't stand the heat of this summer. // 참고 견뎌라 Hang in there. /Hang on. /Hang tough. /Tough it out. /Stick it out. ② [유지하다] bear ; wear ; last ; stand 《against》 ; withstand ; hold out ; be proof against ¶ 열에 견디다 stand〔bear up against〕 heat // 10년간의 사용에 견디다 be good for ten years // 유혹에 견디다 resist〔be proof against〕 temptation // 폭풍우와 지진에도 견디다 stand against storm and earthquake // 먼 여정을 잘도 견디다 withstand a long journey well // 이 금고는 불에도 견딘다 The safe is proof against fire. // 이 신발은 오래 견디지 못할 거요 I am afraid these shoes won't wear well. // 그렇게 하면 몸이 견디어 낼 수가 없다 You cannot keep yourself in good health if you do so.

③ [생계를 꾸리다] eke out 《with》 ¶ 근근히 생계를 견디다 eke out a scanty livelihood ; eke out a miserable existence

견딜성 —性 patience ; perseverance ; fortitude ; endurance ¶ 견딜성 있는 patient ; persevering // 견딜성 없는 lacking in patience // 무슨 일에든지 견딜성이 있어야 성공하는 법이다 Perseverance is the mother of success.

견딜힘 endurance ; patience

견련 牽連 connection ; joining ; linking **—하다** be related〔affiliated〕 《to》

— 사건 a case closely related to ; an affiliated case

견마 犬馬 ① [개와 말] dogs and horses ② [낮춤말] my humble self ; I ; me ¶ 견마지성 one's faithfulness 《to the king》

견마지로 犬馬之勞 one's humble service 《to the king》 ¶ 견마지로를 아끼지 않다 render what little service one can ; do as much as one can

견문 見聞 [지식] information ; knowledge ; [경험] experience ; [관찰] observation **—하다** see and hear ; observe ; experience ¶ 견문을 넓히다 extend〔add to〕 one's knowledge // 친히 견문하다 observe personally // 그 사람은 견문이 넓다 He is well-informed. / He has seen much of life. /He has wide 〔broad〕 knowledge. // 그는 견문을 넓히려 여행에 나섰다 He went on a tour to see more of the world.

—록 a record of personal experience

견문발검 見蚊拔劍 breaking a butterfly on the wheel ; drawing the sword at a mosquito ; making a fuss about trifles

견물생심 見物生心 Seeing is wanting. / The object gives rise to the desire.

견방적 絹紡績 ⇨ 견사 방적

견방직 絹紡織 silk weaving

견본 絹本 silk cloth ; silk canvas

†**견본 見本** [상품의] a sample ; [책 따위의] a sample copy ; [표본] a specimen ¶ 견본〔가두〕 전시품 a floor sample // 무작위 (추출) 견본 a random sample // 견본 한 벌 an assortment of samples // 견본품을 퍼뜨리다 distribute samples // 견본품을 무료로 배포하다 hand out free samples // 견본과 같이 according to the sample ; as per sample // 견본과 같다 be up to the sample // 견본과 다르다 differ from the sample // 견본보다 못하다 be below the sample // 그 잡지의 견본을 1부 보내 주십시오 Will you send me a sample copy of the magazine ? // 견본을 제공하다 furnish a sample // 현물이 견본보다 조금 크다 The actual article is a little larger than the sample.

— 검사 〖상업〗 sampling inspection **—(진열)실** a sample room **—장(帳)** a sample book ; a pattern book (본 견본장) **— 주문** a sample order (소량의 시험용) ; an order by sample **—호(號)** [잡지의] a specimen〔sample〕 number **국제 —시(市)** an international trade fair **상품 —** a trade sample **품질 —** a quality sample

견본 매매 見本賣買 sale by sample

견본쇄 見本刷 a sample copy ; an advance copy ; a specimen page

견본시 見本市 ⇨ 견본 시장

견본 시장 見本市場 a sample〔trade〕 fair

견본 조판 見本組版 a specimen page composition〔typesetting〕 **—하다** put specimen pages into type

견사 絹紗 silk and gauze

견사 絹絲 a silk-thread

견사 繭絲 raw silk-thread

견사 방적 絹絲紡績 silk-reeling ; silk-spinning

견습 見習 apprenticeship ; probation ; [사람] an apprentice ; a probationer **—하다** receive training ; practice oneself 《in a trade》 ; learn 《by observation》 ¶ 사무를 견습하다 learn the business routine of an office ; learn how to conduct business

— 간호사 a nurse in training ; a probationary nurse **— 기관사** an apprentice engineer **— 사관** a cadet ; a probationary officer **— 선원** a landsman **— 운전사** a student driver **— 제도** an apprenticeship scheme ; an on-the-job training system **— 조종사** a student 〔cub (미·구)〕 pilot

견습공 **見習工** an apprentice
견습 기간 **見習期間** a period of apprenticeship〔probation〕; a probationary〔probation〕period ; a term of trial ¶ 견습 기간 중 during one's probationary〔probation〕period ; during probation
견습생 **見習生** an apprentice (student) ; a trainee ; a probationer
견식 **見識** [의견] a view ; [안식] discernment ; insight ; [지식] knowledge ; information ¶ 견식이 있는 사람 a man of insight ; a discerning man // 견식이 높다 have a broad vision ; be farsighted ; have insight
†견실 **堅實** solidity ; steadiness ; soundness **—하다** (be) solid ; steady ; sound ; reliable ¶ 견실한 경영 sound management // 견실한 기업 a sound enterprise // 견실한 사람 a steady〔reliable〕person // 사업을 견실하게 경영하다 run a business on a sound basis // 견실히 solidly ; steadily ; reliably ; soundly // 견실히 재산을 쌓아 가다 accumulate fortunes steadily
견우 **牽牛** 〚천문〛 the "Herdsman" ; the star Altair in the constellation Aquila
—화(花) ⇨ 나팔꽃
견우성 **牽牛星** 〚천문〛 Altair
견우 직녀 **牽牛織女** 〚천문〛 the Altair and the Vega ¶ 견우 직녀의 상봉 the meeting of the two love-stars (on the night of July 7 of the lunar calendar)
견원지간 **犬猿之間** cat-and-dog terms ¶ 그들은 견원지간이다 They lead a cat-and-dog life. /They are on extremely bad terms.
견유 **犬儒** a Cynic ¶ 견유 학파의〔견유적인〕Cynic
견유 학도 **犬儒學徒** a Cynic
견유 학설 **犬儒學說** Cynicism
견유 학파 **犬儒學派** the Cynics
견인 **堅忍** (dogged) perseverance ; fortitude ; stoicism **—하다** endure ; persevere ; bear patiently
—지구(持久) dogged perseverance ; untiring patience
견인 **牽引** traction ; pulling ; hauling **—하다** draw ; pull ; haul ¶ 위반 차량은 위반자의 비용으로 견인될 것이다 Violator's vehicles will be towed away at owner's expense. (경고문)
—기(器) 〚의학〛 a retractor **— 기관차** a traction engine **— 프로펠러** a tractorpropeller **— 하중(荷重)** traction〔tractive〕load
견인력 **牽引力** pulling capacity ; traction (power)
견인불발 **堅忍不拔** perseverance ; tenacity〔singleness〕of purpose ; fortitude ; indefatigability ; untiring patience **—하다** be persevering ; patient ; indomitable ; indefatigable ¶ 견인불발의 정신 an indomitable spirit ; fortitude ; an iron-will
견인차 **牽引車** a tractor ; a tow car〔truck〕; a wrecker ; [총칭] motive power ¶ 경제 발전의 견인차 the motive power for economic development // 그는 우리팀 우승의 견인차였다 He was the driving force behind the victory of our team.
견장 **肩章** a shoulder strap〔ensign〕; a shoulder piece ; an epaulette
*견적 **見積** an estimate ; estimation ; assessment **—하다** estimate ⟪at⟫ ; make an estimate ⟪of⟫ ; calculate ⟪at⟫ ¶ 건물의 견적 an estimate for the building // 세부 견적 an estimate of details // 아무리 많이 견적해도 at the highest estimate ; at most ; at the outside // 아무리 적게 견적해도 at the lowest estimate ; at least // 비싸게〔싸게〕견적하다 estimate ⟪the cost⟫ high〔low〕; overestimate〔underestimate〕// 줄잡아 견적하다 make a conservative〔moderate, low〕estimate // 이것은 당초의 견적과 크게 다르다 This is very much different from the original estimate. // 견적된 비용은 얼마입니까 How much is the estimated cost? // 다음 물품에 대한 귀사의 최저 가격을 견적해 주십시오 Please quote us your lowest〔rock bottom〕prices for the following goods. // 기부금의 총액은 줄잡아 견적해도 100만원은 된다 The total sum of the contributions is conservatively estimated at a million *won*. // 견적 좀 내 주시겠어요 Can you give me an estimate?
개산 — a rough〔rude〕estimate **과대 —** overestimation **과소 —** underestimation **손해 —** an estimate〔assessment〕of damages ; the estimated damage **정밀 —** a close estimate
견적 가격 **見積價格** an estimated〔assessed〕value ; a valuation ; an appraisal ¶ 최초의 견적 가격 이내로 within the original estimates
견적서 **見積書** an〔a written〕estimate ; an estimate〔estimation〕sheet
견적액 **見積額** an estimated amount〔sum〕
견적 원가 **見積原價** an estimated cost
견제 **牽制** [제지] restraint ; check ; [구속] curb ; constraint **—하다** check ; hold〔keep〕in check ; restrain ; [주의 전환] divert ; create a diversion ; 〚야구〛 check ; peg ⟪a runner on the base⟫ ¶ 서로 견제하다 hold〔keep〕each other in check // 적의 증원병을 견제하다 check the arrival of the enemy's reinforcements // 주자를 견제하다 〚야구〛 check a runner ; hold back a runner ⟪to the base⟫ // 주자를 견제하여 아웃시키다 pick ⟪a runner⟫ off // 투수는 1루 주자를 견제했다 The pitcher held the runner on first base. // 사장에 대한 견제책으로 그

사람을 중역 자리에 앉혔다 He was chosen a director to offset the president's influence.

— 공격 〖군사〗 a containing attack —력 a restraining influence — 운동 a diversion — 전술〔작전〕 a diversionary tactics (양동 작전) — 행동 a diversionary move ; delaying tactics

견제구 牽制球 〖야구〗 a pick-off throw ; a feint ball

견제품 絹製品 silk manufactures ; [견직물] silk goods ; silks

***견주다** [비교] compare 《one thing》 with 《another》 ; measure 《one thing》 against 《another》 ; [경쟁] match ; rival 《another in a thing》 ; compete 《with》 ; vie 《with》 ¶ 견주어 보아 판단하다 make a comparative judgment // 실력을 견주다 weigh one's ability against 〔with〕 that of others // 힘〔기술〕을 견주다 measure strength 《with, against》 // 키를 견주다 measure one's height // 견주어서 in comparison with ; (as) compared with ; as against // 견주어 보건대 by comparison // 개인의 살림살이를 나라의 그것에 견주어 말할 수는 없다 It is not proper to compare private home-keeping to state finance. // 경쟁력에서 그 나라와 견줄 만한 나라는 없다 No country can compete with this one. // 두 사람을 견주어 볼 때 한 사람은 어린애에 불과하다 He is a mere boy beside 〔by the side of〕 the other. // 영어에서 그와 견줄 만한 사람은 없다 No one matches him in English. // 화력에서 그것과 견줄 만한 무기는 없다 No weapon can match this one in fire power.

견지 a bamboo fishing frame〔reel〕 used without a rod

‡견지 見地 a point of view ; a standpoint ; a viewpoint ; an angle ¶ 이 견지에서 보면 from this point of view ; viewed in this light // 상업적 견지에서 말하면 from a commercial point of view ; commercially speaking // 문제를 다른 견지에서 보다 look into the problem from different angles // 모든 견지에서 검토하다 examine 《it》 from all angles // 사물을 대국적인 견지에서 보다 look at things from a larger point of view ; take a broad view 《of matters》 // 그 문제를 교육적 견지에서 고려할 필요가 있다 We need to consider the problem from the standpoint of the educational situation.

견지 堅持 —하다 adhere strictly 《to》 ; hold fast 《to》 ; stick 《to》 ; firmly maintain ¶ 낙관적 견해를 견지하다 maintain〔hold fast to〕 an optimistic view // 자기 주장을 견지하다 hold fast 〔strongly〕 to one's opinion // 평화 노선을 견지하다 stick to the peace line // 현 정책을 견지하다 adhere closely to the present policy // 민주주의를 견지하다 hold on to〔adhere to, stick to〕 the idea of democracy

견직물 絹織物 silk fabrics ; silk goods ; silks ; mercery 《영》

— 공장 a silk mill —상 a silk merchant ; a silk mercer 《영》

견진 堅振 〖카톨릭〗 confirmation

견진 성사 堅振聖事 〖카톨릭〗 the sacrament of confirmation ¶ 견진 성사를 받는 사람 a confirmand // 견진 성사를 받다 be confirmed ; receive confirmation // 견진 성사를 베풀다 confirm

견책 譴責 censure ; reprimand ; rebuke ; reproof —하다 censure ; reprimand ; rebuke ; reprove

> 참고 **reprimand** 는 공식적으로 꾸짖는 것 **rebuke**는 사람들 앞에서 호되게 꾸짖는 것 **reprove**는 잘못을 저지른 사람에게 직접 꾸짖는 것

¶ 엄하게 견책하다 deliver a sharp reprimand // 견책을 받다 be reprimanded 《for》 ; receive〔be given〕 a reprimand 〔rebuke〕 // 남의 과실을 견책하다 censure 《a person》 for his error // 그 공무원은 직무 태만으로 엄한 견책을 받았다 The official was sharply reprimanded for his negligence.

— 처분 a reprimand

견치 犬齒 ⇨ 송곳니

견포 絹布 silk cloth ; silk

견학 見學 (learning by) inspection 〔observation〕 —하다 learn by inspection ; visit 《a firm》 for study ; study and observe ¶ 실지 견학〔여행〕을 하다 take a field trip // 조선소를 견학하다 visit〔pay a visit of inspection to〕 a dockyard // 그들은 한국의 자동차 공장을 견학하였다 They paid a visit of inspection to a Korean car manufacturing plant. // 이번 견학이 교육적이었다고 생각하니 Did you find the field trip educational?

— 여행 a trip of inspection ; a study tour 공장 — a tour through a factory 〔studio〕 실지 — a field trip ; on-the-spot study

†견해 見解 an opinion ; a view ; [해석] an interpretation ; a version ¶ 개인적인 견해 a personal opinion // 견해의 차이 divergence of opinion ; discrepancy in opinions // 세계 무역 기구와 OECD 가입에 관한 정부의 견해 the government's stand on the World Trade Organization and entering the OECD // 견해를 같이하다 hold〔have〕 the same view // 견해를 달리하다 differ in opinion ; differ 《with a person about a matter》 ; hold a different view // 그릇된 견해를 가지다 take a wrong view of 《a matter》 // 그것은 견해 차이다 That is a matter of opinion.

//그는 시국에 대한 그의 견해를 말했다 He gave his views on the current situation. //이 문제에 관한 너의 견해는 어떠냐 What is your opinion of this matter? //현 시국에 관한 여야의 견해차 the different views of the government and opposition parties on the current situation

겯고틀다 persist〔hold out〕 to the end; struggle〔dispute, compete〕《over》

겯다[1] ① [기름 따위에 흠씬 배다] become greasy; be oiled; be infiltrated with oil ¶ 때에 결은 옷 a garment greasy with grime //종이가 잘 결었다 The paper has been well oiled. ② [손에 익다] become skilled; be quite at home《in》 ¶ 손에 결은 익숙한 솜씨 adroit craftsmanship ③ [기름이 배게 하다] oil《paper》; infiltrate〔prepare〕《a thing》 with oil ¶장판지를 기름에 겯다 oil the paper for *ondol* floors

겯다[2] ① [짜다] weave; braid; interlace ¶ 삿자리를 겯다 weave a reed mat ② [결쳐 세우다] stack; pile up crisscross ¶ 총을 겯다 stack arms

겯지르다 place《a thing》〔put《a thing》 up〕 crosswise; cross; entwine; intersect

겯질리다 ① [물건이] be crossed〔intersected〕; be placed〔put up〕 crosswise ② [일이] get entangled with each other ③ [힘겹다] get exhausted《at a hard task》

*__결__[1] ① [나무·천 따위] grain; texture ¶ 나뭇결 grain〔texture〕 of wood //돌결 grain〔texture〕 of stone //비단결 a silky〔velvety〕 texture //결이 거칠다 be rough〔coarse〕; be coarse-grained; be of coarse texture //결이 곱다 be fine〔fine-grained〕; be of fine〔smooth〕 texture //살결이 곱다 have a fine〔delicate〕 skin

② [물·숨·소리 따위의] a wave ¶ 물결 a wave //숨결 waves of breath; breathing

③ [성질] disposition; temper; character ¶ 결이 고운 아가씨 a tender-hearted〔softhearted〕 girl //대쪽같이 결이 바른 사람 a straightforward man; a man of frank disposition; a single-minded man

④ [결기] impetuousness; vehemence; a quick〔hot, short, hasty〕 temper; anger (화)

결[2] ① [···하는 길] on one's way; (in) the course of; in passing; while《doing》; at the same time as; when; while; while at it ¶ 지나가는 결에 잠깐 들르다 drop in for a moment on one's way《for》 //어느 결에 그 많은 일을 다했느냐 In what flash have you done so many things?

② [짧은 동안] (as) an incidental result of ¶ 아침결에 in the morning //잠결에 in one's sleep; while asleep //꿈결에 듣다 listen half asleep //어느결에 일주일이 지나갔다 A week has passed in a flash〔an instant〕.

결가부좌 結跏趺坐 〖불교〗 sitting with one's legs completely crossed (and folded over each other) as in Buddhist statues

결강하다 缺講— ① [교수가] do not give one's lecture; cancel a lecture〔class〕 ② [학생이] cut a lecture〔class〕; absent oneself from school

결격 缺格 disqualification; 〖법〗 incapacity **—하다** be disqualified《for a post》 **— 사유** reasons for disqualification; reasons for being disqualified **—자** a disqualified person; a person disqualified《for a position, as a teacher》

†**결과 結果** result; consequence; [결말] issue; outcome; [효과] effect; [성과] fruit; product

> 참고 **result**는 원인에 대한 결과가 아니고 행동이나 수속 따위의 최종적 결과 **consequence**는 어떤 사태에 뒤이어 일어나기도 하고 또는 그 사태에 의해서 필연적으로 일어나는 결과 **effect**는 원인 작용으로부터 생기는 직접의 결과를 말한다

¶ 그 결과 in result //뜻밖의 결과 an unexpected result〔ending〕 //선거의 결과 the results of an election //문의해 본 결과 an inquiry proves that... //지금까지의 결과로 보아 in view of the results so far achieved //원인과 결과 cause and effect //노력의 결과 the product of one's hard work //···의 결과 as a result《of》; in consequence《of》; as a sequel to; as a consequence《of》; with a result that... //결과가 좋다〔나쁘다〕 be successful〔unsuccessful〕 //좋은 결과를 기대합니다 We hope to see good results. //시작이 좋아야 결과도 좋은 법이다 A good beginning makes a good ending. //좋은 결과를 얻다 meet with good results; come to good //이 문제들은 수년간의 부실 경영의 결과이다 These problems are the result of years of bad management. //야구〔축구〕 경기의 결과가 텔레비전에서 방송되고 있다 The baseball〔football〕 results are broadcast on the television. //좋은〔나쁜〕 결과를 낳다 produce good〔bad〕 results //결과가 같아지다 come to〔result in〕 the same thing //시험의 결과를 발표하다 announce the results of an examination //결과가 어떻게 될지 모른다 There is no knowing how it will come out. //결과에 책임을 지다 take〔answer for〕 the consequences //수술의 결과가 좋지 않았다 The surgical operation resulted in

failure. //그의 사업의 성공은 그의 노력의 결과이다 His success in business is a result of his hard work. //협상의 결과 타협이 이루어졌다 The negotiations resulted in a compromise. //결과가 그렇게 되리라 생각했다 I thought it would end up like that〔that way〕. //현 내각의 운명은 그 정책의 결과 여하에 달려 있다 The fate of the present Cabinet depends upon the success (or failure) of that policy. //그의 오늘날의 성공은 오랜 근면과 인내의 결과이다 His present success is the outcome of his years of diligence and perseverance. //겉으로 보기에 그 제휴 회담은 결과가 좋지 않았다 Apparently that talk of a tie-up didn't pan out.
최종 ─ 집계표 the final tabulation

결과론 結果論 criticism 《on past events》 based on the result

결과표 結果表 a result table

결교 結交 ─하다 form a friendship 《with》; associate 《with》

결구 結句 the conclusion ; the concluding part ; 〖문법〗 apodosis

결구 結球 〖식물〗 a head

결구 結構 [구조] structure ; construction ; frame ; [구상] a plan ; a scheme ¶ 단편 소설의 결구 the structure of a short story ─하다 frame ; construct ; map〔plan, work〕 out (a scheme)

‡**결국 結局** [결말에 가서] after all ; in the end ; finally ; ultimately ; in the long run ; in the last analysis ; [결말] conclusion ; close ; end ; a finale ¶ 결국 그녀와 결혼할 것이다 He will marry her after all. //그들은 결국 가지 않기로 결정했다 They ultimately decided not to go. //그 계획은 결국 어떠한 효과도 얻지 못했다 The plan turned out to have had no effect. //그 계획은 결국 실패했다 The plan resulted in failure. /The plan failed after all〔in the end〕. //정직한 사람이 결국 승리한다고 생각한다 I believe that the honest will win in the long run. //그 소문은 결국은 사실임이 밝혀졌다 The rumor turned out〔proved〕 (to be) true. //그는 결국 나타나지 않았다 He didn't show up after all. //결국에 가서는 실력이 승리한다 Real ability will win in the end. //결국은 돈이 문제이다 It is after all〔at root〕 a question of money. //결국은 마찬가지다 After all, it is the same. //결국은 왔구나 So you've come after all ! //결국 우리가 이겼다 At last we won the game. //자 봐 결국 내가 옳았지 So you see I was right after all ! //결국 그것이 싸게 먹는다 That is cheaper in the end. //결국 그는 파면당했다 The payoff〔consequence〕 was that they fired him. //그 문제는 결국 이런 결론이 된다 The question boils down to this. / Boiled down, it simply comes to this.

결궤 決潰 a rip ; a break ; cleavage ; crevasse 《미》 ─하다 break 《down》; burst ; give way ; collapse ¶ 하천의 제방이 결궤했다 The river burst〔broke〕 its banks. /The banks of the river were broken. //제방이 결궤하여 성난 물결이 마을을 덮쳤다 The banks of the river gave way and the raging flood assaulted the village.

결근 缺勤 absence 《from duty, office, school》; nonattendance ─하다 be absent from one's duty ; absent oneself from 《one's office》; stay away 《from》; be away from work ¶ 5일간의 결근 an absence of five days //수차례의 결근 several absences from work //병으로 인한 결근 absence owing to illness //그는 결근을 잘한다 He is irregular in his attendance at the office. //그는 독감 때문에 어제 결근하였다 Yesterday he stayed home from work because of flu. //그 분은 몸이 편찮아서 오늘 결근하셨습니다 He is out sick today. /He called in sick today.
─율(率) the rate of absenteeism ─ 일수 the number of absences〔absent-days〕 무단 ─ absence without notice〔leave〕 장기 ─ a long(-term) absence

결근계 缺勤屆 a report〔notice〕 of absence ¶ 결근계를 내다 report one's absence

결근자 缺勤者 an absent person ; an absentee ; a nonattendant

결기 ─氣 impetuousness ; vehemence ; hot temper ¶ 결기에 사람을 치다 beat 《a person》 in the heat of one's anger

결나다 lose one's temper ; fall into a passion ; be enraged ; have one's blood up ¶ 결나서 얼굴이 붉어지다 become red with anger ; be in a black rage

결내다 become indignant ; get mad ; blow up ; flash up ; give vent to one's anger ; show temper ; get into a rage ¶ 툭하면 결내다 be apt to flare up ; be easily enraged

***결단 決斷** (prompt) decision ; determination ; resolution ─하다 decide ; determine ; resolve ; make up one's mind ¶ 결단력이 있는 사람 a man of decision //결단력이 없는 사람 a man wanting in decision //결단을 내리다 come to〔reach, arrive at〕 a definite decision //결단력이 있다〔없다〕 be quick〔slow〕 to decide //정부는 그 기구에서 탈퇴하기로 결정을 내렸다 The government made a decision to disaffiliate〔withdraw〕 from the organization.

결단 結團 ─하다 organize 《a team, an expedition》
─식 an inaugural meeting〔rally〕 ¶ 결단식을 거행하다 conduct〔hold, perform〕 an inaugural ceremony

결단력 決斷力 the strength of one's mind ; resolution ; determination ¶ 결단력이 있다〔없다〕 be quick〔lack〕 in decision

결단성 決斷性 firmness of character ; determination ; resolution

결단코 決斷— (not) ever ; never ; by any〔no〕 means ; on any〔no〕 account ; for anything ; anything like to decide ; be decisive ¶ 그는 결단코 그런 짓을 할 사람이 아니다 He is the last person to do such a thing. // 결단코 그렇지 않습니다 I am positive that it is not so. // 결단코 양보 않겠다 Never will I make a concession ! // 결단코 그런 짓은 두 번 다시 하지 않겠다 I swear I will never again do such a thing. // 결단코 용서하지 않겠다 I would not forgive you for anything. // 결단코 가지 않겠다 I would not go for anything.

결당 結黨 formation of a party **—하다** form a party

결당식 結黨式 the inauguration ceremony 《of a party》

결딴 ruin ; destruction ; collapse ; fall ; downfall ; wreck ¶ 결딴나다 ruin 《oneself》 ; be ruined ; be done for ; be spoilt ; go to the devil〔dogs〕 ; go to pieces〔ruin〕 // 결딴내다 bring ruin to ; ruin ; bring collapse〔destruction〕 ; make a mess of // 결딴이 난 집안 a ruined family // 시계가 떨어져 결딴났다 The clock fell and broke to pieces. // 은행이 결딴나다 a bank goes bankrupt // 건강이 결딴나다 one's health is ruined // 몸을 결딴내다 ruin one's health // 술로 몸이 결딴났다 Drink brought him to ruin. // 그릇을 결딴내다 break a dish to pieces // 번창하던 사업이 결딴났다 The thriving business collapsed. // 단 한번의 실패로 그의 일생이 결딴났다 Just a single failure ruined his life. // 노름으로 가정을 결딴냈다 Gambling spelled a wreck to his family. // 폭풍으로 농작물이 결딴났다 The crops have been ruined by the storm. // 개들이 꽃을 결딴내 버렸다 Some dogs wrought havoc with the flowers. // 너 때문에 내 인생은 결딴났다 You have made a wreck of my life.

결렬 決裂 rupture ; breakdown **—하다** break down ; be broken off ; rupture ; come to〔end in〕 a rupture ¶ 교섭의 결렬 rupture of negotiations // 회담〔교섭, 협상〕은 결렬되었다 The talks 〔negotiations〕 were broken off. // (정당의) 간부회가 결렬되었다 The caucus has split into factions. // 정상 회담은 핵 실험 금지 문제로 결렬되었다 The summit conference broke down over the nuclear test ban.

결례 缺禮 lack of courtesy ; negligence in etiquette ; failure to pay one's compliments ; want of respect **—하다** omit〔fail, neglect〕 to pay〔offer〕 one's compliments

†**결론 結論** conclusion ; concluding remarks **—짓다** conclude ; close ; perorate ; bring to a conclusion ¶ 필연적인 결론 foregone conclusion // 결론으로서 in conclusion // 잘못된 결론 erroneous〔wrong〕 conclusion // 성급한 결론 hasty conclusion // 피할 수 없는 결론 inevitable conclusion // 근거가 확실한 결론 valid conclusion // 그녀의 편지를 읽고 그녀가 매우 총명하다는 결론을 내렸다 After reading her letter, we came to the conclusion that she was a very intelligent person. // 결론에 도달하다 reach〔arrive at, draw, come to〕 a conclusion // 성급히 결론을 내리다 jump at a conclusion ; jump to conclusion〔a conclusion〕 // 그것은 결국 이런 결론이 된다 It amounts to this〔that〕. // 그의 연설이 결론에 도달하기까지 30분이나 걸렸다 Thirty minutes passed before his speech came to a conclusion. // 배심원들은 증거로 인해 그녀가 유죄라고 결론지었다 The jury concluded from the evidence that she was guilty.

결리다 ① [몸이] have〔feel〕 an ache〔a pain, a stitch〕 《in any part of one's body》 ¶ 가슴이〔옆구리가〕 결리다 feel 〔have〕 a pain in the chest〔left side〕 // 과로해서 온 몸이 결리고 아프다 My every muscle and nerve aches with overwork. // 목이 결린다 I have〔got〕 crick in the neck.
② [기를 못쓰다] shrink 《from》 ; be daunted ; feel timid〔small〕 ¶ 나는 그이 앞에선 괜히 결린다 I feel (myself) small in his presence. /I cannot hold up my head before him.

결막 結膜 〖해부〗 the conjunctiva
— **충혈** hyperaemia conjunctivae

결막염 結膜炎 conjunctivitis
수영장 — swimming pool conjunctivitis
유행성 — epidemic〔contagious〕 conjunctivitis ; pinkeye

†**결말 結末** [끝] an end ; a close ; a conclusion ; [낙착] settlement ; [결과] a result ; an outcome ¶ 공정한 결말 a fair settlement // 불확실한 결말 a tentative settlement // 행복〔불행〕한 결말 a happy〔an unhappy〕 ending // 결말이 안 나다 remain unsettled // 결말이 나다 come to〔reach〕 a settlement // 결말내다 〔짓다〕 bring 《a matter》 to a settlement〔conclusion, an end〕 ; put an end to ; fix up ; wind up 《미》 // 그 문제는 아직 결말이 나지 않았다 The problem is still unsettled. /The matter is yet to be settled. // 그 영화는 어떻게 결말이 날까 How does that movie end ? // 너무 쉽게 결말이 난 승부였다 The match finished with the winner decided all too soon.

//협상의 결말이 났다 An agreement has been reached in the negotiations. //그 분쟁이 마침내 결말이 났다 The dispute was finally settled. //그들은 마침내 지루한 분쟁의 결말을 지었다 They settled 〔put an end to〕 a prolonged dispute at last. //꽤 긴 회의였는데 결말이 났니 That was quite a long conference. Did the discussion come to anything?

결맹 結盟 —하다 [체맹] conclude a treaty; [연맹을] form a league〔federation, union〕

결문 結文 an epilogue; the concluding part; [편지의] the complimentary closing

결미 結尾 the end; the close; the conclusion

결박 結縛 binding; tying —하다 bind; tie; pinion ¶ 결박당하다 be bound〔tied up〕//단단히 결박하다 tie fast〔hard〕//범인을 결박하다 tie a criminal with cords

†**결백 潔白** [순결] purity; [무죄] innocence; [청렴] integrity —하다 (be) pure; upright; innocent; clean(-handed) ¶ 결백한 사람 a man with a integrity; a man with a clean record (경력이)//그들은 결백한 사람을 목매달았다 They hanged an innocent man. //나는 그의 결백을 믿는다 I believe he is innocent (of the charge). //자기의 결백을 입증하다 establish〔prove〕 one's innocence

결번 缺番 a missing〔wanting〕 number ¶ 3번은 결번이다 The number three is blank on the roll.

결벽 潔癖 excessive〔morbid〕 love of cleanliness; fastidiousness; finickiness —하다 (be) fastidious; overnice 《about one's choice》; particular; finical; finicky ¶ 결벽한 사람 a fastidious person; a stickler for cleanliness//그는 지나치게 결벽한 성미 때문에 친구가 없다 His fastidiousness attracted few friends to him.

결별 訣別 [작별] parting; separation; [고별] leave-taking; farewell; good-bye —하다 part from〔with〕 《a person》; take leave 《of》; bid farewell 〔adieu〕 to ¶ 결별의 인사 a farewell address; parting words//결별을 선언하다 declare a separation from//과거와 결별하다 break with the past//여자 친구와 결별하다 break with one's girl friend

결본 缺本 a missing volume; a wanting book 《of a series》 ¶ 제2권이 결본이다 The second volume is missing.

결부 結付 —하다 link〔join, fasten〕 together; connect; combine ¶ 행복과 돈을 결부시키다 associate happiness with riches//그 두 가지 일은 밀접히 결부되어 있다 The two matters are closely linked together. //나를 그 사건과 결부시켜 말하지 마라 Don't associate me with that incident.

결빙 結氷 freezing; frost —하다 freeze over; be frozen over; be icebound; be frostbound; [항구가] be closed by ice ¶ 결빙된 항구 an ice-bound〔ice-locked〕 harbor//한강은 겨우내 결빙한다 The *Han* River is frozen over throughout the winter. //항구는 늦은 봄까지 결빙되어 있었다 The harbor was frozen over until late spring.

결빙기 結氷期 the freezing time〔season〕

결빙점 結氷點 the freezing point

결사 結社 an association; a society; a fraternity —하다 form an association〔a society〕; organize 《themselves》 into a society; club together ¶ 결사의 자유 freedom of association

비밀 — a secret society; an underground organization 정치 — a political organization〔party〕

결사 決死 preparedness for death; do-or-die spirit ¶ 결사적 desperate; death-defying; at the risk of one's life //결사적 용기 desperate courage//결사적 각오로 ready〔prepared〕 to die//결사적 각오로 나아가다 advance in the face of death; go to certain death//결사적으로 싸우다 fight to the last man; fight desperately//결사적으로 시도하다 make a desperate attempt 《to do》

결사대 決死隊 a death-defying〔do-or-die〕 corps; a suicide squad〔corps〕 ¶ 결사대에 참가하다 join a death band// 결사대를 조직하다 organize a do-or-die〔demolition〕 squad organization

결삭다 《one's temper》 soften〔become soft〕; be mollified〔soothed〕

결산 決算 settlement of accounts; closing accounts; liquidation —하다 settle〔balance〕 an account; square accounts; liquidate ¶ 매월말 단위로 매출을 결산하다 settle sales accounts at the end of every month//본사의 결산기는 6월과 12월이다 We settle accounts in June and December.

— 기입 closing entry —액 settled accounts — 위원회 a committee on accounts 반기(半期) — a half-yearly settlement 분식(粉飾) — window-dressing settlement (of accounts) 1/4 분기 — the first quarter settlement 전〔후〕(반)기 — settlement of accounts for the first〔second〕 half

결산기 決算期 a settling term

결산 보고서 決算報告書 balance sheets; [일람표] a statement of accounts

결산일 決算日 a settling day

결석 結石 〖의학〗 a calculus 《*pl.* -li》; a stone 《in the bladder》; a concretion ¶ 결석이 있는 calculous

— 방지제 an antilithic —병 lithiasis — 소식자(消息子) a lithoscope — 용해 litholysis —학 lithology 방광 — a bladder stone 신장 — a renal calculus ; a nephrolith

†**결석 缺席** absence ; nonattendance ; a cut《속》; 〖법〗 default **—하다** be absent《from》; absent oneself《from》; cut ; stay away《from》; fail to attend ; 〖법〗 default ; make a default ¶ 학교를 결석하다 stay away from school // 수업을 결석하다 cut a class // 결석을 허락하다 excuse《a person》from a class // 병으로 3일 동안 결석했다 I was absent from school for three days on account of illness. // 그는 자주 결석한다 He is irregular in his attendance at《school》. // 나는 지난 1년 동안 하루도 결석한 일이 없다 I have never missed a day (of attendance) in the past year.
—률 the rate of absenteeism 무— nonabsence ; regular〔perfect〕 attendance 무단 — absence without leave 장기 — a long absence

결석계 缺席屆 a report of absence〔nonattendance〕 ¶ 결석계를 내다 give a written notice of one's absence

결석 신고 缺席申告 a report of absence

결석자 缺席者 an absentee ; 〖법〗 a defaulter

결석 재판 缺席裁判 〖법〗 judgment by default

결석 판결 缺席判決 judgement by default

결선 決選 ① [투표] a final vote〔ballot, election〕; a runoff **—하다** elect by final vote ¶ 결선 투표에서 in a runoff election // 결선 투표를 하다 take a final〔decisive〕 vote〔ballot〕《on》; take a showdown vote ; hold a runoff ballot ; conduct a runoff election
② [결승] the final contest ; the finals **—하다** play〔run〕 in the finals ¶ 결선에 진출하다 go into〔advance to, move into〕 the finals

결성 結成 formation ; organization ; inauguration **—하다** form ; organize《themselves into》 ¶ 정당을 결속하다 organize a political party // 조합을 결성하다 form a union // 친목 단체를 결성하다 form a social gathering (for friendship)

결성식 結成式 an inaugural meeting〔ceremony, rally〕; an inauguration

결속 結束 union ; unity ; solidarity ; combination **—하다** unite ; band〔stick〕 together ; be united ¶ 당의 결속 party unity // 결속하여 in a body ; in unity // 굳게 결속하다 be closely united // 결속이 무너지다 fail to present a united front // 국민의 결속을 강화하다 strengthen the national unity // 당내의 결속을 꾀하다 solidify the party // 결속하여 적에 대항하다 unite themselves〔band together〕 against the enemy // 회원의 결속을 다지다 strengthen〔confirm〕 members' solidarity // 그들은 교회간의 결속을 논하고 있다 They are discussing church unity. // 노조 지도자들은 노동자들의 결속을 요청했다 The union leaders appealed for workers' solidarity. // 우리는 아직 팀으로서의 결속력이 없다 We haven't quite jelled as a team yet.

결손 缺損 [손실] loss ; [부족] deficit ; shortage ; [손해] damage ; injury ¶ 결손을 메우다 cover the loss〔deficit〕; make up the deficit〔a loss〕; make good the losses // 결손을 보충하다 make good〔make up, cover〕 the losses〔deficit〕 // 생산 과잉으로 결손을 보다 suffer deficits due to overproduction // 50만원의 결손을 가져오다 suffer〔cause〕 a loss〔deficit〕 of 500,000 *won* // 버스는 결손 운행을 하고 있다 The bus service is being operated at a loss.
— 처리〔처분〕 deficits disposal — 충당금〔보충금〕 the reserve fund against losses ; the reserve fund for compensation of deficits

결손액 缺損額 the deficiency ; the amount of loss

결승 決勝 the decision (of a contest) ; [결승전] the finals ; [동점 후의] a run-off ; a play-off
준 — a semifinal game〔round, match〕; the semifinals 준준 — a quarterfinals

결승 문자 結繩文字 a quipu ; a preliterate notation by rope knots

결승선 決勝線 the goal line ; the finish line ; the score

결승자 決勝者 [팀의] a finalist

***결승전 決勝戰** the final round〔game, match, contest〕; the finals ; a run-off (race) ; [동점 또는 비겼을 때의] a play-off ¶ 결승전에서 이기다〔지다〕 win〔lose〕 in the finals // 결승전에까지 이를 줄은 결코 기대하지 못했다 I never expected to get through to the finals. // 한국 축구팀이 월드컵 결승전에 진출하였다 The Korean soccer team advanced to the World Cup finals.
— 출장 선수 a finalist 정구 — the tennis finals

결승점 決勝點 the goal ; home ; the finish line ; the base ¶ 결승점에 다다르다 make〔reach, hit〕 the goal ; breast〔break〕 the tape

결식 缺食 going without a meal **—하다** go without〔skip〕 a meal
— 아동 schoolchildren〔pupils〕 attending school without lunch ; undernourished〔poorly-fed〕 children

결실 結實 ① [열매를 맺음] fruit-bearing ; fructification ; ripening ; fruition **—하다** bear fruit ; fructify ¶ 결실하지

않다 be sterile ; bear no fruit ; be fruitless // 가을은 결실의 계절이다 Autumn is a harvest season〔time〕.
② [일의 결과가 잘 맺어짐] realization ; a result **— 하다** be successful ; achieve〔attain〕 a success ; be realized ¶ 결실을 못보다 [비유적] come to naught ; go wrong // 성공은 노력의 결실이다 Success is the fruits of one's efforts. // 오랜 노력 끝에 그의 꿈이 결실을 보았다 After the years of his efforts his dream came true〔bore fruit〕 // 마침내 우리의 노력이 결실을 맺었다 At last our efforts have come to fruition.

결실기 結實期 the fruiting season ¶ 결실기를 지난 나무 a tree past bearing

†**결심 決心** determination ; resolution ; resolve ; decision **— 하다** determine ; resolve 《on》; make up one's mind ; make a resolve〔resolution〕

> 참고 **determine** 마음을 정하고 그것을 고수하다 **resolve** 숙고한 끝에 확고 부동한 결심을 하다

¶ 굳은 결심 a firm determination〔resolve〕 // 결심하고 있다 be resolved ; be determined // 결심을 뒤집다 go back on〔give up〕 one's resolution // 결심을 흔들리게 하다 shake〔weaken〕 one's resolution // 결심하지 못하고 있다 be irresolute ; hesitate to 《do》 // 그의 결심이 굳어만 간다 His determination increases. // 그는 금주하기로 결심했다 He made a resolution〔resolved〕 to give up drink. // 그녀와 결혼하기로 결심했다 He's set on marrying her. // 나는 두번 다시 그를 만나지 않기로 결심했다 I am determined not to see him again. // 그의 얼굴을 보면 굳은 결심을 알 수 있다 His face tells (itself) of his firm resolution. // 예전에는 한번도 새해 들어 결심한 것을 실천한 적이 없었어 I have never lived up to my New Year's resolution in the past.

결심 結審 〖법〗 the conclusion of a hearing〔trial〕; the decision **— 하다** conclude an examination〔a hearing〕
— 공판 the final trial

*__결여 缺如__ lack ; want ¶ 상호 이해와 협력 정신의 결여 a lack of mutual understanding and spirit of cooperation // 객관성의 결여 a lack of objectivity

결연 結緣 forming a relationship ; making a connection ; 〖불교〗 becoming a believer in Buddhism
자매 — establishment〔setting up〕 of sisterhood relationship〔ties〕 ¶ 자매 결연을 맺은 학교들 sister schools

‡**결연하다 決然—** (be) resolute ; firm ; determined ; decisive ¶ 결연히 resolutely ; firmly ; in a determined manner ; with resolution // 결연한 태도 a determined attitude // 정의를 위해 결연히 일어서다 stand resolute for justice

결원 缺員 a vacancy ; a vacant position 〔post〕; an opening ¶ 결원을 보충하다 fill (up) a vacancy // 결원이 생기다 a position is vacated ; cause a vacancy ; a vacancy occurs // 결원을 그대로 두다 leave a position unfilled〔vacant〕 // 보궐선거에서 채워지게 될 의회의 결원 parliamentary vacancies to be filled at by-elections // 결원이 생기면 연락드리겠습니다 I'll inform you of any openings. // 3학년 반에 결원이 몇 있다 There are some vacancies in the third year class.

결의 決議 a resolution ; a decision ; a vote **— 하다** resolve ; pass〔adopt〕 a resolution ; pass a vote ; decide ; vote ¶ 감사의 결의 a resolution〔vote〕 of thanks // 국회의 결의 a resolution of the National Assembly // 내각 불신임을 결의하다 pass a vote of nonconfidence in the Cabinet // 전쟁 반대〔찬성〕를 결의하다 pass a resolution against〔for〕 war // …을 결의함 Resolved 《that》
— 록(錄) a record of resolutions ; written resolutions **— 서** an act **부대 —** 《pass》 an additional resolution

결의 結義 — 하다 swear to be 《brothers》; take an oath of brotherhood

‡**결의 決意** resolution ; determination **— 하다** determine ; resolve ; make up one's mind ; be determined ¶ 굳은 결의로 with a firm〔determined, unshakable〕 resolution // 단호한 결의 firm resolution ; inflexible determination // 꼭 해내고야 말겠다는 굳은 결의 a firm determination to accomplish〔carry out〕 the objective without fail // 결의를 굳게 하다 confirm one's determination ; be fully determined 《to do》 // 결의를 새로이 하다 make a fresh determination

결의권 決議權 the right to vote ; franchise ; the voting right

결의 기관 決議機關 a voting organ ; a resolutionary organ ; [정당의] a party machine

결의문 決議文 a record of resolutions ; written resolutions ¶ 결의문을 돌리다 present〔hand〕 a resolution 《to》

결의 사항 決議事項 resolutions

결의안 決議案 a (draft) resolution ¶ 불신임 결의안 a nonconfidence resolution // 결의안을 부결시키다 kill〔vote down〕 a resolution // 결의안을 만장 일치로 가결하다 carry a resolution unanimously // 결의안은 절대 다수로 통과되었다 The resolution was carried by a large majority. // 결의안을 제출하다 move 〔introduce〕 a resolution

결의 형제 結義兄弟 sworn〔pledged〕 brothers

결자 缺字 an omitted word ; a missing

character ; a blank type (탈자) ¶ 이 교정지에는 결자가 많다 These proof-sheets are full of blanks.

결자해지 結者解之 One who has tied a knot must untie it. /Solve the problems you yourself create.

결장 缺場 absence ; nonattendance

결장 結腸 〖해부〗 the colon
—부 the colic region

결장염 結腸炎 colonitis

결재 決裁 sanction ; approval **—하다** decide 《upon》 ; sanction ; approve ; authorize ; decide ¶ 결재를 바라다 submit 《a matter》 for 《a person's》 approval // 결재를 얻다 obtain an approval // 결재가 나다 be approved // 아직 장관의 결재를 못 받았다 It remains to be sanctioned by the Minister.
—관 a deciding officer **— 투표** a casting vote

결재권 決裁權 the right of decision ; decisive power ; a casting vote

결전 決戰 a decisive battle ; a settler ; [경기의] a deciding match〔race〕 ; a final ; [동점 후의] a run-off ; a play-off **—하다** fight a decisive battle ; fight it out ; [동점 후에] run〔play〕 off ¶ 일대 결전 an Armageddon // 결전의 시기 the decisive stage 《of a war》 ; the zero hour // 결전 단계에 들어가다 reach a decisive stage
대(大)— an Armageddon ; a most decisive battle

결절 結節 [마디] a knot ; 〖해부〗 a tuber ; a tubercle ; 〖식물〗 a nodule ; 〖병리〗 a node ¶ 결절상의 knotted ; tuberous ; nodose
—나(癩) nodular〔tubercular〕 leprosy **—점(點)** 〖수학〗 a node **—종(腫)** a ganglion **— 형성** tuberculation

결절 문자 結節文字 a string-alphabet

†**결점 缺點** a fault ; a failing ; a weakness ; a defect ; a shortcoming ; [흠] a flaw ; a blemish ; [약점] a weak point ; a drawback ; a disadvantage

> **참고** **fault** 완전이라고 하기에는 아직 결함이 있는 것, 그렇다고 그것은 꼭 비난받아야 할 이유는 없다 **failing** 완전에까지 이르지 못한 것을 의미하며 특히 인격의 결함을 말한다 물론 때로는 용서받을 수 있는 결점이다 **weakness** 의지력의 결여로 생긴 사소한 결함

¶ 결점 있는 defective ; faulty // 결점 없는 faultless ; perfect ; flawless // 결점을 고치다 make up〔cover〕 《a person's》 fault // 결점을 감추다 conceal a defect // 결점을 드러내다 expose one's faults〔defects〕 // 결점을 찾다 find fault 《with》 ; look for a fault // 결점 투성이다 have many faults〔shortcomings〕 // 결점 없는 사람은 없다 No man is free from faults/There is no man but has some faults // 나는 그녀의 결점에도 불구하고 그녀를 사랑한다 I love her despite her faults. // 그에게는 결점이 없다 He is free from faults. /He is above criticism. // 저 친구의 결점은 술이야 He has a weakness for drinking. // 내 자신의 결점은 내가 잘 알고 있다 I am well aware of my shortcomings.

†**결정 決定** decision ; determination ; conclusion ; settlement **—하다** decide 《upon》 ; conclude ; settle ; agree 《upon》 ; fix 《upon》 ; [결정되다] be decided ; be settled ; be fixed ¶ 결정적(으로) decisive(ly) ; definite(ly) ; conclusive(ly) ; final(ly) // 결정적 타격 a decisive blow // (형세를) 결정적으로 만들다 turn the scale // 결정적으로 입증하다 prove it conclusively // 방침을 결정하다 decide on one's policy // 태도를 결정하다 determine one's attitude // 직업을〔학교를〕 결정하다 decide upon one's profession〔a school〕 // 결혼식은 1월 10일로 결정했다 The wedding was fixed for the 10th of January.
— 방정식 a determinating〔an identical〕 equation **—서** 〖법〗 a written decision ; a written verdict ; a written finding

결정 結晶 crystallization ; [결정체] a crystal **—하다** crystallize ¶ 결정형의 crystalline // 노력의 결정 the fruit of one's efforts // 결정하여 설탕이 되다 crystallize into sugar // 이 한 톨의 쌀도 농민이 흘린 땀의 결정이다 This single grain of rice is the crystallization of 〔attests to〕 the farmer's hard labor.
— 계수기 a crystal counter **—기(器)** a crystallizer **— 물리학** crystal physics **— 생성** crystallization **— 석탄산** crystallized carbolic acid **—암〔편암〕** crystalline rock〔schist〕 **—자(子)** crystallite **—점** a crystallization point **—학** crystallography **—핵(核)** a crystalline germ 〔nucleus〕 **—형** a crystal form

결정계 結晶系 a system of crystallization

결정 광학 結晶光學 crystal optics

결정 구조〔조직〕 結晶構造〔組織〕 crystal structure

결정권 決定權 the right to decide ; decisive power ¶ 최종 결정권이 있다 have the final〔last〕 say 《구》 // 그에게는 결정권이 없다 He has no power 〔authority〕 to decide the matter. /He doesn't have the (final) say.

결정론 決定論 〖철학〗 determinism
—자(者) a determinist ; a necessitarian **기계적 —** mechanical determinism **비(非)—** indeterminism

결정면 結晶面 a crystal face

결정수 結晶水 water of crystallization ;

combined water

결정 인자 決定因子 〖의학〗 a factor of determination

‡**결정적 決定的** definite 《reply》; final 《judgment》; decisive 《factor》; definitive 《answer》; conclusive 《evidence》; determinate 《reply》; clinching 《proof》 ¶ 결정적 순간 a decisive moment // 결정적 승리 decisive victory // 결정적 요인 a decisive〔conclusive〕 factor // 그 주전 선수의 부상은 그 시합의 결정적 변수가 될 수 있다 The injury to the key player could be a decisive factor in the game. // 총에 있던 그녀의 지문은 그녀의 죄에 대한 결정적 증거였다 Her fingerprints on the gun were conclusive proof of her guilt.

결정질 結晶質 crystalline structure

결정체 結晶體 a crystal; a crystalloid

결정축 結晶軸 the axis of a crystal

결정타 決定打 [야구의] a winning hit; [권투의] a decisive〔finishing〕 blow; [토론 따위의] a clincher 《구》 ¶ 결정타 한 대에 나가 떨어지다 His finishing blow sent the opponent sprawling on the floor. // 그의 말이 결정타가 되었다 His remark clinched our argument. // 히로시마에 대한 원자탄 투하는 일본을 패배시킨 결정타였다 The dropping of the atomic bomb on Hiroshima dealt〔was〕 the finishing blow to Japan.

결정 투표 決定投票 the casting vote; the decisive〔swing〕 vote

결정판 決定版 a definitive〔a final authoritative, an authorized〕 edition; [역본이] the most authentic version ever published ¶ 법률 용어 사전의 결정판 the most authoritative dictionary of legal terms〔terminology〕 // 이것이야말로 근대 오페라 극장의 결정판이다 This is the last word in a modern opera house.

결정형 結晶形 a crystal form

결제 決濟 settlement; liquidation **—하다** settle accounts ¶ 납품 대금의 결제 payment for goods received // 미결제의 계정 an account outstanding // 대차를 결제하다 settle accounts〔balances〕 **—일** a settlement〔settling〕 day **— 자금** a settlement fund **대차 —** the settlement of accounts **부분 —** partial settlement〔payment〕 **삼각 —** a triple settlement **잔액 —** settlement in full; full settlement〔payment〕 **국제 — 은행** the Bank of International Settlements **대차(貸借) —표** a balance〔clearing〕 sheet **미— 계정** an account outstanding

결제금 決濟金 a settlement fund

결제 통화 決濟通貨 a settlement currency

결증 —症 (a fit of) anger

결집 結集 [모음] concentration; regimentation **—하다** concentrate; collect in mass ¶ 총력을 결집하다 concentrate〔concert〕 all one's efforts // 성난 시민들이 시청 앞에 결집하였다 The angry citizens massed in front of City Hall.

결착 結着, 決着 settlement; conclusion; decision **—하다** be settled; be closed; come to a close〔an end, a conclusion〕; reach an ending ¶ 결착시키다 settle; bring 《a matter》 to a conclusion〔close〕

결체 結滯 〖의학〗 a pause〔an intermission〕 in the pulse **—하다** intermit; be intermittent; stop at intervals

결체 結締 tying up **—하다** tie up; bind

결체 조직 結締組織 connective tissue **— 섬유주(纖維柱)** a trabecula (*pl.* -lae) **급성 —염(炎)** phlegmon

결초보은 結草報恩 —하다 requite〔return, reciprocate, repay〕 another's kindness even after one's death; carry one's gratitude beyond the grave

†**결코 決—** [결코 …않다] never; by no means; assuredly〔positively〕...not; [어떤 경우에도 …않다] under no circumstances; [어떤 이유로도] on no account; [조금도 …않다] not 《bad》 at all; not in the least ¶ 결코 그런 일은 하지 않겠다 I will never do that. // 이것은 결코 나쁘지 않다 This is not bad at all. // 결코 만족스럽다 할 수는 없다 It is by no means satisfactory. // 나는 어떤 일이 있어도 결코 돌아오지 않겠다 I won't get back for the world〔for my life, on any account〕. // 결코 그렇지 않습니다 I am positive that it is not so.

결탁 結託 collusion; conspiracy; complicity **—하다** be〔act〕 in collusion 《with》; conspire 《with》 ¶ …와 결탁하여 in collusion〔league〕 《with》; hand in glove 《with》 // 그들은 결탁하고 있다 They are in collusion.

*****결투 決鬪** a duel; an affair of honor **—하다** fight a duel 《with》; duel ¶ 결투를 신청하다 challenge 《a person》 to a duel; throw down the gauntlet〔glove〕 // 결투에 응하다 accept 《a person's》 challenge to a duel; take up the gauntlet **—법** the code of honor **— 입회인** a second **—장(場)** a field of honor **— 재판** a trial by battle〔combat〕

결투자 決鬪者 a duelist; a dueler

결투장 決鬪狀 a challenge; a cartel

결판 決判 ¶ 결판나다 《a quarrel》 be settled; come to a close; be finished // 결판내다 settle; bring 《a matter》 to a close; put an end to // 담판으로 결판내자 Let's settle the matter by negotiation. // 누가 옳은지 당장 결판을 내자 Let's decide〔find out〕 who is right and who is wrong right now.

†**결핍 缺乏** want; lack; dearth; [부족]

shortage ; scarcity —하다 be〔run〕 short 《of》; run out 《of》; run low ; get scarce〔scanty〕; lack ; want ¶ 식량의 결핍 a shortage of food // 인재의 결핍 a dearth of talent // 자본 결핍으로 for lack of capital // 주택 결핍으로 owing to the dearth of housing ; due to housing shortage // 휘발유가 결핍되어 가고 있다 We are running out of gas. // The gasoline is running low. // 비타민 결핍은 질병의 원인이 될 수 있다 Vitamin deficiency can lead to illness.
비타민 — a vitamin deficiency ; deficiency in vitamins

결핍증 缺乏症 [비타민 따위의] a deficiency disease

결하다 決— [결정하다] decide ; [판정하다] judge ¶ 승부를 결하다 decide a contest ; try conclusion with 《a person》 // 자웅을 결하다 fight to a finish ; try conclusions with one's adversary

결하다 缺— (be) lacking ; deficient ; wanting ; missing

‡**결함 缺陷** a defect ; a fault ; a flaw ; a shortcoming ; [부족] deficiency ; shortage ¶ 결함 있는 defective ; faulty // 사회적 결함 a social defect // 성격상의 결함 a defect in one's character // 성적(性的)〔육체적, 정신적〕결함 a sexual〔physical, mental〕defect〔deficiency〕// 제도의 결함 a defect〔flaw〕in the system // 결함을 메우다 make good〔make up for〕a defect // 교만이 그의 인격에서 가장 큰 결함이었다 Pride was the greatest flaw in his personality. // 그의 논법은 한가지 결정적인 결함을 가지고 있다 His argument has one fatal flaw.

†**결합 結合** combination ; union ; fusion ; cohesion ; 〖전기〗 coupling —하다 unite 《with》; join〔combine〕《with》; bond〔join, club〕together ; weld into 《one body》

> 참고 **unite** 일치 협력하다 **join** 「결합하다」는 동작이 주가 되고 결합의 정도나 시간은 문제되지 않는다 **combine** 공동 목적을 위하여 결합하다

¶ 그들은 결합해서 새 종파를 만들었다 They banded themselves into a new religious sect. // 그 부부는 재결합했다 The couple got back together again. / The couple resumed their former relationship. // 두 파가 결합하여 신당을 수립했다 The two factions combined and formed a new party. // 핑크색은 빨간색과 흰색이 결합된 것이다 Pink is a combination of red and white. // 그 도심의 건축물은 옛것과 새것이 성공적으로 결합된 것이다 The architecture in the town center is a successful combination of old and new.
— 계수(係數) the coefficient of coupling ; a coupling coefficient〔factor〕 —기(器) a coupler —도(度) the degree of coupling —력(力) coherence — 방식 a coupling scheme — 수요 〖경제〗 joint and composite demand — 에너지 bond〔binding〕energy — 전건(電鍵) a combined key —제(劑) a bonding agent —죄 〖법〗 concurrent offences — 직염(織炎) 〖의학〗 cellulitis — 회로 a coupled circuit — 효과 〖물리·화학〗 a packing effect

결합 공급 結合供給 〖경제〗 joint supply

결합범 結合犯 concurrent offences

결합 법칙 結合法則 associative law

결항 缺航 suspension of steamship〔air〕 service —하다 suspend the ship〔air〕 service ¶ 다음 뉴욕발 편은 결항되었다 The next flight from New York has been canceled. // 107 편(便)은 결항되었습니다 Flight 107 has been canceled. // 연락선은 결항되었다 The sailing of the ferry was canceled.

결핵 結核 ① 〖의학〗 a tubercle ; [결핵병] consumption ; tuberculosis 《T. B., t. b.》 ¶ 결핵성의 tubercular ; tuberculous ; hectic // 결핵을 박멸하다 eradicate〔uproot〕tuberculosis // 결핵으로 중태에 빠져 있다 be seriously〔desperately〕ill with tuberculosis // 그녀는 결핵에 걸렸다 She contracted tuberculosis.
② 〖지질〗 concretion ¶ 결핵성의 concretionary
— 결절(結節) a tubercle —약(藥) an antituberculosis drug — 예방 prevention of tuberculosis — 예방 대책 antituberculosis measure — 요양소 a sanitarium〔sanatorium〕for tuberculosis ; a T. B. sanatorium — 형성(形成) tuberculation — 환자 a tuberculosis 《T. B.》 patient 장(腸)〔후두(喉頭)〕 — intestinal〔laryngeal〕tuberculosis 폐(肺) — 〖의학〗 phthisis ; pulmonary tuberculosis ¶ 폐결핵을 앓다 suffer from tuberculosis of the lungs

결핵균 結核菌 tuberculous〔tubercle〕 bacillus ; tuberculous 《T. B.》 germs

결핵질 結核質 a (tubercular) constitution

결행 決行 decisive action ; a resolute step —하다 carry out (resolutely) ; take a resolute step ; carry into effect ¶ 암벽 등반을 결행하다 start rock climbing // 암살 계획을 결행하다 carry out an assassination plot // 총파업을 결행하다 call a general strike

†**결혼 結婚** marriage ; wedding ; union ; matrimony —하다 marry 《her, him》; get〔be〕married 《to》; wed ¶ 갓 결혼한 부부 newlyweds ; a just-married couple // 신분이 다른 결혼 a left-handed marriage // 결혼시키다 marry 《one's daughter》 to ; get 《one's daughter》 married ; make 《them》 man and

wife // 결혼 생활에 들어가다 settle down to married life // 결혼식을 올리다 celebrate a wedding ; solemnize a marriage // 결혼 서약을 하다 take one's marriage vows // 결혼 신청을 하다 make a proposal of marriage《to》; propose to《her》; ask (for) her hand // 결혼을 약속하다 engage to marry ; betroth // 결혼을 주선하다 arrange a marriage《between》; act as go-between // 재산을 노리고 결혼하는 사람 fortune hunter // 평생 결혼하지 않다 remain single all one's life // 결혼은 연애의 무덤이다 Marriage is death to a love affair. // 나는 결혼할 나이의 아들이 하나 있다 I have a son of marriageable age. // 그의 세 번째 결혼은 겨우 한달간 지속되었다 His third marriage lasted only a month. // 그녀의 외국인과의 결혼은 그녀의 가족으로부터 환영받지 못했다 Her marriage to a foreigner was not welcomed by her family. // 그들은 결혼하기로 작정했다 They planned to get married. // 부자와 결혼했다 She is married to a rich man. // 아직 결혼하지 않았습니다 I am not married. // 그의 결혼은 행복〔불행〕했다 He was happily〔unhappily〕married. // 우리들은 작년에 결혼했습니다 We got〔were〕married last year. // 그는 결혼 생활이 행복한가요 Is he a happily married man?

—기(期) ⇨ 혼기 — 날짜 a wedding date — 무효 소송 a nullity suit — 문제 a question of marriage — 보험 marriage insurance — 사기 a matrimonial fraud — 상담소장〔상담원〕a matrimonial agent ; a public love-maker《속》— 상대 a marriage partner — 생활 married life ; marital life — 선물 a wedding present〔gift〕—식장 a wedding hall — 신고 registration of one's marriage — 신청 a proposal of marriage《to》— 의상 a wedding dress ; the outfit of《a girl》on her marriage — 자금 a marriage fund — 중매 matchmaking — 중매인 a matchmaker ; a go-between — 증명서 a certificate of marriage ; marriage lines (주로《영》) — 지참금 marriage portion ; dower(y) — 초야 one's first marriage night — 축가 a nuptial song — 피로(연) an announcement of marriage ; a wedding dinner〔reception〕강제 — (a) forced〔coercive〕marriage〔match〕계약 — marriage by contract 국제 — an international marriage 근친 — a near-kin marriage 매매 — (a) purchase marriage 약탈 — (a) marriage by capture 연애 — a love match〔marriage〕정략(政略) — an expedient marriage ; a marriage forced by political expediency 중매 — an interview marriage 집단 — (a) group marriage 합의 — (a) consensual marriage 혈족(血族) — (a) consanguineous marriage

결혼관 結婚觀 an outlook on marriage

결혼 기념일 結婚紀念日 a wedding anniversary

결혼 반지 結婚班指 a marriage〔wedding〕ring

결혼 비행 結婚飛行 a wedding flight

결혼 사진 結婚寫眞 a wedding picture

결혼 상담소 結婚相談所 a matrimonial agency〔center〕; a public love-maker's office ; a marriage bureau《속》

결혼식 結婚式 a wedding〔marriage〕ceremony ¶ 오늘은 결혼식에 갔었다 I went to a wedding today.

결혼 연령 結婚年齡 one's age at marriage

결혼 적령기 結婚適齡期 a marriageable age ; the age for〔of〕marriage

결혼 행진곡 結婚行進曲 the wedding march

결후 結喉 〖해부〗 Adam's apple

겸 兼 and ; in addition ; combining ; concurrently ; at the same time ¶ 거실 겸 침실 a combination of sitting and sleeping room ; a bed-sitting room // 서재 겸 객실 a room used as study and parlor // 편집인 겸 발행인 the editor and publisher // 그는 국무 총리 겸 외부무 장관이다 He is Prime Minister and (concurrently) the Minister of Foreign Affairs. /He holds the portfolio for Foreign Affairs concurrently〔together〕with premiership.

겸덕 謙德 the virtue of modesty

겸두겸두 at the same time ⇨ 겸사겸사

겸무 兼務 an additional post ; another post〔office〕; plural offices **—하다** hold an additional post《of》; hold also the post《of》; serve concurrently《as》; take the concurrent office ¶ 두 학교에 겸무하다 teach in both schools

겸비 兼備 —하다 combine《one thing》with《another》; have both ; join ¶ 재색을 겸비한 부인 a woman combining wit and beauty ; a lady with both beauty and intelligence // 세 가지 특징을 겸비하고 있다 He combines all the three characteristics. // 그는 문무를 겸비하고 있다 He combines both learning〔He excels at both scholarship〕and the martial arts.

겸비 謙卑 self-abasement ; self-depreciation ; humility **—하다** depreciate oneself ; humble oneself

겸사 謙辭 modesty ; humility ; [말] humble speech ; [사양] declining humbly **—하다** be modest ; be humble ; humble oneself and give way to another ; decline humbly

겸사겸사 partly ... and partly ... ; at the same time ; simultaneously ; for a double purpose ¶ 상용 유흥 겸사겸사로

partly on business and partly for pleasure // 볼일도 보고 해수욕도 즐기러 겸사겸사 부산으로 갈 예정이다 I am going to *Pusan* combining business with a seaside vacation. // 자네도 보고 볼일도 보고 겸사겸사 (서울에) 왔지 I came (to *Seoul*) partly on business and partly for paying a visit to you.

겸상 兼床 a table for two ¶ 겸상을 차리다 prepare〔lay, set〕 the table for two

***겸손 謙遜** modesty ; humility ; diffidence ; self-effacement **—하다** (be) modest ; diffident ; humble ; unassuming ; humble〔efface〕 oneself ¶ 겸손하게 in a modest way ; with modesty // 겸손히 modestly // 겸손한 태도〔사람〕 modest attitude〔a modest person, a self-effacing person〕 // 자신의 결점을 인정할 만큼 충분히 겸손한 사람 the man who has sufficient humility to acknowledge his own imperfections // 지나치게 겸손하다 think too meanly of oneself // 그는 겸손해서 잠자코 있는 거다 Modesty keeps him from speaking. // 겸손이 지나치면 비굴이 된다 Excessive modesty lapses into servility.

겸양 謙讓 humbleness ; modesty ; humility ; diffidence **—하다** (be) modest ; humble ; diffident ; humble oneself and give way to 《another》 ¶ 겸양의 미덕 the virtue of modesty // 지나친 겸양은 오만 Too much humility is pride.

겸양법 謙讓法 the reverent style (of language)

겸양사 謙讓辭 reverent words

겸업 兼業 a side job〔business〕 ; a subsidiary business ; bywork 《미》 **—하다** take up a side job ; pursue〔follow〕 《some trade》 as a side job〔business〕 ; have two jobs at the same time ¶ 겸업의 금지 prohibition of outside work // 그 집은 음식점과 여관을 겸업하고 있다 That house combines restaurant and hotel business.

겸업 농가 兼業農家 a part-time farmer ; a farmer with a side job

겸연쩍다 慊然— be ashamed 《of oneself》 ; be put out of countenance ; be embarrassed ; feel awkward ; be abashed ¶ 겸연쩍게 shamefully ; shamefacedly // 겸연쩍어하다 feel ashamed〔awkward〕 // 겸연쩍게 만들다 make 《a person》 self-conscious ; put 《a person》 out of countenance // 겸연쩍은 얼굴을 하다 be shamefaced ; have a hangdog look // 그가 사람들 앞에서 그런 말을 하여 나는 무척 겸연쩍었다 He put me out of countenance by saying such a thing about me in company. // 겸연쩍어서 그에게 부탁을 못하겠다 I cannot with any grace make the request to him.

겸영 兼營 combining the management of another business **—하다** operate 《a hotel》 in addition to some other business

겸용 兼用 a combined〔double, multiple〕 use **—하다** use in two or more ways ; use (both) as 《A》 and 《B》 ; make 《a thing》 serve a double purpose ¶ 냉난방 겸용 for both heating and cooling // 거실과 식당 겸용의 방 a combined sitting (room) and dining room // 서재를 응접실로 겸용하다 use a study as a reception room

겸유 兼有 —하다 possess (both) 《A》 and 《B》 ⇨ 겸비(兼備)

겸임 兼任 —하다 hold an additional post〔office〕 ; hold also the post〔office〕 《of》 ¶ 두 학교 교사를 겸임하고 있다 He teaches in both schools. // 외상은 수상이 겸임한다 The Prime Minister takes the portfolio of foreign affairs.

겸자 鉗子 〖의학〗 a forceps 《*pl.* ~, -cipes》

— 분만 a delivery with forceps ; a forceps operation **— 지혈(止血)** forcipressure

겸전 兼全 —하다 be perfect in all ; be good at both ¶ 문무가 겸전하다 be good at both literary and military arts // 심신이 겸전하다 be sound both in mind and body

겸직 兼職 a concurrent office〔position〕 ; an additional job〔post, office〕 **—하다** hold 《a position》 concurrently with the principal one ; hold an additional position ¶ 공무원의 겸직에는 제한이 없다 There are no restrictions on civil servants holding other jobs.

— 금지 a ban for holding more than one office

겸치다 兼— combine〔unite, add〕 《one thing with another》 ⇨ 겸하다

†겸하다 兼— [겸용·겸비] combine〔unite〕 《one thing with another》 ; possess both 《A and B》 ; [포함] include ; [겸임] hold an additional post〔office〕 ; concurrently hold another post〔office〕 ¶ 문무를 겸하다 be good at both literary and martial arts // 코치가 선수를 겸하다 He is a coach and a player. // 서재와 객실을 겸하다 It combines a study and a drawing room. /The room serves both as a study and a drawing room. // 그는 지식과 독창력을 겸하여 갖추고 있다 He combines knowledge with originality. /He has both knowledge and originality. // 국무 총리는 다른 직위를 겸할 수 있다 The Prime Minister may hold another office together with the premiership. // 국무 총리는 외무부 장관을 겸하고 있다 The prime minister is also (serving as) the Minister of Foreign Affairs at the same time. // 대

(大)는 소(小)를 겸한다 The greater includes〔serves for〕 the lesser. // 감사역은 이사와 지배인을 겸할 수 없다 An auditor may not at the same time be a director or a manager.

겸행 兼行 ―하다 do〔carry out〕 two different things at the same time ; perform plural duties ¶ 주야 겸행하다 work day and night

겸허 謙虛 modesty ; humbleness ; humility ―하다 (be) modest ; humble ¶ 겸허하게 in a humble way ; with modesty ; modestly // 겸허하게 용서를 구하다 beg humbly for forgiveness // 겸허한 태도 a modest attitude // 정치가는 겸허하게 국민의 소리에 귀를 기울여야 한다 Politicians should listen humbly to the voice of public opinion.

겹 [포개어 거듭됨] fold ; [거듭된 켜] a fold ; a layer ; [쌓아 올린 켜] a pile ; [밧줄 따위의 가닥] a ply ; [두 배] double ; twofold ¶ 두 겹 twofold // 여러 겹 many folds ; over and over again ; repeatedly // 겹으로 지은 옷이나 이불 multi-layered clothes or bedding // 종이를 여러 겹으로 접다 fold a piece of paper over and over again

겹것 something made of two or more piles〔layers〕 ; [겹옷] lined clothes

겹겹이 in many folds ; one over another ; fold after fold ; layer upon layer ¶ 겹겹이 쌓아올리다 lay one upon another ; lay in piles〔layers〕 // 겹겹이 쌓여 있다 be piled high〔thick〕 one over another // 종이로 겹겹이 싸다 wrap 《a thing》 with papers over and over again // 적을 겹겹이 둘러싸다 surround the enemy thick and fast // 산으로 겹겹이 둘러싸이다 be surrounded by range after range of mountains // 그의 집을 경찰이 겹겹이 둘러쌌다 His house was besieged by the police.

겹눈 〖동물〗 compound eyes ; an ommateum 《*pl.* -tea》

겹다 be difficult to stand 《against》 ; be too much for ; be unmanageable ; be beyond one's control〔restraint, ability, power〕 ; be unable to bear up ¶ 흥에 겨워 in an excess of mirth ; driven by one's enthusiasm // 힘에 겨운 일 a task 〔work〕 beyond one's power〔ability〕 // 눈물겨운 광경 a tearful〔pathetic〕 scene // 그는 슬픔에 겨워 소리내어 울었다 He wept loudly in a passion of grief. // 그 일은 젊고 연약한 여자에게는 힘에 겨운 것 같다 The task seems too much for a young and fragile woman. // 이 일은 내 힘에 겨워 못해 내겠다 I find it difficult to deal successfully with this business.

겹말 redundant words ; a pleonasm

겹문자 ―文字 a redundant〔pleonastic〕 passage

겹사돈 ―査頓 a relative doubly related by marriage

겹살림 maintaining more than one household

겹씨 a compound word

겹옷 lined clothes ; clothes with a lining

겹저고리 a lined jacket

겹질리다 be sprained ; 《a joint》 be wrenched ; have a strain in 《one's leg》 ¶ 발목을 겹질리다 have a strain 〔sprain〕 in one's leg

겹집 a house with several wings

겹집다 pick 《them》 up in a pile

겹창 ―窓 a double window ; a storm window

겹쳐지다 lie one upon another ; come one after another ; be folded so that there is more than one fold〔ply, layer〕 ¶ 불행이 겹쳐지다 have misfortune after misfortune ; have a series of misfortunes // 화면이 둘로 겹쳐지다 The screen has two overlapping scenes.

***겹치다** put one upon another ; overlap ; [날짜의 일치] fall on 《another》 ; [늘이다] add ¶ 겹친 불운 repeated ill-luck ; a series of misfortunes ; a run of ill-luck // 불운이 겹치다 A series of misfortunes befalls 《him》. // 손해가 겹치다 suffer loss after loss // 그의 직무와 나의 직무가 겹친다 His duties and mine overlap. // 지붕 위의 기와가 서로 겹쳐져 있다 The tiles on the roof overlap one another. // 공휴일이 일요일과 겹쳤다 A national holiday falls on Sunday.

겹치마 a lined skirt

겻불 a fire made with hulls of rice

겻섬 a sack of rice hulls

경 punishment imposed on thieves ; [심한 고통·교훈] a chastisement ; a bitter experience

경을 치다 관용 have a hard time of it

경 更 a night watch ; [시각] one of the five watches of the night ¶ 삼경 midnight ; 《in》 the dead〔depth〕 of night

경 京 [서울] the capital ; the metropolis

경 庚 [십간의] the 7th of the 10 signs of the heavens in the traditional lunar calendar

경 徑 [직경] a diameter ¶ 반경 a radius

†**경** 頃 about ; toward(s) ; around 《미》 ¶ 두시경 about two o'clock // 이달 말경에 around the end of this month // 금년 말경에 가서 toward the end of this year // 작년 4월경의 일이다 It was in the last spring, sometime in April.

†**경** 卿 Lord ; Sir ; [대신] a minister ; a secretary ¶ 바이런 경 Lord Byron // 이든 경 Sir Anthony Eden

경 景 ① [경치] a view ; a scene ; scenery 《총칭》 ② [경황] a joyful state of things ⇨ 경황(景況) ¶ 관동 팔경 the eight famous spots in Eastern

Korea
경 經 ① [경서] Chinese classics of Confucianism ② 〖불교〗 a sutra ; a Buddhist scripture ③ [피륙의 날] the warp ④ [경도] longitude ¶ 경을 읽다 chant〔recite〕 a sutra
경 境 ① [상태] a state ; a stage ¶ 무아지경에 들다 attain a spiritual state of perfect selflessness ; go into an impersonal state // 황홀경 a trance ; a state of ecstasy
② [지역] a place ; a district ; a region ; an area
무인지— an uninhabited〔a vacant〕 region
경- 硬 hard ; solid ; stiff
—화(貨) hard money〔cash〕 —화(化) hardening
경- 輕 light
—공업 light industries —금속 light metals —기관총 a light machine gun
경가극 輕歌劇 an operetta ; a light opera
경가파산 傾家破産 squandering one's fortune ; bankruptcy —하다 squander one's fortune ; go bankrupt
경각 頃刻 a moment ; an instant ; a second ; a minute ¶ 경각간에 in a moment〔an instant〕 ; within a moment // 경각간의 일이었다 It was a matter of a moment. // 경각도 지체 못한다 There is not a moment to lose.
경각 傾角 〖물리〗 inclination
경각 警覺 warning ; awakening ; remonstration —하다 warn ; awaken ; remonstrate
경각심 警覺心 (self-) consciousness ; (self-) awakening ¶ 경각심을 불러 일으키다 arouse 《a person's》 attention ; bring 《a person》 to 《his》 senses // 전쟁의 참화에 대한 경각심을 불러 일으키다 arouse people's attention to the calamity of war
경간 耕墾 cultivation 《of wasteland》 ; clearing 《the land》 —하다 cultivate wasteland ; clear the land
†경감 輕減 reduction ; mitigation ; [고통 따위의] alleviation ; [형의] commutation —하다 reduce ; lighten ; lessen ; mitigate ; commute ; alleviate 《pain, sorrow》 ¶ 고통을 경감하다 alleviate one's sufferings // 세금을 경감하다 reduce〔lighten〕 a tax // 부담을 경감하다 lighten the burden // 사형을 종신형으로 경감하다 reduce〔commute〕 a death penalty to life imprisonment // 경기 후퇴의 영향을 경감시킬 새로운 경제 정책 new economic measures to help mitigate the effects of the recession
경감 警監 a police inspector〔captain〕
경개 梗概 an outline ; a summary ; a synopsis 《of a play, story》 ; a digest ; an abstract ; an epitome
경거 輕擧 a rash〔hasty〕 action ; a thoughtless〔heedless〕 undertaking ; an ill-considered attempt —하다 behave〔act〕 rashly ; commit a rash act ; act on impulse
경거망동 輕擧妄動 rash and thoughtless action ¶ 경거망동을 삼가다 behave〔proceed〕 prudently ; refrain from rash acts ; be discreet in one's behavior
경건 勁健 strong〔stout〕 health —하다 be in strong〔robust〕 health ; (be) robust ; stout
*경건 敬虔 piety ; devotion ; reverence —하다 (be) devout ; pious ; God-fearing ¶ 경건히 piously ; reverently // 경건한 기독교 신자 a devout〔pious〕 Christian // 경건한 카톨릭 교도 a devout Roman Catholic // 경건하게 기도를 드리다 pray devoutly 《before an altar》 ; offer a most reverential prayer // 경건한 마음으로 옷깃을 여미다 take a pious attitude // 주일은 경건히 지내도록 하세요 Observe the Lord's day〔Sunday〕 piously〔in piety〕.
경건주의 敬虔主義 Pietism
경건파 敬虔派 〖서양사〗 the Pietist
경겁 驚怯 awe ; fright ; scare ; alarm —하다 be awed ; be frightened ; be scared ; be alarmed ; take fright
경결 硬結 solidification ; coagulation ; congelation —하다 solidify ; coagulate ; congeal ; harden ; clot
경경 輕輕 —하다 [경솔] (be) imprudent ; flippant ; careless ; thoughtless ; rash ; frivolous ¶ 경경히 carelessly ; lightly ; hastily ; rashly // 경경한 행동 a rash act // 경경한 짓을 하다 act imprudently
경경 耿耿 —하다 [마음이] be haunted by an anxiety ; feel ill at ease ; feel uneasy 《about》 ; be restless ; [불빛이] flicker ; glimmer ; blink ; [기억이] be vaguely remembered ¶ 경경불매(不寐)하다 Being haunted by anxiety, one sleeps poorly〔passes a bad night〕.
†경계 境界 a boundary ; a border ; a frontier ; 〖불교〗 one's condition given by karma

> **참고** **border** 경계선 자체를 가리키는 경우도 있고 경계선에 연한 어느 정도의 넓이를 가진 지역을 가리키는 경우도 있다 **boundary** 지리적인 경계선 **frontier** 정치적 군사적 견지에서 본 타국과의 국경 지역. 하지만 이런 구별이 절대적 구별은 아니다

¶ 경계를 정하다 fix the boundaries ; border on a 《a place》 // 밤과 낮의 경계 the confines of night and day // 사랑과 우정의 경계 the borderland between love and friendship // 시(市)의 경계 the city limits // 주(州)의 경계 the state

border // 토지의 경계 boundary of the estate // 의학과 생물학과의 경계 the boundary between medical science and biology // 경계를 이루다 form a boundary ; adjoin 《a place》 ; border 《a place》 // 경계를 짓다 draw〔fix, set〕 boundary // 경계를 정하다 demarcate ; delimit ; fix 〔define〕 the boundary 《between》 ; fix the boundaries // 경계를 봉쇄하다 close the borders // 양가의 경계를 이루다 form the boundary between the two houses // 그 울타리는 나의 토지와 그의 토지의 경계를 나타낸다 The fence marks the boundary between my land and hers. // 양자간에 경계를 정해야 한다 A line must be drawn between the two. // 전문 영역간의 경계가 무너지고 있다 The boundaries between specialties are collapsing. // 압록강은 한국과 만주의 경계를 이루고 있다 The Yalu divides Korea from Manchuria. // 그는 그가 사는 주(州) 경계 안에 있어야 한다 He has to stay within his state boundary.
— 분쟁 a boundary〔frontier〕 dispute —선〔표〕 a boundary line〔post, stone〕 — 조건 〚물리〛 a boundary condition — 지(地) the borderland ; a frontier (국경) —층 〚물리〛 a boundary layer

†**경계 警戒** [경비] guard ; lookout ; watch ; [조심] (pre)caution ; [경고] warning ; caution **—하다** guard against ; be on one's guard against ; keep watch ; keep a lookout for ; be on the alert ; take precautions against ; [순찰하다] patrol ¶ 경찰의 엄중한 경계 stringent police precaution // 경계를 게을리하지 않다 keep a sharp lookout 《for》 // 경계시키다 put 《a person》 on guard against ; alert 《the police》 against 《a riot》 // 엄중히 경계하다 keep strict watch ; take strict precaution // 화재를 경계하다 take precautions against fire // 간첩의 침투를 경계하다 guard against the infiltration of spies // 전면 경계 태세에 돌입하다 be on a full alert // 물샐틈없는 경계를 하다 be on strict watch〔guard〕 // 경계를 늦추다 lower one's guard ; let one's guard down // 그는 전군에 특별 경계 태세를 취할 것을 명령했다 He ordered the armed forces to be put on special alert. // 그녀는 경계해야 해 You must be on your guard against her. // 소매치기 경계 Beware of pickpockets. /Watch out. There are pickpockets around.
— 수위(水位) the danger level 《of a river》 — 신호 a warning〔caution〕 signal ; 〚철도〛 a restricted speed signal ¶ 경계 신호를 올리다 put up〔raise〕 a warning signal —심 wariness

경계 驚悸 susceptibility to fright ; sudden palpitation

경계 경보 警戒警報 a preliminary alert ; [공습의] an air-raid alarm〔warning〕 ; [a red alert (공습 경보)에 대하여] a yellow alert ¶ 경계 경보를 발하다 alert 《people》 to ; issue a warning against // 경계 경보를 울리다 sound a warning

경계 관제 警戒管制 an air-raid warning blackout

경계망 警戒網 a cordon of police ; a police cordon ¶ 경계망을 치다 throw 〔lay〕 a police cordon 《around the area》 // 경계망을 빠져 나가다 slip through a police cordon

경계색 警戒色 〚동물〛 warning〔sematic〕 coloration ; a warning〔sematic〕 color

경계석 境界石 a boundary stone

경계선 警戒線 a police line〔cordon〕 ¶ 경계선을 돌파하다 [범죄자가] slip through a police cordon ; [군중이] break through〔across〕 a police line

경계표 境界標 a landmark ; a mete ; a boundary stone〔mark〕 ; a demarcation post

경계 표지 警戒標識 a warning sign

†**경고 警告** warning ; caution ; admonition **—하다** warn 《a person》 against〔of〕 ; give 《a person》 a warning ; caution 《a person》 against ; take warning 《from》 ¶ 경고 없이 without warning〔notice〕 // 접근하지 않도록 경고하다 warn 《a person》 away〔off〕 // 경고하지만 그것은 위험하다 I warn (you) that it is dangerous. // 문에서 떨어지라고 경고했다 He warned me off the gate. // 그 공격은 사전 경고 없이 일어났다 The attack occurred without advance warning. // 그는 품행에 대해서 서면 경고를 받았다 He has received a written warning about his conduct. // 흡연의 위험에 대한 경고가 모든 담배갑에 인쇄돼 있다 A warning of the danger of smoking is printed on every pack of cigarettes. // 그는 그 짐승이 매우 위험하다고 나에게 경고했다 He warned me that the beast was very dangerous. // 테러리스트들은 경찰에게 건물 근처에 가지 말라고 경고하였다 The terrorists gave the police a warning not to go near the building. // 그곳에 가지 말라고 경고하다 give 《a person》 warning not to go there // 위험에 대해 경고하다 give 《a person》 warning of his danger // 국민에게 경고하다 sound a warning to the nation // 경고를 발하다 serve〔give, issue, send〕 a warning on 《a person》 // 큰소리로 경고하다 shout a warning // 경고에 주의하다 heed a warning // 그의 경고는 무시되었다 His warnings were ignored. // 두 번 다시 경고하지 않겠다 I shall not warn you again ! // 경찰은 속도 위반을 경고했다 The policeman gave him a caution for speeding. // 그는 나의 경고를 무시했다 He paid no attention to my warn-

ings. // 위험에 대해 경고받았다 I was warned of the danger. // 그 양식점은 식기가 불결하다고 번번히 경찰의 경고를 받은 바 있다 That restaurant has been repeatedly warned by the police against its unclean tableware.
— 백서(白書) a white paper warning — 사격 warning shots 사전 — an advance warning —선 〖야구〗 warning track〔path〕

경골 硬骨 [굳은 뼈] hard bone ; [기골] firmness ; stubbornness ; inflexibility ; a firm character (사람) ¶ 경골의 firm ; staunch ; uncompromising ; inflexible

경골 頸骨 〖해부〗 the neck bone(s)

경골 脛骨 〖해부〗 the shinbone ; the tibia ¶ 경골의 tibial
— 동맥 the tibial artery

경골 어류 硬骨魚類 〖물고기〗 Teleostei (학명) ¶ 경골류의 Teleostean // 경골류의 물고기 a bony fish ; hard boned fish ; a teleost〔teleostean〕

경골한 硬骨漢 a man of firm character ; a man of principle〔sturdy heart〕

경공업 輕工業 light industry
— 제품 light industry goods〔articles〕

†**경과 經過** ① [시간의] passage ; lapse ; flight ; [기한 만료] expiration —하다 pass ; elapse ; go by ; expire (기한이) ¶ 시간의 경과에 따라 as time goes by ; with the passage of time // 5년이 경과하여 after (a lapse of) five years // 그 후 10년이 경과했다 Ten years have passed〔gone by〕 since then. // 사후 4시간이 경과했다 He has been dead these four hours.
② [사물의] progress ; course ; development ¶ 교섭의 경과 the progress of negotiations // 경과가 양호하다 show satisfactory progress // 경과를 살피다 watch the development of the affair〔event〕 // 지금까지의 경과를 말하다 give 《a person》 an account of all that has passed // 그는 대수술을 받은 후 경과가 좋다 He is progressing favorably after a serious operation.

경과 보고 經過報告 a progress report ; [회의의] a report on the proceedings ; [사건의] report on the development of an affair

경과 시간 經過時間 the time elapsed

경과 조치 經過措置 interim measures

경관 景觀 a scene ; a view ; a spectacle ; scenery 《총칭》 ¶ 일대 경관 a grand view ; a panorama // 빼어난 자연 경관 a site of superb scenic beauty // 경관을 해치다 destroy〔spoil〕 the scenic beauty

경관 警官 a police officer ; a policeman ; a constable (영) ; a cop (속) ; [순찰하는] a patrolman ; the police 《총칭》
—대 a police force〔squad〕 여자 — a policewoman

경교 景敎 〖종교〗 Nestorianism ¶ 경교의 Nestorian

경구 經口 ¶ 경구 백신 oral vaccine // 경구 투여 《doses for》 oral administration // 경구 피임약 an oral contraceptive pill ; a birth control pill

경구 硬球 a hard ball ; a regulation ball

경구 敬具 Sincerely yours ; Yours very truly ; Yours respectfully

*****경구 警句** an epigram ; an aphorism ; an apothegm ; a witty remark ; a witticism —가 an aphorist ; a wit ; an epigrammatist —집 a collection of epigrams

경구 감염 經口感染 an oral infection

경구개 硬口蓋 〖해부〗 the hard palate

경구 면역 經口免疫 oral immunity

경구 투약 經口投藥 《doses for》 oral administration

경구 피임약 經口避姙藥 an oral contraceptive pill ; a birth control pill ; the pill ¶ 경구 피임약을 먹기 시작하다〔상용하다〕 go〔be〕 on the pill

경국 傾國 decline of a nation ; ruining a country

경국 經國 administration ; statesmanship ; running a country

경국지색 傾國之色 a woman beautiful enough to cause the downfall of a country ; a woman of matchless〔peerless〕 beauty ; a Helen of Troy ; a siren

경근 敬謹 modest respect —하다 pay modest respect to 《a person》

경금속 輕金屬 light metals

경기 景氣 ① [형편] times ; things ; condition ; state ¶ 벼락 경기 a boom 《in the market》 // 불경기 a slump ; a depression ; a recession ; bad business ; a dull market // 경기의 내리막 a business slowdown ; an economic downturn // 경기가 좋아 보이다 be prosperous looking ; look prosperous // 시내의 경기를 보다 see how things are in the town // 경기가 좋다〔나쁘다〕 Times are good〔bad, hard〕. // 그는 경기가 좋다 He is prosperous. /It fares well with him. // 경기가 어떤가 How's everything ? /How are you getting on ?
② [상황] business (conditions) ; trade ; (the tone of) the market ¶ 경기의 냉각 cooling down of the economy // 경기가 호황이다 Business is flourishing. // 경기가 상승〔하강〕하고 있다 Business is improving〔falling off〕. // 경기가 회복되었다 Business has rallied. /The market picked〔looked〕 up. // 세계 경기는 명백한 회복의 조짐을 보이고 있다 Global business shows clear signs of recovery. // 내년의 경기 전망도 역시 어둡다 The economic prospects for next year are dark again. // 크리스마스를 앞두고는 경기가 항상 활황이다 Business is always brisk before Christmas.

//우리는 세계 전자산업의 호경기를 이용해야 한다 We must take advantage of the boom in world electronics industry. //석유 시장은 호경기를 누리고 있다 The oil market is enjoying a boom. //경기가 폭등하고 있다 Business is booming. //건설 경기를 타고 아파트 건축 붐이 일다 Apartment building is flourishing along with a boom in the construction business〔a construction boom〕. //경기가 좋다〔나쁘다〕 Business is brisk〔dull〕. //경기가 좋아지다 Business is〔Things are〕 looking up. //어느 시장이나 경기가 좋다 Every market is booming. //우리는 요즘 경기가 좋지 않다 We are kind of slow these days. //이렇게 경기가 좋지않은 상황에서는 보너스도 기대할 수 없을 것 같다 With the economy so bad, I guess we can't expect much in the way of a bonus.
— **동향 조사** a business survey — **부양책** steps to stimulate the economy ; reflation measures〔policy〕; expansionary〔expansionist〕 policy — **상승** a business upturn — **예고 지표** the business warning index 《WI》 — **예측** business forecasting — **자극책** economic measures to boost demand ; measures to stimulate〔pep up〕 the economy — **조정(調整)** business adjustment — **지표(指標)** a business barometer — **침체** stagnancy of business activities ; economic slump — **통계** business cycle statistics — **활성화 시책** an economy-invigorating policy **군수** — a war boom **벼락** — a boom ; a flush **부동산** — the real estate business **전시** — a wartime boom **전쟁(戰爭)** — a war boom **전후** — a postwar boom **투자** — an investment boom ☞ 《p. 159》

†**경기 競技** [시합] a game ; a match ; a contest ; a competition ; a tournament ; [운동 경기] an event ; a sporting event **—하다** have a contest〔game〕; play a game〔match〕 ¶ 근대 오종 경기 the modern pentathlon //십종 경기 ten events ; the decathlon //칠종 경기 the heptathlon //경기에 이겨서 ahead of the game //팽팽한 경기 a close game //중단 경기 called game //경기에 능숙하다〔서투르다〕 play a good〔poor〕 game //이길 가망이 없는〔있는〕 경기를 하다 play a losing〔winning〕 game //경기를 중지시키다 call a game //정정당당한 경기를 하다 play the game //경기에서 이기다〔지다〕 win〔lose〕 a game //경기에 참가하다 take part〔participate〕 in a contest ; take the field //무승부로 경기가 끝나다 《the game》 end in a draw //경기를 포기하다 throw up a game //경기의 승패가 났다 The game is over〔finished〕.
— **시설** athletic facilities — **종목** sport entries **수상(水上)** — water〔aquatic〕 sports ; aquatics **수영** — a swimming competition ; a swim race **실내** — an indoor game **야외** — a field game **주요** — a main event **학교 대항** — an interschool match ; [대학의] an interversity〔a collegiate〕 match

경기 輕機 ⇨ 경기관총

경기 驚氣 ⇨ 경풍(驚風)

경기관총 輕機關銃 a light machine gun **소형** — a submachine-gun

경기구 輕氣球 a dirigible balloon ; a hot-air balloon

경기 대회 競技大會 ① [운동] an athletic meet ; a sports meeting ¶ 경기 대회 당일 the sports day ② [기술 따위] a contest ; a competition ¶ 주판 경기 대회 an abacus contest

경기 변동 景氣變動 〖경제〗 business fluctuation

경기병 輕騎兵 [병사] a light cavalryman ; [부대] light cavalry
— **연대** a light horse regiment

경기 순환 景氣循環 a business〔trade《영》〕 cycle

경기자 競技者 a contestant ; a competitor ; an athlete ; a player ; a racer ; a swimmer (수영의)

경기장 競技場 a sports ground〔field〕; an arena ; a (sports) stadium

경기 지수 景氣指數 a business barometer〔index〕

경기 촉진 景氣促進 [시장의] the artificial enlivening of the market ; [판매의] a promotion stunt

경기 회복 景氣回復 a business recovery ; return to prosperity ; a perk-up

경기 후퇴 景氣後退 business recession

경내 境內 the precincts〔grounds, compound〕 ¶ 경내의 수목 trees in the precincts 《of a shrine》 //사찰의 경내 the precincts of a shrine
— **건물** precinct building

경년 經年 the passing of a year ; the elapse of a year **—하다** pass a year ; a year passes

경노동 輕勞動 light labor〔work〕
—**자(者)** a light worker ; [사무 계통] a business〔an office〕 worker

경농 經農 **—하다** follow the plow ; run a farm

경뇌유 鯨腦油 sperm oil ; spermaceti

경단 瓊團 a dumpling ; a doughboy

경대 鏡臺 a dressing〔mirror〕 stand ; a dresser ; a vanity 《미》; a toilet table 《영》

경도 傾度 gradient ; inclination

경도 傾倒 ① [마음을] **—하다** devote oneself to ; concentrate 《one's attention》 on ; [사람에게] admire ② [넘어짐] **—하다** fall down ; topple ; [쏠음] tilt ; tip ¶ 전력을 경도하다 give all one's energies 《to》; concentrate all one's energies 《on》 //그는 이 사업에 전력을 경도

경 기

▶ 경기(景氣)를 설명하는 표현

경기에 대한 영어 표현은 매우 폭 넓게 사용되므로 딱 한가지로 표현되는 영어는 없다. 상대의 영업 현황을 물을 때는 How is (your) business? 「경기가 나쁘다.」는 Business is slow. 혹은 We're in a bad way. / Things are bad. / Times are hard. 등으로 표현할 수 있다. 경제적 측면에서 묻는다면 The economy is running low. 혹은 The economy is in poor shape. 등으로 쓸 수 있다. 호경기는 good business, business boom 혹은 robust [vigorous] economy 로 쓴다.

¶ (경기가) 호전하다 take a favorable turn; take a turn for the better; turn the corner; pick up; surge ahead // (경기가) 좋아지다 improve; get well; grow better; revive // (경기를) 회복하다 recover; revive // (경기가) 호황이다 prosper; boom; peak // (경기가) 하향전환하다 take a downward turn; take a turn for the worse // (경기가) 후퇴하다 recess; retrogress // (경기가) 나빠지다 deteriorate (further); break down // (경기가) 정체상태가 되다 slump // fall into stagnation; be stagnant // (경기가) 불황이 되다 fall into depression; depress

경기동향 economic performance **경기전망〔예측〕** economic outlook[prospects, forecast] ¶ 내년의 경기전망은 밝지 않다. A poor economy is forecast for next year. **경기변동** economic [business] fluctuation **경기순환** (economic) cycle (★ business cycle 《미》, trade cycle 《영》) **경기대책** countercyclical measures; cyclical countermeasures **경기자극책** step to stimulate the economy; stimulative[reflationary] step **공황** depression; economic panic **호황** (economic) boom; prosperity **불황** recession; depression; slump **구조불황** structural recession **회복기의 경제** reflationary [reflating, recovering, resurgent] economy **과열경기** overheated [overheating] economy **경기의 냉각** cooling of the economy **경기의 하강** decline of the economy **하강경기** declining [sagging, skidding] economy **코스트 인플레이션** cost-push inflation **수요(과잉) 인플레이션** demand-pull inflation **물가·임금 인플레이션** price-wage inflation **임금·물가 인플레이션** wage-price inflation

했다 He gave his all energies to this undertaking.

***경도 經度** ① 〖지리〗 longitude ② [월경] the menses ; menstruation ; monthlies ; menstrual discharge ; monthly sickness (완곡하게) ¶ 경도는 서경 50도이다 The longitude is 50 degrees west. // 그 국가의 수도는 경도상으로 동경 21도에 위치하고 있다 The nation's capital is at longitude 21 degrees east.

경도 硬度 (degree of) hardness ; solidity ¶ 다이아몬드의 경도 the hardness of diamond

경도 輕度 ¶ 경도의 slight ; not serious trifling // 경도의 부상〔화상, 손해〕 a slight injury〔burn, damage〕

경도 驚倒 astonishment **—하다** be astonished ; be amazed ; be dumbfounded

경도계 硬度計 a hardness testing machine ; a durometer

경동 驚動 **—하다** be startled ; be frightened ; stagger in surprise

경동 輕動 a rash action ; rashness **—하다** behave〔act〕 rashly ; act on impulse

경동맥 頸動脈 〖해부〗 the carotid (artery)

경락 經絡 a blood vessel ; [정맥] a vein ; [동맥] an artery

경락 競落 auctioning

—하다 be auctioned off 《to a person》

— 기일 time for objectification

경락물 競落物 objects knocked down

경락인 競落人 successful bidder

경락자 競落者 ⇨ 경락인

경량 輕量 light weight

— 골재(骨材) lightweight aggregate **— 내화물(耐火物)** lightweight refractories **— 내화 벽돌** a light firebrick **— 벽돌** a lightweight brick **— 화물** light freight〔cargo, goods〕

경량급 輕量級 a lightweight 《boxer》

— 선수 〖권투〗 a lightweight ; a light ; lightweights 《총칭》

경량품 輕量品 light goods

†**경력 經歷** a career ; a record ; a personal history ; a curriculum vitae ; antecedents ¶ 경력이 수상한 사람 a man with a dubious past // 다양한 경력을 가진 사람 a man with a varied career // 경력을 조사하다 look into 《a person's》 antecedents ; check up〔trace〕

《a person's》 career〔record〕∥그는 좋은 경력을 가지고 있다 He has a good record. ∥그녀는 어떤 경력을 가진 사람이냐 What is her past career?
— 소개 a biographical introduction 무대 — one's stage career 회사 —서 the historical record of a company
경력 고시 經歷告示 [입후보자의] a career bulletin; a bulletin of candidate's careers
경력자 經歷者 an experienced man
경력직 經歷職 a job for persons with experience
경련 痙攣 〖의학〗 convulsions; a spasm; a jerk; a fit ¶ 경련이 일어나다 be convulsed; fall into convulsions; have a spasm〔cramp〕∥안면〔얼굴〕 경련 a (facial) tic∥경련성의 spasmodic; spastic; conclusive∥격심한 경련을 일으키다 fall into a fit of violent convulsions∥그는 수영하다가 경련이 일어났다 He was seized with a cramp while swimming. ∥내 눈꺼풀이 경련을 하고 있다 My eyelids are twitching. /I have a twitch in my eyelids. ∥다리에 경련이 일어나다 get cramps in one's leg∥그녀는 자주 경련을 일으켰기 때문에 자동차 운전을 할 수 없었다 She could not drive because she sometimes had convulsions.
—제(劑) an antispasmodic; a spasmolytic —학(學) spasmology 강직성(强直性) — a tonic spasm 손가락 — [문필가의] writer's cramp〔palsy, spasm〕; [전신 기사의] telegrapher's cramp 안검(眼瞼) — a nictitating spasm; cillosis
*__경례 敬禮__ salutation; a salute; an obeisance; a courtesy; a bow —하다 salute; bow 《to》; make one's bow; come to the salute; make〔give〕 a salute; make an obeisance 《to a king》 ¶ 거수 경례 a hand〔military〕 salute∥거수 경례를 하다 raise one's hand in salute∥차려 자세로 경례하다 salute at attention; stand at the salute∥경례를 받다 take the salute∥경례에 답하다 return 《a person's》 salute∥군대식 경례를 하다 make a military salute∥장교는 경례를 받았다 The officer took the salute. ∥소령은 하사의 경례에 답했다 The major returned the staff sergeant's salute. ∥국기에 대하여 경례 Salute the National Flag! ∥병사는 장교에게 경례했다 The soldier saluted the officer. ∥경례 [구령] Salute!
*__경로 經路__ a course; a channel; a route; a path; [단계] a stage; [과정] a process ¶ 부정한 경로를 통하여 through illegal channels∥어떤 경로로 through what channel; how∥같은 경로를 밟다 walk in the same path; follow the same course∥발달의 경로를 더듬다 trace the growth 《of》∥이만큼 발달하기까지는 여러 경로를 밟아 왔음에 틀림없다 It must have passed through various stages before the present development was realized. ∥당신은 정부로부터 보조금을 받기 원하면 공식적인 경로를 통해야 한다 You should go through the official channels if you want a grant from the government. ∥너는 어떤 경로로 그 비밀을 입수했느냐 Through what channel did you get the secret?
외교 — a diplomatic channel 전염 — the trace of an epidemic
경로 敬老 respect for the aged〔old〕 —하다 respect the aged; be kind to old men and women ¶ 그 자리는 경로석입니다 The seat is reserved for senior citizens.
— 잔치 a party〔feast〕 in honor of the aged
경로회 敬老會 a respect-for-age association〔meeting〕
경륜 經綸 administration; [국가의] statecraft; statesmanship ¶ 국가 경륜가 executive ability∥국사를 경륜하다 administer state affairs
경륜 競輪 cycling race; a bike race 《미》; a cycle race
— 선수 a (professional) bicyclist; a cycle racer —장 a bicycle race track; a cyclodrome
경륜가 經綸家 a man of great administrative ability
경륜지사 經綸之士 ⇨ 경륜가
경리 經理 [회계] accounting; [처리] management; administration
—하다 take care of accounts; manage; administer ¶ 회사의 경리 관리 the control of corporate accounts 〔finances〕
—부 the paymaster's〔account's〕 department; the Fiscal〔Accounting〕 Division; the general accounting department — 사무 accountant's〔paymaster's〕 business — 사원 an accounting clerk
경리 학교 經理學校 a paymasters' school
경마 a halter; a leading rein; a bridle
경마잡다 [관용] lead a horse; serve as a groom
경마잡히다 [관용] have a groom lead a horse by the halter
*__경마 競馬__ horse racing; a horse race; racing ¶ 경마 순번표 a race card∥경마의 승리마 예상 racing tips∥경마에 나가다 ride a race∥경마를 하다 run a horse race∥경마에 돈을 걸다 bet on horse races; play the races 《미》∥경마에서 돈을 잃다〔따다〕 lose〔make〕 money on the turf〔race〕∥그는 경마로 재산을 날렸다 He raced his property away. ∥말을 경마에 출전시키다 race horses
—계(界) the racing world; the turf —

광(狂) a turf fan ; a racing man — 기수 a jockey — 대회 the races ; race meeting 《영》 —말 a race horse ; a racer ; [집합적] a racing stable —법(法) the Horse Race Act — 팬 a track fan ; race goer

*경마장 競馬場 a racecourse ; a race track ; the turf ; race ground

경망 輕妄 flippancy ; frivolity ; imprudence ; indiscretion ; rashness ; thoughtlessness ; carelessness ; hastiness —하다 (be) rash ; imprudent ; indiscreet ; careless ; reckless ; [까불까불하다] flippant ; frivolous ¶ 경망히 flippantly ; imprudently ; indiscreetly // 경망한 짓 a rash act // 경망한 위인 a hasty〔reckless, shallow, insincere〕 personality // 경망한 언동 frivolities // 경망한 짓을 하다 act imprudently〔hastily〕 // 그렇게 말한 것은 경망한 짓이다 It is rash of you to say so. // 경망한 행동을 삼가시오 Don't act rashly〔hastily〕.

*경매 競賣 auction ; a public〔an open〕 sale ; a sale at auction 《미》 —하다 sell by〔at〕 auction ; auction off ; bring 《things》 to the hammer ¶ 경매되다 be sold by〔at〕 auction ; go under the hammer ; be auctioned off // 경매에 부치다 put 《a thing》 up at〔to, for 《영》〕 auction // 경매에서 값을 매기다 bid a price at auction // 경매에서 물건을 사다〔팔다〕 sell〔buy〕 《a thing》 at〔by 《영》〕 — 가격 a price offered by a bidder ; a bid — 공고 an auction notice — 기일 the date of auction —대(臺) an auction block — 대금 the amount of money obtained for 《an article》 sold by auction —법 〖법〗 the Auction Act — 수속 public auction procedure — 시장 an auction market — 업자 an auction dealer — 중개인 an auction broker — 처분 disposition by public sale〔auction〕 ; (a) tax sale ; selling up —품 an article for sale at auction〔sold by auction〕 강제 — a forced〔compulsory〕 sale by auction 공개 — a public auction 부정〔사기〕 — a mock〔fake〕 auction

경매물 競賣物 an article for sale at auction

경매인 競賣人 an auctioneer

†경멸 輕蔑 contempt ; disdain ; scorn

> 참고 **scorn** 강한 경멸에 노기와 혐오의 감정이 겹쳐 있다 **contempt** 경멸의 감정에 강한 비난의 감정이 겹쳐 있다 **disdain** 경멸의 감정 이외에 자기를 높이 보고 자기는 단연 그런 짓을 하지 않는다는 기분이 섞여 있다

—하다 despise ; hold〔have〕 《a person》 in contempt〔scorn〕 ; look down on〔upon〕 ; scorn ; slight ; think meanly of ; make light of ; put a slight on〔upon〕 《a person》 ; think scornfully of ; pour scorn on〔over〕 ; show contempt for ; have contempt for ¶ …을 경멸하여 in contempt of // 경멸적인 contemptuous ; disdainful ; scornful // 경멸하는 듯한 태도〔웃음〕 a scornful attitude〔smile〕 // 경멸할 만한 contemptible ; despicable // 경멸의 표정 a scornful〔contemptuous〕 look ; a look of disdain // …에 경멸의 감정을 갖다 have〔feel〕 scorn for // …함을 경멸하다 think〔hold〕 it scornful to 《do》 ; think scornfully of // 경멸을 당하다 be held in contempt ; be treated with contempt ; suffer slights // 경멸의 눈길을 보내다 eye 《a person》 with contempt // 그는 그의 급우들의 경멸의 대상이었다 He was the scorn of his classmates. // 그는 경멸할 가치조차 없다 He is beneath contempt. // 경멸하는 투로 말하다 talk〔speak〕 disrespectfully 《of》 // 그는 명예 따위는 경멸한다 He is scornful of honors. // 가난하다고 해서 그를 경멸해서는 안 된다 You should not despise〔look down upon〕 him because he is poor.

경모 輕侮 contempt ⇨ 경멸

경모 敬慕 admiration ; adoration ; love and respect —하다 admire ; adore ; love and respect ; have reverence and affection 《for》 ; worship ¶ 저 여선생은 전교생의 경모를 받고 있다 The whole school adores her. // 선생의 인격과 학문을 경모한다 We admire our teacher's personality and learning.

경모 景慕 worship ; admiration ; respect —하다 look up to ; honor ; respect ; admire ; worship

경묘 輕妙 —하다 (be) light ; free ; ready ; facile ; easy ; clever ; smart ¶ 경묘히 lightly ; freely ; cleverly ; smartly ; adroitly // 경묘한 문체 a light and witty style // 무용수의 경묘한 발동작 the agile 〔adroit〕 steps of a dancer // 경묘한 연설이었다 His speech was in a light vein.

경무 警務 police affairs

경무관 警務官 a police commissioner〔director〕 ; an inspector general

경문 經文 ① [불교 경전] the Buddhist scriptures ; sutras ② [도교 서적] Taoist classics ; [천주교의] Catholic prayers ¶ 경문을 읽다 read a Sutra

경문학 輕文學 light literature

경문학 硬文學 solid reading ; metaphysical literature

경물 景物 the scenery〔natural features〕 of the season

경물시 景物詩 a seasonal poem

경미 輕微 slightness ; triviality —하다 (be) slight ; little ; trifling ; negligible ¶ 경미한 문제 a slight problem ; a trifling〔trivial〕 matter // 경미한

범죄 a minor offense // 경미한 상처 a slight wound // 경미한 손해 a slight damage // 태풍으로 인한 피해는 생각보다 경미했다 Damage caused by the typhoon was much less than feared 〔thought〕.

경미 粳米 nonglutinous rice

경박 輕薄 [천박] frivolity ; fickleness ; levity ; flippancy ; [불성실] insincerity ; untruthfulness **—하다** (be) frivolous ; fickle ; flippant ; light ¶ 경박한 사람 a frivolous person // 경박한 언행 frivolous behavior ; frivolities // 그는 똑똑하지만 경박한 데가 있다 He is clever, but rather frivolous.

경방 庚方 west-by-southwest

경배 敬拜 bowing respectfully ; a respectful bow (절) **—하다** bow respectfully

경백 敬白 ⇨ 경구(敬具)

경벌 輕罰 a light punishment ; a mild penalty

경범죄 輕犯罪 a minor〔light〕 offense ; a misdemeanor ¶ 그는 경범죄 위반으로 벌금을 물었다 He was fined for his misdemeanor.

경범죄 처벌법 輕犯罪處罰法 the Minor Offenses Act

— 위반 a violation of the Minor Offenses Law〔Act〕

경변 硬便 hard excrements〔feces, stool〕

경변증 硬變症 〖의학〗 cirrhosis 《of the liver》

†**경보 警報** an alarm ; a warning ; a signal ¶ 경보를 내리다 give〔raise, issue, sound〕 an alarm ; warn // 폭풍 경보를 발하다 issue a storm warning (공습의) // 경보가 나자 사람들은 곧 집합하였다 People gathered quickly at the alarm. // 공습 경보가 나자 사람들은 모두 지하도로 대피하였다 People took shelter in the underground passage at the air raid alarm.

— 램프 an alarm lamp **— 신호** an alarm signal **— 온도계** an alarm thermometer **— 장치** an alarm device **—종** an alarm bell **— 해제** all clear **경계 —** air-raid warning (공습의) ; preliminary alert **공습 —** an air-raid alarm **비상 —** an alarm (signal) **화재 —** a fire alarm **원거리 조기 —망** the (distant) early warning (system)

경보 競步 [경기] a walking race ; a walking marathon ; a walkathon 《미·캐나다》 ; a 《40-kilometer》 walk (on the track)

— 선수 a walker

경보기 警報器 an alarm (signal)

도난 — a burglar alarm **연기〔화재〕 —** a smoke〔heat〕 sensor

경복 敬服 **—하다** admire ; have a great regard for ; hold 《a person》 in high esteem ; think highly of ¶ 경복할 만하다 be admirable ; be estimable // 직원 일동은 교장에게 경복하고 있다 The whole staff holds the principal in high esteem.

경부 頸部 the neck (area) ; the cervical region

경부 京釜 *Seoul* and *Pusan*

— 고속 도로 the *Kyŏngbu*〔*Seoul-Pusan*〕 expressway〔superhighway, speedway 《미》〕 **—선** the *Kyŏngbu* (Railroad) line

경비 經費 expenses ; cost ; [지출] expenditure ; outlay

> **참고** **expense**는 일상어로서 대개의 경우 복수형 **cost**는 생산 원가 **outlay**는 일정한 목적을 위한 지출 **expenditure**와 outlay는 문어적

¶ 여행 경비 travelling expenses // 영업활동에 필요한 경비 business expenses // 경비 문제가 아니다 Forget the expense ! // 많은 경비를 들여서〔들이지 않고〕 at (a) great〔little〕 cost // 경비 관계로 for financial reasons // 경비를 들이다 go to expense ; make outlay // 경비가 많이 들다 be expensive ; cost 《one》 much ; require〔involve〕 great expense // 경비를 절감하다 reduce〔cut down〕 the expenses ; curtail expenditures // 거기에는 많은 경비가 소요될 것이다 It will involve a heavy outlay. // 자동차를 소유하는 데는 경비가 많이 든다 It's too much of an expense to own a car.

— 삭감 the curtailment of the expenses ; curtailment of expenditure ; cost-reduction **— 절약** (financial) retrenchment **일반 —** general expenses **제(諸)—** overhead expenses〔charges〕 **소요 — 계정** expense account (회사의)

***경비 警備** defense ; guard **—하다** defend ; guard ; police ; keep watch ¶ 경비가 곧 해제되었다 The guard was soon called off. // 국경의 경비를 엄중히 하다 strengthen the defenses of frontiers // (경비선이) 해상을 경비하다 patrol〔police〕 the sea // 대통령의 주위에는 경비원들이 배치되어 있었다 There were guards around the President.

—실 a guardroom ; a guardhouse **—원〔병〕** a guard **과잉 —** excessive policing

경비대 警備隊 a garrison ; guards ; a squad of patrolmen

해안〔연안〕 — coast guards

경비망 警備網 a defense network ¶ 경비망을 뚫다 elude the vigilance of the guard

경비병 警備兵 a guard ; patrol

경비선 警備船 ⇨ 경비정

경비정 警備艇 a coast defense ship ; a patrol boat〔ship〕

경비함 警備艦 a patrol ship

경비행기 輕飛行機 light aircraft ; a light plane
†경사 傾斜 inclination ; slant ; [언덕의] slope ; [배의] a list ¶ 경사지다 incline ; slant ; slope ; lean 《to, towards》; [배가] list // 경사진 inclined ; slant ; sloping // 20도의 경사 a 20° slope ; a slope of twenty degrees // 가파른 경사를 오르다 climb a steep slope // 완만한 경사를 오르다 climb a gentle slope // (배가) 왼쪽으로 경사지다 list to port // 언덕을 오르면서 경사가 급해진다 The slope increases as you go up the hill. // 언덕은 기슭까지 완만히 경사져 있다 The hill slopes gently down to the foot.
—로(路) a slope way ; a ramp —비(比) a rake ratio — 압력계 a pressure inclination gauge — 응력 inclined stress — 조정 slope regulation — 투시도 an angular perspective — 투쟁 [노동 조합의] a graded struggle — 효과 a gap tilt effect
경사 經絲 warp
경사 經史 books on (Chinese) ethics and history
경사 慶事 a happy event ; a matter for congratulation ; an auspicious occasion ¶ 경사스럽다 《an event》 be happy // 경사가 겹치다 have one happy event after another ; have a series of matters for congratulation // 우리 집안에 경사가 났다 A matter for congratulation happened to our family.
경사 警査 a police sergeant
경사각 傾斜角 an angle of inclination ; a dip (angle) ; a tilt angle
경사계 傾斜計 an angle meter ; a clinometer
경사도 傾斜度 a gradient ; grade 《미》
경사면 傾斜面 an incline plane ; an incline
경사 생산 傾斜生産 priority production
경산 京山 mountains around the capital
경산부 經産婦 a multipara 《*pl.* -rae》; [1회의] a primipara 《*pl.* -rae》
경산절 京山— a temple near the capital
경산중 京山— monks from temples near the capital
경상 經常 ¶ 경상의 current ; ordinary ; regular ; working
— 세입 current〔ordinary〕 revenue — 세출 ordinary expenditure〔outlay〕 — 손실 ordinary loss — 예산 the working〔ordinary〕 budget — 이익 ordinary income
경상 輕傷 a slight wound〔injury〕 ¶ 경상을 입다 be slightly injured〔wounded〕; suffer a slight injury
경상 거래 經常去來 ordinary trade 〔transactions〕
경상비 經常費 working〔running〕 expenses ; ordinary expenditure ; operating costs 《미》
경상 수입 經常收入 ordinary earnings 〔takings〕
경상 수지 經常收支 current transactions account ; international accounts ; international payments and receipts
경상자 輕傷者 a slightly injured〔wounded〕 person ; [집합적] the slightly injured〔wounded〕
경색 梗塞 tightness ; blockade ; stoppage ; 〖의학〗 infarct ; infarction ¶ 금융 경색 tight money-market ; monetary stringency // 정국의 경색 a tight political situation
경색 景色 scenery ⇨ 경치
경서 經書 the Confucian classics ; a Confucian classic
경석 輕石 〖광물〗 a pumice(-stone)
경석고 硬石膏 〖광물〗 anhydrite
— 플라스터 hard finishing plaster
경선 經線 circles of longitude ; the meridian
—의(儀) a chronometer 분지(分至) — colure
경선 頸腺 〖해부〗 cervical gland
경성 警醒 — 하다 awake ; rouse ; arouse ; stir ; warn ; bring 《a person》 to 《his》 senses ; open 《a person's》 eyes
경성 硬性 hardness ; solidity ¶ 경성의 hard
— 세제 a hard detergent
경성암 硬性癌 〖의학〗 scirrhus
경성지색 傾城之色 ⇨ 경국지색(傾國之色)
경성하감 硬性下疳 〖의학〗 chancre
경성 헌법 硬性憲法 a strong〔iron〕 constitution
경세 經世 statecraft ; governing ; administration — 하다 administer 《state affairs》; govern
경세 警世 — 하다 awaken the people ; warn the public
—가 a prophet
경세가 經世家 a statesman ; an administrator
경세 제민 經世濟民 administrating the state to relieve the people's suffering
경세지재 經世之才 statesmanship ; executive〔administrative〕 ability ; ability to run a government
경세지책 經世之策 statecraft ; the art of conducting state affairs
*경솔 輕率 rashness ; hastiness ; [부주의] thoughtlessness ; carelessness ; imprudence ; flippancy — 하다 (be) rash ; hasty ; thoughtless ; careless ; imprudent ; flippant ¶ 경솔한 행위 a rash act // 경솔한 판단 a hasty〔rash〕 judgment // 곧 후회할 경솔한 말 hasty words that are soon regretted // 좀 경솔하다 be a little rash // 경솔한 짓을 하다 act hastily ; act on impulse // 경솔하게 약속

하다 make rash promises // 경솔히 판단하다 make a hasty conclusion ; judge hastily // 무슨 일이든지 경솔히 해서는 안된다 Use prudence in whatever you do. // 그녀는 곧 경솔한 결혼 결정을 후회했다 She soon regretted her hasty 〔rash〕 decision to get married. // 네가 그들에게 돈을 빌려 주는 데에 동의한 것은 경솔했다 It was rash of you to agree to lend them your money.

경쇠 磬— [악기] a kind of Korean musical instrument made of stone or jade ; [종] a handbell used by Buddhist monks or fortune-tellers

경수 硬水 〖화학〗 hard water

경수 輕水 light water

경수 鯨鬚 whalebone ; whalefin ; a baleen

경수로 輕水爐 [원자로] a light-water reactor

경순양함 輕巡洋艦 a light cruiser

경승 景勝 picturesque〔superb, beautiful〕 scenery

경승지 景勝地 a picturesque place ; a beauty〔scenic〕 spot ; a place of natural 〔scenic〕 beauty ; a scenic resort ¶ 그 고장은 경승지로 알려져 있다 The locality is known〔famous, noted, famed〕 for its scenic beauty.

†**경시 輕視** contempt ; negligence ; disdain ; slight **—하다** make light〔little〕 of ; take〔treat, hold〕 lightly ; belittle ¶ 인명 경시 풍조 a trend to make light of one's life〔take life lightly〕 // 문제를 경시하다 treat〔take〕 a matter lightly // 공산주의의 영향을 경시하다 belittle 〔make light of〕 the influence of communism // 적의 군사력을 경시하다 minimize the enemy's military power

경시 庚時 〖민속〗 the 18th of the 24 hour periods (4 : 30-5 : 30 p. m.)

경식 輕食 a light meal ; a snack ; a (light) lunch

—당 a lunchroom ; a cafeteria ; a snack bar 《미》

경식 硬式 ¶ 경식의 rigid ; hard // 반경식의 semirigid

— 비행선 a rigid dirigible **— 야구** regulation-ball baseball **— 정구** regulation-ball tennis ; (lawn) tennis **— 탁구** regulation-ball〔hard ball〕 ping-pong

경신 更新 renewal ; [개혁] renovation **—하다** renew ; renovate ¶ 계약을 경신하다 renew a contract // 운전 면허의 경신 renewal of a driver's license // 면허증을 경신할 시기가 되었다 It's time to renew my license. /My license has come up for renewal. // 면허증은 2년마다 경신해야 한다 The license must be renewed every two years.

경신 敬神 reverence for the gods ; piety ; devoutness **—하다** worship 〔revere〕 God ¶ 그는 경신의 마음이 두텁다 He is pious〔devout, God-fearing〕.

경악 驚愕 astonishment ; amazement ; consternation ; fright ; a shock **—하다** be astonished〔shocked, astounded, frightened〕 《at》 ; be thrown into consternation ¶ 경악을 금치 못하다 cannot repress one's astonishment // 그 소식을 듣고 경악하였다 The news gave me a great shock. /I was astonished 〔astounded〕 to hear the news. /The news gave me quite a turn. 《구》 // 나는 그녀의 갑작스러운 죽음에 경악했다 I was shocked at〔by〕 her sudden death. // 나는 그의 행동에 경악했다 I was shocked at his conduct.

경앙 景仰 admiration ; adoration ; reverence **—하다** admire ; adore ; look upon with reverence ; look up to

경앙 敬仰 reverence ; adoration ; admiration **—하다** revere ; adore ; admire ; look up to

경애 敬愛 respect and affection ; love and esteem **—하다** love and respect ; hold 《a person》 in high esteem ¶ 나의 경애하는 A군 (My) Dear Mr. A ! // 워싱턴은 국민에게 경애의 대상이었다 Washington was enthroned in the hearts of his countrymen.

경야 經夜 passing a night ; staying awake for a night ; staying up all night ; keeping vigil ; [초상집 등의] a wake, a vigil **—하다** pass a night ; stay up all night ; keep vigil through the night

경어 敬語 an honorific (expression) ; a term of respect

경역 境域 [장소] a region ; a place ; [경계] a boundary ¶ 신성한 경역 sacred precincts

경연 硬軟 (relative) hardness ; hardness and〔or〕 softness

경연 慶宴 a banquet ; a feast ; a party ¶ 경연을 베풀다 give〔have〕 a party ; hold〔give〕 a banquet

경연 競演 a contest ; a match ; competitive performance ¶ 경연회를 개최하다 hold a contest

민요 — 대회 a folk song concours 〔recital contest〕 ; a hootenanny 《미·속》

경연극 輕演劇 a light theatrical performance

경염 競艶 —하다 vie〔compete〕 with one another in beauty〔splendor〕

*****경영 經營** [관리] management ; administration ; [운영] operation ; running 《of a business, shop》 ; conduct 《of a business》 ; [계획] a program ; a plan **—하다** manage ; conduct ; operate ; run ; plan ¶ 효율적 경영 efficient management // 과학적 경영 scientific management // 다각 경영 multiple business //

경영상의 애로 a bottleneck in management // 국가 경영 기업 government enterprise ; government management // 영국인 경영의 British-run ; British-owned // A씨의 경영하에 under Mr. A's management // 경영이 잘 되지 않으므로 because of bad〔poor, incompetent〕 management // 호텔을 경영하다 [지배인으로서] manage a hotel ; [영업주로서] operate〔run〕 a hotel // 광산을 경영하다 operate〔run〕 a mine // 학교를 경영하다 conduct〔run〕 a school // 상점을 경영하다 keep〔run〕 a shop // 경영이 잘 되다 be well managed // 경영난에 빠지다 be in financial difficulties // 그의 성공은 경영의 수완보다는 행운에 의한 것이었다 His success was attained more by luck than management. // 사업 성공에는 강력한 경영이 필요하다 Successful business requires strong management. // 그는 경영에 실패하여 도산했다 He went bankrupt because he had managed his business badly. // 그들은 아시아에서 다국적 기업을 경영하고 있다 They operate multinational company in Asia. // 우리는 2개의 공장과 1개의 작은 호텔을 경영하고 있다 We run two factories and a small hotel. // 그는 경영진에 든든한 백을 가지고 있다 He has good connections in the management.

— 고문 a management consultant — 공학 industrial engineering — 대리 제도 a managing agency system — 대학원 a (post) graduate school of business administration — 방침 working principle —법 management ; how to run 《its》 business ¶ 과학〔능률〕적 경영법 scientific〔efficient〕 management —비 working expenses ; running expenses ; operating cost — 책임자 the manager of an enterprise ; a chief executive ; a responsible manager — 형태 forms of management 개인 — a private enterprise 다각 — multiple management 집약 — 〖경제·농업〗 intension

경영 競泳 a swimming race〔match, contest〕 **—하다** swim (a race) ¶ 10마일 경영 a ten-mile swimming race

— 대회 a swimming meet — 선수 a (competitive) swimmer ; a merman (남자) 《미》 ; a mermaid (여자) 장거리 — a marathon swim

경영 경제학 經營經濟學 business economics

경영 관리 經營管理 business management

경영권 經營權 the right of management

경영난 經營難 financial difficulty ¶ 그 학교는 경영난에 빠져 있다 The school is in financial difficulties〔finds it difficult to maintain itself〕.

경영 다각화 經營多角化 business diversification

경영 분석 經營分析 business analysis

경영자 經營者 a manager ; an executive ; an operator 《미》 ; the management (경영자측) ; [점주] a proprietor 《영》 ¶ 경영자측은 타협을 거절했다 The management refused to come to terms. // 경영자와 근로자 사이를 중재하다 arbitrate between management and labor

경영 전략 經營戰略 business strategy

경영주 經營主 a manager (가게의) ; a proprietor

경영 참가 經營參加 participation in management

경영학 經營學 business administration 《미》 ; business economics 《영》

경영학과 經營學科 department of business and administration

경영 합리화 經營合理化 business rationalization ; streamlining of management 〔operations〕

경옥 鏡玉 ⇨ 렌즈

경옥 硬玉 〖광물〗 jade ; jadeite

경옥고 瓊玉膏 a restorative herb medicine 《for promoting blood circulation》

경옥암 硬玉岩 〖광물〗 jade ; jadeitite

경외 敬畏 awe ; dread **—하다** dread ; stand in awe 《of》 ; have a dread 《of》 ; be awestruck

경외 京外 outside the capital〔city〕

경외 境外 outside of the premises

경외서 經外書 a non-canonical book

경외성서 經外聖書 the Apocrypha

†경우 境遇 [형편] circumstances ; a situation ; [어떤 때] a case ; an occasion ; an instance ; a time ¶ 이 경우 in this case // 그런 경우 in such a〔that〕 case ; in such circumstances ; on that occasion // 화재의 경우 in case of fire ; in the event of fire // 모든 경우에 on all occasions // …한 경우에는 in case 《of》 ; in the event〔case〕 《of》 ; on the occasion 《of》 ; in time 《of》 // 보통의 경우면 under ordinary circumstances // 대개의 경우에는 in most cases ; generally ; in general // 필요한 경우 in case of need // 사고의 경우에는 in the event of an accident // 경우에 따라서 according to circumstances ; in some cases ; sometimes ; as circumstances require ; when occasion demands ; as the case may be ; case by case // 여하한 경우에도 under all circumstances ; [부정] under no circumstances ; in no case // 내 경우에는 in my case // …한 경우를 제외하고는 except in the case〔event〕 《of》 // …에 흔히 있는 경우지만 as is often the case with // 최악의 경우에 in the worst case ; when (the) worst comes to (the) worst // 경우에 따라서는 거짓말도 방편이 된다 Falsehood is excusable in certain circumstances. /Circumstantial lies may be justified. //이렇게 하지 않으면 안될 경우가 많다 There are frequent occasions when it becomes necessary to do so. //회사는 부정 행위의 경우에 종업원을 해고할 수 있다 The company can dismiss its employees in case of misconduct. //너의 경우를 예외로 할 수는 없다 I can't make an exception in your case. //정직한 사람이 손해보는 경우도 있다 There are instances where honesty does not pay. //만일의 경우를 위해 우산을 가지고 가시오 Take your umbrella with you, just in case. //비가 내릴 경우 경기는 중지된다 In case of rain〔if it rains〕 the game will be called off.

경운기 耕耘機 a cultivator

경원 敬遠 —하다 keep《a person》at a respectful distance ; 〖야구〗 give a batter a walk ; walk a batter intentionally ¶ 서로 경원하는 사이 acquaintances politely shunned by one another //그는 남한테 경원당한다 He is kept at a respectful distance. /He is politely shunned by everybody. //투수는 강타자를 경원하였다 The pitcher intentionally passed the hard hitter.

경위 涇渭 [옳고 그름] good and evil ; vice and virtue ; right and wrong ; [판단·식별력] judgment ; discernment ; good sense ¶ 경위야 어떻든 whether it is right or wrong //경위에 벗어난 짓 an improper act ; unreasonable doings //경위에 어긋나다 be out of reason //그는 경위가 바른 사람이다 He is a man of good sense. /He is a man of fair judgment.

경위 經緯 ① [경위도] longitude and latitude ② [피륙의 날과 씨] warp and woof〔weft〕 ③ [일의 전말] context ; circumstances ; particulars ; details ¶ 사건의 경위를 이야기하다 tell the circumstances of the case ; tell the whole story of the affair //사건의 경위를 알아보다 investigate the details of the accident //경위를 설명하다 give a full account《of》//일이 이렇게 된 경위를 나는 모른다 I don't know how things got this way. //경위가 어떻게 된 것인지 알 수 없다 I don't know how the matter stands.

—도 원점(**度原點**) the origin of longitude and latitude ; the standard datum of geographic coordinates

경위 警衛 ① [경관의 계급] a police lieutenant ② [호위] guard ; patrol ; escort **—하다** guard ; patrol ; escort

경위도 經緯度 longitude and latitude

경위서 經緯書 an account ; a report

경위선 經緯線 lines of longitude and latitude

경위의 經緯儀 a theodolite ; an altazimuth

경유 輕油 light oil ; gasoline

— 발동기 a light oil motor

경유 鯨油 whale-oil ; train oil ; whale fat ; blubber

⁑**경유 經由 —하다** pass〔go〕 through ; go by way of ¶ 경유로 via ; by way of ; through //파리 경유 런던행 (A plane) to London via〔by way of〕 Paris //홍콩 경유 전보 a cable via the Hongkong route //부산 경유의 외국 무역 foreign trade through *Pusan* //파나마 운하 경유로 by way of〔via〕 the Panama Canal

경음 硬音 glottalized sounds

경음 鯨飮 swig ; swill ; heavy drinking **—하다** drink hard〔deep〕 ; drink like a fish ; guzzle ; swig ; swill oneself with 《liquor》

경음악 輕音樂 light music

— 작곡가 a light composer

경음화 현상 硬音化現象 glottalization

⁑**경의 敬意** respect ; regard ; homage ; honor ; reverence ; deference

> 참고 **honor** 타인의 인격·지위·행위 따위에 대한 존경심과 태도 **deference** 타인의 인품·연령·지위·업적 따위를 존경하여 자신을 제쳐 두고 그 사람의 희망과 의견을 세우려는 마음가짐 **homage** 존경·순종의 태도 **reverence** 경애심

¶ 경의를 표하여 out of respect ; as a mark〔token〕 of respect for ; in honor of ; in deference to //경의를 표하다 pay one's respects〔regards〕《to》; show one's respect ; regard〔treat〕《a person》with respect ; do honor《to》; do〔pay〕 homage《to》//경의를 표하기 위해 방문하다 call on《a person》to pay one's respect //용사에 경의를 표하라 All honor to the brave ! //많은 사람들이 고인에게 경의를 표하러 왔다 Many people came to pay homage to the dead man. //우리는 모차르트의 천재성에 경의를 표한다 We pay homage to the genius of Mozart. //당신에게 경의를 표합니다 My hat's off to you. /I take off my hat to you.

†**경이 輕易** lightness ; easiness **—하다** (be) easy ; simple ; light

경이 驚異 wonder ; wonderment ; [경이로운 사물] a wonder ; a marvel ; an eye opener《미》 ¶ 경이로운 wonderful ; marvelous ; phenomenal ; eye-opening《미》//자연계의 경이 nature's wonders //과학계의 경이 a wonder〔sensation〕 in scientific circles //경이의 눈으로 보다 stare in wonder ; open one's eyes in astonishment

경이감 驚異感 wonder ; marvel ; a miracle ; a feeling of doubt〔uncertainty〕

경이롭다 驚異— be curious〔marvelous〕

경이원지 敬而遠之 ⇨ 경원(敬遠)

경이적 驚異的 wonderful ; marvellous ; amazing ; miraculous ; eye-opening 《미》 ¶ 경이적 기록 a distinguished record // 경이적인 사건 an eye-opening event ; an eye-opener ; a miraculous event

경인 京仁 *Seoul* and *Inch'ŏn*
— 고속 도로 the *Seoul-Inch'ŏn* expressway〔superhighway, speedway, freeway〕 —선 the *Seoul-Inch'ŏn* line — 지방 the *Seoul-Inch'ŏn* districts

경일 慶日 a happy day〔occasion〕; a festival day

경입자 輕粒子 〖물리〗 a lepton

†**경작 耕作** cultivation ; farming ; tillage
—하다 cultivate ; farm ; till ; plow ¶ 경작에 종사하다 cultivate the soil ; engage in farming // 경작에 적합하다 be arable ; be tillable
— 기계 farm〔farming〕 tools ; agricultural implement〔machinery〕

경작권 耕作權 the right of cultivation〔to cultivate〕

경작물 耕作物 farm〔agricultural〕 products ; farm crops ; the products of a farm

경작자 耕作者 a tiller (of the soil) ; a plowman ; a farmer

경작지 耕作地 arable land (가능한 땅) ; tillage ; cultivated land ; land under cultivation

경작 한계지 耕作限界地 〖경제〗 marginal land

경장 警長 a police corporal

경장 輕裝 a light dress ; light equipment ; light attire **—하다** be lightly dressed〔equipped, outfitted〕 ¶ 경장으로 여행하다 travel light

경장 更張 reformation ; renovation ; innovation **—하다** renovate ; reform 《the government》; innovate

경재 硬材 hard wood

†**경쟁 競爭** competition ; rivalry ; contest ; struggle ; emulation **—하다** compete with 《a person for a thing》; contest ; rival ; vie〔cope〕 《with each other》; emulate ¶ 선의의 경쟁 competition in good faith // 치열한 국제 경쟁 fierce〔keen, stiff, formidable, bitter, strong, intense〕 international competition // 학문의 경쟁을 하다 compete with 《a person》 in studies // 독일의 상품과 경쟁하다 compete against German goods // 경쟁에 이기다〔지다〕 win〔lose〕 in a contest // 가격 경쟁을 하다 compete in price // 경쟁이 심하다 There is keen competition in 《the industry》. // 몇몇 회사가 그 계약을 따기 위해 서로 경쟁하고 있다 Several companies are competing against〔with〕 each other for the contract〔to gain the contract〕. // 이 다이아몬드에 대한 입찰자들의 경쟁은 치열하다 Competition between bidders for this diamond is keen. // 대학 입학을 위한 경쟁은 치열하다 Competition for admission to the college is keen. // 우리 경쟁사의 제품은 품질면에서 우리 것보다 더 나을게 없는데도 아시다시피 가격은 더 비쌉니다 Our competition's product is no better than ours in quality, but it is more expensive as you know. // 틀에 박힌 방법으로는 경쟁에 이길 수 없다 We'll never beate the competition with conventional methods.
— 무대 an arena of competition — 상대 a rival ; a competitor — 시대 an age of keen competition 가격 — competitive pricing 가격 인하 — a price cutting race ; underselling competition 공개 — open competition 과당 — overcompetition 대외 — foreign competition 생존 — a struggle for existence〔survival〕 자유 — free competition 군비 확장 — an arms〔armament〕 race 무— 선거구 an unopposed constituency ; an uncontested precinct〔district〕

경쟁 가격 競爭價格 a competitive price

경쟁 계약 競爭契約 a competitive contract

경쟁국 競爭國 a competing〔rival〕 country

경쟁력 競爭力 《develop》 competitive power ¶ 가격 경쟁력 a competitive price // 국제 경쟁력 international competitiveness // 경쟁력을 갖춘 상품 competitive goods // 경쟁력이 부족하다 be insufficiently competitive // 경쟁력을 강화하다 strengthen〔sharpen〕 the competitiveness

경쟁률 競爭率 competitive rate ; the ratio of successful (applicants) to total applicants

경쟁 매매 競爭賣買 competitive sales

경쟁 시험 競爭試驗 a competitive〔screening〕 examination ¶ 경쟁 시험으로 선발하다 select by competitive examination

경쟁심 競爭心 a competitive spirit ; a spirit of competition〔emulation〕; a sense of rivalry ¶ 경쟁심이 왕성하다 be full of competitive spirit

경쟁 의식 競爭意識 a sense of rivalry ; a competitive sense ¶ 경쟁 의식이 강하다 have a strong sense of rivalry

경쟁이 經— a person chanting a spell to dispel misfortune ; an exorcist

경쟁 입찰 競爭入札 competitive bid ; a public tender **—하다** make a competitive bid 《for》

***경쟁자 競爭者** a rival ; a competitor ; a contestant ¶ 만만치 않은〔얕잡아 볼 수 없는〕 경쟁자 a formidable〔keen, strong〕 competitor // 비양심적인 경쟁자 unscrupulous competitor // 경쟁자를 물리

치다 outdo〔outdistance, outstrip〕 (all) competitors

†경적 警笛 an alarm whistle ; a honker ; Klaxon《상표》; [경관의] a police whistle ; [자동차의] a horn ; [농무일 때 배의] a foghorn ¶ 경적을 울리다 whistle a warning ; give an alarm whistle ; [자동차가] sound〔blow〕 a horn ; honk — 금지 No horn ! /No honking.

경적필패 輕敵必敗 Don't crow too much over your enemy.

경전 經典 the scriptures ; the sacred book ; [불교의] the Sutras ; [기독교의] the Bible ; [회교의] the Koran

경전 耕田 plowing〔cultivating, tilling〕

경전기 輕電機 light electric equipment ⇨ 중전기(重電機)

경전차 輕戰車 〖군사〗 a whippet (tank)

경절 慶節 a festival ; a national holiday ; a fête day

경정 警正 a police major

경정 更正 correction ; revision ; reassessment (세금의) ; rectification —하다 revise ; correct ; rectify — 결정 [소송] a ruling of rectification ; [세법] a rectification and a decision 추가 — 예산 a supplementary (additional) budget

경정 更訂 revision ; rewriting —하다 revise ; rewrite

경정맥 頸靜脈 〖해부〗 the jugular vein

‡경제 經濟 economy ; [경제 상태] economics ; [재정] finance ; [절약] thrift ; thriftiness ; saving ; economy ; husbandry ¶ 경제적 economic ; financial ; economical

> 참고 **economic**은 「경제의, 경제에 관한」의 뜻이고 **economical**은 「검약한, 낭비하지 않는」의 뜻이다 (보기) 「물건을 파는 사람의 입장에서」 경제적으로 채산이 맞는 값 an economic price ; 「물건을 사는 사람의 입장에서」 경제적으로 이익인 싼값 an economical price

¶ 계획 경제 planned economy // 국가〔가정, 농촌, 사회〕 경제 state〔domestic, rural, social〕 economy // 자립 경제 self-supporting economy ; viable economy // 자유〔자본〕주의 경제 liberal〔capitalistic〕 economy // 규모의 경제 economies of scale // 경제적인〔저연비의〕 차 an economical car // 경제적 견지 an economic point of view // 경제적으로 economically ; financially // 경제적이다 be economical // 비경제적이다 be bad〔poor〕 economy《to do》; be uneconomical // 국내 경제의 회복 추세 the trend toward recovering in the domestic economy // 시간을 경제적으로 사용하다 use one's time economically // 경제적으로 궁핍하다 be financially embarrassed // 그건 비경제적이다 It is uneconomical〔poor economy〕. // 바겐 세일 기간에 구입하면 경제적이다 It's more economical to buy goods on a bargain day. // 빈번한 파업이 그 나라의 경제를 손상시키고 있다 Frequent strikes are damaging the economy of the country. // 서방 국가들의 경제는 대체로 제조업에 기반을 두고 있다 Western economies are largely based on manufacturing. // 그렇게 하는 것이 시간과 돈의 경제이다 It would be economy of time and money to do so. /That will save time and money. // 경제적 관점에서 말하면 그것은 위험한 정책이다 Economically, it is a dangerous policy.

— 감사관〔감시관〕 an economic supervisor〔inspector〕 — 관계 economic relations《between two countries》 — 기자 a reporter of financial news《미》 — 범죄 economic crime (공금 횡령·밀수 등) — 보증 economic security — 부장 〖신문〗 a financial editor ; an editor of financial news — 부흥 회의 the Economic Rehabilitation Congress ; the Council for...《미》 — 분석 economic analysis — 사상 economic thought〔ideas〕 — 사정 the economic〔financial〕 conditions〔situation〕《of Korea》 — 상태 economic〔financial〕 conditions ; [개인의] the state of one's finances — 생활 economic life — 수준(水準) an economic standard〔level〕 — 안정 stabilization of economy ; economic stabilization — 원론 principles of economics — 원조 계획 an economic aid program — 위기 an economic〔a financial〕 crisis — 잠재력 economic potential — 잡지 an economic magazine —전 an economic war ; economic warfare — 정보 economic intelligence — 조정관(실) (office of) Economic Coordinator — 조직 the economic system〔structure〕 — 조치 economic measures —주의 economism — 측정 econometrics — 통계 economic〔financial〕 figures〔statistics〕 — 평론가 an economic critic〔analyst〕 광역 — vast area〔bloc〕 economy 정치 — political economy 지하 — underground economy 통제 — controlled economy 미시〔거시〕 —학 micro-〔macro-〕economics 순수 —학 pure economics 아시아 극동 — 위원회 the Economic Commission for Asia and the Far East《ECAFE》 연차 — 계획 an annual economic plan

경제가 經濟家 an economist ; a man of economy ; a frugal〔thrifty〕 person ; an economizer

경제 각료 經濟閣僚 economic minister — 회의 an economic ministers' conference

경제 개발 經濟開發 economic development〔exploitation〕

—구 economic development zone (중국의) — 5개년 계획 a five-year plan 〔program〕 for economic development
경제 객체 經濟客體 economic objects
경제 경찰 經濟警察 economic police
경제계 經濟界 the economic world ; economic〔financial〕 circles
경제 계획 經濟計劃 an economic plan
경제 고문 經濟顧問 an economic advisor
경제 공황 經濟恐慌 a financial〔an economic〕 panic
경제과 經濟科 [대학의] the economics department
경제 관료 經濟官僚 an economic bureaucrat
경제 구조 經濟構造 an economic structure
경제권 經濟圈 an economic bloc
경제 기구 經濟機構 an economic structure〔setup, buildup〕 ¶ 경제 기구의 개혁 reorganization of the economic structure
경제 기사 經濟記事 〖신문〗 economic 〔financial〕 articles〔news〕 《미》 ; city articles〔news〕 《영》
경제 기획원 經濟企劃院 the Economic Planning Board 《EPB》
— 장관 the Minister of the Economic Planning Board
경제난 經濟難 financial difficulties
경제 단위 經濟單位 economic unit
경제 단체 經濟團體 an economic organization
경제 대국 經濟大國 a great〔major〕 economic power
경제 동맹 經濟同盟 an economic league 〔union, alliance〕
경제란 經濟欄 〖신문〗 the financial section 《of a daily》 ; the financial column(s)
경제력 經濟力 economic power〔might, strength〕
경제림 經濟林 forest of usable〔economical〕 trees
경제 모델 經濟— an economic model
경제면 經濟面 〖신문〗 the financial page
경제 백서 經濟白書 an economic white paper
경제법 經濟法 economic laws
경제 변동 經濟變動 financial fluctuation
경제 봉쇄 經濟封鎖 an economic blockade
경제 블록 經濟— an economic bloc
경제사 經濟史 an economic history ; a history of 《Korean》 economy
경제 사범 經濟事犯 an economic offense (죄) ; a violator of economic laws (사람)
경제 사회 이사회 經濟社會理事會 [유엔] the Economic and Social Council 《ECOSOC》
경제성 經濟性 〖경제〗 economical efficiency
경제 성장 經濟成長 growth of economy ; economic growth ¶ 고도의 경제 성장 high growth of 《Korean》 economy
경제 성장률 經濟成長率 the rate of 《Korea's》 economic growth
경제 속도 經濟速度 an economical speed
경제 수역 經濟水域 economic water (zone)
경제 순환 經濟循環 economic circulation
경제 외교 經濟外交 economic diplomacy
경제 운영 經濟運營 an economic management
경제 원리 經濟原理 an economic principle
경제 원조 經濟援助 economic aid
경제 원칙 經濟原則 economic principle
경제 윤리 經濟倫理 economic ethics 〔morality〕 ; business ethics
— 강령 the Economic Ethics Charter 〔Code〕 — 위원회 the Economic Ethics Commission
경제인 經濟人 an economic man ; a business man
경제재 經濟財 economic goods
경제적 자유 經濟的自由 economic freedom (Alfred Marshall의)
경제전 經濟戰 an economic war ; economic warfare〔competition〕 ; a white war
경제 정책 經濟政策 an economic policy ¶ 대외 경제 정책 a foreign economic policy
경제 정치학 經濟政治學 ecopolitics
경제 제재 經濟制裁 economic sanction
경제 좌표 經濟座標 economic barometer
경제 지리학 經濟地理學 economic geography
경제 지표 經濟指標 an economic indicator
경제 차관 經濟借款 an economic loan
경제 철학 經濟哲學 the philosophy of economy
경제 투쟁 競爭鬪爭 economic strife
*경제학 經濟學 economics ; political economy ; economic science
—과 학생 an economics student — 박사 a doctor of economics ; [학위] Doctor of Economics —사(士) a graduate of the economics department of a university — 원리 the principles of political economy —자 an〔a political〕 economist 거시 — macroeconomics 계량(計量) — econometrics 고전〔정통〕파 — classical〔orthodox〕 political economics 근대(近代) — modern economics 마르크스 — Marxian economics 미시 — microeconomics 소비 — economics of consumption
경제 행위 經濟行爲 economic action 〔activities〕 ; economic life ; economic

behavior
경제 협력 經濟協力 economic cooperation
— 개발 기구(開發機構) the Organization for Economic Cooperation and Development 《OECD》
경제 협조처 經濟協助處 Economic Cooperation Administration 《ECA》
경조 輕躁 rashness ; hastiness ; precipitancy —하다 (be) rash ; precipitant ; indiscreet ; imprudent
—병(病) hypomania
경조 競漕 a boat race ; boat-racing —하다 have a boat race ; row a race
— 대회 a regatta ; a boat race —용 보트 a race〔racing〕 boat
경조 敬弔 condolence ¶ 경조의 뜻을 표하다 express〔offer〕 one's condolence 《to a person about something》
경조 慶弔 congratulations and condolence(s)
—비(費) expenses for congratulations and condolences — 전보 telegrams of congratulations and condolence(s)
경조부박 輕佻浮薄 frivolity ; fickleness ; levity ¶ 경조부박한 사람 a frivolous person ; the fickle and frivolous
경조치 京造— *Seoul*-made imitations of regional specialties
경종 耕種 seedling ; sowing
경종 警鐘 an alarm bell ; [경고] a warning ; a fire-bell (화재시의) ¶ 이것은 현대에 대한 경종이다 It is a warning to the present age. // 방사능이 누출되었다는 뉴스는 널리 국민들에게 경종을 울렸다 The news of the radiation leak caused widespread public alarm.
—대(臺) a fire bell stand
경종을 울리다 (관용) ring〔sound〕 an alarm bell
경죄 輕罪 a misdemeanor ; a minor 〔slight〕 offense
경주 傾注 devotion ; concentration
—하다 devote oneself to ; concentrate on ¶ …에 전력을 경주하다 devote oneself entirely〔one's whole mind〕 《to》 ; put one's whole heart and soul 《into》 ; concentrate one's energies 《on》
†경주 競走 a race ; a run —하다 have 〔run〕 a race 《with》 ; race 《against》 ¶ 경주에 이기다〔지다〕 win〔lose〕 a race
—용 자동차〔자전거〕 a racing car〔bicycle〕 ; a racer — 종목 running events
단거리 — a short-distance race ; a sprint (race) ; a dash 도보 — a foot race 마라톤 — a marathon race 100미터 — a 100 meter dash 2인 3각 — a three-legged race 1만 미터 — the 10,000 meter run 자동차 — an automobile〔a motor〕 race 자전거 — a bicycle〔bike〕 race 장〔중〕거리 — a long-distance〔middle-distance〕 race 장애물 — a hurdle race ; the hurdles (단수 취급) ; an obstacle race 평지 — a flat race
경주로 競走路 a course ; a (race) track
경주마 競走馬 a racehorse
경주자 競走者 a runner ; a racer ; [단거리의] a sprinter
경주장 競走場 the track ; the course ; [자전거 따위의] a velodrome
경중 敬重 respect ; reverence —하다 respect ; revere
경중 輕重 [사물의] relative importance 〔seriousness〕 ; [물체의] weight ¶ 일의 경중을 가리다 weigh (the importance of) a matter
경증 輕症 a slight illness〔attack〕 ; a minor ailment ; a mild〔light〕 case ¶ 경증의 천연두에 걸려 있다 have a slight 〔mild〕 case of smallpox
— 환자 a mild〔light〕 case
경지 境地 ① [상태] a state ; a condition ; a stage ; circumstances ¶ …의 경지에 이르다 attain the stage 《of》 // 무아의 경지에 이르다 attain a state of perfect self-effacement
② [분야] ground ; territory ; sphere ¶ 새로운 경지를 개척하다 break new ground ; open up a new path ; carve out a new career // 독자적 경지를 개척하다 strike out a path of one's own
③ [장소] a land ; a sphere ; a home ¶ 자유를 누릴 새 경지를 찾다 seek a new land where one can enjoy freedom
경지 耕地 [경작지] agricultural〔cultivated〕 land ; plowed land ; farm land ; land under cultivation ; [경작에 적합한] arable land〔soil〕
경지 鯨脂 blubber ; whale fat
경지 면적 耕地面積 acreage under cultivation ; cultivated acreage
경지산 硬脂酸 stearic acid (스테아르산)
경지 정리 耕地整理 readjustment of arable land
경직 硬直 stiffness ; rigidity —하다 stiffen ; get stiff ; become rigid ¶ 경직된 분위기 an uncomfortable atmosphere
사후 — cadaveric rigidity ; rigor mortis
경진 輕震 a weak earthquake
경진 競進 ① [서로 다투어 앞으로 나아감] running neck and neck ; being nip and tuck ② [생산품이나 제품 따위의 우열을 겨룸] ¶ 경진 대회 a competitive exhibition ; an exposition
경진회 競進會 ⇨ 공진회(共進會)
경질 更迭 change ; replacement ; a reshuffle ; [대경질] a shake-up —하다 change ; make a change ; replace ; reshuffle ¶ 장관의 경질 a change in the ministry // 내각의 경질 a Ministerial 〔Cabinet〕 change ; a reshuffle of the Cabinet // 사원의 대경질 a shake-up in the staff // 내각이 경질될 것이다 There will be a change of ministers. /A min-

isterial〔Cabinet〕 change will take place. // 내각의 경질을 단행하다 reshuffle the Cabinet

경질 硬質 ¶ 경질의 hardened ; [물이] hard ; [동물의 피부 따위] scleroid
— 고무 hard rubber — 땜납 hard solder — 비닐 수지 rigid vinyl resin — 섬유 hard fiber

경질 도기 硬質陶器 hard porcelain

경질 유리 硬質— hard glass

경질 자기 硬質瓷器 hard ceramics

경차 經差 a longitudinal difference

†경찰 警察 the police ; the police force ¶ 경찰에 알리다 inform〔report to〕 the police // 경찰에 고발하다 complain to the police // 경찰에 출두하다 report 《oneself》 to the police // 경찰에 자수하다 give 《oneself》 up to the police // (기자가) 경찰에 출입하다 work on the police beat 《for a newspaper》 // 경찰에 붙잡혀 가다 be taken to the police // 경찰은 그를 뒤쫓고 있다 The police are on his track. // 경찰의 수배를 받고 있다 be wanted by the police // 그는 경찰에 유치되었다 He was taken into police custody. // 경찰의 보호를 받고 있다 place oneself under the protection of the police // 수명의 경찰이 그 지역을 순찰하고 있다 Several police are patrolling the neighborhood. // 경찰은 그 살인범을 잡았다 The police have caught the murderer. // 그는 그 사건을 경찰에 신고했다 He has reported the incident to the police. // 그는 경찰이 되고 싶어한다 He wants to join the police force.
— 관할 구역 a police region〔district〕 —국(局) the Police Bureau〔Department, Headquarters〕 —대 a constabulary unit ; the constabulary〔police〕 force ; the constabulary — 대장 a police troop commander —력 police force — 명령 a police order — 법규 the police law — 수첩(手帖) a policeman's pocketbook — 제도 a police system — 직원 police personnel — 출입 기자 a police reporter ; a news reporter on the police beat — 행동 police action 비밀 — the secret police 사법 — the judicial police 청원 — the police specially detailed to protect 《a person's》 body ; private police 서울특별시 —국 *Seoul* Metropolitan Police Bureau〔Headquarters〕 서울특별시 —국장 the Chief of the *Seoul* Metropolitan Police

경찰견 警察犬 a police dog ; a bloodhound 《영》

경찰관 警察官 a police officer 《미》 ; a police constable ; a policeman 《영》

경찰 관서 警察官署 headquarters of the police

경찰 국가 警察國家 a police state

경찰권 警察權 police authority〔power〕 ¶ 경찰권을 발동〔남용〕하다 exercise〔abuse〕 the police authority〔power〕

경찰 대학 警察大學 a police academy〔college〕

경찰 명령 警察命令 a police order

경찰범 警察犯 a police offense

경찰 법규 警察法規 the police laws

경찰 병원 警察病院 a police hospital

경찰봉 警察棒 a truncheon ; a cudgel ; a club

*경찰서 警察署 a police station ; a station house

경찰서장 警察署長 the chief of a police station ; a police chief 《미》 ; a city marshal (시의) 《미》

경찰의 警察醫 a police medical officer ; a police surgeon (외과의)

경찰 지서 警察支署 a police substation ; a branch police station ; a police station branch ; a police box

경찰 처분 警察處分 police disposition

경찰청 警察廳 the Regional Police Headquarters

경찰 학교 警察學校 a police academy

경찰 행정 警察行政 police administration

경찰 허가 警察許可 police authorization

경책 警責 caution ; admonition ; strong warning —하다 rebuke ; reprove ; admonish ; caution

경책 輕責 a censure ; a reproach ; a blame ; reproof ; a rebuke

경척 鯨尺 a cloth-measure 《14. 91 inches》

경천 敬天 worship of Heaven —하다 worship〔revere〕 Heaven

경천동지 驚天動地 ¶ 경천동지의 world-shaking ; astounding ; marvelous ; tremendous ; startling ¶ 경천동지의 대사건 a most sensational〔extraordinary〕 event

경천위지 經天緯地 (the executive ability for) governing the whole world —하다 govern the world ; show great statesmanship

경철 鏡鐵 spiegeleisen ; spiegel〔mirror〕 iron

경철광 鏡鐵鑛 specular iron (ore) ; specularite

*경첩 a hinge ¶ 경첩을 달다 hinge // 경첩을 벗기다 unhinge // 경첩이 달린 문 a hinged door // 문의 경첩이 벗겨져 있다 The door is off its hinges.

경첩 輕捷 agility ; nimbleness ; alacrity —하다 (be) light ; deft ; nimble ; swift ; be free from encumbrances

⁑경청 傾聽 listening closely〔attentively〕 —하다 listen intently〔attentively〕 to ; be all attention ¶ 경청할 만하다 be worth listening to〔one's respectful attention〕 // 그는 그 말을 경청하지 않았다 He did not listen to what was said. // 그녀는 한 마디도 빠뜨리지 않고 열심히 경청하였다 She listened devouring

every word.
경청 敬聽 listening courteously —하다 listen courteously
경추 頸椎 『해부』 the cervical vertebral
경축 慶祝 [축하] congratulation —하다 celebrate ; congratulate 《a person》 on 《his success》 ¶ 광복절 경축 행사 National Liberation Day Celebrations 〔Festivities〕
경축일 慶祝日 a (national) holiday ; a fête day ; a festival〔feast〕 day ; a red-letter day
경축 행사 慶祝行事 commemorative 〔celebration〕 program ; a celebration ; festivities
†경치 景致 a scene ; [한 지방 전체의] scenery ; [조망·전망] a view ; a prospect ¶ 좋은 경치 a picturesque scene ; a fine view // 시골 경치 rural scenery // 그림같은 경치 picturesque scenery // 밤 경치 a night scene // 경치 좋은 곳 a site of scenic beauty // 경치가 좋다 have a fine〔lovely〕 view // 경치의 아름다움에 넋을 잃다 be fascinated〔be carried away〕 by the scenic beauty of // 알프스의 경치는 웅대하다 Alpine scenery is grand. // 그곳은 경치 좋기로 유명하다 The place is noted for its scenic beauty. // 그는 경치가 좋은 방을 원한다 He wants a room commanding a good view.
*경치다 [형벌을 받다] suffer torture ; suffer severe punishment ; be heavily punished ; [혼나다] have a hard 〔rough〕 time of it 《with a person》 ; pay dearly 《for》 ; have bitter experience ¶ 경치게 exceedingly ; awfully ; terribly ; excessively // 너 그런 짓 하면 경친다 If you do (that), you will catch it. /You will have to pay for that. // 시험 치르느라 경쳤다 I had a hard time taking the examination.
경칩 驚蟄 the day on which insects appear from their holes in the earth
경칭 敬稱 an honorific ; a term of respect ; a title (of honor) ¶ 경칭을 생략하고 부르다 call 《a person's》 name without title ; cut out〔leave out〕 prefixes from the names
경쾌 輕快 —하다 [몸이] (be) light ; nimble ; [마음이] lighthearted ; cheerful ; buoyant ¶ 경쾌한 동작 nimble 〔swift〕 movement // 경쾌한 발걸음 light steps // 경쾌한 가락 a cheerful tone // 경쾌한 음악 rhythmical〔lilting〕 music // 경쾌한 복장을 하고 있다 be lightly dressed
경탄 驚歎 wonder ; admiration —하다 wonder〔marvel〕 at ; admire ; be struck with admiration ¶ 경탄할 만한 wonderful ; admirable ; marvelous // 자연의 아름다움에 경탄하다 wonder at the beauty of nature // 사람을 경탄시키다 strike 《a person》 with admiration // 나는 그의 용기에 경탄했다 I admired him for his courage. // 그의 한국 고전에 대한 깊은 조예는 경탄할 만하다 His knowledge of Korean classics is admirable enough to strike us Koreans with admiration.
경토 耕土 rich〔fertile, fine〕 soil
경토 境土 ⇨ 강토(彊土)
경파 硬派 the stalwart〔get-tough〕 faction ; the tough elements ¶ 대외 경파 the chauvinists ; the jingoists ; a strong foreign policy party
경편 輕便 —하다 (be) handy ; convenient ; simple ; [휴대하기에] portable
경편 철도 輕便鐵道 a light railway
경포 輕砲 a light gun
경품 景品 a premium ; a free gift ; a present ¶ 경품부 대매출 a sale with gifts〔premiums〕 ; a gift enterprise 《미》 // 경품을 내걸다 offer premiums
— 인환권 a gift coupon — 증정 『광고』 Customers offered premiums
경품권 景品券 a gift coupon ; a premium ticket
경풍 輕風 『기상』 a light〔gentle〕 breeze 〔air〕 ; a soft wind ; a zephyr
경풍 驚風 convulsions ; (children's) fit ¶ 급성〔만성〕 경풍 an acute〔a chronic〕 convulsion // 경풍을 일으키다 fall into a fit of convulsions ; have a convulsive fit
경하 慶賀 congratulation ; felicitation —하다 congratulate〔felicitate〕 《a person on his success》 ; offer one's congratulation 《on a person's success》 ¶ 경하할 만한 일이다 It is a matter for congratulation 《that》 // 혹서지절에 가내 제절이 두루 무고하시다니 경하하는 바입니다 I am very glad to hear that all your family are in very good health in spite of the intense heat.
경하다 輕— [가볍다] (be) light ; [경미하다] light ; slight ; trifling ; [경솔하다] rash ; imprudent ; thoughtless ; careless ; frivolous ; flippant ¶ 경한 병 a slight illness // 경한 위궤양 a mild stomach ulcer // 경한 부상 a slight wound 〔injury〕 // 경한 짓 a rash act // 책임이 경하다 be not in a very responsible position // 그는 입을 경하게 놀리지 않는다 He weighs〔picks〕 his words.
경학 經學 (the study of) Chinese classics ; the study of Confucian classics 〔Confucianism〕
경합 競合 competition ; struggle ; concurrence ; conflict —하다 concur ; conflict ; contest 《an election》 ; bid against each other ; compete 《with a person for》 ; vie with each other 《for》 ¶ 사정이 경합하다 circumstances concur
— 권리 소송 『법』 an interpleader action —죄 concurrent offenses
경합금 輕合金 a light alloy

경해 驚駭 surprise ; astonishment ; amazement ; consternation **—하다** be surprised〔astonished, amazed〕; be thrown into consternation ; be startled《at》

경향 京鄕 the capital and the country ¶ 경향 각지에 퍼지다 spread over town and country // 경향 각지에서 모이다 come from every corner of the country ; come from far and near

†경향 傾向 a tendency ; a trend ; a drift ; [성향] an inclination ; a disposition ; a propensity ; a leaning ; a turn of mind ; an aptitude ¶ 등귀의 경향 a rising〔upward〕 tendency // 교육계의 경향 the tendency of the educational world // 뚜렷한 보수적 경향 a distinct leaning toward conservation // …의 경향이 있다 tend towards ; tend to《do》; have a tendency to《do, a matter》; be disposed〔inclined〕 to《do》; be apt to《do》// 가격 하락의 경향이 있다 Prices tend downward. // 그녀는 과장해서 말하는 경향이 있다 She has a propensity to exaggerate. // 당시의 학생들은 툭하면 염세 사상에 빠지는 경향이 있었다 The students of those days were too often disposed to develop pessimistic〔Wertherian〕 sentiments. // 소년 범죄는 증가하는 경향이 있다 Juvenile crimes show a tendency to increase.

— 곡선 a trend curve **—극〔소설〕** a tendency play〔novel〕 **— 조사** a trend study

†경험 經驗 experience **—하다** experience ; go through ; undergo ¶ 경험 있는 experienced // 경험 없는 inexperienced ; new《to》// 나의 경험으로는 in〔from〕 my experience // 가르친 경험이 있다 have experience in teaching〔as a teacher〕// 가난의 경험이 있다 know what it is to be poor // 경험이 부족하다 lack〔have little〕 experience // 경험담을 말하다 recount one's experience ; tell《a person》of one's own experience // 경험으로 알고 있다 know《it》by〔from〕 experience // 경험을 쌓다 gain experience《in》// 경험으로 배우다 learn by experience // 경험을 살리다 make use of one's experience // 경험이 풍부하다 have wide experience // 이런 추위는 경험해 본 적이 없다 This is the coldest weather we have ever had〔known〕. // 그 실패는 좋은 경험이 되었다 The failure was a good experience to me. // 내 경험으로는 그렇게 하는 것이 낫다 Judging from my experience, it would be better to do so. // 나는 아직 가르쳐 본 경험이 없다 I am not yet experienced in teaching. // 나도 그런 경험을 해봤기 때문에 그것을 안다 I know it because I've been there.

— 과학 empirical science **—식(式)** 〚화학〛 an empirical formula **— 철학** empirical〔experiential〕 philosophy **— 학파** 〚철학〛 the empiric school **간접 —** indirect〔vicarious〕 experience **내〔외〕—** 〚심리〛 inner〔outer〕 experience **직접 —** direct〔firsthand〕 experience

경험가 經驗家 an experienced man ; a man of experience ; a stager ; [노련가] a veteran ; an old campaigner ; an old-timer《미·속》¶ 풍부한 경험가 a man of ripe experience

경험담 經驗談 a narrative〔story〕 of one's personal experiences ; a rehearsal of one's experience ¶ 경험담을 말하다 tell a story〔give an account〕 of one's experience

경험론 經驗論 〚철학〛 empiricism ; experimentalism ; experiential philosophy

—자 an empiricist ; an empiric ; an experimentalist

경험자 經驗者 a person (who is) experienced《in》; [일의] an experienced hand

경혈 經穴 〚한의〛 spots on the body suitable for acupuncture

경호 警護 guard ; patrol ; escort **—하다** guard ; place under guard ; convoy ; [사람을] escort ¶ 경호의 임무를 맡다 act as escort ; be on guard // 군대의 경호를 받고 under convoy of troops // 그의 집은 경호를 받고 있다 His house is under guard.

경호원 警護員 a bodyguard ; a (security) guard ; a protector ; a secret serviceman ; a muscleman《구》; a bouncer (술집·호텔 등)

대통령 — a secret service man《미》; a presidential guard **무장 —** an armed guard

경홀 輕忽 **—하다** (be) careless ; rash ; hasty ; thoughtless ; imprudent ¶ 경홀히 rashly ; imprudently

경화 京華 the busy streets of the capital〔*Seoul*〕

경화 硬化 hardening ; cementation《of steel》; vulcanization《of rubber》; [의견·태도의] stiffening **—하다** harden ; stiffen ; metalize《rubber》¶ 동맥이 경화하다 the arteries harden // …에 대한 태도를 경화하다 stiffen one's attitude《towards》

— 고무 ebonite ; vulcanite **—유(油)** hardened〔hydrogenated〕 oil **— 작용** a hardening process **— 점토(粘土)** 〚지질〛 [단층간의] bind **—제(劑)** a hardener ; a hardening〔setting〕 agent ; cement ; 〚화학〛 a sclerotic **—증(症)** scleroma **— 지방(脂肪)** hardened fat **동맥 —** sclerosis of the arteries

경화 硬貨 hard money〔cash〕; metallic currency ; effective money

—국 a hard currency country

경화기 輕火器 〖군사〗 light firearms 〔weapons〕
경화학 공업 輕化學工業 light chemical industry
경황 景況 the state of things ; conditions ; an (interesting) situation ¶ 경황없다 [흥이] have no mind for ; have no interest in ; [바빠서] be too busy for // 일에 경황이 없어서 문안 편지도 드리지 못했습니다 I have been so busy that I have failed to write to you. // 남의 일을 생각할 경황이 없다 I have no time to mind other people.
경희 驚喜 a pleasant surprise ━하다 be pleasantly surprised ; be surprised with joy
†**곁** [근처] neighborhood ; vicinity ; [옆] side ¶ 곁의 nearby ; neighboring // 곁에 by ; beside ; [가까이] near ; close〔hard, near〕 by // 곁에서 보고 있는 사람 a bystander ; a looker-on // 창 곁에 by the window // 곁으로 가다 come〔go, draw〕 near // (학교) 곁을 지나가다 pass by 《school》 // 바로 곁에서 보다 see 《a thing》 at close quarters // 곁을 떠나지 않다 keep close to 《a person》 // 부모의 곁을 떠나다 leave one's parents // 곁에 두다 keep 《a thing》 at hand ; have 《one's son》 living with 《one》 // 너 따위는 그의 곁에도 못 간다 You are not to be put beside him. /You are no match for him.
  곁 비다 관용 be without protection ; be not looked after ; be unguarded〔unwatched〕 ; be not cared for
  곁 비우다 관용 leave 《a person》 unattended〔unguarded〕 ; leave one's (guard) post unmanned
곁가닥 a side piece 《of string, thread》
곁가리 false ribs ; spare ribs
곁가지 a side branch ; a lateral branch
곁간 ―肝 a lobe of the liver of cattle
곁길 a side path〔road〕 ; an alley ; a bystreet ; a byway
곁꾼 an extra hand ; a helper ; an assistant
곁노 ―櫓 sculls ; sculling oars
  ―질 sculling
곁눈 a side glance ¶ 곁눈으로 보다 glance sidewise 《at》 ; cast a side glance at 《a person》 ; look askance 《at》
  곁눈 팔다 관용 look away〔off〕 ; take one's eyes off 《a book》 ; look at something else
  곁눈 주다 관용 give a wink ; wink at ; give a suggestion with a look
곁눈질 a side glance ; leering 《at》 ; [눈짓]suggesting by a side glance ; winking ━하다 leer at 《a person》 ; glance sidewise 《at》 ; cast a side(-long) glance at 《a person》 ; look askance 《at》 ; suggest by a side glance ; wink
곁다리 a secondary thing ; someone other than the party concerned
  곁다리(를) 들다 관용 remark〔say〕 from the sidelines
곁두리 snacks for farmhands at work between meals
곁들다 help ; assist ; aid ; lend〔give〕 a hand 《to a person》 ; give a helping hand ; take the part of ; side with ¶ 일을 곁들어 주다 help out with the work // 곁들어 싸우다 take 《a person's》 part in a fight
곁들이다 ① [음식을] put all on one plate ; dress ; garnish ¶ 생선 요리에 야채를 곁들이다 garnish fish with a green vegetable ② [일을] do all at once ; accompany
곁땀 perspiration〔sweat〕 from the armpit ¶ 곁땀이 나다 sweat under the arm
곁마름 an assistant to the supervisor of a tenant farm
곁마부 ―馬夫 an assistant groom
곁말 [빗댄말] an allusive remark (with a bantering simile or metaphor) ; [은어] an argot ; a jargon ; a lingo ; a slang
곁매 an attack by an outsider in an exchange of blows ; blows in assistance of one party in a fighting ; a by-blow ¶ 곁매질하다 deal blows 《at a person》 to help 《the other in a fight》 ; give a by-blow
곁방 ―房 ① [협방] a side chamber ; a small room attached to the main one ② [셋방] a rented room
곁방살이 ―房― living in a rented room ━하다 live in a rented room
곁방석 ―方席 one who frequents the salon of an influential man ; a sycophant ; a toady
곁부축 ━하다 [걸음을] hold 《a person》 under the arms to help walking ; [일을] help ; assist 《a person in doing》 ; back 《a person》 up 《with deeds, with words》
곁붙이 distant relatives
곁뿌리 〖식물〗 a lateral root (측근) ; a rootlet
곁상 ―床 a small (dinner) table set at the side of the main one ; a side table
곁쇠 a passkey ; a duplicate key ; [도둑의] a skeleton key ; a master-key ; a false key ¶ 곁쇠질하다 unlock with a passkey
곁순 ―筍 sprouts〔buds〕 from the side ; extra sprouts〔buds〕 ; lateral buds
곁쐐기 a side wedge ; an accessory 〔additional〕 wedge
곁자리 a side seat ; seats on either side
곁줄기 a side stalk
곁집 the house next door ; an adjoining house ; a neighboring house ¶ 곁집 사람 a next-door neighbor // 곁집에 살다

live next-door
곁쪽 close relatives
곁채 an annex 《of a house》; an attached house; a shed
계 戒, 誡 ① [계율] a precept; a command; an admonition; an injunction ② [불교] Buddhist commandments
계 契 a mutual-aid society; a credit union; a mutual benevolence group; a mutual financing association ¶ 계를 조직하다 organize a fraternity
계 階 official rank; a grade
계 係 [담당] charge; duty; [직제] a subsection 《in charge of》; a desk; [사람] a clerk〔an official〕 in charge
접대— a person in charge of reception
접수— a reception clerk; a receptionist
출납— (부서) the cashier's section; (사람) a teller 《미》; a cashier 《영》
계 計 [합계] the total; the sum total; [합계하여] in total; in all; all told; [계획] a plan; a scheme; [계략] a plot; a stratagem; a trick ¶ 계 3,000원정 total 3,000 *won*∥국가 백년의 계 a permanent national policy
계 系 〚수학〛 a corollary
-계 計 [계기] a meter; a gauge
온도— a thermometer 우량(雨量)— a raingauge
-계 系 [계통] a system; [혈통] a line; lineage; an origin; [당파] a faction; a clique; a party; a group ¶ 라틴계의 국민 people of Latin origin∥S계 극장 the S theater chain∥Y계의 정치가 a politician of the Y faction∥한국계 미국인 a Korean-American; an American of Korean extraction〔ancestry, descent〕
공산당— 신문 a Communist-influenced 〔-inclined〕 paper 피린— 약품 pyrene medicine
-계 界 a world; circles; quarters; a kingdom ¶ 각계의 명사 distinguished figures of all spheres of social activities
동물〔식물, 광물〕— the animal〔vegetable, mineral〕 kingdom
-계 屆 a notice; a report
전출— a moving-out notification 출항— a notice of clearance
계간 季刊 (a) quarterly publication ¶ 계간의 published〔issued〕 quarterly
계간 鷄姦 (anal) sodomy; buggery; pederasty **—하다** commit sodomy ¶ 계간하는 사람 a sodomite; a bugger; a pederast
계간지 季刊誌 a quarterly (magazine)
계계승승 繼繼承承 —하다 succeed generation to generation; be inherited generation after generation
계고 戒告 a warning; a caution; a notification **—하다** warn; give a warning; caution; notify ¶ 그는 직무 태만으로 계고 처분 받았다 He was reprimanded for neglecting his duty.
— 조치 a measure of admonition
계고 稽古 [옛일의] study of antiquities; [공부] study〔learning〕 of literatures **—하다** study antiquities〔literatures〕
계고장 戒告狀 〚종교〛 a monition; 〚법〛 a letter of notification
계곡 溪谷 a valley; a gorge; a glen; a ravine; a dale; a canyon
계관 鷄冠 ① [볏] a cockscomb; a (cock's) crest ② [맨드라미] a cockscomb plant
—초 a cockscomb —화(花) a cockscomb flower
계관 桂冠 a laurel (wreath)
계관석 鷄冠石 〚광물〛 realgar; sandarac
계관 시인 桂冠詩人 a (poet) laureate
†계교 計巧 a scheme; a stratagem; an artifice; a plot; a trick; a will; a design ¶ 계교를 꾸미다 devise a scheme; hatch a plot; invent a trick; scheme a stratagem∥계교 부리지 마라 Don't play a trick.
계구우후 鷄口牛後 Better be the head of an ass〔a dog〕 than the tail of a horse〔a lion〕.
계군일학 鷄群一鶴 ⇨ 군계(群鷄) (—일학)
계궁역진 計窮力盡 —하다 exhaust one's resources; come to the end of one's tether〔wit and strength〕
†계급 階級 [신분] class; estate; caste; [등급] rank; grade; [목사 따위의] order ¶ 계급적 차별 class distinctions ∥계급을 만들다 set up classes∥계급을 타파하다 level classes; break down the barrier of classes∥계급이 강등되다 be degraded; be reduced to a lower grade; be demoted 《미》∥모든 계급의 사람들 people of all classes; [각방면의] men and women in all walks of life∥저 군인의 계급은 무엇입니까 What rank is that soldier?/ What is that soldier's rank?
— 감정 class〔caste〕 feeling — 사회 a hierarchical society — 심리 class psychology — 조직 class organization —층 classes; social strata 무산〔유산〕 — the proletariat〔propertied class, bourgeoisie〕 상〔중, 하〕류 — the upper 〔middle, lower〕 classes 전문 직업 — professional classes 지식 — the intellectual〔educated〕 class; the intellectuals; the intelligentsia; the highbrows 《구》
계급 독재 階級獨裁 class dictatorship
계급 문학 階級文學 proletarian literature
계급 의식 階級意識 class consciousness; a sense of class distinction ¶ 계급 의식이 있는 class-conscious
계급장 階級章 a badge〔an insignia〕 of rank; an ensign
계급 제도 階級制度 a class〔caste〕 sys-

tem
계급 타파 階級打破 class leveling ; demolishing the distinction of classes
계급 투쟁 階級鬪爭 a struggle of classes ; a class strife〔struggle〕
계기 契機 [기회] a moment ; an opportunity ; a chance ; [시초] a start ; a beginning ¶ 이것을 계기로 하여 taking this opportunity ; upon this opportunity ; with this as a momentum // 이탈리아의 참전을 계기로 하여 with Italy's entry into war // 이것이 그의 성공의 계기가 되었다 This paved the way for his success.
계기 計器 a meter ; a gauge ; a scale ; an instrument
—등 [가스·물 따위의] a gauge lamp **—용 변압기** a voltage〔potential《미》〕transformer **—용 변압 변류기(變流器)** a combined voltage current transformer **— 정수(定數)** the calibrating〔meter〕constant **가정용 —** a house-service meter **공업용〔항해용〕 —** industrial〔nautical〕instruments **항공 —** an aircraft instrument
계기 비행 計器飛行 an instrument〔a blind〕flight **—하다** fly〔go〕on instruments
계기 착륙 計器着陸 an instrument〔a blind〕landing
계기판 計器板 an instrument〔a gauge〕board ; a dashboard《구》
†계단 階段 [층층대] (a set of) stairs ; a staircase ; a stairway ; [순서] steps ¶ 긴 계단을 올라가다 go up a long flight of steps〔stairs〕// 계단에서 미끄러지다 slip on the stairs
— 격자(格子) 〖광학〗 echelon grating **— 교실** a theater **— 농업** solid farming **—실(室)** a staircase ; a stair hall **—식 객석** seats arranged in tiers ; tiers of seats ; tiered seats **—식 농장** a terraced farm ; terraced fields **—통**〖건축〗 a stairwell **— 현상** 〖의학〗 a staircase phenomenon **나선(螺旋) —** a spiral〔corkscrew〕staircase ; a winding stair **뒷—** a back stair **만곡(彎曲) —** a geometrical staircase
계대 繼代 succeeding a generation ; succeeding《one's father》**—하다** succeed《one's father》
계도 系圖 genealogy ; lineage ; pedigree ; a genealogical table〔tree〕; a family tree ⇨ 계보(系譜)
—학 genealogy **— 학자** a genealogist
계도 啓導 guidance ; leading ; enlightenment ; illumination **—하다** guide ; lead ; enlighten ; illuminate
계동 季冬 December of the lunar calendar ; late winter
계란 鷄卵 an egg ; a hen's egg ⇨ 달걀
— 덮밥 a bowl of rice topped with scrambled eggs
계란지 鷄卵紙 〖사진〗 albumenized paper
계략 計略 [책략] a stratagem ; a trick ; a ruse ; an artifice ; [음모] a plot ; a design ; [계획] a plan ; a scheme ; [함정] a trap ; a snare

> 참고 **stratagem** 계략에 의하여 자기의 목적을 달성하고 상대방의 목적 달성을 제지하려고 하는 계획 **artifice** 타인을 속여서 자기의 목적을 달성하려고 하는 계략 **ruse** 자기의 목적을 상대방에게 감추고 뒤에서 교묘히 성취시키려고 하는 계획〔음모〕

¶ 계략에 능한 사람 a resourceful man // 깊은 계략 dark designs // 계략을 꾸미다 work out a scheme ; lay〔form〕plans ; devise a stratagem // 계략을 간파하다 see through another's design // 계략에 빠지다 fall into a trap ; be entrapped ; fall a prey to《a person's》plot ; step into a trap laid by《a person》// 계략을 쓰다 use a stratagem〔ruse〕// 계략에 빠뜨리다 entrap ; ensnare // 그는 무엇인가 비열한 계략을 꾸미고 있는 것 같다 I suspect he has some sort of dirty trick up his sleeve. // 나는 너의 계략에 넘어가지 않는다 None of your tricks.
계량 計量 [무게의] weighing ; [길이·부피의] measuring **—하다** measure ; weigh ; gauge
— 경제학 econometrics **— 경제학자** an econometrician **—자** a gauger **— 장치** a register **—컵** a measuring cup **— 탱크** a measuring tank
계량기 計量器 a weighing machine ; a gauge ; scales ; a measure
가스 — a gasometer **수도 —** a water gauge〔meter〕
계루 係累, 繫累 ① [처자 따위] dependents ; (family) ties ; encumbrances ② [연루] implication ; involvement ; complicity **—하다** involve ; implicate ; encumber ; tie《a person》down《to a job》¶ 계루가 없다 have no dependents〔ties〕; [독신이다] be unmarried〔single〕
계류 溪流 a mountain stream〔torrent〕
계류 繫留 mooring **—하다** moor《to, at》; lie ¶ 애드벌룬을 옥상에 계류하다 moor an ad balloon to the top of a building // (배가) 계류 중이다 be riding at her moorings // 계류중인 문제 a pending〔outstanding〕problem ; a question at issue // 배는 부두〔부표〕에 계류되어 있다 The ship is moored at the pier〔to a buoy〕. // 그 사건은 아직도 법원에 계류중이다 The case is still pending in court.
— 기뢰 a moored mine **— 부표(浮標)** a mooring buoy **—삭(索)** a mooring cable ; an anchoring rope **—선(船)** a

moored vessel ; a vessel on the berth —장(場) moorings ; a berthage — 장치 mooring gear —탑〔주(柱)〕 an anchor mast〔post〕

계륵 鷄肋 ① [닭 갈비뼈] chicken ribs ; [비유적] something that one hesitates to give up even though it is of little interest ② [허약] weakness ; feebleness

계리사 計理士 a chartered accountant 《영》; a certified public accountant 《미》

계림 鷄林 Korea ; the Land of Morning Calm

계면 界面 interface
— 장력 〖물리〗 interfacial tension — 화학 surface chemistry — 활성제 a surface active agent

계명 戒名 a Buddhist name (생전의) ; a posthumous Buddhist name (사후의) ¶ 계명을 붙이다 give a posthumous Buddhist name 《to the deceased》

*계명 誡命 〖종교〗 commandments
십— the Ten Commandments ; the Decalogue

계명 鷄鳴 the crowing of a cock〔a rooster〕; cockcrow(ing) 《영》; rooster-crow (ing) 《미》

계명성 啓明星 〖천문〗 Venus ; the morning star ; Lucifer

계명워리 a flirt ; a minx ; a hussy ; a flapper ; a wayward girl

계모 繼母 a stepmother

*⁎계몽 啓蒙 enlightenment ; education ; illumination ; instruction 《of the ignorant》 —하다 enlighten ; educate ; illuminate ; edify ¶ 계몽적인 enlightening ; educative ; [초보의]elementary
—기〔시대〕 the period of enlightenment —대 an enlightenment squad

계몽 문학 啓蒙文學 literature of enlight enment

계몽 사상 啓蒙思想 ⇨ 계몽 철학

계몽 운동 啓蒙運動 an edification〔educational, enlightenment〕 movement ; a campaign for enlightenment ; [18세기 유럽의] the Enlightenment

계몽주의 啓蒙主義 illuminism

계몽 철학 啓蒙哲學 philosophy of enlightenment

계박 繫泊 mooring —하다 moor 《at, to》 ⇨ 계류

*계발 啓發 enlightenment ; illumination ; edification ; education ; improvement ; development —하다 develop ; improve ; enlighten ; edify ; educate ¶ 계발적인 enlightening ; edifying // 계발적 교육 developmental education // 지능을 계발하다 improve one's mind ; develop one's intellect // 나는 그 책을 읽고 크게 계발되는 바가 있었다 The book has enlightened me on many points.
—자 a developer

계방 季方 a man's younger brother

계방 癸方 north-by-northeast

계보 系譜 genealogy ; lineage ; pedigree ; [표] a genealogical table〔chart〕; a family tree ¶ 한국 문학의 계보 genealogy of Korean literature // 계보를 조사하다 look into 《a person's》 genealogy〔pedigree〕 // 그는 계보가 좋은 사람이다 He is a man of good birth./He comes of good stock.

계보 季報 a quarterly (bulletin)

계보학 系譜學 genealogy
—자 a genealogist

계부 季父 the youngest brother of one's father

계부 繼父 a stepfather

계사 繫辭 〖문법〗 a copula ¶ 계사적 접속사 a copulative conjunction

계사 鷄舍 a henhouse ⇨ 닭장

계삭 繫索 moorings ; a fast ; a lasher ¶ 이물〔고물〕 계삭 a head〔stern〕 fast

†계산 計算 calculation ; computation ; reckoning ; figure work —하다 calculate ; compute ; reckon ; figure out ; count ; [합계하다] add up

> 참고 **calculate** 산술적으로 계산해서 결과를 나타냄 **compute** 비교적 간단한 계산으로 따라서 그 결과도 명확하게 나타내는 것을 기대할 수 있다 **estimate** 미리 계산한다는 뜻으로서 계산적 결과를 구한다 **reckon** 구어로서 compute보다 더욱 간단한 계산이다

¶ 이자를 계산하다 compute interest // 계산이 틀리다 calculate wrongly ; miscalculate ; make a mistake in calculation // 거리에 따라 계산하다 reckon by distance // 계산에 넣지 않다 leave 《a thing》 out of account // 계산에 넣다 take 《a thing》 into account ; count 《a thing》 in // 계산에 능하다〔서툴다〕 He is good〔poor〕 at figures. // 비용이 얼마인지 계산해 주시오 Figure out how much it will cost. // 계산은 내게 달아주시오 Put this on my bill./Charge it to my account. // 내가 잘못 계산한 것 같다 I seem to have miscalculated. // 그가 하는 짓은 모두 계산되어 있다 Everything he does is studied. // 그들에 대한 것은 계산에 넣을 필요없다 You need not take them into account. // 계산은 내가 하겠다 I pick up the tap〔check, bill〕.
— 도표 a nomogram —법 a system of measuring —척(尺) a slide rule ; a slipstick 《미·속》 —표 a (ready) reckoner ; a calculating table — 화폐 money of account

*⁎계산기 計算器 a calculating〔counting〕 machine ; an adding machine ; an adder ; a calculator ; a computer
— 공업 the computing industry — 회사 a computer company 고정(固定) 프로그램 — a fixed program computer

동기(同期)〔비동기〕 — a synchronous〔an asynchronous〕 computer 디지탈〔계수형〕 — a digital computer 복합(複合) — a hybrid computer 상사형(相似形) — an analog computer 자기(自己) — a comptograph 전자 — an electronic computer〔brain〕 전자관식 자동 고속도 — a radac《*ra*pid *d*igital *a*utomatic *c*omputation》

계산서 計算書 an account ; a check ; a bill ; (a statement of) accounts ; an account statement ; a tally sheet〔card〕《미》¶ 계산서를 가져오시오 Check〔Bill〕, please./ Fetch〔Get〕 me the bill. // 계산서는 내가 처리할게 Let me take care of the tab.

계산 착오 計算錯誤 miscalculation ; an error〔a mistake〕 in calculation ¶ 계산 착오를 하다 calculate wrongly ; miscalculate ; make an error in calculation

계상 計上 —하다 [충당하다] appropriate《a sum》 for ; put in the budget ; [계산하다] add〔sum〕 up ¶ 이 계획을 위하여 100만원을 예산에 계상하다 appropriate a million *won* for this project in the budget

계색 戒色 sexual abstinence ; continence —하다 abstain from sex ; lead a continent life

계선 繫船 mooring ; [배] a laid-up〔an idle〕 ship —하다 moor a ship ; [짐이 없어서] lay up a ship
—구(具) moorings —닻 a mooring anchor —독 a wet dock —료(料) quayage ; mooring charges — 말뚝 a dolphin — 매듭 a bowline knot — 번호 a berth number — 부표(浮標) a mooring buoy —삭(索) a mooring line —소 moorings ; a berthage ; a moorage —주(柱) a mooring post —환(環) a mooring ring

†**계속** 繼續 continuation ; continuance ; [경신] renewal —하다 continue ; maintain ; go〔keep〕 on with ; keep up ; [경신하다] renew ; [계속되다] continue ; be continuous ; go on ; last(지속하다) ; follow ¶ 계속적(으로) continual(ly) ; uninterrupted(ly) ; continuous(ly) // 계속해서 in succession ; without interruption ; continuously // 5년간 계속해서 for five years together〔running〕 // 며칠이나 계속하여 for days on end // 세 번 계속해서 three times in succession〔in a row〕 // 계속되는 불황 a continuous recession // 사업을 계속하다 go〔keep〕 on with one's work // 비가 계속해서 내리다 keep on raining // 계속해서 서 있다 stay on one's feet // 계속해서 울다 keep on crying // 여행을 계속하다 continue〔proceed on〕 one's journey // (기존) 방침대로 계속하다 continue on one's course // 수업을 계속하다 continue at school // 이야기를 계속하다 continue to talk ; go on talking // 담화를 길게 계속하다 keep up a long conversation // 눈이 계속해서 내렸다 It continued snowing. // 그는 계속해서 걸었다 He walked on and on. // 밤은 낮의 계속이다 Night follows〔succeeds〕 day. // 전쟁은 4년간 계속됐다 The war lasted four years. // 그 계약은 계속하기로 되어 있다 The contract is to run. // 이 길은 공원에 계속되고 있다 This road leads〔goes〕 to the park. // 4면에서 계속 Continued from page 4. // 6면으로 계속 Continued on page 6. // 뒷면에 계속 Over./P.T.O.《Please turn over.》// 다음 호에 계속 To be continued. // 그는 오랫동안 일을 계속했다 He continued working for a long time. // 그의 연설은 한시간 동안 계속되었다 His speech continued for an hour.
— 기간 a period of duration —범(犯) a continuing crime —비(費) a continuing expenditure — 비행 an endurance flight ; a non-stop flight — 사업 a continued program — 상영물 〖영화〗 a holdover — 일수 running days — 주문 a continuation order — 항해 a continuous voyage

계속 繫屬 〖법〗 pendency ¶ 소송의 계속 중에는 during the pendency of action ; when an action is pending

계수 季嫂 a younger brother's wife ; a sister-in-law

계수 計數 calculation ; computation ; figures —하다 number ; count ; calculate ; compute ¶ 계수적으로 numerically // 계수에 밝다 He is good at figures.
— 데이터 enumeration data — 장치(裝置) a scaler — 카드 a tally card —형 전자 계산기 a digital computer — 회로 a scaling circuit 노동 — a labor coefficient 전자식 —기 an electronic counter

계수 係數 〖수학〗 a coefficient ; 〖물리〗 a coefficient ; a modulus ; a factor
— 현상 factorial development — 회로 a counter〔counting〕 circuit 노동 — a labor coefficient 문자 — literal coefficient 미분 — a differential coefficient 분리 — 〖화학〗 a separation factor 숫자 — a numeral coefficient 엥겔 — Engel's coefficient 연결 — a coefficient of coupling 저항〔회전〕 유도 — a coefficient of resistance〔rotary〕 derivatives 증발 — the evaporation factor 탄성(彈性) — the modulus of elasticity 팽창〔수축〕 — a coefficient of expansion〔contraction〕 화학 — a chemical factor 흡수(吸收)〔연결〕 — a coefficient of absorption〔coupling〕

계수관 計數管 [방사능의] a counter
—열(列) a counter array

계수기 計數器 a calculating〔counting〕 machine ; a comptometer

계수나무 桂樹— 〖식물〗 a (Chinese)

cinnamon (tree) ; a cassia (bark) ; Cinnamonum cassia (학명)

계수법 **繼受法** 〖법〗 an adopted law

계술 **繼述** **—하다** succeed to 《one's father's profession》; take over 《one's father's work》; follow one's father's profession ; expound the doctrine of one's master〔predecessor〕

계승 **階乘** 〖수학〗 a factorial

계승 **繼承** succession ; accession ; inheritance **—하다** succeed to ; accede to ; inherit ; take over ; come into ¶ 왕위〔권리와 의무〕를 계승하다 succeed to the throne〔rights and duties〕

— 사채(社債) assumed bonds

계승자 **繼承者** a successor 《to the throne》; an heir 《of liberty》

왕위 — a successor to the throne

계시 an apprentice ¶ 계시살이를 하다 serve one's apprenticeship with〔under〕

계시 **啓示** revelation ; apocalypse **—하다** reveal ¶ 신의 계시 a revelation of God // 요한계시록 The Revelation (of St. John the Divine) // 계시를 받다 receive a divine revelation〔message〕

— 문학 apocalyptic ; apocalypses **— 종교** a revealed religion

계시 **癸時** the 2nd of the 24 hour periods 《0 : 30～1 : 30 a. m.》

계시 **計時** clocking **—하다** [경기 따위에서] check time ; time

—기 a timer **—원(員)** a timekeeper **전자(電子) —** (an) electronic clocking

계시다 《someone esteemed》 be ; stay ; be located ¶ 누님은 댁에 계십니까 Is your sister in ? // (가시지 말고) 좀 더 계십시오 Stay a little longer. // 한국에 얼마나 계셨습니까 How long have you been in Korea ?

계심 **戒心** caution ; prudence ; precaution

계씨 **季氏** 《a person's》 younger brother

계압기 **計壓器** a manometer

†**계약** **契約** a contract ; a compact ; a covenant ; an agreement (협정) ; [매매 계약] a bargain **—하다** contract 《an agreement》; agree ; make〔enter into〕 a contract〔an agreement〕 《with》 ¶ 계약 중이다 be under contract 《to build a ship》// 계약의 만기 expiration〔termination〕 of a contract // 계약의 파기 annulment〔termination〕 of a contract // 계약의 연장 extension of a contract // 계약을 취소하다 cancel〔break off〕 a contract // 계약(기한)이 끝나다 the contract runs out // 계약을 이행하다 fulfill〔carry out〕 a contract // 계약을 지키다 abide by a contract // 계약을 위반하다 break a contract // 이 계약은 유효〔무효〕이다 This contract holds good〔will not stand〕. // …와 구두 계약을 하다 make a verbal〔an oral〕 contract (on) with // 그는 투수로서 이 구단과 계약했다 He signed (on) with this team as a pitcher. // 그 건설 회사는 공사 계약을 따냈다 The construction company has received the contract for the construction work. // 그는 1톤당 만원에 시멘트 납부의 계약을 했다 He made a contract to supply cement at 10,000 *won* a ton. // 1년 안에 준공하겠다는 계약을 맺었다 He has bound himself to complete it in a year.

— 가격 a contract price **— 갱신** renewal of a contract **—고(高)** the contract amount **— 기한** the term of contract **— 기한 초과 일수** demurrage days **— 노동** contract labor **— 당사자** contracting parties **— 도면** a contract plan **— 문서** a charter **—법** the law of contract **— 불이행** nonfulfilment of a contract **—설** the theory of social contract **— 이민** indentured immigrants **—자** a contractor ; a contracting party (일방) ; the parties to a contract (쌍방) **— 조항** contract clause **— 체결** conclusion of contract **가(假)—** a provisional contract **납품 —** a supply contract **단기 —** a short-term contract **단순〔약식〕 —** a simple contract **명시(明示) —** an express promise **무조건 —** a bare contract **불법 —** an illegal contract **비밀 —** a secret agreement (made in connection with a formal contract) **선물(先物) —** 〖상업〗 a forward contract **수의 —** a private contract **쌍무 —** a bilateral contract **용역 —** a service contract **유효 —** a valid contract **장기 —** a long-term contract **적법 —** a legal contract **전세 —** a lease ; a charter **판매 —** a sales commitment **하청 —** a subcontract

계약금 earnest (money) ; a deposit ; bargain money ; down〔initial〕 payment ¶ 계약금은 얼마나 내야 합니까 How much will the earnest money deposit be ?

계약 보증금 **契約保證金** a contract deposit

계약서 **契約書** a (written) contract ; a contract document ; a deed of contract ; an agreement ; a bond ; [상업] an indenture ¶ 계약서에 명기하다 specify in a contract note

계약 위반 **契約違反** breach of contract

계약 조건 **契約條件** terms〔conditions〕 of〔under〕 a contract ; a contract basis

계약 해제 **契約解除** cancellation of a contract

계엄 **戒嚴** guarding against danger **—하다** guard more strictly ; exercise vigilance over

계엄령 **戒嚴令** (the) martial law ¶ 계엄령을 선포〔해제〕하다 proclaim〔lift, withdraw〕 martial law // 전국이 계엄령 아래에 있다 The whole country is under martial law.

계엄 사령관 戒嚴司令官 the chief martial law administrator
계엄 사령부 戒嚴司令部 the Martial Law Enforcement Headquarters
계열 系列 [생물] an order ; a system ; [당파] a faction ; a clique ; a party ; [물리] a series ; [산업] interrelationship 《among industries》 ; [대학] department ¶ 자유당 계열의 정치가 a politician of the Liberal Party // 대학의 계열별 모집 admission of students to a university by department // 기업의 계열화 the systematization of enterprises
— 기업 interrelated enterprises — 회사 the affiliates ; the allied enterprises ; an affiliated company ; a subsidiary company
계원 係員 a person in charge ; a section man ; a clerk
—석(席) a staff enclosure 접수 — an information clerk ; a receptionist
계원 契員 a member of a credit union 〔loan club, mutual-aid association〕
계월 桂月 the moon ; [음력 8월] August of the lunar year
계육 鷄肉 chicken(-meat) ; fowl
계율 戒律 religious commandments ; Buddhist precepts ¶ 계율을 지키다〔어기다〕 observe〔violate〕 the commandments
계음 戒飮 moderation in drinking ; temperance —하다 drink with moderation ; abstain〔refrain〕 from drinking
계인 契印 a tally (impression) ; a joint seal ; the (impression of) a seal over the joint of two papers ¶ 계인을 찍다 affix a seal over two edges ; impress a seal over the joint of two papers
계장 係長 a chief 《*pl.* ~s》 ; a chief clerk
계쟁 係爭 dispute ; contention ; controversy ; [소송] a law suit ¶ 계쟁 중인 문제 a question at issue ; a pending problem ; an issue in dispute // 계쟁 중이다 be in dispute ; be pending in court
— 문제 a matter in dispute —물(건) property under dispute — 사건 a contentious case — 사실 a fact in dispute ; an item of controversy
계쟁점 係爭點 (the point at) issue ; the disputed point
계전 契錢 an installment payment (to one's mutual finance association)
계전기 繼電器 a relay
†계절 季節 a season ; the time of the year ¶ 계절의〔적인〕 seasonal ; in season // 계절에 불구하고 in all seasons ; all the year (round) ; in and out of season // 이 벚꽃은 계절적으로 좀 이르다 The cherry blossoms came out a little too early for the season.
— 고용 seasonal employment — 노동자 a seasonal laborer ; a gandy dancer 《미·속》 —물 seasonal goods ; things in season — 변동 〖경제〗 a seasonal variation — 산업 a seasonal industry — 요리 dishes of the season — 조정 〖경제〗 correction for seasonal fluctuations ; seasonal adjustment — 지수 〖경제〗 a seasonal index
계절감 季節感 a sense of the season
계절풍 季節風 a periodic wind ; a seasonal wind ; a monsoon (인도양의)
계정 計定 an account 《a/c》 ¶ …의 계정에 넣다 place〔pass〕 to the account of. . .
— 과목 a title of account 당좌〔대체〕 — a current〔postal transfer〕 account
⁑계제 階梯 [단계] a step ; a phase ; a stage ; a gradation ; the course〔process〕 《of things》 ; [기회] an opportunity ; an occasion ; a chance ¶ 이 계제에 with this opportunity // 계제가 나쁜 untimely ; ill-timed // 그럴 계제가 아니다 It is not the time to 《do a thing》. // 계제가 되면 찾아 주십시오 Please call on me if you happen to come this way.
계좌 計座 an account ¶ (은행에) 계좌를 트다 open an account (with a bank) // 계좌 번호가 어떻게 됩니까 What's the account number?
대체(對替) — a postal transfer account
계주 契主 the organizer of a mutual finance association〔credit union〕
계주 戒酒 moderation in drinking
*계주 경기 繼走競技 a relay (race) ¶ 400미터 계주 경기 a 400 meter relay
계집 a woman ; a female ; the fair sex ; [아내] one's wife ; [정부] a mistress ; a concubine ¶ 계집을 얻다 get a mistress ; keep a mistress〔concubine〕 // 계집을 버리다 discard〔desert, leave〕 one's wife // 계집이라면 사족을 못 쓰는 남자 a man who has a weakness for woman
계집 입 싼 것 (속담) A woman's tongue wags like a lamb's tail.
†계집아이 a girl ; a lass
계집질 running after women ; whoring ; debauchery —하다 wench ; whore ; dangle after women
계차 階次 the order of rank
계책 計策 a stratagem ; an artifice ; a design ; a trick ; a plan ; a scheme ¶ 계책을 쓰다 adopt〔use〕 a stratagem // 남의 계책을 알아차리다 see through another's design // 계책을 생각해 내다 devise〔think out, work out〕 a plan ; draw up a plan ; invent a scheme
계천 溪川 a stream ; a brook ; a rivulet
계추 季秋 September of the lunar year
계추 桂秋 August of the lunar year
계춘 季春 March of the lunar year ; [만춘] a late spring
계출 屆出 a report ; a notification ; [등

록]registration —하다 report ; notify ; give notice of ; send in a report ; register ¶ 경찰에 계출하다 report to the police

계측 計測 measuring ; measurement —하다 measure ; [토지 따위를] survey
— 공학(工學) instrumentation engineering — 기학(器學) instrumentology —화(化) instrumentation

계층 階層 a class ; a social stratum ; a level

*__계통 系統__ a system ; [계보] lineage ; pedigree ; a family line ; [당파] a party ; a clique ¶ 계통적인 systematic ; methodical // 계통적으로 systematically ; methodically // 계통적으로 조사하다 make a systematic investigation of 《an affair》 // 계통이 끊기다 one's line has died out // 계통을 잇다 [후예가] be descended from ; [기질·병 따위가] be hereditary ; run in the family // 계통을 세우다 systematize // 계통이 서지 않다 be unsystematic // 케네디 계통의 사람이다 He is of Kennedy party〔group〕. // 그의 강연은 계통이 서지 않았다 There was no system in his lecture.
—도(圖) a distribution diagram ; a genealogy — 발생론 phylogeny 근육 — the muscular system 명령 — a chain of command 생식 — the reproductive system 소화 — the digestive system 신경 — the nervous system

계통 繼統 succession to the throne —하다 succeed to the throne

계피 桂皮 cinnamon (bark) ; cassia bark
—산(酸) cinnamic acid — 산염(酸鹽) a cinnamate —수(水) cinnamon water ; aqua cinnamon —유(油) cinnamon oil

계핏가루 桂皮— cinnamon powder

계하 季夏 June of the lunar year

계하 啓下 —하다 obtain royal sanction 《for》 ; be sanctioned by the king

계하 階下 place below the stairs ¶ 계하에 down the stairs〔stone steps〕

계한 界限 [경계] a boundary ; a border ; [한계] a limit ; limitation ; a margin

계행 戒行 〖불교〗 penance ; religious austerities ; ascetic practice

계화 桂花 cassia flowers

†__계획 計劃__ a plan ; a design ; a project ; a scheme ; [의도] an intention ; [예정] a program(me) ; arrangement

> 참고 **scheme**은 이익을 얻기 위한 계획 따라서 사악한 경우가 많다 **project**는 머리 속에서 생각한 계획을 말한다 **design**은 어떤 목적을 수행하기 위한 상세한 고안·준비를 말한다 **plan**은 어떤 일을 하기에 앞서 하는 궁리를 말하며 조직적인 것이 특색이다

—하다 plan ; make〔form〕 a plan ; project ; intend ; contemplate ¶ 계획적인 planned ; premeditated ; deliberate ; intentional // 계획적으로 intentionally ; deliberately ; on purpose // 계획대로 as planned〔scheduled〕 ; as previously arranged // 5년 계획으로 on a five-year plan〔program〕 // 장래의 계획을 세우다 make〔draw up〕 plans for the future // 계획 중이다 It is under consideration. /We have it in contemplation. // 나는 도미할 계획이다 I plan to go to America. // 하루의 계획은 이른 아침에 세워야 한다 The day's plan should be made out early in the morning. // 그는 매사에 계획성이 있다 He always plans ahead. // 강당 건설이 계획중에 있다 Construction of a hall is under consideration.
— 단면 〖토목〗 a designed〔planned〕 section —도(圖) a scheme drawing — 목표 the planned goal — 생산 planned production —선 a projected line (철도 따위의) — 설계도 planning drawing — 입안자 a program planner —자 a projector ; a promoter ; a planner (도시 계획 따위) 기초 — a ground plan 단기〔장기〕 — a short-〔long-〕range plan

계획 경제 計劃經濟 planned economy

계획성 計劃性 《lack》 planning ¶ 계획성이 있는 사람 a man of planning quality

계획안 計劃案 a schedule ; a plan ; a blueprint

곗돈 契— money for〔from, owned by〕 the mutual assistance society〔the credit union〕 ; lodge money

곗술 契— wine provided by a mutual financing association
곗술에 낯내기 속담 Playing the big shot with other people's money

고[1] [끈·옷고름 따위의] a loop 《of string, of ribbon》 ; string〔ribbon〕 ties

고[2] [그] that (little) ; the same ¶ 고 놈 that (little) man // 고 모양이다 be just the same as before ; that is (just) the way it is

-고 ① [대등 연결] and (also) ; as well as ; and then ; both ; as well ¶ 정직하고 근면한 (both) honest and industrious // 바쁘고 피곤하다 be busy and tired // 그는 지식도 있고 경험도 있다 He has experience as well as knowledge.
② [종속의 연결] to do (부정사 용법으로) ; doing〔having done〕 (분사구 용법으로) ¶ 간다고 약속하다 promise to go // 집에 가고 싶다 I want to go home. // 그녀는 아들을 보내고 몹시 울었다 Having seen her son off, she cried bitterly.
③ [진행·완료] be doing ; have done ¶ 나는 책을 읽고 있다 I am reading a book now. // 저녁밥을 먹고 났다 I have just finished my dinner.

고 高 ① [높이] height ② [접미] amount ; sum
매상— the amount sold ; the sales ; the proceeds **생산—** an output ; a yield ; a production **수확—** the yield ; the crop

†**고 故** [이미 죽은] the late ; the lamented ; the deceased ¶ 고 김동원 씨 the late Mr. *Kim Tong-won* ; Mr. *Kim Tong-won* of blessed〔glorious, happy〕memory

고 稿 a manuscript ⇨ 원고

고 苦 [고통] pain ; suffering ; [고난] hardship ; [곤란] difficulty ; trouble

고 庫 [곳간] a warehouse ; a storehouse ; [차고] a garage

고 鼓 a drum

고 膏 plaster ; paste ; ointment
반창— a (medicinal) plaster ; a sticking plaster ; an adhesive plaster

고가 古架 an old song〔poem〕

고가 古家 an old house〔building〕; [폐가] a deserted house ; a dilapidated cottage

고가 高價 a high price ; costliness ¶ 고가의 dear ; expensive ; costly ; high-priced // 고가로 팔다 sell《a thing》at a high price // 고본 고가 매입함 "Second-hand books bought at good prices."
—품 a costly article ; a high-priced article

고가 高架 an elevated construction
—교 an elevated bridge ; an overpass ; a viaduct **— 전차** an elevated electric car

고가 故家 an old〔ancient〕family ; a family of old standing
— 대족(大族) a family with illustrious〔distinguished〕history

고가 雇價 wages

고가 도로 高架道路 a high level road ; an elevated road ; an overpass《미》; a flyover《영》

고가선 高架線 [철도 따위] an overhead〔elevated〕line ; [전선] overhead wires〔wiring〕

고가 철도 高架鐵道 an elevated railroad〔railway《미》〕; the L《미·구》; an overhead railway《영》
— 열차 an elevated train《미》; an L train《미·구》; an overhead railway train《영》

고각 高閣 a tall〔lofty, high〕building ; an edifice

고각 高角 a high〔wide, vertical〕angle ; an altitude
— 발사 a vertical〔a high angle〕fire **— 방사(放射)** 〖전기〗 high-angle radiation
— 측량(測量) altimetry

고각 鼓角 drums and bugles〔trumpets〕

고각포 高角砲 a high-angle gun ; [대공포] an anti-aircraft gun ; an A. A. gun《속》

고간 苦諫 an earnest admonition〔request〕 **—하다** earnestly admonish《a person not to do》

고갈 枯渴 [물의] drying up ; [자원 따위의] exhaustion ; drain **—하다** be dried up ; run dry ; be parched ; [자원 따위가] be〔become〕exhausted ; be drained ¶ 인재의 고갈 a dearth〔lack〕of talent // 그 전쟁은 국가의 인적, 재정적 자원을 고갈시켰다 The war drained the country of its men and money. // 그의 사상은 고갈되었다 He has run dry of all ideas.

고감도 필름 高感度— a fast film

고개 ① the nape〔scruff〕《of the neck》; [머리] the head ¶ 고개를 가로 흔들다 shake one's head ; refuse ; shake one's head no // 그는 마침내 고개를 끄덕였다 At long last, he nodded his assent.
② [언덕·산의] the pass《of a mountain》; a ridge ¶ 고개를 넘다 cross a pass ; cross over the pass // 고개 너머 마을이 있다 The village lies beyond the hill.
③ [절정] the crest ; the summit ; the peak ; the climax ¶ 마흔 고개를 넘다 pass one's forty year milestone ; be on the wrong〔shady〕side of forty // 물가가 고개를 숙인다 The prices are going down〔on the downward path〕. // 추위가 고개를 숙였다 The coldest season is over. // 병세가 고개를 쳐들다 an illness relapses // 이제 나도 육십 고개를 넘어버렸다 So now I'm on the far side of sixty too.
—턱 the head of a slope **—티** a zigzag〔winding〕path over a mountain
곡식은 익을수록 고개를 숙인다 속담 The boughs that bear most hang lowest. /The more noble, the more humble. /Manners maketh man.
고개를 들다 관용 raise〔hold up〕one's head ; keep a straight face ; rise (물가 등이)
고개를 숙이다 관용 hang〔droop〕one's head ; bow〔lower〕one's head ; bend one's face ; bend the neck ; give in ; go down (물가 등이)

고객 孤客 a solitary〔lonely, lone〕traveler

***고객 顧客** a customer ; a client ; a patron ; a buyer ¶ 고객을 만들다 draw custom to《a store》// 고객이 많다 have plenty of custom ; have a large custom // 지나가다 들른 고객 a casual customer

고갯길 an uphill〔ascending〕path

고갯짓 [거부의] a shake of the head ; [찬성의] a nod **—하다** shake one's head (좌우로) ; nod (아래위로)

고갱이 the pith〔medulla, heart〕《of a vegetable》; [핵심] the core ; the essence ¶ 양배추의 고갱이 the heart of cabbage

고거리 a foreleg〔foreshank〕 of beef
고검 高檢 [고등 검찰청] the 《Seoul》 High Public Prosecutors Office
고것 [사물] it ; that ; that one ; [사람] that (little) man〔fellow〕 ; that guy
고견 高見 ① [남의 의견] your opinion 〔views, ideas〕 ¶ 이에 관하여 고견을 듣고자 합니다 Let me know your opinion upon it. /Would you kindly enlighten me on this question ?
② [뛰어난 의견] an excellent opinion ; a capital idea ; a farsighted view
⁑고결 高潔 noble-mindedness ; noble character ; loftiness ; purity ── 하다 (be) lofty ; noble ; pure ; high-minded 〔-souled〕 ¶ 고결한 사람 a man of noble character ; a high-souled person // 누구나 그의 고결한 정신에 경의를 표하였다 Everybody respected him for the nobility of his mind.
고경 苦境 distressed〔adverse, straitened〕 circumstances ; difficulties ; straits ; a dilemma ; a fix ; a sad plight〔predicament〕 ¶ 고경에 있다 be in a fix〔difficulties〕 // 고경에 빠뜨리다 put 《a person》 in a difficult position // 고경을 벗어나다 get〔find a way〕 out of a difficulty〔trouble〕 // 고경에 빠져 있는 사람을 구해 주다 help 《a person》 in trouble // 같은 고경에 처해 있다 be in the same boat
고계 苦界 〖불교〗 the (mundane) world ; this troubled〔suffering〕 world
고고 the go-go〔gogo〕 dance ; go-go ; gogo ¶ 고고를 추다 dance go-go
고고 孤高 a proud loneliness〔isolation〕 ; aloofness ── 하다 stand in lofty solitude ; (be) aloof from others ¶ 고고한 생활 a life of proud loneliness
고고 考古 study of antiquities ¶ 고고적 연구 antiquarian investigations 〔researches〕
고고 呱呱 a baby's cry at its birth
─지성(之聲) the first cry (of a newborn baby)
*고고학 考古學 arch(a)eology ¶ 고고학의 archeological // 고고학상으로 archeologically ; from the archeological point of view
─자 an archeologist ─ 자료 archeological specimens
고골 枯骨 a skeleton
고공 高空 a high sky ; high (up) in the air ; high altitude ¶ 8천 피트의 고공을 날다 fly at an altitude〔a height〕 of 8,000 feet
─병(病) altitude sickness 초(超)─ inner space
고공 雇工 [머슴] a servant ; a farm hand ; a farm laborer ; [품팔이] an extra hand ; a hireling (경멸적)
─살이 the life of a farm hand ; the life of a hireling
고공 비행 高空飛行 high-altitude flying〔flight〕
고공품 藁工品 straw goods
고과 考課 consideration of service〔efficiency〕 ; evaluation of merits
인사 ─ merit〔efficiency〕 rating
고과표 考課表 efficiency report ; [공무원의] a service record ; a personnel record (인사의)
고관 高官 [사람] a high (government) official ; a dignitary ; [직위] a high office
고관 대작 高官大爵 a high office〔rank〕 (벼슬) ; dignitaries (사람)
고관절 股關節 〖해부〗 a hip joint ; a coxa 《*pl.* coxae》 ¶ 고관절염 coxitis ; coxarthritis // 고관절병 a hip(-joint) disease
고광나무 〖식물〗 a mock orange ; a syringa ; Philadelphus schrenckii (학명)
고굉 股肱 one's right-hand (man) ; one's second self
─지신(之臣) one's confidential〔trusted〕 retainer ; one's trusty follower
고교 高校 a high school
─생 a high school student ─ 졸업생 a senior high-school graduate
고교회파 高敎會派 High Church
고구 考究 [조사] research ; investigation ; inquiry ; study ; examination ; [숙고] consideration ── 하다 research ; investigate ; inquire into ; study ; consider
고구 故舊 an old friend
*고구마 a sweet potato 《*pl.* ～es》
─밭 a potato plot 군─ roasted sweet potatoes 찐─ steamed sweet potatoes
*고국 故國 one's native〔home〕 country 〔land〕 ; one's homeland ; one's old home ¶ 고국에 돌아오다 return to one's native country ; return home // 고국을 떠나다 leave one's homeland ; be away from the homeland ; go into exile (망명하다)
─ 산천 (the mountains and rivers of) one's homeland〔native country〕
고군 孤軍 a forlorn force ; an isolated force ; a (small) unsupported army ¶ 고군 분투하다 fight unsupported〔alone〕
고궁 古宮 an ancient〔old〕 palace ; a time-honored palace
*고귀 高貴 nobility ; valuableness ; costliness ; expensiveness ── 하다 [지위·인품이] (be) noble ; exalted ; highborn ; [값이] expensive ; valuable ; rare ¶ 고귀한 사람 a high personage // 고귀한 태생이다 be of high〔noble〕 birth ; [제왕·귀족 따위] be born in〔to〕 (the) purple
고규 古規 an old〔ancient〕 law ; old 〔ancient〕 regulations〔statutes〕 ; an old〔ancient〕 rule
고금 malaria ; malarial fever ⇨ 학질
고금 古今 time past and present ;

ancient and modern ages〔times〕; all ages ¶ 고금의 ancient and modern ; of all ages〔times〕// 고금의 서적 books, ancient and modern // 고금을 통하여 through〔in〕 all ages // 고금을 통하여 가장 위대한 정치가 the greatest statesman of all times

— 독보(獨步) being unique for all times

고금리 高金利 a high rate of interest ; high interest ; usury

고급 告急 —하다 send an urgent〔emergency〕 message〔call〕; raise an alarm ; send out an SOS call ; give〔spread〕 an alarm〔warning〕

***고급 高級** [계급] high rank ; seniority ; [정도] high class〔grade〕

— 관리 higher〔high-ranking〕 officials ; high functionaries — 부관 an adjutant general (군 본부의) ; a senior adjutant (단위 부대의) — 사원 a senior clerk ; a high-grade employee — 상점 a high-class〔a quality, a fashionable, an exclusive〕 store〔shop〕 — 선원 an officer (of a ship) ; [전체] the quarterdeck — 승용차 a deluxe car ; an expensive automobile — 양장점 a high-class dress shop ; haute couture 《프》 — 잡지 a quality magazine ; a magazine of quality ; a slick (magazine) 《미·속》 — 장교 a high-ranking officer ; brass ; a brass hat 《미·속》 — 주철관 〖토목〗 a semisteel pipe — 참모 a senior staff officer — 폭약 high explosives —품 high-grade articles ; an article of quality — 호텔 a deluxe〔a first-class〕 hotel ; an exclusive hotel ; a five-star hotel

고급 高給 a high〔large〕 salary ; high pay ¶ 고급의 high-salaried〔-paid〕// 그는 고급을 받는다 He is highly paid. /He draws a big salary.

†**고기**[1] [짐승의] meat ; [물고기] fish ¶ 불고기 roast meat // 쇠고기 beef // 송아지 고기 veal // 양고기 mutton // 고기 한 점 a slice〔piece〕 of meat ; a chop (of meat) (두껍게 썬 토막) // 고기 다지는 기구 a mincing machine ; a meat grinder // 저민 고기 minced meat // 질긴〔연한〕 고기 tough〔tender〕 meat

—덮밥 rice topped with seasoned beef — 완자 a meat dumpling ; a quenelle —떼 a school of fish —소 stuffing with meat in it (만두의) — 요리 a meat dish — 제품 meat products —칼 a butcher's〔carving〕 knife ; a cleaver ; a meat chopper

고기[2] [장소] that place ; there ; yonder ; [범위] that ; so far ; to that extent ⇨ 거기

고기 古記 ancient documents ; an old record〔account, chronicle〕

고기 古器 antiques ; relics (of antiquity)

고기다 wrinkle ; crumple ; rumple ⇨ 구기다

고기만두 a meat bun ; a rissole

고기밥 fish food ; food given to fish ; [미끼] bait

고기붙이 meats (including fish) ¶ 고기붙이를 먹지 않다 abstain from meat(s)

고기압 高氣壓 high atmospheric pressure ; barometric maximum ; anticyclone ¶ 외몽고는 고기압에 덮여 있다 High atmospheric pressure overlies Outer Mongolia.

— 구역 a high pressure area 대륙성 — the continental high pressure

고기잡이 [어업] fishing ; fishery ; [어부] a fisherman ; a fisher —하다 catch fish ; fish

고김살 a wrinkle ⇨ 구김살

고깃간 —間 a meat〔butcher〕 shop ; a butcher's 《영》

고깃고깃 —하다 (be) crumpled ; wrinkled ; creased

고깃국 a meat〔beef〕 soup

고깃덩어리 a lump of meat ; [비유] a fat person ; a person too poor to wear clothes ; a human flesh

고깃배 a fishing boat〔vessel, craft〕; a fisher-boat

고깃점 a bit〔piece〕 of meat

고까지로 to that (trifling) extent ; with such a trifle (thing) ¶ 고까지로 뭘 울고 있느냐 It is silly of you to cry over such a trifle.

고까짓 such ; so trifling ; so trivial ¶ 고까짓 일로 실망해서야 쓰나 Don't be disappointed at such a trifle. // 고까짓 빚으로 걱정할 것이 뭐 있나 Don't worry about such a nominal debt. // 고까짓 일로 화내지 마라 Don't be offended at such a trifle.

고깔 a peaked hat worn by Buddhist monks and nuns

고깝다 (be) disagreeable ; unpleasant ; offensive ; feel bad 《about a person's lack of kindness》 ¶ 고깝게 여기다 be displeased 《at》; feel bitter 《against a person》// 그가 도와주러 오지 않아서 고까웠다 I thought it cruelly unkind of him not to have come to my rescue.

고꾸라지다 fall ; drop ; [죽다] die

고난 苦難 trouble ; hardship ; suffering ; affliction ; adversity ; distress ; tribulation ¶ 고난을 견디다 bear〔withstand〕 hardships〔a trial〕// 고난을 극복하다 overcome the difficulty // 고난의 길을 걷다 muddle through the bitters of life

고난도 苦難度 the degree of hardship

고냥 as it is〔was〕 ⇨ 그냥

고녀 雇女 a maid (servant) ; a house maid ; a hired girl〔woman〕; a charwoman

고녀 鼓女 a woman with underdeveloped sexual〔genital〕 organs ; a sexually deficient woman

고녀 睾女 a hermaphrodite ; an androgyne

고념 顧念 ━하다 [돌보다] look after ; take care of ; care for ; mind ; [허물을 덮어 주다] cover 《a person's fault》

고논 a paddy field with a good source of water

‡고뇌 苦惱 suffering ; distress ; affliction ; anguish ; agony ━하다 suffer ; be agonized ; anguish ¶ 고뇌의 빛 a look of distress // 고뇌의 생활 a suffering life // 고뇌에 찬 얼굴 a face full of trouble // 그는 심한 고뇌를 맛보았다 The iron entered into his soul.

고니 『새』 a swan

큰— a whooper swan 흑— a black swan

고다 ① [끓이다] boil down ; boil〔stew〕 to a pulp ¶ 물고기를 고다 stew fish to a pulp // 엿을 고다 boil down grains into taffy ② [양조] brew ; distill ¶ 소주를 고다 distill spirits

고다리 branch stretched out over the two legs of an A-frame

고다지 so ; to that extent〔degree〕 ; that much ⇨ 그다지

*고단하다 (be) tired ; fatigued ; wearied ; exhausted ¶ 몹시 고단하다 be tired out ; be worn out ; be tired to death ; be ready to drop (with fatigue) ; be done up 《속》 // 고단해서 자리에 들다 go to bed fatigued // 나는 고단했다 I was tired. // 그는 여행 끝이라 고단해 보였다 He looked tired after his journey. // 아주 고단하신 것 같군요 You look done up.

고달¹ ① [거만] haughtiness ; arrogance ¶ 되지 못한 놈이 고달을 부리는 법이다 A man of straw is likely to put on airs. ② [보챔] fret ; peevishness ; irritation

고달² ① [자루에 박힌 부분] a tang ② [쇠붙이 부리] a ferrule ; a metal cap〔ring〕

고달이 a loop 《on a package》

고달프다 [심신이] (be) very tired ; be utterly exhausted ; be tired out ; be done up ; be fatigued ; [일·시간이] (be) weary ; wearing ; wearisome ; tiresome ¶ 고달픈 일 wearing〔tiring, hard〕 work // 고달픈 인생 a weary〔hard〕 life // 고달픈 나날 wearisome days // 몸이 몹시 고달프다 I am tired out. /I have a tired body. /I am done up.

고담 古談 an old tale〔story〕 ; folklore ; a story from the past ; a legend ¶ 한국의 고담 tales of old Korea

고담 준론 高談峻論 a lofty〔noble〕 and puritanical〔stern〕 discourse ; [자만·과장하는 말] big words ; an exaggerated speech〔statement〕 ; boasting ; bragging ━하다 discourse〔talk〕 in a lofty and severe way ; talk tall〔big〕

고답 高踏 keeping aloof from the madding crowd ; transcending the mundane world ¶ 고답적인 highbrow ; high-toned ; transcendent ; [시적으로] Parnassian // 고답적인 말을 하다 make very abstruse remarks

고답주의 高踏主義 transcendentalism

고답파 高踏派 the transcendentalists ; [프랑스 문학] the Parnassian school

고당 高堂 [높은 집] a high〔tall〕 house〔building〕 ; a mansion ; [양친] father and mother ; parents ; [남의 집] your〔his〕 esteemed house〔mansion, residence〕

고대 just now ; just a moment〔minute〕 ago ¶ 그는 고대 이곳을 떠났다 He left here just now. // 고대 다녀갔다 He has just been here. // 고대 들었다 I have just now heard it.

고대 古代 ancient〔old〕 times ; antiquity ; remote ages ¶ 고대의 ancient ; antique ; of antiquity // 고대로부터 from ancient times ; from time immemorial // 고대의 유물 relics of ancient times

— 모형 an antique pattern — 사라사 cotton prints of antique〔ancient〕 fashion — 지리학 paleogeography — 지질학 paleogeology

*고대 苦待 waiting with impatience ━하다 wait impatiently 《for》 ; wait with a long neck 《for》 ; look forward to 《seeing you》 ¶ 고대했던 소식 the long-awaited news // 그날이 오기를 고대하고 있다 We are waiting impatiently for the day to come.

고대광실 高臺廣室 a grand〔deluxe〕 house ; a palatial mansion

고대 문학 古代文學 ancient literature

고대사 古代史 ancient history

고대 소설 古代小說 a story of ancient times

고대인 古代人 ancient people ; [총칭] antiquity ; the ancients

고도 古都 an ancient city ; [옛 수도] the ancient capital

†고도 高度 [높이] altitude ; height ; [정도] a high power〔degree〕 ¶ 고도의 advanced ; high-powered ; powerful ; intense ; strong ; [문화 따위] highly developed // 고도의 현미경 a high-power〔powerful〕 microscope // 고도의 통제 intensive control // 고도의 문화 수준 a high level〔standard〕 of culture〔civilization〕 // 1,000미터의 고도로 날다 fly at an altitude of 1,000 meters // 고도로 기동화한 육군 a highly mechanized army // 고도를 낮추다 lower its altitude ; fly lower

— 기록 an altitude record —병 altitude

sickness — 성장 high〔rapid, speedy〕 growth —의(儀) an altometer — 제어(장치) 〖항공〗 altitude control (system) — 지역 [건물의 높이를 제한하는] a height district — 측량 〖천문〗 altimetry — 측량기 an altimeter 비행 — flight〔flying〕 altitude 임계(臨界) — the critical altitude 절대 — the absolute altitude 해발 — sea level altitude 자동 — 표시기 an altigraph

고도 孤島 a desert〔an isolated〕 island

고도 高跳 a high jump ; a high leap ; a capriole (말의)

고도계 高度計 an altimeter ; an altometer ; a height indicator

고도리 〖물고기〗 a young mackerel ; a spike

*고독 孤獨 ① [외로움] solitude ; loneliness —하다 (be) solitary ; lonely ; lone ; friendless ; isolated ¶ 고독을 사랑하다 love solitude // 고독한 생활을 하다 live〔lead〕 a lonely〔solitary〕 life // 속세를 떠나 고독하게 살다 live in retirement // 때로는 고독도 즐거운 것이다 I enjoy my own company, too, at times. // 그녀는 평생을 고독하게 보냈다 She led a lonely life. ② [고아] an orphan ③ [자식 없는 늙은이] a childless old person ; an old person without issue

— 공포증 monophobia — 단신 a solitary〔lonely〕 person ; a solitary

고동 ① [요점] the pivot ; the crux ; the main point ② [사이렌] a whistle ; a siren ¶ 고동을 울리다 sound〔blow〕 a whistle ; whistle ③ [기계 가동 장치] a switch ; a starter 《of a machine, of an apparatus》 ; a handle ④ [가락 고동] the two bell-like spindle rings on a spinning wheel

고동 古銅 old copper

*고동 鼓動 ① [심장의] beat ; pulsation ; palpitation ; throbbing —하다 beat ; pulsate ; palpitate ; throb (심하게) ¶ 심장의 고동 the pulsation of the heart // 심장의 고동이 멎었다 His heart stopped beating. // 심장의 고동이 빨라졌다 My heart began to beat fast. ② [고무] encouragement

— 동시 기록기 〖의학〗 a polygraph — 장치 〖기계〗 a pulsator

고동맥 股動脈 〖해부〗 the femoral artery

고동색 古銅色 brown ; reddish brown

*고되다 (be) hard ; tough ; intense ; trying ¶ 고된 일 hard work ; a tough〔hard〕 job ; a trying bit of work // 고된 노동 hard〔intense〕 labor

고두 叩頭 a kowtow ; a bow ; a deep bow —하다 kowtow 《to》 ; bow 《to》 ; make a bow 《to》 ¶ 고두 사죄하다 humbly beg pardon ; make a humble apology

고두리 a blunt tip ; [활] a bow equipped with blunt-headed arrows

고두머리 the pivot pin of a flail

고두밥 rice cooked hard ; hard-boiled〔-steamed〕 rice

고둥 〖조개〗 gastropods ; Gastropoda (학명)

고드랫돌 warp weights ; stones attached to keep the warp ends in place while weaving

고드러지다 be parched ; become hard and dry ; dry up

*고드름 an icicle ¶ 처마 끝에 주렁주렁 달린 고드름 a fringe of ice on the eaves

고들개[1] [방울] a cowbell ; a horsebell ; [채찍의 추] a loaded lash (of a whip) ; [굴레의 턱밑 가죽] ; a throatlatch

고들개[2] honeycomb ; reticulum

고들고들 hard —하다 (be) dry and hard ¶ 고들고들한 밥 hard-boiled rice

고들빼기 〖식물〗 Ixeris sonchifolia (학명) ; a Korean lettuce

고등 高等 high grade ; high class ¶ 고등의 high ; higher ; advanced ; [고급의] high-grade ; high-class

— 동물 a higher animal — 비평 higher criticism — 비행 stunt flying ; advanced flying ; aerobatics ; an aerobatic flight — 식물 higher plant life — 유민 an educated loafer〔idler〕 ; [전체] the idle intelligentsia — 이론 a metatheory — 정책 high politics — 척추 동물 the upper vertebrates — 판무관(辦務官) a high commissioner — 포유 동물 the higher mammals

고등 高騰 [가격의] a rise〔an advance〕 in price ; an increase in value —하다 jump ; soar ; rise ; advance in price ¶ 쌀값의 고등 a rise in the price of rice // 고등을 예기하여 in expectation of increased value

고등 고시 高等考試 the Higher Civil Service Examination

고등과 高等科 an advanced course

고등 교육 高等敎育 (a) higher〔liberal〕 education

— 기관 higher educational institutions〔establishments〕 ; institutions of higher learning

고등 군법 회의 高等軍法會議 a general court-martial

고등 법원 高等法院 a high court of justice ; an appellate court (상고 법원)

고등 수학 高等數學 higher mathematics ; higher math 《구》

고등어 〖물고기〗 a mackerel ; a scombroid ; Scomber japonicus (학명)

*고등 학교 高等學校 a (senior) high school ; an upper secondary school ; a higher school

인문〔여자, 농업〕 — an academic〔a girls', an agricultural〕 high school

*고딕 〖인쇄〗 Gothic
—식 건축 Gothic architecture —체 Gothic type(-face)
고라니 〖동물〗 an elk; a moose 《미》; a wapiti (캐나다 산의)
고라리 a stupid bumpkin〔boor, clodhopper, hick 《미·속》〕
고라말 a chestnut horse with a black back
고락 ① [낙지의 배때기] the belly of an octopus ② [낙지의 먹] cephalopod〔octopus〕ink ¶ 낙지가 고락을 뿜다 an octopus spurts〔ejects〕ink
*고락 苦樂 pleasure and pain; joys and sorrows; weal and woe ¶ 고락간에 for better or for worse // 고락을 같이하다 share one's joys and sorrows〔one's fortunes〕// 인생의 고락 the sweets and bitters of life // 세상의 고락을 다 겪다 have tasted sweets and bitters of life
고람 高覽 your inspection〔perusal, checking reading〕 ¶ 고람하여 주시옵소서 I take pleasure in submitting it for your inspection.
고랑¹ [수갑] handcuffs; shackles; [족쇄] shackles; fetters ¶ 고랑을 채우다 snap handcuffs 《on》; shackle the hands; shackle; fetter
고랑² [두둑 사이] a furrow ¶ 고랑을 짓다 make furrows
—창 a narrow deep trough; a ditch
*고래¹ 〖동물〗 a whale ¶ 고래 같다 be as big as a whale; be huge
— 고기 whale meat — 공선(工船) a whale factory ship — 기름 whale oil — 떼 a herd〔school〕 of whales; a gam — 새끼 a whale calf — 수염 a whalebone; a baleen; a whale fin — 작살 a harpoon; a gaff —잡이 whale fishing; whaling; a whaleman (사람) —잡이 배 a whaling ship; a whale catcher〔chaser〕; a whaler
고래 싸움에 새우등 터지다 [속담] suffer a side blow in a fight
고래² [방고래] hypocaust (heating-system) flues
고랫당그래 rake for cleaning out hypocaust ashes 고랫등 the ridges where hypocaust flues are laid
고래 古來 ¶ 고래로 from ancient〔old, olden〕 times; from time immemorial // 고래지풍(古來之風) an old〔a time-honored〕 custom // 고래로 그런 일은 허다하다 Since ancient times, there have been many examples of this kind.
고래고래 in a loud voice; loudly; at shouting pitch ¶ 고래고래 고함을 지르며 욕하다 roar〔thunder, bark, yelp〕 at 《a person》; shout all kinds of abuses // 화가 나서 고래고래 소리를 지르다 raise one's voice in a huff〔rage〕; cry in a loud voice // 그가 고래고래 소리 지르고 게우고 해서 뒤처리를 하느라고 상당한 시간이 걸렸다 He was ranting and raving and throwing up, we had quite a time trying to keep everything under control.
고래등같다 (be) very large; grand; magnificent; palatial; be as big as a whale's back ¶ 고래등같은 집 a palatial house
고래좌 —座 〖천문〗 the Whale; Cetus
고량 高粱 kaoliang; the sorghum ¶ 고량을 주식으로 하다 live on kaoliang
—밭 a kaoliang field
고량주 高粱酒 kaoliang liquor〔spirits〕
고량진미 膏粱珍味 rich fare; dainty food; all sorts of delicacies; a sumptuous feast; luxurious viands ¶ 고량진미로 손님을 대접하다 entertain 《a person》 with all sorts of delicacies
†고려 考慮 consideration; deliberation; reflection; thinking over —하다 consider; deliberate; take 《a matter》 into account〔consideration〕; give consideration〔thought〕 《to》; reckon with 《a matter》; bear 《it》 in mind; think over; reflect upon ¶ 고려하지 않다 leave 《a matter》 out of consideration〔account〕// 고려할 가치가 없다 deserve little consideration; be not worth consideration // …한 점을 특히 고려하다 special regard will be paid to the fact 《that》; pay due regard to such factors // 고려 중에 있다 have 《a matter》 under consideration; [사물이 주어] be under consideration // 고려할 여지가 충분히 있다 There is much room for consideration. /It leaves much room for consideration.
고려 顧慮 regard; consideration; concern; solicitude —하다 regard; consider; have regard for; be concerned about ¶ 고려하지 않고 regardless〔irrespective〕 of; with little〔no〕 thought of // 고려하지 않다 have no regard 《for》; take no notice 《of》; pay no attention 《to》; be unconcerned about // 그는 남의 이해 관계는 일체 고려하지 않는다 He has no regard〔respect〕 for other's interests.
고려 高麗 *Koryŏ*, an ancient Korean state (918-1392)
— 자기(瓷器) ancient Korean pottery; *Koryŏ* celadon —장(葬) an ancient custom of burying an old man alive —조 the *Koryŏ* dynasty
고령 高齡 an advanced age; a ripe old age ¶ 80세의 고령으로 죽다 die at the advanced age of 80 // 고령에 달하다 attain an advanced age // 그녀는 고령이다 She is advanced in age. // 고령에도 불구하고 in spite of great age
—화(化) aging —화 사회 an aging society
고령자 高齡者 [일반적으로] the aged;

[개인] a very old〔an aged〕 person ; a person of advanced age ¶ 최고령자 the oldest ; the most aged

고령토 高嶺土 Kaolin(e) ; Kaolinite ; china〔porcelain〕 clay

고례 古例 an old practice ; established customs ; tradition

고례 古禮 old manners〔propriety, etiquette, decorum〕

고로 古老 an old person ; an elder ; the aged ; a senior ; an old timer (고참) ¶ 마을의 고로 elders of the village ; village seniors // 고로가 말하는 바에 의하면 according to the aged

고로 故老 old man ; old folks ; a convention-ridden old man

고로 故— and so ; accordingly ; therefore ; for the reason that ⇨ 그러므로

고로 高爐 a shaft〔blast〕 furnace

고로롱거리다 suffer with infirmities of age ; be troubled with a lingering disease

고로여생 孤露餘生 a person who had his parents die in his childhood ; a person orphaned early in life

고론 高論 a lofty〔noble〕 opinion〔view〕 ; [고견] your〔his〕 esteemed opinion〔views〕

고료 稿料 payment〔fee〕 for a manuscript ⇨ 원고료

고루 [같게] equally ; evenly ; [공평하게] fairly ; impartially ; [차별 없이] indiscriminately ¶ 고루고루 나누다 divide equally among all ; divide 《a thing》 equally // 여러 방면의 서적을 고루 섭렵하다 read through books covering all sorts of fields // 음식을 고루 먹다 eat well-balanced meals

고루 固陋 bigotry ; narrow-mindedness ; conservatism ; perversity ; obstinacy **—하다** (be) bigoted ; narrow-minded ; conservative ; obstinate

고루 高樓 a lofty building
—거각(巨閣) a lofty and stately building

†**고르다**[1] [균일] (be) even ; uniform ; equal ; regular ; fair ¶ 고르게 evenly ; alike ; uniformly ; similarly ; fairly // 고르지 않은 uneven ; rough ; rugged // 고르지 못한 길 a rough〔bumpy〕 road // 고르지 못한 보수 inequalities in pay // 고르지 못한 성질 an uneven temper // 복장이 고르다 be dressed all alike〔uniformly〕 // 봄날씨는 고르지 못하다 Spring weather is changeable.

*고르다[2] ① [평평하게] make 《a thing》 even ; level 《it》 off ; flatten ; roll ; bulldoze ¶ 길을 고르다 level the road
② [선택] choose ; select ; pick out ; single out ¶ 잘못 고르다 make a bad choice // 고르고 고른 선수 hand-picked players // 좋은 날을 고르다 fix upon an auspicious day // 가장 좋은 것을 고르다 select the best one // 쌀에서 돌을 고르다 pick sand out of the rice〔grain〕 // 그것은 내가 고른 것이다 It is my choice. // 그 여자는 아버지가 골라준 남자와의 결혼을 거부하는데 있어서 요지부동이었다 She was adamant in refusing to marry the man of her father's choice.

고름[1] pus ; discharge ; (purulent) matter ¶ 고름이 생기다 form pus ; pus is gathered // 고름을 짜내다 press〔squeeze〕 out the pus // 고름이 나오다 The pus is oozing out. /The pimple popped. (여드름 등의)
—집 a pustule

고름[2] a breast-tie ; a coat string ⇨ 옷고름

†**고리**[1] [끼우는] a ring ; a link ; a loop ¶ 고리를 만들다 loop ; form〔make〕 a ring
문— an iron ring fixed on a door (as a handle or fastener)

고리[2] [고리짝 감] willow〔osier〕 branches ; wicker ; [고리짝] a wicker trunk ; a wicker basket

고리[3] [그렇게] so ; so much ; like that ; in that way ; there (그리로) ⇨ 그리

고리 高利 high〔usurious〕 interest ; a high rate of interest ; usury ¶ 고리로 at a high rate of interest
—채 a usurious loan

고리눈 an eye with a white-ringed iris

고리눈이 a person whose eyes have white-ringed irises

고리다 ① [냄새가] (be) fetid ; stinking ; foul-smelling ② [하는 짓이] (be) mean ; low ; petty ; shallow ¶ 고린 생각 a shallow idea ; a foolish idea ; a short-sighted〔narrow-minded〕 view

고리 대금업 高利貸金業 usury ; loan-sharking ¶ 고리 대금업을 하다 practice usury ; lend money at usury
—자 a usurer ; a usury man ; an extortionate creditor ; a loan shark 《미·속》 ; a Shylock

고리못 a ring-shaped nail〔hook〕

고리버들 〖식물〗 an osier ; a red osier ; Salix koriyanagi (학명)

고리삭다 be not sprightly ; be too discreet for one's age ¶ 고리삭기만 한 아이 a child who has an old head on young shoulders

고리장이 a wickerwork maker ; a wickerworker

고리짝 a wicker trunk〔basket, chest〕 ; baggage 《미》 ; luggage 《영》 ¶ 고리짝에 옷을 챙겨 넣다 pack a wicker trunk with clothes

고리타분하다 ① [냄새가] (be) foul〔evil, ill〕-smelling ; stinking ; fetid ; rank ; rancid ; rotten ; offensively strong ¶ 고리타분한 냄새를 풍기다 give〔send〕 out an offensive smell ; emit a foul〔bad〕 odor
② [하는 짓이] (be) low ; mean ; un-

clean ; nasty ; [시원치 못함] sickening ; stale ; hackneyed ; trite ; stock ¶ 고리타분한 수작 a stock remark ; a low act ; pettifoggery

고리탑탑하다 (be) foul-smelling ; mean ⇨ 고리타분하다

고린내 a bad〔foul〕 smell ; an offensive odor ; a stinking smell ; a stench ¶ 고린내가 나다 have a foul odor ; smell bad ; stink

*__고릴라__ 〖동물〗 a gorilla

고림보 ① [늘 앓는 이] a sickly person ; an invalid ② [옹졸한 이] a narrow-minded〔stingy〕 fellow ; a person with insular prejudice ; a stinker ; a niggard

⁑**고립** **孤立** isolation ; helplessness **—하다** be isolated ; stand alone ; be quarantined (정치·질병·예방) ; be cut off ¶ 고립된 isolated ; solitary ; helpless // 고립된 생활을 보내다 play the Robinson Crusoe // 외부로부터 완전 고립되다 be entirely cut off from the outside world // 침략국을 고립시키다 quarantine an aggressor nation

—어 an isolated language **—점** 〖수학〗 an acnode **— 정책** isolationist policy **—지대** 〖군사〗 a pocket **—파(派)** isolationist **—화** isolation ; 〖외교〗 [한 나라의 다른 한 나라 또는 여러 나라에 의한] encirclement

고립감 **孤立感** a sense of isolation

고립주의 **孤立主義** isolationism

—자 an isolationist

고립지세 **孤立之勢** an isolated state〔situation〕

고마리 〖식물〗 the Korean persicary

고마움 [감사] gratitude ; thankfulness ; [가치] value ; blessing 《of health》 ; virtue 《of money》 ; [드높음] sanctity 《of religion》 ¶ 고마움을 알다 know 〔appreciate〕 the value 《of a thing》 〔how much one owes 《to a person》, how good it is to...〕 // 돈의 고마움을 알다 know what it means to have money // 나는 친구의 고마움을 알고 있다 I know what a blessing it is to have a friend. // 이제서야 부모님의 고마움을 알았다 Now I understand how much I owe to my parents. // 병이 나야 비로소 건강의 고마움을 느낀다 It is only after we get ill that we know how blessed it is to be healthy. // 그는 돈의 고마움을 모른다 He is a stranger to the value of money. // 혼자 독립해서 살아보니 부모의 고마움을 알게 되었다 Ever since I started living on my own, I've come to really appreciate my parents.

*__고마워하다__ be thankful〔grateful〕 to 《a person》 for ; appreciate ¶ 그는 나의 사소한 친절을 몹시 고마워했다 He was very grateful to me for the little kindness I had shown him. // 그는 조그마한 일에도 고마워한다 It takes so little to make him thankful.

고막 〖조개〗 an ark shell

고막 **鼓膜** the eardrum ; the drumhead ; the tympanum ; the tympanic membrane ¶ 고막을 터뜨리다 rupture the tympanum

—기(器) 〖동물〗 a tympanal organ

고막염 **鼓膜炎** myringitis ; tympanitis

고만 the best ¶ 이것은 맛이 고만이다 This tastes superb. // 오늘은 날씨가 고만이다 This is ideal weather. /The weather is all that could be wished for.

고만고만하다 be of even size (크기가) ; be of even ability (능력이) ; be of a sort ¶ 모두 그저 고만고만하다 They are of a sort. /There is nothing to choose among them.

고만하다 be much the same ; (be) similar ; be of a sort ¶ 내 모자의 크기도 고만하다 My hat is just as big as that. /My hat is of the same size with it. // 고만한 노력도 안 하고 어찌 성공하기를 바라느냐 How could you dream of success without making that much effort ? // 고만하면 충분하겠지요 That will be enough.

-고말고 There is no doubt that... ; It goes without saying that... ; It is a matter of course that... ; It needs no saying ; It is needless to say that... ¶ 그렇고말고 It is a matter of course. // 내가 가냐고—가고말고 Will I go, you say ? Why, certainly. /Why not ? // 네 말이 맞고말고 It's just as you say. /You are right. /Oh yes, to be sure. /Yes, indeed. /Of course it is. /Sure. 《미·구》 // 그거면 되고말고요 Certainly, that will do. // 괜찮을까요—암 괜찮고말고요 Is it safe ? Oh, it's safe enough. // 전에 여기 다녀가신 일이 있나요—다녀가고말고요 Have you been here before ? Rather ! // 바쁩니까—바쁘고말고요 Are you busy ? Sure, I am.

고맘때 ⇨ 그맘때

⁑**고맙다** ① 《I am》 thankful ; grateful ; appreciative
② (be) kind ; nice ; welcome ; appreciated ; gracious ; helpful ¶ 고마운 말씀 one's kind〔gracious〕 words // 고마운 선물 a much appreciated present // 고맙게 여기다 be thankful〔grateful〕 to 《a person》 for ; feel grateful ; be obliged for // 대단히 고맙습니다 Thank you. /Many thanks. /I appreciate your kindness. / Thanks a lot. // 그렇게 말씀해주시니 고맙습니다 It is kind of you to say so. // 재빨리 회신을 보내 주셔서 고맙습니다 I am much obliged to you for your prompt reply. // 당신의 친절에 대해 매우 고맙게 생각합니다 I deeply appreciate your kindness. // 고맙게도 돈을 꾸어 주

었다 He was kind enough to lend me some money. / He has kindly lent me money. // 내일 왕림해 주셨으면 고맙겠습니다 I'd like you to come to see me tomorrow. / I'd appreciate it if you would kindly call on me tomorrow.

고매 高邁 —하다 (be) noble ; lofty ; highminded ¶ 고매한 이상 a lofty ideal // 그는 고매한 식견을 가졌다 He is a man of broad vision.

고매 故買 fencing ; purchasing stolen goods (knowingly) —하다 purchase stolen goods ; fence

고매자 故買者 a fence ; a receiver of stolen goods ; a hot-goods broker ¶ 고매자의 가게 a fence (shop) 《속》

고매품 故買品 hot goods 《미》

고명 a garnish ; a fixing ; garnishings ; trimmings 《속》 ; a condiment ; a relish ; an ornamental accompaniment ; decorative seasonings ¶ 미나리를 고명으로 얹은 생선회 raw fish garnished with parsley

고명 古名 an old name

고명 高名 ① [명성] fame ; renown ; reputation —하다 (be) noted ; famous ; well-known ¶ 소설가로서 고명하다 win fame as a novelist ; be well known as a novelist
② [경어] your (famous) name ¶ 고명은 많이 들었습니다 I certainly know you by reputation. / I have heard much of you.

고명 高明 [현자] a great man of wisdom ; the wise ; [이름이 높음] fame ; reputation ; renown ; [부귀한 집안] an illustrious family ; a grand mansion (집) —하다 be noble and wise (현명) ; be famous〔renowned, eminent〕(유명)

고명 顧命 deathbed injunctions of a king ; the last words〔will〕of a king
— 대신 a minister entrusted with the king's deathbed injunctions

고명딸 the one and only daughter among one's many sons

고모 姑母 an aunt ; a sister of one's father ; a paternal aunt

고모부 姑母夫 the husband of one's (paternal) aunt

고목 古木 an old〔aged〕tree ¶ 떡갈나무 고목 an old oak (tree)

고목 枯木 a dead〔withered〕tree ; [잎이 떨어진 나무] a bare〔leafless〕tree

고묘 古廟 an ancient mausoleum 《*pl.* -lea》 ; an old ancestral tomb ; a time-honored shrine

고묘 古墓 an old tomb ; an ancient mound

⁑**고무** rubber ; [탄성의] India-rubber ; [수지] gum ¶ 고무를 입힌 rubbered ; rubberized ; gummed // 고무창을 댄 rubber-soled
—공 a rubber ball — 공업 the rubber industry —관(管) a rubber tube — 나무 a rubber〔gum〕tree — 도장 a rubber stamp — 반창고 a rubber (adhesive) plaster — 보트 a rubber boat 〔raft〕 —신 rubber shoes ; gumshoes 《미》 —실 an elastic thread — 인화법 gum printing — 장화 (full-length〔half-length〕) rubber boots — 제품 rubber goods — 테이프 rubber tape —풀 gum arabic ; mucilage — 호스 a rubber hose 생— crude〔raw〕rubber 아라비아 — gum arabic

⁑**고무 鼓舞** encouragement ; inspiration ; stimulation ; incitation —하다 encourage ; inspire ; stimulate ; cheer up ; incite ; stir up 《one's mind》 ¶ 사기를 고무하다 stiffen〔stimulate〕the morale 《of troops》 // 섬유 공업의 전망은 매우 고무적이다 The future〔prospect〕of the fiber industry is very bright〔encouraging〕.

고무끈 an elastic cord〔string〕

고무라기 crumbs of cake ; odd bits of cake

고무래 a rake ; a wooden tool used to spread grain, to rake ashes, or to level soil

고무장갑 a pair of rubber gloves

고무줄 an elastic cord〔string, thread, tape〕; elastic braid ; shir(r)

고무 지우개 a rubber ; an eraser

고무 풍선 a toy balloon

고문 古文 ancient〔archaic〕writing
—체 an archaic style —학 the ancient classics ; paleography

⁑**고문 拷問** torture ; the rack ; third degree 《미》 —하다 torture ; give 《a person》 the third degree ; rack ¶ 고문을 가하다 put to torture ; use torture on 《a person》 // 고문을 당하다 be tortured ; be put to torture
—대 a rack — 치사(致死) torture resulting in death

***고문 顧問** [의견을 물음] asking advice ; [사람] an adviser ; a counselor ; a brain truster ¶ 고문이 되다 become an adviser ; act in an advisory capacity // 외국인 전문가를 고문으로 초청하다 employ a foreign expert as adviser
— 기관 an advisory〔a consultative〕council — 기사 a consulting engineer —의(醫) a medical adviser 기술 — a technical adviser 대통령 — an aide-de-camp to the president 《of Korea》 법률 — a juridical counselor 편집 — an advisory editor

고문관 顧問官 a councilor ; an adviser 〔advisor〕

고문단 顧問團 an advisory group〔body, committee, council〕; brain trusters 《미》

고문 변호사 顧問辯護士 a legal advisor ; [회사의] a corporation lawyer 〔attorney〕 ; [가정의] a family lawyer ; [일반의] a counselor-at-law

고문서 古文書 ancient〔antique〕 documents

고물[1] powdered bean〔sesame, pea〕 (used for covering or coating rice-cake) ¶ 떡에 깨고물을 묻히다 cover rice-cakes with powdered sesame

⁑**고물**[2] [배의] the stern ; the poop ¶ 고물 쪽으로 astern ; aft ; abaft // 이물에서 고물까지 from bow to stern ; fore and aft

***고물 古物** [골동품] antiquities ; antiques ; curios ; bric-a-brac ; [낡은 것] a secondhand〔used〕 article ¶ 저 친구 이젠 고물이라 쓸모가 없어 He is worn-out〔a back number〕 and good-for-nothing. // 너는 이제 고물이 다 되었다 You are a decrepit old man now. // 중고차 매매인에게서 고물차를 산 것 같애 I think I got a lemon from the used car dealer.
— 가격 the price of secondhand goods **—상** an antique shop ; a secondhand shop **— 상인** an antique dealer ; secondhand dealer **— 시장** the flea market **— 자동차** a rickety〔decrepit〕 car ; an old heap 《구》 ; a beat-up car ; a flivver 《미》 ; an old banger 《영》 ; a discarded car (폐차)

고물거리다 wriggle ; dawdle ⇨ 꾸물거리다

고미 a plaster panel ceiling
—받이 a supporting beam for a plaster panel ceiling **—집** a house with an attic **—혀** rafters between supporting beams and boards
고미 누르다 관용 lay〔put in〕 a plaster panel ceiling

고미 苦味 bitterness ; a bitter taste
— 정기(丁幾) 〖약〗 bitter tincture **—제(劑)** bitter〔nasty〕 medicine

고미다락 a kind of attic

고민 苦悶 agony ; anguish ; pang ; worry **— 하다** be in agony〔anguish〕 ; be worried ¶ 고민 끝에 병들다 worry oneself sick // 고민거리 the source of trouble // 청춘의 고민 nameless longings of youth ; torments of awakened love // 고민을 잊으려고 술을 마시다 take a drink to drown one's agony〔mental anguish〕 // 그는 고민스러운 표정을 감추지 못했다 He could not hide his agonized look. // 그는 뇌물 수수 사건으로 고민 끝에 자살했다 Worry about the bribery case drove him to commit suicide. // 그 일로 고민하고 있다 It causes him mental anguish. // 너는 그렇게 고민할 필요 없다 You need not worry so much.

고박 古朴 [질박] timehonored simplicity ; [고풍] old fashions ; antique style **— 하다** (be) old-fashioned and unsophisticated

⁑**고발 告發** 〖법〗 [검사의] prosecution ; indictment ; [민간의] complaint **— 하다** prosecute〔indict〕 《a person for kidnapping》 ; accuse ; charge 《a person with a crime》 ; [민간에서] enter〔file〕 a complaint against

> 참고 **charge** 주로 범죄가 성립되는 일을 경찰 따위에 공식으로 신고하는 것
> **accuse** 부당한 짓을 한 사람에게 직접 신고하는 것 반드시 공식적으로 신고하는 것을 의미하지는 않는다

¶ 언론법 위반으로 고발되다 be prosecuted〔indicted〕 for a press law violation // …의 고발에 따라 on complaint 《of a person》 // 그는 절도 혐의로 고발되었다 He was charged with stealing.
—장 a bill of indictment

고발인 告發人 a prosecutor ; an accuser ; a complainant ; a denunciator ; an informant ; a relator ; 〖법률〗 a plaintiff

고방 庫房 a storeroom ; a lumber room 〔closet〕 ; a go-down ; a boxroom 《영》

고배 苦杯 a bitter cup ; hardships ; a sad defeat
고배를 마시다 관용 drink a bitter cup ; go through an ordeal〔a trial〕 ; drain the cup of sorrow ; [승부에서] be sadly defeated〔beaten〕

***고백 告白** confession ; admission ; [신앙의] profession 《of one's faith》 **— 하다** confess ; own up 《to》 ; admit ; make a confession〔an admission〕 《of》 ¶ 죄상을 고백하다 confess one's guilt ; confess to a crime〔sin〕 // 그것은 너의 무식함을 고백하는 거나 다름없다 That practically amounts to a confession of your own ignorance. /That itself tells of your ignorance. // 그는 그녀에게 사랑을 고백했다 He declared his love for her.
—서 a written confession **— 성사** [카톨릭] the sacrament of penance **— 소설** a confession novel

고백반 枯白礬 〖화학〗 burnt alum

고범 故犯 an intentional crime ; a deliberate offense ; a calculated crime ; a willful transgression

고법 高法 [고등 법원] the High Court

고변 告變 **— 하다** inform 《the authority》 of a rebellion〔mutiny〕 ; report〔bring news of〕 treason

고별 告別 farewell ; leave-taking ; parting ; good-bye ; valediction **— 하다** say good-bye〔farewell〕 ; take leave of ; bid 《a person》 farewell ; pay last respects to ; bid adieu to
—사(辭) [인사] a farewell speech 〔address〕 ; parting words ; valedictory address (졸업생의) ; a funeral oration (弔辭)

고별식 告別式 a farewell ceremony ; [고인에 대한] a farewell〔funeral〕 service

고별 연주회 告別演奏會 a farewell concert
고병 古兵 an older man in the service ; a veteran ; an old-timer ; a senior comrade
고본 稿本 a manuscript ; an MS. 《*pl.* MSS.》; an original draft
고본 古本 a secondhand book ; a used book ; an old book ¶ 고본을 사다 buy 《a book》 at secondhand
— 고가 매입 High prices offered for used books (게시) **— 상인** a secondhand bookseller **— 시장** an old-book market **—점** secondhand bookshop 《영》; a used bookstore 《미》
고봉 高峯 a high〔lofty, cloud-kissing〕 mountain peak
— 절정 the highest peak of a mountain **— 준령** a lofty peak and a steep mountain ridge
고부 姑婦 mother-in-law and daughter-in-law
고부 告訃 an obituary (notice) (신문의) ; the announcement of 《a person's》 death **—하다** announce〔report〕 《a person's》 death
—서 a written〔printed〕 announcement of 《a person's》 death ; an obit(uary) ; a necrology
고부라뜨리다 bend 《one's back》; curve 《a wire》; crook 《one's arm》 ¶ 철사를 고부라뜨리다 bend a wire
고부라지다 bend ; curve ; swerve ; be bent ; be crooked ; turn 《to the right》; [마음씨가] become crooked ; become perverse ; be cross-grained ¶ 고부라지기 쉬운 pliant ; flexible // 그는 나이를 먹어 허리가 고부라졌다 He is bowed with years. /He is bent with age. /He is old and bent. // 길은 거기서 갑자기 고부라진다 There is a sharp bend〔turn〕 in the road there. /The road makes an abrupt turn there. // 이 거리에서 좌측으로 고부라져 곧장 가십시오 Turn to the left at this street and go straight on. // 열차는 산모퉁이에서 고부라져 갔다 The train curved around the hill.
고부랑이 [물건] a bent〔curved, crooked〕 object ; [사람] a person whose back is bent ¶ 늙어서 고부랑이가 되다 stoop〔be bent〕 with years
고부랑하다 (be) bent (잔등) ; crooked (나무 따위) ; twisty ; winding (길이) ; meandering (개천 따위) ; zigzag (진로 따위) ¶ 고부랑고부랑 windingly ; meanderingly // 고부랑한 나뭇가지 a crooked bough // 늙어서 허리가 고부랑하다 be bowed with years ; be bent with age // 길이 몹시 고부랑고부랑하다 The road turns and twists a good deal. // 나는 고부랑한 숲속의 길을 더듬어 갔다 I followed a path meandering through the woods.
고부리다 bend (잔등을) ; curve (철사를) ; crook (팔을) ; inflict〔bend in〕 (안으로)
고부스름하다 (be) somewhat bent ; slightly curved ; be crooked a little
고부장하다 (be) slightly bent (at the waist) ⇨ 구부정하다
고부조 高浮彫 high relief ; alto-relievo ¶ 고부조로 하다 carve 《a thing》 in high relief
고부탕이 ① [꺾인 자리] the fold〔crease〕 of a bolt of cloth
② [고비] a critical point〔moment, stage〕; the peak ; the climax
고분 古墳 an old〔ancient〕 tomb〔mound〕 ¶ 고분을 발굴하다 unearth〔dig up〕 an old tomb
— 시대 the period of ancient burial mounds
고분고분 obediently ; submissively ; gently ; meekly ; pliantly **—하다** (be) obedient ; submissive ; gentle ; meek ; pliable ¶ 고분고분 부모에게 순종하다 be obedient to one's parents
고분자 高分子 a high molecule〔polymer〕
— 물질 a high molecular substance **— 반도체** a semiconductive polymer **— 전해질** a polyelectrolyte **— 화학** chemistry of high polymers ; high polymer chemistry **— 화합물** a highly polymerized compound
고불거리다 wind ; meander ; zigzag ¶ 시내가 여기서부터 고불거리기 시작한다 The brook begins to zigzag from here.
고불고불 windingly ; zigzag **—하다** (be) winding ; zigzag ; meandering ; crooked ¶ 고불고불한 산길 a zigzag〔winding〕 mountain path // 고불고불한 냇물 a meandering stream // 길이 아주 고불고불하다 The road turns and twists a good deal. // 개울이 들 가운데를 고불고불 흐르고 있다 A brook winds 〔meanders〕 through the fields.
고불탕하다 (be) winding ; meandering ; zigzag ¶ 고불탕고불탕 windingly ; meanderingly ; zigzag // 고불탕한 길 a winding road // 고불탕고불탕한 개천 a meandering stream
고붓하다 (be) slightly bent〔curved, crooked〕
고붙 ⇨ 고부탕이
고붙치다 fold〔crease〕 《a bolt of cloth》
고비[1] [절정] the climax ; the crest ; the height ; the peak ; the summit ; [위기] the crisis ; a crucial〔critical, trying〕 moment〔hour〕; [전기] a turning point ¶ 마지막 아슬아슬한 고비에서 at the last moment ; at the eleventh hour // 고비를 넘다 pass the crisis ; turn the corner (병세가) ; pass the peak〔crest〕 of (물가가) // 더위는 지금이 한창 고비다

We are now in the height of summer. /The summer is now at its hottest. //그 환자는 오늘이 고비다 The invalid is passing the crisis today.
—판 a turning point ; a critical moment
고비² [편지꽂이] a letter file〔rack〕
고비³ 〖식물〗 the osmund ; a royal fern ; a flowering fern
고비 考妣 one's deceased parents
고비 高飛 high flight —하다 fly high ; fly at a high altitude ¶ 고비원주(高飛遠走)하다 run away〔off〕; abscond ; elope ; decamp ; take (to) flight
고빗사위 a critical moment〔juncture〕; a psychological moment
고빙 雇聘 employment ; engagement ; invitation ; a call —하다 engage ; employ ; invite ¶ 전문가를 고빙하다 engage the service of an expert ; [의사를] call in a doctor
고뿔 a cold ¶ 고뿔에 걸리다 catch〔take〕cold // 고뿔에 걸려 누워 있다 be laid up〔down〕with a cold
*__고삐__ reins ; a bridle ; a halter ¶ 고삐를 잡다 gather up one's reins // 말의 고삐를 당기다 draw in the reins ; rein in (the horse)
고삐를 늦추다 관용 slacken the reins ; give the reins to (the horse)
고삐 놓은 말 관용 a runaway horse ; a riderless horse
고사 古寺 an old〔ancient〕temple ; a dilapidated temple
고사 古史 ancient history
고사 古事 an ancient happening ; an event of former days
고사 考査 [고찰] consideration ; [시험] examination ; a test ; a quiz 《미》 —하다 consider ; examine ; inquire into ; test ; quiz ¶ 학생의 학력을 고사하다 consider the proficiency of students
—표 a record of merits 기말 — finals 인물 — a character test〔examination〕 중간 — a midterm examination 학력 — an achievement test
고사 苦辭 —하다 decline〔refuse〕cordially ; decline with regret
고사 高士 a man of high〔lofty〕character ; a high-minded person ; a noble character
고사 告祀 offering a sacrifice to spirits —하다 offer a sacrifice to spirits
—떡 rice-cake offered to spirits
고사 固辭 a positive refusal —하다 refuse〔decline〕positively ¶ 고사하고 받지 않았다 He positively declined to receive it.
고사 告辭 an admonitory address (on a ceremonial occasion)
고사 枯死 withering to death —하다 die ; wither ; wilt ; be blighted
고사 故事 [유서] an origin ; a source ; a historical fact〔allusion〕; [민간 전승] tradition ; folklore ¶ 고사 내력 the origin and history // 고사를 인용하다 allude to a historical event
고사 기관총 高射機關銃 an anti-aircraft machine gun ; an A. A. -machine gun
고사리 〖식물〗 a fernbrake ; a bracken
고사본 古寫本 a codex 《*pl.* -dices》
고사 숙어 사전 故事熟語辭典 a dictionary of fables and phrases
고사포 高射砲 an anti-aircraft gun ; an A. A. gun ; an ack-ack 《속》; an Archie (군대에서) 《속》
—대 an anti-aircraft battery〔corps〕 — 조준 산정기(算定機) a predictor — 진지 an A. A. battery position ; an anti-aircraft emplacement —탄 an anti-aircraft shell —화(火) flak
고사풍 [말의 병] stiff limbs
고사하고 姑捨— setting aside ; apart from ; let alone ; to say nothing 《of》; not to speak 《of》; not to mention ¶ 농담은 고사하고 joking aside // 비용은 고사하고 apart from the expense ; let alone the expense ; to say nothing of the expense // 택시는 고사하고 버스도 안 탄다 He does not take a bus, let alone a taxi. // 아침에 일어나면 만사를 고사하고 이것 먼저 해요 Do this the first thing in the morning. // 일등은 고사하고 꼴찌나 면해라 Come out on the bottom, let alone trying for the top.
고삭부리 light eater ; poor eater
고산 孤山 a solitary hill〔mountain〕
고산 高山 a high〔lofty〕mountain ; an alp ¶ 고산의 Alpine
—대 〖식물〗 an alpine belt〔zone〕 — 동물 an alpine animal ; [동물상] an alpine fauna — 생활 an alpine life — 요양소 an alpine sanatorium — 초원 an alpine meadow
고산 故山 one's native place ; one's home (town) ¶ 만년을 고산에서 보내다 pass one's last days〔the remainder of one's life〕in one's old home ; live a retired life in one's home town
고산 기후 高山氣候 a mountain climate
고산병 高山病 mountain〔altitude〕sickness
고산 식물 高山植物 an alpine plant ; [원예] an alpine ; [식물상(相)] an alpine flora
—원 an alpine garden
고산 지대 高山地帶 an alpine region ; the high reaches 《of Tibet》
고살 故殺 〖법〗 manslaughter ; murder in the second degree ; homicide —하다 commit manslaughter ; commit murder
—자(者) a person guilty of manslaughter
*__고상 高尙__ nobleness ; refinement ; elegance ; high-mindedness —하다 (be) noble ; lofty ; high ; [품위가] refined ;

elegant ; high-minded ; high-toned ; elevated ¶ 고상한 사상 a lofty〔noble〕 idea // 고상한 잡지 a high-toned〔high-brow〕 magazine // 고상하게 하다 elevate ; refine ; ennoble // 고상한 체하다 be priggish ; be prudish ; be snobbish // 그녀는 그의 고상한 태도에 반했다 She was impressed by his noble bearing. // 그는 고상한 취미를 가지고 있다 He has an elegant taste.

고상고상 wakeful(ly) ; unsleepingly **— 하다** remain wakeful ; fail to sleep ; stay awake ; make vain effort to get to sleep

고샅 [골목] a narrow alley ; [골짜기 사이] a mountain gorge ; a ravine ; a glen ; a dell

고색 古色 an antique〔a hoary〕 look〔appearance〕 ; patina (청동기 따위의) ¶ 고색을 띤 antique-looking ; hoary ; timeworn ; aged

고색 창연 古色愴然 — 하다 be venerable ; be antique ; be quite black with age ; have a hoary look ; be hoary with antiquity

†**고생 苦生** a hard〔tough〕 life ; privation ; suffering ; hardship ; distress ; adversity ; [수고] toil ; labor ; pain **— 하다** suffer《hardships》; have trials ; [수고하다] toil hard ; have a hard time ¶ 속세의 고생 troubles of life // 고생시키다 give《a person》 much trouble // 가난으로 고생하다 suffer from poverty // 머리가 아파 고생하다 suffer from (a) headache // 가족을 부양하느라 고생하다 be hard put to it to support one's family // 좀 더 고생을 해야 세상을 알아 You ought to know more of life. // 너는 고생한 보람이 있었다 You have not suffered in vain.
—길 a hard row to hoe ; a thorny path **—문** the threshold of a hardship-filled future **—살이** a hard life **— 주머니** a person who has plenty of hardships **—티** traces of a hard life
고생 끝에 낙이 온다 속담 Every cloud has a silver lining. /No pleasure without pain〔repentance〕. /Of sufferance, comes ease〔rest〕.

고생대 古生代 〖지질〗 the paleozoic era ¶ 고생대의 paleozoic

고생물 古生物 extinct animals and plants ; [화석물] fossils

고생물학 古生物學 paleontology
—자 a paleontologist

고생스럽다 苦生— (be) hard ; tough ; trying ; distressful ; afflicting ; bitter ; painstaking ¶ 고생스러운 일 a hard〔tough〕 job // 살아가기 고생스럽다 It is hard to get along.

고서 古書 old〔ancient〕 books ; classics
—전(展) an exhibition of rare old books

고석 古昔 olden〔ancient〕 times

고성 古城 an old〔ancient〕 castle

고성 孤城 an isolated castle ; a solitary castle ; [포위당한] a helpless castle ; a besieged castle

고성 高聲 a loud voice ; loud talking ¶ 고성으로 loudly ; aloud // 고성 방가하다 sing with a loud voice ; sing boisterously

고성 古聖 an ancient sage ; a sage of antiquity ; an old saint

고성낙일 孤城落日 being alone and helpless

고성능 高性能 high effectiveness〔efficiency〕 ¶ 고성능의 highly efficient ; high-powered《gasoline》; high-performance《aircraft》; high-yield《hydrogen bomb》// 고성능의 기계 a highly efficient machine
— 방적기 a super-high draft **— 수신기** a high-fidelity receiver ; hi-fi **— 폭약** a high explosive ; TNT **— 항공기** a high performance aircraft

고섶 right under one's nose ¶ 바로 고섶에 두고 못 찾는다 He can't find it when it is right under his nose.

‡**고소 告訴** a complaint ; a charge ; an accusation ; information **— 하다** bring a charge ; make a complaint against ; proceed〔complain〕 against ; file a bill ; bring〔institute〕 a suit ; accuse

> 참고 **complain** 은 개인에 의한 민사상의 제소 **accuse**는 당국 또는 개인이 제소하는 일로 형사. 민사 양쪽 모두 씀 **charge** 는 당국이 주로 형사 사건에 대하여 기소하며 **sue** 는 당국, 개인의 양쪽에 쓰지만 민사적 사건에 대해 제소하는 경우 사용

¶ 피해자의 고소에 의해서 on a victim's complaint ; on complaint of a victim // 고소를 수리〔기각〕하다 accept〔reject〕 a complaint // 고소를 취하하다 withdraw a complaint // 당신을 고소하겠다 I'm going to take you to court. /I'm going to sue you. /You'll be hearing from my lawyer.
— 절차 an accusatorial procedure

고소 苦笑 a forced〔bitter, ghastly, sardonic〕 smile ; a strained laugh **— 하다** smile bitterly〔grimly〕 ; smile a grim smile ; force a smile ; give a strained laugh

고소 高所 a high place ; the high ground ; an elevation ; a height

고소 공포증 高所恐怖症 〖의학〗 acrophobia

고소득 a large〔big〕 income
—자 a person who earns a large income **—층** the high-income bracket

고소인 告訴人 an accuser ; a complainant ; 〖법〗 an appellant

고소장 告訴狀 a (letter〔bill〕 of) com-

plaint ; a written accusation ; a bill
고소하다 ① [맛이] taste of sesame oil ; have a flavor of nut ; (be) tasty ; sweet ; savory
② [남의 일이] be pleased to see a disliked person make a mistake ¶ 아이 고소해라 Serve you right! // 놀랐지 아이 고소해 They scared you all right.
*고속 高速 high-speed ; rapid transit ¶ 고속으로 at high speed
—강(鋼) high-speed steel — 기관 a high-speed engine —도 드릴 〖치과〗 [고통이 없는] a cavitron —도 수송 rapid transit — 버스 a highway bus ; an express bus — 선반 a high-speed lathe — 시대 a speed age — 역학 high-speed mechanics — 영화 a fast motion picture — 중성자로(中性子爐) a fast neutron — 철도 a rapid transit railway
고속 도로 高速道路 an express〔a high-speed〕 highway ; a freeway ; a super-highway ; a motorway 《영》 ¶ 고속 도로의 통행료 a toll // 고속 도로의 중앙 분리대 a median strip // 고속 도로의 교차점 an intersection ; interchange 《영》 // 고속 도로의 통행료 징수소 a tollgate // 2년 전에 고속 도로에서 사고를 당한 후로는 절대로 고속 도로를 타지 않습니다 I have never driven the freeways since I had an accident on the freeway two years ago. // 나는 고속 도로를 안 타고 일반 도로로만 왔다 I didn't take the freeways. I came by surface streets only.
고속도 사진 高速度寫眞 high-speed photography
고속 촬영 高速撮影 high-speed photography
—용 렌즈 a fast lens
고송 古松 an old pine tree
고송 孤松 a solitary〔lone〕 pinetree
*고수 固守 adhesion ; persistence ; tenacity ; adherence 《to》 —하다 keep〔stick, cling, adhere〕 to ; hold fast to ; stand pat on ; persist in ; [막다] hold out ; defend stubbornly ¶ 자기의 주장을 고수하다 adhere to one's opinion // 주의를 고수하다 hold fast〔stick〕 to one's principle // 진지를 고수하다 cling to〔hold out in〕 a position
*고수 鼓手 a drummer ; a tambour ¶ 소년 고수 a drummer boy
—장(長) a drum major
고수 高手 a better hand ; excellent skill ; a superior 《to another in something》 ; a high-grade player ¶ 그 사람은 바둑〔장기〕의 고수였다 The man was a high-ranking *paduk*〔chess〕 player.
고수레 mixing hot water in flour to make dough —하다 make dough
—떡 a kind of steamed rice-cake
고수련 careful nursing ; care of 《the sick》 ; tending a patient —하다 give 《a patient》 one's best care and service ; tend 《the sick》 // 잠 안 자고 고수련하다 sit up with 《a sick man》 // 고수련하여 완쾌하게 하다 nurse 《a person》 back to health
고수머리 [머리] curly〔frizzled, kinky〕 hair ; [사람] a curl ; a kinky-top
고수부지 高水敷地 the terrace land on the river
고스락 a crisis ; the critical moment ; peak ; extreme ; height
고스란하다 (be) just as it was ; be kept〔left〕 entire ; remain untouched ; be intact ; be as safe and whole as ever ¶ 고스란히 entirely ; wholly ; all ; completely ; with nothing missed〔damaged〕 // 고스란히 그대로 있다 remain intact〔as it was〕 ; left untouched // 고스란히 남다 get a clear grain 《of》 // 창문은 깨지지 않고 고스란했다 The window did not break. It's good as new // 임자가 나서지 않아서 그 돈은 고스란히 그의 것이 되었다 As no one claimed the money, it was all given to him. // 원금은 고스란히 그대로 두고 이자로만 먹고 산다 He lives on the interest keeping the capital intact.
고스러지다 《an ear of grain》 get scraggy
고슬고슬 《rice》 properly cooked —하다 《rice》 be properly cooked
*고슴도치 〖동물〗 a hedgehog ; porcupine ¶ 고슴도치 같은 hedgehoggy
고슴도치 외 따지듯 〔속담〕 be deep〔immersed〕 in debt
고슴도치도 제 새끼는 함함하다고 한다 〔속담〕 The owl thinks her own young fairest. /The crow thinks her own birds fairest.
고습 高濕 high humidity ¶ 고습한 기후 a humid climate
고승 高僧 a high priest ; a prelate ; a bishop
고시 古詩 [옛시] ancient poems ; [중국의] free verse 《in ancient China》
†고시 告示 a notice ; a bulletin ; an announcement ; a notification —하다 notify 《the public of something》 ; give notice 《of》 ; announce ¶ 박물관은 다음 주에 폐관한다고 고시되었다 It has been announced that the museum will be closed next week.
— 가격 an official price ; an officially fixed price — 제2호 Notification No. 2
고시 顧視 looking back ; [고념] looking after ; patronage —하다 look back ; look after (고념)
고시 考試 examination ; a test —하다 examine ; give a test to
— 과목(科目) the subjects for examination ; an examination subject —관 an official examiner —료(料) an examina-

tion fee — 위원 an examiner (한 사람) — 위원회 an examination committee ; the examination board — 제도 an examination system — 준비 preparation for an examination

고시판 告示板 a billboard 《미》; a notice〔bulletin〕 board

고식 姑息 ① [임시 변통] a temporary ease ; a (mere) makeshift ; a stopgap ¶ 고식적인 makeshift ; temporizing ; patchup ; timeserving // 고식적으로 for a shift ; by way of a makeshift ; to temporize // 고식적인 수단 a half〔temporizing〕 measure ; a makeshift // 고식적인 해결 half-way solution // 고식적인 정책 a temporizing policy ; a time-serving policy // 고식적인 수단을 쓰다 temporize ; employ a stopgap policy ; take half-measures

② [처자] one's wife and children

고식 古式 an old rite ; an ancient ceremony

고실 鼓室 〖해부〗 the eardrum ; the atrium ; the tympanic cavity

— 신경 nervous tympanicus

고심 苦心 pains ; efforts ; hard work ; labor ; close application —하다 work hard ; take pains ¶ 고심해서 by hard work with a great deal of trouble // 고심 참담하다 toil and labor ; work hard // 대단한 고심작이다 It is the result of an immense amount of labor. // 모처럼의 고심이 수포로 돌아갔다 All my pains have gone for nothing. // 이것은 고심해서 모은 돈이다 The money has been saved by the sweat of my brow.

고아 古雅 classical grace ; classicality ; antique beauty —하다 (be) classical ; antique and elegant ; have a classic beauty

***고아 孤兒** an orphan ¶ 고아가 되다 be orphaned ; be left〔made〕 an orphan // 그는 고아나 다름없다 He is no better than an orphan.

전쟁(戰爭) — a war orphan ; a child orphaned by the war ; a war destitute child

고아 高雅 elegance ; refinement —하다 (be) elegant ; refined ; graceful ¶ 고아한 필치 an elegant stroke

고아원 孤兒院 an orphanage ; an orphan asylum〔home〕 ; a home for orphans ¶ 고아원을 세우다 build〔establish, found〕 an orphanage

고악 古樂 ancient〔old〕 music

고안 孤雁 a solitary wild goose ; a wild goose flying all by itself

***고안 考案** a design ; a device ; a plan ; an idea ; a contrivance ; a conception —하다 plan ; design ; devise ; originate ; contrive ; conceive ¶ 고안 중이다 [사람이 주어] be working on a plan ; [사실이 주어] be under consideration // …하는 방법을 고안하다 work out a way to 《do》 // 이것은 A씨의 고안입니다 This idea originated with Mr. A.

고안자 考案者 a designer ; a deviser ; an originator

고압 高壓 ① [압제] high-handedness ; coercion ; pressure ; browbeating ; oppression ¶ 고압적인 high-handed ; coercive // 고압적으로 in a high-handed manner ; with the strong hand // 고압적 수단을 쓰다 take a coercive〔high-handed〕 measure

② [전기의] high tension ; high voltage 《미》; [기압 따위의] high pressure

—계(計) a piezometer — 기관(機關) a high-pressure steam engine — 밀봉법(密封法) 〖전기〗 pressurization — 보일러 a high-pressure boiler — 송전 high voltage transmission —솥 a high-pressure kiln〔oven〕 ; an autoclave — 정책 a high-handed policy — 케이블 a high-tension cable — 터빈 a high-pressure turbine —통(筒) 〖기계〗 a high-pressure cylinder — 회로(回路) a high-tension circuit

고압선 高壓線 a high-tension wire〔line〕

고압실 高壓室 a plenum〔high-pressure〕 room

고압 장치 高壓裝置 high-pressure equipment

고압 전기 高壓電氣 high-tension electricity

고압 전류 高壓電流 a high-tension current ; a high-voltage current 《미》 ¶ 위험 고압 전류 "Danger, high voltage!" (게시)

고액 高額 a large amount〔sum〕 (of money) ¶ 고액의 소득이 있다 have a large income

— 납세자 a high〔an upper-bracket〕 taxpayer — 소득자 a large-income earner

고액권 高額券 a large denomination bill〔bank note 《영》〕

-고야 ① [어찌] ¶ 이래가지고야〔이렇고야〕 as〔the way〕 things are ; things being the way they are ; as matters now stand ; in the present state of things ; in〔under〕 the present circumstances // 이래가지고야 어디 외국 가겠나 With the way things stand at the moment, I can't hope to go abroad. // 병세가 그렇고야 어디 오늘 밤 넘기겠나 I'm afraid he may not live over night, judging from his present condition.

② [각오·집념] ¶ 나는 목적을 관철하고야 말겠다 I will move heaven and earth to attain my end. // 기어이 하고야 말겠다 I will do it, or I am a Dutchman. /I will do it come what may. // 무슨 일이 있어도 부닥치고야 말겠다 Whatever may happen, I am prepared for it.

③ [결과] ¶ 그것은 결국 큰 문제를 일으키고야 말았다 It eventually caused a great trouble.

*고약 膏藥 a (piece of) plaster ; an adhesive plaster ; a patch ; [연고] a salve ; an ointment ; an unguent ¶ 고약을 바르다 salve ; dress 《the wound》 with an ointment // 고약을 붙이다 apply 〔stick〕 a plaster 《to》 ; plaster 《a sore place》 // 고약을 떼다 remove〔take off, peel off〕 a plaster

고약하다 [성미가] (be) ill-natured ; evil ; wicked ; crooked ; malicious ; [날씨·냄새·용모 따위가] bad ; ugly ; nasty ; bitter ; grotesque ; [일이] hard ; troublesome ¶ 고약한 사람 a wicked man ; an ill-natured man // 고약한 놈 a rascal ; an unsavory character // 고약하게 생긴 사람 an ill-looking fellow // 고약한 냄새 a stinking〔nasty〕 smell // 읽기가 고약하다 be hard to read ; be a mess to read

고양 高揚 uplift ━하다 enhance ; exalt ; raise

†고양이 〖동물〗 a cat ; a puss ; a pussy (애칭) ¶ 고양이 새끼 a kitten ; a kitty (애칭) // 수고양이 a he-cat ; a tomcat ; a male cat // 암고양이 a she-cat ; a female cat // 도둑고양이 a stray〔an ownerless〕 cat

고양이보고 반찬 가게 지키라는 격 (속담) That's like setting the wolf to guard the sheep. /It's like having the fox guard the henhouse.

고양이소 ━素 a hypocrite ; a wolf in sheep's clothing

고어 古語 [옛말] an archaic word ; an archaism ; classical〔dead〕 languages ; [옛속담] an old proverb

고언 古諺 an old saying ; an old saw ; an old proverb ; an old adage ¶ 고언에 가로되 as the old proverb says 〔goes, has it〕 ; as the saying is

고언 苦言 bitter counsel ; candid〔outspoken〕 advice ; exhortation ¶ 고언을 하다 give 《a person》 candid〔frank〕 advice ; remonstrate with 《a person》 ; give 《a person》 a piece of one's mind ; give bitter-pill advice

고역 苦役 hard work ; a tough job ; toil ; drudgery ; fag ¶ 고역을 치르다 have a hard time of it // 사는 것이 고역이다 Life hangs heavy upon me.

고열 高熱 a high fever ; a high temperature ; a superheat ¶ 고열로 헛소리를 하다 utter meaningless words while sick with a high fever // 고열을 발산하다 emit〔give off〕 superheat

━ 반응 〖화학〗 a pyrogenetic reaction ━ 조정기 a pyrostat

고엽 枯葉 a dead〔withered, dry〕 leaf

고엽제 枯葉劑 a defoliant

고옥 古屋 an old house ; an ancient building ; a dilapidated cottage

고온 高溫 a high temperature ¶ 고온 다습한 기후 a climate of high temperature and high humidity

━계(計) pyrometer ━균(菌) 〖화학〗 thermophilic bacteria ━ 다습(多濕) high temperature and humidity ━ 반응 〖화학〗 a pyrogenetic〔pyrogenic〕 reaction ━ 측정 pyrometry

†고요 silence ; stillness ; tranquillity ; quiet (ness) ; calm (ness) ; quietude ; serenity ; peace ¶ 밤의 고요 the silence 〔dead〕 of the night // 죽음 같은 고요 a dead 〔deathlike〕 silence ; silence like the grave // 폭풍 전의 고요 a calm 〔silence〕 before the tempest

†고요하다 (be) quiet〔silent, still〕 ¶ 고요한 밤 a silent〔quiet〕 night // 고요한 바다 a calm sea // 고요한 아침의 나라 Korea, the Land of the Morning Calm // 주위는 쥐죽은 듯이 고요했다 All was deathly still. /All was so quiet there (that) a pin might have been heard to drop.

고욕 苦辱 hardships and humiliation ¶ 고욕을 당하다 suffer hardships and humiliation

고욤 〖식물〗 a small kind of persimmon

†고용 雇用 employment ; hiring ━하다 employ ; hire ¶ 완전 고용 full employment // 불완전 고용 underemployment // 고용 계약을 맺다 make a hiring contract // 이야기가 복잡해져서 결국 변호사를 고용하게 되었다 The talks started getting unpleasant, so I ended up retaining a lawyer.

피━인〔자〕 an employe (e)

고용 雇傭 employment ; being employed 〔hired〕 ; engagement ━하다 be hired ; be employed ; be engaged

━ 계약 a contract of employment ; an employment agreement ; a hiring (service) contract ━ 관계(關係) employment relationships ; hiring agreement ━ 기간 the period of employment ━ 상태 조사 a survey of employment conditions ; an employment status survey ━ 상황 an employment situation ━자 명부 an employment roll ━ 정책 a hiring policy 공평(公平) ━ [차별 없는] fair employment 장기 ━ long-term employment 종신 ━ lifetime employment

고용 경영인 雇傭經營人 a hired manager

고용살이 雇傭━ the life of an employee ¶ 고용살이에서 벗어나 독립하다 quit a hired job and start one's own business

고용인 雇用人 an employer

*고용인 雇傭人 an employee ¶ 고용인을 두고 가게를 운영하다 hire an employee to run a shop

고용 조건 雇傭條件 employment condi-

tions〔terms〕
‡고용주 雇用主 an employer
고용직 雇傭職 a hired job
고우 故友 ① [오래된 벗] an old friend; a friend of long standing; a long-time friend ¶ 국민 학교 때부터의 고우 one's old friend made in elementary school days // 죽마고우 a childhood friend; an old playmate
② [세상을 떠난 벗] a dead friend
*고원 高原 a plateau; a table-land
고원 高遠 —하다 (be) lofty; noble; high; elevated ¶ 고원한 이상 a lofty ideal
고원 雇員 an employee; a worker; [관청의] a government employee; [은행의] a junior clerk
고원 지대 高原地帶 highlands
고월 孤月 a solitary〔lonely〕 moon
*고위 高位 high rank; distinction
— 관리 high-ranking officials — 당직자 a high-ranking member of a political party — 회담 high-level talks
고위도 高緯度 a high latitude ¶ 고위도의 지방 a district in a high latitude; high latitudes; cold latitudes
— 지방 high latitudes; a district in a high latitude; [한랭 지방] cold latitudes
고위층 高位層 high-ranking officials
†고유 固有 [특유] characteristics; peculiarity; [본질] essence; [천성] inherence —하다 [특유] (be) peculiar 《to》; proper; one's own; [특성] characteristic; [천성의] inherent; inborn; innate ¶ 고유의 말 a language of their own // 한국 고유의 음악 music native to Korea // 동양의 고유 풍습 a custom peculiar to the Orient
*고유 명사 固有名詞 〖문법〗 a proper noun
고유 문자 固有文字 letters native to a country
고유 문화 固有文化 a native culture ¶ 고유 문화를 계승하고 발전시켜 나가다 inherit and develop cultural traditions
고유법 固有法 laws derived from the customs and traditions of a country
고유색 固有色 a local color
고유성 固有性 a characteristic; a peculiarity
고유 식물 固有植物 indigenous flora
고유어 固有語 a native tongue
고유 운동 固有運動 a proper motion
고유 재산 固有財産 a property of one's own
고유종 固有種 an indigenous species
고육 股肉 the flesh of a thigh
고육지계 苦肉之計 ¶ 고육지계를 쓰다 take a desperate countermeasure 《against an enemy》; torture oneself to deceive the enemy
고육책 苦肉策 ⇨ 고육지계 苦肉之計
고율 高率 a high rate ¶ 고율의 이자 a high (rate of) interest; high interest // 고율의 수익을 보장하다 guarantee 〔insure〕 high-rate profits
— 관세(關稅) a high tariff — 배당(配當) high-rate dividend —세(稅) high rate〔percentage〕 taxes — 임금 a high rate of wages; high wages
고은 高恩 great favor; deep kindness; obligations; indebtedness ¶ 고은을 입다 receive great kindness; meet with great favor; be under great obligation 《to a person》
고을 a district (of a province); a country ¶ 우리 고을 사람 a man of our own province〔country〕
고을살이 service as a district headman ¶ 고을살이하다 serve as a district headman〔governor〕
고음 高音 a loud sound; a high key; a high-pitched tone; 〖음악〗 soprano ¶ 고음의 loud; high-pitched; stentorian 《voice》 // 고음 처리가 아주 능란한 가수 a singer who is good at singing in high-pitched tones
—부(部) the treble — 확성기 a tweeter
고음계 高音階 the high scale
고읍 古邑 an ancient town
*고의 故意 intention; deliberation; design; purpose; willfulness ¶ 고의의 intentional; deliberate; designed; studied willful // 고의거나 우연이거나 intentionally or accidentally; whether by design or accident // 고의가 아니다 be unintentional; be accidental // 고의의 살인 wilful murder
고의 高誼 close friendship; your favor
고의 袴衣 summer shorts〔short pants〕
고의 苦衣 〖가톨릭〗 a man's trousers for summer
고의로 故意— purposely; on purpose; intentionally; deliberately; with design; wittingly ¶ 고의로 하다 do 《it》 intentionally〔on purpose〕 // 고의로 의무를 태만히 하다 willfully neglect one's duty
고의범 故意犯 a deliberate〔an intentional〕 offense
고의춤 袴衣— the space between one's abdomen and the belt of one's trousers ¶ 고의춤에 손을 넣다 stick one's hand into one's belt line
고이 [곱게] beautifully; finely; nicely; lovely; well; [편히] peacefully; [조심해서] gently; quietly; carefully ¶ 고이 다루다 handle carefully // 고이 잠자다 sleep peacefully // 머리를 고이 빗다 comb one's hair beautifully // 고이 말을 듣다 obey nicely〔like a good boy〕 // 고이 잠드소서 Rest in peace! // 고이 자라다 grow up nicely // 고이 간직하다 keep 《a thing》 carefully // 고이 돌려보내다 return 《a thing》 carefully

고인 古人 the ancients ; ancient people ; men of old ¶ 고인이 가로되 an old saying goes ((that))
고인 故人 the deceased ; the departed ; the dead ¶ 고인이 된 김씨 the late Mr. *Kim* ; Mr. *Kim* of blessed memory // 고인이 되다 die ; pass away ; be no more ; join the majority // 고인의 명복을 빌다 pray for the repose of the deceased
고인 雇人 an employe(e) ; a hired man [woman]
고인돌 a dolmen
고입 庫入 store goods in a warehouse
고자 古字 letters in ancient writing style
-고자 [욕망] wanting to ; wishing to ; should [would] like to ; going to ; willing to ; intending to ; [목적] (in order) to ; so as to ; with the intention of ; (so) that ~ may ; for (the purpose of) ¶ 그게 내가 말하고자 했던 거다 That is what I was going to say. // 충분한 수면을 취하고자 그는 일찍 잔다 He goes to bed early so as to get plenty of sleep. // 부산에 가고자 한다 I am going to go to *Pusan*. // 더 잘 보고자 안경을 닦았다 He wiped his spectacles in order to see better.
고자 告者 an informant [informer] ; a telltale ; a talebearer
고자 鼓子 a man with underdeveloped genital organs
고자누룩하다 [조용해지다] become quiet ; calm down ; [병세 따위가] lose sharpness ; be alleviated [allayed, mitigated, assuaged, soothed]
고자세 高姿勢 an aggressive [an overbearing, a high-handed] attitude ¶ 고자세를 취하다 assume a high-handed attitude
고자쟁이 a taleteller ; a telltale ; a talebearer ; a tattletale ; a squealer
고자질 talebearing ; taletelling ; tattling ; squealing ((속)) **—하다** tell tales ; tell [tattle, squeal] ((on a person)) ¶ 나를 선생님에게 고자질하다 tell our teacher on me
***고작** at (the) most ; at (the) best ; at the outside ; at the highest [greatest, largest] ¶ 그게 고작이다 That is the limit. // 고작해야 3마일밖에 안 된다 It is three miles at the most. // 고작해야 2만 원의 손해밖에 안 될 것이다 The loss will not be more than twenty thousand *won*. // 그에게 새 외투 한 번 사주는 것이 고작일 것이다 It may be only enough to buy him a new overcoat.
고장 [지방] a district ; [산지] producing center ; [동식물의] the home ; the habitat ; the native place (사람의) ¶ 담배의 고장 tobacco growing district // 유명한 말의 고장 a famous horse-breeding center // 대구는 사과의 고장이다 *Taegu* is the home of the apple. // 나는 그 고장에서 자랐다 I was raised there.
***고장 故障** ① [장해] a hitch ; a hindrance ; an obstacle ; a stumbling block ; [사고] an accident ; trouble ; a break down ; [결함] a defect ; something wrong ¶ 기관의 고장 an engine trouble // 기계의 고장 a mishap to machinery ; mechanical trouble // 고장 없이 without accident [trouble, a hitch] ; without let or hindrance ; well ; all right // 고장이 있다 [생기다] be [get] out of order ; break down // 고장 없이 가다 go well [all right] // 브레이크에 고장이 있다 Something is wrong [the matter] with the brake.
② [이의] an objection ; a protest
—차 a disabled car **— 측정기** a fault finder
고장난명 孤掌難鳴 It takes two to tango. /One needs assistance to accomplish anything.
고장물 [흐린 물] used dirty [filthy] water ; [진물] watery discharge from a sore
고재 高才 great talent [ability] ; genius
고쟁이 drawers [panty bloomers] worn by Korean women
고저 高低 [높이] (relative) height ; [기복] unevenness ; rise and fall ; undulation ; fluctuation (시세의) ; pitch (음성의) ¶ 기온의 고저 the fluctuation of temperature // 토지의 고저가 심한 지방 undulating [rolling] country // 임금의 고저에 따라 according to the wages // 고저가 없다 be even ; be level
— 지도(地圖) a relief map **—차(差)** difference of altitude ; 〖토목〗 difference of elevation
고저각 高低角 〖군사〗 angle of elevation
고저 장단 高低長短 height and length
고적 古跡, 古蹟 historical remains ; ruins ; a place of historical interest ; a historical place [spot] ¶ 명승 고적 scenic spots and places of historic interest // 고적을 탐승하다 visit places of historical interest // 경주 일대에는 고적이 많다 There are many historical remains in *Kyŏngju* and its vicinity.
— 보존회(保存會) a historic spot preservation society
고적 孤寂 solitude ; loneliness ; lonesomeness **—하다** (be) solitary ; lonely ; lone ; lonesome ¶ 고적을 즐기다 love solitude // 고적하게 살다 live in retirement // 고적한 나날을 보내다 live [lead] a lonely [solitary] life
고적대 鼓笛隊 a drum and fife band [corps]
—장(長) a drum major [majorette ((여자))]
고적운 高積雲 〖기상〗 an alto-cumulus

(cloud)
‡**고전 古典** [문학 작품] classics ; classical literature ; [고서] an old book ¶ 동양의 고전 the classics of the Orient
— 건축 classical architecture — 경제학 classical economics — 물리학 classical physics —성(性) classicality — 숭배 a classicalism — 숭배자 a classicist — 예술 classical art
고전 古錢 an ancient〔old〕coin ¶ 고전 수집가 a collector of old coins
—지(誌) numismatography —학(學) numismatics —학자 a numismatist ; a numismatologist
고전 苦戰 hard fighting ; a hard〔tight〕fight ; a desperate battle ; [경기 따위의] a close game ; a tight play ; hard going 《미·속》 —하다 fight hard〔desperately〕; fight against heavy odds ; have a close contest ; be going tough 〔have a tough game〕《미》 ¶ 그는 이번 선거에서 상당한 고전을 했다 He had a close contest in the recent election.
고전극 古典劇 classical drama
고전 문학 古典文學 classical literature ; classics ; humane learning
고전 물리학 古典物理學 classical physics
고전미 古典美 classical beauty
고전 발레 classical ballet
고전어 古典語 a classical language
고전 음악 classical music
고전장 古戰場 an old battlefield〔battleground〕; the scene of an ancient battle
고전적 古典的 classic ; classical ¶ 고전적인 기풍 a classical air // 고전적인 작품 a classic // 고전적인 분위기 a classical atmosphere
고전주의 古典主義 classicism ; classicalism
—자 a classic ; a classicist 신— neoclassicism
고전파 古典派 a classical school
— 경제학 classical economics
고전학 古典學 the classics
—자 a classic ; a classicist ; a classical scholar —파(派) the classical school ; the classicists
고절 高節 lofty virtues ; noble character
†**고정 固定** fixing ; fixation ; [자금의] tie-up ; lockup —하다 be fixed ; be tied 〔locked〕up ; fix ; settle ; solidify [흥분이나 노기를 가라앉힘] calm oneself ; calm down ¶ 고정된〔한〕fixed ; stationary ; immovable // 자금이 고정되다 Capital is tied〔locked〕up. // 이제 그만 고정하십시오 Please calm down now.
— 가격 a fixed〔firm〕price — 간첩 a resident spy —물 a fixed body ; a fixture — 부채 〖상업〗 fixed liabilities — 석 a fixed seat — 손님 a regular customer — 수입 a fixed income —자(子) 〖전기〗 a stator — 자세(姿勢) 〖야구〗 a fixed posture — 질소(窒素) fixed nitrogen — 초점(焦點) 〖사진〗 a fixed focus — 탄소(炭素) fixed carbon
고정 관념 a fixed idea ; idée fixe 《프》
고정급 固定給 a (basic) regular pay ; a fixed pay〔salary〕
고정 독자 固定讀者 a regular reader ; [잡지·신문 따위의] a regular subscriber 《to the Korea Times》
고정란 固定欄 a regular column
고정 부수 固定部數 a fixed number of subscriptions
고정비 固定費 〖회계〗 a fixed charge
고정식 固定式 the way of keeping a thing immobile
고정액 固定液 a fixative ; a fixing fluid
고정 자본 固定資本 fixed capital ¶ (유통 자본을) 고정 자본화하다 immobilize
고정 자산 固定資産 fixed assets〔property〕
— 과세 대장(課稅臺帳) a property tax ledger —세(稅) the municipal property tax — 회전율(回轉率) fixed assets turnover
고정 재산 固定財産 fixed assets〔property〕
고정적 固定的 fixed ¶ 고정적인 수입 a fixed income (salary)
고정주 固定株 a fixed stock
고정표 固定票 a fixed vote
고정화 固定化 fixation ; freezing
고정 환율제 固定換率制 the fixed exchange rate (system)
고제 古制 an old law ; an ancient statute
고제 高弟 an eminent disciple〔pupil〕; one's best pupil
고제 告祭 invoke God's blessing and perform a rite of worship
고조 高調 ① [높은 곡조] a high-toned melody ② [의기를 돋움] elation ; exultation ; encouragement ¶ 고조된 highly-elated ; inspired ; exulting // 고조된 사기 sky-high spirits 〔morale〕// 고조된 분위기 a highly elated atmosphere ③ [역설] emphasis ; stress —하다 emphasize ; lay stress on ; accentuate
고조 高潮 ① [밀물의] high tide 〔water〕; flood-tide ¶ 고조에 달하다 rise to its flood mark ② [정점] the climax ; culmination ; the acme ¶ 고조된 장면 a climax ; a thrilling scene // (최)고조에 달하다 reach〔come to〕a climax ; culminate
③ [감정의] an uprush〔upsurge〕(of emotion) ¶ 감정이 고조되다 become excited // 감정이 고조에 달하다 One's emotion rises to the climax. // 긴장의 고조 an increase〔a buildup〕of tension // 양국간의 긴장이 고조되었다 Tension has built up between the two countries.

—점(點) a high-water mark ; a flood-mark —항(港) a tidal harbor

고조 枯凋 withering ; decay ; decline ; blight —하다 wither ; decay ; decline ; be blighted

고조 高祖 ① the founder of a dynasty〔a sect〕 ② [고조부] a great-great-grandfather

고조 古調 an old tune

고조고 高祖考 one's deceased great-great-grandfather

고조모 高祖母 one's great-great-grandmother

고조부 高祖父 one's great-great-grandfather

고조비 高祖妣 one's deceased great-great-grandmother

고졸 高卒 a high school graduate ¶ 고졸 이상의 학력 educational attainments equal to and higher than those of high school graduate

고종 古鍾 an ancient bell

고종 姑從 a cousin by one's father's sister

고종 사촌 姑從四寸 a child of〔cousin by〕 one's father's sister

고죄 告罪 a confession (of guilt〔sin〕) —하다 confess oneself (to be) guilty ; confess one's sins

고주 孤舟 a solitary boat

고주 雇主 an employer ; a hirer ; a master

— 조합(組合) an employers association〔league〕 — 책임 보험(責任保險) employer's liability insurance

고주망태 (dead) drunkenness ¶ 고주망태가 되다 get〔be〕 dead drunk ; be boozy // 고주망태가 되도록 마시다 continue to drink until becoming dead drunk

고주파 高周波 〖물리〗 high frequency

— 가열(加熱) 〖전기〗 high-frequency heating ; radio(-frequency) heating ; electronic heating — 건조로(乾燥爐) a dielectric-heat dryer — 경화(硬化) 〖화학〗 radio-frequency curing — 무선(無線) high-frequency radio — 저항기 a high-frequency rheostat — 전류 high-frequency current — 전파 high-frequency radio waves — 증폭기 a radioamplifier

고주파로 高周波爐 high-frequency electric heater

고주파 발전기 高周波發電機 a high-frequency generator

고주파 요법 高周波療法 〖의학〗 fulguration

고즈넉하다 ① [잠잠하고 호젓하다] (be) quiet and still ¶ 고즈넉한 정적이 흐르다 A quiet stillness prevails.

② [잠잠하고 다소곳하다] (be) quiet and lonesome ¶ 고즈넉하게 고개를 숙이고 앉아 있다 sit still with a dropping head // 고즈넉이 gently

고증 考證 research ; investigation ; inquiry —하다 investigate ; inquire into ; study ¶ 이 그림의 복장에는 고증상 틀린 곳이 있다 The dress〔costume〕 of the figure in this picture is wrong from the historical point of view. // 왕조실록과 대비하여 일일이 고증하다 ascertain in detail historical evidence in reference to the dynastic annals

시대 — historical research

고증학 考證學 a bibliographical study of Chinese classics

고지[1] [호박 따위의] chopped and dried pumpkins, egg apples, etc.

고지[2] [메주 만드는] a wooden frame for pressing malt, boiled beans, etc. into a lump

*고지 高地 high ground ; [산지] an upland ; [고대] heights ; [고원] a plateau 《*pl.* ~x, ~s》 ; a tableland ¶ 800 고지 the 800-meter Hill // 한랭한 고지에서 재배되는 채소 upland-grown vegetables // 100억 불 수출 고지 the 10 billion dollar goal for exports

고지 告知 notice ; notification —하다 notify〔inform〕 《a person of》 ; announce ¶ 세금 납부 기일을 고지하다 notify the date of tax payment

고지 固持 —하다 persist in ; hold fast to ; stick to ¶ 자기의 의견을 고지하다 persist in one's own opinion ; stick to one's guns

고지 故地 the place where one lived once ; one's native place

고지 高志 a lofty idea

고진공 高眞空 a high-degree vacuum

고지기 a warehouse keeper ; a storekeeper 《영》

고지대 高地帶 the hilly sections

— 주민 hillside residents — 식수난 water shortage in the hilly sections 〔areas〕

고지새 〖새〗 a migratory Chinese grosbeak ; Eophona migratoria (학명)

고지서 告知書 a written notice ¶ 납세 고지서 tax papers ; a tax notice

고지식하다 (be) simple and honest ; guileless ; simple-minded ; unadaptable ; tactless ; formalistic ; naive ; gullible ¶ 그는 고지식한 구식 사람이다 He is a simple and honest fellow of the old form. // 그는 너무 고지식하다 He is stupidly honest. // 고지식해서 남의 말을 곧이 듣는다 He is naive and gullible.

고지 자리품 〖농업〗 rice farming on a subcontract basis

고지판 告知板 a bulletin board

고진감래 苦盡甘來 Sweet after bitter. / Pleasure follows pain. / Pain is gone, and pleasure is come. / No gains without pains.

고질 痼疾 a chronic〔an inveterate〕 disease〔malady, ailment〕 ¶ 고질인 신경통으로 시달리고 있다 He is a chronic sufferer from neuralgia.
고질 固質 solidity
‡고집 固執 stubbornness ; obstinacy ; pigheadedness ; steadfastness ━하다 hold fast 《to》 ; adhere 《to》 ; insist 《on》 ; persist 《in》 ; stand firmly by ¶ 고집이 세다 be stubborn ; be obstinate ; be pigheaded // 자기 의견을 고집하다 hold fast to one's view ; stick to one's gun // 쓸데없이 고집을 부린다 be unduly stubborn // 그는 따라가겠다고 고집을 세운다 He insists upon accompanying us.
고집불통 固執不通 extreme obstinacy〔stubbornness, perversity, bigotry, persistence〕 ¶ 고집불통이다 (be) extremely obstinate〔stubborn, perverse, bigoted, persistent〕 // 고집불통인 영감을 겨우 설득하다 manage to persuade the obstinate old man
고집통이 a stubborn〔stiff-necked〕 fellow ; an obstinate person ; a pigheaded person
고차 방정식 高次方程式 〖수학〗 an equation of higher degree
고차원 세계 高次元世界 a high-dimensional world
고차적 高次的 high-level ; high-degree ; highly developed ¶ 고차적인 문제 a problem of a high order
고착 固着 adherence ; sticking ━하다 adhere〔cohere, stick〕 to ¶ 식물들은 땅(속)에 고착했다 Plants got imbedded in the earth.
━색(色) fast color
고착 관념 固着觀念 〖심리〗 a fixed idea ; a fixation ; an idée fixe 《프》
고착 생활 固着生活 parasitism
고착제 固着劑 a binder
고찰 古刹 an old〔ancient〕 temple
고찰 考察 consideration ; study ; inquiry ━하다 consider ; study ; contemplate ; inquire into ¶ 의회 정치에 관한 고찰 an inquiry into〔a study of〕 Representative Government // 윤리적〔미적〕 고찰 ethical〔aesthetic〕 contemplation // 원주민의 생활 양식을 고찰하다 inquire into the way of living〔life style〕 of the indigenous people // 그것은 여러 가지 각도에서 고찰할 필요가 있다 It involves〔requires〕 consideration from various angles.
고참 古參 seniority ; [사람] a senior ; an old-timer ; a veteran ¶ 고참의 senior // 그는 나보다 훨씬 고참이다 He is many years my senior in service. // 그는 이 회사에서는 고참이다 He is an old-timer in this company.
━병 a veteran conscript ; a senior comrade 최━자 the father ; the doyen
고창 高唱 ① [큰소리로 부름] singing loudly ② [주장] advocating ; urging
고창 鼓脹 〖한의〗 meteorism ; tympanites ; flatulence
고처 高處 heights
고천문 告天文 an announcement to Heaven〔God〕
고철 古鐵 scrap iron ; ferrous scraps ; pieces of old metal ¶ 고철로 팔다 sell 《an old car》 for junk
━상〔상인〕 a junkman ; a junk dealer ; [상점] a junk shop
고체 古體 archaic style〔form〕 ; archaism
‡고체 固體 a solid (body) ¶ 고체의 solid
━ 물리학 solid state physics ; the physics of the solid state
고체 연료 固體燃料 solid fuel
고체화 固體化 solidification
고쳐 again ; over again ¶ 고쳐 쓰다 rewrite ; write over (again) ; [정서하다] copy clearly // 고쳐 짓다 rebuild ; reconstruct // 고쳐 말하면 in other words // 한문을 국문으로 고쳐 쓰다 transliterate〔put〕 classical Chinese into Korean
고초 苦楚 hardships ; difficulties ; trouble ; distress ; sufferings ; affliction ; trials ¶ 고초를 겪다 suffer hardships ; be in trouble ; have a hard time of it ; be in distress
고초 藁草 rice-straw
고총 古塚 an old tomb〔mound〕
고추 red pepper ; cayenne pepper ¶ 작은 고추가 맵다 The smaller, the shrewder.
고추바람 a biting〔piercing, cutting〕 wind
고추박이 a lowborn woman's husband
고추상투 a small topknot (worn by old men)
고추잠자리 a red dragonfly
고추장 ━醬 thick soypaste mixed with red pepper
고출력 高出力 a large output (of power)
고춧가루 powdered red pepper
고충 苦衷 a solicitude ; a painful position ; a predicament ¶ 남의 고충을 동정하다 be sympathetic with 《a person》 in a predicament // 고충을 털어놓다 vent one's mental sufferings〔predicaments〕 // 고충이 있다 be in a dilemma〔predicament〕
고충실도 高忠實度 high-fidelity 《hi-fi》
고취 鼓吹 inspiration ; instillation propagandism ━하다 inspire 《a person》 with ; instil〔infuse, imbue〕 《an idea》 into 《a person》 ; [환기하다] stir up ; arouse ; [선전하다] propagandize ¶ 애국심을 고취하다 instil〔infuse〕 patriotism into the hearts of 《people》 ; imbue a mind with patriotism // 예술 취미를 고취하다 stir up interest in art // 민족 의식을

고취하다 arouse〔stir up〕 national consciousness
—자 an advocate ; a propagator
고층 高層 [건물의] higher stories ; upper floors ; [대기의] the upper layer ¶ 고층의 high-storied 《building》// 고층 아파트 a high-rise apartment building // 새로 지은 고층 건물이 관광 명소가 되었다고 들었습니다 I heard a newly-built high-rise building has become a tourist attraction.
— 기류(氣流) an upper air current **— 기상관측** aerological observation **— 기상대** an aerological observatory **— 기상학** aerology **— 대기(大氣)** the upper atmosphere **— 비행** flying at a high altitude ; a substratospheric flight
고층 건물 高層建物 a multistory〔multistoried〕 building ; a high〔tall, lofty〕 building ; a skyscraper 《미》
고층운 高層雲 altostratus
고치 a (silk) cocoon ¶ 고치에서 실을 잣다 reel silk off cocoons // 누에는 고치를 만든다 The silkworm spins a cocoon.
†**고치다** ① [병을] cure ; heal ; make well ¶ 병을 고치다 cure a disease // 감기를 고치다 cure 《a person》 of a cold // 어린애의 병을 고쳤다 He made the baby well.
② [수선하다] mend ; repair ; make good ; fix (up) ¶ 기계를 고치다 repair a machine ; put a machine in order // 구두를 고치다 mend shoes ; have one's shoes mended // 시계를 고치다 fix a watch ; have one's watch repaired // 빵꾸를 고치다 mend a puncture ; fix a flat (tire) 《미》
③ [교정하다] correct ; rectify ; remedy ; reform ¶ 결점을 고치다 correct one's shortcomings // 버릇을 고치다 get rid of a bad habit ; break〔cure〕 oneself of a bad habit // 잘못을 고치다 correct errors // 틀린 답을 고치다 correct wrong answers // 비뚤어진 자세를 고치다 correct a deformed posture // 밤새는 습관을 고치지 않으면 몸이 상할 것이다 You'll ruin your health if you don't break your habit of staying up so late at night.
④ [변경하다] change ; alter ¶ 계획을 고치다 alter the schedule // 이 외투는 좀 고쳐야 한다 This coat requires some alteration. // 이름을 고치다 change one's name
고치실 yarn spun around a cocoon
고침 高枕 [높은 베개] a high pillow ; [편한 생활] a peaceful life
고침단명 高枕短命 High pillow, short life.
고칭 古稱 an old name〔designation〕 ; an archaic term〔title〕
고콜 a hollow in the wall to place a torch ; a recessed sconce
고콜불 a torch in a niche
고타분하다 (be) fetid ⇨ 고리타분하다
고탑 古塔 an old tower ; an ancient pagoda
고탑 高塔 a high tower
고태 古態 an antique (and unchanged) appearance ; an antique and elegant appearance
고태의연 古態依然 ¶ 고태의연하다 remain unchanged〔as it was〕
고택 古宅 an old house
고토 膏土 rich〔fertile〕 soil
고토 苦土 〚화학〛 magnesia
— 벽돌 a magnesia brick
고토 故土 one's native land ; one's native place ; one's old〔former〕 territory ¶ 고토에 돌아오다 come〔return〕 home
†**고통 苦痛** [아픔] pain ; [괴로움] suffering ; agony ; [마음의] anguish ¶ 정신적 고통 mental anguish // 고통을 느끼다 feel a pain ; suffer (pain) ; be in pain // 고통을 주다 give 《a person》 pain ; pain // 고통을 없애다 remove〔take away〕 a pain ; put 《a person》 out of pain // 고통이 사라졌다 The pain has left me.
고통스럽다 (be) painful ; tormenting ; distressing
고투 古套 an old style ; a conventional form
고투 苦鬪 a bitter struggle ; a hard fight
—하다 fight hard
고판 古版 an old edition ; [책] old books in block print ; [판] an old printing block
⁑**고패** a pulley
— 우물 a wheel well
고팻줄 a pulley rope〔cord〕
고팽이 ① [새끼의 사리] a coil ② [왕복] a round-trip route ③ [고비] the critical moment in a difficult task
고평 高評 [평가] an excellent opinion ; [남의 비평] your〔his〕 esteemed opinion〔criticism〕 ¶ 고평을 듣고 싶습니다 I would like to hear your esteemed opinion〔criticism〕.
고평 考評 review ; comment ; criticism
—하다 review ; comment 《on》 ; criticize
고푸리다 stoop ; lean over ; bend forward (앞으로) ¶ 몸을 고푸리고 꽃을 꺾다 stoop down to pick a flower
고품 古品 antiques
*__고풍 古風__ antiquity ; an antique style ; old fashion〔manner〕 ; [고체] an archaism ¶ 고풍의 antique ; archaic ; old-fashioned ; out-of-date // 고풍의 문체 an antiquated style // 고풍의 건물 an antique building // 고풍을 지키다 follow the old ways ; keep to the old customs
고프다 (be) hungry ; famished 《미》 ¶ 배가 고프다 feel hungry // 배는 고픈데

밥맛은 없고 I am hungry but (have) no appetite.

고필 古筆 old writings ; old writing brush

고하 高下 [지위의] rank ; [품질의] quality ; [시세의] fluctuations ; rise and fall ¶ 신분의 고하를 불문〔막론〕하고 irrespective of rank // 고하를 매기다 grade ; discriminate // 품질의 고하가 여러 가지이다 be various in quality // 값의 고하를 불문하고 사겠다 I will buy it irrespective〔regardless〕 of its price.

고하간 高下間 high and low ¶ 값은 고하간에 일단 사 놓고 보다 buy an article irrespective〔regardless〕 of its price

고하다 告— [말하다] tell (one's superior) ; mention ; speak about ; [통고하다] inform ; announce ¶ 어른께 사실대로 고하다 tell one's superior the truth // 잘못을 고해 바치다 tell somebody about his wrong doings // 군중에게 고하다 announce to the public // 마지막을 고하다 come to an end

*__고학 苦學__ studying under adversity **—하다** study under adversity〔difficulties〕 ; [일하며] work one's way through school ¶ 고학해서 대학을 졸업하다 work one's way through college

고학생 苦學生 a self-supporting student ; a student who is paying his way

†**고함 高喊** a shout ; a yell ; a roar ; a howl ¶ 오라고 고함치다 shout 《to a person》 to come // 고함질러 꿈쩍 못하게 하다 shout 《a person》 down

고해 告解 ⇨ 고해성사

고해 苦海 the bitter human world ; 〖불교〗 this world

-고 해서 saying 《that》 ; on the ground(s) 《that》 ; with the excuse 《that》 ; simply because ¶ 아무리 돈이 많다고 해서 however rich one may be // 가난하다고 해서 남을 경멸해서는 안된다 You should not despise a man (simply) because he is poor.

고해 성사 告解聖事 〖카톨릭〗 confession

*__고행 苦行__ asceticism ; penance ; mortification **—하다** practice asceticism ; do penance

고행자 苦行者 an ascetic

†**고향 故鄕** one's home ; one's home town ; one's native (place) ; one's old home ; one's birthplace ¶ 제2의 고향 one's second home ; one's adopted land (외인의 경우) // 고향에 돌아가다 return to one's old home // 고향을 그리다 be homesick ; long〔pine〕 for home // 고향을 떠나다 leave home〔one's native place〕 // 고향이 어디냐 Where do you come from?

고현 古賢 sages〔wise men〕 of old times

고현학 考現學 the study of modern phenomena

고혈 膏血 sweat and blood ¶ 백성의 고혈을 짜다 squeeze the people

고혈압 高血壓 high blood pressure ; hypertension
— 환자 a hypertensive

고혈압증 高血壓症 hyperpiesia

고형 固形 solidity ¶ 고형의 solid // 고형화하다 solidify ; be solidified
— 물질 a solid body ; a solid **— 식량** compressed food **— 연료** solid fuel **— 음식물** solid food

고형 알코올 solid alcohol

고혹 蠱惑 seduction ; bewitchment ; fascination ; enchantment **—하다** fascinate ; enchant ; bewitch ; charm ; allure ; seduce ¶ 고혹적인 fascinating ; attractive ; alluring // 여인의 고혹적인 눈매 the alluring look of a woman

고혼 孤魂 a spirit for whom there is no one to offer sacrifice ¶ 고혼을 달래다 pray for the repose of the dead // 고혼이 되다 die with no one in attendance ; die in solitude // 수중 고혼이 되다 be buried in a watery grave

고화 古畫 an ancient picture ; an old painting

고환 睾丸 testicles ; a testis 《*pl.* -tes》 ; the balls 《미·속》

고환염 睾丸炎 orchitis ; testitis

고희 古稀 three score and ten ; seventy years of age

고희연 古稀宴 the celebration of one's 70th birthday

곡 曲 a tune ; an air ; a piece ; a melody ; music ¶ 곡을 연주하다 play〔render〕 a tune on 《the violin》 // 가사에 곡을 붙이다 write the music for a song // 곡에 가사를 붙이다 set a poem to music

곡 哭 wailing ; lamentation **—하다** lament about ; bewail ; weep ; keen

곡가 穀價 the price of grain
— 정책 a grain price policy **이중 — 제도** a double-tiered grain price system

곡경 曲境 a difficult〔hard〕 position ; a fix ; a sad plight〔predicament〕 ; difficulties ¶ 곡경에 있는 사람을 돕다 help 《a person》 in trouble

곡곡 曲曲 ① [굴곡] curves ; turns ; twists ② [도처] the whole length and breadth of the land

곡괭이 a hoe ; a pick ; a pickaxe

곡구 曲球 a curve (ball) ; 〖야구〗 a bender ; 〖당구〗 a fancy shot

곡기 穀氣 food ¶ 환자는 이틀간 곡기를 입에 못댔다 The patient was unable to take any food for two days.

곡두 [환영] a phantom ; [환상] a vision ; [착각] an illusion ; a delusion ¶ 곡두 같은 dreamlike // 곡두를 보다 see a phantom // 곡두에게 홀리다 be lured by an illusion

곡론 曲論 sophistry ; a biased argument ; a distorted〔devious〕 argument

곡류 穀類 cereals ; corn ; grain
곡류 曲流 a meander ; a meandering 〔winding〕 stream
곡률 曲率 curvature
—선(線) a circle of curvature — 중심(中心)〔반경(半徑)〕 the center〔radius〕 of curvature 공간(空間) — a space curvature
곡률 반지름 曲率半— the radius of curvature
곡률원 曲率圓 a line of curvature
곡마 曲馬 a circus ; equestrian feats
곡마단 曲馬團 a circus troupe〔company〕
—장(長) the boss of a traveling circus
곡마사 曲馬師 a circus〔stunt, trick〕 rider
곡마장 曲馬場 a circus ; a circus ring
곡면 曲面 a curved surface
곡면체 曲面體 a curved figure
곡명 曲名 the title of a musical composition
곡목 曲目 a program (전체) ; a number (곡)
†곡물 穀物 corn ; cereals ; grain 《미》
— 건조기(乾燥機) a grain drier — 도매상 a grain broker 《미》 ; a corn factor 《영》 — 운반선 a grain carrier — 중매인(仲買人) a grain broker 《미》 ; a corn broker 《영》
곡물상 穀物商 a grain dealer 《미》 ; a corn dealer 《영》
곡물 시장 穀物市場 the grain〔corn〕 market
곡물 창고 穀物倉庫 a granary ; a corn reserve ; a grain elevator 《미》
곡보 曲譜 musical notes ; a score
곡사 曲射 high-angle fire —하다 fire at a high angle
곡사포 曲射砲 a howitzer ; a high-angle gun
*곡선 曲線 a curve ; a curved line ¶ 곡선을 그리다 draw a curved line // 곡선을 그리며 날다 fly through the air forming a hyperbolic curve
— 도표(圖表) a curve ; a graph — 좌표 curvilinear coordinates —주(柱) a cylindroid
곡선계 曲線計 a curvilinear scale curve
곡선미 曲線美 the beauty of one's curves ; curvaceousness ; curvaciousness ¶ 곡선미의 여성 a woman with beautiful curves ; a curvaceous〔curvacious〕 woman 《미·구》 // 다리의 곡선미 the beauty of one's leg line // 그 여자는 미끈한 다리 풍만한 가슴 멋있는 곡선미하며 다 갖췄군 She is leggy, bosomy, curvacious, everything.
곡선 운동 曲線運動 a curvilinear motion
곡선자 曲線— a (French) curve
곡선표 曲線標 a curve sign
곡성 哭聲 a cry ; a wail ; a keen
곡수 谷水 a mountain〔valley〕 stream
*곡식 穀— cereals ; grain
곡신 穀神 the God of Cereals ; Ceres
곡심 曲心 a wicked〔crooked〕 mind
곡예 曲藝 stunts ; (acrobatic) feats ; tricks ; fancy performances ¶ 곡예를 하다 do stunt // 말 곡예를 하다 do equestrian feats ; do stunt on horseback
공중 — stunt flying ; a flying stunt ; aerial acrobatics
곡예 비행 曲藝飛行 stunt flying ; a flying stunt ; an acrobatic flight
기마(騎馬) — equestrian acrobatics 〔feats〕
곡예사 曲藝師 an acrobat ; a tumbler ; a stunt performer ; a circus rider
곡옥 曲玉 a halfmoon-shaped bead
곡인 穀人 a farmer ; a peasant ; peasantry 《총칭》
곡절 曲折 [물리적] winding ; crookedness ; indentation (해안의) ; [우회] meandering ; turns and twists ; [파란] ups and downs ; vicissitudes ; [복잡] complications ; intricacies ; [까닭·사정] circumstances ; reason ; details ; the whys and hows ¶ 우여곡절 ups and downs ; vicissitudes ; complications ; twistings ; meanderings // 사건의 곡절 the complications of an affair // 많은 곡절 끝에 문제는 해결됐다 After many complications the matter was settled. // 무슨 곡절이 있을 것이다 There must be some unknown circumstances〔reasons〕 for it. // 일이 이렇게 된 데는 여러 곡절이 있다 Many circumstances have contributed toward this.
*곡조 曲調 a tune ; an air ; a melody ; a strain ¶ 흥겨운 곡조 a merry tune // 곡조에 맞지 않는 노래 a song out of tune // 한 곡조 부르다 sing a tune // 가사에 곡조를 붙이다 set the song to a music
곡주 穀酒 grain wine
곡직 曲直 right and wrong ; merits〔propriety〕 《of a case》 ¶ 곡직을 가리다 inquire into the rights and wrongs of a case ; judge〔distinguish〕 right from wrong // 불문곡직 without inquiring into the right or wrong
곡차 穀茶 『불교』 rice wine ; wine ; liquor ; alcoholic drinks ; spirits ; intoxicants
곡창 穀倉 [창고] a granary ; a grain elevator 《미》 ; [비유적] a granary
곡창 지대 穀倉地帶 a granary ; a breadbasket 《미》 ¶ 호남 지방은 우리나라의 곡창 지대이다 The *Honam* region is the bread basket of the country.
곡척 曲尺 a metal measure ; a carpenter's square
곡초 穀草 rice straw
곡출 穀出 grain yield
곡피 穀皮 husk

곡필 曲筆 perversion〔falsification, misrepresentation, distortion〕 in writing **—하다** distort the truth〔fact〕《in writing》; pervert in writing ¶ 그는 곡필로 권력에 아첨한다 He flatters the authority by false writing.
무문(舞文)— (a) perversion of the truth
곡학 曲學 prostitution of learning; perverted〔timeserving〕 study; diabolical studies
곡학아세 曲學阿世 perverted〔timeserving〕 study; sophistry
*__곡해 曲解__ misinterpretation; misconstruction; misunderstanding; distortion; [억지 해석] an overstrained interpretation; perversion **—하다** interpret wrongly; misconstrue; misunderstand; strain〔distort, twist〕 into some other meaning (왜곡) ¶ 고의로 곡해하다 misunderstand intentionally // 동료의 호의를 곡해하다 misunderstand one's colleague's kindness
곡향 穀鄕 a rich grain district; a granary ¶ 북미는 세계의 곡향이다 North America is the granary of the world.
곡형 曲形 a curved shape
†**곤경 困境** an awkward〔a hard, a difficult〕 position; a fix; a predicament; a sad plight; straitened circumstances ¶ 곤경에 빠지다 be driven to the wall; be in a fix〔trouble〕; fall into an awkward position
곤고 困苦 hardships; privations; sufferings; adversity ¶ 곤고를 겪다 go through hardships; suffer〔be subjected to〕 privation // 곤고와 싸우다 struggle with adversity // 곤고를 견디다 endure hardships and privations
†**곤궁 困窮** distress; [빈곤] poverty; destitution; penury; want; suffering **—하다** (be) destitute; hard pressed; be in distress; be hard up ¶ 곤궁한 사람들 the poor; the needy // 곤궁한 사람을 도와주다 help a person out of a difficulty // 극도로 곤궁하다 be in extreme distress; be in dire want; sink into the depths of misery
곤대 the stem of a taro
곤댓짓 arrogant〔overbearing, haughty〕 behavior; cocky attitude **—하다** behave in an affected manner; give oneself airs; assume airs
*__곤돌라__ a gondola
‡**곤두박이다** fall〔drop〕 upside down; fall headlong; nosedive; fall head over heels〔top over tail〕
곤두박이치다 fall headlong
곤두박질 falling headlong〔head-over-heels〕 ¶ 계단에서 곤두박질 치다 fall headlong down a flight of stairs
곤두박질 치다 [관용] topple; nosedive; fall (upside) down; fall head foremost〔head-over-heels〕; throw 《it》 upside down
*__곤두서다__ stand on one's head; stand on end; stand upside down ¶ 신경이 곤두서다 one's nerves are on edge // 머리카락이 곤두서다 one's hair bristles up // 그 얘기를 들으니 무서워서 머리털이 곤두서는 것 같았다 That story made my hair stand on end.
곤두세우다 set 《it》 upside down; stand 《it》 wrong way to; set on end; [털을] bristle〔ruffle〕 up ¶ (화가 나서) 머리털을 곤두세우고 with one's hair on end // 신경을 곤두세우고 with one's every nerve bristled up // 한밤중의 전화가 신경을 곤두세우다 A midnight phone call made my nerves stand on end. // 머리털을 곤두세워 화내다 set up one's bristle; bristle with anger // 닭이 고양이를 보고 깃털을 곤두세웠다 The chicken ruffled its plumage as it saw the cat.
곤드기 장원 —壯元 a tie game; a draw (in gambling)
곤드라지다 fall asleep dog-tired〔dead drunk〕; fall down asleep; drop off to sleep ¶ 술에 취해 곤드라지다 sleep due to drunkenness; fall to sleep in overdrinking
곤드레만드레 staggering; [취하여] dead drunk **—하다** stagger; lose one's sense of balance ¶ 곤드레만드레 취하다 be dead〔beastly〕 drunk; be drunk as a lord; be all wet; get boozy (미·속) // 그는 최근에 곤드레만드레 취해 있는 상태라고 한다 I hear he's hitting the bottle recently.
†**곤란 困難** difficulty; trouble; [곤궁] distress; hardship; [난처] embarrassment; perplexity **—하다** (be) difficult; hard; tough; troublesome; trying; [난처하다] embarrassing; awkward; [곤궁하다] needy; distressed ¶ 곤란한 질문 a difficult question // 곤란한 일 a difficult matter; a matter of difficulty // 곤란한 처지 a delicate〔an awkward〕 situation; needy circumstances // 곤란한 사업 a difficult undertaking // 재정 곤란 financial〔pecuniary〕 embarrassment〔difficulty〕 // 해결하기 곤란한 문제 a knotty problem; a problem difficult to settle // 곤란을 느끼다 feel difficult; have〔experience〕 difficulty 《in》 // 생활이 곤란하다 be hard up; live in poverty // 이해하기 곤란하다 be hard to understand // 대답하기 곤란하다 be hard〔awkward〕 to answer // 곤란을 이겨내다 overcome〔surmount〕 difficulties // 여러 가지 곤란을 견디다 endure every hardship // 곤란에 부딪치다 get into difficulty〔trouble〕 // 곤란과 싸우다 struggle with difficulties // 흑백을 가리기가 곤란하다 We find it difficult to judge right from wrong. // 내 이름을 도용하는 그런 일은 곤란하

다 I can't have that-your using my name without my permission. // 이렇게 항상 늦으면 아주 곤란한데 This is too much, your always being late like this.

곤룡포 袞龍袍 a royal robe

†곤봉 棍棒 a club ; a cudgel ; a stick ; a truncheon 《영》

곤봉 체조 棍棒體操 Indian club exercises

곤색 一色 dark〔navy, deep〕 blue ⇨ 감색(紺色)

곤욕 困辱 a bitter insult ; extreme contempt ¶ 곤욕을 치르다 suffer a bitter insult // 곤욕을 당하다 be subjected to humiliation〔disgrace〕 // 곤욕을 참다 put up with an insult ; bear an extreme affront

*곤장 棍杖 a club 《for flogging criminals》 ¶ 곤장을 안기다 flog 《a person》

곤쟁이 a kind of tiny shrimp

곤쟁이젓 tiny shrimps preserved with salt

곤전 坤殿 a queen ; a queen consort
—마마 Her (Royal) Majesty the Queen

곤죽 [진창] quagmire ; muddiness ; [뒤범벅] mess ; utter confusion ¶ 일을 곤죽을 만들다 make a mess of an affair // 장마로 곤죽이 된 길 a road turned into a quagmire // 술에 곤죽이 되다 be soaked with drink

곤줄박이 〖새〗 a titmouse ; a woodcracker

곤지 the red spot on a bride's brow ¶ 곤지 찍다 put rouge on one's forehead ; rouge one's forehead ; wear the brow rouge spot (신부가)

*곤충 昆蟲 an insect ; a bug
—기(記) [파브르의] Entomological Souvenirs (by Jean Henri Fabre) ; *Souvenirs entomologiques* 《프》 —망(網) an insect net — 사육장 an insectarium — 실험실 an insectary — 채집 insect collecting ; entomologizing ; bugging 《구》 ; bug hunting — 표본 상자 an insect cabinet

곤충류 昆蟲類 the insect species ; Insecta

곤충학 昆蟲學 entomology ; insectology ¶ 곤충학을 연구하다 study entomology
—자 an entomologist ; a bughunter 《구》

곤포 昆布 ⇨ 다시마

곤핍 困乏 fatigue ; tiredness ; weariness ; exhaustion —하다 (be) fatigued ; tired ; weary

곤하다 困— (be) weary ; tired ; fatigued ; exhausted ¶ 곤히 in a weary〔an exhausted〕 manner // 곤한 잠 deep〔sound〕 slumber // 몹시 곤하다 be dead tired〔dog-tired〕 ; be exhausted // 곤히 잠들다 fall fast asleep ; drop off into deep slumber // 그는 이층 자기 침실에서 곤히 자고 있다 He is upstairs in his bedroom fast asleep.

곤혹 困惑 embarrassment ; perplexity ; puzzlement ¶ 곤혹스러이 embarrassingly ; perplexedly // 곤혹의 빛을 띠다 wear a worried look ; look troubled〔embarrassed〕

†곧 ① [즉시] at once ; immediately ; directly ; instantly ; without delay ; without loss of time ; right away 《미》 ; soon ; shortly ; before long ; [쉽게] easily ; readily ¶ 곧 떠나라 Leave at once ! // 식사가 끝나면 곧 right〔immediately〕 after the dinner // 서울에 도착하면 곧 as soon as one gets to〔arrives in〕 Seoul // 곧 …하다 lose no time in 《doing》 // 곧 화를 내다 get angry easily // 곧 대답을 하다 give an immediate answer // 곧 가야 한다 I must go at once〔right away〕. // 곧 돌아오겠다 I will be back in a moment. // 그는 나를 보자 곧 뛰어왔다 He ran to me the moment he saw me. // 이제 곧 열시다 It is nearly ten o'clock. // 지금 곧 할 수는 없다 It can not be done at a moment's notice.
② [멀지 않아서] soon ; before long ¶ 그도 곧 오겠지 He will come before long also. // 이제 곧 크리스마스다 Christmas is just around the corner.
③ [즉] namely ; that is (to say) ; or ; in other words ; just ; exactly ¶ 그 사람이 곧 주인이었다 He was the master himself. // 민심이 곧 천심이다 The mind of the people is the mind of heaven.

곧날대패 a straight-blade plane

†곧다 ① [물건이] (be) straight ; upright ; erect ; direct ¶ 곧은 길 a straight road // 곧은 장대 a straight pole // 곧게 하다 straighten
② [마음이] (be) honest ; upright ; straightforward // 곧은 길로 나가다 lead an honest life ; tread the right path // 곧은 나무 쉬 꺾인다 A straight〔upright〕 tree is easily broken〔snapped〕 off.
곧은 나무 먼저 찍힌다 [속담] The good die young.

곧바로 at once ; straight ¶ 일을 끝내자 곧바로 집으로 돌아갔다 Directly after work I went straight home.

곧바르다 (be) straight and right

곧은결 straight grain ¶ 곧은결의 straight-grained

곧은길 a straight road

곧은불림 frank confession —하다 frankly〔candidly〕 confess ; make a frank〔honest〕 confession

곧은창자 ① 〖해부〗 the rectum ② [고지식한 사람] a naive〔tactless〕 person ③ [식후 곧 변소 가는 사람] a person who goes to the toilet right after eating

곧이곧대로 plainly ; straightforwardly ; frankly ; honestly ; tactlessly ; rigidly ;

just as it is ¶ 곧이곧대로 믿다 believe everything just as told // 곧이곧대로의 보고 a tactless account // 곧이곧대로 말하다 give a plain〔straightforward〕 account of 《an affair》; speak out in a straightforward manner; tell the truth // 규율을 곧이곧대로 집행하다 apply a rule tactlessly〔too rigidly〕 // 그는 곧이곧대로의 사람이다 He is a straight〔an honest〕 man.

*곧이듣다 take 《a person's story》 seriously〔as an honest one〕; accept 《a thing》 as true; take 《a person》 at his word; be gullible ¶ 우스갯소리를 곧이듣다 take a joke seriously // 남의 말을 곧이듣다 take another's words as truth // 나는 그의 말을 곧이들었다 I took him at his word. // 그는 그녀의 말이면 뭣이든 곧이들을 것이다 He will swallow any story she tells.

†곧잘 ① [제법 잘] fairly〔pretty〕 well; quite well; well enough ¶ 운동도 곧잘 한다 He plays sports (quite) well. // 그는 영어를 곧잘 한다 He speaks English fairly well. // 약이 곧잘 듣는다 A drug is fairly effective.
② [가끔 잘] frequently; too often ¶ 곧잘 그런 사고가 일어난다 That sort of accident occurs too often. // 그는 곧잘 그런 잘못을 저지른다 He is prone to do that kind of mistake.

†곧장 directly; straightforwardly; straight; without delay ¶ 집으로 곧장 돌아가다 go straight home // 그 길로 곧장 떠나다 leave without delay // 이 길을 곧장 가십시오 Go straight ahead down this street. // 술 마시고 돌아다니지 말고 곧장 집으로 오세요 Don't booze around. Make a beeline for home.

곧추 [일직선으로] straight; in a straight line; [수직으로] perpendicularly; vertically; upright; erect ¶ 곧추 안다 hold 《a baby》 out straight // 곧추 앉다 sit up right〔erect〕 // 곧추 세우다 erect; set upright // 곧추 서다 stand upright // 곧추 가다 go straight on; make straight toward

곧추다 straighten 《a wire》

곧추세우다 hold oneself erect

곧추안다 hold (a baby) out straight

곧추앉다 sit up straight〔erect〕

골¹ [노여움] anger; dander; temper ¶ 골이 나서 in a fit of passion; in anger; in heat // 골나다 get angry; get enraged // 골나게 하다 offend〔provoke〕 《a person》

골² [틀] a block; a mold; a cast ¶ 구둣골 a last; a shoetree // 모잣골 a hat block // 솥 골 a mold for an oven

골³ [금] the crease made when a sheet of cloth, paper, or cardboard is folded into two equal parts; [머리의] an even hair part down the middle of one's head ¶ 골을 타다 part one's hair in the middle

골⁴ [골수] the marrow 《of bones》; the medulla; [머릿골] the brain ¶ 골 아픈 일 a nerve-wracking task
작은— cerebellum (소뇌) 큰— the cerebrum (대뇌)

골⁵ [구멍] a cave; a hollow; [골짜기] a gully; a valley; a dale; [기압] a trough
기압— a trough of low atmospheric pressure

골⁶ the goal; [경마의] the winning post; [농구의] a basket ¶ 골을 얻다 [구기에서] make〔score, win〕 a goal; [농구에서] score a basket; cage
— 라인 a goal line —키퍼 a goalkeeper —포스트 a goal post

골간 骨幹 ① [뼈대] physique; framework ② [골자] gist; substance; essentials

골감 a persimmon with four furrows where the calyx〔stem〕 attaches

골갱이 [심] the core; the heart; [골자] the substance; the gist; the pith

골걷이 〚농업〛 weeding the planted furrows of a field —하다 weed the furrows

골격 骨格 frame; build; physique; bone structure ¶ 골격이 건장한 사람 a man of stout〔sturdy〕 build
— 경화증(硬化症) eburnation — 교착(膠着) anchylosis; ankylosis —성 단백질 albuminoid — 진동(振動) 〚물리〛 (a) skeletal vibration — 해설 skeletography

골격근 骨格筋 skeletal muscles

골계 滑稽 a joke; humor

골고래 [방고래] a hypocaust system with several flue entries

*골고루 evenly among all; indiscriminately; equally ¶ 골고루 나누어 주다 divide evenly〔equally〕 among all

골골 —하다 suffer from a chronic disease; suffer constantly from weak health; be sick all the time ¶ 골골하는 사람 a chronic invalid; an infirm (노인)

골골샅샅이 everywhere; all over; 《look in》 every nook and corner

골김 a moment of anger〔temper〕 ¶ 골김에 in a fit of anger; in the heat of passion; in a rage; in heat // 골김에 사람을 치다 beat 《a person》 in a fit of anger

골나다 be angry; be enraged

골내다 get angry; become enraged

골다 snore ¶ 코를 골며 자다 snore; snore in one's sleep // 코를 골기 시작하다 fall to snoring

골답 —畓 a rich〔productive〕 paddy

골동 骨董 a curio; objects〔articles〕 of virtu; an antique

골동품 骨董品 curios ; antiques ; objects 〔articles〕 of virtu
—상 a curio shop ; an antique shop **—애호가** a virtuoso 《*pl.* ~s, -si》; a curioso 《*pl.* ~s, -si》
골든 디스크 golden disc
골든아워 golden hours ; prime time [라디오·텔레비전] 《at》 (the) peak viewing 〔listening〕 time〔hour〕
골땅땅이 a kind of dominoes
골똘하다 be absorbed〔engrossed, deeply engaged〕 in ; be devoted to ; be given to ; be completely taken up 《with》 ¶ 골똘히 intently ; absorbedly // 연구에 골똘하다 be absorbed in the research // 독서에 골똘하다 be intent on reading a book // 돈 모으기에 골똘하다 be keen〔intent〕 on making money
골 라인 goal line
골라잡다 choose ; select ; take〔have〕 one's choice ¶ 골라잡아 1,000원이오 1,000 *won* a piece at you choice. /Take your choice for 1,000 *won*.
골락새 〖새〗 a woodpecker
골로새서 〖성경〗 (The Letter of Paul to the Colossians)
골마루 a narrow corridor〔hallway〕
골마지 scum
골막 骨膜 〖해부〗 the periosteum
—종(腫) periosteal tumor
골막염 骨膜炎 periostitis
골막이 〖건축〗 plastering between rafters
골막하다 [그릇에] (be) not full ; be but partly filled ; (be) almost full 《with》
골머리 the brain ; the head ¶ 골머리 아픈 일 a headache ; a source of anxiety 〔trouble〕 ; a worry // 그 일로 골머리를 앓고 있다 I have been troubled with the matter.
골머리를 앓다 관용 be annoyed〔troubled〕
골목 a side street ; an alley ; a byway ¶ 뒷골목 a back street 《미》 // 막다른 골목 a blind alley
골목대장 —大將 the boss of youngsters 〔kids〕 of the neighborhood
골몰 汨沒 —하다 give oneself up to ; devote oneself to ; bury oneself in ; be immersed〔absorbed, engrossed〕 in ; be up to the eyes〔ears〕 in ; be hung on ¶ 일에 골몰하다 be engrossed 〔immersed〕 in one's work // 독서에 골몰하다 be absorbed in reading
골무 a thimble
골무꽃 a kind of skullcap plant
골무떡 thimble-shaped pieces of rice-cake
골밀이 a groove in the sash of a window〔door〕
골박다 limit it (to a fixed sphere) ; keep it (to its intended shape)
골반 骨盤 〖해부〗 the pelvis 《*pl.* -ves》
—대(帶) the pelvic arch〔girdle〕 **—벽(壁)** the pelvic wall **—부(部)** the pelvic region
골방 a back room ; a closet ; a small room attached to the main room
골배질 breaking〔crushing〕 the ice over a ferry to pass passengers across the river ; making a ferry channel through the ice to let ferryboats cross the river
골병 a deep-rooted〔-seated〕 illness 〔injury〕 ; an internal injury ; a mortal blow (타격)
골병들다 fall into deep-rooted sickness ; be hurt〔injured〕 internally ; have one's vital parts affected
골부림 losing one's temper readily ; being quick to get angry
골분 骨粉 powdered bones ; bone-dust
골분 비료 骨粉肥料 bone manure
골산 骨山 a rocky mountain
골상 骨相 physiognomy ; one's features ¶ 골상을 보다 tell 《a person's》 fortune phrenologically ; examine 《a person's》 physiognomy
골상학 骨相學 phrenology ; physiognomy ¶ 골상학상으로 phrenologically ; from phrenological point of view
—자 a phrenologist ; a physiognomist
골생원 —生員 [옹졸한 사람] a narrow-minded person ; a man of little caliber ; [허약한 사람] a weak〔delicate〕 person
골속 ① [머릿골의 속] the brains ② [골풀 속] the heart of a rush ③ [왕골 속] the heart of a sedge
골수 骨髓 〖해부〗 the marrow ; the medulla ¶ 그에 대한 원한이 골수에 맺혀 있다 I bear him a bitter grudge.
골수에 사무치다 관용 cut 《one》 to the quick
골수염 骨髓炎 osteomyelitis
골안개 the morning mist in the valley
골 에어리어 goal area
골육 骨肉 flesh and blood ; [육친] blood relations ; kinsfolk ¶ 골육지정 love for one's flesh and blood // 골육지정은 어쩔 수 없다 Blood is thicker than water.
— 형제 a brother of one's own bone and flesh
골육종 骨肉腫 an osteosarcoma ; an osteogenic sarcoma
골인 a finish ; the breasting of the tape ; attainment of the goal **—하다** reach the goal (line)〔winning post, finish line〕 ; breast the tape ; [성공하다] succeed ¶ 결혼에 골인하다 be (happily) married
골자 骨子 the pith and marrow ; the essentials ; the main point ; the gist ; the substance ¶ 논쟁의 골자 the main point〔sum and substance〕 of an argument // 그 논문의 골자 the gist of the article
골재 骨材 aggregate

골절 **骨折** fracture 《of a bone》 ¶ 골절상을 입다 suffer a fracture
단순(單純)〔복잡(複雜)〕— a simple〔compound〕 fracture **세편(細片) —** a comminuted fracture
골절 **骨節** a (bone) joint
골조 **骨組** the (bony) frame ; a skeleton ; a framework ; structure
골질 **骨質** bony〔osseous〕 tissue
— 결합(結合) synost(e)osis **— 연화(軟化)** 〖의학〗 osteomalacia
골짜기 a valley ; a vale ; [협곡] a ravine ; a dale ; a gorge
골창 a ditch
골초 **—草** [저질의 담배] tobacco〔cigarette〕 of inferior quality ; [사람] a heavy smoker ; a chain smoker
골치 the head ¶ 골치 아픈 일 a cause of anxiety ; a worry ; a headache
골치(를) 앓다 관용 worry about 《a matter》 ; be troubled
골치다 put 《a thing》 on the block〔mold, last〕 for shaping
골칫거리 a headache ; a nuisance ; a bother ; a trouble ¶ 그는 가족에게 큰 골칫거리다 He is a great distress to the family.
골켜다 cut the pith out of (wood)
골키퍼 goalkeeper
골 킥 goal kick
골타다 furrow (a field)
골탄 **骨炭** animal〔bone〕 charcoal ; boneblack
—조(槽) a char cistern
골탕 **—湯** [골국] a soup made of fried ox-brain or ox-marrow coated with flour
골탕 great injury〔insult〕
골탕먹다 suffer a big loss ; be cheated ¶ 그 친구를 믿었다가 골탕먹었다 I was taken in, trusting that guy.
골통 the head ; the skull
골통 **骨痛** 〖의학〗 ostalgia ; bone pain
골통대 a kind of tobacco pipe (of short and thick bamboo)
골틀리다 get angry ; be vexed ; be offended ; be displeased ; sulk ; become cross ; get upset 《with a person, at a thing》 ¶ 한 10분 기다리게 했더니 잔뜩 골틀렸다 He was all out of sorts because he had to wait some ten minutes for me.
골파 a variety of leek
골판지 **—板紙** corrugated cardboard
골패 **骨牌** a domino
골퍼 a golfer
골풀 〖식물〗 a rush
골풀무 a kind of bellows
골풀이 **—하다** vent one's anger〔wrath, rage〕 ; give vent to one's anger ; work off one's anger on 《a person》
골프 golf ¶ 골프를 치다 play golf // 골프를 치는 사람 a golfer ; a golf player
—공 a golf ball **—광** a golf maniac **—바지** plus fours 《영》 ; knickerbockers 《미》 **—복(服)** a golf coat **— 연습장** a golf practice range ; a driving range
골프장 a golf course ; (a) golf-links
골프채 a golf club ; a driver
골필 **骨筆** a stencil pen ; an iron pen ; a stylus
골학 **骨學** 〖해부〗 osteology
—자 an osteologist
골함석 corrugated sheet iron
골혹 **骨—** a bone tumor
골회 **骨灰** bone ashes
곪다 [상처가] gather ; fester ; form pus ; [일이] 《an affair》 come to a head ; ripen ¶ 종기가 곪다 a boil festers ; a boil comes to a head // 상처는 곪지 않고 곧 나았다 The wound healed without festering.
곬 [물길] a waterway ; a watercourse ; [방향] a (fixed) direction ; [유래] origin ; source ; cause ¶ 외곬으로 생각하다 see things from only one point of view
물— a channel ; a watercourse ; a drain
곯다[1] [배를] be still hungry ; have not had enough to eat ; have an empty stomach ; 《one's stomach》 be still not full ¶ 돈이 없어서 이틀이나 배를 곯았다 I had to go hungry for two days as I had no money. // 배 곯고 일할 수는 없다 You can't work on an empty stomach.
곯다[2] [그릇에 차지 않다] remain unfilled ; be still not full ; be half-empty ¶ 자루가 좀 곯는다 The bag is only partly filled.
곯다[3] ① [썩다] rot ; spoil ; get stale ; putrefy ; go bad ¶ 곯은 달걀 bad eggs // 참외가 곯다 a melon spoils
② [손해보다] suffer ; sustain damage ; receive injury ; [골병들다] suffer internal injury ¶ 그들의 농간에 아주 곯았다 I suffered heavily from their tricks.
곯리다[1] ① [배를] underfeed ; leave 《a person》 still hungry ¶ 자식들의 배를 곯려서는 안 되겠다 My children must not go hungry.
② [그릇에] underfill ; leave half-empty
곯리다[2] [썩히다] spoil〔addle, rot〕 《a thing》 ; make 《it》 stale ; [해롭게 하다] do harm ; cause damage to ; play trick ; vex ; embarrass ; put in an awkward position ¶ 그녀는 성가신 질문을 해서 나를 곯린다 She embarrasses me by asking bothersome questions. // 그 치가 오면 곯려 주어야겠다 I will take it out of him when he comes.
곯아떨어지다 [술에] drink oneself down ; be dead drunk ; be helplessly drunk ; [잠에] fall into a deep sleep ; drop off into a deep slumber

곯아빠지다 ① [몹시 곯아서 버리게 되다] become utterly rotten〔spoiled, stale〕; be badly addled ② [정신 못 차리다] wallow in vice ¶ 주색 잡기에 곯아빠지다 be given up to wine, women, and dice

*__곰__[1] 〖동물〗 a bear ¶ 곰 가죽 bearskin ; [사람] a regular bear ; a slow-witted person ; a fat-head // 곰 새끼 a (bear's) cub // 곰쓸개 bear's gall // 큰곰자리 the Great Bear // 작은곰자리 the Little Bear **불—** the brown bear **흰—** the white 〔polar〕 bear

곰[2] [국] a thick broth made of thoroughly boiled meat

곰곰이 musing over ; deliberating ; considering carefully ¶ 곰곰이 생각하다 think 《a matter》 over (and over) ; muse on〔over〕; reflect carefully ; ponder over〔on〕; mull 《the matter》 over ; consider carefully ; deliberate // 남의 말을 곰곰이 생각하다 muse on what was said

곰국 a thick beef soup

곰바지런하다 (be) punctilious and diligent

곰방대 a short (smoking) pipe

곰방메 a mallet (used for crumbling clods of earth when covering seeds)

곰배말 a sway-back(ed) horse

곰배팔 a deformed〔mutilated〕 arm

곰배팔이 a person with a deformed 〔mutilated〕 arm

곰보 a pockmarked person ; a person with a pitted face

— 유리 crackled glass

곰비임비 in (rapid) succession ; one after another ; upon heels of another ; manifoldly overlapped ¶ 불행이 곰비임비 닥치다 one misfortune follows on the heels of another

곰삭다 ① [옷이] (old and untouched clothes) reach the point where it will fall apart at a touch ② [젓이] (pickled stuff) gets well〔thoroughly〕 pickled 〔seasoned〕

곰살갑다 [마음이 넓다] (be) generous ; broad-minded ; [다정스럽다] delicate ; tender ; kind ; cordial

곰살궂다 (be) gentle and good ; kind and attentive ; cordial ; warmhearted

곰상곰상 —하다 ① (be) gentle and kind ② (be) meticulous ; narrow-minded

곰상스럽다 (be) punctilious ; meticulous

곰솔 〖식물〗 a Japanese black pine ; Pinus thunbergii (학명)

곰실거리다 wriggle ; writhe ; squirm

곰작, 꼼작, 꼼짝 budging ; stirring ; moving **—하다** budge ; stir ; move ¶ 곰작거리다 stir 《about》; move 《about》; fidget 《about》 // 꼼짝하면 죽는다 One move and you are a dead man. /If you dare budge, I will kill you. // 바위가 꼼짝 않는다 The rock won't budge an inch. // 기계가 꼼짝 않는다 The machine won't work at all. // 그는 꼼짝 않고 서 있다 He is standing motionless. // 그는 꼼짝도 하지 않았다 He refused to budge an inch. // 그는 계속 꼼짝거린다 He is continually stirring. // 꼼짝마 Don't move. /Freeze.

곰지락 ¶ 곰지락거리다 move sluggishly ; stir leisurely ; get about lazily

곰취 〖식물〗 a kind of groundsel

곰치 〖물고기〗 a moray

곰틀 with a wriggle〔wiggle〕 **—하다** give a wiggle ; wiggle ; wriggle ; writhe ; twist ¶ 몸을 곰틀거리다 《a worm》 twist its body // 뱀이 곰틀거리다 a snake twists〔wriggles〕 to and fro // 아파서 몸을 곰틀거리다 writhe in agony

곰파다 dig carefully into (the details of a matter)

곰팡 mold ; mildew ; must ¶ 곰팡(이) 슬다 gather mold ; become〔grow, get〕 moldy ; get musty ; be covered with mold ; mildew

곰팡내 ① mustiness ; fustiness ; frowziness ; a stale〔stuffy〕 smell ¶ 곰팡내가 나다 be musty ; be fusty ; be frowzy ; be stale ; smell musty〔fusty〕; be stuffy ; be mildewed // 곰팡내 나는 방 a stuffy room ② [진부] commonplaceness ; triteness ¶ 곰팡내 나다 (be, grow) stale ; trite ; hackneyed ; commonplace ; banal ; ordinary // 곰팡내 나는 사상 a mossgrown idea

곰팡이 mold ; mildew ; must ¶ 푸른 곰팡이 green mold ; penicillium // 곰팡이 슨 이야기 a hackneyed〔stale〕 talk ; a chestnut 《미·속》 // 곰팡이 피는 것을 막다 keep 《books》 from getting moldy // 장마철에는 여러 물건에 곰팡이가 핀다 During the rainy season many things gather mold.

곱[1] double ; times **—하다** multiply 《a number by》; double 《it》 ¶ 곱 반 one and half a times // 2에 2를 곱하면 4가 된다 Two by two makes four. // 5 곱하기 4는 20이다 Four times five equals twenty. // 8은 2의 몇 곱이냐 How many times two is eight?

두 — double ; twice ; twofold ; two times **세 —** treble ; three times ; thrice ; threefold **네 —** four times ; quadruple

곱[2] [부스럼 따위의] a mucous discharge (usually on a skin wound)

곱걸다 ① [노름에서] double (one's bet) ② [겹쳐 얽다] double-bind

곱꺾다 ① [뼈마디를] bend and stretch a joint

곱꺾이 bending and stretching a joint

곱꺾이다 [뼈마디가] be bent and then stretched ; be flexed

곱끼다 ① [곱살끼다] fret ; be fretful ② [종기나 부스럼이 생기다] form a filmy discharge〔a film of pus〕
곱놓다 double《one's bet》
*곱다¹ (be) beautiful ; lovely ; fair ; fine ; nice ; good-looking ; [가루가] fine ¶ 고운 꽃〔처녀〕 a pretty flower〔girl〕// 고운 옷 fine clothes // 고운 모래〔밀가루〕 fine sand〔flour〕// 고운 말 refined language // 고운 목소리로 in a sweet voice // 곱게 피어 있다 be in beautiful bloom // 얼굴이 곱다 be good〔nice〕-looking ; be fair ; be pretty // 마음씨가 곱다 be kind-hearted ; be noble-minded ; have a heart of gold // 결이 곱다 be fine ; be of close texture // 촉감이 곱다 feel soft to the touch // 살결이 곱다 have a fine〔delicate〕 skin
곱다² [휘다] (be) bent ; stooped ¶ 허리가 곱다 be stooped ; have a bent back // 판자가 곱다 a plank is bent ; a board is warped
곱다³ [손·발이] (be) numb〔benumbed〕《with cold》; [이가] have one's teeth set on edge ¶ 혀가 곱다 be tongue-tied // 추워서 손이 곱다 one's fingers are stiff with the cold
곱다⁴ [손해보다] end up with a loss rather than a profit
곱다랗다 ① (be) quite beautiful ; pretty ; lovely ② [온전하다] (be) whole ; intact ¶ 곱다랗게 quite beautifully ; prettily ; nicely // 곱다랗게 생기다 be beautiful〔pretty〕
곱돌 【광물】 agalmatolite (납석) ; talc (활석)
곱드러지다 stumble over〔upon, against〕《a thing》; trip over〔on〕; lose〔miss〕 one's footing ¶ 돌에 채어 곱드러지다 stumble over a stone
곱들다 [갑절 들다] cost twice as much (as) ; take twice as much (as)
곱들이다 spend〔put out〕 twice as much (as) ; consume twice as much (as)
곱디디다 sprain〔twist〕 one's ankle
곱바 a rope attached to an A-frame to tie a load
곱빼기 ① [두 그릇 몫] double measure《of wine》; a double(-size) drink ; [요리] a double-the-ordinary dish ② [두 번 거듭] double ; two times
곱사등이 a hunchback ; a humpback ; a crookback
곱살끼다 fret ; be fretful
곱살스럽다 [용모가] (be) comely ; pretty ; fair ; good-looking ; [마음씨가] nice ; tender ; gentle
곱삶이 ① [밥] double-boiled〔reboiled〕 rice ② ⇨ 꽁보리밥
곱새기다 ① [곡해하다] misunderstand ; misconstrue ; think ill of ② [거듭 생각하다] think over and over
곱셈 multiplication ━하다 multiply
곱셈 기호 ━記號 the sign for multiplication ; the multiplication sign ; the (sign) ×
곱소리 elephant-tail hair
곱솔 double-stitching (on a sewing machine)
곱송그리다 flinch ; wince ; shrink
곱슬곱슬하다 (be) curly ; curled ; frizzled ; frizzly ; wavy ¶ 곱슬곱슬한 머리 curly〔frizzled〕 hair
곱씹다 [말 따위를] rechew ; repeat (a word) ; [다짐받듯] harp on (a question) ; emphasize
곱은성 ━城 the circular wall protecting a castle gate
곱자 a carpenter's square ; a metal foot-measure
곱잡다 take〔treat, figure〕《it》 double
곱장다리 bowlegs ; a bowlegged person
곱쟁이 double ; doubled amount
곱절 [두 배] double ; [배] times ━하다 double《it》 ¶ 곱절이 되다 double ; be doubled《in value》// 세 곱절하다 treble // A의 곱절이나 크다 be twice〔two times〕 as large as A // 값이 다섯 곱절이나 뛰었다 The price went up fivefold.
곱창 the small intestines of cattle ; [돼지의] chitterlings
곱치다 double ; fold up《a blanket》
*곳 ① [장소] a place ; [좁은] a spot ; [현장] a scene ; [지방] locality ¶ 편리한 곳 a convenient place // 건조한 곳 a dry spot〔place〕// 유명한 전쟁이 있었던 곳 the scene of a famous battle // 그 곳의 명산물 a special product of the locality // 곳에 따라서 in some places // …이 있는 곳에서 in the presence《of》// 곳에 따라 다르다 be different in different locality // 사람이 많은 곳에서 모욕을 주다 insult《a person》 in public // 3미터 되는 곳에서 발포하다 fire at《a person》 from three meter's distance
② [주소] a house ; a home ; an address ¶ 사는 곳이 어디요 What is your address? /Where is your home?
곳간 庫間 a storeroom ; a repository ; a shed ; a warehouse
곳간차 庫間車 a (railroad) boxcar《미》; a covered〔box〕 waggon《영》
곳곳 [부사적] on all sides ; in several places ; in spots ; here and there ; everywhere ¶ 곳곳에 부상병이 쓰러져 있었다 Wounded soldiers were found here and there. // 가는 곳곳마다 환영을 받았다 He was welcomed wherever he went. /He was lionized everywhere.
곳집 庫━ ① [창고] a warehouse ; a storehouse ② [상엿집] a hut where bier and accessories are kept
*̣공¹ [볼] a ball ; a handball ; [원구] a circle ; a sphere ¶ 공을 차다 kick a ball // 공을 튀기다 bounce a ball // 공놀이를 하다 play ball

공² a gong ¶ 공이 울렸다 There is the bell.

***공 空** [영] zero ; cipher ; [무] naught ; nothing (허사) ; [빈 것] emptiness ; vacancy ; [공짜] free of charge ¶ 공구경 an amusement without fee // 공으로 돌아가다 come to naught // 공을 하나 붙이다 put a zero to // 나의 모든 노력은 공으로 돌아갔다 All my efforts came to naught.

***공 功** ① [공로] merits ; services ; credit ; honor ¶ 공에 의하여 in recognition of one's services // 공을 세우다 distinguish oneself ; render distinguished services ; perform a meritorious deed ; win one's spurs // 공을 서두르다 be too eager for success // 공을 다투다 claim credit ⟪for an invention⟫ ② [공력] exertion ; efforts ; labors

***공 公** ① [공사] public〔official〕 affairs ; public business ¶ 공과 사를 구별하다 draw a line between public and private matters ② [공작] a prince ; a duke ⟪영⟫ ③ [존칭] His〔Your〕 Highness

-공 工 [직공] a worker ; a mechanic ; a workman
용접— a welder **인쇄—** a pressman

공가 公暇 an official holiday〔vacation, leave〕

공가 空家 [빈 집] an empty〔a vacant, an unoccupied〕 house ; a deserted house

공간 公刊 publication ; issue

***공간 空間** space ; room (여지) ; the infinite (우주의) ¶ 공간의 spatial // 공간에 spatially // 시간과 공간 time and space // 공간을 날다 travel through space
— 감각 space sense **— 곡선** 〚수학〛 a twisted〔space〕 curve **— 관념** 〚철학〛 space idea ; a notion of space **— 배좌(配座)** 〚화학〛 a conformation ; a configuration **—성(性)** 〚심리〛 extensity **— 속도** space velocity **— 정위(定位)** 〚항공〛 location in space **— 하전(荷電)** 〚전기〛 space charge **물(物)—** object space **상(像)—** image space

공간 예술 空間藝術 space art

공간 지각 空間知覺 〚심리〛 space perception

공갈 恐喝 a threat ; intimidation ; a menace ; blackmail **—하다** threaten ; intimidate ; make a threat ; blackmail ¶ 공갈하여 돈을 빼앗다 blackmail ⟪a person⟫ // 공갈에 복종하다 be intimidated into yielding
— 취재(取財) blackmailing ; extortion by threats **— 취재자** a blackmailer ; a racketeer

공갈죄 恐喝罪 the crime of blackmail ; the crime of intimidation ; extortion ¶ 공갈죄 혐의로 ⟪be arrested⟫ on a charge of blackmailing

공갈치다 恐喝— threaten ; intimidate ; make a threat ; blackmail

***공감 共感** sympathy ; response **—하다** sympathize ⟪with a person⟫ ¶ 공감을 불러일으키다 arouse ⟪a person's⟫ sympathy

공감각 共感覺 synesthesia

***공개 公開** opening to the public **—하다** open ⟪a thing⟫ to the public ; throw open ⟪a thing⟫ to the public ¶ 공개의 open ; public // 공개 석상에서 이야기하다 speak in public // 공개 행사에 참가하다 attend a public function // 정원을 일반에게 공개하다 throw one's garden open to the general public // 주식을 공개하다 offer shares for public subscription // 공개를 금하다 be closed to the public
— 강좌 extension lectures **— 기간** an open period **— 녹음** public recording **— 대학** an open university **— 도서관** a public library **— 시합** an open tournament **— 연설** a public address **— 입찰** a public tender ; an open bid **— 토론회** a〔an open〕 forum

공개 수사 公開搜査 an open criminal investigation

공개 시장 公開市場 an open market ; a market overt

공개장 公開狀 an open letter

공개 재판 公開裁判 a public trial

공개 회의 公開會議 open session (국회 따위의)

공것 空— a thing that can be had for nothing ; a thing got for nothing ; an article obtained without cost ; something free ; a windfall ; a godsend ¶ 그 따위는 공것이라도 안 갖겠다 I would not have it even as a gift. // 공것을 바라지 마라 Don't expect a windfall upon the sudden.

****공격 攻擊** an attack ; an assault ; an onslaught (맹습) ; a raid (급습) ; [비난] an attack ; a charge ; condemnation ; [꾸짖음] scolding ; a rebuke **—하다** attack ; assail ; assault ; make an attack ; [비난하다] attack ; denounce ; say〔speak, write〕 against ¶ 공격적인 offensive ; aggressive // 공격을 가하다 deliver〔make〕 an attack against〔on〕 // 공격을 받다 be attacked ; come under attack // 성을 공격하다 assail a castle // 적의 공격에 대비하다 prepare for the enemy's attack // 신문에서 공격하다 attack ⟪a person⟫ in a newspaper // 연합군은 총공격을 개시했다 The allied forces launched an all-out attack. // 공격은 최선의 방어이다 The most effective defense is offense. /Attack is the best (form) of defense.
—각(角) 〚항공〛 the angle of attack **— 개시 시간** 〚군사〛 H-hour ; zero (hour) **—군** an attacking army〔force〕 **—기(機)** an attack plane ; an air raider (공습의) **—로(路)** a route of attack **— 목표** an

attack objective — 무기 offensive weapons〔arms〕 — 수단 a means of attack —자 an assailant ; an aggressor ; an invader —전 an aggressive war — 전투 (an) offensive action — 정신 fighting spirit ; aggressiveness — 행동 an offensive〔aggressive〕 movement 기습 — a surprise attack 배면(背面)— a rear attack 정면 — a frontal attack 측면 — a flank attack 특별 —대 a "special attack" unit〔corps〕 ; a suicide unit

공격력 攻擊力 striking power

공겸 恭謙 modesty ; humility ; courteousness ; deference —하다 (be) modest ; humble ; courteous ; deferential

공경 公卿 a court noble

공경 恭敬 respect ; reverence ; veneration ; deference —하다 be respectful to 《a person》 ; respect ; revere ; honor ; esteem ; pay deference〔homage, respect〕 to ¶ 공경할 만한 respectable ; venerable // 스승을 공경하다 honor one's master ; show respect to one's teacher // 어른을 공경하다 be respectful to one's elders

공고 公告 a public〔an official〕 announcement〔notice〕 ; a (public) notification ; an (official) announcement —하다 notify publicly ; announce ; give a public notice 《of》
경매 — an auction announcement 특허 — a patent announcement

공고 鞏固 firmness ; soundness ; solidity ; stability —하다 (be) firm ; solid ; sound ; stable ; strong ¶ 공고히 firmly ; strongly ; solidly // 공고히 하다 make solid ; solidify ; strengthen ; consolidate // 공고한 의지 a firm〔strong〕 will // 자기의 지위를 공고히 하다 make one's position secure // 공고한 기초 위에서 있다 It is based on a sound〔solid〕 foundation.

공고 工高 〔공업 고등학교〕 a technical high school ; a higher technical school

공공 空空 ¶ 공공 기지 an undisclosed base // 공공 부대 an unnamed unit

공공 公共 the public ¶ 공공의 public ; common // 공공의 이익 the public good〔interests, benefit〕 // 공공의 이익을 위하여 for the public good〔benefit〕 // 공공심이 강한 public-spirited // 공공을 위하여 힘쓰다 do public service // 공공의 이익을 도모하다 promote the public good〔interests〕
— 관계 법률 public act — 관계 법안 public bill — 기관 a public institution— 기업 보조금 public works subsidies — 부문 public sector — 생활 communal life — 수송 기관 public transport — 용수 water for public use — 위생 public health — 이익(利益) public interests ; the public good ¶ 공공 이익을 도모하다 consult the public interest

공공 경제 公共經濟 public economy —학 public economics

공공 기업체 公共企業體 a public corporation ; a public enterprise ; a public undertaking ; a public utility enterprise

공공 단체 公共團體 a public body

공공물 公共物 public property

공공 방송 公共放送 public noncommercial broadcasting

공공 복지 公共福祉 public welfare

공공 사업 公共事業 a public undertaking〔enterprise〕 ; public work

공공 시설 公共施設 public facilities

공공심 公共心 public spirit ; a spirit of public duty

공공연하다 公公然— (be) open ; public ; overt ; avowed ¶ 공공연히 openly ; publicly ; overtly ; in public ; avowedly ; in the face of the world // 공공연한 비밀 an open secret // 공공연한 애인 one's avowed lover // 공공연한 적대 open〔avowed〕 hostilities // 공공연히 말하다 say in public〔openly〕 // 공공연히 항의하다 make a public protest

공공 요금 公共料金 〔전기 요금 따위〕 public utilities charges

공공 재산 公共財産 public property

공공 투자 公共投資 (a) public investment ; investment(s) in public utilities

공과 公課 public imposts〔duty〕 ; taxes

공과 工科 the engineering faculty〔department〕 of 《a university》

공과 工課 a course of study ; the curriculum

공과 功過 merits and demerits ¶ 공과가 반반이다 His merits and demerits are balanced against each other.

공과 대학 工科大學 an engineering college ; a college specializing in engineering ; an institute of technology
매사추세츠 — Massachusetts Institute of Technology 《M. I. T.》

공관 公館 ① 〔공공의 건물〕 a public hall ② 〔정부 고관의 관저〕 an official residence ③ 〔대사관·공사관 등을 통틀어〕 a legation

공관 복음서 共觀福音書 『성경』 a diatessaron (of the Christian Gospels)

공교롭게 工巧— ① 〔솜씨〕 elaborately ; with fine detail ; skillfully ; deftly ; dexterously ; cleverly ; ingeniously ② 〔마침·우연〕 unexpectedly ; accidentally ; opportunely〔inopportunely〕 ; at a likely〔unlikely〕 time ; luckily〔unluckily〕 ; fortunately〔unfortunately〕 ; by a lucky〔an unlucky〕 coincidence ; as luck would have it ; happen〔chance〕 to ¶ 공교롭게 그날 따라 선편이 없었다 As ill luck would have it, there was no steamer leaving on that particular day. // 공교롭게 그 날 비가 내렸다 The day happened to be rainy. // 공교롭게 돈이 한푼도 없다 It so happens that〔Unfortunately〕 I have no money with me. // 공교롭게 경관이 왔다 As good luck would have it, a policeman came along.

공교롭다 工巧— [뜻밖] (be) coincidental ; unexpected ; accidental ; casual ¶ 공교로운 일치 a chance coincidence // 공교로운 때 a likely〔an unlikely〕 time

공교하다 工巧— ① [솜씨 따위가] elaborate ; complex ; complicated ; fine ; skillful
② ⇨ 공교롭다

공구 工具 a tool ; an implement ; an instrument ¶ 공구 한 벌 a set of tools
—강(鋼) tool steel —실 a toolhouse ; a toolshed — 제작공〔수리공〕 a toolmaker 기계 — a machine tool 목공(木工) — a wood-working tool 절삭(切削) — a cutting tool 정밀 — a precision tool 기계 —점(店) a machine-parts supplier

공구 工區 〖건축〗 a section of works

공구 恐懼 fear ; dread ; awe **—하다** fear ; be overawed ; be struck with awe ; stand in awe

공국 公國 a dukedom ; a duchy ; a principality

공군 空軍 the air force ; a flying corps
— 기지(基地) an air base —력(力) air power ; aerial strength — 부대 an air unit —성(省) the Air Department 《미》 — 작전 an air operation 미국 — the United States Air Force 《U. S. A. F.》 영국 — the Royal Air Force 《R. A. F.》 한국 — the Republic of Korea Air Force 《R. O. K. A. F.》

공군기 空軍機 an air force plane

공군 본부 空軍本部 the Air Force Headquarters

공군 사관 학교 空軍士官學校 Air Force Academy

공굴 〖토목〗 concrete ⇨ 콘크리트

공굴다리 a (reinforced) concrete bridge ; a ferroconcrete bridge

공권 公權 civil rights ; citizenship ¶ 공권을 박탈하다 disfranchise 《a person》 ; deprive 《a person》 of civil rights

공권 空拳 bare〔empty〕 hands ¶ 공권으로 with one's own bare hands ; empty-handed // 적수 공권으로 치부했다 Having nothing to start with, he has made a colossal fortune. /He became a millionaire practically out of nothing.

공권력 公權力 public power ¶ 공권력의 행사 exercise of public power

공권 박탈 公權剝奪 [정지] deprivation 〔suspension〕 of civil rights ; disfranchisement ; civil death

공규 空閨 the bedchamber of a neglected〔bereaved〕 wife

공그르다 sew up with an invisible seam

공극 空隙 an opening ; a gap ; a crevice ; an aperture

공글리다 ① [다지다] harden ; make hard ; consolidate ; solidify ; firm up ; strengthen ; stabilize ② [끝맺다] finish up

공금 公金 public〔government〕 money 〔funds〕 ¶ 공금을 횡령하다 embezzle 〔misappropriate〕 public funds
— 예금 an official deposit — 횡령자 a peculator

공금 횡령 公金橫領 misappropriation 〔embezzlement〕 of public money ; peculation

***공급 供給** supply ; provision ; [가스·수도 따위의] service **—하다** supply〔furnish〕 《a thing to》 ; supply〔furnish, serve, provide〕 《with》 ¶ 수요와 공급 demand and supply // 공급을 받다 be supplied with ; get a supply 《of》 // 공장에 석탄을 공급하다 supply a factory with coal ; furnish coal to a factory // 전력 공급을 끊다 cut off the supply of electric power
—관(管) a supply pipe — 구역 a service area —기(機)〔장치〕 〖기계〗 a feeder — 전압 service voltage — 전원(電源) a source of electric power service

공급 가격 供給價格 a supply price

공급 과다 供給過多 an excessive supply ; an oversupply ; a glut (상품의) ¶ 석탄이 공급 과다이다 We have an oversupply of coal.

공급로 供給路 a channel of supply ; a supply route ; a lifeline ¶ 공급로를 끊다 cut a supply route

공급 부족 供給不足 a short supply ; an undersupply

공급원 供給源 a source of supply

공급자 供給者 a supplier ; a provider

공급지 供給地 a source of supply ; a supply center

공기 [돌] a jackstone ; a pebble ; [놀이] jackstones ; marbles ¶ 공기 놀다 play marbles〔jackstones〕
공기 놀리다 관용 play marbles ; [비유적] make a puppet of 《a person》

†공기 空氣 air ; [분위기] atmosphere ¶ 신선한 공기 fresh air // 오염된 공기 foul air // 상쾌한 산 공기 a refreshing mountain atmosphere // 좌중의 공기 the atmosphere of a meeting // 공기가 든 pneumatic 《tire》 // 공기가 통하지 않는 airtight // 공기를 넣다 let air in ; ventilate 《a room》 ; pump up 《a tire》 // 공기를 빼다 deflate 《a tire》 // 공기의 유통이 좋다〔나쁘다〕 be well〔ill〕 ventilated // 사내의 공기가 매우 험악하다 A tense atmosphere reigns at the office. /There is something tense in the air at the office.
— 가열기(加熱器) an air heater — 건조(乾燥) air drying — 기중기(起重機)

a pneumatic crane —로(路) an air conduit〔duct〕 — 마찰(摩擦) air friction — 받이 〖기계〗 an air receiver — 발동기 an air engine — 방석 an air cushion — 배수기 a pneumatic ejector — 베개 an air pillow — 식물(植物) an air plant — 실(室) an air chamber〔vessel〕 — 압착기(壓搾機) a pneumatic press — 여과기(濾過器) an air filter — 완충장치(緩衝裝置) an air suspension — 요법(療法) aerotherapy ; aerotherapeutics — 정화기(淨化機) an air cleaner — 침대 an air bed — 콘덴서 an air condenser — 터빈 an air turbine —판(瓣) an air valve

공기 空器 [빈 그릇] an empty vessel〔dish〕; [사기 그릇] a bowl ¶ 밥 한 공기 a bowl of rice

공기 公器 a public institution ; [신문 따위] a public organ〔instrument〕 ¶ 공기를 남용하다 abuse public instruments

공기 工期 〖건축〗 a term of works

공기 감염 空氣感染 aerial〔airborne〕 infection

공기 구멍 空氣— [나무통 따위의] a breathing hole

공기 기관 空氣機關 an air engine

공기 냉각 空氣冷却 an air cooling —기 an air cooler — 장치 an air cooling apparatus 실내 —기 a room cooler

공기 동역학 空氣動力學 aerodynamics —자 an aerodynamicist

공기 망치 空氣— an air〔pneumatic〕 hammer

공기 물리학 空氣物理學 aerology —자 an aerologist

공기 브레이크 an air〔a pneumatic〕 brake

공기 세척기 空氣洗滌機 an air washer

공기 압축기 空氣壓縮機 an air compressor

공기업 公企業 public enterprise〔undertaking〕; a government project

공기 오염 空氣汚染 air pollution ; atmospheric pollution (대기 오염)

공기욕 空氣浴 an air bath

공기 저항 空氣抵抗 air resistance

공기 전염 空氣傳染 [병균의] infection (by air) ; aerial〔airborne〕 infection —병 an airborne disease〔malady〕

공기 제동기 空氣制動機 a pneumatic brake

공기 조절 空氣調節 air conditioning — 장치 an air conditioning system 실내 — 장치 a room conditioning system

공기 청정기 空氣淸淨器 an air cleaner

공기총 空氣銃 an air gun〔rifle〕

공기 펌프 an air pump

공납 公納 public imposts ; taxes

공납 貢納 a tribute ; a tributary payment —하다 pay (a) tribute 《to》

공능 功能 [효능] effect ; efficacy ; use ; benefit ; [공적과 재능] merits and abilities

공단 貢緞 woven silk without patterns ; satin

공단 公團 a public corporation

공단 工團 an industrial complex ; an industrial park (미화된)

공담 公談 [공무에 관한] an official talk ; a public conversation〔discussion〕; [공평한] impartial words

공담 空談 an idle〔empty〕 talk ; an empty prattle ; a tittle-tattle ; gossip —하다 talk idly ; gossip ; prattle ; chatter ¶ 공담으로 날을 보내다 pass hours in an idle talk ; gossip away time

공답 公畓 a state〔national, government〕 paddy (field)

공당 公黨 a political party

공대 恭待 [대접] respectful treatment ; [존대] respectful address —하다 receive 《a person》 cordially ; treat 《a person》 with respect ; address with respect (존대하다)

공대공 空對空 air-to-air

공대공 미사일 an air-to-air (guided) missile

공대말 恭待— an honorific (expression) ; a term of respect

공대지 空對地 air-to-surface〔-ground〕

공대지 미사일 an air-to-surface (guided) missile

공덕 公德 public morality〔morals〕; civil virtues ¶ 공덕을 지키다 observe public morals

공덕 功德 〖불교〗 charity ; a pious act ; a charitable deed ; Buddhist merit ; piety ; [공과 덕] merit and virtue ¶ 공덕을 쌓다 accumulate virtuous deeds〔pious act〕// 공덕을 베풀다 do an act of charity ; practice charity

공덕심 公德心 public spirit ; public sense ; a sense of public duty ¶ 공덕심이 없다 be wanting in public spirit

공도 公道 ① [도로] a highway ; a public way ; a highroad ② [정의] justice ; equity ¶ 공도를 밟다 tread the path of justice ; act with justice // 바다는 천하의 공도다 The ocean is an open highway.

공도 公度 a common factor of measurement

공돈 windfall income ; easy-gotten money ; easy money ; gravy 《미·속》 ¶ 공돈은 오래 못간다 Lightly come, lightly go. /Easily got, easily gone. /A thief seldom grows rich by thieving.

공돌다 空— be ownerless〔unattached, free-floating〕; lack an owner

공동 共同 association ; union ; cooperation ; collaboration —하다 work together ; cooperate 《with》; collaborate ; act in concert〔conjunction〕 《with》 ¶ 공동의 common ; joint ; general ; public // 공동으로 jointly ; in con-

cert〔collaboration, association〕《with》 //공동의 이익을 위하여 for the public good ; in the interest of the public //공동으로 사업하다 go into business in partnership with 《a person》
— 각서(覺書) a collective note — 결의(決議) [양원의] a joint resolution — 계산(計算) joint account — 구입 cooperative buying — 방목권 common of pasturage — 보증인 a cosurety ; a joint surety — 숙박소 a public lodging house — 시설 public facilities — 시장 common market — 어업권(漁業權) common fishery rights ; common of piscary〔fishery〕 — 연구 joint research (-es) — 예금 계좌 joint account — 자본 joint stock — 작용(作用) joint action ; 〖의학〗 synergy ; synergism — 재산 joint〔common〕 property — 정신 a spirit of cooperation ; a cooperative spirit — 주권(主權) joint sovereignty ; condominium — 친권 joint custody

공동 空洞 a cave ; a cavern ; a cavity ; [폐의] a vomica 《*pl.* -cae》
— 벽돌 hollow brick — 유리(琉璃) hollow glass —음(音) 〖의학〗 a cavernous whisper〔sound〕 — 척수증(脊髓症) 〖의학〗 syringomyelia

공동 가입 共同加入 〖전화〗 joint subscription
—자 a joint subscriber

공동 가입 전화 共同加入電話 a telephone on a party line ; [시설] two-party telephone service

공동 경영 共同經營 joint management 〔operation〕
—자 a joint manager ; [소유자] a coproprietor ; a joint owner

공동 관리 共同管理 joint control ; 〖국제법〗 condominium
—지 a condominium

공동 기업 共同企業 joint enterprise 〔venture〕

공동 농장 共同農場 a collective〔cooperative〕 farm ; a kol(k)hoz 《*pl.* -zy, ~es》 《러》 ¶ 공동 농장화하다 collectivize 《a farm》

공동 담보 共同擔保 a joint mortgage

공동 모금 共同募金 the community chest
— 운동 a community-chest (fund) drive

공동 모의 共同謀議 〖법〗 conspiracy
—자 a conspirator

공동 목적 共同目的 a common cause 〔objective〕

공동 묘지 共同墓地 a public cemetery

공동 방위 共同防衛 joint defense

공동 변소 共同便所 a public lavatory ; a street latrine ; a (public) comfort station 《미》

공동 사업 共同事業 a joint enterprise

공동 사회 共同社會 a community ; communal society

공동 상속 共同相續 joint inheritance ; (co)parcenary —하다 inherit jointly
—권 coheirship ; joint heirship ; [토지의] coparcenary

공동 상속인 共同相續人 a coheir ; a joint heir ; a coheritor ; [토지의] a coparcener

공동 생활 共同生活 community〔communal〕 life ; communal living ; [남녀의] cohabitation

공동 선언 共同宣言 a joint declaration

공동 성명 共同聲明 a joint statement 〔communiqué〕 ¶ 공동 성명을 발표하다 issue a joint statement〔communiqué〕

공동 소송 共同訴訟 joint action

공동 소유 共同所有 joint ownership ; coproprietorship
—권 joint ownership —자 a joint owner ; a co-owner

공동 원고 共同原告 coplaintiff

공동 의무 共同義務 joint obligations

공동 작업 共同作業 group work ; teamwork ; cooperation —하다 work together ; cooperate 《with》 ; join hands 〔efforts〕 in 《doing》

공동 작전 共同作戰 teamwork ; concerted operation

공동 전선 共同戰線 a common〔united〕 front ¶ 공동 전선을 펴다 form〔make〕 a common front 《against》

공동 전화 共同電話 ⇨ 공동 가입 전화

공동 정범 共同正犯 joint principal offender

공동 제작 共同製作 joint production ; coproduction —하다 produce 《a film》 jointly 《with》 ; coproduce
—자 a joint producer ; a coproducer

공동 조합 共同組合 a cooperative association〔society〕 ; a cooperative ; a co-op 《구》
—원 a copartner

공동 주최 共同主催 joint auspices —하다 cosponsor

공동 주택 共同住宅 an apartment house

공동 책임 共同責任 [위원회·내각 따위의] corporate responsibility ; [부채 따위의 연대 책임] joint liability ¶ 공동 책임을 지다 answer jointly for 《a thing》 ; [부채의] hold joint liability for 《the debt》

공동 출자 共同出資 (a) joint investment ; pooling of funds

공동 취사장 共同炊事場 a community 〔communal〕 kitchen

공동 판매 共同販賣 joint marketing

공동 해손 共同海損 general average ; gross average

공동 협찬 共同協贊 joint auspices —하다 cosponsor ; sponsor jointly

공동화 空洞化 —하다 become hollow ; lose〔become devoid of〕 substance

공들다 功— take much labor〔trouble〕 ;

cost strenuous effort ¶ 공드는 일 hard〔laborious〕 work // 이 작품은 퍽 공들인 것 같다 This work smells of the lamp〔bears traces of labor〕.
공든 탑이 무너지랴 (속담) A man's labors will be crowned with success.

공들이다 功— take trouble 《for》; labor 《for》; work hard 《for》; do careful 〔elaborate〕 work ¶ 공들여 with great effort // 공들인 작품 an elaborate work // 공들인 솜씨 elaborate〔careful〕 workmanship // 여태 공들인 보람이 없어졌다 All my labors have been in vain.

공떡 空— a godsend; a windfall ¶ 이게 웬 공떡이냐 What a welcome windfall!

공뜨다 空— ① lack an owner ¶ 사표는 수리할 사람이 없어서 공뜨고 있다 The resignation paper is making an eternal journey back and forth, with no one to accept it. ② be free-floating

공략 攻落 surrender **—하다** take 《a castle》; capture 《a fort》

공란 空欄 blank; empty space; an empty〔a vacant〕 column; margin ¶ 공란에 기입하다 fill up the blanks // 공란을 메우다 fill in blanks

공람 供覽 display; show **—하다** submit 《things》 to public inspection; exhibit 《things》 before the public

공랭식 空冷式 air-cooling ¶ 공랭식의 air-cooled 《engine》
— 기통(氣筒) an air-cooled cylinder
— 기관총 — 엔진 an air-cooled engine

공략 攻略 capture; reduction; occupation; [침략] invasion; taking by storm **—하다** capture; carry; reduce; take 《a fortress》 by storm; invade 《a country》 ¶ 공략하기 어려운 impregnable 《fortress》 // 적의 진지를 공략하다 capture an enemy position
— 정치 government by aggression

공력 功力 ① [애써 들인 힘] effort; labor; elaboration // 그의 공력도 마침내 허사였다 All his efforts ended in vain. ② [불교에서 이르는] Buddhist merit acquired by practicing austerities

공로 公路 a (public) road; a highroad; a highway

공로 功勞 a meritorious service; merits; a meritorious deed; an exploit ¶ 공로가 있는 meritorious; distinguished // 공로를 세우다 distinguish oneself 《in war》; render a distinguished service 《to the State》; do much 《for》 // 공로에 의하여 for〔in recognition of〕 one's services // 한국 사람으로서 부끄럽지 않은 공로를 세웠다 His service was well worthy of a Korean.
—금(金) a (monetary) reward for (meritorious) services

공로 空路 an airway; an air route; an air lane ¶ 공로로 귀국하다 return home by plane〔air〕 // 공로로 샌프란시스코로 향하다 fly for San Francisco // 공로로 수송하다 send 《cargo》 by plane; 〖상업〗 ship by aircraft
—수송 transportation by airplane

공로상 功勞賞 [철도·경찰의] 《confer》 a distinguished service medal 《on》

공로자 功勞者 a person of merit; a person who has done distinguished service 《to the state》

공로주 功勞株 a bonus stock

공론 公論 [세론] public opinion; consensus; [정론] an impartial 〔unbias(s)ed〕 opinion〔view〕; fair criticism // 나라 일을 공론으로 결정하다 refer all state affairs to public opinion

공론 空論 a desk theory; an academic argument; a paper〔an armchair〕 argument; a futile argument **—하다** talk a desk theory

공론가 空論家 a doctrinarian; a doctrinaire; a futile talker; an impractical theorist

공뢰 空雷 an aerial torpedo

공룡 恐龍 〖고생물〗 a dinosaur

공률 工率 rate of production; 〖물리〗 power; activity

공리 公吏 a public official〔servant〕; a public employee

공리 公利 public〔common〕 welfare 〔interests〕 ¶ 공리를 도모하다 promote public interests

공리 公理 〖수학·논리〗 an axiom; a maxim; [도리] a self-evident truth

공리 功利 utility ¶ 공리적인 utilitarian // 공리적인 사나이 a matter-of-fact fellow // 사물을 공리적으로 생각하다 take a utilitarian view of things

공리 空理 an empty〔impracticable〕 theory; doctrinairism

공리공론 空理空論 ¶ 공리공론에 흐르다 indulge in academic discussion

공리주의 功利主義 utilitarianism
—자 a utilitarian

공리설 功利說 utilitarianism

공리적 功利的 utilitarian
¶ 공리적인 사나이 a matter-of-fact fellow

공립 公立 a public institution ¶ 공립의 public; communal; municipal (시립의)
— 도서관 a public library

공립 학교 公立學校 a public school; a government school

공막 鞏膜 〖해부〗 the sclera
— 절개술(切開術) sclerotomy

공막염 鞏膜炎 sclerotitis; scleritis

공매 公賣 public sale〔auction〕 **—하다** sell by public auction; offer at public sale〔auction〕
—장(場) an auction house〔hall, room〕
강제 — forced sale; sheriff's sale

공매 空賣 〖증권〗 a short sale; short selling **—하다** sell short

공매 처분 公賣處分 (disposition by)

public sale ; (a) public sale of confiscated property ; (a) tax sale ; selling up
공맹 孔孟 Confucius and Mencius
공맹지도 孔孟之道 the doctrines〔teachings〕 of Confucius and Mencius
공맹학 孔孟學 Confucianism ⇨ 유학
공명 公明 fairness ; justice **—하다** (be) fair ; open ; square ; just ; aboveboard ¶ 공명히 fairly ; justifiably
공명 功名 a great〔distinguished〕 achievement ; a glorious deed ; [명예] fame ; renown ; honor ¶ 공명을 세우다 distinguish oneself ; perform a glorious deed // 혁혁한 공명을 세우다 render brilliant services
공명 共鳴 [공감] sympathy ; unison ; response ; echo ; 〖물리〗 resonance ; consonance **—하다** sympathize 《with》 ; echo ; respond 《to》 ; be in sympathy 《with》 ; [물체가] be resonant 《with》 ¶ 그는 나의 사상에 공명하였다 He responded to my thoughts. /He sympathized with my thoughts.
—동(胴) a resonance body **—실(室)** a resonance chamber ; a sound box **—음(音)** sympathetic sound **— 탐침기(探針器)** a resonance probe **—판(板)** [악기의] a sounding board ; a table **— 현상(現象)** [양자 역학적] mesomerism **— 효과(效果)** a resonance〔mesomeric〕 effect **— 흡수(吸收)** resonance absorption **핵자기(核磁氣) —** nuclear magnetic resonance
공명관 共鳴管 a resonance tube
공명기 共鳴器 a resonator
공명 상자 共鳴箱子 a resonance box 〔chamber〕 ; a sound box
공명 선거 公明選擧 a clean〔fair〕 election
공명심 功名心 ambition ; aspiration ; love of fame ¶ 공명심이 많다 be eager 〔thirsty〕 for fame
공명자 共鳴者 a sympathizer
공산주의(共産主義) — a communist sympathizer ; a communist by sympathy
공명 정대 公明正大 fairness ; justice ; (a sense of) fair play ¶ 공명 정대한 square ; open ; fair ; just ; open and aboveboard // 공명 정대하게 행동하다 act fair and square
공모 公募 public subscription **—하다** collect〔invite〕 publicly ; offer for public subscription ; raise 《a fund》 by subscription ¶ 주를 공모하다 offer shares for public subscription // 현상 소설을 공모하다 open a prize list of novels ; invite the public to join in a prize contest for best stories // 공모를 통해서 쓸모있는 사람을 구하기란 쉽지 않다 It's easy to find good people through public announcements.
공모 共謀 conspiracy ; collusion ; complicity 《with a person in a crime》 ; confederacy **—하다** conspire〔plot〕 《with》 ; conspire〔plot〕 together ; collude at ¶ 공모해서 in conspiracy〔collusion〕 《with》
공모자 共謀者 a (co)conspirator ; an accomplice 《in a crime》 ; a confederate
공목 空木, 空目 〖인쇄〗 furniture ; filling material ; lead (인테르)
공무 工務 factory〔workshop〕 affairs ; factory management
공무 公務 official business ; public affairs ; public duties ¶ 공무로 인한 부상 an injury incurred in line of (public) duty // 공무 다망하여 owing to the pressure of official business // 공무를 집행하다 execute〔exercise〕 one's official duties // 공무로 여행하다 travel on official business〔duty〕 // 공무와 사무를 구별하다 discriminate between public and personal affairs
— 재해 보상(災害補償) compensation for accidents in line of duty
공무국 工務局 the Printing Bureau (신문사 따위의)
공무원 公務員 [전체] public service personnel ; civil service ; [개인]a public servant〔employee, official〕 ; a servant of the state ; a public service worker ; a civil servant 《영》 ; an officeholder 《미》 ; a government employee ¶ 공무원이 되다 enter〔go into〕 public service // 공무원을 그만두다 quit〔leave, resign〕 one's public office // 공무원 근성 bureaucratism ; officialism
—법 the National Public Service Law **고급 —** high-ranking public officials **국가 —** a national civil servant **국제 —** an international servant **기술〔기능〕직 —** a public official in technical〔skill〕 post **지방 —** a local civil servant **하급 —** a petty official
공무 집행 公務執行 execution〔performance〕 of one's official duties ; exercise of one's office
— 방해 interference〔intervention〕 with a government official in the execution 〔performance〕 of his duties
공문 公文 [문서] an official document ; [통신] an official correspondence〔note, notice, communication〕
— 서식(書式) formalities for official documents **— 전보(電報)** an official telegram **—체(體)** official style
공문 空文 a dead letter ; a scrap of paper ; a meaningless document ¶ 공문화하다 turn out a dead letter
공문 孔門 the Confucian school
공문서 公文書 an official document 〔paper, note〕 ; a state document ; archives (보존된) ; a communiqué (외교의)

— 위조 forgery of an official document 급송 — a dispatch
공물 公物 government〔public〕 property ; [관급품] government issues
공물 供物 a Buddhist offering ; a votive offering ¶ 공물로 바치다 offer ; make an offering ; devote 《a thing to the Buddhist idol》
공물 貢物 a tribute ; a tributary payment ; tax paid in kind ¶ 공물을 바치다 pay〔offer〕 a tribute // 공물을 바치게 하다 impose a tribute 《upon》; lay 《a country》 under tributes // 통치자에게 공물을 바치다 pay tribute to a ruler
공미 貢米 rice paid as taxes ; rice offered as a tribute
공미리 〖물고기〗 a halfbeak
공민 公民 a citizen ; a denizen ; a freeman ¶ 공민의 의무 civil〔civic〕 duties
—과(科) a civic course ; civics — 도덕 civic virtues — 의식 civil consciousness — 생활 a civil life — 정신 a civil spirit
공민 교육 公民敎育 civic education ; education for citizenship
공민권 公民權 citizenship ; civil〔civic〕 rights ; franchise ¶ 공민권을 주다 enfranchise 《a person》 // 공민권을 얻다 acquire citizenship // 공민권을 박탈하다 disfranchise 《a person》; deprive 《a person》 of rights of citizenship
—법 〖법〗 [미국의] the Civil Rights Act
공민 학교 公民學校 a civil education center ; a citizenship training school
공박 攻駁 refutation ; a wordy attack ; a charge ; denunciation ; confutation —하다 refute ; make a wordy attack 《against》; attack 《by argument》; charge ; denounce ¶ 그녀는 그의 주장을 공박했다 She refuted his argument.
공밥 空— meals one has not paid 〔worked〕 for ¶ 공밥 먹다 take one's reward without working for it ; eat idle bread (놀고 먹다) ; eat 《a person's》 salt (식객이 되다)
공방 攻防 offense〔attack〕 and defense
공방 空房 [빈방] an empty room ; an unoccupied chamber ; [공규] the bedchamber of a woman whose husband is away ¶ 공방을 지키는 아내 a grass widow
공방전 攻防戰 offensive and defensive battle
공배수 公倍數 〖수학〗 a common multiple
최소(最小) — the least common multiple 《L. C. M.》
*공백 空白 a blank ; blank space ; [비유적] a gap ; vacuum ; void ¶ 정치의 공백 a political vacuum // 공백을 메우다 fill up〔in〕 the blank ; bridge the gap // 공백이 생기다 make a blank 《in one's life》; leave a vacuum // 공백에 써 넣다 fill in the blanks
공범 共犯 complicity 《in a crime》 ¶ 공범으로 체포되었다 He was caught as a party to the crime.
— 관계 complicity 《in a crime》
공범자 共犯者 an accomplice 《with〔of〕 a person in a crime》; a confederate 《in a crime》; a partner 《in a crime》 ¶ 그는 그 범죄의 공범자이다 He has had a hand〔is an accomplice〕 in the crime.
공범죄 共犯罪 complicity 《in a crime》
공법 工法 a method of construction
공법 公法 〖법〗 public law
—론(論) publicism — 위반(違反) breach of public law 국제 — international law
공법인 公法人 a public juridical person ; a public corporation
공법학 公法學 (the study of) public law
—자 a publicist ; a specialist in public law
공변되다 (be) fair ; just ; square ; just and fair ; impartial ; even-handed
공변 세포 孔邊細胞 〖식물〗 guard cells
공병 工兵 the (military) engineers ; a sapper 《영》; an engineer ; [기계 공병] a mechanic
— 기계 a mechanic ; a mec 《미·속》 —학(學) military engineering — 학교 the Engineering School 선발(先發) — a pioneer
공병대 工兵隊 an engineer corps〔battalion〕; a construction battalion 《미》
공보 公報 an official report〔notice, communication〕; an official bulletin ; a communiqué 《프》; an official gazette (관보) ; [홍보] (public) information ; publicity ¶ 공보에 의하면 according to an official report ; It is officially reported 《that》 // 공보로 발표하다 publish in a gazette
—계(係) an information service〔unit〕; a publicist (사람) — 비서 a press secretary 《미》 —처(處) the Bureau of Public Information — 활동 information 〔publicity〕 activities 국립 —관〔원〕 the National Information Center 미국 —원 the United States Information Service 《USIS》
공보실 公報室 the Office of Public Information
공복 公僕 a public servant
공복 空腹 an empty stomach ; hunger ¶ 공복을 느끼다 be〔feel〕 hungry // 공복으로 일하다 work on an empty stomach // 공복에 술을 마시지 마라 Don't drink on an empty stomach.
공복 公服 an official uniform〔outfit〕
†공부 工夫 study ; learning ; work (on one's studies) ; scholarly activity —하다 study ; learn ; work at〔on〕 《one's studies》; engage in scholarly activity ¶ 공부한 사람 a learned person // 공부를 못하는 어린이 a boy〔girl〕 who is bad at his〔her〕 books // 공부를 잘하다

be good at one's studies ; learn nicely // 벼락공부를 하다 He is cramming [swotting]. // 열심히 공부하다 study [work] hard ; grind (away) 《구》 // 지나치게 공부하다 overstudy // 공부를 게을리하다 neglect one's studies // 외국에서 공부하다 study abroad // 밤늦게까지 공부하다 study [work] late at [into] night ; burn the midnight oil // 화가가 되려고 공부하다 study to be a painter // 나는 훌륭한 선생님한테 불어를 공부하고 있다 I am learning French from an excellent teacher. // 십년공부 도로아미타불 Ten year's study down the drain !
—방 a study (room) — 시간 study hours ; class (time)

공부벌레 a greasy grind ; a grinder ; a dig 《미·속》 ; a swot ¶ 그는 공부벌레처럼 열심히 공부했다 He studied hard as a grinder. // 그녀의 별명은 공부벌레였다 Her nickname was grinder.

공분 公憤 [의분] righteous [public] indignation ; [민중의 분노] public rage [resentment] ¶ 공분을 느끼다 be morally indignant

공분모 公分母 ⇨ 공통 분모

공비 工費 the cost of construction ; [공임] labor costs ¶ 공비 천만원을 투자해서 at a cost of ten million *won*

공비 公費 public expenditure [expenses] ¶ 공비로 at public expense

공비 空費 waste ; useless expense

공비 共匪 red [communist] guerrillas ¶ 공비를 소탕하다 sweep [mop up] red guerrillas

공사 公司 [중국의] a firm ; a company

†**공사 工事** construction (work) ; (engineering) work ¶ 공사 중이다 be under [in the course of] construction // 공사를 시작하다 start [begin] work // 공사를 감독하다 supervise [superintend] construction [work] // 본 철도의 공사는 내주에 착수한다 Construction work on this railway line begins next week.
—계(係) a person in charge of work —난(難) engineering difficulties —반(班) a construction crew 《미》 ; a gang of navvies 《영》 —별 청부(別請負) a separate contract ; a partial contract — 입찰(入札) a bid for construction work — 현장 a field of construction work 교량 — bridging work 날림 — jerry building ; flimsy [slipshod, shoddy] construction (work) 도로 — road building [construction] ; [수리] road repairing ; street improvement 보수 — repair work 부실 — faulty work ; fraudulent work 철도 — railway [railroad] construction (work) 터널 — tunneling work

공사 公私 official [public] and private [personal] affairs ¶ 공사의 생활 public and private life // 공사가 함께 both in public and private ; officially and privately // 공사를 혼동[구별]하다 mix up [draw up the line between] public and private affairs // 공사를 구별시오 Separate your personal affairs from business.

공사 公事 public affairs ; government affairs

†**공사 公使** a (diplomatic) minister
—직 ministry 각국 — diplomatic representatives ; the heads of foreign missions 대리 — a chargé d'affaires (ad interim) 《*pl.* chargés d'affaires》 《프》 우루과이 주재 한국 — the Korean Minister to [in] Uruguay 특명 전권(特命全權) — an envoy extraordinary and minister plenipotentiary

공사 公社 a public corporation
대한 조선(大韓造船) — the Korea Shipbuilding Corporation 대한 석유 — the Korea Oil Corporation 대한 주택 — the Korea Housing Corporation

공사관 公使館 a legation
— 무관 a military [naval] attaché to a legation —원 [총칭] the staff [personnel] of a legation ; a legation staff ; [한 사람] a member of a legation staff

공사비 工事費 the cost of construction ; construction expenses

공사중 工事中 [게시] Under construction [repair] ; Men working [at work] ; Road Work (s) Ahead

공사채 公社債 bonds ; (public) bonds and (corporate) debentures
— 이율 a yield on corporate and public [municipal] bonds — 투자 신탁 a bond investment trust

공산 共産 common property ; community of property ; [공산주의] communism
—권(圈) the Communist bloc [orbit] —군(軍) the Red Army —권 제국(圈諸國) countries in the Communist bloc [orbit] ; Communist bloc countries [nations] — 세계(世界) the Communist world — 인터내셔널 the Communist International — 분자(分子) a communist element ; a communist fraction —제(制) communism — 조합(組合) a communist association — 지구(地區) a Communist territory ; a Red [Communist] area — 청년 동맹 [소련의] Komsomol ; Comsomol ; the Communist Youth League —촌(村) a communistic village —측 the Communist side 비(非) — 세계 the non-Communist world

공산 公算 probability ¶ 성공할 공산이 크다 bid fair to succeed // 성공할 공산이 적다 have a poor [slim] chance of success // 그 모험이 성공할 공산은 극히 작다 There is very little probability that the venture will succeed. /There is a very slim chance of the venture suc-

ceeding.
— 오차(誤差) a probable error — 인수(因數) a probability factor
공산계 共産系 ¶ 공산계의 Communistic
— 신문 a Communist-influenced〔-inclined〕 paper
공산당 共産黨 the Communist Party《CP》; the Communists
— 기관지 a Communist paper ; a Red paper — 동조자 a communist sympathizer ; a fellow traveler ; a commie ; a commy — 선언 the Communist Manifesto — 세포 a Communist cell — 연차 대회 an annual Communist convention —원 a communist ; a Red〔red〕; a commie ; a commy — 정치국 the Politburo ; the Executive Committee of the Communist Party
공산명월 空山明月 the moon shining on a lone mountain ; [대머리] a baldhead
†공산주의 共産主義 communism ; collectivism ¶ 공산주의의 communistic // 공산주의와 싸우다 battle〔struggle〕 against communism
— 동맹 a communist league〔alliance〕 — 사회 a communitarian society — 운동 a communistic drive for the spread of communism
공산주의 국가 共産主義國家 a communist country〔nation〕 ¶ 공산주의 국가간의 intra-Communist《conflict》
비— a non-Communist country〔nation〕
†공산주의자 共産主義者 a communist ; a Red〔red〕 ¶ 공산주의자가 되다 go communist ; go red
공산 진영 共産陣營 the Communist camp
공산화 共産化 communization ¶ 공산화를 막다 defend《a country》 against Communists
공상 供上 presentation (of local product to the king) —하다 present
†공상 空想 an idle fancy ; imagination ; vision ; a fanciful idea ; a daydream ; a fantasy ; a moonshine —하다 fancy ; imagine ; dream ; daydream ¶ 공상적인 fanciful ; visionary ; dreamy ; romantic ; Utopian // 공상에 잠기다 be given to daydreaming ; indulge in idle fancies // 공상을 그리다 build castles in the air // 요컨대 자네 생각은 공상에 불과하다 Your idea is after all impractical〔Utopian〕. // 미래의 행복을 공상해 보았다 He drew a fine picture of his future happiness.
— 과학 소설 [장르로서] science fiction ; [일편] a science story〔novel〕 — 과학 소설가 a science fictionist — 과학 영화 a science fiction film —력(力) the power of (the) imagination ; the imagination —론(論) a mere ideal ; a fanciful idea ; a (day)dream
공상 公傷 an injury sustained while on duty
공상 工商 [업종] industry and commerce ; [사람] (the classes of) artisans and tradesmen
공상가 空想家 a dreamer ; a daydreamer ; a visionary ; a Utopian
공생 共生 〖생물〗 symbiosis ; commensalism
— 동물〔식물〕 a commensal —체(體) a symbiont ; a commensal
공생애 公生涯 public life ; a public career
공서 共棲 ⇨ 공생
공서 양속 公序良俗 good public order and customs
공석 公席 [회의의] the meeting ; (the presence of) the public ; [공무의] a place where public affairs are attended to
공석 空席 a vacant〔an unoccupied〕 seat ; a vacancy
공선 公選 [공중의 선거] public〔popular〕 election ; election by the people ; [공명 선거] a fair election —하다 elect by popular vote
— 의원(議員) an elective member ; an assemblyman (지방 의회의) — 지사(知事) a publicly-elected (provincial) governor
공설 公設 ¶ 공설의 public ; [시립] municipal // 공설 기관이다 It is a public institution.
— 기관 a public institution — 전당포 a public〔municipal〕 pawnshop — 하수도 public sewerage
공설 시장 公設市場 a public〔municipal〕 market
공설 운동장 公設運動場 a public stadium
공성 攻城 a siege —하다 (be) siege
—군(軍) a besieging army ; besiegers —보루(堡壘) siegeworks — 작업(作業) siege operations —전(戰) siege warfare —포(砲) a siege gun〔piece〕; siege artillery《총칭》
공세 攻勢 the offensive ; the aggressive ; aggression ; an offensive movement〔operation〕 ¶ 공세로 변하다 change to the offensive // 공세를 취하다 take〔assume〕 the offensive〔aggressive〕 // 질문 공세를 하다 assail《a person》 with questions
선전 — a propaganda offensive 외교 — a diplomatic offensive 테러 — a wave of terror
공소 公訴 〖법〗 arraignment ; public prosecution ; accusation ; public action ; a criminal action —하다 arraign ; prosecute ; accuse ; impeach ¶ 공소를 제기하다 institute a public action ; prosecute a case // 공소를 기각하다 dismiss a public action
— 사실 charge — 유지 institution and support of a public action

공소 控訴 an appeal 《to a higher court》 ―하다 appeal against 《a decision》; appeal 《to a higher tribunal》; enter〔file, lodge〕 an appeal against 《a lower court》 ¶ 공소의 appellate // 공소 불능의 inappellable; unappealable // 공소를 기각하다 dismiss〔turn down〕 an appeal // 대법원의 판결은 공소할 수 없다 There is no appeal from the decision of the Supreme Court.

공소권 公訴權 〖법〗 the right of arraignment

공소권 控訴權 the right of intermediate appeal

공소인 控訴人 an appellant of intermediate civil appeal

피― a respondent of intermediate civil appeal

공소장 公訴狀 a written arraignment

공소장 控訴狀 a notice of intermediate civil appeal

‡공손 恭遜 politeness; civility; courtesy; courteousness; respectfulness; reverence; deference ―하다 (be) polite; civil; courteous; respectful; reverent; deferential ¶ 공손한 태도로 in a polite attitude // 공손히 politely; civilly; humbly; courteously; respectfully // 공손히 대하다 treat 《a person》 with civility // 공손히 절하다 salute〔bow〕 politely

공수 〖민속〗 a message from the dead delivered by an exorcist

공수 받다 (관용) get a message from the dead through a medium

공수 주다 (관용) bring a message from the "other side"

공수 攻守 offense and defense; 〖야구〗 batting and fielding

― 동맹 an offensive and defensive alliance ¶ 공수 동맹을 맺다 conclude 〔enter into, form〕 an offensive and defensive alliance 《with》

공수 空手 a bare〔an empty〕 hand

공수 空輸 air transport; an airlift; transportation by air ―하다 airlift; send by plane; carry〔transport〕 by air ¶ 우편물을 공수하다 carry〔send〕 mail by air〔plane〕

― 화물(貨物) airfreight ― 회사 an air transport company 대규모 ― an airlift on a large scale; a massive airlift

공수 拱手 ① placing one's left hand over the right hand 《as a gesture of respect》 ② folding one's arms ―하다 cross one's hands in respect; fold one's arms ¶ 공수 방관하다 look on 《a scene》 with folded arms; remain idle

공수래 공수거 空手來空手去 "come empty, return empty"; the vanity of life

공수병 恐水病 〖의학〗 hydrophobia; rabies ¶ 공수병에 걸린 개 a mad dog; a rabid dog // 공수병에 걸리다 be affected with rabies

― 예방 주사 the Pasteur treatment; anti-hydrophobia serum treatment

공수 부대 空輸部隊 an airborne unit 〔corps, troop, outfit〕; a sky army 〔troop〕; an air transport corps 《A. T. C.》 《구》

공수 사단 空輸師團 〔미군의〕 an airborne division

공수 작전 空輸作戰 airlift〔airborne〕 operations

공수표 空手票 a wind bill; a fictitious bill; a kite; a bad check〔cheque 《영》〕; an accommodation bill ¶ 공수표를 떼다 fly a kite; 〔비유적〕 make an empty promise // 공수표로 끝나다 end in an empty pledge

공순 恭順 obedience; submission

―하다 (be) submissive; gentle; meek

공술 空― free liquor; a gratis drink

공술 供述 a deposition; an affidavit; testimony; a signed statement〔confession〕 ―하다 depose; make an affidavit; testify; confess

―인(人) a deponent; a person who has testified

공술서 供述書 a written statement; an affidavit

*공습 空襲 an air raid〔attack, assault〕 ―하다 air-raid; make an air raid 《on》 ¶ 공습을 받다 be air-raided; undergo〔suffer〕 an air raid

― 감시인 a spotter ―기(機) an air raider ― 부대 a strike force

공습 경보 空襲警報 an air-raid alarm 〔warning, alert〕 ¶ 공습 경보를 발하다 give an air-raid warning // 공습 경보를 해제하다 sound the "all clear"〔a white alert〕

공시 公示 public announcement; a public 〔official〕 notice ―하다 announce publicly; make public; make known to the public

―가격 the declared value ― 송달(送達) 〖법〗 conveyance by public announcement ― 최고(催告) a public summons ― 사항 government notices

†공식 公式 〖수학〗 a formula 《*pl.* ~s, -lae》; 〔의식〕 formality; 〔관청의〕 an official ceremony ¶ 공식의 formal; official; state // 비공식의 unofficial // 공식적으로 formally; officially; in state // 공식으로 표명하다 express in a formula

― 성명 an official statement 《on》; 〔신문 발표의〕 a handout ― 승인 〖국제법〗 〔조약 따위의〕 accession ―주의(主義) formalism (형식주의) ―회합 an official meeting

공식 空食 eating〔getting〕 for nothing; 〖불교〗 feeding people without charge ―하다 eat〔get〕 for nothing

공식론 公式論 formalism
—자(者) a formalist
공식 반응 公式反應 an official response
공식 발표 公式發表 official announcement
공식 방문 公式訪問 a formal〔an official〕 visit ; an official call ; [국가 원수의] a state visit
공식 시합 公式試合 a regular game 〔match〕 ; 〖야구〗 a pennant race ; [선수권 시합] a title match
비(非)— an exhibition game ; [야구] an open game
*__공식화 公式化__ formulation **—하다** formulate
공신 公信 public confidence
공신 功臣 a meritorious retainer〔subject〕 ; a vassal of merit
공안 公安 public peace〔welfare, security〕 ¶ 공안을 해치다 disturb the public peace // 검찰은 공안사범을 검거했다 The prosecution arrested a public safety offender.
— **경찰** public peace police ; security police — **방해범** 〖법〗 a disorderly person — **방해죄** breach of the peace — **방해 행위** breaches of the peace
공안 公案 [공문서의 안] the draft of a public document ; [여론의] a bill drafted in accordance with public opinion ; 〖불교〗 a catechetic question for meditation
공안 위원 公安委員 a public safety commissioner
—**회(會)** a public safety commission **국가 —회** the National Public Safety Commission
공알 〖해부〗 the clitoris
공약 公約 a public pledge〔promise, commitment〕 **—하다** pledge〔commit〕 oneself to 《a policy》 ¶ 정당은 그들의 공약을 지켜야만 한다 The party must keep their public pledge.
선거 — election pledges
공약수 公約數 〖수학〗 a common measure〔divisor〕
최대(最大) — the greatest common measure 《G. C. M.》
공양 供養 [어른에게의] providing one's elders with food ; [부처에게의] offering food to Buddha **—하다** provide one's elders with food ; offer food to Buddha
공양 드리다 관용 offer food to Buddha ; say a mass for the dead
공양미 供養米 rice offered to Buddha
공양주(主) a person who gives alms to Buddhist temple
공양탑 供養塔 a tower erected for the repose of 《a person's》 soul
*__공언 公言__ an open declaration ; profession ; avowal **—하다** declare (openly) ; profess ; proclaim ; avow ¶ 그는 애국자라고 공언했다 He avowed himself (to be) a patriot.
공언 空言 an empty〔a vain〕 word ; prattle ; idle talk ; [거짓] a lie
—**가(家)** a windy speaker ; an idle talker
공얻다 空— get for nothing〔gratis, free of charge〕
†**공업 工業** industry ; the manufacturing industry ; industries 《총칭》 ¶ 공업의 industrial ; technical ; technological ; manufacturing // 공업용의 for industrial use 〔purpose〕
—**가** an industrialist ; a manufacturer — **경영** industrial management — **경제** industrial economy —**계(界)** the industrial world ; industrial circles — **교육** technical education —**규격** industrial standard — **금융** industrial finance — **기사** a technical engineer — **기술자** a technical expert — **디자이너** an industrial designer —**력(力)** industrial might 《of a nation》 — **부기(簿記)** industrial bookkeeping — **분석(分析)** technical analysis — **생산** industrial production — **소유권** industrial property (rights) — **시험소** an industrial laboratory —**염(鹽)** industrial salt — **예술(藝術)** an industrial art — **원료** industrial raw materials — **의장(意匠)** an industrial design — **정책** industrial policy —**주(株)** [증권] industrial stocks〔securities〕 ; industrials — **중심지** a manufacturing〔an industrial〕 center — **지리** industrial geography — **화학** industrial 〔technical〕 chemistry ; technochemistry **가내 —** the household industry **경(중)—** light〔heavy〕 industry **국립 — 연구소** the National Industrial Research Institute **주요 —** key industries **한국 — 규격** the Korean Industrial Standard 《KS》
공업 功業 an achievement ; a meritorious deed〔service〕 ; an exploit ¶ 과학에서의 공업 a scientific achievement
공업 고등 학교 工業高等學校 a technical high school
공업국 工業國 an industrial nation 〔country〕
비(非)— a nonindustrial country **선진 —** advanced industrial nations
공업 단지 工業團地 an industrial complex ; an industrial park (미화된)
울산 — the Ulsan industrial complex 《on the nation's east coast》 **임해〔대단위〕 —** a coastal〔large-scale〕 industrial complex
공업 도시 工業都市 an industrial〔a manufacturing〕 city〔town〕 ; a factory town
공업 약품 工業藥品 industrial chemicals
공업 용수 工業用水 industrial water
공업 제품 工業製品 industrial goods〔products〕
공업 지대 工業地帶 an industrial area ;

a manufacturing district
공업 폐수 工業廢水 industrial effluent〔waste water〕
공업 학교 工業學校 a technical〔technological〕 school
공업화 工業化 industrialization ¶ 아직 공업화되지 않은 지역 a nonindustrialized area // 농촌을 공업화하다 industrialize a village
공역 公役 public service ¶ 공역을 기피하다 evade〔shirk〕 (one's) public service
공역 共譯 joint translation **—하다** translate《a book》in cooperation ¶ …의 공역 translated by《A》and《B》
공역자 共譯者 a joint translator
†**공연 公演** a public performance〔exhibition〕 **—하다** perform ; play ; [연극을] present ; stage ¶ 이 연극은 하루에 3회 공연된다 This play is presented three times a day.
공연 共演 co-acting ; co-starring
—하다 play together ; co-act ; co-star
공연스럽다 空然— ⇨ 공연(空然)하다
공연자 共演者 a co-actor ; a co-star
공연하다 公然— (be) open ; public ; overt ; avowed ¶ 공연한 비밀 an open secret // 공연한 적대 행위 open〔avowed〕 hostilities
†**공연하다 空然—** (be) useless ; futile ; unavailing ; needless ; fruitless ; unnecessary ; ineffectual ; empty ; serve no purpose ¶ 공연한 일 a vain attempt ; a futility ; a trifle // 공연스레 애쓰다 struggle in vain〔for nothing〕 // 공연스레 울다 cry for no reason at all // 공연히 시비걸지 마라 Don't provoke a quarrel uselessly. // 좋아보이는구나 내가 공연히 걱정했구나 You look well. I guess all my worrying was for nothing.
공염불 空念佛 a fair but empty phrase ; cant ¶ 공염불에 그치다 end in an empty talk // 그는 그저 공염불만 외우고 있었다 He chanted empty prayers wildly.
공영 公營 public management ¶ 공영의 public(-managed) ; municipal (시영의)
공영 共榮 mutual prosperity ; co-prosperity
공영 共營 joint management ⇨ 공동 경영
공영 주택 公營住宅 [집합적] public housing ; [한 채의 집] a unit of public housing
공예 工藝 industrial arts ; technology ¶ 공예의 industrial ; technological
—가(家) a technologist **— 공학(工學)** polytechnic engineering **— 미술** applied fine arts **— 연구소** a polytechnic institute **— 유리** art glass
공예품 工藝品 objects of craftwork〔applied arts〕
— 전시회 an industrial arts exhibition
공예학 工藝學 technology ; technics ; polytechnics
—자 a technologist
공예 학교 工藝學校 a polytechnic (school) ; a technological school
공용 公用 public use〔service〕 ; official〔public, government〕 business (용무) ; [비용] public expense **—하다** use publicly ¶ 공용으로 on official business〔duty〕
—물(物) objects for public use **—지(地)** land for public use
공용 共用 common〔joint〕 use **—하다** use《a thing》in common
—물(物) public property **—성(性)** commonality ; commonness **—전(栓)** a common tap ; a water faucet for common use
공용어 公用語 [관청 용어] an official language〔terminology〕 ; [국제 회의 따위의] an official language《of an international conference》
공용차 公用車 an official vehicle
†**공원 工員** a (factory) worker〔hand〕 ; an industrial worker ; [기계의] a machine operator〔hand〕
공원 公園 a park ; a public garden ; [작은 공원] a square
—과(課) [시의] the Parks Section **— 구역(區域)** a park district〔area〕 **— 단속 규칙** park regulations **— 도로** a parkway **— 묘지** a park cemetery **— 청소부** a park cleaner ; a caretaker《of the park》 **국립—** a national park **옥상(屋上) —** a roof garden **자연 —** a wilderness park
공위 攻圍 siege ; investment ; envelopment **—하다** besiege ; invest ; lay siege to ; envelope ¶ 공위를 해제하다 raise the siege
—군(軍) a besieging army **—전(戰)** siege warfare
공위 空位 [빈 자리] a vacancy ; a vacant position〔post〕 ; [이름뿐인] a job〔post〕 in name only
공유 公有 public ownership〔property〕 ¶ 공유의 public ; public(ly)-owned
공유 共有 joint〔common〕 ownership ; 〖법〗 co-ownership **—하다** hold〔own〕《a thing》in common ; own《a thing》jointly ¶ 이 집은 나의 아내와 공유하고 있다 This house belongs to me and my wife.
— 결합(結合) 〖화학〗 a covalent bond **—금(金)** a common purse **— 원자가(原子價)** 〖화학〗 covalence **—자(者)** a joint owner ; a co-owner
공유림 公有林 a public-owned forest
공유물 公有物 public property ; [자산] public assets ¶ 공유물을 사물화하다 use public property for individual purpose
공유물 共有物 common property ¶ 이 책상은 공유물이다 This desk is for

common use.
공유 재산 共有財產 common〔public, community〕 property ; property owned in common
공유 재산 公有財產 public property〔assets〕
공유지 公有地 public〔common〕 land ; land for common use ; public domain ; 〖영국사〗 folkland
*공으로 空— free (of charge) ; for nothing ; gratis ; gratuitously ; for a song ¶ 공으로 얻다 get《it》 for nothing ; get free of charge∥공으로 들어갈 수 없나요 Can we get in free?
공의 公醫 a community doctor〔physician〕
공의 公議 an unbiased view
공이 a pestle ; a pounder
공이치기 the hammer《of a rifle》; a gunlock ; the cock
공익 公益 public interest〔good, benefit〕; common〔general〕 weal ¶ 공익을 꾀하다 promote〔advance〕 the public interest ; work for the public good∥공익을 해치다 be detrimental〔prejudicial〕 to the public interest
— 대표(代表) delegates of〔members representing〕 public interests ; representatives of public interests ; public welfare delegates — 사단(社團) a public utility association — 사업 위원 a public〔neutral〕 member《of a labor relations board》 — 재단 a public utility foundation — 회사 a public service〔utility〕 company
공익 共益 public good ; common benefit〔interest〕 ¶ 공익을 위하여 for the public good ; in the interest of the public
— 비용 〖법〗 expenses for common profit
공익 단체 公益團體 a public corporation
공익 법인 公益法人 a nonprofit foundation ; a juridical person for the public good〔benefit, welfare〕; a public-service corporation《미》
공익 사업 公益事業 public utilities〔works〕; an enterprise for the public good
— 단체 a public utility〔service〕 corporation
공익 우선 公益優先 public interests first ; priority of the public interests over the private
—주의(主義) the principle of "public interests first"
공익 전당포 公益典當鋪 [가게] a municipal pawnshop
— 주인 a public pawnbroker
공인 公人 [사회인] a public man〔character, figure〕; men in public life ; [공직에 있는 사람] a public official ; an officeholder
공인 公印 an official seal
— 위조 forgery of an official seal
공인 公認 authorization ; official recognition〔approval〕 —하다 recognize〔approve〕 officially ; give《a person》 official recognition ; authorize ¶ 공인의 authorized ; official ; officially-adopted∥후보를 공인하다 officially adopt a candidate
— 세계 기록 an officially ratified world record ; an international official record — 중매인(仲買人) a certified〔sworn〕 broker — 풀 a regulation-size pool 학교 — 양복점 a tailor approved by the school
공인 기록 公認記錄 an official record
공인수 公因數 〖수학〗 a common factor
공인 중개사 公認仲介士 a licensed real estate agent
— 시험 the state-sponsored test for licensing real estate agents
공인 회계사 公認會計士 certified public accountant《CPA》《미》; a chartered accountant《C. A》《영》
—법(法) 〖법〗 the Certified〔Chartered〕 Accountant Act
공인 후보자 公認候補者 a recognized〔an official, an authorized〕 candidate
— 명단 the ticket《미》
공일 [거저 하는 일] working for nothing ; a job in vain ; [헛수고] lost labor ; labor lost —하다 work for nothing
*공일 空日 [일요일] Sunday ; [일반] a holiday ; a day off
공임 工賃 [임금] a wage ; wages ; pay ; (cost of) labor ¶ 공임을 올리다 raise〔increase〕 wages∥공임이 비싸서 수지가 맞지 않는다 As labor is very expensive, the work will not pay.
공자 公子 a young nobleman ; a little prince
공자 孔子 Confucius ¶ 공자의 Confucian∥공자의 가르침 Confucianism
공자 앞에 문자 쓴다 속담 Don't teach your grandmother to suck eggs.
공작 工作 [제작] construction ; building ; engineering work ; [수공] handicraft ; [행동] maneuvering ; move ; operation —하다 construct ; build ; [꾀하다] maneuver ¶ 준비 공작을 하다 prepare the ground in advance《for》; pave the way for∥평화 공작을 하다 make a peace move∥막후에서 은밀히 공작하다 maneuver behind the scenes
— 게이지 〖기계〗 a shop〔working〕 gauge —금 operational funds —대(隊) a group of underground activists —도(圖) 〖건축〗 a shop drawing —물(物) a structure ; a building —선(船) a repairship — 시간 the handicraft hour ; a handicraft lesson —장(場) a workshop

*공작 孔雀 〖새〗 a peacock ; a peahen (암컷) ¶ 공작 같은 peacockish // 공작이 날개를 펴고 있다 The peacock is displaying his tail.
— 고사리 〖식물〗 the maidenhairfern — 석(石) 〖광물〗 a malachite
†공작 公爵 a prince ; a duke 《영》
공작 기계 工作機械 a machine tool
—공(工) a machinist
공작 부인 公爵夫人 a princess ; a duchess 《영》
공작품 工作品 handicrafts ¶ 아동의 공작품을 전시하다 show〔exhibit〕 school children's handicrafts
공장 工匠 a craftsman ; an artisan
†공장 工場 a factory ; a plant ; a mill ; a work ; a workshop ; a manufactory ¶ 공장의 일 factory work // 본공장과 분공장 main and branch factories // 공장에서 일하다 work at a factory
— 검사관 a factory inspector — 경영 factory management — 대지 a factory site —부기(簿記) factory bookkeeping — 생산력 production power〔capacity〕 ; productivity — 설계 a plant layout — 용구(用具) a workshop appliance — 위생 factory sanitation — 재단(財團) a factory foundation — 저당법(抵當法) 〖법〗 the Hypothecation of Factories' Property Act — 점거(占據) a sitdown (strike) — 제도 the factory system — 주(主) the owner of a factory ; a mill owner ; a factory proprietor and operator (사업주) — 지대 a factory district〔area〕 — 폐쇄 closure of a factory ; lockout 《미》 — 회계(會計) factory accounting 모직(毛織) — a woolen mill 전시(戰時) — a war plant 조립 — an assembly plant 하청 — an affiliated work shop ; a supplier
공장 감독 工場監督 a factory superintendent ; [현장의] a foreman of machine operators ; a labor foreman ; a supervisor
공장 관리 工場管理 factory〔shop〕 management〔control〕
— 제도 the factory management system
공장 노동자 工場勞動者 a factory worker〔hand〕
공장도 工場渡 [거래] ex factory〔mill, plant, works〕 ; free at factory
— 가격 the factory〔mill〕 price
공장 부지 工場敷地 a factory site
공장 생산 工場生産 [양산] mass production
—품 a manufactured product
공장장 工場長 a factory manager ; a plant superintendent
공장 폐수 工場廢水 industrial sewage〔waste water〕 ; trade waste ¶ 이 강은 공장폐수로 오염되었다 This river was polluted with industrial sewage.
— 처리 장치 a waste water disposal plant
공저 共著 collaboration ; joint authorship ; a joint work —하다 coauthor 《a play》 ; collaborate on ¶ …와 공저로 in collaboration 《with》
공저자 共著者 a coauthor ; a collaborator ; a joint author
공적 公的 (being) open ; [일반의] public ; [공식의] formal ; [관공의] official ; governmental ¶ 공적으로 publicly ; in public ; openly ; officially ; formally // 공적으로 책임을 지다 be publicly answerable 《for》 // 공적인 장소에서는 행동을 조심하라 Be careful of your behavior on a formal occasion. // 그 작품은 아직 공적으로 발표되지 않았다 It was not officially announced yet.
— 기록 an official record — 사업 a public enterprise — 생애 a public career — 생활 public life
공적 公敵 a public〔common〕 enemy
*공적 功績 achievement(s) ; service(s) ; merit(s) ; exploit(s) ¶ 과학적 공적 scientific achievements // 공적을 세우다 render distinguished services 《to the State》 // 그는 공적이 인정되어 승진했다 He was promoted in recognition of his achievement.
— 명부(名簿) a meritorious service register — 조사부 a board of merit ; an awards examining department
공전 工錢 wages ; pay
공전 公電 an official telegram
공전 公轉 〖천문〗 revolution —하다 revolve 《round the sun》 ; move around the sun ¶ 지구의 공전과 자전 the earth's revolution and rotation // 지구의 공전은 1년이 소요된다 The revolution of the earth around the sun takes a year.
공전 空前 unprecedentedness ¶ 공전의 unprecedented ; unheard-of ; record-breaking ; epoch-making // 공전의 대성공〔성황〕 a phenomenal success // 공전의 대전 the greatest war in history〔on record〕 // 공전의 일이다 It has no precedent in history. // 주가가 공전의 오름세를 보였다 The price of stocks have hit an all-time high.
공전 空電 static ; atmospherics
— 장애 atmospheric disturbance — 제거 장치 a static eliminator
공전 空轉 ① skidding (자동차 따위의) ; racing (엔진의) —하다 skid ; race ; run idle (기계 따위가) ¶ 그녀는 자동차의 엔진을 공전시켰다 She raced the engine of her car.
② [일 따위가] ineffective (business) activity ; fruitless effort —하다 prove ineffective ; make a poor show
공전 운동 公轉運動 [천체의] the orbital motion

공정 工程 [진척] the progress of work ; construction progress ; [과정] a process ¶ (제품이) 여러 가지 공정을 거치다 go through various processes // 공정의 중간 과정에 달했다 We are halfway through the work. // 공정이 순조롭다 The work is going smoothy.
— 관리(管理) process control —표(表) progress schedule ; time schedule of work 생산 — a manufacturing process

†공정 公正 impartiality ; fairness ; justice ; equity —하다 (be) impartial ; fair ; just ; equitable ¶ 공정한 처사 a fair〔square〕 deal // 나는 공정한 대우를 받고 싶다 I want to receive fair treatment. // 그 판사는 공정한 판결을 내렸다 The judge gave a fair decision. // 그의 판단은 공정하지 못하다 He does not judge fairly.
— 가격 a fair price — 가격 점포 a fair price shop — 거래 위원회 the Fair Trade Commission — 등본(謄本) an exemplified copy ; an exemplification — 무사(無私) magnanimous candor

공정 公定 official fixture ¶ 공정의 official ; legal ; officially fixed // 한·미화(韓美貨)의 공정 환율 the official *won*-dollar exchange rate // 물가를 공정하다 fix prices officially
— 이율(利率) an official interest rate ; a legitimate rate of interest — 임금(賃金) the regulation fare — 지가(地價) an assessed value of land — 할인율 an official rate of discount — 환율 an official exchange rate

공정 가격 公定價格 an official〔authorized〕 price ; an officially fixed price ; [최고의] a ceiling (price) ¶ 공정 가격으로 팔다〔사다〕 sell〔buy〕 《articles》 at official〔legal〕 prices 〔rates〕

공정 부대 空挺部隊 air-borne troops ; [낙하산 부대] paratroops

공정 시세 公定時勢 an official quotation ; [최고의] a ceiling quotation ; a (price) ceiling ¶ 공정 시세로 거래하다 handle business〔transact〕 at official quotation

공정 증서 公正證書 a notarial〔an authentic〕 deed ; an attested〔an authentic, a public〕 document

*공제 控除 subtraction ; deduction —하다 subtract ; deduct 《from》 ¶ 그가운데서 5,000원을 공제하다 deduct five thousand *won* from the amount // 소득세의 공제 an income tax deduction // 교제비는 임금에서 공제되었다 The entertainment expenses were deducted from wages. // 나는 세금 공제 후의 순수입이 한 달에 5000달러쯤 된다 I make about five thousand dollars after taxes a month. /I net about five thousand dollars a month. // 나는 세금 공제 전의 총수입이 한 달에 5000달러쯤 된다 I make about five thousand dollars before taxes a month. /I gross about five thousand dollars a month.
근로 — earned income exemption 기초 — a basic deduction 부양 — a credit 〔an allowance〕 for dependents 특별 — special deduction

공제 共濟 mutual aid〔relief〕 —하다 aid〔help〕 each other
— 보험 fraternal insurance — 사업 a mutual-aid project —회 ⇨ 공제 조합

공제액 控除額 an amount deducted 《from》 ; a deduction 《from》 ; an abatement
배우자 — the amount exempted from the income tax for the support of one's spouse 소득 — the amount deducted from one's income

공제 저축 控除貯蓄 a deposit through deduction from one's monthly pay

공제 조합 共濟組合 a mutual aid association ; a (mutual) benefit society 《미》 ; a friendly society 《영》

공조 共助 mutual assistance ; cooperation —하다 mutually assist ; cooperate

*공존 共存 coexistence —하다 coexist 《with a person》 ; live together ; live and let live
소극적 — negative coexistence 평화적 — peaceful coexistence

공존 공영 共存共榮 coexistence and coprosperity
—주의(主義) the principle of live-and-let-live ; the idea of give-and-take

공죄 功罪 merits and demerits ; virtues and sins ; services and disservices ; relative merit ¶ 공죄 상반(相半)하다 one's merits and demerits are balanced against each other

공주 公主 a (royal) princess

공준 公準 〖수학〗 a postulate

†공중 公衆 the public ¶ 공중의 public ; common // 공중 앞에서 in public // 공중의 이익 the public interest ; the general good // 공중을 위해서 for the benefit of the public ; for the general good // 공중에게 개방되다 be opened to the public
— 욕탕(浴湯) a public bath(-house)

*공중 空中 the air ; the sky ; space ¶ 공중의 aerial ; in the air // 공중에 in the air〔sky〕 ; in mid-air ; in space // 공중을 날다 fly in the air // 그 비행기는 공중으로 사라졌다 The plane disappeared into space. // 그의 계획은 공중에 떠 있다 His plan is up in the air. // 마치 공중에 떠 있는 기분이었다 I felt as though I were flying in midair.
— 감시 aerial inspection — 관측 〖군사〗 aerial observation — 광고 advertising by airplane ; a sky sign ; sky writing —권(權) an air right — 무선 전화기 an aerophone — 방전(放電) atmospheric discharge — 엄호(掩護) 〖항공〗

an air cover〔umbrella〕 — 열병식 an air review — 전기(電氣) atmospheric electricity — 청음기(聽音機) an aerophone — 충돌 an inflight〔a mid-air〕 collision — 케이블 an aerial ropeway ; a cableway — 투하 airdrop — 현상학(現象學) aerographics

공중 곡예 空中曲藝 [서커스의] an aerialist act ; an aerial stunt performance ; stunt flying
—사(師) [서커스의] an aerialist ; an aerial acrobat〔stunt performer〕

공중 급유 空中給油 air〔air-to-air〕 refueling ; inflight〔aerial〕 refueling
—용 비행기 a tanker (plane)

공중 납치 空中拉致 a skyjack ; hijacking of an airplane ; skyjacking **—하다** highjack (a passenger) plane
—범 a hijacker

공중누각 空中樓閣 [공상] a castle in the air〔in Spain〕 ; an air〔a cloud〕 castle ; a daydream ¶ 공중누각을 짓다 build castles in the air

공중 도덕 公衆道德 public morality〔morals〕 ¶ 공중 도덕을 지키다 take care not to trouble others ; act the gentleman in public

공중 변소 公衆便所 a public〔street〕 latrine ; a public lavatory〔convenience〕 ; a (public) comfort station 《미》 ; a comfort room

공중 보급 空中補給 an airlift ; [연료의] air-to-air refueling

공중 분해 空中分解 disintegration in the air ; a mid-air disintegration **—하다** dismember〔come apart〕 while flying ; break up to pieces in the air

공중 사진 空中寫眞 an air〔aerial〕 photo ; an air scope ; aerial photography
—기 an air〔aerial〕 camera — 측량(測量) aerial photogrammetry ; aerial photographic surveying ; an aerial survey

공중 사찰 空中査察 (an) aerial inspection

공중 생물학 空中生物學 aerobiology
—자(者) an aerobiologist

공중선 空中線 〖라디오·텔레비전〗 an antenna 《*pl.* ~s, -nae》 《미》 ; an aerial (wire) 《영》

공중 수송 空中輸送 air service ; air transportation ; 〖군사〗 an airlift operation
— 부대 airborne troops — 화물 air cargo ; airlift (goods) 《미》

공중 어뢰 空中魚雷 an aerial torpedo 《*pl.* -es》 ¶ 공중 어뢰를 발사하다 discharge〔release〕 an aerial torpedo 《at》

공중 위생 公衆衛生 public health ; public hygiene ; public sanitation

공중전 空中戰 an air battle〔war〕 ; an air combat ; air fighting ; aerial warfare ; an aerial fight〔combat〕 ; an air-fight ; [소형 전투기의] an aerial dogfight

공중 전화 公衆電話 a public〔coinbox〕 (tele)phone ; a pay telephone
—실 (室) a public telephone station〔booth〕 ; a (telephone) pay station〔booth〕 ; a call box 《영》

공중 정찰 空中偵察 air〔aerial〕 reconnaissance〔scout, patrol〕

***공중 제비 空中—** a somersault ; a somerset ; a tumble ; a loop (비행기의) **—하다** turn〔make, throw, cast, cut〕 a somersault ; turn head over heels ; loop the loop (비행기가)

공중 질소 空中窒素 atmospheric nitrogen ¶ 공중 질소를 고정하다 fix nitrogen of〔from〕 the air
— 고정(법) nitrogen fixation

공중 활주 空中滑走 volplane ; gliding **—하다** volplane ; plane ; glide (in the air)

공증 公證 a notarial act ; authentication ; official endorsement **—하다** authenticate ; notarize ; attest
—료 notarial fees〔charges〕 참가 — 수속 a notarial act honor

공증인 公證人 a notary public ; a notary
—법(法) 〖법〗 the Notary (Public) Act
— 사무소 a notary's office

공지 空地 a vacant lot ; vacant land ; [광장] an open space
— 지구(地區) an open area

공직 公職 a public office〔duty〕 ; an official position ¶ 공직에 있는 사람 a public official〔servant〕 ; an officeholder // 공직에 있다〔취임하다〕 hold〔take up〕 a public office // 많은 저명한 사람들이 공직에서 추방됐다 Many a prominent man was purged from public office. // 공직자들이 현재 보이고 있는 근검 절약 행위들을 어떻게 생각하십니까 What do you think of the current austerity practices by the government holders ?
— 생활 a public career〔life〕 ; government service — 희망자 an office hunter

공진 共振 〖물리〗 resonance ; sympathy

공진회 共進會 a competitive exhibition ; a show ; a fair
농업 — an agricultural show 가축 — a cattle show

공징이 〖민속〗 a kind of female fortune-teller

공짜 a thing got for nothing ; free charge ; gratuitousness ¶ 나는 그것이 공짜라도 싫다 I would not take it at a gift. // 공짜 좋아하는 버릇 언제쯤 버릴 건가 When are you going to stop being a sponger ? // 이거 공짜나 마찬가지구나 It's a steal. // 세상에 공짜가 어디 있나 There's no such thing as a free lunch. /There's no free lunch.
— 관람객 a free visitor〔spectator〕 ; a

deadhead 《구》; [총칭] paper 《속》 — 승객 a free passenger —표 a free ticket ; a pass

공차 公差 『수학』 a common difference ; 『기계』 tolerance ; margin ; legal remedy ; [화폐의] allowance ; [도량형의] allowance
— 단위(單位) 『기계』 a tolerance unit
— 한계(限界) 『수학』 a tolerance limit

공차 空車 ① [빈차] an empty vehicle 〔carriage〕 ¶ 마침 공차가 지나갔다 Luckily an empty taxi came along just then. ② [무료로 타는] a free ride ; a stolen ride ¶ 공차 타다 steal a ride on ; get a free ride ; snag a pick up 《미·속》

공창 工廠 an arsenal
해군 — a naval arsenal

공창 公娼 [제도] licensed prostitution ; [창녀] a licensed〔registered〕 prostitute
— 제도 state-regulated prostitution — 폐지 abolition of licensed prostitution
— 폐지 운동 a purification movement 〔campaign〕; an antivice movement

*공채 公債 a public loan〔debt〕; [증권] a government bond ; a public bond ¶ 공채를 발행하다〔사다〕 issue〔buy〕 bonds // 10억원의 공채를 모집하다 float〔raise〕 a loan of a thousand million *won* // 공채를 청약하다 subscribe for a public loan // 공채의 상환을 청구하다 call a bond
—금 수입(金輸入) receipts from public loans — 발행 차입금(發行借入金) a bonded〔funded〕 debt — 상환 자금(償還資金) a sinking fund — 시장(市場) the bond market — 정리(整理) consolidation of public loans — 증권 소지자 a bondholder — 차환(借換) conversion of a public loan 교부(交付) — government compensation bonds 군사 — war bonds 등록 — registered bonds ; an inscribed stock 《영》 5푼 이자(五分利子) — 5 percent bonds ; five percents ; fives 장기(長期) — a long-term government bond 정리 — consolidated public loan bonds

공채 증권 公債證券 government securities ; public loan bond

공책 空册 a notebook

공처 恐妻 (servile〔slavish〕) submission to one's wife
—병 wifephobia

공처가 恐妻家 a hen-pecked〔wife-ridden〕 husband ; a man afraid of his wife ¶ 그는 대단한 공처가다 He is terribly afraid of his wife.

공천 公薦 public nomination〔recommendation〕 —하다 nominate publicly ¶ 후보자를 공천하다 officially adopt a candidate ; nominate a candidate // 공화당 공천으로 입후보하다 stand 《for the Assembly》 on the Republican ticket // 그는 공천 받은 사람이다 He is a nominee.
— 후보자(候補者) a recognized〔an official, an authorized〕 candidate

공첩 公牒 an official dispatch

공청 公廳 a government〔public〕 office

공청회 公聽會 a public〔an open〕 hearing ¶ 공청회를 열다 hold a public hearing
— 속기록 hearings

공출 供出 delivery 《of rice to the government》; offering —하다 offer〔deliver〕 (one's quota of produce to the government at the price fixed by the government)
— 가격 a delivery price 초과 — above-the-quota delivery 할당 — quota delivery

공출 할당 供出割當 allocation of delivery quotas ; [할당된 양] a delivery 〔allocation〕 quota ¶ 공출 할당에 25퍼센트 부족하다 fail to fill the collection quota by 25 per cent

공치기 a ball game ; playing ball

공치다[1] ① draw a circle ; mark down an ○ ② be fruitless〔vain, in vain〕

공치다[2] hit the ball

공치사 功致辭 self-praise ; self-congratulation ; admiration of one's own merit
—하다 praise oneself ; congratulate oneself ; value one's own deed ; admire one's own merit ¶ 공치사는 그만두세요 Don't talk so glibly.

공칙하다 (be) unfortunate ; unlucky ; ill-timed〔chosen, planned〕; be amiss ¶ 공칙하게 unfortunately ; unluckily ; by ill luck ; as ill luck would have it

공칭 公稱 being nominal ; the official name
— 능력 authorized capacity — 마력(馬力) nominal horsepower — 액면 가격 the face value 《of a public bond》

공칭 가격 公稱價格 a nominal price ; the official price

공칭 자본 公稱資本 nominal capital

공탁 供託 deposition ; deposit ; lodgement ; —하다 deposit 《in, with》; place 《money》 on deposit 《in》; lodge 《with》; post 《with》 ¶ 은행에 돈을 공탁하다 deposit money in a bank
—법(法) the Deposit into Justice Offices Act

공탁금 供託金 a (security) deposit ; deposit money ; money on deposit(공탁중의) ¶ 공탁금을 몰수하다 forfeit a deposit

공탁물 供託物 a deposit ; a deposited article

공탁서 供託書 a document that goes with a deposit

공탁소 供託所 a deposit office ; a depository

공탁자 供託者 a depositor

공터 空— an empty〔a vacant〕 lot
†공통 共通 commonness ―하다 be common 《to》 ¶ 공통의 이익 common interest
― 분모(分母) 〖수학〗 a common denominator ―어 a common tongue ―의식 common consciousness ―인자(因子)〔인수〕 a common factor
공통성 共通性 community ; commonness ¶ 사상의 공통성 (a) community of thought
공통점 共通點 a point of sameness ; a common feature〔point〕 ¶ 양자간에는 전혀 공통점이 없다 They have nothing in common with each other.
†공판 公判 a (public) trial ; a public hearing ―하다 hold a court ¶ 공판에 회부되다 be brought to trial ; come to trial ; be tried // 공판에 붙이다 bring 《a case》 to trial ; put 《a case》 on trial // 그 사건은 현재 공판 중이다 The case is under public trial.
― 기일 a fixed day for public trial ; a date for hearing ; a court day ― 수속 procedure in a public trial ― 일정표 a cause list ― 절차 procedure in a public trial ― 조서(調書) a protocol for a public trial ― 청구 a demand for a trial
공판 기록 公判記錄 the record of a trial
공판장 共販場 a joint market
농협 ― an agricultural cooperative's joint market
공판정 公判廷 the court ; a public trial court ; a court in session ; a court room
공편 共編 coeditorship ¶ A씨와 B씨 공편 edited by Mr. A and Mr. B
―자(者) a coeditor ; a joint editor
†공평 公平 equity ; fairness ; impartiality ; justice ―하다 (be) fair ; impartial ; just ; even-handed ; equitable ; unbiased ¶ 공평히 impartially ; fairly ; justly ; without partiality ; squarely // 공평히 말하자면 to do 《a person》 justice ; in (all) fairness to 《a person》 // 공평히 취급하다 give 《a person》 his due // 공평히 분배하다 distribute fairly〔evenly〕 // 공평을 잃다 be unfair ; be partial // 공평한 의견 an impartial opinion // 너는 공평한 판단을 내려야 한다 You have to hand down an impartial judgement.
*공평무사 公平無私 fairness and impartiality
공포 公布 promulgation ; proclamation ; (official) announcement ―하다 promulgate ; proclaim ; announce officially ¶ 법률을 공포하다 promulgate a law
공포 空砲 a blank shot〔cartridge〕 ; blank fire ¶ 세 발의 공포를 쏘다 fire three blank shots
― 사격(射擊) blank firing
공포 空胞 〖생물〗 vacuole ¶ 공포가 있는 vacuolate
― 형성 vacuolation
⁑공포 恐怖 fear ; dread ; terror ; fright ; scare ; horror ; panic (공황) ¶ 공포에 떨게 하다 strike 《a person》 with terror ; terrify // 공포에 휩싸이다 be seized with fear ; be struck with horror // 그녀는 공포에 질려 떨었다 She shivered with fear.
― 관념(觀念) a fear complex ― 소설 a horror story〔tale〕 ― 시대 the Reign of Terror ― 정치 terrorism ; the reign of terror
공포감 恐怖感 (a sensation of) fear ¶ 공포감이 엄습하다 be seized with fear
공포증 恐怖症 a phobia 《against》 ; morbid fear〔dread〕 ; 〖정신병〗 psychasthenia
고독(孤獨) ― monophobia 공습(空襲) ― air-raid psychasthenia 남성(男性) ― androphobia 대인(對人) ― anthrophobia 여성 ― gynephobia
공폭 空爆 aerial bombing ; an air blow ; bombardment from the air ―하다 bomb
†공표 公表 official〔public〕 announcement ; publication ; proclamation ―하다 announce officially ; publish ; make public ; release ; give out ; proclaim ; declare

> 참고 **announce** 정식으로 알리다 **proclaim** 공식적으로 권위를 가지고 알리다 **declare** 명확하게 공표하다

¶ 공표하지 않다 withhold 《a matter》 from the public // 편지를 공표하다 make the letter public
공피증 鞏皮症 〖의학〗 dermatosclerosis ; scleroderma
공하 恭賀 respectful congratulations
⁑공학 工學 engineering ; technology
―과(科) the department of technology ―사(士)〔박사〕 Bachelor〔Doctor〕 of Engineering ― 석사 a master of engineering (사람) ; Master of Engineering (학위) ― 시험로(試驗爐) an engineering testing reactor 《ETR》 ― 제도(製圖) engineering drafting
*공학 共學 mixed education ; coeducation 《미》 ¶ 남녀 공학반 a mixed class // 저 대학은 남녀 공학이다 That college is coeducational.
공함 公函 an official letter
†공항 空港 an airport ¶ 공항에 착륙하다 land at an airport
―장(長) an airport director ― 출입국 관리소 the airport immigration office 국제 ― an international airport 김포 ― *Kimpo* Airport
공해 公海 the open〔high〕 sea(s) ; a marine highway ; international waters

¶ 공해상에서 어업하다 fish in open waters // 그 어선은 공해상을 항해하고 있었다 The fisherboat was sailing in international waters.

공해 公害 environmental pollution (환경오염) ; environmental disruption (환경파괴) ¶ 공해를 제거하다 remove air and water pollutants ; get rid of〔wipe out〕 pollution // 공해를 일으키다 cause harm to the public

— **대책** a measure (to be) taken against environmental pollution ; an antipollution measure — **대책 기본법** the Environmental Pollution Prevention Act — **방지법** 〖법〗 the Environmental Pollution Prevention Act ; a pollution-control〔an antipollution〕 law — **방지 시설** pollution control facilities —**병** diseases caused by environmental pollution ; a public hazard disease — **분쟁 처리법** the Environmental Pollution Disputes Settlement Act — **업소** a pollution-causing factory ; a polluter — **요인** causes of pollution — **조사〔감시〕관** a pollution crime investigator〔watcher〕 — **추방 운동** an antipollution campaign **무— 채소** chemical free vegetables **산업—** industrial pollution **소음 —** noise pollution **열 —** thermal pollution

공해 어업 公海漁業 fishery in the high seas ; ocean〔high seas〕 fishery

*⁑*공허 空虛** emptiness ; futility ; voidness ; vanity ; hollowness ; inanity (내용 없음) ¶ 공허한 empty ; hollow ; void ; futile ; inane // 공허한 생활 a hollow life ; a purposeless life // (사람이 없어서) 공허를 느끼다 miss 《a person》 // 인생의 공허를 느끼다 I feel the emptiness of life. // 그 남자는 공허한 미소를 띠었다 The man gave a hollow smile. // 그의 이야기는 공허하게 울렸다 His story sounded hollow.

공허감 空虛感 a sense of emptiness

공헌 貢獻 contribution ; service **—하다** contribute 《to, towards》 ; do much 《for, towards》 ; make for ; make a contribution 《to》 ; render a service 《to》 ¶ 과학에 크게 공헌하다 render great services to science // 평화에 크게 공헌하다 make a great contribution towards peace ; do much for peace // 그의 연구는 의학계에 크게 공헌했다 His research rendered great service to the medical profession.

공혈 供血 blood donation **—하다** donate〔furnish〕 blood (for transfusion)

공혈자 供血者 a (blood) donor

공화 共和 universal harmony ; republicanism (공화제) ¶ 공화의 republican

— **정체론(政體論)** republicanism

⁑**공화국 共和國** a republic ; a commonwealth

공화당 共和黨 the Republican Party ; the Republicans ; [미국의] the Grand Old Party 《GOP》

—**원** a Republican — **정부** the Republican Administration〔Government〕

공화 정체 共和政體 a republican form〔system〕 of government

공화 정치 共和政治 republican government

공화제 共和制 a republican form of government ; republicanism

공화주의 共和主義 republicanism

—**자(者)** a republican

⁑**공황 恐慌** a panic ; a scare ; consternation ; 〖경제〗 a financial panic〔crisis〕 ¶ 공황을 초래하다 [사람이 주어] be thrown into a panic ; be panic-stricken ; [사건이 주어] cause〔bring on〕 a panic // 공황 상태에 있다 be panicky ; be in a state of panic

— **가격** a panic price — **시세** a panic market **금융 —** a financial panic **주식 —** a stock market panic

공회 公會 a public meeting〔assembly〕

†**공회당 公會堂** a public hall ; a town hall 《미》 ; a community center ; a civic auditorium 《*pl.* ~s, -ria》

공효 功效 success ; fruit(s) ; result(s) ; [보람] virtue ; benefit

***공훈 功勳** merits ; an exploit (of war) ; distinguished services ¶ 혁혁한 공훈 brilliant exploits // 공훈이 있는 meritorious // 공훈을 세우다 perform meritorious deeds ; render distinguished services

공휴일 公休日 [법정의] a legal〔regular〕 holiday ; a bank holiday 《영》 ; [일반적] a holiday ; a day off

⁑**-곶** a point ; a cape ; a headland ; a spit ; a promontory

장산(長山)— *Jangsan* point ; the headland of *Jangsan*

곶감 a dried persimmons

곶감고치에서 곶감 빼 먹듯 〔속담〕 eat away〔up〕 one's savings ; use up one's savings bit by bit

과[1] and ; (together) with ; against ¶ 아들과 아버지 son and father // 곤란과 싸우다 struggle against difficulty // 동생들과 여행하다 travel with one's brothers // 영국은 독일과 싸웠다 The English fought with the Germans. // 그의 세력은 그의 죽음과 더불어 끝났다 His influence ceased with his death. // 그 사람과는 끝이다 I'm through with the man.

과[2] ⇨ 과꽃

과 科 [학과] a course ; a branch ; [분과] a department ; a faculty ; 〖생물〗 a family ; an order ; [병과] an arm ¶ 농과를 공부하다 take an agricultural course

고양이— the cat family **신경 정신—** the department of neuropsychiarty **영어—** the department of English ; [과정] the English course ; [과목] the cur-

riculum of〔in〕 English
†과 課 [학과] a lesson ; [분과] a section ; a department ¶ 제 3 과 Lesson 3 ; the third lesson // 그 국은 여러 과로 나뉘어 있다 The bureau is divided into a number of sections.
—장 the chief〔head〕 of a section 문서(文書)— the Archives and Documents Section
*과감 果敢 resoluteness ; decisiveness ; determination ; daring ; boldness —하다 (be) resolute ; determined ; bold ; daring ¶ 그는 용맹 과감하기로 유명한 장교다 He is an officer pretty well-known for his intrepidity. // 나는 과감히 말했다 I expressed myself daringly.
과객 過客 a passer-by ; a foot passenger ; a wayfarer (나그네)
과거 科擧 the state examination —하다 pass the state examination
†과거 過去 the past (day) ; time past ; bygone days ; 〖문법〗 the past (tense) ¶ 과거의 past ; bygone // 과거의 역사 the history of the past // 과거는 묻지 말자 Let bygones be bygones. // 그것도 이제는 과거의 일이다 It is now a thing of the past.
— 분사(分詞) 〖문법〗 a past participle — 시제(時制) 〖문법〗 the past tense ; the preterite — 역사 the history of the past — 완료 〖문법〗 the past perfect (tense)
과거장 過去帳 〖불교〗 an obituary ; a roster of the dead
‡과격 過激 being extreme〔radical〕 —하다 (be) extreme ; excessive ; violent ; radical ; ultra ; drastic ; rabid 《terrorists》 ; red 《anarchist》 ¶ 과격한 주장 a radical argument // 과격한 사상 radical ideas ; dangerous thoughts // 과격한 언사를 쓰다 employ violent language // 과격한 수단 a drastic measure // 그건 과격하다 You go to extremes. /That's going too far. // 과격한 말을 쓰지 마라 Don't use violent language.
— 분자 an extreme element —주의 extremism ; radicalism ; Bolshevism —주의자 an extremist ; a radical ; a Bolshevik —파 the extremists ; the radicals ; the Bolsheviks
과공 過恭 —하다 (be) overmodest
과공은 비례이다 관용 It is impolite to be too modest.
과꽃 〖식물〗 a (China) aster ; Callistephus chinensis (학명)
과남풀 〖식물〗 a gentian
과납 過納 payment in excess —하다 pay in excess
—액 an amount paid in excess
과냉(각) 過冷(却) supercooling —하다 supercool ; superfuse
‡과녁 a target ; a mark ¶ 과녁에 맞다〔빗맞다〕 hit〔miss〕 the target〔mark〕 // 과녁을 쏘다 shoot at a target
—판 a target board
과녁빼기 the right opposite side〔direction〕 ; a place one faces right ahead ; a place right over against ; the place directly opposite
—집 a house right opposite 《us》
과년 瓜年 ① [여자] marriageable 〔nubile〕 age ② [임기가 다한 해] the last year of one's term of service ¶ 과년한 딸을 출가시키다 marry one's marriageable daughter
과년 過年 getting past the marriageable age ; [지난해] the past year —하다 be overage for the marriage ¶ 과년한 처녀 an old maid ; a spinster
과년도 過年度 the past year ; [역년도] the past calendar year ; [회계 연도] the past fiscal year
— 지출 defrayment belonging to the preceeding financial year
과념 過念 excessive worry —하다 be overconcerned〔overworried〕 about ; worry too much
과다 過多 excess ; superabundance ; superfluity —하다 (be) excessive ; superabundant ; too much〔many〕
공급 — an excessive supply ; oversupply 인구 — overpopulation 지방 — excess of fat ; obesity
과단 果斷 decisiveness ; resoluteness ¶ 과단한 resolute ; decisive ; determined // 과단한 사람 a man of quick decision // 과단한 조치를 하다 take quick〔prompt〕 action ; act quickly ; take resolute steps
*과단성 果斷性 firmness of character ; promptness in action ; decisiveness
과당 果糖 fruit sugar ; fructose ; levulose
과당 過當 —하다 (be) excessive ; be more than needed
— 경쟁 an excessive competition 《in sales》
과대 過大 —하다 (be) excessive ; exaggerated ; extravagant ; too big 〔great〕 ¶ 과대하게 excessively ; extravagantly ; unduly // 과대시하다 overestimate 《a person's ability》 // 과대하게 말하다 exaggerate ; overstate // 과대한 요구를 하다 make an excessive 〔extravagant〕 demand
과대 誇大 exaggeration ; overstatement ; magnification ; hyperbole ¶ 과대한 exaggerated ; bombastic ; extravagant // 과대한 광고 a bombastic〔sensational〕 advertisement // 과대한 말 big〔tall〕 talk ; an exaggeration // 사실을 과대해서 이야기하다 exaggerate a fact // 과대한 기대를 하지 마세요 Don't expect too much of me.
과대 망상 誇大妄想 expansive delusion ; a delusion of grandeur ¶ 과대 망상에 빠지다 fall into expansive delusion

—광(狂) insanity of grandeur ; megalomania ; [사람] megalomaniac

과대 평가 過大評價 overestimation ; overrating ; overvaluation —하다 overestimate〔overrate〕《a person's talent》; overvalue ; think too highly of ¶ 그 사람 너무 과대평가한 것은 아니니 You're giving him too much credit, aren't you?

과도 果刀 a fruit knife

*과도 過度 excess ; immoderation —하다 (be) excessive ; immoderate ; inordinate ; undue ; too much ; too hard ¶ 과도한 공부〔노동〕 excessive study〔work〕; overwork // 과도한 음주 excessive drinking // 과도히 머리를 쓰다 overtax one's brains ; use one's head to excess // 매사에 과도하지 않도록 하여라 Be moderate in everything.

-과도 ¶ 형과도 의논해 봐라 Talk it over with your elder brother, too. // 내 마음은 촛불과도 같다 My heart is just like a candle's flame.

과도기 過渡期 a transition(al) period〔stage〕; an age〔a period〕 of transition ¶ 과도기의 문학 literature in a transition period // 과도기 현상 a transient phenomenon // 우리는 과도기에 있다 We are in a time of transition〔transition stage〕.

과도 정부 過渡政府 an interim government

과동 過冬 wintering ; passing the winter —하다 pass the winter ; winter

과두 정치 寡頭政治 oligarchy ¶ 과두 정치의 oligarchic(al)

과람 過濫 —하다 be too good for one ; be above one's deserts ; be more than one deserves

과량 過量 —하다 an excess (of quantity) ¶ 과량을 주다 give overmeasure (말, 되로) ; give overweight (저울로)

*과로 過勞 overwork ; excessive labor ; overexertion ; strain —하다 work too hard ; overwork oneself ; overtax 《one's brains》; exert oneself too much ¶ 그는 과로로 인해서 건강을 해쳤다 He broke down through overwork. /He fell ill from overwork.

과료 科料 〖법〗 a fine ; a penalty ¶ 과료에 처하다 fine 《a person》// 6,000원의 과료 처분을 받다 be fined 6,000 *won*.

과린산 過燐酸 〖화학〗 perphosphoric acid

— 비료 a superphosphate (fertilizer)

— 석회 superphosphate of lime —염 a superphosphate

과립 顆粒 a granule ; a rash ¶ 과립을 형성하다 granulate

— 형성 〖의학〗 granulation

과명 科名 〖생물〗 a family name

과목 果木 a fruit tree

—밭 an orchard

*과목 科目 a subject ; lesson ; [조목] items ; [전과목] a curriculum ¶ 과목별로 구분하다 itemize ; classify ; break down into details

대학 입학 시험 — the subjects of the entrance examination for a university

선택 — an optional〔elective〕 (subject)

필수 — a required〔compulsory〕 subject

과묵 寡默 taciturnity ; reticence —하다 (be) reserved ; taciturn ; reticent ¶ 과묵한 사람 a taciturn〔reticent〕 person ; a man of few words // 그는 항상 과묵하다 He is usually a man of few words.

과문 寡聞 a poor〔little, scanty〕 knowledge ; limited information —하다 (be) ill-informed ; have little knowledge 《of》 ¶ 과문하여 being poor in knowledge〔information〕// 과문한 탓으로 아직 모르고 있습니다 I've heard nothing about it, I'm sorry to say.

과물 果物 fruit 《총칭》

과물전 果物廛 a fruit store〔shop, parlor〕

과민 過敏 oversensitiveness ; nervousness —하다 (be) nervous ; oversensitive ; touchy ; too keen ¶ 그는 무슨 일로 저렇게 신경 과민이냐 What's he so touchy about?

과민성 過敏性 hypersensitiveness ¶ 과민성의 hypersensitive

과민증 過敏症 〖의학〗 erethism ; hyperesthesia ; anaphylaxis ; hypersensitiveness

과밀 過密 overcrowding ; overpopulation (인구의)

— 도시 an overcrowded city — 시간표 (철도의) a tight schedule for railway transportation

과반 過半 most 《of》; the greater〔best〕 part 《of》; the majority ; the bulk ¶ 재산의 과반 most of one's fortune // 목적의 과반은 성취했다 Our purpose has practically been accomplished.

과반수 過半數 a majority ; a plurality ; [대다수] the greater part 《of》; most of ¶ 과반수를 차지하다 hold a majority // 합격자의 과반수는 대학 출신이었다 The greater part of the successful candidates were university men. // 의결은 과반수로 한다 The decision will be made by majority. // 과반수의 찬성으로 그 법은 통과되었다 The bill was passed by a majority vote.

— 의결 a majority vote 절대 — an absolute majority

과병 寡兵 a small force〔army〕; insufficient army

과보 果報 〖불교〗 retribution ⇨ 인과응보

과부 寡婦 a widow ¶ 과부가 되다 be widowed ; lose one's husband ; be bereft of one's husband // 과부로 지내다 remain a widow // 전쟁으로 많은 과부가 생겼다 The war widowed many wives. /A great many women were widowed by the war. // 과부 사정은 과부가 안다 It takes a widow to know a widow's difficulties.

과부적중 寡不敵衆 The few cannot be a rival to the many. /The few cannot match the many.

과부족 過不足 excess or〔and〕 deficiency ; overs and shorts ¶ 과부족 없는 neither more nor less ; in exact quantities // 과부족이 없도록 하다 avoid extremes ; be moderate

과분 過分 — 하다 (be) above one's deserts ; excessive ; undue ; undeserved ¶ 과분한 상여 a generous〔an undeserved〕 reward // 과분한 칭찬에 송구스럽습니다 I am afraid I hardly deserve such high praise. // 이 선물은 제게 과분합니다 I don't deserve such a gift. // 그 이는 내게 과분한 남편이다 He is too good a husband for me.

과불 過拂 overpayment — 하다 overpay

과불급 過不及 excess or〔and〕 deficiency

과산화 過酸化

—나트륨 natrium peroxide —납 lead peroxide —마그네슘 magnesium peroxide —망간 manganese peroxide —물(物) peroxides —바륨 barium peroxide —벤조일 benzoyl peroxide —수소(水素) peroxide (of hydrogen) ; hydrogen peroxide —수소수(水素水) oxygenated water —수소 표백(水素漂白) (hydrogen) peroxide bleaching —아세틸 acetyl peroxide —아실 acyl peroxide —유기산(有機酸) organic acid peroxide —작용 peroxidation —질소 nitrogen peroxide —철 peroxide of iron

과세 過歲 observation of the New Year — 하다 observe〔celebrate〕 the New Year

‡과세 課稅 taxation ; assessment ; imposition of taxes ; [세금] a tax ; a duty ; a levy — 하다 tax ; impose〔levy, assess〕 a tax〔duty〕 《on》 ¶ 이 상품들은 과세대상입니다 These goods are taxable.

— 가격 the taxable amount — 단위 a unit of assessment — 대상(물건) an object of taxation ; a taxation article — 범위 the scope of assessment — 소득 taxable income — 수량 a quantity〔volume〕 of assessment — 수입(輸入) taxable income — 표준 a standard of assessment 누진 — progressive taxation 배당 — levying tax on stock dividends 분리 — separate taxation 이중 — double taxation 인정 — optional taxation 자본 — a capital levy 중— heavy taxation 종합 — general taxation

과세율 課稅率 a tax rate

과세품 課稅品 a taxable article ; a dutiable〔customable 《미》〕 article (세관의)

과소 過小, 過少 — 하다 (be) too little ; too small

— 생산 underproduction — 소비 underconsumption

과소 寡少 — 하다 (be) little ; few ; scanty

과소 평가 過小評價 underestimation — 하다 underestimate ; underrate ; belittle 《a danger》

과속 過速 overspeed ¶ 과속으로 달리다 overspeed // 당신은 과속 운전을 했습니다 You were speeding.

— 차량 an overspeeding vehicle — 위험, 안전 제일 Speeding is dangerous, safety first (게시)

과수 果樹 a fruit tree

— 재배 fruit-growing — 재배자 a fruitgrower ; a fruiter ; an orchardist

과수댁 寡守宅 an esteemed widow ; a widowed lady

‡과수원 果樹園 a fruit garden ; an orchard ; a fruit farm 《미》

과시 誇示 ostentation ; display ; showing off — 하다 display ; show off ; make a display of ¶ 힘의 과시 ostentation〔a display〕 of one's power

*과식 過食 overeating ; surfeit ; eating to excess — 하다 eat too much ; overeat 《oneself》 ; surfeit on ¶ 과식하여 배탈이 나다 overeat oneself sick

과신 過信 overconfidence ; excessive confidence — 하다 place too much confidence in 《a person》 ; be overconfident ; be credulous ¶ 자기의 힘을 과신하다 overestimate one's own ability // 자신을 과신하지 마라 Don't be too confident of yourself.

과실 果實 a fruit ; [총칭] fruit ; fruitage ¶ 작은 과실 a fruitlet // 과실을 재배하다 grow fruit // 과실을 따다 pick〔pluck〕 fruit // 과실의 껍질을 벗기다 peel a fruit // 법정과실이 생기다 yield a legal fruit

—밭 an orchard ; a fruit garden — 분류학 carpology — 선별기 a fruit grader — 에센스 fruit essence — 운반선 a fruit carrier — 재배자 a fruit gardener〔grower〕 법정 — legal fruit 천연 — natural fruit

†과실 過失 [잘못] a fault ; a mistake ; a blunder ; an error ; [뜻밖의 과실] an accident ; [태만] negligence ; carelessness ; oversight ¶ 과실을 범하다 commit a fault〔an error〕 ; make a mistake // 그것은 나의 과실이다 I am to blame for it. /It is my (own) fault.

—범(犯) (criminal) negligence —사(死) an accidental〔unintentional〕 death —죄 an accidental offense 업무상 — professional negligence

과실 상해죄 過失傷害罪 accidental〔unintentional〕 infliction of injury

과실주 果實酒 fruit wine ; fermented fruit drink

과실 치사 過失致死 accidental〔unpremeditated〕 homicide ; homicide 〔death〕 by misadventure ¶ 그는 과실 치사 혐의로 구속되었다 He was arrested on suspicion of negligence resulting in death.
과액 寡額 a small〔petty〕 sum
과언 過言 intemperate language ; exaggeration ¶ …라 해도 과언이 아니다 It is not too much to say 《that》; It is no exaggeration to say 《that》
과언 寡言 taciturnity ; reticence **—하다** (be) taciturn ; reserved in speech
과업 課業 [학과] lessons ; school work ; [임무] a task ; a duty
과연 果然 just as one thought ; as (was, had been) expected ; sure enough ; in reality ; indeed ; truly ¶ 그것은 과연 거짓이었다 It was false as I had thought. /It turned out indeed to be false.
과열 過熱 overheating ; superheating **—하다** overheat ; get over-hot
— 경보 a temperature alarm **— 경제** an overheated economy **—계(計)** a superheated gauge **—기(器)** a superheater **—도(度)** the degree of superheat **—실** a superheated chamber **— 입시 경쟁** excessive competition for entrance exams (test) **— 증기** superheated steam ; a superhot gas
과염소산 過鹽素酸 perchloric acid
—염(鹽) perchlorate **—칼륨** potassium perchlorate
‡**과오 過誤** a fault ; a mistake ; an error ; a blunder ¶ 과오를 범하다 make a mistake ; blunder // 과오를 뉘우치다 repent one's fault // 과오를 고치다 correct a fault ; mend oneself
과외 課外 extracurricular work ¶ 과외의 extracurricular ; extra-classroom
— 강의 an extracurricular lecture **— 활동** extracurricular activities
과외 수업 課外授業 an extracurricular lesson
과욕 過慾 avarice ; greed ; greediness ; covetousness **—하다** (be) avaricious ; greedy ; covetous
과욕 寡慾 unselfishness ; disinterestedness **—하다** have few desires 〔wants〕 ; content with little ; (be) unselfish ¶ 과욕한 사람 a man of few wants
과용 過用 extravagance ; excessive expenditure **—하다** spend too much ; be extravagant〔prodigal〕 with ; [약을] take an overdose of medicine〔a drug〕 ¶ 그녀는 신경안정제를 과용했다 She took an overdose of a nervine.
과원 果園 an orchard
과원 課員 the staff of a section ; a member of the section staff
과유불급 過猶不及 Too much is as bad as too little.
*****과육 果肉** flesh (of fruit) ; sarcocarp
과율 課率 [세금의] a tax rate
과음 過淫 debauchery ; sexual indulgence〔intemperance〕 **—하다** overindulge in sexual pleasure
과음 過飮 excessive drinking ; intemperance (in drinking) **—하다** drink〔take〕 too much〔to excess〕 ; overdrink oneself ; take〔have〕 a drop too much ¶ 과음으로 병이 나다 drink oneself ill ; drink too much and fall ill
†**과일** (edible) fruit ⇨ 과실(果實)
—가게 a fruit shop〔stand〕 **— 바구니** a fruit basket **— 장수** a fruit dealer〔seller〕
*****과잉 過剩** excess ; surplus ; overabundance ; superabundance ; superfluity ¶ 정력의 과잉 plethora of energy // 과잉의 superfluous ; excessive ; surplus ; more than enough
— 공기 excess air **—금(金)** a surplus (fund) **— 방위** excessive self-defense **— 보호** overprotectiveness **— 생산** overproduction **— 인구** overpopulation ; an overflow of population **— 인원** supernumeraries ; superfluous personnel **— 충성** excessive devotion ; overloyalty **— 투자** overcapitalization **공급 —** an oversupply 《of foods》 **의식 —** overconsciousness
과자 菓子 confectionery 《총칭》; a cake ; [당과] sweets ; candy 《미》; cooky ; pastries (파이 따위)
— 가게 a sweet shop ; a candy store ; a confectionery **— 그릇** a candy 〔sweets〕 dish **— 상자** a box〔package〕 of cake ; a carton of biscuits〔candy〕 **— 장수** a confectioner **— 쟁반** a cake tray **— 접시** a cake dish
과장 科長 the head〔director, chairman〕 of a department 《in a college》
소아 — the head〔chief〕 of the pediatric department
‡**과장 誇張** exaggeration ; overstatement ; grandiloquence ; magniloquence ; magnification ; 『심리』 expansion **—하다** exaggerate ; overstate ; magnify ; overshoot oneself ; overdraw ; make a mountain out of a molehill ¶ 과장된 exaggerated ; bombastic ; inflated ; grandiloquent // 과장해서 exaggeratingly ; bombastically ; grandiloquently // 과장된 말 an exaggerated statement // 사실을 과장하다 overstate fact // 과장하는 버릇이 있다 He is given to exaggeration. /He talks through his hat.
—법 hyperbole **—벽(癖)** mythomania **—성** 『심리』 expansion
과장 課長 the head of a section ; a department chief〔head〕 ; a section chief
— 대리 an acting chief of a section **— 보좌** an assistant section head **판매 —**

the head of the sales department
†과정 過程 process ; course ¶ 과정을 밟다 undergo〔follow〕 a process // …의 과정을 겪다 go through the process 《of》
발전〔생산〕 — a process of development 〔production〕 제조 — a process of manufacture
과정 課程 [학과] a course ; [전과정] a curriculum 《*pl.* -la》 ¶ 고교 과정을 마치다 complete (the course of) high school // 그는 박사 과정에 들어갔다 He went on for a doctorate.
—표 a school timetable ; a schedule 《미》 대학(大學) — a university〔college〕 course ; one's course in a university〔college〕 6년 — a course of six years ; a six-year course
과제 課題 [제목] a subject ; a theme ; a thesis ; [숙제] a task ; homework ; exercise (연습 문제) ; [문제] a question ; a problem ¶ 해결해야 할 과제 a problem awaiting solution〔to be solved〕 // 과제를 내다 set a task 《to students》 // …을 과제로 글을 쓰다 write a composition〔an essay〕 on the subject 《of》
—장 an exercise book ; a (home) work book
과주 果酒 fruit wine ; fermented fruit drink
과줄 a candy prepared by frying sweetened dough
과중 過重 overweight ; being too heavy —하다 (be) too heavy ; burdensome ¶ 그에게는 부담이 과중하다 The burden is too heavy for him.
— 노동 overwork — 부담 too great a burden
과즙 果汁 fruit juice
포도 — grape juice
과찬 過讚 overpraise —하다 overpraise ; give an undeserved reward ¶ 과찬의 말씀이십니다 You overpraise ! /I am so flattered. /This is very flattering.
과태료 過怠料 a fine for default ; a negligence fine
과표 課標 a standard of assessment ; a ratal 《영》
—액 the taxable amount ; [평가액] the assessed value
*과하다 課— [세금 따위를] levy 《a tax on》 ; impose 《a tax》 ; assess ; [일을] assign 《a task to》 ; impose ; take 《a person》 ; give ; set ¶ 중세를 과하다 tax heavily ; impose〔saddle〕 heavy taxes 《on》 // 학생에게 숙제를 과하다 give a student some homework
과하다 過— (be) too much ; excessive ; undue ; unreasonable ; undeserved (과분하다) ; be beyond all bounds〔limits〕 ¶ 과하게 to excess ; excessively ; overly ; unduly // 과한 벌 an excessive punishment // 술을 과하게 마시다 drink too much ; drink to excess // 일을 과하게 시키다 overwork ; overtoil // 그 옷은 나에게는 과하다 The clothes are too much〔fine〕 for me. // 과한 것은 부족한 것이나 다름없다 To go too far is as wrong as to fall short. /Too much is just as bad as too little.
†과학 科學 science ¶ 과학적 scientific // 과학적으로 scientifically // 과학의 진보 the advance(ment) of science // 과학의 연구 scientific research // 비과학적(으로) unscientific(ally) // 과학적으로 경영하다 manage on scientific lines // 농사에 과학을 응용하다 apply science to farming // 과학적으로 생각하다 think scientifically
— 교육 science education —계(界) the scientific world — 기술 scientific technique — 기술 용어 technical and scientific terms — 기술자 a scientific technician — 기술처 the Ministry of Science and Technology — 기술 행정 scientific and technical administration — 만능주의(萬能主義) scientism ; almighty science — 무기 a scientific weapon — 문명 scientific civilization — 박물관 a science museum — 서적 a scientific book — 소설 science fiction — 시대 a scientific age — 심의회(審議會) the Scientific Investigation Council — 연구 a scientific research〔study〕 — 연구비 research expenses ; [문교부의 조성금] a Government subsidy for aiding〔promoting〕 scientific researches — 영화 a science film —자 a scientist ; a man of science — 전(戰) scientific warfare — 지식 scientific knowledge — 체계(體系) a scientific system 사회 — the social sciences 순수〔응용, 자연〕 — pure〔applied, natural〕 science 인문(人文) — the cultural sciences ; the humanities
과히 過— [너무] too ; too much ; excessively ; to excess ; overly ; extremely ; [부정] 《not》 very ; 《not》 quite ; 《not》 much ¶ 나를 과히 믿지는 말게 Don't expect too much of me. // 과히 심한 병은 아니다 It is not a very serious illness.
곽 槨 an outer coffin
곽란 霍亂 〖의학〗 cholera morbus〔nostras〕 ; an intestinal convulsion
곽향 藿香 〖식물〗 a betony
관 冠 a crown ; a coronet ; a diadem ¶ 관을 쓰다 wear〔put on〕 a crown // 배나무 밑에서는 관도 고쳐 쓰지 마라 Avoid every cause of suspicion. /Keep out of any compromising situation.
관 貫 ① [본관] one's ancestral home ; family seat ② [중량] *kwan* ; a unit of weight
관 棺 a coffin ; a casket 《미》 ¶ 관에 넣다 lay 《a person》 to rest in a coffin // 관에 넣을 준비를 하다 lay out a corpse // 관을 메는 사람 a coffin bearer ; a

pallbearer

†관 管 a pipe ; a tube ; 〖해부〗 a tract ; a vas ; [관악기] a wind instrument

관 館 ① [푸줏간] a butcher shop ② [요정] a fancy restaurant ③ [건물] a hall ; a large building

관 款 [조항] an article ; a sub-section ; a part ; a title

-관 觀 an outlook ; a view
사회— a view of society ; a social outlook 세계— a view of the world ; an outlook on the world 인생— a view of life ; an outlook on life

관가 官家 a district office (of the government) ; a public building (건물)

*관개 灌漑 irrigation ; watering —하다 irrigate ; water 《a farm》 ¶ 이 지역은 관개가 잘되어 있다 This district is well irrigated.
— 계획 an irrigation scheme — 공사 irrigation works — 농업(農業) irrigation cultivation — 도랑 an irrigation ditch — 용수(用水) water for irrigation ; irrigation water —용 수로(水路) an irrigation canal —지(地) irrigated land ; land under irrigation

‡관객 觀客 a spectator ; the audience 《총칭》 ; the house ; [입장자] a visitor ¶ 많은〔적은〕 관객 a large〔small〕 audience // 축구 시합의 관객 a crowd of spectators at a football match // 관객이 대단히 많다 It draws a large audience.

관건 關鍵 [문빗장] a bolt ; bolt and key ; [중요점] a key〔pivotal〕 point ¶ 문제 해결의 관건을 쥐고 있다 He holds the key to the solution of the problem. // 최선을 다하는 것이 성공을 위한 관건이다 To do your best is the key to success.

관견 管見 [사견] my (humble) personal views ; my point of view ; [좁은 소견] a narrow view

관계 官界 the official world ; official life ; government circles ; officialdom ¶ 관계에 있는 사람 a man in official life〔in the government service〕 // 그는 관계에 진출했다 He entered government service.
— 쇄신 a renovation of officialdom

관계 官階 an official rank ; a civil service grade

†관계 關係 ① [관련] connection ; relation ; relationship ; a bearing ; [이해 관계] (an) interest ; concern —하다 relate ; be connected with ; be related to ; have something to do with ¶ …와 관계없이 without regard to ; regardless of // 관계가 있다〔없다〕 have some〔no〕 connection with ; have something〔nothing〕 to do with // 관계를 끊다 sever one's connection 《with》 ; break 《with》 // 그는 그 일에 관계하고 싶지 않았다 He wished to stay〔keep〕 out of it. // 나는 이 사고와는 아무런 관계가 없다 I have nothing to do with this accident. // 그녀는 나와 친척관계입니다 She is a relative of mine. // 나이에 관계없이 할 수 있다 You can do it regardless of age. // 두 나라의 관계가 나빠졌다 The relations between the two countries have been turned for the worse. // 회사내의 인간관계가 상당히 복잡해서 오히려 어렵다 Interpersonal relationships in the company are so complex it makes things rather difficult.
② [관여] concern ; participation ; [연좌] implication ; complicity —하다 participate 《in》 ; be concerned 《in》 ; be mixed up 《in》 ; [나쁜 일에] be involved 《in》 ¶ 관계를 끊다 wash one's hands of 《the affair》 // 관계하지 않도록 하다 keep out of 《an affair》 // 뇌물 수수 사건에 관계가 있었다 He was involved in a bribery case. // 나는 이 일엔 관계가 없다 I am not concerned in this affair. /It's none of my business. // 그는 이 사건에 관계되지 않았다 He was not involved in this affair. // 그는 음모에 관계되었다 He was involved in a plot.
③ [영향] influence ; [이유] reason ; account —하다 affect ; influence ; matter ¶ 그것은 나와 관계가 없다 It matters little to me. // 이해에 중대한 관계가 있다 It affects their interests deeply.
④ [남녀의] (sexual) relations ; misconduct —하다 have relations〔liaison〕 with ; misconduct oneself with ¶ 그는 저 여자와 관계하고 있는 모양이다 He seems to have relations with that girl. // 그들은 사랑하는 관계이다 They are in love with each other. // 그녀와의 관계를 끊으시오 Break off your relationship with her.
— 관청 the government office〔agency〕 concerned — 단조(短調) 〖음악〗 the relative minor — 당국 the authorities concerned ; the competent authorities — 대명사〔형용사, 부사〕 a relative pronoun〔adjective, adverb〕 — 법규 the related laws and regulations —사 〖문법〗 a relative — 서류 all the documents related to the matter ; related documents ; necessary papers — 장조(長調) 〖음악〗 the relative major —조(調) 〖음악〗 relative〔attendant, next related〕 keys 거래 — trade connections 외교 — diplomatic relations 인간 — human relationship 적대(敵對) — hostile relations 전후(前後) — [문장의] the context

관계 기관 關係機關 the organs〔agencies〕 concerned ¶ 관계 기관과의 연락 contact with other agencies ; coordination with related agencies

관계자 關係者 the persons〔parties〕 con-

cerned〔interested〕; an interested person 〔party〕; the contracting parties (계약의); a participant; a participator ¶ 관계자에게 To whom it may concern // 범죄 사건의 관계자로 기소되다 be indicted for being party to a crime // 관계자 이외 출입 금지 No Entry〔Off Limits〕 To Unauthorized Persons. (게시)
— 쌍방(雙方) both parties concerned — 일동 all the parties concerned; all interested parties — 회합 a meeting of interested persons 보도(報道) — the press (interested) 제철업(製鐵業) — the iron interested

관계 회사 關係會社 a concern interested; its associated company; [자회사] an affiliated company〔concern〕; a subsidiary company; a subcompany

관곡 款曲 kindness; cordiality **—하다** (be) kind and cordial; warm and cordial

관골 顴骨 the cheekbone; the zygoma ⇨ 광대뼈 ¶ 관골이 나오다 have prominent cheekbones

관공리 官公吏 government and public officials; public servants

관공립 官公立 government and public (institutions)
— 학교 government and public schools

관공서 官公署 government and public offices

관곽 棺槨 the inner and outer coffins
—장이 a coffin maker

†**관광 觀光** sightseeing; tourism **—하다** do〔see〕 the sights《of》; go sightseeing; visit ¶ 새로 지은 고층 건물이 관광 명소가 되었다고 들었습니다 I heard a newly-built high rise building has become a tourist attraction. // 한국의 주요 관광 명소는 어디입니까 What are the major tourist attractions in Korea?
— 가이드 a sightseeing guide — 개발 tourist development — 계절 the tourist season —국(國)〔도시〕 a sightseeing country〔city〕 —단(團) a tourist〔sightseeing〕 party — 도로 a sightseeing road —붐 a tourist〔sightseeing〕 boom — 버스〔선(船)〕 a tourist bus〔ship〕; a rubberneck bus《미·속》 — 사업 the tourist industry〔trade〕 — 시설 the tourist〔sightseeing〕 facilities — 안내소 a travel〔tourist〕 bureau — 업자 a travel〔tour(ist)〕 agent; a tour operator; a travel service man — 업체 a travel bureau; a tourist agency — 열차 a sightseeing〔tourist〕 train — 영화 a travel film —지(地) a tourist resort; a sightseeing resort〔place〕; vacationland; a tourist showplace〔beauty spot〕 — 코스 a tourist route — 호텔 a tourist〔resort〕 hotel 한국 — 공사 the Korea Tourist Service, Inc.《KTS》 미개발 — 자원 tourist potential 시내 — city-sightseeing

‡**관광객 觀光客** a sightseer; a tourist; a visitor; rubberneck《미·속》(특히 단체 여행의); [집합적] tourism ¶ 외국인 관광객 a foreign tourist

관광 여행 觀光旅行 a (sightseeing) tour ¶ 관광 여행을 하다 take a sightseeing trip; sightsee; rubberneck《미·속》
세계 —자 a globe-trotter《구》

관광 자원 觀光資源 tourist attractions

관구 管區 a district (under jurisdiction); the jurisdiction (area)
— 기상대 a district meteorological observatory

관군 官軍 the government troops 〔forces〕; [왕국의] the royal forces

관권 官權 government authority ¶ 관권을 남용하다 abuse government authority; make an improper use of government power

관극 觀劇 playgoing; theatergoing **—하다** go to the theater; go to see a play; enjoy a theatrical performance
—회 a theater party

관급 官給 government supply; government issue《G. I.》
—품(品) an article supplied by the government; a government-issue〔GI〕 equipment《미》

관기 官紀 official discipline
— 문란 a laxity in〔the relaxation of〕 official discipline; corruption of officialdom — 숙정 enforcement of official discipline

관내 管內 (an area) within the jurisdiction 《of》

‡**관념 觀念** [생각] an idea; a notion; intention; thought; [의식] a sense; a spirit; [개념] a conception

> 참고 **idea** 가장 일반적인 말로서 사고·이해·추리·상상 따위의 결과로 마음 속에 생기는 것 **notion** 확연하게 형성되지 않은 생각 **thought** 상상보다도 고찰·추리에 의해서 형성된 생각

¶ 그릇된 관념을 가지다 have a wrong idea《of success》// 시간 관념이 없다 take no thought of time // 책임 관념이 없다 have no sense of responsibility
—가(家) an ideologist — 구성 ideation —력(力) idea force —론 idealism —론자 an idealist —성(性) ideality — 소설 an ideological novel —시(詩) an ideological poem — 연합 association of ideas — 연합설 associationalism — 운동 ideomotor action — 유희 an idle ideological argument —주의 idealism —주의자 an idealist — 투쟁 ideological warfare —학 ideology —학〔론〕자 an ideologist — 형태론 ideology —화(化) ideation 일반 — a general idea 일차(1

次)〔이차(2次)〕 — first〔second〕 intention
관노 官奴 a man slave in government employ
관놈 館— ⇨ 관사람
***관능 官能** [육체의 기능] organic〔physical, bodily〕 functions ; [육체적 감각] (fleshly) sense ; carnal desire (육욕) ¶ 관능적 질병 a functional disease // 관능을 만족시키다 satisfy one's carnal desire // 관능적인 그림 a sensual painting // 관능적인 여자 a glamor(ous) girl
— **장애** a functional impediment —**주의** sensualism
관다발 管— 〖식물〗 vascular bundle ; fibrovascular bundle
관대 款待 a warm〔cordial〕 reception ; hospitality ; welcome —**하다** give a warm reception ; receive 《a person》 hospitably 〔warmly〕 ; make 《a person》 welcome ; treat〔entertain〕 hospitably ¶ 관대를 받다 be kindly and hospitably treated ; be cordially received
***관대 寬大** [너그러움] generosity ; magnanimity ; liberality ; broad-mindedness ; [관용] tolerance ; indulgence —**하다** (be) generous ; magnanimous ; liberal ; broad-minded ¶ 관대한 처벌 a mild punishment // 관대한 태도 a generous attitude // 관대하게도 나를 용서하였다 He was generous enough to forgive me. // 그는 모든 사람에게 관대했다 He was magnanimous to everybody. // 그는 자식들에게 관대하다 He is very permissive with his children. // 그는 여자 사원들의 지각에는 관대하다 He is very lenient about female employees showing up late for work.
관대 寬待 lenient〔generous〕 treatment 〔reception〕 ; hospitality —**하다** give a generous reception ; treat 《a person》 with generosity
-관데 [···이기에] so...that ; such ...that 무슨 일이 있었관데 그녀가 그리 슬퍼하느냐 What makes her so sad ?
관두 關頭 a critical moment ; an emergency ; a crisis
관등 官等 official rank ; civil service grade ¶ 관등이 오르다 be promoted in rank ; be moved up to a senior grade // 관등이 떨어지다 be lowered in grade ; be demoted 《미》
관등 觀燈 the Festival of Lanterns ; celebration of an anniversary of Buddha's birth —**하다** celebrate the anniversary of Buddha's birth ; have the Festival of Lanterns
— **놀이** merrymaking at the Lantern Festival —**절** the Lantern Festival
관디 an ancient court costume ; [신랑의] a bridegroom's attire
관람 觀覽 inspection ; viewing —**하다** see ; inspect ; view ; visit ¶ 일반의 관람을 허가하다[불허하다] It is open 〔closed〕 to the public.
—**권** an admission ticket —**료** an admission fee ; admission ¶ 관람료 500원 Price of admission : 500 *won.* (게시) — **무료** Admission free. (게시) —**자** a spectator ; a visitor ; the audience ; the house 《총칭》 —**차** [유원지의] a Ferris wheel ; a big〔great〕 wheel
관람석 觀覽席 a seat ; a box ; a stand ; a grandstand (정면의) ; a bleacher(s) (지붕이 없는) ; a right 〔left〕-field stand
관력 官力 government power〔authority〕
***관련 關聯** relation ; connection ; reference ; correlation ; association —**하다** be related to ; relate to ; be connected with ; refer to ; have a bearing on ¶ 그것에 관련한 문제 matters connected with it // ···과 관련해서 in connection 《with》 // in relation〔reference〕 《to》
— **기사** a related story —**도(度)** the degree of association — **사항** related matters ; matters relevant to the subject — **산업** allied industries —**성** relation ; relevance ; relevancy — **질문** [의회에서] an interpellation on related matters
관령 官令 a government〔an official〕 order ; an order of the government
관례 冠禮 the celebration of one's coming of age ; the coming-of-age ceremony ; a wedding ceremony
관례 慣例 [풍습] custom ; usage ; usual practice ; a precedent (선례) ; a convention ¶ 관례적 customary ; usual ; timehonored ; conventional // 관례상 conventionally // 관례에 따라서 according to custom // 관례를 어기다 break a custom ; violate usage ; offend against the custom // 관례를 지키다 follow〔observe〕 a custom ; conform to the custom // 한국에서는 ···하는 관례가 있다 It is customary for Koreans 《to do》 // 병문안할 때 과일과 초콜릿을 가져가는 것이 관례이다 It is the custom to take chocolates or fruits when visiting a patient in hospital.
관례법 慣例法 the common law
관록 官祿 stipend ; official salary ¶ 관록을 먹다 receive a stipend
관록 貫祿 dignity ; weight ; commanding appearance ¶ 관록이 있는 사람 a man of dignity // 관록이 있는 실업가 a weighty〔an influential〕 merchant // 장관으로서의 관록이 충분하다 be fully qualified for the portfolio // 그녀는 최근에 관록이 붙었다 She has gained an air of confidence lately.
관료 官僚 bureaucracy ; officialdom ; [동료] a fellow official ¶ 관료적인 bureaucratic ; official // 관료 출신이다 be of bureaucratic origin // 관료화하다 become bureaucratized

— 내각 a bureaucratic Cabinet — 정치 bureaucratic government ; bureaucracy —주의 bureaucratism ; officialism ; bureaucracy —주의자 a bureaucrat ; a bureaucratist —파 a bureaucratic circles ; the bureaucrats 고급 — a high-ranking official 직업 — a career official

관류 貫流 —하다 flow〔run〕 through 《a city》

관리 官吏 a government official ; a public official〔servant〕 ; a civil servant 《영》 ¶ 관리가 되다 enter〔be employed in〕 the government service // 관리를 하고 있다 He is in government service.
고급 — high-ranking officials ; high functionaries 하급〔말단〕 — a petty official — 근성 bumbledom ; officialism ; bureaucratism

†관리 管理 management ; administration ; [지배·감독] control ; supervision ; superintendence ; [보관] charge ; care —하다 manage ; administer ; control ; supervise ; [보관] assume charge of ; care for ¶ 국제〔정부〕 관리하에 있다 be under international〔Government〕 control // 남의 재산을 관리하다 administer〔have charge of〕 《a person's》 estate // 그는 회사의 업무를 관리한다 He manages the business affairs of a company. // 이 동물원은 관리가 잘되어 있다 This zoo is well kept.
— 가격 〖경제학〗 an administered price — 검사(檢査) control inspection —권(權) right of management — 기관 a management agency — 능력 capacity of management — 무역 government-managed trade ; trading business under government control —법(法) [방법] the method of administration ; [법률] the Administration Law —부(部) an executive department — 부장 a principal administrative officer —비(費) management expenses — 사무소 a superintendent's office ; a control office —직(職) [지위] an administrative〔a managerial〕 position 《in an office》 ; [사람] a person holding an administrative〔a managerial〕 position ; a member of the management ; [집합적으로] (the) management ; the management staff ¶ 중간 관리직 people in the middle echelons // 관리직 수당 an administrative allowance — 태만 negligence of administration — 회사 〖경제학〗 a proprietary company 공장 — control〔management〕 of a factory 국제 — international control〔trusteeship〕 법정 — legal management 생산〔업무, 노무〕 — production〔business, labor〕 management 외국환(外國換) — foreign exchange control 정부 — 공장 a government-controlled factory 품질 — quality control

*관리인 管理人 an administrator ; a manager ; a supervisor ; a superintendent ; an executor (유산·유저 따위의) ; a caretaker ; a trustee ; a custodian ; a keeper ; [아파트 따위의] a concierge ; a superintendent 《미》 ; [농장·목장의] a major-domo 《미》 ; [사무소·아파트의] a janitor 《미》 ; a janitress(여자)
—실 a caretaker's room ; a building manager's office〔room〕 가옥 — a house-owner's agent 유산(遺産) — [남자] an administrator ; an executor ; [여자] an administratrix ; an executrix 재산 — a property custodian 토지 — a real estate custodian ; a bailiff 《영》 ; a land agent

관림 官林 a government(-owned) forest

관립 官立 government institution
— 학교 a government school

관망 觀望 observation ; watching —하다 observe ; watch ; wait and see ¶ 형세를 관망하다 watch the development of a matter ; observe the course of events // 대세를 관망하다 observe〔watch〕 developments ; follow the turn of events // 그는 항상 형세를 관망하고 있다 He always sits on the fence.
—주의 a waiting〔wait-and-see〕 policy

관머리 棺— the head of a coffin

관멤 棺— filling the coffin space not taken up by the corpse

관명 官名 an official title

관명 冠名 the name taken on coming of age ; one's adult name

관명 官命 official〔government〕 orders ¶ 관명에 의하여 by official〔government〕 order ; by order of the government // 관명을 띠고 on official business

관모 官帽 an official hat

관모 冠毛 〖새〗 a crest ; 〖식물〗 a pappus 《*pl.* -pi》 ; [민들레 따위의] down

†관목 灌木 a shrub
—림(林) shrubbery ; a bush — 지대 a shrubbery zone

관문 關門 a barrier ; a gateway ; [국경의] a boundary gate ¶ 입학 시험의 관문을 통과하다 get through the barriers of the entrance examination 《to a higher school》

관문서 官文書 an official document
— 위조(僞造) forgery of an official document

관물 官物 government property ; government issues

관민 官民 the government and the people ; officials and private individuals ¶ 관민이 협력하여 by the united efforts of government and people

관발 管— 〖동물〗 a tube〔ambulacral〕 foot

관변측 官邊側 《in》 official〔government〕 circles〔quarters〕 ; government sources ¶ 관변측에 의하면 according to official sources // 관변측에서 나온 정보 a tipoff coming from an official source

관병 官兵 the government forces〔troops〕

관병식 觀兵式 a military review ; a parade ¶ 관병식을 거행하다 hold a grand review of troops〔the army〕
—장 a parade ground

관보 官報 the Official Gazette ; [전보] an official telegram ¶ 관보로 발표하다 gazette ; announce by〔in〕 the Official Gazette // 사직이 관보로 발표되다 be gazetted out // 그의 임관은 관보로 발표되었다 His appointment was gazetted.

관복 官服 an official uniform〔outfit, garb, attire〕

관불 灌佛 〖불교〗 the sprinkling (rite) of perfume on Buddha's statue

관비 官費 government expense ¶ 관비로 유학하다 go abroad at the expense of the government
—생 a government student ; a holder of a government scholarship — **유학생** a student sent abroad by the government ; a government student abroad

관비 官婢 maidservant of the government treated like a slave in olden times

관사 官舍 an official residence ¶ 관사를 배당받다 be provided with an official residence

관사 冠詞 〖문법〗 an article
정(定)〔부정(不定)〕— a definite〔an indefinite〕 article

관사람 館— a butcher ; a meatman 《미·구》

관상 冠狀 ¶ 관상의 coronary ; coronal ; coronate
— 동맥(動脈)〔정맥〕 the coronary arteries〔veins〕 — **동맥 경화증** coronary arteriosclerosis — **봉합(縫合)** a coronal suture — **신경계** 〖생물〗 a tubular nervous system

관상 管狀 ¶ 관상의 tubular ; tubiform ; tubulous
— 기관(器官) 〖곤충〗 a fistula 《*pl.* -lae》 **—물** a tube — **중심주(中心柱)** 〖식물〗 a siphonostele **—화(花)** 〖식물〗 a tubular flower — **화관(花冠)** a tubulous corolla

관상 觀象 meteorological observation **—하다** make meteorological observations
— 특보 a storm warning

관상 觀相 physiognomic judgment of character ; phrenological interpretation **—하다** read〔judge〕 《a person's》 character by the face ; tell fortunes by physiognomy ¶ 관상을 보다 get 《a person》 to tell one's fortune by physiognomy // 관상을 보아주다 read 《a person's》 physiognomy
—가〔쟁이〕 a physiognomist ; a phrenologist ; a reader of faces **—서** a book〔work〕 on physiognomy **—학〔술〕** physiognomy ; phrenology (골상학)

관상 觀賞 viewing with admiration ; enjoyment **—하다** admire ; enjoy 《beautiful scenery》
— 식물 an ornamental〔garden〕 plant **—어(魚)** an aquarium fish **—화(花)** an ornamental garden flower

관상대 觀象臺 a meteorological observatory ; a weather station (측후소)
—원(員) a weatherman **중앙 —** the Central Meteorological Observatory

관서 官署 a government office
중앙 — the offices of the central government **지방 —** local government offices

관선 官線 a government-owned railway line

관선 官選 ¶ 관선의 chosen〔appointed〕 by the government
— 변호사 (an) official counsel ; a court-appointed lawyer〔attorney〕 — **이사** a government-appointed trustee

관설 官設 a government establishment〔installation, facility〕

관섭 關涉 interference ; intervention ⇨ 간섭 **—하다** interfere 《in a matter, with a person》 ; intervene 《in》 ; meddle 《in, with》

관성 慣性 〖물리〗 inertia ¶ 관성의 법칙 the law of inertia
— 기동기(起動機) an inertia starter — **능률〔모멘트〕** the moment of inertia — **승적(乘積)** the product of inertia — **저항** inertia resistance — **조속기(調速機)** an inertia governor — **질량(質量)** inertia mass — **타원(楕圓)** an ellipse of inertia ; a momental

†관세 關稅 customs ; customs duties ; [관세율] (customs) tariff ; tariff rates ¶ 목재에 대한 관세 the tariff on wood // 관세가 붙는 dutiable ; customable 《미》 // 관세가 없는 dutyfree ; free of duty // 관세를 과하다 levy〔impose〕 a duty 《on》 // 관세를 지불하고 화물을 인수하다 clear goods // 관세를 징수하다 collect customs // 관세의 인상〔인하〕 the raising〔the lowering〕 of customs duties // 다국간 관세 인하 교섭 the multilateral tariff negotiations (MTN) // 관세 및 무역에 관한 일반 협정 the General Agreement on Tariffs and Trade (GATT)
— 개정〔개혁〕 tariff revision〔reform〕 — **경찰** customs police — **동맹** custom union — **면세품** dutyfree articles ; an article on the free list — **면제 품목표** a tariff exception list **—법(法)** the Customs Law — **수입** customs revenue — **율(率)** a customs tariff ; a tariff rate — **자주권(自主權)** tariff autonomy — **전쟁** a tariff war — **정책** a tariff policy — **제도** the tariff system — **조약** a tariff treaty **—청** the Office of Customs

Administration — 할당제 a tariff quota system — 협정 a customs agreement — 회의 a tariff conference 가납(假納) — a deposited duty 공통(共通) — a common tariff 국정(國定) — autonomous customs duties ; a statutory tariff 긴급 — an emergency tariff 보복(報復) — retaliatory tariff〔duties〕 보호〔특혜〕 — a protective〔preferential〕 tariff 수입 — import duties 수출 — export duties 종가(從價) — ad valorem duties 종량(從量) — specific duties 탄력 —제 the elastic tariff system 협정 — conventional customs duties ; a conventional tariff

관세음보살 觀世音菩薩 the Buddhist Goddess of Mercy

관세 장벽 關稅障壁 a tariff wall〔barrier〕

관솔 resinous knots of a pine tree

—불 a fire set to pine knots

관쇠 館— a butcher ; a meatman 《미·구》

관수 貫數 the weight in *kwan* ¶ 관수가 나가다 be heavy ; weigh much

†**관습 慣習** custom ; usage ; usual practice ; convention ¶ 관습적 usual ; customary // 관습상 usually ; customarily // 관습에 의하여 according to the usage〔custom〕// 일반화된 관습 acceptable usage // 관습에 얽매이지 않는 사람 a man unbound to custom // 이것은 이 지방의 오랜 관습이다 This is a custom of long standing in this district.

—법(法) 〖법〗 common〔customary〕 law 사회 — the social code ; (social) customs

†**관심 關心** concern ; interest ¶ 교육에 관심을 가진 사람 persons interested in education // 관심을 가지다 be concerned 《about》 ; be interested 《in》// 관심이 없다 be indifferent 《to》 ; take no interest 《in》// 정치에 관심이 없다 be indifferent to politics // 그는 재산이나 명성에 관심이 없다 He cares nothing either for wealth or for fame.

†**관심사 關心事** a matter of concern and interest ; a (matter of) concern

중대 — a matter of grave concern 최대 — a matter of primary concern 공동 — a matter of common interest

관아 官衙 a government office

관악 管樂 〖음악〗 the wind (instrument) music ; pipe music

— 사중주(四重奏) a wind quartet 금— a brass (wind instrument) 목— a woodwind (instrument)

관악기 管樂器 a wind instrument

—부 [오케스트라의] the wind(s) — 주자 a wind player

관업 官業 a government enterprise〔undertaking〕 ; a state enterprise〔business〕 ; a government monopoly (전매)

*‡***관여 關與** participation — 하다 take〔have〕 part in ; participate in ; be concerned in ; play a part in ¶ 정치에 관여하다 mix〔have a part〕 in politics // 사건에 관여하다 be involved in a case ; take part in an affair // 그것은 네가 관여할 일이 아니다 It is no concern of yours. /It is none of your business. // 경영에 관여하다 engage in management

—자 a participant ; a participator ; a party concerned

관역 官役 [공사] official〔government〕 (construction) work ; [부역] levied service〔labor〕 ; corvee ; labor exacted by a feudal lord

관엽 식물 觀葉植物 a foliage plant

관영 官營 government control〔management〕 ; nationalization ¶ 관영의 government(-operated) // 관영으로 하다 nationalize ; put under government control

— 사업 a government enterprise〔undertaking〕

관옥 冠玉 ① [관 꾸미는 옥] jewels or jades attached to the front part of a crown ② [남자의 얼굴] a handsome face

관외 管外 ¶ 관외의 outside the jurisdiction // 관외 출장을 가다 take a business〔official〕 trip outside the jurisdiction ; travel outside the jurisdiction on official business

***관용 寬容** tolerance ; magnanimity ; generosity ; leniency — 하다 tolerate ; bear〔put up〕 with ; forbear ; allow ¶ 관용한 tolerant ; lenient ; generous ; broad-minded // 관용의 정신 the spirit of tolerance // 관용을 바랍니다 Please be patient with us. // 책임 있는 정부는 결코 법의 무시를 관용하지 않는다 No responsible government can tolerate disregard of the law.

—도(度) 〖사진〗 latitude

관용 官用 official〔public, government〕 business ; public use ¶ 관용으로 on official business

—어(語) the official language —차 an official vehicle

관용 慣用 usage ; common use ¶ 관용의 common ; customary ; conventional ; [어구의] idiomatic // 관용상 by usage ; customarily

— 수단 the usual means〔way〕 《to do》 ; an old trick 《of his》 ; an old game — 영어 idiomatic English —음(音) prevalent〔established, popular〕 pronunciation

관용구 慣用句 an idiom ; a common〔an idiomatic〕 expression ; a phrase of common use

*‡***관용어 慣用語** an idiom ; an idiomatic phrase ; a word of established use

—법(法) idioms ; an idiomatic expression

관원 官員 a government official〔clerk〕 ;

a public official〔servant〕; a public functionary
관위 官位 office and rank ; official rank ¶ 관위를 박탈하다 divest 《a person》 of his official rank
관유 官有 government〔state〕 ownership ¶ 관유의 government〔state〕 owned // 관유가 되다 be brought under government ownership
—림 a government〔state〕 forest —물(物) government property
관유 寬裕 generosity ; magnanimity ; liberality ; munificence — 하다 (be) generous ; magnanimous ; liberal ; munificent
관이 the first〔lead〕 player in a game of cards〔gambling〕
관인 官印 an official〔a government〕 seal
관인 寬仁 generosity ; liberality ; magnanimity ; benignancy ; clemency — 하다 (be) generous ; liberal ; broad-minded ; lenient ; merciful ¶ 관인한 사람 a man of generous and magnanimous disposition
관자 貫子 headband buttons (of gold or jade beads)
*관자놀이 the temple ¶ 관자놀이가 쑤시고 아프다 The temples throb with pain.
관작 官爵 office and title
관장 灌腸 rectal injection ; enema ; clyster ; an injection into the bowels — 하다 administer〔give〕 an enema 《to》; apply a clyster 《to》; clyster
—기(器) an enema-syringe ; a clyster pipe —제(劑)〔약(藥)〕 an enema ; a clyster 글리세린 — a glycerine enema
관장 管掌 charge ; management ; control — 하다 take charge of ; have 《a matter》 in charge ; manage ; administer ; control ¶ 사무를 관장하다 take charge of〔supervise〕 business affairs // 그 문제를 관장하다 deal with the question
관장 館長 the director ; the superintendent ; [도서관의] the chief librarian ; [박물관의] the curator
관재 管財 managing property ; property custodianship ; [유산의] administration ; [파산시의] receivership — 하다 manage〔have custody of〕 property ; administer ; put 《property》 under one's custody
—국 the bureau of property custody —인(人) [공공물의] a trustee ; [유산의] an administrator (남자) ; an administratrix (여자) ; [청산의] a receiver ; [정부·점령군의] a property custodian
관저 官邸 an official residence
대통령 — the Presidential residence
관전 觀戰 — 하다 observe〔watch〕 military〔naval〕 operations ; witness a battle ; [경기를] watch a game〔contest, match〕
—기(記) a witness's account 《of a chess match》
*관절 關節 〖해부〗 a joint ; an articulation ¶ 팔의 관절이 빠지다 put one's arm out of joint // 관절을 삐다 have a joint dislocated
—낭(囊) the articular capsule — 동물 an articulate (animal) — 류머티즘 articular〔joint〕 rheumatism —병 a joint〔an articular〕 disease ; arthropathy —부(部) a joint region — 연골(軟骨) the articular cartilage —염 arthritis ; inflammation of a joint —와(窩) the glenoid cavity —인대(靭帶) an articular ligament — 접합 articulation —탈구 dislocation of a joint ; disarticulation —통(痛) arthralgia 가동(可動) — diarthrosis 구와(球窩) — a ball-and-socket joint ; an enarthrosis 《*pl.* -throses》 팔꿈치 — an elbow joint 회전〔환상〕 — a pivot joint
관절 冠絶 — 하다 (be) unsurpassed ; peerless ; unique ; unparalleled ; paramount ; preeminent ; stand peerless〔unchallenged〕
*관점 觀點 a point of view ; a standpoint ; a viewpoint ; an angle of vision ¶ 상업적 관점에서 말하면 from a commercial point of view ; commercially speaking // 이 관점에서 본다면 from this point of view ; viewed in this light // 모든 관점에서 검토하다 examine 《it》 from all angles // 다른 관점에서 보다 view 《a matter》 from a different standpoint
관제 官制 government organization ; official regulations ¶ 관제를 정하다 establish a government organization
— 개혁(改革) reorganization of the government offices ; a reform of government organization
관제 官製 government manufacture ¶ 관제의 government-manufactured〔-made〕
— 담배 tobacco manufactured by the Monopoly Bureau — 데모 a government-inspired demonstration — 민의(民意) a government-fabricated (public) opinion —엽서 a government postcard ; 《미》 a postal card ; an official postcard
관제 管制 control ; contolling
—관(官) a〔an air-traffic〕 controller —기(器) a controller —반(盤) a control board — 장치 controlling gear —판(瓣) a controlling valve 지상〔진입〕 — ground〔approach〕 control
관제탑 管制塔 a control tower (비행장의)
관조 觀照 contemplation ; meditation ; observation ; 〖미학〗 intuition — 하다 contemplate ; meditate ¶ 자연을 관조하다 contemplate nature
관족 管足 〖동물〗 a tube〔an ambulacral〕

foot
ㅡ계 the ambulacral system

관존민비 官尊民卑 respect for the officials and disrespect for the people ; putting government above people ¶ 관존민비의 폐풍 the deplorable custom of putting government above people

관중 貫衆 〖식물〗 a shield fern ; Dryopteris crassirhizoma (학명)

*관중 觀衆 spectators ; onlookers ; the audience 《미》 ¶ 관중이 많다〔적다〕 have a large〔small〕 audience // 관중을 끌다 draw an audience // 관중들은 멋진 공연에 찬사를 보내기 위해 일어섰다 The spectators rose to their feet to pay tribute to the outstanding performance.

관직 官職 a government post〔position, office〕; the government service ¶ 관직에 들다〔있다〕 enter〔be in〕 the government service // 관직에서 떠나다 leave〔resign from〕 government service

†관찰 觀察 observation ; survey ; view ; investigation ── 하다 observe ; make an observation ; view ; watch ; survey ; see ¶ 관찰하는 눈이 있는 사람 a man with an observing eye // 이와 같이 관찰하면 viewed in this light ; considered in this way // 관찰이 날카롭다 be sharp in observation ; have a sharp eye 《for》 // 잘못 관찰하다 make an incorrect observation ; misjudge // 나는 벌의 습성에 대해 관찰했다 I observed the habits of bees.
ㅡ자 an observer ㅡ점(點) a point of view〔observation〕

관찰력 觀察力 (one's power of) observation ¶ 관찰력을 기르다 foster one's power of observation

관찰사 觀察使 a (provincial) governor (in former days)

관찰안 觀察眼 eye 《for》 ¶ 관찰안이 날카롭다 have keen powers of observation // 당신은 관찰안이 있군요 You have an eye.

관철 貫徹 [수행] accomplishment ; fulfillment ; realization ── 하다 accomplish ; achieve ; fulfill ; carry through ; realize ¶ 목적을 관철하다 accomplish one's purpose ; achieve one's end ; realize〔carry through〕 one's purpose // 주장을 관철하다 carry one's point // 초지를 관철하다 attain one's (original) object // 신념을 관철하다 stick to one's belief to the last // 우리들은 끝까지 요구를 관철시켜야 한다 We must push on our demand to the last.

†관청 官廳 a government office ¶ 관청에 근무하다 attend〔serve in〕 a government office // …의 감독 관청 the authorities supervising the affairs 《of》
ㅡ가(街) the civic center ─ 공시 사항 items in a government notice ㅡ식(式) officialism ; red-tapism ─ 용어(用語) official terminology〔jargon〕; officialese ; governmentese 《미》 ─ 집무 시간 official hours of work ; business hours 감독 ─ the authorities supervising the affairs 《of》 당해(當該) ─ the authorities concerned 주무(主務) ─ the competent authorities 행정 ─ an administrative office

*관측 觀測 [관찰] observation ; survey ; [생각, 의견] thinking ; an opinion ── 하다 observe ; make〔carry out〕 an observation ; survey ¶ 희망적 관측 wishful thinking // 나의 관측으로는 in my opinion ; to my mind // 기상을〔천체를〕 관측하다 make a meteorological〔astronomical〕 observation // 일식을 관측하다 observe a solar eclipse
ㅡ값 observed value ; observation ㅡ기(機) an observation plane ─ 기구(氣球) an observation balloon ; a sounding balloon (기상의) ; [비유적] a trial balloon ; ballon d'essai 《프》 ─ 방정식 an observation equation ─ 오차(誤差) an observational error ㅡ자 an observer ─ 판(板) an observation board

*관측소 觀測所 an observatory ; an observation station

관통 貫通 penetration ; piercing ; perforation ── 하다 pass〔go〕 through ; penetrate ; pierce ; perforate ; shoot through (탄환이) ¶ 탄환이 심장을 관통했다 A bullet penetrated his heart. /He was shot through the heart. // 터널을 관통하기에는 아직 1년쯤 걸린다 It will be one year or so before the tunnel is driven through. // 그 군인은 어깨에 관통상을 입었다 The soldier was shot through the shoulder.

관통상 貫通傷 a piercing bullet wound

관포 管鮑 intimate〔bosom〕 friends ¶ 관포지교 an intimate relationship // 그들은 관포지교의 사이였다 They were inseparable friends.

관품 官品 (an) official rank

관하 管下 ¶ 관하의〔에〕 under the jurisdiction〔control〕 of

*관하다 關─ ① [대하다] refer to ; be about ¶ …에 관해서 about ; on ; concerning ; regarding ; with regard 《to》; in connection 《with》; relative 《to》 // 이 일에 관해서 in this connection ; about this matter // 이 점에 관해서 on that score // 그 일에 관해서 그에게 이야기하였다 I spoke to him on the subject. // 그 일에 관해서는 이것으로 그만두자 So much for this. // 환경오염에 관한 토론 a discussion on environmental pollution // 모차르트 곡 연주에 관한 한 저 여자를 알아줘야 해 You've got to hand it to her when it comes to playing Mozart.
② [관계하다] affect ; have 《something》 to do with ; have influence on ; con-

cern ¶ 명예에 관한 문제 a question affecting one's honor // 그것은 생사에 관한 문제였다 It was a matter of life and death.

관학 官學 a national〔government〕 university〔college〕

관할 管轄 jurisdiction ; control ; [영역] province **— 하다** exercise jurisdiction 〔control〕 《over》; control ; govern ¶ 관할에 속하다 be under the jurisdiction 〔control〕 《of》; be within the province 《of》// 그 관청은 북부 지방을 관할한다 The office has jurisdiction over the northern district. // 이 일들은 당 관청의 관할이 아니다 These matters are not within the jurisdiction of this office. // 이 지역은 우리 관할 구역이다 This district is under our jurisdiction.

— 관청 the competent authorities 〔offices〕 — 구역 the extent of jurisdiction — 내(內)〔외(外)〕 within〔outside, beyond〕 the jurisdiction — 다툼 a jurisdictional dispute〔controversy〕 — 범위(範圍) the (sphere〔extent〕 of) jurisdiction — 법원(法院) 〖법〗 a competent court —서(署) the police station concerned ; the competent police authorities — 세무소 the district tax office — 지(地) jurisdiction 경찰 —구(區) a police district

관할권 管轄權 〖법〗 jurisdiction ¶ 관할권이 없다 have no jurisdiction 《over》

제일심(第一審) — original jurisdiction

관함식 觀艦式 a naval review

관항 款項 [관과 항] a title and an item ; [적요] a summary ; a gist ; the point ; the substance

관행 慣行 habitual〔usual, traditional〕 practice ; routine ¶ 관행의 habitual ; customary ; practical // 관행을 따르다 follow a custom

—범(犯) a habitual crime

관향 貫鄕 the birthplace of one's first ancestor

관허 官許 government permission ; license **— 하다** give a government permit〔license〕 ¶ 관허를 얻어 under government license ; with government permission

— 요금 a (government-) licensed charge

관헌 官憲 the (government) authorities ; the officials ; [경찰] the police authorities ¶ 관헌의 간섭 the interference of the authorities ; Government interference // 관헌의 압력 the pressure of the authorities

지방 — the local〔provincial, regional〕 authorities

관현 管絃 wind and string instruments

—악 편곡법(樂編曲法) orchestration

***관현악 管絃樂** orchestral music ; an orchestra

—단(團) an orchestra (band)

관형사 冠形詞 an unconjugated adjective ; a pre-noun (in Korean)

—형(形) a modifier〔an adnominal〕 form

관혼상제 冠婚喪祭 a ceremonial occasion ; the ceremonies of coming-of-age, marriage, funeral, and ancestor memorial

관화 官話 Mandarin ; standard spoken Chinese

관후 寬厚 generosity ; magnanimity ; liberality ; broad-mindedness ; leniency **— 하다** (be) generous ; magnanimous ; lenient ¶ 관후한 인품 a man of magnanimity // 관후한 태도 an air of magnanimity

— 장자(長子) a large-hearted gentleman

괄괄하다 ① [성질이] (be) virile ; spirited ; hot-tempered ; impetuous ; rash ¶ 그는 성미가 괄괄해서 성을 잘 낸다 He is hot-tempered and quick to anger.

② [풀기가] (be) sticky ; be stiff with starch

괄다 (be) strong ; intense ¶ 불이 너무 괄아 밥이 탔다 The rice was scorched 〔charred〕 because the fire was too intense.

괄대 恝待 inhospitality ; a cold reception ; cool treatment **— 하다** treat 《a person》 coldly ; receive 《a person》 with indifference ; be inhospitable to ; give 《a person》 a cold reception

괄목 刮目 — 하다 watch closely ; watch with keen interest ; watch with close attention ¶ 괄목상대하다 look at each other with astonishment ; each rubs his eyes in wonder // 괄목하고 기다리다 wait with keen interest ; look forward with expectation 《to》// 사태의 진전을 괄목하여 주시하다 watch the development of the affair with keen interest // 괄목할 만하다 be worthy of close attention // 괄목할 만한 발전 eye-opening progress

괄선 括線 〖수학〗 a vinculum, a bracket ; a ligature

괄시 恝視 inhospitality ; negligence ; contempt **— 하다** be inhospitable 《toward》; neglect ; contempt ; slight ¶ 괄시받다 be held in contempt ; be treated with contempt

괄약 括約 constriction **— 하다** constrict

괄약근 括約筋 〖해부〗 a sphincter (muscle) ; a constrictor ; a sphincteral muscle

방광 — the sphincter vesicae 항문(肛門) — the anal sphincter

괄태충 括胎蟲 〖동물〗 a slug

괄하다 ① (be) sticky ② be spirited ⇨ 괄괄하다

괄호 括弧 [둥근] a parenthesis 《*pl.* -ses》; [모난] a bracket ; [큰] a brace

[소괄호] parentheses 《미》 (round) brackets 《영》 [중괄호] braces [대괄호] brackets ; square brackets ¶ 괄호 안의 부분 a parenthesized〔bracketed〕 passage // 괄호로 묶다 put 《a word》 in parentheses〔brackets〕 ; parenthesize // 괄호를 없애다 remove the parentheses〔brackets〕

이중 — double parenthesis

괌 Guam

광 a storeroom ; a storehouse ; a cellar (땅광) ; a granary (곡창)

광 光 gloss ; brightness ; sheen ; shine ; luster ; glaze ; polish ; [가구 따위의 윤] patina ; (a) light ; rays (of light) ; a beam ; a ray ¶ 광이 나는 glossy ; lustrous ; bright ; polished // 광이 없는 dim ; dingy ; dull ; dry ; lusterless // 광을 죽이다 dim〔take off, tone down〕 the shine〔luster, gloss〕 ; dull the finish

광 廣 width ; area ; extent ; dimension ¶ 광이 4피트이다 be four feet broad〔in breadth〕

광 壙 the hollow of a grave ; a burial hole

광 鑛 (mineral) ore

철— an iron ore

*‡-광 狂** [열광자] a mania ; a fan ; [광기] madness ; insanity ; [광인] a maniac ; a lunatic a buff 《미》

골프— a golf maniac 경마— a turfman ; a race maniac 낚시— a fishing addict 댄스— a dance maniac 살인(殺人)— homicidal mania ; [사람] a homicidal maniac 야구— a baseball fan 연극— a theatre buff ; an inveterate theatergoer 영화— a movie〔cinema〕 fan ; a film enthusiast 장서(藏書)— bibliomania 재즈— a jazz freak 편집— a monomaniac

광각 光覺 『생물·심리』 the optic sense ; sensation of light〔brightness〕

광각 光角 『물리』 an optic angle

광각 廣角 a wide-angle

— 렌즈 a wide-angle lens ; a pantoscope 초(超)— 렌즈 a super-wide-angle lens

광갱 鑛坑 a mine shaft ; a pit ; a mine

광견 狂犬 a rabid〔mad〕 dog

*광견병 狂犬病** rabies ; hydrophobia ; lyssa ; canine madness

— 공포증(恐怖症) lyssophobia — 바이러스 a rabies virus — 예방법 『법』 the Rabies Prevention Act — 예방 주사 a preventive injection〔shot〕 against rabies ; an antirabies serum injection

*‡광경 光景** a spectacle ; a sight ; a scene ; a view ¶ 처참한 광경 a terrible〔appalling〕 scene ; a wretched spectacle ; a disastrous scene // 하늘에서 본 광경 an aerial view // 그것은 슬픈 광경이었다 It was a sad sight. // 해돋이 광경의 아름다움은 필설로 다 할 수 없다 The beautiful scene of the sunrise is beyond〔beggars, defies〕 description.

*‡광고 廣告** an advertisement ; ad 《미·속》 ; a notice ; an announcement ; [선전] publicity **—하다** advertise ; announce ; publicize ; put in an advertisement ¶ 신문에 광고를 내다 put an ad〔advertisement〕 in a newspaper ; advertise in a newspaper // 잡지에 광고를 내다 take ad space in a magazine // 광고를 보고 찾아오다 answer〔come in answer to〕 an advertisement // 영국에서는 약혼을 신문에 광고한다 In England they announce their engagements in the paper. // 이곳에 광고를 붙이지 말 것 Stick〔Post〕 no bills. // 우리가 한 모든 광고가 아무런 효과도 거두지 못한 것 같다 All that advertising we did seems to have had no effect whatsoever.

— 기관 an advertising medium — 기구(氣球)〔풍선〕 an ad balloon — 대리업자 an advertisement〔ad〕 agent ; an ad collector ; adman 《미》 ; a publicity agent 〔man〕 — 대리점〔업〕 an advertising agency〔business〕 —등(燈) a sign lamp ; advertising lighting〔lights〕 — 문안가(文案家) an ad writer ; a copywriter —비 an outlay for advertisement ; advertising costs —사(社) an advertisement 〔ad〕 agency ; an advertising firm ; a publicity bureau 《*pl.* ~s, -eaux》 《미》 —세(稅) the advertisement tax — 수입(收入) advertising revenue —술(術) the art of advertisement ; advertising technic(s) —판 a billboard ; a notice board ; a signboard — 효과 effectiveness of advertising 과잉 — excess advertisement ; an exaggerated advertisement 구인 — a help-wanted advertisement ; a wanted 사망 — an obituary ; a death notice 삼단 — a three-column advertisement 신문 — a newspaper advertisement ; a classified ad (항목별 광고란의) 안내(案內) — classified ads 자가(自家) — self-advertisement 전면(全面) — a full-page advertisement

광고란 廣告欄 an advertisement〔ad〕 column

삼행(三行) — the classified columns ; a want column 《미·구》

광고료 廣告料 advertisement〔ad〕 rates ; advertising rates〔charge〕 ¶ 3회분의 광고료를 지불하다 pay for three insertions of an advertisement

광고문 廣告文 [게재된] an advertising description ; a written advertisement ; [초안·원문] an advertisement draft ; an original copy of an advertisement

— 작성자 an ad writer ; a copywriter

광고 방송 廣告放送 [라디오·텔레비전] a commercial broadcast ; [문구] a commercial (message) ; a plug 《미·속》

— 프로 a commercial (radio) program ; a sponsor(ed) program
광고부 廣告部 a publicity department
—장 a publicity manager
광고 삐라 廣告— [뿌리는] a (show) bill ; a handbill ; [붙이는] a poster ; a placard
광고업 廣告業 advertising business
—자 an advertisement agent ; an advertising man ; an adman 《미》; [텔레비전] a sponsor ¶ 그 잡지는 광고주가 줄어 경영난에 빠져 있다 The magazine is suffering from financial difficulties owing to a loss of advertising.
광고탑 廣告塔 [가로의] a poster column ; [옥상 따위의] an advertising pillar〔tower〕
광공업 鑛工業 mining and manufacturing industries
광구 匡救 rectification ; redress ; remedy ; correction —하다 rectify ; redress ; remedy ; correct ; reform
광구 鑛區 a mine lot ; a mining area
—세(稅) a mine-lot tax
광구 光球 〚천문〛 photosphere
광궤 廣軌 a broad gauge
—안(案) a gauge-widening plan —제(制) the broad-gauge system
광궤 철도 廣軌鐵道 a broad-gauge railroad 《미》; a broad-gauge railway 《영》
광기 狂氣 madness ; craziness ; insanity ; mental derangement ¶ 그의 열중도는 광기에 가깝다 His zeal verges on madness.
광꾼 鑛— a miner ; a mine worker ; a pitman (특히 탄광의) ; a digger (특히 금광의) ; [경멸적] a grubby miner ; a pitslave
*광나다 光— be glossy ; be lustrous ; be shiny ; have a glaze ¶ 구두가 광나다 the shoes are shiny // 종이가 광나다 the paper is glazed ; the paper has a glaze to it
광내다 光— shine 《shoes》; polish ; make 《a thing》 shine〔bright〕 ¶ 쇳조각을 광내다 burnish a piece of metal
광녀 狂女 a madwoman
광년 光年 〚천문〛 a light-year
광대[1] a performer ; a clown ; a comedian ; a player ; an actor ; an actress (여자) ; [가면·탈] a mask ¶ 광대가 되다 go on the stage // 광대 노릇을 하다 play the jester〔fool〕
광대[2] [얼굴] a face ; a look
— 등걸 a hollow face ; a skinny〔lean, thin〕 face
†광대 廣大 —하다 (be) vast ; immense ; enormous ; extensive ¶ 광대한 제국 a far-flung empire // 미국은 모든 것에서 그 규모가 광대하다 Everything is on a grand scale in America.
광대나물 〚식물〛 a henbit ; a dead nettle ; Lamium amplexicaule (학명)
광대놀음 a farce ; a masque ; a motley show ¶ 그의 행동은 광대놀음에 불과했다 His behavior proved to be a burlesque.
광대 무변하다 廣大無邊— (be) boundless ; unbounded ; vast and boundless ¶ 광대 무변의 천지 the boundless universe
광대버섯 〚식물〛 Amanita muscaria (학명)
광대뼈 the cheekbone ¶ 광대뼈가 나온 사람 a person with high cheekbones
광대수염 〚식물〛 a kind of dead nettle
*광도 光度 intensity of light ; luminous intensity ; (degree of) brightness ¶ 광도의 차이 the different degrees of brightness // 별의 광도 the brightness〔magnitude〕 of a star
—계(階) photometric scale — 측정(測定) photometry — 측정자 a photometrist —표준기(標準器) 〚전기〛 a luminous standard
광도 狂濤 raging waters〔waves〕 ; a stormy sea
광도계 光度計 〚광학〛 a photometer
대색(帶色) — a color photometer 자외선(紫外線) — an ultraviolet photometer
광독 鑛毒 mineral pollution〔poisoning〕
— 피해 damage from mine pollution — 피해자 sufferers from copper poisoning
†광란 狂亂 madness ; craziness ; fury ; frenzy ; raving ; insanity —하다 become mad ; be〔become〕 frantic ; get wild ; be beside oneself ; rage ; rave ¶ 반광란 상태의 half-mad〔-insane〕 // 기뻐서〔슬퍼서〕 광란할 지경이다 be beside oneself with joy〔grief〕 ; be frantic〔wild〕 with joy〔grief〕
광란 狂瀾 raging billows ; angry〔surging〕 waves ; a tumultuous sea
광량 光量 the intensity of radiation
—계(計) an actinometer — 조절기 [필름 현상의] a fader — 측정기 an actinograph — 측정법 actinography ; actinometry
광량자 光量子 〚물리〛 a photon ; a (light) quantum
—설(說) the quantum theory of light
광력 光力 [전등 따위의] light ; 〚물리〛 illuminating power ¶ 광력의 측정 measurement of light
—계(計) 〚사진〛 an actinometer
광림 光臨 your (esteemed) visit〔call, presence〕 —하다 condescend to come〔be present〕 ; honor 《a person, an occasion》 with a visit ¶ 광림하여 주시면 영광으로 알겠습니다 Will you give me the pleasure of your company 《at dinner on…》? /We request the honor of your company 《at dinner on…》.
광막 廣漠 —하다 (be) vast ; extensive ; wide ; boundless ¶ 광막한 땅 an

extensive〔a vast〕 tract of land ; a wide spread of country // 광막한 초원 a vast expanse of grass ; the vast plains 〔prairies〕 《미》

광망 光芒 a beam of light ; a flash of lightning

광맥 鑛脈 a vein of ore ; a lode ; a deposit ¶ 광맥을 찾아내다 strike a vein of ore

—류(瘤) a pocket **—층** a seam〔vein〕 of ore

광면 廣面 wide-spread social connections ; a wide circle of acquaintance **—하다** have a large〔wide〕 circle of acquaintances ; have wide social connections

광명 光明 [빛] light ; [희망] hope ; a bright future〔prospect〕 ¶ 한 줄기의 광명 a ray〔gleam〕 of hope ; a beam of hope 《on the horizon》 // 새로운 광명을 주다 shed〔throw〕 a fresh light 《on》 // 생활에 광명을 주다 brighten 《a person's》 life // 암운 속에 광명의 반면을 보다 see the silver lining in the dark cloud // 그의 앞날에는 광명이 있다 His future prospects are bright. /He has a bright future before him. // 그의 의견은 그 문제에 새로운 광명을 던졌다 His opinion added a new light to the question.

광명도 光明度 brightness (of a binocular)

광명두 a wooden lamp holder

광명 정대 光明正大 fairness ; justice ; openness ; (a sense of) fair play **—하다** (be) fair ; just ; open ; just and fair ; straight ¶ 광명 정대하게 행동하다 act fair(ly) and square(ly) ; behave honorably

광목 廣木 cotton cloth

광무 鑛務 mining (business)

—국 the Bureau of Mining **—소** a mining scrivener's office

⁑광물 鑛物 a mineral ¶ 광물(성)의 mineral // 풍부한 광물 자원 rich mineral resources

—계(界) the mineral kingdom **—면(綿)** mineral〔slag〕 wool **— 섬유** a mineral fiber **—성** mineral **—성 기름** mineral oil **—성 수지(樹脂)** mineral resin **— 시험** a mineralogical examination **— 채취(採取)** extraction of minerals (from the earth) ; diggings (광산의) 《미》

광물질 鑛物質 mineral matter ¶ 광물질의 mineral

— 안료(顔料) a mineral pigment

광물학 鑛物學 mineralogy ¶ 광물학의 mineralogical

—자 a mineralogist

광반 光斑 〖사진〗 a flare (spot)

광범 廣範 ⇨ 광범위(廣範圍)

광범위 廣範圍 a wide scope ; a vast range **—하다** (be) extensive ; broad ; wide ; wide-spread ; wide-ranging ; far-reaching ¶ 광범위하게 extensively ; widely ; comprehensively // 광범위한 개혁 a far-reaching reform // 광범위한 권한 an immense power // 광범위에 걸치다 cover〔extend over〕 a wide range〔area, field〕 // 광범위하게 논하다 discuss 《a subject》 at large ; deal with generalities // 광범위한 영향을 주다 exercise a far-reaching influence 《upon, over》 // 그의 지식은 광범위하다 He is widely informed. // 그녀의 독서 폭은 광범위하다 Her reading is of very wide range〔covers a wide range〕.

광복 光復 the restoration of independence 《to a country》 **—하다** regain its independence

—군 the Independence〔Liberation〕 Army

광복절 光復節 Independence Day of Korea

⁑광부 鑛夫 a miner ; a mine worker ; a pitman ; a digger

—병 miner's disease

광분 狂奔 —하다 ① [분주히 뛰어다니다] be busy 《doing》 ; busy oneself 《about》 ; make desperate efforts ¶ 구직에 광분하다 be busily hunting for a job ; keep oneself busy in search of work // 돈벌이에 광분하다 be busy making money ; be absorbed in money-making // 그는 선거 운동에 광분하고 있다 He is busily engaged in the election campaign.

② [미쳐 날뛰다] run madly about ; run wild ; stampede (말 따위가 놀라서)

⁑광산 鑛山 a mine ; a mine field ¶ 광산을 경영하다 operate〔run〕 a mine // 광산을 채굴하다 mine ; excavate ; work a mine // 광산에 투자하다 invest one's capital in mines

— 공학(工學) mining engineering **— 궤도(軌道)** mine tracks **— 기계** mining machinery **— 기사** a mining engineer **— 노동자** a miner ; a mine worker **— 등(燈)** a miner's lamp **— 보안법(保安法)** 〖법〗 the Mining Safety Act **— 사무소** a mine office **—왕(王)** a mining king〔baron, magnate〕 **— 지방** a mining district **— 채굴권(採掘權)** mining rights〔concessions〕 **—촌(村)** a miners' town ; a camp 《미》 **— 측량(測量)** mine surveying

광산 鑛山 mineral products〔resources〕

—지 a mineralized area ; a district full of mineral deposits

광산물 鑛產物 a mineral product ¶ 광산물이 풍부한 mineral-rich 《province》

광산업 鑛產業 the mining industry ; 《engage in》 mining ; the mines

—자 a mine operator ; a miner

광산학 鑛山學 (the study of) mining ;

mining science
—과(科) the department of mining science
광상 鑛床 ore〔mineral〕 deposits
광상곡 狂想曲 〖음악〗 a rhapsody ¶ 광상곡을 짓다 rhapsodize
*광석 鑛石 an ore ; a mineral (광물) ; a crystal (라디오의)
— 검파기(檢波器) a crystal〔mineral〕 detector — 검파 수신기 a crystal set 〔receiver〕 —법(法) 〖제철〗 an ore process ; a pig-ore process — 운반선 an ore carrier — 운반차 a hutch —체 an ore sieve ; a trommel
광석화 鑛石化 [금속의] mineralization —하다 mineralize
†광선 光線 light ; a ray〔beam〕 of light ¶ 광선의 반사 the reflection of light // 광선이 잘 드는〔안 드는〕 방 a sunny〔an ill-lighted〕 room // 이 사진은 광선의 효과가 좋다 This photo shows fine effects of light and shade.
— 굴절 렌즈(屈折—) a dioptric lens — 분색기(分色器) a disperser — 분석(分析) spectrum analysis —속(束) a pencil of light rays — 여과기 a light filter — 요법(療法) phototherapy ; action therapy — 운동(運動) photokinesis — 전신법(電信法) telegraphing by light — 전화기 a photophone ; a radiophone — 추적(追跡) ray tracing 간접(間接) —an indirect ray of light 굴절(屈折) — refracted light 반사 — reflected light 살인 — a death ray 엑스 — the X〔Roentgen〕 rays 직접 — a direct ray of light 태양 — the sun's rays ; sunbeams
광세 曠世 —하다 (be) rare ; extraordinary ; unparalleled ; [획기적] epoch-making ¶ 광세의 위업 an unprecedented achievement
광속 光速 ⇨ 광속도
광속도 光速度 the velocity of light
광쇠 光— a kind of burin
광수 鑛水 mineral water
광시 狂詩 a comic〔satirical〕 poem, a parody
광시곡 狂詩曲 〖음악〗 a rhapsody ¶ 리스트의 헝가리 광시곡 [곡명] Liszt's Hungarian Rhapsodies
광신 狂信 a religious fanaticism —하다 fanatically believe 《in》 ; be devoted blindly 《to》 ¶ 광신적인 fanatical
광신자 狂信者 a fanatic ; a fanatic believer 《in》
광심 光心 〖물리〗 an optical center
광야 曠野 a wilderness ; a wild〔desolate〕 plain ; a prairie 《미》
광야 廣野 a wide field〔plain〕 ; open country
광어 廣魚 a (dried) flatfish
광언 狂言 unreasonable〔crazy〕 talk ; nonsense

—망설(妄說) absurd nonsense ; incoherent ravings
광업 鑛業 mining (industry)
—가(家) a mine operator 《미》 ; a mine owner —권(權) a mining right〔concession〕 — 기계 mining machinery — 노동자 a mineworker ; a miner — 노동조합 a miners' union ; a mine workers' union —법(法) 〖법〗 the Mines Act —소(所) a mining station〔office〕 —세(稅) the mining tax —저당법(抵當法) 〖법〗 the Mining Hypothecation Act —주(株) mining stocks〔shares〕 ; minings —지(地) a mining area〔center〕 ; diggings —회사 a mining company 국립 — 연구소 the National Mining Research Institute
광역 廣域 a wide〔large〕 area
— 경제 Grossraum-wirtschaft 《도》 ; great-sphere economy — 도시 a megalopolis — 수사(搜査) a search 《for a suspected criminal》 conducted over a very wide area
광열 光熱 light and heat
—비 heat〔fuel〕 and light expense(s)
광영 光榮 honor ; glory
광원 光源 〖물리〗 a source of light
광유 鑛油 mineral oil
광음 光陰 time (and tide) ¶ 광음은 화살같이 흐른다 Time flies (like an arrow). // 광음은 한번 가면 다시 오지 않는다 Lost time never returns. /Time once lost is lost forever. // 광음은 사람을 기다리지 않는다 Time rolls on waiting for no man. /Time and tide wait for no man. // 일촌 광음을 가벼이 마라 Improve〔Make good use of〕 every minute.
광의 廣義 a broad〔wide, large〕 sense ¶ 광의로 해석하다 interpret〔take〕 in a broad sense ; put a wide construction 《upon》
-광이 a person ¶ 느리광이 a slowpoke
광인 狂人 a lunatic ; an insane〔a crazy〕 person ; a madman
광자 光子 〖물리〗 a photon
†광장 廣場 an open space ; a (public) square ; [대광장] a plaza ¶ 광장의 고독 the solitude of wide spaces
— 공포증 agoraphobia 역전 — a station square
광재 鑛滓 slag ; dross
광저기 〖식물〗 the common cowpea ; a black-eyed pea
광적 狂的 ¶ 광적인 mad ; insane ; lunatic ; frantic ; wild // 광적으로 madly ; frantically ; wildly // 광적인 신앙 fanatical devotion // 광적인 행위 an insane act
광전 光電 〖전기〗 photoelectricity
—자(子) a photoelectron —자 방사 photoemission — 효과 the photoelectric effect
광전관 光電管 〖전기〗 a phototube ; a

photoelectric tube
광전지 光電池 〖물리〗 a photovoltaic cell ; a photocell
광점 光點 a luminous point ; a radiant ; a facula (태양의)
광정 匡正 reform ; correction ⇨ 교정(矯正) ―하다 correct ; remedy ; reform
광주 鑛主 the owner of a mine
광주리 a round basket (made of bamboo, wicker, twigs and the like)
광주리장수 a woman carrying a basketload of articles on her head
광중 壙中 the hollow of a grave
광증 狂症 insanity ; madness ; lunacy ; frenzy
광차 鑛車 a mine car ; a coal tub (석탄차)
광채 光彩 luster ; brilliancy ; splendor ¶ 광채를 내다 shed luster ; shine ; cut a dash〔figure〕 (비유적) // 광채나는 황금 lustrous gold // 광채가 찬연하다 be brilliant ; be dazzling ; be glittering // 여왕이 출석하여 무도회는 더 한층 광채가 났다 The queen graced the ball with her presence. // 그녀의 눈은 광채를 잃었다 Her eyes lost their luster.
광천 鑛泉 a mineral spring ; [온천] a spa ; [광수] mineral water(s)
― 요법 hydrotherapeutics ; balneotherapy ― 욕장 a mineral bath place
광체 光體 〖물리〗 a luminous body ; a luminary
광축 光軸 〖물리〗 an optical axis
―각(角) an optic angle
광층 鑛層 an ore bed
광치다 [빛을 내다] glitter ; scintillate ; [자랑하다] show off ; brag ; boast
광탄 光彈 a flare (bomb) ; a star shell ; a light-ball ; a tracer bullet 〔shell〕
광태 狂態 shameful〔disgraceful〕 conduct ; crazy behavior ¶ 광태를 부리다 behave disgracefully〔scandalously〕 ; [취하여] get wild in drink〔on the drink〕 ; [실수하다] get into a mess
*광택 光澤 luster ; gloss ; brilliance ; glaze ¶ 은은한 광택 quiet〔subdued〕 gloss〔sheen〕 // 광택 있는 lustrous ; glossy ; brilliant // 광택 없는 dull ; lusterless // 광택을 내다 polish ; give luster 〔brilliance〕 《to》 // 광택을 잃다 lose luster〔brilliance〕
―계(計) a glossmeter ―도 시험 a brilliance test ―면 a glossy surface ―면사 mercerized cotton yarn ― 사진 a glazed photograph ―제(劑) a brightener ―지(紙) glossy〔slick, coated〕 paper ― 측정 gloss measurement
광파 光波 〖물리〗 a light wave
광포 狂暴 outrage ; frenzy ; fury ; wildness ―하다 (be) furious ; frenzied ; outrageous ; wild ¶ 그는 광포해졌다 He went berserk. /He flew into a frantic rage.
―성 환자 병동(病棟) a violent ward
*광폭 廣幅 ① [넓은 폭] double width ; an (extra-) wide width 《of cloth》 ② [간섭] interference ; meddling
광풍 狂風 a raging wind ; a violent gale
*광학 光學 optics ; optical science
― 공업 optical industry ― 공장 an optical shop ― 기계 an optical instrument ― 기계상 an optician ― 병기 optical weapons ― 유리 optical glass
광한 狂漢 a madman ; a lunatic
광행차 光行差 〖천문〗 an aberration
연주(年週)〔일주(一週)〕 ― annual 〔diurnal〕 aberration 유성(流星) ― planetary aberration
광협 廣狹 relative width ; breadth (and narrowness)
광화학 光化學 〖물리〗 photochemistry
―반응 (a) photochemical reaction
광화학 스모그 photochemical smog
광활 廣闊 spaciousness ; extensiveness ―하다 (be) spacious ; wide ; extensive ; commodious ¶ 광활한 평야 an open field // 광활한 수면 an expanse of water // 광활히 spaciously ; extensively
⁑광휘 光輝 brilliance ; splendor ; glory ; glow ¶ 광휘 있는 glorious〔brilliant, splendid〕 // 광휘 있는 역사 our glorious history // 광휘를 발하다 shine brilliantly ; emit dazzling rays
광희 狂喜 wild joy ; a frenzy of joy ; exultation ; ecstasy ―하다 go〔be〕 wild〔frantic〕 with joy ; be overjoyed ; be beside oneself with joy ; go into raptures
괘 卦 [주역의] a trigram from the Book of Changes ; divination (점괘)
괘경 掛鏡 a hanging〔wall〕 mirror
괘괘이떼다 refuse flatly ; give a flat refusal
괘그르다 卦― have bad luck ; suffer reverses ; have everything go wrong
괘꽝스럽다 be very odd ; be quite queer 〔strange〕 ; be most peculiar 《in behavior》
괘념 掛念 care ; concern ; worry ―하다 mind ; care ; be concerned over ; worry about ¶ 조금도 괘념하지 않다 do not care a bit〔straw〕
괘다리적다 ① [거칠다] (be) boorish ; crude ; unmannerly ② [뻔뻔하다] (be) impudent ; brazen ; unblushing ; barefaced
괘도 掛圖 a wall map〔chart〕 ; a hanging picture
괘력 掛曆 a wall calendar
괘사 a prank ; a practical joke ; a mischievous act〔trick〕 ; a horseplay ¶ 괘사떨다〔부리다〕 play pranks 《on》 ; play a practical joke 《on》 ; crack〔make〕 a joke // 괘사스럽다 be funny〔comic,

amusing〕
괘선 罫線 a rule ; a ruled line ; 〖인쇄〗 a rule mark ¶ 괘선이 있는〔없는〕 종이 ruled〔plain, unruled〕 paper // 괘선을 치다 rule〔draw〕 lines ; rule ⟪paper⟫ with lines
*괘씸하다 (be) insolent ; impertinent ; disgusting ; hateful ; detestable ; unfaithful ; unappreciative ¶ 괘씸한 사람 a disgusting〔an intolerable〕 fellow // 괘씸한 행동 an improper act ; an offensive deed // 나를 이렇게 기다리게 하다니 참으로 괘씸하다 It is perfectly monstrous to keep me waiting like this. // 어른에게 말대답하는 것은 괘씸한 짓이다 It is insolent to retort to the elders. // 괘씸히 생각하다 hold ⟪a person⟫ culpable // 괘씸히 굴다 behave impertinently〔outrageously〕
괘장 a sudden switch〔reversal〕 in attitude ¶ 괘장부치다 suddenly reverse one's attitude ; be whimsical
괘종 掛鐘 a (wall) clock
괘지 罫紙 ruled〔lined〕 paper
*괜찮다 ① [쓸 만하다] (be) passable ; be not bad ; nice ; fine ; good ; fair ¶ 괜찮은 수입 good income // 괜찮은 여자 a good woman ; a fairly pretty woman // 영어를 괜찮게 하다 speak English fairly well // 맛이 괜찮다 taste good (enough) // 그것 괜찮다 That's good. 〔O. K.〕
② [상관없다] (be) permissible ; do not mind ; make no difference ; be all right ¶ 이제 가도 괜찮다 You may go now. // 이 자리에 앉아도 괜찮겠습니까 May I take this seat? /Do you mind if I sit here? // 홍차가 없으면 커피도 괜찮다 Coffee is all right for me if you do not have tea. // 들어가도 괜찮을까요 May I come in? // 어느 쪽이든 괜찮습니다 Either will do. // 괜찮으시다면 if you don't mind (it) ; if it is convenient to you // 괜찮습니다 (사과에 대해) Never mind. /That's all right. // 몇 분 정도는 괜찮다 A few minutes wouldn't hurt. /A few minutes would be all right. // 나 혼자도 괜찮다 I'll be okay by myself.
③ [안심이다] (be) safe ; secure ; be free from danger ; be all right ; be O. K. ⟪미⟫ ¶ (위험을 벗어나) 이젠 괜찮다 Now we are out of danger. // 이 건물은 지진이 일어나도 괜찮다 This building is proof against earthquakes. // 불이 나도 괜찮은 건물 a fire-proof building
괜하다 (be) useless ; pointless ; empty ; idle ; gratuitous ¶ 괜한 소리 useless words ; idle talk // 괜한 욕 groundless censure ; a gratuitous insult
*괜히 in vain ; uselessly ; fruitlessly ; pointlessly ; gratuitously ; without reason〔ground〕 ; for nothing ; to no purpose ¶ 괜히 애쓰다 labor in vain // 괜히 싸우다 fight for no reason at all // 괜히 거짓말하다 tell a lie gratuitously〔to no point〕
*괭이[1] a hoe ; a pick ¶ 괭이로 파다 hoe up the soil ; dig with a hoe
괭이[2] a cat ⇨ 고양이
괴걸 怪傑 a man of extraordinary talent ; a prodigy ; a wonder man ⟪미⟫ ; a mystery man (정체를 알 수 없는)
괴괴망측하다 怪怪罔測— (be) queer ; grotesque ; mysterious ; strange ; odd ¶ 괴괴망측한 일 a strange thing ; an odd thing ; a mystery // 괴괴망측한 풍설 a wild〔scandalous〕 rumor
괴괴하다 (be) quiet ; still ; silent ; deserted ¶ 괴괴한 거리 a quiet〔deserted〕 street
괴금 塊金 a nugget of gold ; gold ingot ; gold bullion
괴기 怪奇 (a) mystery ; (a) wonder — 하다 (be) grotesque ; bizarre ; mysterious ; strange ¶ 괴기하게 eerily
— 소설 a mystery〔spook〕 story ; a thriller
괴까다롭다 ① [문제가] (be) tricky ; intricate ; be difficult (to cope with) ¶ 괴까다로운 문제 a tricky problem ; a difficult question ② [성미가] (be) particular ; fussy ; crotchety ; fastidious ; finicky ; be hard to please ; be difficult (to deal with) ¶ 괴까다로운 사람 a person hard to please ; a difficult 〔fussy〕 person
괴깔 the nap〔the fluff texture〕 of paper, thread, or cloth
괴끼 an awn fragment
괴나리봇짐 —褓— a traveler's knapsack 〔rucksack〕
*괴다[1] [물이] gather ; collect ; form a puddle ; stay ; stagnate ¶ 비가 오면 물이 여기에 괸다 Water stays〔forms a puddle〕 here after a rainfall. // 통분의 눈물이 눈에 괴어 있었다 Tears of vexation were standing in her eyes.
괴다[2] [발효하다] ferment ; undergo fermentation ; be in a ferment
괴다[3] [받치다] support ; [음식을 상에] arrange〔pile up〕 food on the table ¶ 기둥으로 괴다 support〔prop〕 ⟪a wall⟫ with a post // 손으로 턱을 괴다 cup one's chin in one's hands
괴다[4] ① [사랑하다] love ; adore ; favor ② [사랑받다] be loved ; be adored ; enjoy a person's favor
괴담 怪談 a ghost story ; a spooky story ⟪미⟫
괴덕 부리다 act flippantly〔frivolously〕
괴덕스럽다 (be) flippant ; frivolous
괴도 怪盜 a mysterious〔phantom〕 thief
괴란 壞亂 [풍속의] corruption ; demoralization ; [질서의] subversion ; destruction ; disturbance —하다 corrupt ; demoralize ; subvert ; destroy ¶ 풍속을 괴란하다 corrupt〔degrade, be injurious

to〕 public morals ; be detrimental to public decency ; demoralize

괴력 怪力 superhuman〔Herculean, hyperphysical〕 strength ; Amazonian strength (여자의)

***괴로움** [수고] trouble ; annoyance ; [곤란] distress ; trouble ; suffering ; hardship ; affliction ; [시련] trials ; ordeals ; [번민] anguish ; agony ; mortification ; [고통] pain ; pang ¶ 삶의 괴로움 the troubles of life ; life's trials // 양심의 괴로움 pangs of conscience ; the pricks of conscience // 인생의 괴로움 the bitters of life // 가난의 괴로움 the grip of poverty // 죽음의 괴로움 death agony // 괴로움을 주다 inflict pain on 《a person》 // 많은 괴로움을 끼치다 give much annoyance to // 괴로움을 당하다 suffer troubles ; undergo hardships // 괴로움을 견디다 bear one's sufferings // 괴로움을 덜다 alleviate one's sufferings

괴로움이 있으면 즐거움도 있다 속담 Every cloud has a silver lining.

†**괴로워하다** ① [고통을 느끼다] suffer 《from》 ; feel〔be in〕 pain ; be afflicted 《with》 ¶ 괴로워하다가 죽다 die in pain ; die a hard death // 환자는 몹시 괴로워했다 The patient was suffering severely. // 그는 두통으로 괴로워하고 있다 He is suffering from a headache.

② [근심하다] be worried 《by》 ; worry oneself 《about, over》 ; torment with the thought 《of》 ¶ 돈 문제로 괴로워하다 be pinched〔pressed, hard up〕 for money // 그는 생활 문제로 괴로워하고 있다 He is troubled with the question of living.

괴롭다 [고통스럽다] (be) painful ; afflicting ; distressing ; agonizing ; [곤란하다] troublesome ; hard ; difficult ; [난처하다] awkward ; embarrassing ; embarrassed ; [곤궁하다] straitened ; needy ; reduced ; [몸이] be indisposed of ¶ 괴로운 일 hard work ; a tough job // 괴로운 입장 an awkward situation ; a touchy〔delicate〕 situation ; a sad plight // 괴로운 나머지 driven by pain // 괴로운 살림 a needy〔straitened〕 existence〔circumstances〕 // 괴로운 세상 a hard world // 괴로운 표정 an agonized look〔expression〕 // 숨쉬기가 괴롭다 have pain in breathing // 몸이 괴롭다 be out of sorts ; be uncomfortable // 마음이 괴롭다 be ill at ease ; be distressed〔tormented, agonized〕 // 괴로워 소리를 지르다 cry out in anguish // 나는 괴로운 입장에 놓였다 I was in an embarrassing 〔awkward〕 situation. // 그의 일생은 괴로움뿐이었다 His life was full of hardships. // 그 일을 생각하면 지금도 마음이 괴롭다 The matter still troubles my conscience. // 이렇게 추운 날 일찍 일어나기는 괴롭다 It is very hard to get up early on such a cold morning. // 이 제안을 들어주지 않으면 그는 괴로운 입장에 놓이게 된다 He's going to be in a tight spot if this proposal doesn't go through.

†**괴롭히다** afflict〔harass, torment〕 《a person》 ; worry〔annoy, bother〕 《a person》 ; trouble〔molest〕 《a person》 ¶ 마음을 괴롭히다 worry oneself 《about》 ; be concerned 《about》 // 적을 괴롭히다 harass the enemy // 경찰을 괴롭히다 give the police trouble // 부모를 괴롭히다 worry one's parents // 강아지를 괴롭히다 torment a small dog ; be cruel to a puppy // 약자를 괴롭히지 마라 Don't tease the weak.

괴뢰 傀儡 a puppet ; a marionette ; a robot ; [앞잡이] a tool ; a cat's-paw ¶ 괴뢰 노릇을 하다 act as another's tool ; be made a cat's-paw 《of》

—국(國) a puppet〔dummy〕 state **— 정부** a puppet government

괴리 乖離 estrangement ; alienation ; [분리] detachment ; separation ; dissociation **—하다** be estranged 《from》 ; be alienated 《from》

괴망 怪妄 eccentricity ; extraordinariness ; peculiarity ; oddity **—하다** (be) monstrous ; scandalous ; eccentric ; quaint ; queer ; unusual ; odd ; extraordinary ; peculiar ¶ 괴망한 사람 an eccentric person ; an oddity // 괴망한 취미 fastidious tastes

괴멸 壞滅 destruction ; demolition ; ruin **—하다** be destroyed〔demolished, ruined〕 ¶ 괴멸시키다 destroy ; wipe out ; demolish ; ruin // 괴멸적 타격을 주다 give a crushing blow

괴문 怪聞 a strange〔wild〕 rumor ; a scandal (추문)

괴문서 怪文書 reprehensible literature ; irresponsible and slanderous writing ; an anonymous letter

‡**괴물 怪物** a monster ; [유령] a ghost ; a bogy ; [사람] a mysterious man ¶ 정계의 괴물 a political sphinx

괴발개발 sloppily ; clumsily ; at random ¶ 괴발개발 그리다 write clumsily ; write at random

괴배다 塊— 〖한의〗 have〔develop〕 a tumor in one's belly

괴벽 怪癖 oddity ; peculiarity ; eccentricity ; fastidiousness ¶ 괴벽한 사람 a queer man // 괴벽한 취미 fastidious taste(s)

괴변 怪變 a strange accident ; an odd mishap

괴병 怪病 a mysterious disease ¶ 괴병이 퍼졌다 An unidentified disease has spread over.

괴불(주머니) an ornamental purse with strings

괴사 怪死 a mysterious death **—하다**

die a mysterious death
— 사건 a case of mysterious death ; a mysterious murder case
괴사 怪事 [괴이한 일] a mystery ; a strange〔weird〕 event ; [불미스러운 일] a scandal
괴사건 怪事件 ⇨ 괴사(怪事)
괴상 怪常 — 하다 (be) strange ; queer ; peculiar ; odd ; fantastic ¶ 괴상히 strangely ; queerly ; curiously // 괴상한 물건〔일〕 a strange thing ; an oddity // 괴상하게 생각하다 think strange // 나는 지난밤에 괴상한 꿈을 꾸었다 I had a strange dream last night.
괴상야릇하다 怪常— (be) very odd ; quite strange ; most peculiar ¶ 괴상야릇한 표정을 하다 make a quite strange expression
괴석 怪石 an oddly shaped stone
괴수 怪獸 a monster ; a monstrous beast
괴수 魁首 a ringleader ¶ 폭도의 괴수 the ringleader of a mob // 여섯 명의 괴수들은 체포되어 고소되었다 The six ringleaders were arrested and charged.
괴승아 〖식물〗 a wood sorrel ; an oxalis
괴위 魁偉 — 하다 (be) gigantic ; imposing ; commanding ¶ 용모가 괴위한 사람 a man of imposing appearance
*괴이 怪異 — 하다 (be) strange ; mysterious ; weird ; grotesque ; bizarre ⇨ 괴이쩍다
괴이다 get propped ; be supported ; [음식이 상에] be piled up ; be arranged ; [사랑받다] win 《a person's》 favor
괴이쩍다 怪異— (be) strange ; queer
괴이찮다 怪異— be not strange ; be natural ; be in no way peculiar
괴인 怪人 a monster man ; a mystery man
괴인물 怪人物 a mystery〔mysterious〕 person ; a Mr. X.
괴질 怪疾 a mysterious disease ; a strange malady ; [콜레라] cholera ¶ 그 지방에는 괴질이 번지고 있다 An unidentified epidemic is prevalent in the district.
괴짜 怪— an odd person ; an eccentric person ; a character ; an oddball ; a mystery man ; a crank ; an odd fish ; a screwball 《속》 ¶ 그 친구 괴짜야 He is a character (case).
괴철 塊鐵 an iron ingot
—로(爐) a bloomery
괴춤 (the area) between abdomen and belt
괴탄 塊炭 lump coal
괴통 [자루 구멍] the handle hole〔the hold〕 of a pick〔spade, hoe〕
*괴팍하다 乖愎— (be) fastidious ; finical ; fussy ; obstinate ; overnice ¶ 괴팍한 사람 a fastidious〔finical, particular〕 person // 괴팍하게 음식을 가리다 be fastidious about food // 그는 괴팍한 버릇이 있다 He has eccentric ways.
괴하다 怪— ⇨ 괴이하다, 괴이쩍다
괴한 怪漢 a suspicious-looking fellow ; a strange-looking character ¶ 괴한이 집 주위를 어슬렁거리고 있다 A suspicious fellow is loitering around the house.
괴현상 怪現象 a strange phenomenon ; an extraordinary phenomenon (진기한) ¶ 괴현상이 일어났다 A strange phenomenon presented itself.
괴혈병 壞血病 〖의학〗 scurvy ; scorbutus
— 환자 a scorbutic
괴화 怪火 a mysterious fire ; a fire of unknown origin
굄[1] [받침] a prop ; a stay ; a support
굄[2] [사랑] love ; affection ¶ 굄을 받다 be loved
굄대 a prop stick
굄돌 a stone prop〔support〕
굄목 —木 a wooden prop〔support〕
굄새 the way something is propped up ; the propping(s) ; skill at stacking cakes on plates
굄질 stacking〔piling up, heaping up〕 cakes on a plate
굉굉하다 轟轟— (be) roaring ; thundering ; rumbling ¶ 굉굉하게 rumblingly ; thunderingly ; roaringly // 굉굉한 소리 a roar ; a rumble // 굉굉히 울리다 roar
굉대 宏大 — 하다 [광막하다] (be) vast ; immense ; extensive ; [거대하다] great ; huge ; monstrous ; [웅대하다] magnificent ; grand ¶ 굉대 무변한 vast and boundless ; stupendous
굉연 轟然 — 하다 (be) roaring ; thundering ; deafening ; ear-rending — 히 with a roar ; with a roaring〔terrific〕 sound ; thunderously ¶ 굉연히 폭발하다 explode with an ear-rending noise // 대포가 굉연히 불을 뿜었다 The artillery belched fire with a deafening roar.
굉음 轟音 a roar ; a roaring sound ; a deafening roar ; an ear-splitting sound ; a peal ; a rumble ; a booming sound ; a thundering sound ¶ 굉음을 내다 make〔produce〕 a thundering noise
*굉장 宏壯 — 하다 (be) grand ; magnificent ; splendid ; stately ; imposing ; palatial ¶ 굉장한 미인 a strikingly beautiful woman // 굉장한 저택 a palatial residence〔home〕 // 굉장한 부자 an awfully rich man // 불이 굉장한 기세로 퍼졌다 The flames spread with a fearful rapidity. // 저 연극은 굉장한 평판을 듣고 있어 That play is getting fantastic reviews.
굉장히 very ; very much ; exceedingly ; greatly ; immensely ; exceedingly ; magnificently ; awfully ; terribly ¶ 머리가 굉장히 아프다 I have a most beastly headache. // 그는 힘이 굉장히 세다 He

is super strong. // 그는 야구를 굉장히 잘 한다 He is a terrific baseball player. // 오늘은 굉장히 춥다 It's bitterly cold today.

굉침 轟沈 sinking by explosion **— 하다** sink by explosion

굉활 宏闊 spaciousness ; extensiveness **— 하다** (be) spacious ; broad ; wide ; extensive

교 敎 a faith ; a religion ; a teaching ¶ 교를 믿다 believe in a religion

교 驕 haughtiness ⇨ 교만

교가 校歌 a school〔college〕 song ; an Alma Mater (song) ¶ 교가를 합창하다 sing in chorus a school〔college〕 song

교각 交角 〖수학〗 an angle of intersection

교각 橋脚 a pier

교각살우 矯角殺牛 a deadly effect of a good intention ¶ 교각살우다 The remedy is worse than the evil. /You shouldn't burn the house to roast the pig.

교감 校監 a head teacher〔instructor〕 ; an assistant principal ; a vice-schoolmaster

교감 交感 consensus ; sympathy ; mutual response **— 하다** sympathize (with each other) ; respond to each other ; share each other's feeling

교감 신경 交感神經 the sympathetic nerve ¶ [특히 약물이] 교감 신경 파괴의 sympatholytic
—계 the sympathetic system **— 안정제** a sympatholytic **— 파괴** 〖의학〗 sympatholysis **부(副)—** the parasympathetic nerve

교갑 膠匣 a capsule ; a cachet 《프》

교골 交骨 〖해부〗 pubis ; the bones of the pelvis

교과 敎科 a course of study ; the curriculum ; [학과] a lesson ; school work
—목 a subject ; a course (of study)

교과 과정 敎科課程 a curriculum ; a course of study ¶ 4년의 교과 과정을 마치다 finish up〔complete〕 a four-year course of study

†**교과서 敎科書** a textbook ; a schoolbook ; a manual (of instruction)
— 검정 제도 the〔a〕 textbook screening system **검인정 —** an authorized textbook **국정 —** a national textbook

교관 敎官 a teacher ; an instructor ; a professor ; a member of the faculty ; [전체] the (teaching) staff

교교하다 皎皎— [달빛이] (be) brilliant ; bright ¶ 교교히 brightly ; brilliantly // 달빛이 교교하다 The moon shines bright(ly).

***교구 敎區** a parish

교구 敎具 teaching tools〔aids〕 ; instruments of education

교군 轎軍 [가마꾼] a palanquin bearer ; [가마] a palanquin

교권 敎權 [교회의] ecclesiastical authority ; [교육의] educational authority ¶ 교권을 확립하다 establish a teacher's authority

교규 校規 school regulations

교기 校旗 a school banner〔flag〕

교기 校紀 school discipline

교기 驕氣 a haughty〔proud〕 attitude 〔demeanor, air〕 ¶ 교기를 부리다 act proudly ; assume a haughty attitude ; hold one's head high ; ride〔mount〕 the high horse

교내 校內 the school grounds ; the campus 《미》 ¶ 교내에서 in the school (grounds) ; on the campus 《미》 // 교내 대항 웅변〔운동〕 대회 an interclass oratorical contest〔athletic meet〕 // 교내 체육 대회 an intramural athletic meeting

교단 敎壇 the platform ; [목사의] pulpit ¶ 교단 생활 20년 a 20-year experience

교각

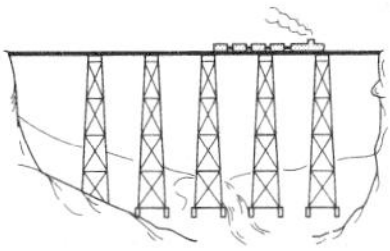
구각교 trestle bridge

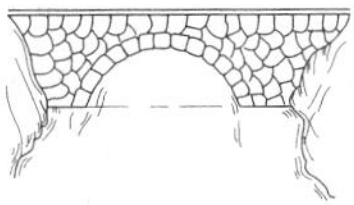
석교 stone bridge

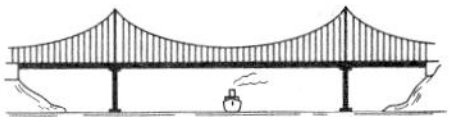
현수교 suspension bridge

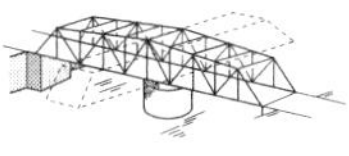
선개교 swing bridge

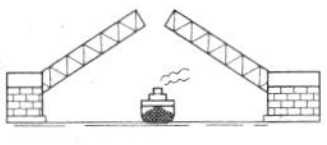
도개교 bascule bridge

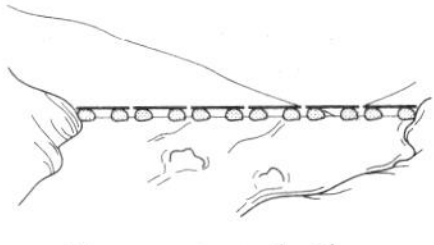
부교 pontoon bridge

of teaching // 교단에 서다 teach (at a school) ; be a teacher // 교단에서 쫓겨나다 be removed from one's teaching post 《at school》 // 교단에서 물러나다 retire from teaching // 교단에 선 일이 있느냐 Have you any experience as a teacher〔in teaching〕?

교단 敎團 a religious body〔association, order, brotherhood〕

교당 敎堂 [교회] a church ; a chapel ; [성당] a cathedral ; [절] a temple

*__교대 交代__ alternation ; change ; relief (보초 따위의) ; shift ; relay **— 하다** take turns 《at a job》 ; take one's turn〔place〕; relieve ; alternate ¶ 교대로 by turns ; in turns ; in shifts〔relays〕; alternately // 3교대로 in three shifts // 10시간 교대로 on ten-hour shifts // 교대로 작업하다 work by turns〔in turn〕; work in shift〔relays〕// 교대로 감시하다 keep watch by turns

— 노동자 a shift worker **—병(兵)** a relief **— 작용** 〖지질〗 metasomatism ; replacement **— 투수(投手)** a relief pitcher **심야(深夜) —** 〖노동〗 a mid-night shift **위병 —** change of guards **주야 —**a day and night shift

교대 시간 交代時間 changing time ; a shift ¶ 나는 다음 교대 시간까지 꼼짝못한다 I'm tied down here until my duty is relieved.

교대 작업 交代作業 〖노동〗 shift operation ; working in shifts ¶ (공장이) 주야 교대 작업을 하다 operate the day and night shift

교대자 交代者 a shift ; a relief ; 〖항해〗 a relief crew ; 〖군사〗 a relief detail

주〔야〕간 — men on the day〔night〕shift

교대제 交代制 the shift system ¶ 2회 교대제로 일하다 work on a two-shift basis

— 근무 shift work **삼(三) —** a three-shift system

교도 敎徒 a believer ; an adherent ; a follower

그리스도— a believer in Christianity ; a Christian **마호메트—** a Mohammedan ; a Moslem **불—** a Buddhist ; a believer in Buddhism

교도 敎導 teaching ; instruction ; training ; guidance **— 하다** teach ; instruct ; train ; guide ¶ 비행 청소년을 교도하다 reform a juvenile delinquent

— 민주주의 guided democracy **—자** a teacher ; an instructor ; a trainer ; a coach ; a coacher

*__교도관 矯導官__ a prison officer ; a warder 《미》; a jailer ; a prison guard ; a gaoler 《영》; a turnkey

†__교도소 矯導所__ a prison 《미》; a correctional institution ; a jail ; a penitentiary ; a gaol 《영》; a pen 《속》

> 참고 **jail**은 《미》에서 미결수, 경범죄용, 《영》에서는 **gaol**로 공용 **penitentiary**는 《미》의 주연방교도소

¶ 교도소에서 나오다 leave prison ; be let out of prison ; be released from prison // 교도소에 수감하다 put 《a criminal》 into prison ; send 《a criminal》 to jail ; put 《a person》 behind bars // 교도소에 들어가다 be put in prison ; be sent to jail〔prison〕

—장(長) the governor of a prison ; the warden of a prison 《미》

교두보 橋頭堡 a bridgehead ; [해안의] a beachhead ¶ 교두보를 만들다〔확보하다〕 establish〔secure〕 a bridgehead〔beachhead〕

‡__교란 攪亂__ disturbance ; derangement ; agitation **— 하다** disturb ; derange ; upset ; stir up ; throw into confusion ; agitate ¶ 평화를 교란하다 disturb peace // 후방을 교란하다 harass the rear

— 전술 harassing tactics

교량 橋梁 a bridge

교련 敎鍊 training ; drill ; exercises ; military exercises〔drill〕 **— 하다** train ; drill ; exercise

— 교관 a drill〔martial art〕 instructor **대대 —** battalion drill **사격 —** target practice

교령 敎令 a King's ordinance

교료 校了 finishing proofreading ; [부호] O. K. ; proofed **— 하다** finish correcting the proofs

—쇄(刷) an OK'd proof ; a press proof ; foundry proofs (연판으로 돌리는 것) **책임 —** O. K. with corrections

교류 交流 ① [교환] interchange ② 〖전기〗 an alternating current 《A. C.》 **— 하다** interchange ¶ 문화의 교류 cultural exchange // 한미간의 문화 교류 cultural interchange between Korea and America // (관청에서) 인사를 교류하다 interchange personnel 《between two ministries》

— 발전기 an AC〔alternating current〕 generator ; an alternator **— 암페어계** an AC ammeter **— 전동기** an AC〔alternating current〕 motor

교리 敎理 a religious doctrine ; a tenet ; a dogma ; a creed

—론 dogmatism **— 문답** catechism

교린 交隣 relations of neighboring countries ; friendship among〔between〕 neighboring countries

— 정책 a good-neighbor policy

교만 驕慢 pride ; haughtiness ; arrogance **— 하다** (be) proud ; haughty ; arrogant ; vainglorious ; conceited ; puffed-up ¶ 교만한 사람 a conceited〔stuck-up〕 person ; a smart aleck 《미》 // 교만하기 짝이 없다 be as proud as

Lucifer〔as a peacock〕// 교만하게 굴다 bear oneself haughtily ; act in a lordly manner // 그녀는 사과하기에는 너무 교만하다 She was too proud to apologize. // 그의 교만한 코를 꺾어 놓겠다 I'll teach him to act so arrogantly !

교모 校帽 a school cap

교모 敎母 a (Catholic) sister

교목 喬木 a (tall) tree ; a forest tree ; an arbor

—대(帶) the forest-tree zone **— 세가(世家)** a family that has been holding prominent posts for many generations

⁑**교묘 巧妙** skill ; dexterity ; cleverness ; ingenuity ; adroitness **—하다** (be) clever ; skillful ; dexterous ; ingenious ¶ 교묘하게 만든 clever-made 〔-wrought〕// 교묘한 장치 an ingenious device // 교묘한 답변 a tactful〔masterly〕 reply // 교묘한 수법 a shrewd〔crafty〕 trick // 교묘한 사기 a subtle deception // 교묘한 세공 elaborate workmanship // 교묘한 솜씨 a deft performance // 교묘한 수단 a clever〔shrewd〕 trick // 교묘히 처리하다 manage 《a matter》 cleverly // 나는 교묘히 속았다 I was nicely taken in. // 그것은 교묘히 짜여진 함정이었다 It was an ingeniously set trap. // 교묘히 환심을 사다 wind one's way into 《another's》 affections〔favor〕// 교묘히 남을 꾀다 be adept at enticing people // 당신이 교묘하게 말꼬리를 돌리지만 않는다면 나도 솔직히 털어 놓겠소 If you cut that fancy footwork out, I'll let it all hang out, too.

교무 敎務 [학교의] school affairs ; [교회의] religious affairs ¶ 교무를 맡아보다 be in charge of class work ; be on the instruction section staff

— 주임 the chief of school affairs ; the director of the instruction section **—과** the educational affairs department ; the instruction section **— 담당자** the official in charge of education **—실** a teacher's room ; a staff room 《영》 **—처** the office of academic affairs **—처장** the dean of academic affairs

교문 校門 a school gate

교문을 나서다 (관용) leave school ; graduate from 《college》

교미 交尾 copulation ; coition **—하다** copulate ; couple ; [새 따위] tread 《a hen》 ; pair ; [짐승이] cover

—기(期) the mating〔breeding, rutting〕 season ; time for pairing

교배 交配 crossing ; cross-breeding ; cross-fertilization (식물의) ; hybridization **—하다** mate 《one breed with another》 ; interbreed ; cross ; cross-fertilize (식물을) ; hybridize

교배종 交配種 a crossbred ; a cross-breed ¶ 교배종의 crossbred

교번 交番 alternation ; change ; (duty) relief ; shift

교번제 交番制 a shift system

교범 敎範 teaching methods ; pedagogics ; pedagogy ; a model for teaching ; a textbook ; 〖군사〗 a drill book〔manual〕

기술 — a technical manual 《TM》 **야전 —** a field manual 《FM》

교법 敎法 a religious doctrine ; a religion ; a creed

—사(師) 〖카톨릭〗 a Catholic missionary

교복 校服 a school uniform ¶ 교복 자율화 the liberalization of the dress code

교본 敎本 a textbook

운전 — a manual for driving

교부 交付 delivery ; transfer ; handing over ; grant ; issue **—하다** deliver ; serve 《a person》 with ; grant ; hand 《a ticket》 to 《a person》 ¶ 통지서를 교부하다 serve a notice on 《a person》 ; serve 《a person》 with a notice // 영장의 교부 a delivery of writ // …에게 여권을 교부하다 issue a passport to 《a person》

교부 敎父 [신부] a (Catholic) father ; [대부] a godfather

— 철학 patristic philosophy

교부금 交付金 《give》 a grant(-in-aid) ; a bounty ; a subsidy

교분 交分 friendship ; friendly relations ; intimacy ¶ 교분을 중히 여기다 value intimacy between friends // 교분이 두텁다 be good friends with ; enjoy a close intimacy with // 교분이 식어지다 grow lukewarm in friendship ; one's friendship cools 《toward》

교빙 交聘 exchange of envoys ; exchange of official visits〔invitations〕 **—하다** exchange envoys ; exchange official visits〔invitations〕

교사 巧詐 craftiness ; cunning ; subtlety ; wiles **—하다** (be) crafty ; cunning ; sly ; deceitful ; wily ¶ 교사한 사람 a crafty person ; a slyboots // 교사스러운 수단 a sharp practice ; a trick // 교사한 행동을 하다 act craftily

교사 校舍 a school house ; a school building ¶ 낡은 교사 a ramshackle school house

⁑**교사 敎師** a teacher ; an instructor ; [국민학교의] a schoolmaster ; a schoolmistress (여교사) ; [가정 교사] a tutor ; a governess (여자) ¶ 교사를 하다 teach (at a) school // 그는 뛰어난 교사이다 He is an excellent teacher. // 교사 티가 나는 schoolmasterish 《attitude》 // 그는 교사로서 빈틈이 없다 He is the complete teacher.

— 자격증 a teacher's license ; a teaching certificate **—직(職)** the teaching profession **영어 —** a teacher of

English ; an English teacher

교사 敎唆 instigation ; incitement ; abetment **—하다** instigate ; incite ; abet ; set〔egg〕《a person》 on ; foment ¶ 나쁜 짓을 하라고 교사하다 abet the commission of a crime // 폭동을 교사하다 instigate a rebellion // 범죄를 교사하다 incite〔instigate〕《a person》 to (commit) a crime ; abet 《a person》 in a crime

— 방조죄 aiding and abetting **—자** an instigator ; an abetter ; 〖법〗 an abettor **—죄** instigation

교사 驕奢 luxury ; haughtiness and extravagance **—하다** (be) luxurious ; haughty and extravagant ¶ 교사를 다하다 live in great extravagance〔in the lap of luxury〕 ; live in grand style

교살 絞殺 strangulation ; strangling ; (death by) hanging **—하다** strangle 《a person》 to death ; hang ; string up ¶ 교살의 흔적 marks of strangulation // 교살당하다 be strangled (to death)

교상 咬傷 a bite ; an injury by biting ¶ 뱀의 교상 《die from》 a snake bite

교생 敎生 a student〔pupil〕 teacher ; a school teacher in embryo

교서 敎書 a message ¶ 대통령의 교서 a presidential message ; the President's message (to Congress) // 미국 대통령의 연두 교서 the President's annual State of the Union Message to Congress

⁑**교섭 交涉** ① [담판] negotiation ; a parley ; bargaining ; an overture **—하다** negotiate 《with a person about a matter》 ; treat〔confer, bargain〕 with 《a person》 ; approach 《a person with a proposal》 ; make an overture to ¶ 교섭 중이다 be in〔under〕 negotiation ; be negotiating // 교섭은 교착 상태에 빠졌다 The negotiations got stalled〔became deadlocked〕. // 그 사건에 관해서 그 여자의 교섭을 받았다 I was approached by her over the matter. // 우리는 교섭을 하기 위해서 더 많은 시간이 필요하다 We need to allow more time for negotiations.

② [관계] connection ; relation ; dealing ¶ 교섭이 있다 have connection with ; have something to do with

— 단체 a bargaining body ; a negotiation body(국회의) **단체 —권** the right of collective bargaining **예비 —** (a) preliminary negotiation〔conversation, discussion〕 ; a pourparler (외교상의) **직접 —** direct negotiation

교섭 위원 交涉委員 a negotiating committeeman ; a walking delegate

—회(會) the negotiating committee ; the labor〔walking〕 delegation

교성 嬌聲 a (woman's) lovely〔charming〕 voice ; seductive tone ¶ 교성이 와자지껄하다 Cackling and chuckling are heard from among women.

교수 絞首 hanging ; strangulation ; strangling **—하다** strangle ; hang ¶ 교수형을 받다 be put to death〔executed〕 by hanging ; be hanged on a gibbet // 그는 교수형 판결을 받았다 He was sentenced to death by hanging.

†**교수 敎授** teaching ; instruction ; tuition ; [사람] a professor ; the faculty 《총칭》 **—하다** teach ; instruct 《in》 ; give instruction 《in》 ; give lessons to 《a person》 in ¶ 사용법을 교수하다 show 《a person》 how to use it // 영어를 교수하다 teach English ; instruct 《a person》 in English // 피아노의 개인 교수를 하다 give private lessons in piano

— 능력 teaching ability〔faculty〕 **—단** the faculty (of professors) ; the professoriate **—안** a teaching plan ; lesson plans **— 자료** teaching aids **—진** professorate ; the teaching staff **개인 —** private lessons **명예 —** a professor emeritus ; an emeritus professor **부—** an associate〔adjunct〕 professor **정—** a (full) professor **조—** an assistant professor **지도 —**an adviser ; tutor 《영》

*__교수대 絞首臺__ gallows ; a gibbet ; a scaffold ; [영국 역사] the Tyburn tree ¶ 교수대의 이슬로 사라지다 be killed by hanging // 교수대에 오르다 mount〔go to〕 the gallows〔scaffold〕

교수법 敎授法 a method of teaching〔instruction〕 ; a teaching method ; how to teach 《German》 ¶ 교수법을 모르다 do not know how to teach 《Korean》

구두(口頭) — an oral method of teaching 《foreign languages》

*__교수형 絞首刑__ death〔execution〕 by hanging ; hanging ¶ 교수형에 처하다 hang 《a person》 ; send〔condemn〕 《a person》 to the gallows

— 집행인 a hangman ; a Jack Ketch 《영》 **— 판결(判決)** a hanging verdict

교수회 敎授會 a faculty meeting〔council〕 ¶ 교수회에 내놓다 submit 《a matter》 to a faculty meeting

교습 敎習 training ; instruction **—하다** train ; drill ; teach ; instruct

— 시간 training hours

교습소 敎習所 a training school〔institute〕 《for》

댄스 — a dancing school **자동차 —** a drivers' school

교시 敎示 instruction ; teaching **—하다** teach ; instruct ; enlighten ¶ 사람에게 …을 교시하다 enlighten 《a person》 as to〔upon〕

⁑**교신 交信** exchange of messages ; communication ; correspondence **—하다** communicate 《with》 ; exchange (radio) messages 《with》 ; conduct a correspondence 《with》 ¶ 교신을 시작하다

start communications 《with》; open correspondence 《with》// 교신이 끊어지다 The communication is cut off〔interrupted〕. // 신호로 배와 교신하다 communicate with a ship by signals

†**교실 教室** a classroom ; a schoolroom ; a lecture room ; a recitation room 《미》; a department (대학)

계단 — a (lecture) theater **물리학** — a physics theater **생물학** — a biology (class) room **콩나물** — an overcrowded classroom **화학** — a chemistry room

교아 절치 咬牙切齒 gnashing of teeth **—하다** gnash one's teeth 《with anger》; grind one's teeth 《with vexation》

교안 教案 a teaching program〔plan〕; lesson plans ¶ 교안을 짜다 form a teaching plan ; form a lesson schedule

†**교양 教養** culture ; education ; refinement ¶ 교양 있는 cultured ; cultivated ; well-educated ; of culture ; refined // 교양 있는 사람 a man of culture ; a well-educated man ; a highbrow 《미》 // 교양 없는 사람 an uneducated person ; an uncultured person ; a lowbrow 《미》; [총칭] the ignorant ; the uneducated ; the illiterate (무식한) // 교양을 위한 독서 reading for culture // 교양이 있다 be cultured ; be well-educated ; be accomplished〔refined〕// 교양을 닦다 enhance the level of one's culture ; cultivate oneself // 그는 꽤 교양이 있어 보인다 He seems to have some cultural background

— **과목** cultural subjects — **과정** the liberal arts course — **소설** a Bildungsroman 《도》 — **프로** a cultural program —**학과** the department of liberal arts and science — **학부** the college of general education ; the liberal arts school

교언 巧言 flattery ; fine〔flattering〕speech ; honeyed〔fair, fine〕words ; blarney ; soft soap **—하다** flatter ; use sweet〔smooth, fine〕words〔blandishments〕; coax ; cajole ; say nice things 《to a person》 ¶ 교언으로 승낙케 하다 cajole〔wheedle〕《a person》 into a consent

—**영색** fine words and insinuating countenance

교역 交易 trade ; commerce ; barter (물물 교환) ; interchange (교환) **—하다** trade〔barter〕《with》; exchange ¶ 외국과 교역하다 trade 《with》 foreign nations

—**선** a trading ship —**소** [미개지의] a (trading) post — **조건** terms of trade

교역 教役 〖종교〗 religious work

—**자** a religious worker

교열 校閱 revision ; revisal ; recension **—하다** revise ; look over 《a manuscript》 ¶ 원고는 아직 교열 중이다 The manuscript is under revision yet.

—**자(者)** a revisor —**부** the proof reading section (신문사)

교오 驕傲 haughtiness ; arrogance ; pomposity **—하다** (be) haughty ; arrogant ; pompous ; overweening

‡**교외 郊外** the suburbs ; the outskirts ; the environs ¶ 교외의 suburban // 교외를 산보하다 go for〔take〕 a walk in the suburbs // 서울 교외에 살고 있다 He lives in the suburbs of *Seoul.*

— **거주자** a suburbanite ; suburbia 《총칭》 — **공업지** an industrial suburb — **산책** 《go for》 a walk in the suburbs 〔countryside〕; a stroll outside the town limits ; a country walk — **생활** a suburban life ; life in the suburbs —**선** the circular line running around the metropolitan zone — **전차** a suburban (electric) train ; an interurban (electric) railway — **주택지** a residential suburb ; a villadom

교외 校外 ¶ 교외의 outside the school ; [대학의] extramural

—**생(生)** [강의록에 의한] an external 〔extension course〕 student — **수업** teaching given outside the school ; extracurricular lessons〔instruction〕 — **활동** extramural activities

교우 教友 〖종교〗 a fellow believer ; a fellow Christian〔Buddhist〕

교우 校友 a schoolfellow ; a schoolmate ; [동창] an alumnus 《*pl.* -ni》 (남자) ; an alumna 《*pl.* -nae》 (여자) ; an old boy 《영》 ¶ 저 사람은 서울 대학교의 교우이다 He is a graduate of *Seoul* National University.

교우 交友 a friend ; a companion ; an acquaintance ; [사귐] making friends 《with》 **—하다** associate 《with》; keep company 《with》; make friends 《with》 ¶ 넓은 교우 범위 a large circle of friends // 교우가 많다〔적다〕 have a large 〔small, limited〕 circle of friends 〔acquaintances〕

교우 관계 交友關係 one's company ; one's associates ¶ 교우 관계를 조사하다 check up 《a person's》 associates ; investigate what company 《a person》 keeps // 교우 관계가 나쁘다〔좋다〕 keep bad〔good〕 company

교우회 校友會 [졸업생의] an alumni〔a graduates'〕 association ; an old boys' association 《영》; [회합] an alumni meeting〔reunion〕

— **잡지** an alumni bulletin〔magazine, gazette〕

교원 教員 a (school) teacher ; [남자] a schoolmaster ; [여자] a schoolmistress ; [전체] the teaching staff ¶ 교원을 하다 teach (at a school) // 교원 자격을 따다 obtain a teacher's license // 그를 그 학교의 교원으로 채용했다 They put

him on the teaching staff of the school. // 그는 중학교의 교원입니다 He is a middle school teacher. /He teaches in a middle school.
— 생활 a teacher's life ; a teaching career —실 the teacher's room〔office〕 — 양성소 a teachers' training school ; a school for the training of teachers

교원 강습회 教員講習會 a teacher's institute 《미》

교원 검정 教員檢定 certification of teachers
— 시험 a teachers' license examination

교원병 膠原病 〖의학〗 a collagen disease

교원 자격증 教員資格證 a teacher's license ; a teaching certificate ¶ 교원 자격증을 교부하다 grant a teacher's license 《to》; issue a teaching certificate 《to》

교유 教諭 [가르침] instruction ; [선생] an instructor ; a teacher

교유 交遊 social intercourse ; association ; friendship ; companionship —하다 associate with 《a person》; keep company 《with》

†**교육 教育** education ; schooling ; [교수] instruction ; [훈련] training ; [교양] culture —하다 educate ; instruct ; train ¶ 교육의 educational ; cultural // 폭넓은 교육 education with wide latitude // 교육의 기회를 균등하게 하다 equalize educational opportunities // 교육상 어린이들에게 좋지 않다 be not good for children from the educational standpoint // 교육을 받은 educated // 교육을 받지 못한 uneducated ; illiterate // 미국 교육을 받다 have an American education ; be American educated // 교육을 보급하다 extend school education // 그는 교육을 충분히 받았다 He is a highly educated man.
—가 an educationist ; an educator —감(監) a superintendent of educational affairs —계(界) the educational world ; educational circles — 공무원 the public educational personnel and staff(총칭) ; an educational public service employee — 공해 educational pollution — 공무원법 〖법〗 the Rules for the Public Educational Personnel and Staff Act — 공학 educational technology — 과정 a course of study ; a curriculum 《*pl.* ~s, -la》 — 기금 an education fund — 기본법 〖법〗 the Fundamentals of Education Act —단체 an educational body — 도서 books for use in schools and colleges — 백서(白書) a white paper on education — 보험 educational endowment insurance — 사업 educational work — 사회학 educational sociology — 시설 educational facilities — 시찰단 a tour group for studying education — 시찰 여행 a trip for observing and studying education ; [시찰관의] a school inspection trip 《by a Ministry of Education official》 — 심리학 educational psychology — 심의회 the Council of Education ; the Education Council — 연도 an educational〔a school〕 year — 연령 〖심리〗 educational age 《E. A., EA》 — 영화 an educational film — 지도 education and guidance — 지수(指數) 〖심리〗 an educational quotient 《E. Q., EQ》 — 철학 educational philosophy — 프로 〖라디오·텔레비전〗 an educational program — 학과 the department of education — 행정(行政) educational administration 가정 — home training〔education〕 domestic science 고등 보통 — liberal education (직업 교육에 대하여) 과학 — science education〔training〕 군대 — military training 대한 — 연합회 the Korean Federation of Education Association 《K. F. E. A》 성인〔평생〕 — adult〔lifelong〕 education 음악 — musical training 의무 — compulsory education 일반 — general education 전문 — professional〔technical〕 education 정규 — formal education〔schooling〕 중등 — secondary education 직업 — vocational education〔training〕 ☞ ◖p. 261◗

교육 개혁 教育改革 reform of the educational system ; (an) educational reform ¶ 교육 개혁을 행하다 reform the educational system // 교육 개혁 심의 위원회 Education Reform Deliberation Commission

교육 기관 教育機關 an educational institution ; an institution of learning ; a teaching institution ; educational facilities
고등 — a higher institution of learning ; an institution for advanced learning

교육 대학 教育大學 a teacher's college

교육 방송 教育放送 educational broadcasting

교육부 教育部 the Ministry of Education ; the Education Ministry ¶ 교육부 장관 the Minister of Education

교육비 教育費 educational〔school〕 expenses ; the cost of school education 《for one's child》 ¶ 요즈음은 아이들의 교육비도 무시할 수 없다 Children's education costs us no small money nowadays.

교육 위원 教育委員 a member of a board of education
—회 a board of education ; a school board

*__교육자 教育者__ an educator ; an educationist ; an educationalist ; a (school) teacher ; [경멸적으로] a pedagogue

교육장 教育長 the superintendent of

교육·학교

1 학교제도

① 미국의 학교제도

미국의 교육정책은 각주와 시를 중심으로 이루어지기 때문에 그 권한도 연방정부보다는 지방교육위원회(board of education)에 위임되어 있다. 의무교육(compulsory education) 연한은 주마다 차이가 있으나 9년(6~14세)이 많다.

▶ 학제(學制)는 6-3-3제와 8-4제로, 「공립학교」(public school)와 「사립학교」(private school)가 있다. 6-3-3제의 경우는 elementary school, junior high school, senior high school이고, 8-4제는 elementary school에서 바로 high school로 된다. 숫자로는 8-4제의 경우가 많다.
▶ 대학의 종류는 종합대학(university), 문리대학(liberal arts college), 2년제의 단과대학(junior college, two-year college), (지방단체가 지역주민을 위해 세운) 지역대학(community college)이 있다. 미국에는 사립대학(private university), 주립대학(state university)뿐이며 국립대학(national university)은 없다. 입학시험은 따로 없고 동부의 College Entrance Examination Board와 SAT(Scholastic Aptitude Test)가 선발 자료로 이용된다. 또한 북동부의 오랜 전통을 가진 Harvard, Princeton, Yale, Columbia, Brown, Dartmouth, Cornell, Pennsylvania 등 8개 명문 대학을 아이비리그(Ivy League)라 일컫는다.
▶ 학기(term)는 2학기제(semester system), 3학기제(trimester system), 4학기제(quarter system, year-round system)가 있다. 개학은 보통 9월.
▶ 직업대학(professional school)으로는 대학원급의 medical school, law school, business school 등을 가리킨다.

② 영국의 학교제도

크게 공립학교(state school)와 사립학교(independent school)로 나뉜다.

▶ 학제는 6년간의 primary school의 교육 후 11세가 되면 능력시험을 치루어 합격자는 대학진학을 목표로 하는 grammar school에 입학한다. 이 외의 학생들은 일반 교양을 익히는 modern school이나 기술 습득을 위한 technical school에 들어간다. 또한 앞에 열거한 modern school이나 technical school 등의 다목적을 지닌 학교로서 7년제의 중등학교를 comprehensive school이라고 한다.
이상의 학교에서 의무교육을 마치고 상급학교에 진학하려면 GCE(General Certificate of Education)의 O Level에 합격하여야 한다(★ General Certificate of Education은 Ordinary Level(O Level)과 Advanced Level(A Level)의 2개급이 있다).
▶ 사립학교 중에는 public school이 있는데 nursery school → preparatory school → public school의 단계를 거친다. 주로 13세부터 18세까지 남학생들을 기숙사제로 교육을 시킨다. (★ 통학제는 day school이라고 함) 최근에는 여학생전문 학교도 생기고 있다. Eton College, Harrow School, Rugby School 등은 명문 public school에 속한다.
▶ 대학은 GCE의 A Level에 합격한 사람이 진학할 수 있다. 수업연한은 스코틀랜드(4년)를 제외하곤 3년이다. 영국에서는 역사·특징·운영방식 등이 서로 다른 college가 모여 university를 이루고 있으며 Eton College와 의무교육 후의 고등학교에 해당하는 technical college, tutorial college, secretarial college 등과 같은 college도 있다.
이 밖에 고도의 공업기술을 배우는 polytechnic이 있으며 방송대학(Open University) 등도 있다.
▶ 영·미의 대학원(postgraduate school 〖略〗 graduate school)의 학생은 graduate student로 부르고 학부(學部) 학생은 undergraduate student라 부른다. 대학원의 석사과정은 M.A.course라 부른다.(★ M.A.는 「석사」(Master of Arts)의 略) 이과계(理科系)는 Master of Science (〖略〗 M.S.)로 부른다.
▶ 박사과정은 Doctor course. 박사는 정식으로는 Doctor of Philosophy (〖略〗 Ph.D.). 또 대학의 학부를 졸업하면 B.A (Bachelor of Arts), 이과계는 B.S. 또는 B.Sc.(Bachelor of Science)라는 학위(degree)를 받는다.

2 교사와 학생

초·중·고교의 교사는 일반적으로 teacher로 부르고, 대학 교수도 teacher라 부르지만 정식으로는 「교수」(professor), 「조교수」(assistant professor), 「강사」(instructor 또는 lecturer)라 부른다.

▶ 미국의 종신교수직(tenure)을 얻기까지는 매년 계약을 갱신한다. 7년에 한번씩 6개월 혹은 1년간의 안식휴가(sabbatical year [leave])를 가진다.
▶ (대학의) 학장·총장 president; chancellor / 학부장 dean / 교직원 faculty / (초·중·고) 교장 principal; headmaster 《영》 / 대학생 university [college] student / 학부생 undergraduate student / 대학원생 graduate student /

(논문집필 중인) 박사 후보생 Ph. D candidate / 유학생 foreign student / 청강생 auditor / 복학생 returnee students

③ 학년

미국에서는 초등학교에서 고등학교까지 통산하여 1학년~12학년으로 부른다. 대학생은 1년생은 freshman, 2년생은 sophomore, 3년생은 junior, 4년생은 senior로 부른다. (★ 실제로는 학년제를 폐지하고 단위제를 도입한 곳이 많다.)
¶ 나는 중학교 1학년이다. I'm in the seventh grade. / I'm a seventh grader. // 나는 고등학교 3학년생이다. I'm a student in the twelfth grade. / I'm a twelfth grader. // 당신은 몇 학년입니까? What grade are you in? (★ 영국에서는 grade, grader를 쓰지 않고 「I'm in the fifth year of a primary school. / I'm in my fifth year at a primary school. (나는 초등학교 5학년생입니다)라고 쓴다.) // 나는 대학 2학년생입니다. I'm in the second year of the University.

④ 강좌·과목

▶ 필수과목 required subject / 선택과목 elective [optional 《영》] (subject) / 문학 literature / 언어학 linguistics / 사회학 sociology / 사회과 social studies / 철학 philosophy / 화학 chemistry / 생물학 biology / 자연과학 natural science / 물리학 physics / 가정학 home economics / (외국어로서의) 영어 English (as a foreign language) / 역사 history / 지리 geography / (중학의) 이과(理科) science / 체육 physical education; P.E. / 수학 mathematics; math

education〔schools〕
교육 정도 敎育程度 a standard of education ¶ 국민의 교육 정도를 높이다 raise〔elevate〕 the educational standard of the people
교육 제도 敎育制度 an educational〔a school〕 system ¶ 민주적 교육 제도 an educational system based on democratic principles // 6·3·3의 교육 제도 the 6-3-3 educational system
교육학 敎育學 pedagogy ; pedagogics ¶ 교육학상 pedagogically
—사 a bachelor of education **—자** a pedagogist
교의 交椅 ① [의자] a chair ¶ 교의에 기대 앉다 lean on a chair // 교의에 앉다 sit on〔in〕 a chair ② [신주(神主)의] a highchair on which the ancestral tablet is put
교의 交誼 friendship ; friendly relations 〔relationship〕 ¶ 교의를 끊다 break friendship with // 교의를 맺다 cultivate 〔promote〕 friendship with 《a person》 // 교의를 두터이 하다 promote friendship 《between》 ; form a close friendship 《with》
교의 校醫 a school doctor〔physician〕
****교의 敎義** a doctrine ; a tenet ; a dogma ; teachings ; a creed ¶ 교의상의 doctrinal ; dogmatic
— 내용 the doctrinal content 《of Buddhism》 **— 문답** catechism **—학(學)** dogmatics
교인 敎人 a believer ; an adherent ; a devotee ; a follower ; 《총칭》 the faithful
예수 — a Christian
교자 交子 food set on a large table
교자상 交子床 a large dining table
교잡 交雜 ① [섞임] confusion ; disorder **—하다** be confused ; be in disorder ; be at sixes and sevens ; be tangled ; be mixed〔jumbled〕 up ② [교배] 〖식물〗 crossing ; 〖동물〗 hybridization
***교장 校長** [국민 학교의] a schoolmaster ; a schoolmistress (여자) ; a headmaster ; a headmistress (여자) ; [중학교의] a principal ; [고교의] a director ; [주일 학교의] a superintendent
— 회의 a headmasters' conference
교장 敎場 [교실] a classroom ; a schoolroom ; [교련장] a (military) drill ground
교장 校葬 a school funeral ; a funeral performed at school expense ¶ 교장을 지내다 give 《a person》 a school funeral
교재 敎材 teaching material ; materials for teaching〔instruction〕 ¶ 신문을 교재로 사용하다 use a newspaper in classes〔school work〕
***교전 交戰** [전투] a battle ; fighting ; an engagement ; an action ; [전쟁 상태] war ; hostilities ; belligerence **—하다** fight ; engage in a battle ; wage war ; be at war 《with》 ¶ 교전 상태에 있다 be in a state of hostilities // 교전 중이다 a battle is going on 《between》 ; be at war 《with》 // 적과 교전하다 engage〔fight with〕 the enemy (troops) // 교전을 중지하다 break off the engagement
— 구역 a war zone ; a zone of hostilities **—군** embattled forces **— 단체** a belligerent body **— 상태** a state of war 《with》 ; belligerency **—지** a battlefield ; a field of battle ; the theater of war **— 회피** 〖군사〗 disengaging action
교전 敎典 a canon
기독교 — (Holy) Scripture ; (Holy) Bible **회교 —** the Scripture of Islam ; the Koran
교전국 交戰國 a warring〔belligerent〕 nation〔power〕 ; a belligerent
비(非) — a nonbelligerent (power)

교전권 交戰權 the right of belligerency ¶ 교전권을 포기하다 discard〔cast off〕 the right of belligerency
교점 交點 a point of intersection ; an intersection point ; 〚천문〛 a node
—월(月) 〚천문〛 nodal month
교접 交接 [접촉] contact ; [성교] sexual intercourse〔union〕 ; coition ; copulation —하다 have sexual intercourse〔connection〕 《with》 ; copulate 《with》 ; [접촉] contact
— 불능 impotency — 불능자 an impotent (man)
교정 交情 friendship ; intimacy ; friendly relations ⇨ 교분 ¶ 그들의 교정은 두텁다 They are on intimate terms.
교정 校正 proofreading ; correction 《of the press》 —하다 read proofs ; correct 《the press》 ¶ 엄밀히 교정하다 read proofs with religious care // 세번 교정하다 read the proofs three times ; make corrections in three proofs // 교정하느라 바쁘다 be busy correcting the proof // 몇번 교정했나 How many times was the proof read? // 교정은 정확히 보았겠지 Do you read proofs with religious care?
— 기호 proof-correction marks ; proofreader's marks —실 a proofroom ; a reading room —자 a proofreader ; a press reader ; a corrector
교정 敎程 a course ; a curriculum 《*pl.* -la》 ; [교수의 정도] a grade ; [방법] a method of teaching ; [교본] a textbook ; a manual
*교정 矯正 correction ; reform ; remedy ; rectification —하다 correct ; reform ; remedy ; cure ; rectify ¶ 교정하기 어려운 incorrigible ; incurable ; irreclaimable // 말 더듬는 것을 교정하다 cure 《a person》 of stammering // 악폐를 교정하다 correct〔remedy〕 evils // 악벽을 교정하다 cure 《a person》 of a bad habit ; [자기의] break oneself of a bad habit // 사회의 악폐를 교정하다 uproot social evils
—법(法) a remedy ; a cure — 시력 corrected eyesight — 시설(施設) a correctional institution —약(藥) a corrective (agent) —원(院) a reformatory ⇨ 소년원 치열 — straightening teeth ; orthodontia
교정 校訂 revision —하다 revise ¶ S 박사 교정 revised by Dr. S // 재판에서 약간의 교정을 했다 Some revisions have been made in the second edition.
—본(本) a recension ; a revised edition 〔text〕 —자 a reviser ; a redactor ; an editor —판 a revised〔critical〕 edition
*교정 校庭 the school grounds ; the campus 《미》 ; [운동장] the (school) playground
교정쇄 校正刷 a (printer's) proof ; a proof sheet ¶ 오식이 많은 교정쇄 a foul proof
봉조(棒組) — a slip ; a galley proof (게라) 저자(著者) — an author's proof 최종 — the final proof
교정필 校正畢 a corrected proof ; [마크] Corrected ; O. K. ¶ 교정필분을 돌려주다 return corrected proofs
†교제 交際 association ; intercourse ; society ; company ; friendship ; acquaintance —하다 associate〔mix〕 《with》 ; have intercourse 《with》 ; keep company 《with》 ; cultivate one's acquaintance ¶ 교제를 싫어하는 사람 a person who loves solitude ; a person who shuns society ; a bad mixer 《미》 // 교제를 끊다 cut 《a person》 ; break off one's friendship 《with a person》 // 교제가 넓다 have a wide〔large〕 circle of friends〔acquaintances〕 // 교제를 맺다 form a friendship 《with》 ; get acquainted 《with》 ; make 《a person's》 acquaintance // 교제를 피하다 avoid company ; keep 《oneself》 to oneself // 좋은〔나쁜〕 사람과 교제하다 keep good〔bad〕 company // 동업끼리 교제하다 associate with people in one's own profession // 교제를 좋아하다〔싫어하다〕 be sociable〔unsociable〕 ; be fond of〔dislike〕 company〔society〕 // 교제가 깊다 be on intimate terms 《with》 ; be closely associated 《with》 // 교제가 얕다 be not well〔be slightly〕 acquainted 《with》 // 그들은 너와 교제하는 것을 주저할 것이다 They will decline to associate with you. // 그 사건 때문에 그들의 친밀한 교제에 금이 갔다 The incident caused a crack in their close relationship. // 그와의 교제는 즐겁다 I enjoy his company. // 그 사람과는 교제하고 싶지 않다 I don't like his society. /I wouldn't seek his acquaintance. // 그와 아직도 교제하고 있느냐 Are you still continuing an acquaintance with him?
—가 a sociable person ; a society man 〔lady〕 ; a club man〔woman〕 《미》 ; a good mixer —법 a social code ; etiquette —술 social tactics
교제 범위 交際範圍 a circle of acquaintance(s) ¶ 교제 범위가 넓다〔좁다〕 have a wide〔narrow〕 circle of acquaintance(s)
교제비 交際費 social〔society, entertainment〕 expenses ; table money ; [회사가 지급하는] 《have》 an expense account ¶ 사교계에 출입하는 데에는 교제비가 든다 It needs a lot of money to be a good society man.
교제상 交際上 as a matter of social courtesy
교조 敎祖 the founder of a religion
*교조 敎條 a tenet ; a dogma ⇨ 교의(敎義)
교조주의 敎條主義 doctrinism ; dogmatism

—자 a doctrinist ; doctrinarian ; a doctrinaire

교졸 巧拙 skill ; tact ; dexterity ; proficiency ; [세공의] workmanship ; [연기의] performance

교종 敎宗 the various non-Zen sects of Buddhism ; non-Zen Buddhism

교주 校主 the proprietor〔founder〕 of a school ¶ 그 학교의 교주는 김씨다 The school is run〔kept〕 by Mr. *Kim*.

교주 敎主 the founder of a religion

교지 校誌 a school magazine

교지 敎旨 [신조] tenets ; [교리] doctrine ¶ 기독교의 교지 the Christian doctrine

교지 校地 a school site ; the site of a school ¶ 새 교지를 물색하다 look for a new site for the school

교지기 校— a school janitor

교직 交織 a mixed weave ; blended fabric ; mixtures

—물 union cloth 면모 — cotton and wool mixtures 마모 —물(物) linsey (-woolsey)

교직 敎職 the teaching profession ; [대학의] professorship ; [종교의] the ministry ¶ 교직에 있다 be engaged in teaching ; be on the teaching staff of 《a school》// 교직에 들어가다 (교직에 몸을 담다) enter the teaching profession ; take up teaching ; enter the ministry (목사)

— 과정 《go through》 a course of study for the teaching profession ; the teacher training course — 수당 a long-service allowance to teachers —자 a school teacher ; those in the teaching profession

교직원 敎職員 school personnel ; the staff of a school ; the teaching staff ; the faculty 《집합적》

— 회의 a faculty conference

교질 膠質 a colloid ¶ 교질의 gluey ; glutinous

— 다이너마이트 gelatinized dynamite —물(物) a jelly ; gelatinoid — 용액 a colloid solution ; a hydrosol — 화약 colloidal powder — 화학 colloid chemistry 소액(疎液) — 〖화학〗 a lyophobic colloid 친액(親液) — 〖화학〗 a lyophilic colloid

†**교차 交叉** crossing ; intersection —하다 cross 《each other》 ; intersect 《each other》 ¶ 두 도로는 거기서 교차한다 The two highways cross each other there. // 두 개의 막대기를 교차시키다 cross the two sticks

— 결합 [원자군] cross-linking ; cross-linkage ; a cross-link — 광맥 〖지질〗 a cross vein — 면역 〖의학〗 cross-immunity —법 〖통신〗 transposition — 승인 cross-recognition 평면 — 〖철도〗 grade crossing 《미》 ; level crossing 《영》 ; crossing at grade (도로와의)

교차 較差 a range ¶ 한란계의 승강 교차 the range of a thermometer

*__교차로 交叉路__ an intersection ; a crossroads ; a cross street ; a crossway ¶ 교차로에서 at the〔a〕 crossroads ; at the intersection 《of two roads》// 사고는 교차로에서 일어났다 The accident took place at the crossroads. // 나는 복잡한 교차로에서 빨간 신호등을 무시하고 달렸다 I ran a red light at a busy intersection.

광화문 — *Kwangwhamun* intersection 완전 정지 — a stop street

교차점 交叉點 [두 선의 교점] a crossing ; the point of intersection ; an intersecting point ; [네거리] a cross ; a crossover ; (a) crossroads ; an intersection ; a crossing ; [선로의] a crossing ¶ 교차점에서 at the intersection 《of》

교착 交錯 [섞임] mixing ; a mixture ; blending ; [착잡] complication ; intricacy ; complexity

—하다 mix ; be complicated〔intricate, entangled〕 ; be involved ¶ 명암의 교착 a mixture of light and shade ; 〖미술〗 chiaroscuro

교착 膠着 agglutination ; adhesion ; stalemate —하다 glue 《to》 ; adhere 〔stick〕 《to》 ; cement ¶ 교착 상태에 있다 be deadlocked ; be at a standstill // 교착 상태에 빠지다 come to a standstill ; bog down // 그들의 계획은 교착 상태에 빠졌다 Their plans got bogged down. // 교착 상태를 타개하다 break the deadlock ; find a way out of the impasse

—어(語) an agglutinative language —제(劑) a binder ; glue ; an adhesive ; an agglutinative agent

†**교체 交替** shift ; change ; replacement ; alternation —하다 shift ; change ; replace ; alternate ¶ 세대의 교체 the change of generations // 8시간씩 3교체로 in three shifts of eight hours // 주야 교체로 by day and night shifts // 교체로 핸들을 잡다 drive by turns ; take turns in driving ; take spells at the (steering) wheel 《미》 // 투수가 교체되다 the pitcher is relieved〔switched〕

— 수석 대표 an alternative chief of the delegation 선수 — 〖경기〗 a change 〔switch〕 of players

교치 咬齒 grinding of the teeth

—하다 grind〔grate〕 one's teeth

교칙 敎則 rules for teaching

—본(本) a manual 《of》 ; a school

교탁 敎卓 a teacher's desk ; a teaching desk ; a desk for the teacher

교태 嬌態 coquetry ; coquettish behavior 〔attitude, ways〕 ¶ 교태를 부리다 play the coquette ; behave coquettishly ; be coy ; display feminine charm // 그녀는 교

태를 부리며 내게 기대었다 She leaned against me flirtatiously〔amorously, coquettishly〕.

†**교통 交通** traffic ; communication ; transportation ; transport ; transit ; navigation **—하다** transport ; commute ; communicate 《with》 ¶ 교통이 두절되다 Traffic is interrupted〔tied up〕. // 교통을 정리하다 regulate〔control〕 traffic // 교통편이 좋다 be easy to reach // 지진으로 교통이 군데군데 마비되어 있다 Traffic has been paralyzed in places by the earthquake. // 차량으로 교통이 막혀 앞으로 나아갈 수 없다 We cannot move because the traffic is blocked. // 교통이 차단되다 be cut off from communication ; [전염병으로] be placed under quarantine // 교통이 좋다〔나쁘다〕 be easy〔hard〕 of access // 교통의 혼잡을 완화하다 relieve〔ease〕 the congestion of traffic // 모두 교통이 편리한 곳들인가요 Are they all easily accessible ? // 교통이 복잡해지기 전에 집에 가는게 좋겠다 I'd better go home before the traffic starts.

— 경제 traffic economy **— 경찰** traffic police **—난** traffic congestion〔a traffic jam〕 **—로** a traffic route ; a line of communication **—망** a traffic network **— 문제** a traffic problem **— 방해** obstruction of traffic〔the public road〕 **—부** the Ministry of Transportation **— 순경** a traffic policeman ; a traffic cop ; a point constable 《영》 ; a traffic warden **— 운수업** communication and transportation undertaking **— 전쟁** traffic warfare **— 정책** a traffic policy **— 조사** the investigation of traffic volume ; a traffic survey ; the checkup of wheeled traffic (차의) 《미》 **— 지옥〔마비〕** a traffic mess〔jam〕 ; (an inferno of) traffic congestion ; hazardous conditions of traffic ; a traffic chaos **— 질서** traffic order **— 체신 위원회** the Transportation & Communication Committee **— 통제 센터** the Traffic Control Center **— 표지** a traffic sign

교통 규칙 交通規則 traffic regulations〔rules〕 ; the rules of the road ¶ 교통 규칙을 범하다 violate〔break〕 traffic regulations // 이것은 교통 규칙 위반이다 This is against traffic rules.

교통 기관 交通機關 means of transportation〔traffic, traveling〕 ; transport〔traffic〕 facilities ; a public conveyance ; public carriers ¶ 교통 기관의 발달 advances in the means〔facilities〕 of transportation // 교통 기관은 혼란 상태에 있다 The transport facilities are upset〔out of order〕.

교통 노동자 交通勞動者 a traffic worker ; a carman ; [철도의] a trainman ; [시가 전차의] a trolleyman 《미》 ; a streetcar worker 《미》

교통 도덕 交通道德 traffic morality〔morals〕 ¶ 교통 도덕을 지키다 follow traffic morals

교통량 交通量 the volume of 《wheeled》 traffic ; traffic volume〔density〕 ; traffic ¶ 교통량이 많은 도로 a road where there is much traffic // 교통량이 가장 많은 시간 the heaviest traffic hours

—도(圖) a traffic discharge map **— 조사** a traffic census〔survey〕

교통비 交通費 traffic expenses ; a carfare ¶ 교통비를 지급하다 provide communication allowances // 버스의 교통비가 많이 든다 It costs me a lot for my bus-rides.

교통 사고 交通事故 a traffic〔street〕 accident ¶ 교통 사고를 일으키다 cause〔bring about〕 a traffic accident

교통 신호 交通信號 a traffic signal ; a traffic light ; blinkers ; a stop-go sign 《영·구》 ¶ 교통 신호를 지키다〔무시하다〕 observe〔neglect〕 traffic signal

—등 a traffic light

교통 안전 交通安全 traffic〔road〕 safety ; the security of smooth traffic ¶ 교통 안전을 도모하다 try to secure〔provide for〕 the safety of traffic〔the streets〕

— 주간 Traffic Safety Week ; Safety First Week **— 지대** a traffic island

교통 위반 交通違反 violation of traffic regulations ; a traffic offense ¶ 교통 위반을 하다 violate traffic regulations ; [도시에서 보행자가] jaywalk 《미·구》 // 교통 위반 스티커를 받다 get a traffic ticket ; be booked 《for speeding》 《영》 // 과속으로 교통 위반 딱지를 떼었다 I got a traffic ticket for speeding.

— 카드 [교통 순경이 주는] 《get》 a traffic ticket **— 즉결 재판소** a traffic court

교통 위반자 交通違反者 a traffic offender〔violator〕 ; [남의 차 앞에 뛰어드는] a road hog ; [속력 위반] a speeder ; [보행의] a jaywalker

교통 정리 交通整理 traffic control〔regulation〕 ¶ 교통 정리를 하고 있는 순경 a policeman directing traffic〔on traffic duty〕

교통 차단 交通遮斷 roadblocking ; isolation ¶ 전염 구역은 교통 차단됐다 The infected area was quarantined〔boarded over〕.

— 구역 a quarantined district ; a closed〔blockaded〕 area ; a barricaded block **—선** [전염병의] 《establish》 a sanitary cordon

교파 敎派 a sect ; a (religious) denomination ¶ 교파적 sectarian ; denominational // 신교파의 교회 churches of the Protestant denominations

—심(心) sectarianism ; denominationalism

교편 教鞭 a teacher's pointer〔ruler〕; [교육] teaching
교편을 잡다 [관용] teach; teach (at a) school; be engaged as a teacher
교포 僑胞 a Korean resident〔national〕 abroad; a Korean residing abroad; [총칭] overseas Koreans
재미〔재일〕 — a Korean resident in America〔Japan〕; a Korean〔Koreans〕 (residing) in America〔Japan〕 **해외 —** overseas Koreans
교풍 校風 esprit de corps of a school; school tradition〔spirit, morals〕 ¶ 교풍을 수립하다 establish〔form〕 the traditions of a school // 교풍을 함양하다 foster〔cultivate〕 the spirit of a school // 교풍에 어긋나다 be against the best traditions of the school // 교풍을 떨치다 enhance the esprit de corps of a school
교풍 矯風 moral reform; reform of morals **—하다** reform popular〔public〕 morals
—회 a temperance union; a society for moral reform
교합 交合 sexual congress〔union, intercourse〕 **—하다** unite sexually; have sexual intercourse
⁑**교향곡 交響曲** 〖음악〗 a symphony ¶ 모차르트의 제25번 교향곡 Mozart's 25th Symphony
교향시 交響詩 a symphonic poem
교향악 交響樂 〖음악〗 symphony
—단 a symphony orchestra **— 단원** a symphonist **서울 —단** the Seoul Symphony Orchestra
교형 絞刑 death by hanging ⇨ 교수형
교호 交互 alternation; reciprocality **—하다** alternate with; be reciprocal
— 작용 reciprocal action; interaction
교호 계산 交互計算 〖상업〗 an account current 《A/C》; a running〔a book, an open〕 account
—부(簿) an account-current book **—서** a statement of account current
⁑**교화 敎化** education; culture; edification; enlightenment; [복음으로의] evangelization; [야만인의] domestication; taming **—하다** educate; enlighten; evangelize; civilize; tame; domesticate ¶ 아프리카 토인을 교화하다 civilize the wild tribes of Africa // 문제 소년을 교화하다 guide a delinquent boy aright
—력(力) educative power **— 사업** educational work **— 운동** an educational〔enlightenment〕 campaign; a drive for people's enlightenment
†**교환 交換** [서로 바꿈] (an) exchange 《for, with》; (an) interchange 《of information》; give-and-take; [물물 교환] barter; trade; substitution; [어음 교환] clearing

> [참고] **exchange** 주고받다 **interchange** 서로 주었다가 받았다가 하다 또는 같은 가치 같은 양의 물건을 주고받다

—하다 exchange〔interchange, barter, substitute〕 《one thing》 for 《another》; swap 《구》 ¶ 의견의 교환 an exchange〔interchange〕 of views // 교환할 수 있는 exchangeable; interchangeable // 교환으로 in exchange〔return〕 《for》 // 의견을 교환하다 exchange〔interchange〕 views 《with a person on a subject》 // 자리를 교환하다 change places〔seats〕 《with a person》 // 밀과 기계를 교환하다 barter wheat for machinery // 신년 축하 인사를 교환하다 wish one another "A Happy New Year" // 한미간에 문화를 교환하다 make a cultural exchange between Korea and America // 영수증과 물품을 교환하여 드립니다 We deliver goods in exchange for a receipt.
— 가격 the exchange price **— 가치** an exchange value; value in exchange **—국** a telephone exchange; a central office 《미》 **—권** an exchange ticket; a coupon **— 렌즈** 〖사진〗 an interchangeable lens **— 무역제** a barter system **— 물자** barter goods **— 사고** 〖전화〗 operating irregularity **—선** a repatriation〔an exchange〕 ship **—실** an operating room; a telephone switchboard room **— 작용** interchangeability **—재(財)** exchange goods **— 전화 회선** operator-assisted circuits **— 조건** a bargaining point **이익 —** reciprocity of benefit **재(再)—** reexchange
교환 交歡, 交驩 an exchange of greetings〔courtesies, good wishes, visits〕 **—하다** exchange greetings〔courtesies, good wishes〕 《with》; fraternize 《with each other》 ¶ 한미 학생간의 교환 an exchange of greetings between Korean and American students
—경기 a good-will match; a courtesy〔friendly〕 game **—비행** a courtesy flight **—회** a get-together meeting; a reception
교환 교수 交換敎授 [사람] an exchange professor; [수업] exchange lessons (어학 따위의)
교환기 交換器 [전화의] a switchboard
복식(複式) — a multiple switchboard
수동식 — a manual switchboard
교환대 交換臺 [전화의] a switchboard ¶ 그 건물에는 교환대가 있다 There is a switchboard service in the building.
교환성 交換性 convertibility ¶ 화폐의 대외 교환성 external currency convertibility // 교환성이 있는〔없는〕 화폐 convertible〔inconvertible〕 currency
비(非)— inconvertibility
교환소 交換所 [어음의] a clearinghouse

¶ 교환소 지불의 payable only through the clearinghouse
교환수 交換手 a telephone〔switchboard〕 operator
장거리 전화 — a long distance operator
교환자 交換子 〖물리·수학〗 commutator
—군(群) a commutator group **—열(列)** a commutator series
교환품 交換品 an exchange ; a thing bartered ; a barter ; a trade-in 《미》 ¶ 이득 있는 교환품 a good exchange
교환 학생 交換學生 an interchange 〔exchange〕 student ¶ 교환 학생으로서 미국의 대학에 가다 attend a U. S. university on an exchange scholarship
†**교활 狡猾** craftiness ; cunning ; artfulness ; slyness **—하다** (be) crafty ; cunning ; sly ; sharp ; wily ; foxy ¶ 교활한 사람 a crafty〔tricky〕 person ; an old fox 《속》 ; a sly dog 《속》 // 교활한 수단 a sharp practice ; a trick // 교활한 꾀 a sly 〔sneaky〕 trick // 교활한 짓을 하다 act craftily ; behave dishonestly
***교황 敎皇** a pope ; [로마의] the Pope ; the Supreme〔Sovereign〕 Pontiff ; [경칭] His Holiness the Pope ¶ 교황의 papal
—관(冠) the Papal crown ; the tiara **—권(權)** the popedom ; the papacy ; the tiara **— 사절** a papal envoy ; a (papal) legate ; a nuncio (대사) ; an internuncio (공사) **— 선거 회의** a conclave **— 절대권주의** Vaticanism ; curialism ; ultramontanism **— 정치** the Papacy ; the popedom **— 제도** papalism ; the papal system **—청(廳)** the Papal court ; the (Roman) Curia ; the Vatican
†**교회 敎會** a church ; a chapel ; a cathedral (대교회) ¶ 교회에 다니는 사람 a churchgoer // 교회원이 되다 join a church // 교회에 가다 go to church // 그는 나와 같은 교회에 다닌다 He belongs to our church. // 교회의 종소리가 울린다 Church bells chime.
—극 [중세의] a church play **— 미술** church art **— 음악(音樂)** church music **—학(學)** ecclesiology **— 회의** an ecclesiastical council ; a 《national, provincial》 synod
교회 敎誨 exhortation ; preaching **—하다** preach 《temperance to a person》 ; show 《a person》 his errors and exhort him to mend his ways〔to reform himself〕
—사(師) a (prison) chaplain
교회당 敎會堂 a church ; a meeting place ; a cathedral (대회당) ; [예배당] a chapel ; a place of worship
교회원 敎會員 a church member ; a member of a church ; a communicant ; [전체] the flock ; the fold ; the congregation ; the ecclesia
†**교훈 敎訓** instruction ; edification ; one's teachings ; a precept ; an injunction ; a lesson ; a moral (우화적인) ¶ 교훈적 instructive ; edifying ; moral ; didactic // 산 교훈 a living lesson // 교훈을 주다 teach ; give 《a person》 a lesson // 교훈에 따르다 follow 《a person's》 precepts // 좋은 교훈을 얻다 learn a good lesson 《from》 // 당신의 교훈은 마음에 사무쳤습니다 Your teachings have gone to my heart. // 그것은 그에게 좋은 교훈이었다 It served as a good lesson to him. // 이것은 모든 사람들이 배워야 할 교훈이다 This is a lesson that every generation has to learn.
—극(劇) a morality play **— 문학** didactic literature **—시(詩)** didactic poetry
교훈 校訓 ¶ school precepts ; a motto for school discipline
†**구 九** nine ; the ninth (제9의) ¶ 구개국 조약 the Nine Power Treaty〔Pact〕 // 십상팔구 ten to one ; in all probability
—각형 a nonagon ; an enneagon
구 灸 ① [구이] roast meat ; grill ② [뜸] moxa cautery ; moxibustion
구 區 [시의] a ward ; a district ; [구역] a territory ; an area ¶ 선거구 an electoral district ; a voting precinct 《미》
†**구 球** a globe ; a sphere ; [전구 따위의] a bulb ; [라디오 따위의] a tube ; [야구 따위의] a ball ¶ 5구 수신기 a five-tube radio (receiver)
‡**구 句** 〖문법〗 a passage ; a phrase ; a clause (절) ; a line (한 줄) ; a verse (시의) ; a stanza (일련) ; a poem (시의) ; [문구] an expression
구- 舊 former ; one-time ; ex- ; outgoing (퇴임한) ¶ 구세대 the old generation // 구사상 old-fashioned idea // 구지사 an ex-governor // 신구시장 the outgoing and incoming mayors
-구 口 an opening ; a mouth ; a window ; a hole ; a wicket
접수— an usher's window〔desk〕 ; an inquiry〔information〕 office ; a reception counter **출납—** [은행] a teller's window〔cage〕
-구 具 a tool ; an implement
운동— athletic〔sport〕 goods
구가 謳歌 glorification ; applause ; eulogy ; paean 《라》 ; a panegyric **—하다** sing the praises 《of》 ; glorify ; admire ; eulogize ; applaud ; extol ¶ 인생을 구가하다 sing the joys of life ; rejoice in life's blessings // 자유를 구가하다 sing the praises of liberty // 청춘을 구가하다 sing the praises of youth
구각 舊殼 ¶ 구각을 탈피하다 break〔discard〕 the tradition 《of》 ; shake off the fetters of old customs and manners
구간 軀幹 [몸] the body ; physique ; build ; [동체] the trunk of the body ; the torso

구간 舊刊 [서적의] an old edition〔publication, printing〕; [잡지의] a back number

구간 區間 the section 《between A and B》; a block (of railroad track) ¶ 버스 요금은 구간 40원이다 The bus fare is 40 *won* a section.
—공(工) 〖철도〗 a section hand〔man〕; a gandy dancer 《미·속》 불통 — a damaged〔disrupted〕 section 승차 — the section of a (railway) line one travels 전차(電車) — an electrized〔electrified〕 section 전 — 운임 a through (freight) rate

구갈 口渴 thirst ¶ 구갈을 느끼다 feel thirsty

구감 口疳 stomatitis

*구강 口腔 〖해부〗 the oral cavity; the mouth
—경(鏡) 〖의학〗 a stomatoscope —근(筋) the muscles of the mouth — 의학(醫學) stomatology; oralogy —암 cancer of the mouth — 외과 dental surgery — 위생 the hygiene of the mouth; dental 〔oral〕 hygiene

*구개 口蓋 〖해부〗 the palate; the roof of the mouth ¶ 구개의 palatal; palatine
—골(骨) the palatine〔palate〕 bones; the palatals —도(圖) 〖음성〗 a palatogram —선(腺) the palatal gland — 신경 the palatine nerve —종(腫) 〖수의〗 lampas (말의) 연(軟)〔경(硬)〕— the soft〔hard〕 palate

구개수 口蓋垂 〖해부〗 the uvula 《*pl.* -lae, ～s》
—염(炎) uvulitis

구개음 口蓋音 〖음성〗 a palatal (sound); a guttural (연구개음)
—화(化) 〖음성〗 palatalization ¶ 구개음화하다 palatalize

†구걸 求乞 begging —하다 beg 《one's bread》; go begging; live by asking alms; ask alms〔charity〕 ¶ 집집마다 다니며 구걸하다 beg from door to door

†구경 an enjoyable sight; an interesting view; a spectacle; an object of interest; an attraction —하다 watch (with interest); look at; enjoy seeing; see the sight〔view〕 of; go sightseeing ¶ 구경스럽다 be worth seeing〔visiting〕// 싸움을 구경하다 watch a fight// 박물관을 구경하다 visit a museum// 구경하러 가다 go sightseeing 《to *Seoul*》// 경주를 구경하다 see〔do〕 the sights of *Kyŏngju*// 연극을 구경하다 see a play; attend a theater// 구경나다 a spectacle takes place〔occurs〕// 서울 구경가다 go to *Seoul* for sightseeing// 강 건너 불구경하듯 하다 remain a mere〔an idle〕 spectator〔onlooker〕// 경주는 구경할 곳이 많다 There are many sights to see in *Kyŏngju*./*Kyŏngju* has many sightseeing attractions.

구경 九經 the Nine Chinese Classics

구경 口徑 caliber; bore; aperture (렌즈의) ¶ 38 구경 권총 a 38-caliber revolver// 구경 16인치의 포 a gun of 16-inch caliber// 대〔중, 소〕구경 대포 a large 〔medium, small〕-caliber gun

구경 究竟 [결국] after all; in the end; finally; ultimately; 〖불교〗 the ultimate fundamental
— 원리 the fundamental〔basic〕 principle — 원인 the final〔ultimate〕 cause

구경 球莖 〖식물〗 a corm; a bulb
— 식물 a bulbous plant; a bulb 《통속》

구경가마리 a laughing-stock; a byword; an object of ridicule

구경감 a sight; a spectacle; an object of interest; an attraction; a highlight 《미》

*구경거리 a sight; an attraction; an object of interest; [흥행] a show; a circus ¶ 구경거리가 되고 싶지 않다 I don't like to be exposed to public view/I don't like to make a show of myself before strangers. // 구경거리로 삼다 put something on show; make a show of

⁑구경꾼 [관광객] a sightseer; a visitor; [관객] a spectator; the audience; [방관자] a looker-on; a bystander; an onlooker; a rubberneck 《미》 ¶ 그 곳을 찾는 구경꾼이 수천 명에 달한다 People visit the place by (the) thousands. // 구경꾼들이 인산 인해를 이루었다 People gathered around, all rubbernecking (to see what happened). // 호기심 많은 구경꾼 curious bystanders; rubbernecks 《미·구》// 그 전에는 가을이 되면 으레 금강산 가는 구경꾼이 많았다 Formerly, many sightseers used to visit Mt. *Kum-gang* in autumn.

구고 舊稿 an old manuscript ¶ 구고를 고쳐 쓰다 rewrite one's manuscript

구곡 舊穀 last year's grain; grain produced in the preceding year

구공탄 九孔炭 a nine-holed (coal) briquet(te)

구관 舊官 the former governor
구관이 명관이다 관용 Better the devil you know than the devil you don't know.

구관 舊慣 old customs〔practices〕; established usages; conventionalities ¶ 구관을 고수하다 keep〔stick〕 to old customs; hold on〔fast〕 to the antiquated〔outmoded〕 system

구관 舊館 the old〔older〕 building

구관 舊觀 the former appearance〔state〕

구관조 九官鳥 〖새〗 a mina; a myna(h)

구교 舊交 old friendship; acquaintance ¶ 구교를 새로이 하다 renew one's old friendship 《with》; brush up one's acquaintance 《with》

구교 舊敎 Roman Catholicism; the

Roman Catholic Church
—도 a (Roman) Catholic

*구구 [닭 부르는 소리] chuck-chuck ; cluck-cluck

구구 九九 the multiplication table (표) ; the rules of multiplication (법) —하다 [셈] calculate by the multiplication table ; [궁리] think over ; consider carefully ; ponder ; mull ; [어림] estimate ; guess

구구하다 區區— ① [변변찮다] (be) trifling ; trivial ; petty ; insignificant ; be of little importance ; be of no account ¶ 구구한 소국 a small〔petty〕 country ; a minor nation // 구구한 이익 immaterial 〔small〕 profit // 구구한 소리 마라 Don't talk nonsense. 《속》
② [각각 다르다] (be) diverse ; various ; different ; divided ; conflicting ¶ 구구하게 severally ; variously // 구구한 보도 conflicting reports // 그 문제에 대해서 의견이 구구하다 They are divided 〔divergent〕 in opinion on that matter. /They have divided views on that matter. // 풍문이 구구하다 Rumors are conflicting. /Conflicting rumors are in the air〔afloat〕. // 그 기원에 관해서 전문가의 설이 구구하다 Expert opinion is divided as to its origin. /The experts disagree in their views regarding its origin.
③ [사소하다] (be) mean ; base ; low ¶ 구구하게 돈을 꾸어 달라고 말하기는 싫다 I should hate to fall so low I have to ask people to lend me money. // 구구한 변명 a lame〔sorry, poor〕 excuse // 구구히 squalidly ; sordidly ; basely

구국 救國 national salvation
— 운동 a save-the-nation drive〔movement〕

구규 舊規 old rules ; conventional regulations

구균 球菌 a micrococcus 《*pl.* -ci》

구극 究極 extremity

*구근 球根 [나리 따위의] a bulb ; [감자 따위의] a tuber ; [뿌리 줄기] rhizome
— 식물 a bulbous〔bulbaceous〕 plant ; a bulb 《통속》

구금 拘禁 detention ; custody ; confinement —하다 detain 《a person》 ; confine ; hold 《a person》 in custody ¶ 구금당하다 be detained (in custody) ; be held in custody ; be placed under confinement // 자택에 구금당하다 be detained in one's home ; be confined to one's own home
—소 a detention〔internment〕 camp —실 [군함 내의] the brig 《미》

*구급 救急 relief ; rescue ; first aid ¶ 구급처치를 하다 administer first aid 《to》
— 병원 an emergency hospital — 붕대 (an) emergency dressing — 상자 a firstaid kit ; an emergency medical kit —소 a firstaid station — 식량 emergency food — 신호 an SOS (call) ; a hurry call — 용구 first aid outfit — 조치 emergency measures —차(車) an ambulance (car) — 치료 a first aid treatment — 환자 an emergency case

구급법 救急法 (knowledge of) first aid ¶ 구급법을 쓰다 give first aid 《to an injured person》

구급약 emergency remedies ; firstaid medicine

구기 a small ladle〔dipper, scoop〕 ¶ 구기로 떠내다 ladle ; scoop (up, out) with a ladle〔dipper〕

구기 枸杞 〖식물〗 a boxthorn ; a matrimony vine ; a Duke of Argyll's tea tree

구기 球技 a game of ball ; a ball game
—장 [볼링장] a bowling alley ; [당구장] a billiard saloon ; [축구 따위의] a soccer〔football〕 ground ; [야구장] a ball park

*구기다 ① [옷 따위를] wrinkle ; crumple ; rumple ; crush ; mess〔muss〕 up ¶ 구겨진 종이 a crumpled sheet of paper // 구겨진 바지 crumpled trousers // 그 여자의 옷이 많이 구겨졌다 Her dress was crushed.
② [운수가] 《circumstances》 take a turn for the worst ; grow bad〔unfavorable, difficult〕

구기박지르다 wrinkle all up

구기자 枸杞子 〖식물〗 (the fruit of) a Chinese matrimony vine

구기적거리다 crumple (up) ; wrinkle ; rumple ; crush 《clothes》 ¶ 구기적구기적 crumpling ; messing up ; to〔in, into〕 a crumpled mess

구기지르다 crumple〔wrinkle, rumple, crease, crush, ruffle〕 up

구김살 creases ; rumples ; folds ; cockles ¶ 구김살 간 crumpled ; rumpled // 구김살 하나 없는 바지 trousers without a crease // 구김살 없는 미소 an angelic smile // 구김살을 펴다 smooth a wrinkle ; iron out (다리미로) // 거기에 앉지 마라 옷에 구김살이 간다 Don't sit on it, it will leave wrinkles.

구깃구깃 —하다 (be) wrinkled ; crumpled ; be full of wrinkles ¶ 구깃구깃한 지폐 a crumpled bank note

-구나 [감탄] how ; what ; indeed ¶ 참 불쌍하구나 What a pity! /Poor thing! /Poor fellow! // 참 아름답구나 How beautiful it is!

구나방 a nut ; a screwball ; a crank

구난 救難 rescue ; salvage
—대 a wrecking crew 《미》 ; a breakdown gang 《영》 —선 a salvage vessel

구난 작업 救難作業 rescue work ; salvage work〔operations〕
해공 — an air-sea rescue

구내 區內 ¶ 구내에 within the section

〔district, area〕

†**구내 構內** premises ; precincts ; a compound ; grounds ; an enclosure ; a close (사원·학교의) ¶ 무용자의 구내 출입을 금함 No admittance except on business. /No trespassing. ∥술이 취한 손님은 구내에 더 있을 수 없습니다 Customers Who had one too many are not allowed to stay on the premises.

— **식당** a dining hall ; a refectory (학교 따위의) ; a refreshment room ; a buffet 《영》 ; a cafeteria 《미》 (역·열차내의) — **전화** an interphone ; an (internal) office telephone — **전화 번호** an extension number **역** — the station compound〔yard〕 **학교** — school grounds ; a campus 《미》

구내염 口內炎 〖의학〗 stomatitis

구년 舊年 the old〔past〕 year ; [작년] last year ¶ 구년을 보내고 신년을 맞이하다 speed the old year and greet the new year ; ring out the Old Year and ring in the New Year

—**묵이** a thing several years old ; an old article

구눌 口訥 awkwardness in speech ; stammering ; stuttering —**하다** (be) awkward in speech ; stammering ; stuttering

구능 〖민속〗 the ninth of the twelve spirits invoked by a shaman

구대륙 舊大陸 the Old World (유럽·아시아) ; the Old Continent ; the European Continent (유럽)

구더기 a maggot ; a grub ; a worm ¶ 구더기가 들끓다 be infested with maggots∥썩은 고기에 구더기가 끓고 있다 The rotten meat is full of maggots.

구덥다 (be) reliable ; dependable ; trustworthy

구덩이 a hollow ; a depression ; a cavity ; a pit ¶ 비가 와서 구덩이에 물이 고였다 The rain water has collected in a depression. /The rain has formed a pool in a sunken place.

구도 舊都 an old〔ancient〕 capital ; a former capital

구도 構圖 composition 《of a painting》 ; planning ¶ 구도가 좋다〔나쁘다〕 it is well〔ill〕 composed

구도 求道 seeking after truth —**하다** seek after truth ¶ 구도심이 있는 religious-minded

—**자** a seeker after truth ; an inquirer

구도 舊道 an old road ; an old highway 〔highroad〕

구독 購讀 subscription —**하다** subscribe 《to, for》 ; take (in) ¶ 잡지를 구독하다 subscribe to a magazine∥구독을 신청하다 send a subscription 《to a magazine》

구독료 購讀料 subscription (rates)

구독자 購讀者 a subscriber ; a reader ; [총칭] the constituency (정기 간행물의) ; the audience (책의) ¶ 구독자가 많다 have a large circulation

—**층** a magazine clientele

†**구두** [단화] shoes ; [반화] boots ; high shoes 《미》 ; footwear ; footgear 《집합적》 ¶ 신사〔여자〕용 구두 men's〔ladies'〕 shoes∥예장용 구두 dress shoes∥고무창이 깔린 구두 rubber-soled shoes∥구두 한 켤레 a pair of shoes∥구두를 닦다 polish〔shine, black〕 shoes ; [시켜서] have one's shoes shined∥구두를 고치다 have one's shoes mended〔repaired〕∥구두를 맞추다 have a pair of shoes made∥구두를 신다 put on one's shoes ; wear shoes∥구두를 벗다 take off one's shoes∥아저씨 구두 닦으세요 Shine, sir ? /Give your shoes a shine, sir ? ∥이 구두는 오래 신을 수 있습니다 These shoes wear long〔well〕. /You can wear these shoes long.

— **상자** a shoe box —**코** the toe 〔point〕 of a shoe **에나멜** — patent-leather shoes

구두

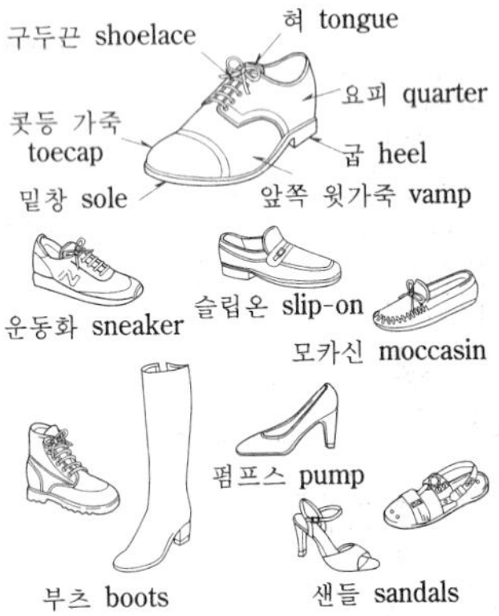

구두 句讀 punctuation ⇨ 구두법, 구두점

*****구두 口頭** word of mouth ¶ 구두의 oral ; verbal ; spoken ; viva voce 《라》∥구두로 orally ; verbally ; by word of mouth ; viva voce 《라》 ∥구두 약속 a verbal promise∥구두로 전하다 communicate 《a fact to a person》 verbally∥구두로 신청하다 make an application by word of mouth ; apply verbally 《for a position》∥구두로 보고하다 make an oral report∥그 소식은 구두로 전달되었다 The news was conveyed verbally〔by word of mouth〕. ∥나는 너의 견해를 위원회 사람들에게 구두로 전하겠다 I will communicate your views verbally to

the members of the committee.
— 계약(契約) a verbal〔parol〕 contract 〔agreement〕 — 교수법 〖교육〗 an oral method ; an oral approach — 유언 〖법〗 an oral〔a nuncupative〕 will — 전언(傳言) an oral〔a verbal〕 message — 주문(注文) an oral order — 통첩(通牒) 〖외교〗 a verbal note (무서명 친서) — 투표 viva-voce voting ; voice vote
구두끈 a shoestring ; a shoelace ; a boot lace (편상화의) 《영》 ¶ 구두끈을 매다 fasten〔tie〕 one's shoes (with strings)
구두닦기 shoe polishing〔blacking〕
—용 도구 shoeshine materials (supplies) —용 헝겊 a shoe rag
구두닦이 a shoeblack ; a bootblack ; a blacker 《미》 ; a shoeshine man ; a boots (호텔의) 《영》
— 소년 a shoeshine boy
구두덜거리다 grumble ⇨ 두덜거리다
*__구두법__ 句讀法 punctuation ; pointing ¶ 구두법이 틀리다 be wrongly punctuated
정밀〔간략〕 — close〔open〕 punctuation
구두 변론 口頭辯論 〖법〗 oral proceedings ; oral argument〔pleadings〕 ; hearing — 하다 debate orally ; plead with〔in〕 words
구두선 口頭禪 a fair word ; mere talk ; an empty slogan ¶ 구두선에 그치다 become mere talk〔an empty slogan〕
‡**구두쇠** a stingy〔close-fisted〕 man ; a miser ; a skinflint ; a tightwad 《미·속》 ; a pinch-penny ; a niggard ¶ 구두쇠 영감 an old screw // 구두쇠로 유명하다 be notorious for parsimony // 그는 구두쇠다 He is a tightfisted type.
구두 수선 —修繕 [일] shoe mending ; cobbling
구두 시험 口頭試驗 a viva voce examination ; an oral test〔examination〕 ; an oral quiz 《미》 ; [면접] an interview ¶ 지원자의 구두 시험 the (oral) quizzing of candidates // 구두 시험을 받다 be interviewed 《for the position of clerk》
구두 심리 口頭審理 a verbal〔an oral〕 trial ; hearing — 하다 have〔hold〕 a verbal trial ¶ 구두 심리를 받다 be orally examined 《by a trial judge》
구두 심문 口頭審問 a verbal〔an oral〕 trial ; hearing ¶ 구두 심문을 받다 be orally examined 《by a trial judge》
구두약 —藥 shoe polish ; (shoe) blacking (검은) ¶ 구두약을 칠하다〔으로 닦다〕 black〔polish〕 one's shoes ; shine one's shoes 《미》
*__구두점__ 句讀點 a punctuation mark 〔point〕 ; a full stop ; a period 《미》 ¶ 구두점을 달다 punctuate ; mark with punctuation marks ; put〔use〕 punctuation marks 《between, after, before》 // 구두점 없이 쓰다 write 《a poem》 without punctuation
구두질 cleaning out〔repairing〕 a Korean hypocaust — 하다 clean〔repair〕 a Korean hypocaust
구두 징 a shoe nail ; a hobnail ¶ 구두 징을 박다 have one's shoes nailed
구두창 the sole of a shoe ; a boot sole ¶ 구두창을 갈다 have one's shoes resoled 《by》
구둣골 [구두를 만들 때 사용하는] a (shoemaker's) last ; a shoe〔boot〕 tree
구둣대 a device for cleaning out hypocaust flues
구둣발 feet with shoes on ; (shoed) feet ¶ 구둣발로 올라오다 enter without taking off one's footgear ; enter with one's shoes on // 구둣발로 차다 kick 《a person》 with boots on // 구둣발로 밟다 tread 《a person》 underfoot // 구둣발에 채이다 be kicked by 《a person's》 boots
구둣방 —房 a shoe store 《미》 ; a shoe 〔boot〕 shop 《영》
구둣주걱 a shoehorn ; a shoeing-horn ; a shoe lift ¶ 긴 구둣주걱 a long shoehorn
구드러지다 dry up ; be parched ; become hard and dry
구들 a Korean underfloor heating system ; a hypocaust ; a Korean floor heater ¶ 구들을 놓다〔고치다〕 install 〔repair〕 a hypocaust // 구들이 덥다 the floor is warm
—고래 ⇨ 방고래 —더께 ⇨ 구들직장 —돌 ⇨ 구들장 —미 burned earth and ashes from the flues of a Korean hypocaust —직장(直長) a person who keeps to the house ; a stay-at-home ; a homebody
구들구들 somewhat dry and hard — 하다 (be) hard-boiled ; dry and hard ¶ 구들구들 마른 입술 parched lips // (연못 따위가) 구들구들하다 be entirely dried up
구들동티 a sudden〔an untimely〕 death from no apparent cause ¶ 구들동티가 나다 die suddenly〔meet with an untimely death〕 from no apparent cause
구들방 —房 a room whose floor is paved with flat stones ; a room with underfloor heating installed
구들장 a piece of flat stone used for flooring a room over a Korean hypocaust
구듭 painstaking service ; undergoing troubles to help 《a person》
구듭치다 [관용] undergo troubles to help 《a person》
구뜰하다 (be) tasty ; appetizing ; savory
구라파 歐羅巴 (the Continent of) Europe ⇨ 유럽
구락부 俱樂部 a club ; a clubhouse (건물) ; [미국 대학생의] a fraternity (남자) ; a sorority (여자) ¶ 구락부에 가입하다 join a club ; become a member of

a club // 구락부를 조직하다 organize a club // 연극 구락부에 가입해 있다 belong to the Drama Club
— 활동 〖교육〗 club〔extracurricular〕 activities ¶ 구락부 활동에 가담하다 take part in extracurricular activities

구랍 舊臘 last December ; the end of last year

구래 舊來 from old times ; from times past ¶ 구래의 old ; traditional ; ancient ; conventional ; time-honored ; long established〔accepted〕 // 구래의 누습을 타파하다 do away with an evil custom〔old abuses〕; get rid of bad practices of long standing // 구래의 습관을 지키다 keep to old customs

구럭 a straw network ; anything made of straw netting ; [망태기] a mesh bag

구렁 [파인 곳] a hollow (place) ; a depression ; a pit ; a cavity ; [비유적] the very bottom ; the depths ; an abyss ; the nadir ; the worst ¶ 깊은 구렁 a bottomless pit // 구렁 생활 a poverty-stricken life ; a life of dire destitution // 구렁에 빠지다 fall into a pit〔hole〕 // 불행의 구렁 속에 빠져 있다 be at the bottom of fortune's wheel // 실망의 구렁 속에 놓여 있다 be in one's darkest days ; be (sunk) in the depths of despair

구렁말 a chestnut〔bay, sorrel〕 (horse)

구렁이 〖동물〗 a big snake ; a huge serpent ; a boa (열대산) ¶ 구렁이 같은 사람 an old fox ; a tricky person
구렁이 담 넘어가듯 하다 속담 play tricks cautiously without arousing suspicion

구렁찰 〖식물〗 a kind of glutinous rice characterized by late-ripening

구렁텅이 an abyss ; a pit ; the depth ; a deep hollow ; a gulf ¶ 불행의 구렁텅이에 빠지다 sink into the depth of misery ; sink into a slough of despondency

***구레나룻** whiskers ¶ 구레나룻이 난 사람 a whiskered man

-구려 ① [감탄] ¶ 참 아름답구려 How beautiful it is ! /What a (beautiful) sight !
② [허용] may ¶ 들어오구려 You may enter. // 좋도록 하구려 Do as you please. // 갈테면 가구려 You may go if you want to.
③ [권유] I advise you《to do, that》; you had better《do》 ¶ 다음 휴가 때 여행을 가려면 경주로 가구려 If you are going somewhere on a trip next vacation, make it *Kyŏngju*.

구력 舊曆 the old calendar ; the lunar calendar ¶ 구력 6월 20일 20th June, old style // 시골에서는 아직도 구력을 사용하는 곳이 많다 The old calendar is still observed in many country places.

구련 拘攣 〖의학〗 convulsions of hands and feet

구령 口令 a (word of) command ; a verbal order **—하다** command ; order ; give a verbal order〔command〕 ¶ 구령이 내리자 전원 차려 자세를 취했다 Everybody stood at attention at the word of command.
—대(臺) a drill platform

구령 救靈 salvation ; the saving of a soul **—하다** save a soul

구례 舊例 an old custom ; a precedent ; a usage

구례 舊禮 ancient manners ; old etiquette

-구료 ⇨ -구려

구루마 a wag(g)on ; a cart ; a dray
—꾼 a wheeler ; a carter ; a drayman ; a wagoner

구류 拘留 detention ; custody ; remand ; commitment **—하다** detain ; hold〔keep, take〕《a person》 into custody ; lock up ; remand ; hold《미》 ¶ 구류 중이다 be in〔under〕 detention ; be kept in custody // 10일간의 구류에 처하다 be sentenced to ten days' detention // 구류되어 취조를 받고 있다 be detained and under examination // 공갈 혐의로 29일의 구류에 처해졌다 He was sentenced to 29 days' detention on a charge of blackmailing. // 그는 구류에서 풀려났다 He was released from custody.
—장(場) a detention house〔room〕; a lockup —장(狀) a warrant of detention
재(再)— 《on》 remand

†구르다¹ ① [데굴데굴] roll (over) ¶ 공이 구르다 a ball rolls // 나에게 행운이 굴러 들어왔다 Suddenly fortune smiled on me. /I had an unexpected piece of good luck. // 그녀에게 큰 재산이 굴러 들어왔다 A big fortune came into her hands. // 그런 것은 아무데나 굴러 다닌다 You can find that kind of thing anywhere.
② [되튀다] recoil ; kick ¶ 대포가 뒤로 구르다 a gun kicks
③ [뒹굴다] tumble ; fall ¶ 계단에서 굴러 떨어지다 fall downstairs ; fall down a flight of stairs
구르는 돌에 이끼 안 낀다 속담 A rolling stone gathers no moss.

구르다² [발을] stamp (one's feet) on《the floor》; tread noisily ; pound ¶ 발을 구르며 울다 cry stamping one's feet on the floor // 발을 굴러 연설을 방해하다 drown a speech by stamping (on the floor)

†구름 a cloud ; the clouds《총칭》
¶ 구름 사이 a break〔rift〕 in the clouds // 구름 한 점 없는 하늘 a cloudless sky ; a sky without a speck of cloud // 솜같은 구름 fleecy clouds // 구름

이 끼었다 Clouds have gathered. // 구름이 개었다 The clouds have broken〔lifted〕. // 하늘이 온통 구름에 덮여 있다 The sky is overcast. // 구름에 뒤덮인 산 a cloud-capped mountain // 구름 사이로 나타나다 break through the clouds // 구름 속에 들어가다 go〔disappear〕 behind the clouds // 구름에 덮이다 be covered with clouds ; be clouded over // 구름이 인다〔걷힌다〕 Clouds rise〔lift〕. // 구름을 보니 폭풍우라도 올 듯한 날씨다 The cloud has an ugly look. /The cloud threatens a storm. // 하늘에는 구름 한 점 없다 There is not a speck of cloud to be seen (up) in the sky. /The sky is cloudless.

—발 a strip of cloud —송이 a cluster of clouds —장 a mass〔sheet〕 of cloud —집 『불교』 a monastery in a mountain ; a mountain monastery

구름다리 a viaduct ; an overpass ; a railway bridge ; a land bridge ; a girder bridge

구릅 a nine-year-old

구릉 丘陵 a hill ; a hillock ¶ 중첩된 구릉 hills piled on hills

— 지대 hill areas ; hilly country ; highland ; downs

***구리** copper ¶ 구리를 입힌 coppered // 구리를 함유한 coppery // 구리를 입히다 copper ; cover〔coat〕 《a thing》 with copper

— 철사 copper wire〔wiring〕

구리 究理 — 하다 inquire into the nature of things ; investigate natural laws

구리 귀신 —鬼神 a tightfisted and stubborn〔obstinate〕 person

구리다 ① [냄새가] (be) ill-smelling ; fetid ; foul〔bad〕-smelling ; stinking ¶ 재래식 변소는 대부분 구리다 Most toilets of conventional type stink.

② [하는 짓이] (be) mean ; low ; nasty ¶ 제 밑이 구리다 have something on one's conscience

구리돈 copper〔brass〕 coins

구리때 『식물』 angelica

구리 철사 copper wire

구리터분하다 (be) foul-smelling ; stinking ; fetid

구린내 a bad〔foul, nasty〕 smell ; stench ; stink ; an offensive odor ¶ 구린내를 풍기다 have〔give out〕 a bad smell ; emit an offensive smell ; smell bad ; stink // 구린내가 코를 찌른다 An offensive smell greets my nose. // 그는 입에서 구린내가 난다 He has bad breath. /His breath smells (bad).

구린입 a foul mouth

구릿빛 copper color ; brown (color) ¶ 구릿빛의 brown ; copper(-colored) ; [햇볕에 타서] bronzed ; (sun)tanned ; sunburnt

***구매 購買** purchase ; buying — 하다 buy ; purchase

—값 a purchasing price —계 purchasing agent〔clerk〕 ; a buyer —과 a purchasing section〔department〕 —부〔점〕 (학교 따위의) a cooperative store ; a co-op 《미·구》 —자 a purchaser ; a buyer

구매 독점 購買獨占 monopsony

소수(少數) — oligopsony

구매력 購買力 purchasing〔buying〕 power ; the buying value (화폐의) ¶ 구매력이 증대하고 있다 Buying power is growing.

— 평가설(平價說) the theory of purchasing power parity 부동(浮動) — floating purchasing power 잉여 — excess purchasing power

구매욕 購買慾 customers' interest ¶ 구매욕을 자아내다 induce 《a customer》 to buy ; arouse customers' interest

구매 조합 購買組合 a purchasing association ; a consumers' purchase cooperative association ; a cooperative (society) ; a co-op 《미·구》 ¶ 구매 조합의 매점 a cooperative (store) ; a co-op 《미·구》

-구먼 ① [-았, -었, -겠 다음에] ¶ 그렇구먼 I see. // 큰일났구먼 That's terrible. /What a business ! /It's no simple matter. // 꽤 크겠구먼 It must be very big, I presume. // 비가 오겠구먼 I see it's going to rain. // 그래 그럼 수재들이었구먼 Really ? Then they were a talented lot !

② [-는, -던, -더 다음에] ¶ 아 눈이 오는구먼 Why, it's snowing. // 그 사람은 그 소식을 곧이듣지 않더구먼 He wouldn't believe the news.

†구멍 ① a hole ; an opening ; a chink (틈)

> 참고 **a slit** 가늘고 긴 구멍 **a slot** 돈 넣는 구멍 **an orifice** 관(管) 등의 구멍

¶ 창(窓)구멍 a chink in a paper window // 바늘 구멍 the eye of a needle // 호스의 구멍 the nozzle of a hose // 빠져나갈 구멍 a loophole ; a way-out ; a way〔means〕 of escape // 구멍을 뚫다 make〔bore〕 a hole 《in the wall》 ; [벌레가] eat a hole 《in cloth》 // 구멍을 메우다 stop〔stuff, chink〕 up a hole // 탈세할 구멍을 막다 plug a tax loophole // 기관이 파열하여 선체에 구멍이 뚫렸다 A boiler explosion blew a hole right through the hull. // 쥐구멍이라도 있으면 들어가고 싶었다 I could have sunk through the floor. /I wished the floor would open and swallow〔engulf〕 me. // 그는 구멍뚫린 회색양말을 신고 있었다 He was wearing grey socks with holes in them. // 웃옷에 좀이 먹어 구멍이 났다

Moths have eaten〔made〕 a hole in my jacket. // 이 우산은 구멍이 났다 This umbrella has a hole in it.
② [팬 곳] a hollow ; a cavity ; a pit ; [움푹한 곳] a socket 《of the eye, ear》; [골프장의] a cup ¶ 깊은 구멍이 생기다 become deeply pitted
③ [결손] a deficit ; a shortage ; a loss ; a hole ¶ 구멍을 메우다 cover a deficit ; make up a loss
④ [결함] a defect ; a blind point (맹점) ¶ 그 계획은 구멍투성이다 There are a number of holes in the scheme.

구멍가게 a small shop〔store〕

구멍새 ① [구멍의] the way a hole is shaped
② [얼굴의] the way a face is shaped

구메구메 on occasion ; at odd moments

구메농사 一農事 [소농] small-scale farming ; [농작] an irregular crop

구메밥 food supplied to a prisoner through an opening in the wall

구면 舊面 an acquaintance (of long standing) ; a familiar face ¶ 그와 나는 구면이다 We have known each other many years. /Our acquaintance is of long standing. /I have known him for a long time.

구면 球面 〖수학〗 a spherical surface ¶ 구면의 면적을 계산하다 calculate the surface area of a sphere
—각 a spherical angle —경 a spherical mirror —계(計) a spherometer — 다각형 a spherical polygon — 삼각법 spherical trigonometry〔geometry〕; spherics — 삼각형 a spherical triangle — 수차(收差) spherical aberration — 운동 a spheric motion — 좌표 〖수학〗 spherical co-ordinates — 천문학 spherical astronomy — 투영법(投影法) a spherical projection —파 a spherical wave — 항법(航法) spherical sailing

*__구명__ 救命 lifesaving ; [죄수의] clemency
— 하다 save one's life ; spare a person's life ¶ 구명을 빌다 beg〔appeal〕 for mercy〔clemency〕
—구(具) a life preserver ; a lifesaving device ; [총칭] survival equipment — 동의(胴衣) a life jacket〔vest〕 —망(網) a life net — 부표 a life buoy —삭(索) a life line —염(焰) a Holmes light 〔signal〕; a life buoy flare ; a self-ignition light —정(艇) a lifeboat —총(銃) a teargas gun

구명 究明 study ; investigation ; inquiry
— 하다 study ; look into 《a thing》; bring 《a thing》 to light ¶ 문제를 구명하다 bring light on a subject ; bring a subject to light // 원인을 구명하다 clear up〔look deep into〕 the cause 《of》 // 원인은 철저히 구명해야 한다 The cause should be thoroughly investigated.

구명 舊名 an old name〔designation, appellation〕

구명대 救命帶 a life belt ; a safety belt ; an air-jacket 《영》

구문 歐文 European language〔letters, writing〕
— 전보 a telegram in a European language ; a Romanized〔Latinized〕 telegram — 타자기 a foreign typewriter — 표기 a Romanized address

구문 舊聞 an old story ; stale〔twice-told〕 news

구문 構文 a construction ; sentence structure ¶ 문법상의 구문 grammatical construction // 불완전한 구문 defective construction
—법(法)〔론(論)〕 syntax

구문 口文 commission ; percentage ; brokerage ¶ 구문을 받다 take a commission 《on the sale of》 // 그는 구문을 받고 기계를 팔았다 He sold the machine on commission.

구문서 舊文書 an ex-proprietor's bill of sale ; a sales note of the prior owner

구물 舊物 ① [옛 것] old things ; antiquities ; antiques ; [골동품] curios
② [상속물] a hereditary article ; heirlooms ; something old and handed down from generation to generation

구물거리다 ① [벌레 따위가] wriggle ; squirm ; wiggle ¶ 구물거리며 나아가다 wriggle along // 구더기가 구물거리다 worms wriggle ② move slowly ; dawdle

*__구미__ 口味 appetite ; taste ¶ 구미에 맞다 suit one's taste ; be nice to the palate // 구미를 잃다 lose one's appetite // 그 음식은 나의 구미에 맞는다 The food is pleasant to my taste. // 운동을 조금 하면 구미가 난다 A little exercise will give you an appetite. // 그것은 구미가 당기는 제안이다 It is a very attractive〔tempting〕 proposal.
구미를 돋우다 관용 stimulate〔sharpen, whet〕 one's appetite ; make one's mouth water

구미 歐美 Europe and America ; the Occident ; the West ¶ 구미의 European and American ; Western
—인(人) Europeans and Americans ; Westerners ; Occidentals — 제국(諸國) Western〔Occidental〕 countries

구미 舊米 old rice ; rice produced in the year before

구미납 舊未納 unpaid taxes from last year ; taxes that are a year overdue

구미수 舊未收 uncollected taxes from last year

구미호 九尾狐 an old fox ; a sly dog ; a tricky〔cunning〕 person

구민 區民 the inhabitants of a ward〔district〕

구밀복검 口蜜腹劍 A honeyed tongue, but a heart of gall. /He has honey in his mouth, but gall in his heart.

구박 驅迫 ill-treatment ; maltreatment ; harsh〔cruel〕 treatment ; mistreatment ; abuse **—하다** ill-treat ; mistreat 《미》; treat badly〔cold, ill, cruelly〕; be hard on〔upon〕 《a person》; use 《a person》 ill ; turn a cold shoulder to ¶ 구박받다 be ill-treated ; be maltreated // 남편을 구박하다 mistreat one's husband ; abuse one's husband // 구박을 참아내다 endure〔bear〕 the severity of the treatment // 며느리를 구박하여 내쫓다 drive one's daughter-in- law away with abuse // 너무 그렇게 구박하지 마오 Don't be so hard on me. / Don't give me a hard time. // 여기는 구박이 너무 심해서 못 견디겠다 I find this place too hot for me. // 남편이 저를 구박한답니다 He is very mean to me〔hard on me〕.

구배 勾配 (경사) an incline ; a slope ; [도로·철도] a grade 《미》; a gradient 《영》; [지붕의] a pitch ⇨ 기울기 ¶ 가파른〔가파르지 않은〕 구배 a steep〔gentle〕 grade // 완만한 구배 a slow grade
— 구간(區間) a grade section **—자** 〖건축〗 a pitch scale **— 철도** 〖철도〗 an incline(d) railway **—표(標)** a grade 〔gradient〕 post

구법 舊法 an old〔ancient〕 law

구벽 口癖 a way of saying ⇨ 입버릇

구변 口辯 speech ; tongue ; eloquence ¶ 구변이 좋은〔나쁜〕 사람 a good 〔poor〕 speaker // 구변이 좋다 have a fluent tongue

†**구별 區別** [차별] (a) distinction ; (a) difference ; discrimination ; [분류] classification ; division **—하다** distinguish 〔discriminate〕 《between A and B, A from B》; tell〔know〕 《A from B》; tell 《two things》 apart ; divide〔classify〕 《things》 (분류하다)

> [참고] **difference**는 일반적인 말 **distinction**은 미묘한 차이 **discrimination**은 가치의 인식이 다른 것을 말함

¶ 구별 없이 indiscriminately ; without distinction 《of》 // 구별하기 어려운 indistinguishable from 《a thing》; hard to tell // 남녀의 구별 없이 without distinction of sex ; irrespective of sex // 분명히 구별하다 draw a clear〔sharp〕 line between 《two things》 // 양서와 악서를 구별하다 discriminate between good and bad books ; discriminate good books from bad (ones) // 공사간의 구별을 분명히 하다 draw a sharp〔clear〕 line between official and private matters // 선악을 구별할 수 있다 I can distinguish right from wrong. /I know right from wrong. // 너는 이제 옳고 그름을 구별못할 나이가 아니다 You are old enough to know right from wrong. // 사실과 소문을 구별하기는 어렵다 It is difficult to tell the difference between fact and rumor. // 모든 사람은 인종이나 신조의 구별 없이 평등하게 대접받아야 한다 Everybody ought to be treated alike without (making any) distinction as to〔of〕 race or creed.

구보 驅步 a run ; [군대의] double-quick ; double time ; [말의] a canter ; a gallop ¶ 구보로 at a run ; at the double ; at a canter (말이) // 구보로 왔다 He came running. // 구보로 행진하다 march at the double // 구보 Double march ! (게시)

구복 口腹 mouth and stomach ; [생계] living ; subsistence ¶ 구복지계 a means of living // 구복을 채우다 satisfy one's appetite ; eat one's fill
구복이 원수다 [속담] Hunger is the source of humiliation. /The devil dances in an empty pocket. /Need makes the naked man run and sorrow makes websters spin. /Need makes the old wife trot. / Poverty is an enemy to good manners.

구부러뜨리다 bend ; twist ; crook ; curve ¶ 철봉을 구부러뜨리다 bend an iron bar ⇨ 고부라뜨리다

⁑**구부러지다** bend ; bow ; curve ; stoop ¶ 활등처럼 구부러진 철도 a railroad line curved like a bow // 허리가 구부러진 노인 an old man stooped〔bent〕 with age // 길이 구부러져 있다 The road is winding.

†**구부리다** bend 《one's back》; stoop ; curve 《a wire》; crook 《one's arm》; bow 《the knee》 ¶ 몸을 구부리다 bend oneself forward ; stoop // 철봉을 직각으로 구부리다 bend an iron rod at a right angle

구부스름하다 (be) rather bent

구부정하다 (be) rather〔slightly〕 bent 〔curved, arched〕; somewhat crescent-shaped ¶ 그는 몸이 수척하고 구부정하다 He is slender and slightly bent.

구분 區分 [분할] a division ; [구획] a section ; [분류] classification ; [한계] demarcation **—하다** divide 《the section》 into 《two》; section (off) ; classify ¶ 우편물을 구분하다 sort mail // 그의 연구실에 있는 책은 조항별로 구분되어 있다 The books in his study are divided〔classified〕 according to subjects. // 한강은 서울을 남과 북으로 구분하고 있다 The *Han* river divides *Seoul* into north and south.
— 색인(索引) 〖도서〗 a sectionalized index **— 애자(碍子)〔스위치〕** 〖전기〗 a section insulator〔switch〕 **— 지도** a sectional map

구분도미 九分搗米 90-percent polished rice

구불구불 meanderingly ; windingly ;

crookedly ; zigzag **—하다** (be) meandering ; winding ; crooked ; zigzag ¶ 구불구불한 길 a winding path // 길이 몹시 구불구불하다 The road turns and twists a good deal.

구불텅구불텅 meanderingly ; windingly ; zigzag **—하다** (be) meandering ; winding ; zigzag

구불텅하다 (be) slowly curved〔bent〕

구붓구붓 all slightly bent〔curved〕

구붓하다 (be) slightly bent〔curved〕

구비 口碑 oral tradition ; legend ; folklore ¶ 구비로 전하는 바에 의하면 according to tradition ; tradition says《that》... // 구비로 전하다 be handed down orally〔by word of mouth〕

구비 具備 **—하다** possess ; have ; be fully equipped ; [재능 따위를] be endowed with ¶ 모든 조건을 구비하다 fulfill all the conditions ; satisfy all the requisites

구빈 救貧 relief of the poor
—법 poor laws **— 사업(事業)** settlement work **—원** a poorhouse ; a workhouse **— 제도** a relief system

구쁘다 feel an appetite

구사 求仕 **—하다** seek a government post〔appointment〕; seek an office

구사 驅使 ① [부림] driving《a person》; ordering about **—하다** have《one's men》at one's beck and call ; turn《a person》round one's little fingers ; order《a person》about ; command the service of《one's subordinates》¶ 부하를 자기 수족처럼 구사한다 He commands the service of his subordinates as willing tools.
② [자유 자재] free use **—하다** command ; have a command of ; use freely ¶ 영어를 구사하다 have a good command of English // 최신 컴퓨터 기술을 구사하다 make full use of the latest computer technology // 외국어를 능숙하게 구사하다 have an excellent command of a foreign language

구사 舊師 one's old〔former〕teacher

구사상 舊思想 old〔out-of-date〕ideas

구사일생 九死一生 a narrow escape from death **—하다** have a narrow〔hair-breadth〕escape ; have a close shave ; escape by the skin of one's teeth ¶ 멧돼지를 만났지만 구사일생으로 살아났다 He had a hair-breadth escape from a wild boar.

구산 求山 **—하다** look for one's graveyard ; look for a mountain to be buried in ; look for a tomb site

구상 求償 claim for compensation〔indemnity, damages〕; reparation ; indemnification
—권(權) a right to indemnity ; a right of demanding〔claiming〕compensation ; a claim for damages **— 무역** compensation trade **—자** a person demanding〔claiming〕compensation **—주의** a compensation system

구상 具象 concreteness ; embodiment **—하다** embody ; express concretely ¶ 구상적 concrete ; tangible ; figurative // 구상화하다 exteriorize
— 개념 a concrete concept **— 명사** a concrete noun **—성(性)** concreteness ⇨ 구체성 **— 예술** the plastic arts

구상 構想 conception ; [작품의] a plot ; a plan **—하다** map out《a scheme》; visualize《a plan》; squeeze out《an idea》¶ 소설의 구상 the plot of a novel // 유럽 합중국의 신구상 the new conception〔idea〕of a United States of Europe // 구상이 떠오르다 conceive an idea〔plan〕// 논문에 대한 구상을 가지고 있다 have a detailed plan for one's thesis // 구상이 웅대하다 be grand in conception // 희곡의 구상이 되어 있다 I've got the plan of a play in my mind. // 소설의 구상은 되어 있으나 아직 집필에 착수하지는 않았다 I have got the plan of a novel in my mind, but have not yet begun to write it. // 구상 단계에 있다 On the drawing board.

구상 鉤狀 ¶ 구상의 hook-shape(d) ; hooklike
—골(骨) an unciform bone **— 기관(器官)** 〖동물〗 a crotchet **— 회전부(回轉部)** 〖해부〗 [뇌의] the uncinate gyrus 《*pl.* -ri》〔convolution〕

구상 球狀 a spherical〔globular〕shape ¶ 구상의 ball-shaped ; spherical ; globular
— 성단(星團) a globular cluster **— 세균** 〖생물〗 a micrococcus 《*pl.* -cocci》 **— 입자** a globule ; a globulet

구상나무 〖식물〗 a Korean fir

구상서 口上書 a verbal note ; a note verbale《프》¶ 구상서로 항의하다 protest through a verbal note〔a note verbale〕

구상유취 口尙乳臭 being babyish〔boyish, puerile〕; [미숙] being green〔unfledged, callow〕¶ 그는 구상유취이다 He still smells of his mother's milk. /He is still in short pants. /His mouth is full of pap.

구상체 球狀體 a spheroid ; a globoid ; a conglobation
— 형성 conglobation

구새 먹다 become hollow ; be eaten hollow ¶ 구새 먹은 나무 a hollow tree

구새통 ① [통나무] a hollowed tree ; the empty〔hollow〕trunk of a tree
② [굴뚝] a wooden chimney

구색 具色 assortment ; an assortment of goods ¶ 구색이 갖추어져 있다 have an assortment of goods ; have a well-assorted stock
— 친구 a wide and varied acquain-

tance

구생 舅甥 ① [외삼촌과 조카] uncle and nephew ② [장인과 사위] father-in-law and son-in-law

구서 口書 ① [입으로 쓴 글] writing done with the brush held in one's mouth
② [구공서] a written confession ; a deposition ; an affidavit

구서 具書 ―하다 write 《a Chinese character》 in the square style

†구석 ① [모퉁이 안쪽] a corner ; a nook ; recess (후미진 곳) ¶ 구석 자리 a corner seat // 마음 한구석 in the innermost recesses of the heart // 구석에 앉다 sit in a corner
② [외딴 곳] a remote〔a retired, a sequestered, an out-of-the-way〕 place 〔corner〕 ¶ 시골 구석에 살다 live in the deepest recesses of the country〔in a remote spot in a country, in the back country 《미》〕
③ [면·점] an angle ; a side ; an aspect ; points ; a way ; a manner ¶ 나쁜 구석도 있다 It has its bad side 〔points〕, too. // 어린 구석이 많다 He has many childish ways. // 그의 이야기에는 다소 미심쩍은 구석이 있다 There are some points in his statement which do not sound quite convincing to me. // 모르는 구석이 없다 know every inch of (the neighborhood) ; know 《a thing》 down to the last detail
―방(房) an inner room ; a sequestered room ; a room way off to itself ―장(欌) a triangular chest of drawers

구석구석 every nook and corner ; everywhere ¶ 세계의 구석구석까지 to the four corners of the globe // 구석구석 찾아보다〔뒤지다〕 look in every nook and corner ; leave no corner unsearched // 이 땅을 구석구석 다 잘 알다 know every inch of this land // 그는 나라의 구석구석까지 여행했다 He has travelled every corner of the country. // 그 방은 구석구석 꽃으로 장식되어 있었다 There were floral arrangements in every corner of the room. // 경찰은 그 건물을 구석구석 뒤졌다 The police searched every nook and corner〔cranny〕 of the building.

구석기 舊石器 a paleolith ; a paleolithic stone implement
― 시대 〖고고학〗 the Old Stone Age ; the Paleolithic Age〔Era〕 ― 시대 사람 a paleolithic man

구석지다 (be) secluded ; recessed ; retired ; sequestered ; out-of-the-way ; be off to one side ¶ 구석진 곳 an out-of-the-way place〔spot〕 ; a recess ; a nook ; the back country 《미》

구설 口舌 malicious gossip ; heated words
―수 the bad luck to be verbally abused

*구성 構成 organization ; constitution ; composition ; make-up ; formation ; lineup 《미》 ―하다 organize ; constitute ; form ; make up ; compose ¶ 문장의 구성 construction of a sentence ; sentence structure // 문장의 구성이 어색하다 The sentence structure is awkward. // (영화 따위의) 이야기의 구성 the framework of a story // 범죄를 구성하다 constitute a crime // 구성되다 be made up〔composed〕 《of》 ; consist 《of》 // 하나의 이론을 구성하다 construct a theory // 사회를 구성하다 form〔constitute〕 society // 팀은 20명의 단원으로 구성되어 있다 The team has twenty members. // 이 논문은 잘 구성되어 있다 This thesis is well constructed〔put together〕.
― 가족 the constituent family members ― 개념 〖심리학〗 a construct ―물 a structure ; an erection ; [심적인] an edifice ― 물질 〖식물〗 structure material ―미 architectonic beauty ― 부분 〖전기〗 a component ― 분자 constituent elements ; components ; a component part 《of》 ―비(比) 〖통계〗 the component〔distribution〕 ratio ―원 a constituent (member) ; a member 《of a community》 ; [계약의] a signatory (member) 인원 ― personnel organization ; lineup 직접 ― 요소 〖언어〗 an immediate constituent 《I. C.》

구성 단위 構成單位 a constituent unit ; a group unit ¶ 사회의 구성 단위 a group unit of society

구성 단체 構成團體 an affiliated body 〔organization〕
―원(員) a member of an affiliated body

구성없다 (be) ill-becoming ; unsightly ; awkward ; clumsy

구성지다 (be) becoming ; tasteful ; elegant ; charming ; attractive ¶ 구성진 목소리로 in a beautiful〔mellow〕 voice

구성파 構成派 〖미술·건축〗 constructivism ; constructionism ¶ 구성파의 미술가 a constructivist ; a constructionist

구세 〖광물〗 porous rock-ore

구세 救世 salvation〔redemption〕 of the world

구세 舊歲 last year ; the old year ; the year passed

구세계 舊世界 the Old World ; the Old Continent

구세군 救世軍 the Salvation Army
― 교지(敎旨) Salvationism ― 군인 a Salvationist ― 사관(士官) an officer of the Salvation Army ; a Salvation Army officer

구세대 舊世代 the old generation

*구세주 救世主 the savior of the world ;

[예수] the Savior ; Christ ; the Redeemer ; the Messiah ; the Messias

*구속 拘束 restriction ; restraint ; shackles ; duress ; [감금] confinement ; detention ; binding —하다 restrict ; restrain ; bind ; be binding on ; put 《a person》 under restraint ; curb ¶ 구속이 없는 free ; unrestrained // 구속을 받다 be bound ; be placed under restraint 〔control〕; suffer restriction // 구속을 풀다 set a person free ; remove restrictions // 언론의 자유를 구속하다 restrict the freedom of speech〔press〕// 그는 일주일 동안 구속되었다 He was kept in custody for a week. // 구속된 용의자는 아직 없습니까 Any suspect in custody yet?

— 연쇄 〖기계〗 a closed chain — 적부 심사 review of legality for confinement — 해제 removal of restrictions

구속 球速 〖야구〗 《a pitcher's》 pace ; the speed of a pitched ball ¶ 구속이 있다 pitch a very swift ball // 구속을 바꾸어 던지다 change one's (pitching) pace // 구속 변화 change of pace

구속 救贖 〖기독교〗 redemption ; salvation

*구속력 拘束力 binding power〔force〕; 〖법〗 vigor ; validity ¶ 구속력 있는 의무 an obligation that binds // 구속력을 잃다 lose 《its》 binding power // 법적 구속력이 있다〔없다〕 carry〔carry no〕 legal binding force

구속 시간 拘束時間 〖노동〗 actual working hours ; portal-to-portal hours ; "portal-to-portal" working hours

구속 영장 拘束令狀 a warrant of arrest ; an arrest warrant

구속자 拘束者 the restrainer

피(被)— a person under restraint ; [전체] the restrained

구송 口誦 recitation —하다 recite ; read aloud

구수 口授 oral instruction ; dictation (받아쓰기) —하다 give oral instruction ; dictate

구수 仇讐 an enemy ; a foe

구수 응의 鳩首凝議 a conference ⇨ 구수 회의

구수하다 ① [냄새·맛이] (be) pleasant ; tasty ; good ¶ 구수한 냄새 savory odor // 맛이 구수하다 taste good // 냄새가 구수하다 smell good

② [말이] (be) interesting ; humorous ; delightful ¶ 구수한 이야기 an interesting〔a humorous〕 story ; an entertaining〔amusing〕 talk // 구수한 사람 a delightful man ; an attractive〔affable〕 person

구수 회의 鳩首會議 counseling together ; a conference —하다 get together to deliberate in a conference ; hold a conference ; counsel together

구순 口脣 [입과 입술] a mouth and lips ; [입술] 〖해부〗 lips ; labis

구순하다 (be) harmonious ; intimate ¶ 둘 사이가 구순하다 They are on good terms.

구순히 harmoniously ; on good terms ; in harmony ¶ 구순히 살다 live happily together ; live in peace〔amity〕 with

*구술 口述 an oral statement ; dictation —하다 state orally ; dictate ¶ 그는 연설을 비서에게 구술하였다 He dictated his speech to his secretary.

— 녹음기 a dictaphone —인 [공청회의] a witness 《before the National Assembly Committee》 — 증거 verbal evidence ; a signed confession

구술 시험 口述試驗 an oral examination 〔test〕; a viva voce examination ; a viva (voce) ; an oral quiz 《미》; [면접] an interview ¶ 지원자의 구술 시험 the oral quizzing of candidates // 구술 시험을 하다 examine〔quiz〕 《a candidate》 by mouth

*구슬 a bead ; a precious stone ; a gem ; a jewel ; a pearl (진주) ; a bijou ¶ 구슬 같은 like a gem ; gemlike ; pearly ; perfect // 구슬의 티 a flaw in a precious stone ; a fly in the ointment 〔amber〕; [인격의] a flaw on one's character ; a hole in one's coat // 구슬이 구르는 것 같은 목소리 a silvery voice

—덩 a sedan chair with beaded screens —백 a beaded handbag — 사탕 toffees ; toffies — 세공 beading ; beadwork —알 a single bead〔pearl〕

구슬이 서말이라도 꿰어야 보배라 (속담) Nothing is complete unless you put it in final shape. /No pains, no gains.

구슬갓냉이 〖식물〗 a kind of horseradish

구슬구슬 —하다 [밥이] be cooked properly〔well〕; be cooked neither too hard nor too soft

구슬땀 beads of sweat ; sweat in beads ¶ 구슬땀을 흘리며 일하다 work with sweat running down in beads

구슬려내다 wheedle〔cajole, coax〕 《a person》 out of 《a thing》; talk 《a person》 into doing 《a thing》

구슬려세다 wheedle〔cajole, coax〕 《a person》 into a good humo(u)r〔a good frame of mind〕

구슬리다 ① [남을] cajole ; wheedle ; dupe ; coax ¶ 구슬리어 만 원을 빼앗다 wheedle〔coax〕 《a person》 out of 10,000 *won* // 자꾸 구슬리어 솔깃하게 만들다 cajole 《a person》 into consenting to 《it》 // 남자를 마음대로 구슬리다 have a man in her pocket ; turn a man round her little finger // 아이를 구슬리어 학교에 보내다 coax a child to school

② [끝난 일을] consider ; deliberate ; meditate 《on》; reflect 《on》; ponder 《over》

구슬붕이 〖식물〗 the squarrose gentian
*__구슬프다__ (be) sad ; sorrowful ; doleful ; touching ; pathetic ; unhappy ; melancholy ; mournful ¶ 구슬픈 노래 a plaintive〔doleful〕 song // 구슬픈 이야기 a sad〔pathetic〕 story // 구슬픈 목소리로 in a sad〔sorrowful〕 voice
구습 舊習 old〔time-honored〕 customs ; old-fashioned〔out-of-date〕 practices ; former ways ¶ 구습을 지키는 사람 a conventionalist // 구습을 고수하다 stick to old customs // 구습을 타파하다 break through〔do away with〕 conventionalities
구시렁거리다 grumble ; nag
구시렁구시렁 grumbling ; nagging
⁑**구식 舊式** an old style〔fashion, type, school〕 ¶ 구식의 old-fashioned ; antiquated ; out-of-date ; outmoded 《미》 // 구식으로 자라다 be brought up in an old-fashioned way // 그 옷은 이제는 구식이다 The clothes are out of style〔fashion〕.
— 교수법 an old-fashioned teaching method **— 무기** an outdated weapon **— 사람** an old-fashioned person ; an old fog(e)y **— 생각** a moss-grown〔an old-fashioned〕 idea **— 혼인** a traditional Korean wedding ; an old fashioned wedding
구신 具申 report(ing) ; a representation **— 하다** report 《on a matter》 ; make a representation to 《a superior》 ; lay 《a matter》 before 《a person》 ¶ 의견을 구신하다 lay one's opinion 《before one's superior》 ; advise
—서 a (full〔detailed〕) report ; a representation
구실 ① [책임·임무] duty ; obligation ; responsibility ② [세금] taxes ; duties ③ [배역] a role ; a part ④ [월경] menstruation ; (monthly) courses ; [홍역] the measles ; morbill ¶ 자식으로서의 구실 a son's duties // 제 구실을 하다 perform one's function〔duty〕 worthily ; discharge one's obligation // 제 구실을 다하지 못하다 fall in〔fall short of〕 one's duty // 사람 구실을 하라 Behave as a person should do. // 대명사는 명사의 구실을 한다 A pronoun serves in place of a noun.
*__구실 口實__ an excuse ; a pretext ; a pretense ¶ 좋은 구실 a good excuse // 그럴듯한 구실 a plausible excuse ; a specious pretense // …을 구실로 하여 under color〔the cloak, the mask〕 of ; on the pretext〔plea, pretense〕 of // 구실을 대다 make〔find, invent, trump up〕 an excuse〔a pretext〕 《of》 ; concoct〔cook up〕 an excuse 《for delay》 // 병을 구실 삼아 on the pretext of illness // 아버지의 병을 구실로 회사에 나오지 않는다 He uses his father's illness as an excuse not to come to the office. // 그것은 구실에 불과해 That's a mere excuse. // 그는 언제나 이러쿵저러쿵 구실을 만들어 할 일을 하지 않으려고 한다 He always tries to shirk his duty on one pretext or another.
구실길 a trip on duty〔official business〕
구실아치 a government employee ; a person in public office
구심 求心 seeking the center
— 력 centripetal force **— 성(性)** centripetalism ; a centripetal tendency **— 성 신경** 〖해부〗 an afferent nerve ; an excitor **— 운동** a centripetal motion
구심 球心 the center of a sphere
구심 球審 〖야구〗 a ball umpire ; a chief umpire (주심)
†**구십 九十** ninety ¶ 구십번째(의) the ninetieth // 구십대의 사람 a nonagenarian
구아주 歐亞洲 Eurasia ; (the continent of) Europe and Asia
구악 舊惡 a past crime〔misdeed〕 ¶ 구악을 폭로하다 expose 《a person's》 past misdeed // 구악이 드러나다 one's past crime comes to light // 구악을 일소하다 make a clean sweep of the old evils
구악 舊樂 old〔ancient〕 music
구안 具眼 a discerning eye ; a critical talent
— 지사 a person with observant eyes ; a man of judgment ; an intelligent observer
구애 拘礙 a hitch ; trouble ; an obstruction ; a hindrance **— 하다** stick to ; adhere to ; be particular 《about》 ¶ 구애하지 않고 freely ; irrespective of // 사소한 일에 구애하다 be scrupulous about trifles // 형식에 구애되다 be particular about formality // 당신은 최초의 계획에 구애될 필요가 없다 You need not adhere to your original plan. // 비용에 구애받지 않고 without regard to cost // 그는 사소한 일에 구애되어 중요한 점을 보지 못하고 있다 He is fussy about minor details and misses the important points. // 법의 문구에 구애되어 그 정신을 잊어서는 안된다 You must observe the spirit, not the letter of the law. // 나는 번역할 때 너무 어구에 구애하는 경향이 있다 I am prone to adhere too closely to the original wording in translation.
*__구애 求愛__ courtship ; love-making **— 하다** court 《a girl》 ; woo ; make love to ¶ 그는 그녀에게 열렬히 구애하고 있다 He's doing everything he can to win her love. /He has been making impassioned advances to her. /He is chasing her like mad. 《구》
구액 口液 spittle ; saliva ⇨ 침
구약 舊約 ① [옛 약속] an old promise〔commitment〕 ② 〖기독교〗 [하나님의 약속] the Old Covenant ⇨ 구약성서
— 시대 the Old Testament era ; Old

Testament days
구약성서 舊約聖書 the Old Testament
구어 口語 spoken language ; colloquial speech ; colloquialism ¶ 구어의 spoken ; colloquial ; conversational // 구어로 in spoken language ; colloquially // 구어체로 하다 colloquialize
—문 a composition written in the colloquial manner〔style〕 **—시(詩)** a poem in a colloquial style ; a poem in simple, spoken form〔language〕
구어박다 ① [사람이] stick at home ; stay inactive in one's place ② [쐐기 따위] drive in
구어체 口語體 a colloquial〔a spoken, a conversational, an oral〕 style ; colloquial〔conversational〕 form of language ; colloquialism ¶ 구어체로 쓰다 write in a colloquial style〔in spoken language〕
†**구역 區域** a zone ; a district ; a territory ; [순회 구역] a beat ; [한계] the limits ; the boundary ; [범위] a sphere ; a scope ¶ 구역을 제한하다 set the limits // 그 경찰은 담당구역을 순찰중이었다 The policeman was on his rounds.
담당 — a district assigned〔allotted〕 to one ; one's rounds ; [경찰관의] one's beat ; one's territory (판매원의) **순찰 —** [경관 따위의] a beat ; a round **안전 —** a safety zone **위험 —** a danger zone
구역 嘔逆 nausea ⇨ 욕지기 ¶ 구역 나는 sickening ; nauseating
구역 나다 관용 have nausea ; feel sick
구역질 嘔逆— nausea ¶ 구역질 나다 feel nausea ; feel sick // 구역질 나는 sickening ; nauseating // 그 사람 얼굴만 보아도 구역질난다 The mere sight of him is quite disgusting. // 그의 태도는 구역질난다 His attitude is nauseating.
구연 口演 an oral narration **—하다** narrate orally ; recite
— 동화 an orally narrated fairy tale
구연 舊緣 old ties ; old relationship
구연 枸 〖식물〗 lemon
—산(酸) 〖화학〗 citric acid
구열 口熱 fever〔temperature〕 in the mouth ¶ 구열을 재다 take one's temperature in the mouth
구왕실 舊王室 the Royal Household
— 재산(財産) the Royal Household properties
구외 構外 outside the compounds〔premises, precincts, grounds〕
구우 舊友 an old friend ; an old pa〔crony〕《구》
구우일모 九牛一毛 a drop in the bucket ; a drop in the ocean
구운 석고 —石膏 plaster of Paris
구움일 drying〔seasoning〕 lumber〔timber〕
구움판 a lumber-drying kiln
구워지다 [빵·김 따위] be baked ; [불에 쬐어] be toasted ; [석쇠로] be grilled ; [고기가] be roasted ; [생선 따위] be broiled ¶ 잘 구워지다 be well-done ; be well-toasted // 설 구워지다 be undone〔half-done〕
구원 久遠 eternity ; permanence ; perpetuity **—하다** (be) eternal ; perpetual ; everlasting ; permanent ¶ 구원의 평화 a lasting peace
†**구원 救援** relief ; rescue ; succor ; salvation ; reinforcement (증원) **—하다** rescue ; relieve ; succor ¶ 구원을 청하다 cry for help // 구원하러 가다 go to 《a person's》 rescue
—군 reinforcements **—대** [조난자의] a relief〔rescue〕 party ; [군대] a relief〔rescue〕 column **— 자금** a relief fund **— 투수** 〖야구〗 a relief pitcher ; a reliefer ; a fireman 《구》
구원 舊怨 an old grudge ; old scores ¶ 구원을 풀다 pay off〔settle〕 old scores
구월 九月 September 《Sep., Sept.》
*__구유__ a manger ; a trough
구은 舊恩 old favor ; old kindnesses ¶ 구은을 갚다 repay 《a person's》 old favors
구음 口音 an oral sound
구읍 舊邑 an old town〔county〕
구의 舊誼 old friendship ¶ 구의를 존중하여 for old acquaintance's sake // 구의를 돈독히 하다 renew one's acquaintance 《with》
*__구이__ meat or fish roasted〔baked〕 with seasonings ¶ 갈비 구이 roasted ribs // 닭구이 fried〔roast〕 chicken // 생선 구이 baked fish // 돼지고기 구이 roast pork
구인 拘引 arrest ; apprehension **—하다** take 《a person》 into custody ; arrest ¶ 구인되어 있다 He is held in custody. /He is under arrest.
— 영장 a warrant of arrest ; a summons
구인 求人 job offering **—하다** offer a job ; seek help
—난(難) a labor shortage ; a shortage of labor **—란(欄)** a help-wanted column (in classified advertisements) **— 신청** application for workers
구인 광고 求人廣告 a wanted 《미》 ; a situation-vacant advertisement 《영》 ; a help wanted ad ¶ 구인 광고를 내다 advertise for (business〔domestic〕) help ; [신문에] put〔run〕 a want ad 《in a newspaper》 // 신문에 난 구인 광고를 보고 전화드리는 겁니다 I'm calling about your help-wanted ad in the newspaper. // 평범한 구인 광고를 적격자를 구하리라고는 생각 않는다 I don't imagine we'd find the right person simply by placing an ordinary want ad.
구일 九日 [아흐레] the ninth day ; [9일

간] nine days ¶ 음력 9월 9일 the ninth day of the ninth month of the lunar calendar
—장 funeral services held on the ninth day following〔after〕《a person's》 death
구입 購入 purchase ; buying ; procurement **—하다** purchase ; buy ¶ …에게서 물건을 구입하다 buy a thing from 〔of〕 a person // 물건을 가게에서〔현금으로, 외상으로〕 구입하다 buy a thing at a shop〔for cash, on credit〕// 새 차를 (1,000만원에) 구입하다 purchase a new car (for ten million *won*) // 싸게 구입하다 make a good purchase
— 가격 the purchase price **—권** [표] a purchasing ticket〔coupon〕; a purchase ticket **— 대금** purchase money **— 도서** books purchased **— 명세서** purchase specifications **— 주문(서)** a purchase order
구입자 購入者 a purchaser ; a consumer ; a buyer
대량 — a heavy buyer
구입(장생) a scanty livelihood ; a bare living **—하다** eke out ; make〔lead〕 a bare living
구작 舊作 one's old work ¶ 구작을 고쳐 쓰다 rewrite one's old work 《for publication》
구잠함 驅潛艦 a submarine chaser ; a subchaser
구장 區長 a village headman ; a ward chairman ; the headman of a ward
구장 球場 a baseball park〔ground〕; a stadium ; a diamond ; a ball park 《미》; a ball ground
구재 ashes and soot settled in the underfloor heating flues
구재 口才 [말재주] eloquence ; the gift of gab ; [노래 재주] singing talent ¶ 구재 있는 사람 an eloquent speaker ; a gifted speaker〔singer〕
구저분하다 (be) shabby ; filthy ; untidy ; rough and dirty ¶ 구저분한 짓 a mean action ; a shameful deed ⇨ 구접스럽다
구적 a thin efflorescent sliver from a stone〔a piece of unglazed pottery〕
구적 口笛 a whistle ⇨ 휘파람
구적 仇敵 a bitter〔sworn〕 enemy ; a foe
구적 舊蹟 a historic spot ; a place of historical interest ; remains ¶ 구적 명승지 place of note and historical interest
구적 求積 〖수학〗 mensuration
구적법 求積法 〖수학〗 mensuration ; planimetry (면적의) ; stereometry (체적의)
*****구전 口傳** information by word of mouth ; (oral) tradition **—하다** inform by word of mouth ; hand down orally ; transmit by word of mouth ; spread ; circulate ¶ 소문이 구전되었다 The rumor was spread by word of mouth.
구전 口錢 commission ; percentage ; brokerage (중개의) ¶ 구전을 받다 take a commission
— 중개인 a commission agent〔merchant〕
구전 舊典 an ancient code of law ; [고전] a classic ; a tradition
구전 俱全 perfection ; completeness ; wholeness **—하다** (be) perfect ; complete ; whole
구절 句節 a phrase and a clause ; a paragraph
구절양장 九折羊腸 a meandering path ; a winding road ⇨ 양장(羊腸)
구절초 九節草 〖식물〗 a kind of wild camomile ; Chrysanthemum sibiricum (학명)
구점 句點 a punctuation (mark)
구접스럽다 (be) dirty ; shabby ; messy ; foul ; filthy ; nasty ; mean ; low
구정 舊情 old friendship〔acquaintance〕 ¶ 구정을 새롭게 하다 renew one's old friendship ; return to one's former love (남녀간에)
구정 舊正 New Year's Day by the lunar calendar
구정물 filthy water ; slops ; sewage (하수) ; seepage from a festered wound (종기에서의) ; used wash water (세탁한 물) ; dishwater (설거지한 물)
—통 a slop pail
‡**구제 救濟** relief ; succor ; help ; aid ; salvation ; redemption ; deliverance **—하다** relieve ; give relief to ; help ; save ; deliver ; redeem ¶ 구제할 수 없는 unrelievable ; unremediable ; past salvation〔redemption〕; beyond remedy // 빈민을 구제하다 relieve the poor // 구제를 받다 receive〔get〕 relief // 남을 위로함으로 그 자신의 절망에서도 구제되었다 Comforting others redeemed him from his own despair.
—비(費) relief expenses **— 사업** relief work(s) **—자(者)** a reliever ; a savior (영혼의) **— 자금** a relief fund **— 조치** relief steps
구제 驅除 extermination ; stamping out **—하다** get rid of ; stamp out ; exterminate ¶ 쥐를 구제하다 get rid of〔exterminate〕 rats // 벌레를 구제하다 stamp out noxious insects // 사회악을 구제하다 uproot〔stamp out〕 social evils
—약 an expellent (medicine) ; insecticide (해충의) ; an eliminator
구제 舊制 [구제도] the old〔former〕 system ; the old order ¶ 구제도를 폐지하다 do away with the old order
— 대학 an university〔a college〕 on 〔under〕 the old system of education
구제책 救濟策 a relief〔remedial〕 measure ; a remedy ¶ 정부의 실업〔빈민〕

구제 the Government measures for the relief of the unemployed〔the poor〕// 적당한 구제책을 강구하다 take〔adopt, find out〕 the proper measures for the relief《of》

*구조 救助 rescue ; aid ; help ; relief ; succor ; [선박이나 적하의] salvage ─하다 save ; rescue ; relieve ; help ; aid ; succor ; [조난자를] pick up ¶ 구조에 임하다 go to《a person's》 rescue〔aid〕// 인질이 구조되었다 The hostage was saved〔rescued〕. // 익사하려는 사람을 구조하다 save〔rescue〕《a person》 from drowning // 인명을 구조하다 save a life // 큰 소리로 구조를 청하다 cry for help ; ask〔call〕 for help〔aid〕// 난파선의 선원들은 지나가던 기선에 의해 구조되었다 The shipwrecked crew were picked up by a passing steamer.
─대(袋) [고층 건물의] an escape chute ─막(幕) [고층에서 뛰어내리게 하는] a life net ─망(網) [전차의] a streetcar〔tram〕 cowcatcher ─선(船) a rescue ship〔boat〕; a lifeboat ─ 자금 a relief fund ─ 작업 relief work ; rescue operations ; [조난선의] salvage work〔operations〕 ─책(策) a relief measure ; a remedy ─총(銃) a teargas gun ; mace 인명(人命) ─《for》 saving a life 해난(海難) ─ sea rescue ; salvage

†구조 構造 construction ; structure ; formation ; make ; [조직] organization ─하다 construct ; build ; make ; fix〔set〕 up ¶ 구조상의 structural // 인체의 구조 the structure of the human body // 사회의 구조 the organization of society // 건물의 철물구조 steel construction of building // 구조적인 모순 the organizational contradiction // 구조는 간단하다 It is simple in construction. // 한국식 구조이다 It is Korean in structure〔style〕.
─ 개혁(改革) structural reform ─ 공학(工學) structural engineering ─물(物) a fabric ; 〖토목·조선·기계〗 a structure ─ 분지 a tectonic basin ─ 설계도 〖건축〗 a structural〔construction〕 drawing ─식(式) 〖화학〗 a structural〔constitutional, graphic〕 formula《*pl.* ~s, -lae》─ 언어학(言語學) structural linguistics ; structurism ─ 역학(力學) 〖건축·기계〗 structural mechanics ; theory of structure ─ 지진 a tectonic earthquake ─ 지질학 tectonic〔structural〕 geology ─호(湖) 〖지질〗 a tectonic lake 건식(乾式) ─ dry construction 문장 ─ the construction of a sentence ; sentence structure 벽(壁)─ 〖건축〗 bearing wall structure 산업 ─ industrial structure 상부(上部) ─ superstructure 심층(深層) ─ 〖언어〗 underlying structure 우주(宇宙) ─ the frame of the universe 이중〔사회〕 ─ (a) dual〔social〕 structure 표면(表面) ─ 〖언어〗 surface structure 하부(下部) ─ understructure ; [단체의] infrastructure ; [경제·토목] substructure

구조개 [굴과 조개] oysters and clams

구조대 救助隊 a relief squad ; a rescue party〔unit〕 ¶ 현장에 구조대를 급파하다 rush〔dispatch〕 a relief squad to the scene // 구조대를 요청하다 ask for a rescue party
항공 사고 ─ an air rescue party

구조상 構造上 structurally ¶ 구조상의 structural ; constructive ; organic // 구조상 결함이 있다 be structurally defective

구조 신호 救助信號 a signal〔call〕 for help ; [조난선의] an SOS (call) ; a distress signal〔call〕 ¶ 구조 신호를 발신하다〔보내다〕 dispatch〔send〕 an SOS〔a distress call〕

구조용 강철 構造用鋼鐵 〖건축·토목〗 structural steel
강력 ─ high-tensile structural steel

구조주의 構造主義 〖언어학〗 structuralism
─ 문법 structural grammar ─자 a structuralist

구족 九族 the nine generations of a family ; one's whole family〔clan〕

구존 俱存 ─하다 have one's parents alive ¶ 그의 양친은 구존하신다 His parents are both alive.

구좌 口座 an account ; a bank account ¶ 은행에 구좌를 두다 open an account with a bank
대체 ─ a postal-transfer account 대체 저금 ─ 번호(番號) the number of a P. O. Savings Transfer Account

구주 歐洲 ⇨ 유럽

구주 救主 [예수] the Savior ; the Redeemer ; Christ

구주 舊主 one's former lord〔master〕

구주 舊株 [주식] an old stock〔share《영》〕

구죽 a pile of oyster shells
─ 바위 petrified oyster shells

구중 九重 [아홉 겹] ninefold ; [대궐] the Royal Palace

구중중하다 (be) dirty ; filthy ; slovenly ; foul ¶ 구중중한 방 a filthy room

구지 舊址 ruins ; historic remains

구지레하다 (be) dirty and untidy ; be squalid ; be in disorder ; (be) filthy ; sordid ¶ 구지레한 방 a dirty and untidy room // 구지레한 집 a squalid〔sordid〕 house // 구지레한 옷차림이다 be slovenly〔shabbily〕 dressed

구직 求職 seeking work〔employment〕; job-hunting《미》 ─하다 seek〔look out for〕 a job ; seek work ¶ 구직 신청을 하다 apply for a position
─자 a job hunter〔seeker〕; an applicant《for a position》

구직 광고 求職廣告 a situation-wanted

advertisement ¶ 구직 광고를 내다 advertise〔put an advertisement〕《in a newspaper》for a (vacant) situation
—란(欄) a situation-wanted column

구진 具陳 a detailed〔minute〕statement **—하다** state in detail ; give a minute statement

구질 九秩 ninety years of age

구질구질 indecently ; in slovenly manners **—하다** (be) indecent ; slovenly

구차스럽다 苟且— ⇨ 구차하다

구차하다 苟且— (be) poor ; be in want needy ; indigent ; destitute ; miserable ¶ 구차한 목숨 an ignoble existence ; a humiliating life // 남에게 구차한 소리를 하다 beg〔plead〕for《a person's》mercy〔sympathy〕// 살림이 구차하다 be badly off ; live in poverty ; be in narrow circumstances // 구차한 변명을 하지마라 Don't make a clumsy excuse. // 그들은 구차하게 살고 있다 They live poorly〔in poverty〕./They are badly off.

구창 口瘡 a sore in the mouth

구채 舊債 an old debt ¶ 구채를 갚다 pay〔clear〕off one's old debt

구척장신 九尺長身 a giant ; a person of extraordinary stature

구천 九天 the highest heavens ; [불교의] the nine celestial bodies

구천 九泉 Hades ; the nether world

***구청 區廳** a ward office ; a district office
—장 the ward head〔chief〕; the district leader〔chairman〕; the mayor of a borough《미》 **— 직원** a ward official **— 청사** a ward office building

구체 球體 a sphere ; a globe

***구체 具體** concreteness ¶ 구체적인 concrete ; definite // 구체적으로 concretely ; in a concrete way // 구체적으로 설명하다 explain concretely // 구체적으로 말하면 to put it concretely ; to be concrete // 구체화하다 take (concrete) shape ; materialize ; put in a definite shape ; give shape to ; embody ; realize // 구체적인 예를 들다 give a concrete example // 일반론만 말할게 아니라 구체적인 대안을 제시하라 Don't give generalities. Give specifics. // 좀 더 구체적으로 말해 주시오 Be more specific./Can you be more specific?
—성 concreteness **—안** a concrete〔definite〕plan ¶ 구체안을 제시하시오 Show me a concrete plan.

구체 久滯 chronic dyspepsia ; long-suffered indigestion

구체제 舊體制 an old structure ; an old order〔system, organization〕

†**구체화 具體化** embodiment ; concretization ; [실현] materialization ; actualization ¶ 구체화하다 embody ; concretize ; give a concrete form to ; [실현하다] materialize ; actualize // 그 계획은 곧 구체화될 것이다 The plan will take concrete shape soon.

⁑**구축 驅逐** expulsion ; ousting ; driving away ; extermination **—하다** drive away〔out〕; expel ; oust《from》; rid of ; exterminate ¶ 적함을 영해에서 구축하다 clear the territorial waters of enemy ships // 시장에서 외래품을 구축하다 drive imported goods out of the market // 악화가 양화를 구축하다 Bad money drives out good money.

구축 構築 construction ; building **—하다** build ; construct
—물 a structure

구축함 驅逐艦 a (torpedo) destroyer ¶ 구축함대 a destroyer-flotilla

⁑**구출 救出** rescue ; save ; help **—하다** save《a life》; help《a person》out of《a dangerous place》; rescue《a person》from ; relieve ; deliver ¶ 승객들을 구출하다 rescue the passengers // 위험에서 구출하다 extricate《a person》out of danger // 물에 빠져 죽어가는 사람을 구출하다 rescue《a person》from drowning // 어린아이를 구출하려다 희생되다 save a child at the cost of one's life ; sacrifice oneself in an attempt to save a child
— 작업 rescue operations ; relief work

구충 驅蟲 extermination of insects ; getting rid of intestinal worms **—하다** exterminate insects ; get rid of worms
—약〔제〕 insecticide ; anthelmintic medicine ; vermifuge ; [회충약] vermicide

구취 口臭 bad〔foul〕breath ; 『의학』 halitosis
¶ 그의 입에서 구취가 난다 He has foul breath (in his mouth).
—증(症) oral odor

구치 灸治 moxa treatment ; moxibustion ; moxa cautery

구치 臼齒 a molar (tooth) ; [작은 구치] a premolar (tooth) ; a false molar

구치 拘置 detention ; confinement ; custody **—하다** detain ; confine ¶ 경찰은 그를 용의자로서 구치시켰다 The police detained him as a suspect.

구치소 拘置所 a detention house〔cell〕; a prison (for confinement) ; a tank《미·속》

구침 鉤針 a hook ; a crochet needle

구칭 舊稱 the old name ; the former title

†**구타 毆打** assault ; a blow ; 『법』 assault and battery **—하다** assault ; strike ; give《a person》a blow ¶ 구타죄로 기소되다 be arraigned〔prosecuted〕on a charge of felonious assault
— 치사(致死) assault resulting in death ; beating to death

구태 舊態 old conditions ; the old state of things

구태여 [일부러] intentionally ; deliberately ; on purpose ; importunately ; [감히] daringly ; positively ; [특히] especially ; particularly ¶ 구태여 그렇게 서둘 건 없네 There is no hurry〔rush〕. // 구태여 회의에 참석할 필요는 없다 You need not necessarily〔don't have to〕 attend the meeting. // 그렇다면 구태여 말리지 않겠다 If you insist, I wouldn't press you to stop it.

구태의연 舊態依然 **—하다** remain as it was ; remain unchanged ¶ 구태의연한 사고방식 an obsolete way of thinking

구택 舊宅 one's old house ; [전에 살던 집] one's former residence ; [대대로 살던 집] an ancestral home

구토 嘔吐 vomiting ; 〚의학〛 emesis **—하다** vomit ; throw up ; puke
— 설사(泄瀉) emesis〔vomiting〕 and diarrhea **—성 독가스(性毒—)** nausea (-producing) gas **—성 두통(性頭痛)** a sick headache **—제(劑)**〔약〕 an emetic

구투 舊套 conventionalism ; an old fashion〔custom〕 ¶ 구투를 벗다 get free from conventionalism ; be unconventional

구파 舊派 the old school〔style, type〕
— 배우 an actor of the old school **— 연극** a play of the old school ; a classical drama

구판 舊版 an old〔a former〕 edition ; [판] an old (printing) plate

구폐 舊弊 old abuses〔evil〕 ; a standing evil ¶ 구폐를 일소하다 sweep away old abuses

구포 臼砲 a mortar

구푸리다 bend ; stoop ; bend 《one's body》 forward ¶ 그는 갑자기 구푸렸다 He stooped down suddenly. // 구푸리고 걷다 walk with a stoop

구피 狗皮 a dogskin

구필 口筆 writing with the brush held in one's mouth

†**구하다 求—** ① [사다] buy ; purchase
② [바라다] demand ; call for ; claim ; request ; desire ; ask for
③ [가지고 싶어하다] look for ; seek ; want ¶ 행복을 구하여 in search〔pursuit〕 of happiness // 책방에서 구하다 get〔purchase〕 《a book》 at a bookshop // 의견을 구하다 seek advice 《from a person》 // 명성을 구하다 seek after fame // 하숙을 구하고 있다 be on a hunt for lodgings // 점원을 구하다 want a clerk // 방을 구하다 look for a room // 사전을 15,000원에 구하다 buy a dictionary for fifteen thousand *won* // 설명을 구하다 call for an explanation // 실업계는 새로운 사람을 구하고 있는 중이다 The business world demands new men.

***구하다 救—** rescue 《a person》 from 《danger》 ; save 《a person》 from 《death》 ; deliver〔extricate〕 《a person》 from 《difficulty》 ; help 《a person》 out of ; relieve 《a person》 from 《suffering》 ; release 《a person》 from 《pain, distress》 ; redeem ; reclaim 《a woman》 from 《a life of sin》 ¶ 구할 길이 없다 be helpless ; be beyond remedy ; be past〔beyond〕 redemption〔salvation〕 // 구할 도리가 없는 hopeless ; desperate ; helpless // 곤경에서 구하다 help 《a person》 out of difficulties ; get 《a person》 out of trouble // 빈민을 구하다 relieve the poor // 목숨을 구하다 save 《a person's》 life // 물에 빠진 사람을 구하다 save 《a person》 from drowning // 위기에 처한 사람을 구하다 deliver 《a person》 out of danger // 노예 생활에서 구하다 redeem 《a girl》 from slavery // 신이여 구해 주소서 Oh God, help me〔save my soul〕!

구학 求學 the pursuit of learning **—하다** pursue learning

구학문 舊學問 classical studies ; Chinese literature ; study of Chinese classics

구험 口險 a foul mouth **—하다** (be) foul-mouthed ; be addicted to ill speaking〔fault-finding〕

구현 具現 embodiment ; materialization **—하다** embody ; realize (실현하다) ; materialize ¶ 언어는 사상을 구현한다 Words embody thoughts.

구혈 灸穴 the parts of the skin suited for moxa cauterization

구혈 九穴 the nine openings of the human body 《eyes, nostrils, mouth, ears, anus, urethra》

***구형 求刑** prosecution **—하다** demand a penalty ; prosecute ¶ 2년의 금고를 구형하다 demand two years' imprisonment 《for the accused》 // 사형을 구형하다 demand the death penalty ; demand a sentence of death // 무기징역을 구형하다 demand life imprisonment 《for the accused》

구형 球形 a spherical shape ¶ 구형의 ball-shaped ; spherical ; globular

구형 矩形 a rectangle ¶ 구형의 rectangular
— 라멘 〚건축〛 a rectangular rigid frame ; a rectangular bent **— 벽돌** 〚화학〛 straight brick **—파(波)** 〚물리〛 a square wave

구형 舊型 ¶ 구형의 outmoded 《cars》 ; old-fashioned

구호 口號 a slogan ; a motto ; catchword ; a catch-phrase ; [군호] a password ; a countersign ; [구점] extemporaneous verse ; composing a poem on the spot ¶ 선거 구호 an election slogan // …의 구호를 내걸고 under the slogan 《of》 // 구호를 그치다 stop shouting

***구호 救護** relief ; aid ; rescue ; [환자·부상자] nursing ; tending ; care ; cure

— 하다 relieve ; give aid to ; save ; rescue ; nurse ; care for ; give 《a person》 a medical treatment ¶ 따뜻한 구호의 손길 a warm helping hand // 부상자를 구호하다 give aid to the injured〔the wounded〕
— 물자 relief supplies **—미(米)** relief rice **—법(法)** the relief law **— 사업** relief work **—소(所)** a medical relief station ; a first-aid station
구호반 救護班 a relief squad〔party〕; an aid station
— 천막 a medical tent **적십자 —** a Red Cross relief squad
*__구혼 求婚__ a proposal〔an offer〕 of marriage ; courtship ; wooing **— 하다** propose 《to》; ask〔sue〕 for 《her》 hand in marriage ; court ; seek 《a lady's》 hand in marriage ; woo ¶ 딸의 구혼자 a suitor to one's daughter // 돈을 목적으로 하는 구혼자 a fortune hunter ; a gold digger (여자) 《미·속》 // 돈을 목적으로 구혼하다 seek a woman's hand for money // 구혼을 승락하다〔거절하다〕 accept〔decline〕 《a person's》 hand〔suit〕
—자 a suitor ; a wooer
구혼 광고 求婚廣告 an advertisement for a spouse ¶ 구혼 광고를 내다 advertise〔put an advertisement〕 《in a newspaper》 for a spouse
구화반자 a ceiling with a chrysanthemum design on it
구화장지 a sliding door with chrysanthemum design on it
구활 久闊 long neglect〔silence〕 in writing〔correspondence〕; remissness **— 하다** neglect one's correspondence for a long time ¶ 구활을 사과하다 apologize for one's long silence
구황 救荒 famine relief **— 하다** relieve famine (sufferers) ; help the famine-stricken people
— 작물(作物) hardy plants
*__구획 區劃__ [구분] a division ; demarcation ; a section ; a compartment ; [한계] a boundary ; a limit
— 하다 divide ; partition ; mark off ; draw a demarcation line ¶ 4구역으로 구획하다 partition off 《an area》 into four districts // 행정구획상 in terms of administrative division
—실(室) 〖조선〗 a compartment **행정 —** an administrative section〔boundary〕
구획 정리 區劃整理 land readjustment ; [도시의] replanning of streets ; readjustment of town lots **— 하다** readjust the division of land ; readjust boundaries ; readjust ¶ 농촌의 구획 정리 the adjustment of partitions of agricultural land
구휼 救恤 relief ; succor **— 하다** relieve ; aid ; succor ¶ 이재민을 구휼하다 relieve the sufferers // 빈민을 구휼하다 administer〔give〕 relief to the poor〔indigent〕
— 사업 relief work **—자** a reliever ; a benefactor
구희 球戲 a ball game ; bowling ; billiards ; pinball
—장 a bowling alley (볼링) ; a poolroom ; a billiard saloon (당구장)
국 soup ; broth ¶ 국을 마시다 sip soup
국에 덴 놈 물 보고도 분다 〔속담〕 A scalded cat〔dog〕 fears cold water. /The burnt child dreads the fire. /Once hitten, twice shy/Once bitten twice shy.
국 國 a nation ; a country ; a state
국 局 [관청의] a bureau ; an office ; a board ; a department [바둑·장기] a game 《of go〔chess〕》 ¶ 1국 3과로 나누다 divide 《an office》 into one department and three sections
사무— a secretariat **업무—** the business department **편집—** the editorial department
†__국가 國家__ a state ; a nation ; a country

> 〔참고〕 **state**는 법률적, 이론적 뜻으로의 국가 **nation**은 국토보다도 그 주민에 중점을 두는 말 **country**는 「나라」의 뜻을 나타내는 가장 일반적인 말로서 국토를 뜻한다

¶ 국가의 간섭 state interference // 국가의 이익 national interests // 국가의 보조를 받다 be granted national assistance // 국가 존망지추에 임하여 at〔on the occasion of〕 a national crisis // 국가에 이바지하다 serve the country ; render service to the country // 국가를 건설하다 build up a nation // 산림 녹화는 국가 백년의 대계이다 Forestation is a long-range project of the State. // 국가를 위하여 목숨을 바친 수백만의 사람들을 잊어서는 안 된다 You must remember that millions laid down their lives for the sake of our country.
— 경륜책 statecraft **— 관념〔사상〕** patriotic sentiment ; a spirit of nationalism **— 권력(權力)** state power **— 기관** the administrative machinery of a state ; a state organ **— 기본권(基本權)** the fundamental rights of a nation **— 대표 선수** a member of the national team ; a national athlete **— 대표팀** the national 《soccer》 team **— 독립권(獨立權)〔평등권(平等權), 자위권(自衛權)〕** right of national independence〔equality, self-preservation〕 **—론(論)** the theory of the State **— 배상법(賠償法)** 〖법〗 the State Tort Liability Act **— 백년 대계** a far-sighted national policy **— 보상(補償)** national indemnities 〔redress〕 **— 복지** a welfare state **— 사업** a national enterprise〔undertaking〕

— 안보 national security — 안전 기획부 the Agency for National Security Planning — 안전 보장법〔보장 회의〕 the National Security Act 《미》〔Council〕 — 연합(聯合) a federation〔union, league〕 of nations — 자본주의 state〔national〕 capitalism — 재정(財政) national finance — 집권주의〔통제주의(統制主義)〕 statism — 총동원(總動員) a national mobilization —학(學) state science ; statecraft ; political science (정치학) — 행정 조직법 〖법〗 the National Government Organization Act — 헌장(憲章) a national charter

국가 國歌 the national anthem ¶ 국가를 연주〔봉창〕하다 play〔sing〕 the national anthem

국가 경제 國家經濟 state〔national〕 economy ¶ 그러한 낭비는 국가 경제의 관점에서 용인될 수 없다 Such wastes cannot be allowed from the standpoint of national economy.

국가 고시 國家考試 a state〔national〕 examination 《for the license of medical practice》 ¶ 국가 고시를 거쳐서 upon〔through〕 the state examination // 국가 고시를 치르다 take〔enter for〕 the state examination

국가 공무원 國家公務員 [전체] national public〔civil〕 service personnel ; government officials ; the Establishment 《영》 ; [개인] a national public official〔servant〕 ; an official in the national public service ¶ 국가 공무원의 직계 a classification of the national public service

— 공제 조합 the Government Official Mutual Benefit Association —법 〖법〗 the Government Officials Act

국가 관리 國家管理 state〔government〕 control ¶ 국가 관리의 state-〔government-〕controlled

국가군 國家群 a group of powers ; a family of nations

민주주의 — a family of democratic nations 서구 민주주의 — the Western democracies

국가보안법 the National Security Law

국가 비상 사태 國家非常事態 a state of national emergency

— 선언 a "state of national emergency" declaration ¶ 국가 비상 사태 선언을 하다 declare a state of national emergency

국가 사회주의 國家社會主義 state〔national〕 socialism

—자 a national socialist

국가 수반 國家首班 the chief〔head〕 of state ⇨ 수반

국가적 國家的 national ; state ¶ 국가적으로 유명한 사람 a person of nationwide fame〔reputation〕 // 국가적 견지에서 from a national point of view // 비국가적 unpatriotic // 초국가적 super national ; supranational

국가주의 國家主義 nationalism ¶ 국가주의적인 nationalistic

—자 a nationalist ; a patriot 초(超)—자 an ultranationalist

국거리 soup makings ; materials for soup

국건더기 ingredients ; stock

*__국경 國境__ the border ; the frontier ; the (national) boundary ¶ 국경 내〔외〕에 within〔outside〕 the border // 국경을 공고히 수비하다 fortify the frontier // 국경을 넘어서 타국으로 가다 cross the border into a country // 사랑에는 국경이 없다 Love has no frontier.

— 경비병 border〔frontier〕 guards〔army〕 ; border posts〔patrols〕 — 도시 a border town — 문제 a boundary issue〔problem〕 — 분쟁(紛爭) a boundary〔border〕 dispute ¶ 국경 분쟁을 해결하다 settle boundary〔border〕 disputes — 사건 a frontier incident — 선(線) a border〔boundary〕 line —전(戰) a border battle ; a frontier war — 지대 a border area〔strip〕 — 협정 a border agreement ; a border demarcation accord 중소(中蘇) — the Chinese-Russian border

국경 國慶 national festival〔feast〕

—일 a national holiday

국경 경비대 國境警備隊 a border garrison ; frontier guards

*__국고 國庫__ the national treasury ; the public purse ; the coffers of the State ; Exchequer 《영》 ; the Treasury Department 《미》 ¶ 국고 수입이 되다 go into the Treasury of the State // 국고 부담이 되다 be provided〔paid〕 from the National Treasury // 국고의 보조를 받다 be supported by state subvention // 의무 교육비는 국고에서 부담한다 The National Treasury will provide the compulsory education expenses.

—금(金) national funds —금 대체(代替) transfer within the Treasury ; remittance by a Treasury order — 부담 state liability ; a charge on the National Treasury — 수입 national revenues ; National Treasury receipts — 잉여금 《leave》 a treasury surplus — 예금(預金) Treasury deposits — 준비금 a treasury reserve fund — 지출 defrayment out of the National Treasury — 지출금 national treasury disbursements — 차입금 a national loan — 채권(債券) a treasury bond〔bill〕 《미》 ; a tap bond ; an exchequer bond〔note, bill〕 《영》

국교 國交 diplomatic relations ; national friendship ¶ 국교의 단절 a severance〔rupture〕 of diplomatic relations // 국교를 맺다〔끊다〕 enter into〔sever〕 diplomatic relations 《with》 // 국교를 더 한층 굳게 하다 establish a closer relationship between two countries // 국교를 회복하다 restore〔reestablish〕 diplomatic relations 《with》

국교 國敎 a state religion〔church〕 ¶ 국교로 정하다 establish 《a church》

— 신봉자 an establishmentarian **영국 —회** the Church of England ; the Anglican Church ; the (Church) Establishment **비—도** a nonconformist ; a dissenter

국구 國舅 the King's father-in-law

국군 國君 the Sovereign ; the King

국군 國軍 the national army ; the government army ¶ 국군의 날 Armed Forces Day // 국군〔한국군〕을 파견하다 dispatch the government army〔the Korean armed forces, the armed forces of the Republic of Korea〕

국궁 鞠躬 prostration

—하다 prostrate (oneself) 《before》 ; bow reverently

국권 國權 national rights〔power, prestige〕 ; the power of the state ¶ 국권을 신장하다 extend〔expand〕 national power〔prestige〕 // 국권을 주장하다 claim national sovereignty

국그릇 a bowl for soup〔broth〕 ; a soup bowl

국금 國禁 national prohibition〔ban〕 **—하다** prohibit by (national) law

국기 國基 the foundation of a nation

국기 國忌 an anniversary of the death of a king〔queen〕

국기 國技 the national sport〔art〕 ; national craftsmanship ¶ 독일에는 국기가 없다 Germany has no national sport.

*__국기 國旗__ the national flag〔colors〕 ; an ensign ¶ 한국기를 게양한 선박 a ship sailing under the Korean flag // 국기를 모욕하다 insult the national flag // 국기를 게양하다 hoist the nation's flag // 국기에 경례하다 salute the national flag

— 게양 flag raising **— 게양식** a flag hoisting ceremony **미국 —** the Stars and Stripes ; the star-spangled banner **영국 —** the British flag ; the Union Jack **프랑스 —** the Tricolor

국기 國紀 national discipline

국난 國難 [위기] a national crisis〔peril, emergency〕 ; [재화] a national calamity〔disaster〕 ¶ 국난에 처하여 용약 출전하다 take up arms for one's country ; respond to one's country's call // 국난에 처한 나라를 구하다 save the nation in a great crisis ; save the country in her darkest hour // 국난을 극복하다 overcome a national crisis // 국난을 면하다 be delivered from a national danger

⁑**국내 國內** the interior of a country ; (within) the country

> 참고 《미》에서는 **domestic**을, 《영》에서는 **home**을 쓰는 일이 많다

¶ 국내에 internal ; domestic ; home // 국내의 within〔in〕 the country ; at home // 국내 수요를 충족하다 fill up the domestic needs ; meet domestic demands // 국내를 순회하다 make a tour of the country

— 경제 domestic〔home〕 economy **— 관세** internal customs ; domestic tariff **— 무역** internal〔domestic, home〕 trade **— 문제** domestic problems〔issues〕 ; internal affairs **— 방송** the home service 《of KBS》 ; domestic broadcasting **—법(法)** 〖법〗 municipal〔civil〕 law **— 보안(保安)** maintenance of internal security **— 산업(産業)** home industries **— 상업(商業)〔통상, 무역(貿易)〕** internal〔inland, domestic, home〕 commerce〔trade〕 **— 생산** domestic production **—선** domestic〔internal〕 air service (항공의) **— 수요** domestic needs〔demands〕 **— 우편물〔우편료〕** domestic mail〔postage〕 **— 정세** the internal〔domestic〕 situation **— 제품** homemade articles〔goods〕 **— 항공 수송** internal〔domestic〕 air transportation **— 항로** a coastwise service (선박의)

국내 사정 國內事情 internal〔domestic〕 affairs ¶ 국내 사정을 감안하여 in view of the present domestic affairs ; for domestic reasons

국내 소비 國內消費 home〔domestic〕 consumption

— 물자 domestic consumption goods ; articles for domestic consumption **—세(說)** the excise (duty)

국내외 國內外 the inside and outside of the country ; home and abroad ¶ 국내외의 internal and external ; home〔domestic〕 and foreign // 국내외 사정 home〔domestic〕 and foreign affairs

국내 항공 國內航空 domestic〔internal〕 air service

— 사업 a domestic air transportation enterprise

국도 國道 a national〔state〕 road ; a national highway

국도 國都 the capital (of a country)

국란 國亂 a civil war〔strife, commotion〕 ; internal〔national〕 disturbance ; a rebellion

국량 局量 [도량] magnanimity ; generosity ; [재간] ability ; talent ; capacity ; caliber ¶ 국량이 있는 high-minded ; tolerant ; able ; talented // 국량이 큰 large-scale ; ambitious // 국량이 좁은 narrow-minded ; small-minded

*__국력 國力__ national power〔strength〕 ; [자원] national resources ¶ 국력의 고갈 the exhaustion of national resources //

국력신장 continued buildup of national strength // 국력을 기르다 build up national power ; develop national resources
국록 國祿 a stipend ; a salary ¶ 국록을 먹다 receive a stipend ; be in government service
국론 國論 public〔national〕 opinion〔sentiment〕 ¶ 국론을 환기하다 arouse public opinion // 국론을 들끓게 하다 excite public opinion ; lead to heated public discussions // 국론을 통일하다 unify public opinion // 국론에 귀기울이다 pay attention〔give ear〕 to the public opinion ; have one's ear to the ground
국리 國利 national interests〔welfare〕 ¶ 국리 민복을 도모하다 promote national interests and the welfare of the people
국립 國立 ¶ 국립의 government-established ; national ; state
— 공원 a national〔state〕 park — 과학 박물관 the National Science Museum — 극장 a national theater — 대학(大學) a national university — 도서관 a national library — 묘지 the National Cemetery — 미술관 the National Museum of Arts — 박물관 the National Museum — 병원 a national hospital — 요양소 a national sanatorium — 은행 a national〔state〕 bank
국말이 cooked rice served in soup
‡국면 局面 the aspect〔phase〕 of affairs ; the situation ; [바둑 따위의] game〔situation〕 on a (checker) board ¶ 전쟁의 국면 the war situation // 정치의 국면 the political chessboard〔situation〕 // 국면을 타개하다 break a deadlock // 국면을 유리하게 타개하다 turn the tables in one's favor // 새로운 국면에 들어가다 enter upon a new phase // 국면의 전개를 기다리다 wait for developments // 그것으로 국면이 일변했다 It changed the situation completely. /It put another face on the matter. // 전쟁의 국면이 일변했다 The war now entered on its new phase.
— 타개 a change in the situation ; a break in the deadlock
국명 局名 the name of a (broadcasting) station ; [무전의] a call sign ; call letters
국명 國名 the name of a country
국명 國命 [사명] a national mission ; [명령] a government order
국모 國母 the mother of the state ; the Empress ; the Queen
국무 國務 State affairs〔business〕 ; the affairs〔business, matter〕 of State ¶ 국무를 맡아보다 administer the affairs of state // 국무를 처리하다 transact〔conduct, attend to〕 state affairs // 국무에 다망하다 be busy with state affairs
— 위원 a state minister ; a minister of state ; a minister without portfolio (무임소 장관)
국무성 國務省 the Department of State 《미》 ; the State Department
국무 장관 國務長官 the Secretary of State 《미》
국무 차관 國務次官 an Undersecretary of State 《미》
—보(補) the Assistant Undersecretary of State 《미》 경제 문제 담당 — the Undersecretary of State for Economic Affairs 극동 문제 담당 —보(補) the Assistant Undersecretary of Cabinet for Far Eastern Affairs
‡국무 총리 國務總理 the Prime Minister ; the Premier
국무 회의 國務會議 a Cabinet council 〔conference, meeting〕 ¶ 국무 회의에 회부하다 submit 《a matter》 to a Cabinet council ; lay 《a matter》 before a Cabinet council // 국무회의를 주재하다 preside over a State Council meeting
임시 — an extraordinary Cabinet meeting 정례 — an ordinary Cabinet council
*국문 國文 [언어] the national〔Korean〕 language ; [문학] national〔Korean〕 literature ; [한글] the Korean alphabet ¶ 국문학을 전공하다 specialize in Korean literature ; major in Korean literature 《미》
—과(科) the Korean literature course
— 타자기 a typewriter with Korean characters
국문 鞠問 a trial for felony —하다 try for a grave offense
국문법 國文法 Korean grammar
국문학 國文學 [한국 문학] Korean literature ; [학문] the study of Korean literature ¶ 국문학을 전공하다 specialize in〔make a speciality of〕 Korean literature ; major in Korean literature 《미》
—과(科) the Korean literature course
—자 a scholar on〔student of〕 Korean literature ; a Korean classical scholar
국문학사 國文學史 the history of Korean literature ; [쓴 것] 《write》 a history of Korean literature
국물 ① [국 따위의] soup ; broth ; gravy ¶ 김치 국물 *Kimchi*〔pickle〕 juice // 멸치 국물 anchovy sauce ; stock made by stewing anchovies
② [부수입] an additional gain〔profit〕 ; an emolument ; a perquisite ; privilege attached to one's position
†국민 國民 [일국민] a nation ; a people ; a nationality ; [인민] the people ; the nation ; [개인] a national ; a member of a nation ; a citizen 《미》 ; a subject 《영》 ¶ 국민의 national // 국민의 의무 a national obligation // 국민의 후원 national backing〔support〕 // 국민을 계몽하다 enlighten one's fellow countrymen // 국

민에게 호소하다 appeal to the country // 주권은 국민에게 있다 Sovereign power resides with the people. // 그 소식을 듣고 온 국민이 환호했다. The whole nation were rejoyiced to hear the news.
— 가요 a popular song — 경제 national〔state〕 economy ; 《strengthen》 the nation's economy — 교육 national education — 국가 a nation-state — 대회 a mass meeting ; a national convention ; a political rally — 도덕(道德) national morality ; civic virtues — 외교 diplomacy by the people ; people's diplomacy — 운동 a national movement ; a popular campaign — 의례 a national ceremony —장(葬) a people's funeral ; a nationally-sponsored funeral (service) — 직업 보도소 a national labor guidance institute — 체육 대회 the National Athletic Meet — 총생산(總生産) gross national product 《GNP》 — 총지출(總支出) gross national expenditure 농업 — an agricultural people 상업 — a nation of shopkeepers 일반 — the general public

국민 감정 國民感情 a national sentiment ; natioinal feeling ¶ 한국에 대한 국민 감정은 좋다〔나쁘다〕 They have no enmity against〔no sympathy for〕 Korea. // 한국인의 국민 감정을 건드리다 provoke the national sentiment of the Koreans

국민 개병 國民皆兵 universal conscription
— 제도(制度) the universal conscription system 《영》

국민 건강 보험 國民健康保險 national health insurance ; National Health Service

국민군 國民軍 a national army ; the (territorial) militia ; armed people ; [독일·스위스의] Landsturm ; [국민 정부의] the nationalists ; Kuominchun

국민당 國民黨 [자유 중국의] the Kuomintang ; the nationalist party

국민병 國民兵 a militiaman 《*pl.* -men》 ; a militia soldier ¶ 국민병에 편입되다 be enrolled into the militia

국민 복지 國民福祉 national welfare

국민 생활 國民生活 national life ¶ 국민 생활에 크게 관계가 있다 be largely concerned with people's living
— 양식 the mode of the people's living

국민성 國民性 the character〔characteristics〕 of a nation ; the national character〔traits〕 《of》 ; nationality ¶ 국민성에 맞다〔안 맞다〕 appeal〔do not appeal〕 to the nation
영국 — English traits

국민 소득 國民所得 the national 〔nation's〕 income ; the annual income of the whole nation ¶ 1인당 국민 소득 the national income per head ; national per capita income
명목(名目) — the nominal national income 분배 — the disposal national income 생산 — the productive national income 실질 — the real national income 지출 — the spendable national income

국민 연금 國民年金 a national pension 〔annuity〕
—법(法) 〖법〗 the National Pensions Act

국민 저축 國民貯蓄 national savings

국민 정부 國民政府 the Nationalist Government (of China) ; the Taiwan Regime

국민 정신 the national spirit
— 총동원 national spiritual mobilization

국민주의 國民主義 nationalism
—자 a nationalist

국민 투표 國民投票 a plebiscite ; a (national) referendum 《*pl.* ~s, -da》 ¶ 국민 투표에 의해서 결정하다 decide (a question) through a referendum 〔plebiscite〕 // 국민 투표에서 가결되다 be approved in a plebiscite // 국민 투표를 실시하다 call〔hold〕 a referendum

국민화 國民化 nationalization ¶ 국민화하다 nationalize

국민 회의파 國民會議派 [인도의] The All-India National Congress Party

국밥 rice served in soup

***국방 國防** national defense ; the defense of a country ¶ 국방상 for defensive reasons // 국방의 충실 the completion of national defense ; preparedness // 국방을 강화하다 strengthen the national defense
— 경제 national defense economy — 계획 a (national) defense program ; a national security plan〔scheme〕 —군(軍) national defense forces ; defensive establishments ; [미국의] a state guard (국내 체류의) —부(部) the Ministry of National Defense ; the Department of Defense 《미》 ; the Ministry of Defence 《영》 — 분과 위원회 [국회의] the National Defense Committee —비(費) national defense expenditure — 예산(豫算) a defense budget — 5개년 계획 a five-year national defense plan — 위원회 [소련의] the Committee of State Security ; the Komitet Gossudarstvennoi Bezopastnosti 《K. G. B.》 《러》 — 장관 [미국의] the Secretary of Defense ; [한국의] the Minister of National Defense — 지령(指令) a defense directive — 지출(支出) defense spending〔expenditures〕 — 차관 [미국의] the Deputy Secretary of Defense ; [한국의] the Vice Minister of National Defense — 회의 the National Defense Council ; [미국의] the National Security Council

《NSC》《국가 안전 보장 회의》 자주 — independent national defense capability
국방 국가 國防國家 military state
고도 — a highly-geared〔-powered〕 military state
국번(호) 局番(號) 『전화』 a telephone office number ; a telephone exchange number ¶ 시외 국번 an out-of-town telephone exchange number
국법 國法 the laws of the land〔country〕; the national law ; federal law 《미》 ¶ 국법으로 금지하다 prohibit by (national) law // 국법을 범하다 violate the law of the land
국보 國寶 a national treasure ; an asset to the nation ¶ 국보로서 보존하다 preserve as a national treasure // 국보적 존재〔인물〕이다 He is a national asset.
— 건조물 a national treasure building
국보 局報 ① [관청의] a government telegram ; [우체국간의] a service telegram ② [방송국의] an official bulletin (of a radio station)
국보 간난 國步艱難 a national crisis 〔emergency〕 ¶ 국보 간난한 때에 in a national crisis〔emergency〕; when the nation's fate is at stake
국본 國本 the foundation〔basis〕 of the state〔nation〕
국부 局部 [분] a part ; a section ; [환부] the affected part ; [음부] the private parts ; the privates ¶ 국부적 local ; sectional // 국부적으로 locally ; sectionally
— 마비 partial paralysis —욕(浴) a local bath — 전류(電流) a local current (of electricity) — 전지(電池) a local battery〔cell〕 — 진찰 an examination of the affected part
국부 國富 national wealth〔resources〕 ¶ 국부를 증진시키다 increase national wealth
—론(論) The Wealth of Nations (아담 스미스의) — 조사 a census〔survey〕 of national wealth
국부 國父 a father of the country ; the founder of a country
국부 마취 局部麻醉 local anesthesia
국부호 局符號 [방송국·전신국의] an office code ; [무전의] a call sign
국비 國費 national expenditure〔expenses, outlay〕 ¶ 국비로 at the expense〔cost〕 of the state // 국비로 유학하다 study abroad at government expense // 국비를 절감하다 cut〔slash〕 governmental spending
— 유학생 a student sent abroad at state expense — 장학생 a state scholarship student ; a student receiving state scholarship
국빈 國賓 a guest of the nation〔state〕; a national〔state〕 guest ¶ 국빈 대우를 하다 accord 《a person》 the treatment of a national guest
— 대우자 a person treated as〔accorded the treatment of〕 a national guest
국사 國士 a distinguished citizen ; [애국자] a patriot ; a patriotic man
***국사 國史** the history of a nation ; a national history
— 연표(年表) a historical calendar of Korea — 자료(資料) historiographical materials
국사 國事 the affairs〔matters〕 of state ; national〔state〕 affairs ¶ 국사를 논하다 discuss the affairs of a nation // 국사에 분주하다 devote oneself to the interests of one's country ; exert oneself in the interests of one's country // 국사에 참여하다 take part in the affairs of state
—범 재판 a state trial
국사 國師 [나라의 스승] the leader of the nation ; [중] the Most Reverend Priest
국사범 國事犯 [행위] a political〔public〕 offense ; high treason ; [사람] a political offender ; a state prisoner〔criminal〕
***국산 國産** home〔domestic〕 production ; [물건] a domestic〔home〕 product ¶ 전자 제품의 국산화 localization of electronic products
— 자동차 a home-manufactured car — 자전거 a bicycle of Korean make〔manufacture〕 — 장려 encouragement of home production〔industries〕
국산품 國産品 a domestic product 〔goods〕; home products ; home-made articles ; [한국의] Korean products ¶ 국산품을 애용하다 use〔buy〕 home-made articles
국상 國喪 state funeral ; national mourning
국새 國璽 the Great Seal of the King
국색 國色 the most beautiful woman in the country
국서 國書 [국가 원수의 문서] credentials (신임장) ; a sovereign's message (친서) ; [일국의 문헌] national literature ¶ 국서를 봉정하다 present one's credentials 《to a sovereign》
국선 國選 ¶ 국선의 chosen〔appointed〕 by the government
— 변호인 a defense counsel assigned by the court ; a court-appointed lawyer 〔attorney〕; a public defender
국세 國稅 a national tax ¶ 국세를 징수하다 collect national taxes
— 부가세 a surtax on the national tax —업무 tax affairs — 체납(滯納) nonpayment〔arrears〕 of national taxes — 체납 처분 disposition of national taxes in arrears ; procedure for failure to pay national taxes 직접(直接)〔간접(間接)〕 — a direct〔an indirect〕 national tax
국세 國勢 the national power ; the national conditions ; the state of a

country ; the strength of the nation ¶ 국세 조사를 하다 take a national census

국세 局勢 the aspect of affairs ; the situation ; phase ; [바둑 따위의] the game on a (chessboard) ¶ 국세가 일변하다 take a new turn ; enter upon a new phase // 승부가 뚜렷하지 않은 국세이다 The game is anybody's guess. /A situation whose outcome is uncertain.

국세청 國稅廳 the office of National Tax Administration ¶ 국세청장 the Director of the Office of National Tax Administration // 국세청 직원 a tax administration agent

국소 局所 a part ⇨ 국부(局部)

국속 國俗 national manners and customs

국수 noodles ; vermicelli ; spaghetti
— 가락〔발〕 a single noodle — 사리 a coil of (boiled) noodles —틀 a noodle maker ; a vermicelli-press

국수 國粹 national characteristics 〔virtues〕 ¶ 국수를 보존하다 preserve the national characteristics
— 보존(保存) the preservation of national characteristics —주의(主義) (ultra) nationalism —주의자 a nationalist

국수 國手 a master〔capital〕 hand ; a national champion [명의] a great doctor ; an excellent physician

국수맨드라미 『식물』 a kind of cockscomb

국숫물 noodle broth

국숫집 [국수 빼는] a noodle factory ; [식당] a noodle shop〔restaurant〕

국시 國是 a national〔state〕 policy ¶ 국시를 정하다 fix〔formulate〕 a national policy ; orientate a government policy // 그 나라는 반공을 국시로 하고 있다 The country takes an anti-communist line.

국악 國樂 national classical music ; Korean classical music ¶ 국립 국악원 the National Classical Music Institute

†국어 國語 [언어] a language ; [자국어] one's mother tongue ; the national 〔native〕 language ; [한국어] the Korean language ; Korean ¶ 2개 국어의 bilingual // 수개 국어를 말하는 사람 a multilingual person ; a polyglot // 제2의 국어 one's second language // 수개 국어로 번역되다 be translated into several languages // 그는 수개 국어에 능통하다 He has a free command of several languages.
— 개량(改良) the language reform — 교사 a teacher of Korean — 독본 (讀本) a Korean reader — 문제 the language question〔problem〕 — 사전 a Korean language dictionary — 심의회 the National Language Deliberation Council —학 the study of the national language —학사 history of the study of the national language

국영 國營 state operation〔management〕 —하다 nationalize 《railways》 ; place under government〔state〕 management ¶ 국영의 state operated
— 기업 state〔national〕 enterprise ; a government enterprise〔undertaking〕 — 농장 a state(-run) farm ; [소련의] a sovkhoz〔sovkhos〕 — 방송국 a government-run broadcasting station

국영화 國營化 nationalization —하다 nationalize ; place (railroads) under government〔state〕 management

국왕 國王 a king ; a monarch ; a sovereign ; a ruler

국외 局外 the outside ¶ 국외의 outside ; external // 국외에 서다 stand outside ; keep aloof 《from》 // 국외에서 관찰하다 observe from the outside
—자 an outsider ; a bystander ; an onlooker — 중립 neutrality ; neutralism

*국외 國外 ¶ 국외로 outside〔out of〕 the country ; abroad ; overseas // 국외로 추방하다 banish〔deport, expel, exile〕 《a person》 from the country ; expatriate ; ostracize 《a person》 // 국외로 추방되다 be expelled from the country
— 발전 overseas expansion — 우편 foreign mail — 추방 deportation — 추방자 an expellee

국욕 國辱 a national disgrace〔humiliation〕 ; a disgrace to the nation

국운 國運 national fortunes〔destinies〕 ; the fate of a country ¶ 국운의 성쇠 the prosperity and decline of a country // 국운을 걸다 stake the national destiny // 국운이 기울어졌다 Fortune deserted the country.

국원 局員 the staff of a bureau (전원) ; a member of a bureau (한 사람)

국위 國威 national prestige〔glory, dignity, honor, power〕 ¶ 국위에 관한 문제 a point of national honor ; a matter of national prestige // 국위를 선양하다 enhance〔heighten〕 national glory ; exalt 〔raise〕 the national prestige // 국위를 손상시키다 compromise〔impair, affect〕 the national dignity ; spot the national prestige

국유 國有 state〔government〕 ownership ; nationalization (국유화) ¶ 국유의 state ; state〔government〕-owned // 기간 산업의 국유화 the nationalization of key industries // 국유화하다 nationalize 《railroads》 ; make 《a thing》 a national possession // 한국의 철도는 대부분 국유이다 Most of the railways in Korea are state-owned.
—림 a state〔national〕 forest —주의(主義) the principle of state ownership — 철도 a government〔state〕 railway 토지 — the nationalization of land ; state ownership of land

국유 재산 國有財産 national〔state〕 property〔resources〕 ¶ 국유 재산법 the National Property Act
국유지 國有地 state〔national〕 land ; a state demesne ; state-owned land
국으로 within one's limitations ; suitable to one's own ability ¶ 국으로 가만히 있다 keep one's place ; stick to〔stay with〕 what one can do
국은 國恩 favors bestowed by one's country ¶ 국은에 보답하다 repay what one owes to one's country
국음 國音 standard national pronunciation ; Korean pronunciation (한국의)
국익 國益 national interests ¶ 국익을 우선하다 give priority to national interests
***국자** a ladle ; a dipper ; a scoop ¶ 국자로 국을 푸다 dip up〔ladle〕 soup
국자 國字 [한 나라의] the national script ; [한국의] Korean characters
국장 局長 the director of a bureau
국장 國章 the national emblem
국장 國葬 a state〔national〕 funeral **—하다** accord 《a person》 a national funeral ; hold a state funeral 《for a person》; inter 《a person》 at state expense
국재 國災 a national disaster〔calamity〕
국적 國賊 a traitor 《to the country》; a rebel ; an insurgent ¶ 국적이라고 비난하다 call 《a person》 a traitor ; call 《a person》 down as a traitor
‡국적 國籍 nationality ; citizenship (미) ¶ 국적 불명의 비행기 a plane of unknown nationality // 국적 이탈 renunciation of nationality // 국적 상실 loss of nationality ; denationalization // 국적 변경 change of nationality // 국적을 속이다 disguise one's nationality // 국적을 취득하다 acquire citizenship // 국적을 박탈당하다 be deprived〔stripped〕 of one's nationality // 그는 한국 국적을 취득했다 He was naturalized in Korea.
—법(法) 〖법〗 the Korean Nationality Act **— 복귀(復歸)** reinstatement of citizenship **— 불명기(不明機)** an unidentified〔an undetermined〕 plane ; a plane of unknown nationality ; a bogy 《군·속》 **— 불명선(不明船)** a vessel of unknown nationality **— 상실** denationalization ; loss of nationality ; expatriation (외국귀화) **— 상실자** a person who has lost his nationality ; a denationalized person **— 포기(抛棄)** renunciation of nationality〔citizenship〕 **무(無)—자(者)** a stateless person **선박(船舶) — 증서(證書)** a certificate of a ship's nationality **영(英)—선(船)** a ship of British registry **이중(二重) —** dual〔double〕 nationality **이중(二重) —자(者)** a person of dual〔double〕 nationality
국전 國典 [법전] the national code; [의식] a state ceremony
국전 國展 the National Art Exhibition ; an art exhibition sponsored by the state
국정 國政 national administration ; government ; [국무] affairs of state ¶ 국정에 참여하다 participate in administration // 국정을 관장하다 administer the affairs of state ; assume the reins of government // 국정을 운영하다 conduct〔administrate〕 state affairs
— 자문 회의 the Advisory Council on State Affairs **— 조사권** the parliamentary right to investigate ¶ 국정 조사권을 발동하다 invoke the parliamentary right to investigate
국정 國定 government authorization ¶ 국정의 statutory ; authorized by the state
— 교과서 state books ; school books compiled by the state
국정 國情 the conditions of a country ; the state of affairs in a country ¶ 중국의 국정에 어둡다〔밝다〕 be ignorant of〔well informed of, posted in〕 Chinese affairs // 친히 국정을 시찰하다 personally inspect the actual condition of a country // 그것은 한국의 국정에 맞지 않는다 It is against the customs of Korea. /It does not harmonize with the actual condition of Korea.
국정 감사 國政監査 inspection of the administration〔government offices〕 conducted by the National Assembly ¶ 국정 감사를 실시하다 inspect the government offices ; conduct inspecting of the government offices
—권(權) authority to inspect the government offices **—반(班)** a team of the National Assemblymen for inspection of the administration affairs
†국제 國際 ¶ 국제적 international ; world ; universal ; cosmopolitan // 국제적으로 internationally ; universally // 국제적 견지 an international point of view // 국제간의 분규 international complications〔disputes〕 // 국제적인 명성을 얻다 win an international reputation // 국제 협조의 정신을 기르다 cultivate the spirit of international cooperation // 국제화하다 internationalize ; become international // 그는 국제적으로 알려져 있다 He is internationally known. // 국제 감각을 익히다 acquire a cosmopolitan outlook // 국제 결혼을 하다 marry a person of a different nationality
— 가격 an international price **— 개발** international development **— 결제 은행** the Bank of International Settlements **— 경기** an international game〔match〕 **— 경쟁력** international competitive power **— 경제** international economy〔economics〕 **— 공법(公法)** 〖법〗 public international law ; the law of nations —

공산당 Comintern ; the Communist International — 공항 an international airport — 관계 international relations — 관례 (an) international usage — 교류 international exchange — 교섭 international negotiations — 금융 공사 the International Development Association 《IDA》 — 기관(機關) an international body — 노동 기구 the International Labor Organization 《ILO》 — 단위 『생물·면역』 an international unit 《IU, I. U.》 — 단체 an international organization — 대차(貸借) international loans — 도덕(道德) international morality〔morals〕 — 도시(都市) a cosmopolitan city — 무선 전신 an international radio〔wireless〕 service — 민간 항공 기구 the International Civil Aviation Organization 《ICAO》 — 박람회 a world's fair ; an international exposition 〔exhibition〕 — 방송 international broadcasting ; an international broadcast (1회의) — 부흥 개발 은행 the International Bank for Reconstruction and Development 《IBRD》 —사법(私法) 『법』 private international law ; the conflict of law — 사법 재판소 the International Court of Justice —선 international lines — 시장 an international market — 신문 편집자 협회 the International Press Institute 《IPI》 — 신의(信義) international fidelity — 아마추어 무선 연맹 the International Amateur Radio Union 《IARU》 — 에너지 기관 the International Energy Agency 《IEA》 — 여행업자 연맹 the International Federation of Travel Agents 《IFTA》 — 연맹 the League of Nations — 영화제 an international film festival — 음표 문자 the International Phonetic Alphabet 《IPA》 — 의례 international etiquette — 의회 연맹 the Inter-Parliamentary Union 《IPU》 — 재단 an international syndicate〔consortium〕 — 저작권(著作權) international copyright — 전화 an international telephone call — 정세 the international〔world〕 situation — 정치 international politics ☞ 《p. 294》 — 질서 an international order — 친선 an international good will — 투자 international investment — 펜 클럽 the international association of Poets, Playwrights, Editors, Essayists, and Novelists 《P. E. N.》 — 항공 수송 협회 the International Air Transport Association 《IATA》 — 해상 물품 운송법 『법』 the International Carriage of Goods by Sea Act — 해양법(海洋法) 『법』 the international law of the sea —환(換) international exchange — 회의 an international conference〔congress〕

국제 경찰군 國際警察軍 an international police force

국제 기능 올림픽 國際技能— the International Vocational Training Competition 《IVTC》 ; the International Youth Skill Olympics 《IYSO》 ; the International Skill Contest

국제 사회 國際社會 international society ; the community of nations ¶ 국제 사회 속의 일원이 되다 join the family of nations

국제 수지 國際收支 『경제』 the international balance of payments ; international payments ¶ 국제 수지 불균형을 시정하다 correct the imbalance of international payments

***국제 연합 國際聯合** the United Nations 《U. N.》 ⇨ 유엔

— 가입(加入) 《the Chinese claim to》 membership of the United Nations — 가입국(加入國) a member of the United Nations — 교육 과학 문화 기구 the United Nations Educational, Scientific and Cultural Organization 《UNESCO》 —기(旗) the United Nations Emblem〔flag〕 — 긴급군(緊急軍) the United Nations Emergency Forces 《UNEF》 — 무역 개발 회의 the United Nations Conference on Trade and Development 《UNCTAD》 — 본부 the United Nations〔UN〕 Headquarters — 식량 농업 기구 the United Nations Food and Agriculture Organization 《FAO》 — 아동기금〔유니세프〕 the United Nations (International) Children's (Emergency) Fund 《UNICEF》 — 안전 보장 이사회 the United Nations Security Council — 원자력 위원회 the United Nations Atomic Energy Commission — 이사국(理事國) a member of the Council of the United Nations —일(日) United Nations Day ; UN Day — 정보국(情報局) the United Nations Information Office — 총회 the United Nations General Assembly — 파견군 the United Nations expeditionary forces — 평화 유지군 the United Nations Peacekeeping Force — 한국(韓國) 대표 (a member of) the Korean delegation to the UN — 헌장(憲章) the Charter of the United Nations ; the United Nations〔UN〕 Charter — 환경 계획 the United Nations Environment Program 《UNEP》 — 회의 the United Nations Congress

국지 局地 a locality ; a limited region 〔area〕 ¶ 국지적 local // 국지적 해결 settlement on the spot ; regional settlement

—전(쟁) limited warfare ; a local war — 해결(解決) localization 《of a disturbance》 —화(化) localization

국채 國債 〔부채〕 a national debt ; 〔공채〕 a national loan ; 〔증권〕 a government bond ¶ 국채를 모집하다

국제 정치

① 국가 (state)

자유 세계 the Free World [the f~ w~] **공산(주의) 세계** the Communist World [the c~ w~] **사회주의 세계** the Socialist World [the s~ w~] **독립국** independent country **주권국** sovereign country **공화국** republic **단일민족국가** single-nation state **복수민족국가** multination state; multiracial state **대국** big power **초대국(超大國)** super power **소국** minor power **위성국** satellite (country) **미국 주정부(州政府)** state government **연방정부** Federal government **영연방(英聯邦)** the British Commonwealth (of Nations) **통일국가** unified country **분열국가** divided country **소국난립(小國亂立)** Balkanization **종주국** suzerain **완충국(緩衝國)** buffer state **완충지대** buffer area [zone] **제 3세력** third force **망명** exile; defection 망명하다 exile; go into exile; defect **망명자** exile; defector; émigré **난민** refugee **선상난민〔보트피플〕** boat people 《베트남 난민》 **근린적대국(近隣敵對國)** confrontation states **내정권(內政權) 부여** devolution **유로커뮤니즘** Eurocommunism 《서유럽 공산당의 자유·민주·자주 노선》 **선진국** developed country **신흥공업국** newly industrializing country 《NIC》 **개발도상국** developing country **미개발국** undeveloped country

② 외교정책 (foreign policy, diplomacy)

대외정책 foreign [diplomatic] policy; foreign relations **강경 대외정책** tough [hard-nosed] foreign policy **유연 대외정책** flexible [soft] foreign policy **굴욕외교** humiliating diplomacy **평화외교** peaceful diplomacy; peace offensive **포함외교(砲艦外交)** gunboat diplomacy **협박외교** warmongering; saber-rattling; blackmail **힘의 외교** power diplomacy **힘의 균형** balance of power; power balance **인권외교** human rights diplomacy **왕복외교** shuttle diplomacy 《제3국의 중재자가 몇 번이고 왕복하여 문제를 조정, 해결하는 것》 **경제외교** economic diplomacy **전방위외교** omnidirectional diplomacy **등거리외교** equidistant diplomacy **극단(極端) 외교** brinkmanship **중립주의** neutralism **중립외교** neutral diplomacy **확대주의** expansionism **확대정책** expansionist policy **불확대정책** non-expansionist policy; retrenchment **유화정책(宥和政策)** appeasement (policy) **고립주의** isolationism **매파(派)** the hawks **비둘기파(派)** the doves
경제보복 economic retaliation **경제단교(經濟斷交)** break off economic relations [ties] **경제봉쇄** economic blockade **경제제재** economic sanction **봉쇄정책** containment policy **반격정책** rollback policy **권력획득경쟁** power game **회색지대(灰色地帶)** grey zone
동맹 alliance; union; league; association; block; front **동맹국** ally **비동맹국** non-allied country **우호국** friendly country [power] **중립국** neutral country [power] **내정간섭** foreign intervention in domestic affairs **부전보장(不戰保障)** non-belligerency guaranty

③ 외교관 (diplomat)

사절단 mission **평화사절** peace mission **대사** ambassador **주한미국대사** the American ambassador to Korea **전권대사(全權大使)** an ambassador plenipotentiary **특명전권대사** an ambassador extraordinary and plenipotentiary
특사 special representative; emissary; special envoy **대통령특사** presidential envoy **대리 대사[공사]** chargé d'affaires / a.i. (=ad interim)
대사관 embassy **대사관부(附) 육군 무관** military attaché **대사관 공보관** press attaché [officer] **영사** consul **영사관** consulate **영사관원** consular staff 《총칭적》 **공사** minister **공사관** legation **1등서기관** first secretary
소환(召還)하다 recall; call back [home, in] **아그레망** agreement; agrément **신임장** credentials 《보통 복수형으로 쓰임》 ¶ 신임장을 제정하다 present credentials **외교특권** diplomatic privilege [immunity] **중국 연구가** Sinologist; China-watcher

④ 조약 (treaty, convention, agreement)

▶ 조약을 교섭하다 negotiate a treaty // 조약을 체결하다 conclude a treaty // 조약을 조인하다 sign a treaty // 조약에 가조인하다 initial a treaty // 조약을 이행하다 observe a treaty // 조약을 위반하다 violate a treaty // 조약을 파기하다 terminate [break off, scrap] a treaty
협정 agreement; convention **규약** pact **헌장** charter **국제 연합 헌장** the Charter of Organization of the United Nations **조약문서** treaty document **조약**

불이행 non-observance of a treaty **2국간[다국간] 조약** bilateral[multilateral] treaty **협정가맹국** signatory; contracting member **WTO 가입국** contracting members of WTO **조약의무** treaty commitment[obligation] **비준(批准)** ratification **구상서(口上書)** note verbale 《상대국에 제출하는 외교 문서》 **친서** personal message **공동성명** joint communique[declaration, announcement, statement] **동시 발표** simultaneous announcement[release, publication] ¶ 경주에서 조인된 한일 공동성명은 서울과 동경에서 동시 발표되었다. The Korea-Japan joint communique, signed in Kyŏngju, was released simultaneously in Seoul and Tokyo.

float〔raise〕 a national loan // 국채를 발행하다 issue national bonds // 국채를 상환하다 redeem a national loan
— **모집 운동** the "buy-national-bonds" campaign — **발행고(發行高)** the amount of government bond issue — **상환 기금(償還基金)** an amortization〔a consolidation〕 fund ; a sinking fund — **소화(消化)** absorption〔digestion〕 of government bonds — **이자 지불 정지(利子支拂停止)** suspension of interest payment on government bonds — **증권(證券)** a national (loan) bond — **현재고(現在高)** the outstanding (amount of government) bonds **내(內)〔외(外)〕—** a domestic〔foreign〕 loan

국책 國策 a national〔state〕 policy ¶ 국책에 따라 in line〔conformity〕 with the national policy // 국책을 수행하다 carry out〔fix〕 a national policy
— **은행** a government-run bank — **회사** a national policy concern ; a state policy corporation〔company〕

국체 國體 national polity〔character〕 ; the structure〔form〕 of the state ; the honor of a country

국초 國初 the beginning of a state (나라의) ; the beginning of a dynasty (왕조의)

국초 國礎 the foundation of a nation

국치 國恥 a national humiliation〔disgrace〕 ¶ 국치를 초래하다 bring disgrace upon one's country
—**일** National Humiliation Day

국태민안 國泰民安 national prosperity and the welfare of the people **—하다** enjoy national prosperity and welfare

국토 國土 a country ; a territory ; a realm ; a domain ¶ 국토를 개발하다 reform〔cultivate〕 the land // 국토를 방위하다 defend one's country 《against》
— **개발(開發)** (national) land development ; national land planning — **개발 계획** a program for land development — **방위** the defense of the country ; national defense — **보존** territorial integrity — **분단** territorial division — **종합 개발법** 〖법〗 the Multiple Purpose Development of the Land Act

국판 菊版 a small octavo ; a medium octavo 《미》 ¶ 국판 300 페이지의 책 a 300-page octavo volume

국폐 國弊 national evils〔vices, abuses〕

국풍 國風 national customs (and manners) ; the Grand Korean Folk Festival ; *Kukpung* ('81)

국학 國學 the national literature ; the national classics
—**자(者)** a scholar of Korean literature

국한 局限 localization ; limitation **—하다** localize ; set limits to ; limit ¶ 오늘의 의제는 이 문제로 국한합시다 Let's confine〔limit〕 today's discussion to this matter.

국한문 國漢文 Korean and Chinese writing〔language〕 ¶ 국한문에 능통하다 be versed in Korean and Chinese literature
—**체** a mixed style of writing Korean with Chinese characters in it

국헌 國憲 a constitution ; the laws of the country ¶ 국헌을 준수하다 respect the national constitution // 국헌을 제정하다 establish a constitution

국호 國號 the name of a country

국혼 國婚 a royal marriage ; royal nuptials

국화 國花 a national flower ¶ 무궁화는 한국의 국화이다 The Rose of Sharon is regarded as the national flower of Korea.

***국화 菊花** a chrysanthemum ; a mum 《미·속》
—**잠** a hairpin with an ornament of chrysanthemum shape

****국회 國會** the National Assembly (한국·프랑스의) ; Parliament (영국의) ; Congress (미국의) ; the Diet (일본·스웨덴의) ¶ 특별 국회를 소집하다 convene〔summon〕 a special session of the National Assembly // 국회를 해산하다 dissolve the National Assembly // 국회가 개회 중이다 The National Assembly is now sitting〔in session now〕. // 국회 회기 중 during the session of the National Assembly
— **도서관** the National Assembly Library ; [미국의] the Library of Congress —**법(法)** 〖법〗 the National Assembly law — **본회의** the Assembly plenary session — **부의장** the vice-speaker — **사무처** the Secretariat of the National Assembly — **사무 총장** the Secretary-General of the National

Assembly — 상임 위원회 the National Assembly Standing Committee — 심의권 legislative prerogatives of the Assembly — 예산 결산 위원회 the National Assembly Budget Settlement Committee — 의사록 the National Assembly record ; Hansard 《영》 — 임시 회기 an extraordinary session of the National Assembly ☞ ⦅p. 297⦆

국회법 國會法 the National Assembly Law

국회 상임 위원회 國會常任委員會 the National Assembly Standing Committee

국회 운영 위원회 國會運營委員會 the Steering Committee of the National Assembly

국회 의사당 國會議事堂 the National Assembly building (한국의) ; the Capitol (미국의) ; the Houses of Parliament (영국의) ; the Diet building (일본의)

†국회 의원 國會議員 a member of the National Assembly ; an〔a National〕 Assemblyman ; a lawmaker ; a Congressman (미국의) ; a member of Parliament (영국의) ; a member of the Diet (일본의)
— 선거 the election of members for〔to〕 the National Assembly ; the Assembly〔parliamentary, general〕 election

국회 의장 國會議長 the chairman ; [하원의] the Speaker ; the President

국회 해산 國會解散 dissolution of the National Assembly

군- extra ; superfluous ; unnecessary ¶ 군음식 a snack // 군걱정 needless anxiety // 군식구 a boarder ; a guest

†군 軍 an army ; a force ; troops ; a team ¶ 미 제8군 the Eighth United States Army // 한국 제1군 the First R. O. K. Army // 백군 the white team // 청군 the blue team // 군 본연의 임무 the military's proper duty // 육해공군 the armed forces // 상비군 a standing army // 군 당국 military authorities // 군에 입대하다 enter〔go into, join〕 the army // 군에서 복무하다 serve in the army

군 君 you ; Mister 《Mr.》 ¶ 김 군 Mr. *Kim*

†군 郡 a county ; a district ¶ 강화군 *Kanghwa* county

군가 軍歌 a war song ; a martial air ; a marching song ¶ 군가를 부르다 sing a war song

군거 群居 a gregarious life —하다 live gregariously ; live in flocks ⇨ 군서
— 본능(本能) a gregarious instinct

군걸음 needless steps

군것 a superfluity ; unnecessary things

군것질 eating between meals

군견 軍犬 a war〔military〕 dog

군경 軍警 the military and the police
— 위문 a consolatory call on〔visit to〕 the military or the police — 유가족 the surviving〔bereaved〕 families of the dead soldiers and policemen

군계일학 群鷄一鶴 the only figure among ciphers ; the sun among inferior lights

군계집 an adulteress ; a (female) paramour

군고구마 roast sweet potatoes

군고기 roast〔grilled, broiled〕 meat

군공 軍功 meritorious service in war ⇨ 전공

군관구 軍管區 a military district ¶ 6군관구 사령부 the 6th Military District Command

군국 君國 ① a monarchy ② [임금과 나라] one's sovereign and country

군국 軍國 a military nation ; a nation at war

*군국주의 軍國主義 militarism
—자 a militarist

군글자 a superfluous〔redundant〕 character ; an expletive

군기 軍紀 military discipline ¶ 군기를 유지하다 maintain military discipline // 군기가 문란하다 Military discipline is slack.

군기 軍氣 morale ; military spirit

군기 軍旗 the colors ; a standard
— 수여식(授與式) the presentation of the colors — 호위병(護衛兵) a color guard

군기 軍器 weapons of war ; arms

군기 軍機 a military secret ; [서류] classification ¶ 군기상 for reasons of military secrecy // 군기를 누설하다 divulge〔disclose〕 a military secret
— 누설 disclosure〔betrayal, leakage〕 of military secrets — 누설 사건 a military secret betrayal case

군기침 a habitual dry cough

군납 軍納 supply of goods and services to the military
—불(弗) dollars earned through supply of goods and services to the U. N.〔U. S.〕 forces —업자 [물품의] a military goods supplier ; [용역의] service contractors for the military — 회사 a military supply contract firm

군납품 軍納品 supplies provided by a purveyor

군내 an unpleasant smell ; a bad smell

군눈 eyes curious for their own good ; an unnecessary heed

‡군단 軍團 corps ; an army corps ¶ 제3군단 the 3rd (Army) Corps
— 사령부 the corps headquarters

군단장 軍團長 the commander〔commanding general〕 of an army corps

†군대 軍隊 troops ; an army ¶ 군대에 들어가다 join〔enlist in〕 the army // 군대에 있다 He serves in the army.
— 교육〔훈련〕 military training〔drill〕 —

국 회

일반적으로 국회는 the (national) assembly [legislature]를 쓴다. 일본·덴마크·스웨덴·헝가리 등의 국회는 Diet, 미국이나 중·남미 공화국에서는 Congress, 영국·캐나다에서는 parliament, 우리나라는 the National Assembly로 쓴다.

미국의 의회 (정식명으로는 연방의회) Congress는 보통 the를 붙이지 않지만 일정하지는 않다. 상원은 the Senate, 상원의원은 Senator, 하원은 정식으로는 the House of Representatives이지만 The House로 줄여 말하는 것이 보통이다. 하원의원은 member of the House (of Representatives) 또는 Representative 등으로 말한다. 상·하원 구별없이 일반적 의원을 지칭할 때는 member of Congress, legislator, lawmaker 등이 주로 쓰인다. Congressman, Congresswoman 도 실제로는 거의가 「하원의원」을 의미한다. 최근에는 성차별을 없애기 위해 Congressperson이라고도 한다. 상원의장은 President of the Senate 또는 Senate President로 쓰고 Vice President of the United States (부통령)가 이것을 맡지만 공무 등으로 등원할 수 없을 때를 대비해 President Pro Tempore 혹은 Pro Tem 으로 불리는 「임시의장」 제도가 마련되어 있다.

하원의장은 정식으로는 Speaker of the House of Representatives이지만 보통은 Speaker of the House, 혹은 House Speaker로 부른다. 의사당은 the Capitol 이고 그 건물이 있는 언덕을 Capitol Hill 이라고 부른다. 「의회에서」라고 말할 때는 in Congress; in the Capitol; on Capitol Hill; on the Hill 등으로 표현한다.

「국회를 소집하다」는 convene [convoke] the National Assembly라 하고 「국회를 휴회하다」는 be in recess로 쓴다.

▶ 관련용어

통상(通常)국회 ordinary National Assembly session; regular (session of the) National Assembly **임시국회** extraordinary session of the National Assembly **특별국회** special session of the National Assembly **변칙국회** abnormal session of the National Assembly **연장국회** prolonged session of the National Assembly

회기 session; term; tenure; life ¶ 60일 회기로 임시국회가 열렸다. The extraordinary session of the National Assembly opened for a 60-day term. / The national Assembly opened for a 60-day extraordinary session.

양원제 two-chamber [bicameral(l)] system **단원제** one-chamber [unicameral(l)] system

하원(下院) the House of Representatives (미국·일본); the Lower House; the House of Commons (영국) **상원(上院)** the House of Councilors; the Upper House; the senate (미국·프랑스); the House of Lords (영국) **하원의원** Member of the House of Representatives; Representative (미국); member of the House of Commons (영국) **상원 의원** Member of the House of Councilors; Councilor; Member of the Upper House; a senator (미국·프랑스); Member of the House of Lords (영국)

정족수 quorum **의장직권** power of the office of the Speaker [the President] ¶ 의장직권으로 본회의가 열렸다. The Speaker, invoking the power of his office, opened the plenary session. / The Speaker, acting *ex officio,* called the plenary into session.

공개심의 open session [hearing] **비공개심의** secret [closed] session [hearing] **시정방침 연설** policy speech **질문** interpellation question ¶ 수상이 야당 질문의 답변에 나섰다. The prime minister took the floor to answer the opposition's interpellation questions. **관련질문** related question **증인** sworn witness **참고인** unsworn witness; expert witness (★ expert witness는 특정 분야의 경험자 혹은 전문가로부터 참고 의견을 듣고자 할 때의 참고인을 말하고, unsworn witness는 「증인」으로서의 참고인으로 쓰인다.)

동의 motion **긴급동의** emergency motion **심의거부** refusal to attend a session; boycott of a session ¶ 야당은 예산위원회에서 심의거부를 하고 있다. Opposition members are refusing to attend the Budget Committee session.

심의미필 failure to act; putting on the shelf ¶ 그 법안은 심의가 끝나지 않았다. The bill was left unacted upon. / The legislature failed to complete action on the bill.

결의(決議) resolution ¶ 양당은 한미 우호를 결의했다. Both parties of the National Assembly resolved for (promotion of) Korea-America friendship.

강행타결 railroading; steamroller ¶ 그들은 강행타결하여 그 법안을 채택시켰다. They were steamrollered into adopting the bill.

▶ 표결 · 채결(採決)

「…을 표결 또는 채택하여 결정하다」 vote on …; take a vote on …; put … to a vote
¶ 법안이 가결되어 법률로 되었다. The bill was voted into law. // 법안이 부결되다. The bill was voted down. (★ 표가 찬·부 동수인 경우는 The vote was evenly split. / It was a tie vote. / The vote was tied. 로 한다. 의장 등이 결정짓는 한 표를 행사할 경우는 cast a tie-breaking vote로 하고 이러한 한 표를 casting vote, 또는 decisive vote라고 한다. 「기립 투표」는 standing vote, 「발성 투표」는 voice vote라 하며 voice vote에서 「찬성하는 사람은 aye라고 말하시오.」라고 동의를 구하는 표현으로는 "Those in favor, say aye."라고 한다.)

▶ **법안 (bill, draft)**

¶ 법안을 제출하다. present [introduce, submit] a bill // 법안을 기초하다. write [draft] a bill // 법안을 심의하다. debate [take up] a bill; deliberate [act] on a bill // 법안심의가 다음 회기로 넘어가다. The deliberation of a bill is carried over to the next session. // 법안을 보류하다. pigeonhole [table, shelve] a bill (★ table은 미국의 의회용어로는 법안의 「심의를 무기 연기하다」의 뜻이며 영국에서는 「심의를 위해 제출하다」의 뜻. 실제로는 미국·영국을 구별하지 않고 「제출하다」의 뜻으로 사용되는 경우가 많다.) // 법안이 위원회에서 본회의로 넘어가다. A committee sends a bill to the plenary session. // 법안이 통과되다. A bill becomes a law. / A bill passes the National Assembly. / A bill is enacted. // 법안이 기각되다. A bill is aborted [killed, rejected]. / A bill dies.
자연 휴회 automatic recess [adjournment] ¶ 예산안이 통과되면 하원은 자연 휴회에 들어갈 것이다. The House of Representatives will automatically recess after the passage of the budget bill.
(국회)해산 dissolution (of the House of Representatives) ¶ 국회해산권은 대통령에게 있어서 중요한 정치적 무기이다. The right to dissolve the Lower House is a vital political weapon for the President.
신임안 confidence motion **불신임안** non-confidence motion
상임위원회 standing committee **특별위원회** special [*ad hoc*] committee **특별조사위원회** select committee ¶ 록히드 특별조사위원회 the Lockheed Select Committee // 위원회가 참고인을 소환하다. A committee calls [summons] a witness. **소위원회** subcommittee **공청회** public hearing
국정조사권 right to conduct investigation in relation to government ¶ 국정조사권을 행사하다 exercise the right to conduct investigation in relation to government

명부 a regimental roll — **생활** an army 〔a military〕 life — **위생** military hygiene — **행진곡** a military march
군대답 —對答 a needless reply
군대식 軍隊式 military fashion; military way
군더더기 [여분] a superfluous one; a superfluity; something superfluous ¶ 군더더기를 붙이다 add something superfluous
군던지럽다 (be) foul; mean; low; nasty
군데 a place; a spot; a point; a part ¶ 한 군데 오래 머물다 stay long in the same place // 여러 군데 상처를 입다 receive several wounds // 몇 군데 들러서 알아보았다 I checked into several places. // 신문은 여러 군데서 새 소식을 취재한다 A newspaper gets news from many sources. // 아직도 얼굴에 몇 군데 상처가 남아 있다 There still remain a few scars on the face.
***군데군데** here and there; sporadically (산재하여); at〔in〕 places ¶ 들판에 군데군데 집이 서 있다 Houses stand scattered in the field. // 서울에는 육교 공사가 군데군데 진행 중이다 Land bridges are being built here and there in *Seoul*. // 전방에 초소가 군데군데 서 있다 Guard posts are placed sporadically along the front line.
군도 軍刀 a saber; a sword
군도 群島 a group of islands; an archipelago (*pl.* ~s, ~es) ¶ 필리핀 군도 the Philippine Islands; the Philippines // 마샬 군도 the Marshall Islands // 말레이 군도 the Malay Archipelago
군도 群盜 a group of robbers
군돈 money spent unnecessarily
군두목 writing in Chinese characters by phonetic equivalents
군두쇠 a large metal ring attached to one end of a log
군드러지다 ⇨ 곤드라지다
군락 群落 〖동물〗 stock ¶ 군락을 이루다 live in stock
군란 軍亂 an insurrection of troops; an army rebellion; a coup (d'état)
군략 軍略 military strategy; a stratagem; tactics ⇨ 전략 ¶ 군략상 strategically; from a strategic point of view
군략가 軍略家 a strategist; a tactician
군량 軍糧 provisions; food; rations
군령 軍令 a military command
군례 軍禮 military honors〔rites〕
‡군림 君臨 reigning —**하다** reign over

《a kingdom, people》; rule over ; lord (it) over ¶ 그 분야에서 군림하다 dominate〔be dominant in〕 the field 《of science, economy》; dominate all the others in the same line // 국민 위에 군림하다 reign over people // 경마계에 군림하다 dominate the turf // 왕은 군림하나 통치하지 않는다 The king reigns, but he does not rule. // 그는 자기 부인에게 군림하기를 좋아한다 He likes to lord it over his wife.

군마 軍馬 [말] a war horse ; a charger ; [군사와 말] men and horses

군막 軍幕 tents for military use ; a military tent

군말 an unnecessary remark ; an expletive ; redundant words **— 하다** say unnecessary things

군매점 軍賣店 a post exchange 《P. X.》; a canteen

군명 君命 a royal command ¶ 군명을 받들어 in obedience to the royal command ; on a royal mission

군모 軍帽 a military cap ; an army〔a navy〕 cap

군목 軍牧 a chaplain ¶ 그는 육군에서 군목으로 복무하였다 He served as a chaplain in the army.

†**군무 軍務** military affairs ; military duties ¶ 군무에 종사하다 serve with the colors ; perform military duties

— **이탈** desertion from military service

군무 群舞 group〔formation〕 dancing ¶ 군무를 추다 dance in groups

군무원 軍務員 a civilian attached to the military

군문 軍門 [문] a camp gate ; [군무] military service ¶ 군문에 들어가다 enlist in the army ; join the colors ; enter the service

군물 [마시는 물] drinking water taken between meals ; [거듭 치는 물] additional cold water added to a boiling liquid

군민 軍民 the military and the people ; the fighting services and the civilians

군민 郡民 the inhabitants of a county

군밤 roast chestnuts

군밥 food for uninvited guests ; rice leftover ; extra rice

군번 軍番 the serial number 《S. N.》; the service number

군벌 軍閥 a military clique〔caste, clan〕; the militarists

— **정치** military dictatorship ; militaristic government ; warlordism

군법 軍法 martial〔military〕 law

군법무관 軍法務官 a military judicial officer

군법 회의 軍法會議 a court-martial

군복 軍服 a military uniform ; regimentals ¶ 군복 차림의 장교 an officer in uniform ; a uniformed officer // 군복을 입고 있다 be in military uniform // 육군 소령의 군복을 입고 있는 사람 a man in the uniform of a major in the army

군부 君父 one's lord〔king〕; one's lord and father

군부 軍部 the military authorities ; army circles ; the militarists ; the military 《총칭》 ¶ 군부의 횡포 militarists' despotism

군불 a fire lit for the sole purpose of heating the floors ¶ 군불을 때다 heat the floors

군불에 밥짓기 (속담) To catch two pigeons with one bean. /To kill two birds with one stone〔bolt, sling〕.

군비 軍備 armaments ; military preparations〔preparedness〕 ¶ 군비를 확장〔축소, 강화, 제한〕하다 increase〔reduce, reinforce, limit〕 armaments

— **경쟁** an arms race — **제한** the limitation of armaments ; arms control — **철폐** disarmament ; demilitarization — **확장 경쟁** an armament race

***군비 軍費** war〔army〕 expenditure ; the sinews of war

군비 축소 軍備縮小 the reduction of〔a cut in〕 armaments ; an armament reduction ; an arms cut

군비 축소 회의 軍備縮小會議 a disarmament conference

군비 확장 軍備擴張 the expansion of armaments ; military expansion

군사 軍士 a soldier ; a private ; the men ; the ranks

군사 軍使 a military envoy ; the bearer of the flag of truce

군사 軍事 military affairs ¶ 군사의 military ; strategic

— **고문단** the military advisory group — **공채(公債)** a war loan〔bond〕 — **교관** a military instructor — **기관** a military agency〔organization〕 — **기밀** military secrets —**범(犯)** a military offense — **시설** military installations〔establishments〕 — **예산** an arms budget — **용어(用語)** a military term — **원조 계획** a military aid〔assistance〕 program — **위원회** [미국의] the Armed Services Committee — **정권** a military junta〔regime〕 — **정세** military situation — **정전 위원회(停戰委員會)** the Military Armistice Commission 《MAC》 — **지출(支出)** military spending — **첩보(諜報)** military intelligence — **체제** military setup — **탐정** a military spy ; a secret service agent — **평론가** a military commentator — **행정** military administration — **회의** a war council — **훈련** military drill

군사 개입 軍事介入 military intervention

군사 고문 軍事顧問 a military adviser

군사 교육 軍事敎育 military education〔instruction〕

군사 기지 軍事基地 an army〔a navy, an air〕 base
군사 동맹 軍事同盟 a military alliance
군사람 a superfluous〔an unnecessary〕 person ; a dispensable employee ; an extra hand
군사력 軍事力 military strength〔capacity, might〕 ; armaments
군사령관 軍司令官 an army commander
군사령부 軍司令部 military headquarters
군사 봉쇄 軍事封鎖 military blockade
군사 분계선 軍事分界線 the Military Demarcation Line
군사비 軍事費 war expenditure〔funds〕
군사설 一辭說 long and superfluous words ; lengthy talk ; a long lecture
군사 우편 軍事郵便 military mail
군사 원조 軍事援助 military aid
군사 위성 軍事衛星 a military satellite
군사 재판 軍事裁判 a military trial ⇨ 군법 회의
군사 정보 軍事情報 military intelligence
군사학 軍事學 military science
군사 행동 軍事行動 military operations ; hostilities
군살 superfluous flesh ; flab ¶ 군살을 빼다 get rid of surplus fat // 배에 군살이 붙다 put on excess weight around the (one's) waist // 요즈음 배에 군살이 붙었다 I've developed a bit of flab around my waistline.
군상 群像 a group ; people
군새 straw used to repair a thatched roof
군색 窘塞 poverty ; destitution ; indigence **—하다** (be) destitute ; poor ; needy ¶ 군색한 집안에 태어나다 be born poor ; be born into a poor family // 군색한 변명 a poor〔sorry, lame〕 excuse // 군색하게 살다 lead a life of want ; make a poor〔scanty〕 living ; earn〔pick up〕 a scanty livelihood
군생 群生 〖생물〗 animate things ; living creatures **—하다** live〔grow〕 in stocks
군서 群棲 gregariousness **—하다** live in flocks ; live gregariously ; live in herds (소 따위가) ; hive (벌이)
— 동물 gregarious〔social〕 animals
군서 群書 various〔many〕 books
군세 軍勢 military power ; the military situation ; [군] an army ; a force ; troops
군소 〖동물〗 a sea hare ; Aplysia kurodai (학명)
군소 群小 minor〔lesser, insignificant〕 persons ; small fry ; [형용사적] insignificant ; minor ; petty
군소리 [군말] an unnecessary remark ; [헛소리] talking in one's sleep〔delirium〕 **—하다** make an unnecessary remark ; talk in one's sleep〔delirium〕
군소 작가 群小作家 minor writers
군소 정당 群小政黨 minor〔lesser-known〕 political parties
군속 軍屬 a civilian attached to the military
군손질 unnecessary trimming〔care〕
군수 郡守 a county headman〔governor〕 ; the magistrate of a county
군수 軍需 munitions (of war)
— 공업가(工業家) a munitions manufacturer ; a war industrialist ; a merchant of death 《미》 **— 보급 기지** a supply dump **— 인플레** military demand inflation **— 자재(資材)** war materials〔supplies〕 **— 회사** a munitions company
군수 경기 軍需景氣 munitions boom
군수 공업 軍需工業 war industry ; the munitions industry
군수 공장 軍需工場 munitions〔an armament〕 factory〔works〕 ; a war plant
군수 물자 軍需物資 war supplies〔materials〕 ; ordnance ; munitions
군수 산업 軍需産業 war industry ; the munitions industry
군수품 軍需品 war supplies〔materials〕 ; ordnance ; munitions
군시럽다 feel creepy〔itchy〕
군식구 一食口 a hanger-on ; a parasite ; a dependent other than a member of one's own family
군신 君臣 sovereign and subject ; the ruler and the ruled
군신 軍神 the god of war ; Mars (로마 신화) ; Ares (그리스 신화) ; [영웅] a war hero
군신 群臣 the whole body of officials
군실거리다 ⇨ 군시럽다
군실군실 all itchy ; all crawly
군악 軍樂 military music
— 대원 a bandsman **— 대장** a military band master
군악대 軍樂隊 a military band
군역 軍役 military service ⇨ 병역
군영 軍營 a military camp
군왕 君王 a king
군용 軍用 military use〔purpose〕 ¶ 군용의 military ; for military use
— 자재(資材) war materials **— 전화** a military telephone
군용 軍容 [진용] a formation of troops ; [형편] military situation〔aspect〕 ¶ 군용을 정비하다 marshal troops for a battle ; complete military preparations
군용견 軍用犬 a war〔military〕 dog
군용금 軍用金 [군자금] war-funds ; a war chest ; [선거 자금] campaign funds ; [용돈] pocket money
군용기 軍用機 a war plane ; a service airplane ; a military〔naval〕 plane
군용 도로 軍用道路 a military road
군용 비둘기 軍用— a carrier pigeon in military service
군용 비행기 軍用飛行機 ⇨ 군용기
군용 수표 軍用手票 ⇨ 군표(軍票)

군용 열차 軍用列車 a troop train
군용지 軍用地 [포·트럭·군수품 따위를 두는] a park
군용 지도 軍用地圖 a military map
군용 철도 軍用鐵道 a military〔strategic〕 railway
군용품 軍用品 military equipment〔supplies〕
군웅 群雄 rival heroes
군웅할거 群雄割據 rivalry of local barons ¶ 군웅할거 시대 the age of rival warlords
군원 軍援 military aid〔assistance〕 ⇨ 군사 원조
— **이관(移管)** transfer of the military Assistance Program(me)
군율 軍律 [군법] martial law ; the articles of war ; [군기] military discipline ¶ 군율을 지키다 observe military discipline // 군율이 엄하다 Military discipline is strictly enforced.
군은 君恩 the royal benevolence〔favor〕; the favor of one's lord
군음식 extra food ; a snack ; food other than meals
군의 軍醫 ⇨ 군의관
군의관 軍醫官 an army〔a naval, a flight〕 surgeon ; a medical officer
†**군인 軍人** military personnel ; a serviceman ; [육군] a soldier ; [해군] a marine ; a sailor ; [공군] an airman ¶ 군인다운 soldierly ; soldierlike
— **사회** military circles — **생활** military life ; soldiering — **연금** a military pension — **정신** the military spirit — **출신** an ex-soldier ; an ex-serviceman **직업** — a professional soldier ; a career soldier 《미》
군일 unnecessary〔futile〕 work ; extra〔needless〕 work
군자 君子 a man of honor〔virtue〕; a true gentleman ¶ 군자인 체하다 assume a virtuous air // 군자는 위험을 멀리한다 The wise man does not court danger. /Discretion is the better part of valor. // 군자는 대로행(大路行)이라 A wise man never takes a short cut. /A man of virtue always sticks to a great cause.
군자국 君子國 a land of gentlemen
군자금 軍資金 war funds ; the sinews of war ; [선거 자금 따위] campaign funds ¶ 군자금을 공급하다 supply the sinews of war ; subsidize // 선거전의 군자금이 부족하다 be short of funds in an election campaign
군자란 君子蘭 〖식물〗 a Kaffir lily ; Clivia miniata (학명)
군자연하다 君子然— assume a virtuous air
군장 軍葬 a military funeral ; [육군장] an army funeral ¶ 군장으로 하다 accord 《a person》 a military funeral ; bury 《a person》 with military honors
군장 軍裝 military uniform ; war outfit ; war attire ; military equipment
— **검사** a kit〔clothing〕 inspection **완전** — full uniform〔gear, kit〕
군적 軍籍 the army〔navy〕 list ; the army register ; the muster roll ¶ 군적에 들다 enlist in the army〔navy〕 // 군적에 몸을 두다 be in the service
군정 軍政 military administration〔government〕; military affairs ¶ 군정하에 두다 put 《a territory》 under military administration
— **고문** a military administration adviser
군정 軍情 military conditions〔circumstances〕; military intelligence
군정청 軍政廳 the Military Government Office
군제 軍制 a military system〔organization〕
군졸 軍卒 soldiers ; the rank and file
†**군주 君主** a sovereign ; a ruler ; a monarch ; a crowned head
— **독재(獨裁)** absolute monarchy ; autocracy — **전제 정체** absolute〔despotic〕 monarchy — **정치 반대자** an antimonarchist **전제(專制)** — an autocrat ; an absolute monarch **입헌(立憲)** — **정체(政體)** constitutional〔limited〕 monarchy
군주국 君主國 a monarchy
***군주 정체 君主政體** monarchism ; monarchy
***군주제 君主制** a monarchial system ; monarchism
†**군중 群衆** a crowd (of people) ; the masses ; a multitude ; a throng ; a swarm ; mob

> 참고 **crowd** 통제되지 않은 사람 또는 물건의 무리 **throng** crowd보다도 더욱 많으며 밀고 밀리는 군중 **swarm** 혼란 속에 움직이고 있는 사람의 무리 **multitude** 다수를 강조하는 말 **mob** 통제가 없고 무법한 군중

¶ 도로상의 많은 군중들 large crowds in the streets // 군중에게 습격당하다 be mobbed // 군중을 헤치고 나아가다 force〔push, elbow〕 one's way through the crowd // 거리는 군중으로 들끓고 있었다 The street was thronged with people.
— **공포증** ochlophobia
군중 대회 群衆大會 a (mass) rally
군중 심리 群衆心理 mob〔mass, crowd〕 psychology ; the group〔crowd〕 mind
군직 軍職 the military〔naval〕 profession ; the profession of arms
군진 軍陣 a military camp
군집 群集 a crowd ; an assembly ; a group **—하다** crowd ; gather ; throng ; congregate

군짓 unnecessary〔useless〕 things ; things done unnecessarily〔in vain〕 **—하다** do unnecessary〔useless〕 things
*__군청 郡廳__ a county office
— 소재지 the seat of a county office
군청 群靑 ultramarine (blue) ; navy blue
군체 群體 〚생물〛 a colony
군축 軍縮 the reduction of armaments ; disarmament **—하다** reduce armaments
— 회담 arms reduction talk
군축 회의 群縮會議 an armament limitation conference ; a disarmament conference
군침 excessive saliva ¶ 군침을 흘리다 drivel ; slaver ; slobber ; salivate ; run〔dribble〕 at the mouth // 군침이 돌게 하는 mouth-watering // 맛있는 요리 냄새가 우리 입에 군침을 돌게 했다 The delicious cooking smell made our mouths water.
군침을 삼키다 관용 swallow〔gulp down〕 one's saliva
군침(이) 돌다 관용 one's mouth waters 《with hunger or greed》
군턱 a double chin
군티 a slight flaw〔defect〕
군표 軍票 military script ; an army note ; military payment certificate 《M. P. C.》
*__군함 軍艦__ a warship ; a man-of-war ; a battleship ¶ 군함을 건조하다 construct a warship // 군함을 폐기하다 scrap a warship // 군함을 파견하다 dispatch a warship // 군함의 승무원 the crew of a warship
군함기 軍艦旗 a naval ensign
군항 軍港 a naval port〔station〕 ¶ 군항 사령부 the headquarters of a naval station
군현 郡縣 counties and prefectures
군호 軍號 a (military) password ; a watchword ⇨ 암호
군화 軍靴 military〔GI〕 shoes ; combat〔army, ammunition〕 boots
군획 —畫 an extra stroke (in writing a character)
군후 君侯 a (feudal) lord
굳건하다 (be) strong and steady ; solid ; reliable ¶ 굳건히 strongly ; firmly ; solidly ; tightly // 굳건한 의지 an iron〔indomitable, adamant〕 will
†**굳다**[1] [굳어지다] harden ; become hard〔solid〕 ; get stiff ; [응결하다] congeal ; curdle (우유가) ; clot (피 따위가) ; set (시멘트 따위가) ; [혀가] be tongue-tied ; lisp ¶ 굳어진 시체 a rigid corpse // 굳어진 빵 hardened bread // 풀이 굳었다 The paste has become hard. // 석고는 빨리 굳는다 Plaster of Paris sets quickly. // 비 온 뒤에 땅이 굳어진다 Ground packs after a rain.
†**굳다**[2] (be) hard ; solid ; stiff ; [견고하다] strong ; secure ; [표정이] stiff ; hard ; [뜻이] firm ; determined ¶ 굳은 결심 a firm resolution〔determination〕 // 굳은 우정 firm friendship // 굳은 신념 strong〔settled〕 convictions // 굳은 표정 stiff〔stern〕 look // 정조가 굳은 여자 a chaste〔virtuous〕 woman // 굳게 믿다 believe firmly // 굳게 결심하다 be firmly resolved // 굳게 맹세를 하다 make a solemn vow // 굳게 약속하다 give a solemn promise // 굳은 악수를 교환하다 shake hands in firm grips // 문을 굳게 잠그다 make the door fast // 마음이 굳어 유혹에 넘어가지 않다 be adamant to temptation // 저 녀석 놀라서 몸이 굳어 버렸군 That guy's scared stiff !
*__굳세다__ (be) strong ; firm ; stout ; vigorous ; steady ¶ 굳세게 undauntedly ; bravely ; stoutly // 굳센 의지 an iron〔a bulldog〕 will // 굳센 신념 a firm conviction // 우세한 적에게 굽히지 않고 굳세게 나아가다 keep advancing in defiance of the overwhelming enemy ; bravely advance against heavy odds
†**굳어지다** harden ; become hard〔solid〕 ; stiffen ; get〔become〕 stiff ; freeze ¶ 굳어진 손 stiff hands // 굳어진 시체 a rigid corpse // 굳어진 빵 hardened bread // 비 온 뒤에 땅이 굳어진다 Ground packs after a rain.
굳은살 hardened skin ; [손의] a callus ; [발의] a corn ¶ 손바닥에 굳은살이 박이다 a callus forms in the palm of one's hand // 발가락에 굳은살이 박이다 get a corn on a toe
굳이 firmly ; positively ; adamantly ; stubbornly ; solidly ; obstinately ¶ 굳이 사양하다 decline once for all // 굳이 원하신다면 if you particularly wish it ; if you insist (upon it) // 네가 굳이 혼자 가겠다면 그렇게 해라 If you insist on going alone, please do so. // 일자리를 굳이 싫다 하고 시골로 갔다 Having flatly turned down the job offer, he retired to the country.
굳히다 harden ; make hard ; stiffen ; solidify ; strengthen ; consolidate ¶ 가열하여 진흙을 굳히다 harden clay by heat // 기반을 굳히다 consolidate the foundation ; secure one's position
‡**굴** 〚조개〛 an oyster ¶ 생굴 a raw oyster
— 껍질 oyster shells **— 양식** oyster farming〔culture〕 ; ostreiculture **— 양식업자** an oyster-culturist ; an oyster farmer **— 양식장** an oyster bed〔farm〕
굴 窟 [동굴] a cave ; a cavern ; a grotto 《*pl.* ~s, ~es》 [터널] a tunnel ; a subterranean passage [짐승의] a den ; a lair ; a barrow〔burrow〕 (토끼 따위의) [탄광의] a drift〔pit, shaft〕 [소굴] a den ; a haunt
굴개 stagnant〔sedimented〕 slime
*__굴곡 屈曲__ winding ; irregularity (해안선

따위의) ; refraction (광선의) ; crookedness ; flexion —하다 (be) bent ; winding ; curved ; refracted ¶ 굴곡이 진 winding ; crooked ; irregular ; indented // 굴곡이 진 해안선 an indented coastline

—부 a bent ; a turn — 분자 〖화학〗 a folded molecule —선 〖수학〗 a broken line — 시험기 a bending tester — 운동 〖생물〗 tropism ; 〖식물〗 curvature movement — 작용 flection (관절 따위)

굴광성 屈光性 〖생물〗 phototropism

굴근 屈筋 〖해부〗 a flexor (muscle)

굴기성 屈氣性 〖생물〗 aerotropism

*굴다 behave ; conduct oneself ; act ; treat (대하다) ¶ 못살게 굴다 treat 《a person》 harshly ; be hard on 《a person》 // 신사답게 굴다 behave like a gentleman // 그는 상관한테 욕을 먹으면 하급자를 못살게 군다 When scolded by his senior, he works off his vexation on his juniors. // 손님에게 친절하게 군다 She receives her visitors kindly. /She is a good hostess.

굴다리 窟— a viaduct ; a land bridge

⁑굴대 an axle ; an axis ; a shaft

굴도리 a round〔cylindrical〕 beam

굴때장군 —將軍 a swarthy giant ; a dark person

굴똥 the axis of a spinning wheel

⁑굴뚝 a chimney ; a smokestack ; a funnel (기선의) ; a stovepipe (난로의) ¶ 굴뚝 소제 chimney sweeping // 굴뚝 소제부 a chimney sweep(er) // 굴뚝을 세 개 갖춘 기선 a three-funneled steamer 〔ship〕 // 굴뚝에서 연기가 난다 The chimney is smoking. // … 생각이 굴뚝 같다 [비유적으로 써서] be quite anxious〔eager〕 《to do》 // 가고 싶은 생각이 굴뚝 같다 I would very much like〔I am dying〕 to go.

아니 땐 굴뚝에 연기 날까 (속담) No smoke without fire.

*굴뚝새 〖새〗 a wren

굴렁쇠 a hoop ¶ 굴렁쇠를 굴리다 drive 〔trundle, roll〕 along a hoop

†굴레 ① [마소의] a bridle ; a halter ¶ 굴레를 씌우다 put a bridle 《on a horse》 ; bridle

② [속박] a yoke ; ties ; bonds ¶ 굴레를 벗다 break〔cast, shake, throw〕 off the yoke

굴레미 a wooden (cart) wheel

†굴리다 ① roll ② [내버려 두다] neglect ; leave 《a thing》 unattended ; lay〔put〕 aside ③ [둥글게 깎다] smooth a log ; cut 《a piece of wood》 round ; round 《an edge》 ④ [운영하다] run ; lend (돈을) ¶ 공을 굴리다 roll a ball // 사람을 굴리다 tumble down 《a person》 // 굴려 떨어뜨리다 roll 《a thing》 down 《a slope》 // 책을 함부로 굴리다 toss a book to one side // 돈을 굴리다 lend one's money out at interest ; invest one's money profitably // 함부로 굴리면 못 쓰게 된다 If you leave it unattended, it will not last. // 버스를 세 대 굴린다 He has three buses running for business purposes.

굴밤 an acorn

굴밥 rice boiled with oysters

†굴복 屈服 submission ; surrender

—하다 submit〔surrender, yield, give in〕 《to》 ; bow one's head 《to》 ¶ 굴복시키다 make 《a person》 give in ; bring 《a person》 to his knees // 남의 의견에 굴복하다 submit tamely to 《a person's》 opinion // 압박에 굴복하다 yield under pressure // 비행기 납치범들은 마침내 경찰에게 굴복했다 The hijackers finally surrendered (themselves) to the police. // 그 성은 오랜 포위 공격 끝에 굴복하지 않을 수 없었다 The castle was forced to yield after a long siege. // 정부는 여론에 굴복하였다 The government has yielded to public opinion.

굴비 a dried yellow corvina

굴성 屈性 〖생물〗 (a) tropism

굴속 窟— the inside of a cave〔den, tunnel〕 ; [어두운 곳] a dark place ; the dark ¶ 굴속 같다 be as dark as a cave

굴수성 屈水性 〖생물〗 hydrotropism

굴신 屈伸 bending and stretching ; extension and contraction —하다 bend and stretch ; extend and contract ¶ 굴신 자재의 elastic ; pliable ; flexible

—율 the flexible rate

굴신 屈身 bending oneself ; [비유적] modesty ; humbleness ; humility

—하다 bend oneself ; humble oneself

굴신 운동 屈身運動 《do》 knee bends

굴왕신같다 (be) old and shabby

*굴욕 屈辱 humiliation ; disgrace ; shame ¶ 굴욕적인 humiliating ; disgraceful // 굴욕을 당하다 be subjected to humiliation // 굴욕을 주다 humiliate ; subject 《a person》 to humiliation ; submit 《a person》 to indignities // 굴욕을 느끼다 feel humiliated〔disgraced〕 // 굴욕을 참다 eat humble pie ; bite〔lick〕 the dust ; pocket an insult // 굴욕적인 강화 조약을 맺다 conclude a humiliating peace

—감 a sense of humiliation — 외교 humiliating diplomacy ; crow-eating diplomacy

굴 우물 窟— a deep〔bottomless〕 well

*굴절 屈折 refraction —하다 be refracted ; bend ¶ 굴절 자재의 flexible

— 렌즈 a refractive lens ; a refractor — 매체 a refractive medium ; a refractor

굴절 屈節 abandonment of one's integrity〔principles〕 —하다 abandon one's integrity〔principles〕

굴절각 屈折角 [광선의] the angle of

refraction ; a refraction angle ; [프리즘 따위의] a refracting angle
굴절계 屈折計 a refractometer
굴절 광선 屈折光線 a refracted ray of light
굴절력 屈折力 refractive power
굴절률 屈折率 a refractive index ; an index of refraction
굴절 망원경 屈折望遠鏡 a refracting telescope ; a refractor
굴절어 屈折語 an inflected〔inflectional〕 language
굴젓 pickled oysters ¶ 어리굴젓 salted oysters with hot pepper
굴젓눈이 a man with only one eye
굴조개 an oyster
굴종 屈從 submission ; surrender —하다 submit (tamely) 《to》 ; yield 《to》 ; succumb 《to》 ; come down ¶ 굴종시키다 bring 《a person》 to his knees ; keep 《a person》 down
굴지 屈指 counting on one's fingers ; eminence ; prominence ¶ 굴지의 leading ; prominent ; distinguished ; foremost // 굴지의 실업가 a leading businessman // 그는 우리 나라 굴지의 부자이다 He is one of the richest men in the country.
굴지성 屈地性 〖생물〗 geotropism
굴진 oily soot that collects in a chimney 〔hypocaust〕
굴진 掘進 digging through —하다 dig through
굴착 掘鑿 digging ; excavation —하다 dig out ; excavate ¶ 굴착 공사 excavation work
굴착기 掘鑿機 an excavator
굴참나무 〖식물〗 an oriental oak
굴총 掘塚 opening〔violating〕 a grave ; digging〔laying〕 a grave open
굴침스럽다 (be) dogged ; determined
굴타리먹다 rot ; get worm-eaten ; become wormy
굴퉁이 a gimcrack ; a trumpery ; a gewgaw
굴피 —皮 an empty pocket〔purse〕 [참나무 껍데기] oak bark
굴하다 屈— [몸을] bend ; stoop ; [마음을] yield〔submit, give in〕 《to》 ; bow one's head 《to》 ¶ …에 굴하지 않고 in spite of ; in the teeth of ; in defiance of ; undaunted // 권력에 굴하다 yield 〔bow〕 to power // 역경에 굴하지 않다 bear up under an adversity // 유혹에 굴하다 yield to temptation // 그는 한 번의 실패에 굴하지 않고 맹진했다 He pushed on undaunted by a single failure.
굴혈 窟穴 a cave ; a tunnel ; a den (소굴)
굴회 —膾 raw oysters ; a dish of fresh oysters
굵기 thickness
*굵다 [몸피가] (be) big ; thick ; burly ; [목소리가] deep ; thick ; [선이] heavy ; [행동 따위가] bold ; strong-nerved ¶ 굵게 thickly ; deeply // 굵은 실 a thick thread // 굵은 연필 a broad pencil // 굵은 팔 a big arm // 몸집이 굵은 사람 a burly man // 굵게 쓰여지는 만년필 a broad-pointed fountain pen // 굵은 목소리로 in a deep〔thick〕 voice // 신경이 굵다 be bold ; be daring // 굵은 글씨로 쓰다 write in bold strokes // 가장 훌륭한 인생은 짧고 굵게 사는 것이다 The best kind of life is one that's short but full.
굵다랗다 (be) very thick ; very big ; [목소리가] very deep
굵어지다 become thick ; thicken
굵직굵직 —하다 be all thick〔big, burly, deep〕 ¶ 굵직굵직하게 썰다 cut into big slices
굵직하다 be somewhat thick〔big, burly, deep, fat〕
굶기다 let 《a person》 go hungry ; starve ; make 《a person》 starve ¶ 처자를 굶기다 let one's family go hungry // 굶겨 죽이다 starve 《a person》 to death
*굶다 starve ; go hungry ; famish ; go without food〔eating〕 ; skip a meal ¶ 굶어 죽다 starve to death ; die of hunger // 나는 하루 종일 굶었다 I have not touched food all day. /I haven't eaten all day. // 욕보기보다는 차라리 굶어 죽겠다 I prefer death by starvation to an insult. /I would rather die of hunger than become subjected to an insult〔humiliation〕. // 굶은 사람은 가리는 게 없다 Nothing comes amiss to a hungry man. // 그들은 사막에서 길을 잃고 굶어 죽었다 They got lost in the desert and starved to death. // 욕되게 사느니 차라리 굶어 죽겠다 I'd rather starve to death than live in dishonor. // 제 3 세계에서는 수많은 사람들이 굶어 죽고 있다 A lot of people are dying of hunger in the Third World. // 그들은 여러 날 굶었다 They went hungry for days.
굶어 보아야 세상을 안다 〔속담〕 The worth of a thing is best known by the want of it. /Wealth is best known by want of it.
굶어 죽기는 정승하기보다 어렵다 〔속담〕 Everyday brings its bread with it.
열흘 굶어 아니 나는 생각 없다 〔속담〕 Hunger and cold deliver a man up to his enemy. /There is no virtue that poverty destroys not.
*굶주리다 be〔go〕 hungry ; starve ; [갈망하다] hunger 《for, after》 ; thirst 《for, after》 ; hanker 《for, after》 ¶ 돈〔사랑〕에 굶주리다 hanker after money〔love〕 // 배움에 굶주리다 thirst for learning // 권력에 굶주리다 hunger for power // 어머니가 없는 아이들은 애정에 굶주려 있다 The motherless children starve for

affection.

‡**굶주림** hunger ; starvation ¶ 굶주림을 면하다 stave〔keep〕 off hunger // 그는 한 덩어리의 빵으로 굶주림을 달랬다 He staved off his hunger with a loaf of bread.

굼닐다 bend and stretch ; do a stretch-up

굼뜨다 (be) slow ; tardy ; sluggish ; dull ¶ 일에 굼뜨다 be slow〔clumsy〕 at the job // 사리에 굼뜨다 be slow to understand // 굼뜬 사람 a laggard

굼벵이 [벌레] a maggot ; [사람] a laggard ; a sluggard ; a slow person

굼벵이도 다치면 꾸풀한다 속담 Tread on a worm and it will turn.

굼슬겁다 be more generous than ⟪one⟫ looks

굼실거리다 writhe ; wriggle ; squirm ¶ 굼실굼실 wrigglingly

굼적거리다 budge ; stir

굼지럭거리다 budge ; stir

굼튼튼하다 (be) steady ; solid ; thrifty ; provident ; tightfisted

굼틀거리다 wriggle ; squirm ; writhe ¶ 굼틀거리며 나아가다 wriggle along // 뱀이 굼틀거리며 길을 건너간다 A snake wriggles across the road.

굼틀하다 wiggle ; wriggle

굽 [마소의] a hoof ; [구두의] a heel ; [받침] the bottom ; a foot ; the base ¶ 사발 굽 the bottom of a dish // 나막신 굽 clog-supports ; the base of a wooden shoe // 굽이 있는 동물 a hoofed animal // 굽이 높은〔낮은〕 구두 high-heeled 〔low-heeled〕 shoes // 갈라진 굽 cloven hoofs // 그의 구두의 굽은 닳았다 The heels of his shoes are worn down.

굽갈다 put new clog-supports on ⟪a pair of wooden shoes⟫

***굽다**[1] (be) bent ; crooked ; winding ¶ 굽은 나무 a crooked tree // 굽은 길 a winding path

굽은 나무가 선산을 지킨다 속담 Crooked logs make straight fires.

†**굽다**[2] roast ; broil ; bake (감자 따위를) ; toast (빵 따위를) ; do (고기 따위를) ; grill (석쇠로) ; parch ¶ 잘 구워진 well-done ; well baked // 덜 구워진 medium (중간) ; rare (설 구워진) // 빵을 굽다 bake bread // 떡을 굽다 toast rice cakes over a fire // 벽돌을 굽다 make 〔burn, bake, fire〕 bricks // 도자기를 굽다 bake〔fire〕 pottery // 빵 한 조각을 굽다 toast a slice of bread // 생선을 굽다 broil fish // 숯을 굽다 burn〔make, bake〕 charcoal // 고기가 설구워졌다 The meat is underdone〔rare〕. // 이 고기는 너무 구워졌다 This meat is overdone.

굽달이 a footed plate〔dish〕

굽도리 the lower parts of the walls of a room

굽슬굽슬하다 (be) curled ; curly ⇨ 곱슬곱슬하다

굽실거리다 cringe ⟪to⟫ ; cower ⟪before⟫ ; fawn ⟪upon⟫ ; bow one's head ; kowtow ¶ 굽실굽실 obsequiously // 머리를 굽실거리다 bob〔bow〕 one's head ; kowtow // 몸을 굽실거리다 make an obeisance // 그는 상관의 비위를 맞추느라고 굽실거린다 He cringes to his superior to make him happy.

굽싸다 tie up the four feet (of an animal) ; tie up by the hooves

굽어보다 [내려다보다] look down ⟪on⟫ ; overlook ; command〔take〕 a bird's-eye view of ; [살피다] take a kindly interest in ; consider ; pay attention to ¶ 골짜기를 굽어보다 look down into a valley // 민정을 굽어보다 look into the condition of the people

굽어살피다 take a kindly interest in ; pay attention to ¶ 하늘이여 굽어살피소서 Heaven be my witness.

굽이 a turn ⟪of a river⟫ ; a bend〔turning〕 ⟪of a road⟫ ; the curve ⟪of a street⟫ ¶ 굽이마다 at every turn〔bend, corner〕

굽이감다 [휘감다] wind ; twist round ; [감돌다] make a curve ⟪around⟫

굽이굽이 [굽이마다] at every turn 〔bend〕 ; [흐르는 모양] windingly ; meanderingly ; in zigzag ¶ 굽이굽이 흐르는 강 a winding〔meandering, serpentine〕 river // 한강은 굽이굽이 흘러 서울을 거쳐 황해로 빠진다 The *Han* River winds its way through *Seoul* to the Yellow Sea.

굽이돌다 wind〔curve〕 around ; make a curve ⟪around⟫ ¶ 굽이도는 시냇물 a meandering stream

굽이지다 make a bend〔turn, curve〕 ¶ 황하는 거기서 동쪽으로 크게 굽이진다 The Yellow River takes its great eastward bend there.

†**굽이치다** wind ; meander ; undulate ; swell (파도가) ; surge ; roll ¶ 물이 굽이쳐 흐르다 a stream meanders back and forth

굽잡다 lay ⟪a person⟫ under restraint ; make ⟪a person⟫ feel uneasy ; have ⟪a person⟫ in one's grasp

굽잡히다 be made to feel small ; be at ⟪a person's⟫ mercy

굽적 with an awe-stricken bow **—하다** make an awe-stricken bow ⟪with one's body⟫

굽정이 a crooked article ; something bent

굽죄이다 have qualms〔misgivings〕 ; have an uneasy conscience ; have a sense of having done wrong ; feel compunction ; be apprehensive ; feel small 〔intimidated, overawed, frightened〕 ; be ashamed〔embarrassed〕 ¶ 부인한테 굽죄여 지내다 be henpecked

굽질리다 run into a snag ; 《a matter》 fail to go smoothly
굽창 a leather reinforcing strip on the heel of a straw shoe
굽통 ① [마소의] a hoof ② [화살대의] the bamboo butt 《of an arrow》
굽통줄 the cords connecting a harrow and the traces
굽히다 bend 《one's back》 ; bow 《one's head》 ; stoop 《one's body》 ; curve 《a wire》 ; twist ; pervert ; deviate〔deflect〕 from 《one's principle》 ; yield ; submit ¶ 허리를〔몸을〕 굽히다 bend one's back ; bend forward ; stoop over ; bend over ; bend down ; bow // 주의를 굽히다 deflect from one's principle // 주장을 굽히다 concede a point // 의지를 굽히다 yield〔submit〕 to another's view // 주장을 굽히지 않다 hold fast to one's own views ; stick to one's guns
굿[1] exorcism **—하다** exorcise
굿[2] [구덩이] a pit ; a hole
굿거리 a tune〔dance〕 performed during exorcism
굿막 —幕 a pit-side hut for miners to rest
굿문 —門 the opening〔mouth〕 of a mining pit
굿바이히트 〖야구〗 a game-ending hit
굿보다 ① [굿을 구경하다] see a performance of exorcism ② [방관하다] remain an unconcerned spectator ; sit on the fence
굿일 digging a pit〔grave〕
굿중 a mendicant monk〔priest〕 **—패** a band of mendicant monks
굿짓다 dig a pit〔grave〕
굿하다 exorcise ; perform an exorcism
궁 宮 a palace ¶ 창덕궁 the *Ch'angdŏk* Palace
궁 窮 [없어짐] exhaustion ; being used up ; [궁박] poverty ; [막힘] being driven to the wall **—하다** be in want ; be reduced to poverty ; (be) destitute ; be driven to the wall
궁 弓 a bow ⇨ 활
궁경 窮境 [가난] poverty ; destitution ; reduced circumstances ; [궁지] a predicament ; a sad plight ; a fix ; an extremity ¶ 궁경에 빠지다 be in great difficulties〔straits〕 ; be driven to the wall ; be cornered ; be in a dilemma ; be in a fix // 궁경에서 빠져 나오다 get out of trouble〔difficulties〕
궁계 窮計 the last shift〔resort〕 ; the last 〔final〕 expedient ; a desperate measure
궁곡 窮谷 an abysmal ravine ; a deep valley
궁곤 窮困 poverty ; destitution ; straitened circumstances **—하다** (be) needy ; destitute ; distressed
궁구 窮究 thorough investigation〔study, research〕 **—하다** investigate thoroughly ; make an exhaustive study of ; study thoroughly ; master
궁굴다 [그릇이] be larger than it looks ; hold more than one might expect
궁굴리다 be tolerant ; forgive with kind words〔remark〕 ; be generous
궁궁이 〖식물〗 Angelica polymorpha (학명)
궁궐 宮闕 the royal palace ¶ 궁궐 같은 집 a palatial residence ; a palace
‡**궁극** 窮極 finality ; extremity ; eventuality ¶ 궁극의 final ; ultimate // 궁극의 목적 one's ultimate purpose〔object〕 // 궁극의 승리 a final victory // 궁극에 가서는 in the end ; in the long run ; in the last analysis ; ultimately
— 목적 the final end〔aim〕 ; the ultimate object **—성** 〖철학〗 finality **— 원인** 〖철학〗 the final〔ultimate〕 cause
궁글다 [속이 비다] (be) hollow ; empty ; be left empty ; [소리가] (be) deep ; hollow ¶ 속이 궁근 나무 a hollow tree
궁글막대 a packsaddle strut
궁금증 —症 anxiety ¶ 궁금증을 풀다 gratify〔satisfy〕 one's curiosity
궁금하다 (be) anxious〔worried, concerned, nervous〕 《about》 ¶ 소식이 궁금하다 be anxious to hear from 《a person》 // 시험 결과가 궁금하다 be worried about the result of the examination // 개표 결과가 궁금하다 be concerned about the result of the ballot counting // 그들의 안부가 궁금하다 I am anxious to know how they are. // 그들에게 무슨 일이 일어났는지 궁금하다 I wonder what happened to them.
궁기 窮氣 a meager appearance ; a wretched look ; wretchedness ¶ 궁기가 낀 poor looking
궁끼다 窮— suffer impoverishment ; be destitute ; be in a fix
궁내 宮內 the royal household ; the palace
궁녀 宮女 a court lady ; a maid of honor
궁노 宮奴 a court servant ; servants in the royal employ
궁노루 〖동물〗 a musk deer ; Moschus moschiferus parvipes (학명)
궁답 宮畓 rice fields owned by the royal family
궁도 弓道 archery ; bowmanship
궁도 窮途 straitened circumstances ; a fix
궁도련님 宮— a green youth ; a young buck ; a rich man's son who is ignorant of the world ; a greenhorn ; a raw stripling ; a novice
궁도령 宮— ⇨ 궁도련님
궁둥방아 a pratfall 《미》 ; a fall on one's

backside〔behind, buttocks〕 ¶ 궁둥방아를 찧다 fall on one's backside〔buttocks〕; come down flop on one's bottom; take a pratfall // 의자에 앉다가 잘못하여 궁둥방아를 찧었다 I missed the chair and sat right down on the floor.

*궁둥이 the buttocks; the hips; the rump; the fundament; the backside; one's bottom〔behind〕 ¶ 궁둥이가 질기다 stay too long; outstay one's welcome

궁둥이가 무겁다 (관용) be lazy; be inactive; be sluggish

궁둥이뼈 〖해부〗 the innominate bone; the hipbone; the hucklebone

궁둥잇바람 lively hip-shaking

궁둥잇짓 shaking one's hips

궁둥짝 either hip; both hips

궁따다 make irrelevant〔absurd〕 remarks; pretend not to know

궁뚱망뚱하다 (be) rustic; mean; miserable; be neglected and shabby (-looking)

‡궁리 窮理 [연구함] study〔research〕 of the laws of nature; [생각함] deliberation; consideration; thinking —하다 deliberate; consider; ponder 《on, about》; mull over; [사물을 연구하다] study the laws of nature ¶ 아무리 궁리해도 좋은 수가 없다 I can think of no better plan.

궁마 弓馬 a bow and a horse; archery and horsemanship

궁민 窮民 poor people; the needy; the destitute; poverty-stricken people

궁박 窮迫 destitution; distress; straitened circumstances —하다 be in needy circumstances; be distressed in a fix; (be) destitute; poverty-stricken ¶ 재정적으로 궁박하다 be in financial difficulty

궁벽 窮僻 —하다 (be) secluded; remote; unfrequented; be out of the way

궁사 弓師 a bowyer; a bow maker

궁상 弓狀 arch ¶ 궁상의 bow-shaped; crescent-shaped; arched

궁상 窮狀 a distressed condition; a sad plight; straitened circumstances ¶ 궁상에 빠져 있다 be in dire〔extreme〕 straits // 농촌의 궁상은 실로 형언할 수 없다 The miserable life of farmers is really hard to describe.

궁상 窮相 a meager face; poor〔wretched〕 outlook ¶ 궁상인 사람 a poor-looking man

궁상맞다 窮相— be miserable-looking; have a look of poverty

궁상스럽다 窮相— be poor〔wretched〕-looking ¶ 궁상스러운 옷차림을 한 여자 a poorly dressed woman

궁색 窮塞 poverty; destitution; want; distress —하다 (be) poor; needy; destitute ¶ 그때가 나의 가장 궁색한 시기였다 That was the worst time of my life.

궁서 窮鼠 a cornered mouse; a rat at bay ¶ 궁서는 오히려 고양이를 문다 A stag at bay is a dangerous foe.

궁성 宮城 a royal palace

궁수 弓手 an archer; a bowman

궁수자리 弓手— 〖천문〗 the Archer; Sagittarius

*궁술 弓術 archery; bowmanship
—가 an archer; a bow-and-arrow man
— 대회 an archery match

궁술사 弓術師 a master of archery

궁시 弓矢 bow and arrow

궁실 宮室 a royal chamber; the royal palace

궁여일책 窮餘一策 ⇨ 궁여지책

궁여지책 窮餘之策 the last resort; a desperate shift〔measure〕 ¶ 궁여지책으로 as the last resort〔expedient〕; as a desperate measure〔shift〕 // 나는 궁여지책을 생각해냈다 I have thought out a plan as the last resort.

궁의 弓衣 a bow case

궁인 弓人 a bowyer; a bow maker

궁인 宮人 a court lady ⇨ 나인

궁전 宮田 fields owned by the royal family

†궁전 宮殿 a (royal) palace ¶ 궁전 같은 집 a palace of a house; a palatial residence; a mansion

궁전 弓箭 bow and arrow

궁절 窮節 a time of straits

궁정 宮廷 the Court; Court circles
— 문학 court literature — 시인 a cavalier poet — 정치 palace politics — 화가 a court painter

궁중 宮中 the Royal Court ¶ 궁중에서 at Court // 궁중에서 봉사하다 serve at Court
— 서열 the order of precedency at Court; a court rank — 예복 a court dress

궁중말 宮中— (royal) court language; a court(ly) term

궁중 문학 宮中文學 court literature

*궁지 窮地 a difficult situation; a fix; a dilemma; a sorry〔sad〕 plight ¶ 궁지에 빠지다 be in a fix〔tight place, sad plight〕; get oneself into a fix; be〔stand〕 at bay // 궁지에 빠뜨리다 drive〔force〕 《a person》 into a corner; put 《a person》 in a hole; drive〔push, thrust〕 《a person》 to the wall; bring〔drive〕 to bay // 궁지에 몰리다 be pushed to the wall; be driven into a corner // 궁지에 몰려 반항하다 turn〔come〕 to bay // 궁지에서 헤어나다 get out of trouble〔difficulty〕

궁진 窮盡 exhaustion —하다 exhaust

궁창 穹蒼 the vault of heaven; the sky; the blue sky

궁책 窮策 the last shift〔resort〕; a desperate measure ⇨ 궁계
궁체 宮體 the court style of writing the Korean script
궁촌 窮村 a poor〔poverty-stricken〕 village ¶ 궁촌 벽지 a poor and remote village
궁춘 窮春 a spring season when peasants are hard up for food ; the period of spring poverty ⇨ 춘궁기
궁태 窮態 extreme straits ; distress ⇨ 궁상(窮狀)
궁터 宮― the site of an old palace
궁핍 窮乏 want ; destitution ; poverty ; penury ; necessitous circumstances
―하다 (be) destitute ; poor ; be in needy〔straitened, necessitous〕 circumstances ¶ 궁핍한 생활 a life of distress 〔want〕; a needy life ; a life of austerity 《영》// 궁핍한 생활을 하다 live in destitution ; live a needy life ; live in poverty // 재정적인 궁핍 financial difficulties // 자금이 궁핍하다 We are in need of funds. // 궁핍에 허덕이다 suffer from〔be tormented by〕 poverty
궁하다 窮― [가난하다] (be) poor ; destitute ; be in want ; be in straitened circumstances ; [난처하다] be at a loss ; be puzzled ; be in difficulties ; be driven to the wall ; be cornered ¶ 궁한 때에 in time of need // 대답에 궁하다 be at a loss for an answer // 돈에 궁하다 be hard up for money // 생활에 궁하다 be unable to make a living // 그는 궁하면 무슨 짓이라도 한다 He would go to extremes if cornered.
궁하면 통한다 속담 There is always a way out. /Want makes wit. /Where one door shuts, another opens. /Necessity is the mother of invention.
궁합 宮合 marital harmony as predicted by a fortuneteller
궁행 躬行 personal practice **―하다** carry out 《by oneself》; exemplify ; do 《something》 personally
궁향 窮鄕 a secluded part of the country ; a remote place
궁형 弓形 a crescent form ; 〖기하〗 a segment of a circle
궂기다 ① [일이] go wrong ; fail ② [죽다] meet one's death ; die
궂다[1] ① [날씨가] (be) bad ; foul ; inclement ; nasty ② [성질이] bad ; ill-natured ; cross-minded ¶ 궂은 날씨 nasty〔bad〕 weather // 암상궂다 be jealous
궂다[2] [눈이 멀다] become blind ; lose one's sight
궂은고기 carrion ; dead and putrefying flesh
궂은비 a long rain
궂은살 superfluous flesh
궂은쌀 rice roughly hulled ; rice of poor quality
궂은일 a misfortune ; a disaster ; an unlucky affair ; an untoward event ¶ 좋은 일이 있으면 궂은일도 있다 Good and evil are interwoven. /Every cloud has a silver lining.
궂히다 be bereaved of 《a person》; lose 《a person in death》; have 《a person》 die ¶ 아버지를 궂히다 lose one's father
†**권 券** [책의] a volume ; a book ; [영화의] a reel ; [한지 20장] 20 sheets of Korean paper ¶ 제1권 the first volume ; book one // 5권으로 된 영화 a five-reel picture〔movie〕// 3권으로 된 저서 a work in three volumes
권 勸 [추천] recommendation ; [권고] advice ; suggestion ; [장려] encouragement **―하다** recommend ; advise ; suggest ; offer ; press (강하게) ; encourage ; invite (권유하다) ¶ 책을 권하다 recommend a book to 《a person》// 담배를 권하다 offer 《a person》 a cigarette // 담배를 피우지 말도록 권하다 advise against smoking ; advise 《a person》 not to smoke ; dissuade 《a person》 from smoking // 손님에게 먹을 것을 무리하게 권하지 마라 You must not press food on your guest. // 의사의 권에 따라 부산으로 전지했다 Following the advice of the doctor, he went to *Pusan* for a change of air.
-권 券 document ; ticket ; card ; bill ; chit ¶ 5,000원권 a 5,000-*won* bill // 우대권 a complimentary ticket
-권 圈 a circle ; a range ; a sphere ; a radius (반경) ¶ 북극권 the Arctic Circle // 태풍권 내에 in the typhoon area
-권 權 [권력] authority ; power ; [권리] a right ; a claim ; [이권] a concession ¶ 부권 the father's authority // 입법권 legislative power // 재산권 the right of property // 채굴권 a mineral power ; a mining concession // 통치권 sovereignty
권계 勸戒 ―하다 admonish ; exhort ; warn ; remonstrate 《with》
권고 勸告 advice ; counsel ; recommendation **―하다** advise ; urge ; recommend ¶ 의사의 권고에 따라 on a doctor's advice // 친구의 권고로 at the urging of friend // 사직을 권고하다 urge〔advise〕 《a person》 to resign
―서(장) written advice ; a letter advising〔urging〕 《a person to do》 **―자** an adviser〔advisor〕; a counselor
권고 眷顧 ―하다 look after ; patronize ; favor
권고 사직 勸告辭職 advice to resign
권내 圈內 ¶ 권내에 within the sphere 〔circle, range, radius〕 《of》// 세력 권내에 있다 be within the sphere of influence // 무전의 통신 권내에 있다 be within the radius of radio communication //

당선 권내에 들어 있다 His election is within the bounds of possibility.

권농 勸農 encouragement of agriculture **—하다** promote〔encourage〕 agriculture〔farming〕

—일 Farmers' Day **— 정책** the farm encouragement policy

***권능 權能** competency ; power ; authority ¶ 권능을 부여하다 empower 《a person》; authorize ; vest 《a person》 with power

권당질 sewing 《it》 together by mistake

권도 勸導 —하다 guide ; lead ; admonish

권도 權道 political expediency ; a policy adapted to circumstances

권두 卷頭 the opening〔beginning〕 page of a book ; the beginning〔commencement〕 of a book

권두사 卷頭辭 a preface ; a foreword ; an introduction ; a preamble

권두언 卷頭言 a preface ; a foreword ; an introduction ; a preamble

†권력 權力 power ; authority ; [세력] influence ¶ 국가의 권력 governmental 〔state〕 power // 권력 있는 powerful ; influential // 권력 없는 powerless ; without authority〔power〕; uninfluential // 권력을 휘두르다 wield〔exercise〕 authority 〔power〕// 권력을 주다 invest 《a person》 with power ; empower // 권력을 잡다 seize power // 권력을 다투다 contend for supremacy

— 구조 《the Soviet》 power structure **— 국가** an authoritarian state **—욕(欲)** desire〔lust〕 for power **— 정치** power politics **—주의** authoritarianism **—형 축재** accumulation of illicit wealth by exercising one's influence

권력가 權力家 a man of power〔influence〕; a person in power ; a power holder

권력 분립 權力分立 division of powers ; respective independence of the legislature, the executive, and the judicature

권력 의지 權力意志 〚철학〛 will to power

권력자 權力者 a man of power〔influence〕; a person in power ; a power holder

권력 투쟁 權力鬪爭 a struggle for power ; a power struggle

권련 眷戀 a deep affection **—하다** have a deep affection 《for》; have a strong attachment 《to》

†권리 權利 a right ; [청구권] a claim ; [소유권] a title ; [특권] a privilege ; [권한] authority ; powers ¶ 권리와 의무 rights and duties // 기득의 권리〔기득권〕 vested rights // 법률상의 권리 legal rights // 평등한 권리로 on terms of equality // 권리를 행사〔남용〕하다 exercise〔abuse〕 one's right // 권리를 주장하다 assert〔insist upon〕 one's rights // 권리를 침해하다 infringe on 《a person's》 rights // 권리를 취득하다 acquire a right // 권리를 상실하다 forfeit〔lose〕 one's rights // 권리를 사다 buy an interest in (경영의) ; buy the good will of (점포의) // 권리를 요구하다 claim one's rights

— 정지 lapse〔suspension〕 of rights **— 증서** a certificate of title **— 포기** the relinquishment〔release〕 of (one's) legal claim 《to》; quitclaim (토지 따위) **— 포기자** a releasor

권리금 權利金 a premium ; key money ¶ 비싼 권리금이 붙은 임대 점포 a rented store〔shop〕 with a high premium

권리 능력 權利能力 capacity of enjoyment of rights

권리락 權利落 〚주식〛 ex rights ; rights off

권리자 權利者 a rightful person

권리증 權利證 ⇨ 등기필증

권리 침해 權利侵害 violation of another's rights ; injury

권리 행위 權利行爲 a rightful act

권말 卷末 the end of a volume〔book〕

권매 權賣 conditional sale **—하다** sell 《a thing》 on the terms that reimbursement will be made in case the goods bought are returned

권면 券面 the face of a bill ; a denomination

권면 勸勉 encouragement **—하다** encourage〔admonish〕 《a person to do》

권모 權謀 a trick ; a scheme ; machination ; an intrigue

—가 a schemer ; a Machiavellian ; a crafty〔wily〕 person **— 외교** Machiavellian diplomacy

권모 술수 權謀術數 trickery ; machination ; diplomacy ; finesse ; Machiavel(lian)ism ¶ 권모 술수를 쓰다 resort to trickery〔machination〕; use diplomacy ; employ every possible form of tactics ; appeal to Machiavellian diplomacy // 권모 술수에 능한 사람 a master schemer

권문 權門 ⇨ 권문 세가

권문 세가 權門勢家 an influential〔a powerful〕 family ; a man of influence

권법 拳法 *tangsu*

권병 權柄 power ; authority ; influence ¶ 권병을 휘두르다 wield power ; exercise authority〔influence〕

권불십년 權不十年 Roses and maidens soon lose their bloom. /All that's fair must fade. /Every flow has its ebb.

권비 眷庇 favor ; protection ; patronage **—하다** favor ; patronize ; take 《a person》 under one's wings

권사 勸士 [기독교] a deaconess ; a Bible woman

권선 勸善 promotion of virtue ; exhortation to righteousness ; [불교의] soliciting contributions for religious purposes **—하다** exhort to righteousness ; encourage to do good ; urge to contribute

권선 捲線 a coil ; winding

권선기 捲線機 a (coil) winding machine

권선징악 勸善懲惡 promotion of virtue and reproval of vice ; encouraging good and punishing evil **—하다** reward 〔promote〕 the good and punish the wicked
—극(劇) a morality play ; a moralizing 〔didactic〕 drama **— 소설** a didactic novel

권세 權勢 power ; influence ; authority ¶ 아버지의 권세로 through the influence of one's father // 돈의 권세는 대단하다 Money is everything.
—욕 the desire〔lust〕 for power ; the will to power
권세(를) 부리다 (관용) wield〔exercise〕 power〔authority〕

권속 眷屬 [식구] a family ; a household ; [아내] one's wife ¶ 일가 권속 a whole family ; one's kith and kin

권솔 眷率 a family ; the members of a household

권수 卷首 ① [첫째 권] the first volume ② [권두] the beginning of a book

권수 卷鬚 〖식물〗 a cirrus 《*pl.* -ri》 ; a tendril

권수 卷數 the number of volumes

권신 權臣 an influential vassal ; a powerful courtier

권애 眷愛 love ; favor ; loving and cherishing

권양기 捲揚機 a winch

권업 勸業 encouragement of industry **—하다** encourage〔promote〕 industry

권연 卷煙 cigarettes ⇨ 궐련

권외 圈外 ¶ 권외에 outside the circle 〔range, radius〕 《of》 // 정치 권외에 outside the sphere of politics ; away from politics // 통신 권외에 있다 be out of the radius of communication // 당선 권외에 떨어지다 be outside the running

권우 眷遇 warm treatment (by the king) **—하다** give warm treatment ; favor

권운 卷雲 a cirrus 《*pl.* -ri》

권원 權原 a title ; the ground of claim

†**권위 權威** [권력] authority ; power ; [위엄] dignity ; prestige ; [권위자] an authority ; an expert ; a master ¶ 권위 있는 authoritative // 권위 있는 잡지 a magazine of authority // 국회의 권위 향상 promotion of the authority of the Assembly // 영문학의 세계적 권위 a world authority on English literature // 이론 물리학에 관한 권위 있는 저작 an authoritative work on theoretical physics // 현대〔사계(斯界)〕의 최고 권위 the highest authority of the day〔in that line〕 // 권위 있는 소식통에게 듣다 learn from authoritative sources // 그의 말에는 권위가 있다 He speaks with authority.
—서(書) an old standard authority

권위자 權威者 an authority ; an expert ; a master

권위주의 權威主義 authoritarianism

*†**권유 勸誘** [운동] canvassing ; solicitation ; [유인] invitation ; [장려] persuasion ; encouragement **—하다** canvass 〔solicit〕 for ; invite ; ask ; persuade ¶ 보험을〔기부를〕 권유하다 canvass for insurance〔subscription〕 // 가입을 권유하다 invite 《a person》 to join 《a club》 // 나는 김 군의 권유로 정구부에 들었다 I have been persuaded by Mr. *Kim* to join the tennis club. // 어떤 사람도 선거에 관하여 기부를 권유하거나 요구하여서는 안된다 No person shall solicit or request others for contributions in connection with elections.
—원(員) a canvasser ; a solicitor **—장(狀)** a canvassing letter ; a letter of solicitation ; an invitation

권유 勸諭 admonition ; counsel **—하다** admonish ; counsel

권의 卷衣 toga ; sari ; saree ; sarong

권익 權益 rights and interests ¶ 우리들의 권익은 보호되어야 한다 Our rights and interests must be protected.
국가 — national interests **기득(旣得) —** vested rights〔interest〕 **특별(特別) —** special interests

권장 勸奬 encouragement ; recommendation ; promotion **—하다** encourage ; recommend ; promote ¶ 임산부에 …할 것을 권장하다 give advice to the expectant and nursing mothers to 《do》

권적운 卷積雲 a cirrocumulus ¶ 권적운이 있는 하늘 a mackerel sky

권점 圈點 a small circle for emphasis ; [종지부] a period ¶ 권점을 찍다 mark 《words》 with small circles ; underline 《the passage》 ; put a period

권좌 權座 the seat of power ; a position of authority〔power〕 ¶ 권좌를 떠나다 resign one's power // 권좌에서 쫓겨나다 be forced from power // 권좌에 있다 hold the seat of power // 권좌에 오르다 come to〔into〕 power

권주 勸酒 offering wine 《to a person》 **—하다** offer 《a person》 wine

권주가 勸酒歌 ① a song to offer wine 《to a person》 ② a Korean drinking song

권지 勸止 dissuasion **—하다** dissuade from 《doing》

권질 卷帙 volumes ; books

권징 勸懲 ⇨ 권선 징악

권척 卷尺 a tape measure

*†**권총 拳銃** a pistol ; a revolver (연발의) ; a gun 《미》 ¶ 구경 38밀리의 권총

a 38 revolver // 권총을 겨누다 point 〔level〕 a gun 《at》 // 권총을 쏘다 fire a pistol 《at》 // 권총으로 협박하다 threaten 《a person》 with a revolver // 아무의 머리에 권총을 들이대다 hold a pistol 〔gun〕 to a person's head // 권총으로 때리다 pistol-whip // 권총 사정 거리 pistol shot

— 강도 an armed robber ; a gunman 《미》 신호 — a Very pistol 6연발 — a sixchambered revolver ; a six-shooter 《미》 자동 — an automatic〔a self-cocking〕 revolver 장난감 — a toy pistol 콜트식 — a Colt (revolver)

권축 卷軸 a scroll

권층운 卷層雲 a cirrostratus

권태 倦怠 weariness ; fatigue ; languor ; tedium ; ennui ¶ 권태를 느끼다 become weary〔tired, fatigued〕 ; feel languor〔languid〕 ; be〔get〕 bored ; have a tired feeling

권태기 倦怠期 a period of lassitude ¶ 권태기에 들다 (부부가) get into the state of ennui in married life

권토중래 捲土重來 —하다 surge back again with fresh〔increased, renewed〕 force ; make another attempt with redoubled〔renewed〕 energies

***권투** 拳鬪 boxing ; pugilism ; a prizefight (흥행) ¶ 권투를 하다 box with 《a person》

—계(界) boxing〔fistic〕 circles — 기술 pugilistic〔fistic 《구》〕 skill — 선수 a boxer ; a pugilist ; [프로의] a professional〔prize〕 fighter — 시합 a boxing bout〔match〕 ; a (glove) fight ; a fistic contest ; a prizefight (현상금부의) —장 a (boxing) ring ; a fistic arena — 장갑 boxing gloves —팬 a boxing fan

권투

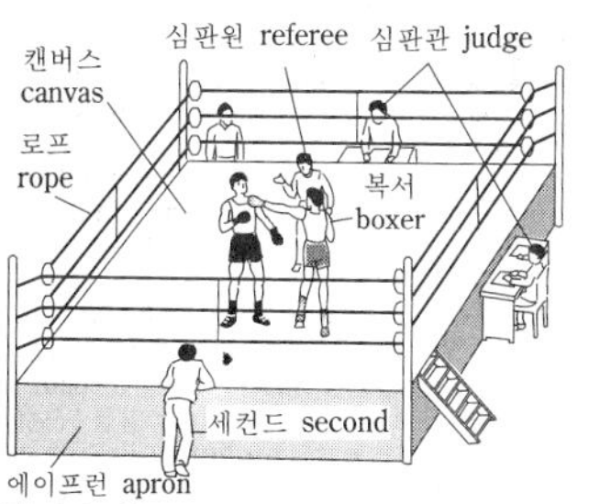

***권하다** 勸— ① [권고] ask ; exhort ; advise ; persuade ¶ 아무한테 회에 들라고 권하다 ask a person to join a society // 담배를 피지 말라고 권하다 advise against smoking ; advise 《a person》 not to smoke

② [추천] recommend ¶ 책을 권하다 recommend a book 《to a person》

③ [음식·물건을] offer 《a person something》 ; present 《a person with something》 ¶ 담배〔차〕를 권하다 offer a cigarette〔a cup of tea〕 // 술을 권하다 offer 《a person》 (a glass of) wine 〔liquor〕 ; ask 《a person》 to have some liquor ; [강권하다] force〔press〕 wine on 《a person》 // 권커니 잣거니 술을 마시다 exchange glasses with each other while drinking

권학 勸學 the encouragement of learning〔education〕 —하다 encourage 〔promote〕 learning

권한 權限 right ; authority ; power ; [관할] jurisdiction ¶ 권한의 위임 delegation of power // 관청의 권한 the competence of a government office // 권한 다툼 conflict of attribution // 권한을 부여하다 empower 《a person》 ; authorize // 권한이 있다 have the right〔authority, power〕 to 《do》 ; be authorized to 《do》 // 권한을 벗어나다 exceed one's authority // 권한을 지키다 observe the limits of competence

권한 대행 權限代行 ¶ 대통령〔총재〕 권한 대행 the acting President

권화 勸化 —하다 [불교에서] solicit contributions for religious purposes

권화 權化 incarnation ; personification ; avatar ¶ 악마의 권화 a devil incarnate 〔personified〕 ; the incarnation of a devil // 자유의 권화 Liberty incarnate // 탐욕의 권화 a perfect picture of avarice ; avarice personified ; the devil of greed // 그는 지혜의 권화이다 He is wisdom personified〔itself〕.

궐[1] 闕 [궁궐] the King's palace

궐[2] 闕 [빠짐] an omission ; a vacancy ; missing —하다 [빠지다] be omitted ; be missing ; [자리가 비다] be left out

궐기 蹶起 —하다 rise ; rouse 《oneself》 to action ; spring up ; stand up 《against》 ¶ 궐기시키다 rouse 《a person》 to action ; stir up // 지금이야말로 궐기할 때다 Now is the time for action.

— 대회 an indignation meeting ; a rally

궐나다 闕— cause a vacancy ; vacate a post

궐내 闕內 the royal palace

***궐련** a cigarette ¶ 궐련을 피우다 smoke a cigarette

— 물부리 a cigarette holder

궐련갑 —匣 a cigarette case

궐문 闕門 the main gate of a palace ; a palace gate

궐문 闕文 missing words ; omitted letters

궐방 闕榜 failure in the examination —하다 fail in the examination

궐석 闕席 [법] non-appearance ; default —하다 make a default

궐석 재판 闕席裁判 judgement by

default
궐식 闕食 skipping a meal —하다 skip〔go without〕 a meal ⇨ 결식
궐위 闕位 a vacancy ; a vacant post〔position〕 —하다 become vacant
궐직 闕直 —하다 fail to keep night watch
궐참 闕參 non-attendance —하다 fail to attend ; absent oneself 《from》
궤 ① an armrest ; an elbow rest ② [책상] a desk ; a writing table ; an altar table
궤 櫃 a chest ; a coffer ; a box
궤간 軌間 a gauge ; a track ¶ 표준 궤간 the standard gauge
궤계 詭計 a trick ; an artifice ; a ruse ; wiles
*궤도 軌道 [천체의] an orbit ; a path ; [기차의] a track ; a rail ¶ 궤도 밖으로〔를 벗어나서〕 out of orbit // 궤도를 선회하는 orbiting // 궤도의 계산 orbital computation // 궤도를 깔다 lay a track // 궤도에 올리다 set 《a matter》 on its way // 인공 위성을 궤도에 올려 놓다 put〔place〕 a satellite in orbit ; orbit a satellite // 일이 궤도에 오를 때 까지는 참고 고생할 상황이다 It's a situation I'll just have to put up with until the work gets on the track.
— 경사 orbital inclination — 기중기 a gantry (crane) —면 〖천문〗 the plane of an orbit — 부설 track construction — 세(稅) the railway line tax — 속도 an orbital velocity — 수준기(水準器) a track level — 요소 orbital element — 용품 permanent way materials ; track appliances — 운동 an orbital motion — 주기 orbital period — 체류 연수 orbital life —축 〖천문〗 the axis of an orbit — 표시기 a track indicator — 회로 a track circuit 단선〔복선〕 — a single〔double〕 (railroad) track 달 — the lunar〔moon〕 orbit 동기(同期) — a synchronous orbit 원(圓)— a circular orbit 전기 — electric tramway 전위(轉位) — a transfer orbit 지구 — the earth's orbit 《(a)round the sun》 타원 — an elliptic orbit 편심(偏心) — an eccentric orbit
궤도를 벗어나다 관용 run off the track ; be erratic
궤도에 오르다 관용 be started along right lines〔in the right direction〕 (회의 따위가) ; [일 따위가] get under way ; get on the track〔on the rails〕
궤도 비행 軌道飛行 an orbital flight ; orbiting
유인(有人) — manned orbiting
궤란 潰爛 decomposition ; decay ; corrosion —하다 ulcerate ; decompose ; decay ; corrode
궤란 潰亂 utter confusion〔disorder〕 —하다 be thrown in a state of utter confusion〔disorder〕
궤멸 潰滅 destruction ; demolition ; [전멸] annihilation —하다 be destroyed ; be ruined ; [궤멸시키다] destroy ; wipe out ¶ 궤멸적 타격을 주다 give a crushing blow
궤배 跪拜 —하다 kneel down and worship
궤범 軌範 an example ; a model ; a pattern ; a standard
궤변 詭辯 sophistry ; sophism ; casuistry ; deceptive talk ¶ 궤변적 sophistic ; casuistic // 궤변을 부리다 quibble ; sophisticate
—술 sophistry
궤변가 詭辯家 a sophist ; a quibbler
궤변 학파 詭辯學派 the sophists
궤복 跪伏 kneeling down —하다 kneel down ; prostrate oneself
궤산 潰散 a rout ; a defeat —하다 be defeated ; be put to rout ; collapse
궤양 潰瘍 〖의학〗 an ulcer
— 대장염 ulcerative colitis —성 구내염(性口內炎) ulcerative stomatitis —암(癌) ulcer cancer ; ulcerocancer (위에 생기는) —학 helcology — 형성 ulceration
궤적 軌跡 [바퀴의] the trace of wheels ; [선인의] the deed of one's predecessors ; 〖기하〗 a locus 《*pl.* -ci》
궤조 軌條 a rail ; a track ⇨ 레일
궤좌 跪坐 —하다 kneel down ; sit on one's feet
궤주 潰走 a rout ; a flight ; [동물군의] a stampede —하다 be routed ; be put to flight〔rout〕 ¶ 적을 궤주시키다 rout the enemy ; put the enemy to flight
궤지기 refuse ; unusable dregs
궤짝 櫃— a box ⇨ 궤 ¶ 사과 한 궤짝 a box of apples // 궤짝에 담다 put 《a thing》 in a box // 궤짝으로 사다 buy 《things》 by the box
궤책 詭策 a trick ; a ruse
궤휼 詭譎 a scheme ; a trick ; an evil design ; wiles —하다 be tricky〔wily, treacherous〕 ¶ 그녀의 상냥한 웃음 속에는 궤휼이 있었다 She cloaked her evil scheme under a friendly smile.
†귀 the ear ; [청각] hearing ; [바늘의] the eye of a needle ; [모퉁이] an edge ; a border ; a corner ; [우수리] an odd sum ¶ 한쪽 귀가 먹었다 be deaf in one ear // 귀가 아프다 have a pain in the ear ; have an earache // 귀를 솔깃하게 하는 것 ear-catcher // 귀를 쑤시다 pick one's ears // …에 귀를 기울이다 bow down〔incline〕 one's ears to ; lend an ear to // 귀를 바짝 기울이다 prick up one's ears // 귀를 기울이고 듣다 listen with strained ears ; listen intently ; bend an ear // …에 귀를 기울이지 않다 turn a deaf ear to // 여론에 귀를 기울이다 have〔hold, keep〕 an〔one's〕 ear to

the ground // 귀에 거슬리다 be offensive〔harsh〕 to the ear ; jar upon the ear // 귀에 익다 be familiar to one's ears // 귀에 들어오다 catch〔fall on, come to〕 one's ears ; meet the ear // 귀에 남다 ring in one's ears // 귀 따가운 이야기 earful // 귀를 익히다 practice oneself in hearing // 귀를 쫑긋거리다 cock〔prick〕 up one's ears // 그는 한 쪽 귀가 안 들린다 He is deaf of one ear. // 한 쪽 귀로 듣고 한 쪽 귀로 흘려 버리다 go in〔at〕 one ear and out (at) the other // 바늘귀를 꿰다 thread a needle // (책장의) 귀를 접다 dog-ear ; dog's-ear ; turn down the corner of a page // 값이 1,000원하고 귀가 달린다 The price is one thousand *won* and a little in addition. // 나의 아버지는 최근에 귀가 어두워지셨다 My father has become hard of hearing lately. // 나는 처음 들었을 때 내 귀를 의심했다 When I first heard, I could hardly believe my ears.

귀가 가렵다 관용 feel one's ear itch ; one's ear burns〔tingles〕

귀가 따갑다 관용 《소문 따위로》 one's ears burn

귀가 멀다 관용 be hard of hearing

귀가 밝다 관용 be quick to hear ; be sharp-eared ; have good ears

귀가 울다 관용 have a ringing in one's ears ; one's ears ring

귀를 의심하다 관용 cannot believe one's ear

귀- 貴- [당신의] your esteemed ; valuable ; noble ; distinguished ¶ 귀교 your school // 귀정부 your government // 귀사 your company

귀가 歸家 returning home ; home-coming **—하다** come〔go〕 home ; return home ¶ 귀가 도중에 on one's way home // 늦게 귀가하다 be late in coming home

귀감 龜鑑 a model ; a pattern ; a paragon ; an exemplar ; a good example ; a mirror ¶ 군인의 귀감 a pattern〔paragon〕 of soldiery ; the flower of chivalry ; a model soldier // 충신의 귀감 a model of loyalty

귀갑 龜甲 a tortoise shell

—형(形) a hexagon ; [모양] a hexagonal〔tortoise-shell〕 pattern ; a honeycomb

귀개 ⇨ 귀이개

귀객 貴客 a distinguished guest ; a guest of honor ; an honored〔important〕 guest ⇨ 귀빈(貴賓)

귀거래 歸去來 homecoming after one's resignation from a government office

귀거슬리다 be offensive〔harsh〕 to the ear ; jar upon the ear

귀거칠다 be unpleasant〔bitter, disagreeable〕 to hear ; be harsh to the ear

귀걸이 [방한용] earmuffs ; an earcap

귀격 貴格 [상] noble features ; dignified appearance ; [체격] a rare physique

귀결 歸結 conclusion ; consequence ; the result ¶ 당연한 귀결로서 It is a logical conclusion 《that》 ; It naturally follows 《that》 ; as a natural consequence

귀결(을) 짓다 관용 bring to a conclusion

귀경 歸京 one's return to *Seoul*〔the capital city〕 **—하다** return to *Seoul*〔the capital city〕

귀고리 an earring ; an eardrop ; a pendant

귀곡새 鬼哭— an owl ; a hoot owl ; a Chinese scops owl

귀골 貴骨 [사람] a person of noble birth ; a high personage ; [골격] noble features

귀공 貴公 you

귀공자 貴公子 a young noble ; a gilded youth ; the scion of a noble family ¶ 귀공자 같은 prince-like ; noble-looking ; aristocratic-looking

귀교 歸校 —하다 return to school ; go〔come〕 back to school

귀국 貴國 your (esteemed) country

귀국 歸國 home-coming ; return to one's country **—하다** go〔come, return〕 home ; return〔go back〕 to one's country ¶ 귀국길에 오르다 leave for home ; start〔set out〕 on one's journey home // 귀국길에 있다 be on one's way home ; be homeward bound // 한국으로 귀국하다 come home to Korea // 귀국 명령을 받다 be ordered home // 귀국차 떠나다 leave for home // 영국에 귀국했다 He is back home in England.

— 보고회 a briefing〔debriefing〕 session after 《a person's》 return from abroad **— 환영회** a welcome-home party

귀글 句— a verse ; a poem

귀금속 貴金屬 precious metal ; noble metal

—상 a jeweller (상인) ; a jewelry store (상점)

귀기 鬼氣 ¶ 귀기가 서린 ghastly ; bloodcurdling ; unearthly

귀기울이다 listen 《to》 ; give ear 《to》 ; listen with attention

귀꿈스럽다 be out of the way ; be remote and uncommon

귀나다 ① [의논이] differ in opinion ; disagree with each other
② [모나다] warp ; be irregular〔uneven〕

귀남자 貴男子 a noble man ; a precious young man ; a young man of noble birth

귀납 歸納 〖논리〗 induction **—하다** induce ; generalize

— 논리학 inductive logic〔philosophy〕

귀납법 歸納法 the inductive method ; induction
귀납적 歸納的 (be) inductive ¶ 귀납적으로 inductively // 귀납적 논리 inductive logic〔philosophy〕// 귀납적 추리 inductive reasoning〔inference〕
귀넘어듣다 listen carelessly ; give no heed to ; take no notice of
귀녀 貴女 [딸] a precious daughter ; [귀한 여자] a woman of noble birth ; a noble woman ; [당신] you
귀농 歸農 ―하다 return to the farm ; resume agricultural pursuits ; go back to soil
―민 the peasantry returned to the soil
― 운동 a back-to-earth movement ; a return-to-the-soil movement
귀느래 a horse with droopy ears ; a flap-eared horse
귀다래기 cattle with small ears
귀담아듣다 listen willingly〔attentively〕; listen carefully ; stuff one's ears with (a person's words)
귀대 歸隊 ―하다 return to one's unit〔company, regiment〕; rejoin one's unit ; rejoin one's command (장교가) ¶ 귀대 명령을 받다 be called in ; be ordered back into the ranks (병졸이) ; be ordered back to one's command (장교가)
귀댁 貴宅 your home
귀돌 〖건축〗 a corner〔an angle〕 stone ; a quoin ; a coigne
귀동 貴童 a beloved〔precious〕 child
귀동냥 information〔knowledge〕 picked up from listening to others ―하다 learn by keeping one's ears open ; learn by the ear ¶ 귀동냥으로 노래하다〔연주하다〕 sing〔play〕 by ear // 그는 귀동냥으로 많은 것을 알고 있다 He has a smattering knowledge of many things.
귀동자 貴童子 a precious〔beloved〕 son
귀두 龜頭 〖해부〗 the glans ; the glans of the penis
―염 balanitis
귀둥대둥 recklessly ; thoughtlessly ; blindly ; indiscriminately
귀둥이 貴― a pet〔beloved〕 child
귀때 a spout ; a tap
― 동이 a jar with a spout ― 항아리 a spouted pot
귀때그릇 a vessel with a lip
귀때기 an ear ¶ 귀때기를 때리다 hit 《a person's》 ear
*귀뚜라미 〖곤충〗 a cricket ; a grig ¶ 귀뚜라미가 울다 a cricket chirps
귀뚤귀뚤 chirring ; chirping ¶ 귀뚤귀뚤 울다 chirr ; chirp ; chirm
귀뜨다 learn to hear things for the first time (after the birth)
귀뜨이다 have one's attention drawn 《to》; have the matter come to one's attention
귀띔 a suggestion ; a hint ; a tip ; an intimation ―하다 give a hint〔tip〕; suggest ; tip off ; intimate ; give〔make〕 a suggestion ¶ 먼저 가라고 귀띔했다 He suggested that I go first. // 한 시민이 자기 집 차고에 그 살인 용의자가 숨어 있다고 경찰에 귀띔해 주었다 A citizen tipped the police that the murder suspect was hiding in his garage.
귀로 歸路 (on) one's way home ; (on) the way home ; (on) one's return trip〔journey〕 ¶ 귀로에 오르다 leave for home ; start homeward ; make toward home
귀룽나무 〖식물〗 a kind of cherry ; Prunus padus
귀류법 歸謬法 〖논리〗 reduction to absurdity
*귀리 〖식물〗 an oat
*귀머거리 a deaf person ¶ 귀머거리이다 be deaf ; be hard of hearing // 귀머거리가 되다 become deaf
귀먹다 become deaf ; be deafened (일시적으로)
귀명 歸命 conversion to Buddhism ―하다 convert oneself to Buddhism
귀명 貴命 your orders〔request, command, instructions〕 ¶ 귀명에 따라 in obedience〔according〕 to your orders
귀목 槻木 [느티나무] zelkova wood
귀문 貴門 [명문] a noble family ; [남의 집안] your〔his〕 family
귀물 貴物 [진품] a rare article ; a curio ; [귀중품] an article of value ; a treasure ; valuables 《총칭》
귀밑 the root of the ear ¶ 귀밑까지 빨개지다 blush to the roots of one's ears
귀밑머리 hair braided behind the ears
귀밝다 (be) sharp-eared ; be quick to hear ; have good ears
귀밝이술 〖민속〗 "ear-quickening wine" (served on the first full moon day of the lunar new year)
귀방 貴邦 your country
귀범 歸帆 a return sail(ing) ; [배] a returning sailboat ―하다 sail back
귀부 龜趺 the turtle base of a stone monument
†귀부인 貴婦人 a lady ; a titled lady ; a noblewoman ; a society dame (사교계의) ¶ 귀부인다운 ladylike
귀부인 貴夫人 your esteemed wife
귀빈 貴賓 an honored〔a distinguished〕 guest ; an important guest
―실(室) a room reserved for special guests ; a room for VIPs 《Very Important Persons》
귀빈석 貴賓席 seats reserved for honored guests ; the royal box
귀뿌리 the root of the ear
귀사 貴社 your company〔firm〕
귀살스럽다 [뒤숭숭하다] be all messed

up ; (be) tangled〔scattered〕; [마음이 산란하다] complicated ; worrisome ; troublesome
귀상어 〖물고기〗 a hammerhead shark
귀서 貴書 your (esteemed) letter ; yours
귀선 歸船 ―하다 return to the ship
귀선 龜船 a turtle-shaped battleship
귀설다 (be) unfamiliar (to one's ear) ; unaccustomed ; strange ¶ 귀선 목소리 a strange voice // 귀선 이름 an unfamiliar name // 귀선 이름들인데요 Their names sound rather strange to me, I think.
귀성 歸省 returning〔going, coming〕 home ; visiting one's parents at home **―하다** visit one's parents at home ; go〔return, come〕 home ¶ 귀성한 학생 a home-visiting student // 3년만에 귀성하다 go home after three years' absence
―객 home-coming people **―일(日)** a home-coming day **― 학생** a home-coming student
귀성 열차 歸省列車 a special train for home-coming people
귀소 본능 歸巢本能 homing instinct
귀소성 歸巢性 homing instinct
귀속 歸屬 reversion ; return ; [소속] possession **―하다** revert to ; return to ; be returned to ¶ 남극 대륙의 귀속 문제 the question of title to Antarctica // 국고에 귀속하다 revert to the State (Treasury)
― 가치 〖경제〗 an imputed value **―물** a revert
귀속 재산 歸屬財産 government-vested property ; properties reverted to the government
귀순 歸順 defection ; submission ; allegiance **―하다** defect ; submit ; give in one's submission ¶ (귀순이 귀속 지위와 붙어 있으므로) 귀순을 맹세하다 swear allegiance 《to》
―병(兵) a soldier returned to allegiance ; a submitted soldier **―자** a 《North Korean》 defector 《to the South》
귀신 鬼神 [죽은 넋] a departed soul ; a spirit ; a ghost ; [마귀] a fiend ; a demon ; a god ¶ …에 관해서는 귀신이다 be a crack hand at // 일에는 귀신이다 be a demon for work // 골프의 귀신 a demon at golf // 귀신도 모른다 No one knows. // 귀신이 곡할 노릇이다 be strange〔mysterious, unaccountable〕 // 몰골이 꼭 귀신 같구나 You are frightfully disfigured.
귀신 같다 [관용] be supernatural ; be unnatural-looking ; be shocking in appearance
귀신들리다 鬼神― be possessed of〔by〕 the devil
귀심 歸心 [집 생각] longing for home ; [사모] attachment ¶ 귀심이 간절하다 long〔yearn〕 for home ; have a great longing for home
귀싸대기 ¶ 귀싸대기를 갈기다 slap 《a person》 on the face ; box 《a person's》 ear
귀아프다 be fed up with ; have heard enough ; be distasteful to one's ears ¶ 귀아프도록 잔소리를 하다 give 《a person》 a long lecture ; give 《a person》 a good scolding // 그 이야기는 귀아프도록 들어 왔네 I have heard enough of the story. /I am fed up with the story.
귀앓이 an earache ; otalgia
귀애하다 貴愛― love ; favor ; treat with love ; be affectionate to
귀약 ―藥 firelock powder
귀약통 ―藥筒 the container of firelock powder
귀얄 a paste〔paint〕 brush
귀얄잡이 a bewhiskered person
귀양 banishment ; exile ; ostracization
―처 a place of exile
귀양가다 go into exile ; be exiled to a distant〔remote〕 place ; be banished to a distant〔remote〕 place
귀양다리 an exile
귀양보내다 condemn 《a person》 to exile ; banish ; ostracize
귀양살다 live in exile
귀양살이 living in exile
귀어둡다 be hard of hearing ; be slightly deaf
귀에지 ⇨ 귀지
귀엣고리 ⇨ 귀고리
귀엣말 a whisper ¶ 귀엣말로 in a whisper〔in whispers〕 // 귀엣말로 소곤대다 talk〔speak〕 in a whisper〔in whispers〕 ; whisper ; speak in 《a person's ear》
귀여겨듣다 listen carefully ; pay careful attention to ¶ 내 말을 귀여겨듣고 명심해라 Listen to what I say and bear it in your mind.
귀여리다 be ready to believe ; be easily deceived〔convinced〕 ; gullible ; credulous
귀여워하다 love ; pet ; hold 《a person》 dear ; be attached〔devoted〕 to ¶ 개를 귀여워하다 treat a dog kindly ; make a pet of a dog // 어린애들을 너무 귀여워한다 They make too much of their children. // 빌리는 선생님이 가장 귀여워하는 아이이다 Billy is the teacher's pet.
귀염 love ; affection ; attachment ¶ 귀염받다 be loved〔petted〕 《by》 ; win one's love〔heart〕 ; be beloved 《of》 ; be favored 《by》 ; be liked 《by》 // 누구에게나 귀염을 받다 be liked by everybody
귀염둥이 one's pet〔beloved〕 child ; one's darling (child)
귀염성 ―性 loveliness ; attractiveness ; amiability ; charm ¶ 귀염성 있는 love-

ly ; cute ; amiable // 귀염성 있는 얼굴 a lovely〔sweet〕 face // 귀염성 있는 성격 an amiable character〔nature〕

†**귀엽다** (be) lovely ; lovable ; pretty ; sweet ; cute ; charming ; attractive ¶ 귀여운 애 a dear child // 귀여운 목소리 a sweet voice // 귀여운 얼굴 a lovely sweet face // 귀여운 태도 a charming manner // 손녀가 귀여워 죽겠다 I have a real soft spot (in my heart) for my granddaughter.

귀영 歸營 —하다 return to barracks ¶ 귀영 시간 the hour for returning to barracks
— **나팔** a call to quarters — **시간** the hour for returning to barracks

귀울다 one's ears ring ; have a ringing in one's ears

귀울음 ⇨ 이명(耳鳴)

귀의 貴意 your will ; your opinion

귀의 歸依 〖종교〗 conversion **—하다** be converted 《to》; embrace ¶ 불문에 귀의하다 be converted to Buddhism ; turn Buddhist
—불(佛) faith in Buddha **—자** a convert ; a new man ; a brand from the burning〔fire〕 (그리스도교의)

귀이개 an ear-pick ; an instrument for cleaning the ears ; an ear swab

귀익다 be familiar to one's ears

귀인 貴人 a noble man ; a noble ; a man of rank ; a high personage ; a dignitary

귀인상 貴人相 a noble face〔visage〕

귀인성 貴人性 (the quality of) nobility ¶ 귀인성스럽다 look〔be〕 noble ; be lovable〔likable, amiable, attractive〕

귀일 歸一 unity ; unification **—하다** be united into one ; be unified

귀일법 歸一法 unitary method

귀임 歸任 return(ing) to one's post **—하다** return to one's post ¶ 귀임 도중에 on one's way back to one's post

귀잠 a deep〔sound〕 sleep
귀잠(이) 들다 관용 fall fast asleep ; sink into a sound sleep

귀재 鬼才 an unusual genius ; a man of remarkable talent ; versatile〔unusual〕 talent ¶ 문단의 귀재 a literary genius

귀적 歸寂 death (of a Buddhist monk)

귀접스럽다 [더럽다] (be) dirty ; filthy ; untidy ; foul ; unclean ; [천하다]mean ; base ; low

귀접이 rounding off the edges ; softening down angularities **—하다** round the edge off

귀정 歸正 coming back to the right way ; returning to the right track **—하다** come back to the right way

귀젖 a skin adhesion near the ear

귀제비 〖새〗 a striated swallow

귀조 歸朝 returning home from abroad ; home-coming **—하다** return 《to Korea》 from abroad ; come〔return〕 home ¶ 귀조의 길에 오르다 leave for home

‡**귀족 貴族** [전체] the nobility ; the aristocracy ; the peerage ; [개인] a noble ; a nobleman ; a peer ¶ 귀족의 noble ; aristocratic ; titled // 귀족의 가문 a noble family // 귀족의 작위 peerage // 그는 귀족 태생이다 He is of noble birth〔blood〕. /He is nobly born. // 귀족의 반열에 오르게 되다 be raised to〔on〕 the peerage
— **기질** aristocratism — **부인** a titled lady ; noblewoman ; peeress — **사회** aristocracy ; aristocratic circles — **정치** aristocracy — **정치론자** an aristocrat — **주의** aristocratism **세습** — a hereditary peer

귀족 계급 貴族階級 the aristocratic class ; noblesse

귀족원 貴族院 the house of Peers ; the Upper House ; the House of Lords 《영》

귀족적 貴族的 aristocratic ; patrician

귀족 정치 貴族政治 aristocracy

†**귀중 貴重** preciousness **—하다** (be) precious ; valuable ; priceless ; costly ¶ 귀중한 인명 precious human lives // 귀중한 시간 valuable time // 귀중한 지식 precious knowledge // 건강은 귀중한 재산이다 Health is a precious possession.
—품실 a strong room

귀중 貴中 Messrs. ¶ 미도파 귀중 Messrs. *Midopa* & Co. // 서울 대학교 귀중 To the *Seoul* National University

귀중중하다 (be) dirty ; filthy ; untidy ; unclean ¶ 옷차림이 귀중중하다 be shabbily clad〔clothed〕

귀중품 貴重品 valuables

귀지 ear-wax ; 〖해부〗 cerumen

귀지 貴地 your place〔district〕

귀지 貴紙 your paper ; your (esteemed) columns ¶ 귀지를 통하여 through the medium of your columns // 6월 10일자 귀지 보도와 같이 as stated in your paper dated June 10

귀지 貴誌 your (valued) magazine

귀질기다 (be) insensitive ; unresponsive ; be slow to understand〔catch on〕

‡**귀착 歸着** ① [돌아옴] return ; coming back **—하다** return ; come〔arrive〕 back ¶ 서울에 귀착했다 He arrived back in *Seoul*. // 자기 집에 무사히 귀착했다 He reached home in safety.
② [귀결] conclusion ; outcome **—하다** arrive at 《a conclusion》; come to ; boil down to ; resolve itself into ¶ 논의의 귀착점 the logical conclusion of an argument // 결국 돈 문제로 귀착한다 After all it is a question of money.
— **갑판** [항공 모함상의] an alighting deck — **장치** [비행기·유도탄 따위의] a homing device

‡**귀찮다** (be) annoying ; irksome ; tire-

some ; troublesome ¶ 귀찮게 annoyingly ; harassingly ; irksomely // 귀찮은 일 troublesome〔irksome〕 work // 귀찮은 듯이 with an annoyed look〔air〕 // 귀찮게 굴다 behave in an annoying way ; annoy〔bother, trouble〕 a person ; make a nuisance of oneself ; make oneself a nuisance // 귀찮게 조르다 ask importunately for 《money》 // 귀찮게 묻다 be inquisitive ; ask 《a person》 an annoying question // 사람을 귀찮게 따라다니다 pay 《her》 cumbrous attentions ; dance attendance on 《a person》 ; tag〔dangle〕 after 《a person》 // 파리가 귀찮다 The flies are annoying. // 여행이란 귀찮은 일이다 A journey is a nuisance. // 귀찮게 하지 마라 Don't bother (me). /Leave me alone. // 얘들아 아빠를 귀찮게 하지 마라 Don't bother your daddy, children.

귀척 貴戚 the royal relation on the queen's side

귀천 貴賤 high and low ; the noble and the mean ¶ 귀천의 차별 없이 high and low alike ; irrespective of rank // 법률 앞에는 귀천이 없다 All men are equal before the law. // 직업에는 귀천이 없다 All legitimate trades are equally honorable.

귀천궁달(貴賤窮達)이 수레바퀴이다 속담 The highest spoke in fortune's wheel, may soon turn lowest.

귀청 the eardrum ; the tympanum 《*pl.* ~s, -na》 ¶ 귀청이 터질 듯이 요란한 deafening ; ear-deafening ; ear-splitting ; ear-rending

귀체 貴體 you ; your health

귀추 歸趨 a tendency ; a trend ; [결과] a consequence ; an issue ¶ 평화 문제의 귀추 the issue of peace // 당연한 귀추로서 as a natural consequence ; as a natural course of events

귀축 鬼畜 [귀신] a devil ; [사람] a brute of a man ¶ 귀축 같은 fiendish ; brutal ; savage

귀축축하다 (be) foul ; mean ; low ; nasty ; indecent ; obscene

귀측 貴側 you ; 《on》 your part

귀태 貴態 a noble〔an august〕 figure ¶ 귀태가 나다 be〔look〕 noble〔elegant, graceful〕

귀택 貴宅 your (esteemed) house〔home〕

귀퉁이 ① [귀 언저리] the root of the ear ② [모퉁이] a corner ; an angle ¶ 책상 귀퉁이 the corner of a desk

귀틀 a frame ; a framework

귀틀집 a log-cabin〔-hut〕

귀하 貴下 ① [편지 등에서] Mr. (남자에게) ; Mrs. (기혼 여성에게) ; Miss (미혼 여성에게) ; Esq. ; Messrs. (상업문에서) ; Mme. (부인에게) ¶ 에이브러햄 링컨 귀하 Mr. Abraham Lincoln ; Abraham Lincoln, Esq. ② [이름 대신] you

귀하다 貴— ① [신분이] (be) noble ; high ; honorable ; venerable ; august ¶ 귀한 가문 a noble family // 귀한 사람 a person of noble birth ; a high personage ② [귀여운] (be) dear ; lovable ; sweet ¶ 귀한 자식 one's precious child ; one's beloved child // 내게 귀한 사람 a person dear to me ③ [드물다] (be) rare ; uncommon ; precious ; valuable ¶ 귀한 손님 a welcome visitor // 귀한 물건 a rarity ; a valuable〔precious〕 thing // 매우 귀한 as scarce as hen's teeth // 그의 우정은 나에게 무엇보다도 귀한 것이다 His friendship is more precious to me than anything else. ④ [소중하다] (be) dear ; precious ¶ 귀한 손님 a welcome visitor

귀한 자식 매 한 대 더 때리고 미운 자식 떡 한 개 더 준다 속담 Spare the rod and spoil the child.

귀함 貴函 your (esteemed) letter〔favor〕 ¶ 귀함을 배수하였습니다 I acknowledge receipt of your letter.

귀함 歸艦 returning to one's warship **—하다** return to one's warship

귀항 歸航 a return trip〔voyage〕 ; a homeward voyage〔trip〕 **—하다** make a return trip ; make a homeward 〔return〕 voyage 《to》 ; sail for home ¶ 귀항 중이다 be on the return trip ; be homeward-bound // 그녀는 한국으로의 귀항 길에 오른다 She starts on the homeward〔return〕 trip to Korea.

귀항 歸港 —하다 return to port ¶ 부산에 귀항하였다 She arrived back in *Pusan*.

—선 a homeward-bound〔a homebound, an inbound〕 vessel〔ship〕 ; a homeward-bounder

귀향 歸鄕 home-coming ; return to one's old home **—하다** go〔come〕 home ; return to one's old home ; arrive home ¶ 귀향 도중에 on one's way home // 휴가로 귀향하고 있다 He is home for the holidays. /He is back home for the vacation.

— 여비 fare for returning home

귀현 貴顯 a distinguished〔an eminent〕 person ; a high personage

— 신사 gentlemen of eminence ; dignitaries

귀형 鬼形 a ghastly figure ; an ugly and haggard appearance

귀화 鬼火 a will-o'-the-wisp ; a jack-o'-lantern ; a corpse-candle

귀화 歸化 [복종] allegiance ; submission ; [국적 이전] naturalization **—하다** surrender ; submit ; yield ; be〔become〕 naturalized ¶ 귀화를 허가하다 confer citizenship 《upon》 // 한국에 귀화

하다 be〔become〕 naturalized as a Korean citizen ; be〔become〕 naturalized in Korea
—국 one's adopted land〔country〕 — 본능 〖동물〗 [귀소 본능] homing instinct ; orientation — 증명서 a naturalization certificate — 캐나다 시민 a Canadian citizen by naturalization

귀화 식물 歸化植物 a naturalized plant

귀화인 歸化人 a naturalized citizen ; a denizen

†**귀환 歸還** return ; repatriation (본국에) —하다 return ; come back (home) ¶ 기지에 무사히 귀환하다 return safely to the base // 그는 일선에서 무사히 귀환했다 He came back from the front in safety.
—병(兵) a returned soldier — 비행 a return〔homeward〕 flight —자 a returnee ; a repatriate

귀휴 歸休 —하다 be released before the expiration of one's service ¶ 귀휴 중이다 be on leave from the service

귀휴병 歸休兵 a soldier (sent) home on leave

귓가 the rim of the ear

귓것 a demon ⇨ 귀신

귓결 ¶ 귓결에 by chance ; by accident ; accidentally ; casually // 나는 귓결에 어느 여인의 울음 소리를 들었다 By chance a woman's sobbing came into my ears.

귓구멍 earhole ; the ear ; the opening of the ear ¶ 귓구멍을 후비다 pick one's ear

귓돌 a cornerstone ; a foundation stone

귓등 the back of an ear ¶ 귓등으로 듣다 do not listen carefully ; take no notice of

귓문 —門 an outer orifice of the ear

귓바퀴 a pinna ; an auricle ; earflap

귓밥 [귓불의 두께] the thickness of an earlobe ; [귀지] ear wax

귓병 —病 an ear disease〔ailment, trouble〕

귓불 an earlobe ; an earlap ; the lobe of an ear ¶ 귓불이 크다〔두툼하다〕 have thick lobes to one's ears // 귓불을 잡아 당기다 pull 《a person》 by his lobe ; pull the lobe of 《a person's》 ear // 그녀는 귓불까지 빨개졌다 She blushed to the roots of her ears.
귓불만 만지다 관용 be at a loss ; do not know 《what to do》 ; be in a quandary ; be fogged

귓속 the inside of an ear ; the inner ear
— 다짐 a whispered definite answer

귓속말 a whisper ¶ 귓속말로 in a whisper〔in whispers〕 // 귓속말로 소곤거리다 talk〔speak〕 in a whisper〔in whispers〕 ; whisper ; speak in 《a person's ear》

귓전 ¶ 귓전에 around the ear rims ; about one's ears // 귓전에도 들리지 않다 pay no attention at all 《to》 ; take no heed 《to》
귓전으로 듣다 관용 hear casually ; happen to hear

귓집 [모자의] earflaps ; earpieces ; earlaps ; [독립한] earmuffs 《미》

규각 圭角 [불일치] disharmony ; discord ; divergence ; [뜻이 다름] dissent ; disagreement
규각 나다 관용 disagree ; dissent ; be disharmonious

규격 規格 a standard ; a norm ¶ 규격외의 non-standardized ; substandard // 규격에 맞다 meet standard requirements // 규격에 맞추다 make a thing meet〔come up to〕 standards
— 검사 inspection of standardization ; normalization — 주택 a standardized house — 통일 standardization

규격판 規格版 a standard size

규격품 規格品 standardized goods〔articles〕

규격화 規格化 standardization ; normalization —하다 standardize

규례 規例 rules and regulations ; a standard

규명 糾明 a close examination ; a searching〔grilling, minute〕 examination —하다 examine 《a matter》 closely ; look〔inquire〕 into 《a matter》 minutely ¶ 죄상을 규명하다 examine into 《a person's》 guilt

⁑**규모 規模** [구조] a scale ; scope ; structure ; plan ; [제도] a rule ; a pattern ; [예산 한도] a budget limit ¶ 대규모로 on a large scale ; in a large way // 돈을 규모 있게 쓰다 make effective use of one's money // 규모를 확장하다 enlarge the scope 《of the project》 // 이 공장은 상당히 규모가 크다 The factory is run on a very extensive scale.

규문 糾問 a cross-examination ; arraignment ; an inquiry ; an interrogation —하다 question 《a person》 closely ; grill ; ply 《a person》 with questions ; cross-examine

규문 閨門 a boudoir

규방 閨房 a boudoir ; a lady's bedroom ; a lady's private sitting room ; [안방] an inner room

규방 문학 閨房文學 literature depicting women's life in feudal society

규벌 閨閥 nepotism ; matrimonial influence

규범 規範 a canon ; a norm ; a standard ; [규모] a pattern ; a rule ¶ 규범적 법칙 normative law
— 의식 norm consciousness

규범 과학 規範科學 ⇨ 규범학

규범 문법 規範文法 normative〔prescriptive〕 grammar

규범학 規範學 the normative science

규사 硅砂 〖광물〗 silica
규산 硅酸 〖화학〗 silicic acid
—겔 silica gel **— 소다** sodium silicate **— 아연광** willemite **—율(率)** silica modulus **— 점토(粘土)** siliceous clay **— 혼합 시멘트** puzzolanic cement
규산나트륨 sodium silicate
규산알루미늄 aluminum silicate ; mullite
규산염 硅酸鹽 a silicate
규산칼륨 potassium silicate
규산칼슘 calcium silicate
규석 硅石 〖광물〗 silex ; silica
— 벽돌 a silica brick
규성 叫聲 a shout ; a cry ; an outcry ; an exclamation
규소 硅素, 珪素 silicon
—강(鋼) silicon steel **—동(銅)** silicon copper **—철** ferrosilicon **— 화합물** a silicide
규소 수지 硅素樹脂 silicone (resin)
규수 閨秀 [처녀] a maiden ; a spinster ; an unmarried young woman ; [글하는 여자] a literary woman ; a bluestocking ¶ 김씨댁 규수 Mr. *Kim's* daughter
규수 시인 閨秀詩人 a poetess ; a female poet
규수 작가 閨秀作家 a woman〔female, lady〕 writer ; an authoress
규수 화가 閨秀畫家 a lady〔woman〕 painter
규식 規式 rules and established forms
규암 硅岩 〖지질〗 quartzite ⇨ 규석
규약 規約 an agreement ; a covenant ; rules ¶ 규약을 정하다 lay out rules // 규약을 맺다 enter into an agreement // 규약을 어기다 break the rules
협회 — the articles of an association **휴전 —** a ceasefire agreement
규운암 硅雲岩 〖광물〗 greisen
규율 規律 [질서] order ; discipline ; [조직] system ¶ 규율 있는 orderly ; disciplined ; systematic // 규율 없는 disorderly ; undisciplined ; unsystematic // 규율 바르게 in good order ; in an orderly manner // 규율이 엄한 사람 a disciplinarian // 규율을 유지하다 maintain discipline // 규율을 지키다〔깨뜨리다〕 observe〔break〕 the rules // 엄격한 규율 rigid discipline // 규율이 엄하다 be under discipline // 군대는 규율이 엄격하다 Discipline is strictly enforced in the army. // 그 학교 학생들은 규율이 썩 잘 잡혀 있다 The students of the school are under perfect discipline.
규장암 硅長岩 〖광물〗 felsite ; felstone
***규정 規定** [조항] a provision ; a stipulation ; [규칙] regulations ; rules **—하다** provide 《for》 ; stipulate 《for》 ; prescribe ; ordain ¶ 도서 대출 규정 library regulations for lending books // 회사의 복무 규정에 따라 in accordance with the terms of service of the company // 현행 규정으로는 under the existing provisions〔standing rules〕 // 회원 입회 규정 a rule for the admission of new members // 금연 규정 a rule against smoking // 융통성 없는 규정 hard and fast rule // 규정의 운임〔요금〕 a regulation fare〔charge〕 // 법률의 규정에 따라 according to (the provisions of) the law ; as prescribed by law // 제1조의 규정에 따라 in accordance with the provision of Article 1 ; under the requirements of Rule 1 // 규정에 반하다 be against the rule // …라고 회칙에 규정되어 있다 It is prescribed in the rules of the association 《that》
—량 [일의] 《fulfill》 the norm **—서** a directory **— 요금** the regulation fare **— 종목** [체조 경기의] compulsory exercise **개정 —** revised regulations **직무 —** the regulation defining the duties of the staff **통행 —** the rules of the road ; the traffic regulation
규정 농도 規定濃度 normalcy ; normality
규정론 規定論 〖철학〗 determinism ⇨ 결정론
규정식 規定食 [환자 따위의] a (prescribed) diet ¶ 환자에게 규정식을 먹이다 put a patient on a special diet
규정액 規定液 〖화학〗 a normal solution
규제 規制 [규칙] regulation ; [제한] restriction ; [통제] control **—하다** regulate ; restrict ; control ¶ 교통을 규제하다 regulate traffic // 소비성 품목의 수입을 규제하다 restrict imports of consumer items
교통 — traffic control **자율 —** voluntary restraint〔control〕 《on》
규조류 硅藻類 〖식물〗 diatom
규조 식물 硅藻植物 ⇨ 규조류
규조토 硅藻土 diatomite ; diatomaceous earth ; silicious marl
규준 規準 a canon ; a criterion
규중 閨中 a boudoir ; a lady's bedroom
규중 처녀 閨中處女 a maiden ; an unmarried young woman ; a virgin
†규칙 規則 a rule ; regulations ¶ 번잡한 규칙 red tape // 융통성 없는 규칙 hard and fast rules // 규칙대로 by〔according to〕 rule // 규칙 투성이의 tied down to rules // 규칙으로 되어 있다 the rule〔regulation〕 says〔requires〕 《that》 // 규칙을 마련하다〔정하다〕 lay down〔make〕 a rule ; establish regulations // 규칙을 지키다 observe〔stick by〕 the rules ; act upon a rule ; keep〔conform〕 to a rule ; follow〔obey〕 a rule // 규칙을 어기다 break〔violate, go against, infringe on〕 the rules // 규칙에 위배되다 be against〔contrary to〕 the rules〔regulations〕 // 규칙을 시행하다 put the rules into effect ; enforce the rules // 규칙을 개정하다 amend〔revise, change〕 the rules // 규칙을 무시하다 disregard the established rules // 규칙에 맞다 conform

to the rule // 규칙에서 벗어나다 deviate from an established rule // 규칙에 따르다 go by rule ; toe the mark〔line, scratch〕// 클럽 규칙 the rules of the club // 교통 규칙 rules of the road // 나는 조반을 규칙적으로 일곱시에 먹는다 I make it a rule to breakfast at seven o'clock. // 이 규칙은 아직도 유효하다 The rule still holds good. // 예외 없는 규칙은 없다 Every rule has its exceptions. / There is no rule without some exceptions. // 사람들이 정해진 규칙대로 행동하리라고 기대하지마 You just can't expect people to go by the book.
— 위반 (a) violation of regulations ; a breach of rules ; an offense against the rule

규칙 동사 規則動詞 〖문법〗 a regular verb

규칙서 規則書 a prospectus ; [회칙] the regulations ¶ 청하시는 대로 규칙서를 보내 드립니다 Prospectus sent on application. (광고)

***규칙적 規則的** (be) regular ; systematic ; methodical ; orderly ¶ 규칙적으로 regularly ; systematically ; methodically // 규칙적인 생활을 하다 have regular habits ; keep regular hours ; live〔lead〕 a well-regulated life ; lead an orderly life

규탄 糾彈 censure ; impeachment ; denunciation **—하다** censure ; impeach ; denounce ¶ 사건을 철저히 규탄하다 search an affair to the bottom // 이 문제로 정부를 규탄하다 censure the Government on the question // 정부의 실정을 규탄하다 impeach〔censure, denounce〕 the government for maladministration // 야당은 정부의 태만을 규탄했다 The opposition parties censured the government for being negligent.

규토 硅土 〖화학〗 silica ; silex

규폐(증) 硅肺(症) 〖의학〗 silicosis

규합 糾合 a rally ; a muster **—하다** rally ; muster ; call〔gather〕 together ¶ 동지를 규합하다 muster〔rally〕 men of the same mind
—점(點) a rallying point

규호 叫號 a shout ; a cry ; an exclamation **—하다** shout ; cry ; shriek

규화 硅華 〖광물〗 siliceous sinter ; geyserite

규화 硅化 silicification **—하다** silicify
—석(石) woodstone

규화목 硅化木 silicified wood

규화물 硅化物 a silicide

규환 叫喚 an outcry ; a shout ; a cry ; a shriek **—하다** cry ; shout ; shriek ¶ 아비 규환의 장면 a terrible scene of confusion ; an agonizing scene

균 菌 a bacillus 《*pl.* -li》; a germ ; bacterium 《*pl.* -ria》 ¶ 균 배양 germ culture ; cultivation of bacteria // 상처에 균이 들어가지 않도록 주의하시오 Take care to keep the wound from being infected.
— 보유자〔보균자〕 a germ carrier 결핵 — tuberculosis bacilli 콜레라— a cholera bacillus

균독 菌毒 mushroom poison

균등 均等 equality ; parity ; evenness ; uniformity **—하다** (be) equal ; even ; uniform ¶ 균등하게 equally ; evenly ; uniformly // …와 균등한 on a parity with // 균등히 하다 equalize ; even ; make equal〔alike〕; render uniform // 균등하게 분배하다 equalize ; distribute equally // 균등한 대우를 받다 obtain parity (of treatment) with 《another》// 비용을 균등하게 부담하다 share the expenses equally // 세금의 부담을 균등하게 하다 equalize the burdens of taxation
— 대우〔처우〕 equal treatment ; parity of treatment —성 uniformity — 화법 〖미술〗 isometric drawing 기회 — equal opportunity ; equality in opportunity 기회 —주의 the principle of equal opportunity

균등 대표제 均等代表制 〖선거〗 an equal representation

균류 菌類 fungi 《*sg.* -gus》
—학 fungology —학자 a fungologist ; a mycologist

균배 均配 division into equal parts **—하다** divide〔share〕 equally

균분 均分 dividing equally ; equal division **—하다** divide equally ; equalize ¶ 유산을 균분하다 distribute the inheritance equally
— 상속 equalized inheritance —원(圓) an equator (적도와 같은)

균사 菌絲 spawn ; a hypha 《*pl.* -phae》

균산 菌傘 an umbrella-shaped top part of fungi ; a mushroom cap ; a pileus ; a capitulum

균열 龜裂 a crack ; a crevice ; a fissure ; a cleft ¶ 균열이 생기다 crack ; be cracked〔cleft〕// 땅에 균열이 생겼다 The ground opened in fissures. // 지진으로 길에 균열이 생겼다 The roads were cracked in places owing to the earthquake.
— 시험 〖화학〗 a cracking test

균일 均一 uniformity ; equality **—하다** (be) uniform ; equal ¶ 균일하게 하다 equalize ; make uniform // 값은 균일합니다 They are of a uniform price. /They are all one-priced. // 값은 100원 균일이다 They are all 100 *won* a piece.
— 가격 a uniform〔flat〕 price —론자 a uniformitarian— 부하(負荷) 〖기계〗 uniform load — 상점 a one-price store ; a uniform price store 〔shop〕 —설 uniformitarianism — 요금〔운임〕 a uniform rate〔fare〕 — 요금 제도 the uniform rate system — 요율 요금제 〖전화〗 the

flat-rate tariff — 종량 요금제 the flat and meter rate schedule 350원 — [버스 요금] three hundred (and) fifty *won* any distance ; three hundred (and) fifty *won* a ride for any distance

균일제 均一制 a uniform system

균점 均霑 equal allotment of profits ; 〖법〗 reciprocity **—하다** share alike ; share in equality

균제 均齊 symmetry ; balance ; equilibrium ¶ 균제가 잡힌 symmetrical ; well-balanced ; proportionate

균질 均質 homogeneity ¶ 균질의 homogeneous // 균질화하다 homogenize // 균질 우유 homogenized milk

—계(系) the homogeneous system **—기(器)** homogenizer **—유** homogenized milk — **물질〔광〕** a homogeneous substance〔light〕

균체 내독소 菌體內毒素 〖생화학〗 endotoxin

균체 외독소 菌體外毒素 〖생화학〗 exotoxin

균평 均平 [균일] equality ; uniformity ; [평평함] evenness ; smoothness **—하다** (be) equal ; uniform ; even ; smooth

균할 均割 equal division〔allotment〕 **—하다** divide〔allot〕 equally

†**균형 均衡** balance ; equilibrium ; poise ; equipoise ¶ 영양의 균형 nutritional balance // 생산과 소비의 균형 the balance of production and consumption // 힘의 균형 the balance of power // 균형이 잡힌 well-balanced // 몸의 균형을 유지하다〔잃다〕 keep〔lose〕 one's balance // 균형을 잃고 off〔out of〕 balance // 균형을 깨뜨리다 upset the balance ; cast the balance // 몸의 균형을 잡다 balance onesef // 한 발로 몸의 균형을 잡다 balance oneself on one leg // 균형을 잡고 책을 머리에 얹다 balance a book on one's head // 그는 몸의 균형을 잃고 넘어졌다 He overbalanced himself and fell. // 이번 예산은 수지 균형이 잡혔다 The current budget is balanced. // 일과 가정 사이에서 적절히 균형을 유지한다는 것은 어렵다 It's hard to maintain the proper balance between work and home.

— **분석** (an) equilibrium analysis **—식(食)** a balanced diet〔ration〕 **—점** the equilibrium point **세력 —** the balance of power **소비 —** consumer equilibrium **수급 —** the balance of demand and supply **축소 —** 〖경제〗 contracted equilibrium **확대 —** 〖경제〗 expended equilibrium

균형 예산 均衡豫算 a balanced budget

귤 橘 an orange ; a wild orange ; a mandarin orange ; a tangerine ¶ 귤껍질을 벗기다 peel an orange

—껍질 an orange peel **—밭** a tangerine orchard〔plantation〕

귤나무 橘— an orange〔a citrus〕 tree

귤색 橘色 orange ; mandarin

귤피 橘皮 an orange peel

그[1] [그이] he ; she ; [그것] that ; it ¶ 그의 his ; her // 그는 나의 아버지이시다 He is my father.

***그[2]** the ; that ¶ 그날 that〔the〕 day // 그 사람 he ; she ; that man ; that woman // 그 이튿날 the next〔following〕 day // 그 학교 that〔the〕 school // 그 근처에 about there // 그 당시에는 in those days ; about that time // 그 때문에 for that reason // 그 자리에서 then and there ; on the spot // 그 즈음 in those days ; at〔about〕 that time // 그 후 after that ; thereafter ; since // 그 일은 그때 가서 봅시다 Then the matter will be given special consideration.

그간 —間 the while ; during that time ; these〔those〕 days ; in the meantime ¶ 그간 어떻게 지냈소 How have you been all these days?

그같이 thus ; so ; like that ; in that manner ¶ 그같이 울어서는 안된다 You must not cry like that. // 그같이 재미있는 소설은 처음이다 I never read a more interesting novel. // 그같이 화내지 마시오 Don't be so angry.

그건 그렇고 by the by(e) ; by the way ; now ; well ¶ 그건 그렇고 네게 물어 볼 말이 있다 Well, now, I have something to ask you.

†**그것** it ; that ¶ 그것만으로 by itself ; that alone // 그것은 그렇지만 it may be so, but // 그것은 그렇다 치고 apart from the question ; setting it aside ; meanwhile // 그것과 이것은 아무 상관이 없다 That's another story. /That is entirely different from this question. // 그것도 그렇군 That is true. // 그것 봐 I told you so. // 그것으로 충분하다 That much is enough for him. // 바로 그겁니다 That's it.

***그곳** that place ; there ¶ 그곳에 in that place ; there // 그곳까지 that far

그글피 four days hence〔from now〕 ; three days after tomorrow

그까지로 to that trifling extent

그까짓 that kind of ; so trifling〔trivial, slight〕 ¶ 그까짓 짓을 누가 하겠소 Who would do that sort of thing? // 그까짓 일은 누구나 할 수 있다 Everyone can do that kind of thing.

그끄러께 three years ago ; two years before last

그끄저께 three days ago ; two days before yesterday ¶ 그끄저께 밤 the night before the night before last ; last night but two ; three nights ago

그끄제 ⇨ 그끄저께

그나마 even so ; still ; nevertheless ; however ; and that ; at that ¶ 그 집에서는 커피 한 잔에 2,000원이나 받는데 그나마 맛이 신통치 않다 They charge

2,000 *won* for a cup of coffee, and not a very good one at that.

*그날 that day ; the same day ¶ 그날의 일 the day's work // 그날 중으로 before the day is over // 그날로 서울에 돌아왔다 I returned to *Seoul* the same day. // 그날이 그날이다 Each day is just like every other day.

그날그날 every day ; daily ; day after 〔by〕 day ; from day to day ¶ 그날그날 겨우 살아가다 eke out a bare existence from day to day ; scrape a living day by day

*그냥 as it is ; as it stands ; as you find it ; in that condition ; all the way ¶ 그냥 두다 leave 《a thing》 as it is ; let 《a thing》 stand as it is ; leave〔let〕 《a thing》 alone ; leave 《a thing》 at that ; leave 《a thing》 intact〔untouched〕 // 그냥 서 있다 stay on one's feet ; keep standing // 그냥 울고만 있다 do nothing but cry // 그 사건을 그냥 내버려 둘 수 없다 The matter cannot be let alone. // 그 집을 그냥 그대로 샀다 I bought the house as it stood. // 도난당한 물건들을 그냥 그대로 되찾았다 The stolen things were all recovered in their original condition. // 집이 쓰러진 채 그냥 있다 The house remains as it fell. // 그냥 서 있다 stay on one's feet ; keep standing

†그네[1] a swing ; a trapeze (곡예용) ¶ 그네를 매다 put up a swing // 그네를 뛰다 swing // 그네를 구르다 propel a swing ; rock a swing back and forth ; (get) on a swing ; sit in a swing

그넷줄 the swing rope(s)

그네[2] those people ; they ; them

†그녀 —女 she

그놈 that fellow〔chap, rogue〕 ; that guy ; 《미》 ; that blighter 《영》 ; that bastard 《속》 ¶ 그놈이 그놈이다 They're all bastards ! /There is little to choose between them.

그느다 《a baby》 show signs of having a call of nature ; give an indication of having a call of nature

그느르다 take care of ; look after ; take under one's wings ; protect

†그늘 ① [응달] shade ¶ 나무 그늘 the shade of a tree // 그늘에서 in the shade // 나무 그늘에서 쉬다 take a rest in the shade of a tree // 모직이니까 그늘에서 말려 주세요 Since it's wool, please dry it in the shade. ② [부모의 슬하] parental care〔protection〕 ③ [잘 드러나지 않는 환경] obscurity ¶ 그늘에서 사는 사람 a person with a shady past ; a social outcast ; an ex-convict ; a fugitive from justice ④ [불행·근심] gloom ; cloud ; shade

†그늘지다 ① [빛이] get〔be〕 shaded ; be shady ; be shadowed ¶ 그늘진 shady ; shadowy // 그늘진 오솔길 a shady〔shadowy〕 path ② [드러나지 않음] (be) in obscurity〔the shadow〕 ③ [성질] feel gloomy ; look dismal ¶ 그늘진 얼굴 gloomy face

그닐거리다 ① [살갗이] feel itchy 〔creepy, crawly〕 ; itch ; be ticklish ② [마음이] feel nervous〔uneasy〕 ; be irritated ; be ill at ease

그닐그닐 ① [살갗이] itching ; tickling —하다 itch ; tickle ; feel itchy ② [마음이] feeling uneasy〔nervous〕 —하다 feel uneasy〔nervous〕 ; be restless ; stir restlessly ; be ill at ease

†그다지 so much ; particularly ; to that extent〔degree〕 ; in that way ¶ 그다지 비싸지 않다 be not so expensive // 그다지 좋아하지 않다 do not care much for // 그다지 예쁘지 않다 She is not so very attractive. // 그다지 할 일이 없다 I have nothing particular to do. // 수술 결과는 그다지 좋지 않다 The result of the operation is far from reassuring.

그달 that month ; [강조하여] the very 〔same〕 month

†그대 you ; thou ¶ 그대들 you ; ye ; all of you

*그대로 like that ; as it is ; as it stands ; thus ; intact ; as ¶ 그대로 내버려두다 leave 《a thing》 as it is ; let 《a person》 alone // 본 그대로 이야기하다 tell as one saw it // 마음먹은 그대로 이야기하다 speak just as one feels // 내 명령 그대로 해라 Do as I tell you. // 그대로 앉아 계시오 Don't get up. /Don't disturb yourself. /Don't bother〔trouble〕. // 그대로 내버려둘 수는 없다 I cannot leave the matter as it is. // 그대로 왔다가 그대로 갔다 He came but just went away. // 있는 그대로를 말하다 tell it like it is ; give an accurate account // 더 좋은 일자리를 찾을 때까지 현 직장에 그대로 있어라 Hang on to your present job until you find a better one.

그도 그럴 것이 because ; for ¶ 아무리 찾아도 없었다 그도 그럴 것이 집에 있었으니까 No wonder we could find him nowhere, for he was at home.

그동안 the while ; during that time ; these〔those〕 days ; in the meantime ¶ 그동안에 어떻게 지냈소 How have you been all these days ? // 그동안에 우리가 할 수 있는 일을 하자 In the meantime, let us do the things we can.

그득하다 (be) full ; filled

그들 they ; them

그들먹하다 be almost〔nearly〕 full

그따위 a thing or person of that kind 〔sort〕 ; such a one ; that kind〔sort〕 (of) ¶ 그따위 일로 울지 마라 Don't cry at such a trifle.

†그때 then ; at that time ¶ 그때의 교장 the then principal ; the principal at that

time // 그때 마침 just at that moment ; just then // 그때까지 by that time ; till then ; up to that time ; theretofore // 그때부터 ever since ; since then // 그때까지 그것을 마쳐라 Finish it by then.

그라비어 〖인쇄〗 (photogravure) ¶ 그라비어 판의 그림 gravure picture // 그라비어 판으로 하다 photogravure
— 인쇄기(용지) gravure press(paper)

그라운드 a ground ; a stadium ; a field ; a playground ; [야구장] a ball park 《미》 ¶ 그라운드를 메운 관중 great crowds of spectators around the stadium
— 관리인 a groundman **— 매너** ground manners **— 스트로크** ground stroke **— 포지션** ground position

그라인더 a grinder

그랑 프리 *grand prix* 《프》 ; the grand prize

†**그래**[1] [대답] Yes. (긍정)/No. (부정)/So it is./That's right.

그래[2] well ; so ; therefore ; accordingly ¶ 그래 그 다음에는 Well, then? // 그래 어쨌단 말이오 So what?/What is it to you?

***그래도** nevertheless ; but ; still ; for all that ; and yet ; even so ¶ 그는 결점이 많지만 그래도 나는 그를 좋아한다 It is true that he has many faults, but I like him none the less. // 그는 열심히 공부하지만 그래도 학교 성적은 별로 좋지 않다 With all his diligence, he still does not make a very good school record. // 그는 악한 사람이지만 그래도 양심이 조금은 있는가 보다 Wicked as he is, he seems to have just a bit of conscience. // 그래도 너만 믿겠다 I believe you even so. // 그래도 이것이 나은 편이다 This is less unsatisfactory than that. // 나는 저금을 꺼낼 수도 있으나 그래도 모자랄 것이다 I could withdraw my savings, but even then we'd not have enough.

†**그래서** so ; therefore ; thereupon ; and ; then ; accordingly ; for that reason ; on that account ¶ 그래서 어떻단 말야 So what? // 너는 그래서 병이 난 거야 That is why you got ill. // 그래서 나는 이렇게 말했다 Therefore, I spoke to him like this.

그래스 코트 a grass court

그래야 only if one does(says) that ; only if it is that way ; only so ; unless so

그래프 a graph ; a (symbolic) diagram
— 대수학 graphic algebra **— 용지** graph(section) paper ; square(d) paper

그래픽 a graphic (magazine)
— 디자이너 a graphic designer **— 디자인** a graphic design **— 아트** the graphic arts

그랜드 grand
— 스탠드(오페라, 피아노) a grand stand(opera, piano)

⁑**그램** a gram(me)
— 당량(當量) gram equivalent **— 분자(원자)** a gram molecule(atom) **— 칼로리** a gram calorie

그러구러 somehow ; in one way or another ; somehow or other ; bit by bit ; little by little ; gradually ; in the meantime ; meanwhile ; already ¶ 일이 그러구러 다됐다 The work got finished somehow or other.

그러그러하다 (be) middling ; so-so ; indifferent ; be neither good nor bad ; be neither better nor worse ; be about the same ¶ 그의 시도 모두 그러그러하다 His poems are none too good, either. // 요즘 기분이 어떤가—그러그러하네 How are you these days? I am neither good nor bad.

†**그러나** but ; still ; however ; and yet ; though ; nevertheless

그러나저러나 at any rate ; anyhow ; anyway ; in any case ; setting aside ; apart 《from》 ¶ 그러나저러나 나는 아무것도 모른다 But, in any case, I know nothing. // 그러나저러나 나는 그것을 말할 수 없다 I cannot say it anyway.

그러내다 take out ; rake out ¶ 난로에서 재를 그러내다 rake out the ashes from a stove

그러넣다 put into ; rake in ¶ 삼태기에 재를 그러넣다 rake ashes into a dust basket // 음식을 그러넣다 eat greedily ; shovel food into one's mouth

그러니까 accordingly ; consequently ; hence ; (and) so ; so that ; therefore ; for that reason ; on that account(score) ¶ 그러니까 친구도 많다 That is why he has so many friends. // 그러니까 가난한 거야 That explains(accounts for) his poverty. // 그러니까 시험에 떨어진거야 That is why you have failed in the examination.

그러니저러니 this or that ; one thing or another ¶ 그러니저러니 할 것 없이 without saying this or that ; without question ; without useless objection ; with a good grace // 그러니저러니 할 것 없이 시작하시오 Begin without making a fuss about it. // 이제 와서 그러니저러니 해봐야 이미 때는 늦었다 It is too late now to make complaints.

그러담다 gather up into ; scrape up into ; rake up into ¶ 낙엽을 가마니에 그러담다 rake up fallen leaves into a straw bag // 불을 화로에 그러담다 rake the fire into a brazier

그러당기다 gather up and pull(draw, drag) ¶ 판돈을 그러당기다 rake in the money on a gambling table

그러들이다 collect ; rake in ¶ 빚준 돈을 그러들이다 collect debts // 닥치는 대로 그러들이다 collect haphazardly

그러루하다 (be) indifferent ; ordinary ¶ 재미는 어떤가—그저 그러루하다 How is the world treating you? Well, the same as usual.

†**그러면** if so ; in that case ; if it is like that ; then ; if that happens ¶ 그러면 내일 오겠습니다 Well then, I shall come tomorrow. // 그러면 담배를 끊는 것이 좋겠다 Then, you may as well give up smoking. // 그러면 나는 어떻게 해야 하지 In that case, what shall I do?

그러면 그렇지 as (was, had been) expected ; it should be so ¶ 그러면 그렇지 It is naturally to be expected. // 그러면 그렇지 자네가 성공할 리가 있나 It is nothing strange that you have failed. // 그러면 그렇지 불평 안 할 리가 있나 No wonder that he makes complaints.

†**그러모으다** gather up ; scrape together ; rake up〔together〕 ¶ 돈을 그러모으다 scrape together a sum of money ; rake up dough 《미·속》 // 낙엽을 그러모으다 rake up fallen leaves // 그러모은 군대 a scratched together〔patchwork〕 army // 그러모은 청중 a motley crowd // 있는 돈을 모두 그러모아 집을 샀다 I scraped up all the money to buy a house.

†**그러므로** so ; hence ; therefore ; on that account ; consequently ¶ 그러므로 병에 걸린 것이다 That is why you got ill. // 그러므로 그는 비관하고 있는 것이다 That explains his pessimism.

그러안다 embrace ; hug ; hold〔take, clasp〕 in one's arms ; fold in one's arms ; press to one's bosom ; hug〔clasp〕 to one's breast ¶ 어린애를 그러안다 hold a baby in one's arms ; hug a baby to one's breast

그러자 thereupon ; thereon ; hereupon ; whereupon ; and ; when ; upon which ; and just then

그러잖아도 even if it were not so ; be it otherwise ; all the more ; in addition 《to》 ; on top of 《it》 ; moreover ; what is more ; to make matters worse ; to add to the surplus ¶ 그러잖아도 나쁜데 to make matters worse // 그러잖아도 딱한데 to add to one's troubles // 그러잖아도 미인인데 그녀는 부자야 She is rich and beautiful as well. // 그러잖아도 미운데 돈까지 꾸어달라네 To make himself more hateful to me, he asks me to lend him money.

그러잡다 grasp ; grip ; clasp ; clutch ; grab ; take hold of ¶ 손을 그러잡다 grasp a person's hand // 머리털을 그러잡다 grasp a person's hair

그러저러하다 be so and so ; be such and such ¶ 그러저러해서 for such and such reasons // 그러저러한 날에 on such and such a day

그러쥐다 seize ; catch ; grasp ; grip ; grab ; take hold of ; hold ¶ 손잡이를 그러쥐다 hold a handle ; grip a strap // 머리털을 그러쥐다 seize 《a person's》 hair // 권력을 그러쥐다 take〔assume〕 power // 확실한 증거를 그러쥐다 have〔get〕 positive proof

†**그러하다** (be) so ; such ; right ¶ 그러한 such ; of the sort ; like that // 그러한 까닭에 so ; accordingly ; for that reason // 그러한 경우에 in such a case ; in a case like that // 그러할 줄 알았다 I should not wonder. // 세상이란 그러한 것이다 Such is the way of the world.

***그럭저럭** one way or another ; in some way ; somehow (or other) ; meanwhile ; by some means (or other) ; by hook or by crook ; barely **—하다** do somehow (or other) ; manage to do in some way ¶ 그럭저럭하는 동안에 in the meantime ; meanwhile // 그럭저럭 살아가다 manage to get along, one way or other // 그러저럭 잘 되겠지 Somehow it will come out all right. // 그럭저럭 일을 끝내다 Somehow, I got the job done. // 그럭저럭 하는 일 없이 하루가 지나갔다 The day has been wasted on this and that (getting nothing accomplished). // 여기서 산 지도 그럭저럭 20년이 된다 It is twenty years since I have lived here.

그런 such ; so ; like that ⇨ 그러하다

그런고로 for that reason ; therefore ; hence ⇨ 그러므로

그런대로 (such) as it is ; anyway ¶ 적은 것이나 그런대로 받아 두시오 It's a small one, but please take what there is of it, anyway. // 그런대로 쓸만한 사람 a good enough man in his way // 경기는 어떻습니까—그런대로 괜찮습니다 How's business? Oh, not too bad〔Just so-so〕.

†**그런데** but ; however ; yet ; though ; for all that ¶ 그는 상냥한 사람이다 그런데 아무도 특별히 그를 좋아하는 이가 없으니 이상한 일이다 He is an amiable man, yet it is strange that no one specially likes him.

그런데도 and yet ; still ; in spite of that ; for all that ; nevertheless ; notwithstanding ; all the same ; none the less ; while

그런듯만듯 likely〔probably〕 or not ; ambiguously ; equivocally ; noncommittally

그런즉 therefore ; so ; then ; accordingly ; such being the case ; hence ; consequently

그럴듯하다 ① [제법 그러하다] (be) plausible ; specious ; likely ¶ 그럴듯하게 들리다 sound reasonable〔plausible〕 // 그럴듯한 거짓말을 하다 lie like the truth // 그럴듯한 말을 하다 tell a plausible story ② [제법 훌륭하다] fair ; passable ; respectable ; decent ¶ 그럴듯한 연설 a speech worth hearing〔listening to〕

그럴법하다 be likely ; probable ; possible ; natural ¶ 그로서는 그럴법하다 He was right in doing so./It was only natural for him to do so.

그럴싸하다 (be) plausible ⇨ 그럴듯하다

그럼 ① [물론] certainly ; of course ; indeed ; yes ; yah ; quite so ¶ 그럼 그렇고 말고 That's right./Certainly it is. //좀 도와주겠니—그럼요 Can you help me? Surely〔Certainly〕! //그러믄요 You can say that again. ② [그러면] if that is so ; if that is the case ¶ 그럼 가자 Then, let us go./OK, let's go.

그렁그렁 —하다 ① [물이] be almost full ; be all watered up ; be suffused with tears ; (be) tearful ② [국물이] watery ; thin ¶ 눈물이 그렁그렁한 눈 eyes suffused〔filled, streaming〕 with tears//국물이 그렁그렁하다 The soup is watery. //항아리의 물이 그렁그렁하다 The water almost fills the jar. ③ [뱃속이] feel bloated〔charged, loaded〕 with water ¶ 그 여자의 눈에는 눈물이 그렁그렁했다 Tears stood〔gathered〕 in her eyes.

그렁성저렁성 this and that ; something or other ; somehow or other ¶ 그렁성저렁성 의견이 많다 There are many different opinions. //거기 관해서 그렁성저렁성 말이 많다 There is a lot of talk about that.

그렁저렁 one way or another ⇨ 그럭저럭

†**그렇게** so ; so much ; that much ; like that ; that way ; in that manner ; particularly ; (not) very (부정) ¶ 그렇게까지 to such an extent ; so far ; that much//그렇게 말하면 if you put it that way ; if you argue it in that way//그렇게 말했을 리가 없다 He cannot have said so. //그렇게 춥지 않다 I do not feel very cold. //그렇게까지 안해도 좋다 You need not go that〔so〕 far. //그렇게 눈에 뜨이는 미인은 아니다 She is not so very attractive. //그렇게 많은 돈을 썼느냐 Did you spend so much money? //그렇게 심한 병은 아니다 It is not a very serious illness. //그렇게 화내지 마라 Don't be so angry. //그럼 그렇게 하기로 정하지 Well, then, let us fix it that way. //그렇게 어렵지는 않았다 It wasn't all that hard.

그렇고말고 indeed ; of course ; certainly ; That's right ; You're right. ; So it is. ; Quite so. ; Sure! 《미·구》 ; You said it.

그렇다 [대답] that is right ; so it is ; you are right ; yes ; no ; [그러하다] (be) so ; such ¶ 그렇다면 if (it is) so ; then//그렇다 하더라도 and yet ; nevertheless ; for all that ; however ; though//그렇지 않으면 otherwise ; else //그렇지 않아도 가난한데 poor enough as he is//그렇다면 얼마나 기쁠까 If so, I shall be very happy. //나는 확실히 그렇다고 생각한다 I feel certain about it. //큰 키는 아니지만 그렇다고 작은 키도 아니다 He is neither tall nor short. //정 그러시다면 좋습니다 All right if you insist. //그렇다고 하더군요 So I heard. //그렇지 않은 사람이 어디 있습니까 Who isn't?

그렇다고 해서 yet ; for all that ; but then ; nevertheless ; be that as it may ; one may well say so, but... ¶ 그렇다고 해서 그만둘 수도 없다 Even so, I cannot give up.

그렇다면 then ; so then ; that granted ; it follows from the foregoing that... ¶ 그렇다면 그렇다고 미리 말해주었으면 좋았을텐데 If that was the case, you might have told me so beforehand.

그렇듯(이) ⇨ 그렇게

그렇지 so it is ; that is right ; you are right

그렇지만 but ; however ; still ; nevertheless ; though ; although ; and yet ; be that〔the matter〕 as it may ; for all that

그렇지 않으면 otherwise ; unless ; if... not so ; (or) else ¶ 이르는 대로 해라 그렇지 않으면 벌을 받을 게다 Do what you are told, otherwise you will be punished. //자유를 달라 그렇지 않으면 죽음을 달라 Give me liberty, or give me death.

그레이드 a grade

그레이프 a grape

— **프루트** a grape fruit

그레인 a grain

그레코로만 〖레슬링〗 the Greco-Roman style

그려 ① ["…습니다" 뒤에서] ¶ 그렇게 많은 피난민들이 몰려들어 왔으니 시내의 식량 배급이 곤란하겠습니다 그려 With so many refugees pouring in, I realize it must be hard keeping the city supplied with food. ② ["…네"·"일세" 다음에] ¶ 자네 말 잘하네 그려 You are very eloquent indeed. //홍씨의 자젤세 그려 Why it's *Hong*'s son! ③ [친근한 명령] ¶ 갑시다 그려 가세 그려 Let's go. //가게 그려 Go on! //한잔 합시다 그려 Let's have a drink, shall we?

그로기 groggy ¶ 그로기 상태가 되다 become groggy ; be done in

그로스 a gross ; 12 dozen

그로테스크 grotesqueness ; bizarrerie ¶ 그로테스크한 grotesque ; bizarre//그로테스크한 물건 grotesquerie//그로테스크한 인간 a freak of nature

그루 ① [농사의] a crop ; a sowing ② [나무의] a root ; a stump ③ [곡식의]

stubble ¶ 한 그루 one crop // 나무 한 그루 a stump of a tree // 벼 한 그루 a stubble of rice plant // 두 그루 심는 농사 two crops a year ; a semiannual crop

그루갈이 [2모작] two crops a year ; semiannual crop ; an aftercrop (두번째 것) **— 하다** raise two crops a year

그루갖추다 《rice plants》 all form ears ; ear up ¶ 호밀이 곧 그루갖출 것이다 The rye should soon be earing up.

그루되다 be stunted (in growth)

그루뒤다 turn over the soil for a second crop

그루들이다 turn over the soil and sow for a second crop

그루박다 ① [거꾸로] drop〔throw down〕 《a thing》 headlong ② [연을] turn a kite upside down ③ [압박하다] oppress ; suppress ; put〔exert〕 pressure upon 《a person》

그루밭 a stubble (field) ; an aftercrop field ; a field used again after a barley crop

그루벼 rice plants raised after harvesting the barley

그루빈대 a bug emerging late for the season

그루빼기 the bottom of a sheaf of straw〔a bundle of firewood〕

그루앉히다 consolidate the foundation for ; solidify the foundation ; make the foundation secure

그루치다 level the headlong stumps by driving them into the ground ; level a field by driving the stumps into the ground

그루콩 an aftercrop of beans

*̣**그루터기** a stump (나무의) ; stubble (벼 따위의)

그루팥 an aftercrop of red beans

그룹 a group ¶ 연구 그룹 a study circle ; a reading circle // 그룹을 지어 in groups // 그룹을 만들다 form a group
— 사운드(樂) a group sound

***그르다** ① [옳지 않다] (be) wrong ; mistaken ; incorrect ; blamable ; be in fault ¶ 그른 일 an evil deed ; a misdeed ; a vice // 마음이 그른 사람 a bad〔a wicked, an evil, an ill-natured〕 person // 그르고 바른 것을 가리다 know right from wrong // 그른 짓을 하다 do a wrong thing ; do wrong // 내가 그르다 The fault lies with me. /I am to blame for it. // 너의 추측이 글렀다 Your guess is quite wide of the mark. // 그런 사람을 믿다니 내가 글렀다 It was my mistake that I trusted him.
② [나쁘다] (be) bad ; foul ; ill ; unwell ; nasty ¶ 건강이 그르다 be in bad health // 날씨가 그르다 weather is foul // 맛이 그르다 taste bad // 안색이 그르다 do not look well〔good〕
③ [가망이 없다] (be) hopeless ; be done for ; be all over ; be all fouled up 《구》 ¶ 성공하기 글렀다 There is no hope〔chance〕 of his success. // 일이 글렀다 I am done for. /It is all up with me. // 환자는 이제 살기 글렀다 The patient has little chance to pull through. /The patient's life is despaired of. // 회복하기 글렀다고 의사는 말했다 The doctor gave no hope of his recovery. // 시험에 합격하기는 다 글렀다 I take it that I am hopeless of success in the examination.

그르렁거리다 wheeze ; purr ¶ 그르렁그르렁 wheezing // (사람이) 목을 그르렁거리다 make a gurgling sound // 고양이가 목을 그르렁거리다 the cat is purring // 목이 그르렁거려 숨쉬기 힘들다 My throat wheezes so much that I find it hard to breathe.

그(르)렁그(르)렁 wheezing ; purring

***그르치다** spoil ; ruin ; destroy ; corrupt ; botch ; mar ; mislead ; make a mess 〔hash, muddle, mush 《구》, mull 《영·구》〕 《of》 ; muff ; muss up ¶ 대사를 그르치다 ruin one's fortune ; ruin oneself ; be ruined // 계획을 그르치다 spoil 〔ruin〕 a plan // 방침을 그르치다 take a wrong course // 일생을 그르치다 make a failure of one's life ; blast one's career // 판단을 그르치다 make an error of judgment // 그와 같은 일은 사회 풍기를 크게 그르치는 것이다 That could be a gross offense against public decency. // 큰일을 그르쳤다 A big job fell through.

*̣**그릇**¹ ① a vessel ; a receptacle ; a container ¶ 놋그릇 a brazen vessel // 질그릇 an earthen vessel
② [기량] caliber ; capacity ; ability ¶ 그릇이 크다〔작다〕 be a man of big〔little〕 caliber ; be a man of great〔small〕 capacity
그릇도 차면 넘친다 (속담) When the well is full, it will run over.

†**그릇**² wrong ; erroneously ; falsely ; by mistake **— 하다** mistake ; err ; do in the wrong way ; make a mistake ¶ 사람을 그릇 보다 misjudge 《a person》 // 그릇 생각하다 misunderstand ; mistake // 그릇 전하다 give false information ; misinform // 남의 말을 그릇 듣다 take 《a person's》 remark in the wrong sense

그릇되다 go〔become〕 wrong ; be spoiled 〔ruined〕 ; fail ; end in failure ; go amiss〔wrong〕 ; be mistaken ; come to naught ¶ 그릇된 wrong ; mistaken ; erroneous ; false ; improper ; incorrect ; errant // 그릇된 생각 a wrong〔an erroneous〕 idea ; a mistaken notion // 그릇된 행실 a misdeed ; an evil doing // 계산이 그릇되다 be wrong in calculation // 판단이 그릇되다 a judgment proves to be wrong

그리 ① [그곳으로] there ; that way ②

[그렇게·그다지] so ; to that extent 〔degree〕 ; in that way ¶ 그리 크지 않다 It is not so big. // 그리 생각하오 Do you think so? // 그리 가겠습니다 I will come there.

†**그리고** and ; and then ; as well as ; and also ¶ 그는 방을 먼저 치우고 공부를 시작했다 First he tidied up his room, and then he began studying. // 그는 연필 둘 공책 둘 그리고 지우개 한 개를 샀다 He bought two pencils, two notebooks, and an eraser. // 그리고 무엇을 했소 And then what did you do?

그리니치 Greenwich
— **천문대** the Greenwich Astronomical Observatory — **표준시** Greenwich mean time 《G. M. T.》

†**그리다**¹ [그림을] picture ; draw ; [채색하여] paint ; [약도를] sketch ; [도안을] describe ; [인물을] portray ; [묘사하다] depict ; describe ¶ 눈썹을 그리다 pencil the eyebrows // 입술을 그리다 rouge one's lips // 마음에 그리다 picture 《a thing》 to oneself ; imagine // 유화를 그리다 paint in oil // 산수화를 그리다 draw 〔paint〕 a landscape // 약도를 그리다 draw a sketch ; sketch // 지도를 그리다 draw a map // 초상화를 그리게 하다 sit for one's portrait // 그것은 현실 생활을 그린 것이다 It is a picture of real life.

그리다² [사모하다] yearn after〔for, toward, to〕 ; pine for〔after〕 ; long for 〔after〕 ; languish for ; thirst for 〔after〕 ; love 《a person》 dearly ; be attached to ¶ 고향을 그리다 pine for home ; be homesick // 도회지를 그리다 be attracted by〔yearn after〕 city life // 애타게 그리다 pine away for love 《for》 ; love 《a person》 to distraction // 애타게 자유를 그리다 have a great yearning〔longing〕 for liberty // 돌아가신 어머니를 그리다 miss one's dead mother

그리드 〖전기〗 a grid
— **검파** grid detection — **전류** a grid current — **축전기** a grid condenser

그리로 ⇨ 그리 ①

그리마 〖동물〗 a millipede ; a house centipede ; Therenonema tuberculata (학명)

그리스¹ [윤활유] grease

그리스² Greece ¶ 그리스의 Greek ; Grecian
— **문명** Hellenic civilization ; Hellenism — **사람** a Greek ; the Greeks 《총칭》 — **신화**〔**철학, 문학**〕 Greek mythology 〔philosophy, literature〕 —**어** Greek

⁑**그리스도** [예수] (Jesus) Christ ; [이명] the Nazarene ; the Messiah ; the Savio(u)r ; the Lord
—**교(教)** Christianity ; the Christian religion〔faith〕 — **재림(再臨)** the second coming of Christ — **재림론자** an Adventist

그리움 yearning ; attachment ; longing ; affection ¶ 그리움을 못 이기다 feel an irresistible yearning for // 떨어져 있으면 그리움은 더해진다 Absence makes the heart grow fonder.

⁑**그리워하다** ⇨ 그리다² ¶ 고향을 그리워하다 be homesick

그리저리 at random ; haphazardly ; in a hit-or-miss manner ; by trial and error
— **하다** try this way and that ; do in a hit-or-miss manner ; do at random ¶ 그리저리하는 동안에 시간이 다 갔다 Time has passed away while I have been messing around doing this and that.

그리하여 [그리고·그런 다음] and ; then ; so ; [이제는] (and) now

그린 [푸른] green
—**백** a greenback —**베레** [특전 부대] Green Beret —**티** green tea —**피스** green peas —**하우스** a greenhouse

그린벨트 a greenbelt ¶ 그린벨트 지역 a greenbelt zone // 그린벨트 지역을 풀다 dissolve a greenbelt zone

그릴 a grill (room)

†**그림** a picture ; a painting ; a drawing (서화) ; a sketch (약도) ; a print (판화) ; an illustration (삽화) ; a diagram (도표) ; a cut (일부 삽화) ; a plate (전면 삽화) ; a figure (도형) ¶ 바다의 그림 a picture of the sea // 그림 같은 picturesque 《view》 // 그림처럼 아름다운 곳 a picturesque place // 그림을 그리다 draw ; paint pie in the sky 《미·속》 // 그림을 잘 그린다 He draws well. // 그녀는 그림처럼 아름답다 She is as lovely 〔pretty〕 as a picture.
— **설명**〔**문구**〕 a caption — **잡지**〔**화보**〕 a pictorial magazine — **전람회** a picture〔an art〕 exhibition — **족자** a picture scroll ; a hanging picture
그림의 떡 속담 a prize beyond one's reach/Pie in the sky.

†**그림 물감** ① pigment ; paint ; coloring materials ; colors 《영》 ② [유화용] oil colors ; oils ③ [수채화용] water〔moist〕 colors ④ [튜브식] tube colors ¶ 그림 물감을 풀다 dissolve colors
—**붓** a color brush —**솔** a paintbrush —**장수** a colorman —**통** a color box —**판** a palette

그림쇠 a rule ; a measure ¶ 그림쇠로 재다 measure with a rule

그림 엽서 —**葉書** a picture〔an illustrated〕 postcard ; a postcard 《미》 ¶ 이 그림 엽서같이 아름다운 도시는 벽이 없는 박물관이라고 불리고 있는데 역사적 유물이 대단히 많기 때문이죠 This postcard-beautiful city is called a museum without walls because it abounds with historical remains.
경치 — scenic cards

†**그림자** a shadow ; a silhouette ; [영상] a reflection ; an image ; [환영] a phantom ; [모습] figure ¶ 호수에 비친 산 그림자 the image of a mountain (afloat) on the lake // 어두운 그림자가 드리우다 an ominous shadow looms 《across》 // 장지에 비친 그림자 the shadow of a man falling on the paper door // 그림자 같은 shadowy // 그림자가 비치다 cast〔throw〕 a shadow // 그림자 같이 따라다니다 go as the shadow follows the form // 사람이라고는 그림자도 보이지 않는다 There is not a soul to be seen. // 그의 얼굴에 죽음의 그림자가 비쳤다 The shadow of death was on his face.
—놀이 a shadowgraph

그림책 一册 a picture book ; a pictorial book ; an illustrated book (삽화가 있는 것) ; an illustrated story book (이야기 그림책)

그립 [손잡이] a grip

그립다 (be) beloved ; sweet ; affectionate ; dear ; missed ; be longed for ; be yearned after ¶ 그리운 사람 a person dear to one ; one's beloved person ; one's darling // 그리운 추억 sweet〔dear〕 memories ; memories dear to one // 고향이 그립다 be sick for one's old home ; be homesick for one's country // 친구가 그립다 I miss my friend. // 그 노래를 들으니 옛날이 그립다 That song conjures up memories of the good old days.

그만[1] [그만한] (a) little (amount of) ; that so little (as that) ; to that (small) extent ; such a ; no more than ; just ; only ¶ 그만 수고를 아끼느냐 Do you begrudge such a small favor ? // 그만 일에 낙심(하지) 마라 Don't be disappointed about such a (trifle) thing. // 그만 일은 삼척동자도 안다 Even a mere child knows it.

그만[2] ① [그 정도까지만] to that extent ; that much and no more ; no more than that ; enough ; by ¶ 그만 울어라 Do not cry any more. // 그만 먹어라 Eat no more than that. /Stop eating. // 오늘은 그만 하자 That is enough for today. /We have done enough for today. // 이제 그만 자는 게 좋겠다. You'd better go to bed now. // 자랑 좀 그만해라 No more of your bragging. // 농담은 그만 하고 너 정말 에베레스트 산에 오를 거냐 Joking aside〔apart〕, are you really going to climb Mt. Everest ?
② [곧] as soon as ; no sooner...than ; hardly〔scarcely〕...when〔before〕 ; the moment〔instant〕 ¶ 그것을 보자 그만 기절했다 She fainted the moment she saw it. // 그 말에 그만 화를 냈다 The remark was provocative enough to him. // 자리에 들자 그만 잠들었다 As soon as he went to bed, he fell asleep. // 그 소리를 듣더니 그만 울음을 터뜨렸다 When he heard the news, he burst right out crying. // 그는 화를 버럭 내면서 그만 가버렸다 He went off immediately in a fit of sudden temper〔anger〕.
③ unavoidably ; of necessity ; under compulsion ; reluctantly ; against one's will ; involuntarily ; unintentionally ¶ 그만 사고로 결석했습니다 Unavoidable circumstances obliged me to absent myself. // 그만 …하다 do by mistake ; be careless enough to do

그만그만하다 be nearly〔about〕 the same ; be much the same ; be of a piece ; be of a sort ; be of a hair 《구》 ¶ 나이가 그만그만하다 be about the same age // 둘 다 그만그만하다 The two are much the same. /There is nothing to choose between the two. // 모두 그만그만하다 They are of a sort.

*__그만두다__ [중지하다] stop ; quit ; cease ; discontinue ; cut out ; [취소하다] call off 《a meeting》 ; [포기하다] give up ; abandon ; renounce ; [사퇴하다] resign ; retire ; leave ¶ 이야기를 그만두다 stop〔cease〕 talking ; drop the subject // 공부를 그만두다 give up one's studies // 술을 그만두다 stop〔give up〕 drinking ; go on the wagon 《미》 // 학교를 그만두다 quit〔give up〕 school // 회사를 그만두다 leave (the service of) the company // 거래를 그만두다 close an account 《with a person》 // 그만두지 않다 go on 《with one's work》 // 갑자기 그만두다 cut short ; break off // 계획을 그만두다 give up a project ; lay aside a plan // 그는 건강 때문에 모든 공직을 그만두었다 He resigned from public life on the grounds of ill health. // 그만둬라 Enough〔None〕 of that ! 《구》 ; Drop it ! // 농담은 그만둬라 None of your jokes ! // 형식적인 것은 그만두자 Let us do away with all ceremony. // 일을 제대로 하든지 그만두든지 하라 Shape up or ship out ! // 그만두려면 적어도 2주일 전에 미리 알려줘 In case you want to quit, give me two weeks' notice. // 장사를 그만두신다면서요 You're going out of business ? // 우선 지각을 그만두는게 어때 For starters, how about cutting out coming to work late ?

그만이다 ① [그뿐이다] be the end 《of it》 ; do not mind ; be no more than that ¶ 헤어지면 그만이다 That's the end of all if they separate. // 늦어도 그만이다 It doesn't matter if you are late. // 그것만 있으면 그만이다 That is all I want. // 해보고 안되면 그만이다 If I try and fail, that's the end of it.
② [최고] the best ; it ¶ 맛이 그만이다 This tastes superb. // 사람이 아주 그만

이야 He's a peach (of a fellow).

그만저만 —하다 be neither good nor bad ; be so-so ; be about the same ¶ (병이) 그만저만하다 be more or less ailing // 내 건강은 그만저만하다 I am in tolerable health.

†**그만큼** that much ; so much〔many〕; as much〔many〕; to that extent ¶ 그만큼 닮은 형제도 드물다 No two brothers can resemble each other more than they do. // 그만큼은 알고 있다 I know as much. // 그만큼이면 충분하다 That will be enough. // 노력하면 그만큼 보답이 있을 것이다 Every effort you make will be rewarded. // 오늘은 그만큼 해둡시다 So much for today. // 한국인으로서 그만큼 영문을 쓰는 사람도 드물다 Few Koreans can write English so well as he. // 그만큼 공부하면 시험에 합격하겠다 You are sure to pass the examination if you go on working at that rate.

그만하다 be about the same ; be neither better nor worse ; be as much〔many〕as ; be not less (than) ; tolerable ; so-so ; be not more (than) ¶ 그의 키도 꼭 그만하다 He is just about the same height. // 그의 병세는 그저 그만하다 His illness is getting neither better nor worse. // 사고가 그만하기 다행이다 You are fortunate that the accident was not so bad. // 이것도 무게가 그만하다 This is as heavy as that. // 당신 것도 좋지만 내것도 그만하다 Mine is as good as yours. // 장사는 어때요—그만합니다 How's business? Oh, not too bad. // 내 신발의 크기도 그만합니다 My shoes are of the same size. // 그만해도 잘했다 That's still pretty good.

그맘때 about that time ; about the same age (나이) ¶ 그맘때까지는 일이 끝날 것입니다 My work will be finished by that time. // 그맘때 일이 조금도 생각나지 않는다 I remember nothing about those times. // 나도 그맘때는 무척 장난이 심했었다 I was quite naughty when I was that age. // 사과는 그맘때가 제일 맛이 있다 That is the time when apples taste most delicious. // 그만큼 충고를 해도 그는 듣지 않았다 All my advice was lost upon him. // 노력하면 그만큼 보답이 있을 것이다 Every effort you make will be rewarded.

⁑**그물** a net ; a seine ; a dragnet ; a network (그물 세공) ¶ 그물의 눈 meshes // 그물을 치다 cast〔shoot〕 a net ; stretch a net ; put up a tennis net (정구의) ; spread a dragnet (수사망을) ; pitch〔stretch〕 a net // 그물을 짜다 net ; make a net // 그물에 걸리다 be caught in a net // 그물을 끌어올리다 haul in a net // 경찰은 범인을 검거하기 위해 그물을 쳤다 The police put out a dragnet for the criminal.

— **선반** [짐 올려 놓는] a luggage〔baggage〕 rack ; a rack —**채** a netted ladle〔scoop〕; a skimmer **고기** — a fishing net (어망) **새**— a fowling net **후릿** — a seine ; a dragnet **챙이** — a cast(ing) net (투망)

그물코 meshes (of a net) ¶ (고기가) 그물코에 걸리다 be trapped〔caught〕 in meshes of a net // 잔고기는 큰 그물코 사이로 빠져 나갔다 Small fish slipped away through large meshes of a net.

그믐 the last day of the month

그믐께 the last days of the month ; around the end of the month

그믐날 the last day (of the month) ¶ 3월 그믐날 the end〔last day〕 of March // 섣달 그믐날 the last day of the year ; New Year's Eve ; the old year's day

그믐달 the old moon

그믐밤 the last night of a lunar month

그믐사리 yellow corvina caught around the end of the month

그믐 초승 the end of the month and the beginning of the following month ; the juncture between months

그믐치 rain〔snow〕 around the end of the month

그믐 칠야 —漆夜 the dark night of the last day of a (lunar) month

그 밖 the rest ; the others ¶ 그 밖의 other ; further ; additional // 그 밖에 besides ; moreover ; further // 그 밖의 여러가지 것 many other things // 그 밖의 일은 아무것도 모른다 I know nothing else. /This is all I know (of). // 그 밖에 누가 오지 Who else is coming?

⁑**그사이** the while ; the meantime ; the interval ¶ 그사이에 in the meantime ; meanwhile ; in the interval // 그사이 안녕하셨는지요 How have you been getting along? // 그사이에 그 소년은 달아났다 The boy ran away in the meantime.

⁑**그슬리다** burn ; scorch ; sear ; roast ; broil ¶ 까맣게 그슬리다 char ; burn to a cinder // 생선을 불에 그슬리다 broil fish over a fire // 고기를 그슬리다 sear the meat ; broil a fish

그악스럽다 (be) fierce ; ferocious ; hard ; rough ; mischievous (장난이) ; excessive (너무하다) ; industrious (부지런하다) ¶ 그악스럽게 돈을 벌다 be engrossed in money-making ; be all eagerness to make money // 그악스럽게 먹다 eat to excess ; overeat oneself // 그악스럽게 부려먹다 drive 《a person》 hard ; sweat 《a person》 // 그악스럽게 굴다 conduct outrageously // 그악스럽게 공부하다 work too hard ; overwork oneself // 우리 아이는 한창 그악스러운 나이입니다 My son is now at his naughtiest age.

그악하다 (be) fierce ⇨ 그악스럽다

그야 it ¶ 그야 그렇지만 It may be so, ⟪but⟫ // 그야 물론이지 It is a matter of course ⟪that⟫ // 그야 그럴 수 있지 That is quite possible.

그야말로 indeed ; really ; quite ; truly ; very ; certainly ¶ 그야말로 아름답다 It is really beautiful. // 그야말로 크다 That is big indeed. // 그야말로 구사일생이구나 You really had a narrow escape. // 그렇다면 그야말로 기쁘다 If so, I shall be very happy. // 그야말로 보람있는 일이다 It is a really challenging job. // 그야말로 네가 잘못이다 Certainly you are wrong. /You are indeed to blame.

그어주다 share ; apportion

그 역시 一亦是 too ; also ; as well ; likewise ¶ 그 역시 사실이다 That also is true. // 그 역시 마음에 들지 않는다 I don't like it either.

그예 at last〔length〕 ; at long last ; in the long run ; in the end ; finally ¶ 그예 실패하다 end in failure // 그예 시험에 합격하였다 He has passed the examination at last. // 그예 빚을 받아냈다 I collected the debt at long last.

그윽이 in secret〔private〕 ; in one's heart ; inwardly ; quietly ¶ 그윽이 기회를 엿보다 be on the lookout for an opportunity ; lie in wait // 그윽이 사모하다 love〔admire〕 ⟪a person⟫ in one's heart // 그윽이 기뻐하다 be pleased at heart

그윽하다 [으늑하다] (be) quiet ; still ; peaceful ; lonely ; solitary ; hidden ; secluded ; [깊다] deep ; profound ¶ 그윽한 곳 a secluded spot ; a solitary place // 그윽한 생각 a deep thought ; a secret idea // 그윽한 마음씨 profound consideration // 그윽한 애정 profound affection // 그윽한 향기 a sweet scent // 먼데서 종소리가 그윽하게 들려왔다 The muffled sound of a distant bell came to my ear. // 그녀의 방에는 꽃향기가 그윽했다 Her room was fragrant with the smell of flowers.

†**그을다** [햇볕에] be sunburned ; be (sun-)tanned ; [연기에] become sooty ; be stained with soot ; be smoke-stained ¶ 햇볕에 그을은 얼굴 a sunburned face // 연기로 그을은 천장 a smoke-stained ceiling // 햇볕에 그을지 않게 하다 keep from being sunburned // 그을은 유리 a glass stained with soot

그을리다 [연기에] cover〔stain〕 with soot ; make (all) sooty ; [햇볕에] sunburn

그을음 soot ; black dirt ¶ 그을음이 끼다 become sooty ; be soot-covered // 그을음을 쓸어내다 sweep away〔wipe off〕 the soot

그이 that person ; he〔him〕 ; [여자] she〔her〕

그 자리 ① [장소] the place ; the spot ② [경우] the occasion ③ [상황] the situation ¶ 그 자리에서 then and there ; there and then ; on the spot ; on that occasion ; extemporaneously (즉석에서) // 그 자리에 있던 사람들 those who happened to be there ; those present // 그의 옷차림은 그 자리에 어울리지 않았다 He was not properly dressed for the occasion.

‡**그저** ① [줄곧] still ; all (the time) ; through ; continuously ; always ; without ceasing ¶ 그저 비가 온다 It keeps on raining. // 그저 책을 읽고 있다 He is still reading a book. // 아침부터 그저 잠만 자고 있다 He has been sleeping all through the morning. // 그는 그저 부모에게 걱정만 끼치고 있다 He is a constant source of anxiety to his parents.
② [목적 없이] recklessly ; casually ; aimlessly ; only ; just ; at random ¶ 그저 앉아 있다 He is sitting down listlessly. // 아무 말도 하지 않고 그저 갔다 He went away without a word. // 그는 그저 웃기만 하였다 He said nothing but smiled.
③ [대단할 것 없이] so-so ; all right ¶ 그저 그럴 줄 알았지 That is about what I thought. /I expected〔thought〕 as much. // 그저 쓸만하다 be just passable
④ [애원] for Heaven's〔God's〕 sake ; for mercy's〔pity's〕 sake please ; I beg of you ¶ 그저 살려 주십시오 Spare me for mercy's sake. // 그저 네가 참아라 Won't you be patient, please ?
⑤ [다른 뜻 없이] only ; merely ; simply ; slightly ; just ¶ 그저 농담으로 한 말이다 I said it just for fun. /I did not mean what I said. // 그저 제가 해야 할 일을 했을 뿐입니다 I only have done what I ought to (do).
⑥ [쉽게] easily ; with no effort ; without trouble ¶ 그런 일은 그저먹기다 It is quite easy to do it. /That is nothing.

***그저께** the day before yesterday ¶ 그저께 밤 the night before last // 그저께 밤부터 눈 한번 붙이지 못 했어 I haven't got any shut-eye since the night before last.

그전 former days〔times〕 ; the other day ; the past ¶ 그전 주소 a former address // 그전같이 as before ; as usual // 그전에 in the past ; formerly ; before ; in old days ; previously // 모든 것이 그전하고는 다르다 Things are not what they used to be. // 우리는 그전부터 아는 사이이다 We have known each other for a long time. // 그전에는 그도 부자였다 He was a rich man in the past.

그제야 for the first time ; only when〔after〕 ; not... until ; at last ; at length ¶ 그는 그제야 바다를 보았다 He saw the sea for the first time in his life. // 며칠 지나서 그제야 그 사실을 알았다 It was not until a few days later that I learned the truth. // 사람들은 건강을 잃고 나서 그제야 그 고마움을 안다 People do not know the blessing of health till they lose it. // 나는 그제야 화재의 무서움을 알았다 Then I realized for the first time how horrible a fire was. // 그는 그제야 입을 열기 시작했다 He began to open his mouth at last.

그중 一中 among the rest ; among them ; of them〔the number〕; between them ; [제일] the most〔best〕 ¶ 너도 그중 한 사람이다 You are (one) of the number. // 부상자는 5명이고 그중 한 사람은 생명이 위험하다 Five were injured, and of these one was as good as dead. // 이것을 그중 좋아한다 I like this better than the others. /I prefer this over〔to〕 others.

그즈음 about that time ; around then ; in those days

그지없다 (be) boundless ; endless ; immeasurable ; limitless ; extreme ; exceeding ; unfathomable ¶ 그지없이 endlessly ; without limit ; exceedingly // 그지없이 소중한 교훈 a lesson of immeasurable value // 불쌍하기 그지없다 be too pitiful for words // 사람의 욕심은 그지없다 There are no bounds〔limits〕 to man's greed. // 유감스럽기 그지없다 be extremely sorry 《for》 // 그 경치는 아름답기 그지없다 I can't fully describe the beauty of the view.

그쯤 ① [그 정도] that much ; that quantity〔degree〕; such a caliber ¶ 그쯤은 문제가 아니다 To that extent〔If that's all〕, there is no problem.
② [장소] around there ¶ 이것은 그쯤에다 놓아라 Put this somewhere (over there).

†**그치다** stop ; cease ; halt ; come to a stop ; end ; abate (바람이) ; die down〔away〕 (소리가) ; be over ¶ 그칠 새 없이 continuously ; unceasingly ; without cease ; with no break // 그칠 새 없는 걱정 constant worry ; ceaseless anxiety // 뚝 그치다 come to a full stop ; cease〔stop〕 suddenly // 비가 오다 그치다 하다 rain off and on // 손님이 그칠 새 없다 have a stream of visitors // 울음을 그치다 stop crying // 내가 방에 들어가자 그들은 이야기를 그쳤다 On my entering the room they suddenly stopped〔ceased〕 talking.

그토록 so (much) ; such ; to such an extent ¶ 그토록 잘해 주시니 고맙습니다 Thank you so much.

*__그 후__ 一後 after that ; afterwards ; later ; since then ; from that time on ; thereafter ¶ 그 후 1주일 a week later // 그 후 나는 서울에서 살았다 I have lived in *Seoul* ever since.

*__극__ 劇 a drama ; a play ¶ 극적인 dramatic // 극적으로 dramatically // 극을 공연하다 play ; give〔stage〕 a play // 극화하다 dramatize // 극을 쓰다 write a play
—문학 dramatic literature **—영화** a film drama ; a play film **—예술** the dramatic art **사회—** a social-life drama

‡**극** 極 [절정] the height ; the extreme ; the zenith ; the climax ; [지구·자석의] the poles ¶ 극에 달하다 be at its height ; reach its climax // 번영의 극에 달하다 be at the summit〔height, zenith〕 of one's prosperity // 절망의 극에 달해 자살하다 kill oneself in despair // 피로의 극에 달하다 be exhausted to the extreme ; be dead tired // 그것은 어리석음의 극이다 It is the height of folly. // 도덕의 퇴폐는 극에 달했다 They are extremely corrupt in morals.
—거리 〖천문〗 codeclination **—지방** the polar regions **이(二)— 발전기〔수화기〕** a bipolar dynamo〔receiver〕

극간 極諫 a strong remonstrance **—하다** severely remonstrate 《with a person on his folly》

극값 極— 〖수학〗 extreme value

극계 劇界 the theatrical world ; theatrical circles ⇨ 극단(劇壇)

극광 極光 the aurora ; the polar lights ; [남극의] the aurora australis ; the southern lights ; [북극의] the aurora borealis ; the northern lights
—대(帶) an auroral zone **남—** an aurora australis 《*pl.* aurorae australes》; the southern lights **북—** an aurora borealis 《*pl.* aurorae boreales》; the northern lights

극구 발명 極口發明 ⇨ 극구 변명

극구 변명 極口辯明 **—하다** spare no pains to defend oneself ; make every sort of excuse

극구 찬송 極口讚頌 the highest praise **—하다** speak highly of ; praise 《a person》 to the skies ; speak in high terms of

극구 칭찬 極口稱讚 the highest praise **—하다** speak highly of ; speak in high terms of ; praise 《a person》 to the skies

극권 極圈 the polar circles
남— the Antarctic Circle **북—** the Arctic Circle

극귀 極貴 **—하다** [드물다] (be) very rare ; [귀중하다] very precious

극기 克己 self-denial〔-control〕; stoicism **—하다** control〔conquer〕 oneself ; be master of oneself ; exercise self-denial
—주의 stoicism ; asceticism **—파** the Stoics

극기 極忌 abhorrence ; detestation ; extreme dislike **—하다** abhor ; detest ; dislike intensely

극기심 克己心 a self-denying spirit ; the spirit of self-restraint ¶ 극기심이 있는 self-denying ; stoic(al) // 극기심이 없다 lack self-denial ; have no command over oneself // 그는 극기심이 강한 사람이다 He is a man of strong fortitude.

극난 極難 —하다 (be) most difficult ; very hard

극년 極年 〖지구물리〗 a polar year

*극단 極端 an extreme ; extremity ; an excess ¶ 극단의 extreme ; excessive // 극단적으로 extremely ; to the extreme degree ; too far // 최극단 the furthest extreme // 극단의 예 an extreme case // 극단의 수단 extreme measures // 극단의 좌경파 ultra-left // 극단으로 흐르다 go to extremes ; go too far ; carry 《it》 too far // 극단에서 극단으로 흐르다 go from one extreme to another

—론 an extreme view —주의 extremism ; ultraism ; radicalism ; maximalism — 주의자 an extremist ; a radical ; an ultraist

극단 劇團 a dramatic〔theatrical〕 company ; a troupe ¶ 지방 순회 극단 a provincial touring company ; a troupe 〔company〕 on the road

—원 a member of a dramatic company

극단 劇壇 the stage ; the theatrical world ¶ 극단에 나서다 come〔go〕 on the stage ; appear before the footlights // 극단을 떠나다 leave〔go off〕 the stage // 저 배우는 극단 출신이다 That actor comes from the legitimate stage.

극대 極大 the greatest ; 〖수학〗 maximum ¶ 극대의 greatest ; maximum

— 극소 the maximum and minimum —량〔수〕 the maximum —치(値) the maximum value

*극도 極度 the extreme ; [최대한] the maximum ; [정상] the zenith ¶ 극도의 extreme ; utmost ; maximum // 극도로 extremely ; in the extreme ; to the utmost // 극도로 흥분하다 be extremely excited ; be excited in the extreme ; be highly wrought up // 극도로 비관하다 be in extreme grief // 번영의 극도에 달하다 reach the zenith of prosperity // 그는 극도의 신경 쇠약에 걸려 있다 He has been suffering from nervous debility 〔neurasthenia〕 of the worst kind.

극독약 劇毒藥 a deadly poison ; a most drastic〔powerful, terrible〕 poison

*극동 極東 the Far East ¶ 극동의 Far Eastern

— 공군 [미국의] the Far Eastern Air Force 《FEAF》 — 문제 the Far Eastern question — 위원회(유엔의) the Far Eastern Commission 《FEC》 — 자문 위원회 the Far Eastern Advisory Commission 《FEAC》

극락 極樂 paradise ; heaven ; Elysium ; the abode of the blessed ; [무상의 행복] bliss ¶ 지상의 극락 an earthly paradise ; an Eden // 극락에 가다 go to heaven // 극락과 같았다 It has been heaven〔heavenly〕.

— 생활 an Elysian life — 정토(淨土) the Land of Happiness〔Perfect Bliss〕 ; the Elysian fields

극락 세계 極樂世界 paradise ⇨ 극락

극락 왕생 極樂往生 euthanasia ; a gentle and easy death ; an easy passage into eternity ¶ 극락 왕생을 하다 pass away peacefully ; die an easy and peaceful〔painless〕 death

극락조 極樂鳥 〖새〗 a bird of paradise ; a king bird

극량 極量 [약의] the maximum dose ; a fatal dose

극력 極力 one's utmost exertion ; the utmost ; [부사적] to the best of one's ability ; with all one's might ; as best one may —하다 exert oneself to the utmost ; make an all-out effort ¶ 극력 반대하다 oppose stubbornly〔stoutly〕 // 극력 힘을 쓰다 do one's utmost ; use every means in one's power ; make every effort // 극력 응원하다 cheer with all one's might

극렬 劇烈 violence ; severity ; intensity ; vehemence ; fierceness —하다 (be) violent ; severe ; keen ; acute ; vehement ; drastic ¶ 극렬히 violently ; severely ; intensely ; vehemently ; keenly ; acutely // 극렬한 언사 vehement language ; high words // 극렬한 경쟁 keen competition ; a sharp contest // 극렬의 도를 더하다 grow in intensity // 극렬한 시위 a violent demonstration

극렬 분자 極烈分子 a radical ; an extremist

극론 極論 an extreme〔exhaustive〕 argument ; sophistry —하다 make 〔advance〕 an extreme argument ¶ 그는 그럴 필요가 없다고까지 극론했다 He went so far as to deny the necessity of it.

극류 極流 〖해양〗 a polar current

극무 劇務 a severe duty ; hard work ; an arduous task〔duty〕 ¶ 극무로 쓰러지다 succumb to the strain of overwork ; break down under the strain of the hard work required // 극무를 맡다 undertake an arduous task

극미 極微 an atom —하다 (be) infinitesimal ; atomic ; microscopic ; ultramicroscopic

— 동물 an animalcule ; an animalculum 《*pl.* -la(e)》 — 동물학자 an animalculist

극복 克服 conquest ; subjugation —하다 overcome ; conquer ; surmount ; subjugate ; cope with ; deal successfully with ¶ 곤란을 극복하다 overcome the difficulty // 약점을 극복하다 overcome one's weaknesses // 위기를 극복하다 weather a crisis // 시국을 극복하다 cope with the situation // 그들은 재정상의 곤란을 잘 극복했다 They successfully tided over their financial difficulties.

극복 克復 restoration ; return **—하다** return ; be restored ¶ 평화 극복시에 on the restoration〔return〕 of peace

극본 劇本 the script of a play ; a drama ; a scenario ¶ 극본을 쓰다 write a play

극북 極北 the Far North ; the North Pole ¶ 극북의 땅 the arctic region ; the top of the world

***극비 極秘** strict〔complete, absolute〕 secrecy ; a top secret 《미》 ¶ 극비의 closely guarded ; in strict secrecy // 극비리에 with utmost secrecy ; in the greatest secrecy // 극비리에 진행되다 The proceedings were conducted in strict secrecy. // 극비에 부치다 keep 《a matter》 a strict secret ; guard 《a matter》 with great secrecy // 그에게 극비의 서한을 보냈다 I have sent him a top secret letter. // 그 제조 방법은 극비다 The process of manufacture is a jealously guarded secret.

극비 서류 極秘書類 a confidential document

극비 정보 極秘情報 a highly confidential information ; hush-hush information

극빈 極貧 extreme poverty ; destitution **—하다** (be) extremely poor ; be as poor as a church mouse ; (be) destitute ; indigent

—자 a needy〔destitute〕 person ; a pauper ; [총칭] the destitute〔indigent〕

극상 極上 the first ; the best ; the highest quality ¶ 극상의 extra fine ; of the highest〔finest〕 quality ; exquisite ; excellent ; extraordinary // 극상의 장소 a tiptop place

—품 the finest〔choicest〕 stuff ; an article of the best quality ; an A 1〔a choice〕 article

극서 極暑, 劇暑 intense〔severe, extreme〕 heat

극선 極線 〖수학〗 a polar

극성 極性 〖전기〗 polarity ¶ 극성의 polar // 극성을 부여하다 polarize // 극성을 없애다 depolarize

극성 極星 the north polestar (북극성) ; the south polestar (남극성)

극성 極盛 [매우 성함] the height of prosperity ; [성질] extremity ¶ 극성스럽다 be highly flourishing〔prosperous, rampant〕 ; [성질이] be extreme〔impatient, impetuous, frantic, furious〕 // 극성스러운 사람 an impatient person // 극성스러운 언동 intemperate conduct // 극성스럽게 일하다 work like mad ; work furiously

극성 떨다 관용 grow impatient ; be impetuous ; run to extreme ; be mad ; be frantic〔furious〕

극세 極細 —하다 (be) very fine 〔minute〕 ; infinitesimal ¶ 극세한 만년필 a superfine-pointed (fountain) pen

극세포 極細胞 〖생물〗 a polar cell

극소 極小 the smallest ; 〖수학〗 minimum ¶ 극소의 smallest ; minimum ; infinitesimal

—량 the minimum **—수** the minimum number ; a small minority **—치(値)** the minimum value

극시 劇詩 a verse drama ; a drama in verse ; dramatic poetry

극심 極甚 —하다 (be) extreme ; enormous ; heavy ; intense ; excessive ; severe ; serious ; tremendous ; terrible ; gross ¶ 극심한 더위 an intense heat // 극심한 추위 a severe cold // 극심한 피해 a heavy damage // 후진국들은 극심한 인재난을 겪고 있다 Underdeveloped countries are faced with serious shortages of talented people. // 오늘 밤은 모기가 극심하다 The mosquitoes are terrible tonight.

극악 極惡 atrocity ; brutality ; villainy **—하다** (be) heinous ; atrocious ; most wicked ; villainous ; diabolical ; flagrant ; infernal ¶ 극악한 사람 an accomplished villain ; a devil ; a fiend // 극악한 행위 infernal deed // 극악한 범죄 a flagrant crime

극악무도 極惡無道 atrocity ; brutality ; enormity

극약 劇藥 a powerful drug ; [독약] a poison ; a deadly poison

극양 極洋 the polar seas

— 어업 the polar-sea fishery

극언 極言 unreserved criticism **—하다** go so far as to say〔declare〕 ; be bold enough to say ; speak in unsparing words ; utter an extreme view ; give unreserved criticism ¶ 극언하자면 to be more exact ; to put it strongly ; strictly speaking // 그는 나를 반역자라고 극언했다 He went so far as to brand me as a traitor.

극영화 劇映畫 a dramatic movie

극우 極右 [사람] an ultra-rightist ; an extreme right-winger

— 단체 a far-right(-wing) organization ; a group of the ultraright〔far right〕 **—파** the extreme right ; an extreme right wing ; the ultranationalists ¶ 당내의 극우파를 일소하다 clear the party of its extreme right wing

극작 劇作 play writing ; dramatic authorship **—하다** write a play 〔drama〕 ¶ 극작상의 dramaturgic(al)

—가 a dramatist ; a playwriter ; a playwright **—법** dramaturgy

***극장 劇場** a theater ; a playhouse

—가 a theater district〔quarter〕 ; a rialto 《미》 — 경영자 a theater manager ; a theatrical producer 《미》 — 안내원 a theater attendant ; an usher —주(主) a theater owner ; the proprietor of a theater 개봉 — a first-run theater 국립 — the National Theater 오페라 — an opera house 영화 — a movie theater〔house〕 ; a cinema 《영》 원형 — an amphitheater

극적 劇的 theatrical ; dramatic ¶ 극적으로 dramatically // 극적인 장면〔정경〕 a dramatic scene〔sight〕 // 극적 효과를 노리다 aim at a dramatic effect // 극적인 만남 a dramatic meeting // 그는 극적인 삶을 살았다 He had an eventful life.

극점 極點 the extreme (point) ; the height ; the climax ; [절정] the summit ; the zenith ; [밑바닥] the bottom ; the nadir

극젱이 〚농업〛 a kind of plow which is used for light plowing

극존 極尊 [임금] His Majesty ; [지위가 높음] prominence ; the highest reverence

극좌 極左 the extreme left ; an extreme left wing ; an ultra-leftist ¶ 극좌의 leftmost ; ultra-leftist // 당내의 극좌파를 일소하다 clear the party of its extreme left wing

— 당원 an extreme leftist〔left-winger〕 ; an ultra-leftist — 분자 the extreme elements on the left ; extreme-leftist elements ; the extreme left ; communistic elements

극중 劇中 ¶ 극중의 사건 an incident in the play // 극중에 등장하는 인물 the characters in the play

극중 極重 —하다 (be) very heavy (무게) ; critical (병세) ; grave (범죄)

‡**극지** 極地 the pole ; the polar region

—법 〚등산〛 a polar method — 탐험 a polar expedition — 탐험가 a polar explorer — 횡단 비행 a transpolar flight

‡**극진** 極盡 cordiality ; heartiness ; utter devotion —하다 (be) very cordial ; kind ; devoted ¶ 극진히 kindly ; cordially ; heartily ; devotedly // 극진히 사랑하다 love deeply ; love 《a person》 to distraction // 극진히 대접하다 treat 《a person》 very cordially ; entertain 《a person》 with warm hospitality

극찬 極讚 ¶ 극찬을 받다 win high praise

극초단파 極超短波 microwave

극치 極致 perfection ; the acme ; the culmination ; the height ¶ 미의 극치 ideal beauty // 문화의 극치 the culmination of civilization // 예술의 극치 the highest reach of art // 완벽한 극치 the acme of perfection // 극치에 이르다 attain the highest perfection // 그것은 어리석음의 극치이다 It's the height of folly.

극치 極値 〚수학〛 the extreme value ; the extremum 《*pl.* -ma》

극터듬다 grope one's way up ; climb up with much difficulty

극통 劇痛, 極痛 an acute〔intense〕 pain ; a severe〔sharp, keen〕 pain ; a pang

극평 劇評 drama〔theater〕 criticism

—가 a drama〔theater〕 critic

극피동물 棘皮動物 an echinoderm

극하다 極— go to extremes ; run to an extreme ; be most 《cruel》 ¶ 참상이 극하다 present a most miserable sight // 포학을 극하다 act with extreme violence ; be most tyrannical // 사치가 극하다 be most luxurious

극한 極寒, 劇寒 intense〔severe〕 cold

극한 極限 a limit ; a bound ; limitation ; 〚기하〛 limit ¶ 극한에 달하다 reach the limit // 극한을 넘다〔넘지 않다〕 go beyond〔keep within〕 the bounds〔limits〕 《of》

— 강도(强度) the ultimate strength — 설계 〚건축〛 a limit design —값 a limiting value

극한 상황 極限狀況 an extreme situation

극한 투쟁 極限鬪爭 struggle to the extremes ; fight to end ; resort to the extremism

극형 極刑 [사형] capital punishment ; [최대한의 형] the maximum〔extreme〕 penalty ¶ 극형에 처하다 condemn 《a person》 to capital punishment

극화 劇化 dramatization ; (a) dramatic 〔stage〕 version —하다 dramatize ; make a dramatic version of a 《story》 ¶ 소설을 극화하다 dramatize a novel

극흉 極凶 —하다 [성질이] (be) extremely wicked ; atrocious ; [얼굴이] very ugly ; very bad-looking

***극히** 極— exceedingly ; excessively ; extremely ; remarkably ; greatly ; immensely ¶ 극히 미묘한 most delicate // 극히 아름다운 very beautiful // 극히 드물게 once in a blue moon // 극히 어려운 과제 an extremely hard task // 극히 유감이다 be most regrettable // 극히 중요한 문제 a very important matter // 극히 좋은 날씨 unusually fine weather // 나는 극히 운이 좋았다 I had capital luck.

근 斤 a *keun* 《0.6 kilogram》 ; a pound 《영》 ¶ 설탕 한 근 a pound of sugar

근 根 ① [종기의] a core ② 〚화학〛 a radical ; 〚수학〛 a root ; a radical

기수(우수)— an odd〔even〕 root 세제곱— a cubic root 제곱— a square root

근 筋 a muscle ; [힘줄] a sinew ; a tendon

—경련 a muscular spasm —디스트로피 〚병리〛 muscular dystrophy —운동 muscular movement〔motion〕 —조직

muscular tissue 복(腹)— an abdominal muscle 후두(後頭)— a posterior head muscle
근 近 about ; near(ly) ; almost ¶ 근 만 원 about 10,000 *won* // 근 삼백 리 nearly 300 *ri*
근간 近刊 [신간] a recent publication [issue] ; [근일 출간] forthcoming publication ¶ 근간의 recently published ; latest ; forthcoming ; in preparation
— 도서 [최근 나온] a recent publication ; [곧 나올] a forthcoming book — 서평 a review of recent publications ; a book review for the month (매월의) — 예고 an announcement of books in preparation [forthcoming books]
근간 近間 [부사적] recently ; lately
근간 根幹 [근본] the basis ; [뿌리와 줄기] root and trunk ; the root ; [기조] the keynote ; the fundamental ¶ 사물의 근간을 모르다 have no knowledge of its basic theory ; have no idea of its basic theory ; have no idea of its background // 한국 외교의 근간이다 It is the keynote of Korean diplomacy.
근거 根據 a basis ; a base ; a foundation ; authority ¶ 근거 있는 well-founded // 근거 없는 baseless ; groundless ; unfounded // 근거 없는 풍설 a groundless [an unfounded] rumor // …에 근거를 두다 base 《one's argument》 on // 이 풍설에는 다소의 근거가 있다 There is some ground for the rumor. // 역사적 근거가 없다 It is not supported by history. // 무슨 근거가 있어 그렇게 말하느냐 What is your authority for that statement? // 무엇을 근거로 나를 의심하느냐 On what grounds do you suspect me?
근거리 近距離 a short distance ; a close range ¶ 근거리에서 at close quarters ; at a close range // 학교는 근거리에 있다 It is not far to school.
— 경주 a short-distance race — 사격 short-distance firing [shooting] — 전화 a short-distance (telephone) call
근거지 根據地 a base (of operations) ; headquarters ; a stronghold ¶ 근거지를 마련하다 establish a base
근검 勤儉 diligence and frugality ; thrift and industry —하다 (be) thrifty and industrious ; frugal ; economical ¶ 근검한 가정 주부 a frugal housekeeper
— 저축 thrift and saving — 저축 운동 a saving movement [campaign]
근검하다 be blessed with many children
근경 根莖 a rootstock ; a subterranean stem
근경 近景 a near [close-up] view
근경 近境 [곳] neighboring districts ; [경우] the recent condition ; the present state of affairs
근계 謹啓 [편지 서두에 쓰는 말] Dear Sir ; Dear Mr... ; My dear Mr... ; Dear Madam (여자 앞) ; [회사·단체 앞] Dear Sirs ; Gentlemen ; Messrs ; Messieurs ; Mesdames [Ladies] (여자 단체 앞)
근고 近古 the early modern age
—사 the history of the early modern age
근고 勤苦 working hard [diligently] —하다 work hard ; apply oneself assiduously ¶ 그의 성공은 다년간의 근고의 결실이다 His success is the result of years of hard work.
근고 謹告 —하다 announce ; respectfullyinform with respect
근골 筋骨 bones and sinews ; [체격] build ; physique ; setup ¶ 근골이 늠름한 powerfully [strongly]-built ; sinewy ; muscular ; brawny
근공 勤工 hard study —하다 study hard ; work hard at one's studies
근교 近郊 a suburb ; the suburbs ; suburbia ; outskirts ¶ 서울 근교에 살고 있다 I live in the suburbs of *Seoul*.
— 철도 a suburban railway — 농업 agriculture in suburban areas
근국 近國 a neighboring country
근근 僅僅 barely ; narrowly ; with difficulty
근근 近近 shortly ; before long ; in a few days ; in the near future
근근득생 僅僅得生 —하다 pick up a scanty living ; eke out one's living
근근부지 僅僅扶持 —하다 maintain [manage] with difficulty
***근근이 僅僅—** barely ; only ; merely ; narrowly ; with difficulty ; no more than ¶ 근근이 달아나다 have a narrow escape // 근근이 살아가다 make a scanty living ; make a bare living ; live barely ; scrape along // 근근이 생계를 세워 나가다 be eking out a scanty livelihood // 근근이 시험에 합격하다 scrape through the examination
근근자자 勤勤孜孜 diligence ; industry and assiduity —하다 (be) industrious and assiduous ; diligent
근근하다 ① [물이] (be) full ; brimful ② [가렵다] (be) itchy
근기 根氣 perseverance ; patience ; endurance ; stamina ¶ 근기 있는 patient ; persevering // 근기를 요하는 일 work requiring patience // 근기 있게 기다리다 wait patiently // 근기를 잃다 lose one's patience ; come to the end of one's endurance
***근년 近年** recent years ; late years ¶ 근년에 of late years ; in recent years // 근년에 보기 드문 큰 불 the biggest fire we have had for some years // 근년의 걸작 one of the best literary works in recent years // 지난해의 벼농사는 근년에 없던 풍작이었다 The rice crop of last year was the largest for the past sev-

eral years.
근념 勤念 a kind consideration —하다 give a kind consideration ((to))
근농 勤農 diligent farming —하다 farm diligently
—가 a most efficient farmer
근대 [식물] a (red) beet ; a sugar beet ; a (Swiss) chard
†근대 近代 modern[recent] times ; the modern age ¶ 근대의 modern ; late ; up-to-date // 근대적인 modernistic // 근대화하다 modernize ; be modernized // 어딘지 근대적인 데가 있다 There is an air of modernity about it.
— 과학 modern science — 국가 a modern state[nation] —극(劇) a modern drama ; the modern theater — 도시 modern cities and towns — 문학 modern literature —사 modern history — 사상 modern ideas — 산업 modern industries — 생활[문명] modern life [civilization] —성 modernity —어 modern language — 여성 modern women — 영어 Modern English ((Mod. E., ModE)) — 예술 modern art — 5종 경기 modern pentathlon — 음악[건축] modern music[architecture] —인 modern people ; moderns — 장비 modern equipment —전 modern warfare —주의 modernism —주의자 a modernist — 한국 modern Korea —화(化) modernization —하다 modernize
근대다 bother ; tease ; annoy
근동 近東 [지리] the Near East
근드적거리다 shake slightly ; sway slightly ; rock ¶ 근드적 근드적 shaking slightly ; swaying gently ; rocking
근들거리다 rock ; sway ¶ 근들근들 rockingly ; swayingly // 근들거리는 건물 a flimsy[jerry] building
*근래 近來 [부사적] of late ; lately ; recently ; in these days ¶ 근래의 recent ; late ; modern // 근래에 드문 큰 비다 This is the heaviest rain we have had for some time.
근량 斤量 weight ¶ 근량을 속이다 give short weight
근력 筋力 muscular strength ; physical strength ; brawn
근로 勤勞 labor ; exertion ; service —하다 labor ; work ; toil ; exert oneself ; serve ¶ 근로에 대한 보수 a remuneration for one's service
— 계급 the salaried class ; the wage earning classes — 봉사 labor service — 봉사대 a labor service corps — 소득 an income from personal service ; an earned income — 소득세 earned income tax — 의욕 the will to work —자 a worker ; a laborer ; ; a working man[woman]a daily-breader ((영·구)) ; [임금의] wage earner
— 조건 working[labor] conditions — 포장(褒章) the Labor Medal
근로 기준법 勤勞基準法 [법] the Labor Standard Act
근류 根瘤 [식물] a root nodule[tubercle]
— 박테리아 root nodule bacteria
근리 近理 reasonableness —하다 (be) reasonable
근린 近隣 the neighborhood ; the vicinity
‡근면 勤勉 industry ; assiduity ; diligence ; application —하다 (be) diligent ; industrious ; hardworking ¶ 근면하게 industriously ; diligently // 근면한 사람 a hardworking man ; a hard worker // 근면은 부의 근원이다 Industry leads to wealth. // 그의 성공은 근면 덕택이다 His success is due to industry.
—가 a hard worker ; a diligent man ; a wheelhorse
근멸 根滅 eradication ; extirpation ; extermination —하다 eradicate ; extirpate ; exterminate ; root out ; eliminate ((a thing)) root and branch
근모 根毛 [식물] a roothair ; a fibril
†근무 勤務 duty ; service ; work —하다 do duty ; be on duty ; work ; serve ¶ 근무 중에 while on duty // 근무를 게을리하다 neglect[slight] one's duties // 근무를 끝마치다 wind up one's service // 근무를 충실히 하다 serve faithfully ; be faithful to one's duty // 그는 그 회사에 근무하고 있다 He is with[in the service of] the company. /He is in the employ of the company. // 나는 런던 지점 근무를 명받았다 I was appointed to duty with the London branch office. // 우리 회사는 7시간 근무제이다 We have a seven-hour day in our company.
— 능률 service efficiency — 당번표 [군사] a roster ; a rota — 성적 one's service record[merit] — 소집 reserve training recruitment ; service call — 시간 office[business, working] hours ; on-duty hours ; hours of duty — 실적 service record — 연한 the length of one's service — 예정표 a desk schedule —자 men in service ; men on duty ; workers — 조건 working conditions[terms] —지 수당 an area[a duty place] allowance —처 one's place of employment — 평점 efficiency rating ; a work performance appraisal — 평점서 an efficiency report 시간외 — overtime (work) 야간 — night duty ; a night shift 육상[해상] — shore[sea] service 주간 — day duty 초과 — 수당 allowance for overtime work 특별 — 수당 specific duty allowance 해외 — 수당 a foreign service allowance
근무 태도 勤務態度 one's conduct ; assiduity ¶ 근무 태도에 따라 승급(昇給)시키다 increase ((a person's)) salary

in accordance with his assiduity
근묵자흑 近墨者黑 He who touches pitch shall be defiled therewith.
*__근방 近方__ the neighborhood ; vicinity ; environs ¶ 근방의 neighboring ; nearby ; close-by // 이 근방에 near here ; around here ; in this neighborhood // 근방의 아이들 neighborhood children // 서울과 그 근방 *Seoul* and its environs // 근방에 살고 있다 live close to 《a person》 ; live close at hand // 이 근방에 우체국이 있습니까 Is there a post office in this neighborhood ?
근배 謹拜 [편지의 끝말] Yours truly ; Sincerely yours ; Faithfully yours
근변 近邊 neighborhood ; the vicinity ¶ 이 근변에 in this neighborhood ; about here ; near here
⁑**근본 根本** [기초] the foundation ; the basis ; [근원] the origin ; the source ; [원인] the cause ¶ 근본적인 fundamental ; radical ; basic ; drastic ; thorough // 근본적으로 radically ; fundamentally ; essentially ; thoroughly // 근본적 개혁 a radical reform // 근본을 밝히다 trace 《a thing》 to its origin〔source〕// 근본부터 틀렸다 It is quite〔radically〕 wrong.
— **문제** a fundamental〔root〕 problem ; a key question — **원인** the basic cause — **원칙** the bedrock absolutes ; the fundamental〔basic, guiding, underlying〕 principle — **자료** original〔primary〕 sources ; source materials
근사 近似 approximation ; resemblance **—하다** (be) approximate ; be closely akin 《to》; (be) closely resembled ; be very similar to ; [훌륭함] fine ; splendid ¶ 근사한 건물 a superb building // 근사한 생각 a happy idea // 근사한 소리를 하다 say nice things // 그의 약혼녀는 근사한 여자인 것 같다 His fiancée seems to be quite a catch.
—법 approximation **—값** an approximate value〔quantity〕
근사 近寫 〖영화〗 a close shot
근사모으다 make continued efforts for
근사치 近似値 ⇨ 근사값
근상 近狀 the recent state〔condition, situation〕; the recent state of affairs
근생엽 根生葉 radical leaves ; a rosette
근서 謹書 written respectfully 《by…》 **—하다** write respectfully
근섬유 筋纖維 a muscular fiber
근성 根性 nature ; disposition ; spirit ¶ 근성이 악한 ill-natured ; crooked // 근성이 썩은 depraved ; base ; mean // 상인 근성을 드러내다 betray a mercenary spirit // 노예 근성 a servile spirit // 섬나라 근성 an insular spirit〔prejudice〕// 속물 근성 snobbery ; philistinism // 그는 근성이 썩었다 He has a mean disposition. /He is rotten at heart. // 근성이 있는 사람 a man who has guts
근세 近世 modern times〔age〕; recent times ¶ 근세의 modern ; recent // 근세의 한국 작가 Korean writers of modern times
—사 modern history
†**근소 僅少** **—하다** (be) a few ; a little ; scanty ; trifling ¶ 근소한 수입 a mere pittance // 근소한 위자료 a nominal solatium // 근소한 차이 a shade of difference // 비용은 근소하다 The expense is trifling. /It costs very little. // 근소한 차로 이기다 win by a narrow margin
근속 勤續 continuous service **—하다** continue in the service ; be in 《a person's》 service ; serve ¶ 10년 근속 ten years of continuous service // 20년 근속했다 He has been in the company's service for twenty years.
— **수당** a long-service allowance — **연한** the length of (one's) service ¶ 근속 연한에 따라 in proportion to the length of service ; on the basis of the length of service **—자** a person in long service ; a long-service man
근수 根數 〖수학〗 a root ; a radical
근수 斤數 the weight ; the poundage ¶ 근수를 달다 weigh 《a commodity》 on a scale // 근수가 모자르다 be short of weight
근시 近侍 an attendant ; a page ; a chamberlain ; an entourage 《프》
근시 近時 of late ; lately ; recently
근시 近視 near〔short〕-sightedness ; near vision ; 〖의학〗 myopia ¶ 근시의 near〔short〕-sighted ; myopic // 나는 근시이다 I am short-sighted.
—경 glasses for near vision〔short sight〕 — **안** a myopia ; near-sightedness ¶ 근시안의 사람 a short〔near〕-sighted person // 근시안적 정책 a short-sighted policy
근신 近臣 a personal attendant ; one's trusted vassal
근신 近信 the latest news ; a newly arrived letter
근신 謹愼 good behavior〔conduct〕; prudence ; discretion ; [자제] self-control ; self-restraint ; [개전] penitence ; [벌] disciplinary confinement **—하다** behave oneself ; be on one's good behavior ; be prudent 《in speech and action》; be penitent ; be confined to one's home ¶ 근신의 뜻을 표하다 show one's penitence // 근신을 명하다 put 《a person》 on good behavior ; place 《a person》 in home confinement // 그는 근신 중이다 He is on his good〔best〕 behavior. // 금후 근신하겠습니다 I will behave myself better after this.
근실 勤實 diligence ; faithfulness ; sincerity **—하다** (be) diligent ; faithful ; sincere ¶ 근실히 일하다 work diligent-

ly ; serve faithfully // 근실한 생활을 하다 live straight ; live honestly
근실거리다 feel itchy
†**근심** anxiety ; concern ; solicitude ; uneasiness ; fear ; apprehension ; care ; worry ; trouble **—하다** be anxious 〔concerned〕 about ; be afraid of〔for〕 ; worry about ; be uneasy about ; be alarmed ; care for ; trouble〔worry〕 oneself about ; be troubled〔worried〕 about ¶ 근심거리 cares ; troubles // 근심의 원인 a cause for anxiety ; a source of anxiety // 쓸데없는 근심 unnecessary anxiety ; meddling (간섭) // 가정의 근심 family cares // 근심스럽게 anxiously ; with a worried air // 근심한 나머지 in an excess of anxiety // 근심을 끼치다 cause 《a person》 anxiety ; give 《a person》 trouble // 쓸데없는 근심을 하다 overworry oneself // 근심스러운 표정을 하고 있다 He looks worried. /He wears an anxious〔a worried〕 look. // 그는 근심이 없다 He is free from cares 〔troubles〕. // 그는 근심이 있다 He is in trouble. /He has something to worry about. // 그는 그 소문을 듣고 대단히 근심했다 He was deeply concerned at the news. // 뭘 그리 근심하고 있는가 What are you worrying about ?
근압 根壓 root pressure
⁑**근엄 謹嚴** sobriety ; sternness ; gravity ; austerity ; seriousness **—하다** (be) stern ; serious ; grave ; solemn ¶ 근엄한 사람 a serious-minded person ; a sobersides ; a man of strict morals // 근엄한 태도 a dignified mien // 그는 매우 근엄하다 He is as grave as a judge.
근역 槿域 Korea ; the Land of Roses-of-Sharon
근염 筋炎 〖의학〗 myositis ; inflammation of a muscle
근엽 根葉 roots and leaves
근영 近影 one's latest photograph
근왕 勤王 loyalty to the King ; royalism
⁑**근원 根源** the origin ; the root ; the source ; [원인] the cause ; [정수] the essence ¶ 사회악의 근원 the root of social evil // 근원을 이루다 lie at〔be〕 the root of 《a thing》 // 근원을 캐다 trace 《a thing》 to its origin〔source〕 ; get at the root of 《a thing》 // 이 습관의 근원은 중국이다 The practice owes its origin to the Chinese. // 금전욕은 모두 악의 근원이다 Love of money is the root of all evil.
근원 벨 칼 없고 근심 없앨 약 없다 〔속담〕 There is a crook in the lot of everyone.
근위대 近衛隊 the Royal Guards ; the court guards
근위병 近衛兵 a Life Guardsman
⁑**근육 筋肉** muscles ; sinews ; thew(s) ¶ 근육질의 muscular ; sinewy ; brawny // 근육의 발달 muscular development // 단단한 근육 solid muscle(s) // 축 늘어진 flabby muscles
— 노동 muscular〔physical〕 labor **— 노동자** a manual worker **—미** muscular 〔physical〕 beauty **— 운동** muscular motion〔movement〕 **— 조직** the muscular system〔tissue〕 ; musculature
근육 주사 筋肉注射 an intramuscular injection
근육질 筋肉質 muscularity
근육통 筋肉痛 muscular pain ; 〖의학〗 myalgia ; myodynia
근읍 近邑 a near town ; a neighboring town
근인 近因 the immediate cause 《of a war》 ; the proximate cause ; the immediate occasion
근일 近日 soon ; shortly ; before long ; in a few days ; one of these days ; at an early date ¶ 근일 중에 shortly ; in a few days ; one of these days // 그는 근일 돌아올 것이다 He will be back in a few days.
근일점 近日點 〖천문〗 the perihelion
근자 近者 ¶ 근자의 recent ; late ; latter-day // 근자에 lately ; of late ; recently ; these days
근작 近作 one's latest work ; one's recent work
근잠 〖농업〗 a kind of rice-plant blight
근저 近著 one's recent literary work
근저 根底 the foundation ; the bottom ; the root ; the basis ¶ 근저를 이루다 lie at the bottom〔root〕 《of》 // 사회의 근저까지 뒤흔들다 shake the society to its very foundation
근저당 根抵當 flexible mortgage ; a collateral security ; fixed collateral
근전도 筋電圖 an electromyogram
근절 根絶 eradication ; extermination ; annihilation ; extirpation ; stamping out **—하다** eradicate ; exterminate ; root 〔stamp〕 out ; uproot ¶ 근절할 수 있는 eradicable // 부패 정치가들을 근절하다 eradicate〔root out〕 corruptionists // 악의 씨를 근절하다 nip evil in the bud // 그는 행정부의 악패를 근절하려 했다 He tried to stamp out the evils of the Administration.
근점 近點 [가까운] a near point ; [근지점] the perigee ; [근일점] the perihelion
⁑**근접 近接** nearing ; approach ; close contact ; approximation ; 〖천문〗 appulse ; 〖심리〗 contiguity **—하다** get near ; near ; approach ; come into close contact ¶ 근접한 neighboring ; adjacent
— 지역 neighboring districts **— 효과** an proximity effect
근정 謹呈 presentation ; [책에] With the compliments of the author. **—하다** give ; present 《a person with a thing,

a thing to a person》
근제 謹製 making carefully ; [명사 뒤에 서] made〔produced, prepared〕 carefully by **—하다** make〔prepare〕 carefully
근조 condolence ; sympathy **—하다** offer〔present, express〕 one's condolence(s) 《to》 ; express sympathy 《with》
근족 近族 a near relative ; a kin
근종 筋腫 〖의학〗 a myoma 《*pl.* -ta, ~s》
근중 斤重 weight
근지 近地 a near district ; a neighboring place
근지럽다 (be) itchy ; scratchy ¶ 등이 근지럽다 My back itches. /I feel itchy in my back. //근지러워 죽겠다 The itching is quite unbearable〔unendurable〕.
근지점 近地點 〖천문〗 the perigee
근직 謹直 conscientiousness ; scrupulousness **—하다** (be) upright ; faithful ; sincere and honest ¶ 근직한 사람 a man of integrity//근직하게 근무하다 be faithful to one's duties ; work conscientiously
근질거리다 feel itchy〔creepy〕
근질근질 —하다 feel creepy ; feel itchy ; be impatient ; be spoiling 《for》 ¶ 등이 근질근질하다 feel one's back itchy//사실을 말하고 싶어서 속이 근질근질하다 burn to tell the truth//그를 한대 먹이고 싶어 내 손이 근질근질하다 My hands itch to deal him a blow.
근착 近着 ¶ 근착의 recently received ; just〔recently〕 arrived
—품 new〔latest〕 arrivals
근채류 根菜類 edible〔esculent〕 roots ; rootcrops
근처 近處 the neighborhood ; the vicinity ; the surroundings ; the environs ¶ 근처의 neighboring ; nearby ; close by //이 근처에 near here ; around〔about〕 here ; in this neighborhood//혹시 이 근처에 오거든 if you happen to come this way//역 바로 근처에 within a stone's throw of the station//근처에 살다 live close to 《a person》 ; live close at hand //이 근처에서 쉽시다 Let's rest somewhere around here.
근척 近戚 a near maternal relation
근청 謹聽 close attention ; listening with attention **—하다** listen attentively 〔intently〕 《to》 ; listen with eager 〔close〕 attention ; be all ears〔attention〕 ¶ 근청 ! Hear〔Let〕 him talk ! /That's right〔the talk〕 ! 《미·구》//그들은 근청하고 있다 They are all attention.
근촌 近村 a nearby〔neighboring〕 village
근축 根軸 〖기하〗 a radical axis
근치 根治 radical〔permanent, complete〕 cure **—하다** cure completely〔radically〕 ¶ 근치되다 be completely〔radically〕 cured
근친 近親 a near〔close〕 relative〔relation〕 ; an immediate relative ; kin ¶ 그와 나는 근친간이다 He is nearly〔closely〕 related to me.
— 결혼 (a) consanguineous marriage
— 상간 incest
근친 覲親 a bride's (first) call at her maiden home ; a bride's post-marital visit to her parents **—하다** make one's first call on one's parents after marriage ; go〔come〕 home for the first time after one's marriage
근태 勤怠 diligence and laziness ; diligence and indolence
근통 筋痛 〖의학〗 myalgia
근풀이 斤— [근으로 팖] selling by the pound ; [값을 따짐] figuring out the cost of a pound **—하다** figure out the cost of a pound ; sell by the pound
근하 謹賀 cordial congratulation ; congratulation with respect **—하다** congratulate cordially〔respectfully, with respect〕
근하 신년 謹賀新年 (I wish you) a Happy New Year ; Allow me to offer you my hearty congratulations on the arrival of the New Year.
근학 勤學 hard study ; diligence ; hard work **—하다** study hard〔diligently〕
근해 近海 the neighboring waters ; the home waters ; the coast ; the adjoining seas ¶ 근해의 coastal ; coastwise ; near sea ; inshore ; offshore//인천 근해에서 in the sea near *Inchon*//한국 근해에서 in Korean waters//그 배는 한국 근해를 순항하고 있다 The ship is cruising in Korean waters.
—어 a shorefish **— 어업** inshore fishery〔fishing〕 **— 항로** a coasting line **— 항행** coasting
근행 勤行 〖불교〗 a religious service **—하다** hold〔conduct〕 a religious service ¶ (부처님에 대한) 나날의 근행 daily Buddhistic service//아침 근행을 하다 hold〔conduct〕 the morning service
근화 槿花 the Rose of Sharon
근화향 槿花鄕 [근역] Korea
근황 近況 the recent condition ; the present state of affairs ¶ 무역의 근황 the present state of trade//근황을 알려 주십시오 Please tell me how you are getting along.
글 ① [공부] learning ; studies ; letters
② [글자] writing ; script ; alphabet ; characters
③ [쓴 것] a piece of writing ; a composition ; an article ; a sentence ; a style ; literature ¶ 글 있는 사람 an educated man//좋은 글 good writing 〔style〕//글을 쓰다 write//글을 짓다 write a composition ; compose a piece

//글을 배우다 learn ; study ; pursue one's studies//글이 있다 be learned ; be educated//글을 잘 쓰다 be a stylist ; write a good style//글깨나 배웠다고 뽐내다 be proud of one's learning//글을 모르다 be unlettered//세련된 글 a polished sentence〔style〕//알기 쉬운 글 an easy〔a simple〕 style//글을 다듬다 elaborate〔polish〕 one's style

글겅이 a currycomb

글겅이질 [털빗기기] currying ; [착취] exploitation ; squeezing **—하다** [빗기다] curry ; [착취하다] exploit ; squeeze

글구멍 literary talent ¶ 글구멍이 크다 have a talent for learning

글귀 —句 a passage ; a line ; a verse ; a couplet ¶ 글귀를 잇다 complete a verse//글귀를 외다 memorize a passage

글그렁거리다 [목이] be wheezy ; purr ; wheeze ; [목을] make wheeze ; make purr ¶ 고양이가 목을 글그렁거린다 The cat is purring.

글동무 a schoolmate ; a schoolfellow ; a fellow student ; a classmate

글라디올러스 〖식물〗 a gladiolus

글라스 ① [잔] a glass ; a glass container ; a cup ② ⇨ [유리]

⁑글라이더 a glider ¶ 글라이더로 날다 fly in a glider

글래머 glamor

—걸 a glamor〔an enchanting〕 girl

글러브 a (baseball) glove ; a mitt

글러지다 [병이] become critical ; fall into a critical condition ; [일이] fail 《to》 ; go wrong ; come to naught ; grow worse ¶ 사이가 글러지다 become estranged//맛이 글러지다 lose its flavor//건강이 글러지다 one's health declines//그 계획은 글러졌다 The plan went wrong.

글로빈 〖생화학〗 globin

글루타민 〖화학〗 glutamine

—산(酸) glutamic acid

글리사드 〖등산〗 glissade

글리산도 〖음악〗 glissando

글리세린 〖화학〗 glycerine

— 연고 glycerine ointment

글리코겐 〖화학〗 glycogen

글발 ① [글씨] jottings ; notes ② [글씨 모양] the appearance of one's letters ¶ 글발이 고르다 The letters are even. ③ [문맥] coherence ¶ 글발이 서다 be coherent

글방 —房 a private school ; a village school

글벗 a literary friend ; a comrade in letters

글썽글썽 with tearful eyes **—하다** be about to cry ¶ 눈물이 글썽글썽한 눈 tearful eyes ; eyes filled with tears//눈물이 글썽글썽하다 tears stand〔gather〕 in one's eyes

†글쎄 now ; well ; let me see ¶ 글쎄 어떻게 할까 What shall I do now?//글쎄 모르겠는데 Well, I am sure I don't know.//글쎄 언제 도착할까 I wonder when he will arrive there.//글쎄 곤란한데 Well, I'm in a fix.

글쎄요 Well, let me see ¶ 몇 사람이나 됩니까—글쎄요 한 200명쯤 되겠죠 How many people are there? Well, I should say about two hundred.

글쓰다 write

†글씨 a letter ; a character ; an ideograph ¶ 갈겨쓴 글씨 a scribble ; a hasty writing//글씨를 잘〔못〕 쓰다 write a good〔poor〕 hand//굵은〔가는〕 글씨 a heavy〔slender〕 character//글씨연습을 하다 practice penmanship

—본 (a book of) model handwriting ; a writing book **—체** a style of penmanship〔handwriting〕

글월 [글] a writing ; a sentence (문장) ; [편지] a letter ; a note ; a message

글자 a letter ; a character ; an ideography (표의 문자)

글재주 literary talent ¶ 글재주가 있다 have a talent for writing

글제 —題 the title〔subject, theme〕 of an article〔a composition, a poem〕

글줄 a line〔some lines〕 of writing

글짓기 composition ; writing **—하다** write〔make〕 a composition ; write a theme 《미》

글쪽지 a card〔slip〕 with writing on it

글피 three days from now ; the day after the day-after-tomorrow ; two days after tomorrow

글하다 engage in studies

⁑긁다 ① [가려워서] scratch ; scrape ¶ 머리를 긁다 scratch one's head//가려운 데를 긁다 scratch an itchy spot〔place〕//구두 흙을 긁다 scrape the mud off one's shoes ; scrape one's shoes//솥밑을 긁다 scrape the bottom of an oven//벌레 물린 데를 긁다 scratch an insect bite

② [끌어 모으다] rake ; scrape up ; gather up ¶ 낙엽을 긁어 모으다 rake up dead〔fallen〕 leaves//흙을 긁다 paw the ground (말이) ; scratch the ground ③ [사람의 감정을] offend ; provoke ; irritate ; nag ; pick on ; needle ¶ 사람을 긁다 pick on〔nag〕 《a person》 ; irritate〔offend〕 《a person》//바가지를 긁어 남편을 못살게 굴다 nag one's husband to death

④ [착취하다] exploit ; squeeze money from 《a person》 ; fleece 《a person》 of his money ; soak 《속》 ; sweat 《미·속》 ¶ 돈을 긁어 내다 squeeze money from 《a person》 ; bleed 《a person》

긁어 부스럼이다 〔속담〕 Let sleeping dogs lie.

긁어 내다 〔관용〕 rake out

긁어 당기다 rake in ; scrape in ¶ 판돈을 긁어 당기다 rake in the money on the gambling table

긁어 먹다 gnaw《upon》; nibble《at》; bite《at》; munch ; [남의 것을] live off《a person》; exploit ; live on the money squeezed out of others ¶ 뼈에서 고기를 긁어 먹다 gnaw the meat off a bone // 가난한 사람의 것을 긁어 먹다 live off poor people ; live on the money squeezed out of poor people

긁적거리다 scratch〔scrape〕 successively ¶ 머리를 긁적거리다 scratch one's head over and over again

긁적긁적 scratching and scratching ; scraping and scraping

긁정이 a kind of plow with a base less bent than that of the usual plow

긁혀미다 be scratched ; be abraded ; be chafed ¶ 긁혀민 상처 a scratch ; an abrasion ; a chafe

긁히다 ① be scratched ; be clawed (발톱에) ¶ 얼굴을 긁히다 be scratched on the face
② [끌어 모음을 당하다] be raked ; rake ¶ 낙엽이 잘 긁히다 the leaves are raked easily
③ [감정을 상하다] be offended〔provoked〕; be picked on
④ [착취 당하다] be exploited ; be fleeced〔squeezed out〕 of《money》

금¹ [값] a price ; a cost ; value ; worth ¶ 적당한 금 a moderate〔reasonable〕 price // 금이 맞으면 if the price is satisfactory〔moderate, reasonable〕 // 금을 올리다 raise〔put up〕 the price // 금을 내리다 lower〔cheapen, put down〕 the price // 비싼 금으로 팔다 sell at a high price // 금이 비싸다 The price is high.
금을 놓다 관용 name〔bid〕 a price ; set a price

****금**² [선] a line ; [접은 자국] a fold ; a crease ; [흠] a crack ; a crevice ¶ 손금 the lines of the palm // 금간 찻잔 a cracked teacup // 금이 가다 be cracked ; crack // 이 공기는 금간 소리가 난다 This bowl sounds cracked.
금을 긋다 관용 draw a line

†**금 金** gold ¶ 금의 gold // 금반지 a gold ring // 금시계 a gold watch // 금을 입힌 gold-plated ; gilded // 금을 입히다 plate《a thing》 with gold // 번쩍이는 것이 다 금은 아니다 All is not gold that glitters.

금- 今— the present《time》; this《year》

금가다 crack ; split ; cleave ; fissure ; be cracked ¶ 금간 그릇 a cracked dish // 금간 바위 a cleft rock // 금간 피부 cracked〔chapped〕 skin // 벽에 금이 갔다 The wall had a crack on it. // 뜨거운 물로 컵에 금이 갔다 The hot water has cracked the glass. // 그 일로 그들 우정에 금이 갔다 The affair impaired their friendship.

금가락지 金— a large gold ring

금가루 金— gold dust

금강 金剛 [금강력] adamantine might ; Herculean strength
—사(砂) 〖광물〗 emery (powder) **—신(神)**〔**역사(力士)**〕〖불교〗 a Deva king

금강산 金剛山 the Diamond Mountains
금강산도 식후경이다 속담 It takes a full stomach to appreciate even the best of scenery. /A loaf of bread is better than the song of many birds. /Better are meals many than one too merry.

***금강석** 〖광물〗 a diamond

금계 禁戒 a commandment

금계 禁界 the limits of a restricted area ; the forbidden ground

금계 錦鷄 〖새〗 a golden pheasant

금계랍 金鷄蠟 〖약〗 quinine

금고 今古 ancient and modern ages

금고 金鼓 ① [싸울 때 쓰는] a war drum and a war gong ② [북 모양의 종] a drum-shaped bell

금고 禁錮 〖법〗 imprisonment ; confinement ¶ 20년의 금고형을 받다 be sentenced to 20 years' imprisonment // 금고형에 처하다 imprison ; confine ; incarcerate
중〔경〕— major〔minor〕 imprisonment

†**금고 金庫** a safe ; a strongbox ; a vault (은행 따위의) ; a coffin 《미·속》; a cashbox ; [국고금 취급소] a depository ; a cash office ¶ 금고용 경보기 a safe alarm // 방화 금고 a fireproof safe // 금고에 넣다 keep〔put〕《a thing》 in a safe // 금고를 잠그다 lock a safe
—털이 [행위] safebreaking ; safecracking ; safeblowing ; [도둑] a safebreaker ; a safeblower **금융 —** a financial bank **내화(耐火) —** a fireproof safe **중앙 —** Central Depository

금곡 金穀 money and corn

금공 金工 ① [공예] metalwork ② [사람] a metalworker ; a worker〔an artist〕 in metals ; a metalsmith

금과옥조 金科玉條 a golden rule ¶ 창설자의 교훈을 금과옥조로 삼고 있다 They follow the teachings of the founder as their golden rule.

금관 金冠 a golden crown

금관 악기 金管樂器 (a) brass

금광 金光 golden color ; luster of gold

금광 金鑛 [광산] a gold mine ; [광석] gold ore ¶ 금광을 발견하다 discover gold deposits

금괴 金塊 a lump〔nugget〕 of gold ; gold bullion ; a gold ingot ; a gold bar
— 밀수 smuggling of gold

금권 金權 the power of money ; money power ; financial〔monetary〕 influence ¶ 요즈음은 금권 만능의 세상이다 Money

rules the world. /Money is everything nowadays.
— 정치 plutocracy ; timocracy — 정치가 a plutocrat
금궤 金櫃 a cash box ; a money chest ; a money box ; a strongbox ; a coffer
금귤 金橘 〖식물〗 a kumquat ; a cumquat ; Citrus japonica (학명)
금긋다 draw a line
금기 今期 this〔the present〕 term〔period〕
금기 禁忌 taboo ; 〖의학〗 contraindication **—하다** avoid ; abstain from ¶ 배합금기 약품 medicines that must not be prescribed together ; incompatible drugs
금나다 ① [잔금이 가다] be〔become〕 creased〔wrinkled〕 ② [값이 정해지다] be priced ; the price is fixed
금난초 金蘭草 〖식물〗 the helleborine
금남 禁男 ¶ 금남의 집 a home without any men // 금남의 섬 an isle of women
금납 金納 cash payment ; payment in money **—하다** pay in money
금낭화 錦囊花 〖식물〗 a dicentra ; a bleeding heart
금년 今年 this year ; the current〔present〕 year ¶ 금년 겨울 this winter // 금년 여름 방학 the coming summer vacation // 금년 중에 in (the) course of this year ; before the end of this year // 금년은 풍년이다 This is a plenteous〔bumper〕 year. // 금년도 다 갔다 The year is drawing to a close. // 금년은 윤년이다 This is a leap year.
금년생 今年生 a baby born this year ; 〖식물〗 a plant new this year
금니 金— a gold tooth ¶ 금니를 하다 have a gold tooth put in
금니박이 金— a man who has gold teeth
금단 禁斷 withdrawal prohibition **—하다** prohibit 《a person from doing》 ; forbid 《a person to do》 ¶ 금단의 열매 the forbidden fruit // 이곳은 살생 금단의 장소이다 Catching fish or hunting birds is prohibited here.
금달맞이꽃 〖식물〗 the evening primrose
금닿다 be reasonable (in price)
금대 今代 the present age ; today
금대 金帶 a golden band〔belt, girdle〕
금덩이 金— a (gold) nugget
금도 襟度 magnanimity ; generosity ; broad-mindedness ¶ 금도가 넓은〔좁은〕 broad〔narrow〕-minded // 금도를 보이다 show one's magnanimity
금도금 金鍍金 gilding ; gold plating **—하다** gild ; plate with gold ¶ 금도금한 반지 a gold-plated ring // 동에 금도금하다 plate copper with gold
금돈 金— a gold coin
금돌 金— 〖광산〗 gold-bearing rock ; ore rock
금동 今冬 this winter
금딱지 金— a gold case 《of a watch》 ; a gold lid
— 시계 a gold watch
금띠 金— a golden band〔belt, girdle〕
금란지계 金蘭之契 close〔old〕 friendship
금력 金力 money power ; the power of money〔wealth〕 ; the influence of money ¶ 금력에 의해 through the influence of financial power // 금력에 좌우되다 be influenced by money
—가(家) a plutocrat ; a gold bug — 결혼 marriage forced by the influence of money — 만능〔숭배〕 mammonism — 정치 plutocracy
금렵 禁獵 prohibition of shooting〔hunting〕 **—하다** prohibit hunting〔shooting〕 ; ban hunting
—기 the closed season 《미》 ; the close time〔season〕 《영》 — 조수(鳥獸) forbidden game —지〔구〕 a (game, hunting) preserve ; a (wildlife, bird) sanctuary
금령 禁令 prohibition ; a ban ; an embargo ; an interdict ¶ 금령을 내리다 put〔issue〕 a ban 《on》 // 금령을 해제하다 lift the ban〔embargo〕 《on》 ; remove the prohibition // 금령을 위반하다 violate the prohibition
금리 金利 interest ; money rates ¶ 금리를 올리다〔내리다〕 raise〔lower〕 the rate of interest // 연 8%의 금리로 at an annual interest rate of 8 percent // 금리를 지불하다 pay interest on a loan // 금리가 싸다〔비싸다〕 Money is cheap〔dear〕.
— 자유화 the liberalization of interest rates — 재조정 readjustment of bank interest rates — 정책 a bank-rate policy — 특혜 preferential interest rates — 하향조정 downward readjustment of bank interest rates 대출 — loan rate 은행 — a bank rate
금맞추다 adjust the price of 《an article》 ; set the price
금맥 金脈 a vein of gold
금메달 金— a gold medal
금명간 今明間 [부사적] today or tomorrow ; in a day or two
금모래 金— ① [사금] gold dust ② [금빛의] golden sand(s)
금몰 金— gold braid〔lace〕 ¶ 금몰이 달린 gold-braided
금문 禁門 ① [출입 금지한 문] a forbidden gate ② [궁궐의 문] the gate of the royal〔imperial〕 palace
금문자 金文字 gilt〔gold〕 letters ¶ 금문자의 gold-lettered // 금문자로 새겨진 간판 a gilt-lettered sign ; a signboard inscribed in gilt letters
금물 禁物 prohibition ; a taboo ; a tabooed〔prohibited〕 thing ¶ 밤늦게까지 안 자는 것은 금물이다 Late hours

are taboo. // 이곳에서 흡연은 금물이다 Smoking is strictly forbidden here. // 천식 병자에게 담배는 금물이다 Smoking is injurious to the cases of asthma.

금박 金箔 gold foil ; gold leaf ¶ 금박이 벗겨지다 the gilt comes〔is rubbed〕 off
금박을 박다 관용 mount with gold
금박을 입히다 관용 plate 《a thing》 with gold ; gild

†**금발 金髮** golden hair ; flaming hair ; fair hair ; blonde (여자의) ; blond (남자의) ¶ 금발의 예쁜 소녀 a lovely, fair-haired girl // 금발 벽안의 with golden hair and blue eyes

금방 今方 just now ; a moment ago ; in a moment ; at once ; immediately ; every moment ¶ 그녀는 금방 울음을 터뜨릴 기색이었다 She was about to cry. /She was on the verge of tears. // 그리로 금방 갈게 I'll be right over.

금방 金房 a goldsmith's shop

금방망이 金— 〖식물〗 a groundsel

금배 金杯 a gold cup

금번 今番 this time ; lately ; recently ¶ 금번에 미국으로 떠나게 되어 on this occasion of my departure for America // 금번 우리 회사는 기구 개편이 있었다 Our company was reorganized recently.

금법 禁法 a prohibitive law ; a ban

금보다 bid a price on ; put a value on

금본위 金本位 the gold standard ¶ 금본위를 정지하다 suspend the gold standard // 금본위를 이탈하다 go off gold
—국 a gold-using country **— 복귀** return to〔restoration of〕 the gold standard **국제 —제** the international gold standard

금뵈다 ① [물건값을] get an appraisal 《of》 ¶ 물건을 …에게 금뵈다 get a person to appraise some goods ② ⇨ 금맞추다

금분 金粉 gold dust

금불 金佛 a gold image of Buddha ; a gilded statue of Buddha

금불초 金佛草 〖식물〗 an elecampane

⁑**금붕어 金—** a goldfish ¶ 금붕어를 기르다 keep goldfish
— 어항 a goldfish basin〔bowl〕 **— 장수** a breeder of goldfish ; a goldfish vendor

금붙이 金— gold ware ; an article made of gold

금비 金肥 [인조 비료] artificial fertilizer ; [화학 비료] chemical manure

금비녀 金— a golden hairpin ; an ornamental hairpin

†**금빛 金—** golden color ¶ 금빛이 찬란하다 glitter with golden colors // 금빛으로 빛나다 give off a golden gleam

금사 金絲 gold thread ; spun gold ¶ 금사 박힌 크레이프 비단 silk crèpe

금사작 金絲雀 〖새〗 a canary

금산 禁山 a forest reserve ; a reserved forest

금산 金山 a gold mine

금상 今上 the present king (Emperor) ; His Majesty the Emperor

금상 金像 a gold statue ; a gilt statue

금상첨화 錦上添花 —하다 add luster to what is already brilliant ; add something more to the beauty〔honor, grace〕 ; give an added grace to what is already beautiful ¶ 그것은 금상첨화다 That's icing〔frosting〕 on the cake.

금새 price ¶ 금새가 비싸다〔싸다〕 be dear〔cheap〕 ; be high〔low〕 in price ; be high〔low〕-priced

금색 金色 a golden color ¶ 금색의 golden ¶ 지는 해가 하늘을 금색으로 물들였다 Sunset gilds the sky. /The sky is tinted with a golden color as the sun is sinking.

금서 禁書 a banned book

금석 今夕 this evening ; tonight

금석 今昔 the past and the present ¶ 금석지감 a sentiment caused by the contrast between the past and the present

금석 金石 ① [쇠붙이와 돌] metals and minerals〔rocks〕 ; [비석 따위] a stone monument ② [굳음] being adamant 〔firm, unyielding〕 ¶ 금석지교 a firm friendship // 금석지약 a firm promise
—문 an inscription on a stone monument ; an epigraph **—학** studies in ancient monumental inscriptions ; epigraphy

금선 金線 gold thread ; [복장의] gold stripes ; gold braid

금설 金屑 gold dust

금성 金星 〖천문〗 Venus ; Hesperus ; the evening star ¶ 금성의 태양 경과 the transit of Venus over the sun's disc

금성철벽 金城鐵壁 an impregnable fortress ; a citadel ; a stronghold

금세 [금시에] in a moment ; at once ; immediately ; without delay ¶ 금세 돌아오다 come back immediately // 금세 가겠다 I'll go at once.

금세 今世 〖불교〗 this〔the mundane〕 world

금세공 金細工 gold-work
—사〔장이〕 a goldsmith **—점** a goldsmith's shop

금세기 今世紀 this century ¶ 이것은 금세기 최대의 행사이다 This is the greatest event of the century.

⁑**금속 金屬** a metal ¶ 금속의 metal ; metallic // 금속성의 소리 a metallic sound // 이 금속은 열에 녹는다 This metal melts with heat. // 철은 유용한 금속이다 Iron is a useful metal.
—공 a metal worker **— 공업** the metalworking industry **— 공학** metal engi-

neering — 광택 metallic luster — 세공 metalwork — 원소 metallic elements — 제품 metal goods ; hardware —판 [인쇄의] metallograph — 화폐 metallic currency 중〔경〕— heavy〔light〕 metals

금속 가공 金屬加工 the processing of a metal
—소 a metal processing shop —학 metallurgical technology

금속 정련 金屬精鍊 metal refinery
—업 metal refining work

금쇠 a line-cutter ; a tool used to make lines on board ; a kind of burin

금수 禽獸 birds and animals〔beast〕 ; a brute ; a beast ¶ 금수 같은 bestial ; beastly // 금수와 같은 행위 a beastly conduct // 금수만도 못한 놈 a fellow little better than a brute ; a person worse than a brute

금수 禁輸 an embargo on the exportation〔importation〕 《of》 —하다 embargo ; forbid export〔import〕 of
—품 contraband (goods) ; articles under embargo

금수 錦繡 [비단과 수] brocade and embroidery ; embroidered brocade (천) ; [자연] a brocade of nature ; rich autumnal tints

금수강산 錦繡江山 a beautiful land ; a country noted for the beauty in the landscape

금수출 金輸出 the export of gold
— 금지 a ban on gold export ; a gold embargo — 해금(解禁) lifting〔removing〕 the gold embargo

금슬 琴瑟 ① [거문고와 비파] a Korean harp and a Korean lute ② ⇨ 금실(琴瑟)

금시 今時 the present time〔moment〕 ; [부사적] a moment ago ; at once ; immediately ¶ 금시에 in a moment ; at once ; without delay // 금시에 마음이 변하다 change one's mind in a flash

금시계 金時計 a gold watch

금시발복 今時發福 —하다 rise to wealth and honor in a day ; spring at a bound into wealth and honor ; make a fortune overnight

금시초문 今時初聞 hearing 《a matter》 for the first time ¶ 이것은 금시초문이다 This is news to me. /I have never heard of this before. /This is a revelation to me.

금식 禁食 fasting ; a abstinence 《from food》 —하다 fast ; abstain ; go without food ¶ 그는 5일간의 금식에 들어갔다 He went on a five day fast.
—일(日) a fast day

금실 金— gold thread ; spun gold ¶ 금실로 수놓다 embroider with gold threads

금실 琴瑟 [부부의 화목] conjugal harmony ; connubial bliss ¶ 금실지락 a happily married life ; the happiness of conjugal harmony // 금실이 좋다 live in conjugal harmony ; lead a happily married life

금싸라기 金— a thing of great value

금압 禁壓 suppression ; prohibition ; a ban ; an embargo ; taboo —하다 suppress ; taboo ; ban ; prohibit ; place 《a thing》 under a ban〔an embargo〕 ; interdict ¶ 정치 운동을 금압하다 suppress a political movement // 언론의 자유를 금압하다 lay an embargo on free speech

†**금액 金額** an amount〔a sum〕 of money ¶ 상당한 금액 a considerable〔good〕 sum of money // 손해 금액은 500만 원에 달한다 The damage amounts to five million *won*. // 전부 합하면 상당한 금액이 된다 The whole comes to an enormous sum.

금야 今夜 this evening ; tonight

금어 禁漁 prohibition of fishing〔fishery〕
—구〔장〕 an area closed to fishing ; no-fishing area〔zone〕 ; a marine preserve —기 the closed season (for fishery) 《미》 ; the close time〔season〕 《for trout》

금언 金言 a wise〔golden〕 saying〔saw〕 ; a proverb ; a maxim ; an adage ¶ 옛사람의 금언 wise sayings of the ancients
—집 a collection of maxims and proverbs

금연 禁煙 prohibition of smoking ; No Smoking
—하다 smoking ; abstain 〔refrain〕 from quit smoking ¶ 교내에서는 금연입니다 Smoking is prohibited within the school compound. // 절대 금연 Positively No Smoking. // 차내 금연 No Smoking in this car. (게시) // 의사는 내게 금연하라고 권했다 The doctor advised me to quit smoking.
— 운동 an antismoking〔anti-tobacco〕 campaign —자 a non-smoker 《미》 —차 a nonsmoking car ; [찻간] a nonsmoking compartment

금오 金烏 the sun
—옥토(玉兎) the sun and the moon

금옥 金玉 gold and gems ; jewels

****금요일 金曜日** Friday 《Fri.》 ¶ 13일의 금요일 Friday the thirteenth

금욕 禁慾 abstinence ; ascetic practice ; self-denial ; continence (성욕의) —하다 repress the passion ; practice asceticism〔continence〕 ¶ 금욕 생활을 하다 lead an ascetic life

금욕주의 禁欲主義 stoicism ; asceticism
—자 a stoic ; an ascetic

금원 禁苑 a palace garden

금월 今月 this month ; the present〔current〕 month ; instant 《inst.》 ¶ 금월 10일 (on) the 10th inst. // 금월 중에 in the course of this month ; before the

end of this month
금융 金融 the money situation〔market〕; finance ; monetary circulation ¶ 금융의 money ; monetary ; financial ; banking // 금융이 완만하다〔핍박하다〕 Money is easy〔tight〕. // 금융 긴축이 행해지고 있다 The money situation is tightened.
— 긴급 조치령 the Emergency Financial Measure Ordinance — 긴축 정책 a tight-money policy — 어음 a finance bill — 여신 a loan advance — 완화 정책 an easy-money policy — 전문가 a financial specialist — 정세〔상태〕 the (financial) situation — 정책 a financial policy — 조직 the banking system — 채(債) a bank debenture — 통제 monetary〔financial〕 control — 핍박 tightness of money situation ; monetary stringency — 협정 a financial agreement ; a credit pact — 회사 a financial company〔firm〕 개발 — development credit 수출〔수입〕 — export〔import〕 financing
금융경색 金融梗塞 monetary stringency ; tightness of money ; a tight-money situation〔market〕
금융계 金融界 the financial world ; the financial〔banking〕 circles ¶ 금융계의 불황 stringency in the money market
금융 공황 金融恐慌 a financial crisis ; a banking〔financial〕 panic ¶ 금융 공황에 부딪치다 be struck by a financial panic
금융 기관 金融機關 a banking organ ; banking〔monetary〕 facilities ; a financial agency〔institution〕
— 예금 an interbank deposit
금융단 金融團 a syndicate
금융 시장 金融市場 the money〔financial〕 market
금융 실명제 金融實名制 The real-name financial (transaction) system ; real-name accounting
금융업 金融業 financial〔banking〕 business ; money lending (business)
—자 a moneylender〔broker〕; a financier ; a moneyman 《미》; a Shylock 《속》; the moneyed interests 《총칭》
금융 자본 金融資本 financial capital
—가 a financial capitalist —주의 financial capitalism
금은 金銀 gold and silver
—괴 gold and silver ingots —방 a jeweler's (shop) — 보화 money and valuables ; treasures ; worldly goods — 복본위 제도 bimetallism ; the gold and silver standard —붙이 things made of gold and silver — 세공 work in gold and silver — 세공자 a gold-and-silversmith
금의 錦衣 clothes of silk brocade
금의옥식 錦衣玉食 gorgeous dress and dainty food ; a good living ; an epicurean life
금의환향 錦衣還鄕 —하다 go home loaded with honors ; return to one's old home in glory
금인 金刃 an edged tool ; cutlery
금인 金印 a gold seal
금일 今日 today ; this day ¶ 금일의 신문 today's newspaper // 금일 오후 this afternoon
금일봉 金一封 an enclosure〔a gift〕 of money ¶ 금일봉을 주다 make 《a person》 a gift of money // 금일봉을 받다 get a gift of money
금자 金字 gold〔gilt〕 letters ; illuminated characters
금자둥이 金子— a precious child
금자탑 金字塔 a pyramid ; a monumental achievement ¶ 출판계의 금자탑 a monument of the publishing business ; a monumental publication
금작화 金雀花 〖식물〗 a (common) broom ; Cytisus scoparius (학명)
금잔 金盞 a gold cup ; a golden goblet ¶ 금잔 한 벌 a set of gold cups
금잔디 金— "golden"〔beautiful autumnal〕 turf
— 동산 soft golden hills
금잔화 金盞花 〖식물〗 the common marigold ; the yellow ox eye ; Calendula arvensis (학명)
금잠초 金簪草 〖식물〗 a dandelion
금잡인 禁雜人 —하다 forbid the access of those who are not authorized
금장 襟章 a collar badge〔mark, ensign, bar〕
금장 禁葬 prohibition of burying dead bodies —하다 prohibit to bury dead bodies
금장 金裝 ornamentation〔decoration〕 with gold
금장도 金粧刀 a gold pocketknife ; a gilded pocketknife (도금한)
금장식 金粧飾 gold(en) decoration —하다 decorate with gold
금전 金錢 money ; cash ; a gold coin ¶ 금전상의 money ; monetary ; pecuniary // 금전상의 원조 monetary〔pecuniary〕 aid // 금전상의 이익 pecuniary profit // 금전상의 일 money matters // 금전적 가치 cash value // 금전을 목적으로 한 mercenary // 금전을 취급하다 handle money // 금전으로 환산하여 비교하다 measure in terms of money ; estimate in dollars and cents // 그와는 금전상 관계가 없다 I have no money relations with him.
— 대부업 money-lending business — 대부 업자 a moneylender
금전 등록기 金錢登錄器 a cash register
금전 신탁 金錢信託 cash in trust ; trust cash fund
금전옥루 金殿玉樓 a palatial residence ; a stately mansion ; a palace
금전 채무 金錢債務 debt 《to be paid in

money》
금전 출납계 金錢出納係 a cashier ; a treasurer ; a teller (은행의)
금전 출납장 a cashbook ; an account book
금점 金店 a gold mine
금정틀 金井— a square timber frame for measuring the proper size of a grave ⇨ 금정(金井)
금제 金製 (what is) made of gold ; goldwork
—품 goldwork
금제 禁制 prohibition ; interdiction ; a ban ; taboo —하다 forbid ; prohibit ; taboo ; place 《things》 under a ban ¶ 여인 금제 be closed for female visitors ; No women admitted. (게시) // 금제되어 있다 be under a ban // 금제를 풀다 lift a ban ; remove a prohibition
— 원리 〖원자 물리〗 the exclusion principle (of Pauli) —품 prohibited〔contraband〕 goods
금조 今朝 this morning
금조개 金— the shell of an abalone
금족 禁足 confinement ; detention ¶ 5일간의 금족을 명하다 order 《a person》 to stay away for five days ; place 《a person》 under five days' confinement // 3일간 금족되다 be placed in three days' confinement
금족령 禁足令 a standstill order
금종이 金— golden paper
금주 禁酒 abstinence from drink ; total abstinence ; temperance ; teetotalism ; prohibition (법률에 의한) —하다 abstain from drinking ; give up〔stop〕 drinking ¶ 금주를 장려하다 promote temperance
—가 a total abstainer ; a teetotaler ; a teetotalist ; a nondrinker 《미》 —국 a prohibition country ; a dry country 《미》 —당 [미국의] the Prohibition Party —동맹 a temperance union〔society, league〕 — 운동 a temperance movement ; a dry campaign ; a crusade 〔campaign〕 against alcohol —주 [미국의] a dry state —회 a temperance society — 회원 a temperance member
금주 今週 this week ¶ 금주 중으로 within〔in the course of〕 the week // 금주 내내 병을 앓았다 I have been ill during this week.
금주법 禁酒法 the prohibition law ; the Volstead Act〔the Dry Act〕 《미》 (1933년 폐지)
미성년 —안 a prohibition bill for minors ; a bill to prohibit the sale of intoxicating liquors to persons under age
금주주의 禁酒主義 teetotalism ; prohibitionism
—자(者) prohibitionist ; anti-alcoholist
금준비 金準備 〖경제〗 gold reserves
금줄[1] 金— ① [시계줄] a gold chain 《on a watch》 ② [계급장 따위의] a gold stripe ③ [금실] gold threads
금줄[2] 金— [금맥] a vein of gold
금중 禁中 the Royal Palace ; the Court
**금지 禁止 prohibition ; inhibition ; a ban ; an embargo ; taboo ; interdiction ; [발행의] suppression —하다 prohibit ; forbid ; ban ; place a ban 《on》 ; put an embargo 《on》 ¶ 벽보 금지 No Posters Allowed. (게시) 《미》 // 주차 금지 No parking. /Parking prohibited. (게시) // 상연 금지 a stage ban // 흡연 금지 No smoking. (게시) // 판매 금지 ban on sales // 통행금지 No thoroughfare. (게시) // 통행금지구역 a restricted area // 판매금지시키다 place〔put〕 《a thing》 under a ban ; prohibit〔ban〕 the sale 《of a thing》 // 금지를 해제하다 remove〔withdraw〕 the prohibition 〔embargo〕 ; lift the ban 《on》 // 법률로써 금지하다 prohibit by law // 음주를〔아편을〕 금지하다 prohibit the use of alcoholic beverages〔opium〕 // 교내에서는 끽연이 금지되어 있다 Smoking is forbidden within the school compound. // 이 약품의 판매는 법으로 금지되어 있다 The sale of this chemical is prohibited by law.
— 구역 a restricted area — 조항 a forbidden clause 금수출 — an embargo on the export of gold ; a gold embargo 상연 — a stage ban 판매 — prohibition of sale 수출입 — 품목 items on the contraband list
금지 禁地 a restricted area ; an off-limits area
**금지령 禁止令 a prohibition order ; a prohibitory〔an interdictory〕 decree ; a negative order〔command〕 ; an interdict ; a law forbidding 《juvenile smoking》 ¶ 무기 인도 금지령을 선포하다 impose an embargo on weapons deliveries // 금지령을 해제하다 issue〔lift, remove〕 the ban〔embargo〕 《on》
금지옥엽 金枝玉葉 [임금의 집안·자손] a person of royal birth ; [귀한 자손] precious sons and daughters ¶ 금지옥엽으로 자라다 be brought up like a prince
금지환 金指環 a gold ring
금차 今次 this time ; the present time
금창 金瘡 a cut ; a wound inflicted by a blade
금쳐놓다 foretell ; predict ; prophesy ; make a prediction
금촉 金— a gold pen
금추 今秋 this〔coming〕 autumn〔fall〕
금춘 今春 this〔coming〕 spring
금치다 name a price for ; appraise
금치산 禁治産 incompetency
— 선고 interdiction ¶ 금치산 선고를

받다 be declared incompetent ; be interdicted from the management of one's property
금치산자 禁治産者 〖법〗 an incompetent ; an interdict
금침 衾枕 bedclothes and a pillow ; bedding ¶ 원앙금침을 펴다 prepare the marriage bed
금탑 金塔 a tower made of gold ; a gold-plated tower
금탑산업훈장 金塔産業勳章 Gold Tower Trlelal 《of the Order of Industrial Service Merit》
금테 金― [안경의] gold rims ; [액자의] a gilt frame ; [책 따위의] gilt edge
― 안경 gold spectacles ; gold-rimmed spectacles **― 액자** a gilt-framed picture
금파리 金― a green bottle fly
금패 金牌 a gold plaque
금품 金品 money and other valuables 〔articles〕; cash and other possessions ¶ 금품을 강탈하다 fleece 《a person》 of money and other articles // 금품을 증여하다 make a gift of money and other articles〔valuables〕// 금품을 증회하다 bribe 《a person》 with money and other articles
금풍 金風 an autumnal breeze〔wind〕
금하 今夏 this summer
금하다 agree on a price of ; fix the price of
*** 금하다 禁―** forbid ; prohibit ; ban ; taboo ; debar ① [못하게 하다] suppress ; repress ; abstain〔refrain〕 from ; check ¶ 끽연을 금하다 prohibit〔prescribe〕 smoking // 관광객의 촬영을 금하다 prohibit〔bar〕 tourists from taking pictures // 도박을 금하다 prohibit gambling ; prohibit 《a person》 from gambling // 학교에서는 극장 출입을 금하고 있다 The school forbids us to go to the theater. / The students are debarred by the school from going to the movie. // 이 저수지에서는 수영과 뱃놀이를 금하고 있다 No one is permitted to swim or row in this reservoir. /Swimming and boating are banned in this reservoir. // 그것은 법으로 금하고 있다 It is prohibited by law. // 기독교에서는 일부다처를 금하고 있다 Polygamy is tabooed〔under taboo〕 in Christianity. ② [억누르다] suppress ; repress ; restrain ; check ; keep under〔back〕 ¶ 그 참상을 보고 동정을 금할 수 없었다 I could not restrain my sympathy at the disastrous sight. // 웃음을 금할 수 없다 I cannot help laughing. // 눈물을 금하지 못했다 I could not keep back my tears. /I could not repress my tears. // 기쁜 마음을 금할 수 없었다 I could not contain myself for joy. // 분노를 금할 길이 없었다 I could not repress my anger. ③ [욕망을 끊다] abstain from ; refrain from ¶ 나는 술을 아주 금하고 있다 I have wholly given up drinking. /I have been strictly on the wagon. 《미·속》
금혼식 金婚式 a golden wedding ¶ 금혼식을 올리다 celebrate one's golden wedding
금화 金貨 a gold 300coin (낱개의) ; gold currency〔coin, coinage〕《총칭》; (gold) specie (정화) ¶ 금화로 지불하다 pay in gold
― 본위 the gold (currency) standard
― 본위 제도(制度) the gold coinage system
금환 金環 ① ⇨ 금지환 ② 〖천문〗 an annulus
금환식 金環蝕 an annular eclipse of the sun
금회 今回 this time ; lately ⇨ 이번
금후 今後 after this ; from now (on) ; in future ; hereafter ¶ 금후의 계획 the future plans // 금후 5년 내지 10년 from five to ten years from now // 금후 조심하라 Be careful after this〔in future〕.
급 急 ① [위급] (an) emergency ; (an) exigency ; a crisis 《*pl.* crises》; (a) danger ; (a) peril ② [긴급] urgency ; an urgent〔a pressing〕 need〔necessity〕 ¶ 급을 요하는 urgent ; pressing ; demanding immediate attention ; admitting of no delay // 급을 고하다 give 〔raise, sound〕 an alarm ; dispatch 〔send〕 an SOS ; send an emergency call 《for》
*** 급 級** ① [등급] a class ; a grade ¶ 3,000톤급의 배 a vessel in the 3,000 ton class // 장관급의 인물 a man of ministerial caliber // 급이 오르다 be moved up to a higher grade // 2계급 특진되다 be promoted by two grades at a time
② [학급] a class ; a grade 《미》; a standard (국민 학교의) 《영》; a form (중학교의) 《영》
③ [수준] a class ; a grade ; a level ¶ 그는 세계 정상급 선수이다 He is an internationally famous player.
대사― 회담 a conference on the level of ambassadors〔at the ambassadorial level〕; an ambassador level conference
메가톤― 핵폭발 a nuclear explosion in the megaton range
*** 급각도 急角度** an acute〔a sharp〕 angle 〔turn〕 ¶ 급각도로 sharply ; with a sudden turn // 급각도의 전환을 하다 ta350ke a sudden turn
† **급강하 急降下** a sudden drop ; a dive
―하다 drop suddenly (온도가) ; dive (비행기가)
― 폭격 dive bombing ¶ 급강하 폭격을 하다 dive-bomb
급거 急遽 hurriedly ; hastily ; in haste ; in a hurry ¶ 급거 상경하다 hurry up to *Seoul* ; rush〔fly〕 to *Seoul* // 급거 회의

를 열다 plunge into a conference // 급거 귀국하다 speed homeward from abroad

급격 急擊 a sudden raid〔attack〕; a surprise《attack》 **—하다** take《the enemy》by surprise

급격 急激 —하다 (be) rapid ; sudden ; abrupt ; hasty ; radical ¶ 급격히 rapidly ; suddenly ; abruptly ; hastily // 급격한 변화 a sudden〔radical〕change // 급격한 진보를 하다 make great〔rapid〕strides〔progress〕// 급격히 악화되다 take a sudden turn for the worse // 급격히 온도가 내리다 The temperature drops rapidly. // AIDS에 의한 사망자의 수가 급격히 증가했다 The number of deaths from AIDS has increased rapidly.

급경사 急傾斜 a steep slope ; [치받이] steep ascent〔acclivity〕; [내리받이] steep descent〔declivity〕; a heavy list (배의) ¶ 급경사의 steep ; rapid // 주의 급경사 커브 지역임 Sharp curve. Steep hill ! (게시)

급고 急告 an urgent notice **—하다** give an urgent notice ; notify urgently ; make an immediate announcement

급구 急求 Wanted ! ; Help wanted. (게시)

급급하다 汲汲— be intent〔bent〕on ; be engrossed〔absorbed〕in ; busy oneself about ¶ 명리에 급급하고 있다 be striving hard after fame and riches〔fortune〕; be hungry for fame ; be thirsty for reputation // 그는 돈벌이에 급급하고 있다 He is bent on making money. // 그는 언제나 노는 데 급급하다 He is always busy seeking pleasure.

급급하다 急急— (be) urgent ; pressing ; imminent

급기야 及其也 in the end ; after all ; finally ; eventually ; ultimately ; in the long run ¶ 돈을 물 쓰듯 하더니 급기야 빈털터리가 되었다 He went on squandering his money until (at last) he became penniless. // 급기야 타협하고 말았다 The upshot of the matter was that they came to a compromise. // 급기야 그 여자는 이혼당하고 말았다 The final outcome was that she was divorced. // 급기야 파면되고 말았다 To crown all, he lost his place. // 급기야는 범행을 자백하고 말았다 He finally confessed his crime.

급난 急難 ① [급박한] an imminent danger ; an impending calamity ② [불의의] an unexpected〔unforeseen〕disaster〔mishap〕

급등 急騰 a jump ; a sudden rise **—하다** rise suddenly ; jump ; skyrocket ¶ 물가의 급등 a speedy rising of prices // 물가가 급등한다 Prices shoot up. // 올해는 전세값이 급등했다 Rental deposits have skyrocketed this year.

급락 急落 a sudden drop ; a slump ; a sharp decline〔fall〕; a sharp break ; a crash **—하다** decline heavily ; slump ; fall suddenly ; toboggan《미》¶ 물가의 급락 a sharp decline in prices // 시세의 급락 a slump in the market // 주식의 급락 a slump in stocks // 물가가 급락하고 있다 The prices are tobogganing.

급락 及落 success or failure (in an examination) ; the result of an examination ¶ 급락을 판정하다 judge the result of an examination // 급락은 아직 모른다 I don't know whether I have passed or failed.

— 판정 회의 a final judgment conference

급랭 急冷 rapid〔quick〕cooling ; 〖화학〗 quenching

†**급료 給料** a salary ; wages ; fee ; pay

> 참고 **salary** 정신적인 일을 하는 사람들에게 지불되는 급료 봉급 **wages** 주로 육체 노동을 하는 사람들에게 지불되는 임금 **fee** 의사 변호사 등 전문가에게 주는 보수 **pay** 일반적 특히 군인에게 주는 봉급

¶ 급료를 많이 내다 pay《a person》well // 급료가 싸다〔비싸다〕be poorly〔well〕paid // 급료를 받다 receive a salary ; get one's pay // 급료를 올리다 raise《a person's》pay〔salary〕// 급료 인상을 요구하다 demand an increase〔a raise ; rise (영)〕in salary // 급료를 내리다 lower〔reduce〕《a person's》wages ; cut〔slash〕《a person's》pay // 그 회사는 급료가 좋다〔나쁘다〕The company pays good〔poor〕salaries. // 급료를 주고 해고하다 pay off // 급료가 얼마입니까 What〔How much〕salary do you get ? // 급료를 올려 주시오 Give us a raise in salary.

— 봉투 a pay envelope ; a pay〔wage〕packet (영) **—일(日)** a pay day (미) ; a wage day (영) **— 지불 수표** a paycheck **—표** a payroll

*__급류 急流__ a swift〔rushing〕stream〔current〕; rapids ; a rapid stream ; a torrent ¶ 급류를 내려가다 shoot the rapids ; shoot down rapids

급모 急募 an urgent〔a pressing〕invitation《to subscribe to a fund》; [신병·신입 회원 따위의] hurried recruiting《of personnel》**—하다** recruit〔enlist〕hurriedly〔in great haste〕; issue〔send〕《a person》an urgent invitation《to subscribe to a relief fund》¶ 간호사 3명 급모 Three nurses urgently wanted. (게시)

*__급박 急迫__ urgency ; imminence **—하다** (be) urgent ; imminent ; pressing ¶ 급박한 문제 a pressing〔burning〕question // 아시아의 급박한 정세 an acute situation in Asia // 급박해지다 become〔grow〕 acute〔critical, tense〕 // 식량 문제가 급박해졌다 The food question has become acute. // 사태가 급박해졌다 The situation has become critical.

급변 急變 ① [갑작스런 변화] a sudden change〔turn〕; an accident; an emergency **—하다** change suddenly; undergo a sudden change; take a sudden turn ¶ 급변하는 국제 정세 the rapidly changing world situation // 병세가 급변하였다 His condition has taken a sudden turn for the worse. // 그의 태도가 급변하였다 His attitude changed suddenly. // 기후가 급변하였다 The weather suddenly changed. ② [갑작스런 변고] an emergency; an accident ¶ 급변에 대비하다 prepare for emergencies

급보 急報 an urgent message〔dispatch〕; an alarm; an express (message) **—하다** report promptly〔at once〕; send an urgent message; [화재 따위를] give the alarm ¶ 급보를 받고 경찰대가 현장에 달려갔다 At the report a police squad was dispatched〔rushed〕 to the scene.

급부 給付 presentation; [지급] delivery; [지불] payment **—하다** make a presentation 《of》; deliver
— 연한 a benefit year **반대 —** a benefit in return 《for》; [비유적으로] a compensation 《for》 **의료 —** medical benefit

급부금 給付金 a benefit ¶ 급부금을 교부하다 give〔grant〕 a benefit 《to》 // 급부금을 지불하다 pay 《a person》 a benefit // 급부금을 받다 receive〔get〕 a benefit 《from》

급비 給費 supply of expenses **—하다** furnish 《a person》 with expenses; allow 《a person》 expenses

급비생 給費生 a scholarship student〔holder〕; a student on scholarship; a scholar ¶ 급비생이다 be a scholarship student

†**급사 急死** sudden death **—하다** die suddenly; die a sudden death ¶ 그는 심장 마비로 급사하였다 He died suddenly of heart failure.

급사 給仕 [식사의] a waiter; a waitress (여자); [사무실의] an office boy; [여관의] a bellboy; [일반적] a bellhop; a page (여자)

급사 急使 an express messenger; a courier ¶ 급사를 보내다 send an express messenger

급사면 急斜面 a steep hill; a steep slope〔decline〕

급살 急煞 the most unlucky star; the worst fate ¶ 급살맞다 die suddenly; meet a sudden death // 이 급살맞을 놈아 Go to hell! / Drop dead! / Curse you! / Go to the deuce!

***급상승 急上昇** a zoom **—하다** zoom; chandelle ¶ 제트 비행기가 급상승하는 소리를 들었다 We heard a jet plane zooming overhead.

급선무 急先務 a matter of immediate necessity; an urgent business; an urgent〔a pressing〕 need〔necessity〕; an emergency; a pressing need; an exigency; a matter requiring immediate attention ¶ 당면한 급선무 the pressing need of the hour // 우리 나라의 당면한 급선무는 북한 핵문제 해결이다 The pressing need for our country is to solve the North Korean nuclear problem.

급선회 急旋回 quick turning; rapid revolving〔circling〕; [방향·태도를 바꿈] a sudden change of direction〔one's course; one's attitude〕 **—하다** turn〔circle〕 quickly; revolve rapidly; change one's attitude〔tune〕

급설 急設 rapid〔hasty, hurried〕 installation **—하다** hastily install〔provide, set up〕

급성 急性 ¶ 급성의 acute // (병이) 급성이 되다 run an acute course // 급성 염증을 일으키다 become acutely inflamed
— 간염(肝炎) acute hepatitis **—병** an acute disease **— 맹장염** an acute attack of appendicitis **— 인플레** a galloping inflation **— 폐렴** acute pneumonia

급소 急所 ① [신체의] a vital spot〔part〕 ¶ 급소의 일격 a fatal〔mortal〕 blow; a home thrust // (탄환이) 급소를 빗나가다 miss a vital spot ② [가장 중요한 곳] the main point ¶ 급소를 찌른 질문 a question to the point; a home question // 그의 비평은 급소를 찔렀다 His remarks hit home. ③[약점] a vulnerable spot ¶ 급소를 찌르다 hit 《a person》 in a vulnerable spot // 급소를 건드리다 hit 《a person》 where it hurts

†**급속 急速** rapidity; swiftness; promptitude **—하다** (be) rapid; swift; prompt; fast ¶ 급속한 발전 the rapid growth 《of a town》 // 급속한 실현을 바라다 hope for the prompt materialization // 급속히 rapidly; swiftly; promptly; in a hurry // 급속히 진보하다 make rapid progress // 문제를 급속히 풀다 settle the matter quickly // 서울시의 자동차 수가 급속히 증가하고 있다 The number of cars in *Seoul* is increasing rapidly.
— 냉동〔동결〕 quick freezing

급속도 急速度 rapidity; high〔lightning〕 speed; swiftness; promptitude ¶ 전염병이 급속도로 번져나갔다 The epidemic is spreading fast〔rapidly〕 to the whole country.

급송 急送 sending in haste **—하다** send 《a thing》 in haste; send 《a thing》 by express ; dispatch 《a thing》; rush 《a thing》《to》《미》 ¶ 소화물을 급송하다 rush a package 《to》《미》; [항공편으로] fly a package 《over》

†급수 給水 water supply〔service〕 —하다 supply 《a town》 with water ¶ 시간 급수를 하다 ration the supply of city water // 급수부족으로 고통받다 suffer from a water famine〔shortage〕 // 급수를 제한하다 restrict the water supply

— 구역 a service area —난 water shortage —량 the amount of water supplied — 본관 a water〔service〕 main — 설비 water-supply facilities ; waterworks —소 a water station —판(瓣) a feed valve — 펌프 a feed(ing) pump 시간 — a water supply restricted to certain hours

급수 級數 〖수학〗 progression ; a series 기하〔등비(等比)〕 — geometric progression〔series〕 대수〔로그〕 — logarithmic series 무한 — an infinite series 부정규(不正規) — abnormal series 산술〔등차(等差)〕 — arithmetic progression〔series〕 ¶ 산술〔기하〕 급수적으로 증가하다 grow (in number) in an arithmetical〔a geometrical〕 progression ; increase at the ratio of arithmetical〔geometric(al)〕 progression 삼각 — a trigonometrical series 수렴(收斂) — a convergent series 순환 — a recurring series 유한 — a finite series 지수 — an exponential series

급수관 給水管 a water〔service〕 pipe ; a feed(-water) pipe 《on a boiler》

급수선 給水船 a water boat〔tender〕

급수 시설 給水施設 a water(-supply) system

급수 장치 給水裝置 a water-supply system ; the feed system (보일러 따위의)

급수전 給水栓 a water tap 《미》; a hydrant (가로의) ; a (water) faucet ; a feed cock (보일러 따위의)

급수차 給水車 a water-supply wagon ; a water wagon

급수 탱크 a feed tank ; a feed trough

급습 急襲 a surprise〔sudden〕 attack ; a raid ; a round-up (일제 단속) —하다 make a sudden attack 《on》; make a raid 《on》; make a surprise attack ; surprise 《the enemy》; take 《the enemy》 by surprise ¶ 적진을 급습하다 make a raid on〔upon〕 the enemy line // 경찰은 어젯밤 도박장을 급습했다 The police made a raid on〔upon〕 the gambling house last night.

급식 給食 supply of food ; meal service —하다 provide meals 《for》; furnish 《a person》 with food ¶ 학교 아동들에게 급식하다 provide (free) lunch for schoolchildren ; feed schoolchildren

— 시설 feeding facilities ; equipment for cooking — 아동 children provided with (school) lunch 학교 — 제도 (provision of) a school lunch〔meals〕 program

급신 急信 an urgent message ; a dispatch ; express mail —하다 rush a message

급양 給養 supplies such as food, clothing, bedding, and the like ; provisions ; the care and feeding 《of person》 —하다 feed and clothe ; provide〔supply〕 《the soldiers with necessaries》

급여 給與 [봉급] pay ; salary ; wages ; [지급] allowance ; grant ; supply —하다 grant ; allow ; supply〔provide, furnish〕 《a person with a thing》 ¶ 상여금을 급여하다 allow 《a person with》 a bonus

—금 an allowance ; a grant ; a dole (실업의) — 수준 a pay〔wage〕 level ; a salary level — 준칙 a pay schedule — 체계 a wage〔pay〕 structure〔system〕 임시 — an extra allowance〔pay〕 특별 — 〖노동〗 fringe benefits (주택·건강·보험·질병·휴가 따위의)

급여 소득 給與所得 an 《annual》 income 《of a white-collar worker》

급용 急用 urgent〔pressing〕 business ; [약속] an urgent appointment ¶ 급용으로 on urgent business // 급용으로 부산에 갔다 Urgent business called him away to *Pusan*. /He rushed〔hurried〕 to *Pusan* on business.

급우 級友 a classmate

급유 給油 oil supply ; supply of oil ; refueling —하다 supply oil ; refuel ; fill (자동차에) ; feed ¶ 공중 급유 air-to-air refueling ; in-flight〔midair〕 refueling

—기(機) [비행기] a tanker plane — 장치 an oiler — 탱크 an oil-feeding tank —함 a naval tanker〔fuel ship〕

급유기 給油器 an oil feeder

급유선 給油船 a tanker ; a tank vessel ; an oiler

급유소 給油所 an oil〔a filling〕 station 〔depot〕; a gas〔service〕 station 《미》

급인 汲引 —하다 [물을] draw up ; pump up (펌프로) ; [인재를] appoint 《a person》 by merit ; select 《a person》 for ability

급자기 suddenly ; all at once

급작스럽다 (be) sudden

급전 急錢 money for immediate use ; urgently needed money

급전 急電 an urgent telegram ¶ 급전을 치다 wire an urgent message ; dispatch a radio message

급전 急轉 a sudden change〔turn〕 —하다 change suddenly ; take a sudden turn ¶ 형세의 급전 an unexpected turn of events // 형세가 유리하게 급전했다

frantically ; as hard as one can ; with all one's might // 기를 쓰다 exert oneself to the utmost ; do one's utmost ; make every effort // 기를 쓰고 반대하다 be bent on opposing 《a person》 // 기를 쓰고 덤벼들다 tackle with all one's might
③ [숨] breath ; wind
④ [정신력] spirits ; heart ¶ 기를 펴지 못하다 cower ; feel ill at ease ; feel constrained
⑤ 〖철학〗 natural passion ; the life force
⑥ [객기] ill-advised bravery ; temper ; spirit ; blind valor ¶ 기가 과하다 be violent-tempered ; be rough
⑦ [냄새] a smell ; a scent ; a hint
⑧ [감·기운] feeling 《of》 ¶ 시장기 hungriness ; a feeling of hunger // 물기 moisture ; dampness // 핏기가 없다 look pale ; have a bad complexion // 그 음식은 기름기가 너무 많다 The food〔dish〕 is too greasy.
기가 나다 (관용) feel triumphant ; swell up ; be puffed 《at》
기가 막히다 (관용) be stifled ; [비유적] be at a loss for words ; be dumbfounded ; be taken aback
기가 죽다〔꺾이다〕 (관용) feel cheap ; lose heart〔courage〕 ; be dejected〔depressed, disheartened, dispirited〕 ; be crestfallen ; be cast down
기를 펴다 (관용) make oneself comfortable ; put oneself at home

기 基 〖화학〗 a radical ; 〖수학〗 a radix 《*pl.* ~es, -dices》 ¶ 산기 an acid radical

†**기 旗** a flag ; a standard ; a banner ; the colors (연대기) ; a streamer ; an ensign (함선기) ; a pennant (우승기) ; bunting 《총칭》 ; a national flag (국기) ¶ 기를 날리며 with banners flying // 기를 흔들다 wave a flag // 기를 올리다 hoist〔run up〕 a flag // 기를 내달다 hang out a flag // 기를 내리다 lower a flag // 기를 접다 furl a flag // 기가 바람에 펄럭이고 있다 The flag is streaming〔fluttering〕 in the wind.
—행렬 a flag procession

-기 記 an account ; a narrative ; [역사] a history ; a chronicle ; [기록] annals ; a record ¶ 여행기 an account of travels ; a traveler's journal // 전쟁기 an account of a battle

-기 期 [기일] a date ; a time ; [시대] an age ; [기간] a period ; a term ; [계절] a season ; [병의] a stage ¶ 2기생 the second-term students // 폐병 1기 tuberculosis in the first stage

-기 紀 〖지질〗 a period
석탄— the Carboniferous period

-기 機 a machine ¶ 비행기 an airplane // 세탁기 a washing machine

-기 [명사형 전성 어미] doing ; being ; to do ; to be ; that it does〔is〕 ¶ 경고하기 위하여 by way of warning // 읽기 시작하다 begin reading〔to read〕 // 배우기 쉽다 be easy to learn // 쓰기에 알맞다 be fit for use ; can be used // 사람은 먹기 위하여 살지 않고 살기 위하여 먹는다 Man does not live to〔that he may〕 eat, but eats to live〔that he may live〕. // 네가 오기를 바란다 I wish you will come.

기가 起家 —**하다** resuscitate a ruined family ; resuscitate〔restore〕 the family to its former prosperity

기가 妓家 a *kisaeng* house

기각 棄却 abandonment ; renunciation (권리 따위의) ; dismissal (소송의) —**하다** abandon ; renounce ; dismiss 《a suit》 ; throw 《a suit》 out of court ¶ 공소를 기각해서 하급심으로 넘기다 remand 《a case》 to a lower court // 신청을 기각하다 reject〔turn down〕 an application

†**기간 期間** a period ; a time ; a term ¶ 유효 기간 a term of validity // 일정한 기간내에 within a certain〔given〕 period of time // 기간을 단축〔연장〕하다 curtail〔extend〕 the period
임대차 — a term of lease **장〔단〕(長〔短〕)—** a long〔short〕 term〔period of time〕

기간 起墾 —**하다** bring under cultivation ; break up the soil ; cultivate 《wasteland》

기간 旗竿 a flag staff

기간 基幹 a nucleus 《*pl.* -clei》 ; a mainstay
— 산업 key〔basic〕 industries **— 요원** key〔cadre〕 members〔personnel〕 **— 중대〔연대〕** a skeleton company〔regiment〕

기간 旣刊 ¶ 기간의 previously published ; already issued
— 도서 목록 a list of books already published ; a backlist **—호(號)** back〔previous〕 numbers ; an earlier issue

기갈 飢渴 hunger and thirst ; starvation ¶ 기갈에 허덕이다 suffer from〔be pressed by〕 hunger and thirst // 기갈을 겨우 면했다 They were narrowly saved〔released〕 from starvation.
기갈든 놈이 돌담조차 부순다 (속담) Hunger breaks stone walls.

기갑 부대 機甲部隊 armored units ; a panzer unit

기강 紀綱 [관기] official discipline ; [질서] public order ; law and order ; the laws ¶ 기강 숙정 enforcement of official discipline // 기강 문란〔퇴폐〕 a breach〔the laxity〕 of official discipline // 기강을 바로잡다 improve the moral fiber 《of》 // 기강을 유지하다 maintain public discipline

기강 氣腔 [세포내의] an air chamber

〔cell〕

기개 氣槪 spirit ; mettle ; pluck ; guts ; backbone ; pride ; self-respect ; pep 《미》 ¶ 기개 있는 high-spirited ; mettled ; plucky ; go-getting 《미》 // 기개 있는 사나이 a man of spirit〔mettle〕 ; a high-spirited man ; a go-getter 《미》 // 기개 없는 사나이 a man lacking (in) spirit ; a spiritless〔spineless〕 man ; a sissy 《미·속》 // 기개를 보이다 show one's mettle

기거 起居 [건강 상태] one's state of health ; [일상 생활] one's daily life ¶ 기거를 묻다 inquire after 《a person's》 health ; ask after 《a person》 // 기거를 같이하다 live together 《under the same roof》 ; live with ; make one's home with 《a person》

— 동작 movement ; behavior ; carriage ; [범절] manners ; bearing

기걸 奇傑 a character ; a remarkable〔an extraordinary〕 man

기결 旣決 ¶ 기결의 decided ; settled ; convicted (죄가)

— 사항〔안〕 a matter settled〔decided on〕 — 서류함 an out-tray —수(囚) a convict ; a convicted prisoner

기경 起耕 farming ; tillage ; plowing ; cultivation ; husbandry —하다 farm ; till 《a field》 ; plow 《land》 ; cultivate 《wasteland》

기계 奇計 a trick ; a clever scheme ; a ruse ¶ 기계를 꾸미다 map out a clever scheme ; cook up a smart idea

†기계 機械 a machine ; [기계류] machinery ; [기관] an engine ; [장치] mechanism ; [기계의] works ¶ 기계적인 mechanic // 기계적으로 mechanically ; automatically // 기계적인 일 mechanical work // 기계적으로 일하다 work mechanically〔in mechanical fashion〕 // 기계를 설치하다 install a machine ; set up machinery // 기계를 운전하다 operate〔work〕 a machine // 기계를 조립하다 assemble a machine ; put a machine up〔together〕 // 기계를 분해하다 take a machine to pieces // 기계를 검사하다 overhaul a machine // 기계가 섰다 The machine has come to a standstill. // 이 기계는 어딘가 고장이다 Something must be wrong with the works. // 이 시계는 스테인리스 케이스지만 기계는 참 좋다 Though stainless-cased, this watch has very good works.

— 가공 machine work ; machining —공 a mechanic ; a mechanician ; machine hand〔operator〕 ; a machinist ; a machiner 《미》 — 공구 a machine tool — 공업 the machine industry — 공장 an engineering works ; a machine 〔mechanics〕 shop — 공학 mechanical engineering ; practical mechanics — 공학과 a course in mechanical engineering —과(科) department of mechanical engineering ; a mechanical course —관(館) [박람회 따위의] a machinery building 〔hall, section〕 —끌 a power chisel — 기술자 a mechanical engineer ; a machinist — 나사 a machine screw — 날염(捺染) machine printing — 냉동 mechanical refrigeration — 능률 mechanical efficiency —력 mechanical power —론(論) 〖철학〗 mechanism —론자 a mechanist —류 machinery — 마무리 machine finish — 만능주의 mechanism — 문명 machine civilization — 부품 a machine part —사(絲) filature silk —설 〖철학·생물〗 the mechanical theory — 설계 the design of a machine — 수뢰(水雷) a mechanical 〔submarine〕 mine — 수리공 a machine mender ; a repairman ; a repairer ; a machinist — 시대 a machine age ; the age of machinery — 시동기 a mechanical starter —실 a machine〔machinery〕 room ; an engine room —(언)어 machine language — 에너지 mechanical energy — 염색 machine dyeing —유 machine〔lubricating〕 oil — 인형 a robot — 작용 mechanical action〔work〕 — 장치 mechanism ; works ; a machine — 제도 mechanical drawing — 제작소 a machine shop — 주조 machine casting — 지레 a mechanical lever —톱 a power saw —학(學) mechanics

‡기계 器械 an instrument ; an appliance ; an apparatus

—실 [물리학의] an apparatus room 물리 — a physical apparatus 의료 — a medical appliance

기계 棋界 [바둑계] *baduk* circles ; [장기계] *janggi* circles

기계 뜨기 機械— knitting by machinery ; machine knitting

— 레이스 a machine lace — 스웨터 a machine-knit(ted) sweater ; a machine-made sweater

***기계적 機械的** ¶ 기계적인 mechanical // 기계적으로 by rote ; routinely

— 기억 rote — 노동 mechanical labor — 작용 mechanical action — 행동설 [동물의] automatism

기계제 機械製 ¶ 기계제의 machine-made 《toy》 ; made by machinery

—품 a mechanical〔machine〕 product

기계 체조 器械體操 heavy gymnastics ¶ 기계 체조를 하다 perform gymnastics on the bar // 기계 체조를 잘하다 be good in〔at〕 heavy gymnastics

기계화 機械化 mechanization —하다 mechanize ¶ 농업의 기계화 farm mechanization ; mechanized farming

— 농업 mechanized farming — 병기 mechanized arms — 부대 a mechanized unit ; a panzer division

기고 起稿 drafting ; a draft **—하다** draft ; frame a draft ; begin to write

*__기고 寄稿__ a contribution **—하다** contribute 《to》 ; write for 《a magazine》 ¶ 잡지에 기고하다 contribute articles to a magazine ; write for a magazine
—가 a contributor **특약 —가** a columnist

기고 旗鼓 colors and drums ; [군대] an army ; a troop ¶ 기고 당당히 with colors flying (and band playing) ; with flying colors ; triumphantly

기고만장 氣高萬丈 elation ; high spirits **—하다** ① [뽐내다] be in high〔roaring, towering〕 spirits ; be elated ; be puffed up ; be on one's high horse ¶ 웅변 대회에서 일등을 하여 기고만장하다 His spirits were sky-high winning the first prize at the speech contest.
② [성나다] be〔get, become〕 excited ; be exasperated ; be enraged ; be infuriated ; be worked up ¶ 그 말을 듣고 화가 나서 기고만장하였다 He was in full tide of his passion at the information.

기골 氣骨 backbone (of character) ; spirit ; mettle ; grit ; soul ¶ 기골 있는 mettlesome ; of firm character // 기골 없는 backboneless ; spineless ; weak ; feckless // 기골 있는 사나이 a man of spirit ; a strong-willed person ; a man of firm character ; a solid-minded person 《미》 // 기골을 보이다 show one's mettle

기골 肌骨 flesh and bones

기공 技工 a craftsman
치과(齒科) — a dental technician

기공 奇功 a signal〔phenomenal〕 success ¶ 기공을 세우다 achieve a signal success ; make a hit ; achieve a much better result than expected // 그 방책으로 기공을 세웠다 That measure did the trick〔proved a signal success〕.

기공 起工 commencement of construction work **—하다** begin〔start〕 construction 《on》 ; [토목 공사의] break ground 《for》 ; [선박의] lay down ¶ 내주에 기공한다 Construction work begins next week. // 이 배는 작년 인천 조선소에서 기공됐다 The ship was laid down at the *Inchon* Dockyard last year.

기공 氣孔 〖식물〗 a pore ; a stoma ; 〖동물〗 a stigma ; a spiracle
—률 porosity **— 증산(蒸散)** 〖식물〗 stomatal transpiration

기공비 紀功碑 a monument to distinguished services

*__기공식 起工式__ the ceremony of laying the cornerstone〔foundation stone〕 (건축의) ; a ground-breaking ceremony (토목 공사의) ; the ceremony of laying down the keel (배의)

기관 奇觀 a wonder ; a wonderful sight ; a strange〔novel〕 sight ; a singular spectacle ¶ 천하의 기관 a wonder of the world ; a wonder on earth ; an eye-opening sight // 기관을 나타내다 present a wonderful sight

기관 汽管 a steam pipe

기관 汽罐 a boiler ; a steam boiler
—사 a boilerman **—실** a boiler room ; [배의] a stokehold ; a fireroom

기관 氣管 the trachea ; the windpipe
— 절개(술) tracheotomy ; bronchotomy

*__기관 器官__ an organ ¶ 감각 기관 sense organs // 호흡 기관 the respiratory organs // 신체의 중요 기관 vital organs of the body ; members
— 계통 the organic system **— 질환** an organic disease **—학** organology ; organography **— 형성** organogenesis **소화 —** the digestive organs〔apparatus〕 **운동 —** a locomotive organ **조정 —** a regulating organ **중요 —** a vital organ

*__기관 機關__ ① [기관] an engine ; a machine ② [수단] an organ ; means ; an agency ③ [설비] facilities ; service ; machinery ; an institution ¶ 기관을 설치하다 set up an agency
— 공장 an engine workshop〔shop〕 **— 장교** 〖해군〗 an engineer **—대** an engine bed〔bearer, seat〕 **— 배치** machinery arrangement **—병** a fireman **—실** the engine department ; 〖선박〗 the engineering crew **—부(夫)** an engine cleaner ; a fireman **— 실습생** an apprentice engineer **—원** a fireman ; a stoker **— 일지** an engineer's logbook **—장** a chief engineer **— 조수** a locomotive fireman ; an assistant engine driver〔engineman〕 **— 효율** engine efficiency **가솔린 —** a gasoline engine **가스 —** a gas engine **관리 —** the governing body **광고 —** an advertising medium **교육 —** educational facilities ; a means of education ; an educational institution ¶ 교육 기관으로서의 영화 the cinema as an educational agency **교통〔운수〕 —** facilities for transportation ; transportation facilities **국제 —** an international agency **금융(金融) —** banking facilities **기압 —** an atmospheric engine **내연 —** an internal combustion engine **대행 —** an agency **디젤 —** a Diesel engine **선박용 —** a marine engine **송풍 —** a blast engine **수압 —** a hydraulic engine **심의 —** a deliberative body **언론 —** organs of public opinion ; mass media **열—** a caloric engine ; a heat〔thermic〕 engine **입법 —** a law-making organ **자치 —** a self-government body ; municipalities ; a municipality ; municipal corporations **전기 —** an electric engine **정부〔정치〕 —** the apparatus〔wheels〕 of government ; government agencies **증기 —** a steam engine **첩보 —** a secret

service 통신 — a means of communication 특무 — the military secret service ; the counter-intelligence corps 《C. I. C.》 행정 — administrative machinery〔agencies〕

기관고 機關庫 〖철도〗 an engine shed〔house〕; a locomotive shed〔depot〕《미》; a roundhouse 《미》

기관 단총 機關短銃 a submachine gun 《SMG》

†기관사 機關士 [기선의] an engineer ; [기차의] an engineman ; an engine driver ; a (locomotive) engineer 《미》; a locomotiveman 《영》

일등 — a first engineer

기관실 機關室 a machinery room〔space〕; [배의] an engine room

기관지 氣管支 a bronchus 《*pl.* -chi》

—경(鏡) a bronchoscope —염 bronchial trouble〔bronchitis〕 — 천식 bronchial asthma — 카타르 bronchial catarrh — 폐렴 bronchopneumonia ; alveobronchiolitis

기관지 機關紙 an organ ; a bulletin

사내 — [회사 따위] a house organ 정당〔조합〕 — a party〔union〕 organ 정부 — a government organ

†기관차 機關車 an engine 《영》; a locomotive 《미》; a loco ¶ 기관차를 운전하다 operate〔run〕 a locomotive

— 기관 a locomotive boiler — 승무원 a locomotive〔an engine〕 crew — 연통〔기통, 보일러〕 a locomotive funnel〔cylinder, boiler〕 보조 — a booster 선구(先驅) — a pilot engine 전기 — an electric locomotive ; an electromotive ; motive power (집합적) 증기 — a steam locomotive (engine)

*기관총 機關銃 a machine gun ; a Maxim gun ¶ 기관총 소사를 하다 sweep by machine-gun fire ; machine-gun

— 사수 a machine-gunner ; an air gunner (비행기의) —좌(座) [진지] a machine-gun emplacement〔position, nest〕 경— a light machine gun 소형 — a submachine gun ; a burpgun 《미군·속》 중— a heavy machinegun

기관포 機關砲 a (heavy) machine gun ⇨ 기관총(機關銃)

*기괴 奇怪 —하다 (be) strange ; mysterious ; weird ; uncanny ; wild ¶ 기괴한 풍문 a strange〔wild〕 rumor // 당신이 그것을 듣지 못했다니 기괴한 일이다 How strange that you should not have heard it ! // 그날 밤 기괴한 일이 일어났다 A strange thing happened that night.

기괴망측 奇怪罔測 —하다 [이상하다] (be) very strange ; [고약하다] outrageous ; scandalous ; monstrous

기괴 천만 奇怪千萬 —하다 (be) extremely strange〔mysterious, monstrous〕; outrageous

*기교 技巧 art ; craftsmanship ; technical〔artistic, mechanical〕 skill ; [예술의] technics ; mechanism ; [책략] an artifice ; a trick ; finesse ¶ 기교를 부리다 use a trick ; employ〔resort to〕 artifice // 기교를 다하다 exert one's technical skill // 기교가 뛰어나다 be technically accomplished // 그는 외교적 기교에 능하다 He has a great diplomatic skill. // 음모의 기교에 뛰어나다 He has much skill in intrigue.

—가 a technician (회화·음악의) ; a mannerist (나쁜 의미의) —주의 [예술상의] technicalism ; mannerism

기교 機巧 resources ; tact

기교질 氣膠質 〖물리·화학〗 aerosols

⁑기구 氣球 a balloon ¶ 기구를 띄우다 fly〔send up〕 a balloon // 기구를 타고 올라가다 ascend in a balloon

— 계류소 a balloon bed〔moor〕 —고(庫) a balloon house —대(隊) a balloon corps — 조종사 a ballooner ; a balloonist 계류(繫留) — a captive balloon 고공 — 관측 an upper-air balloon observation 관측 — an observation balloon 광고 — an ad balloon 기류 관측 — an observation balloon 무인 관측 — a pilotless balloon 유동(遊動) — a dirigible balloon 헬륨 — a helium-filled balloon

기구 崎嶇 ① [운명의] adversity ; vicissitudes ; ups and downs —하다 (be) unlucky ; unfortunate ; checkered ; varied ; ill-fated ¶ 기구한 운명 strange fate ; adverse fortune // 기구한 일생 a checkered career // 기구한 운명에 희롱되다 be a sport of fortune ; be the puppet of fate ; have a varied career ② [산길의] steepness —하다 (be) steep ; rugged ; precipitous

기구 機構 structure ; framework ; mechanism ; organization ; machinery

— 개혁 the reorganization of the system 경제 — an economic structure〔setup〕 국제 — an international organization 당(黨)— the organization of a political party ; party apparatus 사회 — the scheme〔frame(-work)〕 of society 정치 — a political framework ; the frame〔wheels〕 of government ; government machinery 중간 — an intermediate organization 행정 — an administration setup〔structure〕

기구 起句 the opening line of a poem

*기구 器具 a utensil ; a tool ; an implement ; [고정된] an apparatus ; a fixture

주방 — kitchen utensils ; kitchenware ; [총칭] kitchen equipment

기구 부리다 〔관용〕 show off one's well-equipped household

기국 器局 caliber ; capacity ; ability ; competency ; talent ; parts ¶ 기국이 크

다〔작다〕 be a man of large〔small〕 caliber ; be a man of great〔small〕 capacity // 장이 될 기국이다 He has the caliber of leadership. /He is smart enough to lead others. /He is fit to be a leader. // 큰 일을 할 기국이다 He shows a capacity for great achievement.

기궁 奇窮 extreme〔abject, dire〕 poverty ; destitution ; indigence **—하다** (be) very poor ; destitute ; indigent

기권 棄權 abstention 《from voting》 ; renunciation 《of one's right》 ; [경기의] absence ; cancellation 《of the〔one's〕 entry》 **—하다** abstain 《from voting》 ; [권리를] renounce〔waive〕 《one's right》 ; [경기에서] give up 《the race halfway》 ¶ 다리 경련으로 도중에서 기권하다 A cramp in the legs forced him to withdraw from the contest.

— 방지 prevention of abstention from voting **—율** an abstention rate **—자** an absentee 《from voting》 ; a nonvoter ; an abstentionist ; 〖법〗 a releasor **—표** a blank ballot ¶ 기권표를 던지다 cast a blank ballot

기권 氣圈 〖기상〗 the atmosphere ⇨ 대기(大氣) (대기권)

*‡***기근 饑饉** a famine ; failure of crops ; dearth ; [결핍] scarcity ; (a) shortage ¶ 기근이 든 해 a lean year // 기근을 당하다 suffer from a famine

— 구제 자금 a famine relief fund **대—** a great〔big, severe, huge, grievous〕 famine **물—** shortage of water supply ; a water famine〔dearth〕 ; water shortage **석탄 —** a coal famine ; a famine of coal **종이 —** a paper famine ; paper dearth

기근 氣根 〖식물〗 an aerial root

기금 基金 a fund ; an endowment ¶ 기금을 설정하다 create〔establish〕 a fund // 기금을 모집하다 raise a fund

— 모집 collection of a fund ; raising fund **— 모집 운동** a drive for raising funds 《미》 ; a campaign〔drive〕 for collection of funds **감채(減債) —** a sinking fund **구제 —** a relief fund **국제 통화 —** the International Monetary Fund 《IMF》 **공동(共同) —** a common purse **전도 —** a mission fund **카네기 평화 —** the Carnegie Endowment for International Peace

기기 器機 machinery and tools

— 제작소 a machinery shop〔works〕

기기괴괴 奇奇怪怪 —하다 (be) abominable ; monstrous ; extremely strange ; fantastic ; mysterious

기기묘묘 奇奇妙妙 —하다 (be) extremely strange ; very curious〔queer, odd〕 ; marvelous ; fabulous

-기까지 to ; to the extent of 《doing》 ; so far as 《to do》 ; until〔even〕 it does ¶ 빚을 지기까지 해서 even going to the extent of incurring a debt // 훔치기까지 하다 go to the length〔extent〕 of committing theft ; go so far as to commit theft

기꺼워하다 ⇨ 기뻐하다

†**기꺼이** willingly ; with pleasure ; joyfully ; delightfully ; cheerfully ; heartily ; readily ; with (a) good grace ¶ 기꺼이 …하다 would gladly〔fain〕 《do》 ; be willing to do ; take great satisfaction in 《doing》 // 기꺼이 맞이하다 welcome with joy ; receive 《a person》 with open arms // 기꺼이 맡다 be delighted to undertake 《the work》 // 기꺼이 승낙하다 give a ready consent 《to》 // 기꺼이 도와드리겠습니다 I am only too glad to help you. // 기꺼이 그렇게 하겠습니다 I am quite prepared to do it. // 그분을 위해서라면 무슨 일이나 기꺼이 하겠습니다 He is welcome to any service I can do.

†**기껍다** [기쁘다] (be) joyful ; joyous ; glad ; delightful ; happy ; [유쾌하다] (be) pleasant ¶ 기꺼운 날 a happy〔glad〕 day // 기꺼운 대답 a pleasing〔favorable〕 answer

기껏 to the best of one's ability ; to the utmost ; as far〔much〕 as possible ; as far as one can ¶ 기껏 빨리 as soon as possible // 기껏 노력하다 do one's best ; exert oneself as hard as possible // 기껏 공부하다 study as hard as one can

*****기껏해야** at (the) most ; at (the) best ; at the utmost ; at the (very) outside ¶ 그는 기껏해야 스무 살이다 He is twenty at the most〔outside〕. // 기껏해야 한 열흘 걸리겠지요 I should think it will take about ten days at the longest. // 기껏해야 그 정도이지요 That is the utmost〔limit〕 I can do.

기나수 幾那樹 〖식물〗 a bark tree ; a cinchona

기나염 幾那鹽 salt of quinine

기나피 幾那皮 cinchona〔Peruvian quinine〕 bark

기남자 奇男子 a genius ; a man of no common ability

기낭 氣囊 ① [물고기의] an air bladder ② [가스 주머니] a gas bag ; an envelope

기내 畿內 the districts around the capital city

기내 機內 [항공기의] the inside of a plane ; the cabin ¶ 기내에 on board (the plane)

— 통신 〖항공〗 intercommunication ; intercom 《속》 ¶ 기내 통신을 하다 speak over the intercom

기녀 妓女 ① [관비] an official dancing girl ② ⇨ 기생(妓生)

기년 期年 one year ¶ 기년도 안 되어 before a year has passed ; within one year

기년 朞年 ① [복] one year of mourning ② [돌] one year ; the first anniversary

기년 耆年 age over sixty years

*기념 記念 commemoration ; remembrance ; memory ― 하다 [사물을] commemorate ; [사람을] be in memory of (사물이 주어) ¶ 기념하는 in commemorative ; memorial // 기념으로 in remembrance of ; as a memento〔keepsake〕; in token of ; in commemoration of (사물을) ; in memory of (사람을) // 기념할 만한 날 a memorable day // 창립 기념으로 in commemoration of the founding of《a school》// 기념 식수를 하다 plant a commemorative tree // 승리를 기념하다 commemorate the victory // 이것은 초대 교장을 기념하는 비석이다 This monument is built in memory of the first principal of the school.

― 강연회 a commemorative lecture meeting ―관 a memorial hall ― 그림엽서 a souvenir〔commemoration〕picture postcard ; a picture postcard in commemoration《of》― 논문집 essays (contributed) in celebration of《the 10th anniversary of...》― 도서관 a memorial〔commemoration〕library ― 만찬회 a testimonial dinner ― 메달〔배지〕a commemoration〔commemorative〕medal〔badge〕―문 a memorial arch ― 박물관 a memorial museum ― 사진 a commemorative〔souvenir〕photograph ― 우표 a commemorative〔memorial〕stamp ― 전람회 a commemoration〔memorial〕exhibition ― 출판 a commemorative publication ―패(牌) a memorial tablet 전쟁 ― war commemoration

*기념물 紀念物 a souvenir ; a remembrance ; a memorial ; a monument ; a trophy《of the hunt》¶ 기념물로서 보존하다 keep《a thing》as a substantial reminder《of》

기념비 紀念碑 a monument ; a memorial ; a marker commemorating《Nehru's visit》¶ 기념비를 세우다 erect a monument《of a war》// 고 김씨를 위해서 기념비를 세우다 erect a monument to the memory〔in memory〕of the late Mr. Kim

기념식 紀念式 exercises marking the occasion ; commemoration exercises ¶ 우리 학교는 어제 개교 25주년 기념식을 가졌다 Our school celebrated the 25th anniversary of its founding yesterday.

*기념일 紀念日 a memorial day ; a commemoration day ; an anniversary ; a day of remembrance ¶ 독립 기념일 (미국의) Independence Day ; the Fourth of July // 그 날은 그 사건의 기념일이다 The day commemorates the event. // 어제가 우리 결혼 기념일인데 깜박 잊어버렸다 Yesterday was our wedding anniversary and I forgot about it.

기념제 紀念祭 a commemoration (day) ; an anniversary ; a memorial festival〔service〕¶ 기념제를 거행하다 celebrate the anniversary《of》

창립 10주년 ― the 10th anniversary of the founding《of a school》

*기념품 記念品 a souvenir ; a memento《*pl.* ~(e)s》; a memorial ; a remembrance ¶ 기념품 증정이 행해졌다 Presentations were made.

송별 ― a parting memorial

기념호 紀念號 a commemoration number ; [고인의] a special number issued in memory of《the late Mr...》

-기는 but ; however ; though ; (and) yet ; still ; nevertheless ; for all that ; in spite of ¶ …이기는 하지만 although it is that ; Being it were... // 가기는 갔으나 I did go but... // 가난하기는 해도 거짓말은 안한다 Though (he is) poor〔Poor as he is〕, he is above telling a lie. // 나쁜 줄 알기는 알지만 그를 막을 길이 없다 Despite of recognizing it an evil, I cannot stop him to do it.

*기능 技能 ability ; capacity ; skill ¶ 기능이 있는 able ; competent ; skilled

― 검사 skill measurement ― 교육 technical education ―상 a prize for skill ; the technique award ― 양성 cultivation of technical skill ― 올림픽 Olympics in Technology ; [정식명] the International Vocational Training Competition ―자 양성 apprenticeship training ; the training of skilled laborers ―직 technical service ―직 공무원 a technical official 특수 ― expert skill

기능 機能 function ; faculty ¶ 기능적 functional // 기능을 발휘하다 function // 신문의 기능은 사회에 정보를 제공하는 데 있다 The major function of the press is to give information to the public.

― 구조 functional structure ― 기관 a functional organ ―도(圖) a functional diagram ― 변천 change of function ―성 질환 a functional〔dynamic〕disease ― 심리학 functional psychology ―어(語)〘문법〙a function word ― 장애 impaired functioning ; a functional disorder ; dysfunction ; ¶ 기능 장애를 일으키다 be functionally disordered ― 저하 malfunction ;〘의학〙depression ― 적응 functional adaptation ― 전이(轉移) a functional shift ―주의 functionalism 기관 ― organic functions 생식 ― generative functions 소화 ― digestive functions

*기다 crawl ; creep ; go on all fours ; [초목이] trail ; train ; [꼼짝 못하다] cringe ; crouch ; grovel ¶ 상사 앞에서 설설 기다 cringe to one's superior ;

humble〔abase〕 oneself before one's superior // 고양이가 새를 보고 살금살금 기어갔다 The cat crept silently toward the birds. // 담쟁이가 담을 기어 올라갔다 Ivy trailed over the wall. // 우리는 암벽을 기어 올라갔다 We climbed up the side of a cliff. /We clambered over a rocky hillside. // 사다리를 타고 성벽을 기어올랐다 They scaled the wall by ladder〔with a ladder〕. // 조종사는 비행기 속으로 기어 들어갔다 The pilot climbed into his plane. // 공사는 굼벵이 기어가듯 진행하고 있다 The work is proceeding at a snail's pace.

기지도 못하면서 뛰려 한다 속담 First creep and then go.

기다랗다 (be) rather long ; lengthy ; long winded ; long-spun ; long and boring〔tedious〕 ¶ 기다란 장대 a long pole // 기다란 설명 a long(-winded) explanation // 기다란 이야기 a long (-spun) story ; a shaggy-dog story

†기다리다 wait 《for》 ; await ; abide ; watch 《for》 ; [기대] expect ; look for ; look forward to ; anticipate ¶ 기다리고 기다리던 long-awaited ; long-desired // 이제나저제나 하고 기다리다 be on the tiptoe of expectation ; expect 《a person》 every moment // 기다렸다는 듯이 초대에 응하다 jump at an invitation // 기회를 기다리다 wait〔watch〕 for an opportunity // 사람을 기다리다 wait for a person // 자지 않고 기다리다 wait〔sit, stay〕 up for 《a person》 // 끝까지 기다리다 wait out 《the long hours》 // 기다리다가 지치다 grow〔get〕 tired〔weary〕 of waiting 《for》 // 아버지가 돌아오기를 기다리다 wait for one's father to return // 너 때문에 3시간을 꼬박 기다렸다 I kept waiting for three whole hours for you. // 기다리게 해서 미안합니다 I am sorry to have you kept waiting. // 잠깐 기다려 주십시오 Please hold the line a second. (전화에서) // 답장을 기다리겠습니다 Awaiting the pleasure of your reply. (편지에서) /Please oblige me with an answer. // 본건은 당국의 인가를 기다릴 뿐이다 This matter only awaits the approval of the authorities. // 그들은 방학을 기다리고 있다 They are looking forward to the vacation. // 기다리시겠습니까 나중에 다시 거시겠습니까 Would you hold on or call back later? // 그는 그의 방문객을 20분이나 기다리게 했다 He made his visitor cool his heels for twenty minutes. // 다른 심부름 할게 있으니 준비하고 기다려 Stand by for another errand. // 이제 슬슬 네가 올 때가 되었다고 생각하고 숨어서 기다리고 있었다 I thought it was about time for you to come along, so I was lying in wait.

기다마하다 (be) very long ; lengthy ¶ 기다마한 장대 a long pole // 기다마한 캥거루의 꼬리 the long tail of a kangaroo

기단 基壇 〖건축〗 the stylobate ; the stereobate

기단 氣團 air mass

기담 奇談 a strange story ; a weird story ; an interesting anecdote〔episode〕

기담 奇譚 a strange and interesting story ; an interesting anecdote〔episode〕

기답 起畓 **—하다** reclaim 《a plot》 into paddy fields

기대 〖민속〗 ① [무동을 따라다니는] a woman who takes a child dancer around to perform ② [굿에서] the person in charge of music for a shaman's exorcism rite

†기대 期待 expectation ; anticipation **—하다** expect ; look forward to ; look for ; look to 《a person》 for ; anticipate ; count on ; reckon on〔upon〕 ¶ 기대에 반하여 contrary to one's expectations // 기대하고 있던 hoped for 《support》 // …을 기대하여 in expectation〔anticipation〕 of // 기대를 등지다 let 《a person》 down ; fail 《a person》 // 기대에 미치지 못하다 fall short of one's expectations // 기대에 부응하다 live〔come〕 up to one's expectations // 남의 원조를 기대하다 look to others for help // 승리를 기대하다 look for victory // 그들은 지나치게 사회에 기대한다 They expect too much of the world.

기대강이 旗— a flag tip

†기대다 ① [물건에] lean (against) ; rest against ; stand against ; recline on ; [앞으로] lean over ¶ 벽에 기대다 lean〔rest〕 against the wall // 책상에 기대다 lean on〔over〕 a desk // 베개에 기대고 앉다 sit up against one's pillows // 문에 기대어 서 있었다 He stood leaning (with his back) against the door. // 의자에 기대어 깊은 생각에 잠겨 있었다 He was lost in deep thought leaning back in his chair. // 난간에 기대어 강물을 내려다보았다 He gazed down on the stream leaning over the railing.
② [의지] rely upon ; lean on ; depend on ; place dependence upon ; trust to ; count on ¶ 기댈 사람이라곤 너밖에 없다 I have no one but you to turn to. // 남에게 기대지 않겠다는 것이 그의 주의였다 Self-help〔-reliance〕 was his motto. / He made it a rule not to depend upon others.

†기도 祈禱 a prayer ; an invocation ; [식사 전후의] grace **—하다** pray ; offer a prayer ; say grace ¶ 마음에 고이 간직한 기도 an unspoken prayer // 기도하고 있다 be at one's devotions〔prayers〕 // 아침 기도 Morning Prayer ; matins // 저녁 기도 vespers
—문 a prayer **—서** a prayer book ; the Book of Common Prayer (영국 국교의)
—자 a prayer ; a supplicant ; a suppli-

ant ; a supplicator **—회** a prayer meeting ; a devotional service

*__기도 企圖__ an attempt ; a plan ; a try ; a scheme ; a project **—하다** plan ; contemplate ; intend ; undertake ; try ¶ 자살을 기도하다 attempt suicide

기도 氣道 the〔an〕 airway ¶ 환자의 기도가 막히지 않도록 보호하다 protect a patient against obstruction of the airway

-기도 하다 ① do〔be〕 indeed ¶ 춥기도 하다 be really cold // 참 단풍이 아름답기도 하다 My, the autumn leaves are so pretty! // 공부만 하기란 어렵기도 하다 It is pretty tough to do nothing but study all the time. // 그 학생은 부지런하기도 하다 He is really a hardworking student.
② do〔be〕 both... and... ¶ 좋기도 하고 나쁘기도 하다 It has its good points and its bad points. // 배고프기도 하고 목마르기도 했다 I was hungry and thirsty.

†**기독교 基督教** Christianity ; the Christian religion〔faith〕 ¶ 기독교의 Christian
— 교회 a Christian church **—국(國)** a Christian country ; Christendom 《전체》 **—도(徒)** a Christian ; a son of light **— 사회주의** Christian socialism **— 선교사** a Christian missionary **— 여자 청년회** the Young Women's Christian Association 《Y. W. C. A.》 **— 청년회** the Young Men's Christian Association 《Y. M. C. A.》

기동 起動 moving ; stirring ; starting **—하다** move ; stir ; start ; get started ¶ 몸이 아파서 자리에 누운 채로 기동을 할 수 없었다 I was so sick that I had to be confined to bed.
—관 a drive pump **—기** a starter motor ; a starter ; starting gear **—력** motive power **— 저항기** a starting rheostat **— 전력(電力)** starting current **—질(質)** 〖화학〗 an activator

기동 奇童 a remarkable child ; a wonder boy

*__기동 機動__ maneuver ; 〖군사〗 movement **—하다** maneuver
— 경찰 mobile police forces ; [데모 진압 따위의] the riot police **— 경찰 대원** a riot policeman **—력** mobility ; mobile power **— 부대** a mechanized unit ; mobile troops ; a task force 《T. F.》 **— 야포** a mobile field gun **— 연습** maneuvers **— 작전** mobile operations **—전** a war of movement ; mobile warfare **—화** mechanization

기동차 汽動車 a diesel train

기두 起頭 [일의] the beginning ; the start ; [글의] a foreword ; a preface **—하다** begin ; start ; introduce ; write a preface

⁑**기둥** ① a pillar ; a post ; a pole ; a column (원주) ¶ 불기둥 a pillar of fire // 기둥을 세우다 erect〔set up, put up〕 a pillar ② [사람] a support ; a prop ; a stay ¶ 한집안의 기둥 the support〔prop and stay〕 of a family ; the breadwinner // 나라의 기둥 the pillar of the state

기둥목 —木 logs suitable for pillars

기둥서방 —書房 a pimp ; a pander

기드림 旗— a streamer ; a pennon ; a pennant (돛대 끝의) ; a banderole ; 〖군사〗 a sleeve target ; a drogue (비행기가 끄는 대공 사격 연습용)

기득 既得 ¶ 기득의 already acquired〔obtained〕 ; vested

기득권 既得權 vested rights ; vested interests (권익) ¶ 기득권의 침해 infringement of 《a person's》 vested rights

기라 綺羅 a fine〔gorgeous, gaudy〕 dress ; fine clothes

-기라도 ¶ 모든 것을 알기라도 하듯 말하다 talk as if 《a person》 knew everything // 갈 수 있기라도 했으면 좋겠다 I want even a slight possibility to go there.

기라성 綺羅星 glittering〔bright〕 stars ¶ 기라성처럼 늘어선 고관들 a galaxy of dignitaries // 기라성같이 늘어서다 There is a galaxy〔a fine array〕 of...

⁑**기략 機略** resources ; tact ¶ 기략이 종횡무진한 사람 a resourceful man // 기략이 풍부하다 be full of resources ; be tactful

기량 技倆 skill ; talent ⇨ 기능(技能)

기량 器量 capacity ; caliber

기량계 氣量計 〖기상〗 an aerometer

기러기 〖새〗 a wild goose 《*pl.* geese》

기러기발 [현악기의] a bridge

기력 氣力 energy ; vigor ; spirit ; vitality ; virility ; nerve ; pep 《미·속》 ¶ 기력이 있는 사람 an energetic person ; a man of full push // 기력이 왕성한 energetic ; vigorous ; full of vigor // 기력이 없는 spiritless ; lifeless // 기력이 부족하다 be lacking〔deficient〕 in energy // 기력이 쇠퇴하다 lose one's vigor〔energy〕 ; become enervated // 잠은 피로한 몸의 기력을 회복해 준다 Sleep restores energy to the tired body. // 천천히 목욕이라도 하고 식사한다면 다시 기력이 생길 것이다 After a leisurely soak in the tub and dinner, you'll perk up again.

기력 機力 machine power ⇨ 기계(機械)(-력)

기력 汽力 steam power ¶ 기력으로 움직이는 기계 a machine worked by steam ; a steam engine // 기력을 올려서 속력을 내다 raise steam for higher speed
—계 a steam gauge〔indicator〕 **— 발전소** a steam power plant〔station〕

-기로 ① [···로써] with ; as for ¶ 그는

기지가 있기로 유명하다 He is famous 〔noted〕 for his wit. ② [까닭] because ; as ; since ; so ; owing to ; due to ; on account of ; seeing ; considering ¶ 비가 오겠기로 우산을 가져갔다 It threatened to rain and I took an umbrella with me. // 날씨가 꽤 따뜻하기로 밖에 나갔다 Now (that) the weather was much warmer, I went outside. // 네가 떠난다기로 전송을 나왔다 Hearing that you are leaving, I have come to see you off. ③ [아무리 …하다 하더라도] ⇨ -기로서니

기로 岐路 [갈림길] a forked road ; a branch road ; a by-path ; [십자로] a crossway ; a crossroad ¶ 인생의 기로에 서다 face〔stand at〕 the crossroads of life

기로 耆老 a person aged over sixty

-기로서니 even though ; although ; admitting〔granting, supposing〕 that ¶ 그가 아무리 부자이기로서니 however〔no matter how〕 rich he may be // 그렇기로서니 admitting〔granting〕 that it is so ; even if it were so // 그것이 사실이기로서니 어떻단 말인가 Say it were true, what then ?

-기로 하다 fix (up) ; decide (on) ; determine ; make ; arrange ; agree upon ; choose ; set ; appoint ¶ …하기로 하고 있다 be bound on 《doing》 ; make it a rule 《to do》 // …하지 않기로 하다 decide against doing 《something》 // 그는 자신이 하기로 하였다 He determined to do it〔on doing it〕 in person. // 나는 그 집을 빌리기로 하였다 I have arranged to rent the house.

***기록 記錄** a record ; [관청의] a document ; archives ; [의사록] minutes ; [학회의] transaction **—하다** record ; write down ; put〔place〕 on record ; register ¶ 기록적인 record-breaking // 기록에 오르다 be recorded ; be (put) on record // 기록에 남기다 put〔place〕 on record ; keep a record of 《events》 // 기록에서 빠지다 fail to be recorded // 기록을 깨뜨리다 break〔beat, smash〕 the record // 〔신, 세계〕기록을 세우다 make 〔establish〕 a〔new, world〕 record // 기록을 경신하다 better〔renew〕 one's record // 기록에 남기지 마라 This is off the record.

—계(係) a recorder ; [경기의] a scorer ; a timekeeper ; a timer **—계(計)** a recorder **— 문학** documentary literature **— 보관소** the archives **— 보유자** a record holder **— 서류** dossier **인생 —** human documents

기록 영화 記錄映畫 a documentary film 〔movie〕 ; a record film

기록적 記錄的 ¶ 기록적인 사건 an occurrence worth recording ; one for the book 《미·구》 // 기록적 숫자를 보이다 show a record figure

기롱 譏弄 derision ; ridicule ; scoff **—하다** befool ; ridicule ; jeer 《at》

***기뢰 機雷** a mine ¶ 기뢰를 부설하다 lay〔place〕 mines 《in the sea》 // 기뢰에 닿다 strike a mine // 기뢰 방지의 장치를 하다 provide 《a ship》 with an anti-mine device

— 부설함 a mine layer〔boat〕 **계류(繫留) —** a moored mine **부설 —** a submarine mine **부유(浮遊) —** a floating 〔surface〕 mine **수압 —** a pressure〔an oyster〕 mine **자기(磁氣) —** a magnetic mine **촉각 —** an antenna mine

기뢰원 機雷原 a minefield ¶ 기뢰원을 부설하다 place〔plant〕 a field of mines

기루 妓樓 a brothel ; a house of ill fame

기류 氣流 an air current〔stream〕

상승 — an ascending current **상승 온난 —** a thermal **상층〔하층〕 —** the upper〔lower〕 air

기류 寄留 temporary residence **—하다** reside temporarily 《at》 ; live (with a person)

—자 a temporary resident ; a sojourner **—지** a place of temporary residence 〔domicile〕 ; 〖법〗 one's domicile of choice

기류계 寄留屆 report of one's temporary residence ¶ 기류계를 내다 send in a notice of one's temporary domicile

†기르다 [양육하다] bring up ; feed ; breed ; foster ; nurse ; nurture ; [사육하다] rear ; raise ; [교육하다] cultivate ; train ; educate ; [수염 따위를] grow ¶ 우유로 아이를 기르다 bring up〔raise〕 a child on cow's milk // 돼지를 기르다 raise pigs // 새끼 때부터 기른 개 a dog kept from young // 꽃을 기르다 raise flowers // 도의심을 기르다 cultivate moral sense // 좋은 습관을 기르다 cultivate a good habit // 용기를 기르다 cultivate courage // 인재를 기르다 foster men to be great // 이성을 기르다 develop one's mind // 수염을 기르다 grow a mustache // 더 이상 기를 수 없는 개가 한 마리 있다 We have a dog we can't keep any more.

†기름 oil ; fat ; grease ; lard (돼지의) ; blubber (고래의) ; suet (소의) ; tallow (비누 따위를 만드는) ¶ 기름에 튀긴 생선 fried fish // 기름 묻은 oily ; oil-stained // 기름으로 뒤덮인 (수면) oil-slicked // 기름을 바르다 rub with oil // 기름을 짜다 squeeze〔press〕 oil 《from》 // 기름이 묻다 become oily ; be stained with oil〔grease〕

—걸레 oilcloth **—때** oil stain ; a grease spot **—병** an oil bottle **—복자** a measuring cup for oil **— 분리기** an oil separator〔extractor〕 **—챗날** the top part of an oil press **—체** an oil strain-

er〔filter〕 ―통 an oil cask〔barrel〕
기름 먹인 가죽이 부드럽다 〈속담〉 who greases his way travels easily.
기름을 치다 〈관용〉 lubricate ; grease ; oil ; pour oil
기름기 [고기의] the fat ; [기름 기운] oiliness ; greasiness ¶ 기름기가 많은 oily ; greasy ; fatty
기름매미 『곤충』 a large brown cicada
기름 먹이다 oil ¶ 기름 먹인 종이〔헝겊〕 oiled paper〔cloth〕 // 종이를〔헝겊을〕 기름 먹이다 oil paper〔cloth〕
기름물감 oil paint ; oil colors ; oils
기름지다 ① [기름이 많다] (be) greasy ; fatty ; oily ; fat ; rich ¶ 기름진 국 fat soup // 기름진 음식 greasy〔fatty, rich〕 food ; fat diet ; nourishing〔nutritious〕 food
② [비옥하다] (be) fertile ; rich ; productive ; fruitful ; fat ¶ 기름진 땅 fertile land〔soil, field, plains〕 ; fruitful soil ; fat land(s)
기름콩 sprouting beans
기름투성이 ¶ 기름투성이의 oily ; oil-stained ; greasy ; grease-stained // 기름투성이가 되다 be stained〔smeared〕 all over with grease〔oil〕
기름틀 an oil press
기름하다 (be) longish ; be somewhat long ¶ 얼굴이 기름한 long-faced ; with an oval〔egg-shaped〕 face // 기름한 얼굴 a longish〔a rather long〕 face
*기리다 applaud ; praise ; admire ; commend ; extol ; speak highly of ¶ 기릴 만한 laudable ; commendable ; admirable ; praiseworthy // 본교의 창설자의 유덕을 기리기 위하여 이 동상을 건립함 We erect this statue to pay (a) tribute to the memory of the founder of this school.
기린 麒麟 『동물』 a giraffe
― 자리 『천문』 the Giraffe ; the Camelopard
기린아 麒麟兒 an infant prodigy ; a wonder child ; a (child〔young〕) prodigy ; a wizard ¶ 정구계의 기린아 a tennis marvel
기린혈 麒麟血 [수지] dragon's blood
*기립 起立 standing up ―하다 stand up ; rise (to one's feet) ; [호령] Stand up! /Rise! ¶ 기립을 부탁하다 ask 《a person》 to stand up
― 투표 a standing vote
기마 騎馬 horse riding ¶ 기마로 가다 go on horseback // 기마전을 하다 play a cavalry-battle game
― 경찰 a mounted policeman ; trooper ; the mounted police 《총칭》 ―대 a mounted party ― 민족 a horse-riding people ; horsemen ―전 《play》 a mock cavalry battle ― 행렬 a cavalcade
*기막히다 氣― ① stifle ; be suffocated ; feel choked ② [비유적] be stunned ; be struck dumb ; be dumbfounded ; be aghast ; be at a loss for words ; [형용사] be breathtaking ; stunning ; amazing ¶ 기막힌 미인 a stunning〔breathtaking〕 beauty // 기막히게 좋은 날씨 glorious weather // 기막히게 잘하는 연주 a breathtaking performance // 기막힌 사정 a matter hard to tell // 기막히게 awfully ; terribly ; surprisingly ; strikingly ; shockingly // 기막혀서 in blank amazement ; in speechless wonder ; with a vacant look of astonishment // 어린애가 그런 소리를 하다니 기막혔다 I was (struck) dumb with amazement to hear a child say such a thing. // 그 생각을 하니 기막힌다 The thought makes me feel miserable. // 나보고 도리어 거짓말한다니 기막힌다 I am simply aghast to hear that you think I am lying
*기만 欺瞞 deception ; imposition ; a deceit ; an imposture ―하다 deceive ; impose on 《a person》 ; cheat ; play 《a person》 a trick ; draw〔pull〕 the wool over 《a person's》 eye ¶ 기만적인 deceptive ; tricky // 세인을 기만하다 deceive the world // 자신을 기만하다 deceive oneself // 거짓말과 기만으로 생활하다 make a living by lying and imposture // 기만적인 수단 fraudulent measure
―책 a deceitful〔deceptive〕 policy
-기만 ① [전적으로] entirely ; wholly ; solely ¶ 놀기만 하다 be always playing〔idle〕 ; do nothing but play // 물가는 오르기만 한다 Prices go on rising. /Prices are on the increase. ② [적어도] if only... ; so long as... ¶ 너는 그저 열심히 공부하기만 하면 된다 All you have to do is (to) work hard. // 재미있기만 하면 무슨 책이든 좋다 Any book will do so long as it is interesting.
-기 만큼 as ; as ... as ; [부정] not so〔as〕 as ; less... than ¶ 사람을 기다리기만큼 힘든 일은 없다 There is nothing so trying as waiting for a person. // 맑게 갠 봄날에 산책하기만큼 유쾌한 일은 없다 Nothing is pleasanter than〔not so pleasant as〕 to take a walk on a fine spring day.
기말 期末 the end of a term ; a term end
― 시험〔수당〕 a term-end examination〔allowance〕 ― 회계 a term-end account
기망 企望 hope ; expectation ; anticipation ―하다 hope ; anticipate ; expect
기망 欺罔 fraud ; deception ―하다 deceive ; commit fraud
기망 旣望 the sixteenth night of a lunar month
기맥 氣脈 ¶ 기맥이 통하다 be in collusion〔concert〕 《with》 ; communicate with each other ; have a secret〔tacit〕

understanding 《with》 // 적과 기맥을 통하다 have a dark connection with enemy // 두 사람은 서로 몰래 기맥을 통하고 있다 There exists a secret understanding between them.

기면 嗜眠 lethargy ; sopor ; torpor ; deep sleep ¶ 기면성(性)의 〖의학〗 soporose // 기면 상태에 있다 be lethargic ; be in lethargy ; be in a state of somnolence
—성 뇌염 〖의학〗 sleeping sickness ; encephalitis ; lethargica

기명 記名 signature ; register ; subscription **—하다** sign 《one's name》 ; register ; inscribe ; put one's name to ¶ 기명 조인하다 sign and seal
—식 지참인불 payable to order and bearer **—장** a register (book) **—주(권)** a name share ; a registered〔inscribed〕 stock ; stock certificate **— 채권** registered bond **— 투표** an open vote〔ballot〕 ; write-in vote **단기 — 투표** an open vote with single entry **연기 — 투표** an open vote with plural entry

기명 器皿 tableware ; dishes

기모 奇謀 an ingenious scheme ; a clever trick〔strategy〕

기모 起毛 [보풀 세우기] napping ; nap raising **—하다** nap ; raise a nap 《on》 ; fluff
—기 a napping〔nap-raising〕 machine ; a gig (모직물의)

기모 機謀 a stratagem ; a scheme ; a plan ¶ 기모가 있다 be an able strategist

기묘 奇妙 **—하다** (be) strange ; curious ; queer ; singular ¶ 기묘하게 strangely ; curiously ; oddly // 기묘하게도 strange to say ; oddly〔curiously〕 enough // 기묘한 모양의 oddly-shaped // 그것을 기묘하게 생각하다 think it strange ; it strikes 《one》 strange 《that》

기묘 己卯 〖민속〗 the 16th binary term of the sexagenary cycle

기문 氣門 a stoma ; stigma ; spiracle (곤충, 거미 따위)

기문 奇聞 strange news ; [기담] a strange story

기물 器物 [용기] a vessel ; [기구] a utensil ; [기구] furniture

기미 [얼굴의] a discoloration on the face ¶ 얼굴에 기미가 끼다 have discoloration on the face

기미 己未 〖민속〗 the 56th binary term of the sexagenary cycle ¶ 기미 독립 운동 the Korean Independence Movement of 1919

기미 氣味 ① [냄새와 맛] smell and taste ② [심기] feeling ; sensation ③ [취미] taste ; relish

기미 機微 secrets ; inner workings ; penetralia ¶ 외교의 기미 a diplomatic secret // 인정의 기미에 통하다 have a rare knowledge of human nature // 기미를 알아차리다 get a hint〔an inkling〕 of 《a matter》 ; be slightly acquainted with

기민 機敏 promptness ; readiness ; smartness ; shrewdness **—하다** (be) smart ; shrewd ; quick ; prompt ; be wide-awake (미) ¶ 기민하게 smartly ; quickly ; promptly // 기민한 상인 a shrewd businessman // 기민하게 행동하다 act smartly〔cleverly〕 // 기민하게 기회를 포착하다 be prompt〔quick〕 to seize an opportunity

기민 饑民 starved people ; the famished
기민 먹이다 관용 provide the famished with food ; feed the starving people

기밀 機密 secrecy ; a secret ; secret 〔inside〕 information ¶ 기밀의 classified ; confidential ; secret // 군사상의 기밀 military secret // 기밀을 누설하다 divulge〔let out, leak out〕 a secret ; tell an inside story // 기밀을 지키다 observe secrecy ; keep a secret ; keep 《a matter》 under wraps
—비 secret service funds **— 사항** a confidential affairs ; classified information (군대의) **— 서류** secret〔confidential〕 documents **국가 —** a state secret

기밀 氣密 airtight(ness)
—복(服) an airtight garment〔suit〕

기밀실 氣密室 〖항공〗 an airtight chamber

기박 奇薄 **—하다** (be) unfortunate ; unlucky ; hapless ; luckless ; ill-fated ; ill-〔evil-〕starred ¶ 기박한 운명을 타고나다 born under an unlucky star // 기박한 팔자를 한탄하다 grieve over one's tough luck // 그 여자는 한평생 팔자가 기박했다 She led an ill-fated life. /She was hapless throughout her life.

기반 羈絆 a yoke ; fetters ; bonds ; shackles ; ties ¶ 기반을 벗어나게 하다 free 《a nation》 from the fetters〔yoke〕 of // 영국의 기반을 벗어나다 throw〔cast, shake〕 off the British yoke

기반 基盤 a foundation ; a base ; a basis ; bedrock (지질) ¶ …을 기반으로 하다 stand on the basis 《of》 // 종교는 신앙을 기반으로 한다 Religion is based on faith. // 공업은 한국 발전의 기반이다 Industry is the basis of the development of Korea.

기발 奇拔 uncommonness ; extraordinariness ; originality ; novelty **—하다** (be) novel ; clever ; smart ; original ¶ 기발한 의견 a novel view // 기발한 취향 a novel〔an original〕 idea // 기발한 말을 하다 say a clever〔smart〕 thing

기백 氣魄 spirit ; soul ; character ¶ 호쾌한 기백 an intrepid spirit

기백 幾百 hundreds ¶ 기백만 millions

기범선 機帆船 a steam-and-sail-driven boat

기법 技法 techniques ¶ 기법을 터득하다

acquire〔master〕 the technique 《of》
기법 記法 (a) notation
기벽 氣癖 unwillingness to own〔admit, acknowledge〕 one's defeat ¶ 기벽이 세다 refuse to admit one's defeat
기벽 奇癖 an eccentric habit ; an eccentricity ; a peculiarity ; a singularity ¶ 기벽이 있는 사람이다 He is quite a character.
*기별 奇別, 寄別 news ; tidings ; word ; information ; notice ; a letter —하다 let 《a person》 know ; tell ; inform 《a person》 of〔that〕 ; advise 《a person》 of ; give 《a person》 notice ; make 《a matter》 known ; send word ¶ 기별을 듣다 hear of ; have〔receive〕 news of ; get word from // 미리 기별하다 give notice beforehand ; forewarn // 오래도록 기별이 없다 keep silent for a long time // 일주일 전에 기별하다 give 《a person》 a week's notice // 그가 오거든 기별해 주게 Please let me know if he comes. // 며칠이 지나도 그로부터 기별이 없다 Days passed without a line from him. // 무사히 도착하거든 기별해 주게 Please send me word of your safe arrival.
기병 奇兵 a strategic detachment ; a storming party ; a flying corps〔column〕 ; 〖군사〗 shock troops ; a commando 《*pl.* -(e)s》 《영》 ⇨ 기습(奇襲) (-부대) ¶ 기병을 풀어놓다〔쓰다〕 send 〔dispatch〕 a flying corps〔column〕 ; 〖군사〗 take 〔use〕 a shock action (기동 부대의)
기병 起兵 raising an army ; rising in arms ; an uprising (봉기) —하다 raise an army ; rise in arms
*기병 騎兵 [한 사람] a cavalry soldier ; a cavalryman ; a horseman ; cavalry 《총칭》
— 연대 a regiment of horse — 장교 a cavalry officer ; a cavalry — 중대 a cavalry squadron 경— light cavalry
기보 既報 a previous report ; a prior information ¶ 기보한 바와 같이 as already〔previously〕 reported〔announced〕 ; as stated in a previous issue
기보 碁譜 the record of *Baduk* (game) ; a manual of *Baduk* ¶ 명(名) 기보를 남기다 leave an authentic record of celebrated *baduk*〔*go*〕 games
기보법 記譜法 〖음악〗 music notation
기복 起伏 ups and downs ; undulation ; 〖지리〗 accident —하다 undulate ; roll ; be uneven ¶ 기복이 있는 undulating ; rolling // 기복이 많은 생애 a checkered〔a colorful, an eventful〕 career ; a life full of ups and downs // 기복이 있는 평야 an undulating〔a rolling〕 plain
⁑기본 基本 [기초] a foundation ; a basis ; [기준] a standard ¶ 기본을 이루다 be fundamental 《to》 ; form the groundwork 《of》 // 기본에서 시작하다 begin with the ABC 《of》
— 계획 general planning ; a master plan — 과목 basic subjects of study — 과정 an elementary course (of study) —금 an endowment (fund) — 단위 a standard〔fundamental〕 unit — 대사 〖생리〗 basal metabolism — 방침 a keynote —법 an organic law — 사항 basic data — 산업 basic〔key〕 industries — 설계 a basic design — 설계도 a general drawing —수 a basic number ; 〖수학〗 a radix 《*pl.* -es, radices》 — 수준선 a datum line —어 the most important words — 연습 basic exercises — 영어 basic English — 요금 base rate — 원료 basic raw materials — 원리 a basic〔fundamental〕 principle ; fundamentals —음 a fundamental tone — 전술 elementary tactics — 조건 a basal〔fundamental〕 condition — 주파수 fundamental frequency — 측정 a fundamental law —파(波) 〖물리〗 a fundamental wave ; a fundamental — 협정 a basic agreement —형 a fundamental form
기본급 基本給 a basic〔base〕 salary ; basic 〔base〕 wages ; basic〔regular〕 pay ¶ 기본급과 제수당 basic pay and allowance
— 표준 a basic pay level
기본 재산 基本財産 permanent property ; an endowment ¶ 기본 재산이 있는 학교 an endowed school // 기본 재산을 몰수하다 disendow 《a church》
기본적 基本的 ¶ 기본적인 fundamental 《rules》 ; basic ; standard ; cardinal ; 〖생리〗 basal // 기본적으로 fundamentally ; basically
— 인권 the fundamental human rights
— 인권 선언 the Declaration of (Fundamental) Human Rights
기봉 起峰 a towering peak
기부 肌膚 flesh ; skin
⁑기부 寄附 contribution ; donation ; subscription —하다 contribute 《to, toward》 ; donate ; subscribe ; make a donation〔contribution〕 《to》 ¶ 기부를 모으다 raise〔get up〕 a subscription ; collect contributions // 그는 자선 사업에 만 원을 기부했다 He contributed 10,000 *won* for the society for charity work.
기부 基部 the base ; the foundation ; the basal part 《of a column》 ; the subbase (토대의) ; the basement (원기둥의 토대의) ¶ 기부를 향해서 자라는 〖식물〗 basipetal // 기부의 basal ; 〖해부〗 basilar // 두개(頭蓋) 기부의 basicranial // 부리 기부의 basirostral
기부금 寄附金 a contribution ; a donation ; an endowment ; a gift of money ¶ 기부금을 보내다 give〔make〕 a donation 《towards》 // 기부금을 할당하다 levy

contributions 《on》// 기부금을 모으다 collect〔raise〕 a purse 《for》
— 모집 raising contributions **전도(傳道) —** a missionary collection

기부자 寄附者 a contributor ; a subscriber ; a donator ; a donor ¶ 거액의 기부자 a large giver ; a generous donor
자선 사업 — a subscriber to a charity

기부 행위 寄附行爲 an act of endowment ; a contribution ¶ 기부 행위를 하다 make a 《1,000,000 *won*》 contribution 《to》

*__기분 氣分__ feeling ; sensation ; a frame of mind ; mood ¶ 기분이 좋은 pleasant ; agreeable ; comfortable ; refreshing // 기분이 나쁜 unpleasant ; disagreeable ; uncomfortable // 기분 좋게 with a good grace ; willingly // 일시적인 기분으로 on the spur of the moment // 기분에 따라서 as one's humor〔whim〕 dictates // 기분이 좋아지다 feel better // 기분이 나쁘다 feel unwell〔nervous, uneasy〕 // 기분을 나쁘게 하다 hurt 《a person's》 feeling // 울고 싶은 기분이다 feel like crying // 이상한 기분이 들다 have a strange sensation ; feel strange // 자네가 그런 기분이면 If that is the way you feel 《about》 // 무엇인가 불길한 일이 일어날 것 같은 기분이다 I have a feeling that something evil will happen. // 기분이 어떠십니까 How do you feel? // 나는 유쾌하게 떠들고 놀 기분이 나지 않았다 I was in no mood to make merry. // 가끔 기분 좀 내는 게 뭐가 어때서 그래 What's wrong with living it up once in a while? // 오늘은 사장님 기분이 좋지 않은 것 같다 The boss seems to be in a bad mood today. // 기분 내키는 곳으로 여행하고 싶다 I'd like to try taking a trip to whatever places my fancy leads me.
—극 an atmosphere play **—파(派)** a man〔creature〕 of moods ; a whimsical 〔temperamental〕 person

기분 전환 氣分轉換 (a) diversion ; a pastime ; (a) recreation ; (a) relaxation ; [거주의] change of surroundings
— 하다 refresh oneself 《with a song》 ; divert oneself〔one's mind〕 ; recreate〔amuse, unbend〕 oneself ¶ 기분 전환이 되다 [일이 주어] serve as diversion ; [사람이 주어] be amused 《with》 ; be diverted 《by》 // 나는 오랜만에 기분 전환을 한다 This is my first recreation for a long time. // 기분 전환 삼아 이부자리 좀 펴줄래 Why don't you lay out the bedding for a change?

기불 旣拂 ¶ 기불의 paid (up) ; settled

기브앤드테이크 give-and-take

기비 基肥 ⇨ 밑거름

†**기뻐하다** be pleased〔delighted〕 with 〔at〕 ; be happy with ; be glad for ; rejoice over〔at〕 ; congratulate oneself on ¶ 성공을 기뻐하다 be pleased with 《a person's》 success // 껑충껑충 뛰며 기뻐하다 jump for joy ; dance with joy // 모두 그 소식을 듣고 기뻐하였다 Everybody was delighted at the news. // 이 선물은 누구나 기뻐할 것이다 This gift would be acceptable to anyone. // 나는 꿈이 아닌가 하고 기뻐했다 My rapture was so intense that I could scarcely believe my sense.

†**기쁘다** (be) happy ; joyful ; joyous ; glad ; delightful ; pleasant ; gratifying ; [기쁘게 생각하다] delighted ; pleased ; gratified ¶ 기쁜 소식 a glad〔delightful, pleasant, joyful, welcome〕 news〔tidings〕 // 기쁜 날 a joyous occasion〔day〕 // 기뻐서 for〔with〕 joy // 몹시 기뻐하여 in high glee ; full of glee // 기쁘게도 to one's joy // 기쁜 듯한 happy-looking // 기쁜 마음으로 with a glad heart ; with joy〔delight, pleasure〕 ; willingly // 기쁜 얼굴로 with a delightful look ; with a glad air ; in gleeful mood // 기쁘게 하다 gladden ; please ; delight // 기뻐서 어쩔 줄 모르다 be beside oneself with joy ; be entranced〔transported〕 with joy ; be in a transport of joy // 기쁘기도 하고 슬프기도 하다 have mixed feelings of joy and sorrow // 그녀를 만나서 기쁘다 I am glad to see her. // 그 소식을 듣고 기쁘다 I am pleased at the news. /The news is delightful to hear. // 기뻐서 못 견디겠다 I cannot contain myself for joy. // 울고 싶도록 기뻤다 I nearly wept for joy. // 대단히 기쁘신 것 같습니다 You look so happy. // 당신의 편지를 기쁘게 읽었습니다 I have read your letter with great pleasure. /I was very pleased to read your letter. // 이렇게 기쁜 일은 없다 Nothing gives us so great a pleasure. / Nothing can give greater pleasure than this. // 당신이 기부한 돈으로 많은 배고픈 사람들이 밥을 먹게 된다는 사실을 알면 매우 기쁘실 것입니다 You'll be tickled pink to know that your donation will help feed quite a few hungry people.

†**기쁨** joy ; delight ; pleasure ; gladness ; ecstasy ; rapture ; exultation ; glee ; rejoicing ¶ 인생의 기쁨 pleasure〔joys〕 of life // 커다란 기쁨 great pleasure // 기쁨을 참지 못하다 be unable to contain one's joy // 기쁨으로 가슴이 뛰놀다 one's heart pounds with delight

기사 己巳 〖민속〗 the 6th binary term of the sexagenary cycle

†**기사 技師** an engineer ; a technician
—장 a chief engineer **건축 —** a building engineer ; an architect **토목〔기계, 선박, 전기, 광산〕 —** a civil〔a mechanical, a marine, an electrical, a mining〕 engineer

기사 記事 an article ; an account ; news ; [기술] a statement ; [서사]

description ¶ 선거에 관한 기사 election news // 마감 후의 중대 기사 a stoppress // 화재 기사를 싣다 give an account of a fire // 기사 게재를 막다 prohibit printing the news
— 금지 a press ban〔embargo〕; a ban on the publication of news —문 a description ; a descriptive composition — 문체 a descriptive style — 폭주 a congestion〔plethora〕 of news〔reading matter〕 사망 — an obituary (notice) ; a necrology 사회 — social news〔items〕 삼단 — a three-column article 신문 — a newspaper account〔report〕; press news 지방 — local news 특종 — a scoop ; a beat 《미》

기사 記寫 a record —하다 record ; put on record ; write down

기사 棋士 a *baduk* player ; [장기의] a Korean chess player

†기사 騎士 a rider ; a horseman ; [무사] a knight ¶ 우수의 기사 the Knight of the Rueful Countenance 《돈키호테》

기사 騎射 shooting (a bow) on horseback ; equestrian〔mounted〕 archery

기사 饑死 death by starvation —하다 die of hunger ; starve to death ¶ 기사시키다 starve 《a person》 to death ; starve out 《a person》

기사 거리 記事— [신문의] a news item ; (a piece of) news ; a newsbreak ; news matter ; dope 《on》 《속》 ¶ 기사 거리가 되다 be in the news ; become a topic for the newspapers

*기사도 騎士道 knighthood ; chivalry ¶ 기사도는 아직 살아 있다 The age of chivalry is not dead.

기사회생 起死回生 resuscitation ; revival ; restoration from death —하다 restore from death ; revive ; resuscitate ¶ 기사회생의 영약 a wonderful〔magic〕 medicine ; a wonder(-working) drug

기산 起算 —하다 reckon〔compute〕 from ; measure from ¶ 이자는 이달 초하루부터 기산한다 Interest is charged from the first of this month.
—일 the initial date in reckoning ; the day from which a reckoning is made —점 the starting point of reckoning ; the point where one starts counting

*기상 氣象 atmospheric phenomena ; [천후] weather ¶ 기상을 관측하다 make meteorological observation
— 개황 general weather conditions ; the overall weather picture — 관제 [공항의] the meteorological〔met〕 control — 기호 〖기상〗 sky symbols —대 a meteorological observatory ; a weather station (측후소) — 대원 a weatherman —도 a weather chart〔map〕 — 레이더 weather radar — 업무 weather service — 위성 meteorological satellite ; weather satellite — 자동 기록기 a meteorograph — 통계 meteorological statistics — 특보 a special weather report — 현상 atmospheric〔meteorological, weather〕 phenomena 세계 — 기구 the World Meteorological Organization 《WMO》 ☞ ◖p. 367◗

‡기상 氣像 [성질] nature ; disposition ; temper ; [기력] spirit ¶ 과격한 기상 a fiery temper // 쾌활한 기상의 사람 a man of cheerful disposition // 독립적〔진취적〕 기상 an independent〔enterprising〕 spirit

기상 氣相 [기체 모양] gaseity ¶ 기상의 gaseous ; in gaseous form
— 인화(燐化) 수소 phosphin(e)

기상 起床 rising (in the morning) —하다 rise ; get up ; roll out 《미·속》
—벨 a getting-up bell ; a bell for rising — 시간 the hour of rising ; the turnout

기상 奇想 a fantastic idea ; a fanciful notion ; a clever idea ; a conceit ¶ 기상천외의 most fantastic // 그것은 기상천외의 생각이다 It is a most unexpected idea.
—곡 a capriccio 《*pl.* ~s》 《미》 ; a caprice

기상 機上 ¶ 기상에 오르다 get on〔board〕 an airplane // 기상에서 내려다보다 look down from an airplane 《over a city》

기상 관측 氣象觀測 (a) meteorological〔weather〕 observation ; a weather survey ¶ 기상 관측을 하다 make meteorological observations
—기 a weather research craft —선 a weather ship —용 기구 a sounding balloon

기상 나팔 起床喇叭 the reveille ; the morning bugle ; 〖군사〗 the rouse 《영》 ¶ 기상 나팔을 불다 sound〔blow〕 the reveille

기상 통보 氣象通報 weather news ; a weather report〔bulletin〕 ¶ 호남 지방에 관한 기상 통보 a bulletin on weather conditions as they affect *Honam*

기상학 氣象學 meteorology ; aerology (고층의) ¶ 기상학적〔상의〕 meteorological
—자 a meteorologist ; a weather expert ; a weatherman 미(微)〔거(巨)〕— micrometeorology〔macrometeorology〕 총관(總觀)〔이론(理論)〕 — synoptic〔theoretical〕 meteorology

기색 氣色 a look ; a countenance ; (facial) expression ; [기분] mood ; humor ; feeling ¶ 기색이 좋다 look good〔well〕 // 기색이 나쁘다 look unwell〔out of sorts〕 // 기색이 변하다 change color〔countenance〕 // 기색을 살피다 read 《a person's》 face ; study the pleasure of 《a person》 // 불안한 기색을 하다 look uneasy〔anxious〕 // 기뻐하는 기색이 나타났다 A look of pleasure came to her

기상 · 기후

① 기상관측 (meteorological observation)

기상레이더 weather [meteorological] radar / 기상위성 weather [meteorological] satellite / 기상현상 weather phenomenon
기상대 meteorological observatory / 관측소 weather station / 기상청 Meteorological Agency
기상예보 weather forecast [report] / 기상예보관 weatherman; forecaster / 기상정보 (공식 발표된) weather bulletin; (관측자료) weather data
기상경보 weather warning / 기상주의보 weather advisory / 홍수경보 flood warning / 호우경보 heavy rain warning / 해일경보 tidal wave warning
한란계 thermometer / 기압계 barometer / 풍속계 anemometer / 풍향계 weather vane; weathercock / 건습계 psychrometer / 백엽상 instrumental screen / 기압 air pressure / 풍속 wind velocity / 강우량 (the amount of) rainfall; precipitation / 인공강우 rainmaking, artificial rain / 연강우량 annual precipitation / 연적설량 annaual snowfall / 불쾌지수 temperature-humidity index (〖略〗 T.H.I.); discomfort index

② 기후 (climate)

열대 tropical zone / 한대 frigid zone / 아열대 subarctic zone (북극쪽); subantarctic zone (남극쪽) / 온대 temperate zone
대륙성 기후 continental climate / 해양성 기후 oceanic climate / 고산 기후 alpine climate / 건계 dry season
장마 rainy season / 계절풍 seasonal wind / 몬순 monsoon / 무역풍 trade wind / 태풍 typhoon / 국지풍 local wind / 선풍(旋風) tornado
열대성 저기압 cyclone《인도양 방면의》/ 폭풍설 blizzard / 허리케인 hurricane《대서양 서부에서 발생하는 풍속 74마일 이상의》/ 미스트랄 mistral《프랑스 남부의 건조하고 차가운 북풍》/ 시로코 sirocco《사하라 사막에서 지중해 쪽으로 부는 모래섞인 바람》

③ 일기예보의 표현

내일 날씨는 흐린 날씨에 때에 따라 비가 오겠습니다. The outlook for tomorrow is for cloudy skies with intermittent rain. (★ sky는 복수형으로 쓰는 것이 보통. 맑은 하늘은 fair [clear; sunny] skies, 때로 흐림은 occasionally cloudy skies로 한다.) // 오늘은 하루종일 비가 오다가 밤부터 북서풍을 동반한 맑은 날씨가 되겠습니다. Today we'll have rain during the day, and the fair skies toward night with Northwest winds. // 내일 최고 기온은 20도, 최저 기온은 5도가 되겠습니다. Tomorrow's high will be 20°C, and the low, 5°C. (★ The expected temperatures (for) tomorrow will range between a high of 20°C and a low of 5°C. 라고도 표현할 수 있다.) // 기상예보에 의하면 제주지방은 오늘 대체로 맑고 따뜻할 것이라고 합니다. The weather report [weatherman] says that for the Cheju district today, the weather will be generally fair [clear] and mild. // 서울은 부분적으로 구름이 끼겠으나 따뜻하겠습니다. In Seoul, it will be partly cloudy but warm.

His face did not show any emotion. /His countenance betrayed nothing. // 기색으로 보아 그가 성난 것을 알았다 I read anger in his countenance.

기색 基色 the three primary colors ⇨ 원색

기생 妓生 a *kisaeng* (-girl) ; a singing and dancing girl ¶ 기생집 a *kisaeng* house // 기생을 부르다 call in a *kisaeng* **각관 기생 열녀되랴** 〔속담〕 Once a devil, always a devil. /Once a knave, and ever a knave.

기생 氣生 ¶ 기생의 aerial
— 식물 an aerial plant ; an aerophyte

기생 寄生 parasitism **—하다** be parasitic 《on》; live upon ; be a parasite 《on》
—근(根) a parasitic root ; a haustorium 《*pl.* -ria》 **— 동물** a parasite ; an inquiline ; a guest ; a parasitic animal **— 미생물** a microparasite **— 상태** 〖병리〗 parasitism **—음** a parasitic sound ; a parasite **— 전류(電流)** a parasitic (current) **— 화산(火山)** a parasitic volcano ; a parasitic cone ; a new volcanic hump **공(共)—** 〖생물〗 symparasitism **이종(異種) —** heteroecism **일시 —** temporary parasitism

기생물 寄生物 a parasite
—학자 a parasitologist

기생 식물 寄生植物 a parasitic plant ; a

내부 — an endophyte
기생체 寄生體 a parasite
—학(學) 〚동물·식물〛 parasitology 내부(內部) — an endoparasite 외부 — an ectoparasite
*기생충 寄生蟲 a parasite ; a parasitic insect〔worm〕; vermin (집합적) ¶ 사회의 기생충 a parasite living off the community // 기생충이 끓다 [숙주가 주어] get (parasitic) worms ; verminate
— 구제제 a parasiticide —병 〚병리〛 helminthiasis ; vermination ; worms — 보유자 a parasite carrier —학 parasitology ; helminthology (장내) 식물 — insect (parasitic) on a plant ; [수목의] a parasite on a tree 장내 — an intestinal worm ; a helminth 진정 — an obligate parasite 체내 — an entozoon 《pl. -zoa》; an endoparasite 체외 — an epizoon 《pl. -zoa》; an ectozoon 《pl. -zoa》
기서 奇書 a rare〔strange〕 book
기서 寄書 [편지] sending a letter ; [기고] a contribution —하다 [편지를] send a letter ; write to 《a person》; [기고하다] contribute to ; write for
기석 碁石 a *paduk* stone〔piece〕
⁑기선 汽船 a steamship ; a steamer ; a steamboat ; an ocean liner (대양 항로의) ¶ 미국행 기선 a liner for〔to〕 America // 인천에 입항한 기선의 톤수 the tonnage of steamshipping that entered *Inchon* // 기선을 타다 take a steamer // 기선으로 가다 go by steamer
— 회사 a steamship company 정기 — a regular liner ; a steam packet
기선 基線 〚측량〛 the basic line
기선 機先 taking the initiative ; forestalling
기선을 잡다 관용 forestall 《a person》; steal a march on 《a person》; beat 《a person》 to the punch 《미·속》
기선을 꺾다 관용 damp 《a person's》 ardor
기선 機船 a motor boat
기설 旣設 ¶ 기설의 existing ; established // 기설 설비를 이용하다 utilize the existing facilities
—선 lines in operation
기성 氣盛 high spirits〔morale〕; vigor —하다 be in high spirits ; be full of energy〔vigor〕; be full of life
기성 旣成 —하다 be in existence ; be already established ¶ 기성의 accomplished ; existing (현존의) ; ready-made ; established
— 개념 a preconceived idea — 관념 ready-made ideas — 교리 accepted tenets — 도덕 the established moral principles — 문단 the existing literary circle — 시가지 a built-up area — 작가 a writer of established fame ; an established〔a well-known〕 writer〔author〕; a writer of standing —화(靴) ready-made shoes
기성 期成 resolution to carry out 《a plan》 —하다 determine to bring 《a plan》 to success ; resolve to carry out 《a plan》
기성 奇聲 a peculiar〔queer, weird〕 voice ¶ 기성을 발하다 raise a queer voice
⁑기성복 旣成服 ready-made clothes ; a ready-made suit ; store(-bought) clothes 《미》; hand-me-downs ; reach-me-downs 《영》; slops (값이 싼 것) ¶ 기성복을 사다 buy 《a suit》 off the peg
—점 a ready-made shop ; a slopshop (값이 싼)
기성암 基性岩 〚지질〛 basic rocks
기성 작용 氣成作用 〚지질〛 pneumatolysis
⁑기성품 旣成品 manufactured goods ; ready-made articles〔goods〕 in stock
기성회 期成會 an association for the realization of a plan ; an action committee
†기세 氣勢 spirit ; vigor ; ardor ; [형세] a position ; a situation ¶ 무서운 기세 a threatening attitude ; an angry look // 기세가 올라가다 be in high spirits // 기세를 올리다 arouse one's enthusiasm ; show one's nerve // 기세를 꺾다 dispirit ; discourage ; throw a wet blanket on // 기세가 죽다 be in low spirits ; be depressed // 기세가 좋지 못하다 be in an unfavorable position // 그는 무서운 기세로 나에게 대들었다 He turned on me with an angry look.
기세 棄世 —하다 [죽다] pass away ; die ; [세상을 버리다] isolate oneself from the world ; stand aloof from the world ; reject the world
기세양난 其勢兩難 a predicament ; a dilemma —하다 be in a dilemma ; find oneself between two fires
*기소 起訴 prosecution ; indictment ; legal proceeding (민사상의) —하다 [검사가] prosecute〔indict〕 《a person for》; proceed 《against》; charge 《a person with a crime》; [민간인이] bring an action 《against》; take legal proceedings 《against》; bring in an indictment ; have the law 《on a person》; institute an action ; go to law 《with》 ¶ 불기소 처분 a disposition not to institute a public action // 기소되다 be under indictment // 살인죄로 기소하다 indict 《a person》 for murder // 법률 위반으로 기소하다 prosecute 《a person》 for the violation of the laws
— 각하 dismissal of an indictment —자 a prosecutor ; an indictor
기소 유예 起訴猶豫 〚법〛 suspension of indictment ; stay of prosecution —하

다 dispense with a public action ; shelve an indictment ; drop a case 《구》 ¶ 기소 유예가 되다 have one's indictment suspended

기소장 起訴狀 〖법〗 an indictment ; a written indictment ; an information ¶ 기소장을 부인하다 ignore the bill (불기소로 하다)

기송 氣送 [우편의] pneumatic dispatch
—관 a pneumatic tube〔carrier〕; a dispatch tube

기송 記誦 recitation —하다 recite from memory

기송 寄送 sending ; forwarding ; remittance —하다 send ; forward ; remit

기수 技手 an assistant engineer〔technician〕

*기수 奇數 an odd〔uneven〕 number ¶ 기수의 날짜 odd(-numbered) days

기수 氣數 fate ; destiny ; luck ; fortune

기수 基數 a cardinal〔simple〕 number

기수 旗手 a standard-bearer ; an ensign (군대의)
연대 — a bearer of the regimental colors

기수 機首 the nose of an airplane ¶ 기수를 서울로 돌리다 nose one's plane for *Seoul*
— 차륜(車輪) a nosewheel

기수 騎手 a rider ; a horseman ; a jockey (경마의)

기수 旣遂 consummation ; completion ¶ 기수의 consummated ; perpetrated
—범 a consummated crime

기수법 記數法 (the scale of) notation

*기숙 寄宿 lodging ; boarding ; board and lodging —하다 lodge〔board〕《at, with》; take up one's lodgings 《in》 ¶ 삼촌 집에 기숙하다 lodge at one's uncle's // 기숙료를 지불하다 pay for one's board〔lodgings〕
—생 a boarding〔resident〕 student ; a boarder —인 a boarder ; a lodger — 제도 학교 a boarding school

*기숙사 寄宿舍 a boarding house ; a residence hall ; [학교 기숙사] a hostel (대학의) ; a house ; a dormitory ; a dorm 《구》 ¶ 기숙사 생활을 하다 live in a dormitory // 우리 학교에는 기숙사가 있다 Our school has boarding houses attached to it.
— 관리인 a dormitory manager〔supervisor〕; a proctor ; a superintendent of a dormitory —비 boarding expenses — (여자) 사감 a (lady) superintendent of a dormitory ; a dormitory inspector

†기술 技術 art ; technique ; [기량] ability ; skill ; [과학·공업의] (a) technology ; (technical) know-how 《미》; [학과목] manual training ¶ 기술상의 technical // 기술적으로 technically // 기술상의 곤란 a technical difficulty // 기술의 진보 technical improvement // 그것은 기술적으로 불가능하다 It is technically impossible. // 그것은 전문적인 기술을 필요로 한다 It requires technical skill. // 밥을 짓는 것도 일종의 기술이다 There is art in cooking rice.
— 감사(監査) technical supervision — 개발 technical development — 격차 disparity in technique — 고문 a technical adviser — 도입 introduction of know-how〔technology〕 — 수준 the level of one's skill〔technique〕; a technological level ; the standard of 《Korea's》 technology — 수출 export of know-how〔technology〕 — 원조 a technical aid ; technological assistance —자 a technical expert ; a technician ; an engineer — (전문)어 technical terms — 정보 technical know-how — 직원 a technical employee — 집약 산업 a technology-intensive industry — 축적 the accumulation of technology〔industrial know-how〕 — 혁신 technical 〔technological〕 innovation〔revolution〕 — 협력〔제휴〕 technical tie-up 〔cooperation〕 생산 — manufacturing technology 첨단〔최신〕 — up-to-date-technology

기술 奇術 conjuring tricks ; jugglery ; magic ¶ 기술을 부리다 juggle ; play conjuring tricks ; perform a sleight-of-hand tricks
—사 a juggler ; a conjurer ; a magician

기술 記術 description ; an account —하다 describe ; give an account 《of》 ¶ 기술적 descriptive // 기술적 문법 descriptive grammar // 기술하기 어렵다 be beyond description
— 천문학 descriptive astronomy —체 a descriptive style

기스락 the edge (of the eaves) ¶ 기스락물 eavesdrop

기슭 the edge ; the foot ; the base ; the border ; the corner ¶ 강 기슭 the edge 〔brink〕 of a river // 산 기슭 the foot of a mountain // 처맛기슭 the eaves of a roof // 한쪽 기슭에 서다 stand in a corner

기습 奇習 a strange〔rare〕 custom〔habit〕

기습 奇襲 a surprise〔treacherous〕 attack ; a sudden raid〔attack〕 —하다 make a surprise attack〔raid〕; surprise ; take 《a town》 by surprise
— 방지 위성 an early-warning satellite — 부대 〖군사〗 shock troops ; a surprise party ; commandos ; storm troops (특히 나치스의) ; a raiding force —전 a surprise attack〔raid〕; guerrilla warfare

기습 氣習 manners ; customs ; practices

기승 奇勝 a place of scenic beauty ; a beauty spot ¶ 천하의 기승이다 be a place of rare scenic beauty

기승 氣勝 an unyielding spirit ; strong-mindedness —부리다〔하다〕 (be)

unyielding ; unbending ; spirited ; strong-minded ; brave ¶ 기승한 여자 a woman of spirit ; a strong-minded 〔-hearted〕 woman

기승전결 起承轉結 [한시의] introduction, development, turn and conclusion

기식 氣息 breath ; breathing ¶ 기식엄엄하다 gasp for breath ; be at one's last gasp ; be at death's door

기식 寄食 boarding and lodging **—하다** live〔sponge〕 on ; hang on ; be a parasite to

—자 a hanger-on ; a sponger ; a parasite

기신 起身 [일어남] rising〔getting〕 to one's feet ; standing ; moving ; stirring ; [관계를 끊음] withdrawal ; secession **—하다** stand〔get〕 up ; rise〔get〕 to one's feet ; move ; stir ; [관계를 끊다] secede 〔withdraw〕 from ; break away from

기신거리다 move limply ; stir languidly ¶ 기신기신 languidly ; sluggishly ; wearily ; listlessly

기신없다 氣神— [서술적] have not the heart 《to do》 ; be in low spirits ; be out of energy〔spirits〕

기신호 旗信號 flag signaling ; flag-wagging ¶ 기신호를 하다 signal with a flag // 기신호를 올리다 raise〔hoist, put up〕 a signal

기실 其實 [그 사실] the fact ; the truth ; [사실상] really ; as a matter of fact ; to tell the truth ⇨ 사실

기심 欺心 —하다 deceive oneself ; do violence to one's conscience

기쓰다 氣— put forth all one's strength ; do one's best ; exert oneself to the utmost ¶ 기써서 일하다 work with all one's might ; work to the best of one's ability // 기써서 달려들다 tackle with all one's strength ; grapple with 《a person》 desperately // 기써 고함지르다 shout at the top of one's voice

기아 棄兒 abandoning a child ; [버린 아이] an abandoned child ; a deserted child **—하다** abandon〔desert〕 a child

***기아 饑餓** hunger ; starvation ¶ 기아에 허덕이다 be at the point of starvation ; face starvation // 기아로 고통을 받다 suffer from hunger // 많은 사람들이 기아에 처해 있다 Many people are starving. // 그의 현재의 수입은 겨우 기아를 면할 정도이다 His present earnings are barely sufficient to keep the wolf from the door.

— 동맹 파업 a hunger strike **—선** the verge of starvation **— 임금** starvation wages **— 행진** a hunger march

기악 器樂 〖음악〗 instrumental music

—부 instrumental parts **— 연주가** an instrumentalist ; an instrumental musician **— 편성법** instrumentation

기안 起案 drafting **—하다** draft ; draw up in written form ¶ 법률을 기안하다 draft〔draw up〕 a bill

기안자 起案者 a drafter

기암 奇岩 a curious rock ; fantastic rock

기암 괴석 奇岩怪石 fantastic rocks and stones

기압 汽壓 steam pressure

—계(計) a steam gauge

기압 氣壓 atmospheric〔air〕 pressure ¶ 기압 관계로 owing to atmospheric conditions // 제주도 남방 해상에는 980 밀리바의 저기압이 있다 There is a low pressure of 980 millibars over the sea south of *Chejudo*.

— 경도(傾度) a pressure〔barometric〕 gradient **— 급수 탱크** a pneumatic pressure tank **— 기록** a barogram **— 단위** atmosphere **— 배치** the distribution of atmospheric pressure **— 측정기** 〖항공〗 a variometer **— 측정법** barometry **고〔저〕—** high〔low〕 atmospheric pressure ; barometric maximum〔minimum〕 **절대 —** absolute atmosphere

‡**기압계 氣壓計** a barometer ; a manometer ; a baroscope ; an air gauge

—시도(示度) barometric height **미(微)—** a statoscope **아네로이드 —** an aneroid (barometer) **자기(自記) —** a barograph

기압골 氣壓— a trough of atmospheric pressure ; a low pressure trough

기약 期約 promise ; pledge ; appointment ; engagement **—하다** promise ; pledge ¶ 우리는 재회를 기약하고 헤어졌다 We parted, pledging to meet again. // 내주말 그녀와 만날 기약이 있다 I have a date with her next weekend.

기약 氣弱 —하다 (be) faint-hearted ; timid ; timorous

기약 분수 旣約分數 〖수학〗 a simple〔an irreducible〕 fraction

†**기어** a gear ; gears ¶ 기어를 넣다 put 〔set, throw〕 《the car》 into gear ; engage the gears ; let in one's gears ; thrust the gear lever 《영》 // 기어를 바꾸다 [고속으로] gear〔change〕 up ; [저속으로] gear〔change〕 down

감속 — a reduction gear **후진 —** reverse (gear)

기어 奇語 flowery language ; flourishes ; flattery ; fair words

‡**기어오르다** ① [기어서 높은 곳으로 가다] climb〔shin〕 (up) 《a tree》 ; claw one's way up 《a cliff》 ; scramble (up) ; clamber (over, up) ; crawl〔creep〕 up ¶ 가파른 경사면을 기어오르다 clamber up the steep slope ; work one's way up the steep slope // 그는 바위 산을 기어올랐다 He scrambled〔climbed〕 up the rocky mountain. ② [버릇없이 굴다] presume on ; take liberties 《with》 ; be overfamiliar 《with》 ¶ 친절히 대해 주면

기어오른다 have one's kindness taken advantage of

*기어이 期於— by all means ; by heaven and earth ; whatever may happen ; under any circumstances ¶ 이 일은 기어이 성취하고 말겠다 Nothing shall hinder me from accomplishing my purpose. // 그는 기어이 성공하고 말 것이다 He is sure to succeed in the end. // 그들은 만나면 기어이 싸우고야 만다 They never meet without quarreling.

기어코 期於— ⇨ 기어이

†기억 記憶 memory ; mind ; memorization ; remembrance ; recollection (회상) **—하다** remember ; bear in mind ; remain〔live〕 in one's memory ; commit 《a thing》 to memory ; [회상하다] recollect ; recall ; [암기하다] memorize ; learn〔get〕 by heart ¶ 확실〔불확실〕한 기억 an unfailing〔a treacherous〕 memory // 기억할 만한 memorable 《day》 // 내 기억에 착오가 없다면 if my memory serves ; if I remember right // 기억도 새로운데 while memory is green // 나의 기억으로는 as far as I can remember // 기억을 상실하다 lose one's memory // 기억을 되살리다 bring back one's memory // 똑똑히〔어렴풋이〕 기억하고 있다 have a clear〔dim〕 recollection of ; remember clearly〔vaguely〕 // 기억력이 좋다 have a good〔retentive〕 memory // 기억력이 나쁘다 have a bad〔poor, short〕 memory // 기억을 더듬다 trace back in memory // 기억에 남다 remain〔linger〕 in one's memory // 기억을 불러일으키다 call to mind ; recall to one's mind ; recollect // 나는 확실히 기억하고 있다 I remember it clearly. /I have a clear recollection of it. // 그는 아주 기억력이 없다 He has a memory like sieve. // 그를 한 번 만난 것을 기억하고 있다 I remember seeing him once. // 그것은 기억에 새로운 일이다 It is fresh in our memory. // 결국 그 사건은 사람들의 기억에서 사라져 갔다 Eventually the event vanished〔slipped〕 from memory. / Eventually the event was forgotten. // 이것만은 기억해 두십시오 Never forget this. / Be sure to keep this in mind.

—법 a mnemonic system **— 소자** a storage cell〔element〕 **—술** the art of memory ; artificial memory ; mnemonics **— 장애** defects of memory **— 착오** 〖심리〗 paramnesia ; illusion of memory

*기억력 記憶力 (one's powers of) memory ; the retentive faculty ¶ 놀랄 만한 기억력 splendid〔marvelous〕 memory // 기억력이 좋다〔나쁘다〕 have a good〔poor〕 memory

— 감퇴 failure of one's memory **— 이상 증진(異常增進)** 〖의학〗 hypermnesia

기억 상실 記憶喪失 loss of memory ; 《have》 a memory blackout

—증 〖의학〗 amnesia **—증 환자** an amnesiac ⇨ 건망증

기억 장치 記憶裝置 [전자 계산기의] memory tubes ; memory bank ; memory storage

전자 — an electronic memory machine ; a ticketer **주—** a main storage unit ; a main memory unit

기언 奇言 a paradox ; a puzzle ; a sophism ; a bit of sophistry ¶ 기언을 지껄이다 be paradoxical ; be sophistic

기엄기엄 crawling 《along》 ; creeping 《up, down, about》 ; on hands and knees ¶ 산꼭대기에 기엄기엄 기어오르다 climb up to the top of a mountain on hands and knees

‡기업 企業 an enterprise ; an undertaking ; a business ¶ 기업의 합리화 rationalization of enterprises // 기업화하다 produce 《it》 on a commercial basis ; industrialize // 기업을 일으키다 set up a business ; go into business

— 공채 an industrial loan **— 광고** corporate advertising **—농** market farming **— 연합** a cartel **—열** a mania for enterprise ; industrial fever **— 이미지 통합 전략** corporate identity 《C. I》 **— 정비** industrial readjustment ; business reorganization **— 조합** a syndicate **— 진단** management consulting **— 진단원** a business consultant **— 체질 개선** improvement of industrial structure **— 합동** a trust ; a combine (미·구) **— 합리화** rationalization of enterprises **— 합병** amalgamation ; an industrial merger **— 형태** a type〔form〕 of (business) enterprise **대—** a large enterprise〔corporation, company〕 **복합 —체** a conglomerate (corporation〔company〕) **부실 —(체)** an insolvent〔an improperly-run〕 enterprize **중소 —** smaller business ; small and medium-sized enterprises

기업 起業 promotion (of an enterprise) ; organization **—하다** start an enterprise ; promote〔organize〕 an undertaking

— 공채 an industrial loan **—비(費)** initial expenses

기업 機業 the weaving〔textile〕 industry

—가 a textile manufacturer〔man〕 **—지(地)** a weaving center〔district〕

기업가 企業家 an enterpriser ; a man of enterprise ; an enterprising man ; an industrialist ; a captain of industry ¶ 기업가적인 entrepreneurial

소〔대〕— a small-〔big-〕business man

-기에 ① [···하는데, 하느라고] for〔in, by, from〕 doing ; to do ¶ 일하기에 바쁘다 be busy at work // 준비하기에 간단하다 be simple to prepare // 다루기에 편하다 be simple to handle // 아직 자기에는 이르다 It's too early to go to bed.

② […(하)기 때문에] as ; because ¶ 책이 싸기에 한 권을 샀다 As the book was cheap, I bought a copy. // 지배인이 외출중이었기에 전갈을 비서에게 부탁하고 왔다 The manager was out, so I left a message with his secretary.

-기에는 for〔in, by, from〕 doing ¶ 내가 보기에는 the way I see it ; [내 생각에는] in my opinion // 다른 사람 보기에는 the way others look at it

-기에 망정이지 fortunately... otherwise ; it is fortunate that... ; only owing to〔because of〕 ¶ 일찍 돌아왔기에 망정이지 하마터면 비를 맞을 뻔했다 If we had not returned early, we would have been caught in the rain. // 돈이 있었기에 망정이지 아니면 창피당할 뻔했다 It was good that I had money with me, otherwise I would have been put to shame.

기여 其餘 the rest ; the remainder

기여 寄與 contribution ; service **—하다** contribute 《to》 ; be conducive 《to》 ; add (much) to ¶ 문명에 기여한 바가 없다 It has contributed in no way to civilization. // 그 문제 해결에 기여할 것이다 It will go far toward solving the problem.

기역 name of the first letter of the Korean alphabet
낫 놓고 기역자도 모른다 〔속담〕 do not know A from B〔one letter from another〕 ; be completely illiterate

기역니은순 —順 Korean alphabetical order ⇨ 가나다

기역시 其亦是 that too ; also ; as well ; likewise ¶ 기역시 좋다 That is also good.

기연 奇緣 a strange fate〔chance〕 ; a curious coincidence ; an irony of fate ¶ 이렇게 만나다니 참 기연이다 What a strange chance it is that has brought us together !

기연 機緣 [기회] chance ; opportunity ; occasion ; [인연] relation ¶ 이것을 기연으로 taking this opportunity // 이것이 기연으로 두 사람은 친밀해졌다 This led them to an intimate friendship.

기연미연하다 其然未然— (be) ambiguous ; confusing ; uncertain

기연히 期然— for sure ; by any means ; in any case ; without fail ; whatever may happen

기염 氣焰 [기세] high spirits ; enthusiasm ; [큰소리] tall〔big〕 talk ; bombast ¶ 기염을 토하다 talk big〔tall〕 ; blow off steam ; blow hot air 《미·속》
—만장 full of spirits〔enthusiasm〕 ; a very big talk

기영 機影 the sight of an airplane

기예 技藝 arts ; [수예] handicrafts ; [예능] accomplishments
—가 an artist **— 학교** a craft school ; a technical〔polytechnic〕 school ; a practical arts school

기예 氣銳 impetuousness ; spiritedness **—하다** (be) spirited ; energetic ; active ; impetuous ¶ 신진 기예의 young and energetic ; up-and-coming 《미》

기온 氣溫 temperature ¶ 기온의 급상승〔급강하〕 a sudden rise〔fall〕 in temperature // 기온의 변화 a change of temperature // 기온이 오르다〔내리다〕 The temperature rises〔falls〕.
— 경도(傾度) 〖기상〗 a temperature gradient **— 조절(調節)** air conditioning **— 체감률(遞減率)** 〖기상〗 lapse rate **— 파** temperature waves **평균 —** the average temperature

⁑기와 a tile ¶ 기와 굽는 가마 a tile-kiln // 기와 굽는 사람 a tile manufacturer ; a tiler // 기와 얹은 담 a tile-capped wall // 기와로 지붕을 이다 roof 《a house》 with tiles ; tile a roof
— 공장 a tilery **— 이기** tile-roofing ; roof-tiling **—장이** a tiler ; a tile-layer **— 지붕** a tiled roof **기왓고랑** a furrow in a tiled roof **기왓장** a tile **용마루 —** a ridge〔crest〕 tile **평(平)—** a plain〔flat〕 tile
기와 한 장 아끼려다 대들보 썩힌다 〔속담〕 To spoil〔lose〕 the ship〔sheep, ewe, hog〕 for a half penny worth of tar.

기와 起臥 one's daily life **—하다** get up and lie down ¶ 기와를 같이하다 live together under the same roof

기와집 a tile-roofed house

기왕 旣往 the past ; bygones ; [부사적] already ; since ¶ 기왕의 past ; bygone // 기왕이면 if it is done ; if it has already happened // 기왕의 일은 묻지 말자 Let bygones be bygones. // 기왕 늦었으니 자고 가자 Let's sleep here as it is already late.

기왕증 旣往症 [질병] a disease which one had in the past ; a previous illness ; [병력] the medical history 《of a patient》 ; a case history ; 〖의학〗 an anamnesis 《*pl.* -ses》 (기왕력)

기외 其外 the rest ; the others ; [부사적] besides ; else ; moreover ; further ; in addition ¶ 기외의 많은 나라들 many other countries // 기외에 할 일이 별로 없었다 Little else remained to be done. // 기외의 것은 말할 것도 없다 The rest needs no telling.

기요 起擾 —하다 raise a disturbance ; start a riot

기용 起用 appointment ; employment **—하다** appoint ; promote ¶ A씨가 그 직책에 기용될 것이다 Mr. A will be appointed to the post.

기우 杞憂 unfounded〔groundless, imaginary〕 fears〔apprehensions〕 ; baseless anxiety ¶ 그것은 기우에 지나지 않는다 His fears are groundless〔unfound-

ed〕./He is troubling himself unnecessarily. // 그것은 기우로 그쳤다 The apprehensions proved unnecessary. // 나의 기우가 현실화되었다 My apprehensions were realized.
—가 an alarmist
기우 奇遇 a chance〔strange〕 meeting ; a strange encounter **—하다** meet by chance ; meet unexpectedly ¶ 우리들의 해후는 정말 기우였다 Our meeting was a mere chance.
기우 祈雨 praying for rain **—하다** pray 〔offer prayers〕 for rain
기우 寄寓 **—하다** live with ; lodge 〔stay〕 with ; make one's home with 《a person》 ¶ 우리 집에 기우하고 있다 He lives with us.
—자 a lodger ; a paying guest
기우 氣宇 large-mindedness ; magnanimity
기우듬하다, 끼우듬하다 (be) somewhat slanting〔aslant, oblique〕; slant ; be inclined a little ¶ 기우듬히 aslant ; slantwise ; obliquely // 기우듬하게 하다 slant ; lean // 기우듬하게 베다 cut off aslant〔obliquely〕 // 오른쪽으로 기우듬하다 have a tilt to the right // 동쪽으로 기우듬하다 leans to the east // 저 그림은 왼쪽으로 기우듬하다 That picture slants to the left. // 피사의 사탑은 한쪽으로 기우듬하다 The Leaning Tower of Pisa is leaning to one side.
기우뚱거리다, 끼우뚱거리다 rock ; totter ; shake ; roll ; sway from side to side ¶ 기우뚱기우뚱 totteringly ; shakily // 몸을 기우뚱거리다 sway one's body // 기우뚱거리며 걷다 walk along swaying one's body // 의자가 기우뚱거린다 A chair is rocking. // 배가 기우뚱거린다 A boat is rolling〔rocking〕. // 버스가 기우뚱거린다 A bus is swaying〔joggling〕. // 차가 몹시 기우뚱거렸다 The car received a tremendous jolting.
기우제 祈雨祭 a shamanist service to pray for rain ; a ritual (praying) for rain
***기운** ① [힘] strength ; force ; might ; energy ; power ¶ 기운이 센 strong ; mighty ; energetic ; powerful // 기운 없는 weak ; of little strength ; spiritless ; depressed ; feeble // 기운을 다해서 with all one's might // 기운만으로 by sheer strength alone // 기운이 나다 gain in strength ; feel strong // 기운을 내다 put forth〔out〕 one's strength // 기운이 빠지다 be spent up ; be exhausted ; one's strength is gone // 기운차다 be full of life ; be high-spirited // 그는 기운이 아주 세다 He is as strong as a horse./ He is of Herculean strength. // 그는 쇠약해져서 걸어다닐 기운도 없었다 He was so weak that he had not the strength to walk.
② [원기] vigor ; cheerfulness ; spirit ; courage ; vitality ; energy ; life ; get-up-and-go ; pep 《속》 ¶ 기운 있는 cheerful ; vigorous ; energetic ; [노인이] spry ; hale and sturdy // 헛기운 a show of courage ; lion's skin // 기운이 없는 cheerless ; downhearted ; dejected ; crestfallen // 기운을 잃지 않고 without being discouraged ; hopefully // 기운이 있다 be going strong // 기운이 없다 be in low spirits ; be off color ; be disheartened // 기운을 내다 take courage 〔heart〕; pluck〔muster〕 up courage ; buck up // 기운을 회복하다 recover one's strength ; be refreshed // 기운을 잃다 lose heart ; be discouraged // 기운이 왕성하다 be in high spirits // 기운이 넘치다 brim over with good spirits ; be full of vigor〔pep〕 // 기운을 돋우다 buck a person up ; put fight into a person // 그는 이 말에 갑자기 기운이 났다 He was suddenly encouraged by these words./ These words suddenly filled him with new energy. // 커피 한 잔 하면 기운이 날 것이다 A cup of coffee will refresh you./ A cup of coffee will put you in good spirits. // 저 노인은 아직도 기운이 정정하다 The old man still remains hale and hearty〔sturdy〕. // 나는 오늘 기운이 없다 I am feeling low today./I feel mean today. // 기운을 내라 Pull yourself together ! / Don't let yourself get depressed〔discouraged〕! /Cheer up ! /Pep up ! 《미·구》/Show your nerve ! (스포츠에서)/Be of good cheer ! /Perk up ! /Snap out of it ! // 요즘 기운이 없어 보인다 You seem listless lately.
③ [기미] a touch ; a dash ; a tinge ; an air ; a look ; a symptom ; a sign ¶ 독한 기운 poisonous fumes ; a deadly breath // 감기 기운 a touch of cold ; a slight cold // 약 기운 virtue(s) of a medicine // 술 기운에 under the influence of liquor // 불 기운이 있다 show signs of warmth // 그는 오늘 술 기운이 좀 있다 He is a little tipsy today.
기운 氣運 a tendency ; a trend ; the tide ; a movement ¶ …의 기운이 점차 높아지다 there is a growing tendency to 《do》 // 그것이 혁명의 기운을 조성했다 That paved the way for the revolution.
기운 氣韻 [멋] 《artistic, literary》 atmosphere ; elegance ; tone
기운 機運 ① [기회] an opportunity ; the time ② [운] fortune ; luck ③ [경향] a tendency ¶ 기운이 익어가다 the time is ripe for // 드디어 개혁의 기운이 무르익었다 At last the time is ripe for a reform.
기울 bran ; offal
기울다 ① [경사지다] tilt ; incline ; lean ; slant ; list (배가) ; lurch (갑자기) ;

bank (비행기가) ¶ 기울은 inclined ; slant // 탑이 한쪽으로 기울었다 The tower leans to one side. // 배가 좌현으로 기울었다 The ship lists to port. // 그 책상은 잘 기운다 The desk is apt to tilt over.
② [경향이 있다] incline 《to, toward》; lean 《toward》; tend to 《do》; be apt to 《do》 ¶ 사치스러운 방향으로 기울다 be inclined to luxury // 숙명론에 기울다 lean toward fatalism // 국민은 차차로 주전론에 기울어졌다 The people were gradually coming round to jingoism.
③ [쇠하다] decline ; wane ; be reduced ; fall (away) ; ebb ¶ 운이 기울다 be down on one's luck ; one's star is on the wane // 국운이 기울어지고 있다 The national prestige is on the decline. // 그 집은 가세가 기울어지고 있다 Their fortune is waning〔beginning to ebb〕.
④ [해 따위가] decline 《toward》; slant 《toward》; be sinking ; go down ; set ¶ 서쪽에 기운 해 the westering sun // 해가 서쪽에 기울었다 The sun declined toward the west.

기울어뜨리다 tip ; tilt ; lean ; incline ; list ; slant ¶ 병을 기울어뜨리다 tip a bottle

‡**기울어지다** incline ; slant ⇨ 기울다

‡**기울이다** tip ; tilt ; slant ; incline ; lean ; ruin ; [경주하다] devote oneself to ; concentrate 《one's energy, power, etc》 ¶ 고개를 기울이다 incline one's head // 귀를 기울이다 listen to ; give ear to // 술잔을 기울이다 have a drink // 공부에 정신을 기울이다 devote oneself to one's study // 주의를 기울이다 pay attention 《to》 // 연구에 정열을 기울이다 concentrate〔focus〕 one's energies on the research // 재산을 기울이다 squander one's fortune // 나라를 기울이다 ruin one's country // 그것에는 특별한 주의를 기울여야 한다 You should pay special attention to that.

기웃거리다 repeatedly incline〔lean〕; busily crane〔stretch one's neck〕; frequently get a peep 《at》 ¶ 이방 저방 기웃거리다 peek〔snoop〕 around this room and that // 모두 신부를 보려고 고개를 기웃거린다 Everybody is craning to see the bride.

기웃기웃 peeping ; snooping

기웃이 ① [기우듬히] aslant ; slantly ; at a tilt ② [고개를] peeping ; snooping ¶ 빈틈으로 기웃이 들여다보다 peep through a crevice 《in the wall》

기웃하다¹ [형용사] ⇨ 기우듬하다.

기웃하다² incline〔tilt, slant〕 《something》 a little ; put 《a thing》 a little askew ; place 《a thing》 a little out of line ¶ 몸을 왼쪽으로 기웃하다 lean one's body to the left

기원 技員 an assistant engineer〔technician〕

기원 紀元 an era ; an epoch ¶ 서력 기원 1970년 the year 1970 of the Christian era ; 1970 (A. D.) // 서력 기원전 80년 80 B. C. // 신기원을 이룩한 사건 an epochmaking event // 신기원을 이룩하다 make an〔a new〕 epoch

†**기원 祈願** a prayer ; a petition ; supplication **—하다** pray ; supplicate ; petition ; wish ¶ 평화의 기원 a prayer for peace // 병의 회복을 하느님에게 기원하다 pray to God for one's recovery // 꿇어앉아 신에게 기원하다 kneel before God in prayer // 그를 살려달라고 기원했다 I prayed that he might be saved. // 당신의 성공을 기원합니다 I wish you success.
—문 an optative sentence **—자** a supplicant ; a prayer

‡**기원 起源, 起原** origin ; beginning ; genesis **—하다** originate in ; have its origin in ; be stemmed from ; take the rise in ; derive 《its》 origin 《from》 ¶ 지구의 기원 the origin of the earth // 생명의 기원 the beginnings〔origin〕 of life // 종의 기원 The Origin of Species (저서명) // 기원 불명의 of unknown origin // 기원을 캐다 trace 《a thing》 to its origin // 그 기원은 오래다 It is of ancient origin. // 그 풍습의 기원은 봉건시대부터 시작된다 The custom can be traced back to the feudal period. // 그 풍습의 기원은 16세기이다 The custom dates from the sixteenth century.

기월 期月 one full month

기위 旣爲 already ⇨ 이미

기유 己酉 〖민속〗 the 46th binary term of the sexagenary cycle

기율 紀律 order ; discipline

기음 氣音 〖음성〗 an aspirate

기음기 記音器 an oscillograph ; a kymograph

기음매다 ⇨ 김매다

기음 문자 記音文字 phonetic letters

‡**기이 奇異 —하다** (be) strange ; odd ; queer ; singular ; peculiar ; curious ; eccentric ; extraordinary ¶ 기이한 광경 a curious sight // 기이한 행동 an unaccountable action ; eccentric conduct // 기이한 풍속 an odd custom // 기이한 풍설 a strange rumor // 세상에는 기이한 일도 많다 The world is full of mysteries, indeed.

기이다 keep〔hide, conceal〕 《a matter》 from 《a person》; keep 《a matter》 secret 《from》; cover ; veil ¶ 나이를 기이다 conceal one's age ; make a secret of one's age // 사실을 기이다 cover up a fact

기인 奇人 an eccentric person ; a strange person ; a crank ; a queer fish

기인 起因 the cause ; the root **—하다** originate 《in》; have its origin 《in》; arise 《from》; be due to; come from; result from ¶ 일의 기인 the root of the matter // 이 병은 과로에 기인한다 This disease is caused by overwork.

기인 基因 a fundamental cause; the basic origin ―하다 be caused by; have its origin in; be fundamentally 〔basically〕 attributable to

기인 棄人 an abandoned person; a socially rejected person; a disabled person ⇨ 폐인

기일 忌日 an anniversary of 《a person's》 death; the deathday ¶ 조부의 기일 an anniversary of the death of one's grandfather

†기일 期日 the fixed〔given, due〕 date; the appointed day; [기한] a time limit ¶ 시험 기일 the date for the examination // 기일까지는 by the appointed date // 기일을 정하다 fix a date; set a time limit // 기일까지 지불하다 pay 《the bill》 when due // 어음의 지불 기일이 되다 The bill falls due. // 기일을 지키다 keep one's day; be punctual // 기일을 단축하다〔연장하다〕 shorten〔extend〕 the date〔term〕

― 지정 정기예금 a maturity designated deposit

†기입 記入 entry; filling up (용지에); recording ―하다 write 《in》; enter; make an entry 《in》; fill up; register 《미》 ¶ 기입이 끝난 entered // 이름을 기입하다 enter〔fill in〕 one's name; register 《one's name》 《미》 // 장부에 기입하다 make an entry in a book; enter in a book // 용지에 기입하다 fill in a form; fill up a blank 《미》 // 그날 일기에는 아무런 기입도 없었다 There was no entry for the day in his diary. // 이 용지에 기입해 주십시오 Fill this form out, please.

― 누락 an omission ―장 〖부기〗 an entry book

*기자 記者 a writer; a journalist; [신문 기자] a pressman 《영》; a newspaperman 《미》; a reporter (탐방 기자); a correspondent (특파원) ¶ 기자 회견을 하다 meet the press // 그는 동아일보의 기자이다 He is a reporter for the *Dong-A Ilbo*. // 기사의 책임은 기자에 있다 The writer is responsible for wording of the articles. // 그는 기자 생활 20년의 노련한 신문인이다 He is a veteran newspaperman with a 20-year career of journalism.

―단 a press corps; the press association ―석 a press table; a press 〔reporters'〕 gallery (국회의); a press stand (경기장의); a press box (극장·회의장·경기장의) 수습〔올챙이〕 ― a junior reporter; a cub reporter 《미·속》 신문 ―증 a press card 여― a woman〔lady〕 journalist; a newspaperwoman 《미》; a newswoman; a newshen 《속》 외교 ― a diplomatic correspondent; a diplomatic editor; a writer on foreign affairs 잡보(雜報) ― a paragrapher 《미》; a paragraphist 《영》 종군 ― a war correspondent 체육 ― a sports writer〔reporter〕 취재 ― a legman; a legger 탐방 ― a (newspaper) reporter; an interviewer

기자 譏刺 cynicism; a satire; a sarcasm ―하다 satirize; innuendo

기자감식 飢者甘食 Nothing comes amiss to a hungry man. /Hunger is the best sauce.

기자 회견 記者會見 a press interview; a news〔press〕 conference (기자단과의) ¶ 기자 회견을 하다 have〔hold, call〕 a news〔press〕 conference 《with》 // 즉석 기자 회견 an impromptu conference with newsmen

텔레비전 ― a televised news〔press〕 conference

기장¹ length ⇨ 길이

기장² 〖식물〗 millet; Panicum miliaceum (학명)

기장 記章 a badge; an insignia; a medal ¶ 기장을 달다 wear a badge

기장 機長 a plane captain; the crew chief

기장차다 (be) long and straight

‡기장하다 記帳― make an entry 《in》; register; book; [대장에] post up accounts

‡기재 奇才 genius; remarkable talent; a genius (사람) ¶ 문단의 기재 a literary genius

기재 記載 statement; mention; [장부에] entry; [신문에] publication ―하다 state; mention; record; [신문에] print; report; carry; [장부에] enter ¶ 허위 기재 a false entry // 별항에 기재한 바와 같이 as stated〔reported〕 elsewhere // 조간에 기재되어 있다 It is reported〔printed〕 in the morning report. // 그 사항은 장부에 기재되었다 They made an entry of the item in the notebook.

― 누락 an omission ― 사항 mentioned items

기재 機材, 器材 materials; mechanical equipment; machine parts

기저 基底 a base; a basis; a foundation

― 상태 〖물리〗 [원자의] the ground 〔normal〕 state ― 수정(受精) 〖식물〗 basigamy ― 요율 〖화재 보험〗 the basis rate ― 요율표(料率表) the basis schedule ―형 〖언어〗 an underlying form

기저귀 a diaper; a wet napkin; swaddling cloths; clouts ¶ 기저귀를 채우다 diaper 〔put a diaper on〕 the baby

†기적 汽笛 a (steam) whistle; a siren ¶

기적을 울리다 sound〔give, blow〕 a whistle ; whistle // 기적 소리가 울린다 A whistle is sounded. /A whistle blows. // 기차는 건널목으로 오면서 기적을 울렸다 The train whistled at the crossing.

‡기적 奇蹟 a miracle ; a wonder ; a marvel ; a mystery ¶ 기적적 miraculous // 기적적으로 miraculously ; by a miracle ; to a miracle // 기적을 행하다 work〔perform〕 miracles ; do〔work〕 wonders // 기적적으로 살아나다 escape death by a miracle ; have a miraculous escape // 기적이 일어난다 A miracle occurs. // 기적적으로 살았다 God saved us.

—극(劇) [영국 중세의] a miracle play ; a mystery

기전 其前 beforehand ⇨ 그전

기전 起電 〖전기〗 electric generation ; generation of electricity

기전기 起電機 an electric motor

기전력 起電力 electromotive force 《EMF》

역(逆)— counter electromotive force **유기(誘起) —** induced electromotive force

***기절 氣絶** fainting ; a swoon **—하다** faint ; swoon ; lose one's senses〔consciousness〕 ¶ 기절시키다 deprive 《a person》 of his senses ; make 《a person》 insensible // 놀라서 기절할 뻔하다 be frightened out of one's senses〔wits〕 // 기절하여 쓰러지다 fall senseless〔unconscious〕 ; fall〔drop〕 in a faint // 한 대 맞고 기절했다 The blow knocked him senseless. // 그 여자는 아들이 죽었다는 소식을 듣고 거의 기절할 지경이었다 She nearly fainted at the news of her son's death.

기절 氣節 ① [지조] integrity ; principle ; honor ; purpose ; chastity ¶ 기절이 있는 사람 a man of integrity ② [기후] weather ; climate

기점 起點 the starting point ; [도로의] the top ; the head ; [배의] the home port ; [철도의] the terminus ¶ …을 기점으로 하다 start 《from》 // 이 건물을 기점으로 하여 거리를 측정하다 measure the distance with this building as its starting point

기점 基點 cardinal point ¶ 토론의 기점 basic points of discussion

방위(方位) — the cardinal points of the compass

기정 起程 departure ; start **—하다** depart 《on a trip》 ; start ; set out ; leave

기정 旣定 ¶ 기정의 already decided〔settled, fixed〕 ; established // 기정의 결론 a foregone conclusion // 기정의 방침 a prearranged plan // 기정 방침에 따르다 conform to a prearranged program

— 사실 an established〔accomplished〕 fact ; a settled matter **— 세입** established revenue **— 세출** established expenditure **— 예산** the established budget

기정 汽艇 a (steam) launch

기제 忌祭 a memorial service held on an anniversary of 《a person's》 death

기제 旣濟 ¶ 기제의 already finished〔established, settled〕 ; paid-up

기제류 奇蹄類 〖동물〗 Perissodactyla ¶ 기제류의 동물 a perissodactyl

기조 基調 the keynote ; the basis ¶ 재정의 기조 basic financial conditions // 기조를 이루다 form the keynote 《of》

경제 — basic economic condition

기조력 起潮力 the tide generating force

기조 연설 基調演說 [정당의] a keynote address〔speech〕

기존 旣存 ¶ 기존의 existing ; established // 기존의 시설 the existing facilities

기종 氣腫 [의학] emphysema

폐— pulmonary emphysema

기종 機種 kinds〔types〕 of airplanes〔machines〕

기주 嗜酒 love〔fondness〕 for liquor ; a taste for drink **—하다** be fond of liquor〔alcohol〕

***기준 基準** a standard ; a basis ; [규범] a criterion 《*pl.* -ria, ~s》 ; a canon ¶ 취미의 기준 the canons of taste // 새 기준을 정하다 set a new standard 《for》 // 기준에 맞추다 standardize

— 가격 a standard price **—량** a norm ; a standard amount **—면** 〖측량〗 a datum plan〔level〕 ; 〖물리〗 a base level **—선** 〖물리〗 a base〔datum〕 line **— 시세(時勢)** 〖외국환〗 the central rate **— 연도** the basic period〔year〕 **—율(率)** the basic rate **— 임금** standard wages **—점** a datum〔fiducial〕 point

기중 其中 among the rest ; most (가장) ⇨ 그중

기중 忌中 (in) mourning ¶ 기중이다 be in mourning

‡기중기 起重機 a crane ; a derrick ; a hoist ; a jack ¶ 기중기로 들어올리다 crane ; lift 《a thing》 with a crane

고정식 — a stationary crane **수동식 —** a hand operated crane **운반식 —** a portable crane **이동식 —** a travelling crane

기중기선 起重機船 a floating crane

***기증 寄贈** presentation ; contribution ; donation **—하다** present ; contribute ; donate ¶ 상품을 기증하다 donate prizes

—본 a complimentary〔presentation, free〕 copy ; a gift book **—서** a presentation 〔complimentary〕 copy〔given by the author〕 **— 잡지** a gift periodical **—품** a gift ; a donation ; a present

기증자 寄贈者 a contributor ; a donor ; a giver ; a donator

— 명부 a free list (잡지 따위의) 혈액 — a blood donor
기지 奇智 acumen ; rare wisdom
기지 旣知 ¶ 기지의 (already) known ; familiar ; well-known // 기지의 사실 a well-known fact ; an established fact
— 사항 a datum ⟪*pl.* data⟫
†기지 機智 wit ; ready wits ; resources ¶ 기지있는 witty ; tactful ; resourceful ; smart // 기지의 번쩍임 a flash of wit // 기지가 많다 He is keen-〔quick-〕witted. /He is resourceful. /He is a wit.
기지 基地 a base ¶ 무사히 기지에 돌아오다 return safely to the base
—국 a base station — 사령관 a base commanding officer — 협정 a bases agreement 공군 — an air(-force) base 군사 — a military base 연료 보급 — a fueling base 영구 — a permanent base ; an infrastructure 작전 — a base of operations ; an operating base 전초 — a garrison base 중계 — a relay base 해군 — a naval base
기지개 straightening one's back ; stretching oneself ¶ 자고 일어나서 큰 기지개를 한번 켜다 stretch oneself after a sound sleep
기지수 旣知數 a known quantity〔number〕; a datum ⟪*pl.* data⟫
기지촌 基地村 a military campside town
기직 a rough mat ; a coarse straw-mat
기진 氣盡 exhaustion ; (overwhelming) fatigue —하다 be exhausted ; be tired out ; be worn out
— 맥진 complete〔utter〕 exhaustion ¶ 긴 행군으로 군대는 기진 맥진했다 The long march has quite exhausted the troops.
‡기질 氣質 disposition ; temperament ; temper ; nature ¶ 온순한 기질 mild disposition // 학자 기질의 사람 a man of a scholarly turn of mind // 영국 사람 기질 Anglo-Saxonism // 미국 사람 기질 Americanism ; Yankeeism // 기질이 좋은 사람 a good-tempered〔-natured〕 man ; a man of good disposition // 기질이 맞지 않는다는 이유로 이혼 소송을 제기하다 sue for divorce on the ground of incompatibility of temper // 아버지의 기질을 타고나다 inherit one's father's disposition
상인 — the spirit of the tradesman ; mercenary spirit 학생 — the spirit of the student
기질 基質 a stroma ¶ 암의 기질 a cancer stroma
*기차 汽車 a train ; [객차] a railway carriage ; a railroad car ⟪미⟫ ¶ 서울행 기차 a train for *Seoul* // 기차의 발착 시간 train time // 아침 기차 a morning train // 2시 20분발 기차 the 2 : 20 train // 기차로 by train ; by railway ; by rail // 기차를 타다 get on a train ; board a train ⟪미⟫ // 기차에서 내리다 leave〔get off〕 a train ; alight from a train // 기차를 놓치다 miss a train // 기차편으로 보내다 send ⟪a thing⟫ by rail // 기차가 들어오다〔떠나다〕 The train pulls in〔out〕. // 기차가 정시에 도착했다 The train arrived on time.
— 멀미 train sickness — 시간표 a railway timetable schedule — 여행 a railway〔train〕 travel〔journey〕
기차다 氣— be amazed ⟪at⟫ ; stand aghast ⟪at⟫ ; be struck dumb ⟪by⟫ ; be taken aback ; be flabbergasted ; be dumbfounded ; be disgusted ⟪at a person's behavior, with a person⟫ ¶ 기차서 말문이 막히다 be struck dumb with amazement // 어찌 어리석은지 기찰 노릇이다 Your stupidity really beats〔shocks〕 me. // 하도 기차서 서로 얼굴만 마주보았다 We all gazed at each other in blank dismay.
기차 요금 汽車料金 a railroad〔railway〕 fare ¶ 기차 요금을 할인하다 reduce railroad fares ⟪for parties⟫
기차표 汽車票 a (railroad) ticket ¶ 기차표를 끊다 buy a ticket ; punch〔clip〕 a ticket
— 매표소 ticket office ⟪미⟫ ; a booking office ⟪영⟫ — 매표인 a ticket agent ⟪미⟫ ; a booking clerk ⟪영⟫ 왕복 — a return ticket ; a round-trip ticket 편도(片道) — a single ticket ; a one-way ticket ⟪미⟫
기착 寄着 a stopover ; (a) stop-off —하다 stop over〔off〕 ; make a (brief) stop
기찻길 汽車— a railway (line) ⟪영⟫ ; a railroad track ⟪미⟫
기채 起債 floatation of a loan ; a bond issue ; financing —하다 float〔raise〕 a loan ; issue bonds ; finance
— 시장 the capital〔bond〕 market ; the new issue market
기척 a sign ; an indication ; traces ; a hint ¶ 인기척이 있다 There is a sign of somebody present. // 아무도 다녀간 기척이 없다 There is no sign of anyone having been here. // 그 사람 기척도 보이지 않는다 There is no trace of him at all.
기천 氣喘 asthma
기첩 奇捷 an unexpected〔a signal〕 victory
†기체 氣體 gas ; vapor ; a gaseous body ¶ 기체의 gaseous ; aerial ; pneumatic
— 물리학 aerology — 반응의 법칙 〚화학〛 law of gaseous reaction — 역학 aeromechanics ; aerodynamics — 연료 gaseous fuel — 온도계 a gas thermometer — 측정 aerometry —화 vaporization ; gasification ¶ 기체화하다 vaporize ; gasify
기체 機體 a machine ; a plane (비행기

의) ; a fuselage ¶ 비행기의 기체 the body of an airplane // 기체에 고장이 났다 Something went wrong with the machine.
— 수리 공장 a fuselage repair shop
기체후 氣體候 (your) state of health ; the condition of one's health
기초 起草 drafting — 하다 draft ; draw up ¶ 헌법〔법안〕을 기초하다 draw up 〔draft〕 a constitution〔bill〕// 기초 중이다 It is being drafted.
— 위원회 a drafting committee
†기초 基礎 the foundation ; the basis 《*pl.* -ses》 ; the groundwork ¶ 기초적 fundamental ; basic // 문법의 기초 지식 elementary knowledge of grammar // 기초가 없는 groundless ; baseless // …에 기초를 두다 be based〔founded, established〕 on ; base 〔establish〕 《a thing》 on // 기초를 만들다 lay the foundation(s) 《for, of》 // 기초를 공고히 하다 place 《a school》 on a firm 〔solid〕 base // 기초가 되다 form the foundation 〔basis〕 of // 국가의 기초를 위태롭게 하다 undermine the foundation of the State // 공고한 기초 위에 서 있다 It rests on a firm〔solid〕 basis.
— 산업 a basic〔key〕 industry — 영어 the elementary course of English ; a fundamental knowledge of English — 지식 a 《good》 grounding 《in》 ; an elementary 〔basic, fundamental〕 knowledge 《of》 — 학과 the fundamental studies〔courses〕 ; a primary subject (of study) ; a basic subject
기초 공사 基礎工事 foundation work ; ground-making ¶ 기초 공사를 하다 lay the foundation 《of》 // 기초 공사를 단단히 하다 solidify the groundwork 《of》
—용 기계 foundation work equipment
기초 공작 基礎工作 spadework ¶ 기초 공작을 하다 lay the groundwork
기초 공제 基礎控除 basic deduction
기초 대사 基礎代謝 〔생리〕 basal metabolism
—율 a basal metabolic rate 《BMR》
기초 시계 記秒時計 a stop watch
기초자 起草者 a drafter ; a draftsman ¶ 법률 기초자 the sponsor of a law // 평화 조약의 기초자 the architect of the peace treaty // 한국 헌법 기초자의 한 사람 one of the drafters of the Korean Constitution
기초적 基礎的 fundamental ; elementary ; basic ¶ 기초적 요소 the elements 《of》 ; the factors 《of》 // 기초적인 지식 a basic〔fundamental, elementary〕 knowledge 《of》
기총 機銃 a machine gun ⇨ 기관총
— 소사 strafe ; machine-gunning
기축 己丑 〔민속〕 the 26th binary term of the sexagenary cycle
기축 氣縮 discouragement — 하다 be discouraged ; be daunted
기축 機軸 〔중추〕 an axis 《*pl.* -es》 ; an axle ; 〔방안〕 a plan ; a device ; a contrivance ¶ 신기축 a new departure ; a novel contrivance ; a new device // (신)기축을 이루다 make a new departure ; strike out a new line ; introduce a novelty ; give a new twist 《to》 // 상업 선전에 (신)기축을 세우다 devise a new form of commercial propaganda
기축 통화 基軸通貨 key currency
‡기치 旗幟 ① a flag ; an emblem ; a banner ; an ensign ; a pennant ; a standard ; colors (군기) ¶ 기치를 높이 들고 with banners flying // 독립의 기치 아래 under the flag〔banner〕 of independence // 자유의 기치를 내걸고 with "Freedom" as the slogan
② 〔비유적〕 one's attitude〔position〕 ; one's stand ¶ 기치를 선명히 하다 define〔clarify〕 one's attitude〔position〕 ; show one's hand
‡기침 a cough ; coughing — 하다 cough ; have a cough ¶ 마른 기침 a dry cough // 기침약 cough medicine ; a remedy for cough // 연거푸 기침을 하다 have a fit of coughing // 몹시 심한 기침을 하다 have a bad cough // 헛기침하다 clear one's throat // 기침이 그치다 get over one's cough // 기침을 하고 방에 들어섰다 He entered the room with a cough.
기침 起枕 getting up ; rising from the bed ⇨ 기상
기침 감기 —感氣 a cold on the chest 〔lungs〕
‡기타 其他 the others ; the rest ; and others ; and so forth ; and the like ; etc. ¶ 피복 서적 기타 품목 clothes, books, and so forth // 기타 여러 가지 and many other things
기타 a guitar ¶ 기타를 치다 play (on) the guitar
— 연주가 a guitarist
기탁 寄託 deposition ; 〖법〗 bailment — 하다 deposit 《a thing with a person》 ; entrust 《a person with a thing》 ; leave a thing to 《a person's》 care
—금 trust money ; money consigned — 도서 a deposited book —물 a deposit ; a trust ; a thing entrusted ; 〖법〗 goods deposited ; deposited articles —식 the ceremony of depositing the instrument of ratification 《of the Treaty of Peace with Korea》 —자 a depositor ; a truster ; a bailor — 증서 (證書) a deposit certificate
기탄 忌憚 scruple ; reserve ; hesitation — 하다 hesitate ; hang back ; withhold ; be reserved ¶ 기탄없는 frank ; outspoken ; candid // 기탄없는 비평 candid criticism // 기탄없이 without reserve ; unreservedly ; frankly ; candid-

ly // 기탄없이 말하자면 to be frank 《with you》; plainly speaking // 기탄없이 말하다 speak freely ; do not mince matters 〔words〕

기태 奇態 an odd〔a fantastic〕 appearance 〔shape〕

기통 氣筒 a (steam) cylinder

— 용적 piston displacement ; cylinder capacity **—유** cylinder oil **6— 엔진** 6-cylindered engine

기특하다 奇特— (be) praiseworthy ; laudable ; commendable ¶ 기특한 마음씨 a praiseworthy intention // 기특하게도 자진해서 하겠다고 나섰다 He had the grace to offer to do it.

기틀 the key〔pivotal〕 point ; the crux (of a matter)

기틀이 잡히다 관용 the pivotal part functions ; get a firm stand

기펴다 氣— feel〔be〕 relieved〔relaxed〕; feel at ease ; be at peace ; feel animated ¶ 선생님이 엄해서 학생들이 기펼 수 없다 The teacher is so stern that all students are frightened. // 빚을 다 갚으니 이제 나도 기펴고 살 수 있겠다 I feel relieved of a great load as I have paid all my debts off.

기포 氣泡 a bubble ; a blowhole

—관 a bubble tube **— 수준기** a spirit 〔bubble〕 level **— 유리** foam glass **—제(劑)** a foaming agent **— 펌프** an air lift pump

기포 氣胞 an air bladder〔cell〕; [물고기의] a fish sound ; a swimming bladder ; [식물의] an air vesicle

—음(音) a vesicular murmur **—체** 〖동물〗 a pneumatophore

기폭 起爆 detonation ; detonator

—약(藥) the initial explosive **— 장치** a triggering device

기표 記票 balloting ¶ 기표소 a polling booth // 기표하다 fill in a ballot (paper)

기품 氣稟 disposition ; nature ; character ; temperament

***기품 氣品** dignity ; nobility ; grace ; refinement ¶ 기품 있는 noble ; dignified ; graceful // 기품 있는 사람 a refined gentleman ; a dignified lady // 그는 어딘지 기품이 있다 There is something noble about him. // 이 그림은 기품이 없다 This painting is lacking in grace.

기풍 氣風 character ; disposition ; temper ; [단체의] morale ; tone ; [특성] traits ; characteristics ; [정신] spirits ¶ 국민의 기풍 the traits〔characteristics, tone〕 of a nation // 학교의 기풍 the spirits 〔morale〕 of a school

***기피 忌避** evasion ; shirking ; avoidance ; 〖법〗 challenge **—하다** evade ; shirk ; dodge ; challenge (재판관을) ¶ 병역을 기피하다 evade military service // 책임을 기피하다 shirk responsibility // 판사를 기피하다 challenge a judge

— 인물 an unwelcome〔unacceptable〕 person **—자** an evader ; a shirker ; a challenger (법률상의) **병역 —자** a draft dodger

기필 期必 assurance of fulfilment **—하다** assure the fulfil(l)ment of ; be determined to bring about ¶ 기필코 without fail ; by all means ; under any circumstances ; certainly // 기필코 성취시키고야 말겠다 I will have it done one way or the other.

***기하 幾何** ① [얼마] how many〔much〕 ② [기하학] geometry ; Euclid ¶ 기하학적 geometrical // 기하의 문제 a geometrical problem

— 광학 geometrical optics **— 급수** a geometric series〔progression〕 ¶ 기하급수적으로 증가하다 increase by geometric progression **—비(比)** a geometric ratio **— 평균** geometric average 〔mean〕 **— 화법** descriptive geometry **입체 —** solid geometry **평면 —** plane geometry **해석 —** analytical geometry

기하다 忌— loathe ; detest ; avoid ; shun

기하다 期— ① [기약하다] promise ; pledge ¶ 두 사람은 재회를 기하고 헤어졌다 The two parted, pledging〔promising〕 to meet again. ② [시일을 정하다] fix〔set〕 《the date, time》 ③ [확실히 하다] ensure ; secure ¶ 절대 정확을 기하다 ensure the absolute accuracy 《of》 ④ [목표로 하다] aim at ; set〔fix〕 a goal of ¶ 철저하게 완전을 기하다 aim vigorously at perfection // 시험에 완전 합격을 기하다 set a goal of complete success in the examination

기하학 幾何學 geometry ¶ 기하학적 geometric(al) // 기하학적으로 geometrically // 기하학적 도형 a geometrical figure

—자 a geometrician ; a geometer **유클리드〔비유클리드〕 —** Euclidean〔non-Euclidean〕 geometry **평면〔입체, 구면, 해석, 계량, 순정〕 —** plane〔solid, spherical, analytic(al), metrical, pure〕 geometry

***기한 期限** a period ; a time limit ; a term ¶ 공채의 지불 기한 the term of a loan // 일정한 기한내에 within a definite period of time // 기한 전에 before the time set ; before maturity // 기한이 되다 fall 〔become〕 due ; mature (부채 따위가) // 기한을 정하다 set a time limit // 기한이 지나다 be overdue // 지불 기한이 지났다 The time for the payment expired. // 그 표의 유효 기한은 10일간이다 The ticket is good〔effective〕 for ten days. // 그 계약의 기한은 1년간이다 The contract holds good for a year.

— 만료 the termination〔expiration〕 of a term **예정 —** the target date **유효 —** the term of validity

기한 飢寒 hunger and cold ¶ 기한으로

죽다 die from starvation and exposure
기함 旗艦 a flagship
기합 氣合 ① [호흡이 맞음] breathing in harmony ② [기세·소리] concentration of spirit ; will power ; a yell ③ [제재] disciplinary punishment ¶ 기합이 충만한 일격 a stroke full of vitality // 기합을 걸다 shout at 《a person》 ; mesmerize 《a person》 with a yell
단체 — disciplinary punishment upon a group
기합술 氣合術 the art of mesmerizing by one's will power
기항 寄港 a call (at a port) **—하다** call〔touch, stop〕 《at》 ; put in 《at》 ¶ 부산에 기항하다 touch at *Pusan* // 배는 항해 도중에 많은 곳에 기항했다 The vessel called at many ports on her route.
기항지 寄港地 a port of call
기해 己亥 〖민속〗 the 36th binary term of the sexagenary cycle
기행 紀行 an account of travels ; a traveler's journal
기행 奇行 a strange〔an eccentric〕 conduct ; an eccentricity ¶ 그는 기행으로 알려진 사람이다 He is notorious for his eccentricity.
기행렬 旗行列 a flag procession
기행문 紀行文 an account of one's trip ; one's travel sketches
— **작가** a travel writer
기형 畸形, 奇型 deformity ; malformation ; abnormality ; monstrosity ; deformation ; abnormality (형태상의) ¶ 기형의 deformed ; malformed ; abnormal // 선천성 기형 congenital malformation
—물 a monster ; a monstrosity
기형아 畸形兒 a deformed〔malformed〕 child ; a freak of nature
†**기호 記號** a sign ; a mark ; a symbol ; 〖음악〗 a clef ; a note ¶ 기호를 붙이다 mark 《with a symbol》 // 언어는 사상의 기호이다 Words are the sign of ideas. // 그것은 무슨 기호이냐 What does it stand for ?
— **논리학** symbolic〔mathematical〕 logic — **달기** marking **—법** notation ; 〖전기〗 a symbolic method — **순서** the sequence〔order〕 of signs — **풀이** a key **삭제** — a deletion mark〔sign〕 **서사(書寫)** — a graphic symbol **수학** — a mathematical symbol **음성** — a phonetic symbol **음악** — a musical sign **화학** — a chemical symbol
기호 嗜好 taste ; liking ; likes and dislikes ; (a) preference ¶ 기호품 a favorite food // 기호에 맞다 be to one's taste ; suit one's taste // 대중의 기호에 맞다 capture〔strike, hit, catch〕 the public fancy
***기혼 旣婚** ¶ 기혼의 married // 기혼자 a married person ; the married

기화 奇貨 [물건] a curiosity ; a rarity ; [호기] a rare〔good〕 opportunity ¶ …을 기화로 하여 taking advantage of
기화 奇禍 an accident ; a misfortune ; a mishap ; a calamity ¶ 기화를 당하다 meet with an accident
기화 氣化 evaporation ; vaporization ; gasification **—하다** evaporate ; vaporize ; gasify
—기 a vaporizer ; an evaporator ; a carburetor **—성** vaporability **—식 연소기** a vaporizing combustion chamber **—열** evaporation heat ; the heat of vaporization **—점** the evaporation point
기화요초 琪花瑤草 the flowers and plants of fairyland ; beautiful flowers and plants
기황 饑荒 a famine ⇨ 기근
†**기회 機會** an opportunity ; a chance ; an occasion ¶ 좋은 기회 a good chance 〔opportunity〕 // 일생에 다시 없는 기회 the chance of a lifetime // 절호의 기회 a golden〔rare〕 opportunity // 아주 우연한 기회에 by the merest chance // 기회가 있는 대로 at the first opportunity ; at the earliest convenience // 기회를 포착하다 seize a chance // 기회를 얻다 get 〔gain〕 an opportunity 《to do》 // 기회를 기다리다 wait for a chance // 모든 기회를 이용하여 영어로 이야기하다 take every opportunity of speaking English // 기회를 놓치다 miss〔lose, let pass〕 an opportunity // 그와 말할 기회가 없었다 I had no chance of speaking to him. // 이 나라에서는 입신 출세의 기회가 많다 This is a country of great opportunities. // 이 기회를 이용하여 한마디 하겠다 I take this opportunity〔occasion〕 to say a word. // 그것은 다음 기회로 미루겠습니다 I will reserve it for another occasion. // 이런 기회는 평생에 다시 없을 것이다 A chance like this comes but once in a lifetime. /There will never be another opportunity like this. / It's now or never.
— **원인론** 〖철학〗 occasionalism **—주의** opportunism ; timeserving
기회 균등 機會均等 equality of opportunity ¶ 교육의 기회 균등 equal educational opportunities // 기회 균등을 요구하다 call for〔demand〕 equal opportunities
— **고용** equal opportunity employment **—주의** the principle of equal opportunity ; the open-door principle
⁑**기획 企劃** planning ; a plan ; a project **—하다** plan ; make a plan ; work out a program ¶ 기획을 세우다〔짜다〕 make〔draw up〕 a plan ; come up with a plan 《구》 // 기획성이 있다〔없다〕 be gifted with the〔have little〕 ability to make plans
—과 the planning section — **관리** planning and management **—부〔실〕**

planning department〔office〕 **—성** the ability to make plans **—자** a planner ; a plan maker **— 조정실** the Office of Planning & Coordination

기후 其後 after that ; afterward ; thereafter ; ever since ; since that ; later ; thenceforth ; from that time on

***기후 氣候** climate ; weather (날씨) ¶ 기후의 변화 a climatic change // 불순한 기후 unseasonable weather // 온화한 기후 a mild climate // 기후가 변할 때 at the change of season // 이곳 기후는 온화하여 건강에 좋다 The climate here is mild and good for health.

— 순화(順化)〔순응〕 acclima(ta)tion ; acclimatization **— 요법** climate treatment ; climatotherapy ; climatotherapeutics **—학** climatology **—학자** a climatologist **대륙성〔도서성〕 —** a continental 〔an insular〕 climate **해양성 —** a marine〔an oceanic〕 climate

기휘 忌諱 avoiding things **—하다** avoid ; shun ; loathe ; detest ; abhor

기흉 요법 氣胸療法 〖의학〗 a pneumothorax〔chest-airing〕 treatment

†긴급 緊急 emergency ; urgency ; exigency ; [서류 따위에 쓸 때] "Rush" 《미》 ; "Urgent" 《영》 **—하다** (be) urgent ; pressing ; burning ; crying ¶ 긴급한 경우 in case of emergency // 긴급한 용무로 on urgent business // 긴급 상정하다 lay an urgent bill 《before the Congress》 // 긴급 수배하다 make immediate arrangements // 돈이 긴급히 필요하다 I need money very badly.

— 대책 an urgent countermeasure **— 동의** an urgent motion ; emergency motion **— 명령** an emergency order ; a rush order 《미》 **— 문제** an urgent〔a burning〕 question **— 물자** materials urgently needed for the relief 《of》 ; emergency goods **— 사건** an urgent matter ; a pressing affair ; an emergency **— 사태** a state of emergency ; an emergency ; an exigency ; a crisis 《*pl.* crises》 **— 수배** immediate arrangements 《for》 **— 신호** an urgency signal **— 조치** an emergency measure **— 출동** [영공 침범기에 대한 요격기의] a scramble **— 피난** emergency evacuation **— 회의** an urgent conference 〔meeting〕

긴긴날 a long day ¶ 봄철 긴긴날에 in spring time when the days are long ; on the long spring day

긴긴밤 a very long night

긴담 緊談 an important conference 〔talk〕 ; a talk of vital importance

긴대답 —對答 a long-drawn reply ; a rambling answer〔reply〕 **—하다** make a long-drawn reply

긴등 a long ridge

긴말 a long talk〔conversation〕 ; a tirade ; a longwinded〔prolonged, lengthy〕 speech ; a tedious talk **—하다** speak long-windedly ¶ 긴말을 늘어놓다 spin a yarn // 긴말하지 않겠다 I'll cut it short. /I'll not bother you with a long talk. /I shall not enlarge〔expatiate〕 upon the subject.

긴맛 〖조개〗 a razor shell〔clam〕

†긴밀 緊密 compactness ; closeness ; strictness ; rigidity ; tightness **—하다** (be) close ; intimate ; rigorous ; strict ; tight ¶ 긴밀한 접촉 close touch〔contact〕 // 긴밀한 협력 close cooperation // 긴밀한 연락을 취하다 keep in close touch 《with》 // 긴밀히 연결되어 있다 be closely connected 《with》

긴박 緊迫 tension ; strain **—하다** (be) tense ; imminent ; impending ; pressing ¶ 긴박한 아시아 정세 an acute situation in Asia // 긴박한 용건으로 on urgent business // 긴박해지다 grow strained ; become acute // 긴박한 상태를 완화하다 ease the tension

긴박 緊縛 tight binding **—하다** bind 《things》 tight

긴병 —病 a long disease ; a lingering illness ; a chronic disease (고질) ¶ 긴병을 앓다 suffer from a long illness

긴사설 —辭說 a lengthy〔longwinded〕 talk ; a tedious speech ; a tirade

긴살 [볼기긴살] rump roast (of beef)

긴소리 a long-drawn sound〔voice〕

긴요 緊要 importance ; burning necessity **—하다** (be) important ; vital ; [필요하다] necessary ; essential ; [긴급하다] urgent ; pressing ¶ 긴요한 문제 an important matter // 생활상 긴요하다 It is vital〔essential〕 to life. // 더욱 긴요한 문제로서 해결을 요하는 것이 있다 There are problems of more importance which require immediate settlement.

긴용 緊用 **—하다** make good use of 《a thing》 ; put 《a thing》 to good use

†긴장 緊張 tension ; tenseness ; strain ; seriousness **—하다** be〔become〕 tense ; be strained ; be on the strain 〔stretch〕 ; be keyed up ¶ 긴장된 표정 a tense look ; an expression of tension // 긴장된 상황 a tense situation // 이상하게 긴장된 공기 an unusually tense atmosphere // 양국간의 긴장된 관계 strained (diplomatic) relations between the two countries // 긴장시키다 strain 《relations》 ; brace 《up》 // 지나치게 긴장하다 overstrain oneself ; be strained to the limit // 긴장이 결여되다 lack seriousness // 긴장을 완화하다 ease〔relax, loosen, relieve〕 the tension // 청중은 긴장하여 연설을 들었다 The audience followed the speech with the tension of suspense. // 그들의 얼굴에는 긴장의 빛이 보였다 They were all flushed with seriousness〔tension〕. // 긴장할 것 없다

Relax ! /Take it easy.
— 감각 strain —력 tensible force —병 [정신병] catatonia — 상태 a state of tension

긴절 緊切 —하다 (be) urgent ; pressing ; be of vital importance

긴중 緊重 —하다 (be) important ; main ; vital ; momentous

긴지름 ⇨ 장경(長徑)

긴짐승 reptiles ; a snake

긴찮다 緊— (be) unimportant ; unnecessary ; be of little importance

긴촉 緊囑 an urgent request —하다 request urgently

긴축 緊縮 strict economy ; retrenchment ; curtailment ; contraction (통화, 신용 따위의) ; shrinkage (수축) —하다 reduce ; retrench ; curtail ; contract ; cut down ; shrink ¶ 재정을 긴축하다 retrench in finances
— 예산 an austerity budget — 재정 a reduced budget — 정책 a tight-money policy ¶ 긴축 정책을 취하다 adopt a retrenchment policy

긴치마 a long skirt ; a maxi (skirt) ; a trailing skirt

긴팔원숭이 〖동물〗 a long-armed ape ; a gibbon

긴하다 緊— (be) important ; useful ; necessary ; essential ; indispensable ; urgent ; pressing ¶ 긴한 문제 an important problem // 긴한 물건 a useful article // 긴한 부탁이 있어 왔다 I came with an important 〔urgent〕 favor to ask of you. // 사치품은 일상 생활에 긴하지 않다 A luxury is of no immediate importance to our daily life.

긴헐 緊歇 importance and unimportance

긷다 draw ; pump ¶ 우물에서 물을 긷다 draw〔pump〕 water from a well // 두레박으로 물을 긷다 draw water with a well bucket

길¹ the height of a man ; a fathom ¶ 다섯 길 되는 물 water five fathoms deep // 길이 넘는 갈대 a reed taller than one's height // 아이가 길이 넘는 깊이까지 들어갔다 The boy got out of his depth.

*__길²__ ① [윤] polish ; luster ; gloss ; shine ¶ 길이 나서 반들반들한 patinous // 가구를 길들이다 polish furniture // 책상이 길들었다 The desk has a nice gloss to it. // 마루를 자꾸 닦아 길이 들었다 The floor has got a polish from constant rubbing.
② [숙련] skill ; dexterity ¶ 길이 난 솜씨로 skillfully ; with clever hands
③ [가축 따위] domestication ; tameness ¶ 길들인 원숭이 a tame monkey // 길들이기 힘든 짐승 animals hard to domesticate // 짐승을 길들이다 tame an animal
길이 나다 관용 get used〔accustomed〕 to ; become skillful ; be skilled〔experienced〕

*__길³__ ① a way ; a road ; a route ; a street ; a highway ; a thoroughfare (큰길) ; [통로] a path ; a lane ; a passage ; an aisle ; [고갯길] a pass ¶ 가로수 길 an avenue ; a tree-bordered road ; a boulevard // 지름길 a shorter way ; a shortcut // 길 건너편 집 a house across the street 〔road, way〕 ; 길 없는 들판 pathless fields // 길을 내다 make〔build〕 a road ; cut a path // 길을 잘못 들다 take the wrong road // 길을 묻다 ask one's way 《to a place》 // 길을 가로막다 stand in the way // 길을 잃다 lose〔miss〕 one's way ; get lost // 길을 트다 clear the way 《for a person》 ; keep a passage 《for》 // 길에서 사람을 만나다 meet 《a person》 in〔on〕 the street // 다른 길로 귀가하다 go home another way // 먼 길을 오다 come all the way 《from》 // 정거장에 가는 길을 가르쳐 주십시오 Please show me the way to the station. // 이 길을 따라 가시다가 두 번째 신호등에서 왼쪽으로 도십시오 Go down this street and make a left at the second signal.
② [도중] ¶ 길에서 on the way ; en route // 학교 가는 길에 on one's way to school // 오는 길에 만나다 meet 《a person》 on the way back 《from》 // 이쪽으로 나오는 길에 꼭 한 번 우리집에 들러 주세요 When you are out our way, be sure and look us up.
③ [방법·수단] a means ; a way ¶ 생활의 길 a means of livelihood // 성공의 길 a road to success // 그것을 행하는 길 the means〔way〕 of doing it // 살아갈 길이 막연하다 can hardly find a means of livelihood ; be at a loss how to make one's living
④ [진로] a course ; a road ; a path ; a way ; a step ¶ 안전한 길 a safe course // 살아갈 길 a means of living ; a (means of) livelihood // 멸망의 길 the way to ruin // 승진에의 길 an avenue for promotion // 공자의 길 the doctrines 〔teachings〕 of Confucius // 우리들의 갈 길 our path of duty // 스스로의 길을 가다 go one's way // 승진의 길을 열어 주다 open the door to promotion // 후배를 위하여 길을 열어 주다 make way for one's junior ; give the young people a chance // 그 길밖에 다른 도리가 없다 There is no other way. /We have no alternative. // 젊은 사람들을 위해서 길을 열어줘야 한다는 생각이 든다 I just feel that I should make way for new blood. // 나는 의사가 되려고 했으나 길을 잘못 들었다 I intended to become a doctor, but I took a wrong turn along the way. // 빠져 나갈 길이 없다 There is no way out〔through〕.
길을 무서워하면 범을 만난다 속담 Who

fears to suffer, suffers from fear.
모든 길은 로마로 통한다 [속담] All roads lead to Rome.
아는 길도 물어가라 [속담] Better ask the way than go astray.
☞ 《p. 384》

길⁴ [등급] a grade ; a class ¶ 길이 좋다 have a good rating ; be a good grade // 이것은 그것에 비하면 아랫길이다 This is inferior to that in quality. // 이 물건은 윗길이다 The goods are of good quality.

길⁵ [책 한 벌] a set〔series〕 of volumes ¶ 이 책은 열 권이 한 길이 된다 This book is complete in ten volumes.

길⁶ [옷의] the large section(s) of cloth forming the body of a Korean coat or jacket

*****길가** the roadside ; the wayside ¶ 길가의 wayside ; roadside // 가게가 이쪽 길가에 있습니까 Is the store on this side of the street?

길거리 a street ; a road ; an avenue 《미》 ; a thoroughfare ¶ 길거리를 쏘다니다 roam about the street

길경 吉慶 a matter for congratulations ; an auspicious event ; a happy occasion

길경 桔梗 a Chinese balloon flower

길길이 ① [높이] high ; tall ; to a great height ¶ 길길이 쌓인 보고서 vast heap of reports // 길길이 쌓아 올리다 pile up high ; heap 《goods》 high // 잡초가 길길이 자라고 있다 Weeds are growing tall. ② [성난 꼴] very ; extremely ; exceedingly ¶ 화가 나서 길길이 뛰다 be very angry ; hit the ceiling 《미》 ; blow one's top 《미》

길꾼 a skilled gambler

길나다 ① [도로가] A road is open. /A road runs. ② [습관이 되다] become accustomed〔habitual〕 ③ [윤나다] become glossy〔shiny〕

길년 吉年 an auspicious year

길눈¹ [방향 감각] one's sense of direction
길눈이 밝다〔어둡다〕 [관용] have a good 〔poor〕 sense of direction

길눈² [적설] snow deep as a man's height

†**길다** (be) long ; lengthy ; prolonged ; protracted ¶ 긴 막대 a long pole // 긴 세월 long years〔times〕 // 긴 장마 a long rainy season // 긴 세월을 두고 사귄 친구 a friend of long standing ; an old friend // 길어지다 become〔grow〕 longer ; be lengthened // 길게 하다 make longer ; lengthen ; draw long // 긴 안목으로 보다 take a long(-range) view 《of》 // 그의 여생도 길지 못하다 He will not last long. // 거기에는 긴 사연이 있다 There is a long story behind it. // 인생은 짧고 예술은 길다 Life is short, art is long. // 사람은 길게 두고 봐야 안다 It takes a long time to understand a person. // 가지가 긴 붉은 장미 12송이만 보내 주세요 Send a dozen long-stemmed red roses, please.

길닦이 road repairing **—하다** improve 〔repair〕 a road

길더 [네덜란드의 화폐 단위] a guilder ; a gulden

길동무 a traveling companion ; a fellow traveler **—하다** keep 《a person》 company ; travel together ¶ 우연히 행상인과 길동무가 되다 happen to travel together with a peddler ; happen to fall into company with a peddler

길둥글다 (be) long and round 《like a log》

길드 a guild
— 사회주의 guild socialism

*****길들다** ① [익숙해지다] get〔be〕 used to ; grow〔get, become〕 accustomed to ; grow familiar with ; familiarize oneself ¶ 길든 practiced ; experienced ; familiar // 길들지 않은 new ; unfamiliar ; unexperienced // 길들지 않은 일 unaccustomed work // 사치에 길들다 be lapped in luxury // 곧 길들게 될 것이다 You will soon get used to it.
② [동물이] become〔grow〕 tame ; become domesticated ¶ 길든 tame ; domesticated // 길들이기 힘든 shy // 길들지 않은 새 a wild bird // 이 개는 잘 길들어 있다 This puppy is quite tame with me.
③ [윤나다] take a good polish〔shine, gloss, luster〕 ; get glossy ¶ 노상 닦아서 마루가 길들었다 The floor has a shine from constant polishing.

†**길들이다** ① [동물을] tame ; domesticate ; subdue ; charm 《a snake》 ; train 《a dog》 ; break in (말 따위를) ¶ 길들인 동물 a property animal (영화 출연을 위한) // 길들인 원숭이 a trained monkey // 야수를 길들이는 사람 a trainer of wild animals // 개를 길들이다 train a dog 《to do tricks》 // 말을 길들이다 break a horse to the rein ; train〔break in〕 a bronco // 잘 길들여졌다 be kept well under
② [익숙해지게 하다] inure ; accustom ; habituate ; make 《a person》 used to ; train〔improve〕 《a person》 in 《a thing》 ¶ 일에 길들이다 accustom 《a person》 to work〔labor〕 // 곤란한 일에 길들이다 inure 《a person》 to hardships ; habituate 《oneself》 to difficulties ; harden 《a person》 to trouble
③ [윤나게 하다] put a polish on ; polish up ; make 《it》 glossy ; bring out the luster ; give a gloss〔shine, polish〕 to ; glaze

길라잡이 a guide (who shows the way)

길래 forever ; for good ¶ 길래 잘 살다 live happily for good // 은혜는 길래 잊지

길을 물을 때

1 길을 물을 때

① 방향

¶ 역으로 가는 길을 가르쳐 주십시오. Please tell [show] me the way to the station. / Please direct me to the station. // 실례지만 시청으로 가는 길을 가르쳐 주시겠습니까? Excuse me, but could you tell me the way to the city hall? // 국립박물관으로 가려면 어떻게 가면 됩니까? How can I get to the National Museum? / Will you please tell me how to get to the National Museum? // 평화은행이 어디에 있는지 아십니까? Do you happen to know where the Peace Bank is? // 115번지가 어디입니까? Please tell me how I can get to the house no. 115. // 가장 가까운 우체국을 가르쳐 주십시오. Please tell me how to get to the nearest post office.

② 거리 · 시간

¶ 공항까지 얼마나 걸립니까? How far is (it to) the airport from here? 《거리》/ How long will it take (me) to get to the airport? // 택시로 얼마나 걸릴까요? How long will it take (me) (if I go) by taxi? 《시간》// 서울 호텔까지는 걸어서 갈 만한 거리입니까? Can I walk to the Seoul Hotel? / Is the Seoul Hotel within walking distance?

③ 교통편

¶ 국립극장을 가려고 하는데 어디서 내려야 합니까? I'm going to the National Theater. Where do I have to get off? // 종로 3가까지는 몇 정거장이나 남았습니까? How many (more) stops is it to Chongno 3-ga? // 이 (직행) 버스는 서울역으로 갑니까? Does this bus go to the Seoul Station? / Is this the through [direct] bus to the Seoul Station? // 어디서 갈아 타야 합니까? Where do I have to transfer [change]?

④ 기타

¶ 안내소가 어디 있습니까? Where is the information (office)? // 이 부근에 경찰서가 있습니까? Is there a police station around [near] here? // 화장실이 어디에 있습니까? Could you tell me where the rest room is?

2 길을 가르쳐줄 때

① 방향

¶ 두 블럭 더 가면 오른쪽에 있습니다. Walk two more blocks and you'll find it on your right. // 두번째 모퉁이 [건널목, 교차로] 에서 좌회전하면 바로 정면에 보일 것입니다. Turn left at the second corner [crossing, intersection], and you'll find it right ahead of you. // 세 블럭을 더 가면 5번가에 이르게 됩니다. 거기서 좌회전해서 두 블럭을 더 가서 다시 우회전하십시오. Walk three more blocks, and you'll come to the fifth street. Turn left and walk another two blocks, then turn right. // 나도 같은 방향으로 갑니다. 나를 따라오시면 안내해 드리겠습니다. I'm going (in) the same direction. Please come (along) with me. I'll show you where it is. // 미안합니다. 나도 여기 초행길입니다. 다른 사람에게 물어보시지요. I'm sorry, but I'm a stranger here (myself). Please ask somebody else.

② 거리 · 시간

¶ 여기서 공항까지는 약 8킬로미터입니다. It's about eight kilometers from here to the airport. // 택시로 약 20분 걸립니다. It'll take (you) about twenty minutes by taxi. // 걷기에는 너무 먼 거리입니다. It's too far to walk. / It's not within walking distance.

③ 교통편

¶ 길 건너편에서 12번 버스를 타십시오. Take a no. 12 bus on the other side of the street. // 여기서 다섯 정거장입니다. It's five stops from here. // 거기까지 직행버스는 없습니다. 신촌에서 갈아타십시오. There is no through [direct] bus there. Transfer [Change] at shinchon.

않겠습니다 I shall not forget your kindness as long as I live.

-길래 ⇨ -기에 ②, -관데

길례 吉禮 a happy〔a congratulatory, an auspicious〕 ceremony

길로틴 a guillotine ⇨ 단두대

길리다 be brought up ; be bred〔fed〕; be reared〔raised〕 ¶ 우유로 길리다 be brought up on the bottle // 유모 손에 길리다 be fed by a wet nurse

길마 a packsaddle

길마 지우다 관용 put a packsaddle on ; fix a packsaddle

***길모퉁이** a street corner ; a corner ¶

길모퉁이에 있는 파출소 a police box at the corner
길목¹ [버선] high-necked〔high-cut〕 socks
길목² ① [골목의] a corner ; a turn ; a turning ¶ 길목에서 두번째 집 the second house from the corner // 길목에 있는 약국 a corner drug store // 길목을 돌다 turn a corner
② [중요한 어귀] an important〔a key〕 point ; a point of vantage ¶ 무장한 순경이 길목마다 경비했다 Armed policemen mounted guard at every key point of the street.
길목버선 walking〔walker's〕 socks ; secondhand socks for a long travel on foot
길몽 吉夢 a lucky dream ; a dream of good omen
길미 interest on money
길바닥 [길의 바닥] the roadbed ; the road surface ; [길 가운데] the middle of a road
길바로 on the right way〔path〕 ¶ 길바로 들다 go the right way〔track〕 ; keep to the right path
길벗 a traveling companion ⇨ 길동무
길보 吉報 good news ; glad news〔tidings〕 ; a good word
길사 吉事 an auspicious event ; a happy affair
길상 吉祥 a lucky omen〔sign〕 ; a good auspice ; an auspicious sign ¶ 길상이다 be of good omen
길상 吉相 a lucky face ; lucky physiognomy ¶ 길상을 한 사람 a man of lucky physiognomy
길서 吉瑞 a good omen ; a lucky〔an auspicious〕 sign
길섶 the roadside ; the wayside ; the edge of a road ; the shoulder of a road
길속 the inner workings《of a job, of a line of business, *etc.*》
길손 a travel(l)er ; a wayfarer
길쌈 weaving **—하다** weave《on a loom》
—꾼 a weaver
길안내 —案內 showing the way ; guidance of the road ; [사람] a guide **—하다** show《a person》 the way《to》 ; guide〔direct〕《a person to a place》 ; act as (a) guide
길어지다 lengthen ; extend ; be lengthened ; become〔grow, be made〕 longer ; draw out (해 따위가) ¶ 해가 점점 길어진다 The days are lengthening〔growing longer〕. // 한국 사람의 수명이 길어졌다 The lifespan of Koreans has been extended.
길운 吉運 lucky〔good〕 fortune ; luck
†**길이¹** length ; extent ¶ 길이 일곱 자의 뱀 a seven-foot snake ; a snake seven feet long〔in length〕 // 각각 1미터 길이로 잘라 주시오 Cut them in lengths of one meter each. // 길이는 얼마나 How long is it ? / What is its length ? // 길이는 다 같다 They are of the same length. // 이것은 저 길이의 두배 이다 This is twice as long as that. // 이 정도 길이로 잘라 주세요 Leave〔Make〕 them this long. (이발)
†**길이²** long ; for a long time〔while〕 ¶ 길이길이 forever ; for ages ; for good ; permanently // 길이 보존하다 preserve〔cherish〕《a thing》 for good // 그의 이름은 청사에 길이 빛날 것이다 He will live〔remain〕 long in history. // 그분의 은혜를 길이 못 잊겠다 I shall never forget his kindness.
길이불 traveler's portable bedding
길인 吉人 [착한 사람] a good man ; [복 많은 사람] a lucky person
길일 吉日 a lucky〔a propitious, an auspicious〕 day ¶ 길일을 택하다 choose an auspicious day
†**길잡이** a guide ; a trailblazer ; a beacon ; a guidepost ; a signpost ; a guideline ; a handbook ¶ 학계의 길잡이 the guiding〔leading〕 star of the scientific world // 작문의 길잡이 hints on composition // 길잡이 서다 act as a guide ; show the way
길제 吉祭 a memorial service held in the 27th month after《a person's》 death
길조 吉兆 a good〔lucky〕 omen ; a good〔happy〕 augury ; an auspicious sign ¶ 길조를 보이다 be of good omen
길짐 government goods transported in relay by peasants who live along a main road
길짐승 a crawling animal ; a furred animal
길쭉길쭉 —하다 (be) long ; all longish ; all rather long ¶ 길쭉길쭉한 막대 longish stick
길쭉스름하다 (be) longish ; somewhat long
길쭉이 long ; somewhat long
길쯔막하다 ⇨ 길쯤하다
길쯤길쯤하다 be all appropriately long ; (such that) each is nicely on the long side
길쯤이 so that it is nice and longish
길쯤하다 (be) quite longish ; be quite on the long side
길찍이 rather long ; somewhat long ; quite long ¶ 막대를 길찍이 자르다 cut a stick long〔on the long side〕
길찍하다 ⇨ 길쭉하다
길차다 ① (be) overgrown ② be thick〔dense〕 with vegetation
길처 the area bordering on one's way
길체 a corner ; a nook
길초산 —草酸 〖화학〗 valeric〔valerianic〕

acid

길카리 one's distant relatives who may or may not have the same family name; one's distant relatives in blood and law 〔by blood and marriage〕

길하다 吉— (be) auspicious; lucky; propitious; fortunate ¶ 길한 꿈 a lucky dream

길항 拮抗 rivalry; contention; antagonism; competition

—하다 rival; contend〔compete〕 with; stand against; struggle with 《a person》 for supremacy ¶ 충분히 길항할 수 있다 can compare favorably 《with》

—근(筋) 〖해부〗 an antagonist **— 작용** [생물] antagonism

길흉 吉凶 good or ill luck; fortune; lights and shadows ¶ 길흉을 점치다 tell 《a person's》 fortune

김¹ laver; dried laver

‡**김²** steam; vapor ¶ 김이 나는 요리 steaming dishes // 김이 나다 steam; reek; emit〔give off, send up〕 steam // 주전자에서 김이 나고 있다 The kettle is steaming.

김³ [기회] chance; opportunity; occasion ¶ 김에 while; when; as; taking opportunity of // 술김에 under the influence of liquor; emboldened by liquor // 홧김에 in a fit of anger // 생각난 김에 as I am reminded of 《a matter》 // 온 김에 since 〔now that〕 I am here // 이 문제를 토의하는 김에 while on this subject // 홧김에 그릇을 깨뜨렸다 I broke a plate in my anger. // 이 동네에 온 김에 인사나 하고 갈까 해서 들렀습니다 I happened to be in the neighborhood and thought I'd stop by and say hello. // 하는 김에 이 편지를 부치고 와주지 않을래 Would you mail this letter for me while you're at it?

김나가다 lose its taste〔flavor〕; become tasteless; become dull〔insipid〕; fall stale ¶ 김나간 맥주 stale beer // 김나간 이야기 a dull story

김매다 weed; root out〔remove〕 weeds; pick weeds out of ¶ 밭(을) 김매다 weed a field

김빠지다 become tasteless ⇨ 김나가다

김의털 〖식물〗 a sheep's fescue; Festuca ovina (학명)

김장 pickled vegetables prepared for the winter; preparing pickles for the winter **—하다** pickle vegetables for the winter ¶ 김장철 the season for preparing pickles for the winter

—독 a pickle jar

김지이지 *Kim* and *Lee*; certain persons; every Tom, Dick and Harry

김치 pickles; pickled vegetables ¶ 배추〔무·오이〕 김치 cabbage〔radish, cucumber〕 pickles

김포 (국제) 공항 金浦(國際)空港 *Kimpo* (International) Airport

깁 silk gauze

‡**깁다** sew; stitch; mend; patch up (헝겊을 대고); darn (양말을) ¶ 더덕더덕 기운 full of patches; patchy // 손으로 깁다 sew by hand // 옷을 깁다 patch up clothes // 신을 깁다 mend one's shoes // 양말을 깁다 darn stockings // 터진 데를 깁다 stitch up a tear // 해진 곳을 깁다 sew〔stitch〕 up a rip

깁바탕 a piece of silk on which a painting 〔writing〕 is made

깁스 a (plaster) cast ¶ 깁스를 하다 ware a (plaster) cast // 이 팔의 깁스를 풀어도 되겠습니까 의사 선생님 May I remove this cast from my arm, Doc?

깁옷 a garment made of silk gauze

깁창 —窓 a window screened with silk gauze

깁체 a silk sieve; a lawn sieve ¶ 깁체로 거르다 strain through a silk sieve

깃¹ [몫] a share; a portion

깃² [옷깃] a collar; a neckband; a lapel ¶ 깃 없는 블라우스 a collarless blouse // 선〔접은〕 깃 a stand-up〔turn-down〕 collar // 옷깃을 세우다 turn up one's (coat) collar // 옷깃을 잡다 seize〔take, hold〕 《a person》 by the collar〔coat lapels〕; collar 《a person》

깃³ [날개털] a feather; a plume; plumage ¶ 깃을 넣은 베개 a pillow filled with feathers // 아직 깃이 나지 않은 unfledged // 깃이 나다 fledge // 깃이 빠지다 shed feathers; feathers come off // 깃을 뽑다 pluck feathers 《from a fowl》 // 깃이 예쁘면 새도 예쁘다 Fine feathers make fine birds. // 새가 깃을 다듬는다 Birds plume themselves〔their feathers〕.

***깃⁴** [가축의] litter; bedding for animals ¶ 외양간에 깃을 깔아 주다 litter a barn down // 마른 풀로 두껍게 깃을 깔아 주다 cover the floor with thick layer of hay

깃고대 the place where the collar attaches to a garment

깃광목 —廣木 unbleached muslin

깃다 [잡초가 무성하다] be overgrown 〔overrun〕 with weeds

깃다듬다 《birds》 plume themselves〔their feathers〕; smooth down the feathers 《of a bird》

깃달이 sewing on a collar〔neckband〕 to improve the looks of a garment

깃대 [새] a shaft; a scape

***깃대 旗—** a flagstaff; a flagpole ¶ 깃대에 기를 달다 run a flag up the flagpole

깃들다 ⇨ 깃들이다

***깃들이다** [새가] build a nest; nest; roost; [짐승이] lair; dwell ¶ 건전한 정신은 건전한 신체에 깃들인다 A sound mind (dwells) in a sound body. // 새가 나무에 깃들이고 있다 Birds roost in the trees.

깃발 旗— a flag ; a banner ¶ 깃발을 흔들다 wave a flag // 깃발이 바람에 펄럭인다 A flag is fluttering in the wind. // 깃발이 휘날린다 A banner is streaming 〔fluttering〕.

깃옷 a raw-cotton garment, worn for the first three months of mourning one's parents

깃이불 a feather quilt

깃저고리 clothes with no collar

깃주다 litter ; supply 《an animal》 with litter for bed ; cover 《a floor》 with litter ¶ 외양간에 깃주다 litter a stable down

깃촉 —鏃 a quill

†깃털 feathers ; bird down ⇨ 깃[3]

— 이불 feather-quilt ; a quilt of down

깃펜 a quill pen

†깊다 ① (be) deep ¶ 깊이 deeply // 깊은 곳 a depth ; a deep place // 깊은 연못 a deep pond // 깊은 산 a remote mountain ; the depths of the mountain // 깊은 숲 a dense〔deep〕 forest // 한없이 깊은 bottomless ; fathomless // 깊이 파다 dig deep // 깊은 데로 가다 go out of one's depth // 이 늪은 한없이 깊다 This swamp is unfathomably deep. // 너무 깊은 곳에 가지 마라 Don't go out too deep.

② [심오하다] (be) deep ; profound ; [친밀하다] close ; intimate ; thick 《속》 ¶ 학문이 깊은 사람 a man of profound learning // 깊은 애정 deep affections // 깊은 관계 close connections // 깊은 관심 a keen interest // 깊은 뜻 a deep〔profound〕 meaning // 깊은 생각 a deep thought〔reflection〕 // 깊은 인상 a strong 〔a deep, a profound, an indelible〕 impression // 깊이 사랑하다 love 《a person》 deeply〔dearly〕 // 여자와의 관계가 깊다 be deeply in love with a girl // 깊이 연구하다 study〔go〕 deep into a subject // 사물을 깊이 생각하다 have deep views of things // 깊은 흥미를 느끼다 take a deep interest in // 의심이 점점 깊어 갔다 There has prevailed a profound suspicion.

③ [잠이] (be) deep ; sound ; heavy ¶ 깊은 잠 a deep〔sound, heavy〕 sleep // 깊은 잠이 들다 fall into a deep〔sound〕 sleep

④ [밤이] (be) late ¶ 깊은 밤 midnight ; the dead of night // 밤이 깊어서 late at night ; at midnight // 밤이 깊어감에 따라 as the night goes on // 밤이 깊어지다 grow late ; wear on

깊다랗다 (be) somewhat deep ; rather deep

깊드리 a low-lying paddy field

깊숙이 deep ; far ¶ 골짜기 깊숙이 들어앉은 집 a house set deep in a valley // 장 밑 깊숙이 넣다 put deep into a chest // 모자를 깊숙이 눌러쓰다 jam one's hat on // 깊숙이 들어앉다 take a seat far in the corner

깊숙하다 (be) deep ; retired ; recessed ; secluded ; quiet ¶ 깊숙히 deep ; far // 깊숙한 눈 deep-set eyes // 깊숙한 곳 a retired spot // 깊숙한 숲 a deep forest // 깊숙한 골짜기 a deep valley // 장 속 깊숙히 넣다 put 《a thing》 deep into a chest // 깊숙히 들어 앉다 take a seat far in the corner

깊어지다 ① [깊어지다] deepen ; become deeper ; [짙어지다] become thick 〔heavy〕 ; [심원해지다] become profound ; [강해지다] become intense 〔strong〕

② [시간이] be advanced ; be well on ; ripen ¶ 밤이 깊어질 때까지 till the night is far advanced ; into the depth of night // 가을도 깊어졌다 Autumn has ripened〔is well on, is well advanced〕.

③ [관계가] grow〔be〕 intimate 《with》 ; become deeper ¶ 여자와의 사이가 깊어지다 become thick with a woman

⁑깊이[1] [명사] depth ; deepness ; profundity ¶ 생각의 깊이 profundity of thought // 애정의 깊이 the depth of affection // 깊이가 한없는 bottomless ; fathomless // 깊이가 없다 be shallow ; be superficial ; be thoughtless // 깊이를 재다 sound〔plumb〕 the depth 《of》 // 깊이가 5 피트이다 It is five feet deep〔in depth〕.

⁑깊이[2] deeply ; profoundly ; thoroughly ¶ 깊이 뿌리박은 증오심 a deep-rooted hatred // 깊이 감동하다 be deeply moved // 깊이 생각하다 think deeply // 깊이 파다 dig deep // 도랑을 깊이 파다 deepen a ditch // 깊이 연구하다 study〔go〕 deep into 《a subject》 ; make a thorough 〔close〕 study 《on》 // 깊이 잠들다 fall fast asleep // 깊이 사귀다 be on intimate terms with // 깊이 숨을 쉬다 breathe (in) deep(ly) ; take〔draw〕 a deep breath

까까머리 a shaven(-bald) head ; a close cropped head ; a head shaved bald

까까중 (a person with) a head shaved bald ; a monk-headed person

까뀌 an adz(e) ¶ 까뀌로 찍어내다 hew with adz(e) ; adze

까끄라기 [이삭의] an awn ; a beard ; an arista 《*pl.* -tae》

*까놓다 [털어놓다] open one's heart 《to》 ; speak one's mind ; unbosom oneself ; confide 《a secret to another》 ; [껍질을 벗기다] peel〔pare〕 off ¶ 까놓고 말하면 to be frank with you ; frankly speaking ; to speak honestly ; in plain terms // 까놓고 말하다 speak without reserve ; exchange confidences with 《each other》 // 까놓고 말해라 Speak your mind. // 자네에게 까놓고 이야기하고 싶네 I want to confide in you. // 너의 계획을 까놓고 말해봐라

Come out with your plan. // 그는 그 일의 전말을 까놓았다 He opened the whole affair.

†**까다¹** ① [벗기다] peel ; husk ; pare 《an apple》 ; break ; skin ; crack ; shell ; strip ¶ 귤을 까다 peel an orange // 밤을 까다 crack〔shell〕 a chestnut // 달걀을 까다 break an egg // 정강이를 까다 crack 《a person's》 shin
② [부화하다] hatch ; incubate ¶ 암탉이 병아리를 깐다 A hen hatches out chickens.
③ [치다] beat ; strike ; hit ; slug ; slap ; criticize (신문 따위에서)
④ [결점을 말하다] speak ill of ; run down ; criticize ; write down ¶ 그는 선거 연설에서 상대방을 호되게 깠다 In his campaign speech he really blasted the other party.

⁑**까다²** ① [제하다] take (away, out) 《from》 ; deduct 《from》 ; subtract 《from》 ¶ 봉급에서 까다 deduct 《a sum》 from 《a person's》 salary // 세금을 까고 월 50만원의 수입 an income of 500,000 *won* after tax (reduction) ; a take-home pay of 500,000 *won*
② [가산을 축내다] reduce one's fortune
③ [줄다] get thin ; diminish ; dwindle ¶ 살이 까다 get〔become〕 thin // 가산이 까다 one's fortune dwindles

까다³ [입이] talk glibly ; quibble ; sophisticate ; have a clever tongue ¶ 입만 까고 실천이 없는 사람이다 He is all talk and no action. /He does not mean what he says.

까다롭게 ① [성미가] critically ; captiously ; harshly ; severely ; punctiliously ; strictly ; stringently ; fastidiously ; fussily ; difficulty ② [일이] vexingly ; difficultly ; involvedly ; intricately ; delicately ; trickily

*__까다롭다__ ① [성미가] (be) particular ; be hard to please ; (be) fastidious ; overnice ; humorsome ; moody ; critical ; captious ; harsh (엄격하다) ¶ …에 까다롭게 굴다 be particular about〔over, as to, in〕 // 성미가 까다로운 사람 a man hard to please // 맵시에 관해서 까다로운 취미 a fastidious taste in styles // 옷에 까다롭다 be particular〔fastidious〕 about one's clothes // 음식에 까다롭다 be particular〔fastidious〕 about one's food 〔what one eats〕 // 그렇게 까다롭게 굴지마 Don't be so fastidious. // 그 여자는 입맛이 매우 까다롭고 옷을 고르는 데도 매우 까다롭다 She is very fussy about food and very picky about clothes.
② [문제 따위가] (be) complicated ; tangled ; troublesome ; perplexing ¶ 까다로워지다 become complicated〔troublesome〕 // 까다로운 절차를 밟아 비자를 얻다 go through a complicated procedure〔rigmarole〕 to get a visa // 일을 까다롭게 만들다 complicate matters // 이 문제는 까다롭다 This question is hard to solve. /This is a hard nut to crack. // 이 문제는 좀 까다롭다 This problem is a little too hard to solve.

까닥이다 bob one's head up and down ; nod 《the head》 again and again ⇨ 끄덕이다

⁑**까닭** ① [이유] a reason ; a ground ; why ; [원인] a cause ¶ 까닭 없이 without reason〔good cause〕 ; without provocation ; without rime or reason // 까닭에 on the ground of〔that〕 // 무슨 까닭으로 why ; for what reason ; on what ground // 지각한 까닭을 말하다 tell why one was late // 그렇게 생각한 까닭이 있다 I have every reason to think so. // 이제야 까닭을 알았다 That explains. // 거기에는 무슨 까닭이 있음에 틀림없다 There must be some reason for it. // 무슨 까닭으로 사직했습니까 What is your reason for resigning? /How come you left your company? // 까닭 없이 사람을 죽이다 commit murder without provocation
② [연유] a circumstance ; a case ¶ 그런 까닭에 so ; such being the case // 그런 까닭에 그렇게 된 거야 That is how it came to happen. // 그를 알게 된 까닭을 말씀드리지요 I'll tell you how I came to know him.

까대기 a temporary side shed〔shelter〕 ; a makeshift shack

까딱수 一手 a speculative〔risky〕 move ; a shallow trick ; a risky measure ¶ 까딱수를 쓰다 resort to a risky move ; venture ; run a risk

까딱없다 (be) safe and sound ⇨ 끄떡없다

까라지다 get languid ; go limp

까르륵 with a yelp〔bawl〕 **—하다** 《a dog》 let out a yelp ¶ 까르륵거리다 bawl away

⁑**까마귀** 〖새〗 a crow ; a raven (갈가마귀) ; a rook (땅가마귀) ; a bird of ill omen (별명) ¶ 까마귀 떼 a flock of crows // 까마귀 눈에도 제 새끼가 제일 곱다 The crow thinks her own bird fairest, too. // 까마귀 고기를 먹었나 Why are you so forgetful?
까마귀 날자 배 떨어진다 속담 It is just a coincidence that the two events have happened at the same time.
까마귀가 울면 사람이 죽는다 속담 The croaking raven bodes death.
까마귀 학이 되랴 속담 Once a devil, always a devil. /Once a knave, and ever a knave.

까마득하다 be far off ⇨ 까마아득하다

까마무트름하다 (be) dark and chubby

까마반드르하다, 까마반지르하다 (be) black and glossy〔sleek〕

까마아득하다 [공간] (be) far-off ; far-away ; be a long way off ; (be) far 〔distant, remote〕《from》; [시간] (be) remote ; far ; distant ¶ 까마아득히 far away ; afar off ; in the〔at a〕distance // 까마아득한 옛날에 in the far-off〔old〕days ; a long, long time ago ; in remote antiquity ; in the dim past // 까마아득히 먼 곳에서 깜박거리는 빛 a glimmer far in the distance // 까마아득히 보이는 섬 an island dimly seen in the distance // 서울까지 갈 길이 아직 까마아득하다 It is a long way yet to *Seoul*.

까마종이 『식물』 a black〔common〕nightshade ; a morel ; a garden huckleberry

까막거리다 [등불 따위가] flicker ; waver ; [눈을] blink ; wink 《one's eyes》

까막까치 a crow and a magpie

까막눈 the eye of an ignoramus

까막눈이 an illiterate ; an ignoramus ; an unlettered person

까막잡기 blindman's buff

까매지다 get dark ; darken ; become 〔turn〕black ; blacken ; tan (in the sun) ; get〔become, turn〕bronzed (by the sun) ¶ 햇볕에 타서 까매지다 be (sun-)tanned ; be sunburned〔sunburnt〕// 볕에 까매지지 않도록 하다 keep oneself from getting sunburnt // 햇볕에 타서 까매진 얼굴 a face bronzed by the sun

까먹다 ① [까서 먹다] crack〔peel, shell〕and eat ¶ 굴을 까먹다 shell〔shuck〕an oyster and eat it // 바나나를 까먹다 peel and eat a banana
② [밑천을] go〔run〕through 《a fund》 ¶ 밑천을 다 까먹다 be out of funds ; go through all one's funds ; lose both principal and interest ; fail to return the original investment // 재산을 다 까먹다 lose〔run through〕one's fortune // 그는 아버지의 유산을 다 까먹었다 He used up〔squandered〕all the money he had inherited from his father.
③ [잊다] forget 《to fulfil a request》 ¶ 그 일을 깜빡 까먹었다 It has entirely slipped from my mind.
④ [어린이가 돈을] spend all one's money on food

까무러뜨리다 ① [남을] deprive 《a person》 of his senses ; make insensible ; cause 《a person》 to lose consciousness ; [때려서] stun ② [까무러치다] swoon ; faint dead away

까무스름하다 (be) blackish ; darkish ; swarthy ; sunburnt

까무잡잡하다 (be) darkish ; dusky ; dark complexioned〔colored〕

까바치다 tell〔carry〕tales 《about, against, upon》《a person》; inform 《a person》 against 《another》; tell〔squeal〕on 《a person》; sneak (학생 용어) ¶ 친구를 까바치다 peach against one's partner // 나를 까바치지 마라 Don't tell on me. // 아버지한테 까바칠 테야 I am going to tell father on you.

까발리다 pop〔shuck, shell〕《a thing》 out ; [폭로하다] expose ; disclose ; reveal

까부라지다 ① [부피가 줆] run〔get〕low ; lessen
② [나른해짐] feel languid〔weary〕; [쇠약해짐] become weak ; lose vigor

까부르다 winnow ; fan ¶ 곡식을 까부르다 winnow grain ; winnow away chaff from the grain

까불까불 moving up and down lightly ; frivolously ; flippantly

까불거리다 act rashly〔imprudently, on impulse, carelessly〕; behave flippantly

까불다 ① [위아래로] toss ; heave ¶ 물결이 심해서 배가 몹시 까분다 The ship is pitching and tossing in the heavy sea. ② [경망하게] act rashly ; behave flippantly〔frivolously〕 ¶ 까불지 마〔건방진 소리 마라〕 None of your cheek 〔sauce〕! // 까불지 말고 가만있거라 Keep quiet and don't be so boisterous.

까불리다[1] [재물을] waste ; dissipate ; squander ; spend 《money》 wantonly ; run〔go〕through 《one's fortune》 ¶ 금전을 까불리다 spend one's money recklessly ; play ducks and drakes with one's money

까불리다[2] [키질] be winnowed ; let winnow

까불이 a flippant〔frivolous〕person

까붐질 winnowing ; fanning

까옥 caw ; croak ¶ 까옥거리다(-대다) keep crawing〔croaking〕

†**까지** ① [때] till ; until ; to ; up to ; before ; by ¶ 지금까지 till〔until〕now ; up to now〔the present〕; to date ; hitherto // 밤 늦게까지 till late at night // 오늘날까지 up to this day ; up to date // 새벽까지 till dawn // 일몰 후까지 till after dark // 그때까지 till then // 최후까지 to〔till〕the last // 오후 늦게까지 아무것도 안 먹었다 I had not eaten anything till late in the afternoon. // 지금까지 그 일에 대해서 조금도 몰랐다 Till now I knew nothing about it. // 부를 때까지 기다리시오 Wait till called for. // 버스 정류장이 나올 때까지 곧장 걸어가시오 Walk straight ahead till you come to a bus stop. // 소녀는 숨이 찰 때까지 달렸다 The girl ran till she was out of breath. // 바람이 잘 때까지 떠나지 않았다 We did not start until the wind subsided. // 숨이 찰 때까지 계단을 올라갔다 He clambered the stairs until he was breathless. // 지금까지는 좋다 So far, so good. // 다음달까지 [계속] till next month ; [마감] by next month // 세

시부터 다섯시까지 from 3 to 5 o'clock // 죽을 때까지 싸우다 fight till death // 기차가 떠날 때까지는 아직 한 시간이 남았다 There is an hour before the train starts. // 3시까지는 돌아오마 I'll be back by 3. // 전람회는 언제까지 계속되나요 How long will the exhibition be open? // 제가 올 때까지 기다리시오 Wait till I come. // 바로 얼마 전까지만 해도 키 큰 사람이 좋다고 했었잖아 Until just recently you were saying that someone tall would be nice.
② [장소] to ; up to ; as far as ; so far as ¶ 부산까지 to[as far as] *Pusan* // 5페이지까지 읽다 read to[as far as] page 5 // 어디까지 가십니까 How far are you going? // 마지막 한 방울까지 마시다 drink 《the wine》 to the very last drop // 5피트의 깊이까지 가라앉다 sink to a depth of five feet
③ [정도·강세] even ; so far as ¶ 길이 바쁜데 차까지 고장났다 I was in a hurry[pressed for time] and, to make matters worse, even the car broke down. // 누구인지 물어 볼 필요까지는 없다 It is needless to ask who he is. // 심지어 나를 광신자라고까지 불렀다 He went so far as to call me a fanatic. // 옷까지 다 타 버렸다 Even my clothes were burnt.

까지다 [피부가] be grazed ; be chafed ; peel off ; come off ; [몸·재산이] get [become] thin ; waste away ; 《one's fortune》 dwindle ¶ 무릎이 까지다 have one's knee skinned // 바위에 손이 까지다 skin one's hand on the rock // 꺼칠꺼칠한 벽에 살갗이 까지다 graze against a rough wall

까치 〖새〗 a magpie
— **걸음** a bouncy walk[gait] — **두루마기[저고리]** many-colored outer coat [jacket] worn by children on New Year's Day — **설날** New Year's Day — **설빔** (children's) dressing up for New Year's Eve

까치눈 a chap in the bend of a toe

까치무릇 〖식물〗 Amana edulis (학명)

†**까치발** ① [받침] a bracket ; an arm ; a cross-arm ; a crosspiece (전신주의) ; roof truss (처마의) ② [눈 가장자리의] crow's feet ③ 〖식물〗 a kind of poppy plant ; Bidens paviflora (학명)

까치선 —扇 a four-colored fan (used by ladies)

까치콩 〖식물〗 an Egyptian bean

까칠하다 (be) haggard ; emaciated ¶ 까칠한 얼굴 a haggard〔worn〕 face

까탈 [방해] a hindrance ; a hitch ; an obstacle ; an obstruction ; an impediment ; a stumbling block

까탈부리다 raise problems ; make trouble ; put a spoke in another's wheel ; throw an obstacle in 《a person's》 path

까탈스럽다 ① [복잡하다] complicated ; complex ; intricate ② [어렵다] difficult ; hard ¶ 이 문제는 좀 까탈스럽다 The problem is a little too hard to solve. ③ [골치아프다] troublesome ¶ 일이 생각보다 까탈스럽다 The work is more troublesome than I expected.

까탈지다 run into problems〔obstacles, hindrances, objections〕; be frustrated ; come〔be brought〕 to a standstill ; bog down

까투리 a hen pheasant

까팡이 fragments〔broken pieces〕 of unglazed pottery ; potsherds

까풀 skin ; film coat ; scum ; skim ¶ 눈까풀 an eyelid ; a wrinkle on the eyelid (주름) // 까풀지다 get a skin on it ; be coated // 눈까풀이 지다 get wrinkles on one's eyelid // 죽에 까풀이 졌다 The gruel has a skin on it.

깍 caw ; croak ¶ 깍깍 Caw-caw! // 깍깍거리다 caw ; croak

깍두기 sliced〔cubed〕 white-radish *kimchi*

깍둑거리다 cut in uneven slices

깍둑깍둑 cutting in uneven slices

깍듯하다 (be) courteous ; polite ; civil ; respectful ¶ 인사가 깍듯하다 be polite in one's greetings // 깍듯이 politely ; courteously ; respectfully ; civilly // 깍듯이 인사를 드리다 greet 《a person》 politely

깍쟁이 ① [인색한 사람] a stingy fellow ; a miser ; a skinflint ② [약은 사람] a crafty〔shrewd〕 fellow ; a sly dog ; a shark 《속》 ¶ 서울 깍쟁이 a shrewd Seoulite ; a *Seoul* slicker ③ [어린 땅꾼] a young snake-catcher

깍정이 〖식물〗 [도토리의] an acorn cup ; a cupule

깍지¹ [활쏠 때의] a horn ring for the thumb ; [손을] clasping one's hands

깍지² [껍질] an empty pod ; a shell ; a husk

깍지끼다 ① [열 손가락을 서로 끼다] clasp (one's hands so as to link the fingers of both hands) ; lock one's fingers together ② [화살을 쏠 때 끼는 기구] put the archer's thimble on

***깎다** ① [물건을 얇게] shave 《wood》; chop ; cut ; [대패로] plane 《a piece of board》; [뾰족하게] sharpen ¶ 손톱을 깎다 pare〔trim〕 a nail // 연필을 깎다 sharpen a pencil // 얇은 조각으로 깎아내다 shave (off) thin slices // 깎아버리다 shave away〔off〕
② [머리 따위를] cut ; clip ; trim ; [풀을] mow ; [수염을] shave ; [양털을] shear ¶ 머리를 깎다 have〔get〕 one's hair cut ; get a haircut // 수염을 깎다 shave oneself ; have〔get〕 a shave // 양털을 깎다 shear wool from sheep // 잔디를 깎다 shave〔cut〕 a lawn // 짧게 깎은 잔디

the lawn closely shorn // 머리를 짧게 깎다 cut one's hair close // 적당한 길이로 잘라 주세요 Medium cut, please. (이발) // 짧게 깎아 주세요 Short cut, please. (이발) // 군인 스타일로 깎아 주세요 Grew cut, please.
③ [값을] cut〔beat, knock〕 down《the price》; have the price reduced ; [깎아 주다] reduce ; come down ; lower ; take〔knock〕 off ; abate ; make《it》 cheaper ¶ 악착같이 값을 깎다 drive the hardest bargain《with the dealer》// 500원으로 깎다 beat down the price to 500 *won* // 1할을 깎다 have《a person》 come down by ten per cent // 좀더 깎아 주시오 Come down a little more. / Can't you make it cheaper? // 더 이상 깎을 수 없습니다 I can go no lower. // 정가는 40000원인데 그가 5000원을 깎아 줬다 It was ticketed at 40000 *won*, but he knocked off 5000 *won*. // 흥정해서 5000원 깎았다 I haggled 5000 *won* off it.
④ [비용 따위를] cut down ; curtail ; reduce ; whittle down〔away〕 ¶ 비용을 깎다 curtail〔cut down, reduce〕 the expenses // 예산을 깎다 reduce the budget
⑤ [체면 따위를] stain〔compromise, injure, hurt〕《one's honor》; disgrace ; run down
⑥ [벼슬 따위를] demote from《a rank》; dismiss from《an office》 ¶ 벼슬을 깎다 dismiss《a person》 from his office // 관등을 깎다 demote《a person》 to a lower rank
⑦ [공을 비켜 치다] spin ; chop

깎아지르다 (be) extremely steep ; precipitous ; bluff ¶ 깎아지른 듯한 암벽 a precipitous wall of rock

깎은서방님 —書房— a smartly dressed young man

깎은선비 a handsome〔fine-looking〕 gentleman

깎이다 ① [사역] make〔have〕 someone trim〔cut〕 ¶ 뜰의 풀이 깎이다 have the lawn mowed // 이발사에게 머리를 깎이다 have one's hair cut
② [수동] be trimmed ; be cut (down) ; be peeled〔pared〕 ¶ 연필이 잘 깎인다 This pencil sharpens nicely.
③ [값이] be reduced ; be bargained down ; be cut ¶ 예산이 깎이다 A budget is cut.
④ [명예를] be disgraced ; lose face
⑤ [관직 따위를]《an office, a rank》 be taken away ; get demoted

깐 [가늠] calculation ; estimation ; judgment ; [짐히는 생각] recollection ; remembrance ; awareness ; realization ; recognition ¶ 우리들 깐에는 in our own eyes // 내〔네〕 깐에는 by my〔your〕 account // 좋지 않게 말하던 깐이 있어서 얼굴을 붉혔다 I blushed with shame at the thought of my having spoken ill of him. // 제 깐에는 대학자나 된 줄 안다 He is a self-styled scholar. / He is a savant in his own estimation. // 제 깐에는 옳은 줄 안다 He believes himself in the right. // 그녀는 제 깐에는 미인이라고 생각하고 있다 She fancies herself beautiful.

깐깐이 a man of hard-grained character ; a particular person ; a picky person

깐깐하다 [끈질기다] (be) sticky ; [완고하다] pertinacious ; tenacious ; [세심하다] meticulous ; inquisitive ; [엄격하다] strict ; overnice ; [까다롭다] fastidious ; particular ¶ 깐깐한 사람 a particular person ; a picky person ; a man of hard-grained character // 깐깐한 기질 a fastidious mind // 깐깐히 carefully ; scrupulously ; strictly ; exactly ; meticulously // 깐깐히 캐묻다 grill《a person》; dig up all the details to ask about ; inquire in great detail

깐보다 ① [가늠하다] make〔form〕 a conjecture ; give〔make〕 a guess ; tap a person's view ¶ 깐보고 결정하자 Let us see how things turn out before we decide.
② [깔보다] look down upon

깐작거리다 stick《to》; be tenacious

깐작깐작 being tenacious〔persistent, sticky〕

깔개 [방석] a cushion ; [돗자리류] matting ; [융단] a carpet ; [바닥의 일부에 까는] a rug ; [융단 대용의] a floorcloth ; a footcloth

깔기다 discharge《excrements》 indiscriminately〔at random〕 ¶ 길가에다 오줌을 깔기다 do〔have, take〕 a leak by the side of the road ; make〔pass〕 water by the side of the road // 똥을 아무데나 깔기다 use a fresh-air toilet

깔깔 screaming with laughter ⇨ 껄껄 ¶ 깔깔거리다〔대다〕 laugh loudly ; scream with laughter ; guffaw

깔깔하다[1] ① [감촉이] (be) coarse ; rough ¶ 깔깔한 피부 a rough skin // 종이가 깔깔하다 The paper is rough. // 혀가 깔깔하다 The tongue is rough.
② [성미가] (be) particular ; fastidious ; moody ; touchy ; fussy ¶ 성미가 깔깔한 사람 a touchy person

깔끄럽다 (be) rough ; ruckle ; prickly ; prickling

깔끔거리다 prick ; stick ; irritate

***깔끔하다** [매끈하다] (be) sleek and clean ; smart ; neat and tidy ; [성질이] sharp ; harsh ¶ 깔끔한 성질 a sharp temper // 깔끔한 옷차림을 하다 be neatly dressed ; tidy oneself up // 깔끔하지 못한 slovenly ; untidy

***깔다** ① [밑에 펴다] spread ; cover《a thing》 with ; [돌 따위를] pave《streets》 with ¶ 도로에 아스팔트를 깔다 pave 《streets》 with asphalt // 마루에 돗자리를 깔다 lay mats on the floor // 상자 안에 종이를 깔다 line a case with paper ; cover the bottom of the box with paper // 잠자리를 깔다 make the bed // 먼저 신문지를 깔 테니까 잠깐 기다려 Wait a second. Let me spread out some newspapers first. // 5년 후에 새로운 철도가 깔린다고 한다 They say a new railway line's being put through here in five year's time.

② [타고 앉다] sit on

③ [늘어 놓다] spread (out) ; [돈을] invest 《in》 ; put 《money》 in ; loan ; lend ¶ 빚을 몇 군데 깔아놓다 lend money to several persons // 여러 가지 사업에 돈을 깔아놓다 invest〔put〕 money in various business

④ [눈을 아래로] look downward ; cast down one's eyes

⑤ [억누르다] under the thumb of (a person)〔under (a person's) thumb〕 ; dominate ¶ 남편을 깔고 앉다 keep one's husband under one's thumb ; dominate one's husband

깔딱 [삼키는 소리] with a gulp ; [뒤집히는 소리] cracking ; crackling ; popping ; snapping ; [숨이] with gasps ¶ 깔딱거리다(-대다) keep gulping ; gulp repeatedly

깔딱거리다 keep gulping ; gulp repeatedly

깔딱하다 《one's eyes》 be drawn with fatigue〔hunger〕

깔때기 a funnel ¶ 깔때기 모양의 funnel(l)ed ; funnelform ; funnel-shaped

깔리다 ① [흩어지다] be spread ; overspread ② [밑에] be held down ; be sat on 《by》 ③ [돈이] be lent out widely ¶ 부인에게 깔려 사는 남편 a henpecked husband // 방안에 종이가 지저분하게 깔렸다 The room was littered with scraps of paper. // 수많은 경찰이 길에 깔려 경비하고 있다 Hundreds and thousands of policemen stand on guard all along the street. // 깔려 죽다 be crushed〔squeezed, pressed〕 to death // 내려앉은 대들보에 깔려 죽다 be crushed to death under a fallen beam

깔밋하다 (be) simple and neat

***깔보다** look down on ; slight ; regard with contempt ; hold 《a person》 cheap ; think meanly of ; undervalue ; think〔make〕 little〔nothing〕 of ; despise ; disparage ; depreciate ; belittle ; show contempt ; have a contempt for ¶ 남의 능력을 깔보다 underrate another's ability // 병을 깔보다 make light of one's illness // 가진 것이 없다고 깔보지 마라 Do not hold me so cheap〔in contempt〕 only because I have nothing〔I am penniless〕. // 사람을 그렇게 깔보지 마라 Don't look down on me so. // 사람들은 그를 어린애라고 깔보았다 They made light of him as a mere child. // 내가 가난하다고 깔보지 마라 Don't put me down because I'm poor.

깔아뭉개다 [눌러 뭉개다] press down ; compress ; squeeze ; [일을] shelve ; pigeonhole ; table 《미》 ; side track 《미》 ¶ 제안을 깔아뭉개다 shelve〔smother up〕 a proposal

깔쭉이 a milled silver coin

깔쭉깔쭉 —하다 (be) coarse ; rough 《surface》 ; sandy ¶ 가장자리를 깔쭉깔쭉하게 하다 notch ; make notches on the edge

깔쭉거리다 be rough (표면이) ; be coarse (천이) ; be granular ; feel rough to the touch ¶ 이 종이는 깔쭉거린다 This paper feels rough.

깔축없다 show no deficiency ; have no loss

깔치 a gal 《속》 ; a chick 《미·속》 ; a girl friend (여자 친구)

***깜깜하다** ① (be) very dark ; pitch-black ; be as dark as pitch ¶ 깜깜한 밤 a jet-black〔pitch-dark〕 night // 깜깜한 속에서 in utter〔dead, total, thick〕 darkness // (어지러워서) 눈앞이 깜깜해진다 Everything is going black.

② [아는 것이 전혀 없다] (be) ignorant ; blank ¶ 나는 한학에는 깜깜하다 I am utterly ignorant of the Chinese classics.

깜깜 밤중이다 속담 There is no blindness like ignorance. /As blind as a bat. /Blind as a mole. /Blind as a owl.

깜냥 what little ability one has ; one's ability〔capacity〕

깜둥이 ① [살빛이 까만 사람] a dark-faced person ② [흑인] a Negro ; a colored man ; a nigger ; a darky ; a blackie ; a blacky 《구》

깜박, 깜빡 ① [불빛이나 별빛 따위가] with a flash ; with a twinkle ¶ 촛불이 바람에 깜박 한다 The candle flickered in the wind.

② [눈을] with a blink ; with a wink ¶ 눈을 깜박 하다 blink one's eyes // 눈 깜박할 사이에 in the twinkle of an eye ; in a twinkle ; in a blink ; in a wink ; in a flash

③ [정신이나 기억이 잠깐 흐려지는 모양] ¶ 깜박 잠들다 fall into a doze ; doze off // 깜박 잊다 slip one's mind for the moment ; clean〔completely〕 forget // 깜박깜박, 깜빡깜빡 flickeringly ; waveringly ; faintly ; dimly // 깜박거리다(-대다) flicker ; waver ; wink ; twinkle ; blink ; be dim〔indistinct, vague, obscure, hazy〕

깜박등 —燈 an on-and-off light ; a flasher

깜박불 glowing points on a charcoal fire

깜부기 [곡식의] smut ; black ; [숯의] charcoal from the burnt remains of firewood
—불 a dying〔low〕 fire **—숯** cinders ; charred firewood ; used charcoal
깜부기병 —病 smut ; dustbrand ; bunt
†**깜짝** [놀람] with surprise ; with a start ; all of a sudden ¶ 깜짝 놀라다 be startled all of a sudden〔out of one's wits〕; bat an eyelid ; eyebrows go up ; be rocked on one's heel // 깜짝 놀라게 하다 knock one's hat off ; lift eyebrows ; razzle-dazzle // 깜짝 놀라 눈뜨다 start from one's sleep ; awake with a start // 깜짝 놀라 기절하다 faint from fright // 아이구 깜짝이야 What a surprise ! /What a start you gave me ! // 자네를 깜짝 놀래줄 일이 있다 I have a surprise (in store) for you. // 깜짝깜짝 [놀라다] with repeated starts ; [움직이다] budging repeatedly ; [눈을] with repeated blinking // 깜짝깜짝 놀라다 be startled again and again // 그는 우리를 보고 깜짝 놀랐다 He was struck dumb when he saw us. // 깜짝깜짝 [눈을] with repeated winking〔blinking〕; [놀라는 모양] with repeated starts // 깜짝깜짝 놀라다 be startled again and again ; [눈을] keep winking ; [놀라다] repeatedly start up with surprise ; jump with a start again and again
*__깜짝이다__ ① [눈을] wink ; blink ② [몸을] budge ; stir ; make a movement
깜짝이야 Oh my ! /Oh, shocks ! /Goodness gracious ! /What a surprise !
깜찌기실 fine〔thin〕 but durable〔strong〕 thread
깜찍스럽다 (be) precocious
*__깜찍하다__ [영리하다] be clever for one's age ; (be) precocious ; too sharp ; overly shrewd ; [단작스럽다] cunning ; crafty ; sly ; selfish ; [놀랄 만하다] surprising ; unexpected ; [비참하다] piteous, sad ; wretched ; [아주 작다] surprisingly small ¶ 깜찍이 exceedingly ; surprisingly 《clever, small》; shrewdly ; cunningly ; selfishly // 깜찍이 굴다 behave shrewdly ; play fox // 그 계집애 참 깜찍하다 The girl is quite precocious. / What a clever girl ! // 그 개 깜찍하게도 작다 What a tiny dog it is !
깝대기 ⇨ 껍데기
깝작거리다 behave〔act〕 frivolously
깝죽거리다 behave frivolously ; act flippantly
깝죽깝죽 frivolously ; flippantly ; imprudently
깝질 skin ; bark ; shell ⇨ 껍질
깡 〖광산〗 a percussion cap
*__깡깡이__ a fiddle ; a Korean musical instrument somewhat like a violin
깡그리 all ; wholly ; entirely ; utterly ; without (an) exception ¶ 깡그리 자백하다 make a clean breast of ; make a complete confession // 깡그리 잊어 버리다 forget utterly // 그는 깡그리 먹어 치웠다 He ate it all up.
깡그리다 finish ; get through
깡마르다 (be) lean ; haggard ; skinny ¶ 깡마른 사람 a skinny person ; a living skeleton
깡창거리다 hop ; skip ; gambol ¶ 깡창깡창 hopping
깡총하다 (be) lanky ; tall and slender ¶ 학은 다리가 깡총하다 A crane has long slender legs.
*__깡통__ ① [통조림] a can 《미》; a tin 《영》; an empty tin can ② [사람] an empty-headed fellow ; rattlebrain ; rattlehead ; rattlepate
— 따개 a can〔tin 《영》〕 opener
깡통차다 be reduced to begging ; go〔become〕 bankrupt ; go bust 《구》; go to pot
깡패 hoodlums ; a hoodlum ; a good-for-nothing ; a hooligan ; a gangster ; a heavy 《속》; a hood ; a tough ; a villain ¶ 깡패의 세계 the outskirts of society // 깡패가 날뛰는 거리 a gangster-ridden street
— 기질 hooliganism ; hoodlumism **— 사회** gangdom **— 일제 소탕** a round-up of gangsters
깨 [참깨] sesame ; Sesamum orientale (학명) ; a gingili (plant) ; [들깨] wild sesame ; Perilla frutescens (학명) ; [씨] sesame seeds ; perilla seeds ¶ 깨를 빻다 grind sesame-seeds // 그 신혼 부부는 깨가 쏟아진다 The newly-married couple live very happily together.
깨갱 whine ; yelp ; yip ; yap ¶ 깨갱깨갱 whine ; yelp ; yip ; yap // 깨갱거리다 (-대다) whine ; yelp ; yip ; yap
깨기름 sesame oil
깨깨 ¶ 깨깨 마르다 become extremely emaciated ; be reduced to a mere skeleton〔to skin and bones〕// 깨깨 마른 얼굴 a haggard face
*__깨끗이__ ① [청결] clean ; cleanly ; neatly ; tidily ¶ 깨끗이 하다 clean ; cleanse ; tidy (up) ; put in order ; make neat // 몸을 깨끗이 하다 keep oneself clean // 깨끗이 닦다 wipe 《a thing》 clean // 방을 깨끗이 하다 keep one's room clean ; clean a room // 방을 깨끗이 쓸다 sweep a room clean // 흰 옷을 깨끗이 입었다 She has been dressed in white neatly 〔tidily〕.
② [공정] fairly ; clean ; cleanly ¶ 깨끗이 이기다 win fairly // 깨끗이 지다 be fairly beaten ; be a good loser // 깨끗이 처리하다 deal fairly with 《a matter》
③ [완전히] clean ; completely ; entirely ; wholly ; all ¶ 깨끗이 거절하다 refuse flatly // 깨끗이 빚을 갚다 clear off

one's debts // 깨끗이 잊어 버리다 clean 〔quite〕 forget 《it》 // 깨끗이 청산하다 settle the accounts completely〔in full〕 // 깨끗이 손을 떼다 make a clean break 《with》; sever all ties 《with》 // 그는 용돈을 깨끗이 써 버렸다 He spent his pocket money to the last penny.
④ [결백] clean; cleanly; purely; fairly ¶ 깨끗이 교제하다 have a real friendship 《with》; [남녀간에] be in Platonic love 《with》 // 깨끗이 양보하다 make a clean concession; concede to 《a person》 without self-interest

깨끗잖다 ① [더럽다] (be) dirty; soiled; unclean ② [몸이] (be) unwell; sick; out of sorts

†**깨끗하다** ① [청결] (be) clean; pure; unsoiled; [맑음] clear; limpid; transparent; [참함] tidy; neat ¶ 깨끗한 눈 clear eye // 깨끗한 물 clear〔pure〕 water; clean water // 깨끗한 공기 fresh air; unpolluted air // 하늘은 맑고 깨끗하다 The sky is bright and clear. // 그녀의 차림은 깨끗하고 참하였다 Her appearance was tidy and neat. // 호수는 바닥이 보이도록 깨끗하다 The lake is clear to the bottom. // 모든 것이 깨끗하고 잘 정돈되어 있었다 Everything was clean and in perfect order.
② [공정] (be) fair; clean; square ¶ 깨끗한 승부 fair〔fine〕 play // 깨끗한 처리 clean〔fair, just〕 transaction // 깨끗한 한 표 a clean〔an honorable〕 vote
③ [완전] (be) clean; complete; entire; all; whole ¶ 깨끗한 청산 clean liquidation // 깨끗한 영어로 말하다 speak in perfect〔faultless〕 English // 그의 태만은 드디어 깨끗한 실패를 가져왔다 At last his idleness gave rise to a complete failure. // 병이 완치되어 깨끗한 몸이 되었다 He recovered from illness and felt well in his mind and body. // 깨끗한 이력 a clean record〔slate〕
④ [결백] (be) clean; pure; innocent; noble; chaste ¶ 깨끗한 마음 a pure heart〔soul〕 // 깨끗한 사랑 Platonic love // 깨끗한 인격 an innocent personality // 깨끗한 여자 a chaste woman; a nice girl // 깨끗한 일생 a career with a clean record // 마음이 깨끗한 사람은 행복하도다 Blessed are the pure in heart. // 모든 혐의를 벗고 깨끗한 몸이 되었다 He cleared off all suspicion of him, and became a man with a clear record.

깨끼 [깨끼옷] an early summer outfit for ladies which has silk gauze lining, hemmed with elaborate seams
— **저고리** the jacket to a outfit

깨끼춤 a suggestive dance

-깨나 just because of 《a trifle》 ¶ 주먹깨나 쓴다고 까불지 마라 Don't come at me just because you can use your fists. // 돈깨나 있다고 재지 마라 Don't be so stuck up just because you've got some money.

깨나다 ⇨ 깨어나다

깨나른하다 (be) languid; weary; dull; wearisome

‡**깨다¹** ① [잠이나 꿈이] wake up; awake from sleep〔a dream〕 ¶ 깨어 있을 때에 in one's waking hours // 잠이 깨다 awake〔be roused〕 from〔out of〕 sleep; have one's sleep interrupted // 자주 잠이 깨다 be a light sleeper; have a broken sleep; awake often from one's sleep // 잠이 덜 깨다 be sleep-drunk; be half-asleep〔-awake〕 // 자나깨나 awake or asleep; night and day; waking or sleeping // 나는 아기 울음 소리에 잠을 깼다 I was awakened〔aroused〕 by a baby's crying. // 그녀는 깊은 혼수에서 깨어났다 The woman was roused from a long lethargy. // 벌써 아기가 깨었느냐 Has the baby waked〔woken〕 yet? // 그는 깨어보니 벤치에서 자고 있었다 He woke to find himself on a bench.
② [술이] become〔get〕 sober; sober off〔up〕; take off the effects of drink; recover from one's intoxication ¶ 술이 깰 때까지 자시오 Sleep yourself sober. / Sleep and get sober.
③ [미몽에서] awake 《from》; be aroused; become sensible; come to one's senses; be disillusioned ¶ 망상에서 깨다 awake〔be awakened〕 from an illusion // 악몽에서 깨어나다 《a person》 awake from〔come out of〕 a bad 〔an evil〕 dream // 이로써 생각이 깰 테지 This would bring him to his senses.
④ [개화] become civilized; become modernized; be enlightened; open one's eyes ¶ 못 깬 사람 a person not used to the world's way; an unsociable person // 그는 깬 사람이다 He talks senses. /He is quite a man of the world. /He is a civilized man. // 그는 깬 사상을 가지고 있다 He has enlightened 〔civilized〕 thought. // 그 여자는 깬 사람이다 She is modern. /She is a sensible woman.

깨다² ① [물건을] break; crack; crush; smash ¶ 산산이 깨다 break 《a thing》 to pieces; smash 《a thing》 to bits; crash 《a thing》 to atoms // 돌을 깨다 break〔crush〕 a stone; [석공이] cut a stone into small pieces // 머리를 깨다 crack one's head // 접시를 깨다 smash〔break〕 a dish // 호두를 깨다 crack a nut // 유리를 쳐서 산산이 깨었다 He beat the glass and broke〔smashed〕 to〔into〕 pieces. // 호두는 잘 깨어지지 않는다 The nut is very hard to crack. // 하녀는 접시를 마루에 떨어뜨려 깨뜨렸다 The maid let the dishes smash (up) on the floor.
② [일을] upset; frustrate; mar;

spoil ; foil ; disconcert ¶ 상담을 깨다 frustrate〔spoil〕 the business talk〔bargaining〕 // 혼담을 깨다 mar〔upset〕 the matchmaking // 흥을 깨다 spoil one's sport〔pleasure〕; kill joy ; cast a chill over // 침묵을 깨다 break (the) silence // 십 년 만에 세계 기록을 깨다 break〔beat〕 the world record in 10 years

깨다³ [알이] be hatched ; hatch ; [알을] make hatch ; cause 《a chicken》 to hatch 《eggs》 ¶ 갓 깬 새 nestling birds ; a hatch // 알 깨는 데 3주일 걸린다 It takes three weeks for eggs to hatch. // 병아리가 깨었다 The brood are out〔hatched〕./Some chicks are hatched.

깨단하다 realize〔understand〕 all of a sudden ; catch on

†깨닫다 ① [알다] see ; read ; sense ; perceive ; apprehend ; comprehend ; awake to ; be aware of ¶ 사실을 깨닫다 perceive the truth // 형세가 용이치 않음을 깨닫다 be awake to the gravity of the situation // 그는 위험이 닥쳐오는 것을 깨달았다 He sensed the approaching danger. // 그는 차차 깨달을 것이다 He will apprehend better by and by〔next time〕. // 그 일을 깨닫지 못하고 있었다 It did not come under my notice. // 그는 죽을 때가 온 것을 깨달았다 He saw that his time had come. // 어딘가 잘못되어 있음을 깨달았다 I was aware that something was wrong.
② [자각] realize ; grow conscious of ; awake to ; be convinced of ; be aware of ¶ 의무를 깨닫다 grow conscious of one's duty // 잘못을 깨닫다 see the error of one's ways ; be convinced of one's error ; find out one's mistake ; come to one's senses // …을 깨닫게 하다 convince 《a person》 of ; waken 《a person》 to ; open 《a person's》 eyes to // 나는 나의 어리석음을 깨닫고 있다 I am conscious of my own folly. // 나는 깨달은 바 있어 담배를 끊었다 Realizing the harmfulness of the practice, I have given up smoking. // 그 나라의 고도의 정신 문화에 접하여 크게 깨달은 바가 있었다 Their eyes were opened by the high level of moral culture of the country. // 뒤늦게 그 여자는 내가 좋아하는 그런 여자가 아니란 걸 깨달았다 I belatedly found out that she was not my kind of girl. // 나는 그가 자신의 어리석음을 깨달았으면 좋겠다 I wish he'd wake up to his folly.
③ [도를] become enlightened ; be spiritually awakened ; have spiritual awakening ; find true philosophy ¶ 나는 인생의 무상함을 깨달았다 I realized the transience of life. // 깨달은 이 〖불교〗 a man who has attained the highest state of enlightenment ; a philosopher

깨두드리다 break (into pieces) ; smash ; crush

깨드득 with a smashing sound **—하다** sound smashed

깨떡 steamed rice cake coated with sesame seeds

†깨뜨리다 ① [물건을] break ; crush ; destroy ; crash ; smash ¶ 그릇을 깨뜨리다 break〔smash〕 a dish ⇨ 깨다²
② [일을] baffle ; frustrate ; thwart ; disturb ; spoil ; break ¶ 계약을 깨뜨리다 break a contract // 계획을 깨뜨리다 frustrate〔thwart〕 《a person》 in his plan // 세계 평화를 깨뜨리다 disturb world peace // 약속을 깨뜨리다 break one's promise // 침묵〔정적〕을 깨뜨리다 break silence〔stillness〕 // 행복을 깨뜨리다 disturb one's happiness // 혼담을 깨뜨리다 break up marriage talks ; undo a match

***깨물다** crunch ; bite ; gnaw ¶ 혀를 깨물다 bite the tongue // 입술을 깨물고 할 말을 참다 bite back // 입술을 깨물어 화를〔웃음을〕 꾹 참다 bite one's lip(s) // …을 한 입 깨물다 have a chew at

깨소금 powdered sesame mixed with salt

깨알 a grain of sesame ; sesame seed ¶ 동정심이라곤 깨알만큼도 없다 He does not have a grain〔an ounce〕 of sympathy.

깨알같다 be tiny as a grain of sesame

깨어나다 ① [의식이] return to consciousness ; recover〔regain〕 consciousness ; recover oneself ; come to (one's senses) ; come round (to oneself) ; come to oneself ; be brought(back) to life ; be restored from apparent death ¶ 기절했다가 깨어나다 regain one's consciousness after a faint spell ; come out of a faint // 마취에서 깨어나다 come out from under the anesthesia
② [미몽에서] be disillusioned ; be undeceived ; come to one's senses ¶ 그녀는 아직도 환상에서 깨어나지 못하고 있다 She is not yet awakened from the illusion.
③ [술에서] become sober ; sober up〔off〕 ¶ 술에서 깨어나 보니 도랑에서 자고 있었다 When I came to, I found myself lying in the ditch.
④ [소생하다] be refreshed ; be freshened ¶ 비가 오자 초목이 깨어났다 The grass and plants were freshened after a rainfall. / The rain has reinvigorated the withered plants.

깨어지다 be broken ⇨ 깨지다

†깨우다 ① [잠을] wake up ; awake(n) ; arouse 《a person out of sleep》 ; call 《a person》 ; raise 《a person》 out of sleep ¶ 학교에 가도록 사람을 깨우다 call 《a person》 for school // 잊지 말고 7시에 깨

워 주시오 Don't forget to call me at seven o'clock. // 몇시에 깨워 드릴까요 When shall I call〔wake〕 you ? // 아침 일찍 깨워 주시오 Please wake me up early tomorrow morning. // 날카로운 고함 소리가 나를 잠에서 깨웠다 A shrill cry awoke me from〔out of〕 my sleep.
② [각성시키다] bring 《a person》 to his sense ; undeceive ; disillusion ¶ 미몽을 깨우다 disillusion 《a person》 of his dreams
③ [술을] get sober ; make sober ; take off the effects of drink ; sober up from one's liquor ¶ 잠으로써 술을 깨우다 sleep off one's liquor〔drink〕

깨우치다 call 《a person's》 attention ; remind ; make realize ; reason with ¶ 사람의 잘못을 깨우치다 make 《a person》 realize his mistake // 사리를 깨우치다 reason with 《someone》 on the fact of a case // 사실임을 깨우치다 convince 《a person》 of a truth ; awake 《a person》 to the truth 《of》 // 그가 틀렸다는 것을 깨우칠 수가 없다 I cannot convince him of his error.

깨이다 ① [잠이] come to an end ; wake up ② [부화] be hatched ③ [···을] awaken 《a person》 ④ [부화시키다] make 《a chicken》 hatch 《an egg》

깨죽 —粥 a gruel made of powdered sesame

깨죽거리다 grumble ; chew dryly ⇨ 께죽거리다

†**깨지다** ① [물건이] break ; be〔get〕 broken〔smashed〕 ; fall to pieces ; be wrecked ¶ 깨진 사발 a broken bowl 〔dish〕 // 깨지기 쉬운 easily breaking ; brittle ; fragile ; frail // 산산이 깨지다 be broken to pieces ; be smashed into atoms // 얇은 유리는 깨지기 쉽다 Thin glasses are brittle. // 이미 깨진 사발이다 It is no use crying over spilt milk.
② [일이] fall through ; be upset ; be baffled ; be frustrated ; be ruptured ; be broken off〔up〕 ; [흥이] be dampened ; cool down ¶ 담판은 깨지고 말았다 The negotiation was broken off. // 친목회는 깨지고 말았다 The get-together meeting was broken down. // 싸움 때문에 흥이 깨졌다 The quarrel cast a chill over the merrymaking. // 그들의 약혼은 부모의 반대로 깨졌다 Their engagement was broken off because of their parents' opposition. // 양군간의 힘의 균형이 깨졌다 The balance of power between the two countries was upset. // 정상 회담은 핵실험 금지 문제로 깨지고 말았다 The summit talks blew up over the nuclear test ban. // 휴가가 계속되면 생활 리듬이 깨져 버린다 As the vacation goes on, the rhythm really goes to pot.
③ [일정 수준이 돌파되다] be broken 〔beaten, smashed〕 ¶ 세계 기록이 깨졌다 The world record was broken.

깨지락거리다 do〔go at〕 《a thing》 unconcernedly〔half-heartedly, listlessly, with little interest〕

깨치다 [해득] understand ; comprehend ; realize ; perceive 《a truth》 ; master ; learn ¶ 한문을 깨치다 learn 〔master〕 Chinese classics

깩 shrieking ; screaming ; shouting ¶ 깩하고 쓰러지다 fall down with a shriek // 깩깩 screaming ; screeching // 깩깩거리다 (-대다) scream harshly ; screech // 원숭이가 깩깩 운다 A monkey chatters. // 거위가 깩깩 운다 A goose squawks.

깩소리 a word of protest〔complaint〕 ; a peep 《of protest》 ¶ 깩소리 못 하다 cannot let out a peep 《of protest》

깰깩거리다 shriek with giggles

깰깰거리다 giggle (and giggle) ; titter (away)

깻묵 sesame dregs 《what remains after pressing the oil from sesame seed》 ¶ 콩깻묵 bean cake

깻잎 a sesame leaf ; a perilla leaf (들깻잎)

깽 with a moan〔whimper〕 ¶ 깽깽 yap, yap, yap // 깽깽거리다 (-대다) yelp ; yip ; yap

깽깽이풀 〖식물〗 a kind of barber(r)y shrub

꺄룩 craning (one's little neck) ¶ 꺄룩거리다(-대다) crane and crane (one's little neck)

꺄우뚱 moving slantwise again and again

꺅 ① [비명] shrieking ⇨ 깩 ② [꽉] full

꺅도요 〖새〗 a (fantail) snipe

꺼끄러기 awns and bits of rice〔barley〕 husks

꺼끙그리다 hull unhulled grain lightly in a mill

***꺼내다** ① [밖으로] pull〔draw〕 out ; take 〔bring〕 out ¶ 은행에서 예금을 꺼내다 draw one's money from the bank // 호주머니에서 지갑을 꺼내다 take one's purse out of one's pocket // 방에서 가구를 꺼내다 carry furniture out of a room // 지갑에서 돈을 꺼내다 take out some money from a purse ; take some money out of a purse // 그는 지갑에서 10달러짜리 한 장을 꺼냈다 He took out a ten-dollar bill from his wallet. // 강도가 호주머니에서 식칼을 꺼냈다 The robber whipped out a kitchen knife from his pocket. // 불이 빨리 번져서 아무것도 못 꺼냈다 The fire spread so fast that we could not save anything. // 이제 슬슬 겨울옷을 꺼낼 때가 되었다고 생각하니 Do you suppose it's about time to take out the winter clothes ?
② [이야기를] start talking ; introduce 《a subject, topic》 ; bring forward 《a

plan》; draw out 《conversation》; broach 《a matter with a person》; [말하기 어려운 것을] break the ice ¶ 꺼내기 어려운 말 a matter hard to broach //난문제를 꺼내다 bring up a difficult problem //그가 기분이 언짢기에 그 얘기를 꺼내지 않았다 As he was out of temper, I did not broach the subject. //그 얘기를 꺼내기가 곤란했다 I felt embarrassed how to break the ice about it. / I found it difficult to broach the matter.

꺼당기다 pull ; draw ; haul ; tug ; drag ¶ 아무의 머리털을 꺼당기다 pull a person's hair //밧줄을 꺼당기다 tug a rope //아무의 소매를 꺼당기다 pull〔tug〕 at a person's sleeve //그물을 꺼당기다 drag 〔draw〕 a net

꺼두르다 grasp and pull about ¶ 머리채를 꺼두르다 drag 《a woman》 by the hair and pull about

꺼둘리다 get grabbed and pulled about ; get dragged

꺼들다 take up ; pick up ; hold up ¶ 옷자락을 꺼들다 hold up the edge of one's skirt

꺼들이다 take〔bring〕 in ; pull〔draw〕 in ¶ 나무를 광에 꺼들이다 take firewood into a storeroom //아무를 집에 꺼들이다 take a person into one's house

꺼떡거리다 strut ; give oneself airs ; assume an air of importance ; be high-browed ; be high-hatted ; [뽐내다] boast ; brag ; talk big ; be proud of ; pride oneself on ¶ 꺼떡거리고 걷다 swagger ; strut (about) ; stalk about //그는 꺼떡거리는 버릇이 있다 He has a habit of holding his head too high. //하급 관리들은 시골에 가면 꼭 꺼떡거리게 마련이다 Petty officials cannot help putting on airs in the provinces.

꺼뜨리다 let 《a fire》 die〔go〕 out ; put out 《a fire, a light》 by mistake ¶ 불을 꺼뜨리지 마라 Don't let the fire die〔go〕 out.

꺼리다 avoid ; shun ; eschew 《a woman》; alienate ; be reluctant to ; keep aloof from ¶ 사람 접촉을 꺼리다 shun society //세상의 이목을 꺼리다 avert people's eye //나쁜 벗을 꺼리다 shun〔avoid〕 bad company //사람을 꺼리다 shun people ; keep aloof from people //고통을 꺼리지 않고 regardless of pains //수고를 꺼리지 않다 spare no efforts //거기에 가는 것을 꺼리고 있다 He is reluctant to go there. //그녀는 사진 찍기를 꺼린다 She is shy of camera〔is camera-shy〕. /She is reluctant to be photographed. //그녀는 사실을 인정하기를 꺼려했다 She was reluctant to admit the truth.

꺼림칙하다 feel uneasy ; feel uncomfortable 《about》; 《a thing》 weigh on one's mind ¶ 꺼림칙한 꿈 an ominous dream //뒷맛이 꺼림칙하다 leave an unpleasant〔a bad〕 taste behind ; leave an uncomfortable taste in the mouth //그 일이 꺼림칙해서 잠이 오지 않았다 The matter weighed so heavily on my mind that I could not get to sleep.

꺼림하다 feel uneasy 《about》 ⇨ 꺼림칙하다

꺼벙하다 (be) big but shaky

꺼병이 [꿩 새끼] a young〔chick〕 pheasant ; [사람] a man of unsightly appearance

꺼오다 pull in ; draw 《it》 this way

***꺼지다**[1] ① [불이] go〔die〕 out ; be put out ; be extinguished ¶ 꺼져 가는 등불 a failing light //꺼질 듯한 목소리로 in a faint voice //꺼질 듯한 목소리로 in a faint voice //꺼져 가는 불 a dying fire //불이 꺼지지 않게 하다 keep 《a fire》 alive ; keep 《a light》 burning //불〔전등〕이 꺼졌다 The fire〔light〕 was out.
② [분이 풀어지다] be appeased〔softened〕
③ [사라지다] disappear ; vanish ; be gone ¶ 꺼져 Beat it ! /Get lost ! /Scram ! /Split ! /Buzz off ! /Take a walk !
④ [거품이] break ; burst ¶ 거품이 꺼지다 A bubble breaks〔bursts〕

꺼지다[2] [들어가다] cave in ; sink ; subside ; be depressed ; become dented ¶ 눈이 꺼지다 One's eyes become hollow. //얼음이 꺼지다 ice breaks //그의 발 밑에서 갑자기 땅이 꺼졌다 Ground suddenly sank〔gave〕 under his feet. //지면이 꺼졌다 The earth caved in. //오랜 장마 끝에 도로가 꺼졌다 After the long rain the road caved in. //기초 부분이 약해서 그 집은 땅 속으로 꺼졌다 Weak foundations caused the house to subside.

꺼펑이 a cover ; a covering ; a cloak ; a hood

꺼풀 skin ; coat ; outer layer ⇨ 까풀

꺼풀리다 get a skin on it ; be coated

꺽 with a burp〔belch〕

꺽꺽 ¶ 장끼가 꺽꺽 운다 A cock-pheasant cries.

꺽꺽하다 (be) rough ; stiff ; hard ; harsh-tasting

꺽다리 a tall person ; a longlegs

꺽두기 [가죽신] oiled leather shoes ; [나막신] clogs

꺽둑거리다 cut in uneven slices

꺽둑꺽둑 cutting in uneven slices ¶ 무를 꺽둑꺽둑 썰다 cut radish in uneven bits

꺽저기 〖물고기〗 Coreoperca kawamebari (학명)

꺽죽거리다 behave brashly ; push 〔shove〕 oneself forward ; show cheek ; get fresh ; be brash〔forward, fresh, pushy, cheeky〕 ¶ 꺽죽거리는 젊은이 a forward youth

꺽지다 (be) stout ; firm ; tough ; bold ; dauntless ; heroic

꺽짓손 means〔measures〕 that are bold and compelling ; a heroic measure ¶ 꺽짓손 세다 have the means to be bold and decisive ; be indomitable ; be heroic

꺾꽂이 planting a cutting ; a cutting —**하다** take a cutting and plant it

*__꺾다__ ① [휘어서 부러뜨리다] break (off) ; snap ¶ 꽃을 꺾다 pluck〔pick, pull off〕 a flower∥나뭇가지를 꺾다 break off a branch of a tree
② [방향을 틀다] make a turn〔bend〕 ; turn ; shift ; veer (round) ; change direction ¶ 오른쪽으로 꺾다 turn 〔strike〕 to the right ; turn right∥핸들을 오른쪽으로 꺾다 wheel right∥핸들을 꺾을 때에 주의하라 Be careful when you turn the steering wheel.∥그는 핸들을 꺾어 충돌을 모면했다 He cut the wheel sharply (in the other direction) and avoided a collision.
③ [접다] fold ; double (up, over) ; turn down ¶ 칼라를 꺾다 turn down the collar∥표시를 하기 위해 페이지를 꺾다 double over a leaf to mark the page ; turn down a leaf to mark the page∥이부자리를 꺾어 포개다 turn down the bedclothes
④ [기운·생각·말 따위를] discourage ; squelch ; daunt ; unnerve ; dishearten ; dispirit ; dampen ¶ 기를 꺾다 break〔damp〕《a person's》 spirit∥적의 예봉을 꺾다 break the brunt of the enemy∥사기를 꺾다 depress〔sap〕 the morale∥강자를 꺾고 약자를 돕다 side with the weak and crush the strong

*__꺾쇠__ a clamp ; a cramp ; a staple ¶ 꺾쇠를 치다 fix a cramp iron

꺾쇠묶음 〖인쇄〗 (square) bracket

꺾어지다 [부러지다] break ; be broken ; snap ; [접히다] be doubled ; be folded ; 《it》 fold ⇨ 꺾이다

꺾은선 —線 a polygonal〔broken〕 line

꺾은선 그래프 a graph of broken line

꺾이다 ① [부러지다] break ; be broken ; snap ¶ 잘 꺾이지 않는 가지 a tough branch of a tree∥수양버들은 휘기는 하지만 잘 꺾이지는 않는다 The weeping willow may bend, but will not break.
② [방향이] turn ; make a turn ; bend ; be bent ; curve ¶ 길은 여기서 갑자기 꺾인다 There is a sharp turn in the road here.∥크게 꺾인 커브 a sharply breaking curve ; a curve which breaks well
③ [접히다] be folded ; be doubled ¶ 주름이 꺾인 치마 a skirt whose pleats are folded
④ [기운·생각·말 따위가] be discouraged ; be depressed ; be disheartened ; be dispirited ; be daunted ; be dampened ; be squelched ; be unnerved ; lose heart〔courage〕 ¶ 용기가 꺾이다 One's courage is shaken∥기력이 꺾이다 One's spirits become depressed/One is broken in spirit∥한 번 실패로 꺾일 사람이 아니다 He is not a man to be daunted by a single failure.∥소년은 온갖 고생에도 기가 꺾이지 않고 훌륭한 청년으로 성장했다 Not beaten〔discouraged〕 by hardships, the boy grew into a fine young man.∥여간해서는 기가 꺾이지 않는 것이 그의 장점이다 His strong point is that things don't easily get him down.

꺾임새 the fold ; the way it is folded back〔turned down〕

꺾자 —子 [지우는 줄] crossing out ; striking out

꺾자놓다〔치다〕 cross〔strike〕《it》 out

껄껄 ha-ha ; haw-haw ¶ 껄껄 웃다 laugh outright〔uproariously〕 ; roar with laughter ; burst into a roar of laughter ; laugh aloud∥껄껄거리다(-대다) guffaw and guffaw ; keep laughing loudly ; roar with laughter

껄껄하다 (be) rough ⇨ 깔깔하다

껄끄럽다 [깔깔하다] (be) rough ; coarse ¶ 촉감이 껄끄럽다 feel prickly ; be bristly to the touch

껄끄렁베 coarse hemp cloth

껄끄렁벼 rice grains with lots of bits of awns in them ; husky rice grains

껄끔거리다 feel prickly ; prick ; stick ; irritate ¶ 셔츠에 머리털이 박혀 껄끔거리다 Bits of hair are stuck in one's shirt and prick 《one's back》.

껄떡 [삼키는 소리] gulpingly ; with a gulp ; [숨소리] gasping(ly) ; panting(ly) ; out of breathing ; [뒤집히는 소리] crackle ; snap ; pop ¶ 껄떡껄떡 with a gulp ; cracking∥껄떡거리다(-대다) [목이] gulp ; drink with a gulp ; [숨이] pant ; gasp (for breath) ; [얇은 물체가] crackle ; snap ; pop ; [걸근거리다] be greedy〔covetous, avaricious〕

껄떡이 a greedy〔a covetous, an avaricious〕 person

껄떡하다 《one's eyes》 be drawn with fatigue〔hunger〕

껄렁껄렁하다 (be) poor ; worthless ; trashy ; good-for-nothing ¶ 껄렁껄렁한 사내 a good-for-nothing〔wretched〕 fellow ; a worthless scamp∥껄렁껄렁한 학생 a student lacking discipline∥껄렁껄렁한 작품 a cheap novel ; a dime novel 《미》∥껄렁껄렁한 학교 a third-rate school∥나는 그런 껄렁껄렁한 짓은 안 한다 I am worthy of better course./I know much better.

껄렁이 a wretched〔good-for-nothing〕

fellow ; a silly〔stupid〕 fellow ; a shiftless character
껄렁패 a good-for-nothing crew ; a shiftless lot ; a stupid crowd
껄렁하다 ⇨ 껄렁껄렁하다
껄머리 a wig ; a false hair ; chignon worn by the bride at a wedding
껄쭉껄쭉 rough
껌 chewing gum ; [막대기 모양] a stick of gum ; [알약 모양] a tablet of gum ¶ 껌을 씹다 chew gum ; have a chew of gum
풍선— bubble gum
껌껌하다 (be) pitch-dark ; be as dark as pitch ; [마음씨가] evil-hearted ; black-hearted ¶ 마음이 껌껌한 사람 a black-hearted person // 껌껌한 밤 a jet-black〔pitch-dark〕 night // 곧 껌껌해졌다 Soon darkness settled down. // 껌껌해서 아무것도 보이지 않았다 Nothing was to be seen in the utter darkness.
껍데기 [곡물의] husks ; hulls ; [조개의] a shell ; [밤 따위의] a nutshell ; [화투] a blank ; a cipher ¶ 달걀 껍데기 an eggshell // 굴 껍데기 an oyster shell // 모밀 껍데기 buckwheat husk // 밤 껍데기 a chestnut shell // 빵 껍데기 bread crust // 껍데기를 벗기다 take the shell off ; husk ; shuck // 나무 껍데기를 벗기다 peel the bark off a tree
껍죽거리다 [잘난 체하다] put on airs ; hold one's head high ; [까불거리다] behave frivolously
†껍질 [나무의] bark ; [과실의] skin ; rind ; peel ; peelings (벗긴) ; [깍지] husk ; shell ; [얇은 껍질] skin ; film ; cream ; [견과의] nutshell ¶ 귤 껍질 orange-peel // 바나나 껍질 a banana peel // 대나무 껍질 bamboo sheath // 빵 껍질 the crust of bread // 사과〔수박〕 껍질 the rind of an apple〔a watermelon〕 // 옥수수 껍질 the husk of maize // 파 껍질 the coat of an onion // 포도 껍질 grape-skin // 껍질을 벗기다 peel 《a potato》 ; pare 《an apple》 ; shell 《peas》 ; bark 《a tree》 // 껍질째 삶은 감자 potatoes boiled in their jackets ; jacket potatoes
-껏 ① [있는 대로 다] as far〔much〕 as possible ; to the best 《of》 ; at the top 《of》 ; to the full extent 《of》 ; to the utmost 《of》 ¶ 성의껏 whole-heartedly ; heartily ; sincerely ; from one's heart // 힘껏 as far as possible ; as far as one can ; to the best of one's ability ; with all one's strength // 힘껏 일하다 work as far as one can // 마음껏 먹다 eat to one's heart's content ; make 〔have〕 a hearty meal of ; eat one's fill ; eat as much as one can // 마음껏 울다 cry one's heart out ; have a good (long) cry ; weep to one's heart's content ; weep one's fill // 마음껏 마시다 drink one's fill // 재간껏 하다 do〔try〕 one's best // 힘껏 싸우다 fight for all one is worth // 힘껏 일을 해도 생계를 유지 못하는 자가 있다 Some find it difficult to make a living however hard they (may) work. / Work hard as they may, some cannot make both ends meet.
② [까지] (right) up to 《now》 ¶ 여태껏 all this while ; this long while 여태껏 한 것이 이것뿐이냐 It this all you have done up to now? // 대체 여태껏 어디에 있었느냐 Where have you been all this while? // 그는 여태껏 오지 않았다 He has not come as yet.
껑거리 a crupper
껑까다 tell a lie
껑짜치다 feel awkward ; (be) ashamed ; embarrassed
껑충 with a jump〔leap〕 ¶ 깡충거리다(-대다) walk in a leaping manner // 담을 껑충 뛰어넘다 jump over〔hop〕 a fence // 물가가 껑충 뛰어올랐다 Prices have jumped (up).
껑충이 a lamp-post ; a gangling fellow ; a lanky and fickle man
껑충하다 (be) tall and slender ; lanky ¶ 키가 껑충한 사내 a man with a tall, trim form // 두루미는 다리가 껑충하다 A crane has long, slender legs.
께 [에게의 높임말] to〔by, for〕 《a person》 ¶ 선생님께 to the teacher // 어머니께 온 편지 a letter for my mother // 자네 아버님께 이 글을 전하여 주게 Please hand this note to your father. // 이선생님께 올림 To〔Presented to〕 Mr. Lee with best wishes from...
-께 ① [시간] about ; around 《미》 ; toward (s) 《a time》 ¶ 보름께 about 〔towards〕 the middle of the month // 그믐께 about〔towards, near〕 the end of the month // 정오께쯤에 around noon-time ; towards noon ② [장소] around ; in the vicinity 〔neighbo(u)rhood〕 of ; near 《a place》 ¶ 시장께 near the market ; in the vicinity of the market // 우리집께 around〔in the neighborhood of〕 my home
께끄름하다 [사물이 주어] weigh on one's mind ; lie at one's heart ; get on one's nerves ; [사람이 주어] be anxious 《about》 ; feel uneasy 《about》 ¶ 뒷맛이 께끄름한 꿈 a dream remembered with discomfort // 뒷맛이 께끄름하다 leave an unpleasant taste behind // 그 문제로 마음이 언제나 께끄름했다 The question hung heavily on my conscience.
께끔하다 feel uneasy 《about》 ⇨ 께끄름하다
께끼다 [절구질할 때] put overflowing grain back into the mortar ; [노래·말할 때] chime in with 《a person's song 〔remark〕》
께느른하다 (be, feel) languid ; lan-

guorous ; dull ; listless ; tired
께서 [⋯가, ⋯이의 높임말] from《a person》 ¶ 춘부장께서는 무고하신가 Is your father well?/How is your father?
께옵서 ¶ 상감께옵서 영을 내리셨다 The king issued a proclamation.
께적거리다 do〔go at〕 something halfheartedly ⇨ 께지럭거리다
께죽거리다 ① [중얼거리다] grumble ; growl ; complain
② [음식을] chew with apparent disrelish ; chew dryly at《one's food》 ¶ 께죽 께죽 grumbling ; sluggishly
께지럭거리다 do〔go at〕 something halfheartedly〔listlessly, unenthusiastically, with little interest〕 ¶ 께지럭거리지 말고 빨리 먹어라 Stop picking〔dawdling〕 at your food—eat it up.
께지럭께지럭 halfheartedly ; reluctantly ; listlessly ; unenthusiastically ; inattentively ; [식사를] dawdling《over one's 〔a〕 meal》
껴들다 [두 팔로] hold《a thing》 between one's hands〔arms〕 ; [두 물건을] hold both at once
‡**껴안다** [두 팔로 끼어서 안다] embrace ; hug ; hold《a person》 to one's breast 〔in one's arms〕 ; take into one's arms ; [혼자서 일을 맡다] undertake《many responsibilities》 ¶ 서로 껴안다 embrace〔hug〕 each other ; be in each other's arms // 애인을 껴안다 embrace 〔hug〕 one's beloved // 두 사람은 서로 껴안고 울었다 The two threw themselves into each other's arms and wept. // 아무의 목을 껴안다 fling one's arms round a person's neck // 아무를 꼭 껴안다 hug a person tight // 그는 떠나기 전에 그의 딸을 껴안았다 He embraced his daughter before leaving.
껴입다 wear《a shirt》 underneath one's outer clothes ; wear extra (layers of) clothing ¶ 내의를 두 장 껴입다 wear two underwears
꼬기꼬기 wrinkled with handling **——하다** be all wrinkled
꼬기다 wrinkle
꼬기작거리다 crumple (up) ; wrinkle (up) ; rumple ; crease ⇨ 꾸기적거리다
꼬기작꼬기작 wrinkled with handling ¶ 꼬기작꼬기작 구겨진 종이 a crumpled piece of paper
꼬깃꼬깃 crumpled ; wrinkled ; creasy
꼬까옷 children's gala dress
***꼬꼬** [닭] a chicken ; [꼬끼오] cock-a-doodle-doo
***꼬꼬댁** cackling (of a hen after laying an egg) ¶ 꼬꼬댁 소리 (the sound of) cackling // 꼬꼬댁거리다 cackle // 암탉이 알을 낳고 꼬꼬댁 하고 울었다 The hen cackled after laying an egg.
꼬끼오 cock-a-doodle-doo ; cock-a-doodle ¶ 꼬끼오 하고 울다 cry cock-a-doodle ; crow // 먼동이 틀 무렵 어디선가 닭이 꼬끼오 하고 홰치며 우는 것을 들었다 It was dawn, and I heard a cock crowing somewhere.
‡**꼬다** ① [새끼 따위를] twist ; twine ¶ 새끼를 꼬다 twist a rope〔cord〕 // 실을 꼬다 twist a thread〔yarn〕 // 종이를 꼬다 twist paper《into a spill》 // 노끈을 꼬다 twist threads into a string ; braid a cord // 짚으로 새끼를 꼬다 twist pieces of straw into a rope
② [몸을] writhe ; wriggle ; squirm ¶ 고통스러워 몸을 비비꼬다 writhe in agony // 그녀는 온 몸을 비비꼬며 누구에게나 아양을 떤다 She makes herself delightful〔pleasant〕 to every person with her whole body motion.
꼬드기다 ① [부추기다] tempt ; allure ; seduce ; entice ; incite ; abet ; instigate ; agitate ; put《a person》 up to ; egg《a person》 on to《an act, do a thing》
② [연줄을] tug at the string of a kite (to get the kite to go up higher)
꼬등 the first ; first and foremost
— 딸기 early strawberries **—배** early pears ; pears just in
꼬락서니 [상태] a state ; a condition ; [외양] appearance ; [광경] a spectacle ¶ 꼬락서니 좋다 Serve you right!/It serve(s) you right! // 그 꼬락서니라니 Shame on you!/ What a plight he is in! // 꼬락서니 좀 봐라 How dirty you are! // 그 꼬락서니가 뭐냐 Look at you!/What a sight!/How dreadful (of you)!
꼬랑이 a tail
꼬랑지 the tail of a bird
†**꼬리** a tail ; a tag ; [여우·다람쥐 따위의] a brush ; [토끼·노루 따위의] a scut ; [공작새 따위의] a train ; [지느러미] a caudal fin ¶ 혜성의 꼬리 the tail〔train, trail〕 of a comet // 연 꼬리 the tail of a kite // 꼬리 끝 the tip of the tail ; a tag
꼬리(를) 감추다 관용 hide〔conceal〕 oneself ; cover one's trace
꼬리(를) 밟히다 관용 give a clue to《the police》 ; furnish a clue to the discovery ; be traced by
꼬리(를) 잡다 관용 find another's faults ; catch《a person》 tripping
꼬리날개 the empennage《of an aircraft》 ; the tail (assembly, group, unit)
꼬리보 〖건축〗 a beam bent at one end so as to touch a purlin(e)
꼬리지느러미 the caudal fin
꼬리치다 wiggle its tail ; [유혹하다] seduce ; entice ; allure ; lure ; tempt
꼬리치레 〖새〗 a N. China hill-warbler
‡**꼬리표** —票 a label ; a tag ; a docket ¶ 꼬리표를 달다 fasten〔attach, fix〕 a

label 〔tag〕 to ; tag〔label〕 《one's baggage》 ; put on a tag

꼬마 a very small man ; a dwarf 《*pl.* ~s》 ; a runt ; [난쟁이] a pigmy ; [아이] a kid ; a tot ; [소형] baby ; midget ; miniature ¶ 꼬마야 Hey junior !
— **전구** a miniature (electric) bulb ; a midget-lamp — **사진기** a midget 〔miniature〕 camera — **스타** a starlet — **자동차** a baby-auto〔car〕

꼬마둥이 a small child ; a little darling ; a midget

꼬무락거리다 move sluggishly ⇨ 꾸무럭거리다

꼬물거리다 wriggle ⇨ 꾸물거리다

꼬박[1] nodding ; bowing ; kowtowing ¶ 꼬박거리다(-대다) [졸다] doze ; nod ; fall into a doze ; snooze ; [절을] kowtow ; bow ; make (a bow) // 책을 읽다가 꼬박 졸다 nod〔doze〕 over a book

꼬박[2], **꼬빡** without sleeping a wink ⇨ 꼬박이

꼬박꼬박 ① [순종하는 모양] humbly obeying ; obediently ¶ 꼬박꼬박 어른의 말을 잘 듣다 readily obey one's elders ; be very obedient to one's superiors // 세금을 꼬박꼬박 내다 pay one's taxes regularly
② [몹시 기다리는 모양] waiting intently 〔anxiously〕 ¶ 세 시간을 꼬박꼬박 기다리고 있었다 I have been waiting〔keeping my eyes open〕 for you for three hours straight.
③ [차례를 거르지 않는 모양] continuously ; without fail ; faithfully

꼬박이 [계속] straight through ; [밤을] without sleeping a wink ¶ 꼬박이 밤을 새우다 pass a sleepless night ; sit up for the whole night without sleeping a wink // 하루 종일 꼬박이 기다리다 wait for 《a person》 to come all day long // 꼬박이 나흘 동안 (for) a full〔whole〕 four days ; (for) four whole〔clear〕 days // 그 일은 꼬박이 하루가 소요되는 작업이다 It is a good day's work. /It will take a whole day to finish that job.

꼬부라뜨리다 bend 《one's back》

***꼬부라지다** bend ; curve

***꼬부랑꼬부랑** (be) winding ; meandering ; crooked ; sinuous ; serpentine ¶ 꼬부랑꼬부랑한 길 a winding〔crooked〕 road ; a meandering path ; a road that winds every now and then // 좁은 길이 산을 꼬부랑꼬부랑 누비고 있다 A narrow path leads on through the hills with twists and turns.

꼬부랑 글자 —字 [졸필] a poor hand ; "hen tracks〔scratches〕" ; [서양 글자] alphabetic letters ; Roman or Cyrillic script

꼬부랑길 a winding〔tortuous〕 path 〔course〕

꼬부랑 늙은이 a bent〔stooped〕 old person

꼬부랑이 a bent object

꼬부랑하다 (be) bent

꼬부랑 할머니 a bent old woman ; an old woman bent with age

꼬부랑 할아버지 a bent old man ; an old man bent with age

‡**꼬부리다** bend

꼬부스름하다 (be) somewhat bent

꼬부장하다 (be) slightly bent

꼬불거리다 wind ; zigzag ¶ 꼬불대다 wind ; zigzag

꼬불꼬불 winding ; zigzag

꼬불탕꼬불탕 winding ; zigzag

꼬불탕하다 winding

꼬붓하다 (be) slightly curved

꼬이다[1] ① [일이 뒤틀리다] go wrong 〔amiss〕 ; get fouled up ; suffer〔meet with〕 a setback ¶ 일이 꼬였다 Things have gone awry.
② [마음이 뒤틀리다] become perverse 〔peevish, crooked, distorted〕 ; get cranky

꼬이다[2] [꼬다의 수동] [실 등이] be〔get〕 snarled〔twisted〕 ; be entangled ; be in a tangle

꼬장꼬장하다 ① [물건이] (be) straight and strong ¶ 꼬장꼬장한 회초리 a straight and strong switch ; a straight and stiff whip
② [늙은이가] hale and hearty ; vigorous ¶ 그 노인은 아주 꼬장꼬장하다 The old man carries his frame upright.
③ [성미가] stern ; unbending ; upright ¶ 성미가 꼬장꼬장하다 He has a stern character.

‡**꼬집다** ① [살을] pinch ; give a pinch to 《a person》〔give 《a person》 a pinch〕 ; nip ¶ 세게 꼬집다 give 《a person》 a sharp pinch // 남의 팔을 꼬집다 give 《a person》 a nip on his arm // 꼬집어 멍이 들게 하다 pinch 《a person》 black and blue // 꿈이 아닌가 하고 꼬집어 보다 pinch oneself to see if it is real〔not a dream〕
② [비꼬아 말하다] be sarcastic〔cynical〕 《about》 ; make cynical〔cutting, sarcastic, ironical〕 remarks ; say spiteful things

꼬창모 〖농업〗 rice plants set out with a dibble〔stick〕

꼬챙이 a spit ; a skewer ; a spear ; a prod ; a broach ¶ 생선을 꼬챙이에 꿰다 skewer〔spit〕 a fish ; thread a fish on a skewer〔a spit〕 ; skewer a fish // 생선을 꼬챙이에 꿰어서 굽다 skewer a fish and grill it ; roast 〔grill〕 fish on skewer 〔broach〕

꼬치 ① ⇨ 꼬챙이 ② [꼬챙이에 꿴 음식물] food on a skewer ; skewered

food〔stuff〕
꼬치꼬치 ① [몸이 몹시 마른 모양] ¶ 꼬치꼬치 야위다 be nothing but skin and bones ; be worn〔wasted, reduced〕 to a shadow〔skeleton〕 ; be as thin as a lath
② [자꾸 파고들며 물어 보는 모양] inquisitively ¶ 꼬치꼬치 캐묻다 be inquisitive 《about》 ; make a searching inquiry ; ask inquisitively
***꼬투리** ① [담배꼬투리] the unusable refuse of tobacco leaves
② [깍지] a pod ; a legume ; a hull ; a shell ; a sheath ; a shuck ¶ 콩의 꼬투리를 까다 shell〔pod〕 peas〔beans〕
③ [실마리] cause ; reason ; a lead ; a beginning ; a start ; origin ¶ 꼬투리를 잡다 invent〔make up〕 a pretext ; trail one's coat tails
†**꼭** ① [단단히] tightly ; fast ; firmly ; securely ¶ 꼭 묶다 bind〔tie〕 《a thing》 tightly ; fasten tight // 꼭 쥐다 grasp ; grip ; hold 《a thing》 tightly 〔fast〕 ; take fast hold of // 꼭 붙잡다 hold on fast to 《a strap》 // 문을 꼭 닫다 shut the door tight ; fasten the door tightly 〔securely〕 // 꼭 참다 suffer patiently ; stand up bravely // 눈을 꼭 감다 squeeze the lids over the eyeballs // 끈을 꼭 묶다 tie〔fasten〕 the strings tight(ly) // 수건을 꼭 짜다 wring a towel tightly 〔hard〕 // 그는 아들의 손을 꼭 쥐었다 He pressed his son's hand hard. /He squeezed his son's hand. // 어머니는 자기 아이를 꼭 껴안았다 The mother hugged〔embraced〕 her child tightly. // 이 창문은 꼭 닫히지 않는다 This window doesn't shut tight.
② [빠듯이] tight(ly) ; closely ¶ 꼭 끼는 모자 a tight cap // 꼭 끼는 구두〔장갑〕 tight shoes〔gloves〕 // 꼭 맞는 뚜껑 a close lid // 꼭 끼다 be tight〔close〕 // 새 신발이 꼭 낀다 My new shoes pinch. // 이 옷은 나에게 너무 꼭 낀다 This dress is too tight for me.
③ [정확히] just ; exactly ; right ; precisely ¶ 꼭 1시간 just an hour ; one hour to the minute // 꼭 3일 three days to the hour // 꼭 3마일 exactly three miles ; three miles to an inch // (끝전을 버리고) 꼭 1,000원 a round thousand *won* // 꼭 다섯 개 neither more nor less than five // 꼭 알맞은 사람 a suitable person ; the right man // 꼭 5시에 just 〔exactly〕 at 5 o'clock ; at 5 (o'clock) sharp // 이 시계는 꼭 맞는다 This watch keeps correct 〔good〕 time. // 그 모자는 자네에게 꼭 맞는다 That cap fits you exactly〔like a glove〕. // 계산이 꼭 맞는다 The accounts are perfectly correct. // 제 시간에 꼭 맞게 왔군. You've come just in time〔in the nick of time〕. // 그것은 꼭 내가 원하는 물건이다 That is just〔exactly〕 the thing I want. // 그의 옷이 내게 꼭 맞는다 His clothes fitted me to perfection. /His clothes were tightly fitting. // 강연은 꼭 1시간이 걸렸다 The lecture lasted for just〔exactly〕 an hour. /The lecture lasted for one hour to the minute.
④ [반드시] surely ; certainly ; for sure ; without fail ; no doubt ; by all means ; at any cost ; in any case ¶ 꼭 해야 할 일 a must // 꼭 오게 Never fail to come. /Come without fail〔by all means〕. // 꼭 가마 I will come, you may depend upon it. // 아침은 꼭 6시에 일어나기로 하고 있다 I make it a rule to get up at six in the morning. // 그 두 사람은 만나기만 하면 꼭 싸운다 The two never meet without quarreling. // 오시기 전에 전화를 주십시오 Please be sure to telephone us before you come. // 서울 근교에 위치한 민속촌은 관광객들이 꼭 가봐야 할 곳입니다 The Folk Village located in a suburb of the capital city is a must for tourist. // 약속은 꼭 지켜야 한다 No backing out, now — I want you to promise.
⑤ [마치] as if ; as though ; just like ; much〔nearly〕 as ; quite ¶ 꼭 죽은 사람 같다 look as if dead ; be more dead than alive // 꼭 미친 사람 같다 look as if one were mad // 하는 짓이 꼭 어린애 같다 He acts just like a child.
⑥ [애써 참거나 견디는 모양] patiently ¶ 아픈 것을 꼭 참다 endure the pain stoically // 웃음을 꼭 참다 hold back one's laughter
꼭꼭[1] ① [어김없이] without fail ; for sure ; regularly ; precisely ; exactly ; punctually ¶ 빚을 꼭꼭 갚다 pay one's debt regularly ; never fail to pay one's debt // 꼭꼭 들어맞히다 hit the mark (right on the nose) without fail ; always guess right ; always hit the nail on the head ; never miss // 시간을 꼭꼭 지키다 be punctual // 약속을 꼭꼭 지키다 keep one's promise scrupulously ; never fail to keep〔live up to〕 one's promise
② [바싹] without giving 《in》 ; without giving an inch ; firmly ; patiently ; [단단히] so that it won't give an inch ; hard ; tight ¶ 꼭꼭 매다 pull one's belt up right
③ [꽉] with no room〔not an inch〕 to spare ; full ; tight ; hard ¶ 꼭꼭 눌러 담다 fill chock-full ; pack in tight // 허리띠를 꼭꼭 졸라매다 pull one's belt up tight
꼭꼭[2] [암탉이] cluck-cluck ¶ 꼭꼭거리다 (-대다) cluck
†**꼭대기** ① [맨 위쪽의] the top ; the summit ; the peak ; the crest ; the crown ; the apex ; the spire ¶ 산꼭대기 a mountaintop ; the top of a moun-

tain ; the summit of a peak ; the crest of a mountain // 나무 꼭대기 a tree-top ; the top of a tree // 머리 꼭대기 the crown // 지붕 꼭대기 a rooftop ; the top of a roof
② [우두머리] a boss ; the leader ; the chief ; the head ; a topman ; a top sawyer ¶ 사람들의 꼭대기에 서다 be a leader of men ; stand above others

꼭두각시 ① [인형] a puppet ; a marionette
② [비유] a cat's paw ; a tool ; a robot ¶ 남의 꼭두각시 노릇을 하다 act as another's tool〔instrument, cat's paw〕// 그는 꼭두각시처럼 행동한다 He behaves〔acts〕 just like a puppet. // 그는 정부의 꼭두각시가 되었다 He was made a puppet of the government. // 그는 그들의 꼭두각시에 지나지 않는다 He's nothing but their puppet.

꼭두각시놀음 [인형극] a puppet show〔play〕; a marionette show〔play〕; puppetry

꼭두놀리다 manipulate a puppet

꼭두새벽 daybreak ; dawn ; the peep of day ¶ 꼭두새벽부터 from early morning

꼭뒤 ① [뒤통수의] the back of the head ② [활의] the (bow) nock ¶ 꼭뒤 눌러서 억지로 승낙시키다 force〔push, thrust, cram〕《a thing》 down 《a person's》 throat // 그는 경쟁자를 꼭뒤 질러 현재의 지위를 차지했다 He got the start of his rivals and secured the present position. // 그 책을 사려고 했는데 다른 사람한테 꼭뒤 질렸다 I was going to buy the book, but I got beaten to it〔someone bought it ahead of me〕.
꼭뒤(를) 누르다 관용 oppress ; repress ; keep〔hold, put〕 down ; have 《a person》 under one's thumb〔control〕
꼭뒤(를) 눌리다 관용 be oppressed ; be repressed ; be dominated ; be under 《a person's》 thumb
꼭뒤(를) 지르다 관용 go ahead 《of》; precede ; forestall 《a person》; be beforehand with 《a person》; get the start of 《a person》; steal a march upon 《a person》
꼭뒤(를) 질리다 관용 be forestalled 《by》; get beaten to something

⁑**꼭지**[1] ① [그릇 뚜껑의 손잡이] a knob ; a handle ¶ 주전자 꼭지 the handle of a kettle ② [식물의] a stem ; a stalk ③ [연의] a decorative strip pasted near the top of a kite ④ [거지나 딴꾼의 우두머리] a boss〔head〕 (of a band of beggars) ⑤ [도리깨의] the pivot of a flail

꼭지[2] [물건을 세는 단위] a bunch ; a bundle ¶ 미역 두 꼭지 two bunches〔bundles〕 of seaweed

꼭지각 一角 〖수학〗 a vertical angle

꼭지점 一點 〖수학〗 an apex ; a vertex ; the angular point

꼭하다 (be) honest and guileless

꼰질꼰질하다 (be) over-meticulous ; excessively scrupulous ; be too fussy ¶ 그는 무슨 일에나 너무 꼰질꼰질하다 He is too meticulous in everything.

꼲다 mark ; give marks ; grade ; rate ¶ 선생님들은 답안을 꼲기에 바쁘다 The teachers are busy looking over the (examination) papers.

†**꼴**[1] [모양] shape ; form ; [외양] appearance ; [복장] clothes ; [체재] respectability ; [상태] a state ; a condition ; a situation ; [광경] a sight ; a spectacle ; a scene ; [경멸적] face ; countenance ¶ 참담한 꼴 a horrible sight〔spectacle〕// 꼴사납다 (be) ugly ; unbecoming ; unsightly ; disgusting ; detestable ; shameful ; indecent // 꼴이 말이 아니다 be out of shape ; look miserable ; be put out of countenance // 네 꼴이 그게 뭐냐 Look at you ! / What a sight ! /What bad shape you are in ! /How dreadful (of you) ! // 피난민들이 사는 꼴이란 비참하다 The refugees are in a wretched plight. // 꼴 좋다 It serves you right. // 그 놈은 꼴도 보기 싫다 I hate the very sight of him. // 네가 먹는 꼴을 보니까 체중이 줄 가능성은 거의 없겠다 The way you eat, you have a fat〔slim, little〕 chance to lose any weight.

꼴[2] [풀] pasture ; forage ; fodder ¶ 꼴을 먹이다 pasture (animals) ; feed fodder (to animals) // 꼴을 베다 cut fodder (for animals)

-꼴[1] [물건의 낱개의 값] at the rate of ; per unit ¶ 한 다발에 700원 꼴로 at the rate of 700 *won* a bundle // 쇠고기는 한 근에 8000원 꼴로 판매되고 있다 Beef is sold at the rate of 8,000 *won* a *keun*.

꼴간 一間 a hay loft

꼴깍 gulping down ⇨ 꿀꺽

꼴꼴 trickling ¶ 꼴꼴 흐르다 trickle ; ripple ; bubble // 시냇물이 오솔길을 따라 꼴꼴 흐르고 있다 The brook is trickling along the alley.

꼴꾼 a fodder mower

꼴딱 ⇨ 꿀떡

꼴뚜기 〖물고기〗 a kind of octopus ; Octopus ocellatus (학명) ¶ 장마다 꼴뚜기 나랴 Good luck does not always repeat itself.

꼴뚜기장수 ① [꼴뚜기를 파는 사람] an octopus dealer ② [비유] a man of broken fortunes ; a bankrupt man

꼴뚜기젓 salted〔pickled〕 octopus

꼴랑 ⇨ 꿀렁

꼴리다 ① [생식기가] stand erect ; become stiff〔rigid〕 ② [부아가 치밀다] be roused to anger ; flare up (in anger) ¶ 밸이 꼴리다 one's temper flares up

꼴머슴 a servant on a farm ; an odd-job〔a chore〕 boy on a farm

꼴보다 examine a person's face〔personal appearance〕 ; look 《a person》 over ; see how things stand ; see how a situation is ; see how the wind blows ; look things over

꼴불견 —不見 unsightliness ; unpresentableness ; shabbiness ; indecency ¶ 꼴불견이다 be unsightly〔ugly, indecent〕 ; cannot bear to see ; be unable to stand the sight 《of》// 자네 나이에 그렇게 화려한 옷은 꼴불견이네 It is bad taste〔not proper〕 for a man of your age to go about in such a gallant suit. // 늙은이가 그런 식으로 여자를 쫓아다니는 것은 꼴불견이다 It is obscene for an old man to chase around after women that way.

*꼴사납다 (be) ugly ; unbecoming ; disgusting ; shameful ; unsightly ; detestable ; indecent ¶ 꼴사나운 짓 a shabby thing to do ; a shameful act ; unbecoming behavior // 꼴사납게 굴다 behave in a shameful fashion ; act dreadfully // 주제가 꼴사납다 be shabbily dressed

꼴좋다 It serves you right !

꼴짝 ① [소리] squelching ; squashing ; squishing (sound) ② [우는 모양] sniffling ¶ 꼴짝거리다(-대다) squash and squash ; sniffle and sniffle

*꼴찌 the last ; the bottom ; the tail end ; the tail ender ; the last man 《in a race》 ¶ 꼴찌에서 두 번째 the last but one ; the second to last // 그는 달리기에서 꼴찌로 들어왔다 He finished last in the race. // 그는 언제나 학급에서 꼴찌였다 He was always at the bottom of his class. // 그는 꼴찌로 졸업했다 He graduated last on the list. // 꼴찌상 a booby prize

꼴찌락 ¶ 꼴찌락거리다 splash ; splatter ; plop

꼼꼼쟁이 a meticulous person ; a stickler (for details)

*꼼꼼하다 (be) very careful ; scrupulous ; meticulous ; elaborate ; conscientious ; deliberate ; attentive ; detailed ¶ 꼼꼼히 carefully ; scrupulously ; minutely ; elaborately ; in detail // 꼼꼼한 솜씨 elaborate〔careful, conscientious〕 workmanship // 일을 꼼꼼히 하다 work conscientiously ; put great care into one's work // 꼼꼼한 성격 a meticulous nature

꼼바르다 (be) niggardly ; stingy

꼼바리 a meticulous〔scrupulous〕 person ; an attentive〔a conscientious〕 person

*꼼짝못하다 ① [움직이지 못하다] cannot move at all ; cannot move〔budge, stir〕 an inch ; be in a fix ; be quite helpless ; be in a dilemma ; stick in the mud ¶ 그는 그 자리에서 꼼짝도 못했다 He was rooted to the spot. // 내 차는 눈속에서 꼼짝도 못했다 My car got stuck〔got stalled〕 in the snow. // 그 회사는 자금난으로 꼼짝못하고 있다. That company gets into a fix on account of financial difficulty. // 나는 늘 보너스가 나올 때까지는 빚으로 꼼짝못한다 I'm always up to my neck in debt until bonus time.
② [기를 못 펴다] be under 《a person's》 thumb ; be cowed ; be intimidated ¶ 그는 주인 앞에서는 꼼짝못한다 He is always cowed〔too humble〕 in the presence of his master. // 마누라한테 꼼짝못한다 He is henpecked by his wife. // 꼼짝못하고 졌다 We were beaten all hollow. // 그 말 한 마디에 꼼짝못했다 He was silenced by that one word.

꼼짝없다 (be) helpless ; inevitable ; unavoidable ¶ 꼼짝없이 helplessly ; with no way out ; without any means ; without recourse ; inevitably ; unavoidably ; without moving ; without the slightest stir ¶ 꼼짝없이 붙잡히다 be held〔arrested〕 with no way out // 꼼짝없이 죽게 되다 face the inevitable death // 꼼짝없이 굶고 있다 be starving helplessly

꼼치 [작은 것] a tiny〔small〕 thing

꼽꼽쟁이 a person who is punctilious and neat

꼽꼽하다 be a bit damp

*꼽다 [셈하려고 손가락을 하나씩 구부리다] count 《on one's fingers》 ; number ; reckon ; take a count 《of》 ¶ 손꼽아 세다 count on one's fingers // 참된 애국자는 손꼽을 정도야 True patriots may be counted on the fingers. // 이 마을에서 부자로는 그를 첫째로 꼽는다 He is the richest man in the town.

꼽재기 ① [때] dirt ; filth ; grime ; [눈곱] gum ② [아주 작은 물건] a bit〔trifle, mite〕 ¶ 그에게는 품위라고는 꼽재기만큼도 없다 There is no dignity about him.

꼽추 ⇨ 곱사등이
—춤 a comic dance with pillow on one's back

꼿꼿이 ① [곧다] (be) straight ; upright ; erect ¶ 꼿꼿이 서다 stand upright〔erect〕 ② [언행을] honestly ; in a straightforward 〔forthright〕 manner ; strongly ; firmly ¶ 꼿꼿이 대답하다 answer forthright ; give a straight answer ; answer firmly ③ [빳빳이] hard ; hard and dry ; stiff(ly) ¶ 꼿꼿이 얼다 be frozen solid ④ [꼼짝없이] helplessly ; with no recourse ¶ 꼿꼿이 굶다 starve helplessly

꼿꼿하다 ① [곧다] (be) straight ;

upright ; erect ¶ 꼿꼿한 자세 straight posture
② [마음이나 뜻이 굳세다] (be) honest ; upright ; straight ; straightforward ; firm ; strong ¶ 언행이 꼿꼿하다 be upright in one's conduct // 의지가 꼿꼿하다 have strong〔iron〕 will ; be firm // 꼿꼿이 straight ; upright ; erect ; honestly ; in a straightforward〔forthright〕 manner ; strongly ; firmly

꽁꽁¹ ① [언 모양] frozen hard ¶ 꽁꽁 얼어붙다 be thickly frozen (over) ; be frozen stiff〔hard, solid〕 // 땅이 꽁꽁 얼었다 The ground is frozen hard.
② [숨은 모양] hiding oneself good ; getting well hidden ¶ 꽁꽁 숨어라 Hide yourself good. /Get well hidden. // 짐을 꽁꽁 묶다 tip up a parcel // 그는 강도를 꽁꽁 묶었다 He bound the thief firmly hand and foot.

꽁꽁² [앓는 소리] moaning ; groaning

꽁무니 ① [등마루뼈의 끝 부분] the lower end of a backbone ; the rear end
② [엉덩이] the buttocks ; the rear
③ [맨 끝] the tail (end)
꽁무니를 따라다니다 관용 dangle after ; hang about ; chase ; run after
꽁무니(를) 빼다 관용 flinch 《from》 ; shrink (back) 《at, from》 ; hold〔hang〕 back 《from》 ; turn tail ; back down ; run away ; run off ; beat a retreat

꽁무니뼈 〖해부〗 the coccyx

꽁보리밥 boiled barley taken as a meal (instead of rice)

꽁지 a tail ; a train (공작 따위의)

꽁지벌레 〖곤충〗 a maggot

꽁지별 [살별] a comet

꽁초 —草 a cigarette-butt〔-end〕 ; [엽궐련의] a cigar end snip 《미·속》 ¶ 꽁초 줍는 사람 a cigarette-butt picker ; a stub collector // 복도에 꽁초를 버리지 마시오 Don't throw away a cigarette-butt on the floor.

꽁치 〖물고기〗 a saury ; Cololabis saira (학명)

꽁하다 introvert and narrow-minded ; reserved and unsociable ; moody ; hidebound ; reticent and unadaptable ¶ 꽁하게 생각하다 bear in mind ; feel badly〔sore〕 《about》 ; have 〔harbor〕 a grudge against 《a person》

꽂다 [박다] stick 《in, into》 ; put 《into, through, at》 ; fix 《in, into, at》 ; drive 《into》 ; stab ; pierce ; thrust ; prick (바늘을) ; pin 《up, down》 (핀을) ; [끼우다] insert 《in》 ; inset ; impale ¶ 국기를 꽂다 fix the national flag // 생일 케이크에 초를 꽂다 stick candles in a birthday cake // 감자에 포크를 꽂다 stick a fork into a potato // 말뚝을 꽂다 drive in a stake // 병에 꽃을 꽂다 put flowers in a vase // 스위치를 꽂다 plug in ; insert a plug 《in》 // 펜에 펜촉을 꽂다 put a pen into a pen holder // 서류를 핀으로 꽂아 철하다 pin papers together // 헝겊에 바늘을 꽂다 stick a needle into cloth // 상투를 꽂다 wear a topknot // 원수의 가슴에 비수를 꽂았다 He thrust a dagger into his enemy's heart. // 모자에 장미꽃을 한 송이 꽂았다 He stuck a rose in his hat. // 단춧구멍에 장미꽃을 꽂다 stick a rose in one's buttonhole

꽂을대 a rammer ; a ramrod ; a cleaning rod

꽂히다 [박히다] get inserted ; be stuck ; be driven in ; be pinned ; be impaled ; be stabbed ; be pierced ; [끼이다] get between ¶ 타이어에 못이 꽂혀 있었다 I found a nail sticking in the tire. // 화살이 과녁 한가운데에 꽂혔다 The arrow alighted〔was fixed〕 in the very center of the target.

†꽃 ① [식물] a flower (초목의) ; flowerage (집합적) ; a blossom (과수의) ; a floral tribute (헌화)

> 참고 **flower**는 가장 널리 쓰이는 말 **blossom**은 결실을 기대하는 뜻을 포함하고 있다

¶ 꽃 피는 시절 the flower season // 꽃이 피다 bloom ; blossom ; flower ; open ; come to flower // 꽃을 가꾸다 raise〔grow〕 flowers // 꽃을 따다 pluck 〔pick〕 flowers ; break off a spray of flowers // 꽃의 floral // 꽃같은 flowery ; flowerlike // 꽃이 핀다 Flowers open. / Trees blossom〔bloom〕. /Buds come into flower〔bloom〕. // 꽃이 시든다 Flowers wither〔shrivel, fade〕. // 꽃이 졌다 The flowers are gone. // 테이블 위에 꽃이 장식되어 있다 The table is decorated with flowers〔florally decorated〕. // 꽃피어 in flower
② [정수] essence ; flower ; spirit ; pride ¶ 인생의 꽃 the flower of life ; bloom of youth ; the springtime of life
③ [아름다운 여자] a fair woman ; a beauty ¶ 사교계의 꽃 the flower〔the belle〕 of society ; a prominent society woman

꽃가게 a flower〔florist's〕 shop ; a flower stall (노점) ¶ 꽃가게 주인 a florist ; a flower man

꽃가루 〖식물〗 pollen ; anther dust ; farina ¶ 꽃가루 주머니 pollen sac ; a theca

꽃게 〖동물〗 a blue crab ; Portunus trituberculatus (학명)

꽃구경 flower-viewing ¶ 벚꽃 구경하러 가다 go to see the cherry blossoms

꽃구름 glowing〔iridescent〕 clouds

꽃꼭지 ⇨ 꽃자루

꽃꽂이 flower arrangement — **하다** arrange〔set〕 flowers ; put flowers in a vase

꽃나무 a flower plant ; a flowering plant ; a flowering tree
꽃놀이 flower〔blossom〕 viewing ; a picnic under the blossoms ; a picnic for viewing flowers ¶ 꽃놀이 가다 go to see the blossoms 《at》 ; go on an outing to see the flowers ; go flower-viewing
꽃눈 a flower bud
***꽃다발** a bouquet 《프》 ; a bunch of flowers
꽃다지[1] 〖식물〗 a whitlow grass
꽃다지[2] 〖첫열매〗 the first fruit (of cucumber, eggplant, etc.)
꽃답다 be lovely〔pretty, beautiful〕 as a flower ; (be) flowery ; flowerlike ; fine ; worthy ¶ 꽃다운 처녀 a flower of a girl // a girl (as) fair as a May rose // 꽃다운 죽음 a fine death ; an honorable death // 꽃다운 나이이다 be in the flower of maidenhood ; be sweet seventeen〔sixteen〕 // 그녀는 꽃다운 청춘에 죽었다 She was cut off in the flower of her youth.
꽃대 〖식물〗 a flower stalk ; a floral axis ; a r(h)achis 《*pl.* -chises, -chides》 ; a peduncle
꽃덮이 〖식물〗 the perianth ; the floral envelope ; the perigonium 《*pl.* -nia》
꽃돗자리 a figured mat ; fancy matting
꽃동산 a flower garden ; a flowery hill
꽃말 flower〔floral〕 language ; the language of flowers
꽃망울 a flower bud〔button〕 ¶ 꽃망울이 서다 have〔bear〕 buds ; put forth〔shoot out〕 buds ; be in bud ; bud
꽃맞이 a shamanistic ceremony to welcome the new blossoms
꽃맺이 unripe fruit in its early stage (immediately after the falling of the petals)
꽃무늬 floral design ; flower〔flowery〕 patterns ; flowerings ; 〖인쇄〗 a printer's flower ¶ 장미꽃 무늬 a rosette // 꽃무늬의 floral-patterned
꽃물 a kind of thick soup
꽃바구니 a flower basket
꽃받기 〖식물〗 the receptacle (of a flower) ; the torus ; the thalamus
꽃받침 〖식물〗 a calyx ; a (flower) cup ; a receptacle ; a torus ; a thalamus
***꽃밥** the anther
꽃방 一房 ① a shop which deals in imitation〔artificial〕 flowers ② a flower shop ; a florist
꽃방석 一方席 a fancy〔figured〕 cushion ; a flowered mattress
꽃밭 [많은 꽃이 핀 곳] a flower garden 〔carpet, bed〕
†**꽃병** 一瓶 a flower vase
꽃보라 flowers falling in the wind ; a "flower drift" ; a storm of falling 《cherry》 blossoms
꽃봉오리 ① [망울만 맺히고 아직 피지 아니한 꽃] a (flower) bud ; a button ; a budding flower ¶ 꽃봉오리가 맺히다 bear〔have〕 buds ; put forth〔put out〕 buds // 꽃봉오리가 피다 A bud develops into a flower〔bursts into blossom〕. // 꽃봉오리를 꺾다 pluck a flower in the bud ; pluck the bud of maidenhood ; deflower a girl ② [젊은 세대] the youth
꽃부리 〖식물〗 the corolla of a flower
꽃불 ① [이글이글 타는] a blazing fire ② [화약으로 만든] fireworks ; a fireworks display ¶ 꽃불을 올리다 let〔set〕 off fireworks // 오늘밤 꽃불 놀이가 있다 There will be a fireworks exhibition this evening. /Fireworks will be let off this evening.
꽃샘 a cold (windy) weather in the blooming season **—하다** suddenly get cold in the flowering season
— 바람 a chill breeze〔wind〕 in the flowering season
꽃송이 an open flower ; a blossom
꽃수레 a car decorated with flowers ; a flower-bedecked car〔streetcar〕 ; a decorated car ; a float (in a parade)
꽃술 a stamen (수술) ; a pistil (암술)
꽃시계 **一時計** a floral〔flower〕 clock
꽃시장 **一市場** a flower market〔fair〕
꽃식물 **一植物** a flowering plant ; a phanerogam
꽃싸움 ① [꽃 수효의 다수를 겨루는 장난] a flower gathering game ② [화전(花戰)] a flower wrestle
꽃잎 a petal ¶ 꽃잎 넷 있는 quartopetalous ; 4-petaled // 꽃잎 열 있는 decapetalous ; 10-petaled // 꽃잎이 없는 apetalous ; petalless
꽃자동차 **一自動車** a floral car ; a flower-bedecked automobile
꽃자루 〖식물〗 a peduncle ; a flower stalk ; a footstalk
꽃자리 a figured〔fancy〕 mat
꽃장식 **一裝飾** a floral decoration ; a flower piece (탁상 따위의)
꽃재배 **一栽培** floriculture ; flower gardening
꽃전 **一煎** griddle cake of glutinous rice prepared in the form of a flower ; griddle cakes made in flower patterns
꽃전차 **一電車** an illuminated〔a decorated, a floral〕 car ; a streetcar float
꽃주일 **一主日** the first Sunday of June
꽃줄기 the stem〔stalk〕 of a flower
꽃집 a flower〔florist's〕 shop
— 주인 a florist
꽃차 **一車** a car with floral decorations ⇨ 꽃수레
꽃차례 an inflorescence
꽃창포 〖식물〗 ① Russian iris ② a kind of bunchflower
꽃철 the blossom season

꽈르르 gurgling(ly) ; with a gurgle

꽈리 〖식물〗 a ground cherry ; a strawberry tomato ; [물집] a blister

꽉 ① [단단히] tightly ; firmly ; fast ; closely ¶ 꽉 쥐다 grasp〔grip〕 with force ; hold fast ; take fast hold of // 꽉 붙들다 hold on fast to 《a thing》 // 꽉 묶다 bind〔tie〕 fast // 손을 꽉 쥐다 squeeze a 《person's》 hand // 허리띠를 꽉 죄다 wear a belt tight
② [가득히] closely ; tight(ly) ; to the full ; to (full) capacity ; chock-full ¶ 꽉 채워 넣다 cram ; fill to the full ; pack 《a trunk》 close // 꽉 차다 be closely packed ; [승객 따위] be jam-packed 《with》 ; be packed like sardines // 책장에 책이 꽉 차 있다 The bookcase is closely packed with books. // 스탠드에는 관중이 꽉 차 있었다 The stands were solid with the audience〔filled solidly〕. // 홀은 사람으로 꽉 차 있다 The hall is bursting with people.
③ [참는 모양] patiently ; stoically ¶ 그는 이가 아픈 것을 꽉 참았다 He bore〔stood〕 the toothache stoically. // 그녀는 울고 싶은 충동을 꽉 참았다 She resisted an impulse to cry out.

꽉꽉 ① [힘을 주어] tight ; hard ; fast ; firm(ly) ; securely ¶ 꽉꽉 눌러 넣다 squeeze into // 밥을 꽉꽉 눌러 담다 stuff 《a bowl》 full of rice // 짐을 꽉꽉 동여매다 tie a load several times around with tight ropes // 문이 꽉꽉 닫혀 있다 All the doors are shut fast〔are closed tight, are secured〕.
② [가득] full ; chock-full ; compactly ¶ 방은 모두 사람으로 꽉꽉 들어차 있다 All the rooms are crowded〔packed, jammed〕 with people.

†**꽉차다** closely packed ; jam-packed ; full up ; crowded (to capacity) ; filled solidly ¶ 이 버스는 사람이 꽉차서 탈 수가 없군 This bus is quite full up—we can't get in.

꽐꽐 gurgling ; gushing ; with a gurgle ; with a gush

꽝[1] with a bang〔boom〕 ; with a thud〔bump, thump〕 **—하다** bang ; boom ; thump ; thud ; bump ; crash ; slam ¶ 문을 꽝 닫다 bang〔slam〕 a door (shut) // 꽝 떨어지다 fall with a thud // 총소리가 꽝하고 났다 Bang! went the gun.

꽝[2] a blank

꽝꽝 bang-bang ; boom-boom **—하다** go bang bang ¶ 대포를 꽝꽝 쏘다 boom a cannon repeatedly

꽝꽝나무 〖식물〗 holly

***꽤** fairly ; pretty ; quite ; tolerably ; rather ; considerably ¶ 꽤 많은 돈 a sizable〔considerable〕 sum of money // 꽤 많은 수입 a handsome income // 꽤 많은 시간 a considerable time // 꽤 먼 거리 a good distance // 꽤 오래 전에 quite a while ago // 꽤 여러 날이 걸렸다 It took a good many days. // 영어를 꽤 잘한다 He speaks English fairly well. /He is quite a good speaker of English. // 오늘은 꽤 덥다 It's rather hot today. // 꽤 추운 날씨다 It is pretty cold. // 환자는 오늘 꽤 나은 편이다 The patient is much better today. // 그녀는 정구도 꽤 잘한다 She is not half bad at tennis. // 이 그림은 꽤 잘되어 있다 This picture is done pretty well. // 오늘은 꽤 바빴습니다 We have had quite a busy day today. // 공원에는 꽤 많은 사람들이 와 있었습니다 There were quite a number of people in the park. // 그들은 꽤 좋은 집에 살고 있다 They live in a fine house.

꽥 with a shout〔scream, shriek, yell〕 **—하다** utter〔give〕 a shriek〔shout, yell〕 ¶ 화나서 꽥 소리치다 shout with anger // 꽥소리 못하다 be silenced ; be put to silence ; be cowed

꽥꽥 screaming ; screeching ; quack-quack (오리 소리) ; shouting and shouting **—하다** shout ; yell ; quack

꽥꽥거리다 ① [소리치다] cry ; shout ; yell ; roar ; give an angry word ¶ 사소한 일로 꽥꽥거리다 roar at trifles ② [토하려고] keck ; retch ③ quack (오리가) ; gaggle (거위가) ; squawk (갈매기가) ; croak (개구리가)

꽥지르다 cry ; shout ; roar ; thunder ; bawl ; growl ; bark 《속》 ¶ 큰 소리를 꽥지르다 cry aloud ; cry in a stentorian voice // 「누구냐」 하고 큰 소리를 꽥질렀다 "Who's there?" cried the man in a voice of thunder.

꽹 Bong! ; Boom! ; Clang!

꽹과리 a gong ¶ 꽹과리를 치다 beat〔hit〕 a gong

꾀 [지혜] wise counsel ; wit ; resources ; [계략] a stratagem ; an artifice ; a trick ; a ruse ; [계책] a device ; a design ; a scheme ; a subtlety ¶ 꾀가 많은 crafty ; resourceful ; full of shifts and devices ; tactful // 꾀 많은 사람 a resourceful man ; a man of resources ; a tricker // 꾀가 없는 사람 a man of no resources ; a shiftless man // (남의) 꾀에 넘어가다 fall a prey to another's stratagem ; fall into a snare ; be entrapped // 좋은 꾀가 생각나지 않는다 I can't think of any clever resources. // 그 꾀에 속으면 안된다 Don't fall for that ploy.

꾀꼬리 a (Korean) nightingale ; a bush warbler ; an oriole

꾀꼴꾀꼴 warbling and warbling ; singing away (of an oriole) **—하다** 《an oriole》 warble away ; trill ; sing

꾀꾀 ¶ 얼굴이 꾀꾀 마르다 One's face is drawn and haggard. // 병으로 몸이 꾀꾀

마르다 become worn out from illness ; be pulled down by one's illness // 볼품없이 꾀꾀 말랐다 be worn to a shadow ; be a mere shadow of one's former self **—하다** lean〔thin, meager〕

꾀꾀로 [틈틈이] at odd moments ; in one's spare moments ; [살짝] quietly ; secretly ; stealthily

꾀다¹ swarm ; crowd ; gather ; flock ; be infested with ¶ 파리가 꾀지 않도록 하다 keep flies away from 《the food》// 음식에 파리가 꾄다 The food is swarmed with flies. // 설탕에 개미가 꾄다 Ants swarm upon the sugar. // 장마당에 사람이 꾄다 A market place is crowded with lots of people. // 꽃에 진딧물이 꾄다 The flower is infested with aphides. // 썩은 고기에 파리가 꾀어 있었다 Flies were swarming over the rotten meat.

†**꾀다²** [유혹하다] tempt ; entice ; lure ; decoy ; seduce ¶ 꾀어내다 lure 《a person》 out // 돈으로 꾀다 allure 《a person》 with money // 꾀어서 돈을 울거 내다 coax 〔wheedle〕 《a person》 out of money // 달콤한 말로 소녀를 꾀다 seduce〔entice, allure〕 a girl with fair words // 뱀은 이브를 꾀어 금단의 열매를 따게 했다 The serpent tempted Eve to pick the forbidden fruit. // 그는 그녀를 꾀어 돈을 훔치게 했다 He enticed her to steal money.

꾀바르다 (be) crafty ; be clever 《at getting out of hard work》 ; shrewd ; cunning ; sly ; smart 《미》

꾀배 fake stomachache ¶ 꾀배를 앓다 pretend to have a stomachache

꾀병 feigned〔pretended, fake〕 illness ¶ 꾀병 부리다 feign〔sham〕 illness ; pretend to be ill〔sick〕 // 꾀병 부려서 쉬다 be absent 《from work, from school》 with a feigned illness ; malinger (병사들이)

꾀보 a man of quick wit ; a man of resources ; a tricky〔wily〕 person ⇨ 꾀쟁이

꾀부리다 shirk 《one's duty》 ; shuffle off 《responsibility》 ; dodge ; evade ; spare oneself ; be stingy of effort ¶ 꾀부리는 사람 a shirk // 꾀부리고 숙제를 하지 않다 shirk one's homeworks

꾀쓰다 use〔play〕 tricks ; resort to wiles 〔a ruse〕 ; shirk (꾀부리다) ¶ 목적 달성을 위해 꾀쓰다 use tricks to achieve one's object

꾀어내다 lure〔decoy〕 《a person》 out ; entice away

꾀어 들이다 decoy〔lure〕 《a person》 in 〔into〕

꾀음꾀음 with honeyed〔fair〕 words ; tempting 《a person》 with fine words **—하다** seduce ; tempt ; lure

꾀이다¹ tempt ; seduce ⇨ 꾀다

꾀이다² [꾐을 당하다] be lured ; be enticed〔tempted, seduced〕

꾀자기 a crafty〔sly, wily〕 person ; an old fox

꾀잠 sham〔feigned〕 sleep ; fox-sleep ¶ 꾀잠을 자다 feign to be asleep ; sham sleep

꾀쟁이 a man of resources〔ideas〕 ; a tricky〔wily〕 person

꾀죄(죄)하다 (be) shabby ; seedy ; miserable ; untidy ; poor〔wretched〕 looking ¶ 꾀죄한 집 a poor〔shabby, humble〕 house // 옷차림이 꾀죄죄하다 be shabbily 〔poorly〕 dressed ; be of seedy appearance ; be in seedy clothes ; be ill-clad // 너 정말 그런 꾀죄죄한 옷차림으로 데이트하러 갈 거냐 Are you really going on a date in that scruffy outfit ?

꾀피우다 resort to petty tricks ; play〔use〕 tricks ; frame up 《an ill design》 ⇨ 꾀부리다

†**꾀하다** plot ; plan ; attempt ; conspire ; design ; project ; scheme ; devise ; seek ; intend 《to do》 ; aim at ; labor 〔work, strive〕 《for》 ; exert oneself 《for》 ¶ 사리를 꾀하다 look to〔seek〕 one's own interests ; have an eye to the main chance ; be self-seeking // 자살을 꾀하다 attempt suicide // 살해를 꾀하다 form a plot to murder 《a person》 // 독립을 꾀하다 strive for national independence // 공익을 꾀하다 work for the good of the public ; serve the public interest

꾐 temptation ; allurement ; enticement ; seduction ¶ 꾐에 빠지기 쉽다 be easily overcome by temptation ; be weak 〔fragile〕 // 꾐에 빠지다 fall before〔yield to〕 temptation // 악우들의 꾐에 빠져 나쁜 길로 들어갔다 Bad companions tempted him into wrong ways. // 그는 꾐에 빠질 사람이 아니다 He is proof against temptation. // 꾐에 빠지지 마라 Beware of sweet words.

꾸구리 〖물고기〗 Gobiobotia macrocephalus (학명)

꾸기다 wrinkle, crumple

꾸기적거리다 crumple (up) ; wrinkle ; rumple

꾸깃꾸깃 wrinkled ; crumpled

꾸다¹ [꿈을] dream ; dream〔have〕 a dream ¶ 고향의 꿈을 꾸다 dream about one's home // 아버지의 꿈을 꾸다 see one's father in a dream // 다이아몬드를 줍는 꿈을 꾸었다 I had a dream in which I picked up a diamond.

***꾸다²** [돈 따위를] borrow ; have〔get〕 the loan 《of》 ¶ 1,000원을 꾸다 borrow 1,000 *won* from 《a person》 // 돈을 꾸러 오다 come for a loan 《of 1,000 *won*》 // 토지를 잡히고 돈을 꾸다 raise〔borrow〕 money on one's estate // 꾼 돈은 갚아야 한다 One must pay what one owes. //

꾼 돈은 좀 참아 주십시오 Please let me stay a little longer in your debt. // 돈 좀 꿔 줄 수 있습니까 Could you loan me some money?
꾸어다 놓은 보릿자루 (속담) being like a cat in a strange garret.

꾸드러지다 dry up ⇨ 구드러지다

꾸들꾸들 ⇨ 구들구들

-꾸러기 an overindulger
말썽— a burden; a bother; a handful; a nuisance; an imp; a bully 심술(心術)— a cross-grained〔an ill-natured〕 fellow; a dog in the manger; a cynic; a crosspatch 잠— a late riser; a sleepy head; a slugabed; a heavy sleeper 장난— a mischievous boy; an urchin; a little monkey; a limb of the devil〔Satan〕; slyboots

†**꾸러미** a bundle (in a wrapper); [작은] a package; a parcel; a packet; [큰] a bale

> (참고) **bundle** 운송이나 저장에 편리하도록 한묶음으로 만들어 놓은 것 **parcel** 수송이나 판매의 목적으로 비교적 조그맣게 꾸려 놓은 것이며 **package** 는 보통 상자나 용기 안에 담은 것을 말한다

¶ 책 한 꾸러미 a packet of books // 달걀 한 꾸러미 ten eggs in a straw wrapper // 꾸러미로 만들다〔꾸리다〕 make a bundle〔parcel, package, packet〕; bundle《clothes》; pack《goods》// 꾸러미를 풀다 unpack; undo a package〔bundle〕// 책을 20권씩 꾸러미로 묶었다 The books were tied up in bundles of twenty.
가마니 — a package wrapped in straw matting 솜 — a bale of cotton 종이 — a paper package

꾸르륵 [배가] rumbling; with a rumble (of one's bowels); [물이] with a gurgle (of water); [닭이] with a cackle ¶ 뱃속이 꾸르륵거린다 The bowels rumble.

꾸르륵꾸르륵 ① [뱃속이] with rumble; with growl; with gurgle —하다 rumble; growl; gurgle
② [닭이] with cackle —하다 cackle
③ [물이] with much gurgling《of water》—하다 gurgle

꾸리[1] a spindle〔bobbin〕 of thread; a spindle with its thread (뭉치)

꾸리[2] beef from the back of the front leg; foreshank

†**꾸리다** ① [짐을] pack〔wrap, do, tie〕 up; bundle; package (미) ¶ 짐을 꾸려 떠나다 pack up and leave // 짐이 잘 꾸려지다 be well packed // 슈트케이스에 옷을 잔뜩 꾸려 넣다 cram one's suitcase with clothes // 소지품을 꾸리다 pack up one's belongings
② [일을] manage; make do《with》; make shift; arrange ¶ 살림을 꾸리다 manage a household // 쥐꼬리만한 봉급으로 겨우 꾸려 나가다 eke out on meager pay // 그것으로 이럭저럭 꾸려 나가겠습니다 I will make do〔shift〕 with it.

꾸무럭거리다 move slowly〔sluggishly〕; be slow〔long〕; waste time; loiter; linger; dally; delay; hesitate ¶ 꾸무럭거리지 말고 without (a moment's) delay; right〔straight〕 away; quickly (빨리) // 뭘 꾸무럭거리고 있는 거야 What are you all loitering about over there for? /Don't be long about it. /Why have you been so long? // 꾸무럭거리고 있을 때가 아니다 There is no time to lose. /It admits of no delay. // 꾸무럭거리지 말고 대답해라 Answer me and be quick about it. // 꾸무럭거리다가는 기차를 놓치겠다 Hurry up or you will miss the train.

꾸무럭꾸무럭 slowly; tardily; lazily; sluggishly; lingeringly; with delay; with hesitation; dawdling

꾸물거리다 wriggle

꾸물꾸물 ① [벌레 따위] wiggling; wriggling ② slowly ⇨ 구무럭구무럭

꾸미 beef shreds (for soup)

꾸미개 ornamental strips along edges or borders

⁂**꾸미다** ① [치장] decorate; ornament; adorn; bedeck; [얼굴을] make up; touch up ¶ 눈썹을 곱게 꾸미다 touch up one's eyebrows // 몸을 꾸미다 dress up; deck up; adorn oneself // 방을 꾸미다 decorate a room // 얼굴을 예쁘게 꾸미다 make one's toilet; [배우가] make up one's face // 젊어 보이게 꾸몄다 She was youthfully made up.
② [조작] make up; invent; fabricate; forge; coin; concoct; [음모] plot; frame; [가장] affect; pretend; make a show; disguise oneself ¶ 꾸민 말 a made-up story; an invention // 꾸민 태도 an affected attitude // 사전에 꾸민 일 a deliberate〔put-up〕 job // 거짓을 꾸미다 invent〔coin, make up〕 a fictitious story〔lie〕 // 반정부 음모를 꾸미다 plot《with a person》 against a government // 그것은 전부 내가 꾸며낸 이야기다 I made it all up.
③ [조직] organize; form; make ¶ 가정을 꾸미다 make a home // 신내각을 꾸미다 form a new Cabinet
④ [작성] prepare; draw up; make out ¶ 작전을 꾸미다 map out a plan // 서류를 세 통 꾸미다 make out in triplicate // 증서를 꾸미다 draw up a deed // 유언장을 꾸미다 make〔draw up〕 one's will〔testament〕
⑤ [가장하다] affect; be affected; feign; pretend; assume; disguise ¶ 꾸민 태도로 in an affected manner

⑥ [수식하다] embellish ; garnish ¶ 문장을 꾸미다 use a flowery style ; embellish one's style

꾸민잠 —簪 an ornamental hairpin

꾸민족두리 a woman's jeweled hairdress

꾸밈 an ornament ; a decoration ; [의상의] trimmings ; [문장의] flourishes ; [조작] a fabrication ; a fake ; an invention ; a misrepresentation ¶ 꾸밈 없이 말하면 in plain words // 꾸밈 없이 사실대로 진술하다 make an uncolored 〔unvarnished〕 statement ; state a fact just as it is

꾸밈새 [장식] decoration ; [장식법] the way one decorates〔fixes up〕; [모양] a shape ; form ; appearance ¶ 꾸밈새가 좋은방 a decently furnished room

꾸벅 ⇨ 꼬박 ¶ 꾸벅 절〔인사〕하다 make a bow ; bob (one's head) 《at a person》

꾸벅거리다, 꾸뻑거리다 ① [졸려서] nod in a doze ; nid-nod ; doze off ; drop (off) into a doze
② [머리숙이다] bow and bow ; repeatedly make respectful bows ¶ 꾸벅거리고 있는 동안에 while dozing // 윗사람에게 꾸벅거리다 cringe to one's superiors // 나는 사람에게 꾸벅거리는 것을 싫어한다 I don't like bobbing my head to others. // 꾸벅거리다가 바로 잠들었다 Doziness〔A drowsy feeling〕 coming over me, I soon fell asleep.

꾸벅꾸벅, 꾸뻑꾸뻑 bowing ; dozing ¶ 꾸벅꾸벅 졸다 doze off ; fall into a doze // 꾸벅꾸벅 절하다 make repeated bows

꾸부러뜨리다 bend ; twist

꾸부러지다 bend ; curve

꾸부리다 stoop ; curve

†**꾸불꾸불** windingly

꾸불텅꾸불텅 windingly

꾸불텅하다 (be) slowly curved

꾸붓꾸붓 all slightly bent

꾸붓하다 (be) slightly bent

꾸역꾸역 in a steady stream ; in (rapid) succession ; one after another ; one upon the heels of another ¶ 꾸역꾸역 모여들다 come swarming about ; storm 《a place》; rush on 《a place》// 많은 사람들이 꾸역꾸역 나왔다 Large crowds of people poured out.

꾸이다[1] dream ; have a dream

꾸이다[2] lend ; loan ; advance ; accommodate 《a person》 with money ¶ 꾸인 돈을 받다 draw in the debts

꾸정꾸정하다 (be) straight and strong ⇨ 꼬장꼬장하다

꾸준하다 (be) steady ; unflagging ; untiring ; constant ; persistent ¶ 꾸준히 untiringly ; indefatigably ; steadily ; unflaggingly ; constantly // 꾸준한 노력 steady〔ceaseless〕 efforts // 꾸준한 우정 a constant friendship // 꾸준히 공부하다 study indefatigably // 꾸준한 노력이 드디어 결실을 보았다 Constant efforts bore fruit at last.

꾸중 ⇨ 꾸지람

꾸지나무 〖식물〗 the paper mulberry

꾸지람 a scolding ; a rebuke ; a lecture ; a reprimand ; faultfinding **—하다** scold ; rebuke ; lecture ; give 《a person》 a lecture ; find fault 《with》; chide ¶ 꾸지람 듣다 be scolded ; catch a scolding ; catch it // 들키면 꾸지람을 듣는다 If you are found out, you will catch it. // 저 녀석은 실수가 발각되어 상사한테 실컷 꾸지람을 들었다 That guy was really raked over the coals after the boss found out about his mistake.

‡**꾸짖다** scold ; rebuke ; lecture ; chide ; give 《a person》 a scolding〔lecture, lesson〕 ¶ 호되게 꾸짖다 give 《a person》 a good scolding ; give 《a person》 a long lecture ; treat 《a person》 to a sermon // 지각했다고 학생을 꾸짖다 scold a student for being late // 그가 협상에 실패해서 부장이 그 문제로 그를 꾸짖은 것 같다 He failed to bring off the negotiations, and apparently the boss raked him over the coals for it.

꾸푸리다 bend

꾹 [누르는 모양] tightly ; firmly ; hard ; [참는 모양] patiently ¶ 꾹 누르다 press hard // 혁대를 꾹 조르다 tighten a belt // 모욕을 꾹 참다 bear an insult patiently // 치통을 꾹 참다 bear a toothache with stoical resignation // 웃음을 꾹 참다 hold back one's laughter // 그는 울고 싶은 것을 꾹 참았다 He resisted an impulse to cry out.

꾹꾹 ⇨ 꼭꼭[1] ②, ③

-꾼 [길꾼] a (skilled) gambler ; an expert ; [성원] a member ; a man ; a hand

†**꿀** honey ; nectar (꽃의) ; molasses ; honeydew ¶ 꿀 같이 달콤한 사랑 honey-sweet love // 꿀 같이 달다 be sweet as honey
—떡 honey cake **—물** honeyed water **— 범벅** honeyed pudding
꿀 먹은 벙어리 〔속담〕 a person who could not open one's heart to another
꿀은 달아도 벌은 쏜다 〔속담〕 Bees that have honey in their mouths have stings in their tails.

*__꿀꺽__ [삼키는 모양] at a gulp ; [참는 모양] patiently ¶ 꿀꺽 마시다 drink at a gulp ; gulp down // 노여움을 꿀꺽 참다 contain one's anger ; master one's wrath // 모욕을 꿀꺽 참다 swallow an insult ; pocket a humiliation // 침을 꿀꺽 삼키다 swallow one's saliva

꿀꺽꿀꺽 gulping **—하다** gulp away ; swig ; swill ¶ 꿀꺽꿀꺽 마시다 drink 《water》 in big swallows〔heavily〕

꿀꿀 ① [물이 흐르는 소리] bubbling ; gurgling ② [돼지의] grunting **—하다**

bubble ; grunt

꿀꿀이 a greedy person ; a pig ; a swine ; a hog

꿀떡 [삼킴] swallowing eagerly ; gulping hungrily **—하다** swallow〔gulp〕《a thing》 down ; quaff ¶ 한 입에 꿀떡 삼키다 swallow〔drain〕 at one〔a〕 gulp // 침을 꿀떡 삼키다 swallow one's saliva ; be greedy for food ; make one's mouth water

꿀떡거리다 swallow and swallow ; gulp away ¶ 침을 꿀떡거리다 swallow one's saliva again and again ; be very eager to eat ; be very greedy for food

꿀렁 —하다 ① [물이] splash ; slush ; slosh ② [부풀어서] be baggy ; be puffy ¶ 바지 무릎이 꿀렁하다 The trousers are baggy at the knees.

꿀렁꿀렁 ① slushing〔sloshing, splashing〕 around inside **—하다** slush〔slosh, splash〕 around inside ② loosely **—하다** be loose

꿀리다 ① [쭈그러지다] be crumpled ; be rumpled ; be wrinkled ; cave in ; fall in ¶ 꿀린 모자 a crumpled hat ; a caved-in hat // 꿀린 바지 a crumpled trousers // 자리가 편해서 바지가 꿀리지 않았다 It was a comfortable seat and it didn't wrinkle my trousers.
② [형편이] be impoverished ; be hard up ; be in needy〔straitened〕 circumstances ¶ 돈에 꿀리다 be hard up for money // 집안 형편이 꿀리다 be in straitened circumstances // 재정적으로 꿀리다 be in financial difficulties // 살림이 꿀리다 be in needy circumstances
③ [켕기다] have something on one's conscience
④ [기세·형세가] be overwhelmed ; be cornered ; give in ; yield ; succumb ¶ 조금도 꿀리지 않고 nothing daunted ; without flinching // 누구에게나 꿀리지 않다 be second to none // 수에 꿀리다 be overwhelmed by numbers // 말에 꿀리다 be cornered in an argument // 적에게 꿀리다 give in to the enemy // 저런 녀석에 꿀릴까 봐 I will not give in such a man.

꿀물 honeyed water

†**꿀벌** 〖곤충〗 a honeybee ; a bee ¶ 꿀벌집 a honeycomb ; a beehive

꿀수박 a sugared and iced watermelon

꿀쩍 squashing ; sniffling ⇨ 꼴짝

꿀찌럭 with a splatter〔splash, plop〕 **—하다** make a splatter〔splash, plop〕

꿀찌럭꿀찌럭 with splatter after splatter **—하다** splatter and splatter

꿀풀 〖식물〗 the Asiatic self-heal ; Prunella vulgaris (학명) ; a self-heal

꿇다 bend one's knees ; go down on one's knees ; kneel down ; fall〔throw oneself〕 on one's knees ¶ 무릎을 꿇고 on one's knees // 무릎을 꿇고 앉다 sit on one's knees // 무릎을 꿇고 기도를 드리다 kneel in prayer

꿇리다 make 《a person》 kneel down ; bring 《a person》 to his knees ; force to yield

꿇어앉다 kneel (down) ; fall〔drop〕 on one's knees ; genuflect (예배하기 위해) ¶ 꿇어앉아 탄원하다 implore on one's knees

†**꿈** a dream ; [공상] a vision ; an illusion ; a day dream (백일몽) a delusion ; a chimera (망상) ¶ 꿈의 세계 a dream land // 청춘의 꿈 the dream of youth // 불길한 꿈 an evil dream // 헛된 꿈 an empty dream ; a crushed hope // 꿈을 꾸다 dream 《of, about》 ; have 〔dream〕 a dream // 무서운 꿈을 꾸다 have a terrible dream ; have a nightmare // 고향 꿈을 꾸다 dream of 〔about〕 one's old home // 꿈을 해몽하다 interpret a dream // 꿈에 나타나다 appear in a dream // 꿈에서 깨어나다 wake up from a dream // 단꿈에서 깨다 be aroused from a sound sleep // 꿈에서 어머니를 보다 see one's mother in a dream // 오랫동안 간직해 온 꿈을 실현시키다 realize〔give shape to〕 one's long-cherished dream〔vision〕 // 용꿈을 꾸다 have a good dream // 꿈이 들어맞았다 A dream came true. // 그런 일을 하리라고는 꿈에도 생각 안했다 I never dreamed of doing such a thing. // 모든 것이 꿈만 같다 Everything seems to me like a dream. // 파리에 가게 되다니 꿈만 같다 It's like a dream to be able to go to Paris. // 인생은 꿈에 불과하다 Life is but a dream. // 그의 꿈은 산산이 깨졌다 His dream has been shattered. // 헛된 꿈 꾸지마 stop pipe-dreaming.

꿈같다 be like a dream ; (be) dreamlike 〔dreamy〕 ; visionary ; illusory ; chimerical ¶ 꿈같은 이야기 a fantastic story ; a wild tale // 꿈같은 dreamlike ; dreamy ; visionary // 꿈같이 as in a dream // 꿈같은 여행이었다 It was a dream of a trip.

꿈결 [꿈꾸는 동안] (the midst of) a dream ; a dreamy state ; [덧없음] emptiness ; uncertainty ¶ 인생을 꿈결같이 보내다 dream away one's life ; live 〔go about〕 in a dream // 인생은 꿈결같이 허무하다 Life is but an empty dream. // 꿈결에 불이야 하는 소리를 들었다 Half asleep and half awake, I heard the cry, "Fire!"

†**꿈꾸다** dream 《of, about》 ; have〔dream〕 a dream ; [바라다] dream of ; fancy ; hope ; imagine ¶ 미래의 대통령을 꿈꾸다 dream of〔fancy oneself〕 becoming a president // 앞날의 행복한 생활을 꿈꾸었다 He drew a fine picture of his future happiness. // 꿈꾸는 듯한 기분이었다 I felt as if I were in a dream.

꿈나라 a dreamland ; sleep ¶ 꿈나라로 가다 go to dreamland ; [잠들다] fall asleep

꿈땜 ―하다 console oneself that one's bad luck is simply the result of a bad dream that had foretold it

꿈자리 a dream ; the happenings in a dream ¶ 꿈자리가 사납다 《a dream》 be of bad omen // 꿈자리 사나운 꿈을 꾸다 have a bad dream

꿈적이다 budge ; stir ; move slow in a squirming movement ; twist the body around in slow motion

꿈쩍 않다 be unperturbed ; keep cool and calm ; remain unmoved ¶ 총소리에도 그는 꿈쩍 않았다 In spite of the rifle shots, he didn't turn a hair. // 나는 한두 번의 실패로는 꿈쩍 않는 사람이다 I am not a man to be daunted by a failure.

꿈쩍없다 remain motionless ; do not move at all ; safe and sound ¶ 지진에도 그 집은 꿈쩍없었다 The house withstood the earthquake perfectly.

꿉꿉하다 be a bit damp

*__꿋꿋하다__ [견고하다] (be) strong ; firm ; solid ; tough ; hard ; [쪽 바르다] straight ; upright ¶ 꿋꿋한 결심 a firm resolution〔determination〕// 꿋꿋한 자세 a straight posture // 꿋꿋한 의지 a strong〔firm〕 will // 꿋꿋이 버티다 take a firm stand ; show a firm〔an unyielding〕 front // 꿋꿋이 저항하다 make〔offer〕 a stubborn resistance ; put up a stiff resistance // 자기 주장을 꿋꿋이 관철시키다 hold fast to one's views ; stick to one's guns

꿍 [떨어지는 소리] with a thud〔thump, bang〕; [북·총 따위의 소리] with a boom〔bang〕 ―하다 thud ; thump ; bang ; boom ¶ 꿍하고 떨어지다 fall plump〔heavily〕

꿍꽝 rattling and booming ; popping and booming ―하다 be rattling and booming ; be popping and booming ¶ 대포가 꿍꽝거리다 The cannon is roaring.

꿍꿍[1] moaning ; groaning ―하다 groan with pain ; utter a groan ¶ 꿍꿍 앓다 moan with one's ailment

꿍꿍[2] ⇨ 쿵쿵

꿍꿍이셈 a secret design〔scheme〕 of one's own ; secret intention

꿍꿍이속 an underhand scheme ; an underlying motive ; a secret design ¶ 꿍꿍이속이 있다 have a plot in mind ; have an ax to grind // 틀림없이 꿍꿍이속이 있다 There must be something secret behind the scene.

꿍심 a secret ambition

꿍하다 (be) glum ; sullen ; moody and silent ; be in a bad humor

꿜꿜 gurgling ; gushing ; with a gurgle ; with a gush ―하다 gurgle〔gush〕 out

꿩 〖새〗 a pheasant ¶ 수꿩 a cock pheasant // 암꿩 a hen pheasant

꿩 먹고 알 먹고 (속담) To catch two pigeons with one bean. /To kill two birds with one stone〔bolt, sling〕.

꿩의다리 〖식물〗 the columbine meadow rue

꿩의비름 〖식물〗 the blush stonecrop ; an orpine

꿰다 ① [구멍에] pass〔run〕 through ; thread ; string ¶ 바늘 구멍에 실을 꿰다 thread a needle ; run a thread through a needle // 구슬을 꿰다 thread bead ② [찔러 꽂다] pierce ; thrust ; put through ¶ 꼬챙이에 꿰다 skewer ; transfix // 꼬챙이에 생선을 꿰어 굽다 roast fish on skewers ③ [입다] put on ; wear ¶ 신을 꿰다 put on one's shoes // 옷을 꿰다 wear one's clothes

꿰들다 ① [꿰어 들다] spear〔pierce〕 《a thing》 and hold it up ¶ 물고기를 창끝으로 꿰들다 hold up a fish on the end of a spear ② [드러내다] disclose ; expose ; reveal

†__꿰뚫다__ [관통하다] pierce ; pass〔run〕 through ; shoot through (총알이) ; [정통하다] be well versed〔informed〕 《in, on》 ; be expert 《in, at》 ; be conversant 《with》 ¶ 창으로 옆구리를 꿰뚫다 pierce 《a person's》 side with a spear // 마음을 꿰뚫다 be aware of 《a person's》 motive // 총탄이 그의 가슴을 꿰뚫었다 A bullet shot through his breast.

꿰뜨리다 puncture ; break ; burst ; wear out〔down〕 ¶ 공을 꿰뜨리다 burst a ball // 신을 꿰뜨리다 wear out one's shoes // 옷을 꿰뜨리다 wear out one's clothes // 창문을 꿰뜨리다 break a window

꿰매다 [깁다] sew ; stitch ; darn (양말 따위를) ; mend ; [탈없이 하다] patch up ; make shift ¶ 터진 곳을 꿰매다 sew up a rip // 양말을 꿰매다 darn stockings // 상처를 세 바늘 꿰매다 close the wound with three stitches ; put three stitches in the wound // 옷에 조각을 대어 꿰매다 mend〔patch up〕 one's clothes // 듬성듬성 꿰매다 sew with large stitches

꿰미 a string 《for coins, fish, persimmons, mushrooms》 ; [꿴것] things on a string ¶ 생선 꿰미 a string of fish // 돈 꿰미 a string of coins

꿰지다 [미어지다] rip (open) ; be torn ; tear ; [터지다] rend ; burst ; be broken ; [해지다] wear out ; [드러나다] be exposed ; lay bare ; be disclosed〔revealed〕 ¶ 쉬 꿰지다 tear easily // 일이 꿰지기 전에 손을 쓰다 take a counter-measure before something goes wrong with it // 자루가 꿰지다 A bag bursts.

†**꿰찌르다** thrust through ; run through ; pierce ¶ 단도로 가슴을 꿰찌르다 plunge a dagger into 《a person's》 breast

꿰차다 ① [매달다] sew 《a dangling thing》 on ② [제 것으로 하다] make 《a thing》 one's own ; latch on to 《미·속》

꿱 shrieking ; yelling ; shouting ¶ 꿱 소리를 지르다 utter a cry ; yell

꿱꿱 yelling

꿱꿱하다[거리다] shout and shout ; yell and yell ; quack and quack ; [오리가] go "quack ! quack ! quack !" ¶ 꿱꿱 소리지르다 shout away noisily ; yell and yell at the top of one's lungs // 화나서 꿱꿱 소리지르다 roar with anger

뀌다 release ¶ 방귀를 뀌다 break [make] wind ; let a fart ; fart

끄나풀 [끈] a piece of string ; a cord ; [앞잡이] a tool ; an agent ; a cat's paw ; a stool pigeon 《미·속》 ; a pawn ; [관계] connections ; influence ; medium ; good offices ¶ 끄나풀로 잡아매다 fasten with a string // 끄나풀 노릇을 하다 be made a cat's paw of ; work as an agent

끄느름하다 (be) cloudy ; gloomy ; overcast

*****끄다** ① [불을] put out ; extinguish ; blow out (불어서) ; turn[switch] off (전기를) ; snuff (초를) ¶ 불을 끄다 put out a fire ; put a fire under control // 촛불을 끄다 blow out a candle // 전기를 끄다 put[turn, switch] off the light // 라디오를 끄다 turn off[out] the radio // 불을 밟아 끄다 tread out a fire // 물[모래]로 불을 끄다 quench a fire with water[sand] // 두들겨서 끄다 beat out 《the flame》
② [덩어리를] break ; crush ; crack ; smash ¶ 흙덩어리를 끄다 break a clod of earth ; crush a lump[bit] of clay // 얼음을 끄다 break[smash] ice
③ [빚을] pay back ; repay ¶ 빚을 꺼나가다 clear[pay] off one's debt

끄덕거리다, 끄떡거리다 nod ; make a slight movement ¶ 끄덕끄덕 with a nod // 동의하는 뜻으로 끄덕거리다 nod in assent // 끄덕거리는 것은 동의의 표시다 A nod is a sign of agreement.

끄덕이다, 끄떡이다 nod ; nod approval ; approve 《of》 ¶ 고개를 끄덕이다 nod the head // 고개를 가볍게 끄덕이다 nod lightly ; give a slight nod

끄덩이 [머리털] the end of a bunch of hair ; [일의 실마리] the beginning ; the clue ; a general plan (대요) ¶ 머리 끄덩이를 그러잡다 seize[grab] 《a person's》 hair ; seize 《a person》 by the hair // 실 끄덩이를 잡아당기다 pull out a thread from a bunch // 머리 끄덩이를 잡고 질질 끌다 drag 《a person》 by the hair

끄덩이(를) 잡다 [관용] grab[catch, hold] 《a person》 by the hair

끄떡 ¶ (머리를) 끄떡하고 인사하다 nod (a greeting) to 《a person》 // (동의하는 뜻으로) 끄떡하다 nod (in) assent // 혼자서 끄떡이다 nod one's head to oneself // 넌지시 끄떡이다 give a slight nod // 나는 작별의 인사로 머리를 끄떡했다 I nodded adieu to her. // 머리를 끄떡하여 그를 방에서 내보냈다 I nodded him out of the room.

끄떡없다 [안전하다] (be) safe ; secure ; strong ; [병 따위에] immune 《from》 ; [물 따위에] proof 《against》 ; [태연하다] unmoved ; calm ¶ 언제 기습해 와도 끄떡없다 be prepared for any possible surprise attack // 그 건물은 지진에도 끄떡없었다 The building perfectly withstood the earthquake.

끄르다 undo ; untie ; unfasten ; unpack ; loosen ; [잠근 것을] unlock ; take off ¶ 매듭을 끄르다 untie a knot // 구두끈을 끄르다 unlace one's boots // 보자기를 끄르다 undo a package // 양복 단추를 끄르다 unbutton one's coat // 꾸러미를 끄르다 open[undo] a parcel

끄르륵 with a burp[belch] **—하다** keep burping[belching]

끄르륵거리다 keep burping ; belch continually

끄르륵끄르륵 with repeated burps ; burping ; belching

끄무러지다 cloud up ; get[become] cloudy ; get dim[smoky]

끄무레하다 (be) cloudy ; overcast ; dull ; be clouded over ¶ 끄무레한 날씨 cloudy weather ; a cloudy day

끄물거리다 remain unsettled ; become cloudy now and again ¶ 끄물거리는 날씨 unsettled weather // 앞으로 며칠 동안 날씨가 끄물거리겠다 The weather may remain unsettled for the next few days.

끄물끄물 —하다 be unsettled ; be fickle ; be cloudy ; be changeable ; be liable to change ¶ 날씨가 끄물끄물하다 The weather is unsettled.

끄지르다 busy oneself doing nothing ; gad about ; go about idly

끄집다 take[pick] up ¶ 여럿 가운데서 하나를 끄집다 take one among many

끄집어내다 ① take out ; pull[draw] out ; pick out ¶ 호주머니에서 편지를 끄집어내다 take a letter out of one's pocket
② [이야기를] start 《a conversation》 ; make a beginning 《of conversation》 ; draw out 《conversation》 ¶ 말을 끄집어내다 bring up a subject

끄집어내리다 take[bring, carry] down ¶ 사람을 의자에서 끄집어내리다 drag 《a person》 out of a chair // 책을 이층에

서 끄집어내리다 bring down books from upstairs

끄집어당기다 pull ; drag ; draw ¶ 사람의 소매를 끄집어당기다 pull 《a person》 by the sleeve // 머리를 끄집어당기다 pull 《a person's》 hair

끄집어들이다 pull〔take, carry, bring〕in ; [자기 편으로] win〔bring〕over ¶ 짐을 끄집어들이다 carry luggage in // 사람을 자기 편으로 끄집어들이다 win 《a person》 over to one's side // 사람을 방으로 끄집어들이다 draw 《a person》 into a room

끄집어올리다 take〔pull, bring, carry〕up ; [승진시키다] promote ¶ 높은 지위에 끄집어올리다 promote 《a person》 to a high position

끄트러기 ① [나무 조각] chips ; strips ; scraps ② [나머지] odd pieces ; odds and ends

끄트머리 ① [끝] a point ; a tip ; the edge ; the tail end
② [단서] a clue ; the beginning ¶ 끄트머리가 뾰족하다 be pointed〔sharp〕at the end // 끄트머리에 서다 stand at the tail end

†**끈** ① [줄] a string ; a cord ; a ribbon ; a lace ; [꼰 끈] a braid ; [가죽 끈] a strap ¶ 구두 끈 shoestrings ; shoelaces // 구두 끈을 매다〔풀다〕 lace〔unlace〕 one's shoes // 끈을 매다 tie the strings // 끈을 풀다 untie〔undo〕 the strings // 끈이 풀렸다 The strings came untied〔loose〕.
② [연줄] influence ; medium ; connection ¶ 끈을 타고 출세하다 get〔obtain〕 one's high post through connection ; owe one's high position to influence

끈기 一氣 ① [끈끈한 기운] tenacity ; adhesiveness ; stickiness ¶ 끈기 있는 쌀 glutinous rice
② [참을성] perseverance ; patience ; endurance ¶ 끈기가 없다 lack tenacity // 그는 끈기 있는 사람이다 He is patient. /He is of a patient disposition. // 끈기있게 공부하다 stick to one's studies // 그에게는 끈기가 없다 He lacks tenacity.

끈끈이 birdlime ¶ 끈끈이로 새를 잡다 catch a bird with birdlime

끈끈이주걱 〖식물〗 a kind of pitcher plant〔sarracenia〕

끈끈하다 ① [차지다] (be) sticky ; adhesive ; viscous ; gluey ¶ 끈끈한 송진 gluey pine resin // 끈끈한 풀 sticky〔gluey〕 paste // 셔츠가 땀으로 끈끈하다 one's shirt is sticky with sweat.
② [검질기다] (be) tenacious ; persistent ; glutinous ¶ 끈끈한 사나이 a man of great tenacity ; a tough guy 《미》 // 끈끈하게 캐묻다 ask questions persistently〔inquisitively〕

끈덕거리다 be loose ; be rickety ; shake ¶ 끈덕끈덕 loosely // 이가 끈덕거리다 A tooth is loose. // 층계가 끈덕거린다 The staircase is shaky.

끈덕지다 (be) sticky ; tenacious ; persevering ; patient ; tough ; persistent ¶ 끈덕지게 persistently ; tenaciously ; perseveringly ; patiently // 그는 매사에 끈덕진 데가 없다 He sticks to nothing. // He is a rolling stone. // 끈덕지게 질문하다 pester 《a person》 with questions // 정말 끈덕진 아이군 What a pest you are !

끈떨어지다 lose one's means of livelihood〔living〕

끈목 a braid ; a plaited cord ; a gimp

끈붙다 get a means of livelihood

끈적거리다 [들러붙다] be sticky ; be gluey ; be gooey 《미·속》 ; be adhesive ; [검질기다] persevere ; stick 《to》 ; persist 《in》 ; be tenacious ¶ 끈적거리는 흙 sticky soil ; heavy ground // 끈적거리는 사람 a person of tenacity // 사람에게 끈적거리다 stick like glue to 《a person》 // 셔츠가 땀에 끈적거리다 One's shirt is sticky with sweat.

끈적끈적하다 ① [물체가] be sticky ; adhesive ¶ 끈적끈적한 물건 a goo ; a gooey 《당밀 따위》 ② [깐작깐작하다] be tenacious〔persistent〕

끈지다 be sticky

끈질기다 (be) strong and sticky ; (be) strongly adhesive ¶ 끈질긴 punchy // 끈질긴 병 an inveterate disease // 끈질기게 협상하다 negotiate indefatigably // 그는 참으로 끈질긴 녀석이다 What nerve he's got !

끈질끈질하다 ① [오래 끌다] (be) long-pending ; prolonged ; dragging ② [끈질기다] (be) strong and sticky ; strongly adhesive

끈히 tenaciously ; persistently ; pertinaciously

끊기다 be cut ; be broken ; be snapped ; be severed ; be stopped ; be killed

*__끊다__ ① [자르다] cut ; cut off ; sever ; break ; chop off ¶ 줄을 끊다 cut the rope // 둘로 끊다 cut in two // 불에 녹여 끊다 burn off
② [단절하다] sever ; cut〔break〕 off ¶ 관계를 끊다 sever one's connection with 《the company》 ; break off relations with 《the woman》 // 전류를 끊다 switch off the electric current // 회로를 끊다 kill a circuit // 적의 퇴로를 끊다 cut off the enemy's retreat // 연락을 끊다 sever〔cut off〕 the connection // 발을 끊다 stop visiting ; cease to visit // 외교관계를 끊다 break off all diplomatic relations // 전기〔가스〕를 끊다 cut off electricity〔gas〕 // 나는 그와의 교제를 끊었다 I've broken with him. // 그런 남자와는 관계를 끊는 것이 좋다 You're better off

washing your hands of a man like that.
③ [그만두다] cut ; give up ; leave off ; refrain from ¶ 술을 끊다 give up drinking ; be〔go〕 on the wagon 《미》 // 담배를 끊다 give up smoking // 사실은 나도 한때 술을 끊었는데 지금은 다시 마신다 As a matter of fact, I once quit drinking, but I'm off the wagon now.
④ [사다] buy ; purchase ; get ¶ 옷감을 끊다 buy〔purchase〕 dress material // 차표를 끊다 get a ticket ; book passage 《to *Seoul*》
⑤ [죽이다] kill ¶ 목숨을 끊다 take 《a person's》 life ; kill 《a person》
⑥ [그치다] pause ; stop ; break off ; [전화] cut off ; switch off ; disconnect ; hang up 《미》 ; ring off 《영》 ¶ 그는 갑자기 전화를 끊었다 He suddenly hung up.
⑦ [문장을 자르다] punctuate ; mark off by a comma ¶ 이야기를 끊다 punctuate a story
⑧ [발행하다] issue ; write out ; draw ¶ 전표를 끊다 sign a chit // 수표를 끊다 issue a check

끊어뜨리다 ⇨ 끊다

끊어맡다 contract for ; have a contract for ; undertake ¶ 끊어맡는 일 job work ; piecework ; a contract job

끊어주다 pay 《a person》 off〔out〕 ; square accounts with 《a person》

*__끊어지다__ ① [절단되다] break ; snap ; be cut ; break down ¶ 실이 끊어지다 a string snaps〔breaks〕. // 전선이 끊어지다 An electric wire is down. // 전구가 끊어졌다 The filament of the lamp was off.
② [중단·차단되다] break off ; be cut off ; be〔become〕 broken ; discontinue ; be interrupted ¶ 말이 잠시 끊어졌을 때 in a pause of conversation // 교통이 끊어지다 Traffic is stopped〔interrupted〕. // 소식이 끊어지다 communication is cut off // 연락이 끊어지다 A connection is cut off // 전화가 끊어지다 A telephone is cut off.
③ [관계가] have done with ; break (off) with ; finish with ; be through 《with》 ¶ 그녀와의 관계가 끊어졌다 I am done with her. // 인연이 끊어지다 be separated
④ [기한 따위가] expire ; run out ; be due ; terminate ; run out ¶ 약 기운이 끊어지다 The medicine loses its effect. // 1년이 지나면 계약 기간이 끊어진다 The contract holds good for a year. // 그와는 거래가 끊어졌다 The business with him has been terminated.
⑤ [죽다] end ; die ; expire ¶ 숨이 끊어지다 breathe one's last breath ; die ; gasp one's life away

끊이다 [관계가] A relationship〔connection〕 is severed ; [뒤를 못 대고 떨어지다] run out ; sell out ; be sold out of stock

†**끊임없다** (be) continuous ; ceaseless ; incessant ; endless ¶ 끊임없이 constantly ; continually ; all the time ; incessantly ; without interruption〔a break〕 // 끊임없는 걱정 endless worries // 끊임없는 손님 a constant stream of visitors // 끊임없는 주의 constant attention // 끊임없는 연구 ceaseless〔constant〕 study

끊임없이 constantly ; ceaselessly ; incessantly ; unceasingly ; endlessly ; perpetually ; without intermission ; without a break〔letup〕 ; in succession ; successively ; continually ; continuously ¶ 끊임없이 노력하다 make a constant〔ceaseless〕 effort // 이 거리에는 차가 끊임없이 다닌다 There is a continuous stream of cars on the street. // 끊임없이 지껄이다 talk without a pause

끌 a chisel ¶ 끌로 조각하다 chisel a statue out of 《the marble》

끌꺽끌꺽하다 keep belching

끌끌 belching ¶ 트림을 끌끌하다 belch ; burp // 혀를 끌끌 차다 click〔clack〕 one's tongue

끌끌하다 [마음이] (be) clean and pure ; upright ; honest ; clean-handed

끌끔하다 (be) dashing ; smart ; sleek and clean

†**끌다** ① [잡아당기다] pull ; draw ; give a pull ; haul ; tug ; tow ; jerk (갑자기) ¶ 소매를 끌다 pull 《a person》 by the sleeve // 짐차를 끌다 pull a cart // 양쪽에서 끌다 tug from both sides // 그같이 능력있는 사람은 끌어 가려는 사람들이 많을 거다 Someone as capable as he will find lots of takers
② [주의 따위를] attract〔draw〕 《a person's attention》 ; arouse〔win〕 《a person's sympathy》 (동정을) ; charm ; bewitch ; win ; captivate ; fascinate ¶ 사람들의 이목을 끌다 attract public attention // 인기를 끌다 catch〔win, gain〕 popularity
③ [인도하다] lead ¶ 말을 끌다 lead a horse // 노인의 손을 끌다 lead an old man by the hand // 손님을 끌다 draw customers
④ [늘어뜨리고 가다] drag ; trail ; draggle ¶ 발을 질질 끌고 걷다 walk with dragging feet ; shuffle along ; drag oneself along // 치마를 끌고 걷다 walk with a trailing skirt
⑤ [미루다] prolong ; protract ; delay ; extend ¶ 오래 끌어 온 교섭 long-pending〔drawn-out〕 negotiations // 차일피일 끌다 put off from day to day // 회의를 오래 끌다 The meeting drags on. // 지불을 끌다 put off〔delay〕 payment
⑥ [시설하다] lay on 《gas》 ; install 《a telephone》 ¶ 물을 끌다 have water

supplied // 철도를 끌다 a railway is laid 《to a place》 // 파이프로 물을 끌다 pipe water to 《a place》 // 전화를 끌다 have a telephone installed
⑦ [연행하다] pull along by force ; take 《a person》 to 《a place》 ; walk 《a person》 off to 《a place》
⑧ [인용하다] cite ; quote ; refer to ¶ 예를 끌어오다 cite an example

끌러지다 get〔come〕 loose〔undone〕 ; get untied ; become loosened ¶ 구두 끈이 끌러졌다 My shoestring came untied. // 허리띠가 끌러졌다 My belt came loose.

끌리다 ① be drawn ; be pulled ; be dragged ¶ 범인이 현장에서 붙들려 경찰서로 끌려갔다 The offender was caught red-handed and taken to the police station.
② [바닥에 쓸리다] be trailed ; be dragged ¶ 치마가 끌리다 Her dress sweeps the floor.
③ [이끌리다] be attracted ; be charmed〔fascinated〕 ; be drawn〔moved〕 ¶ 자식 사랑에 끌려 moved〔motivated〕 by the love of one's own child // 인정에 끌리다 be touched with humanity
④ [지체되다] be prolonged ; be protracted ; be delayed

끌밋하다 (be) handsome ; clear-cut ; neat ; attractive

끌밥 sawdust from chiseling ; chisel-dust ; chisel chips

끌방망이 a mallet ; a chisel hammer

⁑**끌어내다** take〔pull, draw, drag〕 out ; bring〔carry〕 out ¶ 마구간에서 말을 끌어내다 take a horse out of a stable // 사람을 집에서 끌어내다 drag 《a person》 out of the house // 친구에게서 사업 자금으로 약간의 돈을 끌어내다 get a little money for one's business out of a friend

끌어내리다 take〔bring, carry, pull, draw, drag〕 down ; haul down (기 따위를) ¶ 기를 끌어내리다 haul down a flag // 배를 암초에서 끌어내리다 get a ship off the rocks // 사다리에서 끌어내리다 drag 《a person》 down from a ladder // 낮은 지위로 끌어내리다 demote 《a person》 to a lower position // 임금을 끌어내리다 cut〔bring down〕 wages

끌어넣다 take〔pull, draw, drag〕 in ; lead in ; tempt in ; entice ; win〔gain〕 over ¶ 소를 외양간에 끌어넣다 drag a cow into a barn // 음모에 끌어넣다 tempt 《a person》 into an intrigue // 미국을 전쟁에 끌어넣다 drag America into the war // 자기 당에 끌어넣다 win 《a person》 over to one's political party

⁑**끌어당기다** draw 《a thing》 near ; pull〔drag〕 up ; draw 《toward》 ; attract ; tug ¶ 소매를 끌어당기다 tug at 《a person's》 sleeve // 재떨이를 끌어당기다 draw an ashtray near // 의자를 가까이 끌어당기다 pull〔draw〕 up a chair // 그는 어딘지 사람을 끌어당기는 매력이 있다 There is something attractive about him. // 자석은 철분을 끌어당긴다 A magnet attracts iron.

끌어대다 ① [돈을] raise money ; put up ¶ 돈을 여기저기서 끌어대다 scrape together a sum of money
② [맞대다] bring two parties together ; join together ¶ 살 사람 팔 사람을 끌어대다 bring buyer and seller together
③ [인용하다] quote ; cite ¶ 전례를 끌어대다 cite precedents

끌어들이다 ① [안으로] draw〔drag〕 in〔into〕 ; pull in〔into〕 ; take〔bring〕 into ¶ 수도를 끌어들이다 have water pipes laid ; have water supplied ; lay on water // 수상한 여자를 끌어들이다 bring in a woman of a doubtful character // 마을에 곧 전기를 끌어들인다 The electricity will soon be brought into the village.
② [포섭하다] win 《a person》 over to one's side ; interest 《a person》 in ; induce ; [유혹] tempt ; entice ¶ 나쁜 일에 끌어들이다 induce 《a person》 to be one's partner to evil doing // 사업에 자본가를 끌어들이다 interest capitalists in an enterprise // 자기편에 끌어들이다 win 《a person》 over to one's side // 음모에 끌어들이다 entangle 《a person》 in a plot

끌어매다 tie ; fasten ; sew〔stitch〕 up ¶ 짐을 끈으로 끌어매다 tie up a bundle with a rope // 소를 말뚝에 끌어매다 tie a cow to a post

***끌어안다** hug ; embrace ; draw 《a person》 closer to one's breast ; clasp 《a person》 in one's arms ; hold〔press〕 《a person》 to one's bosom ¶ 어린애를 끌어안다 hug a child // 서로 끌어안다 embrace〔hug〕 each other // 어머니는 애기를 꼭 끌어안았다 The mother clasped her baby to her breast.

***끌어올리다** pull〔lift〕 up ; [침몰선을] refloat ; salvage ¶ 기중기로 끌어올리다 crane ; lift up with a crane // 보다 좋은 자리로 끌어올리다 raise〔promote, advance〕 《a person》 to a higher position

끌채 a thill ; a shaft ; a pole ; a tongue ¶ 끌채에 맨 말 a thiller

끌탕 ―하다 be much worried〔troubled〕 over

끌텅 a stump ⇨ 그루터기

†**끓다** ① [물이] boil ; simmer ; seethe ; come to a boil ¶ 끓어오르다 boil up // 끓어 넘치다 boil over // 우유가 끓어 넘쳤다 The milk boiled over. // 주전자가 불 위에서 신나게 끓고 있었다 The kettle was boiling away merrily on the fire.

② [마음이] burn ; glow ; be aflame ; seethe ¶ 화가 나서 속이 끓다 burn 〔simmer, seethe〕 with anger〔rage〕 // 젊은이의 피를 끓게 하다 stir the youthful blood // 그의 피가 끓고 있다 His blood is on fire. // 그들의 마음은 애국의 정열로 끓고 있다 Their hearts burn with patriotism.
③ [배가] rumble ¶ 배가 끓다 The bowels rumble.
④ [가래가] wheeze ; make a gurgling sound ¶ 목에 가래가 끓는다 Phlegm obstructs〔sticks to〕 the throat.
⑤ [솟아오르다] surge ; gush out 〔forth〕; spring ; flow out〔forth〕 ¶ 심중에 무언가 끓어오르는 것이 있다 There is something surging in me〔my breast〕. // 그들 가슴에는 새 희망이 끓어올랐다 Hope sprang afresh in their breasts.
⑥ [우글우글하다] swarm ; crowd ; gather ; flock ; collect ¶ 벼룩이 끓다 be infested with fleas // 설탕에 개미가 끓고 있다 Ants swarm upon sugar. // 파출소 앞에 사람이 끓고 있었다 There was a big crowd of people around the policebox.

끓어오르다 boil〔seethe〕 up ¶ 나는 분노로 피가 끓어올랐다 My blood boiled with indignation.

*__끓이다__ ① [끓게 하다] boil ; heat ; make hot ¶ 차를 끓이다 make〔prepare〕 tea // 목욕물을 끓이다 heat the bath
② [음식을] cook ¶ 밥을 끓이다 cook 〔boil〕 rice // 국을 끓이다 make soup // 오늘은 두 끼니를 끓였다 We fixed two meals today.
③ [속태우다] worry ; bother ; trouble ¶ 이 일로 속을 끓였다 This weighed 〔pressed〕 heavy on my mind. // 속을 끓일 만한 일이 아니다 That is nothing serious. /It is nothing to worry about.

끔벅 [불이] flicker ; waver ; dim for a moment ¶ 눈을 끔벅이다 twinkle // 촛불이 바람에 끔벅하다 A candle flickers in the breeze (for a moment). // 불이 끔벅 꺼지다 The light goes out〔off〕 suddenly.

끔벅거리다, 끔뻑거리다 [불빛이] flicker ; twinkle ; waver ; [눈을] wink ; blink ¶ 눈을 끔벅거리다 bat one's eyes // 알았다는 눈치로 눈을 끔벅거리다 give a knowing wink // 불이 끔벅거리다 A light flickers // 별이 끔벅거리다 A star twinkles // 촛불이 바람에 끔벅거린다 A candle flickers in the breeze.

끔벅끔벅 with many a wink ; with repeated blinking〔flickering, wavering〕; closing one's eyes again and again〔time after time〕

끔벅이다 [불이] flicker ; waver : [눈을] wink (and wink) ; blink ; close and open (one's eyes) repeatedly ¶ 먼데서 불빛이 끔벅이는 것을 보았다 I saw a blink of light in the distance.

끔찍스럽다 (be) horrible ⇨ 끔찍하다

끔찍이 terribly ; awfully ; horribly ; [몹시] very ; extremely ; exceedingly ; considerably ; [극진히] kindly ; cordially ; heartily ; devotedly ; wholeheartedly ¶ 끔찍이 사랑하다 love very much // 끔찍이 크다 be extremely big

⁑**끔찍하다** ① [참혹하다] (be) horrible ; terrible ; frightful ; dreadful ; appalling ; [놀랄 만하다] tremendous ; extraordinary ; immense ¶ 끔찍한 광경 a horrible sight // 끔찍한 죽음 a horrible death // 끔찍하게 덥다 be awfully〔terribly〕 hot // 끔찍하게 크다 be extremely big // 끔찍하게 서두르다 be in a great hurry // 끔찍하게 죽다 meet a horrible death // 홍수로 그 지방의 피해는 끔찍하다 The flood caused terrible havoc on〔in〕 the locality. // 생각만 해도 끔찍하다 The mere thought of it makes me shudder.
② [극진하다] (be) wholehearted ; hearty ; sincere ; devoted ; thoughtful ¶ 끔찍이 heartily ; wholeheartedly ; cordially ; warmly ; sincerely ; kindly ; courteously // 끔찍이 대접하다 give a wholehearted treatment〔reception〕 // 그는 아이들을 끔찍이 사랑한다 He dotes upon his children. // 나에 대한 대우가 끔찍했다 He did his utmost to entertain me.

끗수 —數 score ; grade points

끙끙 [신음 소리] groaning ; moaning ; [불평 소리] grumbling **—하다** groan ; moan ; grumble ; complain ¶ 그는 무거운 짐을 지고 끙끙거린다 He moaned under a heavy load. // 무엇 때문에 그렇게 끙끙거리나 What makes you grumble ?

†**끝** ① [마지막] an end ; a close ; a termination ; conclusion (결말) ¶ 끝의 final ; last ; concluding ; ultimate ; terminal // 세계의 끝 the world's end ; the end of the world // 끝없는 limitless ; boundless ; endless // 끝으로 finally ; in conclusion // 끝까지 to the end〔last〕 ; to a finish // 끝순서 the last number of the program // 연설 끝에 at the conclusion of one's speech // 처음부터 끝까지 from beginning to end ; from first to last // 끝까지 남다 sit out 《a play》 // 끝까지 듣다 hear out // 페이지의 끝까지 읽다 read down to the foot of the page // 영화를 끝까지 보다 sit through a movie // 끝을 잘 맺다 come to a good〔happy〕 end ; bring 《a thing》 to a successful issue // 무엇이든지 끝이 있다 All things have an end. // 그 소설을 끝까지 읽었다 I read the novel through〔to the end〕. // 내 이름은 명단 맨 끝에 있다 My name stands at the bottom of the list. // 그는

여러 가지 죄를 지은 끝에 살인까지 했다 He went to the extent of committing murder to top off the varieties of crime he had perpetrated. // 즐거운 여행도 끝이 났다 Our pleasant tour has come to a close. // 끝을 잘 맺다 end well ; come to a good end ; come to a happy ending // 이만 끝 That's that. / That's it. // 흥분하지 말고 내 말 좀 끝까지 들어봐 Don't steam. // 오늘밤은 끝까지 마셔보자 Tonight let's drink till we drop.
② [첨단] the point 《of a pencil》; the tip 《of the finger》; the nib 《of a pen》; the nozzle 《of a pipe》 ¶ 혀 끝 the tip of one's tongue // 붓끝 the tip of a writing brush // 창끝 a spear head // 칼끝 the point of a sword // 코끝 the end〔tip〕 of a nose // 핀끝 a pinpoint // 책상 끝 an edge of the table // 끝에서 끝까지 from end to end // 끝이 뾰족하다 be pointed〔sharp〕 at the end // 끝이 가는 tapering // 끝이 굵은 claviform ; club-shaped // 끝이 가늘어지다 taper (to a point) // 끝이 둥글다 be rounded at the end
③ [사물의 결과] (a) result ; (a) consequence ; an outcome ; an effect ; an end (결말) ¶ 숙고한 끝에 upon〔on, after〕 mature consideration // 끝이 좋다〔나쁘다〕 be successful〔unsuccessful〕 // 끝이 재미없다 The result does not come up to one's expectations〔is not quite satisfactory〕. // 수술 끝이 좋다〔좋지 않다〕 The surgical operation resulted in success〔failure〕. // 그는 방탕한 끝에 돈에 궁하여 도둑질을 했다 Want of money consequent upon his dissipation led him to commit theft. // 서로 양보한 끝에 사건은 바로 가라앉았다 We made mutual concessions with the result that the matter was settled at once. // 욕심에는 끝이 없다 There is no limit to one's desire. /Avarice knows no bounds.
④ [단위] a roll 《of silk》 ¶ 끝으로 사다 buy a whole roll of 《cloth》
끝이 좋으면 만사가 좋다 속담 All is well that ends well.

끝갈망 setting 《matters》 right ; settlement ; winding-up〔windup〕 ; putting 《things》 in order ; putting 《things》 to rights ; after-adjustment **—하다** settle ; set 《matters》 right ; take remedial measures ; wind up 《an affair》 ; deal with the aftermath ¶ 끝갈망을 잘하다 bring something to a successful issue

끝구 一句 ① [시조 따위의] the last line ② [마지막 구절] the last phrase ③ [결구(結句)] the conclusion ; the concluding part ; the apodosis

***끝끝내** to the last ; to the (bitter) end ; to the last extremity ; persistently ; stubbornly ; tenaciously ¶ 끝끝내 반대하다 oppose persistently〔stiffly, stubbornly〕 ; be dead set against // 끝끝내 싸우다 contend〔fight〕 to a finish〔the last ditch〕 ; dispute to the hilt ; fight to the bitter end // 끝끝내 항거하다 offer obstinate resistance // 끝끝내 모른다고 버티었다 He persisted in asserting his innocence. /He persisted to the last, denying his knowledge (of it).

***끝나다** end ; come〔draw〕 to an end〔a close〕 ; close ; be closed ; be over ; be done ; finish 《with》 ; be finished ; wind up ; be through 《with》 ; complete ; be completed ; conclude ; be concluded ; terminate ; expire (만기) ; result in (결과) ; [산회] break up ; rise ; adjourn ; pass off (지나다) ¶ 이번 주일이 끝나기 전에 before the week is out〔up〕 // 실패로 끝나다 end in failure // 방학이 끝났다 The vacation came to a close. // 시험이 끝났다 The examination is over. /I am through my examination. // 근무가 끝나다 be off duty // 언제 일이 다 끝나십니까 When will you be through with your work ? // 기초 공사는 그때까지 끝날 것이다 The groundwork will be finished〔completed〕 by that time. // 그 타자기는 다 쓰셨습니까 Have you done with the typewriter ? // 오늘 일도 끝났다 The day's work is done. /I'm finished for today. /I'm through for today. 《미》 // 그들은 미국 여행이 끝나고 영국으로 가는 중이다. They have finished with the U. S. A. and are now on their way to England. // 식이 끝나려고 한다 The ceremony is going to finish〔wind up〕. // 그 길은 숲에서 끝난다 The road terminates in woods. // 음악회는 애국가 연주로 끝났다 The concert concluded with the National Anthem. // 쓸데없이 탄약과 병사의 소모로 끝났다 Their efforts resulted only in the waste of ammunition and men. // 회의는 아무 성과 없이 끝났다 The conference broke up resultless. // 야당의 회의가 무사히 끝났다 The meeting of the opposition party passed off quietly〔without mishap〕. // 모든 일이 무사히 끝났다 Everything went off all right〔without a hitch〕. // 한 해가 끝날 무렵이면 사람은 지난 해를 돌이켜 보고자 한다 Towards the close of a year, one likes to reflect on the past year. // 장마철이 끝났다 The rainy season is over. // 수술은 무사히 끝났다 The operation was completed successfully. // 지금 내가 하고 있는 일이 끝나는 대로 바로 당신 차를 봐 드리겠습니다 I'll take care of your car as soon as I'm through with what I'm doing now. // 이것은 사과한다고 끝나는 일이 아니다 This isn't something that can be written off with an apology.

끝내기 〖바둑〗 the last〔concluding, clinching〕 moves ; the end game ; an ending ¶ 끝내기를 그르치다 commit an error in the end

†**끝내다** end ; make an end of ; close ; bring to a close ; finish ; get through 《with》 ; complete ; conclude ; break up ; wind up ; [결말짓다] settle ; dispose of ¶ 일을 끝내다 finish one's work ; get a work off one's hands // 이야기를 끝내다 wind up a talk // 용무를 끝내다 finish one's business ; make an end of one's business // 토의를 끝내다 terminate〔end〕 a discussion // 여행을 끝내다 complete〔finish〕 a journey // 회의를 끝내다 break up〔close〕 a meeting // 식을 끝내다 go through the ceremony // 일을 대충 끝내다 break the neck of work // 곧 일을 끝내겠다 I will soon be 〔get〕 through with the work. // 그는 미국 여행을 끝내고 귀국했다 He has lately returned from〔after completing〕 his tour of America. // 회의를 성과 없이 끝냈다 They broke up the meeting without result. // 그녀는 척척 일을 끝냈다 She finished off her work efficiently. // 네 일을 빨리 끝내라 Finish (off) your work quickly. // 이것으로 인터뷰는 끝내겠습니다 This wraps up the interview. // 나 화장 거의 다 끝냈어 I'm almost done with my makeup.

끝닿다 reach the end〔bottom, top〕 ; touch bottom

끝돈 the balance unpaid ; the remainder ; the rest ¶ 끝돈을 치르다 pay the remainder〔balance〕

끝동 a cuff ¶ 끝동을 달다 sew a cuff on a sleeve

끝마감 closing (날짜의) ; finish (일의) ; finishing touches (마지막 손질) ; conclusion **—하다** close ; conclude ; end ; put an end to ; bring to a close ¶ 끝 마감날〔시간〕 the closing day 〔hour〕 ; the dead line // 우편물의 끝마감 the closing of the mail // 신문 기사의 끝마감 시간 the time limit for a copy ; the deadline 《미》 ; the time limit 《영》 // 기부금 모집의 끝마감 the close of the subscription〔a fund-raising campaign〕 // 일의 끝마감 completion of one's work // 끝마감 뒤의 기사 late news ; stop-press news 《미》 // 편집 끝마감까지 아무런 보고도 없었다 No report was received up to the time of going to press. // 예약 끝마감은 이달 말까지이다 The subscription list closes in the end of this month.

끝마치다 finish up 《a job》

끝막다 finish ; complete ; terminate ; close ; put an end to ; bring to a close ¶ 기부금 모집을 끝막다 close the subscription list // 편집을 끝막다 go to press // 신청을 끝막다 close applications

끝맺다 ⇨ 끝내다

끝머리 ⇨ 끄트머리

끝물 the last (farm, sea) products of the season

끝수 **—數** 〖수학〗 a fraction ; an odd sum ; odds ¶ 끝수를 버리다 omit 〔ignore, round off〕 fractions // 끝수를 올리다 raise to a unit ; reckon 《0.5 and over》 as a unit

*****끝없다** [넓이] endless ; boundless ; [깊이] unfathomable ¶ 끝없는 욕망 insatiable〔unbounded〕 desires 《for》 // 끝없는 망망대해 a boundless ocean // 끝없는 걱정 endless worries

끝없이 boundlessly ; endlessly ; without end ; eternally ; infinitely ¶ 끝없이 깊은 바다 a bottomless abyss // 끝없이 지껄이다 have an interminable talk // 그녀는 끝없이 수다를 떨었다 She chattered on endlessly.

끝으로 ① [말] last(ly) ; finally ; at〔in〕 the end ; in conclusion ¶ 끝으로 한마디 더 하겠다 In conclusion it only remains to be said that...
② [순서·차례] at the (tail) end ¶ 끝으로 둘째 the last but one // 맨 끝으로 오다 bring〔close〕 up the rear

끝일 [맨 나중 일] the final job〔affair〕 ; the last work ; [뒷정리] after adjustment ; clearance work ; windup

끝장 an end ; a close ; a conclusion ; [낙착] a settlement ; a termination ¶ 끝장나다 end ; come to an end〔a close〕 ; terminate ; wind up ; be done ; be over ; be settled ; come to a conclusion 〔settlement〕 // 끝장내다 end ; put an end to ; bring to a conclusion〔an end〕 ; settle ; finish ; conclude ; terminate // 원만하게 끝장이 나다 be brought to a happy end〔termination〕 // 아직 끝장이 나지 않았다 be still pending // 싸움을 끝장내다 put an end to a quarrel ; settle a quarrel // 일을 끝장내다 finish one's work // 나는 이제 끝장이다 I'm cornered. /I've got my backs to the wall. /This is the end. /There's no way out. /It is all up with me. /All is over (with me). // 끝장을 보고야 마는 사람 a thoroughgoing person ; a perfectionist

끝판 the last part 《of a job, a game》 ; the end ; the close ; the conclusion ; the finish ; the windup ; the last round 《of a game》 ¶ 일의 끝판 the last part of one's work ; the end of the work // 끝판에 지다 lose a game in the last round // 토론 끝판에 가서 싸움이 났다 A quarrel was started at the end of the discussion.

끼 a meal ; a mealtime ¶ 한 끼를 거르다 skip a meal // 하루에 세 끼 먹다 have three meals a day

끼끗이 smartly ; freshly ; healthily ; exuberantly ; youthfully ; attractively ; stylishly ; becomingly ¶ 끼끗이 생기다 be handsome ; have clean-cut features // 끼끗이 차리다 be smartly dressed

끼끗하다 (be) neat ; smart ; clean ; spruce ; [생생하다] fresh ; lively ¶ 끼끗한 글씨 neat handwriting // 끼끗한 외모 a spruce appearance // 끼끗한 야채 fresh vegetables // 끼끗한 얼굴 clean-cut features ; a nice-looking face

끼니 a meal ; a repast ; fare ; dinner ; a diet ; daily meals ¶ 세 끼니 three meals // 끼니를 잇지 못하다 go without a meal ; fail to keep the pot boiling // 끼니를 이을까 말까 할 정도이다 lead a life of half-starvation ; be on the verge of starvation ; want the bare necessities of life // 겨우 끼니는 이어 간다 manage to live ; live by hook or by crook // 끼니 걱정은 없다 have enough to live on ; be well〔comfortably〕 off ; be assured of livelihood // 실력 있는 자는 끼니 걱정은 하지 않는다 Real ability is sure of market.

끼니때 meal time ; dinner time

†**끼다**[1] ① [연기가] smoke ; smolder ; be 〔become〕 smoky ; [안개 따위가] be 〔become〕 foggy〔misty, hazy〕 ¶ 안개가 낀다 The mist is settling. /It is foggy〔misty〕. /A haze lies〔hangs〕 over 《the hills》. // 아침 안개가 들녘에 아직도 끼어 있었다 The morning mists were still hovering over the field.
② [때가] become dirty ; be soiled ; be stained 《with》 ¶ 옷에 온통 기름때가 끼어 있었다 The clothes were smeared all over with greasy dirt. // 얼굴에 기미가 끼다 have a freckled face // 눈곱이 끼다 Matter forms in the eyes. // 기름기가 낀 바지 greasy trousers

끼다[2] ① [틈에] hold 《a thing》 《under, between, behind》 ; [비유적] favor ; side with ; be partial to ¶ 연필을 귀에 끼고 with〔holding〕 a pencil behind one's ear // 책을 겨드랑이에 끼다 hold a book under one's arm // 담배를 손가락 사이에 끼었다 He held a cigarette between his fingers. // 사람들이 쌍쌍이 끼고 춤을 추었다 They danced holding their partners each. // 그 사람을 너무 끼고 돌지 마시오 Don't favor him too much. // 그는 처와 어머니 사이에 끼어서 어려움을 겪고 있다 He's having a hard time, caught between his wife and mother.
② [장갑·반지 따위를] put on ; pull on ; wear ¶ 안경을 끼다 put on glasses // 장갑을 끼다 put〔get, draw, pull〕 on one's gloves // 반지를 끼다 put〔slip〕 a ring on one's finger // 밖에 나갈 때는 대개 안경〔장갑, 반지〕을 낀다 She usually wears spectacles〔gloves, a ring〕 out of doors. // 그녀는 반지를 끼고 있었다 She had a ring on her finger. // 단추를 끼다 fasten buttons // 골무를 끼다 wear a thimble // 나는 장갑을 끼고 있다 I have gloves on.
③ [팔짱을] fold ¶ 팔짱을 끼고 방관하다 look on with folded arms ; stand by with one's arms (folded) across ; stand idle // 두 사람은 팔을 서로 끼고 걷고 있었다 The pair were seen walking arm in arm.
④ [참가] join ; take part 《in》 ; participate 《in》 ; take〔have〕 a share 《in》 ; be involved〔concerned, implicated〕 《in》 ¶ 명단에 끼다 be on the list // 일행에 끼다 join the party // 남의 싸움에 낄 필요는 없다 Don't take part〔be involved〕 in another's quarrel. // 나도 그 추렴에 한몫 끼어 주시오 Please let me take a share in the expenses. // 음모에 한몫 끼었다 He was privy〔a party〕 to the plot.
⑤ [따라서] ¶ …을 끼고 along ; by ; parallel to ; alongside with // 산〔강〕을 끼고 가다 go along the mountain〔river〕
⑥ [배경이 있다] be backed (up) by . . . ; have 《a person》 at one's back ¶ 권력을 끼다 have an influential person at one's back

끼뜨리다 throw 《water》 away

끼루룩 with a long honking **— 하다** honk a long honk

끼루룩거리다 honk and honk ¶ 기러기가 끼루룩거리다 A wild goose is honking (his long honks).

끼룩[1] ⇨ 끼루룩

끼룩[2] [목을 길게] craning (one's fat neck) **— 하다** crane (one's neck)

끼룩거리다[1] [기러기가] honk and honk

끼룩거리다[2] stretch one's neck to see 《a thing》 ; crane one's neck ; peep ; peer greedily ; rubberneck 《미·속》 ¶ 부엌을 끼룩거리다 peek into a kitchen greedily 《for food》 // 창문 밖을 끼룩거리다 stretch one's neck (looking) out a window

끼룩끼룩[1] [기러기가] honking and honking

끼룩끼룩[2] [목을] craning and craning (one's fat neck)

-끼리 ¶ 같은 학생끼리 among fellow students // 친구끼리 싸우는 것은 좋지 않다 You should not quarrel among 〔between〕 yourselves. // 저희끼리 결혼해 버렸다 They married by mutual consent. // 아이들끼리 논다 The children play among themselves. // 우리끼리만 가자 Let's go separately〔by ourselves〕.

끼리끼리 in groups ; in pairs ; by twos and threes ¶ 그들은 5명 내지 10명씩 끼리끼리 서서 이야기하고 있었다 They stood talking in groups of five to ten. // 아이들이 두셋씩 끼리끼리 걸어갔다 The children walked away by twos and threes. // 사람은 끼리끼리 모이기 마련이다 Birds of a feather flock together. /Like attracts like. /Kind calls to kind. // 끼리끼리 해먹다 Each group looks to its own interests〔feathers its nest〕.

끼어팔기 a tie-in sale

*끼얹다 pour ; shower 《on, over》; splash 《on, over, about》 ¶ 몸에 물을 끼얹다 splash water on oneself ; dash water on one's back // 찬물을 끼얹다 pour 〔throw〕 cold water 《on》

*끼우다 [사이에 넣다] put 《a thing》 between ; insert ; hold between ; [빠지지 않게] fix〔fit〕 into ; set 《in》; inlay ¶ 책 속에 끼우다 stick (a thing) between the leaves of a book // 사진을 틀에 끼우다 fix a picture in a frame ; frame a picture // 창문에 유리를 끼우다 fit a pane in a window // 반지에 금강석을 끼우다 set a diamond in a ring ; set a ring with a diamond // 단추 구멍에 꽃을 끼우다 stick a flower in one's buttonhole // 경품을 끼워 팔다 sell articles with a premium // 이 카메라들은 모두 부속품을 끼워서 판다 All these cameras are sold together with accessories.

끼워팔기 a tie-in〔combination〕 sale

*끼이다[1] ① [물건 사이에] be put〔held〕 between ; be caught in ; get jammed 〔hemmed〕 in ; be sandwiched between ¶ 음식이 잇새에 끼이다 A food particle gets in between the teeth. // 손가락이 문에 끼였다 My fingers were caught in the door.
② [게재하다] be〔lie〕 between ; be sandwiched between ¶ 나는 두 사람 사이에 끼여서 난처하였다 I was perplexed between the two. // 그 나라는 양대국 사이에 끼여 있다 She is sandwiched in between the two great powers.
③ [신발 따위가] be tight〔close〕 ¶ 구두가 너무 꼭 끼인다 My shoes pinch (my feet). // 이 웃옷은 내게 너무 끼인다 This jacket is too tight for me.
④ [참여하다] take one's place among ; rank with ¶ 이 사업에 한 몫 끼이지 않겠니 Don't you want to be in on this business?

끼이다[2] [싫어하다] hate (people)

끼적거리다 scribble ; dash ; scrawl ; dash off ; scratch ¶ 종이에 몇자 끼적거려 놓다 scribble something on a piece of paper ; write a hasty line ; dash off a letter

끼치다[1] [소름이] shudder ; shiver ; thrill 《with horror》; feel a thrill ; feel a chill creep 《over one》; feel one's flesh creep 《all over》; be goose-flesh all over ; [사물이 주어] make one's blood run cold ; curdle one's blood ; send a thrill〔chill〕 ; make one's flesh creep ¶ 무서워서 소름이 끼치다 shudder in horror ; feel one's hair stand on end with terror // 추워서 소름이 끼치다 shiver with cold

*끼치다[2] ① [원인이 되다] cause ; make ; render ; [공헌하다] contribute to ; make a contribution to ; render services to ; do much toward ; tend to ; [폐를] trouble 《a person》; give〔cause〕 trouble to ; be a burden to ; [손해 따위를] injure ; harm ; hurt ; impair ; spoil ; mar ; damage ; cause damage to ; [영향을] influence ; affect ; have influence on 〔upon〕 ¶ 산업계에 끼치는 바 공헌이 크다 render great service to the cause of industry // 건강에 해를 끼치다 do harm to one's health ; injure 〔impair〕 one's health // 농작물에 해를 끼치다 damage 〔spoil〕 the crop // 나이는 시력에 영향을 끼친다 Age tells on sight. // 폐를 끼쳐 미안합니다 I am sorry to have troubled you so much. // 걱정을 끼치다 cause anxiety to 《a person》
② [후세에 전하다] bequeath ; transmit ; leave ; hand down ¶ 유산에 끼쳐 주다 bequeath〔leave〕 one's property 〔fortune〕 // 누명을 끼치다 leave a bad reputation // 아들에게 빚을 끼치고 죽다 die leaving debts for one's son

끽 shrieking ; shouting ; yelling ―하다 give〔let out〕 a yell ; give a scream ; shout ¶ 끽소리를 내고 쓰러지다 fall down with a scream

끽겁 喫怯 being frightened ―하다 be frightened ; be struck with horror

끽경 喫驚 astonishment ; amazement ; fright ―하다 (be) astonished ; amazed ; frightened ; terror-stricken

끽고 喫苦 suffering hardships ; going through difficulties ―하다 go through difficulties ; suffer hardships

끽긴 喫緊 ―하다 [중요하다] (be) very important ; vital ; momentous ; be of vital importance ; [필요하다] necessary ; essential ; indispensable ; [긴급하다] urgent ; pressing

끽끽 shouting one's head off ; yelling away ; shrieking ; screaming ¶ 끽끽거리다 shriek ; scream ; give a scream ; screech ; squeak

끽다 喫茶 drinking tea ―하다 drink tea

끽반 喫飯 eating〔taking〕 a meal ―하다 eat ; take〔have〕 a meal

끽소리 a yell (of protest) ¶ 끽소리 못하다 sing small ; be (completely) silenced ; can't say a thing // 끽소리 못하게 하다 put〔reduce〕 《a person》 to silence ; beat 《a person》 all hollow // 이 말에 그는 끽소리 못했다 He couldn't utter a syllable in reply. // 이번에는 꼭 당신을 끽소리 못하게 하겠소 I'll settle your hash this time for sure.

끽연 喫煙 smoking ―하다 smoke 《tobacco, a pipe》; have a smoke ; use

tobacco ; enjoy the weed ¶ 끽연이 금지되어 있다 Smoking is prohibited.
—실 a smoking〔smoke《영》〕 room ; a smoking saloon (배의) **—자** a smoker **—차(車)** a smoking car《미》; a smoking carriage〔coach〕《영》

끽해야 at (the) most ; at the utmost ; at (the) best ; at the outside ¶ 끽해야 스무 살쯤이다 He is twenty at the most 〔outside〕. // 끽해야 보름쯤 걸리겠죠 I should think it will take fifteen days at the longest.

*****낄낄** giggling ; snickering **—하다〔거리다〕** giggle (and giggle) ; snicker away ¶ 낄낄 웃다 giggle ; snicker // 숨어서 낄낄거리다 laugh up one's sleeve

*****낌새** secrets ; delicate signs ; hint ; secret devices ; inner workings ; a delicate turn ; an inkling ¶ 낌새를 보이지 않다 reveal no secret ; show not the slightest sign〔hint〕 of // 정국이 달라질 낌새가 보이지 않는다 I cannot see any sign of change in the political situation. // 우리가 무엇을 하고 있는지 이제 낌새 챈 모양이다 He seemed to have caught on to what we are up to. // 상대방의 계략을 낌새 채다 get wind of one's opponent's plans ; get wise to one's opponent's tricks《구》
낌새 보다 관용 sound out the secrets of《an affair》
낌새 채다 관용 sense the secrets of 《an affair》

낑 with a groan **—하다** make a groan ¶ 낑하고 힘쓰다 put forth one's strength with a groan

낑낑 groaning and groaning ; groan away (under a burden) **—하다〔거리다〕** groan and groan ; groan away ¶ 무거운 짐을 지고 낑낑거리다 groan under the load of heavy burden

ㄴ

-ㄴ가 ① [의문] ¶ 그게 무언가 What is it? // 그게 누군가 Who is it? // 자네 기쁜가 Are you happy? // 그녀는 예쁜가 Is she pretty? // 저게 학교인가 Is that a school?
② [막연한 장소·시간] ¶ 나는 그것을 어딘가에서 읽은 것 같다 I think I have read it in some book or other. // 언젠가 후회할 거다 You will repent it sooner or later.

-ㄴ가 보다 [처럼 보이다] look (like); appear; seem; sound (like); […로 생각 되다] seem; it seems (to me) that...; […할〔있을〕 법하다] ¶ 그는 아마 아픈가 보다 He seems to be ill. // 이 도시는 번화한가 보다 This town has an air of prosperity. // 그 얘기는 정말인가 보다 The story has the appearance of truth. // 그녀의 설명은 맞는가 보다 Her explanation sounds all right.

-ㄴ 고로 —故— […한 까닭에] as; because; for; for the reason that... ¶ 그는 환자인 고로 그것을 안 해도 좋다 Being sick, he need not do it. // 그 책을 못 읽은 고로 나는 모르겠다 I don't know because I never read the book.

-ㄴ 까닭에 [이유] as; because; for; (for) the reason that... ¶ 바쁜 까닭에 가지 못한다 I can't go because I'm busy.

-ㄴ 끝에 […한 결과, 드디어] (as) the final consequence of 《doing》; in the end; after 《doing》; finally ¶ 잘 생각한 끝에 after much thinking // 오래 앓은 끝에 after a long illness // 갖은 죄를 지은 끝에 사람을 죽였다 He committed a murder to top off the varieties of crimes he had perpetrated.

-ㄴ대서 ¶ 증기선은 증기로 간대서 그렇게 부른다 A steamer is so called because it is run by steam.

-ㄴ대서야 ¶ 네가 그걸 모른대서야 되나 It is a pity that you should not know it. // 그런 정직한 사람을 쫓아낸대서야 되나 The idea of kicking out such an honest fellow!

-ㄴ대야 […해 봤자] even if〔though〕; granting that ¶ 지금 떠난대야 만나기는 글렀어 Even if you start now, you will not be able to see him. // 많이 한대야 5천원짜리지 It is worth five thousand *won* at (the) dearest. // 그런 말을 한대야 아무 소용 없다 It is of no avail to tell him so. // 먹는대야 얼마나 먹을라고 내버려 둬라 Let him eat as much as he likes; he can't eat much anyway.

-ㄴ데 ① [그러나] but; however; still ¶ 그는 겉보기는 온순한데 심지는 굳다 He is gentle in appearance, but strong at heart.
② [그리고] and; when; where; who ¶ 난데 문 좀 열어 줘 It's me. Open the door, please.
③ [감탄] ¶ 날씨가 매우 찬데 It's very cold, isn't it?

-ㄴ들 […일망정] ¶ 난들 못할소냐 I can do it too. /I also can do it. // 넌들 나을게 뭐냐 You are no better than I. // 남들이 뭐라한들 대수랴 I don't care what people say of me. // 힘이 약하다 한들 너보다야 약하랴 I may be weak, but I am sure I am no weaker than you.

-ㄴ바 ⇨ 바[1]

-ㄴ즉 ⇨ -즉

-ㄴ지 [의문] ¶ 그가 누군지 아십니까 Do you know who he is? // 어떻게 하는지 알려 주시오 Tell me how to do it. // 그가 올는지 안 올는지 모르겠다 I don't know whether he will come or not. // (전화에서) 누구신지요 Who is this, please?

-ㄴ체하다 ⇨ 체하다

†**나**[1] I; myself; self; ego (자아) ¶ 나의 my; my own // 나를〔에게〕 me; to〔of, on, for〕 me // 나의 것 mine // 나로서는 as for me; as for my own case; for my part // 나도 Me, too. /So do I. /So am I. /Same here. /Ditto. // 나도 모르게 involuntarily; in spite of myself // 이 사진이 나입니다 This picture is my own self. /This is (the picture of) me. /This is my picture. // 나는 상관 없습니다 As for me, I do not care. /(That's) O.K. by〔with〕 me. // 내가 늦은 건 아니지 그렇지 I am not late, am I? // 나라면 그런 짓은 안하겠다 If I were in your〔his〕 place, I would not do like that. // 잘못한 것은 나다 It is I who am guilty. // 존과 나는 항상 친했다 John and I have always been friends.

나는 바담풍(風) 해도 너는 바람풍 해라 〔속담〕 Do as I say, not as I do. /Practise what you preach.

나[2] ⇨ 이나

-나 ① [전후 내용의 상반] but; though ¶ 가난하나 정직하다 be poor but honest // 가난하나 거짓말을 할 사람은 아니다 Though (he is) poor, he is above telling a lie. // 나는 가지 않았으나 그는 갔다 I didn't go, but he did.

② [선택] either... or; whether... or ¶ 나나 너 either I or you // 존이나 메리가 알고 있다 Either John or Mary knows. // 만나나 마나 매한가지다 It doesn't make any difference whether I see him or not.
③ [의문 어미] ¶ 덥나 Are you warm? // 내말 알아듣겠나 Do you understand what I mean?
④ [한결같이] always ¶ 자나깨나 awake or asleep; day and night // 비가 오나 해가 나나 rain or shine // 자나깨나 그 일을 잊을 수가 없다 I can't forget it waking or sleeping.

*나가다 ① [밖으로] go out; get out; take one's way out; step out ¶ 뜰로 나가다 go out into the garden // 산보 나가다 go out for a walk // 방에서 나가다 go out of a room // 지금 나가고 없다 He has gone out. // 그 여자는 장보러 나갔습니다 She has gone out for shopping. // 여기서 나갈 수가 없다 I can't get out of here. // 얼마나 오랫동안 나가 있었느냐 How long have you been gone?
② [진출] go forth 《into the world》; launch 《into》; go upon 《the world's stage》; enter upon 《a political career》 ¶ 실사회에 나가다 launch〔go〕 into the world // 정계에 나가다 launch into politics // 실업계에 나가다 go into business
③ [근무] work 《in》; serve 《in》; be in the service of; be with; hold an office 《in》 (관청에) ¶ 출판사에 나가다 be with〔work for〕 a publishing company // 학교에 나가다 be teaching in a school // 회사에 나가다 be employed in a company
④ [참가] take part 《in》; join 《in》; enter; go in 《for》; run 《for》 (입후보) ¶ 경기에 나가다 take part〔participate〕 in a game // 대통령 후보로 나가다 run for the Presidency // 100미터 경주에 나가다 enter the 100 meter race // 개그 선발 대회에 나가다 enter〔go in for〕 a gag contest
⑤ [팔리다] sell ¶ 가장 잘 나가는 책 the top〔best〕 seller // 잘 나가다 sell well; go well; get sold well; have a good sale // 이 사전은 잘 나갑니다 This dictionary is a good seller. // 이 집은 10만 달러에 나갔다 This house went for 100,000 dollars. // 이 일요판은 꽤 나갑니다 This Sunday edition enjoys〔has〕 a large circulation.
⑥ [해져 찢어지다] be torn to ribbons 〔tatters〕 ¶ 소년의 바지는 엉덩이 부위가 나갔다 The boy's pants have worn thin at the seat.
⑦ [돈이] be spent; be paid out ¶ 어린이 교육에 많은 돈이 나간다 Children's education costs us a great deal. // 쉽게 번 돈은 쉽게 나간다 Easy come, easy go.
⑧ [가치가] be worth; weigh (무게) ¶ 100원 나가는 물건 an article worth 100 *won* // 무게가 10파운드 나간다 This weighs ten pounds.
⑨ [퇴거] move out; leave; take one's leave; get away; depart 《from》 ¶ 집을 나가다 leave home; get out of the house; leave the house // 나가라 Be off with you! /Be gone! /Get you gone! // 그들은 내달에 이 집에서 나간다 They will move out of this house next month.
⑩ [앞으로] advance; proceed; go forward; make one's way; [진보] improve; make progress; get on with 《one's work》 ¶ 한걸음 더 나가서 taking a step forward // 앞으로 한국이 나갈 길 the course Korea should take in the future // 독본은 진도가 얼마나 나갔습니까 How far have you gone with the English reader?
⑪ [정신이] go out of one's mind; be 〔go〕 off one's head; go mad ¶ 이런 날씨에 조깅을 하다니, 그 여자는 정신이 나갔음에 틀림없다 She must be off her head to go jogging in this weather!
⑫ [못쓰게 되다] be broken; go wrong; get out of order; be dead ¶ 전등이 나갔다 The electric light has gone out. // 내 차 배터리가 나갔다 My car battery is dead.

나가동그라지다, 나가둥그러지다 tumble; fall down〔over, off〕; fall head over heels

나가떨어지다 ① [넘어지다] be thrown down; be knocked down; fall flat on one's back ¶ 한 방에 나가떨어지다 be knocked down at a single blow // 그는 말에서 나가떨어졌다 He was thrown off his horse.
② [녹초가 되다] be exhausted; be done up; be dog〔dead〕-tired ¶ 그는 완전히 나가떨어졌다 He is absolutely done up.
③ [패배·실패하다] fall; lose; fail ¶ 그 도시는 적에게 여러 달 동안 포위된 끝에 나가떨어졌다 The city fell to the enemy after a siege of many months. // 우리들은 경기에서 분투했지만 나가떨어졌다 We played well but we lost.

나가자빠지다 ① [자빠지다] fall flat on one's back; tumble down; be thrown down ¶ 벌렁 나가자빠지다 fall full length
② [손을 끊다] withdraw 《from》; retire 《from》; back 《out of a project》 ¶ 빚을 지고 나가자빠지다 run out on〔fail to pay〕 one's debts // 출판계의 불경기로 많은 출판업자들이 나가자빠졌다 Many a publisher has gone bankrupt owing to the depression in the publishing business. // 회사가 나가자빠지려고 한다 The company is on the verge of bankrupt-

cy. // 약속을 했으니 이제 나가자빠질 수 없다 After all your promise you can't withdraw now.

*나귀 a donkey ; an ass

*나그네 a traveler ; a wayfarer ; a passenger ; a vagabond ; a wanderer ; a stranger ; a visitor〔guest〕 (손)
—길 a journey
나그네 인생 (속담) Life is a pilgrimage.

나근거리다 bend ; give ; flex ; be flexible〔supple〕

나근나근 bending ; giving ; flexing

나긋나긋하다 ① [음식이] (be) tender ¶ 나긋나긋한 고기 tender meat ② [살결이] (be) soft ¶ 살결이 나긋나긋하다 have soft skin ③ [태도가] (be) affable ; mild ; benign ¶ 나긋나긋하게 mildly ; affably

나깨 inner husk of buckwheat
—떡 a coarse cake made with buckwheat husks

나나니벌 【곤충】 a digger wasp ; a mud dauber ; Ammophila infesta (학명)

*나날이 day by day ; day after day ; from day to day ; every day ; daily ¶ 날씨가 나날이 추워지고 있다 It is getting colder day by day.

나녀 裸女 a nude〔naked〕 woman

나누기 dividing —하다 divide ¶ 6 나누기 2는 3 6 divided by 2 is〔gives, equals〕 3.

†나누다 ① [가르다] divide 《into》; separate ; split ¶ 둘로 나누다 divide〔split〕 《a thing》 into two // 사과를 반으로 나누다 divide an apple into halves // 과자를 여러 조각으로 나누다 divide a cake into several pieces // 10을 2로 나누면 5이다 Ten divided by two gives five. // 그들은 그 돈을 똑같이 나누었다 They split the sum equally.
② [분배] divide 《between the two, among the three》; share 《a thing》 with 《a person》; distribute 《among》; allot ; apportion ; portion (out) ¶ 자식들에게 재산을 나누어 주다 divide〔share〕 one's property among one's children // 이익을 종업원에게 나누어 주다 distribute the profits among one's employees // 우리끼리 사탕을 나누었다 We divided the sweets between us.
③ [구별] classify 《into》 ¶ 정확히 나누다 draw an exact line 《between》 // 여러 항목으로 나눌 수 있다 It is to be classified into many items.
④ [함께 하다] share 《with》 ¶ 음식을 나누어 먹다 share food with others // 기쁨〔슬픔〕을 나누다 share one's joy〔sorrow〕 with 《a person》 // 비용을 분담하다 share expenses // 점심을 나누다 have lunch together // 친구와 포도주를 나누다 share wine with a friend // 술을 나누며 이야기하다 have a chat 《with a friend》 over wine cups

나누이다 be〔get〕 divided〔separated, split up〕

나눗셈 (a) division —하다 divide

나뉘다 ⇨ 나누이다

나닐다 fly〔hover〕 about

†나다¹ ① [출생] be born ; come into the world ; come into being ¶ 날 때부터 from birth // 부자로 태어나다 be born rich ; be born to wealth // 가난하게 태어나다 be born poor ; be born to poverty // 그는 일본에서 났다 He was born in Japan.
② [생기다] come out ; grow ; spring up ; sprout ¶ 깃털이 다 난〔아직 깃털이 다 나지 않은〕 새 a full-fledged〔an unfledged〕 bird // 싹이 나다 bud (out) ; sprout ; spring up // 풀이 나다 the grass grows // 아기가 이가 났다 The baby has cut its tooth. // 이 새는 깃이 나지 않았다 This little bird is still unfledged. // 비온 뒤에 죽순이 나다 bamboo shoots〔sprouts, springs up〕 after a rain // 이 식물은 고산 지대에 난다 This plant grows in alpine regions.
③ [발생] break out ; happen ; occur ; take place ; come to pass ; come about ; turn up ; rise ; arise ; spring〔come〕 up ¶ 난리가 나다 a war breaks out // 불이 나다 a fire breaks out // 사건이 나다 have an incident ; an incident happens〔occurs, takes place〕 // 탈이 나다 run into a hitch〔hindrance, trouble〕 // 홍수가 나다 have a flood // 바람이 나다 a wind arises〔comes up〕 // 시계가 고장났다 My watch is out of order. // 그에게 사고가 났음이 틀림없다 An accident must have happened to him.
④ [냄새 따위] come out〔forth〕; smell ; taste ¶ 신맛이 나다 be sour to the taste ; taste sour // 장미꽃 향기가 나다 have scents〔a scent〕 of a rose // 매운맛이 나다 have a hot〔biting〕 taste ; be hot to the taste
⑤ [병 따위] become ; have ; get ¶ 병이 나다 be taken ill ; get〔fall〕 sick ; catch a disease // 기침이 나다 have a cough ; cough // 상처가 나다 get wounded〔hurt〕 // 이름이 나다 win a reputation〔fame〕; come to fame // 열이 나다 become feverish ; run〔develop〕 a fever ; come to have fever // 구역질이 나다 feel like vomiting ; suffer from nausea ; feel sick(ish)
⑥ [생각 따위] occur ¶ 생각이 나다 come into one's mind ; occur to one ; remember ; recollect // 심술이 나다 get cross // 화가 나다 get angry // 싫증이 나다 become sick〔tired, weary〕 《of》; lose interest 《in》 // …할 마음이 나다 be〔feel〕 inclined 《to do》; feel like 《doing》
⑦ [흐르다] flow out ; rush〔gush〕 out

¶ 눈물이 나다 tears flow // 콧물이 나다 one's nose runs // 땀이 나다 sweat
⑧ [산출] be produced〔raised, grown〕 ¶ 한국에서 금이 나다 gold is found in Korea // 미인이 나다 beauties are produced
⑨ [결과] turn out ; turn up ¶ 자국이 나다 leave a trace // 홀수가 나다 an odd number results // 끝장이 나다 come to an end // 잘나다 be handsome〔good-looking〕 // 못나다 be ugly // 동이 나다 become scarce ; run short《of》
⑩ [나타나다] appear ¶ 시장에 채소가 나다 vegetables appear in〔on〕 the market // 신문에 나다 appear in the newspaper
⑪ [구멍 따위] open up ; be open ; become available ¶ 구멍이 나다 a hole is made〔opened〕 // 새 길이 나다 a new road is opened // 자리가 나다 a place 〔job, seat〕 opens up ; become available // 방이 나다 a room〔an apartment〕 is available
⑫ [능률·기세 등이 오르다] ¶ 능률이 나다 become efficient // 약효가 나다 tell 〔act, work〕《on》 // 힘이 나다 gain strength
⑬ [이익] issue《from》; accrue《from》; be derived ; be obtained ¶ 부동산에서 나는 이익 profits issuing 〔accruing〕 from real estate
⑭ [티가] have an air〔a look〕 ; look like ; look ; show ¶ 교수티가 나다 have the air of a professor
⑮ [눈밖에] get out of《a person's》 favor ; be in《a person's》 bad graces
⑯ [인품] be outstanding〔eminent, distinguished〕 ; [잘생기다] be good-looking〔handsome〕 ; be well-favored ¶ 난 사람 an outstanding person ; an extraordinary character ; a bigwig《속》 // 못나다 be ugly〔plain, homely〕
⑰ [명성, 소문 등이] acquire ; circulate ¶ 소문이 나다 a rumor circulates〔gets abroad〕 // …에 대한 소문이 나다 a rumor is abroad〔current, in circulation〕 about...
⑱ [계절을] pass a《season》; tide over ; go〔get〕 through ¶ 겨울을 나다 pass the winter ; see winter through ; winter
⑲ [기타] ¶ 탄로나다 come to light ; get discovered // 그릇에 금이 나다 a plate gets cracked // 아홉 살 난 아이 a child of nine
콩 심은 데 콩 나고 팥 심은 데 팥 난다 속담 You cannot make a silk purse out of a sow's ear.

나다² ① [계속] keep《doing》 ¶ 차차 해나면 if you get used to it ② [완료] have just finished《doing》; come from《doing》 ¶ 하고 싶은 말을 하고 나니 속이 시원하다 Now that I have had my say, I feel the easier for it.

나다니다 go out ; gad〔wander〕 about ¶ 자주 나다니는 사람 a regular gadabout // 자주 나다니다 be always on the gad // 여자가 밤에 나다니는 것은 좋지 않다 I do not approve of girls gadding about at night.

나다분하다 (be) untidy ⇨ 너더분하다

나닥나닥 ⇨ 너덕너덕

나달 four of five days ; about four days

나도그늘사초 Korean sedge

나도댑싸리 Axyris amaranthoide (학명)

나도물통이 Nanocnide japonica (학명)

나도밤나무 Meliosma myriantha (학명)

나도방동사니 Juncellus nipponicus (학명)

나도벌사초 Carex bibba (학명)

나도범위귀 bishop's-cap

나돌다 [밖에] wander about (outdoors) ; [말·소문이] get around ; [상품이] arrive〔appear〕 on the market ; hit 〔come on to〕 the market ; be moving ¶ 지금 감이 나돌고 있다 The persimmon is in season. // 당신이 부인과 이혼할 거라는 소문이 나돌고 있다 There is a rumor going around that you're going to divorce your wife.

나뒹굴다 tumble all about ; be spread 〔scattered〕 all over

나들다 come in and go out

나들이 going out ; an outing ; an airing ¶ 나들이 가다 go on a visit
—옷 a Sunday suit ; a Sunday best ; gala〔holiday〕 dress ; a visiting dress

†**나라** ① [국가] a country ; a state ; a nation ; a land ¶ 나라를 위하여 for the sake of one's country // 나라를 세우다 found〔build up〕 a nation // 나라 자랑을 하다 boast of one's country // 나라를 위하여 목숨을 바치다 lay down〔give up〕 one's life for one's country // 나라를 배반하다 betray one's country // 나라를 다스리다 govern a nation〔state, country〕
② [세계] a world ; a realm
꿈— the dream-world ; the dreamland ; the realm of dreams ; the cloudland **달—** the lunar world ; the moon
별— the starry world

나라지다 ⇨ 늘어지다 ④

나락 奈落 hell ; Hades ; the infernal regions ; the nether world

나란하다 (be) even〔uniform〕 ; equal ; be in a line ; be lined up

†**나란히** ① [한 줄로] in a line〔row〕 ; side by side ; abreast ¶ 나란히 서다 stand in a row ; form a line ; line up // 나란히 앉다 sit side by side with《a person》; sit next to《a person》; take one's seat with《a person》 // 옆으로 나란히 서다 stand abreast // 길에 나란히 서다 line the route // 거리에는 상점이 나란히 줄지어 있다 The street is lined with shops. // 우로 나란히 Right dress!

② [가지런히] evenly ; uniformly ; in order ; running parallel with〔to〕 (평행으로) ¶ 높이를 나란히 하다 make them all of uniform height // 책을 나란히 하다 put books in order // 철로와 나란히 뻗어 있는 길 a road running parallel with〔to〕 the railway // 어깨를 나란히 하다 (비유적) rank〔vie〕 《with》; bear〔stand〕 comparison 《with》; equal
—꼴 〖수학〗 a parallelogram
나랏님 the king ; the sovereign ; the ruler
나래¹ a soil leveler (농기구)
—꾼 a soil-leveler operator —질 leveling soil with a soil leveler
나래² [노] an oar ; a pair of oars
‡**나루** a ferry ; a ferry point ¶ 나루를 건너다 ferry over ; cross a river by ferry boat
—지기 a ferryman ; a waterman —질 ferrying —터 a ferry —턱 a ferry ; ferry moorings **나룻가** the vicinity of the ferry **나룻목** [물목] the ferry narrows
나룻 whiskers ; a beard ; a mustache
‡**나룻배** a ferryboat ¶ 나룻배를 타다 take a ferryboat // 나룻배로 건너다 ferry across ; cross a river by ferryboat
— 사공 a ferryman ; a ferrymaster
†**나르다** carry ; convey ; transport ¶ 짐을 나르다 carry luggage // 석탄을 트럭으로 나르다 transport coal by truck // 화물을 배로 나르다 carry goods in a ship // 우편물을 비행기로 나르다 transport mail by airplane // 그 버스는 승객을 정거장까지 날랐다 The bus conveyed the passengers to the station.
***나르시시즘** narcissism
***나른하다** ① (be) languid ; weary ; feel tired ; listless ; dull ¶ 몸이 나른하여 일할 생각이 없다 I feel too languid to work. // 더운 날에는 몸이 나른하다 A hot day makes me feel languid. // 몸과 마음이 모두 나른하다 I am weary in body and mind. // 오늘은 어쩐지 몸이 나른하다 Somehow I feel listless today.
② [힘없이 보드랍다] (be) delicate ; feeble ¶ 몸매가 나른한 여자 a woman of delicate build
†**나름** depending on ¶ 나름이다 depend on ; hang〔turn〕 on ; be conditional 〔dependent〕 on ; rest〔lie〕 with 자기 나름대로 in one's own way // 그것은 사람 나름이다 That depends on the person. // 모두 값이 다른데 물건 나름이다 We have many prices and they depend upon the quality of articles. // (선택은 당신) 나름이다 It rests with you to choose.
나릅 a four-year-old 《animal》
나룻 a shaft (of a vehicle) ; a thill
—걸이 a shaft rack ; an attachment on the yoke to hold the carriage poles

나리¹ your honor ; sir
나리² [식물] a lily ; Lilium (학명)
나마 [이라도, 아쉬운 대로] though ; but anyway ; however ; if only ; even ¶ 주소나마 알았어도 편지를 냈을 텐데 If only I had known his address, I would have written to him. // 그만한 비나마 와 주니 크게 도움이 된다 Even that much of rain is of great help.
-나마 [불만을 참고] but ; though ; however ; even ; even if ¶ 그는 가난하나마 거짓말은 안 한다 Though (he is) poor 〔Poor as he is〕, he is above telling a lie. // 맛은 좋지 않으나마 하나 드시오 They are not very tasty, but please have one anyway. // 집은 작으나마 자리가 좋다 The house may be small, but it's nicely located.
나막신 wooden shoes with clogs (for rainy weather) ; pattens ; sabots
나맥 裸麥 rye ⇨ 쌀보리
†**나머지** ① [남은 것] the rest ; the remainder ; the remnant(s) ; surplus (잉여) ; the balance (잔금) ; remainings ; leavings ; what is left of ; a leftover ¶ 나머지 돈 the money left 《over》 // 나머지 반 the other half // 나머지 빚 the balance of one's debt ; the balance owed // 나머지 사람 the rest of the people // 나머지 일 the remaining work ; the rest of the work // 먹고 남은 나머지 the remnants〔what was left〕 of the food ; scraps of food ; the rest of the food ; leftover food // 나머지 재산 the residue of one's property // 나머지 돈이 얼마 있나 How much money have you left ?
② [넘침] from an excess of ; driven by ; as a result of ¶ 기쁜 나머지 in the excess〔fullness〕 of one's joy ; elated by joy // 슬픈 나머지 in one's grief ; in a passion of grief // 당황한 나머지 all in a fluster // 질투한 나머지 driven by jealousy // 미워한 나머지 out of hatred // 심한 언쟁을 한 나머지 싸움이 되었다 Their severe quarrel resulted in fighting. /As a result of much quarreling they began to fight〔came to blows〕.
나목 裸木 a bare〔leafless〕 tree
†**나무** ① [수목] a tree ; a plant ¶ 나무를 가꾸다 look after plants // 나무를 심다 plant a tree // 나무를 베다 fell a tree // 나무에 물을 주다 water a plant // 나무가 우거지다 be thickly wooded // 나무에 올라가다 climb (up) a tree // 나무 위에 새집이 있다 There is a bird nest in the tree.
② [재목] wood ; timber ; lumber 《미》
③ [땔나무] firewood ; fuel ¶ 나무 조각 a piece〔chip, block〕 of wood ; a splinter ; a chunk of wood 《미》 // 나무하러 가다 go to gather firewood // 나무를 때

다 burn wood
— 거울 a good-for-nothing (fellow) — 공이 a wooden pestle — 괭이 a wooden hoe —깽이 a piece of a wood ; a splinter — 껍질 the bark of a tree — 꾼 a woodcutter ; a woodman ; a lumberjack 《미》; a lumberman —눈〔순〕 tree buds〔sprouts, shoots〕 —때기 a chip〔piece〕 of wood ; a stick ; a board ; a lath — 막대기 a stick ; a pole ; a rod ; a club —못 a wooden nail〔peg〕 —배 a wooden ship〔vessel〕 — 뿌리 the root of a tree — 상자 a wooden box — 장수 a firewood seller ; a fuel dealer — 젓가락 wooden chopsticks — 좀 〖곤충〗 a (wood) borer — 줄기 the trunk of a tree —진 sap of a tree ; resin — 진디 [곤충] a wood louse — 토막 a piece〔chip, splinter〕 of wood ; a block(큰 것) — 판자 a board — 판장 a wooden wall ; a board fence 나뭇가지 the branches of a tree 나뭇간 a woodshed 나뭇개비 a piece of wood ; a splinter 나뭇결 the grain (of wood) ¶ 나뭇결이 곱다〔거칠다〕 be fine-grained〔coarse-grained〕 나뭇고갱이 the pith〔heart〕 of a tree 나뭇길 a woodman's path 나뭇단 a fagot ; a bundle of firewood 나뭇더미 a woodpile 나뭇동 a large bundle of wood 나뭇등걸 a stump of a tree 나뭇바리 a load of wood 나뭇잎 a leaf ; foliage ; leafage 《총칭》

나무 뚝배기 쇠양푼 될까 (속담) Once a devil, always a devil. /Once a knave, and ever a knave.

나무에 잘 오르는 놈이 떨어지고 헤엄 잘 치는 놈이 빠져 죽는다 (속담) Good swimmers are at length drowned. /The best swimmers are the oftenest drowned.

열 번 찍어 아니 넘어가는 나무 없다 (속담) Little strokes fell great oaks.

나무끝 a tree top ; a head of a tree

나무딸기 〖식물〗 a raspberry

†**나무라다** blame ; censure ; reprove ; reproach ; take 《a person》 to task ; give 《a person》 a piece of one's mind ¶ 나무랄 데 없이 impeccably ; perfectly // 되게 나무라다 give 《a person》 a good talking-to ; give 《a person》 a severe scolding ; give 《a person》 a good scolding // 잘못을 나무라다 censure 〔blame〕 《a person》 for his error〔fault〕 // 버릇없다고 나무라다 reprove 《a person》 for his bad manners // 문을 열어 놓았기에 그를 나무랐다 I scolded him for having left the door open. // 그는 힘껏 했으니 게으르다고 나무라지 마시오 Do not reproach him with laziness, he has done his utmost. // 사소한 실수로 신참을 너무 나무라지 마라 You shouldn't be so hard on a new employee for just a minor mistake. // 그녀는 나무랄 데가 없다 아름답고 지성적이고 게다가 몸매도 매력적이고 She's beyond reproach—beautiful, intelligent and with an attractive figure to boot.

서투른 목수가 연장만 나무란다 (속담) A bad〔An ill〕 workman quarrels with his tools.

나무람 a blame ; a censure ; a reproof ¶ 나무람 듣다 be blamed ; receive a reprimand〔reproof〕 ; be called to task // 그는 불려가서 나무람을 들었다 He was summoned to receive a reproof. // 그런 짓을 하면 나무람을 듣는 정도로 그치지 않을 것이다 If you do a thing like that, you can't get away with a mere scolding.

나무 발바리 〖조류〗 the common tree-creeper

나무 아미타불 〖불교〗 Save us, merciful Buddha ! /May his soul rest in peace ! (명복을 빎)

나무하다 gather firewood ; cut firewood

나문재 〖식물〗 sea-blite
— 나물 seasoned greens made from the young leaves of sea-blite

나물 ① [생것] herbs ; wild greens ; salad makings ¶ 나물을 캐다 gather greens ; pick herbs ② [무친 것] seasoned vegetables〔greens〕 ; a Korean salad ¶ 나물을 무치다 season greens
—국 vegetable soup —꾼 herb picker 콩— (cooked) bean sprouts

나박김치 pickled sliced radishes seasoned with pepper, garlic, onion, ginger and celery

나발 喇叭 ⇨ 나팔

나발대 ① [나발의] the stem of a bugle ② [부리] the snout of a pig

*‡**나방** 〖곤충〗 a moth

나뱃뱃하다 (be) flat-faced

나변 那邊 where ¶ 나변에 where (in the world) // 그 이유가 나변에 있는가 Where is the reason ? // 그가 나를 욕하는 이유가 나변에 있는지 알 수 없다 I can see no reason why he speaks ill of me.

나볏하다 (be) fair and dignified

나병 癩病 〖의학〗 leprosy ; Hansen's disease ¶ 나병에 걸려 있다 be leprous
—균 a Hansen's bacillus 《*pl.* -li》 —원 (院) a leprosarium ; [요양소] a leper house — 환자 a leper ; a leprous patient — 환자 수용소 a leper colony

-나 보다 seem ; it seems that… ; I think that… ; I wonder if… ; I'm afraid that ¶ 비가 오려나 보다 It looks like rain. /It is likely to rain. /It threatens to rain. /I'm afraid (that) it's going to rain. // 그의 집이 이 다리 근처에 있었나 보다 His house seems to have been in the vicinity of this bridge. // 누가 왔나

보다 I think someone is here〔at the door〕.
나부 裸婦 a woman in the nude
나부끼다 flutter ; flap ; wave ¶ 바람에 나부끼다 flutter〔wave, flap〕 in the wind // 커튼이 바람에 나부끼고 있다 The curtain flutters in the breeze. // 기가 바람에 나부끼고 있다 The flag is streaming〔fluttering〕 in the wind. // 버들가지가 바람에 나부끼고 있다 The willows are flowing in the wind.
나부대다 talk glibly and flippantly ; move restlessly ; be in a fidget
나부대대하다 have a round flat little face
나부랭이 ① [조각] pieces ; bits ; scraps ; slips ; strips ; odd pieces ¶ 종이 나부랭이 pieces〔scraps, slips, strips〕 of paper // 헝겊 나부랭이 pieces〔scraps, strips〕 of cloth ② [사람] a petty official ¶ 순경 나부랭이 a petty policeman
나부죽이 bending humbly ; gently ¶ 나부죽이 엎드리다 gently bend low〔down〕 (to bow)
나부죽하다 (be) rather flat ; lowish ; flattish ¶ 나부죽한 접시 a flat〔an open〕 dish // 그의 얼굴은 나부죽하다 He has a flattish face.
나분하다 (be) low(-flying) ; be close to the ground.
나분히 (flying) low ¶ 나비가 나분히 날아간다 A butterfly flies low.
나불거리다 ① [흔들리다] flutter ⇨ 나붓거리다 ② [혀·입을] dart back and forth ; wag one's tongue ; chatter ¶ 입을 나불거리다 wag one's tongue ; chatter // 뱀이 혀를 나불거리다 a snake darts its tongue in and out
나불나불 ① [나부끼다] fluttering ; flapping ② [혀를] wagging one's tongue ; chattering
나붓거리다 keep fluttering〔flapping, blowing〕 ¶ 깃발이 바람에 나붓거린다 The flag is streaming〔fluttering〕 in the wind.
나붓나붓 fluttering ; flapping ; blowing ; wavering
나붓이 gently ; softly ; coming down lightly (앉다) ¶ 나붓이 절하다 bow with a gentle sweep ; make a polite bow // 새가 나무에 나붓이 내려 앉았다 A bird alighted〔perched〕 on a tree gently.
나붓하다 ⇨ 나부죽하다
나붙다 《a notice》 be put〔posted, pasted〕 up ; be placarded 《on the wall newspaper board》
‡**나비**[1] 『곤충』 a butterfly ¶ 나비 모양의 butterfly-shaped // 나비처럼 날다 fly like a butterfly // 나비가 꽃을 찾아 날고 있다 Butterflies are fluttering from flower to flower.
— **넥타이** a bow tie —**류** butterflies ; Rhopalocera (학명) —**채** butterfly net
고산(高山) — an alpine butterfly
나비[2] [폭] width (of cloth) ⇨ 너비
나비[3] [고양이] puss ; tabby ; kitty ¶ 나비야 Here kitty ! /Kitty-kitty !
나비가오리 『물고기』 a (sting) ray
나비매듭 a bowknot ; a (single, double) bow ; a rosette (리본) ¶ 나비매듭으로 하다 tie a bowknot
나비잠 the sleep of a baby with outstretched arms
나비잠 —**簪** a hairpin of a butterfly shape (for weddings)
나비춤 a butterfly dance ; dancing in the manner of a flying butterfly
나빠지다 grow〔get〕 worse ; go bad ; worsen ; go from bad to worse ; become deteriorated ¶ 사태는 더한층 나빠졌다 Things went from bad to worse. // 그의 병세가 더욱 나빠졌다 He has taken a turn for the worse. // 더욱 나빠지기만 하다 grow worse and worse ; be worse than ever
나쁘게 badly ; ill ¶ 남을 나쁘게 말하다 speak ill of others // 그이를 나쁘게 말하는 사람은 아무도 없다 There are none who talk against him. // 나쁘게 말하면 간사한 짓이다 To give it a hard name, it is crafty.
†**나쁘다** ① [불량] (be) bad ; [부정] wrong ; evil ; [악의] wicked ; malicious ; [도덕상] immoral ; sinful ¶ 나쁜 사람 a bad〔wicked〕 man // 나쁜 생각 an evil intention // 나쁜 짓 a wrong ; an evil deed ; a misdeed ; a crime (범죄) ; a sin (죄악) ; a vice (악덕) // 나쁜 짓을 하다 do wrong ; commit a sin〔crime〕 // 나쁘게 생각하다 take 《a matter》 amiss〔in ill part〕 // 나쁘게 말하다 speak ill of 《a person》 ; speak against 《a person》 // 운이 나쁘다 have bad luck ; be unlucky // 평판이 나쁘다 have a bad〔poor〕 reputation // 길이 나쁘다 The road is rough. // 나쁘게 생각 말게 Don't think badly of me. // 그런 나쁜 말을 하면 못쓴다 Don't use bad words. /Don't use four-letter words.
② [품질이] (be) bad ; inferior ; poor ; coarse ; be of low grade ; be of inferior make ¶ 나쁜 물건 inferior goods ; a bad〔defective〕 article // 그 물건은 품질이 나쁘다 The goods are of poor quality.
③ [잘못] (be) wrong ; be in the wrong ; be to blame ; be in fault ¶ 내가 나쁘다 I am to blame for it. /I am in the wrong. /The fault is with me. // 거짓말하면 나쁘다 It is wrong to tell a lie. // 둘 다 나쁘다 Both are to blame.
④ [해롭다] (be) bad 《for》 ; injurious 《to》 ; harmful 《to》 ¶ 몸에 나쁘다 be bad for the health ; be injurious to health // 눈에 나쁘다 be hard on one's

eyes // 흡연은 몸에 나쁘다 Smoking is bad for health.
⑤ [병] (be) bad ; ill ; poor ; unwell ¶ 건강이 나쁘다 be in poor health ; have bad health ; suffer from bad health // 눈이 나쁘다 have a bad eye ; have defective eyesight // 안색이 나쁘다 look unwell // 위가 나쁘다 have a stomach trouble ; have a stomach disorder
⑥ [머리·기억력이] (be) poor ; weak ; feeble ¶ 머리가 나쁘다 be weak〔muddle〕-headed // 기억력이 나쁘다 have a poor〔bad〕 memory
⑦ [불쾌] (be) bad ; disagreeable ; unpleasant ¶ 기분이 나쁘다 feel unwell ; be out of sorts ; feel sick ; feel hurt
⑧ [모자라다] (be) not enough ; insufficient ; inadequate ; unsatisfactory ¶ 너는 무엇이 나빠서 그런 얼굴을 하고 있니 What makes you look dissatisfied like that? // 저녁이 내게는 좀 나빴다 The supper didn't fill me up.
⑨ [날씨] (be) bad ; foul ; nasty ; threatening ; inclement ¶ 나쁜 날씨 bad〔foul, nasty〕 weather
⑩ [소식·징조] (be) sad ; bad ; ill ; unwelcome ; unlucky ; ominous ¶ 나쁜 소식 bad〔sad, ill, unwelcome〕 news // 나쁜 징조 a bad〔an ill〕 omen
⑪ [소문 따위] (be) bad ; ill ; unsavory ¶ 나쁜 소문 an unsavory rumor // 그는 그녀에 대한 악의적인 소문을 퍼뜨렸다 He invented a wicked story about her.

나삐 bad ; ill ; insufficiently ; unsatisfactorily ; not enough ¶ 나삐 보다 look down on ; hold in contempt ; hate ; dislike // 남을 나삐 말하지 마라 Don't speak ill of others. // 나삐 여기지 말아 주십시오 Please don't take ill of me.

***나사 螺絲** ① [못] a screw ¶ 나사 돌리개 a screw driver // 나사를 죄다 screw ; screw up 《a box, a door》 ; screw down 《a board, a coffin》 // 나사를 빼다 unscrew // 나사를 늦추다 loosen a screw
② [나선] a spiral ¶ 나사 용수철 a spiral spring // 나사 층층대 a spiral staircase ; screw stairs
— **돌리개** a screwdriver —**못** a screw — **볼트** a screw bolt — **송곳** a single-twist drill ; a screw auger ; a gimlet — **펌프** a screw pump **기계** — a machine screw **수**— a male〔a positive, an external〕 screw ; a bolt **암**— a female〔a negative, an internal〕 screw ; a nut **나삿니** a screw thread ; the thread〔spiral ridge〕 of a screw

나사 羅紗 woolen cloth
— **상인** a woolen draper〔dealer〕 —**지** [벽지용] flockpaper **격자무늬** — plaid cloth ; balmoral ; tartan **능직** — twilled cloth ; twills

나사 NASA 《the National Aeronautics and Space Administration (미 항공 우주국)》

나상 裸像 a nude figure〔statue〕

나상 螺狀 a screw shape ; spirality
— **계단** a spiral〔corkscrew〕 staircase
— **비행** a spiral (flight)

나서다 ① [나와 서다] come out〔forth〕 ; get out ; leave ; appear ; present oneself ; make an appearance ¶ 줄에서 나서다 step〔get〕 out of line // 집을 나서다 leave home // 무대에 나서다 appear on the stage // 정계에 나서다 make one's debut on the political stage ; launch into politics // 후보자로 나서다 run〔stand〕 as a candidate 《for》 // 지원하고 나서다 present oneself for an application // 이 길로 가면 큰길에 나선다 This path leads to the main road.
② [나타나다] turn up ; be found ; present oneself ¶ 빈 자리가 하나 나섰다 An open job〔a vacancy〕 was found. // 지원자가 나섰다 A volunteer appeared.
③ [간섭하다·맡다] intrude ; interfere 《in》 ; meddle 《in, with》 ; take〔have〕 charge of (맡다) ¶ 저 할머니는 항상 남의 일에 나서서 참견한다 That old woman is always interfering in other people's affairs. // 네가 나설 일이 아니다 This is none of your business. /Mind your own business.

나선 裸線 a bare wire ; a naked electric wire

***나선 螺旋** a screw (나사) ; a spiral ¶ 나선형〔상〕의 spiral ; helical
— **강하** a spiral dive〔descent〕 — **계단** a spiral〔corkscrew〕 staircase —**균** a spirillum 《*pl.* -rilla》 —**사**(絲) 〖생물〗 [염색체의] a spireme — **상승** a spiral climb — **운동** screw motion — **장치** a screw (device) —**잭** a screw jack ; a lifting screw —**체** a helicoid ; a spiral —**총** a rifle — **추진기** a screw propeller — **펌프** a screw pump

나선 螺線 a spiral ; 〖기하〗 a helix, a helical curve

나선상 螺旋狀 screw-shape ; spirality
— **계단** a spiral staircase — **성운**(星雲) 〖천문〗 spiral nebula

나스르르하다 (be) fluffy ; woolly ; soft ; shaggy ¶ 털이 나스르르한 개 a shaggy dog // 털이 나스르르한 담요 a woolly blanket

나슨하다 (be) loose ; not tight ; slack ⇨ 느슨하다

나슬나슬하다 ⇨ 나스르르하다

†나아가다 ① [전진] advance ; progress ; go forward ; move on〔onward〕 ; march ; make way ¶ 목표를 향하여 꾸준히 나아간다 make steady progress toward one's goal // 군중을 헤치고 나아가다 elbow〔push〕 one's way through the crowd // 한걸음 나아가서 going one step forward ; moreover ; besides ;

further // 한 걸음 앞으로 나아가다 make [take] a step forward ; go a step further // 해안 쪽으로 나아가다 advance towards the coast // 하루에 50킬로 나아가다 make fifty kilometers in a day // 그는 정계에 나아가려고 한다 He is planning to launch into politics.
② [진보] make progress ; improve ; advance ; be promoted 《to》 (승진) ¶ 이대로 나아가면 at the present rate of progress // 일이 빨리 나아가다 make rapid progress with one's work // 한국의 경제 사정이 급속히 나아가고 있다 The economy of Korea is making rapid progress.
③ [좋아지다] get better [well] ; change for the better ; take a favorite turn ¶ 그의 건강이 나아가고 있다 His health has taken a turn for the better.

*나아지다 become [get] better ; change for the better ; improve ; be improved ; take a favorable turn ¶ 살기가 나아지다 get to be better off ; be in easier circumstances // 솜씨가 나아지다 become more skillful ; get better in skill [workmanship] // 경기가 나아지고 있다 Business is improving [looking up, picking up]. // 그의 건강이 훨씬 나아졌다 He has improved much in health. // 식량 사정이 크게 나아졌다 The food situation has greatly improved. // 전세가 나아졌다 The tide of war turned in our favor. // 그의 이번 작품은 전번 것보다 별로 나아지지 않았다 His new work is little better' than his previous effort [former one]. // 한국 경제는 점점 나아지고 있다 The Korean economy is picking up. /The Korean economy is on the mend.

나약 懦弱 feebleness ; weak-mindedness ; effeminacy ; emasculation ; enervation —하다 (be) weak ; soft and spiritless ; feeble-minded ; emasculate ¶ 나약한 국민 a soft and spiritless [luxurious] people // 게으른 습관으로 나약해진 사람 a man enervated by slothful habits // 나약해지다 become effeminate ; lapse into effeminacy

나열 羅列 marshaling ; an array —하다 arrange in a row ; place 《things》 in a row ; set forth ; enumerate ¶ 통계적 숫자를 나열하다 numerate statistical figures

†나오다 ① [밖으로] come [go, get] out 《of the room》 ; step out ; leave ; emerge 《from》 (나타나다) ¶ 집에서 나오다 get out of the house ; leave home // 극장에서 나오다 come out of the theater // 욕조에서 나오다 step out of the bath // 산보나오다 come out for a walk // 물건 사러 나오다 be out shopping // 기차가 터널에서 나왔다 The train emerged from a tunnel. // 그는 아침 7시에 집에서 나온다 He leaves home at seven in the morning. // 집을 나온 지 10년이다 It is already ten years since I left home. // 이쪽으로 나오시는 길에 꼭 한 번 우리집에 들러 주세요 When you are out our way, be sure and look us up.
② [유출] issue ; run ; flow out ¶ 눈물이 나오다 tears flow ; tears come to one's eyes // 굴뚝에서 연기가 나오다 smoke issues [rises] from the chimney // 콧물이 나오다 one's nose runs // 코피가 나오다 bleed at the nose // 상처에서 고름이 나오다 pus issues from the wound // 하품이 나온다 It makes me yawn. // 기침이 나와 곤란하다 I am troubled with bad cough. // 재채기가 나오다 have a fit of sneezing // 그의 상처에서 피가 나오고 있다 Blood is running [flowing] from his wound.
③ [나타나다] appear ; be [come] out ; emerge 《from》 ; present itself ; make an appearance ; haunt ; infest ; show itself ¶ 무대에 나오다 appear on the stage // 별이 나오다 the stars are out ; the stars appear in the sky // 딸기가 시장에 나왔다 Strawberries are out on the market. // 그 집에는 귀신이 나온다 A ghost walks [haunts] the house. // 부엌에 쥐가 많이 나온다 The kitchen is infested with [by] rats. // 해가 구름 사이에서 나왔다 The sun emerged from behind the clouds. // 전에 그 여자를 본 일이 있다는 자가 나왔다 A man who remembered seeing [having seen] the woman before came forward. // 이 길을 따라 내려가면 브로드웨이가 나옵니까 If I go down this street, do I run into Broadway? // 사실 이것은 가장 최근에 시장에 나온 최신 제품입니다 As a matter of fact, this is a state-of-the-art product just on the market.
④ [발행] be out ; come out ; be published [issued, brought out] ¶ 이 책은 갓 나왔다 The book has just been published. // 책은 다음달 5일에 나온다 The book will be out on the fifth of next month. // 새 소설책이 매일같이 나온다 New novels come out almost every day. // 그 책은 30년 전에 처음 나왔다 The book was first issued 30 years ago.
⑤ [게재] appear ; be found ¶ 그 말은 어느 사전에나 나와 있다 The word is found [given] in any dictionary. // 그 산은 지도에 안 나와 있다 The mountain is not on the map. // 미터는 100으로 나와 있었다 The meter read 100. // 시험 합격자 발표를 보러 갔는데 내 번호도 나와 있었다 I went to see the announcement of the result of the examinations and found that my number was up. // 그 사건은 오늘 신문에 자세히 나와 있다

The incident is reported in detail in today's newspaper.
⑥ [식탁에] be served ; be brought out ¶ 술과 밥이 나왔다 We were treated with wine and food. // 저녁에는 비프스테이크가 나왔다 Beefsteak was served at dinner.
⑦ [출석·참가] attend ; be present 《at》; join ; take part 《in》; participate 《in》; enter (for) 《a contest》 ¶ 파티에 나오다 attend a party // 회합에 나오다 be present at a meeting // 시합에 나오다 take part〔participate〕 in a game // 그는 사무실에 안 나왔다 He didn't show up in the office. // 사회에 나오다 launch〔go out〕 into the world // 오늘밤 모임이 있는데 좀 나와 주시지 않겠습니까 We have a meeting tonight. Won't you join us〔come along〕?
⑧ [근원] come of〔from〕; originate in ; be derived from ; stem from ¶ 질투에서 나온 싸움 a quarrel originating in jealousy // 이 말은 라틴어에서 나왔다 This word is of Latin origin. // 이 소식은 믿을 만한 소식통에서 나왔다 The news was obtained from reliable sources. // 그 말이 누구한테서 나왔느냐 Who started〔first told〕 the story ? // 비용은 어디서 나오는가 Who is to pay the expenses ?
⑨ [사직] leave ; resign 《one's office》; quit ; [졸업] graduate 《from》; finish ¶ 회사에서 나오다 leave〔resign from〕 a company // 그는 예일대학을 나왔다고 한다 I hear that he graduated from Yale University.
⑩ [산출] be produced ; be turned out ; be raised〔grown〕 ¶ 이 지방에서는 사과가 많이 나온다 The country produces a lot of apples. // 이 나라에서는 위대한 과학자가 많이 나왔다 This country has produced〔turned out〕 a number of great scientists.
⑪ [통하다] lead to 《a place》; come to 〔upon〕; come up to ; find oneself at ¶ 이 길로 죽 가면 정거장이 나옵니다 This road leads you to the railroad station. // 그 길을 따라가니 바다가 나왔다 Following the path, I soon came to the sea.
⑫ [태도] take 《a move》; assume 《an attitude》 ¶ 그가 어떻게 나올까 I wonder what move he will take. // 그런 태도로 나올 줄은 전연 몰랐다 His attitude was quite contrary to my expectations.
⑬ [석방] be released ¶ 그는 교도소에서 갓 나왔다 He has just been released from prison.
⑭ [문제] be given ; be brought up ¶ 시험에 다섯 문제가 나왔다 Five questions were given in the examination.
⑮ [싹] sprout ; shoot out ; bud ¶ 봄에 새싹이 나온다 Plants push out new shoots in spring.
⑯ [돌출] project ; protrude ¶ 이마가 나오다 have a prominent forehead // 눈이 툭 나왔다 His eyes protruded. // 윗니가 툭 나왔다 His upper teeth projected. // 그는 배가 나와 있다 His stomach sticks out.
⑰ [입후보] stand 《for》; run 《for》 《미》 ¶ 서울 용산구에서 나오다 run from the *Yongsan* constituency of *Seoul* // 국회 의원 후보로 나오다 stand for Parliament 〔run for congress 《미》〕
⑱ [결과가] come out 《as a result》; work out ¶ 결론이 나오다 come to 〔arrive at〕 a conclusion
⑲ [사진이] come out ; show ; be taken ¶ 이 사진은 잘 나왔다 This photo has come out well〔is taken well〕. // 그 여자는 사진이 잘 나온다 She takes very good pictures. /She photographs very well. /She is very photogenic.
⑳ [없어진 것이] be found ; turn up ; be restored 《to》; get a thing back ¶ 분실한 책이 아직 나오지 않았다 My lost book hasn't turn up yet.

나왕 羅王 〖식물〗 a lauan ; lauan 《재목》

나우루 [서태평양의 공화국] Nauru

나울거리다 wave ; undulate ⇨ 너울거리다

나위 (hardly) worth 《doing》; necessity ¶ 더할 나위 없다 be the most satisfactory ; be first-rate ; be superb // 말할 나위 없다 be needless to say // 사진은 볼 나위가 없다 The picture is not worth looking at. // 그 여자는 아내로서 더할 나위 없다 She is everything a wife should be. /She is all that can be desired as a wife. /She is a perfect〔an ideal〕 wife. // 그 여자의 요리 솜씨는 더할 나위 없다 She cooks to perfection. // 이 책은 더할 나위 없이 좋은 선물이다 This is the most suitable book for a gift. /This book is most suitable for a gift.

†나이 age ; years ¶ 나이 많은 사람 an old man ; an aged man // 나이 탓으로 due to〔because of〕 one's age // 나이 순으로 according to age〔years, seniority〕 // 내가 나이를 먹음에 따라 as I grow old〔older〕 // 내 나이에 at my age ; at my time of life // 당신 나이 때에는 when I was (of) your age // 나이를 한 살 더 먹다 grow a year older // 나이가 지긋하다 be well up〔advanced〕 in years // 제 나이로 보이다 look one's age // 학교에 갈 나이다 be old enough to go to school // 아직 결혼할 나이가 아니다 be too young to marry // 나이에 비해 젊어〔늙어〕 보이다 look younger〔older〕 for one's age // 보기보다는 나이가 젊다 be not so old as one looks // 보기보다는 나이가 많다 be older than one looks // 당신과 같은 나이다 I am your age. // 우리

는 같은 나이다 We are (of) the same age. // 그는 나이는 많지만 마음은 젊다 He is old in years, but young in vigor. // 사랑과 나이가 무슨 상관이 있습니까 What's age got to do with love?/What does age have to do with love? // 나이 차이가 커서 그들은 별로 다투지 않는다 They're not close in age, so they don't fight very much.
나이 많은 말이 콩 마다할까 속담 Avarice is the only passion that never ages.
나이를 먹다 관용 grow older ; grow 〔get, become〕 old ; get on in years
나이깨 ⇨ 나잇살
나이드라지드 〚약〛 Nydrazid
나이로비 Nairobi
나이배기 a person older than he looks
나이애가라 폭포 ─瀑布 Niagara Falls
나이지리아 ¶ 나이지리아의 Nigerian
─ 사람 a Nigerian
나이터 〚운동〛 a night 《baseball》 game
나이테 [나무의] an annual ring
†나이트¹ [기사] a knight ¶ 나이트 작위를 수여받다 be dubbed a knight
─ 작위 a knighthood
나이트² a night
─ 가운 a nightgown ─ 드레스 a nightdress ─캡 a nightcap ─ 클럽 a night club
나이팅게일 Nightingale, Florence (영 1820~1910)
─ 기장 a Florence Nightingale Medal
나이프 a knife
─ 스위치 a knife switch 잭─ a jack-knife
나인 a court lady ; a maid of honor ; a lady attendant in the palace
나일 강 ─江 the Nile (River)
*나일론 nylon
나잇값 behavior appropriate to〔be fitting〕 one's age ¶ 나잇값이나 하시오 You should know better at your time of life〔at your age〕./You are old enough to be more prudent./Act〔Be〕 your age!/Are you not ashamed, at your age? // 그는 나잇값도 못한다 He ought to know better at his age.
나잇살 a mature〔an advanced〕 age ¶ 나잇살이나 들었는데도 in spite of one's mature〔advanced〕 age/being old enough to know better // 그는 나잇살이나 먹었다 He is pretty old. // 그는 나잇살이나 들었는데도 여전히 방탕한 생활을 하고 있다 He is still leading a fast life at his age.
나자빠지다 ⇨ 나가자빠지다
나자 식물 裸子植物 a gymnosperm ; Gymnospermace (학명)
나전 螺鈿 mother-of-pearl ; nacre ¶ 나전 세공 mother-of-pearl work
나전구 裸電球 a (naked) electric bulb ; an unshaded lamp
나전선 裸電線 a naked electric wire
나전어 羅甸語 Latin
─학자 a Latinist ; a Latin scholar
나절 half a day ; about half the daylight hours ¶ 한나절 half a day // 반나절 a fourth of the day // 아침 나절 the morning // 저녁 나절 the evening
나조 ─調 〚음악〛 B
나장〔단〕조(─長〔短〕調) 《a symphony》 B major〔minor〕
나졸 邏卒 a patrol(man)
나좃대 a kind of reed torch burned at the bride's house as a sort of ceremonial candle
†나중 the last ; the latter part ; the end ; the future ; the consequences ; the next ¶ 나중에 some time later ; in the future ; at last ; in the end // 나중 기차 a later train // 나중 일 the consequences // 나중 생각을 하다 think of the future // 나중 생각을 하지 않고 with no thought of the future // 나중은 어떻게 될 테지 The future will take care of itself. // 나중에는 어떻게 되든 상관 없다 I do not care for the consequences. // 그는 맨 나중에 왔다 He was the very last to come./He came at the tail end. // 나중에 뵙겠습니다 I will see you later. // 나중에 가서 후회할 것이다 You will repent for it later〔in future〕. // 더 자세한 것은 나중에 말씀드리겠습니다 I will tell you further details later on. // 나중에야 어찌 되든 우선 먹고 보자 Let's eat first, whatever may happen afterwards.
나지리보다 look down on ; despise ; scorn ; hold 《a person》 in contempt ; sneeze at 《속》 ¶ 사람을 그렇게 나지리보지 마라 Don't look down upon people so. // 그는 나지리볼 것이 아니다 He is not to be sneezed at.
나지리 여기다 look down on ⇨ 나지리보다
나지막이 somewhat〔rather〕 low ; somewhat〔rather〕 soft
나지막하다 (be) somewhat low ¶ 나지막한 집 a low-built house // 나지막한 소리로 말하다 talk in a low voice
나직나직 in an undertone ; in whispers ; secretly ; softly ¶ 나직나직 말하다 speak in a low voice ; talk in whispers〔a whisper〕
나직이 [높이·정도] low ; humbly ; softly ; modestly ; [소리] low ¶ 집을 나직이 짓다 build a house low // 나직이 말하다 speak in a low〔subdued〕 voice // 라디오의 소리를 나직이하다 tone down the radio
나직하다 [높이가] (be) low ; short (키) ; [소리가] low ; soft ; in an undertone ; subdued ; [신분이] humble ; lowly ; mean ¶ 나직한 목소리 a low 〔subdued〕 voice // 천장이 나직한 방 a room with a low ceiling

ㄴ

*나체 裸體 a naked〔nude〕 body ; nakedness ; nudity ¶ 나체가 되다 become naked ; strip oneself naked // 나체로 만들다 strip 《a person》 naked // 나체로 걷다 walk in the nude
—미 the beauty of the nude —미인〔모델〕 a nude beauty〔model〕 —여인 a nude girl〔woman〕 —주의 nudism —주의자 a nudist 반— seminudity 전— a stark-naked body ; complete nudity ; stark-nakedness

나체화 裸體畫 a nude (picture) ¶ 나체화를 그리다 paint 《a woman in》 the nude

나치 a Nazi 《개인》; Nazis 《총칭》 ¶ 나치의 Nazi
—당원 a Nazi (party member) —문학 Nazi literature —즘 Nazism —화(化) Nazification 비(非)—화 denazification

나치 拿致 —하다 arrest ; apprehend ; take 《a person》 to the police station

나침 羅針 a compass〔magnetic〕 needle
—방위 a compass bearing

‡나침반 羅針盤 a compass
—바늘 the needle of a compass 항공— an aero compass 항해— a mariner's〔steering〕 compass 회전— a gyrocompass

나침의 羅針儀 a compass ⇨ 나침반 ¶ 나침의 없이 항해하다 navigate without compass
선박용— a mariner's compass 전륜(轉輪)— a gyrocompass 조타(操舵)— a steering compass 주(主)— a master compass

나타 懶惰 ⇨ 나태(懶怠)

†나타나다 ① [출현] come out ; appear ; make an appearance ; turn up ; show up ; present〔show〕 oneself ; emerge 《from》 ¶ 청중 앞에 나타나다 appear before the audience // 안개 사이로 나타나다 appear through the mist // 역사의 무대에 나타나다 appear upon the scene of history // 갑자기 나타나다 make an abrupt appearance ; pop out〔up〕 // 달이 구름 사이로 나타났다 The moon came out〔emerged〕 from behind the cloud. // 해가 지평선 위에 나타났다 The sun has shown itself above the horizon. // 때마침 순경이 현장에 나타났다 The policeman made a timely appearance on the scene. // 때마침 그가 나타났다 He showed〔turned〕 up in the nick of time. // 그녀는 런던에서 처음 무대에 나타났다 She made her first stage appearance in London. // 그는 어제 창립 기념일 연회에 조차 나타나지 않았다 He didn't even show up at the Founding Day reception yesterday.
② [보이다] come into view ; come into sight ; appear ; become visible ¶ 육지가 나타났다 Land came in sight. /We came in sight of land. // 북동쪽에 섬이 나타났다 The island came into view to the northeast.
③ [표현] show〔display〕 itself ; be revealed ; be expressed ; be described ; appear 《on》 ; come 《over》 ; pass 《over》 ; take〔produce〕 effect ; have an effect 《on》 (효과) ¶ 그녀의 얼굴에 공포의 빛이 나타났다 Fear showed in her face. /Her eyes showed fear. // 정직이 그의 얼굴에 나타나 있다 Honesty is written on his face. // 옷차림에 저속한 취미가 나타나 있다 His clothes show bad taste. // 술에 취하면 본성이 나타난다 Wine reveals the true man. // 이 소설에는 지방색이 잘 나타나 있다 The local color is well brought out in this story. // 약효가 나타났다 The medicine took effect〔showed its effect〕. // 놀라는 빛이 그의 표정에 나타났다 A look of surprise came over his face. // 그녀의 얼굴에는 심각한 고뇌의 빛이 나타나 있었다 Her face registered profound mental anguish. // 약효가 나타났다 The medicine took effect〔showed its effect〕. // 걱정이 그의 얼굴에 나타나기 시작한다 His troubles are beginning to show in his face.
④ [드러나다] come to light ; be found out ; be disclosed〔revealed〕 ; be exposed ¶ 진실은 나타나기 마련이다 Truth always comes out〔comes to light〕. // 그의 범죄는 곧 나타나게 될 것이다 His crime will soon come to light. // 대통령 암살 음모가 나타났다 An assassination plot against the President has been brought to light. // 잃어버렸던 시계가 서랍에서 나타났다 My lost watch turned up in the drawer. // 그가 죽은 후 두 통의 유서가 나타났다 Two notes of his own writing were found after his death. // 그의 시체가 잿더미 속에서 나타났다 His body was recovered in the debris of the fire. // 결과가 나타나다 produce good results
⑤ [알려지다] become famous〔known〕 ; win fame ¶ 세상에 이름이 나타나다 become known〔famous〕 in the world // 나타나지 않고 숨어 살다 live in obscurity
⑥ [기록 등에] be mentioned ; be given ¶ 외국 문헌에 나타난 한국 Korea mentioned in foreign literature

†나타내다 ① [표시] show ; display ; [드러내다] bare ; lay bare ; expose ; reveal ; betray ; [증명] prove ; indicate ; reflect (반영) ¶ 얼굴을 나타내다 appear ; make one's appearance ; show up ; turn up // 수완을 나타내다 show〔display〕 one's ability // 묘기를 나타내다 exhibit one's skill // 노여움을 나타내다 betray〔show〕 one's anger // 정체를 나타내다 betray oneself ; show one's true

colors // 무지함을 나타내다 expose one's ignorance // 그 사실은 그가 결백함을 나타낸다 The fact proves〔indicates〕 his innocence. // 이것은 그의 성실을 나타내고 있다 This speaks for his sincerity. // 그의 말은 학급의 총의를 나타내고 있다 What he says reflects the general sentiment of the class. // 그는 자기의 분노를 밖으로 나타내지 않았다 He kept his indignation to himself. // 이 숫자들은 무엇을 나타내는 것이냐 What do these figures indicate?
② 〔표현〕 express; give expression 《to》 ¶ 생각을 말로 나타내다 put one's thoughts into words; express one's thoughts in words; express oneself in words // 말로 다 나타낼 수 없다 be beyond description〔expression〕; be indescribable; do not know how to put it; have no word for // 그는 자기 생각을 어떻게 나타내야 좋을지 모르고 있다 He is at a loss how to convey his meaning. // 감사한 마음을 말로 나타낼 수가 없군요 I cannot express the depth of my gratitude in words. / My gratitude is beyond〔too deep for〕 description. // 그 감동은 도저히 말로 나타낼 수 없다 I can't find the words to describe how moving it was.
③ 〔대표·상징〕 represent; stand for; symbolize ¶ 이 기호는 무엇을 나타내느냐 What does this sign represent〔stand for〕? // R.O.K.는 대한민국을 나타낸다 The initials R.O.K. stand for the Republic of Korea. // 지도상의 이 표는 절을 나타낸다 This mark on the map represents a temple. // 한국에서는 소나무가 여자의 정조를 나타낸다 In Korea, the pine symbolizes feminine constancy.
④ 〔명성〕 become famous; make one's name; win〔acquire〕 fame; distinguish oneself ¶ 두각을 나타내다 distinguish oneself; cut〔make〕 a conspicuous figure 《in society》 // 그가 단연 두각을 나타내고 있다 He is head and shoulders above his fellows. // 그는 웅변가로서 이름을 나타냈다 He made a reputation as an orator.

나탈거리다 laugh loudly; flutter ⇨ 너털거리다

†**나태** **懶怠** laziness; sloth; idleness; indolence; sluggishness **— 하다** (be) lazy; idle; slothful; sluggish ¶ 나태한 사람 a lazy〔an idle〕 man; (a) lazybones; an idler; a sluggard; a do-nothing; a drone // 나태한 생활 a lazy〔an idle〕 life // 그는 일을 하려 하지 않는다 그는 너무 나태하다 He won't work. He's just too lazy!
—벽(癖) indolence; an indolent〔idle〕 habit **—심**(心) sloth; a lazy mind; a disinclination to work

나토 the NATO〔néitou〕 《*N*orth *A*tlantic *T*reaty *O*rganization》

*__나트륨__ 〖화학〗 natrium 《Na》

나티 〔귀신〕 a destructive deity that takes the shape of an animal; 〔곰〕 a dark red bear
—상(相) a dreadful〔ghastly〕 face

†**나팔** **喇叭** a bugle; a trumpet ¶ 나팔 모양의 trumpet-shaped // 나팔을 불다 blow〔sound〕 a bugle // 나팔 소리와 함께 with a flourish of bugles // 진군 나팔을 불다 sound the advance
— 소리 a bugle note; a trumpet〔bugle〕 call ¶ 나팔 소리가 들린다 A bugle is sounded.

나팔거리다 flutter ⇨ 나붓거리다

나팔관 **喇叭管** 〖해부〗 the Fallopian tubes; the oviduct
—염(炎) salpingitis

나팔꽃 **喇叭—** a morning glory

나팔나팔 fluttering〔flapping〕 away

나팔바지 **喇叭—** bell-bottom(ed) trousers; bell-bottoms

나팔벌레 **喇叭—** a kind of trumpet-shaped ciliate

나팔 불다 **喇叭—** blow〔sound〕 a trumpet; 〔술 따위를〕 drink 《beer》 from a bottle; 〔떠벌이다〕 make a boast of; brag; talk big〔tall〕

나팔수 **喇叭手** a bugler; a trumpeter
— 대장 a trumpet major

나포 **拿捕** arrest; capture; seizure **— 하다** arrest; capture; seize; make prize of
—령 an order for seizure **—선** a captured ship; a prize **— 조항** a capture and seizure clause **불법 —** illegal seizure

나폴리 Napoli; Naples

나푼거리다 flutter lightly; flap gently

나푼나푼 lightly fluttering; gently flapping

나풀거리다 flutter〔flap〕 roughly

나프타 naphtha
— 분해(分解) naphtha cracking

나프탈렌 naphthalene

나한 **羅漢** Buddha's disciples〔followers〕

나화 **裸花** 〖식물〗 an achlamydeous flower

나획 **拿獲** **— 하다** arrest〔capture, seize〕 《a criminal》

나흗날 the fourth day of the month

나흘 four days; the fourth day of the month

†**낙** **樂** pleasure; delight; joy; happiness (행복); enjoyment (향락); amusement (오락) ¶ 독서의 낙 the pleasure of reading // 인생의 낙 the pleasure〔joy, enjoyment〕 of life // 낙이 없는 사람 a man of few pleasures // 낙을 삼아 for pleasure; by way of amusement; to please oneself; as a hobby // 낙을 삼다 take pleasure〔delight〕 in // 자녀 교육을

유일한 낙으로 삼다 find one's sole comfort in the education of the young // 그는 일요일마다 정원을 손질하는 것이 낙이다 He takes delight in trimming the garden every Sunday. // 그는 낙이라고는 독서밖에 없었다 He had few diversions outside of reading.

낙관 落款 (a painter's) sign and seal ; (a writer's) signature **—하다** sign (and seal) ; affix one's signature〔seal〕 ¶ 낙관이 없는 그림 an unsigned painting // 작가의 낙관이 있다 bear a writer's〔painter's〕 signature

낙관 樂觀 optimism ; an optimistic view **—하다** be optimistic ; take an optimistic view《of》; be sanguine《of》; look on the bright side ¶ 낙관적 optimistic // 장래를 낙관하다 be optimistic about the future ; take an optimistic view regarding the future // 지나치게 낙관적이다 be too optimistic ; paint too rosy a picture of affairs // 정세는 낙관을 불허한다 The situation doesn't warrant optimism. /We must not be optimistic about it.

—론 an optimistic〔rosy〕 view **—론자** an optimist

낙관적 樂觀的 ¶ 낙관적인 optimistic ; rosy ; hopeful ; sanguine ; upbeat // 낙관적인 생각 an optimistic〔a rosy〕 view 〔idea〕 // 낙관적인 인생관을 갖다 have an optimistic〔a cheerful〕 view of life // 너는 언제나 사물을 지나치게 낙관적으로 생각한다 You always take an overly optimistic view of things.

낙구 落句 the concluding〔last〕 line of a poem

낙길 落— a missing〔lacking〕 volume

낙낙하다 (be) enough ; big enough ; sufficient ; adequate ⇨ 넉넉하다

***낙농 酪農** dairy ; dairy farming ¶ 그는 낙농업을 한다 He runs a dairy farm.

—가 a dairy farmer ; a dairyman **—장** a dairy farm ; a milk ranch《미》 **—제품** dairy products

†낙담 落膽 discouragement ; disappointment ; despondency **—하다** be〔get〕 discouraged ; be disheartened〔dispirited〕 ; lose heart ; be disappointed《in》; be cast down ¶ 낙담시키다 discourage ; dishearten // 그렇게 낙담하지 말게 Don't be so cast down. // 외동 자식을 잃고 낙담 천만이다 He is heartbroken over the death of his only child. // 그는 시험에 떨어져서 낙담하고 있다 She is discouraged by his failure in the examination.

낙도 落島 a remote〔distant〕 island ; a deserted island

— 주민 out-islanders

낙락장송 落落長松 a tall and exuberant pine tree

낙락장송도 근본은 종자 〔속담〕 Every oak has been an acorn.

낙뢰 落雷 the falling of a thunderbolt **—하다** be struck by (a bolt of) lightning ¶ 공장에 낙뢰했다 The factory was struck by (a bolt of) lightning.

낙루 落淚 the shedding〔dropping〕 of tears ; weeping **—하다** shed tears ; be moved to tears ; weep ¶ 낙루케 하다 move《a person》 to tears ; bring tears to《a person's》 eyes

낙마 落馬 a fall from a horse **—하다** fall from〔be thrown off〕 one's horse ; fall off one's horse

낙막하다 落寞— (be) dreary ; lonesome ; desolate ¶ 낙막한 황야 a lonesome〔desolate〕 wilderness // 낙막하고 황량한 풍경 a dreary and forlorn scene

낙망 落望 disappointment ; despair ; discouragement ; hopelessness **—하다** be disappointed《at, in, of》; despair《of》; lose one's heart ; be〔feel〕 discouraged ¶ 낙망하지 마라 Keep your heart up ! / Never say die ! // 그는 낙망한 나머지 자살했다 Despair led him to suicide. / Despair drove him to commit suicide. // 그 여자는 외아들이 죽어서 낙망하고 있다 She is disheartened at the loss of her only son.

낙명 落命 losing one's life ; death **—하다** die ; lose one's life ; [재난으로] be killed《in a traffic accident》

낙명 落名 losing one's reputation **—하다** lose one's reputation

낙반 落磐 (a) cave-in ; the fall of roof in a mine ¶ 낙반이 되다 cave in

낙방 落榜 failure in an examination **—하다** fail in an examination ; get plucked《영·속》

낙백 落魄 ① [넋을 잃음] stupefaction ; abstraction **—하다** be stupefied ; be distracted ; be at one's wit's end ② [낙심] disheartenment ; discouragement ; disappointment **—하다** be disheartened〔discouraged〕 ③ [영락] reduced circumstances **—하다** be reduced to poverty ; be in reduced circumstances ; sink in one's fortunes ; descend in the social scale

낙부 諾否 approval and〔or〕 disapproval ; yes and〔or〕 no

낙산 酪酸 〖화학〗 butryc acid

— 망간 manganese butyrate **— 발효(醱酵)** butyric fermentation **—염(鹽)** butyrate

낙상 落傷 a hurt〔bruise〕 from a fall **—하다** get hurt from a fall ; fall and hurt oneself

낙서 落書 ① scribbling ; a scrawl **—하다** scribble ; scrawl ; doodle ¶ 벽에 낙서하다 scribble on the wall // 낙서 금지 No scribbling. /Scribbling forbidden. (게시)

② [빠뜨리고 씀] omission ; skipping

—하다 omit ; skip

*낙선 落選 [선거의] defeat〔failure〕 in an election ; [출품의] rejection —하다 be defeated in an election ; lose an election ; fail in election ; [출품이] be rejected ; be not accepted ¶ 그의 작품은 낙선했다 His work was rejected 〔turned down〕.

— 의원 an unsuccessful〔a defeated〕 candidate 《for the Assembly》 —작 a rejected〔an unaccepted〕 work〔article〕

낙성 落成 completion —하다 be completed ; be finished ¶ 새 교사가 곧 낙성됩니다 Our new school building is nearing completion.

낙성식 落成式 an inauguration ceremony ; a celebration of the completion 《of a building》 ¶ 이 달 3일에 공사 낙성식을 올렸다 The completion of the work was celebrated on the 3rd of this month.

낙세 落勢 〖상업〗 decline ; declining market

낙수 落水 ⇨ 낙숫물

낙숫물 落水— raindrops (falling from the eaves) ; eavesdrops ¶ 낙숫물 소리 the patter of raindrops // 낙숫물이 떨어지다 raindrops fall // 낙숫물이 처마에서 뚝뚝 떨어지고 있다 Rain water is dripping from the eaves.

낙승 樂勝 an easy victory ; a walkaway 《구》 ; walkover —하다 gain an easy victory 《over》 ; ease out ; have a walkover ; win in a breeze ¶ 그는 자기 페이스를 유지한다면 낙승할 것이다 If he keeps up his pace, he'll win hands down.

*낙심 落心 loss of heart ; discouragement ; disappointment ; despair —하다 lose heart ; despair ; be discouraged ; be disappointed ; be downhearted ; be downcast ¶ 낙심하여 자살하다 kill oneself out of despair // 낙심하지 마라 Don't be discouraged.

낙양 落陽 the setting sun

낙양 洛陽 [중국 지명] Loyang ¶ 낙양의 지가(紙價)를 올리다 The book sold immensely well. /The book had a tremendous sale.

*낙엽 落葉 fallen〔dead〕 leaves ¶ 낙엽이 지다 《a tree》 shed〔cast〕 《its》 leaves ; 《a leaf》 fall ; be shed

—기 defoliation —색 russet

낙엽송 落葉松 〖식물〗 a larch ; [재목] larch

미국 — a tamarack

낙엽수 落葉樹 a deciduous tree

—림 a deciduous forest

*낙오 落伍 falling behind ; straggling —하다 drop〔fall〕 out of line〔the ranks〕 ; fall behind 《in a race》 ; drop out 《to the rear》 ; straggle

낙오자 落伍者 a straggler ; a dropout ¶ 인생의 낙오자 a derelict ; a (social) failure ; a social outcast // 인생의 낙오자가 되다 make a failure of one's life

‡낙원 樂園 a paradise ; Eden ; Elysium ¶ 아이들의 낙원 a paradise for children // 우인(愚人)의 낙원 a fool's paradise // 지상의 낙원 an earthly paradise ; heaven on earth // 이 숲은 사냥꾼의 낙원이다 These forests are a hunter's paradise.

낙인 烙印 a brand ; a stigma 《*pl.* ～s, -mata》 ¶ 낙인을 찍다 brand ; stigmatize // 그는 반역자란 낙인이 찍혔다 He was branded as a traitor. // 큰 목장에서는 소유자를 나타내기 위해서 소나 말에 낙인을 찍는다 Cattle and horses on big ranches are marked with brands to show who owns them.

낙일 落日 [태양] the setting sun ; [일몰] sunset ; sundown 《미》

낙자 落字 an omitted word ; an omission ¶ 낙자가 둘 있다 Two letters are left out.

낙장 落張 missing pages ; a missing leaf ¶ 이 책은 낙장이 12페이지나 있다 There are twelve pages〔six leaves〕 missing in this book.

— 조사 〖도서〗 collation

낙장거리 falling outstretched on one's back —하다 fall down outstretched on one's back

*낙제 落第 failure (in an examination) ; [검사에서] rejection —하다 fail (in an examination) ; get plucked 《속》 ; [원학년에 머무르다] stay back in the class ; [검사에] be rejected ¶ 시험에 낙제하다 fail〔get plucked〕 in an examination // 낙제해서 퇴학하다 flunk out // 이 물건은 낙제했다 This article has been rejected. // 그는 교사로서는 낙제야 He is a failure as a teacher. // 그는 고등학교에서 두 번이나 낙제했다 At a high school he slipped back a year, then another.

낙제생 落第生 a repeater 《미》 ; a plucked student 《영·구》 ; a failure ; a flop ; a holdover

낙제점 落第點 a failing mark ¶ 두 과목 낙제점을 받다 fail in two subjects

낙조 落照 the setting sun ; sunset

*낙지 a small octopus ; Octopus vulgaris (학명)

낙진 落塵 fallout

방사성 — (radioactive) fallout ; silent killer 《속》

낙질 落帙 a lacking〔missing〕 volume

낙차 落差 〖물리〗 a head ; a fall ; a water level ¶ 낙차 50피트의 물 fifty feet head of water

고〔저, 중〕위 — a high〔low, medium〕 head 동수(動水) — a dynamic head 수압 — a pressure head 유효 — an effective〔a net〕 head 정수(靜水) — a static head

낙착 落着 a settlement ; an end ; a conclusion ; a termination **—하다** be settled ; come to a settlement〔conclusion〕; come〔be brought〕to an end ¶ 사건의 낙착 the settlement〔winding-up〕of an affair // 낙착짓다 settle ; bring 《a matter》 to an end〔a close〕// 잘 낙착되다 be brought to a happy end〔termination〕// 아직 낙착되지 않다 be still pending

낙찰 落札 a successful bid ; awarding of a contract **—하다** make a successful bid ; be awarded a contract ; have one's tender accepted ; have 《an article》 knocked down to 《a person》 ¶ 나에게 낙찰되었다 My bid was successful〔accepted〕./The contract was awarded to me. // 그 그림은 나에게 낙찰되었다 The picture was knocked down to me.

—인 a successful bidder **—가(價)** a contract price ; the highest bid price **—물** an object knocked down

낙천 樂天 optimism ¶ 낙천적 optimistic ; hopeful ; sanguine

—주의 optimism

낙천 落薦 a failure in an application 《for nomination》 **—하다** fail in (one's) application 《for nomination》

낙천가 樂天家 an optimist ; an easygoing person ¶ 너는 낙천가다 You are a born optimist

낙천자 落薦者 an unsuccessful applicant ; one who failed in his application for nomination

낙천적 樂天的 ¶ 낙천적인 optimistic 《about》; hopeful ; sanguine ; rosy ; rose-colored ; happy-go-lucky

낙천지 樂天地 [낙원] paradise ; [유원지] an amusement center〔place〕

낙체 落體 〖물리〗 a falling body

— 법칙 the law of falling bodies

‡**낙타 駱駝** a camel ¶ 낙타의 혹 a hump

— 셔츠 camel('s)-hair underwear **—천〔지(地)〕** camel's-hair cloth ; camlet **—털** camel's hair ; camel hair **—혹** a camel's hump

낙태 落胎 abortion ; miscarriage ; aborticide ; feticide **—하다** abort ; miscarry ; have an abortion ¶ 낙태시키다 cause abortion ; induce〔procure〕abortion

— 수술 a surgical operation to cause abortion ; an illegal operation **—아(兒)** an abortive offspring **—약** an abortive drug〔medicine〕; an aborticide ; an abortifacient **—의(醫)** an abortionist **—죄** criminal abortion operation ; illegal abortion **인공(人工) —** an induced〔artificial〕abortion

낙토 樂土 paradise ; Heaven ; Elysium ¶ 왕도(王道) 낙토 a realm of peace and prosperity

†**낙하 落下** falling ; dropping ; descent **—하다** drop ; fall〔come〕down (to the ground) ; descend ; make a descent ¶ 낙하의 정률(定律) 〖물리〗 the law of falling // 나선 낙하 a spiral ; a corkscrew descent // 수직으로 낙하하다 fall plumb down

—지점 [미사일 등의] an impact point **나선 —** a spiral ; a corkscrew descent

***낙하산 落下傘** a parachute ; a chute ¶ 낙하산으로 내리다 make parachute descent ; parachute down // 낙하산으로 비행기에서 탈출하다 bail out ; hit the silk // 낙하산을 펴다 release a parachute

—병 a parachutist ; a paratrooper ; a parachute trooper **— 부대** a parachute troop〔unit〕; a paratroop ; airborne infantry ; paratroopers **— 융자** a loan given〔made〕through political influence **— 인사** high-handed personnel administration **부동(浮動) —** [우주용] a drogue parachute **회전 —** a rotochute

낙향 落鄕 rustication ; a leaving for the countryside **—하다** rusticate ; move to the country ; go back to the rural life

낙형 烙刑 branding a criminal as punishment **—하다** brand〔put a hot iron on〕a criminal as punishment

낙화 落花 the falling of blossoms ; fallen〔scattered〕blossoms (진 꽃) ; falling blossoms〔petals〕(지는 꽃) **—하다** flowers〔blossoms, petals〕fall〔scatter〕

낙화 烙畫 a poker work〔picture〕; a poker engraving ; a pyrograph ; pyrography ; poker drawing ¶ 낙화를 그리다 poker

낙화생 落花生 a peanut ; a groundnut ; a monkeynut 《영》; a pignut (유럽산의) ; an earthnut ¶ 낙화생 버터〔기름〕 peanut butter〔oil〕

낙후 落後 falling behind **—하다** fall behind 《others》; drop〔fall〕out of line〔the ranks〕; drop out

낚거루 ⇨ 낚싯거루

***낚다** ① angle for ; fish ; fish with rod and line ; catch 《a fish》 ¶ 지렁이를 미끼로 고기를 낚다 fish with the bait of an earthworm // 강에서 고기를 낚다 fish in a stream ; angle in a river // 잉어를 많이 낚다 get a good catch of carp ② [꾀다] allure ; decoy ; entice ; ensnare ; entrap ; draw on ; attract ; take in ; cheat ¶ 여자를 낚다 entice a woman // 그 여자는 사내를 잘 낚는다 She has a way of drawing men to her.

낚대 a fishing rod ⇨ 낚싯대

***낚시** a (fish-)hook ¶ 낚시에 미끼를 달다 bait a hook // 고기가 낚시에 걸리다 a fish is hooked〔caught on the hook〕

—미끼 a bait

낚시걸이 giving 《a person》 something as bait

낚시꾼 an angler ; a Waltonian ¶ 많은 낚시꾼들이 이 강에서 낚시질을 한다 Many anglers cast their lines in this river.
낚시 도구 —道具 fishing tackle〔gear, rig, equipment, things〕; a rod and line
—점 a fishing store
낚시 바구니 an angler's basket ; a creel
*낚시질 fishing ; angling —하다 fish ; angle ¶ 낚시질하러 가다 go fishing〔angling〕《in a river》; go on a fishing excursion // 낚시질을 잘한다 He is a good angler. /He is good at fishing.
낚시찌 a float ; a cork ; a quill ; a bob ¶ 낚시찌를 달다 tie〔fasten〕a float《to》// 낚시찌가 깜박거리다 a float is bobbing up and down
낚시터 a place for angling ; a fishing place
낚싯거루 a fishing boat〔skiff〕
낚싯대 a fishing rod ; an angling rod
낚싯바늘 a fishhook
낚싯밥 a bait ¶ 낚시에 낚싯밥을 달다 bait the hook ; fix a bait on the hook
낚싯배 an angler's〔a fisherman's〕boat ; a fishing boat
낚싯봉 a sinker ; a lead ; a plumb〔plummet〕; a bullet
낚싯줄 a fishline ; a (fishing) line ¶ 낚싯줄을 드리우다 drop a line
낚아 올리다 fish up ; hook up ; land
낚아채다 ① [물고기를] strike《a fish》② [잡아채다] snatch (away)《from, off》¶ 그는 도둑으로부터〔도둑의 손에서〕칼을 낚아챘다 He snatched a knife (away) from the burglar〔out of the burglar's hand〕.
난 亂 a disturbance ; a war ⇨ 난리
난 難 [곤란] difficulty ; hardship ; trouble ; [부족] a shortage ¶ 주택난 a shortage of houses ; housing shortage // 식량난 a shortage of food // 생활난 difficulty of (making) living // 난문제 a difficult〔hard〕problem〔question〕
난 欄 a column ; a section ¶ 네 난에 걸친 기사 an article occupying four whole columns // 그 잡지에서는 그 사건을 여러 난에 걸쳐 특종기사로 다뤘다 The magazine featured the event, running column after column in reporting it.
난가 亂家 a family in turmoil ; a disturbed family
난각 卵殼 an egg-shell
*난간 欄干 a railing ; a rail ; a handrail ; a parapet ; a banister ; a balustrade (계단의) ¶ 다리의 난간 the parapet of a bridge ; a bridge railing // 배의 난간 the rail of a ship
난감 難堪 —하다 [견디기 어려움] (be) unbearable ; intolerable ; insufferable ; unendurable ; [힘겨움] be incapable of《doing》; be beyond one's power〔ability〕; be not equal to《the task》¶ 나에겐 난감한 일이다 I am not equal to the task. /The task is beyond my power.
난거지 (든부자) a person who puts up a front of poverty but is really rich
난공불락 難功不落 impregnability ¶ 난공불락의 요새 an impregnable fortress // 난공불락이다 defy attack ; be hard of approach
난공사 難工事 difficult construction work
난관 難關 [장애] a barrier ; an obstacle ; [곤란] a difficulty ; [난국] a difficult situation ; [교착] a deadlock ; the crux of the situation ¶ 난관을 돌파하는 길 a way out of the difficulty // 난관에 봉착하다 meet the difficulty ; come to a deadlock ; strike a snag ; be faced with an obstacle // 난관을 타개하다 tide over〔overcome〕a difficult situation ; break a deadlock // 입학 시험의 난관을 돌파하다 pass the barrier of an entrance examination
난국 難局 a difficult〔grave〕situation〔position〕; a crisis ¶ 난국에 처하다 be in a difficult position ; be in a fix // 난국을 수습하다 save a situation // 난국을 타개하다 weather a storm ; break the deadlock
난국 亂國 a disturbed〔disrupted, troubled〕country ; a nation in turmoil
난군 亂軍 a lawless〔disorderly〕army ; rampaging troops
난기류 亂氣流 〖기상〗《air》turbulence ; turbulent air ¶ 비행기는 난기류로 평형을 잃었다 The plane lost its stability in the turbulent air.
난낭 卵囊 an ovisac ; an egg sac
난다긴다하다 be quick〔alert, talented, smart, sharp, nimble〕; have many skills ¶ 난다긴다하는 사람 an expert ; a man of great talent〔ability〕
난당 亂黨 rioters ; a mob (of rioters) ; insurgents
난대 暖帶 the subtropical zone ; the subtropics
*난데없다 (be) unexpected ; sudden ; abrupt ; be out of the blue ; [당찮다] unfounded ; unreasonable ; absurd ; preposterous ¶ 난데없이 unexpectedly ; out of the blue ; absurdly // 난데없이 나타나다 make an abrupt appearance ; appear unexpectedly // 난데없는 소리 말아라 Don't talk nonsense. /Don't be absurd.
*난도질 亂刀— mangling ; hacking ; [고기 따위의] mincing ; chopping ; hashing —하다 mangle ; hack to pieces ; [고기 따위를] mince ; chop ; hash ¶ 시체는 난도질을 해 놓아서 분간할 수 없었다 The body was mangled beyond recognition. // 사람을 난도질하다 slash《a

person》 again and again
난독 亂讀 desultory reading ; random reading ―하다 read desultorily ; read at random
―가 an omnivorous〔indiscriminate〕 reader
난동 亂動 a disturbance ; a commotion ; a riot
난동 暖冬 a warm〔mild〕 winter
이상 ― an abnormally warm winter ¶ 올해는 이상 난동이다 We have an abnormally〔unusually〕 warm weather this winter.
난든벌 home wear and street wear ; clothes for the home and for the street
난든집 나다 get practiced ; acquire skill ; master ; be(come) an old hand 《in》 ; be at home 《on》
난딱 easily ; with ease ; without any trouble〔difficulty, effort〕 ; just like that ; in an instant ; in a jiffy 《구》 ¶ 밥 한 그릇을 난딱 먹어 치웠다 He downed a bowl of rice just like that.
‡난로 煖爐 a stove ; a fireplace ; a heater ¶ 난로를 쬐다 warm oneself at a stove // 난로를 피우다 light a stove ; make a fire in the stove
가스 ― a gas stove〔heater〕 석유 ― an oil stove 전기 ― an electric stove〔heater〕
난롯가 煖爐― the fireside ¶ 난롯가에〔에서〕 by the fireside〔fire〕
난류 暖流 a warm current
난리 亂離 [전쟁] a war ; [반란] a revolt ; a rebellion ; [소요] disturbance ; tumult ; riot ; [혼란] confusion ; commotion ¶ 난리가 나다 a war breaks out ; have a war ; have an uproar // 난리를 일으키다 raise a war ; rise in revolt // 물난리가 나다 suffer from a flood〔water famine (물기근)〕 // 그의 갑작스러운 죽음으로 온 집안에 난리가 났다 His sudden death threw the whole house into utter confusion.
난립 亂立 ―하다 be all running for election at once ; be adding to the election confusion ¶ 후보자가 난립하고 있는 선거구 a constituency flooded with candidates
난마 亂麻 raveled hemp fiber ; [뒤얽힌 상태] chaos ; confusion ; disorder ; anarchy ; imbroglio ¶ 난마처럼 얽히다 be in a chaotic state // 쾌도(快刀)로 난마를 자르다 cut the Gordian knot ; solve a knotty problem once and for all
난막 卵膜 〖동물〗 [물고기·파충류·새·곤충의] an egg membrane ; a chorion
난만 爛漫 ―하다 (be) full-blown ; be at 《their》 glory〔best〕 ; glorious ; splendid ¶ 난만한 벚꽃 full-blown cherry blossoms // 천진 난만한 아이 simple and innocent children // 꽃이 난만하다 be in full bloom ; be at their best // 백화 난만하다 All the flowers are in full bloom〔at their best〕.
난망 難忘 unforgettableness ¶ 난망이다 be unforgettable
난맥 亂脈 chaos ; disorder ; confusion ¶ 난맥에 빠지다 fall into chaos ; be thrown into disorder // 저 회사 내막은 난맥 상태이다 The affairs of the company are in a chaotic condition〔in bad shape, in a mess〕.
난무 亂舞 a wild dance ; a boisterous dance ―하다 dance boisterously 〔wildly〕
난문제 難問題 a difficult〔hard, tough〕 question ; a knotty〔sticky〕 problem ; a hard nut to crack ; a difficult case to advise ; a vexed question ; a crux ; a poser ¶ 난문제를 묻다 ask a hard question ; put a hard question to 《a person》 // 난문제에 부딪치다 meet a hard problem // 난문제를 풀다 solve a hard problem // 그것은 내게는 난문제이다 That is a hard nut for me to crack. // 현재 한국은 여러 가지 난문제에 직면하고 있다 Korea today is beset with perplexing difficulties.
난민 亂民 riotous〔lawless〕 people ; insurgents ; rioters ; a mob
난민 難民 the destitute ; the afflicted people ; refugees (피난민) ; sufferers (이재민) ; displaced persons (고국에서 쫓겨난)
― 구제 the relief of the poor〔destitute〕 ; the relief of the sufferers ; refugee relief
난바다 the far-off sea ; the offing ; the open sea ¶ 난바다에 떠 있는 배 a ship in the offing ; a ship (far) out at sea
난반사 亂反射 〖물리〗 diffused reflection
난발 爛發 ⇨ 난만(爛漫)
난발 亂發 ① random〔reckless〕 firing 〔shooting〕 ② [남발(濫發)] overissue ; excessive issue ―하다 fire〔shoot〕 at random ; issue recklessly〔excessively〕 ¶ 지폐의 난발 an overissue of notes
어음 ― an overissue of bills
난발 亂髮 disheveled〔ruffled, unkempt, uncombed〕 hair
난방 煖房 heating ; a heated room
― 계원 [아파트의] a janitor 《미》 ; a caretaker ― 조절 장치 a thermostat 증기 ― steam〔hot-air, hot-water〕 heating 지역 ― district heating 중앙 ―법 central heating
난방 장치 煖房裝置 heating ; air conditioning ; [기구] a heating apparatus 〔arrangement, system〕 ; a heater ; a radiator (복사 난방기) ¶ 이 건물에는 난방 장치가 없다 There is〔We have〕 no heating in this building.
난백 卵白 the white (of an egg) ; the

albumen

난번 —番 off duty (shift) ¶ 난번이다 be off duty ; be off // 나는 오늘 난번이다 I am off duty today. /This is my day off.

난벌 a street dress ; street wear ; clothes for the street ; one's best clothes ; one's Sunday best

난봉 dissipation ; debauchery ; prodigality ; profligacy ¶ 난봉나다 fall into vicious〔evil〕 courses ; take to fast living // 난봉부리다 be dissipated ; lead a dissipated〔dissolute〕 life ; live fast // 그는 난봉이 나서 술과 노름으로 세월을 보냈다 He led a dissolute life, drinking and gambling. // 진탕 난봉부리다 drain the cup of pleasure to the dregs // 난봉 생활에 푹 빠지다 indulge in〔be given to〕 dissipation〔debauchery〕 ; abandon oneself〔give oneself up〕 to dissipation〔dissolute habits, wild ways〕

— 생활 a fast〔dissipated〕 life ; fast living ; a life of follies — 자식 a prodigal son —쟁이〔꾼〕 a libertine ; a debauchee ; a rake ; a rip ; a Lothario 《*pl.* -s》 ; a fast liver

난부자 (든거지) a person who puts up a front of wealth but is really poor

난비 亂飛 fluttering〔flying〕 wildly around —하다 flutter〔fly〕 around wildly〔boisterously〕

난사 難事 a difficult matter〔thing〕 ; a difficulty ; a hard task ; a tough job ¶ 난사 중의 난사 the most difficult of all things ; the hardest thing to do

난사 亂射 firing〔shooting〕 at random ; a wild〔random〕 shot —하다 fire〔shoot〕 at random ; fire blindly

난사람 an outstanding〔a prominent〕 person ; a distinguished person ; a person of extraordinary ability ¶ 그 고을에는 아직 난사람이 별로 없다 There have been almost no outstanding people in that town.

난산 難產 hard labor ; a difficult delivery〔birth〕 —하다 have a difficult delivery ; have a hard labor ; bring forth with difficulty (사물) ¶ 난산이었다 She had a hard labor. // 새 조각은 난산일 것이다 The formation of a new Cabinet will be attended with much difficulty.

난삽 難澁 difficulty ; distress ; hardship —하다 be in distress〔difficulty〕

난색 難色 disapproval ; reluctance ; unwillingness ¶ 난색을 보이다 show disapproval〔unwillingness〕 ; hesitate 《to do》

난생 卵生 〖생물〗 oviparity ; oviparousness —하다 bear (offspring) by egg ; be oviparous ¶ 물고기는 난생이다 Fish are produced from eggs.

—동물 an oviparous〔egg-laying〕 animal ; [총칭] an ovipara

난생 처음 —生— (for) the first time in one's life ; in all one's born days ¶ 난생 처음 당하는 일 an experience met for the first time in one's life // 난생 처음으로 아버지에게 매를 맞았다 He was flogged by his father for the first time in his life.

난생후 —生後 after one's birth ; since one's birth ; this side of one's birth

난세 亂世 troublous〔troubled〕 times ; turbulent days ¶ 난세의 영웅 a hero in a warlike age // 그 당시 중국은 난세였다 At that time all was anarchy in China.

난세포 卵細胞 〖생물〗 an egg cell ; an ovum

난센스 nonsense ¶ 그런 말은 정말 난센스다 That is sheer nonsense.

난소 卵巢 the ovary ; the ovarium

— 낭포 an ovarian cyst —내 임신 ovarian pregnancy —선(腺) a nidamental gland — 수종(水腫) ovarian dropsy —염(炎) ovaritis — 적출 removal of the ovary — 절제술 ovariotomy ; ovariectomy ; oophorectomy — 호르몬 ovarian〔follicular〕 hormones

난수(표) 亂數(表) 〖수학〗 (the table of) random (sampling) numbers〔digits〕

난숙 爛熟 ① [과일] overripeness ; overmaturity —하다 (be) overripe ; overmature ② [성숙의 극] full maturity ; full development ; mellow ripeness —하다 attain full maturity ; reach complete maturity ; (be) mature ¶ 문화의 난숙기 the full maturity of culture ; the mellow ripeness of culture // 그것은 그의 난숙기에 쓰여진 소설이다 The novel was written when his literary skill was at its ripe maturity.

난시 亂視 astigmatism ; distorted vision ¶ 난시인 사람 an astigmatic person

—안 astigmatism ; astigmatic eyes — 안경 astigmatic glasses — 측정 an astigmometer

난시 亂時 troublous times ; a time of confusion〔disorder, anarchy〕

난신 亂臣 ① a traitorous〔treacherous〕 subject ; a rebellious〔mutinous〕 minister ; a traitor ② [난세의 충신] a loyal subject in turbulent days

— 적자(賊者) a traitor ; a rebel ; a traitorous〔treacherous〕 subject

난심 亂心 a distracted〔disturbed〕 mind ; mental derangement ; insanity ; madness

난외 欄外 the margin ; a marginal column (신문의) ¶ 난외의 여백 marginal space // 난외의 주 marginal notes ; notes on the margin ; marginalia

— 기사 stop-press news — 표제 a running title (일반 도서의)

난용 亂用 abuse ; misuse ; misappropriation ; improper〔unlawful〕 use ; diversion (유용) **—하다** abuse ; misuse ; misappropriate ; use improperly〔unlawfully〕; divert ¶ 직권을 난용하다 abuse one's official authority

난운 亂雲 a nimbus 《*pl.* -bi, ～es》

난원형 卵圓形 an eggshape ; ovalness ; an ovoid figure

난이 難易 hardness and〔or〕 easiness ; (relative) difficulty ; hardness ¶ 일의 난이도에 달려 있다 depend on how difficult the work is // 보수는 일의 난이도에 따라 다르다 Your pay varies with the relative difficulty of the job you take in.

—율(率) 〖체조〗 the degree of difficulty

난입 亂入 intrusion ; trespass(ing) **—하다** break into ; intrude ; trespass ; force one's way into ¶ 사무실에 난입하다 break into an office

—자 an intruder ; a trespasser

난자 卵子 an egg cell ; an ovum 《*pl.* ova》; [식물의] an ovule

난자 亂刺 stabbing violently〔wildly〕; 〖외과〗 scarification **—하다** stab violently〔wildly〕; scarify (피부를)

난작거리다 fall apart at a touch ⇨ 는적거리다

난잡 亂雜 disorder ; confusion ; a mess ; pell-mell **—하다** be in disorder〔in a mess〕; (be) disorderly ; confused ; unsystematic ; pell-mell ¶ 난잡한 옷차림 untidy dress // 난잡한 학생 a student lacking discipline // 난잡하게 in disorder〔confusion〕; in a disorderly fashion ; at sixes and sevens ; in a mess // 난잡하게 만들다 put out of order ; throw into disorder // 난잡해지다 fall into disorder ; get out of order // 방이 난잡하다 The room is untidy〔at sixes and sevens〕. // 책이 난잡하게 쌓여 있다 The books are piled up in a disorderly fashion. // 그는 술을 마시면 난잡해진다 He loses control of himself when in cups.

난장 亂杖 random beating ; reckless〔wild〕 beating ; indiscriminate flogging (형벌) ¶ 난장맞다 get beaten wildly

난장 亂帳 [제본] erratic pagination

난장 亂場 a scene of confusion and disorder ⇨ 난장판

난장초 爛腸草 〖식물〗 a begonia ; an elephant's-ear (추해당)

난장판 亂場— a scene of confusion and disorder ; a turmoil ; disorder ; chaos ; bustle and confusion ; a mess ¶ 화재 현장의 난장판 utter confusion at the scene of a fire // 난장판이 되다 fall into utter confusion // 난장판이 되어 있다 be at sixes and sevens ; be in a mess // 온 집안이 난장판이다 The whole house is in a mess. // 주인이 죽어서 집안이 온통 난장판이 되었다 The master's death threw the whole house into utter confusion. // 그 도시는 3일간 완전히 난장판이었다 Perfect chaos reigned the city for three days.

*‡***난쟁이** a dwarf ; a pigmy ; a midget ; a shrimp ; a manikin ; Tom Thumb ¶ 서커스의 난쟁이 a circus midget // 백설 공주와 일곱 난쟁이 이야기 the story of Snow white and the seven Dwarfs

난적 亂賊 rebels ; rioters ; traitors

난전 亂戰 a confused fight ; a dogfight ; a scuffle ; a melee ; a rough-and-tumble (fight) ¶ 난전을 벌이다 start a confused fight ; engage in a scuffle ; have a melee

난점 難點 a difficult〔knotty〕 point ; a crux of a matter ; a rub ; [결점] a bad point ; a fault ¶ 제일 난점은 …이다 The worse of it is 《that》 . . .

난정 亂政 misgovernment ; depraved〔corrupt(ed)〕 administration

***난제 難題** a difficult〔stiff, tough, puzzling, baffling〕 problem〔question〕; a knotty subject〔problem〕; a hard nut to crack ; a crux ; a poser ; a puzzle ; a floorer ; a teaser (속) ¶ 교육상의 난제의 하나 one of the tantalizing problems in education // 한국의 외교상의 난제 the great crux of Korean diplomacy

난조 亂調 [음악의] discord ; ragtime turn ; [혼란] disorder ; confusion ; [맥박의] irregularity ¶ 난조를 보이다 [투수가] lose control // 난조에 빠지다 be thrown into disorder〔confusion〕; be out of tune

난중 亂中 the midst of turmoil〔commotion〕; time of war ; a tumultuous period ¶ 난중에 during the war ; in the midst of turmoil

난중지난 難中之難 the most difficult of all things ; the hardest thing 《to do》

난증 難症 a serious〔malignant〕 disease〔case〕; an intractable case ; an incurable case

— 학질 a bad case of malaria

난질 wanton behavior by a woman ; having illicit sexual intercourse with a man

난질거리다 feel squashy〔pulpy, soft and mushy〕; (be) flimsy

난질난질 mushily ; squashily ; flabbily

***난처 難處** **—하다** (be) difficult ; hard to deal with ; awkward ; embarrassing ; be at a loss ; be in a dilemma ¶ 난처한 입장 an awkward〔a difficult〕 situation // 난처하다 I am at a loss what to do. // 그렇게 하면 내 입장이 난처하다 That would put me in an awkward position. // 참으로 난처한 일이다 What a most awkward case this is ! // 뭐라고 대답해야 좋을지 난처합니다 I am puzzled for an answer. /I don't know how to answer you. // 그는 난처한 표정을 지

었다 He wore a worried look. /Puzzlement showed on his face. // 너의 의견과 그녀의 의견이 정반대니 내가 난처하다 I'm in a bind because your opinion and hers are diametrically opposed.

난청 難聽 hardness of hearing ¶ 난청의 hard of hearing

— 구역[지역] (라디오의) a fringe area where reception is poor ; a blanket area **—자** a person who has difficulty in hearing

난초 蘭草 an orchid ; an iris ; a canna ¶ 난초 재배가 an orchidist

난추니 〖새〗 the male (Asiatic) sparrow hawk ; Accipiter nisus (학명)

난측하다 難測— (be) inscrutable ; unfathomable ; impenetrable ; uncertain ; hard to foresee[foretell, forecast]

난층운 亂層雲 a nimbo-stratus

난치 難治 incurableness ; incurability **—하다** be hard to cure ; (be) incurable ; fatal ; hopeless ¶ 난치 환자 수용소 a home of incurables

—성 간염 intractable hepatitis

난침모 —針母 a day[non-resident, living-out, visiting] seamstress

‡**난타 亂打** beating at random ; pommeling ; repeated knocking[blows] ; random blows **—하다** beat at random ; strike[knock] violently[recklessly] ; pommel ; give 《a person》 a drubbing ; knock repeatedly ; batter ¶ 화재 경종을 난타하다 strike the firebell violently[wildly] // 문을 난타하다 knock the door violently ; pound on the door

—전 [야구·권투의] a slugfest 《미·구》

난투 亂鬪 a confused fight ; a free fight ; a free-for-all (fight) ; a rough-and-tumble ; a scuffle ; a scrimmage ; a scrum ; a melee 《프》 **—하다** have a confused[free] fight ; scuffle ; scrimmage ¶ 상호간 난투극이 벌어졌다 A free fight developed between both sides.

—극 a scene of violence and confusion

난파 暖波 warm wave ; a current of warm air

난파 難破 a shipwreck ; a wreck **—하다** be wrecked ; wreck ; shipwreck ¶ 그 배는 암초에 걸려 난파했다 The ship was wrecked on a sunken rock. /The ship wrecked on a hidden reef.

— 화물 wreckage ; wrecked cargo [goods]

난파선 難破船 a wreck ; a wrecked ship ; a ship in distress

— 구조선 a wrecker

†**난폭 亂暴** violence ; outrage ; roughness ; rudeness ; wildness ; rowdiness ; rampage ; recklessness **—하다** (be) violent ; outrageous ; rough ; rude ; wild ; unruly ; disorderly ; rowdy ; [무법] lawless ; unlawful ; vandal(ic) ; [무모] reckless ¶ 난폭한 사람 a wild[an unruly, a disorderly] fellow ; a rough ; a rowdy ; a tough nut 《속》 // 난폭한 운전 reckless driving // 난폭한 취급 rough treatment[handling] // 난폭한 행위 disorderly conduct ; rowdyism ; vandalism (예술, 문화의 파괴) // 난폭하게 굴다 behave rudely ; do[use] violence ; be rough[wild] ; commit an outrage ; act in an unruly manner ; commit excesses ; run riot // 난폭한 언사를 쓰다 use violent[abusive] language ; utter wild words // 그는 난폭하다 He has a violent temper. // 토역꾼들은 난폭하다 Navvies have rude ways. // 폭도들은 난폭한 짓을 많이 했다 The rioters committed many outrages[excesses]. // 그는 취하면 난폭해진다 He gets riotous under the influence of liquor. // 그는 난폭하게 행동하고 있다 He is acting violently.

난풍 暖風 a warm wind[blast]

난필 亂筆 a scribble ; a scrawl ; scratchy [bad] writing ; a cursive writing ¶ 난필을 용서하십시오 (편지에서) Please excuse me for my hasty writing. / Please excuse my writing in haste.

난하다 亂— (be) loud ; gaudy ; flashy ; showy ¶ 난한 빛깔 a loud color // 난하게 화장을 한 얼굴 a thickly[flashily] painted face // 너무 난하다 be too gaudy [loud] for 《one》 // 난하게 차려 입고 있다 She is showily[gaudily] dressed. // 이 빨간 스카프는 그 여자에게는 너무 난한 것 같다 The red scarf looks too gay [young] for a woman of her age.

난항 難航 a stormy passage[voyage] ; a rough[hard] flight (항공) **—하다** have a difficult sailing ¶ 협상은 난항이다 The negotiations are proceeding with difficulty[having a hard going]. // 배는 격랑 속에서 난항했다 The ship sailed laboriously in a heavy sea. // 그 세법안은 국회에서 난항 중이다 The tax bill is facing rough going in the National Assembly.

난해 難解 —하다 be hard[difficult] to understand ; (be) hard ; knotty ; (be) hard to make out[solve] ; abstruse (심오한) ; unintelligible ¶ 난해한 글 a difficult passage 《in a book》 ; an article hard to understand // 난해한 문제 a difficult problem[question] ; a knotty problem

난행 亂行 debauchery ; misconduct ; violation **—하다** outrage ; violate ; dishono(u)r ; rape

난행 難行 [불교의] asceticism ; (self-) mortification ; religious austerities **—하다** do penance ; practice asceticism ; [행하기 어려움] be hard to put into practice ¶ 난행의 생애 a life of penance ; a penitential life

난형 卵形 an eggshape ; ovalness ¶ 난형의 egg-shaped ; ovoid ; oval ; ovate 《leaf》
—물 an ovoid **— 장식** 〖건축〗 an ovum 《*pl.* ova》
난형난제 難兄難弟 (being) almost equal ; hard to tell who is better ¶ 난형난제다 There is little to choose between the two. /They are six of one and half a dozen of the other.
난형낭 卵形囊 〖해부〗 [내이(內耳)의] a utricle
—염 〖의학〗 utriculitis
난호어 蘭胡魚 〖물고기〗 a goby (망둥이)
난혼 亂婚 promiscuity ; promiscuous sexual relations〔connections〕
난황 卵黃 the yolk〔yellow〕 of an egg ; 〖생물〗 the deutoplasm
—낭(囊) a yolk sac **—막(膜)** a yolk skin ; a vitelline membrane **—분(粉)** yolk powder **—소(素)** 〖생화학〗 vitellin **—질(質)** deutoplasm
낟 cereal grain(s) ⇨ 낟알
***낟가리** a stack of grain stalks ; a stack of straw〔hay, wood〕
†낟알 a grain ; a grain of hulled rice (쌀낟알)
†날¹ ① a day ; a date (날짜) ; time (시일) ¶ 어느 날 one day // 날로 day by〔after〕 day ; every day // 날을 보내다 pass one's day ; spend one's time // 날을 정하다 fix〔set〕 a date // 날이 감에 따라 as days go by // 날이 밝기 전에 before dawn〔day〕 // 날이 저물어서 after dark // 겨우 그날 그날을 지내다 eke out a living ; make a bare living // 날을 물려야겠다 We have to put off the date. // 날이 밝는다 Day〔Morning〕 breaks. /It dawns. // 날이 저문다 Night〔Evening〕 falls. /It gets dark. // 불이 난 다음날에 on the day succeeding〔following〕 the fire // 그가 떠난 다음 날에 on the day subsequent to his departure // 집에 돌아온 다음날 the day after reaching home // 결혼식 날을 잡다 choose a lucky day for one's wedding // 그의 부친은 그가 태어나던 바로 그날에 돌아가셨다 His father died on the very day that he was born.
② [날씨] weather ¶ 날이 좋건 나쁘건 in fair weather or foul ; rain or shine // 날이 좋으면 내일 출발하겠다 I will start tomorrow if it is fine. // 날이 더워진다 It is getting warmer. // 날이 사납다 It is foul〔bad〕 weather.
③ [경우·때] a time when ; in time〔case, the event〕 of ¶ 내가 성공하는 날에는 when I have succeeded // 작품을 완성하는 날에는 on the completion of the work // 화재가 일어나는 날에는 in case of a fire // 전쟁이 일어나는 날에는 in the event of war // 당신을 만난 날을 기억하고 있다 I remember the day when I met you. // 오늘 무슨 날입니까 What's the occasion ?
날² [칼 따위의] an edge ; a blade ¶ 칼날 the blade of a knife // 쌍날칼 a double-edged knife // 대팻날 the blade〔bit〕 of a plane // 면돗날 a razor blade // 날이 선 칼 a sharp-〔keen-〕edged knife // 무딘〔예리한〕 날 a dull〔sharp〕 edge // 날이 긴 칼 a knife with a long blade
날을 세우다 관용 put an edge on ; sharpen 《a knife》
날³ the warp ; the lengthwise threads ¶ 베틀날 the warp〔fixed threads〕 on a loom // 날과 씨 the warp and woof
날- [익히지 않은] uncooked ; raw ; green ; unseasoned ; crude ¶ 날것 raw〔uncooked〕 food // 날계란 a raw egg // 날고기 raw fish〔meat〕 // 날가죽 raw hide ; a pelt // 날로 먹다 eat raw
날강도 —强盜 a barefaced robber ; a racketeer
날강목치다 〖광산〗 mine for nought ; dig in vain ; make vain effort
†날개 the wings ; 〖항공〗 an airfoil〔aerofoil〕 ¶ 비행기 날개 the wings of an airplane // 날개 달린 winged // 날개 돋치다 fledge ; feather 《its wings》 // 날개를 치다 flap〔clap, beat〕 the wings ; flutter // 날개치는 소리 the flappings〔clappings〕 of the wings // 날개를 펴다 spread〔unfurl〕 the wings // 날개 돋친듯이 팔리다 sell〔go off〕 like hot cakes
— 개미 a winged ant **—옷** a robe of feathers ¶ 선녀의 날개옷 the celestial robe of an angel
날갯죽지 a wing ; the shoulder-joint of a wing
⁑날것 raw stuff ; uncooked food ; raw fish〔meat〕 ; unripe〔green〕 fruits (과일) ; untreated article ¶ 날것으로 먹다 eat 《fish》 raw〔fresh〕
날고기 raw〔uncooked〕 meat
날고치 raw〔unboiled〕 cocoons
날공전 daily wages ; a day's wage ¶ 날공전 일꾼 a day laborer〔worker〕 // 날공전으로 고용되다〔일하다〕 be hired〔work〕 by the day // 하루 30,000원의 날공전으로 일하다 work for a wage of 30,000 *won* a day
날귀 the two edges (of a blade) 《on a plane〔chisel〕》
날기와 an unbaked〔a raw〕 tile
날김치 raw〔unaged〕 pickles〔pickled vegetables〕
날나다 fail ; go to ruin ; collapse ; give way
날날이 ① day by day ⇨ 나날이 ② a kind of clarinet ⇨ 날라리
†날다¹ ① [하늘을] fly ; soar (높이) ; take wing(s) ; be flown off (바람에) ¶ 나는 새 a flying bird ; a bird of the air ; a bird flying in the air ; a bird on the wing // 하늘을 날다 fly in the air〔sky〕 //

높이〔낮게〕 날다 fly high〔low〕 in the air // (나비 따위가) 훨훨 날아다니다 flutter〔flit〕 about // 날아가다 fly away〔off〕; take wings // 떼지어 날다 take wing in a flock // 갈매기가 날고 있다 Gulls are wheeling about. // 비행기는 북극 상공을 날았다 The airplane flew over the North Pole. // 모자가 날려서 시궁창에 빠졌다 My hat flew into the gutter. // 독수리가 골짜기 위로 높이 날아올랐다 The eagles soared high above the valleys.
② [빨리 가다] fly; go very fast; run; rush ¶ 나는 듯이 달리다 run like the wind〔with flying feet〕 // 그 소식을 듣고 그대로 집으로 날아왔다 At the news I flew home like the wind. // 그는 즉시 홍콩으로 날아갔다 He flew〔hurried〕 immediately to Hongkong.
③ [달아나다] fly; flee; run away〔off〕; [몰래] slip off〔away〕 ¶ 정부(情夫)와 함께 날다 elope with a lover // 범인은 택시로 날아버렸다 The culprit made his escape by a taxi.

날다² ① [색이] fade (away); lose color; discolor ¶ 색이 난 faded; discolored // 빛깔이 날기 쉬운 quickly fading; fugitive // 빛깔이 날지 않는 fadeless; fast; standing // 햇볕이 강해서 커튼의 빛깔이 날았다 The strong sunlight had faded the curtains.
② [냄새가] lose odor; vanish; go away; [알코올·수증기 따위] evaporate

날다³ [실을] spin 《a thread》; [베틀에] thread the warp of 《a loom》

날다람쥐 『동물』 a flying squirrel; Sciuropterus russicus (학명)

날도 一度 『지리』 longitude

날도둑놈 a barefaced scoundrel; a shameless swindler〔crook〕

날들다 《it》 clear (up); 《it》 become fine weather ¶ 날들기 시작한다 It is clearing up.

날떠퀴 the day's luck; one's luck on the day

*__날뛰다__ act violently; get rowdy; leap〔jump, bound〕 (up); rave; rage; be on the rampage; run amuck; run riot; go〔run〕 wild; become excited〔furious〕 ¶ 기뻐 날뛰다 jump〔leap, dance〕 for〔with〕 joy; exult // 성나서 날뛰다 rave with fury; raise a row // 미친 듯이 날뛰다 run amuck; be〔go〕 on a wild rampage // 잘난 듯이 날뛰다 ride the high horse; throw one's weight around; swagger

날뛸판 leaping〔jumping〕 up and down; moving excitedly〔violently〕; rage; running amuck

날라리 『음악』 a Chinese clarinet; a charamela (포)

*__날래다__ (be) quick; fast; swift; nimble; agile ¶ 날랜 말 a speedy horse // 날래게 quickly; speedily; swiftly // 범인은 날래게 자취를 감추었다 The culprit disappeared in a flash. // 그는 걸음이 날래다 He is swift of foot. /He has swift feet. /He is nimble in his feet.

날려보내다 ① fly; let fly; make fly; set free; release; have 《a thing》 blown〔snatched〕 off〔away〕 ¶ 새를 날려 보내다 let loose a bird; set a bird free // 바람에 모자를 날려 보냈다 I had my hat blown〔snatched〕 off.
② [재산을] blow; waste; squander; lose ¶ 도박으로 돈을 전부 날려 보내다 blow〔squander〕 the whole money in〔on〕 gambling // 주색에 가산을 날려 보내다 squander〔blow〕 one's fortune on woman and liquor

날렵하다 (be) smart; sharp; cute; shrewd; quick; prompt ¶ 아주 날렵한 as smart as steel-trap

날로 ① [날것으로] raw; uncooked ¶ 날로 먹다 eat 《fish》 raw ② [나날이] daily; every day; day by day ¶ 날씨가 날로 더워진다 It is growing hotter every day〔day by day〕. /It is getting hotter and hotter. // 날로 번창하다 enjoy increasing prosperity as time goes on

날름 ① [날쌔게] with a quick snatch; with a dart; snatching like a flash ¶ 원숭이가 어린이 손에서 과자를 날름 채갔다 The monkey snatched a cake from a boy. ② [혀를] 《a tongue》 darting in and out ⇨ 날름거리다

날름거리다 ① let 《a tongue, an arm》 dart in and out; take 《one's hand》 in and out quickly ¶ 뱀이 혀를 날름거린다 The snake darts its tongue in and out.
② [탐내어 노리다] peep stretching one's neck; crane one's neck to see

날름날름 darting〔taking〕 in and out repeatedly

날름쇠 [무자위의] a valve; [총의] the hammer; [물건의] a spring

†**날리다¹** ① fly; let fly; make fly; blow off (바람이) ¶ 연을 날리다 fly a kite // 비둘기를 날리다 let loose a pigeon // 먼지를 날리다 raise the dust // 바람에 모자를 날렸다 I had my hat blown off. // 그는 2루타를 날렸다 He made a two-base hit.
② [일을] scamp〔skimp〕 one's work; do slipshod; do a hasty job ¶ 저 목수는 절대로 일을 날리지 않는다 That carpenter never scamps his work〔never does slipshod work〕. /The carpenter is very conscientious in his work.
③ [없애다] lose 《all》; waste; throw away; bring to naught ¶ 그는 얼마 안 가서 재산을 노름에 날려 버렸다 He soon lost all his fortune in gambling.
④ [명성을] make famous; distinguish; be popular 《with, among》; be

widely〔well〕 known ¶ 이름을 날리다 get a name ; make〔get, win〕 oneself a name

날리다[2] [바람에] wave ; flutter ; flap ¶ (깃발 따위가) 바람에 날리다 flutter〔wave, flap〕 in the wind // 국기가 바람에 날리고 있다 The national flag is flapping in the wind. // 재가 날린다 Ashes blow.

날림 a slipshod job〔thing〕 ¶ 그에게 방을 깨끗이 치우라고 했더니 그는 날림으로 일했다 I told him to clean up his room, but he gave it a lick and a promise.

—글씨 sloppy handwriting **—일** a gasty〔slipshod〕 job **—집** a jerry-built structure ; a flimsy〔shoddy〕 house

날림치 a thing〔article〕 of coarse manufacture ; a thing made〔a job done〕 in a slipshod manner

*__날마다__ every day ; daily ; day after day ; day by day ; from day to day ; per day (하루에) ¶ 날마다 하는 일 daily routine // 거의 날마다 almost every day // 날마다 당신 생각을 하고 있소 Not a day passes without my thinking of you. // 이런 일은 날마다 있는 일이 아니야 Such things do not happen every day.

날망제 〖민속〗 an unexorcised soul ; a restless spirit ; an unquiet〔a wandering〕 ghost

날목 —木 unseasoned wood〔timber〕

날물 ① [나가는 물] outflowing water ② [썰물] a low tide ; an ebb tide ; the ebb

날밑 a blade-guard ; a sword-guard

날바닥 the bare floor〔ground〕

날바람잡다 [바람이 들어 헤매다] stroll〔ramble, knock about, knock around〕 in high spirits

날반죽 cold-water dough ; kneading with cold water **—하다** knead with cold water

날밤[1] [지새우는] a night one stays up all night ¶ 날밤 새우다 stay up all night ; kill the night

—집 a grogshop open all night

날밤[2] raw〔unroasted〕 chestnuts

날벌레 a winged insect

날변 —邊 daily interest ; interest per day ; per diem 《라》

날불한당 —不汗黨 a barefaced swindlers〔crooks〕 ; shameless scoundrels

날붙이 a cutting-instrument ; an edged tool ; bladeware ; cutlery

날빛 daylight ; sunlight ; sunshine ; sunbeams ; the rays of the sun ¶ 날빛을 가리다 keep off the sun ; screen from the sun // 날빛에 얼굴이 타다 get〔be〕 sunburnt

날사이 (for) the past several days ; for some days now

날삯 daily wages

—꾼 a day labor ; a casual laborer

날상가 —喪家 a house in mourning

날상제 —喪制 a person newly in mourning

날새 (for) the past several days (날사이)

날샐녘 dawn ; daybreak ; the early hours of the morning ¶ 날샐녘에 at dawn ; at the peep of day〔dawn〕 ; at daybreak

날서다 be edged ; be sharpened ; 《edge》 become sharp ; take an edge ¶ 날선 칼 a sharp〔keen〕 knife

날성수 —星數 ⇨ 날수 ②

날세우다 sharpen ; put an edge 《on》 ¶ 칼을 날세우다 sharpen〔whet〕 a knife ; put an edge on a knife

날수 —數 ① [수효] the number of days

② [운수] the luck〔fortune〕 of a particular day ¶ 날수가 좋다〔나쁘다〕 have a lucky〔an unlucky〕 day

날숨 outbreathing ; exhalation ; expiration ¶ 날숨 쉬다 exhale ; breathe out ; expire

날실 ① [경사(經絲)] warp threads

② [삶지 않은 실] raw〔untreated〕 thread

날쌍하다 (be) loose-woven ; be (an) openweave ⇨ 늘썽하다 ¶ 날쌍날쌍 all loose

*__날쌔다__ (be) quick ; swift ; nimble ; agile ; prompt ; fleet ¶ 날쌘 청년 a nimble young man // 날쌔게 quickly ; speedily ; swiftly ; quick as a flash // 행동이 날쌔다 be quick〔prompt〕 in action ; act quickly〔promptly〕 // 일을 날쌔게 해치웠다 He finished his work in quick order.

†**날씨** (the) weather ; weather conditions ; atmospheric conditions ; the elements ¶ 좋은 fine〔fair, good, beautiful, favorable〕 weather ; a fine 〔clear〕 day // 나쁜 날씨 bad〔foul, nasty, wretched〕 weather // 아주 좋은 날씨 perfect〔ideal〕 weather // 온화한 날씨 calm〔mild, genial, serene〕 weather // 변덕스러운 날씨 fickle〔broken, changeable, unsettled〕 weather // 음산한 날씨 gloomy〔oppressive〕 weather // 날씨가 좋으면 if weather permits ; weather permitting ; if it is fine // 날씨가 좋건 나쁘건 in fair weather or foul ; rain or shine ; in all weathers ; regardless of weather // 지금 날씨로는 judging from the look of the sky // 날씨를 보다 read the sky ; look at the weather // 날씨를 예보하다 make a weather forecast // 날씨를 탓하다 put down 《anything》 to the weather // 그는 날씨를 잘 본다 He is weatherwise. // 오늘 날씨는 어떠냐 How is the weather today? // 좋은 날씨다 It

is〔We have〕 fine weather. ∥날씨가 차차 좋아진다 The weather is changing for the better. /The weather is improving. ∥비가 올 날씨다 We'll have falling weather. /We shall have some rain. ∥이와 같은 날씨가 오래 계속되지 않을 것이다 This weather will not hold so long. ∥날씨가 좋으면 오겠다 I will come, but it depends upon the weather. ∥추운 날씨가 여러 날 계속되고 있다 The weather has been cold for several days. ∥지금 날씨 같아서는 오후에 비가 올 것 같다 Judging from the sky, we shall have some rain in the afternoon. ∥요즘 날씨가 변덕스럽다 We have had changeable〔fickle〕 weather lately. /The weather is changeable these days. ∥금방이라도 비가 쏟아질 듯한 날씨다 It is threatening weather. /It threatens to rain. ∥오늘은 봄 날씨 같군요 It is spring weather today, isn't it? ∥이 날씨가 얼마나 갈까 How long will this weather hold〔last〕? ∥날씨가 풀렸다 The weather became warmer. ∥내일 날씨가 좋을지 궁금하구나 I wonder if we'll have good weather tomorrow.

☞ ◖ p. 448 ◗

*날씬하다 (be) slender ; slim ¶ 날씬한 손가락 slender fingers∥날씬한 여자 a slim woman ; a woman with a slender figure∥날씬한 허리 a slender〔supple〕 waist∥그녀는 몸매가 날씬하다 She is trim and slender in figure. ∥옷차림이 날씬하다 be smartly〔sprucely〕 dressed ∥날씬하게 차려 입다 spruce oneself up 《for dinner》; dress oneself neat and tidy∥너 전보다 더 날씬해진 것 같다 You look slimmer. ∥음식을 조심해서 먹지않는 한 뚱뚱한 사람들이 날씬해질 가능성은 거의 없다 There is a fat chance for fat people to get slim unless they really watch what they eat.

날아가다 ① [공중을] fly away ; take wings (날개로) ¶ 구름에 뜬 기분이고 날아가는 듯한 기분이다 I'm on cloud nine. /I'm walking on air.
② [없어짐] be gone ¶ 돈이 어느새 다 날아갔다 My money is all gone already.
③ [파면] ¶ 모가지가 날아가다 be dismissed ; be fired 《속》

날아놓다 allocate everybody's share of the expenses

날아다니다 fly〔flutter, flit〕 about〔around〕

날아들다 fly in〔into〕

날아오르다 [높이] fly high〔up〕; [새가] soar (up) ; take wing〔flight〕; [비행기가] take〔hop〕 off ; [바람에 불려] be blown up

날염 捺染 (textile) printing —하다 print ¶ 날염한 천 printed cotton ; print ; calico 《미》
—기 a printing machine — 옥양목 cotton print 실—기 a yarn printing machine

†날인 捺印 affixing a seal ; sealing —하다 seal ; affix one's seal 《to a paper》 ¶ 서명 날인하다 affix one's signature d seal 《to a paper》; sign and seal
—자 a sealer — 증서 계약 a covenant ; a contract under seal 조건부 — 증서 〖법〗 an escrow

날일 [날품팔이 일] daywork ; day labor
— 변경선 a date line 계약 — the date of a contract 약속 — the date of an appointment

†날조 捏造 (an) invention ; (a) fabrication ; (a) concoction ; (a) frame-up 《미》
— 하다 fabricate ; forge ; invent ; make up 《a story》; frame up 《미》 ¶ 날조된 기록 a forged document∥날조된 기사로 가득찬 신문 newspapers (that are) full of invents∥그것은 전적으로 그가 날조한 이야기이다 The story is a pure invention on his part.
— 기사 a fabrication ; a made-up story ; a cooked-up report —자 a fabricator

날줄 (a line of) longitude

날짐승 winged animals ; the feathered tribe ; birds ; fowls

†날짜¹ ① [작정된] a date ¶ 날짜 소인(消印) a day mark〔stamp〕∥계약〔약속〕 날짜 the date of a contract〔an appointment〕∥9월 10일 날짜로 된 편지 a letter dated September 10∥날짜가 없는 undated ; dateless∥날짜가 적혀 있다 date ; be dated∥앞선 날짜로 하다 antedate 《a letter》∥날짜를 정하다 fix a date ; name the day∥사람을 날짜로 묶어 놓다 bind 《a person》 to date∥날짜를 늦추다 put off the date∥날짜를 앞당기다 move up〔advance〕 the date∥그 편지는 8월 5일 날짜로 되어 있었다 The letter bore the date of〔was dated〕 August 5. ∥두 사람의 결혼 날짜가 정해졌다 The date has been chosen for their wedding. /A day has been set for their wedding.
② [일수] (the number of) days ¶ 날짜는 얼마나 걸립니까 How long〔many days〕 will it take? ∥완성하는 데는 여러 날짜가 걸린다 Days are required for finishing it.

날짜² ① [날것] raw stuff ; uncooked food ; untreated〔unprocessed, unseasoned〕 article ¶ 날짜로 먹다 eat raw∥나무를 날짜로 켜다 saw unseasoned wood
② [미숙한] an unexperienced person ; a greenhorn ; a novice ¶ 그런 날짜는 처음 보았다 I have never seen such a greenhorn.

ㄴ

날씨의 표현

L

1 날씨에 관한 일상적 표현

① 날씨를 표현할 때는 보통 비인칭 it를 주어로 사용한다.

¶ 날씨 좋지 않아요? — 정말 그렇군요. (It's a) beautiful day, isn't it?— Yes, isn't it! / Isn't it a beautiful day? — Yes, it (certainly[sure]) is! (★ Yes, isn't it.나 Yes, it is.나 뜻은 같다. 다만 sure를 쓰면 보다 허물없는 표현이 되고 beautiful 대신에 nice, lovely, wonderful 등을 쓰기도 한다. 위와 같은 표현은 It's fine today.나 It's good weather.보다 감정이 풍부한 표현.) // 비가 퍼붓고 있군요. It's really raining [coming down, pouring], isn't it? / (It's) Raining cats and dogs, isn't it? // 오늘 덥죠? (It's) Hot today, isn't it? / Isn't it hot today? // 날씨가 무덥고 끈적거리지요? — 예, 무척이나 덥군요. Hot and sticky, isn't it? — Yes, awfully muggy. (★ 「무척」이란 뜻으로 awfully, terribly가 쓰인다.) // 고약한[음울한] 날씨로군. Miserable[gloomy] (weather), isn't it?

표현에 따라서는 it를 주어로 할 것인가 이외의 것을 주어로 할 것인가는 화자의 기대와 전후 문맥에 따라 결정된다. 예를 들어 「It's a beautiful day today.」는 「날씨가 좋다.」는 것에 대한 감정적 표현이고 「The weather is good.」는 좋은 날씨에 대한 객관적 표현이다. 그러나 「오늘 날씨 어때요? How's the weather today?」와 같이 it를 주어로 할 수 없는 것도 있다.

② 표현

¶ 비가 내리기 시작했다. The rain began to fall. (= It began[started] to rain.) // 비가 그쳤다. The rain has stopped. (=It's stopped raining.) // 어제는 더웠다. Yesterday was a hot day. (=It was hot yesterday.) // 날씨 어때요? — 가랑비가 내리고 있습니다. How's the weather today[what's the weather like]? — It's drizzling. // 소풍가기에 참 좋은 날입니다. It's a perfect day for a picnic. / It's picnic weather for a picnic. (★ weather의 경우 「오늘…날씨」처럼 특정한 상황을 가리킬 때에는 the가 붙지만 일반적인 날씨의 경우에는 무관사로 쓰인다.) // 날씨가 좋으면 내일 골프를 치겠다. If it's fine[the weather is good], I'll play golf tomorrow. // 오후에는 날씨가 개일 것 같습니까? — 글쎄요, 어떨지 모르겠네요. Do you think it'll clear up in the afternoon? — I doubt it. // 오늘 아침 서리가 많이[조금] 왔다. We had a heavy[slight] frost this morning. // 지난 주에는 눈이 엄청나게 왔다. We had a heavy snowfall last week. / It snowed heavily last week. // 눈이 2미터는 쌓였다. The snow lay two meters deep. // 나는 학교에서 돌아오는 길에 억수같은 비를 만났다. I was caught in a downpour on my way home from school. // 이 마을의 연간 강우량은 1200밀리미터이다. The yearly rainfall[precipitation] in this town is about 1200 millimeters. // 그때는 사나운 바람이 불고 있었다. A violent storm was raging at that time. // 봐라. 날씨가 의심스럽다. 지금이라도 당장 비가 퍼부을 것만 같다 Look. The sky is threatening. We may have a downpour (at) any moment. // 이 날씨가 오래 갈까요? — 예 그럴 것 같은데요. 하지만 또 모르죠. Do you think the weather will hold? — Yes, perhaps. But you never can tell. // 오늘은 꽤 서늘하지요? — 예, 그런데요. 오히려 춥군요. It's rather cool[much cooler] today, isn't it? — Yes, it is. Almost cold. // 기온이 몇 도입니까? — 23도입니다. What's the temperature? — It's 23°C[twenty-three]. // 애석하게도 날씨가 좋지 않네요. — 예 내가 보기에 한 이틀 정도는 좋은 날씨가 유지되겠지만 결국 장마가 들어섰으니까요. It's a pity the weather is bad. — Yes, I thought the fine weather would stay for a couple of days at least. But we are in the rainy season after all.

2 기온

섭씨(centigrade)·화씨(Fahrenheit)

섭씨와 화씨는 온도의 단위이다. Fahrenheit는 the Fahrenheit scale을 고안한 독일의 물리학자 Gabriel Daniel Fahrenheit(1686~1736)의 이름을 딴 것이다. Centigrade는 스웨덴의 천문학자 Anders Celsius(1701~1744)의 고안에 따른 것이다. 섭씨(攝氏) 10도는 10℃, 10 degrees centigrade(Centigrade로도 씀), 화씨(華氏) 10도는 10°F, 10 degrees Fahrenheit로 쓴다. 섭씨는 centigrade로

부르는 경우가 많으나 Celsius로도 부른다. 섭씨와 화씨의 환산 공식은 다음과 같다.

0℃ = 32℉
Centigrade = 5/9(Fahrenheit-32)
Fahrenheit = 9/5(Centigrade+32)

¶ 기온이 섭씨 30도로 올랐다. The temperature rose to 30℃.(★ 급상승인 경우는 shot up; soared; climbed 등을 쓴다.)//오늘 날씨는 맑고 최고 기온은 섭씨 31도, 최저 기온은 섭씨 21도가 되겠습니다. Today will be clear with a high of 31℃, a low of 21℃.// 낮 최고 기온은 섭씨 30도가 되겠습니다. High temperatures expected this afternoon 31 degrees Centigrade.//서울 최고 기온은 30도가 되겠습니다. Highs in Seoul near 30 degrees are expected.// 오늘의 최고 기온은 섭씨 32도였다. The maximum temperature today was 32℃./Today's high was 32℃.//오늘밤 최저 기온은 섭씨 15도 전후가 되겠습니다. Low temperatures are expected tonight around 15℃.//기온이 영하 8도로 내려갔다. The temperature sank to 8 degrees below zero./The temperature sank to a sub-zero 8 degrees.//평년보다 5도 높다. 5 degrees above the normal temperature./5 degrees higher than in a normal year./온도계는 30도를 가리키고 있다. The thermometer read[registered] 30 degrees./The mercury hit 30 degrees.

▶ 냉하 unusually cool summer/혹서 severe heat/열파 heat wave/엄동 severe winter/한파 cold wave/난동 mild winter/한기단(寒氣團) cold air mass/동장군 General Winter; rigors of winter

▶ 기온 temperature/섭씨 centigrade/화씨 Fahrenheit/최고 기온 maximum[highest] temperature/최저 기온 minimum [lowest] temperature/평균 기온 average temperature/영하 below zero; below the freezing point/영하 5도 five degrees below zero; minus five degrees

▶ 비 rain; rainfall/폭우 heavy rain/가랑비 light rain/집중 호우 localized torrential downpour/폭우 downpour/지나가는 비 a (passing) shower/(오후의) 소나기 evening shower/뇌우 thundershower/안개비 drizzle; drizzling [fog] rain/초여름비 early summer rain/봄비 spring rain; drizzle/가을비 au- tumn rain/늦가을 소나기 late-autumn shower

▶ 습도 humidity/습도가 높은 날 humid day/무더운 날 sultry day

▶ 안개 fog; mist/농무 dense fog/스모그 smog/광화학 스모그 photochemical smog

▶ 대설 heavy snow/폭설 tremendous snowfall/가랑눈 powdery snow/함박눈 large flakes of snow/만년설 perpetual snow/눈사태 snowslide; avalanche/눈보라 snowstorm/풍설 wind and snow /눈송이 snowflake/눈의 결정 snow crystal/진눈깨비 sleet/싸라기눈 hail/우박 hail/서리 frost/얼음 ice/고드름 icicle

▶ 구름 cloud/권적운 fleecy cloud/적란운(積亂雲) thunderhead/비구름 rain cloud/버섯 구름 mushroom cloud/권운 cirrus/적운 cumulus/층운 stratus/고층운 altostratus/난층운 nimbostratus

▶ 미풍 breeze/강풍 strong wind/폭풍 storm; windstorm/회오리 바람 tornado; whirlwind/모래 폭풍 sandstorm/삭풍 cold wintry wind

▶ 홍수 flood/대홍수 deluge/해일 tidal wave/우레 thunder/번개 lightning/천둥 소리 roll of thunder/벼락 thunderbolt flash to ground

날짝지근하다 (be) languid; weary; feel lazy ⇨ 늘쩍지근하다

날짱거리다 be idle; be〔get〕 lazy ⇨ 늘쩡거리다

날찍 profit (from business)

날치[1] ① [새사냥] catching〔shooting〕 birds on the wing; [비유적] promptness; quickness (날쌤)
② [사람] an excellent hunter

날치[2] 〖물고기〗 a flying fish

날치[3] [일수 빚] a loan with daily interest to be paid every day

날치기 snatching; a snatcher (날치기꾼)

¶ 날치기를 당하다 have 《a purse》 snatched〔picked〕//날치기를 잡다 arrest 〔round up〕 a snatcher//날치기를 조심하십시오 Beware of purse-snatchers./Be alert for purse-snatchers.//지하철에서 핸드백을 날치기 당했다 I had my handbag snatched on the subway.

— **공사** sloppy works; slipshod construction work

날치꾼 a master shot; an excellent hunter (so skilled as to shoot a bird on the wing)

†**날카롭다** (be) sharp; pointed (끝이);

sharp(-edged) knife // 날카로운 감각 keen〔quick〕 sense // 날카로운 귀 a sharp〔quick〕 ear // 날카로운 눈 piercing 〔keen, penetrating〕 eyes // 날카로운 관찰 a shrewd〔keen〕 observation // 날카로운 비평 a sharp〔biting, cutting〕 criticism // 머리가 날카로운 사람 a quick-witted〔shrewd〕 man // 날카롭게 하다 sharpen // 신경이 날카로워지다 become nervous〔touchy〕 // 그는 퍽 날카로운 머리를 가진 사람이다 He is as sharp as a needle〔razor〕. // 날카롭게 공격하다 make hot〔fierce〕 attacks 《on, against》; [말로] make cutting remarks 《about》 // 의견이 날카롭게 대립했다 Opinion was clearly divided into two. // 그녀의 판단력은 날카롭다 She can make acute judgments. // 나는 오른쪽 옆구리에 날카로운 통증을 느꼈다 I felt a sharp pain in my right side.

날큰거리다 (be) soft and droopy

날큰하다 (be) soft and droopy

날큰하다 (be) soft and droopy ; flabby ; weary ⇨ 늘큰하다 ¶ 몸이 날큰하다 feel weary

날탕 a person with no means ; a penniless〔empty-handed〕 person

날틀 a (10-holed) warp-adjuster for a loom

날파람 ① [서슬에 나는 바람] a gust of wind raised by a swiftly passing object ② [기세] roaring spirits ; keenness ; fierceness

날포 several days ¶ 여기 온 지 날포가 되었다 Several days have passed since I came here.

날품 day labor〔work〕 ¶ 날품으로 일하다 work by the day // 날품으로 고용되다 be hired by the day

一삯 daily wages **一팔이꾼** a day labor ; a casual laborer (임시의)

날피[1] a plowshare (보습)

날피[2] a pauper with no character 〔morals〕

∗**낡다** (be) old ; worn ; old-fashioned ; be out of date ; outmoded ; antique ; stale ; threadbare ; hackneyed ; outdated ¶ 낡아빠진 worn-out ; antiquated ; obsolete ; timeworn // 낡은 가구 worn-out furniture // 낡은 것 an old and useless article ; an article out of date ; an effete matter // 낡은 기계 obsolete machinery // 낡은 모자 a time-worn hat // 낡은 집 an old house // 낡은 차 a used car // 낡은 사상 an old(-fashioned) idea // 낡은 학설 an outdated theory // 낡은 수작 an old story ; a hackneyed remark // 그 건물은 건축 양식과 디자인이 낡았다 The building has become a back number〔outdated〕 in construction and design. // 우리 냉방기는 낡아서 더 이상 잘 작동되지 않는다 Our air conditioner's old and doesn't work very well anymore.

†**남** [타인] others ; other people ; another (person) ; a stranger (낯선 사람) ; an unrelated person (친척이 아닌) ¶ 남모르는 고생 hardships unknown to others // 남모르는 눈물 a hidden sorrow // 남의 입 [세상의 평판] Mrs. Grundy ; Lady Gossip // 생면부지의 남 a perfect〔complete〕 stranger // 남몰래 secretly ; unseen // 남의 앞에서 in the presence of others ; in public // 남 하는 대로 like common run ; like others // 남의 손에 넘어가다 fall into a stranger's hands // 남한테 친절하다 be kind to others // 남의 욕을 하다 speak ill of others // 남한테서 듣다 learn from others // 그들은 나를 남 대하듯 했다 They made a stranger of me. /They treated me like a stranger. // 남의 일에 참견마라 A third party should not thrust his nose into these matters. // 남의 일은 남의 일로 내버려 두어라 Let others mind their own business. // 남보다는 친척이 낫다 Blood is thicker than water. // 먼 친척보다는 가까운 남이 낫다 A good neighbor is better than a brother far off. // 그들은 이혼을 했으니까 이젠 남이다 Since they got divorced, they have nothing to do with each other. // 남의 말에 신경 쓸 것 없다 Let people talk and dogs bark ! // 남의 일 같지가 않다 I feel as if it were my own affairs.

남을 물에 넣으려면 제가 먼저 물에 들어간다 속담 To dig pit for another and fell into it oneself.

남의 고기 한 점이 내 고기 열 점보다 낫다 속담 The apples on the other side of the wall are the sweetest. /Our neighbour's ground〔cow〕 yields better corn〔more milk〕 than ours. /The grass is always greener on the other side of the fence.

남의 눈 속의 티만 보지 말고 자기 눈 속의 대들보를 보라 속담 You can see a mote in another's eye, but cannot see a beam in your eye. /The hunchback does not see his own hump, but sees his companion's.

남의 돈 천냥이 내 돈 한 푼만 못하다 속담 A bird in the hand is worth two in the bush. /Better a sparrow in the hand than a pigeon on the roof.

남의 떡에 설 지낸다 속담 Rob Peter to pay Paul.

남의 떡이 더 커 보인다 속담 The grass is always greener on the other side of the fence. /The apples on the other side of the wall are the sweetest. /Our neighbour's ground〔cow〕 yields better corn〔more milk〕 than ours.

남의 짐이 가벼워 보인다 속담 Every horse〔one〕, thinks his pack〔sack〕 heaviest.

남의 집 금송아지가 우리집 송아지만 못하다 [속담] A feather in hand is better than a bird in the air.
남의 흉이 한가지면 제 흉은 열가지라 [속담] The eye that sees all things else sees not itself.
남잡이가 제잡이 [속담] He who digs a pit shall fall into it. /Curses, like chickens, come home to roost.

남 男 [남자] a man ; a male ; a son (아들) ¶ 남동생 a younger brother // 슬하에 3남 2녀를 두고 있다 He is blessed with three sons and two daughters.

남 南 the south ¶ 남쪽의 south ; southern // 남으로 to the south // 남쪽으로 가다 go south〔southward〕// 경주에서 남쪽 10마일 ten miles south of *Kyongju* // 우리 집은 남향집이다 My house faces (to the) south.

남 藍 [남빛] indigo ; indigo〔deep〕 blue ; Indian blue

남가 일몽 南柯一夢 a vain〔an empty〕 dream ; a daylight dream ; [덧없는 영화] fleeting〔passing〕 glory

남계 男系 male line ; the male issue ; the spear side ¶ 남계의 agnate ; on the male line ; on the father's〔spear〕 side〔line〕// 남계의 친족 agnate ; agnation

남공 男工 a male worker ; a male machine operator

남구 南歐 Southern Europe

남국 南國 a southern country〔land〕; the south countries
—인〔풍습〕 southern people〔habits〕

***남극 南極** the South Pole ; the Antarctic (Pole) ; the South Pole (지남철의)
— 관측대 an Antarctic exploration party —광(光) the aurora australis 《*pl.* aurorae australes》; southern lights —권〔대〕 the Antarctic Circle〔Zone〕 —구(區) [동물·지리학상의] the Antarctic Region —성 the south pole star — 지방 the south pole region — 탐험 an Antarctic expedition〔exploration〕; a south-pole exploration — 포경(捕鯨) Antarctic whaling ; whaling in the Antarctic sea —해 the Antarctic Ocean ; [지리학적] the Antarctic Sea 자(磁)— the South Magnetic Pole

남극 대륙 南極大陸 the Antarctic Continent ; Antarctica

남극점 南極點 ⇨ 남극

남근 男根 the penis 《*pl.* -nes》; the virile member ; a phallus 《*pl.* -li》; a priapus 《*pl.* -pi, -es》; membrum virile 《L. =male member》
— 숭배 phallicism ; phallic worship

†**남기다** ① [뒤에] leave ; leave behind ; [유산을] bequeath ; [안 쓰고] reserve ; save ; spare ¶ 발자국을 남기다 leave one's footprints // 나쁜 인상을 남기다 leave a bad impression behind〔on〕// 그는 종이를 한 장도 남기지 않고 다 써버렸다 He used up all the paper down to the last sheet. // 쪽지를 남기다 leave a note for 《a person》// 재산을 남기다 leave a fortune 《to a person》; bequeath 《a person》 a fortune // 일을 (다하지 않고) 남기다 leave one's work halfdone〔unfinished〕// 이름을 후세에 남기다 leave〔hand down〕 one's name to posterity // 빚을 남기고 죽다 leave a debt behind 《one》// 처자를 남기고 죽다 leave a wife and children behind ; die leaving one's wife and children // 한푼도 남기지 않고 다 써 버리다 spend all one's money // 나 혼자 남겨 놓고 모두 놀러 가버렸다 They went out to play leaving me all alone. // 내 것 좀 남겨 놔라 Spare some for me. // 뒤에 쓰도록 절반은 남겨 두어라 Leave half for future use. // 술을 한 방울도 남기지 않고 마셔 버렸다 He drank every drop of wine. // 그는 많은 재산을 남기고 죽었다 He died worth a million. // 그 사람 전화 번호는 남겼습니까 Did he leave a phone number ?
② [이를 보다] make〔realize, secure, obtain〕 a profit ; gain ¶ 많이 남기다 make a large profit // 50,000원을 남기다 clear 50,000 *won* // 그것을 500원 남기고 팔았다 I sold it at a profit of 500 *won*. // 별로 못 남기다 realize little〔just a bare〕 profit // 3할을 남기다 clear〔net〕 thirty percent

***남김없이** all (together) ; wholly ; entirely ; without exception ¶ 한 사람 남김없이 to the last man ; to a man // 남김없이 먹다 eat up // 남김없이 돈을 쓰다 spend all one's money ; spend one's money to the last penny // 남김없이 털어놓다 make a complete〔full〕 confession of 《a fact》; make a clean breast of

남날개 an ammunition pouch ; a cartridge box ; a cartridge belt (띠)

남남동 南南東 the south-southeast 《SSE》

남남북녀 南男北女 In the South it is the men who are handsome and in the North it is the women (who are beautiful).

남남서 南南西 the south-southwest 《SSW》

***남녀 男女** man and woman ; male and female ; persons of different sexes ; both sexes ¶ 남녀를 막론하고 regardless of sex // 남녀 양성의 of both sexes ; bisexual // 남녀간에 between male and female // 젊은 남녀 Jack and Gill〔Jill〕; crew-cuts and ponytails 《속》// 남녀 회원 members of either sex // (대학의) 남녀 공동 기숙사 coed dorm 《미》
— 관계 sexual relations ; the relation

of the sexes — **동등권** equal rights for both sexes ; the equality of the sexes (in law) — **동등권 주의** feminism — **동등권 주의자** a feminist — **양성 구유(兩性具有)** hermaphroditism ; androgyny — **양성 구유자** a hermaphrodite ; an androgyne — **평등(平等)** the equality of the sexes

남녀 칠세 부동석 관용 A boy and a girl should not sit together after they have reached the age of seven (according to Confucian idea).

남녀 공학 男女共學 coeducation ¶ 남녀 공학의 coeducational // 남녀 공학 대학의 여학생 a co-ed 《미·구》 // 남녀 공학의 교육을 실시하다[받다] coeducate
— **제도** the coeducational method[system] ; coeducationalism — **학교** a coeducational[co-ed 《미·구》, mixed 《영》] school ; a school for both sexes

남녀 노소 男女老少 people of all ages and both sexes ; people, young and old, men and women ¶ 남녀 노소를 막론하고 without distinction of age or sex ; people, young and old, men and women all alike

남녀 동등 男女同等 the equality of the sexes

남녀 유별 男女有別 distinction between the sexes

남녀 추니 男女— a hermaphrodite ; an androgyne

남녀 평등 男女平等 the equality of the sexes

남녘 南— the south ; the south side ; the southern districts

†**남다** ① remain ; be left over[behind] ; stay ; survive (살아남다) ¶ 남은 것 remnants ; leftovers ; remainders ; leavings // 남은 돈 the money left (over) // 남은 일 the remainder of work // 돈이 남아 있느냐 Is there any money left? // 얼마간 남아 있다 There is some money left. // 하나가 남는다 There is one too many. // 바구니 속에 샌드위치가 남아 있다 There are still some sandwiches left over in the basket. // 우유가 남아 있거든 고양이에게 주어라 If there is any milk left (over), give it to the cat. // 지갑 속에 아무 것도 남아 있지 않다 There is nothing left in his purse. // 불이 나고 나서 그의 집에는 남은 것이라고는 없다 After the fire, very little remained of his house. // 10에서 4를 빼면 6이 남는다 Taking 4 from 10 leaves 6. // 죽은 뒤에 빚이 남았다 He has left a debt. // 마마는 자국이 남는다 The smallpox leaves marks behind. // 할 일이 아직 남아 있다 I have got something more to do. // 이 회사는 사람이 남아 돌아간다 This company is overstaffed. // 그 문제에 관해서는 아직도 쓸 것이 남아 있다 So much remains to be written on that subject. // 파티가 끝난 다음 남아서 뒤치다꺼리를 도와주겠는가 Will you remain after the party and help (to) clean up? // 교사는 소년에게 방과후에 남아서 50자의 작문을 지으라고 일렀다 The teacher ordered the boy to stay in after school and write a composition of fifty words. // 이 두 팀이 결승까지 남았다 These two teams were left[remained] after the semifinals. / These two teams survived to the finals. // 그 사건은 오래도록 우리의 기억에 남을 것이다 Perhaps the event will linger long in our memory. // 그의 이름은 길이 남을 것이다 His name will be immortal[will live forever]. // 이 남은 음식 좀 싸 주세요 Can I have a doggy [doggie] bag? / Give me a doggy bag, please. // 결혼식까지 날이 얼마 남지 않았지 There aren't many days left till the wedding, are there? // 우리집 개는 먹다 남은 밥은 쳐다보려고도 하지 않는다 Our dog won't even look at leftovers.
② [이가 남다] [사람이 주어] make a profit ; [사물이 주어] (be) profitable ; lucrative ¶ (이가) 남지 않는 unprofitable // 크게 남는 장사 a profitable[paying] business ; a going concern // 그것을 팔아서 5000원이 남았다 I made a profit of 5000 *won* from it. // 이 물건은 몇 할 남습니까 How much percent do you make on this article? // 그것은 만 원 이하로 팔아서는 남는 것이 없다 It wouldn't pay to sell it for less than 10,000 *won*. // 남는 장사 a profitable business // 남지 않는 장사 an unprofitable business

***남다르다** (be) peculiar ; be different from others ; be unlike other people ¶ 남다른 사람 an eccentric (man) ; an oddity ; a character ; a queer[an odd] fish 《구》 ; a queer bird 《속》 // 그는 어딘지 남다른 데가 있다 He has something out of the common.

남단 南端 the southern extremity[end, tip, rim]

남달리 in a different way than other ; out of the common ; uncommonly ; unusually ; extraordinarily ; especially ; exceptionally ¶ 남달리 노력하다 work harder than others ; make a redoubled effort // 남달리 키가 크다 be outstandingly[exceptionally] tall // 그녀는 남달리 추위를 탄다 She is unusually sensitive to the cold.

남대문 南大門 the South Gate 《of *Seoul*》

남독 濫讀 ⇨ 난독(亂讀)

***남동 南東** southeast

***남루 襤褸** ① [누더기] rags ; shreds ; scraps
② [옷 따위가 너절함] being tattered ; being shabby ; being threadbare ; being

ragged ; being in rags ¶ 남루한 옷을 입고 있다 be (clad)〔go〕 in rags (and tatters) // 옷차림이 남루한 사람 a person in rags〔threadbare clothes〕; a ragged 〔tattered〕 man

남동풍 南東風 a southeaster ; a southeasterly wind

남만 南蠻 southern barbarians

남만북적 南蠻北狄 southern and northern barbarians

*__남매 男妹__ brother and sister ¶ 3남매 a brother and sister threesome // 그는 7남매를 두었다 He has a son-and-daughter sevensome.

남모르다 (be) unknown to others ; unseen ; hidden ; secret ; inward ¶ 남모르는 슬픔 a hidden sorrow // 남모르는 고생 inward trouble ; hardships unknown to others // 그녀에게는 남모르는 걱정이 있었다 She had inner troubles. /She had secret troubles.

남몰래 secretly ; inwardly

남미 南美 ⇨ 남아메리카

남바위 a hood hemmed with fur, in olden days worn by woman against the winter cold

남반구 南半球 the Southern Hemisphere

남발 濫發 overissue ; excessive issue **—하다** overissue ; issue recklessly ¶ 지폐의 남발 an overissue of (bank) notes

남방 南方 the south ; the southward ; the direction of the south ¶ 남방의 southern ; southerly // 남방으로 가다 go south

—인 a southerner **— 지역** the southern regions

남배우 男俳優 an actor

남벌 濫伐 reckless deforestation ; indiscriminate felling 《of trees》 **—하다** deforest〔cut down trees〕 recklessly ; fell trees indiscriminately

남복 男服 ① [남자의 옷] men's clothes 〔wear〕; male attire

② [여자가 남자 옷을 입음] being dressed like a man ; being in men's clothes

남부 南部 the southern part〔district, portion〕; the south (미국의) ¶ 한반도의 남부 the southern part of the Korean Peninsula

남부끄럽다 (be) ashamed ; disgraceful ; shameful ; scandalous ; disreputable ¶ 남부끄러운 짓 a disgraceful〔shameful〕 act // 남부끄럽지 않은 살림 a decent living // 남부끄럽지 않다 have nothing to be ashamed 《of》; be up to the mark ; be worth〔decent, honorable〕 // 그런 짓을 하고도 남부끄럽지 않으냐 Aren't you ashamed of what you have done ?

남부럽다 be envious of others

남부럽잖다 well-to-do ; well-off ; wealthy ; rich ¶ 남부럽잖게 살다 be well〔comfortably〕 off ; be well-to-do ; live in plenty〔abundance〕; have no need to envy others

남부여대 男負女戴 man loaded on the back and woman on the head **—하다** set out on a wandering〔vagabond〕 life ; become poor wanderers〔refugees〕

남북 南北 north and south ¶ 남북으로 가로놓이다〔남북에 걸쳐 있다〕 lie from south to north ; extend north and south // 거리는 남북으로 통해 있다 The street runs north and south.

— 공동 성명 the joint communique of 4 July 1972 between the South and the North of Korea **— 교류** exchange between south and north Korea **— 대화** the South-North dialogue **— 문제** [부국·빈국간의] North-South problems ; problems between the industrialized North and the impoverished South ; [한국의] Korean problems **— 분단** the division of Korea into north and south **— 아메리카** North and South America **— 적십자 회담** the South-North Red Cross conference 〔talks, meeting〕 **— 전쟁** [미국사] the Civil War **— 조절 위원회** the South-North Coordinating Committee 《SNCC》 **— 통일** the reunification of North and South (Korea) **— 협상** the South-North negotiations

남북조 시대 南北朝時代 [중국 역사] the Period of North and South Dynasties

남북한 南北韓 south and north Korea ; the South and the North of Korea ; *Seoul* and *Pyongyong*

— 교류 exchange between south and north Korea

남비 濫費 extravagance ⇨ 낭비(浪費)

남빙양 南氷洋 the Antarctic Ocean Sea

남빛 藍— indigo ; deep blue

남사당 男寺黨 a wayfaring male entertainer ; a strolling actor ; actors on the road

남사당패 男寺黨牌 a troupe of players

남산골 딸깍발이 南山— a penniless scholar

남산골 샌님 南山— a penniless scholar (남산골 딸깍발이)

남산골 샌님이 망하여도 걸음 보수는 남는다 속담 It is hard to make an old mare leave flinging.

남상 男相 a woman with manly〔masculine〕 features ; an unwomanly face ¶ 남상(을) 지르다 have a mannish face

남상 濫觴 the origin ; the beginning ; the rise ; the genesis ; the source ¶ 연극의 남상 the origin〔beginning〕 of the drama

남상거리다 stretch〔crane〕 one's neck avidly (to see a thing) ⇨ 넘성거리다

남새 vegetables ; greens

남새밭 a vegetable garden〔patch〕
남색 男色 sodomy ; pederasty ; buggery
—자 sodomite ; a pederast
남색 藍色 indigo ; deep〔dark〕 blue ¶ 짙은 남색(의) mazarine // 남색물을 들이다 dye 《a cloth》 deep blue
‡**남생이** 〖동물〗 a Chinese pond turtle ; a Korean terrapin ; a spotted turtle〔terrapin, tortoise〕
***남서 南西** the southwest ¶ 남서의 southwest ; southwestern // 남서로 가다 go southwest〔southwestward〕
남서풍 南西風 a southwestern wind
남선북마 南船北馬 constant traveling ; restless wandering ; being on the move
***남성¹ 男性** the male (sex) ; manhood ; the sterner〔stronger, rough〕 sex ¶ 남성의 male ; of the male sex
— 용 영화 a stag movie **— 중심 사회** an androcentric society **—화(化)** virilism
남성² 男性 〖문법〗 the masculine gender
남성 男聲 a male voice
— 4중창 a male quartet **— 성가대** a male-voice choir **— 중음(中音)** baritone **— 중음 가수** a baritone (singer) **— 합창** a male chorus **— 합창곡** a chorus for male voices
남성미 男性美 masculine〔manly〕 beauty
남성적 男性的 masculine ; manly ; virile ¶ 남성적인 여자 a girl of masculine spirit // 남성적인 오락 a manly sport // 남성적인 데가 없다 lack masculiness〔masculinity〕 // 남성적인 문체 a masculine style
남성지다 男性— [여자가] (be) mannish ¶ 목소리가 남성지다 have a mannish voice
남성 호르몬 male hormone ; testosterone
남수 男囚 a male prisoner〔convict〕
남십자성 南十字星 〖천문〗 the Southern Cross ; the Cross ; Crux
남아 男兒 ① [남자] a man ¶ 남아답게 like a man ; in a manly manner // 남아 일언 중천금 A man's word is as good as a bond. ② [사내아이] a boy ; a son
남아돌다 (물건이) be in excess ; be superabundant〔superfluous〕 ; (사람이) have too many〔much〕 ; have more than enough ¶ 남아도는 surplus ; excessive ; superfluous ; superabundant // 사람이 남아도는 회사 an overstaffed firm // 그는 돈이 남아돌 만큼 많다 He has more money than he can spend. / He has money enough and to spare.
남아메리카 南— South America
남아프리카 南— South Africa ¶ 남아프리카 태생의 백인 an African(d)er
— 공화국 the Republic of South Africa **— 연방** the Union of South Africa **— 전쟁** the Boer War (1899～1902)
남안 南岸 the southern coast
남양 南洋 the South Seas
— 군도 the South Sea Islands ; Oceania ; Polynesia **— 무역** the South Sea trade
남여 藍輿 an open palanquin〔sedan chair〕
‡**남용 濫用** misuse ; abuse ; improper〔unlawful〕 use ; misappropriation **—하다** misuse ; abuse ; use improperly〔unlawfully〕 ; use to excess ; misappropriate ¶ 공금을 남용하다 misappropriate public money〔fund〕 // 권력을 남용하다 abuse〔make an improper use of〕 one's power // 권력의 남용 an abuse of power ; an abusive exercise of power // 직권 남용 misfeasance // 직권을 남용하다 abuse one's authority
직권 —죄 〖법〗 oppression
남우 男優 an actor
남우세 disgrace ; ignominy **—하다** bring disgrace upon oneself ; disgrace〔humiliate〕 oneself ; become a laughingstock ; be the butt of ridicule ¶ 남우세스럽다 be disreputable ; be shameful ; be scandalous ; be indecent
남위 南緯 the south latitude〔parallel〕 ; ¶ 남위 15도 15 degrees south latitude // 남위 15도 30분에 in lat. 15° 30′ S 〔latitude fifteen degrees thirty minutes south〕
—선 a line of south latitude
남유럽 南— Southern Europe
-남은 ¶ 여남은 ten odd // 스무남은 twenty odd
남의 눈 notice ; observation ; [주의] attention ¶ 남의 눈을 끄는 attractive ; attracting ; striking // 남의 눈을 기이는 사랑 secret love // 남의 눈에 띄지 않는 곳 a secret〔private〕 place // 남의 눈을 꺼리다 avoid〔shun〕 observation
남의달 the month following the estimated month of childbirth ¶ 남의달 잡다 be a month late in childbirth
남의세 being a laughingstock ⇨ 남우세
남의살같다 (be) benumbed ; senseless
남의집 살다 work〔be employed〕 as a domestic servant of a household
남의집살이 domestic service ; living out 《as a maid》 《미》 ; working as a domestic servant ¶ 남의집살이를 하다 be in domestic service
†**남자 男子** a man 《*pl.* men》 ; a male (sex) ; a gentleman ¶ 남자의 male ; masculine // 남자 중의 남자 a man among men // 남자 옷 man's wear // 남자용 men's ; gentlemen's ; for gentlemen's use // 나도 남자다 I am a man of honor. // 너도 남자라면 그런 짓은 못하겠지 You should be man enough not to do a thing like that. // 남자용 화장실 the men's room〔toilet〕 // 남자 친구 a man〔gentleman〕 friend ; a boy friend ; a male〔masculine〕 companion // 남자 대

남자로 솔직히 터놓고 man-to-man // 그렇게 해주면 나는 남자로서의 체면이 선다 I can save face if you will do that for me. // 이상적인 남자를 찾기란 쉬운 일이 아니다 It's not easy to find a Price Charming. // 아직 적당한 남자를 만나지 못했어요 I haven't met Mr. Right yet.

‡**남자답다 男子—** manly ; manful ; masculine ; virile ¶ 남자답지 않은 unmanly ; unmanlike ; effeminate // 남자답게 manfully ; in a manly manner ; like a man ; gamely // 남자답게 행동하다 behave〔act〕 like a man ; play the man ; be a man // 남자다움 manhood ; manliness

***남작 男爵** a baron (사람) ; baronage (작위) ¶ A 남작 Baron A 《외국인에게》; Lord A 《영국인에게》 // 남작이 되다 be created baron
— **부인** a baroness

남작 濫作 writing to excess ; overproduction ; excessive production ; overwriting **—하다** overproduce ; produce excessively ; write many books〔produce many works〕 recklessly ; overwrite ¶ 그녀는 남작으로 소설의 질을 떨어뜨렸다 She churned out novels too rapidly〔She wrote too many novels〕 to maintain high quality.

남장 男裝 male attire〔disguise〕 **—하다** disguise oneself as a man ; wear men's clothes ; dress oneself in male attire ; be dressed like a man ¶ 남장한 여인 a woman (dressed) in male attire ; a girl masquerading as a man // 남장 미인 a fair woman (dressed) in male attire ; a beautiful girl masquerading as a man

남정 男丁 a man above the age of fifteen ; an adult ; a grown-up

남정네 男丁— menfolk (남자들) ; the husbands (남의 남편들)

남정석 藍晶石 〖광물〗 cyanite

남제 濫製 reckless〔excessive〕 manufacture ; overproduction **—하다** manufacture〔produce, turn out〕 excessively ; overproduce

남조 濫造 excessive production ; overproduction **—하다** produce in〔to〕 excess ; overproduce ; manufacture carelessly ¶ 박사의 남조 reckless conferment of the doctor's degree
조제품 — the overproduction of inferior goods

남존여비 男尊女卑 predominance of men over women ; treatment of women as inferior to men ; subjection of women ¶ 남존여비의 사회 a male-dominated society // 그 지역에는 남존여비의 사상이 아직도 일반화되어 있다 In that district the idea that men are superior to women〔women are inferior to men〕 is still prevalent.

남종 男— a male slave

남종화 南宗畫 a Chinese painting of the Southern School

남중 南中 〖천문〗 southing ; culmination **—하다** south ; cross the meridian

남중일색 南中一色 an uncommonly handsome man ; an Adonis

남지나해 南支那海 the South China Sea

남진 南進 southward advance〔movement, expansion〕 **—하다** go〔advance〕 south

‡**남짓** above ; over ; more than ; upward of ; odd ¶ 4년 남짓 over four years ; more than four years ; four years and more ; four years and upward ; upward of four years // 천원 남짓 1,000 odd *won* ; something like 1,000 *won*

남짓하다 be slightly〔a little, a bit〕 over〔above〕 ; be upward of ¶ 나이가 쉰 남짓하다 be a little over fifty // 만 원 남짓한 돈을 갖고 있다 I have a little more than 10,000 *won*. // 10마일 남짓한 거리다 It is a little over ten miles. // 여기 온 지 5년 남짓하다 It is upward of five years〔five years and more〕 since I came here.

†**남쪽 南—** the south ¶ 남쪽의 south ; southern ; southerly // 남쪽으로 south ; southward // 서울의 남쪽 10마일 지점의 섬 an island ten miles south of *Seoul*

남창 男娼 a male prostitute ; a professional catamite

남창 男唱 ① [여자가 남자 목소리로 부르는 노래] a song sung by a woman in male voice ② [남자가 부르는 노래] a man's song

남창 南窓 a window facing the south

남천[1] **南天** the southern sky

남천[2] **南天** 〖식물〗 a nandin (a)

남첩 男妾 a paramour ; a gigolo

남청 藍靑 indigo blue

남치마 藍— a deep-blue skirt

남침 南侵 a southward invasion ; an invasion of the south **—하다** invade the south ¶ 북한의 남침 a North Korean invasion of the South // 북한의 남침 야욕 a North Korean plot to invade the South ; the North Korean scheme of war against the Republic of Korea

남태평양 南太平洋 the South Pacific

남파 南派 sending〔dispatching〕 to the south **—하다** send〔dispatch〕 《an espionage〔armed〕 agent》 to the south
— **간첩** a spy〔secret agent〕 sent (by the north) into the south

†**남편 男便** a husband ; a hub (by) ; my man 《속》; one's worse half (익살로) ; 〖법〗 a baron ¶ 남편다운 husbandlike // 남편으로 적합한 husbandly // 남편의 권리 marital rights // 남편 있는 몸 a married woman // 남편 없는 single ; unmarried //

사랑하는 남편 the lord of one's bosom //남편을 섬기다 be obedient〔devoted, attentive, faithful〕 to one's husband // 남편을 깔고 뭉개다 wear the pants〔the breeches, the trousers〕//남편을 얻다 get a husband ; get married//남편을 잃다 become a widow ; be widowed//훌륭한 남편이 훌륭한 아내를 만든다 A good husband makes a good wife.

남편은 두레박, 아내는 항아리 속담 Husband is bucket, wife is pitcher. /Man makes house, woman makes home.

남포¹ [다이너마이트] dynamite

남포² ⇨ 남포등

남포등 a lamp ; an oil〔a petroleum, a kerosene〕 lamp

남포질 dynamiting ; shattering〔destroying, blasting, blowing up〕 with dynamite

남폿불 lamplight ; a lamp

남풍 南風 the south〔a southerly〕 wind ; a wind from the south ; the Auster

남하 南下 southward advance〔movement〕 **—하다** go〔come〕 south ; advance southwards ¶ 자유를 찾아 남하하다 come to the south seeking for freedom

남학생 男學生 a schoolboy ; a boy student

남한 南韓 South Korea

남항 南航 sailing south ; southing

남해 南海 the southern sea ; the straits of Korea (현해탄)

남행 南行 going south ; southing **—하다** go (down to the) south

— 열차 a south-bound train

남향 南向 a southern exposure ; facing (the) south

남향집 南向— a house facing〔looking towards〕 (the) south ; a house open to the south ; a house with a southern exposure

남향판 南向— a site facing south ; a place open to the south ; a place of southern exposure

남회귀선 南回歸線 the Tropic of Capricorn

남획 濫獲 overfishing ; overhunting ; reckless〔excessive, indiscriminate〕 fishing〔hunting〕 **—하다** overfish ; overhunt ; fish〔hunt〕 recklessly ¶ 그 코뿔소는 남획으로 멸종의 위기에 처해 있다 That species of rhinoceros is endangered because of overhunting. // 고래를 남획하다 catch whales in excessive numbers

납 鑞 lead ; plumbum ; solder ¶ 납의 leaden

—접착제 (soldering) flux **—정련소** a lead melting works **—판** a lead plate **—화합물** a lead compound

납 蠟 wax ; beeswax ; white〔refined〕 wax ¶ 납으로 형을 뜨다 make a wax impression ⦅of⦆

—인형 a wax doll〔figure〕

납가새 〖식물〗 a caltrop ; a caltrap ; a water chestnut ; Tribulus terrestris (학명)

납거미 〖곤충〗 a spider ; Uroctea compactillis (학명)

납골 納骨 laying ⦅a person's⦆ ashes to rest

납골당 納骨堂 a charnel house ; [교회·묘지의 지하 납골소] a crypt ; a vault

납공 納貢 paying〔offering〕 a tribute〔tax, land tax〕 **—하다** pay in tribute〔tax, land tax〕

납금 納金 [지불] payment of money ; [지불한 돈] money paid **—하다** pay ⦅money⦆

납기 納期 the time〔period〕 for payment (금전의) ; the time limit〔appointed date〕 for delivery (물품의) ; the date of tax payment (세금의) ¶ 수업료는 납기내에 납입할 것 School fees should be paid by the due date. //소득세의 납기 the deadline for paying one's income tax

납길 納吉 (the bridegroom's) notifying the bride of the date set for the wedding

납대대하다 (be) pleasantly flattish ¶ 납대대한 얼굴 a nice flat face

납덩이 a slug〔lump〕 of lead ; a lead ingot

납덩이 같다 관용 [얼굴빛이] be pale ; be (as) pale〔white〕 as a sheet ; as dull as lead ; [몸이] be〔feel〕 as heavy as lead

납도리 a square beam

†납득 納得 understanding **—하다** understand ; persuade oneself ; listen to reason ; be convinced of ¶ 납득하기 어려운 unconvincing ⦅argument⦆ ; hard to understand//납득시키다 win ⦅a person⦆ to consent ; persuade ⦅a person into doing⦆ ; convince ⦅a person⦆ of ; reason ⦅a person⦆ into compliance ; make ⦅a person⦆ listen to reason//납득이 가게 설명하다 explain to ⦅a person's⦆ satisfaction//나는 아직도 납득이 가지 않는다 Still I am not open to conviction. //그 점은 나도 잘 납득하고 있다 I am fully convinced of it. //그의 잘못을 납득시킬 수가 없었다 I could not convince him of his mistake. //내 말을 충분히 납득시킬 수가 없었다 I could not make myself fully understood. //그들에게 그것을 수락할 필요성을 납득시키기는 어려웠다 It was hard to sell them on the necessity for accepting it. //그런 모험을 하지 말도록 그를 납득시켰다 I have dissuaded him from running such a risk. //그것에 대해 네가 나를 납득시켰다

You talked me into it./You sold me on it. //납득하기가 너무 힘든 일이군 I find that pretty hard to swallow. //그 결말은 납득할 수 없다 I just don't buy the ending. //아무래도 그의 설명에는 납득이 가지 않는 데가 있다 Something about his explanation just doesn't sit right with me.

납땜 **鑞—** soldering **—하다** solder

납땜인두 **鑞—** a soldering iron〔copper〕

납량 **納涼** enjoying the cool《of the evening》; cooling oneself in the summer breeze ; cooling and refreshing oneself

납본 **納本** presentation of a specimen copy《to the authorities》; [책] a presentation copy ; a specimen copy for censorship **—하다** present a specimen copy《to the authorities》

납부 **納付** payment (금전) ; delivery (물품) **—하다** pay《taxes》; deliver《goods》; supply《goods》

— 기한 the time limit of payment〔delivery〕 **—서** a statement of payment〔delivery〕 **—액** the amount of payment **— 의무자** an obligor for payment ; a contributor (건강 보험의) **—자(者)** a payer **분할 —** divided payments ; payment on an installment basis

납부금 **納付金** money due

납북 **拉北** kidnap(p)ing〔hijacking, abduction〕 to the north ¶ 납북되다 be kidnap(p)ed to the north

— 어선〔어부, 인사〕 a fishing boat〔a fisherman, a person〕 kidnap(p)ed to north Korea

납빛 gray ¶ 납빛의 gray ; livid //그의 얼굴은 노여움으로 납빛이 되었다 His face turned livid with anger.

납석 **臘石**〖광물〗agalmatolite ; pencil stone

***납세** **納稅** payment of taxes ; tax payment ¶ 납세의 의무 a legal obligation to pay one's taxes ; liability to taxation ; liability to pay taxes //국민은 납세의 의무를 진다 The people shall be liable to taxation.

— 고지서 tax papers ; a notification for tax payment ; a tax notice **— 관리인** a tax payment administrator ; a tax manager **— 기일** the tax day ; the tax due date ; the time limit for paying taxes **— 대장** a tax book〔list, roll〕 **— 연체 이자** interest on a delinquent tax **— 자격** the qualifications of a taxpayer ; tax payment requirements **— 적립금** tax reserves **— 증지** a tax payment stamp **—지(地)** the place of tax payment **—필〔미필〕** Tax〔Duty (물품세)〕 paid〔unpaid, in arrears〕

납세 신고 **納稅申告** income tax returns ¶ 납세 신고를 하다 declare one's (annual) earnings for income tax ; make one's income tax returns

— 용지 a tax form

납세액 **納稅額** the amount of one's taxes

납세자 **納稅者** a tax payer ; a ratepayer (지방세의)《영》

— 이의 신청권 the rights of a tax payer to protest the assessment **신고 —** a self-assessed taxpayer

납세 저축 **納稅貯蓄** savings in preparation for tax payment ; tax savings

— 조합 a citizens' voluntary society for tax savings

납세필증 **納稅畢證** a certificate of tax〔duty〕 payment

납시다 (the king) deign to come out ; appear

납신거리다 talk glibly and flippantly ; chatter ¶ 납신납신 glibly ; flippantly

납월 **臘月** December of the lunar calendar ⇨ 섣달

납입금 **納入金** [지불된] money paid ; [지불해야 할] money due

납작 ① [입을 재빨리 벌렸다가 다무는 모양] with one's mouth wide open ¶ 납작 받아먹다 seize upon〔snatch up, gobble up〕 with one's mouth wide open

② [몸을 바닥에 대며 낮게 엎드리는 모양] flat ; low ¶ 납작 엎드리다 lie down flat《on the found, on one's belly》; fall prostrate

납작코 a flat nose ; a flat-nosed person

***납작하다** flat ; low ; thin ¶ 납작하게 flatly ; level //납작한 얼굴의 flat-faced //납작한 가슴 a flat chest //납작하게 만들다 [형태를] make flat〔low thin〕; [굴복시키다] snow ; put down ; beat《a person》hollow ; bring《a person》to《his》knees //납작해지다 [형태가] be flattened ; become flat ; be crushed flat ; [끽소리 못하다] be shut up ; be nonplus(s)ed ; be dumbfounded ; be snubbed //코를 납작하게 하다 knock〔beat〕《a person》into a cocked hat //나는 그의 코를 납작하게 만들었다 I cut him down to size./I put him in his place.

납중독 **—中毒** lead poisoning

납지 **蠟紙** wax paper

납지 **鑞紙** silver paper ; tin foil (포장용) ; lead foil

납질 **蠟質** waxy substance ¶ 납질의 waxen ; waxy //납질 변성〖의학〗waxy degeneration

납채 **納采** wedding presents sent from the bridegroom's house to the bride's house **—하다** send wedding presents to the bride's house

납촉 **蠟燭** a beeswax candle

***납치** **拉致** [사람의] kidnapping ; abduction ; [물건의] seize by force ; hijack

—하다 kidnap ; abduct ; hijack ¶ 이북으로 납치되다 be kidnapped to North Korea // 런던행 비행기가 납치되었다 A plane (bound) for London was hijacked〔skyjacked〕.

납폐 納幣 sending blue and red silks to the bride's house ; wedding presents of silk **—하다** send blue and red silks to the bride's house

납품 納品 delivery of goods ; delivered goods (납품된 물건) **—하다** deliver 《goods》 ; supply 《the government with goods》 ¶ 납품서 statement of delivery // 납품업자 a supplier

납회 納會 ① [그 해에 마지막으로 여는 모임] the last meeting of the year ② [증권 거래소에서] the last〔closing〕 session of the year

***낫** a sickle (작은 낫) ; a scythe (자루가 긴 큰 낫) ¶ 낫으로 벼를 베다 cut rice with a sickle // 낫으로 풀을 베다 mow grass with a sickle ; sickle down weeds ; scythe grass

낫 놓고 기역자도 모른다 속담 be so ignorant as not to know his ABC ; can hardly read or write ; do not know A from B ; be utterly illiterate ; He cannot say B to a battledore.

낫낫하다 (be) tender ; soft ⇨ 나긋나긋하다

***낫다**[1] [서로 견주어] be better 《than》 ; be superior to〔over〕 ; be preferable 《to》 ; surpass ; excel ; exceed ; best ; have the advantage of, gain〔win〕 an advantage over ¶ …보다 조금 나은 정도의 be just a little better than... // 더 나으면 낫지 못하지는 않다 be in no way inferior 《to》 // 건강이 재산보다 낫다 Health is above wealth. // 내 집보다 나은 곳은 없다 There is nothing like home. // 배반하는 것보다는 가난한 것이 더 낫다 I prefer poverty to treachery. // 무어라도 있으면 없는 것보다는 낫다 Something is better than nothing. // 늦더라도 안하느니보다는 낫다 Better late than never. // 그는 나보다 훨씬 살기가 낫다 He is much〔far〕 better off than I (am). // 그는 누구보다도 낫다 He surpasses〔is superior to〕 all. /He is by far the best. // 이런 생활을 할 바엔 차라리 죽는 게 낫다 I would rather〔sooner〕 die than lead such a life. // 그렇게 돈을 쓰려면 차라리 버리는 것이 낫다 You might as well throw away your money as spend it that way. // 둘 다 마찬가지이지만 그래도 이 사람이 좀 낫다 The two are much the same but this man is a bit better. // 이 점에서는 그 보다 나은 사람이 없다 He is second to none in this respect. /In this respect he is unrivaled. // 직접 해보는 것보다 나은 방법은 없다 There is nothing like trying it. // 그 매력에 있어서 알프스보다 나은 산은 없다 The lure of the Alps is unsurpassable.

낫다[2] [병이나 상처 등] get〔become〕 well ; recover from an illness ; be restored to health ; be cured of 《a disease》 ; heal (up) ; be healed ¶ 낫지 않는 a stubborn disease which will yield to no remedy // 감기가 낫다 get over〔rid of〕 one's cold // 저절로 낫다 get well of itself ; heal by itself ; clear up // 병이 나아가다 be getting better ; be on the mend ; be convalescent // 병이 낫지 않다 An illness is bad as ever. /An illness gets no better. // 자네 머리 아픈 게 나았나 Have you thrown off〔got rid of〕 your headache ? // 당신의 슬픔은 세월이 낫게 해 줄 것이다 Time will heal your grief. // 병이 차도가 있을 때 조심해야 한다 You must take good care of yourself when you are convalescing.

낫살 age ; years ¶ 낫살이나 먹은 사람답지 않게 in spite of one's age ; unbecoming for one's age // 낫살이나 먹다 be advanced〔well up〕 in years〔age〕

낫잡다 ① [평가] estimate high ; rate high ¶ 낫잡아 at the outside ; at most // 값을 시세보다 낫잡다 rate the cost higher than the current price // 낫잡아 3 백원밖에 하지 않을 것이다 It won't cost more than 300 *won* at the highest.
② [여유] leave a margin ; give ample measure to ¶ 여비를 낫잡아 계산하다 allow oneself an ample margin for travel expenses

낫질 using〔wielding〕 a scythe〔sickle〕 **—하다** scythe ; use〔wield〕 a scythe〔sickle〕

낫표 Korean quotation marks 《「 」》 ; corner brackets

낭군 郎君 (my) dear husband

낭도 郎徒 an elite youth corps of *Silla* dynasty

†낭독 朗讀 reading aloud ; declamation ; recitation (시를) **—하다** read aloud ; recite ; give a reading 《of》 ; declaim 《verses》 ¶ 각본의 낭독 dramatic reading ; play reading ; script reading // 셰익스피어의 작품을 낭독하다 give a reading of Shakespeare // 영시를 낭독하다 recite an English poem // 연설문을 낭독하다 read a speech (from notes) ; read an address // 자작시의 낭독회를 열다 give a recital〔public reading〕 of one's own poems
—법 elocution **—자** a reader ; a reciter **—회** a public reading **각본 —** dramatic reading

***낭떠러지** a precipice ; a cliff ; a bluff (바닷가의) ¶ 낭떠러지의 소나무 a pinetree hanging over a cliff // 천만 길 낭떠러지에서 굴러 떨어지다 fall over a precipice // 낭떠러지를 기어올라가다 climb (up) a cliff // 낭떠러지에서 아래를 내려다 보다 look over a precipice

낭랑 朗朗 ① [소리가] (be) clear and ringing ; sonorous ; full ; clarion ; silvery ② [빛이] clear and serene ¶ 낭랑한 목소리로 in a rich, resonant voice // 달빛이 낭랑하다 The moon shines brightly〔brilliantly〕.

낭만 浪漫 being romantic

낭만적 浪漫的 romantic ¶ 낭만적인 생애 a romantic〔checkered〕 career // 낭만적인 생각에 빠지다 indulge in romantics

낭만주의 浪漫主義 romanticism ¶ 신낭만주의 neoromanticism

— 문학 Romanticism **—자** a romanticist

낭만파 浪漫派 [유파] the romantic school ; [사람] a romanticist

— 시인 a romantic poet

낭보 朗報 good〔bright, glad, cheering〕 news ; glad tidings

†**낭비 浪費** waste ; extravagance ; squandering ; wasteful expenditure ; dissipation ; prodigality **— 하다** waste ; squander ; use〔spend〕 wastefully ; use to no purpose ; dissipate ; throw away ; be prodigal of ¶ 낭비가 심한 wasteful ; extravagant // 시간〔돈〕의 낭비 a waste of time〔money〕 // 국가 자원의 낭비 the squandering of the nation's resources // 낭비를 줄이다 eliminate waste // 쓸데 없는 것에 돈을 낭비하다 waste one's money on useless things // 정력을 낭비하다 dissipate〔waste〕 one's energy

—자 a waster ; a spendthrift ; a squanderer

낭비벽 浪費癖 spendthrift habits ¶ 낭비벽이 있는 사람 a spendthrift ; an extravagant〔a thriftless〕 person // 낭비벽이 있다 have〔be in〕 the habit of wasting money 《on luxury》

낭상 囊狀 sac-shape ; sac ¶ 낭상의 sac- shaped ; sacciform

—관 a cystic valve **—선(腺)** a saclike〔saccular〕 gland

***낭설 浪說** a false〔wild〕 rumor ; an unfounded〔a groundless〕 report ¶ 악의에 찬 낭설 an ill-willed rumor // 낭설을 믿다 take rumor as it is // 낭설이 퍼지다 a rumor is abroad〔current, circulated〕 // 낭설을 퍼뜨리다 set a false rumor afloat ; circulate a false report〔rumor〕 // …이라는 낭설이 퍼지고 있다 There is a rumor afloat 《that》 ; Rumor has it 《that》 ; It is noised abroad 《that》 // 그것은 순전한 낭설이다 That is a pure fabrication.

낭성 狼星 〖천문〗 Sirius ; the Dog Star

낭성대 a long bamboo stick used as a tool in a home

낭송 朗誦 recitation ; reading **— 하다** recite ; give a recitation ; read aloud ; declaim ¶ 시를 낭송하다 recite a poem // 각본 낭송 reading a play ; [배우의] rehearsal

낭음 朗吟 recitation ; recital **— 하다** recite 《a poem》 ; sing

낭인 浪人 a man out of employment〔office〕 ; a jobless man ¶ 낭인이 되다 be out of office〔work〕 ; lose one's position

낭자 [머리] a chignon ; a coiffure

낭자 娘子 a maiden ; a virgin ; a girl ; a woman

낭자 狼藉 [물건 따위가] disorder ; confusion **— 하다** be in disorder〔confusion〕 ; be〔lie〕 scattered about ; lie in (wild) disorder ; be littered〔strewn〕 《with》 ¶ 살인 현장에는 유혈이 낭자했다 The scene of murder was covered with blood all over.

낭자군 娘子軍 Amazons ; Amazonian troops

낭종 囊腫 〖의학〗 an encysted tumor

낭중 囊中 one's pocket ; one's purse ¶ 낭중 무일푼이다 be penniless ; be stone-broke ; have not a penny in one's purse // 낭중 무일푼이 되다 become〔go〕 penniless ; go broke 《미·속》

낭중물 囊中物 what is in one's pocket ; things one has with him

낭중지추 囊中之錐 Talent in a man, like a gimlet in a bag, will show itself.

낭창낭창 pliant ; pliable ; flexible ; limber ; supple ¶ 낭창낭창한 대나무 pliant bamboo // 낭창낭창한 나뭇가지 a flexible〔pliable〕 twig〔switch〕

낭충 囊蟲 [촌충의 유충] a bladder worm ; a metacercoid

낭패 狼狽 failure ; frustration ; defeat ; miscarriage ; a blunder ; a fiasco ; a trouble ; straits ; a fix ¶ 머리털이 자꾸 빠져서 낭패다 I am troubled with falling hair. // 입장이 묘하게 되어서 낭패다 I am in an awkward position about it. // 이것 정말 낭팬데 What a most awkward way this is ! /What shall I do (in this case) ? /Good〔Gracious, Great〕 Heavens !

낭하 廊下 ① [복도] a corridor ; passage (way) 《주로 영》 ; [빌딩의] a hall ; [넓은] a gallery ; a hallway 《미》 ; [극장 따위의] a lobby ② [행랑] the servants' quarters

†**낮** ① [해가 떠 있는 동안] day ; daytime ; daylight ¶ 10월이 되면 낮의 길이가 확실히 짧아진다 The days sure get short when it gets to be October. ② [한낮] noon ; noonday ; noontime ; high noon ; midday ¶ 낮 흥행 a matinee // 낮에 in the daytime ; during the daytime ; by day // 대낮에 in broad〔full,

open〕 daylight ; in the daytime // 밤낮 없이 day and night ; night and day ; (a)round the clock // 밤낮을 가리지 않고 일하다 work night and day ; work double tides // 그는 낮에 자고 밤에 일한다 He sleeps by day and works by night. // 눈을 뜨니 한낮이었다 It was full day〔daylight〕 when I awake. // 달이 낮같이 밝다 The moon is as bright as day. // 낮에는 따뜻하지만 밤에는 쌀쌀해진다 It's warm enough during the day, but it gets chilly at night.

낮말은 새가 듣고 밤말은 쥐가 듣는다 속담 Walls〔Pitchers〕 have ears. /Fields have eyes, and woods have ears.

낮거리 sexual intercourse performed in the (broad) daytime **—하다** have sexual intercourse in the daytime

낮결 the first half of the afternoon

†낮다 ① [높이] (be) low ¶ 낮은 언덕 a low hill // 낮은 지면 a low tract of land 〔ground〕
② [지위나 수준 따위가] (be) low ; humble ; mean ¶ 지위가 낮다 be low in position ; be of low standing // 지적 수준이 낮은 사람 a man on a low intellectual level // 생활 수준이 낮다 have a low standard of living
③ [질이 좋지 못하다] (be) low ; poor ¶ 질이 낮은 제품 a product of bad quality
④ [소리나 강도 따위가] (be) low ¶ 낮은 목소리 a low voice // 낮은 목소리로 in whisper ; in a low voice ; in an undertone
⑤ [온도·습도·위도 따위가] (be) low ¶ 체온이 낮다 have a low temperature

낮도깨비 ① [낮에 장난을 한다는 도깨비] a goblin〔ghost〕 haunting in broad daylight
② [염치도 체면도 없이 난잡한 짓을 함부로 하는 사람] a shameless bastard

낮도둑 ① [낮에 훔치는 도둑] a sneak thief ; a noonday thief ② [체면을 가리지 않고 제 욕심만 채우는 사람] a shark ; a shameless hog ; a greedy 〔grasping〕 person

낮은말 a vulgar word ; a vulgarism

낮은음자리표 一音一標 〖음악〗 bass〔F〕 clef

낮일 day work

낮잠 a (midday) nap ; a noon's nap ; a siesta ; forty winks ; a snooze 《속》 ¶ 낮잠을 자다 take〔have〕 a nap〔siesta〕 // 드러누워 낮잠 자다 lie down for a nap

낮잡다 estimate low ; underestimate ; rate low ; underrate ; appraise〔evaluate〕 low ; think little of ; make light of ; treat lightly ; disparage ; hold cheap ¶ 낮잡아서 at a conservative〔safe, moderate〕 estimate ; at the lowest estimates // 집값을 낮잡다 rate the price of a house low // 낮잡아 평가하다 underestimate ; make a conservative estimate

낮참 [점심] a midday meal ; lunch ; [쉬는 시간] a recess after lunch ; a noon recess ; a midday break

낮추 low

†낮추다 ① [낮게 하다] lower ; make low ; let〔bring〕 down ; drop ¶ 목소리를 낮추다 lower〔bring down, slash, subdue〕 one's voice // 생활 수준을 낮추다 lower the standard of living
② [말을 하대하여 쓰다] ¶ 말씀 낮추십시오 Please drop honorifics. /Your words sound too polite to me.

낮추보다 ① [실제보다 더 낮게 보다] undervalue ; make a low estimate of
② [얕보거나 업신여기다] look down upon〔on〕 ; hold 《a person》 cheap〔in contempt〕 ; have a low opinion 《of》 ; belittle ; make slight〔light〕 《of》 ; look down one's nose 《at》 ¶ 가난하다고 해서 그를 낮추보지는 마라 You should not despise〔look down upon〕 him because he is poor.

낮춤말 familiar〔plain〕 speech〔terms〕 ; low〔humble〕 talk

†낯 ① [얼굴] a face ; a visage ; features ; a countenance ; a pan 《속》 ¶ 낯이 희다 have a fair face〔complexion〕 // 낯이 붉다 have a red face ; be red-faced // 낯이 여위다 have a lean〔thin〕 face // 낯을 대하다 face each other ; see each other // 낯을 돌리다 turn one's face away ; look away 《the other way》 ; look〔turn〕 aside // 낯을 들여다 보다 look into 《a person's》 face ; look 〔stare〕 《a person》 in the face // 낯을 찡그리다 make a wry face ; frown ; contort〔wrinkle up, pucker up〕 one's face // 낯을 붉히다 redden ; become red in the face ; color up ; get angry ; blush // 낯을 들다 raise one's face ; lift one's head ; face the world without shame // 부끄러워 낯을 들지 못하다 be ashamed to face 《a person》 // 낯을 씻다 wash one's face ; wash up // 낯을 알다 know 《a person》 by sight ; be familiar with 《a person》 // 낯을 익히다 become acquainted〔familiar〕 with 《a person》 // 웃는 낯으로 사람을 대하다 welcome 《a person》 with a smile // 낯이 설다 be unfamiliar with 《a person》 // 낯이 익다 be familiar with 《a person》 // 낯을 가리다 be afraid〔shy〕 of strangers ; cover 〔hide〕 one's face // 나는 어릴 때에는 몹시 낯을 가렸다 I was painfully shy as a child. // 낯이 넓다 be widely known ; have a wide〔large〕 circle of acquaintance // 그녀는 부끄러워 낯을 붉혔다 Shame flushed her cheeks. /Her face flamed with shame.
② [면목] honor ; prestige ¶ 볼 낯이 없다 have no face ; be ashamed of 《oneself》 // 낯이 깎이다 lose face〔coun-

tenance, reputation, honor〕; be put out of countenance // 낯을 세우다 save face〔reputation, honor〕; relieve one from disgrace // …의 낯을 보아 taking 《a person's》 face〔reputation, honor〕 into consideration ; for 《a person's》 sake // 낙제하여 부모를 볼 낯이 없다 I am ashamed to face my parents after failing the examination. // 무슨 낯으로 또 돈을 꿔 달라는 거냐 Where do you get the gut to ask me to lend you money again?

낯가리다 ① [어린애가] be displeased 〔offended〕 with strangers ; be afraid 〔shy〕 of strangers ¶ 이 애는 낯가리지 않고 낯선 사람을 잘 따른다 This baby takes kindly to any strangers. ② [차별하다] treat 《a person》 with discrimination ; discriminate against 《a person》 ③ [얼굴을 덮다] cover〔veil, overspread, hide, bury〕 one's face ¶ 손수건으로 낯 가리다 cover〔bury〕 one's face with one's handkerchief

낯가림 being displeased〔offended〕 with strangers ; being afraid〔shy〕 of strangers

낯가죽 sense of honor ¶ …하다니 낯가죽도 두껍다 have the impudence〔face, cheek〕 to 《do》

낯가죽(이) 두껍다 관용 be brazen-faced ; be impudent ; be audacious ; be shameless ; be cheeky

낯간지럽다 (be) ashamed ; conscience-stricken ; feel small〔embarrassed〕 ¶ 낯간지러워서도 그런 말은 못하겠다 I am ashamed to say such a thing. /My sense of shame forbids me to say such a thing. // 가진 돈이 적어서 낯간지러웠다 I felt awkward to find myself short of money.

낯깎이다 lose face〔countenance, reputation, honor〕; be put out of countenance

낯나다 gain〔win〕 honor ; get credit ; reflect honor〔credit〕 on 《a person》; feel oneself honored ; 《a thing》 do 《a person》 credit ¶ 그 성공으로 그는 크게 낯났다 The success reflected great credit on him. /The success did him great credit.

낯내다 reflect credit to oneself 《for》; do honor to oneself ; act so as to gain the respect of others ¶ 그런 일을 해도 우리들은 낯내지 못한다 We should not get credit for that. // 그런 일로 낯내지는 못한다 That is nothing to be proud of.

낯두껍다 (be) shameless ; unabashed ; unblushing ; brazen(-faced) ; impudent ; saucy ; audacious ; cheeky 《속》 ¶ 낯두꺼운 요구 an impudent request // 낯두껍게도 …하다 have the nerve 〔heart, face, impudence, audacity〕 to 《do》

낯바닥 ⇨ 낯바대기

낯바대기 a face ; a phiz 《속》

낯부끄럽다 (be) ashamed ; shameful ; disgraceful

낯붉히다 become red in the face ; color up ; blush ; get angry ; be enraged ¶ 성나서 낯붉히다 flush〔redden, turn purple〕 with anger // 부끄러워서 낯붉히다 blush for bashfulness

낯빛 face colo(u)r

†**낯설다** (be) strange ; unfamiliar ; new ¶ 낯선 부인 a strange lady // 낯설은 타향 a strange place ; a place strange〔unfamiliar〕 to one

낯알다 know 《a person》 by sight ; remember 《a person's》 face ¶ 다 낯아는 사람들이었다 I knew them all by sight.

낯없다 be ashamed of ; be put out of countenance ¶ 어리석은 짓을 해서 뵐 낯없다 I am ashamed of my folly. /I blush for what I have done.

낯익다 be familiar 《to》 ¶ 낯익지 않은 strange ; unfamiliar ; new // 낯익은 얼굴 a familiar face // 어딘지 낯익은 사람이다 I think I remember his face. /His face seems familiar to me. // 낯익은 얼굴이지만 이름은 모르겠다 I recognize him but don't know his name.

낯익히다 cultivate the familiarity of ; get 《a person》 familiar with oneself

낯짝, 낯판 ⇨ 낯바대기

낱 a piece ; a unit

낱개 a piece ; each piece ¶ 낱개로 apiece ; each // 낱개로 100원 100 *won* apiece〔each〕 // 여기서는 달걀을 낱개로 판다 They sell eggs by the piece here.

낱개비 each split piece of wood ; a piece of wood

***낱낱이** ① [하나하나] one by one ; individually ; separately ; severally ¶ 낱낱이 조사하다 examine 《things》 one by one
② [모두] in every case ; entirely ¶ 낱낱이 간섭하다 find fault with everything one does ; meddle with everything
③ [상세히] in full ; in detail ¶ 낱낱이 설명〔보고〕하다 explain〔report〕 in detail

낱눈 〖동물〗 an ocellus 《*pl.* -li》; an eyespot

낱단 each〔every〕 bunch

낱돈 small money〔change〕; loose cash ; small coins ; money of small denominations ¶ 낱돈으로 바꾸다 change〔break〕 《a note》 into small money

낱뜨기 articles sold loose ; merchandise sold by the piece

†**낱말** a word ; a vocabulary ¶ 영어 낱말을 몇개나 아느냐 How much of a vocabulary have you got in English?

낱알 each grain

낱장 一張 a sheet〔piece〕《of paper》; a copy 《of photograph》; a leaf

낱흥정 piecemeal transactions; transacting one by one

낳다[1] ① [실을] spin; make yarn ¶ 실을 낳다 spin 《cotton》 into yarn ② [피륙을] weave ¶ 명주를 낳다 weave silk cloth

†**낳다**[2] ① [출산] bear; give birth to; be delivered of 《a child》; bring forth; [동물이] breed; calve (소); drop〔pup〕(개); kitten (고양이); foal (말); farrow (돼지); cub (호랑이·사자 따위); lay 《eggs》; spawn (생선) ¶ 사내 아이를 낳다 give birth to a boy // 그녀는 어젯밤에 첫아이를 낳았다 She became a mother last night. // 그녀는 어린애를 다섯 낳았다 She is the mother of five children. // 그녀는 이제 아이를 낳을 나이가 아니다 She is past the age of bearing.
② [생기다] produce; bear; yield; [발생시키다] give rise to; bring〔call〕 into being ¶ 여러 가지 소문을 낳다 give rise to rumors // 영웅을 낳다 produce a hero // 실직은 불행을 낳는다 Unemployment breeds misery.

-낳이 weaving; woven in... ; the weave of...
봄— cloth woven in spring; a spring weave

†**내**[1] [개울] a stream; a brook; a rivulet ¶ 내를 건너다 go across a river // 내를 끼고 가다 go along a stream // 내를 거슬러 올라가다 swim〔sail〕 against the stream

내[2] [연기] smoke ¶ 담배내 cigarette smoke // 내가 자욱하다 be full of smoke; be smoky // 굴뚝에서 내가 나다 Smoke rises from a chimney. // 기관차가 기통으로 내를 내뿜다 A locomotive puffs smoke out of its stack.

내[3] [냄새] smell; odor; scent ¶ 구운내 the smell of something roasted

내[4] [나의] my ¶ 내 책 my book
내 것도 내 것, 네 것도 내 것 속담 What's mine is yours〔mine own〕 and what is yours is mine.
내 돈 서푼이 남의 돈 칠백냥보다 낫다 속담 A bird in the hand is worth two in the bush. /Better a sparrow in the hand than a pigeon on the roof.
내 배 부르면 종의 밥 짓지 말라 한다 속담 He that is warm thinks all so.

내 內 the inside; within; within the scope of ⇨ 안[1] ¶ 건물 내 the inside of a building // 선박 내에서 on board〔aboard〕 the ship // 기한 내에 within the period 《of》 // 권한 내에 within the scope of authority

내- ① [밖으로] out; outside; outward(s); away; forth ⇨ 내걸다; 내쫓다; 내뻗다; 내보내다 ② [힘을 주어] away; out; down; up; off ⇨ 내던지다; 내빼다; 내닫다

내- 來 [이다음의] next; coming; forthcoming ¶ 내주 next week; the coming week // 내주 오늘 this day (next) week // 내주 월요일 next Monday; 《on》 Monday next; Monday (next) week // 내학기 the coming (school) term〔semester〕

내- 耐 -proof ¶ 내알칼리의 alkali-proof

-내 [내내] all (the time); through(out) ¶ 겨우내 all through the winter // 1년내 all the year round // 아침내 비가 왔다 It rained all through the morning.

내가다 take〔bring, carry〕 out〔away〕; remove ¶ 금고의 돈을 내가다 take the money out of the safe // 책상을 방에서 내가다 take a desk out of the room

†**내각** 內閣 a cabinet; a ministry; the government; the administration; the Council of Ministers ¶ 내각을 조직하다 form〔organize〕 a Cabinet〔Government, Ministry〕 // 내각이 흔들리다 the Cabinet is tottering // 내각을 개편하다 reorganize〔reshuffle〕 the Cabinet // 약체 내각 an effete〔a frail〕 Cabinet // 예비 내각 a shadow Cabinet // 초당파 내각 a nonparty Cabinet
— 각료 Cabinet members **— 개조** the reshuffle〔reconstruction〕 of the Cabinet **— 고시 제1호** Cabinet Notification No. 1 **— 경질** a Cabinet〔Ministerial〕 change; a change in the Ministry; a change of Ministry **— 분열** a split in the Cabinet **— 수반** the head of a cabinet; the Prime Minister **— 총사직** a general resignation of the Cabinet **거국 일치 —** an all-nation Cabinet **연립 —** a coalition cabinet; a fusion administration **정당 —** a party cabinet **현 —** the present Ministry〔Cabinet〕

내각 內角 ① 〖수학〗 an interior〔inside〕 angle ② 〖야구〗 in-corner

내각 內殼 an inner shell; an inner layer of skin; the derma

내각 책임제 內閣責任制 the parliamentary government

내간 內簡 letters between women

내간 內艱 the death of one's mother or grandmother

내갈기다 ① [힘껏 갈기다] strike; hit; thrash; slap ¶ 귀퉁이를 내갈기다 box 《a person's》 ear // 몽둥이로 내갈기다 club; cudgel // 빰을 내갈기다 slap 《a person》 on the cheek // 채찍으로 내갈기다 lash; whip ② [글씨를 아무렇게나 마구 쓰다] scribble; scrawl; dash ¶ 편지를 내갈기다 dash off a letter // 몇 줄 내갈기다 scribble a few lines

내강 內剛 strong-mindedness; a strong will; inner strength **—하다** (be) strong-minded〔-willed〕; have inner strength

내객 來客 a caller ; a visitor ; a guest ; company 《집합적》
— 예상수 an estimated number of guests
내거 [내것] my thing ; mine
*내걸다 ① [밖에 내어 걸다] put〔set〕 up ; hang out ; display 《a flag》 ; hoist ; fly 《a sail》 ¶ 간판을 내걸다 hang out〔put up〕 a signboard // 문패를 내걸다 put up one's nameplate ② [어떤 목표 따위를 내놓다] stand for ; advocate ¶ 슬로건을 내걸고 under the slogan of // 조건을 내걸다 give conditions ; stipulate ③ [희생을 무릅쓰다] risk ; stake ¶ 목숨을 내걸고 at the risk〔hazard, peril〕 of one's life
내경 內徑 the inside diameter ; the caliber (원통의) ; [구경] the bore ; the gauge
— 측정기 a calibrator
내계 內界 the inner world〔sphere〕 ¶ 내계의 inner ; inward
내공 耐空 endurance in flying〔flight〕 —하다 stay up 《in the air》 ; make an endurance flight
— 비행 an endurance flight —성 airworthiness — 시간 duration of flight
내공 內攻 〖의학〗 retrocession ; retrocedence —하다 retrocede ; strike inwards —성 질환 a retrocessive〔retrocedent〕 disease
내공 來貢 coming to pay tribute —하다 come to pay tribute
내공목 內供木 coarse cotton material used for lining
‡내과 內科 〖의학〗 internal medicine ; internal treatment (department) ¶ 내과 권위 an authority on internal diseases // 내과의 병 an internal disease // 내과 치료를 받다 be internally treated
— 병동 a medical ward — 병원 a hospital (for internal diseases) ; a medical establishment —의(醫) a physician ; an internist ; a medical practitioner (개업의) — 질환 an internal disease — 치료 internal treatment —학 internal medicine — 환자 a medical case
내과피 內果皮 〖식물〗 the endocarp
내관 內官 [내시] a eunuch ; an official of the Royal Household ; [고자] a man whose genital organs are underdeveloped
내관 內觀 ① 〖심리학〗 introspection ② 〖불교〗 inward contemplation〔looking〕 ¶ 내관적 introspective // 내관적 작가 introspective writer
내관 來觀 attendance ; inspection ; a visit —하다 attend ; inspect ; visit
내관 內棺 the inner part of a coffin ; the inner coffin
내교섭 內交涉 preliminary〔informal〕 negotiations —하다 hold〔carry on〕 preliminary negotiations 《with》
내구 來寇 an invasion ; an incursion ; an inroad ; a raid —하다 invade ; raid ; make a raid〔an inroad〕 into〔on〕
내구 耐久 [지속] endurance ; sustenance ; persistence ; [지구] permanence ; durability —하다 endure ; sustain ; persist
— 경쟁 an endurance contest — 비행 an endurance flight — 소비재 consumer(s') durables ; durable consumer goods — 시험 [지속] an endurance test ; [지구(持久)] a life test
내구력 耐久力 durability ; persistence ; lasting quality ; staying-power ; [사람 따위의] stamina ¶ 내구력이 있다 be durable ; be lasting ; wear long〔well〕 (의복·신발 따위) // 내구력을 시험하다 test the durability 《of a thing》
내구재 耐久財 durable〔hard〕 goods ; durables
비— nondurable goods ; nondurables
내국 內國 home ; the home country ¶ 내국의 home ; domestic ; internal ; native ; national // 내국제품의 homemade 《articles》
—세 an inland〔internal〕 duty〔tax〕 — 시장 the home〔domestic〕 market — 우편 domestic mail — 우편환 an inland money order — 운수 inland transportation —채 an internal〔a domestic〕 loan〔debt〕 —환(換) domestic〔inland〕 exchange —환 어음 an inland bill
내국법 內國法 municipal〔civil〕 law
내국 소비세 內國消費稅 the excise (duty)
내국인 內國人 a native
내국채 內國債 a national〔an internal, a domestic〕 loan
내국 항로 內國航路 domestic line 〔run〕 ; a coastwise service
내굽다 《it》 bend out ¶ 팔이 들이굽지 내굽지 않는다 Blood is thicker than water (피는 물보다 짙다). /Blood will tell.
내규 內規 private rules〔regulations〕 ; tradition ; unpublished〔customary〕 rules ; bylaws ; 〖군사〗 standard operating procedure 《SOP》 ¶ 회사의 내규 the bylaw of a business company // 내규를 위반하다 violate the bylaw ; offend against the tradition
내근 內勤 desk duty ; inside duty ; indoor service ; office〔desk〕 work —하다 work inside ; be on room duty ¶ 내근 사원 an indoor-service employee ; an office 〔desk〕 worker ; a clerk // 내근 순경 desk policeman ; a policeman on desk〔inside〕 duty // 내근으로 전직되다 be transferred to desk duty〔indoor-service〕 villain
—의(醫) a resident〔house〕 physician —자 an indoor service employee ; a

person on room duty ; an office〔a desk〕 worker ; an inside man
내금 內金 payment on account ; partial payment in advance ; token payment ; a deposit ¶ 내금으로 on account ; as partial payment∥내금으로 5,000원을 받았다 I received 5,000 *won* on account〔as partial payment〕.
‡**내기** betting ; staking ; a bet ; gambling **—하다** bet ; make a bet ; wager ; lay a wager ¶ 내기에 지다〔이기다〕 lose〔win〕 a wager∥크게 내기하다 play for high stakes∥그럼 내기할까요 Will you make a bet on it〔lay a wager〕 then?∥이 야구 시합에서 어느 편이 이기나 내기하자 Let's bet on who's going to win the ball game.
—돈 money at stake ; stakes ; a bet
-내기[1] ① [고장 사람] a person from... ; a person born in〔at〕... ¶ 서울내기 a person from〔born in〕 *Seoul* ; a Seoulite∥시골내기 a person from the country ; a country-born person ② [그 정도의 사람임을 얕잡아 이르는 말] ¶ 풋내기 a greenhorn ; an inexperienced person
-내기[2] merchandise ¶ 전내기 goods in stock ; ready-made articles ; mass-produced articles
내깔기다 discharge forcefully ; eject ; put out ¶ 오줌을 내깔기다 urinate
내남없이 everybody ; anyone ; indiscriminately ; with no discrimination between oneself and others ¶ 그것은 내남 없이 다 아는 사실이다 It is a fact known to everybody.
***내내** all along〔through〕 ; all the time ; from start to finish ; from beginning to end ; for the whole period ; all the way ¶ 아침부터 내내 all through the morning∥내내 선두를 달리다 lead the race from start to finish∥그후 내내 여기서 살고 있다 I've lived here ever since.∥그는 6년 동안 내내 수석이었다 He has been at the top of his class the whole six-year period.∥그는 1년 내내 쪼들리고 있다 He is badly off all the year round./He is always in needy〔straitened, narrow〕 circumstances.
내내년 來來年 the year after next
내내월 來來月 the month after next
***내년 來年** next year ; the coming year ¶ 내년 봄 next spring∥내년 5월 next May ; May next (year)∥내년 이맘 때 about this time next year
내놓다 ① [밖으로] put out ; [주머니 속에서] take out ; bring out ; pull〔draw〕 out ¶ 혀를 내놓다 put〔stick〕 out one's tongue∥주머니에서 돈을 내놓다 take〔pull〕 money out of one's pocket
② [노출] expose ; show ; bare ¶ 무릅을 내놓다 expose one's knees∥어깻죽지를 내놓다 bare〔expose〕 one's shoulders
③ [발간] publish〔issue, bring out〕《a book》
④ [제출] present ; send in《an application》; tender《one's resignation》; bring out《evidence》; give〔set〕《a question》
⑤ [음식을] serve《wine》; offer《tea》; set《cake》 before《a person》
⑥ [기부] contribute ; invest (투자) ¶ 자금을 내놓다 furnish《a person》 with funds ; advance (the) capital ; invest in an enterprise
⑦ [짐승을 우리에서] set free ; let go ; let loose ; set at large〔liberty〕 ¶ 개를 우리에서 내놓다 let a dog out of the kennel∥죄수를 감옥에서 내놓다 let a prisoner out of jail ; set a prisoner free
⑧ [물건을 팔려고] put《a thing》 on sale ; offer《a thing》 for sale ¶ 집을 내놓다 put〔offer〕 a house on sale∥어느 대기업이 우리 것과 유사한 제품을 시장에 내놓을 거라는 소문이 있다 There's a rumor that one of the big corporations is coming out with a product just like ours.
⑨ [혼처를 구하다] look for a suitable match ; hunt a husband for one's daughter ; marry off a daughter
⑩ [제외하다] exclude ; except ; leave out ; omit ¶ 저 서점은 수요일을 내놓고는 매일 영업을 하고 있다 That bookstore is open every day except on Wednesday.
⑪ [차지했던 것을 포기하다] abandon ; give up ; leave ; desert ; part with ; resign ; sacrifice ¶ 재산을 내놓다 deliver up one's possession ; offer〔place〕 one's property at the disposal of another∥목숨을 내놓다 lay down〔sacrifice〕 one's life ; risk〔hazard〕 one's life∥지위를 내놓다 throw up〔resign from〕 one's office〔position〕
내다[1] [연기가] smoke ; smolder ; become smoky ¶ 방구들이 내다 a room smokes ; a room is smoky∥장작이 내기만 하고 타지 않는다 The fagots simply smolder and do not burn.
†**내다**[2] ① [밖으로] put〔let〕 out ; take〔bring〕 out ; [꺼내다] pull out ; draw from〔out of〕 ¶ 책상을 밖으로 내다 take a desk out∥포켓에서 편지를 끄집어내다 take〔produce〕 a letter out of one's pocket∥새장에서 새를 내주다 let a bird out of its cage
② [제출] hand〔send〕 in ; present ; submit ; file ¶ 명함을 내다 present one's card∥사표를 내다 hand in〔submit〕 one's resignation∥원서를 내다 file〔send in〕 an application
③ [발송] send ; dispatch ; [우편] post《영》; mail《미》 ¶ 전보를 내다 send《a person》 a telegram ; send a telegram《to a person》∥편지를 내다 write a let-

ter ; mail〔post〕 a letter (투함하다)// 초대장을 내다 send out an invitation
④ [발행·발표] issue ; publish ; send out ; [말을] start ; set forth ¶ 명령을 내다 issue orders // 새 잡지를 내다 publish a new magazine // 신문에 광고를 내다 publish〔put〕 an advertisement in a newspaper // 내 이름은 내지 말아주시오 Please let me remain anonymous. / Please keep my name out of print. // 화를 내다 get angry 《at a matter, with a person》; take offense 《at》
⑤ [발휘] put forth ; get up ¶ 속력을 내다 get up speed ; put on speed // 용기를 내다 summon〔muster, pluck〕 up one's courage // 60마일 속력을 내다 make 60 miles // 힘을 내다 put forth one's strength // 실력을 내다 display one's ability
⑥ [운행] run ; put ¶ 배를 내다 put out a boat // 임시 열차를 내다 run a special train
⑦ [배출] produce ; turn out ¶ 만명의 졸업생을 내다 turn out 10,000 graduates // 많은 수재를 내다 produce〔turn out〕 many brilliant men // 사태로 많은 사상자를 냈다 The landslide caused heavy casualties.
⑧ [지불] pay ; give ; invest (투자) ; contribute (기부) ¶ 15,000원을 내고 시계를 사다 pay 15,000 *won* for a watch // 자선사업에 돈을 내다 give〔contribute〕 to charity // 학비를 내다 pay one's school expenses // 새로운 사업에 돈을 내다 invest in a new enterprise // 다음엔 크게 한 번 내십시오 I'll let you be a big spender next time. // 저녁 식사 값은 내가 내겠다 The dinner is on me.
⑨ [출품] exhibit ¶ 전시회에 작품을 내다 exhibit one's paintings in an exhibition
⑩ [시작] open ; start ; set up ; begin ¶ 가게를 내다 open〔start〕 a shop // 살림을 내다 set up one's own home
⑪ [음식을] serve ; offer ¶ 점심을 내다 treat 《a person》 to lunch // 손님에게 홍차를 내다 serve guests with tea // 이것은 내가 내지 This is my treat. /This is on me.
⑫ [팔다] offer 《a thing》 for sale ; put 《a thing》 up for sale ¶ 쌀을 시장에 내다 put〔place〕 rice on the market
⑬ [소문을] start ; set forth ¶ 말을 내다 start talk〔a rumor〕 // 소문을 내다 start〔spread〕 a rumor
⑭ [길·시간 따위] open ; set up ; make ; arrange 《for》 ¶ 길을 내다 open a road // 시간을 내다 make〔arrange〕 time for 《a thing》 // 자리를 내다 make〔arrange〕 a seat ; leave room for someone to sit // 창을 내다 put in a window // 구멍을 내다 put in〔make〕 an opening
⑮ [빛] emit ; give out ; [소리] utter ; make ¶ 빛을 내다 emit〔give out〕 light // 이상한 소리를 내다 make a strange noise
⑯ [빚·허가] get〔take out, obtain〕 《a loan, a license》 ¶ 빚을 내다 get〔take out〕 a loan ; raise a loan of money ; borrow money 《from, of》 // 여권을 내다 have a passport issued ; obtain〔get〕 a passport
⑰ [방을] clear〔vacate〕 《a room》 (비우다) ; build 《a room》 (만들다) ; [대표자를] offer〔put forward〕 《a representative》
⑱ [이름을] raise ; distinguish ; attain〔gain, win〕 distinction ¶ (자기) 이름을 내다 distinguish oneself ; make one's name familiar〔known〕 to the public ; make oneself famous
⑲ [모를] transplant 《rice seedlings》 ; plant 《rice》 ; set〔bed〕 out 《rice plants》 [거름을] manure 《a field》

내다³ [조동사] do all the way (to the very end, thoroughly) ¶ 모든 고생을 견뎌 내다 endure all hardships (to the last) // 지갑을 끄집어 내다 draw one's purse 《from one's bosom》

***내다보다** ① [밖을] look out 《of, over, on》 ; see from within ¶ 창밖을 내다보다 look out of a window // 거리를 내다보다 look out on the street // 차창에서 노변 풍경을 내다보다 // 창에서 내다보는 경치가 좋다 The window commands a fine view.
② [앞일을] foresee ; forecast ; look forward to ; look ahead at ¶ 장래를 내다보다 look ahead into the future ; foresee the future ; have an insight into the future

내다보이다 ① [밖이] be〔can be〕 seen from within ; be seen out of ; show through (the window) ¶ 거리가 내다보이다 the street is seen 《from the window》 ② [안이] be seen〔be visible, can be seen〕 from without ¶ 환히 내다보이다 be seen through clearly ; be patently transparent ③ [예견] be foreseen ; be anticipated ; be foretold ¶ 풍년이 들 것이 내다보인다 A good harvest is anticipated. // 네 장래가 빤히 내다보인다 It is easy to see what will become of you.

내다지 〖건축〗 a hole through a column〔pillar〕

내닫다 dart off ; start off ; run away suddenly ; break into a gallop (말이)

내달 來― next month ; the coming month ; the month ahead

내달리다 ⇨ 내닫다

내담 來談 an interview ; (a visit for) a talk **―하다** interview ; visit (for a talk) ¶ 본인 내담 Apply in person. /Personal application (is)

requested. (광고)
내당 內堂 ⇨ 내실(內室)
내대다 give the cold shoulder to ; treat back 《old shoulder》 defiantly ; say coldly in retort ; treat coldly ; defy
†**내던지다** ① [힘껏 던지다] throw〔cast, hurl, fling〕 out〔away〕 ¶ 창 밖으로 내던지다 throw 《a thing》 out of the window//의자를 내던지다 hurl a chair at 《a person》//화가 나서 시계를 내던지다 throw away a watch in (a fit of) rage
② [버리고 돌아보지 않다] abandon ; give〔throw〕 up ; throw up one's hands ; forsake ¶ 재산을 내던지다 deliver up one's possessions ; turn over all one's property//사표를 내던지다 thrust one's resignation at 《the employer》//지위를 내던지다 give up one's position//목숨을 내던지다 lay down one's life 《for》
내도 來到 arrival ; coming **—하다** come 《to》 ; arrive 《at》
내돋다 rise to the surface ; come out ; appear ¶ 여드름이 내돋다 Pimples come out 《on one's face》.
내돌리다 hand〔pass〕 《a thing》 around carelessly〔indiscriminately〕
내두르다 ① [휘두르다] brandish ; wave ; flourish ; wield ; swing ¶ 단도를 내두르다 brandish a dagger ; swing a dagger about//주먹을 함부로 내두르다 resort to force〔violence〕
② [마음대로] lead ; control ; rule the roast ; boss the show ; be in the saddle ; lead 《a person》 by the nose ; have 《a person》 under one's thumb ¶ 당을 마음대로 내두르다 be the leader of a party
내둘리다 ① [남에게 쥐다] be pushed around ; be led by the nose ; be at the mercy of 《a person》 ¶ 아무한테나 내둘리다 be at a person's thumb ② [정신이] get dizzy ; be〔feel〕 dizzy
***내디디다** ① [발을 앞으로 옮겨 놓다] step forward ¶ 한 걸음 앞으로 내디디다 take a step forward//해결을 향해 한 걸음 내디디다 take a step towards solution//방 안에 책이 흩어져 있어 발을 내디딜 곳이 없다 The room is littered with books, leaving no space to plant a foot on.
② [무슨 일을 시작하다] enter upon 《a career》 ; set foot 《on, in》 ¶ 정계에 발을 내디디다 enter upon a political career//인생의 첫걸음을 잘못 내딛다 make a wrong start in life
내떨다 ① [붙은 것을] shake〔knock〕 《a thing》 off ② [사람을] shake〔get rid of〕 《a person》
내뚫다 pierce ; penetrate ; perforate ; run 〔bore〕 through ; shoot through (탄알이) ; cut through ¶ 산에 굴을 내뚫다 cut a tunnel through a mountain//총알로 과녁을 내뚫다 perforate a target with bullets//탄알이 그의 가슴을 내뚫었다 A bullet shot through his breast.
내뜨리다 throw〔cast, fling〕 away ; throw down 《a person》 ; toss〔hurl〕 away 〔aside, out〕 ¶ 휴지를 창문 밖으로 내뜨리다 throw wastepaper out of the window//거지에게 돈을 내뜨려주다 toss a copper to a beggar
내락 內諾 an informal〔a private〕 consent **—하다** give an informal〔a private〕 consent ¶ 내락을 얻다 obtain〔secure〕 《a person's》 informal 〔private〕 consent//…의 내락을 받고 by the private〔informal〕 consent of. . .
내란 內亂 a civil war ; internal disturbances〔troubles〕 ; a rebellion ; an insurrection ; a domestic conflict ¶ 내란을 일으키다 raise a rebellion//내란이 일어났다 A civil war broke out.//내란을 선동하다 instigate〔incite, agitate〕 a rebellion
— 음모 conspiracy of a rebellion **—죄** rebellion ; high treason ; an offense against the safety of a state
내레이션 narration
내레이터 [남자] a narrator ; [여자] a narratress
†**내려가다** ① [낮은 데로] go〔come, get, step, move〕 down ; descend 《from》 ; fall ; drop ¶ 내려가는 기차 a down train//산에서 내려가다 descend 《from》 a mountain//언덕을 내려가다 go〔get, climb〕 down a hill ; descend a hill//지하실로 내려가다 descend into a cellar//시골로 내려가다 move〔go〕 down to the country//양말이 내려가다 My socks slip down.//이 길을 따라 내려가면 브로드웨이가 나옵니까 If I go down this street, do I run into Broadway?
② [값이] fall ; drop ; go down ; decline ; sag ; depreciate ¶ 실은 휴대용 전화기의 가격은 자꾸 내려가고 성능은 점점 더 좋아지고 있습니다 In fact the price of portable phones keep coming down while quality keep going on.
③ [온도가] drop ; fall ; go down ¶ 기온이 영하로 내려가다 fall (down) below zero//온도가 내려간다 The temperature falls〔goes down〕.//열이 내려간다 The fever goes down〔abates〕.
④ [잘 소화되다] digest ¶ 먹은 것이 잘 안 내려간다 The food is slow of digestion.
⑤ [하위가 되다] come down ; drop ; sink down ; be degraded 《from》 ; be demoted 《to》 ¶ 아랫자리로 내려가다 be demoted to a lower rank//석차가 내려가다 come down on the list//시험에서 석차가 15등이나 내려가다 be fifteen places down in class after examination
내려 갈기다 flog down
내려긋다 draw a vertical line ; draw 《a

line》 down ; underscore ; make a downstroke ; stroke downward ¶ 선을 내려긋다 draw a line down ; draw a vertical line // 몇줄을 내려 긋다 strike out a few lines

내려 깔기다 void 《urine, feces》 down ¶ 2층에서 오줌을 내려 깔기다 urinate down from upstairs

*__내려놓다__ set〔put〕 down ; take down ; bring down ; lower ; let 《a person》 off 《a vehicle》 ¶ 책을 책상 위에 내려놓다 put a book down on the table // 냄비를 내려놓다 take a pot off the fire // 배를 내려놓다 lower a boat // 배〔수레〕에서 짐을 내려놓다 unload a ship〔cart〕 // 수화기(受話器)를 내려놓다 leave the (telephone) receiver off 《the hook》 // 다음 정거장에서 내려놓아 주시오 Please let me off at the next station. // 그거 여기 내려놓으세요 Put it down here.

내려누르다 ① [위에서] press down 《on》 ; press upon 《a thing》 ; oppress ② [웃 사람이] force 《a heavy task on a person》 ; urge ; compel ; constrain ; oppress ; be oppressive to ; suppress 《freedom》 ¶ 언론을 내려누르다 shackle speech and writing ; place〔put〕 a gag upon the freedom of speech // 위에서 내려누르니 할 수 없이 맡았다 As I was coerced into it, I had to undertake it.

‡**내려다보다** ① [아래를] look down ; overlook ¶ 창문에서 거리를 내려다보다 look down the street from the window // 이 건물에서는 전시가가 내려다보인다 This tall building overlooks the whole city. // 그 언덕에서는 바다가 환히 내려다보인다 The hill commands a fine view of the sea. // 그 빌딩은 근사한 수족관이 있고 스카이 라운지에서는 서울 시내를 한눈에 내려다볼 수가 있지요 The building has a nice aquarium and from its sky lounge you can have a bird's-eye view of *Seoul*.
② [낮추어보다] look down 《upon》 ; despise ; belittle ; slight ; make light〔little〕 of ; hold 《a person》 in contempt ; hold 《a person》 cheap

내려디디다 step down

내려뜨리다 let fall ; drop ; throw down ¶ 유리잔을 마루에 내려뜨리다 drop a glass 〔let a glass fall〕 to the floor // 책을 아래층으로 내려뜨리다 throw a book downstairs // 아랫자리로 내려뜨리다 demote 《a person》 to a lower rank

내려비치다 shine〔reflect〕 down

내려서다 step〔stand〕 down

내려쏟다 pour 《water》 down

†**내려앉다** ① [아래로] come down to a lower seat ; take a lower seat ¶ 의자에서 내려앉다 come down off the chair (and sit on the floor)
② [무너지다] collapse ; fall〔come〕 down ; give way ; sink ; fall〔cave〕 in ¶ 가슴이 내려앉다 be greatly surprised ; be startled // 천장이 내려앉았다 The ceiling has sagged. // 지붕이 내려앉았다 The roof fell down〔collapsed〕. // 다리가 무게로 내려앉았다 The bridge gave way under the weight. // 오랜 장마 끝에 도로가 내려앉았다 After the long rain the road caved in.

*__내려오다__ come〔get〕 down ; descend 《from》 ; get off ; get down from ¶ 산에서 내려오다 come down〔descend〕 from a hill // 비행기에서 내려오다 get off 〔alight from〕 a plane // 대대로 전하여 내려오다 be handed down from generation to generation // 시골로 내려오다 come down to the country // 명령이 내려오다 an order is given ; an order comes from above

내려조기다 split 《a thing》 with a downward blow

내려쫓다 [높은 곳에서] chase down ; [시골로] drive〔hound〕 from the capital

내려찍다 cut with a downward blow

내려치다 give a down blow ; strike from above ; give a blow from above ; throw down ¶ 책상을 주먹으로 내려치다 hit the table with one's fist // 돌을 내려치다 throw down a stone

내력 來歷 one's personal history ; one's past life ; one's career ; antecedents ; a history ; an origin ¶ 내력을 밝히다 trace 《a thing》 to its origin ; investigate the origin 《of》 ; trace one's family origin // 그의 내력은 부침(浮沈)〔파란〕이 많았다 His career was checkered by success and failure.
—담(談) an account of one's life

내륙 內陸 inland
— 수운(水運) inland water transportation **— 운수** inland transport **— 지방** inland area

내리 ① [줄곧] straight through ; all along〔through〕 ; consecutively ; continually ; from start to last ¶ 책만 내리 읽다 read books constantly // 세시간 동안 내리 연설하다 speak for three hours at a stretch // 비가 사흘 동안 내리 쏟아졌다 It has rained continuously for three days. // 올 겨울은 내리 춥기만 했다 It has been cold all through this winter.
② [마구] unduly ; absurdly ; ridiculously ; terribly ¶ 값을 내리 깎다 beat 〔knock〕 the price down // 비가 내리 퍼붓다 rain pours down
③ [아래로] down ; downward ¶ 지붕에서 내리 구르다 fall〔roll〕 down from the roof

내리긋다 draw a vertical〔longitudinal〕 line

내리깎다 knock down the price ; drive a hard bargain ¶ 펜값을 10원으로 내리깎다 beat the price of a pen down as low as ten *won*

내리깔다 cast one's eyes down ; lower 〔drop〕 one's eyes

†**내리누르다** ① [위에서] press down ; press upon 《a thing》 ; push down ; force down
② [압박하다] oppress ; suppress ; clamp down 《구》 ; [윽박지르다] force ; compel ; urge ¶ 언론을 내리누르다 shackle speech and writing ; place〔put〕 a gag upon the freedom of speech

†**내리다**[1] ① [높은 데서] descend ; come 〔go〕 down ; fall ¶ 연단에서 내리다 come down off the platform // 막이 내리다 The curtain falls〔drops, is dropped〕. // 서리가 내리다 It frosts. /Frost forms.
② [타고 있던 것에서] alight from ; get 〔step〕 off〔out of〕 ; dismount (말에서) ¶ 기차에서 내리다 get off a train // 택시에서 내리다 get out of a taxi // 말에서 내리다 dismount (from) a horse // 버스에서 내리다 get down from〔get off〕 a bus // 비행기에서 내리다 alight from〔get off〕a plane // 여기서 내리시오 Please get off here. /This is your stop.
③ [비·눈·이슬 따위가] fall ; come down ; descend ¶ 서리가 내렸다 It frosted. /Frost fell. /Frost formed.
④ [값이] fall ; drop ; go down ; decline ; sag ; depreciate ¶ 물가가 내린다 Prices go down. /Prices are on the decline. // 쌀 값이 내렸다 Rice has dropped in price.
⑤ [온도가] drop ; fall ; go down ¶ 3도 내리다 fall〔drop〕 by 3 degrees // 0도 이하로 내리다 fall down below zero // 기온이 갑자기 내렸다 The temperature suddenly fell〔dropped, went down〕. // 열이 내렸다 The fever has abated〔subsided〕. // 열은 내렸는데 아직 기침이 심하다 My fever's down, but I still have a bad cough.
⑥ [살이] become〔grow, get〕 lean 〔thin〕 ; fall away (in flesh) ; lose flesh ¶ 부기가 내렸다 The swelling went down. // 내가 살이 좀 내렸나 Am I losing flesh a bit?
⑦ [먹은 음식이] digest ; be digested ¶ 잘 내리다〔안 내리다〕 (be) digestible 〔indigestible〕 ; (be) easy〔hard〕 of digestion〔to digest〕 ; digest well // 빨리〔더디〕 내리다 (be) quick〔slow〕 of digestion
⑧ [신이] (be) possessed 《by》
⑨ [뿌리가] take〔strike〕 root ; root ; put down roots ¶ 뿌리가 길게 내리다 take〔spread〕 deep roof ; root deep

†**내리다**[2] ① take〔bring〕 down ; set〔put〕 down (내려놓다) ; lower 《a flag, a sail》 ; let 《a person》 off 《a car》 ¶ 주전자를 내리다 take a kettle off the fire // 시렁에서 물건을 내리다 take a thing down from the shelf // 기를 내리다 lower〔haul down〕 a flag // 휘장을 내리다 let down〔drop〕 a curtain // 짐을 내리다 set a burden down // 트럭에서 짐을 내리다 unload goods from a truck // 다음 정거장에서 내려주시오 Let me off〔Drop me〕 at the next stop.
② [값·정도를] lower ; drop ; bring down ¶ 값을 내리다 lower〔bring down〕 the price // 계급을 내리다 reduce〔demote〕 《a person》 to a lower rank // 기준을 내리다 lower the standard
③ [윗사람이] grant ; give ; confer ; award (상을) ¶ 특사령을 내리다 grant pardon // 작위를 내리다 confer a title on 《a person》 // 허가를 내리다 give 《a person》 permission // 영예를 내리다 award 《a person》 an honor // 명령을 내리다 give 〔issue〕 an order
④ [뿌리를] take〔strike〕 root ; root ¶ 나무가 뿌리를 내렸다 The tree has taken root.
⑤ [커튼·거적 따위를] drop ; let fall ; let down ¶ 셔터를 내리다 pull〔roll〕 down the shutter // 커튼을 내리다 draw 〔drop, bring down〕 the curtain
⑥ [결말에서 판결 따위를] pass 《judgment on a person》 ; pronounce ; hand down one's decision ; render a decision ¶ 결론을 내리다 draw a decision // 위원회는 논쟁중인 그 문제에 대한 판결을 내릴 것이다 The committee will pronounce on the matter in dispute.

내리다지 [어린이옷] children's overalls with a slit in the seat

내리닫다 run〔leap〕 down

내리닫이 a sash window

*__내리뜨다__ lower〔drop, cast down〕 《one's eyes》

내리막 ⇨ 내리받이

내리매기다 number downward ; start from the top and number down〔back〕

내리밀다 push〔shove〕 down〔off〕

내리받이 a downward slope ; a descent ; a downhill ¶ 내리받잇길 a downhill road // 내리받이가 되다 [길 따위가] run downhill ; slope down ; [사업 따위가] cease to flourish ; go downhill ; [경기가] look down ; [운이] be on the wane // 그의 운도 내리받이다 His fortunes are declining. // 더위도 이제 내리받이다 The heat is on the decline.

내리사랑 love from older toward younger members of a family

내리외다 recite all the way through from memory

내리지르다 ① [물·바람이] flow〔blow〕 down forcefully ¶ 물이 세차게 내리지르다 Water flows down〔rushes along〕 in torrents. ② [주먹·발로] kick〔knock〕 down(ward)

내리질리다 get kicked〔knocked〕 downward

내리쬐다 [햇볕이] beat〔strike〕 down on ; shine〔glare, blaze〕 down upon ¶ 뜨겁게 내리쬐는 햇볕 아래 under a burning〔scorching〕 sun // 햇볕이 온통 그녀의 얼굴에 내리쬐고 있었다 The sun was beating fully into her face. // 햇볕이 쨍쨍 내리쬐고 있었다 The sun was beating down unsparingly. /The sun is pouring down its full strength from the sky.

내리치다 beat down ; give a downright blow ¶ 머리를 내리치다 strike《a person》 a blow on the head ⇨ 내려치다

내리키다 pull down ; lower ; drop ; take〔bring〕 down ¶ 허리춤을 내리키다 lower one's belt // 돛을 내리키다 lower〔take down〕 a sail

내리퍼붓다 [눈·비 따위가] pour down ; rain〔snow〕 heavily ; rain cats and dogs ¶ 내리퍼붓는 비 torrents of rain // 비가 내리퍼붓고 있다 The rain is pouring down. /It is raining in torrents.

내리훑다 thresh down

내릴톱 [세로 켜는] a ripsaw

내림[1] heredity ; inheritance ¶ 정신병은 그 집안의 내림이다 There is hereditary insanity in the family. /Insanity runs in the family. // 내림내림 generations of inheritance ; heredity from way back

내림[2] [간수] frontage ; a width

내림 來臨 an honored visit ; deigning to come **—하다** deign to come ; honor with a visit

내림굿 〖민속〗 an invocatory rite of a would-be (spiritualistic) medium

내림대 a rod used by a shaman (to be possessed by a spirit)

내림새 〖건축〗 concave tiles at the edge of eaves

내림세 —勢 a downward trend ; a falling〔declining〕 tendency ; a drop in price trends ¶ 내림세를 보이다 show a downward tendency // 시세가 내림세다 [물가] Prices show a downtrend. / Prices are on the decline.

내림차 〖수학〗 a descending series

내립떠보다 look down ; cast down one's eyes

내막 內幕 the inside〔confidential〕 facts ; the inside story ; the low-down 《미·구》 ¶ 내막을 알고 있다 be familiar with the situation ; be in the know 《구》 // 내막을 말하다 give 《a person》 the low-down 《on》

— 이야기 an inside account〔dope, report, story〕 ; a behind-the-scenes story ; inside information

내막 內膜 〖해부〗 lining membrane

내맡기다 leave〔entrust〕 《a matter entirely to a person》 ; commit 《a matter》 to 《a person's》 care ; leave〔place〕《it》 in 《a person's》 hand ¶ 애를 식모에게 내맡기다 commit one's child to the care of the maid // 일을 그에게 내맡겼다 I trusted to him for the performance of the task.

내면 內面 the inside ; the interior ¶ 내면적 internal ; inside ; inner ; inward // 내면 생활 the inner life

— 관찰 an inside view ; a view from inside **— 묘사** (an) inner description **— 연삭(硏削)** internal grinding **— 형식** an inward form

내면적 內面的 internal ; inside ; inner ¶ 내면적으로 internally

— 고찰 introspection **— 세계** the inner world **— 지식** inside knowledge

내면화 內面化 internalization ; interiorization **—하다** internalize ; interiorize

내명 內命 an unofficial〔informal, secret〕 order ¶ 내명을 내리다 issue an unofficial order ; issue unofficial instructions

내명년 來明年 the year after next

내몰다 drive out〔away〕 ; force out ; drive ahead ; expel ; turn〔send〕 out ; rout 《a person》 out ¶ 말을 외양간에서 내몰다 drive a horse out of the stable // 사람을 방밖으로 내몰다 drive〔force〕《a person》 out of the room

내몰리다 be driven out〔away〕 ; be forced out ¶ 집 밖으로 내몰리다 be driven〔forced〕 out of the house

내몽고 內蒙古 Inner Mongolia

내무 內務 home〔domestic, internal〕 affairs

—반 〖군사〗 quarters ; barracks

내무부 內務部 the Ministry of Home Affairs ; the Department of the Interior 《미》 ; the Home Office 《영》 ; the Ministry of Internal Affairs

— 장관 the Secretary of Interior 《미》 ; the Home Secretary 《영》 ; the Home Minister ; the Minister for Home Affairs

내무 위원회 內務委員會 [국회의] the Home Affairs Committee

†내밀 內密 privacy ; secrecy ¶ 내밀히 secretly ; off the record ; privately ; in secret ; confidentially ; hush-hush 《미·속》 // 내밀히 조사하다 make confidential inquiries // 내밀로 해주십시오 Keep it secret〔quiet〕, please.

†내밀다 ① [끝이 나오다] protrude ; jut out ; project ¶ 내밀은 이마 a projecting〔protruding〕 forehead // 바다로 내밀고 있는 곳 a cape jutting out into the sea ② [밖으로] push〔thrust〕 out ; stick out 《of》 ; force out ¶ 가슴을 내밀다 throw out one's chest // 혀를 내밀다 stick out the tongue // 손을 내밀다 hold〔reach〕 out one's hand // 창밖으로 머리를 내밀다 stick one's head out of the window ③ [남에게 미루다] shift 《on》 ; throw 《on》 ; switch 《over to》 ¶ 책임을 남에게 내밀다 shift the blame〔responsibility〕 on to another

④ [물리쳐 쫓아내다] drive〔force〕 out ; expel ¶ 사람을 방밖으로 내밀다 push 〔shove, throw, thrust〕《a person》 out of the room

내밀리다 be pushed〔thrust, forced, thrown〕 out ; be pressed ¶ 뜰 밖으로 내밀리다 be thrust〔pressed, pushed, thrown〕 out of the garden // 회사에서 내밀리다 get shoved〔pushed〕 out of one's job with the company

내밀힘 pushing〔forward〕 force ; strength ; drive ; [배짱] self-confidence ; boldness

내박차다 ① [발길로] kick out hard ② [거절] strongly reject

내발뺌 an evasion ; an elusion ; a dodge ; an evasive〔a shuffling〕 answer ; prevarication ; an excuse (구실) **—하다** give an evasive answer ; excuse oneself 《for》 ; explain away ; dodge ; shuffle ; talk oneself out 《of difficulty》 ; quibble ; clear oneself of 《a charge》 ¶ 일시적이나마 간신히 그자리에서 내발뺌하다 talk oneself out of trouble somehow for the time being // 네 말은 내발뺌하는 소리로밖에 안 들린다 What you say seems to me very much like prevarication〔evasion〕.

내방 來訪 a call ; a visit **—하다** call on 《a person》 ; visit ; pay a visit ; call at 《a house》 ¶ 내방중인 미국 실업인들 the American businessmen now on a visit to Korea // 내방을 받다 have a visit from 《a person》 // 내방자를 맞이하다 receive callers〔visitors〕 // 틈이 나는 대로 내방해 주셨으면 합니다 Please come and see me when you are free.

내방자 來訪者 a visitor ; a caller
— 명단 a guest〔visitors〕 book ; a visitors' register ; a calling list

내배다 ooze 《out of》 ; soak through ; exude ; transude ; saturate ; percolate ¶ 붕대에 피가 내배어 있었다 The bandage was saturated with blood. /Blood oozed out of the bandage. // 셔츠에 땀이 내밴다 one's shirt is soaking wet with sweat

*__내뱉다__ spit out ; spew ; spue ¶ 내뱉듯이 말하다 say disdainfully

*__내버려 두다__ [방치] leave 《a matter》 as it is ; neglect ; lay aside〔to one side〕 ; let 《a matter》 take its own course ; [사람을] leave 《a person》 alone ; let 《a person》 do what he wants ¶ 병을 그대로 내버려 두다 let one's disease go untreated // 일을 하지 않고 내버려 두다 leave one's work undone // 책을 방구석에 내버려 두다 leave a book in the corner of the room // 울게 내버려 두다 leave 《a person》 alone and let him cry // 제 마음대로 하라고 내버려 두다 let 《a person》 do what he wants

*__내버리다__ throw away ; cast〔fling〕 away ; dump 《refuse》 ¶ 쓰레기를 내버리다 dump rubbish〔refuse〕 // 돈을 내버리다 throw away〔waste, squander〕 one's money // 현관에 내버린 어린아이 a baby left on the doorsteps // 다 내버려라 Throw them all away.

내벽 內壁 an inside〔inner, interior〕 wall

내보 內報 private〔confidential, advance〕 information ; a secret〔an unofficial〕 report ; a tip 《속》 ; dope 《속》

*__내보내다__ ① [나가게 하다] let out ; let go out ; send ; [쫓아내다] expel ; turn 〔get, put, send, drive〕 out ; kick 《a person》 out 《of the house, army》 ; evict (셋방 따위에서) ; [실외로] turn 《a person》 out-of-doors ; show 《a person》 the door ¶ 야구부를 시합에 내보내다 let the baseball team take part in the game
② [해고] give 《a person》 the sack ; send 《a person》 packing ; fire 《미》 ¶ 식모를 내보내다 dismiss〔fire〕 a maid // 마누라를 내보내다 divorce〔cast forth, abandon〕 one's wife

*__내복 內服__ ① [옷] underwear ; underclothes
② [약] internal use **—하다** take〔use〕 internally ¶ 그것은 피하 주사를 해도 좋고 내복을 해도 좋다 It can be given hypodermically or by mouth.
—약 an internal medicine ; a medicine for internal use

†**내부 內部** the inside ; the interior ; the inner part ¶ 내부의 inside ; internal ; inner ; interior ; inward ; domestic (국내의) // 집의 내부 the inside〔interior〕 of the house // 내부에서 내다보다 look from within // 회사 내부 사정에 통하다 be familiar with inside affairs of the firm // 그 사건은 내부에 있는 사람이 한 짓 같다 The case looks like an inside job.
— 감각 inner sensation **— 규율** internal regulations **— 기생(寄生)** 『동물·식물』 internal parasitism ; endoparasitism **— 도체(導體)** an inner conductor **— 마찰** internal friction **— 사정** the internal affairs ; the inside story (내막) **— 에너지** internal energy **— 저항** internal resistance **— 전압** internal voltage **— 전위(電位)** inner potential **— 질환** an internal trouble **신체 —** the inner 〔internal〕 parts of the body ; [내장] one's inwards ; one's internals 《미·구》

내부딪다 ① [부딪다] strike ; hit ; knock ; bump ② [충돌] run against〔into〕 ; collide with ; crash into〔against, together〕

내부딪히다 get struck〔hit〕 ; get knocked 〔bumped〕

내분 內紛 an internal trouble ; domestic discord ¶ 정당의 내분 internal troubles in a political party ; an intraparty conflict〔strife, friction, collision〕

내분비 內分泌 〖생리〗 internal secretion ; incretion ; endocrine
— **계통** the endocrine system — **기관** an endocrine〔incretory〕 organ —**선** endocrine glands ; a ductless gland — **액** an endocrine〔internal〕 secretion ; a hormone —**학** endocrinology

내불다 [바람이] blow away《from》 ¶ 바람이 서쪽으로 내불다 (the wind) blows away west (from the east) // 입김을 내불다 let one's breath out

내비치다 ① [빛·빛깔이 밖으로] be〔grow〕 transparent ¶ 내비치는 openwork《skirt》// 살이 내비쳐 보이는 가운〔블라우스〕 a see-through〔diaphanous〕 gown〔blouse〕// 옷이 얇아서 그녀의 팔이 내비쳐 보인다 Her arms are seen through her thin dress.
② [말로] hint《at, that》; intimate ; insinuate ; suggest ¶ 사직을 내비치다 hint at resignation // 그는 승낙할 뜻을 내비치고 있다 He gives us to understand that he will consent.

내빈 來賓 a guest ; an invited guest
— **경주** a visitors' race — **명단** a guest〔visitors'〕 book ; a visitors' register —**석** the visitors' seats ; the seats for invited guests —**실** a special room reserved for honored visitors

*__내빼다__ scram《속》; run〔scamper, scoot《속》〕 away ; make〔take, run〕 off ; flee ; bolt ; make a getaway ¶ 이런 때는 내빼는 것이 장땡이다 The wisest thing to do in this case is to run away.

내뻗다 put forth〔out〕; spread〔stretch〕 out ¶ 등넝쿨이 내뻗다 A wisteria puts out its vine.

†**내뻗치다** gush out ; spout (out) ; spurt (out, up) ; jet ; put forth ; stretch

*__내뿜다__ [물·피 등] gush out ; spout ; spurt ; jet ; [불·연기 따위가] blow up ; emit ; send out ; [화산 따위가] belch up ; erupt ; [하늘로] shoot up ¶ 상처에서 내뿜는 피 blood spouting from〔out of〕 the wound // 담배 연기를 내뿜다 blow a cloud of smoke

내사 內査 secret examination〔inspection, investigation〕 —**하다** investigate〔examine, inspect〕 secretly

내사 來社 a visit to a company —**하다** visit a company〔an office〕

내상 內相 ① [내무 장관] the Home Minister ; the Minister of Home Affairs
② [남의 부인] (your, his) esteemed wife

내상 內喪 mourning for one's wife ; the death of one's wife

내상 內傷 an internal injury

내색 —色 expression of one's feeling ; one's facial expression〔countenance〕; betrayal of one's emotion ; a (revealing) look —**하다** betray《one's fear》; look ; show ¶ 화난 내색 a look〔show〕 of anger // 내색에 나타내다 betray one's emotion ; reveal unconsciously one's sentiment // 내색을 보이지 않다 pocket〔suppress〕 one's feelings (감정) ; master one's anger (분노) ; veil one's displeasure (불쾌) ; disguise one's grief (슬픔) // 불안한 내색을 하다 look uneasy〔anxious〕// 기쁜 내색을 보이다 A look of pleasure comes to her face. // 실망한 내색을 드러내다 Disappointment is on his face.

내생 內生 〖생물〗 endogeny
— **균근** endotrophic mycorrhiza — **출아(出芽)** endogenous budding — **포자** endogenous spores ; an endospore

내생 來生 the life to come ; the future life ; life after death ¶ 내생의 행복 happiness in next life〔world〕; one's welfare in another world〔after death〕

내서 耐暑 enduring the heat ; heat-proof ; heat-resistant ; proof against the heat —**하다** endure〔stand〕 the heat ; withstand the heat

내서 來書 a letter (received) ⇨ 내신

내선 內線 [전기의] indoor〔interior〕 wiring ; [전화의] an extension ; [작전상의] an inner line ; [인터폰] an interphone ; an intercom line ; an inside line
— **번호** an extension number — **전화(電話)** an extension (tele) phone

내성 內省 introspection ; reflection ; self-examination ; self-communion —**하다** introspect ; introvert ; reflect on oneself ; turn one's thought inward ¶ 내성적 introspective ; introversive〔introvertive〕// 다감하고 내성적인 기질 a sensitive and introspective nature // 내성적인 사람 an introvert // 깊이 내성하다 exercise deep reflection

내성 耐性 〖의학·식물〗 tolerance《to radioactivity》
—**균** resistant bacteria

*__내세 來世__ the life to come ; the future life ; a better world ; life after death ; kingdom (기독교의) ; kingdom come《속》 ¶ 내세를 믿다 believe in the future existence ; believe in the world beyond the grave // 내세의 명복을 빌다 pray for one's welfare in the future life

내세우다 ① [서게 하다] make《a person》 stand ¶ 대열 앞에 내세우다 make《a person》 stand before ranks
② [대표로] nominate ; designate ; make《a person》 represent ¶ 후보로 내세우다 put up〔nominate〕《a person》 as a candidate ; have《a person》 stand for《the Assembly》
③ [자기에게 유리하게] stand on ; insist ; advocate ; set forth ¶ 권리를 내세우다 stand on one's right // 주전론을 내세우다 advocate war // 이유를 내세우다 give〔set forth, render〕 one's reason //

소인은 자기를 내세우고 남을 헐뜯는 법이다 Mean fellows will advertise themselves at the expenses of others.
④ [남이 보도록] put up〔set up, hang out〕《a sign》; put 《a placard on the sidewalk》
내셔널리스트 a nationalist
내셔널리즘 nationalism
내소박 内疏薄 mistreating〔despising, alienating〕 one's husband ; jilting one's husband **—하다** mistreat〔jilt, despise, alienate〕 one's husband ¶ 내소박당하다 be separated from one's wife who despised〔mistreated〕 one
내손 來孫 a great-great-great-grandchild 〔grandson〕
내솟다 spring〔surge, spurt〕 up〔out〕
내수 內需 〖상업〗 domestic demand 〔requirements〕; home consumption
— 산업(産業) enterprises producing commodities for domestic markets
내수 耐水 ¶ 내수의 waterproof ; watertight ; impervious to water
—성 water-proofing ; water-resisting qualities **—포** waterproof cloth ; tarpaulin
내수장 內修粧 interior decoration ; room decoration **—하다** ornament〔adorn〕 the interior of a house ; decorate a room ; upholster a room
내숭 treacherousness ; trickiness **—하다** (be) tricky ; crafty ; sly ; insidious ; wily ; treacherous ; underhand ; snaky ¶ 내숭한 사람 a tricky〔designing〕 fellow ; a snake // 내숭한 웃음 an insidious smile
내숭스럽다 (be) treacherous ; tricky ; insidious ¶ 내숭스러운 수단 a treacherous〔an underhand〕 method ; crafty means
내쉬다 exhale ; breathe out ¶ 숨을 내쉬다 breathe out one's breath
내습 來襲 an attack ; an invasion ; a raid ; an assault **—하다** attack ; assault ; invade ; raid ; make an attack 〔a raid〕《on》; descend on ¶ 적의 내습에 대비하다 provide〔guard〕 against the enemy's attack ; make preparations against a possible attack by the enemy
내습 耐濕 ¶ 내습의 wetproof ; dampproof
내시 內侍 a eunuch
내시 內示 [관청에서의] unofficial〔informal〕 announcement ; a private〔preliminary〕 showing **—하다** announce unofficially ; show privately〔in private〕
— 정가표 a confidential price list
내시경 內視鏡 〖의학〗 an endoscope
— 검사(법) endoscopy
내식 耐蝕 ¶ 내식의 corrosion-resisting 《alloy》
—성 corrosion resistance〔proof〕
내신 來信 a letter (received) ; a message ¶ 형으로부터 내신이 있었다 I received a letter from my brother. /I heard from my brother.
— 상자(箱子) a letter box
내신 內申 an unofficial report **—하다** report unofficially
내신서 內申書 [학교의] a school report on a pupil's record ¶ 합격 여부는 내신서에 의해 결정된다 Success depends on the report of one's school record.
내실 內室 [안방] women's quarters ; the main room ; [남의 아내] (your, his) esteemed wife
내심 內心 one's inmost heart ; real inward feeling ; one's mind ; one's real intention ¶ 내심으로 at heart〔bottom〕; in one's hearts ; within one ; inwardly ; secretly // 내심 비웃다 laugh at 《a thing》 inwardly〔in one's sleeves〕 // 내심 후회하다 repent at heart 〔inwardly〕 // 내심을 털어놓다 unburden one's mind // 내심 …하고 싶어하다 have a secret desire to 《do》 // 그렇게 말했지만 내심 좋아했다 He was delighted at heart, though he spoke to the contrary.
내앉다 sit forward // 그는 아무렇지도 않은 얼굴을 하고 있지만 내심으로는 어떤 생각을 하고 있을까 He looks unconcerned, but I wonder what he's thinking deep down inside?
내앉히다 let〔have〕《a person》 sit forward ; let 《a person》 come out and occupy a seat
내압복 耐壓服 [비행용] a flying skin
내야 內野 〖야구〗 the infield ; the diamond
—수 an infielder ; a baseman ; [집합적] the infield **— 안타** 《hit》 an infield hit
내약 內約 a private agreement〔contract〕; a secret〔tacit〕 understanding (묵계) ; a secret treaty (밀약) **—하다** make a private agreement ; have a tacit understanding 《with》 ¶ 두사람 사이에는 어떤 내약이 있는 것 같다 There seems to be some private agreement between the two.
내역 內譯 particulars
내연 內燃 internal combustion
내연 內緣 an unregistered〔informal〕 marriage ; a common-law marriage ; a marriage of consent ; a companionate marriage 《미》 ¶ 내연의 처 a common-law wife ; a wife not legally married // 내연의 남편 a common-law husband // 내연의 관계를 맺다 contract a marriage of consent // 내연의 부부로 동거 생활을 하다 live together without being legally married ; live in a marriage of consent ; enter into a private alliance // 내연의 부부가 되다 marry 〔jump〕 over a broomstick ; hop the broomstick

— 관계 common-law marriage
내연 기관 內燃機關 an internal combustion engine ; a motor
—차 a diesel locomotive
내연력 內燃力 〖전기〗 internal-combustion power
— 발전소 an internal-combustion power plant〔station〕
내연 터빈 an internal-combustion turbine
내연 펌프 內燃— an internal combustion pump
내열 耐熱 ¶ 내열의 heat-resisting ; heat-proof ; heat-resistant ; 〖야금〗 refractory // 내열성의 thermostable
—복 an anti-heat suit —성 heat-resisting property ; thermal resistance — 시험 a heat(-resistance) test — 유리 heat resisting glass
내오다 take〔carry, bring〕 out ; remove ¶ 마당으로 의자를 내오다 take a chair out into the garden ; bring a chair into the garden
*내왕 來往 [통행] comings and goings ; traffic ; [교제] intercourse ; association
—하다 come and go ¶ 이 길은 사람의 내왕이 빈번하다 This is a busy street. /There is much traffic on this road. // 그들은 서로 내왕하는 사이다 They are on visiting terms. // 배가 인천 부산 사이를 내왕한다 Ships ply between *Incheon* and *Pusan*.
*내외 內外 ① [안팎] the interior and exterior ; within and without ; the inside and outside ¶ 학교 내외를 깨끗이 청소하다 keep the school clean inside and outside
② [국내외] home and abroad ; home〔domestic, native〕 and foreign ¶ 내외로 다사하다 be eventful〔busy〕 at home and abroad
③ men and women keeping away from each other〔keeping the socially proper distance from each other〕 —하다 《the sexes》 keep their distance (from each other)
④ [부부] husband and wife ; a married couple ¶ 내외간 relationship between man and wife // 내외분 you and your esteemed wife〔husband〕 ; he and his esteemed wife ; she and her esteemed husband ; the esteemed couple
⑤ [약] some ; about ; around ; or so ; thereabouts ; a matter of ¶ 5백원 내외 five hundred *won* or so ; around〔some, about〕 500 *won*
— 동포 our countrymen both at home and abroad — 사정 home〔domestic〕 and foreign affairs ; internal and external affairs —인 native and foreign people — 정책 home〔domestic〕 and foreign policy —채(債) domestic and foreign bonds
내외종 內外從 cousins ; cousins by a paternal aunt (내종) ; cousins by a maternal uncle (외종)
내외척 內外戚 relatives on one's father's side and mother's side
*내용 內容 contents ; substance ; (subject) matter ; import (의미) ; [상세한] details ; depth (깊이) ¶ 책의 내용 the contents of a book // 편지의 내용 the gist of a letter // 이야기의 내용 the import of a story〔statement〕 // 대담의 내용 details of the conversation // 사건의 내용 the facts of an event // 형식과 내용 form and matter〔substance〕 // 내용이 빈약한 책 a book poor in substance // 내용이 충실한 학교 a well-equipped school // 내용이 풍부한 substantial ; solid ; rich in contents // 중요한 것은 내용이다 It is a subject matter that counts. // 회담의 내용은 극비에 붙여졌다 The nature of the conference was kept a top〔strict〕 secret.
교육 — the quality of education 연구 — the substance of one's study 직무 — the substance of one's duties and responsibility
내용 內用 ① [내복] internal use —하다 take〔use〕 internally ② [안살림의] home expenditure
—약 an internal medicine ; a medicine for internal use ; [주의서] To be internally used.
내용 견본 內容見本 sample〔specimen〕 pages ; a prospectus ; advance sheets (출판에 앞서서) ¶ 신청 즉시 내용 견본 무료 우송함 Sample pages will be sent free on〔upon〕 request.
내용 연수 耐用年數 [사용 가능〔내구〕 연한] the life 《of a car》 ¶ 내용 연수가 긴 자산 long-lived assets // 내용 연수가 지난 학교 건물 an old school building no longer safe to use
내용 증명 內容證明 certification of contents
— 우편 contents-certified mail〔post〕
내우 內憂 internal〔domestic〕 worries ; trouble(s) from within
— 외환 internal and external troubles ; troubles from within and without ; troubles at home and abroad ¶ 내우 외환이 갈마들며 닥쳐온다 They〔We〕 are beset with troubles both at home and abroad.
내원 內苑, 內園 the inner garden of the Royal Palace
내원 來援 coming to help ; assistance ; aid ; help ; support —하다 come to help〔a person's aid〕 ¶ 내원을 청하다 get 《a person》 to come and help one ; ask 《a person》 to come to one's assistance
*내월 來月 next month ; proximo〔prox.〕 ¶ 내월 9일에 on the 9th of next

month ; on the 9th proximo

내유 來遊 a visit ; a call **— 하다** visit ; call ; come to see ¶ 관광차 내유한 외국인 a foreign visitor on a sightseeing tour // 한국에 내유하다 visit Korea ; pay a visit to this country

— 자 a visitor ; [관광객] a tourist

내응 內應 a secret communication 〔understanding〕 ; collusion ; betrayal ; treachery **— 하다** conspire〔collude〕 with ; communicate secretly〔hold secret communication〕 with 《a person》 ; betray 《a person》 to 《the enemy》 ¶ 적과 내응하다 communicate secretly with the enemy ; betray 《us》 to the enemy

—자 a betrayer

*__내의 內衣__ an undergarment ; underclothes ; an undershirt ; [부인용] woman's underwears 《총칭》 ; lingerie ; scanties 《미·속》 ; underwear ; underclothing ¶ 내의 위에 잠옷을 걸치다 have nightgown on over some underclothes

내의 來意 the object of one's call 〔visit〕 ; the purpose of one's visit ¶ 내의를 밝히다 state the object of one's call ; indicate the purpose of one's visit // 내의를 묻다 ask the pleasure of one's visitor

내의 內意 [의중] one's mind ; one's (secret) intention ; [견해] one's private 〔personal〕 opinion ¶ 내의를 알아채다 read one's intention〔mind〕

내이 內耳 『해부』 the internal〔inner〕 ear ; the labyrinth ; Auris interna (학명)

—강(腔) the vestibule of the ear **—염(炎)** 『의학』 labyrinthitis ; inflammation of the internal ear

내인 內人 [아낙네] a wife ; [나인] a court lady ; a maid of honor

†**내일 來日** [명일] tomorrow ; [장래] the future ¶ 내일 저녁 tomorrow evening // 내일의 세계 the world tomorrow // 내일을 모르는 운명 one's precarious life // 우리 민족의 내일을 짊어질 사람들 those who will be the support and driving force of our nation

내입 內入 ① [돈의] partial〔part〕 payment ; payment on account **— 하다** pay in part ; pay on account〔as part payment, in part settlement〕
② [궁중으로 물건의] delivery 《of goods》 to the Royal Court〔Household〕 **— 하다** deliver〔supply〕 《goods》 to the Royal Court

—금 money paid on account ; part〔partial〕 payment

내자 內子 my wife

내자 內資 domestic capital〔fund〕

— 동원(動員) the mobilization of domestic capital

내장 內粧 interior decoration〔design〕

내장 內藏 — 하다 have 《a thing》 within ; have 《a thing》 built-in

내장 內臟 the internal organs ; the inward parts of the body ; the intestines ; the entrails ; the viscera (장부) ; the guts ¶ 내장의 고장 an internal disorder

—강(腔) a visceral cavity ; a splanchnocoel(e) **— 신경** the splanchnic nerve **— 외과** internal surgery **— 적출(摘出)** evisceration ; exenteration ; nopleure **— 질환** a trouble of an internal organ ; internal disease〔complaint〕 **—통(痛)** visceral pain **— 파열** a visceral cleft **— 포층(包層)** 『동물』 a splanchnic layer **— 하수증(下垂症)** splanchnoptosit ; abdominal ptosis **—학** splanchnology **— 해부** splanchnotomy

내장

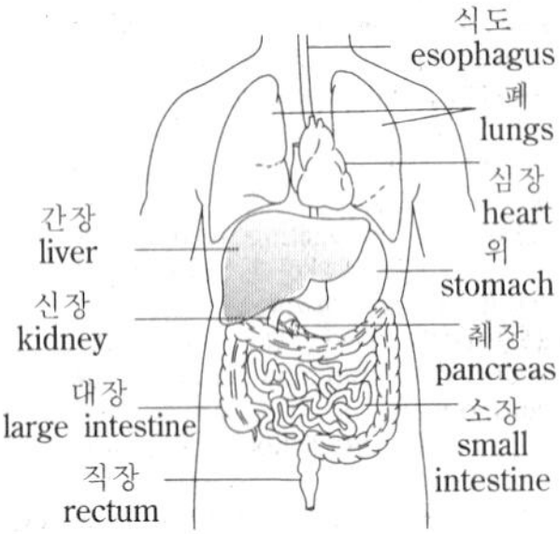

내장 內障 『의학』 cataract (백내장) ; amaurosis (흑내장)

내장 감각 內臟感覺 visceral sensation

내장 공사 內裝工事 interior finish work

내재 內在 『철학』 immanence ; inherence ¶ 내재적 immanent // 신의 내재 divine immanence

— 가치 intrinsic value of 《a thing》

내재 봉소 內裁縫所 a private house in which the housewife earns her living as a seamstress

⁑**내적 內的** [내부의] inner ; internal ; [고유의] intrinsic ; [마음의] mental ; [유전의] inherited

— 가치 intrinsic value **— 경험** inner experience **— 생활** inner life **— 증거** internal evidence

내전 內殿 [왕비] a queen ; an empress

내전 內戰 an internal〔a civil〕 war

내전 來電 an incoming telegram〔dispatch〕 (전보) ; an incoming telephone 〔phone〕 call (전화) ¶ 워싱턴 발 내전 a dispatch from Washington // 런던 2월 12일발 내전에 의하면 a London telegram〔dispatch〕 dated〔of〕 February 12 says

내전 보살 內殿菩薩 feigned ignorance ; pretending innocence ; [사람] a person who feigns ignorance 《about》

내접 內接 ―하다 『수학』 be inscribed ; touch internally

― 다각형 an inscribed polygon ; an inpolygon ―원 an inscribed circle ―형(形) an inscribed figure

내젓다 [손·기] wave ; [팔] swing ; [신체·물병] shake ; [머리·꼬리·손가락] wag ; [배] row out ; pull〔put〕 out 《to sea》

†내정 內定 unofficial〔informal, tentative, private〕 decision ―하다 decide unofficially 〔informally, tentatively〕 ¶ …하기로 내정되었다 It has been unofficially decided to 《do》//그의 후임은 K씨로 내정 되어 있다 It has been informally arranged that Mr. K should succeed him in his post.

내정 內政 ① [국가의] domestic〔internal〕 administration ; domestic policies ; state 〔internal〕 affairs ¶ 타국의 내정에 간섭하다 interfere〔intervene〕 in the domestic affairs of another country

② [가정의] house management ; housekeeping

― 간섭 intervention〔interference〕 in the domestic〔internal〕 affairs of another country ― 문제 a question of home administration

내정 內情 the private〔actual〕 circumstances ; the internal conditions ; the real state 《of affairs》 ; the low-down 《on》 《미·속》 ; tip-off 《속》 ¶ 내정에 밝다 be in touch with the inside of a matter ; be familiar with the inside affairs//내정을 이야기 하다 give 《a person》 the lowdown 《on》//내정을 폭로하다 expose〔reveal〕 an inside story//나는 그쪽의 내정을 잘 알고 있다 I know how things stand with them. //사건의 내정은 아직도 모른다 The real nature of the case is yet to be ascertained

내조 乃祖 one's grandfather

내조 內助 the wife's help〔assistance, aid〕 ―하다 help one's husband ¶ 내조의 공에 의해서 through the assistance of one's wife//그의 성공은 부인의 내조에 힘입은 바 컸다 He owed much of his success to his wife. /His wife was a valuable helper in his work.

내조 來朝 ① [외국 사신의] the arrival 〔visit〕 of foreign envoy ② [왕후의] the visit of a local lord to the King ―하다 《a foreign envoy》 arrive ; visit ; come ; 《a local lord》 visit the King

내종 內從 cousins by a paternal aunt

― 사촌 ⇨ 내종

*내주 來週 next week ; the coming week ¶ 내주의 오늘 this day (next) week//내주 월요일 Monday week ; next Monday

내주다 ① [물건을] take〔bring, put〕 《a thing》 out and give it ; give away〔out〕 ¶ 면허장을 내주다 grant a certificate//돈을 지갑에서 내주다 give money out of one's purse//급료를 내주다 pay wages//이것은 그에게 내줄 돈이다 This money is to him.

② [자리를] resign〔surrender, give up, offer, yield〕 《one's seat to a person》 ¶ 후임에게 자리를 내주다 hand over one's position to a successor//재산을 채권자에게 내주다 make over one's estate to a one's creditor

내주장 內主張, 內主掌 petticoat government ; gynecocracy ―하다 exercise petticoat government ; tie one's husband to one's apron strings ¶ 저 집은 내주장이다 The wife is the ruler in that house. /The wife wears the trousers in that house.

내지 乃至 […부터 …까지] from... to ; between... and ; [또는] or ¶ 100 내지 200 from 100 to 200 ; between one hundred and two hundred//제12조 내지 제16조의 규정 the provisions of Articles 12 to 16 inclusive//A 내지 B A or B//아동의 연령은 8세 내지 18세이다 The ages of the children range〔vary〕 from 8 to 18.

내직 內職 ① [본직 외의] a side job 〔business〕 ; side〔outside, extra, home〕 work ; private〔subsidiary, auxiliary〕 occupation ; extra private work ; a side line (겸업) ; side practice (공직에 있는 의사의)

② [가정 부인의] a job〔work〕 for housewives ―하다 do a side job ; do private〔home〕 work ; earn a second income in spare hours ¶ 내직으로 돈을 모으다 save some money through side issues//내직으로 저작을 하다 write books as a side line//그들은 대개 가정에서 어떤 내직을 하고 있다 Many of them carry on some kind of work at 〔in〕 their homes.

내진 內診 an internal examination ; endoscopy ―하다 make an internal examination 《of》

―경(鏡) an endoscope

내진 來診 ¶ 내진을 청하다 send for a doctor

내진 耐震 ¶ 내진의 proof against earthquakes ; earthquake-proof

― 건물 an earthquake-proof〔-resistant〕 building ― 구조 『건축』 aseismatic structure ― 내화 건물 a fire-and-quake-proof building ―력 resistance against earthquake (shock)

내쫓기다 [밖으로] be〔get〕 driven 〔turned, thrown, forced, kicked〕 out ; [해고] be dismissed〔discharged, fired〕; get the sack ¶ 학교에서 내쫓기다 be expelled from school // 회사에서 내쫓기다 be fired〔sacked〕 by the company

*내쫓다 drive〔force, send, turn, kick〕 out ; bundle off〔out, away〕; expel ; put out ; [지위에서] oust ; relieve ; [퇴거시키다] eject ; evict ; [해고하다] discharge ; dismiss ; give 《a person》 the axe〔sack〕; send 《a person》 packing ; sack 《영·속》; fire 《미·속》 ¶ 고양이〔파리〕를 내쫓다 shoo a cat〔fly〕// 직장에서 내쫓다 dismiss〔remove〕 《a person》 from office〔the service〕; relieve 《a person》 of his post // 집에 세든 사람을 내쫓다 eject〔evict〕 a tenant out of one's home // 집밖으로 내쫓다 turn 《a person》 out of the house ; show 《a person》 the door〔gate〕// 하인을 내쫓다 dismiss〔fire〕 a servant ; send a servant packing

내차다 kick〔boot〕 out ; [냅다] kick hard ; give 《a person》 a hard kick 《on the shin》; give 《a person》 the boot 《속》

내착 來着 arrival ―하다 reach ; arrive 《at, in》; get to

내찰 內札 letters between women

내채 內債 a domestic〔an internal〕 loan 〔debt〕 ¶ 내채를 모집〔발행〕하다 float 〔issue〕 a domestic loan

내처 throughout ; to the very end ; without pause〔intermission〕; at a breath ; at a stretch ; at a heat ; at a dash ; straight ¶ 길을 내처 가다 go on one's way without pause // 일을 내처 끝마치다 finish one's work at one stretch // 여섯 시간 내처 일하다 work for six hours at a stretch // 올라가는 길에 내처 꼭대기까지 올라가다 go on and climb straight up to the top of a hill

내추 來秋 next autumn〔fall〕; the coming autumn

내추럴리스트 a naturalist

내추럴리즘 naturalism

내춘 來春 next spring ; the coming spring

내출혈 內出血 〘의학〙 internal hemorrhage〔bleeding〕 ¶ 내출혈을 일으키다 bleed〔hemorrhage〕 internally

내치 內治 ① [내과 치료] cure by internal treatment〔medicine〕 ② [내정] home administration〔policy〕; internal 〔domestic〕 affairs ―하다 cure by internal medicine ; administer the affairs of state

내치다 throw away ; cast away ; abandon ; desert〔discard〕 《a lover》; reject ; turn down (각하) ; drive back (쫓아 보내다) expel ; drive away ¶ 쓰레기를 내치다 throw away garbage ; dump refuse

내치락들이치락 ① [변덕스럽게] capricious ; whimsical ; frivolous ; fickle ; fitful ; blowing hot and cold ; on-again-off-again ―하다 (be) capricious ; whimsical ; fickle ; fitful ; hot and cold ¶ 내치락들이치락하는 사람 a man of moods ; a capricious〔whimsical〕 person ② [병세가] ―하다 change constantly ; have 《its》 ups and downs ¶ 그의 병세는 내치락들이치락한다 His illness hangs in the balance〔gets better one day and worse the next〕.

내친걸음 having set about doing 《a thing》; having crossed the Rubicon ¶ 내친걸음이니 끝까지 해볼 수밖에 We are in for it. /Over shoes, over boots, let's go through with it. /In for a penny, in for a pound. // 이미 내친 걸음이라 물러설 도리가 없다 Now I've set about it, there is no turning back. /I have gone too far to retreat〔withdraw〕. /The die is cast.

내침 內寢 ―하다 share one's wife's bed ; sleep with one's wife

내켜놓다 remove farther ; set farther ahead

*내키다¹ [마음이] (be) inclined〔disposed, willing〕 《to do》; have an inclination ; care〔like〕 to ; feel like 《doing》; have a mind 《to》 ¶ 마음 내키는 대로 as one's humor dictates ; as the spirit prompts // 마음 내킬 때 하게나 You may do it when you are so inclined. // 어쩐지 일할 마음이 내키지 않는다 I am in no mood for work. // 마음이 내키면 몇 시간이든지 계속해서 공부를 한다 He studies for hours together when the whim is on him. // 기분 내키는 곳으로 여행하고 싶다 I'd like to try taking a trip to whatever places my fancy leads me.

내키다² ① [마음을] bring oneself to ; put one's mind to ¶ 마음을 내키어 공부해라 Put your mind to work.
② [자리를] make〔leave〕 room for ¶ 앉을 자리를 내키어 주다 make a room for 《someone》 to sit

내탄 耐彈 endurance against bullets ; bulletproof

내탐 內探 a private inquiry ; a secret investigation ―하다 make private inquiries ¶ 회사의 사정을 내탐하다 investigate the inside affairs of a company

내탕금 內帑金 a privy〔private〕 purse

내통 內通 ① [남녀의] illicit intercourse ; misconduct ; intimacy ―하다 have improper relations 《with》; misconduct oneself 《with》; fornicate ② [내응] secret communication〔understanding〕; collusion ―하다 communicate secretly〔hold secret communication〕 with 《an outsider》; betray 《one's country》 to 《the enemy》; be in collusion with 《an outsider》

—자 a betrayer
내팽개치다 throw 《a thing》 out (forcefully) ; toss 《a thing》 away
내평 內— the real state 《of affairs》; the internal conditions ; the inside story
*내포 內包 connotation 〖논리〗; intention ; comprehension — 하다 connote ; contain ; involve
내풀로 of one's own accord ; voluntarily ; on one's own initiative
내피 內皮 〖해부〗 endothelium
—종(腫) 〖병리〗 endothelioma —층 〖식물〗 the endoderm
내핍 耐乏 austerity ; voluntary privation ; putting up with poverty — 하다 put up with poverty ; practice austerities
— 예산 an austerity budget ; a retrenchment budget
내핍 생활 耐乏生活 (a life of) austerity ; an austerity life ; austere living ; a hard life ; belt tightening ¶ 내핍 생활을 하다 bear a hard life ; tighten one's belt // 국민에게 내핍 생활을 촉구하다 prescribe more austerity for the people ; impose greater austerity on the people
내한 來韓 a visit to Korea ; arrival in Korea — 하다 visit〔come to〕 Korea
내한 耐寒 proof against the cold ; coldproof ¶ 내한성의 cold-resistant
— 비행 an endurance flight in the cold season — 시험 a cold resistance test — 식물(植物) a (winter) hardy plant — 행군 a cold-weather endurance march — 훈련 training in the cold season
내한 장치 耐寒裝置 winterization ¶ 내한 장치를 하다 winterize // 트럭, 대포, 전차는 영하 10도에서 가동할 수 있도록 내한 장치를 할 수 있다 Trucks, guns and tanks can be winterized to work at 10° below zero.
내항 內航 a coastwise service〔line〕
—로 a coasting line〔route〕 —선(船) a home-waters liner ; a coastwise vessel
내항 內港 the inner harbor
내항 內項 〖수학〗 internal terms
내항 來航 a visit to our shores〔this country〕 — 하다 visit this〔Korea's〕 shore (in a ship) ¶ 영국 함대의 내항 a visit of the British fleet to Korea
내항성 耐航性 ¶ 내항성이 있는 seaworthy
내해 內海 an inland sea ; an arm of the sea
내행 內行 [여행] a journey of a woman ; [행실] the conduct〔behavior〕 of a woman at home
내향성 內向性 〖심리〗 introversion ; [형용사적] introvert ¶ 내향성인 사람 an introvert // 그는 내향성이다 He is apt to turn inward(s).
내형 乃兄 his〔her〕 elder brother
내홍 內訌 internal〔civil〕 disturbance 〔troubles, strife, dissension〕; domestic discord
— 외환 troubles both at home and abroad ; national disturbances from within and without
내화 內貨 domestic currency ; the coin of the realm
내화 耐火 proof against fire ; fireproof — 하다 (be) impervious to fire ; be fireproof
— 건물〔금고〕 a fireproof building 〔safe〕 —도(度) refractoriness —력 fire-resisting qualities — 벽돌 a firebrick ; a refractory brick — 석재 firestone — 시험 a fire-resistance test — 장치 fireproof installation ; fireproofing —재(材) fireproof material ; refractory material ; fire-proofing — 점토 fire clay
내화 구조 耐火構造 fireproof〔fire-resisting〕 construction
반— semi-fireproof〔slow-burning〕 construction
내화성 耐火性 fire resistance ¶ 내화성의 fire-resistant〔-resistive, -resisting〕; 〖야금〗 refractory // 내화성이 있다 be impervious to fire // 내화성이 강하다 have a great resistance to fire
내환 內患 ① [처의 병] the sickness〔illness〕 of one's wife ② [나라 안의] domestic〔internal〕 troubles
외우 — troubles both at home and abroad
내후년 來後年 the year after next ; three years hence
내흉 內凶 wickedness ; treacherousness ; sneakiness ; trickiness ; underhandedness — 하다 (be) wicked ; treacherous ; sneaky ; tricky ; underhanded
*냄비 a pot (깊은) ; a cook-pot ; a pan (얕은) ; a saucepan ¶ 냄비를 불에 올려 놓다 put a pot over the fire // 냄비에 끓이다 boil (a thing) in a pan over the fire
— 검댕 kettle soot — 뚜껑 a pot-lid — 받침 a pot stand — 손잡이 the bail of a pan — 요리 food served in the pot 탁상용 — [풍로가 달린] a chafing dish 프라이 — a frying pan
냄비 국수 pot-boiled noodles ; noodles served hot in a pot
†냄새 smell ; odor ; scent ; [향기] fragrance ; perfume ; aroma ; [악취] stench ; stink ; reek ¶ 좋은 냄새 a sweet〔fragrant, nice, pleasant〕 smell ; an agreeable smell // 나쁜 냄새 a bad〔a disgusting, a vile, a foul, a nasty, an unpleasant, an offensive〕 smell // 냄새가 좋다 smell sweet ; have a good smell ; be sweet-smelling ; be fragrant ; be odoriferous ; be balmy // 냄새가 고약하다

smell bad ; have a bad smell ; stink ; be foul〔ill〕-smelling ; be unpleasant 〔disgusting〕 to the smell // 사향 냄새가 나다 smell of musk ; be scented with musk // 냄새가 없다 be destitute of smell ; be scentless ; be odorless // 냄새가 없어지다 lose the odor // 냄새를 빼다 take the smell ; deodorize (나쁜 냄새를) // 냄새를 풍기다 give out〔send forth, scent, perfume〕 《a sweet fragrance》 ; stink〔reek〕 (악취를) // 냄새를 맡다 smell 《a flower》 ; take a smell 《at》 ; sniff // 냄새를 피워 여우를 몰아내다 stink out a fox // 냄새에 민감한 사람 a person sensitive to odor ; a person of sensitive nostrils // 가스 냄새가 안나오 Don't you smell gas? // 가스 냄새가 난다 I smell gas. /This is a smell of gas. // 그녀는 '라일락'의 냄새를 풍기면서 들어왔다 She came in giving out a sweet odor of lilac. // 입에서 술냄새가 난다 His breath reeks〔smells〕 of wine. // 그의 셔츠에서 땀냄새가 난다 His shirt smells〔reeks〕 of sweat. // 그의 옷에는 신선한 풀냄새가 배어 있었다 His dress was impregnated〔soaked〕 with the odor of fresh grass. // 그릇에는 아직도 술냄새가 남아 있었다 The spirit of the liquor yet hung about the vessel. // 이게 무슨 냄새냐 What's that odor? // 뭔가 타는 냄새가 난다 Something smells like it's burning. // 아무 냄새도 안 난다 I don't smell anything. // 네 양말에서 냄새가 난다 Your socks smell.

냅다[1] [세차게] with force ; hard ; actively ; with all one's strength ; violently ¶ 냅다 후려치다 give a hard blow // 냅다 걷어차다 kick hard // 냅다 달아나다 run away for one's life ; make a quick escape

냅다[2] [연기가] (be) smoky ¶ 방이 냅다 The room is smoky. // 연기가 냅다 smoke stings〔smarts〕

냅뜨다 venture forth ; go full steam ahead 《on a project》 ; sally forth

냅킨 a (table) napkin ; a serviette ¶ 무릎에 냅킨을 펴다 lay one's napkin across one's lap

냇가 a riverside ; the bank (edge) of a river ; a riverbank

냇내 the smell of smoke

냇물 [시내] a stream〔brook〕 ; [물] water of a stream ¶ 냇물을 건너다 wade across a stream

냇버들 〖식물〗 a purple willow ; a purple osier ; Salix Gilgiana (학명)

냇송어 〖물고기〗 a bull trout ; a brook trout

냉 冷 ① [배의] a chill stomach ; a stomach chill ② [하체의 병] a chill ; a body chill ③ [대하증] leucorrh(o)ea ; whites

냉- 冷 [접두어] iced ; cold ; chill(ed) ; cooled ¶ 냉맥주 iced beer // 냉사이다 iced soda pop // 냉커피 iced coffee // 냉육 cold meat

냉가슴 冷— a hidden〔secret〕 pain ; inward pang ; agony unknown to others ¶ 냉가슴 앓다 have a secret troubles

⁑**냉각 冷却** cooling ; refrigeration **—하다** cool ; refrigerate ; be〔get〕 cooled ; cool down ¶ 수증기를 냉각하면 물이 된다 When cooled, vapor is condensed into water. // 남북한의 전쟁위기를 냉각시키다 take the heat out of the war crisis of South and North Korea

— 기간 a cooling-off period (노사간의) ; cooling time **—수** cooling water ; a coolant **— 장치** a cooling device 〔apparatus〕 **—제(劑)** a refrigerant ; a coolant **— 탱크** a refrigeratory **— 효과** a cooling effect 《미》 **공기(空氣) — 발동기** an air-cooled motor

냉각기 冷却器 a refrigerator ; a freezer ; a radiator (자동차 엔진 따위의) ; an air condenser (공기에 의한)

냉간 압연 공장 冷間壓延工場 a cold strip iron mill

냉갈령 coolness ; coldness ; indifference

냉과리 half-burnt charcoal

냉국 冷— soup prepared cold

냉국수 冷— iced noodles

⁑**냉기 冷氣** [찬 공기] cool air ; a chilly draft〔draught〕 ; [찬 기운] cold ; chill ; [기후] a cold wave ; cold weather ¶ 아침 냉기가 몸에 스미다 feel the chill of the morning air // (물의) 냉기를 가셔서 마셔라 Drink the water after taking off the chill.

†**냉담 冷淡** ① [무관심] coolness ; indifference ; lukewarmness ; lack of interest **—하다** (be) cool ; half-hearted ; indifferent ; lukewarm ; apathetic ; phlegmatic ¶ 냉담하게 coolly ; indifferently ; lukewarmly ; half-heartedly ; phlegmatically // 냉담한 태도 an indifferent attitude // 정치에 대해서 냉담하다 be indifferent to〔unconcerned with〕 politics // 그는 교육에 관한 일에는 극히 냉담하다 He is extremely indifferent about 〔takes little interest in〕 educational matters. // 그는 나의 요구에 대해서 거의 냉담했다 He paid but little attention to my request. ② [냉정] cold-heartedness ; heartlessness ; callousness **—하다** (be) cold ; cold-hearted ; heartless ; callous ; icy ; frigid ¶ 냉담하게 coldly ; icily ; cold-heartedly ; heartlessly // 냉담한 성질 a cold temperament ; cold-heartedness // 냉담한 인간 a cold-hearted man ; an unfeeling person // 냉담한 대답 a cold reply // 냉담한 대접 a frigid reception ; cold〔icy〕 treatment // 냉담하게 대접하다 give 《a person》 a cold reception // 냉담해지다 grow cold 《toward a person》

*냉대 冷待 (a) cold〔icy〕 treatment ; a frigid reception ; inhospitality —하다 receive〔treat〕 《a person》 coldly〔with coldness, in a cold way〕 ; treat 《a person》 unkindly ; give〔turn〕 the cold shoulder to 《a person》 ; be inhospitable to ; deal ill with 《a person》 ¶ 냉대를 달게 받다 submit to cold treatment // 냉대를 받았다 He was given a cold reception. / He was treated in a cold way. // 은혜를 입은 사람을 냉대해서는 안된다 You should never be inhospitable to anyone to whom you are indebted.

*냉동 冷凍 refrigeration ; freezing ; cold storage —하다 cool down ; refrigerate ; deep-freeze ¶ 생선을 냉동하다 refrigerate fish
—기 a refrigerator ; a refrigerating machine ; a freezer —선 a refrigerator boat〔ship〕 — 수송 chilled transport — 식품(食品) frozen food —실 a freezer ; a deep freeze — 야채 frozen vegetable —업 the cold-storage business —육(肉) frozen meat —제(劑) refrigerant —차(車) a refrigerator car 〔van〕 ; a chill car 《미》 — 창고 cold storage warehouse —함(函) a deep-freezer 급속 — quick-freeze ; sharp-freeze

냉동 건조 冷凍乾燥 freeze-drying ; lyophilization —하다 freeze-dry ; lyophilize
—기 a freeze dryer

*냉랭하다 冷冷— ① [차갑다] (be) cold ; chilly ; icy ; cool ¶ 방 바닥이 얼음장같이 냉랭하다 The floor is as cold as ice. ② [냉담] (be) cold ; cool ; indifferent ; half-hearted ⇨ 냉담 ¶ 냉랭한 태도 a cold manner // 냉랭히 coldly ; coolly ; indifferently ; half-heartedly // 그들은 나를 냉랭히 대했다 They gave me the cold shoulder. // 그들은 냉랭히 대답했다 They gave a cold〔curt〕 reply.

냉면 冷麵 a cold noodle dish ; iced vermicelli

냉방 冷房 a cold room ; an unheated room (찬 방) ; air conditioning (공기 조절) ; air cooling
—병 《be sick with》 air-conditioningitis — 완비 [게시] Air-conditioned —차 an air-conditioned car

냉방 장치 冷房裝置 an air conditioner ; air conditioning ; an air-conditioning unit ¶ 냉방 장치가 된 건물 an air cooled〔-conditioned〕 building // 냉방 장치가 되다 be air-conditioned ; be equipped 〔installed〕 with an air conditioner

냉소 冷笑 a cold〔sardonic, derisive, cynical〕 smile ; [조소] a sneer ; a jeer ; a derision ; a scornful laugh —하다 smile mockingly ; sneer 《at》 ; jeer 《at》 ; deride ; mock at ; laugh in scorn ¶ 냉소적 mocking ; sardonic ; cynical // 냉소하여 sneeringly ; scornfully ; derisively ; with a derisive smile // 입가에 냉소를 띠우고 with a cold smile on one's lips // 그의 말에는 냉소적인 데가 있었다 There was something derisive in his words.
—자 a sneerer ; a cynic

*냉수 冷水 cold water

냉수 마찰 冷水摩擦 a rubdown with a wet towel ; cold-water rubbing —하다 take a cold rubdown with a wet towel ; rub oneself〔take a rub〕 with a cold wet towel

냉수스럽다 冷水 —(be) dull ; insipid ; uninteresting

냉수욕 冷水浴 cold-water bathing ; a cold bath〔douche, shower〕 ¶ 냉수욕을 하다 take a cold bath〔douche〕 ; bathe in cold water

냉습 冷濕 ① [차고 습함] being cold and damp ; moisture —하다 (be) cold and damp〔moist〕 ② 〖한의〗 a disease caused by cold and dampness ; rheumatism

냉안시하다 冷眼視— look with coldness 〔indifference〕 《at》 ; look askance 《at》

냉엄하다 冷嚴— (be) grim ; stern ; stark ¶ 냉엄한 현실 stark realities of life ; a grim reality〔fact〕 // 냉엄한 조치를 취하다 take stern measures

냉연 冷然 —하다 (be) cold ; indifferent ; icy ; cold-hearted ¶ 냉연한 대답 a cold reply // 냉연히 coldly ; indifferently ; icily ; cold-heartedly

냉온 冷溫 coldness and warmth

냉우 冷遇 cold〔icy〕 treatment ⇨ 냉대(冷待)

냉육 冷肉 cold meat

냉이 〖식물〗 a shepherd's purse ; a mother's-heart ; a pickpurse ; Capsella brusapastoris (학명)

냉장 冷藏 cold storage ; refrigeration —하다 keep 《a thing》 cold ; keep 《a thing》 on ice ; keep 《things》 in cold storage ; refrigerate
—법 refrigeration —선 a cold storage ship — 장치 refrigeration plant —차 a refrigerator car〔van〕 ; a cold-storage car ; a chill car 《미》 — 회사 a cold-storage company

*냉장고 冷藏庫 a refrigerator ; a freezer (냉동용) ; an ice chest ; an icebox ; a fridge 《영·구》 ¶ 냉장고에 넣다 put 《food》 in a refrigerator
전기〔가스〕 — an electric〔a gas〕 refrigerator

냉전 冷戰 a cold war ¶ 냉전의 긴장을 완화하다 ease cold war tensions
— 외교 cold war diplomacy

냉정 冷情 coldheartedness ; heartlessness ; callousness ⇨ 냉담, 냉혹 —하다 (be) cold ; cold-hearted ; hardhearted ;

stony-hearted ; serene ¶ 냉정한 사람 a cold-hearted〔an unfeeling〕 person
†**냉정 冷靜** calmness ; coolness ; serenity ; composure ; presence of mind **—하다** (be) calm ; cool ; cool-headed ; self-possessed ; serene ; composed ; dispassionate ¶ 냉정한 판단 calm〔cool〕 judgments // 냉정을 잃다 lose one's presence of mind ; be perturbed ; be upset // 냉정을 유지하다 keep cool〔collected〕 ; remain serene ; be philosophical // 냉정한 태도를 취하다 take a calm attitude 《toward》 ; assume a dispassionate attitude // 냉정히 검토하다 examine in cold blood // 사물을 냉정히 생각하다 take a cool view of things // 그렇게 흥분하지 말고 냉정하라 Don't be so excited, calm yourself. // 냉정하게 생각하면 자기의 잘못을 뉘우칠 게다 If he thinks about the matter calmly, he will find out his mistake. /Calm reflection will convince him of his error. // 그는 언제나 냉정하다 He always keeps his presence of mind. // 챔피언은 대단히 냉정했다 The champ was as cool as a cucumber.
냉차 冷茶 iced tea
냉채 冷菜 a cold (vegetable) dish dressed with various seasonings ¶ 해파리 냉채 jelly fish and vegetables
냉천 冷泉 a cold (mineral) spring
냉철 冷徹 cool-headedness **—하다** (be) cool-headed ; hard-headed
냉큼 quickly ; briskly ; hastily ; promptly ; without delay ; right away ; readily ¶ 냉큼 대답하다 answer readily ; make a ready answer ; reply on the spot 〔without hesitation〕 // 냉큼 갔다 오라 Come back quick. / Don't tarry on the way. // 냉큼 말하라 Spit it out. // 냉큼 나가라 Get out at once ! / Make yourself scarce ! / Scram ! 《미·속》
냉평 冷評 a sarcastic remark ; scathing criticism ; a jeer ; a sneer **—하다** make a sarcastic remark 《on》 ; jeer 〔sneer〕 《at》
냉풍 冷風 a chilly〔cold〕 wind
냉하다 冷— (be) cold ; chilly ; icy ; freezing ; cold-hearted (마음이)
냉한 冷汗 a cold sweat
냉해 冷害 cold-weather damage ¶ 냉해를 입다 suffer damage due to〔from〕 cold weather // 농작물을 냉해로부터 보호하다 protect crops from being damaged by cold weather
냉혈 冷血 ① [온혈에 대한] cold-bloodedness ¶ 냉혈의 h(a)ematocryal ; poikilothermal ; cold-blooded ② [무정] cold-heartedness ; callousness ; heartlessness ¶ 냉혈의 cold-hearted ; heartless
— 동물 a cold-blooded animal ; a poikilothermic〔poikilothermal, poikilothermous〕 animal ; a poikilotherm
냉혈한 冷血漢 a cold-hearted〔heartless〕 fellow ¶ 저 녀석은 냉혈한이다 His heart is a stone.
†**냉혹 冷酷** cruelty ; heartlessness ; cold-heartedness ; callousness **—하다** (be) cruel ; unfeeling ; heartless ; cold-hearted ; hardhearted ; inhuman ; callous ; merciless ¶ 냉혹한 사나이 a heartless man // 아주 냉혹한 녀석이다 He is as cold as a stone. // 나를 냉혹하다고 그녀는 말한다 She says my heart is a stone.
냉회 冷灰 cold ashes
-냐 [의문] who ; what ; when ; where ; how ¶ 너는 누구냐 Who are you ? // 영어를 할 줄 아느냐 Can you speak English ?
냠냠 Yum-yum ! (How tasty !) ¶ 냠냠거리다 smack one's lips ; go yum-yum
—이 a yummy ; dainty food ; a delicacy
냠냠하다 [먹고 싶어] want〔desire〕 to eat ; [갖고 싶어] wish for ; long〔itch〕 for ; be anxious for ; covet
냥 兩 [화폐 단위] a unit of old Korean coinage ; [중량] a denomination of weight
‡**너**[1] you ; thou 《옛》 ¶ 너의 your ; thy 《옛》 // 너에게 to〔for〕 you〔thee〕 // 너 자신을 알라 Know yourself〔thyself〕
너하고 말하느니 개하고 말하겠다 속담 You tell a tale to a deaf man.
너[2] four ⇨ 넷
너겁 leaves, straws or dirt floating on the surface of the water ; muck floating above the water
너구리 〖동물〗 a raccoon dog
너구리 굴보고 피물(皮物) 돈 내어쓴다 속담 To sell the bear's skin before one has caught the bear.
너그러이 generously ; liberally ; magnanimously ; tolerantly ; leniently ; charitably ; indulgently ; broadmindedly ¶ 잘못을 너그러이 대하다 deal leniently with another's errors〔faults〕 // 너그러이 용서하다 generously forgive // 너그러이 봐주다 overlook 《a person's fault》 ; tolerate ; let 《it》 pass〔go〕 ; shut〔close〕 one's eyes to
***너그럽다** (be) broadminded ; generous ; liberal ; magnanimous ; tolerant ; indulgent ; lenient ; charitable ¶ 너그러운 태도 generous attitude // 반대파에 대하여 너그럽다 be liberal to the opponent // 너그러운 처분을 바라다 plead for leniency 〔clemency〕 // 여자에게 너그럽다 be indulgent with women
너글너글하다 (be) broadminded ; generous ; liberal ; magnanimous ¶ 성미가 너글너글하다 be broadminded
너나들이 intimate friendship **—하다** be on intimate terms ; be on a first-name basis

너나(할것)없다 everybody ; all ; without exception ; equally ; all alike ¶ 우리는 너나없이 그 계획에 반대다 We are (one and) all against the plan. // 우리는 너나없이 같은 운명이다 We are all in the same boat. // 너나없이 점심을 싸왔다 Everybody brought his own lunch.

너더댓 about four or five ¶ 너더댓새 about four or five days

너더분하다 ① [지저분하다] (be) untidy ; be a mess ; be in disorder〔out of order〕; (be) confused ; be in a muddle ; be at sixes and sevens ¶ 이 방은 너더분하구나 This room is in a terrible mess. // 책을 너더분히 쌓아 놓다 pile up books in a disorderly fashion ② [말이] (be) long and boring ; tedious ; lengthy ; long-winded ; diffuse ¶ 너더분한 이야기 an old wives' tale // 너더분하게 말을 한다 He talks tediously. // 그의 문장은 너더분하다 His style is rather wordy. /He writes a prolix style.

너덕너덕 patchily ; in tatters ¶ 너덕너덕 기운 patchy ; full of patches // 벽보가 너덕너덕 붙어 있다 The wall is plastered all over with bills〔posters〕.

너덜거리다 ① [여러 가닥이] dangle〔hang〕 in tatters ② [지껄이다] chatter ; prattle ; gabble

너덜(겅) stony slopes

너덜너덜 in tatters ; in shreds ; in rags and tatters **—하다** (be) tattered ; ragged ; torn ; worn-out ; seedy ; threadbare ¶ 너덜너덜한 것을 입고 있다 He dressed in tatters. // 이 사전은 너덜너덜하게 닳았다 This dictionary has been worn to tatters.

너덧 about four

너도나도 both you and I ¶ 너도나도 불조심 Let's take precautions against fire.

***너도밤나무** 〖식물〗 a beech (tree)

너럭바위 a broad flat rock

***너르다** (be) extensive ; open ; wide ; spacious ; commodious ; spacious and convenient ; roomy ¶ 너른 뜰 an extensive garden // 너른 벌판 an open field // 너른 수면 an expanse of water // 너른 집 a spacious house

너름새 a talent for doing things on a large scale ; managerial ability ; resourcefulness

너리 〖한의〗 a disease of the gums ; pyorrhea alveolaris ; gumboil ¶ 너리먹다 have diseased gums ; suffer from pyorrhea

너머 beyond ; over ; the other〔opposite〕 side 《of a mountain》 ¶ 너머로 across ; over ; beyond // 산 너머로 across〔beyond〕 a mountain // 재 너머 마을 a village beyond〔across〕 the hill // 안경 너머로 보다 look over (the rims of) one's spectacles // 울타리 너머로 보다 look over the fence // 담 너머로 말을 엿들은 것이 사실이냐 Is it true that you overheard〔eavesdropped on〕 what was said on the other side of the wall? // 서산 너머(로) 해가 졌다 The sun has set beyond the mountain. // 한달 너머 걸린다 It takes over a month.

***너무** too ; too much ; ever so much ; excessively ; to excess ; to a fault ; overly 《미》 ¶ 일을 너무 하다 work too hard ; overwork oneself // 그가 공처가라는 것은 너무나 유명하다 It is too well known that he is a henpecked husband. // 나에게 너무 큰 기대는 걸지 마시오 Don't expect too much of me. // 너무 놀라서 말도 못했다 He was speechless with astonishment. // 너무 점잖다 He is gentle to a fault. // 너무 서둘러서 지갑을 두고 왔다 I have forgotten my purse in my hurry. // 너무 안심하지 마라 Don't be too sure of it. // 세상을 너무나 모르는군 How little he knows the world! // 이 책은 너무 어려워서 읽을 수가 없다 This book is so difficult that I cannot read it. // 너무 심한 말이야 What a thing to say!

너무하다 (be) unreasonable ; (too) bad ; too hard ¶ 그건 너무하다 That's too much. /That's going too far.

너벅선 一船 a flat-bottomed boat ; a broad ferryboat

너벳벳하다 [얼굴이] (be) flat and well-looking

너볏하다 (be) nice and neat ¶ 너볏이 nice and neat(ly)

너부데데하다 have an unpleasantly flat face

너부러기 [너부렁이] chips ; scraps ; odds and ends (of cloth)

너부죽이 ① [너부죽하게] somewhat flatly〔evenly〕 ② [엎드리다] 《lie》 prostrate 《before》; 《fall》 prostrate〔flat〕 《upon the ground》

너부죽하다 be somewhat flattish〔even, level〕

너불거리다 flutter ; flap ; wave ¶ 바람에 너불거리다 flutter in the wind

너붓하다 ⇨ 너부죽하다

****너비** width ; breadth ¶ 너비가 넓다〔좁다〕 be wide〔narrow〕 in width // 너비가 5피이트이다 It is five feet wide〔in width〕.

너비아니 slices of roast ; seasoned beef in width

너삼 〖식물〗 Sophora angustifolia (학명)

너새[1] 〖새〗 a great bustard

너새[2] 〖건축〗 a hip[너와] a shingle **— 지붕** a hip(ped) roof

너설 a rock-ribbed place ; a rocky〔craggy〕 spot

너스래미 loose ends〔strips〕 ¶ 멍석 너스래미 loose ends of a straw mat

너스레 ① [아구리에 걸친] a frame-sup-

port made by criss-crossing twigs or sticks (used to cover a hole or to support things at the bottom of a pot) ② a trick ; an artifice ; a catch
너스레 놓다 관용 lead 《a person》 to the (point in) question ; lay some catch in one's question
너스레(를) 떨다 관용 talk nonsense ; make idle remarks ; talk big〔tall〕; brag
너스르르하다, 너슬너슬하다 (be) shaggy and dirty ; rumpled ; tousled
너울 ① [여자가 머리에 쓰는] a thin black hood worn by women for going out ; a lady's veil ② [시든 잎] a withered leaf ; withered grass
너울가지 affability ; sociability ; companionableness ¶ 너울가지가 좋다 be sociable ; be amicable
너울거리다 [파도가] surge ; roll ; swell ; [파도처럼] wave (머리털 따위) ; undulate ; [나무나 풀잎이] swing ; sway ; waver ¶ 파도가 너울거린다 The sea is swelling. / The sea rolls. // 나뭇잎이 바람에 너울거린다 The leaves of the trees tremble〔rustle〕 in the breeze. // 머리카락이 바람에 너울거린다 The hairs swing〔sway〕 around in the wind.
너울너울 waving ; undulating ; surging ; swaying ; swinging ¶ 햇빛이 수면에서 너울너울 춤을 춘다 The sun is dancing on the water.
너울지다 [물결이] be rough in the distance
너저분하다 (be) shabby and untidy ; dirty ; sordid ; filthy ; nasty ; disorderly ; be out of order ¶ 너저분한 거리 an untidy street // 너저분히 책을 늘어놓다 leave books in a mess // 방이 너저분하다 The room is in a awful mess〔jumble〕.
*너절하다 ① [허름하다] (be) shabby ; worn out ; threadbare ; unsightly ; ugly ; unpresentable ¶ 너절한 의복 shabby clothes // 너절한 환경 shabby surroundings
② [변변찮다] (be) shabby ; worthless ; paltry ; petty ; insignificant ; trivial ; unimportant ; trifling ¶ 너절한 선물 a shabby present // 너절한 문제 a trivial matter // 너절한 변명 paltry excuse
③ [품위 없다] (be) shabby ; mean ; vulgar (야비한) ; poor ; despicable (치사한) ; contemptible (비열한) ; deteriorated (타락된) ; disgraceful (창피한) ¶ 너절한 취미 vulgar tastes // 너절한 거짓말쟁이 a despicable liar // 너절한 생각 mean thoughts
너즈러지다 《fallen leaves》 lie scattered all over
너클 볼 『야구』 a knuckle ball
너털거리다¹ ⇨ 너덜거리다
너털거리다² ① [흔들리다] dangle〔sway〕 in a disorderly manner ② [웃다] laugh aloud〔boisterously, heartily〕; roar with laughter ; burst out laughing ; cachinnate ; guffaw
너털웃음 a loud〔hearty, boisterous〕 laugh ; a guffaw ; cachinnation ; a roar of laughter ¶ 너털웃음을 웃다 laugh aloud〔boisterously〕 ⇨ 너털거리다
너테 an added coating of ice on top of ice
너트 『기계』 a nut ¶ 볼트를 너트로 고정하다 fasten a bolt with a nut
너펄거리다 roughly flutter〔wave〕 (in the wind) ; flap rough
너펄너펄 flutteringly
너푼거리다 lightly flutter〔wave〕
너풀거리다 flutter ; wave ; float ; flap ¶ 깃발이 성 위에 너풀거린다 The flag flutters〔floats〕 over a castle. // 깃발이 바람에 너풀거리고 있다 The flag is flapping〔fluttering〕 in the wind.
너풀너풀 fluttering〔flapping〕 away
너희 you ; ye ; you all ; you people ; you folks
*너희들 you ⇨ 너희
넉 four ; fourth (순서) ¶ 넉달 four months // 넉줄째에 in the fourth line 《of the page》
넉가래 a wooden shovel ; a snow shovel ; a snowplow 《미》 ; a snowplough 《영》 ¶ 넉가래질하다 shovel with a wooden shovel
넉걷이 raking out vines ━하다 rake vines off 《a melon field》
*넉넉하다 ① [족하다] (be) enough ; sufficient ; adequate ; plenty〔plentiful〕; ample ; full ¶ 치수가 넉넉하다 have ample measure // 신발이 넉넉하다 One's shoes are big enough〔easy on one's feet〕. // 그 정도의 쌀이면 5인분으로는 넉넉하다 That much rice will be enough for five people. // 천원이면 넉넉하겠다 One thousand *won* (or so) will be sufficient〔will do, will suffice〕. // 시간은 넉넉하다 We have enough〔ample〕 time. /We have plenty of time.
② [살림이] (be) rich〔wealthy, well-to-do, well off〕; comfortably off ¶ 넉넉하게 살다 live comfortably ; be well off // 넉넉한 가정 a well-to-do family // 그 나라에서는 농부들의 살림이 넉넉하다 Farmers are quite well off in that country.
③ [도량이] (be) big-minded〔broad-minded〕; general ; liberal ¶ 넉넉한 마음 a lenient mind
넉넉히 enough ; plenty ; amply ; sufficiently ; fully ; copiously ; plentifully ; well off ; richly ; wealthily ; generously ; liberally ¶ 걸어서 넉넉히 이틀은 걸린다 It is a full〔good〕 two days' journey on foot.

넉살 audacity ; impudence ; shamelessness ; cheekiness ; sauciness ; sassiness ¶ 넉살부리다 behave impudently ; act brazenly〔brashly, with cheek〕; act audaciously ; get fresh // 넉살스럽다 be audacious〔impudent, shameless, brazen(-faced) (철면피)〕; be daring〔bold, cheeky, full of cheek〕// 넉살좋게도…하다 have the impudence〔audacity, cheek〕to 《do》// 넉살 좋은 친구로군 What nerve he's got ! /What a shameless〔cheeky〕fellow he is !

넉살좋다 (be) impudent ; brash ; shameless ; brazen(-faced) ; saucy ; sassy

넉자 a chamois underlay for affixing a seal

넉장 lingering ; tarrying ; slow-moving ; slowness ; tardiness ; dilatoriness ¶ 넉장 부리다 be tardy ; be slow ; be slow-going ; dally ; loiter ; linger ; loaf ; dawdle ; be sluggish ; idle about // 넉장부리다가 기회를 놓치다 dally away one's opportunity // 넉장부리고 있을 때가 아니야 This is no time for sitting idle. /It admits of no delay. // (방문) 시간이 넘었는데도 넉장부리고 돌아가지 않는다 He lingers on past visiting hours.

넉장거리 lying〔falling〕outstretched on one's back **—하다** fall〔lie〕down outstretched on one's back

*__넋__ a soul ; a spirit ; a ghost ; one's spirit(s) (기력) ¶ 죽은 넋 a departed spirit〔soul〕// 너무 기뻐서 넋을 잃다 be beside oneself with joy ; be in an ecstasy〔a rapture〕of joy // 넋이 없다 be absent-minded〔half-hearted〕// 넋을 빼앗기다 be captivated〔enthralled〕《by》// 넋을 잃고 미인을 보다 be lost in admiration of a beauty ; be struck〔enchanted〕by a beauty ; be captivated〔enthralled〕by a beauty

넋을 잃다〔놓다〕 관용 get absentminded ; forget oneself ; swoon ; faint

넋두리 ① [무당의] utterances of a shaman given as those of a deceased spirit **—하다** 《a shaman》 speak in behalf of the dead
② [투덜거림] a complaint ; a grumble ; a murmur **—하다** grumble 《at》; complain 《of》 ¶ 나이를 먹으면 넋두리도 나오는 법 Men become querulous with age.

넌더리 an aversion ; a dislike ; a disgust ; a hatred ; a repugnance ¶ 넌더리 나다 be disgusted with ; be tired of ; get sick of ; be nauseating ; be sickening〔revolting〕// 넌더리 대다 behave disgustfully〔repugnantly〕; make 《a person》 sick of 《a thing》// 그의 지루한 강의에 넌더리가 난다 We are bored by his tedious lecture. // 비에 넌더리가 난다 I am fed up with rain. // 이 일에 넌더리가 난다 I am tired of this work. // 그의 아내는 그가 오로지 일에만 몰두하는 데 넌더리가 나서 그들은 이혼할 것이다 His wife got fed up with his single-minded devotion to work, so they're getting divorced.

넌덕 smooth and witty talk ¶ 넌덕부리다 have a smooth and witty tongue ; speak smoothly and humorously

넌덕스럽다 be witly ; be facile ; be amusing ; be humorous

넌덜머리 ⇨ 넌더리

넌지시 secretly ; indirectly ; tacitly ; allusively ; implicitly ; covertly ; by hints ; quietly ¶ 넌지시 돈을 요구하다 make an indirect demand for money // 넌지시 말하다 hint 《at》; drop a hint ; allude // 넌지시 추파를 던지다 make eyes at 《a person》 secretly // 넌지시 사의를 표명하다 hint at one's resignation // 남의 속을 넌지시 떠보다 beat about〔around〕the bush ; sound 《a person》 about his views ; tap a person's opinion // 넌지시 남을 비난하다 rebuke a person indirectly // 그는 승낙할 뜻을 넌지시 알렸다 He gave us to understand that he will consent.

넌출 a bine ; a vine ; a tendril (호박 따위의) ; a runner (고구마의)
포도 — a grape vine

넌출문 —門 a four-door gate

넌출지다 《tendrils》 dangle down

*__널__ ① [널빤지] a board ; a plank ; planking 《총칭》 ¶ 널을 깔다 lay boards 《on》
② [관] a coffin ; a casket 《미》 ¶ 널 속에 넣다 lay 《a person》 in coffin
③ [유희용] a seesaw
청(廳)— a floor board ; flooring board

널감 ① [널의 감] wood for a coffin ② [죽어 가는 이] an old man ; a person with one foot in the grave

널다[1] [쥐가] gnaw 《a thing》 into shreds〔small pieces〕

*__널다__[2] [펴놓다] spread out ; stretch ; [걸다] hang 《a thing》 out to dry〔air〕 ¶ 빨랫줄에 옷을 널다 hang out clothes on a clothesline // 멍석에 벼를 널다 spread grain out on a straw mat // 옷을 내널다 air clothes // 세탁물을 널다 hang out the washing

널다리 a wooden footbridge

†**널따랗다** (be) rather wide ; extensive ; roomy ; spacious ; broad ¶ 널따란 공지 wide-open spaces.

널뛰기 seesaw ; seesawing ; teetertotter(ing) **—하다** ⇨ 널뛰다

널뛰다 play at seesaw ; teetertotter

널름 ⇨ 날름

⁑**널리** [광범히] widely ; broadly ; extensively ; far and wide ; [대규모] on a large scale ; [보편적으로] universally ; generally ; at large ; [도처에] everywhere ; all over ; throughout ; at every turn ¶ 널리 알려져 있다 be widely known // 널리 광고하다 advertise extensively // 널리 읽히고 있다 be widely read // 명성이 널리 천하에 퍼지다 have a worldwide reputation // 그 사건은 국내에 널리 알려졌다 The case received wide publicity in the country.

널리다¹ [흩어져 퍼지다] be spread 《over》; be scattered 《about》 ¶ 낙엽이 뜰에 널리다 The fallen leaves are spread all over the garden.

널리다² [넓히다] broaden〔widen, extend, enlarge〕 ¶ 길을 널리다 widen〔broaden〕 a road // 옷품을 널리다 make a coat wider // 집을 널리다 enlarge a house // 판로를 널리다 extend the market〔sales channel〕

널마루 a wooden floor

널문 a wooden gate

널반자 a wooden ceiling

널방석 —方席 a large straw mat ; a drying〔an airing〕 mat

널브러지다 spread (out) ; scatter (widely) ¶ 사방팔방으로 널브러지다 scatter in all directions

널빈지 board〔wooden〕 shutters

***널빤지** a board ; a plank ¶ 널빤지 담 a wooden wall ; a board fence // 방을 널빤지로 막다 partition a room off with boards // 널빤지로 지붕을 이다 shingle a roof

널어놓다 spread out ; hang out (a thing to air or dry it) ; stretch out

널음새 way of spreading things out ; the layout ; branching out ; spreading into ; going off (one's topic) on a tangent ; spreading oneself thin ¶ 그는 널음새가 있어 여러 일에 손을 댄다 He has many irons in the fire.

널장 a plank ; a board

널조각 a piece of board

널찍이 rather broadly ; widely ; spaciously ; extensively ; amply ; fully ¶ 앉을 자리를 널찍이 잡다 take an ample space to sit down // 구멍을 널찍이 파다 dig a rather big hole

널찍하다 (be) rather wide ; broad ; extensive ; open ; spacious ; roomy ¶ 널찍한 마당 an extensive garden // 널찍한 집 a roomy〔spacious〕 house

널판때기 a big〔long, broad and thick〕 piece of board

널판자 ⇨ 널빤지

널판장 —板墻 a board fence ; a wooden wall

널평상 —平床 a plank bed ; a wooden bed

†**넓다** ① [폭·면적 따위가] (be) broad ; wide ; roomy ; vast ; extensive ; large ; comprehensive (범위가) ¶ 넓은길 a broad road // 넓은 집 a roomy house // 넓은 풀밭 an extensive meadow // 넓은 이마 a prominent forehead // 넓은 학식 comprehensive knowledge // 시야가 넓은 사람 a man of broad outlook // 교제가 넓은 사람 a person of wide〔large〕 acquaintance // 넓은 의미로 in a broad sense // 넓어지다 widen ; broaden ; become wider〔broader〕 // 교제가 넓다 He has a large (circle of) acquaintance. ② [마음이] (be) broadminded ; large-hearted ; generous ¶ 마음이 넓은 사람 a broad-minded person

넓다듬이 fulling on a fulling stock —**하다** full (on a fulling stock)

넓데데하다 (be) unpleasantly flattish ¶ 넓데데한 얼굴 a flat ugly face

넓둥글다 (be) flat and round

넓삐죽하다 (be) broad〔wide〕 and tapering

***넓이** [폭] width ; breadth ; [면적] extent ; area ; dimensions ¶ 넓이가 여섯자다 have a width of 6 feet ; be 6 feet wide // 이 땅의 넓이는 얼마나 되지 What is the area of this land ?

넓이뛰기 a broad jump 《미》; a long jump 《영》

제자리 — a standing broad jump

넓적 ① [입을] with one's mouth wide open ¶ 어린애가 엄마한테서 과자를 넓적 받아 먹는다 The child gobbles up the sweet his mother gives him. ② [엎드림] flat ; low ¶ 넓적 엎드리다 lay down flat 《on the ground, on one's belly》; fall prostrate ; prostrate oneself 《before a person》

넓적거리다 ① [입을] mouth ; keep one's mouth opening and shutting ② [몸을] keep coming back to a flat position

넓적넓적 [넓적하게] all flat ; so that all are flat ; [입을] with one's mouth wide open ; [서슴지 않고] without hesitation ¶ 그녀는 떡을 넓적넓적 썰었다 She cut rice cake into flat pieces.

***넓적다리** the thigh ; a femur 《*pl.* -mora》; a ham ¶ 총알이 넓적다리를 관통했다 A bullet went through〔penetrated〕 the thigh.

—뼈 the thighbone

넓적부리 〖새〗 a shovelbill ; a spoonbill

— 도요 a spoon-billed sandpiper

넓적스름하다 (be) rather flat〔even, level〕

넓적이 ① [사람] a person with a plane and broad face ② [넓적하게] flatwise ; flatways ¶ 떡을 넓적이 썰다 cut a rice cake into flat pieces

넓적하다 (be) flat ¶ 넓적하게 flatways // 바닥이 넓적한 배 a flat-bottomed boat

넓죽하다 (be) flat and long

***넓히다** [널리다] widen ; enlarge ; expand ; broaden ; stretch〔spread〕 out ¶ 집을 넓히다 build an extension to a house // 사업을 넓히다 expand one's business // 경험을 넓히다 enlarge one's experience // 세력을 넓히다 extend one's influence

넘겨다보다 ① [담너머] look over 《a fence》 ② [탐내다] covet ; look on with envy ¶ 남의 아내를 넘겨다보다 covet another's wife // 담을 넘겨다보다 look over a wall

넘겨쓰다 be made the scapegoat 《for》 ; be falsely charged 《with》 ; have 《a thing》 wrongly imputed to one ¶ 억울하게 남의 죄를 넘겨쓰다 find oneself in the sorry position of being charged with another's crimes // 친구의 잘못을 넘겨쓰다 take the blame for one's friend's fault

넘겨씌우다 put a blame on another ; lay a fault at another's door ; impute ; shift ; shuffle off ¶ 죄를 넘겨씌우다 lay the blame upon another ; shift the responsibility on to other shoulders ; shuffle off the responsibility on to someone else ; impute the fault to another

넘겨잡다 guess ; surmise ; conjecture ; anticipate ; forecast ; foresee ; look ahead ¶ 남의 뜻을 넘겨잡다 anticipate another's wishes // 가격 앙등을 넘겨잡다 foresee〔anticipate〕 higher prices

†**넘겨주다** ⇨ 넘기다 ① ④ ⑥ ⑨

넘겨짚다 guess ; make a guesswork ; make a random guess ¶ 넘겨짚고 말하다 hazard a conjecture // 넘겨짚고 말한 것이 맞다 make a good shot 《at》 ; guess right

넘고처지다 be either too long or too short〔too big or too small, too high or too low, etc.〕 ; be too much one way or too much the other ; be not adequate〔suitable〕 ; be good neither for one thing nor the other ¶ 취직 자리는 몇 군데 있으나 모두 넘고처진다 There are several positions〔vacancies〕, but none of them is suitable for him.

***넘기다** ① [넘어가게 하다] bring〔carry〕 《a thing》 across ; pass over ¶ 담 너머로 넘기다 pass 《a thing》 over a wall
② [넘어뜨리다] throw down ; fell ; trip ¶ 나무를 잘라 넘기다 cut a tree down // 다리를 걸어 넘기다 trip a person
③ [기회·기한을] pass ; spend ; exceed ¶ 해를 넘기다 pass〔speed on〕 the old year ; enter a new year // 60 고개를 넘기다 be on the wrong〔other, shady〕 side of sixty // 출원 기한을 넘기다 pass〔miss〕 the deadline for application
④ [책임·권리를] transfer ; shift ; make over ; turn over ; pass on ; shuffle ¶ 재산을 아들에게 넘기다 make over〔pass on〕 one's property to one's son // 채권을 넘기다 turn one's claim over to 《a person》
⑤ [책장을] turn ¶ 책장을 넘기다 turn a page ; turn the leaves of a book // 사전을 넘기다 leaf through a dictionary
⑥ [인도하다] hand over ; turn over ; pass 《a thing to another》 ¶ 도둑을 경찰에 넘기다 hand over〔turn over〕 a thief to the police // 시체를 유가족에게 넘기다 hand over 《a person's》 remains to the family
⑦ [이월하다] carry〔bring〕 over ; [다음으로 미루다] carry forward ; [연기하다] defer ; postpone ; put off ¶ 전년도에서 넘겨진 일 work brought over from the previous year // 잔액을 다음 회계 연도로 넘기다 carry the balance over to the following fiscal year
⑧ [유지하다] keep〔hold〕 over ; [극복하다] get through〔over〕 ; pass〔go〕 through ; pull through ¶ 겨울을 넘기다 survive〔live through〕 the winter (환자가) // 위기〔고비〕를 넘기다 pass (through) 〔go through〕 a crisis // 용케 그 자리를 넘기다 be master of the situation // 재정위기를 넘기다 weather a financial crisis
⑨ [돌리다] transmit ; send round 《a bill to》 ¶ 서류를 담당자에게 넘기다 send round the papers〔send the papers over〕 to the man in charge

넘나다 be not suitable〔proportionate〕 to one's means ¶ 넘난 생활을 하다 one's style of living is out of keeping with one's means ; live beyond〔above〕 one's means // 넘난 생각을 하다 have ideas above one's station

넘나들다 frequent ; visit here and there 〔many places〕 ; go and come often ¶ 그 댁에 넘나들다 have access to the mansion

넘노닐다 stroll around〔to and fro〕

넘늘거리다 wave〔swing, sway〕 ; droop ; sway at random

넘늘다 act〔speak〕 humorously without losing one's dignity

‡**넘다** ① [건너다] cross ; go across 〔over〕 ; go〔get〕 beyond ; clear ; hurdle (장애물을) ¶ 산을 넘다 go over〔cross〕 a mountain // 고개〔국경〕를 넘다 cross a pass〔the border〕 // 죽을 고비를 넘다 tide over a crisis // 그는 담을 넘었다 He climbed over the wall. // 그는 알프스를 넘어 이탈리아로 갔다 He crossed the Alps into Italy.
② [초과하다] exceed ; pass ; be in excess of ; be over〔above〕 ; be more than ¶ 예순이 넘었다 be over sixty ; be well into the sixties (훨씬) ; be in one's early sixties // 그 교통 사고로 인한 사망자는 10명을 넘는다 More than ten persons were killed in the traffic accident. // 청중의 수는 1,000명이 넘었다 The audience exceeded〔was over〕 one thousand.
③ [고비를] conquer〔overcome, surmount〕 《difficulties》 ; tide over ; pull 〔pass, muddle〕 through

④ [칼날이] be turned ¶ 칼날이 넘다 the edge of a knife is turned
⑤ [넘치다] overflow ; run〔flow〕 over ¶ 강물이 뚝을 넘다 The river overflows the bank.
⑥ [뛰어넘다] jump ; hop ¶ 도랑을 뛰어넘다 hop〔jump〕 a ditch // 줄을 넘다 jump a rope ; play rope skipping

넘버 number
—원 A-1 《구》 ; number one ; first 《미·구》 ; No. 1 《미·구》 ; an ace

넘버링 a numbering machine

넘보다 look down on ; underestimate ; underrate ; undervalue ; hold 《a person》 cheap ; think meanly of ; disparage ; belittle ; make light of ¶ 사람의 재간을 넘보다 underrate 《a person's》 talent // 그를 어린애라고 넘보아서는 안된다 You should not make light of him as a mere boy.

넘성거리다 stretch〔crane〕 one's neck avidly to see 《a thing》 ; rubberneck 《미·속》 ¶ 헌책방을 여기저기 넘성거리며 걷다 walk about looking in second-hand bookstores here and there // 남의 아내를 넘성거리다 covet another's wife

넘실거리다 ① [탐내다] covet ; be greedy for ⇨ 넘성거리다 ¶ 남의 것을 넘실거려서는 못쓴다 You should not covet anything that belongs to others.
② [물·물결이] surge ; roll ; swell ; be brimful ¶ 물이 뱃전에 넘실거린다 The water is about to overflow the side of the boat.

넘실넘실 ① [넘성거림] stretching〔craning〕 one's neck avidly 《to see》 ; rubbernecking ② ⇨ 너울너울

†**넘어가다** ① [지나가다] cross ; go across ; go over ; hurdle (장애물을) ¶ 국경을 넘어가다 cross the border 《into another country》 // 뚝을 넘어가다 go over〔cross〕 a bank // 언덕을 넘어가다 go over〔cross〕 a hill
② [해·달이] sink ; set ; go down ¶ 해가 넘어가기 전에 before dark〔dusk〕 ; before sunset // 해가 서산으로 넘어간다 The sun is sinking beyond the western hills.
③ [남의 소유로] fall into 《a person's》 hands ; pass into〔to〕 another's hands ¶ 그 물건은 다음 사람에게 넘어갔다 The thing passed to the next person.
④ [속다] be taken in ; be imposed upon ; be cheated ; be deceived ¶ 계략에 넘어가다 fall into a trap // 손쉽게 넘어가다 be easily cheated〔deceived〕 // 그런 수작에 넘어갈 줄 아나 So that is your little game ! // 남에게 넘어가다 be cheated〔done in〕 by a person // 너는 상사의 계략에 감쪽같이 넘어갔다 You walked right into the boss's stratagem.
⑤ [쓰러지다] fall down ; collapse ; tumble ; come down
⑥ [때·시기가] pass ; miss ; exceed ; be overdue ¶ 지원 마감 날이 넘어가다 The deadline for application has expired.
⑦ [고비가] tide over ; overcome ⇨ 넘다

넘어다보다 look〔peep〕 over 《a high thing》 ¶ 담을 넘어다보다 look〔peep〕 over a wall

‡**넘어뜨리다** ① throw〔bring〕 down ; [사람을] throw 《a person》 to the ground ; get 《a person》 down ; knock down ; trip up (발을 걸어서) ; [바람이] blow down ; level ; tip down (뒤집어 엎다) ; pull down (무너뜨리다) ; push down (밀어서) ¶ 나무를 넘어뜨리다 fell a tree ; blow down a tree (바람이) // 의자를 넘어뜨리다 tip over a chair // 사람을 때려 넘어뜨리다 knock 《a person》 down // 집을 넘어뜨리다 demolish〔destroy〕 a house (지진 따위가) ; pull〔take〕 down a house // 폭풍이 벼를 넘어뜨렸다 The storm leveled〔blew down〕 the rice plants.
② [지우다] defeat ; beat ¶ 씨름 선수를 넘어뜨리다 beat〔topple〕 a wrestler
③ [전복시키다] overthrow ; undermine ; ruin ¶ 정부를 넘어뜨리다 overthrow〔unseat〕 a government

넘어박히다 be stuck in hard ; be driven into firmly ; be sandwiched tight ; fall down hard.

넘어서다 pass〔get〕 over ¶ 산을 넘어서다 cross the mountain // 어려운 고비를 넘어서다 get over the hump〔the hard period〕

넘어오다 ① fall ; come down ; topple over ¶ 담이 뜰 쪽으로 넘어오다 a wall topples over toward the garden
② [토하다] vomit ; throw〔bring, fetch〕 up 《food》 ; spew ; puke ¶ 아침 먹은 것이 넘어오다 vomit one's breakfast // 먹은 것이 넘어올 것 같다 feel nausea ; feel sick ; feel like vomiting
③ [책임·관리·소유권] be transferred ; be made over ; be turned over 《to one》 ; be passed on ¶ 상속이 아버지한테서 아들에게 넘어왔다 The right of inheritance has been transferred from the father to his son.
④ [넘어서 오다] cross ; go across ; pass ; [고비를] find〔see〕 one's way out of 《difficulties》 ; tide〔get〕 over ¶ 산을 넘어오다 go over〔cross〕 a mountain // 국경을 넘어오다 cross the boundary 《to this country》 // 어려운 고비를 넘어오다 find one's way out of troubles ; struggle through difficulties ; tide over a crisis ; weather the storm // 물이 뚝을 넘어오다 the water overflows the bank
⑤ [자기편에 붙다] come over 《on our side》 ; [투항하다] surrender ¶ 자유진영으로 넘어오다 come over to〔for〕 the

free world

*넘어지다 ① fall ; come down ; collapse ¶ 곤두박이로 넘어지다 fall head over heels ; fall upside down // 넘어지려고 하다 be on the point of falling ; be tottering // 뒤로 넘어지다 fall flat on one's back // 돌에 걸려 넘어지다 fall over a stone // 지진으로 많은 집이 넘어졌다 Many houses were destroyed by the earthquake. // 그는 한방에 넘어졌다 One push sent him tumbling.
② [지다] be defeated ; be ruined ; be overthrown ; go〔become〕 bankrupt (파산) ¶ 넘어져 가는 은행〔정부〕 a tottering bank〔government〕 // 출판계의 불황으로 많은 출판사가 넘어졌다 Many a publisher has gone bankrupt〔broke〕 with the depression of the publishing business.

*넘치다 ① overflow 《the bank》; run 〔flow〕 over 《the brim》; brim over ; flood ; inundate 《the land》; teem ; swarm ¶ 넘칠 만큼 가득히 be full to the brim ; be brimful // 애교가 넘치다 be full of charms ; be brimming with smiles // 투지가 넘치다 be full of fight // 원기가 넘쳐 흐르다 be overbrimming with spirits // 기쁨에 넘치다 be overwhelmed with joy // 호우로 강이 넘쳤다 The heavy rainfall caused the river to overflow. // 한국은 인구가 넘치고 있다 Korea has an overflowing population. // 나는 기쁨이 넘쳐 울었다 I wept overwhelmed with joy. // 플랫폼은 늘 사람들로 넘쳐 있다 The platform is always overflowing with people. // 그는 젊음의 힘으로 넘쳐 있다 He's brimming with youthful energy.
② [지나치다] exceed ; pass ; be more than ; be above〔over〕 ¶ 분에 넘치는 영광 an undeserved honor // 분수에 넘치게 살다 live beyond one's means

넙데데하다 ⇨ 너부데데하다

넙치 〖물고기〗 a flatfish ; a sole
—눈이 a cross-eyed person

넛손자 —孫子 a grandson of one's sister ; a grandnephew on one's sister's side

넛할머니 one's father's maternal aunt ; a great-〔grand-〕aunt on one's father's maternal side

넛할아버지 one's father's maternal uncle ; a great-〔grand-〕uncle on one's father's maternal side

*넝마 rags ; tatters ; shreds ; scraps ; a piece of old cloth
— 장수 a ragman ; a rag-and-bone man ; a junkman ; a junk dealer 《미》
—전 a ragman's store —주이 [사람] a ragpicker ; a ragman ; a guttersnipe 《구》; [일] ragpicking

넝쿨 a vine ; a bine ; a tendril ; a runner

*넣다 ① [속에] put in ; take in ; bring in ; let in ; pour in (액체 따위를) ; pack in (꾸려서) ¶ 책을 상자 속에 넣다 put books in〔into〕 a box // 커피에 우유를 넣다 put milk into coffee // 신선한 공기를 넣다 let fresh air in // 안약을 넣다 drop a lotion into the eye. // 공에 바람을 넣다 pump〔blow〕 air into a ball
② [끼워서] set in ; put in ; insert ; stuff ¶ 반지 속에 보석을 해 넣다 insert a ring with stones // 솜을 넣다 stuff 《a thing》 with cotton // 광고를 신문에 끼워 넣다 insert bills in newspapers // 금니를 해 넣다 have a gold tooth put in
③ [포함] include ; count ¶. 계산에 넣지 않다 leave 《a thing》 out of count // 이것도 계산에 넣어 주세요 Add this to the bill, too. // 애들까지 넣어서 20명이다 There are twenty people, including the children
④ [수용] accommodate ; admit (into) (가입) ; put 《a person》 to (병원 따위에) ¶ 이 회장에 500명을 넣을 수 있다 The hall can accommodate 500 people.
⑤ [보내다] send ; admit ¶ 아이를 학교에 넣다 send a child to school
⑥ [염두에 두다] mind ¶ 마음에 넣어두다 bear〔keep, have〕 in mind
⑦ [기타] ¶ 이자를 넣다 pay interest // 중개인을 넣어 교섭하다 negotiate through an intermediary

네[1] ① [너] you ¶ 네가 해봐라 Try it. / Try it yourself. // 네가 틀렸어 You are wrong. // 네가 잘못했다 You are to blame.
② [너의] your ¶ 네 집 your (own) house // 네 책 좀 빌려다오 Lend me your book.

네[2] [넷] four ¶ 네 살 먹은 소녀 a girl of four (years) // 네 시에 일어나다 get up at four // 네 식구 a family of four

†네[3] [대답] yes ; certainly ; all right ; very well ; surely ; sure ; O. K. 《미·속》; [출석을 부를 때의 대답] yes ; here (sir) ; sir ; present

-네 ① [들] all of ② [가족·친척] ¶ 우리네 we all // 당신네 you all // 그 사람네 his family〔their family〕 // 순이네 little *Sunyee* and her family

*네거리 a crossroads ; a cross ; an X-road ; an intersection ¶ 네거리에 있는 담배집 the tobacconist's at the corner of the street

네거티브 negative

네거필름 negative film

네것 your thing ; yours

네글리제 a negligee ; négligé 《프》

네놈 you

네눈(박)이 a dog with a white spot above each eye

네다리 the limbs ; the legs and arms ; four legs ¶ 네다리를 뻗고 자다 sleep with one's limbs outstretched ; sleep with ease ; have no cares

네다섯 four or five
네댓 about four or five
네덜란드 Holland ; the Netherlands 《공칭》; the Low Countries ¶ 네덜란드의 Dutch
— **사람** a Hollander ; a Dutchman ; the Dutch people 《총칭》 —**어** Dutch
네뚜리 ① [업신여김] looking down on 《a person》; holding 《a person》 in contempt —**하다** look down on 《a person》; disdain ; contempt ② [새우젓의] one fourth of a crock of pickled shrimps
네모 a square ¶ 네모진 square ; four-cornered // 네모나다, 네모지다 be square ; be tetragonal ; be quadrilateral // 네모지게 자르다 cut square
네모꼴 a tetragon ; a quadrangle ; a trapezium ; a quadrilateral
네미 ① [송아지를 부를 때] Here ! ; [욕] Damn it〔you〕! ② [너의 어미] your mother
네발 four feet ¶ 네발 달린 four-footed ; quadruped // 네발 타다 be allergic to (four-legged) meat
—**짐승** four-legged animals ; quadrupeds
네쌍동이 quadruplets
네안데르탈 Neanderthal
—**인(人)** the Neanderthal man ; a Neanderthaler ; Homo (sapiens) neanderthalensis 《라》
네오- neo-
—**로맨티시즘** neoromanticism —**리얼리즘** neorealism — **마이신** neomycin — **클래시시즘** neoclassicism
네온 〖화학〗 neon
— **사인** a neon sign
네이블 오렌지 〖식물〗 a navel orange
네이비 블루 navy blue ; dark blue 《미》
네이팜 napalm
—**탄(彈)** a napalm bomb
네임 a name ¶ 네임밸류가 있는 well-known
— **플레이트** a nameplate
네커치프 a neckerchief 《*pl.* ～s》
네크라인 neckline
네크리스 a necklace ; a choker 《구》
네트 a net ¶ (정구) 네트를 치다 put up a (tennis) net // 네트 플레이를 하다 play close to the net
—**볼** a net ball —**워크** a network
네팔 Nepal ¶ 네팔의 Nepalese
— **사람** a Nepalese —**어** Napali
네활개 four limbs (stretched out) ¶ 네활개 치다 strut ; swagger // 네활개 치며 swaggeringly // 네활개 치며 다니다 strut 〔swagger〕 about a street // 네활개를 뻗다 stretch one's arms and legs // 네활개를 뻗고 자다 sleep at full length ; [편안히] sleep with ease ; have no cares
†**넥타이** a necktie ; a tie ¶ 넥타이를 하다〔매다〕 put on a necktie ; tie〔wear〕 a necktie
—**핀** a tiepin ; a scarfpin 《영》
넨장(맞을) [감탄사] Damn ! ; Damn it ! ; Damn him ! (저주할 때) ; Damn you ; Hang it ! ; [형용사적] damned ; damnable ; wretched ; cursed ; accursed ; deuced ¶ 넨장맞을 녀석 a cursed 〔damnable, damned〕 fellow // 넨장맞을 놈 같으니 Damn you ! / God damn you !
넷 four ¶ 넷으로 접다 fold in four
넷째 the fourth ; No. 4 ; the fourth place ¶ 넷째의 fourth // 넷째로 fourthly
*****녀석** a fellow ; a boy ; a chap ; a guy ; a rascal ; a bird 《속》; a blighter 《영·속》 ¶ 나쁜 녀석 a bad guy // 운 좋은 녀석 a lucky guy // 이 바보 녀석아 You fool ! // 요녀석 You young rascal !
*****년** a woman ; a tramp ; a bitch ; a whore ; a wench ¶ 이 개 같은 년아 You bitch ! // 망할 년 a damned wench // 미친 년 a crazy bitch // 이 년 You wretched slut
*****년 年** year ¶ 1 년 one year
년놈 the man and woman ; the husband and wife
녘 ① [무렵] around ; about ¶ 해뜰〔질〕 녘 at dawn〔sunset〕; towards daylight 〔sunset〕 // 새벽녘 around dawn ; towards dawn ② [방향·지역] (in) the area of (장소) ; (in) the direction of (방향) ; towards ¶ 북녘 the northern district〔region, part〕; the north // 동녘으로 in the direction of the east // 아랫녘 a place in the lower part // 윗녘 a place in the upper part
노[1] [끈줄] a string ; a cord ; a rope ¶ 삼노 a hempen cord
노[2] ⇨ 노상
†**노 櫓** a scull ; an oar ¶ 노를 젓다 paddle ; work a scull ; scull 《a boat》; row 《a boat》; work 《at oars》 // 노를 저어 배를 내다 propel a boat with oars // 노젓는 사람 a rower ; an oarsman
노가주 〖식물〗 juniper ; Juniperus (학명)
노각 老— yellowish overripe cucumbers
노간주 〖식물〗 a juniper
—**나무** a juniper tree
노객 老客 [사람] an aged person ; [손님] an aged visitor
노경 老境 old〔advanced〕 age ; senescence ; one's declining years ¶ 노경에 들다 be advanced in age〔life〕; be well on in years ; be in the decline of one's life ; grow old ; become senescent
†**노고 勞苦** labor ; toil ; pains ¶ 노고를 아끼지 않다 spare no pains // 노고를 치하하다 reward 《a person》 for his labor 〔service〕 // 그의 노고는 보답됐다 Success crowned his labors.
노고지리 a skylark
노곤 勞困 fatigue ; exhaustion ; weariness —**하다** be fatigued ; be tired ;

be exhausted ; be languid ¶ 무더운 날엔 유달리 몸이 노곤하다 A hot day makes us feel languid.

노골 露骨 nakedness ; frankness ; candor ; outspokenness ; openness ⇨ 노골적

***노골적 露骨的** ① [숨기지 않는] naked ; plain ; open ; blunt ; frank ; outspoken ; plainspoken ¶ 노골적으로 plainly ; bluntly ; frankly ; openly ; broadly ; straightforwardly // 노골적인 태도 a blunt manner // 노골적으로 말하면 to be plain with you ; in plain words〔terms〕; frankly speaking // 노골적으로 말하다 speak plainly〔bluntly〕; do not mince words〔matters〕// 노골적인 암시 a broad hint // 노골적인 사람 an outspoken person // 말하는 것이 노골적인 사나이다 He is outspoken.
② [음란한] broad ; indecent ; lewd ¶ 노골적인 농담 a broad joke // 그 그림은 지나치게 노골적이다 That picture is too suggestive. // 그것은 노골적인 장면들이 퍽이나 많았기 때문에 나는 얼굴이 빨개졌다 I found myself blushing because it contained so many explicit scenes.
③ [현저한] conspicuous ; salient ; striking ; acute ¶ 두사람의 알력이 점점 노골적으로 되었다 The friction between them has become salient〔open〕. /Their contention has become rather acute.

노구 老軀 old bones ; old and weak limbs ; an advanced age ¶ 80의 노구에도 불구하고 in spite of one's venerable〔advanced〕 age of 80

노구거리 a pair of inturned ox horns of disproportionate lengths

노구(솥) a brass〔copper〕 kettle

노굿 the flowers of leguminous plants

노그라지다 ① [피로] be tired out ; be worn out ; be exhausted ; be dog-tired ; be dead tired
② [마음이 쏠리다] be given to ; be infatuated with ; give oneself up to ; be bent〔keen〕 on 《a woman》; be mad on ; have a craze for ; be engrossed〔absorbed〕 in ¶ 그는 그 여자에게 아주 노그라졌다 He is off his head about that girl. /He is crazy about that girl.

노그름하다 (be) rather soft ; tender

노글노글 —하다 (be) soft ; pulpy ; mushy ; flabby ; squashy ; flaccid ; limp ¶ 이 풀먹인 칼라는 날씨가 더우면 그냥 노글노글해진다 This starched collar soon gets limp in hot weather.

노급 弩級 the dreadnought class

노급함 弩級艦 a dreadnought
초(超)— a superdreadnought

노긋노긋 —하다 ① [촉감이] (be) supple ; elastic ; soft ; flexible ¶ 촉감이 노긋노긋하다 feel soft ; be soft to the touch ② [성격이] (be) supple ; adaptable ; docile ; compliant

노긋하다 (be) supple ; elastic and soft ; flexible

노기 老妓 an old-woman entertainer ; an old *kisaeng*

노기 怒氣 anger ; wrath ; fume ; indignation ; fury ¶ 노기 띤 말 sharp〔angry〕 words // 노기를 띠다 be in a huff ; be in an angry mood // 노기 등등하다 be in a fit of rage ; be red-hot with anger ; be out of temper // 노기 충천하다 boil with rage ; fury and anger fills one's head // 그는 노기를 띠고 말했다 He said it in an angry tone. // 그의 목소리는 노기로 가득차서 떨렸다. His voice trembled with rage.

노기스 〖기계〗 slide calipers ; Nonius 《도》

노깃 the blade of an oar〔a paddle〕

†노끈 a string ; a small cord ¶ 노끈을 꼬다 make a cord // 삼으로 노끈을 꼬다 twist hemp into a cord // 노끈으로 묶다 tie with a string

노나무 〖식물〗 a catalpa tree ; an Indian bean

노년 老年 old age ; declining years ; the winter of life ¶ 노년이 되어 in one's old age〔later years〕; in the decline〔evening〕 of one's life
—자 the old ; old men ; the aged

노년기 老年期 senescence ; old age ¶ 노년기의 사람 a senescent person // 노년기에 들다 arrive at senescence ; become senescent

노농 勞農 laborers and farmers
— 러시아 Soviet Russia **— 정부** the Soviet government **— 정치** Soviet rule **— 제휴** collaboration of peasants and laborers

노놓치다 let 《a criminal》 escape〔run away〕

노느다 [분배] distribute 《among》; divide 《among》; share ; allot ; apportion ; portion out ; deal out (화투 따위를) ¶ 돈을 둘이〔셋이〕 노느다 divide the money between the two〔among the three〕// 이익을 반반씩 노느다 split 《the profit》 half and half // 음식을 노나먹다 share food with others

노느매기 distribution ; sharing ; division ; allotment ; apportionment ; a share **—하다** distribute 《among》; divide〔split〕 《between, among》; share 《with, between》; share 《a thing》 fifty-fifty ; apportion ; portion ; deal out

노는계집 ⇨ 논다니, 매춘부

노닐다 stroll〔loiter, linger, ramble, wander, saunter〕 about〔along, around〕; hang around ¶ 해변을 노닐다 take a stroll〔ramble〕 on the beach

노다지¹ ① [광맥] a rich mine〔vein〕; (a) bonanza 《미》 ¶ 노다지를 발견하다 discover a rich vein of ore〔a bonanza〕; be in bonanza

② [행운] a bonanza ; a run〔streak〕 of luck ¶ 노다지를 캐다 strike a bonanza ; hit the jackpot 《미》 // 노다지를 캐는 듯한 사업 a get-rich-quick enterprise
—판 a mine where gold is found in nuggets ; a bonanza

노다지² 《속》 ⇨ 언제나, 늘

노닥거리다 make a long and funny talk ; harangue ; keep talking gaily

노닥노닥 in patches ⇨ 누덕누덕

노닥다리 老— an old〔aged〕 person

노닥이다 chat ; chatter ; talk away one's time ; say funny things

노대 露臺 a balcony ; a gallery ; an open-air platform

노대가 老大家 an old master ; a veteran authority 《on》 ¶ 서예의 노대가 a past master of calligraphy // 국문학의 노대가 a veteran student of Korean classics // 문단의 노대가들 men grown gray in the literary profession

노대국 老大國 a senile great nation ; a declining old empire

노도 怒濤 raging billows ; angry〔surging〕 waves ; turbulent waves ; a high〔boiling〕 sea ; rough waters ¶ 노도처럼 밀려오는 군중 surging crowds // 노도를 무릅쓰고 나아가다 advance in the face of high seas // 배는 노도를 헤치고 나아갔다 The ship advanced in the face of raging billows. /The ship ploughed the high seas. // 적이 노도처럼 밀어닥쳤다 The enemy surged upon us.

노독 路毒 the fatigue of a journey ; travel sickness ; fatigue of travel ¶ 노독을 풀다 banish fatigue of travel ; relieve one's fatigue of a journey ; take a good rest after a journey // 잠으로써 긴 여행의 노독을 풀다 sleep away〔off〕 the fatigue of a long journey

†**노동** 勞動 labor ; work ; toil ; industry
—하다 labor ; work ; toil ; engage in labor ; work with one's hands ¶ 8시간 노동 eight-hour labor ; an eight-hour workday // 노동으로 생활하다 live by labor // 그는 노동을 해본 일이 없다 He hasn't done any manual labor.
— 가치설 the theory of labor value — 경제〔경제학〕 labor economy〔economics〕 —계 the labor world — 계급 the working〔laboring〕 class(es) — 계약 labor contract — 공급 the labor supply — 공세 a labor offensive — 과학 labor science — 관리(管理) labor management —권(權) the right to labor〔work〕 — 귀족 a labor aristocrat — 규약 a union constitution 《미》 ; constitution of a trade union 《영》 — 능률 labor efficiency — 대중 the labor〔laboring〕 masses ; masses ; masses of workers — 대책 a labor policy — 동맹 a labor federation — 문제 a labor question〔problem〕 ☞ 《p. 491》 — 배치 assignment of labor — 법규 labor laws ; industrial laws 《영》 — 법안 a labor bill — 보험 labor insurance —복 work clothes — 봉사 labor service — 부족 labor shortage — 분배 division of labor — 소개 day labor referral — 소개소 a labor exchange — 손실 일수 time lost due to strike and lockout ; man-day of idleness — 수요 demand of labor — 심리학 labor psychology — 연맹 a labor league — 용어 labor terms — 원가 labor cost — 위원회 a labor relations commission — 이동 labor turnover — 이동률 rate of labor turnover ; labor turnover rate — 인구 labor population ; working population — 재해 a labor accident — 전문가 a labor specialist — 전선(戰線) a labor front — 정착 immobility of labor — 조건 working〔labor〕 conditions — 조사 a labor survey — 총동맹 the Federation of Labor — 통계 labor statistics〔figures〕 — 행정 labor administration — 행정비 labor administration expenses — 협동 the union of labor — 협약 a labor agreement — 환경 labor environment — 회관 the Labor Hall 강제 — compulsory〔forced〕 labor 경〔중〕— light〔heavy〕 labor 계절 — seasonal〔migrant〕 labor 국제 — 회의 the International Labor Conference 근육 — muscular labor 두뇌 — brain work 생산적〔비생산적〕 — productive〔unproductive〕 labor 시간외 — overtime work 육체 — physical work〔labor〕 1일 8시간 — 《work》 an eight-hour day 정신 — mental work〔labor〕 조직 — organized labor

노동 관계법 勞動關係法 〖법〗 [미국의] the National Labor Relations Act ; the Wagner Act

노동 관계 조정법 勞動關係調整法 〖법〗 the Labor Relations Adjustment Act

노동당 勞動黨 the Labo(u)r Party (영국의) ¶ 노동당의 정책 laborism
— 내각 a Labor ministry〔cabinet〕 —원 a Laborite ; a member of the Labor Party

노동력 勞動力 labor ; manpower ; labor power〔force〕 ; working power〔force〕 ¶ 노동력의 부족 a shortage of manpower〔labor〕 // 그 지방에서는 노동력이 비쌀뿐만 아니라 얻기 힘이 든다 Labor is not only expensive but hardly obtainable in the locality.

노동 시간 勞動時間 working hours ; the hours of labor ; man-hours (연 노동 시간수) ¶ 노동 시간의 단축을 요구하다 demand shorter working hours // 노동 시간을 단축〔연장〕하다 shorten〔lengthen〕 the working hours

노동 시장 勞動市場 the labor market
— 상황 the labor market situation —

노동 문제

노동이나 고용을 둘러싼 광의의 여러 관계를 일반적으로 industrial relations이라 부르며 이것이 개개 종업원의 인사관계에 대해 말하는 「종업원 관계」(employee relations)와 집단으로서의 「노동조합과의 관계」(labor(-management) relations)의 크게 두가지로 나뉘어진다. 전자의 employee relations는 「인사관리」(personnel management[administration]와 거의 동의어로 최근에는 「인적자원관리」(human resources management)라고 불리워지고 있다.

후자의 labor-management relations는 집단적인(collective) labor[trade] union과의 관계를 가리키는 것이기 때문에 단체교섭을 collective bargaining이라고 부르고 있다.

노동조합의 조직(organization of trade unions)의 형태로서는 같은 직종의 노동자들로 조직된 직능별 조합(craft union), 산업내의 모든 노동자로 조직된 산업별 조합(industrial union), 산업간에 걸쳐 결성된 일반조합(general union), 그리고 개별의 기업간에서 정규 종업원으로 결성된 기업별 조합(enterprise(-based) union)의 3종류가 있다. 이 표현으로 company union을 쓰기도 하지만 이것은 company 측이 말하는 대로 되는 union, 즉 「어용조합」의 의미이기때문에 노조를 company union이라 하는 것은 부적절할 때가 있다. 또 같은 (in-)house union이라든가 independent라는 말투로 기업별 노조를 표시하는 경우도 있지만 그 어느것이나 company union과 비슷한 뉘앙스가 포함되어 있기때문에 용법에 주의해야 한다.

▶ 노동 운동 labor movement / 노동3법 the three major labor legislations / 노동조합법 the Labor Union Law / 노동관계 조정법 the Labor Relations Adjustment Law / 노동3권 labors three primary[major] rights / 단결권 right to organize / 단체교섭권 right to bargain collectively / 노동조합 labor union / 노사(勞使) labor and management / 비조합 노동자 unorganized labor[workers] / 노사관계 labor-management relations; industrial relations / 노사협의 labor-management consultation system / 노사협의제 labor-management council / 노동협약 labor contract / 근로기준법 Labor Standards Law / 조합지부 local / 노동자의 경영참가 worker representation on the board; labor participation in the management / 노무관리 labor management / 노동력 labor force / 노동생산성 labor productivity

▶ 파업 strike; walkout / 단식투쟁 hunger strike / 전면파업 all-out strike / 부분파업 partial[local, localized] strike / 시한부 파업 limited-time strike; time-limited strike / 무기한파업 indefinite strike / 노동쟁의 labor dispute / 쟁의권 right to strike / 준법투쟁 work-to-rule strike[struggle, slowdown]

▶ 병가(病暇) sick leave / 산휴(産休) leave for childbirth / 생리휴가 monthly sickness leave / 유급휴가 paid vacation; paid day-off / 주휴(週休)2일제 five-day work week / 직업병 vocational [job-related] disease / 초과근무 overtime work

▶ 고용 employment / 고용대책법 Employment Measures Law / 견습 probation; apprenticeship / 맞벌이 가구(家口) two-income[two-career] family [household]; two-paycheck family / 인사고과제도 merit rating system / 임시고용 노동자 temporary[casual] worker; part-time worker / 숙련[비숙련]노동자 skilled[unskilled] worker / 신규채용 hiring of new graduates / 실근무 시간 actual hours worked

▶ 퇴직 retirement / 퇴직금 retirement allowance; severance pay / 임의퇴직 voluntary retirement

▶ 임금 wage / 임금교섭 wage talk [negotiation] / 임금동결(凍結) wage freeze / 임금가이드라인 wage guideline [guidepost] / 임금격차 wage differentials / 임금타결 wage settlement[agreement] / 최저임금제 system of minimum wage law / 승급 wage raise; raise / 정기승급 periodic[regular, mandatory] pay raise

▶ 취직 getting[being] employed; getting employment; taking a job / 취직난 job scarcity / 취업알선 job placement

▶ 실업 unemployment / 휴직 leave of absence (from office) / 부당해고 unfair dismissal / 인원정리 workforce reduction; personnel retrenchment; employment adjustment / 면직(免職) dismissal; discharge / 복직(復職) reinstatement of a worker / 정년 (mandatory) retirement age

▶ 수당 allowance / 가족수당 family allowance / 근속수당 seniority allowance / 배우자수당 spouse allowance / 고령수당 age allowance

정보 labor market information — 조사 a labor market survey

노동 운동 勞動運動 a labor movement 〔campaign, drive〕
—자 a labor agitator — 지도자 a labor leader

노동 임금 勞動賃金 wages ; pay ¶ 노동 임금을 인상〔인하〕하다 raise〔reduce〕 wages // 노동 임금의 인상을 요구하다 demand higher wages〔a wage hike〕

†노동자 勞動者 a laborer ; a worker ; a workingman ; wage earner work people ; a labor (총칭) ¶ 노동자를 착취하다 exploit laborers // 노동자의 생활을 개선하다 improve the lot of the workingmen // 노동자의 권익을 보호하다 protect the interests of labor
— 가계 조사 a worker's family income survey — 계급 the working classes — 모집 labor recruitment — 모집 지역 a (labor) recruitment area — 보호 protection of laborers — 부족 labor famine ; a shortage of labor — 생활 laborers' life — 수용소 a labor camp — 재해 보상 보험법 〖법〗 the Workmen's Compensation Insurance Act — 주택 계획 a labor housing project 계절 — a seasonal laborer 근육 — a muscular laborer 날품팔이 — a day laborer 임금 — a wage earner ; a wage worker 자유 — a casual laborer 조직 — organized workers〔labor〕 지능(知能) — a mental〔brain, white-collar〕 worker

노동 장관 勞動長官 [미국의] the Secretary of Labor ; the Labor Secretary ; the Minister of Labor ; the Labor Minister

노동 쟁의 勞動爭議 a labor dispute 〔trouble, strife, struggle〕 ; [파업] a strike ; a walkout ; a turnout 《영》
— 조정 mediation in a labor trouble — 중재 arbitration in a labor trouble

노동절 勞動節 [근로자의 날] Labor Day ; May Day (5월 1일) ; [미국·캐나다] Labor Day (9월 첫째 월요일)

노동 조합 勞動組合 a labor union 《미》 ; a trade union 《영》 ¶ 노동 조합을 조직하다 organize a union
— 간부 a union leader — 규약 the constitution of a labor〔trade〕 union ; a union constitution —법(法) 〖법〗 the Labor〔Trade〕 Union Act — 우대 공장 a preferential shop —원 a member of a labor union ; a (trade) unionist ; a union man 《미》 — 임원(任員) a union official —주의 unionism ; laborism — 협의회 a council of trade〔labor〕 unions 반—주의 nonunionism 세계 — 연맹 the World Federation of Trade Unions 《WFTU》 한국 — 총연맹 The Federation of Korea Trade Unions 《FKTU》

노두 露頭 〖광물〗 an outcrop ; a basset ; a crop

노둔 魯鈍 stupidity ; dullness ; imbecility ; muddleheadedness —하다 (be) stupid ; dull ; imbecile ; muddleheaded ; dense ; thickheaded

노둣돌 a horse block (for mounting and dismounting)

노드리듯 in torrents ; in streams —하다 rain in torrents ; rain cats and dogs ; rain in streams

†노랑 yellow
—감투 a mourner's cap —나비 a yellow butterfly —머리 a yellow head ; yellow hair —참외 a yellow melon —퉁이 a person with an unusually yellow complexion

노랑매미꽃 〖식물〗 a Japanese〔yellow〕 rose ; a multiflora rose

노랑이 a yellow thing〔stuff〕 ; [개] a small yellow dog ; [구두쇠] a niggard ; a miser ; a tightwad ; a skinflint ; a pinchpenny

†노랗다 (be) yellow ¶ 얼굴이 노랗다 one's complexion is yellow ; look poor // 싹수가 노랗다 have a slim chance of success ; show no promise of success ; have a dog's chance

†노래 [가요] a song ; [민요] a ballad ; [시가] a poem ; a verse ; an ode (송시) ; poetry 《총칭》 —하다 sing (a song) ; recite (시가를) ; chant (찬송가를) ¶ 가을을 노래한 시 a poem about autumn // 피아노에 맞추어 노래하다 sing to the piano. // 노래를 배우다 take lessons in singing ; take vocal lessons // 노래부르자 Let's have a song. // 그는 노래를 잘한다 He is a good singer. /He is good at singing

노래기 〖동물〗 a millipede ; a myriapod ; Nipponoiulus truncatus (학명) ; a wireworm

노래자랑 an amateur singing contest ; [라디오·TV 프로그램] Amateur Singers on the Air

노래지다 turn yellow

노랫가락 [속요] a popular〔folk〕 song

노랫소리 singing ; a singing voice ; the voice of a singing person ¶ 여명을 알리는 새의 노랫소리 the song of birds that ushers in the dawn

노략 擄掠 [노략질] plunder ; pillage ; looting ; despoilment ; depredation ; spoliation ; sack —하다 plunder ; pillage ; despoil ; loot ; sack ; ravage 《a land》 ¶ 사람으로부터 물건을 노략하다 despoil 《a person》 of a thing // 도시에서 미술품을 노략하다 plunder a city of works of art // 해적들이 연안의 도시를 노략하였다 Pirates pillaged the town along the coast.

놀량목 a very high soprano voice

⁑노려보다 glare〔stare〕 at ; look angrily 〔sharply〕 at ; look sharply in the face ; scowl 《at》 ; stare fiercely 《at》 ;

look daggers at ; throw 《a person》 a furious look ; give a strong stare at ¶ 서로 노려보다 stare fiercely at each other // 기분 나쁘게 노려보다 stare 《a person》 down〔out of countenance〕 // 그녀는 나를 무섭게 노려보았다. She gave me a fierce scowl. /She scowled at me terribly.

노력 努力 effort ; endeavor ; hard work ; exertion ; labor **— 하다** strive ; endeavor ; exert oneself ; make an effort ; work hard ¶ 최선의 노력을 하다 do one's best〔utmost〕 ; make every effort〔endeavor〕 ; spare no effort // 노력을 아끼다 be sparing of one's labor 〔pains〕 // 명성을 얻으려고 노력하다 strive for fame // 피눈물 나는 노력 blood-and-tears endeavor // 헛된 노력 fruitless〔futile〕 effort // 끊임없이 노력하다 persevere in one's efforts // 조금도 노력하지 않다 do not lift a hand // 필사의 노력을 하다 make desperate efforts ; strain every nerve // 나의 노력은 수포로 돌아갔다 All my efforts went for nothing. /My efforts came〔amounted〕 to nothing after all. /After all, my efforts were fruitless〔in vain〕. // 마침내 노력한 보람이 있었다 Efforts were finally rewarded. /My efforts bore fruit at last. // 그는 노력형의 사람이다 He is a man of industry.

—상 a prize awarded in recognition of 《a person's》 efforts

†**노력 勞力** [노동] labor ; [수고] effort ; trouble ; toil ; labor ¶ 노력을 절약하다 economize of one's labors // 노력을 절약하는 기계〔장치〕 a laborsaving machine 〔device〕 // 노력을 제공하다 offer personal labor〔service〕 // 노력이 많이 들다 require a great deal of〔much, hard〕 labor // 노력을 덜다 save one's trouble

— 부족 a shortage of labor **—비** expenses for labor **— 활용** labor utilization

노력가 努力家 a hard worker ; a hardworking〔an industrious〕 person ; a man of industry

***노련 老練** being experienced〔skilled〕 ; mature experience ; expertness ; skillfulness **— 하다** (be) experienced ; veteran ; expert ; skilled ¶ 노련한 솜씨 masterly skill // 노련한 외교관 an old hand at diplomacy // 노련한 작가 a practiced writer // 노련한 교사〔배우〕 a veteran teacher〔actor〕 // 노련한 선수 a veteran player // 노련한 의사 an experienced doctor // 노련한 수부 an old salt 〔sailor〕 ; an old sea dog // 노련한 목수 a skilled carpenter

—가 an expert ; a veteran ; an old hand ; a master hand ; a man of experience ; a master hand ; an old-timer 《미》

노령 老齡 old age ; advanced age ¶ 노령에 이르다 attain an advanced age ; reach a great age

노령 露領 Russian territory

노루 〖동물〗 a deer ; a roe deer ¶ 수노루 a roebuck

노루발[1] [쟁기의] the two triangular pieces under the metal handle of a plow-blade

노루발[2] 〖식물〗 pyrola

노루발장도리 a claw hammer

노루삼 〖식물〗 black baneberry

노루오줌 〖식물〗 the Chinese astilbe

노루잠 a broken sleep ; an unsound slumber ; a catnap

노루종아리 [소반의 다리] the unornamented lower part of a table leg ; [문살의] the part of a doorframe with sparsely-spaced rails

노르께하다 be tinged〔stained〕 with yellow

노르끄레하다 ⇨ 노르께하다

노르다 (be) yellow

노르딕 종목 —種目 〖스키〗 the Nordic events

노르마 a norm ; a standard (amount) ; a work quota ¶ 노르마를 완수하다 fulfill the assigned task

생산(生産) — a production norm

노르만 ¶ 노르만 사람 a Norman ; the Normans

노르무레하다 be a little on the yellow side

노르스름하다 (be) yellowish ; somewhat yellow

노르웨이 Norway ¶ 노르웨이의 Norwegian

—어 Norwegian ; [고대의] Old Norse

— 사람 a Norwegian

노른자위 the yolk〔yellow〕 of an egg ; the vitellus ; the deutoplasm ; the cream ; the best

⁑**노름** gambling ; gaming ; gambling game **— 하다** gamble ; play for money ¶ 노름해서 돈을 잃다 gamble away one's money // 노름에 몰두하다 indulge in gambling ; be given to gambling // 노름을 크게 하다 play for heavy〔high〕 stakes // 노름해서 재산을 탕진하다 lose one's fortune at dice

—돈 a bet ; wager ; stakes **—방** a gambling room ; a gambling den〔joint〕 **— 상습자** a confirmed〔habitual〕 gambler

***노름꾼** a gambler ; a gamester

— 두목 a boss gambler **사기 —** a card sharper ; a rook

노름빚 a gambling debt

노름판 a gambling house〔place, room〕 ; a gambler's den ; a casino ; a gambling joint ; a place where people can gamble ¶ 노름판을 차리다 open a gambling house

노름패 ① a (playing) card ¶ 노름패가 좋다〔나쁘다〕 have a good〔poor〕 hand ② a gang of gamblers〔gamesters〕

*노릇 a job ; work ; duty ; function ; an office ; a post ; a role ; a part ; an occupation ¶ 선생 노릇 a teaching job ; teaching // 간사 노릇 하다 act as a manager ; perform the duties of a manager // 춘향이 노릇을 하다 act〔play, perform〕 the part of *Chunhyang* // 입노릇하다 munch ; eat

노릇노릇 yellowish ; spotted with yellow —하다 (be) yellowish ; spotted yellow ¶ 벼가 노릇노릇하게 익어간다 The rice (plant) is ripening yellow.

*노리개 ① [장신구] trinkets〔ornaments〕 worn by a woman ; trinketry ② [장난감] a plaything ; a toy ¶ 여자를 노리개로 삼다 make a plaything of a woman // 사내의 노리개가 되다 be trifled with by a man ; be made a man's plaything ; be seduced by a man
—첩 a young and beautiful concubine
노리갯감 a plaything ; a toy

노리다[1] ① [냄새] smell of furscorching ; (be) foul-smelling ; rank ; smell like burning fat〔a skunk〕 ; stinking ; fetid ② [마음씨가] (be) mean ; sordid ; stingy ; niggardly ; miserly ; pinchpenny 《미·속》

*노리다[2] stare〔glare〕 at ; watch 《for》 ; keep an eye on ; have an eye to 〔on〕 ; set one's eyes upon ; fix the eye on ; aim at ; be after ; watch for ¶ 기회를 노리다 watch for a chance // 목숨을 노리다 attempt the life of 《a person》 // 돈을 노리다 have designs on 《a person's》 money // 그는 그 여자의 재산을 노리고 있다 He has his eye upon her property. // 그는 은근히 그 자리를 노리고 있다 He has a quiet eye on that position. // 뱀이 개구리를 노리고 있다 The snake is fixing its eyes on a frog. // 그는 도망칠 기회를 노리고 있었다 He was watching for a good chance to run away.

노리다[3] slice crosswise

노리착지근하다, 노리치근하다 be somewhat stinking〔fetid〕

노린내 a fur-scorching smell ; a foul smell ; the smell of burning fat〔hair〕 ; the smell of a skunk

노릿하다 smell somewhat of fur-scorching ; (be) somewhat stinking

노망 老妄 dotage ; second childhood ; senility ; anility ; decrepitude —하다 be in one's dotage〔second childhood〕 ; be senile ¶ 노망한 노인 a dotard ; an old man in his dotage // 노망부리다 dote ; behave like a dotard ; behave childishly // 나이가 들어서 노망기가 있다 Age has begun to tell on him. /His second childhood has come over him. // 아마 노망이 시작되나 보다 Maybe senility is starting to set in.

노면 路面 road surface ¶ 노면을 보수하다 resurface the road
— 개량 street improvement — 교통 surface traffic — 도장 surface treatment — 전차 a surface car ; a streetcar ; a tram(-car) 《영》 — 철도 a surface railway — 포장 surfacing the road ; road surfacing ; pavement — 포장공 a road surfacer — 포장기 a road surfacer

노모 老母 one's old〔aged〕 mother

노목 老木 an old〔aged〕 tree

노무 勞務 labor ; work ; service ¶ 노무를 제공하다 offer one's service(s) // 노무에 종사하다 give〔render〕 one's services
— 공급 사업 a labor supply project — 관리 personnel〔labor〕 management — 기본 계약 a master labor contract — 동원 mobilization of labor — 물자 commodities for labors —비 labor expenses〔cost〕 — 수급 labor demand and supply — 수첩 a labor's card ; a worker's booklet — 시찰 labor inspection — 이동 labor mobility〔turnover〕 — 출자 investment of work and labor ; capitalization with work and labor ; service contribution

노무과 勞務課 the labor section

노무자 勞務者 a worker ; a laborer ; a workman
— 관리 labor control — 모집 labor recruitment

노물 老物 [사람] a superannuated person ; [물건] an old and decrepit stuff ; a worn-out thing

노뭉치 a ball of string〔cord, twine〕

노박덩굴 〖식물〗 the Oriental bittersweet

노박이다 stick to ; be stuck ; be immovable ; be stuck〔fastened〕 for good

노박이로 always ; steadily ; firmly ; unmovingly ; fastened〔stuck〕 for good

노반 路盤 roadbed

노발대발 怒發大發 wild rage ; a big blowup ; flaring up ; enragement ; wrath ; fury —하다 be enraged ; be infuriated ; be transported with rage ; be in a towering rage ¶ 모욕을 당하여 노발대발하다 be enraged at an insult // 그는 노발대발하고 있었다 His rage was boiling over. /He was in hot anger.

노방 路傍 the roadside ; the wayside
—초 grass at the roadside〔by the wayside〕

노벨 상 —賞 a Nobel prize ¶ 노벨상 수상자 a Nobel prize winner

노벨 평화상 —平和賞 the Nobel prize for peace

노변 路邊 the roadside ; the wayside

*노변 爐邊 the fireside ¶ 노변 담화 a fireside chat〔talk〕 // 노변에 앉다 be seated by the hearth〔fireplace〕

노병 老兵 an old soldier ; a war veteran ; a vet 《미·속》 ¶ 노병은 죽지 않고 다만 사라질 뿐이다 Old soldiers never die./they just fade away.

노병 老病 the disease of old age ; senile infirmity ; decrepitude ¶ 그는 노병으로 죽었다 He died of old age.

노복 奴僕 a servant ; a man servant

노부 老父 one's old〔aged〕 father

노부모 老父母 one's aged parents

노부인 老婦人 an aged〔old〕 woman

노비 奴婢 male and female servants

노비 路費 traveling expenses ; travel money ¶ 노비는 자기 부담이다 You must pay your own traveling expenses. ∥부산까지 가는 데 노비가 얼마 듭니까 How much will it cost to travel to *Pusan* ?

노사 勞使 labor and management ; capital and labor

— **간담회** a round-table conference between labor and management — **관계** the relations between labor and capital ; labor-〔union-〕management relations ; industrial relations — **분규** a labor-management dispute ; a conflict between labor and capital — **분규 조정 위원회** a labor dispute mediation committee — **비율** a capital-worker ratio — **협의회** a joint labor-management conference — **휴전** labor-management truce

노사 협조 勞使協調 cooperation〔collaboration, harmonization〕 of capital and labor ; cooperation between labor and management ; industrial conciliation 〔peace〕

— **정책** the capital-labor conciliation policy

노산 老産 delivery in one's old age —**하다** deliver a child in one's old age

***노상** always ; all the time ; at all times ; usually ; habitually ; constantly ; ever ¶ 노상 책만 읽다 always read books∥그는 노상 거짓말만 한다 He is a habitual liar. ∥둘은 노상 싸운다 The two are always quarreling. ∥그는 노상 담배만 피운다 He is smoking all the time. ∥그는 노상 학교에 지각한다 He is habitually late for school. ∥나는 노상 그렇게 생각하였다 I thought so all along. ∥나는 노상 사람의 이름을 잊는다 I am constantly forgetting people's names.

노상 路上 (on) the road ¶ 노상에서 놀다 play on the road∥그가 죽자 그의 가족은 노상을 헤매게 되었다 His death has turned his family adrift.

— **강도** a highwayman ; a footpad ; a holdup man ; a stickup (man) ¶ 노상 강도를 만나다 fall in with footpads ; be held up in the street∥노상 강도가 출몰하다 be infested with footpads∥노상 강도질을 하다 rob wayfarers ; hold up 《미》∥노상 강도를 당했다 I was mugged. — **사고** an accident on the road ; a road accident — **시험 운전** a road test — **안면** a casual acquaintance

***노새** 〚동물〛 a mule

노색 怒色 anger ; an angry face〔look〕 ¶ 노색을 띠우다 have an angry expression ; wear an angry look

노서아 露西亞 ⇨ 러시아

노선 路線 a route ; a course ; a line ¶ 서울-동경 노선에는 하루에 몇 번 비행기가 있습니까 How many flights a day do you have on the *Seoul*-Tokyo route ?

—**도(圖)** a route map — **설정** alignment — **트럭** a truck on a regular delivery route **강경** — a tough〔hard〕 line **버스** — a bus service route **정책** — a policy line **정치** — a political line **항공(航空)** — an airline

노성 怒聲 an angry〔excited〕 voice

노소 老少 young and old ; age and youth ¶ 노소를 막론하고 without distinction of age ; both young and old

노송 老松 an aged〔old〕 pine tree

노쇠 老衰 infirmity of old age ; senility ; dotage ; decrepitude —**하다** grow senile ; become decrepit ; grow old and senile ; become decrepit ; grow old and infirm ¶ 노쇠하여 죽다 die of old age ∥노쇠현상을 보이다 show signs of decrepitude

—**기** senescence —**학** geratology

노숙 老熟 matured experience ; maturity ; mellowness —**하다** (be) mature ; matured ; mellow ; attain maturity ¶ 노숙한 mature ; experienced ; practiced ; veteran∥노숙한 사상가 a mature thinker∥노숙한 경지에 이르다 attain 〔reach〕 maturity ; attain a stage of perfect maturity

노숙 露宿 camping ; camping-out ; sleeping outdoors ; bivouac (군대의) —**하다** camp out ; sleep in the open air

노스탤지어 nostalgia 《for》 ; homesickness ; longing

노승 老僧 an old〔aged〕 priest ; an old Buddhist monk

노심 勞心 anxiety ; care ; worry ; solicitude —**하다** be anxious ; be worried 〔troubled〕 ; worry oneself ; exert one's mind ; rack one's brains ¶ 노심초사 끝에 after taking great pains ; with a great deal of trouble∥노심초사하다가 죽다 worry oneself to death

노심초사 勞心焦思 ⇨ 노심

노아 〚성경〛 Noah ¶ 노아의 방주 Noah's Ark∥노아의 홍수 the Deluge ; Noah's flood ; the Noachian deluge ; the Flood

노아가다 ① [배가] sail fast ; scud ② [말이] run fast ; gallop

노아웃 〚야구〛 no out ¶ 노아웃에 만루이다 The bases are loaded with no outs.

노안 老眼 〖의학〗 long-sightedness ; presbyopia ¶ 노안의 presbyopic // 노안인 사람 a presbyope // 노안이 되다 one's eyes get dim with age
—경 spectacles for the aged

노앞 the starboard〔right〕 side of a boat

노약 老弱 infirmity with age **—하다** be infirm with age ; old and infirm ¶ 노약한 사람 an old and feeble person

노어 露語 Russian ; the Russian language

†**노여움** anger ; indignation ; rage ; fury ; wrath ; displeasure ¶ 노여움을 억누르다 repress〔suppress, contain〕 one's anger // 노여움을 풀다 relent toward 《a person》
노여움을 사다 관용 incur 《a person's》 displeasure〔anger〕 ; give offense to 《a person》 offend〔incense〕 《a person》
노여움 타다 관용 be quick to take offense ; be easily hurt

노여워하다 be offended ; be given offense ; feel hurt 《at》 ; be displeased 《at》 ; be indignant 《at》 ¶ 그는 푸대접을 받고 그들에게 노여워하고 있다 He is indignant with them over the treatment he received. // 그애 말을 너무 노여워하지 마시오 Please do not be offended by the boy's remark. // 오랫동안 소식을 전하지 않았더니 그는 노여워하고 있다 He is offended at my long silence. // 제 말씀에 노여워 마십시오 I hope you will not take any offense at my words.

노역 老役 the part〔role〕 of an aged person ¶ 노역을 하다 play the part 〔role〕 of an aged person

노역 勞役 labor ; toil ; drudgery **—하다** labortoil ; work
—장(場) a workhouse ; a labor house

노염 anger ⇨노여움

***노엽다** be offended ; be given offense ; feel hurt ; be displeased 《at》 ; be displeased 《at》 ¶ 나는 그의 무뚝뚝한 말이 노여웠다 I was offended by his blunt speech. // 나보고 인색하다니 노엽다 I am hurt that he should say I am stingy.

노영 露營 encampment ; camping-out ; bivouac **—하다** encamp ; camp out ; pitch camp ; bivouac ¶ 우리들은 숲 속에서 노영하였다 We pitched camp in the forest. // 우리는 모래 언덕 위에서 노영하였다 We camped out on a sand hill.
—지(地) a camping ground〔site〕 ; a campsite ; the site of a bivouac

†**노예 奴隸** a slave ; slavery (신분) ¶ 술의 노예 a slave to〔of〕 drinking ; a thrall to drink // 노예로 만들다 enslave ; enthrall ; make a slave // 노예처럼 부리다 use 《a person》 like a slave // 노예로 팔리다 be sold into slavery // 노예같이 일하다 work like a slave // 습관의 노예가 되다 be enslaved to a habit // 금전의 노예가 되다 let oneself be a slave of mammonism // 노예를 해방하다 set a slave free // 정욕의 노예가 되다 become a slave to passion // 사랑의 노예가 되다 be a slave to love // 그는 직원들을 노예같이 부려먹는 사람이다 He is a slave driver.
— 근성 a servile spirit **— 노동** slave labor **— 매매** slave trade ; flesh 〔human〕 traffic **— 무역선** a slaver ; a slave ship **— 상인** a slaver **— 생활** slavery ; bondage ; thraldom ; serfdom **— 신세** slavery ; bondage ; peonage ; thral(l)dom ; serfdom **— 폐지론** abolitionism ; antislavery **— 폐지 운동** an antislavery movement **— 해방** emancipation of slaves **반— 상태** a condition of semi-slavery

노예 제도 奴隸制度 slavery ¶ 노예 제도 지지의 proslavery 《states》 // 노예 제도 반대의 antislavery 《movement》
— 국가 a slave state

노오라기 a piece of string

노옹 老翁 an elderly gentleman ; an old 〔aged〕 man

노유 老幼 the young and old ; old age and juvenility ¶ 노유를 불문하고 without distinction of young and old ; irrespective of age

***노이로제** 〖의학〗 (a) neurosis (*pl.* -ses) ; (a) nervous breakdown ¶ 노이로제에 걸린 (사람) (a) neurotic // 노이로제에 걸리다 have a neurosis // 노이로제를 앓다 suffer from neurosis // 노이로제기가 있다 be very nervous ; be highly strung
— 환자 a neurotic

노익장 老益壯 a vigorous old age ¶ 노익장을 자랑하다 enjoy a green old age ; be hale and strong

***노인 老人** an old〔aged〕 man ¶ 노인 같은 소리를 하다 talk as if one were quite old // 노인을 공경하다 respect 〔revere〕 old age
—병 geriatric diseases ; the diseases of old age **—병 전문 병원** a geriatrics hospital **—병 전문의(醫)** a geriatrician **—병학** geriatrics ; geriatric medicine **—정신병** senile psychosis **—학** gerontology

노인경 老人鏡 glasses for old folks ; spectacles for the aged

노인단풍 老人丹楓 〖식물〗 the Korean maple

노일 露日 Russo-Japanese ; Russia-Japan
— 전쟁(戰爭) the Russo-Japanese War

***노임 勞賃** wages ; pay ¶ 비싼 노임을 받다 draw high wages // 노임이 싸다 labor is cheap
— 인상 a rise〔increase, raise〕 in wages ¶ 노임 인상을 요구하다 demand

higher wages — 제도(制度) the wage system 기본 — basic wages 실질〔명목〕 — real〔nominal〕 wages 최저〔최고〕 — minimum〔maximum〕 wages
노자 勞資 capital and labor ; labor and management ⇨ 노사(勞使)
노자 路資 traveling expenses ; travel money ⇨ 여비(旅費)
노작 勞作 [노동] toil and moil ; [역작] a laborious work ; a work involving much labor ¶ 다년간의 노작 a laborious work taking years to finish ; a work completed after many years' labor
*노장 老將 a veteran general
*노장 老壯 young and old ; the old and the young
노적 露積 a stack〔rick〕 of grain ; stacked grain
—가리 stacks of grain
⁑노점 露店 a street stall ; a roadside stand ; a booth ¶ 노점을 벌이다 open a street stall ; engage in street stalling // 노점이 일제히 철거되었다 All the street stalls were pulled down simultaneously. // 노점상 금지 No Peddling. (경고문)
—가(街) open-air stall quarters — 상인 a stall〔booth〕 keeper ; a stallman ; a pitchman
노점 露點 〖물리〗 the dew point
노정 露呈 exposure ; disclosure —하다 be exposed〔disclosed〕 ; come to light ; begin to show
노정 路程 [이수] distance ; mileage ; [여정] an itinerary ; a course ; a journey ¶ 10마일의 노정 a distance of 10 miles // 하루의 노정 a day's journey
—계(計) a measuring wheel ; an odometer —표 a table of itinerary
노조 勞組 a trade union ; a labor union ⇨ 노동 조합
노즐 a nozzle
노질 櫓— rowing ; paddling ; pulling an oar ; sculling —하다 row 《a boat》 ; paddle ; pull an oar ; scull
노처녀 老處女 an old maid ; a spinster
노천 露天 the open air ; the open ¶ 노천에서 in the open air ; out of doors // 노천의 open-air ; outdoor
— 극장 an open-air theater — 수업 open-air classes — 시장 an open-air〔outdoor〕 market — 채굴 open-air mining — 채굴장 a strip mine
노천굴 露天窟 open-air mining ; openwork ; opencut (mining) ; strip mining ; opencast mining
— 탄광 an open-pit coal mine ; an open mine
노체 老體 an old body ; an old〔aged〕 person
노총 the secret of a (fixed) date〔an appointed time〕
노총 지르다 관용 let the (secret) date out ; reveal the secret of the time
노총각 老總角 an old bachelor
노출 露出 exposure ; disclosure ; outcrop (광맥의) —하다 expose ; disclose ; lay bare ; leave 《a thing》 to view ; crop out (광맥이) ¶ 노출된 exposed ; bare // 대중 앞에 육체를 노출하다 expose one's body in public // 이 사진은 노출이 부족하다 This picture is underexposed. // 가슴 노출이 심한 옷을 삼가해 주십시오 Discreet cleavage is advised. // 나는 교회에 노출이 심한 옷을 입고 가는 여자들이 싫다 I don't like women who wear low-cut dresses to church. // 이 카드에는 여성들은 가슴 노출이 너무 심한 옷을 입고 오지 말라고 써 있다 This card says that women are advised not to wear a dress cut too low.
—계(計) an actinometer ; a photometer ; an exposure meter — 공사 open work — 광상(鑛床) an exposed deposit — 배관 〖건축〗 open piping — 부족〔과도〕 under-〔over-〕exposure — 시간 the time of exposure — 전선 a bare wire —증 exhibitionism 국부 —증 a mania for indecent exposure
노친 老親 one's old〔aged〕 parents
노카운트 no count ¶ 노카운트가 되다 be called no count
노커 a (door) knocker ; a rapper ; 〖야구〗 a knocker
노 코멘트 no comment
노크 a knock —하다 knock 《at, on》
노킹 knocking
— 방지제 an antiknock
노타이 셔츠 a wing-collared shirt ; an openneck(ed) shirt
노퇴 老退 superannuation ; old-age retirement —하다 retire (from active life) for one's old age ; be superannuated
†노트[1] a knot (of ship speed) ¶ 30 노트 낼 수 있는 배 a ship good for 30 knots // 배는 한 시간 8노트로 달렸다 We sailed eight knots an hour.
노트[2] a note ¶ 네 노트 좀 빌려다오 Lend me your lecture notes, will you? —하다 note down ; take〔make〕 notes of〔on〕 ¶ 강의를 노트하다 take notes of a lecture
노트북 a notebook
노티 老— signs of (old) age ; looking old ¶ 나이에 비해 노티나다 look old for one's age ; look older than one's age
노파 老婆 an old woman ; [나쁜 뜻으로] a beldam ; a hag
노파심 老婆心 grandmotherly〔old-womanish, excessive〕 solicitude ; solicitude for another's welfare ¶ 나는 노파심에서 이렇게 말한다 I say this out of kindness〔for your (own) good〕.

노폐 老廢 superannuation ; decrepitude ; senescence **—하다** (be) superannuated
—물 effete〔waste〕 matter ; waste material〔product〕 **—보험** invalid insurance
노폭 路幅 the width of a street〔highway〕
*노하다 怒—** get angry ; be offended ; lose one's temper ; take offense ; get mad 《미》 ; show temper ; get into a rage
노하우 know-how (기술적 지식)
노햇사람 people living in the open country by the seashore
노형 老兄 you
노호 怒號 a roar (of anger) ; a bellow **—하다** roar in anger
노화 老化 ag(e)ing **—하다** age
노화 현상 老化現象 symptoms of senility
노환 老患 the infirmities of old age ; senile infirmity ¶ 노환으로 죽다 die of old age
노회 老獪 craftiness ; astuteness ; old roguery **—하다** (be) crafty ; foxy ; cunning ; astute ; wily ¶ 노회한 사람 an old〔a cunning〕 fox ; a sly old dog
노획 鹵獲 capture ; seizure ; plunder ; pillage **—하다** capture ; seize ; plunder ; grab ; pillage
—물 loot 《총칭》 ; booty ; spoils ; a prize ; a trophy of war
노획 虜獲 capturing alive **—하다** capture alive ; take 《a person》 captive
노후 老朽 superannuation ; decrepitude ; senescence **—하다** (be) antiquated ; superannuated ; senescent ; old and decrepit
—도태 elimination of superannuated officials ; superannuation **—선(船)** a hulk ; an old〔a superannuated, a worn-out〕 vessel ; an overage ship **—시설** outworn〔superannuated〕 equipment **—화** deterioration ¶ 노후화되다 become superannuated〔obsolete〕
노후 老後 one's old age ; one's declining years ; the winter〔evening〕 of life ¶ 노후의 낙 consolation of one's old age // 노후에 대비하다 provide for 〔against〕 one's old age // 노후를 편하게 하다 make one's old age comfortable // 노후를 편하게 살다 live comfortably in one's old age ; spend one's declining years in peace
노히트노런 no hit no run
녹 祿 a stipend ; pay ; a salary ; a ration of rice
녹을 먹다 [관용] receive a stipend
녹¹ 綠 green
녹² 綠 rust ; tarnish ¶ 녹슨 rusty // 녹슬다 gather rust ; get rusty ; rust // 쇠는 녹이 슬기 쉽다 Iron is apt to rust. // 금은 녹이 안 슨다 Gold resists rust. // 녹을 방지하다 proof 《a thing》 against rust // 물이 쇠를 녹슬게 하는 것처럼 게으름은 마음을 녹슬게 한다 As water rusts iron, idleness rusts the mind.
녹각 鹿角 an antler ; a deer horn
녹나무 〖식물〗 camphor tree ; Cinnamomum camphora (학명)
녹내장 綠內障 〖의학〗 glaucoma
녹녹하다 (be) damp ⇨ 눅눅하다
녹느즈러지다 get soft and loose
녹는점 —點 a melting〔fusing〕 point ; the point of fusion
녹니석 綠泥石 〖광석〗 chlorite
†**녹다** ① [열에] melt ; thaw ; fuse ¶ 용광로의 쇠가 녹다 The iron in the blast furnace melts. // 금년에는 눈이 일찍 녹았다 It thawed early this spring. // 서리가 하루 종일 녹지 않았다 The frost did not give all day.
② [용해] dissolve ; melt ; liquefy ¶ 물에 녹는다 be soluble in water // 소금은 물에 녹는다 Salt dissolves in water. // 설탕은 화씨 239도에서 녹는다 Sugar melts at 239°F.
③ [주색에] be dissipated ; get ruined by dissipation ¶ 주색에 녹다 ruin one's health with dissipation
④ [혼나다] have a hard time of it ; have a hell of time ; pay dearly for ; have bitter experiences ; be done ; have had it ¶ 등산 갔다가 녹았다 I went hiking and it was just awful. // 악질 고리 대금업자한테 걸려서 녹았다 I had a hell of time dealing with a bad usurer. // 그는 담배 장사하다 녹았다 He lost his shirt in the tobacco business. // 그는 한 펀치에 녹아 버렸다 He was knocked out by only one punch.
⑤ [반하다] be madly in love with ; be fascinated ; be stuck on ; be captivated by ; be gone on 《a girl》 ; be infatuated 《with》 ; be over head and ears in love ¶ 그는 그 여자한테 녹았다 He is stuck on her. // 그에게 걸려들면 어떤 여자라도 녹아 버린다 He could easily win the love of any woman he came to deal with. // 나는 그 노래에 아주 녹았다 That song really melts me.
⑥ [손·발이] warm up ; be warmed ; get warm ¶ 손이 녹다 one's hands warm up // 몸이 녹다 one gets warm
녹다운 a knockdown ¶ 녹다운시키다 knock down ; floor 《미》 // 녹다운 된 후 카운트 9 만에 일어나다 survive a nine-count knock-down
—수출 knockdown exporting
녹두 綠豆 mung beans ; green gram ; Phaseolus radiatus (학명)
—묵 mung-bean jelly **—죽** mung-bean gruel
녹렴석 綠簾石 〖광석〗 epidote
녹록하다 碌碌— (be) poor (in talent) ; worthless ; good-for-nothing ; tri-

fling ; of little value ¶ 녹록잖은 적 a formidable enemy

녹림 綠林 ① [숲] a green forest ② [도적 소굴] a den of bandits
—객〔호걸〕 a bandit ; a brigand ; a mountain robber **—당** robbers ; brigandage

***녹말 綠末** starch ; 〖화학〗 dextrin ; farina 《영》
—당 starch sugar **— 당화 효소(糖化酵素)** diastase **— 시험지** starch paper

녹말질 綠末質 starchiness ¶ 녹말질의 starchy ; farinaceous

녹망간광 綠—鑛 〖광업〗 manganosite

녹물 綠— rust stain

녹반 綠礬 〖화학〗 green vitriol ; sulphate of iron ; copperas ; ferrous sulphate ; melanterite

녹밥 cobbler's thread ; thread used in sewing leather shoes

녹변 綠便 green stool
— 작물 a green manure crop

녹봉 祿俸 ⇨ 녹(祿)

녹비 綠肥 green manure

녹사 綠砂 〖광석〗 greensand

†**녹색 綠色** green ; a green color ¶ 녹색의 green ; verdant ; emerald // 푸른기가 도는 녹색 leekgreen

녹색 신고 綠色申告 [납세 자진 신고] a green return ; a green-paper report 《on business income》
—업체 a green return corporation **—제** a green return〔green tax report〕 system

녹색 혁명 綠色革命 the green revolution

녹선 綠腺 〖동물〗 [갑각류의] a green gland

녹수 綠樹 a green tree ; a green-leaved tree ; greenery 《총칭》

녹슬다 ① [금속이] rust ; get rusty ; gather〔form〕 rust ¶ 녹슨〔녹슬지 않는〕 칼 a rusty〔rustproof〕 knife // 수분은 철을 녹슬게 한다 Water rusts iron ② [기능이] become dull〔blunt〕 ; weaken ; be weakened ¶ 내 영어는 다소 녹슬어 버렸다 My English has gotten a bit rusty.

녹신녹신하다 (be) very soft and flexible ; very elastic ; limp (녹초가 되어)

녹신하다 (be) soft and flexible ⇨ 눅신하다

녹실녹실하다 (be) pliant ⇨ 눅신하다

녹십자 운동 綠十字運動 a tree-planting movement symbolized by a green cross

†**녹아웃** a knockout 《K. O.》 ¶ 녹아우트시키다 〖권투〗 knock out 《a boxer》 ; 〖야구〗 knock out 《a pitcher》 ; clip a pitcher ; drive a pitcher from the mound

녹암 綠岩 〖광석〗 greenstone

녹양 綠楊 a green-leaved willow

녹연광 綠鉛鑛 〖광석〗 phromorphite ; green lead ore

녹엽 綠葉 green leaves ; green foliage 〔leafage〕 《집합적》

녹옥 綠玉 〖광석〗 greenstone ; zonochlorite ; chlorstrolite (녹성석(綠星石)) ; californite (캘리포니아석) ; [연옥] nephrite
—수(髓) chrysoprase **농(濃)—수(髓)** plasma

녹용 鹿茸 the young antlers of the deer

녹음 綠陰 the shade of a tree ; a leafy recess〔shade〕 ; bower ¶ 녹음에서 in the shade of a tree // 녹음이 우거진 거리를 산책하다 go for a walk down a well-shaded street
— 방초 green shades and fragrant plants

†**녹음 錄音** sound recording ; phonographing ; transcription **—하다** record ; phonograph ¶ 음악을 녹음하다 record the music // 테이프에 녹음한 audio-taped 《lecture》 // 녹음으로 전국에 방송하다 broadcast throughout the country by electrical transcription
— 감독 a sound director **— 계원** a record man ; a recordist **— 구성** 〖라디오〗 (a program of) arranged transcription **— 기사** a recordist ; a recording engineer **— 뉴스** a broadcast of 《the day's》 recorded events **—반(盤)** a record **—실** a recording room **— 연설** a transcribed speech **— 장치** recording〔sound〕 equipment **— 재생** transcription playback **— 재생기** a transcription machine **— 테이프** a (sound) recording tape **가두(街頭) —** a "man in the street" interview ; a curbside interview **동시 —** synchronous recording

***녹음기 錄音器** a recorder ; a recording 〔transcribing〕 machine ; a tape recorder (테이프식의) ; 〖라디오〗 a transcription machine
와이어식 — a wire recorder **자기식(磁氣式) —** a magnetic recorder **테이프식 —** a tape recorder

녹음 방송 錄音放送 〖라디오〗 transcription (broadcast) ; broadcast transcription ; broadcasting of recorded speech (etc) ¶ 녹음 방송을 하다 broadcast 《a program》 by electrical transcription ; transcribe 《a drama》

†**녹이다** ① [고체를] melt ; fuse ; smelt 《ore》 ¶ 철을 녹이다 melt〔fuse〕 iron // 광석을 녹이다 smelt ore
② [용해] melt ; dissolve ; liquefy (액화하다) ¶ 얼음을 녹이다 melt ice // 물에 녹이다 dissolve 《a thing》 in water
③ [주색으로] ruin ; blast ; play havoc with ; dissipate ¶ 주색은 젊은 사람을 녹인다 Women and drink play havoc with young men.

④ [혼내주다] teach 《a person》 a lesson ; give 《a person》 beans ; make 《a person》 pay for ; make 《a person》 have a hard time (of it) ; give 《a person》 a hell of a time ¶ 못나게 굴기에 녹여 주었다 I have made him smart for his nasty behavior. /I have made him pay for his nasty behavior.
⑤ [반하게 하다] enchant ; charm ; bewitch ; fascinate ; captivate ; steal the heart of ; enslave ; kill 《a man》 ¶ 남자의 간장을 녹이다 captivate〔fascinate〕 a man // 살살 녹이는 눈짓 a killing wink // 그녀는 한번 눈짓으로 남자를 녹일 만한 여자였다 She belonged to the type of those who enslave men at a glance.
⑥ [손이나 몸을] get warm ; warm up ; take warmth ; warm oneself up ; make oneself warm ¶ 앉아서 난로에 몸을 좀 녹여요 Sit down before the fire and warm yourself.

녹주석 綠柱石 『광석』 beryl

녹죽 綠竹 a green bamboo

녹지 綠地 a green tract of land ; greens (초원)
— **계획** a plan for afforestation —**대(帶)** a greenbelt ; a greenzone ; a tree lawn (가로와 보도 사이의) —**화** afforestation

녹진녹진하다 be all soft and sticky ¶ 갓풀을 녹이면 녹진녹진해진다 Glue gets all soft and sticky when it is heated.

녹진하다 (be) soft and sticky

녹차 綠茶 green tea

녹채 鹿砦 an abatis ; an entanglement ; a palisade

녹초 ① [물건] (being) all tattered ; worn out ¶ 옷이 떨어져 녹초가 되다 one's clothes are worn to tatters 〔shreds〕 // 모자가 비맞아 녹초가 됐다 The rain ruined my hat.
② [사람] (being) utterly exhausted ; dog-tired ¶ 피로해서 녹초가 되다 be utterly worn-out ; be fagged out ; be thoroughly spent ; be reduced to pulp ; be wearied to death ; be dead 〔dog-〕 tired ; be pooped (out) 《미·속》 ; be knackered 《영·속》 // 녹초를 부르다 die ; kick the bucket ; bite the dust ; drop in one's tracks // 그는 아주 녹초가 됐다 He is dead tired. /He is done up. /He is tired out. // 그녀는 녹초가 되어 돌아왔다 She came back exhausted.

녹초 綠草 green grass

녹턴 [야상곡] a nocturn(e)

녹토 綠土 『광석』 green earth

녹피 鹿皮 deerskin

녹화 綠化 tree-planting ; afforestation ; (a) filming —**하다** plant trees ; afforest ; plant 《an area》 with trees
— **계획** a plan for afforestation — **운동** a tree-planting campaign〔drive〕 — **장려** encouragement of afforestation

†**녹화 錄畫** telerecording ; video recording —**하다** record 《a scene》 on video tape

***논** a rice field ; a paddy field ; a rice paddy ¶ 논을 갈다 till〔plow〕 a rice field // 논 농사를 짓다 cultivate〔crop〕 a rice field // 논에 물을 대다 water〔irrigate〕 a rice field // 논을 풀다 make land into rice fields // 논(을) 매다 weed a rice paddy

⁑**논 論** [논의] an argument ; a discussion ; a debate (토론) ; a dispute (논쟁) ; a discourse ; [평론] a comment ; (a) criticism ; [논설] an essay ; a treatise ; [이론] a theory ; [문제] a question ; a problem —**하다** argue ; discuss ; debate ; comment on ; treat of 〔deal with〕 (다루다) ¶ 정치를 논하다 discuss politics // 시사를 논하다 comment on current topics // 이 책은 논할 가치가 없다 This book is beneath criticism. // 이 문제에 관하여 여러 가지 논이 대두되고 있다 Opinion is divided on this question. // 이 책은 노동 문제를 논하고 있다 This book treats of〔deals with〕 the labor question. // 법은 사람을 논하지 않는다 The law has no respect of persons. /All men are equal in the eyes of the law. ⇨ —론(論)

논갈이 plowing〔ploughing 《영》〕 a rice field —**하다** plow〔till〕 a rice field

논객 論客 a controversialist ; a disputant ; a polemic

논거 論據 the basis〔grounds〕 of an argument ; data ¶ 논거가 확실하다 one's argument is well grounded // 논거가 될 몇 가지 사실이 있다 There are some facts in favor〔support〕 of my argument. // 논거가 아주 박약하다 Your ground is anything but convincing.

논결 論決 conclusion ; a peroration ; a decision —**하다** come to a decision 〔conclusion〕 ; conclude

논고 論考, 論攷 a study 《on〔in〕 Korean literature》

논고 論告 the state's address ; the prosecutor's argument ; prosecution —**하다** prosecute ; 《the prosecutor》 address the court ¶ 준엄한 논고 a scathing address // 논고를 개시하다 open the arguments 《on a case》 // 다음에 검사의 논고가 있었다 Then the prosecutor addressed the court.

논공 論功 estimating the merits ; the examination of service ; the weighing of merit ; the evaluation of a meritorious deed —**하다** estimate the merit ; examine 《a person's》 service ; weigh 《a person's》 merit ; evaluate 《a person's》 meritorious deed

논공 행상 論功行賞 a grant of rewards 〔honors〕 after examination of services

〔according to a person's merits〕; the distribution of honors ; weighing《a person's》merit and making appropriate award ; the official recognition of distinguished services ; citation —하다 award〔reward〕 according to 《a person's》merits ; grant honors ¶ 논공행상이 부당했다 The conferment of honors was not strictly fair./The honors were not justly〔fairly〕distributed.

논과 論過 ① refutation ② 〖논리〗 paralogism

논구 論究 an exhaustive discussion —하다 discuss thoroughly〔exhaustively〕; make a full discussion of 《a matter》; conduct an exhaustive discussion

논급 論及 reference ; referral ; mention ; allusion —하다 refer to ; allude to ; enter into ; touch on〔upon〕; make reference to ¶ 타임지는 그 사건에 관하여 논급하였다 Reference was made to the event in The Times.

논길 a lane through rice fields ; a footpath between rice fields ; a paddy path ¶ 논길을 걷다 walk along a lane across paddy fields

논꼬 an irrigation gate〔a sluice〕for irrigating a paddyfield

논난 論難 adverse criticism ⇨ 논란

논농사 —農事 rice farming ; rice cultivation〔culture〕 —하다 do rice farming ; cultivate rice ; cultivate a paddy field〔paddy rice〕

논농사짓다 ⇨ 논농사하다

논다 divide up ; share (노느다) ⇨ 나누다

논다니 a prostitute ; a courtesan ; a harlot ¶ 논다니 노릇을 하다 practice prostitution ; prostitute oneself

논단 論壇 [연단] a platform ; a forum ; [평론계] the world of public criticism ; publicists' circles ¶ 논단의 거물 a great literary critic (문예 비평가) ; an eminent publicist (평론가) ; a leading figure in the press circles (언론계의 거물) // 그 문제는 논단을 떠들썩하게 하였다 The question evoked much controversy among the publicists.

—인 a publicist

논단 論斷 a conclusion ; a verdict —하다 conclude ; pass a verdict upon

논담 論談 discussion ; discourse ; debate ; dispute ; controversy —하다 discuss ; discourse ; debate ; dispute

논도랑 a ditch around a paddyfield

논두렁 a ridge between rice fields ; a levee

논두렁길 a footpath between rice fields

논둑 the bank around a rice field

논란 論難 adverse criticism ; charge ; denunciation ; censure ; disproof ; refutation —하다 criticize ; denounce ; refute ; attack (by arguments)

논리 論理 logic ¶ 논리적인 logical ; dialectic // 논리적으로 logically ; dialectically // 비논리적인 illogical ; fallacious // 논리상 불가능한 일 a logical impossibility // 논리가 맞지 않는다 be illogical ; be contrary to logic // 너의 주장은 논리가 서지 않는다 Your argument has not a leg to stand on. // 논리가 정연하다 One's logic is sound. // 당신의 논리에는 비약이 있다 There is a leap in your logic.

—성 logicality

논리적 論理的 ¶ 논리적인 logical ; dialectic // 논리적인 의론〔결론〕 a logical argument〔conclusion〕// 비논리적 illogical ; fallacious // 논리적 타당성 logicality

논리주의 論理主義 〖철학〗 logicism

**논리학 論理學* (the study of) logic

—자 a logician 기호 — symbolic logic 수리 — mathematical logic 순수 — pure logic 연역〔귀납〕 — deductive〔inductive〕 logic 형식 — formal logic

논마지기 some acres of rice field ; a small amount of paddy land ¶ 그 여자는 논마지기나 가지고 있다는 소문이다 They say she is something of a landowner.

논머리 the border of a rice paddy

†논문 論文 [일반적] a treatise ; a dissertation ; [연구상의] a thesis ; [학회의] a paper ; [신문·잡지의] an article ¶ 한국 문학에 관한 논문 a treatise〔an essay〕 on Korean literature // 논문을 쓰다 write a paper〔thesis, monograph〕《on》// 논문을 심사하다 examine《a person's》paper《on》// 대학에 학위 논문을 제출하다 submit a dissertation to a university // 논문을 제출해서 박사 학위를 받다 obtain a doctorate by presenting a thesis // 그의 제출 논문은 입상 수준에 달하지 못하였다 The paper submitted by him did not measure up to a reasonable standard of merit. //

— 시험 a thesis examination — 심사 the examination of a thesis — 제출 the presentation of a thesis —집 a collection of learned papers 박사 — a thesis for a doctorate〔doctor's degree〕; a doctor's thesis 졸업 — a graduation thesis

논문서 —文書 the title deed of a paddy field

논물 water in a rice field ¶ 논물을 대다 irrigate a rice field

논박 論駁 refutation ; confutation ; disproof ; a wordy attack —하다 disprove argue against ; refute ; confute ; make a wordy attack against

†논밭 paddyfields and dry fields

논밭 전지 —田地 paddyfields and dry fields

논배미 a strip of paddy field ; a parcel

of rice field

논법 論法 argument ; reasoning ; logic ¶ 그릇된 논법 a false argument // 논법에 맞다〔맞지 않다〕 be logical〔illogical〕 // 묘한 논법이군 That's strange logic, isn't it? // 그는 논법에 맞지 않는 말을 한다 He is not governed by logic.
삼단 — 〖논리〗 a syllogism **이단** — 〖논리〗 an enthymeme

논변 論辯 an argument ; a discussion ; a debate

논보리 barley planted in a paddy field as a second crop

논봉 論鋒 the force of an argument ¶ 예리한 논봉 a keen〔an incisive, a trenchant〕 argument // 논봉을 돌리다 turn the force of one's argument against // 그는 마침내 김씨의 논봉에 말문이 막혔다 He was finally silenced by Mr. *Kim's* argument.

논설 論說 [논문] a discourse ; a dissertation ; [사설] a leading article ; a leader ; an editorial ¶ 국제 정의에 관한 논설 an editorial〔a leading article〕 on international justice // 사건을 논설로 취급하다 devote a leader to a matter ; editorialize on a topic 《미》
— **기자〔위원〕** a leader writer ; an editorial writer 《미》 ; an editorialist **—란** the editorial column

논술 論述 discourse ; statement ; enunciation **—하다** discourse upon ; state ; set forth

논어 論語 the Analects of Confucius

논외 論外 irrelevancy to the subject ¶ 논외의 out of the question ; beside the question ; irrelevant ; impertinent // 그것은 논외다 It is out of the question.

‡**논의 論議** discussion ; debate ; argument **—하다** discuss ; debate ; argue ¶ 정치상의 논의 a political discussion // 논의할 여지가 없다 be incontestable ; admit of no argument // (안건이) 논의 중이다 be under discussion〔debate〕 // 논의할 여지가 있다 That is still a matter of debate.

논일 a rice farming ; work in a rice paddy

논자 論者 [논객] a disputant ; a debater ; [주창자] an advocate ; an apostle ; [필자] the (present) writer
개혁— an advocate of reform **산아 제한** — an advocate of birth control **평화** — a pacifist

†**논쟁 論爭** a controversy ; a dispute ; argument ; a contention **—하다** dispute ; argue ; contend ; have an argument with ¶ 법률상의 논쟁 a dispute over a point of law // 논쟁을 시작하다 go into a dispute // 논쟁에 참가하다 enter into〔join in〕 a dispute // 그 문제는 논쟁의 여지가 없다 The matter is beyond dispute. // 이 문제에 대하여 논쟁이 일어나고 있다 There is a controversy on this subject.
—자 a disputant ; a controversialist ; a debater **—점** a point of dispute **미소** — the dispute between America and the Soviet Union

논적 論敵 an opponent〔adversary〕 (in argument)

논전 論戰 [입씨름] a verbal battle ; a battle of words ; wordy warfare ; [논쟁] a controversy ; an argument ; a disputation **—하다** fight with words ; wage a battle of words ; engage in a debate ; argue ; dispute ¶ 지상의 논전 a paper war

†**논점 論點** a disputed〔moot〕 point ; the point at issue〔in question〕 ¶ 몹시 시끄러운 논점 a very moot point // 그의 주장은 논점을 벗어나고 있다 His argument is beside the point.

논제 論題 a subject 《of discussion》 ; a theme ; a topic ¶ 논제에서 벗어나다 digress from one's theme

논조 論調 the tone〔tenor, drift〕 of an argument ¶ 이 문제에 관한 각 신문의 논조는 모두 같다 The press comments on this question are the same in tenor.
신문 — the tone of the press

논죄 論罪 ruling ; finding ; judg(e)ment ; decision **—하다** rule ; find ; pass judgment on ; decide (guilt)

‡**논증 論證** proof ; demonstration **—하다** demonstrate ; prove ; bear it out by fact〔proof〕
—자 demonstrator **직접〔간접〕** — direct〔indirect〕 demonstration

논지 論旨 the point〔drift〕 of an argument ¶ 논지를 명백히 하다 make one's point (of argument) clear // 그의 논지는 철저하지 못하다 His argument is not convincing〔to the point〕.

논진 論陣 ¶ 논진을 펴다 argue 《for, against》 ; take a firm stand 《for, against》

논총 論叢 a collection of treatises

논틀밭틀 twisting paths along the ridges of fields and paddy fields

논파 論破 confutation ; refutation ; controversy **—하다** confute ; refute ; controvert ; disprove

***논평 論評** criticism ; a comment ; a review **—하다** criticize ; review ; comment on ¶ 이 문제에 관한 신문 논평 newspaper〔press〕 comments on this subject // 남의 작품에 논평을 가하다 make a review of 《a person's》 work

논풀다 clear〔cultivate〕 《land》 into a rice field ; make land into a rice field

논프로 nonprofessional

***논픽션** nonfiction

‡**논하다 論—** ⇨ 논(論)

놀¹ a glow (in the sky) ¶ 저녁놀 an

evening glow ; an afterglow of sunset ; a sunset glow // 아침놀 a morning glow // 서쪽 하늘에 저녁놀이 붉게 타오르고 있다 The western skies are lit up with the glow of the setting sun.

놀² [파도] a big wave ; a billow ¶ 잇따른 놀이 배의 갑판을 휩쓸었다 Heavy waves washed〔broke〕 over the deck of the ship.

놀금 a rock-bottom price ; an absolutely minimum take-it-or-leave-it price

†놀다¹ ① [유희] play ; amuse〔enjoy〕oneself ; divert oneself ; make an excursion ; visit ¶ 놀러 나가다 go out to play // 뛰어다니며 놀다 play jumping 〔romping〕 about // 숨박꼭질하며 놀다 play hide-and-seek // 장난감을 가지고 놀다 play with toys // 장기를 두며 놀다 amuse oneself playing chess // 노는 데에 여념이 없다 be given to play // 놀며 시간을 보내다 idle away one's time // 제주도로 놀러 가다 go on an excursion to *Cheju-do* // 휴가 중에 무엇을 하며 놀았니 How did you amuse yourself during the vacation ? // 어린애들이 즐겁게 놀고 있다 The children are having a merry time. // 공부만 하고 놀지 않으면 애가 못쓰게 된다 All work and no play makes Jack a dull boy.
② [유흥] make merry ; have a spree ; revel ¶ 오늘 저녁 한잔 먹고 놀자 Let's have a spree tonight. // 어제 저녁은 밤새껏 마시며 놀았다 Last night we caroused around till dawn. // 그는 젊었을 때 놀아 먹었다 He indulged in youthful follies. / He led a dissipated life while young. /He sowed his wild oats. // 요새 너 좀 너무 노는 것 아니냐 Haven't you been living it up a little too much lately ?
③ [허송 세월] be idle ; idle ; loaf 《one's time》 away ; be doing nothing ; take one's ease ¶ 노는 사람 an idle man ; an idler // 놀고 먹다 live idle ; eat the bread of idleness // 하루 놀다 take a holiday // 그는 놀며 지낸다 He is idling away his time. /He lives in idleness.
④ [실직] be out of work〔job〕 ; be unemployed ¶ 놀고 있는 사람 an unemployed person ; a jobless man ; the unemployed 《총칭》 // 그는 요즘 놀고 있다 He is out of work these days.
⑤ [유휴] be not in use ; lie〔stand〕 idle ¶ 놀고 있는 땅 land lying idle // 놀고 있는 기계 an unused machine ; a machine not in use // 그는 은행에 놀고 있는 돈이 많이 있다 He has a lot of money lying idle in the bank. // 그 공장은 놀고 있다 The factory is lying idle. // 너의 재주를 놀려 두지 말아라 Don't let your talent lie idle.
⑥ [움직임] be loose ; shake ; be rickety ¶ 이가 놀다 A tooth is loose. // 나사못이 놀다 A screw is loose. // 의자가 논다 A chair is rickety.
⑦ [멋대로의 행동] behave as one likes ; act〔have, take〕 one's own way 〔pleasure, course〕 ¶ 멋대로 놀게 하다 give 《a person》 a free hand ; allow 《a person》 to go his way

놀던 계집이 결딴이 나도 엉덩이 짓은 남는다 속담 It is hard to make an old mare leave flinging.

†놀다² [던지다] throw 《dice *yut* sticks》 ; play ; shoot 《dice》 ¶ 주사위를 놀다 throw dice ; play at dice ; shoot craps // 윷을 놀다 throw *yut* sticks ; play *yut*

†놀라다 ① [경악] be surprised〔astonished, amazed, shocked〕 ; be startled ; be astounded 《at》 ; be stunned ; jump ; be taken aback 《by》 ¶ 놀라서 in surprise // 놀랍게도 to one's surprise〔astonishment〕 // 놀란 빛을 보이지 않다 exhibit no surprise // 총소리에 놀라다 be startled at the sound of a gun // 친구의 사망 소식을 듣고 놀라다 be stunned by the news of a friend's death // 뱀을 보고 놀라다 jump at the sight of a snake // 그는 놀라서 쳐다보았다 He looked up in surprise. // 놀라서 말이 안 나왔다 Astonishment deprived me of my power of speech. // 그 소식에 약간 놀랐다 The news took us rather by surprise. // 너 때문에 깜짝 놀랐다 You gave me quite a start. // 그는 우리를 보고 깜짝 놀랐다 He was struck dumb when he saw us.
② [공포] be frightened〔startled, alarmed〕 at ; be horror-struck ; be terrified ; have a fright ¶ 놀라서 in one's fright // 놀라 달아나다 be frightened away // 놀라 기절하다 be frightened out of one's senses // 놀라서 병들다 be ill with〔from〕 fright // 놀라서 말을 못하다 be too much frightened to speak ; be struck dumb
③ [경탄] wonder at ; marvel at ¶ 그의 박학에는 놀랐다 I marvel at his profound scholarship. // 누구나 그 건축의 장려함에 놀란다 Everyone marvels at the splendor of the structure. // 그녀의 목소리의 아름다움에 놀랐다 I wondered at her beautiful voice. // 그런 일에는 놀라지 않는다 I shouldn't wonder at it. // 별로 놀랄 것이 못된다 Well, that's no wonder. /That's nothing wonderful. // 그의 학력은 조금도 놀랄 것이 없다 His attainments are nothing out of the way. // 저래도 대학 출신이라니 놀랐어 He a university man ? Well, I'm dashed. // 그는 놀랄 만큼 유창하게 영어를 말한다 He speaks English with surprising〔amazing〕 fluency.

†놀라움 [경악] surprise ; astonishment ; [공포] fright ; horror ; [경탄] wonder ;

amazement ; admiration ¶ 이 소식을 들었을 때의 양친의 놀라움은 어떠 했으랴 You can imagine the surprise of the parents when they heard it.

놀란 가슴 a startled state of mind
자라보고 놀란 가슴 소댕 보고 놀란다 〔속담〕 Once bitten, twice shy.

‡**놀랍다** (be) surprising ; startling ; [경탄] wonderful ; marvellous ; amazing ; [두렵다] fearful ; dreadful ; frightful ; terrible ¶ 놀랍게도 to one's surprise〔astonishment, amazement〕// 놀라운 소식 surprising news // 놀라운 학식 marvellous learning // 놀라운 무식 astonishing ignorance // 놀라운 무기 a formidable weapon // 놀라운 기억력을 가지다 have a remarkable memory // 산소 요법은 놀라운 효과가 있다 Oxypathy does wonders. // 그녀가 겨우 서른 살이라니 놀랍다 It comes as a surprise to learn that she is only thirty years old.

‡**놀래다** surprise ; astonish ; amaze ; startle ; spring a surprise 《on》 ; [공포감을 주다] frighten ; terrify ; scare ; alarm ; shock ; throw 《people》 into a panic ¶ 너를 놀래 줄 일이 있다 We have some surprises in store for you. // 패전의 보도가 사람들을 놀라게 했다 The news of the defeat threw people into a panic. // 놀라게 해드려 죄송합니다 I am sorry for alarming you. // 그 뉴스는 전시민을 몹시 놀라게 했다 The whole citizens were panic-stricken at the news.

†**놀리다** ① [조롱하다] banter ; tease ; chaff ; laugh at ; make fun〔game, sport〕 of ; poke fun at ; jeer 《at》 ; kid 《미·속》 ¶ 그녀는 아버지를 대머리라고 놀려댔다 She teased her father about his bald head. // 말을 더듬는다고 해서 어린아이를 놀려서는 안된다 You must not tease a child because it stutters. // 나를 놀릴 셈이야 Are you kidding me? // 사람을 놀려도 분수가 있지 There is a limit in befooling one. // 아이들은 그를 울보라고 놀려댔다 The children jeered at him, calling him a crybaby. // 사람을 놀리지 말라 Quit〔Stop〕 your kidding. // 그는 자네를 놀리고 있는 거야 He's fooling〔making a fool of〕 you. // 모든 사람이 그 일로 나를 놀리고 있다 Everybody is giving me a hard time about it.
② [쉬게 하다] give a holiday ; have〔leave〕 《a person, a thing》 idle ; give play to 《a fish》 ¶ 직공을 놀리다 lay off workers // 학생들을 하루 놀리다 give schoolboys a holiday // 돈을 놀려 두다 have one's money lying idle // 자식을 놀려 둘 수는 없다 I cannot afford to have my son idle. // 차를 쓰지 않고 놀려 두는 것은 낭비다 It is a waste to leave a car idle.
③ [움직이다] move ; set〔put〕 in motion ¶ 발을 놀리다 move one's legs // 기계를 놀리다 operate a machine // 레코드를 놀리다 play a record // 입 좀 작작 놀려라 Don't talk rubbish! /Stop your nonsense.

†**놀림** banter ; raillery ; chaff ; fun ; joke ; teasing ; kidding ; making fun of

***놀림감** an object〔a butt〕 of ridicule〔derision〕 ; a mockery ; a laughingstock ¶ 놀림감으로 삼다 make fun〔sport〕 of ; make a plaything of // 놀림감이 되다 be made〔make oneself〕 a laughingstock ; be made fun of by people // 그는 동료간의 놀림감이다 He is the laughingstock of his companions. // 그는 남의 놀림감이 되고 있다 He is exposed to the ridicule of the public.

놀림거리 an object of ridicule ⇨놀림감

놀면하다 (be) rather yellow ; (agreeably) yellowish

놀부 심사 —心思 wickedness ; ill-naturedness ; perverseness ; crossness

놀소리 a baby's babbling **—하다** babble

놀아나다 ① [방탕] lead a fast life ; take to fast living ; indulge in dissipation ; become a playboy ¶ 얌전하던 사람이 갑자기 놀아나기 시작했다 He used to be so nice, but now he has started on the life of a playboy.
② [남의 장단에] act imprudently〔thoughtlessly〕 ¶ 남의 장단에 놀아나다 dance after〔to〕 a person's tune〔pipe, piping〕

놀아먹다 live idle ; lead a fast〔dissipated〕 life ¶ 놀아먹는 사람 a libertine // 젊을 때는 제법 놀아먹은 사람이다 He has sown his wild oats.

놀음 merrymaking ⇨ 놀음놀이
—판 the scene of a spree ; merrymaking

놀음놀이 play ; merrymaking ; amusements ; diversion ; a spree ; fun ; sport

놀음차 a tip ; a gratuity

†**놀이** [유희·경기·오락] play ; game ; sports ; pleasure ; amusement ; pastime ; [소풍] a picnic ; an outing ; an excursion ¶ 단풍놀이를 가다 go maple-viewing
꽃— flower viewing **화투 —** a game of picture cards

놀이꾼 a merrymaker ; a carouser ; a junketer ; a picnicker ; an excursionist

놀이쇠 [총의] a breechblock

***놀이터** a playground ; a pleasure resort ; an outing place ; a picnicking place

놀잇배 a pleasure boat ; an excursion barge

놀지다 a big wave rises〔billows up〕

놀치다 billow ; swell ; surge ; 《big waves》 rise roughly ; 《the water》 grow rough ¶ 바다가 놀치다 The sea gets rough〔high〕.

⁑놈 [사람] a fellow ; a chap ; a creature ; a guy 《미》 ; a bimbo ; a wretch ; a bloke《구》 ; [동물·물건] thing ; one ; case ¶ 고약한 놈 an unsavory character ; a loathsome creature // 불쌍한 놈 a poor wretch // 묘한 놈 an eccentric fellow ; a queer fish // 더러운 놈 a dirty bastard ; a mean guy // 미친 놈 a crazy guy ; a screwball // 재수 좋은 놈 a lucky dog // 암놈 a female // 이놈의 옷 this wretched coat // 그 놈을 이리 주시오 Pass that to me, please.

놈팡이 [남자] a man ; a fellow ; a guy ; [건달] a bum ; an idler ; a sluggard ; a drone ; [여자의 상대] a girl's boyfriend

놉 a casual laborer paid by the day ; a day laborer

놉겪이 hiring a casual laborer by the day ; employment of day laborers

⁑놋 brass (놋쇠)
—단추 a brass button **—대야** a brass basin **—대접** a brass bowl **—세공** brass-work **—숟가락** a brass spoon **—요강** a brass chamber pot **—젓가락** brass chopsticks **—타구** a brass spittoon

놋갓장이 a brazier ; a brass-smith

놋그릇, **놋기명** brassware ; brass tableware

⁑놋쇠 ⇨ 놋

놋점 —店 a brassware shop ; a braziery

놋좆 櫓— a rowlock〔oarlock〕; an oar pivot

놋칼 a brass knife ; a brass sword

농 弄 [장난] a sport ; a prank ; a trick ; a practical joke ; [농담] a joke ; a jest ; pleasantry ⇨농담(弄談) ¶ 농으로 in〔for〕 fun ; in sport ; for amusement // 반농으로 half in fun ; by way of amusement // 그건 농이다 I said so only in fun. /I did it for fun. // 농이 싸움으로 변했다 The joke ended in a quarrel.

농 籠 a basket ; a cage ; a clothes-box

농 膿 pus ⇨ 고름

***농가** 農家 a farmhouse ; a farm household ¶ 그는 농가에서 자랐다 He was reared on a farm.

농간 弄奸 a trick ; an artifice ; a wicked design ; a plot ; an evil scheme ¶ 농간에 빠지다 fall a victim to another's scheme
농간을 부리다 관용 revolve〔devise〕 wicked designs ; lay plot ; play〔use〕 tricks ; machinate

농게 籠— 〖동물〗 a rock crab

농경 農耕 farming ; cultivation ; tillage
— 민족 an agricultural people **—법** agricultural techniques ; farming methods **— 시대** 〖역사〗 the Agricultural Age **—용 가축** farm animals **—용 트랙터** an agricultural motor tractor ; an agrimotor **— 적지** arable〔tillable〕 land ; an arable **—지** farm land **— 지방** a well-cultivated region

농공 農工 agriculture and industry ; [사람] farmers and manufacturers
—업 agriculture and industry

농공상 農工商 agriculture, industry and commerce ; [사람] farmers, artisans and tradesmen

농과 農科 the agricultural department ; an agricultural course ¶ 농과를 수료하다 complete a course in agriculture

농과 대학 農科大學 an agricultural college

농구 農具 farm〔agricultural〕 implements ; farming tools ; farm appliances

⁑농구 籠球 basketball ; a cage game
— 선수 a basketball player ; a cage star ; a cager 《미·구》 **— 시즌** basketball season **—화** sneakers ; basketball shoes

농군 農軍 a farmer ; a peasant ; a farm hand

농구

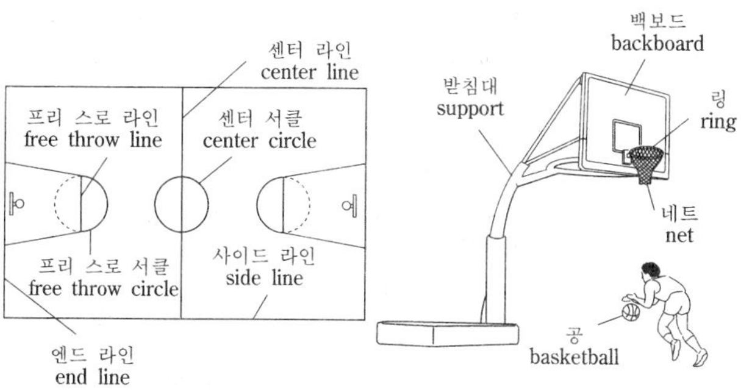

농기 農器 farming tools ⇨ 농구(農具)

*__농노 農奴__ a serf ; a villein ; serfdom (신분)

— **신분** serfdom ; serfhood ; serfage ; villeinage — **해방** emancipation of serfs

농단 壟斷 ① [독점] monopoly ; monopolization ; assumption of an exclusive right ② [절벽] a precipice ; a cliff — **하다** monopolize ; engross ; make a monopoly of ; have 《things》 to oneself ¶ 농단적 monopolizing ; exclusive // 이익을 농단하다 monopolize the profit

—**자** a monopolizer

†**농담 弄談** a joke ; a jest ; a pun ; fun ; pleasantry — **하다** joke ; jest ; crack 〔make〕 a joke ¶ 농담으로 in〔for〕 fun ; in jest ; jestingly // 반농담조로 out of fun ; half in jest // 농담은 그만두고 joking apart ; to be serious // 농담을 주고받다 exchange pleasantries // 농담으로 돌리다 take 《a thing》 as a joke ; make sport of 《a serious matter》 // 농담으로 얼버무리다 turn 《a thing》 into a laughing remark // 그건 농담이다 I don't mean what I say. // 농담이 아니다 It's no joke. /I mean what I say. // 농담이 지나친 것 같습니다 You are carrying the joke too far, I am afraid. // 농담으로 말한 것을 곧이 들었다 What I meant for a joke was taken seriously. // 농담으로라도 그런 말은 말게 Don't say such a thing even in jest. // 기분 나쁘게 생각하지 마시오 농담으로 말했을 뿐이니까 Don't be offended, I only said it in play. // 저 사람하고는 농담도 못한다 He can't take a joke. // 농담이겠죠 You are pulling my leg, aren't you ? / You're putting me on, aren't you ? /You must be joking. // 이렇게 바쁜 시간에 농담이나 하고 다니면 업무량을 늘려 주겠다 Joke around at a busy time like this and I'll increase your work load.

농담 속에 진담 있다 속담 Mows may come to earnest.

농담 濃淡 shading ; light and shade ¶ 빛깔의 농담 a shade of color // 농담을 나타내다 shade 《a drawing》

—**도(度)** depth —**법** 《a picture in》 chiaroscuro ; shading ; gradation — **전지** a concentration cell

농대석 籠臺石 the foundation〔support〕 stone of a tombstone〔monument〕

농도 濃度 thickness ; density ; consistency ; depth of 《color, shade》 ; [화학] concentration ¶ 국물의 농도 the consistency of soup // 빛깔의 농도 the depth〔strength〕 of color // 농도가 높다〔낮다〕 be in high〔low〕 concentration

—**계(計)** 〖사진〗 a densitometer — **분극(分極)** concentration polarization

농들다 膿— form〔generate〕 pus ; fester ; suppurate ; maturate ; 《pus》 be gathered ¶ 상처가 농들었다 Pus has been formed〔gathered〕 in a wound.

농땡이 a lazybones 《구》 ; an idler ; a man of sloth ; a sluggard ¶ 농땡이 부리다 shirk one's duty〔task〕 ; loaf on the job ; lie down on the job 《구》 // 그는 농땡이를 부리느라고 다방에 있는게 분명해 I bet he's playing truant from work at some coffee shop.

농락 籠絡 cajolement ; inveiglement — **하다** cajole ; inveigle ; entice ; trifle 〔toy, sport〕 with 《a person》 ; make 《a person》 one's puppet ; get round 《a person》 ¶ 여자를 농락하다 make sport of a woman ; sport with a woman // 남자에게 농락 당하다 fall prey to a man's lust ; be seduced by a man

— **수단** a means of cajolement

농로 農路 a farm road

농루 膿漏 〖의학〗 pyorrh(o)ea

—**안(眼)** ophthalmoblennorrh(o)ea ; gonorrh(o)eal ophthalmia

농림 農林 agriculture and forestry

— **사업** agricultural and forestry industries — **위원회** the Committee for Agriculture and Forestry — **정책** a policy toward agriculture and forestry — **행정** administration of agriculture and forestry

농림수산부 農林水産部 the Ministry of Agriculture and Fisheries

— **장관** the Minister of Agriculture and Fisheries ; the Agriculture and Fisheries Minister

농림 학교 農林學校 an agricultural and forestry school

농막 農幕 a farmer's hut

농무 濃霧 a dense〔thick〕 fog ¶ 농무가 끼었다 A thick fog came on. // 농무는 뱃사공의 가장 무서운 적이다 A dense fog is the sailor's greatest enemy.

— **경보** a dense fog warning

농무 農務 agricultural affairs ; farming

—**국** the Bureau of Agricultural Administration

*__농민 農民__ a farmer ; a peasant ; peasantry 《총칭》

—**당** an agrarian party — **문학** peasant 〔agrarian〕 literature — **봉기** a peasants' uprising ; an agrarian disturbance — **사회** a farming〔rural〕 community — **생활** peasant life — **심리** peasant psychology — **예술** peasant art — **운동** a peasant movement — **폭동** an agrarian outrage〔disturbance〕 ; a peasant uprising

농번기 農繁期 the farmers' busy season ; the (busy) farming season

— **휴가** school holidays in the (busy) farming season (학교) ; a leave in the (busy) farming season

농병 農兵 agrarian soldiers

농병아리 〖새〗 a little grebe ; a dadchick ; Podiceps ruflcollis poggei (학

명)
농본주의 農本主義 physiocracy ; the 'agriculture-first' principle
*농부 農夫 a farmer ; a peasant ; a plowman ; a farm hand ; peasantry 《총칭》
농사 農事 farming ; husbandry ; agriculture ; agricultural affairs —하다 engage in farming ; do farming ; cultivate the soil ; follow the plow ; farm ¶ 올해 벼농사는 평년 이하라고 한다 This year's rice crop is estimated to be below the average.
— 개량 실험소 an agricultural improvement experiment station — 기계 agricultural implements and machinery —꾼 a farmer — 시험장 an agricultural experiment station —일 farm work ; farming ; husbandry ; peasant labor — 전화(電化) farm electrification —철 the farming season
농사 지도 農事指導 guidance in farming —원 an agricultural agent ; a country 〔an extension〕 agent 《미》
농산물 農産物 agricultural products ; farm produce ¶ 농산물이 풍부하다 be rich in agricultural products
— 가격 farm prices — 가격 유지 제도 a system for shoring up farm prices — 규격 심의회 the Agricultural Products Standards Examination Council — 수출국 an agricultural exporter — 응용 화학 chemurgy
농상 農桑 agriculture and sericulture ; farming and silk-farming
농상 農商 agriculture and commerce ; farmers and merchants (사람)
농상 農相 the Minister of Agriculture
농성 籠城 ① [성을 지킴] holding a castle —하다 be besieged ; be sieged ; hold a castle
② [버티는 일] a sit-in ; a sit-down (strike) ; a stay-in (strike) 《영》 —하다 go on a sit-down (strike) ; stage a sit-down demonstration
— 투쟁 a sit-down (strike) ; a stay-in (strike)
농수산물 農水産物 agricultural and marine products
농수산 위원회 農水産委員會 the (National Assembly) Agriculture-Fisheries Committee
농숙 濃熟 overripeness ; full maturity —하다 be overripe ; mature fully ; attain full maturity
농아 聾啞 deaf and dumb ; a deaf and dumb person ; a deaf-mute
— 문자 sign language ; the deaf-and-dumb alphabet〔signs〕 — 학교 a school for the deaf and dumb ; a deaf and dumb school
농악 農樂 instrumental music of peasants
농액 濃液 a thick liquid
농액 膿液 pus ⇨ 고름
농약 農藥 agricultural medicines〔chemicals〕
— 사용 경작(使用耕作) chemicultivation
농양 膿瘍 〖의학〗 an abscess
농어 —魚 〖물고기〗 a (sea) bass ; a perch ; Lateolabrax japonicus (학명)
농어민 農漁民 farmers and fishermen
농어촌 農漁村 farming and fishing villages〔communities〕
— 개발 공사(開發公社) the Agriculture and Fishery Development Corporation 《A. F. D. C.》
*농업 農業 agriculture ; farming ; agricultural industry ¶ 농업에 종사하다 engage in agriculture〔farming〕 ; follow the plow
— 경영 agricultural〔farm〕 management — 경제 agricultural economy — 경제학 agricultural economics — 공동 경영 cooperative management of agriculture — 과학 agricultural sciences —국 an agricultural〔a farming〕 country — 기계 an agricultural〔a farm〕 machine — 기계화 mechanization of agriculture — 기사 an agricultural engineer — 노동자 a farm worker〔laborer, hand〕 — 보험 agricultural insurance — 용수 agricultural water — 위기 an agricultural crisis — 인구 the agricultural〔farming〕 population — 입국주의 agriculturism — 자금 대부 a rural loan — 재해 보상법 〖법〗 the Agricultural Disaster Compensation Act — 정책 agricultural policy — 지구 a farming region — 토목 agricultural civil engineering — 학교 an agricultural school — 혁명 an agricultural revolution 고도 기계화 — highly mechanized agriculture 조방(粗放) — extensive agriculture 집약 — intensive agriculture
농업 개량 農業改良 agricultural improvement
농업 개발 계획 農業開發計劃 an agricultural development project
농업 경영학 農業經營學 agronomics ; agronomy
—자 an agronomist
농업 기상학 農業氣象學 agricultural meteorology ; agrometeorology ¶ 농업 기상학의〔적〕 agrometeorological
—자 an agrometeorologist
농업 기술 農業技術 agricultural techniques ¶ 농업 기술의 개선 improvement in agricultural technique ; agricultural improvement
농업 단체 農業團體 an agricultural〔a farmers'〕 organization
농업 생물학 農業生物學 agrobiology ¶ 농업 생물학의〔적〕 agrobiologic(al)
농업 생산 農業生産 agricultural〔farm〕 production〔output〕

농업 지질학 農業地質學 agricultural geology ; agrogeology
—자 an agrogeologist
농업 협동 조합 農業協同組合 an agricultural cooperative (association)
— 중앙회 the National Agricultural Cooperative Federation 《NACF》
농예 農藝 agricultural technology ; agriculture and horticulture
농예 화학 農藝化學 agricultural chemistry
농우 農牛 farming cattle ; a plow ox ; a draft ox
⁑농원 農園 a farm ; a plantation
— 농업 estate agriculture —주 the proprietor of a farm ; a farmer 자작 — a home farm (지주의)
농익다 be overripe ; be overmature
농작 農作 farming ; husbandry ; cultivation of land ; tillage of the soil
†농작물 農作物 the crops ; a harvest ; farm produce ¶ 농작물을 해치다 injure [damage] the crops // 농작물이 잘되었다 The harvest turned out well. // 금년 농작물은 잘 안되었다 The crops are very bad this year. // 이 한발이 오래 계속하면 농작물은 큰 해를 입는다 If this drought lasts long, the crops will suffer greatly.
†농장 農場 a farm ; a plantation ; a farmstead (건물 포함) ; a ranch (목축 농장) ¶ 농장에서 일하다 work on a farm // 농장을 경영하다 run [operate] a farm
— 경영 farm management — 관리인 a farm-bailiff — 노동자 a farm hand ; a farm worker [laborer] — 부속 주택 a farmhouse — 작업 farm working —주 [경영자] a farmland proprietor ; a farmer ; [면화 따위의] a 《cotton, coffee, sugar》 planter 국영 — a state farm 실험 — an experimental farm 집단 — a collective farm
농정 農政 agricultural administration
농종 膿腫 『의학』 an abscess
*농지 農地 agricultural land ; farmland
— 개혁 a farmland [an agrarian] reform —법 the Agricultural Land Act — 제도 the farmland system — 증권 agricultural land securities
농지 개발 農地開發 development of farmland [agricultural land]
—법 『법』 the Farmland Exploitation Act
농지거리 弄— joking ; bantering ; jesting ; pleasantry —하다 joke ; banter ; jest ; pass pleasantries 《with》
*농촌 農村 a farm [farming] village ; a rural community ; an agricultural district ¶ 농촌의 rural ; agrarian ; agricultural // 농촌의 쇠퇴 the impoverishment of rural communities // 농촌의 공업화 industrialization of agricultural villages
— 경제 rural economy — 구제 relief to rural communities ; farm relief — 문제 a rural [an agrarian] problem — 생활 life in rural communities ; farm life — 시간 『라디오』 the farmers' hour — 인구 the rural [agricultural, agrarian] population — 전화(電化) rural electrification — 지대 a farm area ; a farm belt 《미》 ; a farming region — 진흥 agrarian improvement ; development [advancement] of an agricultural community — 진흥청 the Agrarian Development Office ; the Office of Rural Development — 청년[여성] farm [rural] youth [women]
*농축 濃縮 concentration ; enrichment
—하다 concentrate ; enrich
— 우라늄 enriched uranium — 우유 condensed milk
농탕 弄蕩 lascivious conduct [life] ; debauchery
농탕 치다 관용 lead a lascivious life ; indulge in debauchery [dissipation]
농토 農土 farmland ; agricultural land ¶ 메마른 농토 barren [sterile] land
— 개량 improvement of farmland
농하다 濃— [빛깔이] (be) dark ; deep ; [액체가] thick ; dense ; heavy ; strong
농하다 弄— joke ; jest ⇨ 농(弄)
⁑농학 農學 (the science of) agriculture
— 박사 [사람] a doctor of agriculture ; [학위] Doctor of Agriculture 《D. Agr.》 —부(部) the department of agriculture —사(士) [사람] a bachelor of agriculture ; [학위] Bachelor of Agriculture 《B. Agr.》 —자 an agriculturist ; an agriculturalist
농한 農閑 spare time on the farm
—기(期) the farmer's slack [leisure] season
농협 農協 ⇨ 농업 협동 조합
농후 濃厚 thickness ; density —하다 (be) thick ; dense ; heavy ; strong ; rich ¶ 농후한 빛깔 rich [gorgeous] colors // 살인의 혐의가 농후하다 There are strong suspicions that he has committed murder.
— 비료 a concentrated fertilizer — 사료 concentrated fodder [feed] —액 dope (윤활제·흡수제로서의)
높낮이 high and low ; unevenness ; undulations
†높다 ① (be) high ; lofty ; tall ; elevated ; prominent (코 따위) ¶ 높은 건물 a high [tall] building // 높은 곳 a high place ; an elevated place ; a height // 높은 코 a prominent nose // 하늘 높이 high up in the air ; way up in the sky 《미·구》 // 높아지다 be raised ; become higher // 파도가 높다 The sea is running high. // 저 산은 얼마나 높은가 How high is the mountain ? /What is the height of the mountain ? // 고도가 높아질수록

기온은 내려간다 The higher you go, the colder it grows.
② [지위·명성이] (be) high ; lofty ; noble ; elevated ¶ 신분이 높은 사람 a person of high positions ; a man of rank // 높은 이상 a lofty〔noble〕 ideal // 명성이 높은 사람 a person of high reputation // 명성이 높아지다 win a reputation // 눈이〔희망이〕 너무 높다 aim〔set one's hopes〕 too high // 지위가 높아지다 rise in position // 높은 지위를 차지하다 occupy a high position
③ [값이] (be) dear ; high ; expensive ; costly ¶ 높은 생활비 a high cost of living // 물가가 너무 높다 prices are too high // 소금이 높은 가격에 팔리고 있다 Salt is selling at a high price.
④ [소리가] (be) loud ; high-pitched ; shrill ¶ 높은 소리로 in a loud voice ; loudly // 소리를 높이다 raise one's voice // 높은 소리로 말하다 speak in a shrill voice // 라디오 소리가 크지 않아 볼륨 좀 높여 줄래 The radio isn't loud enough. Could you turn it up?
⑤ [정도·비율이] (be) high ¶ 열이 높다 have a high temperature // 기온이 높아지다 the temperature rises〔goes up〕
높은 가지가 부러지기 쉽다 [속담] The highest tree has the greatest fall. /The highest branch is not the safest roost.
높은 나무에는 바람이 세다 [속담] A great tree attracts the wind. /Great wind blow upon high hills.

높다랗다 (be) rather high〔tall〕 ; lofty ; towering ¶ 높다란 명동 성당의 첨탑 the soaring spire of *Myŏngdong* Cathedral

높드리 ① [골짜기의] the higher part of a ravine ② [논밭] a high and infertile farmland

높으락낮으락 unevenly ; undulatingly ; high and low ; up and down

†**높이¹** [고도] height ; altitude ; elevation ; [소리의] loudness ; tone ; [도(度)] pitch ¶ 높이 2미터이다 be two meters high // 200미터의 높이를 날다 fly at a height of 200 meters // 이 탑의 높이는 10미터 이상이다 This tower rises to a height of over 10 meters. // 이 나무는 높이 50피트쯤까지 자란다 This tree grows to a height of about 50 feet. // 그 높이에서는 공기가 매우 희박하다 In those altitudes the air is extremely thin. // 이 건물의 높이는 얼마입니까 How tall〔high〕 is this building?
— 제한(制限) [육교 밑을 지나는 차에 대한] a height limit

높이² ① [부사] high ; highly ; aloft ¶ 하늘 높이 high up in the air // 높이 뛰다 jump high // 손을 높이 들다 hold〔raise〕 one's hand high // 높이 평가하다 highly appreciate ; set a high value 《on》 ; esteem // 하늘 높이 날다 fly high up in the air〔sky〕 // 그는 너의 작품을 매우 높이 평가하고 있다 He speaks very highly of your work.
② [소리] loud ; loudly ; high-pitched ; in a loud voice ¶ 소리 높이 in a loud voice ; loudly ; in a shrill voice

***높이다** raise ; heighten ; elevate ; lift ; enhance ; promote (증진하다) ; increase ; improve (개선하다) ; hold 《a person》 in reverence (존대하다) ; boost (전압을) ¶ 뚝을 높이다 build a bank higher ; raise a bank // 가치를 높이다 enhance the value 《of》 // 명성을 높이다 increase one's reputation // 정도를 높이다 raise the standard〔level〕 // 지위를 높이다 promote (in rank) ; raise 《a person's》 position // 품질을 높이다 improve〔raise〕 the quality // 언성을 높이다 raise one's voice ; speak in an angry voice // 사람을 높이다 hold 《a person》 in reverence〔in high esteem〕 // 사회적으로나 정치적으로나 여성의 지위를 더 높이지 않으면 안된다 The position of women should be elevated〔raised〕 higher both socially and politically.

높이뛰기 a high jump ; a high leap ; a capriole (말의)
— 선수 a high jumper **—용 모래밭** a high jumping pit **장대—** a pole vault〔jump〕 ¶ 장대높이뛰기 하다 pole-vault〔-jump〕 **장대— 선수** a pole vaulter〔jumper〕 **제자리—** the standing high jump

높임말 an honorific (term)

높직이 rather〔somewhat〕 high ; rather loud (목소리)

높직하다 (be) rather〔somewhat〕 high ; rather loud (목소리가)

†**놓다¹** ① [두다] put ; lay ; place ; set ¶ 펜을 놓다 lay down the pen // 의자를 그리 놓아라 Put a chair there. // 그것을 어디에 놓을까요 Where shall I put it? // 다 쓴 후에는 제자리에 놓아라 Put it back where it was when you are through. // 명함을 놓고 갔다 He left his card. // 내 모자를 어디에 놓았느냐 Where have you left my hat?
② [해방하다] set free ; release ; unloose ; turn〔let〕 loose ; [손을] let go〔off〕 ; take off one's hand ; let go one's hold 《of》 ; quit one's grasp ¶ 개를 놓아주다 let the dog loose ; unleash a dog // 놓아주시오 Let me go! // 그는 그녀의 손을 쥐고 있다가 놓았다 He held her hand and then let it go. // 지금은 손을 놓을 수가 없다 My hands are full. / I am engaged just now. // 그녀는 새장을 열어 새를 놓아주었다 She opened the cage and set the bird free.
③ [총포를] fire ; discharge ¶ 총을 놓다 fire a gun
④ [불을] set 《fire》 ¶ 불을 놓다 set

fire to 《a house》; set 《a house》 on fire
⑤ [가설하다] build; construct ¶ 전화를 놓다 install a telephone // 강에 다리를 놓다 build〔throw〕 a bridge over a river // 덫을 놓다 set a trap // 철도를 놓다 lay down a railroad
⑥ [주사를] inject; inoculate 《a person with》; syringe ¶ 캠퍼 주사를 두 대 놓다 give〔administer〕 《a person》 two camphor injections
⑦ [마음을] ease; set 《one's mind》 at ease〔rest〕; give 《one's mind》 relief ⇨ 마음놓다
⑧ [자수를] embroider ¶ 금실로 수를 놓다 embroider figures on 《velvet》 in gold thread // 그녀는 손수건에 자기 이름 첫 글자의 수를 놓았다 She embroidered the handkerchief with her initials.
⑨ [주판을] work; use ¶ 주판을 놓다 use〔work〕 the abacus; reckon〔figure it out〕 on the abacus; be calculating (타산적이다) // 비용을 놓다 estimate the expense
⑩ [값을] offer 《a price》; bid; name 《a price》 ¶ 5만원의 값을 놓다 offer 〔bid〕 50,000 *won*.
⑪ [돈을] lend〔loan〕 (at interest); [세를] hire (out); let (out); let 《a room》 on hire; rent; lease (부동산을) ¶ 돈을 5푼으로 놓다 lend〔loan〕 money at 5 percent interest // 집을 세놓다 rent〔let〕 a house // 방을 세놓다 let a room on hire
⑫ [속력을] accelerate; increase ¶ 속력을 놓다 accelerate〔increase〕 speed; speed up
⑬ [말을] lower one's style of speech ¶ 말씀 놓으시지요 Please don't hesitate to drop your honorifics in talking to me, sir.
⑭ [거간을] put in 《as an intermediary》; send 《a person》 ¶ 사람을 놓아 수소문하다 send 《a person》 for information; get information through an agent
⑮ [기르다] keep 《a dog》; raise〔rear〕 《silkworms》 ¶ 참외를 놓다 sow melon seed; grow melon // 닭을 놓다 raise chickens
⑯ [침을] apply 《acupuncture, a needle》
⑰ [솜 따위를 채우다] stuff〔pad〕 with cotton ¶ 방석에 솜을 놓다 stuff a cushion with cotton
⑱ [목을] unrestrainedly ¶ 목을 놓아 울다 cry unrestrainedly
⑲ [바둑에서] ¶ 두 점을 놓고 시작하다 accept a two-stone handicap

놓다² [조동사] ① [...해 두다] ¶ 표를 사 놓아 주셔요 Buy the tickets in advance (now). // 논 갈아 놓고 비를 기다린다 We have finished plowing the paddy field and are waiting for rain.
② [...한 상태] ¶ 잠 못 자게 해 놓다 keep 《a person》 awake // 길이 너무 질어 놓아서 걸어가기 힘들다 The road is so sloppy that it is very hard to walk on.

놓아두다 leave 《a thing》 as it is; let 《a person》 alone ¶ 그대로 놓아두어라 Leave it as it is. // 개를 그냥 놓아둬 놀리면 물 테니까 You had better leave that dog alone, it will bite you if you tease it. // 마음대로 하게 놓아둬 Let him have his own way. // 다 썼으면 있던 자리에 놓아두어라 Put it back where it was when you are through.

놓아먹다 be badly brought up; be ill-bred ¶ 놓아먹은 자식 an ill-bred boy

놓아 먹이다 graze 《cattle》; put 《cattle》 to grass; (put to) pasture; keep loose; leave 《pigs》 at large ¶ 놓아먹이는 닭 yard fowls; fowls ranging freely // 소를 놓아먹이다 pasture cattle

놓아주다 let go; set free; let loose; release; liberate; set at large ¶ 새를 놓아주다 let the bird loose; free the bird // 죄수를 놓아주다 set a prisoner free; give a prisoner his freedom // 이번만은 놓아준다 I will let you off this one time. // 그는 일단 붙잡으면 놓아주지 않는다 Once he gets hold of you, he doesn't let go.

놓이다 ① [얹히다] be put〔laid, placed, set〕 ¶ 테이블 위에 꽃병이 놓여 있다 A vase is placed on the table.
② [마음이] feel relieved; feel at rest; feel reassured ¶ 마음이 놓일 때가 없다 have no moment of ease // 그 소식을 듣고 한결 마음이 놓였다 I was greatly relieved at the news.

†놓치다 [기회 따위] miss; let slip; [범인 따위] let escape; lose; fail to catch ¶ (낚은) 고기를 놓치다 lose a fish // 공을 놓치다 miss a ball; fail to catch a ball // 기차를 놓치다 miss〔lose〕 a train // 그릇을 놓치다 drop a dish; let a dish fall // 도둑을 놓치다 fail to catch a thief // 손님을 놓치다 miss a customer // 좋은 기회를 놓치다 miss a good opportunity // 저 놈을 놓치지 말라 Don't let him get away. // 놓친 고기는 항상 큰 법이야 It is the fish you lose that are the biggest. // 3분 늦어서 막차를 놓쳤다 I missed 〔failed to catch〕 the last train by three minutes. // 한 자리 숫자 때문에 100만 달러 상금을 놓치다니 안됐군 Too bad you missed one million dollar lottery jackpot by one digit. // 저런 땅볼을 놓치다니 믿을 수 없다 I can't believe he let that grounder get by him.

†뇌 腦 the brain; brains (지력); a cerebrum ¶ 뇌의 cerebral // 뇌를 쓰는 일 brain work // 뇌를 쓰다 tax〔rack, overtax〕 one's brains // 뇌가 나쁘다 have

brain trouble // 과도한 공부로 뇌를 상하게 하다 hurt one's brains with overstudy // 그녀는 교통사고로 뇌에 큰 손상을 입었다 She suffered severe brain damage as a result of the traffic accident.
—연화증(軟化症) softening of the brain —작용 cerebration ; brain action —졸중 (cerebral) apoplexy ; stroke
뇌간 腦幹 〚해부〛 the brain stem
뇌개골 腦蓋骨 〚해부〛 the brainpan
뇌격기 雷擊機 a torpedo plane〔bomber, carrier〕
뇌관 雷管 a percussion cap ; a detonation cap ; a detonator ; a snap cap
— 약포(藥包) a percussion cartridge — 장치 a percussion lock — 화약 percussion powder 뇌홍(雷汞)— a fulminate detonator
뇌교 腦橋 〚해부〛 the pons 《*pl.* pontes》
뇌까리다 repeat〔reiterate〕 the same remark unpleasantly ; harp on the same string 《구》 ¶ 화려했던 옛날을 자꾸만 뇌까리다 harp upon the glories of one's former days
뇌꼴스럽다 (be) disgusting ; detestable ; loathful
뇌다 ① [체로] put through a sieve of finer mesh ② [말을] repeat ; say over again ; reiterate ¶ 같은 말을 되뇌다 repeat oneself ; say over again ; harp on the same string 《미·구》
뇌동 雷同 —하다 follow 《another》 blindly ; follow suit without reflection ; echo 《another's view》 ; chime in with
—자 a blind follower
뇌동맥 경화 腦動脈硬化 cerebral arteriosclerosis
뇌락 磊落 —하다 (be) frank ; openhearted ; jolly ; jovial ; free and easy ; unaffected
뇌랗다 (be) sickly yellow
뇌력 腦力 mental capacity ; brain power ; intellectual quotient 《I. Q》
뇌리 腦裡 the brain ; one's mind ; one's memory ¶ 뇌리에 깊이 새겨지다 make a deep impression〔be deeply impressed〕 on one's mind // 뇌리에 떠오르다 come across one's mind ; flash upon one〔one's mind〕 ; occur to one // 그 생각이 뇌리에서 사라지지 않는다 The thought haunts me.
뇌막 腦膜 meninges 《*pl.* -ninx》
—염 meningitis ; brain fever
뇌명 雷鳴 thunder ; a thunderclap ; a roll〔peal, clap, crack〕 of thunder ; the rumbling of thunder
뇌문 雷紋 a fret ; a meander ; a key pattern ; a Greek fret
— 세공 fretwork ; fretting
****뇌물** 賂物 a bribe ; palm oil〔grease〕 《속》 ; golden〔silver〕 key ; boodle 《미·속》 ¶ 뇌물을 주는 사람 a briber // 뇌물을 받다 take〔accept〕 a bribe 《from》 ; be bribed // 뇌물이 통하지 않다 be proof against corruption // 뇌물을 주다 bribe 《a person》 ; offer a bribe ; grease 《the palm of a person》 // 뇌물로 매수하다 buy off 《a person》 // 그는 뇌물 따위를 받는 사람이 아니다 He is above〔beyond〕 bribery. // 뇌물의 효과가 있었다 The bribe has worked.
— 수회 acceptance of a bribe ; bribery ; corruption — 수회자 a bribee ; a boodler 《미·속》 ; a sell-outer
뇌병 腦病 a brain disease
뇌병원 腦病院 a hospital for brain diseases ; a mental hospital
뇌빈혈 腦貧血 〚의학〛 cerebral anemia ; anemia of the brain ¶ 뇌빈혈을 일으키다 have an attack of cerebral anemia
뇌사 腦寫 〚의학〛 encephalgraphy
뇌사 腦死 〚의학〛 brain death
뇌산 雷酸 〚화학〛 fulminic acid
뇌색전증 腦塞栓症 〚의학〛 cerebral embolism
뇌석 腦石 〚광물〛 brain coral
뇌성 雷聲 thunder ; a peal〔cracks, the rumbling, roars〕 of thunder ¶ 뇌성벽력 thunder and lightning // 뇌성대명 worldwide fame ; a resounding name ; a name heard round the world // 먼 곳에서 뇌성이 들렸다 Rolls of thunder were heard in the distance.
—대명(大名) worldwide fame ; 《a person's》 great name —벽력 thunder and lightening
뇌성 腦性
— 마비 cerebral palsy ¶ 뇌성 마비의 spastic 《children》 — 소아마비 cerebral infantile paralysis
뇌쇄 惱殺 —하다 captivate ; fascinate ; enchant ; bewitch ; charm ; steal the heart of ; kill 《a man》 ¶ 뇌쇄적인 눈으로 보다 cast a killing glance 《at》
뇌수 腦髓 the brain
— 마비 cerebral palsy
뇌수술 腦手術 brain surgery ; a surgical operation on brain
뇌수종 腦水腫 〚의학〛 hydrocephalus ; water on the brain ¶ 뇌수종에 걸린 hydrocephalic
뇌신 雷神 the god of thunder ; Thor ; the Thunderer ; Jupiter
뇌신경 腦神經 a cranial〔cerebral〕 nerve
— 세포 a brain cell — 쇠약 nervous prostration〔debility〕 ; brain fag — 외과 neurosurgery ; [병원의] the department of neurosurgery — 외과의(外科醫) a neurosurgeon —절(節) a cerebral ganglion
뇌실 腦室 〚해부〛 a ventricle of the brain ; a cerebral ventricle
—경(鏡) a ventriculoscope —염(炎) 〚의학〛 ventriculitis — 촬영법 ventriculography

뇌염 腦炎 brain inflammation ; encephalitis ; cerebritis ; phrenitis
기면성(嗜眠性) — 〖의학〗 sleeping sickness 유행성 — epidemic encephalitis

뇌우 雷雨 a thunderstorm ; a thundershower ¶ 심한 뇌우 a heavy〔severe〕 thunderstorm // 뇌우를 만나다 be overtaken by a thunderstorm

뇌운 雷雲 a thunder cloud ; a thunderhead

뇌일혈 腦溢血 cerebral hemorrhage ; (a stroke of) apoplexy ; an apoplectic stroke ; a stroke ; effusion of blood on the brain ¶ 뇌일혈로 죽다 die of apoplexy

뇌장 腦漿 the brains

뇌장애 腦障碍 a brain injury ; brain trouble

뇌전 雷電 thunder and lightning ; thunderbolts

뇌조 雷鳥 a snowgrouse ; a ptarmigan

뇌종양 腦腫瘍 〖의학〗 a brain tumor

뇌진탕 腦震蕩 concussion of the brain ; cerebral concussion ¶ 뇌진탕을 일으키다 have a concussion of the brain

뇌척수 腦脊髓 〖해부〗 the brain and spinal chord

뇌척수막 腦脊髓膜 〖의학〗 meninges

뇌척수막염 腦脊髓膜炎 〖의학〗 cerebrospinal meningitis ; brain fever ; spotted fever

뇌척수액 腦脊髓液 〖의학〗 the cerebrofever fluid

뇌척수염 腦脊髓炎 〖의학〗 encephalomyelitis

뇌천 腦天 the crown of the head ; the pate 《속》

뇌출혈 腦出血 〖의학〗 cerebral hemorrhage (뇌일혈)

뇌충혈 腦充血 〖의학〗 congestion of the brain ; cerebral hyper(a)emia

뇌파 腦波 〖의학〗 a brain wave
—계(計) an electroencephalograph —도(圖) an electroencephalogram

뇌하다 (be) low and dirty ; mean and foul

뇌하수체 腦下垂體 〖해부〗 a pituitary gland〔body〕 ; pituitary ; a hypophysis 《*pl.* -ses》
— 기능 부전(機能不全) hypopituitarism — 기능 항진(機能亢進) hyperpituitarism — 이식 transplanting of the pituitary gland ; hypophysedil 〔hypophysial〕 implantation — 절제술 hypophysectomy — 호르몬 pituitary hormone

뇌혈전 腦血栓 cerebral thrombosis

뇟보 a low-down person ; a mean bastard

누 who ⇨ 누구

누 累 implication ; involvement ; trouble ; evil influence〔effect〕 ¶ 남에게 누를 끼치다 bring〔cause〕 trouble to others ; compromise〔affect〕 others ; implicate〔involve〕 others in trouble

누 樓 ① a two-storied house ; an upper story ; a tower ; a turret ; [성의] a lookout ; [망루] belvedere ② a palace ⇨ 누각

누 壘 [야구] a base ; a bag ; a sack 《미·속》
일— the first base 일—수 the first baseman

누가 累加 accumulation ; progressive 〔cumulative〕 increase ; acceleration —하다 accumulate ; increase progressively ; accelerate

누가 복음 —福音 the Gospel of Luke ; Luke

누각 樓閣 a palace ; a tower ; a castle ; a many-storied building ; a tall 〔high〕 building ¶ 모래 위에 누각을 짓다 build a house on (the) sand

누감 累減 [과세의] degression
—세〔과세〕 degressive tax〔taxation〕

누계 累計 the cumulative total ; the total ; the aggregate —하다 total ¶ 누계가 10만원이다 total〔amount to〕 100,000 *won*

누관 淚管 〖해부〗 the tear duct(s) ; the lachrymal duct
— 소식자(消息子) a lac(h)rimal probe —염(炎) dacryosolenitis — 협착(狹窄) dacryostenosis

†누구 ① [의문] who (누구가) ; whose (누구의) ; whom (누구에게, 누구를) ; who 《구》 ¶ 누구가 그렇게 말하더냐 Who told you that ? // 누구세요 Who's there ? / Who is it ? // 누구가 한 짓이라고 생각하느냐 Who do you think has done it ? // 누구를 만났느냐Who〔whom〕 did you see ? // 누구의 연필이냐 Whose is this pencil ? /Whose pencil is this ? // 여 누군가 했더니 김군이군 Well, well, if it isn't Mr. *Kim.* // 이 편지는 누구한테서 온 거죠 Who is the letter from ? // 그 사람이 누구인지 말해주게 Tell me who he is. // 누구를 데리고 갔느냐 Whom〔who〕 did you take with you ? // 수취인을 누구 앞으로 만들어 드릴까요 Who will it to be made out to ? /Who should I make it out to ?
② [누군가] someone ; somebody ; [의문·부정(不定)의 경우] anyone ; anybody ¶ 누군가 딴사람 someone else // 누군가 적당한 사람 some suitable person // 누구 누구 Mr.〔Mrs., Miss〕 So-and-so // 누군가 문을 닫아 주게 Close the door, somebody. // 누군가 자네를 부르고 있네 Someone is calling you. // 누군가 있더냐 Was there anybody there ? // 누구 이 사전이 필요한 사람 있어요 Is there anybody who wants this dictionary ?
③ [누구라도] anyone ; anybody ; [부정의 경우] nobody ; none ¶ 누구도 모른

다 Nobody can tell. // 누구나 약점은 있다 We all have weak points. // 그런 문제는 누구나 풀 수 있었다 Anyone could solve such a problem. // 전쟁이 끝난 것을 누구 한 사람 기뻐하지 않는 사람이 없었다 Everyone was glad that the war was over. // 누구든지 그 책을 원한다면 가져도 좋아 Whoever wants the book may have it. // 누구도 예측을 못할 상황이다 It's anybody's guess. /Your guess is as good as mine.

누구누구 ¶ 누구누구 할 것 없이 every last man ; every man Jack ; without distinction of person // 누구누구 왔나 Who all is here ? // 누구누구 할 것 없이 다 나쁘다 You are all to blame, every last one of you.

누군 as for anyone〔everyone〕 ¶ 누군 그것을 모르나 Who doesn't know that ? / There is no one but knows it. // 누군 그 자리에 없었나 I was there, too.

누군들 whoever ; anyone ; everyone ; even I ¶ 누군들 그런 생각을 했겠는가 Whoever〔Who〕 would have thought of it ?

누군지 who ; someone or other ; so-and-so ¶ 누군지 모른다 I don't know who it is. // 누군지 비밀을 누설했다 Someone has disclosed the secret.

†**누굴** who(m) ; someone ¶ 누굴 찾느냐 Who are you looking (out) for ? // 누굴 보냈느냐 Whom did you send ? /Did you send someone ?

‡**누그러뜨리다** soften 《one's attitude》 ; appease 《one's anger》 ¶ 그녀는 목소리를 누그러뜨렸다 She softened her voice. /She spoke gently〔in a gentle voice〕.

누그러지다 [날씨 따위가] get milder ; ease up ; [값이] get lower ; decline ; [성질 따위가] soften ; cool down ; be mollified ; be soothed ¶ 바람이 누그러지다 The wind goes down〔abates〕. // 날씨가 누그러지다 The weather gets milder. // 추위가 누그러지다 The cold weather eases up. // 물가가 누그러지다 Prices are on the decline. // 마음〔안색〕이 누그러지다 One's heart〔look〕 softens. // 노여움이 누그러졌다 One's anger was softened. // 그의 부드러운 말에 내 마음이 누그러졌다 His tender words melted my heart. // 그녀가 우는 것을 보고 그의 마음이 누그러졌다 His heart melted when he saw her crying.

누글누글 **—하다** (be) tender ; soft ; pulpy ; pasty ¶ 갖풀을 누글누글하게 끓이다 boil the glue soft

누긋누긋하다 ⇨ 노긋노긋하다

누긋하다 [물건이] (be) supple ; soft and flexible ; [성질이] placid ; calm ¶ 누긋한 성질 a placid temper

누기 **漏氣** dampness ; damp ; moisture ; humidity ; wetness ; dankness

누기 차다 (be) damp ; dampish ; wet ; moist ; humid ¶ 누기 찬 방 a damp room

누기 치다 become damp〔humid, moist, wet, soppy〕 ¶ 방에 누기가 치다 A room becomes damp.

누나 《a boy's》 elder〔older〕 sister ; a big sister ¶ 큰누나 the oldest sister

누년 **累年** many years ; several years ; successive years ; a series of years
— 통계 annual statistics〔figures〕

*__누누이__ **屢屢—** repeatedly ; frequently ; many times ; a number of times ; time after time ; time and again ; over and over again ¶ 누누이 말하다 speak repeatedly ; dwell upon 《a matter》 // 같은 말을 누누이 하다 say the same thing over and over again // 이 책의 가치에 대해서는 누누이 말할 필요가 없다 There is no need to dwell upon〔reiterate〕 the value of this book.

누님 an elder sister

*__누다__ evacuate ; pass ; let out ¶ 똥을 누다 have a bowel movement ; defecate ; relieve〔ease〕 nature〔oneself〕 ; evacuate (the bowels) ; shit 《비》 // 오줌을 누다 urinate ; pass water〔urine〕 ; relieve〔ease〕 nature ; piss 《비》

누대 **屢代** successive generations ; a number of generations ¶ 누대로 내려온 보물 a family heirloom

누대 **樓臺** a tower ; a lookout ; a turret

누더기 tattered clothes ; rags ; tatters ¶ 누더기를 걸친 사람 a person in rags ; a ragamuffin ; a tatterdemalion // 누더기를 입고 있다 be (clad) in rags // 그의 옷은 누더기가 되었다 His clothes were worn to rags.

누덕누덕 in patches ; full of patches ; patched and repatched ¶ 옷을 누덕누덕 깁다 patch and repatch one's clothes

누되다 **累—** (be) harassing ; troublesome

누드 (the) nude
—모델 a nude model **—사진**(寫眞) a nude photo ; a nude picture **—쇼** a nude show

누두 **漏斗** a funnel

누락 **漏落** an omission ; a lacuna 《*pl.* -nae, ～s》 ; a hiatus 《*pl.* ～es, ～》 **—하다** be left out ; be omitted ; be missing ; omit ; leave out ¶ 몇자 누락하다 miss out several words // 누락이 많다 There are many omissions.

누란 **累卵** imminent danger ; a delicate〔dangerous〕 situation ¶ 누란의 위기에 처하다 be in imminent peril ; be in a most precarious situation ; be touch-and-go // 누란의 위기에서 나라를 구하다 save the nation in a great crisis ; save the country from threatened ruin

누렁 yellow ; yellow dyes (물감)

누렁물 yellow water ; dirty water
누렁우물 a contaminated〔an impure〕well
*__누렇다__ (be) quite yellow ; a golden yellow ¶ 보리가 누렇게 익었다 The barley is ripe and golden.
누룩 yeast ; leaven ; malt
—덩이 yeast cake **—밀** malt made of glutinous rice
누룩곰팡이 〖식물〗 an aspergillus 《*pl.* -gilli》; leaven
누룽지 scorched rice (from the bottom of the pot)
*__누르께하다__ be tinged〔stained〕with yellow ¶ 세월의 흐름과 함께 원고도 누르께해졌다 The manuscript was yellowed with age.
†__누르다__[1] (be) yellow ; golden ¶ 누른 빛 a yellow〔golden〕color // 누른 잎 a yellow leaf // 누른 빛이 되다 turn yellow
*__누르다__[2] ① press (down) ; push down ¶ 국수를 누르다 make noodles ; squeeze out noodles (through a perforated press) // 도장을 누르다 stamp 《a document》 with one's seal ; set〔fit, affix, stamp〕 one's seal 《to》 // 발로 누르다 step〔tread, trample〕 on // 초인종을 누르다 press the bell ; push the button
② [무거운 것을 얹어서] weigh down ¶ 서진으로 종이를 누르다 keep papers down with a paperweight
③ [억압] suppress ; oppress ; put down ; [위압] overawe ; overpower ; overwhelm ; repress ; subdue ; domineer over ¶ 백성을 누르다 oppress the people // 위력으로 누르다 press 《a person》 by a show of one's power
④ [억제] suppress ; check ; restrain ; repress ; keep〔hold〕 back ; keep〔get〕 under (control) ¶ 누를 길 없는 분노 uncontrollable〔irrepressible〕 anger // 감정을 누르다 control〔suppress〕 one's feelings〔emotions〕 // 노여움을 누르다 master〔control〕 one's anger // 욕망을 누르다 suppress〔repress〕 one's desire ; put a curb upon one's desire // 웃음을 누를 길 없었다 I could scarcely suppress a laugh. // 그는 복받쳐 오는 화를 누를 수 없었다 He could not restrain his temper.
⑤ [경쟁에서] beat 《a person, a team, etc.》; defeat ¶ 첫 세트에서 상대팀을 누르다 defeat the opponent team in the first set
누르락붉으락 turning〔becoming〕 red with anger ; changing countenance with anger
누르락푸르락 turning〔becoming〕 pale with anger ; changing countenance with anger
누르스름하다 (be) yellowish ; a bit yellow
누르퉁퉁하다 be an unpleasant〔unhealthy〕 yellow ¶ 얼굴이 누르퉁퉁하다 look sallow
누른도요 〖새〗 a woodcock 《*pl.* -s》; woodcock 《총칭》
누름단추 [초인종의] a bell push ; a push〔press〕 button ¶ 누름단추식의 pushbutton
누름적 —炙 a kind of egg-coated shish kebab
누릇누릇 **—하다** (be) yellowish ; be spotted yellow ; be yellow here and there
누리[1] hail (우박)
누리[2] 〖곤충〗 a kind of locust ; Pachytilus migratorius (학명)
누리[3] the world (세상) ¶ 온 누리에 all over the world
누리다[1] [냄새가] (be) rank ; rancid ; stinking ; offensive ; smell spoiled〔bad〕 ¶ 누린 고기 rank meat // 국이 누리다 The soup smells bad.
누리다[2] enjoy ; have ; be blessed with ¶ 행복을 누리다 enjoy happiness // 행복을 누리고 살다 live a happy life ; live happily
누린내 a stench ; a fetid〔stinking〕 smell ; a rancid smell
누마루 樓— an upper floor ; a loft ; a garret ; an attic
누만 累萬 tens of thousands ; many thousands
누명 陋名 dishonor ; disgrace ; infamy ; a stigma ; a slur ; a bad name 〔repute〕; ill fame ; disrepute ¶ 누명을 남기다 leave a bad name behind 《one》 // 누명을 씻다 wipe off〔out〕 a dishonor ; clear oneself of a dishonor ; live down one's bad reputation ; purge 〔clear〕 oneself of a false charge
누명을 쓰다 관용 be dishonored ; be stigmatized ; incur disgrace ; be branded with infamy
누문 漏聞 overhearing **—하다** overhear ; know 《it》 by〔from, on〕 hearsay
누범 累犯 repeated offense ; the repetition of offenses ; cumulative offense
—자 an old〔a repeated〕 offender
누벨바그 the new wave 《movement》; la nouvelle vague (프)
누비 quilting ; quilted work
—옷 quilted clothes **— 이불** a quilt **— 포대기** a baby quilt
누비다 quilt ¶ 이불을 누비다 quilt ; form into a quilt // 화장복을 누비다 quilt a dressing gown
누비질 quilting **—하다** quilt ; do quilting
누상 樓上 on the loft〔tower, turret〕 ¶ 누상에 오르다 go up a tower
누선 淚腺 〖해부〗 the lachrymal gland
— 낭종(囊腫) dacryops **—염**(炎) dacryoadenitis
*__누설__ 漏泄 leakage ; disclosure ; divulgence

—하다 leak ; let out ; reveal ; disclose ; be revealed〔disclosed〕; give away ; divulge ; betray ¶ 군기 누설 a leakage of amilitary secret // 비밀을 누설하다 let out〔divulge〕 a secret // 비밀이 누설되었다 The secret is out〔has leaked out〕. // 시험 문제가 누설되어서 큰 소동이 났다 The leakage of some examination papers led to a grave complication. // 누설해서는 안된다 Keep it secret. /Don't it breathe a word〔syllable〕 about it to anyone. // 적에게 내부 정보를 누설하다 Leak inside information to the enemy. // 누가 비밀을 누설했을까 I wonder who let the cat out of the bag.

— 전류 a leakage current

누세 累世 successive〔many〕 generations

누속 陋俗 sordid〔corrupt〕 customs ; low practices

누수 漏水 a water leakage ; a leakage of water ; leaking water —하다 《water》 leak ¶ 탱크가 누수하다 Water is leaking from the tank. /The tank leaks.

— 검출기 a hydrostat 지상〔지하〕 — ground〔underground〕 leakage of water

누습 陋習 an evil〔a corrupt〕 custom ; an evil practice ; an abuse ¶ 누습을 타파하다 do away with an evil custom

누승 累乘 〖수학〗 involution —하다 involve

—적(積) a continued product

누심 壘審 a base〔field〕 umpire ; an umpire on bases

*누에 a silkworm ¶ 누에를 치다 rear〔raise〕 silkworms // 누에가 오르다 silkworms begin spinning // 누에를 올리다 put silkworms on mulberry leaves to feed // 누에에서 생사를 뽑다 obtain raw silk from silkworms

—고치 cocoon —나방 a silkworm moth —똥 silkworm droppings —씨 silkworm eggs ; a strain〔breed〕 of silkworms —치기 sericulture ; silkfarming 석잠 — a three-molt silkworm

누옥 陋屋 a humble house ; a wretched〔squalid〕 hut ; a hovel ; my (humble) dwelling〔house〕 (자기 집)

누운단 the lower hem of a coat〔an upper garment〕

누운목 —木 bleached cotton (cloth)

누운변 —邊 interest paid back at the same time as the principal

누울외 —椳 horizontal〔lateral, cross〕 laths

누워먹다 lead an idle life ; eat the bread of idleness

*누이 a sister ; [손위] an elder〔older〕 sister ; a big sister ; [손아래] a younger〔little, small〕 sister

누이다¹ ① [대소변을] hold out 《a child》; make〔have, let〕 《a person》 defecate〔urinate〕 ② [눕히다] lay down ; send〔put〕 to bed ⇨ 눕히다

누이다² [피륙을] 《cloth》 get washed in limewater

누이동생 a younger〔little, small〕 sister

누일 屢日 many days ; day after day ; (for) days on end

*누적 累積 accumulation ; cumulation —하다 accumulate ; be accumulated ; cumulate // 누적된 결과 the cumulative effects 《of》 // 이자가 누적되어 총 200만원이 되었다 The interest went on accumulating till the whole sum reached two million *won*.

— 분포 곡선도 〖통계〗 an ogive — 투표 cumulative voting — 판결〔증거〕 cumulative judgment〔evidence〕

누전 漏電 an electric leakage ; a leakage of electricity ; a short circuit —하다 short-circuit ; 《electricity》 leak ; 《a wire》 fuse ¶ 누전을 일으키다 cause a short circuit // 화재는 누전으로 일어났다 The fire was started by a short circuit. /The fire was caused by a leakage of electricity. // 배선에서 누전이 되고 있다 You have a short in your wiring.

—계(計) a ground detector ; an earth detector ; a leakage indicator —법 the loss-of-charge method

누정 漏精 spermatorrhea ; involuntary emission of semen (without orgasm)

누지 陋地 here ; this place ; my (humble) place

누지다 (be) damp ; wettish

누진 累進 gradual advance ; successive〔gradual〕 promotion to another —하다 be promoted from one position ; be gradually promoted ; advance〔rise〕 step by step

— 대우 progressive treatment —세 a progressive〔cumulative, graduated〕 tax — 세율 progressive rates of tax — 소득세 a progressive〔graduated〕 income tax — 임금 progressive wages

누진 과세 累進課稅 progressive〔cumulative, graduated〕 taxation

—법 a progressive scale system of taxation

누차 屢次 many times ; many a time ; repeatedly ; over and over ; time after time ; time and again ¶ 누차 말한 바와 같이 as I have told you repeatedly

누추 陋醜 filthiness ; dirtiness ; squalidness ; sordidness —하다 (be) filthy ; dirty ; squalid ; sordid ; shabby (의복이) ¶ 누추한 빈민굴 a squalid slum // 누추한 집이지만 humble as our house is // 누추한 옷차림을 하고 있다 be squalid in attire ; be shabbily dressed

누출 漏出 leakage ; leak ; escape —하다 leak 《out》; start〔make, spring〕 a leak ; ooze out ; escape (가스가) ¶ 가스가 누출한다 The gas escapes.

누치 〖물고기〗 a cornet fish ; Hemibarbus

labeo (학명)
누쿠알로파 Nukualofa
누타 壘打 〖야구〗 a base-hit ¶ 3루타를 치다 make a three-base hit〔a three-baser〕
누풍 陋風 a bad〔an evil〕 custom ; vicious manners ; an evil ¶ 세상의 누풍에 물들다 be infected with the evil ways of the world
누항 陋巷 wretched quarters ; slums (빈민굴) ; a dirty〔squalid〕 alley
눅눅하다 (be) damp ; moist ; wet ; humid ¶ 눅눅한 옷 wet〔damp〕 clothes ∥눅눅한 날씨 humid weather
눅느즈러지다 get〔go〕 limp ; become flabby〔flaccid〕
눅늘어지다 go limp ; become flabby
눅다 ① [반죽이] (be) soft ; ductile ; thin ¶ 반죽이 눅다 The dough is soft. ∥쇠가 눅다 The iron is ductile.
② [습해서] (be) damp ; wet ; moist ; soft and damp ¶ 담배가 눅다 The tobacco is damp.
③ [성질이] (be) placid ¶ 성질이 눅은 사람 a man of placid temper
④ [날씨가] become milder ¶ 날씨가 눅어졌다 The weather has become milder.
⑤ [값이] (be) cheap ; low in price
눅신하다 (be) soft and flexible ; elastic ; pliant ; pliable ; supple ¶ 눅신한 가죽 a supple leather
눅실눅실하다 (be) elastic ⇨ 눅신하다
눅이다 ① soften ; make tender ¶ 반죽을 눅이다 soften the dough
② [마음을] soften ; pacify ; soothe ; appease ¶ 마음을 눅이다 soften〔appease〕 《a person's》 heart∥부드러운 말이 굳은 마음을 눅인다 Gentle words will soften a hard heart.
③ [젖게 하다] wet ; damp ; moisten ¶ 다림질하기 위해 옷을 눅이다 damp clothes prior to ironing
④ [목소리를] soften ; tone down ¶ 목소리를 눅여 말하는 게 좋겠다 You'd better modify your tone.
눅지다 become〔get〕 milder〔warmer〕 ; become less severe ; ease up ¶ 날씨가 눅졌다 It has become less cold. /It has become milder. /The cold weather eased up.
눅진- ⇨ 녹진-
눅진하다 (be) soft and sticky
†**눈¹** ① an eye ¶ 날카로운 눈 alert〔keen, sharp〕 eyes∥눈물 어린 눈 tearful eyes ∥흐린 눈 dull〔fishy〕 eyes∥퉁방울눈 goggle-eyes ; goggling eyes∥움푹한 눈 deep-set eyes∥치켜 올라간 눈 peaked 〔slant〕 eyes∥태풍의 눈 the eye of a typhoon∥눈의 ocular ; optic∥눈의 운동 ocular movements∥눈의 근육 an ocular muscle∥파란 눈의 blue-eyed∥눈 깜짝할 사이에 in the twinkling of an eye ; in an instance ; in a trice∥눈을 감다 close〔shut〕 one's eyes ; die∥눈을 뜨다 open one's eyes ; wake up ; awake∥눈을 크게 뜨다 strain one's eyes∥눈을 돌리다 take one's eyes off 《a thing》 ; look away∥눈을 부비다 rub one's eyes ∥눈이 부시다 be dazzling ; 《one's eyes》 be dazzled∥눈을 부릅뜨다 glare in one's eyes∥눈을 흘기다 look askance at ; look angrily〔sharply〕 at∥눈이 아프다 have sore eyes∥눈병이 나다 have (an) eye trouble∥눈에 거슬리다 offend the eye∥눈을 가리다 blindfold ; bandage 《a person's》 eyes∥눈을 내리깔다 lower〔drop, cast down〕 one's eyes∥눈을 깜박이다 blink one's eyes∥눈을 속이다 deceive ; hoodwink ; pull the wool over 《a person's》 eyes∥눈에 들다 [사물이 주어] be in one's favor ; suit〔catch, take, strike〕 one's fancy ; [사람이 주어] like ; take a fancy 《to》∥눈에 선하다 be vivid to one's eyes∥눈에 설다 be unfamiliar ; be strange∥눈에 익다 be familiar ; get〔become〕 used to seeing∥눈에 불이 나다 see stars ; be indignant∥눈이 휘둥그레지다 be pop-eyed ; be surprised∥눈에 차다 be satisfactory∥눈짓을 하다 wink at ; make eyes at∥눈이 맞다 fall in love 《with each other》∥눈에는 눈 이에는 이 An eye for an eye, a tooth for a tooth. ∥돈에 눈이 멀다 be blind with love of money∥허욕에 눈이 멀다 get blind with avarice∥부러운 눈으로 보다 see 《a thing》 with an envious eye∥눈에 넣어도 아프지 않다 be the apple of one's eye∥소매치기가 바로 그의 눈앞에서 그것을 훔쳐 갔다 The pick-pocket took it right from under his nose. ∥그 광경은 눈을 뜨고 볼 수 없을 정도로 비참했다 The sight was too miserable to look at. ∥그녀의 실망한 표정이 눈에 선하다 Her hurt expression rose again in my mind. ∥그저께 밤부터 눈 한번 붙이지 못했어 I haven't got any shut-eye since the night before last. ∥내 눈에 흙이 들어가기 전에는 안된다 Over my dead body! ∥오늘은 그와 눈을 마주치지 않는 것이 좋다 We'd be wise to avoid making eye contact with him. ∥작은 얼룩조차도 흰옷에서는 눈에 잘 띈다 Even a little stain stands out on white clothes. ∥나도 내 눈을 의심했다 I couldn't believe my eyes either. ∥눈으로 보기에는 약 500달러 정도 들 것 같습니다 Offhand, it will cost around five hundred dollars.
② [시력] eyesight ; sight ; vision ¶ 밤눈 night vision∥눈이 밝다 have good eyes〔eyesight〕∥눈이 나쁘다 have bad 〔poor〕 sight ; have bad eyes〔defective vision〕∥눈이 멀다 be〔become〕 blind ; lose one's sight∥눈이 미치다〔닿다〕

one's eyes reach // 눈이 닿는〔닿지 않는〕 곳에 within〔beyond, out of〕 eyeshot // 한 눈이 멀다 be blind in one eye // 최근 눈이 나빠졌다 My sight has become poor recently. // 많은 별들은 사람의 눈에 보이지 않는다 Many stars are invisible to human sight. // 그녀는 사고로 시력을 잃었다 She lost her sight in an accident. // 내 눈이 점점 나빠지고 있다 My eyesight is failing.

③ [주의] notice ; attention ; watch ¶ 눈에 띄다 come in sight ; catch one's eyes ; be found〔noticed〕 // 눈을 끌다 attract one's attention ; arrest one's eyes ; be attractive // 눈을 돌리다 turn one's eyes〔attention〕 《to》 ; bend one's eyes 《on》 // 눈을 거들떠 보지않다 pay no attention to ; take no notice 《of》 ; give no heed〔regard〕 to ; show no interest to ; be indifferent to // 사람의 눈을 피하다 avoid another's observation // 눈을 속이다 pull the wool over 《a person's》 eyes // 서울은 눈 감으면 코 베어갈 데다 Sharp practices prevail among the inhabitants in *Seoul*. // 인구 문제로 눈을 돌려 봅시다 Let's turn our eyes to the population problem. // 우리 아기는 사방으로 돌아다니기 때문에 그 아이로부터 눈을 뗄 수가 없다 My baby wanders all over the place, so I can't take my eyes off her.

④ [입장·견지] one's eyes ; a point of view ; a standpoint ; a viewpoint ¶ 서양 사람의 눈으로 보면 from a Western point of view // 고객의 눈으로 보면 from the standpoint of the customer // 신의 눈으로 보면 in the sight of God // 공평한 눈으로 보다 look upon 《a person, a matter》 with an impartial eye // 그들의 쾌락의 관념은 외국 사람의 눈에는 좀 이상하게 보인다 Their ideas of enjoyment are rather strange to foreign eyes. // 그네들의 눈으로 보려고 그래봐 Try to look at it from their point of view.

⑤ [안식] an eye ; discrimination ; insight ; judgment ¶ 전문가의 눈 an expert's eye ; a professional eye // 예술가의 눈으로 보다 see with an artist's eye // 눈이 높다 have a keen eye ; aim high ; be desirous of things beyond one's means // 보는 눈이 있다 be a good judge of〔have an eye for〕 《art》 // 내 눈은 틀림 없다 I have an unerring eye. // 그는 그림 보는 눈이 높다 He has a good eye for painting. // 그는 골동품을 보는 눈이 있다〔없다〕 He is a good〔poor〕 judge of antiques.

제 눈에 안경 (속담) Beauty is in the eye of the beholder.

*__눈²__ ① [싹] a bud ; a sprout ; a shoot ; a germ ¶ 눈이 나오다 the buds come out ; 《a plant》 push out new shoot ; bud〔bud out, come into bud〕 ; sprout ; shoot 《up, out》

② [눈금] graduation ; scale ¶ 저울눈을 새기다 graduate ; mark with degrees // 저울눈을 속이다 give short weight // 저울눈이 모자라다 be short in weight

③ [그물·체의] a mesh (그물의) ; a stitch (편물의) ¶ 눈이 50개인 체 a 50 mesh screen // 눈이 가는〔거친〕 체 a sieve of close〔coarse〕 mesh // 눈이 성긴〔촘촘한〕 그물 a wide-〔fine-〕mesh(ed) net

그물— the meshes of a net

†__눈³__ snow ; snows (쌓인 눈) ; a snowfall (강설) ¶ 큰눈 a heavy snow(fall) // 바람이 날리는 눈 snowflakes that come riding on the wind // 눈같이 희다 be as white as snow ; be snowwhite // 눈에 갇히다 be snowbound ; be snowed up〔in〕 // 눈에 덮이다 be covered〔laden〕 with snow // 눈에 묻히다 be buried under〔in〕 the snow ; be snowed under // 눈이 많이 오는 지역 a region of heavy snows〔snowfall〕 // 눈싸움을 하다 have a snowball fight ; have a game of snowballs // 눈을 치다 sweep〔rake, shovel, clear〕 away snow ; clear 《a road》 of snow ; remove snow // 눈을 털다 knock snow off 《one's coat, the fence》 // 눈을 헤치고 나아가다 plow one's way through the snow // 눈이 온다 It snows. /Snow falls. /We have 《much, little》 snow. // 눈이 올 것 같다 It threatens to snow. /It looks like snow. /There are signs of snow. // 눈이 펑펑 내린다 It snows heavily〔thick and fast〕. // 눈이 쌓인다 Snow lies〔piles up, heaps〕 《on the ground》. // 눈이 다섯자 왔다 The snow fell to a depth of five feet. /Five feet of snow fell. /There was a five-foot snowfall. // 눈이 10인치 쌓여 있다 The snow is〔lies〕 ten inches deep. // 금년에는 눈이 많이 왔다 We have had much snow this year. // 20년 만의 큰 눈이다 It is the heaviest〔biggest〕 snowfall we have had in twenty years. /Such a snowfall has not been known for twenty years. // 어떤 산은 일년 내내 눈으로 덮여 있다 Some mountains are covered with snow all year around. // 강원도에는 큰눈이 왔다고 한다 Heavy snowfall is reported in *Kang-won* Province.

—구경 snow-scene viewing **—구름** a snow cloud **—뭉치** snowball **가루—** powdery snow **첫—** the first snow(fall) 《of the season》 **함박—** large flakes of snow

눈가 the eye rims

눈가늠 ⇨ 눈대중

눈가리개 an eye bandage ; blinkers ; blinders (말의) ¶ 눈가리개를 하다 blindfold 《a person》 ; put an eye bandage over 《a person's》 eyes // 눈가리개

를 풀다 unblindfold // 눈가리개를 하고 끌려가다 be taken away blindfold
눈가림 hoodwinking ; deceiving ; camouflage ; deception ; [미봉책] a temporizing measure ; a stopgap ; a makeshift **—하다** hoodwink ; deceive ; camouflage ; temporize ; pull the wool over 《a person's》 eyes ; cover up ¶ 눈가림으로 하는 일 a stopgap work // 정부의 고용 정책은 눈가림에 지나지 않는다 The government employment policy amounts to nothing more than stopgap measures.
눈가죽 (the skin of) an eyelid ¶ 눈가죽이 두텁다 have thick eyelids
*__눈감다__ ① [눈을] close〔shut〕 one's eyes ② [죽다] die ; breathe one's last ¶ 그런 나이 어린 애들을 두고 그는 편안히 눈감을 수 없었다 He could hardly die in peace leaving behind such young children.
*__눈감아주다__ overlook ; wink at ; connive at ; shut one's eyes 《to》 ¶ 죄를 눈감아주다 overlook〔wink at〕 an offense // 노름을 눈감아주다 connive at gambling // 경찰은 범인들을 눈감아주었다 The police winked at the offenders. // 네가 회사 돈을 가져가는 것을 눈감아 줄 수 없다 I can't close my eyes to your taking company money.
눈거칠다 be offensive to the eye ; (be) unsightly ; be hateful to see
눈겨룸 a staring match〔contest〕 **—하다** have a staring match // 처진 눈꺼풀 a drooped eyelid
눈결 a glance ; a glimpse ¶ 눈결에 보다 see 《a thing》 out of the corner of one's eye
눈경치 a snow scene ; a landscape of snow
눈곱 ① a discharge from the eyes ; eye discharges ; eye-wax ; gum〔matter〕 in the corner of the eye ¶ 눈곱이 끼다 one's eyes are gummy〔mattery〕 ; gum collects
② [소량] a bit ; a whit ¶ 눈곱만한 양심 a whit〔bit〕 of conscience // 눈곱만해서 보이지 않다 be so tiny that one can't see it ; be too small to be seen
눈곱자기 a discharge from the eyes ⇨ 눈곱
눈구덩이 a pit in heaped snow ¶ 눈구덩이에 빠지다 slip〔tumble〕 in the snow
눈구멍[1] [안공] the eye socket ; the orbit of the eye ; [눈] an eye
눈구멍[2] [눈구덩이] pit in a snowdrift ¶ 눈구멍에 빠지다 fall into a snowdrift ; slip in the snow
눈구석 the corner of the eye
눈금 ① [자의] graduation ; scale ; a notchmark on a scale ¶ 눈금을 긋다 graduate ; arrange in grades ; divide ; mark with degrees ; calibrate
② [눈짐작으로 그은 금] a line drawn by eyesight
—대 [저울의] a scale beam **—선** a scale mark
눈기이다 hoodwink ; deceive ; pull〔draw〕 the wool over 《a person's》 eyes
눈길[1] [시선] line of vision〔sight〕 ¶ 눈길을 모으다 attract public gaze // 눈길을 피하다 avoid a person's eye ; escape another's gaze // 눈길을 돌리다 turn one's eyes 《upon》 ; turn one's eyes away 《from》
눈길[2] [눈덮인 길] a snowy road
*__눈까풀__ an eyelid (눈꺼풀)
눈깔 an eye ⇨ 눈
— 바구니 an open-work basket **— 사탕** taffies ; tobbees
눈깜작이 a blinkard
눈꺼지다 one's eyes shrink〔droop〕 ; one's eyes become hollow ¶ 배가 고파 눈이 꺼지다 one's eyes are hollow with hunger
눈꺼풀 an eyelid (눈까풀) ¶ 윗〔아랫〕눈꺼풀 the upper〔lower〕 eyelid
눈꼬리 ⇨ 눈초리
눈꼴사납다 ① [아니꼽다] be offensive to the eye ; be hateful to see ; (be) disgusting ¶ 그의 뽐내고 걷는 꼴이 눈꼴사납다 I hate to see him swaggering. /I am sick of seeing him swaggering
② [모양이] (be) evil-looking ; unsightly
눈꼴시다 ⇨ 눈꼴틀리다
눈꼴틀리다 hate to see ; be disgusting ; besick of ¶ 나는 그가 뽐내는 것이 눈꼴틀린다 I hate to see him assuming an air of importance. // 그가 사장에게 아첨하는 꼴이 란 눈꼴틀려 볼 수 없다 I am sick of seeing him licking at his boss's heels.
눈꽁댕이 the corner of the eye (눈초리)
눈높다 ① aim high ; be desirous of things beyond one's means ¶ 그 여자는 눈이 높아 웬만한 사람과는 결혼하지 않으려 한다 She aims high and won't marry a nobody. // 그는 눈이 높아 보통 것으로는 만족치 않는다 He loves nice things and is never satisfied with commonplace stuff.
② [안식] be a good judge 《of》 ; (be) appreciative ; be a connoisseur ; have an eye〔a keen eye〕 《for》 ¶ 눈높은 청중 an appreciative audience // 그는 미술품에 눈높다 He is a good judge of the fine arts. // 자네는 미술에 대해서 보는 눈이 높군 You are a good judge of art indeed. /You have an eye for art indeed. // 너무 눈이 높아도 탈이다 If you go too far in your choice, you will fare worse.
눈다랭이 〖물고기〗 a kind of tuna
눈대중 eye measure **—하다** measure

《a thing》 with the eye ; estimate by looking ¶ 눈대중으로 by (the) eye
눈덩이 a snowball
눈독 eyeing ; having an eye to ; running one's eyes over (a thing with a view to buying or stealing it later)
눈독들이다 eye ; have an eye to ; set one's eye on ; can't keep one's eyes off ¶ 그는 그녀의 재산에 눈독을 들이고 있다 He has an eye on her property. // 나는 이 집을 사기 오래 전부터 눈독을 들이고 있었다 I had my eye on this house long before I bought it. // 그 애가 장난감에 눈독을 들이고 있는 것을 보니 언제고 훔쳐갈 생각을 하고 있을지도 모른다 The way he has been eyeing that toy he may be planning to carry it off some day.
***눈동자** 一瞳子 the pupil (of the eye) ; the apple of the eye
눈두덩 the protuberant parts of the eyelids ¶ 눈두덩이 붓다 have swollen eyes
눈딱부리 a bug-eyed person ; a person with huge〔bulging〕 eyes ; a pop eye
눈딱지 ugly〔sinister〕 eyes ; an ugly〔sinister〕 look
***눈뜨다** open one's eyes ; wake up ; awake ; [깨닫다] be awakened 《to》 ; be awake 《to》 ; become aware 《of》 ¶ 성에 눈뜨다 be awakened to sex ; become aware of sex
눈뜬장님 [장님] an amaurotic person ; [문맹] an illiterate ; an unlettered person ; an ignoramus ¶ 그는 눈뜬장님이다 He is an illiterate. /He cannot read or write. // 그것도 알아보지 못하다니 눈뜬장님이로구나 You are a blind fool not to recognize it. // 눈뜬장님이라 편지 한 장 읽지 못한다 He is so ignorant that he can't even read a letter.
눈띄다 be found ; catch the eye ; be attractive ; be conspicuous ; stand out ¶ 눈띄는 미인 an attractive beauty // 그녀의 수영복은 눈에 잘 띈다 Her bathing suit attracts our attention〔is attractive〕.
눈망울 an eyeball
눈맞다 fall in love with each other ¶ 둘은 눈이 맞아 달아났다 They fell in love with each other and ran away together.
눈맞추다 exchange glances ; look at each other ; [사랑] make eyes at each other ; make silent love to each other
눈매 ⇨ 눈맵시
눈맵시 the shape of one's eyes ¶ 사랑스러운 눈매 charming eyes // 눈매가 곱다 have beautiful eyes
†**눈멀다** become〔go〕 blind ; lose one's sight ¶ 눈먼 사람 a blind man // 눈먼 사랑 blind love
눈 먼 자식이 효도한다 속담 Crooked logs make straight fires.
†**눈물**[1] ① a tear ¶ 거짓 눈물 crocodile tears // 피눈물 bitter tears // 눈물겨운 이야기 a pathetic〔an affecting, a touching〕 story // 눈물젖은 얼굴 a tearful face ; a face wet with tears // 눈물을 흘리며 with tears in one's eyes ; tearfully // 눈물을 흘리다 shed tears ; weep // 눈물이 나오다 tears well up in one's eyes ; tears come to one's eyes ; [병리적] one's eyes water // 눈물이 많다 be easily moved to tears ; softhearted ; sentimental // 눈물이 쏟아지다 one's tears gush out // 눈물이 비오듯하다 shed a shower of tears ; tears stream down one's face ; tears flow thick and fast // 눈물이 그렁그렁하다 tears stand in one's eyes ; one's eyes are full of tears // 눈물에 젖다 be drenched with tears // 눈물겨워지다 be moved to tears // 눈물로 목이 메다 be choked with tears // 눈물을 거두다 stop weeping ; hold one's tears // 눈물을 씻다 wipe one's tears away // 눈물을 참다 repress〔keep back, hold back〕 one's tears // 눈물을 삼키다 gulp down tears ; repress〔hold back〕 one's tears // 눈물이 나도록 웃다 laugh till the tears come out // 눈물로 세월을 보내다 lead a sorrowful life // 뜨거운 눈물이 두 뺨에 흘러내렸다 Burning tears flowed〔ran〕 down his cheeks. // 나는 눈물을 참을 수 없었다 I could hardly keep from tears. // 그 영화의 마지막 장면으로 인해 눈물이 쏟아졌다 The last scene in the movie brought tears to my eyes.
② [동정심] sympathy ; tender heart ¶ 눈물이 없는 사람 a tearless person ; a stone-hearted person ; a cold-blooded person
눈물[2] [녹은 눈] melted snow
눈물겹다 (be) tearful ; sad ; pathetic ; touching ; heartrending ¶ 눈물겨운 이야기 a pathetic〔touching〕 story
눈물지다 shed〔drop〕 bitter tears
눈물짓다 produce tears ; weep
눈바람[1] snow and wind ; [찬바람] an icecold wind
눈바람[2] [설풍] a snow-chilled wind ; a wind blowing over the snow ; an icy wind
눈발 streaks of snow ; snow flakes ¶ 굵은 눈발 big flakes of snow
눈방울 an eyeball ; the globe of an eye ¶ 눈방울을 굴리다 goggle
눈밭 snow-covered ground
눈병 an eye disease〔trouble〕 ; sore eyes ¶ 눈병이 나다 have an eye trouble ; be afflicted with an eye disease ; suffer from the affection of the eyes (눈병을 앓다)
***눈보라** a snowstorm ; a shower of snow ; a drifting〔driving〕 snow ; a blizzard ¶ 눈보라 치다 have a snowstorm ; snow drifts hard // 밤새도록 눈보

라가 몰아쳤다 The snowstorm raged all through the night.

눈부라리다 glare ; look with ; glaring eyes ¶ 노해서 눈을 부라리고 보다 stare〔glare〕in anger at《a person》

***눈부시다** ① [빛이] (be) dazzling ; glaring ; blinding ; radiant ¶ 눈부시게 희다 be dazzling white // 눈부신 태양 the glaring〔radiant〕sun // 빛이 세어서 눈이 부시다 The strong light dazzles my eyes. // 눈부셔서 눈을 뜰 수가 없다 My eyes are so dazzled that I can't open them.
② [모습이] (be) brilliant ; gorgeous ; showy ; gaudy ¶ 눈부시게 푸른 하늘 a brilliant blue sky // 눈부시게 아름다운 여인 a lady of dazzling beauty ; a radiant beauty // 얼마나 눈부신 날인가 What a dazzling day it is !
③ [혁혁하다] (be) brilliant ; striking ; remarkable ; splendid wonderful ¶ 눈부신 발전 remarkable〔striking〕development // 눈부신 업적 a brilliant〔striking, wonderful〕achievement // 눈부신 연출〔효과〕a striking display〔effect〕// 눈부신 활약 remarkable activities // 눈부신 일을 하다 achieve splendid work ; do a spectacular thing // 그는 사건 해결에 눈부신 역할을 했다 He played a conspicuous role in settling the matter.

눈부처 a person's image reflected in the pupil of one's eye

눈비음 dressing up for others' eyes **—하다** dress up for others' eyes

눈빛[1] ① [안광] the glitter of one's eyes ¶ 눈빛이 날카롭다 be sharp〔keen〕-sighted ; eagle-eyed ; be of piercing eyes
② [기색] the expression in one's eyes ¶ 애원하는 눈빛 a look of appeal // 술이라면 눈빛이 달라진다 He is strongly tempted when a liquor is before him.

눈빛[2] (snow) white

***눈사람** a snowman ¶ 눈사람을 만들다 make〔build〕a snowman

눈사태 —沙汰 an avalanche ; a snowslide ¶ 눈사태가 났다 Avalanches rushed down the mountainside.
— 방지 설비 a snowshed **표층 —** a surface snowslide

***눈살** the furrow〔wrinkles〕between one's eyebrows ; furrowed brow ¶ 눈살을 찌푸리고 with a frown ; with knitted eyebrows // 그녀는 눈살을 찌푸리고 시험지를 바라보았다 She looked at the exam paper with a furrowed brow.
눈살을 찌푸리다 관용 knit〔bend〕one's brows ; frown ; make a penthouse of the eyebrows

눈석이 water from the thawing snow

눈석임 thaw ; the thawing of snow ; snowbreak ; snow broth ; melting〔melted〕snow **—하다** thaw ¶ 눈석임철 a snowthawing season ; a thaw // 눈석임(철)이 시작됐다 A thaw has set in. // 눈석임으로 길이 형편없다 The roads are bad on account of the slush〔thaw〕. // 눈석임으로 강물이 불었다 The melting snow caused the river to rise.
—물 thawing〔melting〕snow ; slush ; sludge ; snow broth (질척질척한 눈)

눈설다 (be) unfamiliar ; strange ; different ; new ¶ 눈선 땅 a strange country ; a land one has never set eyes on before // 그 경치가 눈에 설었다 The sight was strange to me.

눈속이다 pull the wool over one's eyes ; deceive《a person》; take in ; impose upon ; play a trick upon

눈속임 hoodwink(ing) ; deception ; cheat(-ing) ; pulling the wool over《a person's》eyes

눈송이 a snowflake

눈시울 the edge of an eyelid ¶ 눈시울이 뜨거워지는 광경 a heart-warming〔pathetic, moving〕sight // 눈시울이 뜨거워지다 be moved to tears ; the tears are ready to well up in one's eyes

눈싸움[1] [설전(雪戰)] a snow-ball fight ; a snowfight **—하다** have a snowfight ; play (at) snowballs

눈싸움[2] [눈겨룸] a staring match〔contest〕

눈썰미 sharp〔dexterous〕eyes ; keen observation ¶ 눈썰미가 있다 have dexterous eyes ; be quick in visual learning // 눈썰미가 없다 be slow in visual learning ; have a dull eye for learning things

***눈썹** the eyebrow ¶ 눈썹 그리개 an eyebrow pencil // 그린〔가짜〕눈썹 painted eyebrows // 짙은 눈썹《a pair of》thick〔heavy, bushy, shaggy〕eyebrows // 반달 같은 눈썹 arched〔crescent-shaped〕eyebrows // 팔자 눈썹 slanted eyebrows // 눈썹을 찌푸리다 knit〔bend〕one's brows // 눈썹을 치켜올리다 raise〔arch〕one's eyebrows // 눈썹을 그리다 pencil one's eyebrows // 눈썹이 짙다 have abundant〔thick〕eyebrows // 눈썹도 까딱하지 않고 with a poker face ; without changing one's expression
눈썹도 까딱하지 않다 관용 remain unperturbed

눈썹차양 a narrow awning along the eaves

눈씨 the force of one's stare ; the power of one's eyes

눈아래 under one's very eyes ; just〔right〕below one's eyes ¶ 눈아래에 내려다보다 overlook ; command (a view of) // 전시가를 눈아래에 내려다 보다 see the whole city under one's eyes ; overlook〔command a view of〕the whole city

***눈알** an eyeball ; the globe of an eye ¶

눈알이 큰 popeyed ; big eyed // 눈알을 굴리다 goggle (one's eyes) ; roll one's eyes
눈알을 부라리다 [관용] goggle (one's eyes) ; stare one's eyes out ; glare ⟪at, upon⟫

눈앞 ① [면전] before one's face〔eye〕; under one's (very) nose ; in one's presence ; before one ¶ 바로 눈앞에서 under one's very nose // 바로 사람의 눈앞에서 물건을 훔치다 steal something in one's presence
② [시간적으로 직전] close at hand ; just ahead ; immediate ¶ 눈앞에 임박하다 be close at hand // 눈앞의 이익을 추구하다 seek immediate gains ; take a short-sighted policy

눈약 ⇨ 안약

눈어리다 have dim〔blurred, bleary〕 eyes ; (be) bleary ; blear-eyed

눈어림 eye-measurement **—하다** measure with the eye ⇨ 눈대중

눈언저리 parts around the eye ; an eye ¶ 눈언저리 around the eye

눈엣가시 an eyesore ; an obstruction 〔offense〕 to the eye ¶ 눈엣가시가 되다 become an eyesore ; offend〔be offensive to〕 the eye // 계모는 언제나 나를 눈엣가시처럼 여겼다 My stepmother regarded me as an eyesore〔as if I always stood in her way〕.

눈여겨보다 observe closely ; watch 〔eye, look at〕 carefully ; take a good look at ; pay〔give〕 attention to ; take notice of ¶ 눈여겨볼 만하다 be worth notice ; be worthy of attention // 행동을 눈여겨보다 observe ⟪a person's⟫ behavior // 지금 당장은 그 자리에 추천할 만한 사람이 생각나지 않지만 앞으로는 눈여겨 보겠다 I can't think of anyone recommendable for the job at the moment, but I'll keep my eyes open for you.

눈요기 —療飢 feasting one's eyes **—하다** feast one's eyes on ⟪a thing⟫ ; delight one's eyes ¶ 눈요기가 되다 be a feast〔joy〕 to the eye

눈웃음 a smile in〔with〕 one's eyes ; a smile about one's eyes ¶ 눈웃음치다 wear a smile in〔about〕 one's eyes ; smile with one's eyes

눈익다 [사물이 주어] be familiar ⟪to a person⟫ ; [사람이 주어] get〔become〕 used to seeing ; become familiar with (the sight of) ¶ 눈익은 얼굴들 familiar faces // 그 애는 동물원에 자주 가기 때문에 사자는 눈익어 있어요 As the child often goes to the zoo, he is familiar with the lion./The lion is familiar to the child because he often visits the zoo.

눈인사 —人事 greeting with one's eyes **—하다** nod ; greet with a nod ¶ 서로 눈인사하다 exchange nods

눈자라기 a baby who is not old enough to sit up

눈자위 the fringe〔rim〕 of an eye
눈자위꺼지다 [관용] be dead

눈정기 —精氣 the glitter of one's eyes ; the keenness of one's eyes ¶ 눈정기가 있다 be keen-eyed ; have glittering〔keen〕 eyes

눈주다 give ⟪a person⟫ the eye ; wink ⟪significantly⟫ at ; make a sign with the eyes ; give an eye signal ; glance a message ; eye ⟪a person⟫ meaningly

눈짐작 ⇨ 눈대중

*****눈짓** a wink ; winking **—하다** wink ⟪one's eyes⟫ ; wink at ; make a sign with the eyes ; give ⟪a person⟫ the eye ; give an eye signal ; eye ⟪a person⟫ meaningly ¶ 서로 눈짓을 하다 exchange glances〔significant looks〕 // 그가 눈짓을 하자 여인은 방에서 살짝 빠져 나왔다 At the sign from his eyes she glided out of the room.

눈초리 the outer corner of the eye

눈총 a glare ; a sharp look ; looking daggers ⟪at⟫ ⇨ 눈총맞다

눈총기 —聰氣 keenness of the eye ; power of observation ¶ 눈총기가 있다 have keen eyes ; be good at remembering by seeing

눈총맞다 be hated ; make oneself hated ; be detested ; be seen as an eyesore ¶ 뭇사람의 눈총을 맞다 be a common eyesore ; become a common object of hatred

†**눈치** ① [감지] sense ; tact ; intuition ; flair ; perceptiveness ; hunch ¶ 아무에게도 눈치 채이지않고 without exciting suspicion ; without attracting any attention // 눈치가 빠르다 be quick-witted ; have quick wits // 눈치가 없다 have no sense ; be tactless // 눈치채다 become aware of ; suspect ; sense ⟪danger⟫ ; notice ; get wind〔scent〕 of ; have an inkling of // 눈치채이다 be suspected ; excite suspicion // 그가 그러한 수작을 부리는 데에는 속셈이 있다는 것을 간파할 만한 눈치가 그녀에게 있었다 She had the sense to see that he had design in doing so. // 얼마나 눈치없는 발언인가 What a tactless remark ! // 나는 눈치로 그가 믿을 만한 사람이 아니란 걸 알았다 My intuition told me he wasn't to be trusted. // 어떻게 알아냈습니까 — 눈치지요 How did you make it out ? It was a hunch.〔I know it in my bones〕.
② [기색] sign ; an indication ; [태도] a manner ; (facial) expression ; a look ¶ 놀란 눈치로 with an air of surprise // 눈칫밥 먹다 eat another's salt ; feed on another // 눈치보다 try to read one's mind ; probe one's motive ; see how the wind blows // 성나지 않았나 눈치보다 study one's face to see if he is angry

//좋아하는 눈치를 보였다 give〔show〕 signs of pleasure//눈치가 보이지 않았다 He showed no sign of 《leaving》. //눈치가 좀 이상하다 He is somewhat strange in his manners. //그녀는 슬쩍 남편의 눈치를 살폈다 She secretly studied her husband's facial expression.
—작전 a wait-and-see policy —지원 (대학의) speculative choice of schools

눈치레 mere show ; showy appearance ; putting on a good front ; vain ornamentation —하다 dress up to appeal to the eye ; stress eye-appeal ; put on a good front ¶ 눈치레로 for show ; for appearance sake

눈치보다 try to read one's mind〔face〕; probe one's motives ; study one's face 〔pleasure〕; grasp a situation ; see how the wind blows ¶ 성내지 않았나 눈치보다 study one's face to see if he is angry//눈치보아 가며 일을 하다 act according to the situation

눈치채다 become aware of 《a person's intention, motive, design, etc.》; get a hint 《of》; scent ; sense ; get wind 《of》; have an inkling 《of》; take a hint 《of》 ¶ 말이 위험을 눈치채고 멈췄다 The horse sensed danger and stopped. //우리 경쟁자들이 우리 계획을 눈치채게 해서는 안된다 Our competitors must not be allowed to get wind of our plans.

눈칫밥 a dinner for a guest〔dependent〕 who is not entirely welcome ¶ 눈칫밥을 먹다 eat 《a person's》 salt ; eat salt with 《a person》

눈코 eye and nose ¶ 눈코 뜰 새 없이 지내다 live in a whirl 《of business》
눈코 뜰 새 없다 관용 be very busy ; have no time〔leisure〕

눈트다 bud out ; come into bud ; sprout ; shoot 《up, out》

눈허리시다 ① [우습다] (be) very funny ; ridiculously amusing ; sidesplitting ② [아니꼽다] (be) disgusting ; loathsome

눈흘기다 glance sideways at〔look askance at〕 《a person》 with hate in one's eyes ⇨ 흘기다

***눋다** scorch ; be〔get〕 scorched〔burned〕; burn ; singe ¶ 눋은 밥 scorched rice//새까맣게 눋다 get scorched black//솥바닥에 눌어 붙다 get scorched and stick to the bottom of a pot//무엇인가 눋는 냄새가 난다 I smell something burning. //밥이 눌었다 The rice has got burned〔scorched〕. //눋지 않도록 자꾸 저어라 Stir it constantly to prevent burning〔scorching〕.

눌눌하다 be a dull yellow

눌러 [곧 이어서] in succession ; consecutively ; repeatedly ; [관대히] generously ; tolerantly ; kindly ¶ 눌러 용서하다 forgive generously//눌러앉다 continue to stay ; remain in the same position (유임) ; stay on

눌러보다 treat with generosity〔kindly, with good grace〕 ¶ 철없는 아이이니 눌러보고 용서하십시오 Kindly forgive him since he is just a boy with little sense.

눌리다[1] ① be squeezed ; be pressed (down) ; be pushed ¶ 초인종이 눌리다 a bell is pressed ; a button is pushed//눌려 죽다 be squeezed to death
② [위압] be overpowered ; be repressed ; be oppressed ¶ 다수에 눌리다 be overwhelmed by the superior number//말에 눌리다 be overwhelmed by the eloquence ; be overpowered by the argument//마누라에게 눌리다 be henpecked ; be tied to one's wife's apron strings

눌리다[2] [눋게 하다] burn ; scorch ; singe ¶ 옷을 눌리다 burn〔singe〕 one's clothes//밥을 눌리다 burn the rice

눌면하다 (be) rather yellow

눌변 訥辯 being poor〔clumsy〕 in speaking ; being awkward in speech
—가 a poor〔an awkward〕 speaker

눌어 訥魚 a cornet fish (누치) ; Hemibarbus labeo (학명)

눌어붙다 ① [타서] get scorched and stick to ¶ 밥이 눌어붙다 rice gets scorched and sticks to the bottom of the pot
② [한자리에] stay on ; settle down ; cling to ; hold on to ; stick to ; adhere to ¶ 한자리에 눌어붙다 stay on in the same place ; remain in the same position//집에 눌어붙다 stick at home

눌언 訥言 a stammering〔stuttering〕 speech

눌외 —椳 horizontal laths (누울외)

눌은밥 scorched rice

눌하다 訥— have an impediment in one's speech ; stammer ; stutter

†**눕다** lie down ; lay oneself down ; recline 《on》; lie reclined ; stretch oneself ¶ 자리에 눕다 lie in one's bed//반듯이〔모로〕 눕다 lie on one's back 〔side〕//풀밭에 눕다 lie on the grass ; lie reclined on the grass//앓아 눕다 be ill in bed ; lie sick in bed//감기로 눕다 be laid up with a cold//당분간 누워 있어야 한다 You must keep to your bed. /You ought to be in bed for the present. //그 노인은 중풍으로 10년간 누워 있다 The old man has been laid up with palsy for ten years. //배를 대고 누우세요 Lie on your stomach.
누울 자리 봐 가며 발을 뻗는다 속담 Stretch your arm no further than your sleeve will reach. /Everyone stretches his legs according to the length of coverlet.

누워서 떡 먹기 [속담] a piece of cake ; as easy as lying
누워서 침 뱉기 [속담] Curses, like chickens, come home to roost.
*눕히다 lay down ; make〔have〕《someone》 lie down ¶ 자리에 눕히다 put to bed // 때려 눕히다 knock 《a person》 down // 상자를 눕히다 lay a box on the side
눙치다 soothe (with nice words) ; appease ¶ 눙쳐서 남의 노염을 풀다 soothe〔calm〕 down an angry man
뉘[1] [쌀의] unhulled rice (in hulled rice)
뉘[2] [누이] a sister ¶ 오뉘 brother and sister
뉘[3] who ; whose ; someone's ⇨ 누구
뉘[4] [자손에게서 받는 덕] blessings from one's offspring
뉘다 ⇨ 누이다[1,2]
뉘렇다 (be) sickly yellow ; sallow
뉘른베르크 Nuremberg ; Nürnberg
뉘반지기 chaffy rice ; rice containing many grains of unhulled rice
뉘앙스 nuance ¶ 말의 뉘앙스 a shade of difference in meaning〔expression〕
뉘연히 with a good〔clear〕 conscience ; fairly ; openly ; in the open ⇨ 버젓하다
뉘엿거리다 ① 《the sun》 be ready to set ; be about to set〔sink〕 ¶ 해가 뉘엿거린다 The sun is going down. /The sun is about to set〔sink〕. ② [속이] feel sick ; feel nauseated ; have a desire to vomit ¶ 보기만 해도 속이 뉘엿거린다 The mere sight makes me sick〔turns my stomach〕.
뉘엿뉘엿 ① [해가] ready to set ② [속이] nauseating ; sickening
뉘우쁘다 (be) penitential ; repentant ; regretful ¶ 뉘우쁜 생각 repentant mood
*뉘우치다 regret ; repent 《of》 ; be sorry 《for》 ; be penitent 《for》 ; feel remorseful ¶ 뉘우침 regret ; repentance ; remorse // 자기가 한 짓을 뉘우치다 be sorry for what one has done ; regret one's act // 죄를 뉘우치다 be penitent for one's sin ; repent one's sin // 뉘우쳤을 때는 이미 늦었었다 I repented too late. /It was too late for me to be sorry. // 법률 공부 안한 것을 뉘우친다 He regrets now he did not study law. // 뉘우칠 일이 조금도 없다 I have nothing to repent of.
뉴기니 New Guinea
뉴델리 New Delhi
뉴룩 a new look ¶ 뉴룩의 new-look ; new-style 《hat》
뉴멕시코 New Mexico 《N. Mex., N. M., New M.》
뉴미디어 new media ☞ ◖ p. 524 ◗
†뉴스 news ; [방송의] news events ¶ 좋은 뉴스 good news // 뉴스(거리)가 되다 make news // 그 기사는 뉴스로서의 가치가 높다 That story is highly newsworthy. // 재미있는 뉴스가 있어요 Here's an interesting piece of news. // 오늘은 큰 뉴스가 없는 날입니다 Today is a slow news day.
— 가치(價値) news value — 방송(放送) newscast — 소스 the news source — 수신기(受信機) a news ticker — 아나운서 a newscaster — 영화(映畫) a newsreel ; a newsfilm ; a news picture — 카메라맨 a newsreel cameraman — 해설(解說) 《radio, TV》 news commentary — 해설자(解說者) a (news) commentator 국내(國內)〔해외(海外)〕 — home〔foreign〕 news
무소식이 희소식 [속담] No news is good news.
뉴욕 ① [미국의 주] New York 《N. Y.》 ② [시] New York City
— 사람 a New Yorker
뉴잉글랜드 New England
뉴저지 New Jersey 《N. J.》
뉴질랜드 New Zealand
— 사람 a New Zealander
뉴타운 a new town
뉴트론 〖물리〗 a neutron
뉴펀들랜드 Newfoundland
뉴페이스 a new face
뉴햄프셔 New Hampshire 《N. H.》
느근- ⇨ 나근-
느글거리다 feel sick (to one's stomach) ; feel nausea〔nauseated〕 ; gag ; keck 《at food》 ; retch ; have a sick stomach ; one's stomach turns ¶ 보기만 해도 속이 느글거린다 The very sight turns my stomach.
느긋거리다 feel sick ; feel queasy ; nauseate stomach ; keck ; retch ¶ 느긋느긋 nauseating ; sickening
*느긋하다 be greatly pleased〔satisfied, gratified〕 ; be relaxed ; comfortable ; carefree ¶ 저녁을 잘 먹고 나니 느긋하다 After such a good dinner, I feel wonderful. // 그는 항상 느긋해 보인다 He always looks carefree. // 엄마와 함께 있으면 마음이 느긋해진다 Being with my mother puts me at ease〔makes me feel at home〕. // 나는 사장이 늘 모든 일에 너무 느긋했기 때문에 회사가 재정적으로 곤란한 상태에 있었으리라는 생각이 들지 않았다 The president always acts so laid-back about everything I never imagined they could be in financial difficulties. // 로비에 잠시 있다가 모두 나간 후에 느긋하게 나가자 Let's relax for a few minutes in the lobby and then head out leisurely after everyone's gone.
†느끼다 ① [지각] feel ; be conscious of ; experience ; be sensible 《to, of》 ; realize ¶ 고통〔공복〕을 느끼다 feel pain〔hungry〕 // 곤란을 느끼다 find〔have〕 difficulty in 《doing》 // 불편을 느끼다 feel inconvenience ; experience inconve-

뉴미디어

뉴미디어(new electronics media)란 새로운 전자기술을 이용한 정보통신매체를 말한다. 뉴미디어 전체의 큰 경향으로는 ① 방송·통신계 미디어 ② 매스컴·퍼스널계 미디어 ③ 전기통신·비전기통신계 미디어 ④ 비지니스 뉴스·홈뉴스계 미디어 ⑤ 정보처리·정보통신 등을 들 수 있다.

1 뉴미디어 시대의 가정

홈오토메이션 home automation / 홈버스(가정내 폐쇄통신회로) home bus / 원격조종 telecontrol / 원격측정 telemetering / 홈뱅킹 home banking / 홈쇼핑 homeshopping / 고화질 TV HDTV; high-definition television; hivision / 전자신문 electronic newspaper / 전자우편 electronic mail / 전자출판 electronic publishing / 전산기원용(援用) 학습 CAI; computer assisted instruction; CMI; computer managed instruction / 시청각교육 audio-visual education / 콤팩트 디스크 CD; compact disc / 광디스크 optical disc

2 뉴미디어 시대의 직장

사무자동화 OA; office automation / 영상회의 video[tele] conference / 이동통신망 계획 Iridium project / 워크 스테이션 work station / 광파일 optical disc memory / 화상전화 videophone / 전략정보 시스템 SIS; strategic information system / 경영정보 시스템 MIS; Management Information System / 그룹웨어 (공동작업지원 시스템) group ware / 자동 번역 automatic translating / 유연(柔軟) 생산방식 flexible manufacturing system / 공장 자동화 FA; factory automation / 인공지능빌딩 intelligent building

3 뉴미디어 시대의 통신

위성방송 satellite broadcasting; broadcasting via satellite / 직접방송위성 DBS; direct broadcasting satellite / 정지위성 geostationary satellite / 정지궤도 geostationary orbit / 방송위성 broadcasting satellite / 통신위성 communication satellite / 오픈스카이계획 open sky project policy / 국제 통신 위성기구 INTELSAT; International Telecommunications Satellite Organization / 국제해양위성기구 INMARSAT; International Marine Satellite Orgnanization / 광통신 optical telecommunication / 광섬유 optical fiber / 광케이블 optical fiber cable / 데이터 통신 data communication / 통신규약 protocol / 디지털데이터 통신망 DDX; digital data exchange / 펄스부호변조 PCM; pulse code modulation / 통합서비스 디지털망 ISDN; integrated service digital network / 고도정보통신 시스템 INS; information network system / 비디오텍스 videotex / 유선방송 CATV; cable TV; community antenna television / 쌍방향 케이블TV Two-way CATV / 부가가치 통신망 VAN; Value Added Network / 셀 방식 전화 cellular phone / 자동차전화 mobile phone / 근거리 통신망 LAN; local area network; 전자게시판 BBS; Bulletin Board System / 화상응답 시스템 VRS; Video Response System / 랜덤억세스(임의접근) random access / 이동통신 mobile communication / 이동무선통신 시스템 MCA; multichannel access radio / 문자다중방송 teletext / 정지화면방송 still picture broadcasting

---

nience ; find it inconvenient 《to do》 // 가슴속 깊이 슬픔을 느끼다 realize true sorrow // 자기의 무식을 통절히 느끼다 keenly realize one's ignorance // 자극을 느끼다 respond to a stimulus // 필요를 느끼다 see〔feel〕 the necessity // 별안간 우리는 기온이 급격히 상승하는 것을 느끼게 되었다 We suddenly become conscious of a sharp increase in the temperature. // 그는 생명의 위험을 느꼈다 He sensed that his life was in danger. // 아내와 헤어지고 나서야 그녀가 얼마나 훌륭한 여자였는가를 절실히 느꼈다 Only after I broke up with my wife did it come home to me what a wonderful woman she was.

② [감동] be impressed 《by, with》; be moved〔touched, affected〕 《by》; be stirred 《by》 ¶ (사물에) 느끼기 쉬운 sensitive 《to》; emotional ; excitable ; nervous 《about》 // 깊이 느끼게 하다 touch 《a person》 to the heart ; impress 《a person》 profoundly // 비애를 느끼다 be seized with grief // 느끼는 바가 있어 for reasons of one's own // 그 수필을 읽고 느끼는 바가 많았다 I was stirred by the essay. // …을 보고 크게 느끼는 바 있다 one's eyes are opened greatly 《by》; learn something〔much〕 《from》 // 세상의 덧없음을 느끼다 realize the uncertainty of life // 느끼는 바 있어 술을 끊었다 I gave up drinking for a certain reason.

③ [흐느끼다] be moved to tears ; sob ; weep silently ; be choked with 〔drowned in〕 tears

느끼하다 be too fatty〔greasy, oily〕; be too rich ¶ 느끼하게 먹다 eat to satiety 〔till it is coming out of one's ears〕

†**느낌** ① [감각] touch ; feel(촉감) ; sense ; sensation ¶ 피곤한 느낌 a sensation of weariness // 뭐라고 말할 수 없는 느낌 an indefinable〔indescribable〕 sensation // 맹인들은 많은 것을 느낌에 의존한다 Blind people rely a lot on touch.

② [인상] an impression ; sentiment 〔feeling〕; a mood ¶ 좋은 (나쁜) 느낌을 주다 make a favorable〔an unfavorable〕 impression on 《a person》; impress 《a person》 favorably〔unfavorably〕 // 괴로운 나그네의 느낌이 잘 표현되어 있다 The feeling of a lonely traveler is well expressed〔described〕.

—씨 an interjection ; an exclamation —표 the exclamation mark〔point〕

-느냐 ¶ 가겠느냐 Are you going? // 무슨 일로 왔느냐 What has brought you here?

-느니 ① [···-느니 ···-느니] ¶ 하느니〔그러느니〕 어쩌느니 핑계를 대어서 with suchlike excuses

② [차라리] rather ; as soon ; sooner than ¶ 항복하느니 차라리 죽는 편이 낫다 I would sooner〔rather〕 die than give in.

느닷없다 (be) abrupt ; unexpected ¶ 느닷없는 짓 unexpected and improper behavior ; strange behavior // 느닷없는 말 an abrupt remark

느닷없이 suddenly ; abruptly ; all of a sudden ; unexpectedly ; without notice ; without warning ; out of the blue ¶ 느닷없이 나타나다 appear unexpectedly // 느닷없이 치다 hit 《a person》 without warning〔provocation〕 // 느닷없이 사직하다 resign without notice // 느닷없이 해고하다 dismiss 《a person》 without notice

-느라고 ① [결과] what with 《doing》; as a result of 《doing》 ¶ 점심 먹느라고 늦었다 Lunch made me late. ② [의도] with the idea to 《do》; with the intention of 《doing》 ¶ ···느라고 애를 쓰다 make an effort to 《do》

-느라면 ¶ 사느라면 별일 다 당하는 법이다 You have to put up with a lot of things to stay alive.

느럭느럭 sluggishly ; idly ¶ 느럭느럭 일하다 work slowly // 느럭느럭 움직이다 move sluggishly // 밥을 느럭느럭 먹다 eat slowly ; take one's time at the table

느런히 in a row (나란히)

느렁이 〖동물〗 a doe ; a hind

*‡**느른하다** [나른하다] (be) languid ; lazy ; weary ; listless ; dull ; feel tired ¶ 피로해서 느른하다 feel languid with weariness // 느른해서 일하기가 싫다 I feel too lazy to work. // 더워서 몸이 느른하다 The heat makes me feel languid. // 다리가 느른하다 My legs feel heavy.

*__느릅나무__ 〖식물〗 an elm (tree)

느리광이 a sluggard ; an idler ; a lazy fellow

느루 (stretched out) over a long period of time ; so that 《it》 lasts ¶ 느루 먹다 eat 《it》 sparingly ; make 《it》 last

†**느리다** ① [속도·동작이] (be) slow ; tardy ; dull ; sluggish ¶ 느린 걸음 a slow pace // 말이 느리다 talk slowly ; drawl // 일이 느리다 be slow in one's work // 진보가 느리다 make slow progress // 만사에 느리다 He is dull in everything. // 이해가 느리다 be slow to understand〔grasp〕 things ; be dull of understanding

② [성글다] (be) loose ; slack ; coarse 《in weave》 ¶ 짜임새가 느린 천 loose 〔coarse〕 fabric

느림 a tassel ; a streamer ; a tail ; a tag

느림보 a laggard ; a dawdler ; a slow coach 《속》 ⇨ 느리광이

*__느릿느릿__ [속도가] slowly ; sluggishly ; idly ; [짜임새가] loose ; slack ¶ 느릿느릿 걷다 walk slowly ; walk at a slow 〔snail's〕 pace // 느릿느릿 말하다 speak slowly ; drawl // 느릿느릿 일하다 work idly // 이 천은 느릿느릿 짜였다 This cloth〔textile, fabric〕 was woven loosely.

느물거리다 talk or behave insidiously ; act craftily

느물느물 insidiously ; craftily ; snakily ; trickily ; treacherously

†**느슨하다** ① [밧줄 따위가] (be) loose ; slack ; lax ; hang slack ; be loosened ¶ 느슨한 밧줄 a slack rope // 느슨한 매듭 a loose knot // 밧줄이 느슨했다 The rope hung slack.

② [언행이나 마음이] (be) relaxed ; easygoing ¶ 성미가 느슨한 사람 an easygoing〔a placid〕 person // 느슨한 교수법 a relaxed style of teaching // 마음을 느슨하게 먹어라 Take it easy.

느즈러지다 ① [느슨해지다] become loose ; loosen ; [마음이] slacken ; relax ; be unguarded ¶ 띠가 느즈러진다 The belt becomes〔gets〕 loose. // 구두 끈이 느즈러졌다 The shoestring has become loose. // 기계의 볼트가 느즈러졌다 A bolt has loosened on the machine.

② [기한이] be postponed ; be put off ;

be prolonged ; be delayed ; be deferred ¶ 길게 느즈러진 long-deferred // 기한이 느즈러졌다 The term has been prolonged. // 출발이 느즈러졌다 My departure has been put off.
느지감치 rather late ¶ 느지감치 일어나다 get up rather late in the morning
느지막이 rather late ¶ 느지막이 자다 go to bed rather late at night
느지막하다 (be) rather late
느직이 rather late
느직하다 be somewhat〔rather〕 late
느치 〖곤충〗 a cadelle ; Tenebroides mauritanicus (학명)
느타리 〖식물〗 an agaric ; Agaricuss subfunereus (학명)
느티나무 〖식물〗 a zelkova (tree) ; Zelkova acuminata (학명)
느헤미야서 一書 〖성경〗 The Book of Nehemiah ; Nehemiah 《Neh.》
늑간 肋間 〖해부〗 intercostal ; between the ribs
— 동맥 the intercostal artery — 신경〔근〕 the intercostal nerve〔muscle〕 — 신경통 intercostal neuralgia ; costalgia
*늑골 肋骨 〖해부〗 a rib ; a costa 《*pl.* -toe》 ¶ 늑골의 costal // 늑골 밑의 subcostal
— 동맥 the intercostal artery —통 costalgia 유리(遊離) — 〖해부〗 a floating rib
†**늑대** a wolf 《*pl.* wolves》 ¶ 늑대의 lupine // 늑대 같은 인간 a wolfish man
늑막 肋膜 〖해부〗 the pleura
— 삼출액 pleural effusion —성 폐렴 pleurogenic pneumonia — 천자(穿刺) pleurocentesis
늑막염 肋膜炎 pleurisy ¶ 늑막염의 pleuritic
건성〔습성〕 — dry〔moist〕 pleurisy
늑목 肋木 wall-bars ; Swedish bars
늑연골 肋軟骨 〖해부〗 costal cartilage
늑장부리다 dawdle ; linger ; slow up work ; loaf 《on the job》 ; dally away ; tarry ; loiter ; dillydally ¶ 늑장부리지 말고 promptly ; without delay〔hesitation〕 ; straight off // 늑장부리다가 기회를 놓치다 dally away one's opportunity // 돌아갈 때가 됐어도 늑장부리고 가지 않다 linger on past visiting hours
늑줄 주다 relax supervision〔control〕 ; ease up 《on continuous bombing》
늑탈 勒奪 plunder ; pillage ; spoliation ; looting ; despoilment〔despoliation〕 — 하다 plunder 《a person of something》 ; pillage ; depredate ; despoil ; loot ; (put to) sack ; strip 《a person of something》
늑하다 (be) satisfactory ⇨ 느긋하다
는 〔조사〕 ¶ 우리 학교는 언덕 위에 있다 Our school is〔stands〕 on the hill. // 이 문제에 관해서는 후에 이야기 하자 With regard to this matter, we will talk with you later.
-는 〔어미〕 ¶ 흐르는 물 running water // 신문을 읽고 있는 신사 a gentleman who is reading a paper // 내가 사랑하는 사람 a person whom I love
-는가 ¶ 어디에 살고 있는가 Where do you live? // 무엇을 하고 있는가 What are you doing?
-는가 보다 ¶ 비가 오는〔왔는, 오려는〕가 보다 It seems to be raining〔to have rained, to be about to rain〕.
-는가 하면 ¶ 내가 무엇을 찾고 있었는가 하면 바로 이것이다 This is just what I have been looking for. // 머리 위에서 지저귀는 새들이 있는가 하면 발 밑을 스쳐 가는 다람쥐들도 있다 Not only are there birds chirping overhead but also squirrels darting underfoot.
는개 a fine drizzle
-는구나 ¶ 열심히 공부하는구나 You are studying hard, aren't you? // 글쎄 그가 나에게 거짓말을 하는구나 To my astonishment, he told me a lie.
-는군 ⇨ -는구나
-는데 ¶ 우체국에 가는데 당신의 편지를 부쳐드리지요 I am going to the post office and I will mail the letter for you. // 옛날에 왕이 한 분 계셨는데 그의 이름은 마이다스였다 Once upon a time, there was a king whose name was Midas. // 저 책을 사야겠는데 지금은 돈이 없다 I have to buy that book, but I have no money with me now. // 김씨가 그러는데 당신 장사가 잘 된다면서요 Mr. *Kim* said your business was prosperous. // 시간이 없는데 서두릅시다 Let's hurry up since we haven't got enough time. // 참 맛있는데요 How delicious this is! // 비가 점점 더 오는데 It rains heavier. // 해외로 갈 수 있으면 좋겠는데 I wish I could go abroad. // 비가 몹시 오는데도 그는 외출했다 He went out in spite of the heavy rain.
-는데도 though ; although ; in spite of ; despite ; with all ¶ 비가 오는데도 in spite of the rain // 몇 차례나 거절했는데도 날더러 받으라고 성화였다 Though I declined it repeatedly, he insisted on my accepting it. // 시험이 임박했는데도 그는 놀고만 있다 He keeps on idling when the examination is in sight.
-는둥 ¶ 밥을 먹는둥 마는둥 하다 just make a gesture of eating one's rice // 책을 보는둥 마는둥 하다 read a book half-heartedly ; give the book a cursory reading
는실난실하다 behave lasciviously〔licentiously〕 ; take liberties〔be too familiar〕 《with a woman》
는적거리다 fall apart at a touch ; feel squashy〔pulpy〕 ; 〔피륙 따위가〕 be flimsy ; 〔상한 생선이〕 be crumbly ; be

crumby ¶ 는적는적 flimsily ; all crumby ; crumbly ; decomposed

-는족족 every occasion that it happens ; whatever time (that) ; whenever ; every time (that) ; as often as ¶ 낳는족족 아들이다 give birth to sons every time

-는지 ① [인지 아닌지] if ; or ; either or ; whether or ¶ 목욕물이 준비됐는지 알아봐 주시오 Please ask if the bath is ready. ∥비가 올는지 안 올는지 모르겠다 I can't tell whether it will rain or not.
② [의문·불안] I wonder ¶ 그 사람은 어떻게 됐는지 I wonder what has become of him. /How is he getting along, I wonder? ∥대체 언제 가야 될는지 It pains me to think when it will be ready.

는지렁이 sticky〔viscous〕 liquid ; mucus ; mucilage ¶ 는지렁이가 있는 slimy ; viscous

는질거리다 feel squashy〔pulpy, soft and mushy〕; be flimsy〔crumbly, crumby, decomposed〕

는질는질 squashy ; pulpy ; soft and mushy to the touch ; flimsy ; crumbly ; crumby ; decomposed

*__늘__ [언제나] always ; ever ; all the time ; usually ; habitually (습관적) ; constantly (부단히) ¶ 늘 하는 농담 usual jokes∥늘 그가 변함이 없다 He is ever the same. ∥그는 늘 담배를 피우고 있다 He is smoking all the time. ∥선생님에게 늘 그렇게 들어왔다 We have been constantly told so by our teacher. ∥그는 늘 나에게 친절하다 He has always been kind to me. ∥이 약을 늘 먹으면 몸에 좋다 The habitual use of this medicine is good for the health. ∥이런 일이 늘 있는 것이 아니다 Such things do not occur everyday. ∥내가 방문했을 때는 그는 늘 집에 없었다 He was not at home every time〔whenever〕 I called on him.

늘그막 one's old age ; one's declining years ; the winter of one's life ¶ 늘그막의 낙 a consolation of one's old age ∥늘그막에 이르러 in one's old age ; in the decline of one's life∥늘그막에 고생하다 have a hard time late in one's old age∥늘그막에 아들을 얻다 have a son in one's old age

†__늘다__ ① [수·양이] increase ; gain (힘·무게 등) ; grow ; multiply ; breed (번식) ; augment (증대) ; swell (팽창) ; mount〔pile〕 up (쌓이다) ; accrue (증식) ¶ 늘어가다 go on increasing ; be on the increase∥10배로 늘다 multiply ten times〔tenfold〕∥가족이 늘다 the family grows larger∥늘지 않도록 하다 keep 《the population》 from increasing ; check the (further) increase 《of》 ∥연 5부의 이자로 늘어간다 Interest accrues at the rate of 5 percent per annum. ∥비용이 늘어간다 Expenses are on the increase. ∥시내에 영화관이 자꾸 늘어간다 Movie theaters are mushrooming in the town. ∥지식이 늘어간다 One's knowledge increases. ∥체중이 점점 늘어간다 I am gaining in weight. /I am putting on weight. ∥자금이 3할 5부 늘었다 The capital has increased by 35 percent.
② [진보] make (good) progress 《in》 ; advance 《in one's learning》 ; improve ¶ 수완이 늘다 improve one's skill 《at, in》∥영어가 늘다 make progress in one's English ; attain proficiency in English ; improve in one's English

늘름 ① [날쌔게] with a quick snatch ; with a dart ; snatching like a flash ¶ 늘름 집어 들다 snatch 《a thing》 up
② [혀를] 《a tongue》 darting in and out

늘름거리다 let 《one's arm, one's tongue》 dart out and in ; take one's hand out and in ¶ 뱀이 혀를 늘름거리다 A snake's tongue darts out and in.

*__늘리다__ ① [양을] increase ; add to ; multiply ; augment ¶ 재산을 늘리다 increase〔add to〕 one's fortune∥인원수를 늘리다 increase the personnel〔the number of men〕; increase hands ; add to a staff
② [면적을] spread ; extend ; enlarge 《a building》; build an addition ¶ 집을 다섯 칸으로 늘리다 enlarge one's house to five chambers〔rooms〕∥구두를 늘리다 stretch one's shoes ; have one's shoes stretched
③ [고무줄 따위를] stretch ¶ 고무줄을 늘리다 stretch a rubber band

늘보 a sluggard (느리광이)

늘비하다 be in a row〔line〕; be drawn up ; be arrayed ¶ 늘비하게 늘어서다 stand in a row∥거리에 가게가 늘비하다 There are shops lined up along the street.

늘썽하다 [짜임새가] (be) coarse ; loose-woven ; open-weave ¶ 늘썽늘썽 all loose〔slack, open〕∥늘썽한 천 (a) coarse texture ; (a) loose fabric ; loose-woven cloth ; (an) open-weave fabric∥늘썽늘썽한 그물 a net with large meshes

늘씬하다 (be) slender ; slim ; slender and elegant ; smart ¶ 늘씬한 허리 a slender〔slim〕 waist∥늘씬하게 얻어맞다 get a sound thrashing (to be stretched out)

늘어가다 ① [수량이] go on increasing 〔growing, swelling〕; be on the increase ⇨ 늘다 ¶ 시내에 건물이 자꾸 늘어간다 Buildings are mushrooming in the town. ∥소비가 늘어간다 The con-

sumption is swelling. // 세계 인구가 늘어간다 The world's population goes on increasing.
② [실력 따위가] be in progress ; be advancing ; be improving

†**늘어나다** lengthen ; grow longer ; stretch ; extend ; expand ¶ 늘어나는 extensible ; expansible ; elastic // 햇볕에 엿가락이 늘어난다 A gluten candy expands〔grows longer〕 under the sun's heat. // 고무는 잘 늘어난다 Rubber stretches easily.

늘어놓다 ① [여기저기] scatter about ; put in disorder ; leave 《things》 lying about ¶ 방에 옷을 늘어놓다 leave one's clothes lying about in the room // 왜 이렇게 온 방안에 옷을 늘어놓았니 Why have you got your clothes laid out all over the room like this?
② [줄지어 놓다] arrange ; place 《things》 in a row ; line up ; draw up ; [진열] display ; lay out ¶ 상품을 선반에 늘어놓다 arrange goods on the shelf // 진열장에 상품을 늘어놓다 display〔lay out〕 goods in the show window // 책상을 3열로 늘어놓다 arrange desks in three rows // 접의자를 뒤에 3열 정도 늘어놓자 Let's line up three rows of folding chairs in the back.
③ [말을] talk away ; rattle on ; way one's tongue〔chin, jaws〕 ; mention ; enumerate ¶ 남의 결점을 늘어놓다 enumerate〔dwell on〕 another's faults // 불평을 늘어놓다 make complaints 《about》 ; spell one's complaints out // 이야기를 장황하게 늘어놓다 speak longwindedly // 그 자동차 판매 사원은 새 모델에 관해 장황한 선전을 늘어 놓기 시작했다 The car salesman started a song and dance about the new model.
④ [사업을] put one's hand to 《various enterprises》 ; attempt 《tasks》 ; extend one's business in all directions ¶ 아버지는 여러 가지 사업을 늘어놓았다가 실패 했다 My father took a hand in various enterprises only to fail.

늘어뜨리다 hang (down) ; suspend ; dangle ¶ 팔을 축 늘어뜨리고 with dangling arms // 막을 늘어뜨리다 hang down a curtain // 머리를 늘어뜨리다 let one's hair down one's back

*__늘어서다__ stand〔be〕 in a row〔line〕 ; be in line ; line up ; form a line ; be drawn up ; [차례로] queue up ; line up in a queue ¶ 두 줄로 늘어서다 form〔stand in, be drawn up in〕 two rows // 극장 입구에 늘어서다 line〔queue〕 up at the entrance of a theater // 길가에 늘어서다 line up along the street // 네 집이 한 줄로 늘어서 있다 Four houses stand in a row. // 거리에는 큰 가게가 늘어서 있다 The street is lined with big shops. // 저 가게는 언제 보아도 앞에 사람이 늘어서 있다 Whenever I pass by it, that restaurant's always got a line out in front.

늘어앉다 sit in a row ; sit in line ; sit around ¶ 많은 사람이 방에 죽 늘어앉아 있다 Many people are sitting around in the room.

⁑**늘어지다** ① [길어지다] be lengthened ; grow longer ; extend ¶ 늘어지게 기지개를 켜다 stretch oneself // 고무는 탄력이 있어 잘 늘어진다 Indian rubber is easily lengthened due to its elasticity.
② [처지다] hang (down) ; droop ; dangle ; sag ; be suspended ¶ 귀가 늘어진 개 a button-〔drop-, flap-, lop-〕 eared dog // 축 늘어진 버드나무 a drooping willow // 천장이 늘어지다 a ceiling sags // 나뭇가지가 늘어지다 the branches of a tree droop // 머래채가 어깨까지 늘어졌다 Her hair hangs down on her shoulder.
③ [시간이] be prolonged (연장) ; be postponed (연기) ; be extended ¶ 기간이 늘어졌다 The term has been prolonged. // 나의 출발이 늘어졌다 My departure has been put off〔postponed〕.
④ [몸이] droop ; languish ; get exhausted ; grow languid ¶ 늘어지게 lazily ; leisurely // 피곤해서 축 늘어지다 sink exhausted ; collapse dead-tired // 늘어지게 자다 sleep oneself out // 그녀는 축 늘어져 의자에 주저앉았다 She went limp and crumpled in the chair. // 병사들은 모두 지쳐서 땅 위에 늘어졌다 Soldiers sank exhausted on the ground all together. // 피곤으로 그의 어깨가 축 늘어졌다 His shoulders drooped with tiredness.

늘옴치래기 an elastic thing ; a thing flexible ; a thing〔an object〕 that shrinks and expands

†**늘이다** ① [길이를] lengthen ; extend ; stretch ; make 《something》 longer ; draw out ¶ 쇠를 늘여서 철사로 만들다 draw out iron into wire // 고무띠를 늘이다 stretch a rubber band // 3미터를 늘이다 lengthen (by) three meters ; make three meters longer
② [아래로] hang (down) ; droop ; suspend ¶ 커튼을 늘이다 hang down a curtain // 목을 늘이다 hang〔lower, drop〕 one's head (down) // 꼬리를 늘이다 drop its tail

늘임새 drawl ; dragging one's words out

늘임표 一標 〖음악〗 fermata 《𝄐》 《이》

늘자리 a bulrush-mat

늘쩍지근하다 feel languid ; feel tired ; (be) dull ; heavy ¶ 더워서 몸이 늘쩍지근하다 The heat makes me feel languid. // 늘쩍지근해서 일하기 싫다 I feel too lazy to work.

늘쩡거리다 be slow-moving ; be lazy 〔slow〕 in doing something ¶ 일을 늘쩡거리다 be lazy in doing one's work ; fiddle at〔poke about〕 one's work
늘채다 be supernumerous ; be far more than the expected number
늘컹거리다 act〔be〕 all soft and doughy 〔droopy, flabby〕 ¶ 뭔지 늘컹거리는 것을 밟았다 I stepped upon something squashy.
늘컹늘컹 (all) soft and doughy〔droopy, flabby〕
늘컹하다 ⇨ 늘컹거리다
늘큰거리다 act〔be〕 soft and droopy ; act 〔be〕 flabby〔pasty, doughy〕 ¶ 늘큰거리는 떡 very soft rice cake
늘큰늘큰 (all) soft and droopy ; pasty ; doughy ; flabby
늘큰하다 (be) soft and droopy ; (be) flabby ; pasty ; doughy ¶ 떡이 늘큰하다 The rice cake is doughy.
늘키다 sob gulping down tears
늘품 —品 potential for improvement in the future ; a promising character
*__늙다__ grow old ; age ¶ 늙은 사람 an old man ; an aged man // 늙어감에 따라 as one grows older ; with (the advance of) age // 곱게 늙다 grow old gracefully ; age with gentleness // 나이보다 늙어 보이다 look older than one's age ; look old for one's age // 늙어도 정정하다 be still hale and hearty ; enjoy a green old age // 늙어서 허리가 굽다 be bent with the weight of years // 당신은 조금도 늙지 않았군요 You haven't aged a bit.
늙고 병든 몸은 눈먼 새도 앉지 않는다 속담 Long life has long misery.
늙으면 아이 된다 속담 Old men are twice children.
늙으면 아이탈 쓴다 속담 Old men are twice children.
늙은 개가 문 지키기 어렵다 속담 When bees are old, they yield no honey.
늙은 소 콩밭으로 간다 속담 Avarice is the only passion that never ages.
늙다리 [사람] a silly old man ; a dotard ; [짐승] an old animal ¶ 늙다리 할멈 a withered woman ; a hag // 늙다리 소 an old ox
늙마 ⇨ 늘그막
늙바탕 old age ; one's declining years
늙수그레하다 (be) fairly old ; oldish ; be rather advanced in age
늙어빠지다 (be) very old ; be old as (old) can be ; be ever so old ¶ 늙어빠진 노인 a decrepit old man
늙으신네 an old person ⇨ 늙은이
늙은이 an old〔aged〕 man ; the old 〔aged〕《총칭》 ¶ 늙은이의 망녕 an indiscretion of an old man // 늙은이를 돌보다 tend an old man ; be kind to old people
늙은이 잘못하면 노망으로 치고 젊은이 잘못하면 철없다 한다 속담 Young men think old men fools, and old men know young to be so.
늙정이 an old man
늙히다 make《a person》 old ; age《a person》 ¶ 처녀로 늙히다 let a girl become an old maid
늠그다 hull (barley)
늠렬 凜烈 [추위] severity ; [늠름] forbiddingness — **하다** [추위] (be) severe ; intense ; [늠름하다] gallant and forbidding ; commanding
늠름하다 凜凜— [위풍 있다] (be) dashing ; mettlesome ; manly ; high-spirited ; imposing ¶ 늠름한 태도 an imposing attitude // 늠름한 기상 a manly mien
늠실거리다 leer ⇨ 넘실거리다
늠연하다 凜然— (be) commanding ; decisive ; imposing ; dignified
늡늡하다 (be) large-minded ; openhearted ; liberal ; magnanimous
능 能 [재능] ability ; capacity ; capability ; talent
능 綾 a kind of thin silk
능 陵 a royal mausoleum〔tomb〕
능 稜 〖기하〗 an angle ; an edge
__능가__ 凌駕 — **하다 surpass ; excel ; exceed ; outdo〔outstrip, outshine〕; be superior to ; stand high above ; get ahead of ¶ 힘이 남을 능가하다 surpass〔excel〕《a person》 in strength // 영어로 급우들을 능가하다 excel one's class in English // 이 제품은 질적으로 저 제품을 능가한다 This product is superior to that in quality.
능간 能幹 capability ; ability ; talent
능갈치다 devise clever excuses〔pretexts〕
능구렁이 ① 〖동물〗 a yellow spotted serpent ; Dinodon rufozonatum (학명) ② [사람] a snaky person ; an old fox ; a sly dog ; a deceitful person ; an insidious person
능그다 hull (barley)
능글능글 — **하다** (be) deceitful ; sneaky ; cunning ; sly ; insidious ; wily ; impudent
능글맞다 (be) tricky ; sly ; snaky ; cunning ; wily ; crafty ; insidious ; foxy ; slick ¶ 능글맞은 웃음《make》 an insidious smile // 능글맞은 놈 a tricky guy ; a crafty fellow ; a sly dog // 무엇 때문에 능글맞게 웃고 있느냐 What are you smirking about?
능금 ① a crab apple ② an apple ⇨ 사과
— **나무** a (crab) apple tree ; Malus asiatica (학명)
능놀다 do《something》 slowly ; take one's time《at a piece of work》

능동 能動 activeness ; activity ¶ 능동적 active ; voluntary
— 면역 〖의학·생물〗 active immunity — 주의 activism —태 〖문법〗 the active voice

능두다 leave enough 《room, food, etc.》 to spare

능라금수 綾羅錦繡 silk fabrics ; silk goods ; silks

능란하다 能爛— (be) dexterous ; deft ; adroit ; expert ; ingenious ¶ 능란한 기수 an expert rider // 계산이 능란하다 be expert at figures // 매우 능란한 솜씨를 보이다 display a great adroitness 《in》 // 사람을 능란하게 다루다 be dexterous in handling men // 그는 호텔 경영에 매우 능란하다 He is very dexterous in hotel management.

†**능력 能力** [역량] ability ; capability ; [지력] mental faculties ; brain power ; [성능] capacity ; [기능] faculty ¶ 지적 능력 intellectual capacity〔faculty〕// 영어의 독해〔작문, 회화〕 능력 reading〔writing, speaking〕 ability in English // 능력 있는 able ; competent ; capable // 능력이 있다 be able to 《do》 ; be capable of 《doing》 ; be competent for 《work》 // 능력이 없다 be unable to ; be incapable of 《doing》 ; be powerless 《to do》 ; be incompetent for // 자기 일에 전능력을 경주했다 He put all of his brain power in to his work. // 제인은 가르칠 능력이 있다 Jane is competent for teaching. // 우리는 미래를 아는 능력보다도 과거를 아는 능력을 더 많이 갖고 있다 We have more capacity for knowing the past than for knowing the future.
—급(給) pay according to ability —별 학급 편성 ability grouping ; grouping by〔according to〕 ability ; streaming 《영》 — 상실 disability ; disqualification —자 a person of great capacity ; a competent〔capable〕 person 생산 — productive〔production〕 capacity ; productivity 정신 — the mental capacity 〔faculty〕 지불 — solvency ; the ability to pay 《one's debts》

‡**능률 能率** efficiency ; 〖물리〗 moment ¶ 능률적 efficient // 비능률적 inefficient // 능률의 증진 increase〔improvement〕 of efficiency ; efficiency progress // 능률의 저하 lowering〔diminution〕 of efficiency // 능률을 올리다 increase〔improve, enhance, develop〕 efficiency // 최소의 노동으로 최대의 능률을 올리다 secure the maximum of efficiency〔get the highest state of efficiency〕 with the minimum of labor // 능률을 수배로 올리다 multiply efficiency severalfold // 능률적으로 일을 처리하다 do one's work efficiently // 이렇게 하면 능률이 올라간다 This will make for〔conduce to〕 efficiency. // 인원은 많지만 능률이 올라가지 않는다 Sufficient efficiency is not obtained in spite of the large numbers of workers.
— 곡선 efficiency curve —급(給) efficiency wages — 승급 제도 proficiency salary raise system — 시험 efficiency test — 저하 lowering〔decrease, diminution〕 of efficiency —주의 the 'efficiency first' principle ; the gospel of efficiency — 증진 increase〔improvement, enhancement〕 of efficiency ; promoted〔higher〕 efficiency —화 the promotion of efficiency 노동 — efficiency of labor ; labor efficiency 작업 — efficiency of work 행정 — administrative efficiency ; efficiency of administration

능멸 凌蔑 ⇨ 능모

능모 凌侮 contempt ; disdain ; scorn —하다 despise ; scorn ; disdain ; slight ; contempt ; look down (up) on 《a person》 ; have contempt for 《a person》 ; throw contempt on ; bring 《a person》 into contempt

능변 能辯 eloquence ; fluency ; oratory ¶ 능변이다 have a fluent〔well-oiled〕 tongue ; speak fluently // 능변일 뿐 아니라 기지도 있다 He has not only a fluent tongue but ready wit.
—가(家) an eloquent speaker ; an orator ¶ 청산유수 같은 능변가다 His tongue runs on the wheel.

능사 能事 proper and suitable work ; one's line of business ; one's work 〔business〕 ; (something within) one's competency ¶ 능사로 삼다 consider 《something》 as one's work ; make it one's business 《to do》 // 먹고 마시는 것만이 인생의 능사가 아니다 There is something in life besides eating and drinking.

능선 稜線 [산의] a ridgeline

능소 陵所 a royal mausoleum

능소능대 能小能大 —하다 (be) able and adaptable ; versatile ; be good at everything ¶ 능소능대한 작가 a versatile writer

능소니 a bear cub ; a cub bear

능수 能手 ① [수완] ability ; capacity ; capability ; talent
② [사람] an expert ; a good hand ; an able man ¶ 실무에 있어서는 능수라 하겠다 He is a shrewd man〔a veteran〕 of business.

능수버들 a weeping willow

†**능숙 能熟** skill(fulness) ; proficiency ; expertness ; adeptness ; dexterity —하다 (be) skilled ; skillful ; expert ; adept ; experienced ¶ 능숙한 사람 an expert ; a practiced hand ; an old stager // 능숙한 사격수 a master shot // 능숙하지 못하다 be unskilled〔inexperienced〕 // 능숙해지다 become skillful 《in》 // …에 능숙하다 be skilled in ; be

experienced in ; be a good hand at ; be an expert〔adept〕 in〔at〕 ; be at home〔well up〕 in // 모든 일에 능숙하다 be skillful in everything ; be a good hand at all things // 교수 방법이 능숙하다 be tactful in teaching // 그는 좌담에 능숙하다 He has great conversational power. // 그는 주판에 능숙하다 He is clever with the abacus. // 그는 테니스에 능숙하다 He is a crack tennis player. // 그는 그림 그리는 데 능숙하다 He is (an) expert at〔in, on〕 drawing.
—도(度) degree of skill〔proficiency〕 ; quality of workmanship (기능)

능에 〚새〛 a Siberian bustard

능욕 凌辱 ① insult ; affront ; indignity ; contempt **—하다** insult 《a person》 ; offer〔level〕 《a person》 an insult ; put an indignity on 《a person》 ; put 《a person》 to shame ¶ 능욕을 참다 bear〔brook, pocket, swallow〕 an insult ② [여자를] violation ; outrage ; rape ; assault **—하다** violate ; commit rape on ; outrage ; force ; ravish ¶ 능욕당하다 be violated ; be outraged ; be attacked // 유부녀를 능욕하다 violate 《a person's》 wife // 처녀를 능욕하다 deflower // 폭행으로 능욕하다 assault and rape 《a woman》

능준하다 (be) sufficient ; more than enough ; abundant

능지기 陵— the caretaker of a royal mausoleum

능지처참 陵遲處斬 hacking a criminal to pieces **—하다** hack 《a criminal》 to pieces

능직 綾織 twill ; diagonal cloth ; figured cloth ; lease ; leash ; twilled fabrics 〔weaves〕 ¶ 능직 천 figured cloth // 능직의 diagonal ; twilled ; figured // 능직으로 짜다 twill

능철광 菱鐵鑛 siderite ; spathic iron ; lodestone

능청 guile ; wile ; wiliness ; deceit(-fulness) ; hypocrisy ¶ 능청부리다〔떨다〕 display guile ; wear an air of innocence // 능청맞다 ⇨ 능청스럽다
—이 a guileful〔wily〕 person ; a sly one

능청거리다 ① [막대기 따위] sway ; (be) pliable ; pliant ; flexible ¶ 능청거리는 지팡이 an elastic cane
② [밧줄 따위] swing ; vibrate ; quiver ; tremble

능청능청 [휘는 모양] swayingly ; flexibly ; pliantly ; [흔들리는 모양] swingingly ; tremblingly ; quiveringly **—하다** ⇨ 능청거리다

능청맞다 ⇨ 능청스럽다

능청스럽다 (be) deceitful ; cunning ; artful ; sly ; crafty ; wily ; insidious ; hypocritical ¶ 능청스러운 사람 an old fox ; a sly dog // 능청스러운 웃음 sly 〔insidious〕 laughter // 능청스러운 짓 a hypocritical act ; a make-believe

능통 能通 proficiency ; mastery ; skill ; a full knowledge **—하다** (be) proficient ; skillful ; be versed ; have a full knowledge 《of》 ¶ …에 능통하다 be proficient in ; be a master of ; have a mastery of ; be versed〔well up〕 in ; be expert in // 영어에 능통하다 be versed 〔well up〕 in English ; have a (great) command of English // 그는 외국어에 상당히 능통하다 He gained tolerable proficiency in foreign languages.

능필 能筆 good writing ; good handwriting ; [사람] a good penman ; a skilled calligrapher ¶ (자네는) 능필이군 You write a good hand.

능하다 能— excel 《in English》 ; (be) capable ; able ; be expert 《in》 ; skilled ; proficient 《in》 ; be well up 〔versed〕 《in》 ¶ 만사에 능하다 He is a man of the world. // 문장에 능하다 He writes well. // 불어에 능하다 He is very good at French.

능형 菱形 a rhomb ; a lozenge ; a diamond (shape) ¶ 능형의 rhombic ; lozenge ; diamond-shaped // 능형 무늬 a diaper pattern // 능형 자수(刺繡) crow's-foot

능히 能— ably ; capably ; competently ; skillfully ; proficiently ; perfectly ; easily ; freely ¶ 능히 할 수 있다 be easily able to do it // 너 혼자서도 할 수 있다 You can do it for yourself. // 내가 능히 할 수 있는 일이면 무엇이고 하겠다 I will do anything in my power.

늦- late ; belated ¶ 늦곡식 late crop

늦가을 late autumn ; late fall 《미》 ; the latter part of autumn

늦겨울 late winter ; the latter part of winter

†늦다¹ ① [시각이] (be) late ¶ 늦게 late // 밤 늦게 at a late hour ; late at night // 늦어도 at (the) latest ; at (the) farthest // 늦은 봄 late spring // 밤 늦게까지 앉아 있다 sit up late at night ; stay up till late // 늦도록 안 돌아오다 be long in returning // 아침 늦게까지 잠을 자다 sleep late into the morning // 늦게 자고 늦게 일어나다 keep late hours // 아침 일찍부터 밤 늦게까지 일하다 work early and late // 귀가가 늦다 come home late // 지금 가선 너무 늦다 It is too late to start now. // 지금이라도 늦지 않다 Even now it is not too late. // 그는 하루 늦게 왔다 He came a day too late. // 늦어도 월요일까지는 돌아온다 I shall be back by Monday at latest. // 저녁을 늦게 먹지 않았더라면 좀 더 먹었을 겁니다 If I hadn't had a late dinner, I'd have had more.
② [느슨하다] (be) loose ; slack ¶ 고삐가 늦다 The rein is slack. // 허리띠가 늦다 The belt is loose.

†**늦다²** [소정 시간에] be〔get, become〕 late ; be behind time ; be delayed ; be overdue (정각에) ¶ 기차 시간에 늦다 be late for a train // 약속 시간에 두 시간 늦다 be two hours late for one's engagement // 기차가 20분 늦었다 The train was twenty minutes behind time. // 비행기가 1시간 늦었다 The plane was delayed one hour. // 빨리 가지 않으면 늦는다 Unless we hurry, we will be late. // 시계가 5분 늦다 Your watch is five minutes slow. // 열차가 꽤 오래〔한 시간〕 늦어지고 있다 The train is long 〔an hour〕 overdue. // 답장이 늦어 죄송합니다 We apologize for our tardy response to your letter. // 죄송합니다만 손님 한 발 늦으셨습니다 세일은 어제 끝났습니다 Sorry, sir, you missed the boat〔bus〕. The sale ended yesterday.

늦더위 late (summer) heat ; the lingering summer heat ¶ 금년에는 늦더위가 심하다 The heat of late summer is severe this year.

늦동이 ① [늦게 난] a child had late in one's life ; a child born of an old couple ② [늦된] a retarded child

늦되다 grow〔ripen, mature〕 late ; be ripe late ; reach〔come to〕 late maturity ; be slow in growing ; grow late ¶ 늦되는 과일 late-maturing fruits ; late fruit // 늦된 아이 a retarded child // 금년은 작물이 늦된다 The crops ripen 〔mature〕 late this year. /The crops come to late maturity this year.

늦바람 ① [저녁 바람] an evening breeze ② [빠르지 않은 바람] a gentle〔light, soft〕 breeze ; a breeze
③ [난봉] dissipation in one's later years ; going wild late in one's life ¶ 늦바람을 피우다 have a secret love affair in one's old age ; take to amours in one's later years

늦배 [짐승의] offspring born〔hatched〕 late
— **돼지** a litter of pigs born late — **병아리** late-hatched chickens

늦벼 a kind of late-ripening rice

늦복 —福 good fortune in one's later days

늦봄 late spring ; the latter part of spring

늦부지런 ① [뒤늦게] belated hasty diligence ¶ 늦부지런내다 make an effort almost too late ; make an eleventh hour effort
② [늙어서] becoming diligent in one's old age

늦새끼 ① [늙어서 난] offspring born of an old animal ② [늦배의] a late litter ③ [사람] a lazy ne'er-do-well

늦서리 a late frost

늦심기 planting late ; late planting

늦여름 late summer ; the last〔latter〕 part of summer

늦잠 late rising ; morning sleep ; sleeping late into the morning ¶ 늦잠꾸러기 a late riser ; a slugabed ; a sleepyhead // 늦잠자다 rise〔get up〕 late ; sleep late into the morning ; oversleep oneself

늦잡죄다 exercise belated〔lax〕 control 〔supervision, management〕 ; be (too) easy with〔on〕

늦장마 a late rainy season ; the rainy spell in late summer

늦추 [늦게] late ⇨ 늦다 ¶ 늦추 오다 come late

†**늦추다** ① [띠·고삐를] loosen ; slacken ; [마음을] relax ; ease ¶ 조금 늦추다 make 《one's belt》 a little looser // 고삐를 늦추다 slacken the rein ; let the rein go ; keep a slack〔loose〕 rein ; give 《a horse》 the rein〔the bridle〕 // 허리띠를 늦추다 loosen one's belt // 경계를 늦추다 relax one's guard〔vigilance〕 ; let down one's guard // 줄을 좀 늦추어라 Ease off that rope a bit.
② [속력을] slack ; slacken ; slow down ; reduce one's speed ; ease (up) 《the speed》 ¶ 걸음〔속도〕을 늦추다 slacken 〔slow down, reduce〕 one's pace 〔speed〕 // 기차가 속력을 늦추었다 The train slackened its speed. /The train slowed down.
③ [미루다] postpone ; put off ; extend ; delay ; defer ; protract ¶ 시간을 늦추다 extend the limit // 이틀 늦추다 put it off for two days // 일요일까지 늦추다 put off〔defer〕 till Sunday // 파티를 일주일 늦추다 delay a party (for) a week // 결심을 늦추다 defer making a decision // 그들은 방문을 몇 주 늦추었다 They put off their visit for some weeks.

늦추위 late cold ; a late chill ; a late cold-spell

⁂**늪** a swamp ; a marsh ; a bog ; a pond

-니¹ ¶ 그가 말하니 모두들 잠잠해졌다 He spoke and all was still.

-니² [의문 어미] Is it? ; Does it?

-니³ ⇨ -으니

-니까 ⇨ -으니까

⁂**니그로** a negro 《*pl.* ～es》 ; a black (man, woman)

> 참고 **Negro** 현재 미국에서는 보통 경멸적으로 쓰이므로 대신 black을 씀

***니스** [바니시] varnish
¶ 니스칠하다 varnish (over) 《the surface》 ; put varnish on

⁂**니켈** nickel 《Ni》 ¶ 니켈 도금의 nickel-plated ; nickelled
— **시계(時計)** a nickel watch

니코시아 Nicosia (키프로스의 수도)

니코틴 nicotine ¶ 니코틴이 없는 담배 a denicotinized〔nicotineless〕 cigarette

— 중독(中毒) nicotinism
니크롬선 —線 nicrome wire
니트로화 —化 〖화학〗 nitrification **—하다** nitrify
니힐 nihil
—리스트 a nihilist **—리즘** nihilism
닉네임 a nickname
†**님** [실] pieces of (sewing) thread
-님 [존칭] ¶ 아버님 Dear father // 주인님 my honorable master ; Sir ! ; Mr. Smith 《미》 // 임금님 Your Majesty (2인칭) ; His Majesty (3인칭) // 선생님 Sir ! ; Mr. Brown 《미》 // 신부님 Rev. 〔Mr., Dr.〕 Smith ; Father ! (호칭) // 소월님 [서신] Mr. *Sowol;Sowol*, Esq.
*님프** a nymph
닢 ¶ 가마니 두 닢 two straw bags // 동전 한 닢 a piece of copper // 엽전 열 닢 ten brass coins

ㄷ

다¹ 〖음악〗 ¶ 내림 다조 C-flat // 올림 다조 C-sharp // 다 장조〔단조〕 C major 〔minor〕

다² ① [모두] all ; everything ; everybody ; everyone ¶ 다해서 in all ; all told // 아이들은 다 all the children // 다 같이 가자 Let us all go together. // 우리들은 다 그 계획에 반대한다 We are (one and) all against the plan. // 나의 친구는 다 좋은 사람들뿐이다 All (of) my friends are 〔My friends are all〕 good fellows. // 인간은 다 행복을 원한다 All (people) want to be happy. /Everyone wants to be happy. // 누구나 다 자기의 의무를 다하지 않으면 안 된다 Everybody must do his duty. // 준비가 다 되었다 Arrangements have been thoroughly made. // 다 마셔라 Drink up.
② [거의] almost ; nearly ; all but ¶ 다 죽어가는 목소리로 in a feeble〔faint〕 voice // 다 죽어가다 be dying ; be in a dying condition ; be on the verge of death // 서울에 다 왔군요 We're approaching *Seoul*.
③ [강조·조소] ¶ 별 일 다 봤다 Now I've seen everything. // 별 꼴 다 보겠네 What a spectacle〔sight〕! /What a mess ! // 별소리 다 듣겠네 None of your nonsense now ! // 별 말씀 다 하십니다 Don't mention it. /Not at all.
④ [고작] at best ; at (the) most ; as much as one can ¶ 빚 안지고 지내는 게 다다 It is as much as I can do to keep out of debt.

-다 be ; do ¶ 먹다 eat // 춥다 It is cold. // 높다 It is high. // 그 여자는 아름답다 She is beautiful. // 나의 동생은 선생이다 My younger brother is a teacher.

다가 [장소] ¶ 어디다가 두었느냐 Where did you put it ? // 어디다가 놓을까요 Where shall I place this ?

-다가 [상태·동작의 이행] ¶ 울다가 잠들다 cry oneself to sleep // 책을 읽다가 잠들었다 I fell asleep reading. // 고기를 다 잡았다가 놓쳤다 I almost caught the fish.

-다가는 ¶ 공부만 하다가는 바보된다 All work and no play makes Jack a dull boy. // 실수했다가는 큰일난다 A miss, and all is up〔over〕. // 한 발 삐끗했다가는 끝장이다 A single false step would be fatal.

다가놓다 bring near ; draw (up) near ; put〔place, lay〕 closer ¶ 책을 다가놓다 put a book closer 《to》 // 재떨이를 앞으로 다가놓다 draw an ashtray near // 그는 내 옆에 그의 의자를 다가놓았다 He placed his chair next to me.

-다가도 but then ; but anyway ; nevertheless

다가붙다 stick nearer 《to》

다가서다 step〔come〕 up to ; go〔come〕 near ; approach ; get near(er) ¶ 다가서서 보다 see 《a picture》 close at hand // 바싹 다가서라 Come close to me. // 위험하다 다가서지 말라 Danger ! Keep away !

다가쓰다 [앞당겨] spend〔use〕 in advance 〔beforehand〕 ¶ 봉급을 다가쓰다 get 〔receive〕 one's salary in advance

다가앉다 take one's seat closer ; sit close ¶ 비좁으니 서로 다가앉아 주십시오 Sit close to each other, please, as there is very little room left. // 얘기 좀 하게 다가앉아라 Sit a little closer, so we can have a talk.

-다가야 and (only) then ; only when ¶ 그와 한참 이야기하다가야 비로소 그의 이름이 생각났다 It was only after I had conversed with him a good while that I remembered his name.

다가오다 come〔go, walk, step〕 up to ; approach ; near ; get near 《a place》 ; move on toward ; [일·날짜가] draw 〔come〕 near ; draw close 《to》 ¶ (배가 육지에) 다가오다 approach land ; draw toward the shore // 종말이 다가오다 draw to a close // 점점 다가오다 get nearer to 《a place》 // 시험이 다가온다 The examination is near at hand. // 방학이 다가온다 The vacation is drawing near. // 크리스마스가 다가온다 Christmas is coming on us. // 초여름이 다가온다 Early summer is just ahead.

다각 多角 many-sidedness ¶ 다각의 many-sided ; multiple ; multilateral ; diversified
— 경영 multiple〔diversified〕 management〔operation〕 **— 농업** diversified farming **— 무역** multilateral trade **—화** diversification

다각적 多角的 many-sided ; versatile ; diversified ; multilateral ¶ 다각적 취미의 사람 a man of diverse interests // 다각적인 취미 many-sided interests // 다각적인 농업 diversified farming // 다각적인 천재 a versatile genius

다각형 多角形 〖기하〗 a polygon ¶ 다각형의 polygonal

다갈색 茶褐色 (yellowish) brown ; liver color ¶ 다갈색의 brown ; livercolored

다갈증 多渴症 〖의학〗 polydipsia ; polydipsia ¶ 다갈증의 polyipsic

다감 多感 sensibility ; susceptibility ; sentimentality **—하다** (be) sensitive ; susceptible ; sentimental ¶ 다감한 청년기 impressionable youth // 다정 다감한 시인 a passionate poet // 다정 다감한 기질이다 be of a sentimental〔emotional〕 nature
다공성 多孔性 porosity ¶ 다공성의 porous
다과 多寡 many and〔or〕 few ; [양] a quantity ; [수] number ; [액] an amount ¶ 손해의 다과에 따라서 in proportion to the damage suffered // 팁의 다과에 따라 대우를 달리하다 treat《guests》differently according to the amount of tip
다과 茶菓 tea and cake ; light refreshments ¶ 다과를 대접하다 serve light refreshments
다과회 茶菓會 a tea party ¶ 다과회에 초대하다 ask《a person》to come in to tea
다구 茶具 tea-things ; tea utensils ; a tea set ¶ 다구 한벌 a set of tea-things
다국어 多國語 many languages
다국적 多國籍 multination ¶ 다국적의 multinational
다그다 ① [당기다] bring near ; draw near 〔close up〕 ; set ahead ; make《anything》earlier ¶ 기일을 다그다 advance the date // 책을 다그다 bring a book nearer〔closer〕 // 이틀 다그다 shift two days ahead ; advance《the date》by two days ② [숨이] pant
다그치다 bring near ⇨ 다그다
다극 多極 ¶ 다극의 multipolar // 세계 정치의 다극화 시대 the age of multipolarized world politics
— 발전기 a multipolar generator
†**다급하다** (be) imminent ; impending ; pressing ; urgent ¶ 다급한 용무로 on urgent business // 다급한 문제 a pressing question // 다급한 경우에는 in case of emergency // 시간이 다급하다 be pressed for time ; time presses // 시험이 다급해졌다 The examination is near at hand. // 식모는 다급하지 않다 I have no immediate need of a maid servant.
다기 多岐 the many branches of a road ; [다방면] many divergences
다기 多氣 boldness ; daring ; intrepidity ; pluck ; nerve(s) **—하다** ⇨ 다기지다
다기지다 多氣— (be) brave ; gallant ; heroic ; courageous ; daring ; plucky ¶ 다기진 사람 a courageous〔brave〕 person ; a person of (great) prowess // 다기지게 bravely ; gallantly ; heroically ; valiantly ; courageously // 다기지게 싸우다 fight bravely ; fight a gallant〔valiant〕 fight
다기차다 多氣— ⇨ 다기지다
다난 多難 **—하다** be full of difficulties 〔troubles〕 ; be fraught with difficulties ; (be) eventful ¶ 다난한 해 a tumultuous year // 국가적으로 다난한 때에 in national crisis〔emergency〕 // 지금은 참 다난한 시대이다 This is indeed a hard world (to live in).
다녀가다 drop in for a short visit ; call at《a house》; stop at《a place》; drop 〔look, blow〕 in《on a person》; look《a person》up ¶ 전주에 다녀가다 stop at *Chonju* ; drop over〔off〕 at *Chonju* ; break one's journey at *Chonju* // 상경하시거든 다녀가시오 Look me up when you are in *Seoul*.
다녀오다 drop in (on a person and then come back) ; go round to see《a person》(and then return) ; get back ; be back ¶ 곧 다녀오너라 Don't tarry〔be long〕 on the way. /Come back quick(-ly). // 곧 다녀오겠다 I shan't be long. // 다녀왔습니다 I'm home.
다년 多年 many years ; a number of years ¶ 다년간 for many years // 다년간의 지기 an acquaintance of many year's standing // 다년간의 노력 years of labor 〔efforts〕 // 다년간의 연구 many years' study ; long-continued study // 다년간에 걸친 전쟁 a war of long duration // 다년간의 희망을 이루다 realize a long-cherished desire
다년생 多年生 〖식물〗 다년생의 perennial
—근(根) a perennial root **— 식물** a perennial (plant) **— 야채** perennial vegetables **— 초본(草本)** a perennial herb
다뇨증 多尿症 〖의학〗 polyuria
다뉴브 강 —江 the Danube river
-다는 ¶ 만병에 좋다는 약 a medicine, what is called a cure-all // 신문에서 당신이 외국에 간다는 것을 알았다 I have learned through the papers that you are going abroad.
다능 多能 versatility ; many accomplishments **—하다** (be) versatile ; many-sided ; accomplished ¶ 다능한 사람 a man of great versatility ; a many-sided person
-다니 [의외] how〔why〕 should ; I am sorry《that》; I regret ; It is a pity《that》 ¶ 여기서 자네를 만나다니 This is the last place where I expected to meet you. // 저렇게 정직한 사람을 내쫓다니 The idea of kicking out such an honest fellow ! // 그가 그러한 편지를 쓰다니 It is inconceivable that he should have written such a letter.
†**다니다** ① [왕복하다] go to and from《a place》; go to《a place》and back ; make a trip to and from《a place》; run (전차 따위) ; ply《between, from...to》(배) ; walk about〔around〕《the street》; [개통하다] be opened to traffic ; be open for traffic ¶ 부산 마산 간을 다니는 배 a ship plying between *Pusan* and *Masan* // 오른쪽으로 다니다 keep to the right // 여기와 서울 사이에 버스가 다니고 있다 Buses run between here and *Seoul*. // 지금은 그 지방에 기차가 다니고 있다 A railroad is now open to that locality. // 곧 다녀와야

한다 You have to come back without delay. // 사례〔답례〕하러 다니다 make round of calls to return thanks // 그 여자는 매일 교회에 다닌다 She goes to church every day. // 버스가 얼마나 자주 다닙니까 How often do the buses run?
② [통근·통학] attend 《school》; go to; commute to 《one's office》 ¶ 교외에서 다니는 사람 a commuter // 학교에 다니다 go to〔attend〕 school // 회사에 다니다 work for a company // 관청에 다니다 be in the service of a government agency // 교외에서 시내에 있는 회사에 다니고 있다 I commute from the suburbs to my office in the city. // 어디 다니십니까 Where do you work?
③ [자주 가다] frequent; visit frequently; resort to; hang around; hang out at ¶ 자주 다니는 길 a familiar road // 구경을 다니다 go sightseeing // 사냥을 다니다 go hunting // 술집에 다니다 hang around a saloon // 전당포에 자주 다닌다 He is a frequenter of pawnshops. // 젊었을 때에는 그곳에 잘 다녔다 When young, he used to be a frequenter 〔frequent visitor〕 of the place.
④ [직무·취미로] ¶ 구경을 다니다 go sightseeing // 출장을 다니다 go on a business trip
⑤ [들르다] stop at 《a place》; drop in for a short visit; call at

다니엘 〖성경〗 Daniel
—서(書) the Book of Daniel

다다르다 arrive at〔in, on〕; reach; get to 《a place》; come up to; gain ¶ 목적지에 다다르다 arrive at one's destination // 산꼭대기에 다다르다 gain the summit of a mountain // 현장에 다다르다 arrive on the scene〔spot〕 // 표준에 다다르다 come up to the standard

다다미 a Japanese floor mat
—방 a room with a *tatami* floor

다다이스트 a Dadaist

다다이즘 Dadaism; Dada

다다익선 多多益善 속담 the more, the better

다닥다닥 in clusters

다닥뜨리다 draw near ⇨ 다닥치다

다닥치다 [닥치다] draw near; approach; come near; be (near) at hand; be imminent ¶ 시험이 다닥치다 an examination is at hand // 연말이 다닥친다 The end of the year is drawing near. // 죽음이 다닥쳤다 Death stared him in the face.

다단 多端 [다항목] many items; ramification; divergence; digression; [다망] pressure〔press〕 of business **—하다** (be) busy; complicated ¶ 공무 다단하여 owing to the pressure of official business // 업무 다단하다 be pressed with business; have one's hands full // 복잡 다단하다 be complicated 〔intricate〕; be a great deal of complexity 《about》

다단식 로켓 多段式— a multistage〔multiple-stage〕 rocket

다닫다 arrive at ⇨ 다다르다

다달이 every month; monthly; per month; a month ¶ 다달이 두번씩 twice a month

다당 多黨 ¶ 다당화의 경향 a multiparty trend // (의회가) 다당화하다 be split into many different parties
—제 a multiparty system

다대 [옷의] a patch; a piece of cloth ¶ 다대를 댄 바지 patched trousers // 다대를 대다 patch up 《a cloth》; put a patch 《on》 // 옷에 다대를 대다 patch up 〔mend〕 one's clothes

*__다대 多大__ a great quantity〔number, volume, amount〕 **—하다** (be) much; great; heavy; considerable; a great deal of; numerous; huge; serious ¶ 다대한 이익 a considerable amount of profit // 다대한 손해 a heavy〔great〕 loss // 다대한 희생자 a huge cost of life // 다대한 동정을 얻다 obtain one's hearty sympathy // 다대한 손해를 입다 suffer a heavy loss // 다대한 원조를 받다 receive a great deal of assistance // 다대한 이익을 얻다 get a great〔a considerable amount of〕 benefit〔profit〕 // 다대한 영향을 입다 be seriously affected; be hard hit // 나라에 대한 다대한 공적으로 표창됐다 He won commendation for his great services to the State.

다도 茶道 the tea ceremony〔cult〕; the art of ceremonial tea-making

다도해 多島海 [에게 해] the Aegean Sea; [보통 명사로서] an archipelago

다독 多讀 extensive〔wide, much〕 reading **—하다** read much〔a great deal, widely, extensively〕
—가 an extensive reader; a voracious reader

다독거리다 gather 《things》 up and press into order

다듬거리다, 따듬거리다 stammer; stutter; falter

다듬다 ① [나무·돌 따위를] trim〔prune〕 《trees》; plane (대패로); shave (칼로); face〔trim〕 《a stone》 ¶ 잘 다듬어진 돌 a stone properly faced // 나무를 다듬다 shave a piece of wood smoothly; [판자를] plane a piece of board smoothly; [각재를] trim a square timber // 돌을 다듬다 face a (building) stone smoothly
② [푸성귀를] nip 《off》; trim 《away, off》; sort out ¶ 죽은 잎을 다듬어내다 nip off dead leaves // 무를 다듬다 clean a radish
③ [깃·머리를] plume (깃을); trim (머리를) ¶ 날개를 다듬다 plume one's feather // 머리를 다듬다 trim one's hair 《with a comb》; smooth one's hair down 《with hair tonic》

④ [땅바닥을] even ; make even ; level ; smooth ; roll ¶ 롤러로 땅을 다듬다 smooth the field with a roller ; roll the ground // 불도저로 땅을 다듬다 level the ground with a bulldozer ; bulldoze the ground
⑤ [옷 따위를] smooth clothes by pounding with round sticks
⑥ [글이나 문장을] refine ; polish ; embellish ; elaborate ; file ¶ 말을 다듬다 refine the language // 문장을 다듬다 polish one's writing

다듬이 ① [옷감] cloth to be fulled 〔smoothed〕 《by pounding》 ② ⇨ 다듬이질

다듬이질 fulling〔smoothing〕 cloth by pounding **—하다** smooth 《starched cloth》 by beating it on a fulling block ; full〔beat〕 《cloth》 ¶ 다듬이질 소리 the sound of fulling cloth

다듬잇돌 a fulling block ; a block of stone used for pounding cloth on

다듬잇방망이 clubs for fulling cloth ; round sticks for pounding cloth with

다듬질 〖조각〗 finishing ; finishing touches **—하다** give the final touch to ; do up **— 대패** a finishing〔smoothing〕 plane

다디달다 (be) very sweet

다따가 suddenly in the middle of the road ; suddenly in the midst of something ; abruptly ; all of a sudden

다라엽 茶羅葉 〖식물〗 a holly ; an ilex ; Ilex latifolia (학명)

다라지다 (be) bold ; daring ; dauntless ; fearless ; hardy ; plucky ; spunky ¶ 그는 다라진 사람이다 He has iron nerves.

다락 a loft〔an attic〕 over a kitchen

다락같다 be very high in price ; be very dear ; be expensive ; be very costly

다락다락 importunately ⇨ 더럭더럭

‡**다락방** —房 a garret ; an attic ; aloft ¶ 다락방에 살다 live in a garret〔an attic〕

다락집 a two-storied house ; a tower

‡**다람쥐** 〖동물〗 a squirrel ; chipmunk
다람쥐 쳇바퀴 돌 듯하다 속담 go round and round ; repeat the same thing forever ; be in a vicious circle

다랍다 (be) dirty ; stingy (인색) ⇨ 더럽다

다랑귀 뛰다 [매달리다] cling to ; hold on fast to ; clutch ; [조르다] press 〔tease〕 《a person》 for something ; badger 《a person》 to do ; clutch ¶ 목에 다랑귀 뛰다 hang on another's neck ; throw〔lock, fold〕 one's arms around another's neck

다랑어 〖물고기〗 a tunny ; a tuna (fish)

다랑이 a small lot of rice-paddy field

다래 ① [다래나무의 열매] the fruit of Actinidia arguta ② [목화의 열매] a cotton boll

다래끼 ① [눈의] a sty(e) in one's eye ; a hordeolum ② [작은 바구니] a basket with a small opening ¶ 오른 눈에 다래끼가 났다 A sty has formed〔I have got a sty〕 in my right eye.

다래나무 Actinidia arguta (학명)

다래다래 dangling in clusters ¶ 마당에 있는 감나무에 감이 다래다래 열렸다 The persimmon tree in the garden has borne abundant fruit.

†**다량 多量** much ; a great quantity ¶ 다량의 much ; plenty of ; a great〔large〕 quantity of ; a large supply of ; abundant // 다량으로 plentifully ; abundantly ; in abundance ; in great quantities 〔numbers〕 ; a great deal // 다량의 물 much〔a great quantity of〕 water // 다량의 독약 a large dose of poison // 다량의 출혈 profuse〔copious〕 bleeding/excessive loss of blood // 비타민을 다량으로 포함하다 be rich〔high〕 in vitamins // 석탄을 다량 수입하다 import coal in great quantities // 우리는 최신형 구두를 다량 구입해 놓았다 We have a large stock of the latest styles in shoes.
— 구입 quantity buying **— 수요** heavy demand **— 주문** a large order

†**다루다** ① [사람을] treat ; deal with ; [손으로] work 《a machine》 ; manipulate ; handle ; [처리] manage ; conduct〔carry on, transact〕 《business》 ¶ 다루기 쉬운 manageable ; easy to handle〔to deal with〕 // 거칠게 다루다 handle 《a thing》 roughly // 문제를 다루다 deal with a problem〔question〕 // 사무를 다루다 conduct〔transact〕 business // 전람회의 사무를 다루다 deal with the affairs of the exhibition // 기계를 다루다 handle〔operate〕 a machine // 공평히 다루다 deal justly with 《a person》 // 정중히 다루다 treat 《a person》 courteously // 총을 다루다 handle a gun // 함부로 다루다 treat 《a person》 with a sneer〔contempt〕 ; turn up one's nose at 《a person》 // 다룰 수 없다 be out of care // 그는 다루기 힘든 사나이다 He is a difficult man to handle. // 여자를 마음대로 다루다 control a woman at will // 그 여자는 환자를 잘 다룬다 She is an expert at humoring invalids. // 그는 책을 조심해서 다루었다 He handled books with care. // 나는 카메라를 다룰 줄 모릅니다 I'm not familiar with cameras.
② [가죽 따위를] tan ; dress 《a skin》 ; taw (희게) ; soften ; make pliant ; work (smooth) [별개이다] distinct ; ¶ 다루지 않은 untanned〔raw〕 《hide》 // 다룬 가죽 tanned leather〔skin〕 ; leather ; chamois leather ; shammy (양·사슴의) ; lambskin (새끼 양의) // 나무를 다루다 work wood

다룸가죽 (a) tanned〔dressed〕 skin ; leather ; [양·사슴의] chamois (leather)

†**다르다** [상이하다] differ 《from, with》 ; be different 《from, with》 ; vary 《from》 ; [유별나다] extraordinary ; uncommon ; peculiar ; unusual [불일치] disagree ; do not correspond 《with》 ; be not in accordance 《with》 ; be contrary 《to》 ;

be not in keeping with ¶ 다른 different ; dissimilar ; unlike ; diverse ; divergent ; another ; other // 크기가 다르다 be different in size // 통례와 다르다 diverge from the normal standard // 그것은 아주 다른 문제다 That's quite another pair of shoes. // 그 점 너와 의견이 다르다 I differ with you on that point. // 사본이 원본과 다르다 The copy does not correspond with the original. // 습관은 나라에 따라 다르다 Customs differ from country to country. // 옛날과 전혀 다른 사람이 됐다 Now he is quite another man. // 운임은 거리에 따라 다르다 The rates vary according to the distance. // 저놈들은 짐승과 별로 다를 바 없다 They do not differ much from the beasts. // 품질은 값에 따라 다르다 Quality varies with 〔according to〕 the prices. // 그것은 다른 문제다 That is another problem. // 천재는 역시 다르다 There is something extraordinary in a genius. // 나는 자신이 다른 사람처럼 느껴졌다 I felt myself quite another man. // 알고 있다는 것과 가르친다는 것은 다른 것이다 To know is one thing ; to teach is quite another. // 형과는 달리 그는 야심가였다 Unlike his brother, he was an ambitious person. // 기대와는 달리 그는 낙선했다 Contrary to our expectations, he failed in the election. // 그 소년은 다른 사람과는 다른 재능을 갖고 있다 The boy has unusual talent. // 다른 데도 알아보겠다 I think I'll get a second opinion. / I think I'll shop around. // 이상한데 다른 길로 온 것 같아 Something's wrong here. Aren't we on the wrong road ?

다름아니라 be no more than ; be nothing but ; be nothing less than ; be none other than ¶ 다름아니라 nothing but ; for no other reason than ; just // 다름아닌 당신이니까 Since it is you of all people // 다름아닌 당신의 부탁이니까 나의 힘을 다하지요 Since it is you who ask it, I will try my best. / Since the request comes from you and none other, I will try my best. // 여기 내가 온 것은 다름아니라 자네를 보러 온 것일세 I came here for nothing else but to see you. // 다름아니라 부탁할 것이 있어 왔네 I have come for no other reason than to make a request of you.

다름없다 (be) similar ; like ; be as good as ; be not different 《from》 ; be the same ¶ 전과 다름없는 우정 a steady 〔everlasting〕 friendship // 그는 거지나 다름없다 He is no better than a beggar. // 그 건축은 완공된 거나 다름없다 The building is nearly〔almost, all but〕 completed. // 그것에 관해서는 모르는 거나 다름없다 Very little is known about it. // 그 따위 놈한테 돈을 주는 것은 돈을 버리는 거나 다름없다 You might as well throw away your money as give it to such a fellow. // 그는 죽은 거나 다름없다 He is as good as dead. // 너나 나나 음치임에는 다름없다 You are no more musical than I. // 원숭이나 다름없다 He is for all the world like a monkey. // 이 모자는 신품이나 다름없다 This hat is just as good as new. // 이 말은 협박이나 다름없다 This amounts to a threat. // 받은 거나 다름없습니다 I will take the will for the deed. // 이것은 나에게 마치 사형 선고나 다름없다 This is as much as a death sentence to me. // 그 게임은 진 것이나 다름없다 The game's as good as lost.

다름없이 equally ; similarly ; alike ; in like manner ; in the same way〔manner〕 《as》 ; likewise ; without a change ¶ 전과 다름없이 아름답다 be as beautiful as ever // 전이나 다름없이 애호하여 주십시오 Please favor me as usual.

다릅나무 〖식물〗 Maackia amurensis (학명)

†**다리**[1] a leg ; a limb (사람·동물의) ; a paw (발톱 있는 동물의 앞 다리) ; suckers (문어의) ; a leg ; a leg piece (물건의) ¶ 굵은〔무〕 다리 pudgy〔thick〕 legs ; piano legs // 책상 다리 the leg of a table // 두 다리 동물 a two-legged creature // 세 다리 의자 a three-legged stool // 의자의 다리 chair legs // 다리가 긴 long-legged // 다리가 짧은 short-legged // 다리를 헛딛다 lose〔miss〕 one's footing // 다리를 물리다 be bitten on the leg 《by a dog》 // 다리를 꼬부리다 bend one's legs〔knees〕 // 다리를 뻗다 stretch one's legs // 다리를 꼬다 cross one's legs // 책상다리를 하고 앉다 sit with one's legs crossed ; sit cross-legged

—뼈 a leg bone **—살** the inner part of a thigh **—통** the girth of the leg **— 훅치기** 〖씨름〗 a double right-leg hook **닭—** a drumstick (of chicken) (요리한)

다리

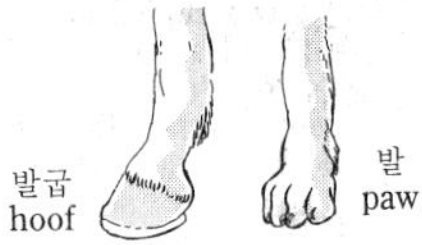

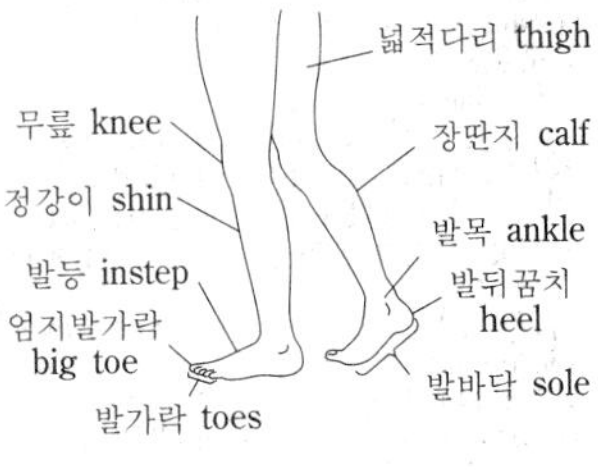

다리[2] ① [교량] a bridge ; [구름다리] a viaduct ; [현수교] a suspension bridge ¶ 궁형 다리 an arch bridge // 다리의 교각 a bridge post // 다리 난간 a bridge rail // 다리 통행세 a bridge toll // 다리를 놓다 build〔throw, lay〕 a bridge across 《a river》 ; span 《a river》 with a bridge ; bridge 《a stream》 // 다리를 건너다 cross a bridge ; go across a bridge // 그 강에는 다리가 두개 놓여 있다 There are two bridges across the river. /Two bridges span the river. // 무거운 차에 다리가 무너졌다 The bridge gave way under a heavy wagon. // 이 다리의 길이는 얼마냐 How long is the span of this bridge?
② [중개] mediation ; good offices
돌― a stone bridge 홍예 ― an arch bridge
다리를 놓다 (관용) mediate〔intermediate〕 《between》 ; act as an intermediary 〔go-between〕

다리[3] [머리의] a false〔an artificial〕 lock of hair ; a toupet〔toupee〕 (프) ; a switch ¶ 다리를 넣다 put on a lock of false hair

다리걸고돌기 〖기계체조〗 knee circling ; the knee circle〔swing〕

다리걸이 〖씨름·유도〗 the scissors ; the leg lock

다리낚아채기 〖씨름〗 a tactic of holding the opponent's foot in one's hand and throwing him

다리다 iron 《clothes》 ; press ; do the ironing ¶ 바지를 다리다 iron out a pair of trousers〔pants〕 ; crease one's trousers neatly (주름잡다)

다리미 an iron ; a flatiron ¶ 전기 다리미 an electric iron // 다리미질하다 iron 〔press〕 《clothes》 ; do the ironing // 밥상보를 다리미로 다렸다 The tablecloth was smoothed out with an iron.
―판 an ironing stand〔board〕

다리바퀴 [무거운 가구의] a caster ; a castor ; a trundle

다리쇠 a trivet ; a tripod ; a spider ; a kettle holder ; fire irons ; a footman

다리품 expenditure of leg energy ; walking ¶ 공연히 다리품만 들이다 use one's leg in vain

다림 plumbing

다림방 a butcher shop

다림보다 ① [겨냥대어] plumb 《the length》 ② [이해 관계를] keep alert to one's own interest ; reckon in advance one's interests and losses

다림살 the path of an iron ; the ease of ironing

다림줄 a plumb line

†다림질 ironing ―하다 iron out 《shirts》 ; press ; do the ironing ¶ 다림질한 ironed ; pressed // 이건 다림질해야겠다 This needs ironing.

다림추 ―錘 a plummet ; a plumb

다림판 ―板 a leveling plate ; a carpenter's level

다릿돌 stepping stones ¶ 다릿돌을 건너다 walk over the stepping stones

다릿목 the approach〔path〕 to a bridge

다마스쿠스 Damascus

†다만 ① [오직] only ; merely ; simply ; alone ; nothing but ; just ¶ 다만 한번 only〔but〕 once // 다만 당신을 위하여 그렇게 했을 뿐입니다 I did it only〔just〕 for your sake〔benefit〕. // 다만 문제는 어떻게 해서 돈을 모으느냐 하는 것뿐이다 The only question is how to get the money. // 다만 웃을 뿐이었다 He did nothing but smile. // 어학의 습득은 다만 연습에 있을 뿐이다 Practice is the only way of mastering a language. // 다만 말한 대로 하면 된다 You have only to do as you were told. // 다만 내 의무를 다했을 뿐이다 I have done nothing but my duty. // 그는 다만 진실을 알고 싶어한다 He merely wants to know the truth.
② [그러나] but ; however ; still ; and yet ; nevertheless ; only ; [조건] provided〔except〕 《that》 ; on condition that ¶ 그는 좋은 결심을 한다 다만 지키지 못할 뿐이다 He makes good resolutions, only he never keeps them. // 무엇을 해도 좋다 다만 남에게 폐를 끼치지 마라 You may do anything you like, provided (that) you do not give trouble to others. // 피로하지는 않다 다만 배가 고플 뿐이다 I am not tired, but I am hungry. // 같이 가도 좋은데 다만 시간이 없다 I would like to go with you, only I have no time.

다망 多忙 pressure〔stress, press〕 of work〔business〕 ; busyness ―하다 (be) busy ; busily engaged ; be pressed by business〔work〕 ¶ 다망한 사람 a busy man // 다망한 1주일 a busy〔rush〕 week // 다망하므로 owing to the pressure〔stress〕 of work〔business〕 // 다망함에도 불구하고 in spite of one's busy life // 나는 여러 가지 일로 극히 다망하다 I am fully occupied with lots of work. // 온종일 다망하였다 I've been kept busy all day long.

다망 多望 a bright future ⇨ 유망 (有望)

다매 多賣 a large sale〔turnover〕

다면 多面 many sides ; many faces 〔phases〕 ¶ 다면적인 many-sided ; multilateral // 다면적인 문제 a many-sided subject
―각(角) a polyhedral angle

다면체 多面體 a polyhedron 《*pl.* -dra, -s》 ¶ 다면체의 polyhedral ; polyhedric // 다면체의 한 면 a facet
정(正)― a regular polyhedron

다모 多毛 hairiness ; hirsuteness ¶ 다모의 hairy ; hirsute
―증(症) 〖의학〗 hirsutism ; hirsuties ―충(蟲) 〖동물〗 a polychaete

다모류 多毛類 〖동물〗 polychaeta (학명)

다모작 多毛作 multiple cropping

다목 〖식물〗 a Brazilwood ; a sappan-

wood ; Caesalpinia sappan (학명)
다목다리 a leg that is blue with the cold
다목장어 多目長魚 a brook lamprey
다목적 多目的 multipurpose
—댐 a multipurpose dam
다못 only ⇨ 다만
다문 多聞 much information ; being well-informed ¶ 다문 박식 much information and wide knowledge // 다문 박식한 사람 a man of various information and wide knowledge ; an erudite
다문다문 once in a while ⇨ 드문드문
다물다 shut ; close 《one's lips》 ¶ 입을 꼭 다물고 with one's lips firmly〔tightly〕 closed // 입을 다물다 be silent ; be shut up ; keep silent ; hold one's tongue ; shut one's mouth ; keep one's lips tight shut // 그의 꼭 다문 입은 강인한 의지를 나타내고 있다 His firm-set〔well-knit〕 lips bespeak an iron will. // 행동을 하든지 입 다물고 있든지 하라 Put up or shut up.
다미씌우다 put〔thrust〕《a blame》 on another ; shift 《a responsibility》 on 《a person》 ¶ 죄를 남에게 다미씌우다 lay the blame on 《a person》 // 실패의 책임을 남에게 다미씌우다 blame 《a person》 for the failure ; lay the failure at another's door // 전책임을 처에게 다미씌우다 throw 〔shift〕 the entire blame on one's wife ; pass the buck to one's wife 《미·구》
다민족 국가 多民族國家 a multiracial nation〔country〕
다박나룻 a bushy〔shaggy〕 beard ; unkempt whiskers ¶ 다박나룻이 난 얼굴 a bushy-bearded face // 다박나룻이 나다 have a shaggy growth of beard
다박머리 disheveled〔unkempt〕 hair ¶ 다박머리 아이 a child with unkempt hair
다반사 茶飯事 a matter of no importance
일상 — a daily event ; an everyday occurrence〔affair〕
****다발** a bundle ; a bunch ; a sheaf (나락 따위) ; a faggot (장작) ; a stack ; a coil (새끼 따위의) ¶ 꽃다발 a bunch of flowers // 다발로 하다 bundle 《things》 up together ; tie 《things》 into a bundle // 짚한 다발 a bundle of straw // 장작은 다발로 판다 Firewood is sold by the bundle.
다발 多發 —하다 [사고 따위가] occur frequently〔often〕 ; [질병 따위가] occur in many places〔localities〕
다방 茶房 a tea room ; a tea house ; a coffee house ; a tea shop 《영》 ; a coffee shop 《미》 ; a coffee room (호텔의)
다방면 多方面 [방면] many quarters ; [방향] many directions ; [측면] many sides ¶ 다방면의 varied ; many-sided ; versatile ; various // 다방면으로 in many quarters // 다방면의 학식 one's many-sided learning // 다방면의 작가 a versatile 〔many-sided〕 writer // 다방면에 취미가 있는 사람 a person of many-sided tastes 〔interests〕 // 다방면에 친구를 가지다 have a varied circle of company // 다방면으로 활동하다 work in various fields of activity
다변 多邊 many-sidedness ¶ 다변적 multilateral
— 외교(外交) a multilateral diplomacy
— 무역(貿易) multilateral trade
다변 多辯 talkativeness ; garrulity ; volubility ¶ 다변의 talkative ; garrulous ; voluble ; long-tongued ; loquacious // 다변에 능사 없다 Great talkers are little doers. // 다변은 웅변이 아니다 A wealth of words is not eloquence.
—가 a great talker ; a prattler ; a chatterbox
다변형 多邊形 〖수학〗 a polygon ¶ 다변형의 polygonal
다병 多病 sickliness **—하다** (be) weak ; infirm ; fragile ; sickly ; frail ; del icate ; be prone to illness ¶ 다병한 사람 a sickly person // 재자(才子) 다병 Men of talents are apt to be of delicate health〔are proverbially frail in health〕.
다보록하다 (be) bushy ⇨ 더부룩하다
다복 多福 great happiness ; great fortune
—하다 (be) happy ; blessed ; blissful ; fortunate ; be favored with good luck
다복다복 in bunches ; in groves ; thickly ; densely ; luxuriantly ; in luxurious growth ¶ 소나무가 다복다복한 언덕 a hill thickly wooded with pine trees
다복솔 a bushy young pine tree
다부닐다 come together in a friendly way ; fraternize ; socialize ; get together
다부 일처 多夫一妻 polyandry ¶ 다부 일처의 polyandrous
다부지다 ① [과단성] (be) determined ; resolute ; firm〔solid〕 (야무지다) ¶ 다부진 여자 a stouthearted woman // 다부진 사람 a tough guy 《미》 // 다부지게 따지다 argue on solid ground // 사람됨이 다부지다 He is a man of firm character. ② [보다 어렵다] be harder than expected ¶ 다부진 일감 a tougher work than expected
다북쑥 ⇨ 쑥[1]
다분히 多分 — much ; a good deal 《of》 ; mostly ; for the most part ¶ 그에게는 시인의 소질이 다분히 있다 He has very much of the poet in him. // 그런 염려가 다분히 있다 It is a matter much to be apprehended. // 그는 다분히 자기 본위이다 He has a very selfish disposition.
다불과 多不過 at (the) most ; at the utmost ; at (the) best ; at the largest ; at the greatest ¶ 다불과 500원 five hundred *won* at most ; no more than five hundred *won* // 다불과 5,000원 정도의 손해일 게다 The loss will not be more than five thousand *won*. // 불과 3마일 정도이다 It is three miles at the most.

다불다불 abundantly ; richly ; [머리털이] in tufts ; [꽃·열매가] in clusters〔bunches〕 **—하다** (be) tufty ¶ 다불다불한 머리털 tufty〔flowing〕hair ; a wealth of hair // 금발이 다불다불한 소녀 a girl with a wealth of golden hair

다붓다붓 at short intervals ; close(ly) ; densely ¶ 다붓다붓 앉다 sit close together

다붓하다 (be) close ; dense ; be at short intervals ¶ 다붓하게 놓다 put〔place〕《books》close together

다붙다 come (close) together ; close in together ¶ 옆에 바싹 다붙다 draw close to each other ; stick together

다붙이다 bring《two things》together〔close〕.

다비 茶毘 『불교』 cremation **—하다** cremate ; reduce the body to ashes
—소(所) a crematory ; a crematorium

다뻑 ⇨ 더뻑

다뿍 to the full ; overflowingly ; brimfully ; to the brim ; plenty《구》

-다뿐 certainly ; indeed ; sure ¶ 우리와 같이 가겠나—가다뿐이겠나 Will you go with us ? Sure !

다사 多事 ① [일이 많음] eventfulness ; storm and stress ; pressure〔press〕of business (다망) **—하다** (be) busy ; eventful ; have much to do ¶ 다사 다난한 해 an eventful year // 나라의 다사 다난한 때를 당해서 in these eventful days ; in these times of storm and stress ; in a critical hour for the country // 그의 일생은 다사하였다 He has an eventful life. // 내외 정세가 다사 다난하다 Event after event is taking place at home and abroad. // 작년은 다사한 해였다 Last year was an eventful one.
② [간섭이 많음] ¶ 다사한 사람 a meddler ; a busybody ; a Nosy Parker《속》; a spoilsport // 다사스럽다 be meddlesome ; be officious // 너도 어지간히 다사스럽구나 How meddlesome you are !

다사다단 多事多端 eventfulness **—하다** (be) eventful ; busy

다사 제제 多士濟濟 a galaxy of intellect〔able men〕;《a party》full of political stars〔talent〕

‡**다산 多産** fecundity ; bearing many young ; [동물의] multiparacity ; [생산의] productivity ; prolificity ¶ 다산의 fecund ; multiparous ; productive ; prolific ; fruitful // 다산 작가 a productive writer // 그녀는 다산계(系)의 여자이다 She is a prolific woman.

다색 多色 many colo(u)rs ¶ 다색의 polychromatic ; versicolor ; multicolored
— 장식(裝飾)〔화법(畫法)〕 polychromy

다색 茶色 light brown ; drab ¶ 다색의 light brown ; brownish

다선 의원 多選議員 a Congressman〔an Assemblyman〕elected for many〔consecutive〕terms

다섯 five ¶ 다섯 배(의) fivefold ; quintuplet // 다섯째 the fifth

다소 多少 ① [많고 적음] large and〔or〕small ; big and〔or〕small ; any ; some ; number (수) ; quantity (양) ; amount (액) ¶ 기부금은 다소간에 고맙게 받습니다 We shall be glad to receive any amount of contribution. // 신청자의 다소에 의해서 결정된다 According to the number of applicants, it shall be settled.
② [얼마만큼] more or less ; somewhat ; a little ; to some extent〔degree〕 ¶ 영어를 다소 한다 speak English a little // 기분이 다소 좋아지다 feel〔get〕somewhat better // 다소 피곤하다 I am a little〔somewhat〕tired. // 그 일에는 너도 다소 책임이 있다 You are also more or less responsible for the matter.

다소곳이 [머리를 숙이고] with one's head drooped〔dropped, bowed〕; with a drooping〔hanging〕head ; [온순하게] obediently ; submissively ; quietly ; gently ¶ 다소곳이 남의 말을 듣다 listen to another's advice with a hanging head〔obediently〕// 수줍은 신부는 다소곳이 앉아 있었다 The shy bride sat mum with downcast eyes.

다소곳하다 be quite courteous with one's lowered head ; (be) modest ; quiet ; gentle ; obedient ¶ 다소곳한 태도 a courteous and obedient attitude

-다손 치더라도 (even) if ; (even) though ; supposing that ; granting〔granted〕that ; however〔no matter how〕... may ; whatever〔no matter what〕... may ¶ 그렇게 말했다손 치더라도 even if one did say so // 아무리 돈이 있다손 치더라도 however〔no matter how〕rich one may be // 설사 무슨 일이 있다손 치더라도 whatever〔no matter what〕may happen ; come what may // 실패한다손 치더라도 해볼 가치가 있다 It is worth attempting though we fail. // 누가 그렇게 말한다손 치더라도 믿지 않겠다 Whoever may say so〔No matter who say so〕, I won't believe it.

†**다수 多數** ① [수] a large〔great〕number ; numbers ; a multitude ; a heap ; a multiplicity

> 참고 **many** 일반어 **innumerable** 헤아릴 수 없을 만큼 다수의, 무수한 **numerous** many와 동의어이지만 딱딱한 말 **manifold** 종류가 많은, 가지가지의 **multifarious** 서로 다른 종류의 것들이 많이 모인

¶ 다수의 many ; innumerable ; numerous ; manifold ; multifarious // 다수의 사람들 a great number of〔great many〕people // 다수의 노동자가 필요하다 Laborers are wanted in large numbers.
② [대부분] a great part ; the majority ;

the mass ; numbers ¶ 국민의 다수 the large mass〔majority〕 of the people // 다수를 믿다 trust to numbers // 다수의 의견에 따르다 agree to the views of the majority // 다수를 위해 소수를 희생하다 sacrifice the few to the many // 그들은 다수를 믿고 횡포를 부렸다 They acted high-handedly by force of numbers. // 학생의 다수는 귀가하였다 The greater part of the students have gone home.
③ [과반수] a majority ; a predominance ; a great part ¶ 근소한 차의 다수 a small〔narrow〕 majority // 압도적 다수 an overwhelming majority // 절대 다수 an absolute majority // 최대 다수의 최대 행복 the greatest happiness of the greatest number // 다수의 횡포 tyranny of the majority // 다수를 점하다 command a majority ; get〔win〕 a majority // 다수결하다 decide by majority // 3분의 2의 다수를 요하다 require a two-thirds majority // 3분의 2 이상의 다수에 의한 의결을 요한다 It is necessary to pass a resolution by a majority of two-thirds or more. // 주민의 다수는 농업에 종사하고 있다 Most〔The greater part〕 of the inhabitants are occupied with agriculture.

다수결 多數決 decision by majority **—하다** decide by majority ¶ 다수결로써 부결하다 vote down by a majority vote // 다수결에 좇다 abide by the decision of the majority.

다수굿하다 (be) obedient ⇨ 다소곳하다

다수당 多數黨 a majority〔dominant〕 party ¶ 그 당은 국회에서의 다수당의 지위를 상실했다 The party lost its majority in the Diet〔Assembly〕.
— 당수 the majority leader

다수표 多數票 majority vote ¶ 다수표를 획득하다 poll a majority

다수확 多收穫 a high yield 《per acre, of rice》 ; abundant yield
— 품종 a high-yield variety 《of grain》

†다스 a dozen (*pl.* ～(s)) 《doz., dz.》 ¶ 연필 한 다스 a dozen pencils // 맥주 두 다스 two dozen bottles of beer // 열 다스 a small gross // 반 다스 half a dozen // 여러 다스의 (many) dozens of... // 다스로 팔다 sell 《things》 by the dozen // 그걸 두 다스만 주시오 I will take two dozens of them.

†다스리다 ① [통치] rule〔reign〕 over ; govern ; [관리하다] manage ; administer ; arrange ; marshal ; regulate ; order ; direct ; preside over

> **참고** **rule**은 「권력을 가지고 지배하다」 **govern**은 「정치를 하다」의 뜻이며 rule은 govern보다 강권적인 의미가 짙다 **reign**은 「주권을 가지고 군림하다」의 뜻

¶ 나라를 다스리다 manage a state ; rule over a country // 무력으로 나라를 다스리다 rule the nation by the sword // 집안을 다스리다 manage〔regulate〕 a household // 물을 다스리다 control flooding ; take river conservancy measures
② [평정하다] put down ; suppress ; pacify ; quell ; subdue ¶ 내란을 다스리다 subdue a rebellion // 싸움을 다스리다 make up a quarrel // 폭도를 다스리다 suppress〔put down, quell〕 the rioters
③ [병을] heal ; cure ; remedy ; set right ; make whole ¶ 병을 다스리다 cure a disease // 상처를 다스리다 heal 《a person》 of a wound
④ [죄를] punish ; bring 《a person》 to punishment〔justice〕 ; penalize
⑤ [통제] control ; keep control over ; regulate ; keep under control ¶ 엄중히 다스리다 exercise strict control over ; control strictly // 홍수를 다스리다 control floods // 물을 다스리다 take flood-control 〔river conservancy〕 measures
⑥ [바로잡다] put 《things》 in order 《trim》 ¶ 교내를 다스리다 keep the school in order

다스하다, 따스하다 (be) warm ; mild (날씨가) ¶ 방안의 다스한 공기 the warm air in the room // 다스한 겨울 a warm〔mild, green〕 winter // 날씨가 다스하다 The weather is mild〔warm〕.

다습 多濕 much moisture ; high humidity ¶ 고온 다습의 hot and humid // 고온 다습한 기후 humid weather **—하다** (be) humid ; damp

다습다, 따습다 (be) nice and warm ; comfortably warm ¶ 몸을 다습게 하다 keep oneself warm // 방이 다습다 The room is nice and warm. // 좋은 난로가 있어서 정말 따스웠어요 With a good stove I was as warm as toast.

†다시 ① [되풀이해서] again ; over again ; once again ; once more ; another time ; a second time ; repeatedly ; twice ¶ 다시 한 번 once more ; a second time // 몇 번이고 다시 many times over ; over and over (again) // 언제 다시 한 번 some other time ; another time // 다시 말하자면 in other words ; that is to say ; namely // 다시 하다 do over again〔once more〕 ; try again ; have another go〔try〕 《at》 // 다시 한 번 해보다 make a second attempt // 다시 쓰다 write over again ; rewrite // 세 번 다시 쓰다 write three times // 일을 다시 시작하다 begin one's work again ; resume one's work ; be back at work // 다시 읽다 read 《a book》 all over again // 고국을 떠난 뒤 다시 돌아오지 않았다 He left his home country never to return. // 그것을 다시 하지 않으면 안 된다 I must do it over again. // 그와는 다시 안 만났다 That was the last I saw of him. // 다시 한 번 말해 보시오 Now say it once more. / Just repeat once more. // 다시는 내집에 들어오지 마시오 Don't darken my doors

again. // 다시 전화하겠습니다〔찾아 오죠〕 I will call 〔come〕 again. // 다시 한 번 말해 주시오 Excuse me? / Pardon me? / I beg your pardon. / What was that again? / Come again? // 사실은 나도 한 때 술을 끊었는데 지금은 다시 마신다 As a matter of fact, I once quit drinking, but I'm off the wagon now. // 당신이 모든 것을 정확히 받아 썼는지 확인하기 위해서 그것을 다시 좀 읽어 주시겠어요 Will you read it back to me to make sure you got everything correct? // 다시 한번 생각해봐 Think twice.
② [새로이] again; anew; afresh; over again ¶ 다시 시작하다 begin anew 〔afresh〕; start all over again // 다시 출발하다 make a fresh〔new〕 start // 다리를 다시 놓다 rebuild a bridge // 나는 라틴어를 다시 하지 않으면 안 된다 I must brush up my Latin. // 모든 연구를 처음부터 다시 하지 않으면 안 되게 되었다 He was forced to go back over all his researches. // 박수 갈채가 다시 일어났다 The cheering was renewed. // 월요일에 배달을 다시 시작해 주세요 Resume delivery on Monday, please.

다시금 again; for the second time; a new ⇨ 다시

다시다 smack one's lips at; [불쾌할 때] click one's tongue at ¶ 입맛을 다시다 smack one's lips; lick one's chops 〔lips〕; [불쾌·분할 때] click one's tongue; regret

다시마 kelp; sea tangle; devil's apron; Laminaria japonica (학명)

다시없다 (be) unique; matchless; unequaled; unparalleled; have no like 〔equal, parallel〕; be never again 〔more〕 ¶ 다시없는 일품 a unique article; only one of its kind // 다시없는 기회 a golden opportunity // 이런 기회는 다시없다 Such an opportunity knocks but once at the door. // 이렇게 경치가 좋은 곳은 다시 없다 The place is unequaled〔has no equal〕 in point of scenic beauty. // 저런 사람은 다시 없으리라 We shall never set eyes on his like. // 저렇게 무자비한 사람은 다시 없으리라 You would scarcely find another so heartless as he.

다시증 多視症 〖의학〗 polyopia

-다시피 [마찬가지로] as; like; sort of; similar to; in the same way 《that》; [같은 정도로] almost; nearly; all but; as good as ¶ 보다시피 as you see // 알다시피 as you know // 무상으로 일하다시피 하다 work for next to no wages // 거의 죽다시피 되었다 He was as good as dead. // 물에 빠져 죽다시피 되었다 I was nearly drowned. / I came near being drowned. // 함대는 거의 전멸하다시피 했다 The fleet was all but annihilated.

다식 多食 gluttony; voracity; hearty appetite; heavy feeding **—하다** overeat; gluttonize; make a pig of oneself

다식 茶食 a kind of pattern-pressed candy made of sesame, chestnut, greenpea flour, honey, etc.

다식증 多食症 〖의학〗 polyphagia; bulimia

다신교 多神敎 polytheism

다실 茶室 a teahouse ⇨ 다방 (茶房)

다심 多心 overcautiousness; excessive scrupulosity; meticulousness **—하다** (be) overcautious; overanxious; nervous; fussy; too meticulous; be given to worries

다액 多額 a large sum〔amount〕 ¶ 다액의 a large sum of 《money》; considerable; huge 《cost》 // 다액의 비용 a huge cost // 다액의 자본〔자금〕 large capital 〔funds〕
—성(性) diversity; multiplicity

다양 多樣 variety; diversity **—하다** (be) various; diverse; manifold ¶ 다양화하다 diversify // 그는 취미가 다양하다 He has many-sided interests. / He is a man of catholic taste.

다언 多言 ① [다변] garrulity; loquacity; volubility; verbosity ¶ 다언은 화근이다 Out of the mouth comes the evil.
② [여러 말] many words ¶ …에 대하여서는 다언할 필요가 없다 There is no need to dwell upon 《the subject》.

다염기산 〖화학〗 polybasic acid

다엽 多葉 ¶ 다엽의 식물에서 multifoliate

다예 多藝 versatility

다오 ① [물건을] give me; let me have ¶ 종이 한 장만 다오 Give me a piece of paper. // 차 한 잔만 다오 Will you give me a cup of tea?
② [···해다오] ¶ 조심해다오 I would have you be on your guard. // 이 문제를 좀 풀어다오 Will you help me (to) do this problem? // 그 얘기 좀 해 다오 Let me hear the story.

다용 多用 **—하다** spend lavishly; use much

다우존스식 —式 the Dow-Jones formula
— 평균 주가(平均株價) the Dow Jones stock industrial average

다운 〖권투〗 a knock-down ¶ 다운시키다 knock down; floor 《미·속》 // 다운되다 be knocked down // 다운됐다가 일어나다 climb off the canvas

다원 多元 〖철학〗 pluralism ¶ 다원적 plural; pluralistic // 다원적 국가론 pluralistic conception of the State
—론 pluralism **— 묘사** descriptions from different viewpoints **— 방송** a broadcast from multiple origination **— 방정식** plural equation

다육 多肉 fleshiness **—하다** (be) fleshy; pulpy; succulent

†**다음** ¶ 다음의 next; following; ensuing; coming; [인접한] adjacent;

adjoining 《room》; [제2위의] second; the rest // 다음에 next; secondly; subsequently; in the second place; after 《me》; next to; second to // 다음 일요일 next Sunday // 다음 정거장 the next station // 다음 주 the next week; the following week // 다음 일요일 (현재에서 보아) next Sunday; (과거 또는 미래의 어느 날에서 보아) the next〔following〕 Sunday // 다음 세대 the next generation // 다음부터는 from now on // 다음 기사 the subjoined〔following, adjoined〕 article // 이 다음에 next time // 하나 다음 next but one // 다음 호에 계속 To be continued (in the next issue) // 다음은 누구 차례입니까 Whose turn comes next? /Who's next? // 동물원에는 이 다음에 가자 Let's go to the zoo some other time. // 다음부터는 조심해라 Be careful in (the) future. // 다음에는 부산에서 만납시다 Let's meet in *Pusan* next time. // 다음과 같다 It is as follows. // 다음에 뭣을 할까요 What shall I do next? // 다음에 뭣을 했습니까 What was done next? // 다음과 같이 말하였다 He spoke as follows. // 다음 사람들이 출석하였다 The following persons were present. // 연설이 끝난 다음에 음악이 있었다 The speech was followed by music. // A씨 다음에 B씨가 국무총리가 되었다 Mr. B succeeded Mr. A as Premier. // 자네 다음에 누가 연설했나 Who spoke after you? // 출석자 중에는 다음 사람들이 있었다 Among those present were the following. // 그러면 다음에 찾아 뵙지요 I'll come back another time then.

다음 多淫 lasciviousness; lustfulness; prurience **—하다** (be) wanton; lustful; lascivious; prurient

다음가다 be second〔next〕 to; come after; rank next〔second〕 to; be in the second place ¶ 뉴욕 다음가는 대도시 the greatest city next to〔second only to〕 New York // 밀턴은 셰익스피어 다음간다 Milton is placed after Shakespeare.

*__다음날__ [이튿날] the following〔next〕 day; [훗날] someday; some time later; another〔some other〕 day ¶ 도착한 다음날 the day after〔following〕 one's arrival // 다음날 아침 일찍이 early the next morning // 그것은 다음날로 미루기로 합시다 Let us leave that for another time. // 다음날 다시 보자 I will see you someday again.

다음다음 next but one; the one after the next ¶ 다음다음 날 the next day after one; the day after next; two days after // 다음다음 역 the next but one station // 다음다음 일요일에 on the Sunday after next

다음 달 the next〔following〕 month ¶ 다음 달 초하루에 on the first day of the coming month // 다음 달로 이월하다 carry 《a thing》 forward to the next month

다음자 多音字 a polyphone

다음절어 多音節語 a polysyllable; a polysyllabic word ¶ 다음절어의 polysyllabic

다음해 the next〔following〕 year; the ensuing year; the year ensuing ¶ 지진의 다음해 the year after the earthquake // 문제를 다음해로 넘기다 carry the matter over to next year

다음호 —號 the next number〔issue〕 ¶ 다음호에 계속 To be continued. // 다음호에 완결 To be concluded (in our next issue).

다의 多義 various〔diverse〕 meanings; polysemy ¶ 다의의 multivocal; equivocal // 다의의 말 a word with many meanings; a multivocal word

다이내믹하다 (be) dynamic

*__다이너마이트__ dynamite ¶ 다이너마이트로 폭파하다 blow up〔shatter〕 《a thing》 with dynamite; dynamite 《a rock》

다이빙 diving ¶ 다이빙을 잘하다 be a good diver; be good at diving
— 경기 a fancy dive〔diving〕 **—대(臺)** a diving〔spring〕 board

다이아 ① [보석] a diamond ② [열차의] a schedule; a diagram; a time(-table) 《시간표》 ¶ 다이아대로 on schedule; on time // 다이아를 변경하다 revise the timetable
— 반지 a diamond ring; a ring set with diamonds

다이아나 Diana

†**다이아몬드** a diamond ⇨ 다이아 ①
— 바늘 [전축의] a diamond stylus **— 혼식(婚式)** a diamond wedding anniversary **— 게임** Chinese checkers

다이아진 〖약〗 diazin(e); sulfadiazine

다이어그램 ① [도표] a diagram ② [예정표] a schedule; a timetable ⇨ 다이아 ②

‡**다이얼** a dial; a radio dial ¶ 다이얼을 돌리다 turn a dial; dial // 다이얼을 맞추다 tune in // 다이얼을 돌려 112번을 부르다 dial 112

다이얼로그 a dialog(ue)

다이오드 diode ¶ 반도체 다이오드 a crystal diode

다이제스트 a digest; [잡지] a magazine digest

다이 캐스팅 〖야금〗 die casting

다인 〖물리〗 a dyne

다작 多作 abundant production; prolificacy in writing **—하다** produce〔write〕 abundantly; be prolific (in writing)
—가 a prolific writer〔author〕

다잡다 ① [감독] exercise rigid〔strict〕 control 《over》; exercise close supervision 《over》; tighten the control 《of students》 ¶ 학생들을 다잡다 put the pupils under strict discipline
② [마음을] brace oneself up; brace〔tighten, strain〕 one's nerves; sober oneself; turn over a new leaf

다잡이 supervising strictly; exercising

strict supervision ―하다 ⇨ 다잡다

*다재 多才 versatile talents ; versatility ―하다 (be) versatile ; talented ; gifted ; many-sided ; have many talents ¶ 다재한 사람 a man of versatile talents ; a many-sided man ; an all-(a)round person ; a person of varied accomplishments〔attainments〕

다정 多情 ① tenderness ; humaneness ; warm-〔kind-, tender-〕heartedness ; affection〔passion〕 (애정) ; emotion (감정) ―하다 (be) affectionate ; warm-hearted ; tender-hearted ; kindhearted ; have a kind〔warm〕 heart ; tender ; passionate ¶ 다정한 사람 a warm-hearted man ; a man of heart // 다정하게 tenderly ; warmly ; affectionately ; sympathetically // 다정하게 손을 잡다 affectionately press 《a person's》 hand ② [우정] a close friendship ; intimacy ―하다 (be) intimate ; familiar ; close ; friendly ; chummy ; thick 《속》 ¶ 다정한 친구 an intimate friend ; a good〔close, great, fast〕 friend ; a familiar ; a chum 《구》 // 다정하게 지내다 be on intimate terms with ; be friends with ; be thick with // 다정한 사이가 되다 make friends with ; become intimate with ; get in with ; get thick with ; get to know 《a person》 better ; come into close association with // 두 사람은 매우 다정한 사이이다 They are hand and〔in〕 glove with each other.

다정다감 多情多感 sentimentality ―하다 (be) passionate ; sentimental ; emotional ; ardent ¶ 다정다감한 사람 a man of sentiment ; a sentimentalist ; an emotional person

다정다한 多情多恨 sensibility ; susceptibility ; sentimentality ; tears and regrets ¶ 다정 다한의 지사 (志士) emotional patriots ; ardent patriots ; a chauvinist // 다정다한한 일생을 보내다 lead a life full of tears and regrets ; lead a life checkered with ardent loves and deep sorrows

다정 불심 多情佛心 tender-heartedness ; kind-heartedness ; compassion

다정자 茶亭子 a tea table

다조지다 exercise strict control over ; make a double-sure ; urge〔press〕 in haste ⇨ 조지다

다족류 多足類 『곤충』 millipeds ; myriapods ; Myriapoda (학명)

다종다양 多種多樣 variety ; multifariousness ―하다 (be) various ; diverse ; multifarious ; variegated ; diversified ¶ 내용이 다종다양하다 contain a wide variety

다죄다 tighten〔stiffen〕 《a thing》 up tautly〔hard〕

다주식 多柱式 ¶ [건축에서] 다주식의 polystyle ; hypostyle
― 건축 a polystyle〔hypostyle〕 building

다주파 多周波 ¶ 다주파의 polycyclic ; multi-frequency

다중 多重 ¶ 다중의 multiplex ; multiple
― 전신법 『무선』 multiplex telegraphy ― 채널 multichannel

다중 多衆 a crowd ; a great〔large〕 number of people ; a host ; hosts ; a multitude

다지다 ① make sure ; make it doubly sure ; keep after 《a person》 ; press 《a person》 for 《a definite answer, promise》 ② [눌러서] harden〔make hard〕 (by stamping, pounding) ¶ 땅을 다지다 harden the ground (by ramming) ③ [음식을] press (seasoned food) ④ [고기를] mince ; hash ; chop up (fine)

다지르다 make sure ; press 《a person》 for a definite answer ; demand assurance ; ask 《a person》 emphatically 《about》 ⇨ 다지다

다질리다 get pressed for a definite answer

다짐 a promise ; a pledge ; an oath ; assurance ; vouching ―하다 pledge ; vow ; swear ; assure ; pledge oneself 《to》 ; give one's word ¶ 다음 주에 다시 오겠다고 다짐했다 He gave his word that he would come back next week.

다짐받다 put 《a person》 on his oath ; make 《a person》 pledge〔promise〕 ; get an assurance from 《a person》 ¶ 다시는 죄를 짓지 않겠다는 다짐을 받고 놓아 주었다 They set him free on his oath that he would never commit a crime again. // 다짐을 받고 준 돈인데 갚을는지 모르겠다 I don't know whether he will pay back the money I lent him on the promise he would pay it back. // 갚겠다는 다짐을 받고 돈을 빌려 주었다 I lent him money on the promise (that) he would pay it back.

다짜고짜로 with neither rhyme nor reason ; peremptorily ; arbitrarily ; whether one will or not ; allowing no excuse ; willy-nilly ; [예고없이] without notice〔warning〕 ¶ 다짜고짜로 뺨을 치다 slap 《a person》 on the cheek all of a sudden // 다짜고짜로 끌고 가다 walk 《a person》 off by force // 다짜고짜로 집을 비우라고 하다 order 《a person》 out of the house without notice // 다짜고짜로 해고하다 dismiss 《a person》 without any reason

다채롭다 多彩― (be) colorful ; varicolored ; variegated ¶ 다채로운 행사 variegated functions

다처 多妻 many wives
일부 ― polygyny ; polygamy

다출혈 多出血 much bleeding ; 『의학』 [산후 따위의] flooding

†다치다 hurt oneself ; get〔be〕 hurt〔injured〕 ; get wounded ; sustain〔suffer〕 an injury ; be damaged ¶ 다친 발 an injured leg // 다치기 쉬운 fragile ; delicate // 다치게 하다 hurt ; injure ; inflict

an injury on 《a person》; do 《a person》 an injury // 몹시 다치다 be badly hurt ; be seriously injured // 발을 다치다 get hurt in the leg // 다행히도 그는 다치지 않았다 Luckily, he escaped unhurt.

-다치더라도 even though ⇨ -다손치더라도

다크 호스 a dark horse ; a sleeper 《미》

다탁 茶卓 a tea table

‡**다투다** ① [싸우다] quarrel〔have a quarrel〕《with a person over a matter》; brawl ; have words with ; argue ; dispute ; have a dispute〔an argument〕; squabble ; wrangle ; engage in a controversy ¶ 쓸데 없는 일로 항상 다투고 있다 They are always at odds about little things. // 울타리 문제로 심히 다투었다 The neighbors had a violent dispute on〔about〕 the boundary. // 그 두 사람은 서로 다투지 않았습니까 Didn't those two have a falling-out with each other?
② [겨루다] contend 《with others for a prize》; compete〔vie〕《with a person for》; struggle 《for》 ¶ 승패를 다투다 contend for victory // 의석(議席)을 다투다 contest an election ; contest a seat in the Assembly // 시간을 다툴 때다 There is no time to lose. // 앞을 다투어 …하다 strive to be first 《for, in doing》; scramble for ; vie with one another 《for, in doing》 // 그들은 주도권을 다투었다 They struggled〔vied with each other〕 for supremacy.

다툼 [싸움] a quarrel ; [논쟁] a dispute ; an argument ; a controversy ; a wrangle ; a brawl ; a squabble ; a row ; [경쟁] a contest ; a competition ; a rivalry ; a contention ¶ 학문상의 다툼 academic controversies // 공명 다툼 a contention for honors // 자리 다툼 the competition for a position // 집안 다툼 a family trouble ; an internal trouble

다툼질 [싸움] quarreling ; wrangling ; squabbling ; having words ; [논쟁] controverting ; arguing ; disputing

다팔다팔 《one's hair》 bouncing up and down ; flowing (in the wind)

다팔머리 bouncing hair

†**다하다**[1] [소모되다] become exhausted ; be used up ; be consumed ; run out ; be all gone ; be spent ; spend itself ; [끝나다] end ; terminate ; come to an end ; come to the end of ; be out〔up, over〕 ¶ 수가 다하다 come to〔be at〕 one's wits' end // 군량이 다하다 the provisions have given〔run〕 out // 수단이 다하다 have played one's last cards // 식량이 다하다 run out of food/The food is all gone. // 힘이 다할 때까지 while〔as far as〕 one's energy lasts // 시간이 다했다 Time is up. // 힘이 다했다 My strength is gone. // 목숨이 다할 때까지 as long as one lives

†**다하다**[2] ① [마치다] finish ; go through ; be through 《with》; accomplish〔achieve〕; fulfil ; perform ; keep ¶ 사명을 다하다 carry out〔perform〕 one's mission // 자기의 의무를 다하다 discharge〔do, perform〕 one's duty // 일을 다하다 finish one's work ; get one's work done // 정치가로서의 일생을 마치다 finish a successful career as a politician
② [다 들이다] exhaust ; use up ; run out of ¶ 수단을 다하다 try〔exhaust〕 every means in one's power ; try everything ; leave no stone unturned〔no means untried〕 // 효도를 다하다 serve one's parents with devotion // 전력을 다하다 do one's best ; do all one can // 필설로 못다 하다 be beyond description // 그는 조국을 위해 할 수 있는 일을 다했다 He did all he could for his country. // 최선을 다해보고 안되면 다시 생각하겠다 I'll give it my best shot, and if I can't hack it, I'll decide what to do then.

다한 多恨 many regrets ; great discontent

다한증 多汗症 【의학】 excessive sweating ; hyper(h)idrosis

다항 선택법 多項選擇法 a multiple choice system

다항식 多項式 【수학】 a polynominal〔multinominal〕 expression

다핵세포 多核細胞 【생물】 a coenocyte

‡**다행 多幸** (good) luck ; good fortune ── **하다** (be) lucky ; fortunate ¶ 다행히도 fortunately ; luckily ; by good luck〔fortune〕; as (good) luck would have it ; in a happy hour〔moment〕 // 다행히 일이 잘되면 with luck on one's side // 불행 중 다행 a happy feature of a misfortune // 다행히도 그는 집에 있었다 I had the luck to find him at home. /By good luck, I found him at home. // 다행히도 근처에는 아무도 없었다 No one happened to be about. // 서울에 친척이 있는 것은 다행이다 It is lucky for you to have a relation〔relative〕 living in *Seoul*. // 당신에게 도움이 된다면 다행입니다 I shall be happy to be of service to you. // 다행히 기차가 늦었기 때문에 탈 수 있었다 Luckily for me the train was late, so I just caught it. // 비가 오지 않아서 다행이었다 It was a good thing〔luck〕 (that) it did not rain. // 그는 좋은 아들을 가져서 다행이다 He is blessed with a good son. // 네가 안 간 것이 다행이다 It is a mercy〔a good thing〕 that you did not go. // 그 사고에서 살아난 것이 다행이다 You are lucky to be alive after being in that accident. // 다행히도 나는 늘 건강하다 Fortunately I am always healthy. /I am always blessed with good health.

다행증 多幸症 [심리] the sense of well-being ; euphoria ; euphory

다혈 多血 sanguineness ; full-bloodedness ¶ 다혈의 sanguine ; full-blooded ; plethoric

—질 a sanguine temperament —한(漢) a hot-blooded fellow

다혈증 多血症 [의학] plethora ; repletion ¶ 다혈증의 plethoric

다홍 —紅 deep red ; crimson ¶ 다홍치마 a crimson skirt

다화 茶話 (a) gossip ; a tea-table talk —회 a tea party

닥나무 〖식물〗 the paper mulberry ; Broussonetia kazinoki (학명)

닥닥 ① [긁는 모양] scraping again and again ; scratching hard ② [갑자기 어는 모양] 《freeze》 solid all over ¶ 닥닥 얼다 freeze up solid all over ③ 《drawing a line》 again and again forcefully

닥뜨리다 ① [직면하다] be faced with ; be confronted by ; meet with ; come upon〔across〕; hit upon ; encounter ; run up against ¶ 곤란에 닥뜨리다 be faced with difficulty ; run〔bump〕against a wall ; strike〔hit, run〕against a snag (불의의 곤란) // 죽음에 닥뜨리다 be confronted by death ; face〔confront〕death ② [몰아치다] press hard ¶ 돈을 빨리 갚으라고 닥뜨리다 dun 《a person》 to repay the money

닥작닥작 thickly covered ⇨ 덕적덕적

닥지닥지 ⇨ 덕지덕지

닥치는대로 at random ; at〔by〕hazard ; randomly ; in a desultory way

*****닥치다** [다가오다] approach ; draw〔come〕near ; be near〔close〕at hand ; come round ; be in the offing ; [임박하다] impend ; be impending ; hand over ; overhang ; be at hand ; gain upon ; be imminent ¶ 눈앞에 닥친 위험 a pressing danger // 시간이 닥치다 time is pressing ; one is pressed for time // 파멸이 그의 눈앞에 닥쳐왔다 Ruin stared him in the face. // 죽음이 닥쳐온다 One's time is drawing near. /One is on the verge〔brink〕of death. // 시험 날이 닥쳐온다 The examination is (near) at hand. // 재난이 그에게 들이닥치다 A misfortune befell him.

닥터 a doctor ; 《속》 a doc.

*****닦다** ① [윤내다] polish 《ware》; give 《anything》 a polish ; burnish 《a metal》; brighten ; scour 《a brass button》; shine 《shoes》; grind 《a lens》; cleanse 《a watch》 ¶ 이를 닦다 brush teeth clean // 구두를 번적번적하게 닦다 put a good shine on one's shoes // 구두를 닦이다 have one's shoes shined
② [훔치다] wipe ; wipe clean ; mop ; wash ; brush ; dry (물기를) ¶ 접시를 닦다 dry a dish with a cloth // 걸레로 마루를 닦다 scrub a floor // 엎지른 물을 닦다 mop up spilt water // 손을 닦다 wipe one's hand 《on, with》 // 눈물도 닦고 안경도 닦아라 Dry your tears and clean your glasses. // 그는 접시를 닦은 뒤에 마루를 닦았다 He wiped the floor after drying dishes.
③ [고르다] level ; make even ; roll ; improve ; smooth ¶ 길을 닦다 improve a road
④ [연마하다] train ; improve ; cultivate ; practice ; harden ; pursue ; drill ; school ¶ 기술을 닦다 improve one's skill ; practice an art // 덕을 닦다 cultivate one's character ; improve upon one's virtue
⑤ [기초·토대를 마련하다] prepare the ground 《for》; pave the way 《for》; solidify one's footing
⑥ [셈을 맞추다] do accounts ; settle〔square〕accounts 《with a person》

닦달 ⇨ 닦달질

닦달질 ① [나무람] scolding ; rebuking —하다 scold ; rebuke ; take 《a person》 to task ; give 《a person》 a good talking-to ② [닦음] polishing ; cleaning —하다 polish ; burnish ; shine ; clean

닦아세우다 scold〔rebuke, rate〕《a person for》; give 《a person》 a scolding〔a good talking-to, a piece of one's mind〕; dress down ; call 《a person》 to account ; speak roughly 《to a person》; reprove 《a person》 to his face ; take〔call, bring〕《a person》 to task 《for》 ¶ 배은 망덕함을 닦아세우다 rebuke 《a person's》 ingratitude ; upbraid〔reproach〕《a person》 for ingratitude // 약속 불이행을 닦아세우다 reproach 《a person》 for breaking his promise // 나는 그가 지각한 것을 닦아세웠다 I gave him a good talking-to for being late.

닦음질 cleaning ; wiping ; clean-up ; sweeping ; scrubbing —하다 clean ; wipe ; mop ; scrub

닦이다 ① [윤냄] be polished ; be burnished ; be shined ; be brightened ; [훔침] be wiped〔scrubbed, washed, cleaned〕 ¶ 이 쟁반은 잘 닦이었다 This tray is well polished.
② [홀닦이다] be rebuked ; be given a good scolding ; be given a good talking-to ¶ 호되게 닦이다 have〔be given〕a good scolding

닦이장이 a polisher ; a shiner ¶ 구두닦이(장이) a shoeshine (boy) ; a shoeblack 《영》

닦이질 polishing ; shining ; burnishing —하다 polish ; shine ; burnish

* **단**[1] a bundle ; a bunch ; a sheaf ; a load ; a faggot ¶ 장작 한 단 a load of firewood // 무 두 단 two bunches of radish // 단으로 팔다 sell by the bunch // 단을 짓다 tie up in a bundle ; make into a bundle

단[2] ⇨ 옷단

단 段 ① [지적의 단위] a *tan* 《about 0.245 acres》 ¶ 밭 2단보 two *tan* of farmland ? ② [신문의 난] a column ¶ 3단 표제 a three-column heading // 이 신문은 1면이

10단이다 This paper consists of ten columns a page.
③ [계급] a grade ; a class ; a rank ¶ (바둑 따위) 9단의 사람 a ninth grader // 단수가 다르다 be not in a class with 《a person》; be not in the same street 《with》《구》; stand on different levels ; be widely apart in ability
④ [문장의] a paragraph ; a passage
⑤ [계단] a step ; a stair (1단) ; a flight of steps ¶ 사닥다리의 단 a rung // 3단의 계단 three flights of stairs

ㄷ

†**단 單** only (one) ; single ; sole ; alone ; once ; no more than ¶ 단 한 사람 only one man ; alone // 단벌 옷 the only suit one has // 단 한 번 only once // 단 한 번도 …않다 never once // 사고의 단 하나의 원인 the only〔sole〕 cause of the accident // 거기에는 잘못이 단 하나도 없다 There is not a single mistake in it. // 단 둘이서 조용히 말씀드리고 싶은데요 I want to talk to you in private.

‡**단 壇** a platform ; a raised floor ; a stage ; a rostrum 《*pl.* ~s, -ra》 (연단) ; a dais ; a pulpit (설교단) ; a terrace (대지) ; a podium ; an altar (제단) ¶ 단에 서다 occupy the platform 〔pulpit〕 // 단상에 나타나다 appear on the platform // 단에 오르다 take the rostrum // 단 위에서 내려오다 descend〔step down〕 from a podium

†**단 但** but ; however ; only ; [조건] provided 〔except〕 《that》 ¶ 단서(但書) a proviso 《*pl.* ~s, ~es》; a provisory clause // 무엇을 해도 좋아 단 남에게 폐를 끼치지 마라 You may do anything you like, provided (that) you do not give trouble to others. // 어디에 가도 좋다 단 저녁때까지는 돌아오너라 You may go wherever you like, provided (that) you come back by evening.

단 團 a band ; a group ; a party ; a body ; a team (경기단) ; a gang (악인 따위의) ¶ 일단의 군중 a crowd of people // 일단의 도적 a band of robbers // 일단이 되어 in a body〔party〕; en bloc 《프》 // 듀이 박사를 수반으로 하는 교육 사절단이 지난 달에 내한했다 The educational mission headed by Dr. Dewey came to Korea last month.

단 斷 decision ; judgment ; resolution ¶ 단을 내리다 make a decision

-단 —端 ¶ 섬의 최남단에 있다 lie on the southern tip〔at the southern extremity〕 of the island

-단 —壇 the world ; circles
문— the world of literature ; the literary circles

단가 單價 a unit cost〔price〕 ¶ 단가 30원에 at 30 *won* a piece // 단가를 절감하다 reduce the unit cost of 《an item》
생산 — the unit cost of production

단가 短歌 a *tanga* ; a kind of short poem

단가 檀家 a parishioner ; a supporter of a Buddhist temple

단가 團歌 the official song of an association

단가살이 單家— the house of a small family ; the life of a small family

단간제 單刊制 a single edition (system) ; a one-edition-a-day system ¶ 복간제에서 단간제로 바뀌다 switch from two editions a day to single daily edition

단갈 短碣 a miniature tombstone〔gravestone〕

단강 鍛鋼 forged steel

단거리[1] [재료] the only material one has〔being available〕

단거리[2] [나무] firewood in bundles〔faggots〕

단거리 短距離 a short distance
— 경주 a short-distance race ; a sprint (race) ; a dash **— 선수** a sprinter ; a dashman **— 수송** short-haul transportation **— 탄도 미사일** a short-range ballistic missile **— 폭격기** a close-range bomber

단검 短劍 a dagger ; a dirk ; a short sword ; a stiletto

단것 sweet things ; sweets ; a sweet

단견 短見 ① [좁은 견해] short-sightedness ; a narrow〔short-sighted〕 view 〔opinion〕 ¶ 단견자 short-sighted persons ; superficial observers ; the shallow-brained〔-hearted〕
② [자기의] my humble opinion ; my personal views

단결 團結 unity ; union ; combination ; solidarity **—하다** unite (together) ; combine ; stand〔hold〕 together ; band together ¶ 국민의 단결 national solidarity // 단결하여 solidly ; in a body ; in union ; in combination // 단결하여 일하다 work with perfect unity // 굳게 단결하고 있다 be closely banded together ; be strongly united // 단결하여 싸울 길밖에 없다 The only way is to unite and fight. // 단결하여 그들에게 대항했다 We banded ourselves against them. // 단결하면 살고 흩어지면 망한다 United we stand, divided we fall. // 단결은 힘이다 Union is strength.

단결에 at a breath ; at once ; at a stretch ; at a stroke ; at a heat ; without missing a chance ¶ 단결에 들이키다 empty 《the glass》 at a draft〔at one gulp〕 // 단결에 일을 끝내다 finish one's work at a stretch // 쇠뿔도 단결에 빼라 Strike while the iron is hot.

단경 斷經 menopause ; natural cessation of menstruation **—하다** go through menopause ; one's menstruation ceases

단경 短徑 〖기하〗 the minor axis

단경기 端境期 a between season ; an off crop〔a pre-harvest〕 season

단계 段階 a step ; a phase ; a stage ; a

gradation (순서) ¶ 교섭은 최후의 단계에 도달했다 Negotiations reached their final stage. // 여론은 이미 이 단계를 지났다 Public opinion has already passed this phase. // 혁명은 새로운 단계에 들어갔다 The revolution entered a new phase.

단곡 短曲 a short piece of music〔poetry〕; a morceau《프》

단골[1] custom ; connection ; patronage ¶ 단골 손님 (거래처) a customer ; a patron ; a client // 단골 술집 one's favorite drinking house // 단골 무당 one's regular shaman // 단골 손님이 많다 have a large connection〔custom〕; enjoy a large patronage // 좋은 단골을 만들다 establish a good connection // 단골을 넓히다 extend one's business connection // 단골 손님 하나 잃은 줄 아시오 You've just lost a steady customer. // 내가 아는 단골집이 한 군데 있지 I have a place, I'm partial to.

단골[2] 〖건축〗 a half-sized tile《기와》

단공 鍛工 a metalworker ; a hammersmith **—소** a smithy

단공류 單孔類 〖동물〗 Monotremata (학명) ¶ 단공류의 동물 a monotreme

단과 單果 a simple fruit

단과 대학 單科大學 a college

단광 單光 〖물리〗 monochromatic light

단광색 單光色 a monochrome ; a single hue

단교 斷交 a rupture ; a severance ; a break of relations **—하다** cut〔break〕off with《a country》; sever the relation with ¶ 두 나라 사이가 단교됐다 Diplomatic relations between the two countries were severed.

단교 경주 斷郊競走 a cross-country race

단구 短句 a phrase ; a short sentence

단구 短軀 short〔small〕stature ¶ 단구의 of short stature ; stocky // 단구의 사람 a stockily built man

단구 段丘 〖지리〗 a bench ; a terrace

단군 檀君 *Tangun*, the founding father of the Korean nation

단권 單卷 a copy ; one volume ; a one volume edition

단궤 單軌 monorail
— 철도 [단선의] a single track(ed) railway ; [외선로의] a monorail

단극 單極 [전기] single pole〔electrode〕

단근 單根 [화학] a simple radical ; [생물] a simple root

단근질 torturing《a person》with a red-hot iron **—하다** torture《a person》with a red-hot iron ; brand a criminal

단금 鍛金 beating gold

단금지교 斷金之交 close friendship

단급 單級 [교육] one class

단기 單騎 a lone horseman ; a single rider ¶ 단기로 적진을 돌파하다 break through the enemy's line on horseback single-handed

단기 短期 a short time〔term〕¶ 단기의 short ; short-term ; short-dated

단기 單機 a single〔lone〕plane ¶ 단기로 적진에 돌입하다 dive into the enemy's position single-handed

단기 團旗 an association banner ; the official flag of an association

단기 單記 single entry

단기 檀紀 [단군 기원] the *Tangun* Era

단기간 短期間 a short period (of time) ; a short space〔span〕of time ¶ 단기간의 체재 a short stay

단기 강습 短期講習 a short(-term) course ¶ 여름 휴가 이용의 영어 단기 강습 a special class of English for the summer vacation

단김에 at a breath ; at a stretch ⇨ 단결에

단꿈 a sweet dream ¶ 단꿈을 꾸다 dream 〔have〕a sweet〔happy〕dream

단나무 bundled firewood ; firewood sold by the bundle〔faggot〕

단내 ① [눌어서] burning〔scorching〕smell ¶ 단내가 나다 smell burning ; give a burning smell
② [코에서 나는] a stuffy smell from one's nostril when one has a high fever

단념 斷念 abandonment ; relinquishment ; despair **—하다** give up ; abandon ; forgo ; relinquish ; despair《of》¶ 단념시키다 dissuade《a person》from 《doing》; make《a person》give up《an attempt》// 그는 성공을 단념했다 He despaired of success. // 그를 설득해서 단념시켰다 I talked him out of the idea. // 미국에 가는 것을 단념했다 I have given up the idea of going to America. // 어떤 일이 있어도 단념 않는다 Nothing can make me give this up.

단단 상약 斷斷相約 a firm pledge ; a solemn promise

단단하다, 딴딴하다 ① [굳다·여무지다] (be) hard ; solid ; adamantine ; [견고하다] firm ; strong ; stout ; stable ¶ 단단한 땅 the solid ground // 단단한 돌 a hard stone // 단단한 방비 the strong defense // 단단한 결심 a firm〔an unshakable〕resolution // 단단한 약속 a solemn promise // 단단한 땅에 물이 괸다 Only a frugal man can save money.
② [매듭 따위가] (be) tight ; strong ; compact ¶ 단단한 매듭 a tight knot
③ [대단하다] (be) great ; extraordinary ¶ 단단한 재미 great fun // 단단한 재산가 a very rich person

단단히, 딴딴히 ① [여무지게] hard ; solidly ¶ 땅을 단단히 다지다 stamp 〔tramp〕the earth down hard // 상자를 단단히 짜다 make a box solidly // 짐을 단단히 꾸리다 pack securely
② [꽉] tight(ly) ; fast ; firmly ¶ 고를 단단히 매다 tie the knot tight // 손발을 단단히 묶다 bind hand and foot tightly // 문을 단단히 잠그다 shut the door tight ; make the door fast

ㄷ

③ [견고히] firmly ; strongly ; solidly ; steadily ; stably ¶ 단단히 결심하다 be firmly resolved ; be grimly determined ; make a firm resolution // 기초를 단단히 하다 lay the foundation firmly 《of》 ④ [크게] greatly ; severely ¶ 단단히 꾸지람 듣다 be severely scolded // 단단히 재미보다 have great fun ; have a good time

단당류 單糖類 [화학] a monosaccharide

단대목 單— a turning point ; a critical point ¶ 단대목에 가서 포기하다 give up at a crucial〔critical, decisive〕 moment

단도 短刀 a dagger ; a dirk ; a short sword ; a poniard ; a stiletto ¶ 단도를 품고 with a dagger in one's bosom // 단도로 찌르다 stab 《a person》 with a dagger ; give a thrust of cold steel

단도직입 單刀直入 straightforwardness ¶ 단도직입적으로 directly ; frankly ; point-blank ; straightforwardly ; without preamble ; without beating about the bush ; without mincing matters〔words〕 // 단도직입적인 질문 a pointblank question // 단도직입적으로 말하면 frankly speaking ; to be frank with you // 단도직입적으로 묻다 ask without preamble // 단도직입적으로 요점을 말하다 come straight to the point

단독 丹毒 [한의] the rose ; erysipelas ¶ 단독성의 erysipelatious

단독 單獨 independence ; singleness ; separateness ¶ 단독의 single ; solitary ; lone ; solo ; sole ; [개개의] individual ; [독립의] independent ; [별개의] separate ; [독력의] single-handed // 단독적으로 independently ; separately ; [독력으로] single-handed ; [혼자서] alone ; by oneself ; singly ¶ 단독 강화를 맺다 conclude a separate peace // 단독으로 그들을 격파하다 beat them single-handed // 단독 비행을 하다 make a solo flight ; fly solo // 단독 행동을 취하다 take an independent action ; act independently〔individually, single-handed, by oneself〕

— **개념** an independent conception — **경제** independent economy — **기관** an exclusive organization — **내각** a one party cabinet —**범** a single-handed offense — **운영** unilateral operation 《of the National Assembly》 — **재판** a single-judge system — **책임** sole responsibility — **회견** an exclusive〔a single〕 interview

단독 강화 單獨講和 a separate peace ¶ 단독 강화를 맺다 conclude a separate peace

단독 비행 單獨飛行 a solo〔lone〕 flight ; a (flying) solo ¶ 단독 비행을 하다 fly solo ; make a solo flight

—**가** a solo flier ; a soloist

단독일신 單獨一身 a person all alone

단독 해손 單獨海損 [상업] particular average 《P. A.》

— **담보** with particular average 《W. P. A.》 ¶ 단독 해손 담보에 대한 약관 an average clause — **부담보(不擔保)** free from〔of〕 particular average 《F. P. A.》

단독 행동 單獨行動 (an) independent action ¶ 단독 행동을 취하다 take independent action

단돈 the small amount of some money ¶ 단돈 백원도 없다 haven't even got a hundred *won*

단동 기관 單動機關 a single-acting engine

단두 斷頭 beheading ; decapitation ; decollation

단두대 斷頭臺 a guillotine ; a scaffold ; a block ¶ 단두대에 오르다 mount the scaffold // 단두대의 이슬로 사라지다 die on the scaffold ; be guillotined

단둘 only two persons ¶ 방엔 단둘밖에 없다 There are only two persons in the room. // 우리 단둘(이)만 가자 Let just the two of us go.

단락 段落 [일의] settlement ; conclusion ; an end ; [문장의] a full stop ; the end of a paragraph ¶ 단락짓다 settle ; finish ; dispose of ; bring 《a matter》 to a conclusion // 이것으로 일단락 지었다 The work has been disposed of for the time being.

단락 短絡 [전기] a short circuit —**하다** short-circuit ; short ; have a short circuit

단란 團欒 harmony(화합) ; a happy (home, family) circel ; a fire-side circle —**하다** sit in a happy circle ; (be) harmonious ¶ 일가 단란한 즐거움 the pleasure of a happy〔sweet〕 home circle // 일가 단란하다 be in the bosom of one's family

단량체 單量體 [화학] a monomer

단려 端麗 grace ; elegance ; beauty —**하다** (be) graceful ; fair ; elegant ; attractive ¶ 단려한 용모 a graceful figure

⁑**단련 鍛鍊** ① [금속을] temper ; forging —**하다** temper ; forge ; anneal ¶ 쇠를 단련하다 temper iron ② [심신을] training ; drilling ; discipline —**하다** train ; drill ; discipline ¶ 단련된 tempered ; trained // 심신을 단련하다 train〔discipline, harden〕 one's mind and body // 신체를 단련하여 고난에 견디다 harden the body against〔inure oneself to〕 hardships // 고난〔전쟁〕에 단련되다 be schooled by adversity〔in war〕 // 태권도는 심신 단련에 도움이 된다 *Taekwondo* is helpful in training one's body and spirit.

단로 短路 〖전기〗 a short circuit

단로 斷路 〖전기〗 a disconnection ; disconnecting

— **스위치** a disconnecting switch ; a disconnect — **플러그** a disconnect(ing) plug

단리 單利 〖경제〗 simple interest
단리 單離 〖화학〗 isolation
단마비 單痲痺 〖의학〗 monoplegia
단막 單幕 one act
—극〔물〕 a one-act drama〔play〕
단말마 斷末魔 one's last moments〔gasp, breath〕; the hour of death ; the point of death ¶ 단말마의 고통 agonies 〔throes〕 of death ; the last agonies ; dying struggles // 단말마의 고함 a death cry // 단말마의 한마디 one's dying words // 단말마에 이르다 be at death's door
단맛 sweetness ; a sweet taste ¶ 단맛이 나다 be〔taste〕 sweet ; have a sweet taste ; be sweetened (감미료를 써서) ; be sugar-coated (당의를 씌워서)
단맥 斷脈 〖광산〗 a leap
단면 斷面 a section ; a sectional diagram (그림) ¶ 사회 생활의 한 단면 a slice 〔phase〕 of social life
단면도 斷面圖 a cross section ; a cross-sectional view
— 부분 a cutaway view〔picture〕
단면적 법칙 斷面積法則 〖항공〗 the area-rule concept
단명 短命 a short life ; a brief span of life ; an early death ¶ 거인은 단명한다 Giants are short-lived. /Giants die young. // 재사 단명 Whom the gods love die young.
단명수 單名數 〖수학〗 a single-unit number
단명 어음 單名— 〖상업〗 a single-name paper
단모음 單母音 a single vowel
단무지 pickled radish
단문 短文 ① [문장] a short sentence ; [작문] a short piece〔composition〕 ② [천학] little knowledge ; superficial learning
단문 單文 〖문법〗 a simple sentence
단물 ① [담수] fresh water ¶ 단물고기 fresh-water fish
② [잇속 있는 부분] the best portion 〔part〕; lion's share ¶ 단물은 혼자서 다 빨아 먹다 take the lion's share ; get all the profit for oneself
③ [맛이 단] sweet water
단물나다 wear out ; be worn out ; become threadbare〔ragged, tattered〕
단박 at once ; immediately ; promptly ; instantly ; directly ; outright ; on the spot ; in another instant ; without delay ; without loss of time ; right away 《미》 ¶ 일을 단박 해치우다 finish a job at a sitting // 군대가 단박 출동했다 The troops were called out without delay〔loss of time〕. // 단박에 답장을 드릴 수는 없습니다 I cannot give you an immediate answer.
단발 單發 ① [한 발] a shot ; a pop 《구》 ¶ 단발에 at a shot ② [발동기] a single engine
—기(機) a single-engined plane **—총** a single-loader
단발 短髮 short〔cropped〕 hair ; crop
단발 斷髮 bob ; bobbed hair ; short hair
—하다 cut〔bob〕 one's hair ; have one's hair bobbed ; wear bobbed hair ¶ 단발 머리 소녀 a bobbed-haired girl // 단발 미인 a beautiful woman with bobbed hair ; a bobbed-haired belle
단방 斷房 sexual abstinence ; continence
—하다 abstain from sexual intercourse ; practice continence
단방 單放 [총포의] a single shot ; [시도] a single try ; a single effort ; [일격에] at a stroke ¶ 단방에 맞히다 kill 《a bird》 at a shot ⇨ 단번
—치기 a single try ; a single effort
단방 單方 [한 가지 약의 처방] a single-medicine prescription ; [효력이 있는 약] an effective medicine
단배 a strong〔keen〕 appetite ; strong desire to eat
단배 주리다 관용 be underfed ; go hungry in spite of a good appetite
단배 單拜 a single ceremonial bow
단배식 團拜式 the New Year's Day celebration 《of an organization》
단백 蛋白 protein ; [흰자위] albumen
—뇨(尿) albuminuria
단백석 蛋白石 〖광물〗 opal ¶ 단백석의 opaline
***단백질 蛋白質** 〖화학〗 protein ; proteide ; [동물·야채의] albumin ¶ 단백질의 proteinic ; proteinous ; proteidic ; albuminous // 단백질이 많은 음식 highly protein food ; protein-rich food // 동물성〔식물성〕 단백질 animal〔vegetable〕 protein // 단백질이 풍부하다 be rich in albuminous substances
단번 單番 only once ; once for all ¶ 단번에 at a stretch〔sitting, stroke, breath〕; at one coup ; at one try // 단번에 시험에 합격하다 succeed in an examination at one's first attempt // 단번에 일을 정하다 decide the issue at a stroke ; settle〔fix〕 a matter once for all
단벌 單— one's only suit 《of clothes》 ¶ 단벌 나들이옷 one's sole Sunday best
단병전 短兵戰 a hand-to-hand fighting
단병 접전 短兵接戰 a fight at close quarters with short weapons ; a hand-to-hand fight
단복 團服 a uniform 《of an association》
단본위제 單本位制 〖경제〗 monometallism ; single standard system ¶ 단본위 화폐 monometallic currency
단봇짐 a handy bundle
단봉낙타 單峯駱駝 ⇨ 단봉약대(單峯—)
단봉약대 單峰— 〖동물〗 an Arabian〔a single-hump〕 camel ; a dromedary
단분수 單分數 〖수학〗 simple fraction
단불용대 斷不容貸 —하다 never admit〔allow〕 of
단비 a welcome〔timely, seasonable〕 rain ; a good〔long-awaited〕 rain ; a gentle

rain
칠 년 대한에 단비 온다 [속담] Long looked for comes at last.
단비 單比 〖수학〗 simple ratio
단비례 單比例 〖수학〗 simple proportion
단사 丹砂 〖광물〗 cinnabar
단사리별 單舍利別 simple syrup
단산 斷産 natural cessation of childbearing **—하다** stop one's childbirth ; suspend one's childbearing ; pass the age of childbearing ¶ 내 처는 몸이 허약해서 서른에 단산했다 My wife has stopped her childbirth at the age of thirty because she was weak.
단삼 丹蔘 a kind of sage plant ; Salvia miltiorrhiza (학명)
단상 斷想 fragmentary〔stray, random〕 thoughts
단상 短喪 short-period mourning (of one year instead of three years)
단상 壇上 ¶ 단상에서 on the platform // 단상에 오르다 take〔be on〕 the platform // 의정 단상에 서다 become a member of the National Assembly
단상 교류 單相交流 〖전기〗 a single-phase current
단색 單色 a single〔simple〕 color ; monochrome ¶ 단색의 unicolored ; monochromatic // 단색으로 그리다 paint in one〔a single〕 color
—광 monochromatic light **—화** a monochrome **— 화법** monochromy
단색 丹色 a red color ; red
단서 但書 a proviso 《*pl.* ~s, ~es》 ; a provisory〔conditional, saving〕 clause ¶ 단서를 붙이다 add the proviso 《that》
단서 端緖 [기원] the birth ; the origin ; [시작] the beginning ; the start ; [초보] the first step ; [실마리] a clue 《to》 ; a trace ¶ 문제 해결의 단서 the first step toward the solution of the question ; a clue for solving a problem // 단서를 열다 begin ; make a beginning ; start ; initiate ; originate // 단서를 잡다 have〔get, gain〕 a clue 《to, for》 ; have a key 《to》 // 문제 해결의 단서를 잡다 get a clue to the solution of the problem // 범인 수사의 단서를 얻다 gain some clues to the criminal's whereabouts // 아직 단서는 못 잡았다 Not a clue has yet been found to it. // 수건이 경찰의 단서가 되었다 The towel put the police on the scent. // 그것이 개혁의 단서가 되었다 It led up to the reform. // 그 비밀에는 단서가 없다 The mystery has no clue to it. // 이것이 그의 출세의 단서가 되었다 This paved the way for his future success. // 단서 조항을 읽어 봐요 Read the fine〔small〕 print.
단서법 斷敍法 〖수사〗 anacoluthia
단석 旦夕 ⇨ 조석 (朝夕)
단선 單線 [한 줄] a single line ; [단궤] a single track ; monorail (외줄의 선로)
단선 斷線 〖전기〗 disconnection ; breaking〔snapping〕 of a wire **—하다** a wire snaps〔is down〕 ¶ 단선으로 on account of broken wires // 눈 때문에 각처에서 단선되었다 Owing to the snow, wires were down in several places.
단선 團扇 a round fan
단성 單性 〖생물〗 unisexuality ; one sex ¶ 단성의 unisexual
— 생식 unisexual reproduction ; monogenesis, parthenogenesis **— 잡종** 〖유전〗 a monohybrid **—화** a diclinous flower
단성 丹誠 sincerity ; devotion
단성 單聲 〖음악〗 a single voice
단세 單稅 the single tax
단세포 單細胞 〖생물〗 a single cell ¶ 단세포의 unicellular
— 동물〔식물〕 a unicellular animal 〔plant〕 **— 생물** a monad
단소 短小 **—하다** (be) small and short ; little ; small ; stunted
단소 短簫 a short bamboo flute
단소 壇所 an altar
단속 團束 [관리] control ; regulation ; management ; [감독] supervision **—하다** control ; regulate ; manage ; supervise ; oversee ; keep〔preserve〕 order ; keep 《something》 in order ¶ 단속의 대상 a subject of control // 단속의 강화 rigid enforcement of regulations // 가사를 단속하다 manage household affairs ; do housekeeping // 교내를 단속하다 keep the school in order // 규칙을 세워 단속하다 control with regulations // 단속이 잘 되어 있다 be well controlled ; be in good order // 단속 불철저로 책망받다 be reprimanded for lack of supervision // 엄중히 단속하다 regulate strictly ; maintain strict control 《over》 // 직공을 단속하다 oversee workmen // 화기를 단속하다 manage (heat of) fire // 네가 그래서야 하급자를 어떻게 단속하겠느냐 If such is the case with you, how can you keep control of those under you ? // 시 당국은 거리에 침 뱉는 사람들을 단속하기로 결정했다 The city government has decided to crack down on people who spit on the streets. // 아마도 극심한 단속을 하지 않아서 그랬을 거야 It's probably because they don't crack down hard enough.
단속 斷續 intermittence **—하다** intermit ; be intermittent ¶ 단속적 intermittent // 단속적으로 fitfully ; intermittently ; by snatches ; off and on ; by fits and starts // 말 소리가 단속적으로 들렸다 I heard snatches of their conversation.
단속곳 a slip ; an under-petticoat ; a Korean underskirt
단속기 斷續器 an interrupter ; a rheotome
단손 but one hand ; one stroke ¶ 단손으로 for oneself ; single-handed // 단손으로 때려 눕히다 knock 《a person》 down with a (single) blow // 단손에 이 일은 다 못한다 I can't do these things all by myself.

단솥 a heated iron pot
단수 斷水 suspension of water supply
—하다 cut〔shut〕 off the water supply ; stop the supply of water ¶ 그들은 전시내의 물을 단수했다 They shut off the water supply over the whole city. // 오늘은 단수합니다 The water is shut off today.
— 구역 a section from which to cut off water supply
*단수 單數 〖문법〗 the singular (number) ¶ 단수의 singular // 단수와 복수 singular (number) and plural (number) // 3인칭 단수 the third person singular // 이 말은 단수로 쓰여 있다 This word is in the singular.
단수 短壽 a short life
단수 端數 odds ; a fraction ; a fractional amount ; an odd sum ¶ 단수를 버리다 omit〔ignore, round off〕 fractions
단수로 短水路 〖수영〗 a 25-meter course
— 기록(記錄) a short-course record
†단순 單純 simplicity —하다 (be) simple ; simple-minded〔-hearted〕 ; uncomplicated ; plain ¶ 단순히 simply // 단순한 생각 a simple idea // 단순한 사람 a simple-minded person // 단순한 생활을 하다 lead a simple life // 단순하게 하다 simplify ; make 《a thing》 simple // 좀더 단순하게 생각하는 편이 좋을지도 모르겠다 It might be better if I take a simple approach.
— 개념 a simple concept —림(林) a pure forest — 점유 〖법〗 naked possession
단순호치 丹脣皓齒 red lips and white teeth ; a beautiful face
단순화 單純化 simplification ¶ 지나친 단순화 oversimplification ; simplism // 단순화하다 simplify // 그는 일을 너무 단순화하는 경향이 있다 He is apt to oversimplify things.
단술 a sweet drink made from fermented rice
†단숨에 單— at a stretch ; at a breath ; at a stroke ; by one effort ; without a break ; at a heat ; at a draught〔gulp〕 (마시다) ¶ 단숨에 마시다 empty〔swallow〕 the glass at a gulp ; toss off 《a glass of wine》 // 단숨에 일을 끝내다 finish one's work straight out // 단숨에 일을 결정짓다 decide a matter by one effort // 단숨에 읽어버리다 finish 《a book》 at a sitting // 단숨에 서울까지 비행하다 make a non-stop flight to *Seoul* ; fly straight to *Seoul* // 단숨에 집까지 달려가다 rush to home without stopping for breath // 독한 술을 그렇게 단숨에 마시면 몸에 좋지 않다 Tossing off hard drinks like that is bad for the health.
단승식 單勝式 a winning system
단시 短詩 a short poem〔verse〕 ; a sonnet
— 작가 a writer of short verses
단시간 短時間 a short time ¶ 단시간에 in a short (space of) time
단시일 短時日 a short (space of) time ¶ 단시일에 in a short (period of) time ; in a day // 사회 개혁은 단시일에 이루어지는 것이 아니다 Social reform is not to be effected in a day.
단시합 單試合 〖정구〗 a single match ; singles
*단식 單式 ① [단일의 방식] a simple system ② 〖부기〗 [단식 기입법] single entry ③ 〖수학〗 a simple expression ④ [정구·탁구의] singles
— 부기 bookkeeping by single entry ; the single-entry system of bookkeeping
— 투표 single vote
단식 斷食 a fast ; fasting —하다 fast ; observe a fast ; abstain from food ¶ 7일간의 단식을 하다 perform a fast of seven days' duration // 단식을 중지하다 break one's fast // 그 여자는 그 날 하루 단식했다 She went without food the whole of that day.
단식구 單食口 a family of one
단식 요법 斷食療法 a starvation cure ; a fasting treatment〔cure〕 ¶ 단식 요법을 하다 practice〔do〕 a fasting cure
단신 單身 alone ; single-handed ; by oneself ; unattended ; solitarily ; without a companion ; [가정에서 떠나] apart from one's family ¶ 단신 남미를 여행하다 travel in South America alone // 단신 적지에 잠입하다 penetrate single-handed into the enemy's territory
단신 短信 a short〔brief〕 letter ; a brief note ; a brief message〔news〕
단신 短身 ⇨ 단구(短軀)
단심 丹心 single-heartedness ; devotion ; sincerity
단심제 單審制 〖법〗 single-trial system
단아 端雅 grace ; elegance ; refinement
—하다 (be) graceful ; elegant ; refined
¶ 단아한 모습 a graceful figure
단안 斷案 [결정] a decision ; [결론] a conclusion ¶ 단안을 내리다 form 〔make〕 a conclusion ; conclude 《that》 // 단안을 내리지 않다 offer no conclusion // 최후의 단안을 내렸다 He made〔gave, brought in〕 a final decision〔verdict〕.
단안 單眼 〖곤충〗 a stemma ; an ocellus
단안경 單眼鏡 a monocle ; [망원경] a monocular telescope
단애 斷崖 a precipice ; a cliff ; a bluff ¶ 단애 위의 등대 a lighthouse on a bluff // 단애를 기어 오르다 clamber up〔scale〕 a cliff // 단애에서 떨어지다 fall over a precipice
— 절벽 a precipitous〔an overhanging〕 cliff ; a sheer precipice
단야 短夜 a short night ; [여름 밤] the short nights of summer
단야 鍛冶 forging
단어 單語 a word ; a vocabulary (어휘) ¶

기본 단어 basic words ; a basic vocabulary // 중요 단어 most frequently used words // 단어를 많이 알고 있다 have a large〔rich〕 vocabulary
— 빈도 word frequency —장 a vocabulary ; a glossary —집 a collection of words ; a word book

†**단언 斷言** affirmation ; (positive) assertion ; averment ; asseveration ; declaration —하다 affirm ; assert ; asseverate ; declare ; aver ; say〔state〕 positively ; avouch ; give one's word ¶ 단언하기를 꺼리다 hesitate to say ; fear to affirm ; refrain from asserting // 단언할 수는 없지만 I cannot say positively〔for sure〕, 《but》 // 그것이 사실임을 단언한다 I affirm〔assert〕 it to be a fact. // 그 일은 단언할 수 없다 I am not positive about it. // 나는 간다고 단언하지 않았다 I did not say definitely that I would go. // 어느 쪽이라고 단언할 수 없다 I cannot commit myself either way. // 그는 그녀의 주장이 허위라고 단언했다 He declared that her allegation was a lie. // 그는 우리에게 내일은 날씨가 좋을 것이라고 단언했다 He assured us that it would be fine tomorrow.

단역 端役 a minor part〔role〕 ; a bit ; a walk-on (part) ; [사람] an extra ; a super 《구》 ¶ 단역을 하다 play a minor part

단연 斷然 ① [단호히] decisively ; resolutely ; firmly ; flatly ; without hesitation ¶ 단연 거절하다 refuse flatly ; give a flat〔point-blank〕 refusal // 단연 반대다 be dead set against // 단연 금연하다 give up cigarettes altogether // 단연 금주하다 swear off drinking
② [결정적으로] decidedly ; definitely ; positively ; absolutely ; by far ; far and away ; by a long way ; (부정) never ; by no means ; on no account ¶ 단연 뛰어나다 show decided superiority ; be a class in itself // 단연 일등이다 be by far the best of all // 단연 유리하다 have a decided advantage // 전체 중에서 단연 이것이 크다 This is far and away the largest. // 단연 두각을 나타내다 cut a conspicuous figure

단연 斷煙 abstention from tobacco ⇨ 금연

단열 斷熱 〖물리〗 ¶ 단열 변화〔압축, 팽창〕 adiabatic change〔compression, expansion〕 // 단열선 an adiabatic curve〔line〕 // 단열 체감 adiabatic lapse

단엽 單葉 〖식물〗 unifoliate

단엽 비행기 單葉飛行機 a monoplane

단오 端午 the *Tano* festival (on the fifth of the fifth month of the year according to the lunar calendar)

단옥 斷獄 judgment of a grave crime ; conviction ; condemnation —하다 convict〔condemn〕 for a grave〔major〕 crime

단운 斷雲 shreds of cloud ; scattered clouds

단원 團員 a member 《of a party, of an association》

단원 單元 〖교육〗 a unit ; 〖철학〗 the monad ⇨ 단자(單子)
—론 monadism ; monadology ; singularism — 제도 the unit credit system

단원제 單院制 the single chamber〔unicameral〕 system ¶ 단원제의 의회 the unicameral legislature

*__단위 單位__ ① [기준 수치] a unit ; a denomination ; 〖철학〗 a monad ; a module (측정하는) ¶ 계산〔매매〕의 단위 the unit of calculation〔trading〕 // 화폐의 단위 a monetary unit // 단위가 같다 be commensurable 《with, to》 // 단위는 천으로 하다 be expressed in (terms of) thousands // 너의 계산은 단위가 틀린다 You calculate on a wrong unit.
② [기준 수량] a unit ¶ 가족을 사회의 단위로 인정하다 take the family as the unit of society // 인구는 천 단위로 표시되어 있다 The population is shown in thousands. // 회사 주식 청약의 단위는 10주이다 The shares of the company are to be sold in blocks of ten.
③ [학습량] a unit ; a credit 《미》 ¶ 필수 단위 required credits // 독어에서 3단위〔학점〕를 따다 take three credits in German
— (노동) 조합 a local (labor) union — 면적 the unit area —원(圓) a unit circle —원(元) the unit element —제(도) the accrediting system — 행렬 〖수학〗 a unit matrix 기본 — a standard〔fundamental〕 unit 절대 — an absolute unit 화폐 — a monetary unit

단위 생식 單爲生殖 〖생물〗 parthenogenesis

단음 短音 〖음악〗 a short sound ¶ A의 단음 short A

단음 單音 single sound ; 〖음악〗 monotone — 하모니카 a monotone harmonica

단음 斷音 〖음성〗 a stop ; 〖음악〗 a staccato 《*pl.* ~s, -ti》
—부(符) a staccato mark — 장치 [피아노의] a damper

단음 斷飮 giving up drinking ; abstinence from drinking ⇨ 금주

단음계 短音階 〖음악〗 the minor (scale) ; the minor mode
선율적 — the melodic minor scale 자연 — the natural minor scale 화성적(和聲的) — the harmonic minor

단음악 單音樂 monophonous music ; monophony

단음절어 單音節語 a monosyllable ; a monosyllabic word

단음정 短音程 〖음악〗 a minor interval

단의 短衣 a jacket ; a waistcoat

†**단일 單一** [단독] singleness ; unity ; [간단] simplicity —하다 single ; singular ; sole ; simple ; individual (개별적)

¶ 단일 항목 a singular item // 단일 주장〔정책〕의 single-issue // 이 물질은 단일 성분이다 This substance consists of one element.
— 경작 monoculture — 국가 a unitary state — 기계 a machine unit — 변동 환율 제 the unitary fluctuation foreign exchange system — 세율 single tariff — 신교(神敎) henotheism — 호봉 single pay(roll) — 환율 a single exchange rate — 후보 a sole candidate

단일화 單一化 simplification ; unification ; unitization **—하다** simplify ; unify ; unitize ¶ 여러 기구의 단일화 the unification of various organizations // 복잡한 절차를 단일화하다 simplify complicated procedures

단자 單字 [글자] a letter ; a character ; [단어] a word

단자 單子 ① 〖철학〗 a monad ② [부의록] a list of gifts ; [후보자 따위의] a list of candidates

단자 短資 a short-term loan ; a call loan 《미》
— 시장 the short-loan market — 회사 a short-term financing company

단자 團子 a dumpling〔doughboy〕 stuffed with honey and sesame

단자 端子 〖전기〗 a terminal
—판(板) a terminal plate

단자론 單子論 〖철학〗 monadology ; monadism

단자엽 單子葉 〖식물〗 a monocotyledon

단작 單作 a single-crop
— 지대 a one-crop area〔belt〕

단작스럽다 (be) dirty ⇨ 던적스럽다

단잠 a sweet〔sound, good〕 sleep ¶ 단잠이 들다 drop off into sound sleep // 단잠을 깨다 wake up from a sound sleep

***단장 丹粧** [화장] toilet ; make-up ; [장식] ornament ; decoration **—하다** make one's toilet ; dress oneself ; make up 《one's face》 ; pretty〔smarten〕 up ; doll oneself up ; [꾸미다] decorate ; ornament ; deck (up, out) ; refurnish ; do over ¶ 정성들여 한 단장 an elaborate toilet // (사무실 따위) 새로 단장하다 furnish up ; give a new look to ; remodel // 새로 단장한 사무실 a newly finished office room // 곱게 단장하고 나서다 go out beautifully dressed up // 그녀는 단장하는 데 몇 분도 걸리지 않았다 She spent only a few minutes on her toilet.

단장 短杖 a walking stick 《영》 ; a cane 《미》

단장 斷章 a literary fragment

단장 斷腸 heartbreak ; a lacerated heart ¶ 단장의 heartrending ; heartbreaking // 단장의 비애 heartbreaking grief // 단장의 비애를 느끼다 feel one's heart rent〔torn to pieces〕 ; one's heart bleeds // 그것을 듣고 단장의 비애를 느꼈다 I felt my heart would break〔bleed〕 to hear that. /My heart was fit to break when I heard it. /It was heartrending news to me.

단장 團長 a commandant ; a leader ; a boss ; a head ¶ …을 단장으로 하여 a party headed by 《a person》

단장 短墻 a low fence

단재 短才 little talent ; want of talent

단적으로 端的— directly ; flatly ; plainly ; frankly ; straightforwardly ¶ 단적으로 말하면 frankly speaking ; to be frank // 내적 생활을 단적으로 나타내다 go full into the inner life 《of》 ; be truly descriptive of the inner life

단전 丹田 the abdomen ¶ 단전에 힘을 주다 strain the abdomen

단전 斷電 [전기가 나감] power failure ; [전력 공급의 중단] suspension of power supply **—하다** suspend power supply ; shut〔cut〕 off electricity

단절 斷切, 斷折 cutting ; severance ; section ; amputation **—하다** cut ; cut off ; chop ; sever ; amputate

단절 斷絶 [가문 따위의] extinction ; [국교의] rupture ; severance ; a break ; [중단] interruption ; stoppage ; discontinuation **—하다** become extinct ; die out ; cease to exist ; [관계가] be broken off ; be severed ¶ 교섭의 단절 the rupture of negotiations // 국교의 단절 the severance〔rupture〕 of diplomatic relations 《between》 // 세대간의 단절 a generation gap // 국교를 단절하다 break off diplomatic relations 《with》 // 그 가문은 단절되었다 The family has died out 〔become extinct〕.
—감 a sense of alienation ; a credibility gap ¶ 그녀는 남편과의 단절감으로 괴로워했다 She was troubled by a sense of alienation from her husband.

단점 短點 a weak point ; a shortcoming ; a defect ; a fault ; a demerit ¶ 단점을 고치다 make up for〔remedy〕 one's defects // 단점을 찌르다 get at 《a person's》 weak point // 그 계획은 장점도 있고 단점도 있다 The plan has both merits and demerits. // 너의 장단점을 다 알고 있다 I know your faults as well as your virtues. // 시골 생활의 단점 the drawbacks of country living // 그 남자에게는 단점이 많다 He is full of shortcomings.

단접 鍛接 welding **—하다** weld

⁑단정 端正 correctness ; rightness ; justness ; uprightness ; decency ; propriety **—하다** (be) correct ; right ; neat ; decent ; proper ; just ; upright ; (정조가) chaste ; constant ¶ 품행이 단정한 사람 a man of upright character〔good moral〕 // 단정히 upright ; straight ; properly ; neatly ; tidily ; smartly // 단정히 앉다 sit up square // 용모가 단정하다 have classical〔neat〕 features // 옷차림이 단정치 못하다 be slovenly〔slatternly, disorderly〕 dressed // 품행이 단정하다 be of upright conduct ; be virtuous // 그는 항상 행실이 단정하다 He is always proper〔correct〕 in his behavior. // 그녀는 몸가짐이 단정했다 She carried herself with grace and dignity.

단정 斷定 [결론] conclusion ; [결정] decision ; [판단] judgment **—하다** conclude ; decide ; judge ; come to a conclusion ¶ 단정을 내리다 draw〔form〕 a conclusion ; conclude 《that》 ; make one's decision ; pass judgment 《upon》 그는 정신이 착란되어 있었다고 단정치 않을 수 없다 I must conclude that he was deranged in mind. /My decision is that he was not mentally sound. // 성급하게 단정해서는 안된다 We must not jump at conclusions. // 그를 도둑이라고 단정하기에는 아직 이르다 It is too early to conclude〔jump to the conclusion〕 that he is the thief.

단정 短艇 a boat ; a cutter (군함의) **— 경조** a boat race ; [대회] a regatta **— 훈련** a lifeboat drill

⁑**단조 單調** monotony ; monotonousness ; dullness ; humdrum ; [음악의] monotone ¶ 단조롭다 (be) monotonous ; dull ; flat ; humdrum ; drab ; monotonic (음악) ; singsong (억양) ; simple ; tactless (방법) // 단조로움을 깨뜨리다 break the monotony // 단조로운 생활을 하다 lead a monotonous〔dull〕 life // 단조롭지 않다 be varied ; be full of variety // 단조로운 빛깔 a dull〔flat〕 color // 단조로운 연설 a dull speech ; a drone // 단조롭게 읽다 read in a monotonous〔singsong〕 tone // 이 경치는 단조롭다 The scenery here is monotonous. /The scene lacks variety. // 그 여자의 작품은 단조롭다 Her works lack diversity〔follow one and the same pattern〕.

단조 短調 〖음악〗 a minor (key) ¶ A 단조 A minor // 마단조의 교향곡 a symphony in E minor

*__단조 鍛造__ forging **—하다** forge

단종 斷種 〖의학〗 sterilization ; castration (거세) ¶ 단종 수술을 하다 sterilize 《a man》

단좌 端坐 —하다 sit straight〔upright〕 ; sit up properly ; [할 일 없이] idle away

단좌식 單坐式 single-seated ¶ 단좌식 비행기 a single-seated plane ; a single-seater

단죄 斷罪 judgment of a crime ; conviction ; condemnation **—하다** convict ; condemn ¶ 단죄되다 be〔stand〕 convicted of a crime

단주 端舟 a boat ; a small ship

단주 端株 〖주식〗 odd-lot〔broken-lot〕 stocks ; an odd lot ; a fractional〔broken〕 lot

단주 斷酒 giving up drinking ; (total) abstinence from alcohol **—하다** stop〔give up, quit〕 drinking ; abstain from liquor ; leave off alcohol ; go dry 《미》 ; be on the wagon 《미·속》

†**단지** a jar ; a pot ; a crock ; an earthenware pot〔jar〕

단지 斷指 —하다 cut off a finger (as one's pledge)

⁑**단지 但只** simply ; merely ; only ; no more than ; just ; alone ¶ 단지 시간의 문제이다 be merely a question of time // 단지 …의 이유로 simply because ; for the sole reason 《that》 // 그는 단지 한 병사에 불과하다 He is a mere private soldier. // 그것은 단지 나 한 사람뿐 아니라 우리 가족 전체에 도움이 된다 It will benefit not only myself, but also all my family. // 그 남자는 단지 웃을 뿐이었다 He did nothing but laugh.

단지 團地 a (public) housing development ; an apartment development 〔area〕 ; a development ; a housing〔an apartment (-house)〕 complex ; a housing estate 《영》 ; a housing project
— 생활 living in a development apartment house **— 아파트** a development house ; a housing-development apartment **공무원 —** a government employees' housing area **공업 —** an industrial park

단지증 短肢症 〖의학〗 phocomelia ; phokomelia

단짝 an intimate friend ; a chum ; one's pal〔partner, mate, fellow〕 ; a crony ; a sidekick 《미·속》

단찰 短札 a short〔brief〕 letter

단참에 單站— at a stretch ⇨ 단숨에

단창 短槍 a short spear ; a javelin

단채화 單彩畫 (a) monochrome
—가 (家) a monochromist **— 화법** monochromy

단처 短處 a weak point ⇨ 단점

단척 短尺 a bolt〔piece〕 of cloth short of standard length〔wanting in length〕

단철 鍛鐵 wrought iron

단청 丹靑 [채색] colors ; [그림] a picture of many colors and designs ¶ 단청의 묘 the exquisite beauty of the painting

단체 單體 〖화학〗 a simple substance ; a simple ; a single element

단체 團體 a body ; a band ; a group ; a company ; a corps ; a party ; [조직체] a corporation (법인체) ; an organization (업자의) ; a community (사회) ; an association ; a unit ¶ 단체를 만들다 form an organization ; make up a party // 단체를 해산하다 dissolve an organization // 단체 여행을 하다 travel in a party ; make a group tour // 단체 행동을 하다 act collectively // 50명 이상의 단체에는 차비를 할인해 준다 For a party of not less than fifty reduced fares are allowed. // 우리들 20명은 단체로 서울 구경을 갔다 Twenty of us made up a party and went to *Seoul* for sightseeing.

— 경기 ⇨ 단체전 (團體戰) — 경주 a team race — 관념 a sense of community life — 관람 a group viewing — 보험 collective insurance — 생활 a group 〔corporate〕 life — 운동 a collective movement — 쟁의 a collective dispute — 정신 a team spirit — 할인 a party- trip reduction (여행의) ; a group reduction — 협약 a collective agreement — 활동 group activity — 훈련 mass training 교섭 — a negotiation body 자선 — a charity organization

단체 교섭 團體交涉 collective bargaining ¶ 단체 교섭을 하다 bargain collectively
—권 the right to bargain collectively ; the right of collective bargaining

단체 여행 團體旅行 traveling in a party ; a group tour ¶ 단체 여행을 하다 travel in a party

단체전 團體戰 〚경기〛 a team sport 〔event〕 ; a team competition ¶ 단체전에서 1등을 하다 lead the team standings // 단체전에서 2등을 하다 place second as a team

단체 행동 團體行動 a collective action ¶ 단체 행동을 하다 act collectively 〔together〕 ; act as a group

단총 短銃 a pistol ; a revolver
기관 — a submachine gun 6연발 — a six-shooter ; a six-chambered revolver

†**단추** a button ; a stud (셔츠 따위의) ¶ 단추를 끼우다 button up 《one's coat》 // 단추를 채우다 fasten a button // 단추를 달다 put on buttons ; sew buttons 《on a coat》 // 단추를 끄르다 unbutton 《a coat》 ; undo〔unfasten〕 buttons // 단추를 떼다 take off a button // 단추가 떨어지다 a button is off〔comes off〕 // 단추가 벗겨져 있다 The button is undone. // 단추가 잠겨져 있지 않소 You've got a button undone. // 바지 단추가 벗겨져 있네요 (완곡하게) Your stable door is open. // 단추 끼워 줄게 이리 온 Come on, my dear. I will button you up. // (초인종의) 단추를 누르다 push〔press, touch〕 the button
금— a gold button 배자 — a vest〔an amber〕 stud 자개 — a shell button

*__단축 短縮__ reduction ; shortening ; curtailment ; condensation —하다 reduce ; shorten ; cut (down) ; curtail ; contract ; condense ; abridge ; abbreviate ¶ 거리를 100마일을 단축하다 cut the distance by 100 miles // 노동 시간의 단축을 요구하다 demand a reduction of working hours ; demand shorter hours // 시간을 단축하다 reduce the time 《of》 // 3페이지로 단축하다 compress〔condense〕 《an article》 into three pages // 여름 방학을 한 달로 단축하다 shorten〔cut down〕 the summer vacation to a month // 학년을 단축하다 shorten the school years // 비행기는 세계의 거리를 단축시켰다 Flying machines have shortened〔cut〕 the distance of the world. // 그곳은 매우 추웠기 때문에 여행 일정을 단축해서 집에 돌아왔다 It was so cold there that I cut my trip short and came back home.
— 수업 shortened school hours —형 〚문법〛 a contracted form 생산 — output reduction ; a cut〔cutback〕 in production 조업 — reduction〔curtailment〕 of operation

단축 短軸 〚수학〛 the minor axis

단출하다 ① [식구가] 《a family》 be small ¶ 그는 식구가 단출하다 He has a small family. /His family is small.
② [일·차림] (be) simple ; handy ; convenient ¶ 단출한 옷 a handy〔convenient〕 garment // 단출한 살림 a simple menage〔household〕

*__단춧구멍__ a buttonhole ; an eye ¶ 단춧구멍을 내다 make a buttonhole // 단춧구멍을 감치다 work buttonholes

단충 丹忠 a true〔perfect〕 loyalty ; an utter devotion

단취 團聚 a happy (family, home) circle ; a happy gathering of close relatives〔friends〕

단층 斷層 〚지질〛 a dislocation ; a fault ; a throw ; a shift ; a jump (광맥의) ¶ 단층으로 되어 있다 be faulted
—면 a fault plane — 산맥 fault mountains — 지진 a dislocation earthquake 사행(斜行) — an oblique fault 소— a slip ; a small fault

단층 사진 斷層寫眞 〚의학〛 [뢴트겐에 의한] a tomogram
—법 tomography

단층집 單層— a one-story(ed) house 《영》 ; a one-storied house 《미》

단침 短針 the short〔hour〕 hand

단칭 單稱 singular
— 명사 a singular term — 명제 〚논리〛 a singular proposition

단칸 單— a single room
—마루 a 6-foot square floor —방 a 6-foot square room ; a single room —살림 (a poor family) living in a single room ; a oneroom household

단칼에 單— with one stroke of the sword〔knife〕 ¶ 단칼에 목을 베다 cut off 《a person's》 head with one stroke (of one's sword)

단타 單打 〚야구〛 a single (hit) ; a base hit

단타 短打 〚야구〛 chopping ¶ 단타를 치다 chop (the ball)

단파 短波 a shortwave ; a shortwave length
— 무전 a shortwave radio — 방송 shortwave broadcasting

단파 수신 短波受信 shortwave reception

단판 單— a single round〔game〕 ¶ 단판 씨름 single-round wrestling // 단판 승부 a one-game〔-bout〕 contest decided by a single round

단판 單瓣 a single valve ¶ 단판의 〖동물〗 univalve(d) ; 〖식물〗 a single-petaled ; unilobed
단판에 單— in a single round ; easily ; at once ¶ 단판에 알아맞히다 make a good guess at once ; guess right easily
단팥죽 sweet red-bean soup (with rice dumplings)
단패 單牌 a single couple〔pair〕
단편 短篇 a short story〔piece〕; a sketch ; a morceau 《프》
— **영화** a short film —**집(集)** a collection of short pieces
단편 斷片 a piece ; a fragment ; a fraction ; a scrap ; a shred ; a snippet ; odds (and ends) ¶ 단편적인 fragmentary ; scrappy ; piecemeal // 단편적으로 in fragments ; scrappily ; 《think》 in patches // 단편적인 개혁 piecemeal reforms // 단편적인 지식 fragmentary knowledge // 단편적 뉴스 snippets of news // 단편적으로 말하다 talk in fragments of words // 그의 지식은 단편적이고 일관성이 없다 His knowledge is fragmentary and unconnected.
단편 소설 短篇小說 a short novel〔story〕; a novelette ; a sketch ; a story (novel에 대하여)
—**가(家)** a (short-) story writer — **선집(選集)** a selection〔a choice collection〕 of short stories
단평 短評 a short comment〔criticism〕; a brief review ¶ 단평을 내리다 make a brief comment 《on》; comment briefly 《on》
시사 — brief comments on current events
‡**단풍 丹楓** [나무] a maple ; [잎] tinged autumnal leaves ; red〔crimson-tinted, scarlet-tinged〕 leaves ; autumnal tints ; crimson foliage ¶ 단풍 들다 turn red〔yellow〕; be tinged with red ; put on autumnal tints // 설악산은 가을 단풍으로 유명하다 Mt. *Sŏrak* is noted for the glorious tints of its autumn foliage. // 산들은 온통 단풍이 들어서 마치 불바다와 같다 The hills are ablaze with autumnal tints. // 그 산의 아름다운 단풍에 감탄할 것입니다 You'll marvel at the beautiful fall foliage of that mountain.
단풍나무 丹楓— a maple (-tree)
단풍놀이 丹楓— an excursion for viewing scarlet maple leaves〔autumnal leaves〕 ¶ 내장사에 단풍놀이를 가다 go to *Naejang* temple to see the scarlet maple leaves there
단풍 들다 丹楓— turn red〔yellow〕
단합 團合 union ⇨ 단결
단항식 單項式 〖수학〗 a monomial (expression)
단핵 單核
—**증(症)**〔구증(球症), 백혈구 증가증(白血球增加症)〕 mononucleosis **전염성(傳染性)** —**증(症)** infectious mononucleosis
단행 斷行 decisive action ; resolute enforcement ; execution —**하다** carry out〔through〕; carry into effect ¶ 계획〔내각 개편〕을 단행하다 (resolutely) carry out a plan〔the reshuffle of the cabinet〕 // 한번 기도한 일은 꼭 단행한다 He carries through anything which he has undertaken.
단행범 單行犯 〖법〗 a single offense (against the law)
단행법 單行法 a special law
단행본 單行本 a book ; a separate volume ; an independent volume ¶ 단행본으로 발간하다 publish in book form // 단행본으로 발간할 가치가 있다 deserve a volume to itself
단현 운동 單弦運動 simple harmonic motion
†**단호 斷乎** —**하다** (be) firm ; resolute ; determined ; decisive ; flat ¶ 단호히 firmly ; resolutely ; positively ; squarely ; conclusively ; in a determined manner ; with a set purpose // 단호한 거절 a flat〔square, obdurate〕 refusal // 단호한 태도로 in a firm〔determined〕 attitude // 단호한 조처를 취하다 take a decisive〔drastic〕 step 《against》 // 단호한 태도를 취하다 throw away one's scabbard ; put one's foot down // 단호히 거절하다 refuse flatly〔absolutely, squarely〕 // 단호히 반대하다 set one's face 《against》; be dead 《against》 // 단호히 배격하다 reject positively
단화 短靴 shoes ; low shoes
단화 單花 〖식물〗 ¶ 단화의 one-flowered ; uniflorous
닫다[1] [사람이] run ; rush ; dash ; dart ; [말이] gallop ¶ 빨리 닫는 말 a swift horse // 전속력으로 닫다 run at full speed
†**닫다**[2] [닫치다] shut ; close ¶ 문을 닫다 close the door〔gate〕 // 창문을 닫다 shut〔close〕 the window // 문을 닫아 두다 keep the door shut // 서랍을 닫다 push a drawer shut // 가게를 닫다 close the shop ; close up shop (폐업하다) // 문을 쾅하고 닫다 bang〔slam〕 the door ; shut the door with a bang // 창문을 닫고 잔다 He sleeps with the windows closed. // 들어오면서 문을 닫으시오 Shut the door after you. // 사용한 후에는 뚜껑을 닫아 주십시오 Put the lid back on after you have used it.
닫아 걸다 fasten〔bolt, latch〕 《a door》 ¶ 문을 안으로〔밖으로〕 닫아 걸다 lock a door from within〔without〕
닫집 a canopy
닫치다 shut〔close〕 《the door》 up ¶ 문을 쾅하고 닫치다 slam〔bang〕 the door ; shut the door with a bang
†**닫히다** be shut〔closed〕; shut ; close ¶ (문이) 저절로 닫히다 shut of itself // 대문이 닫혀 있다 The gate is shut. // 문이 잘 닫히지 않는다 The door does not shut

well. /The door will not shut. // 만나러 가니 문이 닫혀 있었다 I went to see him, but I found his house shut up. // 문이 쾅하고 닫혔다 The door slammed to〔closed with a bang〕.

†**달**[1] ① the moon ¶ 달이 없는 moonless 《night》 // 달빛 moonlight ; moonshine // 달에 비춰진 moonlit 《trees》 // 달의 여신 Diana // 달의 궤도 the lunar orbit // 달 착륙선 the lunar landing〔excursion〕 module // 달 탐험 a lunar expedition // 스무날의 달 a moon twenty days old ; a twenty-day-old moon // 달의 뒷면 the other〔hidden, dark〕 side of the moon // 달이 뜨다 The moon rises〔comes out〕. // 달이 떴다 The moon is up 〔out〕. / There is a moon. // 오늘은 달이 며칠째이지요 How old is the moon?

② [달력의] a month ¶ 큰〔작은〕 달 an odd〔even〕 month // 한 달에 네 번 four times a month // 두 달에 한 번 every other month // 한 달에 5,000원 5,000 *won* per month // 매달의 지불 monthly payment // 책상 위에는 그 달의 잡지가 몇 권 있었다 On the desk there were several periodicals of the current month.

③ [해산할 달] ¶ 달이 차감에 따라 as pregnancy advances // 달이 차지 않은 해산 premature birth // 달이 차지 않은 아이 a premature infant ; a baby born prematurely // (임신) 석 달째다 be three months pregnant // 달이 찼다 Her time came. // 달이 차서 계집아이를 낳았다 At (full) term she gave birth to a girl.

달이 차다〔이지러지다〕 [관용] The moon waxes〔wanes〕.

달도 차면 기운다 [속담] Every flow has its ebb.

달[2] 〖식물〗 a kind of wild reed ; Phragmites japonica (학명)

달[3] [연의] the frame of a kite

⁑**달가닥** with a rattle ¶ 방에서 달가닥 소리가 났다 There was a clatter in the room.

달가닥거리다 rattle ; clatter ¶ 달가닥거리는 접시 소리 the clatter of plates and dishes // 바람에 문이 달가닥거리다 A window rattles in the wind. // 수레가 달가닥거리며 지나간다 A wagon is clattering along the road.

달가닥달가닥 rattling ; clattering ; with a rattle〔clatter〕

달가당 with a clang〔clink, bang〕 ¶ 문이 달가당 잠기다 A door is shut with a bang.

달가당거리다, 딸가당거리다 clang ; clink ; tinkle ¶ 달가당달가당 clinking ; clanging ; tinkling

달가락거리다 rattle ; clatter ¶ 달가락달가락 rattling ; clattering

달가시다 an unlucky〔evil〕 month passes

달각거리다, 딸각거리다 make a rattling sound ; rattle ; clatter ¶ 달각거리는 수레바퀴 소리 the clattering of the wheels // 짐 수레가 달각거리며 지나간다 A cart rattles along.

달갑다 (be) satisfying ¶ 달갑지 않은 손님 an unwelcome guest // 달갑잖은 친절이다 It is a misplaced kindness. /It is an unwelcome favor. /[상대방에게] Thank you for nothing.

달강어 達江魚 〖물고기〗 a sea robin ; Lepidotrigla microptera (학명)

달개 a projection added on to a house ; a penthouse

—집 a penthouse

†**달걀** an egg ¶ 갓낳은 달걀 a new-laid egg // 달걀 껍질 an eggshell // 달걀의 흰자〔노른자〕 the white〔yolk〕 of an egg // 반숙한 달걀 a soft-boiled egg // 날 달걀 a raw egg // 썩은 달걀 an addled〔a rotten〕 egg // 달걀 부침 fried eggs ; an omelet // 달걀색 a light-yellowish color // 달걀술 egg-nog // 달걀 껍데기 an eggshell // 달걀 모양의 egg-shaped ; oval // 달걀을 낳다 lay eggs // 달걀을 부화하다 hatch an egg // 달걀을 품다 sit on eggs // 달걀을 풀다 beat (up) eggs // 달걀을 부치다 fry an egg // 달걀을 깨다 break〔open〕 an egg

바위에 달걀 부딪치기 [속담] It's no use kicking against the pricks.

달거리 ① [열병] monthly fever ② ＝월경(月經)

달게 굴다 badger 《a person to do》 ; tease〔importune, press〕 《a person》 for 《a thing》 ¶ 용돈을 달라고 달게 굴다 tease 《a person》 for pocket money // 그는 아저씨한테 카메라를 사달라고 달게 굴었다 He badgered his uncle to buy him a camera.

달게 받다 submit (tamely) to 《pain, privation, insult》 ; put up with ; be resigned〔reconciled〕 to 《one's fate》 ¶ 모욕을 달게 받다 submit tamely to an insult ; swallow〔put up with〕 an insult // 처벌을 달게 받다 submit to punishment // 학대를 달게 받다 suffer oneself to be ill-treated // 이런 대우는 달게 받을 수 없다 I cannot suffer myself to be treated in this way.

달견 達見 foresight ; clear-sightedness ; excellent〔capital〕 ideas〔views〕

달곰새금하다 (be) sour-sweet

달곰씁쓸하다 (be) bittersweet

달곰하다 ① [맛이] (be) sweetish ; have a sweet flavor ; sweet-flavored ; nicely sweet ¶ 설탕을 넣어서 달곰하게 하다 sweeten 《a thing》 with sugar

② [말이] (be) honeyed ; sugary ; sweet ; fine ; fair ; flattering ¶ 달곰한 말 honeyed〔fine〕 words ; fair speech ; soft things ; cajolery ; flattery // 달곰한 말을 하다 say sweet things 《to》 // 달곰한 말에 속다 be caught〔be imposed upon〕 by another's honeyed words

달관 達觀 a far-sighted view ; a philosophic view ; philosophic ripeness **—하다** take a far-sighted view 《of》 ; see far into the future ; take a philosophic view 《of》 ¶ 그는 세태를 달관하고 있다 He views〔considers〕 human affairs with a philosophic eye. // 그는 모든 것을 달관한 사람이다 He is a philosopher.

달구 a ground rammer

달구경 enjoying〔viewing〕 the moon ; a moonlight〔moon-watching〕 party ¶ 달구경을 하다 enjoy the moonlight

달구다 heat 《metal, stone》 ; make hot ¶ 쇠붙이를 달구다 heat a piece of iron

달구지 a cart ; a wagon ; an ox-cart (소달구지) ¶ 달구지를 끌다 draw a cart

달구질 ramming —하다 ram ; beat down〔pound〕 earth

달굿대 a pole attached to a ground rammer

달궁이 〖물고기〗 a gurnard (달강어)

달그락거리다, 딸그락거리다 rattle ; clatter ¶ 달그락달그락 rattling ; clattering

달그랑거리다, 딸그랑거리다 clang ; rattle ; tinkle ; clink ¶ 달그랑달그랑 with a clang〔clink〕 // 풍경이 바람에 달그랑거린다 A wind-bell is clanging in the wind.

달금하다 (be) sweetish ⇨ 달곰하다

*달기 達氣 a personal appearance that shows promise

달기씨깨비 〖식물〗 a spiderwort ; a dayflower ; Commelina communis (학명)

†달다[1] ① [맛이] (be) sweet ; sugary ; sweet-flavored ¶ 단것 sweet things ; sweets (과자) // 달게 하다 sweeten 《coffee with sugar》 // 과자가 달다 The candy tastes sweet. // 그는 단것을 좋아한다 He is fond of sweets. /He has a sweet tooth. /He goes in for sweets. // 나는 커피를 달게 해서 마신다 I like my coffee sweet. // 그는 단맛 쓴맛을 다 맛본 사람이다 He has tasted the sweets and bitters of life.

② [입맛이] have a keen〔good〕 appetite ¶ 달게 먹다 eat with a good appetite ; eat with gusto〔keen relish〕 // 음식을 참 달게 먹었다 I enjoyed my meal. /I made a good dinner of it.

③ [잠이] satisfactory ; gratifying ¶ 단잠 sweet sleep // 달게 자다 sleep soundly

*달다[2] ① [뜨거워지다] get hot ; become heated ; burn ; glow ; (몸이) feel hot 〔warm〕 ; flush ; burn ¶ 빨갛게 단 부젓가락 red hot tongs // 화끈하게 단 모래 땅 burning sand // 벌겋게 단 숯 glowing charcoal // 빨갛게 달다 become red-hot // 열로 몸이 달다 be burning up with fever ; feel feverish // 부끄러워서 얼굴이 달다 blush for〔with〕 shame // 얼굴이 화끈 달아오른다 My face burns 《with shame》. // 술을 마셔서 얼굴이 달아오른다 My cheeks are flushed with wine.

② [너무 익다] be overboiled〔overdone〕 ¶ 달아지다 be boiled down〔dry〕 // 국물이 다 달았다 The soup is parched up.

③ [마음이 타다] fret ; be fretful ; be nervous ; become impatient ; be irritated ; be anxious to 《see》 ; be tantalized ¶ 애인이 보고 싶어 몸이 달다 be anxious to see one's sweetheart // 시간이 가지 않아 애가 달다 be impatient for the time to pass // 일이 잘 안되어서 마음이 달았다 Failure irritated him greatly.

달다[3] ① [걸다] put〔set〕 up 《a sail》 ; hang out ; suspend ; hoist ; display 《a flag》 ; fly 《a sail》 ¶ 기를 달다 hoist 〔raise〕 a flag // 태극기를 단 배 a ship flying the Korean flag // 문패를 달다 put up one's nameplate // 간판을 달다 hang out〔put up〕 a sign // 태극기를 달고 항해하다 sail under the Korean flag

② [붙이다] attach ; fix ; put on ; tag ; fasten ; stick ; join ; [착용하다] wear ¶ 열차에 식당차를 달다 attach a dining car to a train // 단추를 달다 sew a button on 《a coat》 // 훈장을 달다 wear a decoration〔medal〕 // 너는 단추 하나도 달 줄 모르는구나 You can't even sew on a button.

③ [가설하다] install ; fix ; furnish ¶ 전화를 달다 install a telephone ; fix a telephone 《by the bedside》 // 문에 벨을 달다 fix a bell on the door // 집에 전등을 달다 furnish 《a house》 with electric lamps // 집에 전화를 달았다 We have had a telephone installed in our house. /We are on the phone.

④ [주(註)를] annotate ; annex 《notes to a book》 ; make notes on ; comment 《on》 ; append ; add (something to) ¶ 주석이 달린 교과서 an annotated textbook ; a textbook with notes // 토를 달다 supply the particle(s) // 단서를 달다 annex a proviso (to a deed)

⑤ [장부에] charge 《in a bill》 ; charge to one's account ¶ 외상을 달다 put down〔charge〕 to one's credit account // 내 앞으로 달다 charge 《it》 to my account // 달아놓고 물건을 사다 buy a thing on credit

달다[4] [무게를] weigh ; measure 《the weight》 ¶ 저울로 달다 weigh 《a thing》 in the balance〔on the scales〕 // 체중을 달다 weigh oneself (on a weighing machine) ; take one's weight // 달아서 팔다 sell 《a thing》 by weight // 소금을 저울에 달다 weigh salt (on a scale)

달단 〖역사〗 Ta(r)tary

달달 trembling ⇨ 덜덜

달달 볶다 ① parch 《beans》 ② annoy 《a person》 ⇨ 들들

달떡 a round rice-cake

달뜨다 grow restless ⇨ 들뜨다

달라다 beg ; ask ; request ; appeal ; call upon 《a person》 to 《do》 ; plead 《for》 ; solicit 《for》 ¶ 해달라는 대로 at one's request ; as requested // 하룻밤 재워 달라다 ask for a night's lodging // 출석해 달라다 ask〔request〕 《a person》 to attend // 도와 달라다 appeal 《to a person》 for aid ;

call for help ; call to 《a person》 to help // 연설을 해 달라다 call upon 《a person》 to make a speech

‡달라붙다 stick〔adhere, cling〕 to ⇨ 들러붙다

달라지다 [변화하다] change 《to, from》 ; undergo a change ; alter ; vary (갖가지로) ; shift ; [변형하다] change 〔turn〕 into ; be transformed into ; [수정되다] be revised ; be amended ¶ 달라지지 않다 be〔remain〕 unchanged ; be the same ; be constant // 주소가 달라지다 have one's address changed // 의견이 달라지다 veer round in opinion // 세상이 달라졌다 The world has undergone a change. / We are now in a different world. // 서울의 거리도 많이 달라졌다 *Seoul* has changed a great deal. // 그는 이제 사람이 아주 달라졌다 He is quite another man now. // 바람결이 달라졌다 The wind shifted 《to the west》. // 메뉴가 매일 달라진다 The menu varies from day to day.

달랑, 딸랑 ―하다 ① [가슴이] be much surprised〔startled, frightened, shocked〕 ⇨ 덜렁하다 ② [방울이] 《a bell, ring》 tingle ; jingle

달랑거리다, 딸랑거리다 jingle ; (be) restless ⇨ 덜렁거리다

달랑달랑 ① [방울이] ringing ; tinkling ; jingling ② [까불어 댐] frivolously ; restlessly

달랑달랑하다 ① ⇨ 달랑거리다 ② [돈이] be about to run out

달래 〖식물〗 a wild garlic

‡달래다 [진정시키다] calm (down) ; quiet ; pacify ; placate ; appease ; mollify ; comfort ; [어르다] soothe ; coax ; dandle ; try to please 《a baby》 ; humor ; fondle ; nurse ¶ 달래기 쉬운 placable ; appeasable // 달래기 어려운 inappeasable ; implacable // 슬픔을 술로 달래다 drown one's grief〔sorrows〕 in drink // 화낸 사람을 달래다 calm down 〔pacify〕 an angry man // 우는 아이를 달래다 soothe a crying child // 달래서 승낙시키다 coax 《a person》 into compliance // 가까스로 그를 달래어 집으로 돌려보냈다 I had great difficulty in persuading him to return home. // 그 정도로는 국민의 분노를 달래기에 충분치 않다 That won't be enough to mollify the public's ire. // 네가 그들을 좀 달래주지 않을래 Can't you do something to calm them down ?

†달러 a dollar 《$》 ; a buck 《미·속》 ; a simoleon 《미·속》 ¶ 5달러 지폐 a five-dollar bill〔note〕 ; a fiver 《속》 // 5달러 금화 a half eagle // 10달러 지폐 a ten-dollar bill〔note〕 ; a sawbuck 《속》 // 10 달러 금화 an eagle // 20달러 금화 a double eagle // 1천 달러 a grand 《미·속》 // 달러를 벌다 earn dollars // 달러를 크게 벌어들이는 상품 a big dollar earner 〔winner〕 // 달러로 지불하다 pay in dollars // 달러가 900원으로 내렸다〔올랐다〕 The dollar has fallen〔risen〕 to 900 *won*. // 100달러짜리 두 장, 50달러짜리 다섯 장, 그리고 20달러짜리 열 장 주십시오 Give me two hundreds, five fifties and ten twenties, please. // 주머니에 1달러짜리 지폐를 잔뜩 넣고 다니는 게 낫겠다 I think I'd better carry a bunch of singles in my pocket. **―권** a dollar bloc **― 기근〔위기〕** a dollar gap〔crisis〕 **― 대출〔차관〕** a dollar loan **― 박스** [수입원] a money box ; cashbox ; strongbox ; box- office ; [전주] one's patron〔financial backer〕 **― 부족** dollar shortage〔deficit〕 **― 시세** the exchange rate of the dollar **― 외교** dollar diplomacy **― 자금** dollar funds **― 지역** the dollar area

달려가다 run ; rush ; dash ; dart ; hasten 《to》 ¶ 학교로 달려가다 run to school // 말이 달려가다 A horse is running along. // 현장으로 달려가다 rush to the scene 《of murder》 // 병원으로 달려가다 hasten to the hospital // 아이가 엄마 품으로 달려갔다 The child run to his mother for protection.

‡달려들다 attack〔fall on〕 《the enemy》 ; go at 《a person, a job》 ; spring on 《a person》 ; jump at〔on〕 ; leap on ; fly oneself upon ; rush〔fly〕 at ; grapple with ; pounce upon ; dart at ¶ (물고기가) 먹이에 달려들다 rise at the bait // 전원이 달려들어 with combined〔united, concerted〕 efforts // 세 사람이 나에게 달려들었다 Three men sprang〔leaped〕 at me. // 개가 그에게 달려들었다 A dog flew〔jumped〕 at him. // 세 사람이 달려들어 일을 하루 만에 끝냈다 The three men grappled with the work, and finished it up in a day.

달려오다 hasten〔hurry, rush〕 to 《a place》 ; come running ¶ 사람이 달려오다 A person comes running. // 말이 달려오다 A horse gallops over.

†달력 ―曆 a calendar ; an almanac (책력) ¶ 걸어 놓는 달력 a hanging〔wall〕 calendar // 매일 들춰보는 달력 a block-calendar // 매일 찢어내는 달력 a daily pad calendar // 달력을 넘겨 보다 consult〔refer to〕 the calendar // 달력 상으로는 우기에 들어갔다 According to the calendar, the rainy season has set in.

달로켓 a lunar〔moon〕 rocket ; a mooncraft ¶ 달로켓의 발사 launching of a lunar rocket ; a moonshot

달리 [다르게] differently ; dissimilarly ; in a different〔another〕 way ; in some other way ; distinctively ; [따로] apart ; separately ; [그밖에] extra ; additionally ; in addition ; besides ; [각별히] especially ; particularly ; in particular **―하다** differ 《from》 ; be different 《from》 ; vary 《with》 ¶ 글 뜻을 달리 해석하다 construe the meaning of a sentence differently // 이 돈과 저 돈은 달리 계산되어야 한다 This money must be accounted for separately. // 사장은 그에게 달리 만원을 주었다 The president gave him 10,000 *won* of extra payment. // 달리 취급하다 give 〔accord〕《a person》special〔preferential〕treatment // 그 호텔은 인종에 따라 손님의 대우를 달리한다 The hotel practices race discrimination. // 달리 갈 곳이 있다 I have another place to go to (visit). // 그의 기대와는 달리 그녀는 자금을 마련할 수가 없었다 Contrary to his expectations, she could not raise the money.

달리기 a run ; a spin (탈것으로) ; [경주] a race ; footrace ⇨ 경주(競走)
—선수 a runner ; a racer ; a sprinter **단거리 —** a dash ; a sprint **장거리 —** a (long-) distance race

달리다[1] [부족] run short ; fall short ; run low ; be insufficient ; be in short supply ; be〔come, drop, fall, run〕short《of》; want ; lack ; be lacking《in》; [힘에 부치다] be not equal to ; be not up to ; be not enough ; be no match 〔equal〕for ; be〔fall〕behind ; be inferior to ¶ 능력이 달리다 be wanting in ability ; be incapable // 수학 실력이 달리다 be deficient〔poor〕in mathematics // 힘이 달리다 be not strong enough // 사람 손이〔양식이〕달리다 be short of hands〔provisions〕// 돈이 좀 달리겠는데 I am afraid this money will not go so far. // 우유의 공급이 달린다 The supply of milk is getting tight.

달리다[2] [기운이] sag ; feel languid ; be tired ; be droopy ; [눈이]《one's eyes》feel heavy ¶ 더워서 몸이 달린다 The heat makes me feel languid. // 잠을 자지 못해서 눈이 달린다 My eyes feel heavy from lack of sleep.

†**달리다**[3] [뛰다] run ; rush ; dash ; dart ; hurry ; gallop (말이) ; canter ; [몰다] drive《a car》; urge《a horse》on ; motor《to》¶ 말이 달리다 a horse runs 〔gallops〕// 자동차를 달리다 drive a car // 말을 달리다 gallop a horse // 시속 60마일로 달리다 tear away at sixty miles an hour // 힘껏 달리다 run as fast as one's feet carry one // 전속력으로 달리다 run〔scoot, dash〕at full speed ; drive (a car) at top speed // 급행 열차는 그 거리를 15분에 달렸다 The express covered the distance in 15 minutes. // 이 배는 한 시간에 20노트의 속력으로 달리고 있다 This ship is making twenty knots an hour.

달리다[4] ① [걸리다] hang《on, from》; be suspended《from》; [매달리다] hang down《from》; be hung ; dangle ¶ 높은 가지에 큼직한 감이 한 개 달려 있다 A persimmon as big as a ball hangs high on a branch of the persimmon tree.
② [붙다] be attached ; be fixed ; be coupled ; be appended〔fixed, tagged〕; be added〔annexed〕¶ 주(註)가 달리다 be added with notes // 꼬리표가 달린 트렁크 a trunk with a tag attached〔fixed〕// 이 열차에는 식당차가 달려 있다 There is a dining-car attached to this train.
③ [의존하다] depend on〔upon〕; hang ; hang on ; turn《on, upon》; rest《with》; hinge《on》¶ 상황에 달려 있다 depend upon the situation // 달린 가족이 많다 have many dependents // 장래의 일은 너의 노력에 달려 있다 Your future depends on your efforts. // 결정하는 것은 네게 달렸다 It rests with〔is up to〕you to decide. // 이제 나머지는 전적으로 운명에 달려 있다 Now the rest is entirely up to fate.
④ [가설되다] be built ; be laid ; be installed ; be fitted (up) ; be set〔put〕up ¶ 전등이 달려 있다 an electric lamp is fixed ;《a house》be furnished with an electric lamp // 전화가 달려 있다 A telephone is installed. / The telephone service is operated.

달리아 〖식물〗 a dahlia

달마 達磨 dharma《범》; Dharma (달마 대사)

달 마 다 every month ; monthly ; per mensem《라》

달막거리다, 딸막거리다 move up and down ⇨ 들먹거리다, 뜰먹거리다

달맞이 enjoying〔viewing〕the moon **—하다** welcome〔view〕the first full moon of the new year

달맞이꽃 〖식물〗 an evening-primrose ; a sundrops

달무리 a halo ; a ring〔circle〕around the moon ¶ 달무리가 섰다 The moon has a halo.

달문 達文 a clearly written composition

달밤 a moonlight〔moonlit〕night ¶ 달밤의 moonlit ; moonshiny // 달밤에 산보하다 walk under〔in〕the moonlight

달변 —邊 monthly interest

달변 達辯 eloquence ; fluency
—가 a glib talker ; a fluent speaker

달병 疸病 〖의학〗 jaundice

****달 빛** moonlight ; moonshine ; a moonbeam (한 줄기의) ¶ 달빛을 받은 뜰 a moonlit garden // 달빛을 받은 호수 the lake in the moonlight // 부드럽고 아름다운 달빛 the soft mellow rays of the moon // 달빛이 뜰에 비치다 the garden is bathed in〔is flooded by〕the moonlight

달삯 monthly wage(s)

†**달성 達成** achievement ; attainment ; accomplishment **—하다** accomplish ; achieve《a purpose》; attain《one's object》; carry through〔out〕¶ 세계 평화의 달성 the achievement of world peace // 목표 달성 the attainment of one's goal // 그 목표는 달성하기 힘들다 The object is beyond attainment.

달식 達識 a great insight ; a long sight

달싹거리다 shake ⇨ 들썩거리다

달싹하다 [움직이다] move slightly ; budge ¶ 몸이 아파 달싹도 할 수 없다 I am sick and can't move at all. // 바위가 달싹도 하지 않는다 The rock won't budge an inch.

†달아나다 ① [도망가다] escape ; flee ; abscond ; run away ; take to flight ; make one's escape ; make off ; take to one's heels ; show one's heels ; get 〔break〕 loose (가축 따위가) ; fly away (새가) ¶ 자동차로 달아나다 make one's escape in a car // 살짝 달아나다 sneak away // 달아나는 적을 쫓다 pursue the fleeing enemy // 애인과 함께 달아나다 elope〔run away〕 with a lover // 말이 달아난다 The horse runs away. / The horse gets〔breaks〕 loose. (매어둔 말이) // 새가 새장에서 달아났다 The bird flew out of its cage. // 공항에서 누군가가 내 지갑을 갖고 달아났다 Someone walked away with my purse at the airport.
② [빨리 가다] speed ; scud ; scuttle ; scurry 《away, off》 ; run fast ; run off 〔away〕 ; fly off〔away〕 ¶ 차는 쏜살같이 달아났다 The car sped away. // 학생들은 선생님을 보자 허둥지둥 달아났다 The boys scuttled away〔off〕 when they saw the teacher.

*달아매다 [매달다] hang 《a thing》 up ; suspend ; sling ; [묶다] tie 《a thing》 up ¶ 그네를 달아매다 put up a swing // 공을 실로 달아매다 suspend a ball by a thread

달아보다 [무게를] weigh 《a thing》 ; check the weight 《of》 ; [마음을] fathom ; gauge ; plumb ; size 《a person》 up ; [역량을] evaluate 《a person's》 ability

†달아오르다 ① [뜨거워지다] become red-hot ; glow ; get very hot ¶ 달아오른 쇠 red-hot iron ② [얼굴이] feel hot 〔warm〕 ; burn ; flush ¶ 빨갛게 달아오른 그녀의 얼굴 her face glowing〔aglow〕 with red // 귀가 달아오른다 My ears are burning.

달음박질 running ; a run —하다 run ; rush ; dash ; dart ⇨ 달음질

달음질 ① [경주] a race ; a running race —하다 race ; run a race ② [달음박질] running ⇨ 달음박질

†달이다 boil down 《into》 ; decoct ; infuse ; make a decoction〔infusion〕 《of》 ; brew ; reduce by boiling ¶ 한약을 달이다 boil down medical herb ; decoct herb 《into medical juice》 ; prepare a decoction // 차를 달이다 make〔brew〕 tea

달인 達人 a master 《of》 ; an expert 《at, in》 ; an adept 《at, in》 ; [철인] a mastermind ; a great mind ; a farsighted person

달장근 —將近 about a month ; a month or so ; nearly a month's time ¶ 떠난 지가 달장근이나 된다 It is about a month since he left (home).

달짝지근하다 (be) rather sweet ; sweetish

달착지근하다 (be) rather sweet ; sweetish

달창나다 [해지다] wear out ; 《one's shoes》 be worn out ; 《one's clothes》 become threadbare ; be used up ; [없어지다] run out 《of provisions》 ; be exhausted ; be all gone

달치다 ① [너무 달다] be piping〔steaming〕 hot ; get〔be, become〕 too hot ② [바싹 졸이다] boil 《a thing》 hard 〔dry〕 ; condense 《a thing》 by boiling ; boil down〔away〕

달카닥 with a click —하다 click ¶ 달카닥달카닥 rattling ; clattering // 창문이 달카닥 닫히다 a window shuts with a click

달카닥거리다 keep clicking ; rattle ; clatter ¶ 달카닥거리는 소리 a rattling sound

달카당 with a bang ; with a crash ; rattling ; clattering —하다 bang ; crash ; thud ; bump ¶ 달카당하고 땅에 떨어지다 fall to the ground with a crash // 문을 달카당 닫다 shut a door with a bang

달칵 with a click ⇨ 달카닥

*‡달콤하다 (be) sweetish ; sweet ; have a sweet flavor ; (be) sugary ; honeyed ; saccharine ¶ 달콤한 사랑 sweet love // 맛이 달콤하다 taste sweet ; have a sweet flavor // 달콤새콤하다 sweet and sour ; sour-sweet // 이 오렌지는 달콤새콤하다 This orange has a sour-sweet taste. // 달콤한 말 soft things ; honeyed words // 달콤한 문체 a sugary〔sentimental〕 style // 달콤한 아양 saccharine flattery // 달콤한 재즈곡 a sweet jazz piece // 달콤하게 말하다 talk in honeyed accents ; talk in a wheedling tone // 달콤한 말에 넘어가다 be caught by 《a person's》 sweet talk // 그의 달콤한 말에 주의하는 것이 좋다 You'd better watch out for his sweet talk.

달통 達通 mastery ; conversance ; expertness ⇨ 통달

*‡달팽이 〖동물〗 a snail ¶ 달팽이 껍데기 a snail shell // 달팽이 걸음 a snail's gallop 〔pace〕 // 달팽이 뿔 the horns of a snail // 식용 달팽이 an edible snail // 달팽이처럼 느릿느릿 (walk, proceed) at a snail's pace

달포 about a month ¶ 그가 떠난 지 달포가 된다 It is about a month since he left.

달품 work paid for by the month

달필 達筆 [솜씨] a good〔skillful〕 hand ; [글씨] skillful penmanship ; facile pen ¶ 달필로 쓰여 있다 be written in a good hand〔with a facile pen〕 // 달필을 휘두르다 wield a facile pen

달하다 達— ① [달성하다] accomplish ; achieve ; gain ; secure 《one's end》 ; carry 《one's point》 ; realize 《one's desire》 ¶ 목적을 달하다 accomplish one's purpose ; achieve one's end
② [도달하다] reach ; gain ; attain ; arrive at〔in, on〕 ; get to〔at〕 ; come up

to 《the standard》 ¶ 성년에 달하다 attain〔reach〕 one's majority ; come of age // 산정에 달하다 attain〔reach, gain〕 the summit // 절정에 달하다 come to the climax // 기준에 달하지 못하다 fall short of the standard // 서울시의 인구가 1,200만 명에 달했다 The population of *Seoul* reached 12 million.

③ [수량·정도가] reach ; amount to ; come to ; run up into ; work out at ; cover ; range 《over》 ¶ 1,000만원에 달하다 amount to 10 million *won* ; reach 10 million *won* // 천문학적 숫자에 달하다 run into astronomical figures // 표준에 달하다 come up to the standard // 지원자가 천명에 달하다 the number of applicants mount up to one thousand // 환영회에 초대된 사람은 500명에 달했다 As many as five hundred people were invited to the reception.

†**닭** [암탉] a hen ; [수탉] a cock ; a rooster ; [병아리] a chicken ; [총칭] the fowls 《영》 ; a domestic〔garden〕 fowl ; a barndoor fowl ¶ 닭을 치다 keep〔raise〕 chickens ; keep poultry // 닭이 알을 안다 a hen broods // 알을 잘 낳는〔못 낳는〕 닭 a good〔bad〕 layer

닭 벼슬이 될 망정 쇠 꼬리는 되지 마라 〔속담〕 Better be the head of a dog〔fox, mouse, lizard〕 than the tail of a lion. / Better be the head of a pike than the tail of sturgeon. /Better be first in a village than second at Rome. /Better be the head of the yeomanry than the tail of the gentry.

닭의 새끼 봉이 되랴 〔속담〕 Once a devil, always a devil. /Once a knave, and ever a knave.

†**닭고기** chicken ; fowl

— 수프 chicken soup

닭고집 —固執 a stubborn〔an obstinate, a stiff-necked〕 fellow

닭띠 the zodiacal sign of the Fowl under which one was born

닭백숙 —白熟 boiled chicken

닭볶음 chopped roast chicken ; sautéed chicken

닭싸움 cock-fighting ; a cock-fight

닭의어리 a hencoop ¶ 병아리를 닭의어리로 덮어두다 place〔put〕 a coop over chickens ; coop chickens

닭의장풀 〖식물〗 a spiderwort ; a dayflower

닭의홰 a perch ; a roost ; a hen-roost ¶ 닭의홰에 앉다 be on the perch

*__닭장__ —欌 a henhouse ; a hencoop ; an aviary (대규모) ¶ 닭장에 넣다 house chickens〔fowls〕

닭잦추다 crow repeatedly〔in rapid succession〕 ; crow busily

†**닮다** be〔look〕 like 《a thing》 ; be alike ; resemble ; take after ; bear a resemblance to ; present〔bear〕 similarity to ; have a likeness to ; be similar to ; be the very image of ¶ 꼭 닮다 be as like as two peas ; be the exact counterpart of ; be the spitting image of // 닮지 않다 bear no resemblance to ; look different // 다소 닮은 데가 있다 bear some resemblance to ; have some similarities 《between》 // 그는 아버지를 꼭 닮았다 He is the perfect image of his father. /He is the spit of his father. // 나는 아버지보다 어머니를 많이 닮았다 I take after mother more than father. // 코가 닮았다 They have the same nose. // 아버지 닮지 않은 아들은 없다 Like father, like son. /As the father, so the sons. // 이 두 여행 가방은 서로 닮았다 These two suitcases look alike. // 아드님이 선생님을 닮아 미남인 것 같군요 I think your son inherited your good looks. // 너는 네 아버지를 많이 닮았다 You look very much like your father.

†**닳다** ① [해지다] wear out〔away, down, through〕 ; be worn ; be rubbed off ; be abraded ¶ 닳은 구두 worn-out shoes // 구두 뒤축이 닳았다 The heels are worn down. // 치마끝이 다 닳았다 The skirts are quite worn out. // 전지가 닳았다 The battery went dead. // 타이어는 골고루 닳지 않는다 The tires do not wear evenly.

② [졸다] boil away ; boil down 《to》 ; be boiled down ; be boiled dry ¶ 국이 닳는다 The soup boils down to nothing.

③ 《one's cheeks》 flush with cold

닳리다 ① [해뜨리다] wear 《a thing》 away ; rub 《the nap》 off〔down〕 ; abrade ¶ 연필을 닳리다 wear down the lead of a pencil

② [졸이다] boil down 《the juice》 ; boil 《salt》 dry ; boil away〔off〕 ; condense 《milk》 ¶ 국물을 닳리다 boil the soup away // 약을 다 닳리다 let herb tea boil away

③ 《cold》 make 《something》 flush

†**담**[1] a wall ; a fence (울타리) ¶ 돌〔벽돌〕담 a stone〔brick〕 wall // 흙 담 a mud 〔an earthen〕 wall // 담을 두른 집 a walled-in house // 담을 타고 넘다 climb〔jump〕 over a wall // 담너머로 보다 look over a wall // 담을 두르다 wall 《a place》 in ; surround 《a place》 with a wall

담[2] [머리털 결] ease of combing ¶ 담이 좋다 comb nicely

담 痰 phlegm ; sputum 《*pl.* ~s, -ta》 ¶ 담이 생기다 have〔raise〕 phlegm // 담을 뱉다 expectorate phlegm ; bring〔cough〕 up phlegm // 담이 많이 나다 expectorate much ; cough up much phlegm

—약 an expectorant (medicine)

담 膽 [담낭] gall (bladder) ; liver ; [담력] courage ; spunk ; pluck ; nerve ¶ 담이 크다 be plucky ; be spunky ; be daring ; be bold ; be audacious // 담을 서늘하게 하다 frighten ; make one's blood run cold ; curdle the blood

-담 談 [이야기] a talk ; a story ; a tale ¶ 경험담 a narrative〔story〕 of one's personal experience // 모험담 a tale of an adventure // 성공담 a success story // 여행담 an account of one's travels

담가 擔架 a stretcher ; a litter ⇨ 들것

담갈색 淡褐色 light-brown color ; biscuit ; tan ; ecru

담결석 膽結石 [의학] a gallstone ⇨ 담석(膽石)

***담그다** ① [액체에] soak〔steep, immerse, dip〕 《in water》 ; souse 《something in water》 ¶ 해면을 더운 물에 담그다 soak a sponge in hot water // 옷을 물에 오래 담가두다 give the clothes a long soak // 욕조에 몸을 담그다 lower oneself into a bathtub
② [김치·술 따위] pickle 《greens》 ; brew ; make 《into》 ; salt(절이다) ; preserve with salt ¶ 김치를 담그다 pickle vegetables 《into *Kimchi*》 // 술을 담그다 brew〔make〕 rice wine // 콩으로 간장을 담근다 Soybean is made into soy. // 젓갈을 담그다 preserve fish with salt

담금질 quenching ; tempering ; annealing **—하다** harden ; quench ; temper ; anneal

담기 膽氣 pluck ⇨ 담력(膽力)

†담기다 ① [그릇 따위에] be put in ; be dished up ; be served ; be filled ; [병에] be bottled ; hold ; be barreled〔casked〕 ¶ 이 그릇은 물이 많이 담긴다 This vessel holds a lot of water.
② [의미가] be included〔comprised〕 in ; be put into ¶ 어머니의 사랑이 담긴 편지 a letter filled with my mother's love // 그녀의 말에는 진심이 담겨 있었다 She spoke from the heart.

담낭 膽囊 〖해부〗 the gall (bladder)
—염 〖의학〗 cholecystitis ; inflammation of the gall

†담다 ① [어떠한 물건을] put 《a thing》 in〔into〕 ; bottle (병에) ; [음식을] dish up ; fill ; serve ¶ 반만 담다 fill 《it》 half-full // 사과를 광주리에 담다 put apples into a basket // 음식을 접시에 담다 serve food on a plate〔in a dish〕 // 좀더 많이 담아 달라고 해라 Ask for a larger helping.
② [욕설 따위를] employ 《foul language》 ; speak 《ill, foul》 ; have 《words of abuse》 ¶ 입에 담지 못할 욕을 하다 abuse〔revile〕 《a person》 ; call 《a person》 hard name ; give a scurrilous scolding ; rate 《one's servant》 in foul language
③ [사상이나 감정 따위를] put into ; incorporate 《in》 ; include ; comprehend ¶ 정성을 담은 선물 a gift from 《a person》 with one's best wishes // 그냥 가슴속에 담아 둘 생각이었다 I was going to keep it to myself.

담담하다 ⇨ 덤덤하다

담담하다 淡淡— ① [물이] (be) clear ② [달빛이] (be) bright ¶ 밤하늘에 달빛이 담담하다 A bright moon shines in the sky. ③ [맛이] (be) flat ; plain ¶ 담담한 맛 plain taste ④ [음식이] (be) light ⑤ [심경이] (be) unconcerned ; disinterested ; serene ; tranquil ¶ 담담한 심경 a serene state of mind // 담담한 태도로 임하다 assume a disinterested attitude 《toward》

†담당 擔當 charge ; undertaking **—하다** take charge 《of》 ; be in charge 《of》 ¶ 담당 부서를 지키다 stand by〔stick to〕 one's post // 담당시키다 give 《a person》 charge 《of》 ; put 《a person》 in charge 《of》 // 사건을 담당하다 take charge of the affair // 그는 3학년생을 담당하고 있다 He is in charge of a 3rd-year class. // 그는 수출부를 담당하고 있다 He is in charge of the Export Department
— 변호사 the lawyer in charge **— 업무〔사무〕** the business under one's charge ; one's duty

담당 구역 擔當區域 a district assigned〔allotted〕 to one ; one's round ; [경관 따위의] one's beat ; one's territory (외무원의) ; one's walk (배달원의) ¶ 담당 구역을 순찰하다 make one's rounds

담당 시간 擔當時間 [학교의] one's class hours

담대 膽大 —하다 (be) daring ; bold ; dauntless ; stout-hearted ¶ 담대한 사람이다 He is a man of great courage.

담략 膽略 courage and resourcefulness ¶ 담략이 있다 be courageous and resourceful

†담력 膽力 courage ; pluck ; nerve ; mettle ; grit (미·구) ; guts (속) ¶ 담력 있는 사람 a man of steady nerve〔cool courage〕 ; a daring man // 담력이 있다 (be) courageous ; plucky ; daring ; bold ; nervy ; gritty ; mettlesome // 담력을 기르다 cultivate〔foster, build (up)〕 courage // 담력을 시험하다 put 《a person's》 courage to the test // 그는 담력이 있다 He has plenty of pluck. /He has steady〔iron〕 nerves.

담록색 淡綠色 light〔pale〕 green

담론 談論 discussion ; argument ; discourse **—하다** discuss ; argue ; discourse

담박 淡泊 ① [맛·빛깔이] lightness **—하다** (be) light ¶ 담박한 색 a light color // 담박한 음식 light food〔diet〕
② [마음이] indifference **—하다** (be) indifferent ¶ 금전에 담박하다 be indifferent about money ; do not care much for money

담방 ⇨ 덤벙

담방거리다 act frivolously〔lightly, rashly, carelessly〕 ; bustle ; make a fuss ¶ 그는 담방거리기만 했지 실지 해놓은 일이 없다 He is just bustling around not to get things done.

†담배 tobacco 《*pl.* ~(e)s》 ; [식물] a tobacco plant ; [궐련] a cigarette ; a fag

ㄷ

《속》; [여송연] a cigar; [쌈지 담배] cut〔pipe〕 tobacco; chewing tobacco (씹는 담배); snuff (코담배) ¶ 담배 한 갑 a pack〔package〕 of cigarettes // 담배 한 대 a smoke; a fill (of tobacco) // 담배 한 대 피우다 have a smoke; have a pipe // 담배를 두세 번 뻑뻑 빨다 take a few pulls on one's cigarette // 담배 연기를 둥글게 내뿜다 smoke〔puff〕 rings of smoke; blow a smoke ring // 담배를 끊다 give up smoking // 담배에 불을 붙이다 light a cigarette // 담배에 취하다 smoke oneself sick // 담배로 시간을 보내다 smoke one's time away // 담배를 연달아 피우다 chain-smoke // 담배가 순하다〔독하다〕 the tobacco is mild〔strong〕 // 담배를 피워도 괜찮습니까 Do you mind smoking? // 담뱃불 좀 빌려 주십시오 Please give me〔Let me have〕 a light. / May I ask〔trouble〕 you for a light? // 담배 피우십니까 Do you smoke? // 그 남자는 담배를 피우지 않는다 He is a nonsmoker. /He doesn't smoke. // 이 한 갑만 피우고 담배 아주 끊어 버릴게 I will quit smoking after finishing this pack.

담배 가게 a cigar store 《미》; a tobacco shop 《영》

담배꽁초 a half-smoked〔-consumed〕 cigarette〔cigar〕; a cigarette butt

담배물부리 [담뱃대의] a mouthpiece of a pipe; [궐련의] a cigarette holder

담배설대 a bamboo-stem of a pipe

담배 쌈지 a tobacco pouch

담배칼 a tobacco-leaf cutter

담뱃갑 —匣 a cigarette case; a tobacco box

담뱃값 money for tobacco; cigarette money; [적은 사례금] a small amount of money as reward; a tip ¶ 담뱃값으로 1,000원 주다 give 《a person》 ten hundred *won* for tobacco〔smokes〕; tip 《a person》 1,000 *won* // 담뱃값도 없다 I haven't even enough for a cigarette.

담뱃대 a tobacco pipe; a pipe ¶ 담뱃대를 입에 물고 (with a) pipe in (one's) mouth // 담뱃대를 털다 knock the ashes out of one's pipe // 담뱃대에 담배를 담다 fill one's pipe

담뱃불 a light for one's cigarette〔pipe〕; the light(glow) of a cigarette ¶ 담뱃불 좀 얻을 수 있습니까 May I trouble you for a light? /Would you give me a light?

담뱃재 tobacco ashes ¶ 담뱃재를 털다 flick the ashes off a cigarette

담뱃진 tobacco tar(s); nicotine

담벼락 [담] (the surface of) a wall; [사람] a blockhead

담벼락하고 말하는 셈이다 속담 Talking to the wall.

‡**담보** 擔保 security; mortgage; a guarantee; a warrant; a surety; a cover; a hypothec; collateral **—하다** give〔lay, put〕 to pledge〔in security〕; give〔offer〕 as a security; put up as security ¶ 무담보로 without security; unsecured // 담보로 잡다 take〔receive〕 《a thing》 as security; mortgage; hypothecate // 점포〔토지〕를 담보로 잡히다 mortgage one's store〔land〕; offer one's store〔land〕 as a security // 그는 집을 담보로 잡고 돈을 빌려 주겠다고 제의했다 He offered a mortgage on house property as security. // 그 상품은 모두 담보로 잡혀 있다 All the goods lie〔are〕 in pledge. // 나는 다만 자네가 나한테 돈을 빌리려면 담보를 하나 설정하라는 것뿐이야 I just want you to put up collateral for a loan.

— 계약 a warranty **—권** a security right **—금** a security **—물** a security **— 물권** real rights granted by way of security **—부(付) 대부** secured〔covered〕 loan **—부 사채** a secured debenture **—부 채권** a mortgage bond **—인** a guarantor; a voucher **— 증서** a warranty deed **— 책임** responsibility for security **대물 —** impersonal security **대인 —** personal security **이중 —** double securities **제일 —** the underlying mortgage

담북장 —醬 a bean paste made by mixing and steaming powdered beanpaste, powdered rice with red pepper, and mashed ginger

담불[1] a stack〔rick〕 of grain; a pile 〔heap〕 of corn〔cereals〕

담불[2] a ten-year-old 《ox, horse》

담비 〖동물〗 a marten; a Korean sable

담뿍 full; brimful; to the brim; [많이] much; a great deal ¶ 담뿍 붓다 fill 《a glass》 to the brim // 담뿍 먹다 eat one's fill; stuff and cram plentifully; have a big 《lunch》 // 돈을 담뿍 모으다 make lots of money

담색 淡色 a light color

담석 膽石 〖의학〗 a gallstone; a bilestone; a biliary calculus

담세 擔稅 bearing tax **—하다** bear tax **— 능력** tax-bearing capacity; taxpaying ability **—자** a tax-bearer; taxpayer

***담소** 談笑 a chat; chatting; friendly talk; familiar talk; confabulation **—하다** chat 《with a person》; have a pleasant chat; confabulate ¶ 문제는 담소하는 가운데 해결됐다 The question was settled by friendly talk.

담소 膽小 timidity; faint-heartedness **—하다** (be) timid; faint-hearted; poor-spirited; chicken-hearted; timorous

담소자약하다 談笑自若— [서술적] be laughing and talking unconcernedly

담수 淡水 fresh-water

—어 a freshwater fish **—호** a freshwater lake

담쌓다 ① [담을 두르다] wall; surround 《a place》 with a wall ② [관계를 끊다] break off with 《a person》; have done with 《a matter, a person》; be through with 《미》 ¶ 나는 그 집 사람들과는 담 쌓았다 I have done with that family. /I am through with that family. ∥그들은 서로 담쌓았다 They have nothing to do with each other any more. ∥그녀와는 담쌓은 지 이미 오래다 I broke with her long since.

담쏙담쏙 full ; greedily ¶ 과자를 담쏙담쏙 그러쥐다 grasp a greedy handful of cake

*담요 毯 — a blanket

담임 擔任 charge ; duty **—하다** be in charge 《of》; take charge 《of》 ¶ 담임을 시키다 put 《a person》 in charge of 《a class》∥2학년 영어를 담임하다 teach English in the 2nd-year class∥금년 우리 반 담임 선생은 어느 분이냐 Who is in charge of our class this year? ∥3학년은 내가 담임하고 있다 I have charge of the 3rd-year class. /I'm in charge of a 3rd-grade class. ∥그 여자는 내가 담임하는 학생이다 She is a pupil under〔in〕 my charge.

— 교사 a class teacher ; the teacher in charge 《of a class》; a homeroom teacher — 학급 the class under〔in〕 one's charge

담자색 淡紫色 light purple

*담쟁이 〖식물〗 ivy ¶ 담쟁이 덩굴 ivy vines ∥담쟁이 덮인 벽 an ivy-covered wall∥벽에 담쟁이가 뻗어가게 하다 let ivy creep〔trail〕 on the wall

담적색 淡赤色 a rose color

*담즙 膽汁 bile ; gall ; choler ¶ 담즙의 bilious ; biliary∥담즙질의 사람 a man of choleric temperament

—병 a bilious complaint ; biliousness ¶ 담즙병〔증〕에 걸려 있다 have an attack of biliousness —산 bile acid

담차다 膽— (be) daring ; bold ; plucky ; fearless ; dauntless ; audacious

담채 淡彩 thin〔light〕 colo(u)ring ¶ 담채의 light-colored∥담채를 칠하다 apply light coloring

담천 曇天 an overcast〔a clouded〕 sky ; cloudy weather

담청색 淡青色 light blue

담타 痰唾 [가래와 침] spittle and phlegm

담타기 ⇨ 덤터기

담판 談判 negotiation ; bargaining ; conference ; conversations (외교상의) ; parley ; talks **—하다** bargain ; confer ; have talks ; converse 《with》; negotiate with 《a person》 about〔for〕; hold parley 《with》 ¶ 담판중이다 be under negotiation∥직접 담판을 하다 have direct negotiations 《with》∥담판이 결렬되었다 The negotiations broke down〔were broken off, fell through〕. ∥강경하게 담판하다 press hard ; make strong〔peremptory〕 demands

강화 — peace negotiations 외교 — diplomatic negotiations

담합 談合 [의논] consultation ; conference **—하다** consult〔confer〕 with ¶ 입찰에 관해 담합하다 confer on the bidding

— 입찰 prearranged bidding

담해 淡咳 a moist cough

담홍색 淡紅色 rose pink ; pink ; pale rose-color ; blush tint ; salmon-red 〔-pink〕

*담화 談話 a talk ; colloquy ; conversation ; a statement ; an informal comment **—하다** talk 《with a person》; converse 《with a person》 ¶ 담화 중이다 be in conversation 《with》∥담화의 형식으로 발표하다 issue a statement in the form of conversation∥담화를 나누다 talk together

—실 a conversation room ; a social hall 특별 —문 a special statement

담화체 談話體 a conversational style ; a colloquial style ¶ 담화체의 colloquial∥담화체로 in (a) colloquial style

담황색 淡黃色 lemon yellow ; straw color ; citrine

†답 答 [대답] an answer ; a reply ; [응답] a rejoinder ; a response ; [해답] an answer ; a solution ¶ (문제의) 정확한 답을 내다 get〔work out〕 a correct solution〔answer〕∥답할 수 없는 질문 an unanswerable question

답 畓 a rice field ; a paddy field

답곡 畓穀 grain from the paddy fields ; rice

답농 畓農 cultivation of a paddy field ; rice culture ; rice farming

답다 (be) like ; becoming ; worthy of ¶ 답지 않다〔못하다〕 (be) unlike ; unbecoming ; unworthy of ; improper∥사내다운 manly∥여자다운 womanly ; lady like ∥신사답지 않은 짓을 하다 do a thing unworthy of a gentleman∥사내답게 굴어라 Be a man. ∥꼭 그 사람다운 짓이야 It's just like him. /It's his way. ∥길다운 길이라고는 없다 There is no road to speak of. ∥역시 여자다운 데가 있다 There is something feminine in her after all. ∥학생이면 학생답게 굴어라 If you are a student, behave like one. ∥이 근처는 도시답다 The place bears〔has〕 an urban character.

*답답하다 沓沓— ① (be) stuffy ; close ; stifling ; suffocating ¶ 답답한 방 a stuffy room∥답답한 날씨 close〔oppressive〕 weather∥숨막힐 듯이 답답한 분위기 the stifling atmosphere 《of the spot》∥비좁고 답답한 고을 a small hole of a town∥가슴이 답답하다 feel oppressed in one's breast ; feel heavy in the chest ; feel a pressure on one's chest∥방이 무덥고 답답하다 The room is close and hot. / The room is stuffy. ∥(옷이) 어깨가 답답하다 The coat is too tight in the shoulders.

② [사람이] lack adaptability ; have no resources ; (be) hidebound ; (be) unadaptable ; drawling ; clumsy ; awkward ; sluggish ¶ 답답한 사람 an unadaptable per-

ㄷ

son ; a man of no resources ; a narrow-minded person // 말을 답답하게 하다 drawl ; speak with a drawl
③ [심정이] 《feel》 impatient ; irritated ; anxious ; restless ; uneasy ¶ 답답하게 여겨지다 feel irritated〔be impatient〕《at a person's slowness》// 그는 답답한 녀석이다 He is irritatingly slow. // 집에서 소식이 없어 답답하다 There are no letters from home so I am concerned about my family.

답례 答禮 [인사] a return courtesy ; a return salute〔call〕; [답례품] a return present **—하다** [인사] return〔answer〕a salute〔call, visit, courtesy, compliment〕; salute back ; take the salute (특히 국가 원수가) ; answer (축포 따위에) ; [선물] make 《a person》 a present in return ; make a return present ¶ 답례로 in acknowledgment of ; in return for ; to return the courtesy of // 답례로 무엇을 드릴까요 What shall I give him in return for his present ?

답례포 答禮砲 a return gun salute ¶ 답례포를 쏘다 fire a gun salute in return

답방 答訪 a return visit **—하다** return one's visit ; make a return visit

답배 答— a reply〔an answer〕 to (a letter from) one's inferior **—하다** answer〔reply to〕a letter from one's inferior

답배 答拜 a return salute

답변 答辯 [대답] an answer ; a reply ; [변론] defense ; a plea ; [변명] an explanation **—하다** answer ; reply ; explain ; defend oneself ; make a plea ¶ 질문에 답변하다 answer〔reply to〕《a person's》 question // 답변에 궁하다 be at a loss for an answer〔explanation〕// 답변을 요구하다 demand an answer ; call 《a person》 to account // 답변을 잘하다 be clever in reply // 답변을 못했다 He had no answer for that. // 어떻게 답변해야 좋을지 모르겠다 I don't know what to say to that.

답보 踏步 stepping ; stamping ; a step ; a tread ; [정체] a stalemate ; a standstill **—하다** step ; stamp ; mark time (군인들이) ; [정체하다] come to a standstill ; remain stationary ¶ 답보 상태에 있다 be at a standstill ; be in a stalemate

답사 答辭 a (formal) reply ; an address in reply ; a response ¶ 답사를 하다 make an address in reply ; read the reply // 지사의 축사에 대해서 답사하다 make a formal reply to the governor's congratulatory address

***답사 踏査** survey ; exploration ; field investigation ; reconnaissance **—하다** survey ; explore ; investigate ; go over ¶ 사적을 답사하다 explore a historic scene // 현지를 답사하다 survey ; make a field investigation ; make a survey 《of》 ; make an on-the-spot survey

답서 答書 a reply ; an answer ¶ 답서를 내다 reply to a letter ; answer a letter ; send a reply // 답서를 내지 않다 leave a letter unanswered

답습 踏襲 following **—하다** follow ; follow suit ; follow in the steps 《of a person》 ; follow in 《a person's》 footsteps ¶ 전내각의 정책을 답습하다 follow the policy of the former Cabinet

-답시고 [···인 체] under (the) pretence of ; posing as ; [···할 양으로] with the intention of ; with a view to

답신 答信 a reply ; an answer

답신 答申 a report ¶ 답신을 내다 submit a report

답안 答案 an examination paper ; an exam paper ; a paper ¶ 백지 답안 a blank paper // 영어 답안 a paper in English // 답안을 내다 hand in one's paper // 답안을 채점하다 mark〔look over〕 examination papers

답인 踏印 —하다 stamp one's seal 《on》 ; stamp with one's seal

답장 答狀 a reply ; an answer **—하다** answer〔reply to〕 a letter ; send a reply to 《a person, a person's letter》 ¶ 답장을 내다 answer〔reply to〕 a letter // 답장을 내지 않다 leave a letter unanswered // 답장을 기다립니다 Expecting a response to this letter. // 즉시 답장하여 주십시오 Please answer my letter by return of post.

답전 答電 a reply telegram ; an answer to a telegram **—하다** answer by telegraph〔cable〕; telegraph in return ; wire in answer

답주 畓主 the owner of a paddy field

답지 遝至 rush ; flood ; influx ; onrush ; storming **—하다** rush in ; pour in ; be flooded〔deluged〕 with ; throng to ¶ 감사장이 사방에서 답지했다 Letters of thanks poured in from all quarters. // 신청이 사무실에 답지했다 The office is flooded〔deluged〕 with applications 〔offers〕. // 주문이 답지했다 There was a rush of orders. /Orders poured in. // 축전이 답지했다 Congratulations came snowing in.

답치기 a rash〔reckless〕 act ; a blind act
답치기 놓다 관용 act recklessly ; act on impulse ; go it blind

답토 畓土 paddy ; rice-field

답파 踏破 traveling on foot **—하다** travel on foot ; tramp ; traverse ¶ 전국을 답파하다 tramp all over the country ; travel over the length and breadth of the land

답하다 答— ① [대답하다] answer ; reply ; respond 《to》 ; make answer ; give a reply ② [해답하다] answer ; solve ; do

닷 five ¶ 닷말 five *mal*

닷곱장님 an extremely weak-sighted person

닷새 five days (5일간) ; the fifth day of the month (5일)

닷샛날 the fifth (day) 《of the month》

당 黨 [당파] a party ; [도당] a faction ; a clique ¶ 당간부 party leaders ; senior party members // 당에 가입하다 join the party // 당에서 탈퇴하다 secede from the party ; leave the party ; rat // 당을 조직하다 form a party ; form a clique // 당을 해산하다 dissolve the party // 당에 끌어들이다 win 《a person》 over to one's party

당 當 ① [정당] justice ; righteousness ; propriety ¶ 당 부당은 여하간에 rightly or wrongly // 당치 않은 처사 an improper step // 당치 않은 판결 an unjust sentence // 당치 않다 be wrong ; be unjust 〔unfair, improper〕
② [당해의] this ; our ; [위에 말한] the said ; that ; [문제의] in question ; at issue ¶ 당교 this school // 당자 the person in question ; the said person ; the person concerned // 당년 20세 20 years old at the time in question

당 堂 ① shrine ⇨ 당집 ② a hall ⇨ 대청

당 糖 sugar ⇨ 설탕

당- 當 [이] this ; [그] that ; the said ; [현재의] the present ; the current ; [문제의] in question ; at issue

-당 當 per... ; (for) each ¶ 1인당 per capita 《라》〔head〕 ; for each person // 인구 1인당 per head of population // 톤당 per ton // 1페이지당 낱말 수 the number of words to a page // 비용은 1인당 2천원이었다 The cost came out as two thousand *won* a head.

당개나리 〖식물〗 a tiger lily ; Lilium tigrinum (학명)

당고 當故 **—하다** lose one's parents ; go into mourning for one's parents

당고모 堂姑母 an aunt (who is one's father's cousin)

당과 糖菓 sweetmeats ; comfit ; bonbon ; candy 《미》 ; sweets 《영》

***당구 撞球** billiards ; pills 《영·속》 ; [공] a billiard ball ¶ 당구를 치다 play (at) billiards // 당구치는 사람 a billiard player // 당구에서 이기다〔지다〕 win〔lose〕 a game of billiards
—공 a billiard ball ; a cue ball **—대** a billiard table ; a pool table **—장** a billiard room〔hall〕

†**당국 當局** the authorities (concerned) ; official quarters ; persons in charge (사람) ¶ 당국의 지시에 의하여 by order of the authorities ; by police order (경찰 당국) // 당국의 허가를 얻다 obtain the sanction of the authorities // 관계 당국과 접촉하다 contact the authorities concerned // 당국에 진정하다 complain〔report〕 to the authorities // 시 당국은 거리에 침 뱉는 사람들을 단속하기로 결정했다 The city government has decided to crack down on people who spit on the streets.
—자 a person in authority **군—** the military authorities **군 수사 —** the Army investigation authorities

당권 黨權 party hegemony

당규 黨規 the party regulations

***당근** a carrot

당금 當今 nowadays ; these days ; today ; at present

당기 當期 this〔the current〕 term
— 배당 the dividend for this term

당기 黨紀 party discipline ¶ 당기 문란 a breach of party discipline

†**당기다**[1] ① [끌어서] pull ; draw ; tug ; haul ; [팽팽히] brace up 《a bow》 ; strain ; tighten ; stretch ② [날짜·시간을] advance ; move〔carry〕 up ; make earlier ¶ 잡아 당기다 pull 《a person》 by the sleeve // 그물을 당기다 haul in a net // 기일을 두 달 당기다 advance the date by two months // 결혼 날짜를 하루 당기다 shift the wedding date one day ahead // 너무 팽팽하게 당기면 끊어진다 If you strain it too hard, it will break.

†**당기다**[2] [입맛이] stimulate〔appeal to〕 one's appetite ; 《one's appetite》 be stimulated ¶ 환자가 입맛이 당기기 시작했다 The patient has begun to have a good appetite. // 그 사과가 입맛을 당긴다 The apple appeals to my appetite.

‡**당나귀** a donkey ; an ass ¶ 수탕나귀 a male ass ; a jackass // 암탕나귀 a jenny donkey ; a jennet

당내 堂內 near relatives

당내 黨內 within the party ; (intra-)party ¶ 당내의 알력 intraparty conflict〔trouble〕 // 당내의 의견을 통일하다 unify opinions inside〔within〕 the party

당년 當年 [금년] this year ; [그해] that year ¶ 당년 18세이다 She is eighteen years old (this year). // 나이는 먹었으나 아직 당년의 기운은 잃지 않고 있다 Though old in years, he is as vigorous as in those days.

당년치기 當年— goods which last only one year ; one year's wear

당뇨병 糖尿病 〖의학〗 diabetes ; glycosuria ¶ 당뇨병에 걸리다 be diabetic

당닭 唐— 〖새〗 a bantam (fowl) ¶ 당닭처럼 작은 사람 a short, fat man

***당당하다 堂堂—** (be) dignified ; grand ; imposing ; commanding ; [훌륭한] brilliant ; [공정한] fair ; square ; open ¶ 당당히 stately ; in a dignified manner ; in style // 정정당당히 fairly and squarely ; openly ; boldly and fearlessly // 풍채가 당당한 신사 a grand〔distinguished〕-looking gentleman ; a gentleman of a commanding presence // 당당한 저택 a stately〔an imposing〕 mansion // 당당한 권리 a lawful〔legitimate〕 right // 당당히 겨루다 play fair // 자동차를 타고 당당하게 도착하다 arrive in style in a motorcar // 그는 회사에서는 당당하지만 부인 앞에서

는 양순한 것 같다 He puts on a big show at work, but apparently he's pretty meek around his wife.

당당히 堂堂— ① [훌륭히] grandly ; splendidly ; magnificently ; majestically ; in a dignified manner ; with (great) dignity ; with an imposing air ; with pomp and glory ¶ 당당히 개선하다 return from a victorious campaign in glory // 시험에 당당히 급제하다 pass an examination with flying colors ② [떳떳이] fairly ; justifiably ; squarely ; openly ¶ 당당히 싸우다 fight openly〔on the square〕; play fair // 의견을 당당히 주장하다 defend one's opinion like a man

*당대 當代 the present age ; the day ; today ; one's lifetime ¶ 당대의 present ; contemporary ; of the day ; of our time ; of the age // 당대의 대음악가 a great musician of the day // 당대의 위인 a great man of the present age 〔day〕// 당대 제일의 미인 the reigning beauty // 당대의 미술가들 contemporary artists

당대발복 當代發福 —하다 get rich in one's own lifetime

당도 當到 arrival ; coming —하다 arrive 《at, in》; reach ; get to ; gain 《one's destination》 ¶ 목전에 당도한 위험 a pressing danger // 기회가 당도하다 a chance presents itself

당돌하다 唐突— (be) blunt ; forthright ; bold ; audacious ; presumptuous ¶ 당돌한 언사 blunt〔bold〕language // 당돌하게 굴다 behave boldly // 당돌하오나… Excuse my abruptness, 《but》...

당두 當頭 —하다 draw near ; be near at hand ; be imminent ¶ 시험 기일이 당두하였다 The date of the examination is near at hand.

당락 當落 the result of an election ; success or defeat at the polls ¶ 당락 선상에 있다 have a fifty-fifty chance of being elected

당랑 螳螂 a (praying) mantis ⇨ 버마재비 —거철(拒轍) It is like a fly trying to bite a tortoise.

당략 黨略 party politics ; a party policy

당량 當量 〖화학〗 an equivalent

당로 當路 ① ⇨ 요로(要路) ② [집권] rising to power ; getting〔coming〕 into power

당론 黨論 the view〔platform〕 of a party ; a party platform ; a party opinion

당류 糖類 sugars ; 〖화학〗 saccharoid

당리 黨利 party interests ; partisan politics ¶ 당리를 도모하다 promote 〔advance〕 party interests // 당리 당략에 치우치다 be too much swayed by the party interests ; pursue the party interests 《at the cost of those of the nation》// 당리 당략을 일삼다 play partisan〔party〕 politics

당먹 唐— a Chinese〔fine quality〕 ink stick

당면 當面 —하다 face ; confront ¶ 당면한 present ; immediate ; urgent // 당면한 일 immediate work ; work in hand // 당면한 과제 the present question ; a question of the day〔hour〕; an urgent problem // 당면의 급선무 the need of the hour

당면 唐麵 Chinese noodles

당명 黨命 an order of a party ; a party order〔policy〕

당목 唐木 Chinese cotton goods ; cotton (cloth)

당무 黨務 party affairs ¶ 당무를 처리하다 manage〔conduct〕 party affairs

— 위원 an executive member of a party

— 회의 the executive committee of a party

당무자 當務者 a person in charge〔authority〕

*당밀 糖蜜 molasses 《미》; treacle 《영》

당방 當方 ① [우리들] I ; we ② [이 쪽] our part ¶ 당방의 실수 an oversight on our part // 당방은〔에서〕 on our side ; on our part ; at this end

당번 當番 being on duty ; being on guard ; being on watch ; [사람] the man on duty —하다 be〔go〕 on duty ¶ 당번이 끝나다 be off duty // 오늘 당번은 누구냐 Who is on duty today? // 내가 당번이다 I am on duty〔watch〕. // 내일은 네가 당번이다 It is your turn to be on duty tomorrow. // 매주 한번씩 당번을 해야 한다 I have to be on duty once a week.

—표 a roster 청소 — one's turn for sweeping

당벌 黨閥 a faction ; a clique ; a circle ; a league

당부 當否 propriety ; right or wrong ; suitability

당부 當付 —하다 ask〔request, tell, bid〕 《a person》 to 《do》 ¶ 당부받다 be told to 《do》// 뒷일 봐달라고 당부하다 ask 《a person》 to take care of one's future affairs // 신신 당부하다 request earnestly ; make an earnest request 《to a person for a thing》// 이 말씀을 전하라는 당부를 받았습니다 I was told to see you and tell you this. // 한 가지 당부할 일이 있습니다 I have a favor to ask of you.

당분 糖分 (the amount of) sugar ¶ 콩의 당분 the sugar content in the pea // 당분을 함유하다 contain sugar ; be sugary // 오줌의 당분 유무를 검사하다 examine the urine for sugar

— 측정기 a saccharometer

*당분간 當分間 for the present ; for the time being ; until further notice ¶ 당분간 비는 오지 않을 게다 It will not rain for some time. // 당분간 이곳에 살 작정이다 I will live here for the time being. // 당분간은 그것으로 족하다 It will do for the present. // 당분간 그대로 두라고 합니다 He says it must be left as it is until further

notice.
당비 黨費 party expenditure〔expenses〕
당비름 唐— 〖식물〗 a Ganges amaranth ; a Joseph's-coat
당사 當事 —하다 face〔deal with〕 a problem ; attend to the business ; be concerned in the affair
당사 黨舍 the headquarters of a party
당사국 當事國 the country concerned
†**당사자 當事者** the person〔party〕 concerned ; a concerned party ; a party to an affair ¶ 결혼의 당사자 the contracting parties in a marriage // 소송의 당사자 the parties to a suit // 당사자간의 해결 settlement out of court // 당사자에게 물어보다 ask the person in question // 당사자들이 모이면 사태가 감정적으로 된다 Things get emotional when the parties involved get together.
— 신문(訊問) examination of parties **— 일동** all concerned
당상 堂上 [궁중의 대청] the floor of the Royal Palace
*__당선 當選__ getting〔being〕 elected ; winning an election ; [의원의] return 《영》; [현상의] winning **—하다** be elected ; win〔carry〕 an election ; be returned ; [현상에서] win a prize ; be accepted (소설 따위가) ¶ 당선 가능성이 있는 후보자 a candidate in the winning ; a strong candidate // 국회 의원에 당선하다 be elected to the House of Representatives ; be returned to Parliament 《영》 // 시장〔의장〕에 당선하다 be elected mayor〔chairman〕 // 당선 권내에 들다 be〔come〕 within range of being returned ; be in the running // 현상 소설에서 일등으로 당선하다 win the first prize in a contest for best novels // 그는 최고점으로 당선하였다 He was returned at the head of the poll. // 보선의 결과 김씨가 당선하였다 The by-election resulted in the return of Mr. *Kim*. // 이번만은 당선하고 싶다 I hope I shall get in this time. // 그의 당선은 무효가 되었다 His election was invalidated〔declared void 《영》〕.
— 무효 invalidity of election〔return〕 **— 소설** a prize novel **—율** the ratio of winning numbers **—자** an elected person ; a successful candidate ; the elected ; a prize winner (현상 모집의) **—작** a prize winner **무투표 —** return without voting
당세 當世 the present time〔day, age〕; the day ; the time ¶ 당세풍 modernism ; the latest〔up-to-date〕 fashion ; the fashion of the time
당세 黨勢 party influence ; party strength〔prestige〕 ¶ 당세를 확장하다 enhance (the) party prestige ; increase〔expand〕 (the) party strength // 당세가 신통치 않다 The party is at a low ebb.
당세풍 當世風 modernism ; the latest〔up-to-date〕 fashion ; the fashionable style ¶ 당세풍의 up-to-date ; modish ; stylish
당수 黨首 the party leader〔boss, head〕; the leader of a party ; the president〔head〕 of a political party
당숙 堂叔 an uncle (who is one's father's cousin)
당시 唐詩 the poems of *Tang* age ; *Tang* poetry
*__당시 當時__ at that time ; in those days ; then ¶ 그 당시 at that time // 내란 당시 in those days of civil war // 당시의 여론 the then current opinion // 당시의 학생들 the students of those days // 그 소설은 발표 당시 대단한 인기를 얻었다 The novel had a great vogue in its day. // 당시의 일은 조금도 기억이 안난다 I remember nothing about those days.
†**당신 當身** [2인칭] you ; [3인칭] he ; she ; [부부] dear ; my dear ; (my) darling ; (my) honey 《미》 ¶ 당신의 your ; [3인칭] his ; her
†**당연 當然 —하다** (be) rightful ; proper ; fair ; reasonable ; natural ; be no wonder ¶ 당연히 rightly ; properly ; deservedly ; naturally ; as a matter of course // 당연한 결과 a natural result〔outcome〕; a logical conclusion // 당연한 의무 one's bounden duty // 당연한 일 a matter of course // 당연히 받아야 할 것을 받다 get〔have〕 one's due〔deserts〕 // 그는 당연히 상〔벌〕을 받아야 한다 He deserves praise〔punishment〕. // 그 재산은 당연히 자네 것이다 The property is yours by right. // 빚진 것을 갚는 것은 당연하다 One ought to pay what one owes. // 자네가 그것을 믿는 것도 당연하다 It is natural for you to believe it. /You are justified in believing it. // 화를 내는 것도 당연하다 It is natural for him to get angry〔that he should get angry〕. // 당신이 그렇게 말하는 것도 당연하다 You may well say so. /You are quite right in saying so. // 그녀의 말은 아주 당연했다 What she said was most proper〔reasonable〕.
당원 黨員 a member of a party ; a party man ; a partisan (열성적인)
— 명부 a list of the party members
당월 當月 [이 달] this〔the current〕 month ; [그 달] that month ; the said month
당의 糖衣 sugar-coating ¶ 당의를 입히다 sugar-coat 《the tablet》
—정(錠) a sugar-coated pill〔tablet〕
당의 黨議 [회의] a party council ; [결의] a party decision ¶ 당의에 의해서 결정되다 be decided at a party council
당인 黨人 a party man ; a partisan ; a member of a party〔clique〕
— 근성 party〔partisan〕 spirit
당일 當日 the day ; that day ; the day appointed ; on that day ¶ 당일의 연사 the speaker of the day // 당일한 통용표 a

day ticket // 당일치기 공부 cramming 《before an exam》 // 당일치기 여행 a day's trip ; a one-day trip // 발행 당일만 유효하다 be valid for the day of issue only ; be good only for the day of issue

당자 當者 the person concerned〔in question〕; the concerned party

†당장 當場 on the spot〔instant〕; immediately ; offhand ; then and there ; at once ; impromptu ; in no time ; here and now ; right away ; promptly ; directly ¶ 당장에 필요한 것 an immediate need // 당장에 처형하다 execute 《a person》 on the spot // 지금 당장(은) for the present ; for the time being ; at present // 당장 해야 할 일 business〔work〕 in hand // 당장 나가라 Get out right now. // 당장 시작하라 Start it without delay. // 돈이 당장 필요하다 I want the money right now.

당쟁 黨爭 party strife〔rivalry〕 ¶ 당쟁을 일삼다 be given up to party squabbles

당적 黨籍 the party register ¶ 당적을 가지다 affiliate oneself to〔with〕 a political party // 당적에서 떠나다 leave the party ; disaffiliate oneself from one's party // 당적에서 제적하다 strike 《a person's》 name off the party register

당점 當店 this shop〔store 《미》〕; we

당조짐하다 exercise strict control over 《a person》 by nagging and scolding ; supervise strictly

당좌 當座 [예금] a current deposit ¶ 당좌를 트다 open a current account 《with a bank》 // 당좌에 예금하다 deposit 《one's money》 on current account
— 계정 a current account — 대부금 a call loan — 대월 (an) overdraft ; an overdrawn account — 수표 a check 《미》; a cheque 《영》

당지 唐紙 rice-paper

당지 當地 this place〔district, locality〕; these parts ; here ¶ 당지의 실업계 business circles here // 당지에 오시거든 꼭 들러주십시오 Please drop in when you happen to come in these parts.

당지기 堂— the janitor of a private school〔a temple〕; a sexton

당지다 harden ; become hard ; stiffen ; become solid〔firm〕 by pressure

당직 當直 being on duty〔watch〕 —하다 be on (night) duty ; keep watch ¶ 당직을 인계하다 hand〔take〕 over a duty
— 수당 night duty pay —원 a person on duty — 장교 an orderly〔a duty〕 officer —표 a watch bill

당직 黨職 a party post
— 개편 reorganization of a party's hierarchy

당직자 黨職者 a party executive ; the party leadership 《총칭》

당질 堂姪 a first male cousin once removed

당질녀 堂姪女 a first female cousin once removed

당집 堂— a temple ; a shrine

당차다 be of small but sturdy〔stout, solid〕 build

당착 撞着 contradiction ; inconsistency ; conflict —하다 be contradictory 《to》; be inconsistent 《with》; conflict〔collide〕 《with》; be in conflict 《with》 ¶ 상호 당착하는 가정 inconsistent hypotheses
자가 — self-contradiction ; intellectual suicide ¶ 자가 당착하다 cut oneself

당찮다 (be) unreasonable ; improper ; preposterous ; absurd ; be out of the question ¶ 당찮은 짓 an unreasonable〔improper〕 act // 당찮은 생각 an absurd idea // 당찮은 소리 Absurd ! / Nonsense ! / Never happen ! 《미》

당책 唐冊 a Chinese book ; a book printed in China

당처 當處 [이곳] this place ; here ; [그곳] that place ; there

당철 當— the (right) season ¶ 지금은 수박이 당철이다 Watermelons are now in season.

당첨 當籤 prize winning ¶ 당첨되다 win a prize ; draw a lucky number // 일등에 당첨되다 win the first prize // 그는 복권에 당첨되어서 차를 사는 데 돈을 썼다 He won in the lottery and spent the money on a car.

당초 當初 the beginning ; the outset ; the start ¶ 당초의 original ; initial ; early // 당초에 at first ; at the start〔outset, beginning〕; initially ; [원래] primarily ; originally // 당초의 계획〔의도〕 one's〔the〕 original plan〔intention〕 // 당초부터 전망이 흐렸다 From the outset the prospects were poor.

당치않다 當— [불합리하다] (be) unreasonable ; absurd ; [부당하다] undeserved ; unfair ; unjust

당칙 黨則 the party rules〔regulations〕

*당파 黨派 [정파] a party ; [당내의] a faction ; [도당] a junto〔junta〕; [파벌] a clique ; a league ¶ 당파적 partisan ; factional // 당파적 감정 party〔partisan〕 feeling // 비당파적인 nonparty ; nonpartisan // 당파로 분리되다 split into factions // 당파를 만들다 form a party〔clique〕; establish〔found〕 a party // 당파를 만들어 싸우다 dispute in factions // 당파에 속하다 belong to a party〔faction〕
—심〔근성〕 party feeling〔spirit〕 — 싸움 party dispute〔strife〕; faction ; factional wrangling 초— 외교 supra-party diplomacy

*당하다 當— ① [겪다] have ; encounter ; experience ; be faced〔confronted〕 《with》; confront ; come upon〔across〕 ¶ 불행을 당하다 experience〔encounter〕 a disaster // 일을 당하다 be faced with a problem // 상을 당하다 have a death in

the family ; have a sad bereavement in one's family // 모욕을 당하다 suffer an insult〔affront, indignity〕; be insulted // 그것은 당해보지 않은 사람은 모른다 It is beyond the imagination of anyone who has not experienced it. // 감쪽같이 당하다 be fairly caught ; be fooled ; be taken in // 나는 그녀의 꾀에 꼼짝없이 당했다 She outwitted me. // 나도 오늘 사고를 당했다 I was involved in an accident myself today. // 앉아서 당하고만 있을 건가요 Are you going to take it lying down ?
② [감당하다] match〔equal, rival〕《a person》; be a match for ; keep up with 《a person》; stand 《against, up to》; face confront ; resist ; cope with ¶ 당할 수 없다 be no match for // 힘이 두명을 당하다 be strong enough to be a match for two men // 완력이 그를 당할 사람은 없다 No one is match for him in brute〔physical〕strength. // 이 난국을 당해내기에는 그는 너무 심약하다 He is too weak-minded to stand up to this difficult situation. // 달리기에서는 그를 당할 자가 없다 He has no equal for running.

-당하다 當— suffer ; undergo ; be afflicted with ¶ 거절당하다 be refused ; get turned down // 구타당하다 be struck ; get licked ; receive a blow // 공격당하다 be attacked

당한 當限 —하다 come to a close〔fixed term〕; become〔fall〕due

당해 當該 proper ; concerned ; competent ¶ 당해 관청 the competent〔appropriate, proper〕authorities ; the authorities ; the authorities concerned

당헌 黨憲 the party constitution

당혹 當惑 [곤혹(困惑)] perplexity ; puzzlement ; embarrassment ; [진퇴양난] dilemma ; [혼란] confusion **—하다** (be) perplexed ; embarrassed ; puzzled

당혼 當婚 —하다 reach a marriageable age

*****당황 唐惶, 唐慌** confusion ; consternation **—하다** be confused ; be thrown into confusion ; be upset ; be perplexed ; be puzzled ; be bewildered ; be embarrassed ; be discomfited ; be disconcerted ; be perturbed ; lose one's composure ; lose one's head ; lose one's presence of mind ¶ 당황하여 in confusion ; in panic ; [허둥지둥] in a flurry ; [놀라서] in consternation // 당황하지 않다 remain calm ; keep one's presence of mind ; keep one's composure〔head〕// 당황하게 하다 throw 《a person》 into confusion ; confuse ; disconcert // 그는 조금도 당황하지 않았다 He kept perfect composure. // 당황하지 마라 Take it easy. / Don't panic.

*****닻** an anchor ¶ 작은 닻 a kedge-anchor // 배는 닻을 내리고 있었다 The ship was at anchor.

닻을 감다 관용 weigh〔pull up〕anchor
닻을 주다 관용 cast〔drop〕anchor

***닿다** ① [접하다] reach ; reach to ; get to〔at〕; touch ; touch with ¶ 손 닿는〔닿지 않는〕곳에 within〔beyond, out of〕one's reach // 천장에 닿다 reach to the ceiling // 허리까지 닿다 reach to 《a person's》 waist // 사전을 손 닿는 데에 두다 have a dictionary within reach // 그 줄은 절반밖에 닿지 않는다 The rope reaches only halfway. // 그의 머리가 거의 천장에 닿는다 His head nearly touches the ceiling. // 어린이들 손이 닿지 않는 곳에 두십시오 CAUTION ; keep out of reach of children.
② [이르다] reach ; arrive at〔in, on〕; get to ¶ 무사히 닿다 arrive in safety ; [물건이] arrive in good condition〔order〕// 화재 현장에 닿다 arrive on the scene of a fire // 서울에 닿다 reach *Seoul* ; arrive in *Seoul* // 육지에 닿다 reach〔gain〕land // 그는 내일 이곳에 닿는다 He is due here tomorrow. // 그는 드디어 목적지에 닿았다 He found his way to the place at length.
③ [관계가] have pull ; have connections with 《a person》; get in touch 《with》 ¶ 도지사하고 줄이 닿다 have a pull with the governor
④ [이치에] hold good ; hold water ; be consistent with 《reason》 ¶ 이치에 닿다 stand to〔accord with〕reason // 그의 설교는 가슴에 와 닿았다 His sermon came home to my heart.

닿소리 a consonant ⇨ 자음

***대¹** a bamboo ¶ 대쪽 같은 사람 a straight〔an open-hearted〕man
—껍질 a bamboo sheath **—마디** a bamboo joint〔node〕 **—숲** a clump of bamboo ; a bamboo grove

†**대²** ① [줄기] a stem ; a stalk ; a pipe ; [벼 따위의] a halm〔haulm〕; [대나무·등나무 따위의] a cane ; a pole ; a rod ; a staff ; [붓·펜의] a holder ; [담뱃대] a tobacco pipe ¶ (사람이) 대가 약하다 be weak-kneed ; be faint-hearted ; be timid // 대가 생기는 culmiferous
② [담배의] a smoke ; a fill (양) ; a puff ; a whiff ¶ 담배를 한 대 권하다 offer 《a person》 a smoke // 담배를 한 대 피우다 have〔take〕a smoke ; smoke a pipe // 담배 한 대 피우시지요 Will you have a smoke〔a cigarette〕? // 들어와서 담배 한 대 피우시지요 Won't you come in for a smoke ?
③ [주먹 따위] a blow ; a stroke ; a hit ; a punch ; [주사위] a shot ; an injection ¶ 한 대에 at a〔one〕blow ; with one stroke〔blow〕// 한 대 먹이다 strike 《a person》 a blow ; deal〔give〕《a person》 a blow

대 大 greatness ; largeness ; bigness ; large size (크기) ¶ 대참사 a terrible accident // 대음악회 a grand concert // 실

물대 as large as life ; life-size // 큰 대자로 누워 있다 lie at full length ; lie sprawled // 대를 살리고 소를 죽이다 renounce the small in order to secure the great ; amputate a limb to save the body // 대 중 소의 세가지 종류가 있다 There are three sizes— large, medium and small.

대 代 ① [시대] an age ; an era ; [세대] a generation ; [치세] a reign ; [일대] a lifetime ¶ 고생대 the Paleozoic era // 신생대 the Cenozoic era // 10대들 teenagers ; the teens // 80대의 사람 an octogenarian // 우리 아버지 대에는 in my father's time〔days〕// 1960년대에 in the 1960's // 대를 잇다 succeed 《a person》// 대를 끊다 let the family die out // 그녀는 30대이다 She is in her thirties. // 그 집은 그의 아버지 대에는 번창했었다 The house prospered in his father's days. // 링컨은 미국의 몇대 대통령입니까 Where does Lincoln stand in the order of the American presidents? /What number in the order of presidents is Lincoln?
② [대신] a substitute
③ [값] a charge ; a rate ; a fee ; a cost ¶ 도서대 a book fee // 식사대 food expenses

대 隊 [일행] a party ; [군인의] a company 《of soldiers》; a corps 《*pl.* corps》; a body 《of troops》; a squad ; [악대의] a band ; [대오] the ranks ; a line ; formation ¶ 구조대 a rescue party // 육군〔해군〕 군악대 a military〔marine, naval〕 band

대 臺 ① [밑받침·걸이] a stand ; a rest (총가 따위) ; [시렁 따위] a rack ; [탁자] a table ; [지주] a support ; a stool ; [걸] a bench ; [비석 따위의] a pedestal ; [기초] foundation ; a base ¶ 세면대 washstand
② [단위] a car ; a cart ; a plane ¶ 소달구지 2대 two ox-carts // 6대의 자동차에 분승하다 ride in six separate cars
③ [액수] a level ; a mark ¶ 100원대에 달하다 rise to the level of 100 *won* ; reach the 100 *won* mark // 50원대를 넘어서다 pass〔exceed〕 the 50 *won* mark // 수입이 1억불대를 돌파하다 Imports have broken through the $100 million mark. // 수억대의 자본가 a capitalist with billions
④ [대지(臺地)] a tableland ; a plateau ; a height ; an eminence ; a hill

*__대 對__ ① [짝] a pair ; a counterpart ; a parallel ; [쌍] a couple ¶ 대가 되다 make〔form〕 a pair ; form a counterpart〔parallel〕
② [상대] versus 《v., vs.》; against ; between ; [비율] to ¶ 3대1의 스코어 a score of 3 to 1 // 민주주의 대 공산주의 democracy versus communism // 베어스 대 라이온즈의 야구 경기 a baseball game between the Bears and the Lions // 1대1 동점으로 끝나다 《the game》 end in a tie, 1 to 1 ; 《they》 play a 1 to 1 tie // 3 대 2로 우리 팀이 이겼다 The score was three to two in favor of our team.
공—공 미사일 an air-to-air missile **공—지 미사일** an air-to-ground〔-surface〕 missile **지—공 미사일** a ground〔surface〕-to-air missile **지—지 미사일** a ground-〔surface〕-to-ground〔-surface〕 missile

대 帶 a zone ; a belt
견갑(肩胛)— the shoulder girdle **열—** the tropical zone **온〔한〕—** the temperate〔frigid〕 zone

*__대가 大家__ [대가옥] a big house ; a mansion ; [큰 집안] a wealthy family ; an illustrious〔a distinguished〕 family ; [권위자] an authority ; [대학자] a distinguished scholar ; a savant ; [거장] a (great) master ; virtuoso ; maestro ¶ 그림의 대가 a master painter // 문단의 대가 a distinguished writer // 영문학의 대가 an authority on English literature // 음악의 대가 a great〔celebrated〕 musician // 대가연하다 pose as〔set up for, pretend to be〕 an authority ; put on the airs of a great master // 대가의 설을 인용하다 quote authorities

대가 大駕 a royal palanquin

*__대가 代價__ a price ; [비용] a cost ; [희생] a price ¶ 대가를 치르다 pay the price ; pay for 《a thing》// 비싼 대가를 치르다 pay dear // 어떤 대가를 치르더라도 at any price ; at all costs

대가 貸家 a house to let ; a house for rent 《미》 ¶ 대가 표찰 a "To Let" sign〔card〕

대가 對價 an equivalent ; compensation ; prices

대가극 大歌劇 grand opera

대가다 [시간에] arrive on time (정각에) ; be〔arrive〕 in time 《for》 (늦지 않게) ¶ 수업 시간에 대가다 arrive at school on time // 11시 35분 열차에 대갈 수 있었다 We were in time for the 11 : 35 train. /We made〔could catch〕 the 11 : 35 train. // 그 열차에 대갈 수 없었다 We missed〔couldn't catch, were late for〕 the train. // 기차는 5시에 떠난다 대갈 수 있겠나 The train leaves at five. Can you make it? // 아직도 대갈 수 있다 We shall be in time yet.

대가리 the head ; the top〔tip〕
생선 — the jowl **소—** the head of an ox **콩나물 —** the tips of bean sprouts

대가족 大家族 a large family
— 제도 an extended family system

대각 對角 〖기하〗 the opposite angle ¶ 대각의 방향으로 diagonally ; obliquely
—면(面) a diagonal plane **— 행렬** a diagonal matrix **내(內)—** the interior opposite angle

대각 大覺 attainment of divine enlightenment ; perception of absolute truth **—하다** attain divine enlightenment ; perceive absolute truth

대각거리다 crack ; clatter ; rattle ; keep snapping ¶ 대각대각 with cracks〔snaps〕; with a clatter ; cracking ; snapping // 그릇이 대각거리다 dishes are clattering

대각선 對角線 a diagonal (line) ¶ 대각선적인 diagonal ; catercorner ; cater-cornered // 대각선적으로 diagonally ; cater-cornered // 대각선을 긋다 draw a diagonal (to the opposite angle)

대간첩 작전 對間諜作戰 a counter-espionage operation
— **대책본부** the Counter-Espionage Operations Headquarters

대갈 a horseshoe nail

대갈 大喝 —**하다** cry out loudly ; thunder《out》; roar ; yell

대갈마치 ① [마치] a farrier's hammer ② [사람] a person hardened through adversities ; a person schooled in〔steeled against〕adversity

대갈못 a nail with a big head

대감 大監 His〔Your〕Excellency

대감독 大監督 an archbishop ; a primate (영국 교회)

대갓집 大家— a distinguished family ; a wealthy house

†**대강 大綱** ① [대강령] general〔basic, fundamental〕principles ; [개요] an outline ; main lines ; general features ; [골자] the substance ; the essence ¶ 사건의 대강 줄거리 the (sum and) substance of the case // 대강을 말하다 outline ; give an outline of ; sketch out the general features // 대강을 정하다 lay down fundamental principles // 외교 정책의 대강을 정하다 formulate the main lines of foreign policy // 대강을 파악하다 have a general idea《of》
② [대충] generally ; in general ; roughly ; approximately ; summarily ¶ 대강 어림잡다 make a rough estimate // 대강 훑어보다 glance over《a letter》; run over《papers》; skim through〔over〕《a letter》; take a cursory view of ; give《a thing》the once-over (미·구) // 일을 대강대강 하다 do a passing job // 대강 이야기하다 give a short sketch《of》// 대강 합의를 보다 practically come to an agreement // 그는 누가 했는지 대강 짐작하고 있다 He has a pretty good idea who did it. // 대강 완성됐다 It is nearly〔almost〕finished. // 그것은 대강 다음과 같다 It may be summarized as follows. // 그 일은 대강 끝났다 I'm just about finished with them. // 누구 짓인지 대강 안다 I have a rough idea who it could be.
—**령 (領)** general rules〔principles〕; basic〔fundamental〕principles

대강 代講 —**하다** teach〔lecture〕as a substitute ; act as a substitute teacher ; teach for〔in place of〕《another》

대강풍 大强風 〖기상〗 a strong gale

대갚음 對— return ; repay ; requital ; [보복] retaliation ; tit for tat ; an eye for an eye —**하다** return ; repay《a person's kindness》; requite《a person's service》; [보복] retaliate ; give《a person》tit for tat ; revenge《an insult》; revenge oneself on《a person》; be revenged on《a person》; pay off old scores ; pay《a person》in his own coin ¶ 은혜를 대갚음하다 return a favor ; repay《a person》for his kindness

†**대개 大概** [대략] mostly ; for the most part ; [일반적으로] generally (speaking) ; in general ; [거의] nearly ; almost ; [주로] mainly ; in the main ; principally ; chiefly ; [대요] an outline ; the gist ¶ 대개의 경우 generally ; in most cases // 대개 모두 nearly all ; practically all // 대개의 학생 most students // 나는 대개 7시에 일어난다 I usually get up at seven. // 대개 끝났다 It is almost〔nearly〕finished. // 미국 사람은 대개 사교적이다 As a rule, Americans are outgoing.

대개념 大概念 [논리] a major concept

대객 待客, 對客 reception ; entertainment —**하다** receive〔entertain〕《guests》

대거 大擧 [대기획] a great undertaking〔enterprise〕; [한꺼번에] in a body ; in (great) force ; in large〔great〕numbers ; en masse (프) ; [대규모로] on a grand scale ¶ 대거 공격하다 attack《the enemy》in great force ; take the offensive on a large scale // 대거 상경하다 go up to *Seoul* in a body

대거리 代— a change ; a shift ; alternation

대거리 對— ① [대갚음] repayment ② [대들다] talking back —**하다** talk〔answer〕back ; retort ; contradict《a person》

대검 帶劍 a sword at one's side ; side arms —**하다** wear a sword〔saber〕; wear side arms ; be armed with a sword ¶ 대검을 빼다 draw one's sword // 대검을 허락〔금〕하다 allow〔forbid〕《a person》to wear a sword

대검찰청 大檢察廳 the Supreme Public Prosecutors Office

대겁 大怯 a great fear ; dread —**하다** fear ; dread ; cower《before》

대견하다 ① [흡족] (be) sufficient ; enough ; [유익하다] helpful ; useful ¶ 대견하게 여기다 think〔make〕much of《a person》; take good care《of》
② [견디기가] be hard to bear ; be hard to put up with ; (be) intolerable ; insufferable

대결 代決 —**하다** decide for《another》

***대결 對決** confrontation ; a showdown (미) ; a face-to-face meeting ; [승부] a contest ; a match ; a game ; a bout —**하다** confront ; have a showdown《with》; stand face to face《with》¶ 대결 장면 a confrontation scene∥백주의 대결 a showdown in broad daylight∥대결시키다 confront 《a person》 with 《another》; bring 《a person》 face to face with 《another》∥1대1로 대결하다 engage in a man-to-man fight; fight man to man∥아무리 자신이 있어도 어떻게 저런 큰 회사와 대결할 수 있냐 No matter how much confidence you have, how could you take on a big company like that?

대경 大慶 (a) great happiness; a great joy〔pleasure〕 ¶ 대경할 일이다 Congratulations! /I sincerely congratulate you on it.

대경 大驚 **—하다** be greatly astonished; be startled

대경대법 大經大法 fair principles and fair laws

대경 실색 大驚失色 **—하다** turn pale with horror; lose one's color with astonishment; be greatly startled

대계 大計 a long-range plan; a grand design; a far-reaching plan ¶ 국가의 백년 대계를 세우다 make a national policy on a long-range basis; make a farsighted national policy

대계 大系 an outline ¶ 서양사 대계 An Outline of European History

대고 persistently; importunately; unceasingly; keeping after 《a person》; keeping at 《a thing》 ¶ 대고 조르다 press〔importune, keep after〕 《a person to do something》∥대고 공부하다 keep at one's studies; keep studying without letup∥대고 재촉한다 He is dunning incessantly.

대고모 大姑母 a grandaunt〔great-aunt〕 on one's father's side
—부 the husband of a grandaunt on one's father's side

대공 〖건축〗 a king post

대공 大功 a great merit; meritorious〔distinguished〕 services; a signal deed ¶ 대공을 세우다 achieve great things; render meritorious services; distinguish oneself

대공 對空 anti-air(craft); ack-ack 《속》
— 감시병 a spotter **— 레이더** an air search radar **— 방어** anti-aircraft defense **— 속도** an air speed **— 십자포화** 〖군사〗 a box barrage **— 진지** an anti-aircraft position〔emplacement, installation〕 **—포화** anti-aircraft〔AA〕 fire; flak

대공 大公 a grand duke
—국(國) a grand duchy **—비(妃)** a grand duchess

대공사 大公使 ambassadors and ministers

대공산권 對共產圈 ¶ 대공산권 무역 trade with the Communist bloc

대공지정 大公至正 **—하다** (be) fair and just; just and proper

대과 大過 a serious error; a grave mistake; a blunder ¶ 대과 없이 20년간 근무할 수 있었다 I have been able to serve for twenty years without any serious mistake.

대과거 大過去 〖문법〗 the past perfect tense; the pluperfect (tense)

대관 大觀 [개관] a general survey 〔view〕; an overall view; [장관] a magnificent view **—하다** take a large view 《of》; view broadly; make a general survey 《of》

대관 大官 a high-ranking official; a (governmental) dignitary; high executives of the State

대관 戴冠 coronation **—하다** be crowned (king)

대관식 戴冠式 a coronation ¶ 대관식을 거행하다 perform a coronation (ceremony)

대관절 大關節 on earth; in the world; in the name of God〔wonder〕; the devil; the deuce; the dickens; the blazes ¶ 대관절 그는 무슨 소리를 하고 있는거요 What on earth does he mean?∥대관절 너는 누구냐 Who on earth are you?∥대관절 너는 어디에서 왔으며 누구냐 Wherever do you come from and whoever are you?∥대관절 어디 갔다 오는 거요 Where the blazes 〔hell〕 have you been?∥대관절 무슨 일인가 What the deuce is the matter? /Whatever is the matter?∥대관절 이건 어떻게 된 거야 What is the meaning of all this?

대괄호 大括弧 〖수학〗 (square) brackets

대교 大橋 a large〔big〕 bridge

*__대구 大口__ 〖물고기〗 a codfish; a cod; a gadid; a haddock
— 간유 cod-liver oil **—알** the cod roe **—어선** a cod fisher **— 유어(幼魚)** a parr **—잡이** cods fishery

대구루루, 때구루루 rolling; rumbling; with a rolling〔rumbling〕 sound **—하다** roll; rumble; make a rolling〔rumbling〕 sound ¶ 대구루루 굴러가다 roll over and over∥때구루루 굴리다 roll 《a ball》 over 《the floor》

대국 大局 the general〔whole〕 situation; the issue ¶ 대국적으로는 on the whole; generally speaking∥대국적으로 보면 on a broad survey∥대국에 중대한 영향을 미치다 have an important bearing on the whole situation∥대국을 잘못 판단하다 take a wrong view of things; miss the main point〔issue〕 of things∥사물을 대국적으로 관찰하다 take a long-range view of things∥대국에는 변화가 없다 There is no change in the general situation.

대국 大國 a big country; a great country〔nation〕; a great power (강대국)

대국 對局 ① [바둑 따위의] playing a game 《of *badook*》 **—하다** play (a game of) 《*badook*, chess》 《with》
② facing a situation **—하다** face a situation; confront a difficulty

대군 大軍 a big〔great〕 army ; a large force ; a host of troops ¶ 적의 대군 a big enemy force // 대군을 거느리다 lead〔command〕 a large force
대군 大君 a (royal) prince
대군 大群 a large crowd〔herd (소·돼지의), flock (양 따위의), shoal (물고기의), school (물고기· 고래의)〕《of》
대꾼하다, 때꾼하다 [눈이] be sunken 〔hollow〕 (from exhaustion) ¶ 그는 눈이 때꾼하다 His eyes have sunken.
대굴대굴, 때굴때굴 rolling〔rumbling〕 continuously ¶ 대굴대굴 구르다 keep rolling // 솔방울이 때굴때굴 굴러오다 pine cones come rolling down
대궁 leavings〔remains〕 of a meal ; scraps of waste food ; left-over rice
대권 大權 [왕권] the sovereign authority ; the supreme power ; prerogative ; sovereignty ; an imperium《*pl.* -ria》; [통치권] the governing power ¶ 대권의 발동 exercise of the governing power // 국왕의 대권 the powers and prerogatives of the king // 병마의 대권 the supreme authority over the army // 대권을 장악하다 reign supreme ; wield 〔sway〕 the scepter
대권 大圈 a great circle
— **항로** the great-circle track〔route〕 — **항법(法)** great〔globular〕 circle sailing〔navigation〕; orthodromy
대궐 大闕 the royal palace
*__대규모 大規模__ a large〔big, grand〕 scale ¶ 대규모의 large〔big〕-scale // 대규모로 on a large〔a big, an extensive, a grand, a gigantic〕 scale ; in a big 〔large〕 way // 대규모 검거 a wholesale roundup // 그들은 대규모 방공 연습을 실시했다 They staged a full-scale air defense drill.
— **작전** large-scale (military) operations
대그락거리다 keep clattering〔rattling〕 ¶ 그릇이 대그락거린다 Dishes are clattering away. // 상자 속의 연필이 대그락거린다 Pencils rattle in a box.
대그르르하다 (be) rather thick〔big〕 (among thin〔small〕 things)
대그릇 bamboo ware ; a bamboo bowl
대극 大戟 〚식물〛 a spurge ; Euphorbia pekinensis (학명)
대극 對極 opposite poles
대근하다 (be) unbearable ; intolerable ; insufferable
대근하다 代勤— take over the duties of 《a sick colleague》
대글대글하다 be rather thick〔big〕 among all the thin〔small〕 things
대금 大金 a large〔a big, an enormous〕 sum of money ; a lot〔great deal〕 of money ; a large amount of money ; [고가] a great cost ¶ 대금을 내다 pay a big sum // 대금을 벌다 make a lot of money ; realize a large profit // 대금이 들다 cost a great deal of money // 대금을 소비하다 spend a large sum of money // 대금을 투자하다 invest a large sum《in》// 천만원이라면 대금입니다 Ten million *won* is a mint of money.
대금 代金 price ; the money ; charge ; cost ; a bill ; a fee ¶ 대금을 치르다 pay the price ; pay for《a thing》// 대금 상환 우편으로 보내다 send a parcel C. O. D. 〔cash on delivery《영》; collect on delivery《미》〕// 구두 수선 대금이 얼마요 How much do you charge for mending a pair of shoes? // 대금을 주시겠습니까 Please pay for it. // 여기 대금이 있습니다 Here is the money for it. // 대금은 선불하여 주십시오 Please pay in advance.
— **감액** a reduction in price — **지불 보증 수수료** a del credere commission — **지불 인환증** a document against payment — **징수** collection of bills — **징수 어음** a bill for collection
대금 貸金 [돈놀이] money-lending ; [고리의] usury ; [돈] a loan **—하다** make a loan〔an advance〕 to ¶ 대금을 회수하다 collect〔call in〕 loans
—**업** money-lending business —**업자** a money-lender — **주선료(周旋料)** a procuration fee ; procuration (money) — **취급소** a loan office **단기** — short-term loan **당좌** — a call loan 〔money〕; money at〔on〕 call — **인환(引換)** cash on delivery post《C. O. D.》《영》; collect on delivery《C. O. D.》《미》 **장기** — long-term loan **정기** — a time loan **회수 불능** — bad debts **회수 확실** — good debts
대금 大笒 [악기] a kind of clarinet
대기 大忌 strong aversion ; abhorrence **—하다** abhor ; have a great aversion to ; loathe ; detest ; hate《a person》 like the viper
‡**대기 大氣** the atmosphere ; the air ¶ 대기의 압력 atmospheric pressure // 대기권 밖에 나가다 venture into outer space
—**계(計)** an aethrioscope —**권(圈)** the atmosphere ¶ 대기권내의 핵실험 a nuclear test in the atmosphere ; an atmospheric nuclear test —**론(論)** aerology — **오염** air pollution — **오염 방지법** 〚법〛 the Air Pollution Control Act ; 〚영미법〛 the Clean Air Act — **정력학(靜力學)** aerostatics —**지(誌)** aerography —**차(差)** astronomical refraction
대기 大朞 the second anniversary of《a person's》 death
대기 大器 [큰 그릇] a large vessel ; [큰 인물] a great talent〔man〕; a genius ; a man of great caliber
— **만성** Late fruit keeps well. /Soon ripe soon rotten. /Great success does not usually occur early. /Great talents mature late〔are slow in maturing〕. ¶ 대기 만성형의 사람 a late-bloomer
*__대기 待機__ **—하다** watch and wait《for a chance》; stand by ; stay ready for ; be

on call ; hold oneself in readiness ; be on standby ; wait for an opportunity ; be on the waiting list ¶ 대기를 명하다 order 《a person》 to stand by // 대기 태세를 위하다 assume a posture of standing by ; assume a watch-and-wait attitude // 명령을 대기하다 await orders // 경찰을 대기시키다 alert the police // 상시 대기하고 있다 be on constant alert // 해안 경비대가 대기중이다 The coast guard is standing by. // 택시를 대기시켜 놓았습니다 I have a taxi waiting for you.

— 기간 waiting period —료 the fee for the waiting time — 발령 being placed on the waiting list — 상태 standby status — 실 a waiting room ; an antechamber — 차관 a standby credit

대길 大吉 excellent luck ; a great stroke 〔piece〕 of luck —하다 (be) very lucky 〔auspicious〕 ; have good luck

대길일 大吉日 a most auspicious day

대꼬챙이 a pointed bamboo pole〔stick〕

대꾸 a retort ; back-talk ⇨ 말대꾸

대끼다 be (hard) put to it ; be tried ; see hardships ; rough it ; be driven from pillar to post ¶ 세상 풍파에 대끼다 go through life's vicissitudes

대나무 〖식물〗 a bamboo ⇨ 대¹

대낚시 pole-and-line fishing

대난 大難 a great misfortune〔calamity〕 ; great difficulties

대남 對南 ¶ 대남의 against〔toward〕 the South

— 간첩 an espionage agent against the South — 공작 operations against the South — 방송 broadcasting toward the South

대납 代納 [대신] payment by proxy ; [물건으로] payment in kind

***대낮** broad daylight ; the middle of the day ; high noon ¶ 대낮에 생긴 일이었다 It occurred in broad daylight〔the daytime〕.

대내 對內 ¶ 대내의 domestic ; interior ; home

— 문제 domestic issues — 정책 a domestic〔home〕 policy

대농 大農 [대농업] large-scale farming ; [사람] a big〔wealthy〕 farmer

대뇌 大腦 〖해부〗 the cerebrum 《*pl.* ~s, -bra》 ; the brain proper

—각(脚) a cerebral peduncle —막(膜) the cerebral membrane — 반구(半球) a cerebral hemisphere —엽(葉) a cerebral lobe — 피질(皮質) the cerebral cortex

대님 trouser-cuff bands ; ankle bands ¶ 대님을 매다 tie ankle bands ; tie one's trousers around the ankles

†**대다¹** ① [닿게 하다] put ; place ; lay ; apply ¶ 수화기를 귀에 대다 hold a receiver to one's ear // 눈을 망원경에 대다 apply one's eyes to a telescope // 잔을 입술에 대다 set a glass to one's lips // 구두에 창을 대다 fix a sole on one's shoes // 피가 흐르지 않도록 상처에 가제를 대다 apply gauze on the wound so as to prevent bleeding // 그 여자는 문에 귀를 대었다 She pressed his ear against the door. // 이 기둥에 등을 대고 서십시오 Stand against this post, please. // 호텔 입구에 차를 댈까요 Shall I pull up to the hotel door, sir? // 그것은 조금 손을 대면 사용할 수 있다 A little touching up and it'll be quite usable.

② [비교] compare 《a thing》 with ; make a comparison with ¶ 길이를 대 보다 compare length // 번역문을 원문과 대보다 compare a translation with the original // 원고와 대 보다 check 《it》 with the manuscript // 이것은 그것과는 댈 수도 없다 This cannot bear 〔stand〕 comparison with that. // 수학에서는 그녀에 댈 사람이 없다 No one can touch her in mathematics.

③ [손을] feel ; touch ; lay 《one's hand》 on ; put 《one's hand》 to ¶ 이마에 손을 대다 lay〔put〕 one's hand on one's forehead // 남의 돈에 손을 대다 make free with another's money // 손을 대지 않다 leave 《a thing》 untouched 〔alone〕 // 여자에게 손을 대다 get hold of a girl ; have carnal connection with a girl ; enter 〔come〕 into sexual relation with a girl // 손 대지 마시오 Hands off. 《미》/Please don't touch it. // 자네가 먼저 손을 댔나 Did you strike the first blow?

④ [일에 손을] take to ; put one's hand to 《a task》 ; set to work ; start 《an enterprise》 ; set about 《a thing》 ; attempt ; begin ; try one's hand 《at》 (시도) ¶ 투기에 손을 대다 take to 〔dabble in〕 speculation // 일에 손을 대다 start an enterprise // 정치에 손을 대다 meddle in politics // 술은 입에도 대지 않습니다 I don't touch alcohol.

⑤ [대면] bring 《a person》 into contact with 《another》 ; link (together) 《with》 ; connect 《with, to》 ¶ 김씨를 대주십시오 May I talk to Mr. *Kim*, please? // 소방서를 대주십시오 Put me through to the fire department. // 베이커씨 방 좀 대주시겠습니까 Would you connect me with the room of Mr. Baker?

⑥ [의지] lean 《one's back》 against 《the wall》

⑦ [향해서] aim at ; point〔present〕 《a pistol》 at ; level 《a revolver》 at 〔against〕 ; direct 《a gun》 ¶ 그것은 누구에게 대고 하는 말이오 And who is that remark aimed at?

⑧ [시간에] arrive on time ; make it ; [장소에] bring〔pull up, draw up〕 《a car》 《to, alongside》 ; berth〔moor〕 《a boat》 ¶ 차를 현관에 대다 pull up a car at the entrance ; bring〔draw up〕 a car alongside the porch // 배를 강가〔선창〕에 대다

bring a boat to the shore ; lay a ship alongside the pier // 제 시간에 서울에 대다 get to *Seoul* on time // 기차 시간에 대지 못하다 miss〔be too late for〕 a train
⑨ [구실·성화를] do ; make ¶ 핑계를 대다 find〔make〕 an excuse for oneself

***대다²** ① [돈·물건을] furnish〔supply, provide〕 《a person》 with 《a thing》 ; furnish〔supply〕 《a thing》 to ¶ 재료를 대다 furnish 《a person》 with material ; supply 《a factory》 with material // 학비를 대다 furnish a student with his school expenses ; supply a student with a fund to pay his school expenses
② [물을] water ; draw water 《into》 ; irrigate 《the rice paddy》

***대다³** ① [사실대로] tell 《the truth》 ; speak up〔out〕 ; confess ; own ¶ 사실을 대게 하다 make 《a person》 confess〔own〕 the fact // 그가 알고만 있다면 사실을 기어이 대게 하겠다 If he knows, I will have it out of him. // 누가 유리창을 깨뜨렸는지 대라 Spit it out. Who broke the window ?
② [길을] show〔tell〕 the way ; direct 《a person to a place》

대다⁴ [심히] 《do》 terribly ; awfully ; a lot ¶ 울어대다 cry a lot // 먹어대다 stuff oneself with food

***대다수 大多數** a large〔great, crushing, thumping〕 majority ; an overwhelming〔enormous〕 majority ; the greater part 《of》 ¶ 대다수는 for the most part ; mostly // 대다수를 차지하다 hold〔form〕 a large majority // 대다수의 지지를 받다 be supported by the majority

대단원 大團圓 denouement ; the (grand) finale ; the end ; a catastrophe (주로 비극적인) ¶ 대단원의 막이 내리다 come to an end

대단찮다 be not many〔much, big〕 ; (be) ordinary ; common ; commonplace ; mediocre ; be not serious ; be not grave ; (be) trivial ; slight ¶ 대단찮은 추위 a mild cold spell // 대단찮은 일 a trifle ; a trifling affair ; a matter of no importance // 대단찮은 병 a slight illness // 대단찮은 돈 not much money // 대단찮은 사건 a commonplace event // 손해가 대단찮다 There is no great damage. // 그는 대단찮은 학자다 He is not much of a scholar.

†대단하다 (be) considerable ; immense ; enormous ; severe ; intense ; grave ; serious ; great ; grand ¶ 대단히 very ; seriously ; exceedingly ; awfully ; horribly ; remarkably ; greatly ; a great deal // 대단한 추위 a severe cold // 대단한 학자 a great scholar // 대단한 재산 a considerable fortune // 대단한 눈 much snow ; a big snow // 대단한 미인 a stunning beauty // 병이 대단하다 be seriously ill // 질투가 대단하다 be intensely jealous // 평판이 대단하다 be highly spoken of ; be well received by // 대단히 보고 싶었다 I wanted to see you very badly. // 대단히 미안합니다 I am awfully〔terribly〕 sorry. // 저래 뵈도 고향에 가면 대단하지 He is a hero in his native province. // 그도 대단한 정치가는 아니지 Not much of a statesman, is he ?

†대단히 very ; much ; so ; most ; greatly ; seriously ; terribly 《구》 ; awfully 《구》 ; unusually ; wonderfully ; considerably ; highly ; immensely 《속》 ; extremely ; strikingly ; exceedingly ; excessively ; tremendously 《구》 ; to the utmost extent ; in a high degree ; (in) the worst way 《미·속》 ¶ 대단히 아름다운 경치 a rare〔very〕 fine view // 대단히 큰 사람 a great big man // 대단히 가난하다 be awfully poor // 대단히 아름답다 be strikingly beautiful // 대단히 맛이 있다 It's deliciously tasty. // 그는 대단히 좋은 사람이다 He is such a good man. // 그는 대단히 화를 내고 있다 He is ever so angry. // 그는 대단히 기뻐하였다 He was delighted〔pleased〕 beyond measure. // 나는 대단히 피곤하다 I am tired to death. // 대단히 재미있었다 We had an awfully〔a rattling〕 good time. // 대단히 당신을 만나고 싶었다 I wanted to see you very badly. /I was dying to see you.

대담 對談 a talk ; a conversation ; an interview ; a dialog **—하다** have a talk〔conversation〕 《with a person》 ; have an interview 《with a person》
—자 an interlocutor ; an interviewer

⁑대담 大膽 boldness ; daring ; intrepidity ; hardihood **—하다** (be) bold ; daring ; intrepid ; dauntless ; undaunted ; fearless ; stout-hearted ; courageous ; [모험적] adventurous ¶ 대담하게 boldly ; intrepidly ; fearlessly ; daringly ; courageously ; dauntlessly // 대담하게 소신을 말하다 have the courage of one's opinion ; speak up // 대담하게 행동하다 act boldly // 대담한 녀석이다 He has iron nerves〔nerves of steel〕. // 대담하게도 단신 적진으로 돌입했다 He was bold enough to make an entry into the enemy's camp all alone.

†대답 對答 an answer ; a reply ; [응답] response ; rejoinder **—하다** answer ; reply ; respond 《to》

> 참고 **answer**는 가장 일반적인 말 **reply**는 다소 딱딱하고 형식적인 말 **respond**는 때리면 울리는 것처럼 「응답하다」의 뜻

¶ 확실한〔애매한〕 대답 a definite〔dubious〕 answer // 환호에 대답하다 raise〔wave〕 one's hat to people's cheering ; bow to a cheering crowd // 거침없이 대답하다 answer briskly ; give brisk answers // 물음에 재치있게 대답하다 deal skillfully with a person's inquiry // 문을 두드렸으나 대답이 없었다 I knocked at the door but there was no response. // 그 말에는 대답할 수 없다 That is more than I can answer. // 부르면 대답할 만한 거리다 It is within a hailing distance〔within earshot〕. // 뭐라고 대답해야 좋을지 몰랐다 I was at a loss for an answer.

대당 對當 correspondence ¶ 대당액 corresponding〔equivalent〕 amount〔sum〕// 대당의 corresponding ; equivalent ; homologous

***대대 大隊** a battalion ; a squadron
—기(旗) the battalion flag **—장** a battalion commander **공병 —** an engineering battalion **비행 —** a squadron **비행 —장** a squadron commander **— 부관** a battalion adjutant

대대 代代 successive generation ¶ 대대의 hereditary ; successive // 대대의 신하 a hereditary vassal // 대대로 generation after generation ; from generation to generation ; for generations // 그의 집안은 대대로 의사다 They have been doctors from father to son〔have been in medicine for generations〕. // 그 집안에는 대대로 병신이 태어난다 The family is cursed with deformity in each generation.

대대적 大大的 big ; extensive ; large scale ; wholesale ; sweeping ; grand ; immense ¶ 대대적으로 extensively ; on a large scale ; in a large way // 대대적인 검거 a wholesale arrest ; a roundup // 대대적으로 선전하다 advertise extensively ; place〔put in〕 a large advertisement 《in a newspaper》 // 사업을 대대적으로 했다 He engaged in business on a large scale.

대도 大道 ① [큰길] a highway ; a main road〔street〕; a thoroughfare ; a public street ¶ 대도를 활보하다 swagger along〔strut on〕 the road
② [도의] a great moral principle ¶ 박애는 인류의 대도이다 Benevolence is the great principle of humanity.

대도구 大道具 [연극의] a (set) scene ; stage-setting ¶ 대도구계(係) a sceneshifter

***대도시 大都市** a big city
—권(圈) the metropolitan area ; conurbation

대도회 大都會 a large city ; metropolis

대독 代讀 —하다 read for〔on behalf of〕 《another》 ¶ 대통령의 축사를 국무총리가 대독하였다 The congratulatory address of the President was read by the Prime Minister.

대돈변 —邊 a loan〔an advance〕 of 10 percent interest per month

대동 大東 Korea〔the great land of the East〕

대동 帶同 accompaniment **—하다** be accompanied by ; take〔have〕 《a person》 along 《with》

대동 단결 大同團結 unity ; union ; solidarity **—하다** unite ; be united

대동맥 大動脈 〖해부〗 the aorta 《*pl.* ~s, -tae》; the main artery
—류(瘤) 〖해부〗 an aneurysm of the aorta **—염(炎)** aortitis **—호(弧)** the aortic arch **상행〔하행〕 —** the ascending〔descending〕 aorta

대동사 代動詞 〖문법〗 pro-verb

대동소이 大同小異 substantial identity with negligible〔minor, insignificant〕 differences ; general similarity **—하다** be almost identical〔nearly alike〕; be substantially the same ¶ 대동소이한 much〔nearly〕 alike ; almost〔very nearly〕 identical ; substantially〔practically〕 the same // 양자(兩者)는 대동소이하다 There is little to choose between the two. /They are in substantial agreement with each other.

대두 大斗 a ten-*doe* measure ; a large (dry) measure ¶ 대두 닷말 five *mal* by large measure

대두 大豆 a soy bean ⇨ 콩

대두 擡頭 rise **—하다** raise〔show〕 its head ; become〔get〕 influential ; gather strength ; come to the front ; become a prominent figure ; come to the fore〔the front〕; come into the limelight ; gain force〔power〕 ¶ 금주 운동이 대두하고 있다 The temperance〔prohibition〕 movement is gathering strength. // 우리 나라에 민주주의가 대두한 지는 그리 오래지 않다 It is only a short time since democracy became powerful in this country.

대두리 [큰 다툼] a great dispute ; a big scene ; [크게 벌어짐] aggravation ; spread ; becoming serious〔aggravated〕

대들다 oppose ; put〔set〕 oneself against 《one's superior》; defy ; turn upon〔against〕: set at defiance ; bid defiance to ; rebel against ; stand against ¶ 윗사람에게 대들다 defy〔set against〕 one's superiors // 상관에게 대들다가 해고되다 be discharged for insubordination

대들보 ① 〖건축〗 a girder ; a crossbeam ; a summer
② [사람] a pillar ; a prop (and stay) ¶ 집안의 대들보 the breadwinner〔prop, supporter〕 of a family

***대등 對等** equality ; an equal〔a level〕 footing ; equal terms ; parity ; par ; equivalent **—하다** (be) equal ; level ; even ; be on a level〔par, an equal footing, equal terms〕 with ; stand on an equality with ¶ 대등하게 on equal terms ; on an equal footing // 대등하게 하다 level ; even ; equalize 《a person》 to〔with〕 《another》 // 대등한 교제를 하다 associate on an equal footing // 승부없이 대등하다 have a game on equal terms ; play an even game ; be a good match for each

other
— 교섭 negotiations as equals〔as man to man〕 — 권리 equal rights — 조건 equal terms — 조약 a treaty on equal terms

대뜸 at once ; outright ; forthwith ; on the spot ; then and there ; immediately ; promptly ; instantly ; impromptu ; extempore ; offhand (즉석에서) ¶ 대뜸 승낙하다 give a ready consent ; accept 《an invitation》 immediately // 대뜸 의견을 말하다 give an offhand opinion 《on a matter》

대란 大亂 a serious〔great〕 disturbance ; a great commotion〔rebellion〕 ; an upheaval

†대략 大略 ① [뛰어난 계략] a great strategy
② [개요] an outline ; [적요] a summary ; a gist ; an epitome ¶ 대략을 말하자면 to sum up ; to give a general account of // 대략을 파악하다 have a general 〔rough〕 idea 《of》 // 사건의 대략을 말하다 give an outline of the case ; sum up 〔summarize〕 the case // 그것은 대략 다음과 같다 It may be summarized〔briefly summed up〕 as follows.
③ [대충] approximately ; roughly ; in the main ; cursorily ; about ; on the whole ¶ 대략 말씀드리면 roughly〔broadly〕 speaking // 이 책을 1만 부 찍는 데 필요한 비용을 대략 제시해 줄 수 있습니까 Can you give me a ballpark figure for the cost of printing ten thousand copies of this book ?

†대량 大量 a large〔great〕 quantity ; enormous volume ; a lot 《of》 ¶ 대량으로 in large〔great〕 quantities ; in bulk // 대량 수출하다 export 《a thing》 in large quantities
— 거래 a large transaction — 검거 a mass〔wholesale〕 arrest — 구입 bulk purchase ; heavy buying — 소비 mass consumption — 수요 a large demand — 실업 mass unemployment — 정보 매체 a mass medium ; mass media 《총칭》 — 주문 bulk〔large〕 order — 파괴 mass destruction — 파괴 무기(武器) a weapon of mass destruction ; a mass destruction weapon — 해고 mass dismissal〔discharge〕 ; voluminous dismissal

대량 생산 大量生産 mass〔quantity〕 production ; production on a large scale — 하다 mass-produce ; produce 《a thing》 in commercial quantity ¶ 대량 생산의 mass produced // 대량 생산의 법칙 the law of mass production

대량 학살 大量虐殺 mass murder ; genocide (인종·문화의 절멸을 목적으로 하는)
— 무기 [원·수폭 따위의] a genocidal weapon

‡대령 大領 a colonel (육군) ; a captain (해군) ¶ 대령의 직위 colonelcy ; captaincy
공군 — a flight colonel ; a group captain 《영》

대령 待令 — 하다 wait for an order〔a command〕 ; stand ready to carry out an order ; present oneself (before an official)

대례 大禮 [국가의] a state ceremony ; an august ceremonial ; [결혼식] a wedding ceremony

†대로 ① […같이, …에 따라서] like ; according to ; in accordance with ; as ; as it stands ; after ; true to ; in pursuance of ¶ 규칙대로 according to the rule // 내 명령대로 as I tell you ; according to my orders // 법률대로 in accordance with the law // 본 대로 얘기하다 tell as one saw // 시키는 대로 하다 do as one is told〔instructed〕 // 그것 봐 내가 말한 그대로지 I told you ! // 어머니 말씀대로 비가 왔다 Mother was right about the rain. // 자네는 그대로 하기만 하면 되네 You have only to follow it out.
② […하면 곧] as soon as ; directly ; immediately after ¶ 날씨가 좋아지는 대로 on the first fine day // 형편이 좋아지는 대로 at your earliest convenience // 동경에 닿는 대로 전보를 치시오 Wire me as soon as you arrive at Tokyo. // 기회가 닿는 대로 찾아뵙겠습니다 I will call on you at the first〔earliest〕 opportunity.
③ [할 때마다] every〔each〕 time ; each occasion ; as often as ; whenever ¶ 하는 대로 실패했다 He failed every time he attempted. /He made several attempts and failed as many times.
④ [분리] apart ; separately ; in one's own way〔manner〕 ¶ 그것을 그것대로 두어라 Keep it apart from others. // 그녀는 그녀대로 행동을 취했다 She acted in her own way.

대로 大路 a broad way ; a highway ; a main〔principal〕 street ; a main thoroughfare

대로 大怒 great anger ; rage ; fury ; wrath ; exasperation — 하다 get angry ; rage ; be enraged ; be exasperated ; be furious ; be in the fume〔huff〕 ; fly into a passion ; flare〔flame〕 up ¶ 대로한 나머지 in the fury of one's passion

대롱 a slender bamboo tube ; [물레의] a spinning bobbin

대롱거리다 dangle ; swing ; sway (to and fro) ; hang and swing loosely ¶ 대롱대롱 dangling ; dingle-dangle // 사과가 나무에 대롱대롱 매달려 있다 Apples dangle on the tree. // 초롱이 바람에 대롱거린다 The lantern is swinging in the wind.

대류 對流 〖물리〗 convection current
— 굴절(屈折) convective refraction — 전류(電流) a convection current — 지면(止面) 〖기상〗 the tropopause 난방(暖房) — 기(器) a convector

대류권 對流圈 〖기상〗 the troposphere ¶ 대류권의 tropospheric

†대륙 大陸 a continent ¶ 대륙의 continen-

tal // 대륙간의 intercontinental // 대륙적 사상 continentalism // 그에게는 대륙적인 데가 있다 He is somewhat continental in manner. // 경치가 대륙적이다 The landscape is characteristic of a continent. /The landscape has something continental about it.

—간 사정핵(射程核) 로켓 an intercontinental-range nuclear rocket —간 탄도탄 an intercontinental ballistic missile 《ICBM》 —도(島) a continental island —문학 Continental literature — 여행 a continental tour — 이동설 『지리』 the theory of continental drift — 정책(政策) continental politics —풍〔주의, 사상〕 continentalism — 횡단 고속 도로 a coast-to-coast highway — 횡단 철도 a transcontinental railway ; a coast-to-coast railroad 《미》 아세아 — the Continent of Asia ; the Asian Continent 유럽 — the Continent of Europe ; the European Continent

대륙붕 大陸棚 a continental shelf

— 선언 the Continental Shelf Declaration 한일 — 공동 개발 협정 The Korea-Japan Agreement on Joint Continental Shelf Development

⁑대륙성 大陸性 ¶ 대륙성의 continental

— 기후 a continental climate

대륙적 大陸的 [대륙 특유의] continental ; [비유적으로] large-minded ; carefree ; easygoing ¶ 대륙적 사상 continentalism // 중국 사람은 어딘지 모르게 대륙적인 기풍이 있다 The Chinese are somewhat continental in manner.

†대리 代理 [행위] representation ; agency ; proxy ; [법률] procuration ; attorneyship ; subrogation ; [사람] a proxy ; a deputy ; an agent **—하다** act as substitute for ; act in place〔in behalf〕 of ; act in another's name〔as another's agent〕; represent 《another person》; stand proxy for ¶ 대리로(서) by proxy ; by deputy ; by procuration (법률) // 대리의 acting ; vicarious ; deputy // 누가 김씨의 대리를 할 것인가 Who will stand in the place of Mr. *Kim*? // 많은 사람들이 대리를 시켜 투표했다 A large number of people voted by proxy. // 그의 대리로 투표했다 I voted on his behalf〔as his proxy〕.

— 경작 the cultivation by proxy —권(權) the right〔power〕 of representation〔attorney〕; agency —모〔씨받이〕 a surrogate mother — 목사 a locum tenens 《*pl.* locum tenentes》 — 소송 a lawsuit by proxy〔attorney〕 —업 surrogate business — 위임권 the power of attorney — 위임장 a letter of attorney — 전쟁 a proxy war — 투표 voting by proxy 교장 — an acting principal (of a school) 의장 — a deputy chairman

대리 공사 代理公使 a chargé d'affaires 《*pl.* chargés d'affaires》 《of a legation》; a chargé d'affaires and acting minister 임시 — a chargé d'affaires ad interim

대리 대사 代理大使 a chargé d'affaires 《of an embassy》

대리석 大理石 marble ¶ 대리석 기둥 a marble pillar // 대리석 상 a marble statue ; statue of〔in〕 marble

인조 — scagliola

대리업 代理業 agency ; an agent's business ; commission agency ; factorage

—자 an agent ; a factor

대리 영사 代理領事 an acting consulage

†대리인 代理人 a representative ; a proxy ; an agent ; 『법』 a procurator ; an attorney (소송의) ¶ 대리인이 되다 act as an agent // 본인 또는 대리인 출두하시오 He shall himself report personally or send a proxy.

법정 — a legal representative 전권 — a universal agent 총(總)— a general〔solo〕 agent 특별 — a special attorney〔representative〕

⁑대리점 代理店 an agency ; an agent ¶ 대리점이 되다 act as (an) agent 《for》 // 대리점을 설치하다 establish an agency // 각 도에 대리점을 가지고 있다 maintain an agency in every province

— 계산 an agent's account — 계약 an agency contract — 독점 판매 an exclusive〔a sole〕 (selling) agent 《for a company〔a product〕》 부— a subagent 수출 — an export agent 총— the general agent 판매 — a selling agent

***대립 對立** opposition ; confrontation ; standing face to face ; [반목] antagonism **—하다** be opposed to 《each other》; be confronted with 《each other》; be pitted against ; stand face to face ; be antagonistic to 《each other》 ¶ 대립적 opposing ; rival // 고용주와 피고용인 간의 대립 antagonism between the employer and the employed // 날카롭게 대립된 의견 opinions sharply divided // 양당이 대립하고 있다 The two political parties are pitted against each other〔set up in opposition〕. // 이 문제에 관하여 의견들이 대립하고 있다 There are rival〔opposing〕 opinions on this problem.

— 감정 a feeling of confrontation〔rivalry〕 — 개념 a coordinate concept — 계약 an agency contract —성(性) 『유전』 allelomorphism — 의견 an opposing〔a rival〕 opinion —자(者) an opponent —절(節) coordinate clauses 민족 — the antagonism of one race against another

대마 大馬 [바둑] large group of stones

***대마 大麻** a hemp ¶ 대마제의 hempen

—유(油) hempseed oil —인(仁) hemp seed

대마루 the ridge (of a roof)

대마루판 the crucial〔decisive, critical〕 moment

대마초 大麻草 [식물의] hemp ; [흡연물의] a hemp cigarette ; hashish ; marijuana
— 밀매자 an illegal dealer in hemp — 사범(事犯) an offender of the law on hemp control — 흡연자 a hemp〔marijuana〕 smoker
대막대기 a bamboo stick〔pole〕
대만 臺灣 Taiwan ; Formosa ¶ 대만의 Formosan
— 사람 a Taiwanese ; a Formosan — 해협(海峽) the Taiwan〔Formosa〕 Strait
*대만원 大滿員 a full house ; a crowded〔large〕 audience ¶ 대만원의 chockful ; galleryful // 대만원을 이루다 have a crowded audience ; draw a large〔crowded〕 house // 아침 저녁의 러시아워에는 모든 교통 기관이 대만원을 이룬다 Vehicles of all types are rampacked during the morning and evening rushes. // 극장이 대만원이다 The theater is bursting with people.
대말 a child's hobbyhorse ; stilts ; a bamboo horse 《for children》
‡대망 大望 a great ambition ; a great desire ; an aspiration ¶ 대망을 이루다 realize one's great ambition // 대망을 품다 be full of ambition ; have〔cherish, harbor, nourish〕 an ambition // 대망을 품은 사람 an ambitious〔aspiring〕 man // 그는 대망을 품고 있다 He aims high. / He aspires to greatness. // 그는 대망을 이루지 못한 채 세상을 떠났다 He died without attaining the object of his ambition.
*대망 待望 expectation ; anticipation —하다 expect ; wait for ; look forward to ¶ 대망의 hoped-for ; long-awaited ; long-expected ; long-cherished // 대망의 경기 회복 the hoped-for business recovery
대매 ① [매질] a single lash〔slap〕 of the whip ② [승부의] a final match〔game〕 ; tie-breaking —하다 play a final match ; break a tie
대매출 大賣出 a great〔big〕 sale ; a special bargain sale ¶ 반액〔사은〕 대매출 a half-price〔thank-you〕 bargain sale
대맥 大麥 barley ⇨ 보리
*대머리 a bald head ; a baldheaded person ; a baldpate ¶ 젊어서 벗어진 대머리 a premature bald-head // 대머리 벗어지다 become baldheaded // 일찍 대머리가 된 prematurely bald // 그 남자는 대머리다 He is bald.
대머리 大— the most important part of a work ; the essentials ; an outline
*대면 對面 an interview ; meeting —하다 interview ; meet ; see ; have an interview with ¶ 부자가 20년 만에 대면했다 Father and son met after twenty years' separation.
대면 교통 對面交通 facing traffic ; vis-à-vis〔face-to-face〕 traffic ; walking on the left side of a street facing the oncoming vehicular traffic ; Walk on (the) left side of (the) street facing traffic. (게시)
대명 大命 a Royal〔an Imperial〕 command ; a Royal〔an Imperial〕 mandate ¶ 대명을 받들어 in obedience to the king's command
대명 待命 awaiting orders ; pending appointment ¶ 대명중의 특명 전권 공사 a minister plenipotentiary in reserve // 대명이 되다 be placed on the waiting list ; be ordered to await further orders // 대명중이다 be on the waiting list〔orders〕
‡대명사 代名詞 〖문법〗 a pronoun ¶ 대명사의 pronominal // 그의 이름은 겁쟁이의 대명사이다 His name has become a synonym for cowardice. /He became the personification of cowardice.
관계〔지시, 의문, 인칭, 재귀〕 — a relative〔demonstrative, interrogative, personal, reflexive〕 pronoun
대명사 大名辭 〖논리〗 the major term
대명일 大名日 a grand festival (day) ; a public〔legal〕 holiday
*대모 代母 〖카톨릭〗 a godmother
대모 玳瑁 〖동물〗 a hawksbill (turtle) ; a tortoise shell (대모갑)
대모집 大募集 [고용] wholesale employment ; extensive employment ; [광고] a big〔large-scale〕 advertisement —하다 invite a large number of ; advertise widely for
남녀 공원 — 〖광고〗 Wanted—a large force of factory workers
대모한 [중요한] important ; vital ; momentous ; [주요한] main ; essential
대목 ① [고비] the most important occasion ; the vital moment ; the very time ¶ 섣달 대목 the very end of the year // 위험한 대목에서 at a critical moment // 대목에 가서 앓다 get sick at the very time 《when》
② [자리] the most important position〔spot〕 ¶ 여기가 곤란한 대목이다 This is where the trouble comes in.
—장(場) a fair at the very end of the year
대목 大木 a (master) carpenter
대목 臺木 a stock (tree) ; a parent stock (어미 그루) ; a block (목수의)
대못 a bamboo peg〔nail〕
대못 大— a large nail〔peg〕
대못박이 a fool ; a simpleton ; a dunce ; a blockhead
대묘 大廟 the royal mausoleum
대문 大文 [원문] the text ; the body ; [글의 부분] a passage
대문 大門 a gate ; the front〔main〕 gate〔entrance〕 ¶ 대문을 걸다 bolt the front gate ; close a gate ; lock a gate (자물쇠로 잠그다)
대문 밖이 저승이라 〔속담〕 Death keeps no calendar. /At every hour death is near.
대문띠 大門— a crosspiece of a gate
†대문자 大文字 a capital letter ; a big letter

¶ 대문자로 쓰다 capitalize ; write in capitals〔capital letters〕
대문장 大文章 [글] masterful writing ; [사람] a master writer ; a great master of (literary) style
대문짝 [문짝] a flap ; a (door) leaf ; [문] a door ; a gate ¶ 대문짝만하게 in huge〔bold〕 letters ; conspicuously
대물 代物 a substitute
— **변제(辨濟)** payment in substitutes
대물 對物 ¶ 대물의 real ; objective
— **계약** a real contract — **담보** security against a thing — **대부(貸付)** a loan on security — **렌즈** an object lens —**세(稅)** a real tax — **소송** 〖법〗 real action — **신용** real credit
대물리다 代— hand down〔leave, transmit, bequeath〕 to one's posterity ¶ 손자에게 재산을 대물리다 bequeath one's property to one's grandson
대미 大尾 the end ; the finale ; the dénouement 《프》
대미 對美 ¶ 대미의 with〔toward〕 (the United States of) America // 대미 무역을 촉진하다 promote〔improve〕 the trade with America
— **관계** relation with (the United States of) America — **무역** trade with America — **일변도** total〔complete〕 dependence upon the United States ; being out-and-out pro-American — **정책** policy toward America — **환율** the exchange rate on America ; the *won* dollar rate
대민 對民 ¶ 대민 봉사 활동 service for public welfare // 대민 사업 a project for the people
대바구니 a bamboo basket
대바늘 a bamboo (knitting) needle
대반 大盤 a large tray
대받다 answer〔talk〕 back ; contradict 《a person》 ; retort
대받다 代— succeed 《a person, to the property》 ; accede〔come〕 to 《a person's property》 ; inherit 《the property》
대발 a bamboo blind〔screen〕
대발회 大發會 〖증권〗 the first session of the new year
대밭 a bamboo grove〔thicket〕
대백로 大白鷺 〖새〗 the great white egret
대번 代番 being on duty for〔on behalf of〕 《another》 ; a substitute **—하다** be on duty for〔on behalf of〕 《another》
＊**대번에** [곧] at once ; immediately ; directly ; promptly ; instantly ; [단숨에] at a breath ; at a stroke ; [서슴지 않고] without hesitation ; [쉽사리] easily ; readily ¶ 대번에 알아 맞히다 guess right at once // 그는 대번에 승낙하지 않을 것이다 I am afraid he will not give a ready consent. // 그는 대번에 잔을 비웠다 He emptied the glass at a draft. // 이 물건은 대번에 팔릴 것이다 This article will find quick buyers.

대범 大凡 in general ; on the whole ; generally (speaking) ; as a (general) rule
대범 大泛 —하다 be not overly fussy 《about trifles》 ; be not particular〔fastidious〕 《about》 ; be large-hearted〔openhanded, broad-minded, liberal-minded〕 ¶ 대범한 태도 an air of magnanimity ; lofty manners
대범스럽다 ⇨ 대범하다
대법 大法 fundamental principles ; the law of the land (국법) ; the immutable law ¶ 대법에 어긋나다 be contrary to the law of the land
＊**대법관 大法官** a justice of the Supreme Court ; Lord (High) Chancellor 《L. (H.) C.》 《영》
대법원 大法院 the Supreme Court ; the Supreme Court of Judicature 《영》
—**장** the Chief Justice〔President〕 of the Supreme Court — **판사** a justice of the Supreme Court
대법회 大法會 ① [설법회] a large Buddhist lecture meeting ② [재올림] a great memorial service
＊＊**대변 大變** a serious trouble ; a terrible accident ; a disaster ; a calamity
＊**대변 大便** feces ; excrement ; evacuation ; stool ; dung ¶ 대변을 보다 move〔empty〕 the bowels ; go to stool ; evacuate 《the bowels》 ; relieve〔ease〕 oneself ; do one's needs ; respond to the call of nature ; have a motion // 대변을 보러 가다 go to the lavatory〔toilet〕 // 대변을 의사에게 보이다 send a specimen of one's stool to the doctor // 어제는 대변을 두번 보았다 My bowels acted twice yesterday.
— **검사** an examination of the feces — **불통** constipation
대변 代辯 speaking by proxy **—하다** speak for ; act as spokesman of ; be a spokesman〔mouthpiece〕 of ¶ 국방부의 대변인 spokesman for〔of〕 the Ministry of National Defense
대변 貸邊 the credit side ; account in one's favor ¶ 대변에 기입하다 credit a sum to 《a person》 ; enter on the credit side
— **계정** a credit account ; accounts of the creditor side — **기입** credit entry — **잔고(殘高)** a creditor balance — **재산** positive property —**표(票)** a credit note
대변 對邊 〖기하〗 the opposite side ; subtense
대변인 代辯人 a spokesman ; a mouthpiece ¶ 외무부 대변인 a Foreign Ministry spokesman ; a spokesman for〔of〕 the Ministry of Foreign Affairs
대변자 代辯者 ⇨ 대변인(代辯人)
대별 大別 a general〔broad〕 classification **—하다** classify〔divide〕 roughly 《into》 ; make a general classification ¶

세 종류로 대별하다 classify〔divide〕 into three groups∥두 종류로 대별할 수 있다 may be divided broadly into two categories

대병 大兵 a large military force ⇨ 대군(大軍)

대병 大病 a serious〔severe, critical〕 illness ; a dangerous disease ¶ 대병을 앓다 be in a serious〔critical〕 condition ; be seriously ill

대보 大寶 ① [보물] a treasure of great value ; a priceless treasure ② [옥새] the Royal〔Privy〕 Seal

대보다 compare 《one thing with another》 ; balance ; measure ; contrast (대조하다) ¶ …과 대보면 in comparison 《with》 ; as compared 《with》 ; if weighed against∥번역을 원문과 대보다 compare a translation with the original∥두 사람을 대보면 한 쪽은 마치 어린애 같다 One is a mere child beside〔by the side of〕 the other. ∥그것에는 대볼 만한 것이 없다 It stands unchallenged〔unparalleled, without a peer〕. ∥길고 짧은 것은 대보아야 안다 You can't always tell from appearances.

대보름 大— the 15th of the first month (lunar)

대복 大福 great happiness ; great fortune〔luck〕

대본 大本 the great foundation ; the primal basis ; the basic〔cardinal〕 principles ¶ 국가〔인륜〕의 대본 the foundation of the State〔human morality〕

⁑대본 臺本 [극의] a play-book ; [영화의] a scenario 《*pl.* ~s》 《이》 ; a script ; [가극의] a script ; a libretto 《*pl.* ~s, -ti》 ¶ 대본에 없는 대사를 말하다 ad-lib
— 작가 [영화의] a scriptwriter ; a screenwriter ; a continuity writer ; a scripter ; a scenarist ; [가극의] a librettist 방송용 — 〖라디오·텔레비전〗 a script 회화 — a dialogue script

대본 貸本 books to loan out ; books for lending ; [빌린 책] a hired book
— 서점 a circulating library ; a lending library —업(業) booklending business — 업자 the keeper of a circulating 〔rental 《미》〕 library

대본산 大本山 the headquarters〔cathedral〕 《of a sect》 ; the home temple

대봉 代捧 —하다 be paid in substitutes ¶ 대봉치다 fill up〔supply, replace〕 in substitutes ; substitute with

대부 大富 a millionaire ; a wealthy man

*대부 代父 〖카톨릭〗 a godfather

⁑대부 貸付 loaning —하다 lend ; loan ; advance ; make a loan〔an advance〕
—계(係) [은행의] loan teller ; a loan clerk — 계정 a loan account —금 a loan ; an advance — 기한 the term of a loan — 시장 a loan market — 원부(原簿) a loan ledger ; a loan book — 은행 a credit bank — 이식률 the interest rate on a loan — 잔고(殘高) a debit balance 당좌 — a call loan ; a loan at call ; a day-to-day loan 《미》 ; a demand loan 《영》 신용 — a loan on personal pledge ; a personal〔credit〕 loan ; an open credit 예금 — a deposit loan 은행 — a (commercial) bank loan 익일불(翌日拂) — an overnight loan 장기〔단기〕 — a long-〔short-〕term loan〔credit〕 정기(定期) — a time loan

대부대 大部隊 a large troop

대부등 大不等 extra large sized timber
대부등에 곁낫질이라 (속담) As oak is not felled at one stroke.

대부모 大父母 godparents

†대부분 大部分 ① [전체에 가까운 수효나 분량] most 《of》 ; the greater〔best〕 part 《of》 ; (a) great part 《of》 ; a great〔large, major〕 portion 《of》 ; a large percentage 《of》 ; the bulk 《of》 ; the majority 《of》 ¶ 비용의 대부분은 회원들의 기부였다 The bulk of the expenses was collected from the members. ∥마을 사람들의 대부분은 빈곤했다 Most of the villagers were poor.
② [거의다] mostly ; largely ; for the most part ; in large part ; mainly ; in the main ; on the whole ; nearly ; practically ¶ 참석자는 대부분 주부들이었다 Those present were, for the most part, housewives. ∥그들은 대부분 이민의 후손이다 They are mostly〔mainly〕 descendants of immigrants.

대부인 大夫人 your〔his〕 esteemed mother

대북 臺北 Taipeh ; Taipei

대북 對北 ¶ 대북 방송 propaganda broadcast beamed at North Korea ; broadcast to the north

대분수 帶分數 〖수학〗 a mixed number

대불 大佛 a colossal〔huge, big〕 statue of Buddha ; a great image of Buddha

대불행 大不幸 a great misfortune ; a calamity ; a disaster

대붕 大鵬 a roc ¶ 대붕의 웅지(雄志) a great ambition

대비 a bamboo broom

대비 對比 [비교] comparison ; [대조] contrast ; [심리] correlation —하다 compare〔contrast〕 《two things, A with B》 ; make a comparison 《between two things》 ; correlate 《with》
— 광도계(光度計) a contrast photometer — 논법 〖논리학〗 analogy

대비 大妃 a Queen Dowager ; a Queen Mother

대비 貸費 a loan ; an advance ; a loan scholarship (학비) —하다 loan 〔advance〕 expenses ; make a loan
—생(生) a loan scholarship student ; a holder of a loan scholarship — 자금 a loan fund (to provide scholarships for

students) — 제도 the scholarship system

†대비 對備 provision ; preparation ; preparedness — 하다 provide 《for, against》; prepare (oneself) 《for》; be ready 《for》; make preparation 《for, against》 ¶ 노후에 대비하여 저축하다 save money for one's old age // 비상시에 대비하다 provide against emergencies 〔contingencies〕; prepare for the worst ; lay up against a rainy day // 시험에 대비하다 prepare oneself〔get oneself ready〕 for an examination // 장래에 대비하다 provide〔make provisions〕 for the future // 적침에 대비하여 국방력을 강화하다 strengthen the national defense against possible aggression // 흉년에 대비하여 쌀을 저장하다 store rice away against a famine // 오늘밤에 굉장히 추워질 것 같으니까 단단히 대비를 해야겠어요 We'd better brace for a big chill tonight.

대빈 大賓 a guest of honor ; an important〔a special〕 guest

대빗 a bamboo comb

대사 大事 [큰일] a great thing ; [큰 사업] a great undertaking ; a great enterprise〔task〕; [중요한 일] an important matter ; a serious affair ; [대례] a marriage ceremony ¶ 대사를 이루다 achieve a great thing〔deed, work〕; set the Thames on fire

대사 大師 a great (Buddhist) priest ; a saint

대사 大赦 an amnesty ; a general pardon — 하다 amnesty ; pardon ; grant an amnesty to

—령(令) a decree of amnesty〔oblivion〕 ¶ 대사령을 내리다 grant an amnesty 《to》

대사 代謝 replacement

대사 臺詞 speech ; dialog ; words ; one's lines ¶ 대사를 말하다 speak one's part ; read the lines // 대사를 잊어 버리다 forget one's lines

독백 — a monolog ; a soliloquy

대사 大寫 『영화』 a close-up

‡대사 大使 an ambassador ; an envoy ¶ 대사 일행 the ambassadorial party // 주미 한국 대사 the Korean Ambassador to America // 대사를 특파하다 dispatch a special envoy 《to》

—급 회의 an ambassadorial〔ambassador-level〕 conference ; talks on the ambassadorial level — 부인 an ambassadress 대리 — a chargé d'affaires 무임소 — an ambassador-at-large 이동 — a roving ambassador 전권 — an ambassador plenipotentiary 주미(駐美) — an ambassador to the United States 주영(駐英) — an ambassador to the Court of St. James's〔to Great Britain〕 특명 전권 — an ambassador extraordinary and plenipotentiary

대사 大蛇 a big snake ; a huge〔large, monster〕 serpent ; an anaconda

대사관 大使館 an embassy ¶ 주미 한국 대사관 the Korean Embassy at Washington

—부 육군 무관 a military〔an army〕 attaché to an embassy —부 해군 무관 a naval attaché to an embassy — 사무국 a chancellery ; a chancery — 서기관 a secretary of an embassy — 참사관 a councillor〔counsellor〕 of an embassy 미국 — the American Embassy 영국 — the British Embassy

대사관원 大使館員 (a member of) the embassy staff

대사닥다리 a bamboo ladder

대사무소 貸事務所 an office for rent〔to let 《영》〕; a rented office room

대살 代殺 — 하다 execute a murderer ; put a homicide to death

대살지다 (be) thin and tough ; lean and hard ; sinewy

대삿갓 a conical bamboo hat

대상 大喪 death of the king ; mourning for the king

대상 大祥 the second anniversary of a death

대상 代償 ① [변상] compensation ; reparation ; indemnification ; a consideration ; quid pro quo 《라》 — 하다 compensate〔indemnify〕 《a person for a loss》; pay an indemnity ¶ …의 대상으로 in compensation〔in return〕 《for》 // 이들 모든 것의 대상으로 in return for all this ② [대신하는 변상] vicarious compensation — 하다 compensate on behalf of another ③ [딴 것으로 하는] compensation in substitutes — 하다 compensate in substitutes

— 부전(不全) 『의학』 [심장의] decompensation — 수입 compensatory imports

‡대상 隊商 a caravan

†대상 對象 an object ; the subject ; a target (목표) ¶ 대상적 objective // 과세의 대상 property liable for taxation // 연구〔조사〕의 대상 the subject of study 〔investigation〕 // 공격의 대상 a target 〔subject〕 of criticism // 학생을 대상으로 하는 잡지 a student-oriented magazine // 선망의 대상이 되다 become the object of envy

대상 大商 a wealthy〔an influential〕 merchant ; a merchant prince ; a trader

대상자 —箱子 a bamboo box

대상 작용 代償作用 『생물·정신 분석』 compensation — 하다 compensate

대상 지수 帶狀指數 a zonal index

대생 對生 『식물』 symmetry ; opposition ; dichotomy

—엽(葉) opposite leaves

대서 大署 the Korean midsummer day (occurring about July 23rd) ; an intense heat (혹서)

대서 代書 writing for a person **—하다** write〔draw up〕 for 《a person》
—소 a scrivener's office ; a scrivenery **—업** scrivenery **—인(人)** a scrivener ; a scribe ; a public letterwriter
대서 代署 signing per procuration **—하다** sign〔set a seal〕 by proxy
대서다 ① [뒤에] stand close behind 《another》 ; [가까이] stand close to ¶ 뒤에 대서서 가다 follow at another's heel // 자동차들이 대서서 가다 Cars crawl along bumper to bumper.
② [대들다] stand against ; turn against 〔upon〕 ; defy 《one's superior》
*__대서양 大西洋__ the Atlantic (Ocean) ¶ 대서양의 Atlantic
— 조약 the Atlantic Pact〔Treaty〕 **— 함대** the Atlantic Fleet **— 항로** an Atlantic line **— 헌장** the Atlantic Charter **— 회담** the Atlantic Conference **— 횡단 비행** a transatlantic flight **북(北)— 조약 기구** the North Atlantic Treaty Organization 《NATO》
대서 특필 大書特筆 a feature (story) ; a cover story ; a wide news coverage ; special mention **—하다** publish 《the news》 with heavy headlines ; crack the headlines ; play up 《the event》 with a banner ; splash the news 《영》 ; headline ; banner ; feature ¶ 대서 특필할 만한 《a deed》 worthy of special mention // 신문은 모두 이 사건을 대서 특필했다 The newspapers bannered this incident. // 신문들은 워터게이트 사건을 대서 특필하고 있다 The newspapers are headlining a story about the Watergate scandal. // 그 지방 신문들은 대통령의 방문을 대서 특필했다 The local newspapers featured the President's visit.
대석 臺石 a pedestal (stone)
대석 對席 **—하다** sit facing each other ; sit face to face ; sit opposite ; attend together (회견·회의)
대선 大船 a large vessel ; a big ship 〔boat〕
대선거구 大選擧區 a major constituency **—제** a major constituency system ; a multimember-district system
대선풍 大旋風 a tornado ; a whirlwind ; a waterspout
대설 大雪 [큰 눈] a big〔heavy〕 snow 〔snowfall〕 ; [절후] (the season of) great snow (occurring about December 8th)
대설대 a pipestem
대성 大成 ① [완성] completion ; accomplishment **—하다** complete ; accomplish ; be brought to completion ¶ 사업을 대성하다 accomplish one's task successfully
② [인격의] attain〔come〕 to greatness ¶ 대성할 인물 a man full of promise ; a person with the makings of a great man
대성 大聖 a great sage ; a mahatma ¶ 대성 간디 the Mahatma Gandhi // 대성 소크라테스 the great sage Socrates
대성 大姓 a noted family (거족) ; a noted 〔an illustrious〕 family name (거성)
대성 大聲 a loud voice ; a stentorian voice ¶ 대성으로 loudly ; in a loud voice ; at shouting pitch // 대성을 지르다 bawl ; shout ; yell ; speak〔cry〕 in a loud voice ; give a loud scream // 대성 질호하다 thunder ; fulminate 《against》 ; denounce vehemently // 대성 통곡하다 wail loudly ; lament at the top of one's voice ; mourn bitterly
대성공 大成功 a great〔brilliant〕 success ; smash hit (영화 따위) ⇨ 성공(成功)
대성황 大盛況 prosperity ; a flourishing condition ; a great success ; a boom ⇨ 성황 ¶ 그 가게는 대성황을 이루고 있다 The shop is doing a roaring business.
대세 大勢 ① [형세] the general situation ; [추세] the general trend〔drift〕 《of affairs》 ; the general tendency 《of the world》 ; the main current ; the tide ¶ 대세를 따르다 go with the tide ; run with the times ; follow the general trends ; swim with the current // 대세에 역행하다 go against the current ; swim against the stream // 세계의 대세를 전망하다 realize〔take in〕 the trends of international affairs // 천하 대세를 살피다 study the general tendency of the world // 대세는 이미 정해졌다 The final issue is now certain. /It〔The thing〕 is as good as settled. ② [병의] a serious〔grave〕 condition ; a critical state〔stage〕 《of a disease》 ③ [권세 따위] power (권력) ; influence (세력) ¶ 대세를 잡다 take〔assume〕 the power ; come into power
대소 大小 [대와 소] great and small sizes ; bigness and smallness ; [크기] size ; dimension ; magnitude ¶ 대소의 large and〔or〕 small ; of all〔various〕 sizes // 달의 대소 the number of days in a month ; an odd month and an even month // 대소에 따라 according to size // 대소를 막론하고 regardless〔irrespective〕 of size
대소 大笑 loud laughter ; a roar of laughter ; convulsive laughter ; a cachinnation **—하다** laugh aloud ; burst out laughing ; roar with laughter ; laugh broadly ; cachinnate ¶ 가가 대소하다 break 〔burst〕 into a roar of laughter ; laugh heartily ; enjoy a hearty laugh
대소 代訴 litigation by proxy **—하다** sue〔bring suit〕 on behalf of another
대소 對訴 a counter action〔suit〕
이혼 — a counter divorce action
대소 對蘇 ¶ 미국의 대소 정책 an American policy toward the Soviet Union
— 협상 a negotiation with the U. S. S. R

대소동 大騷動 turmoil ; tumult ; great excitement ; great trouble ; a row ; a shindy ; a great uproar ; a big stir ; a clamor **—하다** be in a turmoil ; make 〔raise〕 a great uproar ; kick up a row 〔dust, shindy〕 ; raise the devil ; cause excitement〔a great stir〕 ; whoop《it》up 《미·속》 ¶ 장내는 대소동이 일어났다 The chamber was thrown into an uproar. // 집안은 대소동이 일어나고 있다 All is confusion in the house. /The house is topsy-turvy〔in a great bustle, in a turmoil〕.

대소변 大小便 [변] urine and feces ; [배설] urination and defecation ¶ 대소변을 보다 relieve oneself〔nature〕 ; ease nature

대소사 大小事 matters great and small ; all sorts of matters

대소상 大小祥 the first two anniversaries of a death

대소수 帶小數 『수학』 a number with a decimal

대소월 大小月 odd and〔or〕 even months

대소장 大小腸 the large and small intestines

대소쿠리 a bamboo basket

대속 代贖 redemption〔expiation, atonement〕 on behalf of another ; 『성경』 the Atonement

대손 貸損 a bad debt ; a dead loan ¶ 대손이 되다 《돈이 주어》 become uncollectable〔irrecoverable〕

대솔 大— a big pine tree

대수 大水 a flood ⇨ 큰물, 홍수

대수 大數 ① [큰수] a big〔great, large, high〕 number ② [대운] good luck ; great fortune

— 법칙 『통계』 the law of large numbers

*__대수 代數__ algebra ; literal arithmetic ¶ 대수적 algebraic(al) // 대수적 해법 an algebraical solution // 대수로 풀다 solve 《a question》 in algebra ; work out 《a problem》 algebraically

— 기호 an algebraic symbol〔sign〕 **—식**〔**함수, 방정식**〕 an algebraical expression〔function, equation〕 **—학자** an algebraist **논리 —** algebra of logic

대수 對手 an opponent ⇨ 적수(敵手)

대수 對數 『수학』 a logarithm ; a log

— 계산척 a logarithmic scale **—율(率)** the modulus of a logarithm **—표(表)** a table of logarithms ; a logarithmic table **— 함수** a logarithmic function

*__대수롭다__ (be) important ; valuable ; useful ; be deserving of respect ¶ 대수롭게 여기다 make〔think〕 much of 《a person》 ; attach importance 《to》 ; have regard for // 대수롭지 않다 be trivial〔trifling〕 ; be insignificant ; be of little importance ; be of no account〔consequence〕 ; be valueless〔unworthy, worthless, useless〕 // 대수롭지 않게 여기다 have no regard 《for》 ; make little 〔light〕 《of》 // 목숨보다도 이름을 대수롭게 여기다 value〔prize, esteem, put〕 honor above life // 그들은 남의 감정 따위는 대수롭지 않게 여긴다 They have no regard for other's feelings. // 대수롭지 않은 일로 떠들지 마라 Don't make a fuss about trifles. // 사람들은 그를 대수롭지 않게 생각한다 He receives scant consideration.

대수술 大手術 a major (surgical) operation

대숲 a bamboo grove〔thicket〕

대승 大乘 Mahayana 《범》 ; the greater vehicle ¶ 대승적 견지에서 문제를 해결다 settle a matter from a broad point of view

— 경전 the Mahayana Sutras **— 불교** Mahayanist Buddhism

대승 大勝 ① a great victory ; a sweeping 〔complete, signal, decisive〕 victory ; a landslide (선거에서) ② great superiority **—하다** win〔get〕 a great〔sweeping〕 victory ; [낫다] surpass ; excel ; be much better 《than》

대승리 大勝利 a sweeping〔complete, signal〕 victory ; [선거에서] a landslide ¶ 공화당의 대승리 a Republican landslide

대승정 大僧正 『불교』 an archbishop ; a chief abbot ; a cardinal (카톨릭교의)

대시 ① [부호] a dash ② [역주(力走)] a dash **—하다** dash

대식 大食 ① [아침 저녁의 끼니] main meals 《breakfast and supper》 ② [많이 먹음] gluttony ; voracity ; heavy feeding **—하다** eat heavily ; eat much ; eat a heavy meal ; eat gluttonously ; gluttonize ; gorge ; gormandize ; cram 〔stuff〕 oneself ; eat like a horse

—가 a big〔large〕 eater ; a glutton ; a gourmand ; a heavy〔huge〕 feeder ; a trencherman **—기(期)** [누에] the gluttonous period of the last age of a silkworm **—증(症)** 『의학』 bulimia ; binge-purge syndrome (식욕 이상 항진증)

†**대신 代身** ① [대리·대용] vicariousness ; substitution ; [사람] a substitute ; a deputy ; a proxy ; an alternate 《미》 ; a relief (교대자) ; a sub 《속》 **—하다** relieve 《another》 ; take the place of ; take 《a person's》 place ; act as a substitute ; be substituted 《for a person》 ¶ 대신에 vicariously ; for ; in place of ; instead (of) ; on behalf of ; in substitute for ; in lieu of ; in the name of ; as (a) substitute for ; in the room of // 대신으로 as a substitute // 주인을 대신하여 for〔in place of〕 one's master // 대신하여 일을 보다 act for 《a person》 ; act on behalf of ; do duty for 《a person》 // …의 대신이 되다 serve as〔for〕 ; do duty for // 협회를 대신해서 on behalf of the association // 대신할 사람을 찾다 look for someone to

take one's place // 그 사람 대신 그 여자가 왔다 She came in his place. // 내 대신 그가 했다 He did it on my behalf. // 내 아들이 나를 대신할 것이다 My son shall be my proxy. // 당신 대신 내가 갈까 Shall I go for you? // 자네가 없는 동안 내가 대신 일해 주지 I'll fill in for you while you're gone.

② [대상(代償)] compensation; return; exchange (교환) ¶ 대신(에) by way of compensation; in return 《for》; in exchange 《for》 (교환); in compensation for; to make up for (보상) // 대신 무엇을 받을까 What do we get in return? // 일해 주는 대신 그에게 영어를 가르쳐 주었다 I taught him English in exchange for his service.

③ [한편] but; though; while ¶ 적도 많지만 대신에 친구도 많다 I have as many friends as enemies. // 값이 비싼 대신 질이 좋다 It is dear but the quality is good.

대신 大臣 a minister 《of State》; a Cabinet〔State〕 minister; a cabinet member

대실 貸室 a room〔hall〕 on〔for〕 hire

대심 對審 〖법〗 confrontation ¶ 대심하다 confront 《the accused with the accuser》

대심원 大審院 the Supreme Court of the United States 《미》

대아 大我 〖철학〗 the higher self; 〖불교〗 Atman 《범》

대악 大惡 atrocity; outrage; heinousness; [대악인] a consummate villain; an arrant knave; a thorough rascal

대안 對岸 the other side of a river; the opposite bank ¶ 대안에 on the opposite bank 《of a river》; on the other side 《of a river》 // 대안의 적 the enemy on the opposite bank // 대안의 화재 구경하듯 하다 play the part of a spectator; look on 《a trouble》 nonchalantly〔unconcernedly, with utter indifference〕

*__대안 代案__ an alternative plan〔proposal〕; a substitute (measure, bill) ¶ 대안을 제시하다 make〔propose〕 an alternative plan〔measure〕 // 무슨 대안이라도 있습니까 Do you have any alternative proposal?

대안 對眼 for the eye

―경(鏡) an ocular **― 렌즈** an eye lens; an eye glass; an eyepiece

대안 對案 a counterproposal ¶ 대안을 제시하다 make a counterproposal

대액 大厄 a great misfortune〔calamity, disaster〕

*__대야__ a basin; a washbasin; a washbowl 《미》

대양 大洋 the ocean; the main 《시》 ¶ 대양의 oceanic // 대양 한 가운데서 in the middle of the ocean // 대양을 항해하다 sail the ocean

―학(學) oceanography **― 항로** an ocean line **― 항로선** an oceangoing vessel; an ocean liner **― 횡단 비행** a transoceanic flight

대양주 大洋洲 Oceania ¶ 대양주 사람 an Oceanian

대어 大魚 a big〔large〕 fish ¶ 대어를 놓치다 miss a capital chance

대언 大言 big talk; big words; a brag ⇨ 대언 장담

대언 代言 ―하다 speak for 《another》

대언장담 大言壯談 tall〔big〕 talk; loud-mouthed boasting; a loud boast; bragging **―하다** talk big〔tall〕; boast of〔about〕; talk in a grandiose style; use bombastic language; be full of hot air; rant

대업 大業 a great achievement〔deed〕; a great enterprise〔undertaking〕; a great〔monumental〕 work; a great〔mighty, gigantic〕 task ¶ 건국의 대업 the great work of founding the State

대여 貸與 lending; a loan **―하다** loan; lend; lease ¶ 무료로 대여하다 lend free; loan 《a thing》 without charge

대여섯 about five or six

대역 大逆 (high) treason

―무도(無道) heinous treason **― 사건** a lese-majesty affair; a high treason case **―죄** high treason; lese majesty

대역 大役 an important task〔mission, role〕; a heavy trust ¶ 대역을 맡다 undertake〔take up, accept〕 an important part // 대역을 완수하다 perform〔discharge, accomplish〕 an important duty

대역 代役 a substitute (actor); a stand-in; a double; an understudy **―하다** play as a substitute for; play the part of 《another actor》

대역 對譯 a translation with the original; parallel versions ¶ 이 영문학 총서는 영한 대역으로 되어 있다 In this English literature series the English original has its Korean translation on the opposite page.

영한 ― 회화 사전 an English-Korean conversation dictionary **―판(版)** a bilingual edition; an interlinear edition

대연 大宴 a big feast; a grand banquet

대연습 大演習 grand maneuvers ¶ 대연습을 하다 hold grand maneuvers

대열 隊列 a line; ranks ¶ 대열을 짓다 form ranks〔in line〕 // 대열을 정돈하다 dress〔align〕 ranks // 대열을 짓고 행진하다 march in rank and file on the street; parade a street (데모 행진 따위)

대엿새 about five or six days

대영 對英 ¶ 대영의 toward〔with〕 Great Britain

― 무역 trade with Great Britain〔the British Commonwealth〕 **― 정책** policy toward Britain **―환(換)** the *won*-sterling exchange

대영 제국 大英帝國 the British Empire

대오 大悟 spiritual awakening〔enlight-

enment〕; 〚불교〛 divine enlightenment
— 하다 attain spiritual awakening; find one's philosophy of life

대오 隊伍 〔대열〕 the ranks; a line; 〔진열〕 an array; formation; 〔행렬〕 a procession ¶ 대오를 짓고 in line〔column, procession〕; in ranks〔files〕; in formation; in regular order // 대오를 짓다 form ranks〔a column〕; form in line // 대오를 흐트러뜨리다 break the line; fall into disorder // 학생들은 대오를 지어 거리를 행진했다 The students marched in rank and file on the street.

대오다 come〔arrive〕 on time; get〔be〕 《here》 on time ¶ 약속한 시간에 대오다 come by the appointed time // 여섯시에 대오겠다 I will be here by six.

대오리 a bamboo strip

대왕 大王 the Great King ¶ 알렉산더 대왕 Alexander the Great

대외 對外 foreign; international; abroad; outside (외부)
— 거래 foreign transactions — 권익(權益) foreign〔overseas, international〕 rights and interests — 무역 foreign trade; overseas trade — 문제 international issues — 방송 broadcasting abroad — 지불 foreign payment — 채권 foreign credit — 채무 foreign liabilities — 친선 promotion of friendly relations with foreign countries — 투자 overseas investment

대외 관계 對外關係 foreign〔international〕 relation; diplomacy ¶ 대외 관계를 사장에게 일임하다 leave everything diplomatic to the president's discretion

대외 원조 對外援助 foreign aid; aid to a foreign country
—법 〚법〛 〔미국의〕 the Foreign Assistance Act

대외 정책 對外政策 a foreign〔an external, an exterior〕 policy ¶ 대외 정책의 수행 the (Government's) conduct of foreign policy // 대외 정책을 결정하다 formulate a foreign policy

대요 大要 a summary; a gist; substance; a syllabus; a compendium; an epitome; a (brief) résumé 《프》; an outline ¶ 사건의 대요 the sum and substance of the matter // 한국 역사의 대요 an outline of Korean history; an outline history of Korea // 질문에 대한 회답의 대요 the general tenor of the answers to a question // 대요를 설명하다 describe 〔give〕 the outline 《of》 // …의 대요를 말하다 epitomize; summarize; outline; give a summary〔an outline〕 of; sum up

대욕 大慾 avarice; cupidity; covetousness; greed; avidity ¶ 대욕의 avaricious; covetous; greedy

대용 代用 substitution — 하다 use 《a thing》 as a substitute; substitute A for B; use A for〔instead of〕 B ¶ 대용의 substitute // 이것은 책상의 대용이 된다 This will serve as a desk. / We can use this for a desk.
— 가능성 substitutability —식(食) substitute food; a rice substitute 《미》 —어(語) 〚문법〛 a substitute — 커피 a substitute for coffee; a coffee substitute —품 a substitute 《for》; a substitute article〔product〕

대용 貸用 using on loan; borrowing — 하다 take〔use〕 on loan; borrow

대우 〚농업〛 planting 《beans》 in〔between〕 the rows of wheat〔barley〕 field

대우 大雨 a heavy rainfall; a pouring rain; a downpour; a deluge of rain; torrents (of rain); a cloudburst 《미·속》

†**대우 待遇** 〔취급〕 treatment; 〔접대〕 reception; entertainment; 〔급료〕 pay; salary; remuneration — 하다 treat; receive; entertain; pay; remunerate ¶ 공정한 대우 fair treatment // 차별 대우 discriminative treatment // 대우가 좋다 pay 《a person》 well; treat〔receive〕 《a person》 well; be paid well〔liberally〕; be hospitable (여관 등이) // 대우가 나쁘다 underpay; be underpaid〔poorly paid〕 // 대우를 개선하다 improve working conditions (조건을); increase pay (급료를) // 노동자의 대우를 개선하다 improve labor conditions // 극진한 대우를 받다 be kindly treated; be received warmly〔cordially〕 // 동등하게 대우하다 treat 《a person》 on the same footing with 《another》 // 신사의 대우를 하다 treat 《a person》 as a gentleman // 파격적인 대우를 하다 make an exception of one's case〔in one's favor〕 // 전관 대우를 받다 be accorded the treatment due to one's late office // 지위에 상당하는 대우를 하다 do 《a person》 the honor due to his position; do 《a person》 due honor // 이 회사는 대우가 좋다〔나쁘다〕 This company pays their employees liberally〔scantly〕.

대우 對偶 ① 〚수학〛 contrapositive (proposition) ② 〚논리〛 opposition; antithesis ③ 〔짝〕 a pair
—법(法) antithesis — 법칙 the law of contraposition — 정리(定理) a contraposition — 주제(主題) 〚음악〛 a countersubject

대우 개선 待遇改善 improvement〔betterment〕 of labor conditions; increase of pay; raising salary ¶ 대우 개선을 외치다 shout〔cry〕 for a raise〔rise〕 in pay

대우주 大宇宙 〚철학〛 the great universe; a macrocosm

대우콩 beans planted as a catch crop with wheat or barley

대운 大運 (a) great fortune; good luck

대울 a bamboo fence〔hedge〕

대웅성 大熊星 (stars of) the Great Bear

대웅전 大雄殿 〚불교〛 the main〔inner〕 temple; the main building〔sanctuary〕

(of a temple)
대웅좌 大熊座 〖천문〗 the Great Bear ; the Big Dipper ; Ursa Major
대원 大願 an earnest prayer ; an intense desire ¶ 마침내 그녀의 대원이 성취되었다 At last her earnest prayer was answered.
— **성취** the attainment of one's desire
대원 隊員 a member ⟪of a fire brigade⟫
대원수 大元帥 the generalissimo ; the commander-in-chief (of the Army, Navy)
대원칙 大原則 the broad〔dominant〕 principle
대월 貸越 an outstanding account (미불) ; an overdraft (은행의) ¶ 대월이 되어 있다 be〔remain〕 unpaid〔due, outstanding〕 ; overdraw one's accounts ; be overdrawn
— **계정** a creditor account
*__대위 大尉__ [육군·공군] a captain ; [해군] a first lieutenant ¶ 대위의 직 a captaincy ; a lieutenancy
대위 代位 〖법〗 subrogation **—하다** subrogate
— **납부** payment in subrogation — **납부 의무자** a subrogator — **변제** subrogated performance ; subrogation
대위 對位 contraposition ; coordination ; counterpoint
대위법 對位法 〖음악〗 counterpoint ¶ 대위법의 contrapuntal
— **작곡가** a contrapuntist **이중** — double counterpoint
대유 大儒 a great confucianist ; a great scholar
대유성 大遊星 the major planets
대은 大恩 a great favor〔obligation〕 ⇨ 홍은(鴻恩)
대음 大飮 heavy〔deep〕 drinking ; a carouse **—하다** drink heavily ; carouse ; have a carouse〔spree〕 ; go on a spree〔bender, binge〕
대읍 大邑 a big town
대응 對應 [마주 대함] confrontation ; facing each other ; opposition ; [상응] correspondence ; [도형의] homology ; [상등] equivalence **—하다** confront〔face〕 each other ; cope with ; correspond to ; be homologous to ; be equivalent to ¶ 시국에 대응하다 cope with the situation
—각(角) a homologous〔corresponding〕 angle **—〔역〕 무역** countertrade **—부(部)** a counterpart — **악절** 〖음악〗 an antithesis **—책** countermove ; countermeasure ; counterplot
대의 大意 [요지] the substance ; the gist ; [개략] a general idea ; an outline ; a summary ; a résumé ⟪프⟫ ¶ 경제학 대의 the elements of economics // 연설의 대의를 간추려 말하다 give the substance〔gist〕 of ⟪a person's⟫ speech
대의 大義 the law of justice ; the great duty〔moral obligation〕 ; loyalty and patriotism ; righteousness ; the just and righteous cause ; a cardinal〔an important〕 principle ; one's first cause ; a noble cause ; a great cause ¶ 대의를 위하여 for the great cause of ⟪a country⟫ // 대의에 죽다 sacrifice oneself for justice ; sacrifice one's life in the great cause
대의 代議 representation
— **정치** representative〔parliamentary〕 government
대의명분 大義名分 the true relations of sovereign and subject ¶ 대의명분을 위해서 진력하다 work for a just〔good〕 cause // 대의명분이 서지 않다 cannot be justified
대의원 代議員 a representative ; a delegate
—단 a delegation **—회** [회의체] a board of representatives ; [모임] a representative conference ; a (general) meeting of representatives
대의제(도) 代議制(度) a representative 〔parliamentary〕 system
— **민주주의** representative democracy
대이름씨 a pronoun ⇨ 대명사
대인 大人 ① [어른] an adult ; a grown-up ¶ 대인용 for an adult ② [군자] a man of virtue ; a noble gentleman ③ [존칭] your〔his〕 esteemed father ④ [관대한 사람] a bighearted〔broad-minded, generous〕 person
대인 代印 signing〔signature〕 per〔by〕 procuration **—하다** sign〔set a seal〕 by proxy ¶ 대인도 무방하다 Signature 〔signing〕 per procuration would do. /You may get somebody to sign it for you.
대인 對人 ¶ 대인의 personnel ; personal
— **관계〔신용〕** personal relations〔credit〕 **—권(權)** personal right — **담보** personal security — **무기** an antipersonnel weapon
대인기 大人氣 a great popularity 〔vogue〕 ; a great success ; a big hit ¶ 대인기를 끈 소설 a best seller // 그 여배우는 지금 대인기다 The film actress is now in the full flush of her popularity. // 그는 지금 학계에서 대인기를 끌고 있다 He enjoys great popularity in academic circles. // 그 소설은 대인기를 끌었다 The novel took the public by storm. /The novel rapidly made its way into universal favor.
대인물 大人物 a great man〔figure〕 ; a man of great caliber ; a prominent 〔leading〕 figure ; a big man〔gun〕 ¶ 정계의 대인물 a great figure in politics
대일 對日 ¶ 대일의 towards〔with〕 Japan // 한국의 대일 외교 정책 Korea's diplomatic policy towards Japan // 대일 감정은

극히 나쁘다 The anti-Japanese sentiment is mounting〔growing〕《in South Asia》. /The feeling is very bad toward the Japanese.
— 강화 조약 the peace treaty with Japan
— 관계 relations with Japan — 무역 trade with Japan

대일 감정 對日感情 the feeling〔sentiment〕 toward Japan

대임 大任 [임무] a great task ; an important charge〔duty〕; [책임] a heavy responsibility ; [사명] an important mission ; [요직] an important office〔position〕 ¶ 대임을 띠고 on a most important mission // 대임을 다하다 fulfill a great mission ; carry through a great task // 대임을 맡다 undertake a great task // 대임을 맡기다 entrust 《a person》 with a great task

대자 a bamboo measure〔rule, scale〕

대자 大字 a large character ; a capital letter (대문자)

대자리 a bamboo mat

대자보 大字報 [중공의] a big-character paper〔poster〕; a wall-poster

대자연 大自然 Mother Nature ; (Mighty) Nature

대작 大斫 large splits of firewood

대작 代作 ① ghost-writing ; vicarious writing ; writing〔composing〕 for another ; [작품] a vicarious work — 하다 ghostwrite ; ghost 《for a person》 ¶ 소설을 대작하다 ghostwrite a novel
② sowing a substitute plant in a dried rice-paddy ⇨ 대파
—자(者) a ghost(-writer)

대작 大作 a great work ; a major work ; a masterpiece (걸작) ; a work〔picture, sculpture〕 of large size (미술)

대작 對酌 — 하다 drink together〔facing each other, across the table from one another〕; hobnob 《with》

대잠 對潛 ¶ 대잠수함의 anti-submarine
— 미사일 an anti-submarine missile

*__대장__ [대장장이] a smith ; a blacksmith ; the knight of the hammer (해학적으로)
—간 a smithy ; a forge ; a blacksmith's shop
대장간에 식칼이 논다 [속담] The tailor's wife is worst clad. /The shoemaker's son always goes barefoot.

*__대장 大將__ a (full) general (육군·공군) ; an admiral (해군) ; [우두머리] a chief ; a head ; a boss ; a master ; a captain ; a kingpin 《미·구》; a governor 《미·속》 ¶ 골목 대장 the king〔boss〕 of the kids 〔youngsters〕 of the neighborhood

대장 大腸 〚해부〛 the colon ; the large〔great〕 intestine
—균 a colon bacillus 《*pl.* bacilli》; a coli (bacillus) —염 colitis — 카타르 catarrh of the colon

대장 隊長 a captain ; a leader ; a commander
대— a battalion commander 소— a platoon leader 중— a company commander
탐험— the leader of an expedition

대장 臺帳 a ledger ; a register ¶ 대장에 기입하다 register ; enter in the ledger
토지 — a cadastre〔cadaster〕

대장경 大藏經 the complete collection of Buddhist Sutras, Laws and Treatises ; a collection of all the sacred writings of Buddhism

대장부 大丈夫 a hero ; a brave〔chivalrous, manly〕 man ¶ 대장부답게 굴라 Behave like a man. /Play the man. // 대장부라면 그런 짓은 못 한다 You should be a man enough not to do a thing like that.

대장일 smithery ; blacksmith work

*__대장장이__ a smith ⇨ 대장

대재 大災 a grave disaster ; a calamity

대저 大著 a great work〔book〕

대저 大抵 generally speaking ; in general

대저울 a beam(-type) balance

대적 大敵 a great〔formidable〕 foe 〔enemy〕; [경쟁자] a great〔formidable〕 rival〔opponent〕 ¶ 민주주의의 대적 the most deadly foe of democracy

대적 對敵 ① [적대] hostility ; antagonism ② [적수] a (good) match ; a worthy opponent ; a rival ; matching — 하다 fight against ; oppose ; be antagonistic to ; contend against ; match ; equal ; rival
— 갱도(坑道) a countermine — 행위 hostile action ; hostilities

대전 大典 [의식] a great function ; a state ceremony ; [법전] a code ; a statute ; a canon (종교의)

대전 大全 [완전] perfection ; completeness ; [전집] a complete collection

대전 大殿 His Majesty the King ; a royal palace ; a king's palace

대전 大戰 a great war ; a great battle (전투) ¶ 제 2 차 세계 대전 the Second World War ; World War Ⅱ
— 기념비 a cenotaph ; a war memorial

대전 帶電 〚물리〛 electrification ; electric charge — 하다 charge with electricity ; electrify
— 미립자 a charged corpuscle —체(體) a charged〔an electrified〕 body

대전 對戰 [전쟁] waging war ; engagement ; [경기] competition ; a match ; a bout — 하다 be pitched 《against》; fight ; meet ; [경기] compete 《with》; be matched 《against》 ¶ 대전시키다 match 《a person against another》 // 작년도 패자와 대전하다 have〔play〕 a game with the championship holder of last year // 양군이 서로 대전했다 The two armies were pitched against each other.

대전어 大錢魚 〚물고기〛 a gizzard shad

대전제 大前提 〚논리〛 the major premise

〔proposition〕
대전차 對戰車 antitank
— 지뢰 an antitank mine —포 antitank gun —호(壕) an antitank trench
대절 貸切 reservation —하다 reserve ; engage ; book
— 버스〔비행기, 열차〕 a chartered bus〔plane, train〕 —석(席) a reserved seat —차 a reserved car〔carriage〕 — 취급 carload consignment〔shipment〕 — 취급 운임 a carload rate — 취급 화물 a carload lot
대절 大節 a great〔lofty〕 principle〔cause〕
대접 a soup bowl
†**대접 待接** treat ; treatment ; entertainment ; hospitality ; reception —하다 treat ; treat 《a person》 to 《a drink》 ; entertain ; receive ; give〔show〕 《a person》 hospitality ¶ 은근한 대접을 받다 be given〔accorded〕 hospitable treatment〔a cordial reception〕 ; receive hospitality // 다과의 대접을 받다 be served tea and cakes // 오찬의 대접을 받다 be entertained at luncheon // 후하게 대접하다 give 《a person》 warm hospitality ; lavish hospitality to ; exercise great hospitality // 대접이 변변치 못해서 죄송합니다 I am sorry I have not been much of a host to you.
대정각 對頂角 〖기하〗 vertically opposite angles
대정맥 大靜脈 the vena cava 《*pl.* venae cavae》
대정자 大正字 a capital〔majuscule〕 letter in Roman type〔letters〕
대제 大帝 a great emperor ¶ 피터 대제 Peter the Great
대제 大祭 a great festival ; a great fete ; a fiesta
대제사장 大祭司長 a high〔chief〕 priest
*__대조 對照__ contrast ; antithesis ; comparison (비교) —하다 contrast〔compare〕 《A》 with 《B》 ; set 《A》 against 《B》 ; check 《A》 up with 《B》 ¶ 명암의 대조 the contrast between light and shade // …와 대조하여 보면 in contrast 《to》 ; as contrasted 《with》 ; in comparison 《with》 // 원문과 대조하다 compare 《it》 with the original〔text〕 // 원서와 대조하다 compare with〔refer to〕 the ledger // 영·미를 비교대조하다 compare and contrast England and America // 뚜렷한 대조를 이루고 있다 be in〔form a〕 striking contrast 《to another》 ; stand out in sharp contrast 《to》 // 빨강은 초록과 아름다운 대조를 이룬다 Red makes a beautiful contrast with green. // 참 재미있는 대조인데요 What a contrast !
— 계정 a contra account — 실험 〖생물〗 a controlled experiment — 악절 〖음악〗 the antistrophe —표(表) a calculating table 명암 — the contrast between light and shade
대조 大潮 the spring tide ; the flood tide ; the major tide
대족 大族 a mighty clan〔family〕 ; a flourishing〔prosperous〕 family
대종 大宗 the main stock〔family line〕 ; the lineage of the head family
—가(家) the head family —손(孫) heir(s) to the head family
대좌 對坐 —하다 sit facing each other ; sit face to face with ; sit opposite each other
대좌 臺座 a pedestal
대죄 大罪 [도덕상의] a grave〔deadly, great〕 sin ; [법률상의] a capital crime ; a high〔serious, foul〕 crime ; a felony ; a heinous offense
—인(人) a felon ; a great offender ; an atrocious criminal
대죄 待罪 —하다 await the official decision on one's punishment ; wait for the judgment
대주 大酒 heavy〔deep, hard〕 drinking ; carousal ; a binge ; a bender
—가 a heavy〔hard, deep〕 drinker ; a toper ; a sot ; a soaker
대주 貸主 the lender ; the creditor ; the lessor
대주 代走 〖야구〗 ¶ 대주자 a pinch runner —하다 run for another
대주교 大主教 〖카톨릭〗 an archbishop ; a primate (수석 대주교)
대주다 supply〔provide, furnish, find〕 《a person with a thing》 ¶ 일감을 대주다 provide 《a person》 with work ; provide〔furnish〕 work to 《a person》 // 한 달에 2만원씩 대주다 allow 《a person》 20,000 *won* a month // 아들에게 학비를 대주다 provide one's son with school expenses
대주 시장 貸株市場 〖주식〗 the stock loan market
대줄거리 大— the essentials ; a summary ; the gist ; an outline (개요)
대중 ① [어림] a rough estimate〔calculation〕 ¶ 대중잡아 at a rough estimate // 비용은 대중잡아 얼마나 들까요 About how much do you expect the expense to be ? /What is your rough estimate of the cost ?
② [기준] a standard ¶ …에 대중을 잡다 set〔fix〕 《wages, price》 on the basis 《of》 // 무슨 말인지 대중을 잡을 수가 없다 I can't make out what he is saying.
대중잡다 관용 estimate roughly ; make a rough estimate〔calculation〕 《of》
†**대중 大衆** the masses ; the mass of people ; the multitude ; the populace ; the general public ; a crowd of people ; the public at large ; grassroots (속) ¶ 근로대중 the working masses〔classes〕 ; the masses of workers // 노동자 대중 the laboring mass // 대중 취향의 popular // 대중의 지지를 얻다 have the support of

the public ; have mass support // 대중에게 호소하다 appeal to the masses // 대중에게 인기가 있다 be popular 《with, among》; win popularity

— 가요 a popular song — 과세 mass tax ; mass taxation ; taxation upon the general public — 교육 public〔mass〕 education — 단체 교섭 mass bargaining ; a mass bargaining session — 문학 popular literature — 문화 pop culture — 물(物) a popular story — 미술 pop art — 사회 『사회』 mass society — 시장 a mass market — 식당 an eating place〔house〕; a cheap restaurant ; [간이 식당] a lunch counter — 오락 mass entertainment — 운동 a popular movement — 작가 a popular writer ; a dime novelist — 잡지 a magazine for the lowbrows ; a popular magazine — 전달 mass communication — 정당 a mass party — 정책 a policy toward the masses — 집회 a mass rally — 투쟁 a mass struggle — 획득 운동 a drive to win (general) public support 근로 — the working masses〔classes〕; the masses of workers 노동자 — the laboring masses

대중 對中 ¶ 한국의 대중 관계 Korea's relations with China // 한국의 대중 외교〔무역〕 Korea's policy toward〔trade with〕 China

대중공 對中共 ¶ 대중공의 toward〔with〕 Communist China

대중말 the standard language ⇨ 표준어

대중성 大衆性 popularity ¶ 예술의 대중성 the popularity of fine arts

대중 없다 (be) inconsistent ; irregular ; unpredictable ; lack a standard ¶ 그의 말은 대중 없다 His remarks are inconsistent. // 그는 하는 짓이 대중이 없어 믿을 수가 없다 He is so inconsistent in his behavior that you can never depend upon him.

대중용 大衆用 ¶ 대중용의 for the masses ; for everybody ; popular ; appealing to the masses // 대중용 요금의 popular-priced 《concerts》 // 대중용의 시계 a watch for popular use // 대중용으로 기획되어 있다 be intended for the lowbrows〔less intellectual people〕

대중화 大衆化 popularization 《of science》 —하다 popularize ; make popular ; be popularized ¶ 과학의 대중화 popularization of science

대증 對症 allopathy ¶ 대증의 allopathic — 약제 allopathic medicine

대증 요법 對症療法 symptomatic〔expectant〕 treatment —하다 treat symptoms ; meet symptoms as they call for attention

대지 大旨 the substance ; the gist ⇨ 대의(大意)

†**대지 大地** the earth ; the ground ; the solid earth ; firm ground ; 『시』 Mother Earth ¶ 대지를 밟다 tread on the ground

대지 大志 an ambition ; a great ambition ; an aspiration ¶ 대지를 품다 have〔cherish〕 a great ambition

⁑**대지 垈地** a site ; a lot ; a plot ; ground ¶ 대지의 선정 the selection of a site 《for》 // 대지를 물색하다 look for a site 《for a building》

— 면적 plottage 건축 — a building site〔lot〕

대지 臺紙 pasteboard ; board ; ground paper ; a mount (사진의) ; a mat (그림의) ¶ 대지 없는 사진 an unmounted photograph // 사진을 대지에 붙이다 mount a photograph

대지 臺地 a plateau ; an eminence ; a tableland

용암 — a lava plateau

대지 對地 anti-ground

— 공격(攻擊) a ground attack — 속도 [비행기의] anti-ground speed 공— 공격 an air-to-ground attack 지— 미사일 a ground-〔surface-〕to-ground〔-surface〕 missile

대지 貸地 land to let〔for rent〕; a lot to let〔for rent〕

대지 大指 the thumb

대지르다 defy ⇨ 대들다

⁑**대지주 大地主** a great landlord ; a large〔big〕 landowner ; a squire ; a lord of board acres

대지팡이 a bamboo cane〔stick〕

대진 代診 examination of a patient on behalf of another doctor —하다 examine〔diagnose〕 a patient on behalf of another doctor ; act as a locum tenens ¶ 대진 의사 a doctor's assistant ; a locum tenens 《영》; an intern 《미》; a locum 《속》

대진 對陣 the confrontation of armies —하다 confront〔face〕 each other ; be encamped facing each other ¶ 강을 끼고 대진하다 face〔confront〕 each other across a river

대질 對質 confrontation ¶ 증인 상호간의 대질을 명하다 order witnesses to confront with each other

대질리다 be defied

대집행 代執行 『법』 execution by proxy

대짜 大— a big one ; big game (사냥감 따위의) ¶ 대짜가 걸렸다 (낚시에서) I have got a bite from something big !

대짜배기 a big〔gigantic〕 one ; an awfully big one ¶ 대짜배기로 in〔with〕 a big one ; [일이] on a big scale ; in a large〔big〕 way // 대짜배기로 한 잔하다 have a drink in a large mug

대쪽 (a piece of) split bamboo ¶ 성미가 대쪽 같은 사람 a straightforward person ; a single-minded person

대차 大差 a great〔material, wide〕 difference ; a great discrepancy〔disparity〕; a great〔striking〕 contrast ¶ 대차가 있다 be much〔very〕 different from ; differ much〔a great deal〕 from ; a great contrast exists 《between》// 대차가 없다 make little〔no great〕 difference ; be much〔about, pretty, nearly〕 the same ; be practically equal // 대차가 생기다 make a great difference // 양자 사이에는 대차가 있다 There is a wide difference between the two. // A와 B는 대차가 없다 There is little difference between A and B. /A is much〔about〕 the same as B. // 출원자 수는 예년과 대차 없다 The number of applicants has practically come up to the level of the average year.

대차 貸借 borrowing and lending ; letting and hiring ; a loan ; [장부상의] debit and credit ¶ 대차를 결산하다 strike a balance ; sum up the debtor and creditor account // 그 사람과는 대차 관계가 없다 I have no account to settle with him. // 학생 간의 금전 대차는 엄금되어 있다 Loans between the students are strictly forbidden.

— 계약서 [버스 따위의] a charter **— 계정** debtor and creditor accounts ; a current account **— 관계** the relations arising from a loan ; accounts **— 기한** the term of a loan **— 대조표(對照表)** a balance sheet 《B/S, b. s.》 **— 소송** an action for debt **—인(人)** debtor and creditor ; [물건의] lessor and lessee **사용 —** loan of use **국제 — 결제** the balance of international payments

대찰 大刹 a large〔great, noted〕 Buddhist temple ; a Buddhist cathedral

대창 the gut of a big animal ; tripe

대창 大漲 a heavy flood **— 하다** be heavily flooded〔inundated〕

대창 —槍 a bamboo spear

— 전술 bamboo-spear tactics

대책 對策 a countermeasure ; a counterplan ; a countermove ¶ 인플레 대책 a measure to counter inflation ; an anti-inflation policy // 대책으로서 as a countermeasure // 대책을 강구하다 consider a counterplan ; devise a countermove ; take a measure to meet the situation ; study how to cope with the situation ; counterplot

대책 大册 a bulky volume ; a big book ¶ 2천 페이지의 대책 a bulky volume of two thousand pages

대처 對處 disposal **— 하다** meet ; deal with ; cope with ; tackle ¶ 정세에 대처하다 meet〔cope with〕 the situation

대처승 帶妻僧 a married Buddhist priest

대척 對蹠 [정반대의 위치] diametrical opposition ; [지구상의] antipodism ¶ 대척적 antipodal ; antipodean ; diametrically opposite ; just the opposite // 사회적 지위로 보아 대척적인 at the opposite social pole

—자(者) an antipode **—점(點)** 〖무선〗 an antipode ; the nadir **—지(地)** the antipodes

대천 大川 a big〔large〕 river

대첩 大捷 a signal〔great, sweeping〕 victory **— 하다** win a signal victory

대청 the white membrane inside bamboo

대청 大廳 the main floored room ; a hall

대청소 大清掃 general (house) cleaning ; great〔giant〕 housecleaning ¶ 춘계〔추계〕 대청소 a spring〔an autumn〕 house cleaning // 같이 일하면 봄맞이 대청소를 금세 끝낼 수 있을 것이다 If we all work together, we'll be finished with spring cleaning in no time.

***대체 大體** ① [개요] an outline ; a summary ; an epitome ; the gist ; the substance ; the purport (취지) ; the principal parts (요점) ; the main〔chief〕 points ¶ 대체적인 general 《idea》 ; main 《points》 ; rough ; loose // 대체를 말하다 give an outline ; outline 《a case》 ; give a summary 《of》 ; summarize 《a matter》 ; epitomize 《a plan》

② [대체로] generally ; in the main ; on the whole ; in general ; as a rule ; by and large ; for the most part ; practically ; almost ; roughly〔summarily〕 (대략) ¶ 대체로 말해서 generally speaking ; in a loose sense of the world ; in round 〔broad〕 terms ; roughly speaking // 대체로 맑음 generally fair // 대체로 흐림 generally〔mostly〕 cloudy // 대체로 다음과 같다 It is substantially as follows. // 대체로 다 되었다 It is practically finished. // 대체로 성공이었다 On the whole we have succeeded. // 이 지역의 기후는 대체로 따뜻하다 The climate in this area is generally mild.

③ [도대체] on the earth ; in the world ; the blazes ¶ 대체 너는 어디서 온 누구냐 Where(ever) do you come from and who(ever) are you? // 대체 너는 한국어를 아느냐 Do you know any Korean at all? // 대체 무슨 일인가 What the deuce is the matter? /Whatever is the matter? // 대체 어디 갔다 왔느냐 Where the blazes have you been?

대체 代替 alternation ; change ; [대용] substitution **— 하다** alternate ; change ; substitute ¶ 대체의 법칙 the principle of substitution // 대체되다 be substituted 《for》

—물(物) 〖법〗 a substitute ; a fungible (대체 가능물) **— 법칙** the principle of substitution **— 식량** substitute food 《for rice》 **— 에너지** alternative energy **— 직업** an alternative occupation **— 효과** 〖경제〗 substitution effect

대체 對替 (ex)change ; transfer **—하다** exchange 《a bill》 ; transfer ¶ 가불금을

손익 계정으로 대체하다 transfer temporary payments to a profit and loss account // 정기 예금으로 대체하다 change to a fixed deposit
— 계정 a transfer account — 계정 거래 a transfer account transaction — 저금 transfer savings — 전표 a transfer slip

대초 大— a large candle

대추[1] a jujube ; a Chinese date
— 나무 a jujube tree ; a Chinese date tree

대추[2] [물려낸 것] a hand-me-down ; a used〔second-hand〕 thing

대축 對軸 a countershaft

대출 貸出 lending — 하다 lend out ; loan out ; advance 《money》 ; let out on hire ¶ 도서관의 대출을 이용하다 use the lending service of a library // 도서관의 책은 누구에게나 대출하여 드립니다 Books in the library will be loaned〔lent〕 out to anybody.
—계 a lending clerk ; [장소] the lending section 《of a bank》 —금(金) loaned 〔advanced〕 money — 능력 banking power —액(額) an amount of loans — 초과 an over loan 부당 — an illegal advance 비상 — an emergency advance

대출혈 大出血 copious〔excessive〕 bleeding ; [손해] a great loss〔casualty〕

†**대충** almost ; nearly ; about ; roughly ; loosely ; grossly ; approximately ; briefly ; cursorily ¶ 대충 예산을 잡아 보다 make a rough estimate of expenses // 일이 대충되다 one's work is almost done // 대충 끝나다 be almost〔practically〕 finished // 대충 짐작하다 make a rough guess ; have a general idea // 대충 얼마 정도의 가격을 생각하고 계십니까 What's your general price range ? // 대충 찾지 않은 것이 확실하냐 Are you sure you aren't being too haphazard in your search ?

대충 代充 — 하다 supplement〔replenish〕 with substitutes

대충 자금 對充資金 the counterpart fund

대취 大醉 dead-drunkenness — 하다 be〔get〕 dead-drunk ; be drunken ; be drunk as a piper〔fiddler, lord〕

대치 代置 replacement ; 〖사회〗 succession — 하다 replace 《A with B》

대치 對峙 standing face to face 《with》 ; confronting each other ; [적대] keeping up rivalry ; holding one's ground against 《the enemy》 — 하다 stand face to face with ; confront each other ; stand opposite to each other ; [적대하다] keep up rivalry ; hold one's own against 《one's antagonist》 ; hold one's ground against 《the enemy》 ; take a stand against ; hold out against 《the government forces》 ¶ 쌍방이 대치하여 굽히지 않는다 Neither would yield to the other in their rivalry.

대침 大針 a big needle

대칭 對稱 ① [제 2 인칭] the second person ② 〖수학〗 symmetry
— 도형(률) 〖수학〗 a symmetrical figure 〔law〕 —면(面) planes of symmetry — 배열(排列) 〖전기〗 symmetrical arrangement — 삼각형 a symmetrical triangle —식(式) 〖수학〗 a symmetrical expression —점(點) a point of symmetry —축(軸) an axis of symmetry — 함수 a symmetrical function 선 — line symmetry 평면 — plane symmetry

대칼 a bamboo-knife

대컨 as a whole ; generally ⇨ 대체

대타 代打 〖야구〗 pinch-hitting

대타자 代打者 a pinch hitter

대테 a bamboo hoop

대토 代土 [바꿈] exchange of land ; substitute land (땅을)

대통 —桶 [담뱃대의] the bowl of a tobacco pipe

대통 大通 — 하다 be wide open ¶ 운수가 대통하다 have a spell of extremely good luck ; fortune turns in one's favor

대통 大統 the Royal line ¶ 대통을 계승하다 succeed to the Royal line〔Throne〕

†**대통령** 大統領 the President ; the Chief Executive 《미》 ¶ 대통령의 presidential // 대통령에 취임하다 be sworn in as President // 대통령에 선출되다 be elected President // 대통령 선거에 출마하다 run for the Presidency
— 경호실(장) (the Chief of) the Office of the Presidential Security — 관저 the Executive〔Presidential〕 Mansion ; the Presidential residence ; the White House 《미》 — 교서 a Presidential message ; the President's message — 당선자 the president-elect —령(令) a Presidential decree ; an executive order — 비서 a presidential secretary — 비서실 the Presidential Secretariat — 비서실장 the Chief Presidential Secretary ; the Secretary-General — 선거 a presidential election — 연두 교서 the State of the Union Message 《미》 — 영부인 the President's wife ; the first lady (of the land) 《미》 — 임기 a presidential term — 주최 만찬회 a State Dinner — 지위 presidency ; the presidential chair〔office〕 — 특별 보좌관 the Special Assistant to the President 《for Foreign Affairs》 — 특사 a special envoy of the President ; a presidential envoy — 후보 a candidate for the presidency ; a presidential nominee〔candidate〕

대통령 선거인 大統領選擧人 the presidential electoral college deputies
—단 the electoral college —(단) 선거 the presidential electoral balloting 〔vote〕 ; the election of the presidential electoral college ; the election of the deputies to the presidential electoral

college
대퇴 大腿 the thigh ; the femur
—골(骨) a thighbone ; a femur **—부(部)** the femoral region **— 절단** amputation below the femoral region
대파 大破 [파손] dilapidation ; ruin ; decay ; serious damage **— 하다** [건물 따위가] be greatly〔badly, seriously〕damaged ; be in ruins ; [손해를 입다] be wrecked〔smashed〕; be heavily damaged〔crippled〕 ¶ 배가 대파했다 The ship was badly damaged.
대파 代播 — 하다 sow〔plant〕 in substitution 《for》 ¶ 논에 보리를 대파하다 plant a paddy-field with barley in substitution 《for rice》
대판 代辦 management of another's affairs ; agency ; commission **— 하다** manage another's affairs ; act for another ; handle as agent〔on commission, by proxy〕
—업 agency
대판 大— a large〔big〕 scale ¶ 대판으로 on a large scale ; in a big way // 대판으로 싸우다 fight〔have〕 a big fight ; fight hard〔furiously〕 // 그 사람 간밤에 부인하고 대판 싸웠다고 하던데요 He said he had a big fight with his wife last night.
대판 大版 large size ¶ 대판의 large-sized ; of large size
대패 a plane ¶ 대팻날 a plane blade // 대팻밥 (wood) shavings ; planing refuse // 마무리 대패 a smoothing plane // 대패질하다 plane 《a board》
대패 大敗 a crushing〔heavy, serious, disastrous, terrible〕 defeat ; an utter rout ¶ 대패를 당하다 meet a crushing defeat ; be beaten hollow // 대패시키다 defeat utterly ; put to rout // 적은 대패했다 The enemy was disastrously defeated〔put to rout〕. // 적어도 그같은 대패를 당하면 패배를 받아들이기가 쉬운데 At least a slaughter like that makes is easier to admit defeat.
대포 grog ; drinking from a large cup〔a goblet, a bowl〕
—잔 a large cup〔a goblet, a bowl〕 **—집** a grogshop ; a groggery
†대포 大砲 ① [병기] a gun ; a cannon ; (a piece of) ordnance ; artillery ¶ 대포소리 the boom〔roaring〕 of guns // 대포를 쏘다 fire a gun
② [거짓말] a (big) lie ; a falsehood ; an untruth ; [허풍] a boast ; tall〔big〕 talk ; a brag ; hot air 《미·속》 ¶ 대포를 놓다 lie ; boast ; tell a lie ; brag ; talk big〔tall〕; tell a tall tale
대폭 大幅 ① [폭이 넓음] full breadth ; double width ¶ 삼베 대폭 한자 one foot of full width hemp // 대폭 한 야드 a yard of broadcloth
② [부사적] sharply ; steeply ; by a large margin ¶ 대폭 삭감 a drastic cut〔curtailment〕 ; a sharp cut // 대폭 인상 a steep raise ; a sharp increase ; a heavy boost // 대폭 하락 a big fall〔reduction〕 ; sharp reductions in prices // 지출을 대폭 삭감하다 cut an appropriation sharply // 미곡의 공정 가격이 대폭 인상됐다 The official prices of rice have been raised〔revised upward〕 by a large margin.
†대표 代表 [대표함] representation ; [대표자] a representative ; a delegate ; a delegation 《집합적》 **— 하다** represent ; be representative of ; stand for ; sit for ; act for ¶ 대표적 representative ; typical (종류의) ; [모범적] model ; exemplary // 대표적 학생 a model〔typical〕 student // 그는 학급을 대표해서 조문을 했다 On behalf of the whole class he conveyed a message of condolence.
— 번호 〖전화〗 a key number **— 사원** a representative partner ; an acting〔a senior〕 partner **—작(作)** the masterpiece ; the most important work 《of》 **— 화폐** representative money **노동자〔자본가〕 —** a labor〔capital〕 delegate **다수〔소수, 비례〕 — 제도** a majority〔minority, proportional〕 representation system **무역 —단** a trade mission **학생 —** a student representative
대표부 代表部 a mission
무역 — a trade mission **유엔 한국 —** the Korean mission to the United Nations
대표제 大標題, 大表題 a big〔splash〕 headline
대푼 a penny ; a tiny sum
—변(邊) one percent interest **—중** a pennyweight **—짜리** a thing of little value
대품 代— exchange〔substitute〕 work
대품 代品 a substitute article
대풍 大豊 an abundant harvest ; a bumper〔heavy〕 crop ¶ 미작은 대풍일 것이다 The rice crop will be very large.
대풍 大風 a high〔big, strong, violent〕 wind ; a gale (질풍)
대풍자 大楓子, 大風子 a chaulmoogra seeds
—유(油) chaulmoogra oil
대피 待避 — 하다 〖철도〗 shunt ; [공습 따위를] take shelter 《in, under》
—로 [자동차 도로의] a pull-out ; a lay-by **—소** a turnout **—선(線)** a sidetrack 《미》 ; a siding ; a shunt line **—역** a shunting station **—호** a shelter ; a dugout
대필 代筆 ghostwriting **— 하다** ghost-write ; write 《a letter》 for 《a person》 ; write 《a letter》 to another's dictation ¶ 어머니의 대필을 하다 write for one's mother
—자(者) a person who writes a letter for another ; an amanuensis 《*pl.* amanuenses》

대필 大筆 a big writing brush ; [명필] excellent handwriting ; noble calligraphy
대하 大厦 an edifice ; a large building ; a mansion
대하 大蝦 〖동물〗 a lobster
대하 大河 a large river
— **소설** a river〔saga〕 novel ; a roman-fleuve 《프》
대하 帶下 a discharge from the womb
—**증(症)** leucorrh(o)ea ; whites (백대하)
대하 고루 大厦高樓 tall and large buildings
†**대하다 對—** ① [마주보다] face ; confront ; be opposite ; be over against ¶ 적을 대하다 confront an enemy ; deal with an enemy // 서로 얼굴을 대하다 face〔confront〕 each other ; be over against each other // 절이 언덕을 대하고 서다 a temple stands facing a hill
② [향하다·관하다] toward ; to ; in ; by ; in regard to (관하여) ¶ 물음에 대한 대답 an answer to a question // 문학에 대한 흥미 interest in literature // 어버이에 대한 의무 one's duty toward〔to〕 one's parents // 주인에 대한 예의 respect due to one's master
③ [대조] as opposed to ; in opposition to ; in contrast to ¶ 구어체에 대한 문어체 written〔literary〕 style as opposed to spoken〔colloquial〕 style
④ [응대하다] address ; receive ; see ; face ; treat ¶ 교만한 태도로 손을 대하다 receive a visitor with a haughty style // 부드러운 얼굴로 학생에게 대하다 address oneself to one's students with a kindly look // 사람을 대하기 싫어하다 don't like to see people
⑤ [대항하다] against ¶ 결정에 대한 항의 a protest against a decision // 적은 전력을 다하여 우리에게 대하였다 The enemy directed his whole strength against us.
⑥ [비교·비례] as compared with ; as against ; per ; to ; against ¶ 100에 대하여 20 twenty per hundred // 100에 대한 150표 150 votes against 100 // 사망률은 1,000명에 대하여 5명의 비율이다 The death-rate is 5 per 1,000. // 수수료는 1,000원에 대하여 100원이다 We charge 10% as commission out of every thousand *won*.
⑦ [보수로서] for ; in return for ¶ 그는 그 발명에 대하여 500만원의 보수를 받았다 He received a reward of five million *won* for the invention.
†**대학¹ 大學** [종합 대학] a university ; [단과 대학] a college ¶ 대학의 자유 academic freedom // 대학 시절에 while in college 《미》 ; while at university 《영》 // 대학 교육을 받지 못한 사람들 those who have been denied college opportunities // 그는 대학을 다니고 있다 He is in a university. /He is in college. 《미》
—**가(街)** a university〔college〕 town — **구내** a university campus — **노트** a large-sized notebook —**모(帽)** a college cap ; a square〔trencher〕 cap — **병원** a university hospital ; a teaching hospital — **분규** a campus dispute ; campus strife — **설치 심의회** the University Chartering Council — **수학 능력 시험** the government-sponsored scholastic aptitude test (for university admission) ; the national〔state-run〕 academic aptitude test — **일〔이, 삼, 사〕년생** a freshman〔sophomore, junior, senior〕 — **총장** a university president ; the president 《of a university》 ; the chancellor 《영》 — **출신 기술자** an engineer with college training — **출신자** a college-bred man ; a college graduate ; a university man〔graduate〕 ; a collegian 《미》 — **학생 클럽** a fraternity (남자의) ; a sorority (여자의) — **학장** a dean ; a president
국립 — a national university **의과〔문리과, 법과, 공과, 농과, 상과, 사범, 미술, 음악, 치과, 약학, 수의과, 수산, 항공〕** — a college of medicine 〔liberal arts and sciences, law, engineering, agriculture, commerce, education, fine arts, music, dentistry, pharmacy, veterinary medicine, fisheries, aviation〕
대학² 大學 the Great Learning
대학 교수 大學敎授 a university〔college〕 professor ¶ 대학 교수답지 않은 unprofessorial 《manner》
—**단(團)** the faculty of a university ; the college staff
대학 교육 大學敎育 a university〔college〕 education ; college training ¶ 대학 교육을 받은 기사 a college-〔university-〕 trained engineer // 대학 교육을 받다 get a college education
대학생 大學生 a university〔college〕 student ; a college man〔woman〕 ; an undergraduate ; a collegian
대학원 大學院 a graduate〔postgraduate〕 school ; the postgraduate course ¶ 대학원에 들어가다 become a graduate student
—**생** a graduate〔postgraduate〕 student ; a grad student 《미·속》
대학자 大學者 a great〔prominent, profound〕 scholar ; a man of great education
대한 大韓 Korea
— **민국(民國)** the Republic of Korea 《ROK》 — **무역진흥공사** the Korea Trade Promotion Corporation 《KOTRA》 — **상공 회의소** the Korea Chamber of Commerce and Industry — **석유공사** the Korea Oil Corporation — **석탄공사** the *Dai Han* Coal Corporation — **체육회** the Korean Amateur Athletic Association — **항공** Korean Air Lines 《KAL》 —

해협(海峽) the Straits of Korea
대한 大寒 midwinter〔the coldest season〕 occurring about January 21st ; [지독한 추위] intense cold
대한 大旱 a severe drought ; a long spell of dry weather
칠년 대한(大旱)에 단비 온다 (속담) Long looked for comes at last.
대합 大蛤 〖조개〗 a clam ; Mertrix lamacki (학명)
— 조가비 a clamshell
*대합실 待合室 a waiting room (역 등의) ; a lobby (은행 등의)
†대항 對抗 opposition ; rivalry ; confrontation ; antagonism ; emulation ; counteraction (저항) — 하다 oppose ; set up (against) ; pit oneself (against) ; stand 《against》 ; rival ; meet ; cope 《with》 ; encounter ¶ …에 대항하여 in opposition 《to》 ; against ; in rivalry 《with》 // 힘에는 힘으로 대항하다 meet〔counter〕 force with force // A와 B를 대항시키다 pit〔set〕 A against B // 정정 당당하게 대항하다 fight openly and squarely ; play square ; attack openly // 웅변가로서 그에게 대항할 만한 사람이 없다 He has no equal as an orator. // 금력으로서는 그에 대항할 수 없다 I am no match for him in money power.
— 단체 a counter organization — 동맹 a counter alliance —력(力) opposing power — 시합〔경기〕 a match — 운동 a countermovement —자(者) an antagonist ; a rival ; an opponent ; an emulator —품(品) competitive goods — 행위 a counteraction
대항책 對抗策 a counterplot ; a countermeasure ; a countermove ¶ 대항책을 강구하다 take a countermeasure ; promote a rival scheme
대해 大害 great harm ; great injury ; great damage
대해 大海 an ocean ; the open sea ; the high seas ; the deep〔main〕 《시》 ¶ 대해의 일적(一滴) a drop in the bucket 〔ocean〕 // 우물 안의 개구리가 대해를 모른다 He who is in the well knows not what heaven is. /The frog in the well knows nothing of the great ocean.
대행 代行 vicarious execution — 하다 carry out〔execute〕 as proxy
— 기관 an agency ; a substitute machinery — 업무 agency business — 자(者) a proxy ; an agent — 회사 a (stock exchange) clearing corporation 대통령 권한 — the Acting President 수출〔수입〕 —업자 an export〔import〕 agent
대헌장 大憲章 The Magna Charta ; The Great Charter
대현 大賢 a man of great wisdom ; a sage
대형 大兄 Mr. ; you
대형 大形 a large〔full〕 size ¶ 대형의 large〔full, over〕-sized ; of a large size ; big ; large // 대형의 배 a large vessel
—주 capital stock ; a giant-capital stock
— 합병 megamerger
대형 隊形 formation ; order ¶ 전투 대형을 갖추고 in battle formation // 대형을 유지하다 keep the formation in order // 대형이 흐트러져 있다 The formation is in disorder.
밀집 — (a) close formation
대혼 大婚 the Royal wedding
—식 a Royal marriage〔wedding〕 ceremony
대화 大火 a big〔great〕 fire ; a conflagration ; a disastrous〔destructive〕 fire ; a holocaust ¶ 대화가 되다 a fire spreads 〔becomes serious〕 // 대화를 입다 be visited by a disastrous fire
대화 大禍 a great disaster ; a calamity ; a woe ¶ 대화를 입다 meet with a calamity〔misfortune〕
*대화 對話 conversation ; a chat ; a dialogue ; a dialog 《미》 — 하다 talk〔converse〕 with ; have a talk with 《a person》 ¶ 두 사람의 대화 a dialogue // 세 사람의 대화 a trialogue // 플라톤의 대화편 the Dialogs of Plato // 그들은 영어로 대화했다 They talked in English.
—극(劇) a dialogic play — 극작가 a dialogist —체 dialogic〔conversational〕 style ¶ 대화체의 dialogistic(al) ; interlocutory 남북 — a South-North dialogue
대환 大患 affliction ; a disaster ; a great misfortune〔trial〕 ; a serious〔major〕 illness
대황 大黃 a kind of rhubarb ; Rheum undulatum (학명)
대회 大會 a great〔grand〕 meeting ; a mass〔grand〕 meeting ; a rally ; [총회] a general meeting ; [회의] a conference ; a convention ; [경기의] a meet ; a tournament ; a tourney ¶ 대회를 열다 hold a mass meeting ; meet in (a) convention // 직장 대회를 열다 hold a workshop rally // 당 대회를 소집하다 call a party convention // 대회에서 연설하다 address a large assembly // 전국 각처에서 대회가 열렸다 Mass meetings were held all over the country.
— 출석자 a conventioneer 국민 — a popular mass meeting ; [정당 주최의] a political rally 《미》 국제 소년단 — a world jamboree 기념 — a commemoration meeting (on a grand scale) 시민 — a mass meeting of citizens 전국 — [정당의] a National Convention 전국 정구 — an all-Korea tennis tournament 추계 — the great autumn meeting
대회전 경기 大回轉競技 〖스키〗 giant slalom
대효 大孝 [효도] great filial piety〔devotion〕 ; great filial duty ; [효자] a dutiful

〔an obedient〕 son
대후비개 a pipestem cleaning rod
대훈위 大勳位 the Grand Order
대흉 大凶 [불길] singular ill fortune ; a black omen ; [극악] atrocity ; brutality ; [흉년] an unusually bad harvest〔crop〕 **—하다** (be) extremely unlucky ; ill-omened ; extremely bad
—일(日) the most unlucky day ; the worst of all days
대희 大喜 exultation ; a transport ; an unalloyed delight **—하다** be overjoyed ; be transported with joy
댁 宅 [남의 집] your〔his〕 esteemed house〔residence, home〕 ; [가족] your family ; [상대자] you ; [남의 부인] the wife of 《a person》 ; Mrs. 《*Kim*》 ¶ 김씨 댁 Mr. *Kim's* (house) // 댁의 아이들 your children // 댁은 어디입니까 Where do you live? // 내일 댁에 가겠습니다 I will call at your house tomorrow. // 김씨 댁은 여기입니까 Is this where Mr. *Kim* lives?
댁내 宅內 your family
댁네 your wife
댁대구루루, 땍대구루루 rolling ¶ 댁대구루루 굴러 가다 roll over and over // 댁대구루루 굴리다 roll 《a pencil》 over 《the floor》
‡**댄서** a dancer ; a dancing girl ; a woman dancer
댄스 a dance ; dancing
— 교사〔교습소(敎習所)〕 a dancing instructor〔school〕 **— 파티** a dancing party ; a dance ; a ball ¶ 댄스 파티를 열다 give a dance〔ball, dancing party〕 // 댄스 파티에 가다 go to a dance ; go dancing **—홀** a dance hall 《미》 ; a dancing saloon 《영》
‡**댐** a dam ¶ 강에 댐을 만들다 build〔construct〕 a dam across a river ; dam a river
다목적— a multipurpose dam **수력 발전용 —** a hydroelectric dam **저수용 —** a water-storage dam
댐나무 a piece of wood attached to a wooden implement to prevent scars when hammering on it
댓 about five ¶ 댓번 about five times
댓가지 a branch of bamboo
댓개비 a slender piece of split bamboo
댓구멍 a pipestem hole ¶ 댓구멍같이 막히다 be narrow-minded
댓닭 a kind of fighting cock
댓돌 臺— 〖건축〗 terrace stones
댓바람 at a stroke〔blow〕 ; at once ; immediately ; in no time ; easily ; quickly ¶ 아무를 댓바람에 때려 눕히다 knock down a person with the first blow // 일을 댓바람에 해놓다 finish one's work at a stroke
댓새 about five days
댓조각 a piece of bamboo
댓줄기 a bamboo stalk〔stem〕
댓진 nicotine〔tar〕 accumulated in a pipe ¶ 댓진이 끼다 be choked with nicotine
댓집 the hole between the stem and the bowl of a pipe
댕가리 dried stalks of turnip〔cabbage〕 with seeds on them
댕가리지다 (be) sly ; cunning ; crafty ; shrewd
댕강- ⇨ 댕그랑-
댕그랑거리다, 땡그랑거리다 tinkle ; jingle ; clang ; cling ¶ 댕그랑댕그랑 tinkle-tinkle ; ting-ting ; ting-a-ling ; jingling ¶ 호주머니의 돈을 댕그랑거리다 clink one's money in one's pocket // 풍경이 댕그랑거리기 시작했다 A hanging bell〔wind bell〕 began to tinkle.
댕그랑댕그랑 cling-cling ; clang-clang ; tinkle-tinkle ; ting-ting ; ting-a-ling ; jingling
댕기 a pigtail ribbon ¶ 댕기를 매다 wear 〔put on〕 a pigtail ribbon
댕기다 [불이] catch〔take〕 fire ; [불을] light〔make, kindle〕 a fire ¶ 불은 이웃집에 댕겼다 The flames caught〔spread to〕 the adjoining building. /The neighboring house caught fire.
댕댕, 땡땡 clanging ; jingling ; ding-dong ; tinkling ; clang clang ¶ 종이 땡땡 친다 The bell clangs. /The bell is ringing.
댕댕이덩굴 〖식물〗 Cocculus trilobus (학명)
댕댕하다, 땡땡하다 (be) tight ; taut ; compact ; hard ; solid ¶ 땡땡한 근육 a hard muscle // 밧줄을 댕댕하게 매다 spread a rope tight〔taut, tense〕 // 젖가슴이 땡땡히 불었다 The breast is swollen. /The breasts fill.
댕돌같다 (be) very solid ; firm ; be as hard as a brick
†**더** [수량·정도] more ; some more ; [시간] longer ; [거리] farther ¶ 더 많이 [양] much〔a lot〕 more ; [수] (a good) many more // 더 중요한 more important // 더 한층 more and more ; still more // 그것에 대해서는 더 말하지 마시오 Please don't say any more about it. // 그러나 더 나쁜 일이 남아 있다 But worse remains. /I have worse to tell. /The worst is yet to come. // 그는 그 일을 더 생각해 보고 싶었다 He wanted more time to think it over. // 더 걷자 Let's go farther. // 더 공부하시오 Be more diligent. /Work harder. // 더 연구할 필요가 있다 It requires further research. // 더 주시오 Give me some more. // 더 참을 수 없다 I can't stand it any longer. // 1마일 더 가서 섰다 We rode a mile further before we stopped. // 더 할 말 없느냐 Do you have anything further to say? // 그 여자는 책값을 500원 더 지불했다 She paid five hundred *won* too much for the book. // 더 드세요 Please have seconds. // 더 드시겠어요 Care for sec-

onds ? // 자네가 문에서 더 가까운 침대를 쓰게나 You take the bunk nearer the door. // 더 이상 말하고 싶지 않다 Period ! // 얼마나 더 가야 되나 How much farther should we go ?

더가다 [거리] go〔walk〕 past〔beyond〕; [시계가] go too fast ; gain time ; [정도] exceed ; go further ; last longer ; be more than ¶ 버스에서 졸다가 두 정거장이나 더가버렸다 I was carried two stops beyond my destination while napping. // 이 모자가 저 모자보다 값이 더간다 This hat is more expensive than that. // 이 내의가 저것보다 더갈 겁니다 This shirt will wear〔keep〕 longer than that.

더구나 in addition ⇨ 더군다나

더군다나 besides ; moreover ; further ; into the bargain ; in addition ; what is more ; to add to 《one's miseries》 ¶ 그녀는 못났고 더군다나 다리까지 전다 She is plain-looking and crippled into the bargain. // 그녀는 부자요 더군다나 미인이다 She is rich and beautiful as well. // 더군다나 비마저 퍼부었다 To make things〔matters〕 worse, it was raining hard. // 더군다나 상처까지 하였다 To crown his misery, he lost his wife. // 더군다나 집까지 태워 버렸다 On (the) top of this, I had my house burnt down in a fire. // 더군다나 한쪽이 귀머거리다 Added to that, he is deaf of 〔in〕 one ear. // 재간도 있고 더군다나 돈도 있다 He has good abilities and plenty of money over and above.

더그매 an empty space between the roof and the ceiling

더그아웃 〖야구〗 a dugout

더금더금, 더끔더끔 in heaps ; on and on ¶ 더끔더끔 쌓아 올리다 pile up high // 마른 풀을 더끔더끔 쌓다 pile hay in heaps

더기 a plateau

더껑이 film ; skin ; scum ; cream ; scab (상처 따위의)

더께 layers of dirt ; accumulated dirt

더넘 troubles〔worries〕 undertaken from others

더넘스럽다 be a little too large

더느다 brail 《string, thread》 in two piles

-더니 ¶ 마구 노름을 하더니 결국 가산을 탕진하고 말았다 He went on gambling until at last he lost all his fortune. // 말다툼을 하더니 끝내 주먹다짐이 되고 말았다 The quarrel ended in their coming to blows.

-더니만 ⇨ -더니

더듬거리다¹, 떠듬거리다 [말을] stammer ; stutter ; falter ¶ 글을 더듬거리며 읽다 falter over a passage // 떠듬거리며 변명하다 stammer out an apology // 약간 더듬거리긴 하십니다만 흠잡을 데 없는 영어를 하십니다 You can speak English a little haltingly, but you speak it flawlessly.

더듬거리다² [찾다] keep groping for〔feeling about for〕; be feeling after 《the handle》 ¶ 어둠 속을 더듬거리며 가다 feel〔grope〕 one's way in the dark

†**더듬다** ① [손으로] grope ; fumble 《in the darkness》 for 《a thing》; feel〔grope〕 about for 《a thing》; feel after 《the handle》 ¶ 어둠 속에서 성냥을 더듬다 grope 〔feel, fumble〕 for the matches in the darkness // 포켓 속의 손칼을 더듬다 feel 〔fish, fumble〕 in one's pockets for his knife // 더듬어서 뭐든지 하지 않으면 안 되었다 I had to do everything by the feel. // 무슨 좋은 해결책이 없느냐고 더듬고 있다 They are now groping in the dark for a solution.
② [길을] feel〔grope〕 one's way ; pick one's way ; [근원을] trace ; tread ; follow ¶ 근원을 더듬어 올라가다 trace back 《a thing》 to its origin // 산길을 더듬다 struggle along a mountain path // 더듬어서 문까지 걸어 갔다 I felt my way to the door.
③ [기억 따위를] ¶ 기억을 더듬다 retrace one's memory ; try to recall ; recollect // 어린 시절을 더듬다 recall memories of one's childhood // 역사를 더듬다 trace the history // 옛일을 더듬다 look back on the past ; recall old times
④ [말을] stammer ; stumble ; stutter ; falter ; have an impediment in one's speech ¶ 그는 심히 더듬는다 He stammers badly. // 그는 말 더듬는 버릇이 있다 He is apt to stutter〔falter in speaking〕. // 초초해서 말을 더듬었다 I panicked and kept stumbling over my words.

더듬더듬 [말을] stammering ; stuttering ; faltering ; [손으로] by feel ; gropingly ¶ 더듬더듬 읽다 falter over 《a passage》 // 나는 그와 더듬더듬 영어로 이야기했다 I talked with him in halting English.

더듬이¹ [말더듬이] a stammerer

더듬이² feeler

더듬적거리다, 떠듬적거리다 be stammering〔stuttering, faltering〕 《in one's speech》

더디 late ; behind time〔schedule〕 ¶ 목적지에 더디 가 닿다 reach one's destination late〔behind time〕

***더디다** (be) slow 《in, of, at》; tardy 《at》; retarded ; late (늦다) ; behind schedule ¶ 걸음이 더디다 be slow of foot ; be heavy-footed ; be a slow walker // 일손이 더디다 be slow in one's work // 진보가 더디다 be slow in progress ; make slow progress

-더라 I have found that ; it is known that ; I hear〔have been told〕 that ¶ 그는 다음 주에 미국에 간다더라 I hear that he is going to America next week. // 그는 아까 자고 있더라 I found him sleeping a little while ago. /He was noticed to be sleeping a moment ago. // 그는 고아라고 하더라 They say〔It is said〕 that he is an orphan.

-더라도 even if ; even though ; supposing that ; whatever may ; although ; however ¶ 그렇게 말했더라도 even if he did say so // 농담이더라도 even in joke // 설령 그렇더라도 supposing〔admitting〕 that it is so ; even if it were so // 아무리 부자더라도 however〔no matter how〕 rich one may be // 어떠한 일이 있더라도 whatever〔no matter what〕 may happen // 싫더라도 꼭 해야 한다 Even if you do not like it, you must do it. // 장관이더라도 그냥 두지 않는다 Minister or no, he shall smart for it. // 틀린 데가 있더라도 아주 적다 There are few mistakes, if any.

-더라면 [가정·희망] if one had done... ; if only... ; if it had been... ¶ 그 신이 좀더 컸더라면 내 발에 맞을 텐데 If the shoes had been a little bigger, they would have fit my feet. // 그가 그 일을 했더라면 좋았을 것을 I wish he had done it (but he didn't).

더러 ① [어쩌다] once in a while ; occasionally ; now and then ; from time to time ; sometimes ; at times ; at moments ¶ 더러 오다 come occasionally〔now and then〕 // 그에게서 더러 소식이 있다 I hear from him once in a while.
② [얼마쯤] some ; a little ; somewhat ; to some degree ; more or less ¶ 그에게도 더러 염치는 있다 He has some sense of honor. // 유학을 갔다 와서 더러 배운 것도 있다 He has been abroad and has learned a thing or two. // 나도 그 문제에는 더러 책임이 있다 I am also more or less responsible for the matter.

-더러 to 《a person》 ¶ 선생님이 나더러 공부 잘 하라고 하셨다 My teacher gave the advice to me that I should work hard. /My teacher told〔advised, ordered〕 me to work hard. // 누구더러 오라고 했니 Whom did you tell to come here ?

더러워지다 be stained ; be soiled ; be polluted ; be defiled ; get dirty ¶ 더러워진 돈 tainted money ; ill-gotten money ; filthy lucre // 더러워진 마음 a polluted mind ; an impure heart // 더러워진 여자 an unchaste〔a defiled〕 woman ; a woman of stained character // 더러워진 옷 dirty〔soiled〕 clothes // 더러워진 일생 a life full of sins ; a dirty life ; a crooked life // 네가 있으면 이 집이 더러워진다 Your presence pollutes the house.

더럭 all at once ; all of a sudden ; in〔with〕 a burst ¶ 겁이 더럭 나다 be seized with fear〔struck with awe〕 all of a sudden ; get into a funk

더럭더럭 importunately ; pertinaciously ; tenaciously ; persistently ; with persistence ¶ 돈을 달라고 더럭더럭 조르다 importune 《a person》 for money ; ask importunately for money // 더럭더럭 재촉하다 make an importunate demand for 《payment》

* **더럼** [불결] dirt ; uncleanness ; filth(iness) ; impurity ; pollution ; soil ; [얼룩·오점] a stain ; blot ; a tarnish ; a blemish ¶ 더럼타는 옷 clothes easy to get soiled
더럼타다 관용 be easy to dirty〔soil, stain〕 ; be easily soiled

⁑ **더럽다** ① [불결] (be) dirty ; filthy ; foul ; unclean ; soiled ; squalid ; shabby ; grimy

참고 **dirty** 일반어 **filthy** 너무나 더러워 불쾌한 느낌을 주다 **foul** 오물, 부패물 따위로 충만되어 강렬한 불쾌감을 주다 **grimy** 때, 그을음 따위로 더럽다

¶ 더러운 옷 soiled〔shabby〕 clothes // 손이 더럽구나 Your hands are dirty.
② [추잡] (be) indecent ; obscene ¶ 더러운 계집 an unchaste〔obscene, impure〕 woman // 더러운 화제 a filthy〔a ribald, an indecent〕 conversation〔topic〕
③ [야비] (be) mean ; base ; low ; sordid despicable ; dirty 《미》 ¶ 마음이 더러운 사람 a person of base mind ; a mean-spirited person ; a man of low character // 보수를 바라다니 더럽구나 It is mean of you to wish for recompense.
④ [인색] (be) stingy ; niggardly ; sordid ; closefisted ; be greedy of money ¶ 돈 쓰는 게 더럽다 spend money sparingly ; mince money matters // 돈을 많이 가지면 가질수록 사람이 더러워진다 The more one has, the stingier one will be.
⑤ [비겁] (be) foul ; unfair ; ignominious (수치스럽다) ¶ 더럽게 이기다 win by foul play

† **더럽히다** ① [때묻히다] make unclean〔dirty〕 ; stain ; soil ; blemish ; foul ; defile ; taint ¶ 책을 더럽히다 soil a book // 피로 더럽혀진 옷 blood-stained clothes // 바지를 더럽히다 have〔get〕 one's pants dirty
② [명예 따위를] bring disgrace upon ; disgrace ; dishonor ; sully ; tarnish ; [모독하다] desecrate 《a shrine》 ; profane 《a temple》 ¶ 가명을 더럽히다 bring disgrace on one's family ; sully〔stain, disgrace〕 one's family name // 조상의 이름을 더럽히다 disgrace the good name〔reputation〕 of one's ancestors // 말석을 더럽히다 be given a seat among the rest // 그 따위 짓은 국가의 체면을 더럽힌다 It is prejudicial〔compromising〕 to the country's reputation〔prestige〕.
③ [여자를] dishonor ; outrage ; violate ; deflower ; rape 《a woman》 ¶ 몸을 더럽히다 lose her chastity〔purity〕 ; stain her virtue // 남자에게 몸을 더럽혔다 Her honor fell a sacrifice to the passion of the man. // 몸은 비록 더럽혀져 있을지 모르지만 마음은 그렇지 않다 Her body may have been soiled〔polluted〕 but her mind is not.

더리다 ① [떠름하다] (be) awkward ; poor ; inadequate ; be out of place ② [어리석다] (be) silly ; soft-headed ; asinine ③ [야비하다] (be) mean ; low ; gross ; dirty

†**더미** a heap ; a pile ; a stack ; a rick ; an accumulation ¶ 쓰레기 더미 a rubbish〔trash〕heap // 볏짚 더미 a stack of straws // 황금 더미 a mountain〔heap〕of gold // 산더미같은 파도 mountainous waves // 산더미처럼 많은 a mountain of ; lots of ; a world of // 짐을 산더미처럼 실은 차 a high-laden cart // 산더미처럼 쌓다 pile《things》mountain high ; gather《things》into a heap // 시체가 산더미를 이뤘다 The corpses lay in heaps. // 할 일이 산더미처럼 쌓여 있다 I have lots of things to do. /I have stacks of work to do.

더미씌우다 ⇨ 다미씌우다

더버기 heaps of ¶ …더버기가 되다 be covered〔smeared〕《with》; be stained《with》// 온몸이 흙 더버기가 되다 be covered with mud from top to toe〔head to foot〕; be muddy all over the body // 책상은 먼지 더버기다 The desk is covered with dust.

더벅머리[1] dishevelled〔unkempt〕hair ; [소년] a lad with dishevelled hair

더벅머리[2] [갈보] a prostitute〔who is still very young〕

더부룩더부룩 all in tufts ; all tufty〔fringy, bushy, thick〕**—하다** (be) all tufty〔bushy〕

더부룩이 in tufts ; tufty ; bushy ; fringy ; thick(ly) ¶ 머리털이 더부룩이 자라다 One's hair grows thick. /One's hair gets tufty.

더부룩하다 (be) tufty ; fringy ; bushy ; thick ¶ 더부룩한 머리 tufty〔thick〕hair

더부살이 a resident〔live-in〕servant ; a domestic (servant) ¶ 더부살이 환자(還子) 걱정 worrying about things which are none of one's concern ; worrying (oneself) unnecessarily

더북더북 ⇨ 다복다복

더불다 ① [함께하다] join in《a thing》; do together ; partake of
② [동행하다] take《a person》with (데리고 가다) ; bring《a person》with (데리고 오다) ; be accompanied by ; go with ; go hand in hand with ¶ 가족을 더불고 피난가다 flee with one's family

더불어 together ; with ; together with《a person》¶ 나이와 더불어 as one grows older ; with one's years // 그와 더불어 기쁨〔슬픔〕을 같이하다 share one's joy〔sorrow〕with him // 더불어 운명을 같이하다 share one's fate ; cast in one's lot《with》// 더불어 일하다 work together ; work side by side with // 더불어 행동하다 cooperate with《a person》; act in concert with《a person》// 천지와 더불어 무궁하다 be eternal as heaven and earth ; be coeval with heaven and earth // 시대와 더불어 나아가다 keep pace with〔abreast of〕the times

더블 double
— 베드 a double bed **— 상의(上衣)** a double-breasted coat **— 스틸** 〖야구〗 a double steal **— 플레이** a double play **— 헤더** 〖야구〗 a double-header

더블린 Dublin

더빙 〖영화·TV〗 dubbing(-in) **—하다** dub ¶ 그 영화는 우리말로 더빙되어 있다 The movie is dubbed in Korean.

더뻑 rashly ; recklessly ; blindly ; thoughtlessly ¶ 일에 더뻑 달려들다 tackle a job recklessly // 돈을 더뻑 쓰다 spend money recklessly

더뻑거리다 act〔behave〕thoughtlessly〔rashly〕

더뻑더뻑 rashly ; recklessly ¶ 더뻑더뻑 행동하다 be rash ; act recklessly ; proceed without regard to consequences ; take a leap in the dark ; go it blind

더뿌룩하다 feel stodgy ; feel〔sit〕heavy on the stomach ; remain undigested

더새다 stay for the night ; spend〔pass〕a night《on one's way》

더없이 most of all ; best (of all) ; supremely ¶ 더없이 아름다운 꽃 the finest flower imaginable // 더없이 기뻐하다 be delighted beyond measure

더욱 more ; still more〔less〕; all the more ; more and more ; less and less ¶ 더욱 공부하다 work harder // 더욱 노력하다 make a greater effort // 더욱 작아지다 grow less and less // 같이 갈 수 있으면 더욱 좋다 If you would go with me, so much the better. // 높이 올라갈수록 공기는 더욱 희박해진다 The higher we go, the thinner the air is. // 막내여서 더욱 귀엽다 I love him the more because he is my youngest child. // 그녀는 더욱 심히 울어댔다 She cried worse than ever〔all the more〕. // 혼자 남으니 더욱 슬퍼졌다 Left all alone I felt all the more sad. // 빠르면 더욱 좋다 The sooner the better. // 더욱더 그들에게 감사해야 한다 We ought to be all the more grateful for them.

더욱더욱 more and more ; increasingly

† **더욱이** besides ; moreover ; furthermore ; further ; in addition ; what is more ; particularly ; especially ; into the bargain ; on top of《that》; to boot ¶ 더욱이 곤란한 것은 to make matters worse ; what is worse // 더욱이 좋은 것은 what is better // 그녀는 불어를 읽지도 못하고 더욱이 쓰지도 못한다 She cannot read French, much less write it. // 더욱이 날씨가 안 좋았다 Besides, the weather was bad. /To make things worse, the weather was bad.

더운무대 a warm current

더운물 hot water

더운점심 a hot lunch

더워하다 be sensitive to the heat ; feel the heat ; complain of the heat ; swelter ¶ 몹시도 더워하는구나 How you feel the heat ! // 어린애가 더워하는 것 같다 The baby seems to feel hot.

†**더위** ① [날씨] the heat ; hot weather ¶ 더위를 견디다 stand〔bear〕 the heat // 더위를 피하다 avoid〔escape〕 the heat // 숨막히는 더위 suffocating〔stifling〕 heat // 찌는 듯한 더위 steaming heat // 나는 더위에 약하다 I am sensitive to the heat. /I am easily affected by hot weather. // 더위에는 아무렇지도 않다 I don't mind the heat. // 오늘은 더위가 심하군 How hot it is today ! // 더위가 물러가다 Hot weather comes to an end.
② [병] heatstroke ; illness from the (summer) heat ; sunstroke ; heat prostration ¶ 더위를 먹다 be affected by the heat ; suffer from hot weather
더위 먹은 소 달만 보아도 허덕인다 〔속담〕 A scalded cat〔dog〕 fears cold water. / The burnt child dreads the fire. /Once bitten twice shy.

더위잡다 clutch 《a thing》 ; grasp at 《a thing》

더치다 ① [병세가] become worse ; be aggravated ¶ 병이 더치다 one's illness worsens ; take a bad turn ; take a turn for the worse ② ⇨ 덧들이다

더킹 [권투에서] ducking **— 하다** duck 《to avoid blows》

더펄이 a scatterbrain ; a madcap ¶ 더펄이 처녀 a madcap〔scatterbrained〕 girl

더펄개 a shaggy dog

더펄거리다 bounce up and down ¶ 머리가 더펄거리다 one's hair is bouncing up and down

더펄더펄 bouncing up and down

더펄머리 bouncing hair

더하기 〖수학〗 addition ; adding up ¶ 간단한 더하기를 하다 do sums in simple addition

†**더하다**[1] ① [심해지다] get worse ; grow harder ; increase in violence ; get serious ; go from bad to worse ; gather strength ; grow intense〔severe〕 ; beat up ¶ 그의 병세가 날로 더한다 His illness gets serious. /He gets worse and worse. // 그의 난행이 점점 더한다 His unruly conduct is getting worse and worse. // 더위가 하루하루 더한다 It is growing warmer every day〔warmer and warmer〕. // 비바람이 더한다 The storm is gathering. // 애정은 해마다 더했다 My love grew with the years.
② [보태다] add 《up》 ; sum up ; add 《one number to another》 ¶ 둘에 둘을 더하면 넷이다 Two and two are〔make〕 four. // 5에 6을 더해라 Add 6 to 5. // 15에 25를 더하면 40이다 Twenty-five added to fifteen makes〔is, equals〕 forty.
③ [늘이다] increase ; augment ; add to ; enlarge ; gain ; grow ¶ 건강은 미를 더한다 Health enhances beauty.

더하다[2] [비교해서] (be) more ¶ 수가 더하다 be superior in number ; be numerically superior ; exceed in number // 독하기는 그것보다 이 술이 더하다 This liquor is stronger than that.

더할 나위 없다 (be) perfect ; the best ; the finest ; excellent ; fine ; ideal ; splendid ; likely ¶ 더할 나위 없이 perfectly ; supremely ; extremely ; immensely // 더할 나위 없는 물건 choice articles ; A-1 articles // 더할 나위 없는 피서지 an ideal summer resort // 더할 나위 없는 한 쌍 a well-matched couple // 날씨는 종일토록 더할 나위 없었다 The whole time the weather was the pink of perfection. // 더할 나위 없는 연구 자료다 This is just the thing we need for our studies. // 소풍에는 더할 나위 없는 날씨였다 It was an ideal day〔weather〕 for hiking. // 일을 더할 나위 없이 소중히 여긴다 He is all in all to the business.

덕 a shelf for drying grain

†**덕 德** ① [덕행] virtue ; morality ; goodness ; moral excellence ¶ 덕이 높은 사람 a virtuous man ; a man of virtue 〔high moral character〕 // 덕을 닦다 cultivate virtue〔moral character〕 // 덕을 행하다 practice virtue ; do good // 온 마을이 그의 덕에 감복했다 The whole village was impressed by his virtue.
② [덕분] favor ; indebtedness ; kindness ; mercy ; [진력] efforts ; good offices ; [조력] assistance ¶ 덕으로 by 《a person's》 favor ; thanks to ; due to ; through 《a person's》 efforts ; owing to // 내가 성공한 것은 당신의 덕이오 I owe my success to you. /Thanks to your assistance, I succeeded in the attempt. // 이것도 과학의 덕이다 We are indebted to science for this. // 저 사람 덕으로 직업을 얻었다 I got a position through his good offices.

덕교 德敎 moral〔ethical〕 teachings

덕기 德氣 virtuous mien ; virtue ; goodness ¶ 덕기 있다 have a virtuous mien ; be virtuous

덕담 德談 well-wishing remarks

덕대 [어린애 무덤] a child's rough-dug grave

덕대 德大 a miner who rents part of a mine to work

덕량 德量 broad-mindedness ; large-heartedness ; a virtuous mind ; generosity

덕망 德望 moral influence ¶ 덕망이 있다 have a moral influence 《over》 ; be renowned for 《one's》 virtues ; enjoy a good reputation
— 가(家) a man of high moral repute (of fair name).

덕분 德分 indebtedness ⇨ 덕택

덕석 a straw mat for covering the back of an ox (to protect against cold)
덕석밤 a big〔large〕 chestnut
덕성 德性 moral character ; virtue ; moral nature ¶ 덕성스럽다 be good-natured ; be kind-hearted ; be virtuous // 덕성을 기르다 build character ; cultivate 〔foster〕 moral character
덕스럽다 德— look virtuous ; (be) virtuous ; respectable ; benignant ; gracious ¶ 덕스럽게 생기다 have respectable features
덕업 德業 virtuous achievements〔deeds〕
덕육 德育 moral training〔culture, education〕 ; character building
덕의 德義 morality ; integrity ; probity ¶ 덕의를 존중하다 have a high sense of honor
덕의심 德義心 moral sense ; a sense of honor ; probity
덕적덕적 thickly covered ¶ 때가 덕적덕적 묻다 be thickly covered with dirt
덕정 德政 [선정] benevolent〔benign〕 administration〔government〕
덕지덕지 thick 《with dirt》 ¶ 때가 덕지덕지 끼다 be covered thick with dirt
****덕택 德澤** indebtedness ; favor ; grace ; patronage ; boon ; [조력] help ; aid ; assistance ; [후원] support ; backing ¶ 근면의 덕택 the fruit〔result〕 of one's labor // 덕택으로 due to ; owing to ; thanks to 《a person's》 patronage ; by 《a person's》 favor〔help, aid〕 ; by 《a person's》 kind influence // 노력한 덕택으로 through hard work // 그의 도움 덕택에 나는 성공하였다 Thanks to his assistance I succeeded in the attempt. // 내가 오늘 이만큼 된 것은 그의 덕택이다 I am indebted to him for what I am. // 덕택으로 아주 건강합니다 Quite well, thank you. // 맹렬히 싸운 덕택으로 이겼다 They won by virtue of hard fighting.
덕행 德行 virtuous〔moral〕 conduct ; virtue ; goodness ¶ 덕행이 높은 사람 a man of lofty character ; a noble-minded man // 덕행으로 알려지다 be renowned for one's virtue
덕화 德化 moral influence〔reform〕 ¶ 덕화시키다 influence〔reform〕 by virtuous example
덖다[1] become dirty〔filthy〕 ; be soiled 〔stained〕 ¶ 때가 덖다 get dirty
덖다[2] [익히다] roast 《tea, coffee beans, etc.》
-던가 [의문·의심] whether it was (observed to be or happen) ; (did you notice) was it? ; (did you hear or find) was it? ¶ 어디 두었던가 Where did I leave it? // 그것이 크던가 작던가 Was it large, or small (I wonder)? // 얼마나 크던가 How big was it? // 내가 왜 그리 했던가 후회됩니다 I have come to worry over why I did that.
-던걸 [회상·감탄] indeed ; really ; certainly ; quite ; I tell you ; you know ¶ 굉장한 미인이던걸 She was a stunning beauty, indeed.
-던데 ① [연결 어미] though ; although ; in spite of ; notwithstanding ; but ¶ 젊은 친구던데 똑똑하더라 Young though he was, he was very wise.
② [종결 어미] I found... ; you see 〔know〕 ¶ 책은 쉽던데 I found the book easy.
-던들 [결과의 반대 가정] granted that ; even if (it had been known to happen that) ; if it had happened that ¶ 빨리 의사에게 보였던들 안 죽었을 터인데 If he had seen the doctor right away, he wouldn't have died. // 당신의 도움이 없었던들 나는 실패했을 것이다 If it had not been for〔But for, Had it not been for 《문》〕 your help, I should have failed.
던적스럽다 [비열] (be) mean ; base ; sordid ; despicable ; [추잡] indecent ; obscene ; filthy ¶ 던적스러운 사람 a man of low character ; a meanspirited person // 던적스러운 행실 despicable behavior 〔conduct〕 // 보수를 바라다니 던적스럽다 It is mean of you to wish for recompense.
던져두다 ① [방치] put〔throw〕 to one side ; leave ¶ 책을 방구석에 던져두다 put a book to a corner of the room ② [하던 일을] lay〔put〕 aside ; leave unattended ¶ 하던 일을 던져두다 lay aside one's work unfinished
-던지 [지난 일의 회상·의심] whether it was (observed to be or happen) ¶ 값이 얼마였던지 기억이 안 난다 I don't remember how much it was.
†던지다 ① [내던지다] throw ; [세게] hurl ; fling ; cast ; [위로] toss ; [공을] pitch ¶ 공을 던지다 throw〔pitch〕 a ball // 돌을 던지다 throw〔fling〕 stones 《at》 ; pelt 《a person》 with stones // 몸을 던지다 drown oneself ; throw oneself into 《a well》 // 주사위를 던지다 cast a die // 창을 던지다 throw a spear〔pike〕 ; 〖경기〗 throw a javelin // 개에게 뼈다귀를 던져 줬다 I threw bones to the dog.
② [투표하다] vote 《for, against》 ; cast 《a vote》 ; poll ; ballot ¶ 깨끗한 한 표를 던지다 cast an honest〔a clean〕 vote 《for》 // 그에게 한 표를 던졌다 I voted for him.
던지럽다 (be) mean ⇨ 던적스럽다
던테 ① [너테] an added coating of ice on top of ice ; a layer of ice
② [더뎅이] a scab ; a slough ¶ 종기에 던테가 앉다 A scab forms over a boil.
③ [문둔테] a door pivot panel
덜 less ; incompletely ¶ 덜 구운 underdone ; half-done ; half-roasted (생선, 고기) ; half-baked (빵) // 덜 마른 half-dried // 덜 삶은 underdone ; half-done ; half-cooked // 덜 취한 half-tipsy ; half-drunk // 덜 마른 나무 unseasoned wood // 덜 익

은 과일 unripe〔green〕 fruit // 덜 죽인 뱀 a halfkilled snake a scotched snake // 이 고기는 덜 익혔다 This meat is underdone. // 잠을 덜 자서 피곤하다 I am tired for lack of sleep. // 실수를 하나만 덜 했어도 되는 건데 I made one too many mistakes. // 아내가 돈을 조금 덜 쓰면 도움이 될텐데 It would help if my wife would spend a little less.

덜거덕거리다, 떨꺼덕거리다 rattle ; clatter ¶ 바람에 문이 덜거덕거린다 A window rattles in the wind.

덜거덩거리다 clang ; rattle ¶ 기차가 그 지점 위를 덜거덩거리면서 지나갔다 The train rattled over the point.

덜걱, 떨걱 rattling ; clattering

덜걱마루 〖건축〗 a rickety wooden floor

덜그럭, 떨그럭 with a rattling〔clattering〕 noise ⇨ 달가닥

덜그럭거리다, 떨그럭거리다 rattle ; clatter

덜께기 an old cock-pheasant

덜꿩나무 〖식물〗 beech viburnum

덜다 ① [절약하다] save ; cut down ; clip ; slash ; [감하다] lighten ; mitigate ; allay ; diminish ; reduce ; lessen ; ease ; alleviate ; relieve ¶ 고통을 덜다 lighten〔mitigate〕 one's pain〔affliction〕 // 근심을 덜다 relax one's attention ; give relief to the mental strain // 생활의 낭비를 덜다 leave out〔omit, eliminate〕 the squandering〔waste〕 of life // 시간〔손〕을 덜다 save time〔trouble〕 ; 고통을 덜다 ease〔allay〕 the pain // 기계는 많은 노력을 던다 Machinery dispenses with much labor. // 이같이 하면 비용을 덜 수 있다 You will be able to cut down your expenses in that way.
② [빼다] subtract ; deduct ; take off ; remove ¶ 스물에서 열다섯을 덜다 subtract 15 from 20 // 열에서 여섯을 덜면 넷이 남는다 Six from ten leaves four. / Ten less〔minus〕 six leaves four. // 너무 많으니 좀 덜어라 It is too much, remove some.

덜덜[1] trembling (ly) ; shivering (ly) ¶ 덜덜 떨다 tremble all over (like an aspen leaf) ; be all of a tremble ; [이가] chatter 《one's teeth》 // 온몸이 덜덜 떨리다 tremble in every limb // 무서워서 덜덜 떨다 tremble for fear ; shudder at 《the sight of》 ; shiver with fright // 추워서 덜덜 떨고 있다 They are trembling with〔shivering from〕 cold.

덜덜[2], **떨떨** rattling ; rolling ¶ 수레가 덜덜 굴러가다 a cart rattles along

덜되다 ① [미완성] (be) incomplete ; unfinished ¶ 아직 덜된 연구 unfinished studies // 아직 덜된 원고 unfinished manuscript // 덜된 채 두다 leave 《a thing》 unfinished // 밥이 아직 덜되다 the rice is not ready〔cooked〕 yet // 조사가 아직 덜되었다 The investigation is not thorough-going enough.
② [사람됨이] be no good ; be a failure ; be a complete botch ; be wretched 〔poor, green〕 stuff ; be not up to the mark ; leave much to be desired ¶ 덜된 놈 a good-for-nothing fellow // 덜된 수작을 하다 talk nonsense

덜렁거리다, 떨렁거리다 ① [소리] tinkle ; jingle ; clink ¶ 덜렁덜렁 jingling ; ding-dong ; tinkling ; jingle-jangle
② [행동] be restless ; conduct〔behave〕 oneself flippantly ; act frivolously ; be always on the go ¶ 덜렁덜렁 돌아다니다 go around restlessly

덜렁말 a skittish horse

덜렁쇠 a careless person ; a flighty 〔hasty, bustling〕 person ; a restless person ; a scatterbrain

덜렁이 ⇨ 덜렁쇠

덜렁이다 be restless ⇨ 덜렁거리다

덜렁하다 ① [겁먹다] feel a shock ; get a start ; be much surprised〔startled, alarmed, frightened〕 ; feel one's heart stop ; get the wind up ; have one's heart in one's mouth ¶ 소식을 듣고 마음이 덜렁했다 The news gave me a shock. /The news came as a surprise to me. // 서장이 나를 부르러 보냈을 때 나는 가슴이 덜렁했다 When the police chief sent for me, I had my heart in my mouth. ② [덜렁거리다] 《a bell》 ring ; jingle

덜름하다 (be) rather short

덜리다 be reduced ; be decreased ; be subtracted ; be deducted ; be removed ¶ 고통이 덜리다 one's pain is mitigated 〔eased, lightened〕 // 걱정이 덜리다 one's anxiety is eased

덜먹다 ① [다 안 먹다] do not eat all (served) ② [실컷 안 먹다] do not satisfy one's hunger ③ [행동이] act improperly and waywardly ④ [나이를] be younger than 《a person》

덜미 the scruff〔nape〕 of the neck ⇨ 뒷덜미

덜미잡이 —하다 take〔seize〕 《a person》 by the scruff of the neck ; catch 《a person》 around the neck

덜미짚다 ① ⇨ 덜미잡이 (—하다)
② [재촉하다] press 《a person for a thing》 hotly ; urge 《a person to do》

덜밉지 않다 be not so bad (in looks) ; be rather good-looking

덜밋대문 —大門 a back〔rear〕 gate ; a postern (gate)

덜어내다 take out of〔from, away〕 ¶ 가마니에서 쌀을 덜어내다 take some rice out of a straw rice-bag // 그릇에서 밥을 덜어내다 take some rice out of a bowl

덜커덕 clattering (ly) ; rattling (ly) ¶ 창문을 덜커덕 닫다 close〔shut〕 a window with a click // 덜커덕덜커덕 clattering (ly) ; rattling (ly)

덜커덕거리다 keep clicking〔rattling, clattering〕 ¶ 덜커덕거리는 창문 a rattling window

덜커덩거리다 keep banging〔crashing, rattling, clattering〕 ¶ 덜커덩덜커덩 with bangs ; with crashes ; rattling ; clattering

*__덜컥__ ① [의외로 빨리] suddenly ; unexpectedly ¶ 덜컥 죽어 버리다 die suddenly ; pop off 《속》 ; drop dead // 덜컥 겁이 나다 be struck with awe〔get into a funk〕 all of a sudden

② [소리] a thump ; plump ; bump ¶ 덜컥 소리내며 with a thud〔thump〕 ; with a bump〔flump〕 ; plump heavily // 덜컥 떨어지다 fall plump〔with a flump〕 ; fall heavily ; flump // 덜컥 마룻바닥에 떨어지다 come down bump on the floor // 덜컥 떨어뜨리다 bump〔flump, flop〕 down ; drop down with a bump

덜퍽부리다 rant ; rave ; stamp with fury

덜퍽스럽다 (be) buxom ; portly ; ample ¶ 몸이 덜퍽스럽다 be buxom

덜퍽지다 (be) plentiful ; rich ; [몸집이] ample ; plump ; portly ; corpulent ; buxom ; stout

덜하다 ① [자동사] lessen ; diminish ; decrease ② [타동사] lessen ; diminish ; decrease ③ [견주어서] (be) less

덤 an extra ; anything thrown in ; an addition ; a throw-in ; a premium (상금, 경품 따위) ; giveaway 《미》 ¶ 죄다 사시면 그것을 덤으로 드리겠습니다 I will throw it into the bargain, if you buy the lot. // 이것은 덤으로 드립니다 This is a free〔an uncharged〕 addition. // 덤으로 몇 개 더 주시오 Throw in a few more, please.

덤덤탄 —彈 a dumdum bullet ; a soft-nosed bullet

덤덤하다 (be) speechless ; taciturn ; closemouthed ; remain〔keep〕 silent ; hold one's tongue ; keep dumb〔mum〕 ¶ 아무 말없이 덤덤하게 앉아 있다 sit in silence〔without saying anything〕

덤받이 a child brought by a second wife ; a child of one's wife by her previous marriage

덤벙 [물속에] splashing ; with a plop ¶ 덤벙 물에 떨어지다 drop in the water with a plop ; fall plop into the water

덤벙거리다 ① [경솔하게] act frivolously ¶ 덤벙거리며 일을 함부로 하다 do one's work carelessly

② [물속에서] splash ; splatter ; bespatter ¶ 덤벙거리면서 걷다 go splashing 《through the mud》 // 발을 물에 담그고 덤벙거리다 dabble one's feet in the water

덤벙덤벙 ① [경솔히] frivolously ; rashly ; lightly ; hastily ; carelessly ¶ 아무 일에나 덤벙덤벙 대들다 poke one's nose into everything ② [물을] splashing ; splattering

덤벼들다 ① [새·짐승이] spring〔leap, jump, pounce, fly〕 upon〔at〕 ; make a spring at ; rush〔bounce〕 upon

② [사람이] throw〔hurl, fling〕 oneself upon ; be〔come〕 down on〔upon〕 ; lunge at〔for〕 ; [치려고] strike (out) at 《a person》 ; [공격하다] attack ; assault ¶ 그는 화가 잔뜩 나서 나에게 덤벼들었다 He turned upon me in a fury.

③ [일을 시작하다] set〔go〕 about 《one's task》 ; get〔set, go, fall〕 to work 《on something》 ; get started on 《one's work》 ; set oneself to 《doing》 ; set〔put〕 one's hand to ¶ 모두 다 덤벼들어 순식간에 일을 끝냈다 All of us tackled the work and finished it in a blink〔made short work of it〕.

덤부렁듬쑥 thick ; dense ; luxuriant ; in luxurious growth **—하다** (be) thick ; overgrown ; luxuriant

*__덤불__ a thicket ; a bush ; a scrub ; a jungle ¶ 가시 덤불 a thorny bush

덤불자작이 〖식물〗 a birch

덤불혼인 marriage between matrimonial relations ; marriage between in-laws 《미·구》

덤비다 ① [달려들다] attack ; assault ; spring on 《a person》 ; leap on ; fling oneself upon ; rush〔fly〕 at ; turn upon ; fall on ; set upon ¶ 비호같이 덤비다 spring at 《a person》 with tiger-like ferocity // 적에게 덤비다 attack〔fall on〕 the enemy // 세 놈이 나에게 덤볐다 Three men sprang〔leaped〕 on me. // 자 덤벼라 Now, come on ! /Make my day ! // 자 몽땅 덤벼라 Go ahead, the whole pack of you !

② [서둘다] be hasty ; be in a hurry ; hurry ; make undue haste ; bustle〔act helter-skelter〕 (당황) ¶ 덤비지 마라 Don't be so hasty〔in a hurry〕. /Take your time. /Steady ! /Take it easy ! / Keep your shirt on ! 《속》

덤뻑 rashly ; recklessly ¶ 덤뻑 내닫다 dash off ; run off recklessly

덤터기 blame-shifting ¶ 덤터기(를) 쓰다 have the blame shifted on to oneself // 덤터기를 씌우다 shift the blame on to another

덤턱스럽다 (be) large and copious

덤퍼 [차] a dumpcart ; a dump truck ; [장치] a dumping device

덤프차 a dump truck ; 〖철도〗 a dump car

덤핑 dumping **—하다** dump ¶ 과잉 물자를 외국 시장에서 덤핑하다 dump the surplus goods in foreign markets

— 방지 관세 anti-dumping duties

덥다 [온도가] (be) hot ; heated ; [덥게 느끼다] 《I》 feel hot ¶ 국을 덥게 하다 heat up the cold soup // 더울 때 먹다 eat 《food》 hot ; drink 《*sool*》 hot // 몸이 덥다 have a fever ; have a temperature // 더운 한낮에 in the heat of the day // 더워지다 get〔grow〕 hot〔warm〕 // 더워지기 전에

before the heat of the day comes on // 더워 죽겠다 The heat is unbearable. /I can't stand the heat. /I'm dying of the heat. // 오늘도 덥겠다 We're going to have another hot day. // 지금이 한창 더울 때다 The summer〔air〕 is now at its hottest.

⁑덥석 quickly ; suddenly ; tightly ; firmly (단단히) ¶ 손을 덥석 쥐다 suddenly clasp〔grasp〕 another's hand ; give 《a person》 a grip // 개가 고깃점을 덥석 물었다 The dog snapped up a piece of meat.

덥적 meddling ; ingratiating, etc.

덥적거리다 interfere 《in a matter, with a person》 ; meddle 《in, with》 ; step in ; butt in ; put in a word ; poke one's nose into ¶ 덥적거리기 좋아하는 사람 a meddlesome person ; a busybody // 그는 남의 일에 덥적거리기 좋아한다 He pokes his nose into another's business.

덥적덥적 ① [남의 일에] meddlesomely ; interferingly ; officiously ¶ 남의 말다툼에 덥적덥적 나서다 interfere with the disputes of others ② [붙임성 있게] amiably ; affably ; sociably ; winningly ; graciously

덥절덥절하다 (be) amiable ; affable ; sociable ; winning ; cordial ; hospitable

덧 [짧은 시간] a short space of time 〔while〕 ; a spell ⇨ 어느덧

덧가지 a double branch

덧거름 fertilizer given to growing plants

덧거리 ① [추가물] an additional thing 〔work〕 ; extra thing〔work〕 **—하다** put〔throw〕 in an additional thing〔work〕 ② [말] an exaggeration **—하다** exaggerate ; overstate ¶ 그는 덧거리가 심하다 He is prone to exaggerate. /He always exaggerates.

—질 [덧얹음] putting〔throwing〕 in an additional thing ; [말의] exaggeration ; overstatement

덧거칠다 (be) unsmooth ; unfavorable ; worsening ¶ 덧거칠 것은 아무것도 없다 Nothing goes wrong〔amiss〕. /All is well.

덧걸다 hang 《a thing》 over〔upon, on top of〕 《another thing》

덧걸리다 be added on

덧걸이 [씨름] an armlock trip ¶ 덧걸이를 걸다〔덧걸이질하다〕 trip a wrestler with an armlock

덧게비 an extra thing〔person〕 ; a burden ; a nuisance

덧게비 치다 [관용] make oneself a nuisance ; interfere ; give trouble

덧깔다 spread 《a thing》 over〔upon, on top of〕 《another thing》 ¶ 요 위에 담요를 덧깔다 spread a blanket over the mattress

덧나다[1] ① [병이] take a bad turn ; take a turn for the worse ; be aggravated ¶ 병이 덧났다 One's condition takes a turn for the worse. // 종기가 덧났다 The boil has gathered〔ripened, inflamed〕. ② [성나다] be offended ; get one's back up ; have one's blood up

덧나다[2] [이가] grow on top 《of another》 ; grow extra ; grow from the common root ; grow to one side ; shoot off ; deviate ¶ 이가 덧나다 have a double〔side〕 tooth ; grow a snag tooth

덧날 a wedge (of a plane) ; back iron ¶ 덧날이 달린 대패 a plane with a back iron

덧내다 ① [병을] cause to take a bad turn ; make worse ; aggravate ; inflame (종기를) ¶ 여드름을 만져서 덧내다 make a pimple inflamed by fiddling with it ② [사람을] make 《a person》 angry ; tread 〔step〕 on 《a person's》 toes ; put 《a person》 out of temper〔humor〕

덧니 a snaggletooth (미) ; a snag tooth ; a double tooth (겹친) ; an oblique tooth

—박이 a person with a snaggletooth

덧달다 hang on top 《of another》 ¶ 덧달리다 be hung on top 《of another》

⁑덧대다 add〔join〕 《on a board, a prop, a layer》 ; put〔attach, place〕 over〔upon, on top of〕 another

덧두리 the cash supplement (in a barter deal)

덧드러나다 be〔get〕 found out ; come〔be brought〕 to light ; come〔be〕 out

덧들다 [잠이] be wakeful ; be hard to get to sleep again

덧들이다 ① [사람을] make 《a person》 angry ; offend ; incense ; give offense 《to》 ; provoke ; get 《a person's》 back up ; tread on 《a person's》 toes〔corns〕 ; put 《a person》 out of temper ¶ 그는 결코 남을 덧들이는 말을 하지 않는다 He never says anything that might give offense to another. // 그것이 그를 덧들였다 That was provocation enough to him. /That put him out of temper. ② [잠을] keep 《a person》 from getting back to sleep ③ [병을] make worse ; aggravate

덧머리 a wig

⁑덧문 —門 an outer〔a double〕 door〔window〕 ; a storm〔rain〕 door〔window〕 ; a shutter

덧물 water formed on an icy surface

덧방붙이다 add a splice plate〔piece〕 《on》

덧버선 outer socks

덧붙다 adhere〔stick, attach, cling〕 to 《a thing》 in addition

덧붙이다 [보탬] add 《a thing》 to ; append ; [붙임] attach〔stick, fix, put〕 (on top of another) ¶ 덧붙여 말하다 add ; make an additional remark // 벽에 널판자를 덧붙이다 fix planks of wood on a wall // 한 말씀 덧붙여 두겠다 Let me add a few more words to make sure.

덧빗 the comb attachment of a hair clipper

덧셈 addition **—하다** add (up figures)

덧소금 overlaid salt (before setting to pickle)
* 덧 신 overshoes ; rubbers ; galoshes ; gumshoes
덧신다 put on〔wear〕《a thing》 over one's shoes
덧쓰다 wear 《a cover》 on one's headgear
덧양말 —洋襪 outer socks
*덧없다 ① [무상하다] (be) short-lived ; be all too soon ; passing ; fleeting ; transient ; transitory ; evanescent ; ephe meral ; momentary ; fugitive ; fugacious ; caducous ; fickle ¶ 덧없는 인생 transient〔ephemeral〕 life〔existence〕 ; mutable life // 덧없는 사랑 a short-lived love // 덧없는 세월 flying〔quick, passing〕 time // 덧없는 세상 the fleeting〔uncertain, changeable〕 world ② [자취·근거 없음] (be) unfounded ; groundless ; baseless ; false ; be without leaving any trace ; be gone
덧없이 fleetingly ; transiently ; transitorily ; evanescently ; ephemerally ; all too soon ; before one knows it ¶ 세월이 덧없이 지나간다 Time flies fleetingly 〔before we know it〕. // 인생은 초로와 같이 덧없이 가버린다 Life is as evanescent as morning dew.
덧입다 put on〔wear〕《a coat》 over a garment
덧저고리 overwear ; overalls ; a wrapper ; a duster 《미》 ; a covert coat 《영》 ; [어린이의] a smock (frock)
덧짐 an added〔extra〕 load
덩거칠다 [우거지다] be thick with vines
덩굴 a vine ; [곱슬 덩굴] a tendril ; [땅바닥에 퍼지는] a runner〔creeper〕 ¶ 고구마 덩굴 (sweet) potato runners 〔vines〕 // 포도 덩굴 grapevines // 덩굴이 퍼지다 a vine creeps〔climbs, trails〕
덩굴걷이 [걷어치움] ingathering of runners ; [열매] young fruits picked while gathering in runners
덩굴손 〖식물〗 a tendril ; a cirrus
덩굴지다 grow creepers ; put on vines ; creep ¶ 포도가 덩굴지다 A grape vine grows〔puts out〕 creepers.
덩그렇다 [높이] (be) high and big ; stately ; imposing ; [텅비다] big and hollow ¶ 덩그렇게 빈 집 a big and empty house // 언덕 위에 집 한 채가 덩그렇게 서 있다 A lonely〔solitary〕 house towers high over the hill.
덩달다 do the same as 《a person》 does ; follow suit ; echo 《another's view》 ; chime in with ; follow 《another》 blindly ; tag along ¶ 덩달아 웃다 laugh following suit ; smile in sympathy // 그녀가 노래를 부르기 시작하자 딴 사람들도 덩달아 불렀다 She began to sing and the rest chimed in.
덩더꿍 tum-tum ; tum-tumming ; tumdedum
덩더꿍이 소출 [속담] "easy-come, easy-go" ; a happy-go-lucky way of life
덩덕새머리 shaggy〔unkempt〕 hair
덩덩 a tum-tum ; tum-tumming ¶ 덩덩 북을 울리다 beat a drum tum-tum
덩덩그렇다 ① [헌거롭다] (be) ever so high and big ; most imposing ② [텅비다] (be) huge and empty
덩두렷이 remarkably ; conspicuously ; strikingly ; obviously
덩둘하다 (be) foolish ; stupid
덩드럭거리다 put on airs〔frills〕 ; give oneself airs ; assume an air of importance ; hold one's head high ; act stuck-up ¶ 그는 덩드럭거리는 버릇이 있다 He has a habit of holding his head too high.
덩실거리다 skip about ; dance lively 〔sprightly〕 ¶ 덩실덩실 (dancing) lively 〔spiritedly, joyfully〕 // 기뻐서 덩실거리다 dance about with joy
덩싯거리다 loll about lazily ; wallow ¶ 종일 누워 덩싯거리다 loll about in one's room〔bed〕 all day
†덩어리 ① [뭉쳐진] a lump ; a mass ; a clod ; a gobbet 《of meat》 ; a dollop 《of butter〔pudding〕》 ¶ 얼음 덩어리 a lump of ice ; pack ice (큰 것) // 핏덩어리 a clot of blood // 흙 덩어리 a clod 〔clump, lump, mass〕 of earth // 땅덩어리 a land mass 《on the earth》
② [떼] a clump ; a cluster ; a group ; a crowd ; a knot ; a flock ¶ (사람들이) 한 덩어리가 되어 in a body〔group〕
③ [바로 그것] ¶ 거짓말 덩어리 a tissue of falsehoods〔lies〕 ; a pack of lies // 욕심 덩어리 a very greedy person ; a lump of avarice〔selfishness〕 ; 《be》 avarice itself // 골칫덩어리 a troublesome fellow
덩어리지다 lump ; mass ; form a mass ; conglomerate ¶ 흙이 덩어리지다 dirt lumps // 얼음이 덩어리지다 ice forms into a mass // 전분은 너무 급히 끓이면 덩어리진다 Cornstarch will lump if boiled too fast.
덩이 a lump ; a mass ; a clod ; a nugget ; a piece
덩지 bulk ; size ; volume ¶ 덩지가 큰 사람 a big〔bulky〕 person // 덩지가 큰 짐 a big〔bulky〕 piece of luggage // 덩지가 크다 be bulky ; be big ; be voluminous
덩치 ⇨ 덩지
⁑덫 a trap ; a snare ; a hook ; a gin ¶ 덫을 놓다 set a trap ; lay a snare // 덫에 걸리다 be caught in a trap ; fall into a snare ; be trapped // 덫으로 잡다 entrap ; snare ; gin ; ensnare ; catch in a trap // 제가 놓은 덫에 제가 걸리다 be caught in one's own snare ; be hoist with one's own petard
†덮개 ① [이불 따위] bedding ; bedclothes ; a quilt ; (bed) covers ; a coverlet ; a comfort(er) 《미》 ② [뚜껑] a lid

⇨ 뚜껑 ¶ 덮개가 있는 covered // 덮개가 없는 차 an open car // 상자의 덮개를 열다 take off the lid of a box

†**덮다** [씌우다] cover ; veil ; overspread ; hang over ; [은폐] hide ; conceal ; cover up ; bury ; [닫다] shut ; close ; put on the lid (뚜껑으로) ¶ 이불을 덮다 put on a quilt〔bedclothes〕; cover oneself with bedclothes ; draw bedclothes over 《a person's body》// 뚜껑을 덮다 put a lid on // 책을 덮다 close a book // 죄를 덮어 주다 cover up 《a person's》 crime ; keep 《a person's》 crime secret // 구름이 하늘을 덮었다 The sky is overcast〔overspread with clouds〕. // 구름이 해를 덮었다 The sun is obscured by a cloud. // 자는 아이에게 당신의 저고리를 덮어 주시오 Cover this sleeping child with your coat.

덮두들기다 pat 《a child》 affectionately

덮밥 ¶ 계란 덮밥 a bowl of rice capped〔topped〕 with eggs // 장어 덮밥 a bowl of boiled eel and rice

덮어놓고 without any reason〔cause〕; causelessly ; without asking or giving any reason〔explanation〕; without inquiring into the truth of the matter ; arbitrarily ; out of a clear blue sky (느닷없이) ¶ 덮어놓고 가자고 하다 ask 《a person》 to go without telling why // 덮어놓고 사람을 치다 hit 《a person》 without giving any explanation

덮어놓고 열 엿냥 금이다 속담 give a random judgement.

덮어두다 ① pass 《a matter》 over unnoticed ; take no notice of ; shut one's eyes to ; overlook ; let 《a matter》 go unchallenged ; ignore ; wink at ; connive at ¶ 잘못을 덮어두다 shut one's eyes to 《a person's》 fault ; overlook 《a person's》 mistake // 이건 그냥 덮어둘 수 없다 We should not let this pass without protest. /This should not be passed unmentioned. // 불쌍하니까 이번만은 덮어둔다 For pity's sake I will let the matter pass for this time.

② [비밀로] keep 《a matter》 secret〔dark〕 ¶ 이 일을 좀 덮어두어 주십시오 Please don't reveal〔disclose〕 this fact. /Please make it a secret. /Please keep it to yourself.

덮어쓰다[1] take (another's guilt) on oneself ¶ 애매한 죄를 덮어쓰다 be falsely accused // 남의 죄를 덮어쓰다 take another's blame on oneself ; take the rap for someone else

덮어쓰다[2] [글씨본을] trace an under copy letter by letter ¶ 글씨본을 덮어쓰다 trace penmanship models

덮어씌우다 ① [가림] cover 《a thing with...》; put 《a thing》 over〔on〕; plate 《a thing with gold》 ② [죄를] charge 《a person with a fault》; pin 《a blame on a person》

덮이다 be covered ; be put on ; be veiled ; be hidden ; be concealed ; be wrapped ; be enfolded ; be closed ¶ 눈에 덮이다 be covered with snow // 담쟁이에 덮이다 be overgrown with ivy ; be hidden by ivy // 뚜껑이 덮이다 a lid is put on ; be lidded // 안개에 덮이다 be enveloped in〔shrouded by〕 mist // 얼음에 덮이다 be coated〔covered〕 with ice // 푸른 잎에 덮이다 be clothed in green leaves ; be clad with verdure // 클로버에 덮이다 be carpeted with clover // 극동의 형세는 암운에 덮여 있다 The whole situation in the Far East is shrouded in darkness. // 산꼭대기가 구름에 덮여 있다 The mountain peak is wrapped in clouds. // 하늘이 구름에 덮여 있다 The sky is overspread with clouds. /The sky is overcast.

덮치기 a large fowler's〔fowling〕 net ; a bird net with double handles

덮치다 ① [겹쳐누르다] hold〔get〕 《a person》 down ; pin 《a person》 《to the floor》; force down ; [습격하다] attack ; raid ; fall on ; set on ; descend on ; swoop upon ¶ 솔개가 병아리를 덮치다 an eagle swoops〔falls〕 down on a chicken // 산적이 길손들을 덮쳤다 The highwaymen fell on a party of travelers. // 폭풍우가 그 배를 덮쳤다 A storm overtook the ship. // 사내가 여자를 덮쳤다 The man attacked a woman. // 태풍은 해안가를 덮치기 직전에 진로를 바꾼 것 같다 The typhoon apparently shifted course just before hitting the coast.

② [한꺼번에] come〔happen〕 all at the same time ¶ 불행이 덮쳤다 We had one misfortune after another〔a series of misfortunes〕. // 엎친 데 덮친다 Misfortune never comes singly. /Out of the frying-pan into the fire. // 혼사에 장사가 덮쳤다 They had a wedding and a funeral one after the other.

데 [곳] a place ; a point ; a spot ; [특징] a feature ; an aspect ; [대목] a passage (문장 따위의) ; a part (부분) ; [경우] case ; a circumstance ¶ 강한 데 a strong point ; one's strength (사람의) // 이것은 머리 아픈 데에 먹는 약이다 This is the medicine you take when you have a headache. // 그녀에게는 여자다운 데가 없다 There is nothing womanly about her.

데걱거리다, 떼꺽거리다 clatter ; rattle ¶ 데걱데걱 clattering ; rattling ; [서슴지 않고] immediately ; on the spot // 자물쇠를 데걱데걱 잠그다 lock the doors with a rattling〔clicking〕 sound

데구루루, 떼구루루 rolling ; rumbling ¶ 데구루루 구르다 roll over and over // 데구루루 굴리다 roll 《a ball》 over 《the floor》; rumble over 《a barrel》

데굴데굴, 떼굴떼굴 rolling〔rumbling〕(continuously) ¶ 계단에서 데굴데굴 굴러 떨어지다 tumble down the stairs

데그럭- ⇨ 대그락-

데꺽 ① [소리] cracking ; snapping ; with a crack ; with a snap ¶ 지팡이가 데꺽 부러지다 one's stick breaks with a snap ② [손쉽게] without any trouble ; with ease ; quickly and easily ; just like that ; in a snap ¶ 그는 그 문제를 데꺽 풀었다 He solved the problem just like that. /The problem was a snap for him. // 이 일을 데꺽 해치우고 한 잔 하러 가자 Let's clear away this work right quick and go out for a drink.

데꺽데꺽 clattering ; rattling

데꾼하다, 떼꾼하다 《eyes》 (be) hollow 《from exhaustion》 ¶ 눈이 데꾼하다 one's eyes have sunken

데님 *denim*

*‡***데다** ① [화상 입다] be〔get〕 burnt ; suffer a burn ; scald〔burn〕 oneself ; get〔be〕 scorched (부젓가락 따위에) ; get〔be〕 scalded (끓는 물에) ¶ 덴 자국 the scar of a burn〔scald〕 // 손을 데다 get burnt in the hand〔burn one's hand〕 《on the stove》 ; scald one's hand 《with hot water》
② [진저리나다] have had enough of 《a thing》 ; know 《a thing》 to one's cost ; have a bitter experience ; find 《a thing》 troublesome〔difficult〕 to deal with ¶ 그놈에게는 아주 데었다 I won't have anything to do with him. // 너의 장난에는 아주 데었다 I have had enough of your mischief. // 빚에는 아주 데었다 I know to my cost what it is to be in debt.

데데하다 (be) poor ; trashy ; good-for-nothing ; worthless ; unsatisfactory ¶ 데데한 사람 a good-for-nothing person // 데데한 수작 useless remarks ; nonsense // 데데한 물건 poor stuff ; trash ; rubbish // 데데하게 굴다 act foolishly // 누가 그런 데데한 이야기를 퍼뜨려 Who's spreading such hogwash ?

데되다 be unsatisfactory in quality ; lack something of〔be short of〕 perfection ; leave something to be desired ; be somewhat defective

데드볼 〖야구〗 a dead ball ¶ 데드볼을 맞다 be hit by a pitched ball // 데드볼로 나가다 get a walk on a dead ball

데려가다 take 《a person》 with ; walk 《a person》 off (연행) ; take 《a person》 back with 《one》 ; take 《a person》 home ¶ 너를 길잡이로 데려가지 I'll take you along as guide. // 데려가 주세요 Let me go with you. // 아이를 학교에 데려갔다 He took a child to the school (with him).

데려오다 bring 《a person》 along ; bring 《a person》 with one ; come in company with ; fetch ; make 《a person》 come back ¶ 왜 그를 데려오지 않았어요 Why haven't you brought him along ?

데리다 be〔get〕 attended〔accompanied〕 《by》 ¶ 종 다섯 사람을 데리고 attended〔accompanied〕 by five servants // 그는 많은 하졸을 데리고 있다 He has a large following. /He is attended by a large retinue. // 그녀를 데리고 산 지가 10여 년이 되었다 We have been married more than ten years.

데릴사위 a son-in-law taken into the family ; one adopted as husband for one's daughter

데릴사윗감 ① [얌전한 젊은이] a young man of good〔irreproachable〕 conduct
② [미운 놈] a detestable fellow ; a repulsive〔an odious〕 wretch

데림추 followers ; adherents ; hangers-on ; one's admiring satellites ; ward-heelers

데마 demagoguery ; demagogism ; demagogy ; a groundless story ; a false〔an unfounded〕 rumo(u)r ; grapevine 《미·구》 ¶ 데마를 퍼뜨리다 set a false rumor afloat ; circulate a false rumor〔report〕

데면데면하다 (be) careless ; thoughtless ; heedless ; negligent ; inattentive ; absent-minded ; harum-scarum ¶ 그들은 어쨌든지 데면데면한 행동을 하는 것 같았다 They seemed somehow to be acting distant.

*‡***데모** a demonstration ; a rally ; a demo 《구》 **—하다** demonstrate 《against》 ; hold〔stage〕 a demonstration ¶ 전쟁 반대 데모 an antiwar demonstration // 데모에 가담하다 join a demonstration // 데모를 해산시키다 disperse a demonstration
—대(隊) (a group of) demonstrators **—만능** almighty demonstration ; all powerful demonstration **— 만능 풍조** the almighty demonstration trend **— 행진** a demonstration parade **가두 —** a street demonstration

데모크라시 democracy ⇨ 민주주의 ¶ 데모크라시의 democratic

데밀다 push in ; force in

*****데뷔** a debut 《프》 **—하다** make one's debut ; come out ; debut ¶ 그녀는 가을에 음악계에 데뷔할 것이다 She will make her debut in the musical world this autumn.

데삶기다 be half-done〔-boiled〕 ; be parboiled

데삶다 parboil ; boil 《an egg》 soft〔lightly〕 ¶ 데삶은 underdone ; half-done ; half-cooked ; half-boiled ; rare // 데삶은 달걀 a half〔soft〕-boiled egg ; a half-done egg ; a half-poached egg // 달걀을 데삶다 boil 《eggs》 soft (반숙)

데생 〖미술〗 dessin 《프》 ; a (rough) sketch

데생각하다 be poor〔immature, shallow〕 in one's thinking ; be imprudent〔indiscreet〕

데생기다 be immature

데설궂다 (be) rough ; rude ; unrefined ; loose

데설데설하다 be rude〔unrefined〕 in nature ;

(be) loose ; unrefined
데스 마스크 a death mask ¶ 데스 마스크를 뜨다 make a death mask 《of》
데스크 [책상] a desk ; [호텔의] the (registry) desk ; [신문사의 편집부] the desk 《미》; a copyreader 《편집부원》
데시- deci- ¶ 데시그램 a decigram // 데시미터 decimeter // 데시리터 a deciliter
데시기다 eat reluctantly〔unwillingly〕 ¶ 그녀는 입맛이 떨어져 음식을 데시기만 했다 She had no appetite and only picked at her food.
데알다 have superficial〔little〕 knowledge 《about》 ; know superficially ; get a smattering of 《literature》 ; smatter ; dabble in
데억지다 [너무 크다] (be) too big〔large〕 ; [너무 많다] excessive ; superabundant ; be in excess
데우다 warm ; heat ; heat〔warm〕 up ; reheat (식은 것을) ; hot up 《속》 ¶ 국을 데우다 heat up the cold soup // 밥을 데워 먹다 eat a rice meal made warm over again〔reheated〕 ; eat a heated-up rice meal
데이비스컵 〖정구〗 the Davis cup
— 선수 a Davis cup teammate **— 쟁탈(爭奪)**〔**쟁탈전**〕 the Davis cup tournament
*__데이터__ data (*sg.* -tum) ¶ …에 관한 데이터를 모으다 gather data on...
— 뱅크 data bank **—베이스** database (DB) **— 전송** data transmission〔transfer〕 **— 처리(장치)** data processing (machine) **— 통신** data communications
데이트 a date ¶ 안면이 없는 남녀간의 데이트 a blind date // 데이트의 상대 one's date **—하다** date (with) 《a girl》 ; have〔make, get〕 a date 《with》 ¶ 그 여자는 나와의 데이트에 응해 주었다 She gave me a date. // 낸시에게 데이트 신청을 했다가 거절당했어 I asked Nancy out, but she turned me down. // 어젯밤 베티가 어떤 남자하고 데이트하는 것을 보았다 I saw Betty dating a guy last night.
데익다 (be) half-cooked〔-done〕 ; rare
데치다 ① [끓는 물에] boil (slightly) ; parboil ¶ 야채를 데치다 parboil vegetables (in hot water) ② [혼내주다] punish severely ; chastise
데카당 〖문학〗 decadence ; a decadent
— 문학 decadent literature **—파** the decadents
데카리터 a decaliter
데카미터 a decameter
데칸 고원 —高原 Deccan Plateau
데커레이션 (a) decoration
크리스마스 — Christmas decoration
데퉁바리 a clumsy oaf
데퉁스럽다 (be) clumsy ; awkward
덱데구루루 rolling ⇨ 데구루루
덴가슴 a horror-stricken state of mind ; a nightmarish memory 《of》
덴겁하다 be confused ; fluster oneself ; be flurried ; be thrown into confusion ; be disconcerted ; lose one's head〔presence of mind〕 ¶ 덴겁해서 in confusion ; helterskelter
덴덕스럽다 [서술적] feel nausea〔unfresh〕 ; be disgusted 《by》 ; get sick of
덴덕지근하다 [서술적] feel quite disgusted ; feel very unfresh
덴마크 Denmark ¶ 덴마크의 Danish
—말 Danish **— 사람** a Dane
델리 Delhi
델리킷 ¶ 델리킷한 delicate // 델리킷한 입장 delicate situation
델린저 현상 —現象 〖물리〗 the Dellinger phenomenon
델타¹ a delta ¶ 델타 지대〔평야〕 a delta land〔plain〕
델타² delta ¶ 델타선 delta rays
뎅그렁거리다, 뗑그렁거리다 tinkle ; jingle ; clang ¶ 뗑그렁뗑그렁 clang! clang! // 풍경이 바람에 뗑그렁거린다 A hanging bell is tinkling in the wind.
뎅뎅, 뗑뗑 clang-clang ; ding-dong ; jingle-jangle
†**도¹** ① [및] and ; as well as ; both... and ; […도 역시] too ; also ; […도 …이 아니다] not... either ; neither... nor ¶ 그는 영어도 알고 불어도 안다 He understands both French and English. // 나는 불어도 영어도 못한다 I can speak neither French nor English. // 그는 불어를 말할 수도 있고 쓸 줄도 안다 He speaks French, and writes it as well. // 돈도 주고 옷도 주더라 He gave me clothes as well as money. // 자네도 거기에 있었나 Were you there also? // 당신이 안 가겠다면 나도 안 가겠다 If you will not go, I will not go, either. // 배고프지 —나도 그렇단다 Are you hungry? So am I. // 아유 목말라—나도 그래 I'm very thirsty. I〔Me〕, too. // 난 그 사전을 살 여유가 없어—나도 그래 I can't afford to buy that dictionary. Neither can I. // 그도 나를 알고 있다 He knows me, too. /He also knows me.
② [까지도] even ; without so much as ¶ 지금도 even now // 그 책은 펴도 안 봤다 I have never even opened the book. // 그는 간다는 인사도 없이 떠났다 He went away without so much as saying goodbye. // 아무도 안 왔다 Nobody came at all. // 아무 것도 없다 We have nothing. / There is nothing. // 근심이 돼서 밤에 잠도 안 온다 I feel so anxious (that) I cannot sleep even at night.
③ [어느 것도] whether... or not ; either... or ¶ 펜으로 써도 좋고 연필로 써도 좋다 You may write it either with a pen or a pencil.
④ [아무리…이라도] even if ; although ; though ; in spite of ; notwithstanding ; no matter 《what, how, who, etc》 ¶ 적어도 at least // 많아도 at (the) most // 아

무리 비가 심히 오더라도 however〔no matter how〕 hard it may rain // 아무리 결점이 많아도 with all one's faults // 가 봐도 그 사람은 없을 거다 You might find him absent, even if you went. // 누가 뭐라 해도 난 찬성 못하겠다 No one will persuade me to approve of it.

도² 〖음악〗 do

⁑도¹ 道 [행정 구역] a district ; a province ¶ 도립의 provincial // 도내의〔에서〕 inside〔in〕 the province // 도외의〔에서〕 outside (of) the province

— 당국 the provincial authorities **—령(令)** a provincial ordinance〔order〕 **—지사** a provincial governor **—행정** provincial administration **경기 —** *Kyunggi* Province

도² 道 ① [도로] a road ② [술] an art ; a craft ③ [가르침] teachings ; doctrines ; truth (진리) ; morality (도의) ; justice (정의) ; reason (도리) ¶ 공자의 도 the doctrines〔teachings〕 of Confucius // 공자의 도를 펴다 expound the teachings〔doctrines〕 of Confucius ; preach〔propagate〕 Confucianism // 도를 구하다 seek after truth // 도를 닦다 cultivate one's moral〔religious〕 sense // 도를 깨닫다 perceive a truth ; realize a religious truth // 접시 닦기에는 도가 텄구나 You've got your dishwashing down to a science.

†도 度 ① [온도·경〔위〕도] a degree ; [각도] degree ; diopter (렌즈의) ¶ 섭씨 5도 five degrees〔5℃〕 // 45도의 각 an angle of 45 degrees // 북위 38도 38 degrees〔38°〕 north latitude // 동경 27도 longitude 27°E // 도수가 높은 안경 spectacles of a high degree ; powerful spectacles ; glasses with heavy lenses // 18도의 안경 spectacles of 18 degrees // 그 여자의 열은 39도 3분이었다 Her temperature was 39.3 degrees. // 아시고 계시는지 모르겠는데요 이 지방에서는 영하 20도의 기온이 보통이에요 You know, in this region temperatures of 20° below zero are common. // 한란계는 그늘진 곳에서 60도였다 The mercury stood at 60 degrees in the shade.

② [정도] a degree ; an extent ; a measure ; a limit (한도) ¶ 도를 넘다 carry 《things》 to excess〔too far〕 ; be intemperate ; have too much of a good thing ; break〔go beyond〕 bounds ; overshoot oneself ; exceed the limits ; overstep the bounds // 모든 일에는 도가 있다 There is a limit to everything. // 만사에 도를 넘지 말아라 Be moderate in all things. // 술은 도를 넘으면 몸에 안 좋다 Excessive〔Too much〕 drinking impairs one's health. // 어떤 일이고 도를 넘으면 해가 된다 If you go beyond bounds in anything, it will do you harm.

도 都 a capital city ; a metropolis ; a city (도회지)

도 徒 a clique ; a set ; a gang ; a pack ; a ring

-도 度 [연도] a year (period) ; a term ¶ 금년도 the current year // 내년도 next year

도가 都家 a club house of businessmen in the same field

도가니¹ a crucible ; a melting pot ¶ 흥분의 도가니가 되다 turn into a scene of wild excitement

도가니² [무릎 도가니] the kneebone of cattle ; the meat on the kneebone of cattle ; [볼기살] rump

도가머리 a crest 《of a bird》 ; a bird with a crest ; [사람] a person with crested hair

도가자류 道家者流 a Taoist ; members of the Taoist school

도각 倒閣 unseating〔overthrowing〕 the Cabinet ¶ 도각 운동을 일으키다 start〔initiate〕 a movement to unseat〔throw out〕 the Cabinet

도감 圖鑑 a pictorial〔an illustrated〕 book 《of the Korean flora》

도강 渡江 crossing of a river **—하다** cross a river

— 훈련 a river-crossing exercise

도개교 跳開橋 a bascule bridge

도거리 the gross ; bulk ; mass ¶ 도거리로 in a lump ; in one lot ; in the gross ; in bulk ; en masse ; together // 도거리로 사다 buy 《things》 in (the) mass〔lot, bulk〕 // 도거리로 보내다 send 《things》 in a bundle

도검 刀劍 swords ; cold steels

도경 道警 the provincial police (headquarters)

도계 道界 the boundary line between provinces

도고 都庫 an exclusive sale ; an exclusive〔a sole〕 agency ; the franchise 《미》 **—하다** make an exclusive sale 《of》 ; sell 《goods》 as the sole outlet

도공 刀工 a swordsmith

***도공 陶工** a potter ; a ceramist ; a porcelain-maker ; a pottery worker

—술(術) ceramics ; pottery

도관 導管 a conduit ; a pipe

— 조직 〖식물〗 a vascular〔tracheal〕 tissue

도괴 倒壞 collapse ; destruction **—하다** collapse ; be destroyed ; fall (down) ; crumble ¶ 가옥 도괴로 인해서 부상하다 be injured in the collapse of a house // 많은 가옥이 지진으로 도괴되었다 Many houses collapsed〔crumbled to the ground〕 in the earthquake.

— 가옥 houses collapsed ; fallen houses

—물(物) debris ; wreckage

도교 道敎 Taoism

— 신자 a Taoist

***도구 道具** ① [연장] an instrument ; an appliance ; an implement ; a utensil ; a tool (공구)

> 참고 **implement** 뜻의 범위가 가장 넓으며 가구, 기물 (종교 의식용), 의류까지 가리킬 수 있다 **tool** 손으로 하는 일에 쓰는 도구 **instrument** 정교한 일 또는 과학적, 공예적 작업에 쓰는 도구 **utensil** 부엌에서 쓰는 도구와 용기

¶ 청소 도구 a cleaning outfit // 가재 도구〔가구〕 furniture ; household belongings (집합적)

② [불교의] utensils used in Buddhist services

③ [수단·방편] a means ; a tool ; a vehicle ; a stepping-stone ¶ 선전 도구 an instrument of propaganda // 남을 도구로 이용하다 make a tool of a person // 언어는 사상 전달의 도구다 Language is the vehicle of thought.

— 상자 a toolbox ; a tool chest ; a (workman's) kit ; a workbox ; a ditty box (영화 촬영 기사의) **—주의** instrumentalism

도구 渡歐 —하다 go to Europe

도굴 盜掘 ① [무덤의] grave robbery ¶ 도굴범 a grave robber **—하다** rob a grave ② [광물의] illegal〔bootleg〕 mining

도규 刀圭 ① [의술] medical arts〔skills〕 ② [약 숟가락] a medicine spoon

—가(家) a medical man ; a physician **—계(界)** the medical world〔profession〕 ; medical circles **—술(術)** the art of medicine〔healing〕 ; the medical art

도그마 a dogma 《*pl.* -s, -mata》 ; dogmatism (주의)

*__도금 鍍金__ gilt ; plating ; gilding ; coating **—하다** plate ; gild ; engild ; wash ¶ 금으로 도금한 반지 a gold-plate ring // 도금이 벗어지다 the gilt comes off // 동에 금을 도금하다 plate copper with gold

—공(工) a plater **—술(術)** the art of plating〔gilding〕 **—액(液)** a plating solution **— 제품** plated ware ; plate ware **전기 —** electric gilding ; electroplating

도급 都給 a contract 《for work》 ; undertaking ¶ 도급 맡다 contract for ; have a contract for ; undertake // 도급으로 일시키다 have a work done by contract

—인 a contractor ; 〖법〗 an independent contractor **—일** contracted work〔job〕 ; piecework

도급 주다 관용 give 《a person》 a contract for 《building a house》 ; contract 《a work》

*__도기 陶器__ [토기] earthenware ; china ; chinaware ; crockery ; [오지그릇] porcelain ; pottery ; ceramic ware ¶ 도기 한 점 a piece of earthenware

—류(類) crockery ; pottery **— 사진술** photoceramics **—상(商)** a crockery 〔china〕 dealer ; [점포] a chinashop **— 제조** pottery **— 제조소** a pottery **— 제조술** ceramics ; the art of pottery

도깨비 a bogy ; a bugbear ; a bugaboo (미) ; a goblin ; a hobgoblin ; an apparition ¶ 그 집에는 도깨비가 나온다 The house is haunted.

—집 a haunted house ; an enchanted house ; a spookish house

도깨비바늘 〖식물〗 a Spanish needles ; Bidens bipinnata (학명)

도깨비부채 〖식물〗 a Rodger's bronzeleaf ; Rodgersia podophylla (학명)

도깨비불 a will-o'-the-wisp ; an ignis fatuus 《*pl.* ignes fatui》 《라》 ; a jack-o'-lantern ; an elf fire ; a corpse-candle (묘지 따위의) ; a death fire (사람의 혼) ; [인화] phosphorescence

도꼬마리 〖식물〗 a cocklebur ; Xanthium strumarium (학명)

도꼭지 a chief ; a head ; a leader ; a boss ; a foreman ¶ 목수 중의 도꼭지 a chief carpenter

⁑**도끼** an ax (미) ; a hatchet (손도끼) ¶ 큰 도끼 a broad-ax ; a big hatchet // 얼음 깨는 도끼 an ice ax

—자루 an axe handle **—질** wielding an axe

도끼는 날 달아 써도 사람은 죽으면 그만 속담 Death is the end of all.

믿는 도끼에 발등 찍힌다 속담 In trust is treason.

도끼눈 glaring eyes ; staring with hatred ¶ 도끼눈을 한 사람 an eagle-eyed person // 도끼눈으로 보다 glare at ; glower at ; look angrily at ; scowl at〔on〕

도끼집 a shack ; a roughly-built house

도난 盜難 robbery ; theft ; burglary ¶ 도난 당하다 be robbed ; be burglarized (구) ; fall a victim to a theft ; be stolen (물건이 주어) // 도난계를 내다 report a burglary to the police // 이웃에서 수 건의 도난 사건이 있었다 There were several burglaries in the neighborhood.

— 경보기 a burglar alarm **— 방지 자물쇠** a burglarproof〔an antitheft〕 lock **— 사건** a burglary ; a robbery ; a theft **—품** a stolen article ; stolen goods **— 피해자** a victim of theft

도내 道內 the inside of a province ; [도내의] within a province ; provincial

도내기 〖건축〗 a groove in the upper frame of a window (to hold the window)

*__도넛__ a doughnut

도닐다 go〔walk〕 round 《a yard》 ; walk up and down〔to and fro〕

도다녀가다 drop in and go back soon ; drop in (here) briefly

도다녀오다 drop in and come back soon ; drop in (there) briefly

도다리 〖물고기〗 a flounder ; a sole

†**도달 到達** arrival ; reaching **—하다** arrive in〔at, on〕 ; reach ; come to ; get to ; attain ; touch ; make it 《to》 ¶ 같은 결론에 도달하다 come to〔reach〕 the same conclusion // 목적에 도달하다 attain one's object // 목적지에 도달하다 reach

the destination
— 거리 『물리』 [힘의] range (of force)
— 지점 the (place of) destination

도담도담 《growing up》 well ; nicely

도당 徒黨 conspirators ; a conspiracy ; a league ; a faction ; a junta〔junto〕; a cabal ¶ 도당을 지어서 in faction〔cabal〕// 도당을 짓다 conspire ; band together ; form a clique〔faction〕
— 근성 cliquishness — 선동자 a factionalist —주의 factionalism ; cliquism

*__도대체 都大體__ in the world ; on earth ; under the sun ; in the name of God ; the dickens ; the hell〔heck〕 ¶ 도대체 그는 무슨말을 하고 있는가 What on earth does he mean ? // 도대체 너는 누구냐 What on earth are you ? // 도대체 어떻게 된 거냐 What the deuce is the matter ? / Whatever is the matter ? // 도대체 누가 그런 소릴 했느냐 Whoever told you a thing like that ? // 도대체 어떻게 하란 말이냐 What on earth do you expect me to do ? // 도대체 그녀는 재산이 있는 거요 Has she any property at all ? // 도대체 네가 나쁘다 Really you are to blame for it. // 도대체 그는 영어를 알고 있느냐 Does he know any English at all ?

†**도덕 道德** morality ; ethics ; morals

> 참고 **ethics**는 도덕의 원리 면을 말하고 **morals**는 그 원리의 실천적 면을 말한다 특히 후자는 남녀간의 도덕을 가리키는 수가 많다

¶ 공중 도덕 public morals // 교통 도덕 traffic manners // 도덕적 moral ; moralistic ; ethical
— 관념 a moral sense ¶ 도덕 관념에서 벗어나다 offend the moral sense — 교육 moral education —률 (a) moral law ; an ethical code — 문제 a moral question — 시간 [학교의] a good citizenship class — 심 a sense of morality 사회〔상업〕 — social〔business〕 morality — 재무장 운동 the Moral Rearmament movement 《MRA movement》

도덕가 道德家 a virtuous man ; a man of virtue ; a moralist ¶ 도덕가인 체하다 assume a virtuous air

도덕상 道德上 morally ; from a moral point of view ¶ 도덕상의 moral ; moralistic ; ethical // 도덕상의 죄인 a moral offender ; a sinner // 도덕상의 문제 a moral question

†**도덕적 道德的** virtuous ; moral ; moralistic ; ethical ¶ 도덕적 감화〔기준〕 moral influence〔standards〕 // 도덕적 교훈 a moral lesson ; a moral // 도덕적 제재〔구속〕 moral restraint〔sanctions〕 // 도덕적으로 설명하다 moralize

도덕 철학 道德哲學 moral philosophy ; ethics
—자 a moral philosopher ; moralist

도도록하다 (be) swollen ; raised ; heaved ¶ 도도록도도록 full of knobs ; rough ; ragged // 도도록한 젖가슴 full〔rich〕 breast (of a woman) // 종기가 도도록하다 a boil is swollen up

도도하다 (be) arrogant ; haughty ; proud ; puffed-up ; stuck-up 《구》 ; uppish ; overbearing ; lordly ; toplofty 《미》 ¶ 도도한 태도 a lofty air ; a haughty bearing // 도도하게 굴다 behave oneself haughtily ; hold one's head very high

도도하다 陶陶— (be) happy ; jolly ; be pleased ¶ 취흥이 도도하다 be gay with wine ; be gloriously drunk

도도하다 滔滔— ① [물이] (be) rushing ; rapid ; swift ¶ 도도히 with a rush ; rapidly ; swiftly // 도도히 흐르다 flow with a rush ; run〔flow〕 in a large stream〔in rushing torrents, in a broad expanse, majestically〕 // 탁류가 도도히 흐른다 The muddy water rushes on in a vast expanse.
② [말이] (be) eloquent ; fluent ; flowing ; effusive ¶ 도도히 eloquently ; fluently ; effusively ; flowingly // 도도한 변설 a flood of eloquence〔words〕 ; flowing eloquence // 그의 변설은 도도하여 그칠줄 몰랐다 His tongue went nineteen to the dozen.

도독 渡獨 going〔a trip〕 to Germany — 하다 go (over) to Germany

도두 high ¶ 둑을 도두 쌓다 build a dike high // 볏가리를 도두 쌓다 heap the sheaves of rice high

도두뛰다 jump as high as one can

도두보다 see with a favorable eye ; see in a favorable light ; place 《a thing》 in good light ; think much of ; think highly of ¶ 너는 저 사람을 도두보고 있다 You estimate his worth too highly. // 나를 도두보고 있는 모양이다 It seems he takes me for better than I am.

도두보이다 look better (than actually is) ; be shown to advantage ; be presented in a favorable light ¶ 유화는 좀 떨어져서 보아야 도두보인다 Oil paintings show to better advantage at a distance. // 찬장을 그렇게 놓으니 훨씬 도두보인다 The cupboard looks much better in that position.

‡**도둑** [도둑놈] a thief ; a burglar ; a robber ; [좀도둑] a sneak ; a pilferer ; a filcher ; a shoplifter ; [도둑질] theft ; burglary ; robbery ; stealing ; pilfering ; filching ¶ 도둑맞다 be stolen ; be robbed 《of》 // 나는 시계를 도둑맞았다 I had my watch stolen. // 나는 도둑이야 하고 고함쳤다 I raised a hue and cry. // 도둑이야 Stop thief ! // 어젯밤 나의 집에 도둑이 들었다 My house was robbed〔broken into〕 last night. /A thief broke into my house last night.

도둑맞고 사립문 고친다 속담 It is too late

to shut the stable when the steed is stolen.
도둑에도 의리가 있고 딴꾼에도 꼭지가 있다 속담 There is honor among thieves.
도둑의 때는 벗어도 화냥의 때는 못 벗는다 속담 Once a whore, ever a whore.
도둑의 씨가 없다 속담 Opportunity makes the thief.
도둑이 제 발 저리다 속담 He that commits a fault thinks everyone speaks of it./He that has a great nose thinks everybody is speaking of it.
바늘 도둑이 소 도둑 된다 속담 He that will steal a pin, will steal a better thing./He that will steal an egg will steal an ox.

도둑고양이 a stray cat ; an alley cat

도둑놈 a thief《*pl.* -ves》⇨ 도둑 ¶ 말 도둑놈 a horse-thief // 도둑놈에게 열쇠를 맡긴 셈이다 He sets the wolf to guard the sheep.
— **근성** a thievish propensity ; a sneaking spirit — **장가** ⇨ 도둑 합례

도둑맞다 get〔have〕《a thing》 stolen ; have《a thing》 pilfered〔filched〕

†**도둑질** theft ⇨ 도둑 —**하다** steal《a thing》 from《a person》; commit theft ; pilfer ; filch ; burglarize《the house》; [강탈] rob《a person》 of《a thing》; rifle《a person》 of《a safe》 ¶ 가난에서 저지른 도둑질 theft through poverty // 도둑질한 혐의로 (be arrested) on a theft charge // 도둑질하여 벌을 받다 be punished for stealing // 도둑질하러 들어가다 break into a house ; burglarize《a house》// 도둑질 행각을 하다 go round against the sun

도둑합례 —合禮 a secret marriage ; a secret consummation —**하다** get married secretly

도둔 逃遁 running away ; flight ; bolting —**하다** run away ; flee ; bolt

도드라지다 [또렷하다] (be) prominent ; salient ; outstanding (현저하다) ⇨ 두드러지다 ; [내밀다] swell ; protrude ; project ; jut ; stick out ¶ 도드라진 눈 protuberant bulging〕 eyes // 길 가운데가 도드라졌다 The middle of the road is high.

도드미 a riddle ; a coarse sieve

도뜨다 be above reproach in word and deed

도라지 〖식물〗 a (Chinese) balloon flower ; a Chinese bellflower ; Platycodon grandiflorum (학명) ¶ 도라지 뿌리 platycodon
— **나물** cooked roots of balloonflowers

*****도락** 道樂 ① [방탕] dissipation ; prodigality ; debauchery ¶ 도락하다 lead a dissipated life ; live fast ; play the prodigal ; debauch oneself ② [취미] a pleasure ; a hobby ; a pastime ; one's favorite amusement

도란거리다 murmur together ; whisper in a group ; have a talk〔chat〕 together in a whispering〔subdued〕 tone ; bill and coo (연인끼리) ¶ 도란도란 murmuring together ; in whispers

⁑**도랑** ditch ; a drain ; a gutter ¶ 도랑을 파다 dig a ditch // 도랑을 치다 clear out a ditch // 도랑에 빠지다 fall into a ditch
—**물** ditch water —**창** a (dirty, filthy) ditch ; a drain ; a gutter

도랑도랑하다, 또랑또랑하다 (be) very clear

도랑이 mange

도랑치마 a short skirt ; a miniskirt

도래 渡來 [사람의] a visit ; [사물의] introduction ; importation ; influx —**하다** come over〔across〕 the sea ; cross over《to Korea》; visit ; be introduced《into a country》 ¶ 불교의 도래 the introduction of Buddhism《into Korea》// 외국 물품의 도래 the influx of foreign goods

*****도래** 到來 arrival ; advent ; visitation ; influx —**하다** come ; arrive ; [기회가] offer〔present〕 itself ; occur ¶ 죽음의 도래 the advent of death // 때가 도래하면 in (course of) time

도래떡 a large-sized round rice cake

도래매듭 a double knot

도래목정 beef neck

도래방석 —方席 a round cushion

도래샘 a swirling fountain〔spring〕

도래솔 pine trees around a grave

도래송곳 a double-edged drill ; a single twist drill (나사 송곳)

도량 跳梁 rampancy ; domination —**하다** (be) rampant ; dominant ; prevalent

†**도량** 度量 magnanimity ; liberality ; generosity ; broad-mindedness ; [수완] ability ; resourcefulness ; talent ; capability ; caliber ¶ 큰 도량 a mind of great capacity // 도량이 큰 generous ; magnanimous ; broad-minded // 도량이 작은 ungenerous ; narrow-minded ; small-minded ; meanspirited ; pusillanimous // 도량이 작은 사람 a narrow-minded fellow

도량형 度量衡 weights and measures
— **검사관** a sealer (of weights and measures) — **검정소** the Weights and Measures Examination Institute —**기** (器) measuring instruments —**표** tables of weights and measures —**학** metrology **미터** —**법** the metric system of weights and measures ☞《p. 617》

도레미파 the musical scale ; [음계명] do, re, mi, fa, sol, la and si ¶ 도레미파로 노래하다 (sing) sol-fa // 도레미파를 연습하다 practice scales《on the piano》

*****도려내다** scoop〔scrape〕 out ; gouge (둥근 끌로) ; cut out〔off, away〕; hollow out ; excise (종기 따위를) ¶ 도려내는 듯한 아픔 poignant〔lancinating〕 pain // 눈을 도려내다 gouge〔scoop〕 out《a person's》 eyes // 사과의 썩은 곳을 도려내다 scrape out spoiled〔sour〕 parts of apples

도량형의 표현

영·미에서는 미터법(Metric System)과 병행하여 전통적인 계량 단위가 널리 사용되고 있다.

미터법에는 길이(length)를 나타내는 meter(metre 《영》), 용적(capacity)을 나타내는 liter(litre 《영》), 무게(weight)를 나타내는 gram 등 세 가지가 쓰인다. 이에 대하여 전통적인 계량법은 일상생활에 의거한 것을 단위로, 명칭도 제각각 다르며 10진법은 취하지 않는다.

① 길이·폭·깊이·높이

¶ 그것은 3미터 길이 [높이, 넓이, 깊이]이다. It is three meters long [high, wide, deep]. / It is three meters in length [height, width, depth]. // 그 상자의 길이 [폭]는 2피트이다. That box is two feet long [wide]. / That box is two feet in length [width]. / The length [width] of the box is two feet. // 그 도로의 폭은 24피트이다. The road is 24 feet broad. // 그 담의 높이는 4피트이다. The wall is 4 feet high. // 그 아이의 키는 4피트이다. The child is four feet tall. (★ 건물 등의 지상으로부터의 높이는 tall, 공중에서의 높이는 high로 표현) // 시냇물의 폭은 6피트이다. The stream is 6 feet across. // 빨리 걷는 사람은 시간당 4마일을 걸을 수 있다. A fast walker can walk 4 miles an hour. // 이 호수는 깊이가 얼마나 됩니까? — 가장 깊은 곳이 약 25미터입니다. How deep is this lake? — At its deepest, it's about 25 meters. // 그는 5미터 높이에서 떨어졌다. He fell down from a height of five meters.

② 직경·원주

¶ 이 구멍의 직경은 2미터이다. This hole is two meters across [in diameters]. / The diameter of this hole is two meters. // 이 원의 둘레는 5미터이다. This circle is five meters around [in circumference]. / The circumference of this circle is five meters.

③ 면적

¶ 우리 학교 운동장은 넓다[좁다]. The playground of our school is large [small]. (★ 넓다의 뜻은 large로 표현, wide는 폭이 넓다의 뜻.) // 그 축구장의 면적은 2에이커가 조금 더 된다. The football field measures a little more than 2 acres. // 방 크기가 얼마나 됩니까? — 약 15제곱 미터입니다. How large is your room? — It's about fifteen square meters.

④ 중량

¶ 무게가 10킬로그램 나간다. It weighs ten kilograms. / It is ten kilograms in weight. // 그는 몸무게를 재보고 0.5킬로그램이나 는 것을 알았다. He weighed himself and found that he was half a kilogram heavier. // 그녀는 먹지 않더니 몸무게가 빠졌다. She never eats and is losing weight. // 이 돌은 크기에 비해 무겁다 [가볍다]. This stone is heavy[light] for its size.

도련 **刀鍊** trimming ; cutting the edge 《of paper》 even
 —칼 a paper-trimming knife ; a paper cutter
 도련치다 관용 trim ; cut the edge 《of paper》 even

도련님 ① [주인의 아들] a young master ; [호칭] Master ; sonny
② [남의 아들] your〔his, her〕 son
③ [시동생] an unmarried younger brother of one's husband
 —천량 a tidy sum saved up by frugality

도련지 **擣鍊紙** calendered paper

도령 ① [미혼자] an unmarried young man ; a bachelor ; [젊은이] a lad ; a youth ; a youngster ¶ 도령귀신 the ghost of a bachelor ② [굿] a shaman's exorcism rite for a bon voyage of the soul of a dead person to the other world ¶ 도령 돌다 perform a ritual dance for the repose of the deceased

도령 **道令** [행정 명령] a provincial ordinance

도로 [되짚어] back ; [먼저대로] as ever 〔before, usual〕 ; as it was ; [또다시] (over) again ¶ 도로 가다 go back ; turn back ; retrace one's steps // 오던 길을 도로 가다 go back over one's way // 도중에서 도로 가다〔오다〕 turn back halfway // 도로 데려오다 bring back // 도로 주다 give 《a thing》 back ; return 《a thing》 // 딸을 도로 데려오다 bring the daughter home (시가에서) // 뺏긴 물건을 도로 찾다 take back 《a thing》 from 《a person》 ; win back (도박에서) // 제자리에 도로 갖다 놓다 put 《a thing》 back in its place〔where it was〕

*__도로__ **道路** a road ; a way ; [가로] a street ; [주요 도로] a thoroughfare ; a high way ¶ 도로를 따라서 along the street // 도로상에서 on the road ; on〔in〕 the street // 도로를 만들다 build a

road ; open a road 《through a jungle》// 도로를 수리하다 repair〔improve〕 a road〔street〕
— 계획 a road plan — 공사 road repairing〔building〕 — 공채(公債) a public loan for the improvement of roads — 교통법 『법』 the Road Traffic Act —망 a road system — 방해 obstruction of traffic〔the public road〕; a roadblock — 번호 a route number — 수송 road transport — 인부 a roadman ; a road mender〔repairer〕; a street repairman — 정비 계획 a road maintenance and improvement project — 청소부 a street cleaner ; a scavenger — 포장 pavement of a road 〔street〕 — 표지 a road sign 한국 — 공사 the Korea Highway Corporation ☞ 《p. 619》

도로 徒勞 a lost labo(u)r ; vain effort ¶ 도로에 그치다 prove fruitless ; end in a waste of labor ; come to nothing
— 무익(無益) vain〔sterile〕 effort ; toiling in vain

도로 건설 道路建設 road building ; street〔road〕 construction
— 계획 a road-building program — 기계 road-building equipment — 기사 a road engineer

도로아미타불 —阿彌陀佛 a relapse ; ending in a failure〔in smoke〕 ¶ 병세가 좀 나아지는 듯하더니 도로아미타불이 되고 말았다 He seemed to have recovered from his illness but had a relapse. // 실험 결과는 도로아미타불이었다 The experiment proved a failure. // 십 년 공부 도로아미타불 Ten year's study down the drain !

-도록 ① [목적] so that ; in order that ; that ; (so as) to ; in order to ¶ 하지 않도록 (so as) not to ; that... may not // 그 여자에게 말하지 않도록 주의하라 Take care not to tell her. // 급행 열차에 댈 수 있도록 빨리 일어났다 I got up early so as to be〔in order to be〕 in time for the express. // 가옥은 신선한 공기와 광선이 많이 들어 오도록 지어져야 한다 Houses should be built so as admit plenty of light as well as fresh air.
② [···때까지] till ; until ; to the point where ¶ 밤이 늦도록 till late at night // 죽도록 사랑하다 love 《a person》 to death // 백살이 되도록 살다 live to be a hundred

도롱고리 『식물』 a kind of millet

도롱뇽 『동물』 ① a (giant) salamander ② a water lizard

도롱이 a rain cape (made of straw)

도롱태[1] ① [수레] a simple wooden wheel ② [바퀴] a wheel

도롱태[2] 『새』 ① Falco columbarius (학명) ② [새매] an Asiatic sparrowhawk

도료 塗料 paints ; pigments
— 분무기 a paint spraying appliance ; a sprayer — 희석제(稀釋劑) a thinner ; a paint diluent 야광 — luminous paint

도루 盜壘 『야구』 a stolen base ; base stealing —하다 steal a base ¶ 도루에 실패하다 be caught stealing // 2루에 도루하다 steal second ; steal into the second base

도루묵 『물고기』 a kind of sandfish ; Arctoscopus japonicus (학명)

도륙 屠戮 massacre ; slaughter ; butchery —하다 slay ; massacre ; slaughter ; butcher ¶ 일가족을 도륙하다 murder 〔slaughter〕 the whole family (in cold blood)

도르다[1] [게우다] vomit ; cast up ; spew ; throw up ; gag

도르다[2] [분배] distribute ; pass round ; serve out (food) ; deal out ; [배달] deliver ; send out ¶ 신문을 도르다 deliver newspapers // 화투장을 도르다 deal cards 《to players》// 초대장을 도르다 send out invitations // 빈민에게 먹을 것을 도르다 measure out food to the poor

도르다[3] [변통] make shift ; tide over ; manage 《with what one has》; [융통하다] accommodate 《a person with money》; advance 《money to a person》; lend ¶ 돈을 도르다 accommodate 《a person》 with a loan ; advance 《money to》; spare 《a person》 《1,000 won》// 자금을 도르다 finance 《an enterprise》

도르다[4] [속이다] cajole〔wheedle, coax〕《a person》《out of, into》; take 《a person》 in with fair words

*__도르래__ a pulley ; a block ; [장난감] a pinwheel

도르르, <u>또르르</u> round and round ; with a twirl ; coiling ; [구르는 모양] rolling ¶ 종이를 도르르 말다 roll paper up round and round // 도르르 감기다 coil 〔twine, wind itself〕 around 《a tree, pole》// 실이 도르르 풀리다 thread is twirled off a reel

도리 a purlin(e)
— 나무 purlin wood

†**도리 道理** ① [이치] reason ; propriety (타당) ; truth (진리) ; justice (정의) ; principle (원리) ¶ 도리상 in reason ; in〔by, from〕 the nature of things ; as a matter of course // 도리에 맞다 be reasonable ; stand to reason ; be consistent with reason // 도리에 벗어나다 be unreasonable ; be contrary to〔inconsistent with〕 reason // 네 말은 충분히 도리에 맞다 There is good reason in what you say. // 네가 그렇게 행동해도 도리에 어긋나지 않는다 It is quite reasonable〔right〕 for you to act that way.
② [방도] a way ; a method ; a process ; a means ¶ 기다릴 수밖에 딴 도리가 없다 You have nothing to do but wait. // 나는 잠자코 있을 수밖에 별 도리가 없었다 There was nothing for it but to hold my tongue. // 울어도 별 도리가 없다 Weeping will mend nothing. // 그에게는 어찌 해볼

도로와 교통

① 도로

도로 road; street; avenue (★ road는 마을과 마을을 연결하는 도로, street는 도로 옆에 가게나 집들이 늘어서 있는 도로, avenue는 도로 양 옆에 가로수가 늘어선 도로, boulevard는 《미》에서 대로라는 뜻으로 통한다. 뉴욕에서는 동서 관통도로를 street, 남북을 가로지르는 도로를 avenue라고도 한다.)

중심가 도로 main street 《미》; high street 《영》/ 주요 도로 thoroughfare / 좁은 길 lane; alley / 오솔길 path / 보행자·자전거 전용 도로 greenway / 뒷골목 back street / 상점가 shopping street / 보도 sidewalk 《미》; pavement 《영》/ 산책로 promenade; mall / 환상 도로 ring [loop, circular] road / 간선 도로 trunk road; arterial highway (★ 미국의 국도 U.S. highway)

고속 도로 express highway; motorway 《영》; expressway 《미동부》/ 유료 고속 도로 toll road; turnpike / 고가도로 elevated highway / 대륙횡단도로 transcontinental highway / 주간(州間) 고속 도로 interstate highway / 진입 램프 entrance ramp / 출구램프 exit ramp / 진입로 entrance lane / 연락도로 access road / 휴게지 rest area / (차도변의) 서비스 구역 service area / 요금 계산소 toll booth; turnpike

산길 (mountain) pass / 옆길 by(-)pass; by(-)road; by(-)path / 우회로 circuit; detour / 진입로 approach / 통로 passage / 회랑 arcade / 지름길 shortcut / 복도 corridor / 포장도로 paved road; pavement / 자갈길 gravel road / 덜컹거리는 길 rough [bumpy] road

② 교통

우측[좌측]통행 keep to the right [left] / 횡단보도 pedestrian's crossing / 적신호에 우회전 금지 No (Right) Turn on Red / 과속방지턱 bump / 속도위반 speeding / 교차점 intersection; crossing; crossroad(s) / 교통신호 traffic signal [light] / 청신호 green light; proceed signal / 황색신호 yellow light; caution signal / 적신호 red light; stop signal / 로터리 rotary; roundabout 《영》/ 신호무시 ignoring a traffic light; crossing the intersection on a red light / (보행자용) 지하도 underground (passage); subway 《영》/ 육교 overpass / 일방통행 one-way traffic / 일방통행로 one-way street / 차선 lane (★ 8차선 도로 an 8-lane highway) / 버스전용로 bus lane / 중앙분리대 median (strip); central reserve 《영》/ 갓길 shoulder / 자전거전용도로 bikeway / 사이클링도로 cycleway / 주차장 parking lot; car park 《영》/ 주차위반 illegal parking / 주차위반 딱지 parking ticket / 주차미터기 parking meter / 주차금지구역 (견인지역) towaway zone; no parking zone / 주유소 gas station 《미》; service [filling] station; petrol station 《영》 (★ full service는 주유, 세차, 엔진오일 체크까지 하는 일괄 서비스, mini-service는 급유만 하는 서비스, self-service는 주유 셀프 서비스) / 자동차 운전 학원 driving school

---

도리가 없다 I couldn't hold a candle to him.
③ [의리] duty ; obligation ; [정의] justice ¶ 자식의 도리 filial duty〔piety〕// 도리를 모르다 have no sense of duty 〔justice〕// 도리와 인정 사이에서 꼼짝 못하다 be torn between love and duty // 어버이된 도리로서 아이를 학교에 아니보낼 수 없다 It is in the nature of things that parents should send children to school.

도리기 a Dutch treat **—하다** have the meals as a Dutch treat ; go Dutch

도리깨 a flail
—질 flailing **—채** ⇨ 도리깻장부 **—침** mouth watering ; saliva〔spittle〕 of appetite **도리깻열** a swingle ; a swip(p)le **도리깻장부** the handle of a flail

도리다 scoop out ⇨ 도려내다

도리도리 [아기에게] Shake (your) head.

도리머리 shaking one's head as a sign of negation〔denial〕

도리사 —紗 a Chinese hemp gossamer

도리스식 —式 〖건축〗 Doric (type, style)

도리암직하다 [사람이] (be) short but slim〔smart〕; dapper

***도리어** [반대로] on the contrary ; instead ; [오히려] rather ; all the more 〔better, worse〕 ¶ 도리어 좋다〔나쁘다〕 be so much the better〔worse〕// 그것은 도리어 곤란하다 It is still more difficult. // 좋기는 커녕 도리어 해롭다 It does more harm than good. // 도리어 병세를 악화시켰다 It only made the patient worse. // 너무 엄하게 대하면 도리어 아이에게 좋지 않다 Too strict〔severe〕 discipline will do more harm than good to children. // 부정한 수단으로 돈을 버는 것보다는 도리어 가난이 낫다 I would rather be poor than get money by dishonest means.

도리질 shaking one's head for fun ;

headshake **—하다** 《a baby》 keep shaking one's head for fun

도린결 [외진 곳] an out-of-the-way place ; secluded place ; a nook

도림장이 a wood engraver

도림질 engraving (wood)

도립 倒立 standing on one's head ; handstanding (체조) **—하다** stand on one's head ¶ 도립해서 걷다 walk on one's hands

도립 道立 ¶ 도립의 provincial
— 병원 a provincial hospital

도마 a chopping board ; a kitchen board
도마에 오른 고기 속담 Like a fish out of water.

도마름 都— a head supervisor of tenant farmers

***도마뱀** 〖동물〗 a lizard ; a blue-tail (미국산)

도마뱀붙이 〖동물〗 a gecko 《*pl.* ~es, ~s》 ; a wall lizard

***도막** a bit ; a cut ; a chop ; a fragment ; a chip ; a slice ¶ 나무 도막 a chip of wood // 고기 한도막 a piece〔slice, chop〕 of meat // 그녀는 물고기를 여러 도막으로 썰었다 She cut a fish into several pieces.

도말 塗抹 —하다 ① [지우다] paint out ; blot out ; [칠하다] paint over ; smear (기름으로) ② [변통하여 꾸림] patch up ; make shift ; temporize
—제 a liniment ; an ointment ; an embrocation **— 표본** a smear

도맛밥 wood chips from a chopping block

†**도망 逃亡** escape ; abscondence ; flight ; getaway ; decampment ; elopement ; [탈영] desertion ; running away **—하다** escape ; run away ; flee ; make 《one's》 escape ; take to flight ; take to 《one's》 heels ; get away ; desert 《a ship》 ; decamp 《for, to》 ; abscond 〔bolt〕 《from a place》 ; elope 《from》 ; [가축 따위가] get free ; break loose ¶ 말이 도망치다 the horse runs away ; the horse gets 〔breaks〕 loose // 국외로 도망하다 fly the country // 돈을 가지고 도망하다 make away with 《a person's》 money // 그는 슬금슬금 도망쳤다 He sneaked away. // 남편은 그녀를 버리고 도망쳤다 She was deserted by her husband.
— 범인 a fugitive from justice ; a fugitive criminal〔prisoner〕 **— 범인 인도** [국제간의] extradition **— 병** a runaway soldier ; a soldier over the hill 《속》 **— 용자동차** a getaway car **—자** a runaway ; an absconder ; a deserter ; a fugitive ; an escapee

도망길 逃亡— an escape ; [수단] a way 〔means〕 of escape ; [빠져나갈 데] a loophole ¶ 도망길을 남겨 두다 leave room for retreat // 도망길을 잃다 lose all means of escape ; have one's escape cut off

도망꾼 逃亡— an absconder ; an escapee ; a refugee ; a runaway ; a fugitive ; a bolter ; [탈영병] a deserter ; a fugitive〔runaway〕 soldier

***도맡다** ① [책임을] take all on oneself ; shoulder 《a thing》 alone ; answer for ; hold oneself responsible for ¶ 빚을 도맡다 hold oneself liable for a debt ; shoulder another's debt // 그는 책임을 도맡았다 He assumed all responsibilities alone. // 나는 재정 문제를 도맡고 있다 I am responsible for the financial matter. // 거래상의 손실은 회사에서 도맡는다 The losses on the transactions will be met by the company.
② [도거리로] take over 《the whole》 ¶ 가게의 물건을 도맡다 take over all the goods in the store

도매 都買 buying wholesale **—하다** buy wholesale

***도매 都賣** wholesale **—하다** sell wholesale ¶ 도매와 소매 wholesale and retail // 물건을 도매로 사다〔팔다〕 buy〔sell〕 goods wholesale // 도매 가격으로 드리겠습니다 We will give it to you at wholesale (price). // 현재 달걀은 도매로 한 줄에 1000원이다 Now eggs sell wholesale for 1,000 *won* a *jul*.
— 물가 지수 wholesale price index **—상** [영업] a wholesale business 〔trade〕 ; [장수] a wholesaler ; a wholesale dealer ; a jobber ; a factor 《영》 ¶ 도매상을 하다 carry on a wholesale trade **— 시세** a trade〔wholesale〕 price **— 시장** a wholesale market

도면 圖面 a drawing ; a sketch ; a plan ; a map
건축 — a blueprint

도모 圖謀 planning ; devising ; contriving ; designing ; scheming **—하다** plan ; devise ; scheme ; plot ¶ 그들은 다만 사리만을 도모했을 뿐이었다 They did nothing but seek their own interests. // 그들은 공익을 도모해야 했었는데 They should have promoted the public interest.

***도무지** ① [전혀] utterly ; entirely ; quite ; altogether ; [근본적으로] fundamentally ; essentially ; [절대로] absolutely ; [부정적으로] never ; 《not》 at all ; 《not》 in the least ; 《not》 a bit ; never once ; not even once ¶ 도무지 알 수 없다 I cannot understand it at all. // 무슨 말씀인지 도무지 이해할 수가 없습니다 I don't understand in the least what you mean. // 도무지 간 일이 없소 I was never there at all. // 독서할 시간이 도무지 없다 I have absolutely no time for reading.
② [도시] all ; all in all ; totally ; whatever ¶ 도무지 재미가 없다 It has no interest whatever for me.

도미 〖물고기〗 a sea bream ; a gold bream ; a red snapper
도밋국 sea-bream soup

도미 掉尾 ① one's crowning labor ; final

efforts ② waving one's tail —하다 put one's crowning labor to ; make a final effort ; wave one's tail

*도미 渡美 going to America ; a visit to America —하다 go (over) to America ; visit America ; emigrate to America (이주하다) ¶ 이달 3일에 도미합니다 I am leaving for America on the 3rd instant.
— 실업단 a party of businessmen visiting〔to visit〕 America — 안내 a visitors' guide to America — 의원단 a parliamentary mission to America

도미 稻米 hulled rice

도미노 a domino
— 이론 the domino theory

도미니카 Dominica ¶ 도미니카의 Dominican
— 공화국 the Dominican Republic — 사람 a Dominican

도민 道民 the inhabitants〔citizens〕 of a province ; the provincial people ; the provincials

도민 島民 the islanders ; the inhabitants〔natives〕 of an island

도박 〖식물〗 a kind of red algae

*도박 賭博 ① [노름] gambling ; gaming ; a gambling game —하다 gamble ; play for money ¶ 사기 도박을 하다 swindle at cards∥도박으로 살림을 망치다 lose one's fortune at dice∥그는 도박으로 돈을 잃었다 He gambled away his money.
② [모험] a speculation ; a venture ; a hazard ¶ 도박을 하다 take the risks〔a chance, chances〕 ; chance〔risk〕 it
—군 a gambler ; gambling fraud —성 an inclination to gambling —죄 the crime of gambling ¶ 도박죄로 체포되다 be arrested on a charge of gambling 사기 — fraudulent〔crooked〕 gambling 상습 —자 a confirmed〔habitual〕 gambler

도박장 賭博場 a gambling place〔room, house〕 ; a gambler's den ; a gaming house〔room〕 ; a casino 《*pl.* -s》 ; a gambling joint 《미·구》

*도발 挑發 provocation ; excitement ; incitement —하다 arouse ; excite ; provoke ; stir up 《sedition》 ; incite ; stimulate ; be provocative of ¶ 도발적 provocative ; suggestive 《play》 ; lascivious 《picture》∥호기심을 도발하다 excite 《a person's》 curiosity∥도발적 언사를 쓰다 employ provocative language ; make inciting〔inflammatory〕 remarks

도배 徒輩 a set ; a lot ; a company ; a group

도배 島配 exile ; banishment —하다 exile〔banish〕 《a criminal》 to an island ; maroon

도배 塗褙 papering 《walls, ceiling》 —하다 paper 《walls, ceiling》 ; hang papers on the walls〔ceiling〕
— 반자 papering and paneling —장이 a paper hanger —지 wallpaper

도배 장판 塗褙張板 papering walls, ceiling, and hypocausted floor —하다 paper walls, ceiling, and hypocausted floor

도벌 盜伐 the secret felling of trees —하다 fell〔cut down〕 trees in secret ; steal timber
산림 — 사건 a forest tree theft scandal

도범 盜犯 [절도범] theft ; larceny ; [강도범] robbery ; burglary

도법 圖法 drawing ; draftsmanship
평면〔투영〕 — projection

도벽 盜癖 kleptomania ; a propensity for theft ; a proclivity to steal ¶ 도벽이 있다 be larcenous ; be kleptomaniac

도벽 塗壁 covering 《a wall》 with plaster ; plastering —하다 plaster a wall

도별 道別 classification〔classified〕 by province
— 인구표 a population chart (broken down) by province

*도보 徒步 walking ; going on foot ; afoot ¶ 도보로 on foot ; heel-and-toe∥도보로 가다 walk 《to a place》 ; go on foot ; foot it ; tramp∥도보로 통학〔출근〕하다 walk to school〔office〕 ; go to school〔office〕 on foot
— 경주 a foot race — 운동 pedestrian exercise —자 a pedestrian —주의 pedestrianism

도보 여행 徒步旅行 a walking〔pedestrian〕 tour ; a walking trip ; a tramp ; a hike ; hiking —하다 travel on foot〔afoot〕 ; do a walking tour ; make a journey on foot
—가(家) a pedestrian〔foot〕 traveler ; a tramp

도복 道服 Taoist garb

도본 圖本 a drawing ⇨ 도면

*도부 到付 ① [공문의] arrival of an official document ② [행상] itinerant hawking ; peddling ¶ 도부치다 peddle ; hawk ; go around hawking〔peddling〕 ; engage in an itinerant trade∥도붓장수 a peddler ; a hawker ; an itinerant vendor〔trader〕

도불 渡佛 going (overseas) to France —하다 go (over) to France

도비 徒費 wastefulness —하다 waste

도사 道士 a Taoist ; an enlightened Buddhist (도승)

도사 導師 a spiritual guide〔teacher〕 in Buddhism

도사공 都沙工 a chief boatman

도사리 ① [과일] an unripe windfall〔fallen fruit〕 ② [잡풀] weeds that have sprung up in the seedbed

도사리다 [앉다] sit〔squat〕 cross-legged ; sit with one's legs crossed ; [마음을] calm 《one's mind》 ; calm down ; compose oneself ¶ 뱀이 몸을 도사리다 a snake coils itself

도산 逃散 dispersion —하다 disperse ;

scatter (away) ; fly in all directions
도산 倒産 〖의학〗 cross birth ; [파산] bankruptcy ; failure **—하다** have a cross birth ; fail ; be bankrupt(ed) // 만일 이게 팔리지 않으면 우리는 도산할 것이다 If this thing doesn't sell, we'll be out of business.
도산매 都散賣 wholesale and retail
*__도살 屠殺__ slaughter ; butchery ; massacre (학살) **—하다** butcher ; slaughter 《cattle》
—자 a butcher ; a slaughterer **—장** a slaughterhouse ; a butchery ; shambles ; an abattoir 《프》 **무통(無痛) —기** a humane killer **밀—** illegal butchery
도상 途上 ① [도중] ¶ 발전 도상에 있는 나라들 developing countries ; countries on their way to development ② [노상] on the road
도상 道床 roadbed
도색 桃色 pink color ; rose (color) ; love ; [외설] obscenity ; indecency ¶ 도색의 rosy ; pink ; rose-colored
— 문학 pornography **— 사진** an obscene picture **— 영화** a sex film ; pornography ; X-rated film ; blue movies 《속》 **— 영화관** a sex kino **— 잡지** a yellow journal
도색 유희 桃色遊戱 sex play ¶ 도색 유희에 빠지다 indulge in sex play
도생 倒生 〖식물〗 ¶ 도생의 anatropous ; obverse
도생 圖生 **—하다** earn 《one's》 livelihood ; make a living
— 배주(胚珠) an anatropous ovule
도서 島嶼 islands
—군 an island group
도서 圖書 books ; [간행물] publications ; [문헌] literature
—비 a book budget **—실** a library ; a book room ; a bibliotheca **— 열람료** a library admission fee **— 열람실** a reading room **— 열람 용지** a call slip **— 열람자** a reader ; a visitor (to a library) **— 장정술** bibliopegy **— 전사 필름** a bibliofilm **— 청구표** a call slip **— 출판자** a publisher **— 출판 회사** a publishing company〔concern〕; a book concern **— 카드** a book card **—학** bibliography ; bibliology **— 해제(解題)** a bibliography **교양 —** cultural books **번역 —** translated books **성인 —** adult books **수입 —** imported books **신간 —** new books **아동 —** children's books **외국 —** foreign books **일반 —** general books **전문 —** special books **참고 —** reference books **학술 —** scholarly books
도서관 圖書館 a library ¶ 도서관에 다니다 frequent a library // 도서관에서 책을 빌리다 take a book from a library ; get a book out of a library
— 교육 library education **— 상호 대출 협정** interlibrary loan arrangements **— 운영 위원회** a committee for library management **—원** a librarian ; a library clerk **—장** the chief〔head〕 librarian ; the director〔curator〕 of a library **—학** library science **— 할인** library discount **— 행정** library administration **공공 —** a public library **국립 —** a national library **국회 —** the Library of the National Assembly ; the Library of Congress 《미》 **대출 —** a lending library **대학 —** a university library **무료 —** a free library **순회 —** a circulating〔itinerant〕 library ; a library on wheels **시립 —** a city〔municipal〕 library **참고 —** a reference library **학교 —** a school library
도서다[1] ① [바람이] change ; shift ; veer (round) ¶ 바람이 남쪽으로 도섰다 The wind shifted〔veered round〕 to the south. ② 《a fetus》 quicken ③ 《mother's milk》 start flowing after childbirth ④ [가던 길을] turn back
도서다[2] (smallpox) heal up
도서 목록 圖書目錄 a publication list 〔catalog(ue)〕 ¶ 과학 서적의 도서 목록 a catalog(ue) of scientific literature
신간 — a list of new publications **신착 —** an accession(s) book
도서 전시회 圖書展示會 a book exhibition ; a book fair ; a book show ¶ 도서 전시회를 열다〔참관하다〕 hold〔visit〕 a book exhibition
도선 導線 the leading〔conducting〕 wire
도선 渡船 a ferry ; a ferry boat ; [직업] ferry service
—업 ferriage **—장(場)** a ferry
도선 導船 [일] pilotage ; piloting ; [배] a pilot boat **—하다** pilot 《a boat》
—료(料) pilotage (dues) **—사(師)** a pilot
도설 圖說 an explanatory diagram ; an illustration
곤충 — explanatory diagrams of insects
도섭 caprice ; fancy ; whim ¶ 도섭스럽다 be capricious ; be whimsical
도성 都城 a capital city
도소주 屠蘇酒 spiced liquor drunk on New Year's Day
도수 徒手 an empty hand ; bare hands ¶ 도수로 with one's own bare hands ; with no capital to start on ; with one's naked fists (무기 없이) // 그는 도수공권으로 제주도에 건너 갔었다 He was literally penniless when he went over to *Chejudo*.
— 체조 free gymnastics **— 훈련** 〖군사〗 a foot drill (초보 교련의)
도수 度數 ① [회수] (the number of) times ; frequency ; incidence ② [온도·안경 따위의] the degree ¶ 안경 도수 the power of glasses // 도수가 높은 안경 powerful〔strong, thick〕 spectacles ; glasses with heavy lenses ③ [알코올의] the percentage of alcohol in liquor ; the alcohol content ¶ 술 도수가 높다 《liquor》 have

a high percentage of alcohol
—계[통화의] a message〔call〕 register ; a service meter **—료** the call charge **—요금** [전화의] message rates **—제(制)** [전화의] the message-〔call-〕 rate system ; time-charge system
도수공권 徒手空拳 ¶ 도수공권으로 without capital ; with nothing to start with // 그는 도수공권으로 미국에 건너 갔다 He was literally penniless when he went over to America.
도수로 導水路 a raceway
도수리구멍 〖공학〗 a fire-hole on the side of a kiln
도수 분포 度數分布 〖통계〗 frequency distribution
도수장 屠獸場 a slaughterhouse ; shambles ; a butchery ; an abattoir 《프》
도숙붙다 have a narrow forehead ; be low-browed
도술 道術 Taoist magic
도스르다 brace oneself (up) ; gird oneself up 《for something, to do something》 ; gird up one's loins ; strain 〔tighten〕 one's nerves 《to do something》 ¶ 그 놈이 돌아오면 혼을 내주려고 도스리고 기다렸다 I was impatient for his return fully prepared to rebuke him.
도습 蹈襲 —하다 follow 《a former policy》 ⇨ 답습(踏襲)
도승 道僧 a Buddhist priest who has attained spiritual enlightenment
†**도시 都市** cities ; towns and cities ; urban communities

> 참고 **city**는 크고 중요한 town을 가리키고 **town**은 큰 고을이지만 아직 시가 되지 않은 것을 가리킨다 이 구별은 영국에서는 비교적 지켜지고 있지만 미국에서는 city를 주로사용한다

¶ 도시의 municipal ; city ; urban // 인구의 도시 집중 경향 the cityward tendency of the population
— 가스 city gas **— 개량** civic improvement **— 개발** urban development **— 개조** urban renewal **— 경제** urban economy **— 계획** town planning ; city planning 《미》 **— 공학(과)** urban engineering〔construction〕 (department) **— 교통 기관** urban transport〔transit〕 systems **— 국가** a city state **— 문제 평론가** an urban critic **— 사회학** urban sociology **— 위생** urban sanitation **— 인구** urban population **— 재개발** urban redevelopment **— 전입** inflow into urban areas **— 집중 경향** the cityward drifting 《of population》 **— 행정** municipal administration **—화** urbanization **— 생활** city〔town, civic〕 life ; urban life **—인** a townsman ; a city man ; a city-dweller **— 재개발** urban renewal **— 재정** municipal finance **— 지구** urban areas〔districts〕 **공업 —** an industrial〔a manufacturing〕 town〔city〕 **국제 —** a cosmopolitan city **대—** a large 〔big, great〕 city **대학 —** a university 〔college〕 city **매머드 —** a megalopolis ; a megapolis **상업 —** a business town **중소 —** small towns
도시 圖示 illustration ; graphic(al) representation **—하다** illustrate ; show by 〔in〕 a diagram ; show in a graphic form **— 계기** a self-registering meter **— 마력〔효율〕** indicated horsepower〔efficiency〕 **—법** the graphic method
도시 都是 (not) at all ⇨ 도무지
도시다 shave 《wood》 ; plane 《a plank》 ; whittle ; trim 《one's nails》 ; finish 《a surface》 ¶ 나뭇가지를 도셔서 매를 만들다 whittle a small branch for a whip
***도시락** [점심] lunch ; luncheon ; [그릇] a lunch package〔basket〕 ¶ 도시락을 싸다 pack a lunch-basket // 도시락을 가지고 가다 take〔carry〕 a lunch with 《one》
도시하다 圖示— illustrate ; [그래프로] show in a graphic form
도식 圖式 〖논리〗 a scheme ; a schema 《*pl.* -mata》 ; a diagram ; a plan ; a figure ¶ 도식으로 나타내다 schematize ; diagrammatize
— 계산 graphic algebra ; graphics **— 해법** graphical solution **—화** schematization ; diagraming ; graphing
도식 徒食 idle life **—하다** lead an idle life ; live in idleness ; eat the bread of idleness ; idle away one's time ; be without employment ; vegetate
—배 idlers ; the drones of society
도식 倒植 〖인쇄〗 a reversed character 〔letter〕
도신 刀身 a sword blade
도신 逃身 escape ; flight ; abscondence **—하다** escape ; run away ; flee ; fly ; take flight
도실 桃實 a peach
⁑**도심 都心** the heart〔center〕 of the Metropolis〔the city〕 ; the downtown ; the urban center ¶ 도심지에 있는 호텔 a downtown〔midtown〕 hotel
—지〔지대, 지역〕 the downtown〔midtown〕 area
도심질 whittling ⇨ 도시다
†**도안 圖案** a design ; a sketch ; ornamental designs ; a plan ; a device **—하다** design ; draw a design 《of》 ; make a design 《of》 ¶ 도안을 작성하다 design // 도안화하다 make a design of 《a flower》
—가 a designer ; a patternmaker (직물 따위의) **—과** the design course **— 용지** design paper
도야 陶冶 cultivation ; training ; education **—하다** cultivate ; train ; educate ¶ 인격을 도야하다 build up〔form, mold〕 one's character
—성 educability ; tractability ; educatability

†도약 跳躍 a jump ; a spring ; a leap ; a skip ; jumping (경기) ; a curvet (말의) ─하다 jump ; leap ; spring ; skip ; cut a curvet (말이) ¶ 한국의 경제 도약 Korea's economic take-off
─ 경기 jumping ─근 a jumping muscle ─기 [곤충의] a spring (organ) ─ 선수 a jumper ─ 운동 a jumping exercise ─ 종목 a jumping event (경기의) ─ 진행 〖음악〗 a skip ─판 a springboard ; a leaping board ─ 회전 〖스키〗 a jump turn
도양 渡洋 [형용사적] transoceanic
─ 작전 transoceanic〔oversea(s)〕 operations ─ 폭격 transocean(ic) bombing ; oversea(s)〔ocean-hopping〕 bombing ; a transoceanic raid
도어 倒語 〖문법〗 inversion ; transposition
도어 a door ⇨ 문(門)
도연하다 陶然─ be flushed with liquor ; feel mellow and gay (from drinking) ; be gloriously drunk
도연하다 徒然─ (be) tedious ; boring ; leisurely ; dull ¶ 도연한 세월 an insipid 〔a boring〕 daily life
도열 堵列 [줄] a line 《of men》 ; [늘어섬] lining up ─하다 line〔be drawn〕 up ; form a line ¶ 도열시키다 line 《people》 along 《a street》// 길의 양편에 도열하다 line up on both sides of a road
도열병 稻熱病 〖식물·병리〗 rice blast disease ; rice blight
도영 渡英 going to England ; a visit 〔trip〕 to England ─하다 go to England
도예 陶藝 ceramic art
─가(家) a potter
도와 陶瓦 an unglazed tile
*도와주다 help 《a person do, to do》 ; assist〔aid〕 《a person in doing》 ; lend 〔give〕 a (helping) hand ; render 《a person》 assistance ¶ 옷 벗는 것을 도와주다 help 《a person》 off with his clothes // 전차에서 내리는 것을 도와주다 help 《a person》 out of a tramcar // 일을 도와주다 help 《a person》 in〔with〕 his work // 돈을 도와주다 help with money
도외 道外 ¶ 도외의〔에서〕 outside the province
도외시 度外視 ─하다 disregard ; ignore ; neglect ; leave 《a thing》 out of consideration〔account〕 ¶ 도외시해서 irrespective 《of》 ; in disregard 《of》 // 여론을 도외시하다 disregard public opinion
도요새 〖새〗 a snipe ; a longbill
도용 盜用 [금전의] appropriation ; embezzlement ; peculation ; [그 외의] surreptitious use ; using by stealth ─하다 appropriate ; embezzle ; peculate ; use by stealth ; steal ¶ 전기를 도용하다 make fraudulent use of electricity ; steal electric current // 사인을 도용하다 use another's private seal by stealth
도우 屠牛 slaughtering cattle ─하다 slaughter cattle
─장 a butchery ; a slaughterhouse ─탄(坦) a slaughterman ; a butcher
†도움 ① [조력] help ; aid ; assistance ; [후원] support ; [응원] reinforcement ; [효용] use ; service ; utility ¶ 도움이 되다 be of help〔service, use〕 to ; be a help to 《one》 ; help 《a person》 to // be useful〔serviceable〕 // 크게 도움이 되다 be a great help to 《one》 ; be of much service〔great help〕 // 도움을 받다 have 〔receive〕 help 《from》 // 도움을 청하다 ask 《a person》 for help // 그는 어려울 때에 도움이 될 것이다 He will stand by me in time of need. // 그는 누구의 도움도 받지 않았다 He had no help from anyone. // 군대에서의 경험이 사회에서 큰 도움이 되더군요 My experience in the military service comes in pretty handy in my civilian life. // 그것은 상당히 도움이 될 것입니다 It'll come in pretty handy.
② [구조] rescue ; help ¶ 도움을 청하다 call〔cry〕 for help
③ [구제·구원] relief ; deliverance ; succor ¶ 수해지역에서 도움을 청해왔다 Aid was requested from the flooded area.
도원경 桃源境 Shangrila ; Shangri-La
도음 導音 〖음악〗 a leading tone〔note〕 ; the subtonic
도읍 都邑 the capital ¶ 도읍을 정하다 set up the capital 《at》 ; 《a dynasty》 hold its court 《at》
─지 the seat of government
도의 道義 morality ; morals ; moral principles ; (principles of) moral justice ¶ 도의의 퇴폐 demoralization // 도의적인 원조 moral support // 도의적으로 봐서 from the moral point of view // 도의에 벗어나다 be against public morals // 도의가 땅에 떨어졌다 Morality has lost its hold on the people. /People have no concern for morality today.
도의심 道義心 moral sense〔scruples〕 ; a sense of morality ¶ 도의심에 호소하다 appeal to 《a person's》 moral sense
도의회 道議會 a provincial assembly
도인 道人 ⇨ 도사(道士)
도일 渡日 a visit〔trip〕 to Japan ─하다 visit〔go to〕 Japan
도임 到任 ─하다 arrive to (assume) one's new post
⁑도입 導入 introduction ; induction ; invitation ; importation ; import ─하다 introduce ; induce ; invite ; bring in ; import ¶ 기술 도입 the introduction of technology // 외자 도입 the induction 〔introduction〕 of foreign capital // 모자에 새 유행을 도입하다 introduce a new fashion in hats
─부(部) 〖음악〗 the introduction (part)
도자기 陶瓷器 ceramic ware ; pottery ; china and porcelain
─공 a ceramist ─ 제조법 ceramics
도자성 導磁性 〖물리〗 permeability

도작 稻作 rice farming ; rice culture

도작 盜作 plagiarism ; piracy ; abstraction ; [도작품] a plagiarism ; a crib 《구》 **—하다** pirate ; plagiarize

도장 刀匠 a swordsmith

도장 道場 a drill hall ; a gymnasium ; a gym 《구》 ; a Buddhist preaching court (불교도의)
유도〔레슬링〕 — a judo〔wrestling〕 hall

*도장 圖章 a seal ; a stamp ¶ 도장 파는 사람 a stamp〔seal〕 engraver // 도장을 파다 engrave a seal // 나는 그 서류에 도장을 찍었다 I put my seal on〔to〕 the documents. /I signed my name to the documents.
— 주머니 a seal case —칼 a seal graver —포〔방〕 a seal-engraver's〔-maker's〕 shop 인감 — a registered seal

도장 塗裝 coating ; painting **—하다** coat with paint
—공 a painter (and decorator) — 공사 painting ; painter's work — 공장 a painting shop — 재료 coating materials

도장방 —房 a lady's private sitting room ; a boudoir 《프》

도저하다 到底— ① [썩좋다] (be) fine ; good ; excellent ¶ 업적이 도저하다 show a remarkable〔an excellent〕 result
② [끝까지 이르다] (be) perfect ; thorough ¶ 조국에 대한 충성이 도저하다 be devoted〔faithful〕 to one's mother country

*도저히 到底— (not) at all ; possibly ; by any possibility ; not nearly 《so》 ; utterly ; absolutely ¶ 도저히 갈 수 없다 I cannot possibly go. // 그것은 도저히 불가능하다 It is absolutely impossible. // 그런 것은 도저히 생각할 수 없다 It is beyond our thinking. /I can hardly think of it. // 누가 이길는지 도저히 알 수 없다 There is no saying who will win. // 이것으로는 도저히 안 되겠다 This will not do at all.

도적 盜賊 a thief ⇨ 도둑

*도전 挑戰 challenge ; defiance **—하다** challenge 《a person to a fight》 ; make〔give〕 a challenge ; give〔offer〕 battle to 《a person》 ; call to a combat ; fling〔throw〕 down the gauntlet〔glove〕 to ; defy 《to》 ¶ 도전적 aggressive ; defiant ; provocative // 도전에 응하다 accept〔take up〕 the challenge ; take up〔pick up〕 the gauntlet // 도전적 태도로 나오다 take〔assume〕 a defiant attitude // 세계 기록에 도전하다 challenge the world record // 이번에는 내가 그에게 도전해 보겠다 I'll take him on next time.
—장 a (written) challenge ; a cartel

도전 盜電 surreptitious use〔stealing〕 of electricity〔electric current〕 **—하다** make surreptitious use of electricity

도전 導電 electric conduction ; conduction of electricity
—률 conductivity —체 an electric conductor

도전자 挑戰者 a challenger ¶ 도전자의 자격을 획득하다 fill the requirements for challenging (a champion)

도정 道政 provincial government〔administration〕

도정 道程 the distance ; mileage ; [길] a course ; a route ; a path ¶ 100마일의 도정 a distance of 100 miles

*도제 徒弟 an apprentice ¶ 도제가 되다 be apprenticed to ; apprentice oneself to ; be articled to ; go apprentice // 목수의 도제가 되다 be apprenticed to a carpenter // 도제를 두다 take apprentices
— 교육 education of apprentices — 기간 the period of apprenticeship — 양성 apprenticeship training — 제도 apprenticeship ; an apprentice system

도제 陶製 ¶ 도제의 ceramic ; earthen
— 파이프 a clay pipe

도조 賭租 sharecrop

*도주 逃走 fleeing

도중 道中 on the way

*도중 途中 [도중에서] on the way ; on one's way 《to》 ; on the road ; en route 《to, for》 《프》 ; in transit (수송 도중) ; [중도에서] halfway ; before finishing ¶ 집에 돌아오는 도중(에) on one's way home ; en route home // 도중에서 포기하다 give up halfway // 그 사람은 지금쯤 오는 도중일 것이다 The man must be on the way. // 도중까지 같이 갑시다 I will go part of the way with you. // 도중에 큰 곤란이 있었다 There lay much difficulty in the way. // 말씀 도중입니다만 지금 몇시쯤 되었습니까 Excuse me for interrupting you, but what time is it now?
—역 stations on the way〔along the line〕 ; stations on〔along〕 the route ; way〔intermediate〕 stations — 계시(計時) clocking part-way times 《in a race》 ; [잰 시간] times clocked part-way 《in a race》

도중하차 途中下車 a stopover ; a layover 《미》 **—하다** stop over〔make a stopover〕 《at a way station》 ; stop off ¶ 도중하차에 관한 규정 rules governing stopover privileges
—역 a stopover station 무제한 — unlimited stopover privileges

도지 賭地 sharecrop land ; [도조] share crop

도지다¹ [심하다] (be) extreme ; intense ; severe ; [몸이] hard ; strained ¶ 도진 감기 a bad cold // 욕이 도지다 be extreme in abusing 《a person》 // 길을 걸어 다리가 도지다 have a strained legs from walking

도지다² [사람이 주어] relapse ; have a relapse ; be seized with a relapse ; [병이 주어] grow worse ; take a turn for the worse ¶ 늑막염이 도졌다 He has relapsed into〔had a relapse of〕 pleurisy. // 그의 병세가 도졌다 His condition grows worse〔takes a turn for the worse〕. // 그 열병은 도질 염려는 없다 There is no fear of a return 〔relapse〕 of the fever. // 과로로 그의 병세가 도졌다 He got a relapse through strain. /Strain brought on a relapse of his illness.

도지사 道知事 a provincial governor ; the governor of a province

도짓소 賭地― a rented ox paid for in crops

도차지 monopoly ⇨ 독차지

†**도착 到着** arrival **―하다** arrive 《in, at》 ; reach ; get to ¶ 도착순으로 in the order of arrival // 도착하는 대로 on 〔upon〕 arrival ; immediately on one's arrival ; as soon as one arrives // 정각에 도착하다 arrive on time〔schedule〕 // 무사히 도착하다 arrive in safety ; arrive in good condition〔order〕 (물품이) // 서울〔한국〕에 도착하다 arrive in *Seoul* 〔Korea〕 // 현장에 도착하다 arrive on the scene 〔spot〕 // 열차는 7시에 도착할 것이다 The train is due at seven o'clock. // 편지는 오늘 도착했다 Your letter came today. // 늦어도 출발 2시간 전에 공항에 도착하도록 해 주십시오 Please plan to arrive at the airport at least two hours before departure.

― **가격** ; a C. I. F. price〔quotation〕 ― **선객 명부** an arrival list ― **성명** an arrival statement ― **승객** an incoming passenger **―역** [최종의] an arrival station ; a destination (station) ― **열차** an arriving train ; an in train **―지** one's destination **―항** a port of arrival **―불** payment on delivery ― **예정 시간** estimated time of arrival 《ETA》

도착 倒錯 perversion ; inversion

성욕 ―자 a sexual pervert〔invert〕

도찰 塗擦 anointment ; embrocation ; inunction **―하다** anoint ; rub in ; embrocate

― **요법** treatment by inunction **―제** an embrocation ; a liniment

†**도처 到處** everywhere ; wherever one goes ; all over ; throughout 《the world》 ; in every quarter ; far and wide ; in all directions ; on all sides ; on every hand ; here, there, and everywhere ¶ 국내 도처에서 all over the country ; throughout the country // 세계의 도처로부터 from all parts of the world // 그는 도처에서 사고를 일으킨다 He makes troubles anywhere he goes.

도처 낭패 到處狼狽 ―하다 fail in every attempt ¶ 그는 도처 낭패했다 Everything he put his hand turned out to be a failure.

도청 道廳 the office of provincial government ; the provincial office〔government〕

― **소재지** the seat of a provincial government

도청 盜聽 [전화의] wiretapping ; bugging ; [라디오의] radio poaching〔bootlegging〕 **―하다** tap a telephone wire ; wiretap ; listen to the radio without a license ; bug ; eavesdrop

― **방지** telesecurity ― **사건** a wiretap scandal **―자** a wiretapper ; bugger 《속》

도청 장치 盜聽裝置 [회화의] a concealed microphone ; [전화의] a wiretapping device ; [벽에 장치된] a wall snooper ; a hidden (electronic) listening device ; a bug 《미·속》 ¶ 도청 장치가 되어 있다 be fitted〔rigged〕 with a concealed microphone ; be bugged (up) // 범죄 수사에 도청 장치를 사용하다 use a wiretap in detecting a crime

도체 導體 〚물리〛 a conductor (열, 전기의) ; a medium (매개)

반― a semiconductor **부―** a nonconductor **양〔불량〕―** a good〔bad〕 conductor **양전기** ― [마찰 전기기의] a prime conductor

도취 陶醉 intoxication ; fascination ; rapture **―하다** be intoxicated ; be fascinated〔charmed〕 ; be lost in the rapture of ; be in the ecstasy of 《music》 ¶ 승리의 환희에 도취하다 be intoxicated with 〔lost in the rapture of〕 the joy of victory

자기 ― narcissism **자기 ―자** a narcissist

도치 倒置 turning upside-down ; 〚문법〛 inversion **―하다** invert ; reverse ; put upside-down

―법 〚문법〛 inversion ; hyperbation

도칠기 陶漆器 lacquered pottery

도침 擣砧

도침 맞다 관용 be calendered ; be mercerized

도킹 [우주선의] docking ; space link-up **―하다** dock 《with the command module》 ¶ (우주선의) 도킹을 풀다 undock

도탄 塗炭 misery ; distress ¶ 백성을 도탄에서 구하다 save the people from distress

도탄에 빠지다 관용 fall into extreme distress ; be reduced to the greatest misery

도탑다 (be) warm-hearted ⇨ 두텁다

도태 淘汰 selection ; weeding out ; a comb-out ; a shake-up 《미·속》 **―하다** select ; comb out ; weed out ; sift 《the good from the bad》 ¶ 노후자를 도태하다 weed out〔dismiss〕 superfluous〔superannuated〕 officials

―반(盤) a buddle ; a strake ― **작용** a sifting-〔weeding-〕out process **자연〔인위〕** ― natural〔artificial〕 selection **자웅(雌雄)** ― sexual selection

도토 陶土 kaolin ; china-clay ; porcelain-clay ; potter's clay

― **제품** a figurine

⁑**도토리** an acorn ; Quercus dentata (학명)

― **깍정이〔받침〕** the cup of an acorn ―

묵 acorn-starch jelly〔paste〕
도톨도톨 unevenly ; ruggedly ; lumpily ; rough(ly) ━하다 (be) rugged ; uneven ; rough ; lumpy ; [여드름 따위가] pimply ; pimpled ; [조직·표면 따위가] granular ; granulated ¶ 도톨도톨한 표면 a lumpy surface // 도톨도톨한 나무껍질 a rugged bark // 여드름이 도톨도톨하게 난 얼굴 a pimpled〔pimply〕 face
도톰하다 (be) rather thick ⇨ 두툼하다
도통 道通 spiritual enlightenment ━하다 attain enlightenment ; be spiritually enlightened ¶ 그 일에 도통하다 be well 〔deeply〕 versed in the matter ; be conversant with the matter
도통 都統 in all ; all together ; totally ; all told ¶ 도통 15개였다 There were fifteen in all.
도투락댕기 a hair ribbon worn by a little girl
도투마리 a warp beam of a loom
도파니 in all ; (in) all told ; altogether ; in the total
*도판 圖版 a plate ; a figure ; an illustration
도포 塗布 ━하다 spread ; apply《an ointment to》
━약 [연고] an ointment ; [물약] a liniment
도포 道袍 Korean full-dress attire (in olden days)
*도표 道標 a signpost ; a milestone ; a road sign ; a guidepost ; a fingerpost ¶ 도표를 따라 나아가다 follow the signposts
도표 圖表 a chart ; a diagram ; a graph
━선 a diagram line 면적 ━ an area chart〔diagram〕 문법 ━ a grammar chart 선(線)━ a line graph 역사 ━ a historical chart 점(點)━ 〖통계〗 a scatter〔dot〕 diagram 통계 ━ a statistical chart
도품 盜品 a stolen article ; stolen goods 〔things, property〕 ; swag《속》; hot goods
*도피 逃避 escape ; evasion ; flight ━하다 escape ; evade ; flee ¶ 자본의 도피 방지가 시급하다 It is urgent for us to prevent the flight of capital.
━ 결혼 a runaway marriage ━ 문학 escapist literature ; literature of escape ━ 생활 a life of escape from the world ━소 a place of refuge ; a bolt-hole ━ 여행 an escape journey ━주의 escapism ━ 주의자 an escapist 망명자 ━지 a sanctuary of political refugees ━처 hideout
도핑 doping ; drug use
━ 테스트 a dope test ; a drug check 〔test〕
도하 都下 the capital ; the metropolis ¶ 도하의 각 중학교 the middle schools in the capital〔metropolis〕
도하 渡河 the crossing〔fording〕 of a river ━하다 cross a river
━ 기재(器材) river-crossing materials ━작전 river-crossing〔fording〕 operations 적전(敵前) ━ the forced crossing of a river against an enemy 전차 ━교(橋) a tank crossing ━점 a crossing (point) ; a point of passage
도학 道學 ethics ; moral philosophy ¶ 도학 군자 a virtuous gentleman
━자 a moralist (학자) ; a moralizer (도덕에 구애되는 사람)
도한 盜汗 night sweat(ing) ; nightly sweats ¶ 그는 밤에 도한이 난다 He sweats at night. /He has night sweats.
도합 都合 [총계] the total ; the sum 〔grand〕 total ; the gross ; [전부 합해서] in all ; all told ; altogether ¶ 도합 5만원이다 The total comes to fifty thousand *won*. /It amounts to fifty thousand *won*.
도항 渡航 a passage ; a voyage ; a sailing ━하다 make a passage ; make a voyage to ; cross the water ¶ 도항 수속을 끝마치다 go through the formalities for going abroad // 미국에 도항하다 go over to America ; sail for America
━권 passage ━ 면허장 a passport (for a foreign voyage) ━자 a passenger ; a foreign traveler ; a visitor ━증 a passport for foreign travel 자유 ━ unrestricted passage
도해 渡海 crossing the sea ; a passage ; a voyage ━하다 cross the sea ; take a passage ; make a voyage
도해 圖解 an explanatory diagram ; an illustration ━하다 illustrate ; diagram ; show by a diagram ; show in a graphic form
━ 백과 사전 an illustrated〔iconographical〕 encyclopedia ━법 iconography ━ 사전 a picture〔a pictorial, an illustrated〕 dictionary ━ 역학 graphical statics 곤충 ━ explanatory diagrams of insects
도형 徒刑 penal servitude
*도형 圖形 a figure ; a device ; a diagram ¶ 도형으로 나타내다 show in〔by〕 a diagram
━ 기하학 descriptive geometry ━ 인식 pattern recognition 기하학적 ━ a geometrical figure 평면〔입체〕 ━ a plane〔solid〕 figure
도홍색 桃紅色 rose (colo(u)r) ; pink
도화 桃花 a peach blossom
도화 圖畫 drawing ; [그림] a picture ; a drawing
━ 용지 drawing paper
도화 導火 ① [불] a fuse ; a fuze《미》② [불씨·동기] a direct cause ; an impetus ; an incentive ; an agency
━관 a fuse ; a fuze ; a primer
도화사 道化師 a clown ; a buffoon ; a comic ; a funnyman《미·구》
도화선 導火線 [탄약의] a fuze《미》; a fuse ; a blasting〔detonating〕 fuse ; a train of powder ; a primer ; [유인] a cause ; an agency ; an impetus ; an incentive ; an

occasion ¶ 도화선을 붙이다 lay a train (of powder) ; put fuze to // 반란의 도화선이 되다 prove an incentive to〔lead up to, give rise to〕 mass revolt
도회 都會 a city ; a town ¶ 도회의 city ; town ; urban // 도회에서 자란 아이 city-bred children // 도회화하다 urbanize ; citify // 도회 생활에의 동경 the passion for city life ; a wish to live in a city
— **문학** urban literature —**병** a city disease — **정서** an urban atmosphere —**지** urban areas〔district〕 —**화(化)** urbanization
도회 생활 都會生活 urban〔town, city〕 life ; urban〔city〕 living ¶ 특히 도회 생활을 좋아하다 have a predilection for town life
도회인 都會人 a townsman ; a city man ; a city-dweller ; an urbanite ; residents in a city ; city-dwelling people
도회풍 都會風 urban〔city〕 manners ; urbanity ¶ 도회풍의 urban ; urbane ; citified ; townified // 도회풍으로 urbanely // 도회풍으로 하다 urbanize ; citify ; townify
도흔 刀痕 a sword cut〔scar〕
도흥정 都— a wholesale transaction〔deal〕 **—하다** wholesale
독[1] a jar ; a vat (양조·염색용) ¶ 그는 독 안에 든 쥐다 He is like a rat in a trap.
독[2] a dock ¶ 독에 넣다 dock《a ship》; put《a ship》 into dock // 독에 들어가다〔에서 나오다〕 come into〔out of〕 dock
‡**독 毒** [독물] poison ; poisonous substance ; [병독·독소] virus ; toxin ; [독약] poison ; a toxicant ; [독사의] venom ¶ 독사의 독 the virus of a venomous snake // 독이 있다 be poisonous ; be virulent ; be toxic〔noxious〕 // 독이 없다 be innoxious〔innocuous〕 ; be harmless (무해) // 독(약)을 마시다 take poison // 독을 제거하다 neutralize〔counteract〕 a poison // 독으로 독을 다스리다 meet evil with evil ; like cures like // 독이 전신에 돌았다 The poison passed into the system.
독이 오르다 관용 become spiteful〔venomous, malicious〕
—**선(腺)** 〖동물〗 a poison gland — **예방** protection against poisoning **뱀—** snake venom
독가스 毒— poison gas ; asphyxiating〔poisonous〕 gas // 독가스를 사용하다 use poison gas // 독가스로 적을 공격하다 gas the enemy
— **공격** a gas attack — **공격 경보** a gas alarm — **마스크** a gas mask — **사형 집행실** a gas chamber —**전(戰)** (poison)-gas warfare —**탄** a poison-gas shell〔bomb〕 ; a gas shell
독감 毒感 influenza ; flu《구》; a bad cold ; grippe ¶ 독감에 걸리다 be attacked by influenza // 독감이 돌고 있다 There's a bad cold going around.

독거 獨居 solitude ; solitary life **—하다** live alone〔by oneself〕 ; live in solitude ; lead a solitary〔secluded〕 life ; keep to oneself
—**성 동물** a solitary animal ; a hermit
독경 讀經 sutra-chanting **—하다** chant a sutra ; chant the Buddhist scripture〔sutra〕
독과점 獨寡占 monopoly and oligopoly
— **품목** monopolistic and oligopolistic items — **회사** oligopolists
독기 毒氣 virulence ; venom ; noxiousness ; [악의] venomousness ; malignance ; malice ¶ 독기 있는 noxious ; venomous ; poisonous ; virulent // 독기 없는 innoxious ; harmless // 독기 있는 말 stinging words ; malicious〔malignant〕 remarks
독나방 毒— 〖곤충〗 an Oriental tussock moth ; Euproctis subflava (학명)
— **피부염** dermatitis caused by the sting of an Oriental tussock moth
독납 督納 tax dunning **—하다** dun for taxes ; press for tax payment
독농 篤農 a most efficient farming producer ; a diligent〔productive〕 farmer
독농가 篤農家 a diligent〔productive〕 farmer ; a most efficient farming producer
***독단 獨斷** arbitrary decision ; [독단적 주장] dogmatism ¶ 독단적 arbitrary ; dogmatic // 독단으로 arbitrarily ; dogmatically ; on one's own authority〔responsibility〕 // 독단으로 회사에 전보를 쳤다 He telegraphed to the office on his own responsibility. /He took upon himself to telegraph to the office.
—**가** an arbitrary person ; a dogmatist —**론** a dogma ; dogmatism
독담당 獨擔當 **—하다** take sole charge of ; assume sole responsibility for
독두 禿頭 [머리] a bald head ; [사람] a baldheaded person ; a baldpate
—**병** 〖의학〗 alopecia (areata)
독려 督勵 encouragement ; stimulation **—하다** encourage ; stimulate ; urge〔spur〕《a person to do》
독력 獨力 one's own efforts ; single-handed efforts ¶ 독력으로 by one's own efforts ; on one's own account ; for oneself ; single-handed ; unaided // 독력으로 성공한 사람 a self-made man // 독력으로 하다 do《a thing》 single-handed ; do《a thing》 off one's own bat〔for oneself〕
‡**독립 獨立** [자립] independence ; self-help ; self-support ; self-reliance ; [분리] separation ; isolation (고립) **—하다** become independent《of one's own parents》; stand on one's own legs ; become (free and) independent ; support oneself (자활) ; paddle one's own canoe ¶ 경제적 독립 economic independence // 독립해서 장사를 시작하다 start business inde-

pendently // 독립시키다 set 《a person》 on his feet // 독립을 선언하다 declare independence // 독립 생활을 하다 support oneself ; earn one's own living // 독립을 위협하다 threaten one's independence
— 가옥 separate house — 구문 〖문법〗 an absolute construction — 기념일 Independence Day ; the Fourth of July (미국의) — 부정사〔분사구〕 〖문법〗 absolute infinitive〔participial phrase〕 — 선언 [미국의] the Declaration of Independence — 세 an independent tax — 운동 an independence〔a separatist〕 movement — 정신 a spirit of independence

독립국 獨立國 an independent state ; a sovereign nation
신흥 — a newly independent nation 〔country〕

독립 독보 獨立獨步 independence ; self-reliance ; self-help — 하다 rely on oneself ; help oneself ; be self-reliant ¶ 독립 독보하는 사람 a self-reliant person

독립 독행 獨立獨行 independence ; self-reliance ; self-help — 하다 rely on oneself ; be self-reliant ; paddle one's own canoe ; cut one's own way ; be one's own master

독립심 獨立心 an independent spirit ; a spirit of independence ¶ 독립심이 없다 lack the spirit of independence // 독립심을 불러일으키다 inspire 《a person》 with the spirit of independence

독립 자영 獨立自營 independence and self-support — 하다 support oneself

독립 자존 獨立自尊 independence and self-respect ¶ 독립 자존의 self-reliant // 독립 자존의 정신 the spirit of independence and self-respect
—주의 the principles of independence and self-respect

독립 자활 獨立自活 independence and self-support — 하다 support oneself

독립 전쟁 獨立戰爭 [미국] the Revolutionary War ; the War of Independence ; the (American) Revolution ¶ 독립 전쟁 이전의 prerevolutionary 《furniture》

독립주의 獨立主義 separatism ; secessionism
—자 a separatist ; a secessionist

독립 채산제 獨立採算制 a self-supporting accounting system ¶ 독립 채산제로 on a self-paying basis

독메 獨— a loan mountain ; a solitary mountain

독무 獨舞 a solo dance ; a pas seul 《프》

독무대 獨舞臺 ① [혼자서 연기하기] playing alone〔by oneself〕 ② [한 사람의 연기가 특히 뛰어난] the sole master of the stage〔field〕 ¶ 그 연극은 그의 독무대였다 In the play he outshone all other actors. ③ [경쟁자가 없는] one's unrivaled sphere of activity ; one's monopoly ¶ 독무대의 without a rival // 그후 정계는 그의 독무대였다 After that, the whole political situation was entirely in his hands.

독물 a dark blue color ; blue-black

독물 毒物 [독] poisonous stuff ; a toxicant ; [사람] a vicious person ; a spiteful person ¶ 그 과자 속에서 독물이 검출되었다 Some poisonous substances were detected in those candies.
— 검출 detection of poisonous matter — 공포증 〖의학〗 toxiphobia —학 toxicology

독미나리 毒— 〖식물〗 a water hemlock

독방 獨房 [혼자서 거처하는 방] a single room ; a room to oneself ; [감방] a cell ; a prison〔jail〕 cell ; a solitary〔an isolation〕 cell ¶ 그는 독방에 감금당했다 He was put in solitary confinement.
— 감금 solitary confinement —제 the solitary imprisonment system

독백 獨白 a soliloquy ; a monolog(ue) ; an aside (무대의) — 하다 talk to oneself ; soliloquize ; perform a monolog
—극 a monodrama 내적 — 〖문학〗 an interior〔inner〕 monologue

독버섯 毒— a poisonous mushroom ; a toadstool

독법 讀法 [읽는 법] (the way of) reading ; [해석] (a) reading ; [발음] pronunciation

독보 獨步 ¶ 독보의 unique ; unrivaled ; unequaled ; peerless ; unchallenged // 그는 현 문단에서 독보적 지위에 있다 He stands unchallenged in the present literary world.

독보 讀譜 〖음악〗 reading music

독본 讀本 a reader ; a reading book
부— a supplementary〔side〕 reader 영어 — an English reader

독부 毒婦 a wicked woman ; a vampire ; a she-devil ; a witch

독불 獨佛 France and Germany ¶ 독불의 Franco-German ; German-French 《dictionary》 ; French-German 《relations》

독불장군 獨不將軍 [독부] an isolated person ; a person left out ; [고집쟁이] a man of self-assertion〔self-will〕

독사 毒蛇 a venomous snake〔serpent〕 ; a nocuous snake ; a viper ; an adder ; an asp

독살 毒殺 ① [죽임] poisoning — 하다 poison ; kill 《a person》 by poison
② [살기] venomousness ; spitefulness ; malignancy ¶ 독살스러운 여자 a spiteful〔vicious〕 woman // 독살스럽다 be venomous ; be spiteful ; be malicious ; be acrimonious // 독살스런 말을 하다 use spiteful〔virulent〕 language
— 사건 a poisoning case —자 a poisoner

독살림하다 獨— live independently ¶ 부모를 떠나 독살림하다 live independently of one's parents ; support oneself with-

out relying on one's parents
독살부리다 毒殺— act spitefully ⇨ 독살피우다
독살스럽다 毒殺— (be) venomous ; malicious ; spiteful ; wicked ; vicious ; furious ; ferocious ; savage ; bloodthirsty ¶ 독살스럽게 spitefully ; malignantly ; virulently // 독살스러운 여자 a spiteful woman ; a vicious woman
독살풀이 毒殺— giving vent to one's spite ; going at 《a person》 in a wicked manner **—하다** give vent to one's spite
독살피우다 毒殺— act spitefully〔acrimoniously〕; give vent to one's spite ; vent one's spite on〔upon〕《a person》; act wickedly〔in a vicious manner〕; act furiously ; say something spiteful
독생자 獨生子 Jesus Christ
†**독서 讀書** reading **—하다** read 《books》 ¶ 널리 독서하다 read widely〔extensively〕// 독서를 좋아하다 be fond of reading ; take kindly to books // 독서 삼매경에 잠기다 be absorbed in reading // 독서로 눈을 피로케 하다 pore one's eyes out
— 경향 조사 〖도서〗 a survey of the readers' interests **—계(界)** the reading public **—광** a bookworm ; a literary glutton **—기(機)** [환자용의] an automatic page-turner **—대** a reading desk **—등** [여객기 내의] an individual reading light **—법** a method of reading (a book) ; a choice of books (선택) **—벽(癖)** the reading habit **—실** a reading room **—욕** a desire for reading **—인** a reader of books ; a book man **— 주간** Book Week **—회** a reading club〔party, circle〕
독서가 讀書家 a book reader ; a great reader ; a well-read person ; a person of wide reading ¶ 그는 상당한 독서가다 He is quite well read.
독서력 讀書力 reading ability ¶ 영어의 독서력을 기르다 cultivate〔improve〕 one's reading ability in English // 오늘날의 학생은 일반적으로 영어의 독서력이 부족하다 The present-day students are mostly lacking in the ability of reading English.
독선 獨善 self-righteousness ; self-importance ; self-complacence ¶ 독선적 self-righteous ; self-complacent ; self-satisfied ; self-justified
—주의 self-righteousness ; self-complacence〔-complacency〕; self-flattery ¶ 관료의 독선주의 bureaucratic self-righteousness
독설 毒舌 a stinging〔an acrimonious〕 tongue ; a venomous〔virulent, devilish〕 remark ; malicious〔abusive〕 language ; vituperation ¶ 독설을 퍼붓다 wag one's slanderous tongue ; speak with acrimony ; speak venomously to 《a person》; vituperate
독성 毒性 virulence ; poisonous character ¶ 독성의 virulent ; poisonous ; toxic ; toxicant
— 궤양 (a) virulent ulcer **— 완화** mollification of virulence **— 완화제** a safener
독소 毒素 a toxin ; poisonous matter
독소 獨蘇 Germany and Soviet Russia ¶ 독소전(獨蘇戰) the Russian-German War
독수 毒手 a vicious clutch ; a vicious means ; a trick ; a trap ¶ 독수에 걸리다 fall a victim〔prey〕 to 《an assassin's dagger》; fall into the clutches〔fangs〕《of》// 독수를 벗어나다 get out of the clutches 《of a usurer》
독수 공방 獨守空房 living in solitude ; 《husband and wife》 living apart ; (especially) a woman's leading solitary life in her husband's absence **—하다** live alone ; lead a solitary life ; live apart
*‡**독수리** 〖새〗 an eagle ; a vulture ; Accipitridae (학명) ¶ 독수리 같은 vulturous
— 새끼 an eaglet **—좌** 〖천문학〗 the Eagle ; Aquila **—집** an eagle's nest〔aerie, aery, eyrie, eyry〕
독순술 讀脣術 lip reading
독습 獨習 self-study ; self-teaching **—하다** study by oneself ; teach oneself ¶ 영어를 독습했다 He learned English by himself.
—서(書) a self-study manual ; a teach-yourself book ; [자습서] a horse 《미》; a pony ; a crib 《영》 **—자** a self-taught person ; an autodidact
독시 毒矢 a poisoned arrow
독시 毒弑 —하다 poison 《one's superior》; kill 《one's superior》 by poison
독신 獨身 a single life ; celibacy ; [남자] bachelorhood ; [여자] spinsterhood ¶ 독신의 single ; unmarried // 독신으로 지내다 live single ; live a bachelor's〔spinster's〕 life // 일생을 독신으로 지내다 remain single all one's life ; remain unmarried for life ; live and die single
— 생활 a single〔unmarried〕 life ; celibacy (종교적 이유에 의한) **—자** a single〔an unmarried〕 person ; [남자] a bachelor ; [여자] a spinster **—주의** celibacy **—주의자** a celibate
독신 瀆神 blasphemy ; desecration ; sacrilege ; profanity ; profanation
독신 篤信 devotion ; earnest belief **—하다** believe earnestly ; be devoted to 《a religion》
—자 a devotee 《of religion》; a devout person
독실 獨室 a single room ; a private room ; [침대차의] a roomette
독실 篤實 sincerity ; faithfulness **—하다** (be) sincere ; faithful ; true ¶ 독실히 sincerely ; faithfully // 독실한 사람 a true gentleman
독심 毒心 malice ; spite ; venom ¶ 독심먹다 be filled with spite
독심술 讀心術 mind〔thought〕 reading ; telepathy

독아 毒牙 a poison fang ; a fang ¶ 독아에 걸리다 fall into《a person's》clutches ; fall a victim〔prey〕《to》
*독액 毒液 poisonous liquid ; poisonous juice (과실즙) ; poisonous sap (나무진)
독약 毒藥 poison ; a poisonous drug〔medicine〕¶ 독약을 마시다 take poison // 독약을 타다 put poison into《food》; poison《food》; mix a poison《with a thing》
—학 toxicology
독어 獨語 ① [독일어] German ; the German language ② [혼잣말] soliloquy ; monolog(ue)
독연 獨演 a solo performance ; a single ; a recital (음악) ; [연극] a one- man show ; a one-man stage play ; monodrama —하다 give a solo performance ; perform alone ; do a single
—자(者) a solo performer —회(會) [음악의] a solo recital ; [코미디 따위] a one-man show
독염 毒焰 a poisonous flame
독영 獨英 England and Germany ¶ 독영의 Anglo-German ; German-English《Dictionary》
독오르다 毒— become spiteful〔venomous〕
독와사 毒瓦斯 poison gas ⇨ 독가스
독이 獨— alone ; by oneself ; single-handed
독인 毒刃 an assassin's dagger ¶ 독인에 쓰러지다 fall a victim to the dagger of《an assassin》; be foully murdered
†독일 獨逸 Germany ¶ 독일의 German ; Germanic
—계 미국인 a German-American —어 German ; the German language —인 a German ; the Germans《총칭》동부(東部) — Eastern Germany 서부 — Western Germany ; the Federal Republic of Germany
†독자 讀者 a reader ; [구독자] a subscriber ; [일반의] the reading public ¶ 그 신문은 백만 독자가 있다 The paper has a circulation of a million. // 그 책은 많은 독자가 애독하고 있다 The book is widely read〔very popular〕.
—란 the reader's column ; the correspondence column ; letters to the editor —수 readership (신문 따위의 독자의 총수) 일반 — general readership
독자 獨子 the only son
독자 獨自 ¶ 독자의 [개인적] individual ; personal ; [독특한] original ; of one's own ; unique ¶ 독자적인 생각 one's personal〔own〕idea // 독자적인 행동을 취하다 follow one's own line of conduct ; go one's own way
—성 individuality (개인적) ; originality (독특한)
독자층 讀者層 a class of readers ¶ 이 잡지들은 각기 독자층이 다르다 Each of these magazines has its own class of subscribers.
독작하다 獨酌— drink alone ; drink without a companion ; drink by oneself
독장수셈 a fruitless〔vain〕effort ; exerting〔straining〕oneself in vain
독장치다 獨場— have the whole field〔stage〕to oneself ; be the sole master of the stage〔field, situation〕; stand without rivals ¶ 정계에서 독장치다 reign supreme in the political world
*독재 獨裁 dictatorship ; absolute rule ; autocracy ; despotism —하다 have《a country》under one's despotic rule ; hold absolute authority《over》
— 국가 a despotic〔an autocratic〕state — 군주 a despotic monarch ; a despot ; an absolute ruler — 군주국 an absolute monarchy ; a royal dictatorship — 정치 dictatorship ; dictatorial government 개인 — personal dictatorship 무산 계급 — proletarian dictatorship
독재자 獨裁者 a dictator ; an arbiter ; an autocrat ; a monocrat ; a despot
독재적 獨裁的 ¶ 독재적인 dictatorial ; despotic ; autocratic(al) // 독재적으로 dictatorially ; autocratically ; despotically
독전 督戰 —하다 urge the soldiers to fight still more vigorously
—대 a supervising unit
독점 —店 a pottery shop
*독점 獨占 monopoly ; monopolization ; exclusive possession —하다 monopolize ; hold〔have〕monopoly《of》¶ 독점적 monopolistic ; exclusive // 방을 독점하다 have a room to oneself // 시장을 독점하다 monopolize a market
— 가격 a monopoly price —권 (the right to) a monopoly ; an exclusive〔a sole〕right — 기업 a monopoly undertaking —도(度) the degree of monopolization —력 monopolistic strength — 사업 a monopolistic enterprise —욕 a desire to have entire possession《of》—자 a monopolizer ; a monopolist ; a sole owner —주의 monopolism — 판매 an exclusive sale — 판매인 a sole agent〔distributor〕— 판매점 a sole agent〔agency〕—화 monopolization — 회사 a monopoly 수요 — a monopsony 순수 — pure monopoly 완전 — complete monopoly
독점 금지법 獨占禁止法 〚법〛the Antimonopoly〔Antitrust〕Act ¶ 독점 금지법에 저촉되다 be against the Antimonopoly Act ; the Antitrust Act forbids《the merger》
— 찬성론자 an antitruster
독점 자본 獨占資本 monopolistic capital ¶ 독점 자본이 지배하고 있는 산업 monopoly-controlled industries
—가 a monopolist —주의 monopolistic capitalism

독종 毒種 [종자] malicious offspring ; a bad seed ; [사람] a malicious person
독주 毒酒 [독한 술] hard liquor ; strong spirits ; [독을 탄 술] poisoned liquor
*독주 獨奏 a recital ; a solo —하다 play a solo ; play alone
—곡 a solo —자 a soloist ; a solo —회 a recital ; a solo 피아노 — a piano solo〔recital〕
독주하다 獨走— run alone ; leave others far behind ; have a walkover 《구》
독지 篤志 [자선] benevolence ; charity ; a charitable spirit ; [열심] interest ; zeal
—간호원 a volunteer nurse —사업 a labor of love ; a charity work —행위 a gratuitous act
독지가 篤志家 a volunteer ; a person interested ; a supporter (후원자) ¶ 익명의 독지가 an anonymous benefactor
독직 瀆職 (official) corruption ; corrupt practices ; bribery ; a graft 《미》 —하다 practice corruption ¶ 독직죄로 on a charge of receiving a bribe
—관리 a corrupt official ; a grafter —사건 a corruption scandal ; a bribery〔graft, corruption〕case —죄 bribery ; a charge of misconduct in office —행위 corrupt practices
독차지 獨— exclusive possession ; monopolizing —하다 have〔keep〕all to oneself ; possess exclusively ; monopolize ¶ 사랑을 독차지하다 engross another's love // 한 방을 독차지하다 have a room all to oneself
*독창 獨唱 a (vocal) solo —하다 sing a solo ; give a vocal solo
—곡 a solo piece —자 a soloist
‡독창 獨創 originality ¶ 독창적 original ; creative // 그는 독창력이 풍부하다 He is rich in〔fertile of〕originality. // 이 방법은 그의 독창이다 This method is original with him.
독창력 獨創力 creative talent〔power, faculty〕; originality ¶ 독창력이 풍부하다 be rich in creative talent // 독창력을 기르다 develop originality
독창성 獨創性 originality ¶ 독창성이 있는 original // 독창성이 없는 unoriginal // 독창성을 나타내다 display originality
독창회 獨唱會 a (vocal) recital ¶ 독창회를 열다 hold〔give〕a (vocal) recital
독채 獨— an unshared house
독천 獨擅 surpassing others ; lacking rivals —하다 surpass others 《in》; be the master of ; lack rivals ; be unrivaled
독천장 獨擅場 one's unrivaled sphere of activity ; one's monopoly ¶ 그 연극은 그의 독천장이었다 In the play he outshone all the other actors.
독초 毒草 [풀] a poisonous〔noxious〕plant〔herb〕; [담배] strong tobacco
독촉 督促 urge ; demand ; pressing ; importunity ; dunning —하다 press〔dun〕《a person for》; urge 《a person to do》 ¶ 지불을 독촉받았다 He was pressed for payment.
—수수료 charge for call〔the demand〕; reminder〔demanding, collection〕fee —장 a demand note ; a (letter of) reminder ; [차용금의] a dunning letter〔note〕
독충 毒蟲 a poisonous〔noxious〕insect
독침 毒針 [곤충 따위의] a poison sting(er) ; [독을 칠한 바늘] a poisoned〔venomous〕needle ¶ 독침에 쏘이다 get stung 《by a bee》 // 독침으로 찌르다 prick with a poisoned needle
독탕 獨湯 a private bath —하다 take a private bath
†독특 獨特 —하다 (be) unique ; peculiar 《to》; characteristic 《of》; be all one's own special ¶ 독특한 기능 a special ability // 한국의 독특한 풍습 a custom peculiar to Korea // 그의 독특한 방법으로 in the way of his own ; in his own way // 그 문체는 그의 독특한 것이다 The style is peculiarly his own.
독파 讀破 —하다 finish 《a book》; read〔go〕(all the way) through ¶ 만권의 서적을 독파하다 read a world of books
독판 獨— monopoly ¶ 독판치다 monopolize
독풀이 毒— ⇨ 독살풀이
독필 禿筆 ① [붓] a stumped pen ; a worndown writing brush
② [자기 글의 겸칭] my writing〔composition〕¶ 독필을 무릅쓰고 though I am a bad writer
독필 毒筆 a spiteful pen ¶ 독필을 휘두르다 dip 《one's》 pen in gall ; wield a spiteful pen ; write〔attack〕with acrimony ; satirize
독하다 毒— ① [독기 있다] (be) poisonous ; noxious ; [해독] harmful ; injurious ¶ 독한 가스 poisonous gas
② [진하다] (be) strong ; severe ¶ 독한 술 strong liquor
③ [잔인하다] (be) spiteful ; vicious ; venomous ; atrocious ¶ 독한 여자 a spiteful woman
④ [굳세다] (be) firm ; dogged ; tough ; unflinching ¶ 독한 마음을 먹고 공부하다 study with firm resolve
독학 獨學 self-teaching ; self-education ; self-study —하다 teach〔educate〕oneself ; study〔learn〕by oneself ¶ 독학한 사람 a self-educated〔-taught〕man // 독학으로 대학을 마쳤다 He gave himself a college education.
독학 篤學 a love of learning ; devotion to one's studies ; earnest scholarship
—하다 study assiduously ¶ 독학의 studious ; assiduous ; given〔devoted〕to study // 독학지사 a devoted scholar
독항 獨航 [단독 항해] sailing alone ; a lone voyage

—선(船) an independent fishing boat
독해 毒害 poisoning ⇨ 독살
독해력 讀解力 ability to read and understand ; comprehension
독행 篤行 good〔golden〕 deeds ; goodness ; upright conduct ; an act of charity
독행 獨行 —하다 [가다] travel alone ; go by oneself ; [행동] act independently ; be self-reliant
독혈 毒血 bad〔poisoned〕 blood
독혈증 毒血症 〖의학〗 toxaemia
독회 讀會 a reading ¶ 의안은 독회 생략으로 가결되었다 The bill was passed, the discussion stage having been dispensed with.
제 1 — the 1st reading ; the committee stage 제 2 — the 2nd reading ; the discussion stage 제 3 — the 3rd reading ; the voting stage
독후감 讀後感 one's impressions of〔after reading〕 a book
†돈[1] [금전] money ; cash ; currency ; coin ; funds ; [재산] wealth ; riches ¶ 돈의 pecuniary ; monetary // 돈줄 financial supporter // 돈벌이 money-making // 돈 문제 money matters // 돈 걱정 financial anxiety // 미국의 돈 American money ; [자금] American fund ; [화폐] American currency // 돈 많은 사람 a rich man ; a well-to-do person // 돈에 궁한〔부유한〕 사람 a hard-up〔well-to-do〕 person // 돈을 헤프게 쓰는 사람 a spendthrift ; a free〔heavy〕 spender // 돈만 아는 사람 a money grubber // 돈이 얼마가 들든지 regardless of expenses ; at any cost // 돈 힘으로 by force of money // 돈에만 움직이는 mercenary // 돈이 남는 profitable ; paying ; lucrative // 돈 한푼 없는 penniless // 돈이 많이 들다 cost a lot of money〔a pretty penny〕 ; be very expensive〔costly〕 // 돈으로 바꾸다 turn 《things》 into money ; realize 《one's stock》 ; cash 《a check》 // 돈으로 치면 10만원의 가치가 있다 be worth 100,000 *won* in value // 돈을 내다 pay 《for》 (치르다) ; contribute money 《to》 (기부하다) ; finance〔subsidize〕 《a project》 (출자하다) // 돈을 모으다 make money // 돈을 마련하다 raise money ; [빚을 얻다] get a loan ; put up dough 《미》 // 돈이 없다 have no money ; be short of money // 돈이 넉넉하다 be well off ; have a heavy purse // 돈을 받다 charge 《a person》 for // 돈을 쓰다 spend money 《on》 // 돈에 곤란을 당하다 be hard up for money ; be in financial difficulties ; be short of money // 자기 돈으로 외유하다 go abroad at one's own expense // 돈맛을 알다 come to love money // 돈을 물쓰듯하다 squander〔lavish〕 money // 돈이 하늘에서 떨어지는 줄 아니 You think money grows on trees ? // 내가 정가보다 돈을 더 낸 것 같다 I think I was overcharged. // 지금 수중에 돈 가진 것 있니 Do you have money on you ? // 돈을 많이 버십니까 Do you make a lot of money ? /Do you make good money ? /Is the money good ?
돈만 있으면 개도 멍첨지이다 〔속담〕 Money often makes the man.
돈만 있으면 귀신도 부릴 수 있다 〔속담〕 Money rules the world. /Money makes the mare to go.
돈만 있으면 처녀 불알도 산다 〔속담〕 Rich men may have what they will. /He that has money has what he wants. /A golden key can open any door.
돈에 범이 없다 〔속담〕 Money makes the mare to go. /What cannot gold do ?
돈에 침 뱉는 놈 없다 〔속담〕 Money is welcome, though it come in a dirty clout.
돈은 돌고 돈다 〔속담〕 Money changes hands.
돈이 돈을 번다 〔속담〕 Money begets〔makes〕 money. /Money draws money. /He that has plenty of goods shall have more. /He that has a goose, will get a goose.
돈이라면 뱃속의 아이도 나온다 〔속담〕 A silver Key can open every door.
돈이 많으면 장사를 잘하고 소매가 길면 춤을 잘 춘다 〔속담〕 Money draws money. /Money makes(begets, breeds) money. /He that has plenty of goods shall have more. /He that has a goose, will get a goose.
돈이 없으면 적막강산이요, 돈이 있으면 금수강산이라 〔속담〕 Money makes a man free everywhere.
돈이 원수다 〔속담〕 Money is the root of all evils.
돈이 장사라 〔속담〕 Money is power. / Money will do anything. /What will not money do ?
돈[2] [무게 단위] a *don* (0.1325ounces, 3.7565 grams)
돈 噸 a ton ; [톤수] tonnage ¶ 영〔미〕돈 a long〔short〕 ton // 중량돈 dead weight tonnage // 미터돈 a metric ton // 용적돈 capacity tonnage // 총〔배수, 적재〕 돈수 gross〔displacement, freight〕 tonnage // 석탄 3돈 three tons of coal // 10돈짜리 배 a ten-tonner // 만돈의 배 a ship of 10,000 tons // 적재량 5돈의 트럭 a five- ton truck // 이 배는 몇돈입니까 What is the tonnage of this ship ?
돈-강 —江 the Don River
돈견 豚犬 ① [돼지와 개] a pig and a dog ② [미련한 사람] a dull〔stupid, senseless〕 person ; a blockhead
돈구멍 [돈이 생기는 길] a source of income〔profit〕 ; a source of money
돈궤 —櫃 a money box ; a strongbox
돈까스 豚— a pork cutlet
돈꿰미 a string for threading coins with holes in them
돈냥 —兩 some money ; a pretty〔fine〕

penny ¶ 돈냥이나 있는 집안 a family with a fine fortune ; a well-to-do family
돈놀이 moneylending ; usury (고리의) **—하다** run a moneylending business ; practice usury ¶ 돈놀이해서 돈을 모으다 make money by usury
돈단무심 頓斷無心 —하다 pay no attention to ; (be) indifferent to〔about〕
돈대 墩臺 high ground ; heights ; an eminence
돈독 —毒 an unhealthy taste for money ¶ 돈독들다 acquire an unhealthy taste for money
돈독 敦篤 ⇨ 돈후(敦厚)
돈돈쭝 —重 a weight equivalent to several *don*
돈들막 elevated ground with a sharp dropoff
돈만 —萬 tens of thousands of coins ; quite a sum of money
돈맛 a taste for money ; a love of money ¶ 돈맛을 알다 come to love money // 돈맛을 들이다 get〔acquire〕 a taste for money ; love money
돈머리 ① [액수] an amount of money ; a sum (of money) ¶ 돈머리 수가 크다 be a large amount of money ; be a tidy sum ② [일정액] a given〔definite〕 amount〔sum〕 of money ¶ 돈머리가 들어맞는다 A sum is correct. // 돈머리가 부족되다 be short (a certain sum) // 돈머리를 맞추다 round the sum off
돈목 敦睦 cordiality ; affability ; friendly terms **—하다** (be) cordial ; affable ; be on good terms 《with》
돈바르다 (be) narrow-minded ; fussy ; be hard to please
돈백 —百 hundreds of coins
***돈벌이** money-making **—하다** make〔earn〕 money ¶ 이 장사는 돈벌이가 안 된다 We can't make money out of this business. /There is no money in this business. // 그는 돈벌이의 천재야 He is a genius for money-making. // 돈벌이가 어떻습니까 How's the money ?
돈벼락 sudden wealth ¶ 돈벼락을 맞다 strike it rich
돈복 —福 luck with money
돈사 豚舍 a pigsty ; a pigpen
돈사 頓死 a sudden〔an abrupt〕 death **—하다** die suddenly ; die a sudden death ; drop〔fall〕 dead
돈수 頓首 ① [편지에서] Yours very respectfully ; Yours sincerely **—하다** close one's letter
② [절] a bow of the head ; a kotow **—하다** bow one's head ; ko(w)tow
돈수 頓數 tonnage ; tons ; burden ¶ 이 배의 돈수는 3천돈이다 This steamer is 3,000 tons burden. /This ship displaces 3,000 tons.
— 증서 〖조선〗 a tonnage certificate **등부(登簿) —** registered tonnage **만재배수(滿載排水) —** load displacement **재화 중량(載貨重量) —** deadweight capacity〔tonnage〕 **적재 —** capacity tonnage **중량 —** dead weight tonnage **총—** gross tonnage ; the total tonnage 《of a company's fleet》 (회사가 소유한 배 전체의)
돈아 豚兒 my son
돈오 頓悟 〖불교〗 sudden enlightenment **—하다** be suddenly enlightened
돈육 豚肉 pork
돈 융통 —融通 financing ¶ 돈 융통을 하다 finance ; raise funds
돈절 頓絶 a sudden interruption〔discontinuation, cease〕 ; an abrupt stop **—하다** interrupt〔discontinue〕 suddenly ; stop abruptly
돈점박이 —點— a brindled〔mottled〕 horse〔leopard〕 ; a dapple ; a dapple grey horse
돈좌 頓挫 a check ; a hitch ; a standstill ; a deadlock ; a setback **—하다** be checked ; receive〔sustain, meet with〕 a check
돈주다 point out one of the coins 《in chuck-farthing》
⁑**돈주머니** a purse ; a moneybag ; a pocket book ¶ 돈주머니를 털어서 주다 give all the money one has // 한집안의 돈주머니를 쥐고 있다 hold the purse strings of a family ; manage the money matters〔affairs〕 of a family // 돈주머니를 졸라 매다 tighten the purse strings
돈줄 financial resources ; [전주] a rich patron ; a capitalist ; a financial backer〔supporter〕 ¶ 돈줄을 잡다〔잃다〕 find〔lose〕 a supplier of funds〔a financial supporter〕
돈지 頓智 wit ; ready〔quick〕 wit ¶ 돈지가 있는 witty ; ready-witted // 돈지가 있는 사나이 a man of ready wit
돈지갑 —紙匣 a coin purse ; a pocketbook
돈지랄하다 spend money in a crazy way
돈질하다 conduct gambling on a cash basis ; gamble in cash
돈천 —千 [천만원] a tidy sum of ten millions
돈치기 chuck-〔pitch-〕farthing **—하다** play chuck-〔pitch-〕farthing
돈키호테 Don Quixote ¶ 돈키호테식의 quixotic
돈팔이 the "money-is-almighty" principle ; mammonism
돈표 —票 [환] money order ; exchange ; 〖상업〗 transfer ; a check (수표) ; a bill (어음)
돈푼 a small sum of money ; a snug hoard of money ; a small fortune ¶ 돈푼이나 모으다 save a pretty penny ; lay by little fortune〔a sizable sum of money〕
돈하다 ① [도지다] (be) sturdy ; be very hard and strong ② [무겁다] (be) too〔overly, excessively〕 heavy

돈후 敦厚 sincerity
돋구다 make (a degree or standard) higher ¶ 안경의 도수를 돋구다 make one's eyeglasses stronger
*__돋다__[1] ① [해·달이] rise ; come up ¶ 해가 돋는다 The sun is coming up. /The sun rises above the horizon.
② [싹 따위가] grow ; sprout ; come up ; bud ¶ 날개가 돋다 wings grow // 움이 돋다 it buds ; buds come〔are〕 out // 뽕잎이 파릇파릇 돋기 시작했다 The mulberry trees have put forth their young green leaves.
③ [종기 따위가] break out ; erupt ; come out ; form ¶ 발에 종기가 돋다 get a boil on one's foot ; a boil forms on one's foot // 온몸에 두드러기가 돋았다 He has a rash all over the body. /The eruption broke out all over him.
돋다[2] raise ⇨ 돋우다
돋보기 [안경] glasses ; spectacles ; [노인경] glasses for the aged
돋보다 see in a favorable light ⇨ 도두보다
*__돋보이다__ look better (than actually is) ¶ 검은색 드레스를 입으니까 너의 흰 피부가 돋보이는구나 The black dress brings out the fairness of your complexion. ⇨ 도두보이다
돋우다 ① [높이다] make higher ; raise ; exalt 《one's tone of voice》 ¶ 심지를 돋우다 turn up the wick // 땅을 돋우다 raise the ground ; bank the road
② [감정 따위를] excite ; stimulate ; stir ; incite ; provoke ; aggravate ¶ 부아를 돋우다 provoke 《a person》 to anger ; offend 《a person》 ; aggravate 《a person's》 anger // 호기심을 돋우다 excite〔incite, evoke〕 《a person's》 curiosity // 식욕을 돋우다 stimulate 《a person's》 appetite // 이것은 당신의 식욕을 돋우어 줄 것입니다 This will whet your appetite. / This will pep up your appetite.
③ [용기·힘을] raise ; lift ; elevate ; heighten ; encourage ; fan ; inflame ¶ 기운을 돋우다 raise〔lift〕 《a person's》 spirit ; cheer up // 용기를 돋우다 encourage ; embolden ; give 《a person》 courage ; put 《a person》 on his mettle
돋움 a support ; an underlay ; an underlayer ; a stand
돋을볕 the morning sunshine
†**돋을새김** relief ; relievo ; embossed carving
돋치다 ① [내밀다] put forth〔out, up〕 ; pop out〔forth〕 ; stick out ; [새로 생기다] grow 《out》 ; spring out ¶ 날개가 돋치다 wings sprout ; fly away (비유적)
② [값이 오르다] rise〔jump〕 《in price》 ; go〔run〕 up
†**돌**[1] a stone ; a pebble ; a small rock (작은 돌) 《미》 ; [석재] stone ¶ 돌집 a stone building // 라이터돌 a flint for the lighter // 돌같이 생긴 stony ; lithic // 돌이 많다 be stony ; be full of stone // 돌을 새기다 carve〔cut〕 in stone // 돌을 잘라내다 quarry stone // 길에 돌을 깔다 pave 《the road》 with stone // 돌을 던지다 throw a stone at 《a dog》 ; pelt 《a person》 with stones ; pelt at 《a person》 // 돌을 갈다 dress stone
―둑 a bank of stone **―문** a stone gate
돌[2] ① an anniversary ; [첫돌] the first anniversary ¶ 다섯돌 the fifth anniversary 《of》 // 오늘이 동생의 첫돌이다 Today is the first anniversary of my brother. // 결혼한지 꼭 한돌이다 It is just full one year since we were married. ② one full year ; a full day ; [출생의] the first anniversary of one's birth ¶ 고향을 떠나온 지 한 돌이 된다 It is a full year since I left home.
돌가루 crushed rock
돌감 a wild persimmon
― 나무 a wild persimmon tree
돌개바람 a whirlwind ; an eddy wind ; a cyclone ; a tornado ; a twister
†**돌격 突擊** a charge ; a dash ; a rush ; an assault **―하다** charge (at, on) ; dash〔rush〕 at ; make an assault upon ¶ 돌격로를 열다 make a breach for 《the advancing infantry》 // 적의 진지에 돌격하다 rush at〔charge〕 the enemy's position
―대 a storming party ; a shock troop〔battalion〕 **―전** a charge ; an assault ; an onslaught ; a raid
돌결 the grain of a stone ¶ 돌결이 곱다〔거칠다〕 The stone has a fine〔coarse〕 grain.
돌계단 ―階段 [층계] a stone step (한 단) ; a flight of stone steps (전부) ¶ 돌계단을 오르다〔내리다〕 climb〔go down〕 a flight of stone steps
돌계집 a barren〔sterile, childless〕 woman
돌고기 〖물고기〗 Pungtungia herzi (학명)
돌고드름 a stalactite
*__돌고래__[1] a dolphin ; a porpoise ; a sea hog
돌고래[2] [방고래] all-stone flues (of a Korean hypocaust)
돌곰기다 《a tumor》 fester within
돌공이 a stone pestle
돌관 突貫 a charge ; a rush ; a bayonet thrust **―하다** charge 《on the enemy》 ; rush〔dash〕 《at the enemy》
― 공사 rush〔speedy construction, lightening〕 work ¶ 돌관 공사를 하다 rush〔push〕 the construction work
†**돌기 突起** a projection ; a protrusion ; a rising ; protuberance ; [동·식물의] a process ; 〖해부〗 an appendix **―하다** rise ; project ; protrude
돌기둥 a stone pillar
돌기와 a slate ; slabs of stone for roofing ¶ 돌기와 집 a slate-roofed house
돌김 〖식물〗 laver〔sloke〕 grown on the underwater rock
돌꼇 a thread winding reel shaped like an

anemometer
돌꼈잠 a disturbed sleep
돌나물 〖식물〗 a sedum ; a stonecrop ; Sedum sarmentosum (학명)
— 김치 sedum pickles
돌날 one's first birthday
돌능금 a wild apple ; a crab apple
†**돌다** ① [회전하다] go round ; turn ; spin ; gyrate ; revolve ; rotate ¶ 뺑뺑 돌다 turn round and round // 팽이가 돌다 a top spins // 오른쪽으로 돌다 turn to the right // 무대가 돌다 the stage revolves // 바퀴가 돌다 a wheel turns // 지구가 태양을 돌고 있다 The earth revolves〔goes〕 round the sun.
② [순회하다] go round ; go〔make〕 one's round ; make a tour 《of》 ¶ 선거 유세를 돌다 take〔go on〕 the stump ; make a stumping tour // 시골을 돌다 make a tour of the provinces ; tour the provinces // 경관이 순찰을 돌다 a policeman makes round of his assigned block
③ [우회하다] go〔come〕 around ; go by roundabout route ; make a detour ¶ 뒷문으로 돌아오다 come round to the back door // 희망봉을 돌아서 오다 round〔get round〕 the Cape of Good Hope // 캐나다로 돌아서 귀국하다 go〔come〕 home via〔by way of〕 Canada
④ [순환·유통하다] circulate ; run ; be current ; [소문이] get abroad ; spread ¶ 소문이 돌다 rumors spread〔are circulated〕 // 새 돈이 지난 6월 1일부터 돌았다 The new currency has been circulated since June 1. // 피는 혈관을 통하여 온몸을 돈다 The blood circulates in the body through the veins.
⑤ [술·약 따위의 효과] take effect ¶ 독기운이 전신에 돌았다 The poison has passed into one's system.
⑥ [현기가 나다] be〔feel〕 dizzy ; be〔feel, turn〕 giddy ; 《one's head》 spin
⑦ [소생] come round ; be restored ¶ 정신이 돌다 come to ; recover one's senses // 맥이 돌다 one's pulse regains its beat
⑧ [정신] go out of one's head ; go〔run〕 mad〔crazy〕 ¶ 좀 돌았다 He is batty〔crazy〕.
⑨ [전염병이] prevail ; be prevalent ; widespread ¶ 유행성 감기가 돌고 있다 Influenza is making the round.
돌다리[1] [조그만 다리] a low flattish bridge built over a brook
돌다리[2] a stone bridge
돌다리도 두들겨 보고 건너라 (속담) Look before you leap.
돌담 a stone wall
돌담불 a pile of stones ; a rock pile
돌대 the axis of rotation ; a pivot
돌대가리 a stupid person ; a stubborn person
돌덩이 a piece of stone ; a stone
돌도끼 a stone ax(e)
돌돌, 똘똘 rolling up ; curling up ; with a twirl ¶ 종이를 똘똘 말다 roll up a piece of paper // 실이 돌돌 풀린다 A thread is unwound with a twirl.
돌돌하다, 똘똘하다 [똑똑하다] (be) bright ; smart ; very clever ¶ 똘똘한 사내아이 a bright boy
돌떡 rice cake made for one's first birthday
돌띠 a coat belt that goes around a child's waist
돌라가다 pilfer ; filch ; pick ; sneak ; steal ¶ 볏단을 돌라가다 sneak a sheaf of rice // 우산을 돌라가다 filch an umbrella
돌라놓다 ① [둘러놓다] put 《things》 in a circle ② [돌려놓다] set 《a thing》 aside ; put 《a thing》 aside
돌라대다 ① [변통하다] swing a loan ② make a ready remark ⇨ 둘러대다
돌라막다 fence in ; put a fence around ⇨ 둘러막다
돌라맞추다 fix 《a thing》 as a substitute ; make 《a thing》 a substitute ; substitute ; use 《a thing for》 ; turn 《a thing into》 ¶ 책상을 식탁으로 돌라맞추다 turn a desk into a dinner table
돌라매다 ① [새끼를] tie 《a thing》 around ¶ 허리에 새끼를 돌라매다 tie a rope around one's waist ② [이자를] convert interest into principal
돌라방치다 replace ; substitute
돌라버리다 vomit on purpose ; bring oneself to vomit up
돌라붙다 change sides ⇨ 둘러붙다
돌라서다 stand in a circle
돌라싸다 ⇨ 둘러싸다
돌라앉다 sit round ⇨ 둘러앉다
돌라주다 hand round ; distribute ; share ; serve round ; deal out〔round〕 ¶ 선물을 돌라주다 deal out〔round〕 gifts
돌라치다 replace ⇨ 돌라방치다
돌려내다 ① [부당 취득] obtain 《a thing》 by dishonest trick ; defraud 《a person of a thing》 ; swindle 《money out of a person》 ¶ 돈을 돌려내다 obtain money by false pretenses ; swindle money 《out of a person》
② [사람을] leave 《a person》 in the cold ; leave out ; cast out ; ostracize 《a person from a group》
돌려놓다 ① [방향을] turn 《around》 ; change direction ; put the other way round ¶ 시계를 돌려놓다 turn the hands of a clock // 책상을 돌려놓다 put a table the other way round
② [사람을] leave out
†**돌려보내다** return ; give back ; [반송] send back〔away〕 ¶ 그것을 당신에게 돌려보내겠다 I will return it〔give it back〕 to you.
돌려보다 have a look 《at a thing》 by turns ; passing 《a thing》 around ¶ 책을 돌려보다 pass a book around reading it

in turns
돌려쓰다 borrow《money, things》
†**돌려주다** ① return ; give back ; send back ¶ 책을 돌려주다 return a book
② [변통] advance ; lend ; let out ; accommodate《a person》with《a loan》¶ 5만원을 돌려주다 accommodate《a person》with 50,000 *won* ; lend〔advance〕《a person》50,000 *won*
†**돌리다**[1] ① [병 따위를] improve ; turn the corner ; take a turn for the better ; pass the crisis ; be over the hump ¶ 병이 돌리다 one's illness improves // 숨을 돌리다 get out of difficult situation ; be over the hump
② [변통] lend ; advance
③ [사람을] leave out in the cold ; be left over (in the cold) ; be ostracized ⇨ 돌려내다 ¶ 모든 사람한테 돌리다 be hated〔shunned〕by everybody
④ [속다] be gotten around《by fair words》; be deceived
†**돌리다**[2] ① [회전] turn ; revolve ; roll ; spin ¶ 핸들을 돌리다 turn a handle // 팽이를 돌리다 spin a top
② [보내다·넘기다] pass (round) ; hand round ; forward《to》; send round《to》; transfer《to》¶ 술잔을 죽 돌리다 pass a glass round // 차를 사무실로 돌리다 send a car round to the office // 모자를 돌리다 pass round the hat《to》// 그를 판매부로 돌렸다 He was transferred to the sales department.
③ [방향을] turn ; change ; divert ; convert ; avert〔turn away〕《from》¶ 방향을 돌리다 change one's course // 화제를 돌리다 change the subject // 주의를 딴 데로 돌리다 turn one's attention《from one thing to another》// 발꿈치를 돌리다 turn one's heels // 눈을 돌리다 avert〔turn away〕one's eyes《from》// 한숨돌리다 take breath ; pause for breath ; take a rest ; [위급을 면하다] turn the corner ; avert〔turn away〕from《dangers》// 당신이 교묘하게 말꼬리를 돌리지만 않는다면 나도 솔직히 털어 놓겠소 If you cut that fancy footwork out, I'll let it all hang out, too.
④ [감정을] change《one's mind》; relent《toward a person》; calm down ¶ 생각을 돌리다 change one's mind // 노여움을 돌리다 calm down one's anger // 돌려서 생각하다 think on reflection
⑤ [돈을 빌리다] borrow ; have《money》on loan ; [빌려 주다] let out ¶ 돈 만원을 친구에게서 돌렸다 I obtained an accommodation of 10,000 *won* from one of my friends.
⑥ [원인·책임을] attribute to ; ascribe to ; [죄 따위를] impute《the evil motive》to ; set〔put〕down to ¶ 실패를 운으로 돌리다 ascribe〔attribute〕the failure to bad luck // 의사는 그의 병을 과음의 탓으로 돌렸다 Doctors attributed the cause of his illness to his overdrinking.
돌리다[3] [따돌리다] leave out (in the cold) ; keep《a person》away ; shun ; ostracize ; blackball ; make an outcast of ; [경원] keep《a person》at respectful distance ; give《a person》a wide berth ¶ 그는 모든 사람에게 돌리고 있다 He is politely shunned by everybody.
돌리다[4] [속다] be gotten around (with fair words) ; be talked out of〔into〕; be deceived〔duped, taken in〕
돌림 ① [교대] turn ; rotation ¶ 돌림으로 by turns ; by〔in〕rotation ; alternately ② [돌림병] an epidemic
돌림감기 —感氣 influenza ; flu《속》¶ 돌림감기에 걸리다 be seized with influenza ; have an attack of influenza
돌림병 —病 a contagious〔an infectious, a catching〕disease ; an epidemic
돌림자 —字 a part of a name which is common to the same generation of a family
돌림쟁이 a person left out in the cold ; an outcast
돌림턱 a treat given by turns
돌림통 the period of prevalence of an epidemic ; [병] an epidemic ¶ 돌림통에 어린애를 잃다 lose a child during a siege of epidemic
돌림 편지 —片紙 a circular letter
돌매 a (stone) hand mill ; a quern
돌멘 [고인돌] a dolmen
돌멩이 a stone ; a piece of stone
돌멩이질 stone-throwing, stone-slinging **—하다** throw a stone at《a dog》; pelt《a person》with stones ; pelt at《a person》
돌무더기 a pile〔heap, mound〕of stones
돌무덤 a stone grave
돌묵상어 〖물고기〗 a bone shark ; a basking shark
돌물레 a rope-making wheel (stabilized with a stone weight)
돌미나리 〖식물〗 wild parsley
돌미륵 —彌勒 a stone image of Buddha
돌반지기 low-grade rice full of sand〔grits〕; rice mixed with sand
돌발 突發 outbreak ; (out)burst **—하다** occur ; happen ; break out ¶ 돌발적으로 suddenly ; unexpectedly
— 사건〔사고〕 an unforeseen〔unexpected〕accident〔incident〕; a sudden happening
돌방 —房 a room made of〔carved out of〕stone
돌배, 똘배 〖식물〗 a wild pear
돌벽 —壁 a stone wall
*__돌변__ 突變 a sudden change〔turn〕; an accident **—하다** change suddenly ; undergo a sudden change ¶ 돌변에 대비하다 prepare for emergencies // 병세가 돌변하다 one's condition takes a sudden turn for the worse

†**돌보다** take care of ; care for ; look after ; attend to ¶ 일을 돌보다 take care of one's work ; attend to one's work // 어린애를 돌보다 take care of〔watch〕 a child // 환자를 돌보다 look after〔tend to〕 a patient

돌부리 a jag of rock

돌부리를 차면 발부리만 아프다 속담 Don't kick against the pricks.

돌부처 ① [석상(石像)] a stone Buddhist image ② [감정이 없는 사람] a creature〔man〕 with a stony heart ; a man deaf to emotional appeals ; [고집이 센 사람] a stubborn person

돌비 —碑 a tombstone ; a gravestone ; a stone slab ; a (stone) monument

돌비늘 〖광물〗 mica ; isinglass

돌비알 a cliff ; a rockwall

돌사닥다리 a stony mountain path

돌사막 —砂漠 〖지리〗 a stony desert

돌산 —山 a stone mountain

돌삼 a wild hemp

돌상 —床 a table laid in celebration of a baby's first birthday

돌샘 a spring gushing out of stony ground ; a rock spring

돌소금 rock salt

돌솜 〖광물〗 asbestos

— **타일** an asbestos tile

돌순 —筍 〖지질〗 a stalagmite

돌싸움 a mock fight with stone missiles ¶ 돌싸움을 하다 play at war with stone missiles

*__돌아가다__ ① [다시 가다] go back ; return ; find one's way back ; turn back ¶ 집으로 돌아가다 return home // 온 길을 돌아가다 return one's step ; turn back // 네 자리로 돌아가라 Go back to your seat.

② [원상으로] return 《to》 ; be restored to ; resume ¶ 정상 상태로 돌아가다 return to normalcy

③ [우회하다] go round ; make a detour ; take a roundabout way ; [경유하다] go to 《a place》 via ¶ 그를 만나지 않기 위해서 돌아가다 take a roundabout way〔circuitous route〕 to avoid him // 캐나다를 돌아 미국으로 가다 go to America via Canada

④ [되어가다] turn 《out》 ; develop ¶ 일이 돌아가는 꼴을 주시하다 watch the development of the event ; wait for the turn of the events // 일이 나쁘게〔좋게〕 돌아가다 take a turn for the worse〔better〕 // 사태가 엉뚱하게 돌아가고 있다 The situation takes a turn for an unexpected result. // 이 일이 돌아가게 하기 위해서는 많은 일손이 필요하다 We need a lot of help to get this job going.

⑤ [···의 결과가 되다] come to ; turn out ; result in ; be reduced to ; end 《in》 ¶ 실패로 돌아가다 turn out (to be) a failure ; result in failure ; prove (to be) a failure // 수포로 돌아가다 come to naught〔nothing〕 ; end in smoke

⑥ [귀속하다] fall into one's hand ; be ascribed〔attributed〕 to ¶ 승리의 영광은 한국팀으로 돌아갔다 The laurel of victory fell into the hand of the Korean team. // 실패의 책임이 그에게로 돌아갔다 The failure was ascribed to his fault.

⑦ [죽다] die ; pass away ; depart from this life ¶ 돌아가신 김 선생 the late Mr. *Kim* // 김 선생이 어제 심장병으로 돌아가셨다 Mr. *Kim* died of a heart attack yesterday. // 아버님이 돌아가셨다니 참 안됐습니다 I'm so sorry your father has passed away.

⑧ [작용하다] work ; operate ; come into play ¶ 잘 돌아가지 않다 fail to operate〔work〕 properly

⑨ [차례로 하다] do 《a thing》 by turns ; take turns ¶ 돌아가며 in (regular, due) order ; in turn ; by turns ; by〔in〕 rotation

⑩ [분배되다] go (a)round ¶ 음식은 모두에게 돌아갈 만큼 있다 There is enough food to go (a)round.

돌아내리다 ① [일부러 사양하다] pretend hesitation〔reluctance〕 ② [연이] 《a kite》 hesitate in its circling

돌아눕다 turn (over) on one's side ; roll ¶ 잠결에 돌아눕다 turn over〔roll〕 in bed ; turn in bed〔one's sleep〕 ; turn on one's side in sleeping // 왼쪽으로 돌아누우세요 Lie on your left side.

†**돌아다니다** ① [쏘다니다] wander〔roam〕 about ; walk〔go〕 about ; hang about ; fool about ; knock about 《구》 ; [순회] make a round ; go one's round ; patrol (순찰) ; [여행] (make a) tour ; travel about ¶ 거리를 이리저리 돌아다니다 wander about in the streets ; knock about〔gad about〕 here and there in the streets // 학교를 시찰하러 돌아다니다 make a round of schools for inspection // 호남지방을 돌아다니다 make the tour of *Honam* district // 단골 손님 집들을 돌아다니다 go the rounds of one's customers

② [병이] prevail ; be prevalent ; be raging ¶ 유행성 감기가 돌아다닌다 Influenza is prevalent. /A bad cold is going around.

③ [소문 따위가] 《the rumor》 be abroad 〔current, in circulation〕 《about》 ¶ 뜬소문이 돌아다니다 an idle rumor gets abroad

돌아들다 return ; come back ; find one's way back 《to》 ¶ 새들이 제집으로 돌아들다 birds fly back to their nests

*__돌아보다__ ① [뒤를] look back 《at》 ; turn one's head ; look over one's shoulder ; turn round ; look back〔round〕 ¶ 잠깐 돌아보다 cast a hasty glance behind ; look back for a second // 부르니까 그는 돌아봤다 He turned when I called. // 그녀는 상당한 미인이어서 길을 가면 사람들이 누구나 돌아보는 정도다 She is such a beauty that everybody turns to look at her when she

passes.
② [회상] look back upon 《the past》; review; retrospect; recollect; reflect upon ¶ 학창 시대를 돌아보다 look back upon one's school days // 1950년을 돌아보다 review 1950
③ [고려] have regard to; take notice of; think of; take 《a matter》 into consideration〔account〕; pay attention to; give heed to ¶ 전후를 돌아보지 않고 without reflecting on the circumstances // 돌아보지 않는다 disregard; ignore; neglect; pay no attention to; leave 《a thing》 out of consideration; take no account〔notice, thought, heed〕 of // 외양 따위는 돌아보지도 않는다 He has no regard to appearance.
④ [살피며 돌다] make a round; go one's round; patrol ¶ 공장을 돌아보다 visit〔go〕 round a factory

*돌아서다 ① [뒤로] turn on one's heels; turn right round ¶ 돌아서 있다 stand with one's back toward 《another》
② [등지다] turn one's back on; turn against; become estranged 《from》; quarrel〔fall out, disagree〕 《with》 ¶ 그의 최근의 행동으로 말미암아 많은 친구들이 그로부터 돌아서고 말았다 His recent conduct has estranged many of his friends.
③ [병이] improve; take a turn for the better; get better ¶ 병세가 많이 돌아섰다 The patient is much better. /His illness has improved quite a bit.

돌아앉다 sit the other way round

*돌아오다 ① [귀환] return; come〔get, be〕 back (home) ¶ 돌아오지 않는 청춘 one's irrevocable youth // 부자가 돼서 고향에 돌아오다 return to one's native place as a rich man // 곧 돌아오겠소 I shan't be long. // 길을 몰라서 돌아오지 못했다 I could not find my way back. // 그는 집에 돌아와 있다 He is home now. // 떠나간 후 다시는 돌아오지 않았다 He left never to return. // 한번 지나간 날은 다시 돌아오지 않는다 Yesterday never comes again. // 잃어버린 물건이 다시 돌아왔다 The lost article was restored to its owner.
② [차례가] come around ¶ 드디어 그의 순번이 돌아왔다 At last his turn came around.
③ [곧장 오지 않고] go around 《to》 ¶ 유럽으로 돌아오다 come home via Europe // 옆문으로 돌아와 주시오 Step around to the side door.
④ [결과가] fall on; be brought ¶ 책임이 돌아오다 a responsibility falls on one's shoulders // 욕이 돌아오다 disgrace is brought upon 《him》
⑤ [몫 따위가] fall 《to》; be allotted 〔apportioned〕 ¶ 돌아온 몫 one's lot 〔portion, allotment, quota〕
⑥ [회복] return 《to》; revert 《to》; recover ¶ 제정신이 돌아오다 come 〔return〕 to (oneself)

돌알 ① [안경알] a crystal lens ② [숙란] a hard-boiled egg

*돌연 突然 suddenly; abruptly; all of a sudden; unexpectedly; without notice; without warning —하다 (be) sudden; unexpected; unlooked-for ¶ 돌연 도착하다 arrive unexpectedly // 돌연 덤비다 spring at 《a person》 without any warning // 돌연 사직하다 resign without notice // 돌연 해고하다 dismiss 《a person》 without notice

돌연 변이 突然變異 〖생물〗 (a) mutation —하다 mutate; sport ¶ 돌연 변이에 의한 mutant // 돌연 변이를 일으키는 mutagenic
—설 the theory of mutation —종 a mutant species —체 a mutant; a sport —체 유전자 a mutant gene — 편향 mutation pressure 전진 — forward mutation 전체 — systemic mutation

돌옷 rock moss

돌우물 a stone well; a stone-built well

돌이키다 ① [고개나 몸을] turn around; turn the head; look over one's shoulder ¶ 고개를 돌이키다 turn round; turn one's head
② [마음을] change 《one's mind》 (자기의 마음) ¶ 돌이켜 생각건대 on second thought; on reflection // 사람의 마음을 돌이키다 make 《a person》 change his mind // 돌이켜 생각하고 안하기로 했다 On second thought, I have made up my mind not to do it.
③ [원상 회복하다] get back; regain; recover; retrieve; restore ¶ 돌이킬 수 없는 irrevocable; irreparable // 저지른 일은 돌이킬 수 없다 What is done cannot be undone. /What is done is done.

돌입 突入 inrush —하다 dash〔rush〕 in〔into〕; charge into ¶ 적진에 돌입하다 dash〔charge〕 into the enemy's position // 자동차가 가게에 돌입했다 The automobile dashed into the shop.

돌자갈 a gravelstone ⇨ 조약돌

돌잔치 the celebration of a baby's first birthday; the birthday party for one's one-year-old baby

돌잡이 ① [돌맞이 아기의 선택] a baby's selection of his preference from among his first birthday presents ② [돌맞이한 아이] a one-year old baby

돌잡히다 let the baby celebrate his first birthday by choosing one thing from the table where the food and gifts are spread

돌장이 [석수] a mason; a stonemason; a stonecutter

돌쟁이 [돌이 된 아이] a one-year-old baby

돌절구 a stone mortar

돌제 突堤 a breakwater; a jetty

돌중방 —中枋 a stone sill at the entrance to an alley

†돌진 突進 a rush; an onrush; a dash; a charge —하다 rush; make a dash; charge in 《upon》 ¶ 문을 향해서 돌진하다 rush for

the door // 적을 향해서 돌진하다 charge in upon the enemy ; charge〔rush at〕 the enemy ; make a dash at the enemy
돌질 ⇨ 돌멩이질
돌집 a stone house〔building〕
돌짬 a crevice between rocks
돌쩌귀 a hinge
***돌출 突出** projection ; protrusion ; prominence **—하다** project ; protrude ; jut out ; pop out ¶ 돌출한 projected ; projecting ; prominent // 돌출한 바위 뒤에 숨어서 폭풍우를 피했다 A protrusion of rock gave us shelter from the storm.
—물 a projection **—부** a projecting part ; a protrusion ; a salient (part) ; 〖군사〗 a salience ; a bulge ; [전선의] a perimeter ; 〖지리〗 [산·바위 따위의] a spur ; 〖동물·식물·해부〗 a ramus 《*pl.* -mi》 **—점** a projecting point ; a jut
돌층계 —層階 (a flight of) stone steps ; a stone stairway ; [한 계단] a stone step ¶ 돌층계를 올라가다〔내려가다〕 go up〔down〕 the stone steps
돌탑 —塔 a stone tower ; a pagoda
돌파 突破 —하다 [깨뜨림] break through ; smash through ; [초과] pass ; top 《1,000 tons》 ; [극복] surmount 《a difficulty》 ; overcome ; exceed ; rise above 《a level》 ¶ 난관을 돌파하다 overcome〔surmount〕 the difficulty // 8백원대를 돌파하다 pass the 800 *won* mark // 입학 시험을 돌파하다 pass an entrance examination // 적의 방어선을 돌파하다 break through the enemy's line
— 작전 〖군사〗 breakthrough operations ; a breakthrough **중앙 —** a frontal breakthrough **포위 —** 〖군사〗 a breakout
돌파구 突破口 a breach ; a break through ¶ 돌파구를 만들다 breach 《a barrier》 ; break through 《a barricade》
돌팔매 a throwing stone **—하다** throw stones
—질 stone throwing
돌팔이 an itinerant trader〔fortuneteller, craftsman〕
— 선생 an unqualified〔incompetent〕 teacher **— 의원** a quack (doctor) ; a (medical) charlatan ; an ignorant practitioner
돌팥 a wild red bean
***돌풍 突風** a (sudden) gust (of wind) ; a strong blast
돌피 wild millet ; Panicum crus (학명)
돌함 —函 a stone box ; a box made of stone
돌확 a stone mortar
돔 〖건축〗 a dome ¶ 철근 돔 an iron dome // 철근 돔 경기장 a steel-roofed stadium〔diamond, bowl, amphitheater〕
돔바르다 ① [인색한] (be) stingy ; niggardly ; close-〔tight-〕fisted ; grasping ② [무정한] (be) heartless ; hard-〔cold-〕 hearted ; unfeeling ; cruel
돔발상어 〖물고기〗 a dogfish ; Squalus mitsukurii (학명)
†**돕다** ① [조력하다] help ; aid ; give〔lend〕 a helping hand ; assist ; stand by ; second

> 참고 **help** 남에게 필요한 것을 주어 조력한다는 뜻의 일반어 **assist** 타인의 곁에 있어 주로 그 사람의 일에 협력하다 **aid** 개인을 직접적으로 돕는다기보다는 단체·주의 따위를 찬조하다

¶ 일을 돕다 help 《a person》 in his work // 타는 것을〔내리는 것을〕 돕다 help 《a person》 into〔out of〕 《a carriage》 ; help 《a person》 on〔off〕 《a horse》 // 하늘은 스스로 돕는 자를 돕는다 Heaven helps those who help themselves. // 하늘은 용기 있는 자를 돕는다 Heaven favors the brave. // 거기 그렇게만 서 있지 말고 좀 도와줘 Don't just stand there. Lend me a hand.
② [구제하다] relieve ; give relief to ; give 《a person》 a helping ; help 《a person》 out of difficulties ¶ 가난한 사람을 돕다 relieve〔extend a helping hand to〕 the poor ; succor the needy // 궁지에 빠진 자를 돕다 draw 《a person》 out of the mire
③ [조장하다] promote ; contribute to ; conduce to ; be conducive to ¶ 소화를 돕다 aid〔promote〕 digestion // 성공을 돕다 contribute to success // 휴식은 건강을 돕는다 Rest conduces to health. // 이 운동은 아동의 발육을 크게 돕는다 This sport will greatly promote〔be very conducive to〕 the physical development of children.
돗바늘 a matting needle
돗자리 a mat ; matting 《총칭》 ¶ 돗자리를 깔다 spread a mat
꽃— a figured mat
돗총이 a legendary dark-blue horse
돗틀 a mat frame
동[1] ① [조리] reason ; logic ; [일관성] a chain of reasoning ; a thread of connection ¶ 동이 닿는 요구 a reasonable demand // 동이 닿지 않다 [조리가] be illogical ; be unjustifiable ; be unreasonable ; [일관성] be incoherent ; be inconsistent ; be irrelevant // 동이 닿지 않는 말을 하다 make disjoined remarks ; talk incoherently
② [한동안] a period ; an interval ¶ 밤이 늦어 전차가 동뜨다 The hour is late and the streetcars are few and far between.
③ [저고리의] a cuff
④ [줄기] a stalk ¶ 상추동 a lettuce stalk
끝— the cuff of a sleeve
동이 닿다 관용 [조리가] be reasonable ; be logical ; be justifiable ; [일관성] be coherent ; be consistent ; be relevant
동이 뜨다 관용 have an interval between ; have a space between
동[2] [묶음] a bundle〔bunch, load〕 ¶ 붓 한 동 a bundle of writing brushes〔10 writing brushes〕 // 감 한 동 a load of persimmons ; 1,000 persimmons
동 東 east ¶ 동으로 가다 go east〔eastward〕

동이 트다 관용 day breaks
동 同 the same ; the said (상기의) ; corresponding (부합하는) ¶ 작년 동일 the corresponding〔same〕 date of last year
— 번지 the same house〔street〕 number — 회사 the same company ; (the) said corporation
동 洞 a *dong* 《an administrative unit》 ; a street ; a block ; a village
*동 銅 copper
—관 a copper tube〔pipe〕 —광(鑛) copper ore —선 copper wire — 세공 copper work — 세공인 a coppersmith —화(貨) a copper (coin)
동 棟 ¶ 2동 two houses〔buildings〕 // B아파트 6동 118호 Rm. 118, B Apt. No. 6
동 胴 [몸] the trunk of the body ; the body ; [검도복의] the body armor ; the plastron
동가 同價 the same price
동가리톱 a crosscut saw
동가식서가숙 東家食西家宿 vagabondism ; vagrancy —하다 lead a vagabond 〔wandering〕 life ¶ 동가식서가숙하는 사람 a wanderer ; a vagabond ; a tramp
동감 同感 [같은 의견] agreement (in opinion) ; concurrence ; [같은 감정] the same feeling ; sympathy —하다 [같은 감정] sympathize〔think〕 with ; feel the same way 《as》 ; share 《a person's》 feelings ; [같은 의견] agree〔concur〕 with ; be of the same opinion ; see eye to eye 《with a person over an issue》 ¶ 너와 동감이다 I agree with you. /You can say that again. /You said it. /You're telling me. /You don't say. /That makes two of us.
*동갑 同甲 the same age ; a person of the same age ¶ 우리는 동갑이다 We are of the same age.
동갓 〖식물〗 a kind of mustard
동강 a piece ; a part ¶ 칼이 두 동강 나다 a sword is broken into two pieces // 엿을 셋으로 동강치다 break a rice-candy bar into three pieces
— 치마 a short〔knee-length〕 skirt
동강동강 into pieces ; piece by piece ¶ 동강동강 자르다 cut 《a stick》 into pieces // 동강동강 부러지다 《a rice-candy bar》 be broken into pieces
동개 a quiver
—살 a large-feathered arrow for the cavalry bow —철 metal strip to reinforce the tenon joint of a gate —활 a cavalry bow
동갱 銅坑 a copper mine
*동거 同居 —하다 live together ; live under the same roof ; reside 《with》 ; share the same house
동거리 an iron piece covering the mouthpiece of a (tobacco) pipe
동거리 同距離 the same distance ; an equal distance
동거인 同居人 an inmate ; a lodger ; a paying guest ; a roomer 《미》 ; a roommate

⁑동격 同格 [같은 지위] the same rank 〔status, standing〕 ; an equal footing ; equality ; 〖문법〗 apposition ¶ 나와 동격이다 He ranks equally with me.
— 명사 a noun in apposition —어 an appositive
동결 凍結 freezing —하다 freeze ; be frozen
— 건조 lyophilization — 방지제 an antifreezing mixture — 수술 〖외과〗 cryosurgery —실 a freezing room — 자산 frozen assets —제(劑) a freezing mixture 임금 — 정책 a wage-freeze policy 자산 — freezing of assets〔credits〕
동경 銅鏡 a copper mirror
⁑동경 憧憬 yearning ; longing ; aspiration ; [숭배] adoration ; admiration —하다 long 《for》 ; yearn 《for》 ; hanker 《after》 ; aspire 《after》 ; adore ; worship ¶ 도시 생활을 동경하다 yearn for city life // 자유를 동경하다 have a longing for liberty // 영국 방문이 나의 오랜 동경이었다 To visit England has been my long-cherished desire.
동경 東經 the east longitude ¶ 동경 30도 15부 30 degrees 15 minutes of east longitude 《Long. 30° 15 E》
동경이 東京— a short-tailed dog
동계 冬季 the winter season〔term〕
— 방학〔휴가〕 the winter holidays〔vacation〕 — 올림픽 the winter Olympic games
동계 動悸 palpitation ; thumping ; throbbing ¶ 동계치다 palpitate ; throb ; beat ; thump
동계 同系 ¶ 동계의 akin ; agnate ; of the same stock
— 교배(交配) inbreeding — 회사 an affiliated concern
동고 동락 同苦同樂 —하다 share one's joys and sorrows 《with》 ; share the pleasures and pains of life 《with》
동고리 a round wicker suitcase〔trunk〕
동고비 〖새〗 a nuthatch
동곳 a top-knot pin
동곳(을) 빼다 관용 surrender ; capitulate
동공 瞳孔 the pupil ; the apple of the eye
—막(膜) the pupil(l)ary membrane — 축소 contraction of the pupil ; miosis 〔myosis〕 — 축소제 a miotic〔myotic〕 — 확대 dilatation of the pupil ; mydriasis
동공이체 同工異體 equal excellence in workmanship though different in style ¶ 동공이체이다 be practically the same ; there is little to choose between the two ; it is six of one and half-a-dozen of the other
동관 同官 a fellow officer〔official〕 ; a colleague ; a coworker
동광 銅鑛 copper ore ; crude copper ; [광산] a copper mine
동구 東歐 Eastern Europe
동구 洞口 the entrance to a village
동국 東國 an eastern country ; [우리 나라] Korea ; the Nation of the East
동국 同國 the same〔said〕 country

—인 a fellow countryman ; a man of one's own nation ; a compatriot
‡동굴 洞窟 a cave ; a cavern ; a grotto 《*pl.* ~(e)s》
— 벽화 a wall painting in a cave —어(魚) a cave fish — 탐험(探險) spelunking — 탐험가 a spelunker
동궁 東宮 [세자] the Crown Prince ; [세자궁] the Palace of the Crown Prince
— 전하 (His Highness) the Crown Prince —비 전하 (Her Highness) the Crown Princess
동권 同權 the same right ; equal rights ; isonomy (법률상의)
남녀 — equal rights for both sexes ; the equality of the (both) sexes (in law) 남녀 —주의 feminism 남녀 —주의자 a feminist
†동그라미 a circle (원) ; a zero (영) ; [돈의 은어] chink ; tin ; the needful ¶ 동그라미를 그리다 draw〔describe〕 a circle // 동그라미를 맞다 《the paper》 be marked〔rated〕 "Good"
—표 the circle symbol
동그라지다 fall over ; fall〔roll〕 head over heels ¶ 미끄러져 나가 동그라지다 slip and fall head over heels
동그랑쇠 ① [굴렁쇠] a hoop ② ⇨ 삼발이
*동그랗다, 똥그랗다 (be) round ; circular ; [구형] globular ; spherical ¶ 동그랗게 round ; in a circle // 동그란 눈 round eyes // 동그랗게 앉다 sit in a circle〔ring〕 // 동그랗게 자르다 cut 《a thing》 round
동그마니 ① [홀로] (round and) separate ; all alone ② [홀가분히] easily ; lightly
동그스름하다 (be) roundish ; somewhat round ¶ 동그스름한 무 a roundish radish
동근 同根 the same roots ¶ 동근이다 have the same roots
동글납대대하다 (be) round and flat
동글납작하다 (be) round and flat ¶ 동글납작한 얼굴 a round and flat face
동글다 (be) round ; circular ⇨ 둥글다
동글동글 ① [구르는 모양] rolling ; turning ¶ 동글동글 굴러 가다 roll over and over ② [여러 모양이] all round ¶ 감들이 동글동글하다 The persimmons are all round.
동글반반하다 (be) round and flat
동글붓 a dull-tipped brush ; a round-tipped brush
동급 同級 the same class〔grade〕 ; [동등] equality ; same rank ¶ 나는 그와 동급이다 I am in the same class with him. /He is my classmate.
—생 a classmate ; a classfellow
동급체 同級體 〖물리〗 an isolog(ue) ¶ 동급체의 isologous
동긋하다 (be) roundish ; rather round
동기 同期 the same period ; the corresponding period ; [동창] the same class ¶ 작년의 동기에 비해서 as compared with the corresponding period of last year
— 복임신(複妊娠) 〖생리〗 superfecundation —생 a classmate ; graduates in the same class (졸업생)
‡동기 同氣 siblings ; brothers and sisters ¶ 우리는 동기간〔형제 자매〕입니다 We are siblings〔brothers and sisters〕. /We are brothers〔sisters〕.
—간 sibling relationship
동기 銅器 a copper〔bronze〕 vessel〔utensil〕 ; copper ware
—류 copperware ; coppers — 시대 the Bronze Age — 제조자 a coppersmith
동기 動機 a motive ; an inducement ; incentive ¶ 불순한 동기 a mixed motive ; an ulterior motive // …이 동기가 되어 motivated〔prompted〕 《by》 // 행동의 동기는 좋았다 You have acted from worthy motives. // 그는 어떤 동기로 자살했을까 What moved〔motivated〕 him to commit suicide?
동기 冬期 the winter (terms) ; the winter season
— 강습 a winter school〔class〕 — 휴가 the winter holidays〔vacation〕
동기 童妓 a child *kisaeng* ; a young apprentice entertainer
동끊기다 ① [동안이] break (off) ; be interrupted ; become broken ; pause ¶ 소식이 동끊겼다 The correspondence dropped. ② [공급 따위가] be cut off from the supply 《of》 ¶ 학자금이 동끊기다 be stopped school expenses
동나다 run out ; be exhausted ; be out ; fail ; [상품이] sell out ; be sold out ; be out of stock ; [사람이 주어] be out of 《the article》 ¶ 기름이 동났다 The oil is used up. /We are out of oil. // 마침 그 물건은 동났습니다 That article is unluckily out of stock. // 휘발유가 동났다 We are getting out of gas〔gasoline〕. /The gas is running short.
동나무 firewood sold by the bundle
동남 東南 the southeast ¶ 동남의 southeast ; southeastern
—풍 the southeast〔southeasterly〕 wind ; a southeaster —향 facing southeast
동남 아시아 東南— Southeast Asia
— 경제 개발 각료 회의 the Ministerial Conference for Development of Southeast Asia — 연합 the Association of Southeast Asia 《ASA》 — 제국 연합 the Association of Southeast Asia Nations 《ASEAN》 — 조약 기구 the Southeast Asia Treaty Organization 《SEATO》
동내 洞內 inside a village ; the whole village ¶ 온 동내가 뒤집히다 the whole village is in an uproar
*동냥 [동냥질] begging ; mendicancy (탁발승의) ; [시물] alms —하다 beg one's bread ; beg food〔rice, money〕 ¶ 동냥(질)을 하다 go (about) begging ; live as a beggar
— 자루 a beggar's〔mendicant's〕 bag —중 a mendicant ; a begging priest
*동냥아치 a beggar

*동네 洞— a village ¶ 동네 사람 [한사람] a villager ; [총칭] village folk〔people〕; the inhabitants of a village ; the whole village // 이 동네에 이사 오신 것을 환영합니다 Nice to have you in the neighborhood.

동넷집 洞— a house in the village ; a neighbor

동녀 童女 a young girl ; a lass ; a maiden

동년 同年 [같은 해] the same year ; [나이] the same age

—배(輩) the same age bracket ¶ 동년배의 사람 one's contemporary // 거의 동년배다 be about the same age // 동년배의 사람들 people (of) about the same age ; people in the same age bracket

동녘 東— the east ¶ 동녘 하늘이 밝아 온다 Day〔Morning〕 dawns. /The light of day is peeping in the east.

동단 東端 the eastern end ¶ 아시아의 동단에 위치하다 be situated at the eastern extremity of Asia

동당(거리다) ⇨ 둥덩(거리다)

동당치기 a kind of gambling game (with cards)

동닿다 ① [조리가] be reasonable ; be logical ; be justifiable ; [일치하다] fit in ; coincide with ; [일관되다] be coherent ; be consistent ; be relevant ¶ 동닿지 않는 말 illogical〔incoherent, unreasonable〕 remarks ; (self-) contradictory statements // 동닿지 않는 변명 a lame apology // 동닿지 않다 be illogical ; be unjustifiable ; be unreasonable ; be incoherent ; be inconsistent ; be irrelevant // 동닿는 대답을 하다 answer relevantly // 방금 네 말은 동닿지 않는다 There is no logic〔neither rhyme nor reason〕 in your last remark.

② [차례가] come〔follow〕 in succession

동대다 ① [조리를] make《one's story》 consistent〔reasonable, coherent〕; try to give a show of truth ; fix《it》 up ; make《it》 look plausible ¶ 이야기를 동대다 make a story consistent〔plausible〕

② [계속] make follow in regular succession ; [계속 제공] send〔pay〕 regularly ; keep in stock ¶ 이자를 동대어 갚다 pay the interest regularly〔punctually〕 // 이 쌀을 가지고는 연말까지 동댈 수가 없을 것 같다 I am afraid we shall have run out of rice before the end of this year. /The rice won't last until the end of the year.

동댕이치다 [내던지다] throw〔cast, fling〕 away ; [포기하다] throw over〔up〕; give up ¶ 화가 나서 책을 동댕이치다 throw away the book in anger // 하던 일을 중간에서 동댕이치다 give up one's work halfway through

동동[1] boom-boom ⇨ 둥둥

동동[2] floating ⇨ 둥실둥실

동동[3] [발을] jumping up and down《from cold, impatience》 ¶ 추워서 발을 동동 구르다 jump up and down for cold // 발을 동동 구르며 분해 하다 stamp with vexation〔chagrin〕

동동거리다 jump up and down ¶ 추워서 발을 동동거리다 jump up and down with cold // 돈을 어서 달라고 발을 동동거리다 ask for money jumping up and down impatiently

†동등 同等 equality ; the same rank (지위가) ; equivalence ; par ; parity ¶ 동등의 equal ; of the same rank ; equivalent // 동등의 권리 equal rights // 동등의 대우 equal treatment // 고교 졸업 또는 동등의 학력 graduation from a high school or the equivalent // 동등하게 하다 make equal ; equalize // 동등하게 대우하다 treat《all》 equally

*동떨어지다 be far《between》; have〔get〕 a space《between》; be wide apart ; be pole apart ; [관계가] be irrelevant ; be wide of the mark ; be off the point ; be out of the place ¶ 동떨어지게 by far ; far and away // 5마일이나 동떨어진 곳 the place 5 miles away from here // 두 사람의 나이는 너무나 동떨어진다 There is such a great disparity of age between the two. // 그 길로 갔더니 가야 할 길과는 동떨어진 데로 나오고 말았다 The road took us far out of our way. // 그건 이것과는 동떨어진 추측이다 Your guess is out of the mark.

동떨어진 소리 a statement wide of the mark (거리가 먼) ; an absurd〔a nonsensical〕 remark (어리석은) ¶ 자네 얘기는 그것과는 동떨어진 소리야 What you say is irrelevant to it.

동뜨다 ① [뛰어나다] (be) superior《to》; far better ; be out〔far〕 and away ; (be) extraordinary ; exceptional ¶ 동뜨게 out of the common〔ordinary〕; exceptionally ; out〔far〕 and away ; a long way // 성적이 학급에서 동뜨다 be out and away 〔by far〕 the best student in the class // 키가 동뜨게 크다 He is exceptionally tall.

② [동안 뜨다] be far apart ¶ 두 동네 사이가 동떠 있다 The two villages are far apart from each other.

동락 同樂 —하다 enjoy together ; share one's joy《with》

동란 動亂 a disturbance ; an upheaval ; a commotion ; a riot ¶ 국내의 동란 internal disturbances // 동란의 유럽 war-torn Europe // 세계적 동란 a world cataclysm // 동란을 일으키다〔진압하다〕 cause〔quell〕 a riot

한국 — the Korean War ; a disturbance in Korea

동량 棟樑 ① [기둥과 들보] a beam and a pillar ② [큰 인재] the pillar ; the chief support (of the State) ¶ 장래의 국가 동량 a future leader of the State

동량지재 棟樑之材 great ability ; the pillars《of a state》

†동력 動力 〖기계〗 (motive) power ; 〖역학〗 dynamic force ; 〖물리〗 moment ¶ 동력의 공급 a supply of power // 동력으로 움직이

는 power-driven
— 공급 시설 power equipment —로(爐) a power reactor (원자로) —료(料) power rate — 사정 power condition —선(船) a power vessel ; a powerboat —선(線) a power line — 송곳 a power drill —원(源) a power source — 장치 the power plant — 측정법 dynamometry —학 power science ; dynamics — 회선 a power circuit

동력계 動力計 a dynamometer
제동기 — a brake dynamometer 응차(應差) — a differential dynamometer

동렬 同列 the same rank〔file〕 ¶ 동렬에 두다 put in the same category 《with》

동록 銅綠 verdigris ; copper〔green〕 rust
동록이 슬다 관용 form green rust

동뢰연 同牢宴 a wedding reception〔feast, dinner 《미》〕; an after-wedding celebration

†동료 同僚 an associate ; a colleague ; a co-worker ; a comrade (동지)

동류 同流 [같은 유파] the same style ; the same school ; [동배] a person of (about) the same age

동류 同類 [같은 종류] the same class〔kind, category〕; [공모자] an accomplice ; a confederate ; [동류의 것] the like(s) ¶ 그도 그 동류에 틀림없다 He must be one of the set〔party〕. // 저 많은 사람들이 다들 그 동류이다 The whole lot of them are tarred with the same brush.
— 상종(相從) Like draws like. /Birds of a feather flock together. — 의식 〖사회〗 consciousness of kind — 의식설(意識說) theory of consciousness of kind —항(項) 〖수학〗 a similar term ; a like term

동륜 動輪 a driving〔traction〕 wheel

동률 同率 the same ratio ; a tie

동리 洞里 a village ¶ 동리 사람들 the village folk ; the villagers

동마루 the ridge of a tiled roof

동매 a straw rope

***동맥 動脈** 〖해부〗 an artery ¶ 동맥의 arterial // 동맥 절개 수술 arteriotomy
—관 an arterial tube —류(瘤) 〖해부〗 an aneurysm〔aneurism〕 —염(炎) arteritis — 절개술 arteriotomy —학 arteriology 경(頸) — the carotid artery 안면(顔面) — the facial artery 요(腰)— the lumbar arteries

동맥 경화증 動脈硬化症 〖의학〗 arteriosclerosis 《*pl.* -roses》; arterial sclerosis ; hardening of the arteries

동맥혈 動脈血 〖해부〗 arterial blood
—화 arterialization

†동맹 同盟 an alliance ; a union ; a league ; combination ; confederation —하다 ally oneself 《with》; league with ; be leagued〔allied〕 with〔together〕; conclude〔form〕 an alliance with ¶ 학생들은 동맹 휴교를 했다 The students went on strike.
—군 an allied army ; allied forces ; [제 1·2차 세계 대전의] the Allies — 운임률 [배의] conference rates —자 an ally ; a confederate ; a friend — 조약 a treaty of alliance 군사 — a military alliance 비—국 a nonaligned〔an unaligned, an uncommitted〕 nation〔country〕

동맹국 同盟國 an ally ; an allied power〔country〕; a confederate ; a confederacy

동맹 파업 同盟罷業 a (labor) strike ; a turnout ; a walkout 《미》 —하다 have a strike ; go on (a) strike ; walkout 《미》; quit work in a body ¶ 시한〔무기한〕 동맹 파업 a strike for a definite〔an indefinite〕 period // 총 동맹 파업 a general strike // 동맹 파업을 중지하다 call off a strike // 동맹 파업 중이다 be on a strike

동맹 휴교 同盟休校 a strike of students ; a school〔college〕 strike —하다 strike ; go on (a) strike ¶ 동맹 휴교 중이다 be on strike
—자 a striker ; a turnout 《영》 — 파괴자 a strike breaker ; a blackleg 《영》; a scab ; a rat 《속》

동메달 銅— a copper medal (작은) ; a copper medallion (큰) ; [경기에서] a bronze medal

동면 冬眠 winter sleep ; hibernation
— 동물 hibernating〔hibernant〕 animals ; hibernants ; sleepers — 장소 winter quarters ; a hibernaculum 《*pl.* -la》; a hibernacle

동명 同名 the same name
— 이물(異物) a homonym — 이인(異人) a person of the same name ; a namesake ; a homonym ¶ 그는 동명 이인이었음이 밝혀졌다 He was found (to be) a different person of the same name.

동명 洞名 the name of the village〔community〕

동명사 動名詞 〖문법〗 a gerund ¶ 동명사의 gerundial

동명태 凍明太 a frozen pollack

동몽 童蒙 a child ; a boy

⁑동무 a friend ; a mate ; a companion ; a comrade (주로 남자의) ; a pal〔chum〕 《속》 —하다 keep company 《with》; keep 《a person》 company ; accompany ; be a companion to ¶ 말동무 a companion to talk with // 술동무 a boon companion // 여자동무 a girl friend ; a date // 동무가 되다 become friends ; fall into company ; find a company 《in a person》; join company // 동무가 없다 be friendless ; have no friend // 나쁜 동무들이 생기다 fall〔get〕 into bad company // 동무해서 갑시다 Let's go together.

동무장사 business〔trade, commerce〕 in partnership —하다 do business with 《a person》; do business in partnership

동문 同文 ① [문자나 문장의] an identical passage〔phrasing〕 《of writing》 ② [언어로서의] a common〔the same〕 script ¶ 이하 동문 The rest is the same as above.
— 전보 a multiple〔an identical〕 telegram — 통첩 an identical note ; a circular note

동문 同門 ① [동창] a fellow pupil〔student,

disciple〕; a classmate ; [졸업생] an alumnus 《*pl.* -ni》; an alumna 《*pl.* -nae》(여자) ¶ 우리는 같은 학교를 나온 동문입니다 We went to the same school.
—회 an alumni association ; an old boys' association
② [같은 문중] the same clan ; [사람] a clansman ; a clanswoman (여자)
동문동종 同文同種 the same script and the same race
동문생 同門生 a fellow student〔disciple〕; pupils under the same master
동문서답 東問西答 an irrelevant answer ; an incoherent reply —하다 answer incoherently ; reply irrelevantly ; say nothing to the purpose〔point〕
동문 수학 同門受學 —하다 study under the same teacher 《with》
**동물 動物 an animal ; a (living) creature ; brute ; a beast (짐승) ; animal life 《총칭》

> 참고 **animal**은 일반적인 말이며 식물(plant)이나 무생물과 반대되는 말 **beast**는 조류·곤충 따위와 구별되는 말 **brute**는 이성을 결한 짐승의 야만스러운 점을 강조하기 위한 말

¶ 동물적 animal ; brutal ; beastly
—계 the animal kingdom〔world〕 — 구조학 zoophysics — 문학 animal literature — 분류학 zootaxy ; zoological taxonomy — 사육장 [자연의 서식 상태에 가깝게 만든] a vivarium 《*pl.* ~s, -ria》 — 생리학 animal physiology — 생태학 zoo-ecology — 세포 an animal cell ; a zooblast — 실험 an animal experiment — 심리학 zoopsychology ; animal psychology — 애호가 an animal lover — 애호일 Be-Kind-to-Animals Day — 애호회〔학대 방지회〕 the Society for the Prevention of Cruelty to Animals 《S. P. C. A.》 — 역학 zoodynamics — 질환 a zoonosis 《*pl.* -ses》 — 측정학 zoometry — 해부학 zootomy ; animal anatomy —화(畫) an animal painting — 화가 an animal painter — 화학 zoochemistry 고등〔하등〕 — the higher〔lower〕 animal ; [개개의] a high〔low〕 animal 양족(兩足)〔사족(四足)〕 — a biped〔quadruped〕 육식〔초식〕 — a carnivorous〔herbivorous〕 animal
동물 공원 動物公園 a park zoo ; a game park
자연 — a wildlife park 용인 — *Yong-in* Zoological Park
동물상 動物相 fauna 《*pl.* ~s, -nae》
연안(沿岸) — littoral fauna 해산(海産) — marine fauna
동물성 動物性 animal nature ; animality ; bestiality ¶ 동물성의 animal
— 단백질 animal protein — 섬유 an animal fiber — 식품 animal food — 지방 animal fat(s)
동물 숭배 動物崇拜 animal worship ; zoolatry ¶ 동물 숭배의 zoolatrous
—자 a zoolater
동물 시험 動物試驗 a biological test —하다 subject 《a medicine》 to a biological test
동물원 動物園 zoological gardens ; a zoo (구) ; [영업용의] a menagerie ¶ 동물원에서 난 표범 a zoo-born leopard
— 원장 the curator of a zoo
동물 조직 動物組織 animal tissue ¶ 동물 조직의 인체 이식 zoografting
동물 지리학 動物地理學 zoogeography ; zoography ; geographical zoology ¶ 동물 지리학의 zoogeographic(al) ; zoographic(al)
—자 a zoogeographer
동물질 動物質 animal matter ¶ 동물질로 변하다 animalize ; be animalized
동물학 動物學 zoology ¶ 동물학(상)의 zoological // 동물학상 zoologically ; from the zoological point of view
—자 zoologist
동물 학대 動物虐待 cruelty to animals
— 방지회 the Society for the Prevention of Cruelty to Animals 《S. P. C. A》
동물화 動物化 animalization —하다 [동물적으로 화하다] animalize ; [동물적으로 되다] be animalized
동민 洞民 the inhabitants of a *dong* ; people of a community ; the villagers ; the village folk
동바 a pack rope of an A-frame
동바리 [마루의] a supporting post ; a puncheon ; [갱도의] a timber ; a post ; a prop ; a puncheon
동박새 〖새〗 a white〔silver〕 eye
동반 同伴 company —하다 accompany ; attend ; escort ; take 《a person》 with

> 참고 **accompany** 다른 사람과 동반하다 **attend** 아랫사람 또는 시중드는 사람으로서 따르다 **escort** 보호자로서 또는 경의를 품고 따르다

¶ 그는 가족 동반이다 He is accompanied by his family.
—석 the family seats〔circle〕 —자 a companion
동반구 東半球 the Eastern hemisphere
동발 ⇨ 동바리
동방 東方 the east ¶ 동방의 eastern ; easterly // 동방에 towards the east ; in an easterly direction
동방 洞房 ① [침실] a bedroom ② [신방] the bridal〔nuptial〕 room
—화촉 sharing bed on the bridal〔first〕 night
동방 東邦 [동방의 나라] an eastern country ; an Oriental nation ; [동양] the Orient ; the East ; [한국] Korea ¶ 동방의 Oriental ; Eastern
—인 an Oriental
동방구리 a fat-bellied jar
*동배 同輩 one's equal ; a social equal ; an

associate ; a colleague ; a comrade ¶ 동배 중 뛰어나다 rise above one's fellows // 우리는 동배간이다 We are equals 〔friends〕.

동백 冬柏 camellia seeds
—기름 camellia oil —나무 a camellia ; Camellia japonica (학명)

동병 同病 the same disease ¶ 동병상련하다 Grief is best pleased with grief's company. /Fellow sufferers have sympathy for each other.

동병 動兵 military mobilization —하다 mobilize《an army》

동복 冬服 winter clothes〔clothing〕; winter wear ; a winter suit ; a winter dress (부인의) ; a winter jacket (학생의)

동복 同腹 children born of the same mother ¶ 동복의 uterine
— 형제〔자매〕 uterine brothers〔sisters〕; brothers〔sisters〕 of the same venter〔mother〕

동복 童僕, 僮僕 a servant boy ; a boyservant ; a page

*동봉 同封 —하다 enclose《영》; inclose《a letter》《미》 ¶ 동봉한 편지 the enclosed〔accompanying〕 letter // 사진을 편지에 동봉하다 inclose a picture in a letter // 200불 수표를 동봉합니다 Enclosed please find a check for two hundred dollars. /I enclose herewith a check for $200.

동봉 動蜂 a worker bee

동부 〖식물〗 a (ripe) cowpea
— 고물 ground-up cowpeas (used to coat cakes) —묵 cowpea paste〔jelly〕

동부 東部 the eastern part ¶ 동부에 있다 lie〔be situated〕 in the east〔the eastern part〕《of》

동부동 動不動 [꼭] for sure ; without fail ¶ 명령이니 동부동 거기에 갈 수 밖에 없다 I have no alternative〔choice〕 but to go there because it is the order.

동부새 東— an east〔easterly〕 wind

동부인 同夫人 —하다 go out with one's wife ; take one's wife along ; accompany〔be accompanied by〕 one's wife

*동북 東北 the northeast
—동 east-northeast — 지방 the northeastern district —풍 the northeast(erly) wind ; a northeaster

동북향 東北向 facing northeast ; having a northeast exposure ¶ 동북향 집 a house facing northeast ; a house open to the northeast

동분모 同分母 〖수학〗 the same denominator

동분서주 東奔西走 —하다 busy oneself about《something》; bestir oneself《in a matter》; be on the move〔go, run, rush〕; take an active interest in《anything》

동빙 凍氷 freezing —하다 freeze

*동사 動詞 〖문법〗 a verb ¶ 동사의 verbal
— 변화 conjugation 규칙〔불규칙〕 — a regular〔an irregular〕 verb 완전〔불완전〕 — complete〔incomplete〕 verb 자〔타〕— an intransitive〔a transitive〕 verb

동사 凍死 death from cold —하다 be frozen to death ; perish from cold ; freeze to death
—자 a person frozen to death

동사 同社 [같은 회사] the same company ; [앞서 말한 회사] the said〔aforesaid, above(-mentioned), aforementioned〕 firm ; [그 회사] they ; it

동사 同事 a joint enterprise〔undertaking〕; business〔trade〕 in partnership —하다 do〔engage in, go in〕 business with ; run〔operate〕 a business in partnership with

동사무소 洞事務所 the office of a *dong* ; a *dong* office ; a village office

동산 [작은 산] a hill〔hillock, knoll〕 near a village ; [정원의] an artificial forest 〔hill〕; a mound ; a garden
—바치 a gardener

동산 動產 movable estate ; personal property ; personalty ; movables ; chattels
— 차압 distrainment 불법 점유 — 반환 소송 a detinue 유류(遺留) —세(稅) 〖법〗 a probate duty《영》 유체(有體)〔무체(無體)〕 — corporeal〔incorporeal〕 movables

동산 銅山 a copper mine

동살 〖건축〗 the cross-strips of a lattice

동살 東— [빛] the faint rays of dawn ¶ 동살이 잡히기 시작했다 The eastern sky is gradually turning gray. /The dawn began to whiten the sky.

동삼삭 冬三朔 October, November and December of the lunar calendar ; the winter season

동상 同上 the same as the above ; ditto《*pl.* ～s》

동상 銅像 a bronze statue〔image〕 ¶ 동상을 세우다 erect a statue

동상 凍傷 frostbite ; chilblains ¶ 동상에 걸리다 be frostbitten ; have chilblains
—자 a frostbitten person ; a case of frostbite

동상례 東床禮 a wedding reception at the bride's house after the wedding ceremony

동색 同色 the same color ; [파벌] fellow members of a party ; the same faction

동색 銅色 copper color
—인(人) a redskin — 인종 a copper-colored race

동생 同生 a younger brother〔sister〕

동생공사 同生共死 —하다 share the fate with others ¶ 우리는 모두 동생공사의 운명이다 We are all in the same boat.

동서 同壻 [자매의 남편] the husband of one's wife's sister ; [형제의 아내] the wife of one's husband's brother

동서 東西 [동과 서] the east and the west ; [동서양] the East and the West ; the Orient and the Occident ¶ 동서로 from east to west ; east and west // 고금동서를 막론하고 in all ages and countries // 동서 약 14 마일 about 14 miles from east to west // 동서도 분간 못하다 do not know one's right

hand from the left ; do not know chalk from cheese // 동서로 흐르다 run east and west // 고금동서로 통하다 be applicable to all times and places
— 관계 the East-West relations — 긴장 the East-West tensions — 대립 the East-West confrontation
동서 同棲 living together ; cohabitation —하다 live together ; live〔cohabit〕 with 《a person》 ; share bed and board with ¶ 부부로서 동서하다 live together as man and wife
—자 a cohabitant ; a bedfellow
동서 同書 [같은 책] the same book ; [그 책] the said book ¶ 동서에서 [출처를 표시할 때] ibidem 《ib., ibid.》
동서고금 東西古今 all ages and countries ; all times and places
동서남북 東西南北 the (four) cardinal points ; north, east, south, and west ¶ 동서남북에서 from all directions〔all quarters, all parts of the country〕
동석 同席 —하다 sit together ; sit in company with ¶ 그 사람과는 동석하고 싶지 않다 I must be excused from being in his company. // 그 사람과 동석하면 불안하다 I feel ill at ease in his company.
—자 those present ; the company ; [탈것의] a seat companion
동석 凍石 〖광물〗 soapstone ; steatite
동선 同船 [배] the same ship ; [타는 일] taking the same ship —하다 take the same ship ; sail on〔in〕 the same vessel ; be in〔on〕 the same vessel ; be a fellow passenger
—자 a shipmate ; a fellow passenger
동선 銅線 copper wire〔wiring〕
동설 同說 the same〔said〕 theory〔opinion, view〕
동성 同性 [이성에 대해] the same sex ; [같은 성질] homogeneity ; homogeneousness ; congeniality ¶ 동성의 homosexual ; [동성질의] homogeneous ; congenial
—(연)애 homosexual love ; homosexuality ; unnatural love ; [여성간의] lesbianism ; sapphism
동성 同姓 the same family name ; the same surname ¶ 동성의 사람 a namesake ; a person of the same name
— 동명(同名) the same family and personal name — 동본 the same surname and the same family origin — 이인(異人) different persons of the same name
동소 同所 ① [같은 장소] the same place ; the same address ② [그 장소] the said place ; the above address
동소체 同素體 〖화학〗 an allotrope
동수 同數 the same number ¶ …와 동수의 as many 《as》 ; of the same number
동숙 同宿 lodging together —하다 lodge in the same house 《with another》
—인 a fellow lodger〔boarder〕 ; a fellow guest ; [전부] inmates 《of a hotel》

동승 同乘 —하다 ride together (말에) ; ride with 《a person》 in the same 《carriage》
—자 a fellow passenger
*동시 同時 the same time〔period〕 ¶ 동시의 simultaneous ; concurrent ; synchronous ; contemporary 《with》 // 동시에 at the same time ; simultaneously 《with》 ; [일시에] at a time ; at once // 등산은 유쾌한 동시에 위험이 따른다 Mountaineering is a pleasant sport, but on the other hand it is attended with danger. // A와 B는 동시에 영국에 갔다 A went to England at the same time as B. // 아버지가 귀가하시는 것과 동시에 나는 외출하였다 I went out the moment father came home. // 그 책은 흥미있고 동시에 유익하다 The book is both〔at once〕 interesting and instructive.
— 방송 simultaneous broadcasting ; a simulcast —성(性) simultaneity ; synchronism — 송수 전신(送受電信) duplex telegraphy
동시 同視 —하다 regard 《A》 in the same light with 《B》 ; class 《A》 with 《B》 ; put 《A》 on a par with 《B》 ; [같이 대우함] treat alike ; do not discriminate ¶ 동시할 수 없다 cannot be regarded in the same light 《as》
동시 凍屍 a frozen corpse ; the corpse of a person frozen to death
동시 童詩 children's verse ; nursery rimes
동시 녹음 同時錄音 synchronous recording —하다 synchronize ¶ 동시 녹음 촬영 sound shooting // 동시 녹음 상영(上映) a double feature〔bill〕 ; a two-picture program
동시대 同時代 the same age〔period〕 ; [시대를 같이 함] contemporaneousness ¶ 동시대의 사람 a contemporary ; a coeval // 동시대의 작가들 contemporary〔coeval〕 writers
동시 통역 同時通譯 simultaneous interpretation —하다 make simultaneous interpretation
—자 a simultaneous interpreter
동식물 動植物 animals and plants ; [어느 지역·시대의] fauna and flora
동실 同室 [같은 방] the same room 〔chamber〕
동실동실[1] floating ; buoyant(ly) ¶ 배가 동실동실 뜨다 a boat is floating buoyantly
동실동실[2] —하다 (be) plump ; [얼굴이] plump and round ; chubby ; chubby-faced ; buxom ¶ 동실동실 살찐 어린이 a chubby child
동심 同心 ① [한마음] the same mind ; [마음의 일치] like-mindedness ; accord ; unanimity ; concord ; agreement ¶ 두 사람은 동심 일체이다 The two are practically of a mind.
② 〖기하〗 concentricity
— 협력 harmonious〔hearty〕 cooperation ¶ 동심 협력하다 cooperate in harmony ; work with one mind // 이 사업의 성공을 위

하여서는 동심 협력이 긴요하다 Perfect unity of purpose is essential to the success of this undertaking.

동심 童心 the child's mind〔heart〕; the juvenile mind ¶ 동심을 상하게 하고 싶지 않다 I don't want a child's hopes crushed./I don't want to disillusion the child.

동심원 同心圓 〖수학〗 a concentric circle

동아 〖식물〗 a wax gourd ; a white gourd-melon

동아 冬芽 winter buds

동아 東亞 East〔Eastern〕 Asia ; [동양] the East ; [극동] the Far East ¶ 동아의 East-Asian ; Far Eastern // 동아의 문제 the Far Eastern question

동아 凍餓 cold and hunger

동아따다 [떨어지다] fall down ; [떨어뜨리다] drop 《a thing》

동아리 ① [부분] a part ; a portion ; ¶ 웃동아리 the upper part // 아랫동아리 the lower part

② [무리] a group ; faction ; companions composed of the people with the same purpose

동아줄 a rope ; a hawser ; a stay

†**동안** ① [기간] a period ; a span ; an interval ; [부사적] for 《an hour》; between 《12 and 1 o'clock》; during 《the night》; [이내에] within 《ten minutes》; [사이에] in the course of 《the dinner》; while ; as〔so〕 long as ¶ 과거 5년 동안 for the past five years // 그 동안 meanwhile ; in the meantime // 잠깐 동안 for a little while ; for a short time // 오랫동안 for a long time 〔while〕 // 살아 있는 동안은 as long as one lives ; while one lives // 5분의 동안을 두고 at intervals of five minutes // 일정한 기간 동안에 within a certain〔given〕 period of time // 자리를 비운 동안에 during one's absence ; while one is out // 닷새 동안에 끝마치다 finish 《a thing》 in five days

② [간격] an interval ; a space ¶ 동안을 띄우다 leave space 《between》

동안 童顔 a boyish face ¶ 동안의 boyish-looking ; juvenile-looking

동안 東岸 the east coast ; the east bank 《of a river》

동안 뜨다 be an interval〔a space〕 between ; be few and far between ; be far apart ¶ 다음 열차 출발 시간까지는 상당히 동안 뜨다 《we》 have plenty of time〔it will be a long time〕 before the next train departs // 두 동네 사이가 동안 뜨다 the two villages are far apart from each other

동압 動壓 dynamic pressure

동액 同額 the same amount〔sum〕 《of money》; a like sum ¶ 동액의 equivalent in amount

동야 凍野 〖지리〗 the tundra

동양 東洋 the Orient ; the East ¶ 동양의 Oriental ; Eastern

—구(區) 〖생물〗 the Oriental region **— 문명** Oriental civilization **— 문학** Oriental literature **— 미술** Oriental art **—사(史)** Oriental history **— 사상** Orientalism **— 인종** Oriental race **— 취미** Orientalism ; orientalism **—학** Oriental studies **— 학자** an Orientalist **—화(畫)** an Oriental painting

동양 動陽 man's sexual impulse

동양인 東洋人 an Oriental ; the Orientals ; the Eastern〔Oriental〕 people ¶ 동양인의 동양 the Orient for the Orientals

동양풍 東洋風 Orientalism ; orientalism ¶ 동양풍의 Oriental // 그것은 크게 동양풍을 띠고 있다 It has a strong Oriental flavor 〔flavor of the Orient〕.

동어 —魚 〖물고기〗 [숭어 새끼] a young mullet

동어 鮦魚 [가물치] a snakehead mullet

동업 同業 the same trade〔profession, calling〕 **—하다** do business in partnership ; run business together

— 조합 a trade association ; (craft) guild

동업자 同業者 [총칭] the profession (의사·변호사 따위의) ; the trade〔craft〕 (상인·직업인의) ; [개인] a person in the same line of business ; a fellow trader 〔business-man〕; a friend ; a colleague 《of doctors》; a brother (tradesman) ; [동업 신문·잡지] a contemporary ¶ 동업자간의 시세 the trade price // 동업자간의 예의 professional courtesy // 동업자가 많은 장사 a crowded profession〔trade〕 // 동업자에 대해서는 2할의 할인이 있다 Twenty per cent〔20%〕 discount is allowed to those in the trade.

동여매다 ① [묶다] bind 《a person to a stake》; bind 《things》 together ; tie ; fasten ; truss ¶ 기둥에 동여매다 fasten 〔lash〕 《a thing》 to a post

② [속박하다] restrain ; restrict ; trammel ; lay〔place〕 《a person》 under restraint

동역학 動力學 kinetics ; dynamics

동옷 a man's coat

†**동요 動搖** [불안정] unsettledness ; [소요] disturbance ; commotion ; [배의] rolling (좌우로) ; pitching (상하로) ; [차·마차 따위의] jolting ; [물가의] fluctuation ; [인심의] agitation ; unrest **—하다** roll ; pitch ; jolt ; fluctuate ; shake ; be agitated ; [생각이 흔들리다] wobble ; waver ¶ 동요하는 사람 a wobbler ; a waverer // 배의 동요 the rolling of a ship // 정계〔경제계〕의 동요 political〔financial〕 disturbances // 국가 경제의 기초를 동요시키다 shake the national economy to its foundations // 이 문제에 대하여 인심이 동요하고 있다 The people are agitated over the question.

—계(計) 〖항해〗 an oscillometer **—병(病)** [탈것의 멀미] motion sickness **— 제지 장치** [배·비행기의] a stabilizer

동요 童謠 child verse ; a children's song ; a nursery rhyme (song)

— 작가 a writer of juvenile songs ; a poet of the nursery **—집(集)** nursery rhymes

동우 同友 like-minded friends ; a fellow member ; a mate ; an associate ; a comrade
동원 凍原 the tundra
동원 動員 mobilization **— 하다** mobilize ; call to the colors ¶ 동원을 해제하다 demobilize // 점원을 전부 동원하다 mobilize all shop assistants // 미국은 총동원을 실시했다 America mobilized her entire army.
— 계획 a mobilization plan **— 해제** demobilization ; redeployment (군사) **노동력 —** labor mobilization **산업 —** industrial mobilization **인력 —** labor mobilization
동원 同原 〖생물〗 isogeny ¶ 동원의 isogenous
동원령 動員令 mobilization order(s) ¶ 제 1 사단에 그날 동원령이 내렸다 Orders for the mobilization of the First Division were issued on that day.
동월 同月 the same month
동위 同位 the same rank〔position〕; the same location ¶ 동위의 coordinate ; corresponding
—각 a corresponding angle
동위 원소 同位元素 an isotope
방사성 — radioactive isotope **안정(安定) —** a stable isotope
동유 桐油 tung oil
—지 oil paper
동육 凍肉 frozen meat
동음 同音 the same sound ; 〖음성〗 homophony
—어(語) a homophone **— 이의어(異議語)** a homonym **이구(異口) —** one voice ; chorus
†**동의 同意** [찬성] consent ; assent ; agreement ; approval ; [동의견] the same opinion **— 하다** consent〔assent, agree〕《to》; approve《of》; subscribe《to》; agree《with a person, to a proposal》; fall in《with》; accede ; acquiesce

> **참고** **consent** 제의 또는 청구된 일에 대하여 동의하다 **assent** 다른 사람의 진술이나 의견에 대해서 동조하다 **accede** 제의에 대해서 찬성하다 **agree** 의견의 차이를 조정해서 동조하다 **acquiesce** 반론을 누르고 찬성하다

¶ 동의를 얻다 obtain《a person's》consent〔approval〕// 너의 의견에 동의한다 I subscribe to your opinion. /I agree with you. // 독일은 영국의 제안에 동의하였다 Germany assented to the British proposal. // 아버지는 우리의 결혼에 동의하지 않는다 My father does not agree to our marriage. // 그 점은 동의할 수 없다 I cannot agree with you on this point.
동의 同義 synonymy ; synonymity ; the same meaning ¶ 동의의 synonymous ; synonymic(al) ; of the same meaning
—서(書) a written consent **—자** an assentient ; an approver
동의 胴衣 [조끼] a vest ; a waistcoat
동의 動議 a motion **— 하다** move《for, that》; make〔bring in, bring forward, propose, introduce〕a motion ¶ 동의에 찬성하다 second a motion // 동의가 가결〔부결〕되었다 A motion was adopted〔rejected〕.
— 제출자 the mover (of a motion) **긴급 —** an urgent〔urgency〕motion
⁑**동의어 同義語** a synonym ; an equivalent ¶ 동의어의 synonymous // 이 말은 그 말의 동의어이다 This word is a synonym for that. // 그 말과 정확히 같은 동의어의 한국어는 찾을 수 없다 We cannot find a precise Korean equivalent for the word.
— 연구 synonymy
동의 인자 同義因子 〖유전〗 multiple factors
동이 a jar
물— a water jar
*__동이다__ bind《a box》; tie up《in a bundle》; fasten ; bundle ; truss ; cord (끈으로) ; chain (사슬로) ; strap (가죽으로) ¶ 끈으로 짐을 동이다 tie up a bundle with string // 기둥에 동이다 tie〔bind〕《a person》to a pillar // 아이를 등에 동여업다 have a baby tied to〔up on〕one's back // 죄인을 박승으로 동이다 tie a criminal with cords
동인 同人 ① [같은 사람] the same person ¶ A와 B는 동인이다 A and B are one and the same man. ② [뜻이 같은 사람] associates ; colleagues ③ [그 사람] the said person ; the person in question ; the subject ; he
— 잡지 a literary coterie magazine ; a little magazine
동인 動因 a motive ; a cause ; an inducement
동인도 東印度 the East Indies
동인종 同人種 the same race
†**동일 同一** [꼭 같음] identity ; sameness ; oneness ; [무차별] nondiscrimination ; equality **— 하다** (be) identical ; (one and) the same ; [무차별] equal ; nondiscriminatory ¶ 사람을 동일하게 다루다 treat men without discrimination // 영과 혼은 동일하다 The spirit is one〔identical〕with the soul.
— 개념 an identical conception **— 원리** 〖논리〗 the principle of identity **—화(化)** identification
동일 同日 the same day〔date〕; the said day
동월 — the same day of the same month
동일류 同一類 〖논리〗 identical classes
⁑**동일시 同一視 — 하다** regard《A》in the same light with《B》; class《A》with《B》; put《A》on a par with《B》¶ 동일시할 수 없다 cannot be regarded in the same light《as》
동자 cooking of rice ; kitchen work **— 하다** cook rice
—아치 a kitchen maid〔woman〕
동자 童子 a child ; a youngster ; a young boy ¶ 그 여자는 옥동자를 낳았다 She gave birth to a boy.

— 기둥 a post —중 a young〔boy〕 monk 〔bonze, priest〕; a priestling ; an acolyte

동자꽃 〖식물〗 a lychnis ; Lychnis cognata

동자력 動磁力 〖물리〗 magnetomotive force

동자르다 ① [관계를] sever〔cut off〕 one's connection with ; dissociate〔break off, sever〕 oneself from ; disconnect ; [교제를] be through with 《미》; break off friendship with ; have done with ¶ 외교 관계를 동자르다 break off〔sever〕 all diplomatic relations // 연락을 동자르다 sever〔cut off〕 the connection〔communication〕 《between the two》 // 본부와의 연락을 동자르다 cut off 《a party》 from the main body

② [길게 끊다] cut〔chop off〕 in long pieces

동자 생식 同子生殖 〖생물〗 homogamy

†동작 動作 action ; movements ; motions ; [거동] carriage ; manners ; behavior ; deportment ; [몸짓] gestures ¶ 완만한 동작 slow motion〔movement〕 // 동작이 느린 사람 a slow coach // 동작이 민활하다 be quick in action // 동작이 우아하다 Her movements are graceful.

동장 洞長 the chief of a *dong* office ; a *dong*〔village〕 headman

동장군 冬將軍 the rigors of winter ; General Winter ; Jack Frost

동저고리 a (man's) coat ; a jacket

동저고릿바람 dressing without an outer coat ¶ 동저고릿바람으로 나다니다 go around without wearing an outer coat ; go around in one's shirtsleeves

동적 動的 dynamic ; kinetic ¶ (인구의) 동적 밀도 dynamic density

— 동일 조건 〖항공〗 dynamic similarity — 밀도 [인구의] dynamic density

동전 銅錢 a copper coin ; a copper ¶ 동전 한푼 없다 be penniless ; have not a penny at all ; be utterly broke 《미》

동전 同前 the same (as before, as above) ; ditto

동전기 動電氣 〖물리〗 current〔dynamic, voltaic, kinetic〕 electricity

동절 冬節 the winter (season) ; winter time

†동점 同點 [점수] the same grade〔mark〕; [경기] a tie ; a draw ¶ 동점이 되다 tie〔draw〕 《with》 // 동점으로 비기다 halve a match // 시합은 6 대 6 동점으로 끝났다 The game ended in tie, 6 to 6.

— 결승 시합 a playoff

동점 東漸 eastern penetration〔drive〕; eastward advance〔movement〕; eastern expansion —하다 proceed east by steps and stage ; move〔advance〕 eastward ; expand eastward ¶ 서방 문명의 동점 the eastward advance〔movement〕 of Western civilization

서력(西力) — the eastern penetration of Western powers

동정 a collar (attached to the top border of a Korean coat)

†동정 同情 sympathy ; fellow feeling ; compassion ; pity ; commiseration —하다 sympathize 《with a person》; have sympathy 《for a person, for a person's death》; feel 《for》; have compassion 《on》; pity ; take pity 《upon》 ¶ 동정적 sympathetic ; warm-hearted ; compassionate // 동정적으로 sympathetically // 심심한 동정 deep 〔profound〕 sympathy // 충심으로부터의 동정 hearty〔heartfelt, sincere〕 sympathy // 동정심이 없다 be unsympathetic ; be cold // 크게 동정받다 find active sympathy // 동정심에 호소하다 appeal to 《a person's》 sympathy // 동정을 구하다 enlist〔court〕 《a person's》 sympathy // 남의 불행을 동정하다 commiserate 《a person》 on his misfortune // 그녀에게 동정이 간다 My heart goes out to her. // 동정을 끌려 해도 소용이 없다 It's useless to play on my sympathy.

—금 alms ; charity funds —자 a sympathizer ; a friend ; a well-wisher (호의자) —표 《win》 a sympathy vote

동정 童貞 chastity ; virginity ; 〖카톨릭〗 a sister ¶ 동정을 지키다〔잃다〕 keep〔lose〕 one's chastity // 동정이 되다 become a sister of chastity // 그는 죽을 때까지 동정이었다 He had no carnal knowledge of woman all his life. /He kept his virginity throughout his life.

—남 a (male) virgin —녀 a virgin ; [성모] the Virgin (Mary) —설 the Virgin Birth

동정 動靜 movements ; a state of things ; conditions 《of the political world》 ¶ 정계의 동정 the development of political affairs // 동정을 감시하다 keep watch on 《a person's》 movement // 자기의 동정을 알리다 inform 《a person》 of one's movements // 적의 동정을 살피다 watch the movements of the enemy // 동정을 알려 주십시오 Let me know how he is getting on.

동정서벌 東征西伐 subjugation〔conquest〕 of many countries —하다 subjugate 〔conquer〕 many countries

동정심 同情心 a sympathetic feeling ; sympathy ¶ 동정심이 있는〔없는〕 sympathetic〔unsympathetic〕; feeling〔unfeeling〕 // 동정심에 호소하다 appeal to 《a person's》 sympathy // 그런 이야기로 내 동정심을 이용하려 해봤자 먹혀들지 않을 것이다 Trying to play on my sympathies with a story like that isn't going to work.

동정 파업 同情罷業 a sympathy strike ¶ 동정 파업을 하다 go on a sympathy strike ; strike in sympathy 《with》

동제 銅製 ¶ 동제의 copper(y) ; made of copper

— 메달 a copper medal —품 copper goods

동조 同調 alignment ; 〖전기〗 tuning ; 〖무선〗 syntony ; 〖음악〗 the same key〔pitch, tune〕 —하다 align oneself 《with》; side 〔ally oneself〕 《with》; fall in 《with》; follow suit ; act in concert 《with》

—자 a fellow traveler ; a sympathizer — 행동 〖심리〗 conformity

동족 同族 [종족] the same race〔tribe〕; [일족] the same family ; [혈족] the same

blood ; consanguinity
— 결혼 endogamy ; consanguineous marriage — 관계 〖화학〗 homology —애 brotherly〔fraternal〕 love —어 related languages —열(列) 〖화학〗 homologous series —체(體) 〖화학〗 a homologue — 회사 a family partnership〔concern, business〕; [동계 회사] an affiliated concern〔company〕

동족 상잔 同族相殘 dog-eat-dog ; a fratricidal war ¶ 동족 상잔의 비극을 겪다 experience the tragedy of fratricidal war —하다 engage in a fratricidal war

†**동종 同種** the same kind〔sort, description〕 ¶ 동종의 kindred ; allied ; of the same kind // 동문 동종의 나라 nations of the same race and language // 동종의 식물 allied plants // 이것들은 동종에 속한다 These things are of the same kind.
— 기생(寄生) 〖식물〗 autoecism —물(物) the like — 요법 〖의학〗 homeopathy ; homeotherapy — 응집소(凝集素) 〖의학〗 an isoagglutinin — 응집원(凝集原) 〖의학〗 an isoagglutinogen — 항원(抗原) 〖면역〗 an isoantigen

동죄 同罪 the same crime

동주 同舟 —하다 take the same boat ; be in the same vessel ; be a fellow passenger ¶ 오월(吳越)동주 implacable〔bitter〕 enemies (placed by fate) in the same boat

동줄기 a packsaddle〔pack〕 rope

동지 冬至 the winter solstice ; the shortest day of the year
—선(線) the Tropic of Capricorn —섣달 November and December in〔by〕 the lunar calendar ; the last two lunar months —점 〖천문〗 the point of winter solstice ; the solstitial point —팥죽 adzuki bean gruel taken on the winter solstice

동지 同志 [마음] the same mind ; the congenial spirit ; a kindred mind ; [사람] a like-minded person ; kindred spirits ; comrades ; fellow thinkers ¶ 동지를 규합하다 muster men under one's banner ; rally kindred spirits

동지 同地 the same place〔district, locale〕; the said place (그 곳)

동질 同質 the same quality〔nature〕; homogeneity ¶ 동질의 of the same quality〔substance〕; homogeneous ; coessential ; cognate

동질량 원소 同質量元素 〖화학·물리〗 an isobar

동짓달 冬至— the 11th month of the lunar calendar

†**동쪽 東**— the east ¶ 동쪽의 east ; eastern ; easterly // 동쪽으로 in the east ; to the east // 동쪽에서 부는 바람 an east 〔easterly〕 wind // 동쪽으로 가다 go east 〔eastward〕 // 바람은 동쪽이다 The wind blows from the east. // 해는 동쪽에서 뜨고 서쪽으로 진다 The sun rises in the east and sets in the west.

동차 童車 a perambulator ; a baby carriage 《미》

동차식 同次式 〖수학〗 a homogeneous expression

동차적 同次積 〖수학〗 a homogeneous product

동창 東窓 a window facing (to the) east

동창 同窓 a fellow student ; a schoolmate ; a schoolfellow ; an alumnus ¶ 우리는 동창이었다 We were at school together. /We were at the same school. // 우리는 동기 동창입니다 We went to school together.

***동창생 同窓生** a fellow student ; a schoolfellow ; a schoolmate ; [졸업생] a graduate ; an alumnus 《*pl.* -ni》; [여자] an alumna 《*pl.* -nae》

동창회 同窓會 [조직] a graduates' association ; an alumni association ; an old boys' 〔pupils'〕 association ; [회합] an alumni meeting〔reunion〕; a meeting of old boys
— 잡지 an alumni bulletin

동천 東天 the eastern sky ; the sky in the east ¶ 동천이 붉게 물들었다 The eastern sky was tinged with crimson.

동천 洞天 a beauty〔scenic〕 spot ; a garden spot

동천 冬天 a winter sky (하늘) ; winter weather (날씨)

동철 銅鐵 copper and iron

동철 冬鐵 [신의] crampons ; [편자의] horseshoe spikes

동체 動體 a body in motion ; a moving body
— 사진 a chronophotograph ; a photochronograph — 사진 녹초기(錄秒器) a photochronograph — 사진법 chronophotography ; photochronography

동체 胴體 the body ; the trunk ; [조상의] the torso 《*pl.* ~s, -si》; [비행기의] the fuselage ; [비행정의] hull ¶ 동체가 두 동강이 났다 The body was severed in two.

동체 同體 the same substance ; one body
일심— one flesh ; being one in body and spirit

동축 動軸 a live spindle

동치 同値 〖수학〗 the equivalent

동치다 bind up ; tie up

동치미 turnips pickled in salt water ; watery radish *kimchi*

동침 —鍼 an acupuncture needle

동침 同寢 —하다 sleep〔lie〕 with 《a person》; share a bed with 《a person》

동태 凍太 a frozen pollack

동태 動胎 quickening fetal movement —하다 《the fetus》 quicken

동태 動態 movement
— 경제 dynamic economy — 통계 dynamic statistics 인구 — the movement of population

동통 疼痛 a pain ; an ache ¶ 오른쪽 다리에 심한 동통을 느끼다 have〔feel〕 an acute 〔a terrible〕 pain in one's right leg

동트기 dawn ; daybreak

*동트다 《it》 dawn ; 《the day》 break ¶ 동틀 무렵에 at dawn ; at daybreak // 동틀 무렵 출발했다 I started at the first gray of dawn.

동티 ① retribution from the earth gods ② [자초한 말썽] trouble brought on oneself

동티나다 ① suffer the wrath of the earth gods ② get into trouble ; incur trouble ③ 《the secret》 be out〔revealed, disclosed〕

동파 同派 [유파] the same school ; [당파] the same faction ; the same junta ; [종파] the same sect ; [파벌] the same clique ; [그 파] the said faction

동파 冬播 winter-sowing

동판 銅版 a copperplate print ; a mezzotint — 인쇄 (copper) plate printing ¶ 동판 인쇄하다 print from copperplates — 조각 copperplate engraving ; mezzotint engraving ; etching ; chalcography — 조각사(彫刻師) a copperplate engraver ; a chalcographer ; a chalcographist —화(畫) a copperplate print

동패 銅牌 a copper medal ; a copper medallion (큰 것)

동편 東便 the east〔eastern〕 side

*동포 同胞 [형제] brothers ; [동국민] brethren ; fellow countrymen ; one's countrymen ; compatriots ; fellow creature (인류) ¶ 5천만 동포에 고하노라 A word for fifty-million compatriots ! // 5천만 동포여 일어나라 Arise, ye fifty million compatriots !

—애 brotherly〔fraternal〕 love ; fraternity ; fellow feeling 사해(四海) — universal〔world〕 brotherhood

동풍 東風 the east wind ; the wind from east ; an easterly wind

동하다 動— ① [행동] go out ; turn out ; move out ; be on the move ; be mobilized ¶ 군대가 동하다 troops turn out ; troops are put on duty // 수십 대의 소방차가 동하다 dozens of fire engines turn out

② [마음이] waver ; fluctuate ; vacillate ; be inclined to 《do》 ; be itching to 《do》 ; be shaken ¶ 동하지 않는 마음 an imperturbable mind // 식지가〔구미가〕 동하다 one's fingers itch 《to do》 ; feel an appetite for ; feel a strong desire 《to do》

동학 同學 a fellow student ; a classmate ; one's schoolfellow ; a fellow scholar ; fellow researcher

동항 凍港 an icebound port ¶ 부동항 an ice-free port

동항 同行 the same generation(al) (bracket) ¶ 동항이다 belong to the same generation

동해 東海 the East Sea ; The Sea of Japan (공식 명칭)

동해 凍害 frost damage

동해안 東海岸 the east coast

동행 同行 going together ; traveling together —하다 go (along) with ; go in company with ; accompany 《a person》 ; go in 《a person's》 company ; travel together ¶ 경찰서에 동행을 요구하다 request 《a person》 to come to the police station // 동행케 해 주시오 Let me go with you. // 동행은 5인이었다 We were a party of five. /The party was formed of five persons. // 경찰관은 그 사람을 경찰서까지 동행했다 The policeman took〔walked〕 him to the police station.

—자 fellow travelers ; a companion

동향 同鄕 the same province〔town, village〕 ¶ 그는 나와 동향입니다 He comes from the same province as I (myself).

—인 a person from the same province 〔town, village〕

동향 東向 an eastern exposure〔aspect〕 ; facing east 《from the west》 —하다 face east ; look toward the east ¶ 동향집 a house facing east ; a house with an eastern aspect〔exposure〕

동향 動向 a tendency ; a trend ; a movement ; an attitude ¶ 경제 동향 an economic trend // 세계의 동향을 보라 See how the world is moving. // 정계는 그것에 대하여 아무런 동향도 나타내지 않았다 There are no signs in the political circles of doing anything about it. // 그 당시의 학생들은 자칫하면 염세 사상에 물드는 동향이 있었다 The students of those days were too often disposed to develop pessimistic sentiments.

동혈 洞穴 a cave ; a cavern ; a grotto

동형 同型 the same〔said〕 type〔pattern〕 ; a similar type ¶ 동형이다 be of the same type〔kind〕

동형 同形 the same shape ¶ 동형의 of the same shape

동호 同好 the same taste —하다 share the same taste ¶ 음악 동호회 a music-lovers' society

—자 men of similar taste (취미) ; interested persons (이해 관계) —회 an association of like-minded persons

*동화 同化 assimilation ; [순응] adaptation ; 〖생물〗 anabolism —하다 assimilate 《with》 ; adapt oneself to (순응) ¶ 동화하기 어렵다 be hard to assimilate ; be unassimilable // 외국 이민을 동화시키다 assimilate foreign immigrants // 외국의 풍습에 동화하다 adapt oneself to foreign customs

—성 assimilability — 세포 an assimilatory cell —수 〖생물〗 metabolic water — 조직 an assimilation tissue

동화 銅貨 a copper coin〔piece〕 ; a copper ; a red (cent) 《미》 ; [전체] copper coinage ¶ 5원 동화 a five *won* copper coin

동화 童話 a fairy tale ; a nursery story 〔tale〕 ; a juvenile story〔tale〕 ; a juvenile story

—극 a juvenile play — 작가 a writer of juvenile stories ; a fairy tale writer ; a nursery tale writer

동화 動畫 [만화 영화] an animation ; an animated film〔cartoon〕

— 제작자 an animator〔animater〕

동화력 同化力 assimilative power ¶ 동화력이 있는 assimilative
동화 작용 同化作用 assimilation ; metabolism (세포의) ; anabolism (음식물의)
동활자 銅活字 a copper type ; the copper types
동활차 動滑車 a movable pulley
동홰 a large torch
동회 洞會 [동의 임] a *dong*〔village〕 council〔meeting〕; [동사무소] a *dong*〔village〕 office
—장 the head of a *dong* office
†**돛** a sail ; a canvas ; muslin 《속》; a jib (삼각형의) ¶ 돛을 내리다 lower〔take down〕 a sail ; strike a sail (급히) // 돛을 펴다〔감다〕 unfurl〔furl〕 a sail // 돛을 달고 달리다 be under sail〔canvas〕 // 순풍에 돛을 달고 달리다 sail before the (fair) wind ; be under easy sail
돛을 달다 관용 hoist〔spread, put up〕 a sail
***돛단배** a sailing ship〔sailing boat, sailing vessel〕; a sailer
****돛대** a mast ; a stick ¶ 돛대를 잃은 배 a dismasted vessel
돠르르, 똬르르 gurgling ; gushing ; copiously ¶ 돠르르 흘러나오다 gush out 《of》; flow out (copiously)
돨돨, 똘똘 [배가] rumble (because of indigestion)
†**돼지** a pig ; (a) swine ; [거세한] a hog ; [암컷] a sow ; [수컷] a boar ; [비유적] a greedy person ¶ 돼지 같은 piggish ; hoggish ; swinish // 돼지같이 piggishly ; hoggishly ; swinishly // 돼지 같은 생활 a dog's life ; an animal life // 돼지같이 살찐 fat as a pig // 돼지를 치다 keep〔breed〕 pigs ; raise hogs
—고기 pork **—기름** lard **—우리** a pigsty ; a pigpen **—치기** a swineherd **새끼—** a pigling ; a hogling ; a piglet ; a shoat (한 살 미만의) ; a young pig ; a piggy
돼지 목에 진주 속담 To cast pearl before swine.
그슬린 돼지가 달아맨 돼지 타령한다 속담 The pot calls the kettle black. /Ill may kiln call the oven burnt-tail. /The frying-pan said to the kettle, 'Avaunt, black brows.'/ The kettle calls the pot burnt-arse.
되[1] [계량기] a measure ; a dry measure (곡식용) ; a liquid measure (액체용) ; [한되] a *doe* 《a unit of measure, 10 *hop*》 ¶ 다섯 되들이 되 a five *doe* measure // 되를 속이다 give short measure // 되글을 가지고 말글로 써먹다 turn one's learning to best advantage ; make the most of meager education
되로 주고 말로 받는다 속담 To sow the wind and reap the whirlwind.
되[2] [만주인] a Manchurian ; [중국인] a Chinese
되[3] [도로·다시] back ; again ; [도리어] on the contrary ; instead ¶ 되묻다 ask in return // 되사다 buy back // 되돌아가다 return ; go back // 되씹다 chew again ; ruminate // 되풀이하다 say again ; repeat ; reiterate // 칭찬하기는 커녕 되나무라다 blame 《a person》 far from〔on the contrary to〕 praising him
-되 ① though ; although ; even though ; but ¶ 아름답기는 하되 지성미가 없다 Although she is beautiful, she lacks intellectual beauty. /It is true (that) she is beautiful, but the intellectual appeal is undesirable. // 그는 학자이되 상식이 없다 He is a learned scholar, to be sure, but lacks common sense.
② [조건] if ; when ¶ 보기는 보되 만지지는 말아라 You may look at it, but don't touch it !
③ [부연] and that ¶ 그는 그것을 하되 훌륭하게 해냈다 He did it, and that very well.
되가지다 take〔get〕 《a thing》 back
되갈다 [논밭을] replow ; replough 《영》; retill ; plow〔till〕 again ; [가루를] regrind ; grind again
되감다 rewind ¶ 되감는 기계 a rewinder
되걸리다 be seized with a relapse ; have〔suffer〕 a relapse ; relapse 《into illness》 ¶ 감기에 되걸리다 catch cold again // 과로로 말미암아 병에 되걸렸다 He got a relapse through strain. /Strain brought on a relapse on his illness.
되게 [몹시] very ; exceedingly ; extraordinarily ; hard ; severely ; heavily ; bitterly ; extremely ; awfully ¶ 되게 덥다 be very hot // 되게 걱정되다 be much worried
되깎이 〖불교〗 ① [승려직에 복귀] returning to the Buddhist priesthood (after having once left it) ; [사람] a reinstated monk ② [재혼] remarriage of a woman ; [사람] a remarried woman
되나오다 come out again ; appear
되내기 [땔나무의] firewood rebundled to look nice〔bulky, large〕
되넘기 brokerage ; reselling **—하다** act as (a) broker ; resell
—장사 broking ; brokerage
되넘기다 resell ; pass round
되넘기 장수 a reseller ; a middleman ; a jobber ; a broker
되놈 [만주인] a Manchurian ; [중국인] a Chinese
되다 keep repeating 《words》 ¶ 남의 말을 되뇌다 echo〔repeat〕 a person's words
되는 대로 ① [되어가는 대로] ¶ 되는 대로 지내다 ride with the tide ; trust to chance // 세상 되는 대로 따라가다 take the world as it is // 세상일을 되는 대로 내버려두다 leave 《a matter》 to take its own course
② [마구] at random ; without thinking ¶ 되는 대로 지껄이다 talk irresponsibly

; say at a venture // 되는 대로 살다 live in a happy go-lucky way // (일을) 되는 대로 하다 do 《things》 at random ; take chances // 되는 대로 대답하다 answer at haphazard ; make a random answer

***되다¹** ① [빡빡하다] (be) thick ; tough ; hard ; stiff ¶ 되게 thickly // 된 죽 thick gruel // 된 밥 hard-boiled rice // 밥이 좀 되다 The rice is rather hard-boiled. // 이 셔츠의 풀이 너무 되다 This shirt is starched too stiff.
② [줄 따위가] (be) taut ; tense ; be stretched tight ¶ 되게 동이다 tie tightly
③ [심하다] (be) severe ; intense ; bitter ; heavy ; foul (병이) ¶ 된 서리 heavy frost // 된 추위 intense〔bitter, severe〕 cold // 되게 얻어맞다 be beaten hard // 되게 아프다 be very〔extremely〕 painful // 된 감기에 걸리다 catch〔get〕 a bad cold
④ [힘들다] (be) hard ; tough ; bitter ; be beyond one's capacity〔power〕 ¶ 된 일 hard〔heavy〕 work ; a tough job // 된고비 the worst〔hardest〕 part ; a crisis ; a crucial moment // 일이 좀 되었던 모양이군 The work seems to have been a little too hard for him. // 이 일은 내게는 되다 This work is beyond my capacity.

되다² [되질] measure ¶ 쌀을 되다 measure rice // 되어 팔다 sell by measure

†**되다³** ① [지위·신분·상태 따위가] be ; become ; get ; grow ; make ; [때가] come ¶ 겨울이 되면 in winter ; when winter comes // 남의 입장이 되어보다 put oneself in another's position // (성장하여) 위인이 되다 grow up to be a great man // 부자가 되다 become〔grow〕 rich // 선원이 되다 go to sea // 어른이 되다 grow into a man // 곧 여름 방학이 된다 We shall soon have the summer holidays. // 그녀는 좋은 아내가 될 것이다 She will make a good wife. // 봄이 되었다 Spring has come. // 아주 미인이 되었군 그래 You have grown a beauty. // 내 나이 오십이 되었으니 나도 한물갔어 I turned fifty, so I'm over the hill now. // 목소리만 좋다고 해서 가수가 되는 것은 아니잖아요 A good voice alone doesn't make a singer. // 나도 그처럼 되어 보았으면 What I wouldn't give to be in his shoes !
② [변하다] turn〔change〕 《into》 ; develop ¶ 노랗게 되다 turn yellow // 중이 되다 turn (to be) a monk // 합쳐서 하나가 되다 unite into one // 재화를 바꾸어 오히려 복이 되게 하다 turn one's misfortune to account // 달걀이 병아리가 된다 An egg develops〔changes〕 into a chicken. // 머리가 거의 백발이 되었다 His hair had gone nearly white. // 지식이 당장에 돈이 될 수는 없다 Knowledge cannot be turned to immediate account.
③ [성립하다] consist of ; be composed of ; be made up of ; form ; constitute ¶ 국회는 양원으로 되어 있다 The National Assembly consists of two Houses. // 그 회는 250명의 회원으로 되어 있다 The association is composed of 250 members. // 사회는 개인의 집합체로 되어 있다 A community is composed of individuals. // 지중해는 영국의 생명선이 되어 있다 The Mediterranean constitutes Britain's life line.
④ [성취하다] succeed ; be realized ; be accomplished ¶ 계획이 제대로 됐다 A plan is effected. /A plot is carried out. // 공사가 다 되었다 The work is finished〔completed〕. // 돈이면 안될 일이 없다 Money is everything. // 되고 안되고는 자네에게 달렸다 Its success or failure solely rests〔depends〕 upon you. // 만사가 제대로 되었다 All went well (with us).
⑤ [결과가] turn out ; result ; prove ¶ 될 대로 되게 내버려 두다 leave 《things》 to their own course // 무죄가 되다 prove innocent ; be found not guilty // 실현이 되다 come true // 그 분은 어떻게 되었지요 What has become of him ? // 그 상처가 치명상이 되었다 The wound proved fatal. // 될 대로 되기 마련이다 What must be, must be. // 선거가 어떻게 될까 How will the election turn out ? // 차차 알게 됩니다 You will come to understand by and by. // 될 대로 되라 Go to the devil ! /I don't care a damn about it.
⑥ [수량이] come to ; amount to ; reach ¶ 몇 천길이나 되는 깊은 물 water (that is) several thousand fathoms deep // 결혼한 지 10년이 된다 It is ten years since we got married. /We have been married for ten years. // 얼마나 되지요 How much does that come to ? // 합계 3,000원이 됩니다 It amounts to 3,000 *won* in all. // 합계하면 2,000원 이상이나 됩니다 It totals more than 2,000 *won*.
⑦ [구실을 하다] act 《as》 ; play ; serve 《as》 ; play the role 《of》 ¶ 중매인이 되다 act as (a) go-between // (연극에서) 오델로가 되다 play the part of Othello // 알코올은 소독약이 된다 Alcohol acts as a disinfectant.
⑧ [연령·시일] attain ; reach ; turn ; [경과] elapse ; pass ; it is 《a week》 since ¶ 몇 백년이나 된 고목 a tree centuries old // 그가 죽은 지 3년이 된다 It is three years〔Three years have elapsed〕 since he died. // 그는 꼭 16세가 됐다 He has just turned sixteen. /He has just attained the age of sixteen. // 이번 생일로 30살이 된다 I shall be thirty years old next birthday. // 이 식탁보는 간 지 사흘이 된다 This tablecloth is three days old. // 일주일이면 만 1년이 된다 Another week will make a full year.
⑨ [시작하다] begin to ; come to ; learn to ; set in ¶ 관심을 갖게 되다 begin to pay attention 《to》 // 좋아하게 되다 begin〔get, come, grow〕 to like 《a thing》 // 그

에 대한 흥미를 점차 잃게 되었다 My interest in it is flagging more and more.
⑩ [가능하다] can 《do》; be able to 《do》; be equal to 《the task》; [사물이 주어] be possible ¶ 될 수 있으면 if (it is) possible〔practicable〕; if one can help it // 안될 일을 부질 없이 바라다 cry for the moon // 무엇이든 사람의 힘으로 안될 일이 없다 Human power is equal to anything.
⑪ [자라다] grow; thrive; prosper ¶ 그런 과일은 여기서는 잘 안된다 Those kinds of fruit do not grow well here. // 올해는 쌀이 잘 됐다 We have had a good crop of rice this year. // 이 언덕에는 포도가 잘 된다 Grapes grow well on this hill.
⑫ [쓸만하다] (will) do〔work〕; serve the purpose; be all right ¶ 이 의자면 될까요 Will this chair do you? // 그거면 돼 That will do me very well.
되면 더 되고 싶다 (속담) The more a man has, the more he desires.

-되다 ① [동사적 명사에 붙어] become; get to be; be ¶ 근심되다 be worried〔anxious〕 about // 시작되다 begin; have a beginning // 해결되다 get solved〔resolved〕
② [형용사·부사적 어근에 붙어] be ¶ 망녕되다 be silly; be nonsensical; be unreasonable; be preposterous // 속되다 be vulgar〔common〕 // 참되다 be true // 헛되다 be false; be in vain; be futile

되다랗다 (be) rather heavy and thick

되대패 a round plane; a circular plane

되던지다 throw〔hurl, cast〕 back

되도록 ① [될 수 있는 대로] as...as possible; as much as you can ¶ 되도록 빨리 달려라 Run as fast as possible〔you can〕. // 되도록 시간을 유효하게 쓰시오 Make the best (use) of your time. ② [될 수 있게] ¶ 일등이 되도록 힘써 봐라 Try hard for the first place.

되돌다 turn back around

되돌려주다 return; give back; bring back; [부쳐서] send back; [떨어 뜨린 주인에게] restore ¶ 돈을 되돌려주다 give back the money 《one borrowed》

되돌리다 ① ⇨ 되돌려주다 ¶ 되돌려지다 be sent back (반송); be restored〔recovered〕 (도난품·분실물 따위가) ② [원상태로] restore ¶ 원위치로 되돌리다 put 《a thing》 back in its place〔where it was〕 ③ [뒤로 물리다] put〔turn〕 back; back ④ [각하하다] reject; turn down; dismiss ¶ 청원서를 되돌리다 reject a (written) petition

†되돌아가다 ① [오던 길로] turn〔go〕 back; retrace one's steps; turn on one's heels; put back 《to》 (선박이); go back where one came ¶ 도중에서 되돌아가다 turn back halfway // 배는 폭풍 때문에 부산으로 되돌아갔다 The ship put back to *Pusan* owing to the storm.
② [원상으로] return 《to》; go back 《to》; revert 《to》 ¶ 예전 직업으로 되돌아가다 return to one's former business // 본론으로 되돌아가다 revert〔return〕 to the subject

되돌아들다 [사람이] come back; return; find one's way back

되돌아오다 come back; retrace one's steps ⇨ 되돌아가다 ¶ 잃어버린 물건이 주인에게 되돌아왔다 The lost article was restored to its owner. // 빌려준 돈이 전부 되돌아왔다 All the loans were paid back.

되들고 되나다 《people》 come in and out continuously〔in succession〕

되들다 raise one's face defiantly

되때까치 〖새〗 a red-tailed shrike 〔butcherbird〕; Lanius cristatus (학명)

되똑거리다 totter; be unstable; shake; be shaky ¶ 책상 다리가 되똑거린다 The leg of a table is shaky. // 하이힐을 신고 되똑거리다 totter (along) on high heels

되똑되똑 tottering; unstable; unsteady; shaky ¶ 어린애가 되똑되똑 걷다 child is tottering (along)

되뜨다 (be) irrational; illogical; unreasonable; go against reason

되롱거리다 dangle; sway; swing ¶ 되롱되롱 dangling; swaying // 사과가 바람에 되롱거린다 Apples are dangling in the wind. // 등이 바람에 되롱거린다 A lantern is swaying in the wind.

되룽거리다 hold one's head high; be haughty; act stuck-up〔high-hatted, high-browed〕 《구》

되리 a woman with no pubic hair

되매기 a reclaimed comb

되모시 a divorcee who alleges to be a virgin

되묻다 ① [다시 묻다] ask again ② [반문] counter a question by asking another; ask back

되밀다 push back

되바라지다 ① [얕다·노출되다] (be) open; shallow; exposed ¶ 되바라진 접시 a shallow dish // 되바라진 장소 an exposed place ② [편협하다] (be) shallow-brained; narrow-minded; intolerant; illiberal ③ [너무 똑똑하다] (be) overly smart〔bright〕; too sharp; sophisticated; pert; saucy; forward; cheeky ¶ 되바라진 사람 a pert〔sophisticated〕 person; a pert〔saucy〕 girl (여자)

되박다 print〔inlay, drive in, *etc.*〕 again; reprint

되박이 a reprint(ing) ── 하다 reprint

되받다 stand up to a scolding; scold back

되부르다 call back; recall

되사 about one *doe* of grain left over when measuring with a *mal*

되살다 ① [먹은 음식이] remain undigested in the stomach; be heavy on one's stomach; feel uncomfortable because of indigestion
② [소생하다] revive; return〔come back〕

to life ; come to oneself〔to one's sense〕; resuscitate ; be freshened ; 《a dying fire》 be rekindled ; flame up again ¶ 죽어가던 사람이 되살다 a dying person comes back to life〔rises from the dead, is brought back to life〕// 가사 상태에서 되살아나다 resuscitate〔be restored〕 from apparent death // 되살리다 restore 《a person》 to life ; raise 《a person》 from the dead // 기억을 되살려 드려야겠군요 I think I should refresh your memory.

되살피다 reexamine ; look back over it again

되새 〖새〗 the brambling

되새기다 [음식을] chew over and over again ; [소 따위가] ruminate ; chew the cud; [마음 속으로] meditate 《on, upon》 ; digest 《an idea》 ; remember ; bear in mind

되새김질 rumination ; cud-chewing

되세우다 make 《a fallen thing》 stand again ; stand〔erect, raise〕 《a thing》 again ; [건조하다] build again〔anew〕; rebuild ; reerect

되솔새 〖새〗 a pale-legged willow-warbler

되술래잡다 counterattack ; put the blame on another ; retort 《on》 ; give a retort 《on》 ; turn the table 《on》

되술래잡히다 be counterattacked ; be counterblamed

되쏘다 [총·화살 따위를] shoot back ; [반사하다] reflect ; [말로] retort

되씌우다 put〔lay, fix〕 《a blame》 on another ; lay 《a fault》 at another's door ; fix〔put〕 《one's responsibility》 on another

되씹다 ① [말을] reiterate ; say over again ; repeat oneself ; repeat the same thing ; harp on the same thing ¶ 추억을 되씹다 carry one's thought back to the past // 그는 같은 말을 되씹을 뿐이었다 He did nothing but repeat himself. // 같은 말을 몇 번씩이나 되씹니 You have been saying that so long. ② [음식을] chew over and over

되알지다 [무리한 고집] (be) forcing ; coercive ; aggressive ; high-handed ; pushing ; [힘에 벅차다] be more than one can do ; be beyond one's power

되양되양하다 (be) flippant ; frivolous

되어가다 be turning out〔shaping up, panning out, becoming of〕 ¶ 뜻대로 되어가다 be coming up to one's expectations // 잘 되어가다 be going well〔all right〕; be working well // 일이 되어가다 one's work is getting done ; an attempt is going to be successful

되우 very ; exceedingly ; extraordinarily ; heavily ; severely ; bitterly ; extremely ; awfully ; hard ¶ 되우 춥다 be very cold // 되우 무식하다 be quite ignorant // 되우 근심되다 be much worried

되우새 〖새〗 a spectacled teal ; Anas formosa (학명)

되작거리다 ransack ; rummage ; fumble〔feel〕 for ⇨ 뒤적거리다

되잖다 be no good ; (be) good-for-nothing ; poor ; wretched ; worthless ; be a failure ; be a complete botch ; [엉터리없는] (be) absurd ; nonsensical ¶ 되잖은 물건 poor〔wretched〕 stuff // 되잖은 수작 absurd remark ; nonsense // 되잖은 일 trifling matter ; a worthless plan // 되잖은 핑계 a poor〔lame〕 excuse

되잡다 lay the blame on another ⇨ 되씌우다

되장이 a person who measures grain at a rice-dealer's

되지기[1] [밥] reheated rice

되지기[2] [논밭] 《a field》 wide enough to plant one *doe* of seed

되지못하다 ① [미달] be short of ; be not up to ; be less than ; be under ¶ 성년이 되지못하다 be under age ② [미완성] be not made ; be not finished〔completed, attained, accomplished〕; (be) unsuccessful ; fall through ¶ 식사가 다 되지못하다 a meal is not ready ③ [격이] be not able〔fit〕 to become ; be not successful (in being) ; be not worthy of ¶ 학자가 되지못하다 be not worthy of being called a scholar ④ [사람답지 못함] be no good ; (be) good-for-nothing ; be not up to the mark ; be not proper ; be not decent ; [건방짐] (be) impudent ; presumptuous ; pert ; saucy ¶ 되지못한 녀석 a good-for-nothing ; a failure ; a presumptuous fellow

되지빠귀 〖새〗 a gray-backed thrush

되직하다 (be) somewhat thick〔heavy〕; a bit too hard ¶ 풀이 되직하다 The paste is a bit thick.

되질 measuring with a *doe* **—하다** measure with a *doe*

되짚어 back ; retracing at once ; returning soon〔right away〕 ¶ 되짚어 가다 retrace one's steps〔way〕 right away ; go〔turn〕 back right away // 되짚어 보내다 send right back ; send back at once // 되짚어 오다 come right back

‡되찾다 [도로 찾다] get〔take〕 back ; regain ; retake ; resume ; restore ; recover ; repossess

되채다 enunciate distinctly and easily

되치이다 be counterattacked ; go for wool and come home shorn ; have the tables turned upon 《one》 ¶ 되치인 격이로군 It is a case of the biter having been bit.

되통스럽다 (be) clumsy ; bungling ; thick ; thick-headed ; obtuse ¶ 되통스러운 사람 a bungler ; a botcher // 그가 하는 짓마다 되통스럽다 He does everything in a clumsy way. // 그는 되통스러워 일을 잘 저지른다 He is such a thick-headed fellow he makes a bungle of everything he does.

되튀다 rebound 《upon》; resile ; recoil 《on》; spring back ; boomerang 《on》; [힘차게] bounce ; spring〔jump〕 up
되티티 ⇨ 되지빠귀
†**되풀이**[1] repetition ; reiteration ; doing over again **—하다** do 《a thing》 over again ; repeat ; reiterate ¶ 되풀이하여 repeatedly ; over again ; over and over again ; again and again // 잘못을 되풀이하다 repeat〔duplicate〕 one's mistake // 그는 연설할 때 같은 말을 되풀이하는 버릇이 있다 He often repeats himself in his speech. // 역사는 되풀이한다 History repeats itself. // 유행은 되풀이된다 Fashions repeat themselves.
되풀이[2] [되로 계산] figuring out the cost 《of a thing》 by the *doe* ; [되로 팔기] selling by the *doe* **—하다** figure〔sell〕 by the *doe*
된똥 hard stool〔feces〕
된마파람 [뱃사람 말] a southeast wind
된매 a severe beating ¶ 된매를 맞다 be severely beaten
된바람 [강풍] a rushing wind ; a gale ; a hurricane ; a violent wind ; [북풍] a northerly wind
된밥 hard-boiled〔overcooked〕 rice
된비알 a very steep slope〔hill〕
된새(바람) [뱃사람 말] a northeast(erly) wind
된서리 a heavy frost ; a severe frost
된서리를 맞다 관용 suffer from a heavy frost ; [혼나다] suffer a great blow ; receive a setback ; be hit hard
된서방 —書房 a hard〔severe, harsh〕 husband
된서방 맞다 관용 marry a hard husband ; [어려움을 당함] suffer an ordeal ; have a great trouble ; be faced with a great difficulty
된장 —醬 soybean paste
—국 bean-paste potage〔soup〕 **—찌개** beanpaste pot stew
된침 —鍼 a painful needle
된풀 thick paste〔starch〕
된하늬 [뱃사람 말] a northwest(erly) wind
될뻔댁 —宅 a person who narrowly missed a chance of success
될성부르다 promising ; auspicious
될성부른 나무는 떡잎부터 알아본다 속담 First impressions are the most lasting./ The first blow is half the battle.
됨됨이 ① [사람] one's character〔nature, personality, disposition〕 ¶ 됨됨이가 정직하다 He is honest by nature〔in character〕. ② [물건] the make ; the makeup ; workmanship ¶ 그 가구의 됨됨이가 멋있다 The set of furniture is of excellent workmanship.
됫밑 leftover grain after measuring with a *doe* measure
됫박 a gourd bowl used as a measure
됫박질 **—하다** measure with a gourd bowl
됫수 —數 the quantity 《of grain》 stated in *doe* ¶ 됫수가 틀리다 The measure is wrong.
됫술 about one *doe* of rice wine
*****두** two ; a couple ¶ 두 배 double ; two times // 두 번 twice ; again ; two times // 두 내외 husband and wife ; a couple // 두 번째 아내 the second wife // 같은 실패를 두 번 거듭하지 마라 Don't repeat the same failure (again). // 이력서를 두 통 내십시오 Turn in your résumé in duplicate.
두 손뼉이 맞아야 소리가 난다 속담 It takes two to make a quarrel.
두 頭 a head 《of cattle, horses》 ¶ 소 5두 five heads of cattle
두각 頭角 top of the head ; prominence ; conspicuousness ¶ 과학계에 두각을 나타내다 become distinguished in science // 단연 두각을 나타내고 있다 He is head and shoulders above his fellows. // 그는 학생 때부터 두각을 나타내더니만 역시 진짜 실력이 있었군 He shone as a student, and I guess he was for real after all.
두각을 나타내다 관용 distinguish oneself ; become distinguished ; obtain distinction ; cut a conspicuous figure ; stand out ; lead all the rest ; come to the front
두개 頭蓋 the cranium 《*pl.* ~s, -nia》; the brainpan
—골 a skull ; the cranium ; a cranial bone **—골(骨) 측정법** craniometry **— 동물** a craniate animal **— 수술** craniotomy **— 시수(示數)** a cranial index **— 측정기** a cephalometer **— 측정법** cephalometry **—학(學)** cranilogy
두건 頭巾 a mourner's hempen hood ¶ 두건을 쓰다 put on a hempen hood
두겁 an ornamental cap at the tip of a long and slender object ¶ 붓 두겁 a sheath of a writing brush
두겁조상 —祖上 one's most distinguished ancestor
두견 杜鵑 ① [소쩍새] a cuckoo ② [진달래] an azalea
두고가다 leave 《a thing》 behind 《one》; leave 《a thing》 for 《a person》; forget
두고두고 many times ; from time to time ; over and over again ; over a long period ; [영원히] forever ; for good and all ; [잊히지 않고] hauntingly ; unforgettably ¶ 두고두고 먹다 keep 《a thing》 and eat it sparingly // 그것은 두고두고 쓸 수 있다 It can be used a number of times. // 이룬 업적에 대하여 두고두고 칭찬받는다 He is praised occasionally for the achievements he once made. // 이 원한은 두고두고 잊지 못하겠다 I shall carry the resentment to the grave. // 두고두고 잊히지 않는다 The memory always haunts me./It haunts my memory.
두고보다 [지켜보다] watch (intently) ;

keep (a good) watch (over) ¶ 어디 두고 봅시다 Let's wait and see. // 너 어디 두고 보자 You'll pay for this. /You won't get away with this.

두고오다 mislay ; misplace ; leave《a thing》(behind) ; forget

두골 頭骨 the cranial bones ; the skull

두그르르, 뚜그르르 rolling ; tumbling ; rumbling

두근거리다 go pitapat ; palpitate ; throb《with emotion》¶ 가슴을 두근거리며 with a beating heart ; in a flutter // 가슴이 두근거리다 one's heart palpitates ; one's heart throbs // 두근거리는 가슴을 가라앉히다 calm one's agitated breast // 그 소식을 듣고 나는 가슴이 두근거렸다 I fell into a flutter at the news. /My heart beat quick at the news. // 가슴이 심하게 두근거려서 어젯밤에는 잠을 거의 못 잤다 My heart was pounding so hard I could hardly sleep last night.

‡**두근두근** pitapat ; palpitating ; throbbing

두글두글 rolling continuously ; with a continuous rolling

두길마보기 double-dealing ; duplicity ; opportunism ; a wait-and-see policy

두길마보다 straddle ; sit on the fence ; try to face both ways

***두꺼비** 〖동물〗 a toad ¶ 두꺼비 같은 toadish // 두꺼비 꽁지만하다 be shallow 〔superficial〕 in one's learning〔talent〕
— **씨름** a tie game
두꺼비 파리 잡아먹듯 (속담) be ready to eat anything ; eat up anything in a twinkling

두꺼비집 [전기] a fuse box ; [보습의] the depressed part of a plow blade where the handle fits

†**두껍다** (be) thick ; heavy ; bulky ; stout ¶ 두꺼운 판자 a thick board // 두꺼운 벽 a heavy wall // 두꺼운 책 a bulky〔stout〕 book

두껍다랗다 (be) somewhat thick ; rather heavy

두껍다리 a small stone bridge (over a ditch)

두껍닫이 〖건축〗 a sliding door pocket ; a box(ing) (창의)

***두께** thickness ¶ 두께가 5인치이다 be five inches thick〔in thickness〕 // 두께 1인치의 합판 one inch plywood

두남두다 [편역들다] be partial to ; show favoritism〔partiality〕 to ; have a bias for ; [가엾게 여겨] sympathize and help

두뇌 頭腦 a head ; brains ¶ 치밀한〔산만한〕 두뇌 a close〔loose〕 head // 두뇌가 명석하다 have a clear head ; be clearheaded // 그의 두뇌는 실무에 적합하다 He has a good head for business.
— **노동** brain work — **노동자** a brain 〔mental〕 worker **인공** — a mechanical brain **전자** — an electronic brain

†**두다** ① [놓다] put ; place ; lay ; set ; deposit (일정 장소에) ¶ 방 안을 정돈해 두다 put〔set〕 a room in order // 그것을 책상 위에 두시오 Lay〔Put〕 it on the table.
② [보관·저장하다] keep ; store ; hold ¶ 돈을 금고에 두다 keep money in a safe
③ [남겨두다] leave (behind) ¶ 메모를 써서 두다 leave a note for《a person》// 우산을 버스에 두고 내리다 leave one's umbrella in a bus // 책을 집에 두고 오다 come leaving one's book at home
④ [주둔·배치하다] station ; post ; put ; arrange ¶ 보초를 세워 두다 post〔put〕 a sentry // 연도에 경관을 배치하여 두다 station〔post〕 police along the route
⑤ [고용하다] keep ; employ ; engage ; adopt ; have ¶ 개〔고양이〕를 두다 keep a dog〔cat〕 // 사람을 두다 employ〔hire〕《a person》; keep a servant〔housemaid〕 // 하숙인을 두다 keep〔take, take in〕 a boarder // 양자를 두다 adopt a son // 형제를 두다 have brothers
⑥ [설치] set up ; establish ; place ; appoint (임명) ¶ 부산에 지점을 두다 set up〔have〕 the branch office in *Pusan* // 근거를 두다 establish grounds ; base《one's argument》 on // 차이를 두다 make a difference // 중점을 두다 put emphasis《on》 // 각부에 장관을 두다 place〔appoint〕 a minister for each department
⑦ [간격을] leave (an interval) ¶ 5피트 간격을 두고 leaving an interval of 5 feet // 10년을 두고 못 보았다 have not seen for ten years
⑧ [품다] hold ; entertain ; cherish ; set on ; have ; bear ; harbor ¶ 희망을 두다 entertain a hope // 확신을 두다 hold a conviction // 앙심을 두다 harbor hatred ; bear《a person》 ill will ; bear a grudge 《against a person》; bear malice《to a person for a thing》// 마음을 두다 have a mind to ; be determined to ; fix〔set〕 one's mind on // 애정을 두다 have an affection 《for, toward》
⑨ [장기 따위를] move《a chessman, checker》; play ¶ 장기를 한 판 두다 play one round of chess // 어서 두어라 Go on and move.
⑩ [넣다] put into ; add ; stuff ¶ 밥에 팥을 두다 put beans in the rice // 이불에 솜을 두다 stuff a quilt with cotton
⑪ [조동사로서] have ; get ; let ; allow ; keep ; leave ¶ 그대로 놓아 두라 Leave it as it is. // 먹어 두자 Let's eat it up anyway. // 그는 이렇게 해두고 싶은 거야 He wants it this way. // 그의 이름은 존 브라운이라고 해두자 His name, let us say, was John Brown. // 아이를 자게 해두어 Keep the child asleep.

두다리 ¶ 두다리 걸치다 have〔play〕 it both ways ; play (a) double (game)

두대박이 a two-masted ship ; a two-master

***두더지** 〖동물〗 a mole ¶ 두더지 가죽 mole-

skin
두덜거리다, 뚜덜거리다 grumble 《about, at》; complain 《of, about》; mutter 《at, against》; murmur 《at, against》; gripe 《미·속》 ¶ 자기 맡은 일에 대하여〔식사에 대하여〕 두덜거리다 grumble over one's task〔at the food〕// 그는 연해 두덜거렸다 He kept on muttering and complaining. // 그들은 하고 싶은 것을 할 틈이 없다고 두덜거린다 They complain that they cannot find time to do what they want to do.
두덜두덜 grumbling; complaining; griping; bitching; nagging
두덩 ① [둑] a bank; an embankment; a levee (논의) ¶ 논두덩 a levee; a ridge between rice fields // 밭두덩 a bank around a field ② [신체의] a raised part of the body; a mound ¶ 눈두덩 an upper eyelid
두동지다 (be) (self-) contradictory; inconsistent 《with》; incoherent ¶ 그것은 그의 이상과 두동진다 It conflicts〔is inconsistent〕 with his ideal.
두두룩이 ① [돋아 오른 모양] protuberantly; protrusively; into a swell〔an elevation〕 ¶ 흙을 두두룩이 쌓아 올리다 pile earth up into a small mound // 젖가슴을 두두룩이 내밀다 her breasts stand out from the chest
② [많이] much; plenty; satisfactorily ¶ 돈을 두두룩이 집어주다 give plenty of money
두두룩하다 (be) swollen; bulged (out); protuberant; puffy ¶ 두두룩한 지갑 a well-filled purse // 두두룩이 much; plenty; satisfactorily // 돈을 두두룩이 주다 give plenty of money
두둑 a ridge between fields; a levee (두덩)
두둑하다 [두텁다] (be) thick; heavy; [넉넉하다] ample; plenty; satisfactory ¶ 두둑한 사례 an ample reward // 호주머니에 두둑한 돈 a pocketful of money
***두둔** —하다 back 《the weak》; give support to; stand by; side〔take sides〕 with 《a person》 ¶ 죄인을 두둔하다 shelter a culprit // 약자를 두둔해 말하다 talk in favor of〔in defense of〕 the weak // 친구가 두둔해 주었다 My friend stood〔spoke〕 up for me.
두둥둥 tee-dum-dum
두둥실 floating gently〔lightly〕; in an airy manner ¶ 두둥실 뜨다 waft // 하늘 높이 두둥실 뜬 기구 a balloon floating on high
두드러기 nettle rash; hives; (allergic) urticaria ¶ 두드러기가 돋다 have urtication; form wheals (in urticaria); break out in a rash; have a breaking-out
***두드러지다** ① [내밀다] swell; bulge out; stick out; project; jut; protrude ¶ 종기가 두드러지다 a boil is swollen up
② [뚜렷하다] (be) prominent; salient; [현저하다] striking; remarkable; distinguished; conspicuous; outstanding ¶ 그의 성격의 두드러진 특징 the salient traits of his character // 그는 한국전 당시 두드러진 공적을 세웠다 He rendered distinguished services in the Korean War.
†**두드리다, 뚜드리다** beat; hit; strike; knock; tap; pat; rap; pound (연타·난타); pommel (주먹으로); thresh (도리깨로); thrash (몽둥이·채찍으로); slap〔clap〕 (손뼉으로) ¶ 문을 두드리다 knock at the door; tap at〔on〕 the door (가볍게); pound on the door (연거푸) // 책상을 두드리다 rap on the table (가볍게); bang〔pound〕 the table (세게) // 그 여자의 어깨를 가볍게 두드리다 pat〔slap〕 her on the shoulder
두들기다 beat; hit; knock ¶ 북을 두들기다 beat a drum // 늘씬하게 두들기다 beat〔pommel〕 《a person》 to a jelly // 신문에 두들겨 맞다 be attacked〔criticized〕 in the newspaper // 그는 턱을 한 방 두들겨 맞고 뻗었다 He was knocked down by a blow on the chin.
두량 斗量 measuring 《grain with a *mal* or *doe* measure》 —하다 measure
두럭 [사람의] a gambling group; [집의] a cluster of houses
두런거리다 murmur; make a murmurous〔murmuring〕 sound ¶ 두런거리는 소리 a murmuring (sound); a murmurous sound
두렁 a levee; the bank of a rice-paddy; a ridge
—길 a levee path; a footpath between rice fields
두렁이 swaddling clothes; a baby's skirt
두렁허리 〖물고기〗 a kind of eel; Fluta alba (학명)
두레 [연장] a water scooper used in irrigation; [모임] a farmer's cooperative group
두레박 a well-bucket ¶ 두레박으로 우물에서 물을 긷다 draw water from a well with a bucket
—틀 a (well) sweep
두레박줄 a well-rope
두레박질 —하다 draw water from a well with a bucket
두레우물 a deep well; a draw well
두레질 irrigation by scooping —하다 irrigate 《paddy fields》 by scooping
두려빠지다 come off (from a center); an entire area sinks
***두려움** [공포] fear; dread; horror; [걱정] apprehension; anxiety; concern; [어른에 대한] reverence; veneration; awe; [위험] danger; risk ¶ 두려움을 모르다 be a stranger to fear; be fearless 《of》 // 다른 병이 병발할 두려움이 있다 There is a fear of complications arising.
†**두려워하다** ① [무서워하다] fear; be afraid of; dread; be scared 《at》; be in fear

of ; be in a fright ; be timid 《of》 ¶ 죽음을 두려워하지 않는 국민 a death-defying people // 뱀을 두려워하다 dread 〔have a horror of〕 snakes // 그녀는 조금도 두려워하지 않고 거기에 갔다 She went there nothing daunted. // 조금도 두려워할 것 없다 You have nothing to fear.
② [걱정하다] fear ; be afraid of ; apprehend ; be apprehensive of ; feel a danger of ; be nervous about ¶ 두려워서 from 〔with〕 fear ; in horror ; in awe ; in apprehension // 낙제할까 두려워하다 be afraid 〔apprehensive〕 of failing in an examination // 잘못한 일이 없으니 조금도 두려워할 것이 없다 My conscience is perfectly at ease, as I am quite innocent.
③ [어른을] stand in fear〔awe〕 of ¶ 어른을 두려워할 줄 모르다 be defiant of one's elders // 나를 두려워할 것이 없다 You need not stand in fear of me.

⁑**두렵다** ① [무섭다] be afraid of ; (be) scared ; frightened ; terrified ¶ 벼락이 두렵다 My dread is thunder. /I am afraid of thunder. // 죽음 따위는 조금도 두렵지 않다 I am not afraid of death in the least.
② [걱정이다] (be) feared ; apprehended ; be in danger (of) ¶ 자네의 인기가 떨어질까 두렵다 There is the risk of your being unpopular. // 사고가 있을까 두렵다 I am afraid that an accident might happen.
③ [어른이] be awed by ¶ 어른이 두렵다 be overawed by one's elders

두렷이, 뚜렷이 clearly ; distinctly ; plainly ; vividly ; evidently ; obviously ; decidedly ; doubtlessly ; undoubtedly ¶ 그는 그 일에 전연 관계가 없다는 것을 뚜렷이 하였다 He made it quite clear that he had nothing to do with the matter. // 한푼이라도 용도를 뚜렷이 하여야 한다 You must account for every penny spent. // 그를 뚜렷이 볼 수가 있었다 I could see him plainly.

두렷하다, 뚜렷하다 (be) clear ; distinct ; vivid ; plain ; evident ; obvious ; manifest ; apparent ¶ 뚜렷한 사실 an obvious〔plain〕 fact // 뚜렷한 기억 a vivid recollection // 뚜렷한 대답 a definite answer // 뚜렷한 목소리 a clear voice // 뚜렷한 증거 a positive proof // 그 뜻은 아주 뚜렷하다 The meaning is quite plain. // 화재의 원인은 뚜렷하지 않다 The cause of the fire is unknown. // 그 자신이 그 편지를 쓴 것이 뚜렷하다 It is apparent that he wrote the letter himself.

두령 頭領 a leader ; a boss ; a head

†**두루** [빠짐없이] without exception ; thoroughly ; [전면적으로] all over ; all around ; [일반적으로] generally ; universally ; [널리] widely ; extensively ; far and wide ¶ 두루 찾다 make a wide search ; comb // 온 세계에 두루 알려지다 be known all over the world // 도시를 두루 안내하다 take 《a person》 all over the city // 그의 명성은 두루 알려져 있다 His reputation is known far and wide.

두루마기 a Korean overcoat

*__두루마리__ a roll of paper ; rolled letter paper ; scroll
—문 a rolling shutter **— 수건** a roller towel (통 속에 말아넣고 쓰는) **— 화장지** a toilet roll

두루뭉수리 ① [엉망] a mess ; a blunder ¶ 두루뭉수리를 만들다 make a mess out of it ② [변변치 못한 사람] a good-for-nothing fellow ; a worthless fellow ; a nobody // 그 여자는 두루뭉수리하고 결혼했다 She has married a nobody.

두루미 〚새〛 a (white) crane ; a sacred crane ; Crus japonensis (학명)
— 자리 〚천문〛 the Crane **재—** a white-naped crane **흑—** a hooded crane

두루미냉이 〚식물〛 a Chinese artichoke ; Stachys sieboldii (학명)

두루주머니 a pouch ; a money purse of cloth ; a purse

두루춘풍 —春風 always being genial to everybody ¶ 두루춘풍이라 누구에게도 원한 사는 일이 없다 He is always genial to everybody, so he never has any enemies.

두루치기[1] [돌려쓰기] using a thing for various purposes

두루치기[2] [음식] a kind of bouillabaisse 〔shellfish-octopus stew〕

두룽다리 a fur cap〔headdress〕

두르다 ① [싸서 가리다] put around ; enclose ; encircle ; surround ; [옷을] wear about 《one》 ¶ 치마를 두르다 wear a skirt // 뜰을 나무 판자로 두르다 fence a garden with wooden boards
② [원형으로 돌리다] turn ; wheel ; revolve ¶ 둘레를 두르다 turn a spinning wheel
③ [변통하다] borrow〔raise〕 《money》 ¶ 만원을 둘러주다 lend 《a person》 10,000 *won* ; accommodate 《a person》 with 10,000 *won*
④ [사람·칼·붓을] control ; command ; wield ; manage ¶ 사람을 마음대로 두르다 have people under perfect control ; have people well in hand // 칼을 두르다 wield〔brandish〕 a sword // 붓을 두르다 wield one's writing pen
⑤ [속이다] deceive ; cheat ; mislead ; swindle ; play a trick on ; take in 《a person》

두르르, 뚜르르 [말리는 모양] round ; with a twirl ; [바퀴 소리] rolling ; rumbling

두르풍 —風 a cape ; a shawl

두름 a string 《of fish, of dried vegetables》 ¶ 굴비 한 두름 a string of 20 dried corvinas

두름성 resourcefulness ; versatility ;

adaptability ¶ 두름성 있는 사람 a resourceful man ; an adaptable person ; a quick-witted man // 그는 언제나 두름성이 있어 잘 꾸려 나간다 He can adapt〔adjust〕 himself to any circumstances.

두릅 aralia shoots

두릅나무 〖식물〗 Aralia elata (학명)

두리기 dining together

—상 a round table set for a group of people

두리기둥 a rounded column

두리목 —木 rounded lumber

두리반 —盤 a large round dining table

***두리번거리다** stare around ; look about ¶ 누가 보지 않나 하고 두리번거리다 look around with one's eyes wide open to see whether anybody is watching him

두리번두리번 looking around wonderingly〔curiously, restlessly〕 ; staring around

두마음 duplicity ; double-dealing ; treachery ; divided loyalty ; a double heart ; two hearts ¶ 두마음을 품다 have two faces ; play (a) double game // 두마음이 있는 double-hearted // 두마음이 없는 single-hearted ; sincere ; devoted

두말 duplicity ; a double tongue ; equivocation ; **—하다** be double-tongued〔-faced〕 ; break one's word ; keep two tongues in one mouth ; tell a lie ¶ 두말하지 않는 사람 a man of his word // 두말 않고 frankly ; honestly ; without complaint ; without objection ; immediately // 두말할 것 없이 of course ; without saying anything further // 두말 말고 어서 돈을 내라 Pay me the money here and now.

두말없이 without saying anything further ; without any complaint〔trouble〕 ; on the spot ; immediately ; with no further ado ¶ 두말없이 승낙하다 consent readily ; give a ready consent

두멍 a water tub ; [큰동이] a large water jar

두메 an out-of-the-way mountain village ; a secluded village in the mountain ; the remote countryside ; the backcountry 《미》 ; the backwoods 《미》 ¶ 두멧사람 a deep countryman ; a backwoodsman 《미》 // 두메에 살다 live in the backcountry〔remote countryside〕

두메오리나무 a kind of alder

두멧구석 a remote village ; an out-of-the-way corner of a mountain district ; a remote backwood

⁑**두목** 頭目 a chief ; a head ; a leader ; a ringleader ; a boss 《미·속》 ¶ 도둑의 두목 a bandit leader〔captain〕

두문불출 杜門不出 confining oneself at home ; a stay-at-home life ; a seclusive life (at home) **—하다** confine oneself at home ; lead a stay-at-home life ; be in the seclusion of one's own home ¶ 두문불출하는 사람 a stay-at-home

두문자 頭文字 ① [처음의 한 자] the first letter 《of a word》 ; [이름의] an initial letter ; initials ② [성명의 두문자] the initials 《of one's name》

두미 頭尾 the head and the tail ; beginning and end

두미 없다 頭尾— (be) incoherent ; inconclusive ; desultory ; rambling ; disorganized ¶ 두미 없는 이야기를 하다 tell an incoherent story

두발 頭髮 the hair ; the hair of the head **— 탈락증** alopecia

두방망이질 beating with both hands ; pounding (of) one's heart

두번 [2회] twice ; two times ; [재차] again ; [두번째] a second time

두벌갈이 a second sowing ; a second crop **—하다** sow twice ; raise a second crop

두벌솎음 thinning (out) vegetables 〔greens〕 for the second time **—하다** thin (out) vegetables for the second time

두벌주검 an examined〔a dissected〕 corpse **—하다** undergo〔be subject to〕 an autopsy

두부 豆腐 bean-curd ¶ 두부 한 모 a cake of bean-curd // 두부 장수 a bean-curd seller〔dealer〕

두부 頭部 the head ¶ 두부의 cephalic // 두부를 다쳤다 He was injured in the head.

두사이 ① [간격] a space between two 《objects》 ; an interval between two points ② [관계] the relation〔relationship, terms〕 between two persons

두상 頭上 [머리 위] the top of the head ; [머리] the head ¶ 두상에 over〔above, upon〕 the head ; overhead // 두상에 떨어지다 fall on one's head

두상화 頭狀花 〖식물〗 a capitulum ; a capitate flower ; a flower head

두서 頭書 a superscription ¶ 두서의 superscribed ; above-mentioned (전기의)

두서 頭緖 ① [단서] a clue ; the first step ; the beginning ¶ 일의 두서를 잡다 get a clue to a matter ② [순서] consistence ; coherence ; order ¶ 두서 없는 inconsistent ; incoherent ; self-contradictory // 너의 말에는 두서가 없다 There is no logic in your remark. /You say incoherent things.

두서너 two or three ; a few ¶ 두서너 사람 a few people // 책을 두서너 권 읽었다 I have read a few books.

두서넛 two or three ; a few

두서 없다 [종잡을 수 없다] (be) wandering ; rambling ; incoherent ; discursive ; vague ; absurd ; wild ¶ 두서 없는 이야기 a rambling〔wild, silly, winding, skimble-scamble〕 talk

두세 two or three ; a few ¶ 두세 번 two or three times

두셋 two or three ¶ 두셋쯤은 당해낼 수

있다 I can cope with two or three.
두손매무리 doing one's work slapdash —하다 do one's work slapdash〔in a hasty, haphazard manner〕; scamp one's work
두약 杜若 〖식물〗 an alpine tree ; Alpinia japonica (학명)
두어 about two ; a couple of ¶ 두어 마디 a few words
두어두다 ① [두다·간직하다] put ; keep ; put away ; store ; leave (behind) ¶ 책을 방에 두어두다 put〔leave, keep〕 a book in the room ② [내버려둠] leave《it》 alone ; [물건을] leave《it》 as《it》 is ¶ 울라, 가만 두어두라 Leave him alone, or he will cry.
두억시니 a demon ; a devil
두엄 manure ; muck
—걸채 a compost rack (carried over the back of an ox) —더미 a manure pile —발치 a compost pit —자리 a compost yard〔dump〕 —풀 compost grass
두엇 about two ; a couple of ¶ 사과 두엇 갖다 주시오 Get me a couple of apples.
두옥 斗屋 a hut ; a shack ; a shed
두우 斗宇 heaven and earth ; the universe ; the cosmos ; the macrocosm
두운 頭韻 alliteration ¶ 두운체의 alliterative // 두운을 맞추다 alliterate
—법 alliteration
두유 豆油 soy (bean) oil
두이레 the fourteenth day after《a baby's》 birth
두절 杜絶 stoppage ; cessation ; interruption ; suspension (중절) —하다 stop ; cease ; be interrupted ; be paralyzed ; be cut off ; be blocked ¶ 폭풍으로 교통이 두절되었다 The traffic was held up〔tied up, cut off〕 by the storm. // 해외 여행은 완전히 두절되어 있다 There was a total cessation of foreign travel. // 심한 폭설로 기차 운행이 두절되었다고 한다 The train schedule has been disrupted by the heavy snowfall.
전신 — telegraphic〔transmission〕 interruption
두족류 頭足類 Cephalopoda (학명) ¶ 두족류의 동물 a cephalopod
두주 頭註 marginal notes ; headnotes
두주 斗酒 kegs of wine ¶ 두주를 불사하다 be capable of downing kegs〔gallons〕 of wine ; drink like a fish
두진 痘疹 the smallpox and the measles ; pustules
두찬 杜撰 ① [허술한 작품] careless〔slipshod, imperfect, inaccurate, faulty〕 literary work ; a book without good authority ② [틀린 곳이 많은 책] a book with many mistakes in it
두창 痘瘡 〖의학〗 smallpox ; pock ; pox ; variola ⇨ 천연두(天然痘)
*두텁다 (be) warm ; cordial ; affectionate ; close ; deep ; hearty ; familiar ; intimate ¶ 두터운 우의 a warm〔deep, close〕 friendship // 두터운 친분 close relations // 친분이 두터운 사이다 be familiar〔fast, good〕 friends ; be on familiar〔intimate〕 terms〔relations〕 with ; be deeply in love《with》 (남녀가)
두텁떡 steamed rice cake coated with honeyed red beans
⁑두통 頭痛 a headache ¶ 깨어지는 듯한 두통 a splitting〔racking〕 headache // 두통이 나다 have a headache // 두통을 앓다 worry about《a matter》 (걱정) // 두통이 있어서 하루 쉬었으면 한다 I have a headache, so I'd like to take the day off.
두통거리 頭痛— a headache ; a source〔cause〕 of constant anxiety〔trouble〕; a worry ; a thorn in one's side ¶ 인구 문제는 아주 두통거리다 The population problem is a real headache. // 그게 두통거리란 말이야 It is a chronic headache to me.
두툴두툴 —하다 (be) uneven ; pimply-rough ; lumpy ¶ 길이 몹시 두툴두툴하다 The road is awfully rough.
두툼하다 (be) somewhat thick ¶ 두툼한 판자 a rather thick board
두편 —便 both sides ; two sides
두한족열 頭寒足熱 keeping the head cool and the feet warm
두호 斗護 protection ; patronage ; looking after —하다 protect ; patronize ; look after ; favor ; take《a person》 under one's wing ¶ 두호 아래 under the patronage《of》 // 약자를 두호하다 protect the weak // 그가 나를 두호하여 주었다 He stood up for me.
두흔 痘痕 a pockmark ; a pit ¶ 두흔이 있다 be pitted〔pockmarked〕
†둑 a bank ; a dike ; an embankment ; a levee (논둑) ¶ 강둑 the bank of the river // 둑을 쌓다 build a bank ; embank《a river》; construct an embankment // 둑이 터지다 a levee breaks down
—길 a causeway ; a bank path ; a dike
둔각 鈍角 〖기하〗 an obtuse angle
— 삼각형 an obtuse-angle triangle
둔감 鈍感 insensibility ; stolidity —하다 (be) dull ; insensible ; obtuse ; dumb ¶ 그 여자는 자기에 관한 소문 일체에 둔감하다 She is impervious to all the gossip about her.
둔갑술 遁甲術 occult arts ; the art of invisibility
둔갑하다 遁甲— disappear ; [변신] change〔transform〕 oneself《into》; take the form〔shape〕《of》 ¶ …로 둔갑하여 in〔under〕 the disguise of... // 여우가 여자로 둔갑했다 The fox took the form of a woman.
둔기 鈍器 a blunt〔dull〕 weapon
둔덕 a hilly spot ; a hill
둔병 屯兵 stationary troops ; a garrison
⁑둔부 臀部 the buttocks ; the rump ; the

posterior ; the hip
둔사 遁辭 an excuse ; a pretext ; an evasion ; an evasive answer ¶ 좋은 둔사를 찾아내다 find a good excuse
둔세 遁世 seclusion from the world ; escape〔retirement〕 from the world **—하다** seclude oneself from society ; escape 〔retire〕 from the world ; renounce the world ; go into seclusion ; live in seclusion
둔영 屯營 a military camp〔station〕 ; military quarters ; barracks ; a cantonment **—하다** be quartered ; be stationed ; be cantoned
둔재 鈍才 dullness ; stupidity ; [사람] a dull-witted person ; a dunce ; a dullhead ; a blockhead ¶ 둔재의 dull-witted ; dull-headed ; dull
둔전 屯田 a farm cultivated by stationary troops ; a farm cultivated by the militia
둔주 遁走 running away ; flight **—하다** run away ; take (to) flight
—곡 〚음악〛 a fugue
둔주곡 遁走曲 〚음악〛 a fugue ¶ 베토벤의 「대 둔주곡」 Beethoven's "Grosse Fuge"
— 작곡자 a fuguist
둔중 鈍重 dullness ; bovinity **—하다** be thickheaded ; fatheaded ; dull
둔질 鈍質 stupidity ; dullness ; imbecility ¶ 둔질의 stupid ; dull ; imbecile ; doltish
둔치 the edge of the water ; the waterside ; a beach
둔탁 鈍濁 dullness ; slowness **—하다** (be) dull ; slow ; stupid ; dull-witted ; thick-witted
둔통 鈍痛 a dull pain ; an obtuse pain
둔팍하다 鈍— (be) thick-headed ; slow-witted ; stolid ; stupid
둔패기 a slow-witted〔dull〕 person
둔필 鈍筆 a poor handwriting ; a poor hand
†둔하다 鈍— [머리가] (be) dull ; slow ; stupid ; thick-headed ; talentless ; dull-brained ; [칼날이] blunt ¶ 둔한 사람 a dolt ; a dull〔stupid〕 fellow ; a slow-coach // 수학의 머리가 둔하다 He is slow at mathematics.
둔해지다 become〔grow〕 dull ; become blunt ; lose one's astuteness ; [약해지다] weaken ; be weakened ¶ 술을 마시면 머리가 둔해진다 Drinking dulls the senses〔muddles one's brains〕. // 팔림새가 둔해졌다 The sale became dull.
둔화 鈍化 blunting 《of sensibility》 ; slowdown 《in the U. S. economy》
†둘 two ¶ 둘째 the second // 둘째로 secondly ; in the second place // 둘씩 two at a time ; by twos ; in pairs // 둘로 접은 two-fold ; twicefolded // 둘 걸러 in〔at〕 every third place // 둘 중 하나 one of the two ; one between the two // 둘도 없는 unique ; peerless ; matchless ; the only ; unrivaled ; sole // 둘로 나누다 divide 《a thing》 in〔into〕 two ; divide by two // 둘다 괜찮다 Both are all right. /Either will do. // 둘 중 어느 쪽에나 앉으십시오 Sit on either side. // 둘 중 어느 이야기도 진실이 아니다 Neither story is true. // 나는 보통 물건이 둘로 보이기 시작할 때까지 마시지 I usually drink until I begin to see double.
둘- [접두어] sterile ; barren
—암소 a sterile cow **—암캐** a barren bitch **—암탉** a sterile hen
둘되다 (be) stupid ; dull ; stolid ; thick(-headed) ; curt ; unpolished
둘둘, 뚤뚤 ① [말거나 감는 모양] round and round ; with a twirl ¶ 둘둘 감다 wind 《a rope》 ; round 《a thing》 ② [구르거나 돌아가는 소리] rolling ; rumbling ¶ 둘둘 굴리다 roll 《a thing》 over and over // 물레바퀴가 뚤뚤 돌아간다 A spinning wheel turns round and round.
둘러대다 ① [변통하다] manage to get a loan ; swing a loan ¶ 집을 사려고 돈을 둘러대다 swing a loan in order to buy a house ② [꾸며대다] put〔cook〕 up 《a good reason, excuse》 ; make a ready remark (to get around a situation) ¶ 돈 못 갚는 이유를 둘러대다 put up good reasons why one hasn't been able to return the money // 그는 말 둘러대는 데는 아주 명수이다 He is good at ready remarks to meet a situation.
둘러막다 surround 《with, by》 ; enclose 《with, in》 ; fence off around (울타리로) ; rope off (밧줄로) ¶ 집을 담으로 둘러막다 surround a house with a wall // 그의 토지는 철조망으로 둘러막혀 있다 His land is fenced with barbed wire.
둘러메다 fling around one's shoulders
둘러보다 look round〔around, about〕 ; give〔take〕 a look round ; survey ; make a survey of ¶ 차내의 사람들을 둘러보다 look around at the people in the car // 공장을 둘러보다 make a survey of a factory
둘러붙다 change front ; turn around ; change sides ; go〔flop〕 to the other party ¶ 유리한 쪽에 둘러붙다 turn around to the favorable side
둘러서다 stand in a circle
†둘러싸다 besiege ; lay siege to ; surround ; invest ; enclose ; environ ¶ 바다로 둘러싸인 나라 a sea-girt country // 요새를 둘러싸다 lay siege to a fortress // 탁자를 둘러싸고 앉다 sit〔gather〕 around a table
둘러싸이다 be besieged〔invested, surrounded, enclosed, girded〕 ¶ 바다에 둘러싸인 나라 a sea-girt country // 산에 둘러싸이다 be surrounded by mountains // 그 집은 수목에 둘러싸여 있다 The house is shut in by trees.
둘러쌓다 pile 《a thing》 up in a circle
둘러쓰다 ① [머리에] wear 《it》 around

one's head ② [몸에] get ⟪it⟫ all over oneself ¶ 담요를 둘러쓰다 wrap oneself up in a blanket ③ [변통] borrow ⟪money, things⟫

둘러앉다 sit in a circle ; sit around ⟪the table⟫

둘러엎다 overturn ; capsize ; upset ; overthrow ; [하던 일을] do away with ¶ 밥상을 둘러엎다 overturn a dining table // 살림을 둘러엎다 do away with a home ; break up a household

둘러차다 [몸에] attach〔tie〕⟪a thing⟫ around one's waist

둘러치다 ① [두르다] put ⟪a screen⟫ around ; surround ; enclose ⟪with, in⟫ ; encircle ; engirdle ¶ 군사 분계선에 방책을 둘러치다 palisade the line of military demarcation // 집에 돌담을 둘러치다 enclose a house with a stone wall ② [내던지다] throw hard ; fling ; hurl ¶ 사람을 땅에 둘러치다 hurl〔throw〕⟪a person⟫ to the ground

†**둘레** circumference ; girth ¶ 못의 둘레 the circumference of a pond // 둘레 5 피트 five feet round〔in circumference〕// 그 나무는 둘레가 9 피트이다 The tree has a girth of 9 feet. // 그는 호수 둘레를 걸었다 He took a walk around the lake. // 집 둘레에 나무가 많이 자라고 있다 Many trees are growing around the house.

둘레둘레 round ; around ; about ; in a circle (빙 둘러) ¶ 둘레둘레 보다 look around ; stare about // 둘레둘레 앉다 sit round in a circle

둘리다 ① [둘러 막히다] be surrounded ; be enclosed ; be encircled ; be environed ; be embosomed ; be fenced ; be encompassed ¶ 사방이 산으로 둘린 마을 a village surrounded〔shut in, hemmed in〕 by mountains on all sides
② [쌓여 가리어지다] be put round ; be wrapped in ; be worn ¶ 머리에 수건이 둘리다 wear a towel around one's head ; one's head is wrapped in a towel〔turban〕
③ [휘둘리다] be controlled ; be swayed ; be wielded ¶ 사람에게 둘리다 be swayed by ⟪a person⟫ ; be wrapped around ⟪a person's⟫ finger

둘소 a barren〔sterile〕 cow

둘이 two people ; a couple ; a pair ¶ 둘이 같이 가자 Let us go together, you and I. // 둘이 다 다녀 갔다 Both of them have been here. // 둘이 서로 뜻이 맞지 않는다 They do not see eye to eye with each other.

*__둘째__ the second ; number two ⟪No. 2⟫ ¶ 그는 둘째로 왔다 He was the second to come. /He came in second. // 그는 마라톤 경주에서 둘째로 들어왔다 He came in second in the marathon race.
— 손가락 a forefinger ; an index finger

둘치 a sterile female animal

둘친 〖화학〗 dulcin

둔하다 (be) stupid ; dull ; dull-witted ; slow ; clumsy ; awkward ¶ 둔한 솜씨 poor skill ; clumsy hand

둥¹ 〖음악〗 the second note of the native Korean musical scale

둥² tomtom ; with a tum ; boom ¶ 북을 둥 치다 rataplan ; tomtom ; thump〔beat〕 a drum

둥³ ¶ 허둥지둥 in a flurry ; in confusion ; in one's hurry ; losing one's head〔presence of mind〕// 그는 갈둥말둥하고 있다 He is thinking over going there. /He hesitates to go. // 그는 조반을 먹는둥 마는둥 외출하였다 He went out, taking his breakfast in a flurry. /He went out, taking almost nothing for his breakfast. // 늦잠을 자서 아침식사도 하는둥 마는둥 집에서 뛰쳐나왔다 I overslept, so I rushed though breakfast and tore out of the house.

둥개다 struggle ; take pains ; labor〔slave〕⟪over⟫ ; have a hard time ; find difficulty to deal with ; be at a loss ; be puzzled ¶ 구속에서 벗어나려고 둥개다 struggle to free oneself from one's bonds // 문제를 해결하려고 둥개다 be at a loss how to unravel the problem // 숙제를 하느라고 둥개다 have a hard time doing one's homework ; slave over one's homework

둥구나무 a large old shade tree

둥굴대 a rounded strickle〔grain-leveller〕

둥굴이 a barked log

둥그러지다 fall ⟪down, over⟫ ; tumble ⟪over, down⟫ ; have a tumble ¶ 그는 돌에 채여 둥그러졌다 He stumbled over a stone〔tripped over a stone〕 and fell down.

둥그렇다, 뚱그렇다 (be) round ; circular ; globular ¶ 둥그렇게 round ; in a circle // 그들은 둥그렇게 앉았다 They sat in a circle〔ring〕.

둥그레 모춤 〖농업〗 four handfuls of rice seedlings bound in a bundle

둥그스름하다 (be) roundish ; somewhat round〔circular, globular〕

둥근대패 a circular〔compass〕 plane

둥근천장 —天障 a dome ; a vault

둥근톱 a circular saw

†**둥글다** (be) round ; circular ; globular ¶ 둥근 탁자 a round table // 둥근 달 a full moon // 얼굴이 둥근 round-faced // 모양이 둥근 round-shaped

둥글둥글, 뚱글뚱글 ① [둥그렇게] round ; roundly ; in a circle ② [원만하게] peacefully ; amicably ; smoothly ; harmoniously ; satisfactorily ¶ 둥글둥글한 가정 a happy home // 둥글둥글하게 살다 live in harmony ⟪with⟫ // 그는 아직 둥글둥글하지 못한 점이 있다 He has corners yet to be rounded off.

둥글리다 round ; make round ⟪into a

ball》; round off (깎아서) ¶ 그는 책상 모서리를 둥글렸다 He rounded off the corners〔edges〕 of the table.

둥글뭉수레하다 (be) roundish ; round and blunt-tipped

둥글번번하다 (be) round and flat

둥당, 뚱땅 ¶ 뚱땅거리다 play musical instruments and make sounds beating things ; enjoy oneselves playing music and beating things∥뚱땅거리며 놀다 make merry ; enjoy oneself ; go on〔have〕 a spree∥그들은 밤새껏 뚱땅거리며 놀았다 They reveled all night long.

둥덩 ¶ 둥덩거리다 keep beating a drum ; rataplan ; tomtom ; beat boom-boom

둥덩실 floating high up in the air ; buoyantly ⇨ 둥실둥실

둥둥[1] [북소리] rub-a-dub ; rat-a-tat ; rat-a-plan ; tom-tom ; boom-boom ; drumming ; thumping ¶ 북을 둥둥 울리다 beat a drum boom-boom

둥둥[2] floating ⇨ 둥실둥실

둥둥[3] [어린아이를 어를 때] peep-bo ! ; bopeep ! ; peekaboo !

둥실둥실 [뜨다] buoyantly ; floating ¶ 배가 둥실둥실 뜨다 a boat is floating buoyantly

둥실둥실하다 [살찌다] (be) rotund ; plump ; corpulent ¶ 둥실둥실한 얼굴 a round〔plumpy〕 face∥둥실둥실한 사람 a rotund〔corpulent, portly〕 person∥둥실둥실하게 살찌다 be plump〔portly, corpulent, fat〕

둥싯거리다 move slowly〔sluggishly, lazily〕

둥싯둥싯 slowly ; sluggishly ; lazily ¶ 둥싯둥싯 걷다 walk slowly〔sluggishly〕

둥어리막대 a packsaddle rack

둥우리 a basket (made of straw, bamboo) 대— a bamboo basket

둥이 child ; one
귀염— one's dear〔precious〕 child ; a pretty〔dear〕 little thing 《구》 막내— the youngest son 쫄래— a frivolous urchin 해방— a chid born in the year of Liberation of Korea in 1945

둥주리감 a round persimmon

둥지 a nest
둥지를 치다〔틀다〕 관용 build a nest

둥치 the base of a tree trunk

둥치다 ① [휩싸서 동이다] tie up together ; pack〔wrap〕 up ② [깎아버리다] cut off the worthless part

뒈지다 kick the bucket ; bite the dust ; drop dead ¶ 너 같은 건 어서 뒈져라 Drop dead, you bastard.

뒝벌 〖곤충〗 a bumble-bee

†**뒤** ① [후방] the back ; the rear ¶ 뒷방 a back room ; a room at the back∥뒤에 있는 사람 a person behind∥집 뒤에 숨다 hide behind a house∥뒤에 남다 stay〔remain〕 behind∥쑥 뒤에 앉다 sit far back∥뒤로 넘어지다 fall backward∥뒤로 물러서다 step back∥뒤에서 부르다 call 《a person》 from behind∥뒤돌아 서다 turn back ; turn on one's heels∥뒤돌아 보다 look back ; look behind∥뒤따라 가다 walk behind 《a person》; follow 《a person》∥뒤를 맞대고 앉다 sit back to back∥고국을 뒤로 하다 leave one's home country∥뒤로 돌아 Right about turn〔face〕! /About turn ! /About face ! ∥내 차가 뒤에서 받혔습니다 I was rearended.
② [미래·장래] the future ; the time to come ¶ 뒤에 in future ; hereafter ; some day〔time〕; later on∥뒷날을 생각하다 think of the future∥뒷날에 대비하다 provide for the future∥뒷일을 예언하다 foretell〔predict〕 the future∥내가 그 유족의 뒤를 돌보겠다 I will look after〔take care of〕 the bereaved family. ∥그는 뒤에 큰 사람이 되었다 He became a great man later on. ∥나는 시계 바늘을 한 시간 뒤로 돌려놓는 것을 깜박 잊어버렸다 I forgot to set my watch one hour backward.
③ [나중·다음] ¶ 뒤에 after ; after doing ; later ; next ; later on ; afterward ∥조반 뒤에 after breakfast∥5일 뒤에 after five days ; five days after∥텔레비전을 본 뒤에 after watching television∥뒤로 미루다 postpone ; put off∥뒤에 전화를 하겠습니다 I'll call you up later. ∥당신은 뒤에 후회할 것이다 You'll be sorry afterwards. ∥뒤로 미루어라 That can wait. /Let it wait.
④ [결과] the end ; the conclusion ; consequences ; results ¶ 사건의 뒷처리를 하다 settle〔wind up〕 an affair ; get an affair straightened∥뒷일이야 알게 뭐야 I do not care what may come of it. /After me the deluge. ∥그렇게 하면 뒤가 재미없을 것이다 You will have to pay dearly for doing so. ∥뒤는 내가 맡겠다 I will answer for the consequences.
⑤ [배후] background ¶ 누군가 뒤에서 그를 조종하고 있는 것 같다 Somebody seems to be pulling the wires behind him. ∥뒤에서 남의 욕을 하지 마라 Don't speak ill of others behind their backs.
⑥ [배경] backing ; support ¶ 뒤를 밀어주는 사람 a backer ; a patron ; a sponsor ∥뒤를 밀어주다 back up〔support〕 《a person》∥그는 뒤가 든든하다 He has strong backing.
⑦ [후계] a successor ; [자손] a descendant ; descent ; posterity ¶ …의 뒤를 이어서 as successor 《to》; to succeed 《another》∥아버지의 뒤를 잇다 succeed one's father 《in his business》∥사장직의 뒤를 잇다 succeed to the presidency∥김씨 집안의 뒤라곤 그 하나밖에 없다 He is the last〔only〕 descendant of the *Kims*. ∥그가 죽으면 그집 뒤가 끊어진다 The family will become extinct with his death.
⑧ [대변] feces ; excrement ; stools ; a

bowel movement ¶ 뒤가 마렵다 have an urge to go to the bathroom ; feel like having a bowel movement // 뒤가 순하다〔굳다〕 have an easy〔a hard〕 bowel movement
뒤를 대다 관용 keep in supply ; supply one's needs ; supply money
뒤를 보다 관용 evacuate ; go to stool ; relieve〔ease〕 oneself ; relieve nature ; have a bowel movement
뒤구르다 ① [반동] recoil ; kick ; rebound ¶ 총이 몹시 뒤구른다 The gun kicks badly. ② [일의 뒤끝을] wind up〔fix, settle〕 with care ¶ 일을 뒤구르다 wind up a job and make sure that everything is all right
뒤까불다 behave rashly ; bear oneself frivolously ; shake up and down
뒤꼍 the backyard ; the back (side) ; out in back ¶ 집 뒤꼍에서 놀다 play in the backyard ; play out in back
뒤꼭지치다 be discouraged ; be dejected ; get disappointed ; get disheartened
뒤꽂이 a hair-ornament
†뒤꿈치 the heel ¶ 구두 뒤꿈치 the heel of a shoe // 뒤꿈치가 높은〔낮은〕 구두 high-〔low-〕heeled shoes
뒤끓다 ① [끓다] seethe ; boil up ¶ 주전자의 물이 뒤끓는다 The kettle boils〔sings〕. ② [소란하다] swarm ; be crowded ; infest (해로운 것이) ¶ 도둑이 뒤끓는 지방 a country infested with robbers // 사람들이 극장 둘레에 뒤끓었다 People swarmed around the theater. // 장마당에 사람들이 뒤끓었다 The market place was crowded with people.
뒤끝 an end ; the conclusion ; termination ; settlement ; result ¶ 뒤끝이 나다 be settled ; come〔be brought〕 to a conclusion〔an end〕 // 뒤끝을 맺다 put an end to 《a strife》 ; settle 《a problem》 ; fix up 《a schedule》 ; wind up 《one's service》 ; be through with 《미》 // 뒤끝이 어떻게 될까 How will the matter end ?
뒤내다 renege ; fail to keep one's promise later ; recede from 《an agreement, a contract, a bargain》 ; back out of 《an agreement》
뒤넘기치다 [넘겨뜨리다] throw down ; throw 《a person》 to the ground ; get 《a person》 down ; [뒤집어 엎다] upset ; overturn ¶ 식탁을 뒤넘기치다 overturn a dining table
뒤넘다 [엎어지다] turn over ; overturn ; [넘어지다] fall on one's back ; fall down ; tumble down ¶ 병풍이 뒤넘었다 The screen has turned over.
뒤넘스럽다 (be) self-conceited ; affected ; presumptuous ; overbearing ; audacious ; cheeky ; forward ; impudent ; stuck-up
뒤놀다 ① [흔들리다] be shaky ; shake ; totter ; reel ; be rickety ; [배가 파도에] roll〔pitch〕 heavily ¶ 뒤노는 의자 a shaky〔rocky, rickety, crazy〕 chair // 책상 다리가 뒤놀다 The legs of the table are groggy. // 배가 뒤놀아서 기분이 나쁘다 The pitch and roll make me seasick.
② [방랑하다] wander ; roam ; rove ; knock around 《미·구》
뒤놓다 upset ; overturn ; overthrow ; turn over
뒤늦다 (be) delayed ; be too late ; be behind time ¶ 뒤늦게 too late // 뒤늦은 사과를 하다 offer a belated apology // 기차 시간에 뒤늦게 오다 arrive too late for a train
뒤대 [북쪽 지방] the northern part 《of》 ; the northern district ; the northland ¶ 뒤대에서 피난 온 사람 a refugee from the north
뒤대다[1] [공급] supply〔provide, serve, furnish〕 《a person》 with ; support ; finance ; give financial aid ; assist in getting a living ¶ 아들의 학비를 뒤대다 supply one's son with school expenses // 당신에게 계속 사업 자금을 뒤대 주겠다 I will keep you furnished with business funds.
뒤대다[2] [틀리게] misinform ; make a false statement ; tell a lie
뒤덮다 ① [덮다] cover with ; veil ; overspread ; put on ; hang over ¶ 그는 이불을 뒤덮고 잤다 He pulled〔drew〕 the bedclothes over his head and fell asleep. // 그는 길을 걸으며 먼지를 뒤덮어 썼다 He was covered with dust while walking along the road. // 하늘은 검은 구름으로 뒤덮여 있다 The sky is overspreading with black clouds.
② [감싸주다] cover 《a guilty person》 ; shield ; screen ¶ 어머니는 딸을 뒤덮어 주었다 The mother covered up her daughter.
뒤덮이다 be covered 《with》 ; be put on ; be overspread ¶ 땅바닥은 눈으로 뒤덮였다 The ground was covered with snow. // 봄이 되면 들과 산은 신록으로 뒤덮인다 In spring, the fields and hills are clothed in fresh verdure.
뒤돌아보다 turn one's head ; look back〔around〕 《at》 ; look over one's shoulder ¶ 반생을 뒤돌아보다 look back one's past // 나의 일생을 뒤돌아보아 그리 즐겁지 않은 것도 있다 One portion of my life is not very pleasant to look back to.
뒤두다 [남겨 두다] keep ; reserve ; leave for the future ; set aside for later ; [마음속에] keep later dealings〔consideration〕 in mind ¶ 이것을 내 몫으로 뒤두지 않겠니 Will you kindly put it aside for me ? // 내일 것으로 뒤두자 Let's save that for tomorrow.
뒤둥그러지다 [뒤틀리다] be twisted (all out of shape) ; be distorted ; be contorted ; [생각·성질이] be perverse ; be

twisted ; become crooked
뒤따르다 follow ; accompany ; continue ; [행렬 등을] bring〔close〕 up the rear ¶ 한 떼의 기마 순경이 뒤따랐다 A group of mounted policemen brought up the rear.
뒤딱지 the back lid 《of a watch》
뒤떠들다 stir ; disturb
뒤떨다 tremble ; shiver ; shake ; shudder ¶ 무서워서 몸을 와들와들 뒤떨다 tremble with fear
†뒤떨어지다 ① [처지다] be〔fall, drop, lag, get〕 behind ; be backward 〔behind-hand〕 ; be outstripped ¶ 문화에 뒤떨어진 나라 a backward〔an underdeveloped, a developing〕 country // 경주에서 다른 선수들한테 뒤떨어지다 fall behind〔be outstripped by〕 the other runners in a race // 영어에 뒤떨어져 있다 be behind the other students in English // 시대〔유행〕에 뒤떨어지다 be behind the times〔fashion〕 // 시대에 뒤떨어지지 않도록 하다 keep abreast of the times ; keep up with the times // 한국은 아직 몇 가지 면에서 유럽에 비해 뒤떨어진 점이 있다 Korea still lags behind Europe in some respects.
② [남다] remain ; stay〔drop〕 behind ; be delayed ; fall out of the ranks ¶ 도중에서 뒤떨어지다 be delayed on the way // 모두 떠났으나 그만이 뒤떨어졌다 All left but he was staying behind.
뒤뚝거리다 stagger ; walk unsteadily ; totter ; reel ; falter ; shamble ¶ 뒤뚝거리는 걸음걸이로 with faltering〔tottering〕 steps // 뒤뚝거리며 걷다 waddle ; shamble ; reel along
뒤뚱거리다 be shaky 《on one's legs》 ; totter ; stagger ; falter ; waver ; be loose ¶ 뒤뚱뒤뚱 totteringly ; unsteadily // 뒤뚱뒤뚱 걷다 walk with faltering steps
뒤뚱발이 a person who totters along
뒤뜨다 [들뜨다] warp and become loose ; [반항하다] oppose ; resist ; stand up
뒤뜰 a backyard ; a back garden
뒤란 a backyard ; a kitchen garden in the back of the house
뒤룩거리다, 뛰룩거리다 ① [눈을] glare 〔goggle〕 《one's eyes》 ② [몸을] sway 〔waddle〕 《one's body》 ③ [성나서] look with glaring eyes
뒤룩뒤룩 [눈알을] glaring ; [몸을] swaying ; waddling ; [성이 나서] jerking with anger ¶ 뒤룩뒤룩 걷다 walk swaying one's body
뒤룽거리다 swing ; sway ; hang swinging loose ¶ 뒤룽뒤룽 swingingly
뒤미처 soon〔shortly〕 after ; right after ; at once ; immediately ; promptly ; without delay ¶ 점심 후에 뒤미처 그는 일을 시작했다 He set to work immediately after lunch. // 그는 서울에 도착하자 뒤미처 남산 공원에 갔다 As soon as 〔Soon after〕 he reached *Seoul*, he went to *Namsan* Park. // 그는 뒤미처 도둑의 뒤를 좇았다 He lost no time in pursuing the thief.
뒤바꾸다 invert ; reverse ; switch ¶ 순서를 뒤바꾸다 reverse the order ; make a mistake in the sequence
*뒤바뀌다 be mistaken ; be reversed ; be inverted ; be switched ; be mixed up ¶ 순서가 뒤바뀌다 the order is reversed 〔inverted〕 ; be out of order // 책이 모두 뒤바뀌다 the books are all mixed up // 형세가 뒤바뀌었다 The situation has taken a new turn.
뒤바르다 [종이 따위를] paste all over ; [분 따위를] paint〔powder〕 one's face thick(ly) ; put on thick make-up
뒤받다 ① [반항하다] oppose ; rise against ; raise one's hand against ; lift a finger against ; turn on〔upon〕
② [말을 받다] answer 《a person》 back ; talk〔speak〕 back 《to a person》 ; make a retort〔repartee, riposte〕 ; riposte ; retort ; give〔pay〕 《a person》 tit for tat
뒤발하다 pour 《a thing》 on and rub 《it》 all over 《a person》 ; smear oneself 《with》 ; be smeared〔soiled〕 《with oil》 ; be covered 《with dust》
뒤밟다 track ; shadow ; dog 《a person's steps》 ; follow 《in a person's track》 ; follow along〔back of〕 《a person》 ; trail ¶ 경관이 도둑을 뒤밟다 a policeman tracks a robber (down) // 뒤밟게 하다 put a dog on the trail
뒤버무리다 ① [섞다] mix up ; mix together ② [말을] equivocate ; pre-varicate ; quibble
*뒤범벅 a mess ; a hotchpotch ; a jumble ; a medley ; a mixture ; a muddle ; a confusion ¶ 뒤범벅되다 be mixed up ; be jumbled together // 뒤범벅을 만들다 mix up ; make a mess ; jumble together // 방안은 뒤범벅으로 흩어져 있었다 The room was in a terrible mess.
뒤변덕스럽다 (be) very capricious ; fickle ; fanciful ; whimsical ¶ 뒤변덕스러운 여인 a fickle woman
*뒤보다[1] [용변] go to stool ; have a bowel movement ; ease nature ; evacuate the bowels
뒤보다[2] [잘못 보다] mistake ; misread ; misjudge ; misview ; miss ¶ 사람을 뒤보다 take 《a person》 for another // 사람의 진의를 뒤보다 misread 《a person's》 motives〔intention〕 // 날짜를 뒤보다 mistake the dates
뒤보아 주다 take care of ; look after ; help ¶ 공부하는 아우를 뒤보아 주다 help〔supply〕 one's brother with school expenses // 자금 융통은 지방 은행이 뒤보아 준다 The financing is taken care of by a local bank.
뒤뿔치기 hack work ¶ 뒤뿔치다 work for another ; do hack work for
뒤서다 stand behind ; fall behind ; be

backward ; be outstripped ¶ 뒤서서 가다 go in the rear // 누구에게도 뒤서지 않다 be second to none ; yield to no man

*뒤섞다 mix up ; mingle〔jumble〕 together ; add in ; make a mess ; put in disorder ¶ 흙과 모래를 뒤섞다 mix earth with sand ; add sand to earth

*뒤섞이다 be mixed (up) ; be jumbled together ; be mingled ; be adulterated ; be put in disorder ¶ 몇 가지의 과일이 뒤섞이다 several kinds of fruits are mixed up // 우유에 물이 뒤섞이다 milk is adulterated with some water // 서류가 뒤섞이다 the papers are put in disorder

뒤숭숭하다 ① [혼란] (be) noisy ; troublous ; be disturbed ; be confused ; be in disorder〔a muddle〕 ¶ 세상이 뒤숭숭해졌다 Times have become troublous. // 쓰레기가 흩어져 집안이 뒤숭숭하다 The house is scattered with rubbish and I feel nervous.
② [마음이] (be) restless ; disturbed ; nervous ; uneasy ; troubled ; be ill at ease ; have a bee in one's bonnet〔head〕 ¶ 그는 아버지의 병환 소식을 듣고 마음이 뒤숭숭하였다 He felt restless〔was disturbed〕 to hear of his father's illness.

뒤스럭거리다 ① [뒤지다] fumble〔feel〕 《for, after, in, about》 ; rummage ; ransack
② [변덕부리다] (be) fickle ; capricious ; whimsical

뒤스럭스럽다 (be) frivolous ; fidgety ; fussy

뒤스르다 arrange ; move around to ; put 《things》 in order

뒤어보다 look for ; hunt up〔after〕search 《for》 ; ransack ; rummage ; fumble for ; seek for ¶ 집안을 샅샅이 뒤어보다 look for 《a thing》 all over the house ; ransack a house // 나는 열쇠를 찾으려고 호주머니를 뒤어보았다 I searched〔felt in〕 my pockets for the key. // 도둑은 서랍을 샅샅이 뒤어보았다 The thief ransacked the drawer.

뒤어쓰다 ① [눈을] roll one's eyeballs back ; show all the white of one's eyes
② ⇨ 들쓰다

*뒤엉키다 ① [밧줄·실 따위가] get〔become〕 entangled ; get〔become〕 raveled ¶ 뒤엉킨 실을 풀다 untie entangled knots
② [이야기 따위가] get confused〔mixed〕 ; get tangled ; [사건 따위가] get complicated ; become involved

⁑뒤엎다 upset ; overturn ; overthrow ¶ 판결을 뒤엎다 reverse a judgment〔decision〕

뒤웅박 a gourd ; a calabash ; a cucurbit

뒤웅스럽다 (be) unshapely ; ugly-looking ¶ 뒤웅스럽게 생겨 먹다 have ugly features

뒤잇다 follow ; succeed ¶ 뒤이어 later on ; following that

뒤재주치다 [던지다] throw ; hurl ; fling ; [뒤집다] turn over at random

뒤적거리다 rummage ; ransack ; fumble ; feel ; finger ; browse (책을) ¶ 편지를 찾으려고 서랍을 뒤적거리다 rummage a drawer for a letter // 책상 위의 서류를 뒤적거리다 finger the papers on the table // 책을 뒤적거리다 browse in a book ; browse among the books (이 책 저 책을) // 잔돈을 꺼내려고 주머니를 뒤적거렸다 I fumbled in my pockets for change.

뒤적뒤적 rummaging ; fumbling ; fingering ; browsing

뒤적이다 rummage ⇨ 뒤적거리다

뒤져내다 rummage 《out》 ; hunt out ; seek〔search〕 out ¶ 서랍에서 돈을 뒤져내다 rummage〔scrounge〕 money from a drawer

뒤져보다 look for ; rummage〔fumble〕 for ; search ; hunt (up) ¶ 돈이 있나 서랍을 뒤져보다 rummage in a drawer to see if there is any money

뒤조지다 call one's (special) attention to ; remind 《a person》 of 《a thing》 ; make sure of〔that〕 ; emphasize ; doublecheck ; confirm 《a contract》 ¶ 그 일에 대해선 일꾼들을 뒤조졌습니다 I called the special attention of the workers to that point.

뒤좇아가다 [추종] follow 《the fashion》 ; go after ; pursue ; [추적] pursue (after) ; chase ; give chase to ; run after ; hunt up ; course (사냥개가) ¶ 나는 전속력으로 그를 뒤좇아 갔다 I made after〔ran after, pursued〕 him as fast as I could.

뒤주 a rice-chest ; a rice-bin ; a grain-chest

뒤죽박죽 topsy-turvy ; higgledy-piggledy 《구》 ; pell-mell ; all mixed up ; all jumbled up ; in mess〔confusion, disorder〕 ¶ 그는 나의 계획을 뒤죽박죽으로 만들어 놓았다 He has made a mess of my plans. // 그는 뒤죽박죽으로 흩어진 서류를 정리했다 He put the papers scattered pell-mell in order.

뒤쥐 『동물』 a shrew ; a shrewmouse

뒤지 —紙 toilet paper ; a toilet roll (두루마리로 된) ; bumf 《영·속》

*뒤지다¹ search 《for》 ; look for ; hunt up ; rummage ; ransack ; fumble〔feel〕 for ¶ 경찰은 범인을 찾으려고 그 집을 뒤졌다 The police searched the house for the culprit. // 나는 지갑을 찾으려고 주머니를 뒤졌다 I felt〔fumbled〕 in my pocket for my purse. // 도둑은 서랍을 샅샅이 뒤졌다 The thief ransacked〔rummaged〕 the drawer.

뒤지다² be〔fall, lag〕 behind ; be backward ; be outstripped ¶ 경주에서 뒤지다 fall behind〔be outstripped by〕 the others in a race // 남에게 뒤지지 않도록 하다 try to keep abreast of〔keep up with〕

others // 시대〔유행〕에 뒤지다 be behind the times〔fashion〕 // 한국은 아직 과학에 있어서 유럽에 뒤졌다 Korea still lags behind Europe in science.

뒤짐 [문화·조류 따위의] a lag ; [일 따위] arrears ¶ 문화의 뒤짐 a cultural lag

뒤집개질 turning 《a thing》 over〔upside down〕 **—하다** turn 《it》 over

뒤집고 핥다 know thoroughly ; understand thoroughly〔in detail〕

†**뒤집다** ① [안을 밖으로] turn over ; turn 《a coat》 inside out ; turn wrong side out ; turn upside down ; turn up 《a card》 ; turn out 《the pocket》 ¶ 상의를 뒤집다 reverse a coat // 옷을 뒤집어 입다 wear one's clothes wrong side out
② [순서를] reverse ; invert ; switch ¶ 정상적 순서를 뒤집다 reverse〔change〕 the normal order
③ [전복시키다] overturn ; overthrow ; upset ; reverse ; turn over ; change ; capsize (배를) ¶ 배를 뒤집어엎다 capsize〔overturn〕 a boat // 자동차를 뒤집어엎다 upset a motorcar // 의자를 뒤집어엎다 overthrow a chair // 정부를 뒤집어엎다 overthrow the government // 학설〔계획〕을 뒤집어엎다 upset〔overthrow〕 a theory〔plan〕 // 판결을 뒤집어엎다 reverse a judgment
④ [혼란시키다] throw into confusion ¶ 그 소식은 장내를 발칵 뒤집어 놓았다 The news threw the audience into utter confusion.

뒤집어쓰다 ① [머리에] put on ; wear ; cover ¶ 그는 모자를 뒤집어썼다 He put on a hat. /He put a hat on. // 그 여자는 수건을 뒤집어썼다 She covered her head with a towel.
② [온몸에] cover with ; put on ; draw〔pull〕 over ; pour on ¶ 이불을 뒤집어쓰다 cover oneself with bedclothes ; pull〔draw〕 the quilt over one's head // 흙탕물을 뒤집어쓰다 be covered〔splashed〕 all over with muddy water
③ [뒤집어서] put on〔wear〕 《a hat》 inside out ; turn over and put on
④ [죄를] take 《a person's blame, fault》 upon oneself ¶ 그는 내 죄를 뒤집어썼다 He took my fault〔guilt〕 upon himself.

뒤집히다 ① [물건이] be turned inside out ; be turned over ¶ 책장이 바람에 뒤집히다 the leaves of a book are turned over by the wind
② [순서가] 《the order》 be reversed ; be switched〔changed〕
③ [전복] be overturned ; be turned over ; be upset ; be overthrown ; capsize (배가) ¶ 정부가 뒤집히다 a government is overthrown // 학설이 뒤집히다 a theory is upset // 형세가 뒤집혔다 The situation was reversed. // 배가 뒤집혀서 세 명이 익사했다 The boat capsized and three men were drowned. // 주인이 죽자 온 집안이 발칵 뒤집혔다 The master's death threw the whole house into utter confusion.

*__뒤쫓다__ follow up ; pursue ; run after 《a person》 ¶ 범인을 뒤쫓다 pursue a criminal

뒤차 一車 [다음 차] the next〔later〕 train ; the following car ; [끝 차] a car in the rear

뒤채[1] a wing in the back (of a house) ; the back wing ; a backhouse

뒤채[2] [가마의] the rear handlebars of a sedan chair

뒤채다 ① [많다] be in excess ; (be) superabundant ; superfluous ② [발에 채다] obstruct the way ; be obstructive ; get in the way

뒤처리 一處理 after-measures ; putting 《things》 to rights〔in order〕 ; settlement 《of an affair》 **—하다** wind 《an affair》 ; put 《things》 in order ; dispose of ⇨ 뒷갈망, 뒷수습 ¶ 사건의 뒤처리를 하다 settle an affair // 너는 언제나 문제만 일으키고 뒤처리는 항상 나에게 떠맡기는구나 All you ever do is cause problems and then force me to clean up your mess.

뒤척거리다 search ; rummage ; ransack ; fumble ; browse ⇨ 뒤적거리다

뒤쳐지다 be turned over

뒤축 the heel 《of the shoes》 ¶ 뒤축이 높은 신 high-heeled shoes

뒤치다 turn over ¶ 책장을 뒤치다 turn over the pages of a book ; leaf through a book

뒤치다꺼리 ① [돌봄] taking care of ; looking after ¶ 어린애들의 뒤치다꺼리를 하다 take care of the children ; look after the children ② [정리] clearing ; clearance ; straightening (out) ; fixing up ; settlement ¶ 연회의 뒤치다꺼리를 하다 put things in order after a party // 밥먹은 뒤치다꺼리를 하다 wash up the dishes ; clear the (dining) table // 분쟁의 뒤치다꺼리를 하다 settle〔wind up〕 a strife ; get a trouble straightened

뒤탈 later trouble ¶ 뒤탈이 두려워 for fear of later troubles // 뒤탈을 없애려면 이런 일은 깔끔히 처리되어야 한다 To avoid future trouble, things like this have to be taken care of properly. // 돈 관계 따위에서 뒤탈이 없도록 모든 것을 깔끔히 처리하도록 하시오 Make sure you get everything straight as far as money and all that's concerned so you won't have any trouble later on.

뒤터지다 have uncontrollable looseness of one's bowels ; lose control of one's bowels

뒤턱 [노름판에서의] a side bet
뒤턱 놓다 관용 《a spectator》 make a side bet

뒤통수 〚해부〛 the occiput ; the occipital region ; the back of the head ¶ 뒤통수를 때리다 strike 《a person》 on the back of

his head
뒤퉁스럽다 (be) clumsy ; blunt ; thick ; thickheaded ; senseless
뒤틀다 ① [비틀다] twist ; wrench ; screw ¶ 팔을 뒤틀다 twist〔wrench〕《a person's》 arm ; give a twist to 《a person's》 arm // 나뭇 가지를 뒤틀어 꺾다 wrench a branch off a tree ; break off a branch by twisting // 나사를 뒤틀다 screw a screw in ② [일을] baffle ; frustrate ; thwart ; obstruct ; foil ¶ 그의 부주의가 내 계획을 뒤틀었다 His carelessness frustrated〔balked〕 me in my plan. // 그는 내 일을 뒤틀었다 He foiled me in my attempt.
뒤틀리다 ① [비틀어지다] be twisted ; be wrenched ; be screwed ; be sprained (삐다) ; [휘어지다] be warped ; be distorted ; go awry ; [마음이] be perverse ; crossgrained ¶ 무릎이 뒤틀리다 get one's knee wrenched // 책뚜껑이 열로 뒤틀렸다 The book cover was warped by heat. // 겹친 불행 때문에 그 여자의 성격이 뒤틀렸다 Her character was warped by repeated misfortunes. // 때로는 사실이 역사가에 의하여 뒤틀린다 Sometimes the facts are distorted by the historians.
② [일이] be thwarted ; be baffled ; be frustrated ; be foiled ; go wrong〔amiss〕 ¶ 계획이 뒤틀렸다 He was thwarted〔obstructed, frustrated, foiled〕 in his plan.
뒤틀어지다 [물건이] be twisted ; go awry ; warp 《with heat, with dampness》 ; [일이] fail ; miss ; go amiss〔wrong〕 ¶ 일이 뒤틀어지다 a plan is thwarted〔misses, goes wrong, falls〕
뒤틈바리 a blunt rude fellow ; a rough
뒤편 —便 the back side
뒤폭 —幅 ① [옷의] the back (piece) of a garment ② [세간의] the back (piece) of a box〔chest〕
뒤표지 —表紙 the back〔reverse〕 cover
뒤품 the shoulder width of a garment
***뒤흔들다** ① [사물을] shake violently ; sway hard ¶ 과일을 따려고 나무를 뒤흔들다 shake the tree for fruit // 그 발명은 공업계를 뿌리째 뒤흔들어 놓았다 The invention rocked industry to its heels.
② [마음을] disturb〔stir, agitate〕《one's mind》
뒤흔들리다 ① [사물이] be shaken〔swayed〕 hard ¶ 지진으로 집이 뒤흔들리다 houses are shaken by an earthquake // 길이 나빠 차가 뒤흔들리다 a car sways because of the rough road
② [교란] be disturbed ; be stirred ; be agitated ¶ 마음이 뒤흔들리다 one's mind is disturbed
뒵들다 wrangle ; quarrel ; argue ; brawl ; dispute
뒷가지 ① [길마의] the back stick on a packsaddle ② [접미사] a suffix
뒷간 —間 a toilet ; a men's〔ladies'〕 room ; a lavatory ; a water closet 《W. C.》 ; a rest room ; a privy ; a latrine (공장, 군대의) ; the head (배, 군함의) ⇨ 변소 ¶ 뒷간 출입이 잦다 have loose bowels
뒷간 기둥이 물레방앗간 기둥을 더럽다 한다 속담 The kettle calls the pot blackbrows.
뒷갈망 winding up (a mess) ; setting right ; after-adjustment ; straightening ; putting in order ; liquidation **—하다** conduct〔deal with〕 the aftergrowth〔aftermath〕 ; settle ; wind up 《one's affairs》 ; straighten up ; put in order ¶ 뒷갈망이 아직도 되어 있지 않다 The matter awaits winding-up. // 뒷갈망이 큰 일이다 It will be a terrific task to straighten things up. // 그는 연회의 뒷갈망을 했다 He put things in order after the party.
뒷갈이 after-plowing〔-ploughing 《영》〕
뒷갱기 the heel padding of a straw sandal ; straw stiffener for a sandal heel
뒷거래 —去來 backdoor〔illegal〕 dealing〔business〕 ⇨ 암거래, 뒷구멍
뒷거름 (an) additional manuring
뒷걱정 after-worries **—하다** worry afterward
뒷걸음 a backward step
‡**뒷걸음질** stepping backward ; taking backward steps **—하다** step backward ; step back (약간)
뒷걸음치다 step〔walk, move〕 backward ; retrograde ; back down ; [무서워서] flinch ; shrink back〔away〕 《from》 ; draw back 《from danger》 ¶ 말이 뱀을 보고 뒷걸음치다 a horse shies〔jibs〕 at the sight of a snake
뒷경과 —經過 the aftercourse ; later development
뒷곁 a backyard ; the back (side) (뒤쪽)
뒷고대 the back of a collar
***뒷골목** an alley ; a backlane ; a back street 《미》 ; an alleyway (좁은) 《미》 ; a bystreet ¶ 한적한 뒷골목을 피하십시오 Stay away from lonely back streets.
뒷공론 —公論 [소문] gossip in private ; [험담] backbiting ; malicious gossip ; scandal ; [일이 끝난 후의] idle discussion after something is over **—하다** gossip in private ; backbite 《a person》 ; speak ill of 《a person》 behind his back ; stab 《a person》 in the back ; discuss 《a thing》 after it is over ¶ 남의 뒷공론을 하는 게 아니야 Don't speak ill of the absent.
뒷구멍 ① [뒷문] a back door〔way〕 ; the kitchen door ; a rear entry ; backstairs channels ; an illegitimate way ; an irregular〔unfair〕 way ; [부정 수단] unjust〔unlawful〕 means ¶ 뒷구멍 계약 a back door contract // 그는 뒷구멍으로 입학했다 He obtained admission to the college by unfair means. /He entered the school

through backstairs channels.
② [항문] the anus ¶ 뒷구멍의 병 anal diseases
뒷굽 ① [동물의] the back hoof of an animal ② [신의] the heel of a shoe
뒷귀 먹다 (be) stupid ; dull-witted ; be slow of understanding
뒷그림자 ① [그림자] a shadow behind ② [뒷모습] the sight〔appearance〕 of one's back
뒷길[1] a back street ; a byroad (샛길) ; [장래] one's future (prospects)
뒷길[2] [옷의] the back piece of an upper garment
뒷날 (in) the future ; later ; (in) afterdays ; the days to come ; someday ; another day ¶ 뒷날을 위해서 for future reference (참고) ; as a warning for the future (교훈) // 언젠가 뒷날 그것을 후회할 것이다 Someday or other you will repent it. // 그에게는 빛나는 뒷날이 있다 He has a brilliant〔bright〕 future before him.
뒷눈질 glancing back **—하다** glance back
뒷다리 a hind leg ¶ 뒷다리로 서다 (말 따위) stand on its hind legs ; rear up
뒷다리 잡히다 관용 fall into 《a person's》 clutches ; be caught in a snare
뒷담 the wall in back
뒷담당 一擔當 answering for the aftermath ; taking care of the rest of 《it》 ; taking responsibility for the future **—하다** answer for the aftergrowth ; take care 〔charge〕 of the rest ¶ 뒷담당은 내가 하겠다 I will answer for the consequences. /I will handle the rest. // 자네가 손해를 보면 내가 뒷담당하겠네 I'll answer for your possible losses.
뒷대문 一大門 the back-entrance 〔-gate〕 ; a rear gate
뒷대야 a basin for bathing the private 〔posterior〕 parts of the body ; a bidet 《프》
뒷덜미 the nape〔scruff〕 ; the back of one's neck ¶ 뒷덜미를 잡다 take 〔grasp, seize〕 《a person》 by the nape 〔scruff〕 of his neck
뒷도랑 the ditch in back
뒷돈 [자금] capital ; funds ; [비상금] reserve funds ; extra funds ¶ 뒷돈을 대다 supply 《a person》 with capital 《for business》
뒷동산 a hill at the back 《of one's house, of a village》
뒷마감 winding-up ; bringing to a finish ; completion ; conclusion **—하다** wind up ; bring to a finish ; complete ; conclude ¶ 일을 뒷마감하다 wind up a job ; finish one's work
뒷마구리 the rear crossbar of a saddle rack
뒷마당 a backyard ; a back garden ; ground at the back of a house
뒷마루 a rear floor ; the floor in the back
뒷막이 ① [세간 따위의] the back piece 〔plank〕 《of a piece of furniture》
② ⇨ 뒷마감
⁑**뒷말** backbiting ⇨ 뒷공론
****뒷맛** aftertaste ¶ 뒷맛이 좋다 leave a pleasing〔clean〕 taste in one's mouth // 뒷맛이 나쁘다 leave a bad〔unpleasant〕 taste behind ; have a bitter aftertaste // 그것은 뒷맛이 산뜻하다 It left a very pleasant aftertaste
뒷맵시 one's appearance〔figure〕 from the back ; the sight of 《a person's》 back ¶ 뒷맵시가 있다〔없다〕 look fine 〔poor〕 from behind ; look smart〔plain〕 when seen from the back // 뒷맵시를 보다 adjust 〔make up, fix up〕 one's appearance from the back
뒷머리 ① [물건의] the back part 《of》 ; the back end ¶ 책상 뒷머리 the back part of a table ② [행렬의] the rear ; the end ¶ 줄의 뒷머리 the end 〔rear〕 of a row // 행렬의 뒷머리 the rear of a procession ③ [머리] back hair (여자의) ; the back of the head
뒷면 一面 ① [이면] the reverse〔wrong〕 side ; the back (side) ; [내면] the inside ¶ 엽서의 뒷면 《on》 the back of a postal card // 뒷면에도 써 있습니다 [주의서] Please turn over. 《P. T. O.》
② [동전의] the tail ; the reverse 《of a coin》
뒷모습 the appearance from behind ; the back ⇨ 뒷모양 ①
뒷모양 一模樣 ① [모양] the appearance 〔figure〕 from behind ; the sight of 《a person's》 back ¶ 뒷모양을 바라보다 gaze after 《a person》 // 그는 뒷모양이 그의 삼촌과 비슷하다 He looks like his uncle from behind.
② [체면] face ; honor ¶ 뒷모양이 안되다 《a person》 loses his face〔is put out of countenance〕
뒷목 [타작 후의 마당 쓰레기] grain tailings (on a threshing floor)
뒷문 一門 a back door〔gate〕 ; a back entrance〔way〕 ; a rear gate
뒷물 bathing one's private parts ; a hip bath ; a sitz bath **—하다** bath one's private parts ; take a sitz bath
뒷밀이 [밀어주기] pushing 《a cart》 from behind (일) ; [사람] a pusher ; a push-man **—하다** push 《a cart》 from behind
뒷바닥 the back of a shoe sole
뒷바라지 looking after ; giving aids ; a help ; taking care of **—하다** help (out) ; take care of〔care for〕 ; look after ¶ 아들 살림의 뒷바라지를 하다 provide one's son with daily necessaries ; help one's son's family out // 그 여자는 애들의 뒷바라지에 바쁘다 She is busy with the care of her children.
뒷바퀴 the back〔rear〕 wheel(s)

*뒷받침 backing ; support ; boosting 《구》 ; [사람] a backer ; a supporter ; a booster 《구》 —하다 back ; support ; boost 《구》 ¶ 의무의 뒷받침이 없는 권리 rights not backed〔unaccompanied〕 by duties // 영국의 뒷받침이 있다 have Britain at her back // 그는 나의 사업에 뒷받침이 되어 주었다 He backed me up in my business. /He gave his assistances to me in my business. // 시저는 배후에 민중의 뒷받침이 있었다 Caesar had the people at the back.

뒷발 ① [동물의] a hind leg ¶ 뒷발로 서다 stand on its hind legs ; rear up (말 따위) // 뒷발로 흙을 차다 scratch up the dirt with its hind legs
② [발길] kicking with one's heel ¶ 뒷발길질하다 kick behind with one's heel

뒷발굽 a back hoof

뒷발막 a kind of leather shoe with seamless heel

뒷발질 kicking with one's heel —하다 kick with one's heel

뒷발톱 ① [마소의] a back hoof ② [며느리발톱] a spur ; a calcar

뒷방 —房 a back〔an inner, a rear〕 room ; a room at the back
—마누라 a wife shoved into the back room (in favor of a concubine) ; a grass widow

뒷배 backing ; support ; helping from behind ¶ 뒷배를 부탁하다 ask〔come upon〕 《a person》 for help〔support〕
뒷배(를) 보다 관용 support ; back up 《a person》

뒷배포 —排布 [검도] preparing to face a retaliatory attack (in fencing)

뒷벽 —壁 a back wall

뒷보증 —保證 endorsement ; visa (여권의) —하다 endorse ; visa ¶ 뒷보증 있는〔없는〕 endorsed〔unendorsed〕 // 어음에 뒷보증하다 endorse a note ; back a bill

뒷북치다 rush〔fuss〕 around fruitlessly after the event ¶ 미련한 놈 뒷북친다 Fools are wise after the event.

뒷사람 a person behind ; [뒷세대] a person of a later generation ; generations to come

뒷산 —山 a mountain in back

뒷생각 afterthoughts

뒷소리 ① [응원] a yell ; a cheer ¶ 뒷소리 치며 응원하다 yell〔root〕 for a team
② [뒷말] gossip ; backbiting ⇨ 뒷공론
뒷소리 치다 관용 cheer up ; yell ; root 《구》

뒷소문 —所聞 gossip about some past event

뒷손 illegal〔false〕 reach ; a dirty hand 《for money》 ; acceptance 《of something》 on the sly
뒷손을 벌리다 관용 demand money〔a thing〕 under a counter ; be ready to accept on the sly

뒷손가락질하다 point after 《a person》 ; point a finger of scorn at 《a person》 ¶ 뒷손가락질받다 have depreciating words uttered behind one's back ; be talked of (in contempt) // 남에게 뒷손가락질당하지 않도록 해라 Keep yourself above suspicion.

뒷손 없다 (be) careless ; loose ; negligent ; slovenly ; slipshod

뒷수쇄 —收刷 putting things in order ; setting matters right ; clearing up ; rearrangement ; after adjustment ; winding-up —하다 put things in order ; rearrange ; clear up ; settle ; wind up ; take remedial measures ; deal with 〔conduct〕 aftermath〔aftergrowth〕 ¶ 식사의 뒷수쇄를 하다 clear the table after the dinner is over // 불탄 자리의 뒷수쇄를 하다 clear the scene of the debris of a recent fire

뒷수습 —收拾 settlement 《of an affair》 ¶ 사건〔빚〕의 뒷수습을 하다 settle an affair〔one's debts〕 // 파산한 회사의 뒷수습을 하다 wind up the affairs of an insolvent company

뒷심 backing ; help〔aid, assistance〕 from behind ¶ 뒷심이 든든하다 have a good backing // 뒷심이 있다 have 《a person》 at one's back

뒷이야기 a sequel to the story

뒷일 [장래] future affairs ; affairs after one's death (사후의) ; [남의 일] later happenings ; the rest ; the aftermath 〔aftergrowth〕 ¶ 친구에게 애들의 뒷일을 부탁하다 entrust the care of one's children to a friend ; entrust a friend with the care of one's children // 뒷일이 어떻게 되든 개의하지 않는다 I do not care for the consequences. // 당신이 없는 동안 뒷일을 돌보겠다 I will look after your affairs while you are away.

뒷입맛 an aftertaste ⇨ 뒷맛

뒷자락 the rear train〔trail〕 (of one's clothes)

뒷자리 a back seat

뒷자손 —子孫 later descendants

뒷전 ① [뒤쪽] the back ; the rear ¶ 뒷전에 멀찍이 앉다 sit far back
② [배후] the back ¶ 뒷전에〔몰래〕 in secret ; [남이 없는 데서] in 《a person's》 absence
③ [뒤로 미루어지는 일] ¶ 뒷전으로 돌리다 lay aside 《one's work》 ; neglect 《one's home》
④ [굿의] the last of 12 stages of an exorcism ¶ 뒷전풀이 performance of the last stage of an exorcism

뒷전놀다 ① [뒤치다꺼리하다] clear up ⇨ 뒤치다꺼리 ② [무당이] perform the last stage of an exorcism

뒷정리 —整理 arrangements for the conclusion〔end〕 —하다 arrange to end 〔conclude〕 ; put 《things》 in order ;

clear away 《청소》; dispose of 《처리》; clear the table 《식사의》
뒷조사 —調査 a detailed investigation —하다 thoroughly investigate
뒷질 pitching ; rocking —하다 《a ship》 pitch ; 《a boat》 rock back and forth
뒷짐결박 —結縛 —하다 tie〔bind〕《a person's》 hands behind his back ¶ 도둑은 뒷짐결박당하였다 The thief has his hands tied behind his back.
뒷짐지다 fold one's hands behind one's back
뒷집 the house adjoining in the back ; the house right back of one's own
*뒹굴다 ① [누워서] roll〔tumble〕 about 〔over〕; [고통으로] writhe ¶ 잠자리에서 뒹굴다 toss〔tumble〕 about in one's bed //잔디 위에 뒹굴다 roll about on a lawn
② [빈들빈들 지내다] idle〔loaf〕 one's time away ; be on the loaf ; eat the bread of idleness ; loaf around 《미》 ¶ 일요일을 집에서 뒹굴며 지내다 pass Sundays idly at home //평생을 뒹굴며 지내다 drift aimlessly through life
뒹굴 자리 보고 씨름에 나간다 속담 Stretch your arm no further than your sleeve will reach. /Everyone stretches his legs according to the length of his coverlet.
듀랄루민 〖화학〗 duralumin
듀스 〖정구〗 deuce ¶ 듀스가 되다 go to deuce
듀엣 〖음악〗 a duet
드나나나 whether (one is) in or out ; whether one is at home or stays out ¶ 드나나나 걱정뿐이다 I have nothing but trouble, out and home.
드나들다 ① [출입] come in and go out ; go〔come〕 in and out ; enter and leave ; [방문] visit (frequently) ; frequent ; [바뀌다] be frequently changed ¶ 나는 그곳을 자유롭게 드나들고 있습니다 I have free access to the place. //이곳은 군인들이 드나들지 못하게 되어 있다 The place is off limits to the soldiers. //그 집은 식모가 자주 드나든다 Cooks are frequently changed in that house.
② [고르지 못하다] zigzag ; crooked ; bent ; go in and out ¶ 해안선이 드나들다 a coast line is much indented
드난 ¶ 드난살다 live in a family as a servant〔charwoman〕
드날리다 ① [이름이] 《one's name》 resound〔echo〕 far and wide ; come to fame ; become famous〔popular〕
② [이름을] have one's name up ; make 〔win〕 a name for oneself
③ [날리다] (hold a thing and) fly〔let fly, make fly〕
*드넓다 (be) spacious ; extensive ; open ¶ 드넓은 들 an open field //그는 드넓은 들판에서 말을 달렸다 He galloped his horse in an open field.
드높다 (be) high ; lofty ¶ 하늘에 드높이 high up in the air ; way up in the sky 《미》
드다르다 (be) quite〔entirely〕 different
드던지다 throw at random〔wildly〕
*드디어 finally ; at last ; eventually ; at length ; in the end ; after all ; in the long run ¶ 그는 드디어 성공했다 At last he succeeded. //그는 드디어 회복했다 At length he got over his disease.
드라마 a drama ; a play
라디오 — a radio play 텔레비전 연속 — a television serial drama
드라이 밀크 powder(ed) milk ; dry milk
드라이버 ① [운전사] a driver ② [나사돌리개] a screwdriver ③ [골프] a driver
†드라이브 a drive ; a motor ride ; a joyride 《미·구》 —하다 drive ; take 〔have〕 a drive 《to》
—웨이 a driveway
드라이 아이스 dry ice
드라이어 a drier ; a dryer ¶ 헤어 드라이어 a hair drier //그냥 드라이어로 말려 주세요 Just blow-dry it, please.
드라이 클리닝 dry cleaning ¶ 드라이 클리닝업자 a dry cleaner —하다 dry-clean ; dry-cleanse
‡드러나다 ① [유명해지다] become known ; become famous〔prominent, conspicuous〕 ¶ 드러나게 유명한 학자 a world-famous scholar
② [표면에] show〔display〕 itself ; reveal 〔assert〕 itself ; be expressed ; be revealed ; come in evidence ¶ 표면에 드러나다 come to the front ; appear on the surface //술에 취하면 사람의 본성이 드러난다 Wine reveals the true man. //이 소설에는 지방색이 잘 드러나 있다 The local color is well brought out in this story. //희색이 얼굴에 드러나 있었다 His face was expressive of joy.
③ [노출] be exposed ; be disclosed ; be bared ; crop out (광맥이) ; be open to the view ¶ 드러난 bare ; exposed ; naked ; uncovered // 어깨가 드러나다 one's shoulders are exposed〔bare〕
④ [비밀이] be found (out) ; be disclosed ; be exposed ; be detected ; be laid bare ; come to light ; be brought to light ¶ 거짓말이 드러나다 one's lie is detected ; one's falsehood is found out // 비밀이 드러났다 The secret got out. //그의 죄상을 말해주는 여러 사실이 드러났다 Various facts were brought to light telling his crimes.
†드러내다 ① [유명하게 하다] distinguish ; make famous ¶ 싸움에서 이름을 드러내다 distinguish oneself in the battle
② [표면에] diplay 《one's ability》; exhibit 《one's skill》; show 《anger》; prove ; express ; [증명하다] speak for ; bespeak ¶ 정직함을 드러내다 《this fact》 speak for his honesty //이것은 그의

현명함을 드러내고 있다 This fact points to his sagacity.
③ [노출] show 《one's true colors》; expose 《one's ignorance》; disclose; reveal; betray 《emotion》; bare 《one's arm》 ¶ 정체를 드러내다 betray oneself; give oneself away // 그녀는 맨발인데다 가슴까지 드러내고 있었다 She was barefooted, and, what is more, her chest was completely bared.
④ [비밀을] reveal〔disclose, divulge〕 《a secret》; expose 《another's crime》; lay bare 《an evil design》; nail 《a lie》 《속》

†**드러눕다** lie down; lay oneself down; throw oneself down; lie on one's back ¶ 병으로 드러눕다 be laid up with illness; take to〔be confined to〕 one's bed // 그는 긴 의자에 드러누웠다 He lay at full length on a sofa.

드러쌓이다 accumulate; be piled (up); [눈 따위가] lie; [많다] be plentiful; be full of ¶ 눈이 10센티미터나 드러쌓였다 Snow lay ten centimeters deep on the ground.

드러장이다 be piled (up); be stacked; be heaped evenly ¶ 쌀가마가 드러장여 있다 Bags of rice are piled up high 《in a warehouse》.

드럼[1] [큰북] a drum

드럼[2] [통] a drum ¶ 드럼통 a drum (can) // 석유 세 드럼 three drums of petroleum

드렁거리다 snore away (through one's nose)

드렁드렁 snoring loudly ¶ 코를 드렁드렁 골다 snore loudly〔terribly, horribly〕

드레 dignity; weight of character

드레나다 [바퀴가] a wheel of a machine wobbles〔gets loose〕

드레드레 dangling(ly); swaying

‡**드레스** a dress
—메이커 a dressmaker

*__드레싱__ 〖요리〗 (a) dressing ¶ 샐러드〔프렌치〕 드레싱 (a) salad〔French〕 dressing

드레지다 (be) dignified; weighty; imposing ¶ 그의 태도에는 어딘지 드레진 데가 있다 There is something dignified in his bearing.

드레질 sizing up; weighing **—하다** size up 《a person》; weigh 《a thing》

드르렁 with a snore

드르렁거리다 keep snoring (loudly) ¶ 드르렁거리기 시작하다 fall to snoring

드르렁드르렁 ⇨ 드렁드렁

드르르[1], **뜨르르**[1] ① [미끄럽게] without stopping; rolling; rumbling ¶ 전차가 드르르 소리를 내며 다리를 지나갔다 A streetcar rumbled over the bridge.
② [떠는 모양] trembling(ly); shivering(ly)

드르르[2], **뜨르르**[2] [거침없이] smoothly; without a hitch; swimmingly; without any difficulty ¶ 어려운 문제를 드르르 풀다 solve a hard question easily // 일이 드르르 진행되었다 The matter went on swimmingly.

드리다[1] give; offer; let 《a person》 have; make 《a person》 a present of 《a thing》 ¶ 웃사람에게 물건을 드리다 present a thing to the superior // 기도를 드리다 offer〔put up〕 one's prayer // 어머니께 진지를 드리다 serve one's mother dinner

드리다[2] [꼬다] braid; plait; twist 《into a rope》 ¶ 댕기를 드리다 plait one's hair into a pigtail // 밧줄을 드리다 braid〔make〕 a rope

드리다[3] [방·마루 따위를] set; put in; make; construct ¶ 방을 드리다 set a room

드리다[4] [가게 문을] close the shop; put up the shutters; close up shop ¶ 가게를 하루 드리다 close the store for the day

드리다[5] [곡식을] winnow away〔off〕 the chaff from the grain

드리블 〖구기〗 a dribble **—하다** dribble

드리없다 [일정하지 않다] (be) irregular; variable; changeable; be subject to change; be not fixed; be in flux ¶ 드리없이 irregularly; variably

드리우다 ① [늘어뜨리다] hang (down); let (hang) down ¶ 장막을 드리우다 hang down a curtain // 머리를 잔등에 드리우다 wear one's hair hanging down on one's back
② [베풀다] grant; bestow on ¶ 가르침을 드리우다 grant a favor of giving lesson; give lesson〔instruction〕 in // 은혜를 드리우다 bestow a favor on 《a person》
③ [후세에 전하다] hand down; leave; bequeath ¶ 자손들에게 드리우다 hand down 《a thing》 to posterity

‡**드릴** ① [송곳] a drill ¶ (도로 공사용) 수동 드릴 a jackhammer ② [훈련] a drill

드림 [기(旗) 드림] a streamer; a pennon; a pennant; a banderole

드림셈 payment by installments; an installment plan ¶ 드림셈으로 가구를 사다 buy furniture on an installment plan

드림흥정 transaction by installments **—하다** sell〔buy〕 on installments

드맑다 (be) very clear

드문드문 ① [시간적] occasionally; once in a while; now and then; from time to time ¶ 드문드문 찾아오다 come once in a while // 그런 일이 드문드문 일어난다 Such things happen from time to time. // 그의 소식을 드문드문 듣는다 I hear from him now and then.
② [공간적] sparsely; thinly; at intervals; sporadically; scatteredly; here and there ¶ 나무를 드문드문 심다 plant trees at intervals // 털이 드문드문 나다 be thinly haired // 들에 집이 드문드문 서 있다 The field is sparsely dotted with houses.

†**드물다** (be) rare; unusual; uncommon; few; scarce; few and far between ¶ 드물게 rarely; seldom; at rare intervals //

아주 드문 물건 a black swan ; a white crow // 그녀는 보기 드문 미인이다 She is a rare beauty. // 그는 드물게 보는 웅변가다 He is a man of rare eloquence. // 이렇게 잘되어가는 일도 드물다 Such a success is quite phenomenal. // 물론 사고도 일어나지만 그것은 아주 드문 일이다 Accidents might occur, of course, but they are few and far between.

드새다 pass the night 《at an inn》

드세다 (be) powerful ; influential ; important ; very strong ¶ 그는 당 내에서 상당히 세력이 드세다 He has 〔wields〕 much power〔influence〕 in the party.

드잡이 ① [싸움] a scuffle ; a handgrip ; a grapple ; a scrimmage ② [차압] seizure ; attachment ; distraint **—하다** come to grips 《with each other》 ; scuffle ; gripple ; seize 《one's kitchen utensils for a debt》 ; attach ; distrain 《upon》 ¶ 가구를 드잡이하다 attach 〔seize〕 《a person's》 furniture // 드잡이를 당하다 have one's property seized 《for a debt》

드티다 [자리나 날짜가] be extended ; be protracted ; be lengthened ; be stretched out ; [자리나 날짜를] extend ; protract ; make an interval longer ¶ 방문 기간을 드티다 protract one's stay // 사이를 드티다 leave space // 지불 기한을 드티다 extend the term of payment // 교섭이 드틴다 Negotiations are protracted.

드팀전 一廛 a drygoods store ; a draper's shop 《영》

득 ① [긋다] 《draw a line》 forcefully ; with pressure ¶ 줄을 득 내려 긋다 draw a forceful line downward
② [긁다] scraping hard ¶ 솥 밑을 득 긁다 give the bottom of the oven a hard scrape
③ [얼다] 《freeze》 hard ; solid

득 得 [이익] gain ; profit ; benefit ; [유리] advantage ; [절약] saving ¶ 득을 보면 봤지 손해는 보지 않는다 You have everything to gain and nothing to lose. // 아무 득도 되지 않는데 왜 빈 깡통을 줍고 있지 Yor're not getting anything in return, so how come you're out picking up empty come ?

득남 得男 begetting a son

득녀 得女 begetting a daughter

득도 得道 attainment of Nirvana (불도) ; spiritual awakening〔enlightenment〕 **—하다** attain Nirvana ; achieve spiritual enlightenment

득돌같다 (be) quite satisfactory ; perfect ; gratifying ¶ 그는 라디오를 득돌같이 고쳐 놓았다 He got the radio in perfect working order.

득득 ① [줄을 긋는 꼴] 《draw a line》 firmly〔fast, forcefully〕 ¶ 줄을 득득 긋다 draw lines fast
② [얼어붙는 꼴] 《freeze》 hard〔solid〕 ¶ 득득 얼어붙다 be frozen hard
③ [긁는 꼴] scratching hard ¶ 득득거리는 소리 a scratching sound // 모기가 문 데를 득득 긁다 scratch a mosquito bite

득롱망촉 得隴望蜀 limitless greed ; Give him an inch, and he will take an ell.

득명 得名 —하다 gain fame ; make a reputation ; make a name for oneself ; become famous ; distinguish oneself ¶ 이 작품으로 그는 크게 득명했다 The work won〔secured〕 him great fame.

득병 得病 —하다 get〔fall, become, be taken〕 ill

득보기 a blockhead ; an ass ; a fool ; a dunce ; an idiot ; a moron

득세 得勢 —하다 ① [세력을 얻음] rise to〔gain, acquire〕 power ; become powerful〔influential〕 ¶ 그 의견이 점점 득세하고 있다 The view is gaining ground 〔gathering weight〕.
② [형편이 유리함] turn to one's advantage ; get an opportunity ¶ 그는 만사에 득세하였다 Everything turned to his profit.

득승 得勝 a victory ; a win ; a success ; a triumph **—하다** win ; win a victory ; end in one's victory ¶ 시합에서 득승하다 win a game

득시글득시글 in swarms ; swarming **—하다** swarm 《with》 ; wriggle about in a swarm ; be alive with 《fish》 ¶ 사람이 득시글득시글하다 be thickly populated // 거지가 득시글득시글하다 swarm〔be overflowing, be crowded〕 with beggars // 연못에 고기가 득시글득시글하고 있다 The pond is alive with fish.

득실 得失 [장단점] merits and demerits 〔defects〕 ; [손익] advantages and disadvantages ; gain and loss ; [성패] success and failure ¶ 득실을 떠나서 without considering personal interest // 득실을 생각하다 weigh〔ponder on〕 the merits〔relative advantages〕

득실득실 ⇨ 득시글득시글

득의 得意 ① [성공] prosperity ¶ 득의의 시절에 in one's bright〔best, palmy〕 days // 득의의 절정에 있다 be at the summit〔height〕 of one's prosperity ; be in one's glory
② [자랑] elation ; self-complacency ; triumph ; pride ¶ 득의의 elated ; triumphant ; self-complacent ; self-satisfied // 득의 만면이다 be proud 《of》 ; pride〔plume〕 oneself 《on》 ; take a pride 《in》

득의 양양 得意揚揚 —하다 [서술적] be as happy as a king ; be as pleased〔proud〕 as Punch〔a peacock, a turkey〕 ; be on (a) cockhorse ; be all set up ; be in the skies ¶ 득의 양양하여 proudly ; in triumph // 득의 양양한 태도〔얼굴〕 a triumphant air ; a complacent look // 그는 금방 득의 양양해 한다 It always goes right to his head.

득인심 得人心 **— 하다** win the hearts of the people
†**득점** 得點 marks ; [경기의] a point ; [총괄적] a score **— 하다** score 《a point》 ¶ 득점이 없다 be scoreless // 득점을 기록하다 score the runs (야구에서) // 4대 3의 득점으로 이기다 win with a score of 4 to 3 // 우리의 득점은 15점이었다 Our team scored 15 points.
— 게시판 [야구 따위의] a scoreboard **— 기입부** a scorebook **— 자** a scorer **— 표** a scorecard ; a points table **개인 —** an individual score **팀 —** a team score
득죄 得罪 **— 하다** take the guilt upon oneself ; hold oneself blamable ; bear guilt
득책 得策 the best〔profitable〕 plan, good policy ; advisability
득표 得票 the number of votes polled 〔obtained〕 ; a polling score ; one's poll ¶ 김씨의 득표는 8만이었다 Mr. *Kim* polled〔got〕 80,000 votes.
— 수 the number of votes obtained 〔polled〕 ; a polling score ; one's poll **법정 — 수** the legally required
득하다 [날씨가] grow cold suddenly
득효 得效 **— 하다** 《a medicine》 have an effect 《on a person》 ; get the effect 《of medicine》
-든 either... or ; whether... or ⇨ -든지
-든가 (either...) or else ⇨ -든지
든거지 난부자 — 富者 a person who looks rich but is really poor
든난벌 (garments for) house wear and street wear
든든하다 ① [굳세다] (be) strong ; firm ; stout ; robust ; hardy ; solid ; durable ¶ 든든한 사람 a strong person // 든든한 기둥 a stout pillar // 발걸음이 든든하다 have a firm step〔steady gait〕
② [미덥다] (be) secure ; reassuring ; safe ; reliable ; trusty ; trustworthy ¶ 든든한 자리 a safe position // 그것을 들으니 마음이 든든하다 It is quite reassuring to hear that. // 너와 같이 있으면 마음이 든든하다 I feel safe as long as you stay with me. /Your presence will inspire me with great confidence.
③ [배가] (be) stomachful ; 《one's stomach》 full ¶ 든든히 먹다 eat a substantial meal ; fortify oneself with meal
든든히 ① [굳세게] strongly ; robustly ; stoutly ; firmly ; solidly ; steadily
② [미덥게] securely ; safely ; confidently
③ [배부르게] fully ; to repletion
든번 — 番 one's turn ; one's time
든벌 home〔everyday〕 wear ; weekday 〔work〕 clothes
든벌이 earning〔making〕 money out of a casual job〔odd jobs〕 **— 하다** earn 〔make〕 money by doing odd jobs
든부자 난거지 — 富者 — a person who looks poor but is really rich
든손 ① [단번에] at a stretch ; without a break ; at a breath ; right away ; on the spot ; immediately ¶ 든손으로 읽어 버리다 finish 《a book》 at a sitting // 든손으로 다 마셔버리다 empty the glass at a gulp // 든손으로 일을 끝내다 finish one's work straight out
② [하는 김에] while ; when ; as ; by the way ; by the by(e) ; at the same time ; apropos ; while one is about it ; while one is at 《a thing》 ¶ 든손에 내 편지도 좀 써주십시오 While you are writing 〔While you are at it〕, please write a letter for me.
†**-든지** either... or ; whether... or ¶ 가든지 말든지 내가 알게 뭐냐 Whether you go or not, I don't care about it. // 그가 죽든지 살든지 모른다 I don't care whether he lives or dies. // 어느 쪽이든지 좋다 Either will do. // 펜으로 쓰든지 연필로 쓰든지 좋도록 해라 You may write it either with a pen or a pencil.
든직하다 (be) calm ; composed ; dignified ; weighty ; sedate ; quiet ; self-possessed ¶ 든직한 사람 a self-possessed person ; a staid〔steady〕 person // 든직한 태도 a quiet attitude ; a calm manner
든침모 — 針母 a resident seamstress 〔needlewoman〕
듣그럽다 (be) noisy ; clamorous ; vociferous ; uproarious ; boisterous
†**듣다**¹ ① [소리를] hear ; listen 《to》 ; give an ear to ; lend an ear to ; learn ; hear of ; be informed〔told〕 of ¶ 끝까지 듣다 hear 《a person》 out // 라디오를 듣다 listen to the radio ; listen to 《a speech》 on the air // 강의를 듣다 attend a lecture // 풍문에 듣다 learn by hearsay // 듣는 바에 의하면 they say ; I am told // 내말을 좀 들어요 Hear me. /Mark my word. /Give heed to what I say. // 내가 듣는 자리에서 그렇게 말했소 He said so in my hearing. // 듣자니 서울에 큰 소동이 있었다구 There were, we learn, great disturbances in *Seoul*. // 듣는 것과 보는 것은 크게 다르다 Rumor and fact are miles apart. // 듣기 싫다 I don't want to hear about it ! // 그렇다고 들었습니다 So I heard. // 세상 오래 살다 보니 별소리를 다 듣겠군 Now I've heard of everything. // 내 말 좀 들어 볼래 You know what ? // 흥분하지 말고 내 말 좀 끝까지 들어 봐 Don't steam. Hear me out. // 얘기는 누구에게 들었습니까 Who did you hear that from ?
② [칭찬·꾸지람을] receive ; suffer ; be given ¶ 잔소리를 듣다 be scolded ; catch a scolding // 칭찬을 듣다 be praised 〔applauded〕 // 칭찬을 듣고 화낼 사람은 없다 Nobody feels offended at compliment.
③ [충고·청 따위를] obey ; follow ; mind ; heed ; grant ; comply with ¶ 충고를 듣다 take〔follow〕 《a person's》 advice

// 말을 듣지 않다 be naughty ; be obstinate // 요구를 듣다 comply with 〔accede to〕 《a person's》 request // 소원을 들어보자 I will attend to your wishes.
④ [효험이 있다] take〔have〕 effect 《on》 ; be efficacious ; do 《a person》 good ¶ 잘 듣는 약 a very efficacious medicine ; a drug of great virtue // 듣지 않다 be no good 《for》 ; have no effect 《on》 // 약이 들었다 The medicine has done me good. // 약이 듣지 않게 됐다 The drug has lost its effect on me.
⑤ [작용하다] work ; act ; operate ; tell ¶ 브레이크가 안 듣는다 The brake refuses to act〔work〕. /This brake will not work well.
들은 말 들은 데 버리고 본 말 본 데 버려라 속담 Hear and see and say nothing.

듣다² [물·눈물 따위가] drip ; drop ; trickle ¶ 빗방울이 듣다 raindrops fall ; it is dripping

듣다못해 being tired of listening to

듣보기장사 speculative business ; a venture

듣보다 search ; seek ; look for ; keep an eye 《on》

듣잡다 [듣다] hear ; listen to ; [들어서 알다] be told ; know ; be informed ; understand ; [분부를] receive 《a command》

*__들¹__ a field ; [전답] the fields ; [평야] a plain ; the plains ; [농지] a farm ¶ 들에서 자란 wild // 들꽃 wild flowers ; flowers of the field // 들에서도 산에서도 in the mountains as well as on the plains // 들에서 일하다 work in the fields
—장미 a wild rose

들² [등등] and other things ; and others ; and so forth〔on〕 ; and the like ; and what not ; etcetera 《etc.》 《라》 ¶ 책상이나 의자들 팝니다 We sell tables, chairs, and other things. // 책상 위에 노리개며 그림들이 많이 놓여 있었다 The table was loaded with toys, pictures, and what not. // 동물원에 가서 코끼리와 범, 곰들을 보았다 We went to the zoo and saw elephants, tigers, bears, and the like.

들- [몹시] hard ; violently ; thoroughly

들가뢰 〖곤충〗 a kind of tiger beetle

들개 a cur ; an ownerless〔a homeless〕 dog ; a stray dog

*__들것__ a stretcher ; a litter ¶ 들것으로 나르다 carry on a stretcher

들고나다 ① [간섭] interfere 《in a matter, with a person》 ; meddle 《in, with》 ; step in ; butt in ; put in a word ; poke one's nose 《into》 ¶ 무슨 일에든지 들고나는 여자다 She meddles with everything. // 부부 싸움에는 들고나지 않는 것이 좋다 One should not meddle in a quarrel between man and wife.
② [세간을] carry out 《household articles》 for sale to raise money

들고뛰다 [도망치다] flee ; run away ; take to flight ; make one's escape ; take to one's heels ; [가축이] get free ; break loose ¶ 돈을 가지고 들고뛰다 make away with another's money // 자동차를 타고 들고뛰다 make one's escape in a car // 말이 들고뛴다 The horse runs away. /[매두었던 말이] The horse gets〔breaks〕 loose. // 순경을 보더니 도둑놈은 들고뛰었다 At the sight of the police the thief took to his heels.

들고빼다 ⇨ 들고뛰다, 들고주다, 들고튀다

들고주다 [달아나다] run away ; [낭비하다] squander ; dissipate ; waste

들고튀다 [달아나다] run away ; flee ; take to flight ¶ 그들은 어둠을 타서 들고튀었다 They made their escape under cover of darkness. /They left the place between dark and daylight. /They shot the moon. 《속》

들고파다 study hard〔untiringly〕 ; work hard〔steadily〕 《at》 ; plod ; dig (into, at) 《미》 ¶ 들고파는 사람 a grind 《미》 ; a swot 《영》 ; a sap 《영》

들국화 一菊花 〖식물〗 a wild camomile 〔chrysanthemum〕

들기름 perilla oil

들까부르다 ① [키질하다] winnow〔fan〕 briskly ② [위아래로 흔들다] move 《a thing》 up and down briskly ; [아기를] dance ; dandle

들까불다 ① [위아래로 흔들(리)다] move up and down briskly ; dance ② [방정맞게] act frivolously〔flippantly, lightly, rashly〕

들까불리다 be winnowed〔fanned〕 briskly ; be moved up and down briskly

들깨 〖식물〗 Perilla japonica (학명)

들꽃 a wild〔field〕 flower

들꾀다 ⇨ 들끓다

들꿩 〖새〗 a hazel grouse

*__들끓다__ swarm ; crowd ; [이 따위가] be infested with ¶ 거지가 들끓다 be crowded with beggars // 집에 쥐가 들끓다 a house is swarming with rats // 개미가 설탕에 들끓다 ants swarm upon the sugar // 파출소 앞에 사람이 들끓고 있다 There is a big crowd of people about the police-box.

들날리다 [이름·세력 따위를] make〔be〕 famous〔well known〕 ; be popular ; win reputation〔renown〕 ; resound ; enjoy a great prosperity ¶ 명성을 전세계에 들날리다 be known all over the world ; win〔enjoy〕 world-wide fame〔reputation〕 // 시인으로서 이름이 온 세상에 들날리다 be famous all over the world as a poet ; be a poet of world-wide fame 〔renown〕 // 그의 이름은 국내외에 들날린다 His name is known both at home and abroad. // 최근 S씨는 가요곡으로 이름을 들날리고 있다 Mr. S has gained his musical reputation by popular songs.

들내 the smell〔scent〕 of perilla
들녘 a plain ; an open field ; flat country
들놀다 swing〔sway〕 up and down〔back and forth〕
들놀이 a picnic ; an outing **—하다** have a picnic ; be on a picnic ¶ 들놀이 가다 go on a picnic ; go picnicking
들놓다[1] [일손 놓다] leave the fields (at a mealtime) ; leave off〔stop〕 work in the fields ; have〔take〕 a break in the fields
들놓다[2] [들었다 놓았다 하다] take《a thing》 up and down
†**들다**[1] ① [날씨가] clear (up) ; become clear ; stop《raining, snowing》 ¶ 날이 든다 It stops raining. /The rain stops〔lets up〕. //안개가 들었다 The fog lifted. //장마가 들었다 The rainy season〔wet weather〕 is over.
② [땀이] stop〔cease〕《sweating》
*__들다__[2] [칼날이] cut (well) ; be keen ; be sharp ¶ 잘 드는 칼 a sharp knife
†**들다**[3] [나이가] grow older ; take〔put〕 on years ; be advanced in years〔ages〕 ¶ 나이가 들음에 따라서 with advancing years //더 나이가 들어서 at a ripe old age //나이가 들면 지혜가 생긴다 Wisdom comes with age. /Years bring wisdom.
†**들다**[4] ① [손에] hold《in one's hand》; carry〔have, take〕《a thing》 in one's hand ; have ¶ 칼을 빼 들고 with a naked sword in one's hand //백을 들고 있다 have a bag with〔about〕《one》//양산을 들고 가다 take an umbrella with《one》//권총을 들고 있다 He is armed with a pistol.
② [사실·예를] give《an example》; cite ; mention ; state ; produce ¶ 예를 들다 give an example〔instance〕//이유를 들다 state the reason //증거를 들다 produce〔adduce〕 evidence //알고 있는 꽃 이름을 들어라 Name the flowers that you know. //이와 똑같은 경우를 하나 더 들 수 있느냐 Can you cite another case at all like this one ?
③ [높이다] raise ; lift (up) ; hold up ; put《a thing》 on ; hoist ; heave ¶ 돌을 들다 raise〔lift〕 a stone //손을 들다 hold〔lift〕 up one's hand ; raise one's hand //얼굴을 들다 look up ; lift one's face //머리를 들다 put up〔lift〕 one's head //상자가 너무 무거워서 들 수 없다 The box is too heavy for me to lift.
④ [음식을] take ; have ; eat ; drink ¶ 그는 어제부터 아무 것도 들지 않았다 He hasn't touched food since yesterday. //더 드시지요 Will you take another helping ? //자 사양 말고 드시지요 Please help yourselves without ceremony. //더 드세요 Please have seconds. //잘 드셨습니까 Did you enjoy your meal ? //더 드시겠어요 Care for seconds ? //커피 한 잔 드시겠습니까 Would you care for a cup of coffee ?
*__들다__[5] ① [들어가다] enter ; go in〔into〕; get in〔into〕; step〔walk〕 in ; put up ; [살다] settle《in a new house》; live ; dwell ; reside ¶ 사람이 들지 않은 집 a vacant〔an unoccupied, an empty〕 house //여관을 들다 put up〔stop〕 at an inn //잠자리에 들다 go to bed ; take to one's bed //병상에 들어 있다 be confined to one's bed ; be laid up //그 집은 누가 들어 있느냐 Who is the occupant of the house ? //그 집엔 사람이 들지 않고 있다 The house is unoccupied.
② [가입하다] join ; go into ; enter ; become a member《of》; associate oneself《with》 ¶ 군대에 들다 enlist in the army //대학에 들다 enter a college ; become a freshman at college //보험에 들다 be insured //조합에 들다 join an association //편에 들다 make the team //어때요 안 들겠어요 Won't you make one ? //100만원의 생명 보험에 들어 있다 I am insured for a million *won*. /I carry a million *won* life insurance.
③ [풍·흉·절기 따위가] set in ; begin ; come (around) ¶ 금년에는 윤달이 들어 있다 A leap month sets in this year. //금년에는 풍년이 들 것 같다 We shall probably have a good harvest this year. //금년에는 흉년이 들었다 The year's crop has turned out a failure. /The crop has failed〔is short〕 this year. //이달에 춘분이 들어 있다 This month contains Spring〔Vernal〕 Equinox Day. //장마가 들었다 The rainy season has set in.
④ [염색되다] dye ; be dyed《with》; take color ; be tainted ; be tinged ¶ 까맣게 들다 be dyed black //물이 잘 들다〔안 들다〕 dye well〔badly〕//피로 물들다 be stained with blood //악에 물들다 be stained with vices ; sink in vices
⑤ [버릇 따위가] take to a habit ; get〔fall〕 into a habit《of》 ¶ 끽연이라는 나쁜 버릇이 들다 take to the bad habit of smoking ; get〔contract〕 the bad habit of smoking
⑥ [마음에] suit《one》; like ; suit〔strike, take, catch〕 one's fancy ; suit one's book《구》; meet (with) one's wishes ; be pleased《with》; be satisfied《with》; be acceptable ; be satisfactory ¶ 마음에 드는 집 a house to one's taste ; a house one likes //마음에 드는 여자 a woman after one's heart〔fancy〕//마음에 들도록 to one's satisfaction ; so as to please《a person》//마음에 들지 않다 be not to one's taste〔liking〕; be unsatisfactory //누구의 마음에나 다 들기는 어렵다 It is hard to suit everybody. //이것이 가장 마음에 든다 This suits my taste best. //저 그림이 마음에 든다 That picture appeals to my taste.
⑦ [포함하다] contain ; hold ; [들어 있다] be included ; be among ¶ 3,000원이 든

지갑 a purse with 3,000 *won* in it // 그 병은 두 홉이 더 든다 The bottle holds two *hop* or so. // 이 지갑에 5,000원이 들어 있다 This purse has 5,000 *won* in it. // 그 속에는 내 몫도 들어 있었다 My part〔share〕 was included in it.
⑧ [병이] be taken ill ; get ill ; catch ; suffer from ¶ 폐병이 들다 get a lung disease〔consumption〕 ; suffer from tuberculosis〔T. B.〕 // 그 여자는 가벼운 감기가 들었다 She had a slight attack of influenza.
⑨ [잠이] fall asleep ; go to sleep ; [정이] fall in love ; [철이] come to have good sense ; become sensible ; attain the age of discretion
⑩ [맛이] 《a taste》 set in ; get a taste 《to it》 ; get tasty ; be seasoned〔flavored〕 with ; ripen ; be〔get〕 ripe ¶ 김치 맛이 들었다 The *kimchi* has ripened. // 한번 돈을 주면 맛을 들여서 또 온다 Once you give him money, he is sure to come round again and again to ask for more. // 음식이 맛이 들기 시작한다 The food is getting taste.
⑪ [수용] can accommodate〔house〕 ¶ 이 방에는 100명이 들 수 있다 This room can accommodate 100 guests. / This room seats 100 persons.
⑫ [필요] take ; cost ; be needed ; be required ; be spent ¶ 돈이 들다 take〔cost〕 money // 시간이 들다 take (up) time // 힘이 들다 be hard〔difficult〕 ; be tough〔trying〕 ; take effort // 얼마 들었소 How much did it cost you? // 이 차를 사는 데 이천만원 들었다 This car cost 20 million *won*. /This car set me back 20 million *won*.

들다람쥐 a ground squirrel ; a spermophile

들대 a nearby plain〔flat, open field〕

들돌 a lifting stone (for weight lifting) ; a barbell stone

들두드리다 pommel〔beat〕 《a person》 to a jelly ; beat recklessly ; strike blow after blow ; trounce ; pound 《on a door》

들뒤지다 ransack

들들 ① [볶는 모양] stirring ; turning upside down ¶ 깨를 들들 볶다 parch sesame-seed turning upside down
② [사람을] annoyingly ; tiresomely ; 《ask》 importunately ¶ 사람을 들들 볶는다 importune a person 《for money》 ; trouble〔pester, plague〕 a person 《with questions》
③ [뒤지는 모양] ransacking ; rummaging ¶ 집안을 들들 뒤지다 ransack the house ; search the whole house

들때밑 an insolent〔arrogant〕 and wicked servant of a powerful〔an influential〕 family

들떠들다 make noise ; be noisy ; make a racket ; raise a clamor ; make a fuss ; be boisterous〔clamorous, uproarious〕 ¶ 종업원들이 들떠들다 the employees are clamoring 《for》 // 그렇게 들떠들지 마라 Don't make such a noise〔fuss〕.

들떼놓고 roundaboutly ; indirectly ; hintingly ; insinuatingly ; in a roundabout way ¶ 들떼놓고 말하다 suggest ; insinuate ; speak in a roundabout way ; drop 《a person》 a hint ; hint at ; beat about the bush // 들떼놓고 빈정거리다 satirize ; make an insinuating remark 《at》 ; give an indirect cut

들떼리다 hurt 《a person》 ; offend 《a person》 ; hurt 《a person's》 feeling

들뜨다 ① [떨어져서] get loose ; come off ; curl up at the end ¶ 장판이 들뜨다 a layer of oil paper comes off the floor // 구들장이 들뜨다 a slab of floor stone gets loose
② [마음이] grow restless ; 《one's mind》 wander〔drift〕 ¶ 봄날이 되면 마음이 들뜨기 쉽다 One's mind is apt to wander when spring comes. // 그건 그가 들떠 있는 걸 보니까 금방 알겠다 That's easy to see from the way he's keyed up.
③ [안색이] 《one's skin》 look yellow and swollen

들뜨리다 ⇨ 들이뜨리다

들락날락 going in and out incessantly
—하다 come and go incessantly ; go in and out frequently ; come in and out incessantly ¶ 저 집엔 무시로 많은 사람들이 들락날락한다 The house is frequented by many visitors. // 쥐가 들락날락 밤을 다 물어 갔다 Going in and out, back and forth, the rats carried away all the chestnuts.

들랑거리다 keep coming and going ; frequent

들러리 [신랑의] a best man ; a groomsman ; [신부의] a bridesmaid
들러리 서다 관용 serve as a best man〔bridesmaid〕

*__들러붙다__ adhere〔stick, cling, cleave〕 to ; attach〔fasten〕 itself to ¶ 벽에 들러붙다 hold on fast to the wall // 찰싹 들러붙다 stick fast 《to》 // 손가락에 들러붙는다 It sticks to my finger. // 집들이 들러붙어 있다 Houses stand close to each other.

들레다 clamor ; make a noise ; be boisterous ; be uproarious

들려주다 [알리다] tell ; inform 《a person of》 ; let 《a person》 hear〔know〕 ; [읽어서] read to 《a person》 ; [연주하여] play for 《a person》 ; give 《a person》 a tune ; [노래불러] sing for 《a person》 ¶ 군가를 들려주다 sing a martial song〔marching song, war song〕 for 《a person》 // 편지를 읽어서 들려주다 read a letter to 《a person》 // 노래를 하나 들려 주십시오 Favor us with a song. // 이것은 아이들에게 들려줄 이야기가 아니다 This is not a story for children. // 피아노를 몇 번이나 들려 주셨다

He played us some tunes on the piano.

*들르다 [도중에] drop in at ; stop off in 〔at〕; look in at ; call at〔on〕 ¶ 아무 곳에도 들르지 않고 without stopping anywhere // (도중에) 대구를 들르다 stop at *Taegu* ; stop over〔off〕 at *Taegu* ; drop off 《the train》 at *Taegu* // 부산에 이틀간 들르다 stop〔stay〕 two days at *Pusan* // 들를 장소도 없다 have no place to stay in // 차 마시러 다방에 들르다 stop〔drop〕 in for tea at a coffee house // 잠깐 집에 들르시지 않겠어요 Won't you come in just for a moment? // 이 기선은 여기에 들르지 않는다 The ship does not call here. // 돌아올 때 그걸 가지러 들르겠소 I shall call for it on my way back. // 지나는 길에 한 번 들르세요 When you happen to pass by, drop in and see us.

†들리다[1] ① [소리가] be audible ; be heard ; meet〔greet〕 the ear ; fall on one's ears ; can hear ; [울리다] sound ; ring ¶ 들리는 소리 an audible sound // 들릴 정도로 audibly // 들리는〔안 들리는〕 데서 in〔out of〕 one's hearing ; within〔out of〕 hearing〔earshot〕; within〔out of〕 the sound 《of》 // 안 들리게 되다 lose one's hearing (귀가) ; die away (소리가) // 들려오다 reach one's ear ; come into hearing // 역설적으로 들리다 sound paradoxical // 내 말이 안들리나 Don't you hear me? // 아름다운 음악이 들려 왔다 Sweet music greeted my ear. // 큰소리로 말하므로 안 들릴 수 없다 They spoke so loud that we couldn't help overhearing what they said. // 900－1234에 전화를 걸려고 하는데 통화중 신호만 들려요 I'm trying to reach 900－1234, but all I get is a busy signal. // 너무 좋은 소식이라 곧이 들리지 않는다 It sounds too good to be true. // 그의 목소리는 잘 들린다 His voice carries well.
② [소문이] come to one's ear〔knowledge〕; be said ; be rumored ¶ 들리는 바에 의하면 according to a report 〔rumor〕 // 소문에 들리다 be talked〔gossiped〕 about // 너의 소식이 종종 들렸다 I've often heard of you. // 전쟁이 난다는 말이 들렸다 There was talk of war. // 그의 장사가 잘 안된다는 소문이 들린다 It is whispered that his business is falling.
③ [듣게 하다] tell ; inform 《a person》 of ⇨ 들려주다

들리다[2] [고갈되다] run out ; be exhausted ; be out of stock ; be used up ¶ 석유가 들리다 run out of kerosene ; the kerosene is all gone // 돈이 들리다 be out of money

들리다[3] ① [병이] suffer from ; be attacked ; get ill ; be inflicted with ¶ 감기가 들리다 catch a cold // 그는 중병이 들렸다 He is seriously ill. /He is suffering from a serious illness.
② [귀신이] be possessed 《by》; be obsessed 《by》; be haunted 《by》 ¶ 귀신이 들린 possessed ; bewitched ; devil-possessed // 그는 귀신이 들렸다 He is possessed by〔with〕 the evil spirit.

들리다[4] [올려지다] be lifted ; be raised ; [들게 하다] let 《a person》 raise〔lift〕; [운반시키다] get 《a person》 to take 〔carry〕 《a thing》 ¶ 보따리를 들리다 have 《a person》 carry a bundle // 하인에게 선물을 들려 보내다 send〔offer〕 a present by the manservant

들맞추다 humor ; soothe ; please 《a person's humor》; lick 《a person's》 boots ; flatter ; say pretty things

들머리 entrance point ; point of entry

들머리판 the final stage of dissipation 〔extravagance〕; bankruptcy ; smash

들먹거리다, 뜰먹거리다 ① [물건이] move up and down ; shake ; totter ¶ 기뻐서 어깨가 저절로 들먹거리다 one's shoulders move up and down with joy // 초조해서 궁둥이가 들먹거리다 one becomes restless ; become unable to settle down
② [무거운 물건을] move〔shake〕 《a heavy thing》 up and down
③ [마음이] become excited ; become restless ; feel nervous ; feel out of place ¶ 봄이 되면 왜 그렇게 마음이 들먹거리는지 모르겠다 I can't find the reason why I feel so out of place in spring. // 가고 싶어 들먹거리고 있다 He is impatient〔all eagerness〕 to go.
④ [남의 마음을] excite 《a person》; fire one's interest ; make 《a person》 restless ¶ 민중을 들먹거려서 폭동을 일으키다 instigate people to violence
⑤ [남을 들추다] mention ; refer to ; specify by name ¶ 그 사람까지 들먹거릴 필요야 없지 않니 You don't have to mention his name.

들먹다 (be) crooked ; dishonest ; perverse ; cross-grained ¶ 들먹은 사람 a crooked person

들먹들먹 ① [움직임] moving up and down ; shaking ② [불안정] restlessly ; [마음이] buoyantly ; excitedly

들메 —하다 fasten〔tie〕 straw sandals to one's feet

들메끈 string used to tie straw sandals to one's feet

들메나무 〖식물〗 an ash tree

들메다 tie 《straw sandals》 to one's feet

들무새 ① [재료] material 《to support a project, used to make a thing》; stuff
② [도움] —하다 vigorously help 《a person》 (to) do rough〔hard, heavy〕 work〔labor〕

들바람 a prairie wind

들배지기 a body-twist throw (in wrestling)

들병장수 a peddler of bottled wine

들보[1] a crossbeam

들보[2] a sanitary napkin〔belt〕; a loincloth

들볶다 annoy ; torment ; harass ; be hard

on 《a person》; treat 《a person》 harshly ¶ 들볶이다 be teased ; be tormented // 며느리를 들볶다 be cruel to one's daughter-in-law // 나를 제발 들볶지 마라 Please, do not bother me, would you ? // 그 여자는 남편을 항상 들볶는다 She henpecks her husband all the time.

들부드레하다 (be) sweetish ; [서술적] have a sweetish taste

들부딪다 hit〔strike〕 hard ¶ 벽에 들부딪다 hit〔bump, bash〕 against the wall

들부셔내다 clean up ; cleanse ; wash up 〔out, off〕 《filthy things》 ¶ 요강을 들부셔내다 clean a chamber pot

들부수다 break 《a thing》 to pieces ; knock to pieces ; smash up ; crush

들비비다 rub hard

들뽕나무 a wild mulberry tree

들살 a prop ; a stay ; a support

들새 wild fowl ; wild birds

*⁑*들소** a wild ox ; a bison

들손 a handle ; a bail

들쇠 [문을 거는] an iron hook to raise and hold up a door ; [손잡이] a handle ; [서랍의] a drawer handle

들쇠통 一筒 a (metal) bucket

들숨 inspiration ; inhalation ¶ 들숨과 날숨 inhalation and exhalation

들썩거리다 ① [움직이다] move up and down ; rise and fall ; raise and lower ¶ 들썩들썩 moving up and down

② [마음이] be restless〔nervous, fidgety〕; be in a flutter〔fidget〕; [충동하다] stir up 《to》 ¶ 들썩들썩 restlessly ; in a fidget // 기분이 들썩거리다 feel restless // 그들은 들썩거리고 있었다 They were flurried and nervous. ⇨ 들먹거리다

들썩하다¹ [그럴싸하다] (be) plausible ; specious ; verisimilar ; sound plausible 〔good〕 ¶ 들썩하게 거짓말을 하다 lie like the truth

들썩하다² ① [떠들려 있다] be turned up 〔lifted, raised〕 slightly ¶ 책 귀가 들썩하다 the corner of a book is a bit turned up

② [물건을] lift〔raise, move〕 《a thing》 slightly ; [물건이] move slightly

들썽거리다 itch ; feel itch ; be impatient ; be nervous ¶ 가고 싶어 마음이 들썽거리다 be impatient〔all eagerness〕 to go // 때리고 싶어 팔이 들썽거리다 one's hands itch to strike at 《a person》; one's hands itch to deal a blow ; feel impatient to attack // 그는 사실을 말하고 싶어 들썽거렸다 He was burning to tell the truth.

들썽들썽 impatiently ; anxiously ; eagerly ; burningly ; itchingly

들썽하다 be impatient ; itch ; burn 《with impatience, eagerness》

들쑤시다 ① [마구 쑤시다] poke〔pick〕 at 《a thing》 at random〔haphazardly〕; stick into 《a thing》 rashly ; pack 《a hole》; prod ¶ 덤불 속을 들쑤시다 stick into the bush〔thicket〕 every nook and corner // 벌집을 들쑤시다 poke at the beehive〔honeycomb〕 at random

② [들썩이다] set 《a person》 on 《to do》; egg 《a person》 on 《to do》; instigate ; incite ; goad ¶ 그 여자를 들쑤셔서 그렇게 하게 하다 set her on to do it // 처녀를 들쑤시다 entice a girl 《away from home》 // 누가 뒤에서 들쑤시는 사람이 있을 거야 Someone must be at the bottom of the affair.

③ [고통] smart ; tingle ; fester ; ache ⇨ 쑤시다

들쓰다 ① [이불 따위를] pull up all over oneself ; put 《a thing》 on all over oneself ¶ 이불을 들쓰다 pull bedclothes over oneself ; pull the bedspread over one's head

② [물을] pour 《water》 《on oneself》; [먼지를] be covered with 《dust》 ¶ 갑판이 파도를 들쓰다 the deck swims with water

③ [모자를] wear on one's head casually

④ [허물·책임을] take 《blame》 upon oneself ; be charged 《with a crime》 ¶ 남의 죄를 들쓰다 take upon oneself another's guilt

들씌우다 ① [이불 따위를] pull 《bedclothes》 over 《a person's》 head

② [물을] pour 《water》 all over 《a person》; [먼지를] cover 《a person》 all over with dust

③ [모자를] put 《a hat》 on 《a person's》 head casually

④ [죄 따위를] impute ; lay〔put, fix〕 blame on 《a person》; shift 《responsibility》 to others

†**들어가다¹** ① [안으로] enter ; go in 〔into〕; get in〔into〕; step〔walk〕 in ¶ 몰래 들어가다 steal into 《a room》 // 창문으로 들어가다 enter by a window // 침입해 들어가다 force one's way into ; break into // 함부로 들어가다 intrude into // 현관〔뒷문〕으로 들어가다 enter at the front door〔back door〕 // 바람이 들어가도록 창문을 열어라 Open the window to let in air. // 그것은 자루 속에 들어가지 않는다 It will not go into the bag. // 한길에서 조금 들어간 곳이다 It is a little way aside from the road. // 어젯밤에는 집에 잘 들어갔니 Did you manage to make it home all right last night ?

② [가입하다] join ; enter ; be employed ¶ 군대에 들어가다 enlist in the army // 대학에 들어가다 enter a college // 실업계에 들어가다 go into business // 클럽에 들어가다 join a club // 외교계에 들어가다 enter on a diplomatic career // 김군은 재정 경제원에 들어갔다 Mr. *Kim* has found a position in the Board of Finance and Economy.

③ [포함하다] contain ; hold ; include ; [수용] accommodate ¶ 그 회관은 1,000명이 들어간다 The hall accommodates

〔seats〕 1,000 persons. //이 과자에는 설탕이 너무 들어갔다 This cake has too much sugar in it. //이 상자에는 책이 몇 권 들어가겠습니까 How many books will this box hold? //이자도 계산에 들어가 있다 The interest is included in the account. //이 병에는 4홉쯤 들어간다 This bottle holds four *hop* or so.
④ [사이에] go through ; be inserted ¶ 바늘귀에 실이 들어가다 a thread goes through the eye of a needle ; a needle is threaded
⑤ [비용이] be spent ; cost 《a great deal》
⑥ [시작] begin ; set in ¶ 우기에 들어가다 the rainy season sets in
⑦ become hollow ; be sunken ; sag ¶ 눈이 쑥 들어가다 one's eyes grow hollow //배가 조금 들어가지 않았니 Has my stomach gotten a little flatter?

들어가다² [가져가다] take away ; make off with ; filch ; steal ; swipe ¶ 남의 우산을 들어가다 make off with another's umbrella //누가 내 칼을 들어갔다 Somebody has taken away my knife.

들어내다 ① [쫓아내다] drive〔send, turn〕 out ; [지위에서] oust ; [셋방에서] eject ; evict ; [해고하다] sack 《구》 ; fire 《미》 ¶ 세든 사람을 들어내다 eject〔evict〕 a tenant out of one's home //집에서 들어내다 turn 《a person》 out of the house //저 놈 들어내라 Out with him! //제발로 안 나가면 들어낼 테다 If you won't go yourself, I shall turn〔rush〕 you out.
② [내놓다] take〔carry〕 out ; remove ; [화재 때] save 《furniture》 ¶ 뜰로 의자를 들어내다 take a chair out into the garden //불이 빨리 번져서 아무것도 들어내지 못했다 The fire spread so fast that we could not save〔remove〕 anything. //화재가 나면 이 상자를 먼저 들어내야 한다 In case of fire, this box must be removed for safety first of all.

들어맞다 ① [알맞다] fit〔suit, be fitted〕 perfectly ; fit like a glove ¶ 들어맞는 옷 well-fitting clothes //꼭 들어맞는 옷 a perfect fit //들어맞는 신발 perfect-fitting shoes //들어맞지 않는 ill-fitting //이 옷은 너에게 꼭 들어맞는다 This coat fits you perfectly〔to a nicety〕. //이 모자는 나에게 꼭 들어맞네 This hat is a right fit for my head.
② [맞추어지다] fit in ; fix into ¶ 이 문이 들어맞지 않는다 This door does not fit in.
③ [명중] hit ; hit the mark ; [실현하다] come true ; turn out true ¶ 화살이 과녁에 들어맞다 an arrow hits the mark //너의 예언은 들어맞았다 Your prophecy came true. //너의 예상이 꼭 들어맞았다. You guessed right. /You hit it.
④ [해당하다] apply 《to》 ; be applicable 《to》 ; hold true〔good〕 ; conform 《to》 ¶ 모든 경우에 들어맞는다 It applies to〔in〕 all cases. //같은 규칙이 여기에도 들어맞는다 The same rule applies here.
⑤ [똑같다] agree with ; be in accord with ; tally with ; square with ; conform with ; answer to ; meet ¶ 두 사람의 말이 들어맞다 Their accounts tally with each other. //그 사나이의 얼굴은 인상서와 들어맞는다 The man meets〔answers to〕 the description.

들어먹다 ① [탕진하다] squander ; dissipate ; eat up〔out〕 ; use up ¶ 가산을 모두 들어먹다 squander〔make ducks and drakes of〕 one's fortune //돈을 다 들어먹다 run through all one's money
② [남의 것을] pocket ; peculate ; appropriate 《a thing》 to oneself ; embezzle ¶ 공금을 들어먹다 embezzle〔misappropriate〕 public funds〔money〕 //남의 재산을 들어먹다 seize another's property ; dispossess 《a person》 of his property

들어박히다 ① [빠지다] fall〔stick, sink, slip〕 into ¶ 도랑에 들어박히다 be mired in a ditch //물 속에 들어박히다 fall into a river〔pool〕 //진창에 들어박히다 stick in the mud
② [촘촘히] be packed ; be stuffed ; be chock-full ¶ 책이 가득 들어박힌 서가 a shelf closely packed with books
③ [나오지 않다] be confined indoors ; keep to the house ; keep one's room ; be shut up 《in》 ; shut oneself up 《in》 ; live in seclusion ; confine oneself in one's house ¶ 집에만 들어박혀 있는 사람 a home-immured person ; a stay-at-home //병으로 집에 들어박히다 be confined indoors with illness //병실에 들어박히다 be shut up in a sickroom //방에 들어박히다 keep one's room //서재에 들어박히다 shut oneself up in one's study //서울을 떠나 먼 시골에 들어박혔다 He withdrew to a country village far from *Seoul*.

들어붓다 ① [비가] pour down ; fall heavily ; rain in torrents ; 《it》 rain cats and dogs ¶ 들어붓는 비 a heavy〔pouring, torrential〕 rain ; a downpour //비가 사뭇 들어부었다 It rained cats and dogs. /It rained in torrents.
② [술을] drink hard〔deep〕 ; drink like a fish ; guzzle ; swill oneself with wine ¶ 술을 들어붓는 사람 a guzzler ; a soaker ; a deep drinker
③ [액체를] pour 《water》 into ; pour 《water》 out of ¶ 주전자의 물을 들어붓다 pour water out of a kettle

들어서다 ① [안쪽으로] enter ; go〔get〕 into ; step in ¶ 구내에 들어서다 enter the premises //한걸음 들어서다 get in by a step //처마 밑에 좀 들어서야겠습니다 Just let me take shelter under your eaves.
② [꽉 차다] be full 《of》 ; be filled 《with》 ; be crowded 《with》 ¶ 번화가에

는 큰 건물들이 쭉 들어섰다 Many great buildings stood in a row on the busy street. // 작은 섬에 나무가 꽉 들어섰다 The islet is thickly wooded. // 회관에는 사람이 많이 들어섰다 The hall was crowded with people.
③ [사람에게] step up to ; move up ¶ 한마디 하려고 사람에게 들어서다 step up to 《a person》 to have a word with him
④ [수효가] come up to 《a certain fixed number》 ¶ 수가 들어서다 the number 《of persons》 is made up
⑤ [제시간에] come in〔arrive〕 on time

들어앉다 ① [안쪽으로] get nearer ; sit nearer ; sit inside closer ¶ 화로 있는 데로 들어앉아라 Take a seat nearer to the fireplace.
② [퇴직하다] retire from business ; retire from〔leave〕 the service ; resign an office ¶ 정년이 되어서 들어앉다 retire under the age limit // 아버지는 병 때문에 들어앉아 계신다 My father retired 《from office, from business》 on account of illness.
③ [지위에 앉다] take up one's post 〔duties〕 《as》 ; find service in ; be installed 〔inaugurated〕 ; settle down ¶ 지배인으로서 들어앉다 take up his post as a manager // 그는 이선생 자리에 들어앉았다 He succeeded Mr. *Lee.* /He stepped into Mr. *Lee's* shoes. // 그 대학의 교수 자리에 들어앉았다 He took an appointment as a professor at the university.

들어열개 〖건축〗 a door that opens upward ; a lifting door

‡**들어오다** ① [안으로] enter ; come〔get〕 in ; walk〔step〕 in ¶ 기선은 내일 들어올 것이다 The steamer will be in tomorrow. // 내 우산 안에 안 들어오겠소 Share my umbrella, won't you? // 들어오시오 Come in. /Come on in. // 이 신은 물이 들어온다 These shoes let in water〔are leaky〕. // 일 없는 사람은 들어오지 마시오 No admittance except on business. /No unauthorized entry allowed. // 비맞지 말고 내 우산 속으로 들어와 Don't get wet. Get under my umbrella. // 베이커 씨께서 오늘 날짜로 예약은 하셨는데 아직 들어오시지 않았습니다 Mr. Baker made a reservation for today, but he hasn't checked in yet.
② [수입이] earn ; get ; have ¶ 그는 한달에 4만원이 들어온다 He earns 40,000 *won* a month.
③ [직업·자리로] join ; enter 《a company》 ¶ 새로 사원 하나가 들어왔다 A new member〔freshman〕 joined our company.
④ [사이에] come in 《between》 ; be inserted ¶ 이것이 두 말 사이에 들어올 말이다 This comes〔is to be inserted〕 between these two words.

†**들어올리다** lift (up) ; raise ; hold up

들어주다 grant 《a request》 ; answer 〔hear〕 《a person's prayer》 ¶ 청을 들어주지 않다 turn one's deaf ear to a person's request

들어차다 become full ; be filled up ; be full 《of》 ; be packed ; be stuffed ¶ 꽉 들어차다 be chock-full ; be packed (to the) full // 집이 꽉 들어차다 be crowded with houses // 못에 고기가 들어차다 a pond swarms with fish // 홀은 사람으로 꽉 들어차 있었다 The hall was bursting with people.

들엉기다 coagulate ; congeal ; solidify ; condense

들엎드리다 confine oneself to 《a room》 ; shut oneself up ; remain indoors ; stay in〔indoors〕 ; be kept 〔cooped up〕 in the house ¶ 하루 종일 집에 들엎드려 있을 테냐 Are you going to stay in all day?

들여가다 ① [안으로] take〔bring〕 in ; carry in ¶ 화물을 차내에 들여가다 take 〔bring〕 luggage into the carriage
② [사다] buy ; purchase ; lay in ¶ 대량으로 들여가다 lay in a large stock of 《coal》 // 좀 들여가시지요 Would you take〔buy〕 some, please?

‡**들여놓다** take〔carry〕 in (and put down) ; [발을] set foot 《in》 ; put one's foot 《into, inside》 ; step into ¶ 책상을 이 방에 들여놓아라 Bring the table in the room.

***들여다보다** ① [밖에서 안을] look into 〔through〕 ; peep into〔through〕 ; peek ¶ 우물을 들여다보다 look in〔peep into〕 the well // 창문에서 안을 들여다보다 peep〔look, peek〕 in at the window // 틈사이로 들여다보다 peep through a crevice 《in the wall》 at 《a person》 // 담 너머로 뜰을 들여다보다 peep into a garden over a wall
② [자세히] look hard 《at》 ; stare 《at》 ; gaze 《at》 ; watch intently ; examine closely ¶ 사람 얼굴을 자세히 들여다보다 watch 《a person's》 face intently 〔closely〕 ; look hard at 《a person's》 face ; stare at 《a person's》 face ; fix one's eyes on 《a person's》 face // 책을 들여다보다 look into a book ; read a book // 사건의 전말을 들여다보다 examine an event in detail // 속이 빤히 들여다보이는 그런 거짓말하지 마라 Don't tell such a transparent lie.

들여디디다 set foot in ; put one's foot into〔inside〕 ; step〔walk〕 in ¶ 진창에 발을 들여디디다 step into a mire ; fall in the mire // 위험한 곳에 발을 들여디디다 tread on dangerous ground ; set foot in a dangerous spot // 이미 들여디딘 발인데 이제 와서 그런 소릴 하면 뭘하니 It is already under way. What's the use of referring to it at this stage?

***들여보내다** send 《a person, a thing》 into ; let 《a person》 in〔into〕 ; see 《a person》 to 《his house》; admit 《a person》 into ¶ 아이를 학교에 들여보내다 put〔send〕 a child to school // 선물을 들여보내다 send in a present // 사람을 뒷문으로 들여보내다 let〔allow〕《a person》 into a house by the back door // 그 사람을 들여보내라 내가 말하겠다 Send the man in, and I'll speak to him.

들여앉히다 ① [손님을] show 《a person》 in and seat him ② [여자를] have 〔make, let〕 a woman settle down in one's home

†**들여오다** ① [안으로] take〔bring, carry〕 in ¶ 상을 들여오다 carry in the dinner table // 비가 오니 빨래를 얼른 들여오너라 Take in the washings quickly because it is raining (outside).
② [사다] get ; buy 《things at a shop》; [수입하다] import ¶ 고철을 미국에서 들여오다 import scrap iron from the U. S. // 채소는 모퉁이의 채소 가게에서 들여온다 We get vegetables from the greengrocer at the corner.

들은귀 picked-up experience ; useful knowledge picked up by keeping one's ears open

들은풍월 一風月 learning by (the) ear ; ideas〔manners〕 picked up from others ¶ 들은풍월로 여러 가지 노래를 알고 있다 He knows many songs which he has picked up by hearing others sing.

들음직하다 (be) worth hearing ¶ 들음직한 것 something worth hearing // 그의 연설은 정말 들음직하다 His speech is certainly worth hearing.

-들이 ¶ 4홉들이 병 a bottle capable of containing 4 *hop* // 이 병은 1파운드들이입니다 This bottle holds a pound.

들이갈기다 hit hard

들이굽다
팔이 들이굽지 내굽나 〔속담〕 Blood will tell. /Blood is thicker than water.

들이긋다 [줄을] draw 《a line》 inwards ; [병독이] strike inwards

들이끌다 pull in

들이끼우다 put 《a thing》 into an opening〔a gap〕; put 《a thing》 in between

들이끼이다 be put〔caught, wedged〕 in between 《two objects》; be put into a gap ; wedge in

†**들이다** ① [안으로] let 《a person》 in ; allow in ; admit ; show〔usher〕 in ¶ 사람을 집에 들이다 let 《a person》 into one's house // 손님을 응접실에 들이다 show a guest into the drawing room // 새 회원을 들이다 admit a new member // 사람을 방에 들이지 않는다 admit no one to one's room
② [물건을] take in ; bring in ; carry in ¶ 장작을 들이다 bring in firewood ; buy firewood // 볏섬을 뜰에 들이다 bring the rice bags into the yard
③ [비용·힘을] put in ; spend ; lay out ; make efforts ¶ 큰돈을 들여서 at a great cost // 힘들여서 with great efforts ; with difficulty // 100만원을 들여서 집을 짓다 spend a million *won* to build a house // 이 책상을 만드는 데 많은 공을 들였다 I have put a lot of work into making this table.
④ [고용·입용] hire ; employ ; take ; engage ; adopt ¶ 새 식모를 들이다 hire 〔engage〕 a new cook // 조카를 양자로 들이다 adopt one's nephew as a son
⑤ [맛을] acquire〔get〕 a taste for ; take to ¶ 돈에 맛을 들이다 get a taste for money // 계집에 맛을 들이다 take to running after women
⑥ [잠을] invite (sleep) ; put 《a person》 to sleep ¶ 자장가를 불러서 어린애를 잠을 들이다 sing〔lull〕 a baby to sleep
⑦ [물감을] dye ; color ¶ 옷에 검정 물감을 들이다 dye one's clothes black // 머리에 물을 들이다 dye one's hair
⑧ [길을] tame ; domesticate ; subdue ¶ 사자를 길을 들이다 tame a lion // 말을 길을 들이다 train〔break in〕 a horse // 가구에 길을 들이다 polish the furniture

***들이닥치다** approach ; draw〔come〕 near ; near ; be (close, near) at hand ; gain upon ; be imminent ; be impending ¶ 코앞에 들이닥친 위험 a pressing danger // 적에 들이닥치다 come 〔close in〕 upon the enemy // 적병이 들이닥치다 be suddenly attacked by the enemy // 뜻하지 않은 손님이 들이닥치다 be visited by unexpected guests // 파멸이 그의 코 앞에 들이닥쳤다 Ruin stared him in the face. // 시험이 들이닥치다 The examination is near at hand.

†**들이대다** ① [반항하다] resist openly ; defy ; protest ; challenge ; attack ; go at ; put〔set〕 oneself against ¶ 윗사람에게 들이대다 set oneself against one's superior
② [물건을] thrust 《a thing》 before 《a person》; put〔place〕 under 《a person's》 nose ; point 《a gun》 at ¶ 권총을 들이대다 point a revolver at 《a person》 // 주먹을 코 앞에 들이대다 thrust one's fist in〔into〕 another's face // 증거를 들이대다 thrust proofs before 《a person》 // 단도를 들이대고 협박하다 threaten 《a person》 with a dagger
③ [공급하다] supply continuously ; provide constantly ¶ 장사 밑천을 들이대다 keep 《a person》 supplied with business fund
④ [물을] bring 《water》 in ; channel in

들이덤비다 ① [남에게] fall〔turn〕 upon 《a person》; defy ; challenge ; flare up 《at》; set upon〔attack, assault〕 furiously ¶ 맹렬한 기세로 들이덤비다 spring at 《a person》 with tigerlike ferocity // 상관에게 들이덤비다 challenge one's superior // …이라고 말하면서 나에게 들이덤볐다 He challenged saying 《that》

② [서둘다] act very hurriedly ; be terribly flustered ¶ 만사에 들이덤비다 busy oneself with everything

들이덮치다 《all sorts of things》 happen at once

들이떨다 shake hard

들이뜨리다 toss〔throw, hurl, fling, cast〕 in casually ¶ 돈을 서랍에 들이뜨리다 toss money into a drawer

들이마시다 [기체를] breathe〔draw〕 in ; inhale ; [액체를] suck in ; drink in ; gulp down ; [술 따위를] guzzle ; swing ; swill ¶ 담배 연기를 들이마시다 inhale〔draw in〕 the smoke // 산소를 들이마시고 탄산가스를 내뱉다 inhale oxygen and exhale carbonic acid gas // 술을 들이마시다 drink up〔off〕 wine ; drink hard〔deep〕 // 단숨에 들이마시다 drink off at a draught

들이맞추다 fix 《it》 in ; put 《it》 in

들이몰다 [안으로] drive in ; [마구] drive violently ; [책하다] blame heavily ; call to account ; censure ; reproach ¶ 골목으로 들이몰다 drive 《a thief》 into a blind alley // 책임을 등한히 했다고 들이몰다 scold 《a person》 for neglecting his duty

들이몰리다 ① [안쪽으로] be driven in ; be shoved in ② [호되게] be called to account ; be taken to task ; be blamed heavily ; be censured〔reproached〕 severely ; be roundly scolded ; be lit into ③ [떼지어] crowd ; throng ; flock together ; swarm

들이밀다 ① [안으로] push in ; thrust in ; shove in ② [냅다] push hard ; thrust hard ; shove hard ¶ 아무를 들이밀다 give a person a shove〔push〕

들이밀리다 ① [안으로] be pushed〔thrust, shoved〕 in ¶ 방구석에 들이밀리다 be pushed into the corner of a room ② [한곳으로] crowd ; flock ; swarm ; come〔get〕 together ; rush ¶ 사람들이 한곳에 들이밀리다 People crowd into〔rush to, storm〕 one place.

들이박다 drive〔pound, press, strike〕 《it》 in ¶ 못을 들이박다 drive a nail into 《a wall》

들이받다 run〔bump, ram〕 《a thing》 into ; butt ; bunt hard ; knock 《a thing》 against ; [뿔 따위로] horn ¶ 기둥을 들이받다 run〔bump〕 against a post // 자동차가 나무를 들이받다 run one's motorcar into a tree // 머리로 문을 들이받았다 He knocked〔bumped〕 his head against the door.

들이불다 [안으로] 《a wind》 blow this way ; blow in ; [마구 불다] 《a wind》 blow hard

들이붓다 pour 《water》 into 《an oven》 ; keep pouring (계속해서)

들이빨다 suck in ; inhale ; imbibe ¶ 젖을 들이빨다 suck the breast hard // 담배를 들이빨다 inhale the smoke of a cigarette // 해면은 물을 들이빤다 A sponge sucks up water. // 나는 연기를 들이빨지 않고 담배를 피운다 I puff〔suck〕 cigarettes without inhaling the smoke.

들이세우다 ① [안에] take〔bring, carry〕 《a thing》 in and stand 《it》 up ② [지위에] place ; install 《a person in a position》 ¶ 새 사람을 교장으로 들이세우다 appoint a new principal for the school

***들이쉬다** breathe in ; inhale ; inspire ¶ 숨을 크게 들이쉬다 breathe deeply ; draw a deep breath ; practice deep breathing // 해녀가 숨을 깊이 들이쉬었다 The woman diver drew a deep breath.

들이쌓이다 lie in a heap ; heap〔be heaped〕 up ; collect ; accumulate ¶ 창고에 쌀이 들이쌓인다 Rice lies heaped up in a warehouse. // 책상 위에 먼지가 들이쌓인다 Dust collects〔is thick〕 on the table. // 휴지가 방에 들이쌓인다 Wastepaper is piled up in a room.

들이쑤시다 ① [아프다] smart ; tingle ; throb with pain ; fester ; rankle ; ache ¶ 골머리가 들이쑤시다 have a severe headache ② [구멍 따위를] poke hard at ; pick ; peck ; prod ¶ 담뱃대를 들이쑤시다 poke the stem of a pipe ; clean a pipe ③ [뒤지다] dig up ; rummage 《for》 ; poke and pry 《into》 ¶ 남의 비밀을 들이쑤시다 poke and pry into another's secret

들이조르다 importune〔beg, press, ask〕 《a person for a thing, a person to do》 relentlessly ; clamor for

들이지르다 ① [때리다] give 《a person》 a sound thrashing ; strike 《a person》 hard〔a blow〕 ; [찌르다] push hard ; thrust 《a knife》 into 《a person's chest》 ¶ 얼굴을 들이지르다 strike 《a person》 in the face // 머리를 들이지르다 punch 《a person》 on the head
② [발로] kick away〔off〕 ; give 《a person》 a kick ; kick at ¶ 발길로 옆구리를 들이지르다 kick 《a person》 on the side ; give a kick on the side
③ [소리를] shout ; cry ; utter a cry ; yell ; raise〔lift up〕 one's voice ¶ 목청이 쉬도록 들이지르다 shout oneself hoarse // 고래고래 들이지르다 cry at the top of one's voice ; yell out loudly

들이차다 [안으로] kick in ; [세차게] kick hard

들이치다[1] sweep into 《a room》 ; drive 〔be driven〕 into ¶ 비가 들이치다 rain into 《the eaves》 // 비가 바람으로 방에 들이치다 rain is blown into a room by the wind // (비바람이) 틈새로 들이치다 blow in through the crevices

들이치다[2] ① [습격] attack ; assault ; storm ; raid ¶ 경관이 도박 소굴을 들이친다 Policemen raid〔make a raid on〕 a gambling den. ② [안으로] hit 《a thing》 this way ; bat in

들이켜다 drink (down) ; drink deep ;

drink heavily〔in large draughts〕; gulp; quaff; take〔have〕 a pull at《liquor》 ¶ 꿀꺽꿀꺽〔벌떡벌떡〕 들이켜다 drink draughts《of》; gulp // 단숨에 들이켜다 swallow at one〔a〕 gulp; gulp down; toss off // 쭉 들이켜다 take a long pull; gulp down // 쭉 들이켜게 Bottom up! /No heeltaps!《구》

*들이키다 [다그다] bring〔put〕《a thing》 close《to》; bring《a thing》 near (to); tug〔draw, take, pull〕 in ¶ 발을 들이키다 draw in one's legs // 책상을 한구석으로 들이켜 놓다 draw a desk over into the corner of a room

들이퍼붓다 [그릇에] pour《water》 hard; [쏟아짐] rain upon hard; bombard hard; pour〔rain〕 down hard ¶ 비가 들이퍼붓는다 The rain pours down. /It rains cats and dogs.

들일 farm work; field labor ¶ 들일을 하다 do farm work; work in the fields

들입다 forcibly; violently; strongly; hard; relentlessly; [계속적으로] continually; ceaselessly ¶ 들입다 패다 beat《a person》 hard // 들입다 달아나다 scamper away〔off〕; take to one's heels; show one's〔a clean pair of〕 heels // 들입다 들이키다 drink up《whisky》 in rapid succession〔straightly〕 // 들입다 조르다 entreat《a person》 to do

들장대 supplementary (side) poles for a palanquin

들장미 —薔薇 〖식물〗 a wild〔multiflora〕 rose; a brier〔briar〕; Rosa Multiflora (학명)

들쥐 〖동물〗 a field rat

들짐승 wild animals; wild game

들쩍지근하다 (be) somewhat sweet; sweetish

들쭉 〖식물〗 blueberries

—나무 the blueberry

들쭉날쭉 —하다 (be) uneven; jagged; rugged; indented; humpy ¶ 가장자리가 들쭉날쭉한 잎 serrated leaves // 톱니가 들쭉날쭉하다 The teeth of a saw are notched.

들차다 be sound in mind and body; (be) strong and firm

들창 —窓 a window which can be raised〔propped〕 open; a push-up window

—눈이 a person with lifted upper eyelids

들창코 —窓— a turned-up nose; a person with a turned-up nose

들척지근하다 (be) somewhat sweet; sweetish

들추다 ① [뒤지다] rummage; ransack; seek (for) ¶ 호주머니 속을 들추다 fumble in one's pocket《for》 // 책을 찾느라고 온 방을 들추다 turn a room upside down looking for a book

② [들어올리다] raise; lift ¶ 이불을 들추다 raise the corner of the bedding // 감자 덩굴을 들추다 dig up the potato vines // 한 손으로 돌을 들추다 lift the stone with one hand

③ [드러내다] reveal; expose; disclose〔divulge〕《a secret》; lay bare〔open〕; bring to light ¶ 잘못을 들추다 expose《a person's》 fault // 남의 비밀을 들추다 disclose another's secret // 회사 내정을 들추다 make a public disclosure of the inside affairs of a company

④ [흔들리다] shake; jolt ¶ 배가 가로세로로 들추다 a boat pitches and rolls

*들추어내다 ① [파내다] dig up〔out〕《potatoes》

② [찾아내다] find out; hunt out; rummage out ¶ 서랍에서 돈을 들추어내다 rummage money out of a drawer

③ [드러내다] expose; disclose; lay bare; unmask; bring to light ¶ 비밀을 들추어내다 lay bare《a person's》 secret; give away // 세상 밖에 들추어내다 make a public disclosure of《a matter》 // 자기의 무지를 들추어내다 betray〔expose〕 one's ignorance // 그의 비행을 들추어냈다 I exposed his dark deed〔wicked act〕.

들치기 [행위] shoplifting; [사람] a shoplifter; a lifter《속》; a booster《미·속》

들치다 raise; lift; hold up (the end of) ¶ 이불을 들치다 hold up an end of a blanket

들큰거리다 [비위를] say disagreeable things; make irritating remarks

들큰들큰 disagreeably; irritatingly; exasperatingly

들큼하다 (be) sweetish; unpleasantly sweet

*들키다 [발견되다] be found (out); be discovered〔detected〕; be caught; come out; be laid bare ¶ 들킬까봐 lest it should be found out; for fear of detection // 복숭아를 훔치다가 들켰다 He was caught in the act of stealing peaches. // 들키지 않도록 조심해라 Be cautious to avoid observation〔being seen〕. // 음모가 들켰다 The plot was detected out〔laid bare〕. // 사기를 치다가 들켰다 He was detected in a fraud. // 변장을 하고 가면 들키지 않을 거다 If you go in disguise, you will not be recognized. // 들치기하는 것을 들켰다 He was caught in the act of shoplifting. // 아이들에게 들키지 않도록 살짝 빠져 나가겠다 I'll slip out quietly so the children don't catch on.

들타작 —打作 thrashing in the fields

*들통 —筒 a pail; a bucket

들통나다 be detected; be revealed; be disclosed; come〔be brought〕 to light ¶ 그가 사기를 친 것이 들통났다 He was detected in fraud.

†들판¹ a field; a plain ¶ 허허들판 a wilderness

들판² ⇨ 들머리판

들피 emaciation from hunger ¶ 들피지다 be〔get〕 emaciated from hunger
‡**듬뿍** to the brim ; brimfully ; to the full ¶ 돈이 듬뿍 든 지갑 a purse full of money // 밥을 듬뿍 담다 serve rice brimful ; fill 《the bowl》 heaping full of rice
듬뿍듬뿍 (severally) much ; plenty ; lots ; full
듬성듬성 sparsely ; thinly ; scatteredly ; sporadically ; stragglingly ¶ 털이 듬성듬성 나다 hair grows thinly // 나무를 듬성듬성 심다 plant trees sparsely // 거기에는 인가가 듬성듬성 있다 There are scattered cottages there. // 그 언덕에는 나무가 듬성듬성 심어져 있다 The hill is sparsely 〔thinly〕 wooded.
듬쑥 full ; greedily ¶ 듬쑥 손을 잡다 clutch ; give 《a person》 a grip // 동전을 한 주먹 듬쑥 움켜쥐었다 He seized all the coppers that his fist can hold.
듬쑥하다 ① ⇨ 든직하다 ② [많다] fill ; be full of ¶ 밥이 그릇에 듬쑥하다 Rice fills a bowl. // 밥을 그릇에 듬쑥히 담다 fill a bowl full of rice
듭시다 ① [들어가다] go in ; enter ¶ 임금께서 침소에 듭시다 the king goes to bed ② [들자] let's enter ; [먹자] let's take
듯 ¶ 너무 적어서 먹은 듯 만 듯하다 I ate so little that I am hardly satisfied. // 비가 올 듯 말 듯했다 I was not sure if it would rain or not. /There was no telling whether it would rain or not. // 짙은 안개로 앞이 보일 듯 말 듯했다 We could scarcely see through the thick fog. // 화병에는 물이 있을 듯 말 듯하다 There is little〔hardly any〕 water in the vase. // 흡사 나무에서 고기를 구하는 듯하다 You might as well go to a tree for fish.
듯싶다 [것 같다] ⇨ 싶다
듯이 like ; as ; as... as ; as if〔though〕 ¶ 그는 네가 생각하듯이 그렇게 대학자는 아니다 He is not such a great scholar as you think. // 그는 백만장자인 듯이 생활하고 있다 He lives as if he were a millionaire. // 그는 죽은 듯이 보였다 He seemed as if dead. // 음식이 몸을 기르듯이 독서는 정신을 기른다 Reading is to the mind what food is to the body. // 네 형이 하듯이 해라 Do as your brother does. // 눈물이 비 오듯이 흐른다 Tears pour down like rain.
***듯하다** look like ; seem ; appear ; give every appearance of ¶ 외국인인 듯한 사람 a man looking like a foreigner // 금방 비가 올 듯하다 It threatens to rain. // 배는 침몰할 듯했다 The boat was ready to sink. // 회사는 파산할 듯하다 That firm is on the brink〔verge〕 of bankruptcy. // 쥐 죽은듯하다 Not a sound is to be heard. // 학생인 듯하다 He looks like a student.
†**등** the back ¶ 의자의 등 the back of a chair // 등을 두들기다 pat 《a person》 on the back // 등을 대고 앉다 sit back to back with 《a person》
등을 돌리다 관용 turn one's back to〔on〕
등 等 ① [등급] a class ; a grade ; a degree (도) ; quality (질) ¶ 1등 the first class〔grade〕 // 상등품 goods of superior quality // 죄를 한등 감하다 reduce the penalty by one degree
② [따위] and so on ; and so forth ; and the like ; and what not ; et cetera 《etc.》 ; and others ; and all that ¶ 서울대학 연세대학 등 *Seoul* University, *Yonsei* University, and so on // 모자 장갑 신발 등 hats, gloves, shoes, etc. // 사과나 배 등 apples, pears, and what not // 우리는 경제 풍기 쾌적 등의 이유로 방을 같이 했다 We shared a room for reasons of economy, morality, coziness, and so forth. // 그는 그림 음악 산수 등을 배웠다 He studied painting, music, arithmetic, and the like.
등 燈 a light ; a lamp ; a lantern ¶ 등불 lamplight // 등을 켜다 light a lamp
등 藤 〖식물〗 a rattan ; a cane
—의자 a rattan〔cane〕 chair
등가 等價 〖화학〗 equivalence (원자의) ; 〖경제〗 parity 《of exchange》 ¶ 등가의 equivalent
—량(量) an equivalent **— 원리** 〖물리〗 the principle of equivalence **공정(公定)** — mint par of exchange
등각 等角 〖기하〗 equal angles ¶ 등각의 equiangular
— 다각형 an isogon **— 삼각형** an equiangular triangle **—선** an isogonic line **—형** an equiangular figure
등갈퀴나물 〖식물〗 a tufted〔cow〕 vetch ; Vicia cracca (학명)
등갓 燈— a shade ; a lampshade
등거리 a sleeveless jacket ; a lady's fur coat
등거리 等距離 equal distance ; equidistance ¶ 등거리의 equidistant // 등거리에 at equal distances
—선 〖수학〗 an equidistant curve **— 외교** equidistance diplomacy **— 지점** equidistants
등걸 a stump ; a stub ¶ 등걸을 캐내다 dig up the stump of a tree
등걸불 a stump fire
등걸숯 charcoal made from stumps
등걸음치다 [시체를] remove〔carry away〕 a corpse ; [끌고 가다] pull〔drag〕 《a person》 by the scruff of the neck
등걸잠 sleeping with clothes on (without covering)
등겨 rice chaff
등겨 먹던 개가 말경에는 쌀을 먹는다 속담 Habits are at first cobwebs, at last cables.
등겻섬에 생쥐 모이듯 속담 Whatsoever the carcase is, there will the eagles 〔ravens〕 be gathered together.
등경걸이 燈檠— a lantern stand
등고선 等高線 a contour line

— 경작 contour plowing — 농법(農法) contour farming — 지도 a contour map
등골 ① [등줄기] the line of the backbone ¶ 등골에 땀이 나다 be given a hard time ; be awfully ashamed // 등골이 오싹해지는 광경 a spine-chilling sight // 등골이 오싹해졌다 I felt my spine〔back〕 go cold. /I felt a chill go〔I felt a shiver〕 down my spine. /A cold shiver ran〔It sent cold chills〕 down my spine.
② [척수] the spinal cord〔marrow〕; pith ; the medulla 《*pl.* -lae》
등골나물 〖식물〗 a joe-pye weed ; Eupatorium chinense var. simplicifolium (학명)
등골뼈 the backbone ; the spine ; the spinal column ¶ 얼빠진 녀석 등골뼈를 분질러 놓을 테다 I'll crack your bones, you poor simp !
등골뽑다 squeeze〔wring, extort〕 money out of 《a person》; sweat ; exploit ; fleece〔bleed, soak〕《a person》 (of his money) ¶ 마지막 한푼까지 등골뽑다 bleed 《a person》 white // 고용주는 고용인을 등골뽑았다 The employer sweat his worker. // 그는 그 여자에게 아주 등골뽑히고 말았다 He was squeezed dry by that woman.
등과 登科 passing the higher civil service examination —하다 pass the higher civil service examination
등교 登校 attending school ; school attendance —하다 go to school ; attend school ¶ 수험자는 매일 오전 8시까지 등교해야 한다 All candidates are requested to be at the school before eight every morning.
등귀 騰貴 a price rise ; an advance ; appreciation —하다 rise ; go up ; advance ; appreciate ¶ 달러의 등귀 appreciation of the dollar // 원료의 등귀로 인해서 owing to the advance on the raw material // 등귀의 경향을 나타내다 show an upward tendency // 물가는 등귀하고 있다 Prices are going up. // 물가는 점점 등귀의 경향에 있다 The prices are on the rise〔on the advance, looking up〕.
물가 — a rise in prices
등극 登極 accession to the throne ; enthronement —하다 accede to〔ascend〕 the throne ; mount the throne ; be enthroned
—령(令) the Regulations Governing the Accession to the Throne
등근 等根 〖수학〗 equal roots
등글개첩 —妾 a young mistress〔concubine〕 of an old man
등글기 [행위] copying〔imitation〕 of a painting ; [작품] a copied〔counterfeit〕 painting ; a counterfeit
등긁이 a (wooden) backscratcher
†등급 等級 a class ; a grade ; a rank ¶ 등급을 정하다 graduate ; grade // 1, 2, 3으로 등급이 붙어 있다 be graded 1, 2, and 3
‡등기 登記 registration ; registry —하다 register ; have 《a thing》 registered ; effect〔make〕 registration ¶ 등기된〔필의〕 registered // 등기되어 있다 be registered ; be on the record // 정식으로 등기하다 register in proper form
—계(係) a registrar ; a recorder —료 a registration fee — 말소 cancellation of registration — 명의인(名義人) a person registered ; the registered holder of right ; the person in whose name the registration is made — 번호 the registered number ; a registration number —부(簿) a register (book) — 사항 matters required to be registered —소 a registry (office) — 수속 the formalities of registration — 용지 a registry folio ; a registration form — 우편 registered mail — 증서 a registered〔an inscribed〕 bond —필증 a registration certificate 변경(變更) — registration of an alternation 선적(船籍) — registration of nationality (of a ship)
등꽃 藤— wisteria blossoms ¶ 등꽃빛 light purple ; lilac
*등나무 藤— 〖식물〗 a wisteria ¶ 등나무 덩굴 wisteria-vine
— 시렁 a wisteria trellis ; a wisteria arbor
등날 the vertebral〔spinal〕 column
등널 the back (board) of a chair
등넘기 leapfrog ¶ 등넘기를 하다 leapfrog
등단 登壇 —하다 go on〔take, ascend, proceed to〕 the platform ; take the rostrum ; mount the rostrum
등달다 be overanxious ; be nervous ; fret ; jitter ; get all hot and bothered ; chafe 《under》; be irritated ; be much concerned 《about》; stew〔be in a stew〕 《구》 ¶ 등달아서 병나다 fret〔worry〕 oneself ill // 언제 돌아오나 하고 등달다 wait in anxious suspense for one's arrival // 사업의 진행이 여의치 않아 그는 등달아 있다 He is quite nervous because his undertaking is not making satisfactory progress. // 그렇게 등달지 않아도 좋다 Don't fret yourself like that. // 네가 늦어서 그는 등달았다 He was vexed〔impatient〕 at your delay.
등닿다 ① [마소의 등이] 《the skin of a horse》 come off ; be grazed ; be abraded ; be rubbed raw
② [의지하다] have backing ; be supported ; lean on ; depend on 《the man of influence》
등대 等待 waiting —하다 wait for ; await
‡등대 燈臺 a lighthouse ; a beacon ; a pharos 《시》
—선(船) a lightship ; a lightboat ; a floating lighthouse —세(稅) light dues 〔duties〕 —지기 a lighthouse keeper ; a

lighthouseman ; a lightkeeper **등댓불** a beacon lamp ; lights

등대다 lean on〔upon〕; depend on ; rely on ; fall back on ; count on ¶ 미국에 등댄 정권 the U. S. -backed regime // 아들에게 등대다 lean on one's son ; depend upon one's son for support // 친척을 등대고 상경하다 come〔go〕 to *Seoul* counting on one's relative's help // 그는 돈에만 등대고 있다 He has nothing to fall back on except money. // 그는 정부에 등댈 만한 유력자 몇 사람이 있다 He has several men of influence he can count on in the government.

등덜미 the upper part of the back ¶ 등덜미를 붙잡다 seize〔take〕《a person》 by the nape〔scruff〕 of the neck

등도 登途 —하다 start〔go, set out, set forth〕 on a journey ; set off ; hit〔take to〕 the road ; leave《for》; depart

*__등등 等等__ etc. ; and so on ; and others ; and all that sort of things ⇨ 등

등등거리 藤— a rattan shirt (worn in summer to keep sweat from coat)

등등하다 騰騰— [서슬푸르다] (be) mighty ; powerful ; influential ; [의기양양하다] triumphant ; exultant ; [도도하다] overbearing ; imperious ; stuck- up ; be on one's high horse ¶ 기세 등등하다 show one's spirit〔nerve〕; be in high spirits〔feather〕; be in high〔towering, roaring〕 spirits // 노기 등등하다 be filled with fury and anger ; look black with anger ; turn purple with rage // 살기 등등하다 reek of murder ; look menacing

등락 騰落 fluctuations ; rise and fall ; ups and downs ¶ 등락하는 물가 fluctuating market〔prices〕

등량 等量 〖화학〗 equivalence ¶ 등량의 equivalent

등렬 等列 the same rank

*__등록 登錄__ registration ; record ; enrollment ; entry **—하다** register《with an office》; make an entry ; enroll ; put on record ; inscribe ¶ 유권자의 대장에 등록하다 enter in the cadaster // 등록돼 있다 be registered ; be on record // 상표를 특허국에 등록하다 register a trademark with the patent office

— 공채 registered〔inscribed〕 bonds **—과** the registration section **— 권리자** an obligee of registration ; a person privileged to register **—금** a registration fee **—료** a registration fee **— 말소** cancellation of a registration **—법** the registration law **—부(簿)** a register ; a roster **— 상표** a registered trademark **—세** a registration tax **— 세대 인원** the number of registered household members **— 세법** 〖법〗 the Registration Tax Act **— 의무자** an obligor of registration ; a person subject to registration **—인〔자〕** a registrant **—제** a registration system **— 증서** a certificate of inscription **—필(畢)** Registered (게시) **사전(事前)—제** an advance registration system **선적(船籍) —** registration of nationality **선적 —항(港)** a port of registry **의장(意匠) —** a registered design **판권 —** registration of copyright

등롱 燈籠 a hanging lantern ; a garden lantern ; a sacred〔dedicatory〕 lantern (신전의) ¶ 등롱에 불을 켜다 light a hanging lantern

등루 登樓 ① [누각에 오름] going up a tower〔an edifice〕 **—하다** go up〔climb〕 a tower
② [창루에] **—하다** visit a brothel〔house of ill fame〕 ¶ 등루객 a visitor to a brothel〔house of ill fame〕

등마루 the ridge of the spine ; the spinal column ; [정상] the (mountain) ridge ; the top ; the summit
산— the ridge〔summit〕 of a mountain
지붕— the ridge of a roof

등메 a rush mat fringed with cloth

등명 燈明 a sacred light ; a taper (light) offered to a god ¶ 제단에 등명을 올리다 offer〔place〕 a sacred light〔taper〕 on the altar
—접시 a light dish

등밀이 ① 〖건축〗 [창살] the fluted ribs of a window lattice ② [깎는 연장] a tool used to trim the bottoms of woodenware or wooden clogs

등바대 a neckband sewed in unlined garments

등반 登攀 —하다 climb (up) ; scale ; make the ascent of
—대(隊) a climbing party **—자(者)** a climber

등받이 the back of a chair

등번호 —番號 〖경기〗 a player's (uniform) number ¶ 등번호 11번 선수 a player with Number 11 on the back of the uniform

등변 等邊 〖수학〗 equal sides ¶ 등변의 equilateral
— 삼각형 an equilateral triangle **—형(形)** an equilateral (figure)

*__등본 謄本__ an attested〔a certified〕 copy ; a transcript ; a duplicate ; 〖법〗 a tenor
공인(公認) — an office copy **인증(認證)〔증명부(證明附)〕 —** 〖법〗 an exemplification **호적 —** a copy of one's family register ¶ 호적 등본을 뜨다 get〔obtain〕 an attested〔a certified〕 copy of one's family register

*__등분 等分__ equal parts ; division into equal parts **—하다** divide equally〔in equal parts〕; share〔deal out〕 equally ¶ 비용을 등분하다 share the expenses equally with《a person》// 재산을 자식들에게 등분하다 divide the property equally among one's children // 이익을 3등분하다 divide〔share〕 the profit among the three
사(四)— quadrisection **삼—** trisection
이—선(線) an internal bisector

†**등불 燈―** a lamplight ; a lamp ¶ 등불을 켜다 light a lamp // 등불 밑에서 글을 읽다 read by lamplight

등비 等比 〚수학〛 equal ratio ; geometric ratio ; analogy
　― 수열(數列) geometric(al) series

등비 급수 等比級數 〚수학〛 (a) geometric(al) progression ; a geometric(al) series ¶ 등비 급수적으로 증가하다 grow in (the manner of) geometrical progression ; increase in (a) geometric ratio

‡**등뼈** the backbone ; the chine ; the spine
　―동물(動物) a vertebrate

등사 謄寫 copy ; transcription ; reproduction ; mimeographing ; dittoing **―하다** transcribe ; mimeograph ; get mimeograph copies ; reproduce ; ditto
　―료 a copying fee **―물** mimeographed material (for distribution) **―지** carbon paper (복사용의)

등사기 謄寫機 a mimeograph ; a ditto 〔copying〕 machine ⇨ 등사판

등사판 謄寫版 a mimeograph ¶ 등사판으로 인쇄하다 mimeograph ; get mimeograph copies
　― 원지(原紙) stencil paper

***등산 登山** mountain climbing ; mountaineering **―하다** climb〔scale〕 a mountain ; go up〔ascend〕 a mountain ; make the ascent 《of a mountain》 ¶ 등산의 계절 the mountaineering season // 그는 등산을 좋아한다 He is fond of mountain climbing.
　―가 a mountaineer ; an alpinist ; a cragsman (암산의) **―대** a mountaineering party ; a team of mountain- climbers **―로** a path up a mountain **― 설비** arrangements〔accommodation〕 for mountain-climbers **―열(熱)** a craze for mountaineering **―용 장비** mountain-climbing equipment **―자** a (mountain-) climber **― 지팡이** an alpenstock **― 철도** a mountain railway ; a funicular railway **―화** mountain-climbing boots

등살 the flesh〔muscle〕 of one's back ¶ 등살이 꼿꼿하다 feel one's back stiff

등살바르다 have stiff back muscles ; have a stiff back

등색 橙色 orange ; orange color ¶ 연한 등색 reddish-yellow

등성마루 the (mountain) ridge ; the top of the back ; the line of the backbone

등성이 the back (잔등) ; a (mountain) ridge (산의)

등세 騰勢 a rising〔an upward〕 trend〔tendency〕 ; 〚증권〛 a rise

등세공 藤細工 rattanwork ; canework
　―품 a rattanwork ; a canework

등속 等屬 and so forth〔on〕 ; and the like ; et cetera 《etc.》 ¶ 보리 밀 등속 wheats, oats, and the like

등속 等速 〚물리〛 uniform velocity
　― 운동 uniform motion

등솔기 a seam on the back of a coat

등수 等數 ① [차례] a grade ; a rank ; a class ¶ 등수를 정하다 grade ; classify ② [같은 수] an equal number ¶ 찬반이 등수이다 The vote is equally divided.

등시 等時 ¶ 등시의 isochronic
　―성(性) 〚물리〛 isochronism

등식 等式 〚수학〛 an equality
　절대적 ― an absolute equality **조건부 ―** a conditional equality

등신 等身 life-size ¶ 등신의 life-size
　― 동상 a life-size bronze statue

등신 等神 a fool ; a dunce ; an ass ; a nincompoop ; a moron ; a silly ; a stupid person ¶ 등신 같은 foolish ; silly ; stupid ; absurd // 등신 같은 짓을 하다 do a foolish〔silly〕 thing ; make a fool〔an ass〕 of oneself ; play the fool // 이 등신아 You fool〔idiot〕! // 이런 등신은 본 적이 없다 I've never come across such a fool in my life. // 그런 일에 찬성하는 등신은 없다 No one is foolish enough to support it.

등심 燈心 a wick

등심 ―心 sirloin ; meat around the backbone of cattle

등심초 燈心草 〚식물〛 a rush

등쌀 botheration 《구》 ; harassing ; annoying ; annoyance ; pestering ¶ 계모가 등쌀대다 a stepmother is so hard upon one // 저 놈 등쌀에 못 견디겠다 I am much annoyed with him. // 모기 등쌀에 잠을 잘 수가 없다 The mosquitoes are so annoying that I can't sleep. // 어디를 가나 거지 등쌀에 못 견디겠다 Beggars bother me wherever I go.
　등쌀대다 관용 treat 《a person》 cruelly ; tease 《a person for》 ; annoy ; pester ; harass ; needle

등압선 等壓線 an isobaric line ; an isobar

등어리 the back ⇨ 등

등에 〚곤충〛 a horsefly ; a gadfly

등온 等溫 ¶ 등온의 isothermal
　― 변화 〚기상·물리·화학〛 isothermal change **―선** an isothermal (line) ; an isotherm **― 압축** 〚기상·물리·화학〛 isothermal compression **―층** the isothermal region ; the stratosphere **― 팽창** 〚기상·물리·화학〛 isothermal expansion

등외 等外 ¶ 등외의 under the regular grades // 등외가 되다 fall under the regular grades // 그는 등외가 되었다 He failed to win the prize. /He was an also-ran.
　―마(馬) 〚경마〛 an also-ran

등용 登用 [임용] appointment ; engagement ; [승진] promotion ; elevation ; preferment **―하다** appoint ; engage ; elevate ; promote ; prefer 《a person to some office》 ¶ 인재를 등용하다 engage men of ability ; raise men of ability to higher position // 재판관에 등용되다 be appointed (as a) judge ; be elevated 〔raised〕 to the bench

공무원 — 시험 a civil service examination
등용 燈用 ¶ 등용 가스 illuminating 〔light〕 gas // 등용 석유 kerosene (oil) // 등용의 for illuminating purpose
등용문 登龍門 an opening to all honors ; the only door to eminence ¶ 문단에의 등용문 the only door to the literary world // 청년의 등용문 the gate to success in life for young people // 이 나라에서는 시험만이 등용문이다 In this country examinations alone open careers to young men.
등원 登院 attendance at the House — 하다 attend the House ¶ 등원을 독려하다 whip in // 등원 명령을 내리다 send〔issue〕 a whip around
등위 等位 class ; grade ; rank ; scale ; 〖전기〗 equipotential
—절 〖문법〗 a coordinate clause — 접속사 〖문법〗 a coordinate conjunction
등위 登位 ascension to the throne ; [교황의] the exaltation 《of the Pope》
*등유 燈油 lamp-〔burning-, illumination-〕 oil ; kerosene ; paraffinoil 《영》
등의자 籐椅子 a rattan〔cane〕 chair
등자 橙子 〖식물〗 a bitter orange
—꽃 orange blossoms —나무 an orange tree —색 orange (color)
*등자 鐙子 stirrups
등잔 燈盞 an oil cup for a lamp ; a lamp-oil container
— 기름 a lamp oil —불 a lamplight ; a lantern light
등잔 밑이 어둡다 속담 At the foot of the candle it is dark. /One has to go abroad to get news of home. /The beacon does not shine on its own base. /You must go into the country to hear what news at London. /Go abroad and you'll hear news of home. /If you will learn news, you must go to the oven or the mill.
등장 登場 [무대에] entrance on the stage ; entry ; [출현] advent ; appearance — 하다 enter the stage ; appear on the stage ; appear ; make one's appearance ¶ 등장 순서 the order of appearance // 신무기의 등장 the advent of new weapons
— 인물 characters ; the cast (역할) ; persons connected 《with an affair》 ¶ 이 사건의 등장 인물은 누구인가 Who are the men that figure in this affair ?
등재 登載 registration ; record — 하다 register ; record
등정 登頂 — 하다 reach the top〔summit〕 of a mountain ¶ 한라산 등정에 성공하다 conquer the summit of Mt. *Hanla*
등정 登程 departure ; starting〔setting out〕 on a journey — 하다 depart ; start〔set out〕 on a journey
등줄기 the protruding parts of backbone
등지 等地 (and) like places ¶ 서울·부산 등지 *Seoul*, *Pusan*, and like〔other〕
등지느러미 the dorsal fin
*등지다 ① [틀어지다] become estranged 〔alienated〕 from ; fall out with ; break up with ; be on bad terms 《with》 ; be at odds 《with》 ; disagree with ¶ 그 두 형제는 요즘 서로 등졌다 The two brothers have lately become estranged. // 그는 친구들과 등지고 있다 He has been estranged from his friends. // 그들은 언제나 서로 등지고 있다 They are always at loggerheads〔odds〕 with each other.
② [배반하다] turn against〔on, upon〕 ; turn traitor to ; betray ¶ 나라를 등지다 betray〔turn against〕 one's country ; turn traitor to one's country // 벗을 등지다 turn against one's friend // 세상을 등지다 turn one's back on the world
③ [등뒤에 두다] 《one's back》 lean against ¶ 관중을 등지고 with one's back to the audience // 벽을 등지다 lean one's back against the wall // 벽을 등지고 앉다 sit with one's back against the wall // 산을 등지고 사진을 찍다 take a photograph with mountains in the background // 서울은 북악산을 등지고 있다 *Seoul* lies with Mt. *Pugag* at the back.
등질 等質 homogeneity ¶ 등질의 homogeneous
등짐 a pack〔burden〕 carried on one's back ¶ 등짐을 지고 with a burden on one's back // 등짐을 지다 carry a burden on one's back
—장수 a packman ; a peddler
등차 等差 [균등한 차] equal difference ; equality and difference ; [등급] a gradation ; a grade ¶ 등차를 정하다 grade ; graduate ; discriminate ; classify
— 급수 〖수학〗 arithmetical progression 〔series〕 —세 discriminating duty ; graded duty〔tariff〕
등창 —瘡 an abscess〔a tumor〕 on one's back ; a swelling on one's back
등청 登廳 office attendance ; attendance at office — 하다 go to〔attend〕 one's office ; go to one's official post of duty
—일 the day for one's attendance at office
등초 謄抄 copy ; reproduction ; transcription — 하다 copy ; reproduce ; transcribe
등촉 燈燭 a lamplight and a candlelight ; a lantern light
등치기 〖씨름의〗 a shoulder-throw
등치다 ① [치다] strike〔slap〕 《a person》 on the back
② [빼앗다] extort 《money from a person》 by intimidation ; blackmail 《a person》 of 《his money》 ; wring〔screw〕 money out of 《a person》 ; pinch ; squeeze ; racketeer 《미·속》 ¶ 등쳐먹는 놈 a blackmailer ; an extortioner // 등쳐먹고 살다 live by racketeering // 남을 등쳐먹

다가 잡혀 갔다 He was arrested on a charge of blackmailing.
등치고 간 내먹다 속담 drive 《a person》 into an awkward situation and proceed to take advantage of it. /To give one〔a dog〕 roast meat, and beat him with the spit.
등친 等親 the degree of consanguinity 〔kinship〕 ¶ 결혼 금지의 등친 forbidden〔prohibited〕 degree // 5 등친 a relation〔kinsman〕 of the 5th degree of consanguinity
등칼키나물 〖식물〗 cowvetch
등타다 go along the ridge of a mountain
등태 a (straw) back pad (used for carrying a burden on the back)
등토시 藤— a pair of rattan wristlets (to protect sleeves from perspiration)
등판 登板 going up〔to〕 the mound **—하다** 〖야구〗 take the plate〔mound〕; go to the mound〔hill 《미·속》〕; [구원 투수로] come in〔up〕 to pitch
등표지 —表紙 the backbone〔spine, shelfback〕 《of a book》
등피 燈皮 a lampshade; a lamp
등하불명 燈下不明 At the foot of the candle it is dark. /One has to go abroad to get news of home. /The beacon does not shine on its own base.
등한 等閑 negligence; carelessness **—하다** (be) negligent; careless ¶ 등한히 하다 neglect; slight; ignore; leave to chance; disregard // 일을 등한히 하다 slight〔neglect〕 one's work // 직무를 등한히 하다 neglect one's duties // 등한히 할 수 없다 cannot be left untouched 〔ignored〕 // 등한히 할 수 없는 문제다 The matter must not be left as it is.
등한시 等閑視 negligence; neglect; disregard **—하다** neglect; be negligent in; be neglectful of; overlook; slight; make light of
등허리 [등과 허리] the back and the waist; [허리의 등쪽] the small of the back
등화 燈火 a light; a lamp light
— 설비 a lamp device **— 신호** signaling with a flashlight〔lantern〕
등화 燈花 the snuff of a wick
등화 藤花 wisteria flowers
등화 관제 燈火管制 control of lights; control over lighting; a blackout; a brownout; a dimout ¶ 등화 관제는 해제되어 있었다 The blackout was up.
—용 커튼 a blackout curtain ¶ 창에는 등화 관제용 커튼이 쳐 있었다 The windows were blacked out.
-디 ① [강조] awfully; terribly; mighty; striking; very ¶ 검디검은 deep-black; 《as》 black as coal〔pitch〕 // 차디찬 《as》 cold as ice; icy-cold // 짜디짠 terribly salty // 춥디 춥다 be awfully〔precious〕 cold
② [의문] ¶ 여기서 얼마나 멀디 How far was it〔What was the distance〕 from here? // 모자는 얼마나 하디 How much did the hat cost you? // 그는 온다디 Is he coming?
디글디글하다 be rather thick〔big〕 among all the thin〔small〕 things
디기탈리스 〖약〗 digitalis; 〖식물〗 a foxglove 《영》
디데이 (the) D-day 《for a military coup》
디도서 —書 〖성경〗 The Epistle of St. Paul to Titus; [약칭] Titus 《Tit.》
***디디다** ① [밟다] step on; tread (on) ¶ 땅을 디디다 step on the ground; tread the ground // 이국 땅에 발을 디디다 set foot on foreign soil; visit a foreign land // 한 발짝 잘못 디디다 take a false 〔wrong〕 step // 남을 디디고 일어서다 make a stepping stone of 《a person》 // 정계에 발을 내어 디디다 enter upon a political career
② [누룩·메주를] tread malted flour paste into cakes
디 디 티 D. D. T. 《*d*ichloro-*d*iphenyl-*t*richloro-ethane》
디딜방아 a treadmill (pestle); a mortar worked by treading
디딤돌 a stepping stone; a stepstone; a step
디렉터 a director
디룽거리다 dangle; swing; sway ¶ 디룽디룽 dangling; dingle-dangle // 바람에 디룽거리다 dangle in the wind
디모데 〖성경〗 Timothy
— 전서〔후서〕 〖성경〗 The First〔Second〕 Epistle of St. Paul (the Apostle) to Timothy; Ⅰ〔Ⅱ〕 Timothy 《Tim》
디밀다 ⇨ 들이밀다
디스카운트 discount
— 세일 discount sale
디스코테크 a discotheque (레코드 연주로 춤을 추는 나이트클럽 따위)
디스크자키 〖방송〗 a disk jockey; a record spinner 《속》
디스토마 [편충] a distoma; flukes; [병] distomiasis
간(肝)— distoma hepaticum
디아스타아제 〖화학〗 diastase
***디자이너** a designer
공업 — an industrial designer
†**디자인** design; designing **—하다** design; make〔draw〕 a plan 《of》
***디저트** dessert
— 코스 the dessert course
디젤 기관 a diesel engine
디젤 기관차 a diesel(-electric) locomotive; a diesel(-electric)
***디프테리아** diphtheria
— 혈청(血淸) antidiphtheria serum
디플레(이션) 〖경제〗 deflation
— 정책 deflationary measures
딜러 a dealer ¶ 그는 딜러였다 He was the dealer.

딜럭스 deluxe 《cars》
―판(版) an edition deluxe ; a deluxe edition **― 호텔** a hotel deluxe
딜레마 a dilemma ¶ 딜레마에 빠지다 fall into〔be on the horns of〕a dilemma
딜레탕트 a dilettante (*pl.* -ti, -tes)
딩딩하다, 띵띵하다 ① [힘이 세다] (be) strong ; robust ; mighty ; stout ; sturdy ¶ 그 노인은 아직도 딩딩하다 The old man is still hale and hearty.
② [핑핑하다] (be) taut ; tense ; tight ¶ 배가 불러 딩딩하다 have a full stomach ; have eaten stomachful // 젖이 불어 딩딩하다 a breast is swollen with milk
③ [기반이 튼튼하다] (be) stable ; secure ; firm ; hard ¶ 살림이 딩딩하다 be well off // 재정적 배경이 딩딩하다 have a stable backing of finance // 종기가 밑이 들어 딩딩하다 The abscess is deep-rooted and hard.
따갑다 ① ⇨ 뜨겁다 ② [쑤시다] (be) stinging ; tingling ; prickly ; pricking ¶ 뙤약볕에 살이 따갑다 One's skin smarts under the sun's rays. // 벌한테 쏘인 데가 따갑다 The spot stung by the bee is tingling.
따귀 ¶ 따귀를 때리다 slap 《a person》 on the cheek ; spank
따귀 떨다 strike on the cheek
따끈따끈 ⇨ 뜨끈뜨끈
따끈하다 ⇨ 뜨끈하다
따끈히 (so that it is) hot ; good and hot ¶ 물을 따끈히 끓이다 boil water good and hot // 술을 따끈히 데워 마시다 drink rice wine hot // 우유를 따끈히 데우다 scald milk warmly
따끔거리다 sting ; prick ; tingle ; be stinging ; be tingling ; be piercingly painful ; be excruciating ¶ 종기가 따끔거린다 A boil is excruciating.
⁑**따끔하다** ① smart ; prick ; bite ; have a tingling pain 《in》 ¶ 상처가 아직 따끔하다 The wound smarts still. // 볕에 탄 등이 따끔하다 My sunburnt back smarts 〔tingles〕. // 피부가 따끔했다 The skin smarted (with pain).
② [느낌이] (be) cruel ; harsh ; hard ; rough ; severe ¶ 따끔한 비평 harsh criticism // 따끔한 맛을 보이다 handle 《a person》 roughly ; treat 《a person》 badly // 따끔한 맛을 보다 have bitter experiences ; have a hard time of it
따님 your〔his〕(esteemed) daughter
†**따다**[1] ① [잡아 떼다] pick ; pluck ; nip ; clip ; trim ; [모으다] gather ; cull ¶ 꽃을 따다 pick flowers ; gather flowers // 나무 열매를 따다 gather nuts // 뽕잎을 따다 pick mulberryleaves // 봉오리 때에 따다 nip 《a thing》 in the bud (미연에 방지하다)
② [찔러 터뜨리다] open ; lance ; cut out 《affected parts》 ¶ 종기를 따다 open an abscess // 병마개를 따다 pull out a top 〔bung〕; unstopper ; uncork a bottle // 포도주를 한 병 따다 open〔uncork〕a bottle of wine // 이제 맥주의 뚜껑을 따도 좋겠습니까 Shall I go ahead and open the beer ?
③ [얻다] get ; take ; obtain ¶ 노름판에서 돈을 많이 따다 gain much money in gambling // 백점〔만점〕을 따다 get 100 points〔a full mark〕// 법학 박사의 학위를 따다 obtain the degree of Doctor of Laws
④ [인용·발췌·표절하다] quote ; make selections ; pick out ; extract ; sum up ; summarize ¶ 그의 시에서 따온 아름다운 몇 줄 beautiful lines culled from his poems // 밀턴의 글에서 따다 extract 〔excerpt, quote〕 from Milton's writings ; make an extract from Milton's writings
따다[2] (be) different ; another ; separate ; irrelevant ¶ 딴 사람 another person // 딴 말 an irrelevant remark // 딴 상자에 넣다 put 《a thing》 in another box // A와 B는 딴 문제다 A is one thing and B (is) another.
따다[3] ① [면회·거절] pretend not to be in ; pretend to be out ; be not at home 《to a caller》; refuse to 《see a caller pretending to be away from home》
② [따돌리다] leave 《a person》 out ; exclude
따다 쓰다 [말·글을] steal ; misappropriate ; take 《over》; borrow 《from》; plagiarize ¶ 남의 글귀를 따다 쓰다 steal another's words ; plagiarize
*__따돌리다__ exclude 《a thing》; leave 《a person》 out in the cold ; neglect ; ostracize (배척) ; cut 《a person》 out ; send 《a person》 to Coventry ¶ 따돌려지고 있다 be out of it 《구》// 그는 급우들한테 따돌림을 받고 있다 He is the pest to his classmates. /He is left out in the cold by his classmates. // 누구나 따돌림을 받는 것을 싫어한다 No one likes to be left out. // 그들은 나를 따돌리고 말 상대를 하지 않았다 They left me entirely out of their conversation.
*__따뜻이__ ① [열로] warmly ¶ 몸을 따뜻이 하다 (옷을 입고) keep oneself warm ; dress warmly // 따뜻이 간직하다 keep 《a thing》 warm
② [온정으로] warmly ; warm-heartedly ; kindly ¶ 따뜻이 맞아들이다 welcome warmly〔with warm affection〕; receive 《a person》 with warm hands
†**따뜻하다** ① [온도] (be) mild ; warm ; genial ¶ 따뜻한 겨울 a soft〔mild, green〕winter // 따뜻한 햇빛 genial sunshine // 점점 따뜻해진다 It is getting warmer. // 난로가 좋아서 여간 따뜻하지 않다 With a good stove I was as warm as toast.
② [온정] (be) kindly ; genial ; heartwarming ; cordial ¶ 따뜻한 환영 a cordial〔genial〕welcome ; a warm reception // 따뜻한 동정 warm sympathy // 마음이

따뜻한 사람 a person of a genial disposition ; a warm-hearted person // 따뜻한 손을 뻗치다 extend friendly help to 《the poor》 // 사람을 따뜻하게 맞다 receive 《a person》 with warm hands

따라 according to ⇨ 따라서

*__따라가다__ ① [동반] go with ; accompany ; go in the wake of ; [뒤를] follow ; follow at another's heel ¶ 길을 따라가다 follow a path // 그대가 좋아하는 데라면 어디고 따라 가겠다 I will follow you anywhere you like to stay.
② [모방·복종] obey ; follow ; act upon 《one's advice》 ; follow suit (after) ; model 《a person》 ; copy after〔from〕 ; yield to ¶ 따라가지 않다 disobey ; act contrary to // 남이 시키는 대로 따라가다 bow to another's will
③ [뒤지지 않도록] keep up with ; catch up with ¶ 자네를 좀처럼 따라갈 수 없네 I can't keep up with you. // 영어에 있어서는 아무도 그를 따라갈 수 없다 No one can equal〔rival, compete with〕 him in English.

‡**따라다니다** ① ⇨ 따르다¹ ② [귀찮게] follow 《a person》 about ; dangle about 〔after, round〕 《a person》 ; shadow

‡**따라붙다** overtake ; catch〔come〕 up with ; [점차] gain upon

†**따라서** ① […대로] in accordance with ; in conformity with〔to〕 ; according to ; agreeably to ; true to ¶ 국법에 따라서 in accordance with the national law // 전통에 따라서 true to the tradition 《of》 // 약속에 따라서 in compliance with the promise // 귀하의 신청에 따라서 agreeably to your proposal // 명령에 따라서 in obedience to 《a person's》 orders // 습관에 따라서 according to custom // 그는 자기 주의에 따라서 행동했다 He acted up to his principle.
② [비례해서] in proportion to〔as〕 ; proportionately with ¶ 수입이 증가함에 따라서 according to〔in proportion as〕 one's income increases ; in proportion to the increase of one's income // 문명이 발달함에 따라서 as civilization progresses ; with the progress of civilization // 나이가 들어감에 따라서 지혜가 생긴다 Sense〔Wisdom〕 comes with age. // 공기는 지상의 높이에 따라서 차가워진다 The air becomes cooler in proportion to the height of the ground.
③ [그러므로] accordingly ; consequently ; in consequence ; therefore ; so that ; hence ¶ A는 B와 같고 B는 C와 같다 따라서 A는 C와 같다 A is equal to B, B is equal to C, therefore A is equal to C. // 그는 매일 놀고만 있다 따라서 학교 성적도 나쁘다 He is idling all the day with the consequence that his school record is very poor.

*__따라오다__ [뒤를] follow ; come with ; accompany ; tag along with ; [모방하다] follow ; follow suit ; do likewise ; [좇아서] keep〔catch〕 up with ¶ 이 개는 어디를 가나 나를 따라온다 This dog follows me everywhere I go. // 누군가 나를 따라오는 듯 느껴졌다 I thought I heard somebody following me.

‡**따라잡다** ⇨ 따라붙다

따라지 ① [땅보] a shorty ; a dwarf ② [노름판의] one point ; the lowest point in a card game ③ [따분한 존재] a miserable existence ¶ 따라지 신세 a wretched life ; a bare living (살림) // 따라지 생활을 하다 live a wretched life ; eke out a scanty livelihood

*__따로__ ① [별개로] separately ; apart ¶ …과는 따로 apart〔separately〕 from ; independently from // 따로 만나다 see 《them》 separately // 따로 걷다 walk apart // 따로 몫을 두다 set〔put〕 apart 《for》 // 나는 아버지와는 따로 영업을 하고 있다 I run my own business independently from my father's. // 나는 후일을 위하여 그것을 따로 젖혀두었다 I set that apart for the future use.
② [별도·여분] additionally ; in addition ; besides ; apart〔aside〕 from ¶ 요금을 따로 받다 charge extra 《for》 // 그는 월급 외에 따로 한 달 2만원의 수입이 있다 He has an additional income of 20,000 *won* a month apart from his monthly salary.
③ [특별] especially ; particularly ; in particular ¶ 따로 말할 것이 없다 I have nothing particular to say. // 따로 들어 말할 이유가 없다 I have no particular reason for it.

따로나다 [살림을] establish〔set up〕 a separate branch of the family ; make a separate home

따로내다 [살림을] make 《a person》 establish a separate home

†**따로따로** [떨어져] separately ; apart ; [개별로] each ; severally ; respectively ; individually ; one by one ¶ 따로따로 걷다 walk apart 《from one another》 // 따로따로 살다 live separately 《from》 // 따로따로 퇴장하다 exeunt severally // 따로따로 간직하다 keep 《things》 apart // 그들은 각자 따로따로 자기의 길을 갔다 They went their respective ways.

‡**따르다¹** ① [뒤따르다·수행하다] accompany ; follow ; go after ; go with 《a person》 ¶ 비서가 그를 따랐다 A secretary accompanied him. // 그를 따라 다방으로 들어갔다 I followed him into a coffee shop. // 시세(時勢)에 따르다 go with the stream // 유행을 따르다 follow〔run after〕 the fashion
② [수반·병행하다] be followed by ; be attended by ; keep (in) step with // 세상이 진보하는 데 따라서 with the progress of the world // 수입이 증가하는 데 따라서 (in proportion) as one's income increas-

es // 나이를 먹는 데 따라 as one grows older ; with advancing years // 여러 가지 폐단이 따르다 be attended with various evils // 성공에는 고생이 따르기 마련이다 Success and hard work go together. / Success attends hard work. // 자유에는 책임이 따른다 Freedom carries responsibility with it.

③ [복종하다] obey ; follow ; yield〔submit, give in〕《to》 ¶ 명령을 따르다 obey 《a person's》 orders // 남의 뜻을 따르다 yield〔bow〕 to another's will // 통제〔명령, 당규〕를 따르다 toe the line 〔mark, scratch〕 // 그는 나의 의견에 따랐다 He has given in to my views.

④ [응하다] comply with ; accede to ; agree to ; [지키다] follow ; act on 〔upon〕 ; take ; conform to ; abide by ¶ 신문 보도에 따르면 according to a newspaper report // 충고를 따르다 take〔follow, act upon〕 《a person's》 advice // 법률을 따르다 conform to the law ; observe the law // 습관을 따르다 follow〔conform to〕 the custom // 결정을 따르다 abide by the decision

⑤ [붙좇다] become endeared〔attached〕 ; cling to ; take (kindly) to 《a person》 ; love ; like ; be fond of ; be tamed (동물이) ¶ 아이들이 그녀를 몹시 따라 한시도 놓아주지 않는다 The children love her and just cling to her. // 그녀는 아주 매력적이어서 뭇 남성들이 따랐다 She was so attractive that a great many gentlemen used to court her. // 저 사람은 아동들이 자연히 따르는 사람이다 He is the sort of person that children take to instinctively. // 개는 모르는 사람에겐 잘 따르지 않는다 Dogs do not take kindly to strangers.

†**따르다²** pour 《out, in》 ; fill 《a cup with coffee》 ; put 《water in a bowl》 ; feed 《a lamp with oil》 ¶ 차를 따르다 pour (out) tea // 컵에 따르다 fill a glass ; pour 《wine》 into a glass // 병에서 우유를 따르다 pour milk out of a bottle // 내가 따르겠습니다 Let me serve. // 더운 물을 좀더 따라 주십시오 Please pour in some more hot water.

따르르 ① [구르는 꼴] rollingly ; rumbling ; over and over ¶ 따르르 구르다 roll over and over

② [작은 종 소리] clink ; tinkle ; tingling ; jingle

따름 only ; merely ; simply ; alone ¶ 그 일을 해낼 사람으로는 오직 그가 있을 따름이다 He alone can do it. /He is the only man that can do it. // 그는 일개 학생일 따름이다 He is a mere student. / He is nothing but a student. // 저는 저의 의무를 다했을 따름입니다 I have done nothing but my duty. // 신은 단지 하나 있을 따름이다 There is but one God.

따리 flattery ; toadying ; fawning ; adulation ; lip salve ; apple-polishing ; soft-soap 《구》

―꾼 a flatterer ; a sycophant ; a toady

따리붙이다 관용 flatter ; curry favor with ; fawn upon

따먹다 ① [과실을] pick 《an apple》 and eat ② [장기·바둑 따위에서] take ; catch ; get ; seize ③ [여자를] defile 〔trifle with〕 《a girl's》 chastity ; seduce 〔dishonor, ruin〕 《a girl》

*__따분하다__ ① [느른하다] (be) languid ; listless ; dull ; heavy ¶ 날씨가 더워서 따분하다 The heat makes me feel languid.

② [지리하다] (be) boring ; tedious ; dull ; unpleasant ; gloomy ; disagreeable ¶ 따분한 사람 a dull〔tedious, boring〕 fellow // 따분한 문체 an enervated style // 휴일을 따분하게 보냈다 He spent his holiday gloomily.

③ [난처하다] (be) embarrassing ; awkward ; helpless ¶ 돈이 없어 따분하다 be hard up for money ; be embarrassed to find oneself without money

따비 a kind of small plow ; a weederplow

따비밭 a field of so small acreage as to be plowed with a small plow

따오기 〖새〗 a sacred ibis ; a crested ibis

따옴표 ―標 quotation marks

*__따위__ such as ; the like ; any〔some〕 such ; 《a thing》 like that ; that sort〔kind〕 《of thing》 ; [등등] and so forth〔on〕 ; and〔or〕 the like ; and what not ; and such like ; et cetera 《etc.》 ¶ 그 따위 것 a thing ; a thing like that ; that sort of thing // 너 따위 your likes // 나 따위 people in my position // 사과 배 따위 apples, pears, and what not // 장난감 따위 toys or the like // 가령…따위 such as ; for example // 너 따위가 할 수 있을 것 같애 You never could do it. // 나는 정치적 야심 따위는 없다 I have no political ambition. // 그는 그림과 음악과 산수 따위를 배웠다 He studied painting, music, arithmetic, and the like. // 우리는 동물원에 가서 코끼리와 범 및 사자, 곰 따위를 보았다 We went to the zoo and saw elephants, tigers, lions, bears, and the like.

따지다 ① [시비를] call 《it》 in question ; distinguish between right and wrong ¶ 잘 잘못을 따지다 distinguish between right and wrong ; bring it out who is wrong // 뉴스의 진위를 따지다 verify the news // 신원을 따지다 inquire into 《a person's》 antecedents // 미심한 점을 따지다 inquire into a doubtful point ; have a doubtful point explained

② [숫자를] calculate ; reckon ; count ; compute ; figure up ¶ 이자를 따지다 compute interest // 원가를 따지다 figure out the cost // 위성의 궤도를 따지다 compute the orbit of a satellite

따짝거리다 scratch (and tear off) ; claw

딱 ① [정확하게] accurately ; exactly ;

precisely ; [꼭] just ; punctually ; [들어맞게] perfectly ; [꽉] tightly ; closely ¶ 딱 한 잔만 더 먹다 have just one more glass // 그 옷은 너에게 딱 맞는다 The clothes fit you perfectly. // 두 사람이 딱 들어 붙어 있다 The two men cling to each other tightly. /The two men united closely. // 당신의 견해는 나와 딱 들어 맞는다 Your views exactly correspond to〔coincide with〕 mine. // 딱 2만원 줬다 I paid twenty thousand *won* even.
② [버티는 꼴] firmly ; stiffly ¶ 딱 버티고 서다 stand firm 《against》 ; won't yield〔budge〕 a step〔an inch〕
③ [단호히] definitely ; resolutely ; flatly ; squarely ¶ 딱 거절하다 refuse flatly ; decline squarely
④ [벌린 꼴] wide ¶ 입을 딱 벌리고 with one's mouth wide open // 눈을 딱 부릅뜨다 open one's eyes widely ; strain one's eyes ; look angrily at // 가슴이 딱 바라지다 have a strong〔an out-thrust〕 chest
⑤ [소리가] with a bang〔slam, smash, crush〕

딱다그르르 rolling ; rumbling ; thundering ¶ 딱다그르르하는 소리 a rumbling sound ; a rolling noise (구르는 물건의) ; a peal〔clap〕 of thunder (뇌성)

딱다기 ① [연장] wooden clappers ¶ 딱다기를 치다 beat〔strike〕 clappers ② [사람] a night watchman

딱다깨비 〖곤충〗 a kind of grasshopper

*__딱따구리__ 〖새〗 a woodpecker

딱딱 ① [꺾이는 꼴] with a snap〔crack〕 ¶ 딱딱 부러지다 break with snaps // 손가락 마디를 딱딱 꺾다 crack one's fingers ② [마주치는 소리] with repeated claps〔cracks, raps〕 ¶ 손벽을 딱딱 치다 clap one's hands

딱딱거리다 [을러대다] speak harshly〔roughly〕 ; be strict〔severe〕 with ¶ 너무 딱딱거리지 말라 Don't speak so harshly.

‡**딱딱하다** ① [나무·돌 따위가] (be) hard ; solid ; [야채·고기 따위가] tough ; stiff ; rigid ; stark ¶ 딱딱한 나무 hard wood // 쇠고기가 딱딱하다 This beef is tough.
② [엄하다] (be) strict ; rigid ; stern ; formal ; stiff ; ceremonious ; starchy ¶ 딱딱한 규율 rigid〔strict〕 discipline // 딱딱한 주인 a hard master // 딱딱한 생활 a hard life // 아이들에게 딱딱하게 굴다 be stern to one's children // 그는 사소한 일까지도 매우 딱딱하게 군다 He is exacting even in trifles.
③ [글 등이] (be) stiff ; bookish ; classical ¶ 딱딱한 문장 a bookish〔formal〕 style // 그는 늘 대화를 딱딱하지 않게 한다 He always keeps the conversation going in a light vein.

딱바라지다 ① [몸이] (be) stocky ; sturdy ; pudgy ; thickset ; chunky ; squab ; short and stout ¶ 딱바라진 사람 a short and stout person ; a stocky man ; a chunky fellow
② [물건 모양이] (be) wide and shallow

딱부리 a bug-eyed person ; a person with huge and bulging eyes

딱새 〖새〗 a redstart ; a flycatcher

딱성냥 a lucifer match ; a kind of friction match ¶ 딱성냥을 긋다 strike〔light〕 a match

딱장대 a hard〔harsh, severe, strict, rigorous, stern〕 person ; a rude〔rough〕 person (사나운 사람)

딱장받다 torture ; use torture on 《a person》 ; give 《a person》 the third degree ; put 《a person》 to torture〔the rack〕 ¶ 딱장받아 …을 불게 하다 make 《a person》 confess under torture〔sweating〕 that...

딱정벌레 〖곤충〗 a beetle ; a ground beetle

딱지¹ ① [부스럼의] a scab ; a crust ¶ 종기에 딱지가 앉다 a scab forms over a boil // 딱지가 떨어지다 a scab peels away〔comes off〕 ② [종이 티] a fleck in paper ③ [게·소라·거북 따위의] a shell ; carapace ¶ 거북 딱지 a tortoise shell ④ [시계의] a watch case ⑤ [거절] rejection ; refusal ¶ 딱지 맞다 be refused〔rejected〕

딱지² a label ; a (postage) stamp (우표) ; a tag (꼬리표) ; a picture card (아이들의) ¶ 딱지 치기 game of slap-match // …라고 딱지가 붙은 사람 a person labeled as 《a pro-communist》 ; a notorious person〔scoundrel, lady-killer〕 // 그는 무단도로 횡단으로 받은 교통 위반 딱지를 교통 경찰관 앞에서 찢어 버렸다 He tore up a traffic citation for jaywalking in front of the police officer who'd ticketed him.

딱지놀이 playing with picture cards ; a game of slap-match

딱총 ―銃 a popgun ; [폭죽] fire cracker

딱총나무 ―銃― an elder (tree)

딱하다 ① [가엾다] (be) pitiable ; pitiful ; poor ; miserable ; [안되다] sorry ; regrettable ¶ 딱한 사정 a pitiable circumstance // 딱하게도 sorry〔sad〕 to say // 딱하게 여기다 be〔feel〕 sorry (for) // 참 딱하게 되었군요 I am sorry for you. /I am sorry to hear that. // 매우 딱한 생활을 하고 있다 He lives a very wretched life.
② [난처하다] (be) annoying ; embarrassing ; be at a loss ; be at one's wits' end ¶ 딱한 입장 an awkward position // 나는 어떻게 해야 할지 매우 딱하다 I am at a loss what to do. // 뭐라고 말을 했으면 좋을지 퍽 딱하다 I am quite at a loss for words. // 싸우는 두 친구 사이에 끼어 매우 딱하다 I am in a very delicate position between the two rivaling friends.

딴¹ […로서는] as ; as for (oneself) ; on one's part ; in one's own estimation ; in one's own way ¶ 내 딴은 as for myself ;

on my part // 제 딴은 잘한다고 생각하고 있다 He fancies himself to be doing it well.

†**딴²** [다른 하나] another ; [다른 여러 개] other ; different ; separate ¶ 딴 것 other things ; something else ; the rest (나머지) ; another (다른 어떤 것이나) ; the other (둘중의 나머지) // 딴 데 another place ; some other place(s) ; elsewhere ; somewhere else // 딴 방법 another〔different〕 method(s) // 언젠가 딴 날 some other day // 딴 수작 irrelevant remark // 딴 때에 at another time // 딴 종이에 쓰다 write on another sheet // 그는 그 사건에 대하여 아주 딴 이야기를 들려주었다 He told me another〔a different〕 account of the event. // 그 아버지와 아들은 각기 딴 살림을 한다 The son and the father make a separate livelihood.

딴것 another one ; something else ; a different thing

딴군 —軍 a police underling ; a police spy〔agent〕 ; the terrier〔hound〕 of the law

딴따라패 [배우를 낮추어] a player ; an actor ; [여자] an actress ; theater folk 《총칭》 ; theatrical people

딴마음 [타의] another motive〔intention〕 ; [악의] ill will ; malice ; malicious intent ; [속셈] an ulterior motive ; a secret purpose ; [반심] double-heartedness ; a treacherous intention ¶ 딴마음 있는 사람 a double-dealer // 딴마음 있는 double-faced ; double-dealing ; treacherous ; perfidious // 딴마음 없는 single-hearted ; sincere ; devoted // 딴마음이 없다 bear no malice ; mean no harm 〔mischief〕 // 딴마음을 품다 harbor treacherous intention ; carry two faces (under one hood) ; play a double game

딴말 an irrelevant〔improper〕 remark (관계 없는) ; an absurd remark (어리석은) ; a double-tongue ; a lie **—하다** make an irrelevant〔improper, absurd〕 remark ; evade the issue ; beat around the bush ; tell a lie ¶ 나중에 딴말 해야 소용 없다 You know, it's no use regretting afterwards〔crying over spilt milk〕. // 딴말 하지 마 You are talking nonsense. (어리석은 말)/You are telling a lie. /I want no more of your absurd remarks. /Don't change the subject.

딴맛 a different taste ; a particular〔peculiar〕 taste (특이한 맛) ; a changed taste (음식이 변해서) ¶ 이 술은 어쩐지 딴맛이 난다 This liquor tastes changed.

딴머리 a wig ; a false hair

딴사람 ① [타인] another person ; someone else ; others ; a different person ¶ 딴사람들 the others ; the rest 《of the company》 // 딴사람은 모르거니와 나로서는 for my own part ; I don't know about others, but. . .
② [새사람] a changed being〔man〕 ; a new〔different〕 being ¶ 그는 아주 딴사람이 되었다 He is quite another man now. /He became a new man. /He is now a new being.

딴사설 —辭說 a different〔another〕 story ; irrelevant remarks

딴살림 a separate living〔livelihood〕 ; [부부의 별거] a separation ; limited divorce **—하다** live in a separate house ; live separately ; live apart 《from》 ¶ 형제는 각기 딴살림한다 Each brother has his own home.

딴생각 another thinking〔idea, motive, concept, plan〕 ; a different intention ; [엉뚱한] a secret purpose ; an ulterior motive ¶ 딴생각을 먹다 have an ulterior motive

딴소리 an irrelevant remark ; a lie (거짓말) ⇨ 딴말

딴은 ① [하기야] well ; I see ; indeed ¶ 딴은 그렇소 Well, so it is. /Indeed you are right. // 딴은 네 말도 그럴 듯하다 Hearing what you say, it sounds quite reasonable.

딴전 quite another business ; an irrelevant matter ; irrelevant remarks
딴전 보다 [관용] do another work ; neglect one's main duty
딴전 피우다 [관용] feign〔pretend〕 ignorance ; play the innocent ; speak of a different subject ; say what one does not mean ; make irrelevant remarks

딴죽 [씨름에서] a "leg-bracket"
딴죽 걸다 [관용] bracket one's leg with a foot

딴죽 치다 ① [발로] hit 《a person》 on the leg with one's foot ② [어기다] back out of〔disregard〕 an agreement

딴 쪽 another〔different〕 direction ; the other side (반대 쪽)

딴청 ⇨ 딴전

딴판 a completely different state of affairs ¶ 딴판이다 be quite〔widely, entirely, diametrically〕 different 《from》 ; differ entirely 《from》 ; be poles apart〔asunder〕 《in opinion》 // 성격이 아주 딴판이다 Their characters are opposed to each other.

†**딸** a daughter ¶ 귀염둥이 딸 one's pet daughter ¶ 첫딸 one's first daughter // 딸을 시집보내다 marry off one's daughter

딸가닥 ⇨ 달가닥

***딸기** a strawberry ; a raspberry (나무 딸기)

딸깍발이 a penurious〔poor〕 scholar who has to wear wooden shoes all the time

딸꾹거리다 hiccup ; keep hiccuping

딸꾹딸꾹 with repeated hiccups

딸꾹질 a hiccup ; a hiccough **—하다** hiccup ; hiccough ; have hiccoughs ¶ 딸꾹딸꾹 with repeated hiccups

딸년 a daughter ; my daughter

딸따니 one's dear〔precious〕 little daughter
딸리다 be attached to ; belong to ¶ 가스와 수도 시설이 딸린 집 a house with gas and city water laid on // 나에게 딸린 식구 my (own) family ; a family depending upon me // 할머니에게 딸린 하녀 a maid attached to my grandmother ; a maid waiting on my grandmother ; a maid attending my grandmother // 이 뚜껑은 저 냄비에 딸린 것이다 This lid belongs to that pot.
딸막- ⇨ 들먹-
딸보 [난쟁이] a dwarf ; a pigmy ; [소견 좁은 사람] a narrow-minded person
딸자식 —子息 a daughter ; [자기의] my daughter
‡땀[1] sweat ; perspiration ¶ 땀내가 나다 smell of sweat // 땀을 마구 흘리다 sweat〔perspire〕 profusely ; be dripping with sweat // 땀이 나다〔흐르다〕 the sweat comes out ; the perspiration oozes out ; [흘리다] sweat ; perspire ; be in a sweat // 땀을 닦다 wipe the perspiration from 《one's face》 // 땀이 배어 끈적거리다 be clammy with sweat ; become moist with perspiration // 땀이 줄줄 흐르다 be dripping〔running〕 with sweat // 땀투성이가 되다 be wet〔soaked〕 with perspiration ; be bathed in perspiration ; be all in the sweat // (바빠서) 땀을 빼다 be busy 《writing》 ; be busily occupied in 《writing》 // 땀을 많이 내면 감기가 떨어지는 수가 있다 A good sweat often cures a cold. // 땀을 흘려 벌어먹다 He works hard. /He earns his bread by the sweat of his brow. // 땀을 뻘뻘 흘렸다 I broke out in sweat. // 이마에 구슬 같은 땀이 맺혔다 Great beads of sweat stood on his forehead. // 정말 땀뺐다 It was really a horrid sweat. // 아침에 땀을 흘리면 기분이 좋다 It feels good to work up a sweat in the morning.
땀[2] [바느질] a stitch
땀기 a bit of sweat ¶ 땀기가 있다 be a little bit in sweat ; have a bit of sweat 《in one's palm》
땀나다 ① sweat ; perspire ; the sweat〔perspiration〕 comes〔oozes〕 out
② [힘들다] (be) hard ; toilsome ; take pains ¶ 그 숙제는 정말 땀나더라 The homework was really a horrid sweat.
땀내 a smell of sweat ¶ 땀내 나다 smell sweaty ; stink of sweat // 땀내 나는 옷 garments stinking with sweat
땀내다 induce perspiration ; work up a sweat ; throw 《a person》 into a sweat ; sweat 《a patient》 ¶ 땀내서 감기를 낫게 하다 sweat out a cold // 땀내서 체중을 줄이다 sweat away one's surplus weight
땀들이다 cool oneself ; dry one's sweat
땀등거리 an undershirt for sweat
땀띠 prickly heat ; heat rashes〔spots〕 《미》 ¶ 땀띠가 나다 have prickly heat
땀띠약 —藥 prickly heat powder ; talcum powder
땀받이 an undershirt (땀등거리) ; sweat clothes (말의 안장 밑에) ; a sweatband (모자의)
땀방울 beads of sweat ¶ 이마에 땀방울이 맺히다 beads of sweat stand on one's brow
땀 빠지다 ⇨ 땀 빼다 ¶ 땀 빠지게 일하다 work hard ; sweat away at a job
땀 빼다 [수고] sweat 《with heavy work, etc.》 ; [애먹음] suffer severely ; sweat (it out) ; have a hard time of it ¶ 일 하느라 땀빼다 have a hard time in doing a job
땀질하다 chisel〔knife, cut〕 out〔off, away〕 unnecessary parts of 《wood》
†땅[1] ① [대지] the earth ; [육지] land ; [땅바닥] the ground ¶ 땅을 파다 dig in the ground
② [영토] territory ; land ¶ 한국땅을 밟다 set foot on Korean soil // 만리 타국 땅에 묻히다 be buried in a remote foreign〔strange〕 land
③ [토지] land ; [택지·대지] a lot ; realty 《영》 ; real estate 《미》 ; [소유지] landed property ; estate ¶ 100 평의 땅 a lot of 100 *pyong* // 땅에 투자하다 invest in realty 《영》 ; invest in real estate 《미》 // 그는 경상도 일대에 큰 땅을 많이 가졌다 He has many big estates around the *Kyungsangdo* provinces.
④ [흙] soil ; land ¶ 메마른 땅 poor〔barren〕 soil // 땅을 일구다 till〔cultivate〕 the soil〔land, ground〕 // 땅을 걸우다 enrich〔fertilize〕 the soil
땅[2] [총소리 따위] bang ; with a bang ¶ 땅 하고 총알이 나갔다 "Bang!" went the gun. /The gun went with a bang.
땅가뢰 〖곤충〗 a blister beetle
땅가물 a drought ; dry weather
땅강아지 〖곤충〗 a mole cricket
땅거미[1] 〖동물〗 a ground spider
***땅거미**[2] dusk ; twilight ; crepuscule ¶ 땅거미 진 twilight ; crepuscular // 땅거미가 질 때 at dusk ; in the gathering darkness ; when the evening closes in // 땅거미가 진다 Dusk falls. /The dusk gathers.
땅광 a cellar ; an underground storeroom ; a go-down
땅굴 —窟 a tunnel ; an underground way〔passage〕 ¶ 북한이 비무장 지대에 몰래 파놓은 땅굴 a tunnel the North Korean infiltrators have secretly dug under the Demilitarized Zone〔DMZ〕
땅그네 a swing
땅기다 have a convulsive fit ; be cramped ; have a cramp〔stitch〕 《in one's side》
땅꽈리 〖식물〗 a ground cherry
땅꾼 a snake-catcher
땅내 the smell of dirt ; smelling of the ground ¶ 땅내 맡다 [동물이] settle down in a place ; [식물이] take root

땅덩이 the earth (지구) ; a territory (지역) ¶ 미국은 땅덩이가 크다 America has a large territory.
땅딸막하다 (be) short and fat ; stocky ; thickset ; dumpy ; pudgy ; stodgy ; chunky ; squabby ; stumpy
땅딸보 a dumpy (person) ; a stocky man ; a chunky fellow
땅땅 bang-bang (총소리) ; clang-clang (쇠붙이소리)
땅땅거리다 ① [큰소리] talk big〔tall〕; brag ; swagger ; boast ; be a big talker ¶ 대학에 들어갈 자신이 있다고 땅땅거리고 있다 He is bragging that he is confident to pass the college entrance exam.
② [호화롭게] live in grand〔extravagant〕 style ¶ 땅땅거리며 살다 live in great splendor ; live in luxury ; live on the fat of the land
땅뙈기 a small plot of field〔rice paddy〕
땅띔 lifting 《a thing heavy》 off the ground ¶ 땅띔 못하다 cannot lift〔get〕 《a thing》 off the ground ; [모르다] cannot understand at all ; cannot do at all (못하다)
땅마지기 a few acres of field
땅바닥 the (bare) ground ¶ 땅바닥에 주저앉다 sit〔squat〕 on the (bare) ground
땅버들 〖식물〗 a sallow ; a goat-willow
땅버섯 〖식물〗 a mushroom
땅벌 〖곤충〗 a digger wasp ; a sphex ; Sphex umbrous (학명)
땅벌레 a grub ; the larva of a ground beetle
땅볼 〖야구〗 a grounder ; a bounder ¶ 땅볼을 잡다 field〔take〕 a grounder // 땅볼 안타를 치다 hit into the dirt
땅비싸리 〖식물〗 a kind of indigo plant
땅빈대 〖식물〗 a spurge ; a euphorbia
땅세 一稅 land rent
땅울림 earth tremor ; a rumbling of the earth ¶ 땅울림이 난다 The ground rumbles.
땅임자 a landowner ; a landlord
땅재주 tumbling ; acrobatic feat〔performance〕 ¶ 땅재주를 넘다 give acrobatic feat ; tumble ; somersault
***땅콩** a groundnut ; a monkey-nut 《영》 ; a peanut 《미》
땅파기 a fool ; an idiot ; a dunce
땅파다 dig the soil ; dig into the ground ¶ 땅파먹다 do farm〔mine〕 work for a living ; make one's living off the soil (as a farmer)〔out of the ground (as a miner)〕; dig (dirt) for a living
땅풍뎅이 〖곤충〗 a kind of ground beetle ; Anomala rufocuprea (학명)
***땋다** braid 《one's hair》 ; plait ¶ 머리를 땋다 wear one's hair in braids
†**때**¹ ① [시간] time ; hour ; [익살] Father time (시간의 신) ¶ 점심때 lunch time // 때를 정해서 [정시에] at fixed time ; [일정한 사이를 두고] at regular intervals // 때를 놓치지 않고 immediately ; at once // 때를 어기지 않고 punctually ; on time 《미》 // 때를 가리지 않고 at all times // 때를 같이해서 at the same time // 때가 지나다 time passes // 때가 지나는 것도 잊다 lose count of time ; be unconscious of the passage of time
② [그때·당시] the time ¶ …할 때 when (접속사) ; […하는 동안] while // 어릴 때부터 since childhood ; from the time when I was a child // 화재가 났을 때 at the time of the fire // 내가 파리에 있을 때 when〔while〕 I was in Paris // 바로 이 때 at this moment ; at this juncture // 나는 그 때 워싱턴에 있었다 I was in Washington at that time. // 멀지않아 나라가 통일되고 평화롭게 살 때가 올 것이다 The time will come soon when we shall live peacefully in the unified fatherland.
③ [시기·기회·경우] time ; occasion ; case ; season ; opportunity ¶ 언제 좋은 때를 보아서 at a favorable opportunity // 어떤 때는 sometimes ; occasionally // 때에 따라서는 as the occasion demands // 마침 좋은 때에 just at the right time ; in good time ; in the nick of time // 불이 났을〔내가 없을〕때에 in case of fire〔my absence〕 // 때에 맞는 timely ; well-timed ; opportune // 때에 맞지 않는 untimely ; inopportune ; illtimed // 때 아닌 unseasonable ; out of season // 때 아닌 더위 unseasonable heat // 때를 만나다 have a favorable opportunity ; have one's day // 때를 놓치다 miss an opportunity〔a chance〕 // 때를 기다리다 wait for an opportunity ; bide one's time // 졸업식 때가 됐다 The time〔season〕 has come for graduation. // 탁상 공론을 벌일 때가 아니다 This is no time for vain discussion. // 지금이야말로 일어설 때다 Now is the time for us to rise up. // 모든 것이 다 때가 있는 법이다 There is a time for everything.
④ [시대·당시] an age ; a period ¶ 그때의 of the time ; then ; of the day // 그때의 수상 the then Premier // 때를 같이 한 인물들 contemporary figures
⑤ [끼니] a meal ¶ 때를 거르다 go without a meal // 간신히 때를 잇다 eke out a scanty livelihood〔poor existence〕
***때**² ① [더러움] dirt ; filth ; grime ; [오점·얼룩] a stain ; a spot ; a blot ¶ 때투성이의 dirty ; filthy ; begrimed // 때를 벗은 refined ; elegant ; chic 《프》 ; smart ; polished ; [취미가] in good taste ; [도시풍의] urban // 때를 못 벗은 unpolished ; unrefined ; raw ; uncouth ; countrified // 때가 묻다 become dirty ; become filthy〔soiled〕 // 때를 씻다 wash oneself // 때를 빼다 clean 《a thing》 of a blot〔an ink〕 ; remove stain 《from the coat》 ; [문질러서] rub〔scrape〕 off dirt // 식모가 아직 때를 벗지 못했다 The maid hasn't got the hayseed out of her hair.
② [인색] meanness ; stinginess ¶ 하는

짓이 때가 묻었다 There is something mean in what he does.
③ [오명] a false charge ; a slur ; a blot ; disgrace ; dishonor ¶ 때를 벗다 clear oneself of a false charge

때가다 be taken up ; be taken to ((the police station)) ; be caught ; be arrested ; get〔be〕 nabbed ; be rounded up ((구)) ¶ 경찰에 때가다 be taken〔walked off〕 to the police station ; be taken up by the police

때그락- ⇨ 대그락-

때깔 the color and charm ((of cloth)) ; the colorful pattern ((of cloth))

때꼽재기 bits of dirt〔filth, grime〕

때다[1] [배척당하다] be rejected ; be ostracized ; be boycotted ; be left out ((in the cold))

때다[2] [잡히다] be caught ; be arrested ; be rounded up ; be taken〔walked〕 off ((to the police station))

때다[3] [불을] make〔build〕 a fire ; burn ; kindle ; heat with a fire ¶ 아궁이에 불을 때다 make a fire in the kitchen ; light the kitchen fire // 방에 불을 때다 heat a (hypocausted) room // 땔 것이 없다 We have nothing to make a fire with.

때다[4] ⇨ 때우다

†**때때로** occasionally ; now and then ; sometimes ; at times ; from time to time ; once in a while ; off and on ¶ 때때로 오다 come occasionally ; come now and then // 때때로 방문하다 call on ((a person)) from time to time

때때옷 a colorful dress for children

때때중 a young Buddhist monk

때려눕히다 knock〔batter〕 ((a person)) down ; floor ((a person)) (with a fist) ; beat〔strike〕 down

*__때려부수다__ ① [두드려 부수다] smash up 〔in, down〕 ; shatter ; break〔tear〕 down ② [비유적] give a crushing defeat ; put down

때려죽이다 knock〔strike, beat〕 ((a person)) to death

때려치우다 give〔throw〕 up ; quit ; abandon

†**때로(는)** according to circumstance ; on occasion ; sometimes

†**때리다** ① [치다] strike ((a person)) ; hit ; give a blow ; thrash ; beat ; knock 〔rap〕 ((at, on)) ; slug ; slap ; flog ; whip ; smack ; smit ; wallop ; whack ; pound〔batter〕 ; [가볍게] tap ((at, on))

> [참고] **beat** 가장 일반적인 말이며 계속해서 때리다 **hit** 강력하게 일격으로 때리다 **pound** 주먹이나 해머로 계속해서 때리다 **pommel** 주먹으로 난타하다 **thrash** 몽둥이를 휘둘러 강타하다 **flog** 와 **whip**은 벌로서 때리는 것 **strike** 손이나 손에 든 것으로 강하게 때리다

¶ 때려 눕히다 knock ((a person)) down ; beat ((a person)) to pulp ; strike down // 때려 부수다 knock ((a thing)) to pieces ; smash ((a thing)) up // 때려 죽이다 strike ((a person)) dead〔to death〕 // 호되게 때리다 give ((a person)) a sound thrashing ; strike ((a person)) a sound thrashing ; strike ((a person)) hard // 지팡이로 때리다 strike〔hit〕 ((a person)) with a stick // 얼굴〔머리〕을 때리다 beat ((a person)) in the face〔on the head〕 // 빰을 때리다 slap ((a person's)) face
② [비난·공격] attack ; charge ; denounce ¶ 신문에서 때리다 attack 〔pound, traduce〕 ((a person)) in the press // 그는 어제 나를 때리는 말을 여러 사람에게 하였다 He publicly denounced me yesterday.

때마침 just at the right time ; at the right moment ; in the (very) nick of time ; in good time ; just in time〔season〕 ; timely ; seasonably ; opportunely ; fortunately ; luckily ; as good luck would have it ¶ 때마침 택시가 지나가서 다행이다 What a break! Here's a taxi just when we needed it.

때맞다 (be) timely ; well-timed ; seasonable ; opportune ¶ 때맞은 바람 a timely wind // 때맞은 말 a seasonable〔an opportune〕 remark

†**때문** ground ; reason ; because (of) ¶ 때문에 on account of ; because of ; owing to ; due to ; by reason of ; through ; in view of ; for ; from ; by ; with ; thanks to (덕분에) // 그 때문에 on this account // 부주의 때문에 because of〔through〕 carelessness // 전쟁 때문에 owing to the war ; as a result of the war (결과로) // 부지런 때문에 due to one's hard work // 날씨가 좋았기 때문에 thanks to good weather // …때문이다 be due〔owing, attributable〕 to ; attribute ((a matter)) to // 무엇 때문에 나를 욕하는가 Why do you slander me ? // 신병 때문에 못 갔다 I couldn't go on account of my illness. // 그는 술 때문에 말썽을 일으켰다 He got into trouble through drink. // 그것 때문에 출발이 늦었다 The consequence was that my departure was delayed.

⁑**때묻다** [더러워지다] get dirty〔soiled, stained〕 ; [인색하다] (be) stingy ; mean ; dirty-minded

때물 unrefinedness ; rusticity ; boorishness ; dirt ¶ 때물 벗은 식모 a servant girl free from vulgarity // 때물을 벗다 be refined〔urbane, smart, polished〕 ; be free from boorishness

*__때아닌__ untimely ; unseasonable ; inopportune ¶ 때아닌 꽃 [핌] unseasonable flowering ; [꽃] a blossom out of season

때없이 at any time ; regardless of the time ; "just any old time" ; irregularly ; at irregular intervals ¶ 때없이 밥을

달라 하다 ask for food at any time
때우다 ① [깨어진 곳을] solder (up) ; braze ; tinker (up) ¶ 솥을 때우다 solder〔braze〕a pot
② [깁다] patch (up) 《the trousers》; darn 《stokings》; put〔add〕a patch on 《a coat》; sew (in) a patch
③ [끼니를] substitute ¶ 식빵 하나로 점심을 때우다 substitute a loaf of bread for regular lunch // 이들 피해자들은 그들의 전통 음식인 밥 대신 라면으로 끼니를 때우고 있다 These victims make do with instant noodles instead of their traditional rice.
때움질 ⇨ 땜질
때죽나무 〖식물〗 a snowbell
때찔레 〖식물〗 a sweet brier ; Rosa eglanteria (학명)
땔감 fuel ; firewood (장작)
땔나무 [장작] firewood ; [섶] brushwood ¶ 땔나무를 하다 gather firewood
땜[1] soldering
땜[2] [액운의] an escape 《from》 **—하다** forestall 《a disaster》 with a lesser sacrifice
땜납 solder ; pewter ¶ 땜납으로 붙이다 solder
땜인두 a soldering iron
땜일 soldering ; tinkering
*__땜쟁이__ a tinker
땜질 soldering ; brazing ; patching 《the trousers》; [수선] tinkering ; repairing ; mending **—하다** solder ; tinker ; repair ; patch up ; mend ¶ 이 쇠주전자의 금간 데를 땜질해 주시오 Please solder the cracked spot of this iron pot./ Please mend this iron pot.
땟국 dirt ; filth ; grime ¶ 얼굴에 땟국이 끼다 have dirt on one's face
땟물 ① [자태] figure ; shape ; appearance ¶ 땟물이 훤하다 be handsome ② [씻어낸] dirty water ; washings
땟솔 a bath brush ; a scrub brush
땡[1] ① [땡땡구리] a card-matching game
② [행운] a lucky break falling with a windfall ; meeting with an unexpected good fortune ; having a stroke of good luck
⁑**땡**[2] [소리] with a clang
땡감 an unripe and puckery〔astringent〕persimmon
땡강- ⇨ 댕그랑-
땡땡이 a paper tambourine with beads inside ; a kind of rattle
땡땡이중 a mendicant priest who goes around hitting a gong
땡잡다 hit the jackpot ; make a lucky〔big〕hit ; strike oil〔a bonanza〕; make a killing 《구》; [장사에서] make a good deal ; [투기] strike it rich ¶ 그는 그 사업에 투자하여 땡잡았다 He had invested in the business and made a killing.
땡추절 a temple controlled by unworthy priests
땡추중 a priest only in name ; an unworthy priest
떠가다 float away
떠꺼머리처녀 —**處女** an old maid with a pigtail
떠꺼머리총각 —**總角** an old bachelor with a pigtail
†**떠나다** ① [출발] start ; leave ; depart ; set out〔off〕; set forth〔forward〕; go off to ; (set) sail (배가) ¶ 미국으로 떠나다 leave〔depart, sail〕for America // 한국을 떠나다 leave〔depart from, sail from〕Korea // 여행을 떠나다 start on a journey // 나는 도쿄를 향해 부산을 떠났다 I left *Pusan* for Tokyo.
② [관계를 끊다] break off〔with〕; part from ; cut off ; leave ; be estranged ; be away 《from》 ¶ 그는 관계를 떠났다 He left his official life./He quitted his office. // 그 생각이 머리에서 떠나지 않는다 The idea haunts my mind. // 차마 떠나올 수가 없었다 I could not tear myself away.
③ [세상을] die ; depart (from this life) ; pass away ¶ 불쌍한 김노인은 마침내 세상을 떠났다 Poor old *Kim* has departed at last.
떠내다 scoop (out) ; dip ¶ 그물로 떠내다 scoop 《fish》 with a net // 국자로 국을 떠내다 ladle〔scoop up〕soup
떠내려가다 be washed〔swept, carried, borne〕away ; drift away〔down〕; be driven (바람에)
떠다니다 [공중으로] float in the sky ; hang in the air ; [물 위로] drift ; be adrift ; [방랑하다] wander about ; roam ¶ 이틀 간이나 물결 가는 데로 떠다녔다 We dirfted about at the mercy of the waves〔were tossed about by the waves〕for two days. // 하늘에는 구름이 떠다니고 있다 Clouds are floating in the sky.
떠다밀다 ① [손으로] thrust〔shove〕aside〔away〕¶ 사람을 떠다밀다 push people aside // 떠다밀고 들어가다 break into // 그는 사람들을 떠다밀고 지나갔다 He elbowed his way through a crowd.
② [남에게] put 《the blame》 on another ; shift 《the blame》 on someone else ; lay 《a fault》 at another's door
떠대다 untruthfully reply with
⁑**떠돌다** ① [소문이] get about〔abroad〕¶ 내각 개편의 소문이 떠돌고 있다 Rumor has it that there will be a change in the Cabinet.
② [물 위에] drift about ; be adrift ; float ¶ 그 선박은 9일 동안 물결을 따라 이리저리 떠돌았다 The vessel was tossed about in the waves for nine days.
③ [방랑] wander (about) ; roam ; knock about 《the country》
떠돌이 a wanderer ; a vagabond ; a waif ; hobo 《*pl.* ~s, ~es》 《미》
— 고아 a rootless little orphan **— 노동**

자 a wandering laborer — 생활 a wandering life

떠둥그뜨리다 lift up a corner of an object and bring〔throw, push〕 it down〔away〕

*떠들다¹ ① [큰 소리로] make a noise ; be noisy ; make a fuss ; make an outcry ; [술렁거리다] clamor ; kick up a row ; raise a dust ; make a disturbance ¶ 교실에서 떠들지 마시오 Please don't make a disturbance in the classroom. // 쓸데 없는 일로 떠들지 마시오 Don't make a fuss about nothing! // 이것은 신문에서 떠들었던 문제입니다 This matter was noised about in the newspaper. // 그들은 그가 사직해야 한다고 떠들고 있다 They are clamoring for his withdrawal. // 너는 정말 잘 떠드는구나 You're a real life-of-the-party type of guy.
② [소문이 나다] be rumored ; be gossiped about ; create a public sensation

떠들다² lift〔raise〕 the corner of 《an object》; lift〔take off, undo〕 《the lid》; jack up ¶ 뚜껑을 떠들고 한 숟가락의 설탕을 넣었다 I lifted the lid and put a spoonful of sugar.

떠들썩하다¹ 《a corner》 be lifted up ; be raised ¶ 이불귀가 떠들썩하기에 들여다 보니 고양이란 놈이 자고 있었다 Wondering why the end of the quilt was raised, I peeked in and found a cat sleeping under it.

⁑떠들썩하다² ① [시끄럽다] (be) noisy ; boisterous ; [왁자하다] uproarious ; clamorous ; turbulent ; tumultuous ¶ 떠들썩하게 noisily ; boisterously ; uproariously ; clamorously // 떠들썩하게 하다 make a noise〔racket〕 // 세상이 떠들썩하다 Times are troublous. // 임금 인상 문제로 세론이 떠들썩하다 The people are clamorous for better pay.
② [소문이] 《a rumor》 (be) abroad ; be noised about ¶ 그가 면직당했다는 소문이 떠들썩하다 The rumor is that he has been fired.

떠들어대다 make a terrible noise〔an uproar, a disturbance〕 ¶ 쓸데 없는 일로 떠들어대다 make much ado about nothing

떠들치다 ① [비밀을] reveal ; disclose ; divulge ; expose ¶ 비밀을 떠들치다 divulge〔let out〕 a secret // 그는 돈을 받고 자기 나라의 비밀을 떠들치었다 He disclosed the secret of his country to the man for money.
② [물건을] lift up 《one side of a stone》

떠름하다 ① [맛이] (be) astringent ; puckery ¶ 이 감 맛은 떠름하다 These persimmons are astringent.
② [내키지 않다] be indisposed to ; (be) reluctant ; be unwilling to ¶ 나는 어쩐지 마음이 떠름하여 춤을 거절했다 I didn't feel like dancing and rejected it.
③ [꺼림하다] feel uneasy ; feel uncomfortable 《about》

떠맡기다 leave 《a matter》 to others ; saddle 《a thing》 upon 《a person》; impose 《a matter》 on others ¶ 빚을 남에게 떠맡기다 saddle one's debts upon another // 그는 그 비용을 나에게 떠맡겼다 He charged the expense to me.

떠맡다 be saddled with ; be charged with 《a duty》; hold oneself responsible for ; take 《a matter》 in one's hands ; take 《a task》 upon oneself ; take over 《another's business》 ¶ 부채를 떠맡다 hold oneself liable for a debt ; shouder another's debt // 내가 그 일을 떠맡았다 I took the affair into my own hands. // 누구든지 이 일을 떠맡아 주면 좋겠는데 I wish someone would take the work off my hands.

떠메다 lift 《a thing》 up and shoulder it

떠밀다 ⇨ 떼밀다

떠받다 [머리나 뿔로] butt ¶ 소가 아무를 떠받는다 A bull butts a person. // 대가리로 아무를 떠받다 butt a person with one's head // 책상을 떠받다 hit one's head against a desk

떠받들다 ① [쳐들다] lift (up) ; raise (high up) ; heave ; hold (up high) ¶ 그는 그 돌을 한 손으로 떠받들었다 He lifted the stone with one hand.
② [공경] serve faithfully ; take good care of ; have a (high) regard of ¶ 남편을 떠받들다 take good care of one's husband ; be devoted to one's husband
③ [소중히 다루다] think〔make〕 much of ; hold 《a person》 dear

⁑떠받치다 support ; bolster ; prop〔shore〕 up ¶ 벽을 기둥으로 떠받치다 support a wall with a post // 지붕을 떠받치다 give support to a roof

떠버리 a prattler ; a chatterbox (아녀자) ; a braggart ; a gasbag ; a rattler ¶ 그는 떠버리다 He has a big mouth.

떠벌리다 ① [과장] brag ; exaggerate ; talk big ; draw a long bow ¶ 소문을 떠벌리다 exaggerate a rumor
② [규모를] set 《it》 up on a large scale〔big way〕 ¶ 사건을 떠벌려 놓다 make too much of the matter ; carry the matter to a foolish extent

떠보다 ① [무게를] weigh ; check the weight
② [사람됨을] measure ; size up the caliber of a person ¶ 사람됨을 외모로 떠보기란 불가능하다 A man's character cannot be measured by his appearance.
③ [속뜻을] sound ; fathom ¶ 남의 의향을 떠보다 sound (out) 《a person》〔another's view〕; fathom another's thoughts ; tap 《a person's》 opinion // 그가 도와줄지 어떨지 떠보겠다 I'll sound him as to whether he will help us.

떠세 —하다 make use of another's influence ; shelter oneself under another's influence

†**떠오르다** ① [해·달이] rise (up) ; be up ② [생각이] come〔flit, flash, shoot〕 across one's mind ; occur to 《a person》 ; hit 《a person》 ; burst upon 《a person》 ¶ 그 일이 곧 떠올랐다 It flashed through 〔on, across〕 my mind. // 좋은 생각이 머리에 떠올랐다 A capital idea suggested itself to me〔burst upon me〕. /I hit upon an excellent plan.
③ [물위에] rise〔come up〕 to the surface ; surface (잠수함 따위가) ; refloat ¶ 나무 토막이 물위에 떠오르다 a block of wood pops up out of the water

떠죽거리다 ① [젠 체하고] boast ; talk big ② [거짓 사양] pretend to decline in a flowery way

떠죽떠죽 boastfully

떠지껄하다 be noisy ; vociferous ; boisterous ; clamorous ¶ 바깥쪽이 떠지껄하다 There is a commotion outside. /It is noisy outside.

*****떡**¹ ① [먹는] rice cake ¶ 가래떡 bar rice cake // 구운 떡 roast〔toasted〕 rice cake // 쑥떡 rice cake seasoned with mugwort // 갓 빚은 떡 rice cake fresh from the dresser // 그림의 떡 (a) pie in the sky // 떡해 먹을 집안 a troubled〔trouble-ridden〕 family // 떡을 치다 pound steamed rice into cake ; pound rice for cake ; make rice-cake
② [아주 쉬운 것] an easy task〔job〕 ; a piece of cake 《구》 ¶ 그것은 누워서 떡 먹기다 It's〔That's〕 nothing. /It is a cinch.
떡줄 사람은 아무 말도 없는데 김칫국부터 마시지 마라 속담 Catch the bear before you sell his skin. /Don't spread the cloth till the pot begins to boil. / Make not your sauce, before you have caught the fish.

떡² ① [버티는 꼴] firmly ② [벌리는 꼴] wide (open) ⇨ 딱

떡가래 a piece of rice cake

떡가루 rice flour (for making rice cakes) ¶ 떡가루를 빻다 pound rice into flour // 떡가루를 찌다 steam rice flour // 떡가루를 반죽하다 knead dough

떡갈나무 〖식물〗 an overcup oak ; Quercus dentata (학명)

떡고물 covering or coating for rice cake

떡국 rice-cake soup (prepared with slices of rice cake, beef, eggs, etc.) ¶ 떡국점 rice-cake slices (to put in soup)

떡무거리 rough rice flour sieved out as unsuitable for making rice cakes

떡방아 a rice-flour mill ¶ 떡방아를 찧다 make rice flour ; pound rice into flour
떡방아 소리듣고 김칫국 찾는다 속담 Don't spread the cloth till the pot begins to boil. /Make not your sauce, before you have caught the fish.

떡벌어지다 ① [퍼지다] be side open ¶ 어깨가 떡벌어지다 be square-〔broad-〕 shouldered ; have broad shoulders ② [소문이] 《the rumor》 get abroad ; be in the everybody's mouth ③ [잔치가] 《a banquet》 be given〔held, thrown〕

떡볶이 a broiled dish of sliced rice cake, meat, eggs, seasoning, etc.

떡산적 —散炙 spit-roasted〔skewered〕 rice cake

떡살 a wooden rice-cake pattern

떡소 stuffing (for rice cakes)

떡심 [고기의] tendons and tough parts of beef ; [근력] muscular strength ; [억센 사람] a tough〔brawny〕 person ; a man of mighty sinews

떡쑥 〖식물〗 a cottonweed ; a cudweed

떡잎 a seed leaf ; a cotyledon ; a sprout
될성부른 나무는 떡잎부터 알아본다 속담 Genius displays itself even in the childhood.

떡치다 pound steamed rice into cake ; [성교] have sex 《with》

떡판 a pounding board for making rice cakes ; [엉덩이] a woman's buttocks

떡팥 boiled redbeans to be used in stuffing rice cake

떨거둥이 a person left out in the cold ; [사회의] an〔a social〕 outcast ; [추방자] a purgee

떨거지 one's relatives

떨기 [한 송이] a bunch ; a cluster ; [한 뿌리] a root ; a plant ¶ 한 떨기 꽃 a bunch of flowers // 국화 나무 한 떨기 one chrysanthemum plant

†**떨다**¹ [몸을] tremble ; quiver ; quake ; shake ; shiver ; [전율] shudder ; thrill ; [현악기의 줄이] vibrate ¶ 추워서 떨다 shiver with〔from〕 (the) cold ; quiver from (the) cold // 무서워서 떨다 tremble for fear ; shudder at 《the sight》 ; shiver with fright // 사지를 떨다 tremble in every limb // 니코틴 중독으로 손을 떨다 one's hands tremble from oversmoking〔tobacco-poisoning〕 // 입술을 떨다 one's lips quiver

떨다² ① [먼지 따위] sweep〔brush〕 off 《dust》 ¶ 먼지를 떨다 clear dust away ② [덜어내다] take off〔away〕 ; deduct ¶ 세금을 떨고 95,000원의 수입 an income of 95,000 *won* after tax reduction // 봉급에서 떨다 deduct 《a sum》 from one's salary // 그 비용은 내 월급에서 떨렸다 The cost was taken away 〔deducted〕 from my pay.
③ [죄다 팔다] sell off〔out〕 ; dispose of ; clear out〔off〕 ; get out of stocks ; close out 《a stock of shoes》 ; [죄다 사다] buy up ; have a clearance sale
④ [부리다] act ; do ¶ 애교를 떨다 sprinkle compliment ; be all smiles (to everybody) ; do the pretty (아가씨 따위가) // 극성을 떨다 get upset〔mad〕
⑤ [주머니나 돈을] empty ¶ 주머니를 떨다 empty one's purse // 가산을 떨다 squander one's fortune

떨떠름하다 ① [맛이] (be) astringent ; puckery
② [내키지 않다] (be) indisposed ; uninterested ; reluctant ; unwilling ; disinclined
③ [꺼림칙하다] (be) uneasy ; concerned ; anxious ; [서술적] weigh on one's mind ; lie at one's heart

떨떨하다 ① [천하다] (be) mean ; shabby ; humble ; wretched ; indecent ¶ 떨떨한 사내 a good-for-nothing fellow ② [내키지 않다] (be) disinclined ; leery 〔wary〕; don't feel like doing ; feel uneasy at doing ¶ 그 음식 먹기가 떨떨하다 I don't feel like eating the food.
③ [덜익다] (be) unripe ; immature ; green

떨뜨리다 act haughty ; give oneself airs ; hold one's head high ; stand upon one's dignity

†**떨리다**[1] [몸이] tremble ; quiver ; shiver ; quake ; shake ¶ 다리가 떨리다 one's legs tremble (under one) // 이가 떨리다 one's teeth chatter // 말소리가 떨렸다 His voice trembled as he spoke.

떨리다[2] ① [먼지 따위가] be swept 〔brushed〕 off ; 《the dust》 come〔fall〕 off
② [떨려서 빠져 나오다] be rejected 〔plucked, excluded, eliminated, left out, skipped over〕 ¶ 일등품으로서는 떨리었다 The goods were rejected as firsts. // 20명 이상의 지원자가 시험에서 떨리었다 More than 20 candidates were rejected in the examination.

떨새 a bird-shaped silver ornament on a woman's (ceremonial) headgear

떨어내다 shake off ; beat off〔out of〕 ¶ 담요에서 먼지를 떨어내다 beat dust out of a blanket // 나뭇가지에서 죽은 나뭇잎을 떨어내다 shake dead leaves off the branches of a tree

*****떨어뜨리다** ① [낙하] drop ; let fall ; throw down ¶ 컵을 마루에 떨어뜨리다 drop a glass〔let a glass fall〕 to the floor // 폭탄을 떨어뜨리다 drop bombs 《on》 // 비행기를 떨어뜨리다 shoot down an airplane
② [놓치다] miss ¶ 공을 떨어뜨리다 miss a ball ; fail to catch a ball ; 〚야구〛 fumble 《a grounder》 ; muff
③ [잃다] lose ; drop ¶ 지갑을 떨어뜨리다 lose one's purse // 인기〔명성, 신용〕를 떨어뜨리다 lose one's popularity 〔reputation, credit〕
④ [함락] take ; capture ; reduce ; carry ¶ 적의 요새를 떨어뜨리다 reduce an enemy's fort // 진지를 떨어뜨리다 capture a position
⑤ [지위를] debase ; abase ; degrade ; reduce ; lower ¶ 직위를 떨어뜨리다 reduce 《an officer》 to lower grade
⑥ [실추] depreciate ; detract 《from one's merit》 ; take from 《the value》 ¶ 품격을 떨어뜨리다 demean oneself ; lose dignity // 물건의 가치를 떨어뜨리다 detract 〔take〕 something from the value // 위신을 떨어뜨리다 lose one's prestige // 행복한 환경이 오히려 그의 성공의 가치를 떨어뜨리고 있다 His fortunate circumstances attenuate〔lessen〕 the merit of his achievement.
⑦ [낮추다] lessen ; decrease ¶ 속력을 떨어뜨리다 slow down〔up〕 《a car》
⑧ [품질을] make worse ; deteriorate ; debase ¶ 품질을 떨어뜨리다 lower in quality ; deteriorate
⑨ [남기다] leave behind ¶ 미국의 관광객이 떨어뜨리고 가는 돈 the dollars 〔money〕 left behind〔spent〕 by the American tourists
⑩ [경매에서] knock down 《an article》 (in price at an auction)
⑪ [경쟁자를] outstrip ; outrun ; cast 《one's rival》 behind ; push ahead ; get ahead of 《one's comrades》 ; outsail 《another ship》 ¶ 결승점에서 그를 떨어 뜨렸다 I outstripped him near the goal.
⑫ [시험에서] fail 《a student》 ¶ 학생을 시험에서 떨어뜨리다 fail a student in an examination
⑬ [해뜨리다] wear out ¶ 옷을 떨어뜨리다 wear out one's clothes
⑭ [구두의 뒤축을] have the heels of one's shoes worn down ; have one's shoes down at the heels
⑮ [뒤가 딸리게 하다] exhaust ; run out ; use up ; run through 《one's money》 ; run short〔low〕 ¶ 쌀을 떨어뜨리다 use the rice up ; run out of rice ; run short of rice

떨어먹다 squander ; go〔run〕 through 《one's fortune》 ; spend all 《one's money》 ; drain 《the resources》 ; spend the last cent ; eat up ¶ 친구의 돈을 떨어먹다 empty a friend's purse // 소지금은 다 떨어먹었다 I have spent my last penny.

†**떨어지다** ① [낙하·추락] fall ; drop ; get 〔have〕 a fall ; come〔go〕 down ; be down ; crash (비행기 따위가) ¶ 나무에서 떨어지다 fall〔drop〕 from a tree // 계단에서 떨어지다 fall down〔off〕 the stairs // 배에서 떨어지다 fall overboard // 말에서 떨어지다 fall from the horse // 접시가 상에서 떨어져서 깨어졌다 The dish fell off the table and was broken. // 우리아들이 계단에서 떨어져 의식 불명이다 My son is unconscious after falling down the stairs.
② [빗방울 따위가] drop ; come down ; drip ¶ 처마에서 빗방울이 떨어진다 Water drops from the eaves.
③ [해나 달이 지다] set ; sink ; go down ¶ 해는 서산에 떨어졌다 The sun has sunk behind the western mountains.
④ [낙제·낙선] fail〔get plucked〕 《in the exam》 ; lose〔fail〕 《in an election》
⑤ [흘러서 빠지다] slip ; drop ¶ 연필이

손에서 떨어지다 a pencil falls out of 〔drops from〕 one's hand
⑥ [붙었던 것이] come off ; come out ; be broken off ; be removed ¶ 잎이 떨어지다 leaves are shed // 겨울이 되면 대부분의 나무는 잎이 떨어진다 In winter most trees are stripped of their leaves.
⑦ [분리] separate ; be detached ; come off ; fall apart ; become disjoined ¶ 떨어지기 쉬운 separable ; severable // 떨어질 수 없는 inseparable // 책상 다리가 떨어지다 a leg of the table comes off〔is disjoined〕 // 붙어서 떨어지지 않다 stick 〔adhere, cling〕 to ; stick like a bur // 멀리 떨어져 살다 live far apart // 여러해 동안 떨어져 살다 have been separated 《from a person》 for years // 여자가 사내한테서 떨어지다 a woman is separated from her man // 그 애는 항상 어머니의 곁을 떨어지지 않는다 The child is always hanging on her mother's sleeve〔is always at her mother's side〕. // 두 사람은 떨어질 수 없는 사이다 They are inseparable from each other.
⑧ [온도나 열이] fall ; drop ; go down ¶ 온도가 떨어지다 the temperature falls〔drops, goes down〕 // 열이 떨어지다 the fever abates // 서울에서는 수은주가 영하 15도까지 떨어진다 The mercury dips as low as 15 degrees below zero in Seoul.
⑨ [물가가] fall ; drop ; go down ; decline ; sag ; depreciate ¶ 물가가 떨어졌다 Prices have gone down. // 견직물의 값이 떨어졌다 Silk goods have sunken in price. // 시세가 떨어져가고 있다 The market price is on the decline〔goes on declining〕.
⑩ [실추] fall in value〔merit〕 ; depreciate ; be debased ; be impaired ; be detracted ; [쇠퇴] go down ; fall 《in one's estimation》 ¶ 품격이 떨어지다 lose one's dignity ; debase〔degrade〕 oneself // 위신이 떨어지다 lose one's prestige // 신용이 떨어지다 lose public confidence // 인기가 떨어지다 lose one's popularity ; fall in popularity ; fall into disfavor // 손님이 떨어지다 a shop loses its customers ; the customers drop〔fall off〕
⑪ [손 안에] fall into ; be carried away ¶ 남의 수중에 떨어지다 fall into another's hand ; fall into another's trap 〔snare〕 (책략에) // 그 그림은 경매에서 10만원에 내 손에 떨어졌다 The picture was knocked down to me at an auction for 100,000 *won*.
⑫ [딴 것만 못하다] be inferior 《to》 ; do not come up to ; fall short of ¶ 작년의 수확은 예년에 비해 떨어진다 Last year's harvest fell short of the average. // 이것은 견본에 비해 질이 떨어진다 This does not come up to the sample.
⑬ [함락] fall ; be reduced ; be captured ¶ 그 성은 떨어졌다 The castle was seized 《by the enemy》.
⑭ [남아 있다] be left over 《behind》 ; remain ¶ 홀로 집에 떨어져 있다 be left behind alone in the house ; remain 〔stay, stop〕 alone at home // 그 빚을 갚아도 상당한 돈이 떨어진다 We have a comfortable little money left over after paying the debt.
⑮ [경쟁에서] be outstripped 《by》 ; be outrun 《by another runner》 ; be backward ; be behindhandfall〔drop〕 behind 《another runner in a race》 ; ¶ 병으로 공부가 떨어지다 be behind in his studies because of an illness // 시험에서 석차가 5등이나 떨어지다 be five places down in class after examination // 내 성적이 떨어져서 엄마는 몹시 화가 났다 My mom's mad because my grades went down.
⑯ [지위·계급이] come down ; sink down ; drop ; [강등] be broken 《to》 ; be degraded 《from》 ; be demoted 《to》 《미》 ¶ 하급으로 떨어지다 sink down to a lower level // 병졸로 떨어지다 be broken to the level of a private
⑰ [해지다] be worn out〔through〕 ; wear threadbare ; become seedy ¶ 떨어진 옷 seedy〔ragged, worn-out, threadbare〕 clothes // 치마가 다 떨어졌다 The skirts are quite worn out.
⑱ [뒤가 딸린다] be out ; be exhausted ; be gone ; be out of stock ; run out ; run short ¶ 쌀이 떨어지다 run out of rice ; rice is exhausted // 돈이 떨어지다 be out of money〔cash〕 ; come to the end of one's money // 휘발유가 떨어져서 as he ran out of gasoline // 담배가 떨어졌다 My tobacco is out. // 연료가 떨어져가고 있다 The fuel supply is low. /We are short of the fuel. // 양식이 떨어졌다 The provisions have given〔run〕 out. /We have run out of provisions. // 쌀이 떨어졌다 We're out of rice. /Rice is out of stock.
⑲ [거리가] be 《a long way》 off ¶ 조금 떨어져서 at a short distance 《from》 // 멀리 떨어져서 at a long distance ; a long way off ; far away 《from》 // 4마일 떨어졌다 be four miles 《from》 // 길에서 조금 떨어진 곳에 큰 소나무가 서 있다 There stands a big pine tree a little way off the road. // 좀 떨어져서 보면 더 좋게 보인다 It looks better at a distance.
⑳ [터지다] be broken ; be punctured ; be torn ¶ 귀청이 떨어지다 puncture an eardrum
㉑ [낙태] abort ; miscarry ¶ 애가 떨어지다 have an abortion〔miscarriage〕
㉒ [명령 따위가] be given ; be issued
㉓ [숨이] ¶ 숨이 떨어지다 breathe one's last ; expire ; die // 숨이 떨어지려는 사람 a person at the point of death〔at death's door, in his last moments〕 ; a dying man

떨어진 주머니에 어패 들었다 (속담) There's many a good cock come out of a tattered bag.

떨어치다 drop ; let fall ⇨ 떨어뜨리다

떨이 goods for clearance〔rummage〕 sale ; remaining articles offered at market-down〔knocked-down, reduced〕 prices ; a bargain ¶ 떨이책 books sold in remainder ; remaindered〔dumped〕 books // 떨이로 팝니다 Surplus stock for sale at a (great) sacrifice.

떨잠 —簪 a kind of ornamental hairpin

떨치다¹ [명성을] make well-known in the world ; [위세를] wield 《power, influence》 ; make one's influence felt ¶ 명성을 천하에 떨치다 make a noise in the world ; win〔enjoy〕 a worldwide reputation ; one's name resounds 〔becomes popular〕 throughout the land 〔all over the world〕 // 위세를 전 세계에 떨치다 wield power all over the world

떨치다² [흔들어] shake ; beat ¶ 소매를 떨치고 자리에서 일어나다 leave one's seat brusquely

떫다 (be) puckery ; astringent ¶ 떫은 감 a puckery persimmon

떰치 a straw mat under a packsaddle

떳떳이 honorably ; in a honorable way ; fairly (and squarely) ; openly ; with a clear conscience ; like a man ¶ 떳떳이 승부를 겨루다 play fair〔on the square〕 ; fight openly and squarely ; play the game 《구》 ; play square // 할 말이 있으면 뒤에서 욕하지 말고 내 앞에서 떳떳이 말해봐라 If you have anything to say, say it out to my face instead of backbiting.

*떳떳하다 (be) fair ; square ; open ; aboveboard ; honorable ; straight ; have a clean conscience ¶ 떳떳한 경기 fair play // 떳떳한 행동 an honorable act // 떳떳하지 못한 짓 shady conduct // 떳떳한 의론 a fair and square argument // 떳떳하게 행동하다 act fair and square ; behave honorably ; play the game 《구》 // 그의 태도는 떳떳하지 못하다 His attitude lacks fairness. // 나는 떳떳하지 못한 짓은 결코 안한다 I never do a shady thing〔anything underhand〕. /My conscience is clear. // 그의 행동은 떳떳하다 His action is open and aboveboard.

떵떵거리다 live in a grand〔an extravagant〕 style ¶ 떵떵거리며 살다 be quite well off ; live off the fat of the land

†떼¹ [무리] a group ; a multitude ; a crowd ; a throng ; [짐승의] a herd (소, 말 따위) ; a flock (양) ; a pack (승냥이, 엽견) ; a pod (해구 따위) ; [새의] a flock ; a bevy (작은 새) ; a drove (비둘기) ; a skein (날고 있는 야생조) ; [고기의] a school ; [벌레의] a swarm ; a cloud (메뚜기 따위) ; [무생물] a cluster 《of stars》 ; a clump ¶ 거지 떼 a group〔crowd, throng〕 of beggars // 파리 떼 a swarm of houseflies // 떼지어 사는 동물 a gregarious animal // 10명 또는 20명씩 떼지어서 in groups of ten to twenty // 떼를 짓다 form groups ; be found in groups // 떼지어 날다 fly in a flock

떼² [잔디] sod ; turf ¶ 떼를 뜨다 cut out sod // 떼를 입히다 sod ; turf

떼³ [뗏목] a raft ¶ 떼를 짜다 make a raft of // 떼로 나르다 carry 《timbers》 on a raft〔float〕

떼⁴ [고집] an impossible〔unreasonable, unjustified〕 demand〔claim, assertion〕 ; an importunate〔an insistent, a persistent〕 demand〔claim, assertion〕 ; keeping after 《a person for a thing》 ; insisting on ¶ (어린이 따위가) 떼(를) 쓰다 tease〔importune, press〕 《a person for a thing》 ; badger 《a person to do》 // 아버님께 떼를 써서 시계를 샀다 I teased my father into buying me a watch. // 그는 그녀를 꼭 만나야겠다고 떼를 썼다 He insisted on seeing her. // 틀린 것을 옳다고 떼를 쓴다 He stands firm in his error.

떼거리 impossible demand

떼거지 ① [떼지어 다니는] beggars going around in a bunch ② [재해로 생긴] a great number of people who have turned beggars owing to a natural calamity ; a nation of beggars

떼걸다 sever〔cut off〕 one's connections 《with》 ; dissociate oneself 《from》

떼과부 —寡婦 a lot of widows ¶ 전쟁으로 떼과부가 생겼다 The war widowed many women. /A great many women were widowed by the war.

*떼다¹ ① [붙은 것을] take off〔away〕 ; remove ; dismantle 《an equipment》 ¶ 미닫이를 떼다 take out〔off〕 a paper sliding-door ; have a paper sliding off its sill
② [갈라지게] draw〔pull, set〕 《a person, things》 apart (잡아당겨서) ; separate ; cut (asunder) ; detach ; keep 《one thing》 from 《another》 ; keep apart ¶ 2미터씩 떼어서 two meters apart ; at intervals of two meters // 사랑하는 사이를 떼다 separate the pair of lovers // 아이의 젖을 떼다 wean a child // 한 줄씩 떼다 leave a space between lines // 친한 사이를 떼다 keep 《them》 apart ; estrange〔alienate〕 《two friends》 // 맞잡고 싸우는 애들을 떼다 pull apart two grappling children // 두 사람은 뗄려야 뗄 수 없는 사이이다 They are bound up each other.
③ [거절하다] refuse ; reject ; decline ¶ 청을 잡아 떼다 refuse a request ; turn down another's request
④ [봉한 것을] break〔open〕 《the seal》 ; cut 《a letter》 open ¶ 함부로 봉을 떼다 tamper with the seal
⑤ [수표 따위를] issue ; tear off 《a chit》 ¶ 수표를 떼다 issue a check
⑥ [관직 따위를] deprive〔strip〕 《a per-

son》 of 《his official rank》
⑦ [끊다] give up ; stop ¶ 술을 떼다 give up drinking // 나쁜 버릇을 떼다 get over a bad habit
⑧ [끝내다] finish up ¶ 독본을 떼다 finish up a textbook // 그녀는 이번에 새로 구입한 신형 컴퓨터도 떼었다 She's already a whig with a new computer she just got.
⑨ [빼다] subtract ; take off〔away〕; deduct ¶ 봉급에서 떼다 deduct 《a sum》 from one's salary // 수입에서 지출을 떼면 다소의 이익이 있다 When earnings and disbursements are balanced, some profit is left.
⑩ [병을] get rid of ; cure ¶ 학질을 떼다 get rid of malaria ; [비유적] get rid of a nuisance
⑪ [낙태시키다] ¶ 아이를 떼다 commit feticide ; have an abortion ; have an (artificial) abortion performed

떼다² [안갚다] abscond with ⇨ 떼어먹다

떼도둑 a gang〔group〕 of robbers ; a pack of thieves

떼도망 —逃亡 fleeing in a band ; collective abscondence ; a group flight **—하다** flee in a band

떼먹다 ⇨ 떼어 먹다

떼몰이 raft driving ; rafting **—하다** drive rafts ; raft

떼밀다 push ; thrust ; shove ; force out of the way ; elbow 《a person》 out (팔꿈치로) ¶ 팔꿈치로 사람들을 떼밀고 지나갔다 I jostled along〔elbowed my way〕 through the crowd. // 떼밀지 마라 Don't push me so much. /Stop shoving.

떼버리다 ① [뜯다] take away ② [거절] refuse ⇨ 떼다

떼새 〖새〗 a plover (물떼새) ; [새의 무리] birds in flock

떼쓰다 ⇨ 떼⁴

†**떼어놓다** ① [경주에서] run ahead 《of others》; draw away 《from a rival》; outdistance ¶ 2등을 5미터나 떼어놓다 be five meters ahead of the second runner〔the runner-up〕
② [붙었던 것을] draw〔pull, set〕 《persons, things》 apart ; separate ; cut (asunder) ¶ 두 애인 사이를 떼어놓다 separate the pair of lovers // 맞붙어 싸우는 두 애를 떼어놓다 pull apart the grappling children

떼어먹다 bilk ; jump 《a bill》; [횡령하다] embezzle ; welch〔welsh〕; abscond with 《the money》 ¶ 외상을 떼어먹다 bilk〔jump〕 a bill // 빚을 떼어먹고 행방을 감추다 bolt without paying one's debt // 여러 요리점의 음식 값을 떼어먹다 victimize several restaurants // 그는 4,000만원을 떼어먹었다 He bilked them out of forty million *won*.

떼이다 be cheated 《of a debt》; be welched〔welshed〕 on ; be bilked ¶ 빚을 떼이다 a debt is dishonored // 공금을 떼이다 public funds are embezzled // 떼인 외상값 a bill left unpaid

떼쟁이 an insistent person ; a person who always makes impossible〔unreasonable, unjustifiable〕 demands 〔claims, assertions〕; a child who is always after 《a person》 for 《a thing》

떼짓다 form〔make up, constitute, be〕 a group

떼치다 ① [달라붙는 것을] shake oneself loose〔free〕 from 《the grasp》; tear oneself away ; push〔thrust, brush〕 aside 〔away〕 (떠밀어서) ¶ 애인을 떼치다 jilt 〔discard〕 one's lover // 치마에 매달리는 아이들을 떼치고 집을 나갔다 She went out of the house thrusting aside her children clung to her skirts.
② [거절하다] refuse〔brush aside〕 《a request》; reject 《a demand》; spurn 《an offer》; repel 《a plea》; repulse 《advice》; turn down 《a proposal》

뗀둥이 a person marked with burns

뗏말 a herd of horses ¶ 뗏말에 망아지 a person who tags along with the group

*__뗏목__ —木 a (log) raft ¶ 뗏목을 짓다 make a raft of log // 뗏목을 지어서 목재를 운반하다 carry timbers on a float

뗏밥 earth given on the turf of a grave for fertilization
뗏밥 주다 관용 scatter〔give〕 earth on the turf of a grave

뗏일 a sodding〔lawning〕 work

뗏장 a piece〔chunk〕 of sod〔turf〕

또 ① [다시] again ; once more ; another time ; for the second time ; repeatedly (반복해서) ; in succession (계속해서) ¶ 승리 또 승리 victory after victory // 또 언제든지 (나중에) some other time ; in another time // 또 일을 시작하다 begin one's work again ; resume one's work ; be back at work // 또 부산에 불이 났다 There was another fire in *Pusan*. // 며칠 사이에 또 들르겠습니다 I will call again one of these days. // 그를 또 만났다 I met him for the second time. // 또 시작이야 You are at it again ! // 또 수고를 끼쳐드려서 죄송합니다 I am sorry to put you to repeated troubles. // (세상에) 저 사람 같은 사람이 또 있을까 Shall we ever see the like of him again ? // 거짓말을 한번 하면 또 하게 된다 One lie leads another.
② [그 위에] and ; moreover ; besides ; further(more) ; what is more ¶ 그는 어학자요 또 음악가이기도 하다 He is both〔at once〕 a linguist and musician. // 비가 오는데 또 바람까지 분다 It is raining and, what is more, the wind is blowing. // 거기다 또 감기까지 걸렸다 What is worse, I have a bad cold.
③ [한편] on the other hand ; in turn ; while ¶ 형은 공부하기를 싫어 하는데 동생은 또 책 읽기를 좋아한다 The elder

brother does not like studying, on the other hand the younger brother is very fond of reading. // 나는 또 누구라구 Well, it's you. (I thought it was somebody else.)

또그르르 rolling ¶ 또그르르 구르다 roll over and over

또깡또깡 clearly ; distinctly ; precisely **—하다** (be) clear ; distinct ; precise

또다시 [한번 더] again ; once more ; over〔once〕 again ; [재차] for the second time ; [새로] afresh ¶ 또다시 일어나다 recur ; renew // 또다시 시작하다 resume ; return to // 또다시 하다 repeat ; do over again // 같은 실수를 또다시 저지르다 repeat the same error // 또다시 박수 갈채가 일어났다 The cheering was renewed.

또닥거리다 tap ; rap ; beat ; knock ; pat ¶ 창문을 또닥거리다 tap against the window // 귀여워서 가볍게 또닥거리다 give it an affectionate little pat // 누가 문을 또닥거리고 있다 Someone is knocking at the door. // 비가 지붕을 또닥거리며 온다 The rain is pattering on the roof.

또닥또닥 tap-tap ; rap-tap-tap ; rat-tat-tat

또드락장이 a goldbeater

또래 (of) the age ; (of) the size ¶ 고 또래 몇이 찾아 왔었다 A group of boys of that age had been here to see me. // 그 또래를 몇개 더 사다 주오 Buy a few more of that size. // 모두 그 또래다 All of them are of the same age〔size〕.

또렷또렷 all vividly〔clearly, distinctly〕 **—하다** (be) all vivid〔clear, distinct〕 ¶ 글씨를 또렷또렷 쓰다 write a clear hand // 옛일이 또렷또렷하게 생각나다 Old memories come vividly to mind.

또렷이 vividly

또렷하다 (be) clear

또바기 without fail (꼭) ; always (한결같이) ; completely (완전히) ¶ 식전에 또바기 한 시간씩 산보를 한다 I make it a rule to take an hour's walk before breakfast. // 신문을 또바기 매일 읽는다 He never misses an issue.

또박거리다 swagger ; strut ; mince (along) ⇨ 뚜벅거리다

또박또박 ① [정확히] neatly ; exactly ; carefully **—하다** (be) neat ; exact ; careful ¶ 또박또박 쓴 글씨 neat writing ; a neat hand // 글씨를 또박또박 쓰다 write neatly // 개수를 또박또박 세어 받다 count the number exactly and then take them

② [거르지 않고] punctually ; regularly ¶ 또박또박 제시간에 대 오다 come on time punctually // 빚을 또박또박 갚다 pay one's debt regularly

또아리 a ring-shaped (coiled) head pad (for bearing loads) ¶ 뱀이 또아리치다 a snake coils itself

†**또한** ① too ; also ; as well ; likewise ; both... and ; at once... and ; and at the same time... ; as well as ¶ 그는 정치가요 또한 시인이기도 했다 He was a statesman and poet. /He was at once a statesman and a poet. /He was a statesman and at the same time a poet. // 그 책은 흥미도 있거니와 또한 교훈적이었다 The book was interesting and instructive as well. /The book was both interesting and instructive. /The book was as instructive as interesting. /The book was not only interesting but also instructive. // 그의 양친도 또한 연회에 초대 받았다 His parents, too, were invited to the banquet. /His parents were invited to the banquet, too. /His parents also were invited to the banquet. // 그는 거기에 가지 않았으며 나도 또한 가지 않았다 He didn't go there, neither did I.

② [그 위에] and ; moreover ; besides ; further(more) ; what is more ¶ 그는 약속을 했으며 또한 그것을 실행했다 He made a promise and kept it. /Besides making a promise, he kept it.

똑[1] [두드리는·떨어지는 소리] with a rap ; with a tap ; with a flop ; [부러지는 소리] with a snap ; snappingly ¶ 책상을 똑 두드리다 rap on a table // 똑 부러지다 break with a snap ; crack // 책상 위의 책이 방바닥으로 똑 떨어졌다 The book on the desk dropped on the floor with a rap. // 나뭇가지가 똑 부러졌다 The branch was broken with a snap.

똑[2] [꼭] exactly ; just ; precisely ; punctually ; sharp ; [완전히] completely ¶ 똑 100 원 neither more nor less than 100 *won* ; just 100 *won* // 똑같다 be exactly alike // 똑 제시간에 right on time // 돈이 똑 떨어졌다 We have run out of money completely. /We have spent our last money.

똑같다 (be) just〔exactly〕 alike ; absolutely identical 《with》 ; exactly the same 《as》 ; equal 《to》 ; [닮다] be the exact image〔likeness〕 《of》 ; be 《a person's》 double ¶ 똑같은 날에 on the very same day // 어제 들은 이야기와 똑같다 It is the same story that I heard yesterday. // 나도 그와 똑같은 사람이다 I am no less a man than he is.

똑같이 [한결같이] equally ; evenly ; [공평하게] impartially ; [차별없이] indiscriminately ; alike ; similarly ; in the same way ; likewise ¶ 똑같이 보이다 look alike

똑딱거리다 ① [소리] tick ; rap ; knock ; hammer ; bang-bang ; patter ; clatter ¶ 똑딱똑딱 [시계가] tick-tock ; tick-tack ; [기계가] click-click ; clack-clack ; [장도리로] rap-rap ; bang-bang // 문을 똑딱거리다 rap〔knock〕 at〔on〕 the door // 빗방울이 유리창을 똑딱거리고 있었다 Raindrops were pattering on the window panes. ② [가슴이] go pitapat ; palpitate ; throb

똑딱단추 a snap ; a snap fastener〔hook,

link〕
똑딱선 一船 a steamboat ; a motorboat ¶ 똑딱선이 똑딱거리면서 지나간다 A steamboat chugs along.
똑똑 [떨어지는 소리] dropping one by one ; dripping ; [부러지는 소리] with snaps ; [두드리는 소리] rapping ; knocking ¶ 나뭇가지가 똑똑 부러지다 branches are broken with snaps // 책상을 똑똑 두드리다 rap on a table // 빗방울이 똑똑 떨어지기 시작했다 Drops of rain began to fall. // 처마에서 물이 똑똑 떨어진다 The eaves are dripping. // 눈물이 똑똑 떨어진다 Tears drop one by one.
†**똑똑하다** ① [명백하다] (be) clear ; distinct ¶ 똑똑한 구별 a sharp〔clear, clear-cut〕distinction // 똑똑한 발음 clear〔articulate〕pronunciation // 똑똑한 목소리로 in a clear〔distinct〕voice〔tone〕
② [영리하다] (be) bright ; smart ; intelligent ¶ 똑똑한 아이 a bright boy // 똑똑하게 처리하다 adopt〔take up〕a wise policy ; act wisely ; show wisdom in handling a matter
똑똑히 ① [분명히] clearly ; distinctly ; definitely ¶ 똑똑히 인쇄하다 print clearly // 똑똑히 발음하다 pronounce clearly〔distinctly〕// 똑똑히 말하다 speak clearly ; say definitely // 똑똑히 들리다 be clearly heard
② [영리·현명하게] brightly ; smartly ; intelligently ; well ¶ 사람이 똑똑히 생기다 look bright〔smart〕// 일처리를 똑똑히 하다 dispose of a matter intelligently
똑바로 ① [모양·방법] straight ; in a straight line (직선으로) ; [꼿꼿이] upright ; erect ; [수직으로] perpendicularly ; vertically ; [직행으로] straight ; direct(ly) ¶ 똑바로 서다〔앉다〕 stand〔sit〕upright〔erect〕// 똑바로 걷다 walk straight // 똑바로 가다 go〔keep〕straight on ; make straight toward〔for〕; follow one's nose // 똑바로 집으로 가다 go home straight〔direct〕// 몸을 똑바로 하라 Hold yourself straight. // 똑바로 놓아라 Place it on end. // 이 길을 똑바로 가시오 Go straight ahead down this street. // 그 사이의 거리는 똑바로 가서 5 마일이 된다 The distance between them is 5 miles in a straight line.
② [정직] honestly ; frankly ; straightforward ; candidly ¶ 말을 똑바로 하는 사람 an outspoken person // 똑바로 대다 tell the truth ; confess straightforwardly〔frankly〕// 세상을 똑바로 살다 lead an honest life ; pursue an honest career ; live straight // 만사를 똑바로 하다 be straight〔square〕in all one's dealings
†**똑바르다** ① [곧다] (be) (dead) straight ; (as) straight as an arrow ; straight direct ; [위로] upright ; erect ¶ 똑바른 자세로 in a correct posture ; sitting〔standing〕erect
② [올바르다] (be) right ; (as) right as nails ; righteous ; just ¶ 똑바른 행동 right conduct // 행실이 똑바르다 behave properly〔correctly〕; do a right thing
똑하다 [고지식하다] (be) simple ; frank ; [정직하다] very honest
똘기 unripe fruits
똘똘이 a bright child
똥 excrement ; ordure ; feces ; dung (말·소의) ; droppings (새의) ; shit 《속》 ¶ 그것 때문에 똥쌌다 I had a hell of time of it. /I paid dearly of it. /It cost me dear.
똥 묻은 개가 겨 묻은 개 나무란다 속담 The pot calls the Kettle black. /Ill may kiln call the oven burnt-tail. /The frying-pan said to the kettle, 'Avaunt, black brows.'/The kettle calls the pot burnt-arse.
똥을 누다 관용 have a bowel movement ; evacuate〔move〕 the bowel ; evacuate〔void〕excrement ; relieve oneself ; shit 《속》
똥값 a nominal price ; a dirt-cheap price ¶ 똥값으로 팔다 sell for almost nothing
똥개 ① [개] a mongrel (dog) ; a dog of nondescript breed ② [체중] (body) weight 《속》
똥거름 night soil ; dung-manure ; manure〔muck〕(농장에서 얻는) ¶ 똥거름을 치다 remove (the) night soil // 똥거름을 주다 apply dung-manure to 《land》; dung〔manure〕the ground
똥겨주다 enlighten ; let 《a person》 know ; [남 모르게] tip off ; hint ; suggest ; intimate ¶ 경찰에 똥겨주다 tip off the police // 그의 의도가 뭔지 저를 똥겨주시겠습니까 Will you enlighten me as to his intentions ?
똥구멍 the anus ; the anal passage〔orifice〕
똥구멍이 찢어지게 가난하다 속담 As poor as a church mouse. /As poor as Job.
똥그라미 ① [원] a circle ; a ring ② [돈] money ; coin
똥끝 the tip(s) of excrement ¶ 똥끝 타다 feel anxious〔worried〕; worry oneself (sick) ; be fidgety
똥기다 inform ; tip off ⇨ 똥겨주다
똥누다 have a bowel movement ; relieve oneself ; move〔evacuate〕 the bowel ; shit 《속》
똥독 [뒷간의] a night-soil jar
똥독 一毒 poison (virulence) in excrement ; rash caused by excrement ¶ 똥독 오르다 get a rash from touching excrement
*****똥똥하다** [생김새가] (be) short and corpulent〔fat〕; plump ; chubby ; [불룩하다] be full ; be swollen up ¶ 똥똥한 여자 a short and corpulent woman // 똥똥한 볼 (round and) plump cheek // 배가 똥똥하다 be pot-bellied (살이 쪄서) ; be big with child (임신)

똥마렵다 [서술적] feel a motion ; feel like defecating ; feel one's bowels urge ; be taken short (갑자기) 《구》
똥물 ① [똥이 풀린 물] excremental water ② [구토가 심할 때 나오는] yellow water coming out in a heavy vomiting ; bile
똥바가지 a dung dipper
똥배 a potbelly ; a protuberant〔protruding〕 belly ; a big paunch
똥싸개 a child who is not able to control his bowel movements ; a pants-soiler
똥싸다 ① [똥을] have an uncontrollable bowel movement ; pass evacuations uncontrollably ② [혼나다] have a hard 〔bad〕 time of it 《with a person》 ; have a bitter〔terrible〕 experience ¶ 숙제를 다 하느라고 똥쌌다 I had a hell of time finishing my homework.
똥오줌 feces and urine ; excretions ; body wastes ; "night soil" ¶ 환자의 똥오줌을 받아내다 take care of the body wastes of a patient
똥요강 a stool ; [요강] a chamber pot
똥주머니 [쓸모 없는 사람] a trash ; a good-for-nothing ; a tomfool
똥줄 ¶ 똥줄 빠지다〔당기다〕 be frightened out of one's wits ; be scared to death ; be scared shitless 《비》
똥집 ① [대장] the large intestine ② [체중] body weight ¶ 똥집이 무겁다 stay too long ; overstay〔outstay〕 one's welcome
똥차 一車 a night soil〔manure〕 car(t) ; [고장 잘 나는 차] a ramshackle car(t) ; a shabby car ; a jalop(p)y
똥창 맞다 be of one mind ; be in complete sympathy〔agreement〕 《with》
똥칠하다 smear dung ; disgrace ¶ 얼굴에 똥칠하다 disgrace one's name ; bring disgrace on 《a person》 ; stain one's good name
똥탈나다 ① [배탈] have stomach trouble ② [사고] have a great trouble 《with》 ; be in real trouble ; [급한 병] have an attack of an acute disease
똥털 anal hair
똥통 一桶 a "honey bucket" ; a dung tub ; a manure pail
똥파리 a bottle-green fly ; a dung fly
똥항아리 a chamber pot ; [비유적] a useless person in superior position
똬리 ⇨ 또아리 ¶ 똬리쇠 a (metal) washer
뙈기 [논밭의] a piece〔section, patch〕 (of a field, paddy) ; [조각] a piece ; a sheet ; a mat ¶ 자리 두 뙈기 two mats // 논발 뙈기나 가졌다 He has a few patches of rice paddy.
뙤다 snap off ; break off ¶ 그물코가 뙨다 The mesh of a net breaks off. // 바늘귀가 뙨다 The eye of a needle snaps〔breaks〕 off. // 책상귀가 뙨다 The edge of a table breaks off.
뙤뙤 stammering **— 거리다** stammer
뙤약볕 strong〔dazzling, blazing, scorching, broiling, burning〕 sunshine ¶ 뙤약볕을 쪼이다 expose oneself to strong sunshine // 뙤약볕을 쪼이며 under burning 〔sweltering〕 sun
뙤창 一窓 a door with a small window in it
뚜 hooting ; with a toot ; honking (자동차가) ; with a honk ¶ 기적이 뚜 울리다 a steam whistle hoots // 오정 사이렌이 뚜하고 울린다 The noon siren blows with a toot.
†**뚜껑** a lid (솥, 상자의) ; a cover (덮개의) ; a back (책의) ; a cap (병·만년필의) ; a shield (붓 따위의) ; a flap (호주머니의) ; a case (시계 따위의) ¶ 뚜껑 달린 lidded ; covered // 뚜껑 없는 lidless ; open // 뚜껑을 열다 open〔lift, take off〕 a lid〔cover〕 ; uncover
뚜껑을 닫다 관용 close〔cover up, put on, shut down〕 a lid
뚜껑을 덮어 두다 관용 keep 《a thing》 secret (비밀로 하다)
뚜껑이불 padded quilts without sheets
뚜덕거리다 knock ; tap ; rap ¶ 뚜덕뚜덕 rapping ; tapping ; rap-tap-tapping
뚜뚜 toot-toot ; hoot-hoot ¶ 나팔을 뚜뚜 불다 blow a trumpet // 기적을 뚜뚜 울리다 a whistle is sounded with hoot-hoot
뚜벅거리다 swagger ; strut ; walk gingerly〔in affected manner〕 ¶ 뚜벅뚜벅 swaggeringly // 그는 연단에 뚜벅뚜벅 걸어갔다 He walked to the platform in surefooted steps.
뚜쟁이 a pimp ; a pander ¶ 뚜쟁이 짓을 하다 act as a pimp ; pander
뚝 ① [갑자기] suddenly ; unexpectedly ¶ 음악이 뚝 그쳤다 The music stopped dead. // 울음을 뚝 그쳐라 Stop crying ! // 전화가 도중에 뚝 끊어졌다 The telephone was suddenly cut〔switched〕 off during the speaking.
② [떨어지는 소리] with a thump〔thud, whack, plump〕 ¶ 뚝 떨어지다 drop with a thud
③ [부러지는 소리] with a snap ¶ 사과를 뚝 따다 snatch an apple off a tree // 지팡이가 뚝 부러지다 a stick is broken with a snap ; a stick is snapped
뚝딱거리다 [소리] clatter ; rattle ; [가슴이] go pit-a-pat ; palpitate ¶ 가슴이 뚝딱거린다 My heart beats〔throbs〕 violently.
뚝뚝 ① [물방울 소리] dropping one by one ; pattering ; dripping ; trickling 《down, out, along》 ¶ 눈물을 뚝뚝 떨어뜨리다 shed big drops of tears ② [부러지는 소리] with snaps ; with creaks ¶ 지팡이가 뚝뚝 부러졌다 The sticks were broken with snaps. ③ [두드리는 소리] rapping ; knocking ¶ 그는 계속 문을 뚝뚝 두드렸다 He kept knocking at the door.

뚝뚝하다 ① [굳다] (be) hard ; tough ; stiff ; rigid ② [성질이] (be) harsh ; rough ; tough ; unaffable ; rude ; unsociable ; blunt ¶ 뚝뚝하게 bluntly ; curtly // 뚝뚝한 응대 a stiff reception // 뚝뚝한 사람〔성질〕 an unsociable person〔nature〕 // 뚝뚝하게 거절하다 give a flat refusal ; reject point-blank // 그는 태도가 뚝뚝하다 He is blunt in his bearing.

뚝발이 a cripple

뚝배기 earthen(ware) bowl ¶ 뚝배기보다 장 맛이 좋다 Appearances are often deceptive. /You can't tell a book by its cover.

뚝별나다 (be) quick-tempered ; testy ; touchy ; peevish ¶ 그 여자는 나이 이야기만 나오면 매우 뚝별나게 군다 She is most touchy on the subject of age.

뚝별씨 hot temper ; quick temper ; touchiness ; testiness ; peevishness

뚝심 physical strength ; staying power ; [당해 내는 힘] endurance ; tenacity ¶ 뚝심이 센 사람 a man of mighty sinews // 그는 뚝심이 있어 어떤 곤란도 버티어 나갈 수 있을 것이다 He is so strong that he will be able to endure any difficulties.

뚝지 〖물고기〗 a sea fish (Aplocyclus ventricosus)

뚝하다 ⇨ 뚝뚝하다

***뚫다** ① [구멍을] bore ; punch ; make〔drill〕 a hole ; perforate ; [관통하다] pierce〔perforate〕 into〔through〕 ; cut〔pass〕 through ; shoot through (탄환이) ; penetrate (침투하다) ¶ 구멍 뚫는 기구 a drill ; a perforator ; a punch // 벽에 구멍을 뚫다 make〔bore〕 a hole〔an opening〕 in the wall // 법망을 뚫다 evade〔get round〕 the law ; slip from the grip of the law // 적진을 뚫다 penetrate into enemy position // 강이 시내 가운데를 뚫고 흐르고 있다 The river runs through the city.
② [길을] bore ; cut ; excavate ; build ; open 《up》 ¶ 터널을 뚫다 cut〔bore, drive〕 a tunnel // 산길을 뚫다 build〔open〕 a mountain path
③ [이치에 통하다·통찰하다] pierce ; penetrate ; attain ; get at ; master ¶ 영원한 진리를 뚫다 attain to the eternal truth // 학문의 깊은 이치를 뚫다 master〔gain, reach, penetrate〕 the secrets of learning // 가면을 뚫어 보다 pierce〔penetrate〕 a disguise // 사물의 진상을 뚫어 보다 pierce beneath the shows of things
④ [틈을 비집다·무릅쓰다] go〔elbow〕 through ; penetrate ; weather (곤란을) ; brave (무릅쓰다) ¶ 인파 속을 뚫고 나아가다 penetrate a crowd ; elbow one's way through the crowd ; push through the crowd // 폭풍우를 뚫고 나아가다 ride out〔weather〕 a storm // 곤란을 뚫고 나아가다 get through〔tide over, cut one's way through, find one's way out of〕 a difficulty
⑤ [굸을 알아내다] find a way ¶ 돈구멍을 뚫다 find a way to get money // 장사구멍을 뚫다 explore the business possibilities // 일자리를 뚫다 look for work〔a job, a position〕 ; seek a job〔an employment〕

뚫리다 ① [구멍이] be pierced〔bored, perforated, drilled, penetrated〕 ; get opened up ¶ 구멍이 뚫린다 A hole is made. /A way is found. // 터널이 뚫린다 A tunnel is made〔bored, cut, driven, excavated, built〕.
② [이치가] be attained ; be mastered ¶ 학문의 깊은 이치가 뚫린다 The secrets of learning are mastered〔penetrated〕.

뚫린골 [뚫린 골목] an open〔a passable〕 alley

뚫어내다 pierce out ; bore out ; [학문의 이치를] manage to master 《the secret of learning》 ¶ 험한 산길을 뚫어내다 open a path through a steep mountain // 목수가 두꺼운 판자에 구멍을 뚫어냈다 The carpenter bored out a hole through a thick board.

뚫어뜨리다 succeed〔manage〕 to bore〔pierce, perforate〕 ; pierce〔bore〕 out ¶ 마침내 그 철판에 구멍을 뚫어뜨렸다 Finally I have drilled out a hole through the iron plate. // 나는 신발을 뚫어뜨렸다 I have worn out my shoes.

뚫어새기다 cut out a fretwork pattern

뚫어지게 보다 stare 《at》 ; look hard 《at》 ; scrutinize ¶ 사람을 뚫어지게 보다 stare at 《a person》 // 사람의 얼굴을 뚫어지게 보다 stare in 《a person's》 face

뚫어지다 [송곳 따위가] bore ; drill ; pierce ; perforate ; [물건에 구멍이] be bored ; be drilled ; be pierced ; be perforated ; 《a hole》 be made ; be torn〔broken, worn out〕 ¶ 이 송곳은 안 뚫어진다 This drill won't bore. // 이 펀치는 안 뚫어진다 This punch doesn't work〔pierce〕. // 험한 산에 긴 터널이 힘들게 뚫어졌다 A long tunnel in a steep mountain has been laboriously excavated〔driven out〕.

뚱기다 ① [튀기다] bounce ; bound ; rebound ; resile ; spring back ② [깨닫게 하다] inform ; notice ; tip off

뚱기치다 give a hard bound ; bounce hard

뚱딴지 [사람] a blunt〔dull〕 person ; a dolt ; a blockhead ; a log ; an ass ; a pumpkin head 《미》 ; [전기 기구] an insulator ¶ 뚱딴지 같은 preposterous (터무니 없는) ; absurd (불합리한) ; laughable (우스꽝스러운) ; foolish (어리석은) ; senseless (몰상식한) ; nonsensical (되지 못한) ; unexpected (뜻밖의) // 뚱딴지 같은 소리 하지 마라 Don't talk rot ! / Nonsense !

뚱뚱보 a corpulent fellow ; a fatty ; a plump person ¶ 야 뚱뚱보 Hello, fatty ! // 그 여자는 뚱뚱보다 She is a fat piece.

뚱뚱이 ⇨ 뚱뚱보
⁑뚱뚱하다 (be) fat ; corpulent ; [포동포동하다] plump ¶ 그는 배가 뚱뚱하다 He is a pot-bellied man.
뚱보 ① [뚱한 사람] a taciturn〔glum, uncommunicative〕 person
② [뚱뚱보] a plump person ; a fatso ⦅속⦆
뚱하다 ① [말이 적다] (be) taciturn ; silent ; uncommunicative ; quiet ; reserved ; reticent ¶ 뚱한 사람 a man of silence ; a reticent person
② [못마땅하다] (be) moody ; glum ; sullen ¶ 뚱한 얼굴 a glum look // 그는 뚱해서 말도 안 하고 앉아 있었다 He sat sullen and silent.
*뛰놀다 [뛰어 놀다] skip〔jump〕 about ; romp ; gambol ; frisk ; frolic ; caper ¶ 새끼 양들이 들에서 뛰논다 Lambs are skipping about in the field.
†뛰다[1] ① [물·진흙 따위가] splash ; spatter ; sputter ; spark (불꽃이) ¶ 옷에 기름이 뛰다 have splashes of grease on one's clothes
② [도망가다] run away ; escape ; flee ; take to flight ¶ 남의 돈을 갖고 뛰다 make away with ⦅a person's⦆ money // 국외로 뛰다 fly the country
③ [두근두근하다] beat ; palpitate ; throb
뛰다[2] ① [달리다] run ; dash ; rush
② [도약하다] jump ; leap ; spring ; bound ; vault ; hop ; skip (차례를) ¶ 기뻐서 뛰다 leap〔jump, dance〕 for joy // 갑자기 뛰다 make a sudden leap // 2미터를 뛰다 jump〔vault〕 two meters // 화가 나서 펄쩍 뛰다 jump up with anger // 10페이지에서 15페이지로 뛰다 skip from page 10 to 15
뛰다[3] [그네를] swing ⦅on a swing⦆ ; have a swing ; [널을] seesaw ; play seesaw
뛰다[4] [가슴이] beat ; throb ; palpitate ; [맥박이] pulsate ¶ 가슴이 뛴다 one's heart beats // 맥박이 뛴다 one's pulse beats ; pulsate
†뛰어가다 run ; rush ; dash ; dart ¶ 갑자기 뛰어가다 break into a run // 단숨에 뛰어가다 dash in a breath〔with one breath〕 // 그는 1마일을 4분에 뛰어갔다 He ran a mile in 4 minutes. // 학교까지 쭉 뛰어갔다 He ran all the way to school.
뛰어나가다 run〔rush〕 forward ; run out ; jump〔leap〕 out ¶ 앞으로 뛰어나가다 run〔dart〕 forward ⦅from the rear⦆
*뛰어나다 excel ; surpass ; tower〔stand〕 above ; be superior to ; be distinguished〔prominent outstanding〕 ¶ 뛰어나게 extremely ; exceedingly ; strikingly ; by far // 지능이 뛰어난 사람 a man of excellent intelligence // 뛰어난 재주 a distinguished talent ; an unusual ability // 뛰어난 학자 an outstanding scholar // 그는 영어에 뛰어났다 He excels in English. // 공부에 있어서 반에서 가장 뛰어났다 He is by far the best in studies in his class.
뛰어내리다 jump〔leap, spring〕 down ¶ 달리는 차에서 뛰어내리다 jump off a running car // 2층에서 뛰어내리다 jump〔leap〕 from the second floor // 말에서 뛰어내리다 fling oneself from one's horse ; vault〔swing〕 from a saddle // 5층에서 뛰어내려 자살하다 leap to one's death from the fifth floor ; commit suicide by leaping from the fifth floor
†뛰어넘다 ① [넘다] jump〔leap, vault, skip, pass〕 over ¶ 울타리를 뛰어넘다 jump over a fence ; clear ⦅a fence⦆ (말이) // 도랑을 뛰어넘다 leap over a ditch
② [거르다] skip〔jump〕 over ¶ 10페이지를 뛰어넘다 skip ten pages // 한 계급 뛰어넘어 승진되다 be jumped one grade in rank
⁑뛰어다니다 ① [겅중겅중] jump〔bounce, skip〕 about
② [바삐] run about 〔round〕 ; fly about ; hustle about ; dash around ; kick up one's heels ⦅구⦆ ; busy oneself ⦅about⦆
⁑뛰어들다 ① [몸을 내켜] jump〔leap〕 into ; rush into ; run into ; dive into (물 속으로) ¶ 방 안으로 뛰어들다 jump into a room // 물속에 뛰어들다 plunge〔dive〕 into the water // 배에서 물에 뛰어들다 jump overboard // 품 안으로 뛰어들다 fly to ⦅a person's⦆ arms // 선로에 뛰어들다 throw oneself on a track
② [끼어 들다] thrust oneself into ⦅the scene of dispute⦆ ; [참견] thrust one's nose〔oneself〕 in ; butt into ¶ 그는 아무데나 뛰어들기를 좋아한다 He is too fond of thrusting himself forward.
뛰어오다 run〔rush, dash〕 along this way ; come running ; come back at a run ¶ 애들은 그에게로 뛰어왔다 The children ran up to him. // 집에서 쭉 뛰어왔다 He ran all the way from home.
†뛰어오르다 jump〔leap, spring〕 up ; jump on ; bounce ; bound ; [값이] rise ; go up ; be raised ¶ 연단에 뛰어오르다 spring up on a platform // 달리는 차에 뛰어오르다 jump on a running car // 기뻐서 뛰어오르다 leap〔jump, dance〕 up for joy // 공이 뛰어오른다 A ball bounces. // 개가 사람에게 뛰어오른다 A dog jumps up to a person. // 물가가 뛰어오른다 Prices take a jump. // 값이 갑자기 500원에서 1,000원으로 뛰어올랐다 The price was suddenly raised from 500 *won* to 1,000 *won*.
뛰엄젓 [개구리젓] salted frogs
†뜀 [달리기] running ; rushing ; dashing ; [뛰기] jumping ; leaping ; skipping ; springing ; vaulting
뜀뛰기 〖경기〗 jumping ; leaping ; skipping
— 선수 a jumper — 운동 a jumping exercise — 종목 a jumping event —판 a springboard ; a leaping board

뜀뛰다 [달리다] run ; race ; run a race ; [뛰다] jump ; leap ; spring

뜀박질 [달리기] a race ; running ; [뛰기] jumping ; leaping

뜀틀 a vaulting horse

뜨 개 것 knitted work ; knit goods ; knitwear ; knitting

뜨개바늘 a knitting needle ; a knitting pin 〔stick〕 ; [코바늘] a crochet hook

***뜨개질** knitting ; knitwork **—하다** knit ; do knitting

뜨거워하다 feel 《it》 hot ; find 《it》 hot ¶ 어린애가 국을 뜨거워한다 The child finds the soup too hot.

†**뜨 겁 다** (be) hot ; heated ; burning ; scorching ¶ 뜨거운 국 hot soup // 뜨거워지다 become hot // 햇볕이 뜨겁다 The sun is hot. // 부끄러워서 얼굴이 뜨겁다 My face burns with shame. // 나는 뜨거운 음식이 좋다 I like my food hot.

-뜨기 one ; guy ; thing ¶ 사팔뜨기 a cross-eyed〔squint-eyed〕 person // 시골뜨기 a hick ; a country bumpkin // 칠뜨기 a moron ; an idiot // 얼뜨기 a half-wit

뜨끈뜨끈 —하다 (be) burning hot ⇨ 따근따근 ¶ 뜨끈뜨끈한 감자 steaming 〔piping〕 hot potatoes ; potatoes hot from the oven

뜨끈하다 (be) fairly hot ¶ 뜨끈한 국 hot soup

뜨끔하다 (be) stinging ; prickly ⇨ 따끔하다 ¶ 양심이 뜨끔하다 prick at one's conscience

뜨 내 기 ① [방랑자] a wanderer ; a vagabond ; a vagrant ; a tramp ; a hobo ¶ 뜨내기 일꾼 a wandering laborer ② [일] an odd job ¶ 뜨내기 일을 해서 지내다 get along by doing odd jobs

뜨내기손님 a chance〔casual, stray〕 customer ; a chance comer ; a transient guest

뜨내기장사 a casual〔temporary〕 business ¶ 그는 뜨내기장사로 많은 돈을 모았다 He has amassed a lot of money by doing a casual〔an odd〕 business.

†**뜨다¹** ① [느리다] (be) slow ¶ 걸음이 뜨다 be slow-footed ; be slow of foot // 시계가 10분 뜨다 The watch is ten minutes slow. // 그 나라는 진보가 뜨다 The country is slow in progress.

② [둔하다] (be) dull ; slow ; slow-witted ; sluggish ¶ 배움이 뜨다 be slow in learning lessons

③ [입이 무겁다] (be) taciturn ; reticent ¶ 입이 뜬 사람 a man of few words

④ [무디다] (be) blunt ; dull ¶ 칼날이 뜨다 the edge of a knife is blunt

⑤ [사이가] be separated ; have an interval ; be estranged (애정이) ¶ 10년 사이가 뜨다 be at an interval of ten years // 부부 사이가 뜨다 the man and wife are estranged from each other

⑥ [다리미 따위가] be slow to heat up ¶ 다리미가 뜨다 an iron is slow to heat up

뜨다² ① [물·하늘에] float ; keep afloat ¶ 하늘에 구름이 뜨다 clouds float in the sky // 물에 거품이 뜨다 bubbles float on the water

② [해·별이] rise ; come up ¶ 해가 뜬다 The sun rises. // 별이 뜬다 Stars appear (in the sky). // 보름달이 중천에 떠 있다 The full moon is high up in the sky.

③ [공간적 사이] be distant ; be apart (from) ; be separated ¶ 우리 집과 그의 집은 상당히 사이가 뜨다 My house and his are quite separated from each other.

④ [붙어 있던 것이] get loose ; come off 〔apart〕 ; be detached ; be disjoined ¶ 구들장판이 뜨다 A layer of oil paper comes off the floor.

⑤ [돈이] be lost for good ¶ 그에게 빌려 주었던 돈이 떴다 The money I lent him is gone.

⑥ [연이] 《a kite》 float away free (after disentangled)

⑦ [열 따위가] 《fever》 rise ; go up

뜨 다³ ① [썩다] become stale ; grow moldy ; go musty and fusty ; [발효] ferment ; undergo fermentation ¶ 날이 더워 창고의 쌀이 떴다 The rice stored in the warehouse has become stale〔moldy〕 because of the hot weather.

② [얼굴빛이] become〔grow〕 sallow ¶ 누렇게 뜬 얼굴 a sallow face // 너무 집에만 들어 박혀 있어서 네 얼굴이 다 떴다 Since you have shut yourself in the house all the time, your face has grown all sallow.

뜨다⁴ [뜸을] cauterize 《the skin》 with moxa ; apply cauterizing〔moxa cautery〕 ¶ 머리 꼭대기에 뜸을 뜨다 cauterize the top of one's head 《with moxa》

뜨다⁵ [자리를] leave ; quit (그만두다) ; [옮기다] move ; clear out ¶ 학교를 뜨다 leave school // 관직을 뜨다 throw up〔quit, retire from〕 office // 그는 지금 살고 있는 집에서 뜨려고 하고 있다 He is thinking of moving out of his house.

뜨다⁶ ① [잔디·얼음 따위를] cut out ; shovel ¶ 잔디를 뜨다 cut sod // 그들은 흙을 삽으로 떠냈다 They shoveled up clods of earth.

② [물·국] scoop up ; ladle ¶ 국을 뜨다 ladle soup // 배 안에서 물을 떠내다 scoop water out of a boat

③ [소·돼지를 잡아서] cut up ¶ 소를 잡아 뜨다 cut up a slaughtered cow

④ [포를] slice 《meat》 ; cut into slices ¶ 포를 뜨다 slice and jerk meat

⑤ [옷감] cut out ; cut ; buy ¶ 옷감을 뜨다 cut out〔buy〕 a piece of cloth for one's clothes

⑥ [풀·종이를] make 《paper》 ¶ 종이를 뜨다 make paper // 풀을 뜨다 make paste cakes

뜨다[7] ① [눈을] open 《one's eyes》; be awake ¶ 눈을 뜨다 open one's eyes // 성에 눈을 뜨다 be awakened to sex ② [귀를] hear ; catch ; begin to understand ¶ 음악에 귀를 뜨다 begin to appreciate music

뜨다[8] ① [그물·편물 따위를] net ; knit ; crochet ¶ 그물을 뜨다 make〔knit〕 a net // 털실로 양말을 뜨다 knit stockings out of wool
② [바느질] stitch ; sew ¶ 터진 데를 한두 바늘 뜨다 put one or two stitches in a rip
③ [문신] tattoo ¶ 팔에 용의 문신을 뜨다 have a dragon tattooed on one's arm

뜨다[9] [본을] copy ; imitate ¶ 버선 본을 뜨다 copy the pattern of socks from the original model // 아버지 본을 뜨다 imitate one's father ; follow one's father's example

뜨다[10] [받다] horn ; toss ; butt ¶ 소가 아무를 뿔로 뜨다 a cow tosses a person with his horns

뜨더귀 tearing apart (to pieces) **—하다** tear〔pull〕 apart (to pieces) ; dismantle

뜨더귀판 a place where〔an occasion when〕 tearing〔pulling〕 to〔in〕 pieces is going on ; the (scene of) dismantling

뜨덤뜨덤 falteringly ; with difficulty ¶ 글을 뜨덤뜨덤 읽다 read falteringly〔with difficulty〕

뜨듯하다 ⇨ 뜨뜻하다

뜨뜻미지근하다 (be) lukewarm〔tepid〕

뜨뜻이 (pleasantly) warm ; hot ¶ 구들을 뜨뜻이 때다 heat a room warm // 옷을 뜨뜻이 입다 wear oneself warm // 난로 앞에 앉아서 몸을 뜨뜻이 녹이시오 Sit down before the fire and have a warm.

뜨뜻하다 (be) warm ; (pleasantly) hot ¶ 뜨뜻한 옷 a warm clothes // 뜨뜻한 날씨 warm weather // 점점 뜨뜻해진다 It is getting warmer.

뜨막하다 be long 《since》; have a long interval 《between》; be few and far between ¶ 오늘은 일요일이 되어 버스가 뜨막하다 Since it is Sunday, the buses are running few and far between.

뜨물 the washing water of rice ; water from the first washing of rice

뜨악하다 (be) reluctant ; disinclined 《to do》; unwilling ; unappealing

뜨음하다 (be) infrequent ; [서술적] have a rather long interval ; be in a lull〔break〕《in the rain》 ¶ 뜨음해지다 hold〔let〕 up ; abate ; subside ; become light

뜨이다 ① [눈이] 《one's eyes》 open ; awake ; wake up ; be opened ; 《one's ears》 prick up ¶ 아침 다섯시에 눈이 뜨이다 awake at five in the morning // 성에 눈이 뜨이다 be awakened to sex // 그 보도는 사람들의 눈을 번쩍 뜨이게 하였다 The report was an eye-opener to the people. // 그 소식을 들었을 때 귀가 번쩍 띄었다 My ears pricked up with surprise on hearing the news.
② [눈에] be seen〔found〕; be conspicuous〔prominent, striking, remarkable〕; meet〔greet〕 one's eyes ; catch 〔arrest〕 one's eyes ; attract one's attention ; strike the eye ; come to〔under〕 one's notice ¶ 눈에 뜨이는 특징 conspicuous characteristics // 눈에 뜨이는 미인 an attractive beauty // 눈에 뜨이지 않게 in a quiet〔an inconspicuous〕 way // 눈에 뜨이게 좋아지다〔나빠지다〕 grow better〔worse〕 every moment // 눈에 뜨이게 건강이 쇠약해지다 One's health declines noticeably. // 내 눈에 먼저 뜨인 것은 카메라였다 The first object on which my eyes rested was a camera.

뜨직하다 (be) indisposed 《to do, toward(s) a something》; reluctant 《to do》; [서술적] have no inclination 《to do》; take little interest 《in》; be in no mood 《to do》

뜬것 [귀신] a wandering demon〔devil, evil spirit, fiend〕

뜬계집 a woman with whom one has a casual affair

뜬구름 ① [구름] a drifting〔floating〕 cloud ; a cloud drift ; a drift of cloud ¶ 하늘에는 한 조각의 뜬구름도 없었다 There was not a speck of cloud to be seen (up) in the sky.
② [덧없는 일] mutability ; transience ; evanescence ¶ 뜬구름과 같은 인생 transient〔mutable〕 life ; the transience of human life // 인생은 뜬구름과 같은 것이다 Nothing is certain in this world. /All is vanity in life. /Life is an empty dream.

뜬눈 ¶ 뜬눈으로 밤을 새우다 pass a sleepless night ; cannot get a wink of sleep

뜬돈 money earned unexpectedly ; a windfall

뜬세상 —世上 the (transitory) world ; (transient) life ; the earth ; this weary world

뜬소문 a groundless rumor ; a wild 〔false〕 rumor ; an unfounded〔a groundless〕 report ; a canard 《프》 ¶ 뜬소문이 돌다 a groundless rumor is current〔afloat, in the air〕

뜬숯 used charcoal ; cinders

뜬재물 —財物 a windfall ; an unexpected income ¶ 뜬재물이 굴러 들어오다 have a fortune drop in one's lap

뜬저울 an areometer ; a hydrometer ; a hydrostatic balance ; a gravimeter

뜯게 worn-out clothes

뜯기다 ① [물리다] be bitten 《by fleas, mosquitoes, insects》 ¶ 벌레에 뜯긴 자리가 부풀어 올랐다 The sting of an insect has swollen up.
② [빼앗기다] be extorted ; be squeezed ; be divested〔stripped, deprived〕 of ¶ 돈을 뜯기다 have one's money taken // 재산

을 뜯기다 be stripped of one's wealth // 그는 고리 대금업자에게 그의 돈을 다 뜯기었다 He was squeezed dry by a usurer.
③ [머리털 따위를] be plucked ; be pulled out ; be torn out〔off〕 ¶ 머리털을 뜯기다 one's hair is torn〔pulled〕 out by the roots // 공작이 깃을 뜯기다 a peacock is plucked of his feathers
④ [풀을] put 《a cow》 on grass ; graze ; pasture ¶ 소에게 풀을 뜯기다 put a cow on grass ; put cattle to feed on growing grass

†**뜯다** ① [떼다] take away ; take〔pull, tear〕 down ; break up ; take 《a machine》 to pieces ; dismantle《equipment》 ; remove ; disassemble ; demolish ; [풀·털 따위를] pluck ; pick ; tear〔pull〕 out ¶ 시계를 뜯다 take a clock apart〔to pieces〕 // 공장을 뜯다 dismantle a plant // 집을 뜯다 pull〔take, tear〕 down a house // 잡초를 뜯다 pluck out weeds
② [현악기를] play 《a harp》 ; touch 《the strings》 ; thrum (on) 《a mandolin》 ; strum (on) 《a guitar》
③ [빼앗다] extort ; squeeze ; fleece ¶ 백성들한테 돈을 뜯다 extort money from the people // 노름판에서 돈을 뜯다 receive a tip from gamblers

뜯어고치다 ① [해체하여 고치다] tear〔take〕 apart and mend〔repair〕 ; [개조하다] reconstruct ; rebuild ; adapt (문장 따위를)
② [검토하여 시정하다] look over and change〔alter〕 ; examine and improve ¶ 원고를 뜯어고치다 revise a manuscript // 행실을 뜯어고치다 mend one's ways

뜯어내다 ① [붙은 것을] remove ; take〔tear, pick〕 off ; take away ; dismantle ; dismount
② [돈을] extort ; squeeze ; pluck ⇨ 뜯다
③ [분해하다] disjoint ; dismantle ; disassemble ; disintegrate ; take〔pull〕 《a thing》 to pieces ; take 《a machine》 apart〔down〕

뜯어말리다 pull apart 《fighters》 ¶ 맞붙어 싸우는 아이들을 뜯어말리다 pull the grappling children apart

*‡***뜯어먹다** ① [붙은 것을] take it off and eat ; pluck〔tear〕 and eat ; [뼈·고기를] nibble at ; gnaw off ¶ 뼈에 붙은 고기를 뜯어먹다 gnaw the meat off a bone // 물고기가 먹이를 뜯어먹다 the fish nibbles (at) the bait // 소가 풀을 뜯어먹다 a cow grazes
② [남의 것을] live off〔on〕 ; sponge 《on》 ¶ 친척을 뜯어먹고 살다 live off one's relatives // 남의 것을 뜯어먹고 살다 live at another's expense ; live off another

뜯어버리다 tear 《a thing》 off and throw 《it》 away ; remove ; clear away

뜯어벌리다 ① [벌리어 놓다] take〔tear〕 《a machine》 to pieces〔apart〕 ② [이야기를] talk in a disagreeable manner ; tell in an irritating fashion

뜯어벌이다 ① [뜯어서 벌여놓다] take〔tear, pull〕 《a thing》 to pieces and spread 《it》 out 《on the ground》 ② [얘기를] spin a story (in a disagreeable manner) ; give a long talk

뜯어보다 ① [열어보다] open and look at it ; undo ¶ 편지를 뜯어보다 tear〔break〕 a letter open ; undo a sealed letter // 통조림을 뜯어보다 cut a can〔tin〕 open
② [살펴보다] look at it from every angle ; scrutinize ; examine minutely ; inspect ¶ 안경을 쓰고 사람의 얼굴을 뜯어보다 scrutinize 《a person》 through one's spectacles // 집을 이모저모로 뜯어보다 look a house over thoroughly
③ [겨우 읽다] read〔construe〕 with difficulty ; decipher 《a manuscript》 ¶ 뜯어보기 힘든 필적 a handwriting difficult to decipher // 글이 워낙 힘들어서 뜯어볼 수가 없다 The passage is so difficult I can't make it out at all.

뜯적거리다 scratch (and tear off) ; claw

뜯적뜯적하다 ⇨ 뜯적거리다

†**뜰** a garden ; a yard ; a courtyard ; a ground ¶ 뜰에 심은 나무 a garden tree // 뜰에는 나무를 심어야 한다 The yard must be planted with trees.

뜰뜰 ① [수레 소리] clattering down ② [잘 시행됨] with proper〔admirable〕 exercise of authority

뜰아래채 an outhouse ; a detached minor wing of a home

뜰아랫방 a room in a minor, outer wing of a house ; a room in an outhouse separated by a garden from the main building

뜰층계 —層階 steps from the yard to the veranda(h)

뜸[1] a rain〔sun〕 screen〔shelter〕 woven of straw〔cattails〕 ; a cattail mat

뜸[2] moxa cautery ; moxibustion ¶ 머리에 뜸을 뜨다 cauterize the head (with moxa)

뜸[3] being well-steamed〔-cooked〕 ; an interval

뜸[4] a residential section (of a town) ; a block of houses

뜸깃 material to make a mat

뜸단지 a cupping glass〔pot〕

뜸들이다 ① [음식을] cook〔steam〕 thoroughly ¶ 밥을 뜸들이다 steam boiled rice ; allow boiled rice to settle by its own heat // 감자를 뜸들이다 steam potatoes thoroughly
② [일을] give a necessary interval of time ; give a pause ; give time (enough) ¶ 일을 뜸들여 하다 allow enough time to get a job done

뜸베질 horning ; tossing ; butt **—하다** horn ; toss ; butt

뜸부기 〖새〗 a crake ; water rail ; Porzana (학명)
뜸쑥 moxa
뜸지근하다 (be) rather slow and dignified
뜸직뜸직 [언행이] slowly ; gravely ; solemnly ; in a dignified manner ¶ 말을 뜸직뜸직하다 speak solemn words ; measure one's words // 걸음을 뜸직뜸직 건다 walk slowly ; walk with dignified [measured] steps
뜸직이 slowly ; gravely ; solemnly
뜸직하다 (be) dignified ; measured ; imposing ; commanding ¶ 뜸직한 사람 a man of remarkable composure ; a dignified character
뜸질 cauterizing with moxa **—하다** cauterize with moxa ; apply a heat treatment (찜질하다)
뜸집 a thatch hut [shack]
뜸하다 [머춤하다] lull ; let up 《구》 ; [도수가] (be) infrequent ¶ 뜸해지다 come to (a state of) lull ; there comes a lull // 비가 뜸해졌다 The rain is letting up a little.
*__뜻__ ① [의지] a mind ; a wish ; [의향] an intention ; one's idea ; [목적] aim ; purpose ; [희망] hope ; desire ; [야망] ambition ; aspiration ¶ 뜻이 굳은 사람 a man of iron will // 뜻이 큰 사람 a man of great ambition // 뜻을 밝히다 speak one's mind ; express one's intention // 뜻을 세우다 set an object before one ; have a fixed purpose 《in life》 // 뜻을 이루다 attain one's aim ; accomplish one's purpose ; realize one's aspiration // 뜻을 높이 품다 aim high ; hitch one's wagon to a star // 뜻이 서로 통하다 come to [arrive at] an understanding ; understand each other // 장사할 뜻은 조금도 없다 I haven't the slightest intention of going into business. // 연작이 어찌 홍곡의 뜻을 알리오 A man must be a hero to understand a hero. // 그는 뜻을 이루지 못하고 죽었다 He died before he could realize his dream. // 부모의 뜻을 어겨서는 안된다 You shouldn't do anything against your parents' wishes.
② [의미] meaning ; sense ; significance ; effect ; purport ; point ¶ 깊은 뜻 a deep [profound] meaning // 애매한 뜻 an ambiguous [obscure] meaning // 글자대로의 뜻 a literal meaning // 뜻이 없다 be meaningless // 뜻을 곡해하다 pervert [twist] the meaning // 좋은 뜻으로 취하다 take it in a favorable sense ; take it well // 뜻이 분명하다 The meaning is clear. // 그 말에는 두가지 뜻이 있다 The word bears double meaning. // 지체는 위험을 뜻한다 Delay spells danger. // 그의 말뜻을 전혀 알 수 없다 I cannot make head or tail of his discourse. // 이 글의 뜻은 전혀 알 수 없다 I can make nothing of this passage. // 잘 있다는 뜻의 편지를 받았다 I received a letter to the effect that he is getting along well.
뜻이 있는 곳에 길이 있다 〔속담〕 Where there's a will, there's a way.
뜻글자 an ideograph
뜻대로 as one likes [pleases, desires, wishes] ; in one's own way ; just as wished [hoped, intended, meant] ; at one's pleasure ¶ 뜻대로 되다 [안되다] come up to [fall short of] one's expectation // 뜻대로 하다 have [get] one's (own) way 《in a matter》 ; do 《a thing》 (just) the way one wants to // 계획이 뜻대로 되었다 The plan worked as desired. // 만사가 뜻대로 되었다 Everything turned out as I wished. // 만사가 뜻대로 되지 않는다 Everything goes against me.
뜻맞다 ① [의기 상통] (be) congenial 《to, with》 ; be of similar temperament ; be like-minded ; be united in spirit ; hit it off 《with》 《미·속》 ¶ 뜻맞는 친구 congenial friends // 그들은 뜻맞는 친구다 They are congenial spirits [souls]. /They are like-minded. // 우리들은 서로 뜻이 맞지 않는다 We cannot temperamentally agree with each other.
② [마음에 들다] suit one's taste [fancy] ; accord with one's will ; be in one's favor ; take a fancy to 《a person》 ¶ 뜻맞지 않다 be not to one's liking ; be undesirable ; be distasteful 《to》 ; be disagreeable [offensive] ; go against the grain ; be unable to stomach // 좀처럼 뜻맞는 사람을 구할 수 없다 It's hard to find a man to suit me.
*__뜻밖__ unexpectedness ; a surprise ¶ 뜻밖의 unexpected ; unlooked-for ; unanticipated ; surprising // 뜻밖에 unexpectedly ; beyond expectation ; all of a sudden // 뜻밖의 손님 an unexpected guest // 뜻밖의 일 an unexpected happening ; an unforeseen occurrence // 그의 성공은 참으로 뜻밖이다 His success is really surprising. // 그것은 천만 뜻밖이었다 That was a great surprise. /That was a bolt from the blue. // 회의는 뜻밖에 큰 성공이었다 The meeting was a greater success than we had expected. // 뜻밖의 방면에서 구원이 왔다 Help came from an unexpected quarter. // 당신을 여기서 만나다니 참으로 뜻밖이다 It's quite a surprise to see you here. / You are the last man I expected to meet here. // 그는 뜻밖에도 전과자였다 He turned out to be an exconvict. // 형의 병은 뜻밖에도 중하였다 My brother was more seriously ill than I had imagined.
뜻받다 meet 《a person's》 request ; comply with 《a person's》 wish ; obey ¶ 뜻받들어 in obedience to 《a person's order》 // 부모를 뜻받다 yield to one's parents
뜻있다 [의미 있다] (be) significant ; [유의

하다] useful ; [가치 있다] worthwhile ; [함축성 있다] meaningful ¶ 뜻있게 meaningfully ; sensibly ; in a meaningful or sensible way // 뜻있는 미소를 띠고 with a meaning smile // 뜻있는 생활을 하다 lead a life worth living

†**뜻하다** ① [계획하다] plan ; intend 《to go abroad》 ; aim at 《distinction》 ; aspire to〔after〕 《honor, fame》 ; have 《a thing》 in view〔mind〕 ; [결심하다] determine 《to rise in the world》 ; make up one's mind 《to go to sea》 ¶ 외교관이 되기를 뜻하다 aspire〔aim〕 to be a diplomat // 실업계에서 성공할 것을 뜻하다 hope to succeed in the field of business // 나는 그가 뜻하고 있는 바를 이해할 수 없다 I cannot guess what he is driving at.
② [의미하다] mean ; signify ; point ; connote ¶ 뜻하는 바가 분명하다 the meaning is clear // 그것은 무엇을 뜻하느냐 What does it mean ? // D. D. 는 무엇을 뜻하느냐 What does D. D. stand for ?

***띄다** ① [눈에] catch sight of ; meet the eye ⇨ 뜨이다 ② [연·배 따위를] fly ; float ⇨ 띄우다[1]

띄어쓰기 spacing words

띄어쓰다 write leaving space 《between the words》 ; leave spaces ¶ 한 줄씩 띄어쓰다 write on every other line

띄엄띄엄 sparsely ; scattered ; 《walk》 slowly

***띄우다**[1] ① [공중에] fly ; let fly ; make fly ¶ 연을 띄우다 fly a kite // 광고 기구를 띄우다 send up an advertising balloon // 비행기를 띄우다 fly an airplane ; launch an airplane into the air
② [물 위에] float ; set 《a ship》 afloat ; waft (나뭇잎을) ; launch 《a newly-built ship》 ; sail 《a boat》 ¶ 한강에 배를 띄우다 set a boat afloat on the *Han* River // 뗏목을 띄우다 float a log raft 《down a river》
③ [편지를] send (out) ¶ 편지를 띄우다 send a letter // 감사 전보를 띄우다 send a telegram of thanks ; telegraph one's thanks

†**띄우다**[2] [발효시키다] ferment ; leaven ; mold ; make fusty ; [쇠를] cast (iron) ¶ 술을 띄우다 brew wine // 쌀을 창고에 오래 두어 띄워 버렸다 The rice was kept in the warehouse so long that it got stale from the heat.

띄우다[3] [사이를] leave an interval ; leave space ¶ 사이를 띄워서 at intervals // 5피트를 띄워 나무를 심다 plant trees five feet apart // 줄 사이를 띄우다 leave space between the lines ; space the lines // 기둥은 5피트씩 띄워져 서 있다 The poles stand at intervals of five feet.

***띠**[1] ① [허리의] a belt ; a sash (여자용) ; a girdle ; a (waist) band ; belting 《총칭》 ¶ 띠를 매다 tie a belt〔girdle〕 // 띠를 조르다 tighten one's belt ; adjust〔fix〕 one's belt // 띠를 풀다 untie〔undo〕 the sash ; ungird oneself
② [물건의] a band ; a tape ¶ 섬띠 the band of a rice bag // 술통에 쇠띠를 하다 hoop a wine keg with iron
③ [12지간] the zodiacal sign one was born under ¶ 그는 말띠 태생이다 He was born in the Year of the Horse.
④ [아기의] a baby-carrying band

띠[2] 〖식물〗 a kind of reed ; Imperata cylindrica (학명) ¶ 띠로 이은 지붕 a thatched roof

띠그르르 —**하다** be somewhat thick 〔big〕 among all the thin〔small〕 things

†**띠다**[1] ① [띠를] tie a sash〔belt〕 ; do up a sash ; girdle oneself ; wear a belt〔girdle〕
② [지니다] carry ; wear ; be armed with ¶ 칼을 허리에 띠다 wear a sword at〔by〕 one's side ; gird on a sword
③ [사명 따위를] be charged with ; be entrusted with ; be invested〔clothed〕 with ¶ 공무를 띠고 on official business 〔duty〕 // 용무를 띠고 여행하다 go on a trip for business purposes // 중대한 사명을 띠다 be charged〔entrusted〕 with some important mission ; have an important mission // 대사는 조약 체결의 전권을 띠고 있다 The ambassador is vested with full powers to conclude the treaty.
④ [빛·기색 따위를] have ; wear ; assume ; take on ¶ 붉은 빛을 띤 reddish 《cheeks》 // 붉은 빛을 띤 자주색 purple inclining to red ; purple with a dash of red // 붉은 빛을 띠다 be reddish ; be tinged with red // 주기를 띠다 be under the influence of liquor ; be tipsy // 노기를 띠다 look angry // 활기를 띠다 present an animated appearance ; liven up // 입가에 미소를 띠고 with a smile about one's lips // 눈에 기쁜빛을 띠고 with one's eyes beaming〔sparkling〕 with joy // 그는 만면에 희색을 띠고 있었다 His face beamed with joy. // 그 운동은 국제적 성격을 띠게 됐다 The campaign has taken on an international character.

띠다[2] ① let fly ⇨ 띄우다[1] ② make stale ⇨ 띄우다[2]

띠씨름 belt-hold wrestling

띠앗머리 sibling〔brotherly〕 affection ; fraternal love ¶ 띠앗머리 없다 lack in brotherly affection

띠엄띠엄 ① [드문드문] at long intervals ; sparsely ; scatteredly ; sporadically ; scatteringly ; stragglingly ; here and there ¶ 나무를 띠엄띠엄 심다 plant trees at considerable distance from each other // 띠엄띠엄 읽다 read at random〔desultorily〕 ; read skipping here and there // 골짜기에 인가가 띠엄띠엄 있다 The valley is sparsely dotted with houses. // 그 언덕에는 나무가 띠엄띠엄 서 있다 The hill is sparsely wooded.

② [천천히] very slowly ¶ 띠엄띠엄 걷다 walk very slowly // 띠엄띠엄 걸어도 황소걸음 slow but steady ; slow but sure

띠톱 a band〔belt〕 saw

띰목 —木 a prop supporting the ceiling of a mine pit ; timbering

띳장 —杖 〖광산〗 a thick wooden piece laid across the two poles which are on either side of a mine pit ; 〖건축〗 a wooden piece placed sideways across boarding

띳집 an imperata-thatched house

띵하다 [아파서] have a deep-seated〔dull〕 pain ¶ 머리가 띵하다 have a dull headache ; be numb with a headache

ㄹ

-ㄹ ¶ 갈 곳 the place to go // 올 가을 the coming autumn // 폭풍이 올 전조 indications of a coming storm // 그 박물관은 한번 찾아가 볼 만하다 The museum is worth visiting. // 누가 그것을 할 것인가 Who will do it? // 그가 말하는 것을 들으면 그를 촌뜨기라고 생각할 것이다 To hear him talk, one would take him for a countryman.

-ㄹ걸 ① [한탄] ¶ 이 세상에 태어나지 않았으면 좋았을걸 I wish I had never been born. // 시험을 쳤더라면 좋았을걸 I ought to〔should〕 have taken the examination. // 의사의 말을 들을걸 If I had only taken my doctor's advice! // 영어를 배워 두었더라면 좋았을걸 Oh, that I had learned English! // 그때 너의 충고를 들었더라면 지금 나는 행복할걸 If I had taken your advice, I should be happier now.
② [추측] ¶ 네가 더 클걸 I think〔guess〕 you are taller than I. // 이것으로 충분할걸 This will probably be enough. // 그는 꼭 성공할걸 I am sure (that) he will succeed. // 그는 갔을걸 He may have gone. // 아닐걸 I should say not.

*-ㄹ 것 같다 […같이 보이다] look; appear; […라고 생각되다] 《it》 seem 《to me》 that; [아마 …것이다] be likely to; probably ¶ 비가 올 것 같다 It looks like rain./It is likely to rain. // 아무래도 그 내각은 붕괴할 것 같다 Most probably the Cabinet will collapse. // 그는 곧 회복할 것 같지 않다 There is no hope of his recovering soon. // 그는 늦을 것 같다 I am afraid〔I fear〕 he will be late.

-ㄹ게 ¶ 내 곧 돌아올게 I'll be right back. // 내 갖다 줄게 I'll fetch it for you. // 내일 찾아갈게 I'll call on you tomorrow. // 나 먼저 갈게 I'll leave before you.

-ㄹ까 ¶ 그럴까 Really?/You don't say so! // 그와 같은 일이 가능할까 Can such things be possible? // 그 여자는 올까 I wonder if she is coming. // 그가 이 제안을 거절하면 어떻게 될까 If he should refuse the proposal, what would happen? // 창문을 열까요 Shall I open the window? // 나는 그 여자와 같이 가 볼까 한다 I have half a mind to go with her. // 해 볼까 한다 I think I'll try. // 그들은 싸울까 항복할까 망설였다 They hesitated between fighting and submitting. // 벌이 그 여자의 코를 쏘면 어떻게 될까 If the bee were to sting her nose!

-ㄹ까 보냐 ¶ 어찌 그런 일이 있을까 보냐 How can it〔that〕 be?/It's impossible! // 내가 그 게임에서 질까 보냐 There is no reason why I can't win the game./It can't be possible that I lose the game.

-ㄹ까 보다 ① [추측] ¶ 내가 더 클까 보다 I might be taller than you. // 이것이 저것보다 클까 보다 This looks larger than that. // 비가 올까 보다 It looks like rain./It is likely to rain.
② [불확실한 자기 의사] ¶ 그만 갈까 보다 I think I'll go by now. // 책이나 읽을까 보다 I would rather read.

-ㄹ까 봐 ① [우려] for fear 《of doing that》〔lest... should do〕; fearful of 《getting infected, losing it》 ¶ 또 실패할까 봐 걱정이다 I'm afraid I shall fail again. // 그는 살해될까 봐 도망쳤다 He fled lest he (should) be killed.
② [불확실한 자기 의사] I would rather 《do》

-ㄹ까 하다 [예정] intend to 《do》; will 《do》; have a mind to 《do》; mean to 《do》; think of 《doing》; have the intention of 《doing》; expect to 《do》; be going to 《do》 ¶ 할까 하고 with the intention of...; for the purpose of... // 오전 중에 돌아올까 합니다 I expect to come back before noon.

-ㄹ꼬 ¶ 그것이 무엇일꼬 What could〔might〕 it be? // 어떻게 하면 좋을꼬 I wonder what I had better do. // 어찌하여 그는 이렇게 늦을꼬 How is it〔Why is it〕 (that) he is so late?

-ㄹ는지 [의문] if; or; either... or; whether...or ¶ 비가 올는지 안 올는지 모르겠다 I can't tell if it will rain or not.

-ㄹ는지도 모르다 may〔might〕 《be, do》; perhaps; maybe; possibly ¶ 그렇게 될는지도 모른다 It may turn〔come〕 out so. // 그럴는지도 모른다 It may be so./I am afraid so. // 그렇게 말했을는지도 모른다 I may have told you that way.

-ㄹ 듯이 as if〔as though〕 to do〔be〕; tending to ¶ 금방 때릴 듯이 노려보다 glare at me as if he were going to strike me at any moment // 죽을 듯이 신음하다 groan as if he were going to die

-ㄹ **듯하다** be about to ⟪do⟫ ; be on the point of ⟪doing⟫ ; be ready to ⟪do⟫ ; be likely to ⟪do⟫ ¶ 금방이라도 비가 쏟아질듯하였다 It was threatening to rain. // 두 사람은 주먹다짐이라도 벌일 듯하였다 They were (on the point of) coming to blows.

-ㄹ**라** ¶ 빨리 서둘러라 학교에 늦을라 Hurry up, or you will be late for school. // 조심해라 넘어질라 Be careful lest you fall down. // 병날라 그만 먹어라 Stop eating before you get sick. // 비가 올라 우산을 가지고 가거라 Take your umbrella, in case it should rain.

-ㄹ**라치면** whenever ; when ; if ¶ 나는 서울에 갈라치면 언제나 아저씨 댁에 머문다 Whenever I go up to Seoul, I stay with my uncle. // 그는 우리집에 올라치면 뭔지 아이 선물을 가져다 준다 He never calls on me without bringing me some toys or other for my child.

-ㄹ**락말락** ¶ -ㄹ락말락하다 be on the point〔brink, verge〕 of ⟪doing⟫ ; come near ⟪doing⟫ ; be about〔ready〕 to ⟪do⟫ // 꽃망우리가 필락말락하고 있다 The buds are just ready to burst. // 두 나라는 전쟁을 벌일락말락하고 있다 The two countries are on the brink of war.

-ㄹ **만하다** ① [충분하다] be enough ; be sufficient ¶ 천 명을 수용할 만하다 be large enough to accommodate a thousand people ② [값어치가 있다] be worth ; be worthy of ; deserve ¶ 칭찬할 만하다 be worthy of praise // 한번 볼 만하다 be worth seeing〔worthy of inspection〕

-ㄹ**망정** but ; however ; (even) though ; nevertheless ; although ; yet ¶ 그는 나이는 어릴망정 유능한 변호사다 Young as he is〔Though he is young〕, he is an able lawyer. // 굶어 죽을망정 도둑질은 안 한다 Even if I starve to death, I won't steal.

-ㄹ **모양이다** be likely ⟪to⟫ ; probably ; in all likelihood〔probability〕 ; bid fair ⟪to⟫ ¶ 비가 올 모양이다 It looks like rain. /It is likely to rain.

-ㄹ **바에** ¶ 할 바엔 잘해라 Do it well if you do it at all. // 어차피 죽을 바엔 무엇이든 좋아하는 것을 먹이는 것이 좋다 Let him eat what he likes, if there is no hope for his life. // 어차피 헤어질 바에는 친구로 헤어지자 Let us part friends, as long as we are going to part anyway.

-ㄹ **바에야** if you do ⟪it⟫ at all ¶ 어차피 할 바에야 똑똑히 해라 If you do it at all, do it well. // 어차피 지불할 바에야 지금 지불하게 If you are going to pay it at all, you had better pay it now.

-ㄹ**밖에** ¶ 그렇게 할밖에 다른 수가 없다 There is nothing for it but to do so. /It's the only thing we can do. /There is〔We have〕 no choice〔alternative〕 but to do so. /That's the only course open to us. // 놀랄 수밖에 없다 I cannot help being astonished.

-ㄹ **뿐더러** not only〔merely〕... but ; as well as ¶ 영어를 말할 뿐더러 불어도 한다 He speaks not only English but also French. /He speaks French as well as English. // 그는 시인일 뿐더러 화가이기도 하다 He is both 〔at once〕 a poet and a painter.

-ㄹ**세** ¶ 이것이 내 집일세 This is my house. // 오늘이 오월 초하룰세 It is the first of May.

-ㄹ**세라** (there is a fear) lest ; there is a danger of ; it will ; it might ; in a way so as to avoid ¶ 아플세라 it might hurt you ; so there won't be pain ; lest you feel pain

-ㄹ**세말이지** [남의 예상에 대한 부인] ¶ 내가 자네를 도와 줄세말이지 You can hardly expect me to help you. // 비가 올세말이지 It will be all right if it rains, but it won't.

*-ㄹ**수록** [비교] the more... the more (더) ; the less... the less (덜) ¶ 빠를수록 (더) 좋다 The sooner, the better. / The sooner you do it, the better it will be. // 사람이 많으면 많을수록 즐겁다 The more, the merrier. // 가지면 가질수록 더 갖고 싶다 The more you have, the more you want. // 말하지 않을수록 좋다 The less said about it, the better. // 생각하면 생각할수록 더 모르게 된다 The more I think, the less I understand.

*-ㄹ **수 없다** cannot ; be unable ⟪to do⟫ ; be impossible (불가능) ; cannot afford ⟪to do⟫ (여유가 없다) ⇨ 수 없다 ¶ 그 문제는 어려워서 도저히 할 수 없다 The problem is utterly beyond me. // 그것은 어려워서 나는 할 수 없다 It is too difficult for me to do. /It's too much for me. // 무슨 일이든 인간의 힘으로 할 수 없는 것은 없다 Human power is equal to anything. // 그것을 나는 참을 수 없다 It is more than I can bear.

-ㄹ **수 있다** [사람이 주어] can ⟪do⟫ ; be able〔in a position〕 to ⟪do⟫ ; be capable of ⟪doing⟫ ; be equal to ⟪the task⟫ ; have ⟪something⟫ in one's power ; [사물이 주어] be possible ; […해도 상관없다] may ⟪do⟫ ; be permitted to ⟪do⟫ ¶ 그것은 할 수 있다 It can be done. // 할 수 있는 일이면 무엇이나 하겠습니다 I will do anything (that) I can for you.

-ㄹ **양으로** with the intention〔object, aim, idea〕 of ; with a view to... ; with the view of... ; from〔through〕 motives of... ; for the purpose of... ; in the hope〔hopes〕 of... ; in the expectation of... ; by way of··· ¶ 그는 사죄를 할

양으로 뭐라곤가 말했다 He said something by way of apology. // 그는 여생을 딸 내외와 살 양으로 영국으로 돌아왔다 He had come back to England purposing to live with his daughter and her husband for the rest of his life.

-ㄹ **양이면** if it is the intention〔idea〕 to do ; if one is going to do ¶ 한국에 갈 양이면 한 달은 걸리겠다 It will take one month to get to Korea. // 강산 구경을 다할 양이면 몇 날이 될지 모르겠구나 There's no telling how many days it will take if we do all the sightseeing.

-ㄹ**작시면** if ; in case (of) ; supposing ; provided 《that》 ¶ 만일 한국이 외국의 공격을 받을작시면 어떻게 하겠는가 What would you do in case Korea were attacked by foreign arms? // 만일 초목에 꽃이 피지 않을작시면 자연은 얼마나 쓸쓸할까 Suppose plants were not to flower, how dreary nature would be!

-ㄹ **줄** ¶ 그런 못된 놈일 줄은 몰랐다 Who should have imagined him to be such a rascal?

*-ㄹ**지** whether (or not) ; if ¶ 그가 올지 어떨지 모르겠다 I don't know whether he will be here. // 가야 할지 그대로 있어야 할지 모르겠다 I am uncertain whether to go away or stay where I am. // 오실지 안 오실지 여쭈어 보아 주시오 Please ask him if he will come. // 그가 집에 있을지 모르겠다 I wonder if 〔whether〕 he is at home (or not). // 무슨 일이 일어날지 아무도 모른다 There is no saying〔No one can say〕 what may happen. // 어떻게 하면 좋을지 가르쳐 주시오 Tell me what to do.

-ㄹ**지나** though... must〔should〕... ; must〔should, ought to〕 《do》, but... ¶ 당장 갈지나 should go right now, but... // 그의 죄는 죽어 마땅할지나 his crime deserves certain death, but...

-ㄹ **지니라** must ; should ; ought to 《do》 ; shall (2·3인칭) ¶ 부모님 말씀에 순종할지니라 You should〔ought to〕 obey your parents. // 간음하지 말지니라 〖성경〗 Thou shalt not commit adultery.

-ㄹ**지도 모르다** may〔might〕 《be, do》 ; perhaps ; maybe ; possibly ¶ 그렇게 될지도 모른다 It may turn〔come〕 out so. // 그럴지도 모른다 It may be so. /I am afraid so. // 갈지도 모른다 Perhaps he will go. // 그렇지 않았더라면 그는 목숨을 잃었을지도 모른다 Otherwise he might possibly have lost his life. // 그는 회복할지도 모른다 He may possibly recover. // 그렇지 않을지도 모른다 I'm afraid not. // 어쩌면 사실일지도 모른다 It may be true for aught I know. // 내가 그렇게 말했을지도 모른다 I may have told that way. // 그 여자는 40세가 넘었을지도 모른다 She is over forty, I should think〔say〕. // 내가 틀렸을지도 모른다 // I am afraid I am wrong. // 그가 옳을지도 모른다 He is right, I dare say.

-ㄹ**지라** ought to 《do》 ; should ; shall (2·3인칭) ; must ¶ 부모를 사랑할지라 You should obey your parents. // 간음하지 말지라 Thou shalt not commit adultery. // 각자는 그의 직업에 착실할지라 Let every man stick to his calling.

†-ㄹ**지라도** even though ; even if ; although ; however ; no matter 《who, what, whom》 ; regardless of ¶ 비가 올지라도 even if it rains〔should rain〕 // 아무리 고단할지라도 however〔no matter how〕 tired one may be // 어떤 일이 생길지라도 whatever〔no matter what〕 may happen // 사실일지라도 granting it to be true ; granted it is true // 비록 그럴지라도 나는 동의하지 않겠다 It may be so, but I will not agree. // 아무리 바보일지라도 그것쯤은 알고 있다 The veriest simpleton knows that.

-ㄹ**지어다** [명령] ought to 《do》 ; should ; shall (2·3인칭) ; must ¶ 도둑질하지 말지어다 Thou shalt not steal. // 국민된 자는 병역에 복무할지어다 It shall be the duty of everybody to undergo military service.

-ㄹ**지언정** rather than ; sooner than ¶ 죽을지언정 항복하지 않겠다 I would rather〔sooner〕 die than surrender. /I prefer death to surrender. // 낙제를 할지언정 컨닝은 안 한다 I would rather fail than cheat. // 죽을지언정 살아서 치욕은 받지 않겠다 Death is preferable to dishonor. /I would rather〔sooner〕 die than suffer disgrace.

-ㄹ**진대** [가령] if ; in case ; provided that ; [-ㄹ 것 같으면] according to ; judging from ¶ 필요할진대 if necessary // 기왕 싸울진대 끝까지 싸워라 If you do fight, fight it out. // 내가 볼진대 그는 승산이 없다 In my opinion〔From what I know of him〕 the chances are against him.

-ㄹ **터이다** [1인칭] will ; intend to ; expect to ; mean to ; be going to ; [남이] be supposed to ; be expected to ¶ 오전에 돌아올 터이다 I expect to come back before noon. // 그가 7시에 도착할 터이니 기다려 보자 Let's wait because he is supposed to arrive at 7. // 좀더 열심히 공부하였으면 좋았을 터인데 You ought to〔should〕 have studied harder.

-**라**¹ ① [종결 어미] ¶ 인명은 재천이라 Life and death are providential. // 그는 나를 해칠지라도 나는 그를 사랑하리라 Should he injure me, I would love him. // 생명으로 인도하는 문은 좁고 길이 협착하여 찾는 이가 적음이니라 For the gate is narrow and the way is hard, that leads to life, and those who find

it are few.
② [연결 어미] ¶ 우천인지라 시합은 중지되었다 As it was rainy, the game was called off. // 그는 가난한지라 자동차를 살 수 없었다 Since he was poor, he could not buy a car.
③ [명령] ¶ 서두르지 말아라 Don't hurry. // 이웃 사랑하기를 네 몸같이 하여라 Thou shalt〔must〕 love thy neighbor as thyself. // 구하라 그러면 너희에게 주실 것이요 Ask, it will be given to you.

라² 〖음악〗 la
—단조〔장조〕 D minor〔major〕

라고 ¶ 종이 집게라고 써 있는 상자 the box that says "Paper Clips" // 성경에〔신문에〕 …라고 써 있다 The Bible〔paper〕 says 《that》 // 이것은 진달래라고 하는 꽃이다 This is a flower called azalea. // 이 꽃은 영어로 무어라고 하느냐 What do they call this flower in English? // 그들은 그 아기를 메리라고 이름지었다 They named the baby Mary. // 나는 그를 위대한 학자라고 생각하지 않는다 I don't regard him as a great scholar. // 모든 젊은이는 군대에 가야 한다 너라고 예외는 아니다 Every young man has to go to army, you are no exception.

-라고 ¶ 기다리라고 해라 Tell him to wait. // 들어오라고 할까요 Shall I tell him to come in? // 그는 학생들에게 담배를 피우지 말라고 했다 He told the students not to smoke.

라고는 ⇨ 이라고는

라고도 also; in a sense〔manner〕; so to speak ¶ …라고도 하다 be equally said... // 생은 죽음의 시초라고도 할 수 있다 Birth is, in a sense, the beginning of death.

라고 해서 because; as; on the ground 《that...》; on〔under〕 the plea 《of, that...》 ¶ 부자라고 해서 반드시 행복한 것은 아니다 The rich are not always happy. // 가난뱅이라고 해서 남을 멸시해서는 안된다 You should not despise a man because he is poor.

라기 보다 rather 《than》; more of... ¶ 그는 실업가라기 보다 학자다 He is more of a scholar than (of) a businessman. / He is a scholar rather than a businessman. /He is not so much a businessman as a scholar.

라놀린 〖화학〗 lanolin(e)

라는 called; named; styled; titled ¶ 보브라는 소년 a boy, Bob by name; a boy called Bob // 김 모라는 사람 a (certain) *Kim* // 백조라는 책 a book titled "The Swan" // 코리아라는 잡지 a magazine styled〔under the style of〕 the "Korea" // …라는 의미의 which may be thus interpreted; to the effect 《that》

-라는 ¶ 법정에 출두하라는 통고를 받다 receive notice to appear in court // 내가 하라는 대로 하시오 Do as I tell you. // 전쟁이 곧 일어나리라는 소문이 줄곧 돈다 There is a persistent rumor that there will be a war soon.

라니 ¶ A씨라니 누구 말이냐 Whom do you mean by "Mr. A"? /"Mr. A"? whom do you mean? // 김씨가 간첩이라니 나는 깜짝 놀랐다 I am greatly surprised to hear that Mr. *Kim* is a spy.

라도 [⋯까지도] even; [설사 ⋯일지라도] though; even if; however; [어떤 ⋯라도] any ¶ 내가 아니더라도 besides me // 어린아이라도 아는 intelligible even to a child // 아무리 가난할지라도 however poor one may be // 꿈에라도 보고 지고 I wish I could see you even in a dream. // 실패한다 하더라도 해볼 만하다 It is worth attempting though we fail. // 어느쪽이라도 좋다 Either (of them) will do. // 어떤 아이라도 그만한 것은 할 수 있다 Any child can do it.

라돈 〖화학〗 radon 《Rn》

*__라듐__ 〖화학〗 radium 《Ra》
— **광천 요법** a radium spring (treatment) — **방사능** radioactivity — **방사선** radium rays

라드 [기름] lard

-라든지 or; whether〔either〕... or; otherwise ¶ 그에게 그 일을 하라든지 말라든지 결정을 해 줘야 한다 We must decide whether to make him do the work or not.

라디안 〖수학〗 radian

라디에이터 a radiator

†__라디오__ radio 《미》; wireless 《영》; [기계] a radio 《*pl.* ~s》; a radio〔wireless〕 set ¶ 라디오 방송을 하다 broadcast; speak on the radio〔air〕; talk over the radio // 라디오를 틀다〔끄다〕 turn〔switch〕 on〔off〕 the radio // 라디오의 파장을 맞추다 tune in a frequency // 라디오를 듣다 listen to the radio; hear on〔over〕 the radio // 라디오 소리를 크게〔적게〕 하다 raise〔lower〕 the volume of the radio
— **녹음** radio transcription — **뉴스** the news on the radio; radio news — **드라마** a radio drama — **로케이터** a radio locator — **방송** radio broadcasting; a radio broadcast — **방송국** a radio (broadcasting) station — **송신기** a (radio) transmitter; [자동차용] an autoradio 《미》 — **수신기** a (radio) receiver; a radio (set) — **아나운서** a radio announcer — **전파** a radio beam —**존데** 〖기상〗 a radiosonde — **중계** hookup 《미》; relay — **중계 방송** a 《nationwide》 hookup; a relay broadcast — **청취자** a radio listener〔audience〕 — **체조** radio cal(l)isthenics〔exercises, gymnastics〕 — **코미디** a radio comedy — **해설자** a radio commentator

라디오 감도 —感度 the sensitivity〔reception〕 of a radio〔wireless〕

라라 [아시아 구제 연맹] LARA 《Licensed

Agencies for Relief in Asia》
라르고 〖음악〗 largo
라마[1] [라마승] a lama
—교 Lamaism **—교도** a Lamaist ; a Lamaite **— 사원** a lamasery
라마[2] 〖동물〗 a l(l)ama
라면 [국수] Chinese noodles
-라면 [라 하면] if it be (said to be) ¶ 내가 새라면 너한테 날아가련만 If I were a bird, I'd fly to you.
라벤더 〖식물〗 a lavender
‡라벨 a label ⇨ 레테르
-라서 [감히·능히] indeed ; possibly ; by any audacity ¶ 뉘라서 나를 이기리요 Who indeed can beat me?/Who would dare to beat me?
라셀 〖의학〗 a rhonchus 《*pl.* -chi》; a rale ; a murmuring sound 《in the lungs》
라스트 the last
— 신 the last scene
-라야, 라야만 only if it be ; unless it be ¶ 너라야 능히 그 일을 하겠다 It is you that can do the job. // 달은 밤에라야 빛을 낸다 The moon shines only at night.
라우드스피커 a loudspeaker
라운드 〖권투〗 a round ; [둥근] round
라운지 [호텔·클럽 따위의 사교실] a lounge
라이너 〖야구〗 a liner ; a line drive ; [안옷감] (a) liner ¶ 라이너성 싱글히트 a line single // 강한 라이너를 치다 hit a strong liner
라이노타이프 〖인쇄〗 a linotype
라이닝 〖기계〗 lining
라이덴병 —甁 〖물리〗 a Leyden jar
라이벌 a rival
— 의식 the spirit of rivalry
라이선스 (a) license 《미》; (a) licence
라이스 rice
— 페이퍼 rice paper **카레 —** curry and rice ; curried rice
라이온 a lion ; [암컷] a lioness
라이온스 클럽 Lions Club 《*l*iberty *i*ntelligence *o*ur *n*ation's *s*afety의 두문자》
라이카 [상표 이름] a Leica (camera)
라이터 [불켜는] a (cigarette) lighter ; [글쓰는 이] a writer ¶ 라이터를 켜다 snap lighter into flame
— 기름 lighter oil **—돌** a lighter flint **가스 —** a gas lighter
라이트[1] [빛] light ; [등] a (car) light
라이트[2] ① 〖야구〗 the right field ; [우익수] a right fielder ¶ 라이트 플라이를 치다 hit a fly to right ② 〖권투〗 a right
—급 선수 〖권투〗 a lightweight (boxer)
— 윙 〖축구〗 the right wing
‡라이플 a rifle
라인 a line
라인업 a〔the〕 lineup ¶ 라인업을 소개〔발표〕하다 announce the lineup 《of the Yankees》
***라일락** 〖식물〗 lilac
라임라이트 the limelight
라조 —調 〖음악〗 D ¶ 라 장〔단〕조 D major〔minor〕
†라켓 a racket ; [탁구의] a bat
라틴 Latin ¶ 라틴의 Latin
— 문학 Latin literature **— 민족** the Latin races **— 아메리카** Latin America **—어** the Latin language **—어 학자** a Latinist ; a Latin scholar
-락 ¶ 오락가락하다 go〔walk〕 to and fro ; go back and forth ; wander // 비가 오락가락하다 rain off and on // 구름이 오락가락하다 the clouds float back and forth // 정신이 오락가락하다 《one's mind》 wander〔stray〕
-락말락 ¶ 갈매기가 물위에 닿을락말락하게 날아간다 A gull flies skimming the water. // 담이 무너질락말락 한다 The wall is on the brink〔verge〕 of collapse.
락토오스 〖화학〗 lactose ; milk sugar
란 [라고 하는] that〔what〕 is called ⇨ -라는 ; [라고 하는 것은] ¶ 진리란 무엇인가 What is truth? // 날씨란 알 수 없는 것이다 There is no telling about the weather.
란제리 lingerie 《프》
-람 ¶ 내가 가야 할 이유가 뭐람 Why should I go of all things?
랑 and ; or ; and so on〔forth〕; [함께] (together) with ¶ 너랑 나랑 you and me // 친구랑 이야기하다 talk with a friend
랑데부 a rendezvous ; a date 《미》 ¶ 랑데부의 상대 one's date 《미·구》 // 랑데부하다 meet ; have a date 《with》 《미·구》
-래서 ¶ 그를 오래서 같이 놀자 Let's ask him to come to play with us. // 그가 저녁을 먹으러 오래서 그의 집에 갔다 I went to his house, being invited to dinner.
-래서야 ¶ 이래서야 됩니까 You shouldn't do this. // 석 달도 못 되어 그만두래서야 되겠소 It is unreasonable that you should ask me to quit within three months. // 이것이 백 원 어치래서야 될 말입니까 Are you kidding to say that this is worth 100 *won*?
-래야 ¶ 곧 출발하래야 되겠다 I must tell him to start at once. // 그래야 마땅하지 You should do so./It should be so.
래커 lacquer ¶ 래커를 칠하다 lacquer
랙 lac
— 칠 shellac
랜덤 샘플링 random sampling
랜턴 a lantern
†램프 a lamp
석유 — an oil lamp
랩소디 a rhapsody
랩 타임 the lap time ¶ 300미터의 랩 타임 the 300 meter lap time

ㄹ

랭킹 ranking ¶ 국제〔국내〕 랭킹 international〔national〕 ranking // 랭킹 제1위를 차지하다 take the first ranking
-랴 ① [반어] ¶ 그것이 어찌 스스로 부러지랴 It cannot break of itself. /How can it break of itself? ② [문의] ¶ 결혼식은 언제로 하랴 When shall the wedding be? // 돈을 주랴 Do you want some money? /Shall I give you some money?
-량 量 ⇨ 양(量)
교통— (volume of) traffic **생산—** an output 《of a factory》
-러 ¶ 너를 보러 왔다 I have come to see you.
러너 〖야구〗 a runner ¶ 러너를 내보내다〔홈인시키다〕 send〔return〕 a runner // 러너를 일소하다 empty the bases of the runners
러닝 a running (race)
— **메이트** a running mate — **셔츠** a sweatshirt ; a (sleeveless) undershirt
러브 love
— **레터** a love letter —**신** a love scene
러시아 Russia
—**말** Russian (language) — **사람** a Russian
러시 아워 the rush hour(s) ¶ 아침저녁의 러시 아워 the morning and evening rush hours
러키 lucky
— **존** the lucky zone
러프 rough
*__럭비__ 〖운동〗 Rugby (football) ; rugger 《영·속》
—**공** a Rugby ball ; an oval
럭스 〖물리〗 a lux
런던 London
— **사람** a Londoner ; a cockney — **사투리** cockney accent — **영어** cockney (English) —**탑** the Tower of London
런치 lunch ; luncheon
— **타임** lunch time — **파티** a luncheon party
럼 [술] rum
—**주(酒)** rum
레가토 〖음악〗 legato
레귤러 a regular
— **멤버** a regular member — **포지션** regular position
레그혼 a leghorn
레늄 〖화학〗 rhenium 《Re》
레닌주의 Leninism
—**자** a Leninite
레더 leather
레디메이드 ready-made ; ready-mades
*__레모네이드__ lemonade
‡__레몬__ 〖식물〗 a lemon
—**산(酸)** citric acid —**수(水)** ⇨ 레모네이드 — **스쿼시** lemon squash —**유(油)** lemon oil —**즙〔주스〕** lemon juice —**차(茶)〔티〕** lemon tea

레바논 Lebanon ¶ 레바논의 Lebanese
— **사람** a Lebanese
레버 ① 〖기계〗 a lever ② [자동차의] a gearshift
레벨 level ¶ 레벨이 높다〔낮다〕 be on a high〔low〕 level // 높은 레벨에 이르다 attain a high level // 레벨을 높이다〔낮추다〕 level up〔down〕
*__레스토랑__ a restaurant
레슨 a lesson ¶ 피아노 레슨 piano lessons // 바이올린 레슨을 받다 take〔have〕 a violin lesson
레슬러 a wrestler
‡__레슬링__ wrestling
— **선수** a wrestler
레위기 —**記** 〖성경〗 Leviticus
레이 a lei ¶ 레이를 목에 걸다 put a lei round one's neck
*__레이더__ radar 《*ra*dio *d*etecting *a*nd *r*anging》
— **기지** a radar base〔site〕 —**망(網)** a radar fence〔screen network〕
레이디 a lady
레이디 퍼스트 lady first ; deference toward women
레이스 ① [경주] a race ② [수예품] lace ¶ 레이스를 달다 trim with lace
—**실** cotton thread — **장식** enlacement ; lacing — **코스** a race course
레이아웃 a layout
*__레이온__ rayon ; artificial silk
— **펄프** rayon pulp
레이저 〖물리〗 a laser 《light amplification by stimulated emission of radiation》
— **광선** a laser beam
레인지 [조리대] a (kitchen) range ; a cooking stove
가스 — a gas range
‡__레인코트__ a raincoat ; [벨트 달린] a trench coat ; [고무를 입힌] a mac(k)intosh ; [갠 날에도 입는] a weatherall
†__레일__ a rail ; a railway line ; a railroad track ¶ 레일을 깔다 lay rails
레저 leisure
— **산업** the leisure industry
레즈비언 a lesbian
레지 [다방의] a tearoom waitress
레지스탕스 resistance
레지스터 a register ¶ 여자 레지스터 a cash-register girl
레커차 —**車** [구호차] a wrecker ; a tow car 〔truck〕
†__레코드__ ① [기록] a record ; a mark ; ⇨ 기록(記錄) ② [축음기의] a (phonograph) record ; a disk ; a disc ¶ 레코드를 틀다 put〔play〕 a record on the gramophone // 레코드에 취입하다 record 《a speech》 on a disk〔the gramophone〕
— **수집가** a phonophile — **음악(音樂)** recorded〔disk〕 music ; a canned music 《속》 — **콘서트** a record concert ; a disk recital — **플레이어** a record play-

er ; a phonoplayer 어학(語學) — a linguaphone 엘피 — a long-playing〔an LP〕 record
레크리에이션 (a) recreation
— 센터 a recreation center
레터 a letter
레테르 a label ¶ 레테르를 붙이다 label 《a bottle》
레토르트 〖화학〗 [증류기] a retort
레퍼리 a referee ¶ 레퍼리를 보다 referee (a match)
레퍼토리 repertory ; repertoire
레프트 left
— 윙 the left wing — 잽 a left jab — 필더 a left fielder — 필드 a left field
⁑렌즈 a lens ¶ 렌즈의 중심 the optical center // 렌즈를 …에 돌리다 direct the lens to... // 렌즈를 맞추다 train the lens 《on》 // 렌즈를 닦다 clean a lens
대물(對物) — objectives ; a substance lens 오목〔볼록〕— a concave〔convex〕 lens 접안(接眼) — eyepieces ; an ocular lens 합성〔확대〕 — a compound 〔magnifying〕 lens
***렌치** a wrench
렌터카 a rental car
-려 ① [막 …하려 하다] be ready to 《do》 ; be about to 《do》 ; set about to 《do》 ; be going to 《do》 ; be on the point〔brink, verge〕 of 《doing》 ¶ 터지려 하는 꽃봉오리 a bud just ready to burst // 막 그것을 하려던 참이다 I am (just) going to do it.
② ⇨ -려고
-려고 ¶ 산보하려고 나가다 go out for a walk // 무엇 하려고 왔니 What do you come here for? // 떠나려고 한다 He is going to leave. // 좋은 자리를 잡으려고 일찍 갔다 I went early (in order, so as) to get a good seat. // 그는 말을 하려고 입을 열었다 He opened his lips to make some remarks. // 그 사람에게 눈물을 보이지 않으려고 그 여자는 얼굴을 돌렸다 She turned her head away lest he should see her tears. // 그는 아무것도 갖지 않으려고 하였다 He would have none of it.
-려기에 on account of ; owing to ; as ; because ; since ¶ 그가 슬쩍 집에 가려기에 붙들어 두었다 I held him as he was going home furtively. // 비가 오려기에 우산을 갖고 왔다 I took an umbrella with me, because it was going to rain.
-려나 ¶ 언제 돈을 주려나 When shall I have the money? // 언제 떠나려나 When are you going to leave? // 자네 오늘 저녁에 산책하러 오려나 Will you come for a walk this evening?
-려네 I will ; I intend〔mean〕 to 《do》 ; I am going to 《do》 ; I am thinking of 《doing》 ¶ 나는 자려네 I am going to sleep. // 자네가 가면 나도 가려네 I will go if you go. // 나는 내년에 외국에 가려네 I intend〔mean〕 to go abroad next year.
-려느냐 ¶ 그것으로 무엇을 하려느냐 What are you going to do with it? // 무슨 말을 하려느냐 What do you mean to say? // 어디를 가려느냐 Where do you intend going? // 나에게 무엇을 시키려느냐 What do you expect me to do? // 언제 돌아오려느냐 What time will you be back?
-려는 ¶ 너를 속이려는 생각은 털끝만큼도 없다 I haven't the slightest intention 〔the least idea〕 to cheat you. // 이것은 이제 우리가 만나려는 소녀의 사진이다 This is the picture of a girl whom we are going to see.
-려는가 ¶ 언제 떠나려는가 When are you going to leave? /When do you intend to leave? // 얼마나 뉴욕에 있으려는가 How long are you going to stay in New York? / How long do you plan to stay in New York?
-려는데 ¶ 내가 막 외출을 하려는데 그가 들어왔다 He came in just as I was going out.
-려는지 ¶ 그가 직접 오려는지 모르겠다 I am uncertain whether he will come himself or not.
-려니 ¶ 우리들은 그가 시험에 합격되려니 생각했다 We expected that he would pass the examination. // 그들이 진심으로 환영해 주려니 생각했다 I thought that they would give me a hearty welcome.
-려니와 [또한] not only... but... ; as well as ; [한편] on the other hand ¶ 그는 학자도 아니려니와 정치가도 아니다 He is neither a scholar nor a politician. // 취직도 하려니와 곧 결혼도 하겠다 Besides getting a job, I will get married soon. // 그는 영어도 말하려니와 불어도 한다 He can speak not only English but also French.
-려다가 ¶ 소풍을 가려다가 날씨가 흐려서 그만두었다 As it was cloudy, I gave up the idea of going on a picnic. // 처음에 교사가 되려다가 그만두었다 Teaching was my original intention, but I have changed my mind.
-려도 ¶ 아무리 하려도 할 수 없다 However much I may try, I cannot do it. // 죽으려도 죽을 수 없다 I can't die in spite of myself. // 있으려도 나의 건강이 허락지 않는다 My health will not permit of my staying here.
-려면 ¶ 싸우려면 끝까지 싸워라 If you do fight, fight it out. // 고기를 잡으려면 옷이 젖는 것을 꺼리지 말아야 한다 He who would catch fish, must not mind getting wet.
-려면야 ¶ 이기려면야 이길 수 있지만 I could win, if I would.

-**려무나** may ; had better ¶ 여기에 열쇠가 있으니 언제든지 들어오려무나 Here is the key, you may enter at will. // 내 사전을 쓰고 싶으면 쓰려무나 You may use my dictionary if you like. // 좀더 누워 있으려무나 But you had better take a little more rest.

-**려야** ¶ 나는 웃지 않으려야 웃지 않을 수 없었다 I could not help laughing. /I could not but laugh. // 나는 가려야 갈 수 없다 I do wish to go, but I am unable to go.

-**려오** I will〔would〕 ¶ 다시는 그런 짓을 안 하려오 I will never do such a thing again. // 나라를 위해서라면 기꺼이 목숨을 바치려오 I am quite willing to sacrifice my life for my country.

-**력 力** [힘] power ; strength ; [능력] ability ; capability ; capacity
경제— economic power〔strength, might〕 **구매—** purchasing power **영도—** leadership ; the capacity as a leader

련 ⇨ -려느냐 ¶ 커피 한잔 더 하련 Won't you take one more cup of coffee? // 10 달러만 꿔 주련 Would you mind lending me ten dollars?

-**련다** ¶ 나는 내일 가련다 I'm going to go tomorrow.

-**련만** ¶ 내가 차를 운전할 수 있으면 좋으련만 I wish I could drive a car. // 비라도 곧 그쳐 주었으면 좋으련만 If only the rain would stop soon. // 좀 더 열심히 공부를 했으면 좋았으련만 You ought to have〔should have〕 studied harder. // 나에게 몇 자 적어 보내 주었으면 좋았으련만 You might have dropped me a line.

-**렴** may ⇨ -려무나 ¶ 마음대로 해보렴 Do〔Try〕 as you like.

-**렵니까** ¶ 언제 떠나시렵니까 When are you leaving? // 저와 같이 영화를 보러 가시지 않으시렵니까 Won't you go to the movies with me? // 오늘 저녁에 방문하면 댁에 계시렵니까 Shall you be in〔at home〕 if I call this evening?

-**렷다** ¶ 다시는 두말 못하렷다 You will never break your word again, understand? (다짐) /No doubt this will put him to silence. (추측) // 그는 장안 갑부렷다 I understand〔I am given to understand〕 that he is the richest man in the capital city.

†**로** ① [수단·기구] by ; by means of ; with ; in ; on ¶ 기차로 by train // 도보로 on foot // 배로 by ship〔sea〕 // 비행기로 by plane〔air〕 // 영어로 in English // 전보로 by telegraph〔cable〕 // 전화로 by〔over the, on the〕 telephone // 손으로 만들다 make by hand // 연필로 쓰다 write with a pencil〔in pencil〕 // 잉크로 쓰다 write in ink // 칼로 자르다 cut with a knife // 코로 냄새를 맡다 smell with one's nose
② [원인·이유] at ; with ; of ; from ; through ; for ; because of ; on account of ; owing to ; due to ¶ 뇌일혈로 죽다 die of〔from〕 apoplexy // 추위로 떨다 shiver with cold // 공포로 떨다 tremble for fear // 개인적인 이유로 거절하다 refuse from private reasons // 부주의로 실패하다 fail through one's carelessness
③ [원료·재료] from ; of ¶ 이 집은 나무로 만들어졌다 This house is made of wood. // 포도주는 포도로 만든다 Wine is made from grapes.
④ [척도·표준·단위·정도] by ¶ 파운드로 팔다 sell by the pound // 월불로 하숙하다 board by the month // 1분 차이로 기차를 놓치다 miss a train by a minute // 8을 2로 나누다 divide 8 by 2 // 외모로 판단하다 judge by the appearance // 내 시계로는 3시다 It is three o'clock by my watch.
⑤ [방향] to ; for ; forward ¶ 해변가로 가다 go to the seaside // 서울로 떠나다 leave for *Seoul* // 뒤로 돌아 About turn〔face〕!
⑥ [지위·신분·자격] as ; in the capacity〔position〕 of ⇨ 로서 ¶ 대표로 as a representative

로가리듬 〖수학〗 a logarithm

로고 ¶ 참으로 해괴한 일이로고 What a strange thing it is! /What a mystery it is! // 참으로 뻔뻔한 놈이로고 How impudent he is!

로고스 〖철학〗 logos

-**로구먼** ¶ 벌써 한 시로구먼 It is already one o'clock! // 정말 재미있는 광경이로구먼 What a funny sight (it is)!

-**로군** ¶ 정말 아름다운 여자로군 Truly, she is a fair woman. // 그것 좋은 생각이로군 It's a good idea. // 이 진주는 전부 가짜로군 These pearls are all shams. // 기상천외로군 What an idea!

로그 〖수학〗 log

로는 ¶ 영어로는 이것을 뭐라고 하느냐 What is the English for it? /What do you call it in English? // 내 시계로는 약 2시다 It is about two by my watch. // 미모로는 그녀가 최고다 She has no equal for beauty. // 나는 그 후로는 한번도 그녀를 보지 못했다 I have never seen her since then.

-**로다** ¶ 참으로 장관이로다 Really, it is a magnificent view. // 그이야말로 군자로다 He is indeed a remarkable gentleman〔a man of virtue〕.

로도 ¶ 그 곳은 기차로도 배로도 갈 수 있다 You can get there either by train or by ship. // 이 곳은 경치로도 유명하다 This place is famous for its scenery also.

-**로되** ¶ 그는 늙은이로되 힘은 장사다 He is quite strong although (he is) very old.

로듐 〖화학〗 rhodium 《Rh》
로드 게임 a road game
로드 레이스 [자전거의] a road race
로드 쇼 a road show ; a special release
로렐라이 Lorelei
†로마 Roma ; Rome ¶ 로마의 Roman // 로마는 하루아침에 이루어진 것이 아니다 Rome was not built in a day.
—교(敎) Roman Catholicism — 교황 the Pope ; the Holy Father —법 the Roman Law — 사람 a Roman —서(書) 〖성경〗 the (Pauline) Epistle to the Romans — 숫자 Roman numerals —식(式) 〖건축〗 Roman order ; Romanesque —자(字) Roman letters ; the Roman 〔Latin〕 alphabet — 카톨릭 교도(敎徒) a Roman Catholic — 카톨릭 교회 the Roman Catholic Church 신성(神聖) — 제국(帝國) the (Holy) Roman Empire
로마네스크 Romanesque 《architecture》
로망 〖문학〗 a novel 《프》
로망스어 —語 a romance language
‡로맨스 romance ; romantic ; a love affair ; affairs of the heart ; [연애 사건] a love story
로맨티시스트 a romanticist
로맨티시즘 romanticism
‡로맨틱 romantic ¶ 로맨틱한 일생 a romantic career
로봇 [인조 인간] a robot ; [허수아비 같은 사람] a figurehead ¶ 로봇화하다 robotize
로부터 from ; out of ¶ 그리스어로부터 유래된 말 a word derived from Greek
‡로비 a lobby
로빙 〖테니스〗 lobbing
‡로서 ① [지위·신분·자격] as ; for ; in the capacity〔character, position〕 of ¶ 교사로서 있을 수 없는 행위 an act unbecoming to a teacher // 지도자로서 받들다 look up to 《a person》 for one's leader // 보호자로서 행동하다 act in the capacity of (a) guardian // 의사로서 충고한다 I advise you as a doctor.
② [···으로부터] from ; out of ¶ 바람이 남쪽 바다로서 불어온다 The wind blows from the south sea.
로션 lotion
로스 [등심] loin ; sirloin
로스트 (a) roast
— 비프〔치킨〕 roast beef〔chicken〕
로스트 제너레이션 the lost generation
로스트 타임 lost time
로써 [수단] with ; by ; by means of ; using ; [원인] as ; for ; with ; from ; because of ; due to ; [재료] with ; of ; out of ; [결과] as a consequence of ; with ¶ 그의 권력으로써 with his power // 나무로써 짓다 build 《it》 of wood // 썰매로써 가다 go by sled // 그녀의 아름다움은 말로써 표현할 수가 없다 Words cannot express her beauty. /She is too beautiful for words.

로열 박스 a royal box
로열 젤리 royal jelly
로열티 a royalty
로이드 안경 —眼鏡 glasses with thick celluloid rim ; tortoiseshell〔horn-rimmed〕 spectacles
로이터 Reuter
— 전보(電報) a Reuter dispatch — 통신사(通信社) the Reuter News Agency ; Reuter's Ltd.
로제타석 —石 the Rosetta stone
로즈 rose
로카 ROKA 《Republic of Korea Army》
로컬 local
— 뉴스 a local news
로케(이션) 〖영화〗 a location ; a location scene ¶ 로케 가다 go on location // 로케 중이다 be on location
— 헌팅 location hunting
†로켓 a rocket (비행체) ¶ 로켓으로 공격하다 attack 《an enemy base》 with rockets ; rocket 《an enemy fortress》 // 로켓으로 인공 위성을 궤도에 올리다 rocket a man-made satellite into orbit // 로켓으로 날다 fly by rocket 《to》 ; rocket 《to the moon》
— 결합 docking — 발사장〔대(臺)〕 a launching site〔pad〕 — 발사 장치 a rocket launcher —탄(彈) a rocket bomb —포(砲) a rocket gun 달〔우주(宇宙)〕 — a moon〔space〕 rocket 3〔다(多)〕단식 — a three-stage〔multistage〕 rocket 역추진(逆推進) — a retrorocket 증속(增速)〔감속(減速)〕 — a booster 〔retarding〕 rocket
로코코 rococo 《architecture》
로큰롤 rock'-n'-roll ; rock'n-roll
로터리 a rotary ; a traffic circle
— 클럽 a Rotary club ¶ 로터리 클럽 회원 a Rotarian
로테이션 rotation ¶ 로테이션으로 《do something》 by〔in〕 rotation
†로프 a rope
로 하여금 ¶ …로 하여금 …을 시키다 [강제로] make 《a person do》 ; cause 《a person to do》 ; force 《a person to do》 ; compel 《a person to do》 ; [허락·방임] let 《a person do》 ; allow 《a person to do》 ; [의뢰해서] get 《a person to do》 ; have 《a person do》 // 나는 그로 하여금 그 일을 하게 했다 [의뢰] I had him do the work. /I got him to do the work. /I had〔got〕 the work done by him.
로힐 low-heeled〔flat〕 shoes
록클라이밍 rock-climbing
-론 論 ① [논설] an essay ; a treatise ; a comment ; a leading article ② [논의] argument ; discussion ; discourse ; debate ; controversy
국방— the question of national defense 시사— comments on current events 예술— an essay on art 유심— spiritual-

ㄹ

ism 추상— an abstract discussion 한자제한— the question of limiting the use of Chinese characters 화폐— the theory of money
론도 〖음악〗 a rondo
— 형식 a rondo form
론 코트 a lawn court
론 테니스 lawn tennis
*롤러 a roller
— 스케이트 [기구] 《a pair of》 roller skates ; [놀이] roller skating — 스케이트장(場) a roller skating rink
롤링 rolling —하다 roll
롤백 정책 —政策 the rollback policy
롤빵 a roll of bread
-롭다 be ; be characterized by ¶ 호화롭다 be gorgeous〔luxurious, brilliant〕// 새롭다 be new〔fresh〕// 향기롭다 be fragrant // 해롭다 be harmful 《to》 ; be injurious 《to》 ; do harm
롱런 a long run 《of a film》
롱비치 Long Beach
롱플레잉(레코드) a long playing (record)
뢴트겐 roentgen
— 검사 an X-ray examination — 기계(器械) an X-ray apparatus — 기사(技師) a radiographer — 사진 a Roentgen〔an X-ray〕 photograph ; radiogram ; radiograph ¶ 뢴트겐 사진을 찍다 radiograph ; X-ray — 사진술 radiography —선(線) Roentgen rays ; X-rays — 요법(療法) Roentgenotherapy
-료 料 ① [요금] a charge ; a rate ; a fee ② [재료] a material
입장— an admission fee 전화— a telephone charge 조미— a seasoning
루나 파크 a Luna park ; an amusement center
루르 the Ruhr
루마니아 Rumania ; Romania ; Roumania ¶ 루마니아의 Rumanian ; Romanian ; Roumanian
— 사람 a Rumanian ; a Romanian ; a Roumanian
루미네선스 〖물리〗 luminescence
루바슈카 a rubashka shirt〔blouse〕
루블 a rouble
*루비 ① 〖광물〗 a ruby ② 〖인쇄〗 a small size of print ; 5 1/2 pt. size
— 반지 a ring set with a ruby ; a ruby ring
루스 loose —하다 (be) loose ; slovenly
루스 리프 a loose-leaf (book)
루주 rouge 《프》 ¶ 새빨갛게 루주를 칠한 입술 thickly rouged lips // 루주를 바르다 put on rouge
루터파 —派 the Lutheran Church ¶ 루터파의 교리 Lutheranism // 루터파의 교회 a Lutheran church // 루터파의 신자 a Lutheran
루트 ① [경로] a route ; a channel ¶ 정식 루트 legal channels ② [수학] root ¶ 루트 4 the root of 4 《 $\sqrt{4}$ 》
루프 (a) loop
— 안테나 a loop antenna
루피 [인도의 동전] a rupee 《R, Re》
룰 a rule ¶ 룰에 위반하다 be against the rules
룰렛 [도박] roulette ; [기구] a roulette ; [양재용] roulette
룸 a room
—쿨러 a room cooler
룸바 rhumba
룸펜 a hobo 《미》 ; a bum ; a vagrant ; [실업자] a jobless person
룻기 —記 〖성경〗 (the book of) Ruth
-류 類 ① [강(綱)] a class (of insects, ferns) ② [목(目)] an order (of carnivores, hymenoptera) ③ [유파] a type ; a style ; a mode
-류 流 ① [형] a style ; a type ; a mode ; a manner ; a way ; a system ¶ 자기류 one's own fashion // 한국인류의 생각 Korean modes of thought ② [등급] order ; rate ; class ; rank ¶ 2류의 출판사 a second-rate publishing company // 일류 시인 a poet of the first order
‡류머티즘 〖의학〗 rheumatism ; rheumatic trouble ¶ 류머티즘에 걸리다〔의 기가 있다〕 have an attack〔a touch〕 of rheumatism
급성(急性)〔만성(慢性)〕 — acute〔chronic〕 rheumatism
륙색 a rucksack
-륜 輪 [바퀴] a wheel
2—차 a two-wheeled vehicle ; a two-wheeler
르네상스 Renaissance ¶ 르네상스는 근대 문명의 여명이다 Renaissance is the dawn of modern civilization.
— 건축 Renaissance architecture
르포(르타주) reportage 《프》 ; a report 《on》
를 ① [동사의 목적어] ¶ 우표를 수집하다 collect stamps // 나에게 시계를 주다 give me a watch // 나에게 일자리를 구해 주다 find me a job // 그를 의장으로 선출하다 elect him chairman // 바다를 보기를 원하다 want to see the sea // 곧 회복하기를 바라다 hope that one will recover soon ② [전치사의 목적어] ¶ 개를 무서워 하다 be afraid of dogs // 머리를 때리다 hit 《a person》 on the head // 나의 시계를 훔치다 rob me of my watch // 학교를 쉬다〔결석하다〕 stay away〔absent oneself〕 from school // 적에게 수도를 빼앗기다 suffer the loss of the capital city to the enemy // 나를 보라 Look at me.
†리 理 ¶ …리가 없다 cannot be ; must not be ; It is hardly possible 《that》 // 그것이 사실일 리가 없다 It cannot be true. // 그가 병났을 리가 없다 He cannot have been ill. // 늦을 리가 없다 There is

no reason for delay. // 아까까지 여기 있었던 것을 내가 모를 리가 있나 You can't help knowing about a thing that was here a minute ago, can you?

-리 裡 amid(st) ; in ¶ 갈채리에 단(壇)을 내리다 leave a platform amidst〔in〕 the applause of the audience

리골레토 〖음악〗 rigoletto 《이》

리그 a 《baseball》 league

—전(戰) a league game ; the league series〔tournament〕 대(大)〔소(小)〕— the Major〔Minor〕 League

-리까 ¶ 무엇을 하오리까 What shall I do? // 그 여자에게 무엇을 시키오리까 What shall she do?

리넨 linen

*리놀륨 linoleum

-리다 ① [즐거이 하겠소] (I) will gladly do ¶ 내가 하리다〔읽으리다〕 I'll be glad to do〔read〕 it. // 그 일은 내가 맡아 보리다 I'll take care of that matter. ② [···할 것이다] will probably be〔do〕 ¶ 손해를 보신다면 내가 책임지리다 I'll answer for you possible losses. // 빨리 가시오 기차를 놓치리다 Hurry up, or you will miss the train.

리더 ① [지도자] a leader ② [책] a reader

—십 leadership

리드 ① [앞섬] a lead —하다 lead 《a person in a race》 ¶ 근소한 차로 리드하다 lead with a narrow margin // 파트너를 리드하다 lead one's partner ② [악기의] a reed ③ [가곡] a lied

*리듬 rhythm ¶ 리듬 있는 rhythmic ; rhythmical

리딩 히터 〖야구〗 a leading hitter

리라 [이탈리아의 화폐단위] a lira (*pl.* lire) 《L》

-리라 ① [추측] may〔might〕 《be, do》 ; must ; would ; I think〔suppose〕 ¶ 아마 그러리라 It may be so. /I suppose so. // 틀림없이 그는 알고 있으리라 He must be aware of this. ② [자기 의사] I will 〔shall〕 ; I would ; I am going to ¶ 당신을 위해서라면 무엇이든지 하리라 I will do anything for you. // 비가 오면 안 가리라 If it should rain, I shall not come.

리리시즘 lyricism

리릭 a lyric

-리만큼 ¶ 그는 운전사를 두리만큼 부자다 He is rich enough to afford a chauffeur. // 말로 표현할 수 없으리만큼 아름답다 It is too beautiful for words. // 그는 다 쓰지 못 하리만큼 돈이 많다 He has more money than he can spend. // 나는 울고 싶으리만큼 사정이 딱했다 I was so distressed that I felt like crying.

리무진 〖자동차〗 a limousine

리바이벌 (a) revival 《of》

리버럴 liberal

— 아트 liberal arts

리베이트 (a) rebate ; rake-off 《미》

리벳 a rivet ¶ 리벳을 치다 beat a rivet 《into》

*리본 a ribbon ¶ 머리에 리본을 달다 put on a hair ribbon // 머리를 리본으로 매다 tie one's hair with a ribbon

리볼버 a revolver

리뷰 a review

리비도 〖심리〗 libido

리비아 Libya ¶ 리비아의 Libyan

— 사람 a Libyan

*리사이틀 a recital ¶ 리사이틀을 열다 give a 《piano》 recital

*리셉션 a reception ¶ 리셉션을 열다 give reception 《in honor of the new ambassador》 ; hold a reception 《at *Chosun* Hotel》

리스트 a list ¶ 리스트에 올리다 put 《a person》 on the list

리시버 〖무전·경기〗 a receiver

리시브 〖경기〗 receiving —하다 receive 《the served ball》

리아스식 —式 〖지리〗 ria (type) ¶ 리아스식 해안 a ria〔heavily indented〕 coast

리어카 a rear-car ; a bicycle-drawn cart

리얼 real

—리스트 realist —리스틱 realistic —리즘 realism

-리요 ¶ 어찌 말로 다할 수 있으리요 No language can express it. // It is beyond description. // 그 소식을 들으면 얼마나 기뻐하리요 How glad he will be to hear it!

리졸 〖화학〗 lysol

리치 ¶ 리치가 길다 [권투 선수가] have a long reach.

리케차 〖생물〗 a rickettsia (*pl.* -ae)

리퀘스트 (a) request ¶ 리퀘스트 곡 a request tune〔song〕

*리터 [용량 단위] a liter

리턴 매치 a return match

리튬 〖화학〗 lithium

리트머스 〖화학〗 litmus

— 시험지 litmus paper

리포트 report ; a term report (학교의)

리플릿 a leaflet

*리허설 rehearsal ; a dry rum 《속》

린스 a rinse —하다 rinse ; apply a rinse to 《one's hair》

*린치 a lynching ; lynch (law) ¶ 린치를 가하다 lynch 《a person》

*릴 a reel

릴레이 a relay (race) ¶ 400미터 릴레이 400-meter relay

릴리프 relief ¶ 릴리프로 활약하다 work in relief

— 피처 a relief pitcher ; a reliever

림프 〖해부〗 lymph

—관(管) a lymphatic vessel〔duct〕 —샘〔선(腺)〕 a lymphatic gland ; a lymph node —선염(腺炎) inflammation of the lymphatic gland —액(液) lymph

립스틱 a lipstick ; a lip pencil ⇨ 루주
링 ① [반지] a ring ② [권투의] the ring ③ [체조] (the) flying rings ; the rings ④ [피임용] an intrauterine (contraceptive) device 《IU(C)D》
—사이드 《sit at》 the ringside
링거주사 《give》 an injection of Ringer's solution
링크 ① 〖경제〗 a link ② [스케이트장] a rink ¶ …을 링크제로 하다 place... on link system
—제(制) a grouping〔link〕 system
링크스 (golf) links

ㄹ

ㅁ

-ㅁ세 I will gladly《do it for you》; let me ¶ 내 나중 감세 I'll be along later. // 곧 갚음세 I'll pay you back right away.
마¹ [남쪽] the south (뱃사람들의 말) ¶ 마파람 the south wind ; a souther
마² 〖식물〗 a yam
마³ 〖음악〗 mi ¶ 마음(音) E // 내림마 E flat 《E♭》// 올림마 E sharp 《E#》
마 麻 〖식물〗 a hemp
—대(袋) a jute bag —모 교직물 linsey(-woolsey)
마 碼 a yard ¶ 마로 팔다 sell by the yard
마 魔 ① [마귀] a demon ; a devil ; an evil spirit ; evil influence ② [불길함] ill〔bad〕luck ¶ 마의 산 an enchanted〔a haunted, a devil-ridden〕mountain // 마의 손 evil influence // 그가 살인을 하다니 마가 들렸지 He must have been possessed by some evil spirit to commit murder.
살인— a devilish murderer 색— a male flirt ; a wolf
마가 들다 관용 be possessed by an evil spirit〔a demon〕; be bewitched〔bedeviled〕; be tempted by a devil ; come under the influence of an evil spirit ; be jinxed
-마 I will gladly《do》; I shall be glad to 《do》 ¶ 내가 가마 I will go. /I shall be delighted to come.
마가린 margarine ; marge (영·속)
마가목 〖식물〗 a mountain ash ; a rowan (tree) ; Sorbus commixta (학명)
—열매 a serviceberry ; a rowanberry
마가복음 —福音 〖성경〗 (the Gospel of) Mark ; The Gospel According to St. Mark
마각 馬脚 a horse's legs ; one's true character〔colors〕
마각을 드러내다 관용 show the cloven hoof〔foot〕; reveal one's true character ; betray oneself
*마감 磨勘 closing ; finish ; conclusion —하다 close ; bring to a close ; finish ; conclude ; shut off ¶ 일을 마감하다 finish a job // 편집을 마감하다 complete the editing ; go to press // 기부 모집을 마감하다 close the subscription list // 유럽행 우편물은 오늘밤 10시에 마감합니다 The European mail closes this evening at ten o'clock.
—날 the closing day ; the final day 《for》; the deadline 《for》(미) ; the time limit 《for》 끝— the last finish 모집 — [기부 따위의] the close of the subscription 일— finishing a job 장부 — the closing of books 편집 — editorial deadline ; the final editing 기사 — 시간 the copy deadline (of a newspaper)
*마개 a stopper ; a stopple ; a cork ; a plug ; a stopcork ¶ 마개를 막다 cork ; plug ; put a cork〔stopper〕《in》// 마개를 뽑다 uncork 《a bottle》; remove a stopper // 마개로 구멍을 막다 plug up a hole // 귀에 솜으로 마개를 하다 stuff cotton in one's ears
귀— an earplug 병— a cork ; a stopper
마개 뽑이 a bottle opener ; [코르크 마개의] a corkscrew ; a cork extractor ; [맥주병 따위의] a cap opener
마고자 an outer coat worn by men over their jackets
마고 할미 麻姑— a fairy-tale crone
마광 磨光 polish(ing) ; burnish(ing) —하다 polish ; burnish
**마구 ① carelessly ; at random ; without discretion ; without discrimination ; blindly ¶ 글씨를 마구 쓰다 write carelessly // 말을 마구 하다 be rough of speech ; be rough-spoken ; talk at random // 아무 것이나 마구 먹다 eat anything without discrimination // 돈을 마구 쓰다 spend money recklessly
② [세차게] hard ; much ¶ 마구 욕하다 abuse 《a person》 hard // 비가 마구 온다 It rains hard.
**마구 馬具 harness ; trappings (장식) ; horse equipment ; saddlery ¶ 마구를 단 harnessed // 마구를 달다 harness a horse // 마구를 풀다 unharness a horse ; remove the harness from a horse
—류 harnessry —제조 (판매) saddlery — 제조소 a saddlery — 일습 a set〔suit〕of harness
*마구간 馬廐間 a stable ; a barn ¶ 마구간에 넣다 stable 《a horse》; put〔lodge〕a horse in a stable
— 설비 stabling
마구리 end pieces ; caps on both ends
—판 a device for squaring wooden end pieces 베게 — wooden end pieces on a Korean pillow
마구발방 rude speech and wild conduct ; sloppy〔outrageous〕behavior —하다 use wild words ; behave outrageously ; behave in a sloppy way ; be sloppy
마구상 馬具商 [사람] a harness maker ; a saddler ; [점포] a harnessry ; a saddler's shop ; a saddlery
마구잡이 random〔haphazard, careless〕

behavior ; a reckless act
마군 馬軍 the cavalry
마굴 魔窟 ① [마귀의] a lair of devils ② [악인의] a den 《of thieves, robbers》; an underworld hangout ③ [창녀의] the brothel districts ; a brothela house of ill fame ¶ 마굴의 여자들 inmates of a brothel ; street girls
마권 馬券 a pari-mutuel ticket
— **매표소** a ticket window〔office〕; a betting booth **—세** the horse-race tax
마귀 魔鬼 an evil spirit ; a devil ; a demon [기독교] the Devil ; Satan ¶ 마귀같은 demoniac ; fiendish ; diabolic ; cruel ; inhuman ; unnatural // 마귀 같은 인간 a devil incarnate ; a devil of a man
—못 an enchanted〔a haunted, a devil-ridden〕pond **— 할멈** a witch ; a hag ; a harridan ; an ogress
마그나카르타 〖역사〗 Magna C(h)arta
마그네사이트 〖광물〗 magnesite
마그네슘 〖화학〗 magnesium 《Mg》; [사진의] flash powder
—광(光) magnesium light **산화(酸化)—** oxide of magnesium ; magnesia **염화(鹽化)—** magnesium chloride
마그네시아 〖화학〗 magnesia
마기 ultimately ; really ; in reality
마나님 [나이 많은 여자] an elderly lady ; an old woman ; [호칭] madam ; your (good) lady
마냥 till full ; to satiety ; to the full(est) extent ; all the way ; to one's heart's content ¶ 마냥 즐기다 enjoy to one's heart's content // 마냥 먹었다 I have eaten all I wanted. // 해변까지 마냥 걸어갔다 I walked all the way to the beach.
마냥모 [모] rice seedlings transplanted late ; [모내기] belated transplanting of rice seedlings
마네킹 a mannequin ; a manikin
— 걸 a manikin girl
⁑**마녀 魔女** a witch ; a sorceress ; a she-devil ¶ 마녀잡기 a witch-hunt ; witch-hunting
— 재판 a witch trial
마노 瑪瑙 〖광물〗 agate
마누라 [아내] one's wife ; [늙은 여자] an old woman ¶ 마누라를 얻다 take a woman to a wife // 마누라로 삼다 have a woman for one's wife
마는 but ; only ; though ¶ 가고 싶지마는 바빠서 못가겠다 I should like to go, only I'm too busy. // 돈은 있습니다마는 지금 곧 빌려드리진 못하겠습니다 I have the money but I can't lend it to you right now.
마늘 garlic ¶ 마늘 냄새가 나는 garlicky ; smelling of garlic
—모 a trigonal shape **—장아찌** pickled garlics **—종** the stalk〔stem〕of a garlic **—쪽** a clove of a garlic
마니교 魔尼教 Manichaeanism
마니아 [상태] a mania ; a craze ; [사람] a 《dance》 maniac ; a 《baseball》 fan ; a 《camera》 bug 《미·속》
마닐라 Manil(l)a
— 로프 Manila rope **—삼** Manila hemp **—지(紙)** Manila paper
⁑**마님** madam ; My Lady
-마님 Your〔His〕Excellency ; My Lord ¶ 대감〔영감〕 마님 My Lord
마다[1] [짓찧다] hit ; smash ; crush
***마다**[2] each ; every ; all ; at an interval of ; whenever ¶ 날마다 every day ; daily // 집집마다 each and every house ; at every door ; from door to door // 곳곳마다 everywhere // 10년마다 every ten years // 갈적마다 whenever〔as often as〕one goes ; every time one goes // 그때마다 on all such occasions // 상경할 때마다 그는 내 집에서 묵는다 Each time he comes up to *Seoul* he stays with me.
마다다 ① [싫어하다] dislike ; hate ; detest ¶ …하기를 마다지 않다 do not mind 《doing》; be ready〔willing〕to 《do》 ② [싫다고 거절하다] refuse ; decline ¶ 마달 수가 없다 have no words to decline ; do not know how to decline
마담 a madam ; [요정 등의] a proprietress (주인) ; the manageress 《of a saloon》 (고용된)
얼굴 — the manageress 《of a tea room》 **유한(有閑) —** a leisured lady ; an idle, rich woman
†**마당** ① [뜰] a garden ; a yard ; a court ② [타작 마당] a threshing floor〔ground〕; the yard for threshing ③ [경우] an instance ; a case ¶ 이 급한 마당에 무엇을 하고 있는가 What a hell are you doing at this emergency ?
— 맥질 level(l)ing〔smoothing〕 the threshing ground by ramming and daubing it with clay **—비** a yard broom **앞〔뒷〕—** a front〔rear〕 garden
마당발 a wide-sized foot
마당질 threshing〔flailing〕 in the yard ; **—하다** thresh〔flail〕 in the yard
†**마대 麻袋** a gunny bag〔sack〕; a sandbag
마도로스 a sailor ; a seaman
— 파이프 a (tobacco) pipe
마도요 〖새〗 an Indian curlew ; a sabre-bill ; Numenius arquatus (학명)
마도위 馬— a horse broker
마돈나 [성모] the Madonna
마되질 measuring **—하다** measure 《with *mal* and *doe*》
마드모아젤 a mademoiselle (*pl.* mesdemoiselles) 《프》
마들가리 ① [나무의] twigs ; sticks ; dead branches ② [솔기] seams of a worn-out garment ③ [꼬인] kinks in straw-rope〔thread〕
마들다 魔— get possessed by a demon ; be caught by an evil spirit ; be jinxed 〔hoodooed〕; be thwarted by evil influ-

ence ¶ 마들어서 아무 일도 되지 않는다 I am thwarted by evil influences in all I do.

*마디 ① [관절] a joint ; a knuckle (손가락의) ; [결절] a knot ; a knob ; a gnarl ¶ 다리마디 the leg joints // 나무마디 a gnarl ; a knar // 대나무마디 a bamboo joint // 마디가 많다 be full of knots ; knotty ; knobby ; gnarled
② [말·노래] a word ; a phrase ; a song ; a tune ¶ 한마디 하다 say a word // 한마디 부르다 sing a tune // 두 마디 않고 돈을 꾸어주었다 He lent me the money without a word.

마디꽃 〖식물〗 a kind of loosestrife plant

마디다 (be) durable ; long-lasting ; long-wearing ¶ 이런 감은 마디지 못하다 This kind of cloth does not wear well.

마디마디 ① all the joints ; every joint ¶ 마디마디가 아프다 feel pain in every joint ; every joint aches
② [말 따위] all the words〔phrases〕; every word〔phrase〕 ¶ 마디마디에 깊은 뜻이 있다 All the words are pregnant with meaning.

마디지다 have nodes〔joints〕; (be) gnarled ; knotty ; be full of knots ¶ 마디진 솔 a gnarled pine

마디충 〖곤충〗 a rice borer ; a pearl moth

마디풀 〖식물〗 a knotgrass ; Polygonum aviculare (학명)

마따나 according to 《something said》 ¶ 자네 말 마따나 옛날에는 여기에 못이 있었네 As you say, there was a pond here in olden times. // 옛말 마따나 암탉이 울면 집안 망하는 법이다 As the old saying goes, "When the woman wears the trousers the family goes to ruin."

*마땅하다 ① [적합] (be) becoming ; suitable ; befitting ; right ; appropriate ; [상당] fair ; reasonable ; proper ¶ 마땅하지 않다 (be) unbecoming 《of》 ; unworthy 《of》 ; unsuitable 《for》 ; improper 《for》 ; inappropriate 《to》 // 마땅한 집 a suitable house // 마땅한 예 an apt instance ; a good example ; a case in point // 마땅한 조건으로 on fair terms // 마땅한 값으로 at reasonable prices // 마땅한 때에 at a proper〔good〕 time ; at the right moment ; opportunely // 그 자리에 마땅한 인물이다 be the very 〔right〕 man for the place ; be a competent man for the position // 그에게는 수위 정도가 마땅하다 His right place is that of a janitor. // 그 옷은 네게 마땅하지 않다 That suit does not become you.
② [당연] (be) right ; proper ; reasonable ; ought to ; should ; deserve ¶ 마땅한 일 a matter of course // 마땅한 결과 natural results ; a logical conclusion // 그는 죽어 마땅하다 He deserves death. // 빚진 것은 갚아야 마땅하다 One ought to pay what one owes. // 그것을 믿는 것도 마땅하다 You are justified in believing it.

마땅히 ① [당연히] justly ; properly ; naturally ; as a matter of course ; deservedly ; necessarily ; of course ¶ 지금쯤은 마땅히 목적지에 도착해 있어야 한다 He ought to have arrived at his destination by now. // 상관의 명령은 마땅히 복종해야 한다 You must naturally obey the orders of your superiors.
② [적당히] suitably ; adequately ; appropriately ; properly ; reasonably

마뜩잖다 (be) dissatisfactory ; disagreeable ; offensive ¶ 마뜩잖은 소리를 하다 say something disagreeable〔offensive〕

마뜩하다 (be) satisfactory ; agreeable ; acceptable

*마라톤 a marathon (race) ; a crosscountry race
— 선수 a marathon runner

마래미 ① 〖물고기〗 a young yellowtail ② [소작 관리인] the supervisor of a tenant farm

마량 馬糧 fodder ; forage ; provender ; hay ; feed stuff〔supply〕

†마력 馬力 〖물리〗 horsepower 《h. p., Hp》 ¶ 5백 마력의 기관 a 500 h. p. engine // 마력을 올리다 get up steam // 그 발동기는 7천 마력입니다 The motor develops 7,000 horsepower.
실— actual horsepower 유효— effective horsepower 축(軸)— brake horsepower

마력 魔力 magical power〔virtues〕; supernatural powers ; spell ; [여자의 매력] the power to charm ; fascinating 〔captivating〕 power ; charm ¶ 그녀의 눈에는 일종의 마력이 있다 There is something in her eyes that captivates us.

†마련 plan ; arrangements ; management ; preparations —하다 [준비] prepare ; get ready ; arrange ; [조달] supply ; raise (돈을) ; make out〔up〕; [처리] manage ; complete ¶ 일을 마련하다 manage〔handle〕 an affair // 집을 마련하다 get a house // 주문품을 마련하다 supply the article ordered ; execute〔fill〕 the order // 돈을 마련하다 raise money ; make up a sum ; have 《a sum of money》 ready // 설비를 마련하다 complete the arrangements // 필수품을 마련하다 get〔purchase〕 the requisites // 식사가 마련되었다 The meal is ready.

마렵다 feel an urge to urinate〔defecate〕; have a call of nature ¶ 오줌이 마렵다 have to urinate // 똥이 마렵다 have to defecate // 엄마 오줌 마려워 Mommy, I want to do my needs.

마로니에 〖식물〗 a marronnier 《프》; a horse chestnut

*마루 ① [집의] a (wooden) floor ¶ 마루를 놓다 floor ; board the floor ; put in flooring // 마루를 뜯다 break open〔tear up, rip up〕 the floor ② [지붕·산의] a ridge ③ [일의] the final〔most important〕 part of

an event ¶ 마루씨름 the wrestling finals // 마루씨름군 the top wrestlers
—대 a ridge pole ; a ridge beam —면적 the floor area〔space〕 —밑 the space under the floor —방 a floored room ; a room with a wooden floor —씨름 the wrestling finals —씨름군 the top wrestlers 산— the ridge of a mountain 용— the ridge of a roof 지붕— the ridge of a roof

마루청 a floor board ; flooring 《집합적》 ¶ 마루청을 깔다 board a floor ; floor 《a house》

마루터기 the top ; the peak ; the summit 고개— the summit of a pass 산— the ridge of a mountain 지붕— the ridge of a roof

†마룻바닥 the floor ¶ 마룻바닥에 앉다 sit on the floor

†마르다[1] ① [건조] dry ; get dry ; dry up ; wither (꽃·잎이) ; be seasoned (목재가) ; be parched (입술이) ¶ 바싹 마른 입술 parched lips // 마른 가지 a withered 〔dead〕 branch〔twig〕 // 바싹 마르다 be dried up // 눈물이 마를 틈도 없이 울어댄다 She does nothing but cry (all day).
② [여위다] become〔grow〕 thin〔lean〕 ; grow gaunt ; lose flesh ; fall away ; pine away (걱정으로) ¶ 마른 thin ; lean ; skinny ; raw-boned // 대쪽같이 말라빠진 as thin as a lath // 그전보다 훨씬 마르셨습니다 You have got much thinner than you were. /You appear to have lost flesh. // 그는 근심으로 말라서 뼈와 가죽뿐이다 He is a mere skeleton with care. /He is worn to a shadow with care.
③ [목이] be thirsty ; feel thirsty〔dry〕 ¶ 목이 마르다 be thirsty ; have a dry throat // 몹시 목이 마른다 I'm very thirsty. // 입안이 바싹 말랐다 My mouth felt parched.
④ [돈이] run out ; become exhausted ; be used up ¶ 돈이 마르다 money is used up ; have no money left // 자금이 말라서 through scarcity of funds // 금주에는 돈이 말랐다 Money is tight this week.

마르다[2] cut out ; cut ¶ 마름질 cutting // 마르는 법 cutting ; how to cut out // 옷을 마르다 cut out clothes // 재목을 재어 마르다 cut lumber to measure

마른갈이 plowing a rice field while it is dry ; tillage of a dry rice-field

마른걸레 a dry floorcloth ; a dry mop 〔cloth〕 ; a dry house-cloth ¶ 마른걸레질하다 wipe with a dry cloth

마른고기 dried meat〔fish〕

마른국수 [말린] dried noodles〔vermicellis〕 ; [삶지 않은] uncooked noodles ¶ 마른국수로 먹다 eat noodles uncooked

마른기침 a dry cough ; a hacking cough —하다 hack ; emit a short and dry cough ; clear one's throat

마른나무 dried wood ; dried firewood

마른반찬 dried meat or fish eaten with rice as side dishes

마른밥 [주먹밥] a rice-ball ; [국 없는 밥] boiled-rice eaten without soup

마른버짐 〖의학〗 psoriasis ; a kind of ringworm

마른번개 lightning in a clear blue sky

마른빨래 ① drying muddy clothes and then scraping the dirt off ② getting rid of the fleas in one's own clothes by giving them to someone else

마른신 ① [기름에 결지 않은] unoiled leather shoes ② [마른 땅에서 신는] fine 〔dry〕-weather shoes

마른안주 dried meat or fish tidbits to eat as a snack while drinking

마른옴 〖의학〗 the itch ; scabies

마른일 housewife's chores done without wetting her hands ; that part of housework in which one doesn't get one's fingers wet —하다 do the dry part of the housework

마른입 [국물을 안 마신] a parched mouth (after a soupless meal) ; [맨입] a hungry mouth

마른천둥 thunder in a clear blue sky

마른하늘 a clear sky ; a cloudless sky ¶ 마른하늘에는 한 조각의 구름도 없었다 There was not a speck of cloud in the clear sky.
마른하늘에 날벼락 친다 (속담) The unexpected always happens.

마른행주 a dry dish towel

마름[1] [이엉의 단위] a bundle of woven straw for thatching

마름[2] [소작 관리인] the supervisor of a tenant farm

마름[3] 〖식물〗 a water chestnut ; a watercaltrop

마름모 a lozenge ; diamond (shape) ; 〖수학〗 a rhombus ¶ 마름모의 lozenge-shaped ; rhombic ; diamond-shaped ; lozenged // 마름모꼴 ⇨ 마름모

마름모(꼴) a lozenge ; a diamond (shape) ; 〖수학〗 a rhombus ¶ 마름모(꼴)의 lozenge-shaped ; rhombic ; diamond-shaped ; lozenged
—꼴 교차 〖철도〗 a diamond crossing —꼴 무늬 diaper ; lozenge pattern

마름쇠 a caltrop〔caltrap〕

마름자 a yardstick used in cutting out clothes

마름질 cutting out 《clothes》 —하다 cut out ¶ 옷을 마름질하다 cut out a dress

마리 the number of animals ¶ 다섯 마리의 새끼 고양이 five kittens // 새 한 마리 a bird // 말 두 마리 two horses

마리아 Mary ; Maria
성모(聖母)— the (Blessed) Virgin Mary ; the Holy Mother

마리오넷 a marionette 《프》

마리화나 [환각제] marihuana ; marijuana

마림바 [악기] a marimba

마마 〖의학〗 smallpox ; variola ¶ 마마에 걸

리다 suffer from smallpox ; be taken ill of smallpox

—꽃 pox pustules —균 a smallpox germ 〔virus〕 —환자 a case of smallpox 자반성(紫斑性)— black small pox

마맛자국 a pockmark ; a pit ¶ 얼굴에 마맛자국이 있다 one's face is pitted with smallpox

마멋 〖동물〗 a marmot(te)

마멸 磨滅 wear (and tear) ; defacement ; attrition ; abrasion —하다 wear out ; be worn out〔away, down〕; be defaced ; be abraded ¶ 도장이 마멸되었다 The stamp has become defaced.

—시험 an abrasion test —제(劑) an abrasive

마모 磨耗 wear (and tear) ; abrasion —하다 be worn away

†마무르다 ① [일을] finish ; complete ; conclude ; get through with ¶ 흥정을 마무르다 conclude a bargain // 일을 마무르다 finish〔get through with〕one's work

② [둘레·가장자리를] hem ; fringe ; border

마무리 finish ; finishing touch ; completion ; conclusion —하다 finish ; complete ; conclude ; get through with ¶ 마무리가 안된 unfinished ; in the rough // 마무리가 엉성한 roughly finished // 마무리 단계에 이르다 come to the finish // 마무리가 잘 됐다 The finish is good.

—공 a fitter —공장 a fitting〔fitter's〕shop —기계 a finishing machine ; a mangle (세탁의) —대패 a finishing 〔smoothing〕plane —줄 a smooth file

마물 魔物 a thing of evil ; malignant spirits

마미단 馬尾緞 haircloth ; horsehair

마바리 [말] a pack-horse ; [짐] a burden carried by a pack-horse ; 〖농업〗 harvesting two *sem* of grain on a one-*majigi* plot of land ¶ 마바릿군 a pack-horse driver ; a pack-horse man ; a pack-horse peddler

마방 馬房 an inn〔a wineshop〕with stable facilities ; a horse stable

마방집 馬房— a livery stable

⁑마법 魔法 magic ; sorcery ; black art ; witchcraft ; wizardry

> 참고 **magic**은 「초자연적 내지 오묘한 힘을 빌어 놀랄 만한 효과를 만들어 내는 요술」을 나타내는 일반적인 말 **sorcery**는 보통 「해로운 목적 또는 불길한 목적으로 주문을 읊는다든가 요술을 부린다든가 하는 마법」을 뜻하고 **witchcraft**는 여자 마법사(witch)가 쓰는 간계를 그리고 **wizardry**는 남자 마법사(wizard)가 보여 주는 「비범한 기량 및 교묘함」 따위를 내포하는 마법을 뜻한다

¶ 마법을 쓰다 practice the black art ; exercise witchcraft ; use〔work〕magic // 마법을 걸다 cast spells 《upon a person》 // 마법으로 병을 고치다 cure a disease by magic ; conjure away an illness

⁑마법사 魔法師 a magician ; a sorcerer ; a wizard ; a necromancer

여자— a witch ; a sorceress

마병 junk ; odds and ends ; worn-out goods〔articles〕

—장수 a junk dealer〔man〕

마병 馬兵 cavalry

⁑마부 馬夫 a groom ; a horsekeeper ; a stableman ; a coachman ; a footman (말구종)

마분 馬糞 horse-manure〔-dung〕; horse-droppings

—지 strawboard ; millboard

⁑마비 痲痺 paralysis ; palsy ; numbness ; anesthesia (마취) ¶ 마비되다 be paralyzed ; be benumbed ; be palsied ; go numb ; be anesthetized // 마비시키다 paralyze ; benumb ; anesthetize // 국부를 마비시키다 anesthetize locally〔a part〕// 그는 양심이 마비되어 있다 He is dead〔lost〕to conscience. /His conscience is benumbed.

—약 an an(a)esthetic —증 환자 a paralytic 급성— 〖의학〗 foudroyant paralysis 뇌성— cerebral palsy 대(對)— paraplegia 부전(不全)— paresis ; partial paralysis 심장— heart failure 안면— facial paralysis 전신〔국부〕— general〔local〕paralysis 진행성— progressive paralysis ; [매독에 의한] general paresis 〔paralysis〕

마비풍 痲脾風 〖의학〗 diphtheria

—증상 diphtherial〔diphtheric〕symptoms —혈청 serum of diphtheria ; antidiphtheria serum

마사 馬事 horse affairs〔matters〕

한국 —회 the Korean Horse Affairs Association

*마사지 (a) massage ; a rubdown —하다 massage〔rub down〕《a person》; give 《a person》 a massage〔rubdown〕

—사(師) a massagist ; a massager 전기— electromassage

마삭나무, 마삭줄 〖식물〗 a star jasmine

마삯 the fee for hiring a horse

마상 馬上 horseback ¶ 마상에서 on horseback // 마상에서 사람을 부르다 call out to another from on one's horse

—객 a rider ; an equestrian

마상이 a (small) boat ; a skiff ; a canoe ; a dugout

—운임 boatage

마성 魔性 devilishness ; fiendishness

마소 horses and oxen〔cattle〕

마속 the capacity of a *mal* measure-cup

마손 磨損 friction loss ; wear and tear ; abrasion ; attrition

—위험 하주 부담 〖보험〗 the owner's risk of chafing 《ORC》 —학 tribology

마수 ① [그날 운수] the luck of the day judged from the first sale ¶ 마수가 좋다

〔나쁘다〕 the first sale bodes good 〔bad〕 luck for the day's business
② ⇨ 마수걸이
마수 —數 quantity measured in *mal*
마수 魔手 evil influence ; an evil hand ¶ 마수를 뻗치다 exert one's evil influence
마수걸다 make the first sale of the day ; sell for the first time
마수걸이 the first sale of the day ; the first transaction at the beginning of a business **—하다** make the first sale of the day ¶ 마수걸이로 감 한 개를 팔다 sell a persimmon as the first sale of the day∥당신이 마수걸이하면 오늘 내 재수는 좋을 텐데 If you are my first customer, I shall have good luck for the day.
*__마술 魔術__ magic ; the black art ; sorcery ; witchcraft ¶ 마술을 쓰다 practice sorcery ; use magic∥마술을 걸다 throw a spell 《over a person》
—사 a magician ; a wizard ; a sorcerer
마술 馬術 horsemanship ; equitation ; the art of riding ¶ 마술의 연습 riding practice∥마술의 명수 a master horseman
— 경기 an equestrian〔riding〕 event **— 경마장** dressage
마스크 a mask ; a gauze mask over the mouth and nose ; a flu mask ¶ 마스크를 쓰다 wear a mask
마스터 [주인] a master ; [경영자] the proprietor **—하다** master 《English》 ; get the thorough knowledge 《of》
마스터 플랜 [기본계획] a master plan
마스트 a mast ¶ 마스트가 셋인 배 a three-masted ship
†**마시다** ① [액체를] drink ; take ; have ; [들이키다] swallow ¶ 먹지도 마시지도 않고 without bite or drop∥물〔술〕을 마시다 drink water〔wine〕∥냇물을 마시다 drink at a brook∥한 컵의 물을 마시다 drink a glass of water∥단숨에 들이 마시다 quaff ; drink off at a draught∥한 입에 마시다 swallow at a mouthful gulp∥꿀꺽꿀꺽 마시다 guzzle ; swig ; swill ; swallow ; gulp down∥한 잔 마시다 have a drink ; have a wet ; wet one's whistle∥술을 마시러 가다 go for a drink∥뭣을 마실래 (홍)차냐 커피냐 Which do you take, tea or coffee ? ∥마시면서 이야기하자 Let us talk over our cups. ∥그 사람 마시기만 하면 재미있거든 He is merry in his cups. ∥그는 마시면 다루기가 힘들다 When drunk, he gets out of control. /Liquor makes him ugly. ∥술을 마시면 마음이 풀린다 The heart opens under the influence of wine. ∥사실은 나도 한때 술을 끊었는데 지금은 다시 마신다 As a matter of fact, I once quit drinking, but I'm off the wagon now.
② [호흡] breathe in ; inhale ; imbibe ; inspire ¶ 담배 연기를 들이마시다 inhale tobacco-smoke∥나는 신선한 공기를 마시기 위해 창문을 열었다 I opened the window to get a draught of fresh air.
마신 魔神 a devil ; an evil spirit
마신 馬身 a horse's length ¶ 그 말은 3 마신의 차로 이겼다 The horse won by three length.
마치 a march
웨딩— the wedding march
마켓 a market
슈퍼— a supermarket
마약 痲藥 a narcotic ; an anesthetic ; an opiate ; a dope ¶ 마약을 쓰다 administer an anesthetic
— 남용 drug abuse **— 남용자** a drug abuser **— 단속** narcotic control **— 단속반** a narcotics squad **— 단속법** the Narcotic Control Act **— 밀매** drug traffic 〔trade, business〕 ; dope peddling〔trafficking〕 《구》 **— 밀매자** a narcotic trafficker ; a drug〔dope〕 peddler ; a (dope) pusher 《미·구》 ; a junker 〔runkie〕 《미·속》 **— 상습자** a drug 〔narcotic, dope〕 addict ; a narcotic ; a drug〔dope〕 fiend 《미·구》 ; a junker 《미·속》
마약 중독 痲藥中毒 narcotics〔drug〕 addiction ; narcotism ¶ 마약 중독이 되다 become addicted to (the use of) narcotics ; go on the needle
— 환자 치료소 a narcotics-withdrawal clinic
마왕 魔王 the Devil ; Satan ; Beelzebub ; the Prince of Darkness ; 〖불교〗 an evil spirit
마운드 〖야구〗 the mound ; the pitcher's plate ¶ 마운드를 밟다 play as a pitcher ; take the mound
마유 麻油 hempseed oil
*__마을__ ① [동리] a village ; a hamlet ; a rural community ¶ 마을 언저리에서 on the outskirts of a village
② [옛 관청] a government office
— 사람 villagers ; village people **이웃 —** a neighboring village
마을가다 visit one's neighboring village ; visit one's neighborhood
마을꾼 a habitual frequenter 《to one's neighborhood》 ; a woman who never stays home
†**마음** ① [정신] mind ; spirit ; heart ; soul ; idea ; thought ; mentality

> 참고 **mind**는 body, heart, soul에 대한 일반적인 말로서 「지력·기억」 따위를 나타낸다 **heart**는 「정」에 해당하는 말이며 「정애·열의」 따위를 나타낸다 **soul**은 어떤 경우에는 spirit를 대신할 수 있는 말이지만 spirit보다 감정 감성의 깊이가 더하고 body와는 성질상 다르며 「영혼·넋」을 말한다 **spirit**는 flesh와 상대되는 말로서 soul보다도 더욱 육체와의 독립을 강조한 말이며 생의 에너지도 soul보다 더욱 강하게 나타내고 있어 육체를 갖지 않은 「정신」에 대해서도 쓰인다

¶ 어린 마음 young ideas ; a juvenile 〔puerile〕 mind // 어머니 마음 maternal affection ; a mother's love ; a mother's feeling // 마음이 고운 tenderhearted ; kind-hearted // 마음이 큰 broad-minded ; liberal ; generous // 마음이 좁은 narrow-minded ; ungenerous // 마음이 곧은 right-hearted // 마음 속으로 inwardly ; secretly ; in one's heart // 마음 깊이 deep down in the heart // 마음에 품다 cherish ; harbor ; entertain // 마음을 터놓다 unbosom oneself ; lay bare one's thought ; open one's heart // 마음에 그리다 image ; visualize ; picture to oneself // 마음을 가라앉히다 calm down one's feelings // 마음에 새기다 print 《a fact》 on one's mind〔on one's memory〕 ; be laid to one's heart // 좋은 생각이 마음에 떠오른다 A good idea occurs to me. /I hit upon a good idea. // 마음이 흐뭇해지는 이야기이다 It is a heartwarming story. // 그는 마음은 좋은 놈이다 He is a good fellow at bottom. // 마음을 가라앉히시오 Calm yourself. /Calm down your feeling. // 조금은 내 마음도 알아주시오 Kindly think about the matter from my point of view. // 마음 약한 소리를 하는군 You are talking like a weak character. // 그는 마음 속으로 웃고 있다 He is laughing in his sleeve. // 너의 제의는 고맙지만 마음으로만 받아들이겠어 I appreciate your offer, but I can accept it in spirit only. // 인간은 외모가 아니라 마음이 중요하다 It's not a person's looks that counts, it's what's inside.

② [사려] consideration ; sympathy ; tenderness ; heart ; kindness ¶ 마음 있는 〔없는〕 사람 a thoughtful〔thoughtless〕 man ; a considerate〔an inconsiderate〕 person ; a human〔an inhuman〕 mortal // 그런 일은 마음 있는 사람이 할 짓이 아니다 A man who can think at all wouldn't do such a thing. // 만사는 마음 먹기에 달렸다 Everything has its two sides to look at.

③ [주의] mind ; attention ; interest ; care ¶ 마음을 기울이다 direct one's attention to // 마음을 쓰다 give attention to ; be attentive // 그가 말한 것을 마음에 두지 마라 Don't mind what he says.

④ [의지] will ; intention ; design ; inclination ¶ 마음대로 at will ; as one pleases ; at one's pleasure ; of one's free will // 이것은 그의 마음에서 나온 것은 아니다 It has not come of his own free will. // 저 사람은 입과 마음이 같지 않다 He talks one thing and means another. // 그는 남에게 마음에도 없는 말을 한다 He speaks to others what is quite apart from his real motive.

⑤ [취미] fancy ; taste ; liking ; [기분] a mood ; humor ; a frame of mind ¶ 마음에 드는 집 a house to one's fancy 〔after one's heart〕 // 마음에 드는 여자 a woman after one's heart // 마음내키는 대로 as fancy dictates〔strikes, leads〕 one ; as the humor takes〔dictates, strikes〕 one ; as one feels inclined // 마음 내키지 않다 be in no mood to ; be unwilling 《to do》 // 그 소녀는 그의 마음에 들었다 The young maiden captivated his heart. // 그 일에는 마음이 내키지 않았다 I was not in the humor for the job.

마음을 끌다 관용 attract ; allure ; appeal to

마음에 걸리다 관용 weigh upon one's mind ; trouble one's mind ; [사람이 주어] be worried about

마음에 들다 관용 be to one's liking ; be after one's fancy ; be in one's favor ; impress favorably

마음이 화합하면 부처도 본다 속담 Where there's a will, ther's a way.

마음에나 있어야 꿈을 꾸지 속담 What the eyes sees not, the heart rues not.

마음가짐 ① [마음 태도] one's mental attitude ; one's state of mind ② [결심] determination ; resolution ; resolve

마음결 a turn〔cast〕 of mind ; grain ; temper ; nature ; disposition ; temperament ¶ 마음결이 좋은 good-natured ; good-tempered ; tender-hearted ; kind-hearted // 마음결이 나쁜 ill-natured ; 《a man》 of coarse grain // 마음결이 곱다 have a sweet temper ; be of gentle disposition // 온화한 마음결을 가진 사람 a man of a gentle disposition

***마음껏** ① [실컷] to one's heart's content ; to the full ; to the utmost〔hilt〕 ¶ 마음껏 울다 weep oneself out ; weep one's fill ; cry one's heart out // 마음껏 즐기다 enjoy oneself to the full // 마음껏 먹다 eat one's fill // 마음껏 욕하다 abuse to one's heart's content // 마음껏 휴일을 즐기다 enjoy the holiday to one's heart's content // 오늘 저녁은 마음껏 즐겁게 지내자 Tonight let's live it up.

② [충심으로] with one's whole heart ; with devotion ; with a single heart ¶ 부모를 마음껏 섬기다 serve one's parents with devotion

마음놓다 ① [안심] set one's heart 〔mind〕 at ease ; feel easy 《about》 ; feel at rest ; relax ; make oneself easy ¶ 마음놓고 free from all anxiety ; easy in mind ; in peace ; free from care ; with mind at ease ; with security // 그 점에 대해서는 마음 놓으십시오 On that score, make your mind quite easy. // 마음놓고 언제까지든 묵으십시오 Please make yourself at home and stay with us as long as you please. // 우리는 최종 허가를 받을 때까지 마음을 놓을 수 없다 We can't breathe easy until we get the final okay. // 그 소식을 들으니 마음이 놓인다 It's a relief to hear that news.

ㅁ

② [방심] relax one's attention ; slacken one's effort ; be off one's guard ; be inattentive ; be negligent ¶ 마음놓지 않다 be on guard ; be on the lookout ; be wide awake ; have one's wits about one // 그 소식 듣고 마음놓았다 I felt relieved at the news. // 내가 마음놓고 있을 때 때렸다 He hit me when I was off my guard. // 마음놓지 말고 가게 잘봐야 한다 Don't take your eyes off the store even for a moment. // 저 사람 같으면 마음놓고 돈을 맡길 수 있다 You can trust him with money.

*마음대로 as one pleases〔likes, wishes〕; at one's convenience ; [자유 의사로] of one's own accord ; of one's free will ; [독단으로] on one's own authority ; at one's discretion ; [무단으로] without leave〔permission〕 ¶ 자기 마음대로 하다 have one's (own) way 《in everything》// 마음대로 되지 않다 be beyond one's control // 남의 물건을 마음대로 쓰다 make free use of another's thing // 네 마음대로 해라 Do as you please. /Take〔Have〕 your own way. /So you are the emperor. // 마음대로 잡수시오 Help yourself, please. // 이 방을 마음대로 사용해도 좋다 You are at liberty to use this room. // 기후는 사람 마음대로 되는 것이 아니다 One is powerless against the weather. /The weather is beyond man's control. // 가건 말건 네 마음대로 해라 You are at liberty to go or stay. // 마음대로 쓰십시오 It is entirely at your disposal.

마음먹다 ① [의도] intend to ; have a mind to ; mean to ; think of ; plan to ; have the intention of 《doing》 ¶ 나는 이 사건에 간섭하려고는 마음먹고 있지 않다 I have no mind to meddle with this affair. // 만사가 마음먹은 대로 됐다 Everything turned out as I wished. // 나는 하숙을 옮기려고 마음먹고 있다 I am thinking of changing lodgings.
② [결심] be determined ; make up one's mind ; be resolved ; make a resolution ¶ 마음먹은 대로 실행하다 act up to one's resolution // 마음먹은 바를 포기하다 give up one's resolution ; reconsider one's resolution // 우리들은 최후까지 싸울 것을 마음먹었다 We are determined to fight to the last. // 하려고 마음먹으면 못 할 일이 없다 Where there is a will, there is a way. /A resolute will makes the god give way. // 그는 위대한 학자가 되려고 단단히 마음먹고 있다 He is firmly determined to become a great scholar.

마음보 temper ; nature ; disposition ; a cast of mind ¶ 마음보 사나운 사람 an ill-natured person ; a dog in the manger // 마음보 사나운 여자 a scratch cat ; a she-devil ; a grimalkin (할멈) // 마음보가 사납다 be ill-tempered ; be ill-natured ; be ill-disposed // 마음보 사납게 굴다 behave maliciously〔crossly, ill-naturedly〕// 그는 그들에게 마음보 사납게 굴었다 He worked his wicked will upon them.

마음성 [심성] nature ; temper ; temperament ; disposition ¶ 마음성이 좋다 be good-tempered ; be good-natured ; have a good disposition // 어머니 마음성을 닮다 inherit one's mother's disposition

마음속 one's mind ; one's heart ; the bottom of one's heart ; one's innermost thoughts ; one's bosom ¶ 마음속으로부터 우러나온 말 words flowing out of one's heart // 마음속에 사무치다 sink deep into one's heart // 마음속을 털어놓다 unbosom oneself to ; speak one's mind // 네 마음속은 알고 있었다 I knew what was working in your mind. // 그는 마음속으로 웃고 있다 He is laughing in his sleeve.

마음쓰다 work one's brain ; use one's mind〔head〕; study ; think ; [유의하다] pay attention [동정하다] be moved ; feel sympathy

마음씨 a turn〔cast〕 of mind ; nature ; temper ; disposition ¶ 마음씨가 부드러운 사람 a man of a soft〔sweet〕 temper // 마음씨가 좋다 be good-natured ; have a good disposition // 마음씨가 나쁘다 be ill-natured〔-tempered〕; be cross ; be malicious // 그녀는 마음씨는 좋은데 지혜가 부족하다 She has a sweet temper but poor sense. // 그런 마음씨를 가지고는 다른 사람과 같이 일을 해 나갈 수가 없다 With your bad temper, you can't expect people to get along with you.

마음자리 nature ; temper ; disposition ; character ; heart ; mind ¶ 마음자리가 좋은 사람 a good-natured person ; a nice person // 마음자리가 바로 박이다 have a lovely disposition ; have one's heart in right place // 마음자리가 삐뚜로 박이다 be perverse ; be crooked ; have a twisted heart〔disposition〕

마음잡다 calm oneself ; settle (down) ; recover one's composure ¶ 마음잡지 못하다 feel nervous〔uneasy〕; be ill at ease // 마음잡고 일을 시작하다 settle (down) to work

마음졸이다 be anxious about ; be concerned about〔for〕; feel uneasy about ; have misgivings about ¶ 나는 또 실패하지 않을까 마음졸이고 있다 I am afraid I shall fail again. // 그의 모친은 그의 장래에 관해 몹시 마음졸이고 있다 His mother is very anxious about his future. // 그는 시험 결과에 대해서 마음 졸이고 있다 He is concerned about the results of the examination.

마의 麻衣 hemp clothes

*마이너스 『수학』 minus ; a minus ; subtraction ; subtracting ; [결손] a deficit ; a deficiency ; [결점] a defect ¶ 마이너스가 되다 [결손] suffer a loss ; [불리] be disadvantageous 《to》// 8 마이너스 3은 5

Eight minus three leaves〔is〕 five.
— 부호 a minus (sign)

마이동풍 馬耳東風 utter indifference ; praying to deaf ears ¶ 아무리 말해도 마이동풍이었다 All my words fell on deaf 〔heedless〕 ears. /All my advice was just so much sound to him. /All my words fell flat upon〔were unheeded by〕 him.
마이동풍 〔속담〕 Talk to the wind. /To sing psalms to a dead horse. /To whistle psalms to the taffrail. /Knock at a deaf man's door.

마이신 〖약〗 streptomycin

마이크로버스 a microbus

마이크로톰 a microtome

*__마이크(로폰)__ a microphone ; a mike ¶ 마이크 앞에서 말하다 speak at〔over, into〕 a microphone // 아 아 마이크 시험중입니다 One-two-three-four-testing ! Testing !
— 스탠드 a microphone stand — 이동장치 [영화] a sound boom 무선— a wireless microphone 수음(收音)— a (sound) pick-up microphone

마이크로필름 a microfilm
— 리더 a microfilm reader

마인 魔人 a demon of a man

†**마일** a mile 《1.6 km》

마작 麻雀 mah-jong(g) —하다 play mah-jong(g)

마장 [거리] a *ri* ¶ 반마장 half a *ri*

마장 馬場 [목장] grazing land ; pasturage ; [경마장] a riding ground ; a racecourse ; a race track

마장수 a peddler with a horse to carry his wares about

마장스럽다 be a hindrance ; (be) thwarting

마저[1] [부사] with all the rest ; without leaving any ¶ 이것마저 잡수십시오 Please take this last one up, too.

마저[2] [조사] even ; also ; to the extent of ; so far as ; besides ; on top of ; into the bargain ¶ 도둑질마저 하다 go so far as to commit theft ; go to the extent 〔length〕 of committing theft // 빚마저 내서 even going to the extent of incurring debt // 그는 집마저 팔았다 He went so far as to sell his house. // 밤에는 바람마저 불기 시작했다 It began to blow a gale at night into the bargain.

마적 馬賊 mounted bandits〔brigands, thieves〕

마전[1] bleaching —하다 bleach ¶ 마전한 무명 bleached cotton
—쟁이 a bleacher —터 a bleaching establishment

마전[2] a grain-measuring place

마제 馬蹄 a horseshoe ⇨ 말굽

마제형 馬蹄形 horseshoe shape ¶ 마제형의 horseshoe-shaped ; U-shaped

마조 —調 tone E ¶ 마장〔단〕조 E major 〔minor〕

†**마주** face to face ; vis-a-vis ¶ 마주보다 look at each other ; look each other in the face // 그와 마주보고 앉다 sit face to face〔vis-a-vis, tête-à-tête〕 with him

마주놓다 set 《things》 opposite each other

마주르카 mazurka

마주보다 [마주 대하다] be opposite 《to》 ; face each other ; confront ; [눈으로] look at each other ; exchange glances ¶ 마주보고 opposite ; face to face // 놀라서 서로 마주보다 exchange looks of astonishment ⇨ 맞보다

마주서다 stand〔come〕 face to face ; stand right opposite ; stand facing right ahead ; confront ¶ 서로 마주서다 stand face to face with 《a person》 ; stand opposite to 《a person》 // 우편국과 경찰서는 마주서 있다 The post office stands opposite to the police station.

마주앉다 sit face to face〔vis-à-vis〕 with 《a person》 ; sit facing each other 《across a table》 ; take a seat opposite to 《a person》 ¶ 마주앉아서 face to face ; vis-à-vis ; tête-à-tête // 마주앉아 이야기 하다 talk face to face with 《a person》 ; have a tête-à-tête with 《a person》

마주잡다 [서로 잡다] take each other ; take〔hold〕 together ; [드잡이하다] grapple with each other ¶ 손에 손을 마주 잡고 hand in hand 《with》 // 책상을 마주잡고 들다 lift a table together

마주잡이 a bier carried by two bearers

†**마주치다** ① [부딪치다] collide with ; crash with ; run against ; crash into 〔against, together〕 ; knock〔strike, bump〕 against ; dash against
② [우연히 만나다] meet with ; be faced by 〔with〕 ; come across〔upon〕 ; hit 〔chance〕 upon ; butt into ¶ 십자로에서 차가 서로 마주쳤다 At the crossroads the cars collided with each other. /A collision of cars occurred at the crossroads. // 그들은 난문제에 마주쳤다 They are faced by a terrible problem. // 전차를 내리자 박군과 마주쳤다 On getting off the tram car, I came across Mr. *Park*. // 두 사람이 거리에서 우연히 마주쳤다 Two men bumped into each other on the street.

†**마주하다** put opposite ¶ 책상을 마주하고 앉다 sit opposite the table

마죽 馬粥 boiled horse feed

†**마중** meeting ; reception (영접) —하다 meet 《a person》 ; greet ; receive ; go 〔come〕 (out) to meet 《a person》 on arrival ¶ 그는 아버지를 마중하러 역에 갔다 He went to the station to meet his father. // 모든 정부 요인들이 그를 마중나왔다 All the high government officials came out to greet him.

마중물 ¶ 펌프에 마중물을 붓다 fetch the pump

마지기 a patch of field requiring one *mal* of seed ; a *majigi* ¶ 논 한 마지기 a patch of rice paddy // 밭 세 마지기 three *majigi* of fields

마지노선 —線 the Maginot line

†**마지막** the last ; the end ; a close ¶ 마지막날 the closing〔concluding〕 day // 마지막으로 lastly ; finally ; at the conclusion // 마지막까지 to the end〔last〕 // 그것이 내가 그를 본 마지막이었다 That was the last I saw him. // 한번 결심하면 마지막까지 한다 Once I am determined, I never give up. // 마지막에는 싸움이 되고 말았다 It ended in a quarrel.

*****마지못하다** be compelled〔forced, obliged, pressed〕 to《do》; be driven by dire〔sheer〕 necessity to《do》 ¶ 마지못하여 against one's will ; unwillingly ; reluctantly ; with a bad grace ; inevitably ; out of necessity // 마지못해 학교를 그만두었다 He was obliged〔compelled〕 to leave school. // 마지못해 최후의 수단을 썼다 I was driven〔impelled〕 to extreme measures. // 마지못해 단념하였다 He had no alternative〔option〕 but to give it up. // 마지못해 승낙을 하였다 He gave an unwilling consent. // 그녀는 마지못해 그와 결혼한 것 같다 She seems to have got married to him against her will. // 마지못하여 한 일이다 I did it of necessity, not of choice. /This is an outcome of necessity.

마지않다 can never《thank》 enough ¶ 감사하여 마지않습니다 I can never thank you enough. /I have no words to express my gratitude to you. // 경하하여 마지않습니다 I offer you my sincerest congratulations.

마직물 麻織物 hemp cloth

마진 痲疹 〖한의〗 measles

마진 a margin《of profit》
—**제**(制) the margin system

마질 —**하다** measure with a *mal* measure

⁑**마차** 馬車 a carriage ; a coach ; a cab ; a cart ; a wagon ¶ 마차로 가다 go by carriage ; drive《to》 // 말 한 필이 끄는 마차 a one-horse carriage
—**길** a drive(way) ; a carriage-drive —**삯** carriage〔cab〕 fare ; cartage (짐차의) **4륜**— a four-wheeler ; a wagon **쌍두**— a carriage and pair **짐**— a horse and van ; a wagon **포장〔유개〕**— a close carriage ; a covered wagon (대형의)《미》

마차꾼 ⇨ 마부(馬夫)

마차말 馬車— a carriage horse ; a cart horse

†**마찬가지** sameness ; identity ; likeness ; similarity ¶ 마찬가지의 [동일한] the same ; one and the same ; identical ; [동등한] equal ; equivalent ; [유사한] like ; alike ; similar // 마찬가지로 alike ; likewise ; in the same manner ; similarly ; as ever // 그것이나 이것이나 마찬가지다 It is the same as this. // 그의 영어 지식은 나와 마찬가지다 His knowledge of English is on a par with mine. // 그것은 물과 마찬가지 빛깔이었다 It was similar in color to the water. // 그것은 새것이나 마찬가지다 It is as good as new. // 키가 모두 마찬가지다 They are all of the same height. // 우리 살림은 밤낮 마찬가지다 My life is always the same. // 자네도 마찬가진데 뭘 I can say the same thing about you.

*****마찰** 摩擦 ① rubbing ; chafing ② 〖물리〗 friction —**하다** rub《against, with》; chafe《the skin》 ¶ 젖은 수건으로 전신을 마찰하다 rub all the body with a wet towel // 열은 마찰로 생긴다 Heat is produced by friction. ③ [알력] friction ; discord ; feud ; a trouble ¶ 두 파 사이에는 마찰이 끊임없다 There is a perpetual friction between the two factions.
—**계**(計) a tribometer —**계수**(係數) the coefficient of friction —**마력** [내연 기관] friction horsepower —**면** [기계 따위의] the friction surface —**물리학** tribophysics —**부** the part that undergoes friction —**손실** 〖물리〗 friction loss —**열** frictional heat —**저항** frictional resistance —**전기** frictional electricity **건포**—《take》 a rubdown with a dry towel **회전**— 〖기계·물리〗 rolling friction

마찰음 摩擦音 a frictional sound ; 〖음성〗 a fricative sound〔consonant〕 ; a fricative ; 〖동물〗 a stridulating sound (귀뚜라미의 날개 따위의)

*****마천루** 摩天樓 a skyscraper

마철 馬鐵 a horseshoe

마초 馬草 fodder ; hay ¶ 마초를 주다 fodder〔feed, give fodder to〕 a horse

*****마취** 痲醉 an(a)esthesia ; narcotism ¶ 마취시키다 anesthetize ; narcotize ; etherize (에테르로) // 마취에서 깨어나다 come out of the ether〔anesthetic〕
—**법** a method of anesthesia ; narcosis —**분석** narcoanalysis —**요법** narcotherapy —**의**(醫) an anesthetist —**작용** narcosism —**총** [동물의 포획에 사용하는] an anesthetic gun —**최면** narcohypnosis **국부〔전신〕**— local〔general〕 anesthesia **에테르**— etherization **전기**— electronarcosis **척추**— spinal anesthesia

마취목 馬醉木 〖식물〗 a mountain fetter bush ; Lyonia japonica (학명)

마취제 痲醉劑, **마취약** 痲醉藥 an anesthetic ; a narcotic ; a stupefacient ; a soporific ; an opiate ; a (narcotic) drug ¶ 마취제를 넣은 술 drugged wine // 마취제에 취해서 돈을 빼앗기다 be drugged and robbed of one's money
국소〔전신〕— a local〔general〕 anesthetic

마취학 痲醉學 anesthesiology
—**자** an anesthesiologist

마치¹ [장도리] a small hammer ; a claw hammer ; [망치] a hammer ¶ 마치질하

다 hammer // 마치로 못을 박다 drive a nail in with a hammer ; hammer a nail in

*마치² as if〔though〕; as ; just like〔as〕; as... as ¶ 마치 거미처럼 벽을 기어오르다 scale the wall just like a spider // 그것은 마치 눈처럼 희다 It is (as) white as snow. /It is snow-white. // 그는 그녀를 마치 자기 딸처럼 사랑했다 He loved her as if she had been his own daughter.

마치다¹ ① [부딪치다] be struck ; be obstructed ; be stuck ; hit ¶ 말뚝이 바위에 마치어 들어가지 않는다 The stake has hit a rock and won't drive in any deeper.

② [아프다] pinch ; feel an acute pain ¶ 구두가 마치다 one's shoes pinch // 구두에 발이 마치다 one's feet are pinched by one's shoes // 마룻바닥이 등에 마치다 the floor hurts one's back

*마치다² finish ; complete ; get〔be〕through ; end ; conclude ¶ 그는 하루의 일을 마쳤다 He finished〔got through〕his business of the day. // 그는 학교를 마치자 은행원이 되었다 As soon as he completed schooling, he became a banker. // 저녁을 마치고 산책을 했다 I took a walk after dinner.

마침 just ; exactly ; favorably ; fortunately ; opportunely ; in the (very) nick of time ¶ 마침 그때 문을 두드리는 소리가 났다 Just then, there was a knocking at the door. // 마침 잘 만났네 Well met ! // 마침 친구가 와서 나의 곤경을 덜어주었다 As good luck would have it, a friend of mine came and helped me from difficulties.

마침가락 the very thing〔person〕wanted ; the right thing〔person〕; just the thing〔person〕¶ 마침가락으로 just in time ; at the right moment ; fortunately ; luckily // 마침가락으로 그가 왔다 He has come at just the right moment. // 마침가락으로 기차가 연착하여 잡아 탔다 Luckily for me the train was late, so I just caught it. // 그는 그 자리에 마침가락이다 He is the right man for the position.

⁑마침내 finally ; at last ; eventually ; at length ; in the end ; in the long run ; after all ¶ 그는 마침내 내 의견에 동의했다 At length he agreed to my opinion. // 그는 마침내 성공했다 At last he succeeded. // 마침내 일이 끝났다 The work has come to an end at last. // 폭주를 하더니 마침내 건강을 해쳤다 He kept on drinking hard until he ruined his health.

†마침표 —標 a period ; a full stop

*마카로니 macaroni

— 웨스턴 an Italian western ; a spaghetti western

마케팅 marketing

— 리서치 marketing research

마타리 〖식물〗 a kind of valerianaceous plant

마탁 磨琢 ① [연마] polishing ; shining ② [향상] cultivation ; training —하다 polish ; shine ; cultivate ; train ; work hard ; work out ; elaborate

마태 馬太 beans for horse feed ; horse bean

마태복음 —福音 〖성경〗 (the Gospel of) Matthew

마투리 odd measure ; some odd *mal* ¶ 닷섬 마투리 five *sem* and some odd *mal*

마파람 [남풍] the south wind ; a souther

마파람에 게눈 감추듯 (속담) 《eat a thing up》 in a moment〔in no time at all, as quick as a wink〕

마판 馬板 [말 매는] a horse paddock ; [마구간의] floorboards of a stable

마편초 馬鞭草 〖식물〗 verbena

마포 麻布 hemp ; hemp cloth (삼베) ; jute (인도 마포)

마피 馬皮 horsehide

마피아 [미국의 범죄 비밀결사] the Maf(f)ia

마필 馬匹 horses ¶ 마필 개량 horse improvement

마하 〖물리〗 Mach (number)

*마호가니 mahogany

마흔 forty

†막¹ [방금] just ; just now ; [바야흐로] 《be》 about to ; 《be》 on the point of ¶ 그는 막 떠났다 He just left a moment ago. // 배는 막 떠나려 했다 The ship was about 〔just going〕 to start. /The ship was on the point of sailing. // 지금 막 식사를 마쳤습니다 I have just finished dinner. // 막 떠나려 하는데 그로부터 전화가 왔다 I was about to leave when he telephoned. // 그는 시골서 막 올라온 사람이다 He is the man new〔fresh〕 from the country.

막² [함부로] carelessly ; at random ; roughly ; blindly ; recklessly ; [사납게] severely ; violently ; wild ; hard ; terribly ; awfully ¶ 막말 a blunt remark ; a rash speech // 막되다 be ill-bred ; be rude ; be wild // 막살다 lead a rough sort of life // 그는 곤봉으로 개를 막 때렸다 With a stick he struck a dog blindly. // 그는 돈을 막 썼다 He spent money recklessly. // 그는 음식을 막 먹었다 He ate greedily 〔ravenously〕. // 비가 막 퍼붓듯이 왔다 The rain poured down terribly 〔heavily〕.

막³ [마지막] the last

—내 the lastborn —물 the last crop 〔catch〕 —차 the last train

⁑막 膜 〖해부〗 a membrane ¶ 막질의 membranous

†막 幕 ① [집] a booth ; a hut ; a cabin ; a cottage ; a shed ; a shack ; a lodge ¶ 원두막 a look-out shed // 막을 짓다 put up a booth

② [휘장] a curtain ; a hanging screen ; a tent (천막) ¶ 막을 치다 stretch a curtain // 막을 열다 draw the curtains ; draw

〔pull〕 (aside) the curtains // 막을 올리다 raise〔draw up, lift〕 a curtain
③ [연극의] an act ¶ 1막짜리 연극 a one-act play // 3막 4장의 극 a play in three acts and four scenes
④ [끝장] an end ; a close ; a conclusion // 그 원정은 그의 죽음으로써 막을 내렸다 The expedition ended with his death. // 그 음악회는 국가 연주로 막을 내렸다 The concert concluded with the National Anthem.
제2— 제2장 Act 2, Scene 2
막을 내리다 관용 let down〔draw down, lower〕 a curtain

막가다 [행동이] behave rambunctiously

막간 幕間 an interval (between acts) ; an intermission 《미》 ¶ 15분간의 막간 a fifteen minutes' interval // 막간에 가벼운 식사를 하다 eat a light meal between acts 〔during an intermission〕
—극 an interlude ; a middle piece ; a skit between acts

막강 莫強 —하다 be mighty ; have the greatest power ; be enormously powerful ¶ 막강한 군사력 great military strength // 막강한 전함 a mighty battleship

막걸리 *makkoli* ; raw〔unrefined〕 rice wine

막골 膜骨 [해부] a membrane bone

막깎다 cut 《one's hair》 short ; give a crew cut ¶ 머리를 막깎다 have one's hair cut short ; get a crew cut

막나이 [막치 무명] rough muslin

막내 the lastborn ; the youngest of the family
—둥이 one's darling baby child ¶ 막내둥이 응석받듯 humor 《a person》 indulgently —딸 the last〔youngest〕 daughter —며느리 the wife of one's last 〔youngest〕 son —아들 the last 〔youngest〕 son —아우 the last 〔youngest〕 brother —아이 ⇨ 막냇자식 막냇누이 the last〔youngest〕 sister 막냇동생 the youngest brother〔sister〕 막냇사위 the youngest son-in law 막냇삼촌 the youngest uncle 막냇손자 the youngest grandson 막냇자식 the youngest child ; the baby of the family

막노동 —勞動 ⇨ 막일

†**막다** ① [봉하다] stop〔fill〕 up ; close ; plug ¶ 쥐구멍을 막다 stop up a mouse hole // 구멍을 종이로 막다 close up an opening with paper // 병마개를 막다 stop 〔cork, cap, put the stopper on〕 a bottle // 귀를 막다 plug one's ears // 도망갈 뒷구멍을 막다 plug up a loophole
② [차단하다] block (up) ; obstruct ; stop ; check ; intercept ¶ 길을 막다 stand in another's way ; bar〔obstruct〕 the passage ; block the way // 강을 막다 dam a river // 광선을 막다 intercept the light // 바람을 막다 shut out the wind ; shelter〔screen〕 《a person》 from the wind // 소음을 막다 arrest noise // 입을 막다 cover one's mouth ; gag〔silence〕 《a person》 ; buy 《a person's》 silence
③ [간막다] screen off ; partition ; compartment ; wall up ¶ 방의 간을 막다 partition a room // 휘장으로 간막다 screen off part of a room
④ [방어] defend ; protect ; [방지] keep away〔off, out, back〕 ; ward off ; [예방] prevent ; provide against 《a disease》 ¶ 적을 막다 keep off〔guard against〕 the enemy ; defend oneself against an enemy // 적의 진격을 막다 check the enemy's advance ; hold the enemy in check // 추위를 막다 protect oneself from the cold ; keep out the cold // 홍수를 막다 keep water from overflowing // 병의 전염을 막다 prevent infection of a disease // 가지 못하게 막다 stop 《a person》 from going // 집의 출입을 막다 forbid 《a person》 to enter one's house // 아무것도 그것을 막을 수 없다 Nothing can prevent it.

막다르다 be closed at one end ; come to a deadlock〔standstill〕 ; be brought to a standstill ; find no way out ; reach 〔be in〕 an impasse ; come to the end of the road
막다른 골목 관용 a blind alley ; a dead-end road

***막다른골** [골목] a blind〔dead〕 alley ; an impasse ; [사태] a standstill ; a deadlock ; a stalemate ¶ 막다른골에 다다르다 come〔be brought〕 to a stalemate 〔standstill〕 ; reach an impasse ; run〔be driven〕 into a blind alley ; be driven into the corner // 휴전 회담은 포로 교환 문제로 막다른 골에 다다랐다 The truce talks were stalled〔deadlocked〕 over the issue of prisoner exchange.

막다른집 a house at the end of a blind alley

***막대 莫大 —하다** (be) vast ; immense ; huge ; enormous ; tremendous ¶ 막대한 돈 a huge〔an enormous〕 sum of money // 막대한 비용 enormous 〔immense〕 expense // 막대한 빚 a vast 〔mammoth〕 debt // 막대한 재산 an immense wealth〔fortune〕 // 벼 농사에 막대한 피해를 입었다 A vast damage was done to the rice crop. // 수해로 막대한 손해를 입었다 We suffered an enormous loss from the flood. // 100만불은 막대한 돈이다 A million dollar is a mint of money. // 그 영화는 특수 효과에만도 막대한 비용이 들었을 거야 Apparently the special effects alone in that movie cost them a mint.

†**막대기** a stick ; a rod ; a bar ; a club (곤봉) ; a baton (지휘봉) ¶ 그는 막대기로 개를 때렸다 He hit a dog with a stick.
대— a bamboo stick 쇠〔금속〕— a metal bar

막대 사탕 loaf sugar ; a sugar loaf ; [막대

에 붙인 사탕] a lollipop ; a lolly 《영·구》 ; a sucker 《구》
막대잡이 ① [오른쪽] a blindman's right ; the right ② [앞장군] a guide
막대패 a jack plane ; a fore plane ¶ 막대패질 jack-planing // 막대패질하다 use a fore plane
막 되 다 (be) ill-bred ; ill-mannered ; wild ; rude ; rough ; unmannerly ¶ 막되게 굴다 behave rudely〔wildly, badly〕
막둥이 [막내] the last〔youngest〕 son ; [사내 종] a boy servant ; a page
막론하다 莫論— go without question ; be a matter of course ; be needless to say ; there is no need to speak 《of》 ¶ …을 막론하고 not to speak of ; to say nothing of ; as a matter of course // 남녀를 막론하고 regardless of sex ; (no matter) whether it be man or woman // 지위의 고하를 막론하고 irrespective of rank // 결과의 여하를 막론하고 no matter what the consequences may be
막료 幕僚 a staff officer ; the staff 《총칭》
막막 寞寞 —하다 (be) desolate ; deserted ; solitary ; lonely ; forlorn ¶ 막막한 생활 a desolate life
막막 漠漠 —하다 (be) vast ; boundless ; extensive ¶ 막막한 벌판 a vast plain // 막막한 사하라 사막 the vast and boundless Sahara Desert
막말 —하다 speak roughly ; talk at random ; talk wild ; put 《it》 bluntly ; talk without thinking ¶ 막말로 하자면 to put 《it》 bluntly〔curtly, brusquely〕
막무가내 莫無可奈 ¶ 막무가내로 obstinately ; stubbornly ; resolutely ; firmly // 막무가내로 듣지 않다 will not listen to ; turn a deaf ear to ; refuse flatly // 그렇게 막무가내하지 마라 Don't be so obstinate.
막바지 the end ; the very end ; the dead end ; the extremity ¶ 골목 막바지 the end of the alley // 길 막바지 the dead end of a road // 언덕 막바지 the top of a hill
막벌다 earn wages as a day laborer ; earn by doing rough〔hard〕 work ; work as a day laborer
막벌이 earning wages as a day laborer **—하다** earn wages as a day laborer
막벌잇군 a day laborer ; an odd-jobber
막베먹다 [밑천을] eat into ; cut into ; go into ; make an inroad
막부 幕府 Japan's feudal government ; the shogunate (government)
막부득이 莫不得已 ⇨ 부득이
막불겅이 [저질 살담배] cut tobacco of inferior quality ; [익지 않은 고추] halfripe cayenne pepper
***막사 幕舍** a camp ; a barracks
막사리 tidewater (before it is frozen)
막살다 lead a rough〔careless, haphazard, reckless〕 sort of life ; lead a nondescript 〔drab, grubby〕 life ¶ 산골에 있을 때에는 한동안 막살았다 I really roughed it for a while in the mountain village.
막살이 a rough〔haphazard, reckless, planless, heedless〕 life ; a nondescript 〔drab, grubby〕 life ¶ 막살이하다 live a haphazard life
막상 ultimately ; really ; actually ; in reality ¶ 막상 당해 보니 상상과는 달랐다 I found the reality quite different from what I had imagined. // 일이란 막상 당해 보지 않으면 모르는 것이다 The proof of the pudding is in the eating.
막 상 莫 上 the best ; the first-rate 〔grade〕 ; the highest quality
막상 막하 莫上莫—하다 match 《each other》 ; be equal 《to》 ; be even〔on a par〕 《with》 ; be fifty-fifty ; be equally matched ; be well contested ¶ 두 사람은 막상 막하의 접전을 벌였다 The two ran a neck-and-neck race. // 두 사람은 기술에 있어서 막상 막하이다 The two are on a par with each other in skill. / There is little difference between the two in skill. // 세 후보가 막상막하다 The three major candidates are in a dead heat.
막새 ① [수키와] convex tiles at the edge of eaves ② [암·수키와] (both concave and convex) tiles at the edge of eaves
막서다 make a stand 《against》 ; face ; show fight ; lift a hand against 《one's master》 ; turn upon ; rise against 《one's lord》 ; defy ¶ 어른에게 버릇 없이 막서다 defy one's elder rudely // 막서서 대들다 fight against 《a person》
막시목 膜翅目 〖곤충〗 Hymenoptera ¶ 막시목의 hymenopterous // 막시목의 곤충 a hymenopteron 《*pl.* -ra》 ; a hymenopteran ; a hymenopter
막심하다 莫甚— be at the furthest extreme ; (be) immense ; tremendous ; enormous ; heavy ; hard ; terrible ¶ 막심한 손해 a tremendous loss ; a heavy loss // 통상의 불경기가 오늘보다 막심한 적이 없었다 Never before has trade experienced such heavy depression. // 열강의 경쟁이 나날이 막심하여 간다 The competition between the powers is growing in intensity.
막아내다 ward off ; keep away〔out, off, back〕 ; check ; hold in check ; hold off ; keep〔hold〕 《the enemy》 at bay ¶ 적을 막아 내 다 keep off〔guard against〕 the enemy ; defend 《oneself, the country》 against an enemy ; bear the brunt of the enemy // 추위를 막아내다 protect oneself from the cold ; keep off〔out〕 the cold // 병의 만연을 막아내다 check the spread of a disease // 홍수를 막아내다 keep water from overflowing // 아무것도 그것을 막아낼 수는 없다 There is no help for it. /Nothing can prevent it.
막엄 莫嚴 —하다 (be) very severe 〔strict, stern, rigid, rigorous, stringent〕

ㅁ

막역 莫逆 intimacy ; closeness ; familiarity **—하다** (be) intimate ; close ; familiar ¶ 막역한 친구 an intimate friend ; a close friend // 막역한 사이 intimate relations // 막역하게 지내다 be intimate 〔friendly〕《with》; be on good〔intimate, familiar〕terms《with》; be close to each other // 그들은 매우 막역한 사이이다 They are hand and glove with each other. // 그와는 아주 막역하게 지내고 있다 I am one of his best friends.

⁑**막연 漠然, 邈然 —하다** (be) vague ; hazy ; obscure ; dim ; ambiguous ¶ 막연히 vaguely ; obscurely ; hazily // 막연한 말〔대답·약속〕vague words〔answers, promises〕// 그때의 일은 막연히 기억하고 있을 뿐이다 I have but a faint remembrance of those days. // 이 점에 대한 그의 대답은 막연했다 His answer was rather hazy on this point.

막이 protection ; defending ; warding off ; prevention ; damming up ; banking up ; a charm (부적) ; a screen (칸막이) ¶ 보막이 banking up a paddy // 동막이 throwing 〔building〕up levees // 홍수막이 flood protection〔prevention〕work // 서리막이 a protection from frost // 아랫막이 bottom end piece ; bottom garment // 액막이 a charm against evil influence // 칸막이로 방을 막다 partition the room with a screen

막일 rough work ; physical labor ; toil ; heavy work **—하다** labor ; toil ; do rough work

—꾼 a (physical) laborer ; an odd-jobber ; a handyman

막자 a medicine pestle

막잡이 a rough article used for any purpose ; a coarse article

막장 a blind end〔front〕in a mine gallery ¶ 막장군 a miner ; a digger ; a pitman

막전 幕電 〖기상〗 sheet lightning

막중 莫重 —하다 (be) very〔extremely〕precious ; invaluable ; priceless ; costly ; very important ¶ 막중한 인명 precious human lives // 막중한 시간 valuable time // 막중한 물건 valuables〔valuable things〕// 그의 우정은 나에게 막중한 것이다 His friendship is very precious to me. // 그는 막중한 사명을 띠고 있다 He has〔is entrusted with〕an extremely important mission.

막지르다 ① [앞을] interrupt ; stand in one's way ; confront ; block ; bar ¶ 길을 막지르다 block one's way ; bar one's passage // 말을 막지르다 interrupt《a person》; cut《a person》short

② [함부로] thrust〔jab, stab, push, kick〕at random〔with force〕; shout loudly (소리를) ¶ 칼로 사람을 막지르다 stab at《a person》wildly〔hard〕// 소리를 막지르다 yell out ; shout and yell

막질 膜質 ¶ 막질의 membran(e)ous ; 〖식물〗 scarious

— 외피 〖식물〗 a tunic

막질리다 ① [앞을] be interrupted ; be blocked ; be barred ; be confronted

② [함부로] get thrust〔jabbed, stabbed, pushed, kicked〕at random〔with force〕

막차 —車 the last train〔bus〕

막초 —草 coarse〔poor-quality, cheap〕tobacco ; cut tobacco of inferior quality

막치 a coarse〔crude, low-grade〕article ; poor stuff ; coarse manufactures

막판 [마지막 판] the last round ; the final scene ; [중대한 때] the last〔critical〕moment ¶ 막판에 와서 at the last moment

막필 —筆 a coarse writing brush

막하 幕下 [막료] the staff ; [가신(家臣)] a vassal ; a feudatory ; [부하] a follower ; a subordinate ; a subaltern (부관) ; a following《총칭》 ¶ S 대장의 막하 an officer on General》S's staff // …의 막하가 되다 be placed〔place oneself〕under《a person's》command

막후 幕後 behind the curtain ; in the background ¶ 막후의 인물 a man behind the scene // 막후에서 조정하다 pull the wires〔strings〕// 막후에서 활약하다 play an active part in the background // 막후에 무엇인가 있다 There is something behind the scenes.

— 흥정〔교섭〕 [정치의] behind-the-scenes dealing〔negotiation〕

***막히다** ① [폐색] be stopped〔blocked〕up ; be clogged ; be choked ; be stuffy ¶ 숨이 막히다 stifle ; be suffocated 〔smothered〕// 목구멍이 막히다 one's throat contracts // 코가 막히다 one's nose is stuffy // 병마개가 막히다 a bottle is corked〔stopped up〕// 파이프 구멍이 막히다 a pipe is clogged // 도랑이 막히다 a gutter is choked《with debris》// 굴뚝이 막히다 a chimney is choked up《with soot》// 도망갈 뒷구멍이 막히다 a loophole is plugged up

② [차단] be blocked ; be stopped ; be stuck ; be cut off ; be closed ; be shut ¶ 길이 막히다 a road is blocked《with snow》// 교통이 막히다 traffic is held up 〔blocked〕// 앞길이 막히다 be deadlocked ; have no way out ; be stalled ; have no opportunity in future // 말이 막히다 be stuck for a word ; be at a loss for words ; lose one's words《in tears》// 앞에 강이 막히다 a river lies across the path ahead // 뒤에 산이 막히다 be walled in from behind by a mountain // 벽으로 막히다 be partitioned with a wall ; be walled up

③ [생각이] be〔become〕stupid ; be blockheaded ; be thickheaded ; be dull-witted ¶ 막힌 사람 a blockhead ; a halfwit

⁑**만¹** ① [단지] only ; alone ; just ; merely ; simply ; very ; but ; except ¶ 꼭 한번만

only once // 일생에 한번만 for once in one's life // 한번만 더 just once again 〔more〕 // 이번만은 for this once ; for this time only // 서울에서만이라도 in *Seoul* alone // 방에는 그녀와 그 둘만 있었다 He was alone with her in the room. // 하나만 주시오 Give me just one. // 저 사람은 독서하는 것만이 일이다 Reading is his exclusive occupation. // 그것만이 아니다 밤에도 일해야만 한다 Not only that, but I must work at night. // 그의 이름을 듣기만 해도 몸서리가 난다 I shudder at his very name. // 수부들은 매일 바닷물만 보고 지냈다 The sailors saw nothing but water every day.

② [정도·범위] as many as ; as much as ; enough 《to do a thing》 ; to the amount〔extent〕 of ; so far as ; all one has〔can〕 ; all there is ¶ 이만큼만 있으면 사전을 살 수 있다 This amount will be enough to buy a dictionary. // 그만한 길이로 충분합니까 Is it long enough ? // 평판만으로 판단할 때 그는 위대한 사람같다 So far as reputation goes, he seems to be a great man. // 오늘은 이만 해 두자 [수업 시간에] So much for today. // 그런 생각을 가지고 있는 것은 일부 사람들만이다 The idea is limited〔confined〕 to a certain circle. // 자네 차를 오전중만 빌릴 수 없을까 Can't I borrow your car for the morning ? // 잘 모르지만 마누라가 없다는 것만은 확실하다 I am not quite sure, but this much is quite sure that he has no wife.

③ [상당] worth ¶ 500원어치만 설탕을 샀다 I bought five hundred *won's* worth of sugar. // 이 책은 읽을 만하다 This book is worth reading. // 나도 먹고 살 만한 수입이 필요하다 I must have income enough to live on.

④ [적어도] at least ¶ 나는 한 달에 천원만 이라도 저축하고 싶다 I wish to save a minimum of 1,000 *won* a month. // 나는 아들에게 중학만은 보내고자 한다 I will give my boy middle school education at least.

⑤ [비교] as... as ¶ 그의 키는 너만하다 He is as tall as you. // 이 꽃은 그만 못하다 This flower is not so pretty as that.

만² [때] ¶ 이틀 만에 on the second day // 상경 후 5년 만에 five years after he came up to *Seoul* // 그가 떠난 지 꼭 두 해만이다 It is just two years since he left. // 오래간만입니다 It is a long time since I saw you last.

만³ ⇨ 마는

***만 萬** ten thousand ; many ; all ; a myriad (다수) ¶ 수만 tens of thousands // 수십만 hundreds of thousands // 5만분지 1의 지도 a map on the scale of one- fifty-thousandth // 만에 하나 one in ten thousand ; be very rare // 그것은 만인이 인정하는 바이다 It is universally recognized. /Everybody admits it. // 그런 일은 만에 하나도 일어나지 않을 것이다 It is one in ten thousand that such a thing will happen.

†만 灣 a gulf ; a bay ¶ 멕시코만 the Gulf of Mexico // 인천만 *Inchun* Bay // 만을 이루다 form a gulf〔bay〕

만 滿 just ; full ; fully ¶ 만 17세 full seventeen years old // 나이를 만으로 세다 count 《a person's》 age in full // 그 여자는 오는 4월로 만 18세가 된다 She is going to be 18〔will complete her eighteenth year〕 next April. // 그가 미국으로 떠난 지 만 10년이 된다 It is a full ten years since he left for America.

만 卍 the Buddhist cross ; a Buddhist emblem ; a fylfot ; a gammadion 《*pl.* -dia》 ; a swastika ¶ 만기 the swastika flag (나치스 독일의)

만가 挽歌 a dirge ; an elegy ; a lament ; [상여를 메고 갈 때] a funeral song

만감 萬感 a flood〔crowd〕 of emotion ¶ 만감이 북받쳤다 A thousand emotions 〔thoughts〕 crowded on my mind. // 만감이 북받쳐서 말이 안 나왔다 My heart was too full for words. /I could not utter a word with a heart full of feeling.

만강 萬康 peace ; tranquility ; security ; welfare ; health

만강 滿腔 a full heart ; full-heartedness ; whole-heartedness ¶ 만강의 hearty ; heartfelt ; whole-heartedness ¶ 만강의 축의를 표하다 offer one's hearty congratulations // 만강의 사의를 표하다 express 〔tender〕 one's whole-hearted thanks

만개 滿開 full bloom ⇨ 만발

만경 晩景 ① [저녁 경치] an evening scene ¶ 파로호의 만경 an evening view of Lake *Paro*

② [늦경치] a scene behind the season

만경 晩境 one's later years ; the latter part of one's life ; the close〔evening〕 ofone's life〔days〕 ; one's closing days

만경 萬頃 vastness ; enormousness ; extensiveness ; boundlessness ; immensity

— 창파 the boundless expanse of water

만경되다 one's eyes become dull〔lifeless, lusterless〕 ; one's eyes become lacking in vitality

만경 타령 —打令 negligence ; neglect ; disregard ; remissness

만고 萬古 [옛] all antiquity ; [영원] perpetuity ; eternity ¶ 만고의 진리 an eternal truth // 만고의 영웅 a hero for all ages // 만고로부터 from immemorial antiquity // 만고에 유가 없다 be unique for all generation

만고 불멸 萬古不滅 immortality ; imperishability ; everlastingness ; eternity ; perpetuity **— 하다** be immortal〔imperishable, eternal〕 ; do not perish forever ; last forever 만고 불멸의 immortal ; undying ; imperishable ; deathless ; permanent ; eternal

만고 불변 萬古不變 permanence ; constancy ; being unchangeable **—하다** be unchangeable ; be immutable ; be permanent ; be constant ¶ 만고 불변의 진리 immutable truths ; eternal laws

만고 불역 萬古不易 everlastingness ; immutability ; invariableness ; eternity ; perpetuity **—하다** (be) everlasting 〔invariable, immutable〕; eternal〔perpetual〕

만고 불후 萬古不朽 being immortal ; remaining intact〔undecayed〕 for ever ; eternity ; imperishability ; immortality **—하다** be immortal ; be eternal ; be imperishable ; be undying ¶ 만고 불후의 명작 an immortal masterpiece〔work〕; a book of everlasting merit

만고 잡놈 萬古雜— a thorough-paced 〔thoroughgoing〕 libertine〔rake〕; an all-time philanderer

만고 절담 萬古絶談 an immortal saying ; unchangeable maxim ; an eternal truth〔verity〕; a timeless truth

만고 절색 萬古絶色 an unsurpassed beauty ; a (woman of) peerless beauty ; the fairest of the fair ; the loveliest of all

만고 절창 萬古絶唱 [가수] an unparalleled〔a peerless〕 singer ; [노래] a superb song unequalled in its beauty ; [시] a poem unexcelled in its beauty throughout the annals of literature

만고 풍상 萬古風霜 all kinds of hardships and privations ; long trials ¶ 만고 풍상을 겪다 suffer hardships and privations ; undergo〔experience〕 all sorts of hardships and privations

*̣**만곡 彎曲** a curve ; a crook ; a bend ; a bow ; curvature ; flexion **—하다** curve ; bend ; be curved ; be bowed ; be crooked **—부** [무릎 따위의] a genu《*pl.* genua》; [하천의] a bend ; [배 밑바닥의] a bilge **—제어**〖전기〗bulge control **이상(異常)—** abnormal curvature〔curving〕 **척추—** spinal curvature

만구 灣口 the entrance〔mouth〕 of a bay

*̣**만국 萬國** all nations ; the nations of the world ; all countries on earth ; the world ¶ 만국의 international ; universal

— 박람회 an international exposition ; a world fair《미》 **—사** a universal〔world〕 history **— 신호** the international code signals **— 우편 연합** the Universal Postal Union **— 음성 기호** the international phonetic alphabet **— 평화 회의** the International Peace Conference (1899년과 1907년의) **— 표준시** universal time

만국기 萬國旗 the flags of all nations ; bunting《총칭·장식용》 ¶ 만국기로 꾸며져 있다 be decked with bunting

만군 萬軍 a myriad soldiers ¶ 만군은 얻기 쉬워도 일장(一將)은 얻기 힘들다 Workers are earlier〔easier〕 found than masters.

만굴 彎屈 a curve ⇨ 만곡(彎曲)

만궁 彎弓 drawing a bow **—하다** draw 〔bend〕 a bow

만권 萬卷 ten thousand books ; [수많은] many books ; a large library

만귀잠잠하다 萬鬼潛潛— be all quiet 〔silent, still, hushed〕 ¶ 만귀잠잠한 한밤중에 in the unearthly〔ghostly〕 hour ; at the still of the night ; at dead of night

만근 輓近 recent times ; late years ¶ 만근의 recent ; late ; modern ; latter-day // 만근에 recently ; lately ; of late ; in recent times ; of late years

만근 萬斤 great weight ¶ 그의 말은 우리에게는 만근의 무게가 있다 His word carries great weight with us.

만금 萬金 ten thousand pieces of gold ; an immense sum of money ¶ 만금으로도 바꿀 수 없다 be invaluable ; be priceless // 만금을 투자하다 invest an immense sum《in》

***만기 滿期** expiration《of a term, contract》; maturity《of a bill》 ¶ 만기의 matured ; time-expired // 만기가 되다 [임기가] expire ; [어음이] mature ; fall〔be, become〕 due ; [복역이] serve out one's time // 계약이 만기가 되었다 The contract has expired. // 신채권은 10년으로 만기가 된다 The new bonds mature in ten years. // 이 어음은 오는 25일이 만기이다 The note is due on the 25th inst.

— 배당〖생명 보험〗a maturity dividend **—병** time-expired soldiers **— 상환** redemption at〔on〕 maturity **— 석방** release《of a prisoner》 on the expiration of the period of punishment **— 어음** a matured bill **—일** the expiration date ; the date of maturity ; the due date **— 제대** discharge on expiration of term of service

만기 萬機 ① [중요한 정치 사항] all the important matters in politics ; all the affairs of state (임금이 보살피는)
② [비밀] all (sorts of) secret ; all confidential matters ¶ 만기를 보살피다 attend to the affairs of the state // 만기를 총람하다 conduct all state affairs

만끽 滿喫 **—하다** [먹다] have enough 《of》; have one's fill ; eat〔drink〕 to one's heart's content ; do ample justice to 《dinner》; [즐기다] enjoy full〔to the full〕

†**만나다** ① [사람을] see ; meet ; [면담하다] interview ; have an interview《with》; [약속해서] meet ¶ 뜻밖에 만나다 come across《a person》; come〔stumble〕 upon《a person》; 몰래 만나다 meet secretly ; have a secret meeting ; rendezvous // 여자와 만날 약속을 하다 have 〔get〕 a date with a girl《미》 // 그 사람하고는 요새 별로 만나지 않았다 I have not seen much of him lately. // 내일 또 만납

시다 Good-bye till tomorrow. /I will be seeing you tomorrow. 《미》// 저 사람하고 만날 필요가 없다 He is a perfect stranger to me. // 저 사람을 만나지 않도록 해라 Keep yourself out of his sight. // Avoid〔Shun〕 his society. // 얼마나 너를 만나고 싶었는지 모른다 I have been dying to see you. // I have missed you very badly. // 만나 보면 좋은 사람이라는 것을 알 것이다 You will find him a good man. // 직접 본인을 만나 보지 않으면 안된다 You must have a personal interview with him. // 너희 둘은 어떻게 만나게 되었니 How did you two meet?
② [재앙·화·때를] meet with 《an accident》; encounter 《difficulty》; come upon〔across〕; light〔fall〕 upon; be overtaken by 《a storm》; be caught in 《shower》 ¶ 무서운 일을 만나다 have a dreadful experience // 태평 성대를 만나다 fall on〔live in〕 the happy era

만난 萬難 all〔a thousand and one〕 difficulties; all kinds of trials; innumerable difficulties; all obstacles〔hindrances〕 ¶ 만난을 무릅쓰고 at any cost; at all costs〔hazards, risks〕; in spite〔despite〕 of all difficulties; through thick and thin // 만난을 배제하다 surmount〔overcome〕 all difficulties

만날 always; all the time; habitually; every time; invariably ¶ 만날 서로 싸우다 quarrel with each other all the time // 만날 놀다 always idle one's time away // 그는 만날 같은 넥타이만 맨다 He always wears the same tie. // 그는 만날 유쾌한 생활을 하고 있다 He leads a life of continual pleasure.

만냥 萬兩 an immense sum of money

만네리즘 ⇨ 매너리즘

만년 晩年 one's later〔latter, last〕 years; the later part of one's life; late in life; the close〔evening〕 of one's life〔days〕 ¶ 만년에 in the evening of one's life; in one's latter〔later, last〕 days // 만년에 접어들다 enter the twilight of one's life // 만년을 불우하게 보내다 live the rest of one's life in obscurity

만년 萬年 ten thousand years; eternity; perpetuity
—력(曆) a perpetual almanac〔calendar〕 **— 처녀** a fadeless beauty; a perennially youthful woman **— 청년** a man of perennial〔ageless〕 youth; a man who never loses his youthful vigor

만년빙 萬年氷 polar icecaps

만년설 萬年雪 perpetual〔permanent〕 snow (field); [높은 산의] an icecap; 〖지질〗 firn (snow) 《도》; névé 《프》 ¶ 극지의 만년설 polar icecaps

*﹡**만년필 萬年筆** a fountain pen; a self-feeding pen ¶ 만년필에 잉크를 넣다 fill a fountain pen // 만년필의 잉크가 떨어졌다 The fountain pen has run out of ink〔is dry〕.
자동(흡입)식 — a self-filling (fountain) pen

만능 萬能 omnipotence; being almighty; having an all-round capability ¶ 만능의 all-powerful; almighty; omnipotent; all-round // 만능의 신 the Almighty (God)
— 공구(工具) an all-purpose tool **— 마멸기〔분쇄기〕** a universal grinder **— 선반** a universal lathe **— 선수** an all-round〔all-around〕 player〔athlete〕 **— 약(藥)** a (universal) panacea; a cureall; a heal-all; a universal remedy; a catholicon

만다라 曼陀羅 〖불교〗 mandala 《범》; Buddha's picture

만단 萬端 all sorts of affairs; everything; all; every (possible) means (모든 수단) ¶ 만단의 준비가 되어 있다 All〔Everything〕 is ready. /All is in readiness. /Every preparation is made.
— 설화 all sorts of stories; various stories **— 수심(愁心)** all kinds of worries; lots of worries; manifold vexations

만달 〖미술〗 an arabesque design

만담 漫談 a gag; a joke **—하다** gag; joke ¶ 코미디언의 만담에 관중이 폭소를 터뜨렸다 The comedian's gags made the audience laugh.
—가(家) a gagster; a gagman; a gagger; a comedian; a funster; a comic-chat artiste

만당 滿堂 the entire hall; the whole house〔hall〕; [청중] all the audience **—하다** be full; be packed ¶ 만당의 갈채를 받다 carry〔bring down〕 the house // 만당이 물을 끼얹은 듯 조용해졌다 A hush fell over the crowded hall. /Silence reigned over the audience. // 만당이 입추의 여지 없이 꽉 찼다 The hall was closely packed〔filled to overflowing〕. // 만당에 계시는 신사 숙녀 여러분 Ladies and gentlemen!

만대 萬代 all generations; all ages; eternity ¶ 만대 불변의 eternal; everlasting // 만대의 영화 eternal prosperity and glory // 만대에 for all ages 《to come》; through all ages; forever; eternally // 만대에 전해지다 be remembered for ages to come

만도 晩稻 late-ripening rice

만도 滿都 the whole〔entire〕 city ¶ 만도의 시민 all the citizens

만도 晩禱 〖기독교〗 the vespers; the evening prayer

만돌린 [악기] a mandolin ¶ 만돌린을 타다 play (on) the mandolin
— 연주자 a mandolinist

만동 晩冬 late winter; the later part of winter

만두 饅頭 a bun; a dumpling
—소 (a) bun filling〔stuffing〕 **고기 —** a bun stuffed with seasoned meat and vegetables; a bun with a (minced) meat

ㅁ

filling〔stuffing〕 군— a fried dumpling stuffed with minced pork 찐— a steamed dumpling 팥— bun with a bean-jam filling ; a bean-jam bun

만득 晩得 [자식을 낳음] begetting a child in one's later years ; [낳은 자식] a child begotten in one's later years **—하다** beget〔procreate〕 a child in one's later years

†만들다 ① [창조] make ; create ¶ 하느님께서 최초에 하늘과 땅을 만드시었다 In the beginning God created (the) heaven and (the) earth.
② [제작·제조] make ; manufacture ; prepare ¶ 밀가루로 만든 prepared from flour // 넝마로 종이를 만들다 manufacture rags into paper // 대로 여러 가지 기물을 만들다 make bamboo into various goods ; make various vessels out of bamboo
③ [양조] make 《into, from》 ; brew 《beer》 ; distill 《whisky》 ¶ 포도주는 포도로 만든다 Wine is made from grapes. // 보리로 맥주를 만든다 Barley is made into beer.
④ [작성] make ; frame ; make out ; draw up (서류 따위를) ; write (책을) ; lay down (규칙을) ¶ 서류를 만들다 draw up a document // 책을 만들다 write a book
⑤ [건조] make ; build ; erect ; construct ¶ 정원을 만들다 lay out a garden // 신시가지를 만들다 lay out a new street
⑥ [주조] coin ; cast ; strike ; mint ¶ 화폐를 만들다 strike〔mint〕 coins ; coin money // 총포를 만들다 cast guns
⑦ [조성·조직] constitute ; form ; organize ; found ; set up ; establish ¶ 학교를 만들다 found〔establish〕 a school // 회를 만들다 organize an association // 회사를 만들다 set up a company
⑧ [양육] foster ; cultivate ; build (up) ¶ 인물을 만들다 build up a man 《of talent》 // 선량한 시민을 만들다 train good citizens
⑨ [허구] make up ; invent ; fabricate ¶ 만들어 낸 이야기 a made-up〔an invented〕 story ; an invention
⑩ [하게 하다] make 《a person do》 ; cause 《a person to do》 ; induce 《a person to do》 ; get 《a person to do》 ; have 《a person》 do ¶ 믿게 만들다 make believe 《in》 // 명령에 복종하게 만들다 force 《a person》 to obey an order
⑪ [음식을] prepare 《food》 ; cook
⑫ [기타] ¶ 신어를 만들다 coin a new word // 적으로 만들다 make an enemy // 사람을 병신으로 만들다 make a fool of 《a person》 // 사람을 도둑으로 만들다 make 《a person》 into a thief

만듦새 [구조] make ; construction ; structure ; [세공] workmanship ; craftsmanship ; [옷의] cut ; style ¶ 옷의 만듦새 the make of the coat // 만듦새가 좋다〔나쁘다〕 be of fine〔poor〕 workmanship // 저 집의 만듦새가 근사하다 The make of the house is fine.

만록 漫錄 light essays ; random comments ; stray notes ; jottings

만록 萬綠 a myriad of green leaves ¶ 만록 총중 홍일점 the only member of the fair sex present

만료 滿了 expiration ; termination **—하다** expire ; come to an end ; complete ¶ 기한〔임기〕은 오늘 만료한다 The term expires today.
—일 the expiration date 계약 — the termination of an agreement 기한 — the expiration of the term〔period〕 임기 — the termination of one's office

만루 滿壘 〖야구〗 a full〔loaded〕 base ¶ 만루가 되다 The bases are full〔choked〕. /The sacks are tenanted〔sold out〕. // 이사 만루가 됐다 The bases were filled with two out.
— 홈런 a base-loaded homer〔home run〕 ; a grand slam〔homer〕

만루책 滿壘策 〖야구〗 the tactic of deliberately filling the bases ¶ 만루책을 쓰다 deliberately fill the bases

만류 挽留 holding〔keeping〕 back ; check ; detaining **—하다** hold〔keep〕 back ; prevent ; detain ; check (저지하다) ¶ 간곡히 만류하다 detain 《a person》 by the sleeve ; hold 《a person》 by the button ; buttonhole 《a person》 // 사직하려는 사람의 만류책을 강구하다 take measures to induce a person to stay in office // 싸우지 말라고 만류하다 hold 《a person》 back from wrangling ; dissuade 《a person》 from fighting

만류 灣流 the Gulf Stream

만리 萬里 ten thousand ; a long distance ¶ 만리길 a long way〔journey〕
— 장천 the high heavens

만리경 萬里鏡 a telescope ; a field-glass

만리 장성 萬里長城 the Great Wall of China

만만장이 a pushover ; an easy mark ; a softy ; a person easy to deal with

만만하다 ① [보드랍다] (be) soft ; tender ; supple ; plastic ; limp
② [용이하다] (be) easy 《to deal with》 ; be ready to yield ; (be) soft ; not firm ; easygoing ¶ 만만치 않은 stiff ; tough ; stubborn // 만만한 일 an easy job // 만만한 사람 an easy mark ; a pushover
③ [우습게 보이다] (be) negligible ; slight ; be of no account〔importance〕 ; (be) insignificant ¶ 만만히 cheaply ; insignificantly ; slightly // 만만찮은 적 formidable enemy ; an adversary of no mean strength ; an ugly customer // 일을 만만하게 여기다 treat a matter as of little account // 사람을 만만하게 보다 make light of a person // 그는 만만찮은 학자다 He is no mean scholar. // 약한 적일지라

도 만만히 여기지 마라 Don't despise a weak enemy. ∥그는 실제로 만만찮은 사람이다 He's actually a rather formidable character.
만만하다 滿滿— be abundant ; be full of 《ambition》; be filled with 《courage》; be brimming with 《vigor》 ¶ 불평이 만만하다 be thoroughly discontented ; be filled with discontent ∥야심이 만만하다 be full of ambition ; be ambitious ∥자신이 만만하다 be full of self-confidence ; have plenty of confidence in oneself
만망 萬望 an earnest desire ; an eager wish〔hope〕; solicitation ; anxiety **—하다** desire earnestly ; wish eagerly 《for》
만면 滿面 the whole face **—하다** fill〔cover〕 the whole face ; be all over one's face ¶ 만면에 미소를 띠고 with one's face beaming all over ∥희색이 만면하다 smile〔beam〕 all over one's face ; be all smiles
— 수색(愁色) a face full of anxiety **— 희색** a face beaming with joy
만몽 滿蒙 〖지리〗 Manchuria and Mongolia ; Manchu-Mongol
만무 萬無 —하다 cannot be ; be hardly possible 《that》; be not likely at all 《that》; be out of the question ; there is no reason why ¶ 그것은 진실일 리가 만무하다 That cannot be true. ∥그가 그런 어리석은 말을 할 리가 만무하다 He cannot have said such a foolish thing. ∥그럴 리가 만무하다 That cannot be the case. /That's impossible ! ∥네가 그것을 모를 리 만무하다 It is hardly possible that you do not know about it. ∥그런 일을 내가 알 리 만무하지 않나 How should I know about such a thing ?
만무방 rascals ; scoundrels ; outrageous people ; knaves
만문 漫文 [수필] an essay ; [만필] causeries ; stray〔rambling〕 notes ; jottings
만물 the last weeding (of a rice paddy)
만물 萬物 all things (under the sun) ; nature ; creation ¶ 인간은 만물의 영장이다 Man is the lord of all creation.
만물 박사 a well-informed person ; a walking dictionary ; a pantologist
만물상 萬物商 a general store〔shop〕; a grocery (store)
만민 萬民 the whole nation ; all the people
만반 萬般 all things ; all kinds ; all affairs ; all sorts of matters ¶ 만반의 준비를 갖추다 get everything in readiness 《for》
만반 진수 滿盤珍羞 a groaning table ; rich and dainty food
만발 滿發 full bloom **—하다** come into full bloom ; be in full bloom〔blossom〕; be at its best ¶ 만발한 장미 a full-blown rose ; a rose in full bloom ∥벚꽃이 만발했다 The cherry trees are in full bloom. /The cherry blossoms are at their best.
만방 萬方 all directions ; every way ; all possible means ¶ 만방으로 in every way
만방 萬邦 all nations ; the nations of the world ; all nations on earth ¶ 만방의 international ; universal
만백성 萬百姓 all the people ; the whole nation
만병 萬病 all kinds of disease ¶ 만병 통치약 a cure-all ; a panacea ∥감기는 만병의 근원이다 Cold may lead to all kinds of illness.
만병초 萬病草 〖식물〗 a kind of rhododendron
만보 a wage coupon
만보 漫步 a ramble ; a stroll ; a saunter **—하다** ramble ; saunter ; stroll
만복 滿腹 a full stomach ¶ 만복이 될 때까지 먹었다 He ate his fill. ∥이제 만복입니다 I've had enough. /I am full.
만복 萬福 great fortune〔happiness〕; all kinds of good luck ¶ 귀하의 만복을 빕니다 I wish you every happiness.
만복감 滿腹感 a feeling of fullness〔plenitude〕《after a meal》 ¶ 그는 만복감으로 기분이 좋았다 He was feeling comfortably full.
만부당 萬不當 —하다 (be) utterly〔entirely, absolutely〕 unjust ; unlawful ; unreasonable ; absurd ¶ 만부당한 말 an absolutely〔utterly〕 unreasonable remark
만부득이 萬不得已 ¶ 만부득이한 사정으로 under unavoidable circumstances ; in the last extremity ; [필요에 의하여] out of sheer necessity ∥만부득이한 일이었다 That was quite unavoidable. ∥They simply couldn't help it.
만부부당 萬夫不當 ¶ 만부부당의 용사 a matchless〔mighty〕 warrior ∥그는 만부부당지용(之勇)이 있다 He is a warrior of a thousand.
만분지일 萬分之一 one in ten thousand ; a ten-thousandth
만사 萬事 all things ; everything ; all ¶ 만사가 돈이다 Money is everything. ∥만사 오케이다 Everything is O. K. ∥만사가 잘 되었다 All went well (with us). ∥만사가 허사이다 All is up〔over, lost〕 (with me). ∥일사가 만사이다 From one learn all. /The lion is known by his claw. ∥만사가 틀렸어 Everything has gone to the dogs.
만사 여의하다 萬事如意— everything turns out as one wishes ; all goes well
만사 태평 萬事泰平 [일이 잘됨] all going well ; nothing amiss ; [무관심] nonchalance ; indifference ; carelessness **—하다** [일이] all goes well ; nothing goes amiss ; all is quiet ; [성질이] (be) nonchalant ; careless 《about》; do not care a bit 《about》

만사 형통 萬事亨通 ―하다 all goes well ; be prosperous in everything ; everything turns out as one wished
만사휴의 萬事休矣 ¶ 만사휴의다 The worst has happened. /All is over. /All hope is lost.
만삭 滿朔 the month of parturition ; the last month of pregnancy ―하다 be in the last month of pregnancy ; be parturient ; come to one's time of childbirth ¶ 만삭한 부인 a parturient woman ; a woman who has gone her full time ; a woman near her time
만산 滿山 the whole hill〔mountain〕; all the hills ―하다 cover the whole mountain ¶ 벚꽃이 만산에 덮여 있다 The whole hill is covered with cherry blossoms.
만상 萬象 all things in the universe ; the universe ; (all) creation
만생 晩生 begetting a child in one's later years ―하다 beget a child in one's later years
만생종 晩生種 a variety of late ripening
만석꾼 萬石君 a rich man ; a millionaire ; a person who owns fields yielding as much as 10,000 *seog* of rice
만성 晩成 being slow in maturing ; maturing late ―하다 be slow in maturing ; mature late
― 식물 a slow grower 대기 ― Great talents mature late〔are slow in maturing〕. /Big success does not usually occur early. /Soon ripe, soon rotten. 《속담》
*만성 慢性 〖의학〗 chronicity ¶ 만성의 chronic ; confirmed ; inveterate // 그의 거짓말은 만성이 되어 버렸다 He is a habitual liar. // 그의 병은 만성으로 변했다 His disease passed into a chronic state.
―병 a chronic disease ―병 환자 a chronic〔an established〕 invalid ― 위장병 inveterate〔confirmed〕 dyspepsia ― 인플레 chronic inflation ― 전염병 a chronic infectious disease
만성 蠻性 barbarism ; savagery ; wild nature
만성절 萬聖節 All Saints' Day
*만세 萬世 all ages〔generations〕; eternity ¶ 만세에 전해지다 be transmitted into eternity
*만세 萬歲 ① [만년] ten thousand years ; a long time ② [외치는 소리] cheers ; hurrah ; long live ¶ 만세 삼창하다 give three cheers 《for a person》 // 스미스군 만세 Hurrah for Smith !
만세력 萬歲曆 a perpetual calendar ; a thousand-year calendar〔almanac〕
만세 불망 萬世不忘 ―하다 keep in mind forever ; remember long ¶ 당신의 은혜는 만세 불망이올시다 I shall be eternally grateful to you.
만세 불역 萬世不易 everlastingness ; eternity ; perpetuity ¶ 만세 불역의 everlasting ; eternal ; perpetual
만수 萬壽 long life ; longevity
― 무강 a long life ; longevity ¶ 만수 무강하다 live long ; be long-lived ; enjoy longevity // 만수 무강을 빕니다 Long life to you !
만수 滿水 ¶ 만수가 되다 be filled (to the brim) with water
만수받이 ―하다 tolerate〔put up with〕 other's misbehavior
만숙 晩熟 late 《sexual》 maturity ; late ripening ¶ 만숙의 late-maturing ; late-ripening
만시 晩時 being too late ¶ 만시지탄 repenting of one's missing a chance
만신 a female shaman ; a sorceress ; a medium
만신 滿身 the whole〔entire〕 body ¶ 만신에 all over the body // 만신의 힘을 기울여 with all one's might〔strength〕; with might and main
―창이 be covered all over with wounds
만심 慢心 pride ; self-conceit ; a vanity-swelled head ―하다 be proud ; be self-conceited ; be puffed up 《with》; have a swelled head ¶ 그는 성공하여 만심하고 있다 He is puffed up〔swollen〕 with his success. /Success has gone to his head.
만안 萬安 peace ; tranquility ; security ; welfare ; health ―하다 (be) peaceful ; tranquil ; secure ; healthy ; well ; [서술적] be in good health
만약 萬若 if ; in case (of) ⇨ 만일
만억년 萬億年 thousands of millions of years ; eternity
*만연 蔓延, 蔓衍 spread ; diffusion ―하다 spread ; sweep 《over》; diffuse ; prevail ; be prevalent ; be widespread ¶ 만연성의 progressive // 만연을 방지하다 prevent〔check〕 the spread 《of》 // 서울 시내에 이질이 만연할 것 같다 There are signs of dysentery spreading in *Seoul*.
만연 漫然 ―하다 (be) aimless ; rambling ; desultory ¶ 만연히 aimlessly ; discursively ; in a rambling〔desultory〕 way // 만연히 독서하다 read at random
만열 滿悅 great delight ; ecstasy ; satisfaction ―하다 be much delighted 〔satisfied〕; feel ecstatic ; be in ecstasy〔rapture〕
만염 晩炎 the late〔lingering〕 summer heat
만왕 萬王 [신] the God ; the ruler of the universe ; [그리스도] King ¶ 만왕의 왕 (the) King of Kings
만용 蠻勇 brute〔venturous〕 courage ; foolhardiness ; temerity ; force (완력) ¶ 만용을 부리다 resort to force ; act with violence ; show reckless valor
만우절 萬愚節 All Fools' Day ; April Fools' Day

*만원 滿員 a capacity audience〔crowd〕; a full〔packed〕 house ; no vacancy ; [게시] "Full up", "House full" ¶ 만원 사례의 간판을 내걸다 put up a "full up" notice // 만원을 이루다 be full (up) ; be closely packed ; be crowded to the limit〔its full capacity〕; be full to the doors ; have a full audience ; draw a full house (극장) // 극장이 만원이라 많은 관객이 되돌아갔다 The theater was full and turned many away from its doors. // 여관은 만원이다 The hotel is all crowded to the limit〔capacity〕. // 이 식당은 올 때마다 만원이다 This restaurant is packed whenever we come.
— 버스 a jampacked bus

만월 滿月 a full moon

만유 萬有 all things 《under the sun》; the creation ; all things in the universe ; the whole of creation

‡만유 漫遊 a tour ; a (pleasure) trip — 하다 travel 《for pleasure》; tour ; make a tour 《of》; make a pleasure trip ¶ 국내를 만유하다 travel in〔about〕 the country // 세계 만유의 길을 떠나다 start on a tour of the world
—객 a tourist ; a sightseer —기 travel sketches 세계 — a world tour ; a tour round the world ; a round-the-world trip ; globe trotting 세계—자 a round-the-world tourist ; a globe trotter

만유 신교 萬有神敎 pantheism ¶ 만유 신교의 pantheistic
— 신자 a pantheist

만유 인력 萬有引力 universal gravitation ¶ 만유 인력의 법칙 the law of gravitation

만이 蠻夷 barbarians ; savages

만인 萬人 all people〔men〕; everyone ¶ 그것은 만인이 주지하는 바다 It is a matter of universal knowledge.

만인 蠻人 a savage ; a barbarian

만인계 萬人契 a large-scale mutual financing association ; a mutual aid group formed on extensive scale

†만일 萬一 if ; in case 《of》; suppose〔provided〕《that》; by any chance〔possibility〕 ¶ 만일의 경우 emergency ; the worst // 만일의 경우는 if anything should happen ; in (case of) emergency ; if the worst comes (to the worst) // 만일의 경우에 대비하다 prepare for the worst ; provide against a rainy day // 만일 기차 시간에 늦으면 supposing you miss the train // 만일 비가 오면 if it should rain ; in case of rain // 만일의 요행을 바라다 trust to chance〔luck〕; hope against hope // 만일에 대비해서 봉급의 일부를 저축해 두라 Put aside part of your salary for a rainy day. // 만일 그가 여기에 있다면 어쩌겠소 Suppose (that) he were here, what would you do? // 만일 그를 만나면 내가 기다린다고 전해 주게 If by any chance you should see him, tell him that I am waiting for him to come.

만입 彎入 embayment — 하다 《the sea》 penetrate 《into the land》; push a bay (into the land)

만자 卍字 a fylfot ; a gammadion 《*pl.* -dia》; a swastika
—창 a fret window

만장 萬丈 unfathomable depth〔height〕 만장의 계곡 a ravine of unfathomable depth // 만장의 기염을 토하다 give full vent to one's feelings ; talk big ; give an eloquent speech
황진(黃塵) — a cloud of dust

만장 萬障 all kinds of obstacles〔hindrances〕

*만장 滿場 the whole house〔hall〕; the whole company〔assembly, audience〕 ¶ 만장의 박수 갈채를 받다 bring down the (whole) house // 만장의 청중에 감명을 주다 carry the entire audience
— 일치 unanimity ¶ 만장 일치로 unanimously ; with one accord〔consent〕; by a unanimous vote ; without a dissenting voice // 만장 일치로 가결하다 pass 《a bill》 unanimously〔by a unanimous vote〕

만장 輓章, 挽章, 挽丈 an elegy ; a threnody ; a funeral ode ; a funeral streamer

만장봉 萬丈峰 a lofty〔high〕 peak ; an alp

만장이 a large wooden boat with a prow

만재 滿載 full load ; a full〔capacity〕 cargo — 하다 carry a full load 《of》; load 《a ship》 to capacity 《with》; be filled〔packed, crowded〕《with》 (손님을) ; be loaded up ¶ 석유를 만재한 선박 a ship carrying a full cargo of oil
— 흘수(吃水) gauge ; full〔load〕 draft — 흘수선(吃水線) a load line〔water-line〕; the Plimsoll line〔mark〕 (이 표시가 물에 잠길 정도로 적재해서는 안 됨)

만적거리다 finger ; feel ; fumble 《with》; play〔toy〕《with》; tamper 《with》; fidget 《with》 ¶ 넥타이를 만적거리다 finger one's tie // 손잡이를 만적거리다 feel after the handle // 열쇠를 만적거리다 fumble with a key // 그녀는 초조해서 목걸이를 만적거렸다 She fidgeted with her necklace. // 시계를 가지고 만적거리지 마라 Don't fool around with the watch.

만적만적 fumbling ; fingering ; toying ; monkeying with

만전 萬全 perfectness ; perfection ¶ 만전의 perfect ; sure ; safe ; secure // 만전을 기하다 make assurance doubly sure // 만전책을 강구하다 adopt a prudential policy ; use a sure card
—책 a carefully thought-out plan〔measure〕; a prudent〔scrupulous〕 policy

만점 滿點 a full marks ; a perfect score ¶ 만점의 perfect ; impeccable // 영어에서 만점을 받다 win〔get〕 a full mark in English // 그만하면 만점이다 That's perfect. /That

ㅁ

leaves nothing to be desired.

만정 滿庭 ¶ 만정의 사람들 all the persons present in the courtroom

만져보다 feel ; try touching ; finger ; test with one's hand ¶ 손가락으로 만져보다 feel 《a thing》 with one's fingers // 만져 보니 차갑다 It is cold to the touch.

만조 滿朝 the whole court
— 백관(百官) all the (civil and military) officials of the court

만조 滿潮 the high〔full〕 tide ; flood tide ¶ 만조시에 at full〔high〕 tide ; at high water ; when tide is at high level〔at the full〕

만조하다 (be) shabby ; grubby ; seedy ; poor-looking ; unsightly

⁑**만족 滿足** satisfaction ; gratification ; complacency ; contentment

> 참고 **satisfaction**은 「자기의 욕망을 충족시킨 만족」 **contentment**는 「자기가 가지고 있는 것으로써 충족감을 느끼고 불만 걱정을 갖지 않는 만족」 **gratification** 「기쁨이라든가 자기가 바라던 대로의 것을 주는 만족」을 말한다. 그리고 **content**는 명사로서 「만족」의 뜻이 있지만 **in content** (만족하여), **to one's heart's content** (마음껏) 이외에는 쓰는 경우가 드물다

— 하다 be pleased〔satisfied〕 《with》 ; be gratified 《with a person, at a matter》 ; be content 《with》 ¶ 만족한 표정 a pleased expression of countenance // 만족스러운 satisfactory ; gratifying // 만족하게 satisfactorily ; properly (적합하게 // 대단히 만족해서 in perfect content // 만족시키다 satisfy ; gratify // 만족을 주다 give 《a person》 satisfaction // 만족의 뜻을 표하다 express one's satisfaction // 그 소식을 듣고 매우 만족했다 I hear the news with great satisfaction. /It is very gratifying to hear the news. // 나는 그것으로 만족하고 있다 I am satisfied with it. // 지금 하고 있는 일에 만족하는가 Do you satisfy yourself with your present work? // 편지 하나 제대로 만족스럽게 쓰지 못한다 He can't write even a letter properly. // 행복은 만족에 있다 Happiness lies in contentment.
—감 a feeling of satisfaction **자기 —** self-contentment〔-satisfaction〕

만족 蠻族 a savage tribe

만종 晩鍾 the evening bell ; the curfew (-bell)

만좌 滿座 the whole company ; the entire assembled party ¶ 만좌 중에서 창피를 당하다 be put to shame before the whole company ; be insulted publicly

만주 滿洲 Manchuria ¶ 만주의 Manchurian
—말 Manchu ; the Manchu language **— 문자(文字)** the Manchu script **— 사변(事變)** the Manchurian Incident

만지 蠻地 a savage land ; a dark country ; an uncivilized country

†**만지다** finger ; touch ; feel ; brush ; handle ; stroke ; pass one's hand over ¶ 손가락으로 만지다 feel 《a thing》 with one's fingers // 어깨를 만지다 touch 《a person》 on the shoulder // 수염을 만지다 stroke one's beard // 만지지 마시오 Hands off. /Do not touch. (게시)

***만지작거리다** finger 《a button》 ; fumble with 《a key》 ; toy〔play〕 with 《fire》 ; tamper with 《a machine》 ; meddle with 《papers》 ; monkey with 《속》 ¶ 만지작 만지작 fingering ; fumbling ; toying ; monkeying〔fooling〕 around // 그녀는 목걸이를 만지작거리고 있었다 She fidgeted with her necklace.

만질만질하다 be soft to the touch ; feel soft ¶ 만질만질한 비단 soft silks

***만찬 晩餐** supper ; dinner ; the evening meal

> 참고 **dinner**는 하루의 정식 식사로서 미국이나 영국의 중류 이하의 가정에서는 낮에 드는 일이 많고 상류 가정에서는 밤에 든다 **supper**는 「밤참」의 뜻으로 많이 사용된다

¶ 최후의 만찬 the Last Supper // 만찬회를 베풀다 give a dinner party ; entertain 《persons》 at dinner // 만찬에 초대하다 ask〔invite〕 《a person》 to dinner
—식 [주(主)의] the Lord's Supper ; the Eucharist

만찬회 晩餐會 a dinner party ; [공식의] a banquet ¶ 만찬회를 열다 give a dinner (party) // 호화로운 만찬회를 열다 throw a dazzling dinner

만천 滿天 [온 하늘] the whole sky ; the entire firmament

만천하 滿天下 the whole world ¶ 만천하에 in the whole world ; throughout the realm ; under the sun // 만천하에 알려져 있다 be known all the world over ; be universally known // 만천하에 알려져 있는 사실이다 The whole world knows this fact. /It is a matter of universal knowledge.

만초 蔓草 a vine ; a climber ; a creeper

만추 晩秋 late autumn〔fall〕 ¶ 만추에 in late autumn ; in late fall ; towards the end of autumn ¶ 만추의 어느날 one day late in autumn

만춘 晩春 late spring ¶ 만춘에 in late spring ; late in spring ; towards the end of spring

만취 滿醉 dead drunkenness

†**만큼** ① [비교] as...as ; so...as ¶ 눈만큼 희다 be as white as snow // 죽었다고 할 만큼 조용하다 be as quiet as dead // 이것도 그것만큼 좋다 This one is as good as that. // 그녀만큼 영어를 할 수 있으면 좋겠다 I wish I could speak English as well

as she.
② [어느만큼] how much〔many, long, far〕 ¶ 시간이 얼마만큼 걸리느냐 How long does it take? // 보수는 얼마만큼 받을 수 있느냐 What compensation do you offer?
③ [정도] so...that ; so as...to ; enough to... ¶ 이만큼 this much ; thus much ; so much // 그만큼은 나도 알고 있다 I know that much. // 한국 사람으로서 그 사람만큼 영문을 쓸 수 있는 사람은 많지 않다 Few Koreans can write English as well as he. // 이만큼 재미있는 책은 없다 No book is more interesting than this one. /This is the most interesting book.
만큼만 (just) as much as
만태 萬態 a great diversity in form and figure ; various phases
인생 — various phases of life
만판 entirely ; wholly ; [실컷] to the full ; to one's heart's content ; to one's satisfaction ¶ 만판 놀다 enjoy oneself to the full ; spend all one's time loafing (마냥) // 그는 만판 놀기만 한다 He spends all his time loafing. // 나는 만판 먹기만 했다 I have eaten all I wanted.
만평 漫評 desultory〔rambling〕 criticism ; literary gossip —하다 criticize desultorily〔ramblingly〕 ; gossip 《on》
시사 — rambling criticism on current events〔topics〕
만풍 蠻風 a savage〔barbarous〕 custom ; an uncivilized manners ¶ 만풍을 일소하다 do away with the whole barbarous customs〔habits〕
만필 漫筆 causeries (신문·잡지의) ; stray〔rambling〕 notes ; jottings
—가 a columnist
만하 晩夏 late summer
*만하다 ① [정도가] be enough to ; be to the extent of ; be as big〔little〕 as ; be as much〔little〕 as ; be the size of ¶ 새알만하다 be the size of a bird's egg ; be as small as a bird's egg // 불가능이라 해도 좋을 만하다 It is next to impossible. /It is almost〔practically〕 impossible. // 그는 거지라 해도 좋을 만했다 He was little better than a beggar. // 그만한 것쯤 알고 있지 I know as much. // 그만한 것쯤 살 돈은 갖고 있다 I have enough money to buy it with.
② [가치나 힘이] be (well) worth 《doing》 ; deserve ; bear ; be entitled to ¶ 볼 만하다 be worth seeing // 믿을 만하다 be trustworthy // 먹을 만하다 be eatable // 쉴 만한 공원 a park that is a good place to relax in // 그 일은 수고할 만한 가치가 없다 The work is not worth the trouble. // 그 책은 읽을 만하다 The book is worth reading〔is readable〕. // 그것은 능히 1,000명을 먹일 만하다 That is sufficient to feed a thousand men. // 가르쳐서 겨우 일할 만하다 싶으면 그만두어 버린다 You teach them the ropes, and just when you think they may be ready to pull their own weight, they quit.
만학 晩學 learning late in life ; a late education —하다 get a late education ; study late in life ¶ 만학한 사람이지만 어학력이 대단하다 He has a marvelous linguistic knowledge which he acquired in his later years.
—자 a late learner
만학 천봉 萬壑千峰 steep mountains and deep〔dark〕 valleys ; a remote mountainous region
만행 萬幸 good fortune ; good luck —하다 (be) very fortunate ; terribly lucky
만행 蠻行 an act of barbarity ; a barbarism ; a brutality ; an atrocity ; an outrage
만호 萬戶 ten thousand houses ; numerous〔many〕 houses (많은 집)
— 장안 a capital city with many inhabitants
만혼 晩婚 late〔deferred〕 marriage —하다 marry late 《in life》 ; get married late ¶ 저 부부는 만혼이다 The couple married late 《in life》.
만홀 漫忽 negligence ; neglect ; carelessness —하다 (be) negligent ; neglectful ; careless ; thoughtless ; heedless ; a bsent-minded ¶ 만홀히 negligently ; neglectfully ; carelessly
만화 〖해부〗 spleen and pancreas
*만화 漫畫 a caricature (인물 풍자의) ; a cartoon (풍자적인) ; a comic strip (신문, 잡지 연재의) ; funnies 《미·속》
—가 a caricaturist ; a cartoonist ; a comic artist —란 a comic section 《of a newspaper》 ; a funny column 《미》 ; funnies 《미·구》 — 신문 a funny paper — 영화 a cartoon film ; a movie cartoon ; an animated (film) cartoon — 영화 제작 animation — 잡지〔책〕 a comic magazine〔book〕 — 제작 cartooning 불량 — substandard comic books
만화경 萬華鏡 a kaleidoscope
만화 방창 萬化方暢 luxuriant growth of all things in spring —하다 《in spring》 all things grow luxuriantly
*만회 挽回 recovery ; revival ; retrieval 《of one's honor》 ; restoration ; redemption —하다 revive ; recover ; retrieve ; restore ; redeem ¶ 경제 시장의 만회 a trade revival // 만회하기 어려운 irrecoverable ; irretrievable ; beyond 〔past〕 recall // 명성을 만회하다 retrieve one's reputation
—책 a measure for retrieving
†많다 ① [수] (be) many ; numerous ; [양] much ; [수·양] plenty ; abundant ; plentiful ; copious ; exuberant ¶ 사람이 많다 There are many people. // 이 책에는 오식이 많다 This book is full of misprints. // 출석자가 많은 편이었습니까 Were there

ㅁ

many present at the meeting? // 이런 개구리는 한국에 많다 These frogs abound in Korea. // 그것을 믿을 만한 이유가 많다 I have abundant reason to believe it. // 금년 여름에는 비가 많았다 We had a copious rainfall this summer. // 저 사람은 가족이 많다 He has a large family. // 그녀는 많은 역할을 할 것이다 She will wear many hats.

② [도수] (be) frequent ; often ; prevalent ; current ; common ; be rife 《with errors》 ¶ 여기는 언제나 이렇게 화재가 많습니까 Are fires so frequent here? // 질병은 빈민굴에 많다 The plague is rife in the slums. // 이 지방엔 바람이 많다 Winds are prevalent in this district. // 그 꽃은 이 지방에 많다 The flowers are common in this country.

*많이 ① [수량] much ; lots ; plenty ; in abundance ; in profusion ¶ 말을 많이 할 필요가 없다 There is no need to talk much about it. // 그는 돈을 많이 쓴다 He spends much〔a lot of〕 money. // 우리 나라에는 봄이나 가을에 관광객이 많다 Most foreign tourists to Korea come in spring or autumn. // 태풍은 농작물에 해를 많이 주었다 The typhoon did a great deal of damage to the crops. // 돈이 많이 들 것이다 It will cost you an arm and a leg. /It will cost you a fortune. /It will cost you a mint. /It will cost you a pretty penny. /It will cost you a bundle. // 돈을 많이 버십니까 Do you make a lot of money? /Do you make good money? /Is the money good?

② [대개] often ; lots ; frequently ¶ 이 병은 어린애들이 많이 걸린다 This disease prevails much among children. /Children often get〔come down with〕 this disease.

맏 firstborn ; first ; eldest ; oldest ¶ 그이가 맏이다 He is the eldest.

—딸 the eldest daughter ; the first daughter —며느리 the eldest daughter-in-law ; the wife of the eldest son —형수 the wife of the eldest brother

맏물 ① [배추·해초 따위의] the first cut ¶ 맏물 상치 lettuce from the first cut ; the early lettuce ; the first lettuce of the season

② [곡식·과실] the first crop ; the first of the season ¶ 맏물 사과 apples from the first crop // the early apples ; the first apples of the season // 맏물 딸기를 먹다 eat early strawberries

맏배 the firstborn (of animals) ; the first batch〔hatch, lifter〕

— 병아리 chickens of the first hatch — 돼지 the first litter of pigs

맏사위 the husband of one's firstborn〔eldest〕 daughter

맏상제 —喪制 the chief mourner ; the eldest son of the deceased

맏아들 the eldest〔oldest 《미》〕 son ; the first-born son ; a first-born

맏이 the firstborn 《son》 ; the eldest 《child》

맏잡이 [맏아들] one's eldest son ; [맏며느리] one's eldest daughter-in-law ; the wife of one's eldest son

맏파 —派 the descendants of an eldest son ; the eldest son's line of descent

†말¹ a horse ; a stallion (수말) ; a mare (암말) ; a pony (망아지) ; a colt (새끼 수말) ; a filly (새끼 암말) ; a steed (군용마) ; a racer〔race horse〕 (경마용) ¶ 부루〔생〕 말 an unbroken horse // 짐싣는 말 a packhorse // 달구지 말 a carriage horse // 맨 말 a bareback horse // 말을 타고 가다 go on horseback // 말에서 내리다 get off〔alight from〕 a horse ; dismount from a horse // 말에서 떨어지다 fall from a horse // 말에 타다 mount〔get on〕 a horse ; ride a horse // 말을 달리다 gallop a horse ; spur a horse on // 말을 세우다 pull up〔hold in〕 a horse ; draw rein // 말을 길들이다 train a horse ; break in a horse (사나운 말을) // 말에 마구를 채우다〔안장을 놓다〕 harness〔saddle〕 a horse

말 잃고 소 외양간 고친다 (속담) It is too late to shut the stable door When the steed is stolen.

말 죽는데 체장수 모이듯 (속담) Whatsoever the carcase is, there will the eagles〔ravens〕 be gathered.

말 타면 종두고 싶다 (속담) The more a man has, the more he desires.

말² 〖식물〗 a duckweed ; a duckmeat

말³ a unit of measure 《about 18 liters》

†말⁴ ① [회화] a talk ; a conversation ; a chat ; a gossip (잡담) ; [연설] a speech ; an address ; [진술] a remark ; a statement ; what one says ¶ 말이 많은 사람 a wordy〔talkative, loquacious〕 person ; a windbag // 말수가 적은 사람 a reticent〔taciturn〕 person // 말을 하다 speak ; talk ; chat ; have a talk // 말을 끄집어 내다 draw out conversation 《agreeable to a party》 // 말을 그치다 stop〔wind up〕 talking // 말씀 도중 실례입니다만 Excuse my〔me for〕 interrupting you, 《but》 // 네가 말하는 것은 하나도 못 알아듣겠다 I can't make out〔have no idea of〕 what you say. // 그런 나쁜 말을 하면 못쓴다 Don't use bad words. /Don't use four-letter words. // 그 사람 말을 믿어도 좋다 You may take him at his word. // 내 말을 믿어도 좋다 Believe me. /Trust me. /Take my word for it. /You've got my word for it. // 말 좀 잘해 주시겠습니까 Would you put in a word for me, please? // 정치인들은 폭동 피해 보상을 말로만 떠들고 있다 Politicians pay only lip service to compensation for riot victims. // 당신의 말을 행동으로 보여 주시오 Put your money where your mouth is. // 진심으로 하는 말입니까 You mean it? // 진심으로 하는 말

이야 I mean it. /I mean business. // 나는 그들의 말이 옳다고 생각한다 I think they said a mouthful. // 그 말 한번 잘했다 You can say that again. // 내가 하고 싶은 말을 네가 했다 You took the words out of my mouth. // 말허리를 꺾어 미안하다 I'm sorry to break up the conversation.
② [언어] language ; speech ; [단어] words ; [국어] a language ; a tongue ; [방언] a dialect ; [표현] expression ; diction ; phraseology ¶ 정중한 말 courteous 〔polite〕 expressions // 동정의 말 a word of sympathy // 시골말 a local dialect ; dialectal speech // 서울말 *Seoul* speech // 표준말 the standard language // 이별의 말 parting words // 대꾸할 말이 없다 have no word in reply // 말로 다할 수 없다 be inexpressive ; be indescribable ; be unspeakable ; be beyond〔past〕 all description // 자네 자신의 말을 빌자면 to borrow your own words // 말을 삼가다 be careful in one's speech ; weigh〔spare〕 one's words // 처음으로 미국에 갔을 적엔 말이 안 통해서 혼났다 When I first went to America, I had hard work to make myself understood.
③ [소문] a rumor ; a report ; news ; an account ¶ 말이 퍼지다 word spreads // 그 말은 믿을 수가 없다 The report is unfounded. // 전번에 말씀드렸던 A 선생이십니다 This is Mr. A I spoke of the other day.
④ [꾸중] a scolding ; a reprimand ; a lecture ; a rebuke ; [비난] a complaint ; a criticism ¶ 말듣다 be reprimanded ; be scolded // 그 길을 막으면 동네 사람들이 말을 할 것이다 If you block the road, the villagers will complain.
말로 온 공을 다 갚는다. 〔속담〕 A good tongue is a good weapon.
말은 할수록 늘고 되질은 할수록 준다 〔속담〕 A tail never loses in the telling.
말이 많으면 실언이 많다 〔속담〕 Talk much, and err much.
말 잘하고 징역가랴 〔속담〕 A good tongue is a good weapon.
말 한 마디로 천냥 빚을 갚는다 〔속담〕 A soft answer turned away wrath. /Good words are good cheap. /Good words cost nought.
실없는 말이 송사(訟事) 건다 〔속담〕 Many babbling is not without offence.
오는 말이 고와야 가는 말이 곱다 〔속담〕 Soft answer turneth away wrath.
말이 나다 〔관용〕 rumor is started

말⁵ [장기·윷 따위의] a marker in chess ; checkers ; a piece ; a man

말⁶ [받침] a flat piece of wood placed under something to be sawed or planed ; a sawhorse

말 末 ① [종말] the end ; the close ¶ 4월 말에 at the end of April ② [가루] powder ¶ 분말 밀크 powdered milk

말갈기 a horse's mane

말갛다 (be) clear ; clean ; nice ; serene ¶ 하늘이 말갛다 The sky is nice and clear.

말개지다 become clear ; clear up ; get clean

말거리 ① [재료] a topic of〔for〕 conversation ; material of conversation ¶ 말거리가 끊어지다 topics of talk are exhausted ② [말썽] a subject〔a target, an object〕 of criticism ; a cause of complaint ¶ 말썽이 되다 become a source of trouble ; cause trouble

말거머리 〖동물〗 a horseleech ; Whitmania pigra (학명)

말경 末境 ① [끝판] the end ; the close ② [말년] the declining years of one's life

말곁 a word chimed in (동조) ; an interruption (참견) **—하다** chime in ; [참견] interrupt 《a person》 in his talk ; chop in

말고 not... but... ; instead of... ; except ; but ¶ 그 사람말고 그의 부인이 왔다 It was his wife, not he, that came. // 너말고 누가 그런 짓을 하겠느냐 Who would do such a thing but you?

-말고 certainly ; of course ; indeed ; I say ; you know ; to be sure ; rather ¶ 그렇고 말고 Certainly〔Of course〕, it is. /It's just as you say. /You are right. /Oh yes, to be sure! /Yes, indeed. /Sure. 《미·구》

말고기 horsemeat ; horseflesh ; horse beef
— 자반 a red-faced drunk

말고삐 reins ; a bridle ¶ 말고삐를 잡다 take〔hold〕 a horse by the reins // 말고삐를 당기다 tighten〔pull up〕 the reins ; draw rein ; rein in 《a horse》 ; check 《a horse》 with the reins ; tug at the reins (힘껏) // 말고삐를 늦추다 slacken the reins ; give 《a horse》 his head

말공대 —恭待 courteous expressions ; addressing in honorifics **—하다** speak in polite language ; pay respect by addressing in honorifics ; address in honorifics ; pay lip service

말괄량이 a romp ; a hussy ; a minx ; a tomboy ; a hoyden ; a kitten ; a flapper

말구유 a manger ; a horse trough

말구종 —驅從 a groom ; a footman

말굳다 be stuttering ; be stammering ; stammer ; stutter ; falter

말굴레 a bridle ; a halter

말굽 a horse's hoof ; a horseshoe (편자)
— 소리 the sound of a horse's hoofs ; the clatter of a horse's hoofs ; hoofbeat
— 자석 a horseshoe magnet

말귀 ① [말] the import of the words ; words ② [이해하는 힘] sense ; hearing ; understanding ; catching on 《미》 ¶ 말귀가 밝다 be quick of hearing ; be quick-eared ; have sharp ears // 말귀가 어둡다 be dull〔hard〕 of hearing ; have a bad ear ; have difficulty in hearing ; be slow in understanding what one says // 말귀가

ㅁ

빠르다 be quick to understand what one says ; catch on quick

말기 [치마의] the upper waistband of a Korean skirt〔trousers〕

말기 末期 the end ; the close ; the last stage ; the last period〔years, days〕 ¶ 공산주의의 말기 the last stage of communism∥조선 말기에 at the end〔close〕 of the *Chosun* Dynasty∥말기적인 현상을 나타내다 show signs of decadence

말길되다 (a way) is opened to consult with《a person》; have a chance to see

말꼬리 the end of one's words〔speech〕; one's words' ending

말꼬투리 ⇨ 말꼬리

말꼴 hay ; fodder ; feed ; provender ; forage ¶ 말꼴을 주다 fodder〔give fodder to〕 a horse ; feed《green grass》 to a horse

말꾸러기 ① [수다쟁이] a prattler ; a tattler ; chatterbox ; a babbler ; a chatterbug《속》
② [말썽꾼] a troublemaker ; a troublesome person〔child〕

말꾼¹ [말몰이꾼] a packhorse driver〔man〕; a horse driver

말꾼² visitors (from the village) ; (local) callers

말끄러미 with fixed eyes ; staring ¶ 얼굴을 말끄러미 들여다 보다 stare《a person》 in the face ; look hard〔steadily〕 at《a person's》 face

말끔 all ; completely ; entirely ; wholly ; perfectly ; thoroughly ¶ 빚을 말끔 청산하다 pay all one's debt ; clear off one's debt∥준비는 말끔 완료되었다 Every preparation has been made.∥집은 말끔 완성되었다 The house is now completely built.∥가진 것을 말끔 도둑맞았다 I was stripped of all I had in my pocket.

말끔하다 (be) clean ; cleanly ; neat ; tidy ; nice ; [매력적] good-looking ; comely ; attractive ¶ 말끔한 하늘 a clear sky∥말끔한 옷차림을 하다 be neatly〔smartly〕 dressed∥그 여자의 얼굴은 말끔하다 Her face is attractive〔comely〕.∥그의 방은 언제나 말끔하다 His room is always clear and tidy.

말끔히 clean ; clear ; neat(ly) ¶ 마당을 말끔히 쓸다 sweep a garden clean∥방을 말끔히 치우다 put a room in order ; tidy〔do up, straighten up〕 a room neatly∥얼굴을 말끔히 씻다 wash one's face clean∥얼굴이 말끔히 생기다 have a nice face

말끝 the end of words ; the end of one's speech ¶ 말끝에 in conclusion ; by the way ; incidentally∥말끝을 맺다 conclude one's speech∥말끝마다 욕을 한다 He never opens his lips without curse and swear.

말나다 ① [논의] be broached ; be proposed ; be taken up ; be talked about ; be rumo(u)red ¶ 새 학교를 세우자고 말난 것은 사친회 석상에서였다 It was at the P.T.A. meeting that the proposal to found a new school was made.
② [비밀이] get out ; slip〔leak〕 out ; transpire ; be disclosed〔divulged〕 ¶ 말날까 두려우니 아무한테도 이야기 말게 Don't tell anybody about it. I'm afraid of its leaking out.

말남 末男 the youngest〔last〕 son

말내다 ① [이야깃거리를] begin to talk《about》; propose《a plan》; broach《a subject》; draw out conversation ¶ 수영하자고 A군이 말냈다 Mr. A suggested a swim.
② [비밀을] reveal ; let out ; disclose ; divulge ; betray ¶ (비밀로 하는 일을) 말내지 마라 Keep it to yourself. /Don't give the show away.

말녀 末女 the youngest〔last〕 daughter

말년 末年 ① [인생의] one's last few years ; one's declining years ; the last phase of one's life ¶ 말년에 들어서다 enter the twilight of one's life ② [말기] one's last days ; the last period

말눈치 a suggestion ; a hint ; an inkling ; an implication ; a connotation ¶ 그의 말눈치가 다 알고 있는 것 같다 By the way he talks, he seems to know everything about it.

말다¹ [종이 따위를] roll《up》 ¶ 종이를 말다 roll paper∥담배를 말다 roll a cigarette∥기를 말다 roll up a flag

말다² [음식을] put《boiled rice》 into soup〔water〕; mix《food》 with《water, soup》 ¶ 국수를 말다 put noodles into soup∥밥을 국에 말아 먹다 take a meal of rice and soup mixed together

말다³ [중지] stop ; cease ; discontinue ; leave off ; drop ; give up ; lay aside ; quit ; cut out ¶ 이야기를 말다 cease〔leave off〕 talking ; drop the subject∥장사를 말다 go out of〔give up〕 business∥일을 반만하고 말다 give up halfway∥말았더라면 좋았을 것을 I wish I had not done with it.

말다⁴ ① [금지] don't ; had better not ¶ 기다리게 하지 마라 You must not keep him waiting.∥나는 그에게 가지 말라고 했다 I told him not to go.∥더 이상 여기에 머물지 마라 You had better not remain here any longer.∥잊지 말게 Don't forget.
② [필경 …되다] ¶ 그는 드디어 가고 말았다 He went away at length.∥실패하고 말고 He is sure to fail.

말다래 a saddle flap

†말다툼 a dispute ; an altercation ; an argument ; a quarrel ; a wrangle ;《exchange of》 high words **—하다** dispute ; altercate ; bicker ; wrangle ; quarrel ; have an argument《with》; get into argument《with》; bandy words《with》; have a high〔heated〕 exchange of words ¶ 그는

누구와도 말다툼한 일이 없다 He never had words with anybody. // 그와 말다툼했다 I fell wrangling〔had angry words〕 with him. // 말다툼이 격투로 변했다 High words led to hard blows.

†**말단 末端** the end ; the tip ; the rank and file ¶ 말단의 terminal // 말단까지 고루고루 퍼지다 diffuse every inch of 《the country》

— **관절** terminal joints — **기구** terminal organization〔offices〕 ; the smallest unit — **비대** 〖의학〗 [뇌하수체 기능 항진에 의한] hyperpituitarism — **사원** a minor clerk

말단 공무원 a petty〔minor〕 official ; an understrapper ; a humble placeman 《영》 ; a junior clerk

말대 末代 the last generation〔years, stage〕

*__말대꾸 —對—__ a retort ; a severe〔an incisive〕 reply **—하다** retort ; make a retort ; talk〔answer〕 back ; reply in kind to ¶ 날카로운 말대꾸 a sharp retort // 그는 내가 잘못했다고 말대꾸했다 He retorted upon〔against〕 me, saying I was to blame.

말대답 —對答 back talk ; answering〔talking〕 back ; retort ; contradiction **—하다** answer〔talk〕 back ; retort ¶ 어른한테 말대답하는 것은 실례가 된다 Talking back to older people is impertinent.

말더듬 stammering ; stuttering

*__말더듬다__ stammer ; stutter ; falter ¶ 말더듬으면서 stammeringly ; stutteringly ; falteringly // 말더듬는 것은 고칠 수 있다 Stammering can be cured.

말더듬이 a stammerer ; a stutterer

— **교정기** an articulator

말동무 ⇨ 말벗

말되다 ① [이치에 맞다] make sense ; be reasonable ; be logical ¶ 말도 안 된다 It is quite out of the question. /It is quite absurd.

② [말거리가 되다] become the focus〔subject, target〕 of criticism ; be subjected to criticism

말똥 horse dung ; horse droppings ; stable manure

말똥가리 〖새〗 the Korean buzzard

말똥거리다 roll (one's eyes) vacantly ¶ 누운 채 눈을 말똥거리며 천장만 바라보다 lie with a vacant stare at the ceiling

말똥말똥 with wide fixed eyes ; blankly ; with a vacant stare **—하다** have one's eyes wide open (absent-mindedly, blankly)

†**말뚝** a pile ; a stake ; a post ; a picket ¶ 말뚝을 박다 drive in a stake〔pile, picket〕 // 말뚝을 세우다 put〔set〕 up a post

—잠 sleeping while sitting upright **—잠(簪)** [비녀] a kind of metal hairpin

말뜨다 (be) slow-spoken ; be slow in one's speech

말뜻 the meaning of a word

말라깽이 a lean〔skinny, scraggy〕 person ; a living skeleton ; a bag of bones

†**말라리아** 〖의학〗 malaria ¶ 말라리아에 걸린 malarial ; malarian ; malarious // 말라리아에 걸리다 be taken with malaria

—열(熱) malarial fever — **요법** a malarial fever treatment

말라빠지다 become〔get〕 thin〔lean, skinny, emaciated〕 ; grow gaunt ; lose one's weight ; pine away (걱정으로) ¶ 말라빠진 lean ; haggard ; gaunt ; skinny // 말라빠진 사람 a skinny〔thin, lean〕 person ; a living skeleton // 그는 불면 날아갈 만큼 말라빠졌다 He is as thin as a lath〔wafer〕.

말라죽다 [초목이] wither ; dry up ; shrivel ; be blighted〔blasted〕

말랑거리다 feel soft〔tender〕 ; be soft to the touch

말랑하다 [감 따위가] (be) soft ; ripe and tender ; [성질이] soft〔mild, meek〕 ¶ 말랑한 살 tender flesh // 말랑한 감 a ripe〔soft〕 persimmon // 말랑한 사람 a person easy to deal with ; a milksop ; a softy ; a sissy

말래카 해협 —海峽 the Strait of Malacca

말레이(야) Malay(a) ¶ 말레이의 Malay

— **반도(半島)** the Malay peninsula **—어** the Malay(an) language — **사람** a Malay(an)

말레이지아 Malaysia

— **연방(聯邦)** the Federation of Malaysia

⁑**말려들다** be dragged 《into》 ; be〔get〕 involved〔entangled〕 《in》 ; involve oneself in ¶ 싸움에 말려들다 be embroiled〔entangled〕 in a quarrel // 전쟁〔분쟁〕에 말려들다 be involved in a war〔trouble〕

말로 末路 the last days ; the final fate ; the end ¶ 영웅의 말로 the last days of a hero // 그의 말로가 비참했다 He had a miserable end.

말류 末流 ① [낮은 계급] the lower classes

② [혈통의 끝] declining descendants

③ [유파] a sect (종파) ; a lower branch (분파) ; [사람] an insignificant follower

말리 茉莉 〖식물〗 a jasmine ; Jasmium grandiflorum (학명)

말리다¹ be rolled (up) ; be curled (up) ¶ 치마 끝이 말리다 the end of a skirt is rolled

†**말리다²** [건조] make dry ; dry ; desiccate ; dehydrate ¶ 말린 고기 dried fish // 볕에 말리다 dry 《a thing》 in the sun // 불로〔에〕 말리다 dry over〔at〕 the fire // 옷을 불에 말리다 dry clothes over a fire // 그냥 드라이어로 말려 주세요 Just blow-dry it, please. // 집집마다 세탁물을 밖에다 많이 말리고 있다 Every house has lots of laundry hanging out to dry.

*__말리다³__ stop〔dissuade〕 《a person》 from 《doing》 ; make 《a person》 stop ; turn 《a

ㅁ

person》 away 《from a bad habit》 ¶ 말리는 것도 듣지 않고 in defiance〔spite〕 of one's remonstrance // 시끄럽게 구는 것을 말리다 get 《people》 to stop making a noise // 싸움을 말리다 stop a quarrel ; put an end〔a stop〕 to a quarrel ; [중재] get〔intervene〕 between the two men ; make up a quarrel

말림 conservancy 《of forest, pasture》 ; reservation —하다 reserve 《a forest》 ; conserve

말림갓 a reserved forest〔pasture〕 ; a forest reserve

말마디 a talk ; a speech ; a phrase ; a clause ¶ 그 사람 말마디나 할 줄 안다 He knows how to put a talk over. /He is quite a good speaker〔conversationalist〕.

말막음 —하다 hush up ; forestall another's words ; appease ; allay

말말뚝 a horse post

말매미 〖곤충〗 a kind of cicada ; Cryptotympana coreana (학명)

말머리 the beginning of one's speech〔talk〕 ; introductory remarks ; one's first few words ; the subject of one's speech ¶ 말머리를 돌리다 change the subject of one's speech

말머리아이 a child born right after wedlock

말먹이 horse feed ; fodder ; hay ; forage ; provender

말목 抹木 a pile ⇨ 말뚝

말몫 [소작인의] a share of the tenant's grain according to the sharecropping

말몰이꾼 a packhorse driver

말못되다 be in bad shape ; be in very poor condition ¶ 말못되게 indescribably ; beyond description〔expression〕 // 요즘 말못되게 야위었다 He has lately become terribly thin.

말문 —門 one's mouth when speaking ¶ 말문이 막히다 be struck dumb 《with surprise》 ; be dumbfounded ; be tonguetied ; be at a loss for words ; lose one's speech ; be agape 《with wonder》

말미 leave (of absence) ; furlough ; day-off ¶ 말미를 얻다 get leave of absence // 그는 말미를 얻어 고향에 돌아갔다 He went home on furlough〔leave〕. // 하루 말미를 주셨으면 합니다 I should like to get a day's leave〔day-off〕. /Would you please give me a day's leave?

말미 末尾 the end ; the close ; the tip ; finis

말미암다 come from ; arise from ; be derived from ; be owing to ; be due to ¶ …으로 말미암아 owing to ; because of ; in consequence of ; on account of ; in accordance with // 운전 부주의로 말미암은 사고 an accident due to careless driving // 어머님은 폭설로 말미암아 오시지 못했다 My mother couldn't come because of the heavy snow. // 그의 실패는 태만으로 말미암은 것이다 His failure is due to negligence.

말미잘 〖동물〗 a sea anemone

말밑[1] [되고 남은] grain left over after measuring with a mal

말밑[2] ① [어원] the etymology〔origin〕 of a word
② [말밑천] one's stock of words ; one's eloquence〔verbal ability〕

말박 ① [큰박] a large gourd ② [말대용의] a gourd used in place of a *mal* measure

말방울 a bell hung round a horse's neck

말뱃대끈 a bellyband (of a horse) ; a girth (of a horse)

말버둥질 pawing the air ¶ 말버둥질치다 a horse paws the air

말버릇 the manner of speaking ; a way of talking ¶ 말버릇처럼 되다 never fail to say ; always say ; be in the habit of saying // 말버릇이 나쁘다 have a foul tongue ; be rude in speech〔address〕 // 그는 그것을 말버릇처럼 말하고 있다 He never opens his mouth without saying it.

말버짐 ringworm ; psoriasis

***말벌** 〖곤충〗 a (ground) wasp ; a kind of hornet

말벗 a companion with whom one can chat ; someone to talk to〔with〕 ¶ 좋은 말벗 a boon companion ; a crony ; a pal // 말벗이 되다 keep 《a person》 company // 말벗이 없다 have nobody to talk to // 말벗이 있었으면 좋겠다 I want to have company to talk together with.

말보 talkativeness from a usually taciturn person ¶ 말보가 터지다 begin to talk freely ; break the ice

말복 末伏 the last 10-day period of the dog days (beginning around early August) ; the last phase of the dog days〔midsummer heat〕

말본 phraseology ; grammar ; diction

말불버섯 〖식물〗 a puffball ; a smut ball

말뼈 ① [뼈] horse bone(s) ② [거친 사람] a rough person〔fellow〕

말사 末寺 a branch temple

말살 抹殺 erasure ; obliteration ; effacement ; liquidation ; defamation (명예 손상) —하다 erase ; strike〔blot, cross〕 out ; obliterate ; rub out ; efface ; [체면·명예를] blight 《a person's》 honor ; ruin 《a person's》 dignity ¶ 공산주의를 말살하다 liquidate communism // 이름을 명부에서 말살하다 cross out〔erase〕 a name from a list

말살스럽다 抹殺— (be) indifferent ; heartless ; hard-hearted

말상 —相 a long face ; an extremely long face ¶ 말상의 long-faced ; horse-faced

말상대 —相對 a companion ; someone to talk to ; conversational partner ; [상담 상대] an adviser ; a consultant

말석 末席 the lowest seat ; the bottom ¶ 말석을 차지하다 have the honor of being present at ⟪a meeting⟫
말선두리 〖곤충〗 a water beetle
말세 末世 a degenerate〔corrupt〕 age ; these latter〔degenerate〕 days ; the end of the world ¶ 이렇게 되면 세상도 말세다 The world is going to the dogs. /This reminds us of the age of decadence we live in.
말소 抹消 erasure ; cancel ; obliteration **—하다** erase ; cancel ; obliterate ; strike〔cross〕 out ¶ 등기의 말소 cancellation of registration ∥ 소송을 말소하다 withdraw a suit
말소리 a voice ; a whisper (소근대는) ; a murmur ¶ 말소리가 들리다 hear ⟪a person⟫ talk ∥ 말소리가 높다 have a loud voice ; talk in a loud voice ∥ 옆방에서 말소리가 들려 온다 The voices of people in the next room can be heard.
말속 the meaning〔implication〕 of one's words ; one's intention ; what is behind one's words ; the true intent
말속 末俗 customs of a degenerate age ; degenerate customs ; a bad custom
말손 末孫 a distant descendant ; a scion ; [집합적] posterity ; progeny
말솜씨 one's ability to speak〔talk〕 ; eloquence ¶ 말솜씨가 좋다 be good at speaking〔talking〕 ; be a good〔brilliant〕 talker ; be eloquent ; have a ready tongue ; have the gift of gab ∥ 말솜씨가 없다 be poor at speaking〔talking〕 ; be a poor speaker
말수 —數 words ; speech ¶ 말수가 많은 사람 a talkative person ; a prattler ; a chatterbox ∥ 말수가 적다 be taciturn ; be ⟪a man⟫ of few words ; be reticent ; be scanty of words ∥ 말수가 많다 be talkative ; loquacious ; voluble ; verbose ; wordy ∥ 그녀는 말수가 적다 She is scanty of words〔a woman of few words〕.
말술 *a mal* of wine ; [많은 술] kegs of wine ¶ (술을) 말술로 마시다 be capable of downing kegs〔gallons〕 of wine ; drink like a fish
말승냥이 ① [이리] a large wolf ② [키 큰 사람] a tall person ; a gangling fellow
말실수 —失手 a tongueslip ; a slip of the tongue ; an impropriety in speech ; a verbal lapse **—하다** make a tongueslip ; one's tongue slips ; commit an impropriety in speech ; use improper language〔words〕 ¶ 말실수한 것을 사과하다 apologize for one's impropriety in speech ∥ 말실수한 것을 취소하다 retract one's words ∥ 말실수한 것을 따지다 blame ⟪a person⟫ for his improper language
말썰매 a horse sleigh
***말썽** trouble ; complaint ; difficulties ; criticism ; a dispute (분쟁) ; complication (분규) ¶ 말썽을 부리다 complain ; cause〔get into〕 trouble ; lead to a dispute ∥ 말썽이 나고 있다 be in trouble
말썽거리 the cause〔source〕 of trouble ; a matter for complaint ; the origin of a dispute ; a bone of contention ; an apple of discord ; a cause of anxiety ¶ 말썽거리가 되다 become a source of trouble
말썽꾼 a troublemaker ; a black sheep ; a grumbler ; a mischief-maker ¶ 집안의 말썽군 the black sheep of the family
⁑**말쑥하다** (be) clean ; neat ; smart ; nice ; tidy ¶ 말쑥한 얼굴 nice features ; a fair countenance ∥ 말쑥한 방 a clean room ∥ 그녀는 항상 말쑥한 옷차림을 하고 있다 She is always neatly dressed. ∥ 이발을 하고 나니 말쑥하구나 You look sharp after a haircut.
말쑥히 clean ; neatly ; smartly ¶ 옷을 말쑥히 차리다 dress oneself up smartly ∥ 방을 말쑥히 치우다 tidy one's room up neatly
말씀 words ; language ; speech ; talk ¶ 친절한 말씀 your kind words ∥ 감사의 말씀을 뭐라고 여쭈어야 할지 모르겠습니다 I can't thank you enough. /I don't know how to express my thanks. ∥ 당신 말씀이 옳소 What you say is true.
†**말씨** use of words ; way of speaking ; manner of speaking ; choice of words ; wording ; diction ; expression ¶ 점잖은 말씨 refined diction ∥ 야비한 말씨 a mean〔low〕 expression ∥ 정중한 말씨로 in courteous terms ∥ 말씨가 점잖다 be refined〔polite〕 in speech ∥ 말씨가 난폭하다 use harsh〔violent〕 language ∥ 그는 말씨가 투박하다 He is crude in speech.
말씬말씬 —하다 [연하다] (be) soft ; tender ; [물씬하다] flaccid ; flabby
말씹조개 a kind of freshwater mussel
말 아니다 ① [이치에 맞지 않다] (be) unreasonable ; absurd ; ridiculous ; preposterous ; nonsense ¶ 말 아닌 값을 부르다 name an exorbitant price ∥ 말 아닌 말을 하다 talk nonsense ② [형편이] (be) miserable ; wretched ; pitiful ; be in bad shape ; be in very poor condition ¶ 그의 생활은 요즈음 말 아니다 He is leading a miserable〔wretched〕 life these days.
말 안되다 (be) unreasonable ; illogical ; absurd ; nonsense ¶ 자기 자식을 버린다는 것은 말 안되는 소리다 It is outrageous to desert one's own child.
말야 I mean ; you know ; you see ; uh ; that is ; I say ; See what I mean ?
말약 末藥 powdered medicine
말없이 [조용히] in silence ; silently ; without saying anything ; without a word〔comment〕 ; [말썽 없이] without causing any trouble ; without ado ; [무단으로] without leave〔permission〕 ; without notice ¶ 말없이 보고 있다 be looking in silence ∥ 그는 아무 말 없이 이 물건을 놓고

갔다 He left the article without explanation. // 저 부부는 말없이 잘 산다 The couple are getting along well without any trouble between them. // 그는 아무 말없이 결석했다 He absented himself without notice.

말엽 末葉 the end ; the close ¶ 19세기 말엽에 towards the end of the 19th century

말오줌나무 〖식물〗 a red-berried elder ; Sambucus racemosa (학명)

말일 末日 the last day ; the end ¶ 5월 말일에 at the end〔last day〕 of May

말자 末子 the youngest〔last〕 son

말잠자리 a kind of dragonfly ; Sieboldius japonicus (학명)

말잡이 one who measures grain

말장난 a play upon words ; a wordplay ; a pun ; paronomasia ; punning ; word-mongering **—하다** play upon words ; pun 《on, upon》 ; make puns〔a pun〕 ¶ 그것은 소위 우리들의 일부 정치 지도자라는 사람들의 입으로부터 나오는 매우 무책임한 말장난이다 It's a very thoughtless rhetoric that is coming out of some of our quote-unquote leaders in the political arena.

말재기 a gossipmaker ; a gossipmonger

말재주 a talent for words〔language〕 ; eloquence ; the gift of gab ¶ 말재주가 있다 have the gift of gab ; be gifted with eloquence ; have a talent for languages // 말재주가 없다 be poor at speaking ; be no speaker ; be slow in speech

말쟁이¹ [마되질군] a person who measures grain for pay

말쟁이² [수다쟁이] a talkative〔wordy〕 person ; a chatterbox ; a prattler

말전주 tale-telling〔-bearing〕 ; mischief-making **—하다** tell tales ; tell on ; make mischief ¶ 말전주꾼 a tale-bearer〔-teller〕 ; a mischiefmaker

말절 末節 the last paragraph (문장의) ; the last part ; the last stanza (시의)

말제 末弟 one's youngest brother

말조심 —操心 care in speaking **—하다** be careful of one's speech ¶ 말조심하시오 Watch your mouth. /Watch your language.

말좌 末座 the lowest seat ; the bottom ⇨ 말석

말주변 talking ability ; oratorical skill 〔talent〕 ; the gift of gab ¶ 말주변이 좋다 have a ready tongue ; have the gift of gab // 말주변이 없다 be a poor talker 〔speaker〕 ; be awkward in speaking

말죽 boiled horse-feed
—통 a horse-feed tub ; a manger

말증 末症 an incurable〔a fatal〕 disease ¶ 말증을 앓다 suffer from an incurable disease

말직 末職 a small post ; the lowest position ; a petty office

말질 tale-telling ; a dispute ; an argument ; a quarrel ; a wrangle **—하다** tell tale about others ; gossip ; criticize ; have a quarrel ; have words ¶ 말질 잘하는 사람 a telltale ; a gossip (monger) ; a tale-bearer // 그들은 쓸데 없는 일로 말질했다 A mere trifle led to a quarrel between them.

말질 末疾 an incurable disease ; a terminal illness

말집 a house with eaves on all sides

말짜 末— [물건] things of the lowest quality ; [사람] an ill-mannered〔unmanly〕 fellow ; a low character ; an article of inferior quality

말짱하다¹ [흠없다] (be) impeccable ; irreproachable ; be free from blemishes ; [깨끗하다] tidy ; neat ; clean ¶ 말짱한 옷 clean〔spotless〕 clothes // 정신이 말짱하다 be sound in mind // 나는 일을 말짱하게 해치웠다 I have finished the work thoroughly.

말짱하다² [성질이] (be) soft ; sissy

말짱히 safely ; intactly ; in one piece ; without a flaw〔blemish〕 ; in perfect shape

말째 末— the last ; the bottom ; the tail (end) ; the first counting backward 〔from the bottom〕 ¶ 말째로 졸업하다 graduate last on the list ; come out bottom // 저 애는 성적이 학급에서 말째다 The boy is at the bottom〔foot〕 of his class. // 그는 말째로 왔다 He was the last to come. /He came last.

말참견 —參見 interfering ; meddling ; officiousness ; meddlesomeness **—하다** interfere ; intervene in ; meddle in〔with〕 ; break〔chop, cut〕 in ; poke〔put, thrust〕 one's nose into ; put in word ; make comment 《on》 ¶ 말참견하지 마라 Do not poke your nose into my affairs. /Mind your own business.

말채찍 a (horse) weep ¶ 말채찍질하다 whip〔lash〕 a horse

말초 末梢 a tree-top (나무 끝) ; a tip (말단) ; 〖해부〗 the periphery ¶ 말초부의 distal ; peripheral // 말초적인 trifling ; trivial ; insignificant ; minor
—기관 an end-organ **— 혈관 확장증** 〖의학〗 telangiectasia ; telangiectasis

말초 신경 末梢神經 〖해부〗 a peripheral nerve
—계 the peripheral nervous system

말총 horsehair

말치레 nice-talk ; using fair〔fine, pretty, honeyed〕 words ; making a specious remark **—하다** nice-talk ; use fair 〔fine, pretty, honeyed〕 words ; say nice 〔pretty〕 things ; make a specious remark

말캉말캉 softly ; flabbily ; flaccidly **—하다** (be) soft ; flabby ; flaccid ; limp

말코¹ a loom roller

말코² the muzzle〔nose〕 of a horse ; a person's nose shaped like a horse's

말코지 a branched hanger〔hook〕

말투 one's way〔manner〕 of talking ¶ 말투가 사납다 have a nasty way of talking ∥말투가 거칠다 use harsh〔violent〕 language∥그는 무엇이든지 알고 있는 말투다 He talks as if he knew everything. ∥요즈음 젊은 여성들은 말투가 거칠다 Young women these days have such an unrefined way of talking.

말판 a game board ; a dice board

말편자 a horseshoe ¶ 말편자형의 horseshoe-shaped ; U-shaped∥말편자를 붙이다 shoe a horse ; horseshoe

***말하다** ① talk ; speak ; converse ; utter ; remark ; chat 《over》 ; have a talk〔chat〕 《with》 ; tell ; put 《in》 ; state ; mention ; relate ; explain (설명하다) ; describe (상세히) ; say ; bid ; express

> 참고 **speak**는 내용보다도 입을 놀리는 동작에 중점을 두어 「지껄이다」의 의미 **say**는 내용에 중점을 두어 의견이나 보고 따위를 말하는 것 **talk**는 회화나 회담 따위에 쓰이며 **utter**는 소리내어 말하는 것 **express**는 표현하는 것 **state**는 딱딱하고 형식적인 말로서 「진술하다」의 뜻 **remark**는 간단한 의견 따위를 발표하는 말 **mention**은 어떤 것을 특히 들추어서 말하는 것

¶ 영어로 말하다 speak in English∥말하고 싶은 것을 말하다 speak one's mind ; speak out ; give rein to one's tongue∥머리가 아프다고 말하다 complain of a headache∥사람을 좋게〔나쁘게〕 말하다 speak well〔ill〕 of a person ; say good〔bad〕 things about a person ; say a good〔bad〕 word for a person∥당신에게 말하고 싶은 것이 있다 I have something to tell you. ∥이 사람이 당신에게 말한 김군이다 This is Mr. *Kim* I spoke of to you. ∥나는 그일에 대해서 아버지에게 말했다 I laid the case before my father. ∥누구에게도 말하면 안된다 Not a soul must be told. /This is strictly between you and me. ∥모든 것은 나중에 말하겠습니다 I will let you know all about it later on. ∥말하면 이해가 간다 Talk〔Discussion〕 will make the matter clear. ∥이제 내가 말할 차례다 It is now my say. ∥네가 말한 대로다 It is just as you say. /What you say is true. /You are quite right. ∥빨리 말해 Out with it. ∥이렇게 말하면 너는 저렇게 말한다 You contradict everything. ∥말하기는 쉽고 행하기는 어렵다 Easier said than done. ∥그는 죄를 지었다고 말했다 He confessed himself to be guilty. ∥남자답게 졌다고 말해라 Acknowledge your defeat with good grace. ∥이것은 영어로 무어라고 말합니까 ? How do you say〔put〕 this in English ? ∥그때의 마음을 무어라고 말할 수 없다 Words fail to express how I felt at the moment. ∥그것은 세상사람들이 흔히 말하는 일이다 It is a matter of common talk among people. ∥정확히 어떻게 이 사태가 개선될 것인지에 대해서는 남장관은 자세히 말하지는 않았다 Exactly how the situation will improve Minister *Nam* has not elaborated. ∥사람들은 그가 인격자라고 말한다 He is said to be a man of character. ∥다른 사람에게 내가 그렇게 말하더라고 하지 마라 Don't quote me. ∥당신이 그렇게 말할 만도 합니다 I don't blame you. ∥더 이상 말하고 싶지 않다 Period ! ∥적당할 때 그만 달라고 말하십시오 Say when. (남에게 술을 따라줄 때)

② [어린애가] begin to speak〔talk〕 ¶ 어린애가 말하기 시작했다 The child started to babble.

③ [부탁하다] ask ; beg ; wish ; hope ¶ 그녀에게 결혼해 달라고 말했다 I asked her for her hand. /I asked her to marry me.

④ [말리고 꾸짖다] tell ; bid ; advise ; dissuade 《a person》 from 《doing》 ¶ 하지 말라고 말하다 tell 《a person》 not to do ; dissuade 《a person》 from 《doing》∥내가 누차 말했는데도 그는 담배를 끊지 못했다 He kept on smoking in spite of my repeated warning.

말할 수 없는 관용 unspeakable ; unutterable ; indescribable

말하자면 so to speak〔say〕 ; so to call it ; as it were ; in a manner 《of speaking》 ; in a way〔sense, kind, sort〕 ; as one might put it ; in a word (한 마디로 말하면) ¶ 그녀는 말하자면 우리에 든 새다 She may be likened〔compared〕 to a caged bird. ∥그는 말하자면 애어른이다 He is, so to speak, a grownup baby. ∥이 근처는 말하자면 내 집 같다 This neighborhood is kind of like my home.

말할것도 없다 ¶ …은 말할것도 없다 it is a matter of course that. . . ; it goes without saying that. . . ∥…은 말할것도 없이 not to mention〔speak of〕 ; to say nothing of ; not only. . . (but) ∥말할것도 없이 (as a matter) of course ; needless to say ; it goes without saying

말향 抹香 incense (powder)

— 고래 a spermwhale ; a cachalot

말혁 —革 reins attached to both sides of a saddle as decoration

†**맑다** (be) clean ; clear ; pure ; limpid ; transparent ; resonant (소리가) ; innocent (일이) ; lucid ; [살림이] poor ; indigent ¶ 맑은 마음 a lucid (serene) mind ∥맑은 물 clear〔limpid〕 water∥맑은 하늘 a clear sky∥맑은 정신 a fresh〔clear〕 mind ; a good memory∥맑은 살림 a meager living

맑은 샘에서 맑은 물 난다 속담 Parents are patterns. /One sheep follows another. /If one sheep leap o'er the dyke, all the rest will follow.

ㅁ

맑디맑다 (be) very clear ; perfectly clear ; be as clear as can be〔as crystal〕
맑스그레하다 (be) pleasantly thin 〔watery〕; juicy
맑은 소리 〖언어〗 a voiceless sound
맑은술 refined rice wine
맑은 장국 —醬— clear〔thin〕 meat soup ; bouillon
맑히다 make clear ; purify ; make neat ; clean; clarify ; settle ; make clean ; cleanse ¶ 정신을 맑히다 refresh one's mind ; make one's mind fresh // 물을 맑히다 clear the water
맘마 food ; rice —하다 eat
맘보 a mambo
— 바지〔즈봉〕 drainpipe trousers
맙소사 Oh, no ! ; Good God〔Lord, me〕! ; Good gracious〔heavens〕! ; Gracious Heaven〔goodness〕! ; Save us ! ; My eye(s) !

ㅁ

‡맛¹ ① [음식의] taste ; flavor ; savor ¶ 맛이 좋은 nice ; tasty ; palatable ; savory ; delicious ; flavorous // 맛이 없는 ill-tasting ; untasty ; unsavory ; unpalatable // 맛이 변하다 turn sour〔stale〕; get high (고기가)
② [느낌] taste ; relish ; zest ; gusto ; aroma ¶ 맛을 알다 get〔acquire〕 a taste for // 여자의 맛을 알고 있다 have carnal knowledge of women ☞ 《 p. 763 》
맛² 〖조개〗 a solen ; a razor clam
—젓 pickled razor clams
맛김 seasoned laver
맛깔 taste
맛깔스럽다 ① [맛이] (be) palatable ; delicious ; tasty ; edible ¶ 맛깔스러운 음식 an agreeable〔edible〕 food ② [마음에] be pleased〔satisfied〕 with ; (be) satisfactory ; acceptable ; suit〔catch, take, strike〕 one's fancy ¶ 맛깔스러운 집 a house to one's taste // 저 그림은 맛깔스럽다 That picture appeals to my taste. /I take a fancy to that picture. // 이것이 나에게 제일 맛깔스럽다 This suits my taste best.
†맛나다 (be) tasty ; delicious ; sweet ; savory ; palatable ; taste good ; have a good flavor 《of》 ¶ 맛난 요리 a delicious〔palatable〕 dish // 아 맛나다 It tastes good. /Goody ! 《미》
맛난이 ① [조미료] sauce ; flavo(u)ring ; seasoning ; something to bring out the flavor ② [음식] delicious food
맛들다 become tasty ; pick up flavor ; become good to eat〔drink〕; grow ripe ; ripen ¶ 맛든 수박 watermelon ripe enough to eat
맛들이다 ① season 《food》; flavor 《a drink》; give〔impart〕 a flavor to ; add seasoning to ② [재미를] get〔acquire〕 a taste 《for》 ¶ 돈에 맛들이다 get a taste for money // 여자에 맛들이다 have a carnal knowledge of women // 음주를 맛들이다 take to drink // 돈을 구해 주었더니 맛들여 또 찾아 왔다 Emboldened by his first success in borrowing money from me, he has come again for another.
맛맛으로 according to one's taste〔pleasure〕; to one's liking
맛바르다 have not eaten enough ; want to eat more ; have one's appetite still unsatisfied
맛배기 [맛보기 위한 소량의 음식] a taster ; [특제] a special order
맛보기 tasting ; sampling ; foretaste ; prelibation ; degustation
†맛보다 [음식을] try the flavor of ; taste ; sample 《wine》; [경험] experience ; know ; learn ¶ 인생의 쓰라림을 맛보다 experience the bitterness of life // 그는 가난을 맛본 일이 없다 He has no experience of poverty. /He is a stranger to poverty.
맛부리다 behave insipidly ; behave in an insipid manner
맛살 the meat inside a razor clam
맛없다 ① (be) tasteless ; unsavory ; unpalatable ; insipid ; flat ¶ 맛없는 요리 unsavory〔tasteless〕 dishes ② [재미·흥미가] (be) dull ; dry ; insipid ; uninteresting ; irksome ; wearisome ; flat ¶ 맛없는 세상 the dreary world ; wearisome life // 맛없이 살다 lead a wretched life // 맛없이 굴다 behave in an insipid manner
‡맛있다 ① (be) delicious ; sweet ; nice ; tasty ; palatable ; savory ; flavorous ¶ 맛있게 보이는 delicious-looking ; tempting // 맛있는 음식 tasty food ② [재미 있다] (be) interesting ; delightful
맛장수 an insipid〔a prosaic, a dull〕 person
맛적다 ① (be) tasteless ; flavorless ; flat ; dull ; insipid ② [재미적다] (be) unenjoyable ; disagreeable ; unpleasant ¶ 맛적은 음식 flat food // 맛적은 사람 a dull person ; a disagreeable person
맛젓 pickled razor clams
맛피우다 behave insipidly ⇨ 맛부리다
†망¹ 望 ① [살핌] watch ; lookout ; vigilance 〔vigil〕 ¶ 망을 보다 stand guard 《at the door》; watch ; keep watch〔a look-out〕; keep an eye on ; be on the lookout 〔watch, alert〕; picket // 망을 세우다 get an outlook ; place a guard 《at the door》; keep guard 《over the house》
② [명망] good reputation
③ [천망] recommendation
—대 a lookout ; a watch tower ; an observation tower
망² 望 ① [만월] a full moon
② [음력 보름날] the fifteenth day of a lunar month
망 網 a net ; a casting net (투망) ; netting 《총칭》 ¶ 망을 뜨다 make a net // 망을 치다 pitch〔lay〕 a net ; stretch a net // 망에 걸리다 be trapped〔caught〕 in a net // 망

맛의 표현

1 여러 가지 맛

① 단맛

sweet; sugary; luscious (★ sugary는 매우 단맛, luscious는 잘 익은 과일처럼 향기와 단맛이 좋을 때 쓰임)
¶ 단맛이 나다. be [taste] sweet; have a sweet taste // 달콤한 간장 mild soy sauce // 후식으로 맛좋은 과일이 나왔다. Luscious fruits were served for dessert.

② 쓴맛

bitter
¶ 쓴맛이 나다. be [taste] bitter; have a bitter taste

③ 신맛

레몬이나 덜 익은 과일의 신맛을 표현할 때 sour, 초의 신맛은 acid, 와인 등이 시큼해진 것은 sharp.
¶ 이 우유는 시어졌다. This milk has turned [gone] sour. // 이 오렌지는 약간 시다. This orange is [tastes] rather acid.

④ 매운맛

입안이 화끈화끈하게 매운맛은 hot, 치즈 등의 짜릿한 맛은 sharp, 향신료 등의 자극적인 맛은 pungent, 와인 등의 탁 쏘는 듯한 맛은 dry.
¶ 매콤한 소스 a rich and pungent sauce // 이 카레는 무척 맵다. This curry is too hot. // 이 와인은 탁 쏘는 맛이 있다. This wine is dry.

⑤ 짠맛

salty; salted
¶ 살짝 절인 연어 lightly salted salmon // 이 수프는 약간 짜다. This soup is a little too salty.

⑥ 떫은맛

감, 과일 등이 떫은맛이 날 때는 puckery를 많이 쓴다. 술 등의 떫은맛은 rough나 harsh를 쓴다.
¶ 이 감은 떫은맛이 난다. This persimmon has a puckery taste.

⑦ 톡 쏘는 맛

음료수, 음식 등에서 톡 쏘는 맛이 날 때는 tang; tangy.
¶ 그 레모네이드는 톡 쏘는 맛이 일품이었다. The lemonade was a delicious, tangy taste.

⑧ 푸짐한 식사

영양이 풍부한 식사는 rich, 양이 많은 식사는 substantial. **(가벼운 식사)** 소화가 잘 되고 뱃속이 편한 light, 담백한 맛 plain, 식사가 간소한 것은 simple.

⑨ 느끼한 맛

걸쭉하고 진할 때 thick, 기름기가 많은 greasy.
¶ 이 수프는 약간 느끼하다. This soup is a little too thick [greasy].

⑩ 진한 식사

먹고 나서 더부룩한 heavy, 너무 먹어서 물린 cloying, 맛이 진한 strong.
¶ 맛이 진한 블랙 커피 strong black coffee // 거친 음식은 위에 좋지 않다. Heavy food is bad for the stomach.

⑪ 감칠 맛 나는

술 등이 진하고 감칠 맛 날 때 full-bodied; rich; silky.
¶ 그녀는 감칠 맛 나는 적포도주를 내놓았다. She served us full-bodied red wine.

2 맛의 표현

① taste

혀로 느껴지는 맛이며 가장 일반적으로 쓰인다. 「…맛이 난다」는 뜻의 자동사로도 쓰인다.
¶ 이 사과는 달고 감칠맛이 난다. This apple has a sweet, slightly silky taste. // 이것은 쓴맛이 난다. This tastes bitter. // 이 수박은 맛이 없다. This watermelon doesn't have much taste. // 이것은 초콜릿 아이스크림 같은데 커피 맛이 난다. This is supposed to be a chocolate ice-cream, but it tastes of coffee.

② flavor

맛 중에서 음식물 특유의 맛을 의미하며 그것은 혀로 느껴지는 것뿐만 아니라 향기와 기타 요소까지 혼합된 총체적인 의미로 쓰인다.
¶ 그 연어 통조림들은 색과 향이 다르다. The various grades of salmon differ in color and flavor.

③ smack

여러 가지 혼합된 것 중에 하나의 특징적인 맛이 약간 느껴질 때 쓰인다.
¶ 이 수프는 후추맛이 난다. This soup has a smack of pepper.

④ season

소금·후추 등으로 맛을 낼 때 동사 season, spice를 쓴다.
¶ 그녀는 소금, 생강, 마늘로 수프 맛을 냈다. She seasoned [spiced] the soup with salt, ginger, and garlic.

③ 맛이 좋다, 나쁘다의 표현

① 맛이 좋을 때

보통 good, nice를 쓴다. 좀 더 강한 표현은 wonderful, excellent, 약간 과장된 표현은 tasty, 감탄을 표할 때는 delicious, 향기가 좋을 때는 savory, 그럭저럭 먹을 만할 때에는 palatable, 식욕을 돋우는 것일 때는 appetizing.
¶ 그녀가 만든 프랑스 요리는 매우 맛이 있다. The French dishes she made were very good [delicious]. // 저 식당 음식은 그저 먹을 만하다. The food at that restaurant is not so bad [palatable].

② 맛이 없을 때

맛이 없을 때 tasteless; flavorless, 맛이 싱거울 때 insipid, 불쾌한 맛일 때는 unsavory, 맛이 지독할 때는 terrible; disgusting, 맛이 없는 것을 점잖게 표현할 때 have no taste; not taste of anything; not too good.

으로 새를 잡다 net a bird ; catch a bird in a net // 검거의 망을 펴다 spread〔put〕 a dragnet ; post a cordon
통신〔철도, 방송〕— a communications 〔railroad, radio〕 network

망가 亡家 [망한 집] a ruined family ; [결딴냄] ruining a family

*****망각 忘却** lapse of memory ; forgetfulness ; oblivion **—하다** forget ; be forgetful〔oblivious〕 of ¶ 세상에서 망각되다 be buried in oblivion // 사실을 망각하다 lose sight of the fact // 취해서 전후를 망각하다 become quite befuddled with drink // 너무나 화가 나서 전후를 망각하다 forget oneself in a fit of passion

망간 〖화학〗 manganese 《Mn》
—철(鐵) manganese steel〔iron〕

망개나무 [식물] a kind of supplejack

망거 妄擧 a reckless attempt〔undertaking〕 ; a leap in the dark ; an ill-advised attempt

망견 望見 —하다 look out over 《a view》

망계 妄計 a reckless scheme ; a rash plan ; unjust〔unfair, wrong, unrighteous〕 scheme

망고[1] ① [연줄의] letting out〔paying away〕 all the kite string ; come to the end of the kite string **—하다** let loose〔pay away〕 all the string of a kite ② [파산] squandering ; losing all one's fortune ; come to the end of one's fortune **—하다** run through one's fortune ; go bankrupt ③ [끝판] an end ; a conclusion **—하다** come to the end
망곳살 the tooth of a reel after all the kite string has been let out

망고[2] 〖식물〗 a mango 《*pl.* ～es, ～s》

망구다 ruin ; spoil ; destroy ; wreck ¶ 계획을 망구다 spoil〔ruin〕 a plan // 신세를 망구다 ruin oneself ; bring ruin upon oneself // 나라를 망구다 ruin 〔destroy〕 a nation

망국 亡國 national decay〔ruin〕 ; a ruin of one's country ; a ruined country (망한 나라) **—하다** ruin〔destroy〕 one's country ¶ 망국적 ruinous〔dangerous, pernicious〕 to the state // 망국적 문학 antipatriotic literature // 망국적 경제 finances ruinous to the state
— 민족 a ruined people ; a homeless race **— 지탄** lamentation〔grief〕 over the national ruin

망군 亡君 one's deceased〔late〕 king

망군 望軍 a watchman ; a lookout ; a guard ; a keeper ; a picket

망그러뜨리다 break (down) ; destroy ; demolish ; crack ; injure ; impair ; damage ; ruin ; wreck ; batter 《furniture》 ; spoil ; mar ; put out of shape ; crush out of shape ¶ 기계를 망그러뜨리다 break up a machine // 모자를 망그러뜨리다 smash〔squash, batter, stave in〕 a hat // 시계를 망그러뜨리다 get a watch out of order // 자물쇠를 망그러뜨리고 열다 force open a lock

망그러지다 break ; be broken ; be wrecked ; be demolished ; be damaged ; be destroyed ; be put〔crushed〕 out of shape ¶ 망그러진 남비 a broken 〔cracked〕 pan // 망그러진 모자 a battered hat // 망그러진 차 a disabled car // 망그러지기 쉬운 easily breaking ; easy to break ; brittle ; fragile ; frail // 망그러지지 않게 하다 keep〔prevent, protect〕 《a thing》 from breaking // 상자가 망그러졌다 The box was crushed out of shape.

망그지르다 ruin ⇨ 망그러뜨리다

망극 罔極 —하다 (be) immeasurable ; great ; immense ; extreme ; infinite ¶ 망극한 은혜 a great favor〔benefit〕 of one's parents〔king〕

망극지통 罔極之痛 grief beyond expression ; the greatest grief〔lament〕

망나니 ① [사형 집행인] an executioner ② [못된 사람] a rogue ; a wretch ; a villain ; a scamp ; a scoundrel ; an outlaw

망녀 亡女 [죽은 딸] one's deceased daughter

망년 忘年 ① [송년] speeding the old year ¶ 망년 집회 〖종교〗 a watch meeting // 함께 망년 술을 마시다 drink to the parting year together ② [나이 먹는 것을 잊음] indifference to age

망년회 忘年會 a year-end party〔social gathering〕 ¶ 망년회를 열다 give a year-end party ; celebrate the outgoing year

망념 妄念 delusion ⇨ 망상

망녕그물 a net for catching rabbits〔pheasants〕; a fowling net
망대 望臺 ⇨ 망루
망동 妄動 **—하다** act blindly〔on impulse〕; behave rashly
망둥이 〖물고기〗 a goby ; Acanthogobius hasta (학명)
망라 網羅 **—하다** [포함] include ; comprehend ; comprise ; contain ; [모으다] bring together ; collect ¶ 모든 것을 망라한 comprehensive ; exhaustive // 모든 사실을 망라하다 cover〔include〕 all the facts // 이 사전은 현재 사용되고 있는 8만의 어휘를 망라하고 있다 This dictionary comprises〔contains〕 80,000 English words now in use. // 이 회합에는 사회 각층의 사람들이 망라되어 있다 Every class〔rank〕 of society is represented in this society〔at the meeting〕.
망령 亡靈 a departed soul〔spirit〕; manes ; [유령] a ghost ; an apparition ; a spirit
망령 dotage ; second childhood ; senility ; anility ¶ 망령한 senile ; doting // 망령이 든 노인 a dotard ; an old man in his dotage // 망령들다 be in one's dotage〔second childhood〕; be senile ; become infirm with age ; dote // 망령부리다 behave like a child ; behave unreasonably〔foolishly〕// 망령들지 않았다 have one's mental faculties unimpaired // 나이 때문에 망령들었다 Age has begun to tell on him. /His second childhood has come over him.
망령되다 (be) childish ; foolish ; silly ; stupid ; absurd ; ridiculous ; unreasonable ¶ 망령된 소리를 하다 utter an absurdity
망령스럽다 (be) childish ; foolish ; ridiculous ; silly
망론 妄論 an absurd view ; a foolish opinion ; a ridiculous talk ; an irrational〔unfair〕 opinion ; irresponsible utterances ¶ 망론을 하다 make absurd remarks
망루 望樓 a watchtower ; an observation tower ; a lookout ; a belvedere
망륙 望六 fifty-one years of age ¶ 나이 망륙에 이르다 reach〔attain〕 one's 51st year of age
망막 網膜 〖의학〗 the retina
— 검시경 〖안과〗 a retinoscope ; a skiascope **— 검시법** 〖안과〗 retinoscopy ; skiascopy **—상(像)** a retinal image **— 출혈** a retinal hemorrhage **— 화상** 〖군사〗 a retinal burn
망막 茫漠 **—하다** ① [넓다] (be) vast ; boundless ; extensive ¶ 망막한 평원 a vast stretch of lowland
② [막연하다] (be) vague ; obscure ¶ 망막한 전도 vague prospects
망막 세포 網膜細胞 〖동물〗 a retinal cell ; a retinula (*pl.* -lae) ; a retinule ¶ 망막 세포의 retinular
망망하다 茫茫— (be) vast ; broad ; boundless ; limitless ¶ 망망한 바다 a boundless ocean ; a vast expanse of water
망망하다 忙忙— (be) very busy
망명 亡命 a flight from one's own country **—하다** flee from one's own country ; exile oneself ; seek〔take〕 refuge《in a foreign country》¶ 미국에 망명하다 come to America as an exile〔a refugee〕
—객 a political exile **—자** a (political) refugee ; an exile **— 정권** an exiled regime **— 정부** a refugee government
망모 亡母 one's late〔deceased〕 mother
망발 妄發 an ignominious〔disgraceful〕 speech ; an unreasonable〔absurd, reckless〕 speech ; a thoughtless remark **—하다** make an ignominious speech ; make an absurd〔reckless〕 remark ; use improper language
망발 풀이 妄發— a treat given to make up for one's absurd〔reckless〕 remarks **—하다** give a treat〔an entertainment〕 in apology for one's unreasonable remarks
망배 望拜 worshiping from a far〔a distance〕 **—하다** worship from a distance ; bow to the direction of《one's ancestral grave yard》
망백 望百 ninety-one years of age
***망보다 望—** keep watch ; look out for ; be on the lookout〔watch, alert〕; keep sentry ; stand guard ; stand watch ; exercise surveillance ; picket ¶ 엄중히 망보다 keep strict watch ; guard strictly // 저 순경은 합승 정류장에서 소매치기를 망보고 있다 The policeman is stationed at a busstop to look out for pickpockets.
망부 亡父 one's late〔deceased〕 father
망부 亡夫 one's deceased〔late〕 husband
망부석 望夫石 a legendary faithful wife who died and was turned to stone waiting for her husband ; the stone on which a faithful wife stood waiting for her husband until she perished
망사 網紗 gauze
망사 網絲 [그물 뜨는 실] netting thread
망상 妄想 a wild fancy ; a fantasy ; a chimera ; a fantastic idea ; an impossible idea ; a delusion (정신병) ¶ 망상에 잠기다 be lost in wild fancies ; spin a daydream ; be woolgathering ; be lost in lascivious thoughts (음탕한) // 망상을 품다 nurse delusion
—광 paranoia **과대 —증** insanity of grandeur ; megalomania
망상 網狀 net shape ; reticulation ¶ 망상의 netlike ; reticulate ; reticular
—맥 〖식물〗 netted〔reticulate〕 venation **— 섬유** 〖식물〗 a reticulum (*pl.* -la) **— 조직** net ; a network
망상 望床 a large (dinner) table laid with

ㅁ

various foods and fruits

망상스럽다 (be) crafty ; frivolous ; saucy ; tricky ; impertinent ; treacherous ; fickle

망새 a decorative tile standing at either end of a roof ridge ; a gargoyle

망석중이 a puppet ; a marionette ; puppetry (집합적) ; a puppet for another (남의 손에 노는 사람)

망설 妄說 a fallacious speech ; an erroneous idea〔opinion〕; a groundless opinion ; [그릇된 풍설] a false〔baseless〕 report

*망설거리다 hesitate ⇨ 망설이다

망설망설 hesitatingly ; waveringly ; shillyshally ; dilly-dally ¶ 망설망설 결정을 짓지 못하다 hover in indecision ; hang back from making a decision

*망설이다 hesitate ; scruple ; waver ; vacillate ; think twice ; hang〔hold〕 back ; be irresolute ; be hesitant ; shilly-shally ; make two bites at a cherry ; jib〔balk〕 at 《doing》 ¶ 망설이면서 hesitatingly ; reluctantly ; irresolutely // 망설이지 않고 without hesitation ; without scruple 〔wavering, hesitation〕; resolutely // 망설이지 않다 make〔have〕 no scruple of ; do not stick at // 명확히 답하기를 망설이다 hesitate to give a definite answer // 나는 그 사람을 찬양하는 데 망설이지 않는다 I do not hesitate to pay him a tribute. / His action commands my spontaneous admiration.

망솔 妄率 hastiness ; rashness ; recklessness ; precipitancy ―하다 (be) hasty ; rash ; reckless ; precipitate ; headlong

망쇄 忙殺 busyness ; pressure〔stress, press〕 of work ―하다 (be) very busy ; be pressed with work

⁑망신 亡身 shame ; disgrace ; discredit ; dishonor ; infamy ; ignominy ; humiliation ―하다 disgrace oneself ; humiliate oneself ; be put to shame ; be dishonored ¶ 망신을 주다 put 《a person》 to shame ; bring 《a person》 into contempt ; humiliate ; insult // 저 아이는 집안의 망신거리다 That boy is a disgrace 〔discredit〕 to our family. // 그렇게 하면 내 망신이 된다 If you do so, you will bring shame on me.

―살 ill luck to bring disgrace

망신 妄信 blind belief〔faith〕; credulity ―하다 believe blindly ; be credulous

망실 亡失 loss ―하다 lose

망실 忘失 ① [잃음] loss ; missing ② [망각] forgetfulness ; oblivion ; lapse of memory ―하다 lose ; miss ; forget ; be forgetful〔oblivious〕 of

망아 亡兒 [죽은 아이] one's dead child 〔son, daughter〕

⁑망아지 a foal 《총칭》; a colt (수컷) ; a filly (암컷)

망야 罔夜 all night sitting ⇨ 철야(徹夜)

망양보뢰 亡羊補牢 Locking the barn door after the horse is stolen. /After death, the doctor. /To cover the well after the child has been drowned in it.

망양지탄 望洋之歎 lamenting one's inability〔incapacity〕; a feeling of hopelessness ¶ 망양지탄이 있다 feel one's object to be unattainable ; lament one's incapacity

망어 妄語 a falsehood ; a lie ; an untruth ; a prevarication

망언 妄言 an absurd〔improper〕 remark ; a foolish talk ; a reckless remark ; thoughtless words ―하다 make an absurd remark ; talk foolishly

망얽이 a net of ropes

망연자실 茫然自失 ―하다 (be) distrait ; stupefied ; entranced ; dazed ; be at one's wits' end ; feel〔be quite〕 at sea

망연하다 茫然― ① [넓고 아득함] (be) vast ; boundless ; extensive ; limitless ② [멍하다] (be) vacant ; blank ; abstracted ; absent-minded ¶ 망연히 vacantly ; blankly ; absent-mindedly ; in a daze // 어찌할 바를 몰라 망연하다 be quite at a loss what to do

망외 望外 ¶ 망외의 unexpected ; unlooked-for ; unforeseen ; unanticipated // 망외의 기쁨 a pleasant〔pleasing〕 surprise // 망외의 성공 an unexpected 〔unlooked-for〕 success

망우 亡友 one's dead〔deceased〕 friend

망우초 忘憂草 a day-lily ⇨ 원추리

망운 亡運 evil luck which will bring ruin ; decline of fortune ; adversity ¶ 망운이 들다 tend towards decline ; begin to sink〔decline〕; be going downhill

망울 ① [덩어리] a lump ; a ball ; a kernel ; a stone ¶ 망울지다 get lumpy ; have a lump ② [꽃 따위의] a flower bud ; a bud ③ [임파선종] 〚의학〛 inflammation〔swelling〕 of a lymphatic gland ; lymphadenitis ¶ 망울지다 have lymphadenitis

망원 가늠자 望遠― a telescopic sight ¶ 망원 가늠자가 붙은 소총 a telescopic rifle

*망원경 望遠鏡 a telescope ; a field-glass ; a spyglass (소형의) ; binoculars (쌍안경) ¶ 망원경으로 별을 보다 look at the star through a telescope

감마선 ― a gamma-ray telescope 광학 ― an optical telescope 굴절 ― a refracting telescope ; a refractor 반사(反射) ― a reflecting telescope ; a reflector 전파 ― a radio telescope 조준(照準) ― a sighting telescope 지상 ― a terrestrial telescope 천체 ― an astronomical telescope 태양 관측용 ― a helioscope

망원 렌즈 望遠― a telephoto-lens

망원 사진 望遠寫眞 a telephoto(graph) ―기 a telephotographic camera ; a telecamera ―술 telephotography

망월 望月 ① [보름달] a full moon ② [달

을 봄] watching the moon ; gazing at the moon ; viewing the moon **—하다** gaze at〔watch〕 the moon

망은 忘恩 ingratitude ; unthankfulness **—하다** be ungrateful ; lose one's gratitude ¶ 망은한 사람 an ungrateful person ; an ingrate // 망은의 ungrateful ; unthankful // 망은을 사죄하다 ask 《another's》 pardon for one's ingratitude

망인 亡人 a dead person ; the dead ; the deceased

망일 望日 a full-moon day ; the fifteenth day of the lunar month

망자 亡子 one's dead〔deceased〕 son

망자 亡者 a dead person ; the deceased ; the departed

망자 芒刺 a thorn ; a prickle ; a sticker

망자 존대 妄自尊大 haughtiness ; arrogance ; self-importance ; pomposity ; superciliousness **—하다** bear oneself haughtily ; assume an air of importance ; put on the airs of a great man ; hold one's head high ; ride the high horse

망제 亡弟 one's dead〔deceased〕 younger brother

망조 亡兆 omens〔a foreboding〕 of ruin ; signs of declining fortune ¶ 망조가 들다 show signs of ruin

망족 望族 an illustrious〔honorable, a reputable〕 family

망종 亡種 a villain ; a ruffian ; a scoundrel ; a (worthless) scamp ; a bad boy ; a rascal ; a bad egg

망종 亡終 the time〔hour〕 of death ; the last hour of one's life ; one's last moment ; one's deathbed ; the dying hour

망종 芒種 ① [까끄라기가 있는 곡식] awned 〔bearded〕 grain ② [24절기의 아홉째] "the barley harvest season" (as the 9th of the 24 seasonal divisions according to the lunar calendar that falls on about 5th of June)

망주석 望柱石 a pair of stone posts in front of a tomb

망중한 忙中閑 leisure in intervals of one's business ; a moment of relief from pressure of business ; a break in the pressure of one's work ¶ 망중한을 아껴서 저작하다 write a book, making the best of the odd moments saved from one's regular work

망지소조 罔知所措 being at a loss what to do ; not knowing what to do

망집 妄執 a mistakenly held obsession ; a deep-seated delusion

망처 亡妻 one's deceased wife

망초 芒硝 sulphate of soda

망측 罔測 inordinateness ; absurdity ; senselessness **—하다** (be) inordinate ; absurd ; senseless ¶ 망측한 생각 an inordinate idea // 망측한 이야기 an absurd story // 망측해서 말도 안되다 be too absurd to take seriously

⁑**망치** a hammer ¶ 큰 망치 a maul ; a sledge(-hammer) // 망치로 뚜드리다 hammer ; strike with a hammer // 망치로 못을 박다 drive in a nail with a hammer ; hammer a nail 《into》
— 대가리 a hammerhead **— 자루** the handle of a hammer **—질** hammering

***망치 忘置** lapse〔slip〕 of memory ; forgetting ; forgetfulness ; oblivion **—하다** forget ; lose one's memory ; be oblivious

†**망치다** ruin ; spoil ; mar ; destroy ; frustrate ; make a muddle〔mess〕 of ¶ 건강을 망치다 injure〔impair, ruin〕 one's health // 신세를 망치다 ruin oneself ; bring ruin upon oneself // 일생을 망치다 ruin〔blast〕 one's career〔life〕 ; make a failure of one's life // 계획을 망치다 spoil 〔ruin〕 a plan ; frustrate one's plan ; throw a wet blanket over a project // 너 때문에 하루를 망쳤다 You rained on my parade. // 이번 주말은 망쳤군 There goes my weekend ! // 나는 이미 일을 망쳐 놨다 I've already made a big mess of things. // 그는 분위를 망쳐놓았다 He ruined the whole atmosphere. // 눈물을 많이 흘려서 화장을 망쳤다 I shed so many tears I ruined my make-up.

망친 亡親 one's deceased〔late〕 parents

망칠 望七 sixty-one years of age

망태기 網— a mesh〔net〕 bag

⁑**망토** a mantle ; a cloak ; a cape (어깨 망토) ¶ 망토를 몸에 걸치다 fold one's cloak about one

망판 網版 〖인쇄·사진〗 a halftone ; a halftone plate〔block〕

망팔 望八 seventy-one years of age

망평 妄評 a rash comment ; unjust criticism ; abusive〔ill-considered〕 remarks ; poor〔undue, unfair〕 criticism **—하다** comment rashly〔poorly〕 ; criticize unjustly ; make abusive remarks

***망하다**[1] **亡—** go to ruin ; be ruined ; fall ; perish ; cease to exist ; die out ; meet with destruction ¶ 망해가는 민족 a dying race // 나라가 망하다 a country perishes // 집안이 망하다 a family goes down // 회사가 망하다 a company fails // 난 이제 망했구나 I'm washed up. /I'm done for. // 그의 사업은 1년쯤 후에 망할 것 같다. I'm afraid his business will fold in a year or so.

망하다[2] **亡—** [꼴사납다] (be) very ugly ; bad-looking ; unbecoming ; unshapely ; [못되다] wretched ; [다루기 힘들다] be hard to deal with ; [귀찮다] (be) troublesome ; [밉다] hateful ; disgusting ¶ 보기에 망하다 look ugly〔shabby〕 // 그 책은 읽기 망하다 The book is hard to read.

망향 望鄕 homesickness ; nostalgia ¶ 망향병에 걸리다 become homesick〔nostalgic〕 ; yearn〔long〕 for the sight of one's

home
망형 亡兄 one's dead〔deceased〕 elder brother
망혼 亡魂 the spirit〔soul〕 of the dead ; a departed spirit ; a ghost ; an apparition ; a specter
맞- [마주] facing ; directly opposite ; together ; jointly ; each other ¶ 맞대면 a face-to-face interview // 맞부딪다 hit each other // 맞앉다 sit face to face with 《a person》 ; sit opposite 《a person》
—바람 a headwind
맞갖다 be to one's taste〔liking〕 ; (be) agreeable ; satisfactory ; likable ¶ 맞갖은 음식 tasty food // 맞갖은 여자 a girl after one's heart // 맞갖은 집 a house to one's taste
맞갖잖다 (be) distasteful ; offensive ; disagreeable ; unsatisfactory ; undesirable ; go against the grain ¶ 맞갖잖은 음식 distasteful〔unpleasant〕 food // 맞갖잖은 사람 a disagreeable person // 맞갖잖은 수작 an offensive remark ; a remark hard to stomach
맞걸다 stake the same amount 《of money》 as the other party ; stake against
맞걸리다 ① [두 물건이] be linked together ; be coupled ¶ 차량 연결기가 맞걸리다 the couplers of the cars are engaged〔joined〕 ② [두 사람이] be pitted against each other ; be matched〔faced〕 with each other ; be out for fight〔competition〕 ¶ 둘이 결승전에 맞걸리다 the two are pitted against each other in the final match
맞고소 —告訴 a cross〔counter〕 action ; a counterclaim 《for damages》 ; a countercharge **—하다** bring a counter〔cross〕 action 《for, against》 ; counterclaim ; countercharge
맞교군 —轎軍 a sedan chair (carried by two men)
맞교대 —交代 two shifts
— 작업(作業) operating with two shifts
맞구멍 a hole (made) through 《a thing》 ; perforation
맞꼭지각 〚수학〛 vertical angles
†**맞다**[1] ① [옳다] (be) right ; correct ¶ 맞는 답안 correct answers // 시간이 잘 맞다 keep good time // 당신 말이 맞다 You are right.
② [적합·조화하다] harmonize with ; be agreeable to ; agree with ; correspond to 〔with〕 ; answer the purpose ; meet 《one's wish》 ; go with ; match ¶ 격에 맞는 생활 a living harmonized with incomes // 가풍에 맞다 conform with a family custom 〔tradition〕 // 도리에 맞다 stand to reason // 그 타이는 이 양복에 맞지 않는다 That tie doesn't go with the suit. // 합창 연습을 했지만 박자나 음정이 전혀 맞지 않았다 We had choral practice, but we were off the beat and out of tune.
③ [취미·음식이] suit ; be suitable ; be agreeable ¶ 마음에 맞는 여자 a girl after one's heart // 입에 맞다 suit one's palate〔taste〕 ; be palatable ; be to one's taste // 아마도 나는 이런 일에는 맞지 않는 것 같다 Maybe I'm not cut out for this type of work.
④ [물건이] fit ; suit ; be suited ; become (어울리다) ¶ 발에 맞는 구두 fitting shoes // 몸에 맞는 양복 a well-fitting coat // 딱 맞다 fit perfectly ; fit like a glove ; fit to a T〔nicety〕 // (옷을) 잘 맞도록 지어 주시오 Be sure to make me a good fit.
⑤ [합치하다] agree with ; be congruous ; be in accord 《with》 ; tally 《with》 ; be compatible ¶ 마음에 맞는 친구 a congenial friend // 그의 말은 사실과 맞지 않다 His statement does not tally with the facts.
⑥ [수지가] pay ; be profitable ¶ 수지맞는 장사 a paying business ; a good bargain
⑦ [적중] hit ; tell ; catch ¶ 총알이 전부 맞았다 All shots told. // 오늘의 일기예보는 맞았다 Today's weather-forecast proved right. // 총알이 표적의 한가운데에 맞았다 The bullet hit the target right in the center. // 당신도 총을 맞았습니까 You got hit, too ? // 예언이 맞았다 The prophecy came true.
‡**맞다**[2] ① [사람을] receive ; welcome ; greet ; hail 《a person as a leader》 ; meet ; invite 《a person》 in ¶ 사람을 반가이 맞다 welcome 《a person》 ; receive 《a person》 with delight // 아내를 맞다 take a wife ; marry 《a woman》 // 양자를 맞다 adopt a son // 새 선생님을 맞다 have a new teacher come
② [날을] greet ¶ 새해를 맞다 greet the New Year // 이팔 청춘을 맞다 attain one's sixteen years // 서기 2000년을 맞다 enter upon A. D. 2000.
③ [비·바람·눈 따위] be exposed to ; expose oneself to ¶ 비를 맞다 be exposed to rain // 찬 바람을 맞아 취기에서 깨다 air oneself to take off the effects of drink // 그건 네가 벼락에 맞을 가능성보다 더 희박해 That's even slimmer than your chance of being struck by a lightning.
④ [매를] be struck ; be knocked ; be beaten ; be whipped ; be lashed ; be flogged ¶ 종아리를 맞다 be whipped on the calves // 뺨을 맞다 be boxed on the ears ; be slapped across the face // 팔에 총알을 맞다 be shot in the arm
⑤ [도둑을 당하다] be robbed ; have 《a thing》 stolen〔swiped, pilfered〕 ; [퇴짜를] get rejected ; be turned down ; [야단을] be scolded ; get a scolding ; be called on the carpet 《미》
맞닥뜨리다 be faced with ; be confronted with ; happen to meet ; fall across ; come plump upon ; come face to face ; run up

against ; come across ¶ 어려운 문제에 맞닥뜨리다 be faced with a difficult problem // 막다른 골목에 맞닥뜨리다 run 〔come〕 right into a dead end // 길에서 사람을 맞닥뜨리다 come across 《a person》 on the street // 외나무 다리에서 원수를 맞닥뜨리다 encounter an enemy on a log bridge

맞닥치다 encounter ; come face to face with ¶ 난관에 맞닥치다 be confronted with a difficult problem ; hit〔run into〕 a snag // 일요일과 축제일이 맞닥치다 a holiday falls on Sunday

맞담 a stone wall

맞담배 ¶ 맞담배 피우다〔질하다〕 smoke to another person's face ; sit smoking together

맞당기다 pull〔drag, tug, haul〕 from both sides ; draw〔pull〕 each other ¶ 줄을 맞당기다 tug a rope from both sides // 줄이 맞당겨 끊어지다 a rope is pulled apart // 해와 달이 지구를 맞당긴다 The earth feels the pull of the sun and the moon.

맞닿다 come in contact with each other ; touch (with) each other ¶ 하늘과 바다가 맞닿다 sky and water merge into each other // 음극과 양극이 맞닿다 the anode and the cathode are in contact

맞대다 face〔confront〕 (each other) ; bring face to face with ; bring in touch with ¶ 맞대고 face to face ; vis-à-vis ; to 《a person's》 face ; in the presence 《of a person》 // 맞대고 욕하다 abuse 《a person》 to his face // 맞대놓고 칭찬하다 praise 《a person》 to his face // 당신과 맞대고 앉았던 사람은 누구요 Who is your vis-à-vis ? // 그들과 맞대고 앉아 서로 쳐다봤다 They sat face to face and looked at each other.

맞대매 a play-off ; a finish fight ; the finals ; the final game〔contest, match〕 **—하다** play off ; play the finals

맞대면 —對面 a face-to-face interview 〔confrontation〕 **—하다** interview〔confront〕 face to face

맞대하다 come face to face with ; confront 〔meet〕 each other ; stand opposite each other ¶ 맞대하는 각 the opposite angle

맞돈 cash (payment) ; hard cash ; ready money ¶ 맞돈을 내다 pay in cash ; pay on the spot ; pay down ; present ready money // 맞돈으로 사다〔팔다〕 buy〔sell〕 《a thing》 for cash ; purchase〔sell〕 outright // 맞돈으로 거래하다 deal 《things》 in cash

맞들다 ① [마주들다] lift together ; hold up 《a thing》 together ¶ 책상을 맞들다 lift a table together
② [협력하다] cooperate ; unite strength 〔efforts〕 ; work together

맞뚫다 bore〔penetrate〕 straight through ; penetrate each other

맞먹다 be a match for ; match ; be as good as ; be equal to ; equal ; rival ; [···에 상당하다] be equivalent to ; be worth ¶ 맞먹는 자가 없다 have no equal 〔match, parallel〕 ; be without a match 〔peer〕 ; be unrivaled ; be peerless // 영어 실력이 그와 맞먹는 자가 없다 There is no one who can match him in his ability in English. // 그 시절의 100원은 지금의 1000원에 맞먹는다 One hundred *won* of those days is worth one thousand *won* now.

맞모금 a diagonal (line) ¶ 맞모금을 긋다 draw a diagonal (line)

맞물다 ① [이가] bite each other ; 〖치과〗 occlude ② [톱니바퀴 따위가] mesh together ; (inter)lock ; engage 《gears》 ; put into gear ¶ X의 톱니바퀴가 Y 톱니바퀴와 맞물었다 The wheel X engages with the wheel Y.

맞물리다 [기어가] go in gear ; gear 《into, with》 ; engage 《with》 ; set the tooth ¶ 기어가 맞물리지 않다 get out of gear // 윗니와 아랫니가 맞물리다 occlude

맞물림 〖기계〗 gearing ; engagement (기어 따위의) ; bite ; 〖건축〗 toothing ; 〖치과〗 occlusion

맞바꾸다 interchange ; exchange 《one thing for another》 ; barter〔trade〕 《A for B》 ; truck ; trade by barter ¶ 책과 공책을 맞바꾸다 exchange〔truck〕 a book for a notebook // 쌀과 건축자재를 맞바꾸다 barter〔trade〕 rice for building〔construction〕 materials

맞바느질하다 sew with two needles

맞바둑 an unhandicapped match of checkers ; checker players of equal skill ¶ 맞바둑을 두다 play checkers on an even basis

맞바람 a head〔contrary〕 wind ; an adverse wind ; a foul〔a dead, a cross, an unfavorable〕 wind ¶ 강한 맞바람 a dead noser // 배는 맞바람 때문에 발이 묶이었다 The ship was wind-bound.

맞바리 resale of firewood〔brushwood〕

맞받다 [정면으로] receive〔face〕 head-on ; [호응] respond at once ; [들이받다] crash head-on ; crash into each other ¶ 태양빛을 맞받다 receive the direct sunlight // 두 사람이 이마를 맞받다 two people bang their heads into each other

맞받이 an opposite side

맞발기 commercial records kept by buyer and seller alike

맞배지기 〖씨름〗 counter-lifting

맞벌이 working together (for a living) ; working in double harness ; the joint bread-winning 《of husband and wife》 **—하다** work together for a living ; earn a livelihood together ; work〔run〕 in double harness ¶ 부모가 맞벌이하는 집안의 아이 a door-key child ; a latchkey child〔kid, boy, girl〕 // 우리는 맞벌이 부부입니다 Both of us bring home the bacon〔groceries〕.
— 가정 a dual〔two〕-income family — 부

부 husband and wife both working〔contributing to the family income〕; two-paycheck couple
맞벽 the outer layer of a two-layer wall
맞보기 clear glasses ; plane glasses
맞보다 watch each other ; look at each other ; look each other in the face ¶ 맞보고 웃다 smile at each other∥그저 맞보기만 하고 아무 말도 하지 않는다 They are just watching each other without saying a word.
맞부딪다 hit〔scrape against〕 each other
맞부딪치다 hit against ; run into〔against〕; strike〔dash〕 against ; crash〔smash〕 into ; collide with ¶ 버스와 트럭이 맞부딪치다 a bus collides with a truck ; a bus and a truck run into each other
맞붙다 stick〔cling, glue〕 together ¶ 맞붙어 싸우다 come to grips with each other ; grapple with each other∥두 점포가 맞붙어 있다 The two shops stand close to each other. ∥그들은 언제나 맞붙어 다닌다 They always stick together. ∥눈꺼풀이 맞붙어 떨어지지 않는다 I cannot open my eyes. /They are glued together.
맞붙들다 catch〔hold〕 together〔each other〕; detain each other ; help each other ; 〖권투〗 clinch ¶ 어깨를 양쪽에서 맞붙들다 hold 《a person》 by both shoulders
맞붙이 ① [대면] an interview ; a face-to-face meeting ; a direct negotiation
② [옷] a lined garment without filling of cotton
맞붙이다 ① [붙이다] stick〔plaster, affix〕 together ¶ 종이 두 장을 맞붙이다 put two sheets of paper together
② [대면시키다] bring face to face
맞붙잡다 seize〔grasp〕 each other
맞비겨떨어지다 balance ; come out even ; both ends meet ¶ 셈이 맞비겨떨어지다 the accounts balance
맞상 —床 a table for two **—하다** dine à deux〔tête-à-tête〕《프》
맞상대 —相對 direct confrontation ; a man-to-man fight ; a single(-handed) combat〔fight〕; a straight fight
맞서다 ① [마주서다] stand opposite each other ; face〔confront〕 each other
② [버티다] hold one's own《against one's antagonist》; stand against ; hold out against《the government forces》; defy ; pit oneself against ; be pitted against each other ¶ 어른에게 맞서다 defy one's elders〔superiors〕; turn upon one's elders∥서로 맞서서 양보하지 않는다 Neither would yield to the other in their rivalry.
맞선 an interview〔a meeting〕 with a view to marriage ; a marriage meeting ¶ 맞선 보다 see each other with a view to marriage ; have an interview with a prospective bride〔bridegroom〕∥네가 맞선을 보았다는 소문이 있는데 I hear you were formally introduced to a prospective wife.
맞소송 —訴訟 a counter-suit〔-action, complaint〕
맞수 —手 a match ; an equal ; a peer ¶ 장기의 맞수 one's equal in chess
맞쐬다 compare《A with B》; collate〔contrast〕《A with B》; set《one thing》 against《another》
맞아들이다 show〔usher〕《a person》 in
맞아떨어지다 tally ; be correct ¶ 계산이 맞아떨어지다 a calculation is correct ; the figures tally∥내 계산과 네 계산이 맞아떨어진다 My figures tally〔check〕 with yours. ∥네 추측이 정확하게 맞아떨어졌다 Your guess was right on the money. /Your guess was right on the nose.
맞아죽다 be struck dead ; be beaten to death ; be killed by a blow ; [총에] be shot dead〔to death〕
맞욕 —辱 counter-abuse ; answering back with abuse ; calling names right back again **—하다** call names back ; answer back with abuse
맞은 바람 a headwind ⇨ 맞바람
맞은 바래기 the opposite side〔place〕; the other side ¶ 맞은 바래기의〔에〕 in front of ; on the other side ; right over against ∥그의 집은 교회의 맞은 바래기에 있다 His house stands opposite〔over against〕 the church.
†**맞은편** the opposite side ; the other side ; the opposite〔other〕 party (상대편) ¶ 강 맞은편 the other side of the river ; across the river∥길 맞은편 집 a house across the road∥맞은편 팀 the opposite team∥바람이 맞은 편에서 불어 오다 have a headwind
맞이 meeting ; greeting ; reception ; welcoming ; hail **—하다** go to meet ; meet ; greet ; receive ; welcome ¶ 웃는 낯으로 맞이하다 greet《a person》 with a smile ; smile a welcome to∥환호성으로 맞이하다 receive《a person》 with cheers ; hail《a winner》∥이팔 청춘을 맞이하다 attain one's sixteen years∥새해를 맞이하다 greet the New Year∥오늘로서 2001년을 맞이한다 Today we enter upon the A. D. 2001.
맞잡다 ① [서로 잡다] hold together ; hold each other ¶ 손을 맞잡다 hold hands∥손을 맞잡고 울다 take each other's hand and weep∥책상을 맞잡아 들다 lift a table together∥서로 맞잡고 싸우다 come to grips with each other
② [협동] cooperate《with》; work together ; help each other ; get together ; help out ¶ 일을 맞잡아 하다 cooperate in getting a job done
맞잡이 an equal ; a match ; a peer ¶ 장기의 맞잡이 a match in chess

맞장구치다 [동의] chime in with others ; echo another's words ; fall in with 《a person's》 views ; make oneself agreeable to another ; dance to another's tune〔pipe〕 ☞ 《 p. 772 》

맞적수 —敵手 a match ; an equal ; a peer

맞절 mutual bowing ; bowing to each other **—하다** bow to each other ; exchange bows ; greet each other

맞접다 fold together

†**맞추다** ① [조립하다] fix into ; assemble ; frame ; put together ¶ 기계를 맞추다 build〔construct, frame〕 a machine ; assemble〔put together〕 a machine // 책상에 다리를 맞추다 put legs on a table // 자동차를 맞추다 assemble an auto // 분해했던 시계를 맞추다 reassemble a watch // 입을 맞추다 kiss 《each other》 ; give 《each other》 a kiss // 재료를 맞추어 집을 짓다 build materials into a house
② [맞게 하다] set 《it》 (right) ; make 《it》 tally ; correct 《it》 ; put 《a thing》 to rights ¶ 시계를 시보에 맞추다 set a watch by the time signal // 수지를 맞추다 balance one's income and outlay ; make both ends meet // 계산을 맞추다 correct one's calculation ; tally one's figures // 숫자를 맞추다 check figures
③ [적합시키다] adjust ; adapt ; conform ; square ; set ; fit ; suit ; tune ; match 《colors》 (배합) ¶ 안경 도수를 맞추다 adjust one's lens prescription // 자신을 환경에 맞추다 adjust〔accommodate〕 oneself to one's circumstances // 망원경을 눈에 맞추다 adjust〔set〕 a telescope to one's eye // 양복을 몸에 맞추어 만들다 have a suit made to measure〔order〕 // 구두를 발에 맞추어 짓다 make shoes to measure // 악대의 연주에 맞추어 행진하다 march to the playing of the band // 관습에 맞추어 행동하다 conform to custom // 라디오를 런던 방송에 맞추다 tune in the radio to London // 비위를 맞추다 humor〔please, flatter〕 《a person》 ; make oneself agreeable to 《a person》 // 곡조를 맞추다 tune (up) ; put in tune ; attune // 피아노에 맞추어 노래하다 sing with piano accompaniment // 음악에 맞추어 춤추다 dance to the music // 넥타이를 옷에 맞추다 match tie to suit // 나의 휴일의 계획을 너와 맞추겠다 I'll fit my holiday plan in with yours.
④ [주문] order ¶ 맞추어 만든 made to order ; custom-made // 구두를〔양복을〕 맞추다 order shoes〔clothes〕 made
⑤ [약속] promise ; reserve ; arrange ; set ; appoint ¶ 날짜를 맞추다 fix〔appoint, set〕 a date for ; name a date 《for》
⑥ [알아맞히다] guess ; figure out 《a problem》 ; surmise ¶ 나 어디 있는지 맞춰 봐 Guess where I am !

맞춤법 orthography ; the rules of spelling ; orthographical rules
— 통일안 a draft for unified spelling system **— 학자** an orthographer **한글 —** the spelling of *Hangul* ; the rules of Korean spelling〔orthography〕 **현행 —** the current spelling system

맞혼인 —婚姻 [비용을 양분하는] a marriage with equal share of expenses between the two families ; [중매 없는] a consensual marriage

맞흥정 face-to-face bargaining〔chaffering, haggling〕 **—하다** make a direct 〔buyer-to-seller〕 bargain ; bargain〔chaffer, haggle〕 《with a tradesman》 directly ; make a deal without a broker

***맞히다** ① [명중] hit 《the mark》 ; tell ; guess right (알아 맞히다) ¶ 표적을 맞히다 make a bull's eye // 잘 맞히다 make a good hit // 못 맞히다 miss the mark ; guess wrong (추측) // 잘 알아 맞히다 guess right ; hit the mark ; make a good guess ; make a good hit ; hit the nail on the board // 제비를 맞히다 win a prize in a lottery // 거의 모든 총알들이 맞혔다 Nearly all the shots told. // 저 점쟁이는 더러 맞힌다 That fortune-teller often makes good hits. // 이 속에 무엇이 들어 있는지 맞혀 보시오 Just guess what are in there〔there in the box〕. // 바로 맞혔어 You guessed it.
② [눈·비 따위를] expose 《to》 ; subject 《to》 ¶ 비를 맞히다 expose 《a thing》 to the rain // 바람을 맞히다 air ; expose 《a thing》 to the air〔wind〕

†**맡기다** ① [물건을] give 《a thing》 into 《a person's》 keeping〔custody〕 ; place 《a thing》 in another's custody ; deposit 《a thing》 with 《a person》 ; place 《a thing》 in〔under〕 《a person's》 charge ; put 《a thing》 in charge of 《a person》 ; leave 《a thing》 with 《a person》 ; give 《a person》 charge of 《a thing》 ; give 《a thing》 in trust ; entrust 《a person》 with 《a thing》 ¶ 돈을 은행에 맡기다 put〔keep〕 money in a bank ; deposit money with a bank // 돈을 맡기다 trust 《a person》 with one's money // 귀중품을 맡기다 place valuables in 《a person's》 custody ; entrust valuables to〔with〕 《a person》 // 짐을 맡기다 check one's baggage 《미》 ; label one's luggage 《영》 // 어린애를 맡기다 commit a child to 《a person's》 care ; leave a child in the care of 《a person》 ; give 《a person》 charge of a child // 그것은 자네의 판단에 맡기네 I leave it to your judgment〔discretion〕. // 그것은 너의 상상에 맡기겠다 I'll leave that to your imagination.
② [위임하다] entrust 《a person》 with 《a matter》 ; entrust 《a matter》 to 《a person》 ; charge 《a person》 with 《a matter》 ; commit 《a matter》 to 《a person's》 care〔management〕 ; commission 《a person》 to 《do something》 ; place 《a mat-

맞장구치는 표현

영·미에서는 상대방과 대화할 때 보통 이야기 끝에 Do[Did] you?, Are[Were] you?, Right, Is it true? 등과 같이 상대방의 이야기에 관심을 갖고 듣는 것이 예의이다.

1 긍정, 찬성

¶ 예. Yes. // 예, 그럼요. Yes, absolutely certain. / That's quite right. / Certainly. / Sure. / Surely. // 물론이지. Why not? / Of course. // 물론 그렇지 않지. Of course not. 《상대방의 부정적인 의견에 동조를 나타냄》 // 그래, 맞아. Right. / That's true [right]. / Exactly. / Absolutely. // 응, 그래. Yes, that's it. / Yes, that's correct. // 알겠습니다. I see. // 나도 동감이야. I think so, too. // 내 생각도 그래. I (absolutely) agree (with you). // 됐어. All right. / OK. // 그렇고 말고. By all means. / Yes, that's quite right. // 기꺼이 해드리겠습니다. With pleasure. // 물론 좋지. Why not? // 됐어. Fine. / Good. // 이 그림은 너무 비싼 것 같아. — 맞아, 동감이야. (그리고 그다지 좋아 보이지도 않아, 그렇지?) I think these paintings are very expensive. — Yes, I agree, (and they really aren't very good, are they?)

2 부정, 반대

¶ 아니오. No. (it isn't.) // 아닙니다, 그럴 리 없어. 《강한 부정》 Probably not! / Impossible. / No way. / Surely not. / Certainly not. / I'm afraid not. / I'm not sure (actually, in fact). / Not really. / No, that's all wrong. / That's not right. // 절대로 안됩니다. 《강한 부정》 By no means. // 절대로 아니다. Not at all. / Never! / I think that's nonsense (I'm afraid). // 네가 틀렸다. You are mistaken [wrong]. // 동의할 수가 없군요. Oh, I don't agree [disagree] (with you). / I can't agree (with you). // 그렇게 생각하지 않습니다. I don't think so. // 상관없어. It doesn't matter. // 농담이겠지, 설마! You must be joking! / You can't mean that.

3 가벼운 응답

① 질문형

¶ 그렇니? Is that so? // 정말이니? Really? / Is that true? / Are you sure?

② 응답형

¶ 요전 날 그녀를 만났었어. — 정말? I have met her the other day. — Did you? [You did?] // 김선생이 외국에 갈거래. — 그가? Mr. Kim is going abroad. — Is he? [He is?] // 나는 어제 부산에 갔었다. — 아, 그래? I went to Pusan yesterday. — Oh, did you? [You did?]

4 불확실, 의심쩍음

¶ 아마도. Maybe. 《미》 / Perhaps. // 아마 그럴거야. I think [suppose] so. // 그럴 것 같군요. It's quite probable. / That's very likely. // 그때 형편에 달린 거지. That [It] depends. // 글쎄, 어떨런지. I'm not quite sure. // 매우 의심스러운데요. That's very doubtful. // 그럴 리 없어. It cannot be true.

5 놀라움

¶ 원, 저런! Oh, dear! / Oh no! / Dear me! 《주로 여성들이 사용》 // 뭐! What! // 이런! Well, well! // 어머, 이를 어째! What a pity! // 그것 참 묘한 일이로군. (That's) very strange! / That's very odd! // 웃기는군. That's funny! // 멋지군. Wonderful! / Great! // 설마. You don't say! // 그럴 리가, 농담이겠지. You're joking. / You must be joking. / You're kidding (me)! / No kidding! // 그거 안됐군. That's too bad.

---

ter》 in the hands of 《a person》; put 《business》 under 《a person's》 charge; authorize; empower 《a person》 to 《do something》; delegate 《authority》 to 《a person》 (대표로서) ¶ 전권을 맡기다 entrust 《a person》 with full powers; give 《a person》 a carte blanche // 책임을 맡기다 place responsibility on 《a person》 // 그렇게 적은 돈으로 이런 큰일을 맡길 데는 없을 거다 You're not going to find anyplace that'll take on a big job like this for so little pay. // 이런 사람들에게 나라를 맡겨 둘 수 없다 We just can't entrust the country to these people.

†**맡다** ① [보관] keep; receive 《a thing》 in trust〔custody〕; take charge of 《things》; take 《a thing》 in charge; be entrusted with 《a thing》; have the custody of 《a thing》; [담당·감독] take〔have〕 charge of; be in charge of; have 《a child》 under one's charge〔care〕; assume the care of 《children》; take care of 《a matter》 ¶ 그 사무를 맡고 있는 사람 a man in charge of the business // 5학년을 맡고 있다 have charge of the fifth-grade class; take care of fifth-grade class // 그

물건은 내가 맡고 있다 The article has been given into my keeping. // 선장은 수천명의 생명을 맡고 있다 The captain has the safety of thousands of lives in his keeping. // 제가 일체의 사무를 맡고 있소 I am entrusted with all business. /All business is left in my charge.

② [허가·인가를] get ; obtain ; receive ; be permitted ; be authorized ; have 《a license》 issued ¶ 허가를 맡다 obtain permission // 여기서 사진을 찍을 때는 당국의 허가를 맡아야 한다 You must apply to the authorities for permission to take a photograph here.

③ [냄새를] smell ; scent ; sniff ¶ 냄새를 맡아보다 give a sniff 《to》 ; sniff 《at》 ; have〔take〕 a smell 《at》 // 냄새를 맡고 돌아다니다 nose about the ground (개가) // 이 장미꽃 냄새 좀 맡아봐요 Just have a smell of this rose.

④ [눈치채다] suspect ; sense ; scent out ; get wind of ; sniff ; smell out ; detect a secret ; get wise 《to》 (미) ; smoke (속) ¶ 그 친구 냄새를 맡은 것 같다 He seems to have got on it.

＊매¹ ① a whip ; a rod ; a cane ; a lash ¶ 매를 때리다 whip ; flog ; lash ; use a rod ; birch ; cane ; horsewhip // 매를 맞다 be whipped〔flogged, birched, caned, horsewhipped, hit, struck, beaten, slapped〕

② [매질] whipping ; flogging ; birching ; caning ; striking ; beating ¶ 심한 매질 a hard whipping ; a good lick // 사정없는 매질 merciless flogging

매² ① [맷돌] a millstone ; a grind mill

② [매통] a wooden grind mill

매³ 〖새〗 a hawk ; a falcon ; Asturus gentilis (학명) ¶ 매눈 같은 hawk-eyed

매⁴ [맵시] figure ; shape ; form ; cast ¶ **몸매** one's figure〔shape〕 ; one's physique ; one's carriage ; a pose // 눈매 a look ; the expression〔cast〕 of one's eyes ; one's eyes

매⁵ quite ; much (the same) ¶ 매한가지다 be much about the same ; come to the same thing after all ; be all the same

매⁶ [염소의 울음 소리] baa ; bleat

매- 每 each ; every ¶ 매주 every week

-매 枚 sheets 《of paper》

매가 買價 a purchase〔buying〕 price

매가 賣價 a sale〔selling〕 price

매가 賣家 a house for sale ; selling a house **—하다** sell a house

매가오리 〖물고기〗 an eagle ray

매각 賣却 sale ; disposal (by sale) ; selling **—하다** dispose of ; sell

— 공고 a public notice of sale **— 대금** proceeds from sale **—손〔익〕** loss〔profit〕 on sale 《of》 **—인(人)** a seller ; a vendor **— 조건** terms of sale **— 통지** a notice of sale

매갈이 removing the hulls from rice ; hulling rice **—하다** remove the hulls from rice ; hull〔husk〕 rice

— 기계 a (rice) huller ; a husker **매갈잇간(間)** a rice-hulling mill

매개 the course (경과) ; the development〔progress〕 of an event (진전) ; the way things are developing (상태) ¶ 매개보다 see how the wind is blowing ; watch the situation〔development of events〕 ; take stock of situation

매개 每個 each one ; every piece ¶ 이 참외는 매개 당 10센트이다 These melons are ten cents apiece.

매개 媒介 intermediation ; mediation ; agency ; intervention **—하다** mediate ; intermediate ; intervene 《between two parties》 ; act as an intermediary ; serve as a medium ; carry 《germs》 (전파하다) ¶ 모기는 때때로 전염병을 매개한다 The mosquito is often a carrier of infectious disease.

— 동물 [병균의] a vector ; a carrier **— 변수** 〖수학〗 parameter **— 세포** an auxiliary cell **—자** a mediator ; an agent ; an intermediary ; a go-between ; a middleman (상업상의) ; [병균의] a carrier ; a vector (곤충)

매개념 媒概念 〖논리〗 the middle concept ; the mean term

＊매개물 媒介物 a medium ; an agency ; [병독의] a carrier ; a vehicle ¶ 전염병의 매개물 a vehicle of infection

매거 枚擧 —하다 enumerate ; count ; reckon ; mention ¶ 일일이 매거할 수 없다 be too numerous to mention ; it is virtually impossible to exhaust 《the list of》

매고 賣高 the amount sold ⇨ 매상고

매고르다 be all alike ; be even ; be of a sort

매골 a bad〔poor〕 appearance〔look〕

매골 埋骨 burial of 《a person's》 ashes **—하다** bury 《a person's》 ashes

매관매직 賣官賣職 corruption in the government personnel administration ; trafficking of official posts ; [엽관 제도] spoils system **—하다** traffic in government positions ; practice pay-off deals for appointive offices

매국 賣國 selling one's country ; betrayal of〔treachery to〕 one's country **—하다** sell〔betray〕 one's country ; be treacherous to one's country ; become a quisling

— 행위 an unpatriotic act

매국노 賣國奴 a traitor (to one's country) ; a betrayer (of one's country) ; a quisling ¶ 매국노가 되다 turn traitor to one's country ; sell〔betray〕 one's country ; become a quisling

매기¹ ① [수퇘지와 암소의 트기] a cross between a boar and a cow

② [트기] a hybrid ; a mongrel ; a

cross ; a half-breed
매기² 〖건축〗 laying rafters down side by side when building a house
매기 買氣 〖증권〗 bullish sentiment ; a buying disposition ; interest
매기 每期 every season〔semester, time, period〕; each term
†**매기다** [값을] charge 《a price》 on 《an article》; appraise ; value ; offer 《a price on an article》 (살 사람이) ; bid (경매에서) ; [점수·등급] give ; grade ¶ 점수를 매기다 score ; give marks ; rate // 등급을 매기다 grade ; graduate ; classify into grade // 값을 비싸게 매기다 put the price high 《on an article》
매기단하다 wind up one's affairs ; deal with the aftermath ; bring 《a matter》 to a conclusion ; put 《things》 in order ; set matters right
매꾸러기 a mischievous child who has to be whipped all the time
†**매끄럽다** (be) smooth ; sleek ; slick ; slippery ; velvety ¶ 매끄러운 표면 smooth surface // 매끄러운 종이 slick 〔sleek〕 paper // 비단처럼 매끄러운 살결 skin as soft〔smooth〕 as silk
매끈거리다 feel slippery
매끈하다 (be) smooth ; sleek ; slick
매끼 a strip of straw rope 《for binding sheaves, faggots》; a binding rope
매나니 ① [빈손] an empty hand ; a bare hand ¶ 매나니로 with empty 〔bare〕 hands ; empty-handed
② [음식] a meal without side dishes ; a simple〔plain〕 diet ; simple food
매너 manners ¶ 테이블 매너 table manners // 매너가 좋은 well-mannered // 매너가 좋다 have good manners
매너리즘 mannerism ¶ 매너리즘에 빠지다 fall into mannerism ; become stereotyped
‡**매년 每年** every year ; yearly ; annually ¶ 매년의 yearly ; annual // 매년 이 때가 되면 눈이 내리기 시작한다 It always begins to snow at this time of year. // 나는 매년 여름이면 부산에서 지낸다 I stay at *Pusan* every summer.
매니저 a manager
매니큐어 (a) manicure ¶ 매니큐어를 바르다 [스스로] manicure ; [남이] have a manicure 《on one's nails》
†**매다¹** [동여매다] tie ; bind ; knot ; fasten ; link ; join ¶ 개를 매다 chain a dog // 구두끈을 매다 tie (up) one's shoes ; tie a shoestring // 머리를 매다 bind one's hair up // 허리띠를 매다 fasten one's belt // 책을 매다 make〔put together〕 a book // 나무에 목을 매다 hang oneself on a tree // 소를 나무에 매다 tie a cow to a tree // 베를 매다 stiffen threads with paste (for weaving) // 안전벨트를 매 주십시오 Please fasten your seat belt. /Please wear your seat belt. /Buckle up.
매다² [김을] weed (out) ; pick weeds out of ; pull weeds ¶ 논〔밭〕의 김을 매다 weed a rice paddy〔corn field〕
매다³ put 《a price》 on
‡**매달 每—** every month ¶ 매달의 monthly // 매달의 지불 monthly payment // 매달 한 번 once a month ; monthly
†**매달다** ① bind up ; truss up ; hang ; suspend ¶ 밧줄로 매달다 suspend 《a thing》 with rope〔string〕 // 목을 매달다 hang 《a person》 on a tree ② [의지하다] depend on ; lean on 《a person for support》; rely upon ③ [일에] tie oneself down to 《a job》; bind〔chain〕 oneself to
†**매달리다** ① be hung ; be suspended ; be tied down ¶ 시체가 나무에 매달려 있다 A dead body is hanging on a tree. ② [붙들다·늘어지다] hang on 《another's neck》; dangle ; cling to 《one's mother's skirt》; hold on to 《a rope》 ¶ 매달린 가족이 많다 have a big family to support
매대기 smearing〔daubing, besmearing〕 all over ¶ 매대기치다 smear〔daub〕 all over // 벽에 진흙을 매대기치다 smear a wall all over with mud // 얼굴에 분을 매대기치다 daub one's face all over with powder ; powder〔paint〕 one's face thick ; put on heavy make-up
매도 罵倒 condemnation ; denunciation ; scathing ; severe criticism ; abuse **—하다** denounce ; decry ; condemn ; criticize severely ; abuse ; rail 《at》; revile 《at》; cry down
매도 賣渡 sale and delivery **—하다** sell (over) ; [어음 따위를] negotiate 《a bill》; sign away
— 계약 a contract for selling **—인(人)** a seller ; 〖법〗 a vendor **— 증서** a bill of sale ; a sales note (매약서) **—품 목록** a bill of parcels **소하물 — 증서** a bill of parcels
매독 梅毒 〖의학〗 syphilis ; a secret disease 《미·속》; pox ¶ 매독성의 syphilitic // 매독에 걸리다 contract〔get, catch〕 syphilis ; become syphilitic
— 환자 a syphilitic (person) **선천성 —** congenital syphilis **양성 —** florid syphilis **유전 —** hereditary syphilis **음성 —** latent syphilis **제 1〔2, 3〕기 —** primary〔secondary, tertiary〕 syphilis
†**매듭** a knot ; a tie ; a joint (대 따위의) ¶ 댓매듭 the node of a bamboo joint // 매듭을 짓다 knot ; make〔tie〕 a knot // 매듭을 풀다 unknot ; untie〔undo〕 a knot // 매듭이 풀리다 a knot comes untied〔off〕
매듭지어지다 [결말이 나다] be settled 〔fixed〕; be concluded ; be completed ; be brought to completion ; be finished ; [타협되다] reach〔arrive at, come to〕 an agreement ; be brought to an agreement ; be arranged
매듭짓다 ① make a knot ; knot ② [끝맺다] conclude ; complete ; put an end

《to》; close ; finish ¶ 일을 매듭짓다 conclude one's work // 일을 벌려놓고 매듭지을 줄을 모른다 He is ready to start a job but never gets it done. // 지금 기획팀에서 그 계획을 매듭짓고 있다 The project team is putting the final touches on the plans.

‡**매력 魅力** fascination ; charm ; magnetic power 《속》; glamor ; attractiveness ¶ 성적 매력 a sex appeal // 여성적인 매력 feminine attraction // 매력 있는 웃음 a bewitching〔captivating〕smile // 매력이 없는 여자 a plain〔homely〕women // 매력이 있다 be fascinating〔charming, attractive, glamorous, bewitching〕// 매력이 없다 have nothing attractive 《about one》; do not appeal 《to》// 매력을 느끼다 be fascinated〔charmed〕《by》// 저 여자는 무엇인가 매력이 있다 She has something attractive about her. /She has the power to charm. // 나에겐 영화가 별로 매력이 없다 The cinema has little attraction for me.

매련쟁이 a stupid fool ; an ass ; a dullard ; a thickhead ; a coward

매련통이 a dull〔stupid〕fellow ; Mr. Thick Head ⇨ 매련쟁이

매료 魅了 ―하다 charm ; fascinate ; captivate ; cast a spell 《on》; hold 《the audience》 spellbound ¶ 그는 독자를 매료했다 He took the readers with him.

매립 埋立 reclamation ; filling-up ―하다 fill in 《a moat》; fill up 《a pond with earth》; reclaim 《land from the sea》; recover 《land from the sea》 ¶ 해면을 매립하다 reclaim foreshore (from the sea)
― 공사 reclaiming〔reclamation〕work 해안 ― reclamation of the foreshore

매립지 埋立地 a reclaimed〔filled, filled-up, filled-in〕land〔ground〕; a land reclaimed from a lake〔the sea〕

매만지다 adjust ; trim ; tidy ¶ 옷 매무새를 매만지다 adjust〔tidy〕oneself // 대머리를 매만지다 pass one's hand over one's baldhead // 머리를 매만지다 tidy〔arrange〕one's disordered hair ; give a smooth to the hair

매맛 the bitters of a whip ¶ 매맛을 보이다 lash ; flog ; whip ; switch 《a boy》 (with a cane) ; give 《a person》 a hiding 《구》// 매맛을 보다 be whipped〔lashed〕; get the cane ; get a hiding 《구》// 매맛을 알아야 게으름을 피우지 않겠지 I'll flog laziness out of you !

매맞다 [매로] get flogged ; [언어 맞다] be whipped ; be hit ; be struck〔beaten〕; be thrashed ; be knocked ; get licked ; get beans 《속》 ¶ 또 매맞고 싶니 Do you want another thrashing ?

†**매매 賣買** buying and selling ; purchase and sale ; [거래] dealing ; trade ; transaction ; a bargain ; traffic ; a deal 《속》 ―하다 buy〔purchase〕and sell ; trade 《in》; deal ; traffic 《in》; market ¶ 투표의 매매 traffic in votes // 매매 계약하다 strike〔close〕a bargain ; close a contract // 매매 계약을 취소하다 cancel a contract
― 가격 sale price ―고 sales amount ; a turnover ― 당사자 parties to a sale ― 보고서 a bought and sold note ― 수속 transaction procedure ― 조건 sales terms ; terms of sale〔bargaining, transaction〕― 조직 a market organization ― 증서 a bill of sale ; a contract note ― 차익금 a margin ― 통제 marketing control 견본 ― a sale by sample 부정 ― an illegal〔illicit〕bargain 선물 ― a futures sale〔trading〕; a forward bargain 위탁 ― consignment sales and purchases 인신 ― human traffic 직접 ― a direct sale 현금 ― a cash sale 현물 ― a spot sale〔transaction〕

매매 계약 賣買契約 a sales contract ; a bargain ¶ 매매 계약을 하다 make a contract 《with》; conclude a sale
―자 a bargainer ―증 a contract note

***매머드** a mammoth
― 기업 a mammoth enterprise ― 도시 a megalopolis

매명 賣名 self-advertisement ; self-publicity ―하다 publicize〔advertise〕oneself ; seek publicity ; court〔seek〕notoriety ¶ 매명을 위하여 in order to have one's name up ; for publicity's sake ; as a publicity stunt // 매명을 일삼다 strive for publicity ; hanker after notoriety
―가 a self-advertiser ; a seeker of notoriety〔publicity〕; a publicity seeker ― 행위 publicity stunts ; playboy tactics

매명 每名 each〔every〕person ; per person

매목 埋木 bog〔fossil〕-wood ; lignite
― 세공 fossil-wood work ; mosaic

매몰 埋沒 burying ―하다 bury ; be〔lie〕buried 《in the ground, under debris》 ¶ 눈 속에 매몰되다 be buried under snow

매몰스럽다 (be) cold ; unkind ; hard ; harsh ; cruel ; heartless ; callous ¶ 매몰스럽게 heartlessly ; cruelly ; coldly ; harshly ; cold-heartedly // 매몰스러운 태도 a cool〔cold〕attitude ; a distant air // 매몰스럽게 거절하다 give a point-blank〔flat〕refusal

매몰차다 (be) very unkind ; very cold ; hard ; harsh ; callous ; heartless

매몰하다 (be) cold ; icy ; cold-hearted ; unfeeling ; curt 《answer》; harsh ¶ 매몰하게 cold-heartedly ; icily ; curtly ; harshly ; pitilessly ; cruelly ; bitterly // 매몰하게 굴다 treat 《a person》 coldly〔in a cold way〕; deal hardly with ; be unkind to ; be hard upon 《a person》; behave coldly toward 《a person》; be mean〔unfair〕to 《a person》

매무새 dress ; attire ; (personal) appearance ¶ 매무새가 좋다〔나쁘다〕 be well〔ill〕dressed // 그녀는 옷 매무새가 형편 없다 She is slovenly in her dress.

매무시 primping ; dressing up —하다 primp ; primp oneself ; tidy (up) ; dress ; tidy up oneself ¶ 매무시가 단정하다 keep oneself neat and trim ; be careful about one's personal appearance ; look neat and tidy

매문 賣文 literary journeywork ; selling one's writing —하다 sell one's writing ; make a living with one's pen ; peddle out one's knowledge ¶ 매문을 업으로 하다 be engaged in literary journeywork

—가 a literary hack ; a hack writer ; a commercial author ; a penny-a-liner

매물 賣物 an article for sale ; offerings ; For Sale (게시) ¶ 매물로 내놓다 put 《a thing》 on the market ; offer〔put up〕《a thing》 for sale ; place 《a thing》 on sale

*매미 〖곤충〗 a cicada ; a cicala ; a locust 《미》 ¶ 매미 우는 소리 the shrill chirrup of a cicada // 매미의 허물 the cast-off shell of a cicada // 매미가 울다 a cicada sings

매미나방 〖곤충〗 a gipsy〔gypsy〕 moth ; Lymantria dispar chosenensis

매방 買方 a buyer ; a purchaser ; 〖증권〗 bulls ; longs

— 선택 〖증권〗 buyer's option — 시장 buyer's〔buying〕 market 약세 — 〖증권〗 a stale〔weak〕 bull

매방 賣方 a seller ; the selling side ; 〖증권〗 a bear

— 과다 sellers over — 선택 〖증권〗 seller's option — 연합 〖증권〗 a bear pool

매번 每番 every〔each〕 time ; very often ; always ; frequently ; constantly ¶ 거기 갈 때마다 나는 매번 그런 일을 당한다 That sort of thing always happens to me when I go there. /Every time I go there, that sort of thing always happens to me. // 매번 폐를 끼쳐 죄송합니다 I am sorry to trouble you so frequently.

*매복 埋伏 ambush(ment) ; lying in ambush〔wait〕 —하다 ambush ; lie in ; wait in ambush for ; waylay ; conceal oneself in ambush ; lie concealed ¶ 매복했다가 습격하다 attack 《enemy》 from ambush

—치(齒) an impacted tooth

매부 妹夫 the husband of one's sister ; one's brother-in-law

매부리[1] [매를 부리는 이] a falconer ; a hawker

매부리[2] [사람] a hawk's beak ; hawk bill ¶ 매부리 같은 hawk-billed // 매부리 징 a kind of hobnail (구두의)

—코 a hooked nose ; a Roman nose ; an aquiline nose

매사 每事 every matter〔affair, business〕 ; every circumstance ; each undertaking ; each plan ¶ 매사에 in every business〔matter, affair〕

매사 媒辭 〖논리〗 the mean term

매사냥 hawking ; falconry —하다 go hawking ; hawk

매사냥꾼 a falconer ; a hawker ; a falcon hunter.

매사불성 每事不成 —하다 fail in every attempt

매삭 每朔 every〔each〕 month ; monthly

매상 買上 purchase ; buying ; procurement (정부의) —하다 purchase ; buy

매상 賣上 sales ; proceeds ; receipts ¶ 오늘은 50,000원의 매상을 올렸다 The sales of today amounted to 50,000 won. // 오늘 매상은 어제보다 많았다 Today's sale was larger than yesterday's.

— 원장(元帳) a sales〔sold〕 ledger ; a customer's ledger — 장부 a sales book — 전표 a sales ship 정부 — 가격 the Government's purchasing〔buying〕 price

매상 계정 賣上計定 sales account

—서 account sales 《A/S》 ¶ 매상 계정서는 결재 송금액과 함께 매월 제출해 주십시오 Account sales is to be rendered monthly together with a remittance in settlement.

매상고 賣上高 the sales ; the amount sold ; the proceeds of sale ; the turnover ; the returns ; the takings ¶ 그 날의 매상고 the day's proceeds // 그날의 매상고는 5만원이었다 The sales for the day totaled 50,000 *won*.

당기(當期) — the sales for this term 순— the net sales 총— the gross sales〔proceeds〕

매석 賣惜 an indisposition to sell ; holding back ; restricting sales —하다 be unwilling〔indisposed〕 to sell ; hold back 《goods from selling》 ; restrict sales

매설 埋設 laying —하다 lay (under the ground) ¶ 수도관〔가스관〕을 매설하다 lay water-pipes〔gas-pipes〕 underground // 지뢰를 매설하다 lay〔charge〕 a (land) mine

*매섭다 (be) fierce ; severe ; strict ; stern ; sharp ¶ 매서운 눈초리 hard eyes ; fierce eyes // 매섭게 생기다 look sharp〔fierce〕

매세 賣勢 —하다 strut about in borrowed plumes ; bluff under the shelter of another's influence

매소 賣笑 prostitution ⇨ 매음(賣淫)

⁑매수 買收 purchase ; [사람을] bribing ; buying off —하다 buy ; [사람을] buy off ; bribe ; win over (by bribery) ¶ 사설 철도를 매수하다 buy the private railways // 부자에게 매수되다 sell oneself to the rich // 투표를 매수하다 buy votes

— 가격 a purchase price — 계획 a purchasing plan — 운동 an agitation〔effort〕 for buying off〔up〕 —자 a fixer — 전술 money tactics —책 a buying-out policy — 투표 a venal vote — 행위 [선거 때 따위의] corrupt practices

매수 買受 buying over —하다 buy over ; take over ; purchase

— 대금 the price (paid) —인 a purchaser ; a buyer ; a vendee
매수 枚數 the number of leaves〔sheets〕
매스껍다 feel sick ; feel nausea ⇨ 메스껍다
매스 게임 mass calisthenics
매스 미디어 mass (communication) media
매스 커뮤니케이션, 매스컴 mass communication ; the press ; journalism ¶ 매스컴을 경원하다 avoid press publicity // 매스컴에 타고 싶어하다 seek press publicity // 매스컴에 많이 타다〔타지 못하다〕 receive much〔little〕 publicity from the press
— 기 관 the mass〔communication〕 media ; the mass media (of communication) ; the means〔channels〕 of mass communication
매스 프러덕션 mass〔quantity〕 production
매시 每時 every hour ; per hour ¶ 매시 600킬로의 속도로 at a speed of 600 kilometers per hour // 매시 정각 Every hour on the hour // 서울에서 출발은 오전 7시 30분에 시작하여 오후 8시 30분까지 매시 30분마다 한 편씩 있습니다 동경에서는 오전 8시부터 오후 9시까지 매시 정각 출발합니다 The first flight from *Seoul* is at 7 : 30 in the morning and thereafter every hour at 30 minutes past the hour until 8 : 30 in the evening. From Tokyo, the plane departs every hour on the hour from 8 a.m. until 9 p.m.
매시근하다 (be) languid ; wearisome ; tired ; worn out ; exhausted ¶ 매시근해서 일하기가 싫다 I feel too lazy to work.
매식 買食 dining out ; eating at a restaurant〔an inn〕 —하다 dine out ; board out ; be boarded out ; eat at a restaurant〔an inn〕; eat《one's meal》out《미》
매실 梅實 a plum
—주 plum wine
매실매실하다 (be) sly ; crafty ; foxy
매씨 妹氏 [남의] your〔his〕 esteemed sister ; [자기의] one's elder sister
매암 돌다 spin (oneself) round ; whirl
매암 돌리다 spin〔whirl〕《a person》round
매암매암 chirping ¶ 매미가 매암매암 울다 A cicada is singing. /A locust is chirping.
매암쇠 [맷돌의] the rynd (of a millstone)
매약 賣約 a sales contract —하다 conclude〔strike〕 a bargain ; contract to sell ¶ 매약필 "Sold"
매약 賣藥 a patent medicine ; a drug —하다 sell〔deal in〕 patent medicines
—상 a chemist《영》; a druggist《미》— 행상인 a nostrum vendor ; a medicine peddler〔pedlar〕
매양 每樣 always ; all the time ; every time ; constantly ¶ 그는 매양 같은 넥타이만 매고 있다 He always wears the same tie. // 그 여자는 매양 아름답기만 하다 She is as beautiful as ever.
매연 煤煙 smoke ; sooty smoke
— 농도계 a smoke indicator — 차량 a vehicle〔car, bus〕 that discharges exhaust fumes
매염 媒染 mordancy ; color-fixing by means of a mordant ¶ 매염성의 mordant // 매염제를 사용하다 mordant《a thing》; treat《a thing》with a mordant
—성 mordancy — 염료 mordant dyes〔dyestuffs〕 —제 a mordant ; a fixative
매옴하다 (be) rather hot〔pungent〕 (매움하다)
† 매 우 very ; so ; most ; exceedingly ; extraordinarily ; greatly ; remarkably ; much ; much too ¶ 매우 아름다운 여자 a very〔most〕 beautiful woman // 매우 기쁘다〔재미있다〕 be very glad〔interesting〕 // 매우 덥다 exceedingly〔unusually, extremely〕 hot // 매우 감사하고 있다 be much obliged《to you》// 네가 없으면 매우 외롭다 I miss you very much. // 매우 더워서 상의를 벗었다 It was so hot that I took my coat off. // 매우 즐거웠습니다 I enjoyed every minute of it.
매우 梅雨 the long spell of rain in early summer
—기 the rainy〔wet〕 season
매욱하다 (be) stupid ; foolish ⇨ 미욱하다
매운 바람 a sharp〔biting〕 wind
매운탕 a pepper pot soup ; a hot chowder
매움하다 (be) rather hot〔spicy, sharp, pungent〕
매워하다 find《it》hot〔spicy, sharp, pungent〕; feel《it》too hot ¶ 고추를 많이 치지 않았는데 국을 매워한다 Although I didn't put much red pepper in the soup, he finds it too hot.
*매월 每月 every month ; each month ; monthly ¶ 매월 한 번 once a month ; monthly
매음 賣淫 prostitution ; harlotry —하다 practice prostitution ; prostitute oneself
—녀 a harlot ; a prostitute ; a streetwalker〔street girl〕 — 반대 운동 an antivice campaign — 방지법 the Anti-Prostitution Act — 행위 (an act of) prostitution
매음굴 賣淫窟 a house of prostitution〔ill repute, ill fame〕 ; a disorderly house ; a bawdy house ; a cathouse《속》
매이다 be tied ; be fastened ; [일에] be bound up with ; [속박] be chained ; [목을] be strangled ; be hanged ¶ 구두끈이 매이다 shoelaces are fastened ; one's shoes are tied // 나뭇가지에 목을 매이다 be hanged on the branch of a tree // 일에 매이다 be tied down to a job ; be busy ; have one's hands full ; be taken up with one's duties
매인 每人 each person ; every person ¶ 매인당 for each person ; per head ; per capita // 매인당 두개씩 지급하다 supply〔furnish〕 them two apiece
매인 목숨 not being one's own boss ;

being an underling〔a slave〕; an underling ; a slave ¶ 매인 목숨이다 I am not my own boss.

†**매일 每日** every day ; each day ; daily ¶ 매일의 daily ; everyday // 매일 있는 일 daily happenings〔events〕// 매일의 일 daily works // 매일 매일 day after day ; from day to day ; day in (and) day out // 매일 같이 almost every day // 매일 밤 every evening〔night〕; nightly ; night after night

매일반 一般 all the same ; much the same ¶ 엎어지나 잦혀지나 매일반이다 It is six of one and half a dozen of the other. // 오늘 출발하나 내일 출발하나 매일반이다 It makes little difference whether I set out today or tomorrow.

매입 買入 buying ; purchase **—하다** buy ; purchase ; lay in ¶ 대량 매입하다 lay in a large stock of 《coal》// 신선한 야채를 다량 매입하다 lay in a good store of vegetables

— 가격 the purchase〔purchasing〕price ; the cost price ; the buying cost **— 상환** redemption〔repayment〕by purchase **고본 —** "Second-Hand Books Bought"

매자 媒子 a matchmaker ; a go-between ; a mediator

매자기 〖식물〗 a kind of bulrush〔clubrush〕; Scirpus maritimus (학명)

매자나무 〖식물〗 the Korean barberry ; Berberis Koreana (학명)

매자목 賣子木 〖식물〗 a snowbell ; Styrax japonica (학명)

매작지근하다 be tepid〔cool, lukewarm〕; be not warm enough

매잡이¹ ① [매듭의] degree of tightness of a knot ② [일의] finishing up ; winding up 《a job》

매잡이² [사냥] hunting falcon ; [사람] a falcon hunter **—하다** hunt falcon

⁑**매장 埋葬** burial ; interment ; [사회적] social ostracism **—하다** bury ; inter ; lay 《the body》 to rest ; entomb ; [사회적으로] ostracize ; expel from society ; treat 《a person》 as a social outcast ¶ 그의 유해는 여기에 매장된다 His remains will be buried〔interred〕here.

—비 cost of burial **—식** the burial service〔rites〕; the obsequies **— 신고** the report of a burial **—지** a burial〔burying〕ground〔place〕; [묘지] a cemetery ; a graveyard ; [고대 도시 또는 유사 전 유적의] a necropolis **— 허가증** a burial permit〔certificate〕 **가—** temporary burial

매장 埋藏 burying underground ; deposits (of minerals) **—하다** [묻다] hide underground ; bury in the ground ; [묻혀 있다] lie underground ; be deposited

—량 [석탄의] coal reserves ; (the estimated amount of) coal deposits **—물** buried property ; 〖법〗 treasure trove ; deposits (광물의) **— 지대** a field ; a (gold〔coal〕) field

매장 賣場 a counter ; a store ; a shop ; a place which sells

— 감독 a shopwalker 《영》; a floorwalker 《미》 **— 판매원** a sales clerk

매점 賣店 a booth ; a stand ; a stall ¶ 매점을 내다 install a booth ; set up a stand

신문 — a newsstand **역—** a station stall **학교 —** a school store 《미》 **협동 소비 조합 —** a co-op store **회사 —** a company store

매점 買占 cornering ; a corner 《on goods》; 〖주식〗 a bull corner **—하다** corner ; buy up ¶ 쌀을 매점하다 corner rice ; make a corner in rice // 부근의 토지를 매점하다 buy up all lands in the neighborhood

—자 a corner man ; a cornerer ; a rigger ; a regrater ; a monopolist **시장 —** market cornering

매점매석 買占賣惜 cornering and hoarding ¶ 매점매석 행위를 단속하다 crack down on practices of cornering and hoarding

매정스럽다 (be) callous ; hard-hearted ; unfeeling ; pitiless ; harsh ; cruel ¶ 매정스럽게도 heartlessly ; cruelly ; be cold-hearted enough to // 매정스럽게 굴다 be hard on ; treat coldly

매제 妹弟 a younger sister's husband ; a brother-in-law

매조지 (putting on) the finishing touches ; the finish

⁑**매주 每週** every week ; each week ; weekly ¶ 매주 화요일 every Tuesday

매주 買主 a buyer ; a purchaser ; a vendee

— 시장 a buyer's market

매주 賣主 a seller ; a vendor

— 시장 a sellers' market

매죽 梅竹 a plum tree and a bamboo

매지구름 a rain cloud

매지근하다 (be) tepid ; lukewarm ⇨ 미지근하다

매지매지 《divide something》 into several parts

매직 [마술] magic

— 아이 [라디오 따위의] a magic eye **— 유리** one-way glass **— 잉크** (a kind of) marking ink ; [상표] Magic ink

매진 賣盡 selling out ; a sellout **—하다** sell out ; be sold out ; run out of 《merchandise》 ¶ 금일 매진 sold out today // 좌석이 매진되었다 Every seat is booked.

매진 邁進 pushing on ; dash **—하다** push on ; dash〔push〕forward ; strive for ; struggle on ¶ 새로운 한국의 건설에 매진하자 Let all of us strive to build up (a) new Korea.

매질 whipping ; flogging ; lashing ; beating **—하다** whip ; flog ; lash ; beat

매질 媒質 〖이학〗 a medium

매차 每次 each time ; every time
매체 媒體 a medium 《*pl.* -dia》 ¶ 공기는 소리의 매체이다 The air is a medium for sound.
광고 — a medium of advertisement **대중 —** the mass (communication) media ; the mass media (of communication)
매초 每秒 every second ; per second ¶ 매초 20미터의 속도로 at a velocity〔speed〕 of 20 meters per〔a〕 second
매초롬하다 (be) wholesome looking ; possess a healthy beauty ; (be) charmingly healthy
매축 埋築 reclamation ; filling up〔in〕 **—하다** reclaim ; reclaim from the sea ; fill up〔in〕
— 공사 reclamation〔reclaiming〕 work **— 지** filled-up land ; [바다·못] reclaimed land ; land reclaimed from the sea
매춘 賣春 harlotry ; prostitution ; streetwalking **—하다** practice prostitution ; sell one's favors
— 방지법 the Anti-Prostitution Act **— 생활** a life of prostitution ; streetwalking **— 업자** a vice racketeer **— 행위** (an act of) prostitution
매춘부 賣春婦 a prostitute ; a street girl ; a streetwalker ; a woman of the streets〔town〕 ; a tart ; a harlot ¶ 갱생한 매춘부 a magdalene // 매춘부가 되다 become a prostitute ; go on the streets 〔town〕
매출 賣出 a sale ; putting on sale ; [증권 따위의] a public offer **—하다** market ; place 《the goods》 on sale ; offer ¶ (염가) 대매출 a bargain sale // 연말 대매출 the year-end bargain sale // 특가 대매출 a special sale
— 가격 the offering〔sale〕 price **— 광고** an advertisement of the opening sale
매치 ① [경기] a match ¶ 〖정구〗 매치 포인트 the match point // 〖골프〗 매치 플레이 match play
② [조화] **—하다** match 《with》 ; go well 《with》 ¶ 장갑과 머플러를 매치시키다 match one's gloves with one's muffler
매치광이 a madman ; a maniac
매치다 be crazy about ; be eccentric ; lose one's senses
매캐하다 ① [연기내] (be) smoky ; stinging ; burning ¶ 방이 매캐하다 A room is smoky. ② [곰팡내] (be) musty ; mo(u)ldy ; fusty ; stale-smelling ; smelly
매콤하다 (be) somewhat hot-tasting 〔spicy, peppery, pungent, sharp〕
매큼하다 (be) peppery-smelling ¶ 매큼한 냄새 a peppery smell
매탄 煤炭 coal
매통 a wooden mill for hulling rice
*__매트__ a mat
*__매트리스__ a mattress
매파 —派 a hawk ; the hawks ; a hardliner ¶ 매파의 hawkish
매파 媒婆 an old woman go-between 〔match-maker〕
매판 an under mat (for a handmill)
매판 자본 買辦資本 comprador capital
매팔자 —八字 easy circumstances ¶ 매팔자이다 be in easy circumstances
매표 賣票 selling of tickets **—하다** sell tickets ¶ (역에서) 매표를 시작했다 The ticket window is open.
—구 a ticket window **—소** a ticket office 〔cage〕 ; a booking office 《영》 ; [합동의] a consolidated ticket office ; [극장의] a box office ; a paybox 《영》 **—원** a ticket agent 《미》 ; a ticket girl ; a booking clerk 《영》 ; [극장의] a boxoffice girl 《미》
매품 賣品 an article for sale
매한가지 all the same ; much the same ¶ 엎어지나 잦혀지나 매한가지다 It is six of one and half a dozen of the other.
매합 媒合 matchmaking **—하다** bring about a match ; go between
매향 梅香 a fragrance of plum blossoms
매혈 賣血 selling blood (for money) **—하다** sell blood for money
매형 妹兄 an elder sister's husband ; a brother-in-law
매호 每戶 every〔each〕 house〔door, family〕
매호 每號 every number〔issue〕
†**매혹 魅惑** fascination ; captivation ; a lure ; a luring charm **—하다** fascinate ; charm ; captivate ; bewitch ; enchant ¶ 매혹적인 fascinating ; captivating ; enchanting ; glamorous // 그것에는 매혹적인 데가 있다 There is a fascination about it. // 그는 그 여자의 미모에 매혹되었다 He was bewitched by her beauty.
매화 梅花 [나무] a Japanese apricot tree ; Prunus Mume (학명) ; [열매] a Japanese apricot ¶ 매화꽃 an ume flower〔blossom〕
—주 ume brandy
매회 每回 each〔every〕 time ; each〔every〕 round (권투 따위)〔inning (야구 따위)〕
매흙 a fine gray loam
— 모래 fine gray sand
매흙질 plastering a wall with gray loam **—하다** plaster〔face〕 a wall with loam
맥 脈 [맥박] pulse ; pulsation ; [광맥] a vein ; a vein of ore ¶ 맥을 찾아내다 strike a vein of ore // 맥이 뛴다 The pulse beats. // 맥이 빠르다 The pulse is fast. // 맥이 멈추다 The pulse ceases to beat. // 아직 맥이 있다 The pulse is still beating. /There is still some life left. // 맥을 봅시다 Let me feel your pulse.
맥고모자 麥藁帽子 a straw hat
맥관 脈管 a blood-vessel (혈관)
맥노 麥奴 〖식물〗 the black ear (of barley)
맥농 麥農 cultivation of wheat〔barley〕 ; wheat〔barley〕 farming

맥도 脈度 pulse rate ; pulse frequency
맥동 脈動 pulsatory motion ; pulsation
— 전류 a pulsating current
맥락 脈絡 the veins ; the system of veins ; [기맥을 통함] the interconnections ; the intricacies ¶ 맥락을 통하다 be in collusion with 《a person》 ; secretly communicate with each other
—막 〖해부〗 the choroid ; the chorioid ; the chorioidea ; the choroid coat 〔membrane〕 — 집망(集網) 〖동물〗 the choroid plexus
맥량 麥涼 the cool weather at the barley harvest season
맥량 麥糧 barley for summer use〔provisions〕
맥류 麥類 barley ; wheat ; oat
맥류 脈瘤 〖의학〗 an aneurysm ; an aneurism
맥리 脈理 [문맥의] a contextual connection ; the thread of logic ; the context ; [맥의 이치] the theory of the pulse
맥망 麥芒 a wheat beard ; an awn
맥맥하다 ① [코가] (be) stuffed up ; congested ; stuffy ¶ 코가 맥맥하다 My nose is stuffy. /I have got a stuffed-up nose. ② [생각이] (be) stuck ; be at a loss ; be at one's wits' end ¶ 생각이 맥맥하다 be stuck for an idea ; can't think of a thing ; one's mind is blank
맥맥히 脈脈— continuously ; unbrokenly ¶ 천 5백년 이상이나 맥맥히 이어온 전통 an unbroken tradition of over 1,500 years
맥무병 脈無病 〖의학〗 acrotism
⁑**맥박 脈搏** pulse ; pulsation ¶ 약하고 빠른 맥박 a thready pulse // 맥박이 고르지 않다 The pulse is irregular. // 맥박에 이상 없다 The pulse is normal. // 맥박이 75이다 The pulse is 75.
—계 a pulsimeter ; a pulsometer ; asphygmometer —수 (a) pulse frequency ; a pulse〔heart〕 rate — 청진기 a sphygmophone 결체성 — an intermittent pulse
맥반 麥飯 cooked barley (보리밥)
맥반암 脈斑岩 〖지질·광산〗 elvan
맥보다 脈— [맥박을] feel〔examine, take〕 the pulse ; [의향을] sound out 《a person》 ; feel out a situation ¶ 형편이 어떤지 맥보련다 I am going to feel the situation out (to see how the wind blows).
맥분 麥粉 wheat flour (밀가루)
맥비 麥肥 fertilizer for barley farming
맥빠지다 脈— ① [지치다] be tired 〔exhausted〕 ; feel weak〔feeble〕 ; be worn out ¶ 맥이 빠지셨군요 You look done up 〔run down〕. ② [낙심] be frustrated ; be disappointed ; be discouraged ; it makes 《a person》 tired ¶ 시험 결과를 보고 맥이 빠졌다 I felt greatly disappointed at the result of the examination. // 맥이 빠진 얼굴이구나 You look down in the dumps.
맥상 脈相 〖동물·식물〗 nervation ; venation
맥석 脈石 〖광산〗 gangue ; veinstone ; veinstuff
맥소 脈所 [맥이 짚이는 곳] the places (on a human body) where the pulse can be felt〔observed〕 ; [급소] a vital point
맥시 a maxi ; a maxi-skirt
맥시류 脈翅類 〖곤충〗 Neuroptera (학명)
— 곤충 a neuropteron ; a neuropter
맥아 麥芽 malt
—당 maltose ; malt sugar — 제조소 a malthouse
맥암 脈岩 〖지질〗 a dike rock
맥압계 脈壓計 a sphygmomanometer
맥없다 feel tired ; (be) enervated ; dispirited ; be in low spirits ; be in the dumps ; feel blue
맥없이 ① [힘없이] weakly ; tiredly ; spiritlessly ; helplessly ; disappointedly ; in low spirits ¶ 맥없이 앉아 있다 sit exhausted ; sit dejected〔disappointed〕 // 그는 맥없이 땅바닥에 쓰러졌다 He fell down easily on the ground.
② [까닭없이] without much reason ; at the slightest push ¶ 맥없이 울다 start crying at the least little thing
맥우 麥雨 rain coming in the barley ripening season
맥이 풀리다 lose one's energy〔vigor〕 ; fall into low spirits ; be dispirited ; lose interest
맥작 麥作 cultivation of barley〔wheat〕 ; barley growing ; barley crop
맥적다 ① [열적다] (be) bored ; feel ennui ; have a dull time ; find time hanging heavy on one's hands ¶ 할 일이 없어 맥적다 With nothing to do, I am bored to death.
② [대할 낯이 없다] (be) ashamed (of oneself) ; afraid〔hesitant〕 (because of shame) ¶ 돈 더 꾸어달라기가 맥적다 I am afraid to ask for more money.
⁑**맥주 麥酒** beer ; ale ¶ 김빠진 맥주 stale 〔flat〕 beer // 맥주의 거품 beer suds // 김빠진 맥주 같다 be as insipid as stale beer // 맥주에 취하다 be in beer ; be beery // 보통 맥주로 할까요 그렇잖으면 흑맥주로 할까요 (Which will you have,) Light or dark ?
— 냉각기 a beer cooler —병 a beer bottle — 애음가 a beer drinker — 양조 beer brewing — 양조장 a beer brewery ; a beer brewhouse (소규모의) — 여과기 a beer filter — 효모 beer yeast 깡통 — canned beer 병— bottled beer 생— draft beer 저장 — lager (beer) ; stock beer 흑— dark〔black〕 beer ; stout (ale)
맥줄 脈— an artery
맥진 驀進 a dash ; a rush —하다 rush ; dash forward〔onward〕 ; charge in 《upon》 ¶ 적을 향하여 맥진하다 charge in upon 〔make a dash at〕 the enemy
맥추 麥秋 barley〔wheat〕 harvest season

맥파 脈派 a pulse wave
— **묘사기** 〚의학〛 a sphygmograph
맥풀리다 脈— ⇨ 맥빠지다
맨[1] nothing but ; just ; full of ¶ 구경거리는 없고 맨 사람뿐이다 There is nothing to see but lots of people. // 못에는 맨 고기다 The pond is full of fish〔swarms with fish〕.
맨[2] the very ; the extreme ¶ 맨 처음 at the very first ; first of all ; at the very beginning ; right at the start // 맨 왼편 집 a house at the very left ; the house way at the left // 복도 맨 끝에 있습니다 It's way down at the end of the hall.
맨- bare ; naked ; nothing but ; just ¶ 맨머리 a bare head ; bareheaded // 맨발 bare feet ; barefoot(ed) // 맨밥 just rice (without any side dishes)
맨 꼴찌 the very last〔bottom〕
맨꽁무니 without resources ; empty-handed ¶ 맨꽁무니로 장사를 하려 든다 He is going into business without a cent to back him up.
맨끝 the very end ; the very last ¶ 맨끝의 final ; concluding ; closing // 맨 끝에 at the close 《of》 ; at the conclusion ; in conclusion // 소설을 맨끝까지 읽다 read a novel through〔to the end〕 // 맨끝까지 보다 sit out 《a play, a concert》 // 거기가 줄의 맨끝인가요 Is this the end of the line ?
맨 나중 the very last〔end〕 ¶ 맨 나중의 final ; terminal // 맨 나중에 in conclusion ; finally // 그는 맨 나중에 왔다 He arrived last.
맨둥맨둥하다 (be) treeless ; bare ; hairless bald ⇨ 민둥민둥하다
맨 뒤 the very last〔end〕 ; the tail〔end〕 ¶ 줄 맨 뒤에 서다 stand at the tail of a queue
맨드라미 〚식물〛 a cockscomb ; Celosia cristata (학명)
맨드리 [옷맵시] the figure one cuts ; one's appearance ; [모양새] the appearance〔shape, look〕 of something made
맨 땅 bare ground
맨망떨다 act frivolously〔capriciously, flightily〕
맨망하다, 맨망스럽다 (be) fickle ; flighty ; flippant ; frivolous
맨머리 a bare head ; bareheaded ¶ 맨머리 바람으로 외출하다 go out bareheaded ; go out without putting on a hat ; go out hatless
맨 먼저 [최초로] at the very first〔beginning〕 ; [첫째로] first of all ; before anything else ¶ 맨 먼저의 foremost ; first // 그가 맨 먼저 왔다 He was the first to arrive on the scene. // 어머니가 맨 먼저 일어나신다 Mother gets up earliest of all.
맨몸 [알몸] a naked body ; nude ; naked ; [무일푼] being penniless ¶ 맨몸으로 in the nude ; with nothing on ; in one's birthday clothes // 맨몸이 되다 become naked ; strip oneself naked ; [무일푼] become penniless ; go broke ; be stripped // 맨몸으로 시집가다 be married with no dowry at all
맨몸뚱이 a naked body ⇨ 맨몸
맨 밑 the very bottom ¶ 맨 밑의 the lowest ; the bottommost
맨 바닥 the bare floor〔ground〕
*__맨발__ bare feet ; barefoot ¶ 맨발로 barefoot ; in one's bare feet // 맨발로 걷다 go〔walk〕 barefoot // 맨발로 거리를 걸어다니다 walk barefoot through the street
맨밥 boiled-rice served without any side dishes ¶ 맨밥을 먹다 eat rice alone ; eat rice without any side dishes at all
맨션 a mansion
— **하우스〔아파트〕** a mansion house〔apartment〕 ; a ferroconcrete apartment house of a better class
맨손 empty hands ; a bare hand ; naked fists ¶ 맨손으로 empty-handed ; with empty hand ; [무기없이] unarmed ; with bare hands ; with naked fists // 맨손으로 장사를 시작하다 start business without any capital // 맨손으로 적과 싸우다 fight the enemy with naked fists〔bare hands〕 // 맨손으로 방문하다 call on 《a person》 with empty hands ; visit 《a person》 without bringing a present // 맨손으로 돈을 벌 수 없다 cannot make money with an empty purse // 맨손으로 큰 돈을 벌다 make a fortune starting from scratch
맨송맨송하다 ① [털이 없는] (be) hairless ; bald ; bare ¶ 털이 맨송맨송하다 be beardless ; have no beard ; have a bald chin
② [나무가 없는] (be) treeless ; bald ; bare ¶ 맨송맨송한 산 a treeless〔a denuded〕 mountain
③ [술취하지 않은] (be) sober ; unintoxicated ; not drunk ¶ 아주 맨송맨송한 be dead〔cold〕 sober // 술을 얼마나 마셨는지 모르지만 아직 맨송맨송하다 I don't know how much you have drunk, but you seem none the worse for it.
맨아래 the bottom ; the lowest ¶ 맨아래의 the lowest ; the nethermost ; the undermost ; the bottommost ¶ 봉급은 맨아래가 4십만원이다 The salary is 400,000 *won* at the lowest.
맨앞 the head ; the van ; the foremost ; the very front ¶ 맨앞에 at the head of // 맨앞의 차 the foremost car // 맨앞에 서서 가다 go at the head of 《a party》 ; lead the way ; lead the van of // 그의 이름이 맨앞에 나와 있다 His name leads the list.
맨위 the top ; the summit ; the peak ; the maximum (최고) ; the best (최상) ¶ 맨위의 topmost ; uppermost ; highest ; best
맨입 an empty mouth〔stomach〕 ¶ 맨입에

술을 마시다 drink on an empty stomach
맨주먹 empty hands ⇨ 맨손
맨처음 the very first ; the earliest ; the original ¶ 맨처음에 first and foremost ; in the first place ; at the very beginning ; first of all // 맨처음에 무엇을 할까요 What shall we do first ? // 그가 맨처음 달려왔다 He was the first to arrive on the scene. // 어머니가 맨처음에 오셨다 My mother was the first to come. /My mother came before all the rest.
맨투맨 ¶ 맨투맨 방어 〖축구·농구〗 a man-to〔-for〕-man defense
맨틀피스 a mantelpiece
*__맨홀__ a manhole
맴돌다 ⇨ 매암돌다
*__맵다__ ① [맛이] (be) hot ; pungent ; peppery ; sharp ; spicy ¶ 매운 카레 요리 hot curry // 매운 소스 pungent sauce // 국이 맵다 the soup tastes hot ② [독하다] (be) severe ; strict ; intense ; harsh ¶ 매운 추위 severe cold〔weather〕
맵살스럽다 (be) hateful ⇨ 밉살스럽다
†**맵시** figure ; form ; appearance ; shapeliness ; smartness ¶ 몸 맵시 one's figure〔carriage〕 // 옷 맵시 a style of dressing ; the cut of one's clothes // 우아한 맵시 an elegant figure // 걷는 맵시 the walking figure 《of a person》 // 맵시가 있다 be shapely ; be well-formed ; be nicely turned out ; be well cut ; be handsome ; be smart // 맵시가 없다 be ill-shaped〔-formed〕 ; be shapeless ; be unseemly ; be awkward ; be clumsy // 그녀는 언제나 맵시 있게 옷을 입는다 She is always smartly dressed.
맵싸하다 (be) pungent ; acrid ; peppery ; tongue-tingling
맵자하다 have a tight〔firm, solid, becoming〕 shape〔form, figure, look〕
맷가마리 one who deserves a whipping
맷고기 small cuts of beef sold separately
†**맷돌** a millstone ; a hand mill ; a grinding stone
맷돌중쇠 the pivot〔upper plate〕 and gudgeon〔lower plate〕 of a millstone
맷돌질 grinding 《grain in a stone mill》
맷맷하다 (be) straight and smooth ⇨ 밋밋하다
맷방석 a round straw mat which is spread under the millstone
맷손 [맷돌의] the handle of a millstone
맷수쇠 the pivot of a millstone
맹격 猛擊 a hard〔severe〕 blow ; a violent〔fierce〕 attack ; an onslaught ¶ 맹격을 가하다 deal 《a person》 a hard blow ; make an onslaught 《on》 ; make violent attacks 《against the enemy》
맹견 猛犬 a ferocious〔fierce, savage〕 dog ¶ 맹견 주의 Beware of the fierce dog !
맹공격 猛攻擊 a fierce attack ; a violent〔murderous〕 assault ; an onslaught ¶ 맹공격을 가하다 make a vigorous attack〔an onslaught〕 on 《the enemy》 ; 〖야구〗 drive〔bat〕 to the showers
맹그로브 〖식물〗 a mangrove
맹근하다 (be) somewhat warm ⇨ 밍근하다
맹금 猛禽 〖새〗 a bird of prey ; a raptorial bird ¶ 맹금성의 hawk-like ; accipitral
맹금류 猛禽類 birds of prey ; rapacious birds
맹꽁맹꽁 croaking **—하다** croak
맹꽁이 ① 〖동물〗 a kind of small round frog ; Cacopides tornieri (학명) ② [바보] an idiot ; a moron
맹꽁이 자물쇠 a padlock
맹눈 illiterate eyes ; an ignoramus
맹도견 盲導犬 a Seeing Eye Dog ; a guide dog ; a blindman's dog
맹독 猛毒 a deadly poison
맹동 孟冬 [초겨울] early winter ; the beginning of winter ; [음력 10월] the 10th lunar month
맹동 萌動 germination ; budding ; quickening ; signs of forthcoming activity **—하다** germinate ; bud ; start taking shape ¶ 조합 민주화 운동의 맹동이 보인다 There is a quickening of democratization of the union.
맹랑하다 孟浪— ① [허망하다] (be) false ; untrue ; [근거 없다] groundless ; unfounded ; [터무니 없다] absurd ; nonsensical ; preposterous ; fabulous ; [믿을 수 없다] incredible ; unbelievable ¶ 맹랑한 사람 an unreliable person ; a disappointing person // 맹랑한 이야기 an incredible〔a silly〕 story // 맹랑한 소문 wild rumors // 일이 맹랑하게 됐다 My plan was unexpectedly frustrated. /My plan got spoiled so easily.
② [허수롭지 않다] be not negligible ; be tougher than one had expected ; be quite contrary to one's expectation ¶ 맹랑한 적수 no common antagonist
†**맹렬하다 猛烈—** (be) violent ; furious ; fierce ¶ 맹렬히 violently ; furiously ; fiercely // 맹렬한 공격 a heavy attack // 맹렬한 경쟁 keen〔cutthroat〕 competition, a bitter contest // 맹렬한 더위〔추위〕 intense heat〔cold〕 // 맹렬한 반대 strong opposition // 맹렬한 싸움 a hot fight // 맹렬한 속도 a terrific speed // 맹렬한 연습 heavy〔intensive〕 practice〔training〕 // 맹렬한 폭풍우 a violent storm // 맹렬해지다 grow violent〔in violence〕 // 비가 맹렬히 퍼붓는다 It rains cats and dogs〔in torrents, heavily, hard〕. // 적의 포화가 시시 각각으로 맹렬해졌다 The enemy artillery-fire increased hourly in violence.
맹롱아 盲聾啞 the blind, deaf, and dumb ¶ 맹롱아 아동을 위한 시설 a home for blind, deaf and dumb children
⁑**맹목 盲目** blindness ¶ 맹목의 blind ; sightless ; unseeing // 맹목적으로 blindly ; recklessly ; ignorantly // 맹목적 사랑〔복종, 숭배〕 blind love〔obedience, devo-

tion〕
— 비행 blind flying ; a blind flight — 착륙 blind〔instrument〕 landing

†**맹목적 盲目的** blind ; reckless ¶ 맹목적으로 blindly ; recklessly // 맹목적 사랑 blind love // 맹목적 모방 blind〔servile〕 imitation // 맹목적 숭배 blind devotion // 맹목적 시도 a venture made blindly ; a leap in the dark

맹문 the situation ; circumstances ; the state of things ; details ; the matter ; the case ¶ 맹문 모르고 without knowing the case // 맹문 모르고 덤벼들다 rush〔plunge〕 into something without knowing anything about it ; thrust oneself into without knowing the case

맹문 모르다 관용 do not understand the matter〔circumstances〕 at all ; have no grasp of the situation ; have no sense

맹문이 a person who doesn't understand the situation at all ; a person who doesn't know how the wind blows ; a person who has no sense ; a babe in the woods ¶ 그런 맹문이는 처음 보았다 I have never seen a man so utterly devoid of sense as he.

맹물 ① [물] water ; tasteless water ¶ 이것은 술이 아니고 맹물이다 This isn't wine, it's dishwater !
② [사람] an insipid person ; a dull drink of water ; a drip ¶ 그 사람은 맹물이다 He is a dull drink of water.

맹반격 猛反擊 a terrific counterattack — 하다 make a violent counterattack 《on》

맹방 盟邦 an ally ; allied powers ; a confederate (state) ; a confederacy ; a confederation

맹사 盲射 random firing〔shooting〕 ; a shot in the dark — 하다 fire〔shoot〕 at random ; take a potshot 《at》

맹사격 猛射擊 a heavy fire ; severe〔hot〕 firing ; a fusillade〔vehement shower〕 of bullets ; liveliness 《군·속》 ¶ 맹사격을 퍼붓다 rain a heavy fire on 《the enemy》

맹서 盟誓 an oath ⇨ 맹세

맹성 猛省 serious reflection〔reconsideration〕 — 하다 reflect seriously on oneself ¶ 맹성을 촉구하다 urge 《a person》 to reconsider seriously〔to make serious reconsideration〕

***맹세** [신에 대한] an oath ; a vow ; a pledge (서약) ; a promise (약속) — 하다 swear ; pledge ; vow ; take〔make〕 an oath ; make a vow ; pledge oneself 《to do》 ; promise 《to do》 ; give one's word〔honor, pledge〕 ¶ 맹세코 upon my oath〔word, honor, life〕 ; as God is my witness ; by God // 맹세를 지키다〔깨뜨리다〕 keep〔break〕 one's vow〔pledge, oath〕 // 천지 신명께 맹세하다 swear before〔by, to〕 God 《that》 // 마음 속으로 맹세하다 swear to oneself ; promise oneself // 충성을 맹세하다 swear allegiance // 금주〔금연〕를 맹세하다 swear not to touch drinks〔to smoke〕 ; swear off drinks〔smoking〕 // 비밀을 맹세하다 pledge oneself to secrecy // 맹세코 약속을 지키겠다 I swear I will keep my promise. // 그 젊은 부부는 서로 사랑할 것을 맹세하였다 The young couple plighted their love for each other. // 그는 금주의 맹세를 하고 있다 He is under〔bound by〕 a vow to drink no wine〔a vow of abstinence〕.

맹세지거리 swearing in vulgar language ; a profane oath ; a curse — 하다 swear profanely ; utter curses ¶ 그는 거짓말이면 개자식이라고 맹세지거리했다 He swore that he would be a s. o. b. if he was lying.

맹수 猛獸 a ferocious beast ; a fierce animal ; a beast of prey (육식수) ¶ 맹수를 길들이는 사람 a tamer of wild beasts

맹수 사냥 猛獸— big-game hunting ; a safari (동부 아프리카의) ¶ 맹수 사냥꾼 a big-game hunter // 맹수 사냥을 하다 shoot big game ; go big-game hunting

맹습 猛襲 a vigorous〔furious, heavy, hot〕 attack ; a violent assault ; an onslaught — 하다 make〔launch〕 a vigorous attack〔an onslaught〕 on 《the enemy》 ; assault

맹신 盲信 credulity ; a blind faith — 하다 be credulous ; believe blindly

맹아 盲啞 the blind and dumb
— 교육 education for the blind and dumb — 학교 a blind and dumb school

맹아 萌芽 [발아] germination ; [싹] a bud ; a germ ; a sprout
— 기 embryo ; a germinal stage ¶ 맹아기에 있다 be in embryo ; be in a germinal stage — 림 a sprout forest

맹약 盟約 [서약] a pledge ; [협정] a pact ; a covenant ; a compact ; [동맹] an alliance ; a confederacy ; a league ¶ 맹약을 맺다 conclude a pact ; confederate ; form a league〔an alliance〕
— 국 an ally ; a pact member ; a confederate state

맹연습 猛練習 rigorous〔intensive〕 practice — 하다 do hard training ; carry out rigorous practice〔exercises〕

맹우 盟友 a sworn friend

맹위 猛威 fury ; fierceness ; violence ; ferocity ¶ 맹위를 떨치다 rage (with all one's force) ; be rampant ; be at the height of fury // 콜레라가 발생하여 맹위를 떨치고 있다 Cholera has broken out and is raging with all its force. // 태풍이 밤새도록 맹위를 떨쳤다 The typhoon raged in all its fury throughout the night.

맹이 the frame of a saddle

맹인 盲人 a blind person

맹장 盲腸 〖해부〗 the caecum 《*pl.* -ca》 ; the vermiform ; appendix 《*pl.* -dices》 ; the blind gut ¶ 맹장 수술을 받다 have〔undergo〕 an operation〔be operated on〕 for appendicitis

— 주위염 perityphlitis
맹장 猛將 a veteran fighter ; a champion (선수)
맹장염 盲腸炎 〖의학〗 appendicitis ; caecitis ; typhlitis ¶ 맹장염의 typhlitic
— 수술 appendectomy ; an operation for appendicitis 천공성 급성(穿孔性急性) — an acute attack of appendicitis with rupture
맹장질 盲杖— a severe flogging〔whipping〕 —하다 flog severely ; administer a hard whipping 《to》
맹점 盲點 a blind point〔spot〕 ¶ 법의 맹점 a blind point of law // 법의 맹점을 이용하다 make an illicit use of law
맹졸 猛卒 a fierce〔daredevil, courageous〕 warrior〔soldier〕
맹종 盲從 blind obedience〔submission〕 —하다 follow〔obey, submit〕 《a person》 blindly ; follow like a sheep ; be led by the nose
—자 a blind〔thoughtless〕 follower
맹주 盟主 the leader (of a band of confederate states) ; the leading power ¶ 맹주가 되다 become the leader 《of》 ; assume the leadership 《of》
맹진 猛進 a dash ; a drive ; a thrust —하다 dash forward ; make a dash ; make a drive 《on》
맹추 a stupid person ; a fool ; a thick-headed person ; a blockhead ; a hare-brain ; a dullard
맹추 孟秋 [초가을] early autumn〔fall〕 ; [음력 7월] July of the lunar calendar
맹춘 孟春 [초봄] early spring ; [음력 정월] January of the lunar calendar
맹타 猛打 a hard〔severe〕 blow ; 〖야구〗 slugging ; a heavy hit —하다 strike〔beat〕 violently ; give a heavy hit ; hit hard ; slug 《a ball》
—자 a slugger ; a heavy batter
맹탕 ① [국물] insipid〔tasteless〕 soup ; flavorless soup ; unseasoned soup
② [사람] an empty person ; an insipid person ; a dull〔an uninteresting〕 person
맹폭 盲爆 blind〔indiscriminate〕 bombing —하다 bombard〔bomb〕 blindly
맹폭 猛爆 heavy bombing〔bombardment〕 ; an intensive air-raid —하다 bomb〔bombard〕 heavily ; strafe
맹풍 猛風 a violent〔vehement〕 wind ; a furious wind ; a storm ; a hurricane ; a typhoon ; a gale
맹하 孟夏 [초여름] early summer ; [음력 4월] April of the lunar calendar
맹학교 盲學校 a school for the blind
맹한 猛悍 ferocity and intrepidity —하다 (be) fierce and intrepid
맹호 猛虎 a ferocious〔fierce, wild〕 tiger
맹화 猛火 roaring〔raging〕 flames ; a raging〔terrible〕 fire ; a fierce conflagration ¶ 맹화속에 뛰어들다 rush〔plunge〕 into the raging flames // 맹화에 휩싸이다 be enveloped in raging fire
맹활동 猛活動 full〔vigorous〕 activity ; active〔full〕 operation —하다 be in full activity〔swing〕 ; take〔play〕 a very active part 《in》 ; be actively engaged 《in, as》 ; act vigorously ¶ 사회 개혁가로서 맹활동하다 be actively engaged as a social reformer
맹훈련 猛訓鍊 intense〔hard〕 training —하다 carry out intense training ; train hard
맹휴 盟休 [동맹 파업] a strike ; a walkout 《미》 ; [동맹 휴교] a school strike —하다 go on (a) strike ; walkout 《미》 ¶ 학생들이 맹휴했다 The students went on strike.
*맺다 ① [매듭을] knot ; tie ¶ 매듭을 맺다 tie a knot ; knot
② [결실] bear ; produce ¶ 열매를 맺다 bear fruit ; produce a result ; be brought to fruition // 그의 노력은 열매를 맺었다 He was rewarded for his efforts. /His efforts were crowned with success. /Success rewarded his efforts.
③ [관계를] form ; make ; enter into ; contract ¶ 관계를 맺다 enter into a relation ; form a connection // 우정을 맺다 form〔contract〕 a friendship // 계약을 맺다 contract ; make〔establish, conclude〕 a contract // 조약을 맺다 conclude〔enter into〕 a treaty // 동맹을 맺다 ally〔league〕 with // 백년 가약을 맺다 exchange the vows of marriage
④ [완결] finish ; end ; conclude ; close ; wind up ¶ 연설을 맺다 conclude one's speech 《with》 // 편지는 다음과 같이 맺어져 있다 The letter concludes as follows. // 이제 잘 시간이어서 이 편지를 여기에서 맺습니다 It's time to go to bed, and I must now close this letter.
⑤ [원한을] harbor ; bear ; cherish ; nurse ¶ 원한을 맺다 bear a grudge ; harbor an enmity 《toward》
맺음말 concluding remarks ; conclusion
맺히다 ① [열매가] come〔develop〕 into fruit〔bearing〕 ; fruit ; fructify ; seed ; go to seed ¶ 열매가 맺히다 fruit ; be in fruit ; come into bearing
② [매듭이] be tied ; be knotted ¶ 매듭이 맺히다 be knotted ; a knot is tied
③ [원한이] be pent up ; be congested ¶ 맺힌 원한 a deep grudge ; pent-up rancor // 가슴에 맺힌 원한 grudge smoldered in one's heart
④ [눈물·이슬이] form ¶ 눈물 맺힌 눈 eyes suffused〔filled, streaming〕 with tears ; moist eyes // 눈물이 맺히다 tears forms ; have tears // 이슬이 맺히다 dew forms ; be dewy ; be covered with dew // 피가 맺히다 blood gathers ; 《skin》 be bruised // 풀잎에 이슬이 맺힌다 Dewdrops form on the blades.
맺힌데 a bruised spot ; [원한이] a point of

rancor

머 aw ; nyah ; mmh ; huh ; well ; and how ; shucks ; so there ¶ 너 진정으로 하는 말이니? 그럼 머 You mean it? And how.

머구리 a frog ⇨ 개구리

머귀나무 〖식물〗 a paulownia ; Fagara ailanthoides (학명)

머금다 ① [입에] keep〔hold〕《a thing》 in one's mouth ; mouth (음식을) ¶ 물을 머금고 with one's mouth full of water ② [마음에] entertain ; harborbear in mind ; have ¶ 악의를 머금다 entertain ill feeling // 원한을 머금다 bear 《a person》 a grudge ; bear rancor
③ [눈물을] have tears in one's eyes ; tears stand in one's eyes ; be filled with tears
④ [웃음을] have a smile (on one's lips) ; 《one's face》 beam〔shine〕 with joy ; wear a smile

머나멀다 ① [거리] (be) very far 〔long〕 ; distant ; far-off ; remote ; a long way off ¶ 머나먼 곳 a faraway place ; a place far far away // 머나먼 길 a long long road〔distance〕 // 머나먼 길 수고가 많으셨소 It is very kind of you to come all this distance. ② [시간] (be) very old ; ancient ; remote ¶ 머나먼 옛날 a long time ago // 머나먼 옛날을 생각하다 think of the days long past

머다랗다 (be) rather far ; rather long 〔distant〕 ¶ 머다란 길 quite a long way

머드러기 a big〔large〕 one ; a large piece of fruit ; a large fish

머루 〖식물〗 wild grapevines ; wild grapes

머름 〖건축〗 a wainscot

†머리 ① [두부] the head ; the pate (속) ; the noddle (구) ¶ 머리에서 발끝까지 from head to foot ; from top 〔crown〕 to toe // 머리가 벗어지다 become bald // 머리가 어지럽다 one's head swims ; one's brain reels ; feel giddy〔dizzy〕 // 머리를 긁다 scratch one's head // 머리를 들다 lift one's head ; raise〔hold up〕 one's head // 머리를 때리다 strike〔knock〕 《a person》 on the head // 머리를 팔로 감싸다 bury 〔hold〕 one's head in one's arms // 머리를 숙이고 아무 말도 하지 않았다 He did not speak a word with his head drooping 〔down〕.
② [두뇌·사고력] a head ; a brain ; brains ; intellect (지력) ; mind ¶ 머리를 쓰는 일 brain〔head〕 work ; mental 〔intellectual〕 work // 머리가 좋다 have a clean 〔bright〕 head ; be clean〔bright〕-headed ; have a nice brain // 머리가 나쁘다 have a poor〔thick, dull〕 head ; be dull-headed // 머리가 잘 돌다〔돌지 않다〕 have a quick〔slow〕 mind ; be quick〔slow〕-witted ; be fast〔slow〕-thinking // 머리를 쓰다 use one's brain(s)〔head〕 ; work 〔use〕 one's wit // 머리에 떠오르다 [생각이] occur to one〔one's mind〕 ; come 〔flash〕 into one's head // 그는 수학에 머리가 있다 He has good head for mathematics. // 그 일은 머리가 필요하다 The job requires a lot of brains〔intelligence〕.
③ [정신 상태] mind ¶ 그는 머리가 돌았다 He is out of his mind. /He is off his head. /He is wrong in the head.
④ [머리털] hair ¶ 머리를 깎다 have one's hair cut〔trimmed〕 ; get a haircut // 머리를 가르다 part one's hair // 머리를 기르다 let one's hair grow long // 머리를 땋다 braid one's hair // 머리를 쪽찌다 do one's hair in a chignon // 머리를 지지다 frizz〔curl〕 one's hair // 머리를 풀다 [여자가] let one's hair loose ; undo one's hair ; go into mourning (상을 당해서)
⑤ [꼭대기] the top〔head, point, tip〕 《of》 ¶ 기둥 머리 the top of a pillar // 끝머리 the end (part) ; the end piece
⑥ [맨 처음] the beginning ¶ 말 머리 introductory remarks // 일 머리 the beginning of a job
⑦ [우두머리] a chief ; a leader ; a boss ¶ 우두머리가 되다 become a leader ; take the lead ; play first fiddle
머리가 무겁다 관용 one's head feels heavy ; feel heavy in the head
머리가 아프다 관용 one's head aches ; have a headache
머리를 숙이다 관용 bow low ; bow 〔lower〕 one's head 《to a person》 ; droop one's head ; stoop
머리를 썩히다 관용 [생각으로] rack 〔tax〕 one's brain ; [근심·걱정으로] bother one's brain 《about》 ; be worried 《about》 ; worry (oneself) 《about》
머리를 쓰다듬다 관용 pat 《a person》 on the head ; stroke 《a person's》 head

머리감다 wash one's hair ; have a shampoo

머리기름 hair oil ; pomade

머리꾸미개 a hair-ornament

머리끄덩이 a lock〔clump〕 of one's hair ¶ 머리끄덩이를 잡다 grab 《a person》 by the hair

머리끝 the ends of one's hair ; the crown of the head ¶ 머리끝에서 발끝까지 from the crown of the head to the tip of the toes

머리띠 a headband ; a hairlace (여자용) ; a fillet (가느다란) ; a frontlet (장식 있는)

머리말 a preface ; a foreword ; an introduction ; a preamble

머리맡 one's bedside ¶ 머리맡에 at one's bedside ; by one's pillow ; at the head of one's bed ; close to the pillow

머리모양 —模樣 the cut〔style〕 of one's hair ; the way one's hair is worn ; hair-do

머리쓰개 a headpiece ; headgear ; headdress ; a hood ; a kerchief ; a veil

머리악쓰다 do one's best ; make every possible effort

머리얹다 put up one's hair ; do one's hair in a chignon ; [비유적] attain womanhood ; get married ; lose her virginity

머리 염색 —染色 hair dyeing ¶ 머리 염색을 하다 dye one's (gray) hair black

—약 hairdye

머리채 a long tress of hair

머리 치장 hairdressing ; hairdo **—하다** do up one's hair ; dress〔arrange, fix up〕 one's hair

머리카락 a hair (of one's head) ¶ 흰 머리카락 a white hair // 굵은 머리카락 a thick〔coarse〕 hair // 머리카락을 뽑다 pull out a hair

머리칼 ⇨ 머리, 머리카락

†**머리털** the hair on one's head ¶ 머리털이 빠지다 hair falls out〔comes off〕 // 그 무서운 광경을 보고 내 머리털은 곤두섰다 My hair stood on end at the frightful sight.

머리통 the bulk of one's head ¶ 머리통이 크다 have a big head

머리핀 a hair pin

머릿골[1] the brain ; brains ¶ 머릿골 썩히다 [생각하느라고] rack〔tax〕 one's brains ; [걱정으로] bother one's brain 《about》 ; worry oneself 《about》 ; trouble (oneself)

머릿골[2] [기름 짜는] an oil press

머릿기름 [물기름] hair oil ; brilliantine ; hair cosmetic ; [포마드] pomade ; pomatum

머릿니 head lice ; vermin in the hair ¶ 머릿니가 끓다 be swarming with head lice

머릿방 a small back room

머릿살 아프다 have a headache ; (be) troublesome ; troubled ; annoyed ; worried

머릿살 어지럽다 have a headache ⇨ 머릿살 아프다

머릿수 the number of persons ; a head〔nose〕 count ; numerical strength ; quorum (의회의)

머릿장 —欌 a single chest of drawers set at the bedside

머릿줄 ① [연줄] a string tied between the two ends of the top pole of a kite ② [부호] a mark over a word to show a long vowel ; a macron

†**머무르다** ① [묵다] stay ; put up 《at》 ; stop ; lodge 《at》 ¶ 호텔에 머무르다 stop〔put up〕 at a hotel // 오래 머무르다 stay long // 친구 집에 머무르다 stay at a friend's home // 하룻밤 머무르다 stay overnight ; stop the night // 어젯밤은 아저씨 댁에서 머물렀다 Last night I stayed with my uncle〔at my uncle's〕.
② [쉬다] stop ; standstill
③ [남아 있다] remain ; stay ¶ 현직에 머무르다 remain in one's present office

머무적거리다 hesitate ; waver ; wobble ; be irresolute〔hesitant〕 ; linger ; be slow ; dawdle ; shilly-shally ¶ 머무적머무적 hesitatingly ; hesitantly ; waveringly ; slowly // 머무적거리지 말고 without hesitation ; straight off // 결단을 못 내리고 머무적거리다 be hesitant to make a decision

머뭇거리다 hesitate ⇨ 머무적거리다

머슴 a farmhand ; a farmer's man ; a farm servant ¶ 머슴 살다 become〔serve as〕 a farm servant // 머슴을 두다 keep a farmhand

—애 a boy servant ; a boy

머슴살이 serving as a farmhand ; working as a farmhand ; the life of a farmhand **—하다** work as a farmhand ; take service as a farm laborer

머시 something (물건) ; somebody (사람) ¶ 송 머시라는 이 a certain *Song* // 그는 외무부의 머신가 하는 자리에 있어 He is something in the Foreign Office. // 어제 자네가 보여 준 것 말야 그것이 머시드라 What do you call it, the thing you showed me yesterday, I mean?

머쓱하다 ① [키가 크다] (be) lanky ; spindly ; gangling ; rangy ¶ 머쓱한 사나이 a lanky man ; a gangling fellow // 그는 키가 머쓱하니 크다 He is tall and lanky. ② [기가 죽다] (be) discouraged ; dejected ; be in low spirits

머위 〖식물〗 a bog rhubarb ; a butterbur ; a coltsfoot ; Petasites japonicus (학명)

머저리 a fool ; an ass ; a jackass ; a simpleton ¶ 머저리 같은 foolish ; stupid ; dumb 《미·속》

머줍다 (be) dull ; slow ; sluggish ; tardy

머지않아 [이윽고] soon ; presently ; before long ; in a short time ; by and by ; [때가 되면] in due course of time ; in due course〔time〕 ; [불원간] some〔one〕 day ; at no distant date ¶ 머지않아 그들은 결혼할 것이다 Their wedding is in the offing. // 머지않아 이 물건은 제값을 할 거다 Before long, this stuff is going to be worth something.

머츰하다 《it》 stop for a while ; break ; lull ; hold up ; let up ¶ 비가 머츰하다 It stops raining for a while. /It lets up for the moment. /The rain is letting up a little. // 열이 머츰하다 The fever abates.

머큐러크롬 mercurochrome

***머플러** a muffler

***먹** an ink-stick ; Chinese ink ; Indian ink ¶ 먹 한 자루 a cake〔stick〕 of Chinese ink // 먹으로 그린 산수(화) a landscape drawn in black and white // 먹을 갈다 rub (down) an ink-stick // 먹을 묻히다 smear with ink (손에) ; dip in ink (붓에)

먹감 a persimmon blackened by the sun

먹구렁이 〖동물〗 a black snake

먹구름 a black cloud ; dark clouds ; a brewing ¶ 산에 먹구름이 덮이기 시작했다 The mountain is getting wrapped in dark clouds. // 먹구름이 하늘을 덮다 The sky is overspread with dark clouds. // The sky is overcast.

먹그림 a contour picture drawn in India ink

먹놓다 chalk out ; mark (measure lines on lumber) with ink〔inks〕 ¶ 치수를 먹놓다 mark out the measurements

†**먹다**[1] ① [음식을] eat ; take ; have ¶ 다 먹다 eat up all // 조금〔한입〕 먹다 have a bit〔bite, snack〕 of // 배불리 먹다 eat one's fill ; eat to one's heart's content ; take a hearty meal // 알맞게 먹다 eat in moderation // 먹을 수 있다 be edible ; be eatable ; be good to eat // 아무거나 맘대로 집어 먹어라 Help yourself to anything you like on the table. // 오늘 밤엔 집에서 저녁을 먹겠습니다 I am going to dine in this evening. // 어젯밤부터 아무것도 먹지 않았다 I have not tasted anything〔touched food〕 since last night. // 이리 와 잡아 먹지 않을 테니까 Come here, I won't bite you. // 누에는 무엇을 먹느냐 What do silkworms feed on? // 뱀은 개구리나 쥐를 먹는다 The snake lives on frogs, mice and rats. // 너는 피자를 너무 많이 먹는다 You pig out on pizza. // 먹지 말 것 Not to be taken internally. // 너는 밥을 빨리 먹는구나 You're a fast eater.

② [먹고 살다] live (on) ; make a living ; earn one's living〔livelihood〕 ; exist on ¶ 먹고 살 수 없다 be unable to make a living ; be badly off ; have nothing to live on ; find it hard to make a living ; be needy ; be without means of subsistence // 먹기에 걱정 없다 have enough to live on ; be well off // 이럭저럭 먹고 살아가다 manage to live ; keep body and soul together ; make a scanty living ; live by hook〔crook〕 ; manage to keep oneself afloat // 먹기 위해 일하다 work for a livelihood // 남이 번 것으로 먹고 살다 live on《a person's》 earning // 그는 간신히 먹고 산다 He earns a bare living. // 그는 먹는 듯 마는 듯 생활을 한다 He is almost starving. // 뭘 하여 먹고 사나 What do you do for a living? // 혼자 먹고 살기도 빠듯합니다 It's all I can do to feed myself. // 나는 그를 먹고 살게끔 해 주었다 I have put him in the way of earning his own bread. // 그는 붓으로 먹고 산다 He depends upon the pen for his living.

③ [벌레 먹다] eat into ; be worm-eaten ; be moth-eaten ; be decayed ¶ 벌레 먹은 moth-〔worm-〕eaten // 벌레 먹은 이 a decayed tooth // 옷에 좀이 먹다 a garment is moth-eaten // 벌레가 잎을 먹다 Worms nibble green leaves.

④ [담배·물 따위를] smoke ; drink ¶ 담배를 먹다 smoke ; smoke cigarettes // 물을 먹다 drink water // 술을 먹다 drink (liquor) // 약을 먹다 take medicine // 젖을 먹다 suck milk

⑤ [남의 것을] take ; seize ; appropriate ; devour ; swallow up ; make away with ; get ; cheat out of ¶ 공금을 먹다 embezzle〔misuse〕 public funds // 남의 재물을 먹다 take another's property // 뇌물을 먹다 take〔accept〕 a bribe ; graft《미·구》

⑥ [욕을] get a scolding ; be insulted ; be disparaged ; be abused ; be scolded

⑦ [겁을] fear ; dread ; get scared ; be intimidated ; be afraid of

⑧ [마음을] fix ; set ; make ; intend ; plan ; scheme ; contemplate《suicide》 ¶ 그 글을 쓰려고 마음먹었지만 아직 쓰지 못하고 있다 I have been intending to write the article, but I just haven't gotten around to it yet. // 그는 큰 과학자가 되려고 마음먹고 있다 He is firmly determined to become a great scientist.

⑨ [나이를] get (years of age) ; acquire ; grow older ; become old ; advance in age〔years〕 ¶ 보기보다는 나이를 먹지 않았다 be not so old as one looks // 나이 먹어 시력이 약해졌다 My eyesight has become weaker with age.

⑩ [해치다] put〔cast〕 a slur ; hurt ; harm ; injure ¶ 그는 나를 먹지 못해 야단이다 He is upset that he can't harm me. // 나를 잡아 먹으려고 갖은 중상을 다한다 He resorts to all sorts of slander to hurt me. // 여지 없이 한 대 먹었다 I was fairly caught. /I was fooled. /I was taken in.

⑪ [더위를] be affected by the heat ; be ill from the heat

⑫ [상금·판돈 따위를] win〔take〕《the prize, wager》

†**먹다**[2] ① [귀가] become deaf ; lose one's hearing ; go deaf ; be deafened ¶ 왼편 귀가 먹었다 be deaf of the left ear // 시끄러워 귀가 먹겠다 The noise is deafening.

② [대패·톱 따위가] bite ; saw ; plane ; cut (well) ¶ 톱이 잘 먹다 a saw bites〔cuts〕 well ; saw easily ; a saw is sharp // 대패가 잘 먹는다 This tool planes well.

③ [씨아·맷돌 따위가] gin ; grind ¶ 씨아가 잘 먹다 gin well

④ [물감이] dye ; be dyed ; take color ; [풀이] starch ; be starched ; [잉크 따위가] spread ¶ 풀이 잘 먹힌 well-starched《cloth》 ; starchy《cloth》 // 이 천은 물감이 잘 먹는다 This cloth dyes well.

⑤ [소비하다] consume ; spend ; be spent ; be consumed ¶ 돈이 많이 먹다 be costly ; be expensive // 기름이 많이 먹다 oil is consumed in large quantities // 얼마 먹느냐 How much do you charge for it? // 얼마나 먹었소 What did it cost (you)?

먹도미〖물고기〗 a gilthead ; a black porgy

먹두루마기 a garment smeared all over with ink

먹똥 ① [찌끼] dried sediment of India〔Chinese〕 ink ② [자국] a black ink-spot

먹먹하다 (be) deaf ; deafened ; have dif-

ficulty in hearing ; stunned ¶ 귀가 먹먹하다 be deaf ; be deafened
먹물 India ink ; Chinese ink ; inky water (먹물 같은) ¶ 먹물이 들다 be stained with Chinese ink
먹병 —甁 an inkpot ; an ink-bottle
먹빛 an ink(y) black
먹사과 〖식물〗 a kind of melon
먹새 ⇨ 먹음새
먹성 appetite ; capacity for eating ¶ 그는 먹성이 좋다 He has a good〔large〕 appetite. /He is omnivorous. /He is a great〔hearty, heavy〕 eater.
먹실 a string stained with ink ; a string dyed black
먹어나다 accustom oneself to 《some food》 ¶ 먹어난 음식 the food〔dish〕 one is accustomed to
먹은금 [실비] actual expense ; [원가] cost ; the cost price ; the prime cost
먹을알 ① [질 좋은 금광맥] gold ore of good quality ; a superior gold vein ② [쉬운 벌이] easy gain ; exorbitant 〔undue〕 profits
먹음새 ① [요리 솜씨] cooking ; cookery ; style of cooking ; the manner of cooking ¶ 그 집 먹음새가 아주 훌륭하다 Their cooking is simply wonderful. /They serve nice dishes. (식당에서)
② way of eating ; appetite ¶ 먹음새가 좋다 eat heartily ; eat well
먹음직스럽다 (be) delicious looking ; appetizing ; tempting ¶ 이 참외는 먹음직스럽다 This melon looks very tempting.
먹음직하다 (be) delicious looking ⇨ 먹음직스럽다
†먹이 feed ; food ; provisions ¶ 말〔소〕 먹이 feed for horses〔cows〕 // 개〔괭이〕 먹이 dog〔cat〕 food // 먹이가 떨어지다 run out of provisions // 말에게 건초를 먹이로 주다 feed a horse with hay // 오늘밤에는 우리 개에게 먹이를 주지 마시오 Don't feed my dog tonight. // 뱀은 개구리를 먹이로 한다 Snakes prey on frogs.
†먹이다¹ ① [음식을] let someone eat 〔drink〕 ; serve 《a person》 with ; treat 《a person》 to〔with〕 ; entertain 《a person》 with ¶ 배불리 먹이다 let 《a person》 have his fill // 친구에게 술을 먹이다 treat a friend to a drink // 억지로 약을 먹이다 force 《a person》 to take medicine // 환자에게 질긴 것을 먹이지 마라 Be careful not to give tough things to the patient. // 무리하게 먹여서는 안 된다 Food should not be forced upon him.
② [부양·사육] feed ; support ; keep ; provide for ; maintain ; raise ¶ 많은 가족을 먹여 살리다 support a large family ; have a large family to provide for // 가족을 먹여 살릴 수 있을 만큼 벌다 earn enough to feed〔support〕 one's family // 소를 먹이다 raise a cow // 개를 먹이다 keep a dog // 나는 가족을 먹여 살려야만 한다 I must provide for my family.
③ [뇌물을] bribe with ; offer a bribe ; corrupt ; grease the hand of ; grease 《a person's》 palm with ¶ 돈을 먹이다 bribe 《a person》 ; slip money into 《a person's》 hands // 먹여서 입을 막다 buy 《a person's》 tongue ; bribe 《a person》 into secrecy // 선거민에게 돈을 먹이다 temper with the voters
④ [겁을] inflict on 《a person》 ; frighten ; terrify ; scare ; threaten ¶ 겁을 먹이다 scare〔intimidate〕 《a person》 // 욕을 먹이다 let 《a person》 get a scolding ; cause 《a person》 to be abused
⑤ [때리다] give ; administer ¶ 주먹을 먹이다 strike with one's fist // 한 대 먹이다 give〔deal〕 a blow // 빰을 한 대 먹이다 slap 《a person》 on the cheek ; give a box on the ear
먹이다² ① [물감을] dye ; apply ; [풀을] starch ; [초를] wax ; [기름을] oil ¶ 검정 물을 먹이다 dye (in) black // 머리에 물을 먹이다 dye one's hair // 셔츠에 풀을 먹이다 starch one's shirt // 장판에 기름을 먹이다 oil floor paper // 실에 초를 먹이다 wax a string
② [씨아에 솜을] feed ; gin ; put in ¶ 씨아에 솜을 먹이다 feed a gin with cotton ; feed cotton to a gin
③ [돈을] spend ; put 《money》 in ¶ 돈을 많이 먹여 집을 짓다 put a lot of money into building a house // 비용 2만원을 먹이다 spend 20,000 *won* in expenses
④ [연장에 재료를] feed 《a hay cutter》 with 《hay》 ¶ 인쇄기에 종이를 먹이다 feed paper to a printing press
먹자 a carpenter's square for drawing ink lines
먹자판 a scene of riotous eating ; a big feast ; eating what there is
먹장 a piece〔stick〕 of Chinese ink ¶ 먹장 갈아 부은 듯하다 be as if poured all over with ink ; be black as ink
—쇠 hames
먹장 구름 black clouds ; inky clouds ¶ 먹장 구름이 빨리 움직이고 있다 Black clouds are moving fast.
먹줄 an inking line (승묵) ; an inked string (쳐서 낸 줄) ¶ 먹줄을 대다 stretch out an inking line // 곧기는 먹줄 같다 be straight as a carpenter's ink line ; look honest but is wicked at heart
— 꼭지 the tip of an ink-line
먹지 —紙 carbon paper ; copying paper
먹집게 an ink-stick holder
먹초 a black kite with the white top
먹치마 a kite whose lower half is black
먹칠 —漆 smearing with ink —하다 smear with ink ; [명예 따위에] injure ; disgrace ; mar ; [계획 따위] spoil ; throw a wet blanket 《over》 ¶ 가문에 먹칠을 하다 bring disgrace on one's family // 명성에 먹칠을 하다 smear one's reputation

with infamy ; tarnish one's reputation ; cast a slur on one's fame
먹칼 an inking spatula (of a carpenter)
먹통 ① [목수용] an inkpad case ② [먹물통] a kind of inkwell ③ [바보] a fool
먹투성이 a person〔thing〕 smeared all over with ink ¶ 그들의 옷은 먹투성이가 되었다 Their clothes were all smeared〔stained〕 with ink.
먹황새 〖새〗 a black-headed stork
먹히다 ① [먹음을 당하다] be eaten (up) ; get eaten ; be devoured ; be swallowed〔gulped〕; be consumed ¶ 먹느냐 먹히느냐의 싸움 a life-and-death struggle ; a war of survival // 밥이 잘 먹히다 have a good appetite ; can eat much rice // 개구리가 뱀에게 먹히다 A frog is eaten by a snake.
② [빼앗기다] be cheated of ; be taken for ; lose ¶ 사람한테 돈을 먹히다 be cheated of money by 《a person》; lose one's money to 《a person》
③ [돈이] be spent ; be put in ; cost ¶ 비용이 5만원 먹히다 It costs 50,000 *won* in expenses.
먼가래 the provisional burial of a person who has died away from home
먼가래질 —하다 throw earth far away in spadework
먼길 a long way〔journey, distance〕 ¶ 먼길을 가다 make a long journey ; go a long way // 먼길을 오시느라 수고가 많았습니다 It is very kind of you to come all this distance.
먼나라 a faraway〔distant〕 country ; a far-off land
먼눈 [소경의 눈] a blind eye ; [먼 곳을 보는 눈] a far-off〔faraway〕 look in one's eyes ¶ 먼눈을 팔다 have a faraway look in one's eyes
먼데 ① [먼곳] a far-off place ; a distant place ; a distance ¶ 먼데에 in the distance // 꽤 먼데 a good distance off // 먼데로 가다 go faraway // 먼데서 오다 come a long way ② [변소] a toilet
먼데 점이 맞는다 속담 Intimacy lessens fame. / A maid oft seen, and a gown oft worn, are disesteemed in scorn. /Respect is greater from a distance.
먼동 the dawning sky ; the eastern sky of an early morning ¶ 먼동이 틀 때 at dawn ; at daybreak ; at break〔peep〕 of day // 먼동이 트기 전 before dawn〔daybreak〕 // 먼동이 틀 때부터 해가 질 때까지 from dawn till dusk ; from sunup to sundown // 먼동이 트기를 기다리다 wait for the light of day // 먼동이 트다 Day breaks〔dawns〕. /Morning〔It〕 dawns.
먼물 potable〔drinkable〕 well water
먼발치 a distant place ; a spot far-off ¶ 먼발치서 보다 have a distant view 《of》; look 《a thing》 at a distance
먼빛 a distant view ; a spot far-off ¶ 먼빛으로 from a distance ; from afar // 먼 빛으로 보면 when viewed from a distance ; to gaze at a distance // 먼빛으로 보다 view from a distance ; have a distant view 《of》
먼산 —山 a distant mountain
—바라기 a person with a far-away look in the eyes
먼일 the future ; future〔coming〕 events ¶ 먼일을 보지 않고 with no thought of the future // 먼일을 예상하다 anticipate what is to come // 먼일을 내다보다 look far ahead into the future // 먼일을 생각하다 think〔look to〕 the future ; look far〔forward〕 into the future
먼저 ① [순위] first ; ahead ; first of all ; above all ; before anything else ¶ 먼저 가다 go first ; go before 《a person》; go ahead 《of another》 // 먼저 먹다 take〔eat〕 first ; eat before 《a person》 // 먼저 여러분에게 감사의 말씀을 드려야겠습니다 First of all, I must express my heartfelt thanks to you. // 먼저 가겠습니다 Please excuse my going first. // 먼저 가십시오 Please go first. /Let me follow you. /After you, sir. // 내가 맨 먼저 일어난다 I get up earliest of all. // 먼저 빚을 갚아야겠다 I have to pay my debts before anything else. // 몇 가지 이유를 들자면 먼저 돈이 부족하다는 것입니다 There are several reasons, firstly we are short of funds. // 먼저 앉는 사람이 임자다 First come, first served. // 무엇보다도 먼저 부모님께 알려라 Let your parents know first thing.
② [이전에] ago ; previously ; before ; formerly ; earlier ; recently ; lately ; [미리] in advance ; beforehand ¶ 먼저 꾸어간 돈 the money you borrowed from me previously // 먼저 말한 바와 같이 as previously stated // 먼저 떠나다 leave earlier than 《a person》 // 돈을 먼저 준비하다 get the money ready beforehand // 돈을 먼저 치르다 pay in advance // 먼저 그렇게 말한 일이 있지 않은가 Didn't you say that sometime ago? // 내일 아침에는 먼저 수표부터 한 장 보내드리겠습니다 I'll send a check first thing in the morning.
먼저께 the other day ; sometime ago ; [요즈음] lately ; recently ; in the recent past ¶ 먼저께의 recent ; late // 먼저께부터 for some days〔time〕 past // 먼저께 당신에게 말한 바와 같이 as I told you previously // 먼저께는 고마웠소 Thank you for the other day.
†**먼지** dust ; a mote ¶ 먼지가 일다 be dusty ; dust rises // 먼지가 끼다 be covered with dust // 먼지를 일으키다 raise〔stir up〕 dust // 먼지를 털다 brush away〔beat off〕 dust ; dust 《a coat》; brush 《a hat》 // 먼지를 가라앉히다 lay dust // 그 책상은 먼지투성이다 The desk is covered with dust. // 이 먼지 좀 봐 What a dust! // 털어서 먼지 안 나는 사람 어디 있나 Every-

one has a skeleton in his closet.
—떨이 a duster
먼지떨음 ① [살금 때림] flogging 《a boy》 only for form's sake ; giving a slight rod ② [오랜만의 나들이] going out after keeping the house for a long while
먼촌 [일가·친척] a distant relative ; [촌락] distant village
멀개지다 clear a bit ; go from dark to dull ; become paler〔clearer〕
멀거니 absent-mindedly ; blankly ; vacantly ; with a blank look ; with an abstracted air ; with a blank look ; stupidly ¶ 멀거니 바라보다 look〔gaze〕 vacantly 《at》// 멀거니 앉아 있다 be sitting absent-minded
멀건이 an absent-minded person
멀겋다 (be) hazy ; be a bit clear ; be not quite clear ; [묽다] (be) thin ; watery ; washy ; dilute ¶ 멀건 하늘 a hazy sky // 멀건 우유 thin〔washy〕 milk // 국이 멀겋다 Soup is〔looks〕 thin 〔watery, washy〕. // 하늘이 멀겋게 개다 The sky clears up a little.
멀구슬나무 〖식물〗 a "bead" tree ; a bastard cedar ; Melia japonica (학명)
멀끄러미 (looking) vacantly ⇨ 물끄러미
멀끔하다 (be) clean ⇨ 말끔하다
멀다[1] [눈이] go blind ; be blind ¶ 눈 먼 사람 a blind man ; a sightless person ; the blind 《총칭》// 눈이 멀다 be blind ; become blind ; lose〔be deprived of〕 one's sight // 돈에 눈이 멀다 be blinded by money
†**멀다**[2] ① [거리] (be) far ; distant ¶ 먼 길 a long way ; a long distance ; a long journey // 먼 곳에 far away〔-off〕 ; a long way off ; in the distance // 갈 길이 멀다 have a long way to go // 우리 집은 여기서 멀다 My house is far from here. // 마을은 훨씬 멀다 The town is a long way off.
② [시간] (be) remote ¶ 먼 옛날 a long time ago ; remote antiquity ; in the far-off days // 먼 장래에 in the remote〔far-off, distant〕 future // 먼 옛적으로 거슬러 올라가 way back to remote antiquity // 멀고 먼 곳에 산이 보이기 시작했다 A mountain became visible far in the distance.
③ [관계] (be) distant ¶ 먼 친척 a distant relative〔connection〕 ; a remote relative // 먼 친척보다는 이웃사촌 A good neighbor is better than a distant cousin. // 안 보면 멀어진다 Out of sight, out of mind. // 이것은 진짜 프랑스 요리 맛과는 거리가 멀다 This is nowhere near the taste of real French cuisine.
④ [귀가] be hard of hearing ¶ 귀가 멀다 be hard〔slow, dull〕 of hearing
멀면 정도 멀어진다 속담 Far from eye, far from heart.
멀떠구니 [새의] the craw ; the crop
멀뚱멀뚱 vacantly, blankly, absent-mindedly ; with an abstracted air ; with a blank look ; stupidly **—하다** (be) vacant ; blank ; absent-minded ; abstracted ; [국물이] watery ; thin ¶ 멀뚱멀뚱한 표정 a blank〔vacant〕 look ; a moony face 《미·속》// 멀뚱멀뚱 바라보다 look〔gaze〕 vacantly〔blankly〕 《at》
†**멀리**[1] far ; faraway〔-off〕 ; a long way off ; in the distance ; afar ¶ 멀리에서 from a distance ; from afar ; from faraway // 멀리로 to a distance // 멀리 여행하다 travel far // 아주 멀리 집 한채가 보였다 A house was seen at a great distance. // 멀리서 대포 소리가 들려왔다 We heard guns〔Guns were heard〕 afar〔in the distance〕. // 그녀는 역에서 더 멀리는 가지 않는다 She goes no farther than the station. // 도시에서 멀리 떨어진 시골에 산다 He lives in the remote country from the city.
***멀리**[2] **—하다** keep 《a person》 away from ; keep 《a person》 at a distance 〔arm's length〕 ; avoid (피하다) ; shun (싫어서) ; alienate (소외하다) ; abstain 《from liquor》 ¶ 사람을 멀리하다 keep 《a person》 at arm's length ; keep clear of 《a person》// 사람을 멀리하여 이야기하다 have a private talk ; talk〔meet, hold consultation〕 behind the closed doors // 악우를 멀리하다 shun〔avoid〕 bad company ; keep away from bad company ; avoid evil companions // 여자를 멀리하다 keep away from women ; eschew women ; give women up // 주색을 멀리하다 swear off wine and women ; give up liquor and sex ; abstain from sensual pleasures
멀미 ① nausea ; sickness ; queasiness ② [싫증] being fed up with ; being sick of ; an aversion ; dislike ; disgust **—하다** get sick ; feel queasy ; feel nausea ; [싫증] get sick of ; be tired of ; feel a repugnance to ; feel an objection to ¶ 그 일에는 이제 멀미가 난다 I am beginning to get fed up with the work. /I am tired of that business.
—약 antiseasickness pills for the queasy
배 — seasickness ¶ 배멀미하다 get〔feel〕 seasick // 나는 배멀미를 잘한다 I get seasick easily. /I am a bad〔poor〕 sailor. 비행기 — airsickness 차 — carsickness ¶ 나는 차 멀미를 하기 일쑤다 I am prone to motion sickness.
멀쑥하다 ① [키가] (be) lank(y) ; lean and tall ② [국물이] (be) thin ; watery ; washy ③ [모양이] (be) comely ; clean ; neat ¶ 멀쑥한 국물 thin 〔watery〕 soup // 멀쑥한 얼굴 a comely 〔good-looking〕 face // 키가 멀쑥하다 be lanky〔spindling〕
멀어지다 ① [소원] become estranged 《from》 ; be alienated 《from》 ¶ 사이가 서로 멀어지다 be〔become〕 estranged each other // 그들은 점점 서로 사이가 멀어졌다 They drifted farther and farther apart

from each other. // 그 여자는 놀라서 정신이 멀어졌다 She was frightened out of her senses〔wits〕.
② [거리가] become more distant ; go〔get〕 away《from》; withdraw〔recede〕《from》 ¶ 등불은 점점 멀어지더니 드디어 어둠 속으로 사라졌다 The lantern receded and disappeared at last in the dark.
③ [소리가] die away ; grow faint

멀쩡하다 ① [온전] (be) whole ; complete ; intact ; sound ; be free from damage ¶ 멀쩡한 옷 clean〔spotless〕 clothes ; clothes without defect // 멀쩡한 그릇 a whole dish ; a dish in perfect condition // 정신이 멀쩡하다 have a clear mind ; be sound in mind ; be in one's right mind // 폭풍이 불었지만 창고는 멀쩡했습니다 The storm left the barn intact. // 그릇이 하나도 깨지지 않고 모두 멀쩡하다 Not a dish broke, they are all in perfect shape.
② [가식] (be) hypocritical ; pretending ; dissembling ; [뻔뻔하다] impudent ; infamous ; audacious ; bold ; cheeky ; unblushing ; shameless ¶ 멀쩡한 놈 a hypocrite ; a dissembler ; an infamous person ; a person lost to shame // 멀쩡한 거짓말 a hypocritical lie ; an arrant lie // 멀쩡하게 굴다 play the hypocrite ; play possum

멀찌막하다 (be) pretty far ; rather distant ; be some distance away〔apart〕

멀찍멀찍 far apart ; at distant intervals《between》; at a good distance ; some distance apart ¶ 멀찍멀찍 떨어져 앉다 take seats some distance apart // 꽃을 멀찍멀찍 심다 plant flowers at a good distance each other

멀찍이 at a distance ; quite a way off ; far-away ; afar ¶ 멀찍이 떨어진 곳 a distant place // 멀찍이 사이를 두다 leave a pretty long interval《between》// 우리 집은 길에서 멀찍이 떨어져 있다 Our house is quite a way off the street.

멀찍하다 (be) pretty far ; rather distant ; be some distance away〔apart〕

†**멈추다** stop ; cease ; put a stop to ; bring to a stop〔halt〕; halt ¶ 딱 멈추다 stop short〔dead〕; stop suddenly〔completely〕; come to a standstill〔a full stop〕// 일을 멈추다 stop〔cease〕 work(ing) ; stay one's hand // 차를 멈추다 stop a car ; bring a car to a halt // 말을 멈추다 pull up a horse ; bring one's horse to a stop // 싸움을 멈추다 stop a quarrel ; cease fire (전쟁을) // …에 눈을 멈추다 let one's eyes rest on // 비가 멈췄다 It has stopped〔ceased〕 raining. // 비가 잠시 멈추었다 There was a lull in the rain. /The rain let up a little while. // 눈이 멈추지 않고 내렸다 It snowed without a break.

멈칫 ―하다 stop abruptly〔suddenly〕 for a moment ; come to a sudden halt ; flinch ; wince ¶ 하던 말을 멈칫하다 suddenly stop talking for a moment // 비가 멈칫하다 the rain stops for a moment

멈칫거리다 hesitate ; waver ; hang〔hold〕 back ; pause ; mark time ; vacillate ; falter ; shilly-shally ; dilly-dally ¶ 멈칫거리지 말고 네 생각을 말해라 Out with it ! Never stand shilly-shally. // 멈칫멈칫 hesitatingly ; hesitantly ; slowly ; lingeringly // 대답을 멈칫거리다 be slow to answer // 방에 들어오지 않고 멈칫거리다 hesitate to enter a room ; linger at the door

멋 ① [세련된 몸매] smartness ; stylishness ; [맵시 부리기] foppery ; dandyism ; dudism ¶ 멋있는 모자 a fanciful hat // 멋으로 for show // 멋있는 be stylish ; smart ; modish ; fanciful ; chic ; spicy ; gallant ; spruce ; swanky《미·속》; nobby《속》// 아주 멋있다 be as smart as a new pin // 그의 제복은 빨간 선이 들어 있어 아주 멋있다 His uniform looks very smart with the red stripe in it. // 나는 멋있게 차린 그를 만났다 I met him all spruced up. // 그녀에겐 어딘가 멋있는 데가 있다 There is something chic about her.
② [풍취] taste ; charm ; elegance ; flavor ¶ 멋있는 말 an interesting comment ; a witty saying ; a topping remark // 멋없는 말 a vapid〔uninteresting〕 remark // 멋있게 with gusto ; with relish ; delightfully // 멋이 있다 be full of gusto〔interest, flavor〕; (be) wonderful ; fine ; marvelous ; excellent // 멋이 없다 (be) insipid ; uninteresting ; dry ; dull ; flat ; vapid // 그녀의 옷차림은 멋있다 Her dress is in good taste. // 이 정원은 멋이 있다 This garden is tastefully arranged. // 혼자 가기는 좀 멋적다 It's a bit awkward to go there alone.
③ [이유·원인] reason ; ground ; cause ; the case ⇨ 멋모르다 ¶ 멋도 모르고 달려들다 try to go at somebody〔something〕 without knowing anything about him〔it〕

멋거리 dandification ; foppishness ; foppery ¶ 멋거리지다 be foppish ; be dandified

멋내다 smarten〔spruce, preen〕《oneself》 up ; pretty up ; be foppish ; be dandified ; dress stylishly〔smartly〕; try to look pretty〔smart, stylish〕

멋대가리 ⇨ 멋《속》¶ 멋대가리 없는 unrefined ; rustic ; boorish ; uncouth ; clownish ; awkward ; stiff (어색한) ; stupid ; senseless (몰상식한) ; stale《custom》(케케묵은) ; conventional // 멋대가리 없는 녀석 a bungling〔clumsy〕 fellow ; a boor ; a gawk // 기생을 붙들고 설법을 하다니 정말 멋대가리 없는 짓이다 Nothing is more out of place than to preach morals to a *kisaeng*.

*****멋대로** in one's own way ; willfully ; waywardly ; selfishly ¶ 제멋대로 as one likes // 제 멋대로 굴다 have one's own way ; act at one's pleasure ; have everything in one's own way ; act willfully // 네 멋대로 해라 I throw you on your own resources. // 그것은 내 멋대로 정할 수가 없다 I can't settle it on my own authority.

멋들다 be captivating 〔sexy〕 ; be beautiful〔charming, fascinating〕 ; get interesting ; take on flavo(u)r〔charm〕 ¶ 멋든 계집 an exciting girl ; a dashing girl ; a girl ripe for sex

멋들어지다 (be) splendid ; magnificent ; glorious ; grand ; excellent ; superb ; wonderful ; be very nice ; stylish ; smart ¶ 멋들어지게 splendidly ; superbly ; smartly // 멋들어진 미인 a great beauty ; a glamor girl 《미》 ; a chic girl // 멋들어진 생각 a capital〔good〕 idea // 멋들어진 성공 a phenomenal success // 멋들어진 승리 a brilliant victory // 멋들어진 요리 splendid dishes // 멋들어진 풍채 commanding presence ; imposing appearance // 영어를 멋들어지게 하다 have a wonderful command of English // 수양버들이 멋들어지게 늘어지다 a weeping willow droops gracefully

멋모르다 do not know ; know nothing ; be ignorant 《of》 ; have no idea〔conception〕 《of》 ; be innocent 《of》 ; be quite unconscious〔unaware〕 《of》 ¶ 멋모르고 unawares ; unknowing(ly) // 멋모르는 소리 말아 Don't be so unreasonable.

멋부리다 spruce up ; smarten〔prettify, fancy, liven up〕 ; dress smartly ; brush up ¶ 옷에 멋부리다 spruce oneself up // 그녀는 오늘 아침 멋부리고 왔다 She came all dressed up this morning.

멋없다 (be) uninteresting ; dull ; dry ; insipid ; lack flavor ; be poor ; awkward ; be not smart ; be not stylish ¶ 멋없는 사람 an uninteresting〔a dull〕 person // 멋없는 생활 prosaic〔cut-and-dried〕 life // 멋없이 굴다 act awkward ; be ungainly ; be unseemly // 그 아이는 멋없이 키만 크다 The boy has height but that's about all.

*멋쟁이 a dude 《미》 ; a dandy ; a fop ; a swell 《구》 ; a classy dresser ; a cockscomb — 양복 a stylish suit — 아가씨 a body soxer 《미·속》 — 미남자 a dandy ; a handsome boy

†멋지다 be full of beauty〔grace, fun〕 ; (be) splendid ; smart ; fascinating ; exciting ; thrilling ¶ 멋지게 춤추다 dance beautifully ; dance with gusto // 김선생님이 그런 멋진 일을 하다니 It's hard to believe Mr. *Kim* would do something that classy.

멋질리다 become dandified ; get foppish ; take to vanity

멋쩍다 ① [멋없다] lack flavor ⇨ 멋없다 ② [불쾌하다] (be) unpleasant ; distasteful ¶ 멋쩍은 말 작작해라 Away with your distasteful remarks.
③ [어색하다] feel embarrassed〔awkward〕 ; feel small ; feel uncomfortable ; be confused ; feel like a cat in strange attic ; feel ill at ease ¶ 낼 돈이 모자라서 멋쩍은 생각이 들었다 I felt awkward to find myself short of cash. // 또 부탁하기가 멋쩍다 I am embarrassed to ask a further favor.

멍 ① [맺힌 피] a bruise ; a contusion ¶ 멍들다 get〔have, sustain〕 a bruise ; suffer a bruise ; be bruised ; have〔suffer〕 an internal injury // 눈에 멍이 들다 have〔get〕 a black eye // 얻어 맞아〔꼬집혀〕 멍들다 be bruised by a blow 〔pinch〕 // 멍이 들도록 때리다 beat 《a person》 black and blue
② [타격] a hit ; a shock ; damage ; a real snag ¶ 일이 멍들다 a plan suffers a serious hitch〔runs into a real snag, runs into trouble〕 ; get a severe blow ; be hard hit 《by》 // 주가의 폭락으로 멍들다 lose heavily by a slump in the stocks // 사랑에 가슴이 멍들다 be lovesick ; be lovelorn ; languish for love

멍, 멍군 [장기] a defensive against a checkmate ; "out of check" —하다 make a defensive move against a checkmate ; get out of check ¶ 멍군 장군〔장이야 멍이야〕 It is hard to tell which of the two is wrong.

멍게 〖동물〗 an ascidian ; a sea squirt

멍구럭 a straw net of large meshes ; a large, loose-knit straw net

멍들다 ⇨ 멍

멍멍 bowwow ¶ 멍멍 짖다 go〔bark〕 bowwow ; bark

멍멍거리다, 멍멍대다 bark at 《a person》 ; bowwow

멍멍하다 keep being deafened 《by the din》 ; stay stunned〔dazed〕 ¶ 멍멍히 silently ; as if stunned ; blankly ; absent-mindedly ; vacantly

멍석 a straw mat
— 자리 a straw mat seat —짝 an individual straw mat

멍석딸기 〖식물〗 the white-flowering raspberry ; Rubus triphyllus (학명)

‡멍에 a yoke ¶ 소에게 멍에를 메우다 put a yoke on an ox ; yoke an ox // 멍에를 메다 come〔be〕 under a yoke // 멍에를 벗다 cast〔throw〕 off a yoke
—목 a neck of a river across which a bridge is built

멍엣줄 〖인쇄〗 the borderline of a printed page

멍울 [덩이] a lump ; [염증] an inflammation

멍울멍울 every lump ; in a lump —하다 (be) lumpy ; (be) full of lumps

멍청이 a stupid〔thick-headed〕 person ; a dullard ; a dunce ; a fool ; a silly fellow ; a simpleton ; an ass

*멍청하다 (be) stupid ; dull ; dumb ;

thickheaded ; stolid ; slow-〔dull-〕witted ¶ 멍청한 사람 a stupid person // 멍청한 짓을 하다 do a stupid thing ; make an ass of oneself
멍추 a stupid person ; a fool ; a forgetful person ; a weak-minded person
멍텅구리 ① 〖물고기〗 a sea fish ; Aptocyclus ventricosus (학명) ② [사람] a stupid person ③ [병] an ill-shaped bottle
멍하니 absently ; absent-mindedly ; vacantly ; blankly ; abstractedly ; with a faraway look ; in a daze ¶ 멍하니 앉아 있다 be sitting absent-mindedly // 멍하니 바라보다 look〔gaze〕 vacantly〔blankly〕 《at》 ; moon about ; have a vacant stare // 멍하니 정신이 없다 be in a daze // 그는 그 소식을 듣고 너무 충격을 받아 한참 멍하니 있었다 The news was such a shock to him that for a while he remained stupefied. // 무엇을 멍하니 생각하고 있니 A penny for your thoughts ! // 이렇게 멍하니 있을 수만은 없다 This is no time for idling.
⁑**멍하다** (be) abstracted ; absent-minded ; vacant ; blank ; dazed ; woolgathering ; [상심해서] stunned ; stupefied ¶ 멍한 얼굴 a vacant look ; a moony face 《미》 // 귀가 멍하다 be deafened // 멍하고 있어 미안하오 Please excuse my absent-mindedness〔me for being so absent-minded〕.
메[1] [제사밥] rice offered to the gods〔to departed spirits〕
메[2] [메꽃뿌리] the root of a bindweed 〔convolvulus〕
—나물 seasoned roots of bindweed
메[3] [방망이] a hammer (철재) ; a mallet (목재) ; a sledge-hammer (대장간의) ; a mallet (큰것) ¶ 메로 치다 hammer ; strike〔beat〕 with a hammer
메[4] [산] a mountain ; a hill
메- [차지지 않은] nonglutinous ; not sticky ¶ 메조 nonglutinous millet // 메떡 cake made of nonglutinous grain
메가사이클 〖물리〗 a megacycle 《mc, mc., m. c.》
메가와트 〖전기〗 a megawatt 《Mw》
메가톤 a megaton ¶ 메가톤급의 《a hydrogen bomb》 in the megaton range
메가트론 〖라디오·TV〗 a megatron ; a lighthouse tube
*__메가폰__ a megaphone
메공이 a hammer-shaped pounder
메귀리 〖식물〗 the wild oat
메기 〖물고기〗 a catfish ; a sheatfish ; a horned pout
메기다[1] fix 《an arrow in one's bow》 ; put 《an arrow on the string》 ; notch 〔nock〕 《an arrow upon the bow》
메기다[2] ① [소리를] lead 《a song, chant》 ② [톱을] take the lead on a two-man saw
메기입 a big long mouth ; a catfish-like mouth
메기장 nonglutinous (India) millet
메꽃 a convolvulus ; a bindweed ; the flower of convolvulus ; Calystegia japonica (학명)
메꾼 a hammerer ; a blacksmith
메꿎다 (be) willful〔stubborn〕 and illtempered ; headstrong and cross-grained
메뉴 a menu ; a (menu) card ; a bill of fare ¶ 메뉴에 있다 be on the menu 〔card, bill〕
메다[1] [어깨에] shoulder 《a gun》 ; carry 〔bear〕 《a thing》 on one's shoulder ¶ 총을 메고 with a gun on one's shoulder // 무거운 짐을 메다 carry a heavy burden on one's shoulder
메다[2] be stopped up ; be〔get〕 blocked ; get clogged ; be choked ; be closed ¶ 목이 메다 one's throat is choked ; feel choked // 코가 메다 one's nose is stuffy ; have got a stuffed-up nose // 굴뚝이 메다 a chimney is foul〔choked up〕 // 길이 메다 a road is crowded // 파이프가 메다 a pipe is clogged // 눈물로 목이 메다 be choked with tears // 그 하수도는 아주 메었다 The drain is completely stopped 〔bunged〕 up.
⁑**메달** a medal ; a medallion (대형의) ¶ 메달을 획득하다 win〔receive, obtain, carry off〕 a medal 《in〔for〕 the horizontal bar》 ; be awarded a medal 《for second place》 // 이 경기에서 금메달의 행방이 판가름 난다 This match will decide the destination of the gold medal.
— 획득자 a medalist **금〔은, 동〕—** a gold〔silver, bronze〕 medal
메달리스트 a medalist
금 — a gold medal winner ; a gold medalist
메들리 레이스 a medley race
메디나 Medina
메딱다구리 〖새〗 a Korean black-napped green woodpecker ; Picus canus jesoensis (학명)
메떡 cakes made from nonglutinous grain
메떨어지다 (be) rustic ; boorish ; crude ; unrefined ; awkward 《in one's actions》 ; stiff(-mannered)
⁑**메뚜기** 〖곤충〗 a grasshopper ; a locust (벼메뚜기)
메뜨다 (be) sluggish ; slow-moving ; tardy ¶ 모든 일에 메뜨다 He is slow-moving.
메리노 [양모] merino
— 모직물 a merino 《*pl.* -s》 **—양** a merino 《*pl.* -s》 ; a merino sheep
메리야스 knit(ted) goods ; knitwear ; hosiery ; a knit undershirt (셔츠)
*__메마르다__ (be) very dry ; parched ; arid ; sterile ; barren ; waste ¶ 메마른 땅 barren〔sterile〕 land ; wasteland // 메마른 땅을 개간하다 open〔develop〕 wasteland
메모 a memo 《*pl.* -s》 ; a memorandum 《*pl.* -s, -da》 **—하다** take a memo ;

take notes ⦅of⦆ ; jot down
— 용지 scratch paper
메밀 buckwheat
— 가루 buckwheat flour — 껍데기 buckwheat chaff — 국수 buckwheat noodles —묵 buckwheat paste〔jelly〕 —밥 boiled buckwheat
메벼 nonglutinous rice plants
메부수수하다 (be) boorish ; rustic ; countrified
메숲지다 (be) thick ; luxuriant ; dense ; bushy ¶ 메숲진 숲 a dense forest
메스 〖의학〗 a scalpel ; a surgical knife ⦅*pl.* -ves⦆ ¶ …에 메스를 가하다 plunge a scalpel 〔make a searching inquiry〕 into... ; dig into... ; probe ⦅a matter⦆ to the bottom // 날카로운 비판의 메스를 가하다 apply a scalpel of sharp criticism ⦅to⦆
†메스껍다 ① [구역나다] feel nausea ; feel sick〔queasy〕 ; feel like vomiting ¶ 속이 메스껍다 feel sick at the stomach // 떡은 보기만 해도 메스껍다 Even the sight of a rice-cake makes me sick.
② [아주 불쾌하다] (be) sickening ; stomach-turning ; nauseating ; revolting ; disgusting ; abominable ¶ 메스껍게 굴다 act〔behave〕 disgustingly // 메스꺼운 아첨 nauseating〔sickening〕 flattery // 그의 잘난 체하는 꼴만 보면 메스껍다 I am nauseated with his affectation.
메슥거리다 feel like throwing up〔vomiting〕 ; feel sick to one's stomach
메슥메슥 —하다 feel sick (at the stomach) ; feel like vomiting
메시아 [구세주] the Messiah ¶ 메시아의 Messianic
— 사상〔신앙〕 Messianism
†메시지 a message ¶ (본인 부재 중) 메시지를 남기다 leave a message ⦅with the secretary⦆ // 메시지를 낭독하다 read a message // 메시지를 보내다 send〔communicate〕 a message // 메시지를 전달하다 convey〔deliver〕 a message // 메시지를 주고 받다 exchange messages ⦅of friendship⦆
메신저 a messenger
*메아리 an echo ¶ 메아리가 울리다 be echoed ; echo ; resound ; reverberate // 우리가 소리지르자 산이 메아리쳤다 The hills resounded when we shouted.
메어붙이다 throw a person over his shoulder
메어치다 throw ⦅a person⦆ over one's shoulder ; throw ⦅a person⦆ to the ground ; buttock (유도 따위에서)
메역취 〖식물〗 a goldenrod ; Solidago virgaurea (학명)
*메우다¹ ① [빈 곳을] fill up〔in〕 ; plug (up) ; inlay ⦅with⦆ ; reclaim (바다 따위를) ¶ 틈을 메우다 fill〔make〕 up a gap ; stop a gap // 여백을 메우다 fill blanks ; fill in a blank ; fill space // 구멍을 메우다 plug a hole
② [결손을] fill up ; make up for ; make good ; cover ¶ 결손을 메우다 make up 〔make good, cover〕 a deficit
*메우다² ① [통 따위의 테를] put a hoop ⦅on a tub⦆ ② [북통에 가죽을] put a drumskin ⦅on a drum⦆ ③ [쳇바퀴에 쳇불을] fix a sieve net ⦅on its frame⦆ ④ [짐 따위를 사람에게] make ⦅a person⦆ carry ⦅a burden on his shoulder⦆ ¶ 세금을 메우다 impose a tax ; tax ⑤ [소에게 멍에를] yoke ⦅an ox⦆ ; put a yoke ⦅on an ox⦆
메이다 ① [테를] make ⦅a person⦆ put a hoop on a tub ¶ 통에 테를 메이다 make ⦅a person⦆ hoop a tub ② [북을] make ⦅a person⦆ put a drumskin on a drum ③ [체를] have ⦅a person⦆ fix a sieve net on its frame
메이저 [국제 석유자본] majors ; the seven international oil majors
— 판매 가격 sales prices of the majors
‡메이커 a maker ; a manufacturer ¶ 일류 메이커의 제품 an article made by a well-known manufacturer ; name brands
메이크업 ① [얼굴 화장] (a) makeup ; gilding (텔레비전·속) —하다 make (oneself) up ¶ 메이크업한 made-up ⦅complexion⦆ // 짙은 메이크업을 하다 use too much makeup // 메이크업을 지우다 take〔get〕 one's makeup off ② 〖인쇄〗 (a) makeup ¶ 봉조(棒組)에서 메이크업하다 make up the columns of a galley into pages
—공(工) a maker-up ⦅*pl.* makers-⦆ —계(係) a makeup man
메조 〖식물〗 nonglutinous〔regular〕 millet
메조 소프라노 mezzo-soprano
— 가수 a mezzo-soprano (*pl.* ~s, -ni)
메주 fermented soybeans ¶ 재주가 메주다 be a slow-witted person // 메주를 쑤다 boil soybeans // 콩으로 메주를 쑨대도 믿지 않다 deliberately deny the truth of what was said ; shut one's ears〔turn a deaf ear〕 to a person
—콩 soybeans — 덩이 a lump〔ball〕 of fermented soybeans
메지¹ the end of work ; the conclusion of a job ; settling ; concluding ¶ 일을 메지내다 bring a job to a conclusion ; settle // 일이 메지 나다 a job comes to a conclusion〔close〕 ; be settled〔fixed〕
메지² a seam ; a joint ; a juncture
메지다 (be) nonglutinous ; be not sticky ¶ 메진 쌀 nonglutinous rice
메지메지 ⦅dividing something up⦆ portion by portion
메질 —하다 hammer ; strike with a mallet ; pound ⦅stones for road-making⦆
*메추라기 〖새〗 a quail ¶ 메추라기 떼 a bevy of quails
메추리도요 〖새〗 a common snipe
메치다 ⇨ 메어치다
메카 Mecca ; [동경의 땅] a Mecca ⦅for artists⦆

메콩 강 —江 the Mekong (River)
메키하다 ① [곰팡내] (be) musty ; moldy ; fusty ; frowzy ¶ 메키한 빵 moldy bread // 메키한 냄새가 나다 smell musty 〔fusty〕 // 방이 메키하다 A room is musty. ② [연기 냄새] (be) smoky ¶ 방이 메키하다 A room is smoky. // 연기로 눈이 메키하다 One's eyes sting 〔burn〕 from the smoke.
메탄 『화학』 methane
— 가스 methane (gas) ; marsh gas
메탄올 『화학』 methanol ; methyl alcohol
메탕 —湯 [국] broth ; soup ; [제사 때 쓰는] vegetable〔kelp〕 soup offered in a memorial service to one's ancestors
메테나민 『약』 methenamin(e)
메트로놈 『음악』 a metronome
메틸알코올 methyl alcohol ; wood alcohol
멕시코 Mexico ¶ 멕시코의 Mexican
—만(灣) the Gulf of Mexico — 사람 a Mexican — 시티 Mexico City
멘델 Mendel, Gregor Johann (오스 1822–84)
—법칙 『생물』 Mendel's laws
멘스 『생리』 menses ; menstruation
멘탈 테스트 a mental test〔examination〕
멘히르 『고고학』 a menhir
멜대 a carrying pole ¶ 멜대로 메다 carry 《a thing》 on a pole
*‡멜로드라마 a melodrama
*멜로디 a melody
멜론 『식물』 a melon
멜빵 a rope〔strap〕 for carrying something on one's shoulder ; a shoulder strap 〔belt〕 ; [양복 바지의] braces ; suspenders
멤버 [한 사람] a member ; [팀의 전용] a lineup ¶ 정규 멤버 a regular member // 오랜 노력의 보람이 있어 그는 올림픽 팀의 멤버가 될 수 있었다 After a long hard training, he could make the Olympic team.
멤버십 membership ¶ 멤버십을 갖다 hold membership ; belong to 《a club》
— 카드 a membership card
멥새 『새』 a meadow bunting ; Emberiza cioides castaneiceps (학명)
멥쌀 nonglutinous rice
멧갓 a reserved forest ; a forest reserve
멧괴새끼 a wild fellow ; a rowdy ; a rough ; a roughneck 《미·속》
멧굿 an exorcism with musical accompaniment
멧나물 edible mountain herbs ; wild vegetables
멧닭 『새』 a grouse ; a black grouse 〔cock〕 ; Lyrurus tetrix (학명)
멧대추 a jujube
—나무 a jujube tree
멧도요 『새』 a woodcock
멧돼지 a wild boar
멧두릅 『식물』 a spikenard ; Aralia cordata (학명)
멧미나리 『식물』 Ostericum sieboldii (학명)
멧부리 a peak ; a summit ; the top of a mountain
멧부엉이 ① [새] a mountain screech owl ② [사람] a rustic ; a countryman ; a boor ; a hick ; a bumpkin
멧새 ① [산새] a mountain bird ② [멥새] a meadow bunting
멧종다리 『새』 a Chinese mountain hedge sparrow ; Prunella montanella pallas (학명)
멧짐승 mountain animals
며 and ¶ 사과며 포도며 기타 여러가지 apples, grapes and many other fruits
-며 ① [어미] and ; or ¶ 비가 오며 말며 하다 rain off and on
② [면서] while ; as ; over ; during ; with ¶ 웃으며 with a smile ; smiling // 커피를 마시며 이야기하다 linger over one's coffee // 울며 얘기하다 tell between sobs // 술을 마시며 얘기하다 talk over a bottle of wine
*며느리 a daughter-in-law ¶ 며느리를 보다 get a wife for one's son // 며느리가 미우면 손자까지 밉다 He who hates Peter harms his dog.
며느리 자라 시어머니 되니 시어미티 더 낸다 (속담) The mother-in-law remembers not that she was a daughter-in-law.
며느리고금 『한의학』 quotidian malaria 〔ague〕
며느리발톱 spur ; a calcar
며느리밥풀 a 『식물』 a kind of cowwheat ; Melampyrum japonicum (학명)
며래 『식물』 a kind of nettle ; Nanocnide japonica (학명)
며루 『곤충』 the larva of a crane fly 〔mosquito〕
며칟날 what day of the month ¶ 오늘이 며칟날인가 What day of the month is it today ?
며칠 [시일] what day of the month ; [일수] how many days ; how long ; [수일] a few days ¶ 그 일을 하는 데 며칠 걸리겠소 How many days will it take to get the work done ? // 그는 며칠 전에 떠났다 He left here a few days ago. // 며칠이나 서울에 머무르셨습니까 How long did you stay in *Seoul* ? // 이번 일요일은 며칠이냐 What date is this Sunday ?
멱1 [목] a throat ; a gullet ¶ 멱을 따다 cut 《a fowl's》 gullet ; cut 《a person's》 throat // 멱을 졸라 죽이다 strangle 《a person》 to death ; garrotte 《a person》 // 멱을 그러잡다 grasp 《a person》 by the throat〔neck〕
멱2 [목욕] bathing ; a cold bath ¶ 멱감다 bathe ; have〔take〕 a cold bath // 냇가로 멱감으러 가다 go to the river for a bath
멱3 『장기』 a chess piece located in a position which blocks another piece from making a move ¶ 말멱 a piece blocking another piece // 멱장기 a chess move

against the rule ; a chess player who does not know the rules of the game

멱⁴ [멱서리] a bag knitted of straw

멱 冪 〖수학〗 power ¶ 3승 멱 the third power

— **급수** power series **—수(數)** an exponent **이〔삼〕승 —** the second 〔third〕 power

멱둥구미 a straw basket ; a deep round grain-basket woven of straw

멱미레 dewlap (beef)

멱부리 a chicken〔cock, hen〕 with a feathery wattle〔gill〕

멱부지 —不知 a chess player who does not know the rules of the game

멱살 throat ; a collar (옷깃) ¶ 멱살을 잡다 grab 《a person》 by the throat ; grab 《a person's》 throat ; collar 《a person》 ; seize 《a person》 by the collar

멱서리 a straw bag ; a bag knitted of straw

멱신 shoes woven out of straw or hemp

멱씨름 **—하다** grapple at each other's throats ; come to grip with each other

멱통 the throat

†**-면** if ; in case 《of》 ; provided〔supposing〕 that ¶ 비가 오면 if it rains ; in case of rain // 시간이 있으시면 if you have time // 원하신다면 if you like〔want〕 // 그렇지 않으면 otherwise ; or else // 여기서 약 10분이면 간다 It's about ten minutes' walk from here. // 만일 실패하면 어찌하겠소 If you should fail, what would you do ? // 봄이 오면 꽃이 핀다 When spring comes, the flowers bloom.

면¹ [흙] earth dug out by rats, crabs or ants

면² [미동(美童)] a catamite 《남색(男色)의 상대》 ; a queen 《속》

면¹ 面 ① [얼굴] a face ¶ 면전에서 칭찬하다 praise 《a person》 to his face
② [체면] prestige ; dignity ; honor ; reputation
③ [표면] the surface ; a side ; a face ¶ 지구의 표면 the surface of the earth // 입방체는 6면을 갖는다 A cube has six sides〔faces〕.
④ [방면] an aspect ; a phase ; a side ; a field ¶ 재정면에서 in the financial aspect // 어느 면으로 보든지 in every respect // 사물의 밝은〔어두운〕 면을 보다 look on the bright〔dark〕 side of things
⑤ [가면] a mask ; a face guard (검도의) ¶ 면을 쓰다 wear〔put on〕 a mask // 면을 벗다 take〔throw〕 off one's mask
⑥ [지면] a page ¶ 사회면 the society page // 일면 the front page

면² 面 [행정 구역] a *myŏn* (a subdivision) of a *gun*〔county〕) ; a township
— **의회** a *myŏn*〔township〕 council

면 綿 cotton ¶ 면과 인견의 교직 a mixture of cotton and rayon〔artificial silk〕 // 면과 모의 교직 cotton-wool mixture ; half wool

면경 面鏡 a hand mirror ; a small looking glass

면계 面界 the border〔boundary〕 of a township

면관 免官 ⇨ 면직(免職) ¶ (장교가) 면관되다 lose one's commission

면괴 面愧 shamefacedness ; abashment ; shame **—하다** be shamefaced ; be ashamed ; be abashed ¶ 면괴하기 짝이 없습니다 I am deeply ashamed of myself. /I am stricken with shame.

면구 面灸 shamefacedness ⇨ 면괴

면구스럽다 面灸— (be) shamefaced ; abashed ; feel awkward〔embarrassed〕

면급 免急 **—하다** escape a danger〔a crisis, harm〕 ; get〔pass, come〕 through a crisis ; turn the corner ; hold back〔stave off〕 a crisis ; get〔keep〕 out of harm's way

면나다 ① [체면] get credit 《for》 ; win honor ; be honored ; save one's face ¶ 면나는 일 a thing that brings honor to 《a person》 ; a job that brings 《a person》 credit // 그렇게 되면 나도 면난다 That will also save my face.
② [광채] shine ; be prominent ¶ 사교계에서 면나다 shine in society

면내다 ① [흙을 파다] dig out ; gnaw ; nibble ¶ 쥐가 벽에 면내다 A rat makes a hole in a mud wall. ② [도둑질] steal bit by bit ; filch〔pilfer〕 bit by bit ; carry away in small quantity ; make free with 《money》 ; sneak 《미·속》 ¶ 쌀에 면내다 steal rice little by little

면내다 面— save one's face ; win honor ; bring honor to ¶ 남을 면내주다 keep 《a person》 in countenance // 자기 면내느라고 10만원을 기부하였다 He has donated a hundred thousand *won* to do himself proud.

면담 面談 an interview ; a talk ; personal conversation **—하다** have an interview 《with》 ; talk personally 《with》 ¶ 이 문제에 대하여 지배인과 면담했다 I talked over the matter with the manager.

면대 面對 facing **—하다** face each other ; meet〔come〕 face to face ¶ 면대하여 face to face ; to another's face (면전에서) // 면대하여 욕을 퍼붓다 abuse 《a person》 to his face

‡**면도 面刀** ① [면도질] shaving **—하다** shave oneself ; get a shave ; get oneself shaved ¶ 깨끗이 면도한 얼굴 a clean-shaven face // 면도를 하지 않고 지내다 go unshaven ② [면도칼] a razor
—날 a razor blade **— 숫돌** [돌의] a (razor) hone **안전 —** a safety razor **전기 —** an electric razor

면도칼 面刀— a razor ¶ 면도칼을 갈다 sharpen a razor ; whet a razor ; strap a razor

면려 勉勵 ① [근면] diligence ; (close) application ; industry ; assiduity ; exertion

(노력) ―하다 be industrious ; be diligent ¶ 직무에 면려하다 be diligent in one's duty ; apply oneself closely to one's duties ; strive ; exert oneself ② [격려] encouragement ; urging ; incitement ―하다 encourage ; urge ; spur

면류 麵類 noodles

면류관 冕旒冠 the imperial crown ; a diadem

면마 綿馬 〖식물〗 a kind of fern

면먹다 ① [내기에서] leave out debt of honor between two persons ② [편되다] be on the side of ; take sides〔part〕 with ; side with ; join the side of

면면 面面 [방면] all〔various〕 sides ; [각기] all faces ; each one ; every one

면면하다 綿綿― (be) continuous ; unbroken ; endless ¶ 면면히 continuously ; ceaselessly // 면면히 끊이지 않다 be unceasing ; be unending

면모 面貌 [얼굴의] a countenance ; looks ; features ; [일의] aspect ; appearance ¶ 면모를 일신하다 put on quite a new aspect ; be completely changed ; undergo a renewal ; change the appearance〔entire aspect〕

면모 面毛 downy〔fine, soft〕 hair on the face ; down〔fluff, fuzz〕 on the face

면목 面目 ① [체면] face ; countenance ; honor ; dignity ¶ 신사의 면목 a gentleman's honor // 면목을 세우다 save one's honor〔face〕 // 면목을 유지하다 preserve one's honor ; maintain one's dignity // 면목을 손상시키다 injure〔impair〕 one's honor // 면목이 없다 be ashamed 《of oneself》 ; be put out of countenance // 면목을 잃다 lose one's face〔countenance, honor〕 ; disgrace〔humiliate〕 oneself // 무슨 면목으로 집에 돌아갈 것인가 With what face can I go home ? // 바보짓을 해서 면목이 없습니다 I am ashamed of my folly. ② [양상] appearance ; an aspect ¶ 면목을 일신하다 take on quite a new aspect ; change the appearance〔entire aspect〕 ; undergo a renewal // 철도가 통함으로써 시의 면목이 일변하였다 The railway has completely changed the appearance of the city.

면목부지 面目不知 ―하다 be unknown to each other ; be total strangers to each other ; do not know each other's face

면민 面民 people of a township〔*myŏn*〕

†**면밀 綿密** minuteness ; exactness ; carefulness ; elaborateness ; scrupulousness ―하다 [세밀하다] (be) minute ; elaborate ; close ; detailed ; [주의 깊다] careful ; scrupulous ; meticulous ¶ 면밀히 minutely ; closely ; in detail ; carefully ; scrupulously ; elaborately // 면밀한 사람 a scrupulous person // 면밀한 관찰 minute observation // 면밀한 검사 a close examination // 면밀한 주의 close attention // 면밀한 조사의 결과 as a result of close investigation

면바르다 (be) smooth ; clean-cut ; well-formed ; nice and neat ; shipshape ¶ 그는 면바르게 생긴 젊은이다 He is a nice-looking〔clean-cut〕 young man.

면박 面駁 personal reproof ; refutation to 《a person's》 face ―하다 refute〔reproach〕 to 《a person's》 face ; throw the reproach into 《a person's》 teeth ; blame〔reprove〕 《a person》 to his face ; argue 《a person》 down〔into silence〕 ¶ 그는 공석상에서 나를 면박했다 He railed at me in public.

면방적 綿紡績 cotton spinning
―기 a cotton spinning machine

면벽 面壁 〖불교〗 meditation facing the wall

면보다 面― keep up〔maintain〕 the appearance 《of a gentleman》 ; save one's face〔honor〕

면부 面部 the face ; the facial region

면부득 免不得 ―하다 (be) inescapable ; unescapable ; inevitable ; unavoidable ; ineluctable ¶ 천재는 면부득하다 Calamities are inevitable. // 그것은 면부득하다 It cannot be helped.

면분 面分 a casual acquaintance ; knowing by sight ¶ 면분이 있다 know by sight ; be on nodding terms

면사 綿絲 cotton yarn〔thread〕

면사 免死 escape from death ―하다 escape〔be saved from〕 death ; get rid of death ; be snatched from the jaws of death

면사무소 面事務所 a *myŏn*〔township〕 office

면사포 面紗布 a wedding veil ; a bridal veil ; a face veil

면상 面上 (in) one's face ¶ 면상에 미소를 띄우고 with a smile on one's face // (감정이) 면상에 나타나다 show in one's face

면상 面相 looks ; features ; a countenance ; physiognomy (관상) ¶ 무서운 면상의 horrible-looking ; of a forbidding look // 면상이 좋지 않은 사람 an ill-looking person

면새 面― ① [표면] the surface ; appearance ② [체면] honor ; prestige

-면서 ① [불구하고] though ; yet ; notwithstanding ; in spite of ; for〔with〕 all ¶ 부자이면서 for all one's wealth // 싫어하면서 against one's will // 나쁜 줄 알면서 그는 거짓말을 했다 He told a lie though he knew it was wrong. ② [동시에] as ; while ; at the same time that ; with ; between ¶ 방긋 웃으면서 with a smile // 걸으면서 책을 읽다 read a book as one walks // 울면서 말하다 tell between sobs // 즐겁게 한잔 하면서 이야기하다 talk over a cheerful glass // 춤을 추면서 노래 부르다 dance and sing at the same time // 그는 밥을 먹으면서 책을 읽었다 He kept on reading while (he was) eating.

면서기 面書記 a *myŏn* official ; an official of a township office

면세 免稅 exemption form taxation ; tax exemeption ; immunity from taxes **—하다** exempt 《a person》 from taxation ; free 《goods》 from (custom) duties (관세를) ¶ 면세의 tax〔duty〕-free ; tax-exempt // 면세되다 be exempted from taxation

— **기간** a period of tax exemption ; a tax holiday — **수입품** (duty-) free imports ; free goods —**점** the tax exemption limit —**표(表)** a free list 《미》 —**품** articles free〔exempt〕 from taxes ; free goods ; tax〔duty〕-free goods〔articles〕

면세점 免稅店 a duty-free shop

면소 免訴 dismissal 《of a case》 ; acquittal 〔discharge, release〕 《of a prisoner》 **—하다** dismiss 《a case》 ; acquit〔discharge, release〕 《a prisoner》 ¶ 증거 불충분으로 면소되었다 He was acquitted for lack of evidence. // 그 사건은 예심에서 면소되었다 The case was dismissed after the preliminary trial.

면솔 面— a small brush for sideburns 〔side-whiskers〕

면수 免囚 a discharged convict〔prisoner〕 ; a released prisoner〔ciriminal〕

면수 面數 [책의 매수] the number of pages〔leaves〕 ¶ 면수가 잘못되어 있다 be wrongly paginated // 이 책은 면수가 많이 모자란다 This book has many missing leaves.

— **매기기** pagination ; paging — **조사** collation

면숙 面熟 familiarity〔acquaintance〕 with 《a person》 **—하다** be familiar〔acquainted〕 with 《a person》 ; know

면식 面識 acquaintance ¶ 면식이 있는 사람 an acquaintance // 면식이 있다 be acquainted with 《a person》 ; know // 면식이 전혀 없다 He is quite a〔a total〕 stranger to me.

면식 眠食 eating and sleeping ; food and sleep **—하다** eat and sleep

면실 綿實 cottonseed

—**유** cottonseed oil

면양 緬羊 〖동물〗 a sheep 《*pl.* sheep》

면업 綿業 the cotton industry

***면역 免疫** immunity **—하다** render immune ; confer immunity ¶ 면역되다 be〔become〕 immune 《from a disease》 // 면역이 되게 하다 make 《a person》 immune 《from》 ; immunize〔plant immunity into〕 《a person》 《against a disease》 // 그들의 욕설에는 면역이 되었다 I am impervious〔callous〕 to their abuse. // 한 번 그 병에 걸렸으니까 면역이 되어 있다 I am immune from the malady, as I have had it once.

— **요법** immunotherapy — **유전학** immunogenetics —**자(者)** an immune —**제** an immunizing agent — **주사** (a protective) inoculation — **혈청** an immune serum ; an antiserum

면역 免役 [노역의] exemption from public labor ; [병역의] exemption from military service ; immunity for conscription ; [죄수의] discharge〔release〕 from penal servitude〔prison〕 ¶ 면역이 되다 be exempted from 《public labor, military service》 ; be released〔discharged〕 from 《prison》 ; be set free (죄수가)

면역 기간 免疫期間 a period of immunity ¶ 선감 종두(善感種痘)의 면역 기간은 겨우 5년이다 The protective power of a successful vaccination lasts only five years.

면역 반응 免疫反應 an immune reaction 〔response〕

자가 — an auto-immune reaction

면역성 免疫性 immunity ¶ 면역성의 immune 《to, against, from》 ; refractory 《to reinfection》 // 면역성이 없는 nonimmune // 면역성을 주다 confer immunity 《on the patient》 // 면역성을 강하게 하다 raise 《a person's》 immunity 《to consumption》

— **결핍** anergy **후천** — acquired immunity

면역원 免疫原 〖의학〗 an immunogen

—**성** immunogenicity

면역체 免疫體 〖혈청〗 an immune body ; an antibody

자가 — 〖의학〗 an auto-immune body

면역학 免疫學 immunology ¶ 면역학적 방위 기구 the immunological defenses 《of a person》

—**자** an immunologist

면욕 面辱 a personal humiliation ; a personal insult〔offense〕 **—하다** humiliate 〔insult, offend〕 《a person》 to his face

면욕 免辱 escaping a humiliation〔shame〕 **—하다** escape a humiliation〔shame〕

면우 面友 a mere acquaintance

면작 棉作 cotton culture ; cultivation of cotton ; cotton harvest〔crop〕 (수확)

면장 免狀 a license ⇨ 면허장

면장 面長 the head〔chief〕 of a *myŏn* 〔township〕

†**면적 面積** area ; dimensions ; size (of a land) ; floor space (건물의) ¶ 넓은〔좁은〕 면적 a large〔small, limited〕 area // 그 도시의 면적은 100평방 마일이다 The city has〔covers〕 an area of 100 square miles. // 이 토지의 면적은 얼마입니까 What is the area of this land ?

—**계** a planimeter — **속도** 〖물리〗 areal velocity **경작** — area under cultivation **총** — the gross area

면전 面前 《a person's》 presence ¶ 면전에서 before 《a person》 ; in one's presence ; in the presence of 《a person》 // 사람들 면전에서 책망당했다 He was scolded in the presence of people.

***면접 面接** an interview ; a personal interview **—하다** see ; receive ; interview ; have an interview ¶ 면접 시험을 치다 undergo an oral test ; undergo a personal interview

—계 an interviewer **— 시간** hours for interviews **—실** a reception room **개인 —** an individual interview

면접 시험 面接試驗 an oral test〔examination〕; an interview ¶ 면접 시험을 행하다 give an oral test〔examination〕《to an applicant》// 면접 시험을 받다 undergo an oral test

면제 免除 exemption ; immunity ; impunity ; release ; discharge ; remission

> 참고 **exemption** 의무나 이행 따위로부터 해방되는 것 **immunity** 의무 속박 벌 고통 따위로부터 해방되고 보호되는 것 **impunity** 벌을 면제받는 것

—하다 exempt 《a person》 from ; release〔discharge〕《a person》 from ; excuse 《a person》 from ; remit ¶ 수업료를 면제받다 remit the tuition fee // 조세를〔병역을, 시험을〕 면제하다 exempt 《a person》 from taxation〔military service, examination〕// 채무를〔노역을〕 면제하다 release〔discharge〕《a person》 from a debt〔labor〕// 이 물건들은 관세를 면제받고 있다 They are exempt from customs duty.

일부 — partial exemption **입학금 —** exemption of the entrance fee **전부 —** total exemption

면제품 綿製品 cotton goods

면조 免租 exemption from a land tax **—하다** exempt land from taxation

—지 land exempted from taxation ; tax〔duty〕-free land

면종 面從 eyeservice ; pretended〔disguised〕 obedience **—하다** pay eyeservice 《to one's master》; be an eyeservant 《to》; work〔be obedient〕 only under the eyes of one's employer〔only when watched〕; pretend obedience

—복배(腹背) treacherous obedience ; (a) Judas kiss

면종 面腫 a furuncle〔boil〕 on the face

면죄 免罪 〖법〗 acquittal ; exoneration ; remission of sin (종교) **—하다** acquit ; remit

—부(符) an indulgence (카톨릭)

면지 面紙 〖인쇄〗 end paper ; end leaf ; the inside of a book cover

면직 免職 removal〔dismissal〕 from office ; deprivation of office ; discharge **—하다** dismiss〔remove〕《a person》 from office〔post〕; relieve 《a person》 of his office〔post〕; discharge 《a person》 from his duties ¶ 면직이 되다 be dismissed〔removed〕 from office ; be discharged ; be relieved of one's post ; lose one's position ; get the sack 《구》; be fired 《미·구》// 의원 면직이 되다 be relieved of one's post at one's own request

— 사령 a notice of dismissal

면직기 綿織機 a cotton loom

면직물 綿織物 cotton fabrics〔textiles, cloth〕; cotton piece goods

— 업자 cotton weavers

면질 面叱 personal rebuke〔scolding, reproof〕 **—하다** rebuke〔reprove, reprimand〕《a person》 to his face

면질 面質 confrontation ; face-to-face questioning〔controversy〕 **—하다** confront ; question face-to-face

면책 面責 personal reproof **—하다** reprove 《a person》 to his face ; cast a reproach in one's teeth ; reprimand 《a person》 personally

면책 免責 exemption〔immunity〕 from responsibility〔obligation, duty〕 **—하다** escape responsibility〔obligation, duty〕 ¶ 면책되다 become immune from obligation ; be exempted from obligation ; receive immunity from responsibility

— 조항 an exemption〔escape〕 clause ; 〖해상 보험〗 a negligence clause **— 특권** 〔국회의원의〕 the privilege of exemption from liability for one's speech in the National Assembly ; 〔외교관의〕 diplomatic immunity

면치다 面— trim the surface 《of a board》

면치레 面— saving appearances ; a facelifting **—하다** save (one's) face ; facelift ; save〔keep up〕 appearances ; put up a good front ; put a good face on the matter

면포 綿布 cotton (cloth) ; cotton stuff〔tissue〕

—류 cotton piece goods **—상(商)** a dealer in cotton goods

면피 面皮 face skin ; countenance

†**면하다 免—** ① 〔벗어나다〕 escape ; avoid ; get rid of 《trouble》; be relieved of ; get out of 《a difficulty》 ¶ 면할 수 없다 be unavoidable ; be inevitable ; be unescapable // 벌을 면하다 escape〔evade〕 punishment ; go scot-free // 위험을 면하다 escape〔get out of〕 a danger // 죽음을 면하다 escape death ; be saved from death // 도난을 면하다 escape being robbed // 욕을 면하다 save one's face ; avoid dishonor // 책임을 면하다 shirk〔evade, shuffle off, be freed from〕 one's responsibility // 화재를 면하다 be saved from the fire // 난쟁이를 면하다 just miss being a dwarf // 굶주림을 면하다 barely avoid hunger ; just manage to keep body and soul together // 간신히 면하다 have a narrow escape ; narrowly escape ; just miss 《being killed》// 원에 의하여 직을 면하다 dismiss 《a person》 from office at his own request ; be relieved of office at one's own request // 살아 있는 것은 죽음을 면치 못한다 Life is subject to decay. /Man

is mortal. // 그는 굴욕을 면했다 He was spared that humiliation.
② [면제] be exempted〔exempt〕 from ; be released〔relieved〕 from ; be free from ¶ 병역을 면하다 be exempted from military service ; gain immunity from conscription ; exempt 《a person》 from military service // 조세를 면하다 be exempted from taxation ; exempt 《a person》 from taxation // 오늘 밤은 숙제를 면해 주마 I will excuse you from homework for this evening.

면하다 面— face ; front ; look on ; look out on〔into〕 ; open out on 《the street》 ¶ 그 집은 바다에 면하고 있다 The house fronts〔faces〕 the sea.

면학 勉學 study ; pursuit of knowledge ; academic pursuit ; prosecution of studies **—하다** study ; pursue one's studies ; prosecute one's studies ; pursue knowledge ¶ 면학을 위하여 for study
— 분위기 an atmosphere conducive to academic pursuit ¶ 면학 분위기를 조성하다 create an academic atmosphere

‡**면허 免許** license ; permission **—하다** license ; permit ¶ 의사 개업 면허 a license to practice medicine // 면허를 얻다 obtain〔secure〕 a license
—료 a license fee **—세** the license tax ; taxation on a licensed business **— 어업** chartered fishery **— 영업** a licensed business **— 의사** a licensed physician **—제** the license system

면허장 免許狀 a license ; a certificate (증명서) ; a permit (허가증) ; a charter (법인체 설립 허가서) ¶ 면허장을 교부하다 grant〔issue〕 a license〔certificate〕 ; award a license (수여하다) // 면허장을 따다 obtain〔take〕 a license〔certificate〕 // 면허장을 갖고 있다 hold a license // 면허장을 압수하다 forfeit a license // 1개월간 면허장 행사를 정지당하다 have one's license suspended for a month
— 소지자 a license-holder ; a licensee **가—** a temporary license ; [자동차 따위 연습 중의] a learner's permit **본—** a full license **의사 개업 —** a medical practitioner's license **자동차 운전 —** a chauffeur's〔truck driver's〕 certificate〔license〕

면화 棉花 raw cotton ¶ 면화씨 기름 cottonseed oil // 면화 재배 cotton growing

면화 免禍 —하다 escape a disaster〔calamity, mishap, misfortune〕

면화약 綿火藥 guncotton

면회 面灰 lime mortar for the final coating **—하다** give the final coating of lime mortar 《to the wall》

***면회 面會** an interview ; a meeting **—하다** see ; meet ; interview ; have an interview with ¶ 면회를 거절하다 deny〔excuse〕 oneself to (a visitor) ; decline 〔refuse〕 to see 《a person》 // 면회를 청하다 ask 《a person》 to see 《someone》 ; ask for an interview 《with》 // 사장님을 면회하고 싶습니다 I should like to see the president. // 환자는 면회 사절이다 The patient is not allowed to see anyone. // 오늘은 누구에게도 면회를 사절해 주시오 Excuse me to callers today. /I am not at home to callers today. /I'm seeing no one today.
— 사절 No Visitors (allowed). (게시) /Interview declined. /Don't disturb. (병원에서) **— 시간(時間)** the visiting hours **— 실** [형무소 따위의] an interview room **작업중 — 사절** Interviews declined during working hours. (게시)

면회인 面會人 a visitor ; a caller ¶ 면회 왔는데요 Here's a gentleman〔lady〕 who wants to see you.

면회일 面會日 a receiving day ; a reception day ; a visiting day ; an at-home day ¶ 금요일이 면회일로 되어 있다 He sees visitors〔is at home〕 on Fridays. /Friday is his at-home day.

멸 〚식물〛 a kind of pepper plant ; Houttuynia cordata (학명)

멸각 滅却 extinction ; extermination ; destruction ; annihilation **—하다** extinguish ; exterminate ; destroy ; annihilate

멸공 滅共 red hunt ; rooting up communists ; eradication of communism
— 정신 the firm anti-Communist spirit ; the "Defeat Communism" spirit ¶ 멸공 정신을 강화하다 strengthen 《the nation's》 anti-Communist stand

멸구 〚곤충〛 a green leafhopper

멸균 滅菌 sterilization ; pasteurization (살균) **—하다** sterilize ; pasteurize
— 가제 sterilized gauze **—수** sterile water **— 작용** sterilizing action〔power〕

멸도 滅度 〚불교〛 Nirvana 《범》 ; the final emancipation ; the complete annihilation of self

†**멸망 滅亡** fall ; downfall ; ruin ; collapse ; destruction **—하다** fall ; be ruined ; go to ruin ; be destroyed ; cease to exist ¶ 국가의 멸망 the fall of a nation // 멸망의 길을 걷다 be on the road to collapse〔ruin, doom〕 // 그 나라는 멸망의 날이 박두했다 The hour of the doom of the country is at hand.

멸문 滅門 extermination of a whole family ; destruction of all one's kinsfolk **—하다** a whole family is exterminated〔destroyed〕 ; exterminate one's whole kinsfolk ¶ 멸문지화 a disaster that wipes out a whole family

멸사봉공 滅私奉公 self-annihilation for the sake of one's country ; sacrificing one's personal interest to public good

***멸시 蔑視** contempt ; disdain ; disregard **—하다** regard 《a person》 with contempt ; despise ; disregard ; disdain ; hold 《a person》 in contempt ; look down upon ; hold 《a person》 cheap ; make light〔little〕 of ; slight ¶ 멸시 받다 be held in contempt ; be treated with contempt // 가난하다고 해서 멸시해서는 안 된다 You should not despise〔look down upon〕 him because he is poor.

멸여 蔑如 contempt

멸적 滅敵 destruction〔extermination〕 of an enemy **—하다** destroy〔exterminate, conquer〕 an enemy

멸절 滅絶 extermination ; extirpation ; eradication ; extinction

멸족 滅族 extermination of a family〔tribe〕 **—하다** exterminate a family〔tribe〕

멸종 滅種 extermination (of a stock) **—하다** exterminate (a stock)

멸치 〖물고기〗 an anchovy ; Engraulis japonicus (학명)

—젓 salted anchovies

멸치고래 〖동물〗 Balaenoptera borealis (학명)

멸하다 滅— ruin ; destroy ; overthrow ; exterminate ; annihilate ; be destroyed〔overthrown, annihilated〕; cease to exist ; die out ¶ 나라를 멸하다 ruin〔destroy〕 a nation // 적을 멸하다 destroy〔conquer〕 an enemy

명 ① [무명] cotton cloth ② [목화] cotton ; a cotton plant

명 名 ① [인원수] persons ② [이름] name ; fame ③ [유명한] noted《wrestler》; celebrated《place》; distinguished《person》; great《work》; star《actor》; wise《judge》; judicious《decision》 ¶ 30명 thirty persons

—판사 an able judge ; a Daniel

명 明 [중국의 왕조] Ming ⇨ 명조(明朝)

명 命 ① [목숨] life ¶ 명이 길다 live long ; have a long life ; last long // 제 명에 죽다 die a natural death ② [운명] (a) destiny ; fate ③ [명령] an order ; a command ; instructions ; a dictation (지시) ¶ 명에 의하여 at〔by〕 command ; on〔under〕 orders // 당국의 명에 의하여 by order of the authorities ; under government orders〔mandate〕 // 명을 받다 receive orders《from a person》; be ordered // 명을 따르다〔거역하다〕 obey〔disobey〕《a person's》 orders

****명 銘** [기념비의] an inscription ; [묘비의] an epitaph

명가 名家 ① [명문] a reputable family ; an illustrious house ⇨ 명문 ② [사람] an eminent person (명망 있는) ; a great master (대가)

— 수상집 a choice collection of light essays

명가 名價 fame ; reputation ; nominal value

명가수 名歌手 a famous〔renowned〕 singer

명감 明鑑 a broad view and high intelligence (높은 식견) ; bright discernment (올바른 식별)

명개 loam along the riverside

명검 名劍 an excellent〔a fine〕 blade ; a noted〔famous〕 sword

명견 名犬 a fine dog

명견만리 明見萬里 deep insight ; farsightedness **—하다** have deep insight ; be farsighted

명경 明鏡 ① a clear mirror ¶ 마음이 명경 지수와 같다 The mind is as bright and clean as a stainless mirror. ② [분명한 증거] definite〔strong〕 evidence〔proof〕

명계 冥界 the nether world ; the land〔region〕 of the dead ; Hades ; the land beyond the grave

명곡 名曲 famous music ; musical classics ¶ 명곡을 감상하다 appreciate famous music

— 감상 music appreciation

명공 名工 a master hand ; an expert (artisan) ; a skillful workman〔craftsman〕

명과 銘菓 a cake of an established〔a well-known〕 name ; an excellent cake

명관 名官 a celebrated〔an illustrious〕 governor ; a good〔wise〕 magistrate

명관 明官 a wise governor〔ruler〕

명관 鳴管 〖해부〗 a syrinx (of a bird)

명구 名句 a famous〔memorable〕 phrase〔line〕; a fine〔happy〕 expression ; a wise saying ; a well-known adage ¶ 명구집 a collection of a famous sayings ; an anthology of fine expressions〔splendid remarks〕

명군 明君 a wise ruler〔king〕 ; an enlightened monarch ; a benevolent lord

명궁 名弓 [사람] an expert archer ; a famous bowman ; [활] a noted bow

명금 鳴禽 a singing〔song〕 bird ; a songster

명기 名妓 a celebrated〔famous〕 *gisaeng*

명기 名器 [유명한 물건] a famous article ; [일품] an excellent article ; [악기] an exquisite instrument

명기 明記 —하다 write〔mention, state〕 expressly ; write〔put down〕 clearly ; specify ¶ 규칙에 명기되어 있다 be specified〔defined clearly〕 in the regulations

명기 明氣 ① [산천의] the beautiful scenery of landscape ② [안색] bright and cheerful expression〔countenance, complexion〕

명년 明年 next year ; the coming year

명념 銘念 —하다 keep〔bear〕 in mind ; engrave on one's mind〔in one's heart〕

명단 明斷 a judicious decision ; a clear〔wise, convincing〕 judgment ¶ 명단을 내리다 pass a clear judgment《on》

명단 名單 a list of names〔persons〕 ; a roll ; a roster

명담 名談 a wise〔golden〕 saying ; a witty〔sensible, felicitous〕 remark ; a famous remark

명답 明答 [확답] a definite〔decisive〕 answer **—하다** answer〔reply〕 definitely ; give《a person》 a definite answer

명답 名答 [바른] a right〔correct, excellent〕 answer ; [교묘한] a clever〔shrewd〕

answer ¶ 명답이다 You are quite right. /You have guessed right. /You said it. 《미·구》
—안 an excellent paper

명당 明堂 ① [정전] the king's audience hall ② [무덤 앞 땅] the flat space in front of a grave ③ [좋은 묏자리] a propitious site for a grave

명도 明渡 delivery ; surrender ; evacuation ; quitting **—하다** evacuate (비우다) ; quit 《a house》; [인도] deliver 《a castle》 ; surrender ; clear out of 《a house》; give〔yield〕 up 《a castle to the enemy》 ¶ 집을 명도하다 vacate〔quit〕 a house // 명도를 요구하다 ask 《a person》 to quit 《the house》
— 소송 an eviction suit ; dispossession proceedings **— 신청** a petition for eviction **— 통고** eviction notice

명도 明度 brightness ; luminosity ; value 《of color》

명도 冥途 Hades ; the nether world ; the other world ; the realm of shades

명동 鳴動 rumbling **—하다** rumble ¶ 태산 명동에 서일필 Much cry and little wool. /Much ado about nothing.

명란 明卵 spawn of a pollack
— 젓 salted roe of the pollack

†**명랑 明朗** brightness ; clearness ; cheerfulness ; gaiety **—하다** (be) bright ; clear ; cheerful ; merry ; gay ; sunshiny ; lighthearted ¶ 명랑하게 merrily ; cheerfully ; lightheartedly ; in a gay spirit // 명랑한 가정 a merry home // 명랑한 기분 a happy〔light〕 heart // 명랑한 사람 a cheerful〔sunshiny, frank〕 person ; a person of sunny disposition // 명랑한 정치 clean politics // 명랑한 현대 여성 a bright modern woman // 가정을 명랑하게 하다 fill one's home with happiness

†**명령 命令** an order ; a command ; bidding ; a direction (지시) ; instructions (훈령) ; [법령] a law ; an ordinance ; a decree ; laws and regulations **—하다** order ; command ; bid ; give orders〔a command〕 ; direct ; charge ; instruct

> 참고 **command** 군주 사령관 따위의 절대적인 명령으로서 짧은 말로 전달된다 **order** command에 비하여 공식적이 아니며 때로는 성급한 또는 제멋대로의 명령에 쓰인다 **direct** 주로 사무상 공무상의 지시를 말한다 **instruct** direct와 거의 비슷하지만 명령 사항은 확실히 알아듣도록 전해진다 **charge** 의무적인 일을 명령하다

¶ 명령적 imperative ; commanding // 명령적으로 imperatively ; peremptorily // 명령대로 as ordered ; according to an order // 장관의 명령에 의해서 by order of the minister // 명령을 내리다 issue an order〔a command〕 ; give orders // 명령을 받다 receive〔have, be under〕 orders ; get the word 《미》 // 명령에 따르다〔거역하다〕 obey〔disobey〕 《a person's》 order // 명령을 이행하다 carry out〔execute〕 an order // 명령조로 말하다 speak in a commanding〔an authoritative〕 tone // 명령대로 행하다 do as one is told ; act upon 《a person's》 order ; do 《a person's》 bidding // 그에게 무엇이라고 명령했느냐 What order did you give him ? /What did you tell〔order〕 him to do ? // 그것을 하기 싫지만 명령이니 할 수 없지 I hate to do that, but an order is an order. // 그 명령은 이행되지 않고 있다 The order is being ignored. // 나는 네 명령은 받지 않겠다 I will not be dictated by you.
— 계통 a line〔chain〕 of command **—문** 〖문법〗 an imperative sentence **—법** 〖문법〗 the imperative mood **—서** an order ; a (written) directive ; 〖법〗 a warrant ; a precept ; 〖항공〗 a briefing (비행사에게 주는 간결한) **— 위반** violation of an order **—자** a commander ; a dictator ; an orderer **— 항로** 〖항공〗 a government-directed service ; a subsidized line **전투〔전투중지〕 —** a combat〔cease-fire〕 order **특별 —** a special rule

명론 名論 an excellent opinion ; a sound〔cogent, well-founded, telling〕 argument〔view〕 ; an excellent treatise
— 탁설(卓說) an original opinion worth listening to ; a feast of reason (Alexander Pope의 귀절 "the Feast of Reason and the Flow of Soul"에서)

명료 明瞭 clearness ; plainness ; lucidity ; distinctness **—하다** (be) clear ; plain ; lucid ; distinct ; perspicuous ¶ 명료하게 발음하다 pronounce〔articulate〕 《a world》 distinctly // (글씨를) 명료하게 쓰다 write clearly〔legibly〕 // 명료하지 않다 be vague ; be obscure // 명료하게 하라 make clear〔plain〕 ; clarify

명료도 明瞭度 〖통신〗 articulation
— 지수 an articulation index

명류 名流 a celebrated〔prominent〕 person ; a celebrity ; a noted person ¶ 당대의 명류 prominent men of the time

명리 名利 fame and wealth ; name and fortune ; riches and honor ¶ 명리를 초월하다 be above riches and wealth // 명리에 급급하다 be constantly striving after fame and profit ; be over-anxious for gains and fame

명리심 名利心 worldly〔terrestrial〕 aims〔interests〕 ; a carnal ambition ¶ 명리심이 있는〔없는〕 worldly-〔unworldly-〕 minded

명마 名馬 a fine horse ; [군마] an excellent〔a good〕 steed ; a renowned charger ; a Bucephalus

명망 名望 reputation ; repute ; renown (명성) ; popularity ¶ 명망을 얻다 gain fame // 명망을 잃다 fall in public estima-

tion ; lose one's popularity
명망가 名望家 a man of (high) repute 〔renown〕; a popular man ; a man high in public esteem ¶ 이제 그는 상당한 명망가이다 He now enjoys a fairly high reputation.
명매기 〖새〗 the large white-rumped swift ; Micropus pacificus (학명)
명맥 命脈 life ; the thread of life ; existence ¶ 명맥을 이어가다 keep alive ; retain life ; remain in existence // 명맥이 짧다 be short-lived ; have a short life // 겨우 명맥을 이어가다 barely keep oneself in existence
명멸 明滅 **—하다** flicker ; glimmer ; blink
— 신호 a blinking signal
†**명명 命名** christening ; naming **—하다** give a name to ; christen ; name ; call ; designate ¶ 태극호라고 명명하다 christen〔name〕 a ship the *Taegeuk* // 숙모의 이름을 따서 진숙이라고 명명했다 We named her *chinsuk* after〔for〕 her aunt.
—식 the christening〔naming〕 ceremony
—자 a godfather ; the author 《of a scientific name》
명명백백 明明白白 **—하다** (be) clear ; plain ; obvious ; be as clear as day ; be as plain as print
명모 明眸 bright eyes
—호치(皓齒) starry eyes and pearly teeth ; (personal) beauty ; comely features
명목 名木 [유서 깊은 나무] an old tree of historical interest ; [목재] precious 〔choice〕 wood ; fine incense wood
명목 名目 ① [명칭] a name ; a title ; an appellation ② [구실] a pretext ¶ 명목상의 nominal ; titular ; in name only // 명목상으로 nominally ; titularly ; in name only // …의 명목으로 under the pretext 〔name〕 《of》 // 명목을 만들어서 under some pretext or other
— 임금 nominal wages〔prices〕 **— 자본** nominal capital
명목 瞑目 **—하다** [눈을 감다] close one's eyes ; [죽다] die ; pass away ; breathe one's last ; expire
명목론 名目論 〖철학〗 nominalism ; terminism
—자 a nominalist ; a terminist
명문 名聞 reputation ; fame ; honor ; credit ¶ 명문천하 《gain》 world-wide fame〔reputation〕
명문 名文 an excellent〔a beautiful〕 composition ; a literary gem ; a beautiful passage ¶ 명문이다 be well written ; be high in literary merit ; be well composed // 명문을 쓰다 write finely〔beautifully〕 ; write a fine〔beautiful〕 style
—가(家) a fine prose writer ; a master of literary style ; a master stylist **—집** a choice collection of prose ; select pieces 《from an author》 ; an anthology of 《19th century》 prose ; a collection of literary gems
명문 名門 a distinguished〔an illustrious〕 family ; noble lineage ¶ 명문의 자제 children of noble birth〔a good family〕 // 명문 출신이다 come of a noble family ; be high-born ; be a man of high birth ; be blue-blooded
— 거족(巨族) mighty〔powerful〕 clans **— 교(校)** a school of high (academic) reputation ; a prestige〔prestigious〕 school
명문 明文 an express provision〔statement, words〕 ; a specific proviso ¶ 법률에 명문이 없다 There is no provision in the law. /That is not provided for in the law.
— 규정 substantive enactment
명문천하 名聞天下 world-wide fame〔reputation〕 **—하다** be world-famous ; gain world-wide fame
명문화 明文化 stipulation **—하다** stipulate ; put in a statutory form ¶ 명문화되(지 않)다 be (not) provided for in the law ; be (not) expressly stipulated in the text
명물 名物 [산물] a special〔noted〕 product ; a speciality ; [유명한 물건] a feature ; an attraction ; an institution 《속》 ; [사람] an institution ; a popular figure ¶ 대구의 명물 사과 the apple for which *Taegu* is noted // 안개는 런던의 명물이다 The fog is a thing for which London is famous. // 이 지방의 명물은 무엇입니까 What is this locality noted for? // 이 식당의 명물은 냉면이다 This restaurant features iced vermicelli〔noodles〕.
명미 明媚 beautifulness ; picturesqueness **—하다** (be) beautiful ; picturesque ¶ 풍광 명미한 땅 a place of scenic beauty ; a beauty spot
명민 明敏 sagacity ; intelligence **—하다** (be) sagacious ; intelligent ; sharp ¶ 두뇌가 명민하다 have a clear head ; be clearheaded
명반 明礬 alum
—석 alumstone ; alunite ; alumite
†**명백 明白** **—하다** (be) clear ; plain ; obvious ; evident ; manifest ; distinct ; patent ; unmistakable ¶ 명백하게 clearly ; plainly ; evidently ; obviously ; expressly ; explicitly ; distinctly // 명백하게 하다 make clear ; clear up ; explicate ; clarify // 명백해지다 become clear
명복 冥福 happiness in the other world ; heavenly bliss ¶ 명복을 빌다 pray for the repose of 《a person's》 soul ; pray for the souls〔happiness〕 of the dead // 명복을 비는 미사를 올렸다 masses were said 〔read〕 for 《a person's》 soul
†**명부 名簿** a list (of names) ; a register ; a roll ; a roster ¶ 명부를 작성하다 make a list 《of》 // 명부에 기입하다 list ; register

선거인 — a poll book 직원 — a register of the staff ; a roster 참관인 — a visitors' book 총원 — [함선의] a muster roll 학급 — a class list 회원 — a list of members ; a membership list

명부 冥府 the other〔nether〕 world ; the underworld ; Hades

명분 名分 one's moral duty〔obligation〕; (moral) justification ; justice ¶ 명분이 서지 않는 unjustifiable // 명분을 세우다 justify ((oneself, one's conduct)) // 명분을 밝히다 clearly define one's moral obligations ; uphold the cause of loyalty // 전쟁을 일으키는 명분이 서지 않으리라 There would be no justification for a war.

명불허전 名不虛傳 ¶ …은 명불허전이다 It is quite true as I have heard that...

⁑명사 名士 a man of note ; a distinguished 〔noted, prominent〕 person ; a celebrity ; a notable ¶ 명사들의 집회 a gathering of notables ; a distinguished gathering // 정계의 명사 a distinguished politician // 문단의 명사 notabilities in literary circles ; a famous〔noted〕 writer // 당대의 명사 prominent men of the time // 대통령의 초대연에 많은 명사들이 참가하였다 Many notables came to the President's reception.

⁑명사 名詞 〖문법〗 a noun ; a substantive
—구〔절〕 a noun phrase〔clause〕 물질〔추상, 보통, 고유〕 — a material〔an abstract, a common, a proper〕 noun

명사 名辭 〖논리〗 a term ; a name
—주의 〖철학〗 terminism 대〔소〕— the major〔minor〕 term 절대 — the absolute term 중— the middle term

명산 名山 a noted〔celebrated〕 mountain
— 대천 noted mountains and large rivers ; splendid mountains and rivers

명산 名産 a special〔noted〕 product ; a speciality ¶ 그것은 경주의 명산이다 It is a special product of *Kyŏngju*. /*Kyŏngju* is famous for it.

⁑명상 瞑想, 冥想 meditation ; contemplation **—하다** meditate ((on)) ; contemplate ; muse ((on)) ¶ 명상적 meditative ; contemplative // 명상에 잠기다 be lost〔buried, sunk〕 in meditation ; fall into a brown study
—가 a meditator ; a contemplator — 록 meditations

명색 名色 a name ; a title ; a designation

명석 明晳 clearness ; distinctness **—하다** (be) clear ; lucid ; distinct ¶ 두뇌가 명석한 사람 a clear thinker ; a clearheaded person // 두뇌가 명석하다 be clear-headed ; have a clear head

†명성 名聲 fame ; renown ; reputation ; celebrity ¶ 불후의 명성 one's undying fame // 명성이 높다 be renowned ; noted ; celebrated // …로서 명성이 있다 have renown ((for)) // 명성을 얻다 gain fame ; make a reputation ; make a name for oneself // 명성을 잃다 lose one's reputation // 명성을 유지하다 maintain one's reputation // 명성을 손상하다 hurt〔injure, impair, affect〕 one's reputation // 시인으로서 세계적 명성이 있다 be famous all over the world as a poet ; be a poet of world-wide fame〔renown〕 // 명성은 재산보다 낫다 A fair name is better than riches.

명성 明星 〖천문〗 Venus ; [새벽의] the morning star ; Lucifer ; [저녁의] the evening star ; Hesperus ¶ 문단의 명성 a literary star

명세 明細 details ; particulars ; [내역] the items ((of an account)) ; breakdown ; classification ; itemization ; an accounting **—하다** (be) detailed ; full ; minute ; particular ¶ 명세하게 in detail ; fully ; minutely // 명세하게 설명하다 set forth ((something)) in detail ; go〔enter〕 into particulars〔details〕 // 지불〔지불금〕의 명세를 보고하다 render an account for payment of all money spent // 합계 550만원이며 그 명세는 다음과 같다 It totals 5,500,000 *won*, made up as follows.
—표 an itemized account ; a portfolio ((*pl.* -s))

명세서 明細書 a detailed statement ; a minute description ; details ; a list of particulars ; specifications ; a detailed account ¶ 첨부 명세서와 여히 as per specifications attached
선적 — shipping specification 지출 — a bill of expenditures

명소 名所 a place of interest〔note〕; a celebrated locality ; a noted place ; sights (to see) ; a beauty spot ¶ 부여 명소 안내서 a guide to the principal places of interest in *Puyŏ* // 경주의 명소를 구경하다 see〔do〕 the sights of *Kyŏngju* // 진해는 벚꽃의 명소이다 *Chinhae* is famous for its cherry blossoms. // 새로 지은 고층 건물이 관광 명소가 되었다고 들었습니다 I heard a newly-built high-rise building has become a tourist attraction. // 한국의 주요 관광 명소는 어디입니까 What are the major tourist attractions in Korea?

명소 고적 名所古跡 scenic spots and places of historic interest ¶ 명소 고적이 많다 be rich in scenic and historic interest // 명소 고적을 돌다 visit places of natural beauty and historic interest

명수 名數 [인원수] the number of persons ; [명목수] a nominal number

명수 命數 [수명] a person's natural span of life ; a person's (length of) days ; [운명] fate ; destiny ¶ 명수를 알다 know one's doom ; know that one is dying 〔near death〕 // 명수가 다하다 be deserted by fortune (운수)

명수 名手 a master〔capital〕 hand ; a master ; an expert ¶ 피아노의 명수 an accomplished pianist

명수법 命數法 〖수학〗 numeration

명승 名勝 a place of scenic beauty ; a beauty〔scenic〕 spot

― 고적 scenic spots and places of historic interest ¶ 명승 고적을 순방하다 visit〔pay visits to〕 places of natural beauty and historic interest

명승 名僧 an eminent〔a noted, a celebrated〕 Buddhist priest

†**명시 明示** clear statement ; elucidation **―하다** state clearly〔plainly〕 ; express 〔describe〕 clearly ; clarify ; elucidate

명시 明視 clear vision **―하다** see 《a thing》 clearly ; see in a clear light

― 거리 〖물리〗 the distance of distinct vision

명신 名臣 an illustrious retainer〔subject〕 ; a well-known statesman

명실 名實 name and reality〔fact〕 ¶ 명실을 구비한 민주 국가 a democratic country worthy of the name // 명실공히 both nominally and virtually〔really〕 ; both in name and reality ; in fact as well as in name // 명실 상부하다 be true to the name ; be up to 《its》 reputation // 명실이 상부하지 않는다 The reality does not agree with〔falls short of〕 the name. // 명실공히 그 운동의 통솔자이다 He is the leader of the movement in fact〔deed〕 as well as in name.

명심 銘心 bearing in mind **―하다** bear 〔keep〕 《anything》 in mind ; take 《an advice》 to heart ; have 《anything》 stamped〔engraved〕 on one's mind ; impress 《a fact》 on one's mind ¶ 우리들은 이 교훈을 깊이 명심해야 한다 This lesson is what we should deeply impress upon our mind. /We should take this lesson to heart.

명아주 〖식물〗 a goosefoot ; Chenopodium album (학명)

명안 名案 a good〔capital, brilliant〕 idea ; a splendid plan ¶ 그것은 명안이다 That's an idea. /Good idea ! // 명안이 머리에 떠올랐다 A bright idea came to him.

명암 明暗 light and shade〔darkness〕 ¶ 인생의 명암 양면 the bright as well as the dark side of life

―도 brightness ; 〖사진〗 light intensity **― 등〔광〕** 〔항로 표지〕 an occulting light **― 법** 〖제도·미술〗 shading ; clear obscure ; chiaroscuro 《이》

명야 明夜 tomorrow night〔evening〕

명약관화 明若觀火 being as clear as daylight **―하다** be as clear〔plain〕 as daylight ; (be) obvious

명언 名言 a wise〔golden〕 saying ; a sage 〔witty〕 remark ¶ 만고의 명언 an immortal saying

―집 analects

명언 明言 declaration ; a definite statement ; assertion **―하다** 〔공언하다〕 declare ; 〔단언하다〕 say〔state〕 definitely〔positively〕 ; assert ; remark ; distinctly ¶ 지금은 명언할 수가 없다 At present I cannot say anything definite about it.

명역 名譯 an apt〔excellent〕 translation

명연기 名演技 an excellent〔a beautiful〕 performance

†**명예 名譽** honor ; 〔영광〕 glory ; 〔영예〕 distinction ; 〔신망〕 credit ; 〔명성〕 fame ; reputation ; 〔체면〕 dignity ; prestige ¶ 명예로운 honorable ; glorious // 명예를 존중하는 사람 a man of honor // 명예로운 지위 an honorable position // 명예를 얻다 win〔gain〕 fame〔honor〕 // 명예를 손상하다 bring〔invite〕 disgrace on 《a person》 ; injure〔impair〕 《a person's》 honor // 명예를 존중하다 value honor ; have a keen sense of honor // 명예를 회복하다 restore one's honor ; reestablish one's impaired reputation ; retrieve one's character // 명예로운 전사를 하다 die gloriously〔a glorious death〕 at the battle // …하는 것을 명예로 생각하다 esteem it an honor to 《do》 // 학교의 명예가 되다 be a credit〔an honor〕 to the school // 학교의 명예와 관계되다 affect the honor of the school ; cast a reflection on the school // 그것은 결코 그의 명예를 손상하지 않는다 It is by no means a discredit to him. // 이것은 우리들의 명예에 관한 문제이다 This is a point of honor with us.

― 계약 〖해상 보험〗 an honor agreement **―관** one's notions of honor **― 제도** 〔사관학교의〕 the honor system **― 학위** an honorary degree **― 혁명** 〖영국사〗 the Glorious〔Bloodless〕 Revolution ; the English Revolution **― 회복** regaining the impaired reputation **― 회장〔회원〕** an honorary president〔member〕

명예 교수 名譽敎授 an emeritus〔honorary〕 professor ; a professor emeritus ¶ 명예 교수의 칭호를 받다 be granted the title of emeritus professor

명예 시민 名譽市民 an honorary citizen 《of Seoul》

명예심 名譽心 ⇨ 명예욕(名譽慾)

명예욕 名譽慾 love of fame ; ambition ; a desire for fame ; aspiration after fame ¶ 명예욕이 강한 사람 a hunter after fame // 명예욕이 강하다 have a strong desire to win fame ; have an ardent passion for fame // 명예욕을 만족시키다 satisfy one's ambition

명예직 名譽職 an honorary post 〔office〕 ; a post without pay ¶ 그 지위는 명예직이다 The post carries no pay.

명예 훼손 名譽毁損 defamation of character ; (a) libel (문서에 의한) ; (a) slander (구두의) ¶ 명예 훼손의 소송을 제기하다 sue 《a person》 for libel

― 사건 a libel (case)

명왕성 冥王星 〖천문〗 Pluto

명우 名優 a great〔celebrated〕 actor ; a (famous) star ¶ 명우가 되다 rise to star-

dom
명운 命運 one's fate ; one's doom (악운)
명월 明月 a bright moon ; a full moon (보름달) ¶ 중추의 명월 the harvest moon
명유 名儒 a famous〔well-known〕 confucianist ; a prominent scholar ; a scholar of note
명의 名義 ① [이름] name ¶ 명의상의 nominal ; titular∥명의만의 교장 a nominal principal ; a principal in name only∥명의상으로 in name ; nominally ; titularly ∥아들의 명의로 되어 있다 be in〔under〕 the name of one's son∥아들의 명의로 변경하다 transfer 《property》 to the son ② [명분] one's moral duty
— 도용(盜用) an illegal use of other's name — 이전 nominal transfer —인 a nominal person ; the holder of a title deed
명의 名醫 a noted doctor〔physician, specialist〕 ; an excellent physician ; a Hippocrates
명의 변경 名義變更 transfer (of the title) 《trans.》 ; entry of a change of holders ; 〖주식〗 transfer ¶ 주식의 명의 변경을 정지하다 close the transfer books ; suspend transfers of stocks
— 대리인 a transfer agent —료 a transfer fee — 증서 a deed of transfer
†명인 名人 a noted person ; a (past) master ; a master hand ; an expert ¶ 승마의 명인 an accomplished equestrian
—전(戰) [장기의] the professional chess players' championship series
명일 名日 a festive day ; a national holiday ; a fete (day) ; a gala day
명일 明日 tomorrow (내일)
명일 命日 the anniversary〔date〕 of 《a person's》 death (기일)
명자 名字 [이름자] the characters of one's name ; [평판] fame
⁑명작 名作 a masterpiece ; a fine piece 《of literature》 ; an excellent work 《of art》 ¶ 근래의 명작 the greatest masterpiece in recent years
명장 名匠 a master hand ; a master craftsman ; a skilled workman〔artisan, artist〕
명장 名將 a great commander ; a famous 〔a distinguished, an illustrious〕 general
명재경각 命在頃刻 be on the brink〔point, eve〕 of death ; be〔lie〕 at death's door ; be in the hour of death ¶ 그 아이는 명재경각이다 The boy's life hangs by a thread.
명재상 名宰相 an able〔a noted〕 premier
명저 名著 a notable〔famous〕 book〔work〕 ; a great〔fine〕 work ; a masterpiece
명절 名節 festival〔festive〕 days ; big holidays ; gala days ¶ 실상 명절 기분은 그믐날 밤부터 시작된다 In reality, the festive mood begins on the eve of the New Year's Day.
명정 酩酊 intoxication ; drunkenness ; inebriety —하다 get〔be〕 drunk ; be intoxicated〔inebriate(d)〕 ; get tipsy
명정 銘旌 a funeral banner〔streamer〕 ; a streamer with an inscription of the name and the rank of the deceased
명제 命題 ① 〖논리〗 a proposition ; a thesis 《*pl.* -ses》 ② [제목] a given subject for a composition
가언 — a hypothetical〔conditional〕 proposition 긍정〔부정〕 — an affirmative 〔a negative〕 proposition 단칭 — a singular proposition 동일 — an identical proposition 전칭 — a universal proposition 특칭 — a particular proposition
명조 明朝 ① [내일 아침] tomorrow morning ② [명나라] the Ming-dynasty
명조 冥助 divine favor ; providence
명조체 明朝體 Ming-style printing type ; [영자] roman type ; the roman
†명주 明紬 silk ; [견직물] silk fabric 〔cloth〕
—실 silkthread —옷 silk clothes
명주 銘酒 liquor of a famous brand ; high quality liquor
명주 조개 a trough shell ; a surf clam
명줄 命— ⇨ 수명(壽命)
명중 命中 a hit —하다 hit 《the mark》 ; strike ; [예언이] come true ¶ 과녁의 복판에 명중하다 make〔hit〕 the bull's eye∥탄환이 눈에 명중하다 strike 《a person》 in the eye∥명중하지 않다 miss 《the mark》 ; go wide∥탄환은 거의 다 명중했다 Nearly all the shots told.
—수 the number of hits
명중탄 命中彈 a (direct) hit ; a telling shot ¶ 김 중위는 자기 비행기의 오른쪽 날개에 명중탄을 맞았다 Lieut. *Kim* took a hit on the right wing of his plane.
명증 明證 [증거] clear evidence ; a positive proof ; [증명] verification ; clarification —하다 prove clearly ; verify ; clarify
명징 明澄 clearness ; lucidity —하다 (be) clear ; lucid
명찰 明察 insight ; discernment ; penetration ; keen judgment —하다 discern ; have an insight 《into a matter》 ; see through ; penetrate〔pierce〕 to the bottom 《of the matter》 ¶ 명찰하여 주시옵기 바랍니다 I leave it to your good judgment.
명찰 名札 an identification tag ; a place card (자리의) ; a name-〔door-〕plate (문패) ¶ 명찰을 달다 affix〔put on〕 a name tag ; attach a name card
명찰 名刹 a famous〔noted〕 temple
명창 名唱 [노래] a famous song ; [사람] a noted〔great, celebrated〕 singer
명철 明哲 sagacity ; intelligence ; [사람] a wise man ; a sage —하다 (be) sagacious ; wise ; brilliant
명추 明秋 next autumn〔fall〕
명춘 明春 next spring

명충 螟蟲 〖곤충〗 a pearl-moth ; a rice-borer

명치 the pit of the stomach ; the solar plexus

—뼈 the bone above the pit of the stomach

*__명칭 名稱__ a name ; a title ; a term ; a designation ; a denomination (화폐 단위 따위의) ¶ …의 명칭으로 under the name 〔title〕《of》// 명칭을 붙이다 name ; call ; give a name〔title〕; designate // 명칭을 바꾸다 change the name ; rename ; rechristen ; retitle

명콤비 an excellent pair ¶ 명콤비를 이루다 make an excellent pair

*__명쾌 明快__ clearness ; lucidity ; explicitness **—하다** (be) clear ; lucid ; explicit ¶ 명쾌하게 clearly ; lucidly ; explicitly // 명쾌한 문체 a lucid literary style // 명쾌한 설명 a clear explanation

명태 明太 〖물고기〗 the Alaska pollack ; Theragra chalcogramma (학명)

명토 名— pointing out ; indication ¶ 명토 박다 point out ; indicate

명투 明透 mastery ; conversance **—하다** be well-versed《in》; be a master《of》

명패 名牌 [책상 위 따위에 놓는] a nameplate ¶ 명패를 못박아 붙이다 peg one's nameplate《at》// 명패를 달다 attach〔affix〕 a name tag《to》

명필 名筆 ① [필적] an excellent handwriting〔calligraphy〕; [명필가] a good hand《at writing, at painting》; a noted calligrapher ¶ 그는 명필이다 He writes a very good hand. /He is an excellent penman.
② [명화] an excellent drawing〔painting〕; [명화가] a master painter

*__명하다 命—__ ① [명령] order ; give orders ; command ; tell ; bid ¶ 엄중히 명하다 give strict orders ② [임명] appoint ; nominate ; assign

*__명함 名銜, 名啣__ ① a (name) card ; a visiting card ; a calling card《미》; [영업용] a business card ¶ 명함을 주고 받다 exchange cards // 명함을 두고 가다 leave one's card ② [성함]《a person's》esteemed name

명함판 名銜判 the size of a visiting card **— 사진** a card-size photograph ; a quarter plate **— 사진기** a quarter-plate camera

명현 名賢 a noted wiseman〔sage〕

명호 名號 ① [이름과 호] name and pen-name ② [명목] a title ⇨ 명목

명화 名花 a famous〔celebrated〕 flower ; [사람] a beauty ; a celebrated courtesan

명화 名畫 a famous〔celebrated〕 picture ; a notable painting ; a masterpiece ; an old master (고전적 대가의 작품) ; a notable film (영화의) ¶ 루벤스의 명화 a masterpiece of Rubens

†__명확 明確__ clearness ; precision ; definiteness **—하다** (be) clear and accurate ; precise ; definite ; distinct ¶ 명확하게 clearly ; precisely ; definitely ; distinctly/ 명확한 대답〔선〕 a definite answer〔line〕 // 이 점을 명확히 하다 clear up〔clarify〕 this point // 권한과 책임의 한계를 명확히 하다 establish clear-cut lines of authority and responsibility

명후년 明後年 the year after next

명후일 明後日 ⇨ 모레

몇 [약간] some ; a few ; several ; [얼마] how many ¶ 몇 해 how many years ; a few〔several〕 years // 몇 살 how old ; what age // 몇 시 when ; what time // 마흔 몇 개인가의 회사 forty odd corporations // 몇이나 about how many ; about so many ; several // 다만 몇 안되는 only a few // 몇 번이고 many〔several〕 times ; many a time ; over and over again // 몇 사람이든지 좋다 Any number of persons will do. // 몇입니까 How old are you ? // 몇 시 차를 탈까요 What train shall we take ? // 몇 년이나 된 전화기입니까 How old is your phone ? // 몇 시까지 문을 엽니까 How late are you open ?

†__몇몇__ some ; several ; a few ¶ 몇몇 사람 some〔several〕 persons // 몇몇은 죽고 몇몇은 부상했다 Some people were killed, others wounded. // 김군하고 또 몇몇 친구가 같이 간다 I am going with *Kim* and a few other friends.

몇 번 how often ; several times ¶ 몇 번이고 often ; many〔a dozen, a number of〕 times ; over and over again ; repeatedly // 몇 번이든 해 보시오 Try as often as you can〔will〕. // 몇 번 말해도 마찬가지다 This is my last word, I tell you.

모[1] [벼의] a young rice plant ; [모종] a seedling ; [묘목] a young plant〔tree〕 ¶ 모를 심다 (trans) plant young rice plants ; set〔bed〕 out rice plants

모[2] ① [각] an angle ; [모서리] an edge ; a corner ¶ 모난 angular ; angulated ; angled // 모를 세우다 make angular ; sharpen the edge // 모를 죽이다 round off the angle ; trim the corner // 모가 지게 자르다 cut square
② [성질·사물이 모남] angularity ; stiffness ; harshness ¶ 모난 angular ; stiff 《manners》; unsociable ; uncompromising ; not affable // 모가 없는 사람 a smooth-mannered person ; a sociable 〔an affable〕 person // 모난 소리를 하다 speak harshly // 모나게 굴다 behave〔act〕 harshly〔unsociably〕

네— a square ; a quadrangle **세—** a triangle

모[3] [윷] the 5 points made by throwing the four *yuch* sticks so that all four faces are down

모[4] a cake ; a block ¶ 두부 한 모 a cake of bean curd

모 毛 ① [털] hair ; fur ; wool ② [단위] a

mo ⟪one-tenth of a *ri*⟫
모 母 a mother
모 某 [모인] a certain person ; Mr. So-and-so ; someone ; [어떤] a certain ; one ; a ; some ; unnamed ¶ 김모씨 a certain *Kim* ; a person named *Kim* // 모박사 Doctor So-and-so ; Doctor What's-his-name ⟨속⟩ // 모처에서 at a certain place ; at an undisclosed〔unidentified〕 place
모가비 a boss ; a head ; a chief ; a gang leader
모가지 a neck ⇨ 목
모가치 one's share ⇨ 몫
모감주나무 〖식물〗 Koelreuteria paniculata ⟨학명⟩
모개로 all together ; in the lump ; in the gross ; wholesale ; in one lot ; in bulk ; en masse ⟨프⟩ ¶ 모개로 사다 buy wholesale ; buy ⟪things⟫ in mass〔lot, bulk〕 // 돈을 모개로 지불하다 pay in lump sum〔in one sum〕 // 물건을 모개로 보내다 send things together // 모개로 흥정하다 make a package deal〔wholesale dealing〕
모걸음질 walking〔marching〕 off at an angle
모경 暮景 an evening scene ; evening twilight
모경 暮境 one's declining years ; old age
모계 母系 the maternal〔mother's〕 line ; the spindle〔distaff〕 side ; one's mother's side ; the uterine descent ¶ 모계의 maternal ; on the maternal〔mother's, distaff〕 side // 모계에 왕가의 피를 받고 있다 trace one's descent to the Royal family on the mother's side
— **가족** a maternal〔an umbilical〕 family — **사회** a matrilineal〔matricentric〕 society — **친척** the relatives〔relations〕 on the maternal side
모계 謀計 a trick ; a plot ; an artifice ; a machination ; a stratagem ¶ 모계를 꾸미다 plot ; conspire // 적의 모계에 빠지다 fall a prey to the enemy's stratagem ; play into the enemy's hands
모골 毛骨 hair and bone ¶ 모골이 송연하다 shudder ; feel one's hair stand on end
모공 毛孔 ⟨the skin⟩ pores
모과 〖식물〗 a Chinese quince ; a papaya
모과나무 〖식물〗 a Chinese quince ; a papaya tree ; Chaenomeles sinensis ⟨학명⟩
모관 毛管 〖물리〗 a capillary ⟨vessel⟩
모관 현상 毛管現象 capillary action〔phenomenon〕 ⟨모세관 현상⟩
*__모교 母校__ one's alma mater〔Alma Mater〕 ; one's old school
—**애** almamaterism
모교회 母敎會 a mother-church
모국 母國 one's mother country ; the 〔one's〕 homeland ; one's native country ¶ 모국을 방문하다 visit one's mother country // 그는 영어를 모국어처럼 말한다 He speaks English like a native〔one born to it.〕
*__모국 某國__ a certain country〔nation〕
— **관광단** a tourist party on a visit to their homeland
모국어 母國語 one's mother tongue ; [그 나라의 말] the native〔vernacular〕 language ¶ 한국어를 모국어처럼 말하다 [외국인이] speak Korean like a native〔one born to it〕
모군 募軍 ① [인부] a navvy ; a coolie ; a construction worker ¶ 모군서다 become a construction worker ; work as a coolie ② [모병] recruiting
—**삯** construction worker's wages —**일** construction〔coolie〕 work
모권 母權 maternal right ; mother's authority ¶ 모권을 확장하다 raise the status of motherhood
— **사회** a matriarchal society —**설** the theory of metronymy —**제(制)** matriarchy —**제 시대** the matriarchal stage
모근 毛根 〖해부〗 the root of hair ¶ 모근을 이식하다 implant a hair
‡**모금** a draft ; a gulp ; a drop ⟨조금⟩ ; a sip ⟨차 따위⟩ ¶ 물을 한모금 마시다 drink a draft of water // 물을 한모금에 마시다 drink the water down at one gulp // 그후로 술은 한모금도 안마신다 I have not tasted a drop of wine since.
모금 募金 money〔fund〕 raising ; invitation〔collection〕 of subscriptions ; collection of contributions〔donations〕 —**하다** collect contributions ; invite〔raise〕 subscriptions ⟪for⟫
— **상자** collecting〔collection〕 box —**액** the amount of subscriptions to be raised — **운동** a fund-raising campaign ; a drive to raise funds ; a canvass for subscriptions **가두** — a street collection of subscriptions **불우 이웃 돕기 — 운동** a community chest drive ; a "Red Feather" campaign
*__모기__ 〖곤충〗 a mosquito ¶ 모기가 물다 mosquitoes bite〔sting〕 // 모기에 물리다 be bitten〔stung〕 by mosquitoes // 모기가 앵앵거리다 mosquitoes buzz // 모기를 잡다 swat〔slap, catch〕 mosquitoes // 연기를 피워 모기를 쫓다 smoke out mosquitoes // 말라리아는 모기가 매개한다 Malaria is carried by the ⟨anopheles⟩ mosquito.
모기도 모이면 천둥소리 낸다 속담 Weak things united become strong. /Union is strength.
모기둥 an angular〔a square〕 pillar
모기떼 a swarm of mosquitoes
모기방동사니 〖식물〗 a kind of sedge
모기장 —**帳** a mosquito net ¶ 모기장을 치다 put up〔hang〕 a mosquito net // 모기장을 걷다 take down a mosquito net // 모기장을 치고 자다 sleep under a mosquito net
모기향 —**香** a mosquito〔incense-〕 stick

〔coil〕
모깃불 a smudge ; a mosquito-fumigator 〔-smoker〕 ¶ 모깃불을 피우다 smudge ; fumigate to keep off〔out〕 mosquitoes // 모깃불을 피워 모기를 내쫓다 smoke〔fumigate〕 out mosquitoes ; smoke mosquitoes away
모꼬지 a meeting ; a gathering ; a party **—하다** gather together
모끼 a kind of plane used to round off sharp edges
—연 〖건축〗 a rafter laid over a long rafter (placed at both edges of a roof)
모나다 ① [각이 지다] be angular〔angled〕 ⇨ 모² ② [성질이] be angular〔harsh, unsociable〕 ⇨ 모² ③ [유효하다] be useful ; effective ; profitable ¶ 돈을 모나게 쓰다 spend money well〔to good cause〕 ; make the most of one's money
모내기 rice-planting ; setting out rice plants ; rice transplantation **—하다** transplant rice ; set〔bed〕 out rice-plants ¶ 모내기에 바쁘다 be busy planting the rice
—철 the rice-planting season
모내다 ① [벼의] transplant rice seedlings ; set〔bed〕 out rice-plants ② [각을] make angular〔square〕 ; give square〔edges〕 ; put corners on ¶ 기둥을 모내다 make a pillar square
모녀 母女 mother and daughter ¶ 모녀간 between mother and daughter
모년 某年 a certain year
모노드라마 〖극〗 a monodrama
모노레일 [궤도] a monorail ; [차량] a monorail car〔train〕
모노타이프 a monotype
모놀로그 a monologue
⁑**모니터** a monitor
—제(制) 〖방송〗 a monitor system
모다 ⇨ 모으다
모다기- all at once ; from all sides ¶ 모다기령(令) order coming from everywhere all at once // 모다기 포화〔공격〕 a concentrated fire〔attack〕
모다깃매 blows from all sides
모닥불 a bonfire ; a campfire (야영의) ; fire in the open air ¶ 모닥불을 피우다 make a fire 《in the open air》 ; make 〔build〕 a bonfire〔campfire〕
모당 母堂 your〔his, her〕 esteemed mother
모더니스트 a modernist
모더니즘 modernism
모던 modern ; modernistic 《tearoom》 ; (be) abreast of the times
— 아트 the modern art
모데라토 〖음악〗 moderato 《이》
†**모델** a model ¶ 화가의 모델 an artist's model // 모델로 하다 model 《A on B》 // …을 모델로 하여 《work, paint》 from a model // 실제의 모델을 토대로〔보고〕 쓰다 〔그리다〕 work〔draw〕 from a living model // …을 모델로 해서 그린 초상화 a portrait painted from sittings given by... // 모델이 되다 act as a model ; pose for an artist ; sit for〔to〕 a painter // 이 소설의 주인공은 A씨가 모델이다 The hero of this novel is modelled after Mr. A.
— 소설 a roman à clef 《프》 **— 알선소** a model agency **— 인형** a plastic model ; a lay figure **— 체인지** a model change ; restyling ; face-lifting **—카** a miniature model of a car **— 케이스** a model case **— 학교** a model school **패션 —** a fashion model
모도 母道 motherhood
모도록 thickly ; luxuriantly ; densely **—하다** (be) thick ; luxuriant ; dense
모도리 [여무진 사람] a shrewd fellow
모독 冒瀆 defilement ; debasement ; pollution ; [신성 모독] blasphemy ; profanity ; desecration **—하다** profane ; blaspheme ; desecrate ; defile ; debase ; pollute ¶ 십자가를 모독하다 blaspheme (against) the Cross // 존엄(성)을 모독하다 debase 《a person's》 dignity
— 행위 a sacrilegious practice
모동 暮冬 late winter
모되 a square *doi* measure
†**모두** all ; everyone ; everybody ; everything ; [합계] in all ; all told ; [다 함께] all together ; altogether ; in a body ; en masse 《프》 ; [몰아서] in the gross ¶ 애들은 모두 all the children // 우리 세 사람 모두 everyone of us three // 모두 반대다 All are against it. // 모두 내 잘못이다 It's all my fault. // 모두 살해됐다 They were killed to a man〔all of them〕. // 모두 너에게 주겠다 These are for you all. // 그 일은 모두 알고 있다 I have heard all about it. // 모두 같이 노래를 부르자 Let's sing the song all together. // 우리 일행은 모두 10명이었다 There were ten of us, all told. // 모두 가져 가거라 Take the whole lot〔all the lot〕. // 그들은 모두 독신이다 They are bachelors without exception. // 용돈을 모두 써 버렸다 I have spent the last penny of my pocket money. // 그 상품은 모두 500만원으로 평가되었다 The goods were valued in the gross at 5,000,000 *won*. // 나의 형제는 모두 키가 크지 않다 None of my brothers are tall. // 번쩍인다고 모두가 금은 아니다 All is not gold that glitters. // 모두 얼마요 How much altogether ? /How much for the lot ?
— 먹기 winner-take-all
모두 冒頭 the beginning ; the opening ; the outset ; the head paragraph (제 1절에) ; the lead ¶ 연설의 모두에 at the outset of one's speech // 모두에 싣다 give 《an article》 at the beginning // 연설의 모두에 성경의 한 구절을 인용하다 preface one's speech with a quotation from the Bible // 그 장의 모두에 시가 실려 있다 The

chapter opens with a poem.
—문(文) 『신문』 a lead — 서명자 the oversigned — 진술 『법』 arraignment

모두거리 [씨름의 기법] tripping one's opponent by slapping his feet ; [넘어짐] a stumble from having both feet tripped

모두걸이 a fall from having both feet tripped

모두뜀 leaping on both feet

모두머리 a hairdo in a chignon with a strand of braided hair

모드라기풀 『식물』 a (round-leaved) sundew ; Drosera rotundifolia (학명)

모드레짊다 swim with a kind of crawl stroke

†**모든** all ; every ; each and every ¶ 모든 종류의 사람 all kinds〔manner〕 of people // 모든 점에 있어서 in every respect 〔point〕 ; in all points〔respects〕 // 모든 경우에 on all occasions // 모든 것을 젖혀 놓고 before everything // 모든 수단을 다하다 exhaust every means ; adopt all means in one's power ; leave no means untried // 자기의 모든 것을 바치다 offer one's life and all ; give one's all 《to a person》 // 모든 인생은 고투의 연속이다 All life is a series of struggles. // 모든 사람은 자기의 몸을 지킬 권리가 있다 Every person has a right to take care of himself.

모들뜨기 a cross-eyed person ; a convergent squinter
—눈 a cross-eye ; a convergent squint

모들뜨다 turn one's eyes inward〔toward the nose〕 ; have cross-eyes ; squint convergently

모듬냄비 《clam, oyster》 chowder

모뜨다 ① [본뜨다] copy ; reproduce ② [흉내 내다] imitate ; copy ; ape ; mimic ¶ 사람의 행동을 모뜨다 imitate 《a person's》 conduct

모라토리엄 a moratorium

모락모락 ① [힘차게] rapidly ; well ¶ 모락모락 크다 become taller with rapidity〔without ceasing〕 // 모락모락 자라다 grow up quickly〔rapidly〕
② [연기·김이] thickly ; densely ; heavily ¶ 연기가 모락모락 나다 smoke rises up in thick clouds // 향수내가 모락모락 나다 be heavily perfumed ; reek of perfume

모란 牡丹 a (tree) peony ; Paeonid suffruticosa (학명) ¶ 모란 꽃밭 a peony garden

모란채 牡丹菜 『식물』 a kind of cabbage ; Brassica oleracea (학명)

모랄 a moral ; morals ; moral sense ¶ 모랄을 어지럽히다 contaminate the public morals

†**모래** sand ; grit (거친) ¶ 모래 파는 곳 a sand pit // 모래가 많은 sandy // 모래로 닦다 sand 《metal》 // 모래 장난을 하다 play with sand // 모래 위에서 놀다 play on the sand // 모래 위를 걷다 walk on〔in〕 the sand // 모래를 쌓다 pile〔heap〕 sand // 쌀에 모래가 들어 있다 There are grits in the rice. // 눈에 모래가 들어갔다 I have got some sand in my eye.
— 강변 a sandy shore〔beach〕 —땅 sandy soil ; sandy plain ; the sands — 무더기 piles of sand ; sand dunes —사장〔밭〕 a sandy plain ; the sands —자갈 fine gravel — 채취장 a sandpit —펄 a marsh〔swamp〕 covered with sand —흙 sandy soil ; the sands

모래무지 『물고기』 a false〔goby〕 minnow ; Pseudogobio esocinus (학명)

모래 벌판 a sandy plain ; the sands

모래빛 [불그스름한 노랑] a sand color ; sand

모래 시계 —時計 a sandglass ; an hourglass

모래알 a grain of sand

모래 언덕 a sand hill ; [해안의] a dune

모래주머니 [모래를 담은 포대] a sandbag ; 『군사』 an earth bag ; 『동물』 [새 따위의] a gizzard ; a ventriculus 《*pl.* -li》 ; the muscular stomach

모래지치 『식물』 a kind of phlox

모래찜 a (hot) sand bath
— 요법 treatment by the sand bath ; 『의학』 ammotherapy ; arenation

모래집 『해부』 the amnion 《*pl.* -nia》

모래집물 amniotic fluid ; 『의학』 liquor amnii ; forewaters ; waters ¶ 모래집물이 나오다 [해산(解產) 직전에] the water breaks

모래톱 a sandy plain 《along a river》 ; a sand bank ; the sands

모랫길 a sandy road ; a path on the sand

모략 謀略 [음모] an intrigue ; an artifice ; a plot ; a scheme ; a trick ; [계략] strategy ; a stratagem ¶ 모략을 꾸미다 devise〔concoct, work out〕 a plot // 모략에 빠지다 fall into a snare ; be caught in a trap ; be entrapped
— 선전 strategic propaganda

***모레** the day after tomorrow ¶ 모레 아침〔저녁〕 the morning〔evening〕 after next

모로 [비스듬히] diagonally ; obliquely ; [옆으로] sideways ; sidelong ; askance ; askew ; athwart ¶ 모로 걷다 walk sideways // 모로 눕다 lie on one's side // 모로 자르다 cut diagonally // 모로 가도 서울만 가면 된다 The end justifies the means.

모롱이[1] [산의] a spur of a hill

모롱이[2] 『어류』 ① [웅어] a baby *Coilia ectenes* fish ② [숭어] a baby gray〔grey 《영》〕 mullet

***모루** an anvil

모루채 a hammer ; a sledge

†**모르다** ① do not know ; cannot tell ; be unaware〔ignorant〕 of ; be not familiar 《with》 ; be not acquainted 《with》 ¶ 모르는 unknown ; strange ; unfamiliar // 모르는 곳 a strange place // 모르는 사이에 before one is aware〔one knows〕 ; without one's knowledge // 모르고서 without

knowing 《a matter》; ignorantly ; unknowingly // 자기도 모르게 in spite of oneself ; unconsciously ; unwittingly // 모르고 있다 remain ignorant [in ignorance] // 모른다고 잡아떼다 stoutly maintain one's ignorance // 어쩔 줄 모르다 do not know what to do ; be at a loss ; be in a fog ; be at one's wit's end // 전혀 모르다 know nothing of ; have not the slightest [remotest] idea of ; be quite ignorant of // 이유를 모르겠다 I cannot tell the reason. // 그를 모르는 사람은 없다 He is known to everybody. // 그 이상은 모른다 I know nothing beyond it. /My knowledge ends there. // 모르는 게 약이다 Ignorance is bliss. // 하나만 알고 둘은 모른다 You know only one side of the story. // 어느 옷을 사야 할지 모르겠다 I'm at a loss as to which dress to buy.
② [깨치지 못하다] do not understand ; do not know ; do not appreciate 《the value of money》; do not see [get] ; cannot make out ; do not follow ¶ 그 뜻을 모르겠다 do not understand the meaning of it // 조금도 모르다 do not understand at all ; have not the slightest idea of // 당신의 말은 모르겠다 I don't get you. // 왜 안 오는지 모르겠다 I don't see why he doesn't come. // 그의 마음을 모르겠다 I cannot make him out. // 그것은 도저히 모르겠다 It is above my comprehension [head]. /It is beyond me [my reach, my depth]. // 그것은 뭐가 뭔지 나로서는 모르겠다 It is all Greek to me. /I cannot make head or tail of it. // 나는 네가 무슨 말을 하는 지 모르겠다 I don't understand. /I don't know what you are talking about. /You've lost me. /I've lost you. /I don't follow you. /I don't get it. /I don't dig it. /You are talking over my head.
③ [안면이 없다] be not acquainted with ; do not know ¶ 모르는 사람 a stranger // 모르는 얼굴들 [사람들] strange [unfamiliar] faces ; strangers
④ [못 알아차리다] fail to notice [see, perceive, realize, sense] ; be not conscious of ¶ 위험을 모르다 do not realize [sense] the danger // 자기 잘못을 모르다 be blind to one's own faults [mistakes] ; do not realize one's own mistakes // 계략이 있을 줄은 조금도 몰랐다 I little suspected the plot.
⑤ [느끼지 못하다] do not feel ; be unconscious of ; be insensible of [to] ; be impervious to ¶ 부끄러움을 모르다 be dead [lost] to shame ; be impervious to shame // 은혜를 모르다 be insensible of kindness // 추운 줄 모르다 do not feel the cold
⑥ [기억하지 못하다] do not remember ¶ 그 당시의 일을 전혀 모르겠습니다 I cannot remember anything of those days at all.
⑦ [알아보지 못하다] do not recognize ¶ 그가 누군지 모르겠다 I can scarcely recognize who he is. // 그는 길에서 나를 만나고도 모른체했다 He did not recognize me in the street. // 저(를) 모르시겠습니까 Can't you recognize me?
⑧ [관계가 없다] be not concerned with ; have nothing to do with // 그 일은 나는 모른다 I have nothing to do with the matter. /It's no concern of mine. / That's none of my business. /I can't help what you have done. // 죽거나 살거나 나는 모른다 He may be drowned for all I care.
⑨ [경험이 없다] have no experience ; be ignorant of ¶ 가난을 모르다 have never known poverty ; be ignorant of poverty // 여자를 모르다 do not know woman ; have had no experience with woman
모르는 것이 부처 [속담] He that knows nothing, doubts nothing.
모르면 약이요, 아는 게 병 [속담] Where ignorance is bliss, it is folly to be wise. /Ignorance is the peace of life.

모르면 모르되 if my guess is right ; in all probability ; in all (human) likelihood ; [십중 팔구] in nine cases out of ten ; ten to one ; most likely ; nine-tenths 《미·속》 ¶ 모르면 모르되 그는 40세 가량 되었다 If my guess is right, he must be about forty. /I shall guess his age at about forty.

모르몬교 一敎 Mormonism
一도(徒) a Mormon

모르쇠 know-nothingism ; feigned ignorance ; [벙어리 행세] playing dumb ; playing the dummy
모르쇠 잡다 [관용] play dumb ; feign [affect] ignorance ; pretend not to know

*__모르타르__ mortar ¶ 모르타르를 바른 mortared

모르핀 morphia ; morphine
— 중독 morphinism **— 중독 환자** a morphinomaniac

*__모른체__ pretending not to know ; pretended innocence ; an unconcerned air ; feigned ignorance ; indifference ; nonchalance ; a nonchalant attitude **—하다** pretend not to know ; pretend innocence ; look on with indifference ; assume an unconcerned air ; feign [pretend, affect] ignorance ; pretend to be ignorant ; [길에서 만나] cut 《a person》 dead ; refuse to recognize 《a person》; give 《a person》 the go-by ¶ 모른체하고 with an unconcerned air ; with nonchalance ; with an air of innocence (관계가 없는 듯이) ; as if nothing was the matter (아무일도 없었던 듯이) // 간곡히 부탁했으나 그는 모른체했다 He turned a dead ear to my entreaties.

모름지기 by all means ; necessarily ; [사람이 주어] should 《do》 ¶ 학생은 모름지기

공부에 전념해야 한다 It is imperative that students should put their hearts and soul into their studies. // 선생님 나이에는 모름지기 분별이 있어야 한다는 사실을 알지 못하세요 Don't you know that you ought to know better at your age?

모름하다 (be) stale; bad; be not fresh ¶ 조심하세요. 생선이 모름하고 있어요 Be careful. The fish is going.

모리 謀利 profiteering **—하다** profiteer; make undue〔unreasonable〕profits ¶ 모리를 단속하다 control profiteering
—배 a profiteer **전쟁 —배** a war profiteer

모말 a square mal measure

모맥 牟麥 wheat and barley

†**모면 謀免** evasion; shirking; escape; eluding **—하다** evade; shirk; escape; elude ¶ 모면할 수 없다 be unavoidable 〔inevitable〕// 기아를 모면하다 keep body and soul together; scarcely keep off hunger // 위기를 모면하다 just manage to tide over crisis

모멸 侮蔑 contempt; scorn; disdain; slight **—하다** despise; scorn; disdain; slight; look down upon; treat〔regard〕《a person》 with contempt; hold 《a person》 in contempt

모모 某某 some persons; such and such persons
—인 Messrs. So and so; a certain number of persons

모모한 worthy of mentioning; celebrated; well-known ¶ 모모한 인사 a man of mark; a noted person; a celebrity; a notable

모물 毛物 furs; fur goods
—전 a fur store

모물질 母物質 [핵 연료의] fertile material

모밀잣밤나무 〖식물〗 the Japanese chinquapin; Castanopsis cuspidata (학명)

모반 —盤 a small hexagonal〔octagonal〕 dining table

모반 母斑 〖해부〗 a birthmark

*****모반 謀叛** [반란] a rebellion; a revolt; an insurrection; [반역] treason; conspiracy (음모) **—하다** revolt; rebel; conspire; plot treason; plot against; rise in revolt 《against》
—죄 treason

모반심 謀叛心 a spirit of rebellion 〔revolt〕; rebellious〔revolting〕 spirit ¶ 그는 모반심을 품었다 He harbored rebellious designs.

모반인 謀叛人 a rebel; an insurgent; a mutineer; a conspirator ¶ 모반인이 되다 turn traitor

모발 毛髮 hair
—병 trichosis **— 색소 결핍증** 〖의학〗 achromotrichia; canities **— 습도계** a hair hygrometer **— 영양제** a hair tonic **— 탈락** alopecia; loss of hair

*****모방 模倣** imitation; copying; mimicry **—하다** imitate; copy 《from, after》; model 《on, after》; pattern 《after》; follow an example 《of》; mimic ¶ 모방적 국민 an imitative people // 모방하기 어려운 inimitable // 그의 독특한 필치는 도저히 모방할 수 없다 His unique style defies imitation. // 우리는 모방에 의해서 많은 것을 배운다 We learn many things by imitation. // 일본 사람은 모방은 잘 하나 독창력이 부족하다고 한다 It is generally thought that the Japanese are a nation of imitators and lack originality. // 베토벤의 초기 작품의 어떤 것은 모차르트의 모방이다 Some of Beethoven's early works are an echo of Mozart.
— 문명 imitated civilization **—본능** the instinct of imitation **— 예술** imitative arts **—자** an imitator; a copier; a copyist; a copycat (구); an echo(er) (무정견한 경향이 있는)

†**모범 模範** a model; an example; a pattern; a paragon ¶ 모범적 model; exemplary; typical // 모범으로 삼아야 할 사람 a model of what a man ought to be // 모범으로 삼다 model〔pattern〕《after》// 모범을 보이다 set〔give〕《a person》 a good example; set a model to 《a person》// 그의 용감한 행위는 타의 모범이 되었다 His brave deed served as a pattern for others.
— 경기 an exhibition game **— 공무원〔용사, 운전사〕** an exemplary official〔soldier, driver〕 **— 농장** a model farm **—림** a model forest **— 부락** a model village **—생** a model〔an exemplary〕 student **—수** a well-behaved prisoner; a trusty **— 청년** a youngman of exemplary life **— 학교** a model school

모법 母法 a parent law; a mother law

모병 募兵 recruiting; conscription; draft **—하다** recruit〔conscript, draft, enlist〕 《soldiers》
—계 an enlisting〔a recruiting〕 officer ¶ 모병계의 상사 a recruiting sergeant

모본 模本 ① an example ⇨ 본보기 ② a model ⇨ 모형 ③ imitation ⇨ 모방

모본단 模本緞 a kind of Chinese silk

모붓다 sow rice-seeds (on a seedbed)

모비행기 母飛行機 mother aircraft; a mother plane〔ship〕; a parent plane

모빌유 —油 mobile oil

모사 毛絲 wool (1) en yarn; worsted (yarn); wool; [털로 짠] knitting wool ¶ 모사로 양말을 짜다 knit wool into socks
— 내의 woolen〔all-wool〕 underwear **—류 판매점** a wool shop **—상** a woolman; a dealer in wool **— 세공** woolwork **— 스웨터** a jersey; a sweater (미) **— 양말** worsted〔woolen〕 socks 〔stockings〕

모사 茅舍 ① [자기집] my (humble) house ② [모옥] a thatched cottage

모사 模寫 copying; a copy; a reproduction ; a facsimile ; a replica

> 참고 **facsimile**는 「치수는 다를지 모르나 정확한 모사 복사」 **copy**는 가장 널리 쓰이는 말로서 「원물의 복사」이며 흔히 「근사한 모방」의 뜻으로도 쓰인다 **reproduction**은 「원물에 극히 가까운 모사」의 뜻으로서 흔히 재료 크기 성질이 다른 것에 사용된다

—하다 copy ; reproduce ; trace ; make a facsimile of ¶ 밀레의 모사 a copy from Millet

모사 謀士 a strategist ; a tactician

모사 謀事 planning ; making a plan ; [계획] a plan ; a device ; a scheme ; a stratagem (군략) ; [계략] a plot ; a trick **—하다** plan ; make a plan ; scheme ; plot 《against》 ; device a stratagem ; lay 〔form〕 a plan ¶ 모사가 좌절되었다 The plot has been frustrated.
—군 a schemer

모사탕 —砂糖 cube〔lump〕 sugar ; sugar cubes

모살 謀殺 premeditated〔deliberate, wilful〕 murder **—하다** murder ; kill 《a person》 with malice of forethought
— 미수 attempted murder **—범** (the crime of) murder ; petit treason (주인·남편에 대한) **— 사건** a murder case **—자** a murderer

모상 母喪 the death of one's mother ¶ 모상을 당하다 lose one's mother ; be bereaved of one's mother

모새 fine sand ⇨ 모래

모색 暮色 evening twilight〔gloom, dusk〕 ; shades of night

모색 摸索 —하다 grope 《for》 ; feel one's way ¶ 암중 모색하다 grope for ; search blindly ; grope (blindly) in the darkness // 살인 사건의 단서를 모색하다 grope for a clue to the murder

모샘치 〖물고기〗 a goby (fish)

모생약 毛生藥 a hair restorer〔grower〕

모서리 a corner ; an edge ; an angle ¶ 모서리가 서다 be sharp-edged ; be angular // 모서리를 죽이다 round off a corner〔an edge〕

모선 母船 a mother ship〔vessel〕 ; 〖우주항공〗 a command ship (사령선)
포경 — a whaling mother ship ; a whale factory ship

모성 母性 motherhood ; maternity
— 검진 〖의학〗 premarital examination **— 본능** maternal instinct **—애** mother's 〔maternal〕 affection〔love〕 **— 예찬** adoration of motherhood **— 옹호** protection of motherhood **— 옹호 투쟁** a maternity protection struggle **— 유전** maternal inheritance

모세 Moses ¶ 모세의 Mosaic // 모세의 십계명 Moses' Ten Commandments // 모세의 율법 the Law of Moses ; the Mosaic Law

모세관 毛細管 〖물리〗 a capillary tube 〔vessel〕 ; a capillary
—벽(壁) a capillary wall **— 분석** capillary analysis **—수(水)** capillary water **— 인력** capillary attraction **— 작용** (a) capillary action ; 《by》 capillarity **— 전위계** a capillary electrometer **— 척력(斥力)** capillary repulsion **— 현상** capillary ; a capillary phenomenon

모세혈관 毛細血管 〖해부〗 a capillary (vessel)

모션 a motion ; a movement ¶ 모션을 걸다 try to influence 《a person》 ; [구애하다] make love 《to》 ; make a pass 《at》 // (이성에게) 슬쩍 모션을 걸다 make a small pass 《at》 // 모션이 큰 투수 a pitcher with a big motion

모소 某所 a certain place ; somewhere ⇨ 모처

모손 耗損 wearing out ; friction ; wear and tear ; abrasion **—하다** wear out ; undergo friction

모수 母樹 a seed tree

*__모순 矛盾__ contradiction ; conflict ; inconsistency ¶ 모순된 contradictory 《to each other》 ; conflicting ; inconsistent // 모순이 없는 consistent // 모순된 생각 an inconsistent idea // 모순된 증언 conflicting testimonies // 모순되다 be contradictory to ; be inconsistent with ; conflict with ; clash with ; contradict // 모순된 말을 하다 contradict oneself ; make a contradictory statement // 모순이 많은 세상이다 This is a world of contradictions. // 현실과 이상은 모순된다 The actual is often contradictory to the ideal.
— 개념 〖논리〗 a contradictory concept 〔idea〕 **— 명사(名辭)** 〖논리학〗 contradictory terms **—성** contradictoriness **—율** 〖논리학〗 the law〔principle〕 of contradiction **무—성** 〖수학〗 consistency

모순 대당 矛盾對當 〖논리학〗 a contradiction ; a contradictory (opposition)

모숨 a handful 《of grass》 ; a lock 《of straw》

모스부호 the Morse code〔alphabet, signals〕 ; the Morse ¶ 모스 부호로 송신하다 send Morse code ; communicate〔signal〕 by means of Morse code ; morse

모스크 [회교 사원] a mosque

모슬린 [직물] muslin

†**모습** features ; looks ; appearance ; a shape ; a figure ; a visage ; an image ; a face ¶ 걷는 모습 the walking figure 《of a person》 // 아름다운 모습 a graceful figure ; good looks // 어릴 때의 모습 a childhood〔baby〕 face ; one's infant features // 아버지의 모습을 닮다 have a look of one's father ; look like one's father ; be the image of one's father // 모습을 나타내다 show one's face ; make one's appearance ; show oneself ; show up // 어릴 때의 모습을 찾아 볼 수 없다 His infant features are gone. // 그의 모습이 아직 눈에

선하다 His image is still vivid in my mind. // 그 시인은 그 영웅의 모습을 눈에 보는 듯이 그리고 있다 The poet finely images the hero. // 존의 모습이 보이지 않는다 John is missing. // 이것이 현대 한국 교육의 그대로의 모습이다 This is a true picture of education in modern Korea.

모시 ramie fabric ; ramie cloth ; a kind of hemp〔cambric〕 ¶ 모시 옷 clothes of ramie cloth

모시 某時 a certain〔undisclosed〕 time

모시계 母時計 a master〔control, primary〕 clock

모시다 ① [웃어른을] attend (on) ; wait on ; be in attendance on ; serve (under) ; [수행하다] escort ; accompany ¶ 모셔 들이다 show 《a person》 in〔into〕 ; usher in 《a person》 // 부모를 모시다 have one's parents with ; wait upon one's parents ; support one's parents // 주인을 모시고 가다 accompany〔escort〕 one's master // 선생을 회의에 모시다 have one's teacher at a meeting ; invite one's teacher to a meeting
② [신으로] deify ; worship ; [사당에] enshrine ; shrine ; place in a shrine ¶ 조상을 모시다 worship one's ancestors

모시류 毛翅類 『곤충』 Trichoptera ; the caddis flies

모시조개 ① [황합] a shortnecked clam ② [가막조개] a corbicula

모시풀 『식물』 a ramie ; a China-grass ; the ramie plant ; Boehmeria nivea (학명)

모시항라 —亢羅 loosely woven ramie cloth

모신 謀臣 a strategist ; a tactician ; a schemer

모심기 rice-planting ⇨ 모내기

모싯대 『식물』 a ladybell

모씨 某氏 a certain person〔gentleman〕 ; Mr. So-and-so ; Mr. X〔Blank〕 ; an unnamed person ; a man who shall be nameless

모아들다 gather ; come〔get〕 together ; flockcrowd ; swarm ; cluster ; collect ¶ 바닷가에 모아들다 flock to the seaside // 테이블 둘레로 모아들다 draw round a table // 곳곳에서 모아들다 flock from all〔various〕 quarters // 우글우글 모아들다 come swarming about // 떼를 지어 모아들다 come in flocks〔crowds, droves〕 ; gather in crowds〔swarms〕 // 그 곳은 여름에는 많은 사람이 모아든다 In summer the place attracts many visitors.

모야 暮夜 the dead of night ; midnight ¶ 모야에 late at night

†**모양 模樣, 貌樣** ① [형태] (a) shape ; (a) form ; [자태] (personal) appearance ; (a) figure ; looks (맵시) ; an air (태도) ¶ 코 모양 the shape of one's nose // 갖가지 모양의 돌 stones of various shapes // 저고리의 모양 a cut of one's coat // 초라한 모양 a miserable shape〔plight〕 // 모양이 좋다 look nice〔well〕 ; be well-shaped〔-formed〕 ; be shapely ; be well-cut // 모양이 나쁘다 look bad〔poor〕 ; be ill-shaped 〔-formed〕 ; be shapeless ; be unseemly 〔clumsy, awkward〕 // 모양을 내다 adorn oneself ; decorate ; dress up // 모양을 바꾸다 assume another〔a different〕 shape 〔form〕 // 이 소나무는 모양이 좋다 This pine tree has a good figure. // 그 여자는 그 옷을 입으면 모양이 우습다 She looks funny〔awkward〕 in the suit. // 이 모양으로는 사람들 앞에 설 수 없다 I'm not fit to be seen.
② [동태] signs ; indications ; appearance ¶ …한 모양이다 seem to be (현재) ; seem to have done (과거) // …할 모양이다 look like ; seem to do〔be〕 ; show signs of // 그는 돌아오지 않을 모양이다 There is no sign of his return. // 오늘 비가 올 모양이다 It looks like rain today. // 쌀 값이 내릴 모양이다 There are indications that the price of rice will fall. // 일이 되어 가는 형편으로 보아 3시쯤인 모양이군 The way things are going, it should be around three o'clock.
③ [상태] the state of affairs ; [방법] a way ; a manner ¶ 이 모양으로 in this way // 이 모양으로 나가면 if things go at this rate // 그 여자는 펜을 이상한 모양으로 쥔다 She holds a pen in a strange way. // 아버지가 하는 모양으로 하면 된다 You will make it if you do as your father does.
④ [무늬] a pattern ⇨ 무늬

모양다리 貌樣— form ; shape ; figure ⇨ 모양새

모양 사납다 貌樣— look unseemly〔awkward, indecent, improper, unsightly, unbecoming〕 ; be offensive 《to the eye》 ; look bad ; (be) ignoble ; disgraceful ¶ 옷차림이 모양 사납다 be shabbily dressed (초라하다) ; be indecently dressed (점잖지 못하다)

모양새 貌樣— ① [생김새] shape ; form ; appearance ; figure ¶ 모양새가 예쁘다 be nice-looking ; look nice〔pretty〕 ; be shapely // 모양새가 사납다 be bad-looking〔ugly, shapeless〕
② [체면] respectability ; appearances ; dignity ¶ 모양새가 없어지다 lose face ; be put out of countenance // 그것을 말하면 내 모양새가 어떻게 되겠는가 What about my losing face if you tell him about that?

모어 母語 the mother tongue ¶ 라틴어는 근대 로만스어의 모어이다 Latin is the parent of the modern Romance languages.

모여들다 gather ; flock ⇨ 모아들다

모역 謀逆 ① [반역] treason ; conspiracy (음모) ; plotting treason **—하다** plot treason 《against》 ; conspire 《against》 ② [종묘 파괴죄] (the crime of) devastating royal tombs〔palaces〕 **—하다** devastate royal tombs〔palaces〕

모오리돌 a round stone ; a stone with no edges

모옥 茅屋 a hovel ; a straw-thatched cottage

***모욕 侮辱** insult ; contempt ; indignity ; affront

> 참고 **insult** 상대방을 다쳐 모욕하려고 하다 **affront** 고의적으로 행해지는 공공연한 무례 행위 **indignity** 상대방의 위엄을 다치는 무례한 행위

—하다 insult ; affront ; treat ⟪a person⟫ with contempt ¶ 모욕적인 언사 insulting remarks // 모욕을 주다 offer ⟪a person⟫ an insult〔affront〕; level insults ⟪at a person⟫ ; put an indignity〔affront〕 upon ⟪a person⟫ // 모욕을 당하다 be insulted ; suffer an insult ; be slighted // 모욕을 참다 brook〔bear, pocket, swallow〕 an insult ; eat humble-pie ⟪영·속⟫ ; eat crow〔dirt〕 ⟪미·속⟫

—죄 contempt **법정 —죄** contempt of court

모우 牡牛 an ox ⟪*pl.* oxen⟫〔a steer〕 (거세한 소) ; a bull (거세하지 않은 소)

모우 暮雨 evening rain ; rain at nightfall

모월 某月 a certain month

모유 母乳 mother's milk ; breast milk ¶ 모유로 자란 아이 a breast-fed child ; a child reared at the breast // 모유로 기르다 rear ⟪a child⟫ at the breast ; feed ⟪a child⟫ on mother's milk

†**모으다** ① [여럿을] gather ; get ⟪things, people⟫ together ; [수집] collect ; make a collection of ¶ 긁어 모으다 scrape together // 병정을 모으다 recruit〔draft〕 soldiers // 불러 모으다 call ⟪people⟫ together ; assemble // 우표를 모으다 collect〔make a collection of〕 stamps // 자금을 모으다 raise the funds // 증거를 모으다 collect evidence // 모아서 맞추다〔만들다〕 assemble ⟪parts into a car⟫ ; join together
② [집중하다] concentrate ; focus ¶ 정신을 모으다 concentrate〔focus〕 one's attention ⟪on⟫ // 광선의 초점을 모으다 concentrate rays of light into focus // 세상의 이목을 모으다 attract〔absorb, arrest〕 public attention
③ [저축하다] accumulate ; amass ⟪riches, a fortune⟫ ; make ; save ; lay up ; store ¶ 돈을 모으다 make money // 돈을 모아 두다 lay〔store, save〕 up money
④ [쌓아 올리다] heap up ; pile up ; bring together ¶ 재〔쓰레기〕를 모으다 heap up ashes〔rubbish〕 // 재를 그러 모으다 rake up ashes

***모음 母音** 〖음성〗 a vowel (sound) ¶ 모음화하다 vocalize

— 변화 vowel gradation ; mutation ; modification **—자** a vowel (letter) **— 조화** vowel harmony **—화** vowelization **구—** an oral vowel **반—** a semivowel **비(鼻)—** a nasal vowel **전설(前設)〔후설〕 —** a front〔back〕 vowel **중성 —** a mixed〔neutral〕 vowel

모의 謀議 conference ; consultation ; deliberation ; conspiracy (음모) **—하다** hold a conference ; consult ; hold counsel ; deliberate on〔over〕 ⟪a matter⟫ ; plot〔conspire〕 together (음모를)

모의 模擬, 模依 imitation ; copy ¶ 모의의 sham ; mimic ; mock

— 국회 a mock congress **— 법정** a moot〔mock〕 court **— 시험〔고사〕** a sham〔trial〕 examination **— 운동** 〖심리〗 motor mimicry **— 재판** a mock trial (학생의) ; [토론] a moot **—전(戰)** a sham fight〔battle〕 ; (a) mock〔mimic〕 battle ; a dry run **— 전투 연습** exercises under simulated combat conditions **— 투표** a straw vote ⟪미⟫

모의 毛衣 furs ; fur garments ; fur pieces

모이 feed ¶ 모이를 주다 feed ⟪hens⟫ ; give food to ⟪hens⟫

—통 a feed bucket〔box〕 ; a trough **닭—** chicken fee **새—** bird feed

†**모이다** ① [떼지어] gather ; come〔get〕 together ; flock ; crowd ; swarm ¶ 서로 모이다 gather〔flock〕 together ; get together // 장터에 사람들이 모이다 people crowd into a market // 돈 때문에 모인 친구는 믿을 수 없다 You cannot depend upon friends whom money has brought to you.
② [회의에] meet ; assemble ; congregate ¶ 회의하려고 모이다 meet〔assemble〕 for a meeting
③ [돈·물건이] be collected ; be gathered ¶ 모인 돈 the collected money // 눈이 모여 덩이가 되다 snow piles up into a heap // 기부금이 전부 모였다 All the subscriptions have been collected.

모인 某人 a certain person ⇨ 모씨

모일 某日 a certain day ; one day

†**모임** a gathering ; a meeting ; an assembly ; a party ; a congregation (종교적인) ; a social gathering ¶ 모임이 있다 A meeting will be held.

†**모자 帽子** [테 달린] a hat ; [차양이 있는] a cap ; [여자용] a bonnet ; [사냥모] a hunting〔sporting〕 cap ; [중산모] a derby (hat) ⟪미⟫ ; a soft〔felt〕 hat ; a bowler ⟪영⟫ ; headgear ⟪총칭⟫ ¶ 모자 차양 the shade〔visor, peak〕 of a cap // 모자 위의 둥근 부분 the crown of a hat // 모자 테 the brim of a hat // 모자 띠 a hatband // 테가 넓은 모자 a broadbrimmed hat // 모자를 쓰지 않은 사람 a hatless〔bareheaded〕 person // 모자를 쓰다 put on a hat // 모자를 쓰고 있다 wear a hat ; have a hat on // 모자를 벗다 take off one's hat ; remove one's hat ; raise one's hat ⟪to a person⟫ (인사) // 모자를 흔들다 wave

one's hat ⟪to a person⟫ // 모자를 푹 내려 쓰다 pull one's hat over one's eyes // 모자를 빗겨 쓰다 cock one's hat // 모자를 뒤로 젖혀 쓰다 have one's hat on the back of one's head // 우리들은 모두 일어나 모자를 벗었다 All of us stood up and took off our hats.
— 걸이 a hatrack ; [벽의] a hatrail ; [발 달린] a hatstand ; a hat tree ; a hat peg 〔hook〕 (못) —상(商) a hatter ; [여자용] a milliner —점 a hat shop — 제조업자 a hatmaker

모자 母子 mother and son ; mother and child ¶ 모자 모두 건재하다 Both mother and child are doing well.

†**모자라다** be not enough ; (be) insufficient ; deficient ; lacking ; be short of ; (be) missing ; lack ; want ; [사람이] dull ; stupid ; dull〔half〕-witted ¶ 역량이 모자라다 be wanting in ability ; be incapable // 일손이 모자라다 be short of hands ; be short-handed // 식량이 모자라다 be short of provisions // 키가 다섯치 모자라다 be five inches short // 아직 모자라는 점이 많다 Much remains to be done. // 의자가 둘 모자란다 We need two more seats ⟪for the party⟫. // 그 남자는 좀 모자란다 He wants two pence in the pound. /He is a little wanting〔somewhat weak in the head〕. // 나는 키에 비해 체중이 모자란다 I'm underweight for my height. // 우리는 오늘 일손이 모자란다 We're short-handed today. /we're short of workers today. /Workers are in short supply today // 500원이 모자란다 I'm five hundred *won* short.

모자반 〚식물〛 gulfweed

***모자이크** 〚미술〛 (a) mosaic

모자점 帽子店 a hat shop〔store〕; a millinery (여자용 모자의)

모작패 [광산에서의] a share-mining system

모잠비크 Mozambique

모잡이 a rice planter ; a farm worker transplanting rice seedlings

모장 帽章 a cap-badge ; the badge on a cap

모장이 a rice-seedling distributor

모재 母材 [주요 재료] the basic material ; 〚용접〛 the parent metal.

모쟁이 〚물고기〛 a boby gray〔grey ⟪영⟫〕 mullet

모전 毛氈 a rug ; a carpet ¶ 모전을 깔다 lay a carpet // 마루에는 두터운 모전이 깔려 있다 The floor is thickly carpeted.

모정 母情 maternal affection

모정 慕情 longing ; yearning ; love ; affection

모제품 毛製品 woolen goods〔stuff〕

‡**모조 模造** imitation —하다 imitate ; pattern ⟪after⟫ ; model ⟪after⟫ ; reproduce ⟪from⟫ ; counterfeit (위조) ¶ 납유리로 다이아를 모조하다 imitate a diamond in paste
— 가죽 imitation〔artificial〕 leather ; leatheroid ; leatherette —금(金) imitation gold —자 an imitator — 진주 an imitation〔artificial〕 pearl ; a Roman pearl (유리 구슬의) —품 an imitation ; a counterfeit (위조품) ; a fake ; a replica

***모조리** all ; one and all ; wholly ; entirely ; all through ; without an exception ; without reserve ; exhaustively ; completely ; utterly ; thoroughly ¶ 전원 모조리 to the last man ; to a man ; every one of them // 모조리 털어놓다 make a clean breast of ; make a complete confession // 전답을 모조리 팔아치우다 sell all one's real estate ; make a clean sweep of one's real estate // 모조리 사형에 처하다 put every last one of them to death // 가진 돈을 모조리 써버렸다 I spent all the money I had with me. // 내가 맡은 사업은 모조리 실패였다 In everything I undertook I failed.

모조지 模造紙 imitation vellum ; vellum (paper)

모종 〚농업〛 a seedling ; a young plant ; nursery trees —하다 transplant the seedlings of ; bed out ¶ 배추를 모종하다 transplant cabbages
고구마 — a sweet potato cutting 나무 — a sapling ; a seedling ; a young tree 〔plant〕 ; a nursery tree ; a set ; a plantlet

모종 某種 a certain kind〔sort〕 ¶ 모종의 a certain ; one ; some ; unnamed // 모종의 이유로 for a certain reason

모종비 a timely rain for transplanting seedlings

모종삽 a (garden) trowel

모주 a hard drinker ; a confirmed drinker ; a drunkard ; a sot ; a thirsty soul ⟪속⟫

모주 母酒 ⇨ 밑술
—집 a crude liquor shop

모주망태 a (confirmed) drunkard ; a heavy drinker ; a souse ; a (drunken) sot

모지 某地 a certain place

모지다 ① [뾰족하다] (be) angular ; angulated ; pointed ; square ; sharp ¶ 모진 기둥 a square pillar
② [성질·일 따위] (be) angular ; sharp ; pointed ; uncompromising ; unsociable ; stiff ; harsh ¶ 모진 말 a sharp〔biting〕 remark

모지라지다 wear out ; be worn down 〔out〕 ; get stumpy〔blunt〕 ¶ 붓이 모지라졌다 The writing brush is worn to a stump.

모지락스럽다 (be) very harsh ⇨ 모질다

모지랑붓 a worn-out writing brush

모지랑비 a worn-out〔stumpy〕 broom

모지랑이 something worn to a stump ; a stump

‡**모직 毛織** [방모] woolen fabric〔cloth〕 ;

[소모] worsted
— 머플러 a woolen muffler
†**모직물 毛織物** woolen cloth〔goods, stuff, fabrics, textiles〕; stuff goods ; wool ; hair (낙타·알파카의 털로 짠) ¶ 모직물은 명주보다 질기다 Woolen outwears silk. // 모직물을 입고 있다 be dressed in woolen
— 공업 the woolen manufacturing industry — 공장 a woolen mill —상 a woolen draper ; a woolen merchant —업 the woolen textile industry — 제조 업자 a woolen manufacturer
모진 목숨 one's damned〔contemptible〕 life ; one's wretched〔miserable〕 life ¶ 모진 목숨이 아직 붙어 있다 I am still prolonging this damned life of mine.
모질다 ① [잔인] (be) cruel ; brutal ; atrocious ; ruthless ; merciless ; pitiless ; heartless ; hard ; cold-hearted ; harsh ; tough ¶ 모진 사람 a hardhearted person // 모진 짓을 하다 do a cruel thing ; commit cruelties〔atrocities〕 // 사람을 모질게 다루다 treat harshly ; treat 《a person》 with brutality ; be cruel to
② [능히 배겨내다] bear〔stand, endure〕 stoically // 모진 사람 a diehard ; a tough guy // 재난을 모질게 배겨내다 bear one's misfortune with stoical fortitude // 울음을 모질게 참았다 He resisted an impulse to cry out.
③ [정도가 세다] (be) intense ; severe ; extreme ; hard ¶ 모진 추위〔더위〕 intense cold〔heat〕; extreme of cold 〔heat〕
모질음 persistence ; toughness ; harshness ; hardness ¶ 모질음쓰다 fight 〔struggle〕 hard 《against pain》; resist persistently
모집 募集 ① [지원자의] invitation ; collection ; registration (학생의) ; [군인의] recruitment ; enlistment ; [광고로] advertisement —하다 invite ; collect ; raise ; advertise for ; make an invitation 《to》; [군인을] recruit ; enlist ; raise ¶ 모집에 응하다 apply for the position offered ; respond to an invitation // 회원〔직공〕을 모집하다 raise〔recruit〕 members〔operatives〕 // 학생을 모집하다 advertise for students ; receive applications for admission // 학생 모집을 시작〔마감〕하다 open〔close〕 registration of students // 현상 소설을 모집하다 hold a prize contest for novels // 점원 모집 Shop boys wanted. // 신 회원을 모집 New members asked 〔invited〕 to join. // 학생 모집 New students invited.
② [공채·기부금 따위의] flo(a)tation ; subscription ; solicitation —하다 raise ; collect ; float 《a loan》; appeal〔call〕 for ; solicit ¶ 공채를 모집하다 raise〔float〕 a loan // 기부금을 모집하다 raise〔invite〕 contributions ; get up subscriptions // 모집을 시작하다 start a collection // 모집에 응하다 subscribe to 《a fund》
— 광고 an advertisement 《for operatives》 — 방법 a method of recruitment —액 the amount to be raised — 인원 a volume of recruitment ; the number 《of students》 to be admitted — 지역 a recruitment area 기금 — 운동 a drive to raise funds
모집다 ① [지적] point out specifically ; show ② [집다] grasp〔hold〕 all
모집단 母集團 〖통계〗 a population ; a universe
모집 요항 募集要項 a prospectus 《of a school for candidates》
모짝 at one sweep ; all at once ; in one big bite ; in a sweep
모쪼록 as much as one can ⇨ 아무쪼록
모찌기 removing the young rice plants from the seedbed
모착하다 (be) short and fat〔chubby, plump〕
모채 募債 loan flotation ; the flotation 〔raising〕 of a loan —하다 float〔raise, issue〕 a loan
— 가격 the issue price —액 the amount of a loan — 인수 underwriting — 정책 a loan policy — 조건 the terms of loan flotation 비—주의 a non-loan policy
모처 某處 a certain place
모처럼 ① [오랜만에] at long last ; finally ; after long time〔interval, silence, absence, separation〕; for the first time in many days〔years〕 ¶ 그는 모처럼 귀향했다 He returned home after a long absence〔for the first time in many years〕. // 그들은 모처럼 서로 만나서 대단히 기뻐했다 They were very pleased to see each other after a long separation. // 모처럼의 일요일을 비가 와서 망쳤다 Rain spoiled our long-awaited Sunday. // 모처럼 좋은 소식이로군 What good news for a change ! // 그 사람 때문에 모처럼의 상담이 틀어진 것 같다 Because of him, the deal we've gone to so much trouble for is about to fall through.
② [벼른 끝에] at great pains (수고스럽게) ; especially (특별히) ; on purpose (일부러) ; kindly (친절하게도) ; expressly ¶ 모처럼 초대해 주셔서 감사합니다 Thank you for your kind〔special〕 invitation. // 모처럼 모은 돈을 써버리다니 바보짓을 했다 I was foolish enough to spend the money I had saved at no small pains. // 모처럼 왔는데 박물관이 휴관이라 매우 실망했다 Though I came to visit the museum all the way, it was closed to my great disappointment. // 모처럼 좋은 기분으로 듣고 있었는데 Just when I was really getting into it.
모체 母體 the mother-body ; the mother ; [주체] the parent (body) ; the matrix (형성·생장의) ¶ 선거의 모체 an electorate ; the electoral college (대통령

의) 《미》 // 모체 보호를 위하여 for the health of the mother
— 전염 hereditary transmission
모체 발아 母體發芽 〖식물〗 viviparity ¶ 모체 발아의 viviparous
모춤 a bundle of rice seedlings
모춤하다 be a little too much〔many〕 ; be a little too long
모충 毛蟲 a hairy〔black〕 caterpillar ; a wooly bear (caterpillar) ; 〖동물〗 [털 있는 짐승] a furred〔fur-bearing〕 animal ; fur 《총칭》
모친 母親 one's mother ⇨ 어머니
모탕 a (wooden) block on which wood is cut
—세(貰) storage charges
모태 母胎 the mother's womb〔uterus〕 ¶ 모태 내에서의 발육 불충분 defective intrauterine development
†모터 a motor ; an engine
— 보트 a motorboat — 사이클 a motorcycle
모터 풀 a motor pool ; a parking lot
모텔 [자동차 여행자용 숙박소] a motel ; an auto court
‡모토 motto 《*pl.* ～s, -es》 ¶ …을 모토로 하다 make it one's motto to do
모투저기다 save up little by little
†모퉁이 a corner ; a turn ; a turning ¶ 모퉁이의 가게 a corner shop ; a shop at 〔on〕 the corner // 길모퉁이에서 at〔on〕 a street corner // 모퉁이를 돌다 turn (around) a corner // 그 집은 모퉁이에 있습니다 The house stands on the corner. // 첫번째 모퉁이를 왼쪽으로 돌아가시오 Take the first turn〔turning〕 to the left.
—집 a house on〔at〕 the corner 모퉁잇돌 〖건축〗 a cornerstone (주춧돌)
모티브 a motive ; a motif 《프》
†모판 —板 a nursery ; a seedbed ; a seed plot
모포 毛布 a blanket ; a rug
모표 帽標 a cap-badge ; the badge on a cap
모풀 green manure for the rice seedbeds
*모피 毛皮 [부드러운] a fur ; a skin ; a flix (토끼 따위) ; [생피] a pelt ; a fell ¶ 모피로 만든 외투 a fur(-lined) overcoat ; a mink coat // 모피를 팔다 deal in furs
— 모자 a fur hat — 목도리 a fur comforter ; a boa (여자용의) —상 a furrier
— 외투 a fur coat ; a fur-lined overcoat
— 제품 a fur piece ; [집합적] furs
모필 毛筆 a writing〔painting〕 brush ; a hair pencil
—화 a hair-pencil picture ; a wash drawing
모한 冒寒 —하다 brave〔face, defy〕 the cold
모함 謀陷 a plot to entrap 《a person》 —하다 entrap 《a person》 ; ensnare ; land 《a person》 in difficulties ¶ 남을 모함하려다가 자기가 도리어 구렁에 빠지다 hoist with one's own petard ; be caught in one's own trap
모함 母艦 a depot ship ; a tender ; a mother ship
잠수 — a submarine tender ; a nurse ship 항공 — an aircraft carrier
모항 母港 a home port
모해 謀害 a plot to do harm —하다 plot to do harm 《to a person》
†모험 冒險 an adventure ; a hazard ; a risk —하다 adventure ; venture ; hazard ; risk ; run a risk〔hazard〕 ; make a venture ¶ 모험적인 adventurous ; hazardous (위험성이 많은) ; risky // 모험적 사업 a hazardous〔risky〕 enterprise // 모험적 생애 an adventurous life // 목숨을 걸고 모험을 하다 risk〔venture〕 one's life // 모험적으로 해보다 try〔take〕 one's chance ; chance it // 그것은 모험이다 I am afraid it is rather reckless of you. // 이것은 조금도 모험이 아니다 There is no risk in this. /This is by no means (taking) a leap in the dark. // 그것은 모험이라고 생각지 않습니까 Don't you think it's a little too hazardous ? // 다소의 모험이 필요하다 Some risk must be run.
—가 an adventurer — 사업 a hazardous enterprise ; an adventurous〔risky〕 undertaking ; a venture ; [투기] a speculation ; a flier 《미》 — 소설 an adventure novel〔story〕 —심 an adventurous〔a venturesome〕 spirit ; the spirit of adventure
모험담 冒險談 an account of one's adventure ¶ 모험담을 하다 relate one's adventure
*모험적 冒險的 ¶ 모험적 정신 an adventurous〔a venturesome〕 spirit // 모험적인 adventurous ; risky ; hazardous // 모험적으로 adventurously ; at a venture
모험주의 冒險主義 adventurism ¶ 모험주의의〔적〕 adventuristic
—자 an adventurist
모형 母型 [활자의] a matrix 《*pl.* -trices》 ; [원형] a prototype
†모형 模型 a model ; [기계 따위] a pattern ; [주조의] a mold ¶ 모형을 만들다 make a model 《of》
— 군함 a model〔miniature〕 warship — 비행기 a model plane — 제작자 a patternmaker — 지도 a 《three-dimensional》 model map (입체의) 소(小)— a miniature 실물 크기 — [비행기·기계·기구·무기 따위의] a (full-scale) mock-up 실용 — [기계의] a working model 인체 — a model of a human body 축척 — a scale model
‡모호 模糊 dimness ; vagueness —하다 (be) vague ; dim ; ambiguous ; equivocal ; obscure ; indistinct ; hazy ; misty ¶ 모호한 대답을 하다 give a vague answer // 모호한 태도를 취하다 take an equivocal〔dubious〕 attitude
모회사 母會社 a holding company〔corpo-

ration〕; a parent company
†목¹ ① [동물의] a neck ¶ 기다란 목 a long〔slender〕 neck // 짧은 목 a short neck // 목을 움츠리다 shrug one's shoulders // 목에 매달리다 throw both arms round another's neck // 애인의 목에 매달리다 neck her lover // 목을 졸라 죽이다 strangle 《a person》 to death // 목을 매어 죽다 hang oneself // 목을 자르다 cut off 《a person's》 head
② [인후] a throat ; a gullet ; a windpipe ¶ 목이 마르다 be〔feel〕 thirsty ; one's throat〔mouth〕 parches with thirst // 목이 아프다 have a sore throat // 목을 축이다 quench one's thirst ; wet one's whistles // 목을 놓고 울다 weep with abandon // 목이 메게 울다 be choked with tears ; sob // 목에 가시가 걸리다 a bone sticks〔lodges〕 in one's throat
③ [길의] the bottleneck in a way of escape ; a key position (on the road) ; a strategic point ¶ 목을 지키다 fortify the points of strategic importance
④ [물건의] a neck ¶ 버선목 the ankle of a sock // 병목 the neck of a bottle
목을 따다 관용 cut one's throat
목이 메다 관용 one's throat is choked
목이 쉬다 관용 have a hoarse throat ; have a frog in one's throat
목² 〖광산〗 gold ore found (on refining) to contain an admixture of silver or lead ; slag ; dross
목 目 ① [항목] an item ; [생물 분류상의] an order ② [바둑 돌] a piece ; a stone ; [판의 눈] a cross ¶ 한 목 놓다 put a stone ; give a piece
*목가 牧歌 a pastoral song〔poem〕; bucolics ; bucolic verse ¶ 목가적 pastoral ; bucolic
목각 木刻 wood carving ; woodcutting ; wood engraving ―하다 carve〔engrave, cut〕 《a design》 on wood
―화 a woodcut ; a wood-block print ; a wood print ; a wood engraving ― 활자 a block letter
목간 沐間 [목욕] taking a bath ; [목욕간] a bathroom ―하다 take a bath
―통 a bathtub ; a bath basin
목갑 木匣 a wooden box
*목걸이 a necklace ; a rivière (보석의) 《프》; [개의] a collar ¶ 진주 목걸이 a pearl necklace // 목걸이를 하다 wear a necklace
목검 木劍 a wooden sword
†목격 目擊 observation ; witnessing ―하다 witness ; see with one's own eyes ; observe
목격자 目擊者 an eyewitness ; a witness ; an observer ¶ 목격자의 이야기 an eyewitness ('s) account ; a firsthand account // 목격자의 대질 [경찰의] an identification parade ; a choice of faces ; a lineup
목고리 [개의] collar ¶ 목고리를 달다 put a collar on 《a dog》
목곧다 (be) stiff-necked
목곧이 a stiff-necked〔a stubborn ; an obstinate〕 fellow
목골 木骨 ¶ 목골 구조의 건물 a halftimbered building
― 구조 a timber〔wooden〕 frame
목공 木工 [사람] a woodworker ; a carpenter ; [일] woodwork(ing) ; carpentry ; carpentering
― 기계〔공구〕 a woodworking machine〔tool〕 ― 기술 carpentry ; woodcraft ―소(所) a carpenter's shop ―일 carpenter's work ; carpentering ―품 woodwork
목관 木管 a wooden pipe
목관 악기 木管樂器 a woodwind (instrument) ; the woodwind 《총칭》
―부 [관현악단의] the woodwind (section)
†목구멍 a throat ; a gullet ; a windpipe ¶ 목구멍이 아프다 have a sore throat
목구멍이 포도청이다 속담 The hungry belly has no ears. /A full belly counsels well. /The devil dances in an empty pocket. /Need makes the naked man run and sorrow makes websters spin. /Need makes the old wife trot. /Poverty is an enemy to good manners.
목귀질하다 trim (up) the corners of a piece of wood
목근 木根 a tree root
목금 目今 at present ; now ⇨ 목하
목금 木琴 〖음악〗 a xylophone
― 연주자 a xylophonist
목기 木器 a wooden container ; a vessel made of wood ; wooden tableware
―전 a woodenware store〔shop〕
목누름 〖씨름〗 a nape press
목눌 木訥 innocence and lack of eloquence ; artlessness ―하다 (be) innocent〔honest〕 and unstudied ; artless ; naive ; unsophisticated
*목다리 木― 《a pair of》 crutches ¶ 목다리로 걷다 walk on crutches
목단 牧丹 a peony ⇨ 모란
목달이 worn-out socks
목담 〖광산〗 a wall built of oreless rocks
목대야 木― a wooden washbasin
목대잡다 direct ; control ; supervise ; command
목대잡이 a director ; a supervisor ; a commander
목덜미 the nape〔back, scruff〕 of the neck ¶ 목덜미를 잡다 seize〔grab〕 《a person》 by the scruff of his neck
목도 [일] carrying on a shoulder pole ; [몽둥이] a shoulder-carrying pole ―하다 carry on a shoulder pole
―꾼 polebearers
목도 木刀 a wooden sword〔stick〕
목도 目睹 witnessing ⇨ 목격

목도리 a muffler ; a neckerchief ; a neck scarf ; a comforter ; a shawl (여자용) ; a (neck) wrap ; a boa (여자용) ¶ 목도리를 하다 wear a muffler

목돈 a sizable〔tidy〕 sum (of money) ; a good round sum (of money) ¶ 목돈으로 만원 a round sum of 10,000 *won*

목돌림 a catching〔an infectious〕 sore throat

목동 牧童 [양의] a shepherd boy ; [소의] a cowboy ; a cowherd ; a cowpuncher 《미·구》 ; [일반적으로] a herdboy ; a herd 《총칭》

목두기 [목두개비] a wood fragment ; [귀신] a nameless ghost

목랍 木蠟 [옻나무·거망 옻나무의 열매를 짓찧어서 만드는] vegetable wax ; [붉나무에서 채취하는] Japan tallow〔wax〕 ; Japanese wax

목련 木蓮 〖식물〗 a magnolia ; Magnolia liliflora (학명) ¶ 목련꽃 a magnolia blossom

목례 目禮 nod ; nodding **—하다** nod 《to》 ; greet with a nod〔one's eyes〕 ; give 《a person》 a nod ; give a glance in salute ; recognize ¶ 목례를 교환하다 exchange nods

— 술집〔주점, 집〕 a stand-up bar

†**목록 目錄** [상품·장서의] a catalogue ; [목차] (a table of) contents ; [일람표] a list ; a table ; [재산 따위] an inventory ; [색인] an index ¶ 목록을 만들다 catalogue 《one's books, furniture》 ; make a list of 《articles》 // 목록에 올리다 put 《an item》 on〔in〕 the catalogue ; list

—계 a catalog(u)er **— 변경** recatalog(u)ing **— 작업** [도서관의] catalog(u)ing **물품 —** a list of articles **신간 서적 —** a list〔catalog(ue)〕 of new books 〔publications〕 **재산 —** an inventory **총 —** a general catalogue **카드식 —** a card catalogue

목리 木理 ① [나뭇결] the grain of wood ② [연륜] the annual rings of a tree

목마 木馬 a wooden horse ; [어린이용] a rocking horse ; [체조용] a vaulting horse ; a dummy horse 《미》

회전 — a merry-go-round ; a carrousel ; a whirligig ; a roundabout 《영》

목마 牧馬 [일] horse raising ; horse pasturing ; [말] a pasturing horse **—하다** raise〔pasture〕 horse

⁑**목마르다** ① be〔get〕 thirsty ; thirst ¶ 한 병의 맥주로 목마름을 가라앉히다 quench 〔slake, relieve〕 one's thirst with a bottle of beer
② [갈망하다] have a thirst for ; crave 〔long, yearn, thirst, hunger〕 for ; be anxious for ; hanker after ¶ 지식에 목마르다 have a thirst for knowledge // 사랑에 목마르다 crave for affection

목말 riding (on) another's shoulder ¶ 목말을 타다 ride the shoulder of ; ride pickaback 《on another》 // 목말을 태우다 give 《a person》 a ride on one's shoulder ; have〔hold〕 《a child》 on one's shoulder ; have 《a child》 pickaback

목매기송아지 a tethered calf

목매다 ① [남을] strangle 《a person to death》 ② [스스로] strangle oneself 《with a cord》

목매달다 ① [남을] hang 《a person》 by the neck ; strangle 《a person》 to death ② [스스로] hang oneself 《on a tree》 ; strangle oneself 《with a cord》

목매아지 a tethered colt

목맺히다 be choked 《with tears》 ¶ 설움에 목맺히다 be all choked up with sorrow

목메다 be choked 《with》 ; be stuck 《with》 ; choke ¶ 밥이 목에 메다 choke on the rice ; have rice stick in one's throat // 설움에 목메다 be choked with sorrow // 목메어 울다 lose one's voice in tears ; tears choke up one's voice

목면 木綿 ① a cotton plant ⇨ 목화 ② cotton cloth ⇨ 무명

—사 cotton yarn ; cotton (thread) **—상** a dealer in cotton goods **—직** cotton fabrics〔textile〕

목목이 at every strategic point〔position〕 ; at key〔important〕 positions on the road ¶ 목목이 지키다 stand guard at every turn of a road ; watch every strategic point ; fortify the points of strategic importance

목문 木紋 the grain (of wood)

목물 ① [깊이] neck-deep water ② [목욕] a bust bath **—하다** take a bust bath

목민 牧民 governing the people **—하다** govern the people

—관 a governor

목발 木— ⇨ 목다리

목본 木本 trees ; shrubs

목부용 木芙蓉 〖식물〗 a cotton rosemallow ; Hibiscus mutabilis (학명)

목불 木佛 a wooden image of Buddha

목불인견 目不忍見 being unbearable to witness〔see〕 ¶ 목불인견이다 cannot bear to witness〔see〕 ; be unable to stand the sight of ; be too pitiful to look at

목비 a spell of heavy rain in the rice planting season

목사 木絲 cotton thread〔yarn〕

⁑**목사 牧師** a pastor ; a minister ; a parson ; a curate ; a rector ; a curate ; a clergyman ; a chaplain (군목)

> 참고 **clergyman**은 일반적인 말이며 특히 영국 국교회의 목사 **pastor, parson**은 속어적 **vcurate**는 교구 목사의 최하급으로서 「목사보」 **vicar**는 curate의 상급 목사 또한 **rector, minister**는 비국교회의 목사

¶ A 목사님 Reverend A // 목사의 직무 pastoral duties // 목사가 되다 enter the ministry ; take (holy) orders ; [영국 교회의] enter the Church
—직 order(s) ; ministry
목사리 an ox bridle
목상 木商 [재목상] a timber〔lumber〕 dealer ; [화목상] a wholesale firewood dealer
목상 木像 a wooden image〔statue〕; a graven image (우상) ; a wooden figure
목새[1] fine soft sand
목새[2] rice-plant fever
목석 木石 ① trees and stones ; [생명이 없는 것] inanimate objects ; stocks and stones
② [비유적] insensibility ; unsusceptibility ¶ 목석 같은 사람 an insensible〔unsusceptible〕 person // 목석 같다 have no feeling than a stone ; be lost to sense // 나는 목석이 아니다 I am not a stock nor a stone. /I am made of flesh and blood.
목선 木船 a wooden vessel〔ship〕
목성 木星 〚천문〛 Jupiter
목세공 木細工 woodwork ¶ 목세공사 a woodworker
목세루 木— cotton serge
†**목소리** a voice ; a tone (of voice) ¶ 가는 목소리 a thin voice // 굵은 목소리 a deep〔full〕 voice // 커다란 목소리 a loud voice // 아름다운 목소리 sweet〔beautiful〕 voice // 은방울 같은 목소리 a silvery voice // 쉰 목소리 a husky〔hoarse〕 voice // 성난 목소리 an angry voice // 낮은〔작은〕 목소리로 in a low voice ; in a quiet tone ; in an undertone ; in whisper // 높은〔큰〕 목소리로 in〔with〕 a loud voice ; in a high voice ; loudly ; loud // 슬픈 목소리로 in a sad voice ; in accents of grief // 떨리는 목소리로 with a quivering voice // 있는 목소리를 다하여 at the top of one's voice // 목소리가 좋다 have a sweet〔fine, musical〕 voice // 목소리가 나쁘다 have a poor voice // 목소리를 높이다 raise〔lift〕 one's voice ; shout // 목소리를 낮추다 lower〔drop, sink〕 one's voice // 목소리가 쉬도록 외치다 shout oneself hoarse // 목소리가 나오지 않다 one's voice fails ; lose one's voice ; be out of voice // 쉿 목소리를 내지 마라 Hush! Don't make a voice! // 목소리가 안 나왔다 My voice failed me.
⁑**목수 木手** a carpenter ; a woodworker ¶ 목수의 연장 a carpenter's tool〔kit〕 // 배 만드는 목수 a ship-carpenter // 엉터리 목수 a hack〔bungling〕 carpenter // 목수가 많으면 집을 무너뜨린다 Too many cooks spoil the broth.
— 도구 a carpenter's tools〔kit〕 —일 carpenter's work ; carpentering ¶ 목수일을 하다 carpenter ; do carpentering —직 carpentry
목수 木髓 pith
†**목숨** life ¶ 귀한 목숨 one's precious〔dear〕 life // 천한 목숨 one's abject life // 모진 목숨 one's wretched〔damned〕 life // 목숨을 건 일 a desperate〔very dangerous〕 undertaking ; a matter of life and death // 목숨을 걸고 at the risk of one's life ; upon one's life // 목숨을 건 사랑 love at the risk of one's life // 목숨을 버리고 at the cost of one's life // 목숨이 붙어 있는 한 as〔so〕 long as one lives // 목숨을 잃다 lose one's life ; be killed ; die // 목숨을 구하다 save 《a person's》 life // 목숨을 건지다 escape death ; have a narrow escape (겨우) // 목숨을 빼앗다 take 《a person's》 life ; kill // 목숨을 버리다 lay down〔give up〕 one's life ; throw away one's life // 목숨을 살려 주다 spare another's life // 목숨을 바치다 offer〔sacrifice〕 one's life 《for one's own country》 // 목숨을 아끼다 grudge one's life ; be afraid of death // 목숨을 중히 여기다 value one's life highly ; hold life dear // 목숨을 가볍게 여기다 value one's life lightly ; slight one's life // 목숨을 돌보지 않다 disregard one's life ; set one's life at naught // 목숨을 위태롭게 하다 endanger〔imperil〕 one's life // 겨우 목숨만 살아 도망하다 escape with bare life ; have a narrow escape // 그는 교통사고로 목숨을 잃었다 He lost his life〔was killed〕 in a traffic accident. // 제발 목숨만 살려 주십시오 For mercy's sake, please spare me〔my life〕. // 사람의 목숨은 이슬처럼 덧없는 것이다 Man's life is as transient as dew. // 목숨이 붙어 있는 한 희망이 있다 While〔Where〕 there is life, there is hope.
목쉬다 get〔grow〕 hoarse〔husky〕 ¶ 목쉰 소리 a hoarse voice // 목쉬도록 지껄이다 talk oneself hoarse // 그는 소리를 질러서 목쉬었다 His voice was hoarse from shouting. /He shouted himself hoarse.
목야 牧野 pastureland ; grassland ; a pasture ; a ranch
—림 a pasture forest
목양 牧羊 sheep-raising〔farming〕 —하다 raise sheep
—자 a sheep farmer〔raiser〕; a sheepman ; a shepherd —지 a sheep meadow ; sheepland ; a sheep run 《미》
목양 牧養 stock-raising〔-farming〕 ⇨ 목축
목양말 木洋襪 cotton socks〔stockings〕
목어 木魚 ① 〚물고기〛 a sandfish ② [목탁] a wooden clapper ③ [절에서 쓰는 제구] a wooden drum (in the shape of a carp in the Buddhist temple)
목엽 木葉 a leaf ; leaves (of a tree)
†**목요일 木曜日** Thursday ¶ 내주〔지난 주〕 목요일 next〔last〕 Thursday ; Thursday week
†**목욕 沐浴** a bath ; bathing —하다 take〔have〕 a bath ; bathe ; wash oneself ; take tub ; take one's tub ¶ 간단히 목욕하다 have a short〔quick〕 bath // 냉수로 목

욕하다 take a cold bath // 목욕물을 데우다 prepare〔make〕 a bath ; get a bath ready // 목욕물을 긷다 fill the bathtub with water // 아기를 목욕시키다 give a baby a bath ; bathe a baby // 천천히 목욕하다 have a long bath // 목욕물이 차다 The bath is not warm enough. // 피부가 따끔따끔할 만큼 목욕물이 뜨겁다 The bath is tingling〔unbearably〕 hot.

—값 a bath fee —탕 [가정의] a bathroom ; [공중의] a bathhouse ; a public bath —통 a bathtub ; a bath basin 아침 — a morning bath〔tub 《영·구》〕 증기 — a steam〔vapor〕 bath 터키 — a Turkish bath

목욕물 沐浴— water for bath ; bath (water) ¶ 목욕물을 데우다 heat the bath ; prepare a bath ; get a bath ready

목욕 재계 沐浴齋戒 ablution ; purification —하다 perform one's ablutions ; perform purification ¶ 목욕 재계하고 기도하다 offer prayers after performing one's ablutions

목우 木偶 a wooden figure〔image〕 ; a dummy

목우 牧牛 cattle at pasture〔grass〕 ; pasturing〔grazing〕 cattle

—장 a cattle pasture ; a cattle ranch 《미》

목운동 —運動 a neck exercise

목인 木印 a wooden seal

목자 牧者 ① [목양자] a shepherd ; a sheep raiser ② [성직자] a shepherd ; a pastor ; a minister ; a clergyman ; a father ¶ 선한 목자 the Good Shepherd (성경)

목자르다 ① [칼 따위로] cut 《a person's》 throat〔head〕 ; behead ; decapitate ② [해고하다] dismiss〔discharge〕 《an employee》 ; fire 《미》 ; cashier〔sack〕 《속》

목작약 木芍藥 〖식물〗 a peony ⇨ 모란

목잠 [이삭의 병] a grain blight

목잠 木簪 an ornamental wooden hairpin

목잠기다 grow〔get〕 hoarse ; hoarsen ; lose one's voice ¶ 목이 잠기도록 말을 하다 talk oneself hoarse

‡**목장 牧場** a stock farm ; a ranch 《미》 ; a pasture ; a meadow ; a grazing ground〔land〕 ¶ 목장 주인 the owner of a stock farm ; a rancher ; a ranchman 《미》 // 목장에서 일하다 work on a stock farm ; ranch 《미》

—주 the owner of a stock farm ; a cattleman 《미》 ; a (cattle) rancher ; a ranchman

목장갑 木掌匣 (a pair of) cotton work gloves

†**목재 木材** wood ; [건축용] timber ; lumber 《미》

— 건조법 timber seasoning〔drying〕 — 공업 the lumber industry — 공장 a timber〔lumber〕 mill — 벌채업 lumbering — 벌채 인부 a timberman ; a lumberman 《미》 —상 a lumber〔timber〕 merchant —소 a sawmill ; a timber〔lumber〕 mill — 운반선 a lumber〔timber〕 carrier — 운반용 트럭 a logging truck

†**목적 目的** an object ; a purpose ; an aim ; an end (종국적) ; a goal (목표) ; an intention (의도) ¶ 목적이 있는 purposeful // 목적이 없는 purposeless ; aimless // 공동의 목적 a common cause // 인생의 목적 an aim in〔of〕 life // 확고한 목적 a fixed〔set〕 purpose // 목적을 이루는 수단 a means to an end // …할 목적으로 with the object of ; with a view to 《doing》 ; for the purpose of 《doing》 // …을 목적으로 하다 aim at ; have 《a thing》 for one's object ; intend to 《do》 ; have an intention of 《doing》 // 목적을 세우다 set up a purpose〔goal〕 // 목적을 고수하다 stick to one's purpose // 목적에 합당하다 answer〔serve, suit〕 the end〔purpose〕 // 목적을 달성하다 accomplish〔achieve〕 one's purpose ; attain one's object // 목적을 추구하다 pursue〔seek〕 one's object // 본회의 목적은 …에 있다 the object of the association shall be... ; the association has for its object... // 국민의 복지가 정치의 목적이다. National welfare is the object of politics. // 목적을 위해서는 수단을 가릴 필요가 없다고 생각하는 자들이 있다 Some think that the end justifies the means. // 어떤 목적으로 이곳에 왔느냐 What was your purpose in coming here ? /What have you come here for ? // 그가 여기에 온 데는 무슨 목적이 있다 He has some object〔an axe to grind〕 in coming here. // 이 책은 세상에 발표할 목적으로 쓴 것이 아니다 This was written with no eye for publication.

—격 〖문법〗 the objective (case) —물 the object ; the objective ; the game ; the aim —성 〖철학〗 finality —세 an object tax — 소설 a purpose novel — 절 〖문법〗 a final clause —항 the port of destination 공동 — a common cause 직접〔간접〕 —어(語) a direct〔an indirect〕 object

목적 木賊 〖식물〗 a scouring rush ⇨ 속새

목적론 目的論 〖철학〗 teleology ¶ 목적론적 논증 teleological argument

목적인 目的因 〖철학〗 a final cause

목적지 目的地 one's destination ; the end of one's journey ; the goal

목전 目前 ¶ 목전지계 a short-sighted policy ; an expedient // 목전의 immediate ; imminent ; impending // 목전에 under one's eyes〔very nose〕 // …의 목전에서 in the presence 《of》 // 구경꾼의 목전에서 in full view of spectators // 여름 방학을 목전에 두고 with the summer holidays coming soon // 목전에 닥치다 be (close) at hand ; be imminent // 목전의 이익을 좇다 seek immediate gain // 죽음이〔기아가〕 목전에 임박했다 Death〔Starvation〕 stared at him in the face.

목전 木栓 a cork
목정 neckbeef ; chuck ¶ 목정강이 the neck bone ; the cervical vertebrae
목정 木精 wood spirit ; methyl alcohol
목젖 〖해부〗 the uvula 《*pl.* ~s, -lae》
— 염증 uvulitis
목제 木製 ¶ 목제의 wooden ; made of wood
—품 wooden ware ; wooden manufactures〔articles〕; wood products ; woodwork ¶ 목제품 공업 the wooden article industry
목조 木造 ¶ 목조의 wooden ; made〔built〕of wood ; of wood ; frame 《미》 // 그 집은 목조이다 The house is built of wood.
— 가옥 a wooden house〔frame building 《미》〕 —선(船) a wooden vessel
목조 木彫 wood-carving ¶ 목조의 carved in〔out of〕wood
—공 a wood-carver〔-engraver〕; the a woodcraftsman —기 a wood-carving machine — 인형 a wooden doll ; a doll carved in wood
목조 木槽 a wooden manger
목조롱벌 〖곤충〗 a kind of potter wasp ; Eumenes japonica (학명)
목줄기 the lines around the throat ; throat lines
목질 木質 lignum ¶ 목질의 woody ; ligneous
—부 the wood ; the woody parts 《of a plant》; 〖식물〗 the xylem — 섬유 woody fiber
목찌르다 stab in the throat ; pierce one's neck
목차 目次 (a table of) contents ; the contents of a book
목책 木柵 a wooden fence〔picket, barricade〕
목첩 目睫 ① [눈과 눈썹] eye and eyebrow ② [가까움] nearness ; closeness ; imminence ¶ 목첩지간에 박두하다 be near〔close〕at hand ; be imminent ; be directly〔just〕ahead
목청 [성대] the vocal chords ; [목소리] one's voice ¶ 목청껏 at the top of one's voice // 목청을 울리다 vibrate the vocal chords // 목청이 좋다 have a lovely〔sweet〕voice // 목청이 나쁘다 have a poor voice // 목청을 높이다 raise〔lift〕one's voice
목초 牧草 grass ; pasturage ¶ 목초를 뜯어먹고 있다 be at grass ; be grazing 《in the fields》
—권 〖법〗 herbage ; pasturage —림 a grazing forest — 시대 〖역사〗 the pastoral age〔stage〕 —장 a pasture ; a stock farm — 지대 cattle land〔country〕
목촛대 木— a wooden candlestick
목축 牧畜 stock farming〔raising〕; pasturage ; cattle breeding〔raising〕
—림 a grazing forest — 시대 the pastoral age〔stage〕 —지(地) grassland ; meadow ; ¶ 소를 목초지에 풀다 put〔send, turn out〕to grass
목축업 牧畜業 stock-farming ; cattle-breeding〔-raising〕 ¶ 목축업을 하다 engage in stock-farming ; run a ranch 《미》; ranch // 이 나라의 목축업은 아직 초보 단계에 있다 The stock-farming in this country is still primitive〔in an early stage〕.
—자 a stock farmer〔breeder〕; a cattle breeder ; a rancher 《미》; a cattleman ; a stockman
목측 目測 eye-measurement —하다 measure with the eye
— 거리 distance measured with the eye
목침 木枕 a wooden pillow
—찜 beating〔battering〕《a person》 with a wooden pillow
목타르 木— wood tar ; pine tar
목탁 木鐸 ① 〖불교〗 a wooden gong ; a bell with a wooden tongue ¶ 목탁을 두드리다 sound a wooden gong
② [지도자] a leader ; a guide of the public ; a herald of justice and culture ¶ 사회의 목탁 a leader〔monitor〕of society // 사회의 목탁인 신문 the press that should lead the public // 세상의 목탁으로 자처하다 set up for the guide of the times
목탄 木炭 charcoal ; fusain (그림용의)
— 가스 charcoal gas — 자동차 a charcoal-driven automobile ; a charcoal-engine〔-burning〕car —지 charcoal paper —화(畫) a charcoal (drawing) ; a fusain
목통 ① the throat ; the gullet ; the neck ② [욕심쟁이] a greedy person ; a pig ¶ 목통이 굵다 have a thick neck
목통 木桶 a wooden tub ⇨ 나무통
목판 木板 [음식 담는] a wooden platter〔tray〕; a trencher ; 〖제본〗 a wooden board ; [널빤지] a board ; a plank ¶ 과자〔과일〕를 목판에 담다 place cookies〔fruit〕on a wooden plate
—차 an open wagon
목판 木版 a printing block ; a woodcut ; an engraving block
— 문자 〖인쇄〗 a block letter —본 a block〔xylographic〕book —술 woodblock printing ; xylography ; wood engraving
목판화 木版畫 a woodcut ; a wood engraving ; a woodprint ; a wood-block print
목패 木牌 a wooden ticket〔tag, check〕
목포수 —砲手 a hunter lying in wait for game animals
⁑목표 目標 [표적] a mark ; a target ; a sign ; [목적] a goal ; an aim ; an object ; an objective ; [표지] a guide —하다 aim 《at》; take aim 《at》; set the goal 《at》; have 《a matter》 as an object ¶ 어학 학습의 목표 the object of language study // 목표에 달하다 reach〔attain〕the

goal // 목표에 미달이다 be wide of the goal // 100% 증산을 목표로 하다 set〔fix〕 a goal of 100 per cent increase in production // 목표에 훨씬 미달이다 The goal is far off. /We are far from the goal. // 1994 년도 수출 목표는 구백육십이억불로 정해졌다 The export target for 1994 has been set at 96.2 billion million dollars. // 우리는 소나무를 목표로 사격했다 We took aim at the pine tree and fired. // 목표를 너무 높게 잡은 것 아니냐 Maybe you were aiming too high.

— 반경(半徑) 〖군사〗 the radius of target — 시간 the target time — 연도 the goal year — 지역 〖군사〗 the target area — 지점 〖군사〗 the target spot ; the aiming〔objective〕 point —탑 [비행장의] a pylon 공격 — the target for〔of〕 an attack 중간 — 〖군사〗 an intermediate objective

목표액 目標額 a target figure ¶ 목표액에 달하다 realize〔hit〕 the target ; reach the targeted level // 목표액을 돌파하다 pass〔exceed〕 the target〔targeted level〕

월산 — the target for monthly output 저축〔수출〕 — a savings〔an export〕 target

목표일 目標日 [계획 따위의] a target date〔day〕 ¶ 목표일을 정하다 fix the target date // 그 계획은 3년 후를 성공의 목표일로 하고 시작되었다 The project was initiated with a three-year target date for success.

목피 木皮 bark

초근 — roots and barks ; herbs (약초)

목하 目下 now ; at present ; at the present moment ; currently ¶ 목하의 present ; existing ; current // 목하 고려 중인 사항 a matter now under consideration

목합 木盒 a wooden bowl

목향 木香 〖식물〗 an elecampane ; Inula helenium (학명)

목형 木型 a wooden pattern ¶ 구두의 목형 a shoetree ; a boot tree

—공 a patterner — 공업 the wooden-pattern making industry

†목화 木花 a cotton plant ; a cotton wool tree ; [솜] cotton ¶ 목화를 따다 pick cotton // 목화를 틀다 gin cotton

—꽃 a cotton flower —솜 cotton ; cotton wool — 송이 a cotton ball —씨 cottonseed — 재배 cotton growing

목활자 木活字 wooden (printing-) type

목회 牧會 pastoral duties ; cure of souls ; pastorate —하다 take the spiritual care of a congregation ; shepherd a flock of souls ¶ 목회의 pastoral 《duties》

— 방문 a pastoral visit 《to》 —학 pastoral theology

†몫 a share ; a portion ; a lot ; an allotment ; a quota ; a rake-off (미·구) ; a divvy (속) ¶ 내 몫 my share // 한 몫 끼다 have a share 《in》 ; share 《in the profit》 ; get〔take, have〕 one's whack (속) // 한 몫 차지하다 take a share ; get a rake-off // 한 몫 주다 give a share 《to》 ; 몫을 요구하다 claim a share 《in a profit》 // 부당한 몫을 차지하다 take an excessive share〔a lion's share〕 // 한 몫을 받을 권리가 있다 have a share 《in the profit》 // 내 몫은 요것뿐이다 This much has fallen to my lot. // 각각 한 몫을 받았다 A share was allotted to each.

몫몫이 each〔every〕 share〔portion, quota〕 ; into shares〔portions, quotas〕 ; share by share ¶ 몫몫이 차지하다 take each his own share // 몫몫이 나누다 divide into shares

몬다위 ① [우마의] shoulders of a horse〔an ox〕 ② [약대의] a camel's hump

몬닥 falling apart from decomposition ¶ 몬닥 떨어지다 fall apart flabbily〔flaccidly, limply, squashily〕

몬순 [기상] a monsoon

몬존하다 (be) calm ; composed ; collected

몰- [죄다·전부] all ; whole ; total ; entire ; complete ; every ; exclusive

몰- 沒 [없음] lacking ; lack〔want〕 of ; non ; -less ; without ; no

몰각 沒却 disregard ; ignoring ; effacement —하다 [무시하다] disregard ; ignore ; [잊다] forget ; efface ¶ 개성을 몰각하다 sink 《a person's》 individuality // 당초의 목적을 몰각하다 forget〔lose sight of〕 one's original object // 법의 정신이 몰각되어 있다 The spirit of law is ignored.

몰강스럽다 (be) cruel ; merciless ; brutal ; pitiless ; harsh ; inhumane ¶ 몰강스러운 짓을 하다 do a cruel thing

몰골 appearance ; shape ; form ¶ 몰골 사나운 옷 shapeless〔ill-cut, ugly〕 clothes // 몰골 사나운 짓 unseemly〔improper, unbecoming〕 behavior〔conduct〕

몰골스럽다 (be) unshapely ; ill-formed ; ill-shaped ; unsightly ; unseemly ; offensive

몰교섭 沒交涉 ① [무관계] lack of relation —하다 be unconcerned 《in, with》 ; be unrelated 《to》 ; be irrelevant 《to》 ; be independent 《of》 ; have no connection〔relation, concern〕 《with》

② [무간섭] noninterference ; nonintervention —하다 do not interfere〔intervene〕 《in》 ; do not meddle 《in, with》

몰년 沒年 [나이] a person's age at death ; [해] the year of 《a person's》 death

†몰다 ① [자동차 따위를] drive 《a car》 ; urge on 《a horse》 ¶ 차를 몰고 …에 가다 drive to 《a place》 // 소를 몰아 넣다 drive in the cattle ; impound the cattle // 자동차를 몰아 현장에 급히 가다 rush〔hasten〕 to the scene in a car

② [좇다] drive ; chase ; give chase to ; run after ; follow game ; hunt up ; run 《a fox》 ¶ 토끼를 몰다 chase a rabbit ; course a rabbit (사냥개로) // 짐승을 몰고

있다 be on the track〔trail〕 of an animal ③ [궁지에] corner ; drive ¶ 궁지에 몰다 drive 《a person》 to the corner〔wall〕 ; get 《a person》 into a scrape〔fix〕 ; corner 《a person》 ; reduce 《a person》 to extremity ; bring〔drive〕 《a person》 to bay
④ [죄인·역적으로] impute 《a guilt》 to 《a person》 ; charge 《a person》 with 《a guilt》 ; accuse 《a person》 of 《a guilt》 ; denounce ¶ 살인범으로 몰다 charge 《a person》 with murder // 역적으로 몰다 denounce 《a person》 as a traitor
⑤ [한곳으로] gather (up) ; push to one side

***몰두 沒頭** absorption ; preoccupation ; devotion of oneself 《to》 ; engrossment of oneself 《in》 ; giving up oneself 《to》 **—하다** be absorbed〔engrossed, immersed, lost〕 in 《one's studies》 ; devote〔immerse〕 oneself to ; give oneself up to ; bury oneself in ; be up to the eyes〔ears, neck〕 in 《one's work》 ; give oneself up wholly to 《one's work》 ¶ 그는 일에 몰두하려 했으나 허사였다 He attempted vainly to lose himself in work. /He attempted to lose〔bury〕 himself in work, but it was in vain. // 그들은 세속과는 멀리 떨어져 연구에만 몰두하고 있다 They're immersed in their studies far from the vulgar everyday world.

몰라보다 fail to recognize ; [무시하다] ignore ; fail to appreciate ¶ 친구를 몰라보다 fail to recognize a friend ; ignore〔neglect〕 a friend // 남의 수고를 몰라보다 fail to appreciate another's efforts〔kindness〕 // 몰라보게 달라지셨습니다 You sure have changed beyond recognition. // 몰라보게 컸구나 You sure have grown up beyond recognition.

***몰락 沒落** ruin ; fall ; collapse ; downfall ; [파산] bankruptcy **—하다** fall ; go to ruin ; be ruined〔wrecked〕 ; [파산하다] become bankrupt ¶ 몰락한 귀족 ruined peers // 몰락시키다 ruin ; bring to ruin // 토지 개혁으로 많은 지주들이 몰락했다 Many a landowner has become bankrupt due to the land reform. /Many landed proprietors were ruined due to the land reform.

***몰래** secretly ; privately ; quietly ; on the quiet ; stealthily ; by stealth ; surreptitiously ; imperceptibly ; furtively ; clandestinely ¶ 몰래 눈짓하다 give a furtive wink // 몰래 (빠져) 나가다 steal out ; slip out ; sneak off // 몰래 도망하다 steal away // 몰래 뒤를 쫓다 shadow 《a person》 stealthily // 몰래 만나다 have a clandestine meeting ; meet in secret〔clandestinely〕 // 몰래 보다 steal a glance 《at》 ; cast stealthy〔furtive〕 glances 《on》 // 몰래 탐지하다 spy out 《the land》 // 몰래 말해주다 tell 《a person》 secretly // 남 몰래 웃다 laugh in one's sleeve // 기차에 몰래 타다 steal a ride on a train // 몰래 재미를 보다 take one's pleasure on the sly

몰려가다 ① [쫓겨 가다] be driven ; be pursued ; be chased ¶ 모퉁이로 몰려 가다 be driven into a corner
② [떼지어] flock〔crowd, swarm, cluster〕 toward ; go in flocks〔crowds, swarms, shoals〕 ; go en masse ¶ 고기 떼가 몰려가다 a shoal of fish swim together // 사람들이 장터로 몰려 가다 people flock toward the market

몰려나다 ① [쫓겨 나다] be driven〔turned, forced, kicked〕 out ; be expelled ; be ousted ; be ejected ; [해고되다] be dismissed〔fired〕 ¶ 동네에서 몰려 나다 be driven out of one's village ; be ostracized by the community // 회사에서 몰려 나다 be kicked out of a company ② [떼지어 나가다] go out in crowds〔groups, flocks, swarms, shoals〕

몰려다니다 ① [쫓겨 다니다] be driven〔chased〕 about〔around〕 ; be run after ¶ 구름이 바람에 몰려 다니다 clouds are driven about by the wind
② [떼지어 다니다] move〔walk〕 about〔around〕 in crowds〔groups, flocks, swarms〕 ¶ 고기떼가 몰려 다니다 fish move〔swim〕 around in shoals // 새 떼가 몰려 다니다 birds fly about in flocks // 애들이 몰려 다니고 있다 Children are loafing around in groups.

몰려들다 ① [쫓겨 오다] be driven〔chased, pressed, pushed〕 into ¶ 도둑이 골목에 몰려 들다 a thief is driven into an alley // 한편 구석으로 몰려 들다 be driven〔pressed〕 into a corner
② [떼지어] come in crowds〔flocks, shoals, droves, swarms〕 ; crowd〔flock, cluster, swarm〕 in ¶ 사람들이 장터로 몰려 들다 people flock into a market place // 어린애들이 방안으로 몰려 들다 children crowd into a room // 새 떼가 나무로 몰려 들다 birds flock to a tree

몰려오다 ① [쫓겨 오다] come driven〔pushed, pressed, forced, chased〕 back ; [퇴각] retreat ; fall back ¶ …에 몰려 오다 retreat〔fall back〕 on
② [떼지어 오다] come in crowds〔flocks, swarms, packs, shoals〕 ; flock ; throng ; storm 《a place》 ¶ 몰려오는 적군 the surging〔advancing〕 enemy // 벌이 몰려오다 bees come swarming // 새가 몰려오다 birds come flocking // 사람이 몰려오다 people come crowding ; people pour in〔into〕 《a place》 // 사람들이 상점으로 몰려왔다 People stormed the shop. // 예금자들이 은행으로 몰려왔다 The depositors besieged the bank. /The bank had a rush of depositors. /There was a rush (of depositors) on the bank.

몰리다 ① [쫓기다] be〔get〕 driven〔chased, pursued〕 after ; [사냥에서] be

hunted up ; be coursed (사냥개에서) ¶ 방 한구석으로 몰리다 be driven into the corner of a room // 도둑이 몰려서 골목으로 도망했다 The hunted thief rushed into an alley.
② [궁지에] be driven to the wall〔corner〕; be pressed ; be hard up ; be in a straitened circumstances ¶ 대답에 몰리다 be at a loss for an answer ; do not know what to answer〔what answer to make〕// 돈〔시간〕에 몰리다 be pressed〔hard up〕for money〔time〕// 일에 몰리다 be pressed with work ; be driven by business ; be too busy with one's work ; have lots of things to do all at once
③ [한 곳에] get together ; gather together ; group〔flock, crowd, swarm〕together ; throng ; storm ¶ 돈이 한 곳에 몰리다 money flows into one place ; money is poorly distributed // 사람이 한 쪽으로 몰리다 people crowd〔throng, press together〕to one side
④ [죄인·역적으로] be charged with ; be accused of ; be denounced as ¶ 간통죄로 몰리다 be charged with adultery

몰리브덴 〚화학〛 molybdenum 《Mo》
—강(鋼) molybdenum steel —광(鑛) molybdenite

몰매 ⇨ 뭇매

몰몰아 in all ; all together ; all told

몰박다 put〔fix〕all in one place

몰사 沒死 extinction ; dying out ; annihilation —하다 become extinct ; be annihilated ; die to the last man

몰살 沒殺 massacre ; annihilation ; extermination ; a wholesale murder〔slaughter〕—하다 massacre ; annihilate ; exterminate ; kill to a man ; wipe out ¶ 적을 몰살하다 annihilated the enemy // 일가를 몰살하다 murder the whole family

몰상식 沒常識 lack of common sense ; senselessness ; shamelessness —하다 be lacking〔wanting, deficient〕in common sense ; have no common sense ; (be) senseless ¶ 그는 몰상식하다 He has no common sense.

***몰수 沒收** confiscation ; forfeiture ; seizure ; sequestration (가차압) —하다 confiscate ; forfeit ; seize ; sequestrate ¶ 몰수당하다 be confiscated ; be forfeited 《to the government》// 몰수하기로 되어 있다 be forfeitable // 너의 재산은 몰수될 것이다 Your property will be seized.
—물〔품〕a confiscated article〔property〕; a forfeit ; a forfeiture —시합 a forfeited game (운동 경기에서) —자 a seizor ; a confiscator 적산(敵產) — confiscation

몰식자 沒食子 a gall(-nut) ¶ 몰식자성의 gallic
—산(酸) gallic acid

몰씬 [물렁한 모양] soft ; tender ; [냄새가] fragrant —하다 (be) soft ; tender ; [냄새가] nicely〔strongly〕scented ¶ 몰씬한 고기 meat cooked tender // 참외 냄새가 몰씬몰씬하다 a melon smells nice // 향수 냄새가 몰씬거리다 be strongly scented〔reek〕with perfume

몰아 in all ; all ; all together ; en masse ; in the gross ; in the aggregate ; in a lump ; as a whole〔group〕; in bulk ; en bloc ; in the bloc ; by the lot ; collectively ¶ 몰아 사다 buy up all ; buy in bulk ; buy en bloc // 몰아 얼마요 How much is it in all? // 몰아 5만톤이 되는 12척의 배를 갖고 있다 They have twelve ships, aggregating 50,000 tons.

몰아 沒我 self-effacement〔-abnegation, -renunciation〕; selflessness ; self-annihilation ; self-oblivion ¶ 몰아적 self-abnegating ; self-effacing // 몰아의 경지에 이르다 rise above self

몰아가다 ① [몰고 가다] drive ¶ 소를 풀밭으로 몰아가다 drive cattle to pasture // 파도가 그 배를 해안으로 몰아가고 있었다 The waves were driving the ship to the shore.
② [휩쓸어 가다] take away all together ; carry away everything ; [몰아 사다] buy up all ; buy as a lot ¶ 홍수가 많은 집을 몰아갔다 The flood washed many houses away. // 그가 상점에 있는 모든 과일을 몰아갔다 He bought and took away all the fruits in the store.

†**몰아내다** expel ; turn〔get, put, send, drive, press, push, shove〕out ; kick 《a person》 out ; give 《a person》 the sack ; fire ; [토지·건물에서] eject ; evict ; [지위에서] oust ¶ 방에서 몰아내다 put 《a person》 out of the door ; show 《a person》 the door // 선동 분자를 회합에서 몰아내다 eject an agitator out of a meeting // 마을에서 몰아내다 expel 《a person》 from the village // 고용원을 몰아내다 kick an employee out of the firm // 회장 자리에서 몰아내다 oust 《a person》 from the position of chairman // 사냥개가 숲에서 꿩을 몰아내다 a hunting dog〔hound〕chases a pheasant out of the bush

몰아넣다 ① [들어가게 하다] drive in〔into〕; push〔press〕into ; chase into ¶ 돼지를 우리에 몰아넣다 drive a pig into the pigpen
② [궁지에] drive into a corner ; corner ¶ 궁지에 몰아넣다 corner 《a person》 up ; drive 《a person》 into a corner ; put 《a person》 into a fix
③ [휩쓸어] put〔push, press, cram, jam〕all into ¶ 학생들을 한 교실에 몰아넣다 put〔cram〕all the students into one classroom

⁑**몰아대다** ① [재촉] press hard ; hurry 《a person》 up ; urge on 《one's horse, workmen》 ¶ 일을 빨리 하라고 몰아대다 press 《a person》 to make a quick job of

it〔to speed up the work〕// 말을 몰아대다 spur a horse on ; drive a horse hard
② [해대다] rebuke ⇨ 몰아세우다

몰아들이다 ① [쫓아서] drive 《hens》 into the 《henhouse》; chase 《games》 into 《a volley》 ¶ 막다른 골목으로 몰아들이다 drive 《a person》 into a blind alley ; corner 《a person》
② [휩쓸어] take all in bulk ; buy up (all) the lot ¶ 과일을 몰아들이다 buy up all the fruits (in the marketplace)

몰아때리다 ⇨ 몰아치다

몰아받다 ① [한꺼번에] receive〔get〕《it》 all at one time〔in a lump〕 ¶ 빚을 몰아 받다 collect the debt in one lump sum // 편지를 몰아 받다 receive the letter all at one time
② [한 사람이] receive all (as a representative of other people) ; engross ; monopolize ¶ 수석이 동급생의 졸업장을 몰아 받다 the top student receives the diplomas on behalf of his classmates // 막내 아들이 부모의 사랑을 몰아 받는다 The youngest son monopolizes the parents' affection.

몰아붙이다 ① [한쪽으로] push〔put, thrust, shove〕《things》 all to one side ¶ 의자를 방구석에 몰아붙이다 put the chairs to〔into〕 a corner of the room
② [한 군데에 붙이다] stick〔paste, plaster, affix, put, post〕《notices》 all in one place ¶ 그림을 벽 왼쪽에 몰아붙이다 hang all pictures on the left side of a wall

몰아사다 buy in a lump ; buy in bulk

몰아세우다 rebuke 《a person》 strongly ; rate〔berate〕《a person》 roundly ; take 《a person》 roundly to task ; bring〔call〕《a person》 to account ; give 《a person》 a hard time 《of it》 ¶ 그의 실수를 몰아세우다 give him a hard time over his mistake

몰아오다 ① [자동사·한꺼번에] come in crowds〔flocks, droves〕; storm 《a place》; crowd in〔into〕《a house》; [비바람이] come driving 《at》 ¶ 폭풍이 몰아오다 a storm comes up〔on〕
② [타동사·휩쓸어서] drive 《the cows》 along〔this way〕; buy up all 《the fruits》 (휩쓸어 사오다) ¶ 바람이 소나기를 몰아왔다 The wind has brought a shower along.

몰아주다 [한꺼번에] give 《it》〔pay 《it》 up〕 all at once ; give〔pay up〕 the whole amount ¶ 1년 생활비를 몰아주다 give 《a person》 the living expenses for one year in a lump sum

***몰아치다** ① [한 곳으로] put all to one side〔in one place〕
② [급하게] do 《work》 all at once ; speed up 《one's business》; make short work 《of it》; bundle off in quick〔short〕 order 《미》 ¶ 밀린 일을 몰아치다 get caught up on one's work in one big push

몰약 沒藥 〖식물〗 myrrh

몰염치 沒廉恥 impudence ; shamelessness **—하다** (be) impudent ; shameless ; be without shame ; have no shame ¶ 몰염치하게도 shamelessly ; unblushingly ; in a shameless manner ; ignominiously // 몰염치하게도 …하다 have the impudence to 《do》

몰이 [사냥의] chasing ; hunting ; beating ; running 《after》 **—하다** chase 《from, out of, to》; beat ; hunt ; run 《after》
— a chaser ; a hunter 꿩— pheasant beating ; beating for pheasants

몰이꾼 a chaser (in hunting) ; a beater ; a hunter

몰이해 沒理解 lack of understanding〔sympathy〕 ¶ 몰이해한 unfeeling ; heartless ; unsympathizing

***몰인정** 沒人情 lack of human kindness ; inhumanity ; want of sympathy ; heartlessness **—하다** (be) cruel ; inhuman ; pitiless ; cold-hearted

몰입 沒入 ① [빠짐] immersion ; devotion ; absorption ; engrossment ② [몰수] confiscation ; seizure ; forfeiture **—하다** be immersed〔absorbed, engrossed〕 in 《one's work》; get oneself absorbed in ; give oneself up to ; lapse into ; indulge oneself in ; confiscate ; seize ; forfeit ¶ 황홀경에 몰입하다 lapse〔fall〕 into a state of ecstasy

몰지각 沒知覺 lack of discretion ; indiscretion **—하다** be lacking in discretion ; have no sense ; (be) thoughtless

몰취미 沒趣味 lack of taste **—하다** be lacking of taste ; (be) dry ; vulgar ; dull

몰칵 ⇨ 물컥

몰풍 沒風 tastelessness ; dullness **—하다** (be) tasteless ; dry ; dull ; insipid ; vulgar

몰풍정 沒風情 inelegance ; tastelessness ; flavorlessness ; vapidity **—하다** (be) inelegant ; tasteless ; flavorless ; vapid

몰풍치 沒風致 lack of artistic effect ; tastelessness **—하다** be lacking in artistic effect ; (be) tasteless ; unpleasing

몰하다 be less bulky than expected

몰하다 歿— die ; pass away ; perish

몰후 歿後 after one's death ; after the death

†**몸** ① [신체] the body ; the system (전신) ; [체격] physique ; build ; construction ; frame ; [몸집] stature ; size ; [모습] figure ¶ 몸에 맞는 옷 well-fitting clothes // 온몸에 all over the body // 몸이 큰 large(-sized) ; big-bodied ; big ; of imposing〔large〕 figure // 몸이 작은 small (-sized) ; short ; small in stature // 몸이 호리호리한 slim-figured ; thin ; slender 《girl》 // 몸이 뚱뚱한 stout ; corpulent ; fat

//몸이 건장하다 have a strong constitution〔frame, physique〕; have a solid build ; be sturdy〔strong〕//몸이 약하다 have a weak constitution ; be delicately built ; be weak〔delicate, puny〕//몸을 단련하다 harden〔strengthen〕 one's body ; build up one's constitution//몸을 쉬다 have〔take〕 a rest ; rest from work ; rest oneself//몸을 편하게 하다 make oneself comfortable ; ease oneself//몸을 녹이다 warm oneself 《at the fire》//몸과 마음을 일에 바치다 give one's body and soul to the work//몸을 가리다 cover oneself ; clothe oneself//몸을 닦다 clean〔polish〕 oneself ; dry oneself//경찰은 그의 몸에서 칼을 하나 발견했다 The police found a knife on him〔on his person〕.

② [건강] health ¶ 몸이 편치 않다 be ill〔sick〕; be in poor〔bad〕 health ; be out of sorts ; feel unwell//몸조심하다 be careful of one's health ; take good care of oneself//몸에 좋다 be good for one's health ; (be) healthful ; wholesome ; beneficial ; do 《a person》 good//몸에 나쁘다 be bad for one's health ; be harmful〔injurious, unwholesome〕; do 《a person》 harm//몸을 해치다 injure one's health ; break down in health//몸을 회복하다 get well ; improve in health ; regain one's health ; be quite well again ; be restored to health//몸이 견디어 낼 수 없다 I cannot stand the strain. //몸이 좋지 않고는 아무 것도 못한다 You cannot accomplish anything without good health.

③ [몸통] the body ; the trunk ; the torso ¶ 비행기의 몸 the body of an airplane

④ [사람 자신] one's own person ; self ; oneself ¶ 내 몸 my body ; myself ; I//몸가지다 conduct〔behave〕 oneself//첩의 몸에서 난 아들 a son begotten by a concubine//몸에 걸치다 wear ; be in 《a red coat》; put on ; wrap oneself in//몸에 익다 be accustomed to ; be familiar with//몸을 던지다 drown oneself ; throw oneself into ; engage in ; enter into//몸을 두다〔담다〕 stay in ; live in//몸을 의지하다 lean〔rely〕 on ; find shelter with 《a person》//몸을 아끼다 spare oneself 〔one's efforts〕//몸을 그르치다 ruin oneself ; go astray//몸을 감추다 conceal 〔hide〕 oneself//(여자가) 몸을 더럽히다 be sullied ; be dishonored ; lose her chastity〔purity〕; stain her virtue//몸을 팔다 [노예로] sell oneself 《into slavery》; go into bondage ; [악에] sell oneself to vice ; [매음] prostitute oneself ; earn money on the streets//몸을 맡기다 give oneself to 《a man》; place oneself at 《a person's》 disposal//몸을 바치다 devote oneself〔one's life〕 to ; sacrifice oneself〔one's life〕; offer one's life ; give herself to 《a man》; lay down〔sacrifice〕 one's life 《for the country》//중요한 서류는 항상 몸에 지니고 있다 I always keep〔carry〕 my important papers on my person.

⑤ [지위·신분] position ; station ; place ; one's status〔circumstances〕 ¶ 귀한 몸 a person of high〔noble〕 birth ; an important figure ; an august〔exalted〕 personage//천한 몸 a person of low〔humble〕 birth

몸가지다 ① [임신하다] become〔be〕 pregnant ; be with child ; be in the family way ; conceive ¶ 몸가진 지 6개월이다 be six months pregnant〔gone with child〕; be in the sixth months of pregnancy
② [월경하다] have the menses 〔monthlies〕; see the flowers

*⁎***몸가짐** [거동] one's behavior〔conduct〕; deportment ; manner ; bearing ; [태도] an attitude ; a setup ; an air ; a stand ¶ 신사적 몸가짐 a gentlemanly attitude〔bearing〕//위엄 있는 몸가짐 a dignified manner//몸가짐이 점잖다 have gentlemanly behavior ; behave like a gentleman//몸가짐이 얌전하다 behave well〔oneself〕

몸가축 taking care of one's personal appearance **—하다** keep oneself neat〔tidy〕 ¶ 몸가축을 잘하다 be careful about one's personal appearance ; be neat in one's person ; be well-groomed //여자는 몸가축을 잘해야 한다 A woman ought to take good care of her personal appearance.

*****몸값** [화대] money paid for prostitution ; [포로 따위의] ransom ¶ 종의 몸값 the price paid for a slave servant//사람을 억류하고 몸값을 요구하다 hold 《a person》 to〔for〕 ransom//몸값을 치르고 죄수를 구해주다 redeem a prisoner

몸꼴 physique ; frame ; figure ; make ; build ; construction

몸나다 grow fat〔corpulent, stout〕; put on flesh ; gain weight

몸닦달 training oneself ; hardening one's body ; self-discipline **—하다** train oneself ; harden one's body ; harden the body against〔inure oneself to〕 hardships

몸단속 —團束 guarding ; arming oneself **—하다** guard 《against》; arm oneself 《to the teeth》; be on guard

몸단장 —丹粧 decorating〔embellishing〕 oneself **—하다** dress〔equip〕 oneself

*⁎***몸달다** be all hot and bothered ; be too eager ; be overzealous ; fidget ; be in a fidget ; have the fidgets ; be in a bustle ¶ 영화 구경가지 못해 몸달아하다 be all hot and bothered because one wants to go〔because one can't go〕 to the movie //사소한 일에 몸달아하는 상사 밑에서 일하는 것은 괴롭다 It's rough working for a boss who's so fussy about details.

몸두다 stay〔live〕 in ; take shelter with ¶

몸둘 곳이 없다 have no place to live〔stay〕 in ; have no friend to take shelter with∥몸두어 일할 곳을 구하다 look for a place to work in∥(부끄러워) 몸둘 바를 모르다 be deeply ashamed of oneself

몸때 the time of menstruation ; the menstrual period ; [몸의 때] dirt ; filth ; grim

몸뚱이 a body ; a frame ¶ 몸뚱이가 크다 be huge of limb ; have a bulky frame∥몸뚱이가 작다 be small of frame ; be short of stature

몸말 the subject ⇨ 주어

몸매 one's figure〔form, shape〕; one's carriage ¶ 몸매가 예쁘다 have a nice figure∥무용을 하면 몸매가 예뻐진다 Dancing improves one's figure〔carriage〕.

몸맨두리 one's figure ; appearance ; carriage ¶ 몸맨두리를 꾸미다 trim oneself up

몸받다 take《the task of a superior》upon oneself ; undertake《the task of a superior》; take over《father's business》; succeed to《father's business》

몸보신 一補身 tonicking ; nurturing ; restoring health of the body **—하다** improve〔build up〕one's health by taking tonics ; strengthen oneself with a tonic

*__몸부림__ struggle ; wriggle ; kicking and screaming **—하다** struggle ; wriggle ; writhe ; flounce ¶ 고통으로 몸부림치다 writhe in the agony of pain∥결박에서 벗어나려고 몸부림쳤다 I struggled to free myself from my bonds.∥어떻게 해서든지 출세하려고 몸부림쳤다 He strove hard to rise in the world somehow.∥아무리 몸부림쳐봐도 소용없다 It's no use struggling and wriggling.∥육지로 헤엄쳐 가려고 몸부림쳤다 He strained to reach the shore.∥그녀는 미친 여자처럼 몸부림쳤다 She flounced about like a mad woman.

몸빠진살 a slender arrow

몸살 illness from fatigue ¶ 몸살이 나다 suffer from fatigue∥몸살풀이하다 take a good rest

몸상 一床 a small auxiliary table (set in front of the main one at a celebration party)

몸서리 shuddering ; being sick of ; being heartsick ; disgust ¶ 몸서리치다〔나다〕 shudder ; tremble《for fear》; shiver ; be sick of ; be heartsick ; be〔feel〕disgusted《at, by, with》∥듣기만 해도 몸서리나다 shudder at the mere mention of《the name》∥그 말에 그는 몸서리쳤다 At the word every drop of his blood was chilled.∥나는 그의 거짓말 버릇에 몸서리가 난다 I am disgusted by〔sick of〕his habit of lying.∥냄새만 맡아도 몸서리난다 Its smell disgusts me.

†**몸소** in person ; personally ¶ 몸소 가다 go oneself ; go in person∥몸소 검사하다 make a personal inspection∥몸소 지휘하다 take〔assume〕personal command of ; be in personal command of∥그는 몸소 부하에게 모범을 보였다 He personally set an example to his inferiors.

몸솔 a scratcher ; a scratching brush

몸수색 一搜索 a body search ; a frisk(ing) **—하다** search one's person〔a person〕; frisk ¶ 흉기를 숨기고 있지 않는가 몸수색을 하다 search《a person》for concealed weapons

몸시계 一時計 a pocket watch

몸쓰다 perform a feat ; (do) a stunt

몸약 a shot of dynamite ; a mining blast

몸엣것 [피] menstrual blood〔discharge, flow, flux〕; [월경] menses

몸있다 menstruate ; have one's period ; be in the flowers ; be unwell《미》

몸져눕다 be confined to bed ; be ill〔sick〕in bed ; lie in one's sickbed ; be bedridden〔bedfast〕; be laid up ; keep one's bed ¶ 그는 폐병으로 몸져 누워 있다 He is laid up with consumption.∥그의 부인은 망연자실한 나머지 몸져 누웠다 I hear his wife is so devastated she's taken to her bed.

몸조리 一調理 taking care of one's health **—하다** take good care of one's health

*__몸조심__ 一操心 ① [건강에] taking care of oneself ; being cautious about one's health
② [근신] behaving oneself **—하다** take (good) care of one's health ; be careful of one's health ; behave oneself ; be on one's good behavior ; be moderate ; use great moderation ¶ 정치적인 사건에 말려들지 않기 위하여 몸조심하다 exhibit reserve on political matters∥병에 걸리지 않도록 몸조심해라 Take care not to make yourself ill.∥몸조심하시오 I wish you a good journey. (여행을 떠나는 사람에게)/Take care (of yourself).

몸종 a lady's maid ; a handmaid〔slave girl〕《to Mrs. ...》; a waiting〔body〕maid

몸주체 ① [몸가눔] body control ; handling oneself ¶ 술에 취해서 몸주체를 못하다 be so drunk that one can't control oneself
② [몸거둠] taking care of oneself ¶ 그는 너무 늙어서 몸주체를 못한다 He is so senile that he cannot take care of himself.

몸집 a body ; figure ; size ; stature ; a frame ; build ; constitution ¶ 몸집이 매우 큰 사람 such a bulky fellow∥몸집이 홀쭉하다 be slim ; be of slender build∥몸집이 크다 be big of frame ; be large-limbed ; be large-built ; be of large build∥몸집이 뚱뚱하다 be fat〔stout, portly〕

†**몸짓** a gesture ; gesticulation ; motion **—하다** make gestures ; gesticulate ;

motion ; sign ; move one's body ¶ 몸짓으로 찬성〔불찬성〕의 의사를 표시하다 make a gesture of assent〔dissent〕 // 몸짓 손짓으로 의사 표시를 하다 express 《oneself》 by gesture // 그는 몸짓으로 가라고 나에게 명령했다 He motioned me away.

몸차림 dress ; equipment ; outfit ── 하다 dress oneself ; equip oneself 《for》 ; fit oneself up 《for》

몸채 the main house〔building, wing〕

몸치장 ─治粧 dressing up ; trimming oneself up ; decking oneself out ── 하다 dress oneself up ; trim oneself up ; deck oneself out ; be dressed up ¶ 몸치장도 하는둥 마는둥 외출하다 go out without spending much time in dressing ; go out after having dressed oneself in haste〔in a hurry〕 // 보석으로 몸치장하다 deck oneself out with jewels ; bejewel oneself // 그 여자는 말쑥하게 몸치장했다 She trimmed herself up.

몸통 the trunk ; the bulk of one's body ; the body (의복의) ; the barrel (말의) ¶ 몸통이 길다〔짧다〕 have a long〔short〕 trunk (신체의) ; have a long〔short〕 waist (의복의)

몸풀다 be delivered (of a baby) ; give birth (to a baby) ¶ 몸풀 때가 가까웠다 She is nearing her confinement. / She is going to have a child shortly. / She is soon to become a mother. /She is expecting.

몸피 physique ; build ; constitution ; frame

†**몹시** very ; greatly ; highly ; severely ; heavily ; hard ; ever so much ; awfully ; terribly ; deadly ; [과도하게] exceedingly ; excessively ; [극렬하게] severely ; heavily ; intensely ; badly ; [극도로] extremely ¶ 몹시 머리가 아프다 have a severe headache // 몹시 아름답다 be terribly beautiful // 몹시 꾸짖다 scold severely // 몹시 굴다 behave cruelly ; act harshly ; be hard 《on》 // 몹시 취해 있다 be heavily〔dead〕 drunk // 비가 몹시 온다 It rains hard. // 나는 몹시 피로했다 I am dead tired.

몹쓸 bad ; evil ; wicked ; immoral ; vicious ¶ 몹쓸 감기 a bad cold ; a severe cold // 몹쓸 계집 a bad woman // 몹쓸 놈 a wicked guy ; a rascal // 몹쓸 병 a virulent disease // 몹쓸 짓 an evil deed ; a misdeed ; a vice // 남에게 몹쓸 짓을 하다 do evil to others

†**못**[1] [연못] a pond ; a pool (작은) ¶ 못을 치다〔푸다〕 drain〔dry up, pump out〕 a pond ; pump a pond ; dry // 못을 파다 dig a pond // 못을 메우다 fill in a pond

†**못**[2] a nail ; a peg (나무못) ; a screw (나사못) ; a spike (침목용) ; a sprig (대가리가 없는) ; a tack (대가리가 납작한) ¶ 대나무못 a bamboo nail // 못대가리 the nailhead // 못을 박다 drive a nail 《in》 ; nail up 《a box》 (못질하다) ; nail down 《a lid》 ; nail 《a thing》 to 《the door》 // 못을 뽑다 unnail ; extract〔pull out, draw out〕 a nail // 못에 걸다 hang 《a hat》 on a peg〔hook, nail〕 // 발이 못에 찔리다 run a nail into one's foot // 가슴에 못을 박다 hurt〔wound〕 《a person》 deeply in his heart // 꼼짝 못하게 그 약속에 못을 박다 nail 《a person》 down to his promise

못[3] [손발의] a corn (주로 발의) ; a callosity ; a callus ¶ 못 빼는 약 a corn plaster // 못이 생기다 become callous // 못을 빼다 take off〔remove〕 a corn // 발바닥에 못이 생겼다 I have got a corn 〔A callosity formed〕 on the sole of my foot. // 귀에 못이 박히도록 들었다 I am sick of hearing it. /Please, don't drum a lesson into my head. (듣기 싫다)

못[4] not ; never ; can't ; won't ¶ 못 가겠다 I can't go. /I won't go. /I refuse to go. // 못 읽겠다 I can't〔won't〕 read. // 우리는 폭풍우로 출발을 못한다 The storm prevents us from starting. // 나는 그러한 사치는 못한다 I can't afford such luxury. // 이 건물 안에서는 담배를 못 피운다 You are not allowed to smoke in this building.

못가새 〖농업〗 one third of a bunch of rice seedlings

못걸이 a clothes rack ; pegboard (연장용)

못견디다 ① [참지 못하다] be unbearable ; be unendurable ; cannot be borne 〔endured〕 ; be past〔beyond〕 endurance ; [사람이 주어] cannot stand 〔bear, endure〕 ② [억누르지 못하다] cannot help 《doing》 ; cannot but 《do》 ; cannot refrain from 《doing》

못나다 ① [용모가] (be) ugly ; bad-〔ill-〕 looking ; homely ; plain ; ill-favored ¶ 얼굴이 못나다 have an ugly face // 지지리 못나다 be awfully ugly-looking ② [어리석다] (be) dull ; foolish ; silly ; stupid ¶ 못난 생각 a foolish notion〔idea〕 // 못난 짓 a foolish act ; stupidity ; folly ; foolishness ; foolery // 지지리 못나게도 foolishly enough // 못난 짓을 하다 do a foolish〔stupid〕 thing ; commit a folly // 그들은 얼마 안 가서 그 따위 행위가 못난 짓이란 것을 알게 되리라 They will soon see the folly of such a course.

못난이 a stupid person ; a no-good ; a tomfool ; a fool ; a simpleton ; a blockhead ; a good-for-nothing ; a ne'er- do-well

못내 forever ; unforgettably ; always ; eternally ; lingeringly ¶ 못내 잊지 못하다 never forget ; hold 《a person's》 memory ever dear ; be ever present in one's mind // 못내 서러워하다 be in constant sorrow // 그는 그 여자를 못내 그리워하고 있다 He still thinks of her tenderly. /He still retains a lingering love for the girl.

못되다 ① [미완] be not yet done 《through, over, ready》 ; be unfinished

〔incomplete〕 ¶ 그 일이 아직 못되었다 The job is not yet finished.
② [미달] be under ; be below ; be short of ; be not up to ; be not more than ; be less than ; do not reach 〔make〕 ¶ 백만 원이 못되다 be less than one million *won* ∥20세가 못되다 be under twenty years of age∥6개월이 못되어 그만두다 resign within six months
③ [건강·상태] look poor ; be in bad shape ; get worse ; decline ¶ 앓고 나서 얼굴이 못되다 look poor after one's illness∥건강이 매우 못되다 one's health is in very bad shape∥집안이 못되어가다 a family goes downhill∥나라가 못되어가다 a country is on the decline
④ [악하다] (be) bad ; bad-natured ; evil ; wicked ; wrong ¶ 못된 놈 a wicked man ; a rascal ; a rogue∥못된 짓 an evil deed ; a misdeed ; a wrong act ; misbehavior ; a vice∥못되게 굴다 do wrong ; misbehave oneself

못마땅하다 [사물이 주어] (be) unsatisfactory ; be not gratifying ; go against the grain ; (be) disagreeable〔offensive〕《to》 ; distasteful 《to》 ; unacceptable 《to》 ; [사람이 주어] be displeased〔dissatisfied〕 with ; be unable to stomach ¶ 못마땅한 기색이다 look displeased 〔unsatisfied〕∥조건이 못마땅해서 거절했다 I declined it as the terms were unsatisfactory. ∥무엇이 그렇게 못마땅하냐 What makes you so displeased ? / What are you so displeased with ? ∥그 음식이 나에게는 못마땅하다 The food was unsatisfactory〔disagreeable〕 to me. ∥그는 월 80만원의 봉급을 못마땅해한다 He is dissatisfied〔not content〕 with his salary of eight hundred thousand *won* a month.

못바늘 a pin

†**못박다** drive a nail in ; [남의 가슴에] wound a person's feelings ¶ 십자가에 못박다 crucify 《a person》

못박이다 ① [손발에] get〔have〕 a corn 〔callus〕 ¶ 발바닥에 못박이다 have a corn on the sole of one's foot∥손바닥에 못박이다 have a callus on the palm of one's hand
② [가슴에] have a grudge 《against》 ; feel bitter 《against》 ; be hurt deep 《in one's heart》 ¶ 원한이 깊이 못박이다 harbor a deep grudge

못보다 overlook ; make an oversight ; pass by〔up, over〕 ; fail to notice ; lose sight of

못본체하다 pretend not to see ; [관대] connive〔wink, blink〕 at ; overlook ; look over ; let 《it》 pass〔go〕 ; close one's eyes 《to》 ; [돌보지 않음] neglect ; have no regard for ; pay no attention to ; slight ; do not care for ; show indifference to ¶ 그는 길에서 나를 못본체했다 He passed me up cold〔cut me dead〕 in the street. ∥곤경에 처한 친구를 못본체했다 He left his friend in the lurch. ∥이번만은 못본체 해 두마 I will let the matter pass for this once.

못비 a sufficient rain for rice transplantation

못뽑이 pincers ; a carpenter's pincers ; a nail puller〔extractor〕 ; a claw hammer

못살게 굴다 tease ; treat badly ; torment ; be hard upon 《a person》

*__못생기다__ (be) plain ; ugly ; homely ; bad-looking ; ill-favored ⇨ 못나다

못쓰게 되다 [얼굴·건강이] a person becomes poor in health ; a person is in bad shape ; [물건이] be spoilt ; be ruined

못쓰다 ① [좋지 않다] (be) bad ; wrong ; improper ; no-good ; worthless ¶ 몹쓸짓 a bad〔the wrong〕 thing to do ; a misdeed ; misconduct ; misbehavior∥못쓸 사람 a no-good person∥사람이 못쓰게 되다 a person gets bad 〔worse〕
② [금지] must not 《do》 ; shall not 《do》 (2, 3인칭) ; ought not to 《do》 ¶ 너 그런 짓하면 못써 You must not do such a thing. ∥그런 식으로 말하면 못써 Don't talk like that.
③ [사물] (be) bad ; inferior ; poor ; coarse ; unusable ; unsuitable ; inadequate ; be out of order ¶ 못쓸 물건 bad 〔poor〕 goods ; an unusable〔unsuit- able〕 article∥못쓰게 만들다 spoil ; ruin ; destroy ; rot 《속》

못자리 ① [묘판] a rice seedbed〔nursery〕 ¶ 못자리를 내다 prepare a rice seed plot
② [씨뿌리기] sowing rice seeds **—하다** sow rice seeds

못정 a piece of iron used to drive a nail in deep ; [광산용] a pointed chisel

못주다 drive〔put〕 a nail into 《a wall》 ; nail (down) ; hammer a nail into

못줄 〖농업〗 a guide line for setting out rows of rice seedlings

못지 않다 be not inferior 《to》 ; be just as good as ; be no less 《than》 ¶ 그 여자는 자기 언니 못지 않게 아름답다 She is no less beautiful than her elder sister. ∥이것은 외래품에 못지 않다 This compares quite well with foreign-made article. ∥그는 과학 지식에 있어 그 반의 누구에게도 못지 않다 He is second 〔inferior〕 to none in scientific knowledge in his class. ∥신부에게 적어도 남 못지 않은 결혼 준비는 해주고 싶다 I'd at least like her to have the usual items a bride receives.

못질 nailing **—하다** nail ; drive (in) a nail ; nail down

*__못하다__[1] [불능] cannot ; be impossible ; be unable to ; fail to ; cannot afford 《to do》 ; [부정] be not ¶ 사람은 물과 공기가 없으면 살지 못한다 We are unable to subsist without water and air. ∥너무 어려워서 나는 못한다 It is too difficult for me

to do. // 폭풍 때문에 출발을 못한다 The storm prevents us from starting. // 그 문제는 어려워서 도저히 내 힘이 자라지 못한다 The problem is utterly beyond my power. // 내 형편으로는 그런 사치는 못한다 I cannot afford such luxury. // 이 더위는 참지 못하겠다 I can't bear this hot weather. /This hot weather is more than I can bear. // 죽어도 그런 나쁜 짓은 못하겠다 I will not do such an evil deed even if it should cost me my life. // 노력했지만 우리는 상을 타지 못했다 In spite of our efforts, we failed to win the prize. // 물이 맑지 못하다 The water is not clear. // 이 등불은 밝지 못하다 This lamp does not give a good light. // 그는 유능하지 못하다 He is lacking in ability. // 그의 세력이 전국에는 미치지 못한다 His influence does not extend all over the country.

*못하다² [열등] (be) inferior ; be worse than ; be below ; fall behind ; be not as 〔so〕 good as ; be lower 《in》 ; be not on a level with ¶ 그는 학문에 있어서 형만 못하다 He is not quite so learned as his elder brother. // 그는 영어에 있어서 동생만 못하다 He isn't up to his younger brother in English. // 그는 짐승만도 못하다 He is worse than a beast.

몽구리 ① [까까머리] a close-cropped〔-cut〕 head ② [중] a Buddhist priest ; a bonze ; a monk

몽그작거리다 ⇨ 뭉그적거리다

몽근벼 awnless〔beardless〕 rice grains

몽근짐 a heavy〔weighty〕 load for its bulk

몽글다 [낟알이] (be) awnless ; beardless

몽글리다 ① [낟알을] take beard off ; strip an ear of 《rice》 ; remove impurities ; clear grains ② [단련] inure ; harden ; train ; discipline ¶ 추위〔더위〕에 몸을 몽글리다 inure oneself to cold 〔heat〕 ③ [맵시를] trim up ; preen ; tidy oneself ¶ 옷매를 몽글리다 trim oneself up

몽글몽글 ―하다 (be) clotty ; lumpy

몽깃돌 a killick

몽니 [욕심] greed ; avarice ; rapacity ; [심술] perverseness ¶ 몽니사납다〔부리다〕 be cross and greedy〔covetous, avaricious, rapacious, grasping〕

―쟁이 a cross and greedy fellow ; a shark ; a dog in the manger

몽달귀 ―鬼 the ghost of a bachelor

몽당붓 a stubby〔stubbed〕 writing brush

몽당비 a stumpy broom(-stick) ; a worn-out broom

몽당이 ① [실뭉치] a ball of thread ② [닳은 것] worn-down stump

―붓 a worn-out writing brush ― 연필 a stubby pencil ; a stub〔stump〕 of pencil

몽당치마 a ragged short skirt

몽동발이 a worn-down stump

*몽둥이 a stick ; a club ; a cudgel ; [경관의 곤봉] a truncheon ; a baton 《미》 ; a snag 《속》 ¶ 몽둥이로 때리다 club〔cudgel〕 《a person》 ; beat with a stick // 몽둥이로 얻어 맞다 be clubbed ; be cudgeled ; get beaten with a stick

몽둥이 세례 ―洗禮 beating with a stick ; clubbing ; cudgelling ¶ 몽둥이 세례를 주다 beat with a stick ; club ; cudgel // 몽둥이 세례를 받다 get beaten with a stick ; be clubbed

몽둥이찜 beating with a stick ; clubbing ; cudgelling ―하다 beat with a stick ; club ; cudgel

몽따다 pretend ignorance ; pretend to be ignorant ; play the innocent ; dissemble ; feign〔affect, sham〕 ignorance ; face it out

*몽땅 all ; completely ; entirely ; wholly ; in the lump ¶ 빚을 몽땅 갚다 pay all one's debts // 몽땅 살해됐다 They were killed to a man〔all of them〕. // 돈을 몽땅 잘렸다 He lost all the money. / He was cheated out of the entire sum. // 용돈을 몽땅 써버렸다 He has spent the last penny of his pocket money. // 벚꽃이 몽땅 져버렸다 The cherry blossoms have all scattered.

몽땅몽땅 ⇨ 뭉떵뭉떵

몽똑 ―하다 (be) stumpy ; blunt ; dull ; stubby ¶ 몽똑한 연필 a stubby pencil

몽똑몽똑하다 be all stumpy〔stubby, blunt〕

몽똥그리다 bundle it up crudely ⇨ 뭉뚱그리다

몽롱 朦朧 dimness ; indistinctness ; obscurity ; mistiness ; vagueness ―하다 (be) dim ; faint ; indistinct ; vague ; obscure ¶ 몽롱하게 dimly ; faintly ; indistinctly // 몽롱해지다 grow dim // 의식이 몽롱해지다 have a dim consciousness

― 상태 a condition of clouded consciousness ; 〖의학〗 fugue

몽매 蒙昧 ignorance ―하다 (be) ignorant ; unenlightened ; uncivilized ; benighted ¶ (무지) 몽매한 백성 uncivilized 〔benighted, unenlightened〕 people

몽매 夢寐 sleeping and dreaming ¶ 몽매간에도 even while asleep ; awake or asleep ; all the time // 그 무서운 경험이 몽매에도 머리 속을 떠나지 않는다 Awake or asleep, the horrible experience still haunts my memory.

몽상 夢想 a dream ; a day dream ; a vision ; a fancy ; a reverie ―하다 dream 《of》 ; fancy ; indulge in reveries ¶ 몽상도 안해본 사건 an undreamt-of event // 몽상에 잠기다 be given to day dreaming ; indulge in idle fancies ; be lost in wild fancies

―가 a dreamer ; a visionary ; an idealist

몽상 蒙喪 mourning ¶ 몽상중이다 be in mourning ―하다 observe〔go into, take to〕 mourning 《for one's mother》 ;

wear mourning
몽설 夢泄 a wet dream ; a nocturnal pollution〔emission〕 **—하다** have a wet dream ; have an involuntary emission of semen
몽실몽실 plump ; fleshily ; round **—하다** (be) lumpy ; plump ¶ 몽실몽실한 젖가슴 an ample〔a rich〕 breast ; a well-rounded bosom // 몽실몽실한 얼굴 a full face // 몽실몽실한 몸 a fleshy body // 몽실몽실 살이 찌다 be〔grow〕 plump
몽유병 夢遊病 〖의학〗 somnambulism ; sleep-walking
—자 a somnambulist ; a sleepwalker ; a somnambule ; a noctambulist
몽은 蒙恩 receiving a favor〔benefit, grace, kindness〕 **—하다** receive a favor〔benefit, grace, kindness〕 ; be indebted to
몽정 夢精 a wet dream
몽조 夢兆 a dream ; the omen of a dream ; a prognostic from a dream
몽중 夢中 《in》 a dream ¶ 몽중에 보다 see in a dream
몽진 蒙塵 **—하다** [왕이] flee from the Royal Palace〔Capital〕 ; be a fugitive on the dusty roads
몽짜스럽다, 몽짜치다 be more subtle than one might think ; be deeper〔smarter〕 than one looks
몽총하다 ① [냉정] (be) cold ; indifferent ; icy ; frigid ; blunt ② [몽똥] (be) short ; stubby
몽치 a club ; a bar ; a cudgel ¶ 몽치질 clubbing ; wielding a cudgel // 몽치로 때리다 beat with a club // 몽치로 얻어 맞다 be clubbed ; be cudgeled ; get beaten with a club
쇠— an iron club
몽치다 lump together ⇨ 뭉치다
몽키다 gather together ⇨ 뭉키다
몽타주 (a) montage
— 사진 《make》 a composite picture 〔photograph〕 ; a composite ; 《compose》 a photomontage ; a montage picture 〔photo〕
몽탕몽탕 《cut》 in big lumps〔in chunks〕
몽태치다 steal ; take ; purloin ; swipe 《속》
몽톡 —하다 (be) stumpy ; blunt ; dull ; thick
몽학 蒙學 ① [아동의 공부] learning 〔schooling〕 of the young ② [몽고어학] Mongolian studies ; Mongolian philology
몽혼 夢魂 one's soul as it appears in a dream
몽혼 朦昏 〖의학〗 anesthesia ⇨ 마취
몽환 夢幻 dreams and phantasms ; a vision ¶ 몽환의 fantastic ; dreamy ; phantasmal
—경(境) a world of phantasms **—곡** a fantasia **—극** a fantasy play
뫼 [무덤] a grave ; a sepulcher ; a tomb ¶ 뫼쓰다 bury ; use ground for a grave // 뫼를 파내다 dig open a grave // 선산에 뫼를 쓰다 bury in the family ground
묏자리 a grave site ¶ 묏자리를 구하다〔잡다〕 look for〔choose〕 a grave site // 묏자리를 정하다 designate〔fix〕 a grave site
*__묘 墓__ a grave ; a tomb ; a resting place ; a sepulcher

> 참고 **grave** 시체를 매장하기 위한 땅 속의 굴을 의미하며 죽음 자체의 뜻을 이면에 포함하고 있다 **tomb**은 grave를 의미하는 품위 있는 말 특히 grave 위에 있는 묘비 묘석 묘표 따위를 말한다

묘 卯 the Hare 《as the fourth of Terrestrial Branches》
—년 the Year of the Hare **—방** the Direction of the Hare〔East〕 **—시** the Hour of the Hare 《the time between 6 a. m. and 8 a. m.》
묘 廟 [문묘] a shrine ; [종묘] a mausoleum
묘 妙 ① [현묘(玄妙)] a mystery ; a wonder ; a miracle ¶ 조화의 묘 the mystery of nature〔creation〕 ; the wisdom of the creator
② [교묘] cleverness ; adroitness
묘계 妙計 an ingenious trick ; a clever scheme ; a wise〔capital〕 plan
묘구 妙句 an excellent phrase〔expression〕 ; a clever〔witty, happy〕 expression
묘구도적 墓丘盜賊 [도굴자] a grave robber ; a looter〔plunderer〕 of a grave ; [시체 도굴자] a body snatcher
*__묘기 妙技__ exquisite skill (솜씨) ; a wonderful performance (연극 따위의) ; a splendid feat〔a stunt〕 (곡예의) ; a fine play (야구 따위의) ¶ 공중의 묘기 an aerial stunt // 묘기를 보이다 exhibit〔display〕 one's feats ; perform a wonderful feat
묘년 妙年 blooming age ⇨ 묘령
묘당 廟堂 [조정] the Court ; the Government ; the Cabinet ; the Ministry
묘령 妙齡 youth ; blooming age ; the flower of youth ¶ 묘령의 young ; blooming ; youthful // 묘령의 여성 a young lady〔girl〕 ; a woman of eligible 〔marriageable〕 age ; a girl in the flower of maidenhood // 묘령에 달하다 attain budding womanhood ; arrive at a marriageable age
묘리 妙理 an exquisite〔abstruse〕 principle ¶ 묘리를 터득하다 attain to the exquisite principle ; get (into) the knack 《of》 (요령을) ; get at the fundamental principle
묘막 墓幕 a hut built near a grave
묘망 渺茫 **—하다** (be) vast ; limitless ; broad ; boundless
*__묘목 苗木__ a young tree〔plant〕 ; a nursery

tree ; a sapling ; a seedling ; a set

묘미 妙味 beauty ; charm ; exquisiteness ; a nicety ; a nice point ¶ 묘미를 음미하다 appreciate the beauty 《of》 // 그의 문체에는 말할 수 없는 묘미가 있다 There is an indescribable charm in his style. // 그는 이 묘미를 모른다 He cannot appreciate this nice point.

묘방 卯方 〖민속〗 the direction of the Hare ; the east

묘방 妙方 an excellent prescription (처방) ; an excellent means〔method〕 (방법)

묘법 妙法 ① [처방] an excellent means〔method〕 ② [불법] the marvelous〔wonderful〕 law of Buddha

묘비 墓碑 a tombstone ; a gravestone ¶ 묘비를 세우다 set up a tombstone —명(銘) an epitaph ; an inscription on a tombstone —조각사 a monumental mason

†묘사 描寫 description ; delineation ; representation ; depiction ; portrayal —하다 depict ; represent ; delineate 《a character》 ; portray ; [그림으로] draw ; sketch ; paint ; [글로] describe ¶ 묘사적 depictive ; descriptive // 생생한 묘사 a vivid description // 간단히 묘사하다 sketch // 어떠한 말로도 그 혼란을 묘사할 수 없다 No language can depict the confusion. // 인물이 잘 묘사되어 있다 The characters are well drawn〔portrayed〕.

사실적 — a realistic description 성격 — character delineation〔portrayal〕 실물 — model drawing 심리적 — a psychological description 인물 — character portrayal ; characterization 인상 — an impressionistic description 자연 — a naturalistic description〔picture〕 평면 — an objective description

묘산 妙算 a wise plan ⇨ 묘책

묘상 苗床 a nursery ; a seedbed ; a seed plot ; a rice seedbed (못자리)

묘석 墓石 a gravestone ; a tombstone ; a headstone

묘소 墓所 a graveyard ; a burial ground〔place〕

묘수 妙手 [솜씨] excellent skill ; [바둑 따위] a capital move ; [사람] a master hand ; an accomplished person ; a proficient ; an expert ; an adept ¶ 피아노의 묘수 an accomplished pianist ; a wonder on the piano

묘시 卯時 the hour of the Hare 《the period between 5 and 7 a. m.》

묘안 妙案 a capital〔happy〕 idea ; an excellent〔ingenious〕 scheme〔plan〕 ¶ 묘안이 생각나다 hit upon a capital 〔happy〕 idea ; be struck with a happy notion ; a bright idea strikes 《one》

묘안석 猫眼石 〖광물〗 a cat's-eye

묘약 妙藥 a specific ; an excellent 〔sovereign, golden〕 remedy ; a wonder 〔miracle〕 drug ; a cure-all ¶ 암의 묘약 an excellent remedy for cancer // 이 약은 위병의 묘약입니다 This medicine is marvelously effective for indigestion.

묘역 墓域 a graveyard

묘연하다 杳然— [멀어서] (be) faraway ; remote 《from》 ; [기억이] dim ; vague ; indistinct ; [소식이] 《one's whereabouts》 be utterly unknown

묘연하다 渺然— (be) immense ; vast

묘우 廟宇 a shrine

묘의 廟議 a Cabinet council (회의) ; a Cabinet decision (결의)

묘전 墓前 ¶ 묘전에 in front of a tomb 〔grave〕 ¶ 묘전에서 곡하다 weep over 《a person's》 grave

묘제 墓祭 ancestral rites held before the grave

묘주 卯酒 a morning drink

⁑묘지 墓誌 an epitaph ; an inscription on a tomb (묘지명)

묘지 墓地 a graveyard ; a burial ground ; a cemetery ; a churchyard (교회의)

공동 — a (public) cemetery 공원 — a cemetery park 국립 — the National Cemetery 유엔 — U. N. Memorial Cemetery

묘지기 墓— the guardian of a grave ; a grave keeper

묘책 妙策 a clever〔pet〕 scheme ; a capital plan ⇨ 묘안

묘출 描出 depiction ; description —하다 depict ; describe

묘판 苗板 a seedbed ⇨ 못자리

묘포 苗圃 a seedbed ; a nursery

묘필 妙筆 an excellent piece of brushwork〔writing, painting〕

묘하 墓下 a family burial ground ; a family graveyard

*묘하다 妙— ① (be) exquisite ; marvelous ; delicate ② [이상하다] (be) strange ; curious ; mysterious ¶ 묘한 사람 a strange 〔queer〕 person ; an eccentric (기인) // 묘한 말 a strange remark // 묘한 이야기 a mysterious story

묘혈 墓穴 a grave ¶ 스스로 묘혈을 파는 짓 a suicidal〔self-destroying〕 act // 스스로 묘혈을 파다 He digs his own grave. /He brings about his own ruin.

무[1] [옷옷의] a reinforcing cloth strip (as at the armpit of an outer-coat)

무[2] 〖의학〗 an acute periostitis

*무[3] a radish

—김치 radish *kimch'i*〔pickles〕 ; pickled radish —말랭이 dried slices of radish —장아찌 sliced radish soaked in soybean paste —짠지 highly-salted〔salt-preserved, salty〕 radish *kimch'i* —채 radish shreds〔strips〕 ; shredded radish —청 parts of radish ; radish tops 〔leaves〕

무 戊 〖민속〗 the 5th of the 10 Heaven's

무 武 military affairs ; [무예] military arts ¶ 무를 숭상하다 pursue the policy of militarism ; glorify military power // 무를 닦다 train oneself in warlike arts // 문을 버리고 무를 배우다 give up the pen for the sword

*무 無 nothing ; nonexistence ; naught ; nil ; nihility ; zero ¶ 무가 되다 come〔be brought〕 to nothing〔naught〕 ; go for nothing // 무에서 유는 못 만든다 Out of nothing, nothing comes. // 전부가 아니면 무 All or nothing.

무가 武家 a military family〔class〕 ; a warrior (무사)

무가내(하) 無可奈(何) inevitability ; having no alternative ¶ 무가내(하)다 (be) inevitable ; unavoidable ; necessary // 무가내하로 inevitably ; unavoidably ; inescapably ; out of sheer necessity // 무가내(하)의 사정 inevitable〔unavoidable〕 circumstance // 무가내하로 최후 수단을 취하다 be driven to (take) the last resort ; cannot help〔avoid〕 taking the ultimate step // 무가내(하)로 한 짓이지 좋아서 한 짓이 아니다 He did it of necessity, not of choice. // 이제는 무가내하다 There is no help for it.

무가당 無加糖 ¶ 무가당의 sugarless ; nonsugared ; natural
— 오렌지 주스 sugarless orange juice

*무가치 無價値 worthlessness —하다 (be) worthless ; valueless ; be of no value ¶ 그것은 무가치하다 It is worth nothing. /It is worthless.

무간 無間 —하다 (be) intimate ; close 《to one's bosom》 ; friendly ¶ 무간한 친구 a close〔bosom〕 friend // …와 무간하게 지내다 be on an intimate footing with 《a person》 ; be thick with 《a person》 // 그들은 무간한 사이다 They are hand and glove with each other.

무간섭 無干涉 noninterference ; nonintervention
—주의 a policy〔principle〕 of noninterference ; a hands-off〔let-alone〕 policy ; a laissez-faire policy

*무감각 無感覺 [무지각] insensibility ; numbness ; [무관심] indifference ; callousness ; apathy —하다 (be) insensible ; senseless ; callous ; numb ; apathetic ; indifferent ¶ 수족이 무감각하다 My hands and feet are numb〔have no feeling〕. /My limbs are asleep. // 그는 체면 같은 것에 대해선 아예 무감각하다 He is lost to any sense of honor.
—증 『의학』 anesthesia

무감동 無感動 apathy ; indifference ; ataraxy ; ataraxia —하다 (be) apathetic ; indifferent ; stolid ; impassive ¶ 무감동하게 apathetically ; indifferently ; stolidly ; impassively

무감사 無鑑査 ¶ 무감사의 not submitted to the jury〔the selecting committee〕 // 무감사 입선 Not submitted to the jury. (게시)

무감찰 無鑑札 (being) unlicensed ; no license ; without (a) license

무강 無疆 eternity ; immortality ; everlastingness —하다 (be) endless ; everlasting ; eternal ; infinite ; immortal ¶ 만수무강하옵소서 May you live long !

무개 無蓋 ¶ 무개의 without a lid〔cover〕 ; unlidded ; uncovered ; open
— 자동차 an open car ; a breezer 《미·속》 — 화차 an open freight car ; an open goods waggon 《영》

무거리 coarse flour ; shorts of flour

무겁 the mound behind a target
— 활량 the archer in charge of the target mound

†무겁다 ① (be) heavy ; weighty ; burdensome ; ponderous ; massive

> 참고 **heavy** 비교적 무겁다는 뜻으로서 물질적 비유적 어느편의 의미에도 널리 쓰인다 **weighty** 비교해서가 아니라 절대적으로 무겁다는 뜻으로서 비유적 의미로 쓰인다 **burdensome** 무거움이 귀찮은 부담을 줌을 강조한다 **ponderous** 겹쳐서 무겁다는 뜻으로서 비유적으로 그런 느낌을 주는 경우에도 쓰인다

¶ 무거운 돌 a heavy stone // 무거운 짐 a heavy〔weighty〕 burden // 무거운 다리를 끌다 tread heavily ; walk with leaden feet ; drag oneself
② [신중] (be) grave ; serious ; quiet ¶ 사람이 무겁다 be grave and quiet // 입이 무겁다 be taciturn ; be a man of few words ; be slow of speech
③ [우울] (be, feel) heavy ; de pressed ; dull ¶ 머리가 무겁다 have a dull〔heavy〕 feeling in the head // 마음이 무겁다 have a heavy heart ; be depressed in spirits
④ [중하다] (be) serious ; critical ; severe ; grave ; grievous ¶ 무거운 벌 a severe〔heavy〕 punishment // 무거운 죄 a grievous offense ; a serious〔grievous〕 crime // 병이 무겁다 be seriously〔critically, gravely〕 ill
⑤ [중대] (be) important ; weighty ; momentous ; grave ¶ 무거운 책임 a heavy〔grave〕 responsibility // 무거운 사명 an important mission

†무게 ① [중량] weight ② [중요성·위엄] weight ; importance ; dignity ; authority ; prestige ¶ 무게를 달다 weigh 《a thing》 // 무게가 있다 be heavy〔weighty〕 ; be dignified // 무게가 3파운드 나가다 weigh three pounds ; have the weight of three pounds // 무게 있는 말 a remark carrying weight〔authority, conviction〕 // 무게 있는 사람 a dignified person ; a person of dignity // 무게가 없다 lack in dignity
— 중심 『물리』 the center of gravity ; the centroid

무결근 **無缺勤** ⇨ 무결석(無缺席)
무결석 **無缺席** regular attendance ; nonabsence ¶ 일년 내내 무결석이다 He has not missed a day through the year.
—자 a person who is regular in attendance ; a regular attendant
무경쟁 **無競爭** ¶ 무경쟁으로 without contest〔competition, a rival〕// 무경쟁 선거구 an unopposed constituency ; an uncontested division // 무경쟁으로 당선되다 be elected〔returned〕 unopposed
무경험 **無經驗** lack of experience ; inexperience ¶ 무경험의 inexperienced ; green ; untrained // 무경험의 교사 an inexperienced teacher
—자 an inexperienced person ; a green〔an untrained〕 hand ; a greenhorn 《구어》
무계출 **無屆出** ¶ 무계출의〔로〕 without notice // 무계출 결근 absence without notice〔leave〕 // 무계출로 결근하다 absent oneself 《from work》 without notice
무계획 **無計劃** **—하다** (be) planless ; unplanned ; haphazard ; reckless ¶ 무계획적인 지출 reckless expenditure // 무계획한 짓 a rash act
무고 **無故** ① [사유 없음] being without reason ¶ 무고하게 without reason
② [탈 없음] being without mishap ; freedom from trouble ; freedom from a disease〔an accident〕 **—하다** have no trouble ; (be) safe ; well ¶ 무고히 without trouble〔mishap〕 ; safely ; peacefully ; [병없이] well ; in good health ; safe and sound
무고 **無辜** innocence **—하다** (be) innocent ; guiltless ¶ 무고한 백성 innocent people
무고 **誣告** a false accusation〔charge〕 ; slander ; a libel (문서상) ; a calumny **—하다** slander ; calumniate ; make a fake〔false〕 accusation 《against》 ; accuse 《a person》 falsely
—자 a false accuser ; a calumniator **—죄** a calumny ; a false charge〔accusation〕
무곡 **舞曲** dancing and music ; a dance music (무용곡) ; a dance tune
원(圓)— a waltz
무골충 **無骨蟲** ① [벌레] boneless worms ② [사람] a spineless〔wishy-washy〕 person
무골충이 a decorative groove cut on the edge 《of a table〔pillar〕》
무골호인 **無骨好人** the meekest of men ; an excessively good-natured person ; a come-on 《미·속》
무공 **武功** military achievements〔merits, feats, exploits〕 ; distinguished military services ¶ 무공을 세우다 render distinguished military service // 무공을 세워 훈장을 받다 be awarded a medal for outstanding〔meritorious〕 military services
— 훈장 the Order of Military Merit ¶ 화랑〔태극〕 무공 훈장을 받다 be awarded the Order of Military Merit *Hwarang*〔*Taegŭk*〕
무과 **武科** the military service examination (for the royal army)
무과실 **無過失** ¶ 무과실 (손해) 배상 책임 no-fault liability for compensation // 무과실 책임 〖법〗 strict〔absolute, no-fault〕 liability ; liability without fault
무관 **武官** a military〔naval〕 officer ¶ 대사관부 무관 a military〔naval〕 attaché to an embassy
시종 — an aide-de-camp to His Majesty
무관 **無關** having no concern with ⇨ 무관계
무관 **無冠** ¶ 무관의 uncrowned // 무관의 제왕 an uncrowned king〔monarch〕 ; a king without a crown
*__무관계__ **無關係** no connection ; no relation〔concern〕 **—하다** have nothing to do with ; have no connection with ; be not related to ; (be) unrelated ; unconnected ; unconcerned 《in》 ¶ 나는 그것과 무관계하다 I have nothing to do with it. /I have neither part nor lot in the affair. /I am not involved in it〔the crime〕. /I am not implicated in it〔the scandal〕.
*__무관심__ **無關心** indifference ; unconcern ; apathy ; nonchalance

> 참고 **indifference** 어느 편이든 무방하다는 무관심 **unconcern** 걱정이나 주의의 필요성을 느끼지 않는 무관심 **apathy** 자기의 걱정 고통 이외의 모든 것에 대한 무관심

—하다 (be) indifferent 《to》 ; unconcerned 《with, at, about》 ; apathetic ; nonchalant ¶ 무관심한 체하다 pretend to be indifferent 《to》 ; assume the air of indifference // 그러한 일에는 무관심하다 He is indifferent to〔has no interest in〕 that sort of thing. // 그는 당신의 의견에는 무관심하다 He is unconcerned about your opinions. // 그는 골동품에는 아주 무관심하다 He has not the least 〔slightest〕 interest in curios.
무교육 **無敎育** ¶ 무교육의 uneducated ; uncultured ; untaught ; illiterate // 무교육한 사람 an uneducated person
무구 **武具** arms ; weapons of war ; an armor (갑옷)
무구 **無垢** purity ; innocence **—하다** (be) pure ; spotless ; innocent ; genuine ; naive ; simple ; immaculate ; unspoiled ; unpolluted ¶ 무구한 농민 an innocent farmer // 무구한 처녀 an innocent〔immaculate〕 virgin
무국적 **無國籍** loss of nationality ¶ 무국적자 a denationalized person ; a stateless person // 무국적 피난민 a stateless refugee // 무국적자가 되다 lose one's nationality〔citizenship〕 ; be denationalized

무궁 無窮 eternity ; infinitude ; immortality **—하다** (be) eternal ; infinite ; endless ; immortal ¶ 무궁히 eternally ; infinitely ; forever ; immortally
무궁무진 無窮無盡 —하다 (be) infinite ; endless ; boundless ; unlimited ; inexhaustible
무궁화 無窮花 〖식물〗 the rose of Sharon ; Hibiscus syriacus (학명) ; [국화] the national flower of Korea
— 대훈장 the Grand Order of *Mugunghwa* **— 동산〔삼천리〕** the beautiful land of Korea
무궤도 無軌道 ¶ 무궤도의 railless ; trackless ; [상궤를 벗어난] aberrant ; extravagant ; eccentric // 무궤도한 생활 a reckless〔loose, dissipated〕 life // 무궤도한 행동 eccentric act
— 전차 a trackless〔railless〕 tram 〔car〕 ; a trackless trolly car ; a trolley bus
무균 無菌 〖의학〗 asepsis ¶ 무균의 aseptic ; germfree ; without bacilli ; sterilized (살균한) // 무균의 수술 기구 aseptic surgical instrument // 무균의 우유 sterilized〔pasteurized〕 milk
— 배양 sterile culture **—법** 〖의학〗 an asepsis 《*pl.* -ses》 **— 상태** an aseptic 〔a germ-free〕 condition ; an asepsis 《*pl.* -ses》 **— 수술** aseptic surgery
무극 無極 ¶ 무극의 [무한] limitless ; boundless ; endless ; [무전극] without poles ; lacking poles ; nonpolar
— 결합 nonpolar union **— (성) 분자** a nonpolar molecule **— 접전** 〖전기〗 a neutral contact
무근 無根 ¶ 무근의 unfounded ; groundless ; baseless ; false // 그 보도는 사실 무근이다 The report is unfounded 〔a pure fabrication〕. /There is no foundation for the report.
무급 無給 ¶ 무급의 unpaid ; without pay 〔salary〕 ; gratuitous // 무급의 간사 an unpaid secretary // 무급으로 일하다 work without pay ; work for nothing
무기 武技 military arts ⇨ 무예
*̣**무기 武器** arms ; a weapon ; ordnance

> 참고 **arms** 총검 따위 전쟁용으로 만들어진 것을 말한다 낫 칼 따위는 arms가 아니고 **weapon**이라 할 수 있다

¶ 무기와 탄약 arms and ammunition // 무기를 들다 take up arms ; arm oneself // 무기를 버리다 give up one's arms // 무기를 빼앗다 disarm 《a person》 // 무기를 들고 일어서다 take up arms ; rise in arms // 최신식 무기를 갖추다 be armed with weapons of the latest model 〔newest type〕 // 무기라고는 권총밖에 없다 be armed with a revolver only // 눈물은 여자의 무기다 Tears are a woman's weapon. // 어학에 능통한 것이 그의 유일한 무기다 Language proficiency is his exclusive weapon.
—고 an armory ; ordnance stores ; an ordnance department 《미》 **— 원조** arms aid **— 제조** weaponry ; weaponeering **— 탄약** arms and ammunition **— 판매** arms sale ; sales of arms〔military equipment〕 **대항 —** a counterweapon
무기 無期 no (time) limit ¶ 무기의 indefinite ; for an indefinite period ; for life (징역) // 무기 연기되다 be indefinitely postponed ; be postponed sine die // 회의는 무기 연기되었다 The conference was adjourned sine die〔for an indefinite period〕
— 정간 suspension of publication for an indefinite period **—형** imprisonment for life
무기 無機 ¶ 무기의 inorganic
—계 the inorganic world **—물** an inorganic matter〔substance, body〕 **— 안료** a mineral pigment **—질 질소〔인산, 카리〕 비료** inorganic nitrogenous〔phosphoric, potassic〕 fertilizer **— 화학** inorganic chemistry ; abiochemistry **— 화합물** an inorganic compound
무기 舞妓 a dancing gril ; a dancer
무기교 無技巧 ¶ 무기교의 artless ; without art // 무기교의 기교 artless art
무기력 無氣力 enervation ; lethargy **—하다** (be) spiritless ; nerveless ; languid ; sluggish ; supine ; enervated ; emasculated
***무기명 無記名** ¶ 무기명의 unregistered ; uninscribed ; unsigned ; blank
— 공채(公債) a bearer bond **— 사채〔증권〕** an unregistered〔a bearer〕 debenture〔security〕 **—식 이서** (a) blank〔general〕 endorsement **— 어음** a blank bill **— 예금** an uninscribed deposit **— 주권** bearer〔uninscribed〕 stocks〔shares〕 ; a share certificate to bearer **— 투서** an unsigned suggestion ; an anonymous note〔notice〕 **— 투표** a secret ballot ; a secret vote ; secret voting ¶ 무기명 투표로 선출하다 elect by secret ballot
무기 연기 無期延期 (an) indefinite postponement ¶ 무기 연기가 되다 be postponed〔put off〕 indefinitely〔for an indefinite period〕
무기음 無氣音 〖언어〗 unaspirated sounds
무기 징역 無期懲役 life imprisonment ; a life term〔sentence〕 ¶ 무기 징역의 선고를 받다 be sentenced to penal servitude for life
—수 a lifer ; a life-timer
무기한 無期限 an indefinite period ; no time limit ¶ 무기한의 limitless ; indefinite ; without a time limit // 무기한 대부금 a dead loan // 무기한 파업 a strike for an indefinite period // 무기한 연기하다 be postponed indefinitely // 무기한 유효하다 be good at any time
무김치 pickled radish
무꾸리 a shaman's rites ; a kind of

shamanistic divination

무난 無難 ① [쉬움] being easy ; being without difficulty〔trouble〕 ② [안전] safety ; having no trouble ③ [난점이 없음] faultlessness ; passableness ; acceptability **—하다** (be) easy ; simple ; not difficult ; [안전] safe ; secure ; be free from danger ; have no trouble ; [난점이 없음] (be) passable ; acceptable ; fairly good ¶ 그가 5만원을 마련하기는 무난한 일이다 It is an easy thing for him to provide himself with 50,000 *won*. // 그는 무난히 그의 임무를 수행하였다 He performed his duty without difficulty. // 만일의 경우에 대비하는 것이 무난할 것이다 It will be safe for you to prepare for emergency. // 그만하면 그저 무난하다 This is tolerable〔passable〕. /This may pass. /This may be acceptable. // 그는 그 자리에 무난하다 He is faultless for the post.

무남독녀 無男獨女 an only daughter

무너뜨리다 pull down ; tear down ; break down ; destroy ; demolish ¶ 담을 무너뜨리다 pull down a wall // 집을 무너뜨리다 destroy〔tear down〕 a house // 낭떠러지를 무너뜨리고 길을 냈다 A road was cut through the cliff.

*__무너지다__ collapse ; crumble ; fall〔come〕 down ; break down ; give way ; fall〔drop, go〕 to pieces ; be destroyed ¶ 눈〔흙〕이 무너지다 the snow〔earth〕 breaks loose // 벽이 무너지기 시작했다 The wall has begun to crumble. // 둑이 언제 무너질지도 모른다 The embankment may go any moment. // 다리가 무너졌다 The bridge is out.

무녀 巫女 a (female) shaman ⇨ 무당

무녀리 ① [첫새끼] the first-born of a litter ② [사람] a simpleton ; a blockhead ; a dunce ¶ 맏이에 무녀리가 많다고 한다 The eldest son is proverbially a dunce.

무념 無念 freedom from distraction〔all thoughts〕 **—하다** be free from distraction

무념무상 無念無想 freedom from all ideas and thoughts **—하다** be in a frame of mind void of all ideas and thoughts

무느다 demolish ⇨ 무너뜨리다

*__무능 無能__ inability ; inefficiency ; incompetency ; lack of talent〔ability〕 **—하다** (be) incapable ; inefficient ; incompetent ¶ 당국의 무능함을 공격하다 attack the Government for its inefficiency // 무능해서 해고당하다 be dismissed for incompetency

— 교사〔공무원〕 an incompetent teacher〔official〕

무능력 無能力 lack of ability ; incompetence ; incapacity ; disability **—하다** (be) incompetent ; inefficient ; incapable ; lacking in ability

—자 an incompetent (person) ; a person without (legal) capacity ; an incapable (person)

†**무늬** a pattern ; a figure ; a design ¶ 무늬 있는 비단 figured〔patterned〕 silk ; silk with a 《flower》 design on it // 무늬 없는 천 plain〔unadorned, unfigured〕 cloth // 무늬를 넣어 짜다 weave in figures〔pattern〕

줄— a linear design

*__무단 無斷__ ¶ 무단히 [허가 없이] without permission ; without leave ; [예고 없이] without warning〔notice〕 // 그는 무단 도로 횡단으로 받은 교통 위반 딱지를 교통 경찰관 앞에서 찢어 버렸다 He tore up a traffic citation for jaywalking in front of a police officer who'd ticketed him.

— 거주자 a squatter **— 복사본〔해적판〕** a pirate edition **— 출입 금지** No trespassion. (게시)

무단 武斷 militarism ; enforcement (강행) ; high-handedness

—주의 militarism **—주의자** a militarist **—파** a militarist party〔faction〕

무단 결근〔결석〕 無斷缺勤〔缺席〕 absence without leave〔without (due) notice〕 **—하다** be absent without leave〔without (due) notice〕 ; stay from work without leave

무단 외출 無斷外出 [군인의] absence without leave **—하다** be absent without leave ; go AWOL 《미군·속》

—병 a soldier who is absent without leave ; an AWOL 《미군·속》 ; an awol private

무단 정치 武斷政治 military government〔rule〕 ; government by the bayonet ¶ 무단 정치를 하다 govern by the bayonet ; rule one's people with the rod of iron

무담보 無擔保 ¶ 무담보의 unsecured ; naked ; without collateral〔security〕 // 무담보 대부 an unsecured loan // 무담보로 돈을 꾸어주다 grant 《a person》 a loan without collateral

— 대부금 an unsecured loan **— 사채(社債)** an unsecured〔a naked 《영》〕 debenture **— 채권** 〖상업〗 a plain bond

무당 巫— a (female) shaman ; a sorceress ; a witch ; a necromancer ; a spirit medium

선무당이 사람 죽인다 속담 A little learning is a dangerous thing.

선무당이 장고 탓한다 속담 A bad workman always blames his tools.

무당 無糖 ⇨ 무가당

무당가뢰 〖곤충〗 a blister beetle ; a meloid ; a Spanish fly

무당개구리 〖동물〗 a kind of red-bellied frog

무당벌레 〖곤충〗 a ladybird ; a ladybug 《미》

무당새 〖새〗 a yellow bunting

무당 서방 巫堂書房 ① [무당의 남편] the husband of a sorceress ② [공것을 바라

는 사람] a man who likes to have things for nothing〔free of charge〕

무당선두리 〖곤충〗 a water spider

무대¹ a (water) current ; an ocean current

무대² [못난이] an ass ; a fool ; a goose ; a dolt ; a dimwit ; a birdbrain

†**무대 舞臺** [연극의] the stage ; the boards ; [활동의] a sphere〔field〕《of activity》; an arena ¶ 무대 공포증에 사로잡히다 suffer from stage fright // 무대를 떠나다 quit〔retire from〕 the stage // 무대를 장치하다 set the stage // 무대를 처음 밟다 make one's debut // 무대에 서다 appear on the stage ; [배우가 되다] go on the stage ; tread the boards 〔stage〕// 그는 세계를 무대로 활약하고 있다 The wide world is his stage. // 그의 활동 무대가 넓어졌다 He has a larger stage opened to him. // 무대면이 바뀐다 The scene changes〔shifts〕. // 이 소설은 서울을 무대로 하고 있다 The story is laid in *Seoul*.
— 경험 stage experience **— 기교** stagecraft **—극** a stage play 〔drama〕; the speaking stage **— 도구** (stage) setting ; scenery ; a set piece (낱개) ; property ; prop (소도구) **—면** a scene ; scenery **—명** a stage name **— 배우** a stage actor 〔player〕 **— 예술** theatrical art **— 조명** stage illumination ; stage lighting **— 중계** a stage relay ; a drama relayed from the stage **— 효과** stage effect ; scenic effects **— 휴게실** a greenroom **전쟁 —** the theater〔arena〕 of war **활동 —** one's sphere〔arena〕 of activity ; one's field of action ; the stage of one's operations **회전 —** a revolving〔rotative〕 stage

무대 감독 舞臺監督 [일] stage management ; [사람] a stage director〔manager〕 ¶ 무대 감독을 하다 stage-manage

무대 생활 舞臺生活 a stage〔theatrical〕 career ¶ 무대 생활에 들어가다 follow 〔enter upon〕 a stage career ; begin one's theatrical career

무대소 無大小 elastic substances〔fabrics〕; elastics ; an elastic ; the elastic

무대 얼굴〔화장〕 a made-up face ¶ 무대 얼굴〔화장〕이 좋다 look handsomer on the stage than off

무대 연습 舞臺演習 a dress rehearsal ¶ 본무대 연습 a full-dress rehearsal // 무대 연습을 하다 have a dress rehearsal

무대 의상 舞臺衣裳 stage costume ¶ 무대 의상을 입은 배우 an actor in costume

무대 장치 舞臺裝置 stage setting ; decor ; mise-en-scène 《프》 ¶ 무대 장치를 하다 set the stage
—가 a scenic〔stage, theater-set〕 designer

***무더기** a pile ; a heap ; a deposit ¶ 우편물의 무더기 a mountainous pile of mail // 무더기로 쌓이다 be piled〔heaped〕 up // 책상에 책을 무더기로 쌓다 pile a desk with books ; pile books mountain high on the desk // 무더기로 쌓아라 Heap〔Pile〕 up !
—돈 a pile of money ; a lump sum of money **— 해고** mass dismissal〔discharge〕 **돌—** a pile〔heap〕 of stones

무더기무더기 in piles ; in heaps ; heap by heap ¶ 돌이 무더기무더기 쌓이다 stones are deposited in heaps // 쓰레기를 무더기무더기 쌓아 놓다 pile up rubbish〔garbage, refuse〕

무더위 sultriness ; (high) humidity ; sultry 〔sweltering, humid〕 weather

무덕 無德 lack of virtue〔moral influence〕
—하다 be of no virtue ; lack virtue ; be lacking in virtue

무덕 武德 knightliness ; chivalry

무덕지다 (be) plentiful ⇨ 무드럭지다

무던하다 ① [너그럽다] (be) generous ; broad-minded ; liberal ; quite good 〔nice〕 ¶ 그는 사람이 무던하다 His personality is gentle and sincere. /He is good-natured. /He is quite a nice man. / He is broad-minded.
② [충분하다] (be) enough ; sufficient ; satisfactory ; quite good ¶ 그의 영어는 무던하다 His English is quite good. // 그에게는 그만하면 무던하다 I think that will be enough for him. /I am sure that will satisfy him.

무던히 ① [너그럽게] generously ; kindly ; nicely ; satisfactorily ; courteously ; warmly ¶ 그는 우리 애들에게 무던히 잘 해주었다 He was quite nice to our children. // 그 여자는 손님들을 무던히 접대했다 She received her visitors warmheartedly.
② [어지간히] quite ; pretty ; fairly ; considerably ; [매우·몹시] extremely ; exceedingly ¶ 무던히 애를 쓰다 make considerable efforts // 그 사람 키가 무던히도 크다 What a tall man he is ! // 무던히 춥다 It's quite cold.

†**무덤** a grave ; a tomb ; a resting place ; a sepulcher ¶ A씨의 무덤 [묘비명] "Sacred to the Memory of Mr. A" // 무덤에 묻다 entomb ; bury in a grave ; consign 《the body》 to the grave // 무덤을 파헤치다 dig open a grave // 스스로 무덤을 파다 dig one's own grave ; bring about one's own ruin

***무덥다** (be) sultry ; sweltering ; muggy ; close and hot ; hot and damp ¶ 무더운 날씨 sultry weather // 무더워 잠 못 자다 cannot sleep well on account of the oppressive heat // 방이 무덥다 The room is hot and damp〔stuffy〕. // 무더운 7·8월에는 섭씨 35도까지 기온이 올라 갑니다 The temperature climbs as high as 35 degrees Celsius during the sizzling months of July and August.

‡**무도 無道** wickedness ; evil ; atrocity ; inhumanity ; immorality ; brutality
—하다 (be) wicked ; evil ; atrocious ; inhuman ; immoral ; brutal ; cruel ; heartless

무도 武道 military〔martial〕 arts ; military science ; the spirit of chivalry ; knighthood

무도 舞蹈 dancing ; a dance ; a step ; hop (속) **—하다** dance ; shake a leg (속) ; hop (it) (미·속)

—광 the dance craze ; craze for dancing **—곡** a dance music **— 교사** a dancing master **—극** a dance drama **— 복장** a dancing dress **—실** a ballroom **— 연습** step〔dance〕 exercises **—장** a dance hall (미) ; a dancing hall **—화** dancing shoes ; pumps

무도병 舞蹈病 〖의학〗 St. Vitus's dance ; chorea ; the jumps

*__무도회 舞蹈會__ a ball ; a dancing party ; a dance ¶ 무도회용의 드레스 a balldress // 무도회를 열다 give a ball〔dance〕

가면〔가장〕 — a masked〔fancy dress〕 ball ; a masquerade

무독 無毒 ① being nonpoisonous〔nontoxic〕 ; innocuousness ; innoxiousness ; harmlessness ② [성질] gentleness ; mildness

무두장이 a tanner

*__무두질__ ① [모피의] tanning ; tawing ; dressing skin ② [고통] a grinding 〔pricking, gnawing, piercing, stabbing〕 pain **—하다** tan ; taw ; dress ; skin ; [고통이] grind ; gnaw ; prick ; pierce ; stab ¶ 가죽을 무두질하다 tan leather ; dress skin // 뱃속에서 무두질하다 have a gnawing pain in one's stomach

무드 a mood ; an atmosphere ¶ 무드가 있는 멜로디 a romantic and relaxing melody // 무드를 조성하다 create〔set〕 a mood〔an atmosphere〕

— 음악 mood(y) music

무드기 in a pile ; in a heap ; in piles 〔heaps〕

무드럭지다 (be) plentiful ; plenty ; abundant ; heaping

무득무실 無得無失 no gain no loss **—하다** be without gain or loss ; be neither advantageous nor disadvantageous

무득점 無得點 ¶ 무득점의 scoreless // 무득점으로 봉쇄하다 shut out〔whitewash〕 the opposite team (미·속) // 무안타 무득점 〖야구〗 no hit no run // 20회전에 계속 무득점이다 do not score a run in 20 consecutive innings // 무득점으로 끝나다 wind up 〔end〕 scoreless〔with no score〕

무등 無等 (being) peerless ; matchless ; supreme

— 호인(好人) a superb fellow ; a peerless good-natured man ; a very good 〔nice〕 fellow

*__무디다__ ① [칼날이] (be) blunt ; dull ¶ 무딘 면도날 a dull razor blade // 칼날이 무디다 The edge of the knife is blunt.

② [둔하다] (be) dull ; slow ; thickheaded ; slow-witted ¶ 무딘 사람 a dull 〔dense〕 person ; a dullard ; a dolt ; a slow-coach // 정신이 무디다 be dull 〔thickheaded, slow〕 // 경우에 무디다 be insensible to the rights and wrongs of things ; be thick-skinned

③ [말씨가] (be) blunt ; brusque ; curt ¶ 무딘 말 a brusque remark // 말을 무디게 하다 talk bluntly

무뚝뚝하다 (be) blunt ; brusque ; abrupt ; curt ¶ 무뚝뚝한 사람 a blunt 〔brusque〕 person // 무뚝뚝한 말씨 a brusque way of speaking // 무뚝뚝한 대답을 하다 give a curt reply ; reply in a monosyllable // 무뚝뚝하게 굴다 act brusquely // 무뚝뚝하게 거절하다 refuse bluntly ; give a flat refusal // 태도가 매우 무뚝뚝하다 He has a very abrupt manner. // 부장의 무뚝뚝한 성격에 견딜 수 없다 I cannot put up with the boss's gruff personality.

무람없다 (be) impolite ; discourteous ; rude ; impudent

무략 武略 strategy ; military tactics

무량 無量 immeasurability ; infinity ; infinite quantity **—하다** (be) infinite ; full ; immeasurable ; inestimable ; be beyond measure

— 대복 infinite bliss ; infinite〔immeasurable〕 happiness

무량수 無量壽 〖불교〗 immeasurable bliss

—경(經) the Book of Constant Life

무럭무럭 ① [성장] rapidly ; well ¶ 어린 애가 무럭무럭 자란다 The child is growing up rapidly. // 나무가 무럭무럭 자란다 The tree grows well.

② [냄새·연기가] thickly ; densely ; heavily ; in thick clouds ¶ 향수 내가 무럭무럭 나다 be heavily perfumed ; reek of perfume // 연기가 무럭무럭 난다 Smoke rises up in thick clouds.

무럼생선 —生鮮 a jellyfish ⇨ 해파리

무렵다 (be) itchy (from bites) ; itching

무려 無慮 to the prodigious〔vast〕 number of ; as many as ; no less than ¶ 무려 10만명 as many as one hundred thousand people // 무려 1,000명이 회합에 참석했다 No less than 1,000 people were present at the meeting.

*__무력 無力__ [기력이 없음] powerlessness ; impotence ; [능력이 없음] incapacity ; incompetence ; [재력이 없음] lack of funds **—하다** (be) powerless ; impotent ; incapable ; helpless ; incompetent ¶ 공격에 대하여 무력하다 be helpless 〔powerless〕 against an attack

—감 a feeling of helplessness〔ineffectualness〕

†**무력 武力** military power ; force (of arms) ; the sword〔saber〕 ; the mailed fist ¶ 무력에 호소하다 appeal〔resort〕 to arms ; use force // 무력으로 이기다 win by force of arms // 무력으로 해결하다 settle (an affair) by force

— 간섭 armed intervention〔interference〕

— 공격 an armed attack — 외교 power diplomacy ; diplomacy backed by force — 저항 armed opposition〔resistance〕 — 전 armed hostility — 정치 power politics ; militant government ; government by the sword ; rule of force — 행사 the use of armed force — 혁명 an armed revolution

*무렵 the time《when》 ¶ 복숭아꽃 필 무렵 peach-blossom time // 여행이 끝날 무렵 toward the end of one's journey // 무렵에 at〔about〕 the time ; the time《when》; when ; as // 그 무렵에 in those days ; then // 집에 도착할 무렵에는 by the time you get home // 해질 무렵에 도착하다 arrive toward evening // 한창 자랄 무렵이라 많이 먹는다 As he is in that fast-growing stage, he eats a lot. // 매년 이 무렵에는 홍수가 난다 We suffer from a flood at this time〔in this season〕 of the year. // 그 무렵 한국은 비참한 상태에 있었다 Korea was in miserable situation in those days.

⁑무례 無禮 [실례] impoliteness ; rudeness ; discourtesy ; disrespect ; [불손] insolence ; [모욕] insult —하다 (be) impolite ; rude ; discourteous ; disrespectful ; indecent ; uncivil ; insolent ¶ 무례한 놈 a rude fellow // 무례한 짓 (a) breach of etiquette // 무례한 짓을 하다 be rude to《a person》; behave disrespectfully to《a person》// 무례하게도 …하다 have the impertinence to《do》; be rude enough to《do》// 무례한 말을 하다 make an insulting remark ; say a rude thing // 이 무례한 놈아 You insolent fellow ! // 그 놈이 무례하게도 이 따위 편지를 보내 왔다 He had the impertinence to write me such a letter as this. // 매우 무례한 부탁인 줄은 압니다만 저의 취업 추천서를 써 주실 수 있겠습니까 I know it's very forward of me to ask you, but do you think you could write a job recommendation on my behalf ?

무론 無論 naturally ⇨ 물론

무뢰배 無賴輩 sons〔men〕 of Belial

무뢰한 無賴漢 a rogue ; a ruffian ; a bum ; a hooligan ; a villain ; a scoundrel ; a rowdy ; a vagrant ; a hoodlum ; a roughneck ; a desperado

†무료 無聊 tedium ; wearisomeness ; ennui 《프》; dullness —하다 (be) bored ; tedious ; dull ; wearisome ; suffer from ennui ; find time hanging heavily〔heavy〕 on one's hands ; be busy with having nothing to do ¶ 무료함을 달래다 beguile the tedium〔one's time〕

*무료 無料 no〔free of〕 charge ¶ 무료의 free (of charge) ; gratuitous // 무료로 free ; free of charge ; gratis ; for nothing ; without pay〔fee〕 // 무료로 배달하다 deliver《things》 free of charge // 카탈로그를 무료 진정함 Catalogues are sent free. — 관람권 a complimentary〔free〕 ticket — 배달 free delivery《FD》 — 봉사 free〔gratuitous〕 service — 숙박소 a free lodging house — 승차권 a (free) pass — 입장〔관람〕자 a free visitor ; a deadhead《미·구》; paper (집합적) — 진료소 a free clinic ; a dispensary (시료원) 상품 포장(商品包裝) — [게시] Case〔Packaging〕 free. /No charge for case. 운임 — [게시] Freight free. 입장 — [게시] Admission (is) free. /No charge for admission.

무릉태 a soft-headed person

무루 無漏 without exception ; with no omission ; one and all ; for〔to〕 everybody ; in full ; exhaustively ¶ 무루 조사하다 make a thorough〔an exhaustive〕 investigation // 회원에게 무루 통지하였다 We notified every member of the meeting.

무르녹다 ① [무르익다] ripen ; get fully ripe ; mature ; mellow ; be at its best (꽃 따위가) ¶ 복숭아가 무르녹다 The peach is ripe. // 진달래꽃이 무르녹다 Azaleas are in full bloom〔at their best〕.
② [그늘이] be deep ¶ 숲 그늘이 무르녹다 The shade in the grove is thick. // 신록이 무르녹다 The fresh green (of spring) is at its best. /Spring is at its greenest. /The woods are bright〔glistening〕 with fresh verdure.
③ [시기가] be ripe《for》; mature ¶ 기운이 무르녹기를 기다리다 wait for a ripe opportunity // 때가 무르녹았다 The time is ripe for it. /The opportunity has matured. /It is high time (now).

⁑무르다¹ ① [연하다] (be) soft ; tender ; flabby ; flaccid ; limp ¶ 무른 감 a soft persimmon // 무른 고기 tender meat // 무른 살 flabby〔flaccid〕 flesh
② [마음·힘이] (be) weak ; infirm ; pliant ; yielding ; submissive ¶ 무른 성질 yielding disposition〔temper〕 // 무른 체질 an infirm constitution // 그는 사람이 무르다 He has a soft head. // 사람이 물러 좀체로 아니란 말을 못한다 He is a weak sort of person unable to say 'no' on most occasions. // 우리 과장은 정말 여자에게 무르다 Our section chief's really got a soft spot for women.

무르다² ① [익어서] get soft ; become tender ¶ 복숭아가 무르다 the peach has got soft.
② [요리되어] get soft ; become tender ; be well cooked〔done〕; be boiled quite soft ; become stewed ¶ 무른 감자 a well-cooked potato // 고기가 잘 물렀다 The meat has become tender enough.

무르다³ ① [물러 받다] get〔obtain〕 a refund ; [물러주다] give a refund ; make repayment《to》; pay back ; repay ; refund ; reimburse ¶ 대금을 무르다 refund the price paid // 샀던 시계를 무르다 return a watch (and get one's money

back) // 팔았던 시계를 물러주다 accept the return of a watch (and refund the sale price) // 마음에 들지 않거든 언제든지 물러드리겠습니다 We will refund your money at anytime should you find it unsatisfactory.
② [상쇄] cancel each other's accounts ; counterbalance ¶ 주고 받은 것을 무르다 cancel the debts each owes the other
③ [장기·바둑에서] turn around ; retreat ; go back ; withdraw

무르익다 ① [과실 따위가] get ripe ; be fully ripened ; (be) mellow ¶ 무르익은 감 a fully ripened persimmon // 무르익은 술 mellow wine
② [시기가] become ripe for ; (be) ripe 〔matured〕 ¶ 기회가 무르익다 the opportunity is ripe 《for》; it is high time 《for》 // 기회가 무르익기를 기다리다 wait for a ripe opportunity

무르춤하다 halt ; stop short ⇨ 무춤하다

무르팍 a knee ⇨ 무릎

무름하다 (be) rather soft〔tender〕; quite weak〔infirm〕

†**무릅쓰다** risk ; face ; brave ; dare ; defy ; run 《a risk, hazard》; venture ¶ 생명의 위험을 무릅쓰고 at the risk of one's life // 위험을 무릅쓰다 run a risk 《of》; brave〔dare, defy〕 a danger 《of》 // 풍우를 무릅쓰다 brave〔dare, defy〕 the wind and rain ; weather a storm // 폭풍우를 무릅쓰고 나가다 go out in the teeth〔face〕 of a storm // 비를 무릅쓰고 학교에 가다 go to school in spite of the rain // 죽음을 무릅쓰고 저항하다 face death to resist // 일제의 강압을 무릅쓰고 독립 운동을 하다 carry on an independence movement in defiance of Japanese coercion // 다소의 위험을 무릅써야 한다 Some risk must be run. // 자네가 나를 실망시키지 않을 줄 알기 때문에 위험을 무릅쓰고 결심한 거야 I decided to risk my neck because I know you will not let me down.

무릇[1] 〖식물〗 a squill ; a scilla ; Scilla sinensis (학명)

무릇[2] generally speaking ; as a general rule ; in general ; on the whole ¶ 무릇 사람은 자기 본분을 지켜야 한다 All men should be faithful to their duties.

무릇하다 (be) rather soft〔tender〕

무릉도원 武陵桃源 an Arcadia ; a Utopia ; the Happy Valley ¶ 무릉도원의 꿈 a Utopian dream

†**무릎** a knee ; a lap (여자의) ; a genu 《*pl.* -nua》 ¶ 무릎을 꿇다 go down〔fall〕 one's knees ; kneel down ; drop the knee ; bend one's knees 《to》; [굴복하다] yield 《to》; surrender ; be brought to one's knees // 무릎을 꿇리다 make 《a person》 kneel down ; make 《a person》 bend his knees ; bring 《a person》 to his knees // 무릎을 치다 slap one's lap ; hit〔pat〕 one's knee // 무릎 위에 앉다 sit on 《a person's》 lap // 무릎 위에 앉히다 hold 《a child》 in〔on〕 one's lap // 무릎을 베다 pillow〔lay〕 one's head on 《a person's》 lap // 무릎을 치며 감탄하다 express one's deep admiration // 무릎을 맞대고 이야기하다 have a heart-to-heart talk ; get knee to knee with 《a person》 // 눈이 무릎까지 찼다 The snow lay〔is more than〕 knee-deep. // 바지의 무릎이 다 닳았구나 Your trousers are worn out at the knees.
— 마디〔관절〕 the knee-joint **—뼈** the kneecap ; the kneepan

무릎맞춤 a confrontation **—하다** have a confrontation ; be confronted ¶ 두 사람을 무릎맞춤시키다 confront two parties with each other ; bring two parties to a confrontation

무릎베개 —하다 pillow one's head on 〔in〕 《a person's》 lap

무릎치기 ① [바지] shorts ; knickers ; knee breeches ② [씨름] a knee-whack

*__무리__[1] ① [한패] a company ; a band ; a party ; a set ; a lot ; a gang ; a group ; crowd ¶ 무리를 짓다 group ; band together ; form a clique ; conspire (together) ; be banded in party ; gang up
② [떼] a group ; crowd ; throng
③ [철] the season ¶ 청어 무리 the herring season

무리[2] [앙금] ground-up water-soaked rice (which is to be steamed into rice cakes) **—떡** steamed rice cakes made of sedimentary rice **무릿가루** flour of dried settlings of rice

무리[3] [해·달의] a halo 《around the sun》; ring ; corona ¶ 달무리하다 The moon has a ring around it.
달〔햇〕— the halo of the moon〔sun〕

무리 無理 ① unreasonable(ness) ; irrationality **—하다** (be) unreasonable ; unfair ; unnatural ¶ 무리가 아닌 reasonable ; fair ; natural // 무리한 요구 an unreasonable〔unfair〕 demand // 무리가 없는 자세 a natural posture // 무리가 없도록 not to go too far ; not to be too extreme // 그에게 그것을 시키는 것은 무리다 It is not in reason to ask him to do that. // 이 일에 무리가 있다 There is going against nature in this work. / This work is not rationally done. // 자네가 그러는 것도 무리가 아니다 You may well say so. /It is natural for you to say so. // 그가 화를 내는 것도 무리가 아니다 He has good reason to be angry.
② [강제] compulsion ¶ 무리하게 by force ; against 《a person's》 will // 무리하게 결혼시키다 make 《a person》 marry against his〔her〕 will ; force 《a person》 into marriage // 무리하게 앉히다 make 《a person》 sit down by force // 무리하게 잡아당기다 pull by force // 싫다는데도 무리하게 술을 먹였다 He made me drink against my will.

③ [불가능] impossibility —하다 (be) impossible ; be beyond one's power ¶ 무리한 일을 하려고 하다 attempt the impossible ; try to do the impossible 〔something beyond one's power〕 // 이런 일을 자네에게 부탁하는 것은 무리일는지 모르겠다 It will be almost impossible for you to grant my request.
④ [과도·과로] excess ; immoderation —하다 (be) excessive ; immoderate ¶ 무리한 운동 immoderate exercise // 무리하게 공부하다 work too hard〔to excess〕// 무리하게 일을 시키다 overtax 〔overwork〕 《a person》 // 너무 무리를 하다 overstrain 〔overwork, force, overexert〕 oneself // 무리를 했더니 몸에 해로웠다 The over-strain affected my health. // 이 독본은 2학년 학생에게는 무리다 This reader is too difficult for second-year grade pupils. // 그 일은 나에게는 무리다 I am not equal to the task.
— 방정식 an irrational equation —수 an irrational number ; a surd (number) —식 an irrational expression
무리고치 an unclean silk cocoon
무릿매 stone-slinging ¶ 무릿매질하다 sling stones ; throw stones with a sling
무릿풀 rice starch〔paste〕
무마 撫摩 ① [손으로] stroking ; patting ② [달램] soothing ; pacification —하다 [손으로] stroke ; pat ; [달래다] soothe ; coax ; pacify ; appease ; quiet ; placate 《an offended colleague》 ¶ 무마하기 어려운 inappeasable ; implacable // 성낸 사람을 무마하다 calm〔soothe〕 down an angry person
무망중 無妄中 unexpectedly
무면허 無免許 ¶ 무면허의 unlicensed // 무면허 의사 an unlicensed physician // 무면허로 운전하다 drive 《a car》 without a license
무명 cotton (cloth)
—베 cotton cloth ; muslin —실 cotton thread ; cotton yarn (방직용) —옷 cotton clothes ¶ 무명옷을 입고 있다 wear cotton clothes ; be clothed in cotton —활 a bow used in cotton willowing
무명 武名 military fame〔distinction〕 ¶ 무명을 떨치다 obtain military distinction ; win one's spurs
†**무명 無名** [이름이 없음] being nameless ; [익명] anonymity ; [알려지지 않음] obscurity ¶ 무명의 [이름이 없는] nameless ; [알려지지 않은] nameless ; unknown ; obscure ; [익명의] anonymous // 무명의 작품 an anonymous work ; a book by an anonymous author // 무명의 섬 a nameless island // 무명의 편지 an anonymous〔a nameless〕 letter // 무명으로 출판하다 publish anonymously // 이 영역은 무명씨의 손으로 된 것이다 This English version was made by an unknown hand.
—수 〖수학〗 an absolute number —씨 an anonymous person — 인사 an obscure individual ; a person of no distinction 〔reputation, name〕 — 작가 an obscure〔a nameless〕 writer ; a writer unknown to fame
무명 無明 〖불교〗 ignorance ; illusion ; lack of enlightenment
무명 無銘 ¶ 무명의 unsigned ; nameless ; bearing no signature〔inscriptions〕
무명골 無名骨 〖해부〗 a hipbone ; an innominate bone
무명 전사 無名戰士 an unknown soldier ¶ 무명 전사의 묘 [미국 워싱턴의] the Tomb of the Unknown Soldiers
무명조개 a kind of clam ; Cytherea meretrix (학명)
무명지 無名指 the ring finger ; the third finger (thumb을 제외한 셋째 손가락)
⁑**무모 無謀** rashness ; recklessness ; imprudence —하다 (be) rash ; reckless ; imprudent ; thoughtless ¶ 무모하게 recklessly ; rashly ; thoughtlessly // 무모한 계획 an ill-advised〔reckless〕 attempt // 무모한 짓 하지 마라 Don't do anything rash. / Don't take a leap in the dark.
무모 無毛 ¶ 무모의 hairless ; 〖생물〗 glabrous
—증 〖의학〗 atrichia ; atrichosis 《*pl.* -choses》 ; alopecia
무문근 無紋筋 〖해부〗 a smooth muscle ; an unstriated muscle
무미 無味 —하다 ① [맛없음·몰취미] (be) tasteless ; flavorless ; insipid ; flat ; prosaic ; vapid ¶ 무미 건조한 사람 a prosaic person // 무미 건조한 강연 a dry-as-dust lecture // 무미 건조하다 be dry ; be cut and dried ; be dry as dust ; be uninteresting〔vapid, prosaic〕
② [무의미] (be) meaningless ; senseless
무미 건조 無味乾燥 ⇨ 무미(無味)
무미류 無尾類 〖동물〗 an anuran ; Salientia (학명)
무반 武班 the military nobility
무반동총 無反動銃 〖군사〗 a recoilless rifle
무반주 無伴奏 〖음악〗 ¶ 무반주의 unaccompanied 《cello sonata》
*****무방 無妨** no harm ; no hindrance —하다 do no harm ; be no hindrance ; it does not matter〔make a difference〕 ; it is all right ¶ 무방하다면 if you don't mind ; if you have no objection ; if it suits your convenience // 없어도 무방하다 We can do without it. // 창을 열어도 무방한가 Will it bother anyone if I open the window? // 산보는 좀 해도 무방하다 A little walk will do you no harm. // 담배는 피워도 무방하다 Smoking will do you no harm.
무방비 無防備 ¶ 무방비의 defenseless ; unfortified ; open // 무방비 도시 an open city // 무방비 상태 《leave a town in》 a defenseless state
무배당 無配當 ¶ 무배당이다 No dividend is paid 《on the stocks》.

무벌점 無罰點 〖레슬링〗 ¶ 무벌점이다 be clean of penalty marks

무법 無法 [불법] injustice ; unlawfulness ; wrong ; unreasonableness (이치에 어긋남) ; outrageousness (난폭) ; lawlessness **—하다** (be) lawless ; unjust ; unreasonable ; outrageous ¶ 무법한 조치 an unlawful measure // 무법한 요구 an unreasonable〔unlawful〕 demand // 무법 상태에 있다 be in a lawless state〔condition〕 ; be in disorder
—자 an outrageous fellow ; a desperado ; an outlaw **— 천지** a lawless world ; an anarchy

무변 武弁 a military man ; a warrior ; a soldier

무변 無邊 ① [끝없음] infinity ; infinitude **—하다** (be) boundless ; limitless ; infinite ¶ 광대 무변한 vast and boundless ② [변리 없음] (being) free of interest ; bearing no interest
— 대해 the boundless ocean **—전** money free of interest ; a loan without interest

무변화 無變化 changelessness ; [단조] monotony ¶ 무변화의 unchanging ; unchanged ; monotonous

무병 無病 freedom from ailment〔illness〕 ; good health **—하다** be free from diseases ; be healthy and sound

무보수 無報酬 nonpayment ; no compensation ; no pay ¶ 무보수의 free ; unsalaried // 무보수로 without pay 〔salary, recompense, remuneration〕 ; for nothing ; free of charge ; [변호사·의사 따위가] without a fee ; 《teach》 free ; as a labor of love // 무보수로 일하다 work without pay〔recompense〕 ; give one's service free

무복 巫卜 shamans and fortunetellers ; sorceresses and soothsayers

무복친 無服親 distant relatives (for whom one wears no mourning)

무부 武夫 [용맹스런 사내] man of courage ; a brave man ; [무사] a warrior ; a soldier

⁑**무분별 無分別** indiscretion ; imprudence ; recklessness ; thoughtlessness ; rashness **—하다** (be) indiscreet ; injudicious ; reckless ; imprudent ; thoughtless ¶ 무분별하게 thoughtlessly ; indiscreetly ; imprudently // 무분별한 짓을 하다 do a rash thing ; do something rash // 그런 짓을 하다니 무분별하다 It is ill-advised of you to do such a thing.

무불간섭 無不干涉 indiscreet meddling in everything ; indiscreet interference **—하다** poke one's nose into everything ; meddle constantly in all matters ; interfere in everything

무불통지 無不通知 being well informed ; broad and extensive knowledge **—하다** (be) well-informed ; erudite ¶ 무불통지한 사람 a walking dictionary ; a dictionary on legs ; a well-informed person

무비 武備 armaments ; military preparations

무비 無比 incomparableness ; peerlessness **—하다** (be) matchless ; unique ; unparalleled ; unequaled ; peerless ; incomparable ; unrivaled ; unsurpassed ; unchallenged ¶ 세계 무비이다 be unique 〔unparalleled〕 in the world ; have no equal in the world

무비판 無批判 ¶ 무비판적(으로) uncritical(ly) ; [무차별] indiscriminate(ly)

무빙 無氷 non-freezing **—하다** be ice-free ; get unfrozen

무빙 霧氷 frost flowers

무사 武士 a warrior ; a soldier ; a knight
—도 chivalry ; knighthood ; the way of the warrior

*__무사 無事__ [안전] safety ; security ; [평온] peace ; quietness ; tranquility ; [건강] being well **—하다** [안전] (be) safe ; secure ; [평온] peaceful ; quiet ; [건강] (quite) well ; be doing well ¶ 무사히 [안전] safely ; safe ; in safety ; without accident ; all right ; without a hitch 〔trouble〕 ; [평온] peacefully ; in peace ; uneventfully ; amicably ; [건강] well ; all right // 무사 태평한 세상 a peaceful time ; a reign of peace and happiness // 무사히 임무를 수행하다 perform one's duty without any hitch ; acquit oneself of a duty // 무사히 지내다 live in peace (평화) ; get along well ; be〔doing〕 well (건강) // (물건이) 무사히 도착하다 arrive in good order〔condition〕 // (식 따위) 무사히 끝나다 be carried out all right // 전쟁에서 무사히 돌아오다 come back safe from the war // 무사히 해결이 나다 come to a satisfactory conclusion // 나는 무사하다 Nothing is wrong with me. /I am all right. // 무사히 돌아오니 반갑다 I am glad to see you safe home again. // 그 밤도 무사히 지났다 The night passed uneventfully./ Things were quiet that night.
—주의 a peace-at-any-price principle ; prudentialism

무사 無私 impartiality **—하다** (be) impartial ; unselfish ; disinterested ; self-less ¶ 공평 무사한 fair and impartial ; just and fair

무사 無嗣 having no posterity

무사 無死 ¶ 무사 만루이다 〖야구〗 The bases are full〔loaded〕 with no outs.

무사고 無事故 ¶ 무사고로 without a trouble〔an accident〕 // 나는 10년 간의 무사고 운전 기록을 가지고 있다 I have a perfect driving record for ten years.

무사고 비행 無事故飛行 accident-free flying ; flying without an accident

무사마귀 a wart ¶ 무사마귀가 생기다 have a wart ; a wart forms〔grows〕

무사 분주 無事奔走 **—하다** be very busy about nothing

무사 불참 無事不參 poking one's nose into everything ; meddling in everything —하다 meddle in everything ; poke one's nose into everything

무사 안일 無事安逸 ¶ 무사 안일주의 a peace-at-any-price principle ; the principle of "safety first" ; prudentialism

무사 태평 無事泰平 [태평] (perfect) peace ; tranquility ; [낙천적임] easiness ; optimism —하다 (be) peaceful ; tranquil ; easy ; easygoing ; happy-go-lucky

*무산 無産 ¶ 무산의 propertyless ; without property ; proletarian
— 계급 the proletarian classes ; the proletariat ¶ 무산 계급의 독재 the dictatorship of the proletariat —당 a proletarian party —자 a person without property ; a proletarian ; have-nots 《구》

무산 霧散 dissipating〔vanishing〕 like the mists —하다 dissipate ; vanish ; be dispelled ; disperse

무산증 無酸症 〚의학〛 achlorhydria ; anacidity

무삶이 〚농업〛 ① [고르기] softening a rice field with water ② [갈기] plowing 〔ploughing 《영》〕 a rice field wet

무상 無上 ¶ 무상의 (the) supreme ; the greatest ; the highest ; the best ; superative // 무상의 영광 the highest 〔supreme〕 honor // 무상의 행복 consummate happiness
—권 supremacy — 명령 〚윤리〛 the categorical imperative

무상 無常 uncertainty ; transiency ; mutability —하다 (be) uncertain ; transient ; evanescent ¶ 인생의 무상을 느끼다 realize the uncertainty〔vanity〕 of life // 인생이란 무상한 것이다 Man's life is transitory. / Nothing is certain in this world.

무상 無償 no compensation ¶ 무상의〔으로〕 without compensation ; gratis ; free of charge ; [무보수로] gratuitous(ly) ; for nothing
— 계약 a gratuitous contract ; a nude pact〔contract〕 — 교부 〚주식〛 delivery without compensation — 대부 a free loan — 배급 a free distribution — 양도 a gratuitous conveyance — 양도 양수인 〚법〛 a volunteer ; a voluntary grantee — 원조 a grant ; a grant-type aid —주 a stock dividend — 행위 a gratuitous act

무상 無狀 [무례] impoliteness ; rudeness ; discourtesy ; [무형] invisibility —하다 (be) impolite ; uncivil ; rude ; discourteous ; shapeless ; formless

무상 출입 無常出入 —하다 go in and out constantly ; frequent ; have free access to ; visit freely

무색 —色 dyed color
—옷 a dyed dress

*무색 無色 ① [빛깔] lack of color ; colorlessness —하다 (be) colorless ; achromatic ¶ 무색 투명의 액체 a colorless and transparent liquid
② [부끄럼] shame ; disgrace —하다 be ashamed 《of》 ; feel shame ¶ 무색한 얼굴 an ashamed look // 무색해서 머리를 숙이다 hang one's head for shame // 무색하게 하다 put 《a person》 to shame ; make 《a person》 blush with shame ; [빛을 잃게 하다] outshine ; excel // 그녀의 아름다운 용모는 좌중의 여인들을 무색하게 했다 Her graceful appearance threw〔cast〕 all the other girls present into the shade.

무생물 無生物 an inanimate object 〔thing〕 ; a lifeless thing
—계(界) inanimate〔inorganic〕 nature —시대 〚지질〛 the azoic age〔era〕 —학 abiology

무서리 the first frost ; the early frost ¶ 무서리가 내렸다 We have had the first frost of the year.

†무서움 fear ; dread ; horror ; fright ; terror ¶ 무서움을 타다 be easily frightened // 무서움이 없다 have〔know〕 no fear ; be fearless ; fear nothing

*무서워하다 be afraid 《of》 ; fear ; dread ; be frightened〔scared, terrified〕 《at》 ; be fearful 《of》 ; be timid〔in fear〕 《of》 ¶ 지진을 무서워하다 be afraid 〔timid〕 of earthquakes ; dread earthquakes // 무서워서 그 개를 가까이 할 수가 없었다 He was afraid to come near the dog. / Fear kept him from the dog. // 무서워하지 마시오 Don't be afraid. // 무서워할 것 없다 You have nothing to fear〔to be afraid of〕. / You need fear nothing. // 무엇을 그렇게 무서워하니 What are you so scared about?

무석인 武石人 a stone statue〔image〕 of a warrior standing in front of a royal tomb

무선 舞扇 a dancing fan ; a dancer's fan

⁑무선 無線 radio ; wireless
— 검파기(檢波器) a radiodetector ; a detector — 공학 radio engineering —국(局) a radio〔wireless〕 station — 기술자〔기사〕 a radio operator ; a radioman — 등대 a radio beacon — 방송 radio broadcasting ; radiocasting 《미》 — 사진 전송 radio photography — 송신 wireless transmission — 주파수 a radio frequency — 중계 radio relay — 중계국 a radio relay station — 통신 wireless〔radio〕 communications — 항행(航行) radio navigation — 호출기 a beeper ¶ 급하시면 무선 호출기로 불러보시지요 If it's urgent, you may wish to call him through his beeper.

무선 전신 無線電信 wireless (telegraphy) ; radio ¶ 한미 간의 무선 전신 a wireless service between Korea and America // 무선 전신으로 by wireless ; by radio // 무선 전신을 치다 telegraph by wireless ; wireless ; radio // 무선 전신을 갖추고 있다 carry wireless // 무선 전신 통신권 내에 있다 be within a wireless communication ; be within a wireless radius —국 a wireless〔radio〕 station —기 a wireless〔radio〕 apparatus — 기사 a radio 〔wireless〕 operator ; a radio telegraphist ; a radioman ; a sparks (배의) 《구》 —법 the Wireless Law —실 a wireless cabin 〔room〕 (선박의) ; a radioroom —탑 a wireless tower 유선식 — wired wireless telegraphy

†**무선 전화 無線電話** [기계] a wireless 〔radio〕 telephone ; [기술] wireless〔radio〕 telephony ; [통신] a wireless telephone message ¶ 무선 전화 수화기 a wireless 〔radio〕 receiving set // 무선 전화로 말하다 talk over the radiophone // 무선 전화를 걸다 telephone by wireless // A B 간에 무선 전화가 통하고 있다 A radiophone service is opened to public between A and B.
—국 a radio station —실 a radioroom —용 마이크로폰 a radio microphone 유선식 — wired wireless telephony 다통로 —기 a multichannel radiophone 휴대용 —기(機) a walkie-talkie

무선 조종 無線操縱 wireless〔radio〕 control ¶ 무선 조종의 radio-controlled 《plane》
—법 telemechanics — 비행기〔선〕 a radio-controlled airplane〔vessel〕 ; a drone

무선철 無線綴 〖제본〗 unsewn binding

무섬타다 be easily frightened ; scare easily

†**무섭다** ① [겁나다] (be) fearful ; dreadful ; terrible ; frightful ; [사납다] fierce ; ferocious ; [두려워하다] fear ; dread ; be afraid of〔that〕 ; be apprehensiv 《lest》 ; [놀라다] scared ; frightened ¶ 무서운 꿈 a terrible dream // 무서운 광경 a horrible〔frightening〕 sight // 무서운 짐승 a fierce animal // 무서운 무기 a formidable weapon // 무서운 적 a dreadful enemy // 벌이 무서워서 from fear of punishment // 무서운 얼굴을 하다
look fierce ; look〔appear〕 terrible〔horrible〕 // 개가 무섭다 I am afraid of dogs. // 지진이 무섭다 I dread earthquakes. // 감기들까 무섭다 I am afraid of catching a cold. // 지붕이 무너질까 무섭다 I fear the roof may fall in. // 죽음은 무섭지 않다 I am not afraid to die〔of death〕. // 무서워서 죽을 뻔했다 I was scared to death. // 아무것도 무서울 것 없다 There is nothing to fear〔to be afraid of〕.
② [모질다] (be) awful ; terrible ; frightful ; wonderful ¶ 무섭게 awfully ; terribly ; horribly ; frightfully ; wonderfully // 무서운 깍쟁이 an awful miser // 무서운 정력 terrible〔terrific〕 energy // 무서운 기세로 in stupendous force // 무섭게 춥다 be awfully cold // 무섭게 서둘다 be in an awful rush // 일념(一念)이 얼마나 무서운 것인지 알 수 있다 It goes to show what a formidable thing determined mind can be.

무성 無性 ¶ 무성의 sexless ; 〖생물〗 asexual ; 〖문법〗 neuter
— 상태 asexuality — 세대 a sexless generation — 식물 a neuter (plant) —체 〖동물〗 a gemmule ; a gemmula 《*pl.* -lae》 —화(化) desexualization —화(花) 〖식물〗 a neuter〔an asexual〕 flower

*****무성 茂盛** —하다 (be) thick ; exuberant ; luxuriant ; close-grown ; grow in abundance ¶ 잎이 무성한 나무들 trees thick with leaves // 나무가 무성한 산 a thickly-wooded hill // 풀이 무성하다 The grass grows thick. /It is overgrown with grass.

무성 無聲 ¶ 무성의 silent ; voiceless
— 방전 silent discharge — 전광 heat lightning —총 a noiseless firearm〔rifle〕

무성 생식 無性生殖 〖생물〗 asexual reproduction ; monogony ; monogeny ; agamogenesis ; agamogony ; agamy ; 〖식물〗 blastogenesis ; blastogeny ¶ 무성 생식을 하다 be nonsexual in reproduction // 무성 생식의 agamogenetic ; agamic ; agamous ; blastogenetic

무성아 無性芽 〖동물·식물〗 a gemma 《*pl.* -mae》 ; a gemmule ¶ 무성아가 있는 gemmate // 무성아가 나오는〔로 번식하는〕 gemmiferous // 무성아로 번식하다 gemmate
— 번식 gemmation

무성 영화 無聲映畫 a silent film 〔(motion) picture, movie〕
— 시대 the silent picture days

무성음 無聲音 〖음성〗 a voiceless sound ; a breath consonant

무성의 無誠意 insincerity —하다 (be) insincere ; unfaithful ; be lacking in sincerity ; lack sincerity ¶ 무성의하게 insincerely ; unfaithfully // 너의 행위는 무성의하다 Your conduct betrays want of sincerity.

무세 無勢 powerlessness ⇨ 무세력

무세 無稅 ¶ 무세의 free ; tax-free ; untaxed ; free of tax duty ; duty-free // 무세 수입을 허가하다 allow the free entry 《of goods》 ; admit 《goods》 free of (customs) duty
— 수입품 (duty-)free imports ; articles on the free list 《미》 —품 (duty-)free goods ; goods free of duty〔tax〕 ; nondutiable goods

무세력 無勢力 powerlessness —하다 (be) powerless ; uninfluential

*****무소** 〖동물〗 a rhinoceros ; Ceratotherium simum (학명)

무소 誣訴 a false accusation〔charge〕 ; a trumped-up charge —하다 accuse 《a person》 falsely〔unjustly〕 ; make〔bring〕 a false accusation 《against a person》

무소권 無訴權 no right to bring an action in court

무소득 無所得 no gain ; no benefit —하다 gain little 《from, by》 ; get little benefit 《from》 ; be little benefited 《by》

무소부재 無所不在 omnipresence ; ubiquity —하다 (be) omnipresent ; ubiquitous
무소부지 無所不知 omniscience ; infinite knowledge ; extensive learning —하다 (be) omniscient ; know everything ; have infinite knowledge
무소불능 無所不能 omnipotence ; almightiness —하다 (be) omnipotent ; almighty ; all-powerful ; be unlimited in power
무소속 無所屬 independence ; being affiliated with no party ¶ 무소속의 independent
— 의원 an independent member ; a nonpartisan representative ; nonaffiliated members —자(者) a freelancer — 정치인 an independent (politician) ; a maverick 《미·구》
무소식 無消息 no news 《from a person》 —하다 be not heard from〔of〕; have no news from ; receive no words from ¶ 그는 영 무소식이다 Nothing has been heard from him since.
무소식이 희소식이다 속담 No news is good news.
무손 無損 —하다 be without loss ; suffer no loss ; sustain no damage ; (be) undamaged
무솔다 [푸성귀가] decay from the dampness
무쇠 cast iron ; iron ¶ 무쇠를 띄우다 cast iron
— 골격(骨格) a strong frame ; a brawny〔muscular〕build ; an iron constitution
무쇠도 갈면 바늘이 된다 속담 Constant dripping wears away the stone.
무수 無水 ¶ 무수의 anhydrous
—규산 silicic (acid) anhydride ; silicon dioxide —량 〖화학〗 bone-dry weight —물 an anhydride —산 anhydride —식 가스 탱크 a waterless gas holder —아류산 sulfurous anhydride —아비산 arsenic trioxide —알코올 absolute alcohol —유산 anhydrous sulphuric acid —초산 acetic anhydride —탄산 carbon dioxide ; carbonic anhydride —화합물 an anhydrous compound —황산 sulfuric anhydride
*무수 無數 —하다 (be) innumerable ; numberless ; countless ¶ 무수히 without number ; beyond count // 무수한 서적 books without number ; numberless books // 예를 무수히 들다 give no end of examples
무수기 the difference in water level between ebb and flood tides
무수다 beat relentlessly〔without mercy〕; destroy whatever〔anything that〕one can lay hands on
무수리[1] 〖새〗 an adjutant ; an adjutant bird〔crane, stork〕
무수리[2] [궁중의] a maid in charge of the water for the court ladies to wash their faces
무수입 無收入 ¶ 무수입으로 without (any) income
무수정 無修正 ¶ 무수정으로 without revision〔amendment〕
무숙자 無宿者 a homeless wanderer ; a vagrant ; a vagabond
무순 無順 (being) without order ; (in) random〔unalphabetical〕order ; "No special〔particular〕order is observed."
무술 武術 military arts
— 사범 a fencing master
무술 戊戌 〖민속〗 the 35th year of the sexagenary cycle ; the Year of the Dog
무쉬 the 9th and 24th days of a lunar month, when the flood tide sets in
*무슨 what ; what kind of ; some ; some kind of ¶ 무슨 일이나 in anything and everything // 무슨 까닭인지 why ; for what reason // 무슨 일이 있어도 whatever may happen ; come what may // 무슨 일이냐 What is the matter with you?/What's going on?/What's happening?/What's up?/What's cooking? // 무슨 물건을 사러 왔소 What are you out shopping for?/Are you out buying something? // 무슨 일이 생겼소 What happened?/Did something happen?/Has anything happened? // 무슨 일이 생겼음에 틀림없다 Something must have happened. // 무슨 말을 하고 있는 거요 What are you talking about? // 무슨 일이고 열심히 해야 한다 Whatever (kind of) job it is, you should do it whole-heartedly. // 무슨 사람이 그렇게 게으르담 What a lazy man he is! // 무슨 음식을 이렇게 많이 만들었습니까 My, what a lot of nice food you have fixed for us! // 무슨 문제라도 있니 Anything the matter? // 무슨 일로 오셨습니까 May I help you?/May I ask the nature of your business?/May I ask what this is regarding? // 사랑과 나이가 무슨 상관이 있습니까 What's age got to do with love?/What does age have to do with love?
무슨 일이 있어도 [긍정] by all means ; at any cost ; at all costs〔risks〕; whatever one may do ; [부정] by no means ; 《not》 by any means ; on no account
*무승부 無勝負 a draw ; a drawn game ; a tie ¶ 무승부로 끝나다 end in a tie〔draw〕; draw〔tie〕with 《a person》
**무시 無視 —하다 disregard ; ignore ; set at naught ; close one's eyes 《to》; throw to the winds ; take no notice 《of》; leave 《a person》 in the cold ; leave 《a thing》 out of account ¶ 무시해도 좋은 양〔인물〕 a negligible quantity〔person〕 // 규칙을 무시하다 set the rules at naught ; flout〔defy〕the rules // 남의 권리를 무시하다 ignore others' rights // 문법을 무시하다 do violence to grammar // 사실을 무시하다 close one's eyes to the facts // 여론을 무시

하다 disregard〔defy〕 public opinion // 민의를 무시하다 override the wishes of the people

무시근하다 (be) slovenly ; sloppy ; lazy and slipshod ; loose

무시로 無時— at any time ; anytime at all ; irregularly

*__무시무시하다__ (be) dreadful ; frightful ; ghastly ; horrible ; terrible ; awful ; shocking ; gruesome ¶ 무시무시한 광경 a terrible〔dreadful, ghastly〕 scene

무시무종 無始無終 〖카톨릭〗 without beginning and without end ; 〖불교〗 the eternal nature of mahatman **—하다** (be) eternal ; have neither beginning nor end

*__무시험 無試驗__ no〔without〕 examination ¶ 무시험 입학 admission without examination // 무시험으로 without examination // 무시험으로 교원 자격을 얻다 get a teacher's certificate without examination

중학교 — 추첨 제도 the lottery system instead of written examinations in enrolling freshmen at middle schools

*__무식 無識__ ignorance ; illiteracy **—하다** (be) ignorant ; illiterate ; uneducated ¶ 무식의 소치로 due to ignorance // 자신의 무식을 폭로하다 betray one's ignorance

—쟁이 an ignorant man ; an ignoramus

무신 戊申 〖민속〗 the 45th binary term of the sexagenary cycle

무신경 無神經 insensibility ; callousness ; apathy ; stolidity **—하다** (be) insensible 《of, to》 ; callous ; stolid ; thick-skinned ; dull ; apathetic 《to》 ¶ 남이 하는 말 따위에는 무신경이다 He is too thick-skinned to mind what others say.

무신고 無申告 ¶ 무신고로 without no-tice〔leave〕

— 집회 a meeting held without notice

*__무신론 無神論__ atheism ¶ 무신론적 atheistic

—자 an atheist ; an infidel ; an unbeliever

무실 無實 (being) without fact ; groundless ; false ; untrue **—하 다** (be) untrue ; false ¶ 무실한 죄로 on a false charge ; under a false accusation // 무실함을 주장하다 protest one's innocence // 무실하게 고발되다 be falsely charged 《with》 ; be falsely accused 《of》

무실점 無失點 ¶ 무실점으로 without losing a point // 무실점으로 기록하다 record no losing point〔score〕

무심 無心 ① [무의식] inadvertence ; absentmindedness ; heedlessness ; insentience (무감각) ; innocence (순진) ; [무관심] indifference ; being not interested 《in》 **—하다** (be) unwitting ; unintentional ; absentminded ; inadvertent (무감각한) ; unconscious ; innocent (순진한) ¶ 무심히 unwittingly ; inadvertently ; absentmindedly ; unintentionally ; innocently // 무심한 어린이 an innocent〔inoffensive〕 child // 무심히 잠든 얼굴 《her》 innocent sleeping face // 무심한 행동 an involuntary action // 무심히 입 밖에 내다 speak without malicious intent ; speak lightly ; talk unwittingly // 무심히 창 밖을 보다 look casually out of the window ; happen to look out of the window // 무심히 한 말이 친한 친구의 사이를 벌어지게 하는 수가 있다 A few light words sometimes estrange the closest friends.
② [불교에서] absence of the worldly desires ; disinterested beatitude

⁑__무심코__ [별 생각없이] unintentionally ; undesignedly ; unguardedly ; [문득] by chance ; casually ; [부주의하게] carelessly ; [무의식적으로] unconsciously

무쌍 無雙 —하다 (be) peerless ; matchless ; unequaled ; unique ; incomparable ; unparalleled ; unrivaled ; unsurpassed ; unchallenged

*__무아 無我__ self-effacement ; absence of ego ; selflessness ; annihilation of self ¶ 무아경에 들다 attain a spiritual state of perfect selflessness

—경(境) the state of complete absence of ego ; a perfect impersonal beatitude ; ecstasy **—애** absolute altruism **— 의식** 〖정신 분석〗 the id

무악 舞樂 a court dance and music

무안 無顔 shame ; disgrace ; dishonor **—하다** (be) ashamed ; feel shamed at ; lose face ; humiliate oneself by ; blush with shame ¶ 무안주다 put 《a person》 to shame ; humiliate 《a person》 ; put 《a person》 out of countenance // 그는 몹시 무안해 했다 He was filled with shame.

무안타 無安打 〖야구〗 no hit

— 무득점 경기 a no hit, no run game

무애 無涯 boundlessness ; infinity ; infinitude **—하다** (be) boundless ; infinite ; limitless

무애 無碍 freedom (from all obstacles)

무액 기압계 無液氣壓計 〖물리〗 an aneroid barometer

무양무양하다 (be) inflexible 《in personality》 ; hidebound

무어 ① [무엇] what ; something ⇨ 무엇 ¶ 무어 먹을 것 없어요 Have you anything to eat? // 뭐가 뭔지 모르겠다 I can't make anything〔head or tail〕 of it. // 부엌에 좀처럼 오지 않으니까 뭐가 뭔지 모르겠다 I como into the kitchen so seldom I don't know what's what.
② [반문] What? /Huh! ¶ 무어라고 What? /What did you say? // 무어 아우가 죽었다고 What! Brother dead? // 무어 얼마라고 What! How much did you say it is? // 무어 내가 잘못했어 What? I am wrong?
③ but ; but anyway ; somehow or other ; just ¶ 돈이 무어 여간 들어야지 You know it costs a lot of money. // 무어 어려울 것

없어 Why, that's quite easy. /Why, nothing is easier.

④ ¶ 무어니 무어니 해도 say what you will ; indeed ; let me tell you // 무어니 무어니 해도 가난처럼 쓰라린 것은 없다 Indeed there is nothing so hard to bear as poverty.

무어라 ¶ 무어라 말할 수 없다 [단언 못함] One cannot tell. /God〔Heaven only〕 knows ! ; [형용키 어려움] be unspeakable ; be inexpressible〔indescribable〕 // 무어라 사과 드릴 말이 없습니다 I don't know how to apologize to you. // 무어라 감사의 말씀을 드려야 할지 모르겠습니다 I can never thank you enough.

‡무언 無言 silence ; muteness ; taciturnity ; reticence ―하다 (be) silent ; mute ; tacit ; taciturn ; nontalking ; dumb ; speechless ; reticent 《about》 ¶ 무언중 in silence ; mutely ; without (saying) a word // 무언의 동정 unspoken sympathy // 무언의 용사들 silent〔dead〕 war heroes // 무언 중 양해가 성립되었다 There was tacit understanding between them. // 그는 끝내 함구무언이었다 He remained silent throughout.

―가(歌) 〖음악〗 songs without words ; Lieder ohne Worte 《도》 ; romances sans paroles 《프》

*무언극 無言劇 a pantomime ; a dumb show

― 배우 a pantomimist ; a mummer

무언 부답 無言不答 ―하다 have too much to say in answer ; keep silent without answering

무엄 無嚴 imprudence ; indiscretion ―하다 (be) imprudent ; indiscreet ; bold ; forward ; audacious ¶ 무엄한 언동 indiscreet words or actions // 무엄하게도 …하다 have the indiscretion to 《do》 ; be indiscreet enough to 《do》

†무엇 what ; which ; something ; anything ¶ 무엇이나 anything (at all) ; whatever ; everything // 무엇보다도 above all things ; before everything else ; first of all ; of all things // 무엇 때문에 what for // 무엇이라 말할 수 없다 be beyond expression ; be indescribable // 무엇이 어쨌다고 What ? /What did you say ? /What are you talking about ? // 네게 무엇을 감추겠니 Would I hide anything from you ? // 무엇이든지 마음에 드는 것을 가지시오 You may have anything you like. // 무엇인지 사 가지고 왔다 She's bought something or other. // 목에 무엇인지 생겼다 I seem to have some sort of growth on my neck. // 무엇 때문에 그런 짓을 했느냐 What did you do that for ? // 무엇을 좀 먹어야 하지 않소 Surely you have to eat something, don't you ? // 무엇이고 하겠소 I will do anything. // 그는 장사에 관한 한 무엇이나 다 알고 있다 He knows anything and everything about the trade. // 무엇보다도 먼저 그 버릇을 고쳐야 한다 You ought to correct that habit before everything else. // 무엇을 드시겠습니까 What would you like ? /What will it be ? // 무엇이 그리 급하냐 What's the rush ? // 조건이 무엇이냐 What's the catch ? // 네가 도와주어서 무엇보다도 기쁘다 I'm very grateful. Your help made all the difference.

무엇하다 [거북하다] be awkward ; be hard to say〔describe, put into words〕 ; be embarrassing ; be unsatisfactory ¶ 말씀드리기 좀 무엇합니다만 excuse me for my frankness, but ... ; to be frank with you ; to speak frankly ; it may be rude 〔unkind〕 to say so, but ... ; though I say it who shouldn't ... // 좀 무엇한 말이지만 그는 영어는 거의 모른다 I hesitate to speak it out, but he has very little knowledge of English.

무에리수에 the cry of a blind fortuneteller ; Get〔Have〕 your fortune told !

†무역 貿易 trade ; commerce ―하다 trade 《with》 ; have trade relation 《with》 ¶ 우리 나라의 대미 무역 our trade with America〔the U. S. A.〕 // 무역을 개발하다 cultivate a trade 《with》 // 무역을 진흥〔증진〕하다 promote〔increase〕 foreign trade // 무역을 육성하다 foster trade // 미국과 무역하다 trade with America // 직접 무역의 길을 열다 establish a direct trade 《with》 // 크게 무역을 하고 있다 have a large trade 《with》 // 미국의 연간 무역액은 굉장하다 The annual amount of trade done by the U. S. A. reaches very big figures. // 한국의 대미 무역은 근년에 급증하고 있다 Korean trade with America has lately grown by leaps and bounds.

― 경쟁국 a trade rival ―과 the trade department ― 관계 trade relations ― 관습 trade practices ―국 a trading country〔nation〕 ― 균형 〖통상〗 balance of trade ― 박람회 a trade fair ― 사절단 a trade mission ― 상대국 a trade partner ― 신용장 a trade credit〔L/C〕 ―액 the amount of trade ― 연보 annual trade returns ―외 수입 earnings on〔income from〕 invisibles ―외 수지 invisible trade ; invisible exports and imports ― 자금 a foreign trade fund ; a commercial fund ― 자유화 liberalization of trade ― 정책 trade policy ― 통계 trade returns ―품 trade goods ; exports (수출의) ; imports (수입의) ―항 a trade〔treaty〕 port ― 허가장 a permit for trading ― 협정 a trade agreement ― 회사 a trading company〔firm〕 ― 회전 기금 a revolving fund for trade 국내 ― domestic〔home〕 trade 대일 ― Korea's trade with Japan 대한 ― 진흥 공사 the Korean Trade Promotion Corporation 《KOTRA》 바터 ― barter trade 보상 ― compensation trade

삼각 — triangular trade 상품 — trade of goods 국제〔세계〕 — international 〔world〕 trade 수출 — export trade 연안 — coastwise〔intercoastal〕 trade 외국〔해외〕 — foreign trade ; seaborne〔overseas〕 trade ; overseas trade 《영》 외국 — 정책 a foreign trade policy 자유〔보호〕 — free〔protective〕 trade 중계 — transit trade 한국 — 협회 the Korea Traders Association 한일(韓日) — commerce between Korea and Japan 해상 — floating trade ☞ ◖p. 851◗

무역상 貿易商 a trader ; a trading merchant ; an importer (수입상) ; an exporter (수출상) ¶ 무역상을 경영하고 있다 be in the export-import business

무역업 貿易業 trade business ; trading business
—계 trading circles

무역풍 貿易風 a trade wind ; monsoon
동기〔하기〕 — dry〔wet〕 monsoon 반대 — an antitrade wind

무연 無煙 ¶ 무연의 smokeless

무연 無緣 ¶ 무연의 indifferent ; unrelated ; [연고자가 없는] without relations ; having no surviving relatives
— 묘지 a cemetery for those who left no relatives behind — 분묘 an unknown person's grave ; a neglected〔deserted〕 grave

무연 憮然 —하다 (be) disappointed ; disheartened ; discontented ; disconcerted

무연고 無緣故 ⇨ 무연(無緣)

*__무연탄 無煙炭__ anthracite (coal) ; smokeless〔hard, blind〕 coal ; stone coal ; glance coal ¶ 무연탄질의 anthracitic

무연 화약 無煙火藥 smokeless (gun) powder
혼성 — ballistite

무예 武藝 military arts ; feats of arms ¶ 무예를 갖춘 사람 a master of military arts ; a man of martial accomplishments // 무예를 닦다 practice military arts

무오 戊午 〖민속〗 the 55th binary term of the sexagenary cycle

무욕 無慾 freedom from avarice ; generosity —하다 (be) unselfish ; unavaricious ; generous ; disinterested ¶ 지나치게 무욕하다 be disinterested to a fault

*__무용 無用__ ① [용무 없음] ¶ 무용의 without business // 무용자 출입 금지 No admittance except on business. (게시) ② [무익·불필요] ¶ 무용의 useless ; of no use ; good for nothing ; [불필요한] unnecessary ; needless // 무용의 토론 useless discussion

무용 武勇 valor ; bravery ; prowess
—담 a tale of heroism ; a heroic episode ; a martial romance

무용 舞踊 dancing ; a dance —하다 dance ; perform a dance
—극 a dance drama —단 a corps de ballet 《프》 ; (a troupe of) ballet dancers — 선생 a dancing master — 연구소 a dancing school

무용장물 無用長物 a good-for-nothing ; a wasteful adjunct ; a white elephant ; a fifth wheel

무용지물 無用之物 a useless thing〔person〕 ; a good-for-nothing

무우 無憂 freedom from worry〔anxiety〕 —하다 (be) carefree ; be free from care

무우수 無憂樹 〖불교〗 the tree of sans souci

무우주론 無宇宙論 〖철학〗 acosmism

무운 武運 the fortune of war ¶ 무운을 빌다 pray for 《a person's》 success in war ; wish 《a person》 good luck in war // 무운이 다하여 죽다 fall by doom of battle

무운 無韻 〖시〗 (being) unrhymed 〔unrimed〕 ; blank
—시 a blank verse ; an unrhymed poem

무월경 無月經 〖의학〗 amenorrhoea

무위 無爲 doing nothing ; idleness ; inactivity ; inaction ; quietism ¶ 무위의 생활 a life of ease ; an idle life
— 도식 an idle life ; eating the bread of idleness — 도식배 an idler

무위 無違 (being) without mistake 〔error〕 —하다 (be) correct ; right

무위 武威 military prestige〔glory, power〕 ; armed might ¶ 무위를 떨치다 raise〔exalt〕 military prestige ; achieve martial glory

무의무신 無義無信 lack of integrity and trust —하다 (be) unfaithful (and untrustworthy)

무의무탁 無依無托 —하다 (be) helpless ; homeless ; lonely ; forlorn ; have no one〔friends, relatives〕 to depend on〔turn to〕 ¶ 무의무탁한 고아 a helpless orphan

⁑__무의미 無意味__ meaninglessness ; senselessness —하다 (be) meaningless ; senseless ; empty ; absurd ; insignificant ; nonsense ¶ 무의미하게 meaninglessly ; unmeaningly // 무의미한 말 empty words ; words devoid of sense // 무의미한 말을 하다 talk nonsense // 무의미한 생활을 보내다 lead a meaningless life // 그것을 따지는 것은 무의미하다 There is little point in arguing about it.

*__무의식 無意識__ unconsciousness ; involuntariness ¶ 무의식적으로 unconsciously ; involuntarily ; [기계적으로] mechanically // 무의식적 동작 an involuntary action // 무의식적으로 뒤로 물러섰다 He drew back involuntarily. // 자기가 하고 있는 일에 전혀 무의식적이다 She is almost unaware of what she is doing.
— 상태 an unconscious state〔condition〕
— 행동 〖심리〗 automatism

무의의 無意義 meaninglessness ⇨ 무의미

무의촌 無醫村 a doctorless village

무 역

외국[국제] 무역 foreign[international] trade **무역 수지** trade balance ¶ 한국의 대미(對美)무역 수지는 흑자이다. Korea has a favorable trade balance with the U.S.. / Korea has a trade surplus on the U.S.. **무역 제한** trade restrictions **무역 마찰** trade dispute [conflict, friction] ¶ 한·미 무역 마찰 The Korea-U.S. trade dispute[friction] / Korea's trade dispute with the U.S. **무역 불균형** trade imbalance **엔고** yen appreciation **무역 진흥책** trade promotion measures [policy] **무역 자유화** trade liberalization **자유 무역주의** free trade principle **보호 무역주의** (trade) protectionism **대(對) ··· 무역** trade with ... ¶ 한국의 대중국(對中國) 무역 Korea's trade with China **무역 입국(貿易立國)정책** (national) policy to live by trade **가공(加工)무역** improvement trade; processing trade; importing raw materials and exporting manufactured products **상호[다각]무역** two-way [multilateral] trade **삼각 무역** triangular trade **중개 무역** intermediary trade; cross [commission] trade **바터 무역** barter trade **무역협정** trade agreement **관세** tariff; customs duty **관세율** tariff rate **관세 장벽** tariff barrier **비관세 장벽** nontariff barrier **보복 관세** retaliatory tariff **상쇄 관세(相殺關稅)** countervailing [compensating] tariff [duties] **관세 무역 일반 협정** GATT(General Agreement on Tariffs and Trade) **관세의 일괄 인하** across-the-board reduction of tariffs **다국간 관세 인하 교섭** MTN (the multilateral tariff negotiations) **세관** custom(s) house **통관** customs clearance **최혜국 대우** most-favored-nation treatment **채권국** creditor nation(s) **면책 조항** escape clause **통상 대표부** 《미》 Office of the U.S. Trade Representative **통상 대표** Trade Representative **수입 할당제** import quota system **수입 과징금** import surcharge **수입 제한 [규제]** import restriction[control, regulation] **수출 자유 규제** self-restraint in exports; self-imposed export restraint **시장 개방책** market-opening measures **수출 경쟁** export competition **수출 승인** bank validation of export contract **수출 장려책** export promotion measures **수출 장려금 [보조금]** export subsidy **수출 드라이브** export drive; drive to promote exports **플랜트 수출** plant export **적정 수출(適正輸出)** orderly marketing

무이다 fall out (머리털이) ; become bald

무이자 無利子 no interest ¶ 무이자의 without interest ; interest-free ; noninterest-bearing 《bills》 // 무이자로 without 〔free of〕 interest
— **공채** passive bonds

*__무익 無益__ uselessness ; futility —**하다** (be) useless ; futile ; be no good〔use, avail〕 ; (be) vain ; fruitless ¶ 무익한 살생 wanton destruction of life // 무익한 논쟁 a futile argument // 무익한 살생을 하다 kill needlessly // 유해 무익하다 do more harm than good // 더 이상 수색을 계속하는 것은 무익하다 It is useless to continue the search any longer.

무인 拇印 a thumbmark ; a thumbprint ¶ 무인을 찍다 seal with the thumb 《on a document》

무인 戊寅 〖민속〗 the 15th binary term of the sexagenary cycle

무인 武人 a soldier ; a warrior
— **기질** a military spirit

무인 無因
— **계약** an abstract contract —**론** 〖철학〗 indeterminism — **행위** 〖법〗 an abstract act

무인 無人 ¶ 무인의 manless ; unmanned ; uninhabited
— **건널목** an unattended〔unguarded〕 (railroad) crossing — **위성〔역〕** an unmanned satellite〔railroad station〕 — **지대** no-man's-land ; an uninhabited region — **판매기** a self-service stand (신문 따위의)

무인도 無人島 a desert island ; an uninhabited island

무인 비행기 無人飛行機 a pilotless 〔radio-controlled〕 airplane ; a robot plane ; a drone ¶ 무인 비행기를 원격 관제 장치에 의해서 조정하는 사람 〖항공〗 a beeper

무인 절도 無人絶島 a desert islet ; an uninhabited and isolated island

무인지경 無人之境 an uninhabited region ; no-man's-land ¶ 무인지경을 가듯하다 carry〔sweep〕 everything before one ; advance with an irresistible force

무일물 無一物 having nothing ; being penniless ¶ 그의 집엔 무일물이다 He has got practically nothing in the house to claim for his own ! /He is as poor as a church mouse.

*__무일푼 無一—__ (being) penniless ¶ 무일푼이다 be penniless ; have not a penny in

the world ; be utterly broke 《미》 // 무일푼이 되다 become〔find oneself〕 penniless
*무임 無賃 free of charge ; free
— 승객 free passenger ; a deadhead 《구》
무임소 無任所 ¶ 무임소의 without portfolio
— 장관 a Minister of State without portfolio
무임 승차 無賃乘車 a free ride ; deadheading 《구》 —하다 ride free (of charge) ; have a free ride ; steal a ride 〔one's way〕 《on a train》
—권 a free pass
무자 戊子 〖민속〗 the 25th binary term of the sexagenary cycle
무자격 無資格 disqualification ; 〖법〗 incapacity ¶ 무자격의 disqualified ; unqualified ; [무면허의] uncertified
— 교원 an uncertified〔unlicensed〕 teacher —자 an incompetent ; a disqualified person
무자력 無資力 insolvency —하다 be without funds ; (be) insolvent
—자 a person of no resources〔means〕 ; [지불 불능자] an insolvent (person)
무자맥질 diving ; going under the water —하다 dive ; go〔swim〕 underwater ; submerge
무자본 無資本 lack of capital〔funds〕 ¶ 무자본으로 without capital〔funds〕 ; with nothing to start with
*무자비 無慈悲 mercilessness ; cruelty ; harshness ; brutality ; ruthlessness —하다 (be) merciless ; heartless ; pitiless ; cruel ¶ 그는 곤경에 빠진 친구를 무자비하게도 버렸다 He was cold-hearted enough to forsake a friend in need.
무자식 無子息 (being) childless ; heirless —하다 (be) childless ; heirless
무자식 상팔자 〔속담〕 Love of children is an eternal encumbrance.
무자위 a (water) pump
무자치 〖동물〗 a kind of harmless water snake
무작위 無作爲 ¶ 무작위화하다 randomize
— 표본 〖통계〗 a random sample — (표본) 추출 random sampling —화(化) 〖생물〗 randomization
무작정 無酌定 lack of any definite plan ; recklessness ; rashness —하다 lack any definite plan ; have no particular view in mind ; (be) aimless ; (be) without any goal in mind ; (be) rash ; reckless ¶ 무작정 recklessly ; rashly ; thoughtlessly ; blindly ; aimlessly ; at random // 무작정 상경했다 I went up to *Seoul* with no definite object in view.
무작하다 (be) ignorant and boorish ; rude
무장 thin〔watery〕 soy sauce
무장 武將 a military commander ; a general ; a warlord
*무장 武裝 arms ; armament (나라의) ; equipment (개인의) —하다 arm ; be under〔in〕 arms ; bear arms ; equip oneself ¶ 무장한 armed ; armored (장갑한) // 무장한 백만 대군 a million men under arms // 무장 시위 행렬 armed demonstration // 충분히 무장한 be fully armed 《for warfare》 ; be armed at all points〔to the teeth〕 // 권총으로 무장하다 arm〔equip〕 oneself with a pistol // 무장을 해제하다 disarm ; demilitarize ; dismantle (함선을) // 무장 봉기하다 take up arms 《against》 ; rise in arms
— 경관(警官) an armed policeman ; armed police 《총칭》 — 도시 a fortified city —병 an armed soldier ; a man-at-arms 《*pl.* men-at-arms》 — 봉기 rising in arms ; an armed uprising — 상선 an armed merchantman —선 an armed ship — 해제 disarmament ; demilitarization ; dismantlement (군함·포대의) 비—지대 a demilitarized zone 《DMZ》
무장지졸 無將之卒 a leaderless army
무장화 武裝化 militarization —하다 militarize 《a frontier》
비— demilitarization
무재 無才 lack of ability ; being untalented ; incompetence —하다 be lacking in ability ; (be) untalented ; ungifted ; incompetent
무저항 無抵抗 nonresistance ¶ 무저항의 nonresisting ; nonresistant // 소극적인 저항 passive resistance // 무저항 상륙을 하다 make an uncontested landing
—주의 the principle of nonresistance —주의자 a nonresistant
*무적 無敵 ¶ 무적의 invincible ; matchless ; unconquerable ; unrivaled ; unequaled ; all-conquering // 무적의 용사 a man of matchless valor // 무적이다 have no equal〔rival〕 《in》 ; stand alone〔unchallenged〕 《in》 ; be first〔second to none〕 《in》
— 함대 〖역사〗 the Invincible Armada
무적 無籍 absence of a registered domicile ; lack of a record
—자 a person without a registered domicile
무적 霧笛 [고동] a fog siren ; a foghorn
무전 無錢 ¶ 무전의 moneyless ; penniless ; without money // 무전 유흥하다 go merrymaking without money ; leave a pleasure-house bill unpaid
— 여행 a penniless trip ; a vagabond journey ¶ 무전 여행하다 travel without money ; hitchhike 《미·구》 // 세계를 무전 여행하다 work one's way round the world — 취식 jumping a restaurant bill ¶ 무전 취식하다 bilk〔defraud〕 a restaurant
무전 無電 wireless ; radio ⇨ 무전 전신
무절제 無節制 intemperance ; excesses ; immoderation ; incontinence ; incontinency —하다 (be) intemperate ; incon-

tinent ; [서술적] commit excesses ¶ 무절제한 사람 an intemperate person // 무절제로 건강을 해치다 injure〔ruin〕 one's health by intemperance // 무절제한 생활을 하다 lead an intemperate life

무절조 無節操 inconstancy ; unchastity **—하다** (be) inconstant ; inconsistent ; unchaste ; wanton ¶ 무절조한 정치인 an unprincipled politician // 무절조한 여인 a wanton woman

*__무정 無情__ hardness ; heartlessness ; inhumanity ; cruelty **—하다** (be) hard ; heartless ; inhuman ; cruel ; pitiless ; cold hearted ¶ 무정 세월 pitiless〔fleeting, transient〕time // 무정한 사나이 a heartless man ; a man with a heart of stone // 무정하게도 …하다 be cold-hearted enough to 《do》

무정견 無定見 lack of a fixed principle 〔policy〕 ; caprice **—하다** (be) fickle ; inconstant ; wavering ; vacillate 《in one's opinion》 ; have no fixed views of one's own ; have no settled opinion

무정란 無精卵 an unfertilized egg

*__무정부 無政府__ anarchy ¶ 무정부의 anarchic(al) // 무정부 상태이다 be in a state of anarchy ; be in an anarchical〔a chaotic〕 condition // 당시 러시아는 무정부 상태였다 Anarchy prevailed in Russia at that time.

—주의 anarchism **—주의자** an anarchist ; an anarch

무정수 無定數 without a fixed number

무정위 無定位 〖물리〗 astaticism ¶ 무정위의 astatic

— 검류계 an astatic galvanometer **— 스위치** 〖전기〗 a nonhoming switch **— 조속기(調速機)** an astatic governor **—침(針)** an astatic needle

무정차 無停車 nonstop

무정형 無定形 amorphousness ; shapelessness ¶ 무정형의 formless ; shapeless ; amorphous

— 금속 amorphous metal **— 물질** an amorphous substance **— 수정** massive quartz **— 흑연** amorphous graphite

무제 無題 no title ¶ 무제의 titleless ; without a title

무제 無際 infinity ; infinitude **—하다** (be) boundless ; unlimited ; infinite

무제한 無制限 ¶ 무제한의 unrestricted ; unlimited // 무제한으로 without any restriction ; freely // 이민의 무제한 입국 the unrestricted admission of immigrants // 연령〔인원〕은 무제한이다 There are no restrictions as to age〔the number of persons〕.

— 법화(法貨) unlimited legal tender **— 입국** unrestricted admission 《of immigrants》 **— 통화** free currency

*__무조건 無條件__ ¶ 무조건의 unconditional ; unqualified ; absolute ; open 《contract》 // 무조건으로 unconditionally ; unqualifiedly // 무조건 받아들이다 accept 《a person's statement》 without reserve // 무조건 승낙하다 give an unqualified 〔unconditional〕 consent

— 반사 〖심리〗 an unconditioned reflex **— 사면** a free pardon **— 신용장** an open credit **— 항복** unconditional surrender **— 협상** unconditional negotiations〔discussions〕

무족 無足 ¶ 무족의 apodal ; apodous

—류 〖동물〗 Apoda ; Apodes **—류 동물** an apodal ; an apodan

무좀 athlete's foot ; bath-itch ; 〖의학〗 water eczema ¶ 무좀에 걸리다 have athlete's foot

무종교 無宗教 no religion ; being without religion ¶ 무종교의 irreligious ; godless ; atheistic

—자 a person without religion ; an atheist ; an unbeliever

⁑**무죄 無罪** innocence ; guiltlessness ; clean hands **—하다** (be) innocent ; guiltless ; not guilty ¶ 무죄가 되다 be found innocent〔not guilty〕 // 무죄로 하다〔무죄를 언도하다〕 find〔declare〕 《a person》 not guilty ; acquit 《a person》 of the charge 〔crime〕 // 무죄를 주장하다 plead not guilty ; assert 《a person's》 innocence // 무죄 선고를 받다 be given a verdict of "not guilty" // 무죄 석방이 되었다 He was found innocent and acquitted. /He was acquitted of the crime.

— 판결 a judgment of acquittal ; a decision of "not guilty"

무죄 석방 無罪釋放 acquittal (and discharge) ¶ 무죄 석방이 되다 be found innocent and acquitted

무주 無主 being ownerless

— 고혼 a forlorn wandering spirit (that has no posterity to perform the memorial service) **— 공당(公堂)** an ownerless house ; an unoccupied house **— 공처(空處)** an unowned land ; a deserted lot

무주의 無主義 lack of principle ¶ 무주의의 without any principle ; unprincipled

—자 a person without definite principle

무주정 無酒精 ¶ 무주정의 nonalcoholic

— 음료 a nonalcoholic beverage ; a soft drink

무주택 無住宅 ¶ 무주택의 homeless ; houseless

— 서민(층) the homeless masses **— 인구(비율)** the homeless population 〔ratio〕 **—자** a houseless〔homeless〕 person ; houseless people **— 증명서** a certificate verifying a person's homeless status

무중력 無重力 weightlessness ; nongravitation ; nongravity ; zero G

— 상태 a state〔the condition〕 of weightlessness ; a weightless state ; a gravity-free state

무지 [한 섬이 못되는 곡식] grain slightly〔a little〕 less than a *sŏm* ; a short *sŏm* of

grain
무지 拇指 a thumb
†무지 無知 ignorance ; illiteracy ; stupidity —하다 (be) ignorant ; uneducated ; illiterate

> 참고 **ignorant** 일반적으로 널리 쓰이는 말이며 때로는 어떤 일에 지식이 없다는 뜻 **illiterate** 읽고 쓰기를 못한다 **uneducated** 정규 교육을 받지 않다

¶ 무지한 백성 unenlightened people // 잘못이 있었다면 그것은 무지의 소치이다 If he did wrong, it was from〔through〕 ignorance. // 무지는 최악의 적이다 Ignorance is the most fierce enemy. // 자기의 무지를 모르는 것이 무지한 사람들의 폐단이다 To be ignorant of one's ignorance is the malady of the ignorant.
무지각 無知覺 insensibility ; indiscretion —하다 (be) insensible ; indiscreet
*무지개 a rainbow ¶ 무지개를 쫓는 사람 a rainbow chaser // 무지개 다리 the rainbow's arch // 무지개가 섰다 A rainbow appeared〔hung, rose, formed〕 《against the sky》.
—빛 rainbow〔spectral〕 colors ; the hues of the rainbow ; iridescence 쌍— a double rainbow
무지근하다 feel heavy〔dull〕 ¶ 머리가 무지근하다 have a slight〔dull〕 headache ; feel heavy in the head // 다리가 무지근하다 have a heavy〔uncomfortable〕 feeling in one's leg // 뒤가 무지근하다 My bowels are stuffy〔constipated〕. // 감기로 머리가 무지근하다 A cold makes my head feel stuffy.
무지기 an underwear skirt ; a slip
무지러지다 get stumpy〔blunt〕 ; wear down to a stump ; wear out ; be worn out ; be stumped ¶ 무지러진 비 a stumpy broom // 붓이 무지러졌다 The writing brush is worn to a stump.
무지렁이 a dunce ; a moron ; a stupid person
무지르다 cut off〔away〕 ¶ 나뭇가지를 무지르다 cut branches off a tree ; lop off〔down〕 branches
무지막지 無知莫知 —하다 (be) ignorant and uncouth ¶ 무지막지한 짓을 하다 commit an outrage
무지몰각 無知沒覺 —하다 (be) utterly ignorant ; know nothing
무지몽매 無知蒙昧 lack of enlightenment —하다 (be) unenlightened ; ignorant ¶ 그 섬의 토인은 무지몽매하다 The inhabitants of the island are in an uncivilized state〔in the darkest ignorance〕.
무지스럽다 無知— (be) ignorant ; [우악함] cruel ; rough ; rude
무직 無職 ¶ 무직이다 have no occupation ; be without occupation ; [실업] be unemployed ; be out of work〔a job〕
—자 a person out of work〔without a regular occupation〕 ; a jobless man ; the unemployed (집합적)
무직하다 ⇨ 무지근하다
무진 戊辰 the 5th binary term of the sexagenary cycle
무진 無盡 [무궁] (with) no end ; no limit —하다 (be) unending ; unlimited
— 판매 a raffle — 회사 a mutual loan〔mutual financing〕 company
무진동 〖광물〗 rock containing over 50% iron sulfide
무진장 無盡藏 an inexhaustible supply〔treasury〕 ; unlimited resources —하다 (be) inexhaustible ; unlimited ; limitless ¶ 무진장의 보고 an inexhaustible mine of wealth // 무진장의 공급원 unfailing sources of supply // 그 지방의 철광은 무진장이다 The region has an inexhaustible mine〔deposits〕 of iron ore. // 돈을 무진장으로 가지고 있다 He has a mint of money. /He has no end of money.
무질리다 be cut off〔away〕 ¶ 나뭇가지가 무질리다 branches are cut off from a tree
*무질서 無秩序 disorder ; confusion ; [혼돈] chaos ; anarchy —하다 (be) disordered ; confused ; chaotic ; anarchic ; lawless ; higgledy-piggledy 《구》 ; be at sixes and sevens
무집게 a pair of pincers ; nippers
무쩍 all at once ; in one big bite ; in a sweep〔push〕 ¶ 무를 한 입 무쩍 깨물다 bite off a big bite of radish // 일을 한꺼번에 무쩍 몰아 하다 do one's work in one sweep
무찌르다 ① [살육] kill off ; mow〔cut〕 down ; kill recklessly ; slaughter ; butcher ¶ 적 수백을 무찌르다 mow down hundreds of the enemy // 닥치는 대로 무찌르다 strike down everything that comes in one's way
② [공격] attack ; assault ; launch an attack 《on》 ; fall upon ; set upon ; [유린] devastate ; overrun ; conquer ¶ 적의 성을 무찌르다 assault〔devastate〕 an enemy castle
무찔리다 ① [살륙] get killed off ; be〔get〕 mowed down ② [공격당함] be attacked ; be assaulted ; be devastated ¶ 성이 적에게 무찔리다 a castle is assaulted〔devastated〕 by the enemy
무차별 無差別 indiscrimination ; non-discrimination ¶ 무차별의 indiscriminate // 무차별하게 indiscriminately // 남녀 무차별로 without distinction of sex
— 곡선 〖경제학〗 an indifference curve — 급(級) 〖유도〗 the open-weight division — 도표 〖경제〗 an indifference map — 폭격 indiscriminate bombing 신앙 —론 〖종교〗 indifferentism
무착륙 無着陸 nonstop ; without alighting ¶ 무착륙으로 비행하다 fly nonstop 《to》 ;

make a nonstop flight 《to》// 뉴욕에서 파리까지의 무착륙 비행 a nonstop flight from New York to Paris

무참 shame ; disgrace **—하다** be 〔feel〕 ashamed ; feel mortified

무참 無慘 **—하다** (be) cruel ; merciless ; pitiless ; ruthless ; tragical ¶ 무참한 광경 a horrible scene (to look at) // 무참하게 mercilessly ; cruelly ; ruthlessly ; in cold blood ; without pity〔mercy〕 // 무참한 죽음을 당하다 die a horrible death ; meet with〔come to〕 a tragic end

무채색 無彩色 an achromatic color

무책 無策 resourcelessness ; lack of policy〔plan〕 ¶ 속수 무책이다 be resourceless ; have no policy ; lack policy ; lack of means to deal with a situation

***무책임 無責任** irresponsibility **—하다** (be) irresponsible ¶ 무책임하게 irresponsibly ; without a due sense of responsibility // 무책임한 사람〔행위〕 an irresponsible person〔conduct〕 // 그는 무책임한 말은 하지 않는다 He is responsible for what he says. // 저 사람은 무책임하다 He lacks a sense of responsibility. // 그는 어쩌면 그토록 무책임할 수가 있는가 How could he be so irresponsible ?

***무척** very ; highly ; exceedingly ; extremely ¶ 무척 칭찬하다 praise highly // 무척 손해보다 suffer a great loss // 무척 영리하다 be remarkably clever // 무척 피곤하다 be dead tired // 무척 춥다 It is very cold.

무척추동물 無脊椎動物 an invertebrate animal

무체 無體
— 동산(動產) a chose in action **—물(物)** an immaterial being **— 재산** intangible property

무춤하다 halt ; start back ; hold back one's steps ; stop short ; shrink back 《at, from》 ; pull back ; recoil 《from》 ; flinch 《from》 ; hesitate ¶ 뱀을 보고 무춤하다 stop short at the sight of a snake // 밀려오는 적의 대군을 보고 무춤했다 They flinched before the great force marching against them.

무취 無臭 ¶ 무취의 odorless ; inodorous ; scentless

무취미 無趣味 lack of taste ; vulgarity **—하다** (be) dry ; dull ; tasteless ; prosaic ; vulgar ¶ 무취미한 사람 a person of no taste ; a prosaic person

무치다 season ; dress ; add flavo(u)ring to ¶ 나물을 무치다 season vegetable

무턱대고 without rhyme or reason ; for no good reason〔cause〕 ; unreasonably ; with no prearrangement ; with no preparation ; with no resources〔capability〕 ; with nothing to fall back on ¶ 무턱대고 책망하다 scold 《a person》 for no good reason // 무턱대고 찾아가다 call on 《a person》 just like that // 무턱대고 사업을 시작하다 go into a business with nothing to back one up // 무턱대고 시험을 치러 보다 try taking an examination without any preparation // 그가 왜 무턱대고 화를 내는지 모르겠다 I don't see any reason for his anger.

무텅이 planting a newly-developed 〔opened〕 field with〔to, in〕 《rice, barley, wheat, corn, etc.》

무테 無— ¶ 무테의 rimless ; frameless ; unframed ; brimless
— 안경 (a pair of) rimless glasses

무통 無痛 ¶ 무통의 painless ; free from pain ; 〖병리〗 indolent
— 분만 painless delivery〔labor〕 **—성 종양** an indolent tumor

무투표 無投票 ¶ 무투표로 without voting
— 당선 return without voting

무트로 [한목에 많이] in a lump at one time ; a large amount 《of something》 at one time

무패 無敗 no defeat ; a clean record

무표정 無表情 **—하다** (be) expressionless ; blank ; unrevealing ¶ 무표정한 얼굴 an expressionless face ; a dead-pan 《미·속》 ; a poker face 《구》

무풍 無風 a dead〔flat〕 calm ¶ 무풍의 windless ; calm

무풍대 無風帶 the calm latitudes〔belt〕
온대 — the horse latitudes **적도 —** the equatorial calm ; the doldrums

무풍 상태 無風狀態 a (dead, flat) calm ; 〖항해〗 a Paddy's hurricane ; [시세] a featureless market ¶ 정치적 무풍 상태에 있다 be in political doldrums

무학 無學 [무지] ignorance ; [문맹] illiteracy **—하다** (be) ignorant ; uneducated ; illiterate ; unlettered ; unschooled ¶ 무학 몽매한 사람 an illiterate person ; an ignoramus

‡**무한 無限** infinity ; infinitude ; boundlessness **—하다** (be) unlimited ; limitless ; boundless ; infinite ; endless ; immeasurable ; inestimable ; inexhaustible ¶ 무한히 infinitely ; endlessly ; to an unlimited extent ; eternally // 무한의 권력 unlimited power // 무한한 사랑〔자애, 바다〕 boundless love〔mercy, sea〕 // 수요는 무한히 증가될 것이다 The demand will increase to an unlimited extent.
— 급수 〖수학〗 an infinite series **—량** infinite quantity **— 승적** 〖수학〗 an infinite product **— 원점(遠點)** 〖수학〗 the point at infinity ; the infinite point **— 화서(花序)** 〖식물〗 indefinite〔indeterminate〕 inflorescence

무한 궤도 無限軌道 an endless track ; a caterpillar ; a crawler ; a (caterpillar) tread ¶ 무한 궤도를 나아가다 drive on treads
—식 군용 자동차 a half-track **—차** a caterpillar tractor ; a crawler (tractor) ; a tracklayer ; a cat

무한대 無限大 infinity ; an infinite quality ¶ 무한대의 infinite ; infinitely great // 무

한대의 거리에서 at infinity
무한소 無限小 the infinitesimal ¶ 무한소의 infinitesimal ; infinitely small
무한정 無限定 unlimitedness ; infinity **—하다** unlimited ; infinite ¶ 무한정(으로) [언제까지라도] as long as one like ; for any length of time ; [무기한으로] indefinitely ; for an indefinite time ; [영구히] forever ; for good (and all) ; permanently ; eternally // 무한정 그를 기다릴 수는 없다 I can't afford to wait for him eternally.
무한 책임 無限責任 unlimited liability
— 사원 a general partner ; a partner with unlimited liability **— 회사** an unlimited company
무함 誣陷 slander ; backbiting ; calumny ; detraction **—하다** slander ; calumniate ; accuse falsely ; bring a false charge 《against》 ; stab 《a person》 in the back
무항산 無恒產 ¶ 무항산이면 무항심(無恒心)이다 A real property, a real purpose. /Competency is for constancy of mind.
무해 無害 harmlessness ; innocuousness ; innoxiousness **—하다** (be) harmless ; innocuous ; innoxious ; inoffensive ¶ 무해한 약품 a harmless drug // 인축 무해 no harm〔harmless〕 to men and beasts
무해무득 無害無得 —하다 be neither gain nor loss ; be neither harmful nor useful
무허가 無許可 no permit ; without a permit〔license〕
— 판매〔제조〕 nonlicensed sale〔production〕 **— 판자집〔건물〕** an unlicensed shack〔building〕
무혈 無血 ¶ 무혈의 bloodless ; without bloodshed // 무혈의 승리 a bloodless victory
— 상륙 bloodless landing **— 전쟁** a white war 《of propaganda》 **— 점령** a bloodless occupation **— 혁명** a bloodless revolution
무혐 無嫌 being unsuspicious **—하다** be free from suspicion ; be clear (of suspicion) ; (be) unsuspected
무혐의 無嫌疑 ⇨ 무혐(無嫌)
무협 武俠 chivalry ; heroism ¶ 무협적 chivalrous
***무형 無形** ¶ 무형의 [비물질적] immaterial ; incorporeal ; [정신적] moral ; spiritual ; [추상적] abstract ; [보이지 않는] formless ; invisible ; intangible (만질 수 없는) ¶ 무형의 원조 moral support // 무형의 재산 incorporeal〔immaterial, intangible〕 assets〔property〕 // 무형의 손해 immaterial loss // 그에게 유형 무형의 은혜를 입었다 I am indebted to him materially and morally.
— 문화재 intangible cultural properties **—물** an immaterial thing ; an incorporeal entity ; an incorporeity **— 세계** the immaterial world **— 원조〔이익〕** moral support〔gains〕 **— 자산** intangible assets

무호동중 無虎洞中 a Triton among the minnows ¶ 무호동중 이작호(狸作虎) When the cat's away, the mice will play. /Where there are no dogs, the fox is a king.
***무화과 無花果** a fig
— 나무 a fig tree
무환 수입 無換輸入 no-draft import
무환 수출 無換輸出 no-draft export
무환자 無患子 〖식물〗 a kind of soapberry ; Sapindus mukurossi (학명)
—과(科) Sapindaceae〔the soapberry family〕 **— 나무** a soapberry (tree)
****무효 無效** ① [보람 없음] ineffectiveness ; inefficiency ; futility ② [법적] invalidity ; nullity ; unavailability (불통용) **—하다** (be) ineffective ; ineffectual ; inefficient ; futile ; fruitless ; come to nought ; be of no〔little〕 avail ; yield no results ; invalid ; void ; nugatory ; null and void ; [통용 안되는] unavailable ; stale ¶ 무효화할 수 있는 abatable // 무효로 하다 repeal ; annul ; dissolve ; make (null and) void ; avoid ; nullify 《a law》 ; invalidate ; override ; overrule 《veto》 // 무효가 되다 become null〔void, ineffective, unavailable〕 ; be invalidated ; be nullified ; lose effect ; resolve ; lapse // 무효로 간주되다 be regarded as not valid // 무효처분 당하다 be dealt with as invalid // 강제된 약속은 무효이다 A promise made under compulsion is not binding. // 그 투표지는 무효로 한다 That (voting) paper shall not be counted. // 김씨의 당선은 무효가 되었다 Mr. *Kim's* election was declared invalid. // 도중 하차하면 이 차표는 무효가 된다 If you break your journey, this ticket will cease to be valid 〔you will be unable to use your ticket〕.
— 계약 a void contract **— 소송** a nullity suit **— 심리(審理)** mistrial **— 에너지** 〖기계〗 unavailable energy **— 저수량** 〖수력〗 dead storage **— 전력계** a reactive volt-ampere〔VA〕 meter ; a reactive〔wattless〕 power meter **— 차표** an unavailable ticket **— 청구 소송** [계약 따위의] an action of nullity **— 투표(投票)** an invalid〔a spoilt, a null and void〕 vote **결혼 — 소송** a nullity suit **증서 — 확인 소송** a rescissory action
무후 無後 having no posterity **—하다** (be) sonless ; be without offspring
무훈 武勳 a distinguished military service ; military exploits〔merits, feats, achievements〕 ¶ 무훈을 세우다 distinguish oneself on the field of battle ; win one's spurs
무휴 無休 no holiday ; without holiday ¶ 무휴이다 have no holiday // (점포 따위가) 연중 무휴이다 be open throughout the year
무흠 無欠 [흠이 없음] flawlessness ; faultlessness ; perfection **—하다** (be)

flawless ; faultless ; be free from blemish
무희 舞姬 a dancing-girl ; a ballet-girl ; a ballerina 《이》 ; a danseuse 《프》
묵 jelly
녹두— green-pea jelly 도토리— acorn jelly 메밀— buckwheat jelly
묵객 墨客 a calligrapher (서예가) ; a painter (화가)
묵계 默契 a tacit〔an implicit〕 understanding〔agreement〕 —하다 agree tacitly ; make a tacit agreement ¶ 양자간에 묵계가 있다 There is a tacit agreement between the two.
묵고 默考 a silent thought ; (a) meditation ; contemplation —하다 meditate 《on》 ; muse 《on》 ; contemplate ; commune with oneself〔one's soul〕
묵과 默過 connivance —하다 overlook ; look over ; pass over 《a matter》 in silence ; let 《it》 pass〔go〕 ; let 《a person》 go unchallenged〔unpunished〕 ; connive 《at》 ; wink (an eye) 《at》 ; blink 《a fact》 ; give 《a person》 the go-by 《구》
묵념 默念 ① meditation ⇨ 묵상 ② a silent prayer ⇨ 묵도
*__묵다__[1] [오래되다] get old ; get antiquated ; get stale ¶ 묵은 관습 old customs // 묵은 학설 an outdated〔obsolete〕 theory // 묵은 사상 an old-fashioned〔a moss-grown〕 idea // 묵은 빚 an old debt ; a debt of long standing // 케케묵은 생각 a completely outmoded idea // 케케묵다 be hackneyed ; be threadbare ; be stale
*__묵다__[2] [숙박하다] stay 《at, in, with》 ; put up 《at》 ; stop 《at, in》 ; lodge 《in, with》 ; put up〔stop〕 《at a hotel》 ; register 《at a hotel》 ¶ 밤이 늦었으니 자네 집에서 하룻밤 묵고 가겠네 It's late, so I will stay overnight with you. // 아무리 밤이 늦어도 남의 집에서 묵는 일이 없다 I never stay out, but always come home, however late at night. // 오늘은 늦었으니 하루 묵고 가십시오 It's late, so why don't you stay the night?
묵도 默禱 a silent〔tacit〕 prayer ; a silent tribute —하다 pray silently ; offer a silent prayer ¶ 전몰 장병에 대하여 1분간 묵도를 올리다 stand for a minute in silent tribute to the war dead ; offer one-minute prayer for the repose of the souls of the war
묵독 默讀 silent reading —하다 read 《a book》 silently
묵례 默禮 a silent bow —하다 bow to 《a person》 in silence ; make a silent bow ¶ 묵례를 교환하다 exchange bows with 《a person》
묵묵 默默 —하다 (be) silent ; mute ; tacit ¶ 묵묵히 in silence ; silently ; mutely ; tacitly // 묵묵 부답하다 be silent and make no response // 내가 이야기하는 동안 그는 묵묵히 서 있었다 He stood perfectly mute while I talked to him.
묵밭 a fallow field
묵볶이 fried jelly with spices
묵비 默秘 nondisclosure ; nonconfession —하다 keep silent 《about》 ; keep 《a matter》 secret
묵비권 默秘權 the right to keep silent ¶ 묵비권을 행사하다 use the right of silence ; stand mute (of malice) // 묵비권을 행사하겠다 I'll take〔plead〕 the Fifth 〔fifth, five〕. 《미·구》 // 당신은 묵비권을 행사할 권리가 있으며 변호사와 상의할 권리도 있다 You have the right to remain silent and the right to consult a lawyer.
묵비지 the lees from filtering the green-pea liquid to make jelly
묵살 默殺 ignoring (by keeping silence) ; taking no notice ; pretending not to know —하다 ignore ; take no notice 《of》 ; pretend not to know ; have no comment 《on》 ; treat 《something》 with silent contempt ¶ 의안을 묵살하다 pigeonhole 〔shelve〕 a bill // 제안을 묵살하다 smother up a proposal
⁑**묵상 默想** meditation ; contemplation ; musing ; (a) reverie ; a brown study —하다 meditate 《on》 ; contemplate ; muse 《on》 ; brood 《on》 ¶ 묵상적 contemplative ; meditative // 묵상에 잠기다 fall into (a) reverie ; indulge in reveries 《about the future》
묵새기다 make a long stay (eating the bread of idleness)
묵수 默守 adherence —하다 adhere 〔stick〕 to ; cling to ; keep to ¶ 구습을 묵수하다 keep〔cling〕 to old customs
묵시 默示 ① [신의] revelation ¶ 요한 묵시록 the Revelation of St. John the Divine ; the Revelation 《Rev.》 ; (the) Revelations ; the Apocalypse 《Apoc.》 // 묵시를 주다 reveal
② [암시] implication —하다 imply ¶ 명시 또는 묵시의 계약 an agreement expressed or implied
—록 the Book of Revelation ; the Revelation 《Rev.》 ; the Apocalypse 《Apoc.》
묵시 默視 —하다 overlook ; shut one's eyes 《to》 ; wink〔connive〕 《at》 ; tolerate ; pass 《a thing》 over in silence ; remain a mere spectator ; let go unchallenged ¶ 그 사실은 묵시할 수가 없다 I cannot shut my eyes to the fact.
묵약 默約 a tacit agreement〔understanding〕 ; an implicit promise〔contract〕 —하다 agree tacitly ; make a tacit agreement 《with》
묵언 默言 silence ; muteness —하다 keep silent ; utter no words
묵연 默然 —하다 (be) silent ; mute ; tacit ¶ 묵연하게 silently ; without saying anything ; mutely ; speechlessly // 묵연중에 허락하다 give a tacit permission
묵은 세배 —歲拜 bowing one's greeting to elders on New Year's Eve

묵은해 the old year ; the year that has been rung out ; last year
묵음 默音 ¶ 묵음의 silent ; 〖음성〗 mute
묵이 an old thing〔matter〕 ; old stuff
묵인 默認 connivance ; tacit consent 〔admission, permission, approval〕 ; toleration ; implied sanction **—하다** connive 《at gambling》 ; give a tacit consent to 《the marriage》 ; tolerate ¶ 묵인 가격 a permitted price // 묵인하에 행해지다 be done with 《a person's》 connivance // 네가 회사 돈을 가져가는 것을 묵인할 수 없다 I can't close my eyes to your taking company money.
묵자 默字 a mute (letter)
묵정밭 weed-grown fallow (field) ; a fallow that has turned to wasteland ; a deserted〔an abandoned〕 field
묵정이 old stuff ; stuff that has been laid aside for a long time ¶ 묵정이 땅 a fallow land // 묵정이 쌀 old rice
묵종 默從 passive obedience ; acquiescence **—하다** obey passively ; acquiesce 《in》 ; submit tamely〔unprotestingly〕 《to》
묵주 默珠 〖카톨릭〗 a (Roman Catholic) rosary
묵주머니 ① [묵의] a jelly bag ② [일의] a mess ; a wreck ¶ 일을 묵주머니로 만들다 make a mess of 《it》
묵죽 墨竹 a Chinese-ink painting that depicts bamboo
묵중 默重 taciturnity ; reticence **—하다** (be) taciturn ; reticent ; reserved
묵즙 墨汁 India(n) ink
묵지 墨紙 carbon (paper) ; copying paper ¶ 묵지를 받쳐 쓰다 take a carbon copy
묵직이 heavily ; gravely ; seriously ; solemnly ¶ 짐을 묵직이 싣다 load a heavy cargo ; pack a weighty load // 입을 묵직이 열다 talk in a grave〔serious〕 manner
묵직하다 ① (be) rather heavy〔weighty〕 ② [언행이] (be) rather grave〔serious, solemn, dignified〕 ¶ 묵직한 음성으로 in a grave tone // 묵직한 발걸음으로 with a dignified step // 입이 묵직하다 be rather taciturn
③ [뒤가] feel a bit heavy〔constipated〕 ¶ 뒤가 묵직하다 feel as if the bowel movement is still incomplete
묵척 墨尺 a carpenter's inking line
묵철 —鐵 bird shot ; a shot pellet of iron
묵허 默許 tacit consent ; connivance (법률) **—하다** consent tacitly ; give tacit permission ; connive 《at》 ; wink 《at》 ; pass over ¶ 묵허를 얻다 get a tacit consent from 《a person》 // 그것을 묵허하였다 He consented to it tacitly. // 경찰이 그것을 묵허하고 있다 The police authorities simply pass it over〔connive at it〕.
묵형 墨刑 tattooing on the face
묵화 墨畫 a painting in Chinese ink〔black and white〕 ; an Indian-ink drawing
— 화가 a chiaroscurist
묵흔 墨痕 ink marks ; handwriting (필적) ¶ 묵흔이 선명하다 be written vividly ; be written in bold strokes
묵히다 ① [버려두다] leave unused ; leave wasted ¶ 묵혀둔 땅 land lying idle ; land in fallow // 돈을 묵혀 두다 let one's money lie idle // 쌀을 묵히다 leave rice unused // 땅을 묵히다 lay land fallow ; fallow 《land, soil》
② [나그네를] give〔afford〕 shelter ; accommodate 《a person》 with a night's shelter〔lodging〕 ¶ 하룻밤 묵히다 give 《a person》 a night's lodging〔shelter for the night〕
⁑**묶다** ① bind ; tie ; fasten 《together》 ; bundle〔bunch, sheave〕 ¶ 짐을 묶다 tie up a bundle // 단으로 묶다 tie 《a thing》 into a bundle // 볏단을 묶다 sheave rice ; bind rice into sheaves // 개를 나무에 묶다 tie a dog to a tree // 상자를 끈으로 묶다 bind (up) a box with a cord // 일에 묶이다 be chained〔tied〕 to one's business // 시간〔규칙〕에 묶이다 be restricted by time〔rules〕
② [포박] bind ; tie ; fetter ; chain (쇠줄로) ¶ 죄인을 포승으로 묶다 tie a criminal with cord // 손발을 쇠줄로 묶다 chain 《a person》 hand and foot // 사람을 묶어 가다 arrest a person ; take a person away all tied up
묶어치밀다 [감정이] feel a lump rise in one's throat ; be filled 《with emotion》 ; have a fit 《of》 ¶ 가슴속에 묶어치미는 증오 the hatred rising〔heaving〕 within one // 마음속에 묶어치미는 슬픔 the sorrow welling up within one // 노여움이 묶어치밀다 have a fit of anger ; feel a lump rise in one's throat
⁑**묶음** a bundle ; a bunch ; a sheaf (곡물·서류 따위) ; a truss 《of hay》 ¶ 꽃 한 묶음 a bunch of flowers // 서류 한 묶음 a sheaf〔bunch〕 of papers // 한 묶음에 500원 500 *won* a bundle〔bunch〕 // 묶음을 짓다 make a bundle ; bundle 《things》 ; bunch ; do〔tie〕 up in bundles ; bunch into a bundle // 묶음으로 팔다 sell by the bundle〔bunch〕
⁑**묶이다** ① [물건이] be fastened together ; be bound〔tied, trussed, bundled, bunched, sheaved〕 ¶ 짐이 단단히 묶이다 a bundle is tied up tight
② [사람이] be bound〔tied up, fettered, chained〕 ¶ 손발이 묶이다 one's hands and feet are tied up
③ [정·의리 따위에] be tied〔fettered〕 by ; be overcome by ; [규칙 따위에] be bound by 《a rule》 ¶ 의리에 묶이어 in duty bound // 의리에 묶이다 be fettered by the bonds of obligation // 부모의 애정에 묶이다 be fettered by parental affection
문 文 ① [문장] a sentence ② [학문·문화]

literature ; letters ; the pen ¶ 문이 무보다 강하다 The pen is mightier than the sword. ③ [글] (a piece of) writing ; composition
—반 civil functionaries

†**문 門** ① [입구] a gate ; a door ; a gateway ; a portal ¶ 들어가는 문 the entrance ; the gate〔door〕《into a house》 // 나가는 문 the exit ; the gate〔door〕 out // 문으로 들어가다 go〔pass〕 through a gate // 문을 두드리다 knock at the door〔gate〕 // 문을 열어주다 open a gate〔door〕《for a person》 ; [기회] give an opportunity to ; open the gate to // 문을 잠그다 lock a door // 교회는 천당으로 들어가는 문이 아니다 The church is not a gateway to heaven.
② [부류] a department ; a special study
③ [집안] a family ¶ 김씨문 *Kim*'s family ; the *Kims*
④ [대포] cannons ¶ 대포 수문 several pieces of ordnance
방— a door 창— a window

문 紋 stripes ; lines ; streaks ; figures ; pattern ⇨ 무늬

문 問 a problem ⇨ 문제

문간 門間 the entrance〔front door〕 of a house ; the gateway ; [현관 앞] the doorway ; the porch ¶ 손님을 문간까지 전송하다 see a visitor off to the gate
—방 a room beside the entrance

문갑 文匣 a stationery chest (of drawers) ; a papeterie

문견 聞見 one's experience〔knowledge〕 ⇨ 견문

문경지교 刎頸之交 sworn friendship ; devoted friendship ; a friendship unto death ; a sworn〔devoted, bosom〕 friend

문고 文庫 ① [문갑] a box for stationery ; a papeterie ; [책장] a bookcase ; a book chest ; [서고] a library ; archives (기록 보존용) ¶ 마을 문고 a village library ② [문집] a collection of works ③ [총서] a library
—본(本) a pocket〔paperback〕 edition ; a paperbacked book ; a paperback

문고리 a door handle ; a door fastener ; a doorpull ; an iron ring attached to a door ¶ 문고리를 걸다 fasten〔latch〕 a door

문공 文公 [문화와 공보] culture and information ; [문교와 공보] education and information
국회 —위원회 the National Assembly Education-Information Committee

문과 文科 ① [인문과] the department of liberal arts《of a university》 ② [과거] the higher civil service examination ¶ 문과에 급제하다 pass the civil service examination
— 대학 a college of liberal arts

문관 文官 a civilian ; a civil official ; the civil service《총칭》
— 시험 the civil service examination — 우위 the superiority〔priority〕 of civil service to military service

문교 文敎 education ; culture ¶ 문교를 관장하다 be in charge of education // 문교당국 the educational authorities

문구 文具 ① [문방구] stationery ; writing materials ② [문식] rhetorical flourishes ; literary embellishment

문구 文句 a passage ; a paragraph ; a sentence ; words ; a phrase ; a clause ; [표현] an expression ¶ 편지의 문구 the wording of a letter

문구멍 門— a hole in a door〔window〕

문기둥 門— a doorpost ; a gatepost

문내 門內 ① [대문안] the inside of the gate ; within the gate ② [문중] the whole family〔clan〕

문단 文壇 [문학계] the literary world ; literary circles ; the world of letters ; the literati (문학자들) ; [문예란] a literary column ¶ 문단의 거성 a literary magnate // 문단의 스타 a star〔luminary〕 in the literary world〔firmament〕 // 한국의 문단 the Korean literary circles〔scene〕
— 시론 comments on current literary events — 의식 the consciousness of the current situation of the literary world —인 a writer ; a man of letters ; a literary man 기성 — existing literary circles 기성 —인 a writer〔an author〕 of established reputation

문단속 門團束 locking〔fastening〕 doors〔gates〕 ; securing the doors —하다 lock〔fasten〕 the doors securely ; secure the doors ¶ 문단속을 하지 않다 leave a door unlocked // 문단속이 되어 있는가 보러 돌아다니다 go around to see whether the doors are fastened

문답 問答 questions and answers ; a conversation ; a dialogue (대화) —하다 catechize (교리를) ; hold a dialogue ¶ 문답식 교수 catechism (교리상의) // 문답식으로 in the form of questions and answers ; in question and answer form
—식 교수법 the interrogatory method of teaching

문대다 rub ; scrub ; daub ⇨ 문지르다

문덕 falling apart《from》; decomposition ; crumbling〔falling〕 to pieces

문도 門徒 a disciple ; a follower ; an adherent ; a believer

문돋이 紋— patterned cloth ; brocade ; fabric with raised figures

문동개 門— the hole of the hinge panel of a door into which the hinge is put

문둔테 門— the hinge panel of a door

문둥병 —病 leprosy ; lepra ¶ 문둥병 환자 a leper // 문둥병 환자 수용소 a leper colony // 문둥병에 걸려 있다 be leprous

문둥이 a leper ; a lazar (거지) ¶ 문둥이 요양소 a leper hospital〔colony, house〕 ; a lazaret

문드러지다 crumble into decay ; molder away〔down〕; disintegrate ; decompose ; fall to pieces ¶ 비바람을 맞아서 문드러지다 fall to pieces as the result of exposure to wind and rain // 살이 썩어 문드러지다 flesh rots off

*__문득, 문뜩__ suddenly ; unexpectedly ¶ 문득 생각나다 《it》 suddenly occur 〔come〕 to one 《that》; remember 《a thing》 in a flash ; have a flash (of memory) // 사람 만날 약속이 문득 생각났다 It suddenly occurred to me that I had an appointment. // 문득 그들이 사기꾼이 아닐까 하는 의심이 일어났다 The suspicion flashed across his mind that they are impostors. // 지나간 일이 문득 생각난다 Suddenly I am reminded of the old days. // 옛 추억이 문득 머리에 떠올랐다 Old memories unexpectedly recurred to his mind.

문뜩문뜩 hauntingly ; suddenly〔unexpectedly〕once in a while ; at times

문란 紊亂 disorder ; confusion ; chaos ; breach **—하다** be in disorder ; be disorganized〔disordered〕; be in a tangle ¶ 문란케 하다 disorder ; disorganize ; throw 《a thing》 into confusion ; corrupt 《public morals》; derange 《social order》 // 문란해지다 fall into disorder

관기 — a breach of official discipline **풍기 —** an offense against public decency

문례 文例 an example 《for writing, to write after》; a model sentence

문루 門樓 the upper story of a castle 〔city〕 gate ; a tower gate

문리 文理 ① [문과와 이과] liberal arts and science(s) ② [문맥] the construction (style) of classical Chinese ; the context ③ [조리] the line of thought

—과 department of liberal arts and science(s) **—과 대학** the College of Liberal Arts and Science(s) **— 학부** the division of liberal arts and sciences

*__문맥 文脈__ context 《of a passage》 ¶ 문맥상의 contextual // 나는 이 글의 문맥을 알 수가 없다 I cannot make out the construction of this sentence.

문맹 文盲 illiteracy ; ignorance ; [사람] an illiterate (person) ; an ignoramus ; an unlettered person ¶ 문맹의 illiterate ; unlettered ; ignorant ; uneducated

—률 《lower》 the illiteracy rate **— 타파** a crusade against illiteracy ; the eradication of illiteracy

문머리 門— the upper frame of a gate 〔door〕

문면 文面 the contents〔wording〕 of a letter ¶ 문면에 의하면 according to what letter says // 편지의 문면은 다음과 같다 The letter reads as follows.

문명 文名 literary fame〔reputation〕 ¶ 문명을 떨치다 win literary fame ; make a name for oneself as an author

⁑**문명 文明** civilization ; enlightenment ¶ 문명된 civilized ; enlightened // 문명의 시대 a civilized age ; an enlightened age // 문명의 이기 modern conveniences ; facilities of civilization // 문명의 수준이 낮은 나라 a country low in the scale of civilization ; a backward country // 문명이 진보하다 civilization advances〔makes progress〕

— 개화 civilization and enlightenment **—국** a civilized nation〔country〕 **— 국민** a civilized people **—병** diseases incidental to civilization **— 비평** criticism on civilization **— 비평가** a critic on civilization **—사** the history of civilization ; a history of civilization (저술) **— 사회** civilized society **물질〔기계〕 —** material〔mechanical〕 civilization **서양 —** Western〔Occidental〕 civilization **원시 —** primitive culture

문묘 文廟 a Confucian shrine

문무 文武 [일] civil and military affairs ; the sword and the pen ; [직권] civil and military authority ; [기예] civil and military arts

— 겸전 having both literary and military accomplishments **— 백관** civil and military functionaries〔officials〕

문문하다 ① [부드럽다] (be) soft ; tender ; supple ¶ 문문한 고기 tender meat // 문문한 가죽 soft leather ② [우습게 보이다] be easy to deal with ; (be) soft ; be not firm ; (be) easygoing ¶ 문문한 사람 a pushover ; a person easy to deal with ; an easy mark 《속》

문문히 ① [부드럽게] softly ; tenderly ¶ 가죽을 문문히 이기다 tan leather soft // 고기를 문문히 삶다 cook meat tender ② [우습게] as a softy ; not being firm ¶ 사람을 문문히 보다 make light of a person ; look on a person as a softy ; think little of a person

문물 文物 civilization (문명) ; culture

서양 — Occidental civilization ; things Western

문미 門楣 a lintel (of a door)

문밖 門— ① [대문밖] outside the door 〔window, gate〕 ¶ 문밖에서 놀다 play outside near the door

② [성문밖] outside the city gate ; the suburbs〔outskirts〕 of a city ¶ 문밖 사람 a suburbanite ; a suburban resident // 서울 문 밖에 살다 live in the suburbs of *Seoul*

문발 門— a screen ; a blind ¶ 문발을 치다 hang a blind

*__문방구 文房具__ stationery ; writing materials

—점 a stationery shop〔store〕; a stationer's

문방사우 文房四友 the four precious things of the study

문뱃내 [술냄새] the smell of a drink ; a stale smell of wine ; a dead-wine smell

문벌 門閥 lineage ; pedigree ; birth ;

family ¶ 문벌이 좋은 사람 a man of family〔high birth〕; a man of renowned 〔good〕 lineage // 문벌 있는 집안에 태어나다 come of a distinguished family ; be high-born ; be of a noble birth // 문벌도 재산도 없다 He has neither birth nor money.

문범 文範 model composition(s) ; a model sentence

⁑**문법 文法** grammar ¶ 문법상의 grammatical // 문법상의 잘못 a grammatical error 〔mistake〕; a mistake in grammar // 문법에 구애하다〔하지 않다〕 adhere to〔be free of〕 grammar // 문법에 맞다〔맞지 않다〕 be grammatically correct 〔incorrect〕 // 문법적으로 이 글은 완전하나 관용적 어법은 못된다 Grammatically this sentence is all right, but it is hardly idiomatic.

—책 a《French》grammar **—학자** a grammarian **규범 —** prescriptive grammar **기술(記述) —** descriptive grammar **비교 —** comparative grammar **영 —** English grammar **일반 —** general〔universal〕 grammar **학교 —** school grammar

문병 門屛 a screen〔wall〕 in the doorway

*__문병 問病__ a visit to a sick person ; an inquiry after a sick person **—하다** pay a visit to a sick person ; inquire after a sick person ; go to ask after a sick person ¶ 입원중의 친구를 문병하다 visit a friend in hospital

문복 問卜 having one's fortune told **—하다** have one's fortune told ; consult a fortuneteller

문부 文簿 documents ; records ; an account book

문빗장 門— a door latch ; a gate bar ; a bolt ¶ 문빗장을 지르다〔빼다〕 latch 〔unlatch〕 the door

문사 文士 a literary man ; a writer ; a man of letters

문사 文詞, 文辭 expressions ; phraseology ; diction

문사극 文士劇 amateur stage performances by literary men

문살 the frame of a paper sliding door

문상 問喪 condolence ⇨ 조상

문새 門— the look〔style〕 of a door〔gate〕

⁑**문서 文書** a document ; a paper ; a record ; archives ¶ 문서로 in written form ; in writing // 문서를 교환하다 exchange notes // 모든 보고는 문서로 제출하라 Submit all reports in writing.

—과 the archives and documents section (관청의) ; the correspondence department (회사의) **— 놀음** paper transactions **— 위조(죄)** forgery of documents ; falsification **—철** a file **— 훼기** 〖법〗 spoliation **불온 —** dangerous〔inflammatory〕 literature ; subversive documents **외교 —** a diplomatic note **항복 —** an instrument of surrender

문석 文石 ① [마노] agate ② [문석인] the stone image in the form of a civil official erected in front of a royal tomb

문선 文選 ① 〖인쇄〗 type picking ② [선집] a selection of literary works ; an anthology **—하다** select literary works ; pick types

—공 a type picker

문설주 門— the side posts of a door 〔window, gate〕

문세 文勢 the force of (literary) style

— 점락(漸落) anticlimax

문소리 門— the noise made by opening or shutting a door〔window, gate〕 ¶ 문소리가 난다 I hear the door.

문수 文數 shoe size ; the size of shoes

문식 文飾 rhetorical embellishments 〔flourishes, ornaments〕

문신 文身 a tattoo《*pl.* ~s》; tattooing **—하다** tattoo ¶ 등에 용의 문신이 있다 have a dragon tattooed upon one's back

문신 文臣 a civil minister〔vassal〕

문신 門神 the spirit of the door

문아 文雅 elegance ; grace ; refinement **—하다** (be) elegant ; graceful ; refined ; polished

문안 門— ① [문의 안] within the gate ; inside the gate〔door, window〕 ¶ 문안에 들어서다 step inside the gate〔door〕; go〔come〕 into a room

② [성의 안] inside the city gate ; the city proper ¶ 문안 사람 a person who lives in the city // 문안에 살다 live in the city

*__문안 問安__ an inquiry after the health of《a person》; sending kind regards **—하다** inquire after《a person》; send kind regards ; pay a visit of courtesy

—객 a visitor ; a sympathizer ; an inquirer **— 편지** a letter of inquiry after《a person's》 health ; a sympathy card

문안 文案 ① [초안] a draft ¶ 문안을 작성하다 make a draft《of》; draft ② [문부] documents

— 작성자 a drafter ; a draftsman

문약 文弱 effeminacy ; literary indulgence to the neglect of military arts ¶ 문약해지다 become effeminate ; be given to polite pursuits at the expense of military arts

문어 文語 written language ; literary language ; [표현] literary expression

—투 a flavor of literary style

문어 文魚 an octopus ¶ 문어 단지 an octopus trap // 문어 데침 a boiled octopus

문어귀 門— an entry (way)

문어체 文語體 literary〔book〕 style ¶ 문어체의 영어 literary English // 문어체로 쓰다 write in a literary〔dignified, formal〕 style

문얼굴 門— a door frame

문예 文藝 literary art ; literature (문학) ; art and literature (문학 예술) ¶ 문예의 소양 literary accomplishments // 문예

에 조예가 깊다 be well versed in art and literature
— 과학 the science of literature — 기자 a literary writer — 독본 literary selections —란 a literary column〔page, section〕 —부 the literary section — 사조 the trend of literary thoughts — 영화 literary pictures〔films〕 —인 a literary man〔artist〕 — 작품 literary works〔productions〕 — 활동 literary activity

*문예 부흥 文藝復興 the revival of learning ; [유럽의] the Renaissance
— 시대 the period of the Renaissance

문예 비평 文藝批評 literary criticism ; a book review
—가 a literary critic ; a book reviewer

*문외한 門外漢 an outsider ; a layman ; a nonspecialist ¶ 문외한의 의견 an outsider's opinion ; a lay opinion // 그 문제에 대해서 나는 전혀 문외한입니다 I don't know the first thing about the subject.

문우 文友 a literary friend

문운 門運 the fortune of a family

문운 文運 cultural progress ; enlightenment ; civilization

문원 文苑 [문단] the literary world

문의 文義 the meaning〔effect, purport〕 of a passage

‡문의 問議 an inquiry —하다 make inquiry 《about》 ¶ 그에게 문의하다 inquire of him about 《a matter》
—서 a letter of inquiry —처 a reference

문인 門人 a pupil ; a disciple ; a follower

문인 文人 a man of letters ; a literary man
—극 a theatrical performance by men of letters — 사회 literary circles ; the literati 《라》 — 협회 the Literary Men's Association

문인화 文人畫 a painting in the literary artist's style
—가 a painter in the literary artist's style

문일지십 聞一知十 A word is enough to the wise. —하다 judge the whole by a part ; infer the whole from a single

†문자 文字 ① [글자] letters ; figures ; a character (문자 하나) ; an alphabet
② [구·관용구] a phrase ; an idiomatic phrase from the Chinese classics ¶ 문자를 잘 쓰다 be much given to quoting 〔using〕 phrases from classical Chinese // 문자 쓰기를 좋아하다 love to use old Chinese expressions
—반(盤) a dial (plate) ; the face 《of a clock》 ; the clockface
문자 그대로 관용 literally ; to the letter

문자새 門— doors and windows

문장 門帳 a curtain ; a hanging screen

†문장 文章 ① [글] a writing ; a composition ; [논문] an article ; an essay ; [산문] prose ; [문체] a style ¶ 문장에 능하다〔서투르다〕 write a good〔bad〕 style ; write cleverly〔poorly〕 // 문장으로 일세에 이름이 있다 glorify the age with one's writings
② [문(文)] a sentence ¶ 세련된 문장 a polished〔refined〕 sentence // 서투른 문장 a clumsy〔poor〕 sentence // 문장을 고치다〔고쳐쓰다〕 correct〔rewrite〕 a sentence // 다음 문장을 우리말로 옮기시오 Translate〔Put〕 the following sentences into Korean.
— 기예(技藝) the art of writing —론 syntax —어 written〔uncolloquial〕 style —체 literary style

문장 紋章 a crest ; family insignia ; a coat of arms

문장가 文章家 a good〔fine, clever〕 writer ; a stylist (문체가) ¶ 그는 문장가다 He writes a good style. /He is clever with his pen.

문장부 門— a door pivot

문재 文才 literary talent〔ability〕 ¶ 문재가 있는 사람 a person of〔gifted with〕 literary ability // 문재가 있다 have a talent for writing // 문재를 발휘하다 display〔show〕 a talent for writing

문전 文典 a grammar ; a grammar book

문전 門前 《in》 front of a gate ¶ 문전 성시 having a constant stream of callers // 문전 걸식하다 go out begging
문전 나그네 흔연 대접 속담 It is a sin against hospitality, to open your doors and shut your countenance.

문제 門弟 a pupil ; a disciple ; an apprentice ; a follower

문제 文題 the theme ; the subject 《of a composition》

†문제 問題 a question ; a problem ; an issue ; [제목] a subject ; a topic ; [일] a matter ¶ 금전의 문제 a money matter // 토의할 문제 a subject of discussion // 사활의 문제 a vital question // 문제의 인물 the man in question ; a man in the limelight // 문제의 다른 일면 the other side of the shield〔medal〕 // 아무도 손을 대지 아니 한 문제 an untouched subject // 문제를 내다 set 《a person》 a question // 문제에 답하다 answer a question // 문제가 생기다 a question arises // 문제를 일으키다 raise a question〔an issue〕 ; raise discussion ; [싸움을] get into trouble 《about》 // 문제가 안 되다 be out of the question ; do not matter // 문제에서 벗어나다 be beside the question // 문제가 되다 be discussed ; be brought up ; a question is raised 《whether, who》 // 문제를 해결하다 solve a problem // 문제 삼다 call 《a person's conduct》 into question ; take 《a person》 seriously // 문제삼지 않다 take no notice 《of》 ; do not care (a straw) 《about》 ; ignore // 정치 문제화하다 be made a political issue // 그것은 취미의 문제이다 It is a matter of taste. // 저 사람은 문제가 되지 않는다 He counts for nothing. /He's a cipher. // 이것은 별로 문제가 되지 않는다 This is a small matter. // 그가 무엇을 하든 문제가 되지 않는다 It matters little

what he does. // 그것 때문에 문제가 생겼다 This aroused〔caused〕 troubles in the company. // 그것이 중대한 국제적 문제가 됐다 It led to a grave international issue. // 무슨 문제가 생겼어 Is anything the matter? // 그는 어려운 문제를 다루는 것 같다 He appears to be skating on thin ice.
—아 a child who needs special care; a problem child 계쟁(係爭) — the question at〔in〕 issue 긴급 — a pressing 〔burning〕 question; an urgent problem 수학 — a problem in mathematics; a mathematical problem 시험 — an examination question〔paper (전체)〕

문제 의식 問題意識 《have》 a critical mind

문제자 門弟子 a disciple ⇨ 문제(門弟)

문제점 問題點 the point at issue; a controversial〔an open, a moot, a mooted 《미》〕 point ¶ 얼마간의 문제점을 제기하다 raise several points

문제화 問題化 —하다 become an issue; come into question; [표면화] come to a head〔the fore〕; [말썽] cause 〔give rise to〕 trouble ¶ 문제화되고 있다 be at issue

문조 文鳥 〖새〗 a paddybird; a Java sparrow

문죄 問罪 accusation; indictment; arraignment —하다 accuse 《a person》 of a crime; indict 《a person》 for 《murder》; arraign 《a person》 on 《a charge of a murder》

문주란 文珠蘭 〖식물〗 a crinum; Crinum maritimum (학명)

문중 門中 a family; a clan; one's kinsfolk; one's folks; one's kin; one's relatives

****문지기 門—** a gatekeeper; a janitor; a gateman; a doorman; a porter; a guard

문지도리 門— the hinges of a door

****문지르다** rub; scrub; scrape; chafe (손따위를); daub ¶ 눈을 문지르다 rub one's eyes // 문질러 지우다 rub out; erase // 문질러 없애다 rub off 《dirt》 // 찬 손을 문지르다 chafe one's cold hands // 마루를 걸레로 문지르다 scrub a floor with a floor cloth // 벽에 회를 문지르다 daub plaster on a wall // 얼굴에 먹을 문지르다 daub〔smear〕 one's face with Chinese ink // 문에서 페인트를 문질러 없애다 scrape paint from a door

****문지방 門地枋** a door〔window〕 sill; the threshold

문직 紋織 figured texture

문진 文鎭 a paperweight

문질리다 [사역] make〔have〕 《a person》 rub〔scour, scrub〕; get 《one's back》 massaged; [피동] be rubbed〔scoured, scrubbed〕

문집 文集 a collection of works; a prose collection; an anthology ¶ 셰익스피어 문집 a collection of Shakespeare's works

문짝 門— a leaf〔flap〕 of a door ¶ 문짝을 열어 젖히다 push〔pull〕 the door open

문창 門窓 a door and a window

문채 文采, 文彩 ① [문장의 광채] beautiful coloring; a lovely sheen ② [무늬] a figure; a pattern; a design

문책 問責 censure; reproof; reprimand; reprehension; rebuke —하다 censure; reprove; reprimand; reprehend; rebuke; call 《a person》 to account; take 《a person》 to task ¶ 문책받다 be reprimanded〔rebuked, censured〕 // 내각의 실정을 문책하다 censure the Ministry for its misadministration

문책 文責 the responsibility for the wording of an article ¶ 문책 재기자(在記者) The editor is responsible for the wording. /The responsibility for the wording lies with the editor.

문첩 文牒 an official document

***문체 文體** a literary style ¶ 구어적 문체 a colloquial style // 평이한 문체로 in a plain 〔an easy〕 style // A의 문체를 본받아 쓰다 write in the style of A
—론 stylistics 고— an antiquated style

문초 問招 questioning〔interrogating〕 a criminal; an examination —하다 question 《a criminal》; cross-examine 《a criminal》 ¶ 경찰의 문초를 받다 be examined by the police // 문초중이다 be under investigation〔examination〕; inquiry is now in progress

문치 門齒 an incisor; a fore-tooth

문치 文治 civil administration; administration by civilians
—파 a civilian party

문치적거리다 dilly-dally; vacillate; act shilly-shally; dawdle; waver ¶ 문치적거리다가 기회를 잃다 dally away one's opportunity

문치적문치적 shilly-shally; dawdling

문턱 a doorsill; a threshold ¶ 문턱에 걸터앉다 sit on a doorsill

문투 文套 a literary style〔form〕

문틀 門— the framework of a door; a doorframe

문틈 門— a crack〔chink〕 in the door 〔gate, window〕; a door opening ¶ 문틈으로 들어오는 바람 a draft 《미》; a draught 《영》 // 문틈으로 들어오는 바람을 막다 cut off the drafts // 문틈으로 들여다보다 peep〔look〕 in through a chink in the door

문패 門牌 a doorplate; a nameplate ¶ 문패를 내걸다 put up a doorplate

문풍지 門風紙 a weather strip; weather stripping 《총칭》 ¶ 문풍지를 달다 seal up 《a window》; weatherstrip 《the joints of a window》 // 문풍지를 달아 한기를 막다 paper out the cold wind

문필 文筆 literary art; literary pursuits; [신문·잡지업] journalism ¶ 문필로 생활하다 live by one's pen // 문필에 종사하다

be engaged in literary pursuit ; pursue literature ; follow the profession of letters // 문필에 재주가 있다 have a talent for writing
—가 a literary man ; a writer ; a knight of the pen ; a quill-driver (조소적으로)
— 노동 literary work

문필업 文筆業 the literary profession 〔occupation, pursuits〕 ¶ 직업은 문필업이다 I'm a writer by profession.

*문하 **門下** being under 《a person's》 instruction〔guidance〕
—생〔인〕 a disciple ; a student ; a follower ¶ 그는 대학에서 나의 문하생이었다 He was a student under me at the university.

⁑문학 **文學** literature ; letters ¶ 문학의 literary // 영문학을 연구하다 study English literature // 문학에 뜻을 두다 aspire to literary honors ; aspire to be a writer // 문학의 소양이 있다 have literary culture // 문학을 논하다 talk on〔discuss〕 literature
— 개론 an introduction to literature —계(界) the literary world ; literary circles ; the world of letters —과 a literary course —론 comments on literature ; [이론] a literary theory — 박사 [학위] Doctor of Literature 《Litt. D》 ; [사람] a doctor of literature —사(士) [학위] Bachelor of Arts 《B. A.》 ; [사람] a bachelor of arts —사(史) the history of literature ; a literary history ; [서적] a history of literature —상 a literary award — 운동 a literary movement — 작품 literary works〔writings, productions〕 — 잡지 a literary magazine — 청년 a young lover of literature ; a literary youth ; a youthful literary enthusiast〔aspirant〕 — 취미 literary taste ; interest in letters — 혁명 a literary revolution —회 a literary society ; a literary meeting (회합) 고전 — classic literature 근대 — modern literature 아동 — juvenile literature 에로 — erotic literature 통속〔대중〕 — popular literature

문학부 文學部 the department〔faculty〕 of literature ¶ 문학부의 학생 a lit. student〔boy, girl〕
—장 the dean of the literature department

문학서 文學書 a literary work〔book〕
경(硬)〔연(軟)〕— solid〔soft〕 readings

문학자 文學者 a man of letters ; a literary man ; a littérateur 《프》 ; the literati 《총칭》
영〔불, 독〕— a scholar of English〔French, German〕 literature

문한 文翰 ① writing ; literary arts ② [문필가] a writer ; a literary man
—가(家) a literary family

⁑문헌 **文獻** literature ; documentary records ; documents ¶ 프랑스 혁명에 관한 문헌 the literatures of the French Revolution // 지진에 관한 최초의 문헌 the first mention of〔reference to〕 earthquakes in literature // 여러 문헌을 조사하다 refer to sundry records // 그 기원에 관한 참조문헌이 없다 There is no literature to refer to〔consult about〕 its origin.
참고 — literature cited ; a bibliography

문헌학 文獻學 bibliography ; philology ¶ 문헌학적인 philological // 문헌학적으로 philologically

문형 文型 a sentence pattern

문호 文豪 a great〔master, eminent〕 writer〔author〕 ; a great man of letters ; a literary giant ; a literary luminary〔light〕

문호 門戶 the door ¶ 문호를 개방하다 open the door 《to》 // 문호를 폐쇄하다 exclude 《foreigners》 // 문호 개방 기회 균등의 원칙 the principles of the open door and equal opportunities for all nations

문호 개방주의 門戶開放主義 the policy of the open door ; the open-door policy

†문화 **文化** culture ; civilization ; cultivation

> 참고 **culture**는 정신면을 강조하고 **civilization**은 물질면 정신면을 다같이 포함한다 **cultivation**은 culture에 달하는 과정에 중점을 둔 말로서 「교화」라는 의미

¶ 문화적 cultural ; cultured ; civilized // 문화가 진보하다 advance〔make progress〕 in culture // 문화가 뒤떨어져 있다 be backward in civilization // 국가간의 문화 교류를 증진시키다 promote cultural exchange among nations // 한국의 문화 수준을 높이다 uplift the cultural level of Korea
— 국가 a cultural〔civilized〕 nation — 국민 a cultured nation — 교류 cultural exchange〔interchange〕 ; an exchange of culture — 단체 a cultural organization — 사절 a cultural envoy〔ambassador〕 — 시설 cultural facilities〔institutions〕 — 양식 〖사회〗 a culture pattern — 영화 a cultural〔an educational〕 film — 유산 cultural inheritance —인 a cultured man ; a man of culture —제(祭) a cultural festival — 주택 a new-type residence ; a modern dwelling (house) — 협정 a cultural agreement — 훈장 an Order of Cultural Merits ; a Cultural Medal

문화사 文化史 cultural history ¶ 한국 문화사 the history of Korean culture ; the cultural history of Korea

문화 생활 文化生活 a cultural〔cultured, modern〕 life ¶ 문화 생활을 하다 live a civilized life

문화 수준 文化水準 a cultural level ; a level of culture ¶ 문화 수준이 높다〔낮다〕 be high〔low〕 in national standards of culture // 고도의 문화 수준에 달하다 attain a high level of culture // 문화 수준을 높이다 raise the cultural standard

문화인 文化人 a man of culture ; a cultured〔civilized〕 man ; an intellectual ;

[자칭의] an illuminato 《*pl.* -ti》 ¶ 문화인인양 젠체하는 자 a culture snob

문화재 文化財 cultural assets〔properties〕 ¶ 중요 문화재로 지정되다 be designated〔registered〕 as important cultural property

— 보존 위원회 the Cultural Properties Protection Committee **— 보호법** the Cultural Properties Protection Act **무형 —** intangible cultural assets

문화주의 文化主義 culturism ; belief in culture

—자 one who believes in culture ; an advocate〔a devotee〕 of culture ; a culturist

문화 집단 文化集團 【사회】 a culture ¶ 두 개의 다른 문화 집단 two divergent cultures

문화 혁명 文化革命 [중국의] the Cultural Revolution ¶ 문화 혁명을 홍위병이 주도했다 The Red Guards took the initiative of the Cultural Revolution movement.

문후 問候 inquiring (by letter) after another's well-being ; paying one's respect to 《a person》 (by letter) **——하다** write a letter 《to》

†**묻다¹** ① [파묻다] bury ; [매장] inter ; inhume ; lay 《the body, a person》 to rest ; bury 《in a grave, under the ground》 ¶ 시체를 묻다 bury a corpse 〔body〕 ; bury 《a person's》 remains in the grave ② [감추다] cover ; conceal ; keep 《a matter》 from 《a person》 ; keep 《a matter》 under wraps ¶ 살인 사건을 비밀로 묻어두다 keep a murder case secret // 계획을 묻어두고 일반에게 알리지 않다 keep a plan from the general public

묻다² [들러붙다] stick 《to》 ; be stuck ; adhere 《to》 ; be covered ; be stained 《with》 ; be smeared 《with》 ¶ 피가 묻다 be stained with blood // 때가 묻다 be stained with dirt // 잉크가 묻다 be smeared with ink // 그을음이 묻지 않게 하다 keep clean of soot // 떡에 콩가루가 묻었다 Rice cakes are covered with bean flour. // 벽에 잉크가 묻었다 The wall is smeared with ink.

†**묻다³** ① [질문하다] ask ; question ; inquire of 《a person》 about 《a thing》 ; put〔pose〕 a question to 《a person》 ¶ 값을 묻다 ask the price // 글 뜻을 묻다 ask the meaning of a sentence // 역으로 가는 길을 묻다 ask 《a person》 the way to the station // 이름을 묻다 ask (for) 《a person's》 name // 그의 계획을 묻다 ask 《a person》 about his plan // 전문가한테 묻다 consult an expert // 한가지 더 묻겠다 I have another question to ask of you.

② [책임 따위] charge 《a person》 with 《responsibility》 ; call to account ¶ 책임을 묻다 call 《a person》 to account ; charge 《a person》 with responsibility

③ [안부·소식 따위] inquire〔ask〕 after ; inquire about ¶ 안부를 묻다 ask after 《a person, his health》 ; inquire after 《a person's》 safety // 소식을 묻다 ask how 《a person》 is getting along ; ask for news about 《a person》

묻히다¹ smear ; stain ; cover ¶ 손에 잉크를 묻히다 get〔have〕 one's hands stained with ink // 구두에 흙을 묻히다 get〔have〕 mud on one's shoes // 떡에 콩가루를 묻히다 cover a rice cake with bean flour // 붓에 먹을 묻히다 dip a writing brush in Chinese ink

묻히다² get buried ; be concealed ; be kept secret ¶ 눈에 묻히다 be under snow ; be snowed up // 묻혀 살다 live in obscurity // 그는 웨스트민스터 사원에 묻혀 있다 He lies buried at Westminster.

†**물¹** ① water ; the water(s) (강·호수·바닷물 따위) ¶ 물탄 위스키 whisky and water // 물을 긷다 draw water 《from a well》 // 물을 붓다 pour water 《into a kettle》 ; put water 《in》 // 물을 타다 add water 《to》 ; mix with water ; weaken ; dilute with water ; water // 물을 뿌리다 sprinkle water // 물을 주다 water 《flowers, plants》 // 물을 엎지르다 spill water // 물에 빠지다 be drowned // 물 쓰듯하다 spend 《money》 like water // 논에 물을 대다 draw water into a paddy // 물불을 가리지 않다 go through fire and water ; stick to 《a matter》 through thick and thin // 너 돈을 물 쓰듯하는구나 You spend money like water.

② [액체] liquid ; fluid ; [수액 따위] sap ; juice ¶ 잉크물 wet ink // 물약 liquid medicine // 나무에 물이 오르다 the sap rises〔runs〕 in a tree

③ [홍수] a flood ¶ 물이 나다 have a flood

④ [물고기의] freshness ¶ 물이 좋다 nice and fresh // 물이 나쁘다 be not so fresh

—발 the speed〔velocity〕 of flowing water **—비누** liquid soap ; soft soap (반 유동체의) **단—** sweet〔fresh〕 water **빗—** rain water **약(藥)—** medicinal〔mineral〕 water

물 밖에 난 고기 속담 Like a fish out of water.

물에 빠지면 짚이라도 잡는다 속담 A drowning man will catch at a straw.

물에 빠진 놈 건져 놓으니까 내 봇짐 내라 한다 속담 Save a stranger from the sea, and he'll turn your enemy. /Save a thief from the gallows and he'll cut your throat.

물에 빠진 생쥐 속담 Like a fish out of water.

물은 깊을수록 소리가 없다 속담 Still waters run deep.

물² dyed color ¶ 빨강물을 들이다 dye 《a thing》 red // 물이 들다 dye ; be dyed 《with》 ; take color ; be stained 《with》 ; be imbued 《with》 ; be tainted 《with》 // 핏물 들다 be stained with blood // 머리에 물

을 들이다 dye one's hair // 물을 빼다 bleach ; take the color out // 물이 날다 the color fades

물³ ① [빨래의] a wash ; the number of times clothes have been washed ¶ 한물 빤 옷 clothes that have been washed once // 새물 옷〔첫물 옷〕 new clothes that have yet to be laundered // 세물째에 옷이 못쓰게 되었다 The clothes gave way after the third washing.
② [과실·해산물 따위의 산출 시기] a crop ; a catch ; a flush ; the season in which something comes out in plenty ¶ 만물 사과 the first crop of apples // 끝물 고등어 the last catch of mackerel // 참외가 한물 졌다 Melons are in full flush. / Melons are at their best. // 딸기가 한물 갔다 Strawberries are past their best.
첫— the first products of the season

†**물가** the water's edge ; the edge〔verge, brink〕 of the water ; the waterside ; the shore ; the beach ¶ 물가에서 at the water's edge ; close by the water // 물가에 집을 짓다 build a house close by the water

*__물가 物價__ prices (of commodities) ¶ 물가가 오르다 prices advance〔rise, go up〕 // 물가가 내리다 prices decline〔fall, come down〕 // 물가를 내리게 하다 lower〔reduce, bring down〕 prices // 물가를 안정시키다 stabilize prices // 물가를 조절하다 regulate prices // 물가를 통제하다 control prices // 물가가 천정부지로 오른다 The prices are skyrocketing.
—고 high prices of commodities ; the increased cost of living — 대책 a (commodity) price policy — 동결 pegging 〔freezing〕 of prices — 동결령 the price-stop decree — 변동〔파동〕 price fluctuation — 수준 the price level — 악순환 price spiral — 안정 price stabilization 〔stability〕 — 조절 regulation of prices — 지수 a price index — 체계 a price structure〔system〕 —표 a price list — 현실화 price rationalization — 소비자 the consumer(s') price 주요 — prices of staple commodities ☞ ❰ p. 867 ❱

물가 등귀 物價騰貴 a rise〔an advance〕 in prices ; a price rise ¶ 물가 등귀의 경향이 있다 Prices have an upward tendency〔are tending upward〕.

물가 인하 物價引下 a price reduction
— 운동 a cut-price drive

물가 통제 物價統制 price control
—령 the Price Control Ordinance

물갈래 [지류] a branch〔fork〕 of a river ; a tributary 《of》 ; [분기점] a fork ; the point where a river forks ¶ 물갈래가 둘로 되다 fork into two rivers 〔streams〕 // 이것이 두 강의 물갈래이다 This is the point where the two rivers branch off.

물갈이 plowing a paddy with water in it
—하다 plow a paddy with water in it

물갈퀴 a web ; a webfoot

*__물감__ dyestuffs ; dyes ; color ¶ 물감을 들이다 dye // 물감이 날다 discolor ; fade ; become discolored // 물감이 잘 먹다 dye 〔take dye〕 well ; dye fast // 물감이 잘 안 먹다 dye badly
— 제조 dye making〔manufacture〕 합성〔인조〕 — synthetic〔artificial〕 dyes

물개 〖동물〗 a fur seal ; an otter ¶ 물개 가죽 sealskin

물거름 [액체 거름] liquid fertilizer〔manure〕
—통 a night soil bucket ; a honey bucket 《미·속》

물 거 리 sticks (used for fire) ; dead branches ; brushwood

물거리 —距離 distance by water ; navigable distance at high tide

물거미 〖곤충〗 a water spider ¶ 물거미 뒷다리 [비유적] a tall skinny person ; a beanpole

물거품 a bubble ; foam ; froth ¶ 물거품이 지다 bubble ; foam ; froth // 물거품처럼 사라지다 burst like a bubble ; come to nothing ; be brought to naught ; end 〔go up〕 in smoke

†**물건 物件** [물품] a thing ; an article ; stuff ; goods ; an object ¶ 증거 물건 material evidence // 이것은 내 물건이다 This is mine. /This belongs to me. // 물건이 좋다〔나쁘다〕 be of good〔poor〕 quality // 솔직히 말씀드리면 그 물건은 재고가 너무 쌓여서 밑지고 파는 겁니다 Honestly, we are overstocked on that item, so we are selling it below cost. // 우리는 그 물건을 취급하지 않습니다 We don't carry that item.
— 계약 a real contract — 목록 an inventory — 압류 attachment of objects

물걸레 a damp house〔floor〕 cloth ; a wet mop (자루 달린) ¶ 물걸레질을 하다 wipe〔mop〕 with a damp cloth

물것 biting insects

†**물결** a wave ¶ 잔 물결 a ripple // 큰 물결 a billow ; a surge // 거친 물결 wild〔raging〕 waves ; rough〔heavy, high〕seas // 잔잔한 물결 gentle waves // 물결이 일다 waves rise ; the sea gets up // 물결이 가라앉다 the sea goes down ; waves subside // 물결에 휩쓸리다 be washed〔swept〕 away by waves // 물결을 타다 ride (on) the waves〔surf〕 // 물결을 헤치고 나가다 plow through the (heavy) seas ; shear the sea // 시국의 물결을 타다 avail oneself of the situation // 사람들의 물결을 보고 있는 것만으로 눈앞이 빙빙 돌아간다 Just seeing all the people streaming by makes my head spin.
— 마루 the crest of a wave ; a wave crest — 소리 the sound〔roar〕 of the waves ; the booming of the sea — 이랑 the ridges of waves — 타기 surf-riding

물결치다 waves rise ; rise and fall (like waves) ; wave ; roll ; undulate ; dash

물 가

물가수준 price level **물가지수** price index **소비자 물가지수** CPI(consumer price index) **도매 물가지수** wholesale price index **물가상승** price rise [increase] **물가상승률** price increase rate; rate of price increase **물가폭등** price spurt [spiral, climb] **물가하락** price fall [decline, decrease] **물가폭락** price tumble [plunge, nose dive] **물가안정** price stability **물가억제** price suppression ¶ 물가를 억제하다 suppress prices; suppress the rise of prices; suppress higher prices **소매〔소비자〕가격** retail[consumer] price **도매가격** wholesale price **정가** list [fixed] price **시장가격** market price **이중가격** two-tier prices; dual prices **독점가격** monopoly[monopolistic] price **가격통제** price control **가격 동결** price freeze **가격을 유지하다** hold the price line **물가 슬라이드 제(制)** indexation; indexing; index-linking **가격 조작** price adjustment [management]; price fixing [rigging, manipulation] **가격차별** price discrimination **가격협정** price cartel **물가통제위원회** price commission **정가표** price list [tag] **업자동맹** price ring 《가격유지 목적의》 **가격인하 싸움** price war

《against》 ¶ 물결치는 대로 at the mercy of the waves // 물결치는 바다 a rolling sea // 바람에 물결치다 waves rise in the wind // 절벽에 물결치다 waves dash against〔break on〕 the foot of a cliff // 밀이 바람에 물결치다 wheat undulates in the wind

물경 勿驚 surprisingly〔startlingly〕 (enough) ; it will surprise you 《but》 ; you would be surprised 《but》 ; You have got a surprise coming ! ¶ 쌓인 빚이 물경 100만원이었다 The debt went on increasing, reaching at last a surprising amount of one million *won*.

물계 [쌀] low-grade rice mixed with glutinous rice

물계 物— [시세] the current〔selling〕 price ¶ 그는 물계에 환하다 He is well-informed in current prices.

물계 物界 the material〔physical〕 world

물고 物故 death of an eminent〔notorious〕 person ¶ 물고나다 die ; be dead // 물고내다 kill 《a person》 ; execute a criminal

†**물고기** a fish ; fish ¶ 바닷물고기 sea-fish // 물고기 뼈 a fish bone // 물고기 장수 a fishmonger 《영》 ; a fish dealer ; a fish-peddler (행상) // 물고기를 낚다 angle for fish // 물고기를 잡다 catch a fish ; fish

물고기

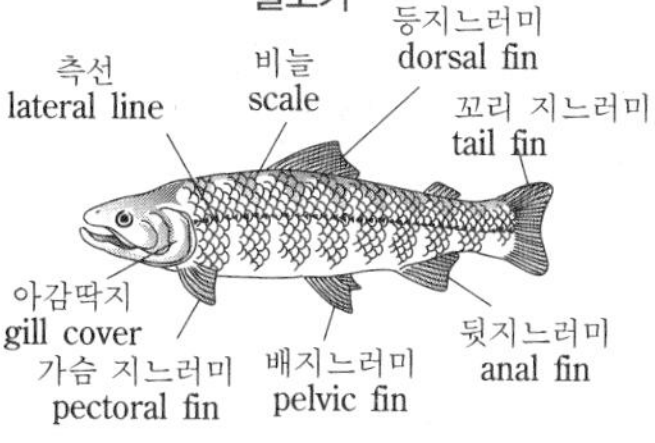

물고기자리 〖천문〗 the Pisces ; the Fishes **—떼** a shoal of fishes

물고 늘어지다 ① [입으로] bite at〔sink one's teeth into〕 something and hang on to it ¶ 개가 그의 목을 물고 늘어졌다 The dog sank his teeth in his throat and hung on.
② [집요하게] stick to ; hang〔hold〕 on 《to》 ; get〔have〕 a firm grip on 《one's rival》 ¶ 끝까지 물고 늘어지다 stick to one's last // 집요한 질문으로 국무 위원을 물고 늘어지다 harass a state minister with repeated interpellations〔questions〕

물고동 a faucet ; a tap

물고랭이 〖식물〗 a bulrush ; a club rush

물고의 —袴衣 shorts for working in water

물곬 a channel ; a water course ; a drain ¶ 도랑에 물곬을 내다 make a drain in a ditch // 물곬이 메다 a drain is stopped up

***물구나무서다** stand on one's (head and) hands ; stand on end ; do a hand-stand ¶ 물구나무서기 hand-standing (체조) // 물구나무서서 걷다 walk on one's hands

물구덩이 a pool ; a (mud) puddle ¶ 물구덩이가 생기다 pools form // 물구덩이에 빠지다 get〔fall〕 into a puddle

물굽성 —性 〖식물〗 hydrotropism **양성(陽性)〔음성(陰性)〕 —** positive 〔negative〕 hydrotropism

물굽이 a bend〔curve〕 in a river〔stream〕 ¶ 물굽이지다 wind (in and out) ; meander ; bend ; have a bend ; curve // 개천이 숲 속을 물굽이져 흐른다 A brook winds〔runs in twists and loops〕 through the woods. // 강이 굽이굽이 물굽이져 흘러간다 The river meanders along with many twists and turns.

물권 物權 a real right ¶ 물권의 이전〔설정〕 the transfer〔creation〕 of a real right **—법** the Law of Reality〔Realty〕

물귀신 a water demon ¶ 물귀신이 되다

drown ; be drowned (to death)
물그릇 a water bowl
물그림자 shadows on the water
물금매 **―金梅** 〖식물〗 a primrose willow ; Jussiaea repens (학명)
물긋물긋하다 (be) very thin ; weak ; watery ; washy
물긋하다 (be) somewhat thin ; watery ; washy
물기 **―氣** moisture ; dampness ; wetness ¶ 물기가 있다 be moist ; be damp ; be wet // 물기가 없다 be dry ; be husky
물기근 **―飢饉** a water famine ; the shortage of water supply
물기둥 a column of water
물기름 hair oil
물길 a waterway ; a watercourse ; a water route ¶ 물길을 따라 항해하다 sail along a waterway
― 측량 a hydrographical survey **― 측량술** hydrography **― 표지** a beacon
물김치 watery plain〔flat〕 *kimchi*
물까치 〖새〗 the blue magpie
물까치수염 〖식물〗 a kind of loosestrife
물꼬 a sluice gate ; an irrigation gate
*__물끄러미__ with a blank〔vacant〕 look ; 《look》 blankly ; vacantly ; absent-mindedly ; abstractedly ¶ 물끄러미 바라보다 look〔gaze〕 vacantly〔blankly〕 《at》 // 얼굴을 물끄러미 쳐다보다 gaze〔look〕 abstractedly〔blankly〕 at 《a person's》 face ; turn bemused eyes toward 《a person》
물난리 **―亂離** ① [수재] a flood disaster ¶ 물난리가 나다 have a flood disaster ② [식수난] trouble〔confusion〕 resulting from a water shortage
물납 **物納** payment in goods〔kind〕 **―하다** pay 《taxes》 in kind
―세 a tax in kind **― 지세(地勢)** a land tax in kind **세금 ―** payment of tax in kind
물내리다[1] [기운빠짐] become weak 《due to an illness, agony, etc.》 ; lose one's strength〔vitality, sap〕 ; be sapped ; be devitalizd
물내리다[2] [체질] resift rice flour on a loose sieve while pouring water over it
물너울 swell on the sea ; rolling of the waves ¶ 바다에 물너울치다 waves roll〔swell〕 on the sea
물놀이 ① [잔 물결] rippling〔wrinkling〕 of water ② [어린이들의] dabbling in water **―하다** 《water》 ripple ; wrinkle ; dabble in water ; splash water playfully
*__물다__[1] ① [깨물다] bite ¶ 개가 문 자국 a mark left by a bite of a dog // 개가 사람을 물다 a dog bites (at) 《a person》 // 물어뜯다 bite off ; gnaw off〔away〕 ; cut off with the teeth // 로프를 물어 끊다 bite a rope in two // 혀를 물어 끊다 bite off one's tongue // 물어 죽이다 bite to death // 오늘은 고기가 잘 문다 The fish are biting well today.
② [물것이] bite ¶ 모기가 물다 mosquitoes bite // 벼룩 문데가 가렵다 The fleabite itches.
③ [이권 따위를] get〔catch〕 《속》 ¶ 계집이 사내를 물다 a woman gets a man // 그는 그 부자를 물었다 He caught the rich man. /He got〔had〕 a stand-in with the rich man. 《미·속》
④ [입에] hold〔put〕 in the mouth ; hold〔have〕 between the teeth ¶ 물을 입에 물다 hold water in one's mouth // 담뱃대를 입에 물다 put〔hold〕 a pipe between one's teeth
⑤ [톱니바퀴 따위가] gear with ; be in gear with ; engage 《in, into》 ¶ 서로 물고 있는 톱니바퀴 engaged wheels
무는 개 짖지 않는다 〔속담〕 A barking dog never bites.
물다[2] ① [갚다] pay ; repay ; return ¶ 입장료를 물다 pay an admission fee〔charge〕 // 책값을 물다 pay for a book // 빚을 물다 pay〔repay〕 one's debt // 세금을 물다 pay a tax〔duty〕 // 벌금을 물다 pay a penalty〔fine〕
② [손해를] pay for ; compensate for ; reimburse ; indemnify ; make good ; make reparations for ; cover 《a loss》 ¶ 손해를 물어주다 indemnify 《a person》 for damage ; compensate 《a person》 for loss ; make up for 《a loss》 // 깨지면 물어드리죠 If it breaks, I will pay for it. // 그 나라는 자국의 침략으로 손해를 입은 나라들에게 배상을 물었다 The country paid reparations to the countries which suffered from its aggression.
③ [대신] pay〔compensate〕 on behalf of 《another》 ¶ 가난한 학생의 공납금을 물어주다 pay a tuition fee for a poor student // 고맙게도 그는 나의 입원비를 물겠다고 제의했다 With beautiful generosity, he offered to pay for my hospitalization.
물다[3] [상하다] go bad (in heat or moisture) ; spoil ; turn sour (우유) ; be stale ; rot ¶ 더위로 물고기가 곧 물었다 The fish soon went bad in hot weather. // 물기 시작했다 Rot has set in.
물덤벙술덤벙 blindly ; aimlessly ; heedlessly ; at random〔haphazard〕 ; in random way **―하다** act blindly〔naively〕 ; go it blind
물독 a water jar ; a water jug
물동 [둑] a dam ; [광산의] a prop〔support〕 used to hold the puddle in a mine
물동 계획 **物動計劃** a materials mobilization plan ; a program for the mobilization of material resources
물동이 a water jar
물두부 **―豆腐** bean-curd cakes cooked in water
*__물들다__ ① [빛깔이] dye ; get dyed ; take color ¶ 거멓게 물들다 be dyed black // 잘 물들다 dye well〔fast〕
② [오염] get stained ; get smeared ¶ 잉

크물이 들다 be stained with ink // 피로 물들다 be stained〔smeared〕 with blood
③ [감염] be imbued with ; be tainted 〔contaminated〕 with ¶ 악에 물들다 be tainted with vice // 도시풍에 물들다 be imbued with urban〔city〕 manners

*물들이다 dye 《a thing》 ¶ 머리를 물들이다 dye one's hair // 장미색으로 물들이다 dye 《a thing》 rose-colored // 손톱을 벌겋게 물들이다 paint〔enamel〕 one's nails red

물딱총 —銃 a water pistol ; a squirt gun ¶ 물딱총 놓다 squirt water

물때[1] ① [조수의 때] tide time ② [밀물때] high tide ¶ 물때를 기다리다 wait for high tide // 물때를 놓치다 miss the high tide // 물때가 이르다 It is too early for the high tide.

물때[2] fur ; incrustation ; slime ¶ 물때가 끼다 fur forms // 물때를 벗기다 clean fur 《from a kettle》 // 주전자의 안쪽에 물때가 끼어 있다 The inside of the kettle is incrusted with slime.

물때까치 [새] a Chinese great grey shrike

물똥 [물찌똥] watery〔loose〕 feces

물똥싸움 a water fight ; splashing water on each other —하다 have a water fight

물똥 튀기다 splash〔spatter〕 water

물량 物量 the amount〔quantity〕 of materials〔resources〕 ¶ 물량의 우세 material odds ; physical superiority // 물량의 힘을 과시하다 let one's material superiority tell on 《the enemy》 // 물량으로 압도하다 overwhelm 《the enemy》 with material superiority
전(全)— 방식(方式) [노동] the market basket formula

*물러가다 ① [뒤로] move backward ; fall〔draw, step〕 back ; back ; retreat ; withdraw ; pull out ¶ 한걸음 뒤로 물러가다 take a step backward // 한 걸음도 안 물러가다 hold every inch of the ground ; do not budge an inch backward ; do not yield a foot〔an inch〕
② [떠나다] withdraw 《from》 ; retire from ; leave ; take one's leave ; [사직] resign ; quit ¶ 어른 앞에서 물러가다 withdraw from the presence of superiors // 왕 앞에서 절하고 물러가다 bow oneself away from the king's presence // 자기 방으로 물러가다 retire to one's room // 공직에서 물러가다 resign〔withdraw〕 from public life // 대학 교수직에서 물러가다 leave〔resign from〕 the faculty of the university // 그만 물러가겠습니다 I think I must be off〔going now〕. // 물러가라 Away with you (from my presence) !
③ [연기] be put off ; be postponed ; be held over ; be set back ¶ 결혼 날짜가 사흘 물러갔다 The marriage date was set back three days.

*물러나다 ① [어긋나다] fall off ; come off ; come loose ; be〔get〕 out of place ¶ 담돌이 물러나다 a stone falls〔comes〕 out of a wall // 책상 다리가 물러나다 a leg of the table comes loose
② [후퇴] fall〔draw〕 back ; withdraw ; retreat ; retire ; leave ; pull out ¶ 식탁에서 물러나다 withdraw〔retire〕 from the table // 물러날래야 물러날 수 없다 I am in for it now. /I have gone too far to retreat. /I cannot withdraw〔turn back〕 now.
③ [은퇴] retire ; resign ; quit ; leave ¶ 실업계〔영화계〕에서 물러나다 retire from active business〔the screen〕 // 관직에서 물러 나다 withdraw from one's office

*물러서다 ① step〔stand〕 back〔aside〕 ; move off ; get out of the way ¶ 한걸음 물러서다 take a step backward // 한걸음도 물러서지 않다 do not budge an inch backward // 뒤로 물러서다 move off to the rear // 사람이 지나가게 물러서다 make way for 《a person》
② [사임] retire ; resign ; leave ; quit ¶ 교수직을 물러서다 retire from professorship // 조정에서 물러서다 leave government service

물러앉다 ① [뒤로] draw one's seat back ; move one's seat backward ② [지위에서] retire ; resign ; leave ③ [내려앉다] collapse ; be flattened ; be crushed ; come〔go〕 to smash

물러오다 retrace 《one's steps》 ; come 〔go, turn〕 back ; retreat ; recede ; retrogress ¶ 가던 길을 물러오다 retrace one's steps〔way〕 // 적이 물러오다 the enemy comes〔falls〕 back in retreat

물러지다 ① [무르게 되다] get soft ; soften ; grow tender ¶ 감이 물러지다 a persimmon softens up // 고기가 물러지다 meat becomes tender // 양초를 불에 대면 물러진다 Wax softens in heat.
② [마음이] soften ; be pacified〔mollified, appeased〕 ¶ 마음이 물러지다 one's heart softens ; one is pacified

물렁팥죽 ① [사람] a softy ; a milksop ; a pushover ② [물건] soft stuff

물렁하다 ① (be) soft ; tender ; juicy ; overripe ¶ 감이 익어 물렁하다 The persimmon is ripe and juicy.
② [성질] (be) yielding ; flabby ; flaccid ; limp ; soft ; weak-kneed ¶ 물렁한 성질 a yielding disposition〔temper〕 // 물렁한 살 flabby flesh〔muscles〕 // 물렁한 사람 a flabby character ; a person easy to deal with ; a pushover ; a softy ; a milksop

*물레 a spinning wheel ¶ 물레질하다 spin on a spinning wheel
—바퀴 the wheel of a spinning wheel 〔water mill〕 —질 spinning ; making yarn
물렛가락 a spindle 물렛돌 a stone put on the base of a spinning wheel (to keep it stable) 물렛줄 a spinning-wheel belt

물레방아 a water mill〔wheel〕

*물려받다 inherit 《from》; take over; obtain by transfer; receive ¶ 아버지의 재산을 물려받다 inherit〔succeed to〕 one's father's property // 왕위를 물려받다 succeed to the throne // 사업을 물려받다 take over the business

*물려주다 hand〔make〕 over; bequeath 《property》 to 《a person》; transfer; abdicate (왕위·권리를) ¶ 전 재산을 아내에게 물려주다 make over all one's property to one's wife

물려지내다 move〔be〕 at another's beck (and call); be kept under 《a person's》 thumb; be at 《a person's》 mercy; be in 《a person's》 clutches ¶ 아내에게 물려지내다 He is under his wife's thumb.

물력 物力 ① physical force; one's resources; wealth ② [재료와 노력] materials and efforts ③ [물역] construction materials

물론 勿論 (as a matter) of course; needless to say; not to mention; to say nothing of; naturally; undoubtedly; to be sure ¶ 물론 그렇다 Of course, it is. // 영어는 물론 불어도 한다 He speaks French, not to speak of〔mention〕 English. // 예외가 있는 것은 물론이다 It goes without saying that there are exceptions.

*물리 物理 [자연의 이법] natural〔physical〕 laws; the laws of nature; 〖물리〗 physics ¶ 물리적 physical // 물리적인 성질 physical properties // 물리적인 현상 a physical phenomenon // 물리적으로 불가능한 physically impossible

—관(觀) physical〔materialistic〕 view of the universe; materialism — 광학 physical optics — 변화 a physical change — 실험 an experiment in physics

물리다¹ [싫증나다] be fed up 《with》; get sick 《of》; have had enough 《of》; be satiated; grow tired 《of》 ¶ 물리도록 to one's fill; to satiety // 물리도록 먹다 eat one's fill; fill up // 냉면에 물리다 be fed up with cold noodle dishes // 단것에 물리다 have had one's fill of sweets // 소설에 물리다 grow weary of reading novels // 아무리 보아도 물리지 않다 never grow weary of gazing 《at》

물리다² [익히다] cook soft〔tender〕; soften ¶ 고기를 푹 물리다 cook meat tender enough // 감자를 물리다 steam potatoes soft

물리다³ ① [미루다] put off; postpone; defer ¶ 이틀 물리다 put it off for two days // 화합 날짜를 물리다 postpone (the date of) a meeting // 일요일까지 물리다 put off〔defer〕 till Sunday

② [옮겨 놓다] change direction; turn; shift; switch over; remove

③ [물려주다] hand〔turn〕 over; leave; bequeath; transfer; yield; convey; abdicate (지위·권리) ¶ 권리를 남에게 물려주다 transfer one's right to another // 조카에게 유산을 물려주다 leave a legacy to one's nephew // 소유권을 아우에게 물리다 yield one's right of possession to one's little brother // 입던 옷을 동생에게 물려주다 pass one's clothes on to one's brother

물리다⁴ [치우다] clear away; put away; take away ¶ 밥상을 물리다 take away the table; have finished eating // 장농을 물리고 책상을 놓다 take away a chest and put a desk in its place

물리다⁵ [쫓다] drive away〔out〕; exorcise; expel; dispel ¶ 악귀를 물리다 exorcise evil spirits 《from, out of》

물리다⁶ get bitten ¶ 미친 개한테 물리다 be bitten by a mad dog // 모기한테 물리다 be bitten by a mosquito

물리다⁷ make pay; make compensate; make reimburse; impose 《a tax, a penalty》 on 《a person》 (세금·벌금) ¶ 깨뜨린 그릇 값을 물리다 make 《a person》 pay for a broken dish // 농작물에 끼친 손해를 물리다 make 《a person》 pay compensation for the damage done to one's crops

물리 요법 物理療法 physiotherapy; physical therapy〔treatment〕

물리치다 ① [거절] decline; refuse; reject; spurn; repel; turn down ¶ 요구를 물리치다 reject 《a person's》 demand; turn down〔refuse〕 《a person's》 request // 선물을 물리치다 decline a gift // 뇌물을 물리치다 spurn a bribe // 제의를 물리치다 turn down 《a person's》 proposal // 충고를 물리치다 ignore 《a person's》 advice

② [격퇴] drive back〔away〕; beat off〔back〕; repel; repulse ¶ 적을 물리치다 repulse〔dislodge〕 the enemy; drive the enemy away // 유혹을 물리치다 thrust temptation away

③ [사람을] keep away ¶ 사람을 물리치고 밀담하다 get 《a person》 off from others for a private talk; be closeted together; have a private talk with 《a person》 behind closed doors

*물리학 物理學 physics; physical science ¶ 물리학적 physical

— 기구(器具) physical instrument —자 a physicist; a natural philosopher 실험 — experimental physics 이론〔응용〕(理論〔應用〕) — theoretical〔applied〕 physics 정신 — psycophysics 지구 — geophysics

물리 화학 物理化學 [물리학적 화학] physical chemistry; chemicophysics

물림 ① [연기함] putting off; postponement ② 〖건축〗 an extra space of half a *kan* added to a regular room as a kind of porch ③ [넘겨받음] property handed down〔bequeathed, transferred〕; a hand-me-down (옷·물건) ¶ 물림 재산 property bequeathed by one's forefathers; the family fortune; the inheritance

물림쇠 a staple ; a metal bend ; a clamp
물마 an overflow ; a flood
물마개 [병 따위의] a stopper ; [코르크로 만든] a cork ; [수도 따위의] a stopcock ; [구멍을 막는] a peg ; a plug ; [배밑바닥 따위의] a bung
물마루 the crest of waves ; a swell
물만두 —饅頭 a stuffed bun boiled in water
물말이 ① [밥] cooked rice served in water ② [젖은 것] a thing drenched with water ; dripping-wet clothes (옷) ¶ 비를 맞아 옷이 물말이가 되다 one's clothes get soaked with rain
물맛 the taste of water ¶ 물맛이 짜다 The water tastes salty.
물망 物望 the hope of the people ; popular favor ¶ 물망에 오르다 win public 〔popular〕 support ; rise in〔to〕 popularity
물망초 勿忘草 『식물』 a forget-me-not
물맞이 drinking〔bathing in〕 mineral water **—하다** drink〔bathe in〕 mineral water ; take the waters ; try the waters for medical purposes
물매[1] [매질] hard flogging〔whipping〕 ¶ 물매맞다 be flogged hard // 물매치다 punish 《a person》 with a good sound flogging
—질 flogging〔whipping〕 hard
물매[2] [경사] the slope〔slant, pitch〕 of a roof ¶ 물매가 싸다 The roof has a steep enough slant to it. // 물매가 뜨다 The roof is not steep enough.
물매[3] [무릿매] a sling (for throwing stones) ; a slingshot ¶ 물매로 과일을 따다 knock off fruits with a slingshot hard
물매질 flogging〔whipping〕 **—하다** flog 〔whip〕 hard
물멀미 dizziness〔vertigo〕 caused by looking at a vast expanse of water ; seasickness **—하다** fell dizzy〔seasick〕 ¶ 저는 물멀미를 잘해요 I am a bad〔poor〕 sailor.
물면 —面 the surface of water
물명 物名 the name of a thing〔an article〕
물목 ① [아귀] a point at which the water flows out ; the fork of a river 〔stream〕 (물갈래) ; the narrows (해협 따위) ¶ 물목을 지키다 stand watch at the fork of a river
② [사광에서] the spot where gold dust pans thickest
물목 物目 a catalog of goods ; a list of articles
물몽둥이 a kind of hammer (used by blacksmiths and masons)
물문 —門 a sluice ; a floodgate ; a lock (gate) ; a penstock ; a flash
— 관리인 a lock keeper — 통행세 lockage
*물물 교환 物物交換 barter ; bartering ; truck ; dicker 《미》 **—하다** barter ; truck ; dicker ; swap 《미》 ¶ 물물 교환으로 by barter ; on the barter system // 소금과 식량을 물물 교환하다 barter〔trade〕 salt for eatables
물미 a spike
— 작대기 a spiked prop on an A-frame
물밀다 rise ; flow ; come in ¶ 물밀 때 the flow of the tide ; tide time // 물밀 듯이 들이닥치다 be deluged 《with tourists》 ; rush like a flood
물밑 [바닥] the bottom of the water 〔sea, river〕 ; [해면 아래] under the water ¶ 잠수함은 물밑을 다닌다 Submarines sail under the water.
물바가지 a gourd for dipping water
물바람 a wind blowing over the water
물박 ⇨ 물바가지
물받이 [세로의] a waterspout ; a downspout ; a downpipe ; a rain leader〔pipe〕 ; a drainspout ; [가로의] a gutter ; an eaves trough
물방개 『곤충』 a Korean water beetle
물방아 ① [물레방아] a water mill ¶ 물방아에 곡식을 찧다 grind grain in a water mill ② [방아 두레박] waterwheel buckets
물방아잠자리 『곤충』 a kind of dragonfly ; Anotogaster sieboldii (학명)
†물방앗간 a water mill
물방울 a drop of water ; a water drop
— 무늬 polka dots
물벌레 a water insect ; a water beetle
물베개 a (rubber) water-pillow
물벼 undried rice
물벼락 sudden down-fall〔pouring〕 of water
물벼락 맞다 관용 get doused〔a dousing〕 ; be suddenly poured over with water
물벼룩 a water flea
물병 —瓶 a water bottle〔flask〕 ; 『불교』 a water bottle dedicated to the image of Buddha
유리 — a carafe
물보낌 a wholesale whipping〔lashing, flogging〕 **—하다** whip〔lash, flog, cane〕 one person after another
*물보라 a spray (of water) ¶ 물보라를 일으키다 raise spray ; send up clouds of spray
물볼기 whipping〔flogging〕 a woman wearing drenched〔wetted〕 underwear
물봉숭아 『식물』 a touch-me-not ; a kind of snapweed
물부리 ① [담뱃대의] the mouthpiece of a pipe ② [궐련의] a cigarette holder ; a mouthpiece
물분 —粉 liquid makeup ; a face-powder fluid ; a liquid cosmetic〔foundation〕
물불 water and fire ¶ 물불을 가리지 않고 through thick and thin // 그녀는 그를 위해서라면 물불을 가리지 않는다 She goes through fire and water〔through thick and thin〕 for his sake.

물비누 liquid soap ; soft soap (반유동체의)
물비린내 a fishy smell of water
물빛 ① [물감의 빛깔] dye color ; dyed color ② [물색] aquamarine ; light blue ; water green ; bluish green
물산 物産 local products ; produce 《총칭》
물살 the current〔flow〕 of water ¶ 물살이 빠르다 The current is swift.
물상 物像 the shape of an object
물상 物象 ① [사물] an object ② [현상] material phenomena ③ [학과] the science of inanimate nature
물상 담보 物上擔保 a secured mortgage ; a real security ¶ 물상 담보부 사채 mortgage bonds // 물상 담보부 장기 차입금 〖부기〗 mortgages payable
물새 a waterfowl ; a water bird ; an aquatic bird
물색 物色 ① [물건의 빛깔] the color of a thing ② [물들인 빛] dyed color ③ [풍경] nature ; scenery ; landscape ④ [고름] selecting ; [찾음] looking for **—하다** [찾다] look for ; search for ; hunt up ; [고르다] select ; pick out ; single out ; take one's pick 《from》 ¶ 일자리를 물색하다 hunt for a job // 후계자를 물색하다 look for a successor
물색없다 (be) unreasonable ; absurd ; extraordinary
물샐틈없다 ① (be) watertight ② [완벽하다] (be) strict ; rigorous ; watertight ¶ 물샐틈없는 상자 a watertight box // 물샐틈없는 변론 watertight argument // 물샐틈없는 경계 a strict watch〔vigil〕 // 물샐틈없는 수비 (야구에서) airtight fielding // 물샐틈없는 경계망을 치다 throw a tight cordon〔net〕 around // 연도는 물샐틈없이 경비되어 있었다 The route was rigorously〔closely, carefully〕 guarded.
물성 物性 〖물리〗 a property of matter
물세 物稅 a real tax ; a tax on goods and possessions ; a property tax
물세례 —洗禮 〖종교〗 baptism (by immersion)
물소 〖동물〗 a water buffalo
물소리 the sound of 《falling, running》 water
물속 in the water ; deep in the water ; at the bottom of the water ¶ 물속 깊이 잠기다 sink deep down to the bottom of the water // 아무를 물속에 처박다 give a person a ducking
물손 ① [반죽의 농도] the degree of wateriness〔the flour-water ratio〕 in dough ② [젖은 손] a wet hand
물수건 —手巾 a wet towel ; a steamed〔hot〕 towel
물수란 a poached egg
물수리 〖새〗 an osprey ; Pandion haliaetus (학명)
물수세미 〖식물〗 the Canada parrotfeather ; Myriophyllum verticillatum (학명)
물수제비 ducks-and-drakes ; skipping stones ¶ 물수제비 뜨다 play ducks and drakes ; skip stones
물시계 —時計 a water clock ; a water gauge (수도 계량기)
물신선 —神仙 an indifferent〔nonchalant〕 person
물실호기 勿失好機 Strike while the iron is hot. /Make hay while the sun shines.
물심 物心 matter and mind ¶ 물심 양면으로 both materially and morally〔physically and spiritually〕
물심부름 —하다 fetch and carry water ; go to fetch water
물싸움 ① [논물의] an irrigation〔a water-rights〕 dispute **—하다** dispute about〔over〕 the water-rights ② ⇨ 물똥싸움
물써다 ebb ; go out ¶ 물이 써고 있다 The tide is ebbing〔at its ebb〕. /The tide is going out.
물썽하다 [만만하다] (be) gullible ; unstubborn ; feeble ; be easy to be fooled
물쑥 〖식물〗 a kind of wormwood ; an artemisia ; Artemisia selengensis (학명)
물쓰듯하다 spend 《money》 like water ; be a free spender ; play (at) ducks and drakes with 《one's money》
물씬 —하다 ① (be) soft ; tender ② [냄새가] be nicely〔strongly〕 scented ¶ 물씬한 고기 meat cooked tender // 향수 냄새가 물씬하다 be strongly perfumed ; reek with perfume // 이상한 냄새가 물씬하다 An offensive smell assails my nostrils. // 그녀한테선 늘 마늘 냄새가 물씬하다 She always reeks of garlic.
물씬거리다 ① [물체가] be〔become〕 soft〔tender〕 ② [냄새가] smell nice〔strong〕 ; be strongly scented with ; reek with ¶ 향수 냄새가 물씬거리다 be strongly scented〔reek〕 with perfume
물아 物我 external objects〔the objective world〕 and self ; the ego and the non-ego ; the subjective and the objective
물아래 a down-river area
물안개 a wet fog ; a rain-fog
물안경 —眼鏡 swimming goggles
물알 soft unripe grain ¶ 물알들다 develop into soft unripe grain
물앵두나무 〖식물〗 a honeysuckle ; Lonicera ruprechtiana (학명)
물약 —藥 a liquid medicine
물어내다 ① carry off in the mouth (짐승이) ; smuggle 《a thing》 out of 《the house》 ¶ 쥐가 밤을 물어내다 a rat carries off chestnuts in its mouth // 주인의 돈을 물어 내다 peculate one's master's money
② [누설] let〔leak〕 out 《a family secret》
③ [변상] pay for ; compensate ; indemnify ; make good
물어내리다 ask 《a senior about something to do》 ; inquire 《of an elder about something》
물어넣다 reimburse ; refund ; repay ;

compensate for ¶ 유용(流用)한 회사 돈을 물어넣다 repay misappropriated company funds

물어떼다 bite off ; gnaw off〔away〕; cut off with the teeth ¶ 떡을 한입 물어떼다 bite off a mouthful of rice cake

***물어뜯다** bite (hard) ; bite〔tear〕off ¶ 개한테 다리를 물어뜯기다 be〔get〕bitten on the leg by a dog // 고기를 물어뜯다 bite off meat // 코를 물어뜯다 bite 《a person's》 nose

물어보다 [묻다] ask ; inquire ; question ; query ; [조회] make inquiries 《about》; refer to ; apply to ; [확인] ascertain (by inquiry) ¶ 사무실에 가서 자세한 것을 물어보다 apply at the office for the particulars // 그것을 물어보아야겠다 I will inquire about it. // 옆집에 가서 물어 보시오 Apply next door.

물어주다 pay 《for》; recompense ; make compensation for ; indemnify for ¶ 잃어버린 책 값을 물어주다 pay〔compensate〕for the book one has lost // 아우의 빚을 물어주다 pay one's brother's debt

물억새 〖식물〗 a common〔ditch〕reed ; Miscanthus sacchariflorus (학명)

물여우 〖곤충〗 a caddis worm
— **나비** a caddis fly

물역 物役 [건축 재료] construction〔building〕materials ; [재료와 노력] materials and labor (in construction)
— **장수** a dealer in construction〔building〕materials

물엿 millet jelly ; molasses

물오르다 ① [초목에] rise ② [가난한 사람이] get rich ; make money ; get ahead (in life) ; rise ¶ 봄이 되니 나무에 물오르기 시작한다 Spring has come and the sap of trees begin to rise.

물오리 〖새〗 a wild duck ; a mallard ; a drake (수컷)

물오리나무 a Siberian alder (tree) ; Alnus sibirica (학명)

물외 a (water) cucumber

물욕 物慾 worldly〔earthly〕desires ; a desire for material gain ¶ 물욕에 사로잡히다 be blinded by love of gain ; be〔get〕worldly-minded〔earthly-minded〕

물위 ① [수면] the surface of water ¶ 물위에 떠오르다 come up to the surface (of the water) // 배가 물위에 뜨다 a boat floats on the water
② [상류] the upper reaches〔courses〕of a river ; an upper stream〔course〕

물유리 —琉璃 water〔liquid, soluble〕glass

***물음** a question ; a query ; an inquiry
—**꼴** the question〔interrogative〕form 《of a verb》 —**표** a question〔an interrogation〕mark

물의 物議 public criticism〔censure〕; public discussion〔comment〕; trouble ¶ 물의를 일으키다 give rise to public criticism ; bring on public criticism ; raise a scandal // 이 박사의 연설이 교육계에 물의를 일으켰다 The speech made by Dr. *Yi* elicited much criticism in educational circles.

물이꾸럭 paying off some other's loss〔debt〕 —**하다** pay off 《for another》

물이끼 a sphagnum 《*pl.* -na》

물자 a (high-)water mark ; a water level gauge

물자 物資 [상품] commodities ; goods ; [원료] materials ; [자원] resources ¶ 물자의 공급 a supply of goods // 물자의 부족 a shortage〔famine〕of materials〔goods〕 // 물자를 보급하다 furnish supplies 《to》; supply goods 《to》 // 물자를 확보하다 secure the supply of goods // 물자가 풍부하다 be rich in natural resources
— **동원** mobilization of materials — **수급** supply and demand of goods — **활용** utilization of materials **구호** — relief goods〔supplies, cargoes〕 **생활** — vital〔essential〕commodities ; daily necessaries

물자동차 —自動車 a street sprinkler ; a sprinkler truck

물자체 物自體 〖철학〗 thing-in-itself ; Ding an sich (도)

물잡다 draw water into (a paddy) ; supply (a paddy) with water ¶ 논에 물잡다 irrigate a paddy

물장구 [헤엄칠 때] treading water ; dabbling ; paddling ¶ 물장구질하다〔물장구치다〕 tread water ; dabble ; paddle

물장난 ① [어린이의] playing〔dabbling〕in water ② [홍수] a flood disaster —**하다** play〔dabble〕in water

물장사 [술집] a gay trade ¶ 물장사하는 여자 a woman of the gay world

물장수 a water-seller ; a water-bearer

물재 物財 goods and money

물적 物的 material ; physical
— **원조** a material help〔support, aid〕 — **자원** material resources — **증거** real evidence — **증권** securities on property

물정 物情 [사물의 상태] the state of things ; the conditions of affairs ; [세상 인심] public feeling ¶ 세상 물정에 어둡다 be ignorant of the world // 물정이 소연하다 There is public unrest. /Public feeling is in turmoil. // 그의 형은 세상 물정을 안다 His brother knows his way around.

물주 物主 ① [자본주] a financier ; a financial backer ; a moneylender ; a finance agency〔man〕 ② [노름의] the banker ¶ 물주서다 become the banker〔bank〕

물주다 give water 《to》; water 《a plant》

물줄기 ① [흐르는] a watercourse ; a stream ; a current ; a flow
② [분출하는] a spout〔jet, gush〕of water ¶ 물줄기가 두 갈래로 갈리다 a water branches off into two streams // 물줄기가 세게 뻗쳐 나온다 Water spouts〔gushes〕out.

물증 物證 [물적 증거] real evidence
물지게 a water-carrying yoke ; an Aframe for carrying water buckets
—꾼 a water carrier
†물질 物質 matter ; substance ; material

> 참고 **matter**는 「정신」 (mind or spirit)에 상대되는 말로서 material보다 널리 쓰이며 「공간을 차지하고 있는 모든 물체」라는 뜻에 사용된다 **material**은 어떤 특정한 종류 성질 양의 matter로서 사용을 주된 목적으로 하는 「원료」 **substance**는 본성과의 관련에서 본 물체의 구성물을 말한다

¶ 물질적인 material ; physical // 물질 불멸의 법칙 the principle of conservation of matter // 그는 물질적으로 나아졌다 His material circumstances improved. /He is better off now. // 그는 물질적으로 윤택하다 He is blessed with material possessions.
—계(界) the material world — 명사 a material noun — 문명 material civilization — 생활 one's material life —욕 a desire for material gain 반(反)— 〖물리〗 antimatter
물질 대사 物質代謝 〖생물〗 metabolism ¶ 물질 대사의 metabolic // 물질 대사시키다 metabolize
*물질적 物質的 ¶ 물질적인 physical ; material ; objective // 물질적으로 physically ; materially ; in a material way // 그 사람의 생각은 너무나 물질적이다 He is very materialistic in his ideas.
— 번영 material prosperity — 우주 the material universe — 원조 material aid 〔help〕 — 이익 《seek》 a material gain — 존재 materiality — 쾌락 physical comfort
물질주의 物質主義 materialism ¶ 물질주의적인 materialistic
—자 a materialist
물집[1] a dyer's ; a dye house ; a dye shop
물집[2] [수포] a (water-)blister ¶ 물집이 생기다 blisters form〔rise〕
물쩍지근하다 (be) stagnant ; dull ; tedious ; standstill
물쩡하다 (be) soft ; weak-willed ; be a milksop ; have no spirit〔backbone〕 ; lack nerve
물찌똥 ① [똥] watery〔loose〕 feces ② [물덩이] splashing waterdrops
물차 —車 a street sprinkler ; a sprinkler cart
물차돌 〖광물〗 pure quartz
물참 the high tide
물체 物體 a body ; 〖법〗 a material object ; a physical solid ; an object ; a substance
— 거리 〖사진〗 the object distance — 심도(深度) 〖사진〗 the depth of field —학 somatology
물초 —하다 get dripping wet ; get wet through and through ; get〔be〕 drenched 〔wet〕 to the skin ; be all wet ; be soaking wet ; be soaked to the bone〔skin〕
물총 —銃 a water pistol〔gun〕 ; a squirt gun ¶ 물총으로 쏘다 shoot 《a person》 with a water pistol ; squirt a water pistol 《at》
물총새 〖새〗 a common Indian kingfisher
물치 〖물고기〗 a frigate mackerel
물침대 —寢臺 a water bed
물컥 stinking(ly) ; with a strong stench ¶ 생선 썩은 냄새가 물컥 나다 stink of rotten fish // 곰팡 냄새가 물컥 난다 The stench of rot hits my nose. /It smells awfully musty. // 거기에 들어서자 고약한 냄새가 물컥 풍겼다 A nasty smell greeted my nose as I entered there.
물컹거리다 be very soft ; become〔be〕 too soft ; lose texture ¶ 고기가 상해서 물컹거리다 meat has gone bad and lost its texture
물컹(물컹) softly ; squashily —하다 (be) soft ; squashy ¶ 무엇인가 물컹(물컹)한 것을 밟았다 I felt something squashy under my feet.
물컹이 ① [물컹한 것] soft〔overripe〕 stuff ; something squashy ¶ 물컹이 복숭아 an overripe peach ② [사람] a softy ; a weakling ; a sissy ; a milksop
물컹하다 (be) very〔too〕 soft ; squashy ; pulpy ; mushy ¶ 물컹한 땅 squashy ground // 무엇인지 물컹한 것을 밟았다 I felt something squashy under my feet. /I stepped upon something squashy.
물쿠다 be〔become〕 sultry〔sweltering, steaming hot〕 ¶ 물쿠는 날씨 sultry weather // 날이 몹시 물쿤다 It is steaming hot.
물크러지다 [과일이] spoil ; rot ; [종기가] fester ; ulcerate ; decompose (시체 따위가)
물큰(물큰) with a strong smell ; piquant ; pungent ; [악취가] stinking ; reeking ¶ 향수내가 물큰 나다 the pungent smell of perfume hits one's nose
물타작 —打作 harvesting cut of rice while still wet —하다 harvest the rice before it dries
물탄꾀 shallow resources〔cunning〕 ; superficial craftiness
물탕[1] —湯 a hot-spring bathing place ; a hotbath
물탕[2] —湯 〖광물〗 a tank in which cyanide is made for extracting gold from slag
‡물통 a water pail〔bucket〕
물퉁이 ① [물건] a thing which is water-soaked and swollen ② [사람] a fatty but frail person
물편 a general name for all kinds of rice (cakes except steamed rice) cake(s)
물표 物票, 物標 a (baggage) check ; a tally ¶ 물표를 받고 맡기다 check // 짐에 물표를 달다 label a parcel ; check a package 《미》

물푸레나무 〖식물〗 an ash tree ; Fraxinus rhynchophylla (학명)

†**물품 物品** [물건] a thing ; an article ; [상품] goods ; commodities
— 기부 donations in kind — 대부업 the business of hiring articles — 보험 property insurance — 임금제 a truck system

물품 목록 物品目錄 a list of goods ; a catalog ; an inventory (재고 조사의) ; itemization ¶ 물품목록을 만들다 itemize

물품세 物品稅 a commodity tax ; an excise tax
—법 the Commodity Tax Act

물할머니 the spirit that lurks in a well or a spring

물행주 a (wet) dishrag〔dishcloth〕

물홈 the groove of a paper sliding door

물화 物貨 goods ; commodities (일용품) ; merchandise (상품)

물활론 物活論 〖철학〗 hylozoism ; animism

†**묽다** ① [농도가] (be) watery ; thin ; weak ; washy ¶ 묽은 국 thin〔washy〕soup // 묽은 우유 watery milk // 물을 타서 풀을 묽게 하다 thin paste with water // 국이 아주 묽다 The soup is like dishwater. ② [사람이] (be) weak ; feeble ; soft ¶ 묽은 사람 a feeble〔weak〕person ; a softy

묽디묽다 ① [물이] be very〔ever so〕watery ; be as thin as can be ② [사람이] (be) awfully feeble〔weak〕; very soft ; be a real sissy〔drip〕《속》

묽숙하다 (be) rather watery〔thin〕

뭇[1] [묶음] a bundle ; a sheaf ; a faggot ¶ 생선 두 뭇 two bundles of fish // 장작 한 뭇 a bundle of firewood // 짚 한 뭇 a sheaf of rice straw // 한 뭇에 50원 50 *won* a bundle

뭇[2] [여러] many ; numerous ; a number of ; all ; all sorts of ¶ 뭇사람이 다 그를 칭찬한다 All the people praise him. // 뭇 짐승이 떼를 지어 다닌다 All sorts of animals move around in groups. // 뭇놈이 달려들어 그를 때려눕혔다 A whole gang went at him and knocked him down.

뭇[3] [큰 작살] a large fish spear

뭇가름 dividing sheares into smaller ones

뭇갈림 going halves〔fifty-fifty〕 in rice sheaves between the landlord and the tenant

뭇나무 firewood in bundles ; a faggot ¶ 나무를 뭇나무로 팔다 sell firewood by the bundle

뭇따래기 [훼방놓는 무리] troublesome〔bothersome〕people ; [쓸모없는 인간들] good-for-nothing〔worthless〕people

뭇매 (several) beating all at one time ¶ 뭇매를 때리다 gang up and give a beating // 뭇매를 맞다 get《it》from all sides ; get a pelting rain of kicks and blows by a gang

뭇발길 kicking《a person》 from all sides ; an attack from all quarters (비난) ¶ 뭇발길을 당하다 get〔be under, be subjected to〕 a pelting rain of kicks by a gang

뭇방치기 ① forwardness ; minding other's business ; meddling ; officiousness ② [사람] a lot of meddlers ; officious persons
—하다 intrude ; intermeddle《with, in》; meddle〔stick one's nose〕 in everything ; poke one's nose into《another's affair》; make uncalled-for meddling

뭇소리 many voices ; many〔all, all sorts of〕 opinions ; gossip ¶ 뭇소리를 무시하고 자기 마음대로 하다 disregard the many opinions to do just as one pleases // 뭇소리가 일치하지 않는다 Opinions are divided.

뭇시선 —視線 everyone's eyes

뭇입 criticism from all〔many, several〕 people ; public rebuke ; popular criticism ; Mrs. Grundy ¶ 뭇입을 두려워하다 fear what people will say ; be afraid of what Mrs. Grundy would say // 뭇입이 시끄러울 테니 그만두게 Don't (do it) or it may cause scandal.

뭇줄 a thick hemp rope ; a Manila rope

뭉개다[1] ① [짓이기다] crumple ; crush ; mash ; squash ¶ 뭉갠 감자 mashed potatoes // 감자를 뭉개다 mash potatoes // 모자를 깔고 뭉개다 sit on a hat (and mash it in) // 뭉개서 못쓰게 하다 squeeze out of shape
② [갈팡질팡] do not know what to do with〔how to deal with〕; be embarrassed ; be at a loss ; make a mess of

뭉개다[2] [자리에서] dawdle ¶ 한 자리에서 뭉개다 dawdle at one place

뭉게구름 〖기상〗 a cumulus《*pl.* -li》; a towering mass of clouds

뭉게뭉게 in thick clouds ; thickly ¶ 구름이 뭉게뭉게 떠오르다 clouds rise up one after another ; thick clouds are gathering // 연기가 뭉게뭉게 나다 smoke rises up〔rolls〕 in thick clouds // 새까만 연기가 하늘로 뭉게뭉게 피어오르고 있었다 Columns〔Volumes〕 of murky smoke overspread the sky.

뭉구리 ① [까까머리] a close-cropped〔shaven〕 head ¶ 뭉구리의 close-cropped ; roundheaded ② [중] a priest ; a bonze

뭉그러뜨리다 crumble ; throw〔knock〕 down ; let fall ; demolish ¶ 담을 뭉그러뜨리다 crumble a wall // 쌓아놓은 과일을 뭉그러뜨리다 throw〔knock〕 down piled-up fruit

뭉그러지다 crumble ; collapse ; break ; fall down ; come down ; drop〔go, fall〕 to pieces ¶ 벽이 뭉그러지다 a wall collapses // 쌓아놓은 과일이 뭉그러지다 piled-up fruit falls down

뭉그적거리다 dawdle ; linger ; move lackadaisically〔listlessly〕 or aimlessly ¶ 몸을 뭉그적거리다 dawdle ; move one's body aimlessly // 한 자리에서 뭉그적거리다 daw-

dle in one place
뭉그적뭉그적 dawdlingly ; listlessly ; aimlessly ⇨ 뭉그적거리다
뭉근하다 《a fire》 be low but steady ¶ 뭉근히 (burn) low〔slow〕 but steady // 불을 뭉근히 때다 keep a low fire going steadily
뭉글뭉글 —하다 (be) clotty ; lumpy ¶ 뭉글뭉글한 과자 a lumpy candy // 임파선이 부어 뭉글뭉글하다 Lymphatic glands are swollen and lumpy.
뭉긋이 [비스듬히] (sloped or warped) gently ; slightly ¶ 고개가 뭉긋이 경사지다 a hill is gently sloped // 막대가 뭉긋이 휘다 a stick is slightly bent
뭉긋하다 ① [비스듬하다] (be) sloping ; inclined ; gently sloped ¶ 고개가 뭉긋하다 a hill slopes gently ② [휘우듬하다] (be) warped ; gently〔slightly〕 bent ¶ 막대가 뭉긋하게 휘다 a stick is slightly bent
뭉기다 throw down ; destroy ; demolish ; let fall
뭉때리다 ① [시치미떼다] pretend ignorance of ; pretend not to know ; pretend innocence
② [기피하다] deliberately shirk 《a job》
뭉떵뭉떵 ¶ 돈을 뭉떵뭉떵 잘리다 lose great chunks of money repeatedly // 떡을 뭉떵뭉떵 자르다 cut a rice cake into big chunks
뭉뚝 —하다 (be) stumpy ; stubby ; blunt ¶ 뭉뚝한 연필 a stubby〔stumpy〕 pencil // 뭉뚝한 끝 a blunt point〔edge〕 // 뭉뚝한 사람 a stubby〔stumpy〕 person
뭉뚱그리다 bundle up crudely ; wrap up in a slipshod way ; throw together hastily ¶ 짐을 뭉뚱그리다 bundle up a package crudely
뭉실뭉실 —하다 (be) plump ; lumpy ; portly ; stout ¶ 뭉실뭉실 살이 찐 아이 a plump baby // 뭉실뭉실 살이 찌다 be 〔grow〕 plump
뭉우리돌 a smooth round stone ; a boulder
뭉치 ① a bundle ; a roll ; a lump ; a clod ; a mass ¶ 편지 한 뭉치 a bundle of letters // 지폐 한 뭉치 a bundle〔roll, wad〕 of bank notes ; a roll of (paper) money
② [쇠고기의] beef round
***뭉치다** ① [덩이지다] lump ; mass ; conglomerate ¶ 풀이 뭉치다 Paste lumps. / Paste forms a hard mass.
② [단결] unite ; combine ; hold〔hang, get, come, stand〕 together ¶ 뭉쳐서 in a body〔force, group〕 ; in one united body // 뭉쳐서 대항하다 stand together against ; be united against // 국가의 위기에 모든 정당이 한데 뭉쳤다 All the political parties stood together in a national crisis. // 한데 뭉치면 살고 헤어지면 죽는다 United we stand, divided we fall. // 반 학생들이 전부 똘똘 뭉쳐 약한 학생들을 상대로 괴롭힌다 The whole class gangs up on the weak ones and taunts them.
③ [타동사] lump together ; mass ; conglomerate ; [단결] unite ; put〔gather, group〕 together ; bind together ¶ 풀을 한덩이로 뭉치다 mass paste into a lump // 눈을 뭉쳐서 덩이를 만들다 mass snow into a ball ; press snow into a lump // 종이를 뭉치다 crumple paper into a ball // 힘을 뭉치다 join efforts // 짚을 뭉쳐 단을 짓다 bind straw together into a bundle
뭉크러지다 ① [뭉그러지다] crumble ; collapse ; fall down ② [종이 따위가] break ; [궤양으로] ulcerate ¶ 문둥병으로 얼굴이 뭉크러지다 have one's face disfigured by leprosy // 뭉크러진 잇몸 an ulcerated gum
뭉클뭉클하다 (be) clotty ; lumpy
뭉클하다 ① [먹은 것이] be〔lie〕 heavy on one's stomach ¶ 먹은 것이 뭉클하고 내리지 않는다 The food I have eaten rests heavy on my stomach.
② [감동] be choked with grief ; have 〔feel〕 a lump in one's throat ¶ 나는 그 광경을 보자 가슴이 뭉클하여졌다 A lump came into my throat, looking at the sight. /I felt a gush〔rush〕 of pity at the sight. // 노여움으로 가슴이 뭉클하여졌다 Indignation surged up within me.
뭉키다 ① [덩이지다] lump ; mass ; conglomerate ¶ 풀이 뭉키어 덩이가 되다 paste masses into a lump // 눈이 뭉키어 단단하게 되다 snow lumps into a hard mass
② [여럿이] gather〔draw, get〕 together ; swarm ; crowd ; cluster (송이송이) ¶ 뭉키어 in a body〔group, band〕 ; in clusters〔crowds〕 // 사과가 한가지에 뭉키어 달렸다 Apples hung on a branch in clusters. // 그렇게 뭉키어 오지 말고 한 사람씩 나와주시오 Come one by one instead of in a group.
뭉텅 in lumps
뭉텅이 a lump ; a mass ; a bundle ; a package ; a clod 《of earth》
금 — a lump of gold **솜 —** a wad of cotton **지폐 —** a bundle〔roll, wad〕 of bills〔paper money〕
뭉툭 —하다 (be) stumpy
†**뭍** land ; dry land ; terra firma 《라》 ; the shore (배에서 본) ¶ 뭍 쪽으로 landward // 뭍이 보이는 곳에 within sight of land // 뭍에서 멀리 떨어진 far off the coast 《of》 ; far away from land // 뭍에 살다 live on land // 뭍에 올라가다 go ashore // (배에서) 뭍이 보이다 come in sight of land
—벼 dry land rice **—짐승** a land animal
뭐 ⇨ 무어
-므로 for ; as ; with ; from ; because of ; due to ¶ 비가 오므로 갈 수 없다 We cannot go, for it is raining. // 돈을 가지고 있지 않았으므로 사지 않았다 As I had no money with me, I did not buy it. // 비가 왔으므로 가지 않았다 I did not go because of the rain.
***미** 美 beauty ; the beautiful ; charm ; grace

¶ 육체미 physical beauty ; bodily charm // 자연의 미 natural beauty ; beauties of nature // 음율의 미 rhythmical charm // 미적 감각 a sense of beauty // 미적 감각이 있다 have an eye for the beautiful

미 未 ① the Sign of the Sheep〔Goat〕 ② [미방] the Direction of the Sheep《south-west-by-south》 ③ [미시] the Watch of the Sheep《the period between 1 and 3 p. m.》

미- 未 not yet ; un- ; in- ¶ 미개 being uncivilized〔savage, barbarous〕// 미완성 being incomplete〔unfinished〕

미가 米價 the price of rice
— 정책 the rice price policy — 조절 control〔regulation〕 of the rice price〔market〕 공정(公定) — the official〔ceiling〕 rice price 적정 — reasonable rice price

미가공 未加工 ¶ 미가공의 raw ; crude ; unprocessed // 미가공의 직물 greige ; gray goods

†미각 味覺 the palate ; the (sense of) taste ; the gustation ¶ 미각을 돋구는 음식 tempting〔appetizing, inviting〕 food ; food tickling the palate // 미각이 예민하다 have a sensitive tongue // 미각을 만족시키다 please one's palate
— 세포 a taste〔gustatory〕 cell — 신경 the gustatory nerve

미간 未刊 ¶ 미간의 unpublished
— 원고 an unpublished manuscript

미간 眉間 the middle of the forehead ; the brow ; 〖해부〗 a glabella ¶ 미간에 흠이 있다 have a scar between one's eyes

미간지 未墾地 uncultivated land ; land in grass ; virgin soil

미감 美感 a sense of beauty ; an esthetic sense〔feeling〕 ¶ 미감이 부족하다 lack a sense of beauty ; be insensible to beauty

미감 味感 the taste ⇨ 미각

미감아 未感兒 [나병의] a child not communicated to leprosy ; [결핵의] a child not infected with tuberculosis

미개 未開 ① [야만] ―하다 (be) uncivilized ; barbarous ; savage ¶ 미개 상태에 있다 be in the state of nature
② [꽃 따위가] ―하다 (be) unblown ; be not in flower
—국 an uncivilized〔a savage〕 country — 사회 (a) primitive society —인 a barbarian ; a savage ; [종족] a savage〔primitive〕 people〔race〕 ; an uncivilized tribe —지 a backward region

미개간 未開墾 ¶ 미개간의 uncultivated
—지 uncultivated land ; land in grass ; land in its natural state ; virgin〔maiden〕 soil

미개발 未開發 ¶ 미개발의 undeveloped ; unexploited《district》; untapped〔dormant〕《resources》; wild《land》
—국 an undeveloped country ; a backward country — 지역 an undeveloped area

*미개척 未開拓 ¶ 미개척의 undeveloped ; unexploited ; untapped ; unreclaimed ; unexplored // 과학계에도 아직 미개척의 분야가 많다 Science has many fields still unexplored.
— 방면 an unexplored field — 시장 a potential market —지 undevelope〔waste〕 land ; untapped territory ; virgin〔maiden〕 soil

미거 美擧 a commendable act ; a praiseworthy undertaking ; good work

미거 未擧 imprudence ; thoughtlessness ; indiscretion ―하다 [생각이 모자라다] (be) imprudent ; thoughtless ; indiscreet ; [아둔하다] silly ; foolish ; unwise

미견 迷見 a mistaken view ; a fallacious opinion ; an erroneous idea

†미결 未決 ¶ 미결의 unsettled ; undecided ; pending ; open ; unconvicted (죄인의) // 미결인 채로 두다 leave《a matter》 unsettled // 그 문제는 여전히 미결이다 The question is still open〔unsettled〕.
— 구류 detention pending trial〔judgment〕 ; unconvicted detention — 구류 일수 the number of the days of unconvicted detention — 문제 a pending〔an open, a moot〕 question — 사항 arrearage ; matters yet to be settled — 서류함 an in-tray〔-box〕 —수 an unconvicted prisoner ; a prisoner under trial —안 an unsettled bill ; an undecided matter

미결산 未決算 ¶ 미결산의 unsettled ; unbalanced ; open
— 계정(計定) open〔unbalanced, outstanding〕 account ; suspense credits (차변) ; suspense debits (대변)

미결정 ⇨ 미결(未決) ¶ 미결정의 undecided ; undetermined // 미결정인 채로 남겨 두다 leave《a matter》 unsettled〔at large〕

미결제 未決濟 ¶ 미결제의 unsettled ; outstanding ; unpaid (미불의)
— 거래 an incomplete transaction — 계정(計定) a suspense〔an outstanding〕 account

미경지 未耕地 uncultivated land ; an area not yet brought under cultivation

미경험 未經驗 ¶ 미경험의 inexperienced ; unexperienced ; green ; new
—자 a novice ; a green hand ; an inexperienced person ¶ 미경험자 환영 Welcome, the inexperienced.

미곡 米穀 rice
— 검사 rice conditioning — 도매상 a rice factor ; a rice commission merchant (미) —상 a rice dealer — 시장 the rice market — 연도 the rice (crop) year — 중매인 a rice broker — 창고 a (rice-) granary

미골 尾骨 〖해부〗 the coccyx ; the tailbone

미공인 未公認 ¶ 미공인의 not yet offi-

cially recognized ; unofficial
— 기록 an unofficial〔a pending〕 record
미관 美觀 a beautiful〔charming〕 sight 〔spectacle〕; a fine〔lovely〕 view ¶ 미관을 손상하다 spoil〔injure〕 the beauty《of》// 자연의 미관 the beauties of nature // 거리의 미관을 해치다 defile the appearance of the street
— 지구 an aesthetic area
미관 味官 the gustation〔taste〕 organ
—구(球) a taste bud〔bulb〕
미관 微官 a petty〔minor〕 official ; a humble placeman《영》
— 말직(末職) the lowest position《of the Government》
미광 微光 faint light ; a glimmer of light ; a shimmer
—등 a dim light
미구 未久 ¶ 미구에 soon ; before long ; shortly ; in the near future // 그는 미구에 돌아올 것이다 It will not be long before he returns. /He will be back soon. // 그는 미구에 도미할 것이다 He will leave for the United States in the near future〔in the not too distant future〕.
미구 불원 未久不遠 near future ¶ 미구 불원에 in the near future ; soon ; shortly ; before long ; at no distant date〔day〕 // 미구 불원에 그 날이 올 것이다 The day will not be far distant.
미국 美國 America ; the United States (of America)《U. S. A.》; [국외의 미국인이 자기 나라를 불러] the States ¶ 미국의 American ; U. S. ; Yankee // 미국제 자동차 an American-made car ; a car made in U. S. A.
— 국기(國旗) the American flag ; the Stars and Stripes ; the Star-Spangled Banner — 군인 an American soldier ; a GI —령(領) American territory ; an American possession —말 American English ; the American language ; [일반 미국어] General American —면(綿) American raw cotton — 본토(本土) stateside ¶ 미국 본토의 stateside // 미국 본토로 stateward — 사람 an American ; [전형적인] Uncle Sam ; [북부나 New England 지방의] a Yankee《속》; the Americans《총칭》— 어법(語法) (an) Americanism —의 소리 방송(放送) the Voice of America —인 기질(氣質) Americanism — 정부(政府) the United States Government ; Washington ; the White House ; Uncle Sam —톤 American〔short〕 ton —화(化) Americanization ¶ 미국화하다 Americanize
미군 美軍 the U. S. Armed Forces ; American Forces ; the U. S. Army
— 점령 지역 the American-occupied area 주한 — the U. S. Armed Forces 〔the American forces〕 stationed in Korea
미궁 迷宮 a labyrinth ; a maze ; mystery ¶ 사건은 미궁에 빠졌다 The case has become shrouded〔wrapped〕 in mystery. // 그 문제는 여전히 미궁에 빠져 있다 The question is as much in dark as ever.
미급 未及 —하다 fall short of ; be not up to par ; be not sufficient ; be no match〔equal〕《for》; be inferior《to》; be unattainable ; do not reach ¶ 영어에 있어서 누구나 그에게는 미급하다 No one can match him in English. // 생각이 거기까지는 미급했다 I was not far-sighted enough to think of it.
미기 美妓 a beautiful〔pretty〕 *kisaeng* 〔girl〕
미기 美技 a brilliant〔beautiful, neat〕 performance ; 〖야구·정구〗 a fine play
미기 [제트기] a MIG jet fighter ; MIG
미꾸라지, 미꾸리 〖어류〗 a loach ; a mudfish ¶ 미꾸라지 같은 놈 a slippery 〔an eely〕 fellow
미꾸라지 한 마리가 온 웅덩이를 흐린다 속담 One ill weed mars a whole pot of pottage. /The rotten apple injures its neighbour.
미끄러뜨리다 let《a thing》 slip〔slide, skid〕 ¶ 발을 미끄러뜨리다 let one's foot slip ; slip
†**미끄러지다** slide ; glide ; slip (발이) ; skid ; [실패] fail《in an exam》; get plucked《in an exam》《미·속》¶ 얼음 판에서 미끄러져 넘어지다 slip and fall on the ice // 미끄러지지 않도록 조심하라 Watch your steps so as not to slip. // 길이 미끄러워 차가 미끄러져 나갔다 The car skidded on the slippery road. // 배가 호수 위에 미끄러져 나간다 A boat glides along the lake. // 그는 사닥다리에서 미끄러져 떨어져서 다리가 부러졌다 He slipped down the ladder and broke his leg.
†**미끄럼** a slide ; sliding ; a slip ; slipping ¶ 미끄럼타다 [얼음 위에서] skate on the ice ; do skating ; [눈 위에서] slide over the snow (in a sleigh)
—대〔판〕 a (playground) slide — 마찰 sliding friction — 방지 타이어 a nonskid 〔skid-proof〕 tire — 운동 a sliding motion ; 〖식물〗 a gliding movement
***미끄럽다** (be) smooth ; sleek ; slippery ; slick ¶ 미끄러운 길 a slippery road // 미끄러운 종이 slick〔sleek〕 paper // 몹시 미끄럽다 be as slippery as an eel
미끈거리다 (be) slippery ; slimy ¶ 길이 미끈거리다 A road is slippery〔slick〕《with mud》. // 뱀장어가 미끈거리다 The eel feels slippery.
미끈둥하다 (be) very smooth〔sleek, slick〕; quite slippery〔oily〕 ¶ 미끈둥한 뱀장어 a very slippery eel
미끈미끈 smoothly ; sleekly ; slickly ; slippery ; oily —하다 (be) very smooth 〔sleek, slimy, slippery, oily〕; be all smooth〔sleek〕; be all slippery〔oily〕 ¶ 미끈미끈한 머리 sleek hair // 비단을 미끈미

끈하게 다듬다 beat silk smooth ; smooth silk // 뱀장어가 미끈미끈하여 손에 잡히지 않는다 The eel is so slippery (that) I can't catch it.

미끈하다 (be) sleek ; well-fed ; well-dressed ; well-groomed ; comely ; handsome ¶ 미끈한 자동차 a sleek car // 미끈한 얼굴 a sleek face ; a good-looking face // 미끈하게 생기다 be good-looking ; have nice features // 옷을 미끈하게 입다 be well-dressed // 그 여자는 미끈한 다리, 풍만한 가슴, 멋있는 곡선미하며 다 갖췄군 She is leggy, bosomy, curvacious, everything.

‡**미끼** ① [낚싯밥] a bait ¶ 낚시에 미끼를 물리다 put a bait on a hook ; bait up // 고기가 미끼를 문다 A fish takes a bite. // 미끼를 떼이다 lose the bait 《to the fish》 ② [유혹물] a bait ; a decoy ; a lure ; an allurement ¶ 미끼에 걸리다 be lured ; get decoyed // 돈을 미끼로 여자를 낚다 decoy〔lure, entice〕 a woman with money // 닭을 미끼로 여우를 잡다 catch a fox with a hen for a decoy // 여자를 미끼로 돈을 끌어내다 get money from 《a person》 using a woman as bait

낚시 — fish bait ; a bait for fish

미나리 〖식물〗 parsley

—꽝 a dropwort field

미나리아재비 〖식물〗 a buttercup ; a crowfoot ; Ranunculus acris (학명)

미남자 美男子 a handsome man ; a good-looking fellow ; an Adonis

미납 未納 default in payment ; nonpayment ; arrearage ¶ 미납의 unpaid ; in arrears ; delinquent ; back

—세 unpaid〔delinquent〕 taxes ; back taxes 《미》 **—액** the amount in arrears **—자** a person in arrears ; a defaulter **— 처분** punishment for failure to pay〔of payment〕 **세금 —자** a tax defaulter

미네랄 minerals ; [광천수] mineral water

미녀 美女 a beautiful woman ; a beauty ; a belle ; a knockout 《미·속》 ¶ 미녀 중의 미녀 the fairest of the fair

— 투표 a beauty contest〔competition〕 **— 투표 당선자** a prizewinner in a beauty contest

미농지 美濃紙 (a kind of) rice paper

미뉴에트 〖음악〗 a minuet

미늘 a barb

미니 mini

— 스커트 a miniskirt **—카** a minicar

미니어처 a miniature

— 세트 〖영화〗 a miniature set

미다[1] get bald ; grow bald ¶ 머리가 미다 become bald ; one's head gets bald // 뒷머리가 미다 one's head gets bald in the back

미다[2] tear a hole in 《paper, leather》 ¶ 잘못해서 종이를 미다 tear a hole in the paper by mistake

미다[3] [따돌리다] ostracize ; leave out in the cold ; give 《a person》 the cold shoulder

미닫이 a sliding door

—창 a sliding window

미달 未達 shortage ; lack ; deficiency ; insufficiency **—하다** be short 《of》 ; be deficient 《in》 ; be less than ; be under ; lack ; want ¶ 아직 정원 미달이다 The number limit has not been reached.

미담 美談 a praiseworthy〔laudable, fine〕 anecdote ; a moving story

효자 — an admirable story of filial piety

미답 未踏 ¶ 미답의 [발을 들여 놓지 않은] untrodden ; [손대지 않은] unexplored

미대다 ① [전가] lay ; throw ; shift 《the blame, the responsibility》 ② [미루다] delay ; put off ; postpone ; defer ¶ 일을 미대다 put work off

†**미덕 美德** a virtue ; a noble attribute ; a good trait ; a grace of character ¶ 미덕을 지닌 사람 a man of virtue ; a virtuous man

***미덥다** (be) reliable ; trustworthy ; trusty ; dependable ¶ 미더운 사람 a reliable〔trustworthy〕 person // 미덥지 않다 be unreliable〔untrustworthy〕 ; be unworthy of trust // 미덥게 여기다 repose〔place〕 trust in 《a person》 ; hope〔expect〕 much from 《a person》 // 미더운 자리에 돈을 빚주다 lend money to 《a person》 of good credit // 미더운 자리에 딸의 혼처를 정하다 get one's daughter engaged to a dependable person

미동 美童 [미소년] a handsome〔good-looking〕 boy ; [남색(男色)의 상대] a catamite

미동 微動 a tremor ; a slight shock ; a quiver ¶ 미동도 하지 않다 do not budge 〔move〕 an inch ; stand as firm as a rock

—계(計) a tromometer **— 기압계** a statoscope **— 측정기** a microdetector

미두 米豆 bucket-shop operation in rice ; speculation in rice

—장(場) the rice exchange

미드웨이 섬 Midway Island

미들급 —級 a middleweight

— 챔피언 a middleweight champion

미들 헤비급 —級 the middle heavyweight

미등 尾燈 a tail-light

미디 a midi ; a midi-skirt

미뜨리다 push〔shove〕 off ; thrust ⇨ 밀뜨리다

***미라** a mummy

미락 微落 〖경제〗 fractional decline

미란 靡爛 [염증] inflammation ; [궤양] ulceration ; fester ; erosion ; [부란] decomposition **—하다** be inflamed ; be decomposed ; decompose ; ulcerate ; fester ¶ 시체가 몹시 미란되어 있었다 The corpse was in a fearful state of decomposition.

—성 가스 irritating〔vesicant〕 poisonous gas ; lewisite

†미래 〖농업〗 a kind of farm implement used to level ground

*미래 未來 [때] future ; time to come ; [내세] the future life ; the next world ; the life to come ; 〖문법〗 the future tense ¶ 미래의 future ; coming ; to come ; prospective // 미래에 in (the) future ; in days to come // 미래의 아내 one's intended wife ; one's future 〔prospective〕 wife // 미래의 일 future 〔coming〕 events // 미래에 무슨 일이 일어날지는 알 수 없다 There is no knowing what the future may bring forth. // 그 작가는 미래가 촉망되고 있다 The writer has a bright〔great〕 future before him.
—사(事) future (coming) events 〔affairs〕 —상(像) an image of the future — 영겁(永劫) forever ; through of eternity ; till the end of time — 완료 the future perfect tense —인 man of the future world ; Homo futurus —학 futurology

미래파 未來派 〖예술〗 futurism ; [사람] a futurist ¶ 미래파의 futurist(ic)

†미량 微量 a very small amount ; extremely small quantities
— 분석 〖화학〗 microanalysis — 영양 micronutrient (비타민 따위) — 원소 〖동물·식물〗 a microelement ; a trace element —천칭 a microbalance ; a delicate balance —측정기 a microdetector —화학 microchemistry

미레자 a T-square

미레질 reverse〔back-hand〕 planing ; smoothing

미려 美麗 beauty ; elegance ; loveliness
—하다 (be) beautiful ; elegant ; lovely

†미력 微力 poor ability ; small ability ; slender means (자력) ; little influence (세력) ¶ 미력을 다하다 do what little one can ; do one's bit ; exert oneself to the full

*미련 stupidity ; dullness, clumsiness ; awkwardness —하다 (be) stupid ; dullwitted ; clumsy ; awkward
—쟁이〔퉁이, 꾸러기〕 a stupid fool ; a dullard ; an ass
미련한 놈 잡아들이라 하면 가난한 놈 잡아들인다 (속담) The poor suffer all the wrong.

미련 未練 [애착] lingering attachment ; reluctance to give up ; regret ¶ 미련이 있다 have a lingering affection 〔love〕 《for》 ; be still attached to // 그 자리에 미련이 있다 I still retain a lingering desire for the position. // 도시생활에는 미련이 없다 I do not regret giving up city life. // 그 여자에게 아직도 미련이 남아 있다 Still he cannot give her up.

미령 靡寧 indisposition —하다 (be) indisposed ; unwell ; ill

*미로 迷路 a maze ; a labyrinth ¶ 미로에 빠지다 be〔get〕 lost in a maze ; be at a loss
— 신경염 〖의학〗 neurolabyrinthitis — 학습 〖심리학〗 maze learning

미료 未了 ¶ 미료의 unfinished ; incomplete ; unsettled ; pending
—안(案) a pending bill

†미루다 ① [연기·지연] put off ; postpone ; delay ; defer 《payment, action》 ; procrastinate ¶ 출발을 2·3일 뒤로 미루다 put off the departure for a few days // 다음 월요일까지 가는 것을 미루다 defer going till next Monday // 빚을 갚지 않고 미루다 delay paying a debt // 일을 하루 이틀 자꾸 미루다 put off a job from day to day // 하찮은 핑계로 약속을 미루다 put 《a person》 off with a frivolous excuse // 세부적인 일들은 다음번으로 미루고 술이나 마시러 가자 Let's leave the details to next time and go have a drink.
② [전가] shift ; shuffle off ; lay〔throw〕 《the blame on a person》 ¶ 일을 남에게 미루다 shuffle off a duty on to someone else // 책임을 남에게 미루다 shift a responsibility on to another's shoulders // 나한테 책임을 미루지 마라 Don't pass the buck to me.
③ [추측] infer ; deduce ; gather ; guess ; surmise ; conjecture ; give〔make〕 a guess ; draw an inference 《from》 ¶ 모든 점에서 미루어 볼 때 all things taken together ; all things considered // 그의 행동으로 미루어 점잖은 사람인 것을 알겠다 I see from his behavior that he is a gentleman. // 이번에 한 일로 다음에 어떻게 할 것을 미루어 알 수 있다 You can guess from what he has done this time what he will do in the future. // 나머지는 미루어 알 수 있는 일이다 The rest is for you to infer.

미루적거리다 postpone ; delay ; defer ; procrastinate ; put off ¶ 일을 미루적거리다 delay one's work // 그렇게 미루적거리다가는 그 일 할 날이 없겠다 Procrastinating that way, you will never get the job done.

미루적미루적 ¶ 미루적미루적 일하기를 싫어한다 He drags his feet on the job, he hates it so.

미류나무 美柳— a poplar

미륵 보살 彌勒菩薩 Maitreya 《범》

*미리 beforehand ; in advance ; previously ; in anticipation ¶ 집세를 미리 내다 pay the rent in advance // 돈을 미리 준비하다 have money ready in advance // 미리 감사하다 thank 《a person》 in advance // 미리 통지하다 give previous notice // 미리 허가를 얻다 obtain a permit in advance // 미리 자리를 잡다 reserve a seat beforehand // 미리 나에게 이야기를 했어야 했다 You ought to have told me beforehand.

미립 a knack ; a trick ; the hang ¶ 미립을 얻다 acquire〔get〕 the knack of ; get the hang of it // 곧 미립이 날거야 You will soon learn the trick of it. // 미립을 얻으면 아주 쉽다 It's quite easy when you have the knack of it.

미립 微粒 a particle ; a small grain
—체 〖생물〗 a microsome

미립자 微粒子 〖전기〗 a corpuscle ¶ 미립자의 corpuscular
—병 [누에의] pébrin 《프》 **—설(說)** the corpuscular theory of light **— 전류** corpuscular current **— 필름** a finegrained film **— 현상** a corpuscular phenomenon **— 현상액** a fine grain developer

†**미만 未滿** under ; below ; less than ; not more than ¶ 5세 미만의 아이 children under 5 // 100원 미만 less than〔not exceeding〕 100 *won*

미만 彌漫 pervasion ; diffusion ; permeation **—하다** pervade ; permeate ; prevail ; extend all round

미망 迷妄 an illusion ; a delusion ; a fallacy **—하다** link to a delusion〔an illusion〕 ¶ 미망을 깨우치다 open 《a person's》 eyes ; bring 《a person》 to his senses ; undeceive ; disillusion // 미망에서 깨어나다 be undeceived〔disillusioned〕 ; come〔be brought〕 to one's senses
—설 illusionism

‡**미망인 未亡人** a widow ; a widowed lady ; a dowager (귀족의) ¶ 김씨의 미망인 the widow of the late Mr. *Kim* ; Mr. *Kim's* widow // 전쟁 미망인 a war widow // 전쟁으로 인해 많은 미망인이 생겼다 The war widowed many women.

미맥 米麥 rice and barley

미명 未明 early dawn ; the gray of the morning ¶ 미명에 before dawn ; in the early dawn ; in the gray of the morning ; before daybreak〔it is light〕

미명 美名 a good〔fair〕 name ; high reputation ¶ 자선이란 미명 하에 under the cloak of charity ; in the name of charity

***미모 美貌** a beautiful〔handsome〕 face ; attractive〔good〕 looks ; pretty features ; personal beauty ¶ 미모의 beautiful ; good-looking ; handsome ; charming ; comely // 미모에 사로잡히다 be captivated〔fascinated〕 by 《a person's》 beauty ; be smitten with 《a person's》 charms // 미모가 그녀의 신세를 망치게 하였다 Her beauty was her ruin〔downfall〕.

미목 眉目 looks ; features ; a face ¶ 미목이 수려한 청년 a handsome young man // 미목이 수려하다 have a handsome face

미몽 迷夢 an illusion ; a delusion ¶ 미몽에서 깨어나다 be disillusioned ; come〔be brought〕 to one's senses ; wake up from a delusion // 그는 아직 미몽에서 깨어나지 못하고 있다 He is not yet awakened from illusion.

†**미묘 美妙** elegance ; exquisiteness **—하다** (be) fine ; sweet ; elegant ; graceful ¶ 미묘한 음악 exquisite music

***미묘 微妙** delicacy ; subtlety ; nicety **—하다** (be) delicate ; subtle ; nice ¶ 뜻의 미묘한 차이 delicate shades of meaning // 정국의 미묘한 동향 a subtle shifting of the political situation // 이 일로 인해 그는 미묘한 입장에 놓이게 될 것이다 This is going to put him in a delicate situation.

미문 美文 elegant prose ; a literary essay **—체** a flowery〔an ornate〕 style ; a florid prose style **—학** polite literature ; belles-letters 《프》

미물 微物 ① [세균] a microbe ; a microorganism ; a microscopic organism ② [하찮은 물건] a trifle
—학 micrology

미미 美味 [좋은 맛] relish ; a good flavor ; deliciousness ¶ 미미의 tasty ; sweet ; nice ; delicious // 미미의 음식 a delicacy ; a dainty ; a rich diet

미미 微微 slightness ; insignificance **—하다** (be) slight ; insignificant ; small ; tiny ; petty ¶ 미미한 증가 an immaterial increase // 그 회사는 처음에는 미미한 존재였다 At first the company was a petty affair.

미미부진하다 微微不振— be at a low ebb ; be in a poor way

미발견 未發見 ¶ 미발견의 undiscovered ; unexplored

미발달 未發達 ¶ 미발달의 undeveloped ; underdeveloped

미발표 未發表 ¶ 미발표의 unpublished ; not yet made public

미방 未方 〖민속〗 the Direction of the Sheep ; southwest-by-south

미병 美兵 an American soldier〔sailor〕 ; a (U.S.) GI 《*pl.* GI's, GIs》

미복 微服 disguise in dress ¶ 미복 잠행하다 travel incognito ; go in disguise

미본토 美本土 the continental U.S. ¶ 미본토의〔에 있는〕 stateside // 미본토로 stateside

미봉 彌縫 temporizing ; patching up ; tinkering **—하다** temporize ; patch up 《a matter》 ; make shift ; gloss over 《a fault》 ¶ 잠시 미봉하다 patch 《things》 up for the moment // 미봉적으로 해결하다 patch the matter up
—책 a makeshift ; a temporary〔time-serving〕 remedy ; a temporizing policy〔measure〕 ; a stop-gap policy 《미》 ¶ 미봉책으로 for a shift

미부 尾部 the tail ; [항공기의] the empennage 《프》 ; tail unit

미분 微分 〖수학〗 differential ; differentiation
— 계수(係數) a differential coefficient〔quotient〕 **— 방정식** a differential equation **— 적분학** differential and integral calculus

미분자 微分子 an atom ; a molecule

미분학 微分學 differential calculus

미불 未拂 arrears ; arrearage ¶ 미불의

unpaid ; outstanding ; unsettled ; back 《미》 // 미불의 공급 back pay〔salary〕 ; pay〔salary〕 in arrears // 아직 미불이다 remain unpaid〔unsettled, outstanding〕
— 계정(計定) an outstanding〔unpaid〕 account ; an account overdue ; [지불할] an account payable —금 an account not yet paid ; arrears ; arrearage — 배당금 accumulated dividends — 봉급 back pay〔salary〕 —액(額) an unpaid〔outstanding〕 amount ; (amount in) arrears — 이자 interest in arrears — 자본 unpaid capital

미불 美弗 ⇨ 미화(美貨)

미불입 未拂入 ¶ 미불입의 unpaid(-up)
— 주〔자본금〕 unpaid stocks〔capital〕 ; uncalled capital

미비 未備 insufficiency ; imperfection ; inadequacy —하다 (be) insufficient ; be not enough ; (be) unsatisfactory ; imperfect ; incomplete ; defective ; inadequate ; be not up to the mark ¶ 제도상의 미비 institutional inertia // 교통 기관의 미비 imperfect means of transportation // 미비한 점이 많다 There is much to be desired. // 서류가 미비되어 있다 The documents are not in order.

미쁘다 (be) trustworthy ; reliable ; trusty

*__미사 美辭__ flowery words〔language〕 ; rhetorical flourishes ¶ 미사 여구를 늘어놓다 marshal all sorts of flowery words // 미사 여구를 쓰다 use honeyed〔fair〕 words
— 여구(麗句) fine phrases ; florid language

미사 彌撒 〖카톨릭〗 a (Christian) mass ¶ 미사를 올리다 say〔read〕 mass // 미사에 참례하다 go to mass
위령(慰靈) — a requiem mass 추도(追悼) — a memorial mass

미사리 a hairy wild man living in the mountains on herbs and berries

‡__미사일__ 〖군사〗 a missile ¶ 미사일을 발사하다 fire〔launch〕 a missile
— 경쟁(競爭) a missile race — 기지(基地) a missile base〔station〕 — 발사 기지(發射基地) a missile launching site — 시설(施設) a missile installation — 실험 the test-firing of a missile 공중 발사 탄도(空中發射彈道) — an air-launched ballistic missile 《ALBM》 대전차(對戰車) — an antitank missile 유도(誘導) — a guided missile 《GM》 작전용(作戰用)〔전략용〕 — an operational〔a strategic〕 missile 지대공(地對空) — a surface〔ground〕(-to)-air missile 《SAM》 탄도탄 요격용(彈道彈邀擊用) — an antiballistic missile 《ABM》 핵(核) — a nuclear missile 대(對) — 방위(防衛) antimissile defense 육군(陸軍) — 부대(部隊) an army missile unit

미산지 米産地 a rice-producing district ; a rice country

미삼 尾蔘 the root hair of ginseng ; tiny-sized ginseng

미상 未詳 —하다 (be) unknown ; unidentified ; be not exactly known ¶ 저자 미상의 anonymous ; unidentified // 신원 미상이다 A person's identity is not established. /A person's name and address are unknown. /A person is unidentified. // 피해 정도는 미상이다 The extent of the damage is not yet known 〔ascertained〕. // 원인 미상이다 The cause still remains a mystery.

미상불 未嘗不 indeed ; truly ; undoubtedly ; certainly ¶ 미상불 이것은 편리한 기계다 This is a handy apparatus, to be sure.

미상환 未償還 non-redemption ¶ 미상환의 outstanding 《debts》 ; unredeemed 《liabilities》
—액(額) outstanding issues

미색 美色 ① [미인] a beautiful woman ; a beauty ; [아름다움] beauty (of a woman) ② [빛깔] a beautiful color

미생물 微生物 a microorganism ; a microbe ; a microscopic organism ; a germ ¶ 미생물의 microbial ; microbic
— 연구소 the Institute of Microbiological Diseases

미생물학 微生物學 microbiology ¶ 미생물학(상)의 microbiological // 미생물학상 microbiologically
—자 a microbiologist

미설 未設 ¶ 미설의 unestablished ; uninstalled ; under project

미성 未成 incompletion ¶ 미성의 unfinished ; uncompleted ; crude // 미성화 a half-finished picture

미성 美聲 a sweet〔beautiful〕 voice

*__미성년 未成年__ minority ; under age ; nonage ¶ 미성년자 a minor ; an infant ; a person under age // 미성년자 금주법 the law for prohibiting minors from drinking // 미성년이다 He is under age. /He is not yet of age.
— 노동 child labor — 범죄 juvenile delinquency — 시대 the preadolescent period

미성숙 未成熟 immaturity ; unripeness —하다 (be) unripe ; immature ; green —아(兒) an immature infant ; a premature baby〔infant〕 ; a premie

미성안 未成案 an unfinished plan ; an uncompleted scheme ; a proposal which has not yet been substantialized

미성품 未成品 an unfinished article 〔product〕

미세 微細 minuteness —하다 (be) minute〔delicate〕 ; fine ; nice ; detailed ; particular ¶ 미세하게 minutely ; in full detail // 미세하게 논하다 discuss 《a matter》 in detail〔minutely〕

미세기¹ [밀물·썰물] ebb and flow ; flux and reflux ; the tide

미세기² 〖광물〗 a hole dug at an angle in a mine
미세기³ 〖건축〗 a double sliding-door
미세화 微細畫 a miniature ; [화법] miniature ¶ 미세화의 초상 a portrait in miniature
—공(工) a miniature painter
미션 missions ; [선교사] a missionary
— 스쿨 a missionary〔mission〕 school
미소 美蘇 America and the Soviet Union ; American-Soviet ; Russo-American
— 공동 위원회 the U.S.-Soviet Joint Commission — 핵무기 제한 회담 Strategic Arms Limitation Talks《SALT》
‡미소 微小 minuteness —하다 (be) minute ; microscopic ; infinitesimal
— 식물 a microphyte — 진화(進化) 〖생물〗 microevolution —체 a minute particle of matter ; a granule ; a corpuscle ; 〖생물〗 a microcyte
미소 微少 a very small amount ; extremely small quantities —하다 (be) very little
—부 측광기(部測光器) a microphotometer
†미소 微笑 a smile —하다 smile ; beam ; crack a smile ¶ 미소를 띄우고 smiling ; with a smile ; with a smiling face
미소년 美少年 a handsome youth ; a comely youth ; a good-looking boy ; a fair-faced youth〔lad〕 ; an Adonis
미속 美俗 a beautiful〔laudable〕 custom
미송 美松 〖식물〗 the Oregon pine ; the Douglas fir〔pine, spruce〕
미수 未收 ¶ 미수의 uncollected ; accrued ; receivable ; unearned ; deferred
—금 an uncollected〔outstanding〕 amount —금 계정 accounts receivable —배당〔이자〕 accrued dividends〔interest〕 receivable —보험료 due and deferred premiums — 수익 uncollected〔accrued〕 income〔revenue〕 —요금 an outstanding fee
미수 未遂 ¶ 미수의 attempted ; unconsummated // 미수로 끝나다 end〔fail〕 in the attempt
—죄 an attempted〔uncommitted, unconsummated〕 crime〔offense〕 ; an attempt to commit a crime ; a criminal attempt ¶ 방화 미수죄로 체포되다 be arrested on a charge of attempted incendiarism 살인 — an attempt at murder ; an attempt to kill〔murder〕 자살 — an attempted suicide ; an attempt to kill oneself
미수 米壽 one's 88th birthday ¶ 미수 잔치 the celebration of one's 88th birthday
미수범 未遂犯 an attempted crime ; an unconsummated crime ; an attempt at an offense ; a criminal attempt ; an infraction not consummated ; a would-be criminal 암살 — a would-be assassin (범인)
*미숙 未熟 unripeness ; greenness ; immaturity —하다 [과실이] (be) unripe ; green ; immature ; [숙달하지 못한] inexperienced ; unskilled ; callow ; raw ; poor ; half-fledged ¶ 미숙한 자 a greenhorn ; a green hand ; an inexperienced person // 나의 그림은 미숙하다 My picture is poor〔far from perfect〕. // 이 배는 아직 미숙하다 This pear is not yet ripe. // 그는 모든 면에서 아직 미숙한 철부지이다 He's still just an immature youth with a superficial view of everything.
—아(兒) an immature infant ; a premature baby〔infant〕 ; a pre(e)mie
미숙련 未熟練 ¶ 미숙련의 unskilled ; unskillful ; untrained
—공 an unskilled workman〔labor〕 ; a green hand ; unskilled labor (집합적으로)
*미술 美術 art ; the fine arts ; polite arts ¶ 미술적인 artistic // 미술적으로 artistically // A씨 소장의 미술품 Mr. A's art collection
—가 an artist — 감독 〖영화〗 an art director — 감정가 a virtuoso《*pl.* ～s. -si》 ; a connoisseur ; an art expert —계(界) the world of art ; art circles ; the art world —관(館) an art gallery — 비평가 an art critic —상(商) a fine art dealer —서 an art book —원(院) the Academy of Art — 자수(刺繡) art needle work — 전람회 an art exhibition 응용 — applied art 장식 — decorative art 조형 — formative arts
미술 감식안 美術鑑識眼 an artistic eye ; an eye for the beautiful
미술 공예 美術工藝 artistic handicraft ; arts and crafts
—가 a handicraftsman ; an artisan —품 artistic handicrafts
미술사 美術史 art history
—가 an art historian
미술안 美術眼 an artistic eye ; an eye for the beautiful
미술품 美術品 a work of art ; an art object〔piece, work〕 ; an object of art ; an object d'art《*pl.* objects d'art》 ¶ 동양의 미술품 objects of Oriental art
미술 학교 美術學校 an art school〔academy〕 ; a school of fine arts ¶ 미술 학교의 학생 an art student
미스 [미혼녀] Miss《*pl.* ～es》 ; a miss ; an unmarried woman ¶ 미스 김 Miss *Kim* // 그녀는 아직 미스다 She is yet unmarried. /She still remains single.
— 유니버스 Miss Universe — 코리아 Miss Korea
미스터 Mister《Mr.》 ; a mister ; a gentleman
미스(테이크) [틀린 데] a miss ; a mistake ; a slip(-up)
미시 a cold drink of roast-grain powder ⇨ 미싯가루
미시 未時 the Watch of the Sheep《the period between 1 and 3 p.m.》
미시 微視 ¶ 미시적인 microscopic
— 경제학 microeconomics — 분석

microscopic analysis
미식 美式 American-style
미식 美食 dainty food ; a luxurious diet ; delicacies ; dainties **—하다** have 〔live on〕 dainty food ; be an epicure
—가 an epicure ; a gourmand ; a gourmet ; a good〔high〕 liver ; a bon vivant 《*pl.* bons vivants》《프》 **—법** gastronomy **—생활** good〔high〕 living ; an epicurean life **—주의** gourmandism ; epicurism
미식 米食 rice diet **—하다** live〔feed〕 on rice ; eat rice
— 인종 a rice-eating people
미식 축구 美式蹴球 American football
‡**미신 迷信** superstition ¶ 미신의〔적〕 superstitious // 미신을 신봉하다 entertain a superstitious belief // 미신을 타파하다 do away with〔break down〕 superstitions
—가 a superstitious person
미심 未審 doubt ; uncertainty **—하다** (be) doubtful ; questionable ; uncertain ¶ 미심한 점 a doubtful point // 미심쩍은 듯이 dubiously ; doubtingly ; suspiciously ; with a suspicious look // 미심히 여기다 doubt 《something》 ; regard as doubtful // 미심쩍은 얼굴을 하다 look dubious〔suspicious〕 // 미심한 데가 좀 있다 There is something that is not clear to me.
미싯가루 powder of roast grain〔rice, barley〕
미싱 [재봉틀] a sewing machine ¶ 미싱으로 박다 sew by machine
미아 迷兒 a lost〔missing〕 child ; a stray child ¶ 미아를 찾다 search for a missing child
***미안 未安 —하다** ① [거북하다] (be) uneasy ; uncomfortable ; feel uneasy ; feel oneself to be blamable ¶ 그 건에 대해서는 지금도 미안하게 생각하고 있다 That matter still troubles my conscience.
② [남에게] be sorry ; be regrettable ; be repentant ; be regretted ¶ 대단히 미안합니다 [사과] I am very sorry. / Please excuse me. /[감사] Thank you very much. // 미안하지만 물 한 잔 주십시오 Give me a glass of water, please. // 미안하지만 편지 좀 부쳐 주시겠습니까 May I trouble you to post this letter for me ? /Do you mind posting this letter ? // 폐를 끼쳐 미안합니다 I am sorry for giving you trouble. // 초대에 응하지 못해서 미안합니다 I'm sorry I can't accept your kind invitation. // 돈을 쓰게 해서 미안합니다 I am sorry for putting you to such expense. // 도와 줄 수 없어 미안합니다 I regret to say that I am unable to help you. // 늦어서 미안합니다 I must apologize for my lateness. /I must apologize to you for coming so late. // 그는 미안하다고 하며 내 청을 거절했다 He declined my request expressing his regrets. // 미안해 할것 없소 Don't give it a second thought. /Don't worry about it. /It doesn't matter. /That's all right 〔OK〕. // 저 사람에게는 정말 미안한 일이다 I'm afraid we've really done him a terrible turn. // 언제나 너에게는 미안하다는 생각이 든다 I always feel I owe you an apology.
미안 美顔 a beautiful〔handsome〕 face ; a fair face ; good〔attractive〕 looks ; pretty features
—료〔화장품〕 beauty aids **—수** a beauty wash〔lotion〕 **—술** beauty culture ; facial treatment ; facial culture
미안쩍다 (be) sorry ; regretful ; be ashamed ; be out of countenance ¶ 바보짓을 해서 미안쩍다 I am ashamed of my folly. // 오라고 초대한 것을 가지 못하여 몹시 미안쩍다 I am awfully sorry that I couldn't accept his invitation.
미안해하다 未安— regret ; be sorry about ; apologize for ¶ 미안해할 것 없소 Don't give it a second thought. / Don't worry about it. /Don't be sorry.
미약 微弱 —하다 (be) weak ; feeble ; faint ; insignificant
미약 媚藥 an aphrodisiac (drug) ; a philter ; a love potion
미양 微恙 an indisposition ; a slight illness
미어 謎語 a riddle ; a puzzle (수수께끼)
미어 美語 American English ; an Americanism ; American 《미》
미어뜨리다 tear a hole in 《paper》
미어지다 [종이·가죽이] be tattered ; be torn ; split ; burst
미역[1] 〖식물〗 brown seaweed ; Undaria pinnatifida (학명)
미역[2] (outdoor) bathing ; swimming ; a bathe ; a swim ¶ 미역감다 bathe (oneself) ; have a swim ; swim // 바닷가에 미역감으러 가다 go to the beach for a swim
미역국 seaweed soup
미역국 먹다 관용 get the sack ; get dismissed〔fired, sacked〕 ; fail an exam
미연 未然 ¶ 미연에 before 《anything》 happens ; before materializing ; previously // 미연에 방지하다 prevent〔keep〕 《anything》 from occurring // 병을 미연에 막다 prevent a disease // 화를 미연에 방지하다 nip the evil in the bud
미열 微熱 a slight fever ¶ 미열이 있다 be a bit feverish ; have a slight fever
미온 微溫 tepidity ; lukewarmness
—계(計) 〖물리〗 a micropyrometer **—수** tepid〔lukewarm〕 water **—욕** a tepid bath
미온적 微溫的 ¶ 미온적인 lukewarm ; tepid ; indifferent ; half-hearted // 미온적으로 with kid glove // 미온적 태도 a lukewarm〔noncommittal〕 attitude
— 수단〔정책, 태도〕 a lukewarm measure〔policy, attitude〕
***미완성 未完成** incompletion ¶ 미완성의 incomplete ; unfinished
— 교향악 the Unfinished Symphony (by

Schubert) — 그림 a picture in the rough 〔in the making〕 —작 an unfinished work 《of art》; a torso 《*pl.* ~(e)s, -si》 (미술·문학의)

미용 美容 ① [미안(美顔)] a beautiful〔handsome〕 face ; good〔attractive〕 looks ; pretty features ② [미장] beauty culture ¶ 미용과 건강에 좋은 good for health and beauty // 미용을 위해 식사를 제한하다 diet for beauty ; go on a beauty diet

—식(食) food for beauty — 성형(成形) cosmetic surgery — 체조 calisthenics ; aesthetic gymnastics — 학교 a beauty school

미용사 美容師 a beauty artist〔expert〕 ; a beauty-culturist ; a beauty doctor〔specialist〕 《미》 ; a cosmetologist ; a beautician 《미·속》

미용술 美容術 beauty art ; beauty culture〔treatment〕 ; cosmetology 《미》

미용원 美容院 a beauty salon〔studio〕 ; a beauty parlor〔shop〕 ; a hairdressing establishment

미우 眉宇 the brow(s)

미욱하다 (be) stupid ; thickheaded ; foolhardy ¶ 미욱한 사람 a foolhardy person // 미욱하게도 그는 병중의 몸으로 거기에 갔다 He had the thoughtlessness to go there in spite of his illness.

미움 hate ; hatred ; enmity ; loathing ; spite ¶ 미움을 받다 be hated ; be detested // 미움을 사다 incur 《a person's》 hatred ; become an object of loathing // 그는 모든 사람들의 미움을 받고 있다 He is a common object of hatred.

†미워하다 hate ; detest ; loathe ; have a spite against ; abhor ; abominate ¶ 적을 미워하다 hate one's enemy // 위선을 미워하다 hate hypocrisy // 죄를 미워하고 사람은 미워하지 않는다 I loathe the offense but not the offender. /Condemn the offense, but pity the offender.

미음 米飮 a thin gruel 《of rice, millet》 ¶ 미음을 쑤다 prepare thin rice gruel // 병자에게 미음을 먹이다 feed a thin rice gruel to a sick person

미음 美音 a beautiful〔sweet, lovely〕 voice ; a melodious sound

미의식 美意識 aesthetic consciousness

미이다 [종이·가죽이] get torn ; be tattered ; be worn out ; split ; burst

미익 尾翼 [비행기의] a tail〔tailwing〕

수직(垂直) — a vertical tail (plane) 수평(水平) — a (horizontal) tail plane

*미인 美人 ① a beautiful woman〔girl〕 ; a beauty ; a belle ¶ 놀라운 미인 a strikingly beautiful woman ② [미국인] an American

— 대회 a beauty contest

미인계 美人計 a badger game ¶ 미인계를 쓰다 pull a badger game

미작 米作 [수확] rice crop〔yield, harvest〕 ; [재배] rice culture〔growing〕 ; cultivation of rice

미장 [한의학] a deconstipating〔laxative〕 suppository

—질 deconstipating oneself, getting sluggish bowels to move ; inserting a laxative suppository ¶ 미장질하다 deconstipate oneself ; get one's bowels to move ; insert a laxative suppository

미장 美粧 beauty culture〔art〕 ; beauty treatment ; cosmetology

—원 a beauty parlor〔shop〕

미장 美匠 [도안 따위의] a decorative 〔an artistic〕 design

미장이 a plasterer

미저골 尾骨 [해부] the coccyx 《*pl.* ~es, -cyges》 ; the tailbone

— 신경 the coccygeal nerve

미적 美的 aesthetic ¶ 미적 감각〔정서〕 an aesthetic sense〔feeling〕 // 미적 가치 an aesthetic value

미적거리다 ① [밀다] keep budging ; push〔shove〕 bit by bit ¶ 돌을 미적거리다 keep budging a stone ② [지연시키다] postpone ⇨ 미루적거리다

미적미적 ① [밀다] budging ; pushing 〔shoving〕 bit by bit —하다 keep budging ⇨ 미적거리다 ¶ 돌을 미적미적 움직이다 move a stone pushing it bit by bit ② [지연] postponing ; delaying ⇨ 미루적미루적

미적분 微積分 differential and integral calculus ; infinitesimal calculus

미적지근하다 (be) lukewarm ; tepid ; half-hearted ¶ 이 맥주는 미적지근하다 This beer is warm. ⇨ 미지근하다

미전 美展 an art exhibition

미절 offal of beef (used for soup)

미점 美點 a virtue ; a merit ; an excellent point ; a good point〔quality〕 ; a beauty ; a point of beauty ; a charm

미정 未定 ¶ 미정의 unsettled ; undecided ; uncertain ; in abeyance ; pending ¶ 계획은 미정이다 My plan is unsettled. // 결혼식 날짜는 미정이다 The date of the wedding is still undecided〔held in abeyance〕. // 아직 미정이다 Not decided yet. /Up in the air.

—고(稿) an unfinished manuscript — 문제 an open question ; a moot point

미정리 未整理 ¶ 미정리의 pending arrangement ; undisposed 《stocks》 ; unsettled 《account》

미제 未濟 ¶ 미제의 unfinished ; outstanding ; unsettled to be settled ; pending ; unpaid

— 계정(計定) an unsettled〔outstanding〕 account ; an unpaid bill — 봉급 a back salary

미제 美製 ¶ 미제의 American〔U. S.〕 made ; of American make ; made in U. S. A.

—자동차 American-made〔U. S. made〕 cars —품 an American article〔product〕

미조 美爪 manicure
—사(師) a manicurist —술 a manicure (손의) ; a pedicure (발의) —원 a manicure parlor
미조직 未組織 ¶ 미조직의 unorganized 《laborers》
미주 美酒 a delicious〔excellent〕 wine ; a good drink
미주 美洲 the continent(s) of America ; the American continent(s)
— 기구(機構) the Organization of American States 《O. A. S.》
미주 신경 迷走神經 〖해부〗 the vagus 《*pl.* vagi》 ; the pneumogastric nerves
미주알 sphincter(ial) muscles of the anus ; the sphincter ani〔vesicae〕 ; the anus (항문)
미주알고주알 inquisitively ; minutely ; thoroughly ; to the last details ¶ 미주알고주알 다 알다 know everything ; know all about a secret // 미주알고주알 캐묻지 말아라 Don't be so inquisitive.
미중 美中 [미국과 대만] America and Taiwan ; [미국과 중공] America and (Communist) China
— 회담 a Sino-American conference
미증유 未曾有 ¶ 미증유의 unheard-of ; unexampled ; unprecedented ; rocord-breaking ; unparalleled ; phenomenal // 미증유의 사건 an unheard-of event // 미증유의 대전쟁 the greatest war on record 〔in history, ever fought〕 // 이것은 이 나라 역사상 미증유의 사건이다 This is absolutely unexampled〔unparalleled〕 in the history of this country.
미지 —紙 wax paper
†미지 未知 (being) unknown ; strange ; unacquainted 《with》 ¶ 미지의 사람 a stranger // 미지의 세계 the unknown world
미지 美紙 [전체] the American press ; [개개의] an American paper
미지 美誌 an American magazine
미지 微志 a little token of one's gratitude〔appreciation〕 ; a small present
*미지근하다 (be) tepid ; lukewarm ; be not warm enough ; [하는 짓이] (be) half-hearted ; lukewarm ; mild ¶ 미지근한 물 tepid〔lukewarm〕 water // 미지근한 대답 a dubious〔vague, non-committal〕 reply // 미지근한 처사 half-way measures // 미지근한 태도를 취하다 assume a lukewarm〔indecisive, undecided〕 attitude ; pussyfoot 《미·속》 // 방이 미지근하다 A room is not warm enough.
미지수 未知數 an unknown quantity ; the unknown ¶ 승패는 전혀 미지수이다 The match is a very open one.
미진 微震 a slight shock (of an earthquake) ; a faint earth tremor ; microseism (지각의)
—계(計) a tromometer ; a microseismograph
미진 微塵 a bit ; an insignificant thing ; a trifle ; a particle ; fine dust ; atoms
미진 未盡 —하다 be unexhausted ; be incomplete ; be unfinished
—처(處) an unfinished part
미착 未着 ¶ 미착의 not yet arrived ; undelivered
—품 goods to arrive〔in transit〕 ; goods not yet delivered
미착수 未着手 ¶ 미착수의 not yet started
— 공사 construction work not yet started
미채 迷彩 camouflage ; dazzle painting ¶ 배에 미채를 하다 camouflage a ship
미처 (not) up to that ; as far as ; to that extent ; far〔early〕 enough ; in time ; in advance ¶ 거기까지는 미처 생각 못했다 I was not far-sighted enough to think of that. // 돈을 미처 갚지 못해서 미안하다 I am sorry not to have returned the money in time. // 바빠서 미처 회합 준비를 하지 못했다 I was too busy to arrange things for the meeting in advance. // 그는 온 지 미처 한 시간도 못 되어서 집에 돌아가고 싶어졌다 He had hardly been there an hour before he wanted to return home.
미처리 未處理 ¶ 미처리의 《business》 yet unattended ; 《papers》 not yet disposed of
미처분 未處分 ¶ 미처분의 unfinished ; unsettled ; undisposed 《articles》
— 이익 undivided profit
미처치 未處置 ① [치료가] ¶ 미처치의 《the wounded》 left untreated ② ⇨ 미처리
미천 微賤 low rank ; obscurity ; humble station —하다 (be) lowly ; humble ; obscure ; be of low〔humble〕 origin ¶ 미천한 몸 a man of obscure birth ; a person in humble station // 미천하게 태어나다 be base born ; be of humble origin // 미천에서 입신하다 rise from obscurity ; rise from the gutter〔ranks〕
미첩 美妾 a beautiful concubine
미추 美醜 beauty or ugliness ; personal appearance (용모)
미추룸하다 (be) healthy and handsome 〔fair〕 ; look young and fresh ; be fresh and comely ; be of healthy beauty
미취 微醉 slight intoxication ; mellowness ; tipsiness —하다 be slightly intoxicated ; be in a cheerful mood with drink
미취학 未就學 ¶ 미취학의 not (yet) attending school
— 아동(兒童) preschool children ; children not attending school
*미치광이 ① [광인] a madman ; a lunatic ; a crazy〔insane〕 man ; a bedlamite
② [열광자] a maniac ; an enthusiast ; a fan 《미》 ; a fanatic (광신자) ; [이상한 놈] an eccentric ; a crazy guy〔duck, bird〕 ¶ 미치광이 짓 the act of a madman ; sheer

insanity // 미치광이 짓을 하다 behave like a madman ; act crazy〔frantic〕// 그는 책 미치광이다 He is a bibliomaniac. // 그는 영화 미치광이다 He is crazy〔mad〕about the movies.

술— an inveterate drunkard ; an alcoholic ; a toper **춤—** a dance maniac

† **미치다¹** ① go mad〔crazy〕; become insane ; lose one's senses ; go out of one's mind ¶ 미친 사람 a madman ; a lunatic ; an insane〔a demented〕person // 미쳐 날뛰다 run amuck〔amok〕; run riot ; rave ; be raving mad

② [열광·흥분] be crazy〔mad〕about ; go crazy〔mad〕over ; run mad after〔over〕; have a rage for ; be beside oneself over〔with〕; lose one's head over ; [이상해지다] become eccentric〔crazy, screwy, cranky〕¶ 미친 놈 a crazy guy〔duck, bird〕// 미친 듯이 like mad ; frantically ; madly // 미친 듯이 날뛰다 rave like a madman ; rush about wildly // 미친 짓을 하다 do crazy〔wild〕things // 여자한테 미치다 be crazy〔mad〕about a girl // 야구에 미치다 go crazy〔mad〕over baseball // 음악에 미치다 run mad about〔after〕music // 우표 수집에 미치다 have a rage for stamps // 정치에 미치다 be all wrapped up in politics // 성나서 미친 듯이 굴다 rave (like a madman) with anger ; be crazy〔mad〕with anger ; get mad and lose one's mind // 기뻐서 미칠 듯이 굴다 be crazy with delight ; be beside oneself〔delirious〕with joy // 질투로 미칠 듯이 굴다 be consumed〔green〕with jealousy

* **미치다²** ① [이르다] reach ; get to〔at〕; attain to ; come to ; come up to《the standard》¶ 손이 미치는 곳에 within one's reach // 힘이 미치는 한 as much as lies in one's power // 손이 미치지 않다 be out of one's reach // 표적에 미치지 않다 fall〔come〕short of the mark // 손이 나뭇가지에 미치다 one's hand reaches the branch // 힘이 미치지 못하다 be beyond one's power〔ability, capacity, reach〕; find oneself unequal《to the task》// 생각이 미치다 be clever〔alert, farsighted〕enough to think of // 품질이 표준에 미치다 the quality comes up to standard // 토지가 국경에까지 미치다 The land reaches the frontier. // 거기까지 생각이 미치지 못했다 I was not farsighted enough to think of it. // 내 힘이 미치지 못하는 일이다 The task is beyond〔out of〕my power.

② [누·영향] fall on ; befall ; happen《to a person》¶ 위험이 미치다 be in danger ; be faced with〔get exposed to〕danger // 재난이 미치다 a misfortune befalls《a person》// 사업에 영향이 미치다 have effect on business ; affect business // 누(累)가 남에게 미치다 others are involved in trouble // 손해가 이웃 마을에 미쳤다 The damage extended to the next village.

미칭 美稱 a euphemism

미크론 a micron《*pl.* ~s, micra》

밀리 — a milli-micron

미타 彌陀 〖불교〗 Amita Buddha

미태 媚態 coquetry ; coquettish behavior ¶ 미태를 부리다 be coquettish ; play the coquet ; purr《at her lover》; cast sheep's eyes at《a person》

‡ **미터** ① [길이] a meter ¶ 길이 5미터 five meters long〔in length〕② [계기] a meter ¶ 택시의 미터 a taximeter // 가스〔수도, 전기〕의 미터 a gas〔a water, an electric〕meter // 미터가 올라가다 [택시 따위의] the meter accelerates // 미터에 나온 요금을 지불하다 pay the meter

— 검사원(檢査員) a meter reader **—법(法)** the metric system **— 사용료(使用料)** meterage

미투리 hemp-cord sandals

‡ **미풍 美風** a laudable〔good, fine〕custom **— 양속(良俗)** established social morals and customs ; public morals

미풍 微風 a breeze ; a gentle〔light〕wind ; a breath of air

미필 未畢 incompletion **—하다** have not finished〔fulfilled〕¶ 미필의 unfinished ; unfulfilled ; incomplete ; unexecuted // 병역 미필자 a person who has not yet completed his military duty

미필적 고의 未必的故意 willful〔advertent, conscious〕negligence ; dolus eventualis《라》

미합중국 美合衆國 the United States of America《U. S. A.》; the States ; Uncle Sam《미·구》

미해결 未解決 ¶ 미해결의 unsettled ; unsolved ; pending ; outstanding // 미해결의 문제 an unsolved problem〔issue〕; a pending〔an outstanding〕question // 쟁의는 미해결인 채로 있다 The trouble has been unsettled〔left open〕.

미행 尾行 —하다 shadow《a person》; follow《up》; tail《after》¶ 형사에게 미행당하다 be shadowed〔followed〕by a detective

—자 a shadow(er) ; a tail ¶ 미행자를 따돌리다 give a shadower the slip

미행 微行 —하다 travel incognito ; make a private visit ; go in disguise (변장하고) ¶ 미행의 왕자 a prince incognito // 미행으로 방문하다 pay an incognito visit《to》

미행 美行 a praiseworthy〔laudable〕conduct ; a commendable act ; a good deed

미혹 迷惑 [헷갈림] confusion ; bewilderment ; [홀림] delusion ; infatuation **—하다** be confused ; be bewildered ; be seduced ; be infatuated《with》; be captivated《by》¶ 여자에게 미혹되다 be infatuated by a woman // 헛소문에 미혹되다 be carried away by rumors // 낭설을 퍼

뜨려 인심을 미혹하다 seduce the public by spreading false reports

†미혼 未婚 ¶ 미혼의 single ; unmarried // 그 여자는 미혼입니다 She is single.
—자 a single〔an unmarried〕 person ; not-yet-weds ; a bachelor (남자) ; a maiden girl ; a bachelor girl (여자)

미화 美貨 American money〔currency〕 ; the American dollar ¶ 미화로 in American money // 미화 5불 five U. S. dollars
— 공채 a dollar bond〔loan〕 —불 한국 공채 a Korean dollar bond — 어음 a dollar bill — 지불 payable in dollars —환 dollar exchange

미화 美化 beautification —하다 beautify ; make 《a matter》 beautiful ; pretty up ; embellish ; adorn (장식) ¶ 도시 미화 운동 a city-beautiful movement

미확인 未確認 ¶ 미확인의 not yet confirmed ; unconfirmed
— 보도 news from an unconfirmed source — 비행물체 an unidentified flying object 《UFO》 — 비행 물체학 ufology

미확정 未確定 ¶ 미확정의 not yet decided ; unsettled ; pending

미흡 未洽 insufficiency ; inadequacy ; unsatisfactoriness —하다 (be) insufficient ; be not enough ; (be) inadequate ; unsatisfactory ; be not up to the mark ¶ 미흡한 점 one's faults ; one's shortcomings〔failings〕 // 미흡한 점이 많다 leave much to be desired // 조사가 미흡하다 The investigation is not thoroughgoing enough. // 혹 미흡한 점이 있으면 말해 주십시오 Please remind us if there is anything amiss on our part.

미희 美姬 a beautiful maiden〔girl〕 ; a beauty

민가 民家 a private house ; a commoner's house

*민간 民間 ¶ 민간의 civil ; private ; civilian ; non-government (관에 대해서) ; nonmilitary (군에 대해서) ; popular // 민간에 큰 영향을 끼친다 He has great influence with the people.
— 공로자 a social benefactor — 단체 a private organization — 대표 위원 nongovernmental delegates —무역 private foreign trade ; foreign trade by private hands — 방송 a commercial broadcast — 방송국 a commercial radio〔TV〕 station — 사업 a private enterprise〔business〕 — 설화 a folktale ; a folk story — 신앙 a popular〔folk〕 belief — 외교 nongovernmental〔people-to-people〕 diplomacy — 요법 folk remedies — 자본 private capital — 회사 a private corporation

민간인 民間人 a non-official civilian ; a non-government person

민간 전승 民間傳承 folklore ; a legend ¶ 민간 전승적 folkloric ; legendary

민간 항공 民間航空 civil aviation
—국 〔미국의〕 the Civil Aeronautics Board

‡민감 敏感 sensitiveness ; susceptibility ; susceptivity —하다 (be) sensitive ; susceptible ; susceptive ¶ 극도로 민감한 hypersensitive // 민감한 귀 a sensitive ear // 색채에 대해서 민감하다 have an unusual sensibility for colors // 더위〔추위〕에 대해서 민감하다 be sensitive〔susceptible〕 of heat〔cold〕 // 나는 민감하다 I am very susceptible. // 이곳의 화재 경보기는 매우 민감해서 담배 연기에도 소리를 낸다 The fire alarms here are so sensitive that they're always being set off by cigarette smoke.
—도(度) 〔계기(計器)의〕 responsiveness

민감성 敏感性 susceptibility ; sensitiveness ; sensibility ¶ 이상 민감성의 allergic
이상(異常) — 〖병리〗 allergy

민국 民國 a republic ; a democratic country〔nation〕 ; a democracy
대한— the Republic of Korea 《R. O. K.》
중화— the Republic of China

민군 民軍 militia

민권 民權 civil rights ; the people's rights ¶ 민권을 옹호〔신장, 주장〕하다 defend〔extend, assert〕 the people's rights // 민권을 유린하다 trample on the people's rights
— (수호)운동 a civil rights movement ; a movement for the protection〔defense〕 of civil rights — 운동가 a civil righter 《미·구》

민꽃식물 〖식물〗 a cryptogam ; a flowerless plant ; the Cryptogamia 《총칭》

민날 the bare blade of a dagger 〔sword〕 ; a naked dagger〔sword〕

민낯 a woman's unpainted face ; a face with no make-up on it ; a naked face

민단 民團 a settlement corporation
재일 한국 거류 — the (pro-Seoul) Federation of Korean Residents in Japan

민대가리 a bald head

민도 民度 the (living, cultural) standards of the people ; the level〔stage〕 of development of the people ¶ 민도가 높다 have a high level of culture〔standard of living〕 // 형편 없는 후진국으로서 그 민도는 말이 아니다 It is a fearfully backward country and the low state of its people surpasses description.

민도리 〖건축〗 a pointed beam

민둥민둥하다 (be) bare ; bald ; hairless ; treeless ¶ 민둥민둥한 산 a bare〔bald〕 mountain // 민둥민둥한 머리 a bald head

민둥산 a bare〔bald〕 mountain ; a barren〔a treeless〕 hill

*민들레 〖식물〗 the dandelion

민란 民亂 a revolt ; an uprising ; a riot ¶ 민란을 일으키다 raise a revolt ; rise in arms 《against》 // 민란을 진압하다 suppress an insurrection of the people // 민란

이 일어나다 A revolt breaks out.
민력 民力 national power〔strength〕; national resources ¶ 민력을 함양하다 foster〔build up〕 national power ; store up national resources
민망 民望 [백성의 희망] public desire ; popular expectation ; [백성의 신망] public confidence〔trust〕; popular favor ¶ 민망을 얻다 enjoy public confidence
민망 憫 **—하다** (be) embarrassed ; sorry ; sad ¶ 그의 초라한 모습이 보기 민망할 정도였다 He looked so miserable that I was embarrassed. // 거 참 민망하군요 That's very embarrassing. // 방 안에 혼자 남게 되었을 때 내가 얼마나 민망했겠나 상상해 보시오 Imagine my embarrassment upon being left alone in the room.
민머리 ① [벼슬 없는 사람] a person without office ② [대머리] a bald head
민며느리 a girl who is brought up by the family of the husband-to-be
***민물** fresh water
—고기 fresh-water fish **— 호수** a fresh-water lake
민박하다 民泊— take lodgings at a private house
민방 民放 ⇨ 민간(-방송)
민방위 民防衛 civil defense〔-ce〕; civilian defense
—대 the Civil Defense Corps **— 대본부** the Civil Defense Corps Headquarters **— 대원** a Civil Defense Corps member **— 체제** the Civil Defense system **— 훈련(의 날)** (the day designated for) Civil Defense training
민법 民法 the civil law ; the civil code (법전) ¶ 민법학의 권위 an authority on the civil law
— 학자 a scholar of the civil law
민병 民兵 a militia ; a militiaman
—단 a militia corps
민복 民福 national〔public〕 welfare ; the well-being〔welfare〕 of the people ¶ 민복을 도모하다 promote the public welfare
민본주의 民本主義 democracy
민비녀 a plain silver hairpin
민사 民事 civil affairs〔matters〕; a civil case〔action〕 ¶ 소송이란 민사상의 투쟁이다 The suit is a civil battle.
— 사건 a civil case **— 원고〔피고〕** a plaintiff〔defendant〕 **— 책임** civil liability **— 회사** a noncommercial company
민사 悶死 death in agony **—하다** die in agony〔convulsions〕; die of vexation
민사 소송 民事訴訟 civil suit〔action〕¶ 민사 소송을 제기하다 bring a civil action〔civil proceedings to bear〕《against》
—법 〖법〗 the Civil Proceedings Act ; the Code of Civil Procedure **— 비용법** 〖법〗 the Costs in the Civil and Administrative Litigation Act
민사 재판 民事裁判 a civil trial
—권 civil jurisdiction **—소** a civil court

민색떡 —色— a colored rice cake
민생 民生 the livelihood of the people〔nation〕 ¶ 민생의 안정 the stabilization of the people's livelihood
—고 the people's economic plight〔difficulties〕 **— 문제** problems concerning public welfare **— 안정** the stabilization of the people's livelihood
민선 民選 popular election ¶ 민선의 elected by popular vote ; popularly elected
— 의원 a representative elected by popular vote
민성 民聲 public opinion ; the voice of the people ¶ 민성에 따르다 obey the dictates of public opinion ; act in accordance with public opinion // 민성을 무시하고 소신대로 하다 go one's way in defiance of public opinion
민속 民俗 ethnic customs ; folk-ways ; folk-customs
— 무용 a folk dance **— 무용가** a folk dancer **— 문학〔예술〕** folk literature 〔art〕 **—자료** 《collection of》 folk material ; folklore data **— 작가** a folk writer **—학(學)** folklore **—학자** a folklorist **국립 — 무용단** the National Folk Ballet Troupe
민속 敏速 quickness ; promptitude ; swiftness ; agility ; alacrity **—하다** (be) quick ; prompt ; swift ; agile ¶ 민속히 행동하다 be prompt in action ; act promptly // 사무를 민속히 처리하다 transact business with dispatch
민속 음악 民俗音樂 folk music
—가 a folk musician
민수 民需 civilian demands〔requirements〕
— 산업 civilian industry **— 생산** production of goods for nongovernmental use **—품** civilian goods ; consumer's goods ; goods for nongovernmental use 〔consumption〕
민수기 民數記 〖성경〗 The Book of Numbers ; [약칭] Numbers 《Num., Numb.》
민숭민숭하다 ① [머리] (be) hairless ; bare ; bald ¶ 털이 민숭민숭하다 be beardless ; have no beard ② [산이] (be) treeless ; bare ; bald ¶ 민숭민숭한 산 a bare〔bald〕 mountain ③ [말짱하다] (be) sober ; unintoxicated ; be not drunk ; be none the worse for drinking ¶ 술을 한 되 마시고도 민숭민숭하다 remain sober after drinking a gallon of liquor ; be none the worse for having drunk a gallon of liquor
민습 民習 popular〔national〕 customs ; folk-ways
민심 民心 popular feelings ; public sentiment ; the mind of the people ¶ 민심을 잃다 lose popularity〔the support of the people〕 // 민심에 역행하다 go against public sentiment // 민심을 선동하다 stir up〔inflame〕 the popular passion // 민심이 동요되고 있다 Restlessness prevails among

the people. // 민심이 점차 정부로부터 이탈되었다 The Government was gradually alienated from the people.

민약설 民約說 the Theory of Social Contract

민영 民營 private management〔operation〕 ¶ 민영의 privately-managed〔operated〕; non-government(al) (관영에 대해서) // 민영화되다 come under private management
— 사업 a private enterprise〔undertaking, business〕 — 아파트 a privately-built apartment house ; an apartment house built by the private sector

민예 民藝 folk arts ; folk crafts
—품 a folk art article

민완 敏腕 ability ; capability ; capacity ; fitness ¶ 민완의 able ; capable ; competent // 민완을 휘두르다 show〔give full play〕 to one's ability // 그는 차관으로서 크게 민완을 휘둘렀다 He proved himself highly capable as a Vice-Minister.
—가(家) an able〔efficient〕 person ; a man of ability〔capacity〕 — 형사 a competent detective

민요 民擾 an insurrection ; a revolt ; a riot ; a popular rising ¶ 민요를 일으키다 rise in revolt〔rebellion〕; revolt against // 민요를 진압하다 get under〔put down, suppress〕 a revolt

*민요 民謠** a folk song ; a ballad
— 가수 a folk singer — 대회 a hootenanny 《미》

민원 民願 a civil application ; a civil appeal〔petition〕
— 공무원 a civil affairs official — 봉사 speedy processing of civil petitions — 비서 a secretary in charge of civil affairs — 상담소 a civil affairs office — 서류(의 간소화) (simplification of) civil affair documents — 업무 civil affairs administration — 창구 a window for civil petitions

민원 民怨 popular enmity ; popular complaint(s) ; public hatred ¶ 민원을 사다 incur the enmity of the people ; provoke the hatred of the people

민유 民有 private ownership ; the people's possession ¶ 민유의 privately owned ; in private possession ; private
—림 a forest under private ownership — 지 private land — 철도 a privately-owned railway

민의 民意 the will of the people ; the popular will ; a consensus of public opinion ¶ 민의를 무시〔존중〕하다 disregard〔respect〕 the will of the people // 민의를 반영하다 reflect the will of the people // 민의를 묻다 consult the will of the people ; seek〔appeal to〕 the judgment of the people

민의원 民議院 the Lower House ; the House of Representatives 《미·일》; the House of Commons 《영》; the Chamber of Deputies 《프》
— 의원 a member of the House of Representative — 의장 the Speaker of the House of Representative

민재 民財 private possessions〔property, good, assets〕

민적 民籍 [등록] census registration ; [등본] a census register ; a family register

민정 民政 civil administration〔government〕; [민주 정치] democracy ; democratic government ¶ 민정을 실시하다 establish a civil government
— 이양 transfer of power to civil〔an elected〕 government — 장관 a civil administrator

민정 民情 the realities of the people's life ; the condition〔state〕 of the people ¶ 민정을 살피다 see how the people live ; observe the conditions of the people
— 시찰 여행 a tour for inspection of the people's conditions

†**민족 民族** a race ; a nation ; a people ¶ 앵글로 색슨 민족 the Anglo-Saxon race // 그들은 모두 독일 민족이다 They are all Germans by race.
— 감정 a race feeling — 기원론 〖인류〗 ethnogeny — 생물학 ethnobiology —성 racial characteristics〔traits〕; the character of a people — 심리학 folk〔ethnic〕 psychology ; ethnopsychology — 언어학 ethnolinguistics — 운동 the racial movement — 의상(衣裳) a folk costume ; 《in》 native dress — 의식 national〔racial〕 consciousness — 이동 racial migration — 자본 native capital ; national capital — 전선(戰線) a people's〔racial〕 front — 정신 racial spirit — 주체성 national identity ; a national pride —지(誌) ethnography — 지상주의 racism — 해방 전선 the National Liberation Front《NLF, FLN》; Front de Libération Nationale 《프》 소수 — a minority race 유태 — the Jewish nation 지배 — a master race ; [나치스가 제창한] the Herrenvolk 다— 국가 a multinational〔multiracial〕 country

민족 음악 民族音樂 folk music
—가 a folk musician

민족 자결 民族自決 self-determination of peoples
—주의 the principle of self-determination of peoples

민족주의 民族主義 [국민주의] nationalism ; [인종주의] racialism
—자 a nationalist ; a racialist

민족학 民族學 ethnology ; ethnography (민족지(誌))

민족 화해 民族和解 national reconciliation

민주 民主 democracy ¶ 민주적인 democratic // 비민주적인 undemocratic
— 공화국 a democratic republic — 사상 democratic ideas — 사회주의 democratic socialism — 전선 a democratic front

— 정당 a democratic party — 정체(正體) democracy ; government of the people (by the people, for the people) — 정치 democratic form of government ; democratic government — 제도 the democratic system — 혁명 a democratic revolution

민주국 民主國 a democratic state ; a democracy
서구 — Western democracies

민주당 民主黨 [미국] the Democratic Party ; the Democrats
—원 a Democrat

민주대다 dislike ; hate ; detest

민주스럽다 (be) embarrassed ; abashed ; ashamed

†민주주의 民主主義 democracy ; democratic principles ; democratism
— 국가 a democratic state ; a democracy —자 a democrat 민족적 — national democracy 사회 — social democracy 의회제〔인민, 대중〕 — parliamentary〔people's, mass〕 democracy

민주화 民主化 democratization —하다 democratize ¶ 민주화된 국가 a democratized country

민주 회복 民主回復 the restoration of democracy —하다 restore democracy ; restore the country's democratic institutions ; have a democratic government

민줄 an unreinforced kite string

†민중 民衆 the people ; the mass of the people ; the masses ; the populace ¶ 민중적인 popular ; democratic
— 대회 a mass meeting ; a people's rally — 심리 popular psychology — 예술 popular arts — 오락 popular amusements — 운동 popular movements — 정치 popular(-based) government

민중화 民衆化 popularization —하다 popularize

민지 民智 the intellect〔intellectual level〕 of the people ; the public intellect

민짜 a plain thing ; an artless article

†민첩 敏捷 quickness ; agility ; alacrity ; shrewdness ; promptitude ; nimbleness
—하다 (be) quick ; agile ; shrewd ; prompt ; nimble ; alert ¶ 민첩하게 quickly ; promptly ; with alacrity // 민첩한 사나이 a shrewd man // 행동이 민첩하다 be quick〔prompt〕 in action

민촌 民村 a commoner's〔grass-roots〕 village

민틋하다 (be) gently-〔smoothly-〕sloping ; even and slant ¶ 민틋한 비탈 a gentle〔an easy〕 slope

민패 ① [민짜] a plain〔simple〕 thing〔article〕 ; an artless〔undecorated〕 thing ② [얼굴·수족] a face without a nose〔an ear〕 ; a hand without fingers ; a foot without toes

민폐 民弊 [권리의 방해] a public nuisance ; private nuisance (특정인 상대의) ; [금전의 갈취] extortionate practices by public officials ; [공직자의 비행] a malpractice

민하다 (be) senseless ; thoughtless ; stupid ; silly ; foolish

민화 民話 a folk story ; a folktale

민활 敏活 quickness ; promptitude ; alacrity ; agility ; activity ; dispatch —하다 (be) quick ; prompt ; active ; nimble ¶ 민활하게 quickly ; promptly ; briskly ; with alacrity〔dispatch〕 // 민활하게 행동하다 act promptly ; be prompt in action // 민활한 조치를 취하다 take prompt action // 사무의 민활을 도모하다 promote promptitude in business // 그 노인은 아직도 동작이 민활하다 The old man still moves with alacrity.

†믿다 ① [의심치 않다] believe ; put belief in ; credit ; give credit〔credence〕 to ; put credit in ; be convinced of 《a fact》 ¶ 믿을 수 없는 이야기 an unbelievable〔incredible〕 story ; a story that passes belief // 내가 믿는 바로는 in my opinion ; to the best of my belief ; my belief is 《that》 // 믿을 수 있다 be credible ; be believable // 믿을 수 없다 be incredible ; be unbelievable ; be doubtful // 남의 말을 잘 믿다 be credulous ; be ready to believe anything one hears // 남의 말을 잘 믿지 않다 be incredulous ; skeptical 《about》 // 굳게 믿다 have a firm belief 《that》 ; firmly believe 《that》 // 남이 말한 대로 믿다 take 《a person》 at his word // 옳다고 믿는 바를 행하다 do anything one believes right // 나는 그것이 거짓이었다고 믿고 있다 I believe it was false. /I believe it to have been false. // 나는 그녀의 말을 진실이라고 믿고 있다 I place credit in her statement as being true. // 나는 그의 죽음이 믿어지지 않는다 I cannot persuade myself that he is dead〔of his death〕. // 그의 말은 믿을 수 없다 I cannot believe him. /I can't give credit to his statement. // 그것 참 믿기 어려운 이야기로군 That's a tall tale〔story〕. // 그 사람 말을 믿어도 좋다 You may take him at his word. // 내 말을 믿어도 좋다 Believe me. /Trust me. /Take my word for it. /You've got my word for it.
② [신뢰] trust ; trust〔believe, confide〕 in ; have confidence in ; put trust〔faith〕 in ; [의지] rely on ; depend upon ; trust to ; place reliance on ¶ 믿을 수 없는 사람 an unreliable〔untrustworthy〕 person // 믿을 만한 보도에 의하면 according to reliable〔trustworthy〕 information // 믿을 만하다 be trustworthy ; reliable ; authentic ; authoritative // 자기 힘을 지나치게 믿다 trust to one's strength too much ; be too confident of one's own strength // 나는 그를 전적으로 믿는다 I have full confidence in him. // 그는 믿을 만한 사람이다

You may rely upon him. /He deserves our confidence. /He is trustworthy. // 그는 믿을 수 없다 He is not to be relied upon. // 당신을 믿고 이 일을 맡긴다 I will trust to you for the performance of the task. // 그는 단 하나의 친구를 믿고 상경했다 He came up to *Seoul,* counting on his only friend for help.
③ [확신] be sure of ; be confident of ¶ 성공을 믿다 be sure of success // 그들은 자기들의 승리를 굳게 믿고 있다 They were confident of their victory. / They were confident that they would win a victory. // 나는 너의 성공을 믿는다 I am sure you will succeed.
④ [신앙] believe in ; have belief〔faith〕 in ¶ 불교를 믿다 believe〔profess〕 in Buddhism // 하느님을 믿다 have faith in God
믿는 나무에 곰이 핀다〔믿는 도끼에 발등 찍힌다, 믿었던 돌에 발부리 채인다〕 속담 In trust is treason. /Trust makes way for tneachery. /Trust is the mother of deceit.

‡믿음 ① [신뢰] trust ; confidence ; credit ; credence ¶ 믿음을 받다 enjoy〔be in〕 《a person's》 confidence // 믿음을 잃다 lose credit 《with》 ; lose the confidence 《of》 // 믿음을 배반하다 betray 《a person's》 trust〔confidence〕
② [신앙] faith ; belief ¶ 믿음이 강하다 be pious ; be devout ; have a strong 〔deep〕 faith // 믿음을 버리다 forsake 〔give up, renounce, abjure〕 one's faith // 그는 믿음이 강하다〔약하다〕 He is strong〔weak〕 in faith.

믿음성 —性 reliability ; dependability ; trustworthiness ¶ 믿음성이 있다 be reliable ; be dependable ; be trustworthy // 믿음성 없다 be unreliable ; be undependable ; be untrustworthy

믿음직하다 (be) reliable ; dependable ; trustworthy ; authentic ; authoritative ¶ 믿음직하게 여기다 place great trust in 《a person》 ; hope〔expect〕 much from 《a person》 // 그는 믿음직한 사람이다 He is to be depended upon.

†밀[1] wheat
—녹말 wheat starch **—밭** a wheat field **—짚** wheat straw **—풍작〔흉작〕** a fine 〔poor〕 crop of wheat

밀[2] [밀랍] beeswax ; wax ¶ 밀먹인 waxed // 밀먹인 종이 wax paper
—초 wax candle

†밀가루 wheat flour
— 반죽 dough ; [버터를 섞은] puff paste ; [우유·버터·달걀을 섞은] batter

밀감 蜜柑 a mandarin orange ; a tangerine ¶ 밀감 껍질을 벗기다 peel an orange
— 껍질 an orange peel **—밭** a tangerine orchard〔plantation〕 **—색** orange ; mandarin

밀계 密啓 a confidential〔secret〕 report to the King **—하다** submit a confidential report to the King ; report secretly to the King

***밀고 密告** secret information 《against》 ; anonymous notice ; betrayal ; report **—하다** inform against ; peach against 《속》 ; blow the gaff 《to the police》 《속》 ; snitch 《on》 ¶ 친구를 밀고하는 것은 옳지 않다 It's not right to lodge an information against your friend.
—자 (者) an informer ; an informant ; a betrayer ; a snitcher 《속》 ; a sneak 《영·구》

밀골무 a wax-thimble

밀교 密敎 Esoteric Buddhism

밀국수 wheat vermicelli ; wheat-flour noodles

밀굽 a deformed〔one-sided〕 hoof 《as of a limping horse》

밀기름 a pomade made of beeswax and sesame oil

밀기울 (wheat) bran ; pollard (밀가루가 들어 있는) ¶ 밀기울을 빼지 않은 밀가루 whole-wheat flour ; whole meal

밀깜부기 a smut ball of wheat

밀나물 ① 〖식물〗 greenbrier ② [멸] lizard's-tail

밀낫 a reaping-hook

†밀다 ① [떼밀다] push ; shove ; thrust ; jostle ; give a push ¶ 수레를 밀다 push 〔wheel〕 a cart // 밀어 넘어뜨리다 push down // 밀어 젖히다 push aside // 밀고 가다 shove along // 문을 밀어 열다 push the door open // 사람을 방에서 밀어 내다 shove〔push〕 a person out of a room // 군중을 밀어 젖히고 나가다 jostle〔elbow one's way〕 through a crowd // 책상을 앞으로 밀다 thrust a table forward // 군중은 서로 떠밀며 극장으로 들어갔다 The crowd jostled into the theater.
② [깎다] shave ; plane ¶ 수염을 밀다 shave one's face ; shave oneself ; have 〔get〕 a shave // 대패로 판자를 밀다 plane a board // 등을 밀어 드릴까요 Shall I scrub your back for you ?
③ [추천] recommend ; support ; back up ¶ 김씨를 회장으로 밀다 recommend Mr. *Kim* as a chairman ; propose Mr. *Kim* for chairman

밀담 密談 a private〔secret〕 conversation ; a confidential talk **—하다** talk secretly ; have a confidential talk 《with》 ; be closeted 《with》

밀대 ① [막대] a push stick ② [총의] the recoil mechanism 《on a carbine》

***밀도 密度** density
—계 a densimeter ; a densitometer **—류** 〖해양〗 a density current **—측정** densimetry **인구 —** the density of population ¶ 이 지방의 인구 밀도는 1평방 마일에 100명 꼴이다 The density of population in the region is 100 person to a square mile.

밀도살 密屠殺 illegal butchery ¶ 밀도살 행위를 적발하다 pick up illegal butchery practices

밀따리 (a variety of) late-ripening rice
밀떡 wheat plaster〔paste〕《to be applied to a wound》
밀똘레 a lump of beeswax
밀뜨리다 push〔shove〕《a person》off ; thrust ; give a shove ¶ 사람을 절벽에서 밀뜨리다 thrust〔push〕a person over a cliff
*밀랍 蜜蠟 beeswax
*밀려들다 advance〔press〕on《a castle》; make〔rush〕for《the door》; [파도가] beat upon《the shore》; surge into ¶ 밀려드는 파도 advancing〔surging〕waves // 입구로 밀려들다 make a rush for the door // 사람들이 그 가게로 밀려들었다 People stormed the shop. // 예금자들이 은행으로 밀려들었다 The depositors besieged the bank. /The bank had a rush of depositors. // 조수가 밀려든다 The tide is flowing.
밀렵 密獵 poaching —하다 poach ; trespass on game〔fish〕; steal game ; take game〔fish〕by illegal method ¶ 꿩을 밀렵하다 poach for pheasants // 남의 수렵지에서 밀렵하다 poach upon another's preserves
—선(船) a poaching-boat〔vessel〕 —자 a poacher
밀리 milli-
—그램 a milligram《mg., mgm.》—리터 a milliliter《ml.》—미터 a millimeter《mm.》—바 a millibar《mb.》
밀리다 ① [일이] be left undone ; be delayed〔retarded〕; be in arrears《with》; be behind《with, in》; pile up ; accumulate ¶ 밀린 일 arrears of work ; work still waiting to be done // 일이 밀리다 get behind in〔be arrears with〕one's work // 주문이 밀리다 orders pile up // 밀린 사무를 정리하다 clear up belated business ; clear off one's arrears of work // 우리는 밀린 일이 많다 We have quite a backlog. /We've got so much work piled up. // 교통 사고 때문에 차들이 수마일이나 밀렸다 Due to an accident, the traffic backed up for miles. // 20km나 차가 밀려 있다고 한다 They say traffic's backed up for the next twenty kilometers. // 일이 산같이 밀려 있다 There is a good deal of work left undone. /There are heaps of work in arrears.
② [지불이] fall into arrears ; be in arrears《with》; be left unpaid ; be overdue ; be outstanding ¶ 밀린 돈 arrears ; arrearages // 밀린 이자 an interest on arrears // 밀린 봉급 back pay〔salary〕// 계산〔지불할 돈〕이 밀리다 get behind in〔be in arrears with〕the payment ; one's account is left unpaid〔unsettled〕// 집세가 밀리다 be in arrears with the rent ; have arrears of rent to pay // 자동차 대금 지불이 밀렸다 I am behind in my auto loan payments.
③ [떼밀리다] be pushed ; be shoved ; be thrust ¶ 밀려나가다 be pushed out ; be forced out ; be squeezed out ; be crowded out // 사장 자리에서 밀려나다 be ousted〔dismissed〕from the position of president ; be squeezed out of the position of president // 요즘은 카세트 테이프조차도 CD한테 밀려나고 있는 판이다 These days even audio cassettes are giving way to CD's.
④ [깎이다] be shaved ; shave (면도가) ; be planed ; plane (대패가) ¶ 수염이 잘 밀리다 one's beard shaves well ; have an easy beard (to shave) // 이 대패는 잘 밀린다 This plane planes well. // 이 판자는 잘 밀리지 않는다 This board planes poorly.
*밀림 密林 a dense〔thick〕forest ; a jungle
— 지대 a jungle area
밀막다 refuse under a pretense ; decline on the pretext《of》
밀매 密賣 illicit sale《of》; illicit traffic《in》; smuggling ; bootlegging (주류의)
—하다 sell secretly ; deal secretly《in》; smuggle ; bootleg (주류를)
—자 a secret〔an illicit〕dealer ; a smuggler ; a runner《미》— 장소 a bootleggery ; a blind pig〔tiger〕《미》—품 smuggled goods
밀매매 密賣買 illicit traffic《in》—하다 engage in illicit traffic《in》; deal secretly《in》
밀매음 密賣淫 unlicensed prostitution —하다 engage in unlicensed prostitution
—녀 an unlicensed prostitute
밀모 密謀 a plot ; an (underhand) intrigue ; [공모] a conspiracy —하다 plot ; conspire
밀무역 密貿易 smuggling —하다 smuggle
—업자(業者) a smuggler
*밀물 the flow ; the flux ; the tide ¶ 밀물이 들어오다 The tide is rising〔coming in〕. /The tide is on the flow. // 밀물이 썰기 시작하다 The tide begins to ebb.
밀방망이 a rolling pin (to flatten dough)
밀벌 〖곤충〗 a kind of yellow-jacket〔wasp〕
밀범벅 wheat-and-pumpkin pudding
밀보리 wheat and barley ; rye (쌀보리)
밀봉 蜜蜂 a honeybee
밀봉 密封 sealing up ; sealing tightly —하다 seal hermetically〔tightly〕; seal up
— 교육 secret〔clandestine〕training
밀사 密使 a secret envoy〔messenger〕; an emissary
밀생 密生 —하다 grow thick〔in clusters〕; be thickly wooded
— 식물 a cespitose plant
밀서 密書 a secret letter ; a confidential message ¶ 밀서를 몸에 지니다 bear a secret message
밀선 密船 a smuggling vessel〔boat〕; a smuggler ; a runner《미》

밀송하다 密送— send〔dispatch〕 secretly 〔in secret〕
밀수 密輸 smuggling ; contraband (trade) —하다 smuggle 《something into, out of》 ¶ 금제품을 밀수하다 run contraband goods
— 감시선 a contraband-control vessel —단 a smuggling gang〔ring〕 —선 a smuggling vessel〔boat〕 ; a smuggler ; a runner 《미》 —입(入) smuggling ; contraband trade ¶ 밀수입하다 import unlawfully〔through illegal channels〕 ; smuggle 《a thing》 (over) —입자 a smuggler ; a contraband trader ; a runner 《미》 —출 smuggling 《goods》 out 〔abroad〕 ¶ 밀수출하다 smuggle 《a thing》 abroad〔out of the country〕 ; export 《an article》 unlawfully ; run 《미》 —품 smuggled goods ; contraband articles ; run goods 《미》
*밀수 蜜水 honeyed water
밀수제비 a piece〔dish〕 of flour dough boiled with (meat) soup ; wheat-flour dough boiled in soup
밀실 密室 a secret room〔chamber〕 ; a closet ¶ 밀실에 감금하다 keep 《a person》 in solitary〔close〕 confinement
— 감금 solitary confinement — 살인 사건 a locked-room murder case
밀쌀 a grain of wheat ; a wheat corn
밀썰물 high tide and low tide
밀약 密約 [약속] a secret promise 〔understanding〕 ; [협약] a secret agreement〔treaty〕 —하다 make a secret promise ¶ 밀약을 맺다 conclude a secret treaty ; contract a secret pact
밀어 [통밀어] on the average ; en masse 《프》
밀어 密語 a confidential〔private〕 talk ; lover's whispers (애인 간의) ¶ 밀어를 속삭이다 talk in whispers
밀어 密魚 poaching (for fish) —하다 poach for fish ; trespass on fish ; take fish by illegal method
—선(船) a poaching boat —자(者) a poacher
*밀어내다 push〔press〕 out〔forward〕 ; push 《a thing》 out ; thrust out ; force out ; squeeze out ; crowd out ; elbow out
밀어넣다 push〔force, squeeze, thrust〕 in
밀어붙이다 push〔drive〕 《a person》 to ; push〔thrust〕 against
밀어올리다 push up ; thrust up ; force up
밀어젖히다 push away〔aside, by〕 ; thrust aside
*밀월 蜜月 a honeymoon
— 여행 a honeymoon trip ¶ 밀월 여행을 하다 make a honeymoon trip ; honeymoon — 여행자 honeymooners
밀음쇠 a snap clasp (on a briefcase) ; a buckle (on a belt)
밀의 密議 a secret conference ; a private consultation ; a chamber-council —하다 confer in private 《with》 ; have a private consultation 《with》 ; hold a secret conference
밀입국 密入國 smuggling ; stowing away —하다 smuggle oneself into a country ; stow away ¶ 중국인을 미국에 밀입국시키다 smuggle a Chinese into the United States
밀장지 a sliding door〔screen〕 ; a sliding partition ¶ 밀장지를 달다 fit in〔put up〕 a paper slide
밀전병 —煎餠 a grilled wheat cake
†밀접 密接 —하다 (be) close 《to》 ; intimate 《with》 ¶ 사제지간의 밀접한 관계 the intimate relations between master and pupil // 밀접한 관계가 있다 be closely connected 《with》 ; be intimately associated 《with》 // 기후와 농작물 사이에는 서로 밀접한 관계가 있다 There is close correlation between climate and crops.
밀정 密偵 a secret agent ; a spy ; an emissary ; an undercover man〔agent〕 ; an agent provocateur
밀조 密造 illicit manufacture ; [술의] unlawful brewing ; illicit distilling ; bootlegging〔moonshining〕 《미·속》 —하다 manufacture illicitly〔secretly〕 ; brew 〔distill〕 unlawfully ; moonshine 《미·속》
밀주 密酒 home-brewed wine ; moonshine 《미·속》 ; bootleg ; home-brew ¶ 밀주를 담그다 brew clandestinely〔secretly, illicitly〕 ; moonshine 《미·속》 ; distil illicitly
— 양조장 a bootlegging〔an illicit〕 distillery
밀지 密旨 secret〔private〕 orders 〔instructions〕
‡밀집 密集 missing ; concentration —하다 crowd ; swarm ; close up ; aggregate densely ; cluster together ¶ 밀집한 close ; massed ; thick ; crowded // 인가가 밀집하고 있다 The houses stand close together 〔roof by roof〕.
— 모자 a straw hat — 서까래 『건축』 a small〔slender〕 rafter — 세공 strawwork ; straw fancy goods
밀집 부대 密集部隊 massed troops ; troops in close formation〔order〕 ; serried ranks of troops〔soldiers〕
밀짚 (wheat) straw
— 대형(隊形) a close order ; (a) close 〔compact〕 formation — 훈련 close-order drill — 화음(和音) 『음악』 close harmony
밀착 密着 close adherence —하다 stick (fast) to ; adhere closely to ; be glued to
—법 『사진』 contact printing — 인화 a contact print〔copy〕 — 인화지 contact paper
밀책 密策 a secret plan
밀초 a beeswax candle
밀초 蜜炒 honeyed medicinal herbs that

are roasted

밀치 a crupper stick

‡**밀치다** push roughly〔forcibly〕; shove ; thrust ¶ 밀쳐 넘어뜨리다 push《a person》 down // 밀치고 나가다 jostle〔shove〕 along ; push〔force, elbow〕 one's way 《through a crowd》 // 옆으로 밀쳐내다 push〔brush〕 aside〔away〕; force out of the way // 차에서 밀쳐 버리다 thrust《a person》 out of a train〔car〕 // 밀치지 마라 Stop shoving.

밀치락달치락 hustling and jostling **—하다** hustle and jostle ; push and shove ; push one another

밀칙 密勅 a King's secret instruction〔order〕

밀크 (cow's) milk ¶ 밀크로 키우다 bring up《a baby》 on the bottle

밀타승 蜜陀僧【약】 litharge

밀탐 密探 spying ; espionage ; secret investigation **—하다** spy《on a person, into a secret》; be engaged in espionage ; do detective work ¶ 행동을 밀탐하다 spy into《a person's》 actions // 적의 움직임을 밀탐하다 spy upon the enemy's movement // 회사의 내정을 밀탐하다 investigate the inside affairs of a company

밀통 密通 adultery ; fornication ; misconduct ; liaison ; intrigue ; an illicit intercourse **—하다** commit adultery with《a person》; misconduct oneself with ; make an illicit love《to》

—자 an adulterer (남자) ; an adulteress

밀펌프 a forcing〔force〕 pump

‡**밀폐 密閉 —하다** shut〔cover up, close up〕 tight ; seal hermetically ; make〔keep〕 airtight ¶ 밀폐한 상자 an airtight box ; a hermetically sealed box // 용기를 밀폐해 두면 내용물은 오래 보존된다 If the receptacle is made airtight, the contents will keep for a long time.

밀푸러기 (wheat) flour soup

밀풀 wheat flour paste

밀항 密航 a secret passage ; stowing away ; smuggling **—하다** stow away ; smuggle oneself《into a foreign country》; go as a stowaway ¶ 그는 미국 배로 밀항하려고 했다 He attempted to go as a stowaway on an American ship.

—선 a smuggler **—자** a stowaway **—자 집단** a smuggling ring

밀행 密行 a prowl **—하다** go secretly〔stealthily〕;［경관이］ patrol in plain clothes

밀회 密會 a clandestine〔secret〕 meeting ; a romantic rendezvous **—하다** have a clandestine meeting ; meet secretly〔in secret〕

— 장소 a place of assignation ; a place of secret meeting ; a secret rendezvous ; a tryst

밉광스럽다 (be) very hateful ; abominable ; detestable ; spiteful ; loathsome ⇨ 밉살스럽다

‡**밉다** (be) hateful ; spiteful ; abominable ; detestable ; disgusting ;［미워하다］ hate ; detest ¶ 미운 짓 a detest-able conduct // 밉게 굴다 behave〔act〕 detestable〔abominably〕 // 이 애는 지금 한참 미울 때다 He is in his naughty boyhood.

밉살머리스럽다 (be) (very) hateful ⇨ 밉살스럽다

***밉살스럽다** (be) (very) hateful ; abominable ; detestable ; disgusting ; spiteful ; odious ; loathsome ¶ 밉살스러운 웃음 a malicious smile // 밉살스러운 녀석 a detestable〔repulsive, odious〕 fellow // 밉살스러운 소리를 하다 say spiteful things // 말투가 밉살스럽다 use malicious language // 그는 밉살스러울 정도로 침착했다 He remained provokingly cool〔calm〕.

밉상 —相 a disgusting face〔appearance, act〕 ¶ 그다지 밉상만은 아니었을테지 You have a fancy for her, haven't you ?

밋밋이 long and slender〔upright〕; plain and smooth ¶ 턱을 밋밋이 밀다 shave one's beard off ; shave one's chin clean // 나무가 밋밋이 자란다 A tree grows long and slender.

밋밋하다 (be) plain and smooth ; long and slender〔upright〕 ¶ 밋밋한 애나무 a young tree long and slender // 밋밋한 턱 a beardless chin

밍밍하다 (be) tasteless ; flat ; insipid ; weak ; thin ; watery ¶ 밍밍한 국 thin soup // 밍밍한 술 flat wine

밍크 코트 a mink coat

***및** and ; also ; as well as ; in addition to ; besides ¶ 영어 및 수학에 있어서 in mathematics as well as in English

†**밑** ①［하부］ the bottom ; the foot ; the base ; the lower part ¶ 밑의 under ; lower ; subordinate // 밑에 under ; beneath ; below ; underneath (바로 밑에) // 밑으로 down ; downward // 밑에서 일곱째 줄 the seventh line from the bottom // 밑의 사람 one's subordinate〔inferior〕 // 밑의 지위 a subordinate position // 산 밑에 at the foot of a mountain // 나무 밑에 under a tree // 방석 밑에 underneath a cushion // 밑으로 내려가다 go〔come〕 down ; go〔come〕 downstairs (아래층으로) // 밑에서 받치다 support《a thing》 from below // 눈 밑에서 below one's eyes // 남의 밑에서 일하다 work under another // 대위는 소령의 밑이다 The captain is beneath the major. // 그는 김씨 밑에서 일하고 있다 He works under Mr. *Kim*. / He plays second fiddle to Mr. *Kim*. // 나는 그의 밑에서 영어를 3년간 배웠다 I studied English under him for three years.

②［근본］ the root ; the foundation ; the basis ; the origin ; the source

③［뿌리］ a root ; a bulb (구근) ¶ 무 밑 a radish root // 밑이 들다 form a root

〔bulb〕; the root〔bulb〕 grows big
④ [음부] one's private parts
⑤ [바닥] the bottom ; the bed (하천, 호수, 바다) ; the sole (구두창) ¶ 바다 밑에 at the bottom〔depths〕 of the sea // 강밑에 in the river bed // 상자의 밑에 빠졌다 The bottom of the box fell〔came〕 out. /The bottom fell〔dropped〕 out of the box.

밑각 —角 〖수학〗 a base angle

밑감 [원료] raw materials

밑거름 〖농업〗 fertilizer used at sowing time

밑거리 [단청의] a light green used as a basic color before painting a building

밑구멍 ① [구멍] a hole at the bottom ; a bottom hole ② [항문] the anus ; [여자의 음부] the vulva

밑그림 a rough sketch ; a draft ; a design

밑글 once-learned knowledge ; knowledge in one's possession

밑널 a bottom board

밑넓이 〖수학〗 the base area

밑돌다 do not amount 《to》; fall short 《of》; be less〔lower〕 than ; be a fraction 《of》 ¶ (결과가) 예상을 밑돌다 fall short of one's expectation(s)

밑동 the lower part ; the base ; a root ; a stump ¶ 기둥 밑동 the lower part〔base〕 of a column // 시금치 밑동 spinach root // 밑동을 다듬다 take off the roots 《of vegetables》

밑둥치 the root 《of a tree》

밑들다[1] [밑이 들다] grow big ; form a root〔bulb〕 ¶ 감자가 밑들다 a potato grows big

밑들다[2] [밑에 들다] 《a kite》 get under another kite

밑머리 original hair ¶ 밑머리를 치다 thin one's hair

밑면 —面 〖수학〗 the base side (of a geometrical figure)

밑면적 —面積 the bottom dimensions

***밑바닥** ① the bottom ; the base ¶ 독의 밑바닥 the bottom of a jar // 구두의 밑바닥 the sole of a shoe // 강의 밑바닥에 at the bottom〔bed〕 of a river ; in the river bed // 밑바닥을 떼어내다 knock the bottom out // 밑바닥이 빠지다 the bottom comes〔falls〕 out
② [마음 속] one's inmost thoughts〔desire〕 ¶ 네 마음 속 밑바닥이 들여다 보인다 I can clearly see through your intention. /Your motive is apparent. /I can read your inmost thoughts.
③ [사회 생활 따위의] the bottom ; the depths ; abyss ¶ 사회의 밑바닥 the bottom of the social scale ; the lowest social stratum
— **생활** a life in the slums ; a poverty stricken life

밑바탕 ① [본질] essence ; [기초] the foundation ; the basis ; the groundwork ; the ground ¶ 서구 민주주의의 밑바탕 the basic ideas of Western democracy
② [본성] the original nature ; the inherent character ; one's true colors ¶ 밑바탕이 좋지 못하다 be bad〔wicked〕 by nature // 밑바탕이 천하다 be of low birth // 밑바탕을 드러내다 reveal one's real nature〔character〕; unmask oneself ; show one's real colors

밑반찬 side dishes pickled, salted, or preserved by other means for longer duration to go with rice at meals

밑받침 an underlay ; an underlying object ; a support ; a rest ; a pad ¶ 기둥 밑받침 a stay at the base of a pillar // 밑받침을 받치고 글씨를 쓰다 write on a paper with a board beneath it

밑밥 [낚시질의] ground bait

밑변 —邊 〖기하〗 the bottom side of a polygon ; the base ; the base line

밑불 [불씨] kindling〔live〕 charcoal〔coal〕 to make a fire ; [항상 점화해 두는] a pilot flame〔light, burner〕

***밑살** [미주알] sphincter muscles of the anus ; [쇠고기의] rump beef ; [보지] the vulva

밑세장 the bottom strut of a A-frame

밑술 crude liquor ; raw spirits

밑싣개 the seat of a swing

밑쌀 the basic grain used in preparing mixed cereals

밑씨 〖식물〗 a germinal vesicle ; an ovule

밑씻개 toilet paper

밑알 a nest egg

밑절미 the base ; the basis ; the foundation ⇨ 밑바탕

밑정 the frequency of a baby's evacuation

밑조사 —調査 [예비 조사] a preliminary investigation ; spadework

⁑**밑줄** an underline ¶ …에 밑줄을 치다 [긋다] underline ; underscore

밑줄기 the lower part of a stem〔stalk〕

***밑지다** lose ; suffer〔take, make, sustain〕 a loss ; do not pay ¶ 밑지는 장사 a losing business〔transaction〕 // 밑지고 팔다 sell at a loss〔sacrifice〕; sell to〔at a〕 disadvantage // 본전을 밑지고 팔다 sell at a price lower than the original cost // 그 값에 팔면 제가 밑집니다 I will be losing money if I sell it at that price. /But I'm losing by it. // 그렇게 하면 크게 밑진다 It involves a big loss. // 이 거래에서 천원 밑지고 있다 I am 1,000 *won* out of pocket by this transaction. // 밑져야 본전이다 Trying wouldn't hurt. /Trying wouldn't do any harm. // 솔직히 말씀드리면 그 물건은 재고가 너무 쌓여서 밑지고 파는 겁니다 Honestly, we are overstocked on that item, so we are selling it below cost.

밑질기다 be slow 《in taking (one's) leave》; stay (too) long ; overstay one's time ; make a long visit ; outstay ; overstay ; outsit

밑창 the bottom piece ; the base piece
구두 — the sole of a shoe
***밑천** ① [자본] capital ; funds ; stock ; principal (원금) ¶ 장사 밑천 business funds // 밑천을 대다 provide capital 《for》; provide〔supply〕《a person》 with capital 〔funds〕; finance // 밑천이 다 떨어지다 run out of funds // 그가 밑천을 대주겠다고 한다 He offers to finance the business〔to supply us with business〕. // 장사를 하려고 해도 밑천이 없다 I have nothing〔no capital〕 to start business with. // 어떤 일을 하든지 밑천이 든다 You must sow 〔give〕 before you can reap 〔take〕. // 그와 같은 경험을 얻는 데는 많은 밑천이 들었을 것이다 He must have paid a high price for his experience. // 말했다가 밑천도 못 찾았다 He cut me down with a sharp rejoinder. // 많은 밑천을 들였다 He put a lot of money 《in》.
② [성기] one's penis
밑층 —層 the ground floor (아래층) ; the bottom layer
밑판 —板 the bottom board
밑화장 —化粧 a makeup base ; a foundation

ㅂ

-ㅂ니까 is 《this, it, he》 . . . ? ; are 《you, they》 . . . ? ; do 《you》 . . . ? ; 《what》 is 《that》 . . . ? ; 《what》 does 《she》 . . . ? ¶ 그는 의사입니까 Is he a doctor? // 그녀를 사랑합니까 Do you love her?

-ㅂ니다 be ¶ 그는 군인인 동시에 정치가입니다 He is a statesman as well as a soldier. /He is a soldier-statesman. // 나는 학교에 갑니다 I am going to school. // 비가 옵니다 It is raining.

-ㅂ디까 did you hear〔notice〕 that . . . ? ; have you found〔been told〕 that . . . ? ; be it known that . . . ? ¶ 내가 언제 그런 계획을 당신에게 제안합디까 When did I suggest such a plan to you? // 그는 몇 시에 여기 오겠다고 합디까 What time did he say he would come here?

-ㅂ디다 I hear〔noticed〕 that. . . ; it is said〔known〕 that. . . ; it has been . . . that ; as it is found ; they say〔said〕 ¶ 그렇다고 합디다 So I hear. /It is said to be so. /So I understand. // 미스 김은 곧 미국으로 간다고 합디다 I am told Miss Kim is going to the United States shortly.

†-ㅂ시다 let us ¶ 갑시다 Let us go. // 한잔 합시다 Let us have a drink.

바[1] 〖음악〗 fa ; F ¶ 올림 바조 F sharp (기호 : F#) // 내림 바조 F flat (기호 : F♭) // 바 장조 F major // 바 단조 F minor

†바[2] a thing ; what ¶ 그가 말하는 바 what he says // 내가 아는 바로는 as〔so〕 far as I know ; to the best of my knowledge ; for all I know // 위에서 말한 바와 같이 as stated〔described, mentioned〕 above // 할 바를 모르다 do not know what to do ; be at a loss what to do // 그가 죽든 말든 내가 알 바 아니다 He may die for all I care. // 내가 본 바로는 그렇지 않다 I look at it differently. // 자네가 관여할 바가 아니다 That is none of your business. /It is no concern of yours. /It is nothing you would know anything about.

†바[3] [밧줄] a rope ; a cord ¶ 바를 쳐서 교통을 차단하다 rope off traffic

바[4] [술집] a bar ; a barroom ; a bar parlor ; a saloon 《미》 ; a public house 《영》 ; a pub 《영·구》 ¶ 바의 단골 a barfly 《미·구》

— 걸 a barmaid ; a B-girl 《미·속》

바[5] [높이뛰기·축구 골문의 가로장] a crossbar ; [금속봉] a bar

바[6] [기압의 단위] bar

밀리— millibar

바가지 a gourd (dipper) ; a calabash ¶ 바가지로 물을 푸다 dip water with a gourd dipper // 바가지를 긁다 snarl 《at》 ; speak crossly 《to》 ; snap〔yap〕 《at》 ; nag // 그 여자는 바가지를 잘 긁는 아내다 She is a nagging wife.

바가지쓰다 pay through the nose ; pay exorbitantly ¶ 어제 나는 바에서 바가지썼다 Yesterday I paid through the nose at a bar. // 당신은 고물차를 가지고 나한테 바가지를 씌웠다 You ripped me off with a junker! // 너 바가지쓴 것 같다 I'm afraid you got ripped off. /I'm afraid you took a beating.

바각, 빠각 gratingly ; with a scrape —하다 scrape ; grate ; make a grating sound ¶ 이를 바각거리다 grate〔grit〕 the teeth // 무엇이 부엌에서 바각거리느냐 What is that scratching〔scraping〕 in the kitchen? // 쥐가 문을 바각거린다 A mouse is scratching at the door.

바각바각 scraping repeatedly

바겐 a bargain

— 세일 a bargain sale

바곳[1] [송곳] a drill〔an awl, a gimlet〕 with a metal sidehandle

바곳[2] 〖식물〗 an aconite ; a wolfsbane ; a monkshood

†바구니 a wicker〔bamboo〕 basket ¶ 손바구니 a handbasket

바구미 〖곤충〗 a rice weevil

바그르르, 빠그르르 [물·거품] simmering ; foamly ; frothily —하다 simmer ; bubble up ; foam ; froth ¶ 물이 바그르르 끓다 Water simmers. // 비누 거품이 바그르르 일어난다 Suds bubble up〔rise in bubbles〕.

바글거리다 [물이] simmer ; seethe ; boil ; [거품이] bubble ; [우글거리다] swarm

바글바글 seething ; boiling ; bubbling ¶ 바글바글 끓다 boil (over) ; simmer // 물을 바글바글 끓이다 boil water ; bring water to a simmer〔boil〕 // 일요일에는 어디나 사람들로 바글바글하였다 Every place swarmed with people on Sundays.

†바깥 the outside ; the exterior ; [문밖] the out doors ; the open (air) ¶ 바깥의 outside ; external ; exterior ; outdoor // 바깥심부름을 보내다 send out on an errand // 바깥에 나가다 go out 《of doors, of the house》 ; go out into the open air // 그는 바깥에 나가지 않는다 He is a regular stay-at-home. /He always keeps indoors. // 바깥이 춥다 It is cold outside. // 바깥에서 총소리가 들렸다 Shots were heard from outside.

— 공기 outdoor air —뜰 an outdoor yard〔garden〕 —문 the outer〔outside〕 gate —방 a room in the outer wing of the house —부모 one's father —사돈 the father of one's son-in-law〔daughter-in-law〕 —소문 (a) rumor ; gossip ; common talk ; hearsay —식구 male members of a family —일 outdoor work —채 an outbuilding ; an outhouse ; an annex

바깥 소식 —消息 news ; the news of the town ; foreign news ¶ 바깥 소식에 어둡다 be unfamiliar with what is going on in the world ; have but little information of the world

바깥 양반 the master (of the house) ; one's husband (남편)

바깥짝 more than 《a certain distance》 away ; beyond ; over 《a certain limit》 ; [둘째줄] the second line of a couplet ¶ 10마일 바깥짝에 있다 be over 10 miles away

바깥쪽 the outside ; the exterior

바께쓰 a bucket ¶ 한 바께쓰의 물 a bucketful of water

†바꾸다 ① [교환] change ; exchange ; [물물교환] trade ; barter ; convert ¶ 남과 좌석을 바꾸다 change seats with another // 다른 물건으로 바꾸다 have an article exchanged for another // 물품을 현금으로 바꾸다 convert goods into money // 미화를 바꾸다 change 《*won*》 into dollars // 수표를 현금으로 바꾸다 cash a check
② [대신·변경] replace ; change ; alter ; modify ; amend

> 참고 **change**는 「근본부터 완전히 바꾸다」「딴 것으로 변화시키다」의 뜻 **alter**는 「부분적으로 바꾸다」의 뜻으로 흔히 사용된다

¶ 바꿀 수 없는 unalterable ; unchangeable // 바꾸어 말하면 in other words // A를 B로 바꾸다 replace A with B ; substitute B for A // 제도를 바꾸다 reform a system // 진로를 바꾸다 change the course // 의견을 자주 바꾸다 blow hot and cold // 베이커 씨를 바꿔 드리겠습니다 I'll put Mr. Baker on. // 나는 그를 온순한 녀석으로 생각해 왔으나 그에 대한 평가를 바꿨다 I'd thought of him as just a mild-mannered guy, but I've revised my opinion of him.
③ [피륙을] buy〔purchase〕 《cloth》

바꾸이다 be〔get〕 changed ⇨ 바뀌다

바꿈질 exchange ; change ; replacement ; switching

바꿔놓다 replace 《A with B》 ; substitute 《B for A》 ; displace

바꿔말하다 say〔express〕 in other words ; change〔alter〕 an expression ; put 《it》 (in) another way ¶ 바꿔 말하면 in other words ; that is (to say) ; to put it (in) another way ; namely

바뀌다 get〔be〕 changed ; [변형] be transformed 《into》 ; [수정] be revised〔amended〕 ¶ 세상이 바뀌다 The times change. // 방침이 바뀌다 The policy has been changed. // 서울도 많이 바뀌었다 *Seoul* has changed a great deal. // 규칙이 바뀌었다 The regulation has been changed. // 해가 바뀌다 The old year goes out and the new year comes in. /The year changes.

바끄러움 [수치] shame ; disgrace ; [수줍음] shyness

바끄럽다 be〔feel〕 ashamed ⇨ 부끄럽다

*바나나 a banana ¶ 바나나 껍질을 벗기다 peel (off the skin of) a banana
— 송이 a bunch of bananas

바나듐 〖화학〗 vanadium 《V》

*바느질 needlework ; sewing —하다 sew ; do needlework ¶ 바느질 그릇 a sewing box // 바느질로 생계를 유지하다 make one's living by one's needle ; earn one's living by needlework // 바느질을 배우다 take sewing lessons // 바느질을 잘한다 She is clever with her needle. // 바느질이 거칠다〔곱다〕 Her needlework is coarse〔fine〕.
—고리 ⇨ 반짇고리 —삯 sewing charges —손 sewer —자 a ruler〔measure〕 for sewing

바느질품 needlework ¶ 바느질품을 팔다 earn one's living by needlework

†바늘 a needle ; a pin ; [낚싯바늘] a hook ; [시계의] a hand ; [벌의] a sting ¶ 머리를 두바늘 꿰매다 take two stitches in one's head // 바늘에 실을 꿰다 thread a needle // (낚시) 바늘에 미끼를 달다 bait a hook // 바늘을 꽂다 stick a pin 《in》 // 바늘 가는 데 실이 간다 The thread follows the needle.
바늘 넣고 도끼 낚는다 속담 You must lose fly to catch a trout. /Venture a small fish to catch a great one. /Throw out a sprat to catch a mackerel〔Herring, whale〕.
바늘 도둑이 소 도둑 된다 속담 He that will steal a pin, will steal a better thing. /He that will steal an egg will steal on ox.

바늘겨레 a pincushion

바늘 구멍 a hole made by a needle
바늘 구멍으로 황새 바람 들어온다 속담 A small leak will sink a great ship. /A little fire burns up a great deal of corn. /Of a small spark, a great fire.

바늘귀 a needle's eye

바늘꼬리도요 〖새〗 a pintail snipe

바늘꼬리칼새 〖새〗 a needle-tailed swift

바늘꽃 a kind of willow-weed

바늘밥 thread remnants

바늘방석 ① [바늘 겨레] a pincushion ② [자리] a mat of needles ¶ 바늘방석에 앉은 것 같다 I feel as if I had sat on pins and needles. /I feel so uneasy.

바늘쌈 a packet of needles

ㅂ

바니싱 크림 vanishing cream
*****바닐라** 〖식물〗 a vanilla ; Vanilla fragrans
†**바다** the sea ; [대양] the ocean ¶ 바다의 사나이 a seaman ; a sailor // 바닷바람 a sea breeze // 거울 같은 바다 a sea smooth as a mirror // 바다로 둘러싸인 나라 a sea-girt〔seabound〕 country ; a country surrounded by the sea // 바다 건너 across 〔beyond〕 the sea // 바다에 떠서 on the sea // 바다와 육지에서 by land and sea // 바다에 가다 go to the seashore // 바다에 나가다 go〔put〕 out to sea // 갑판에서 바다에 뛰어들다 leap overboard
— **거북** a turtle —**밑** the bottom〔floor, bed〕 of the sea ; the seabed **불(피)** — a sea of flames〔blood〕 **바닷길** a sea route **바닷말** seaweed **바닷새** a sea bird ; seafowl 《집합적》
바다는 메워도 사람의 욕심은 못 메운다 속담 Covetousness is always filling a bottomless vessel. /A Poor man wants some things, a covetous man all things.
바다에 가서 토끼 찾기 속담 To seek a hare in a hen's nest. /You cannot get blood from a stone.
바다꿩 〖새〗 a long-tailed duck
바다낚시(질) sea fishing ; angling in the sea
바다매 Peale's peregrine falcon
바다뱀 a sea snake〔serpent〕
바다뱀자리 〖천문〗 (the constellation) Hydra
바다비오리 a red-breasted merganser
바다오리 a guillemot
바다제비 a fork-tailed petrel
‡**바다표범** a seal ; Phoca vitulina (학명)
†**바닥** ① [평면] a flat part〔surface〕 ¶ 땅바닥 the ground // 마룻바닥 the floor // 손바닥 palm ; the flat of the hand // 발바닥 sole (of the foot)
② [밑부분] the bottom ; [강 따위의] the bed ; the ground ; [신의] the sole ¶ 바닥이 이중으로 된 double-bottomed ; double-soled // 이 찻잔은 바닥에 금이 갔다 There is a crack in the bottom of this teacup. // 바닥이 빠지다 The bottom falls 〔drops〕 out 《of a cask》. // 물이 얕아서 발이 바닥에 닿는다 The water is so shallow I can touch the ground〔bottom〕.
③ [끝] the end 《of one's resources》 ; rock bottom ¶ 바닥이 나다 be drained 〔exhausted, used up, consumed〕 ; run out ; come to an end // 양식이 바닥 났다 Provisions have given out. /We have run out of provisions. // 나는 바닥이 났다 I am at the end of my resources〔at rock bottom ; at the bottom of the barrel〕.
④ [짜임새] weave ; texture
⑤ [번잡한 곳] a congested〔built-up〕 area ¶ 서울 바닥 the *Seoul* area // 장 바닥 the market area〔market place〕 // 중 바닥 the central〔downtown〕 area
바닥나다 run〔give〕 out ; be all gone ; be drained〔exhausted〕 ⇨ 바닥
바닥내다 allow 《a thing》 to run out ; run out of
바닥보다 ① [밑천이] run out of capital 〔funds〕 ② [실패하다] fail ; fall through ¶ 올해 보리 농사는 바닥보았다 We had a poor barley crop this year. /The barley crop this year failed.
바닥짐 ballast ¶ 바닥짐을 싣다 take on ballast // 바닥짐을 싣고 항해하다 sail in ballast
바닥 첫째 the first from the bottom ; the last ; at the bottom ¶ 나는 우리 반에서 바닥 첫째다 I am at the bottom of my class.
†**바닷가** the beach ; the seashore ¶ 바닷가에 있는 마을 a village by the sea // 바닷가를 산책하다 take a walk on the beach
바닷개 a fur seal
바닷게 a (saltwater) crab
바닷고기 a sea fish ; a salt-water fish
바닷귀신 —鬼神 a sea goblin〔monster〕
바닷물 sea water ; salt water ¶ 바닷물이 짭짤하다 Sea water is salty.
바닷바람 a sea breeze ; a wind blowing from the sea
바닷사람 a seafarer
바닷장어 —長魚 a salt-water eel
바대 a reinforcement strip sewed inside a jacket〔an undershirt〕
바더리 〖곤충〗 a long-legged wasp ; a kind of yellow-jacket
바동거리다 (kick and) struggle ; wriggle ; writhe ; strain at 《one's bonds》 ; be impatient 《for》 ¶ 괴로워서 바동거리다 writhe in pain〔agony〕 // 바동거리다가 죽다 die in agony // 바동거리지 않고 …하다 have the grace to 《do》 // 바동거려도 소용없다 It is useless for you to struggle. // 바동거리지 마 Don't make a scene! 《미》
바둑 *paduk* (game) ; Korean checkers ¶ 바둑을 두다 play (a game of) *paduk*
—**돌** *paduk* pieces〔stone〕 ; stone checkers —**판** a *paduk* board —**판 무늬** check ; checkers ; chequers 《영》 ; cross stripes
바둑말 a piebald〔dapple〕 ; a dappled horse
바둑무늬 a pattern〔figure, design〕 with black and white spots ; a speckled design ¶ 바둑무늬가 있는 속치마 a petticoat with a speckled design
바둑이 a spotted dog ; a dog with white and black spots ; "Spot(ty)"
바둑 장기 —將棋 *paduk* and *changgi* ; Korean checkers and chess
바둑점 —點 a spot ; a speck ¶ 바둑점이 있는 spotted ; speckled
바드득, 빠드득 with a grating〔grinding, creaking〕 sound —**하다** grind ; creak ; squeak ; grate ¶ 이를 바드득 갈다 grit 〔grate〕 one's teeth

바드득거리다, 빠드득거리다 《the chair》 creak ; 《the floor》 squeak ; emit a squeaky 〔creaky〕 sound ; grate ¶ 내 구두가 바드득거린다 My shoes creak.

바드득바드득 grinding away ; creaking and creaking

바드름하다 protrude ⇨ 버드름하다

바득바득 persistently ; obstinately ; doggedly ; importunately ¶ 과자를 사달라고 바득바득 조르다 clamor for candy // 바득바득 우기다 stand firm on one's opinion ; stick doggedly to one's guns〔opinion〕// 자기 것이라고 바득바득 우긴다 He persistently claims it is his.

바들거리다 quiver

바들바들 ⇨ 부들부들

바듬하다 (be) somewhat prominent

바듯하다, 빠듯하다 ① [겨우 차다] be on the margin 《of》 ; be barely enough ¶ 빠듯한 이익 marginal profits // 빠듯이 barely ; narrowly // 살기가 빠듯하다 eke out a living ; be on the margin of bare subsistence // 그는 월급으로 빠듯이 살아간다 He barely manages to live on his salary. // 1,000원은 차표 사기에 빠듯하다 1,000 *won* will barely pay for the railroad ticket.
② [꼭 맞다] fit perfectly〔exactly, to a T〕; (be) tight〔close〕(꼭 끼다) ¶ 빠듯한 구두 tight shoes // 모자가 좀 빠듯하다 The hat is a little too tight. // 상의가 빠듯하게 잘 맞다 The coat fits〔suits〕 you perfectly〔to a T〕. // 구두가 빠듯이 맞다 The shoes just barely fit.

바디 a reed

바따라지다 (be) rich〔thick〕 and tasty 〔savory〕

바라기 a small porcelain dish ; a kind of small food dish

†**바라다** ① [소원] wish ; desire ; want ; seek ; aspire ; wish for ; long for ; yearn for ; [관심] care for ; [부탁] beg ; request

> 참고 **wish**는 desire만큼 강하게 바라는 것이 아니며 때로는 실현할 수 없는 바람을 뜻한다 **desire**는 want, wish의 격식을 갖춘 대용어로서 쓰이기도 하지만 흔히 강한 바람을 의미하며 그것을 얻기 위하여 노력하는 의욕을 포함하고 있다

제발 바라건대 for mercy's〔God's〕 sake // 행복하기를 바라다 wish for happiness // 관직을 바라다 seek a government post // 평소 바라던 소망을 이룩하다 have one's long-cherished desire fulfilled // 내가 가장 바라던 것이다 Nothing suits me better. // 그는 사업가가 되기를 바란다 His aspiration is〔He desires〕 to be a businessman. // 명예나 부귀를 바라지 않는다 I don't care for fame or wealth. // 목록을 송부해 주시기를 바랍니다 Please oblige 〔favor〕 me with your catalogue.
② [기대·예기] hope ; expect ; look forward to ¶ 용서를 바라다 hope for 《a person's》 pardon // 남자 아이를 낳기 바라다 hope for a son // 남의 도움을 바라다 look to others for help // 도저히 바랄 수 없는 일을 바라다 hope against hope // 그에게 별로 바랄 것이 없다 You cannot expect much of him. // 성공하기를 바란다 I am hopeful of your success. // 모든 일이 잘되기 바란다 I hope everything will come out all right. // 그한테 너무 바라지 마라 Don't expect too much of him.

바라문 婆羅門 a Brahman ; Brahmanism **—교(敎)** Brahmanism

바라밀다 波羅蜜多 〖불교〗 Paramita ; entrance into Nirvana

†**바라보다** ① [건너다 보다] see ; look at ; watch ; [응시] gaze〔stare〕 at ; [관망] view ; get a view 《of》 ¶ 바다가 바라보이는 집 a house with an outlook over the sea // 바라보이다 be in sight ; come 〔heave〕 in sight ; come into view // 경치를 바라보다 see a view ; admire the scenery // 빤히 바라보다 watch 《a person's》 face intently // 우두커니 바라보다 stare blankly〔vacantly〕《at》// 하늘을 바라보다 look up at the sky // 먼산을 바라보다 stare into empty space ; look out the window absent-mindedly // 놀라서 그 광경을 우두커니 바라보았다 He stood aghast at the sight. // 집은 관악산이 멀리 바라 보이는 언덕에 있다 The house stands on a hill commanding a distant view of Mt. *Kwanak*. // 가능하면 시내 중심가를 바라볼 수 있는 방을 주세요 Give me a room looking out on the downtown area, if possible.
② [바라다] expect ; look for ¶ 장래를 바라보다 look forward to the future

바라보이다 look over ; command ; overlook ¶ 멀리 도봉산이 바라보이다 command a distant view of Mt. *Dobong* // 내 집은 바다가 바라보이는 언덕 위에 있다 My house stands on a hill commanding the sea. // 호텔에서 호수가 잘 바라보인다 The hotel has a good command of the lake. // 높은 창문에서 시내의 반이 바라보인다 The high window overlooks half of the city.

바라지 attentive care ; looking after ; assistance ; provision **—하다** take care of ; attend to ; care for ; mind ¶ 자식 바라지하다 look after a child ; take care of children // 옷 바라지하다 provide 《a person》 with clothes

바라지다¹ ① [몸이] (be) short and fat 〔thick〕; stocky ; stumpy ; thickset ¶ 바라진 사람 a stocky fellow
② [그릇] (be) shallow ¶ 바라진 접시 a shallow dish
③ [야무지다] (be) saucy ; cheeky ; stuck-up ¶ 바라진 아이 a forward child // 바라진 말을 하다 say a cheeky thing

바라지다² [갈라지다] split off ; [열리다]

ㅂ

widen ; open out ; broaden ¶ 가슴이 바라지다 He is broad of chest. // 틈이 바라지다 The opening widens.

바라크 a barrack ; a temporary shelter ; a jerry-building ; a shack ¶ 이 집은 바라크처럼 지은 집이다 This is a house run up very cheaply.

바락 ⇨ 버럭

바락바락 desperately ; frantically ; insistently ¶ 바락바락 기를 쓰다 make desperate efforts // 바락바락 덤비다 turn upon 《a person》 desperately ; oppose 《a person》 tooth and nail // 바락바락 화를 내다 be red-hot〔black〕 with rage

†**바람**[1] ① [공기의 유통] a wind ; [미풍] a breeze ; [강풍] a gale ; [폭풍] a storm ; [통풍] a draft〔draught〕 ; [선풍기 따위의] a current ¶ 선풍기 바람을 쐬면서 in the current of an electric fan // 바람을 쐬다 expose oneself to the wind // 바람을 안고 가다 go against〔in the teeth of〕 the wind ; brave the wind // 바람이 잘 통하다 be well ventilated ; be airy // 틈으로 바람이 새어들어오는 곳에 앉다 sit in a draft // 깃발이 바람에 휘날린다 The flags blow in the wind. // 바람이 새어 들어온다 There is a draught. // 바람이 인다 The wind rises. // 바람이 잔다 The wind falls 〔drops, goes down〕. // 바람이 한 점도 없다 There is not a breath of air. // 센 바람이 불고 있었다 It was blowing hard. // 이 방은 틈새로 바람이 잘 들어온다 This is a pretty drafty room.

② [들뜬 마음] fickleness ; inconstancy ; [행위] amours ¶ 바람난 fickle ; wanton ; inconstant ; flirtatious ; unfaithful // 바람난 남편 a flirtatious husband // 바람을 피우다 have a secret love affair ; take to amours // 그는 40이 되자 바람이 가라앉았다 When he reached forty, he settled down.

③ [과장] big〔tall〕 talk ; a whopper ; a whopping lie ¶ 바람이 센 친구 a braggart ; a boaster

④ [풍병] palsy ; paralysis

바람[2] ① [기세] 《in》 conjunction 《with》 ; 《as a》 result 《of》 ; influence ; impetus ; momentum ¶ 충돌하는 바람에 by the force of impact // 술바람으로 떠들다 revel 〔rave, make merry〕 under the influence of alcohol // 앞에서 오는 차를 피하려는 바람에 아이를 치었다 We ran over a child trying to dodge an oncoming car.

② [차림] without one's 《clothing》 on ¶ 셔츠 바람으로 in shirt sleeves ; without one's coat on // 맨머리 바람으로 bareheaded ; without a hat on // 그는 맨발 바람으로 밖에 뛰어나갔다 He ran out into the street barefoot.

바람[3] [길이] the length of an arm-span 《about two yards》 ¶ 새끼 한 바람 two yards of rope

***바람개비**[1] a weather vane ; a weathercock ; [장난감] a toy pinwheel ¶ 바람개비가 바람에 돈다 The vane is turning with the wind.

바람개비[2] 〖새〗 a nighthawk ; a nightjar ; a goatsucker ; Caprimulgus indicus (학명)

바람결 rumor ; hearsay ; report ; talk ¶ 바람결에 들으니 There is a rumor (in the air) 《that》 ; Rumor has it 《that》 ; As I hear tell ; A little bird told me 《that》 // 바람결에 새소리가 들린다 The wind brings the sound of birds.

바람구멍 an air hole ; a wind hole ; a vent

바람기 一氣 ① [바람의 기운] the force 〔feel〕 of wind

② [들뜬 마음] fickleness ; wantonness ; inconstancy ; profligacy ¶ 바람기가 있는 fickle ; wanton ; inconstant ; profligate // 바람기가 있는 여자 a woman of loose morals〔easy virtue〕 ; a wanton woman ; a flirt

바람꽃[1] a hazy atmosphere around the top of a distant mountain presaging a high wind

바람꽃[2] 〖식물〗 a windflower ; Anemone narcissiflora (학명)

바람끼다 [바람기가 들다] become fickle 〔dissipated〕 ; feel like taking to fast living

바람나가다 become insipid ; grow dull ; get lifeless ¶ 바람나간 설교 an empty sermon // 그 놈 바람나갔군 What a dull fool he is !

바람나다 ① lead a loose life ; keep fast company ② [신바람나다] warm up ; get warmed up ; get under way ; really get started ¶ 한번 바람나면 그는 밤낮을 모르고 공부한다 Once he gets warmed up, he studies night and day.

***바람둥이** ① [허풍선이] a braggart ; a boaster ; a windbag〔gasbag〕 ② [바람잡이] a flirt ; an inconstant lover ; a playboy ; a fickle〔wanton〕 woman (여자) ; a light-o'-love 《미》

바람들다 ① [바람나다] play with love ; go wild ; take up a gay life ; become indiscreet ¶ 바람든 여자 a demimondaine ; a fast woman ; a high stepper // 바람든 남자 a gay blade 〔dog〕 ; a man-about-town

② [무 따위가] get pulpy〔spongy, soft, soggy〕 ¶ 바람든 무 a spongy〔pulpy〕 radish

③ [방해가 생기다] go wrong ; be hindered〔spoiled〕 ; fail ; be upset ¶ 우리 계획은 바람들었다 There has been a hitch in our plan.

바람막이 a windbreak ; windscreen ; a shelter from the wind ¶ 무성한 수목이 겨울에 바람막이가 됐다 A dense growth of trees served as a shelter from the wind in winter.

바람맞다 ① [속다] be fooled〔cheated〕 ; be taken in ; [여자에게] be rejected ; be

stood up ; get the cold shoulder ¶ 여자한테 바람 맞다 be spurned〔scorned〕 by a woman
② [풍병에 걸리다] be stricken with paralysis ; have a stroke
바람맞히다 reject《a suitor》; give the cold shoulder《to》; give the gate《to》; [기다리는 사람을] keep《a person》 waiting in vain ; stand《a person》 up
*바람받이 a place open〔exposed〕 to the wind ; a wind-swept place ¶ 바람받이 집 a house exposed to the wind // 바람받이 벌판 a bleak plain // 바람받이에서 놀다 play in the draft
바람벽 a wall ; a partition
바람비 wind and rain ; the elements ¶ 바람비를 맞다 be exposed to the wind and the rain // 바람비가 크게 일다 The elements let loose〔rage〕.
바람세 [풍세] wind force
바람자다 ① [바람이] the wind dies down ; the breeze stops blowing ② [들뜬 마음이] calm down ; quiet down
바람잡다 seek pleasure ; lead a fast way of living ; take up a fast〔wild〕 life ; lead a dissipated life ; burn one's candle at both ends ¶ 그 나이에 벌써 바람잡았다 At that age, he had already begun leading a fast life.
바람잡이 a frivolous character ; a fast liver ; a playboy ; a fast〔loose〕 woman
‡바람직하다 (be) desirable ; advisable ¶ 바람직하지 않은 인물 an undesirable person
바람켜다 dissipate ; lead a fast life ; lead a life of pleasure ; take to fast living
바랑 a knapsack ; a rucksack ; a pack-sack ; a shoulder〔back〕 pack ¶ 바랑을 지다 carry a knapsack on one's back // 바랑을 내려놓다 take one's knapsack off ; put one's knapsack down《on the ground》
‡바래다¹ ① [퇴색] fade ; discolor ; get washed out
② [표백] bleach〔fade〕《cloth》 in the sun ; wash out ¶ 빨래를 햇볕에 바래다 bleach laundry in the sun // 방석이 햇볕에 바랬다 The cushion faded in the sun. // 햇볕에 커튼의 색이 바랬다 The sun has faded the curtains.
바래다² [배웅] see《a person》 off ; escort ; see《a person》 leave《for》; see《a person》 to ; see《a person》 home ¶ 역까지 친구를 바래다 주다 go to the station to see a friend off // 집까지 바래다 주다 see《a person》 home // 대문까지 바래다 주었다 I saw him out to the gate. // 아이를 집까지 바래다 주어라 Take the child home.
†바로¹ ① [바르게] rightly ; honestly ; correctly ; properly ; straight ¶ 바로 말하면 candidly speaking ; frankly ; to tell the truth // 바로 발음하다 pronounce it correctly // 마음을 바로 가져라 Be honest. / Be right-minded. // 모자를 똑바로 써라 Put your hat on straight. // 이 길로 곧장 바로 가십시오 Keep going straight ahead on this road.
② [정확히] just ; exactly ; precisely ; right ; very ¶ 바로 한 시 정각 exactly one o'clock sharp // 바로 그때에 just〔right〕 at that moment // 바로 명중시키다 shoot〔hit〕 straight ; make〔hit〕 the bull's-eye // 그 분이 바로 이 자리에 앉아야 한다 He is the very man for this post. // 바로 그대로다 That is exactly what it is. // 그것이 바로 내 눈 앞에서 사라졌다 It vanished right under my nose. // 오늘이 바로 내 생일이다 This very day is my birthday. // 자네 말이 바로 맞았어 You are right. /You are in the right. // 바로 그겁니다 That's it.
③ [곧] at once ; immediately ; directly ; straight away ; right away ; in a jiffy ; with no delay ¶ 식사가 끝나면 바로 right〔immediately〕 after lunch // 지금 바로 …하다 lose no time in《doing》;《do》 without delay // 지금 바로 가시오 You had better go right now. // 그이가 왔다가 바로 갔다 He came but left immediately. // 집이 바로 무너질 것 같다 The house appears likely to fall any minute.
④ [곧장] straight ; directly ¶ 집에 바로 가시오 Go home straight. // 바로 여관으로 가거라 Go straight to the hotel.
⑤ [구령] Eyes front ! ¶ 우로 나란히 — 바로 Eyes right ! Eyes front !
바로² [곳] right about this〔that〕 place ¶ 그 바로에 우리 집이 있다 Right about there is where our house is located. // 불이 거기 바로에 났다 The fire is somewhere about there.
바로미터 [청우계] a barometer ; [추측의 표준] a barometer ; an indicator ¶ 건축계의 활동은 상황(商況)의 바로미터이다 Construction is a barometer of business conditions.
†바로잡다 ① [굽은 것을] straighten ; make straight ② [잘못을] correct ; reform ; rectify ; amend ; renovate ¶ 교풍을 바로잡다 restore〔renovate〕 the school tradition // 행실을 바로잡다 amend one's conduct ; correct one's behavior ; turn over a new leaf ; mend one's ways // 마음을 바로잡다 reform oneself ; straighten oneself out // 일이 더 악화되기 전에 바로잡아야 한다 We'll have to straighten things out before they get worse.
*바로크 〚건축〛 baroque ¶ 바로크식 건물 a baroque house
바루다 ⇨ 바로잡다
바륨 〚화학〛 barium《Ba》
†바르다¹ ① [곧다] (be) straight ¶ 바른 길 a straight road // 바른 자세 a correct posture〔carriage〕 // 자세를 바르게 하다 straighten oneself

ㅂ

② [옳다] (be) right ; honest ; true ; upright ; straightforward ¶ 바른 사람 an honest man // 마음이 바르다 be honest 〔right-minded〕 // 바른 말을 하다 tell the truth ; tell what is right // 바른 일을 하다 do right ; do a right thing ; do what is right // 그는 모든 일에 바르다 He is aboveboard in all his dealings. // 바른 말을 해라 Give it to me straight.
③ [햇볕이] (be) sunny ¶ 양지 바른 곳 a sunny place

*바르다² ① [붙이다] put《on》; paste ; apply ;《to》stick
② [칠하다] paint ; coat (페인트를) ; varnish (니스를) ; plaster (회반죽을) ; lacquer (옻칠) ; rub (문질러서) ; powder (분을) ¶ 버터를 바른 빵 bread and butter ; buttered bread // 고약을 바르다 apply a plaster // 종이에 풀을 바르다 put paste on a sheet of paper // 벽에 종이를 바르다 paper a wall ; hang wallpaper // 분을 바르다 powder〔paint〕one's face // 빵에 버터를 바르다 spread butter on bread // 벽을 바르다 plaster a wall // 그것을 온 몸에 바르시오 Rub it all over the body. // 먹지 말고 바르기만 하십시오 For external use only.

바르다³ [쪼개다] open ; crack (open) ; split ; shell ; cleave ; husk ¶ 밤을 바르다 crack a chestnut // 콩을 바르다 split peas // 조개를 바르다 open a clam // 닭고기를 바르다 take chicken meat off the bones

바르르 ① [끓다] bubbling ; in bubbles ; seething ; boiling ; fizzing ; sizzling ¶ 물이 바르르 끓다 The water comes to a bubbling boil.
② [성내다] in a (sudden) fit of anger ; in a rage〔huff〕 ¶ 사소한 일에 바르르 화를 내다 fly into a rage〔flare up in anger〕 on the slightest provocation
③ [불타오르다] in a sudden burst of flame ¶ 바르르 타다 burst into flame (s) ; go up in flames
④ [떨다] shivering ; trembling ; quivering ¶ 무서워서 바르르 떨다 shake 〔tremble〕 with〔for〕 fear // 추워서 바르르 떨다 She is shivering with〔from〕 the cold. // 성이 나서 여자의 입술이 바르르 떨렸다 Her lips quivered with anger.

바르바도스 Barbados (서인도 제도의 자치국)

바르작거리다 struggle ; wriggle ; writhe ; strain at《one's bonds》

바르집다 ① [폭로] expose ; disclose ; bring to light〔the surface〕; reveal ¶ 비밀을 바르집다 expose〔disclose〕 a secret // 증거를 들이대고 거짓을 바르집다 nail a lie to the counter // 사람의 결점을 바르집다 bring to light〔explore〕 the chinks in《a person's》 armor ; dwell on《a person's》 failings
② [과장] exaggerate ; make too much of ; overdraw ; lay the praise on thick ; dwell on ¶ 작은 일을 바르집어 말하다 grossly exaggerate ; make a mountain out of a molehill

바른길 ① [곧은 길] a straight way 〔road〕
② [옳은 길] justice ; the right path 〔track〕 ¶ 바른길을 밟다 pursue an honest career ; tread the path of virtue // 바른길로 인도하다 guide《a person》 into the right track〔path〕

바른말 [옳은 말] truth ; a reasonable word ; [직언] a candid〔frank, straightforward〕 remark ; a plain word ¶ 바른말을 하다 tell the truth ; speak in plain words

바른쪽 the right side〔hand〕

바리¹ [밥그릇] a woman's brass rice bowl ; [바리때] a wooden rice bowl used by temple priests
— 뚜껑 the lid of a brass bowl 퉁— a low quality brass bowl of rice ¶ 퉁바리 맞다 be given a flat refusal

바리² [짐] a load ; a burden ¶ 바리 무 turnips loaded on a horse〔an ox〕 // 장작 두 바리를 사다 buy two loads of firewood // 그것을 세 바리로 꾸려야 한다 I must make three loads of it. // 마차에 나무 한 바리를 실었다 He put a load of wood in the cart. /He loaded the cart with wood.

바리나무 firewood loaded on a horse〔an ox〕

바리때 a wooden rice bowl used by temple priests

바리전 —廛 a brassware shop

바리캉 (a pair of) hair clippers

*바리케이드 a barricade ¶ 바리케이드를 치다〔쌓다〕 set up a barricade ; barricade

바리콘 〖전기〗 a variable condenser

바리톤 〖음악〗 baritone (남성 중음부) ; a baritone (가수) ¶ 그의 목소리는 바리톤이다 He has a baritone voice.

바림 〖미술〗 shading

바바리코트 a Burberry coat (상표명) ; a burberry

바베큐 a barbecue ¶ 옥외의 바베큐 요리 outdoor barbecue cooking
—로(爐) a barbecue grate — 비행 a barbecue maneuver (우주선의)

바벨 〖성경〗 Babel
—탑 the Tower of Babel

†바보 a fool ; a dunce ; an ass ; a silly ; a dumb bunny ; an idiot ; a blockhead ; a lunkhead ; a ninny ; a nincompoop ¶ 바보 같은 소리하다 sound like an idiot ; talk nonsense // 바보 같은 짓을 하다 make a fool of oneself ; act like a nitwit ; be silly ; play the fool // 바보 같은 소리 하지마 Don't be silly. // 그런 말을 하다니 그도 바보군 It is very silly of him to say such a thing. // 그 사람이 그런 바보 같은 짓을 할 리 없다 He knows better than that. // 바보 같은 짓 좀 작작 해라 Cut out the foolishness. // 이 바보야 You fool〔idiot〕! // 나는 바보같이 그런 여자를 사랑했었다 I

ㅂ

was a fool to love such a woman.

†**바쁘다** ① [다망하다] be busy〔engaged〕; be not free ; be occupied ¶ 바쁜 일정 a crowded〔heavy〕 schedule // 바쁜 하루〔생활〕 a busy day〔life〕 // 바쁘게 busily // …하기에 바쁘다 be busy《doing》; be closely occupied《with》// 눈코 뜰 새 없이 바쁘다 live in a whirl of business ; be (as) busy as a bee ; be too busy to eat and sleep ; be so busy he doesn't know whether he's coming or going ; be awfully pressed with business // 그는 시험 준비에 바쁘다 He is busy preparing (himself) for the examination. // 오늘은 대단히 바쁘다 I have a great pressure of work today. /I am very busy today. // 늘 바쁘시군요 I see you are busy〔keeping busy〕 as usual.
② [급하다] (be) pressing〔urgent, immediate〕 ¶ 바쁜 일 a pressing matter ; urgent business // 바쁜 걸음으로 with hurried steps ; at a quick pace // 바쁜 용무로 on urgent〔pressing〕 business // 한시가 바쁘다 Time presses. // 우선 바쁜 일을 다 해놓았다 I have gotten all the rush business done for the moment.

바삐 busily ; [급히] in a rush ; in haste ; in a hurry ; quickly ; hurriedly ¶ 바삐 걷다 walk with hurried steps ; put one's best foot forward // 바삐 굴다 hurry ; rush ; behave hurriedly ; hasten ; make haste // 바삐 지내다 lead〔live〕 a busy life // 옷을 바삐 입다 dress hurriedly // 바삐 일하다 work busily ; be hard at work // 바삐 가다〔돌아오다, 들어오다, 내려가다〕 hurry along〔back, in, down〕 // 바삐 굴지 마라 시간이 넉넉하니 Don't hurry, there's plenty of time. // 좀 바삐 굴어라 차 놓치겠다 Hurry up, or we'll miss the train.

바사기 [덜된 사람] a half-wit ; a blockhead ; a dolt ; a stupid person

바삭 with a rustle〔crinkle〕; with a crunch **—하다** give a rustle〔crinkle〕; crunch

바삭거리다 rustle ; crunch (again and again) ; crinkle ¶ 잡목 숲을 바삭거리며 지나가다 go rustling through the thicket // 가랑잎이 바람에 바삭거린다 The fallen leaves rustle in the breeze. // 가랑잎이 밟혀서 바삭거린다 The fallen leaves crunch under foot. // 바람이 불어 나뭇잎이 바삭거린다 The wind rustles the leaves.

바삭바삭 rustlingly ; with a rustle〔crunch〕 ¶ 눈을 바삭바삭 밟으며 가다 crunch through the snow // 자갈을 바삭바삭 밟다 crunch on gravel

바서지다 break ; be broken〔smashed〕; go to pieces ; fall to pieces ¶ 바서져 두 조각나다 break in two // 산산히 바서지다 be smashed〔broken〕 into fragments〔pieces〕 // 사발이 바서지다 A bowl gets broken.

바소 [침] a needle used for lancing a boil

바소쿠리 a basket made of bush clover as a dirt-carrier

바수다 break ; smash ; crush ; grind ; [빻다] pound ; pulverize ¶ 산산히 바수다 break〔smash〕《a thing》 into smithereens // 얼음을 바수다 crush ice

바수지르다 ⇨ 바스러뜨리다

바순 a bassoon
— 연주자 a bassoonist

바스 a bath
— 타월 a bath towel

바스대다 fidget ; move about restlessly ; shift nervously ; be never still ¶ 바스대는 아이 a restless child // 바스대지 마라 Don't fidget.

바스라기 crumbs ; scraps ; odds and ends ; shreds ; bits ¶ 헝겊〔고기〕 바스라기 scraps of cloth〔meat〕 // 빵 바스라기 bread crumbs

바스락 faint(ly) ; indistinct(ly) ; stealthy ; stealthily ; with a low〔soft, muffled〕 sound **—하다** make a muffled〔indistinct〕 sound ; make one faint〔muffled〕 sound after another ; make (re-peated) indistinct sounds ; rustle ¶ 바스락 걷는 소리 the muffled sound of stealthy footsteps // 바스락거리다 rustle ; make a succession of slight and soft sounds // 거기서 무엇이 바스락거리느냐 What is that rustling over there ?

바스락거리다 make (repeated) indistinct sounds ; rustle ¶ 낙엽이 바람에 바스락거린다 That fallen leaves are rustling in the wind.

바스락바스락 with one faint〔muffled〕 sound after another ; rustlingly ; with a rustle

바스러뜨리다 smash ; crush ; break into crumbs ; shatter into splinters

바스러지다 [덩이가] crumble ; fall to pieces ; fall into small pieces ; break into small fragments ; [얼굴이] get thin for one's age ; get emaciated ¶ 바스러진 얼굴 a haggard〔gaunt〕 face // 바스러져 가루가 되다 crumble to dust // 빵이 바스러진다 Bread crumbles. // 앓고 나더니 얼굴이 아주 바스러져 보인다 Since his illness, he looks so emaciated.

바스스 gently ; softly ; lightly ¶ 잠자리에서 바스스 일어나 앉다 gently sit up in bed // 바람에 먼지가 바스스 인다 The wind raises a small cloud of dust. // 산들바람이 머리칼을 바스스 헝클어뜨린다 The breeze softly ruffles her hair.

바스켓볼 『농구』 basketball ; [공] a basketball

바슬바슬 crumbly **—하다** be crumbly ¶ 떡이 너무 말라서 만지는 대로 바슬바슬 부스러진다 The cake is so dry, it crumbles when you touch it.

바실루스 『생물』 a bacillus《*pl.* -li》

바심¹ [풋바심] threshing and milling unripe grain

바심² [재목의] trimming timber **—하다**

ㅂ

trim timber
바싹 [마른 모양] completely ; in a parched manner ; scorched ; burnt up〔off, dry〕; [죄는 모양] closely ; tightly ; step by step ; hard by ; close to ; fast ; [소리] rustlingly ; with a crunch ; [우기는 모양] stubbornly ; doggedly ; stiffly ; resolutely ¶ 바싹 마른 입 a parched mouth // 바싹 마른 얼굴 a shriveled〔wizened, dried up〕face // 바싹 우기다 persist stubbornly ; stick to it // 바싹 껴안다 hug tightly in the arms // 옆에 바싹 다가앉다 sit closer to 《a person》// 몸이 바싹 야위다 lose much weight // 바싹 타고 재만 남다 be (completely) burnt to ashes // 과자를 바싹 깨물다 crunch〔champ〕a cake // 논에 물이 바싹 말랐다 The paddy〔rice〕field has all dried up〔been parched up〕.
바야흐로 [한창] at the height 《of》; in full swing ; [이제 막] about 《to》; almost ; nearly ; on the point 《of》 ¶ 바야흐로 짙은 여름에 in high summer ; at the height of summer // 배가 바야흐로 출항하려고 한다 The ship is about〔just going〕to departure. /The ship is on the point of sailing. // 회사가 바야흐로 파산지경에 이르렀다 The firm was on the verge of bankruptcy. // 휴전 회담이 바야흐로 진행중이다 The truce talks are in full swing.
바에야 [이왕 …이면] at all ; [차라리] rather ; sooner... than ¶ 이왕 포기할 바에야 if you give it up at all // 항복할 바에야 차라리 죽겠다 I would rather die than surrender.
바와 같이 as ; like ¶ 아시는 바와 같이 as you know〔see〕
바운드 bounce ; bound **—하다** bounce ; bound ¶ 바운드시키다 bounce ; bound
†**바위** a rock ; a crag ¶ 바위가 많은 rocky // 바위를 차면 제 발뿌리만 아프다 If one kicks a rock, it only hurts one's own foot. /Obstacles should be attacked with caution.
바위너설 sharp edges of a rock
바위솔 〖식물〗 a houseleek ; a sengreen ; Orostachys japonicus (학명)
바위옷 moss ; lichen ¶ 바위옷이 끼다 be covered with moss ; be mossy
바위옹두라지 the spur of a rock ; a jag of a rock ; a rock with jagged edges
바위제비 〖새〗 a (house) martin ; a black-chinned martin ; Delichon urbica dasypus (학명)
바위종다리 〖새〗 a N. China hedge sparrow
바위채송화 〖식물〗 a kind of sedum ; a stone-crop ; Sedum polystichoides (학명)
바위취 〖식물〗 a saxifrage ; Saxifrage oblongifolia (학명)
바윗돌 a rock block ; a block of rock
바음 기호, 바음자리표 〖음악〗 F〔bass〕clef

바이 at all ; in the least ; absolutely ; (there is no) way 《to》 ¶ 나로서는 방법이 바이없다 I simply do not know how to do it. // 바이없는 일이로다 I cannot help it. /It cannot be helped. /There is no help for it. // 슬프기 바이없다 It is terribly sad.
***바이러스** 〖의학〗 a virus ¶ 바이러스의 viral **—병** a viral disease ; virosis **—학** virology ; virusology **— 혈증(血症)** viremia ; virusemia **항—제(劑)** an antiviral drug
바이어 a buyer ; a buying agent from abroad
바이올렛 〖식물〗 a violet ; [빛깔] violet
바이올리니스트 a violinist
‡**바이올린** a violin ; a fiddle ¶ 바이올린의 명수 a master violinist // 바이올린을 켜다 play the violin
— 독주(獨奏) a violin solo ; a solo on the violin **— 연주자(演奏者)** a violinist ; a fiddler **제 1〔2〕 —** 《play》 the first〔second〕 violin〔fiddle〕
바자 bamboos〔reeds, stalks〕 linked〔joined〕 to make a fence
—문 a twig gate in the bamboo fence **—울** a bamboo〔reed, stalk〕 fence
***바자** [자선시] a (charity) bazaar ; a fancy fair ¶ 바자를 열다 open〔hold〕 a bazaar
바자위다 (be) niggardly ; stingy
바작바작 [소리] crackling ; cracking ; [마음 죄이다] nervously ; fretfully ¶ 바작바작 타다 burn crackling // 속이 바작바작 타다 be torn〔devoured〕 by anxiety ; grow fretful
바장이다 walk idly back and forth ; ramble ; stroll aimlessly
바조 —調 〖음악〗 the note F ¶ 바장조 F major // 바단조 F minor
바주카포 —砲 a bazooka (gun)
‡**바지** baggy trousers worn by Koreans ; trousers ; pants ; slacks ; breeches ¶ 승마용 바지 riding breeches ; peg-tops // 바지를 입다 wear trousers ; put on trousers **—걸이** a trousers hanger **— 멜빵** suspenders 《미》; braces 《영》 **—저고리** coat and trousers ; [비유적] a man of no guts ; a good-for-nothing **— 주머니** a trouser pocket **나팔 —** bell-bottom(ed) trousers ; bell-bottoms ; bags 《영·속》 바짓가랑이 a trouser〔pant〕 leg **반 —** breeches ; shorts ; knicker(bocker)s **속 —** underwear pants ; shorts **솜 —** wadded〔cotton padded〕 trousers **양복 —** trousers **여자 —** slacks
바지락조개 a short-necked clam ; Mactra veneriformis (학명)
바지랑대 a laundry pole
바지런하다 (be) diligent ; industrious ⇨ 부지런하다
바지저고리 coat and trousers ; [비유적] a man of no guts ; a good-for-nothing ¶ 그는 바지저고리다 He has no backbone. /He is a straw man.

바지지, 바지직 with a hiss〔sizzle, fizzle〕; with a hissing〔ripping〕 sound ―하다 hiss; give〔let out〕 a hiss; rip ¶ 바지지바지지 with repeated hissing〔ripping〕

바짝 completely; closely ⇨ 바싹

-바치 a maker; a worker; an artisan; a mechanic

갖― a maker of leather shoes; a shoemaker

†바치다¹ [드리다] give; offer; present; dedicate (책·물건을); devote (헌신); [세금 따위를] pay; clear ¶ 뇌물을 바치다 bribe 《a person》; offer a bribe // 평생을 바치다 give〔devote〕 one's life to 《the study》 // 수업료를 바치다 pay school tuition; pay for instruction // 세금을 바치다 pay a tax // 나라를 위하여 생명을 바치다 sacrifice oneself〔one's life〕 for one's country // 이 책을 A씨에게 바침 Dedicated to Mr. A.

바치다² [즐기다] be mad〔crazy, wild〕 about; be excessively fond of ¶ 계집을 바치다 be sex-mad; be wild about women // 술을 바치다 He is crazy about alcoholic drinks. /He is a tippler〔soaker〕.

바캉스 (a) vacation; holidays

바커스 〖로마 신화〗 Bacchus

†바퀴¹ a wheel; [일주] a round; a turn; a rotation; a cycle; a turn of the wheel ¶ 바퀴에 기름을 치다 grease the wheels // 섬을 한 바퀴 돌다 go round the island; make a tour of the island

― 덮개 a wheel cowling ― 멈추개 a scotch; a scotch-block; [회전을 멈추는] a lock ― 자국 ruts; a (wheel) track; a furrow; the print of a wheel ―통 the hub 《of a wheel》; a nave 앞〔뒷〕― the front〔rear〕 wheel

바퀴² 〖곤충〗 a cockroach; a roach

바퀴살 a spoke

바퀴의자 ―椅子 [환자용] a wheelchair; a wheeled chair; an invalid chair

바탕¹ ① [기질] natural disposition; character; nature; temperament; constitution (체질) ¶ 바탕이 좋은 사람 a man of good disposition // 그와 나는 바탕이 다르다 He is a man of different stamp from me. // 그의 바탕은 예술가다 He has an artistic temperament.

② [품질] material; quality ¶ 그 옷감은 바탕이 거칠다 The dress material is of coarse texture.

③ [기반] background; ground; field ¶ 흰 바탕에 얼룩 무늬 a spotty design on a white ground

바탕² a bout; a turn; a round; a rubber; a set; a spell of action ¶ 씨름 한 바탕 a bout of wrestling // 한바탕 놀았다 We played a round.

바터 barter

― 무역 barter trade; give-and-take trade 《미》 ―용 상품 barter goods ―제 the barter system〔basis〕

바텐더 a barman; a bartender 《미》; a barkeep(er)

바투 closely ¶ 바투 앉다 sit close // 시간이 바투 다가온다 The time draws near.

바특이 a little bit; closely; thick (국물이)

바특하다 [국물이] (be) thick; stodgy; dry ¶ 국이 좀 바특하다 The soup is a bit thick. /The soup needs more water.

*바티칸 [교황청] the Vatican (Palace); [도시] Vatican City

박¹ a gourd; a calabash

―꽃 a gourd flower

박² ① [긁거나 가는 소리] with a vigorous rasp〔grate, scrape, grind〕 ② [찢는 소리] with a rip

박 泊 staying the night ¶ 1박 2식(食)에 30,000원 thirty thousand *won* a night including two meals // 1박하다 stay〔stop 《미》〕 overnight

박 拍 a (musical) clapper

*박 箔 foil; leaf ¶ 금박 gold leaf

*박격 迫擊 a close assault〔attack〕 ―하다 make a close attack 《on》; storm

―포 a trench mortar; a mine thrower; a bomb-gun

*박공 〖건축〗 a gable ¶ 박공 지붕 a gable roof

박구기 a (small) gourd dipper

:박다 ① [못 따위를] drive 《in》; hammer 《in》; thrust 《in, into》; insert ¶ 기둥에 못을 박다 drive a nail into the post // 땅에 말뚝을 박다 drive a stake into the ground // 반지에 보석을 박다 set a stone in a ring; adorn a ring with a stone

② [인쇄·사진] print; get 《a thing》 printed; put into (press); impress; take 《a photograph》; stamp ¶ 명함을 박다 have one's cards printed // 사진을 박다 take a picture // 1,000부 박다 print 〔run off〕 1,000 copies

③ [바느질] sew; make stitches ¶ 이불을 박다 stitch a quilt // 박음질로 박다 backstitch

④ [송편·만두 따위에] fill with 《savory matter》; stuff with ¶ 떡에 소를 박다 stuff a rice cake; fill a rice cake with stuffing; put stuffing〔a filling〕 in a rice cake

⑤ [판에] cut out; make; shape ¶ 다식을 다식판에 박다 cut out honey cakes on the honey-cake board〔mold〕

박다위 a hemp shoulder〔carrying〕 strap

박달나무 〖식물〗 a kind of birch; Betula Schmidtii (학명)

박답 薄畓 a poor〔an unproductive〕 paddy field

박대 薄待 a cold reception〔treatment〕; inhospitality; ill-treatment ―하다 receive〔treat〕 《a person》 coldly ¶ 그는 박대 받았다 He was given a cold reception. /He was treated in a cold way.

박덕 薄德 possessing little virtue ; scanty virtue ; lack〔want〕 of virtue —하다 be of scanty virtue ; be scant in virtue
박도 博徒 a (professional) gambler ; a gamester ¶ 박도의 두목 a boss gambler
*박두 迫頭 pressure ; urgency ; impendence —하다 draw near ; press ; (be) imminent ¶ 박두한 위기 imminent danger // 선거일이 박두하다 The election day draws near〔is at hand〕. // 시간이 박두했다 We are pressed for time.
박락 剝落 peeling off ; exfoliation —하다 come〔fall〕 off 《in layers, in scales》 ; peel〔scale〕 off ; exfoliate
박람 博覽 wide reading ; extensive knowledge ; getting a broad view —하다 read widely〔extensively〕 ; get a broad view 《of》 ¶ 박람 강기한 사람 a man of wide reading with a retentive memory
*박람회 博覽會 an exhibition ; an exposition 《미》 ; a fair ¶ 만국 박람회 an international exhibition ; a world fair
—장 the exhibition〔fair〕 grounds — 출품자 an exhibitor 만국 — an international exhibition ; a world('s) fair 《미》
박래 舶來 importation
—품 foreign-made goods〔articles〕 ; imported goods
박력 迫力 force ; intensity ¶ 박력있는 strong ; powerful ; able ; convincing ; forcible // 사실이 지니는 박력 the irresistible logic of facts // 그 영화는 박력이 없다 That film appeals little to the audience.
박론 駁論 refutation ; confutation ; disproof ; retort ; 〖법〗 rebuttal ; rebutment —하다 refute ; confute ; disprove ; argue ; retort ; rebut ¶ 정부 시책에 박론을 가하다 criticize government policies
박리 剝離 exfoliation ; [표피의] desquamation —하다 come〔peel, scale〕 off ; exfoliate ; excoriate ; desquamate
박리 薄利 meager〔small〕 profits ; a small 〔narrow〕 margin of profit ¶ 박리로 팔다 sell at a small (margin of) profit ; sell at a bargain
박리 다매 薄利多賣 quick sales at small profits ; small profits and quick returns ; nimble sixpence〔shilling〕
—주의 a quick-returns policy
박멸 撲滅 extermination ; eradication ; extirpation —하다 eradicate ; extirpate ; stamp out ; annihilate ; wipe out of existence ¶ 결핵 박멸 운동 a crusade against tuberculosis ; an anti-T. B. drive // 전염병을 박멸하다 stamp〔wipe〕 out epidemics // 해충을 박멸하다 exterminate vermin
—책 an exterminatory measure
박명 薄命 evil〔sad〕 fate ; unhappiness ; misfortune —하다 (be) unfortunate ; hopeless ; unlucky ; ill-fated ; ill-starred ; hapless
가인(佳人) — Beauty is often inconsistent with luck. /Beauty and luck seldom go hand in hand.
박모 薄暮 dusk ; twilight ¶ 박모에 at dusk ; in the twilight hours
박문 博聞 erudition ; wide information —하다 be well〔widely〕 informed 《on》 ¶ 박문한 사람 a well-informed person
박물 博物 ① [지식] wide knowledge ② [박물학] natural history
— 군자 a man of erudition ; a widely informed person — 표본 a specimen of natural history
박물관 博物館 a museum
국립 — the National Museum 대영(大英) — the British Museum
박물학 博物學 natural history ; the study of nature
—자 a naturalist
박박[1], 빡빡[1] [갈다·긁다] scrapingly ; hard ; roughly ; vigorously ; scratch ; [찢다] ripping up ; shredding ¶ 모기가 문 곳을 박박 긁다 scratch a mosquito bite hard // 종이를 박박 찢다 tear paper to pieces
박박[2], 빡빡[2] ① [얽은 모양] 《pockmarked》 all over ; solid 《with pockmarks》 ¶ 빡빡 얽다 be pitted〔pockmarked〕 all over the face
② [머리 깎은 모양] 《having one's hair cut》 close ¶ 중처럼 머리를 빡빡 깎다 have one's hair cut short〔close-cropped〕 like a monk
박복 薄福 misfortune ; ill-luck ; sad fate —하다 (be) unlucky ; unfortunate
박봉 薄俸 a small〔scanty, low, meager〕 salary ; poor pay ; a pittance ¶ 박봉으로 겨우 살아가다 eke out on one's meager pay
—자 an underpaid person
박빙 薄氷 thin (coat of) ice
†박사 博士 a doctor ; [정통한 사람] an expert ; [학식있는 사람] a learned man ¶ A 박사 Dr. A
— 논문 a thesis for a doctorate ; a doctoral thesis〔dissertation〕 — 학위 a doctor's degree ; a doctorate ¶ 박사 학위를 수여하다 confer a doctorate on 《a person》 // 박사 학위를 받다〔따다〕 take 〔receive, obtain〕 a doctorate 《in economics》 만물 — a well-informed person ; a walking〔living〕 dictionary
박사 薄謝 a small consideration ; a slight 〔small〕 token of one's gratitude 〔appreciation〕
박살 撲殺 clubbing〔beating〕 《a person》 to death —하다 club〔strike〕 《a person》 dead ¶ 박살당하다 be beaten to death
박새 〖새〗 a great-tit ; a titmouse
박색 薄色 an ugly face ; a plain woman ¶ 그 여자는 둘도 없는 박색이다 She is ugly enough to stop a clock.
박속 the flesh〔edible part〕 of a gourd
박수 a male diviner〔shaman〕 ; a sorcerer
*박수 拍手 clapping of hands ; hand clap-

ping ―하다 clap one's hands ¶ 우레 같은 박수 속에 amidst a thunderous clapping of hands

―갈채 clapping and cheering ; applause ; plaudits ¶ 박수 갈채하다 clap and applaud // 박수 갈채를 환영하다 greet 《a person》 with loud applause // 한바탕 우뢰와 같은 박수 갈채를 받으면서 무대에 서 있는 기분이 어떤 것인지 한번만이라도 알고 싶어 Just once I'd like to see how it feels to be up on the stage receiving a thunderous round of applause.

박스 [상자] a box ; [좌석] a box ; [가죽] box calf

― 구두 shoes〔boots〕 made of box calf

박식 博識 wide〔extensive〕 knowledge ; erudition ―하다 (be) well-informed 〔-read〕 ; erudite ; learned

박신거리다 swarm ; crowd ; throng ¶ 거리에 사람들이 박신거린다 The street swarms〔is crowded〕 with people.

박신박신 in swarms ; in crowds ―하다 ⇨ 박신거리다 ¶ 박신박신 모여들다 gather in swarms ; flock together

박애 博愛 benevolence ; philanthropy ; charity ¶ 박애의 philanthropic ; benevolent

― 사업 philanthropic work ―주의 philanthropism ―주의자 a philanthropist

박약 薄弱 feebleness ; weakness ―하다 (be) feeble〔weak, flimsy〕 ; [근거·신용이] shaky ; insufficient ¶ 근거가 박약하다 be based on insufficient evidence // 의지가 박약하다 have a weak will ; be weak of purpose

박언학 博言學 philology ; linguistics

박옥 璞玉 an uncut gem

박용 舶用 ¶ 박용의 marine ; for ships 〔vessels, shipping〕

― 엔진〔터빈, 발전기〕 a marine engine 〔turbine, dynamo〕

박은이 [인쇄인] a printer ; a typographer

박음질 sewing ; sewing-machine stitches ; a backstitch

-박이 an inlaid one

덧니― a person who has a side〔double〕 tooth

박이다 ① [끼어 있다] get stuck ¶ 뼈가 목에 박였다 A bone has stuck in my throat. // 하늘에 별이 박여 있다 The sky is studded with stars.

② [배다] remain deep〔embedded〕 《in one's heart》 ; become a habit (담배 따위) ¶ 담배를 피우면 인이 박이어 끊기 어렵다 Once smoking becomes a habit, you can hardly give it up. /The smoking habit stays with you.

③ [인쇄·사진] put into print ; have one's picture taken ¶그는 원고를 인쇄에 박였다 He got his manuscript printed./ He had them print his manuscript.

박이 부정 博而不精 ¶ 박이 부정이라 Jack of all trades, and master of none.

박이옷 clothes sewn with sewing-machine stitches ; clothes sewed entirely by backstitch

박자 拍子 time ; rhythm ; measure ; beat ¶ 2〔3〕박자 binary〔triple〕 time // 박자에 맞추어 in〔keeping〕 time 《with》 // 손으로 〔발로〕 박자를 맞추다 keep〔beat〕 time with the hands〔feet〕

박작거리다 jam ; swarm ; crowd ; bustle ¶ 박작거리는 거리 crowded streets // 그가 그 소식을 전하자 회중은 박작거렸다 When he announced the news, there was a stir in the congregation.

박작박작 in a bustle ; full of stir ; tumultuously ¶ 사람들이 박작박작 모여든다 The people jam together in a crowd.

박장 拍掌 hand-clapping ; clapping ―하다 clap hands ; applaud ¶ 박장 대소하다 laugh aloud clapping one's hands ; engage in applause mingled with laughter

박재 雹災 a hail disaster ¶ 박재를 당하다 suffer from a hail disaster

박절 迫切 ―하다 (be) cold-hearted ; unfeeling ; heartless ; inhuman ; severe ; inconsiderate ; relentless

박절기 拍節機 〖음악〗 a metronome

박정 薄情 cold-heartedness ; heartlessness ; cruelty ―하다 (be) cold-hearted〔heartless, stony-hearted〕 ¶ 박정하게 대하다 be hard on 《a person》 ; ill-treat // 그는 박정한 사람이다 He has a heart of stone. /He has no feelings. // 그렇게 박정한 짓은 할 수 없다 I cannot find it in my heart to do such a thing.

박제 剝製 stuffing ; a stuffed animal〔bird〕 ¶ 박제로 하다 stuff

―술 taxidermy ―자 a taxidermist ― 표본 a stuffed specimen

박주 薄酒 untasty〔poor〕 liquor ; unpalatable *sool*

박주가리 〖식물〗 milkweed ; Metaplexis japonica (학명)

*박쥐 a bat

박쥐 구실 opportunism ; a wait-and-see policy ; a seesaw policy ¶ 그는 박쥐 구실 한다 He is an opportunist.

박쥐우산 ―雨傘 an (Occidental) umbrella ; a parasol (양산)

박진 迫眞 truthfulness to life ; verisimilitude

―하다 be true to life〔nature〕 ; be lifelike ¶ 박진의 realistic 《acting》

박진성 迫眞性 truthfulness to life ; verisimilitude ¶ 박진성 있는 true to life ; realistic

**박차 拍車 a spur ; a rowel spur ; [촉진] acceleration ; speeding up ¶ 말의 옆구리를 박차로 세게 차다 dig one spurs into the horse's sides // 박차 달린 구두를 신고 나타나다 come forth booted and spurred // 새로운 운동에 박차를 가하다 give an impetus to the new movement

박차를 가하다 관용 put〔set, give, clap〕 spurs to ; expedite ; accelerate
박차다 kick away〔off〕 ; give a vigorous kick ; [거절] reject ; turn down ¶ 요구를 박차다 turn down a request ; reject a demand // 자리를 박차고 일어나다 stamp out of the room // 모든 장애를 박차고 나가다 go ahead sweeping aside all obstacles
박찬 薄饌 poor〔unsavory〕 side dishes
박처 薄妻 mistreatment〔ill-treatment〕 of one's wife ―하다 treat one's wife coldly〔cruelly〕 ; abuse one's wife
박치기하다 bump〔knock〕 one's head against 《a person》 ; give a butt (of a head) 《to a person》
박타다 ① [박을 쪼개다] split a gourd in two ; saw a gourd in half ② [낭패되다] fall short of〔do not come up to, be far from〕 one's expectations ; be disappointed in one's expectations ; be frustrated 《in one's ambition》
*박탈 剝奪 deprivation ; divestment ; dispossession ―하다 deprive 《a person》 of 《a thing》 ; strip 《a person》 of 《his clothes》 ; take away ¶ 공민권을 박탈하다 deprive 《a person》 of civil rights // 그는 관직을 박탈당했다 He was divested of his office.
박태기나무 〖식물〗 a redbud ; a Judas tree ; Cercis siliquastrum (학명)
⁑박테리아 a bacterium 《*pl.* -ria》
박토 薄土 barren〔poor, sterile〕 soil
박통 博通 ⇨ 박식
박피 薄皮 a thin skin ; a film (액체의) ; a membrane (박막)
*박하 薄荷 〖식물〗 a peppermint ; mint ―껌 peppermint〔spearmint〕 gum ―뇌〔빙, 정〕 menthol crystals ―담배 a mentholated cigaret(te) ―사탕 peppermint (candy) ―수 peppermint solution ―유 peppermint oil ―정(精) mint camphor ; essence of mint
박하다 薄― ① [인색하다] (be) stingy ; strict ; [인정이 열다] hard ; tough ; coldhearted ; inhuman ¶ 인심이 박한 세상 a hard〔tough〕 world to live in // 점수가 박하다 be severe〔strict〕 in grading // 박하게 굴지 마라 Don't be so stingy.
② [적다] (be) scanty ; meager ; little ¶ 박한 봉급 a meager salary // 이익이 박하다 The profit〔margin〕 is small.
박학 博學 great learning ; erudition ; wide knowledge ―하다 (be) erudite ; learned ; well-informed〔-read〕 ¶ 박학다식한 사람 a well-informed man with broad vision // 박학한 체한다 He pretends to know much.
*박해 迫害 persecution ; oppression ―하다 persecute ; oppress ; torment ¶ 박해의 희생자 victims of oppression // 종교상의 박해 religious persecution // 박해를 받다 be persecuted ; suffer persecution
―자 a persecutor ; a tormentor ; an oppressor ; a molester
⁑박히다 [못 따위가] be nailed ; be driven into ; be stuck in ; [인쇄물이] be printed ; be taken (사진이) ¶ 벽에 못이 박혀 있다 There is a nail stuck in the wall. // 사진이 잘 박혔다 The photo came out good.
†밖 ① [바깥] the outside ; the exterior (외면) ; [호외] out-of-doors ; the open (air) ¶ 밖의 outside ; outdoor ; external ; exterior // 밖에 out ; outside ; out of doors // 밖에 나가다 go out (of doors) ; go out of the house〔into the open air〕 // 밖에서 내다보다 look from the outside // 밖에서 놀다 play outdoors // 밖에서 문을 열다 open the door from the outside // 밖에서 식사하다 dine out // 밖으로 내쫓아 버리다 turn 《a person》 out of the house // 창밖을 내다보다 look out of the window // 밖은 춥다 It is cold outside. // 그는 도무지 밖에 나가지 않는다 He is a regular stay-at-home. /He always keeps indoors.
② [이외] the rest ; the others ; 《with》 exception 《of》 ; outside of (a limit) ¶ 그 밖에 besides ; in addition to that // 가진 돈이라고는 이것밖에 없다 This is all the money I have on me. // 그렇게 생각하는 사람은 너 밖에 없다 Nobody thinks so but you. // 그렇게 할 수밖에 없다 There is no choice〔alternative〕 but to do so. // 그밖에 다른 질문은 없습니까 Are there any other questions ? // 그밖의 사람은 가도 좋다 The rest of you may go home. // 그의 친구라고는 나밖에 없다 He has no friends except me.
반 a flattened sheet〔layer〕 ¶ 솜반 a flattened layer of cotton
반 反 〖철학〗 the antithesis 《*pl.* -ses》 ⇨ 반-(反)
†반 半 a half ; half ; halfway ; partial ; incomplete ⇨ 반-(半) ¶ 한 시 반 one-thirty ; half past one // 반은 무의식 중에 half unconsciously // …보다 반이 더 많은 half as much〔many〕 again as // 반은 불행으로 반은 병으로 인해서 partly through 〔what with〕 illness and partly through 〔what with〕 misfortune // 밥그릇에 반만 채우다 fill the rice bowl halfful // 그는 반야수다 He is half man and half beast. // 그 친구 이야기는 반을 에누리하여 들어라 You had better take what he says with a grain of salt.
시작이 반이다 속담 Well begun is half done.
*반 班 a group〔company, party, unit, circle, class〕 ; [학급] a class ; [군대] a squad ; [동네의] a *pan* 《the smallest unit of a neighborhood association》 ¶ 반장 a class monitor (학급의) ; a group 〔party〕 leader (조) ; a squad leader (군대의) ; a head of a *pan* (동네의) // 2통 3반 3번지

#3, 3-*pan*, 2-*tong* // 인사 행정반 the personnel and administration unit // 합동 조사반을 편성하다 organize a joint investigation party

반- 反 anti-
—공 anticommunist ; anticommunism **—정부 시위** an antigovernment〔antiadministration〕 demonstration **—제국주의** anti-imperialism **—체제 운동** an antiestablishment movement

반- 半 half ; semi- ; demi- ; hemi- ¶ 반반의 half-and-half // 반숙의 half-cooked // 반영구적인 semipermanent
—시간 half an hour ; a half hour **—신(神)** a demigod **—액** half the sum **—원** a half circle ; a semicircle ; a hemicycle **—장화** half boots

반가 半價 half the price ; half-price ⇨ 반값 ¶ 반가로 at half-price ; at 50% off the regular price

반가 班家 a noble family ; a house of nobility

반가공품 半加工品 semi-manufactured〔processed〕 goods

반가부좌 半跏趺坐 sitting with one's legs half-crossed, as in Buddhist statues

반가움 delight ; joy ; gladness

***반가워하다** be glad〔pleased, delighted〕 about 《meeting》 ; rejoice in ; take pleasure in 《meeting》 ¶ 소식을 듣고 반가워하다 be overjoyed at hearing the news // 편지를 받고 반가워하다 be glad to get a letter from home // 그는 나를 보고 반가워했다 He rejoiced to see me.

반가이 joyfully ; gladly ; delightedly ; with joy ; with pleasure ¶ 반가이 맞다 welcome 《a person》 gladly

반간 半間 half a *kan* ; a half-size room (반간방) ⇨ 간

반감 反感 antipathy ; animosity ; ill feeling ; spite ; a feeling of revolt ; an antagonistic feeling ¶ 반감을 사다 rouse 《a person's》 antipathy ; antagonize 《a person》 // 반감을 품다 harbor〔nurse〕 ill feeling against 《a person》 // 반감을 품을 하등의 이유가 없다 I've got nothing against him.

반감 半減 reduction by half ; a 50 percent reduction〔cut〕 **—하다** reduce by half ; cut in half ; halve ¶ 비용을 반감하다 cut the expense by half ; halve the expense // 흥미가 반감되다 lose half one's interest in 《a thing》

반감기 半減期 〖물리〗 a half life ; a half(-life) period ¶ 방사성 탄소의 반감기는 5천 6백년이다 Radiocarbon has a half life of 5,600 years.

***반갑다** (be) happy ; glad ; be pleased〔delighted〕 ¶ 반가운 happy ; glad ; joyful ; delightful // 반가운 손님 a welcome guest // 반가운 소식 happy〔glad〕 news ; good tidings // 반가워서 for joy ; in one's joy // 그 소식을 듣고 반가웠다 I was pleased at the news. // 눈물이 날 정도로 반가웠다 I nearly wept for joy. // 같이 일하게 돼서 반갑습니다 Nice to have you with us.

반값 半— half the sum〔amount〕 ; half-price ¶ 반값으로 at half the price ; at half-price // 반값 이하로 at less than half-price // 반값 이하로 내리다 reduce (the price) by half

반개 半個 half a piece ; half ¶ 사과 반개 half (of) an apple

반개 半開 〔문이〕 (being) half〔partly〕 open ; ajar ; 〔꽃이〕 half in bloom ; half open ; 〔문화가〕 semi-civilized ; semi-barbarous **—하다** be half open ; be ajar ; be half in bloom ; be half-〔semi-〕civilized

반거들충이 半— a half-trained〔educated〕 person ; a smatterer ; a sciolist ¶ 반거들충이의 superficial ; half-learned

반걸음 半— half a step

***반격 反擊** a counterattack ; a responsive attack ; a counteraction ; a counteroffensive **—하다** make〔deliver〕 a counterattack ; drive〔strike〕 back
— 기지 a retaliation base **— 작전** counterattack operations

***반경 半徑** 〖수학〗 a radius 《*pl.* ~es, -dii》 ; a semidiameter ¶ 반경 5마일 이내〔밖〕에 within〔outside〕 a 5-mile radius // 반경을 그리다 describe a radius
비행 — the flying radius **행동 —** 〖군사〗 a radius of action

반골 叛骨 an uncompromising〔a defiant〕 attitude of mind ¶ 반골의 unyielding ; proud
— 정신 a spirit of defiance ; an unyielding spirt

반공 反共 anticommunism ; anticommunist **—하다** oppose communism ¶ 반공 사상을 고취하다 infuse〔instil〕 strong anticommunistic ideas〔sentiments〕 《into the minds of the public》 // 반공 운동을 전개하다 start〔inaugurate〕 an anticommunist movement〔campaign〕
— 교육 anticommunist education **—법** the anticommunist Law **— 사상** anticommunism **— 운동** an anticommunist movement **— 전선** the anticommunist front **— 정책** an anticommunist policy **아시아 — 연맹** the Asian People's Anti-communist League 《APACL》

반공 反攻 a counteroffensive ; a counterthrust
— 기지(基地) a retaliation base **— 작전** counteroffensive operations

반공일 半空日 a half holiday ; Saturday

반관반민 半官半民 semi-governmental management
— 신문 a semiofficial organ **— 회사** a semi-governmental company〔corporation〕

****반구 半球** a hemisphere ¶ 동〔서〕반구 the

ㅂ

Eastern〔Western〕 Hemisphere
반국가적 反國家的 antinational ; antistate 《activities》
반군 叛軍 the rebels ; the rebel〔insurgent〕 army ; rebel troops
반군 反軍 opposition to military authorities 〔the military〕
반군국 反軍國 ¶ 반군국적인 antimilitaristic
—주의 antimilitarism
반기 a tray of eatables to be distributed among guests after a party〔ceremony〕
반기 反旗 the standard〔flag〕 of revolt
반기를 들다 관용 raise the standard of revolt〔rebellion〕; rise in arms against 《a person》
반기 半旗 a flag at half-mast ¶ 반기를 올린다 They display a flag at half-mast. /Flags are (flying) at half-mast.
반기 半期 a half term ; a semester ; a half year ¶ 반기의 half-yearly ; semiannual // 반기 결산 a half-yearly account 〔settlement〕// 반기 배당 the semiannual dividend // 상〔하〕 반기 the first〔latter〕 half of the year
반기다 rejoice 《at, over》; be glad 《of》; be delighted 《at, with》; be pleased 《at》 ¶ 손님을 반기다 be delighted to see a guest // 친구를 만나 반기다 be delighted to meet a friend
반기생 半寄生 『생물』 semiparasitism ¶ 반기생의 hemiparasitic ; semiparasitic
— 생물 a hemiparasite
반깃반 —盤 a tray ; a refreshment tray
반나마 半— more than half
반나절 半— a quarter of a day ; half the morning ; several hours of the day
반나체 半裸體 a half-naked body ¶ 반나체화 a semi-nude picture // 반나체의 half-naked ; semi-nude
반날 半— half a day ; a half day 《미》
반납 返納 return ; restoration —하다 return ; give back ; restore ¶ 정부에 반납하다 return 《a thing》 to the Government
반년 半年 half a year ; a half year 《미》 ¶ 반년마다 half-yearly ; semiannually
반단 半— a half bundle 《of straw》; a half sheaf 《of rice》; half a fag(g)ot 《of firewood》; a half bunch
반닫이 半— a cabinet ; a cedar chest (for storing clothes) which has half of one side hinged
반달 半— [반개월] half a month ; two weeks ; a fortnight ; [달의] a half-moon ; a crescent ¶ 반달분의 급료 semi-monthly pay // 반달형의 half-moon // 잡지를 반달에 한 번씩 내다 publish a magazine semi-monthly
반당 反黨 [반역자] traitors ; [반당 행위] anti-party activities ¶ 반당 행위를 하다 engage in anti-party activities
— 분자 anti-party elements
†반대 反對 ① [반항] opposition ; [이의] objection ; dissension —하다 be against ; be opposed to ; object to ; be hostile to ; be antagonistic to ; dissent from ¶ 반대의 opposite ; contrary // …에 반대하여 in opposition 《to》// 반대를 받다 meet with opposition ; be opposed // 반대 신문을 하다 cross-examine // 반대 운동을 일으키다 start a movement〔campaign〕 against // 의안에 반대하다 vote against the bill // 국민은 전쟁에 반대인 듯했다 The people seemed to be against the war. // 그것에 찬성인가 반대인가 Are you for it or against it? // 존이 내 후임으로 임명되는 것에는 반대이다 I object to John being appointed my successor. // 너는 늘 나에게 반대한다 You always take the side opposite mine.
② [역] reverse ; opposite ¶ 반대의 reverse ; opposite ; contrary // 반대의 소문 a rumor to the contrary // 반대 행동 a counteraction〔movement〕// 반대로 on the contrary ; the other way ; conversely // 반대 방향으로 in the opposite direction // 이것은 저것과 정반대이다 This is diametrically opposed to that. // 바보라니 그 반대이다 He is no fool, but just the opposite〔reverse〕. // 진상은 완전히 그 반대이다 The truth is quite the other way round. // 그것은 그가 생각한 것과는 정반대이다 It is the very reverse to what he intended. // 나는 정반대로 생각했다 I thought quite the opposite. // 꿈은 반대로 풀이된다 Dreams go by contraries. // 「어둡다」의 반대는 무엇인가 What is the opposite of dark?
— 개념 a contrary concept — 급부(給付) consideration —당 the Opposition ; the opposing (party) —론 an opposite view ; an argument against 《a matter》 —방향 the opposite direction —색 an antagonistic〔opponent〕 color — 세력 counterforce ; counterpressure 《to the cold war》 — 신문(訊問) 『법』 cross-examination —어 an antonym —자 an objector ; a dissenter — 투표 a negative〔an adverse〕 vote ; a blackball ; blackballing ¶ 반대 투표하다 vote against 《a measure》; blackball 《an applicant》 —파 the opposing party ; the opposition
반대기 a flattened dumpling ; a cooked vegetable ball
—떡 a rice dumpling
반대표 反對票 a dissenting vote
*반도 半島 a peninsula
한— the Korean Peninsula
반도 叛徒 rebels ; insurgents
반도미 半搗米 half-polished〔-cleaned〕 rice
반도체 半導體 『물리』 a semiconductor
반독립 半獨立 halfway independence ; partial independence ; quasi-independence

ㅂ

—국 a halfway independent〔quasi-independent〕 country ; a quasi-sovereign state
*반동 反動 reaction ; rebound ; [총 따위의] kick ; rebound —하다 react ; rebound ; kick ; recoil ¶ 반동적인 reactionary // 반동적인 정치가 a reactionary politician // 반동이 생겼다 A reaction has set in. // 이 총은 반동이 약하다 This gun kicks only slightly.
—내각〔정치〕 a reactionary cabinet 〔government〕 —력 reaction —분자 reactionary elements —사상 reactionary sentiment〔thought, idea〕 —주의 reactionalism —주의자 a reactionary ; a reactionist —혁명 counterrevolution
무—총〔포〕 a recoilless rifle〔cannon〕
반동강 半— ¶ 반동강나다 be split into two // 반동강으로 자르다 cut《a thing》 right in two
반두 a scoop-net ; a dip-net
반둥거리다, 빤둥거리다 live idle ; idle away one's time ; lounge ; loaf ; loiter ¶ 반둥반둥 idly ; leisurely // 문 근처에서 반둥거리다 hang about the door // 집에서 반둥거리다 loaf at home
†반드럽다 ① [매끈매끈하다] (be) smooth ; glossy ; sleek ; glazed ② [약빠르다] (be) smart ; slick ; wide-awake ; shrewd ; sharpe ¶ 반드러운 사람 a smart〔shrewd〕 fellow〔guy〕 ; a slick operator // 반드러운 머리털 sleek hair // 반드럽게 하다 smooth ; make smooth // 반드럽게 굴다 be wide-awake《to one's own interests》; be keen after one's interests // 대리석같이 반드럽다 be as smooth as marble
반드르르, 빤드르르 glossily ; sleekly ; lustrously ; smoothly —하다 (be) lustrous ; glossy ; bright ¶ 반드르르 윤기 나는 얼굴 a blooming complexion // 마루를 얼음장같이 반드르르하게 닦다 polish a floor as smooth as a sheet of ice
‡반드시 [확실히] (most) certainly ; surely ; [꼭] without fail ; by all means ; at any cost ; [필연적으로] necessarily ; inevitably ; unavoidably ; [늘] always ; [예외없이] without exception ; invariably ¶ 반드시 성공하다 be sure to succeed // 반드시 필요하다 be positively necessary // 반드시 …하지 않다 not always ; not necessarily ; not all〔every〕 // 그는 반드시 출석한다 He never fails to attend the meeting. // 도둑은 때가 되면 반드시 잡힌다 The thief is certain to be caught in time. // 반드시 실패한다 He is sure〔bound〕 to fail. // 아침 여섯 시면 반드시 일어난다 He makes it a rule to get up at six in the morning. // 반드시 그렇지 않다 It is not necessarily so. // 부자가 반드시 행복하지는 않다 The rich are not necessarily happy. // 반드시 시험을 보십시오 Take the examination by all means. // 재군비는 반드시 3차 대전을 초래한다 Rearmament is certain to bring about World War III.
반득, 빤뜩 shining ; flashing ; flickering ; glittering —하다 shine ; flash ; glisten ; shimmer ; glimmer ; gleam ¶ 반득거리다 flicker ; waver ; blink ; twinkle // 기뻐서 눈을 반득이다 one's eyes light up with joy // 회중 전등을 반득거리다 flash a flashlight // 거울을 햇빛에 반득거리다 flash a mirror with〔in〕 the sun // 눈이 달빛에 반득거린다 Snow glistens in the moonlight. // 달빛이 호수에 반득거린다 Moonbeams shimmer on the lake. // 번개가 하늘에 반득이었다 Lightning played in the sky.
반득반득 flickeringly ; twinklingly
반들거리다, 빤들거리다 ① [놀기만 하다] idle away one's time ; idle ; loaf ⇨ 반둥거리다 ② [약게 굴다] be shrewd 〔smart〕; be keen after one's interest ; [매끈하다] glisten ; shimmer ; shine
반들반들, 빤들빤들 ① [윤나게] smoothly ; glossily ; lustrously ; shiningly —하다 (be) smooth ; glossy ; lustrous ; shiny ¶ 소매가 닳아 반들반들한 저고리 a coat worn shiny in the sleeves ② [약게] shrewdly ; smartly ; alertly ③ [게으르게] idly ; lazily ; slothfully
반듯반듯하다 (be) all square and level ; all straight ; all in good order〔shape〕
반듯이 ⇨ 반듯하다
*반듯하다, 반뜻하다 [바르다] (be) straight ; even ; square and level ; be straightened up ; be in an even form 〔position〕; be in good order ; [흠없다] (be) tidy ; neat ; clean ; decent ; [반반하다] comely ; chiseled ; well-shaped ¶ 반듯한 얼굴 regular〔comely, chiseled〕 features // 반듯한 상자 a (perfectly) square box // 네모 반듯한 유리 a perfect square of glass // 반듯이 squarely ; straight ; orderly // 반듯이 눕다 lie face up ; lie on one's back // 반듯이 앉다〔서다〕 sit〔stand〕 square〔straight〕 // 몸이 반듯하다 have a good posture // 방안을 반듯하게 치우다 tidy up the room ; keep the room tidy 〔clean〕 // 판자의 모서리를 네모지게 반듯이 깎다 square the edges of a board // 연필을 반듯이 잡다 hold a pencil right // 몸을 반듯이 가지다 hold oneself straight // 집안을 반듯하게 치웠다 I kept my house neat. // 그 여자는 반듯하게 생겼다 She has comely features.
반등 反騰 『경제』 a sharp rally —하다 rally in price ¶ 주가의 반등 a rally in stocks
반디 a firefly ; a lightning bug
반딧불 the glow of a firefly〔lightning bug 《미》〕 ¶ 반딧불같은 빛 a light as faint as the glow of a firefly // 어둠 속에 반딧불이 반짝인다 Fireflies glow in the dark.
반뜻 in a flash
반락 反落 『증권』 a reaction —하다 react
‡반란 反亂 revolt ; rebellion ; uprising ;

ㅂ

mutiny ; insurrection

> 참고 **revolt** 충성을 버리고 복종을 거부함 **insurrection** 정권에 대해서 일부의 사람들이 무력을 갖고 반항하는 것 **rebellion** 정부에 대한 공공연하고 무력에 의한 반란 과거사에 대하여 말할 경우에는 보통 실패한 반란을 의미한다 **mutiny** 군인 특히 수병의 상급자에 대한 불복종

―하다 rebel 《against》; rise in revolt 《against》 ¶ 반란을 진압하다 quell〔put down, suppress〕 a rebellion〔revolt〕
―군 a rebel army **―자** a rebel **―표** a dissident vote

반려 伴侶 a companion ; a partner ; an associate ; a comrade ; a mate ¶ 일생의 반려 a companion for life ; one's yokefellow ; a life partner

반려 返戾 return ; restoration ; giving back ; retrocession **―하다** give back ; return ; restore ; retrocede ¶ 사표를 반려하다 turn down 《a person's》 resignation

ㅂ

반례 返禮 return ; repayment ; acknowledgment

반론 反論 [의론] an objection ; a refutation ; a dissension ; [의론 전환] switching one's idea ; conversion of one's idea **―하다** object to ; raise an objection 《to, against》; abandon〔switch〕 one's idea〔opinion〕

반만 半萬 half a myriad ; five thousand **―년** five millennia ; 5,000 years

반말 半― [낮춤말] crude language ; rough talk ; insolent〔impolite, slipshod, slovenly〕 speech **―하다** talk roughly〔solvenly〕; speak impolitely ; drop one's particles (in talking)

†**반면 反面** the other side ¶ 반면에 on the other hand // 화려한 도시 생활에도 어두운 반면이 있다 The gay citylife has a seamy side to it.

반면 半面 [사물의] one side ; [타면] the other side ; the reverse ; [얼굴의] a profile ; half the face ; a half face ¶ 달의 반면 the moon's disc〔disk〕 // 반면의 진리 a half-truth // 반면 미인 a beauty in profile // 문제의 반면만을 보다 only look at one side of a question // 사람은 다 약한 반면을 가지고 있다 Everybody has his weak side. // 그의 말에도 반면의 진리는 있다 There is some truth in what he says.

반명 班名 a title of nobility

반모음 半母音 『언어』 a semivowel

반목 反目 antagonism ; antipathy ; hostility ; enmity ; variance **―하다** be set 《against each other》; be hostile 《toward》; be at odds 《with each other》; be antagonistic 《to each other》; do not see eye-to-eye 《with》; be at loggerheads〔enmity, daggers, variance〕 《with》; feud 《with》 ¶ 양자간의 반목 antagonism between the two // 계급간에 서로 반목케 하다 set one class against another // 사람을 서로 반목케 하다 set 《a person》 at odds with 《another》

반몫 半― half a share〔portion〕; a half share

반문 反問 a cross-question〔-examination〕; a counter-question **―하다** ask in return ; retort ; make a retort ; cross-question ; cross-examine

반문 斑紋 a spot ; a speckle

반 물 a deep〔dark〕 blue color ; blue black ; indigo ¶ 반물 치마 a navy blue skirt

반미 飯米 rice for eating ; cooking rice

반미개 半未開 semibarbarian

반미치광이 半― a slightly mad person ; a half-crazed person

반민주주의적 反民主主義的 antidemocratic

반바닥 the base〔root〕 of the thumb

반바지 半― knee trousers〔pants〕; knee〔short〕 breeches ; knickers ; shorts

반박 反駁 refutation ; a retort ; confutation ; contradiction
―하다 refute ; confute ; retort ; contradict ; gainsay

반반 半半 half-and-half ; fifty-fifty ¶ 반반으로 half-and-half ; evenly ; share and share alike // 반반으로 나누다 halve ; divide in two equal parts ; go halves〔shares〕; go fifty-fifty // 반반으로 섞다 mix half-and-half // 반반으로 하자 I will go halves with you. /Let's go fifty-fifty. // 그러면 반반씩 내자 Let's go halves, then.

반반하다 ① [바닥이] (be) smooth ; even ; level ; flat ¶ 반반한 길 a level road // 반반한 표면 an even〔a smooth〕 surface // 길을 반반하게 고르다 level the road
② [생김이] (be) comely ; clear-cut ; chiseled ; handsome ¶ 반반한 용모 comely features
③ [지체가] (be) respectable ; decent ; highborn ; noble ¶ 반반한 집안 태생이다 be of high〔noble〕 birth ; come of a good family

반발 反撥 repulsion ; repelling **―하다** [되튀다] spring back ; [반격] repulse ; repel ; drive back ; resist
―력 repulsive〔repelling〕 power **― 작용** repulsion

반백 半白 [머리털이] (being) gray-haired ; grizzled ; half-white ; [쌀이] polished rice mixed evenly〔half-and-half〕 with unpolished rice
― 노인 a grizzled old man

반백 半百 fifty years of age ; half a hundred

반벙어리 半― a man of inarticulate pronunciation ; a mumbler ; a stammerer

반베 斑― towel cloth woven of indigo

threads mixed with white
반병두리 a flat-bottomed brass soup bowl
반병신 半病身 [불구자] a slightly deformed〔disabled〕 person ; a half〔semi〕-paralytic (반신불수) ; a half-wit (반편이)
반보 半步 half a step ; a half step
*반복 反復 repetition ; reiteration —하다 repeat ; reiterate ; do over again ¶ 반복하여 repeatedly ; over and over again // 늘 반복하는 changeable ; fickle // 몇 번이나 반복하여 읽다 read several times over // 유행은 반복된다 Fashions repeat themselves.
— 기호 〖음악〗 a sign of repetition ; a repeat — 발생 〖생물〗 palingenesis —설 〖철학〗 the recapitulation theory
반복 反覆 fickleness ; inconstancy ; switching (의견) —하다 switch ¶ 반복무상한 changeable ; fickle ; inconstant
반봇짐 半— a small parcel which one can carry in the hand
반봉건 半封建 semi-feudalism
—사상〔사회〕 a semi-feudalistic idea〔society〕
반부새 a gentle gallop ; a canter
반분 半分 half —하다 halve ; divide in two
반불겅이 半— [고추] a half-red pepper ; [담배] reddish tobacco (leaves)
반비 飯婢 a female kitchen worker ; a female cook
반비 反比 〖수학〗 inverse ratio
반비례 反比例 〖수학〗 inverse proportion —하다 be in inverse proportion 《to》
반비알지다 [땅이] be at a slight angle ; be gently sloped
반빗 飯— a female cook (in charge of making side dishes)
—간(間) a kitchen —아치 a court kitchen-maid
반빙 半氷 half frozen ice ; [반취] slight intoxication ; being half-intoxicated
‡반사 反射 reflection —하다 reflect ; reverberate ; [영상을] image ; mirror 《in》 ¶ 전반사 total reflection // 광선을 반사하다 reflect light
—각〔선〕 the angle〔line〕 of reflection —경 a reflecting mirror ; a reflector —광선 reflected rays —광학(光學) catoptrics —기(器) reflector —로(爐) a reverberatory furnace —망원경 a reflecting telescope —면 specular surface —성 reflexibility —신호기 a heliograph —열〔광〕 reflected heat〔light〕 —운동 reflex-movement ; counter-movement —율(率) reflexibility —작용 〖생리·심리〗 reflex (action) —체(體) a reflector —카메라 a reflex camera 조건— a conditioned reflex
반사식 反射式 ¶ 반사식의 스토브 a reflecting stove〔heater〕
반사회적 反社會的 (being) antisocial
반삭 半朔 half a month ; a half month ; a fortnight
반상 班常 the high and the low ; the nobles and the means〔commons〕
반상기 飯床器 a table service ; a dinner-set ; a set of tableware〔table-utensils〕 ; a set of dishes for a table
반색하다 be glad ; rejoice 《in, at》 ; take pleasure〔delight〕 《in》 ; be pleased 《with, by》 ¶ 반색하며 승낙하다 give one's hearty approval ; consent with pleasure // 반색하며 맞이하다 receive 《a person》 with great joy〔open arms〕
반생 半生 half one's life ; half a lifetime
반생반사 半生半死 (being) half-alive and half-dead —하다 be half-dead ; be dying ; be more dead than alive
반생반숙 半生半熟 (being) half-done ; half-baked (빵) ; half-roasted (고기) —하다 (be) half-baked ; half-boiled ; half-raw
반석 盤石 a rock ; a crag ¶ 반석같다 be as firm as a rock // 반석같이 서다 stand as a rock // 어떠한 유혹에도 반석같이 동하지 않았다 He stood adamant to any temptation.
반설음 半舌音 ⇨ 반혓소리
‡반성 反省 reflection ; self-examination ; introspection ; reconsideration (재고) ; meditation (숙고) —하다 reflect 《on》 ; examine oneself ; reconsider ; meditate ¶ 반성해보니 on second thought(s) ; on reflection // 반성을 촉구하다 ask 《a person》 to reconsider 《a matter》 // 자기의 행위를 반성하다 reflect on one's conduct
—회 a meeting for reviewing
반성 유전 伴性遺傳 sex-linkage ¶ 반성유전의 sex-linked
반세 半世 half one's life ; half a lifetime
반세기 半世紀 half a century
4— a quarter century
반소 半燒 partial destruction by fire —하다 be half〔partially〕 burned〔destroyed by fire〕
반소 反訴 a cross action ; a counteraction ¶ 반소를 제기하다 bring a counteraction
—인〔자〕 a counterclaimant —장(狀) a cross-bill
반소경 半— (being) half-blind ; purblind
반소매 半— a half-sleeve ; a half-length sleeve ¶ 반소매 셔츠〔블라우스〕 a shirt〔blouse〕 with short(-length) sleeves
반송 伴送 —하다 send〔deliver〕 《a thing》 along with
반송 返送 —하다 send back ; return
반송장 半— a good-for-nothing old man〔woman〕 ; a dotard ; a person half dead (from age and infirmity)
반수 半數 half the number ; the half ¶ 반수를 넘다 be more than half the number ; show〔hold, obtain〕 a majority // 위원의 반수 개선 the reelection of half the committee

반수반성 半睡半醒 broken sleep ; doze **—하다** have a broken sleep ; doze ; be half-asleep and half-awake

*__반숙 半熟__ [달걀 따위] half-cooked〔-boiled, -done〕; soft-boiled ; [과일] half-ripe ; green **—하다** be half-boiled〔-done〕; be half-ripe
—란(卵) a half〔soft〕-boiled egg ; a half-done egg

반시 半時 [반시간] half an hour ; [잠시] a short time〔while〕; a moment ¶ 한시 반시 놀지 않다 never idle away one's time ; work all the time

반시 a flat persimmon

반시간 半時間 half an hour ; thirty minutes

반시류 半翅類 〖곤충〗 Hemiptera (학명)

반식민지 半植民地 ¶ 반식민지의 semicolonial
— 국가 a semicolonial state **— 상태** semicolonialism

반식민지주의 反植民地主義 anticolonialism
—자 an anticolonialist

반신 半身 one side of the body ; half the body ¶ 반신 사진을 찍다 have one's half-length portrait taken
—불수(不隨) hemiplegia ; paralysis of one side ¶ 반신불수의 paralyzed on one side **— 사진** a half-length photograph **—상(像)** a half-length figure〔statue〕 **상〔하〕—** the upper〔lower〕 half of one's body

반신 叛臣 a rebel courtier〔retainer〕; a traitorous〔rebellious〕 minister

반신 返信 a reply ; an answer **—하다** answer〔reply to〕 a letter ; send a reply to《a person, a person's letter》
—료(料) return postage ; postage for a reply ¶ 반신료를 선납하다 prepay the reply **—료 선납 전보** a reply-paid telegram **—용 엽서** a reply (postal) card

반신 半信 **—하다** be suspicious〔doubtful〕《of》; mistrust ; be half in doubt《about》

반신반수 半神半獸 a half-god and half-beast

반신반의 半信半疑 doubt ; misgivings **—하다** be (half) in doubt ; be dubious〔incredulous〕

반신반인 半神半人 a demigod

반실 半失 **—하다** lose〔waste〕 half ¶ 반실되다 be half-wasted ; be half-lost

반심 叛心 a rebellious〔treacherous〕 intent〔heart〕; the intention to revolt ¶ 반심을 품다 harbor rebellious intention ; be treacherous〔perfidious〕《to, against》

반암 斑岩 〖광물〗 porphyry

*__반액 半額__ half the sum〔amount, price〕; a half-price ¶ 반액으로 at half the price ; at half-price // 반액으로 하다 reduce the price by half // 반액을 물리다 repay half the sum // 12세 미만은 반액임 Children under twelve are allowed half rates.

반야 半夜 ① [한밤중] midnight ; the middle of the night ② half a night ¶ 반야에 at midnight // 반야까지 until midnight ; far into the night

반야심경 般若心經 〖불교〗 Prajna-paramitasutra《범》

반양자 反陽子 〖물리〗 an antiproton

*__반어 反語__ irony ¶ 반어적 ironical ; sarcastic // 반어를 쓰다 speak ironically

‡__반역 叛逆__ treason ; high treason ; rebellion ; insurrection ; revolt ; insurgency ; mutiny **—하다** rise in revolt ; rebel《against》; turn traitor ; revolt ¶ 반역적 treasonous ; rebellious ; treacherous // 정부에 대해서 반역을 꾸미다 plot against the government
—심 a rebellious spirit ; a treasonous intention **—아(兒)** a revolting son ; an apostate **—자** a traitor ; a plotter ; a mutineer ; a conspirator ; an insurgent ; a rebel **—죄** (high) treason **대—** heinous treason

‡__반영 反映__ reflection ; [영향] influence **—하다** reflect ; be reflected《in》 ¶ 국민의 여론은 국회에 반영된다 Public opinion is reflected in the National Assembly. // 신문은 시국을 반영한다 Newspapers are a mirror of the time.

반영 半影 penumbra ; partial〔imperfect〕 shadow ¶ 반영의 penumbral
—식(蝕) 〖천문〗 penumbral eclipse of the sun〔moon〕

반영 反影 a reflection ; a reflected shadow

‡__반영구적 半永久的__ (being) semi-permanent

반올림 半- rounding off to the nearest integer
—하다 round (off) ; count amounts of 5 and over as the next unit and disregard the rest ¶ 소수 둘째 자리에서 반올림하다 round off the numbers to two decimal places

*__반원 半圓__ a half circle ; a semicircle ¶ 반원의 semicircular // 반원을 그리다 make a half circle
—규(規)〔자〕 a semicircle **—기(器)** a semicircumferentor **— 아치** a semicircular〔round〕 arch **—의(儀)** a graphometer **—주(周)** a semicircumference **—형** a semicircle ; a hemicycle

반월 半月 [반달] a half-moon ; a crescent
—기(旗) the crescent **—형** a semilunar shape ; a semicircle ; a half-moon ; a crescent ¶ 반월형의 semilunar ; crescent(ic) ; crescent-shaped ; semicircular

반유동체 半流動體 semiliquid ; semifluid

반유대 反猶太 ¶ 반유대의 anti-Semitic
—주의 anti-Semitism **—주의자** an anti-Semite ; Jew baiter

반음 半音 〖음악〗 (chromatic) semitone
—계 a chromatic scale **— 변화 기호** a

ㅂ

chromatic sign —부〔표〕 a half note《미》; a minim《영》
*반응 反應 ① reaction; response; [효과] effect ② [배반] betrayal; defecting; turning coat; becoming a turncoat —하다 react; act《upon》; respond《to》; affect; [배반] betray; defect; turn coat ¶ 반응이 없다 have no effect《on》// 알칼리의 반응을 보이다 show an alkaline reaction
—기〔로(爐)〕 a reactor —성 reactivity —속도 reaction velocity —시간 reaction time; a latent period —시험 a reaction experiment —체질 reactor 양성〔음성〕— a positive〔negative〕 reaction 투베르쿨린— a tuberculine reaction
반의반 半—半 one fourth; a quarter
반의식 半意識 『심리』 semiconsciousness; subconsciousness (잠재 의식) ¶ 반의식적 half-conscious
‡반의어 反意語 an antonym
반이 搬移 moving; removal —하다 move (house); remove; carry
반일 半— half the work; a half-day's work; a halftime job
반일 半日 half a day; a half day
반일 反日 ¶ 반일의 anti-Japanese
—감정 anti-Japanese sentiments〔feelings〕
반입 搬入 —하다 carry in; take〔bring〕 in
반자 a ceiling ¶ 반자를 도리다 ceil; board a ceiling
—지 the ceiling paper —틀 a crossboard frame for putting up a ceiling
반자 半字 a simplified〔contracted〕 (Chinese) character; a simpler〔an abbreviated〕 form《of》
반자성 反磁性 『물리』 diamagnetism ¶ 반자성의 diamagnetic
반작, 빤짝 glittering; sparkling; in flashes; twinkling —하다 glitter; sparkle; twinkle; glisten; flash; glimmer; gleam ¶ 하늘에 반작거리는 별 twinkling stars in the sky // 반작반작 sparklingly; glitteringly; brilliantly // 반작이다〔거리다〕 glitter; glimmer; gleam; flash; twinkle // 햇빛에 반작거리다 glitter in the sun // 별이 반작인다 Stars twinkle. // 보석이 반작인다 Gems glitter. // 불빛이 물위에 반작거린다 The light glimmers on the water. // 식기가 반작반작한다 The dishes are sparklingly clean.
반작 半作 『농업』 sharecropping; tenancy —하다 sharecrop; tenant《a farm》
*반작용 反作用 reaction ¶ …의 반작용 reaction《to》// 작용과 반작용 action and reaction // 반작용하다 react《upon》// 작용이 있으면 반드시 반작용이 있다 Action is inevitably followed by reaction.
반장 叛將 a rebel leader〔chief〕
‡반장 班長 a squad〔section, group〕 leader; [학급의] a class monitor; [인부·직공의] a foreman; [동네의] the head of a neighborhood association
반장화 半長靴 half boots
반적 叛賊 a traitor; a rebel
반전 反戰 ¶ 반전의 antiwar // 반전을 외치다 cry against war; advocate peace
—론 pacifism; opposition to war —론자 a pacifist; a pacificist《영》; a dove —사상 an antiwar idea〔sentiment〕 —운동 an antiwar movement〔campaign〕 —파 an antiwar faction〔party〕; the dove
반전 反轉 reverse turn —하다 roll〔turn〕 over; make a reverse turn
—기(器) 『전기』 a reverser —성 『물리』 parity —필름 a reversal film —현상 『사진』 solarization 급— 『항공』 a split turn 급상승— 『항공』 a wing over
반전 返電 a reply telegram〔message, dispatch〕; a reply by wire〔cable〕 —하다 answer a telegram; wire back; cable in return; send a telegram in reply
반절 半— a half bow
반절 反切 [한글의] a paradigm of the Korean alphabet arranged as a syllabary
반절 半折 folding in half —하다 fold in half〔two〕; double
—지 a piece of paper folded in half
반절 半切 cutting in half〔into two〕; [종이의] a half sheet of paper; half size —하다 cut in half〔into two〕; halve; divide into halves
—족자 a half-size hanging scroll〔picture〕
†반점 半點 a half point; half a point; [시간] a half hour; half an hour
반점 斑點 a spot; a speck ¶ 반점이 있는 spotted; speckled
반정 反正 [바로잡음] restoration; renovation; [새 임금이 섬] enthronement of a new king subsequent to dethronement of a wicked king —하다 restore; reform; depose〔dethrone〕 a king
반정립 反定立 『철학』 antithesis
반정부 反政府 (being) antigovernment
—당 an opposition party —신문 an antigovernment〔antiministerial〕 newspaper
반정신 半艇身 a half-length (of a boat) ¶ 반정신의 차로 이기다 win a race by a half-length〔by half a length〕
반제 返濟 payment; repayment; refundment; redemption —하다 pay back; redeem; repay; refund; return ¶ 빚을 반제하다 pay back what one owes〔one's debt〕// 반제 기한이 되다 It〔The debt〕 falls due. // 반제 기한이 지났다 It is overdue.
—금 repayment; money repaid —기간 the term of repayment〔redemption〕
반제국주의 反帝國主義 anti-imperialism ¶ 반제국주의의 anti-imperialistic
—사상 anti-imperialist ideas〔thinking〕 —운동 the anti-imperialist movement —

ㅂ

투쟁 the struggle against imperialism
반제품 半製品 half-finished goods〔products〕; partly manufactured articles
반조 返照 reflection
—기(器) a reflector — 램프 a reflecting lamp
반족 班族 a noble family
반주 伴奏 〖음악〗 accompaniment —하다 play 《a person's》 accompaniment ; accompany 《a person on the piano》 ¶ 오케스트라의 반주 an orchestral accompaniment // B의 반주로 노래하다 sing to B's accompaniment // 아코디언의 반주로 노래부르다 sing to the accordion accompaniment 《by Mr. *Kim*》
—부 the accompaniment —자 an accompanist
반주 飯酒 liquor taken at meal time
반주 半周 a semicircle —하다 go half round 《a place》
반주권국 半主權國 a semi-dependent country
반주그레하다 (be) rather nice-looking ; attractive
*반죽 kneading ; dough (덩이) —하다 knead 《flour》; work ; mortar ¶ 반죽 그릇 a large wooden kneading bowl // 밀가루를 반죽하다 knead flour
반죽음 半— half death
반죽좋다 (be) imperturbable ; good-natured
반중간 半中間 half-way ; the middle
*반증 反證 evidence to the contrary ; contrary evidence ; counterevidence ; disproof ¶ 반증을 내걸다 produce contrary evidence ; prove the contrary
†반지 班指, 半指 a ring ¶ 반지를 낀 손가락 a ringed finger // 반지를 끼다 put a ring on one's finger
결혼〔약혼〕— a wedding〔an engagement〕 ring 금— a gold ring 보석 — a ring set with a stone〔jewel〕
반지 半紙 common Japanese writing paper ; rice paper
반지기 adulterated with ¶ 모래〔돌, 겨, 뉘〕 반지기 쌀 hulled rice with sand〔stones, husks, bran〕 in it
반지랍다 (be) smooth and glossy〔lustrous〕; sleek ¶ 반지랍게 하다 smooth ; lubricate (기름 따위로) ¶ 마루가 반지랍다 The floor is well-polished.
반지르르 smoothly ; glossily ; sleekly ⇨ 번지르르
*반지름 半— a radius
반지반 半之半 a quarter ; one fourth
반지빠르다 ① [얄밉도록] (be) affected ; snobbish ; saucy ; stuck-up ; impudent ; cheeky ; pert ¶ 반지빠른 말 a saucy remark
② [어중되다] (be) awkward ; inadequate ; inconvenient
반지화 班枝花 〖식물〗 a kapok tree ¶ 반지화 솜 kapok

반직업적 半職業的 semiprofessional
반짇고리 a workbox〔-basket〕; a housewife
반질거리다, 빤질거리다 ① [매끄럽다] be glossy〔lustrous, smooth, slippery, sleek〕; take on a gloss ; shine with luster ¶ 반질거리는 머리 lustrous〔glossy〕 hair
② [교활하다] be sly〔cunning, crafty, foxy, tricky, wily〕 ¶ 여우처럼 빤질거리다 be as sly as a fox
반질반질, 빤질빤질 sleekly ; smoothly ; lustrously ; glossily —하다 (be) slippery ; smooth ; sleek ¶ 반질반질한 안색 a blooming complexion // 빤질빤질한 녀석 a crafty person ; a sly boots // 빤질빤질하게 굴다 act craftily // 반질반질하게 머리 기름을 잔뜩 칠하다 plaster one's hair with pomade
반짝 ① [쉽게] lightly ; easily ; without effort ¶ 돌을 반짝 쳐들다 lift up a stone easily ② [높이] high ¶ 반짝 들리다 be raised〔lifted〕 high
반짝거리다 ⇨ 반짝이다, 반짝반짝(하다)
*반짝반짝 brilliantly ; glitteringly ; dazzlingly —하다 glitter ; gleam ; twinkle ; flash ; glisten ; sparkle ; shine ¶ 반짝반짝하는 별 twinkling stars // 반짝반짝 빛나는 보석 glittering jewels
*반짝이다 shine ; glitter ; be bright〔brilliant〕; twinkle (별 따위가) ; glimmer (멀리) ¶ 반짝이는 보석 sparkling gems // 반짝이는 눈 twinkling eyes // 금처럼 반짝이다 glitter like gold // 햇빛에 거울을 반짝이다 flash a mirror in the sun(light)
반쪽 半— (a) half
반쯤 半— (about) half ; halfway
반찬 飯饌 a (side) dish ; dishes served to go with rice ¶ 오늘 저녁 반찬은 뭐냐 What are we having for side dishes tonight?
— 가게 a grocery (store) ; a grocer's (shop) —거리 groceries ; materials for making side dishes 고기 — a meat dish
반창고 絆瘡膏 a plaster ; an adhesive plaster〔tape〕 ¶ 반창고를 붙이다 apply a plaster
고무〔아연화〕 — a rubber〔zinc oxide〕 adhesive plaster 테이프 — adhesive tape
반청 半晴 (being) partly clear ¶ 반청반담 partly clear and partly cloudy
반체제 운동 antiestablishment movement
반추 反芻 rumination —하다 ruminate ; chew the cud
— 동물 a ruminant
반출 搬出 —하다 take out ; carry out ; [화재 때] save
반춤 gentle swaying of the body
반취 半醉 slight intoxication —하다 be half drunk ; be half-tipsy ; be slightly intoxicated
반측 反側 —하다 [뒤척거리다] turn over ; toss about ; roll over on one's side
*반칙 反則 a foul ; an irregularity ; foul

play ; violation ; infringement —하다 violate〔break, infringe〕 the rules ; act against the rules ; play foul ¶ 반칙 우편물 banned mail // 축구의 반칙권 penalty area // 반칙의 foul ; against the rules ; contrary to the regulations // 그것은 반칙이다 It is against the rules. /It is a violation of the rules.
—자 an offender ; a transgressor

반침 伴寢 staying at the same hotel ⇨ 동숙

반침 半寢 a closet ; a small room attached to a large room

반코트 半— a half-coat

반타작 半打作 sharing a tenant crop fifty-fifty with the landowner —하다 share the crop equally ; share equally 〔half-and-half〕 with the landowner

반토 礬土 〖화학〗 alumina

반투명 半透明 translucency ¶ 반투명의 translucent ; semitransparent
—체 a translucent ; semitransparent body

반파 半破 partial destruction ¶ 반파되다 be partially〔partly〕 destroyed〔wrecked, demolished〕
— 가옥 a house partially destroyed

반편 半偏 a fool ; a half-wit ; a blockhead ; a simpleton ; a ninny ¶ 반편같은 수작 foolish talk ; an absurd story // 반편스럽다 be slow-witted ; be foolish〔stupid, silly〕 // 반편짓하다 play the fool ; make a fool of oneself // 반편스럽게 굴다 act like a fool ; play the fool ; behave like an idiot 〔a moron〕

반포 頒布 distribution ; promulgation ; circulation —하다 promulgate ; circulate ¶ 널리 반포하다 distribute 《things》 ; broadcast (far and wide)
무료〔유료〕 — free〔charged〕 distribution

반포 反哺 repaying one's indebtedness to parents —하다 feed one's parents in return

반푼 [엽전] ① a half *p'un* ; half a *p'un* ② a Korean half-cent ; half a farthing ¶ 반푼쭝 a half-*p'un* weight

반품 返品 returning〔sending back〕 goods ; [물건] returned goods — 하다 return goods ¶ 반품 사절 All Sales Final. (게시)

반품 半— half a day's work

*__반하다__[1] fall in love with 《a person》 ; become〔be〕 enamored of ; be charmed with ; be fascinated by ; fall for 《미》 ; be stuck on 《속》 ¶ 홀딱 반한 여자 a woman of one's heart // 미모에 반하다 be charmed〔bewitched〕 by 《a person's》 beauty // 한눈에 반했다 He fell in love with her at first sight. // 나는 그 여자에게 반했다 I have a crush on her. /I'm crazy about her. /I'm nuts about her.

반하다[2], **빤하다** ① [환하다] (be) light ; bright ¶ 동쪽이 빤하게 트였다 The east grows faintly luminous. /The first faint streaks of dawn show in the east.
② [틈나다] be at leisure ; be free〔not engaged〕 ¶ 반한 틈 spare moments
③ [병세가] be in a state of lull〔slight improvement〕
④ [분명하다] (be) obvious ; self-evident ; plain ; clear ¶ 빤한 사실 a plain fact // 빤한 이치 a self-evident truth // 빤한 일이다 It is clear〔plain〕 《that》 // 그것은 빤한 사실이다 The fact speaks for itself.

⁑**반하다 反—** be contrary to ; be against ; be opposed to ; run counter to ¶ …에 반하여 against ; contrary to ; in opposition to // 나의 의사에 반하여 against my will // 이에 반하여 on the contrary ; on the other hand

반할인 半割引 a 50% reduction〔discount〕 ; half rate —하다 make a 50% reduction ; discount half of the price

반합 飯盒 a canteen ; a messtin ; a mess kit

⁑**반항 反抗** [저항] resistance ; [반대] opposition ; [불응] disobedience ; insubordination ; [도전] defiance ; [반역] revolt ; [혐오] hostility ; recalcitration —하다 resist ; oppose ; disobey ; defy ; rebel 《against》 ; offer resistance 《to》 ; antagonize ; turn upon 《a person》 ; lift one's hand against ¶ 반항적 defiant ; rebellious // …에 반항하여 in opposition to ; in defiance of ; in the teeth of // 완강히 반항하다 put up a stiff resistance // 여론에 반항하다 fly in the face〔teeth〕 of public opinion // 부모에게 반항하다 defy one's parents // 법률에 반항하다 resist〔defy〕 the law // 반항적 태도를 취하다 assume a defiant attitude 《toward a person》
—기 (期) the period of contrariness ; the negative phase —심 the spirit of insubordination ; a rebellious spirit ; hostility

⁑**반향 反響** an echo ; a reverberation ; [반응] a reflection ; a response ; a repercussion —하다 echo ; reecho ; resound ; reverberate ; be reflected ¶ 대단한 반향을 일으키다 create a sensation // 광고에 대해 아무런 반향이 없었다 The advertisement was not at all responded to by the public. // 논문에 대해 어떤 반향이 있었느냐 Did your article elicit any public comment? // 정부의 이번 조치는 전세계의 반향을 일으킬지도 모른다 The action of the government may have repercussions all over the world.

반혁명 反革命 a counterrevolution ; an antirevolution ¶ 반혁명주의의 counterrevolutionary
— 운동 an anti-revolutionary agitation 〔movement〕 —파 (波) the counterrevolutionaries

반현 半舷 the broadside

반혓소리 半— 〖언어〗 a "semi-lingual"

ㅂ

〔lateral〕 sound ; the Korean "L"
†**반환 返還** return ; restoration **―하다** return ; give back ; restore ¶ 수표의 반환 surrender of a bill // 영토의 반환 the retrocession〔restitution〕 of a territory // 점령지를 반환하다 recede conquered territory
―자 a restitutor **―점** [마라톤의] ⟪at⟫ the turn ; the turning point
반회전 半回轉 a half turn ; [승마의] a caracole
반휴일 半休日 a half holiday
반흘림 半― semi-cursive writing
받걷이 ① [거둬들임] collecting money (or the like) here and there **―하다** collect money here and there ② ⇨ 받자
받고차기 ① [받고참] butting and kicking **―하다** butt and kick ② [다툼] wrangle ; argument ; altercation ; mudslinging **―하다** wrangle ; brawl ; argue
받낳이 buying thread and weaving it **―하다** get thread and weave it
받내다 take care of the urination〔bowel movement〕 of ⟪an invalid⟫
†**받다** ① [수령·수납] receive ; accept ; take

> **참고** **accept**는 제공된 것을 기꺼이 「받아들이다」의 뜻 **receive**는 그저 「받다」의 뜻이며 반드시 만족·승인하지 않는다 따라서 물건을 타인에게 주는 경우에는 Would you please accept this ? 라고 하는 것이 보통이고 receive는 사용하지 않는다 **take**는 자기의 의지·노력·힘을 다하여 「얻다」의 뜻

¶ 교육을 받다 receive an education // 꾸어준 돈을 받다 collect〔call in〕 loans // 상을 받다 take〔win〕 a prize // 신뢰를 받다 enjoy the confidence of ⟪a person⟫ // 존경을 받다 win respect ; command esteem // 주문을 받다 receive〔get〕 an order
② [입다] suffer ; sustain ; receive ¶ 모욕을 받다 be subjected to an insult // 타격을 받다 suffer a blow // 혐의를 받다 be suspected ⟪of⟫ ; incur suspicion
③ [겪다] undergo ; go through ¶ 수술〔건강 진단〕을 받다 undergo a surgical operation〔medical examination〕 // 취조를 받다 be subjected to an examination ; be examined
④ [공·물 따위를] catch ; receive ¶ 공을 받다 catch a ball // 빗물을 받다 catch the rainwater ⟪in the bucket⟫
⑤ [우산을] put up ; hold ¶ 우산을 받다 put up an umbrella
⑥ [뿔 따위로] butt ; gore ; horn ; hit head against ¶ 머리로 문을 받다 knock〔bump〕 one's head against the door // 뿔로 받다 butt〔gore〕 with horns
⑦ [면하다] face ¶ 달빛을 몸에 받다 be bathed in the moonlight
⑧ [아이를] deliver ¶ 아이를 받다 deliver a child
⑨ [음식이] suit ⟪one's taste, palate⟫ ; agree ⟪with⟫ ¶ 음식이 받다 The food agrees with me. /I have a good appetite. // 음식이 속에서 받지 않는다 My stomach revolts at the food.
⑩ [사다] buy ¶ 도매로 받아 소매로 팔다 buy wholesale and sell at retail
-받다 [입다·당하다] receive ⟪an action⟫ ; suffer ¶ 주목받다 receive attention // 협박받다 be threatened
받들다 ① [공경하다] honor ; respect ; hold ⟪a person⟫ in esteem ; pay respect〔deference〕 to ¶ 스승을 받들다 honor one's master ; show respect to one's teacher // 윗사람을 받들다 be respectful to one's elders
② [받쳐들다] hold〔lift〕 up ; uphold ; aid〔assist〕 (보좌) ; support (지지) ¶ 정부를 받들다 support the government // 회장을 받들다 assist〔give counsel to〕 the president〔chairman〕
받들어총 ―銃 [호령] Present arms ! **―하다** present arms
받아넘기다 parry ⟪a blow, a question⟫ ; dodge ; make a ready reply ; sing ⟪after another⟫ readily ¶ 남의 말을 멋지게 받아넘기다 give a repartee ; make a ready〔smart〕 retort
†**받아들이다** accept ; take in ; adopt ¶ 서양 문화를 받아들이다 introduce Western culture into this country // 요구를 받아들이다 accede to ⟪a person's⟫ demand ; comply with ⟪a person's⟫ request // 제안을 받아들이다 approve〔adopt〕 ⟪a person's⟫ proposal // 그는 남의 의견을 받아들이지 않는다 He won't〔refuses to〕 listen to others. /He turns a deaf ear to other's advice. // 아무리 여러 번 경고해도 그는 내 말을 진지하게 받아들일 기미를 보이지 않는다 No matter how often I warn that guy, he shows no sign of having taken it to heart.
*__받아쓰기 ―하다__ have dictation
받아쓰다 write〔take〕 down ¶ 받아쓰게 하다 dictate ⟪a note⟫ to ⟪a person⟫ // 연설을 속기로 받아쓰다 take down a speech in shorthand // 편지 한 장 빨리 받아써요 Take a letter quickly.
받아치다 receive and give back ; [권투에서] counter
받을어음 bills receivable ⟪B/R, b. r.⟫
받자 ① [징세] collecting taxes〔levies〕 ② [관용] being generous〔good-humored〕 in the face of unreasonableness〔vexation, insult〕 ; being "big" 〔big-minded〕 about it **―하다** face unreasonableness〔vexation, insult〕 with good humor〔generosity〕 ; be "big"〔big-minded〕 about it
†**받치다** ① [괴다] support ; prop〔bolster〕 up ; hold up ¶ 기둥을 받치다 support ⟪a wall⟫ with a post // 우산을 받치다 put up an umbrella
② [치밀다] surge up ; have a fit of ; be

filled〔seized〕 with 《emotion》 ¶ 먹은 것이 받치다 feel heavy in the stomach // 분이 받치다 have a fit of anger ; get into rage

③ [닿소리를] put a consonant under 〔after〕 a vowel

†**받침** [괴는] a support ; a prop ; a fulcrum ; a (hot) pad ; a mat ; underpinning ; 〖언어〗 a final consonant (or consonant cluster) on the end of a Korean orthographic syllable ¶ 받침을 괴다〔받치다〕 put a support 《under》 ; underpin // 책상 다리 밑에 받침을 괴다 put a support under a table leg // 지렛대 밑에 받침을 괴다 put a fulcrum under the lever

—대 a prop ; a support ; a strut ; a crosspiece

받히다[1] sell wholesale ; supply ¶ 제품을 소매상에게 받히다 supply a retailer with products // 우리는 쌀을 군대에 받힌다 We handle rice for the army.

받히다[2] be butted ; be gored ¶ 소에게 받히다 be gored by a bull // 내 차가 뒤에서 받혔습니다 I was rear-ended.

†**발**[1] a foot ; a paw (발톱 있는 동물의) ; suckers (문어의) ; a leg (다리) ¶ 네발 달린 책상 a four-legged table // 발로 박자를 맞추다 keep〔beat〕 time with the feet // 발로 짓밟다 trample underfoot ; crush with one's feet // 발을 맞추다 keep〔fall into〕 pace〔step〕 with 《a person》 // 발을 밟다 step〔tread〕 on 《a person's》 foot // 발을 뻗다 stretch out one's legs ; be relaxed (비유적) // 발을 헛디디다 lose 〔miss〕 one's footing // 발 가는 대로 가다 walk on as fancy leads one // 발이 길다 have a long leg ; be in time for a treat (비유적) // 제 발로 서다 stand on one's own feet ; be independent (비유적) // 한 발 늦다 fall a step behind 《a person》

—등 the instep **—바닥** the sole (of a foot)

발 없는 말이 천리 간다 속담 Give a lie twenty-four hours' start, and you can never overtake it.

발[2] [가리는] a bamboo blind〔curtain〕 ; a reed screen ; shade ¶ 발을 치다 hang 〔let down〕 a bamboo blind // 발을 걷다 draw up〔raise, roll up〕 the blinds

발[3] ⇨ 발쇠

발[4] [버릇] a bad habit

발[5] [천의] the texture〔weave〕 of cloth ¶ 발이 굵다〔가늘다〕 be loose-woven 〔close-woven〕

발[6] the span of both arms ; [길이·깊이의 단위] a fathom ¶ 발로 뼘다 span it off // 발이 크다 have a large arm span

발 發 ① [출발] departure ; leaving ; [발송] dispatch ¶ AP 통신발 an AP dispatch // 서울역 6시 20분발 기차 the train leaving *Seoul* at 6 : 20 ; the 6 : 20 train from *Seoul* // 2월 10일 뉴욕발 전신 a New York dispatch dated Feb. 10th.

② [탄수] a volley ; a round ; a shot (소총의) ; a shell (대포의) ¶ 백발백중 a hundred shots and a hundred hits ; perfect marksmanship // 탄약 5천발 5,000 rounds of ammunition // 다섯 발을 쏘다 fire five shots

③ [발동기] ¶ 쌍발 전투기 a twin-engine fighter // 6발 폭격기 a six engined 〔engine〕 bomber

발 跋 an epilogue ; a postscript

-발 [줄·기세] lines ; streaks ; rays ; impression ¶ 빗발 streaks of rain

⁑**발가락** a toe

†**발가벗다** strip〔divert〕 oneself of one's clothes ; strip oneself bare〔stark-naked〕 ¶ 발가벗기다 strip 《a person》 stark-naked // 발가벗고 돌아다니다 go about naked〔without any clothes on, in one's birthday suit〕

발가숭이 a nude ; a naked body

발각 發覺 detection ; disclosure ; discovery ; revelation **—하다** find out ; discoverdetect ¶ 발각될까봐 lest it should be found out ; for fear of detection // 발각되다 come out ; be detected ; come to light ; be brought to light ; be exposed

발간 發刊 publication ; issue **—하다** publish ; issue ; start 《a magazine》

발감개 footcloth ; foot-wrappings ; leggings

발강이 〖물고기〗 a young carp

발강이, 빨강이 [물건] a red-colored article〔stuff〕

발갛다 (be) bright-red ; scarlet ¶ 뺨이 발갛다 have red cheeks // 네온 빛으로 하늘이 발갛다 The sky is tinged with red from the neon lights.

발개지다, 빨개지다 turn red ; redden ¶ 얼굴이 발개지다 blush ; flush // 부끄러워서 귀밑까지 발개지다 blush from one ear to the other with shame // 술을 마셔서 얼굴이 빨개지다 be flushed with wine

발갯깃 a pheasant's plume

발거리 [남을 속임] artifice ; trickery ; cunning ; scheming ; [알려 줌] forewarning ; informing on someone ¶ 발거리 놓다 [남을 속임] trick〔deceive〕 《a person》 ; [알려줌] inform on someone ; forewarn

발걸음 gait ; step ; pace ¶ 가벼운 발걸음으로 with light steps // 그녀는 발걸음이 느리다 She is a slow walker. /She is slow of foot.

발걸이 [의자 따위의] a rung ; [자전거의] a pedal ; [발 놓는 데] a footrest ; a foot rail (바 같은 데서)

발검 拔劍 **—하다** draw〔unsheathe〕 a sword

†**발견 發見** discovery ; [발각] detection ; revelation **—하다** discover ; find (out) ; detect ; recover 《a body》 ; unearth ; [우연히] chance upon ; light upon 《a fact》 ; strike upon 《a theory》 ¶ X광선을

ㅂ

발견하다 discover the X-rays // 과학상의 많은 발견을 하다 make many scientific discoveries // 셰익스피어의 생애에 관해서 새로운 사실을 발견하다 unearth new facts about the life of Shakespeare // 골동품상에서 이것을 발견하였다 I came across this in a curio shop. // 시체가 10구 발견되었다 Ten bodies were recovered. // 어제 어느 고서점에서 좋은 것을 발견하였다 I had a great find in an old bookshop yesterday.
—물 a discovery ; a find — 시대 The Age of Discovery —자 a discoverer ; a finder ; a detector

발고무래 〖농업〗 a kind of rake used to level earth ; a hand rake with four or six prongs

발광 發狂 insanity ; madness ; craziness **—하다** become insane ; go mad ; go out of one's mind

***발광 發光** radiation ; radiance ; emitting light **—하다** radiate ; emit light
—균 a luminous〔photogenic〕 bacteria —도료(塗料) luminous paint — 동물 a luminous animal — 식물 a photogen — 신호 a flash signal —지(紙) luminous paper —체 a luminous body ; a luminary —탄(彈) a luminous projectile ; a light ball

발구 [썰매] a sleigh ; a sledge ; [걸채] a saddle rack

발구르다 stamp one's feet noisily 《on the floor》

발군 拔群 ¶ 발군의 outstanding ; conspicuous ; preeminent ; distinguished ; unsurpassed // 발군의 성적으로 졸업하다 graduate with honors〔an exceptional record〕 // 전쟁에서 발군의 공을 세우다 distinguish oneself at a battle

발군 撥軍 an express messenger ; a fast courier ; a 《military》 dispatch rider ¶ 발군을 보내다 send an express messenger 《to》

***발굴 發掘** unearthing ; excavation ; exhumation (시체의) **—하다** unearth ; excavate ; exhume ¶ 시체를 발굴하다 dig up〔exhume〕 《a person's》 body
—자 an excavator —품 a find 석유 —권 (이 있는 지구) an oil concession

****발굽** a hoof

발권 發券 note issuing
—액 the amount of notes issued — 은행 an issuing bank

발그대대하다 (be) dull red

발그댕댕하다 ⇨ 발그대대하다

발그레하다 be tinged with red ; be flushed ; (be) ruddy ; be aglow ¶ 기뻐서 얼굴이 발그레하다 His face is flushed with joy.

발그림자 a footmark ; a trail ; a trace ; a shadow ¶ 그 후 그는 발그림자도 아니 했다 Since then, there has been no trace of him.
발그림자도 아니 하다 〔관용〕 never come ; do not appear

발그무레하다 (be) reddish

발그스름하다 be tinged with red ; (be) reddish

발그족족하다 (be) meanly〔unevenly〕 reddish ; ruddy

발근 拔根 uprooting ; eradicating ; extirpation **—하다** root up〔out, away〕 ; uproot ; stamp〔wipe〕 out ; eradicate ; extirpate

발금 發禁 sale prohibited

발급하다 發給— issue ¶ 여권을 발급하다 issue a passport

발긋발긋, 빨긋빨긋 —하다 be studded〔dotted〕 with red spots

발기 —記 a catalog(ue) ; a list of articles

발기 發起 [제안] proposal ; suggestion ; [솔선] initiation ; [사업의] promotion ; [주최] auspices **—하다** propose ; suggest ; promote ¶ …의 발기로 at the suggestion of ; under the auspices〔sponsorship〕 of (주최로) // 회사의 설립을 발기하다 promote a company〔an orgainzation〕
—인 [계획의] a projector ; a sponsor ; a promoter (회사 따위의) —인주(人株) a promoter's share, the management share —회 a meeting of promoters

발기 勃起 ① [성남] fury ; rage ; anger ; wrath **—하다** fly into a rage〔temper, passion〕 ; flare〔flame〕 up
② 〖생리〗 erection **—하다** become〔stand〕 erect ; rise up ; become stiff
—근(筋) an erector (muscle) —력 감퇴 impotency —성 erectility

발기계 —機械 a foot-operated machine ; a machine with a treadle

발기다 open up ; crack open ; shell ; split open ¶ 밤을 발기다 crack a chestnut

발기름 fat of the abdominal region

발기발기 to pieces ; to shreds ¶ 발기발기 찢다 tear to pieces

발길 [걷어차기] a kick ; [왕래] coming and going ; association (교제) ¶ 발길로 차다 give a kick 《at a person》 // 발길이 잦다 have frequent contacts with 《a person》 ; frequent
—질 kicking ; a kick 《at something》 ¶ 발길질하다 kick ; give 《a person》 a kick

발김쟁이 a roaming rowdy ; a rascal ; a scamp ; a rogue

발깍 in a sudden outburst (of violent passion) ; [뒤집히는 모양] topsy-turvy ; in aturmoil〔hubbub, mess〕 ¶ 발깍 성이나다 flare up in anger ; boil over ; turn purple 《with anger》 ; become livid 《with rage》 // 발깍 소리지르다 yell out in anger // 발깍 문을 열다 jerk a door open // 집안이 발깍 뒤집히다 a house is all topsy-turvy〔messed up, torn up〕 // 서울 장안이 발깍 뒤집혔다 All *Seoul* was in an uproar.

발깍거리다 [술·빨래 따위] bubble up ; [진흙 따위] make mud squash underfoot ¶ 술이 발깍거리다 the rice liquor is bubbling up (as it ferments) ; be bubbling a brew ; be brewing abubble // 진흙이 발깍거리다 squash mud under one's feet

발깍발깍 bubbling ; in bubbles ; with squashes〔squishes, squelches〕

발꿈치 a heel

발끈 in a fit of rage ; with a burst of anger ¶ 발끈 화를 내다 fly into a rage ; fly off the handle // 사소한 일에 발끈 성을 내다 fly into a rage on the slightest provocation

발끈거리다 be hot-tempered ; get mad easily ; be touchy ; be easily offended ; fly into rage〔passion, temper〕

발끈발끈 bursting into rages readily ; being quick to anger

발끝 the tip of the toes ; a tiptoe ¶ 머리끝에서 발끝까지 from top to toe ; from head to foot // 발끝으로 걷다 tiptoe ; walk on tiptoe // 발끝으로 서다 stand on tiptoe

발노구 a brass or copper kettle with legs

발놀림 footwork (테니스·권투·댄스에서)

*‡**발단 發端** [말의] opening one's mouth ; [일의] origin ; beginning ; opening —하다 open one's mouth ; begin ; commence ; be originated ¶ 사건의 발단부터 이야기하겠다 I shall tell it from the beginning.

†**발달 發達** development ; growth ; [진보] advance ; progress ; advancement —하다 develop ; make progress ; grow ; advance ¶ 공업의 발달 the development of industry // 심신의 발달 physical and mental development // 도시의 발달 the growth of cities // 인지의 발달 the advancement of human knowledge // 잘 발달된 well-developed 《body》 // 발달시키다 develop ; make 《a city》 grow ; advance // 급속히 발달하다 make rapid progress ; experience rapid growth // 발달을 돕다〔저해하다〕 promote〔retard, arrest〕 the development 《of》 // 그 공업이 크게 발달하였다 The industry has made great development〔strides〕. // 마을이 발달하여 도시가 되었다 A village has grown into a large town.

— 심리학 developmental〔genetic〕 psychology

발덧 sore feet from much walking ¶ 발덧이 나다 be footsore ; have a sore foot ; one's feet get sore

발돋움 standing on tiptoe ; [발판] something to stand on —하다 stand on tiptoe ; stretch oneself ¶ 발돋움을 가져오너라 Bring me something to stand on.

발동 發動 [일의] motion ; activity ; [소요] disturbance ; commotion ; [권력의] exercise —하다 move ; be active ; put in motion ; raise a disturbance ; kick up a row ; exercise ; invoke ¶ 연맹 규약 제15조를 발동하다 invoke Article 15 of the League Covenant

—력 motive power〔force〕

발동기 發動機 a motor ; an engine ¶ 100마력의 발동기 a 100-horsepower〔100 h. p.〕 motor

고정식〔공냉식, 내연식, 수냉식〕 — a fixed〔an air-cooled, an internal combustion, a water-cooled〕 engine 기름〔가솔린, 가스, 증기, 석유〕 — an oil〔a gasoline, a gas, a steam, a kerosene〕 engine

발동기선 發動機船 a motorboat ; an autoboat ; a motor ship (디젤 엔진에 의한)

****발뒤꿈치** the heel ; the upper rear portion of the heel ¶ 발뒤꿈치가 높은〔낮은〕 구두 high-〔low-〕heeled shoes // 제인은 메리의 발뒤꿈치에도 못 따라간다 Jane can't stand comparison with Mary. /Jane is not fit to hold a candle to Mary. // 제집 개에게 발뒤꿈치를 물리다 One has one's heel bitten by one's own dog. /It's a case of the dog biting the hand that feeds it.

발뒤축 a heel ¶ 발뒤축이 높은〔낮은〕 구두 high〔low〕-heeled shoes // 구두의 발뒤축이 닳다 one's shoes are worn down at the heel // 양말의 발뒤축이 닳다 one's socks are out at the heel

발등 the instep of a foot ; the top of the foot ¶ 사람의 발등을 디디다 step on 《a person's》 foot ; thwart ; forestall ; steal a march 《on》 ; block // 사람의 발등을 밟다 tread on another's foot

발등거리 a makeshift lantern (used at a house of mourning)

발등걸이 ① [씨름에서] stepping on an opponent's foot to throw him off balance ② [앞지름] forestalling ③ 〖체조〗 (the gymnastic feat of) hanging by the feet from the parallel bars —하다 hang (from parallel bars) by the feet

발딱 [갑자기] suddenly ; with a spring〔jerk〕 ; [반듯이] flat ¶ 발딱 일어서다 jump〔spring〕 to one's feet // 침대에서 발딱 일어나다 jump〔spring〕 out of bed // 발딱 자빠지다 fall flat on one's back

발딱거리다, 빨딱거리다 ① [맥·가슴이] beat ; throb ; go pit-a-pat ; pulsate ; palpitate ¶ 가슴을 발딱거리며 with a beating heart ; in a flutter // 가슴이 발딱거렸다 My heart went pit-a-pat〔throbbed〕. ② [들이마시다] gulp ; guzzle ; drink in large drafts ¶ 발딱거리면서 물을 마시다 gulp down a glass of water

발라내다 tear〔peel〕 off ; strip off ; pare ; hull 《peas》 ; crack 《a chestnut》 ; shell ; clean ¶ 생선을 발라내다 clean fish // 살구씨를 발라내다 remove the stone〔pit〕 from an apricot ; pit an apricot // 콩을 발라내다 shell peas

발라맞추다 cajole ; wheedle ; dupe ; coax ; flatter ¶ 발라맞춰서 만 원을 빼앗다 wheedle 《a person》 out of 10,000 *won*

발라먹다 wheedle ; (sweet-) talk 《a person》 out of 《a thing》 ; coax 《a thing》 out of 《a person》 ; get 《a thing》 by being

ㅂ

nice to 《a person》

발란 撥亂 ⇨ 평정(平正) ¶ 발란반정(反正)하다 put down a disturbance and establish〔restore〕 peace in the country

‡**발랄** 潑剌 ―하다 [약동] (be) lively ; sprightly ; fresh ; vivid ; be full of life ; (be) vigorous ; animated ¶ 생기가 발랄하다 be full of life〔vigor, go, vim, vitality, animation〕 ; be vivid with life ; brim with life ; be full of pep ; be peppy

발랑거리다 act nimbly〔smartly〕 ; move agilely

*****발레** a ballet ¶ 발레를 배우다 take ballet lessons

―광 a balletomane ―단 a corps de ballet (프) ― 댄서 a ballet dancer ; a ballerina 《*pl.* -nas, -ne》 ― 학교 a ballet school〔studio〕 수중 ― water ballet 창작 ― a balletic creation

발레리나 a ballerina 《*pl.* -nas, -ne》 《이》

발령 發令 giving an official order ; gazetting ; [법령을] proclamation 《of a law》 ―하다 give an official order ; announce officially ; gazette ; proclaim 《a decree》 ¶ 그의 임관 발령이 났다 His appointment was gazetted. // 너 해외로 발령났다며 You have been posted overseas ?

―장 a written appointment ; a warrant 〔writ, letter〕 of appointment

발로 發露 expression ; manifestation ―하다 become manifest ; speak for ; manifest ; express ; reveal ¶ 우정의 발로 a manifestation〔an expression〕 of friendship

발록거리다 inflate and deflate〔open and shu〕 alternately ; quiver ; wiggle ; palpitate (가슴이) ¶ 코를 발록거리다 quiver one's nostrils

발록구니 an idler ; a dawdler ; a loafer

발록하다 ⇨ 벌룩하다

발론 發論 a motion ; a proposal ; a suggestion ―하다 move ; make a motion ; propose ; suggest

―자 a proposer ; a mover ; an introducer ; a broacher

발름거리다 quiver

발름하다 (be) wide open ; agape ¶ 입이 발름하다 have one's mouth wide open

발리다¹ [사이를] widen ; broaden ; make wide ; [속을] open ; crack ; shell ; [펴다] unfold ; stretch ; unroll ; [늘어놓다] lay out ; spread out

발리다² be opened ; be cracked open ; be hulled

발리볼 volleyball

발맘발맘 slowly ; step by step ―하다 walk slowly ; be slow

발맞다 keep in step ; be in step ¶ 발맞지 않다 be out of step

발맞추다 keep〔fall into〕 pace〔step〕 with 《a person》 ¶ 발맞춰 가다 walk〔march〕 in step with 《a person》

발매 (timber-) felling ; lumbering ―하다 cut timber ; fell 《trees》

― 검사 a stamp inspection ―나무 felled trees for fuel ― 면적 a cutover area ― 시기 the felling season ; the cutting period ―치 boughs for firewood cut off from a large felled tree ― 허가 a lumber permit

발매넣다 [관용] start (timber-) felling 〔lumbering〕

발매놓다 [관용] lumber an area of a forest

발매 發賣 sale ; putting on sale ; issue ; making available (to purchasers) ―하다 sell ; put 《things》 on sale〔the market〕 ; make available ¶ (상품이) 발매 중이다 be on sale // 책의 발매를 금하다 suppress〔ban〕 a book // 그 책은 곧 발매된다 The book will be put on sale soon. // 현재 발매 중 Now on sale ! // 그 잡지는 발매 금지가 되었다 The sale of the magazine was prohibited.

― 금지 prohibition of sale〔circulation〕 ; suppression 《of a book》 ; [주의서] "Sale Prohibited" ― 부수 circulation ―일〔시기〕 the date of issue ― 처(處) a sales 〔selling〕 agent

†**발명** 發明 invention ; contrivance ―하다 invent ; devise ; originate ; contrive ¶ 발명의 천재 an inventive genius // 신발명의 newly-invented

―가 an inventor

발명품 發明品 an invention ; [신고안품] a contrivance ; a device

― 전람회 an exhibition of inventions

발모가지 ⇨ 발목

‡**발목** an ankle ¶ 발목을 삐다 sprain one's ankle

발목고리 [새의 생태 조사용] a leg band 〔ring〕

발목잡히다 be busy 《with work》 ; be pressed 《with work》

발묘 拔錨 weighing anchor ―하다 weigh〔pull up, raise〕 anchor ; sail 《from》

발문 跋文 an epilogue ; a postscript

발밑 ¶ 발밑에 at one's feet ; close to one's feet // 발밑을 조심하라 Watch your step ! / Look where you are going !

‡**발바닥** the sole of the foot ¶ 발바닥에 티눈이 생기다 get a corn on the sole of one's foot

발바리 a (toy) spaniel ; a Pekingese (dog)

발바심 ―하다 thresh by treading〔stepping〕 《on》

발바투 [잽싸게] 《catch, do something》 smartly ; quickly ; nimbly ; agilely ; alertly ; [바싹] right at one's feet ; right under one's nose

발발¹ shivering ; shaking ; trembling

발발² easily ; asunder ―하다 tear easily ¶ 상보가 낡아서 발발 나간다 The tablecloth is so old that it tears easily.

발발 勃發 outbreak ; outburst ; sudden occurrence —하다 break〔burst〕 out ; occur suddenly ¶ 전쟁의 발발 the outbreak of war

발밤발밤 —하다 walk on aimlessly ; walk on as fancy leads one

발밭다 be quick to take advantage of an opportunity ; "never miss a trick" ; be wide-awake to one's own interests

*발버둥이치다 (kick and) struggle ; wriggle ; stamp 《the ground》 ; be restless ¶ 분해 발버둥이치다 stamp the ground with vexation

†발버둥질 stamping ; (kicking and) struggling ; wriggling —하다 squirm ; struggle ; wriggle

발벗다 be barefoot(ed) ; have bare feet ¶ 발벗고 나서다 throw oneself into a matter with enthusiasm

†발병 發病 an attack (of a disease) —하다 be taken ill ; fall ill〔sick〕

발병 —病 foot troubles ; a foot disease ¶ 발병이 나다 have sore〔tender〕 feet ; be footsore

발보이다 ① [재주를] display one's ability〔skill〕 proudly〔ostentatiously〕 ; show off one's skill
② [일의 끝만을] give a hint ; reveal a part〔something〕 of 《a thing》

발복 發福 a favorable change in fortune —하다 《one's luck》 have turned ; 《fortune》 have begun to smile upon 《a person》

발본 拔本 ① [밑천을 뽑다] —하다 recover〔get back〕 one's capital 《from an investment》
② [뿌리뽑다] —하다 eradicate ; uproot ; root〔stamp〕 out
—적 개혁 a radical〔drastic〕 reform —적 대책 a drastic measure

발본색원 拔本塞源 —하다 eradicate sources of evil ; lay the ax to the root of evil

발부 髮膚 hair and skin
신체 — one's body

‡발부리 the tip of the toes ; tiptoe ; [신발·양말의] a toe

발분 發憤 —하다 be roused to action ; be stirred〔spurred〕 ; bestir oneself

발분망식 發憤忘食 —하다 devote oneself to ; give oneself up to ; be immersed〔absorbed, engrossed〕 in

발빠지다 break away 《from》 ; break off 《from, with》 ; sever one's connection 《with》 ¶ 장사에서 발빠지다 break away from the business

발빼다 quit ; wash one's hands ; break 《with》 ; be through 《with》 ¶ 나는 발뺐다 I washed my hands (of that matter).

*발뺌 an excuse ; a pretext ; an evasion —하다 make〔find, invent〕 an excuse ; dodge ; shirk ; draw back from 《a matter》 ¶ 발뺌을 잘하다 be good at subterfuges〔making excuses〕 // 그것은 발뺌에 불과하다 That is only a pretext.

†발사 發射 firing ; discharge ; shooting ; blast-off (로켓의) —하다 discharge ; fire ; blastoff (로켓을) ¶ 권총을 발사하다 discharge〔fire〕 one's revolver
—각 the angle of fire — 단계 the launch phase —력 projectile force —물〔체〕 projectile — 속도 rapidity of fire — 시험[포신의] proof firing —약 powder —장〔대〕 a launching site〔ramp, pad〕 《of a guided missile》 — 장치 a launcher

발사 跋辭 an epilogue

발사관 發射管 a torpedo〔launching〕 tube
현측(舷側)〔상갑판, 함수(艦首), 함미〕 — a side〔deck, bow, stern〕 tube

*발산 發散 diffusion ; emission ; emanation ; evaporation (증기의) ; radiation (빛, 열의) —하다 evaporate ; radiate ; diffuse ; emit ; exhale ; transpire ; give off〔out〕 ; send forth ¶ 빛〔냄새〕의 발산 diffusion of light〔odors〕 // 좋은 냄새를 발산하다 give off a fragrant odor ; send forth fragrance // 태양은 빛과 열을 발산한다 The sun radiates〔emits〕 light and heat. // 과장은 욕구 불만을 부하 직원들에게 발산함으로써 스트레스를 해소하고 있다 The boss relieves his stress by taking his frustrations out on his subordinates.
— 광속(光束) a divergent pencil of rays — 급수(級數) divergent series — 렌즈 a diverging〔divergent〕 lens

발상 發想 『음악』 expression ; [사상] conception

발상 發喪 announcement of 《a person's》 death —하다 announce a death

발상지 發祥地 [임금의] the birthplace of the founder of a dynasty ; [요람지] the cradle〔birthplace〕 ¶ 문명의 발상지 the cradle of civilization

발샅 the space between the toes

‡발생 發生 [생겨남] birth ; origination ; production ; generation (화학적) ; genesis ; [일어남] outbreak (돌발적으로) ; happening ; occurrence ; 『생물』 development ; growth —하다 originate ; come 《from》 ; be generated ; spring 《from》 ; come into existence〔being〕 ¶ 콜레라의 발생 an outbreak of cholera // 사고의 발생 the occurrence of an accident // 선원 중에 페스트가 발생했다 Plague has broken out among the crew.
—기(期) 『화학』 a nascent state ; a developmental stage —기(器) a generator —론 the evolution〔development〕 theory — 생리학〔심리학〕 genetic biology〔psychology〕 — 유전학 developmental genetics — 장치 [가스 따위의] a producer —지 the place of origin ; the birthplace ; the cradle 《of civilization》 동시 — synchronism ; simultaneity 신— 『생물』 caenogenesis 자연 — spontaneous generation

ㅂ

발생연 發生爐 a gas generator〔producer〕
— 가스 air gas ; producer gas
발생학 發生學 〚생물〛 embryology ¶ 발생학상 embryologically // 발생학적 embryological
발선 發船 ⇨ 출범(出帆)
발설 發說 divulging ; revealing ; disclosing — 하다 disclose ; divulge ; blab ; reveal ¶ 비밀을 발설하다 let out〔divulge, reveal〕 a secret
발섭 跋涉 traversing — 하다 traverse ; rove ; travel about ; hike 《미》 ¶ 산야를 발섭하다 rove〔range〕 over hill and dale // 전국을 발섭하다 travel all over the country ; traverse the length and breadth of the land
발성 發聲 utterance ; ejaculation ; speaking ; exclamation ; sound ; vocalization — 하다 speak ; utter ; shout ¶ 발성 순서로 in the order of speaking // A씨의 발성으로 국왕 만세를 부르다 Mr. A leads a cheer for the King.
—기(器) a vocal organ ; a talking apparatus ; a speaker —법 〚음악〛 vocalization — 연습 vocal exercises — 영사기 a sound projector — 영화 a talking picture〔film〕 ; a talkie ; a sound picture〔film〕 — 장치 a mechanism of voice production
‡**발소리** (the sound of) footsteps ; a footfall ¶ 발소리를 죽이고 with stealthy steps // 발소리가 들렸다 Steps〔Footfalls〕 sounded. /I heard steps. // 발소리가 사라졌다 The footsteps died away.
***발송 發送** dispatch ; delivery ; sending ; shipping ; forwarding — 하다 forward ; dispatch ; send out〔forth〕 ; ship ; [우편물을] post ; mail 《a letter》 ¶ 통지서를 발송하다 send out notices
—계〔원〕 a shipping clerk ; [우편물의] a mailing clerk — 문서 a dispatched document —소〔실〕 a forwarding〔shipping〕 station〔room〕 —역 a forwarding station —인 a sender ; [출하주(出荷主)] a consignor
발송전 發送電 generation and transmission of electricity
발솥 a three-legged〔tripod〕 pot
발쇠 informing on others ¶ 발쇠서다 inform on
발쇠꾼 a spy ; an informer
발수 發穗 — 하다 come into ears ; be in (the) ear
발신 發身 — 하다 rise from obscurity to fame ; rise in the world ; rise to distinction〔prominence〕
발신 發信 dispatch of a message ; an outgoing message ; sending a letter〔telegram〕 — 하다 dispatch ; post ; send ; wire ; telegraph
—국 the sending office ; the office of origin (of dispatch) —기 a transmitter —부(簿) an outgoing letter book —음 a dial tone (전화의) ; a signal (무선의) —인 an addresser ; a sender of message —지 the place of dispatch
발심 發心 ① [의향] a new intention — 하다 intend to do 《something》 ; be inclined to do ; set on a new plan
② [불교에서] spiritual〔religious〕 awakening ; conversion ; a change of heart — 하다 have a spiritual awakening ; turn over a new leaf
발씨 skill with one's feet ; familiarity to one's feet ¶ 발씨 익은 길 a familiar path // 그의 공 차는 발씨가 용하다 He has a splendid kick (in football). // 이 길이 내 발씨에 서투르다 This road is unfamiliar to me〔to my feet〕.
발씨름 ankle〔shin〕 wrestling
발아 發芽 germination ; sprouting — 하다 germinate ; sprout ; bud
—력 germinative power
발악 發惡 — 하다 revile ; abuse ; rave ; rail 《against》
발안 發案 a suggestion ; a proposal ; an initiation ; a motion (동의) ; an initiated idea ; a plan ; a proposition ; a move — 하다 suggest ; propose ; initiate ; originate ; move ; make a suggestion ¶ A씨의 발안 계획이다 The plan originated with Mr. A.
—자 a proposer ; an originator ; an initiator
발암 發癌 carcinogenesis ; the production of cancer ¶ 발암성의 carcinogenic 《chemicals》 ; cancerogenic ; cancer-causing〔-forming〕 《substance, agent》
— 물질(物質) a carcinogenic〔cancerogenic〕 substance ; a carcinogen
발양 發揚 exaltation ; elevation ; enhancement ; promotion — 하다 [높이다] exalt ; raise ; enhance ; [진척시키다] promote ⇨ 선양(宣揚)
†**발언 發言** speaking ; utterance ; proposal — 하다 utter ; open one's mouth ; speak ; take the floor (의원이) ¶ 발언을 얻다 get〔obtain〕 the floor ; catch the Speaker's eye // 발언을 금하다 prohibit 《a person》 from speaking // 발언의 기회를 잃다 lose the opportunity of speaking // 발언을 취소하다 retract one's words
—자 a speaker
†**발언권 發言權** the right to speak〔of speaking〕 ; (the right to) a voice ¶ 발언권이 있다〔없다〕 have a〔no〕 voice 《in a matter》 ; have a〔no〕 say 《in a matter》 《구》 // 발언권을 안 주다 be denied a voice // (의원이) 발언권을 얻다 get〔obtain〕 the floor ; catch the Speaker's eye
발연 發煙 emitting smoke ; fuming — 하다 smoke ; emit smoke
— 병기 smoke arms —제(劑) a fumigant ; a smoke generating agent —탄 a smoke shell —통 a smoke candle — 포탄 a smoke ball — 폭탄 a smoke bomb — 황산〔질산〕 fuming sulphuric〔nitric〕

acid
발연 勃然 ① [갑자기] suddenly ; all at once
② [분연] in a fit of passion ; in a flare ¶ 발연(히) 일어나다 rise suddenly ; break〔burst〕 out // 발연 대로 하다 fly into a passion ; get into a rage ; flame〔flare〕 up ; suddenly fly into a great rage ; burst into a passion // 발연 변색하다 suddenly change one's countenance // 발연 전쟁이 일어나다 A war suddenly breaks out 〔flares up〕.
발열 發熱 〖의학〗 having fever ; pyrexia ; 〖물리〗 generation of heat ; calorification **—하다** have fever ; be feverish ; emit heat ; generate heat
—기(器) a heater **—기(期)** a pyrogenetic〔hot〕 stage (말라리아의) **— 량〔력〕** caloric value〔power〕 **— 물질〔원(原)〕** a pyrogen **— 반응** exothermic reaction **— 신경** a calorific nerve **— 요법** fever treatment ; pyretotherapy **—체** a heating element〔unit〕 ; a pyrogen
발염 拔染 discharging ; discharge printing **—하다** discharge ¶ 발염성(性)의 dischargeable
발염제 拔染劑 a discharge printing agent
†**발원 發源** the origin ; the source ; [수원] the head〔source〕 of a river **—하다** originate 《in》 ; have its origin 《in》 ; take rise 《in》
발원 發願 a prayer **—하다** make a prayer
*__발육 發育__ growth ; development **—하다** grow ; develop ¶ 발육기의 아이 a growing child // 발육 불완전한 underdeveloped // 발육이 좋은 well-developed〔-grown〕 // 충분히 발육한 fully-developed ; full-grown〔-fledged〕 // 발육을 돕다〔방해하다〕 promote〔retard, arrest, stunt〕 the growth 《of》 // 아이들은 발육이 빠르다 Children grow rapidly.
—기(期) the period of development **— 기관** a developmental organ **—병(病)** a developmental disease **— 부전(不全)** underdevelopment ; undergrowth
⁑**발음 發音** pronunciation ; enunciation ; articulation (음절로 나누어서) **—하다** pronounce ; enunciate ; articulate ¶ 발음을 잘못하다 mispronounce 《a word》 // 발음이 나쁘다 His pronunciation is bad. // 이 말을 어떻게 발음합니까 How do you pronounce this word ?
— 기관(器官) the vocal organs **— 기호** a phonetic sign〔symbol〕 ; diacritical marks **— 사전** a pronouncing dictionary **— 연습** drill on pronounciation
발음학 發音學 [음성학] phonetics ; [음운학] phonology
발의 發意 an initiative ; a suggestion **—하다** suggest ; originate
⁑**발의 發議** an instance ; [제안] a proposal ; [동의] a motion **—하다** propose ; move ; make a proposal ; suggest ¶ 모씨의 발의로 at someone's suggestion〔instance〕 ; on someone's motion // 이 집회에 발의하고 싶은 것이 있다 I have a proposal to make to this meeting.
—권 〖정치〗 the initiative **—자** a proposer ; a sponsor ; an introducer ; a broacher
발인 發靷 carrying a coffin out of the house ; the starting of a funeral procession **—하다** carry a coffin out of the house ; carry out a bier for burial ¶ 오전 11시 발인이다 The funeral cortege leaves the residence at 11 a. m.
†**발자국** a footprint ; a footmark ; a track 《미》 ¶ 발자국을 남기다 leave one's footprints // 발자국을 좇다 follow the trail of footprints
발자귀 an animal's footmark〔footprint〕
발자취 [발자국] footprints ; footmarks ; [종적] a trace〔track〕 ; a wake ¶ 발자취를 남기다 leave one's mark 《in history》 // 10년간 걸어온 발자취를 회고하다 think of〔recollect〕 the course one has followed for ten years
⁑**발작 發作** a paroxysm ; a fit ; an access ; a seizure ; a stroke ; 〖의학〗 a spasm **—하다** have a fit〔spasm〕 ¶ 발작적 정신 이상 a temporary derangement of the mind // 발작적으로 spasmodically ; fitfully ; by fits and starts // 발작을 일으키다 have a fit〔paroxysm〕 // 발작적으로 공부하다 study by fits and starts // 발작적으로 울다 cry hysterically
발장구치다 [헤엄] kick ; do one's kick ; [태평하게] pass one's days in indolence ; eat the bread of idleness
발장단 —長短 beating time with the foot ¶ 음악에 맞추어 발장단을 치다 beat time to the music with one's foot
발재봉틀 —裁縫— a sewing machine with a treadle
†**발전 發展** [발달] development ; growth ; [확대] enlargement ; expansion ; [융성] prosperity **—하다** develop ; grow ; advance ; prosper ; flourish ¶ 발전적인 expansive ; developmental ; growing // 도시의 급격한 발전 the rapid growth of cities // 사건의 발전을 주시하다 watch the development of the event // 사태는 우리들에게 유리하게 발전했다 The situation developed favorably for us. // 이 사업은 크게 발전성이 있다 This enterprise has great possibilities.
발전 發電 [전기의] generation of electric power **—하다** [전기를] generate electricity ¶ 10만 킬로와트의 발전력을 가진 발전소 a power house which generates 100,000 kilowatts of power
— 기관(器官) [생물의] an electric organ **—체** 〖물리〗 a charged body **직접 —로** a direct conversion reactor
*__발전기 發電機__ a〔an electric〕 dynamo 《*pl.*

~s》; a (power) generator ; an electric generator
교류〔직류〕 — an alternating〔a direct〕 current dynamo ; an A. C.〔a D. C.〕 generator 수력〔화력〕 — a hydro〔thermal〕 generator 원자력 — an atomic power generator 2극〔다극〕 — bipolar 〔multipolar〕 generator
발전동기 發電動機 a motor dynamo ; a dynamotor (발전기와 전동기의 두 작용을 하는)
발전성 發展性 possibility of future growth ; possibilities ¶ 발전성 있는 산업 promising industries ; industries with a future
발전소 發電所 a power plant〔station〕; a powerhouse ; a generating plant〔station〕 대〔초출력〕— a superpower plant〔station〕 수력 — a hydroelectric power plant 〔station〕; a hydropower plant〔station〕 원자력 — an atomic〔a nuclear〕 power station〔plant〕 자가 — an isolated〔a home〕 power plant 화력 — a thermoelectric power plant〔station〕; a steam power plant〔station〕
발정 發情 sexual excitement ; estrus —하다 come into heat〔season〕; get in heat ; go to (the) rut ; rut ¶ 발정한 암소 a cow in〔on〕 heat // 발정한 사슴 a rutting〔an estrous〕 deer
—기(期) (the age of) puberty ; [동물의] heat ; [새의] the mating season — 주기(週期) an estrous cycle — 호르몬 an estrous〔estrogenic〕 hormone
발정 發程 [출발] departure —하다 start ; set out ; take the road
발족 發足 [출발] starting ; beginning ; [사업의] inauguration —하다 start ; make a start ; start functioning
발주 發注 placing an order ; ordering —하다 place〔give〕 an order for 《goods》; order
발주저리 one's feet wearing tattered 〔filthy〕 socks
발진 發疹 〖의학〗 eruption ; rash —하다 erupt ; break out (in a rash) ; effloresce
—티푸스 eruptive typhus ; typhus fever
발진 發進 [비행기의] departure ; take off ; [로켓의] launching ; blast-off ; lift-off
발진기 發振器 〖물리〗 an oscillator
발진자 發振子 〖통신〗 radiator
발짝 a step ; a pace ¶ 한 발짝 한 발짝 step by step // 세 발짝 내디디다〔뒤로 물러서다〕 take three steps forward〔backward〕
발쪽거리다 pucker 《it》 up ¶ 입을 발쪽거리다 pucker up one's lips // 입을 발쪽거리며 웃다〔울다〕 pucker up and smile〔cry〕
발쪽발쪽 opening slightly and shutting
발쪽이 (with mouth) half open ; with lips slightly parted ; with a smile
발쪽하다 《mouth》 be half open ; lips are slightly parted ; (be) smiling ¶ 입을 발쪽하게 벌리다 half open one's mouth
발차 發車 departure ; [차장의 신호] All aboard ! —하다 leave ; go ; depart ; start ; pull out ¶ 발차의 벨 the warning bell // 발차를 알리다 [역원이] call a train // 2번선에서 발차하다 start from track No. 2 // 열차는 25분마다 발차한다 A train leaves every 25 minutes.
— 시간 departure time — 신호 a starting signal — 플랫폼 adeparture platform
발착 發着 departure and arrival —하다 arrive and depart
— 시간표 a timetable ; a railroad schedule
발채 a mat-like rack
발초 拔抄 an extract ; a selection ; an excerpt —하다 quote 《from》; make extracts 《from》
⁑**발췌 拔萃** an extract ; an excerpt ; selection —하다 extract〔excerpt, quote, select〕 《from》; make an abstract 《of》 ¶ 밀턴 작품의 발췌 a selection from Milton's writings // 편지의 한 구절을 발췌하다 transcribe a passage from a letter
— 개헌안 the selected amendment bill to the Constitution —곡(曲) a (musical) selection
발치 direction of one's feet when one lies down ; a (dark) corner of a room ; [근처] vicinity
발칫잠 sleeping at the feet of others
발치 拔齒 extraction of a tooth ; a tooth extraction —하다 extract〔draw, pull out〕 a tooth
—술 exodontia
발칙하다 [버릇없다] (be) ill-mannered ; ill-bred ; unmannerly ; rude ; mean ; [괘씸하다] (be) hateful ; abominable ; detestable ; cursed ; spiteful ¶ 발칙한 놈 an outrageous〔a rude〕 fellow // 발칙한 말을 하다 say rude things 《to》; make a rude remark 《to》 // 발칙한 짓을 하다 act rudely 《to a person》; behave discourteously 《to a person》; commit a breach of etiquette ; be rude 《to a person》; misbehave oneself // 그 놈은 발칙한 놈이야 He is a detestable fellow. // 이 발칙한 놈아 This cursed fellow !
발칵 ⇨ 발깍
발칸 the Balkans
— 반도 the Balkan Peninsula — 제국(諸國) the Balkan States
⁑**발코니** a balcony ¶ 발코니로 나가다 go out on the balcony // 발코니로 나가 시원한 바람을 쐬다 enjoy the cool air out on the balcony
발타다 《a young animal》 find its legs 〔feet〕; try its legs for the first time
발탄 강아지 관용 a pup just able to walk
발탁 拔擢 selection ; choice —하다 select ; single out ; choose ¶ 수천명의 지원자 중에서 단 30명이 발탁되었다 Out of

thousands of applicants only thirty were chosen.
— 승진 promotion by selection

발탄 강아지 a gadabout (사람)

†발톱 a toenail (사람의) ; a claw (짐승의) ; a talon (맹금의) ; a hoof (마소의) ; a bill (고양이의) ¶ 발톱으로 할퀴다 scratch with one's claws ; claw // 발톱을 갈다 sharpen one's claws // 호랑이는 발톱을 숨긴다 The tiger sheathes its claws. / A powerful man shows his power only when it is needed.
—눈 the lunule〔lunula〕 of a toenail

발트 Balt(ic)
—해(海) the Baltic Sea

발틀 [재봉틀] a treadle sewing machine

발파 發破 blasting —하다 blast
—약 blasting powder — 점화 장치 a portfire

*발판 —板 a footing ; a foothold ; a scaffold (건축장의) ; a stepping stone (수단) ¶ 남을 발판으로 삼다 make a stepping stone of 《a person》 // 발판을 걸다 set〔get〕 up a scaffold // 발판을 잡다 secure a footing // 작가로서의 발판을 굳혔다 He is now established as an author.

발포 發布 promulgation ; proclamation ; issuance —하다 announce ; promulgate ; proclaim ; issue ¶ 헌법의 발포 the promulgation of the constitution

†발포 發砲 firing ; discharge —하다 discharge 《a gun》 ; fire ; open fire ¶ 우리에게 발포하다 fire 《a revolver》 at us ; open fire on us
— 사건 a shooting case〔incident〕

발포정 發泡錠 a foaming〔an effervescent〕 tablet

발포제 發泡劑 a blowing〔foaming〕 agent

†발표 發表 [공표] announcement ; publication ; presentation ; [표현] expression —하다 announce ; make public ; make known ; release ; express ¶ 의견을 발표하다 express one's view ; express oneself // (학회 따위에서) 연구를 발표하다 read a paper 《on a subject》 // 정견(政見)을 발표하다 air〔make a declaration of, set forth〕 one's political views // 그 사람의 이름은 발표하지 않기로 한다 The man shall be nameless. // 그의 이름은 발표되지 않았다 The name has not been made public.
정식 — a formal announcement 미— 작품 an unpublished work

*발하다 發— ① [피다] bloom ; come out ② [떠나다] leave 《a place》 for ; depart for ③ [파견하다] dispatch ; send out ¶ 병력을 발하다 dispatch troops ④ [내리다] issue ; announce ; publish ¶ 명령을 발하다 issue an order ⑤ [내다] utter (소리를) ; [열·빛을] emit ; radiate ; give out ¶ 큰소리를 발하다 give a (loud) cry ; cry out ⑥ [기원하다] originate 《in》 ; spring up ; rise

*발한 發汗 perspiration ; sweating —하다 perspire ; sweat
—제(劑) a diaphoretic ; a sudorific ; a sweater

발항 發航 ⇨ 출항

†발행 發行 [도서의] publication ; issue ; [채권·지폐] floatation ; [출발] departure ; leaving —하다 publish ; issue ; bring out ; float ; depart ; leave ¶ 연 4회 발행의 quarterly // 매주〔매월〕 발행의 weekly〔monthly〕 // 발행을 중지하다 suspend publication // 지폐를 발행하다 issue bank notes // 발행 부수는 2만이다 It has a circulation of 20,000. // 새 잡지가 다음 주에 발행된다 A new magazine will be out next week.
— 가격 the issueprice —권 the right of publication — 부수 a circulation —소 a publishing office —액 the amount issued —인 a publisher — 정지 suspension〔prohibition〕 of publication

발행고 發行高 (the amount of) circulation ; [공채·지폐 따위의] the amount issued
— 한도 the issue limit 《of bank notes》

발행 금지 發行禁止 suspension〔prohibition〕 of publication

발행일 發行日 the date〔day〕 of issue〔publication〕 ¶ 발행일을 늦추다 shift〔move back〕 the date of issue 《to》

발허리 the arch of the foot

발헤엄 treading water —하다 tread water

발현 發現 revelation ; manifestation —하다 be revealed〔manifested〕 ; manifest itself

발호 跋扈 rampancy ; domination ; presumption —하다 (be) rampant ; dominant ; dominate ; prevail ¶ 군벌의 발호 the domination of the militarists

발화 發火 [발산] firing ; the outbreak of a fire ; [점화] ignition —하다 catch〔take〕 fire ; start ; originate ¶ …에서 발화하다 The fire starts〔originates〕 from 《a defective flue》. // 열차의 한 객차에 발화했다 One of the cars of the train caught fire.
—기(器) an exploder —약 a detonator — 장치 an ignition device —전(栓) an ignition plug — 전선(電線) detonating cable —점 the ignition〔combustion〕 point ; [기름의] the burning〔firing, flash〕 point ; [분쟁 따위의] the flash point 자연 — spontaneous combustion 지연 — hangfire

발회 發會 the opening of a meeting ; [거래소의] the first meeting 《of the year》 —하다 open a meeting ; hold〔give〕 the opening〔first〕 meeting
—식 an opening ceremony

발효 醱酵 fermentation —하다 ferment
—관〔실〕 a fermentation tube〔chamber〕 —균 a zymogen — 방지제 an anti-ferment —법 zymotechnics —성〔력〕 fer-

ㅂ

mentability **—소** (素) yeast ; leaven ; ferment **— 작용** zymolysis **—학**〔론〕 zymology ; fermentology

*__발효 發效__ coming into effect ; effectuation **—하다** become effective ; come into effect ¶ 평화 조약이 발효함에 따라 with the effectuation of the peace treaty

*__발휘 發揮__ display ; exhibition **—하다** display ; exhibit ; show ¶ 수완을 발휘하다 show〔display〕 one's ability // 충분히 발휘하다 give full play〔scope〕 to 《one's genius》

발흥 勃興 a sudden rise ; a sudden increase in power **—하다** suddenly rise ; spring up ; rise into power (나라가) ¶ 민족주의의 발흥 the rise of nationalism

밝기 [명도] luminosity

†**밝다**¹ ① [환하다] (be) bright ; light ; rosy ; promising (전망이) ¶ 달 밝은 밤 a bright moonlit night // 밝은 동안에 while it is light ; before (it gets) dark // 밝게 하다 light (up) ; brighten // 등불이 밝다 The lamp gives a good light. // 무역의 전망이 밝다 There is a good outlook for foreign trade. // 얼굴 표정이 밝아졌다 His face brightened〔lit〕 up.

② [눈·귀가] (be) sharp ; keen ¶ 귀가 밝다 have sharp ears // 눈이 밝다 have keen eyesight

③ [능통하다] be versed in ; be well acquainted with ; be familiar〔conversant〕 with ¶ 사정에 밝다 be well-informed // 일본 사정에 밝다 be conversant〔well acquainted〕 with Japanese affairs // 그는 외환 시장에 관해 밝다 He is an expert〔a specialist〕 in the foreign exchange market.

†**밝다**² [날이] dawn ; break ¶ 날이 밝기 전에 before dawn // 날이 밝는다 It dawns. / It gets light. /Day〔Morning〕 breaks.

밝을녘 daybreak ; dawn ; the early hours of the morning ¶ 밝을녘에 at daybreak ; at dawn // 밝을녘까지 공부하다 study into the early morning hours

†**밝히다** ① [밝게 하다] light (up) ; brighten ; lighten ¶ (탐조등으로) 해상을 밝히다 flash over the sea

② [분명히 하다] make 《a matter》 clear ; clear up ; clarify ¶ 도난물이 누구의 것인지를 밝혀 내다 establish the identity of stolen goods // 자기 입장을 밝히다 make one's position clear

③ [밤을] sit up late ; stay up all night ¶ 독서로 밤을 밝히다 sit far into the night reading // 이야기로 밤을 밝히다 talk the night away

밞다 [길이를] measure 《the length》 in double-arm spans ; [거리를] measure 《the distance》 by pace ; pace 《the distance》

*__밟다__ ① [디디다] step 《on》 ; tread 《on》 ¶ 남의 발을 밟다 step on 《a person's》 foot // 모국 땅을 밟다 step〔set foot〕 on one's native country ; return home // 밟고 차고 하다 kick and tread on // 처음으로 무대를 밟다 make one's debut // 방금 당신이 담배꽁초를 버리고 발로 밟아 끄는 것을 보았다 I just saw you throw a cigarette butt and step on it.

② [뒤를] follow〔trail〕 《a person》 ; trail after ; shadow 《a person》 ; dog ¶ 뒤를 밟다 put 《dogs》 on the trail // 경찰이 그의 뒤를 밟는다 He is shadowed by the police.

③ [순서를 거치다] go through ; undergo ; complete〔fulfil〕 (이행하다) ¶ 고등학교 과정을 밟다 complete (the course of) high school // 수속을 밟다 go through 〔comply with〕 formalities // 올바른 길을 밟다 walk in the path of virtue // 정식 과정을 밟다 complete a regular course

밟다듬이 pressing〔smoothing〕 laundry by treading on ; foot pressing **—하다** give the laundry a foot pressing ; tread laundry

밟히다 be stepped on ; be trampled on ; be trodden upon

†**밤**¹ night ; evening (저녁) ¶ 밤에 at night ; by night // 밤이고 낮이고 day and night ; at all hours // 밤이 되기 전에 before dark〔nightfall〕 // 밤이 되어 after dark ; in the evening // 10일 밤에 on the night of the 10th // 월요일 밤에 on Monday night // 밤늦게까지 이야기하다 talk far into the night // 밤이 되다 night falls // 그는 낮에 자고 밤에 일한다 He sleeps by day and works by night. // 밤 11시였다 It was 11 o'clock at night.

밤에 휘파람을 불면 도둑놈이 온다 속담 A whistling maid boded never luck to a house.

*__밤__² 〚식물〛 a chestnut ¶ 밤색의 chestnut-colored ; nutbrown ; maroon

—나무 a chestnut tree

밤³ [놋그릇 틀] a die ; a mold

밤거리 night streets ; the town at night ¶ 밤거리의 여자 a lady of the night ; a streetwalker ; a street girl ; a woman of the streets

밤길 night walking ; a walk at night ; a night trip ¶ 밤길을 가다 go〔walk〕 at night ; make a night trip

밤꾀꼬리 a (European) nightingale

밤낚시 night fishing〔angling〕 **—하다** go fishing by night ; drop a line at night

밤낮 night and day ; at all hours ; always ; day in and day out (늘) ¶ 밤낮으로 일하다 work night and day ; work double shifts

밤놀이 night amusement〔pleasure〕 **—하다** have fun at night ¶ 밤놀이를 다니다 go out in the evening for pleasure

밤눈¹ night vision ¶ 밤눈에도 분명히 보이다 be clearly visible in the dark

밤눈이 어둡다 관용 be night-blind

밤눈² [내리는 눈] snow in the night

밤느정이, 밤늦 a chestnut blossom
밤늦다 it is late at night ¶ 밤늦게 late at night // 이렇게 밤늦게 at this time of (the) night // 밤늦게까지 far into the night ; till late at night // 밤늦도록 공부하다 work 《at one's studies》 far into the night ; burn the midnight oil
밤대거리 a night shift ; a night crew ; a night relief **—하다** be〔work〕 on the night shift ; take night duty ; be on the night turn ¶ 그는 밤대거리로 일한다 He works 《in the mine》 on the night shift.
밤도와 all night ; all through the night ; all hours of the night ¶ 밤도와 책을 읽다 sit far into the night reading
밤들다 《the night》 be advanced ; grow late ; wear on ¶ 깊이 밤들었다 The night was far advanced.
밤똥 having a bowel movement at night ¶ 밤똥누다 move the bowels at night 〔every night〕
밤마다 nightly ; every night ; night after night
밤바람 a night wind
밤볼 a plump〔chubby〕 cheek
밤비 rain in the night
밤비에 자란 사람 속담 a person who is soft in the head〔weak and cowardly〕
밤사이 the night time ¶ 밤사이에 during the night ; overnight // 밤사이에 내린 폭풍우로 on account of the storm that has been raging overnight
*__밤새__ the night time ⇨ 밤사이
밤새껏 all night ; all through the night ; all hours of the night ¶ 밤새껏 마시다 drink all night long ; drink away (the night) // 밤새껏 한잠 자지 못했다 I have been up all night. /I didn't sleep even a wink the whole night.
*__밤새우다__ sit up all night ; keep awake all night through ¶ 밤새워 일을 끝내다 finish 《a thing》 by working all night through // 책을 읽고 밤새우다 stay〔sit〕 up all night over a book // 밤새워 시험 준비를 했다 I sat up all night preparing myself for the examination.
밤새움 being a night owl ; staying up late〔all night〕 **—하다** stay up all night ¶ 밤새움은 건강에 나쁘다 Late hours are bad for your health.
밤색 —色 a chestnut color ; maroon ; brown
밤샘 staying up all night ⇨ 밤새움
밤소경 night blindness ¶ 밤소경이다 be night-blind
밤소일 —消日 night pleasure〔amusement〕 ; sitting up all night playing **—하다** find night amusement 《in》 ; sit up all night playing
밤손님 a burglar ; a night thief ; a night prowler 《속》 ¶ 밤손님이 들다 be broken into by a burglar
밤송이 a chestnut bur
밤안개 a night fog〔mist〕
밤알 a chestnut ¶ 밤알을 줍다 gather chestnuts
밤얽이 a kind of knot
밤얽이를 치다 속담 tie a double bowknot
밤엿 a taffy
밤윷 *yut* sticks small as chestnuts
밤이슬 the night dew ¶ 밤이슬을 맞다 expose oneself to the night air〔dew〕
밤일 night work ; a night shift (야근)
밤자갈 pebbles (for paving)
밤잔물 a bowl of drinking water left overnight at the bedside
밤잠 sleeping at night ; night sleep
밤장 —場 a night market
밤재우다 keep overnight
밤저녁 late evening
밤중 —中 the middle of the night ; midnight ¶ 밤중의 midnight // 밤중에 at midnight ; in the middle of the night
밤중같은 사람 속담 There is no blindness like ignorance. /As blind as a bat. /Blind as a mole. /Blind as an owl.
밤차 —車 a night train ¶ 밤차를 타다 board a night train
밤참 a midnight meal〔snack〕
밤톨 a chestnut ¶ 밤톨만한 돌 a stone as big as chestnut
밤하늘 a night sky
†**밥**[1] ① [쌀밥] boiled rice ¶ 밥을 세 그릇 먹다 eat three bowls of rice // 밥을 짓다 boil rice
② [식사] a meal ; food ¶ 밥을 먹다 have a meal // 하루에 밥을 세 끼 먹다 take three meals a day // 밥 먹었느냐 Have you had dinner?
③ [먹이] feed ; food ; bait (낚시용) ; a prey〔victim〕 (다른 동물의) ¶ 돼지밥 hog feed // 늑대의 밥이 되다 become the prey〔victim〕 of wolves
밥[2] waste material produced in cutting 가윗— scraps of cloth〔paper〕 끌— chisel dust 대팻— shavings 실— bits of thread 톱— sawdust
밥값 food costs ; board
밥그릇 a rice bowl ¶ 밥그릇에 밥을 반만 담다 fill a bowl half-full with rice
밥내다 torture a confession out of 《a criminal》
밥맛 appetite (식욕) ; the flavor of rice
밥물 [끓일 물] water for boiling rice ; [넘는 물] ricewater ¶ 밥물이 넘는다 The ricewater is boiling over.
밥밑 beans〔barley, *etc.*〕 boiled with rice **—콩** choice beans (suitable for cooking with rice)
밥벌레 a lazy bum ; a good-for-nothing ; a useless mouth
밥벌이 means of scanty livelihood ; breadwinning ; one's bread and butter **—하다** earn one's bread ; make a livelihood〔living〕 ¶ 겨우 밥벌이하다 eke out a scanty livelihood ; make a bare liv-

ㅂ

ing // 밥벌이는 되다 earn enough to eat
밥보자기 —褓— a covering over rice bowls and dishes on the table
***밥상** —床 a dinner table ; an eating〔a dining〕table ; a table ¶ 밥상을 내가다 clear away dinner things // 밥상에 고기를 올리다 serve up fish at 《a person's》 table // 밥상을 받다 sit down to table // 밥상을 차리다 set the table ; lay the cloth
밥소라 a large brass food bowl
밥솥 a rice pot〔kettle〕
밥술 a spoonful of boiled rice
밥쌀 rice for boiling ; eating rice
밥알 a grain of boiled rice
밥자배기 an earthen bowl (for boiled rice)
밥잔치 a plain and simple dinner party
밥장사 restaurant business ; running a restaurant —하다 run a restaurant ; serve meals to customers
밥장수 a restaurateur ; the keeper of a restaurant
밥주걱 a spatula (for serving boiled rice)
밥주머니 ⇨ 밥벌레
밥줄 a means of living
밥줄이 끊어지다 [관용] lose one's means of livelihood
밥집 an eating house ; a chophouse ; a snack bar
밥짓다 boil rice ; cook food
밥통 —桶 ① [그릇] a wooden container for boiled rice ② [위] the stomach ③ [밥벌레] a good-for-nothing
밥투정 —하다 grumble〔complain〕about meals〔food〕
밥풀 [밥알] a grain of boiled rice ; [풀] rice paste
밥풀강정 a rice-coated fried cake, made of glutinous rice and honey
밥풀과자 —菓子 a honey cake coated with popped rice
밥풀칠 —하다 put rice paste on ; cover with rice paste
밧줄 a rope ; a cord (가는) ; a line ; 〖항해〗 a stay ; a hawser (굵은) ; [마소용의] a tether (rope)
방 放 [총알 따위의] a shot ; a round ; a shell (대포) ¶ 방귀를 한 방 뀌다 let out a fart // 총을 한 방 쏘다 fire a shot 《at》
†**방** 房 a room ; a chamber ; an apartment ¶ 어린이 방 a children's room // 방을 세내다 rent a room // 방을 예약하다 reserve a room 《at a hotel》
방 榜 ① [방목] the list of successful candidates ② [방문] a placard ; a public notice
방 磅 a pound
-방 方 [방위] direction ¶ 남방 the south ; the direction of the south
-방 房 [댁] care of 《c/o》 ¶ 이영세 씨 방 홍길동 씨 Mr. *Hong Kil Tong*, c/o Mr. *Lee Young Se*
방가 放歌 singing loudly —하다 sing noisily〔loudly〕
방갈로 a bungalow
방값 [방세] room rent ; [호텔 따위의] room charge ; room rate
방갓 方— a wide-brimmed bamboo hat (worn by a mourner) ¶ 방갓쟁이 a man wearing a mourner's bamboo hat
방게 〖동물〗 a kind of small crab ; Helice tridens (학명)
방계 傍系 a collateral line〔family〕 ¶ 방계의 collateral ; subsidiary
— 비속(卑屬)〔존속(尊屬)〕 a collateral descendant〔ascendant〕 — 인족(姻族) collateral relatives-in-law — 친족 a collateral relative — 혈족 a collateral relation by blood — 회사 a subsidiary〔an affiliated〕 company
방고래 房— a flue of a hypocaust
방공 防空 air defense
— 감시원 an air-raid warden — 기구(氣球) a barrage balloon — 대책 air-raid precaution — 부대 an interception force — 시설 air defense facilities — 식별권 an air defense identification zone — 연습〔훈련〕 an anti air-raid drill ; air defense maneuvers〔exercises〕 — 자재 air defense supplies — 지구 an air defense identification zone 《ADIZ》 — 체제 an air defense setup —호 a dugout ; an air-raid shelter 민— 훈련 a civil air defense drill
방공 防共 defense〔-ce〕 against communism —하다 fight〔defend against〕 communism
방과 放課 dismissal of a class —하다 《school》 get out ; let out ; be dismissed ; be over ; break up ¶ 방과후 after school (hours) ; after school is over
— 시간 a recess (hour) ; playtime ; the break ; the end of school hours
***방관** 傍觀 onlooking ; looking on as a spectator —하다 look on ; watch ; sit as a spectator ; remain indifferent〔impassive〕 ; remain a spectator ; stand by idly ¶ 방관적 태도를 취하다 assume the attitude of an onlooker ; assume an indifferent attitude ; remain an idle onlooker
—자 a looker-on 《*pl.* lookers-》 ; a bystander ; a spectator ; an onlooker
방광 膀胱 〖해부〗 the (urinary) bladder ; the vesica ¶ 방광의 cystic ; vesical
— 결석(結石) 〖의학〗 a bladder stone ; a cystolith ; stones in the bladder —경(鏡) a cystoscope —경 검사 cystoscopy —염 〖의학〗 cystitis ; inflammation of the bladder — 절제술 cystectomy — 카타르 catarrh of the urinary bladder — 파열 rupture of bladder
방구들 房— a hypocaust
방구리 a water jug ¶ 옹방구리 a small water jug
방구매기 〖건축〗 producing a bulge in

eaves

방구멍 the center hole in a kite

방구석 房— the interior of a room ; a room ¶ 방구석에 in a room ; indoors // 언제나 방구석에 박혀 있다 I stay indoors at all times. // 방구석에서 뭘 하냐 What are you doing in the room ?

방귀 wind ; a fart ¶ 방귀를 뀌다 break wind ; fart

방그레 smilingly ; beamingly ; with a smile ; with a beaming face ¶ 방그레 웃다 smile sweetly 《at a person》 ; beam 《upon a person》

방글거리다 smile ; beam

방글방글 with a gentle〔bland〕 smile ; smilingly ; beamingly ⇨ 벙글벙글

**방금 方今 just now ; a moment ago ¶ 방금 떠났습니다 He has just left. /He left just now. // 방금 여기 있었는데 He was here a moment ago.

방긋 with a (sudden) smile ¶ 방긋 웃다 smile a beautiful smile ; beam 《upon a person》 ; smile 《at a person》

방긋거리다 beam ; smile

방긋방긋 smiling ; beaming

방긋이 ① [웃으며] smilingly ; with a smile ⇨ 방그레

② [열린 꼴] ajar ¶ 문을 방긋이 열다 open the door a little

방긋하다 be ajar ; be partly opened

방기 放棄 abandonment ⇨ 포기(抛棄)

방나다 become〔go〕 bankrupt ; go into bankruptcy ; be ruined

방나다 榜— 《the list of successful candidates》 be released〔made public〕

방년 芳年 blooming age ; the sweet age (of a young girl) ¶ 방년 20세의 처녀 a girl of sweet twenty

방념 放念 **—하다** set one's mind〔be, feel〕 at ease〔rest〕

방뇨 放尿 **—하다** urinate ; make〔pass〕 water ; relieve oneself

방담 放談 a random〔free〕 speech ; irresponsible〔unreserved〕 talk

—회(會) a gabfest 《미·구》 ; a bull session 《속》

*__방대__ 尨大 **—하다** (be) huge ; vast ; enormous ; bulky ; colossal ; massive ; g igantic ; stupendous ; extensive ; mammoth ¶ 방대한 예산 a huge budget // 방대한 개발 계획 vast plans of development // 방대한 규모의 계획 a scheme of vast scope // 방대한 금액 an enormous sum of money

방도 方途 a way ; a method ; a means ; a measure ¶ 적절한 방도를 취하다 take proper measures // 다른 방도가 없다 There is no alternative〔other way〕.

방독 防毒 protecting oneself from poison ; keeping away poisonous substances **—하다** protect oneself from poison ; keep away poisonous substances

— 마스크〔면〕 a gas mask **—실** a gasproof shelter ; an antigas room

방둥구부렁이 a quadruped with a sagging rump

방둥이 the rump

*__방랑__ 放浪 wandering ; roaming ; roving ; a bohemian life **—하다** wander〔roam, rove〕 about ; tramp ; lead a bohemian life ¶ 방랑 생활을 하다 lead a roving〔wandering〕 life // 세계를 방랑하다 roam〔wander, knock〕 about the world

—객〔자〕 a wanderer ; a vagrant ; a vagabond ; a tramp ; a hobo 《미·속》 ; a bohemian **— 문학** bohemian literature **—벽(癖)** vagrant habits **— 생활** a wandering life ; a bohemian〔Gypsy〕 life ; the life of a vagabond **—시** bohemian poetry **—주의** bohemianism

방략 方略 [정책] a policy ; [계획] a plan ; [책략] a stratagem ; [수단] a means ¶ 전반적인 방략을 꾸미다 map out a general plan〔scheme〕

방령 芳齡 blooming age ⇨ 방년(芳年)

방론 放論 a harangue ; a rant **—하다** speak irresponsibly ; talk bombastically ; declaim ; comment arbitrarily

방류하다 放流— [물을] discharge ; [고기를] stock 《the streams》 with ¶ 강에 잉어를 방류하다 stock a stream with carp

방리 方里 a square *ri*

방만 放漫 laxity ; looseness ; indiscretion (무분별) **—하다** [긴장이 풀린] be lax〔loose, slack〕 ; [멋대로의] be reckless〔wild, random, arbitrary〕

방망이 a club ; a cudgel ; a mallet

—질 beating with a paddle〔club〕 《in washing, smoothing clothes》 ¶ 방망이질하다 beat with a paddle〔club〕

방매 放賣 sale ; selling **—하다** sell off〔out〕 ; keep for sale ; clear out ; put it on sale ; dispose 《of》 ¶ 특가 방매 a special sale // 연말 염가 대방매 the year-end bargain sale

—가(家) a house for sale

방면 方面 ① [방향] a direction ; [부분] a quarter ; [일의 분야] a line ; a field ¶ 문학 방면 the literary field // 각 방면의 활동 무대 various spheres〔fields〕 of activity // 각 방면에서 from all quarters ; from many sources // 그는 여러 방면에 친구를 갖고 있다 He is acquainted with all classes. // 이 방면에는 경험이 적다 I have little experience in this line.

② [국면] an aspect ; a phase ; an angle ; a source ; [견지] a point of view ; a standpoint ¶ 이 방면에서 본다면 viewed from this angle ; from this point of view

③ [얼굴] a square〔squarish〕 face

방면 放免 release ; discharge ; liberation ; [무죄 방면] acquittal **—하다** let 《a person》 go ; set 《a person》 free ; release 《a person》 ; liberate ; discharge ; acquit

ㅂ

《a person》 of 《the charge》
무죄 — acquittal and discharge ¶ 그는 무죄 방면되었다 He was acquitted. 훈계 — release after admonition

방명 芳名 (your, his) honored〔esteemed〕 name ; a good name ¶ 방명은 일찍이 잘 알고 있었습니다 I have known you by reputation.
—록 a list of names〔acquaintances〕; a visitors' book ; a guest book

방모 紡毛 carded wool ; carding (short) wool
—기 a carding machine —사(絲) woolen yarn ; wool

방목 放牧 grazing ; pasturage —하다 graze 《cattle》; turn out 《cattle》 to grass ¶ 방목 중이다 be at grass
—권 herbage ; pasture〔grazing〕 rights
—지 grazing land ; a pasture

방목 榜目 the (filed) list of successful candidates (in the higher civil service examination)

방문 榜文 a placard ; a public notice ; a government notification ¶ 방문을 내붙이다 put up〔post〕 a notice

ㅂ

방문 方文 prescription ⇨ 약방문

방문 房門 a door (of a room)

†방문 訪問 a call ; a visit ; an interview —하다 call on 《a person》; call at 《a person's house》; visit ; look up (구) ; pay 《a person》 a visit ; make a call 《on》 ¶ 인사의 방문 a courtesy call // 방문을 받다 receive a call from 《a person》// 방문을 갔다 He went out for a visit. // 그를 학교로 방문했다 I called on him at his school.
— 비행 《make》 a goodwill flight 《to Taipei》 — 외교 diplomacy through personal visitation 공식 — a formal visit ; an official call ; [국가 원수의] a state visit
☞ 《p. 935》

방문객 訪問客 a caller ; a visitor ; a visitant ¶ 방문객이 있다〔없다〕 have a〔no〕 visitor to receive // 방문객을 맞다 receive a caller〔visitor〕// 방문객을 사절하다 deny oneself to〔refuse to see〕 a caller

방문단 訪問團 a group〔team〕 of visitors

방문차 房門次 a paper door decoration

방물 women's merchandise items ; fancy goods

방물장사 a peddler〔hawker〕 selling women's items

방물장수 a woman selling women's items

방미 訪美 a visit to the United States ¶ 방미길에〔중에〕 on one's way〔while on a visit〕 to America

방밑 枋— the lower part of a wall

방바닥 the floor of a room

방방곡곡 坊坊曲曲 every inch〔nook and corner〕 of the country〔land〕; all over the country ¶ 방방곡곡에 퍼지다 It spreads throughout〔all over〕 the country.

방범 防犯 crime prevention —하다 prevent crimes
—대원 a night guard —벨 a burglar alarm

방범 주간 防犯週間 Crime Prevention Week

†방법 方法 a way ; a method ; a process ; a manner ; a system

> 참고 **method**는 특별한 또는 일정한 체계적 이론적 「방법」으로서 정신적인 활동과 일종의 딱딱함을 포함하고 있다 **way**는 manner보다 형식적이고 명확한 습관적 「방법」이지만 method보다 논리성·명확성이 모자란 「방법·양식」 **manner**는 개인적 활동의 방법으로서 눈에 띄게 특색 있는 「양식」을 뜻하는 이외에 일이 일어나는 「방법」을 의미하기도 한다 **fashion**은 way와 같은 일반적인 말로서 주로 전치사 after, in과 함께 구를 이룬다 **system**은 사상·사실·목적 따위 체계적이고 능률적이며 비교적 복잡한 「방법」 **process**는 일련의 행동·운동·작업으로서 종말에 연결된 정해진 과정의 진행적 「방법」을 의미한다

[수단] a means ; [조치] a step ; a measure ; [연구] a device ; [계획] a scheme ; [제법] a recipe ; a formula 《*pl.* ~s, -lae》 ¶ 여러 가지 방법으로 by various means ; by hook or by crook // 방법을 발견하다 find a way // 방법을 세우다 form〔formulate, draw up〕 a plan // 방법을 정하다 fix upon a plan // 방법을 취하다 take measures // 적당한 방법을 강구하다 take proper measures // 틀린〔올바른〕 방법으로 하다 do 《a thing》 in the wrong〔proper〕 way // 달리 방법이 없다 There is no alternative〔other way〕. // 어떤 방법으로 하는지 모르겠다 I don't know how to do it. // 그것을 하는 데는 이것이 최선의 방법이다 This is the best way to do it. // 우리의 자녀 교육 방법에 문제가 있었다는 건가 I wonder if there was something wrong with the way we raised our child.
—론 methodology — 연구 a study of methods ; method study

방벽 防壁 a barrier ; a protective wall ; a bulwark ¶ 민주주의의 방벽 a bulwark of democracy
— 지대 [국방상의] a security ring

방보라 〖건축〗 [욋가지 대신의] small sticks of wood woven vertically into a thin wall as substitutes for laths ; [설외의] reinforcing wooden pieces for vertical laths in a wall

방부 防腐 prevention against putrefaction ; preservation from〔against〕 decay ; embalmment ; antisepsis —하다 preserve (from decay) ; prevent putrefaction ; embalm ¶ 방부의 antiseptic // 방부처리를 하다 apply antiseptic treatment ; embalm (시체에)

방부제 防腐劑 an antiseptic (substance) ;

방 문

영국이나 미국의 관습으로는 남의 집을 방문할 경우 혹은 만날 약속을 하고자 할 때 미리 날짜와 시간 등을 약속해 둘 필요가 있다. 만일 상대방이 초청해 왔을 때는 서면이나 구두로 의사 표시를 분명하게 전달해야 한다. 거절의 표현으로는 Well, that's very kind of you, but.... / Thank you (very much) for asking me, but.... / I'd like to, but.... / I wish I could, but.... / I'm afraid I've already promised to....(but thank you very much all the same.) 등의 표현을 쓴다.

1 방문 약속의 문의

¶ 다음 일요일에 야구 경기 보러 가지 않을래? Would you like to come and watch a baseball game with me next Sunday? // 오늘 오후 점심 같이 안 할래? Why don't you come to lunch with me this afternoon? // 몇 시에[언제] 만나 뵐 수 있을까요? What time shall we meet? / When can I see you? / When can we get together? // 화요일 오후에 당신 사무실로 찾아뵙겠습니다. I'd like to visit you at [see you in] your office sometime Tuesday afternoon.

2 문의에 대한 응답

¶ 고마워, 기꺼이 가지. Thank you, I'd like to very much. // 일요일은 거의 하루 내내 시간이 비어 있습니다. I am free all day (almost) every Sunday. // 일요일은 언제라도 오십시오. Please come any time any Sunday. // 그 식당에서 수요일 저녁 7시에 당신을 기다리고 있겠습니다. Then I'll be expecting you at that restaurant at seven (on) Wednesday evening. // 저녁 8시 이후에는 항상 집에 있습니다. I am usually at home after eight in the evening. // 당신이 오기를 기다리고 있겠습니다. We'll be [We're] looking forward to seeing you. // 미안합니다. 그날은 선약이 있습니다. I'm sorry, but I have a previous appointment[engagement] that day.

3 방문했을 때

① 방문객

¶ 브라운 씨 집에 계십니까? Is Mr. Brown at home? // 윌리엄 씨 좀 만나고 싶습니다. I'd like to see Mr. William. / Can[May] I see Mr. William? // 스미스라는 사람이 만나고 싶어 한다고 전해 주십시오. Please tell him that Mr. Smith wants to see him.

② 방문객을 맞이할 때

¶ 예, 그는 집에 있습니다. 누구시라고 전해드릴까요? Yes, he's in[at home]. May I have your name, please? / Who shall I say is calling? // 어서 오십시오. Please come in. // 잠깐 기다리십시오. Please wait a minute.

4 헤어질 때

① 방문객

¶ 아쉽지만 이제 헤어져야겠군요. I'm afraid I have to go [must be going] now. / Well, I think I must [have to] say good-by now. / I'm afraid I really must go. / I'm afraid I oughtn't to [shouldn't, mustn't, can't] stay any longer. // 이제 가봐야겠어. I must be off (now). / Well, better be going, I suppose. // 안부 전해 주십시오. Please give my regards to Mrs.... / Please say hello to Mrs.... 《구어적 표현》 // 댁내 모든 분에게 안부 전해 주십시오. Please remember me to everyone in your family.

② 방문객을 맞이한 쪽

¶ 조금 더 계시지요. Can't[Couldn't] you stay a little longer? (★ Couldn't you....가 정중한 표현.) // 벌써 가셔야 합니까? Must you go[be going, be leaving] so soon? // 그렇게 바쁘지는 않죠? You're not in a hurry, are you? / Please don't rush off[be in such a hurry]. // 다시 또 들러 주십시오. Please come and see me again. // 이곳에 오실 일이 있으면 꼭 제 사무실에 들러 주십시오. Please drop by my office whenever you are here.

[용액] an antiseptic solution ; an aseptic ; a preservative ; a resist ¶ 방부제를 바르다 apply antiseptic treatment 《to》 ; [시체에] embalm ; preserve

목재 — a wood preservative

방불 彷彿 close resemblance ; looking alike **—하다** [닮다] resemble closely ; be〔look〕 alike ; indicate faintly 〔dimly〕 ¶ 수천이 방불하다 water and sky merge together

방불케 하다 관용 remind 《a person》 of 《a thing》 ; adumbrate

방비 房— an indoor broom

방비 防備 defense ; fortification ; defen-

ㅂ

sive works ; safeguard ; defensive preparations —하다 defend ; fortify ; guard ¶ 방비가 없는 defenseless ; undefended ; unguarded ; unarmed ; unfortified // 방비를 엄하게 하다 strengthen〔reinforce〕 the defenses

무— 도시 an open city

방사 房事 sexual intercourse ¶ 방사 과도 sexual intemperance

*****방사 放射** [광열의] radiation ; [빛·열·냄새의] emission ; emanation ; [발사] firing ; discharge —하다 radiate ; emit ; discharge ; fire ¶ 방사성 탄소에 의한 연대 측정 C_{14}〔radiocarbon, radioactive carbon〕 dating // 방사상의 radial ; radiated // 방사상으로 (shooting out) in all directions 《from》 ; like the spokes of a wheel // 열을 방사하다 radiate heat

—계(計) a radiometer —관(管) a discharge pipe —기(器) an ejector —물 an emission —상〔형〕 a radial shape ¶ 방사상 도로 a radial road — 화학 radiochemistry ; radiation chemistry

방사 紡絲 [실] a (weaving) thread ; a strand ; [방적] spinning ; [방적사] yarn ; spun cotton〔wool, silk〕

방사 放飼 pasturage ; grazing —하다 pasture ; leave 《cattle》 at large

방사능 放射能 radioactivity ¶ 방사능이 있는 radioactive 《element》 // 방사능이 없는 inactive // 방사능의 강도 a radioactive level ; the intensity of radioactivity // 방사능에 쐰 사람 an irradiated person // 공기 속의 방사능 atmospheric radioactivity

— 검사 a radioactivity check — 검출 radioactivity readings — 구름 a radioactive cloud —비〔눈〕 radioactive rain〔snow〕 — 연구자 a radiologist — 오염 radioactive contamination — 원소 a radioactive element — 장애〔질환〕 a radiation disease〔sickness〕 —재 radioactive ashes〔fallout〕 — 전쟁 radioactive 〔radiological〕 warfare 《RW》 —진(塵) radioactive dust ; radiodust — 측정 radiological monitoring — 측정기 a radiation detector — 허용 한도 the maximum permissible exposure to radiation 내(耐)—복(服) a radiation (-proof) suit

방사림 防沙林 an erosion control forest ; trees for sand arrestation

방사선 放射線 radiation ; [복사 광선] radial〔radiant〕 rays ; [방사능 광선] radioactive rays ¶ 방사선에 민감한 radiosensitive // 방사선 조사(照射)를 받은〔받지 않은〕 an irradiated〔a nonirradiated〕 《person》 // 방사선의 강도 radiation intensity

— 계수관 a radiation counter —과(科) the department of radiology —대(帶) 〚천문〛 the radiation belt ; the Van Allen (radiation) belt —병(病) radiation sickness ; a radiation disease — 사진 a radio (auto) graph ; an autoradiograph ; a skiagraph ; a skiograph — 사진술 radio (auto) graphy ; autoradiography ; skiagraphy — 생물학 radiation biology ; radiobiology — 요법 radiotherapy ; radiotherapeutics ; radiation therapy —의학 radiotherapeutics — 치료 설비 radiotherapy equipment — 치료의(醫) a radiotherapist ; radiotherapeutist —학 radiology — 화학 radiation chemistry ; radiochemistry

방사성 放射性 radioactivity ¶ 방사성의 radioactive // 방사성 탄소에 의한 연대 측정 radiocarbon dating

— 낙진 radioactive〔radiation〕 fallout — 동위 원소 a radioactive isotope ; a radioistope — 물질 a radioactive substance ; radiation material ; a hot material 《속》 — 원소 a radioactive element ; radioelement — 입자 radioactive particles ; Geigers 《구》 — 폐기물 radioactive waste 의약용 — 물질 atomic cocktail

*****방산 放散** ① [헤침] diffusion ; radiation (열, 빛) ; evaporation (수증기) ; emanation (방사능) —하다 radiate ; diffuse ; emanate ② [흩어짐] dispersion ; scattering —하다 disperse ; scatter

—통(痛) [의학] heterotopic〔referred〕 pain

방산충류 放散蟲類 〚동물〛 radiolarian ; Radiolaria (학명)

방생 放生 the release〔setting free〕 of captive animals

방석 方席 a cushion ¶ 방석에 앉다 sit 〔seat oneself〕 on a cushion

수(繡)— an embroidered cushion

방선 傍線 a side line

방설 防雪 protection against〔from〕 snow

—림 a snowbreak ; a snow forest

방성대곡 放聲大哭 weeping loudly and bitterly —하다 cry loudly ; weep bitterly ; lament ; grieve 《over, for》

방성통곡 放聲痛哭 weeping loudly and bitterly —하다 weep loudly and bitterly ; lament ; grieve 《over, for》

방세 房貰 room rent

방세간 房— (room) furnitue

†**방송 放送** [라디오] broadcasting ; a broadcast (1회의) ; [석방] release ; liberation —하다 broadcast ; send (out) 《a drama》 on the air ; speak over the radio (방송자가) ; go on the air ; release ; set free ¶ 해외에 대한 방송 overseas radio service // 강연을 방송하다 broadcast a lecture ; put a lecture on the air // 방송을 듣다 listen in on the radio〔to a broadcast〕 // 방송 중이다〔아니다〕 be on〔off〕 the air // 텔레비전으로 방송하다 [방송국에서] telecast ; televise ; [출연자가] appear〔go〕 on television // 7시 뉴스 방송으로 듣다 hear about 《a thing》 on the seven o'clock newscast 〔broadcast〕

—극 a broadcast play ; a radio drama — 기사(技師) a broadcasting engineer —

기자 a radio〔TV〕 newsman〔reporter〕 —망 a (radio, television) network ; a (radio, TV) circuit — 방해 jamming —부장 broadcasting manager — 사업 the broadcasting industry — 수신기 a broadcast receiver — 순서〔프로〕 a broadcast program ¶ 주요 방송 순서 a radio〔TV〕 highlights — 시간 [방송국의] broadcasting hours ; air time ; [어떤 프로그램의] the time 《for》 ; the length 《of a program》 —실 a radio〔TV〕 studio 《*pl.* ~s》 — 연설 a radio〔TV〕 speech 〔address〕 —원 an announcer — 윤리 위원회 the Broadcasting Ethics Commission — 음악회 an air〔a radio, a TV〕 concert —자 a broadcaster — 종료 sign-off — 주파수 radio frequency — 중단 dead air 《속》 ; a dead spot — 청취자 a (radio) listener ; a listener (-in) ; a radio subscriber — 토론회 a radio〔TV〕 forum — 통신 대학 the university of the air — 프로그램 시청률 조사 Cooperative Analysis of Broadcasting Rating 《C. A. B. rating》 — 협회 Broadcasting Corporation 뉴스 — newscasting ; [텔레비전의] a newscast ; a news show 민간 — commercial broadcasting 생— a live broadcast〔program〕 전국 중계 — broadcasting over a nationwide hookup〔network〕 중계 — relay broadcasting ; rebroadcasting ; a relay broadcast ; a rebroadcast ; hookup 텔레비전 — (a) television broadcast ; (a) telecast

방송국 放送局 a broadcasting〔radio, TV〕 station
중앙〔지방〕 — a key〔local〕 station

방수 防守 defense ; defensive ; guard —하다 defend ; act on the defensive ; guard ¶ 방수 동맹 a defensive alliance // 방수 동맹을 맺다 conclude a defensive alliance

방수 放水 drainage —하다 drain water off
—관 a drainpipe ; an offlet ; an a(d)jutage (분수의) —구(口) 〖토목〗 a spillway —로 a drain ; a (drainage) canal ; a flood control channel ; a sluiceway —문 a flood〔drainage〕 gate — 펌프 drain pump

†방수 防水 ① (being) watertight ; waterproof ; flood control ② [군함의] torpedo defense ¶ 방수의 waterproof ; watertight —하다 make 《cloth》 watertight 〔waterproof〕 ; waterproof ; [홍수의] control〔prevent〕 flood
— 대책 a flood prevention measure ; an antiflood measure —모(帽) tarpaulin ; trap 《미·속》 —문 a watertight door — 설비 flood protection works ; protective facilities against floods — 외투 a waterproof coat ; a mackintosh — 장치 waterproofing ; a waterproof device —제 a waterproof agent ; waterproof stuff — 처리 waterproofing —포(布) waterproof cloth ; tarpaulin ; oilskin —화(靴) rubbers ; rain-shoes

방수 傍受 —하다 pickup ; intercept ¶ 무전을 방수하다 intercept a radio message

방술 方術 method and technique

방습 防濕 damp〔moisture〕 proof

방시레 mildly ; sweetly ; peacefully ¶ 방시레 웃다 smile sweetly 《at a person》 ; beam 《upon a person》

†방식 方式 [형식] a form ; [방법] a method ; a process ; [정식] a formula 《*pl.* ~s, -lae》 ; [수속] formalities ; [관례] usage ¶ 일정한 방식 an established〔a regular, a proper〕 form ; a definite method // 방식에 따라서 in due〔proper〕 form // 방식을 세우다 introduce a method 《into》 ; methodize ; systematize // 방식에 따르다〔위반하다〕 conform〔run counter〕 to the usage

방식제 防蝕劑 an anticorrosive ; a rust preventive ; a resist

방실거리다 smile 《at a person》 ; beam 《upon a person》

†방심 放心 ① absent-mindedness ; abstraction (of mind) —하다 be absent-minded ② [안심] relief ; peace of mind —하다 be relieved ; rest assured ¶ 그 점은 방심해도 좋습니다 Set your mind at rest about it. /You may take it easy on that score.

방심 傍心 〖수학〗 an excenter

방아 a mill ; a mortar
—찧기 milling 디딜— a treadmill 물— a water mill

방아굴대 the water wheel shaft

방아깨비 〖곤충〗 a grasshopper ; a locust

방아다리 a plaything made of gold, silver or precious stone in the shape of a scarecrow

방아두레박 [장치] a (well) sweep ; a shadoof ; [통] a sweep-well bucket

방아살 back ribs of beef

*방아쇠 a trigger ¶ 방아쇠를 당기다 pull the trigger

방아채 a long board holding the pestle of a mill

방아타령 —打令 a kind of folk song

방아풀 〖식물〗 a kind of mint

방아확 the mortar of a mill (partly buried underground)

방안 方案 a plan ; a device ; a scheme ; a program ¶ 대체적인 방안 a general plan // 방안을 세우다 draw up〔formulate〕 a plan

방안지 方眼紙 section〔graph, squared〕 paper

방앗간 —間 a rice(-cleaning) mill ; a mill

방앗공이 a pestle ; a pounder

방약무인 傍若無人 arrogance ; audacity ; overbearance ; effrontery ; outrage ; defiance ; insolence —하다 (be) auda-

ㅂ

cious ; arrogant ; outrageous ; insolent ; overbearing ; domineering ¶ 방약무인한 짓을 하다 behave outrageously 〔audaciously〕; conduct oneself recklessly

†방어 防禦 defense ; protection ; safeguard —하다 defend ; bulwark ; shield ; protect oneself 《against》; safeguard 《against》 ¶ 방어가 없는 defenseless ; undefended // 방어하기 어려운 indefensible // 방어의 위치에 서다 be〔stand〕 on the defensive
— 갑판 an ironclad〔a protective〕 deck — 공사 fortifications ; defensive works ; defense installations — 구역 a defense sector — 동맹 a defense alliance —력 defensive power〔strength〕 —망 a torpedo net — 무기 a defensive weapon —물 a protector ; a cover ; a shield — 병기 defensive equipment —선 a line of defense — 수단 a defensive measure — 수뢰 a defensive torpedo —율(率) 〖야구〗 earned run average 《ERA》 — 자세 guard (무술·권투의) —전 a defensive war(-fare) — 진지 a defensive position — 포화 defensive fire 공세〔수세〕 — active 〔passive〕 defense 밀집 — tight defense 지역 — zone defense 해안 — coast defense

*방언 方言 a dialect ; a provincialism
— 지도(地圖) a dialect map〔atlas〕 — 지리학 dialect geography —학〔연구〕 dialectology — 학자〔연구가〕 a dialectologist 개인 — 〖언어〗 an idiolect 계급 — a class dialect 지역 — a regional 〔local〕 dialect

방언 放言 bombastic〔random, big〕 talk ; unreserved talk ; free speech —하다 talk unreservedly〔big, bombastically〕

방역 防疫 prevention of epidemics 〔infectious disease〕; disinfection ; quarantine —하다 prevent an epidemic of ; take preventive measures against epidemics
—관 a health official ; an epidemic control commissioner — 대책 preventive measures against epidemics — 대책 위원회 Infectious Disease Prevention〔Control〕 Commission —선 a (sanitary) cordon ; a quarantine line

방연광 方鉛鑛 〖광물〗 galena

방열 防熱 protection against heat
—복(服) heatproof clothes〔clothing〕 — 필터 a heat filter

방염제 防染劑 a resist ; a resistant

방영하다 放映— 〖텔레비전〗 telecast

†방울 ① 〖쇠방울〗 a bell ¶ 방울을 울리다 ring〔tinkle, jingle〕 a bell ② 〖물의〗 a drop
— 소리 the tinkling〔tinkle〕 of a bell 눈물 — drops of tears 물— water drops 빗— rain drops 이슬— dewdrops

방울방울 drop by drop ; in drops ; dripping ; dribbling

*방울뱀 〖동물〗 a rattlesnake

방울벌레 〖곤충〗 a bell-ring insect ; a house cricket ; Homoeogryllus japonicus (학명)

방울새 〖새〗 a goldfinch ; a greenfinch ; a green linnet

방울집게 pincers ; a nailpuller

†방위 方位 a direction ; a bearing ; a course ; azimuth (방위각) ¶ 방위를 알다 get〔find〕 one's bearings // 방위를 잃다 lose one's bearings // 방위를 정하다 find one's position〔bearings〕
—각 〖천문〗 an azimuth (angle) ; 〔편각〕 a declination —경(鏡) an azimuth mirror — 계기 orientation instruments —권(圈) an azimuth circle — 기선〔기점〕 〖항해〗 the lubber's line〔mark, point〕 — 나침반〔안정기〕 an azimuth compass〔stabilizer〕 —의(儀) a pelorus — 주점(主點) the cardinal points — 측정기 a radio direction finder ; an azimuth finder — 측정(소) radio direction finding (station) —판 a plotting board ; a director ; an offset angle solver —표 a traverse table 무선 —계(計) a radiogoniometer 진(眞)— 〖항공·항해〗 the true heading 〔bearing〕

방위 防衛 defense ; protection ; safeguard —하다 defend ; protect ; shield ; safeguard ¶ 자기 방위를 위해서 in self-defense // 방위의 자세를 취하다 take 〔assume〕 a posture of defense
— 계획 a defense plan〔program〕 —군 a defense corps —대 a defense corps 〔force〕 —력 defense capacity ; defensive strength —비 defense expenses — 산업 the defense industry — 성금 a donation 〔contribution〕 to the national defense fund —세 a defense tax — 소집 a defensive call-up ; a defense call ; defensive mobilization — 수역 defensive waters — 시설 defense facilities〔installation(s)〕 — 전쟁 a defensive war — 조약 a defense treaty — 지출 defense expenditures — 체제 a defensive system ; a defense setup — 포장(褒章) a Defense Medal — 협정(協定) a defense〔defensive〕 agreement 달러 — defense of the dollar 민— civil defense 민—대 the Civil Defense Corps 자기〔자주〕 — self-defense 정당 — legal defense 지상(地上) — ground defense

방음 防音 sound arresting ; soundproof (-ing) ; sound absorption —하다 arrest 〔absorb〕 sounds ; be soundproof ; make soundproof ¶ 방음의 soundproof
— 구조 soundproof construction —실 a soundproof room — 유리 soundproof glass — 장치 soundproofing ; 〔설비〕 a silencer ; a sound arrester — 재료 soundproofing〔deadening, absorbing〕 material

방일 放逸 ⇨ 방종(放縱)

방임 放任 noninterference ; nonintervention —하다 let《a person》 alone ; leave《things》 to themselves ; let《a matter》 take its own course ; give《a person》 a free hand ; give a free rein to ¶ 사태는 방임을 불허한다 This state of affairs can't be left to itself.
—주의 a principle of noninterference ; a let-alone〔noninterference, permissive, laissez-faire〕 policy ; liberalism ; a liberal〔tolerant〕 attitude ; permissiveness ; laissez-faire《프》 ¶ 아들에게는 방임주의이다 She lets her son do as he likes.

방자 invoking evil〔curses〕 upon《a person》 ; imprecation ; damning —하다 curse ; imprecate ; wish ill of《a person》

방자 房子 a servant ; a footman

*방자 放恣 license ; self-indulgence ; impudence ; rampancy —하다 (be) impertinent ; impudent ; uppish ; licentious ; self-indulgent

방자고기 roasted meat seasoned with salt only

방잠망 防潛網 an antisubmarine net

방장 房帳 a mosquito net〔curtain〕 ; (room) curtains ¶ 방장을 치다〔걷다〕 put up〔take down〕 a mosquito net

방장 方丈 [주지] a chief priest ; an abbot ; [주승의 처소] an abbot's chamber ; the residential quarters of a high priest

방재 防材 a (wooden) boom

**방적 紡績 (cotton) spinning
— 견사(絹絲) spun silk — 공업 spinning industry — 공장 a cotton (spinning) mill — 기계 a spinning machine —사 cotton yarn —업 the spinning industry —업자 a cotton spinner — 여공 a female cotton-mill hand — 회사 a (cotton) spinning company

방전 放電 〖물리〗 electric discharge ; discharge of electricity —하다 discharge (electricity)
— 거리 striking distance —관(管) a discharge tube —등 a discharge lamp —삭(索) a discharge cable —자(子) a discharger — 전류〔전압〕 discharge current〔voltage〕 공중〔진공, 진동성〕 — atmospheric〔vacuum, oscillating〕 discharge 불꽃 — spark discharge

방점 傍點 a side dot〔point〕 ¶ 방점을 찍다 mark with a side dot

방접원 傍接圓 〖수학〗 an escribed circle

방정 a rash〔thoughtless, careless〕 act ; indiscreet behavior
—꾼〔꾸러기〕 a light-headed person ; a flighty person ; a giddy goat ; a madcap ; a rash person ; an impudent fellow

방정 方正 —하다 [언행이] (be) irreproachable ; good ; upright ; [물건이] neat and square
품행 — good moral conduct

방정떨다 act imprudently〔rashly〕 ; act on impulse ; behave in a giddy way

방정맞다 (be) light-headed ; frivolous ; giddy ; rash ; flippant

방정식 方程式 〖수학〗 an equation ¶ 방정식을 세우다 set up an equation ; equate one term with another
고차 — an equation of higher degree 극(極)— a polar equation 대수〔기하, 화학〕 — an algebraical〔a geometric, a chemical〕 equation 미분 — a differential equation 법선(法線) — a normal equation 연립 — simultaneous equations 2항 — a binominal equation 1〔2, 3〕차 — a simple〔quadratic, cubic〕 equation ; an equation of the first〔second, third〕 degree 지수 — an exponential equation

방조 幇助 assistance ; aid ; help ; backing ; countenance ; pander ; 〖법〗 aiding and abetting —하다 aid ; assist ; help ; back up ; pander ; aid and abet
—자 a supporter ; a backer ; [범죄의] an abetter 자살 —죄 being a party to a death pact ; aiding and abetting suicide

방조제 防潮堤 a tide embankment ; a sea wall

*방종 放縱 dissoluteness ; self-indulgence ; license ; looseness —하다 be loose〔unrestrained, unbridled〕 ; be dissolute〔licentious〕 ¶ 방종한 생활을 하다 lead a dissolute〔riotous〕 life

*방주 方舟 an ark ¶ 노아의 방주 Noah's ark

방주 旁註 marginal notes ¶ 방주를 붙이다 margin ; make marginal notes

방죽 an embankment ; a dike ; a bank ¶ 방죽을 쌓다 build〔throw up〕 a dike ; construct an embankment // 방죽이 언제 무너질지 모르겠다 The embankment may go any moment.

방증 傍證 circumstantial evidence
— 수집 collection of circumstantial evidence

*방지 防止 prevention ; check ; preclusion —하다 prevent ; stop ; check ; [미연에] nip in the bud ¶ 야채의 부패를 미연에 방지하다 prevent vegetables from decaying
—책(策) a preventive measure

방직 紡織 spinning and weaving ; textile manufacturing
—기 spinning and weaving machinery ; spindles and looms — (공)업 the spinning and weaving industry ; textile manufacturing —업자 a textile manufacturer

방진 方陣 a square (formation) ; a phalanx

방짜 high quality brass tableware

방책 方策 [계획] a plan ; a scheme ; [방침] a policy ; [수단] a means

방책 防柵 a palisade ; a paling ; a stockade

방천 防川 a dike ; an embankment ; a

levee ; river conservation ; flood protection —하다 shore up the river(s) ; take flood-prevention measures ¶ 방천을 쌓다 build a dike // 방천이 무너지다 a dike breaks

방첩 防諜 prevention of espionage ; anti〔counter-〕espionage ; protection from〔against〕 spying ; the detection of enemy espionage

— 강조 주간 Counterintelligence Week —대 Counter Intelligence Corps 《C. I. C》 — 대책 a counterespionage policy

방청 傍聽 hearing ; attendance ; [입장] admission —하다 hear ; attend ; listen to ; audit ; sit in on ; visit ¶ 다수〔소수〕의 방청자 a large〔small〕 audience // 재판을 방청하다 attend a trial // 일반의 방청을 허락하다 be open to the public // 회담을 방청하다 sit in on a conference // 방청 무료 Admission free. // 국회를 방청했다 They visited the National Assembly in session. // 방청은 금지되었다 The conference was conducted behind closed doors. /The court sat in camera. (법정의)/The public was excluded from the meeting. (회합의) // 방청 자유〔금지〕 The meeting is open〔closed〕 to the public.

—권 an admission ticket —료 an admission fee —석 [회의의] the (visitors') gallery ; seats for the public —인 a hearer ; [전체] an audience

방초 芳草 fragrant〔green〕 grass

방촌 方寸 [사방 한 치] a square *chi* ; [마음] the mind

방추 方錐 a square drill ¶ 방추의 pyramidal

—형(形) a pyramid shape ; pyramid (shaped)

방추 紡錘 a spindle ¶ 방추형의 spindle-shaped

방축 防築 a dike ; an embankment ; a bank ¶ 방축을 쌓다 build a dike // 방축이 무너지다 a dike breaks

방축 防縮 shrink-proofing ¶ 방축의 shrink-proof

— 가공 (처리) non-shrink treatment ; shrink-resistant finish

방축 放逐 —하다 expel 《a person》 from ; drive 《a person》 out of ; oust 《a person》 from ; [국외로] deport ; banish

방축 가공 防縮加工 ¶ 방축 가공한 pre-shrunk ; [상표 이름] Sanforized

방춘 芳春 [봄] the flowering spring ; [방년] blooming age ; the flower of youth

방출 放出 —하다 [방산] emit ; radiate ; [배출] discharge ; release ¶ 정부미를 방출하다 release government rice

— 물자 released goods

방충 防蟲 ¶ 방충 가공의 mothproof

—제 insecticide ; [좀약] a moth ball

방취 防臭 deodorization —하다 deodorize

—제(劑) a deodorizer ; a deodorant —판 a stink〔stench〕 trap ; a gas trap ; a drain trap (하수구의)

방치 放置 leaving alone ; negligence —하다 leave〔let〕 《a thing, a person》 alone ; leave 《a matter》 as it is ; leave 《a person》 to himself ; leave 《a matter》 to chance ; neglect

†**방침 方針** a course 《of action》 ; [정책] a policy ; [주의] a principle ; [계획] a plan ; [목적] a purpose ; an aim ; an object ¶ 국가의 방침 a national policy // 일정한 방침 a definite policy // 명확한 방침을 취하다 take a marked line // 방침을 잘못 잡다 pursue a wrong course of action〔policy〕 // 방침을 정하다 decide on a policy〔course of action〕 // 사업의 근본 방침을 정하다 lay the first lines of the work

근본 — a fundamental policy 시정〔교육, 외교〕 — an administrative〔an educational, a foreign〕 policy 영업 — a business policy〔plan〕 행동 — a course of action

방탄 防彈 (being) bulletproof ; protection against bullets —하다 shield from bullets

— 내각(內閣) a bulletproof cabinet for the Chief Executive —실〔헬멧〕 a bombproof room〔helmet〕 — 유리 bulletproof glass — 조끼 a bulletproof vest〔jacket〕 —창(窓) a bullet-resistant window

***방탕 放蕩** dissipation ; debauchery —하다 be dissipated ; lead a dissipated 〔dissolute〕 life ; [젊은 때의] sow one's wild oats ¶ 방탕한 자식 a prodigal son // 방탕으로 몸을 버리다 impair one's health by dissipation

— 생활 a fast〔dissipated〕 life ; fast living ; a life of follies —자 a libertine ; a rake ; a dissolute person ; a fast liver

방토 邦土 a country ; a land ; a realm

방파제 防波堤 a breakwater ; a bulwark ; a mole ¶ 방파제를 쌓다 build a breakwater

방판 方板 a square board

****방패 防牌** a shield ; a buckler (원형) ¶ 방패 모양의 shield-shaped ; scutellate ; peltate 《leaf》 // 방패삼아 [핑계·구실] on the strength〔ground〕 of ; on the plea 〔pretext〕 of 《illness》 ; on the authority of 《law》 // 나무를 방패로 삼다 use a tree as a shield 《against bullets》 ; hide 《oneself》 behind a tree // 방패막이 하다 defend〔shield〕 from ; ward off ; [구실삼다] make a pretext ; concoct a good excuse

방편 方便 expediency ; an expedient ; [수단] a means ; a device ; [도구] an instrument ¶ 일시적인 방편 a temporary expedient // 방편으로 쓰다 use 《a thing, a person》 as an instrument ; make a cat's-paw of 《a person》

방포 放砲 a blank shot —하다 fire a

blank shot
방풍 防風 protection against wind
—림 a windbreak (forest) ; a shelter belt ; a tree belt
†방학 放學 school holidays ; a vacation —하다 go on vacation ; close for a vacation ; break up for a vacation ; be free from school ; be on vacation ¶ 언제 여름 방학입니까 When are you to break up for the summer vacation ?
여름〔겨울〕— the summer〔winter〕 vacation〔holidays〕 ¶ 우리 학교는 이 달 11일부터 여름 방학이다 Our school breaks up for the summer vacation on the eleventh this month.
방한 防寒 protection against the cold —하다 keep the cold away ; ward off〔protect against〕 the cold ¶ 방한 설비를 한 자동차 a winterized car
—구 protections against the cold ; cold weather gear —모 a winter cap — 설비 provisions against the cold —화〔복〕 winter boots〔clothes〕 ; arctics
방한 訪韓 a visit to Korea —하다 visit Korea ¶ 방한 미국 사절단 an American mission to Korea
⁑방해 妨害 [장애물] an obstacle ; a hindrance ; [훼방] disturbance ; interruption ; obstruction ; interference —하다 obstruct ; disturb ; interrupt ; interfere with ; put obstacles in the way of ¶ 세계 평화에 대한 방해 an obstacle to world peace // 공부에 방해가 되다 interfere with 《a person's》 studies // 교통을 방해하다 obstruct traffic // 생산을 방해하다 obstruct〔hinder〕 production // 성공에 방해가 되다 be an obstacle to 《a person's》 success // 안면을 방해하다 disturb 《a person's》 sleep // 연설을 방해하다 interrupt a speaker // 그들은 하는 일에 방해를 받았다 They were hindered in their work. // 지금 무슨 일을 하시는데 제가 방해가 되고 있는 것은 아닙니까 Am I interrupting anything ?
—물 an obstacle ; an impediment ; an obstruction — 방송 jamming — 운동 obstructionism —자 an obstructor ; an obstructionist (특히 의사 진행 따위의) — 전술 obstructive tactics 공무 집행 — an unlawful interference with an officer in the execution of his duty 교통 — traffic obstruction 의사 진행 — a filibuster 치안 — the disturbance of public peace
방해석 方解石 〚광물〛 calcite ; calcareous spar
†방향 方向 ① [방위] direction ; bearings ; [진로] a course ¶ 반대 방향으로 in the opposite direction // 서울 방향으로 in the direction of *Seoul* // 방향을 잃다 lose one's bearings〔course〕 // 방향을 전환하다 change one's course
② [방침] one's course ; [목적] an aim 〔object〕 ¶ 방향을 바꾸다 change one's object〔course〕 《in life》 // 방향을 잘못 잡다 err from the right path ; [직업의] make an error in the choice of one's occupation
— 지시기 a direction〔traffic〕 indicator ; a turn signal ; a traficator 《영》 ; 〚항공〛 a direction indicator —판 [열차의] a route and destination plate ; [플랫폼의] a destination board 무선 — 탐지 radio direction finding 《R. D. F.》
방향 芳香 a sweet smell ; perfume ; a fragrance ; an aroma ¶ 방향이 풍기는 fragrant ; aromatic ; sweet-smelling // 방향을 풍기다 give out fragrance ; smell sweet ; spread〔send forth〕 fragrance
—제(劑) an aromatic
방향 감각 方向感覺 a sense of direction ¶ 방향 감각의 혼란 disorientation // 방향 감각이 없다 have no sense of direction
방향 전환 方向轉換 ① [방향] a change of direction〔front〕 ; a turnabout ; an about-face ; a turn ② [방침] a change of one's object〔policy, principle〕
방향타 方向舵 a (vertical) rudder
균형 — a balanced rudder
방향 탐지기 方向探知機 radar ; a direction finder
무선 — a radio compass 자동 — [항공기의] an automatic direction finder 《A. D. F.》
방형 方形 a square ¶ 방형의 square(-shaped)
방호 防護 protection ; defense ; custody —하다 protect ; defend ; have custody of
— 기관 〚생물〛 an armature —자 a protector ; a defender ; a custodian
방화 放火 incendiarism ; 〚법〛 arson ; [화재] an incendiary fire —하다 set 《a house》 on fire ; set fire to 《a house》 ¶ 그 불은 방화에 의한 것이다 The fire was incendiary.
—광(狂) incendiary mania ; [사람] an incendiary maniac ; a firebug 《미·속》 — 범(인) an incendiary〔arsonist, arsonite〕 —죄 arson ; incendiarism
방화 邦貨 [화폐] Korean money〔currency〕 ; [화물] Korean goods ¶ 방화로 환산하다 convert 《dollars》 into Korean currency
방화 邦畫 a Korean film〔motion picture, movie〕
*방화 防火 prevention of fire ; fire prevention〔protection〕 ¶ 방화에 힘쓰다 try to prevent (the spread of) a fire
— 구조〔건축〕물 a fireproof construction〔building〕 —대(帶) a firebreak — 도료(塗料) a fireproof paint —막 [극장의] a safety curtain —문〔벽〕 a fire door〔wall〕 —선(線) a firebreak ; a fire arresting line — 설비〔장치〕 fire prevention equipment ; fire protection — 셔터 a fire shutter —전(栓) a hydrant — 주간

Fire Prevention Week —포(布) fire cloth — 훈련 a fire drill

*방황 彷徨 ―하다 wander〔roam〕 about ; rove ¶ 방황하는 사람 a wanderer ; a vagabond ; a hobo 《미》// 세계를 방황하다 roam〔knock〕 about the world // 여러 곳을 방황하다 wander from place to place // 생사의 지경을 방황하다 hover between life and death ; linger on the verge of death ; be at death's door

†밭 a field ; a farm ; a garden ¶ 밭을 갈다 till〔cultivate〕 the soil ; plow
감자— a potato patch 대— a bamboo thicket (숲) 배추— a cabbage patch 보리— a barley field 사과— an apple orchard 솔— a pine grove (작은 숲) 채소— a vegetable garden 풀— a lawn ; a yard

밭갈이 plowing ; tillage ; cultivating ―하다 plow ; till ; farm ; cultivate

밭걷이 harvest ―하다 harvest ¶ 밭걷이에 바쁘다 be busy with the harvest

*밭고랑 a furrow ¶ 밭고랑을 짓다 make furrows ; furrow 《a field》

밭곡식 —穀— dry field grain〔corn〕 ; crops of a field

밭귀 a corner of a field

밭날갈이 a field so large it takes several days to get it plowed

밭농사 —農事 dry field farming

밭다[1] [장소가] (be) very close ; [인색하다] stingy ; miserly ; [시간이] be short of time ; be pressed for time ; [기침이] (be) dry ; hacking ; habitual

밭다[2] [졸아붙다] boil away to nothing

밭다[3] [거르다] filter ; strain ; leach ; percolate ¶ 술을 밭다 strain rice liquor // 모래로 물을 밭다 filter〔percolate〕 water through sand // 커피 찌꺼기를 밭아 내다 strain coffee to remove the grounds

밭도랑 a ditch (for draining or irrigating)

밭두둑 a ridge (making the boundaries between fields)

밭둑 an embankment around the end of a field

밭뒤다 repeatedly plow a field

밭매기 weeding a dry field ―하다 weed (in) a dry field

밭머리 the two sides of a field at right angles to the ridges and ditches

밭문서 —文書 a (title) deed

밭벼 a dry-field rice plant ; upland〔hill〕 rice

밭보리 barley (planted in a dry field)

밭사돈 —査頓 father of one's son-in-law〔daughter-in-law〕

밭어버이 the father ; the male parent

밭은기침 a dry〔consumptive, habitual〕 cough ; a (dry) hack ¶ 그는 밭은기침을 한다 He has a dry hack.

밭이다 be〔get〕 filtered〔strained, drained〕 ; filter 《out》 ; strain 《through, out》

밭이랑 plowed rows in a field

밭일 farming ; field work ―하다 work in the fields

밭장다리 a bow-legged person ¶ 밭장다리의 X-legged ; bow-legged

밭쟁이 a kitchen gardener

밭치다 ⇨ 밭다[3]

*배[1] ① [복부] the abdomen ; the belly ; the bowels ; the stomach

> 참고 **belly**는 「복부」 「위」와 「장」을 포함하는 부분으로서 과히 점잖은 말이 못되고 특히 부인들 앞에서는 사용하지 않는 것으로 되어 있다 **stomach**는 「위」 「속」이라는 뜻으로서 belly에 비하여 점잖고 흔히 쓰이는 말 **abdomen**은 해부학상의 말 따라서 곤충의 복부에 대해서도 쓰는 말 **bowels**는 「장」「내장」이라는 뜻으로 보통 복수형으로 쓰인다

¶ 배가 고프다 be hungry // 배가 부르다 one's stomach is full // 배가 아프다 have a stomachache ; one's stomach aches 〔pains one〕 // 뱃속이 좋지 않다 My bowels are irregular. // 너 요즘 배가 좀 나왔다 You're gotten a bit of a paunch lately. // 배의 어디가 가장 아프십니까 Where does your abdomen hurt most ?
② [뱃속] heart ; mind ; intention ¶ 배가 시꺼멓다 be black-hearted ; be wicked ; be evil-hearted // 배가 맞다 be in cahoots 《미·속》 ; be thick ; fall in love with each other (남녀간) // 배가 아프다 be green with〔out of〕 envy
③ [태] a womb ¶ 후처의 배에서 생긴 자식 a child born of one's second wife // 배가 부르다 be big with child ; be in the family way // 배가 다르다 be born of a different mother ; be half-blooded

†배[2] [선박] a vessel ; a ship ; a boat ; craft 《총칭》 ; a steamer (기선) ; a motor ship (동력선) ; a junk (중국의) ¶ 배에 강한〔약한〕 사람 a good〔poor〕 sailor // 배 안에서 in〔on〕 a ship ; on board a ship // 다음 배편으로 by the next boat // 배를 타다 take〔catch〕 a ship ; embark〔go on board〕 (a ship) // 배를 젓다 row a boat // 배에서 내리다 leave〔get off〕 a ship // 부산에서 배를 타다 take a boat at *Pusan* // 배로 갑니까 Do you go by boat〔steamer〕 ?
—벌레 a shipworm 놀잇— a pleasure boat ; a barge

‡배[3] a pear
—나무 a pear tree

배 胚 〖식물〗 an embryo ; 〖동물〗 an embryo ; a fetus

†배 倍 [2배] double ; twice ; two times ; twofold ; [···배] times ; fold ¶ 3천배의 질산은 용액 a 1/3000 silver nitrate solution // 50배의 망원경 a telescope of 50 magnifications // 배가 되다 double ; be doubled 《in value》 // 배로 하다 double // 3배로 하다 treble // 배반이 길다〔많다〕 be one and a half times as long〔many〕 //

(돈을) 배로 해서 돌려주다 repay double the original amount // A의 2배 크기이다 be twice〔two times〕 as large as A // 5배로 앙등하다 go up fivefold // 그렇게 하면 비용이 배가 든다 It would cost twice as much as that. /It would cost as much again as that. // 이것은 비용이 예전보다 배나 올랐다 This costs double what it did before. // 당신은 내 나이의 두 배다 You are double my age.

배- 排 anti ¶ 배일 정책(排日政策) an anti-Japanese policy

-배 輩 a fellow ; people ¶ 불량배 a hoodlum ; a hooligan

배가 倍加 doubling **—하다** double ; be doubled ; increase double〔twofold〕 ¶ 노력을 배가하다 redouble one's efforts // 수입을 배가하다 double the income // 인구가 배가한다 The population doubles〔is doubled〕.

배갈 a kind of Chinese liquor

배겨나다 bear up 《under》; put up 《with》; suffer patiently 《through》 ¶ 그는 십년 동안 갖은 고생에 배겨났다 He put up with all sorts of hardship for ten years.

배겨내다 ⇨ 배기다²

배격 排擊 rejection ; denouncement
—하다 reject ; denounce ; condemn ¶ 파시즘을 배격하다 reject〔oppose〕 Fascism

배견 拜見 inspection ; looking at **—하다** see ; look at ; inspect ; have a look at ¶ 혜한(惠翰)은 틀림없이 배견하였습니다 Your letter was duly received.

***배경 背景** ① a background ; [무대의] scenery ; setting ; a scene ¶ 지는 해를 배경으로 하여 against the setting sun // 동양을 배경으로 한 소설 a novel with an Oriental setting // 배경을 그리다 paint scenes // 산을 배경으로 해서 사진을 찍다 photograph 《a person》 with a hill for background
② [후원] backing ; support ; [사람] a backer ; a supporter ; a patron ; a booster 《미》 ¶ 배경이 없다 have no pull behind 《one》 // 그에게는 정치적 배경이 없다 He has no political backing.
—막 a backdrop **— 음악** background (music) **—포(布)** a back cloth **—화** scene painting ; a set scene **— 화가** a scene painter

배계 拜啓 Dear Sir ; Dear Madam ; (My) Dear Mr. 〔Mrs.〕《A》; [남성 복수] Gentlemen ; Messrs. 《A and B》; [여성 복수] Mesdames〔Ladies〕

†배고프다 (be) hungry ; feel hungry ; (be) sharp-set ¶ 배고파 죽게 하다 hunger 《a person》 to death // 배고파 죽겠다 I'm simply starving. 《구》/I am dying with hunger. /I am (as) hungry as a hunter〔hawk〕. // 배고파서는 일할 수 없다 You cannot work on an empty stomach.

배고픈 호랑이 중이나 개를 헤아리지 않는다 속담 Beggars must〔should〕 be no choosers. /Never look a gift horse in the mouth.
배고픈 때에는 침만 삼켜도 낫다 속담 A crust is better than no bread. /Poor folks are glad of porridge.

배곯다 have an empty stomach ¶ 그는 배곯고 지낸다 He always goes hungry.

배공 胚孔 〖동물〗 a foramen ; the alimentary cavity of an embryo

배관 配管 pipe laying **—하다** lay a pipe **—공(工)** a plumber **— 공사** piping work

배관 拜觀 inspection ; visit **—하다** (humbly) inspect ; look at ; view ; visit 《a shrine》 ¶ 배관의 영예를 입다 have the honor of seeing // 배관을 허락받다 be allowed to visit

배광 背光 ⇨ 후광

배교 背敎 apostasy ; perversion of faith **—하다** renegade ; become an apostate **—자** an apostate ; a renegade ; a pervert ¶ 배교자가 되다 apostatize

배구 排球 volleyball **—하다** play volleyball
— 시합 a volleyball game

배구 倍舊 ¶ 배구의 increased // 배구의 애호를 바랍니다 I solicit your increased 〔further〕 patronage.

배금 拜金 money worship ; worship of the Almighty Dollar 《미》
—주의 mammonism **—주의자** a money worshiper ; a mammonist

배급 配給 distribution ; supply ; rationing (통제) **—하다** distribute 《things among, to》; supply 《a person with things》; ration ; serve out ¶ 배급제가 되다 be put on rations ; be under the rationing system // 물품이 부족하면 배급받게 된다 Citizens are rationed when supplies are scarce.
—계(원) a supplier ; distributor **— 기관** a distribution organ〔machinery〕 **— 기구** a distribution system〔structure〕 **—량** a ration **— 루트** a distribution channel **—미** rationed rice **— 제도** a distribution 〔rationing〕 system **— 통장** a ration card〔book〕 **— 통제** distribution control **—표** a ration ticket **—품** rationed goods **식량 —** food rationing

배급소 配給所 a distributing〔supply〕 station〔point〕; a distribution〔ration〕 point 〔center〕; a ration board 《미》
영화 — a film-distribution office

배기 排氣 ventilation ; exhaust ; [폐기] used steam
— 가스 waste gas ; exhaust (gas) **—갱(坑)** an upset gallery **—관** an exhaust 〔eduction〕 pipe ; [통풍관] a vent pipe **—구(口)** an exhaust pipe **—기(機)** a ventilator **—량** engine〔piston〕 displacement **— 장치** an air exhauster〔escape〕 **—판(瓣)** an exhaust〔eduction〕 valve ; a

cutout (내연 기관의) — **펌프** an air pump

배기다¹ [마치다] be hard ; pinch ; squeeze ¶ 의자가 등에 배기다 a seat is hard on one's back

*** 배기다²** endure ; stand ; put up with ; withstand ; hold out ¶ 시련에 배기다 bear〔endure, withstand〕 a trial // 공격에 배기다 withstand an attack // 배길 수 없다 be beyond one's perseverance ; be past bearing // 더 이상 못 배기겠다 This is more than I can endure. /This is too much. /I can't stand this any more. // 더 이상 더위에 못 배기겠다 I can't stand this heat any longer. // 그가 그 고통에 배길 수 있을까 Can he stand the pain ? // 그가 끝까지 배길 수 있을까 Can he hold out to the last ? // 폐병 환자도 2·3년은 죽지 않고 배길 수 있다 A consumptive person may hold out for years.

배꼬다 twist ⇨ 비꼬다

배꼽 the navel ; the umbilicus 《*pl.* -ci》 ¶ 내민 배꼽 a protruding navel
—노리 the neighborhood of the navel **—쟁이** a person with a protruding navel **—점(占)** fortunetelling by dominoes **—참외** a melon with a navel-like formation at the top

배끗거리다 ① [어긋나다] fail to fit smoothly ; do not join properly ; will not go in as it should ② [일이] go amiss 〔astray, awry, wrong, haywire 《속》〕 ; get out of line ¶ 일이 늘 배끗거린다 Somehow everything I do seems to go 〔to come out〕 wrong.

배끗배끗 ① [어긋나다] not fitting properly ; not going in as it should ; not joining smoothly ② [일이] (going) amiss ; astray ; awry ; wrong ; (getting) out of line ¶ 일이 배끗배끗 잘 안된다 The thing just doesn't turn out right.

배낭 胚囊 〖식물〗 an embryo sac ; a megaspore

*** 배낭 背囊** a knapsack ; a pack ; a rucksack 《도》 ¶ 배낭을 메다 strap on a knapsack // 배낭을 내려놓다 take off a knapsack // 배낭에 물건을 넣다 pack a knapsack with things ; pack things in a knapsack

배내 breeding animals from another person's stock and sharing the offspring with him ¶ 배냇닭 chickens raised on a share-basis

배내- from birth ; inborn ; a baby's ; of a newborn baby
배냇냄새 the smell of a newborn baby **배냇니** a milk tooth ; the first set of teeth **배냇머리** downy hair of a baby **배냇병** a connate disease **배냇병신** a congenital deformity〔cripple〕 **배냇소경** a person born blind

배내똥 the first feces〔excrements〕 of a newborn baby ; the last feces of a dying person

배내옷 clothes for a newborn infant

배냇짓 the twitching of a newborn baby's face while asleep

배농 排膿 〖의학〗 drainage 《of a wound》 **—하다** drain 《a wound》 of pus

배뇨 排尿 urination **—하다** urinate ; pass one's urine ; pass〔make〕 water
— 과다증 diuresis **—통(痛)** dysuria (곤란)

배다¹ [조밀하다] (be) close ; dense ; thick ¶ 올이 밴 옷감 a cloth of fine 〔close〕 texture // 배게 closely ; compactly ; leaving no space // 나무를 배게 심다 plant trees close together // 씨를 배게 뿌리다 sow seeds thickly

배다² ① [침윤] soak〔sink〕 into ; filter into ; spread (잉크 따위가) ; permeate 《the soil》 ¶ 물이 벽에 배다 water soaks into the wall // 땀이 셔츠에 배다 one's shirt is soaked through with perspiration〔is wet with sweat〕 // 붕대에 피가 배어 있었다 The bandage was saturated with blood. // 독한 냄새가 방안에 배어 있다 A powerful scent permeates the room.
② [익숙하다] be familiar 《with》 ; get used 《to》 ; grow〔become〕 accustomed 《to》 ; become habituated 《to》 ¶ 손에 밴 일 a familiar job ; a job one has had some experience with // (일이) 손에 배다 get one's hand accustomed 《to》 ; get skilled 《in》 // 음주의 습성이 몸에 배다 fall into〔get, contract〕 the bad habit of drinking // 그의 연기는 아직 몸에 배어 있지 않다 There is something unnatural〔artificial〕 in his acting〔performance〕.

배다³ [잉태하다] conceive ; get〔become〕 pregnant ¶ 아이를 배다 conceive a child ; be with child ; be pregnant ; be in the family way ; be in an interesting condition ; be knocked up (미·속) ; be with young (동물이) // 배게 하다 get a woman with child ; put a woman in the family way // 어느 외국인의 아이를 뱄다 She is with child by a certain foreigner. // 저 여자는 아이를 뱄다 She is big with child.

배다⁴ ⇨ 배우다

배다르다 be (born) of a different mother ; be half-blood ¶ 배다른 형제 half-brothers〔sisters〕 ; a stepbrother〔stepsister〕

배다리 a pontoon bridge ¶ 배다리를 놓다 build a pontoon bridge 《across a river》
배다릿집 a house with a pontoon bridge in front of the gate

배달 倍達 (the earliest name for) Korea **—민족〔겨레〕** the Korean race〔people〕

†배달 配達 delivery **—하다** deliver 《things to a person, at a place》 ; distribute ¶ 무료로 배달되다 be delivered free // 물품을 가정에 배달하다 deliver articles at 《a person's》 house // 신문을 배달하다 deliver

newspapers // 대금은 배달시 지불한다 The cash will be paid on delivery. // 우편은 하루에 두 번 배달된다 Letters are delivered twice a day.
— 구역 a delivery zone〔radius〕; [우편] a postal delivery zone〔district《영》〕 —료 delivery charge — 불능 편지 a dead letter ; a blind letter (주소 성명 불명으로) —용 트럭 a delivery van —원 a carrier ; a deliveryman ; a distributor ; [우편] a postman《영》; a mailman《미》; a letter carrier ; [우유] a milkman ; [신문] a newsboy — 증명서 a delivery certificate〔receipt〕 — 증명 우편 certified mail — 착오 misdelivery ; miscarriage 무료 — free delivery 시내 — local delivery 우편 — mail delivery 특별 — special delivery

배당 配當 allotment ; a dividend (주주의) — 하다 allot ; pay a dividend ¶ 이익 배당을 받다 share in the profits // 이익 배당이 없다 pass a dividend // 보통주에 대하여 6부의 이익 배당을 했다 A dividend of 6 percent on the common shares was paid.
— 공제 a tax credit for dividends received —락(落) ex dividend《ex div.》 —률 dividend rate —부(附) cum dividend《cum div.》; dividend on — 소득 income from (stock) dividends —안 a proposed dividend arrangement ; a scheme of distribution — 통지서 a dividend notice 무— non dividend《non div.》 우선 — a preferred dividend 주식 — stock dividend 특별 — an extra dividend《on stocks》; a plum ; a bonus

배당금 配當金 a share ; a dividend ¶ 배당금을 발표하다 declare a dividend
특별 — a bonus《on stocks》; an extra dividend

배덕 背德 immorality ; demoralization ; corruption ¶ 배덕의 immoral ; corrupt —자 an immoral〔a corrupt, a depraved〕 person ; a scoundrel ; a blackguard — 행위 immoral conduct

배돌다 keep to oneself ; avoid mixing with people ; keep aloof from others

배동바지 the time when the rice plant starts bearing grains

배두렁이 a belly band for a baby

배둥근끌 a "round-bellied" chisel (used in sculpture)

배둥근대패 a "round-bellied" plane

*배드민턴 badminton

배듬하다 ⇨ 비스듬하다

배때기 stomach ; belly

배때벗다 (be) arrogant ; haughty ; insolent

배뚜로 aslant ; obliquelys ; slopewise

배뚜름하다, 빼뚜름하다 (be) inclined ; slant ; crooked

배뚤다 ⇨ 비뚤다

배라먹다 ⇨ 빌어먹다

배란 排卵 ovulation — 하다 ovulate

배랑뱅이 a beggar ; a tramp ; a hobo

배래 the offing ; the open sea ¶ 배래에 in the offing ; offshore ; off the shore 〔coast〕; out at sea ; off

배래기 the abdominal region〔belly〕 of a fish ; [옷소매의] strip of cloth along the sleeve-seam

배럴 a barrel《용량의 단위》

†배려 配慮 care ; concern ; consideration ; [진력] trouble ; [알선] good offices — 하다 take the trouble ; consider ¶ 세심한 배려 careful concern ; thoughtful consideration // …의 배려로 through the good offices of《a person》// 배려하여 주셔서 감사합니다 I am very much obliged to you. /Thank you very much for your trouble〔what you have done for me〕.

배례 拜禮 a salutation ; a salute ; worship — 하다 bow down ; salute ; worship

배롱나무 『식물』 a crape myrtle ; Lagerstroemia indica (학명)

배리 背理 unreasonableness ; irrationality ; absurdity ; paralogism ; unnaturalness ¶ 배리의 unreasonable ; irrational ; absurd ; contrary to reason ; unnatural

배리다 (be) fishy ; bloody ⇨ 비리다

배리착지근하다 (be) somewhat fishy

배릿배릿 disgusting ; sickening

배릿하다 (be) somewhat fishy ⇨ 비릿하다

배맞다 have illicit intercourse ; commit adultery《with》

배메기 sharecropping on a fifty-fifty basis《미》; sharing a tenant crop equally with the landlord

배면 背面 the back ; the rear ¶ 배면 공격 an attack from the rear // 적의 배면을 공격하다 attack the enemy in the rear
— 공격 an attack from the rear ; a rear attack — 비행 an inverted flight — 포격 a reverse fire

배명 拜命 — 하다 [명령을] receive an order ; have the word ; [임명] accept an appointment ; be appointed《to》

배목 『건축』 an eyebolt (to receive a door-ring) ; a staple

배문 拜聞 — 하다 hear ; be informed of

배미 a strip〔piece, patch〕 of rice paddy ; an individual rice paddy ¶ 논 두 배미 two strips of paddy ; two paddies // 논배미 an individual rice paddy // 논배미가 크다 have a big (strip of) rice paddy

배밀이[1] [어린아이의] crawl ; creeping — 하다 crawl ; creep

배밀이[2] [대패] a three-groove plane ; [대패질] planing the triple groove on a *changsal*

*배반 背反 ① [위배] going against ; running counter《to》; acting contrary《to》 — 하다 go against ; be contrary to ; run counter to ; act contrary to ; betray ¶ 양친의 의사를 배반하다 go against one's

parents' wishes // 기대를 배반하다 be contrary to《a person's》 expectations // 신뢰를 배반하다 prove false to〔betray〕《a person's》 trust // 약속을 배반하다 go back on〔break〕 one's promise〔word〕
② [반역] betrayal ; revolt ; rebellion **—하다** betray ; rebel〔revolt, rise〕 against ; turn traitor to ; turn against《on, upon》 ¶ 나라를 배반하다 betray one's country ; turn traitor to one's country // 친구를 배반하다 turn against one's friend ; go back on one's friend // 아내에게 배반당하다 be betrayed by one's wife

배반 胚盤 〚생물〛 the germinal disk ; the blastodisk

배반자 背反者 a betrayer ; a traitor ; a double-crosser《미·속》; [변절자] a turncoat ; a quisling ; a rat《속》; a ratter ; [밀고자] an informer ; a squealer《미·구》; [파업의] a strikebreaker ; a scab ; a blackleg《영·구》

배배 ⇨ 비비

배백 拜白 "Yours very truly" ; "From"

배번 背番 a uniform number

배변 排便 a bowel movement **—하다** evacuate〔open〕 the bowels

배복 拜伏 humbly prostrating oneself **—하다** humbly prostrate oneself

배복 拜復 In reply to your letter〔favor〕; Dear Sirs ; This is to acknowledge your letter...〔Thank you for your kind letter, In reply...〕

배본 配本 delivery of a book ; distribution of subscribed books **—하다** deliver a book ; distribute subscribed books

배부 背部 the back ; 〚해부〛 the dorsum《*pl.* -sa》 ¶ 배부의 dorsal ; posterior

배부 配付 distribution ; delivery **—하다** distribute《among, to》; deliver《to》

배부 개가 背夫改嫁 —하다 betray one's husband and marry another man

배부 도주 背夫逃走 —하다 betray one's husband and run away

⁑배부르다 (be) full ; have a full stomach ; (be) replete《with》; have enough of《one's stomach》 ¶ 배부르게 먹다 eat one's fill ; eat heartily ; have enough〔plenty〕; eat to one's heart's content ; make a good square meal ; be satiated with ; do ample justice《to a dinner》; make〔have〕 a hearty meal of《속》// 배부르게 지내다 be well off ; live in comfort // 배부른 소리하다 talk high and mightly // 배부른 흥정을 하다 do not care whether one makes a deal or not ; be indifferent to the outcome of a transaction ; [비유적] adopt an attitude of indifference to《a thing》; do not care whether《a person》 does something or not ; be not particularly interested in〔concerned about〕 doing something ; take a standoffish attitude // 오늘밤은 정말 배부르게 먹었다 I really stuffed myself tonight.

배부른 흥정 관용 a take-it-or-leave-it sale〔deal, proposition〕; indifference to the outcome《of a transaction》

배부장나리 a potbellied person

배분 配分 ⇨ 분배

배불뚝이 a person with a potbelly

배불리 (eating one's fill) heartily ¶ 배불리 먹었습니다 I have had more than enough.

배불리다 fill one's stomach ¶ 남의 것으로 자기를 배불리다 appropriate other's property for〔unto〕 oneself ; take care of oneself〔feather one's own nest〕 at other people's expense

배붙이기 silkcotton fabric ; a fabric woven of〔with〕 silk and cotton in the warp and weft〔with silk on the outside〕

배비 配備 arrangement ; disposition ; placement ; stationing **—하다** arrange ; distribute ; dispose ; place

배사 拜辭 refusal ; declining ; excusing oneself《from》 **—하다** decline ; refuse ; excuse oneself《from》 ¶ 호의는 감사하나 이번 일은 배사하겠습니다 Thank you for your kindness in offering the job, but I wish to be excused from it.

배사 背斜 〚지질〛 anticline ¶ 배사의 anticlinal
— 습곡(褶曲)〔축〕 an anticlinal fold〔axis〕

배사 背射 reverse fire

배상 拜上 ① [올림] sending (a letter) **—하다** send (a letter) ② [편지에서] "Yours truly" ; "From"

⁑배상 賠償 reparation ; indemnity ; compensation **—하다** indemnify《for》; make reparation《for》; compensate《for》 ¶ 손해 배상 소송 a damage suit ; an action for damages // 배상으로서 in reparation《for》// 배상을 청구하다 demand reparation〔compensation〕《for》; claim《against a company》 for compensation ; seek redress // 손해를 배상하다 pay for damage (done) ; indemnify《a person》 for damage // 그를 상대로 손해 배상의 소송을 제기하다 bring an action for damage against him
— 문제《discuss》 the reparations problem **— 요구** claim for compensation **— 의무** liability for reparation **—자** an indemnitor ; a compensator **— 책임** a liability of reparation **— 청구권** the right to demand compensation **— 협정** a reparation treaty **손해 —** compensation ; indemnity **현물〔금전〕 —** reparation in kind〔cash〕

배상금 賠償金 indemnities ; reparations ; damages ; a tender ¶ 배상금을 지불하다 pay indemnities〔reparations〕// 배상금을 받다 recover damages // 다액의 배상금을 요구하다 demand a large indemnity ; claim heavy compensation

배상꾼 an insolent and sly person

배상부리다 act conceited and cunning ; be insolent and sly

배상주의 賠償主義 (the theory of punishment as) social reparation

배색 配色 arrangement of color ; coloration ; coloring ; a color scheme —하다 arrange the colors ; do the colors〔coloring〕 ¶ 배색이 좋다〔나쁘다〕 The colors match well〔badly〕.

배서 背書 (an) endorsement —하다 endorse《a check》; back《a bill》
—인(人) an endorser 피(被)—인(人) an endorsee

배석 陪席 sitting with a superior —하다 act in an associate capacity ; sit with《one's superior》
—자 an attendant — 판사 an associate judge

배선 配船 allocation〔arrangement, assignment〕 of vessels〔ships〕 —하다 place〔assign〕 a ship《on the European route》

배선 配線 wiring ; distributing wires ; [전선] a service wire ; a power line —하다 wire《a house》
—도 a wiring diagram —반(盤) a distributing board ; [전자 계산기의] a plugboard — 손료 a charge for wear and tear on the distributing wires 전기 — electric wiring

배설 排泄 excretion ; evacuation —하다 excrete ; evacuate
—강(腔) a cloaca《*pl.* -cae》 —관 an emunctory ; a nephridium《*pl.* -dia》 —기(器) an excretive〔excretory〕 organ —물 excrement ; excretion ; ejection ; dejection ; evacuation ; egesta ; excreta ; ejecta ; evacuated matter ; ordure ; f(a)eces ; output (분뇨 이외의, 신진 대사에 의한) ; liquid (body) wastes (오줌) ; solid body wastes (똥) —선(腺) an excretory gland — 작용 evacuation

배설 排設 preparation ; arrangement —하다 prepare ; arrange ¶ 연석을 배설하다 prepare banquet seats

배설 排雪 clearing〔removing〕 of snow ; snow clearing〔removal〕 —하다 remove〔clear〕 snow

배성 陪星 〖천문〗 a satellite ; a moon

배속 配屬 attachment ; assignment —하다 attach ; assign
— 장교 a military officer attached to a school

****배수 排水** drainage ; sewerage (하수) ; pumping out (펌프로) —하다 pump out《water》; drain《a place》 ¶ 그 땅은 배수가 잘된다 The ground is well drained. // 그 배의 배수량은 1,500톤이다 She displaces 1,500 tons.
— 공사 drainage works —관 a drainpipe —구(溝)〔로〕 a waterway ; a drainage way ; a drain〔drainage〕 ditch —구(口) an overflow ; 〖건축〗 a beak —기(器) a drainer — 작업 draining (work) ; pumping out — 지역 a catchment area〔basin〕; a drainage area — 톤수 displacement (tonnage) — 펌프 a drainage〔drain〕 pump

배수 拜受 receiving《a thing from a person》 with thanks ; acceptance —하다 receive《a thing, a gift》 with thanks ; accept ; be grateful to receive ¶ 혜서는 배수하였습니다 I acknowledge receipt of your letter. /Your letter has just come to hand. /Thank you for your kind letter.

배수 倍數 a multiple ; a double number
— 비례 multiple proportion — 염색체 a diploid 공— a common multiple

배수 配水 supply〔distribution〕 of water ; water supply —하다 supply〔distribute〕 water
—관 a water pipe ; a conduit pipe —지(池) a water(-supply) reservoir ; a distributing reservoir —탑 standpipe ; a water tower

배수량 排水量 displacement ¶ 배수량이 3만톤이다 have a displacement of 30,000 tons/displace 30,000 tons
수상〔수중〕 — a surface〔submerged〕 displacement

배수성 背水性 〖식물〗 negative hydrotropism

배수진 背水陣 a position taken up with a river behind the troops ; burning the bridges〔boats〕 (behind one)
배수진을 치다 관용 fight with one's back to the wall ; have one's retreat cut off

배숙 —熟 boiled pear preserved in honey

배스듬하다 be slightly inclined ; be a bit askew ; be a bit off-center ⇨ 비스듬하다 ¶ 모자를 배스듬히 쓰다 have one's hat on askew

배승 陪乘 riding in the same car〔carriage〕 —하다 ride in the same carriage〔car〕《with one's superior》; attend on《one's superior》 in the same carriage〔car〕

배시 陪侍 attendance —하다 wait upon〔attend on, accompany, follow〕《one's superior》

배식 陪食 dining with《one's superior》 —하다 have the honor of dining with《one's superior》; partake of a dinner with《one's superior》

***배신 背信** betrayal ; infidelity —하다 betray《a person's》 confidence ; break faith
—자 a betrayer ; a turncoat (변절자) ; an informer (밀고자) — 행위 a breach of faith ; an act of treachery ; a double cross (미·속)

배신 陪臣 an attendant ; a retinue (of attendants)

배심 背心 a traitorous mind ; a treacherous mind

배심 陪審 jury —하다 hold jury ; partic-

ipate in a trial as a juryman
— 재판 a trial by jury — 제도 the jury system
배심원 陪審員 [총칭] a jury ; [개인] a juryman ; a juror
—석 the jury box 대— a grand juror 보결 — a talesman (방청인 중에서 선정한)
배쌈 the sides of a ship and their rims
배아 胚芽 an embryo bud ; a germ
—미 rice with embryo buds ; partly polished rice ; rice with germs ; whole rice
배악비 the cloth lining in Korean leather shoes
배알 entrails ; guts ⇨ 창자
배알 拜謁 an audience 《with the king》; court presentation —하다 be received in audience 《by His〔Her〕 Majesty》; have an audience with 《His Majesty》
배앓이 〖의학〗 colic ; gripes ; stomach trouble(s) ¶ 배앓이를 앓다 have stomach trouble
배액 倍額 double the amount ; twice the cost ¶ 배액의 임금을 받다 receive double pay
— 지불 조항 〖보험〗 the double indemnity clause
배양 培養 cultivation ; culture (세균의) ; nurture —하다 cultivate ; raise ; grow ¶ 굴의 배양 oyster culture
—균 cultured bacteria —기(基) a culture medium ; a medium —법 a method of cultivation ; a method of culture (세균의) —소 a farm ; a nursery ; a culture ground —액(液) a culture fluid〔solution〕 —자 a cultivator ; a culturist — 접시 a culture dish〔plate〕 —종 a cultigen —지 a culture ground 《for microbes》 —토 culture soil 세균 — germiculture ; cultivation of bacteria 시험관 — test-tube culture 인공 — artificial culture 조직 — tissue culture
배어루러기 an animal with a mottled belly
⁑배역 配役 the cast 《of a play》 ¶ 배역을 정하다 cast〔assign〕 a part to 《players》
— 명단 the cast (of characters〔players〕) (연극의)
배역 背逆 betrayal ; turning against 〔upon〕; rebellion —하다 betray ; turn against〔upon〕; rebel against
†배열 排列 arrangement ; disposition —하다 arrange ; dispose ; put〔place〕 in order ; array ¶ ABC순으로 배열하다 arrange in alphabetical order
배엽 排列 〖식물〗 a germinal layer ; a germ layer
배영 背泳 the backstroke (swim) —하다 swim the backstroke ; backstroke
— 선수 a backstroke swimmer
배외 拜外 ¶ 배외의 pro-foreign ; pro-alien ; xenophilous
— 사상 pro-foreign ideas ; pro-alienism —주의자 a xenophile
배외 排外 antiforeign —하다 be antiforeign ; exclude as foreign ¶ 배외의 antiforeign ; anti-alien
— 사상〔감정〕 antiforeign ideas〔feeling〕 —열(熱) antiforeign fever ; xenophobia — 운동 an antiforeign movement〔agitation〕 —주의 exclusionism ; exclusivism ; [맹목적] chauvinism ; [호전적] jingoism —주의자 an exclusionist ; an exclusivist ; a chauvinist ; a jingo 《*pl.* -es》; a jingoist
⁑배우 俳優 a player ; an actor (남자) ; an actress (여자) ; [광대] a minstrel ¶ 배우가 되다 go on the stage ; become an actor〔actress〕
— 학교 a school of acting — 학교 학생 a student of acting 무대 — a stage actor 〔actress〕 영화 — a film actor〔actress〕 인기 — a star ; star actor〔actress〕 일류 — a great〔an eminent〕 actor〔star〕; a headliner 《미》; a topliner 《영》
†배우다 learn ; take lessons 《in, on》; be taught ; study ; [연습] practice ; be trained 《in》

> 참고 **learn**은 「배워 익히다」라는 뜻으로서 꼭히 노력의 뜻이 포함되어 있지는 않다 한편 **study**는 익히기 위하여 노력하며 「배우다, 연구하다」의 의미

¶ 영어를 배우다 learn〔study〕 English // 피아노를 배우다 take lessons on the piano // 수영을 배우다 learn how to swim // 책으로 배우다 learn from books // 완전히 배우다 learn to perfect ; master // 요리 〔꽃꽂이, 양재〕를 배우다 take lessons in culinary art〔flower arrangement, foreign dressmaking〕 // 장사를 배우다 be trained to trade // 나는 김 교수로부터 불어를 배웠다 I was taught French by Prof. *Kim.* // 무슨 과목을 배우고 있습니까 What subjects are you studying? // 수년간 권투를 배웠다 I got training in boxing for years. // 어디서 한국말을 배웠습니까 Where did you pick up korean? // 어린이들은 외국어를 빨리 배운다 Children pick up a foreign language quickly.
*배우자 配偶者 a match ; a mate ; a life partner ; a spouse ; a yokefellow ¶ 적당한 배우자를 고르다 get a suitable match for one
배우자 配偶子 〖생물〗 a gamete
배움 learning ; study ¶ 배움의 길 (the pursuit of) learning // 배움에 뜻을 두다 aspire to learning
배움배움 scholarly attainments ; learning ; scholarship ¶ 배움배움이 없다 be illiterate // 배움배움이 많다 be learned ; be erudite
배움터 a place where learning is taking place ; a school
†배웅 seeing 《a person》 off ; a send-off —하다 see off ; give a send-off ; see 《a person's》 departure ¶ 배웅하러 가다 go

to see 《a person》 off // 현관까지 배웅하다 see 《a person》 to the porch // 배웅하러 정거장에 갔다 왔다 I have been to the station to see 《a friend》 off. // 많은 사람이 김 박사를 배웅하러 나왔다 Many people came to give Dr. *Kim* a send-off.

배유 胚乳 『식물』 an albumen ; an endosperm ¶ 배유가 있는 albuminous

배율 倍率 magnification ; magnifying power ¶ 10배율의 망원경 a fieldglass of ten magnifications

—기(器) a multiplier ; a multiplicator

⁑**배은(망덕) 背恩(忘德)** ingratitude ; ungratefulness **—하다** be ungrateful ; lose one's gratitude 《to》 ; forget kindness〔benefits〕 received ¶ 배은망덕한 ungrateful ; insensible of 《a person's》 kindness // 배은망덕한 짓을 하다 act ungratefully

—자 an ingrate ; an ungrateful person

배음 倍音 『물리』 harmonics ; 『음악』 an overtone ; a harmonic (tone)

배일 排日 anti-Japanese **—하다** exclude 〔oppose〕 the Japanese ; be anti-Japanese

— 감정 anti-Japanese sentiment〔feeling〕 ; Japanophobia **—론자** an anti-Japanist **— 운동** an anti-Japanese movement〔campaign〕

배일성 背日性 『식물』 negative heliotropism ; apheliotropism

배임 背任 misfeasance in office ; misappropriation ; breach of trust ¶ 배임죄로 문초받다 be charged with misfeasance in office

—죄 breach of trust〔faith〕 ; misfeasance in office ; misappropriation **— 행위** an act in violation of one's duty

배자 胚子 an embryo

배자 排字 arrangement of letters **—하다** arrange letters

배자 褙子 a vest

배재기 a pregnant woman

배전 倍前 ¶ 배전의 redoubled // 배전의 애호를 바랍니다 We solicit your increased patronage.

배전 配電 supply of electric power ¶ 배전을 중지하다 cut off the electric supply

—기 a power distributor **—선** a service wire ; a distribution line **—소** a power distribution station ; a lighting plant **—함** a switch box **— 회사** a power distribution company ; an electric power supply company **교류 —** alternating current distribution

***배전반 配電盤** a distributing board 〔plane〕 ; switchboard ; a panel board

배젊다 (be) very young

배점 配點 distribution〔allotting〕 of marks **—하다** allot 《15 points to a question》

배정 配定 allocation ; apportionment ; assignment **—하다** allot〔assign〕 《work》 to 《each student》 ; allocate 《shares》 to 《persons》 ; apportion 《one's property among one's sons》

배정과 —正果 sliced pears preserved in honey

배젖 胚— albumen ; endosperm ¶ 배젖이 있는 albuminous

***배제 排除** exclusion ; elimination ; removal **—하다** exclude ; eliminate ; remove ¶ 그런 가능성을 완전히 배제할 수는 없다 You can't completely rule out the possibility.

—법 『논리』 the method of exclusion **—자** 『법』 an abator

배제 配劑 a prescription ¶ 하늘의 배제 the〔a〕 dispensation of Heaven ; Providence

배좁다 ⇨ 비좁다

배종 陪從 accompanying〔following〕 one's superior ; waiting upon〔attending on〕 one's superior **—하다** wait upon 〔attend on, accompany, follow〕 one's superior

배종 胚種 『식물』 a germ ; a germinal vesicle

— 세포 a germinal cell

배주 胚珠 『식물』 an ovule ; germinal vesicles

배주룩하다 stick〔thrust, jut〕out a bit

배죽거리다, 빼죽거리다 twist one's mouth ; pout (one's lips) ; make a pout 〔lip〕 ; curl〔screw up〕 one's lips (경멸) ¶ 입을 배죽거리면서 말하다 say poutingly (불평) ; say something threatening to cry (어린이가)

배중률 排中律 『논리』 the principle of the excluded middle

배증 倍增 doubling ; growing double **—하다** be doubled ; increase double

소득 — 계획 an income doubling program

⁑**배지** 《wear》 a badge

배지기 『씨름』 a belly grab ; a belly throw

배지느러미 『어류』 the ventral fin of a fish

배지성 背地性 『식물』 apogeotropism ; negative geotropism

배진 背進 backing ; [철수] withdrawal **—하다** fall back ; retire ; withdraw

배질 rowing ; sailing

배짱 ① [버티는 힘] self-confidence ; boldness ; audacity ; effrontery ; hardihood ; imprudence ; assurance ; cheek (미) ¶ 배짱으로 나가다 push on to the front // 배짱이 있다 be pushing ; be unyielding ; be aggressive ; be strong-willed ; be brazen-browed〔-faced〕 // 배짱이 없다 be fainthearted ; have no guts ; lack confidence〔assurance, nerve〕 // 배짱이 없으면 사랑도 못한다 Faint heart never won a fair lady. // 배짱으로 나갈 수 밖에 없다 There is no other way than to push forward.

② [속마음] mind ; heart ; intention ; a hidden thought ; an ulterior motive ¶ 말은 그러나 배짱은 다르다 That's what he

says, but I know better. // 그의 배짱은 알 수 없다 Who can guess at his hidden motives〔at what he's really thinking〕?
배짱이 세다 관용 have got a lot of nerve〔cheek〕
배차 配車 allocation of cars ; marshalling of cars —하다 allocate〔marshal〕 cars
—계〔원〕 a 《train》 dispatcher
배차 排次 [차례] order ; one's turn ; [차례를 정함] ordering —하다 order ; arrange the order
배참하다 vent one's anger〔spite〕 on another ; wreak one's wrath upon another
배척 a crow(bar)
배척 排斥 exclusion ; ostracism ; a boycott —하다 exclude ; ostracize (사회적으로) ; boycott (상품을) ; oust 《a person from a place》 (부정 수단으로) ¶ 외제 물건을 배척하다 boycott foreign goods
— 운동 expulsion agitation ¶ …배척 운동 agitation against...
배추 Chinese cabbage ; celery cabbage
—꼬랑이 cabbage root —김치 pickled (Chinese) cabbage —속대 cabbage heart —찜 cabbage stew ; cabbage boiled with pork and seasoning
배축 胚軸 〖식물〗 the hypocotyl
배출 排出 discharge ; exhaust ; [체외로] pushing out ; elimination —하다 discharge ; transpire ; exhaust ¶ 노폐물을 체외로 배출하다 eliminate waste matter from the system
배출 輩出 coming forward in succession ; appearing one after another —하다 come forward in succession ; appear one after another ¶ 속속 배출하다 come forth〔turn out〕 in great numbers // 그 지방에서 수재가 많이 배출되었다 The place has produced a large number of talented persons.
—관 a discharge pipe ; an exhaust pipe —구 an issue ; an outlet —판(瓣) an exhaust valve
배치 背馳 —하다 be contrary 《to》 ; be opposed 《to》 ; run counter 《to》 ¶ 이것은 사실과 완전히 배치한다 This is utterly opposed to the fact. // 이것은 조약의 정신과 배치된다 This runs counter to the spirit of the treaty.
배치 排置 arrangement —하다 set in ; place arrange
†배치 配置 arrangement ; disposition ; posting ; stationing —하다 arrange ; distribute ; [부서에] post ; station ¶ 경관을 연도에 배치하다 station〔post〕 police along the route
— 계획 block planning (도시 계획 따위의) ; 〖건축〗 plot planning —도(圖) 〖기계〗 an arrangement plan ; 〖건축〗 a plot plan ; a block plan 공격〔방어〕 — offensive〔defensive〕 disposition 부대 — troop disposition 인원 — disposition of men
배치 전환 配置轉換 a reshuffle ; a shake-up ; transposition ; redistribution ¶ 공무원의 배치 전환 relocation of government officials // 노동력의 배치 전환 labor turnover // 사원의 배치 전환 a personnel reshuffle〔shake-up〕
배코 the place right under the topknot where the hair is cut off ¶ 배코 치다 cut off the hair under the topknot
—칼 a small knife used to cut the *baeko* hair off
‡배타 排他 exclusion ¶ 배타적 exclusive ; cliquish
—론자 an exclusionist — 정신 exclusive-mindedness —주의 exclusivism ; exclusionism
배탈 a stomach upset ; a stomach disorder ¶ 배탈나다 have a stomachache ; have a pain in the stomach ; suffer from indigestion // 너는 배탈이 자주 나지 않니 You often have an upset stomach, don't you?
배태 胚胎 [임신] pregnancy ; germination ; [원인] origin ; germ —하다 [임신] be pregnant ; [원인] originate 《in》 ; have origin 《in》 ; arise 《from》 ; result 《from》 ¶ 그것은 심장의 질환에 배태한다 It originates in some disorder of the heart.
*배터리 ① [전지] a battery ¶ 배터리가 떨어져 간다〔떨어졌다〕 The battery dies〔is dead〕.
② 〖야구〗 the battery
배터 박스 〖야구〗 a batter's box ¶ 배터 박스에 두 번째로 서다 be at bat twice
배퉁이 belly ; stomach
†배트 〖야구〗 a (baseball) bat ; a willow 《미·속》 ; a stick ¶ 배트를 휘두르다 swing one's bat // 배트를 길게〔짧게〕 잡다 hold one's bat long〔short〕 // 공에 가볍게 배트를 대다 bat a ball lightly
배틀거리다 stagger ; totter ; reel ; falter ; shamble ¶ 배틀거리며 with faltering〔tottering〕 steps // 배틀거리며 걷다 waddle ; shamble ; reel along〔about〕 // 무거운 짐을 지고 배틀거리다 stagger under a heavy load // 한 대 되게 얻어맞고 배틀거렸다 He reeled under the heavy blow. /The blow staggered him.
배틀다 twist ; wrench ; screw ; wring ¶ 팔을 배틀다 wrench〔twist〕 《a person's》 arm // 그는 내 팔을 배틀었다 He gave my hand a wring.
배틀리다 get twisted ; be distorted ; be wrenched ¶ 넥타이가 배틀리다 have one's tie twisted a little
배팅 〖야구〗 batting
배편 —便 shipping service ¶ 배편으로 by ship〔boat, steamer, water〕 // 배편으로 물건을 보내다 send a thing by boat
배포 配布 wide distribution ⇨ 배부 —하다 distribute widely 《among》
—망 a network of distribution

배포 排布, 排鋪 ① [능력] one's capacity ; scale〔breadth〕 of thinking ; [계획] planning ; scheme ¶ 가슴에 딴 배포가 들어 있다 have some plot in one's mind ; have an axe to grind ② [배치] arrangement
배포가 크다 관용 be magnanimous ; think on a large scale ; have big idea
배포가 유하다 관용 be hard to ruffle 〔discompose〕 ; be unconcerned with trifles ; be nonchalant〔impassive〕 ; be brazen
배풍 背風 a fair wind ; a tail wind
배필 配匹 a spouse ; a consort ; a life partner ; a life's companion ; a companion for life ; a mate ; a wife〔husband〕 ; one's better half ¶ 적당한 배필을 고르다 choose a suitable match 《for one》
배하다 拜— receive 《a government appointment》 ; be appointed to 《a government post》
배합 配合 combination ; mixture ; composition ; arrangement ; match ; harmony **—하다** match ; combine ; mix ; compound ; harmonize ¶ 색의 배합 a color scheme // 그 배합은 잘 어울린다 The combination is a becoming one. // 색의 배합이 나쁘다 These colors don't match.
— 금기(禁忌) incompatibility ¶ 배합 금기 약품 incompatible drugs **— 비료** compound fertilizer **— 사료** assorted feed
배행 陪行 accompanying〔following〕 one's superior ; [배웅] going along partway with a departing person
배혁 背革 a leatherback ¶ 배혁으로 장정한 책 a quarter-bound〔leatherback〕 book
— 제본 quarterbinding
배화 排貨 a boycott (movement) 《against》 ; boycotting **—하다** boycott
배화교 拜火敎 fire-worship ; Zoroastrianism ; Parsiism
—도 a fire worshiper ; a Zoroastrian ; a Parsi
배회 徘徊 loitering (about) ; sauntering ; hovering (about) ; knocking about ; rambling about ; wandering〔roaming〕 about ; hanging around 《미》 **—하다** loiter (about) ; saunter ; knock about ; wander about ; roam〔ramble〕 about ; prowl 《after one's prey》 (맹수가) ¶ 광야에서의 배회 wandering in the wilderness // 이곳 저곳을 배회하다 wander from place to place
†배후 背後 the rear〔back〕 ¶ 배후에 at the rear〔back〕 《of》 ; behind // 적의 배후를 찌르다 attack the enemy in the rear 〔from behind〕 // 그의 배후에는 자본가가 있다 He has capitalists behind him〔at his back〕.
— 인물〔조종자〕 a wirepuller ; a man 〔worker〕 behind the scenes
백 back ; [정구의 후위] backhand
백 [연줄·배경] favor ; patronage ; backing ; connections ; strings ; help ; pull 《미》 ; [후원자] a patron ; a backer ; a supporter ¶ …을 백으로 하여 backed (up) by // 아무의 백으로 회사에 들어가다 enter a company〔obtain a position in the firm〕 through a person's influence〔pull〕 // 그에게는 좋은 백이 있다 He has a powerful supporter〔good backing〕. // 그 사람 백을 쓰기라도 한 모양이지 He must have pulled strings or something. // 나는 백이 없다 I have no connections. /I have no strings to pull. // 그는 경영진에 든든한 백을 가지고 있다 He has good connections in the management. // 나는 백으로 입사하기는 싫다 I don't want to get a job on connections
백 白 white ¶ 경주에서 백이 이겼다 The white won the race.
백 伯 [백작] a count ; an earl 《영》 ; [만형] the eldest brother
†백 百 a〔one〕 hundred ¶ 100번째 the hundredth // 100살 난 사람 a centenarian ; a hundred-year-old person // 수백명의 사람들 hundreds of people // 100에 대하여 per centum // 100단위로 세다 count by the hundred // 여섯 개만 더 있으면 100개가 된다 I need only six more to have a full hundred.
백가서 百家書 the books of various philosophers and scholars
백각 白— 『광물』 white quartz
백건 白鍵 [건반의] a white key ; a natural
백계 百計 all means ; all resources ¶ 백계를 다 써보다 try every〔all〕 means available〔conceivable〕 ; try every possible means ; leave no stone unturned // 백계가 다하다 exhaust all resources 〔means〕 ; be at one's wit's end ; come to the end of one's rope
—무책(無策) helplessness
백계 노인 白系露人 a Russran émigré
백곡 百穀 all kinds of crops
백골 白骨 [뼈] a skeleton ; a white 〔bleached〕 bone ; [목기·목물] wooden vessels (칠하지 않은) ¶ 백골 난망이다 carry《a person's》 favor to the grave ; never forget 《a person's》 favor〔kindness〕
백곰 白— a white〔polar〕 bear
백공 百工 [장색] all sorts of artisans 〔workmen〕 ; [백관] all officials
백과 白瓜 『식물』 a white cucumber 〔muskmelon〕
‡백과 百科 all kinds〔branches〕 of learning
— 사전(事典) an encyclopedia **— 전서** an encyclopedia (set) ; an encyclopedic series of handbooks ; a complete encyclopedia ¶ 백과 전서적 지식 encyclopedic knowledge
백관 百官 all the government officials
문무 — civil and military officers ; all the officials of both services

백구 白鷗 〖새〗 a white (sea) gull
백군 白軍 〖역사〗 the white Russian Army ; [경기에서] the white team ; the white(s)
백귀야행 百鬼夜行 ¶ 백귀야행격이다 be a veritable pandemonium ; present a most scandalous scene〔sight〕
백그라운드 a background
*백금 白金 platinum ; white gold ¶ 백금 상의 platinoid
—속 platinum metals ; things made of platinum
백기 白旗 a white flag ; a flag of truce (항복의 표시) ¶ 백기를 들고 항복하다 display〔raise〕 a flag of truce ; hang〔show〕 the white flag
백날 百— ① [아기의 백일] the hundredth day of a newborn baby ¶ 백날 잔치 the feast〔celebration〕 of a hundred-day-old baby
② [많은 날] a hundred days ; a very long time ¶ 백날이 되도록 for a long time
백납 白— 〖의학〗 vitiligo ; leucoma
백납먹다 (관용) have a leucoma
백내장 白內障 a cataract (in the eye)
노인성 — a senile cataract ; cataracta senilis 선천성〔후천성〕 — congenital〔acquired〕 cataract
백넘버 a uniform number
백네트 〖야구〗 a backstop
백년 百年 ① [한 세기] one hundred years ; a century ② [한평생] one's whole life ¶ 국가 백년의 대계 a far- sighted national policy〔program〕 // 백년해로하다 (a married couple) grow old together // 백년하청(河淸) (격이다) It's like waiting for pigs to fly. /If the sky falls, we shall catch larks.
—가약(佳約) a marriage bond ; a conjugal tie ¶ 백년가약을 맺다 tie the nuptial knot ; become man and wife for weal and woe ; cast in one's lot with a partner for life —대계(大計) ⇨ 대계 —제(祭) a centennial (anniversary) 《미》 ; a centenary 《영》
백년을 다 살아야 삼만 육천일 (속담) Life is but a span.
백년초 百年草 〖식물〗 a cactus 《*pl.* ～es, -ti》
백년해로 百年偕老 growing old together in wedded life ¶ 백년해로를 언약하다 be united as a man and wife for weal or woe ; take each other for better or for worse ; swear to become one flesh ; promise to live together till they shall become Darby and Joan
백단향 白檀香 〖식물〗 white sandalwood
백대 百代 one hundred generations ; a very long time ¶ 100대 자손〔선조〕 one's descendants〔ancestors〕 in the hundreadth generation
백대하 白帶下 〖의학〗 leucorrh(o)ea ; whites 《속》

백도 白桃 a white peach
백동 白銅 [합금] nickel ; [백동화] a nickel (coin) ¶ 백동 딱지 a nickel watchcase // 백동 시계 a watch with a nickel case // 백동전〔화〕 a nickel coin
백두 白頭 a white head ¶ 백두의 노인 a white〔grey〕-haired〔headed〕 old man
백랍 白蠟 [초 원료] white〔refined〕 wax ; [벌레집] insect wax
—벌레 〖곤충〗 a wax(-depositing) insect ; Ericeruspala chauannes (학명)
—초 a candle made of white〔refined〕 wax
백러시아 白— White Russia ; Byelorussia
백련 白蓮 [연꽃] a white lotus (flower) ; [목련] a white magnolia
백로 白鷺 〖새〗 an egret ; a snowy〔white〕 heron
백로 白露 [이슬] white dew ; a white dewdrop ; [계절] the 16th of the 24 seasonal divisions of a year
백리 白痢 〖한의〗 dysentery with diarrhea that becomes white with mucus
백마 白馬 a white horse
백막 白膜 〖해부〗 the sclerotic ; the sclera
—염 scleritis
†백만 百萬 a〔one〕 million ¶ 백만 원 one million *won* // 백만 인 one million persons // 백만 인의 노래 music for the million // 백만 분의 1 one-millionth // 백만 대에 달하다 reach the seven-figure mark
‡백만 장자 百萬長者 a millionaire ; a multimillionaire
백면 白麵 [가루] buckwheat flour ; [국수] buckwheat vermicelli
백면서생 白面書生 a stripling ; a greenhorn ; a novice ¶ 백면서생 시절 one's salad days
백모 伯母 an aunt ; the wife of one's father's elder brother
백목 白木 cotton (cloth)
백목련 白木蓮 〖식물〗 a yulan ; a Chinese magnolia
백묵 白墨 chalk ⇨ 분필
백문 白文 ① [관인 없는 문서] a written statement without government seal ; a document without official seal
② [주석 없는 한문] an unpunctuated Chinese composition〔text〕 ; a straight〔plain〕 text without any marks〔comments〕
백문이 불여일견 百聞不如一見 Seeing is believing. /A thousand hearings are not worth one seeing. /To see for oneself is worth all the books of travel. /There is nothing like seeing for oneself.
백물 百物 all sorts〔kinds〕 of goods〔articles〕 ; various kinds of things
백미 白米 polished〔cleaned〕 rice
—병(病) a disease caused by feeding on polished rice ; beriberi (각기) —상(商) a rice dealer
백미 白眉 a person who excels others ;

the finest example (of the kind) ; the best《of》; the prince〔monarch〕《of》; the pick《of》¶ 저서 중의 백미 the best of one's works // 한국 소설 중의 백미 one of the best Korean novels // 박람회 건축물 중의 백미 the architectural gem 〔crowning glory〕 of the exposition
백미러 a rearview〔rear-vision〕 mirror
백반 白斑 ① [반점] a white spot ¶ 백반이 있는 white-spotted ② [태양의] a facula《*pl.* -lae》; a bright spot ③ [피부의] leucoderma ; leukoderma ; vitiligo ; albinism in patches ; a piebald skin ; a white macula (in the skin)
백반 白礬 alum
백반 白飯 cooked〔boiled〕 rice (not mixed with any other cereals) ; a meal including rice
백발 白髮 white〔gray〕 hair ; snowy hair ¶ 백발의 gray-haired ; white-headed ; hoary ; with a white head // 백발의 노인 a gray-headed old man // 백발이 되다 one's hair turns gray ; one grows gray
백발백중 百發百中 a hundred hits to a hundred shots ; a hundred percent in bull's-eyes ; all hits ; [실패 없음] infallibility **—하다** never miss the target 〔mark〕; (be) infallible ¶ 총알이 백발백중하였다 Every shot told. // 그는 백발백중의 명사수다 He is a dead〔crack〕 shot. /He is an ace marksman. // 그 의사의 진단은 백발백중이다 That doctor never makes a wrong diagnosis.
백방 白放 acquittal ; absolution ; exculpation **—하다** acquit ; absolve ; exculpate ; set free ; release
백방 百方 ① [여러 가지 방법] various ways ; every way ¶ 백방으로 위로하다 console《a person》in every way // 백방으로 손을 쓰다 try all〔every〕 means available ; leave no stone unturned // 백방으로 진력하다 make every effort ; exert oneself to the utmost
② [여러 방향] every direction ; all sides ¶ 백방으로 사람을 구하다 look all round〔all over〕 for a person
백배 百倍 one〔a〕 hundred times ; a hundredfold **—하다** increase《a number》hundredfold〔a hundred times〕; multiply a hundredfold ; centuple ¶ 백배의 centuple ; hundredfold // 용기 백배하다 inspire《the troops》with redoubled courage
백배 百拜 bowing many times〔a hundred times〕 **—하다** bow many times 〔a hundred times〕 ¶ 백배 사례하다 express one's gratitude〔thanks〕 by bowing many times ; bow one's thanks many times ; offer a thousand thanks // 백배 사죄하다 make〔offer〕 an apology by bowing many times
백범 白帆 a white sail
백변 白邊 sap ; sapwood ; alburnum
백병 百病 all kinds of diseases〔illnesses, maladies〕
— 통치약 a cureall ; a panacea
백병 白兵 a naked sword〔sabre〕; sword and bayonets
—전 hand-to-hand fight ; close combat ; fighting with swords and bayonets ¶ 백병전을 벌이다 fight hand to hand
백부 伯父 an uncle ; one's father's elder brother
백부장 百夫長 〚성경〛 a centurion
백분 白粉 face powder ; [가루] flour ¶ 백분을 바르다 powder one's face ; put powder《on》
물— liquid powder
*__백분 百分__ one-hundredth part **—하다** divide《a thing》into a hundred parts ¶ 백분의 20 twenty-hundredths ; 20 percent
— 도표 a centesimal scale **—비(比)〔율〕** percentage
백비탕 白沸湯 plain hot water
백사 白沙 white sand
—기(器) white earthenware **—장(場)** a sandy beach ; a beach with white sands ; the sands **—지(地)** sandy soil
백사 百事 all kinds〔sorts〕 of matters 〔things〕; everything ¶ 백사에 실패하다 fail at everything
백사과 白— 〚식물〛 a white melon
백산호 白珊瑚 white coral
백삼 白蔘 white ginseng
†**백색 白色** white (color) ; [우익] the white〔right〕 wing ¶ 백색의 white ; of white color ; white-colored
— 인종 the white race ; white people **— 테러** the white terror
백서 白書 a white paper ; a white book
경제 —《publish, issue》an economic white paper
백서 白鼠 〚동물〛 a white rat
백석 白晳 white (in complexion) **—하다** (be) white-skinned ; be of white complexion ¶ 백석의 호남 a handsome man of white complexion
백석 白石 a white stone
백선 白癬 〚의학〛 favus
백설 白雪 white snow ; snow ¶ 백설같이 흰 snow-white ; snowy ; white as snow // 백설이 덮인 산 a snow-capped mountain
—총이 a snow-white horse with black lips
백설기 白— steamed rice-cake
백설탕 白雪糖 white sugar ; castor sugar
†**백성 百姓** [국민] the people ; the populace ; the nation ; [서민] the common people ; the commoners ; the commons
만— all the people ; the whole nation
백세 百世 one hundred generations ; forever
백수 白首 a head of white hair ; a white-haired person
백수 白鬚 a white mustache〔beard,

whiskers〕
백수 百獸 all kinds of animals ¶ 백수의 왕 the king of beasts
백수건달 白手乾達 an out-and-out libertine ; a debauchee ; a good-for-nothing
백수풍신 白首風神 a white-haired gentleman of distinguished〔fine〕 appearance
백숙 白熟 fish or meat boiled in plain water
백스트로크 [배영] the backstroke
백십자 白十字 the white cross
백씨 伯氏 your〔his〕 (esteemed) elder brother
백악 白堊 [백회] chalk ; chalkstone ; [흰 벽] a white wall
—계(系) 〖지질〗 the Cretaceous system —기(紀) 〖지질〗 the Cretaceous ; the Cretaceous period —질 [이(齒)의] cement —층 〖지질〗 chalk bed〔pit〕 —토(土)〔암(岩)〕 malm —화(化) cretification
백악관 白堊館 [미국 대통령 관저] the White House
백안시 白眼視 —하다 look coldly upon ; look askance at 《a person》 ; look with ; indifference ; frown upon ; have a prejudiced view 《of》
백야 白夜 a white night
백약 百藥 all kinds of medicines ¶ 백약이 무효하다 All medicines prove useless.
백양 白楊 〖식물〗 a white〔silver〕 poplar
백양 白羊 a white sheep
—궁 〖천문〗 the Aries ; the Ram
백어 白魚 a whitebait ⇨ 뱅어
백업 〖야구〗 backup ¶ 백업하다 back up ; support
백연 白鉛 white lead ; ceruse
—광(鑛) white lead ore ; cerusite
†백열 白熱 [온도의] white heat ; incandescence ; white glow ; [열정의] a climax ; enthusiasm ¶ 백열적 환영 an enthusiastic welcome // 백열적 논전 heated controversy // 백열된 incandescent ; white-hot ; most exciting ; seasaw 《game》 // 백열화하다 glow white ; get excited // 백열점에 달하다 reach a white-heat point ; reach a climax
—광(光) incandescent light —등 an incandescent electric lamp ; a glow lamp —전(戰) hot fighting
백옥 白玉 a white gem ; a white precious stone
백옥 白屋 a hovel ; a humble cottage
백운 白雲 white clouds ¶ 창공에 떠 있는 백운 fleecy clouds floating in the blue sky
백운모 白雲母 〖광물〗 white〔common〕
백운석 白雲石 〖광물〗 dolomite
백의 白衣 a white robe〔dress〕 ¶ 백의의 여자 a woman in white ; a white-robed woman
— 민족 the white-clad folk ; the Korean people — 용사 a hero in white ; a wounded〔disabled〕 soldier in a white robe — 천사 an angel in white ; a ministering angel〔nurse〕 ; a white-clad nurse
백인 白人 a white man ; a Caucasian ; a white 《속》
— 여자 a European woman〔lady〕 —종 the white race ; the whites — 지상주의자 a white supremacist
백인 白刃 a drawn〔naked〕 sword 〔saber〕 ; a naked〔bared〕 blade
*백일 白日 broad daylight ; a bright day ¶ 백일하에 드러나다 be brought to light
—몽(夢) a daydream ; a revery ¶ 백일몽을 꾸는 청년 a youth given to daydreaming
백일 百日 [백일 간] a hundred days ; [어린이의] the one hundredth day
— 잔치 a party〔banquet〕 given to a hundred-day-old baby —천하 a hundred-day reign ; a very brief reign ; a short-lived rule — 치성 a hundred-day worship
백일 기도 百日祈禱 praying for a hundred days
백일장 白日場 a composition〔literary〕 contest ; a contest for composition
주부 — a literary contest for housewives
백일재 百日齋 〖불교〗 a Buddhist memorial service on the hundredth day after 《a person's》 death
백일초 百日草 〖식물〗 a zinnia
백일해 百日咳 〖의학〗 whooping cough ; pertussis
백일홍 百日紅 〖식물〗 a crape-myrtle ; a garden zinnia
*백작 伯爵 a count ; an earl 《영》 ¶ T 백작 및 동부인 Count and Countess T
— 부인 a countess
백장 a butcher ; [욕] a son-of-a-bitch ; a bastard ¶ 개 백장 a dog killer ; a dog-catcher
백저 白苧 grass-cloth〔ramie-cloth〕 bleached white
백전 百戰 [맨손 싸움] fist fighting ; a fist fight ; fighting with bare hands ; [글시합] a verse-writing contest
백전노장 百戰老將 a veteran ; an old timer ; an old campaigner
백전백승 百戰百勝 —하다 be ever-victorious ; be invincible ; be unbeaten ; win every battle
백절불굴 百折不屈 —하다 (be) indefatigable ; unbending ; indomitable ; unflinching ¶ 백절불굴의 정신 an indomitable spirit
백절불요 百折不撓 ⇨ 백절불굴
백점 百點 one〔a〕 hundred points ; full marks〔a full mark〕 (만점) ; a perfect score
백정 白丁 a butcher ⇨ 백장
‡백조 白鳥 〖새〗 a swan (고니) ; a white heron (해오라기)

— 사육자 a swanhead — 사육장 a swannery —자리 〖천문〗 the Swan ; the Cygnus
백종 百種 various kinds ; all kinds
백주 白酒 white liquor〔wine〕
백주 白晝 broad daylight ; the daytime ¶ 백주에 in broad daylight ; in the daytime // 백주에 횡행〔활보〕하다 stalk about at noonday
백중 百中, 百衆 the Buddhist All Souls' Day 《the 15th (day) of the 7th lunar month》
—날 mid July by the lunar calendar —맞이 the Buddhist ceremony for the repose of the dead on *Paekjung* ; [무당의] an exorcism held on the same day —물 rainfall around the time of *Paekjung* —불공 the Buddhist Festival of the Dead
백중 伯仲 [맏형과 둘째형] one's eldest brother and second eldest brother ; [맞섬] being equal 《to》 ; being equally matched ; being even 《with》 ; being on a par 《with》 **—하다** (be) equal ; be even 《with》
—숙계(叔季) the first, second, third, and fourth of brothers
백지 白— the white *paduk* stones ; the whites
백지 白紙 ① [흰 종이] white paper ; Korean paper made from mulberry fiber ② [공지] a clean〔blank〕 sheet of paper ③ [상태] a clean slate ; a mind free from prejudice〔preconception〕 ¶ 백지 답안을 내다 hand in a blank paper // 백지로 돌아가다 start with a clean slate
— 동맹 sending in blank examination papers as a student protest — 위임장 a blank power of attorney ; carte blanche 《프》 ¶ 백지 위임장을 주다 give 《a person》 carte blanche — 투표 (a) blank vote ¶ 백지 투표를 하다 cast a blank vote — 투표지 a blank ballot〔vote〕
백지장도 맞들면 낫다 〈속담〉 Many hands make light work. /Many a little makes a mickle. /Many a mickle makes a mackle.
백지도 白地圖 a blank〔an outline〕 map
백차 白車 a (police) patrol car ; a squad 〔cruise, prowl〕 car ; a cruiser 《미·구》
백척간두 百尺竿頭 extremities ; the last extremity ¶ 백척간두에 서다 be in a dire extremity ; be driven〔reduced〕 to the last extremity // 백척간두에 일보를 더 나가다 go a step further ; take one more step ; make one more effort
백천만사 百千萬事 everything ; all sorts of things
백철광 白鐵鑛 〖광물〗 marcasite ; white iron pyrites
백청 白淸 honey of fine quality
백출 百出 —하다 arise〔appear, pop up〕 in great numbers ¶ 그 문제로 의론이 백출했다 The matter became the subject of heated discussion. /The subject provoked〔led to〕 warm discussion.
백치 白痴, 白癡 [치우] idiocy ; imbecility ; [치인] an idiot ; an imbecile ; a moron
백탄 白炭 fine charcoal ; charcoal of fine quality
백탕 白湯 (plain) hot〔boiled〕 water
백태 白苔 ① [혓바닥의] a coating on the tongue ¶ 백태가 끼었다 The tongue is coated. ② [눈의] a morbid coating on the eyeball that interferes with vision
백태 百態 various phases
미인 — various poses of glamor girls 인생 — various phases of life
백토 白土 white clay ; terra alba 《라》
백통 nickel ; white brass
—돈 a nickel (coin)
백판 白板 ① [흰 널빤지] a white board ② [형편] having nothing
— 건달 a penniless wretch
백팔 百八 one hundred and eight
—번뇌(煩惱) 〖불교〗 the hundred-and-eight torments of mankind —염주(念珠) a Buddhist rosary of 108 beads —종(鍾) a temple bell sounded 108 times each morning and evening
백 퍼센트 百— one hundred percent ; 100% ¶ 효과 백 퍼센트다 be 100 percent efficacious ; be most effective
백편 白— steamed rice-cake
백포도주 白葡萄酒 white wine ; sherry (프랑스 산) ; hock (독일 산)
백학 白鶴 a crane ⇨ 두루미
백합 白蛤 〖조개〗 a kind of clam
백합 百合 a lily ¶ 백합같이 아름답다 be as fair as a lily
백해 白海 〖지리〗 the White Sea
백해무익 百害無益 —하다 do more harm than good
백핸드 〖정구·탁구〗 backhand ; a backhand drive
백혈구 白血球 〖해부〗 a white blood corpuscle ; a leucocyte ; a phagocyte ¶ 백혈구의 leucocytic
— 감소증 leukopenia — 수 leukocyte 〔white〕 count — 증가증 leukocytosis — 형성 leukopoiesis
백혈병 白血病 leuk(a)emia ; leukosis ; leucosis
백형 伯兄 one's oldest〔eldest 《영》〕 brother
백호 白虎 ① 〖천문〗 the white tiger ; a group of Chinese zodiacal constellations that includes 7 constellations in the west ② 〖민속〗 a symbol of the god in charge of the west ③ [지맥] mountains branching off on the right side of the main high mountain
—날 〖민속〗 a mountain ridge branching off on the right side of the main high mountain
백호 白狐 a white〔silver〕 fox ; a blue 〔an

arctic] fox
백호 白濠 White Australia
—주의 the White Australia principle [policy]
백화 百花 all sorts of flowers ¶ 들에 백화가 난만하다 The field is alive [bright] with all sorts of flowers.
백화 白話 colloquial Chinese ; vernacular Chinese ; Chinese as spoken
—문(文) written colloquial Chinese
백화 白樺 〖식물〗 the white birch
*백화점 百貨店 a department store ; the stores ; an emporium [a general store]
밴대, 밴대 보지 the vulva without pubes
밴대질 lesbianism ; sexual practice between women —하다 practice lesbianism
밴댕이 〖물고기〗 a large-eyed herring ; Harengula zunashi (학명)
밴둥거리다 loaf away ; idle away one's time ¶ 밴둥밴둥 on the loaf ; idly
†밴드 ① [띠·끈] a band ; a strap ; [혁대] belt ¶ 밴드를 두르고 있다 wear a band [belt] ② [악단·악대] a band ; a brass band (취주악의)
—마스터 a bandmaster —맨 a bandsman
밴들거리다 loaf [idle] away one's time ; lead an idle life ¶ 밴들밴들 idly ; on the loaf
밴조 [악기] a banjo
밴텀급 —級 the bantamweight class ¶ 밴텀급의 선수 a bantamweight
밸러스트 ballast
모래 — sand ballast
밸런스 balance ¶ 밸런스가 잡힌 well-balanced
밸브 a valve
— 장치 valve gear
*뱀 a snake ; a serpent ¶ 뱀같은 snaky ; [모양] serpentine
— 공포증 ophidiophobia — 부리는 사람 a snake charmer — 허물 the slough of a snake
뱀날 〖민속〗 the Day of the Snake
뱀도랏 〖식물〗 a hedge parsley ; Torilis anthriscus (학명)
뱀딸기 〖식물〗 Indian [mock] strawberry ; Duchesnea indica (학명)
뱀띠 the attributes of (those born in the Year of) the Snake
뱀무 〖식물〗 the Japanese avens ; Geum japonicum (학명)
뱀밥 〖식물〗 a horsetail ; Equisetum arvense (학명)
뱀뱀이 upbringing ; breeding ; training ; discipline ¶ 뱀뱀이가 있다 be well brought up ; have had a good upbringing // 뱀뱀이가 없다 be badly brought up ; have had a poor upbringing // 뱀뱀이를 가르치다 teach manners ; bring up ; discipline
*뱀장어 —長魚 〖물고기〗 an eel
뱀프 [요부] a vampire ; a vamp 《속》 ¶ 뱀프형의 여자 a vamp type woman
뱀해 〖민속〗 the Year of the Snake
뱀혀 〖식물〗 a kind of cinquefoil
뱁대, 뱁댕이 thread-spacer (on a loom)
뱁새 〖새〗 a Korean crow-tit ; Suthora webbiana fulvicauda (학명)
—눈 narrow eyes —눈이 a person with tiny downward-slanted [slitted, narrow] eyes
뱁새가 황새를 따라가면 다리가 찢어진다 속담 If a crow-tit tries to walk like a stork, he will break his legs. /Tailor your ambitions to the measure of your abilities.
뱁티스트 [침례교도] a Baptist
뱃가죽 flesh [skin] of the belly
뱃고동 a boat whistle
뱃구레 the abdomen
뱃길 a (ship's) course ; a waterway ; a channel ; a sealane ¶ 뱃길 안내자 a pilot
뱃노래 a boatman's song ; a boating song ; a barcarol(l)e ; a sailor's song ; a chant(e)y [shanty] ¶ 베니스의 뱃노래 a Venetian gondolier's barcarol(l)e // 뱃노래를 부르다 sing a boating song
뱃놀이 boating ; yachting ; a boat ride ¶ 뱃놀이 가다 go boating [rowing] ; go for a row ; go for a boat ride
뱃놈 a sailor ; a seaman ; a mariner
뱃대끈 [여자용] a woman's bloomer sash ; [마소용] a cinch ; a (saddle-) girth ¶ 뱃대끈을 조르다 tighten the girth
뱃덧 disagreement of food ; foodpoisoning ; indigestion
뱃덧 나다 관용 be poisoned by food ; get [have] indigestion
뱃두리 a kind of jar
뱃머리 the bow ; the prow ; the head ¶ 뱃머리를 돌리다 wind a ship ; put a ship about
뱃멀미 seasickness ; nausea —하다 get seasick ¶ 뱃멀미하는[하지 않는] 사람 a poor [good] sailor
뱃바닥 ① [살] stomach flesh (of animal) ; [바닥] the bottom [underside] of an animal's belly ② [타는 배의] the bottom of a ship ; the bilge ; the floor
뱃바람 a wind that one is sailing directly into ; a head wind
뱃밥 oakum ; pledget ; ca(u)lking ¶ 뱃밥을 만들다 pick oakum // 뱃밥으로 메우다 ca(u)lk a boat ; stop up 《seams》 with oakum
뱃병 —病 stomach trouble ; intestinal upsets ¶ 뱃병이 나다 have stomach trouble ; have a stomach upset
*뱃사공 —沙工 a boatman 《*pl.* -men》 ; a sailor ; a seaman 《*pl.* -men》
뱃사람 a seaman 《*pl.* -men》 ; a sailor ; a shipowner ¶ 뱃사람의 생활 seafaring life // 뱃사람이 되다 go to sea
뱃삯 [승객의] passage ; a fare ; [나룻배의] a ferryboat charge ; [용선료] charter-

age ; [화물의] freight (rates)
뱃살 abdominal muscle ; muscle〔skin〕 of the belly〔abdomen〕 ¶ 뱃살 고부라지게 웃다 be convulsed with laughter ; split〔shake〕 one's sides with laughter // 뱃살 고부라지게 하다 throw 《a person》 into convulsion
뱃소리 a boatman's song ⇨ 뱃노래
뱃속 ① [복부] the inside of the stomach ; the stomach ¶ 뱃속이 아프다 have a stomachache ; have a pain in the stomach // 뱃속이 비다 have an empty stomach ② [속마음] inward thoughts ; intention ; heart ; mind ¶ 뱃속이 검다 be black-hearted ; be evil-minded ; be wicked // 뱃속을 떠보다 sound 《a person》 ; try to fathom the unexpressed intuition of 《a person》
뱃심 brazen effrontery ; impudence ; nerve ; audacity ; self-confidence ; cheek 《미》 ¶ 뱃심 좋게 밀고 나가다 brazen it out ; push on to the front
뱃심 좋다 관용 have got the nerve〔cheek〕 to ; have got plenty of guts ; be brazen-faced
뱃일 work aboard ship
뱃자반 一佐飯 fish salted on board〔at a fishing place〕
뱃장사 peddling wares in a small boat
뱃전 the sides of a boat〔ship〕 ; a gunwale ¶ 뱃전이 기울어진다 A boat tips〔lists〕 to one side.
뱃줄 a boat line〔rope〕 ; a hawser
뱃지게 an A-frame carrier used by stevedores
****뱃짐** a (ship's) cargo ; freight ; freightage ¶ 뱃짐을 싣다 take in cargo ; load a ship // 뱃짐을 부리다 discharge cargo ; unload a ship
뱃집 〖건축〗 a kind of open building with a roof that lacks eaves and has rounded side-boarding at either end ; [배의 부피] the bulk of the abdomen ¶ 뱃집이 크다 have a big belly
뱅, 뺑 round〔around〕 ; in a circle (둘러싼 모양) ¶ 사면이 바다로 뺑 둘러싸인 나라 a country girded by the sea on all sides // 뺑 돌다 turn round ; wheel about // 소문이 뺑 돌다 The rumor has got abroad〔spread in a flash〕.
뱅그래, 뺑그래 smiling ⇨ 빙그레
뱅글거리다 smile ; beam ¶ 뱅글뱅글 smilingly ; with a smile ; beamingly ; with a bland smile // 좋아서 뱅글거리다 beam with delight〔joy〕 // 어린애가 그의 손을 잡고 얼굴을 쳐다보며 뱅글거렸다 The child took his hand and beamed up at him.
뱅글뱅글 ⇨ 빙글빙글
뱅니 〖민속〗 the spouse called by the dead soul through a medium
뱅뱅, 뺑뺑 round and round ⇨ 빙빙
뱅어 一魚 〖물고기〗 an ice fish ; a whitebait
—젓 salted whitebait **—포** dried slices of seasoned whitebait
-뱅이 one ; person ¶ 가난뱅이 a poor man ; a pauper // 비렁뱅이 a beggar ; a tramp ; a hobo ; a mendicant ; panhandler 《미·구》 // 주정뱅이 a bad drunk ; a drunken brawler
뱅충맞다 (be) stupid ; thickheaded ; bashful ; clumsy ⇨ 빙충맞다
뱅충이 a stupid and bashful person ; a clumsy person ; a dolt ; a thickhead
***뱉다** ① spit out ¶ 가래를 뱉다 cough up phlegm // 그는 먹은 것을 다 뱉어 버렸다 He threw〔brought up, vomited〕 all he had eaten.
② [비유적] disgorge ; surrender ; give up ¶ 그는 착복한 돈을 뱉어 놓았다 He disgorged〔surrendered〕 the embezzled money.
뱌비다 ⇨ 비비다
뱌비작거리다 rub and rub ⇨ 비비다
뱌슬거리다 avoid coming to grips with 《a job, a problem》 ; keep aloof
뱐둥거리다 idle away one's time
뱐미주룩하다 (be) slightly bulging out
뱐반하다 (be) handsome ⇨ 반반하다
뱐주그레하다 (be) rather nice-looking ⇨ 반주그레하다
뱐죽거리다 pert ; act flippantly
뱝뛰어가다 caper ; gambol ; jump〔skip〕 about ; run〔dash, rush〕 about
버걱, 뻐걱 creaking ; squeaking ; grating ¶ 버걱버걱 with a squeaking noise // 버걱거리다 creak ; squeak ; grate
버겁다 be beyond one's capacity ; be too much for 《one》 ; be beyond one's control ; (be) unwieldy ; unmanageable ¶ 이 일은 나에게 버겁다 This work is beyond my capacity. /I am not equal to the task.
버그러뜨리다 crack ; split ; loosen ¶ 물동이를 버그러뜨리다 crack a water jug // 의자를 버그러뜨리다 break a chair
버그러지다 loosen ; separate ; split ; fissure ¶ 틈이 버그러지다 a split〔crack〕 gets wider // 마른 나무보다 생나무가 잘 버그러진다 Green wood splits more easily than dry.
버그르르, 뻐그르르 simmering ⇨ 바그르르, 빠그르르
버근하다 be ajar ; (be) open ; gappy ; loose ; fall aprt
버글거리다, 뻐글거리다 ① [끓다] simmer ; boil ; seethe ; come to a boil ¶ 물이 버글거린다 The water is boiling briskly.
② [거품이] bubble up ; rise in bubbles ¶ 비누 거품이 버글거린다 Suds are bubbling up.
③ [많이 모여] be crowded 《with》 ; crowd (together) ; flock together ; swarm〔teem〕 《with》 ¶ 거지가 버글거리

다 [장소가 주어] swarmbe overflowing, be crowded〕 with beggars
버글버글 [물이] seethingly ; [거품이] foamily ; bubbling ; [많이 모여] in swarms〔crowds〕 ¶ 버글버글 끓다 seethe ; boil up // 거품이 버글버글 일어나다 bubble up ; rise in bubbles ; foam up // 광장에는 군중이 버글버글했다 The public square was crowded〔thronged〕 with people.
버금 the second in order ; the next ¶ 버금가다 be in the second place ; be second to ; come second ; rank next to // 런던에 버금가는 대도시 the greatest city next to London // 작가로서 밀턴은 셰익스피어에 버금간다 As a writer, Milton is placed after Shakespeare.
버긋하다 (be) gappy ; open ; be ajar ; be loosened a bit ; be slightly apart ¶ 석류가 버긋하게 벌어졌다 The pomegranate is split a little. // 마루청이 버긋하다 The floorboards have come a little apart.
버꾸 [악기] a kind of small drum
—잡이 a drummer (of a small drum)
버너 a burner
가스 — a gas burner
버덩 a waste land overrun with weeds ; a barren plateau
버둥거리다 squirm ; wriggle ; writhe ; struggle ; flounder ¶ 진창 속에서 버둥거리다 flounder in the mud // 그는 입신 출세하려고 버둥거렸다 He strove hard to rise in the world somehow. // 그는 불을 피하려고 버둥거렸다 He squirmed his way out of the fire. // 아무리 버둥거려도 소용없다 It is no use struggling and wriggling.
버둥버둥 struggling ; wriggling ; floundering —하다 squirm ; wriggle ; writhe ; struggle ; flounder
버둥질 ⇨ 발버둥질
버드나무 a willow
—벌레 a willow parasite
버드러지다, 뻐드러지다 ① protrude (이가) ; project ; jut out ; spread out (가지가) ¶ 버드러진 이 a projecting〔prominent, protruding〕 tooth ; a bucktooth ② [뻣뻣해지다] stiffen ; become rigid ③ [죽다] (stiffen and) die ; drop dead
버드름하다 (be) slightly protruding ; somewhat prominent
버들 a willow ¶ 버들같은허리 a slender waist
버들개지 a pussy willow
버들고리 a willow〔wicker〕 trunk ; a hamper
버들눈 a willow bud
버들치 〖물고기〗 Moroco oxycephalus (학명)
버듬하다 protrude ⇨ 버드름하다
버라이어티 쇼 〖연예〗 a vaudeville 《미》 ; a variety show 《영》
버러지 an insect ⇨ 벌레
버럭 suddenly ; (all) of a sudden ¶ 버럭 소리를 지르다 cry out suddenly ; shout suddenly // 버럭 화를 내다 explode with rage ; burst into a passion ; fly into a great rage
버럭버럭 desperately ; frantically ; insistently
버렁 ① [범위] a scope ; an extent ; a sphere ② [장갑] thick gloves used in hawking
버력[1] 〖광물〗 rock with no mineral content ; low-grade ore
버력[2] divine retribution ; a curse
버력을 입다 (관용) be punished by Heaven ; incur the wrath of God ; incur a curse
버르르 ⇨ 바르르
버르장머리 a habit ; manners ⇨ 버릇
버르장이 a habit ; manners ⇨ 버릇
버르적거리다, 뻐르적거리다 writhe ; squirm ; struggle ¶ 그는 고통스러워서 버르적거렸다 He writhed (his body) under〔with〕 pain. // 사슬에서 빠져나오려고 버르적거렸다 I struggled to free myself from my bonds.
버르적버르적, 뻐르적뻐르적 writhing ; struggling ; wriggling ; squirming ; floundering —하다 writhe ; squirm ; struggle
버르집다 ① [벌려 펴다] stretch ; expand ; enlarge ; push a dent out (오므라진 것을) ¶ 모자를 버르집다 stretch a hat
② [들추어내다] disclose ; reveal
③ [과장하다] exaggerate
버름버름하다 be all loosely fitted ; have many cracks〔crevices〕
버름하다 be ajar ; (be) slightly open ; loosely fitted ; have a crack〔crevice〕 between
†버릇 ① [습관] a habitual practice ; a (personal) habit〔way〕 ; a customary practice ; an acquired tendency ¶ 게으름 피우는 버릇 a habit of idleness // 술마시는 버릇 an intemperate〔a liquor〕 habit // 고치기 어려운 버릇 an inveterate habit // 버릇이 생기다 become a habit ; get into a habit // 버릇을 고치다 cure 《a person》 of a habit (타인의 버릇) ; get rid of a habit (자기의 버릇) // 눈을 깜박이는 버릇이 있다 have a way of blinking // 일단 버릇이 들면 고치기 힘들다 Once you get the habit, it will stay with you. // 담배 피우는 것이 버릇이 되었다 Smoking has grown into a habit with me. // 나는 아침 일찍 일어나는 버릇을 들였다 I have formed〔cultivated〕 a habit of early rising. // 나쁜 버릇은 붙기는 쉽고 고치기는 어렵다 A bad habit is easy to get into and hard to get rid of. // 그는 말을 되풀이하는 버릇이 있다 He has the habit of repeating himself.
② [성벽] a propensity ; an idiosyncrasy ; a characteristic ; a peculiarity ; a

peculiar way ¶ 말버릇 one's peculiar way of speaking // 그는 남의 허물을 캐는 버릇이 있다 He has a propensity for finding faults with others.
③ [예의] manners ; etiquette ; courtesy ; propriety ; decorum ; politeness ; civility ; breeding ; behavior ; respectful deportment ⇨ 버릇없다 ¶ 버릇을 가르치다 give 《a person》 lessons in manners〔etiquette〕; teach 《a person》 manners ; [혼내 주다] teach 《a person》 a lesson ; give 《a person》 a raw deal // 버릇이 없어지다 lapse from good manners ; grow impudent〔insolent〕; be spoilt
세 살 적 버릇이 여든까지 간다 속담 What is learned in the cradle is carried to the tomb. /Custom〔Habit〕 is a second nature. /Old habit dies hard.

버릇소리 〖언어〗 a habitual sound

‡**버릇없다** (be) ill-mannered ; ill-bred ; ill-behaved ; unmannerly ; mannerless ; uncivil ; uncourteous ; discourteous ; impolite ; impertinent ; rude ; churlish ; boorish ¶rurhsu 버릇없는 ill-mannered ; ill-bred ; rude ; wayward ; discourteous // 버릇없이 rudely // 버릇이 없다 be wanting in politeness // 버릇없는 말을 하다 say rude things // 그는 버릇이 없다 He has no manners. /He is ill-mannered. // 나한테 너무 버릇없이 행동하는 것 같다 I'm afraid you're being forward with me.

버릇하다 form a habit ; be〔get, grow〕 accustomed〔used〕 to ; be habituated to ; be in the habit of 《doing》 ¶ 가 버릇하다 visit frequently // 규칙적인 생활을 해 버릇하다 accustom oneself to a regular life // 먹어 버릇하다 be accustomed〔used〕 to eat // 써 버릇하다 be accustomed to use〔to the use of〕

버릇다 dig open ; cut open ; scatter ; kick〔scratch〕 about

†**버리다**[1] ① [내던지다] throw〔fling, cast〕 away ; cast aside ¶ 쓰레기를 버리다 dump refuse // 돈을 그냥 버리는 것과 마찬가지다 It is a mere waste of money. /You are throwing away your money. // 담배꽁초를 함부로 버리지 마세요 Please don't litter with your cigarette butts.
② [포기·방기] abandon ; desert ; discard ; forsake ; give up ; renounce ; leave

> 참고 **desert** 서약·약속·의무 따위를 버린다는 뜻으로서 비난의 뜻이 포함되어 있다 **forsake** 감정적인 유대를 끊는다는 뜻 반드시 비난의 뜻이 포함되어 있지는 않다 **abandon** 결정적으로 버리고 다음은 운명에 맡기다

¶ 현관에 버려진 갓난아이 a baby left on the doorsteps // 버림받은 첩 a castoff mistress // 전재산을 버리다 forsake all the riches // 지위를 버리다 give up one's position // 집을 버리다 leave one's house // 세상을 버리다 renounce the world // 악습을 버리다 renounce bad habits // 궁지에 빠진 사람을 버려 두다 leave 《a person》 in the lurch // 이 문제는 중대하기 때문에 버려 둘 수 없다 The problem is too serious to be left unattended to〔undealt with〕. // 자존심 같은 것은 버리고 때를 기다려라 Swallow your pride and bide your time. // 이 직업을 가졌을 때 자존심 같은 것은 다 버렸다 I pocketed my pride when I got this job.
③ [망그러뜨리다] spoil ; ruin ¶ 매를 아끼면 아이를 버린다 Spare the rod and spoil the child. // 그 소식이 입맛을 버려 놓았다 The news spoilt the dinner.

버리다[2] [끝내다] finish ; get through ; get done ; do completely ; dispose of a job ¶ 나는 돈을 다 써 버렸다 I have spent all my money. // 그는 그 책을 다 읽어 버렸다 He has finished reading the book.

***버림받다** be abandoned ; be deserted ; be forsaken ; be jilted ; be marooned ; be left behind ¶ 남편에게 버림받다 be discarded〔deserted, left〕 by one's husband // 사회에서 버림받다 be cast out from society // 세상에서 버림받다 die from the memory of the public // 그녀는 남자친구에게 버림받았다고 들었다 I hear she was dumped by her boy friend.

버림치 a useless thing ; junk ; an obsolete〔outdated〕 thing ; a discard ; a reject ; waste material

버마재비 〖곤충〗 a (praying) mantis ; a rearhorse

버무리 food mixed 《with》

버무리다 mix〔stir〕 up ; compound ¶ 나물을 버무리다 fix〔mix〕 a salad

버물다 be involved 《in a crime》 ; be implicated ; be mixed up ; link one's name 《with a scandal》 ¶ 나쁜 동무와 버물다 keep bad company // 범죄〔음모〕에 버물다 be involved in a crime〔plot〕

버물리다 ① [피동] get mixed ; mix ② [사역] get 《a person》 to mix ¶ 가정부에게 나물을 버물리다 have〔let〕 the housemaid fix salad // 그는 사람과 잘 버물리지 않는다 He does not mix well.

버새 〖동물〗 a hinny

버석 ⇨ 바삭

버석거리다 rustle ; make a rustle〔a rustling sound〕 ¶ 버석버석 rustlingly ; with a rustle // 낙엽이 바람에 버석거린다 The fallen leaves are rustling in the wind.

버선 Korean socks ; bootees ¶ 버선을 벗다〔신다〕 take off〔put on〕 one's socks
—목 the ankle of a sock **—발** one's feet with socks on ; stocking feet ¶ 그는 버선발로 나갔다 He went out in stocking feet. **—본** a paper pattern for making socks **—볼** the width of socks ; [기울 때]

a piece of cloth sewed on to mend socks ; a sock patch 솜 — wadded 〔padded〕 socks
*버섯 a mushroom ; a fungus ; a toadstool (유독한) ¶ 버섯 따러 가다 go mushroom-hunting // 원폭에 의한 버섯 구름 a mushroom cloud in an A-bomb explosion
— 구름 [핵폭발의] a mushroom cloud — 벌레 a mushroom parasite — 재배업자 a mushroom grower 독 — a poisonous mushroom
버성기다 [틈이] have a crevice〔crack〕; be cracked〔cleft, split〕; be loosened ; be out of order ; [사이가] be estranged ; be alienated ¶ 두 사람 사이가 버성기어졌다 The two became estranged from each other〔had a break in their friendship〕.
†버스 a (motor) bus 《pl. bus(s)es》; an autobus ; a motor coach 《미》 ¶ 버스로 가다 go 《to a place》 by bus ; take a bus 《to》; bus 《to》 《구》 // 버스에 타다 take a bus ; take a bus ride // 버스를 놓치다 miss a bus ; [비유적으로] miss the bus // 이 근처에는 버스 편이 없다 There is no bus service〔no bus running〕 around here. // 그곳까지 버스 편이 있다 A bus service is available as far as there. /You can get there on the bus〔by bus〕. // 여기는 버스가 다닙니까 Is this a bus route? /Do buses pass this road? // 버스가 얼마나 자주 다닙니까 How often do the buses run?
—값 bus fare — 안내양 a (bus) conductress — 여행 a coach tour — 정류장 a bus stop ; a coach station (장거리 버스의) — 터미널 a bus terminal 관광 — a sightseeing bus ; a rubbernecker bus 시영 — a city-operated bus 장거리 — a long distance bus 통근 — a commuter〔commuting〕 bus 통학 — a school bus
버스러지다 ① [분쇄되다] crumble ; be crushed ; be smashed ; break ; go to pieces ¶ 컵이 떨어져 버스러졌다 The glass fell on the floor and went to pieces.
② [벗겨지다] peel off ; come〔go〕 off ; exfoliate ; be worn off ¶ 칠이 버스러졌다 The paint has peeled〔fallen〕 away.
③ [벗어나다] be beside the point ; go wide ; miss ¶ 처음 계산〔의도〕에서 버스러지다 go wide of the mark // 내 희망이 완전히 버스러졌다 My hopes were shattered.
버스럭거리다 rustle ; make a rustle〔a rustling sound〕
버스름하다 [사이가] be a bit strained ; do not get on together ¶ 둘 사이가 버스름하다 The two of them don't get along very well.
버스트 a bust
버슬버슬 ⇨ 바슬바슬
버슷하다 [관계가] be a bit estranged ; do not get on together ¶ 둘 사이가 버슷하다 The two of them don't get along very well.
버저 a buzzer ¶ 버저를 울리다 buzz
버적버적 with a crunching sound ; with crunches ⇨ 바작바작
*버젓하다 (be) fair and square ; be free from shame ; (be) open and aboveboard ¶ 버젓이 fairly ; in the open ; openly ; overtly // 버젓이 말하다 say openly // 버젓이 비난하다 denounce 〔score〕 in public ; openly assail // 그는 그런 일을 하고도 버젓했다 He did it, and yet with a good conscience. // 도둑은 버젓이 앞문으로 들어왔다 The thief entered the house through the main gate in state. // 면허증도 없이 버젓하게 의사인 체한다 He poses as a doctor though he has no license.
버정이다 walk idly back and forth
버지다 ① [베어지다] be cut ; be scratched (긁히다) ¶ 잘 버지는 칼 a knife that cuts well // 대리석이 물러서 칼로 잘 버진다 Marble is soft, and can be scratched with a knife.
② [찢어지다] fray ; be frayed ; be worn out ; wear out ¶ 소매가 버졌다 The cuff was frayed〔became threadbare〕.
버질 Virgil (로마 70-19 B.C.)
버짐 scabs ; a scabby ; eruption ; pityriasis (진버짐) ; psoriasis (마른버짐)
버쩍 ① [마른 모양] 《dried up》 completely ; entirely ¶ 우물물이 버쩍 말랐다 The well has all dried up. ② [죄는 모양] tightly ; firmly ¶ 버쩍 당기다 pull 《a thing》 with a jerk // 버쩍 죄다 tight fast ③ [우기는 모양] stubbornly ; doggedly ¶ 버쩍 우기다 persist stubbornly ; stick to it ④ [느는 모양] a great deal ; considerably ¶ 버쩍 늘다 increase markedly
버찌 a cherry ; a cherrybob
—술 cherry wine ; kirsch(wasser) 《도》 —씨 a cherry stone —편 a heavy cherry sauce cooked with honey and starch
버치 a large bowl
버캐 scum ; crystallized substance
소금 — crystallized salt ; salt 오줌 — dried-up〔crystallized〕 urine
버커리 a withered old woman ; a hag ; a crone
버클 a buckle
†버터 butter
버터플라이 [수영법] the butterfly stroke
버튼 a button
버티다 ① [견디다] endure ; bear ; tolerate ; stand ¶ 모든 어려운 일을 버티다 stand all hardships // 불경기에 버티어 나가다 weather the times of receding trade // 금년 여름의 더위는 버티기 어렵다 I simply can't stand〔bear〕 the heat of this summer. // 피곤해서 더 이상 버틸 수 없다

I am so tired I cannot hold out any longer. // 이 건물은 강한 지진에 버틸 수 있도록 건축되었다 This house is so constructed as to withstand a violent oscillation in an earthquake. // 그럭저럭 버텨 나가고 있습니다 I'm just getting by.
② [겨루다] withstand ; resist ; hold one's ground ; stand ¶ 순경한테 버티다 resist a policeman // 서로 버티다 compete against each other ; vie〔contend〕 with each other // 유혹에 굴하지 않고 버티다 resist temptation // 쌍방은 다 자기 설을 주장하여 버티었다 The two contending parties remained adamant in asserting their own opinions.
③ [괴다] prop (up) ; support ¶ 막대기로 나무를 버티다 prop up a plant with a stick // 지붕을 버티다 give support to a roof
④ [가누다] keep the balance (몸을) ¶ 한 발로 몸을 버티고 서다 balance oneself on one leg
⑤ [졸음을] force one's eyes open ¶ 눈을 버티고 책을 읽다 force one's eyelids open to read

*버팀목 —木 a support ; a prop ; a stay ¶ 버팀목으로 나무를 버티다 prop up the tree with a wooden support

버팅 〖권투〗 a butt ; butting

벅벅[1] hard ; roughly ⇨ 박박[1]

벅벅[2] 《pockmarked》 all over ⇨ 박박[2]

벅벅이 without fail ; surely ; for sure ; undoubtedly

벅신거리다 swarm ; flock together ; throng ; be thronged ; herd (짐승 따위가) ¶ 무수히 벅신거리다 swarm by thousands // 그 회합에는 사람들이 벅신거렸다 The party was thronged with people.

벅적거리다 bustle ; be crowded ; be thronged ; throng ¶ 거리는 몹시 벅적거렸다 The street was full of bustle. // 그 백화점은 손님들로 벅적거렸다 The department store was crowded with customers.

*벅차다 ① [힘에 겹다] (be) unbearable ; be beyond one's power〔capacity〕 ; be too much for 《one》 ¶ 이 일은 나에게 벅차다 This work is beyond my endurance. /I am not equal to this task. // 저 팀은 우리에겐 벅차다 That team is too much for us. ② [넘치다] be too full ; be torrential ; be in great force ¶ 벅찬 기쁨 an overflowing joy // 벅찬 감사의 마음을 누를 수가 없었다 I was overwhelmed with gratitude. // 개울물이 벅차게 흐른다 The stream rushes in torrents. // 가슴이 벅차서 말이 안 나온다 My heart is too full for words.

번 番 ① [당번] duty ¶ 번들다 go on a (night) watch // 당번이다 be on duty // 비번이다 be off duty
② [차례] turn ¶ 번갈아 by turns ; by shifts // 번을 갈다 take a turn ; shift ; change // 그들은 번갈아 이야기했다 They took turns in telling a story.
③ [횟수] a time ¶ 한번 a time ; once ; one time // 두 번 twice // 한번 더 once more〔again〕 // 여러 번 many times ; many a time // 사람은 한번 죽는다 A man can die but once.
④ [번호] number ¶ 1〔2〕번 number one〔two〕 // 5번 교실 classroom No. 5 // 오른쪽으로부터 세번째의 사람 the man third from the right // 너는 학급에서 몇 번이냐 How do you stand in your class ? // 저는 3번입니다 I stand No. 3 in my class.

번가루 extra flour used in kneading dough properly

번각 飜刻 reprinting ; reimpression ; a reprint ; reproduction **—하다** reprint ; reproduce
—물(物) reprinted materials ; a reprint
—자 a reprinter **—판(版)** a reprinted edition ; a reproduction

번갈아 番— alternately ; by turns ; in turn ¶ 번갈아들다 alternate ; take turns // 그들은 여덟 시간마다 번갈아 일한다 They work in eight-hour shifts. // 그들은 나를 번갈아 찾아 왔다 They came to see me by turns.

*번개 (a flash of) lightning ¶ 번개같은 솜씨 a lightning trick // 번개같이 날쌔게 with lightning as lightning ; in a flash // 번개가 번쩍인다 Lightning flashes. // 그 생각이 번개같이 마음속에 떠올랐다 The thought flashed across〔into〕 my mind. // 번개가 번쩍하자 천둥 소리가 울렸다 The lightning flashed and the thunder filled the air.
번개가 잦으면 천둥을 친다 속담 There is lightning lightly before thunder.

번갯불 a bolt of lightning
번갯불에 솜 구워 먹겠다 속담 be telling a barefaced lie〔a whopper〕
번갯불에 콩 볶아 먹겠다 속담 be quick 〔nimble〕 ; be quick-tempered〔rash, hasty〕

*번거롭다 ① [복잡하다] (be) troublesome ; cumbersome ; irksome ; vexatious ; annoying ; complicated ; involved ; entangled ; intricate ¶ 번거로운 규칙 vexatious rules // 그 연극의 줄거리가 너무 번거롭다 The plot of the play is too involved to follow. ② [시끄럽다] (be) noisy ; boisterous ¶ 번거로운 아이들 noisy children

번거롭히다 [귀찮게 함] trouble ; bother ; keep 《a person》 busy ; cause 《a person》 trouble ; put 《a person》 to trouble ¶ 그 일로 그 분을 번거롭혔다 I troubled him with the matter.

번거하다 ⇨ 번거롭다

번극 煩劇 pressure of business〔work〕 ; busyness **—하다** (be) busy ; be fully occupied 《with》 ; be pressed by business〔work〕 ; (be) overbusy ; have one's hands full

번나다 番— be off duty〔watch〕; be through with one's duty

번뇌 煩惱 agony ; anxiety ; anguish ; [욕욕] evil passions ; lust(s) ; carnal desire —하다 be worried about ; be in distress ; be oppressed 《with》; be in agony ; [욕욕에] be harassed by evil passions

번다 煩多 —하다 (be) multitudinous ; troublesome

번답 反畓 converting a (dry) field into a paddyfield —하다 convert a (dry) field into a paddyfield

번데기 a chrysalis 《*pl.* ~es, -lides》; a pupa 《*pl.* ~s, -pae》

번둥거리다 loiter ; loaf ; be idle〔lazy〕; lead an idle life ¶ 번둥번둥 lazily ; idly // 하는 일 없이 번둥거리다 be at loose ends

번드럽다 [미끄럽다] (be) glossy ; smooth ; lustrous ; [약빠르다] clever ; smart ; shrewd ; sharp

번드르르, 뻔드르르 glossily ; smoothly —하다 (be) glossy ; glabrous ; smooth

번드치다 ① [뒤집다] turn over ; upset ; overturn ② [변심하다] change (one's mind) ¶ 초지를 번드치다 desist from one's original intention

번득, 번뜩 with a flash ¶ 번득거리다 flash ; flicker ; glitter // 그들이 자객이 아닌가 하는 의심이 그의 머리에 번득 들었다 The suspicion flashed across him〔his mind〕 that they might be assassins.

번득이다 [번개·칼 따위가] flash ; fulgurate ; [빛이] glitter ; gleam (희미하게) ; [재치가] scintillate ; flash ; sparkle ¶ 재치의 번득임 a flash of wit

번들거리다 be glossy ; be smooth ; be slippery ; be slimy ¶ 번들번들 smoothly ; glossily

번들다 番— be on duty ; go on guard

번듯하다, 번뜻하다 (be) even ; well-balanced ; symmetrical ; be in harmony

번뜻 in a flash ; quickly

번로 煩勞 trouble ; vexation ; worry ; annoyance ; nuisance —하다 (be) troublesome ; vexatious ; irksome

번론 煩論 troublesome〔vexing, complicated〕 arguments

번롱 翻弄 —하다 trifle with ; fool ; make a fool of ; make sport of ¶ 여자를 번롱하다 trifle with a woman // 배는 격랑에 번롱되었다 The ship was tossed about in the heavy seas.

번루 煩累 troubles ; cares ; annoyances ; encumbrance ¶ 인생의 번루 the worries〔curse〕 of life // 가사상의 번루가 없는 free from family cares // 번류를 벗어나다 get rid of one's cares

번망 煩忙, 繁忙 busyness ; pressure of business —하다 (be) busy ; be pressed〔harassed〕 with business ; be hard at work ; be fully occupied 〔engaged〕 in

번무 煩務 troublesome affairs

번문욕례 繁文縟禮 red tape ; red-tapism ; officialism ; circumlocution

번민 煩悶 agony ; worry ; anguish ; pang —하다 be in agony〔anguish〕; agonize ; suffer ¶ 번민을 잊으려고 술을 마시다 drink to drown one's agony〔mental anguish〕 // 그것 때문에 번민한다 It causes him mental anguish.

번바라지 番— food to be delivered to the man on duty —하다 send food to the man on duty

번방 番房 a watchman's room ; a guard room

번번이 every〔each〕 time ; every occasion ; always ; whenever ; as often as ¶ 서울에 올 때마다 번번이 every time I come to *Seoul* // 몇 번 해 보았지만 번번이 실패했다 I made several attempts and failed as many times.

번번하다 [물건이] (be) smooth ; even ; [얼굴이] fair

번복 翻覆 —하다 change ; turn ; reverse ; upset ¶ 결심을 번복하다 change one's mind

번본 翻本 a reprint ; a reprinted book

번분수 繁分數 『수학』 a compound fraction

번서다 番— go on guard ; stand guard ; be on duty

번설 煩屑 annoyance ; vexations ; vexatiousness ; troubles ; harassment ; harassing

번설 煩說 ① [잔말] boring〔tedious〕 talk ; small talk ; twaddle —하다 talk dully〔tediously〕; chatter ; twaddle ② [소문냄] tattling about ; gossiping —하다 tattle about ; tell tales ; blab off ; gossip

번성 蕃盛 prosperity ; abundance ; [수목 따위의] luxuriance of growth ; exuberancy —하다 prosper ; flourish ; [수목 따위가] grow thick ; luxuriate ; exuberate ¶ 국민은 그의 시정하에서 번성을 누렸다 The nation prospered under his administration.

번성 繁盛 prosperity —하다 prosper ; flourish ; thrive ; grow prosperous ¶ 가정의 번성 the prosperity of one's family // 번성하고 있다 be prosperous ; be thriving ; be flourishing ; be roaring ; be brisk // 번성하지 않다 be unprosperous // 사업이 번성하다 one's business prospers ; one's trade thrives // 가게가 번성하고 있다 The shop is doing〔driving〕 a splendid business.

번쇄 煩瑣 troublesomeness ; complicatedness ; (being in) disorder —하다 (be) troublesome ; annoying ; vexatious ; complicated

— 철학 (medieval) Scholasticism ;

scholastic philosophy ─ 철학자 a Schoolman ; a Scholastic
번수 番手 (yarn) count ¶ 가는〔굵은〕 번수 high〔low〕 count 《thread, yarn》// 20번수의 면사 No. 20 count cotton yarn
*번식 繁殖 propagation ; increase ; multiplication ; breeding ─하다 increase ; propagate ; multiply ; breed ¶ 박테리아의 번식 the propagation of bacteria // 파리는 폐물 속에서 번식한다 Flies breed among waste material.
─기(期) a breeding season ─ 기관(器官) a propagative organ ─력 propagation power ¶ 번식력이 왕성하다 be prolific ─률 a breeding coefficient ─지(地) a breeding place 동종(同種) ─ narrow 〔close, in-and-in〕 breeding ; inbreeding 이종(異種) ─ broad〔cross, out-and-out〕 breeding ; outbreeding 인공 ─ artificial fecundation〔spawning〕
번안 翻案 [안건의] change ; reversal ; switch ; [작품의] an adaptation ─하다 [안건을] change ; reverse ; switch ; [작품을] adapt 《from》
─ 소설 an adapted story
*번역 翻譯 translation ─하다 translate 《English》 into 《Korean》 ; render 《into》 ; put 《into》 ; turn 《into》 ; [암호를] decipher ; decode ¶ 번역으로 생활하다 make a living by doing translations // 번역물로 읽었다 I read it in translation. // 그 여자는 번역을 잘한다 She is a good translator. // 이 이야기는 구주 각국어로 번역되었다 The story has been translated into various European languages.
─가〔자〕 a translator ─권(權) The right to translate ¶ 번역권을 얻다〔얻고 있다〕 secure〔be given〕 translation rights ─료 a charge for translation ─서〔물〕 a translation ─ 착오 a mistranslation 전자─기 an electronic translator
번연 翻然, 幡然 ¶ 번연히 suddenly ; with a sudden turn ; clearly // 번연히 개심했다 He turned over a new leaf.
번열증 煩熱症 a fever ; a febrile disease
*번영 繁榮 prosperity ; flourish ─하다 prosper ; thrive ; flourish ¶ 번영의 prosperous ; flourishing ; thriving // 국가의 번영 the prosperity of a nation ; national prosperity // 시의 번영책 a scheme for booming the city
번요 煩擾 ─하다 (be) annoying ; troublesome ; bothersome ; disturbing
번육 燔肉 roast meat ; grill ; grilled food
번의 翻意 changing one's mind ; reversing one's decision ; reconsideration ─하다 change one's mind ; reverse one's decision ; go back on one's resolution ; eat one's word〔take back one's words〕 (식언하다)
번인 藩人 [토착민] an aboriginal 《*pl.* aborigines》 ; [야만인] a savage ; a barbarian
번잡 煩雜 complexity ; intricacy ─하다 (be) complicated ; complex ; intricate ; troublesome ; annoying ; crowded ; confused ¶ 번잡한 거리 crowded streets
번적 with a flash ─하다 give out a flash ; flash ¶ 번적 빛나다 give out a flash // 눈에서 불이 번적 나다 see stars ; see a flash of red
번적거리다, 번쩍거리다 glitter ; glisten (반사로) ; twinkle (별 따위) ; [섬광] glare ; flash ; sparkle (보석 따위) ¶ 번갯불이 북쪽 하늘에서 가끔 번적거렸다 We saw occasional flashes of lightning in the northern sky. // 풀잎의 이슬이 번적거렸다 The dewdrops sparkled〔glistened〕 on the leaves. // 번적거린다고 반드시 금은 아니다 All is not gold that glitters.
번전 反田 converting a ricefield into a (dry) field ─하다 convert a ricefield into a (dry) field
번족 蕃族 the aborigines〔aboriginal tribes〕 of Taiwan
번족 繁族 a prosperous family ─하다 《a family》 prosper
번주그레하다 (be) rather nice-looking ; attractive
번죽거리다 vex ; provoke ; annoy ; get on one's nerves ; behave in an irritating way ¶ 그는 늘 나한테 번죽거린다 He always annoys me.
번지 『농업』 a soil rake ; a kind of farm tool used in level(l)ing soil or in raking up fallen grain
*번지 番地 a house (lot) number ; the number (of an address) ¶ 주소 번지 one's address // 댁은 몇 번지입니까 What is the number of your house ?
번지기 [씨름에서] a (wrestler's) foot-forward defensive stance
번지다 ① [물 따위가] spread ; run ¶ 이 잉크는 종이에 번진다 This ink spreads on〔runs over, blots on〕 the paper. // 불이 번진다 The fire spreads. // 소문이 번진다 The rumor spreads〔gets abroad〕. // 독이 온 몸에 번진다 The poison runs 〔spreads〕 all through the body. // 빨면 색이 번진다 Colors run in washing.
② [사건 따위가] get serious ; assume serious proportions〔a grave character〕 ; worsen ; be aggravated ¶ 폭동은 크게 번지기 전에 진압되었다 The riot was nipped in the bud. // 불은 번지기 전에 진화되었다 The fire was put out before it got serious.
③ [옮아가다] spread ; be diffused ¶ 홍역이 이웃 마을로 번졌다 Measles spread to a neighboring village.
번지럽다 (be) smooth ; sleek ; glossy ; lustrous
번지르르, 뻔지르르 sleekly ; brightly ; glossily ─하다 (be) sleek ; bright ; smooth ; glossy ; lustrous ¶ 번지르르한 머리털 sleek hair
번지질 『농업』 using a *beonji* (=a soil

rake) ―하다 do the soil raking
번질거리다, 뻔질거리다 be sleek ; be slippery ; be slick ; [약게 굴다] be sly ; be cunning ; be crafty ; be wily ; skulk ¶ 일을 번질거리다 shirk one's duty〔task〕// 번질거리는 버릇이 붙다 get〔fall〕into an idle habit
번질번질 greasily ; sleekly ; shiningly ; brightly ―하다 (be) greasy ; sleek ; shining ; shiny ; bright ; glossy
번쩍¹ with a flash ―하다 give out a flash ; flash ¶ 번쩍 빛나다 give out a flash // 눈에서 불이 번쩍 나다 see stars ; see a flash of red
†번쩍² at a breath ; easily ; lightly ; without any effort ¶ 무거운 돌을 번쩍 들다 lift the heavy stone at a breath ; lift up a huge stone as if it were made of cotton
번쩍번쩍 ① [빛나는 모양] ―하다 [섬광이] flash in rapid succession ; [반사광이] glitter ; shine ; sparkle ¶ 번쩍번쩍하는 보석 a glittering〔dazzling〕jewel
② [들어올리는 모양] ¶ 쌀가마니를 번쩍번쩍 들어올리다 lift up rice sacks easily〔lightly〕in rapid succession
†번쩍이다 shine ; glitter ; be bright〔brilliant〕; twinkle (별 따위가) ; glimmer ⇨ 반짝이다
번차례 番次例 an order ; a turn ¶ 번차례로 one after another ; one by one ; in succession // 번차례를 기다리다 wait for〔await〕one's turn
*번창 繁昌 prosperity ; flourish ; success ―하다 (be) prosperous ; flourishing ; thriving ; successful ; do well ; prosper ; flourish ; thrive ; do a good business ¶ 그 상점은 번창하고 있다 The shop is doing〔driving〕a splendid〔thriving〕business.
번철 燔鐵 a frying pan
번초 蕃椒 red pepper
*번트 〖야구〗 a bunt ―하다 bunt 《a ball》 ¶ 1루 쪽에 번트하다 beat out a bunt to first
드래그 ― a drag bunt 희생 ― a sacrifice bunt
번폐 煩弊 a troublesome abuse ; a harassing evil
번하다, 뻔하다¹ ① [훤하다] (be) light ; bright ¶ 동이 번하게 튼다 The day is dawning bright and clear. ② [분명] (be) clear ; evident ; obvious ; distinct ; unquestionable ; plain ¶ 뻔한 사실 an obvious fact ; the plain truth // 뻔한 거짓말 palpable lies // 그가 실패한다는 것은 뻔한 일이다 It is obvious that he will fail. ③ [여가가 있다] have a little leisure time ; (be) free ; unoccupied ¶ 번한 틈을 타다 make use of one's leisure time 《to do》 ④ [병이] be in a state of lull ; improve slightly ; show signs of improvement ¶ 병이 좀 뻔하다 A patient gets a bit better.

†번호 番號 a number ¶ 번호 순서대로 in numerical order // 번호를 붙이다 number ; give a number // 번호가 없다 be unnumbered〔numberless〕; lack a number // 번호 Number ! (호령) // 번호가 틀렸습니다 (You've got the) wrong number. // 그 번호로 지금 한번 걸어 보세요 Try the number now. // 혹시 그 번호가 사용되지 않고 있는 것은 아닌지 알아봐 줄 수 있습니까 Could you check and see if that number is out of service or something?
―표 a number ticket〔plate〕 ―판 〔자동차 따위의〕 a number plate ; a license (number) plate ; a registration number plate 수험 ― an examinee's slat number
자동 ― 날인기 an automatic numbering machine
†번화 繁華 prosperity ; flourish ; bustle ; liveliness ―하다 (be) lively ; busy ; bustling ¶ 번화한 거리 a thriving town // 번화해지다 prosper ; thrive
―가(街) amusement quarters ; a busy street
벋가다, 뻗가다 stray ; go astray ; behave in a contrary〔perverse〕way
벋나다 protrude ; stick out
벋놓다 turn loose ; give a free rein to
벋니 a projecting〔protruding〕tooth ; a bucktooth
벋다¹ be protruding
벋다², 뻗다 [가지 따위가] spread ; stretch ; extend ; [힘이] spread out ; [쭉 펴다] stretch out ¶ 노기가 하늘까지 벋다 one's anger mounts to the sky // 세력이 뻗다 one's influence is extended // 팔을〔다리를〕 뻗다 stretch one's arm〔leg〕// 그 나뭇가지들이 햇빛 쪽으로 벋고 있다 The branches are spreading toward the sun. // 철도가 그 나라 남단까지 뻗어 있다 The railway line extends to the southern end of the country.
벋대다, 뻗대다 [버티다] hold〔stand〕out ; stand firm ; hold fast to ; [맞서다] oppose ; stand against ; resist ¶ 끝끝내 뻗대다 hold out to the last // 적에게 완강하게 뻗대다 hold out obstinately against the enemy
벋디디다, 뻗디디다 [버티어 내다] stand firmly ; [나가 디디다] step out of bounds
벋버듬하다 have a gap between the two ends
벋버스름하다 be at odds with each other ; have a gulf between each other
벋새 〖건축〗 a flat tile
벋서다, 뻗서다 resist ; oppose ; rise against ⇨ 버티다
벋정다리 a stiff leg ¶ 그는 벋정다리로 걷는다 He walks stiff-legged.
벌¹ [들] field ; a plain ; an open field ; a prairie ¶ 황량한 벌 a wilderness ; a moor // 그 지방에는 넓은 벌이 많다 The province has a large expanse of plains.
*벌² a bee ¶ 벌떼 a swarm of bees // 벌의 침

a bee('s) sting // 벌집 a beehive ; a honeycomb ; a nest of hornets // 벌에 쏘이다 be[get] stung by a bee
꿀— a bee ; a honeybee 땅— a wasp 말— a hornet
†벌³ a set 《of dishes》; a suit 《of clothes》; a copy 《of a set documents》 ¶ 옷 한 벌 a suit of clothes // 반상 두 벌 two sets of dishes // 찻잔 한 벌 a tea set ; a set of tea things ; a tea service // 문서 한 벌 a copy of a set of documents
*벌 罰 punishment ; penalty ; [천벌] judgment ¶ 벌을 주다 inflict punishment upon 《a person》; punish 《a person》
벌 閥 a clique ; a faction ; a clan ; a coterie (동인) ; a combine 《미·속》; sectarianism (종교·학문상의) ¶ 학벌 an academic clique // 군벌 a military group[clique] // 재벌 a great industrial family
벌개지다, 뻘개지다 turn red ; redden ; color ; blush 《for》; flush ¶ 얼굴이 벌개지게 하다 put 《a person》 to the blush // 동쪽 하늘이 벌개지다 The eastern sky brightens[gleams]. // 그녀는 부끄러워서 벌개졌다 She blushed[turned red] for shame.
*벌거벗다, 뻘거벗다 strip[divest] oneself of one's clothes ; strip oneself naked ; strip to the skin ¶ 벌거벗은 사내아이 a naked[bare, undressed, stark-naked] little boy // 벌거벗기다 strip 《a person》 of his clothes ; strip 《a person》 naked ; unclothe ; denude // 벌거벗겨지다 be stripped naked // 벌거벗고 돌아다니다 go about naked[without any clothes on] // 벌거벗으면 사람은 다 마찬가지다 All men are equal if stripped of their garments.
*벌거숭이, 뻘거숭이 a nude ; a naked body

> 참고 **bare**는 평상시에도 가려져 있지 않은 상태를 의미하며 **naked**는 평상시에 몸을 가리어 주던 것 특히 옷이 벗겨진 상태를 뜻한다 **nude**는 옷을 입고 있지 않은 상태를 말한다

¶ 벌거숭이의 naked ; bare ; uncovered ; undressed ; nude // 벌거숭이로 nakedly ; in nudity ; in the buff 《구》; in nature's own[one's birthday] clothes ; in the nude
—산 a bare[naked, deforested, treeless] mountain
벌건 [모두·통째] utter ; downright ¶ 벌건 거짓말 a downright[plump] lie ; a barefaced lie ; pure fabrication // 벌건 상놈 an utterly vulgar person
벌겅, 뻘겅 red ; [진홍] scarlet ; crimson
벌겋다, 뻘겋다 (be) red ; crimson ; ruddy (얼굴이) ¶ 벌건 얼굴 a ruddy face // 벌겋게 red ; ruddily // 서쪽 하늘이 벌겋다 The western sky is aglow with the setting sun.
벌그데데하다 be a dirty red ; be a coarse and unpleasant red
벌그뎅뎅하다 be a messy[smeared, dirty] red
벌그레하다 be tinged with red ; be flushed ; (be) ruddy ; be aglow
벌그무레하다 (be) reddish
벌그숙숙하다, 벌그죽죽하다 (be) reddish ; ruddy
벌그스름하다 (be) reddish
*벌금 罰金 a fine ; a penalty ¶ 벌금을 과하다 fine // 3만 원의 벌금이 부과되다 be fined 30,000 *won* // 속도 위반은 5만 원 이하의 벌금에 처한다 The penalty for speeding is a fine not exceeding 50,000 *won*. // 교통 위반으로 2만 원의 벌금을 물었다 I was fined 20,000 *won* for a violation of traffic regulations.
—형 punishment with a fine ; monetary penalty ; 『법』 amercement
벌긋벌긋 ⇨ 발긋발긋
벌기다 open ; crack open ; cut open
벌꺽 outburst ; suddenly ; all of a sudden ¶ 벌꺽 화를 내어 in a rage // 벌꺽 화를 내다 burst[fly] into a rage[passion] ; flare up // 온 집안이 벌꺽 뒤집혔다 The whole house was in a terrible confusion.
벌꺽거리다 [술·빨래 따위가] bubble up ; [진흙 따위를] make mud squash underfoot ¶ 술이 벌꺽거리다 the rice liquor is bubbling up (as it ferments) ; be bubbling a-brew ; be brewing abubble // 진흙을 벌꺽거리다 squash mud under one's feet
벌꿀 honey ; mel (약용의)
—술 mead
벌끈 [성내는 모양] with a burst of anger ; in a rage ; all of a sudden ; [소란한 모양] in an uproar ; in commotion
—하다 fly into a rage[passion, temper] ; flare[flame] up ; lose one's temper ; blow one's top 《미·속》 ¶ 곧잘 벌끈하는 사람 a blowtop 《미·속》 // 벌끈하여 in a fit of rage[passion, anger] ; in hot blood // 그 소식에 온 마을이 벌끈 뒤집혔다 The whole town was thrown into an uproar with the news.
벌낫 a (field) scythe
벌노랑이 『식물』 a bird's-boot trefoil
벌다¹ get wider ; spread ¶ 사이가 벌다 the crack gets wider ; a chink forms // 마루바닥의 틈이 벌었다 The crack in the floor spread wider.
†벌다² ① earn ; make (money) ; make a profit ¶ 고생해서 번 돈 hard-earned money // 용돈을 벌다 make pocket money // 생활비를 벌다 earn[gain, make] one's living[livelihood] // 부업으로 벌다 earn money on the side // 1할을 벌다 clear[net] ten percent // 쉽게 벌다 make easy money // 그는 날품팔이로 겨우 벌어먹고 있다 한다 I hear he is earning a

poor living as a day laborer. // 상거래에서 큰돈을 벌었다 He made a large〔an immense〕 profit on a deal. // 그 물건을 팔아서 만 원 벌었다 I sold the article at a profit of 10,000 *won*. // 누가 돈을 더 법니까 Who brings more bacon〔groceries〕?
② [자초하다] invite ; earn ; court ; incur ; bring upon oneself ¶ 매를 벌다 ask for a whipping // 욕을 벌다 bring slander upon oneself

벌떡 suddenly ; abruptly ¶ 벌떡 일어서다 spring to one's feet ; get up with a jump // 벌떡 엎드리다 lie flat // 의자에서 벌떡 일어서다 jump up from one's chair

벌떡거리다 ① [가슴이] go pit-a-pat ; palpitate ; throb ; beat ; pulsate ¶ 벌떡거리는 가슴 a beating〔palpitating〕 heart // 가슴이 벌떡 거렸다 My heart throbbed violently.
② [마시다] gulp down ; drink at a gulp ; gorge ; take a swig at 《구》 ¶ 맥주를 벌떡거리며 마시다 toss off〔down〕 a glass of beer ; gulp down a glass of beer

벌떡벌떡 ¶ 맥이 벌떡벌떡 뛰다 one's pulse beats // 벌떡벌떡 마시다 gulp down ; drink at a gulp // 가슴이 벌떡벌떡 뛰다 one's heart flutters

벌렁 on one's back ¶ 벌렁 눕다 lie on one's back ; lie supine // 벌렁 자빠지다 fall on one's back

벌렁거리다 behave lightly ; act nimbly

벌렁벌렁 [민첩히] nimbly ; agilely ; quickly ; [들떠서] gadding about

벌렁코 a flaring nose

‡**벌레** [곤충] an insect ; a bug 《속》; [연충] a worm ; [나방] a moth ¶ 벌레 먹은 worm〔moth〕-eaten // 벌레 먹은 사과 a wormy apple // 벌레 먹은 이 a decayed tooth // 벌레가 끓다 be infested with insects ; worms breed // 벌레가 울다 an insect chips〔sings〕 // 벼에 벌레가 끓는다 The rice-plant is infested with noxious insects.
—그물 an insect net **—집** a cocoon **—혹** a gall

벌레잡이 식물 —植物 an insectivorous plant

벌룩거리다 quiver ; palpitate ; inflate and deflate alternately ; [놀며 다니다] idle away one's time

벌룩벌룩 inflating and deflating alternately ; palpitatingly **—하다** quiver ; palpitate ; inflate and deflate alternately ; [놀며 다니다] idle away one's time

벌룩하다 (be) bulgy ; be inflated

벌룽거리다 behave lightly ; act nimbly

벌름거리다 swell and subside alternately ; quiver

벌름하다 (be) wide open

벌리다[1] [돈이] [사물이 주어] be profitable〔gainful, lucrative〕; yield profits ; [수지맞다] pay ; be paying ; [사람이 주어] make a profit ; gain ; earn ¶ 벌리는 장사 a profitable〔lucrative, paying〕 business

***벌리다**[2] [사이를] open ; widen ; leave space ; [펴다] stretch out ; outstretch ; [늘어놓다] lay out ; arrange ; spread ; display ¶ 입을 크게 벌리다 open one's mouth wide // 두 팔을 벌리다 outstretch one's arms // 사이를 벌리다 widen the space between two things // 그는 식료품 가게를 벌렸다 He opened a grocery store.

벌림새 [상품 따위의] the mode of display〔arrangement〕 ¶ 그 진열창의 물건 벌림새가 훌륭하다 They have a striking display of goods in that show window.

벌매듭 a bee-shaped knot ; a kind of bowknot

벌모 young rice plants growing outside the nursery

벌목 伐木 felling ; cutting ; logging **—하다** cut down ; fell ; lumber
—기(期) a felling season **—꾼** a feller ; a woodcutter **—령**(齡) cutting〔felling〕 ages **— 작업** felling operation

벌물 [논·그릇의] spilt water ; slop ; slopped water ; overflowed water

벌물 罰— ① [마구 마시는] water that is swilled ¶ 벌물 켜듯 마시다 take draughts 《of》; drink heavily ; swill ; swig
② [고문하는] water forced on 《a person》 to drink as punishment

벌바람 wind on an open field

†**벌받다** 罰— [처벌] be punished ; take the penalty ; bring a punishment on oneself 《속》; [천벌] suffer a visitation of God ; be visited with divine punishment ; [응보] be overtaken by retribution ; be served right ; pay dearly 《for》

벌배 罰杯 ⇨ 벌주(罰酒)

벌벌 trembling(ly) ; shivering(ly) ; shaking(ly) ¶ 벌벌 떨다 tremble ; shake ; shiver // 무서워서 벌벌 떨다 shake with〔for〕 fear ; tremble for fear ; shiver with fright // 추워서 벌벌 떨다 shiver with〔from〕 the cold ; quiver from the cold // 흥분으로 벌벌 떨다 shake〔quiver, thrill〕 with emotion〔excitement〕 // 손이 벌벌 떨려서 쓸 수 없었다 I could not write as my hand shook.

벌벙거지 a gang fighter's〔contestant's〕 identifying hat

벌봉 罰俸 ⇨ 감봉(減俸)

벌부 筏夫 a raftsman ; a rafter

벌불 a side prong of a flame ¶ 벌불지다 a flame develops〔has〕 a side prong

벌사양, 벌생 a bride's hairdress

***벌써** already ; yet (의문문에) ; long ago ; by now〔this time〕 (지금쯤은) ¶ 벌써 12시다 It's already twelve o'clock. // 기차가 벌써 떠났습니까—벌써 떠났습니다 Has the train left yet? It left some time ago. // 벌써 그 일을 해 놓았어야 했다 I should have done the work before. // 벌써 다 떨어졌다 I have none left over. // 금방 꾸중 듣고도 벌써 이 따위 장난을 하는구나 You got scolded a moment ago, and you are up to mischief!

벌쐬다 get stung by a bee ¶ 벌쏜 사람 같다 be like a man stung by a bee

벌쓰다 罰— be punished ; suffer punishment ; 《a child》 stand a corner

벌씌우다 罰— punish ; penalize ; visit 《a person》 with punishment ; stand 《a child》 in the corner ¶ 선생은 그 아이를 벌씌웠다 The teacher made the child stand in the corner.

벌어먹다 earn one's bread〔living, livelihood〕; work for one's living ; support oneself ¶ 이럭저럭 벌어먹다 live by shifts ; manage to live〔get along〕; make a bare living (간신히) // 벌어먹기 힘들다 find it hard to make a living // 아내가 벌어먹는다 He lives on his wife's earnings.

벌어지다 ① [틈이] widen ; get wider ¶ 그들은 사이가 벌어졌다 They became estranged.
② [일이] get serious ; get enlarged ; spread ; develop ; [터지다] arise ; break out ¶ 원유회가 벌어졌다 The garden party took place. // 두 나라 사이에 싸움이 벌어지려 한다 War is brewing between the two countries. // 귀찮은 일이 벌어졌다 There is mischief afoot.
③ [몸이] grow stout〔firm〕 ¶ 어깨가 딱 벌어졌다 be square〔broad〕-shouldered ; have broad shoulders

벌열 閥閱 a distinguished family〔clan〕

벌윷 a *yut* stick that fell out of bounds

벌이 a livelihood ; a job ; an income ¶ 벌이가 좋다 have a good income // 그날 벌이로 지내다 live from hand to mouth
—터 one's place of work **벌잇길** a means of earning one's bread **벌잇줄** a source of income〔earning〕

*__벌이다__ spread ; arrange ; display ¶ 운동을 벌이다 start〔launch〕 a movement // 사업을 벌이다 embark in〔on〕 an enterprise // 장사를 벌이다 start business ; go into business // 가게를 벌이다 set up in business ; open up the shop ; open a store // 잔치를 벌이다 give a banquet ; spread a banquet // 진열창에 상품을 벌여놓다 arrange goods in the show window // 방에 물건을 벌여 놓다 leave things lying about a room ; scatter things about a room

벌이줄 a cord ; a tie string

벌전 罰錢 a cash penalty ; a fine

벌점 罰點 a demerit ; black marks ¶ 벌점을 주다 give black marks 《for》

벌족 閥族 a distinguished family〔clan〕
— 정치 clan government

벌주 罰酒 the wine forced on 《a person》 to drink as punishment

벌주다 罰— punish ; inflict penalty on 《a culprit》

*__벌집__ a beehive ; a honeycomb ¶ 방안이 벌집 쑤셔 놓은 듯하였다 The room was just a hive of excitement〔in utter confusion〕. // 탄환이 벽을 벌집처럼 뚫어 놨다 Bullets riddled the wall.

벌쩍거리다 ① [움직거리다] squirm ; wriggle ¶ 아기가 일어나려고 벌쩍거린다 The baby squirms to get up. ② [비벼 빨다] rub lazily〔unenergetically〕; scrub softly ¶ 벌쩍거리지 말고 잘 빨아라 Don't scrub with so little energy-rub hard.

벌쩍벌쩍 struggling(ly) ; floundering(ly) ; [빨래를] 《rub, scrub》 roughly ; reluctantly —**하다** ① [움직거리다] squirm ; wriggle ② [비벼 빨다] rub lazily〔unenergetically〕; scrub softly

벌쭉거리다 pucker 《it》 up

벌창 —**하다** [물이] overflow ; run over ; flood ; [물건이] be flooded 《with》; be glutted 《with》 ¶ 시장에 물자가 벌창하다 The market is glutted with commodities.

벌채 伐採 felling ; lumbering ; deforestation —**하다** cut down ; fell 《trees》 ¶ 산림을 벌채하다 exploit〔work, cut down〕 a forest
—량 a fall — 면적 a cutover area — 방법〔순서〕 a cutting method〔order〕 —자 a feller ; a woodcutter

벌책 罰責 reproof ; rebuke ; reprimand ; censure —**하다** reprove ; rebuke ; reprimand ; censure ¶ 잘못을 벌책하다 censure 《a person》 for a fault // 벌책(처분)을 받다 be reprimanded

벌초 伐草 mowing ; cutting the weeds〔mowing the grass〕 around a grave
—**하다** mow ; cut the weeds〔mow the grass〕 around a grave

벌충 recovery ; supplement ; compensation —**하다** recover ; make up 《for》; compensate ; make amends ; make good ¶ 손해를 벌충하다 recover one's losses ; make up for the loss ; make good the loss ; compensate a loss // 충분히 벌충됐다 Full amends were made.

벌치 a wild cantaloupe

벌칙 罰則 penal clauses〔regulations〕; punitive rules〔provisions〕; a disciplinary code ¶ 벌칙에 저촉되다 infringe the penal regulations

벌컥 all of a sudden ⇨ 벌꺽

벌타령 —打令 doing 《things》 at random〔as one pleases〕; acting impetuously

*__벌통__ —桶 a wooden beehive

†**벌판** [평야] a plain ; a field ; [대초원] a prairie 《미》; steppe (시베리아 지역의) ; [황야] a moor ; a wilderness

†**범** a tiger ; a tigress (암컷) ¶ 새끼범 a tiger cub ; a tiger kitten // 범의 굴에 들어가야 범을 잡는다 Nothing ventured, nothing gained. /He who would search

for pearls, must dive below.
범 없는 골에는 토끼가 스승이라 〔속담〕 For want of a wise man, a fool is set in the chair. /In the kingdom of the blind, the one-eyed is King.
범모르는 하룻강아지 〔속담〕 Fools rush in where angels fear to tread.
범 犯 an offense ; a violation ―하다 commit 《a crime, a sin》 ; violate ; infringe
강력― a violent criminal 상습― a habitual criminal ; a recidivist 전과 2― the criminal with two previous convictions 절도― larceny 지능― an intellectual criminal 파렴치― an infamous criminal
범- 汎 Pan- ¶ 범아메리카주의 Pan-Americanism
범계 犯界 a border violation ―하다 violate a border
범고래 〖동물〗 a grampus ; a killer whale ; Grampus orca (학명)
범골 凡骨 an ordinary person ; a mediocre person ⇨ 범인(凡人)
범과 犯過 a fault ; a wrong ―하다 commit a fault ; do a wrong
범국민 汎國民 pan-national
― 운동 a pan-national campaign 〔movement, drive〕
범금 犯禁 violation of bans ―하다 violate a ban ; break a prohibition law ; transgress ; contravene ; infringe
범꼬리 〖식물〗 the common bistort
범나비 〖곤충〗 a (tiger) swallowtail (butterfly)
―벌레 the caterpillar of the swallowtail
범독 泛讀 reading at random ; desultory reading ; skimming ; scanning ―하다 skim ; scan 《미·구》 ; read at random ; read desultorily ; skip through
범띠 the attributes of (one born in the year of) the Tiger
†범람 氾濫, 汎濫 [물의] overflowing ; flood ; inundation ; deluge ; spate ; [제분수에] presumption ; forwardness ―하다 overflow 《the banks》 ; flow over 《the banks》 ; be presumptive ; be forward ¶ 강이 범람하고 있다 The river is in flood〔out of its banks, overflowing its banks〕. // 거리에 자동차가 범람하고 있다 The street is deluged with cars.
범례 凡例 introductory remarks ; explanatory notes
범론 汎論, 氾論 a summary ; general remarks ; an outline ; an introduction
범론 泛論 a vague remark ; vague talk
범류 凡類 ordinary persons ; ordinary minds ; the common run of men ; laymen ; a mediocrity
범리론 汎理論 〖철학〗 Hegelism ; panlogicism
범미 汎美 Pan-America(n)
―주의 Pan-Americanism ― 회의 the Pan-American Conference

범민 凡民 a commoner ; the common people ; a plebeian
범방 犯房 having sexual〔marital〕 intercourse ―하다 have sexual〔marital〕 intercourse 《with》
범백 凡百 ① [모든 것] all things〔matters〕 ② [예절] manners ; etiquette ; breeding ; one's daily behavior ¶ 그는 범백을 모른다 He has no manners〔sense of proprieties〕. /He is ill-mannered. /He knows no etiquette. // 그 여자는 범백이 바르다 She is well-mannered. /She has good manners.
―중생 all creatures
범벅 [음식] pudding prepared with rice ; flour and pumpkin ; [일] a medley ; a mess ; a pell-mell ; a hotchpotch ; a muddle ; a jumble
범벅이 되다 〔관용〕 go to pie ; be jumbled together ; be in a muddle ; be mixed up ; be messed up
범범하다 泛泛― (be) careless ; heedless ; negligent ; inattentive ¶ 범범한 사람 a careless person ; a blockhead ; a simpleton
범법 犯法 violation of the law ; breaking the law ; an offense against the law ―하다 violate〔transgress〕 the law ; break the law
―자 a lawbreaker ; an offender 《against the law》 ― 행위 an illegal act ; [공무원 따위의] an irregularity ; (a) malfeasance ; misconduct
범부 凡夫 an ordinary person ; a mediocrity ; a common mortal ; the common run of people ; a layman ¶ 부처도 본래는 우리와 같은 범부였다 The Buddha was originally a common mortal like one of us.
범부채 〖식물〗 a variety of iris
범분 犯分 ―하다 forget one's own place ; show insolence ; go beyond one's duty ; exceed one's authority
범사 凡事 ① [만사] all matters ; every thing ; all things ② [평범한 일] an ordinary matter ; a common affair
범살장지 〖건축〗 a paper sliding door of crude latticework〔coarse structure〕
범상 凡常 ―하다 (be) ordinary ; common ; commonplace ; normal ; average ; mediocre ¶ 범상치 않은 remarkable ; extraordinary ; uncommon ; 《a thing》 out of the common ; abnormal (병적인) // 범상한 사람 an average〔ordinary〕 man // 범상치 않은 재능 an unusual gift〔talent〕 ; talents above the average ; extraordinary abilities // 일견해서 범상치 않은 사람이라는 것을 알았다 I saw at a glance that he was no ordinary man.
범색 犯色 immoderate sexual intercourse ―하다 have immoderate sexual intercourse

범서 凡書 a mediocre book ; an ordinary book

범서 梵書 Buddhist scriptures (불경) ; a book written in Sanskrit

범선 帆船 a sailing boat ; a sailer

범속 凡俗 mediocrity ; banality ; commonplaceness ; vulgarity —하다 (be) mediocre ; ordinary ; common ; commonplace ; vulgar ¶ 범속을 초탈하다 rise above the common crowd

범수 犯手 ① [손찌검] hitting ; beating ; striking —하다 hit ; beat ; strike ② [범용] peculation ⇨ 범용(犯用)

범신교 汎神敎 pantheism ¶ 범신교적 pantheistic
—도 a pantheist

범신론 汎神論 pantheism ¶ 범신론적 pantheistic
—자 a pantheist

범심론 汎心論 panpsychism

범아귀 the space between the thumb and the forefinger

범안 凡— a layman's〔an unprofessional〕 eye ; the uninitiated (eye) ; an ordinary intelligence (안식) ¶ 범안에게는 그렇게 보일는지도 모른다 It may look so to the uninitiated〔untrained〕 eye.

범애 汎愛 philanthropy ; universal love —하다 love all〔everybody〕
—주의 philanthropism

범어 梵語 Sanskrit ; Pali ¶ 범어의 Sanskrit(ic)
— 학자 a Sanskrit scholar ; a Sanskritist

범연 氾然, 泛然 —하다 (be) indifferent ; careless ; heedless ; inattentive ; sloppy

범용 凡庸 mediocrity ; commonplace ; banality —하다 (be) mediocre ; common(-place) ; ordinary ; banal ; platitudinous

범용 犯用 peculation ; misappropriation ; embezzlement —하다 peculate ; misappropriate ; embezzle ; use illegally ¶ 공금을 범용하다 embezzle〔misappropriate〕 public funds // 그 돈의 약간을 범용했다 Some of the money stuck to his fingers.

범월 犯越 border transgression ; illegal crossing of a border ; violation of the border —하다 violate《a border》; illegally cross《a border》

†범위 範圍 scope ; sphere ; province ; range ; extent ; horizon ; purview ; [제한] limits ; bounds ; compass ; reach

> 참고 **range** 마음 감각 기계 따위가 유효하게 작용할 수 있는 범위 **scope** 이해 시력 적용 따위의 가능한 범위 **compass** 사물의 작용이 미치는 범위 **reach** 능력 유효도의 극한

¶ 내가 아는 범위에서는 as far as I know // 넓은 범위에 걸치다 cover a wide scope〔range〕 // 범위를 한정하다 set limits〔bounds〕 to // 교제 범위가 넓다 He has a large (circle of) acquaintance(s). // 이것은 내가 생각하고 있는 가격 범위를 벗어난 것이다 This is out of my price range.
세력 — a sphere〔an orbit〕 of influence
활동 — the sphere of activity

범의 犯意 〖법〗 criminal intent ; intention of commitment ; malice

범의귀 〖식물〗 a creeping〔strawberry, beefsteak〕 saxifrage

범인 凡人 an ordinary man ; a man of mediocre talent ; the common run of people《총칭》 ¶ 그것은 범인의 힘으로는 할 수 없다 It is beyond the power of a common mortal.

*범인 犯人 a criminal ; a culprit ; an offender ; a convict ¶ 범인을 은닉하다 harbor〔shelter〕 a criminal // 범인은 아직 체포되지 않았다 The criminal is still at large.
— 수사 man〔criminal〕 hunt — (신병) 인도 협정 an extradition agreement〔treaty〕 (국제간의) — 용의자 a criminal suspect — 은닉 concealment of an offender

범일 汎溢, 氾溢 inundation ; overflowing ; flooding —하다 overflow ; inundate ; flood

범입 犯入 illegal entry —하다 trespass ; illegally enter ¶ 개인 주거에 범입하다 forcibly enter a private dwelling

범자 梵字 Sanskrit

범재 凡才 common〔ordinary〕 ability ; a person of common ability ; a (man of) mediocrity

범절 凡節 manners ; etiquette ; decorum ; propriety ; form ; deportment

범종 梵鐘 the bell of a Buddhist temple ; a temple bell

†범죄 犯罪 a crime ; an offense ; a criminal act ; a culpable act ; a delict ; a misdemeanor —하다 commit〔perpetrate〕 a crime ; violate〔offend, infringe〕 the law ¶ 범죄의 현장 the scene of a crime // 범죄적 criminal // 이곳 범죄가 그렇게 심합니까 Is the crime situation that bad here?
— 감식 자료 materials〔data〕 for criminal identification — 건수 the number of offenses〔crimes〕 committed — 과학 criminalistics — 발생률 a crime rate — 사실 the facts constituting an offense〔a crime〕 — 사회학 criminal sociology — 소설 crime stories — 심리 criminal psychology ; crime complex — 예방 the prevention of crime ; crime prevention — 용의자 a suspected criminal — 조직 a criminal syndicate — 통계 criminal〔crime〕 statistics —학 criminology —학자 a criminologist — 행위 a criminal act —형(型) a crime type 발동〔우연〕성 — an active〔occasional〕 crime 상습 —자 a habitual criminal 소년 — a juvenile

delinquency 소년 —자 juvenile delinquent 전쟁 —자 a war criminal 집단 — an organized crime (조직적인) ; a group crime (조직적 단체가 아닌)
범죄 감식 犯罪鑑識 criminal identification
범죄 감정법 犯罪鑑定法 a system of criminal identification
범죄 수사 犯罪搜査 (a) criminal investigation
—계(원) a criminal investigator
*범죄인 犯罪— an offender ; a criminal ; a culprit (미결의) ; a convict (기결의) ; a con (죄수) 《미·속》
범죄자 犯罪者 ⇨ 범죄인
‡범주 範疇 a category ; a class ¶ 미적 범주 an (a)esthetic category // 범주에 넣다 place under the category 《of》 // 범주에 들다 fall under〔come within〕 the category 《of》
범주 泛舟 floating a boat —하다 set a boat afloat
범주하다 帆走— sail
범천 梵天 〖불교〗 Brahma
—왕 Brahma the Creator
범청 泛聽 inattentive listening —하다 listen inattentively
범칙 犯則 infringement〔violation, breach〕 of regulations ; transgression of the law ; default —하다 infringe〔violate〕 regulations ; transgress ; default
— 물자 illegal materials〔goods〕 ; [밀수품] a smuggled article —자 an offender ; a transgressor ; a defaulter
범칭 泛稱, 汎稱 a general title〔term〕 ; a popular name
범타 凡打 〖야구〗 poor batting —하다 make a poor show of batting
범퇴 凡退 —하다 〖야구〗 be easily put out ¶ 삼자 범퇴가 되었다 They went out in a one-two-three order. /Three went out in quick order.
*범퍼 ① [완충 장치] a bumper ② [차번호] an auto licenseplate number
범포 帆布 canvas ; sailcloth
‡범하다 犯— [죄를] commit ; perpetrate ; sin against 《morality》 ; be guilty of ; [규칙·법률을] violate ; infringe ; break ; offend again-st ; transgress ; [여자를] violate ; outrage ; rape ; attack ; assault ¶ 범할 수 없는 위풍 dignified appearance // 교칙을 범하다 break the school regulations // 중립국의 영토를 범하다 violate neutral territory // 특허권을 범하다 infringe patent rights // 신성하여 범할 수 없다 be sacred and inviolable // 법을 범해 가면서 몰래 영업을 하다 run on the quiet in violation of the law ; operate secretly and illegally // 벌이 무서워서 죄를 범하지 않는 사람이 많다 The fear of punishment deters many people from crime.
범행 犯行 a crime ; an offense ¶ 범행을 부인하다 deny〔refuse〕 to admit one's crime // 범행이 발각되다 have one's offense detected
— 현장 the scene of an offense
†법 法 ① [법칙·법률] a law ; [총칭] the law ; [법칙] a rule ; [법전] a code ¶ 법의 힘 the arm of the law // 법에 어그러지지 않는 lawful ; legal // 법에 어그러지는 unlawful // 법에 호소하다 appeal to the law // 법을 위반하다 violate〔break〕 the law // 법을 지키다 observe〔keep, obey〕 the law ② [방법] a method ; a way ¶ 글쓰는 법 how to write
③ [도리] reason ; justification ¶ 법에 어긋나다 be wrong ; be unreasonable
— 집행 기관 a law enforcement agency
교수— a teaching method 서술— indicative mood 장수— a recipe for long life
법은 멀고 주먹은 가깝다 〈속담〉 Where drums beat, laws are silent.
법계 法系 the legal system ; a code of law
로마 — Roman law 중국 — the Chinese legal system ; Chinese law
법계 法界 〖불교〗 the realm of Buddhism ; the universe ; the world〔circles, society〕 of Buddhists ; [법조계] legal circles ; the judicial (world)
법과 法科 [학부] the law department ; the law school 《미》 ; [과정] a law course ¶ 법과를 수학하다 complete a law course
— 대학 the college of law ; a law school
— 출신 a graduate of the law department
— 학생 a law student
†법관 法官 a judicial officer ; a judge ; the judiciary 《총칭》 ; the bench (집합적)
법권 法權 a legal right
*법규 法規 laws and regulations ; legislation ¶ 법규의 불비로 owing to a defect〔fault〕 in legislation // 법규상의 수속을 마치다 go through all legal formalities
현행 — the law in force ¶ 현행 법규를 무시하다 neglect the law in force
법당 法堂 a building that contains a statue of Buddha ; a sermon hall ; the sanctuary
법도 法度 a law ; a rule ; regulations
법등 法燈 〖불교〗 [불법] the light of Buddhism ; the teachings of Buddha ; [전통] Buddhistic tradition〔heritage〕 ; [등불] a light offered to the Buddhist altar
법랑 琺瑯 enamel ¶ 법랑을 칠하다 enamel
—질 enamel (of teeth) — 칠기 enameled ironware
‡법령 法令 a statute ; laws and ordinances ¶ 법령에 정해져 있다 be provided for〔be specified〕 in the law
— 양식 legal forms —집 the complete collection of laws and regulations ; a statute book
법례 法例 the law governing the application of laws ¶ 법례의 정하는 바에 따라서 according to the rule concerning the application of the law
†법률 法律 a law ; a statute ¶ …을 금하는

법률 a law against 《gambling》 // 법률을 잘 지키는 국민 a law-abiding people // 법률상의 legal ; judicial // 법률상 legally ; judicially // 법률에 위반되는 unlawful ; illegal ; against the law // 법률에 맞는 lawful ; legal // 법률상의 견지에서 from a legal point of view ; in the eye of the law // 법률에 규정되어 있다 be specified〔provided for〕 in the law // 법률로써 금하다 prohibit 《a matter》 by law // 법률에 호소하다 have recourse to law // 법률을 배우다 study law // 법률을 제정하다 make〔enact〕 a law // 법률을 지키다〔어기다〕 observe〔break〕 the law // 법률 상담에 응하다 take legal advice // 법률상의 수단을 취하다 take legal steps // 법률에 의해서 처분하다 deal with 《a case》 according to law
—가 a lawyer ; a jurist — 고문 a legal adviser — 문제 a legal question — 사무 the practice of law ; legal work — 사무소 a law office — 사실 a legal matter — 상담 legal advice —서 a lawbook —안 a legislative bill ; a draft of a proposed law — 용어 a legal〔law〕 term — 위반 a breach of the law — 전문가 a legal expert ; a jurist — 제도 the legal system —학 jurisprudence — 행위 a legal act〔action〕
법리 法理 a principle of law
—학 jurisprudence ; the science of law ¶ 법리학의 jurisprudential —학자 a jurisprudent
법망 法網 the net〔hands, clutch, grip〕 of the law ¶ 법망에 걸리다 fall into the hands〔clutches〕 of the law // 법망을 피하다 evade the law ; escape the meshes of the law ; slip from the grip of the law
법명 法名 one's Buddhist name ; a sacred name ; [죽은 사람의] a posthumous Buddhist name.
법무 法務 judicial affairs ; 〖불교〗 clerical duty
—관 a judiciary ; a law officer ; 〖군사〗 a judge advocate —국 the Bureau of Judicial Affairs
법무부 法務部 the Ministry of Justice ; the Justice Department
— 장관 the Minister of Justice ; the Justice Minister
법무사 法務士 a judicial scrivener
법문 法文 〖법〗 the law ; written laws ; [법과와 문과] law and literature ; 〖불교〗 Buddhist writings ¶ 법문에 규정되어 있다 be provided〔specified〕 in the law
—화 legalization ¶ 법문화하다 put on the statute book ; enact into law ; codify
법문 法門 Buddhism ; the Buddhist priesthood ¶ 법문에 들어가다 enter the Buddhist priesthood
법복 法服 [재판관의] a judge's robe ; a gown ; [변호사의] a lawyer's robe ; a barrister's gown ; [승려의] a sacerdotal 〔clerical〕 robe
법사 法師 a Buddhist priest〔monk〕 ; a bonze ; [법주] the teacher of a Buddhist priest
법사 위원회 法司委員會 the Legislation and Judiciary Committee (국회의)
****법석** a noise ; a fuss ; a bustle ; a clamor ; an uproar ¶ 법석떨다 make a lot of noise ; raise a clamor ; make a fuss ; be in a bustle // 사소한 일에 법석을 떨다 make a great fuss about trifles〔nothing〕 ; raise a storm in a teacup // 마을에서는 야단법석이 났다 The village is in an uproar. // 손님을 맞느라고 법석을 부리다 make much ado to receive a guest ; lionize a guest // 법석이 가라앉다 the tumult subsides
—판 a clamorous〔noisy〕 scene ; a clamor ; noise ; pandemonium
법수 法手 a means ; a method ; ways and means
법수 法數 〖수학〗 a divisor
법식 法式 [형식] a form ; [방법] a method ; a process ; [정식] a formula 《*pl.* ～s, -lae》 ; [수속] formalities ; [관례] usage ; 〖불교〗 Buddhist ritual ; formalities of a Buddhist ceremony ¶ 일정한 법식 a regular〔proper〕 form // 법식에 따르다〔위반하다〕 conform〔run counter〕 to the usage // 법식대로 증서를 쓰다 draw up a deed in proper form
†**법안 法案** a bill ; a measure ¶ 법안을 제출하다 introduce〔bring in〕 a bill // 법안을 가결하다 pass a bill ; railroad a bill
법어 法語 〖불교〗 ① [설교] a Buddhist sermon ; Buddhist literature
② Buddhistic terms ; a Buddhist term
법언 法言 canonical remarks
법열 法悅 ecstasy ; rapture ; transport ; 〖불교〗 religious exaltation
법왕 法王 ① [불교에서] Tathagata ; Buddha ② [카톨릭교에서] the pope ; the pontiff
— 정치 papal government ; papacy — 제도 the papal system ; papacy
법요 法要 〖불교〗 a Buddhist service ; a memorial service
법원 法院 a court of justice〔law〕 ; a courtroom ; a tribunal ; the bar
— 서기 a clerk of the court —장 the president〔presiding officer〕 of a court — 행정처 the Office of Court Administration 가정 — the Court of Family Affairs ; the Family Court 고등 — an appellate court ; a court of appeal 대— the Supreme Court 지방 — a district court 지방 — 판사 a district judge
법의 法衣 〖불교〗 a sacerdotal robe ; canonical dress ; canonicals ; a Buddhist priest's robe
법의 法意 the spirit〔intent〕 of the law
법의학 法醫學 medical jurisprudence ; legal〔forensic〕 medicine ¶ 법의학의

medicolegal
— 교실 a legal medicine lecture room — 자 a doctor of forensic medicine〔medical jurisprudence〕; a medicolegal expert

법익 法益 the benefit and protection of the law

⁑법인 法人 〖법〗 a juridical〔legal〕 person ; an imaginary person for legal purpose ; an artificial person ; a corporation ; a body corporate ¶ 법인 조직으로 하다 incorporate 《a firm》
— 과세 taxation on juridical persons —권(權) corporate rights — 단체 a body corporate — 설정 incorporation — 설정 인가증 a certificate of incorporation —세 the corporation tax — 소득 the income of a corporation — 신탁 corporation trust — 이득세 the corporation profit tax — 자본세 corporation capital tax — 자산 corporate assets 공개 — an open corporation 국내 — a domestic corporation 단독 — a corporation sole 사단 — a corporation aggregate 영리 — a business corporation 외국 — a foreign corporation 재단 — a juridical foundation 특수 — a corporation〔juridical person〕 having a special status 공개 — 체제 an open corporate structure

법적 法的 (being) legal ; legalistic
— 근거 a legal basis — 수단 legal procedure〔steps, action, proceedings〕 ¶ 법적 수단을 취하다 take legal steps 〔action〕; institute legal proceedings

†법전 法典 a code of laws ; a statute ; 〖종교〗 a canon ¶ 법전을 제정하다 establish a code // 법전을 편찬하다 codify laws
— 편찬 codification — 편찬자 a codifier 현행 — the code in force

†법정 法廷 a law court ; the court of law ; a tribunal ; the bar ¶ 법정 전술 legal tactics // 법정의 웅변 forensic eloquence // 법정에 나가다 appear in court // 법정에 서다 stand at the bar // 법정에서 싸우다 go to law with 《a person》 // 법정에 소송을 제기하다 bring 《a matter》 into court // 법정을 열다 hold a court (재판관이) // 법정이 개정되었다 The court is sitting.
— 모욕죄 (criminal) contempt of court — 투쟁 court struggle ; 〖노동〗 a litigating struggle 대〔소〕— a Grand 〔Petty〕 Bench 《of the Supreme Court》

법정 法定 — 하다 provide by law ; fix by law ; ordain〔stipulate〕 by law ¶ 법정의 legal ; statutory
— 가격 the legal price — (가독) 상속인 the legal heir to a house ; the heir-at-law — 과실 〖법〗 legal fruits — 기간 a statutory period — 기일 legal deadline — 대리인 a legal representative — 득표수 the legally required minimum number of votes — 선거 비용 the amount authorized by law for election campaign expenses — 세율 statutory tariffs —수 a quorum (출석의) — 신탁 a constructive trust — 의무 a legal duty — 이율 the legal rate of interest — 이자 the legal〔lawful, legitimate〕 interest —일 a legal day — 재산제 the legal property system — 적립금〔준비금〕 legal reserve — 전염병 an infectious disease designated by law ; a legal epidemic — 평가(平價) the mint par of exchange (환의) — 호주 상속인 the legal heir to a house ; the heir-at-law — 화폐 legal tender — 후견인 a statutory guardian — 휴일 a legal holiday

법제 法制 legislation ; laws ; the legislative system
—사 annals of legislation ; a history of laws — 사법 분과 위원회 the Legislation and Judiciary Committee —처 (장) (Director of) the Office of Legislation ; (Director of) the Legislative Office

법조 法曹 judicial officers ; judges and lawyers ; the bench and (the) bar
—계 legal circles ; the legal world〔profession〕; the bench and (the) bar

법주 法主 a Buddhist high priest ; [법사] the teacher of a Buddhist priest

법치 法治 constitutional government ; governing according to the law
— 국가 a constitutional state ; a law-governed country — 사회 a community of law ; a law-abiding society —주의 constitutionalism ; legalism

법칙 法則 a law ; a rule ¶ 자연의 법칙 a law of nature ; a natural law
—론 nomology 자연 — a law of nature ; a natural law

법통 法統 〖불교〗 a religious tradition

법폐 法弊 (a Chinese) legal tender

⁑법하다 have good reason to 《be, do》; It ought to be 《that》; It can be expected 《that》; It seems likely 《that》 ¶ 그가 화날 법도하다 He has every right to be angry. // 비가 올 법도하건만 It should rain but it doesn't. // 그가 왔을 법도하다 He must have arrived. // 그 일이 될법도하다 It seems likely to succeed. // 비가 올법도하다 It looks like rain.

*법학 法學 law ; [법리학] jurisprudence
—도 a law student — 박사 [사람] a doctor of laws ; [학위] Doctor of Laws 《LL. D.》 —부 a law department 〔school〕; the faculty of jurisprudence — 사(士) a bachelor of laws ; [학위] Bachelor of Laws 《LL. B》 — 석사 a master of Laws ; [학위] Master of Laws 《LL. M.》 —자 a jurist — 통론〔개론〕 an outline of law ; a compendium of law ; an introduction to law —회 the Jurisprudence Society

법호 法號 〖불교〗 a (posthumous) Buddhist name

법화 法貨 〖경제〗 legal tender ; lawful

money
법화 法話 a sermon ; a homily
법화경 法華經 〖불교〗 the Saddharmapundarika Sutra
법회 法會 a Buddhist ceremony ; a memorial service ¶ 고인을 위해서 법회를 열다 hold a memorial service〔Buddhist service〕 for the dead ; have a ceremony for the repose of a soul
†벗 a friend ; a companion ; a mate ; a pal〔chum〕《구》 ¶ 친한 벗 an intimate friend ; a chum // 믿을 수 없는 벗 a fair-weather friend // 신앙의 벗 a brother〔sister〕 in faith // 생애의 벗 a lifelong friend // 책을 벗삼다 have books for companions // 벗을 얻기는 어렵고 잃기는 쉽다 A friend is easier lost than found.
벗가다 go beyond the limit ⇨ 벗나가다
벗개다 clear up
*벗겨지다 ① [신·옷 따위] come off ; be taken〔stripped〕 off ; get undressed ; slip off〔down, out〕 ; [단추 따위] be unbuttoned〔unzipped〕 ¶ 구두가 벗겨지지 않는다 My shoes will not come off.
② [칠·비늘 따위] fall〔come〕 off ; [거죽·껍질 따위] get stripped off ; grow〔get〕 bald (머리가) ; peel off〔away〕 ; fret (금박이) ; fade〔discolor〕 (색깔이) ; clear up (구름이) ¶ 옻이 군데군데 벗겨져 있었다 The lacquer was (worn) off in places. // 페인트 칠이 벗겨졌다 The paint has peeled〔fallen〕 away. // 이 색깔은 씻어도 벗겨지지 않는다 This color will stand the wash.
③ [덮개 따위] get removed ; be taken off
†벗기다 ① [옷을] unclothe ; undress ; strip《a person of his clothes》 ; take〔strip〕 off《a person's clothes》 ¶ 빨가벗기다 strip《a person》 to the skin // 아이의 옷을 벗겨 주다 undress a child // 외투를 벗겨 주다 help《a person》 take off his overcoat // 그의 옷을 벗겨서 호주머니를 조사했다 They stripped him and searched his pockets.
② [껍질을] peel ; skin ; pare ; flay ; strip off ¶ 나무 껍질을 벗기다 peel〔strip〕 a tree from the bark // 벽지를 벗기다 strip paper from the wall // 바나나 껍질을 벗기다 peel a banana // 사과 껍질을 벗기다 pare an apple // 토끼 껍질을 벗기다 flay a rabbit // 범의 껍질을 벗기다 skin a tiger
③ [제거하다] remove ; take off ¶ 지붕에서 기와를 벗기다 remove tiles from the roof // 뚜껑〔담요〕를 벗기다 take off the lid〔blanket〕 // 그의 가면을 벗기고 말겠다 I will show up his hypocrisy.
벗기어지다 ⇨ 벗겨지다
벗나가다 deviate ; swerve《from》 ; go astray ; go beyond the limit ; [비유적] behave improperly ¶ 벗나간 짓 an improper behavior ; an outrageous act
벗놓다 let go astray ; let stray from the right path ; have alone ⇨ 번놓다
*벗다[1] ① take〔put〕 off ; divest〔strip〕 oneself of ; remove ; slip off《one's clothes》 ¶ 옷을 벗다 take off one's clothes ; undress oneself // 외투를 벗다 take off〔get out of〕 one's overcoat // 장갑을 급히 벗다 pull one's gloves // 구두를 발로 벗다 kick off one's shoes // 구두를 벗어 던지다 fling〔throw, pull〕 off one's boots // 구두를 벗지 않아도 좋습니다 You may keep your shoes on.
② [누명·빚·짐을] clear oneself of ; remove ; rid oneself of ; unburden oneself of ¶ 짐을 벗다 put one's load down ; take off one's load // 빚을 벗다 free oneself from debts ; clear up one's debts ; pay off one's creditors // 책임을 벗다 rid oneself of responsibility // 누명을 벗다 clear oneself of a false charge // 오해를 벗다 remove a misunderstanding
③ [티를] get rid of ¶ 어린애 티를 벗다 grow out of child // 시골티를 벗다 get polished〔sophisticated, citified〕 ; get free from boorishness
④ [허물을] ¶ 허물을 벗다 [뱀 따위가] slip out of its skin ; change its skin ; [곤충이] leave the cocoon
벗다[2] [벗어지다] come off ; go away ¶ 칠이 벗다 the paint comes〔is worn〕 off
벗바리 a backer ; a supporter
벗바리 좋다 관용 have strong backing ; have a lot of backing
†벗어나다 ① free oneself from ; get out of《difficulties》 ; escape ¶ 구속에서 벗어나다 free oneself from bondage // 위기에서 벗어나다 escape danger // 간신히 벗어나다 have a narrow escape《from》 ; narrowly escape // 벗어날 길을 찾다 find one's way out
② [눈에] lose favor with ; incur《a person's》 displeasure ; fail to find favor in《a person's》 eyes ¶ 그는 사장 눈에 벗어났다 He is out of favor in the eyes of the boss. /He lost favor with the boss. // 하는 짓이 남의 눈에 벗어난다 Everything he does displeases another.
③ [어그러지다] be contrary to ; be against ; deviate from ¶ 도리에 벗어나다 be contrary to reason // 기대에 벗어나다 be contrary to one's expectations // 관습에 벗어나다 deviate from the custom // 규칙에 벗어나다 be against the rule // 이것은 내가 생각하고 있는 가격 범위를 벗어난 것이다 This is out of my price range.
벗어던지다 fling〔cast〕 off ; throw away
벗어버리다 fling〔cast, throw〕 off ; shuffle《one's clothes》 off ; kick off《one's shoes》 ; [누명·책임·빚을] divest〔clear〕 oneself of ; rid oneself of ; pay off ¶ 모자를 벗어버리다 take off one's hat // 빚을 벗어버리다 clear up one's debts ; pay off one's debts // 책임을 벗어 버리다 rid oneself completely of responsibility
벗어부치다 ① [옷을] slip off one's clothes

② [비유적] go at 《it》 taking off the gloves〔with might and main〕

*벗어지다 come off ; slip off ; peel off ; scale off ¶ 햇볕에 탄 살갗은 벗어진다 Sunburnt skin will peel. // 햇볕에 너무 타서 등 가죽이 벗어졌다 The skin of my back peeled off with too much exposure to the sun. // 계단에서 떨어져 무릎이 벗어졌다 I fell down the steps and barked〔skinned〕 my knee. // 장갑이 벗어지질 않는다 My gloves won't come off. // 망또가 자꾸 벗어진다 My cloak keeps slipping off. // 페인트가 점점 벗어진다 The paint is peeling off. // 그는 아직 젊은데도 머리가 벗어졌다 He became baldheaded before his time.

벗장이 a poor〔an unskilled〕 handicraftsman ; a half-learned〔half-trained, half-baked, green〕 person ; a smatterer

목수 — a green carpenter 활량 — a poor archer

벗트다 become intimate ; get so intimate that one can dispense with formalities in talking 《with》

벗하다 become a good friend ; be a companion to ; make a companion of ; keep company with ¶ 책을 읽어 옛사람들과 벗하다 communicate with ancients through their books // 책과 벗하다 have books for companions ; make a companion of one's books // 자연을 벗하다 live with nature ; converse with Nature

벙거지 a hat ; headgear ; [옛 군인의] a soldier's hat in old times

벙그레 ⇨ 방그레

벙글거리다 smile ; beam ¶ 기쁜 듯이 벙글거리다 smile happily // 사람을 보고 벙글거리다 beam upon 《a person》 // 어린애가 그의 손을 잡고 쳐다보며 벙글거렸다 The child took his hand and beamed up at him.

벙글벙글, 벙긋벙긋 with a broad smile ; smilingly ; cheerfully

벙긋하다 be ajar ; be slightly opened ¶ 문이 벙긋하게 열려 있다 The door is left ajar.

벙벙하다 be dumbfounded ¶ 벙벙해서 in open-mouthed amazement ; in mute amazement // 그는 잠시 어안이 벙벙했다 He was nonplused for a moment.

벙벙히 silently ; as if dumbfounded ¶ 벙벙히 서 있지 말고 무엇 좀 해라 Don't stand there like a bump on a log-do something !

벙시레 ⇨ 방그레

벙실거리다 smile

*벙어리[1] [사람] a dumb person ; a deaf and dumb person ; a deaf-mute

벙어리[2] [저금통] a piggy bank ; a saving box

벙어리매미 『곤충』 a female cicada

*벙어리장갑 —掌匣 a mitten

벙태기 headgear ; a hat

벚꽃 cherry blossom

—놀이 a picnic under the cherry blossoms ; a cherry-blossom viewing party

†벚나무 a cherry tree

베 hemp cloth ; [인도베] jute ; [삼] a hemp plant

*베개 a pillow ; [긴 베개] a bolster ; [공기베개] an air cushion ¶ 베개를 베다 rest〔lay〕 one's head on a pillow // 베개를 높이 하고 자다 sleep in peace ; sleep with a clear conscience ; [익살] sleep the sleep of the just // 책을 베개삼아 자다 sleep (with) one's head pillowed on a book

베갯머리 the end of a pillow ¶ 베갯머리에 at〔by〕 《a person's》 bedside

베갯모 a pillow end ; embroidered pads attached to both sides of a pillow for decoration

베갯밑공사 —公事 love talk ; soft nothings ; a private request given by a wife to her husband ; a curtain lecture ¶ 베갯밑공사에 넘어가지 아니 하는 사람이 없다 No husband can fail to comply with his wife's private entreaties.

베갯속 the stuffing of a pillow

베갯잇 a pillow slip ; a pillowcase ; a pillow-cover

베거리 sounding ; probing 《a person's》 mind

베겡이 ⇨ 비경이

베고니아 『식물』 a begonia

*베끼다 copy ; make a copy of ; transcribe ¶ 서류를 베끼다 copy a document // 사람들이 나를 우리 아버지를 그대로 베껴 놓은 것 같다고 그런다 They say I'm a carbon copy of my father. / They say I'm the ditto of my father.

베내다 cut off ⇨ 베어내다

베넬룩스 Benelux 《Belgium, the Netherlands and Luxemburg》

베니어판 —板 [단판] a veneer board ; [합판] plywood ¶ 베니어판을 댄 문 a veneered door

베다[1] [베개를] rest〔lay〕 one's head on 《a pillow》 ¶ 팔베개를 베다 pillow one's head on one's arm

†베다[2] [자르다] cut ; chop ; hash (잘게) ; saw (톱으로) ; shear〔clip〕 (가위로) ; carve (식탁에서 고기를) ; slash (얇게) ; hack 《to pieces》 (난도질) ; slice〔strip, shave〕 (얇게) ; fell〔hew〕 (나무를) ; sever (베어 나누다) ; reap 〔gather in, harvest〕 (곡물을) ; mow (풀을) ¶ 둘로 베다 cut 《something》 in two // 손가락을 베다 cut one's finger // 목을 베다 cut〔strike〕 off 《a person's》 head ; behead ; decapitate // 나무를 베다 cut down〔fell〕 a tree // 가지를 베다 cut〔lop〕 off a branch // 가위로 옷감을 베다 cut material with scissors // 찬바람이 살을 베는 듯하다 The wind is cutting 〔biting, piercing〕 cold.

베돌다 remain apart from ; keep to one-

self ; do not mix with ; keep aloof from
베돌이 an antisocial〔unsociable〕 person ; a poor mixer
베드 a bed
더블 — a double bed
베드로 전〔후〕서 〖성경〗 First〔second〕 Epistle General of Peter
*‡***베란다** a veranda(h) ; a porch 《미》
베레모 a beret ¶ 그는 베레모를 비스듬히 눌러쓰고 있었다 He had a beret pulled on sidewise above his face.
베르무트 [리큐어] vermouth
베르사유 조약 the Versailles Treaty
베리줄 ropes attached to the front and back ends of a *geolchae* loading rack
베릴륨 〖화학〗 beryllium 《Be》
베물다 sever with one's teeth ; bite off
베붙이 hemp cloth
베스트 best ¶ 베스트를 다하다 do one's best
— 셀러 a best seller ; a top seller — 텐 〖야구〗 the best ten hitters 《for the season》
베슥거리다 be reluctant〔averse〕 《to do》 ; be backward 《in doing》 ¶ 베슥거리는 reluctant
베슥베슥 reluctantly ; half-heartedly ; backwardly ; lukewarmly ; shrinkingly
베슬거리다 keep aloof ; shirk one's work
베슬베슬 shirking
베실 twine ; hemp yarn ; linen thread
베어내다 cut off〔away〕 ; cut out ¶ 잔디의 풀을 베어내다 mow the lawn // 나무를 베어내다 cut down〔fell〕 a tree // 신문에서 광고를 베어내다 clip an advertisement from a newspaper // 잡지에서 그림을 배어내다 cut out pictures from magazines // 고기 한 점을 베어내다 cut off a slice of meat
베어링 〖기계〗 a bearing
볼 — a ball bearing
베어먹다 cut off and eat ; [빠지다] cut ¶ 과자를 베어먹다 slice a cake to eat // 역사 시간을 베어먹다 cut one's history class
베어 버리다 cut ; cut down〔off〕 ¶ 나무를 베어 버리다 cut down a tree // 한 칼에 베어 버리다 cut down with one sword stroke // 고기 덩어리를 단번에 베어 버리다 cut down a lump of meat with one stroke
베옷 hemp clothes
베이다 get 《it》 cut ; get cut on ¶ 나는 손가락을 칼에 베었다 I got cut on the finger with a knife.
베이비 a baby
— 장롱 a small-sized chest of drawers
*****베이스¹** ① [기준] a base ; a basis ¶ 베이스를 올리다 raise the base ② [주성분] the base 《of a cocktail》 ③ 〖야구〗 a base ; a base bag ; a bag 《속》 ; a sack ¶ (주자가) 베이스에 들다 be on the base // (주자가) 베이스를 떠나 있다 be off the base // 베이스를 밟다 step on a base ; reach a base
— 히트 a base hit 임금(賃金) — the wage base ; the basic wage rate
베이스² 〖음악〗 bass ¶ 훌륭한〔굵은〕 베이스의 목소리 a fine〔deep〕 bass
— 가수 a bass (singer)
베이스볼 baseball ¶ 베이스볼을 하다 play baseball
베이스 캠프 a base camp
베이지 beige ¶ 베이지색의 beige
*‡***베이컨** [먹는] bacon
베이클라이트 〖화학〗 bakelite
베이킹 파우더 baking powder
*‡***베일** a veil ¶ 신부의 베일 a bridal veil // 수수께끼의 베일 속에 숨겨져 있다 be hidden in a veil of mystery // 베일을 쓰고 있다 wear a veil ; be in a veil // 베일로 얼굴을 가리우다 veil one's face ; muffle one's face in a veil // 베일을 올리다〔내리다〕 raise〔drop〕 one's veil
베정적 defiance ; standing up to a threat 〔to violence〕 —하다 show denance ; bay a denanc ; stand up to a threat
베짱베짱 [베짱이의] chirping ; chirring
*‡***베짱이** 〖곤충〗 a grasshopper
베타 beta ; ß
—선(線) beta rays — 입자 beta particles
베테랑 a veteran ; an expert ; an old hand ; an old-timer ¶ 그 방면의 베테랑 an old-timer in his line
*****베틀** a loom ¶ 베틀로 피륙을 짜다 weave fabric on a loom
—다리 the four legs of a loom —신 the treadle shoe of a loom
†**베풀다** [잔치 따위를] give ; hold ; throw 《속》 ; [조력·은혜 따위를] give ; bestow ; grant ; render ¶ 잔치를 베풀다 give〔hold, throw〕 a banquet〔dinner party〕 // 자선을 베풀다 give alms ; render aid 《to the poor》 // 은혜를 베풀다 bestow a favor 《on a person》
벡터 〖물리·수학〗 a vector
— 공간 the vector space — 함수 a vector function — 해석 vector analysis
벤젠 〖화학〗 benzene ; benzol
—핵(核)〔환(環)〕 benzene nucleus 〔ring〕
벤진 〖화학〗 benzine
†**벤치** a bench ; [야구 선수의] a dugout
벤틸레이터 a ventilator
*‡***벨¹** a bell ; a doorbell, a front-bell (현관의) ¶ 벨이 울리는 소리 the sound of the bell // 요란한 벨 소리 a clamorous〔loud-sounding〕 bell // 벨을 울리다 ring〔touch〕 the bell ; ring at the bell // 벨을 세 번 울리다 ring three bells ; ring the bell three times // 벨을 울려 하인을 부르다 ring for a servant // 벨을 누르다 press〔push, touch〕 the bell〔bell button〕 // 찌르릉 찌르릉 벨이 울렸다 R-r-ring! went the bell. // 벨이 요란하게 울렸다 The bell rang clamorously〔furiously〕. // 벨을 울렸더니 하녀가 나왔다 The maid answered the bell. // 벨을 울렸더니 노파가 문을 열었다 An old woman opened the door in

response to my ring. // 문의 벨이 울리고 있다 There's a ring at the door. // 벨이 울린다〔손님이 왔다〕 There goes the bell. /There's the bell.

벨벳 velvet

†벨트 a belt

— 컨베이어 a belt conveyer

벰베르크 [상표명] Bemberg rayon

*벼 a rice plant ¶ 벼를 심다 plant rice // 벼를 베다 harvest〔reap〕 the rice ; mow〔cut down〕 the rice plants // 벼가 잘 된다 The rice is doing well.

벼농사 —農事 rice farming —하다 do〔engage in〕 rice farming

벼때 〖농업〗 rice harvest (time)

*벼락 thunder ; a thunderbolt ¶ 벼락치는 소리 a clap of thunder // 벼락같은 thunderous // 집에 벼락이 떨어졌다 The lightning has struck a house.

벼락감투 official positions sold to individuals to raise government fund ; government positions given as a political favor ¶ 벼락감투를 쓰다 become a government official overnight ; go from nobody to government official overnight // 벼락감투를 씌우다 make an absurd appointment ; give an office as a political plum 《to someone》

벼락공부 —工夫 cramming ; cram 《구》 —하다 cram up ; get up 《for an examination》 ¶ 시험을 위해서 학생에게 벼락공부를 시키다 cram a pupil for an exam // 그는 역사 시험을 위해서 (역사적) 사실과 연대를 벼락공부하고 있다 He is cramming (up) facts and dates for his history examination.

벼락김치 improvised cabbage pickles

벼락닫이 〖건축〗 a window consisting of a fixed upper section and a movable lower section

벼락대신 —大臣 a tough nut (to crack) ; a tough guy ¶ 그는 벼락대신이다 He is a tough nut (to crack).

벼락덩이 a big clump of mud〔soil〕 turned up in cultivating

벼락맞다 be struck by lightning ¶ 벼락맞은 thunderstruck ; thunderstricken // 벼락맞아 죽다 be struck dead by lightning // 벼락맞을 놈 Drop dead ! // 벼락맞을 것 Hell ! // 너, 그런 짓 하면 벼락맞는다 If you do (that), there will be hell to pay ! // 그건 네가 벼락에 맞을 가능성보다 더 희박해 That's even slimmer than your chance of being struck by a lightening.

벼락바람 a sudden and impetuous charge ; a sudden attack〔brunt〕

벼락부자 a mushroom〔overnight〕 millionaire ; an upstart ; a nouveau riche 《프》 ; parvenu 《프》 ¶ 전쟁 통의 벼락부자 a war millionaire // 벼락부자가 되다 gain sudden wealth // 암상인들이 한국의 벼락부자가 되었다 Black-market operators became the new millionaires of Korea.

벼락불 [번갯불] (a flash of) lightning ; a bolt〔shaft〕 of lightning ; [사나운 명령] a tyrannical decree〔order〕 ¶ 벼락불을 내리다 issue a tyrannical decree

벼락장 —醬 improvised hot pepper bean paste

벼락치기 hasty preparation ; hasty〔hurried〕 job ; a stopgap ¶ 벼락치기의 지식 hastily acquired information ; crammed knowledge

벼락치다 《lightning》 strike ; 《a thunderbolt》 fall ¶ 그 건물에 벼락이 쳤다 A thunderbolt struck the house. // 큰 소나무에 벼락이 쳐서 나무가 결딴났다 The lightning splintered a big pine tree.

벼랑 a cliff ; a precipice ; a bluff

벼루 an inkstone ; [벼랑] a cliff ; a precipice ¶ 벼루에 먹을 갈다 rub an inkstick on the inkstone

‡벼룩 a flea ¶ 벼룩이 물다 a flea bites // 벼룩에 물리다 get bitten by a flea

벼룩이자리 〖식물〗 a thyme-leaved sandwort

벼룻길 a narrow road leading to a precipice

벼룻돌 stone used as an inkstone

벼룻물 ink (stone) water ; water for an inkstone ; ink

벼룻집 a stationery cabinet ; a writing case ; an inkstone case

벼르다[1] intend 《to》 ; plan 《to》 ; contemplate ; be determined to ¶ 벼르고 벼르던 기회 the long-awaited chance // 기회를 벼르다 watch for a chance ; be on the lookout for an opportunity // 사람을 죽이려고 벼르다 have designs upon〔against〕 a person's life // 그 여자는 오랫동안 벼르던 모자를 샀다 The girl bought the hat she had been wanting〔thinking about〕 for a long time. // 그는 미국에 가려고 10년 동안 별렀다 For 10 years he kept his eyes open for an opportunity to go to the States.

벼르다[2] portion out ; apportion ; divide equally ¶ 두 몫으로 벼르다 divide into two // 아이들에게 과자를 별려 주다 divide sweets among children

벼름(질) allotment ; apportionment ; equal division —하다 portion out ; apportion ; divide equally

벼리 [그물의] the guide ropes at the edge of a fishing net ; [책의] index ; contents

*벼리다 put an edge on (a knife by forging) ; forge a blade on ; sharpen ¶ 부엌칼을 벼리다 forge the edge on a kitchen knife

벼릿줄 ⇨ 벼리

벼멸구 〖곤충〗 a rice insect ; a leafhopper

벼슬 a government post ; official rank —하다 take office ; obtain a post in the government ; enter the government service ¶ 벼슬이 높다〔낮다〕 be of high〔low〕 government position ; be high

〔low〕 in rank∥벼슬을 얻다〔잃다〕 secure 〔lose〕 a government position∥임금이 그의 벼슬을 올려 대신을 시켰다 The king promoted him to the rank of a minister.

벼슬길 the way (to get) into the government service ; government employ ¶ 그는 벼슬길에 올랐다 He started his career as an official.

벼슬살이 life as an official ; an official life〔career〕 **—하다** be in government service ; hold an office〔a post〕 under the government

벼슬아치 a government official ¶ 그는 벼슬아치가 되더니 사람을 깔본다 He looks down on other people ever since he became such a fancy official.

— 근성 officialism **— 생활** an official life〔career〕

벼팔이 speculative buying-in〔stocking〕 of rice grain **—하다** buy (in) rice for〔on〕 speculation

벼훑이 a threshing machine ; a thresher

벽 sodomy ⇨ 비역

벽 碧 ⇨벽색

벽 癖 a habit ; a characteristic ⇨ 버릇 ¶ 도벽 a thieving habit ; kleptomania

†**벽 壁** a wall ; a partition ¶ 삼면이 벽으로 둘러싸인 방 a room walled in on three sides∥집을 둘러싼 사방의 벽 the four walls of a house∥벽을 칠하다 plaster a wall∥벽에 그림을 걸다 hang a picture on the wall∥우리는 예산 문제에서 벽에 부딪혔다 We ran up against a brick wall over budgeting costs.

—신문 a wall newspaper **—토** plaster

벽개 劈開 cleavage ; crevice **—하다** cleave

—면 a plane of cleavage

벽걸이 壁— a wall tapestry

벽견 僻見 a prejudiced opinion ⇨ 편견

벽계 碧溪 a blue stream

벽공 碧空 the blue〔azure〕 sky ; the blue heaven ¶ 벽공에는 일편의 구름도 없다 There's not a speck of cloud in the blue sky.

벽난로 壁煖爐 a hearth

벽도 碧桃 ① [과일] a peach that is supposed to exist in fairyland ② [꽃] a blossom of the double-flowering peach

—나무 a double-flowering peach (tree)

⁑**벽돌 甓—** (a) brick ¶ 벽돌을 쌓다 lay bricks

— 가마 a brickkiln **—공** a bricklayer ; a mason ; a hod carrier (조수) **— 공장〔제조소〕** a brickyard ; a brickfield ; a brickworks **—담** a brick wall **— 제조인** a brick maker〔burner〕 **— 조각** a brickbat **—집** a brick building ; a building in brick **공동(空洞)〔나무, 통풍〕 —** (a) hollow〔wood, an air〕 brick **내화 —** (a) firebrick ; (a) fireproof brick **붉은 —** (a) red brick **포장 도로 —** a brick-topped road **화장 —** a dress brick

벽두 劈頭 [글의] the opening ; [일의] the outset ; the start ¶ 벽두에 at the very beginning ; first of all ; at the outset

벽력 霹靂 a (thunder) bolt ¶ 청천의 벽력 a bolt from the blue

벽로 壁爐 a fireplace

— 선반 a mantelpiece

벽론 僻論 a biased〔one-sided〕 argument ; a prejudiced opinion〔view〕 ; a narrow-minded view

벽루 僻陋 [장소] a remote〔an out-of-the-way〕 place ; [성격] eccentricity ; perversity **—하다** (be) secluded ; out of the way ; [성격이] eccentric ; perverse ; cranky ; bigoted

벽면 壁面 the surface of a wall

벽보 壁報 a bill ; a poster ; a wall newspaper ; a placard ¶ 벽보를 붙이다 put up a bill〔poster〕∥벽보를 붙이지 마시오 Post no bills here.

괴— a strange〔mysterious〕 poster ; an illegal bill

벽색 碧色 dark〔deep〕 blue

벽서 壁書 [광고] a placard ; a bill ; a poster ; a hand bill ¶ 벽서를 붙이다 put up a poster ; placard ; stick a bill on (a wall)

벽서 僻書 a rare and curious book ; a literary oddity

벽성 僻姓 an unusual〔odd, rare〕 surname

벽시계 壁時計 a wall clock

벽신문 壁新聞 a wall newspaper

벽안 碧眼 blue eyes ¶ 벽안의 소녀 a blue-eyed girl

—자염(紫髯) blue eyes and a red beard

벽오동 碧梧桐 〖식물〗 a sultan's parasol ; Firmiana platanifolia (학명)

벽옥 碧玉 jasper ; green jade

벽원 僻遠 —하다 (be) remote ; secluded ; out of the way

벽자 僻字 an odd and rare character ; an unusual letter

⁑**벽장 壁欌** a wall closet〔cupboard〕

벽장식 壁裝飾 a mural decoration

벽장코 a snub〔flat, pug〕 nose

***벽지 壁紙** wall paper

벽지 僻地 a remote place ; an out-of-the-way place

벽지다 僻— (be) secluded ; isolated ; remote ; outlying ; out-of-the-way

벽창호 a pigheaded person ; a stubborn 〔obstinate〕 person ; a bigoted person

벽채 a mine hoe〔pick〕

벽촌 僻村 a remote village ; an out-of-the-way hamlet

벽치다 壁— 〖건축〗 construct a wall

벽토 壁土 plaster ; wall mud ; stucco

벽하다 僻— [장소] (be) remote ; out of the way ; isolated ; [성질] eratic ; rare ; odd

벽항 僻巷 a remote village ; an isolated village

벽해 碧海 the blue sea

벽향 僻鄕 a remote〔secluded〕 village
벽화 壁畫 a mural (painting) ; a wall painting ; a fresco 《*pl.* ~es, ~s》
—가 a muralist ; a mural painter
변 [은어] jargon (직업상) ; an argot〔a cant〕 (도둑 따위의) ; a lingo ; a secret language ¶ 장사치의 변 trademen's talk // 판수의 변 fortuneteller's jargon // 변을 쓰다 use jargon
변¹ 邊 ① [각의] a side ; 〖수학〗 a latus 《*pl.* latera》 ¶ 3각형의 변 the three sides of a triangle ② [한자의] a left-hand radical (of a Chinese character) ③ [과녁의] the white (of the target)
변² 邊 [변리] interest (on money) ¶ 변놀이 moneylending ; usury // 비싼〔싼〕 변으로 at a high〔low〕 rate of interest // 빌린 돈에 변이 붙다 pay interest on a loan 〔borrowed money〕
—돈 a loan ; money lent at interest
변 變 [변고] an accident ; a mishap ; a misfortune ; a calamity ; a disaster ; [변란] an uprising ; a rebellion ¶ 변을 당하다 have a mishap ; meet with an accident // 변에 대비하다 provide against emergencies // 이런 변 봤나 Why, I have never known such a thing to happen ! // 무슨 변이 났나 왜 그가 오지 않을까 What can have happened ? Why doesn't he come ?
변 便 motions ; feces ; excrement ¶ 변을 보다 relieve oneself〔one's bowels〕 ; ease oneself // 변 검사를 하다 examine feces ; make a stool test
변개 變改 change ; alteration ; modification **—하다** change ; alter ; modify ; amend
변격 變格 irregularity ; anomaly ; 〖문법〗 irregular conjugation (불규칙 변화)
변경 邊境 the frontier ; the border ; a remote region ; outlying districts
— 개척자 a frontierman 《*pl.* -men》 ; a pioneer **— 개척 정신** frontier spirit
****변경 變更** change ; alteration ; modification ; amendment **—하다** change ; alter ; modify ; shift ; amend ¶ 항로의 변경 deviation // 계획의 변경 a change of plan // 외교 정책의 변경 reorientation of a foreign policy // 변경할 수 없는 unalterable ; unchangeable // 변경할 수 있는 alterable ; changeable ; modifiable // 날짜를 변경하다 change the date // 변경을 가하다 make alterations // 가격은 변경할 수 있다 The prices are subject to alteration〔change〕. // 정책에 변경은 없다 The policy remains unaltered 〔unchanged〕.
변계 邊界 the border (land) ; the frontier ¶ 변계를 침범하다 violate a frontier
변고 變故 an accident ; a mishap ; trouble ; a misfortune ; a disaster ¶ 변고를 당하다 meet with trouble ; have a mishap
변광성 變光星 〖천문〗 a variable star
변괴 變怪 an extraordinary calamity〔disaster〕 ; an extraordinary misdeed
변기 便器 a chamber pot ; a night chair〔stool〕 ; a urinal ; a bedpan
변놀이 邊— usury ; moneylending **—하다** lend money at interest
****변덕 變德** fickleness ; whim ; caprice ¶ 변덕스럽다 be capricious〔fickle, changeable, whimsical〕 // 변덕을 부리다 behave capriciously // 그 여자는 변덕이 많다 She is so changeable.
—쟁이〔꾸러기〕 a man of mood ; a weathercock ; a fickle〔capricious〕 person
변돈 邊— a loan ; money lent at interest
****변동 變動** (a) change ; fluctuation (s) **—하다** change ; show〔undergo〕 a change ; be altered ; alter ; fluctuate ¶ 물가의 변동 fluctuations in prices // 사회적 대변동 a cataclysm ; an upheaval // 변동이 없는 unchanged ; unaltered ; stationary 〔firm〕 (물가) // 조금도 변동이 없다 show no change // 변동을 초래하다 bring about a change ; affect // 시세 변동이 심하다 The market is subject to sharp〔wide〕 fluctuations. /Prices fluctuate very widely. // 내각은 바뀌어도 외교 정책에는 변동이 없을 것이다 The reshuffe〔ministerial change〕 will not affect our foreign policy. // 시세의 변동은 없다 The quotation is〔remains〕 unchanged.
— 소득 fluctuating income **—폭** the range of fluctuation 《in price》 **대—** [사회의] social upheaval〔cataclysm〕 ; 〖증권〗 violent fluctuations
변동 환율 變—換率 〖경제〗 the floating exchange rate 《for the *won*》
—제 a floating exchange rate system ¶ 변동 환율제로 하다 float 《the *won*》
****변두리 邊—** ① outskirts 《of a district》 ; border ¶ 서울의 변두리 the outskirts of *Seoul* ② [가장자리] rim ; brim ; margin ; the outer edge ¶ 찻잔의 변두리 the rim of a teacup // 쟁반의 변두리 the edge of a tray // 이 유리잔은 변두리가 깨졌다 This glass is chipped.
변두통 邊頭痛 〖의학〗 megrim ⇨ 편두통
변란 變亂 a (social) disturbance ; a disorder ; a civil war ; an uprising ; an upheaval ; a rebellion
****변론 辯論** discussion ; argument ; debate ; pleading (법정의) **—하다** discuss ; argue ; debate ; plead ¶ 변론을 잘하는 사람 a good speaker〔debater, pleader〕 // 법정에서 변론하다 plead at the bar 〔before the court〕 // 변론을 종결하다 conclude one's argument // 피고인을 위하여 변론하다 argue on behalf of the accused ; argue the case for the defendant
—가 a controversialist ; a debater **— 기일** the date for pleading **—자** a pleader **구두 —** oral proceedings
변류기 邊流器 〖기계〗 a converter ; a cur-

rent transformer
변리 邊利 interest (on money)
변리 辨理 management —하다 manage ; conduct
변리 공사 辨理公使 a minister resident 《*pl.* ministers resident》
변리사 辨理士 a patent attorney〔lawyer, agent〕
변말 ⇨ 변
변명 變名 an assumed〔a fictitious〕 name ; a false name ; an alias ; changing one's name —하다 [개명하다] change one's name ; [가명을 쓰다] assume another name ¶ 변명으로 under the assumed〔false〕 name
†변명 辯明 explanation ; [변호] defense ; vindication (자기의 정당함을) —하다 explain oneself ; defend〔excuse〕 oneself 《for》 ; explain away ; vindicate
—서 a written explanation ; an explanation in writing
변모 變貌 transfiguration —하다 undergo a complete change ; assume a different aspect ; be transfigured ¶ 변모시키다 transfigure ; transform
변모없다 [변통없다] (be) inflexible ; unadaptable ; [무뚝뚝하다] blunt ; rude ; unpolished ; uncultured
변민 邊民 people in a border district ; residents in an outlying area ; borderers ; frontiersmen ; border folk
변박 辯駁, 辯駮 refutation ; confutation ; contradiction ; rebuttal —하다 refute ; confute ; contradict ¶ 잘못이 너무나 명백해서 변박할 필요도 없다 The error is too obvious to require a particular refutation.
변발 辮髮 a pigtail ; the Chinese queue 〔cue〕 —하다 queue ; plait one's hair into a pigtail ¶ 변발을 한 pigtailed // 변발을 하고 있다 wear a pigtail
변방 邊方 edges ; a remote region ; the border areas ; [변경] a frontier (district)
변변찮다 ① [생김새가] (be) unattractive ② [흠이 있다] (be) unlikely ; unbecoming ; unfitting ; ungainly ; uncouth ; stupid ③ [약소] (be) trifling ; small ¶ 변변찮은 것이지만 받아 두십시오 Won't you accept this little remembrance (unworthy though it is) ?
변변하다 [생김새] (be) handsome ; fairly good-looking ; [성격·사물이] fairly good ; tolerable ; passable ; fair ; decent ; satisfactory ¶ 변변치 못하다 be unattractive ; be unlikely〔unbecoming, ungainly〕 ; be stupid // 변변치 못한 사람 a stupid person ; a good-for-nothing ; an unlikely // 사람이 변변하다 have a fairly good character // 변변하게 생기다 be good-looking ; look pretty // 영어를 변변하게 하다 speak English fairly well ; be quite a good speaker of English // 물건이 변변하다 The thing is tolerably good.
변변히 [잘] well ; [충분히] enough ; sufficiently ; much ; [만족스럽게] satisfactorily ; [알맞게] properly ; decently ¶ 변변히 생각해 보지도 않고 without due consideration // 제 나라 역사도 변변히 모르다 do not have a passable knowledge even of the history of one's own country // 편지 한장 변변히 못쓴다 He can't even write a decent letter. // 변변히 문법도 모른다 He has little knowledge of grammar. // 질문하면 변변히 대답도 못한다 He can't give satisfactory answers to questions. // 어찌나 소심한지 사람들 앞에서 변변히 말도 못한다 He is so timid that he scarcely opens his mouth in public.
변별 辨別 discrimination ; distinction —하다 distinguish 《between A and B》 ; mark〔notice〕 the difference 《between》 ; discriminate 《between, one from the other》 ¶ 시비를 변별하다 discriminate between right and wrong // 양자를 변별 못하겠다 I can not tell one from the other. // 얼른 봐서는 변별하지 못할 것입니다 You will not notice the difference at first sight.
—력 (power of) discrimination ; judgement
변보 變報 news〔a report〕 about an accident〔a disaster, a calamity〕 ; (a piece of) bad news
변복 變服 disguise ; disguising oneself —하다 disguise ; disguise oneself 《as a beggar》 ¶ 여자로 변복하다 disguise oneself〔be disguised〕 as a woman // 그는 신부로 변복하여 여행을 했다 He traveled under〔in〕 the guise of a priest.
변비(증) 便秘(症) constipation ; costiveness ¶ 변비에 걸리다 be constipated ; be costive ; be oppilated ; suffer from constipation // 나는 변비(증)에 걸렸다 My bowels have stopped. // 그것을 먹으면 변비증에 걸린다 It will constipate you〔bind your bowels〕.
변사 辯士 [연설하는] a speaker ; an orator ; [무성 영화의] a film interpreter ; a movie talker
변사 變死 an accidental〔a violent〕 death —하다 meet one's death accidentally ; die in one's shoes〔boots〕 ; die an unnatural〔a violent〕 death
—자 a person who has met〔died〕 an unnatural death ; a person accidentally killed
변사 變事 an accident ; a mishap ; a calamity ; a disaster
변사 變辭 changing one's previous words 〔remarks, statement〕 —하다 eat 〔break〕 one's words ; go back on one's word
변상 辨償 payment ; compensation ; reparation —하다 pay for ; reimburse ; indemnify ; make good ¶ 손해를 변상하다 indemnify 《a person》 against damage ;

compensate 《a person》 for loss ; make up for 《a loss》 // 깨어지면 변상하겠다 If it breaks, I will pay for it.
—금 an indemnity ; a compensation ; reparations ; 〖법〗 tender

변색 變色 ① [빛깔의] discoloration **—하다** fade ; discolor ¶ 그 색은 변색하지 않는다 The color is fast. ② [안색의] change of countenance **—하다** change (one's) countenance ; change color 《at》 ; turn pale ; look black 《at, on, upon》

변설 辯舌 speech ; eloquence ¶ 변설이 유창한 eloquent ; fluent // 변설이 유창하다 have a fluent tongue
—가 an eloquent〔fluent〕 speaker

변성 變成 rebirth ; regeneration ; metamorphosis
— 작용 〖지질〗 metamorphism

변성 變性 denaturalization ; degeneration **—하다** degenerate ; denaturalize ; denature
—제(劑) a denaturant — 주정(酒精) methylated spirit(s) 지방〔전분〕 — fatty 〔amyloid〕 degeneration

변성 變性 [이름] changing one's surname **—하다** change one's surname〔family name〕

변성 變聲 the change of voice **—하다** 《one's voice》 change〔break, crack〕
—기 puberty

변성명 變姓名 changing one's surname and given name **—하다** assume an other name ; change one's full name

변성암 變成岩 〖지질〗 a metamorphic rock
반상(班狀) — porphyroid

*__변소 便所__ a lavatory ; a water closet ; a toilet room 《미》 ; a latrine (공장 따위의) ; a ladies' room (여자용) ¶ 변소에 가다 go to the toilet ; wash one's hands // 변소에 있다 be at stool // 변소는 어디입니까 Where can I wash my hands? / Where's the washroom?
공중 — a public lavatory 남자〔여자〕용 — [회사·역 따위의] a man's〔ladies'〕 room ; a rest room 《미》 ; [게시] Gentlemen〔Ladies〕/Men〔Women〕 수세식 — a flush toilet

변속 變速 change of speed **—하다** change speed ; shift gears
— 장치(裝置) the transmission 《of an automobile, etc.》

변속기 變速機 a gearbox ; a transmission

변속 운동 變速運動 〖물리〗 motion in variable speed

변수 變數 〖수학〗 a variable ; a fluent

변스럽다 變— (be) odd ; queer ; funny ; peculiar ¶ 변스럽게 굴다 behave queerly〔oddly〕

변신 變身 disguise ; transformation **—하다** disguise oneself 《as》 ; be disguised 《as》 ; be transformed

변심 變心 change of mind〔heart〕 ; infidelity ; treachery **—하다** change one's mind ; undergo a change of heart ; [배반하다] play 《a person》 false ; betray 《a person》

변압 變壓 〖전기〗 transformation
—소 a transformer substation

변압기 變壓器 a (current) transformer ; a potential transformer
1차 진동〔삼상, 고정〕 — a primary oscillation〔three-phase, stationary〕 transformer

변역 變易 mutation ; [변경] alteration ; modification **—하다** mutate ; change ; modify ; shift

변온 동물 變溫動物 〖동물〗 cold-blooded animal ; a poikilothermal animal

변위 變位 〖물리〗 displacement
— 전류 a displacement current

변음 變音 〖음악〗 a flat

변이 變異 change ; 〖생물〗 variation ; mutation
—설 the variation theory —종 a variable species 돌연 —(설) (a) mutation (theory)

변이 變移 ⇨ 변천

변자 邊子 [둘레 꾸미개] edging ; frill ; a border ; fringe ; purfling

변작 變作 alteration ; forgery (위조) **—하다** alter ; forge

‡__변장 變裝__ disguise **—하다** disguise oneself 《as》 ; be disguised 《as》 ; wear a disguise ¶ 변장한 탐정 a detective in disguise // 변장해서 in disguise // 여자로 변장하다 disguise〔make up〕 as a woman // 그는 안경과 가짜 수염으로 변장했다 He put on spectacles and a false moustache for a disguise.
—술 the art of disguise

변재 辯才 oratorical talent ; eloquence ; the gift of gab 《속》 ¶ 변재가 있다 be gifted with eloquence ; have an oratorical talent

변재 變災 an accident ; a disaster ; a calamity

변전 變轉 mutation ; change ; vicissitude **—하다** change ; mutate ¶ 국제 정세의 변전 inconstant〔ever-changing〕 international situation

변전소 變電所 a (transformer) substation

변절 變節 apostasy ; treachery ; betrayal **—하다** apostatize ; backslide ; change sides ; change〔turn〕 one's coat
—자 a turncoat ; a backslider ; a renegade ; a traitor ; an apostate

변제 辨濟 repayment ; payment ; reimbursement ; discharge ; settlement ; 〖법〗 performance ; satisfaction 《of one's obligation》 **—하다** repay ; pay back ; reimburse ; pay (off) ; 〖법〗 discharge ; satisfy 《one's debt, an obligation》 ; perform 《an obligation》
—금 〖법〗 tender —기(期) the time for〔of〕 performance ; the time appointed for payment

변조 變造 alteration ; forgery **—하다** alter ; forge ¶ 수표를 변조하다 falsify a cheque ; raise a cheque (금액을 올려서)
— 수표 an altered〔a falsified, a forged, a raised〕check 《미》〔cheque 《영》〕**—자** a falsifier **— 화폐** a counterfeit coin

변조 變調 〖음악〗 a change of tone ; variation ; [불규칙] irregularity ; [이상] abnormality ; anomaly ¶ 변조를 초래하다 become irregular ; show strange symptoms
—관 a modulation tube **—기(器)** a modulator **주파수 —** frequency modulation 《FM》 **진폭 —** amplitude modulation 《AM》

변종 變種 a variety ; a variant ; a sport ; a mutation ; a freak ¶ 변종의 varietal ; sportive ; mutative

변주곡 變奏曲 〖음악〗 a variation (on a theme)

변죽 邊— a rim ; a brim ; an edge
변죽울리다 관용 hint 《at》; intimate ; allude to ; drive at ; glance at ; beat about〔around〕the bush

변증 辯證 demonstration **—하다** demonstrate ¶ 변증적인 dialectic ; dialectical // 변증적으로 dialectically

변증법 辨證法 〖철학〗 dialectic ¶ 변증법적으로 dialectically // 헤겔의 변증법 the Hegelian dialectic
— 유물론 dialectical materialism **유물 —** materialistic dialectic

변지 邊地 a remote place ; the edge of land ; the borderland

변질 變質 change in quality ; deterioration ; transmutation **—하다** change in quality ; degenerate ; deteriorate ; transmute ; go bad (음식물이)

변질자 變質者 a degenerate ; a pervert ; a deviate ; a deviant

변차 變差 〖천문〗 (a) variation ; 〖물리〗 (a) declination

***변천 變遷** change ; transition ; [성쇠] vicissitude ; ups and downs **—하다** change ; undergo a change ¶ 시대의 변천 the changes of the times // 수많은 변천을 거쳐 after many changes

변체 變體 an anomalous state ; anomaly ; abnormality ¶ 변체의 anomalous ; abnormal

변칙 變則 irregularity ; anomaly ¶ 변칙적인 irregular ; anomalous // 변칙적인 발음 incorrect pronunciation // 변칙적으로 영어를 배우다 learn English by an "irregular" 〔an unnatural〕 method
— 교육 an irregular education **— 국회** an abnormal National Assembly session **— 동사** 〖문법〗 an irregular verb **— 영어** broken English

변칭 變稱 changing the name ; a changed name **—하다** change the name〔title〕 《of》; rename ; give another name 《to》

변태 變態 〖생물〗 metamorphosis ; transformation ; [이상] abnormality ; anomaly ¶ 변태적인 abnormal ; anomalous ; perverted // 변태적인 상태 abnormal conditions
— 성욕 abnormal sexuality〔sexual desire〕; sexual perversion **— 심리** abnormal mentality **— 심리학** abnormal psychology

‡**변통 變通** [융통] adaptability ; flexibility ; versatility ; [처리] contrivance ; management ; makeshift ; arrangement **—하다** contrive ; manage ; make shift ; arrange ¶ 돈을 변통하다 raise money // 변통이 없다 be unadaptable ; be hidebound ; be straight-laced
—성 adaptability ; flexibility ; versatility ; resourcefulness ; elasticity ¶ 변통성이 있다 be adaptable ; be versatile ; be resourceful **임시 —** a rough make shift

변통 變通 the action〔movement, motion〕of the bowels ; bowel movement ; a passage ¶ 변통을 고르게 하다 regulate one's stools // 두 번 변통이 있었다 I had two motions.
—약 a laxative ; a purgative

변통수 變通數 a resource ; a contrivance ; an expedient ; a makeshift

변폭 邊幅 hemming ; a hem ; a selvage ; a list

†**변하다 變—** change ; become different ; undergo a change ; vary ¶ 변하기 쉬운 changeable ; unsettled ; fickle // 영원히 변하지 않는 eternal ; everlasting // 변하지 않다 be〔remain〕 unchanged ; be the same (as before) ; be constant // 마음이 변하다 change one's mind // 음식 맛이 변하다 food spoils // 옛날과 지금은 많이 변했다 Things are not what they used to be. // 서울이 많이 변했다 *Seoul* has changed a great deal. // 세상도 참 많이 변했다 We are now in a different world. // 별로 변한 것이 없습니다 There is nothing fresh 〔new〕 to tell. // 참 그도 사람이 변했군 He is quite another man now. // 그가 형무소를 나올 때는 사람이 아주 변해 있었다 He left prison quite a changed man. // 바람이 서쪽으로 변했다 The wind veered〔shifted〕 to the west. // 그는 어찌나 변했는지 알아볼 수가 없었다 He was changed beyond recognition. // 자네 하나도 안 변했군 You haven't changed a bit.

변함 變— a change ; a turn ¶ 변함없이 unchanged ; constantly ; uneventfully ; in peace // 변함없는 사랑 constant love // 변함이 없다 show no change ; be 〔remain〕 unchanged ; be constant

변혁 變革 a change ; a reform ; a revolution (혁명) **—하다** revolutionize ; reform ¶ 기술상의 변혁 a technical innovation

‡**변형 變形** metamorphosis ; transformation ; a variety ; a modification **—하다** change ; turn 《into》; be transformed

《into》
— 문법 〖영문법〗 transformational grammar

‡변호 辯護 defense ; pleading ; justification ; self-defense (자기 변호) —하다 defend ; plead 《for》 ; argue 《for》 ; justify ; hold a brief for 《a person》 ¶ 변호하는 사람 pleader ; an advocate // 변호하여 in defense 《of》 // 자기를 변호하다 defend oneself // 사건을 변호하다 defend〔plead〕《a person's》 case // 변호할 수 없다 be indefensible
—권 the right of defense —료 a lawyer's fee — 위임장 a warrant of attorney — 의뢰인 a client 자기 — self-justification

‡변호사 辯護士 a lawyer ; a barrister (at law) ; a solicitor ¶ 변호사가 되다 be admitted to the bar ; be called to the bar // 변호사를 업으로 하다 practice law // 변호사를 의뢰하다 engage counsel〔a lawyer〕
—법 〖법〗 the Attorneys-at-Law Act — 사무소 a law office — 수수료〔보수〕 a lawyer's〔retaining〕 fee ; [승소했을 때의] a contingent fee — 시험 the examination for the bar —업 the practice of lawyer ; the legal profession —회 a bar association 개업 — a practicing lawyer 고문 — a legal advisor 《to the corporation》 상대편 — the opposing counsel 악덕 — a shyster (lawyer) 《미》 형사〔민사〕 전문 — a lawyer specializing in criminal〔civil〕 cases

변호인 辯護人 a counsel ; a pleader ; a defender ; an advocate ; the (defense) counsel 《총칭》 ¶ 변호인의 도움을 받을 권리 the right to have one's lawyer ; the right to counsel
—단 the defense counsel 《composed of several attorneys-at-law》 —측 증인 a defense witness 국선〔관선〕 — a court-appointed lawyer〔attorney〕 ; a public defender 원고측 — a plaintiff's lawyer ; counsel for the plaintiff 특별 — a special counsel 피고측 — the defense counsel ; counsel for the defense

†변화 變化 change ; [변경] alteration ; [다양] variety ; [변태] transformation ; 〖문법〗 declension〔inflection〕 (격의) ; conjugation (동사의) —하다 change ; turn ; vary ; alter ; transform ; 〖문법〗 inflect ; decline ; conjugate ¶ 무궁한 변화 endless change // 변화하기 쉬운 changeable ; variable // 변화가 없는 stationary ; changeless ; monotonous (단조로운) // 변화가 없는 생활 a monotonous life // 변화를 구하다 seek variety // 다음 동사의 변화를 표시하라 Conjugate the following verbs. // 정세에 변화는 없다 The situation remains unchanged.
—구(球) 〖야구〗 a slow ball〔a curve (ball)〕 pitched for the change of pace — 무궁(無窮) endless change

변환 變換 change ; conversion ; transformation (수학에서) ; diversion —하다 change ; convert ; divert ¶ 변환할 수 있다 be convertible
—기(器) 〖전기〗 a converter ; an inverter ; a transducer

†별 〖천문〗 a star ; the stars ¶ 별이 밝은 밤 a starlit night // 별이 나다 The stars are out. // 별이 떨어지다 A star falls. // 별이 반짝이다 The stars twinkle. // 하늘에 별이 총총하다 The heavens are covered with stars.

-별 別 classified by ¶ 도별(道別) 인구 population by provinces

별가 別家 ① [작은집] a concubine ② [딴집] a separate house

별가락 別— an uncommon tune〔melody〕

별갑 鼈甲 tortoiseshell ¶ 별갑 테의 안경 tortoiseshell-rimmed glasses〔spectacles〕
—색 amber color — 세공 tortoise(-shell) work 모조 — imitation tortoiseshell

‡별개 別個 a different〔distinct〕 one ; a separate one ; another one ¶ 별개의 separate ; distinct ; different ; another // 별개로 회견하다 see 《them》 separately // 그것은 별개의 문제이다 That is another question. // 사랑과 결혼은 별개다 Love is one thing and marriage is another. /Love and marriage are two different things.

‡별거 別居 living separately ; separation ; limited divorce ; legal separation —하다 live separately〔apart〕 from 《one's husband》 ; live in a separate house ¶ 별거 중의 남편〔아내〕 a separated husband〔wife〕 ; a grass widower〔widow〕
— 수당 a separate allowance ; alimony

별건 別件 ① [물건] an unusual thing ; something unusual ② [사건] an unusual event〔case〕

별것 別— a rarity ; a curiosity ; an oddity ¶ 그것은 별것이 아니다 It is nothing peculiar. // 금강석은 별것 아니라 석탄의 일종이다 Diamond is nothing but a kind of coal. // 별것 아니지만 받아 주십시오 This is a little something for you. // 옛날에는 이혼이 수치스러운 일이었으나 요즘은 별것 아닌 일이 되었다 In olden days, divorce was something to be ashamed of, but it's old hat these days.

별격 別格 a special〔exceptional, extraordinary〕 status ¶ 별격의 special ; exceptional ; extraordinary // 그는 별격이다 He is an exception.

별견 瞥見 a glance ; a glimpse ; a cursory view —하다 glance at ; catch sight of ; catch〔take〕 a glimpse of ; glance through ; snatch a brief view of

별고 別故 ① [뜻밖의 사고] an untoward event ; a hitch ; a trouble ¶ 별고 없이 quietly ; without any accident〔mishap, hitch〕 // 별고 없다 be well ② [까닭] a specific reason ¶ 별고 없이 결석하다 absent oneself without any reason〔for no

good reason〕
별곡 別曲 〖문학〗 a new tune ; a special tune
별과 別科 a special course〔department〕
—생 a special student; a special 《미》
별관 別館 an annex ; an extension ; an outhouse ; an outbuilding
재무부 — the detached office of the Finance Ministry
별궁 別宮 a detached palace ; a secondary palace ; a royal villa ; the palace of the queen〔the wife of the heirapparent〕
별기 別記 a separate paragraph〔note〕 —하다 write in a separate paragraph ; make a separate note 《of》 ¶ 별기와 같이 as stated elsewhere ; as stated in a separate paragraph
별꼴 別— an extraordinary spectacle ; an obnoxious〔a disgusting〕 thing〔person〕 ¶ 별꼴이다 What a spectacle (sight) ! / What a mess !
별꽃 〖식물〗 a chickweed
⁑별나다 別— (be) peculiar ; queer ; strange ; eccentric ¶ 별난 사람 an eccentric ; a queer bird ; an odd duck // 별나게 strangely ; oddly ; curiously // 별난 이야기를 하는 것 같지만 it may sound funny // 그의 행동에는 좀 별난 데가 있다 His behavior is rather funny. // 별난 일도 있군 How can a thing like that happen, I wonder. // 나한테 이혼했다는 말을 안 하다니 참 별나기도 하다 It's awfully funny he never told me of his divorce.
별나라 starland
별납 別納 paying〔delivering〕 separately ; an extra payment〔offering〕 —하다 pay〔deliver〕 separately ; make an extra payment〔offering〕
별놈 an eccentric ; an eccentric〔a cranky, a crotchety〕 fellow ; a crank ; an oddity ; an odd〔a strange〕 fish ; a queer fellow〔card〕
별다르다 別— be of a peculiar kind ; (be) extraordinary ; uncommon ; particular ¶ 별다른 일 something in particular // 별다른 일 없이 지냅니다 I am getting along as usual〔with nothing in particular happening〕. // 이것이나 저것이나 별다르지 않다 There is no great difference between this and that. // 유명한 사람에게는 별다른 버릇이 있다 Celebrated men all have their peculiarities. // 그는 별다른 일도 없이 학교에 안 갔다 He absented himself from school without any particular reason. // 그것은 아주 별다른 일이다 That is quite another pair of shoes. // 이 기계는 취급에 별다른 주의가 필요하다 The machine requires special care in handling.
별달리 別— ¶ 별달리 굴다 behave differently // 별달리 굴지 마라 Stop trying to be different ! // 제 말을 별달리 생각하지 마십시오 Don't take my words ill.
별당 別堂 a separate house ; [절에서] the residence of the superior of a Buddhist temple〔a Buddhist teacher, a Buddhist preacher〕
별도 別途 a separate way ; [용도] separate use ¶ 별도의 special ; separate
— 계정(計定) a separate account ; a separate project — 수입 a special〔casual〕 income — 예금 separate deposits — 적립금 a special reserve fund — 지출 a special outlay
별도리 別道理 an alternative ; a choice ; a better way〔means〕 ¶ 별도리 없다 have no choice but to 《do》 ; there is no alternative but to 《do》
별동대 別動隊 a detached force ; partisans ; flying column〔party〕
별똥 a shooting star ; a meteor ¶ 별똥이 떨어지다 A star shoots.
†별로 別— especially ; particularly ; in particular ¶ 별로 좋지 않다 be not particularly good // 별로 이야기 할 것도 없다 I have nothing particular to tell you. // 나는 별로 춥지 않다 I do not feel very cold. // 별로 할 일도 없다 I am not particularly engaged. // 저 사람에게서 별로 이상한 점을 찾아볼 수 없었다 I found nothing very strange about him.
별리 別離 ⇨ 이별(離別)
별말 別— an absurd〔preposterous〕 remark —하다 make an absurd〔extraordinary〕 remark ¶ 별말 다 한다 You talk nonsense. /Be reasonable. /Don't mention it. // 별말씀 다 하십니다 Don't mention it. /My pleasure. /The pleasure was all mine. /Think nothing of it. /Any time. /Not at all. // 별말하지 말고 내 말 들어라 Don't talk nonsense, listen to me.
⁑별명 別名 a by-name ; an alias ; a nickname ; a pseudonym ; another name ¶ 별명을 붙이다 give 《a person》 a nickname ; fasten a nickname upon 《a person》 ; nickname 《a person》 // 별명을 부르다 call 《a person》 by his nickname
별무늬 a star〔starred, starlike, star-shaped, starry〕 design〔pattern, figure〕
별문제 別問題 another〔different〕 question ; another thing ; a different matter ¶ 비용은 별문제로 하고 apart〔aside〕 from expenses // 이것과 그것은 별문제이다 They are two different questions. /These questions must be dealt with separately.
별물 別物 [물건] a peculiar〔an unusual〕 thing ; [사람] a queer duck ; an odd one ; a character ; an eccentric (person)
별미 別味 a delicacy ; a tidbit ; an exquisite flavor ; an extraordinary taste
별미쩍다 別味— (be) queer ; odd ; unusual ; peculiar ; wacky 《구》
별박이 [말] a horse with a white spot on its head ; [연] a highflying paper
별반 別般 particular(ly) ⇨ 별로

별배 別杯 a parting〔farewell, stirrup〕 cup ; a grace cup ; a farewell〔send-off〕 toast
별배달 別配達 special-delivery mail
— 우편(郵便) special-delivery mail
별법 別法 another〔a different, an alternate〕 method
별별 別別 of various and unusual sorts ¶ 별별일 unusual things of all sorts // 별별 사람 all sorts and conditions of people ; all sorts of people in all conditions of life // 별별 경험 a varied experience // 별별 음식 all sorts of rare dishes
별보 別報 [특보] a special report ; special news ; a (news) flash ; [별도 보도] another report〔news〕
별봉 別封 a letter under separate cover ¶ 별봉으로 under separate cover
***별빛** starlight ; the stars ¶ 별빛 속에 in the starlight // 별빛이 밝다 The stars are shining brightly.
별사 別使 a special envoy〔messenger〕 ; another messenger
별사 別辭 a farewell〔send-off〕 address 〔speech〕 ; parting words
별사건 別事件 a queer〔strange, curious〕 event ; an odd affair ; [특별한] some particular event
별사람 別— a queer bird ; an odd duck ; an eccentric ¶ 별사람 다 보겠다 I have never seen such a mess of a man.
별석 別席 another room ; another seat ; a special seat ; a seat apart **—하다** sit apart ; sit in a special seat
별설 別設 special establishment ⇨ 특설
별세 別世 —하다 die ; pass away ; decease ; depart this life
별세계 別世界 another world ; a world of its own ; a different world ; a fairyland ¶ 전혀 별세계이다 It is quite a world apart.
별소리 別— unreasonable remarks ⇨ 별말
별송 소포 別送小包 a package sent by separate post
별송하다 別送— send by separate post 〔under separate cover〕
별수 別數 ① [운수] special luck ; extraordinary good fortune ¶ 별수가 나다 hit a jackpot ; have unexpected luck ; strike gold ; make a fortune // 별수없다 가자 We aren't getting anywhere— let's go. // 거기 가봐야 별수없을 게다 가지 마라 Don't go there—you won't have any better luck there. // 흥 난 별수나 난 줄 알았지 Hm ! I thought you made your fortune.
② [수단·방법] the magic formula ; the magic touch ; the secret 《to》 ; a secret key ; a special〔an effective〕 means ¶ 난 별수나 있는가 했지 I was thinking you would have the magic touch. // 너도 별수 없구나 You don't have any magic formula, either.
별스럽다 別— (be) odd ⇨ 별나다
별식 別食 a rare dish (of delicate flavor) ; specially prepared food
별실 別室 another room ; a special room ; a separate room ; [작은집] a concubine ¶ 각자 별실에서 살다 live each in a separate room
별안간 瞥眼間 suddenly ; all of a sudden ; all at once ; in an instant ; in the blink of an eye ¶ 별안간 날씨가 변했다 The weather changed all of a sudden. // 별안간 비가 오기 시작했다 All at once, it began to rain.
별유천지 別有天地 ⇨ 별세계(別世界)
별일 別— a particular thing ; an odd thing ; a strange thing ¶ 별일 없이 safely ; in safety ; without any accident // 별일 없이 지내다 be well ; live in peace // 별일 없이 잘 지냅니다 I am getting along OK. // 별일 없으면 오늘 저녁 놀러 오십시오 Come and see me this evening if you do not have anything particular to do. // 별일 다 보겠다 Ridiculous !
별자 別者 [사물] a strange〔curious, peculiar, singular, an odd〕 thing ; [사람] ⇨ 별사람
별자리 『천문』 a constellation ; an asterism
***별장 別莊** a villa 《영》 ; a country house 〔place〕 ; a summer house (여름의) ; a cottage 《미》 ¶ 해변의 별장 a seaside villa **—지기** a villakeeper **임대 —** a villa to rent〔let〕
별제 別製 ⇨ 특제
별종 別種 another〔a different〕 kind ; a (special) variety ; a distinct species ; [선물] a special gift
별주 別酒 a specially prepared〔brewed〕 liquor ; [이별주] a farewell drink ; a parting drink
별증 別症 a deuteropathy ; a (medical) complication ; an intercurrent disease ; a secondary〔concomitant, concurrent〕 disease
별지 別紙 an annexed〔accompanying〕 paper ; an enclosure ¶ 별지와 같이 as stated in the accompanying paper〔document〕 ; as per enclosure
별쭝나다, 별쭝맞다, 별쭝스럽다 (be) peculiar ⇨ 별나다
별차 別差 a great〔big, vast, considerable, material, wide〕 difference ¶ 별차 없다 make no great difference ; make little difference ; be much〔about〕 the same ; be practically equal
별찬 別饌 especially tasty sidedishes ; rare〔dainty〕 sidedishes
별채 別— another building ; an outhouse 〔outbuilding〕 ; an annex 《to the main building》
별책 別冊 a separate volume ; an independent〔a supplement〕 volume ; [잡지 따위의] an extra number〔issue〕

별책 부록 別冊附錄 a separate-volume supplement
별천지 別天地 another world ⇨ 별세계
별첨 別添 an annexed〔attached〕 paper ; an accompanying〔a separate〕 sheet ¶ 별첨의 enclosed herewith // 별첨과 같이 as per enclosure
별체 別體 an odd style ; a peculiar style
별칭 別稱 another name ; a by-name
별파 別派 [당파] a different party ; [종파] a separate〔different〕 sect ; [유파] another〔a different〕 school
별판 別— an unexpected improvement of the situation〔things〕 ; a queer turn of fate
별편 別便 separate post ; separate mail 《미》 ¶ 별편으로 by separate〔another〕 post
별표 —票 [별꼴] a star ; a mark ; an asterisk ¶ 별표가 붙은 asterisked // 별표를 붙이다 asterisk 《the word》 ; mark with an asterisk
별표 別表 an attached table ; an annexed list ; an appended chart
— 양식(樣式) an attached form
별항 別項 a separate paragraph〔clause〕 ; special heading ; another clause〔provision, section〕
별행 別行 another〔a new〕 line ; a separate column ¶ 별행에 쓰다 write as〔on, in〕 a new line ; write in a separate column
별호 別號 [호] a pen name ; nom de plume 《프》 ; [별명] a nickname
볍씨 rice seed
***볏[1]** [새의] the crest ; the cockscomb
볏[2] [모습의] the mo(u)ldboard of a plow
볏가락 awns on a rice plant
볏가리 a stack〔rick〕 of rice straw
볏가을 rice harvest **—하다** harvest rice
볏단 a rice-sheaf ; a sheaf of rice
볏모 a young rice plant
볏밥 plowed earth ; the earth turned over by a moldboard
볏섬 a sack of rice
볏자리 the part of a plow to which a moldboard is attached
볏짚 rice-straw ¶ 볏짚을 단으로 묶다 tie up rice-straw in sheaves // 볏짚을 깔다 spread rice-straw
†병 瓶 a bottle ¶ 꽃병 a vase // 작은 약병 a phial // 아가리가 넓은 병 a jar // 목이 가는 양주병 a decanter // 병 주둥이 the neck of a bottle // 맥주 한 병 a bottle of beer // 병에 담다 bottle〔fill a bottle〕 《with wine》 // 병을 비우다 empty a bottle // 한 병에 얼마로 팔다 sell 《a thing》 by the bottle // 이 주스는 한 병에 500원이다 This fruit juice is 500 *won* a bottle.
—맥주 bottled beer
†병 病 ① [일반적으로] (a) sickness 《미》 ; (an) illness 《영》 ; (a) disease ; (a) malady (만성병) ; (an) affection ; [경증] (an) indisposition ; (an) ailment ; [국부적] (a) trouble ; a disorder ; a complaint ; [병원 용어] a case ¶ 아이들의 병 children's troubles // 중병 a serious illness // 가벼운 병 a slight illness〔ailment〕 // 잘 낫지 않는 병 an obstinate disease // 불치의 병 an incurable〔fatal〕 illness // 오래 끄는 병 a protracted〔lingering〕 disease // 병을 앓고 나서 회복기에 있는 사람 a convalescent (person) ; a person in his convalescence // 병문안 a visit to a sick person // 병난 sick 《미》 ; ill 《영》 ; unwell ; ailing ; diseased ; indisposed // 병으로 인해서 for reason of health ; for health reasons ; because of〔owing to, due to〕 one's illness // 병에 걸리다 fall〔be taken〕 ill ; catch〔contract〕 a disease ; be attacked〔seized〕 with a disease ; be affected〔afflicted〕 with a disease // 병이 낫다 the disease is cured : [사람이 주어] get well ; recover from one's disease ; get over one's illness ; be cured of a disease ; be restored to health // 병이 가볍다 (one's illness) be not serious ; be slightly ill // 병을 고치다 cure a disease // 병을 치료하다 treat a disease // 병을 예방하다 prevent〔stave off〕 a disease // 병으로 결근하다 be absent from one's duty〔office〕 owing to illness ; be on sick leave〔the sicklist〕 // 병으로 누워 있다 be sick〔ill〕 in bed ; be laid up (with illness) ; be on one's back // 병으로 죽다 die of sickness〔illness〕 ; die of〔from〕 a disease // 나는 병에 잘 걸린다 I am liable to illness. // 이 병은 특히 유아들이 걸리기 쉽다 Infants particularly are subject to this disease. // 나는 병에 약하다 I easily yield to a disease. // 그는 병에 강하다 He stoutly fights a disease.
② [약점] a weakness ; a fault ¶ 도박이 그의 병이다 He has a mania for gambling. // 술을 좋아하는 것이 그 사람의 병이다 He has a weakness for the bottle.
③ [탈] trouble ; a breakdown ; something wrong 《with》 ¶ 병이 나다 get out of order ; fail ; stall // 병을 내다 put something out of order ; mess something up // 라디오가 병이 났다 The radio is out of order. // 그가 내 라디오를 병냈다 He got my radio out of order.
눈— eye trouble **발—** footsoreness ; a sore foot **심장—** heart trouble **위장—** stomach trouble **정신—** mental trouble **폐—** lung trouble ☞ ◀ p. 986 ▶
병 丙 [등급의] a third class ; the third grade ; C ; [제3의 사람] a third ¶ 징병 검사에서 병종이 되다 be put under class "C" on the physical examination for conscription
병가 兵家 ① [병법가] a tactician ; a strategist ② [군인] a serviceman ; a soldier ; a man of arms
병가 病家 a patient's house

병·병원

일반적으로 「그다지 심하지 않은 병」에는 illness, 병명이 분명한 것, 전염병 또는 의학 연구·치료의 대상이 되는 것에는 disease, 다소 구어적인 표현으로는 sickness, 정신병은 mental illness 등으로 약간의 차이가 있다. 「병에 걸리다」의 일반적인 표현은 get[become] ill, 「갑자기 병에 걸리다」는 be taken ill, 「장기간 또는 심각한 병에 걸리다」는 fall ill 등으로 표현한다. 치료와 관계없이 「좋아지다」의 일반적인 표현은 get well, recover (from an illness)이다.

① 병명

▶순환기 계통의 병 circulatory disease/소화기 계통의 병 alimentary disease; gastrointestinal disease/호흡기 계통의 병 respiratory[pulmonary] disease/유전성 질환 hereditary disease/소아병 infantile disease/성병 venereal disease/신경병 neurosis; neurotic disorder/신장병 kidney disease/폐병 lung disease/위장병 stomach disease/심장병 heart disease (★ 장기의 이름을 딴 병명은 무관사)/피부병 skin disease (★ 구어에서는 disease 대신에 problem이나 trouble을 대신 사용하기도 한다.)/안질환 eye disease/정신병 mental disease [disorder]

▶신장염 nephritis/심장 이식 cardiac [heart] transplant/심부전(心不全) cardiac insufficiency/심근 경색(心筋梗塞) cardiac arrest; heart attack; myocardial infarction/협심증 angina pectoris/뇌졸중(腦卒中) cerebral hemorrhage/뇌사 (腦死) cerebral [brain] death/간염 hepatitis/간경변 cirrhosis (of the liver)/당뇨병 diabetes (★ 당뇨병 환자 diabetic)/카타르 catarrh/알레르기 allergy/건초열 hey fever/천식 asthma/콜레라 cholera/디프테리아 diphtheria/이질 dysentery [dísnteri(:)]/파라티푸스 paratyphoid/폐렴 pneumonia/결핵 tuberculosis/충수염(蟲垂炎) appendicitis/티프스 typhoid (fever)/암 cancer/위암 stomach cancer/백혈병 leukemia/일사병 sunstroke/영양 실조 malnutrition/설사 diarrhea; loose bowels; diarrhoea 《영》/인플루엔자 influenza; flu 《구》/홍역 measles/성홍열 scarlet fever/천연두 smallpox/백일해 whooping cough/기관지염 bronchitis/관절염 arthritis/소아마비 polio/정신 분열증 schizophrenia ; split personality/자폐증 autism/변비 constipation/발진 (發疹) rash/화상 burn scald/염좌 (삠) sprain/(복잡) 골절 (compound) fractures/불면증 insomnia; sleeplessness/신경 쇠약 nervous breakdown

▶꾀병 feigned [pretended] disease/만성병 chronic disease [complaint]/지병 old complaint/난치병 incurable[malignant] disease/희귀병 rare disease; orphan disease

▶전염병 contagious disease ; epidemic/간접 전염병 infectious disease/법정 전염병 legal endemic/직업병 vocational [occupational] disease/공해병 pollution-caused disease/풍토병 endemic disease/방사선병 radiation disease

② 의료 기관 명칭

병원 hospital/의원 doctor's office/진료소 clinic/약국 (큰 병원의) pharmacy; (약방) drugstore 《미》; chemist's shop 《영》; (공장이나 작은 병원의) dispensary/의무실 (구급실) emergency room; first-aid station; (학교 등의) nurse's office [station]/(학교·공장 등의) 부속 진료소 infirmary/외래 환자 outpatient

③ 의료인

의사 doctor (★ 보통 dentist를 제외한 의사의 총칭. physician도 doctor와 같은 뜻이나 내과의로 쓰이는 경우도 있다. medical doctor, doctor of medicine은 「박사」란 뜻의 doctor와 구별하여 쓰임.)/간호사 nurse/수간호사 head [chief] nurse/양호교사 school nurse/의료 기사 medical technician (★ paramedic은 구급 대원과 같이 의료 보조 업무에 종사하는 사람.)/약제사 pharmacist; chemist 《영》/개업의 general practitioner (★약어는 G.P.)/전문의 specialist/가정의 family doctor/수련의 intern (★통근 수련의 extern)/레지던트 resident; registrar 《영》

④ 전문 분야·전문의(專門醫)

내과 internal medicine/내과의 internist; physician **외과** surgery/외과의 surgeon **소아과** pediatrics/소아과의 pediatrician; baby doctor 《구》 **안과** ophthalmology/안과의 ophthalmologist; eye doctor [specialist] 《구》 **이비인후과** otolaryngology; otorhinolaryngology/이비인후과의 otolaryngologist; otorhinolaryngologist; ear, nose, and throat [ENT] doctor [specialist, man] 《구》/이과의 otologist **비뇨기과** urology; urinology/비뇨기과의 urologist **피부과** dermatology/피부과의 dermatologist; skin doctor [specialist] 《미》 **신경과** neurology/신경과의 neurologist **정신과** psychiatry; psychopathy/정신과의 psychiatrist; psychopathist; (임상 심리학자) clinical psychologist; (정신 요법사) psychotherapist **산과** obstetrics / 산과의 obstetrician; (조산사) midwife **부인과** gynecology; gynecology (영) / 부인과의 gynecologist **정형외과** orthopedics; orthopaedics (영); orthopedic surgery / 정형외과의 orthopedist; orthopedic surgeon **성형외과** plastic surgery **방사선과** radiology / 방사선과의 radiologist **마취과** anesthesiology / 마취과의 anesthesiologist **항문과** proctology / 항문과의 proctologist **치과** dentistry; (치열 교정) orthodontics / 치과의 dentist / 치과 교정의 orthodontist

5 병에 대한 표현

① 전신 증상

▶ 열이 높다 I have a (high) fever. / I'm running [I have] a high [an elevated] temperature. // 미열이 있다 I have a slight fever[temperature]. (★ temperature는 구어로 많이 씀) // 잠이 잘 오지 않는다 I'm suffering [I suffer] from insomnia. / I'm an insomnia.

▶ 한기가 느껴진다 I feel cold. / It feels cold to me. // 오한으로 떨다 I have the chills. / I'm shivering. (★ chill은 떨리는 것 같은 느낌이고, shiver는 실제로 떠는 상태) // 늘 피로한 상태이다 I am [feel] tired (out) [weary] all the time. // 어질어질하다 I feel dizzy [giddy]. (★dizzy는 주로 육체적인 상태, giddy는 정신이 제대로 들지 않은 상태)

▶상처가 밤새도록 아팠다 My wounds smarted [throbbed] all night long. (★ smart는 쿡쿡 쑤시는 것, throb는 일정하게 욱신욱신 아픈 것)

② 통증

pain, hurt가 일반적인 표현, ache는 지속적인 통증, chronic [acute] pain [illness, complaint]는 만성[급성] 통증, sore는 피부 등의 상처가 따끔따끔 쑤시는 것, smart는 욱신욱신 쑤시는 듯한 통증, prickle, tingle은 쿡쿡 찌르는 것 같은 통증, twinge는 치통과 같이 순간적으로 찌르는 듯한 통증, dull은 무지근하게 아픈 통증, pang은 에는 듯한 격통.

¶위에 통증이 있다 I feel pain [have a pain] in my stomach. // 나는 무지근하게 머리가 아프다 I have a dull short of headache. // 목구멍이 따끔따끔하다 My throat is sore.

③ 각 부위의 증상

▶ (칼에) 베였다 I got a cut [I accidentally cut myself] (with a knife). / I was accidentally cut (with[by] a knife). // 송곳에 찔렸다 I accidentally stabbed myself with ice pick. / I was accidentally stabbed with [by] an ice pick. // 야구공에 머리를 얻어맞았다 I was hit in the head with [by] a baseball. // 나무 문짝에 팔을 긁혔다 I scratched [bruised] my arm on [against] a rough wooden door. // 꼬마가 떨어져서 무릎을 까였다 My little boy fell down and skinned his knee.

▶ 어제 심하게 햇볕을 쐬였더니 피부가 따끔따끔 거린다 My skin smarts from the bad sunburn I got yesterday. // 발이 가렵다. My feet itch.

▶ 꽃가루 때문에 볼에 뾰루지가 생겼다 I got a rash on my cheek from (the) pollen. / My cheek was poisoned with [by] (the) pollen. // 내 손등에 빨갛게 염증이 생겼다 I have an inflamation [inflamed area] on (the skin on) the back of my hand. / (The skin on) the back of my hand is inflamed. // 무좀이 있다 I have [am suffering from] athlete's foot.

▶ 모기에 팔을 물려서 퉁퉁 부어 올랐다 I have a swollen mosquito bite on my arm. / I was bitten by a mosquito and got a bad swelling [swollen spot] on my arm.

▶ 머리를 맞아서 큰 혹이 생겼다 I was hit on the head and got a (large) bump. / I have a (large) bump from being hit on the head.

▶ 피가 나다 I began to bleed. // 피를 많이 흘리다 I lost a lot of blood. / My wound has bleed [been bleeding] a lot.

▶ 두통이 있다 I have a headache. // 머리가 무겁다 My head feels heavy. // 머리가 욱신거린다 I have a throbbing headache. / My head throbs. // 두통이 멈추지 않다 I have a constant headache [constant headaches]. (★ 복수형을 쓰면 짧은 두통이 주기적으로 계속되는 것을 말함)

▶ 눈에 뭐가 들어간 것 같다 I feel that I have something in my eye(s). / I feel as though [if] there was something in my eye(s). (★ 전자는 눈에 이물질이 들어간 경우, 후자는 그 밖의 원인에 의한 불쾌감) // 눈이 따끔따끔하다 My eyes are smarting. // 스모그 때문에 눈이 따끔거렸다 The smog made my eyes smart. // 눈이 피로하다 My eyes get tired. // 근시가 된 것 같다 I think my nearsightedness [myopia] has gotten worse. / I think I've become more nearsighted. // 약간 원시이다 I'm slightly [a little] farsighted. // 난시가 아닌가 생각합니다 I wonder if I have astigmatism. // 이 안경은 도수가 맞지 않는다 My glasses aren't right for me [don't fit (me)] anymore. // 눈이 충혈됐다 My eyes are bloodshed // 눈곱이 끼었다 I have a discharge (of mucus) from my eyes. // 눈이 가렵다 My eyes feel itchy. // 눈이 부시다 My eyes are easily dazzled by the light. / My eyes are sensitive to the light.

▶코가 막히다 My nose gets [is] stopped up. / I have a stuffy nose. (★ 잘 막히거나 막혀있는 코) // 코가 근질거리다 My nose itches. / My nose feels itchy. // 콧물이 흐르다 I have a runny nose. // 콧물이 계속 나온다 My nose is always running.

▶ 귀가 잘 들리지 않는다 I can't hear well. / I'm a little deaf. // 귀에서 고름이 나온다 My ear is [Ears are] running. / I have a discharge from my ear(s). // 귀에서 울림소리가 난다 My ear rings. // 귀가 아프다 I have an earache.

▶ 충치가 있다 I have a rotten tooth. // 이가 아프다 I have a toothache. // 이가 흔들린다 My tooth [One of my teeth] is (coming) loose. // 찬물이 이에 닿으면 아프다 I feel pain in my tooth when I drink cold water. / My tooth [one of my teeth] is painfully sensitive to cold. // 이빨이 맞부딪히면 잇몸이 아프다 I feel pain in the upper gum when I grit my teeth. // 의치가 잘 들어맞지 않아서 아프다 My jaw is sore because my dentures [false teeth] don't fit properly [right]. // 의치가 흔들린다, 너무 헐거운 것 같다 My dentures rattle; I think they're too loose.

▶목구멍이 따끔따끔하다 My throat feels [is] sore. / I have a bad sore throat. // 목구멍에 가래가 차 있다 My throat is full of phlegm. // 기침이 멈추지 않는다 I have a chronic [persistent] cough. // 말을 할 때 목이 아프다 It hurts when I talk. // 무엇을 삼킬 때 목구멍이 아프다 It hurts when I swallow something. // 목이 쉬었다 My voice is getting husky.

▶뱃속이 묵직하다 My stomach feels heavy. // 배가 쿡쿡 쑤시는 것처럼 아프다 I feel a sharp [biting] pain in my stomach. // 배가 쌀쌀 아프다 I feel a slight but persistent sharp pain in the abdomen. // 식욕이 없다 I have a poor [small, bad] appetite. (★ 식욕이 왕성하다 I have a good [big, hearty, healthy] appetite.) // 토할 것 같다 I'm [I feel] nauseated. / I have nausea. / I feel like throwing up [vomiting]. / I'm sick at [to] the stomach. // 토했다 I threw up [vomited]. // 설사를 한다 I have diarrhea. / I have loose bowels. // 묽은 변을 본다 I have slight diarrhea. / My bowels [bowel movements] are a little loose. // 변비이다 I'm constipated. // 배탈이 나다 I have a problem with my digestion [digestive system]. // 헛배가 부르다 My abdomen [gut] feels swollen [bloated, distended] // 위경련이다 I have severe stomach cramps. / I have cramps in my [of the] stomach

▶고혈압 [저혈압]이다 I have high [low] blood pressure. / My blood pressure is high [low]. // 심장에 통증이 있다 I have [feel] pain (in the chest) around my heart. // 숨이 가쁘다 I can't catch my breath. / I'm very short-winded. / My breathing has become labored [painful].

▶관절이 아프다 I have pain in the joints (of my knee). // 관절염에 걸렸다 I'm developing arthritis. // 오른쪽 팔꿈치가 아프다 I've got a sore right elbow. // 근육통이다 My muscles ache. / My muscles are [feel] sore. / I have muscular aches (and pains). // 어깨가 결린다 I have stiff shoulders. / My shoulders are stiff. // 발목을 삐다 I sprained my ankle. // 발가락을 삐었다 I stubbed my toe. // 넘어져서 왼팔에 골절상을 입었다 I fell down and broke my left arm. // 축구를 하다가 왼쪽 어깨가 탈구되었다 I dislocated my left shoulder playing football.

▶ 요통이 난다 I have lumbago. // 손에 마비 증세가 있다 My hands are numb [palsied] at times. / I have writer's [scrivener's] palsy. // 수영하다가 왼발에 쥐가 났다 I got a cramp in my right leg when I was swimming. // 목 근육에 쥐가 났다 I got a crick in my neck.

⑥ 진료

▶집단 요법 group therapy / 최면 요법 hypnotic therapy / 물리 요법 physical therapy / 화학 요법 chemotherapy / 전기요법 electrotherapy / 침 치료 acupuncture / 침(鍼) 요법 moxibustion / 지압 요법 acupressure / 정골(整骨) 요법 osteopathy / 민간 요법 folk medicine / 예방 의학 preventive medicine / 비타민 요법 vitamin therapy / 식이 요법 dietary therapy (★식이 요법의 전문가는 dietary therapist, dietitian) / 동종(同種) 의학 homeopathic medicine (★ 병원자와 같은 성질을 가진 물질을 소량 투여하는 치료 방식) / 돌팔이 의사 quack; horse doctor

▶진단 diagnosis / 초진 first visit (to a doctor); first medical examination; patient's first visit / 재진 revisit / 왕진 house call; home visit / 오진 malpractice

▶내시경 endoscope / 혈관 내시경 angioscope / 심장경 cardioscope / 심전도 electrocardiogram / CT 촬영 computerized axial tomography / 진찰실 consultation [examination] room / 수술실 operation room / 회복실 recovery room / 분만실 delivery room / 병실 sickroom / 병동 ward

▶가루약 powder / 정제 tablet / 당의정 sugar-coated pill / 연고 ointment / 해독제 antidote / 해열제 antipyretic drug;

antifebrile / 소화제 peptic / 소독제 antiseptic / 진통제 anodyne / 항생 물질 antibiotic / 수면제 sleeping pill / 안약 eyedrops / 좌약 suppository / 탈지면 (absorbent) cotton

병가 病暇 sick leave
병갑 兵甲 arms and armor
병객 病客 a sick person ; a patient
병거 兵車 a (war) chariot
병결 病缺 absence on account of〔due to〕 illness
병고 病故 an illness《영》; a sickness《미》; a disease ¶ 병고로 결석하다 absent oneself《from a meeting》 due to〔owing to〕 an illness
병고 病苦 the pain of sickness〔illness〕; suffering from sickness ; illness ¶ 병고에 몹시 시달리다 suffer acutely from illness // 병고를 위로하다 console《a person》 in his pain of illness
병골 病骨 a sickly person ; a feeble〔weak, delicate〕 person
병과 兵戈 ① [창] a spear ; a lance ② [전쟁] a war ; a conflict ; a meeting of arms ; a crossing of lances
병과 兵科 a branch of the (military) service
보병 — the infantry branch 전투 — 장교 a combatant officer
병구 病軀 a sick body ; ill health ; a sickly constitution ¶ 병구를 무릅쓰고 in spite of one's illness
병구완 nursing ; tending《a sick person》 **—하다** nurse ; tend ; attend on ¶ 밤새도록 병구완하다 sit up with《a patient》; nurse《a patient》 all through the night // 병구완하여 회복시키다 nurse《a patient》 back to health // 그녀의 정성 어린 병구완으로 나는 곧 회복됐다 Owing to her careful nursing, I soon got well.
병권 兵權 military power〔authority〕; control of the armed forces ¶ 병권을 잡다 possess〔assume〕 military power
병균 病菌 a (disease) germ ; a virus
— 보유자 a germ carrier
병근 病根 the cause of a disease ; a morbific agent ; [화근] the cause〔root〕 of an ailment〔a trouble〕; the root of an evil ¶ 병근을 없애다 exterminate the germs of a disease ; strike at〔wipe out〕 the root of an evil
병기 兵器 arms ; ordnance ; weapons〔implements〕 of war
—고(庫) an armory — 공업 the armament industry — 공장 an arsenal ; an ordnance〔an arms, a munitions〕 factory ; an armory《미》 — 과학 an ordnance science — 장교 an ordnance officer —창 an arsenal ; an ordnance department ; an armory《미》 공격〔방어〕 — an offensive〔a defensive〕 weapon 화학〔생물〕 — a chemical〔biological〕 weapon
*__병나다 病—__ ① [질환] get〔fall〕 sick〔ill〕; be taken ill ; get diseased ; lose one's health ; be unwell ¶ 과식으로 병나다 make oneself ill by overeating ; overeat oneself ill // 과로해서 병나다 (over-)work oneself ill // 당신은 소화기가 병났다 You have a digestive trouble. ② [고장] go wrong ; get〔be〕 out of order ; break down ¶ 시계가 병났다 This watch has gone wrong〔is out of order〕.
병내다 病— ① [몸에] make《a person》 sick〔ill〕; bring about〔cause〕 illness ② [사물에] put out of order ; cause a breakdown ; mess《a thing》 up
병단 兵端 hostilities ; war ¶ 병단을 열다 open hostilities《with》; open fire《on》
병단 兵團 an army corps
병대 兵隊 a soldier ; an army ⇨ 군대
병독 病毒 disease germs ; the virus poisons ¶ 병독에 감염되다 be infected《with》 // 병독을 퍼뜨리다 disseminate〔spread〕 infection
— 매개 생물 『생물』 a reservoir — 매개자〔보유자〕 a germ carrier ; a vector — 원(源) a reservoir of a virus
⁑**병동 病棟** a ward ; a sick〔hospital〕 ward ¶ 격리 병동 an isolation ward // 시료 병동 a charity ward // 일반 병동 a general ward
병들다 病— get〔fall〕 sick〔ill〕; be taken ill ; get diseased ; lose one's health ; be sick〔ill〕
병란 兵亂 a war ; a disturbance ; trouble ¶ 병란의 도가니로 변하다 become a scene of war
병략 兵略 strategy ; tactics ; a stratagem
병력 兵力 military power〔force〕; the strength (of an army) ¶ 병력으로 by force of arms // 적의 병력은 10 만이다 The enemy is 100,000 strong./The enemy strength is 100,000 men.
병력 病歷 the history of a case ; a case history
병렬 竝列 a row ; a line **—하다** be in a row ; stand in a line
— 회로 『전기』 a parallel circuit
병리 病理 the pathology (of a disease)
병리학 病理學 pathology ¶ 병리학(상)의 pathological
—자 a pathologist — 총〔각〕론 general〔special〕 pathology
병리 해부학 病理解剖學 morbid〔pathological〕 anatomy
병립 竝立 compatibility ; coexistence ; standing side by side **—하다** stand together ; coexist《with》; (be) consistent《with》; compatible《with》

— 개념 a coordinate concept
병마 兵馬 [병기와 군마] arms and war horses ; [군대] troops ; [군사] military affairs ; [전쟁] war ¶ 병마를 동원하다 raise〔mobilize〕 an army ; appeal to arms // 병마의 대권을 잡다 assume supreme military power
병마 病魔 (the curse of) a disease ; the demon of ill health ¶ 병마에 사로잡히다 be taken ill ; be seized with an illness
병마개 瓶— a bottle cap ; a capsule ; a stopper ; a cork ¶ 병마개를 뽑다 uncork ; open a bottle // 병마개를 막다 put a cap on a bottle ; put a stopper on a bottle ; cork a bottle
—뽑이 a bottle opener ; [코르크 마개의] corkscrew ; a cork extractor ; [맥주병 따위의] a cap opener
병막 病幕 a quarantine station〔camp〕 ; an isolation hospital ; a detention hospital
병명 病名 the name of a disease〔malady〕 ¶ 병명 미상의 병 an unidentified disease // 병명을 붙이다 diagnose〔name, identify〕 a disease // 의사가 병명을 모른다 The doctor fails〔is unable〕 to diagnose a case.
병목 瓶— the neck of a bottle
병몰 病沒 death from sickness ⇨ 병사
병무 兵務 military affairs
—국 the Military Service Bureau — 소집 a call for reserve training —청 the Office of Manpower Administration — 행정 conscription administration
병발 竝發, 倂發 concurrence ; a complication (병의) ; supervention —하다 concur ; occur simultaneously ; take place together ; develop ; happen at the same time ; supervene ¶ 열을 병발하다 develop fever
—증 a complication ; an intercurrent disease ; a deuteropathy
병방 丙方 〖민속〗 south by southeast
병배 瓶— a bottle-shaped pear
병법 兵法— tactics ; strategy ; the art of war
—가 a tactician ; a strategist
병변 兵變 a war ⇨ 병란
병비 兵備 armaments ; military〔warlike〕 preparations ⇨ 군기
†병사 兵士 a soldier ; a private
병사 兵舍 barracks
퀀셋 — a Quonset hut 《미》 ; a Nissen hut 《영》
병사 兵事 military affairs
— 계원 a secretary in charge of military affairs —과 a military affairs section —구 a recruiting district
병사 病死 death from disease ; a natural death —하다 die of illness ; die from a disease ; die in one's bed ; die a natural death
병사 病舍 an infirmary ; a hospital
격리 — an isolation ward ; a quarantine (station)
병살 倂殺 〖야구〗 a double play
병상 病床 one's sickbed ¶ 병상의 노부인 a bedridden old lady // 병상에 눕다 be ill abed ; be confined to bed
— 일지 [병자가 쓴] a sick person's diary ; [병원의] a sickbed record ; a clinical report — 치료 bedside medicine
병상 病狀 the condition of a patient ; one's condition ¶ 병상에 변화가 없다 There is no change in his condition.
병상병 病傷兵 the sick and wounded (soldiers) ; the invalids ; the invalid soldiers
병색 病色 a sick complexion ; sickly appearance
병서 兵書 a book on strategy〔tactics〕 ; a book on military science
병서 竝書, 竝書 writing the same (consonant) characters laterally attached —하다 write the same (consonant) characters laterally attached
병석 病席 a sickbed ⇨ 병상
병선 兵船 a warship ; a military vessel ; an armed vessel
병설 竝設 establishment as an annex —하다 establish 《a primary school》 as an annex 《to the college》
병세 兵勢 military force ; the number of soldiers ; an army ; a force
병세 病勢 the condition of a disease (of a patient) ¶ 병세가 악화되다 take a serious turn ; take a turn for the worse // 병세가 나아지다 get better ; improve // 병세가 나빠지다 be in an advanced stage of illness
병소 病巢 a focus 《*pl.* ~es, -ci》
병소 감염 病巢感染 focal infection
병술 瓶— bottled liquor ; liquor sold by the bottle
병술 丙戌 〖민속〗 the 23rd binary term of the sexagenary cycle
병시 病時 〖민속〗 the 12th of the 24 hour periods 《10 : 30—11 : 30 a. m.》
병신 丙申 〖민속〗 the 33rd binary term of the sexagenary cycle
*병신 病身 ① [불구자] a deformed person ; a maimed person ; a cripple (다리 병신) ; a disabled person ¶ 병신을 만들다 deform ; disfigure ; maim ; cripple ; mutilate // 병신이 되다 be〔get〕 deformed 〔disfigured〕 ; be maimed〔crippled〕 ; be disabled // 평생 병신이 되다 be crippled 〔maimed, disabled〕 for life // 병신으로 태어나다 be born a cripple // 해마다 교통 사고로 수천 명이 병신이 된다 Traffic accidents maim thousands of people every year
② [병자] a sickly person ; a chronic invalid ; an invalid for life (고질 병자)
③ [바보] a stupid person ; a fool ; a dunce ¶ 이 병신아 You blockhead you ! // 병신처럼 굴지 마라 Don't be a fool.

④ [온전치 못한 물건] an incomplete〔a defective〕 thing ; an odd set ¶ 영화가 검열에 잘려서 병신이 돼버렸다 The censor mutilated the film.
병신 자식이 효도한다 〔속담〕 Crooked logs make straight fires.
병신 구실 病身— unworthiness ; uselessness ; behavior to be expected of a defective **—하다** play the part of a defective ; be no good to anybody ; (be) useless ; prove to be a failure ¶ 사내가 아내에게 병신 구실한다 He is tied to his wife's apron strings.
병신성스럽다 病身— (be) foolish ; silly ; iditic ; stupid ; imbecile ; moronic
병실 病室 a sick room ; an infirmary (학교·공장 따위의) ; a (sick) ward (병원의) ¶ 개인 병실 a private ward // 배의 병실 a sick bay
†**병아리** a chick ; a chicken ¶ 쥔 병아리 같다 be like a pecked chick ; be always getting picked on
— 감별사 a chicken sexer — 오줌 a chicken ; a chickenhearted〔fainthearted〕 person ; a dull conservative person ; a stick-in-the mud
‡**병약** 病弱 weakness ; infirmity ; delicate constitution **—하다** (be) sickly ; delicate
병어 —魚 〖물고기〗 a pomfret ; a flatfish ; a butterfish ; a flounder ¶ 병어주둥이 a person with a very small mouth
***병역** 兵役 military service ; service in the army ; conscription ¶ 병역 기간의 단축 a reduction of the length of conscript service // 병역에 부적합한 자 a noneffective // 병역을 기피하다 evade military service // 병역을 복무하다 serve in the army // 병역을 면제하다 exempt 《a person》 from military service
— 기피 evasion of military service — 기피자 a draft evader〔dodger〕 ; a shirker of military service ; a slacker 《구》 — 만기 completion of (military) service — 면제 exemption〔immunity〕 from military service —법 the military service law — 연한 the term of military service — 의무 obligatory〔compulsory〕 military service ; selective service 《미》 — 제도 the conscription system
병영 兵營 barracks
— 생활 an army life ; a barrack life — 연기 student deferment
병오 丙午 〖민속〗 the 43rd binary term of the sexagenary cycle
병와 病臥 **—하다** be ill〔sick〕 in bed ¶ 통풍으로 병와 중이다 He is laid up〔ill in bed〕 with gout.
병용 並用 **—하다** use jointly〔together〕 ; use in combination 《with》
— 치료 a combined treatment
병원 兵員 military personnel ; strength (of an army, troops) ¶ 육군의 병원을 증가〔경감〕하다 increase〔reduce〕 the personnel of the Army
— 명부 [육군] a muster roll ; an army list ; [해군] a navy list〔register〕 《미》
†**병원** 病院 a hospital ; an infirmary ; a nursing home ¶ 병원에 다니다 attend a hospital ; go to hospital // 병원에 데리고 가다 take 《a person》 to (a) hospital // 병원에 입원시키다 send 《a person》 to a hospital ; hospitalize // 병원에 입원하고 있다 be in hospital // 병원에 입원하다 enter〔go into〕 (a) hospital
—선 a hospital ship — 열차 an ambulance train —장 the director of a hospital —차 an ambulance 개인〔사립〕 — a private hospital 구급 — a receiving hospital 야전 — a field hospital ; a clearing hospital 육군 이동 외과 — a mobile army surgical hospital 《MASH》 정신 — a mental institution 종합 — a general hospital 후송 — an evacuation hospital
병원 病原, 病源 the cause〔source〕 of one's illness ; the origin〔etiology〕 of a disease
—균 germs ; a bacillus 《*pl.* -cilli, -lai》 ; a virus —체 pathogenic organ —학 aetiology 《영》 ; etiology 《미》
병유 併有, 並有 combination of one thing with another ; possessing both 〔together〕 **—하다** possess together ; combine 《a thing》 with 《another》 ; enjoy concomitantly
병인 兵刃 bladed weapons ; military weapons ; bayonets
병인 丙寅 〖민속〗 the 3rd binary term of the sexagenary cycle
병인 病人 a sick person ⇨ 병자
병인 病因 the cause of a disease ; an etiological cause〔factor〕 ¶ 그의 병인은 술이다 Wine is at the bottom of his illness.
—론〔학〕 etiology ; aetiology — 학자 an etiologist
병자 丙子 〖민속〗 the 13th binary term of the sexagenary cycle
병자 病者 a sick person ; a patient (환자) ; a case ; the sick 《총칭》 ¶ 그는 병자같다 He looks very ill. // 요즘 가족에 병자가 많이 났다 There has been a great deal of illness in the family.
병작 並作 sharecropping on a fifty-fifty basis 《미》 ; sharing a tenant crop equally with the landlord **—하다** sharecrop on a fifty-fifty basis ; share a tenant crop equally〔half-and-half〕 with the landlord
—농 fifty-fifty sharecropping
병장 兵長 a lance corporal 《영》 ; [육군·해병] a sergeant ; [해군] seaman first class ; [공군] an airman first class
***병적** 病的 (being) morbid ; diseased ; unsound ; pathological ; abnormal ¶ 병적으로 morbidly // 병적으로 좋아하다 have a morbid liking for ; have a weakness〔passion〕 for // 그 정도면 거의 병적이라

할 수 있다 When it goes that far, it's almost a drsease.
— 성격 abnormal character — 소질 diathesis ; pathological predisposition — 흥분 fever heat
*병적 兵籍 military register ; one's military status ¶ 병적에 들다 enlist (in the army) ; be enrolled as a soldier
—부 a muster roll — 편입 enrollment
병점 病占 —하다 《a fortuneteller》 predict〔foretell, prognosticate〕 the course of an illness ¶ 병점을 하다 consult a fortuneteller about one's illness
병정 兵丁 a soldier ; a serviceman
병제 兵制 a military system〔organization〕
병존 竝存 coexistence —하다 coexist 《with》 ; be coexistent 《with》 ; exist together
병졸 兵卒 a private ; a (common) soldier ; an enlisted man 《미》 ; the ranks ; the rank and file 《총칭》 ¶ 일개 병졸에서 대장이 되다 rise from the ranks to be a general
병종 兵種 a branch of the army
병종 丙種 the third class〔grade〕
병주머니 病— a person with many (chronic) diseases ; a bag of woes
병중 病中 ¶ 병중에 during one's illness // 병중임에도 불구하고 in spite of one's ill health
병증 病症 the nature of a disease〔an illness〕
— 불명 acrisia
병진 丙辰 〖민속〗 the 53rd binary term of the sexagenary cycle
병진 竝進, 倂進 —하다 keep abreast of 《a person》 ; keep pace with 《a person》 ; advance side by side
— 운동 〖기계〗 translation
병진 兵塵 the tumult of war ; the dust of the battlefield
병집 病— ① 〔흠〕 a weakness ; the trouble with 《a person》 ; a flaw ¶ 술을 많이 마시는 것이 그 사람의 병집이다 His trouble is he drinks too much.
② 〔병근·화근〕 the cause〔root, source〕 of disease〔trouble〕 ¶ 병집을 없애다 remove the cause of one's disease
병참 兵站 communications ; impedimenta ; supply trains ; logistics
—감 the quartermaster general 《Q. M. G》 ; the commander of the line of communications — 기지 a supply〔commissary〕 base — 보급창 a quartermaster depot 《미》 — 부대 the quartermaster corps — 사령부 Logistic Support Command —선 a line of communications ; a supply line — 업무〔근무〕 logistics ; a logistical job — 장교 a commissary ; a quartermaster 《미》 —학 logistics
병창 竝唱 —하다 sing together〔in chorus〕
병추기 病— a sickly person ; an invalid
병충해 病蟲害 damages by blight and harmful insects
병칭 竝稱 ranking together ; classing 《a person》 with —하다 rank them together ; class〔rank〕 《a person》 with another
병탄 竝呑, 倂呑 absorption ; annexation —하다 annex 《to》 ; absorb 《into》 ; swallow up ; devour
병태 病態 the condition (of a patient)
병통 病— trouble 《with a thing》 ; malfunction ; something wrong 《with》 ; a hitch ; a snag ; a breakdown ¶ 기계〔일〕에 병통이 생기다 have trouble with a machine〔one's work〕
병폐 病廢 disablement〔deformity〕 by an illness〔a disease〕 —하다 be disabled by an illness〔a disease〕 ; be invalided
병폐 病弊 an evil ; a vice ; evil practices ; abuses (악습)
병풍 屛風 a folding screen ¶ 여섯 쪽으로 된 병풍 a six-fold screen // 병풍을 두르다 set up a screen // 연산이 병풍을 두른 듯 절벽을 이루고 있다 A range of precipitous mountains stretches away like a wall.
병학 兵學 military science ; tactics ; strategy
병합 倂合 annexation ; amalgamation ; absorption ; incorporation —하다 annex 《to》 ; amalgamate 《into》 ; absorb 《into》 ; merge ¶ 그 회사는 다른 회사에 병합되었다 The firm was amalgamated into another.
—죄 〖법〗 the concurrence of offenses ; concurrent offenses
병해 病害 blight (농작물의)
병행 竝行 〔나란히〕 going side by side ; parallelism —하다 go abreast 〔side by side〕 ; run parallel 《with》 ; carry out 《two things》 side by side ¶ 선로와 병행하다 run parallel with a railway line // 소비는 생산과 병행한다 Consumption keeps pace with production.
병화 兵火 the fires of war ¶ 병화의 와중 a battlefield // 병화에 짓밟히다 be destroyed 〔devastated〕 by fire in a battle
병환 病患 《your, his》 disease ; illness 《영》 ; sickness 《미》 ; indisposition (가벼운) ¶ 어머님의 병환은 어떠하신가 How's your (sick) mother ?
병후 病後 convalescence ; the convalescent stage ¶ 병후의 convalescent // 병후에 after an illness // 병후(의) 정양 aftercare // 병후(의) 쇠약 weakness from one's illness // 병후 정양 시설 aftercare facilities // 진해에서 병후 정양을 하다 recuperate at *Chinhae* // 병후가 양호하다 convalesce favorably
*볕 sunshine ; the sun ; the warmth of the sun ¶ 볕이 잘 드는 sunny // 볕이 잘 안 드는 unsunny ; gloomy // 볕이 잘 드는 방 a sunny room // 볕에 타다 be sunburnt ; be

tanned // 볕에 말리다 dry in the sun // 볕에 쬐다 expose ⟪a thing⟫ to the sun (바래다) ; bask〔bathe〕 in the sun (일광욕) // 볕에 내놓다 put〔place〕 ⟪a thing⟫ in the sun // 볕을 쬐지 않다 keep〔have〕 ⟪a thing⟫ out of the sun ; protect〔screen〕 ⟪a thing⟫ from the sun // 볕이 따갑다 The sun is burning-hot. // 볕이 잘 든다 The sunshine comes in freely. // 그의 방에는 전혀 볕이 들지 않는다 No sun ever gets into his room.

볕기 一氣 heat of the sun ; the force of the sunlight

볕들다 shine ⟪into, in, upon⟫ ¶ 방에 볕 들다 The sun shines〔streams〕 into the room.

보 [들보] a crossbeam ; a beam

보 步 [걸음] a step ; a pace ¶ 제1보의 the first〔initial〕 step // 한 시간에 3마일의 보속 a pace of three miles an hour // 1보 전진〔후퇴〕하다 make a step forward(s)〔backward(s)〕

보 保 [보증] (a) guarantee ; (a) guaranty ; (a) security ; an assurance ; [보증인] (a) guarantor ; (a) guaranty ; (a) surety (연대의) ; a reference ¶ 보가 붙은 guaranteed ; warranted ; secured // 보를 서다 stand guaranty〔security〕 ; go bond for ⟪a person⟫ // 보를 세우다 give〔find〕 security for ⟪a person⟫

보 洑 a reservoir for irrigation ; a dammed pool for irrigation

***보 褓** a (small) wrapping〔covering〕 cloth

-보 補 assistant ; probationary
서기— an assistant clerk〔secretary〕 외교관— a probationary diplomat 차관— an assistant viceminister

보가지 〖물고기〗 a swellfish ; a blowfish

보각 補角 〖기하〗 a supplementary angle ; a supplement

보각 [술 따위가] with a bubble〔pop〕 ¶ 보각보각 bubbling ; popping // 보각거리다 bubble ; pop

보감 寶鑑 [귀감] an exemplar ; a mirror ; [책 따위의] a thesaurus ; a handbook

***보강 補强** reinforcement ; invigoration —하다 reinforce ; strengthen ; invigorate ¶ 내각의 보강 조치를 취하다 take steps to strengthen the cabinet
— 공사 reinforcement work —제(劑) a reinforcing agent (고무의) — 증거 〖법〗 corroboration — 철재 〖건축〗 armature

보강 補講 a supplementary lecture ; a make-up lesson —하다 give a supplementary lecture ; make up for a missing lecture〔lesson〕

보건 保健 health ; preservation of health ; [위생] hygiene ; sanitation ¶ 이것은 시민 보건에 중대한 문제이다 This is a vital question for the health of the citizen(s).
— 강장제 a tonic (medicine) —과(課) the Health Section —법 a health measure —소 a public health center — 식품 healthful〔sanitary〕 food —원(員) a (public) health〔district, community〕 nurse (여자) — 음료 a hygienic drink —의(醫) a (public) health doctor — 제도 the health system — 지도 health guidance — 체육 healthful and physical education — 체조 health gymnastics — 행정 public health administration 국민 — 운동 a national keep-fit movement 세계 — 기구 the World Health Organization ⟪WHO⟫

보검 寶劍 a precious〔treasured〕 sword ; [의장용] a formal-dress sword

보결 補缺 filling a vacancy ; supplement ; a substitute (사람) ; an alternate ⟪미⟫ —하다 fill a vacancy ; cover a deficiency ; make up for ¶ 보결의 supplementary ; substitute
— 모집 an invitation for filling vacancies ¶ 보결 모집하다 invite ⟪students⟫ to fill vacancies —생 a student for filling 〔admitted to a school to fill〕 a vacancy ; a stand-by〔supplementary〕 student — 선거 a special election ⟪미⟫ ; a by-election ⟪영⟫ — 선수 a substitute player ; a reserve ; a bench warmer ⟪미·속⟫ — 시험 a special entrance examination for stand-by students

보고 ⇨ 더러[2]

†**보고 報告** a report ; information (정보) ; returns (통계적) ; a paper (학술상의) ; a memoir —하다 report to ⟪a person⟫ on ⟪a matter⟫ ; give an account of ; inform ⟪a person⟫ of ; read a paper ⟪on a subject⟫ (학회에서) ¶ 국세 조사 보고 census returns // 사건을 상관에게 보고하다 report the matter to one's superior // 회의에 대해서 보고하다 give a report of the conference
— 문학 reportage ⟪프⟫ —자 a reporter ; one who reads〔presents〕 a paper 연차〔중간〕 — an annual〔interim〕 report 최종 — the final report

보고 寶庫 a treasurehouse ; a thesaurus ⟪*pl.* ~es, -ri⟫

†**보고서 報告書** a (written) report ; [학회의] a paper ; a memoir ; a journal ; [계수의] returns ; [협회 따위의] transactions ; [기사] a record ; a brief ; a briefing ¶ 보고서를 작성하다 make a report ⟪on⟫ // 보고서를 제출하다 send in〔file〕 a report

***보관 保管** custody ; charge ; safekeeping ; deposit —하다 keep ; have ⟪a thing⟫ in one's keeping ; take charge ⟪of⟫ ; take ⟪a thing⟫ in custody ¶ 보관을 의뢰하다 ask ⟪a person⟫ to keep ⟪a thing⟫ ; leave ⟪a thing⟫ in the custody of ⟪a person⟫ // 서류는 A군이 보관하고 있다 The papers are in the custody of Mr. A./The papers are in Mr. A's keeping. // 이 서류 좀 정리하여 보관해 주세요 File

these papers, please.
—료 charges for custody ; storage (창고의) —물 an article in custody —소 a depository —인 a custodian ; a keeper —증 a certificate of custody ; a receipt
보관 寶冠 [왕의] a crown ; [귀족·왕족의] a coronet
보교 步轎 a sedan (chair) ; a palankeen ¶ 보교를 타다 ride〔have a ride〕 in a sedan chair // 보교로 가다 go by palankeen
—꾼 a chair-bearer
보국 報國 patriotism ; service of gratitude to one's country **—하다** place oneself in the service of one's country ¶ 보국의 patriotic
납세 — patriotic service by paying taxes
보국 안민 輔國安民 —하다 promote the national interests and provide for the welfare of the people
보군 步軍 a foot soldier ; a footman
보굿 a piece of bark ; [그물의] a net float (usually made of bark)
보궐 補闕 ⇨ 보결(補缺)
보균 保菌 carrying germs ; being infected **—하다** carry germs ; be infected
—자 a germ〔disease〕 carrier ; a carrier
보그르르, 뽀그르르 ⇨ 부그르르, 바그르르
보글보글 boiling ; simmering ¶ 보글보글 끓다 simmer ; be at a simmer
†**보금자리** a nest ; a roost ; a home ¶ 사랑의 보금자리 a love nest // 보금자리에 든 at roost // 보금자리를 짓다 build a nest ; nest 《in a tree》 // 보금자리에 들다 go to roost ; roost // 보금자리로 돌아가다 fly home to roost
‡**보급 普及** spread ; diffusion ; propagation ; popularization **—하다** spread ; diffuse ; popularize ; propagate ¶ 교육의 보급 the diffusion〔spread〕 of education // 민주 사상의 보급을 도모하다 promote the spread of democracy // 그것은 교육 영화의 보급에 도움이 된다 It aids in popularizing educational films. // 텔레비전이 보급되었다 Television has come into wide use.
—판 a popular〔cheap〕 edition
***보급 補給** supply **—하다** supply ; replenish ¶ 보급이 끊어지다 run out of supplies // 연료를 보급하다 replenish fuel
—관 〖군사〗 a quartermaster — 기지 a supply base —로 a supply route — 부대 the Quartermaster Corps 《미》 —선 a supply ship —품 공수 air supply ; a supply lift —품 저장소 a supply depot 〔dump〕
보급소 普及所 an agency ; a distributing agency〔agent〕 ; a distributor
신문 잡지 — an agent for newspapers and magazines
보기[1] [실례] an example ; an instance ; [예증] an illustration ¶ 보기를 들면 for example〔instance〕 《e. g.》 // 보기를 들다 cite〔give〕 an instance〔example〕
보기[2] [보는 각도] a way of looking at 《things》 ¶ 보기에 따라서는 in a sense ; viewed from another angle
보기 寶器 a treasured article ; a treasure
보기 補氣 invigoration of one's energy 〔vitality〕 by taking medicine **—하다** take a tonic ; pep oneself up with a tonic
보깨다 have a stomach trouble ; suffer from indigestion
보꾹 〖건축〗 the inner part of a roof ; the ceiling
보나마나 needless to say ; (as a matter) of course ; to be sure ; no〔without, beyond, out of〕 doubt ; undoubtedly ; obviously
보내기 洑— making an irrigation ditch
†**보내다** ① send ; forward ; transmit (전신을) ; remit (돈을) ; ship (배·차로) ; consign (탁송) ; dispatch (파견) ¶ 편지를 보내다 send〔write〕 《a person》 a letter ; send〔write〕 a letter to 《a person》 // 심부름을 보내다 send 《a person》 on an errand // 찬사를 보내다 pay 《a person》 a compliment // 돈을 우편환으로 보내다 remit〔send〕 money by money〔postal〕 order // 데리러〔가지러〕 보내다 send 《a person》 for // 군대를 보내다 dispatch troops // 신문을 사러 아이를 보내다 send a boy out for a paper // 역까지 마중나오라는 전보를 보내왔다 He wired me 〔asked me by wire, sent me a telegram asking me〕 to meet him at the station. // 주문하신 물건을 오늘 배편으로 보냈습니다 We have forwarded your order by ship today.
② [전송] see〔send〕 off ; give a send-off ; escort (여자를) ¶ 역까지 보내다 see 《a person》 off to the station // 역에서 보내다 see 《a person》 off at the station // 자동차로 보내 주다 drive 《a person》 to 《a place》
③ [세월을] spend ; pass ; lead ; live ¶ 시간을 보내기 위해서 to kill time // 헛되이 세월을 보내다 idle away one's time // 적적하게 세월을 보내다 lead a lonesome life // 만년을 편히 보내다 live the rest of one's life happily // 묵은 해를 보내고 새해를 맞다 see the old year out and the new year in // 공부를 하며 시간을 보내다 spend one's time (in) studying
보너스 a bonus ⇨ 상여금 ¶ 월급 2개월분의 보너스 a bonus equivalent to two months' pay // 연말 보너스 a year-end bonus
보늬 the inner skin (of a chestnut)
‡**보닛** [모자] a bonnet ; [자동차의] a hood 《미》 ; a bonnet 《영》
†**보다[1]** ① see ; look at ¶ 보아하니〔보매〕 judging from appearances // 어느 모로 보나 to all appearances // 한번 보아 at first glance ; at a glance ; at first sight // …을

보자 at the sight of // 보는 데서 in one's sight〔view〕 // 슬그머니 보다 steal a glance at // 얼핏 보다 catch a glimpse 《of》 // 자세히 보다 have a good look 《at》 // 죽 훑어보다 glance over 《a thing》 ; look through 《a book》 // 사람의 얼굴을 보다 look 《a person》 in the face // 못 본 체하다 pretend not to see〔not to have seen〕 ; wink〔blink, connive〕 《at》 // 잘못을 못 본 체하다 wink〔look through one's fingers〕 at 《a person's》 faults // 차마 볼 수 없다 cannot bear to see ; be unable to bear the sight of // 보기 싫다 hate 《a person》 ; hate the sight 《of a person》 // 그는 보기도 싫다 I hate the very sight of him. // 그는 내가 안 보는 사이에 그 짓을 했다 He did it while I was not looking. // 그는 나를 못 본 체했다 He cut me cold on the street. /He gave me the cold shoulder on the street. // 이것 봐요 Look here ! // 도둑은 순경을 보자 도망갔다 At the sight of the policeman, the thief took to his heels. // 그녀의 슬픔은 보기에도 딱했다 Her grief was painful to behold. // 상자 안에 무엇이 들어 있는지 보고 싶어 죽겠다 I'm dying to see what's inside of this chest. // 좌우간 가서 보고 오너라 At any rate, go and have a look at it. // 좀 더 잘 보기 위해 앞으로 나아갔다 He stepped forward to take a better look at it. // 그는 어느 모로 보나 군인이다 He is a soldier, every inch of him. // 그것 좀 빨리 보고 싶군요 I can hardly wait to see it. // 세상 오래 살다 보니 별것을 다 보게 되는군 Now I've seen everything. // 서울에서는 무엇이 볼 만 한가요 What would you recommend I see in *Seoul*.

② [고찰·간주] consider ; judge ; view ; look 《at》 ; regard 《as》 ¶ 내가 보기에는 from my point of view ; in my opinion ; as I take it ; to my mind // 대체로 보아 on the whole ; considered as a whole // 어느 모로 보나 in every respect ; from every point of view // 보는 바가 다르다 look at 《a matter》 differently ; view differently // 교육적 견지에서 보다 consider 《a matter》 from the educational point of view // 사태가 중대하다고 보다 regard the situation as serious // 정직한 사람으로 보다 take 《a person》 to be an honest man // 눈으로 보기에는 약 500달러 정도 들 것 같습니다 Offhand, it will cost around five hundred dollars. // 나를 몇 살로 보느냐 How old do you take me for ? // 저마다 보는 바가 다르다 Each has his own opinion. /They view the matter from different angles. // 그것은 보는 사람에 따라 다르다 It is a matter of opinion. // 말이 없는 것은 동의하는 것으로 보아 무방하다 His silence can be read as consent. // 그 여자는 사람 보는 눈이 없구나 She certainly is a poor judge of character.

③ [구경] see ; see the sights of 《a place》 ; do 《a town》 ; visit 《a theater》 ; watch ¶ 서울을 보다 see (the sights of) *Seoul* ; do *Seoul* // 영화를 보다 see a movie // 텔레비전을 보다 watch television // 영화를 보러 가다 go to the movies ; attend a movie // 연극을 보러 가다 visit 〔attend〕 a theater // 공장을 보러 가다 visit a factory // 비원을 보러 가다 visit the Secret Garden // 볼 만하다 be worth seeing〔visiting〕

④ [읽다] read ; see ; look through ¶ 신문을 보다 read〔see〕 the newspaper // 책을 보다 look through a book

⑤ [돌보다] look after ; take charge of ; watch ¶ 아이를 보다 look after〔nurse〕 a baby ; baby-sit 《미》 ; keep an eye on the baby (주의해서) // 집보다 look after〔take care of〕 the house // 상을 보다 set the table // 아이를 볼 사람이 없다 I have no one to leave the baby with. // 나 없는 사이에 가게 좀 잘 보아라 Keep an eye on the store while I am away. // 우리가 휴가가 있는 동안 우리 집 좀 봐주시겠습니까 Could you house-sit for us while we are gone on vacation ? // 제가 화장실에 가 있는 동안 아기 좀 잠깐 봐주시겠습니까 Could you please keep an eye on my baby while I'm gone to the rest room ?

⑥ [일을] manage ; transact ; attend to ¶ 사무를 보다 attend to business // 일을 보다 take care of a business ; conduct affairs ; handle a job ; work // 나라 일을 보다 manage〔conduct, administer〕 state affairs // 아내가 집안일을 본다 My wife manages the housework.

⑦ [치르다] take ¶ 시험을 보다 take〔sit for〕 an examination ; undergo an examination

⑧ [당하다] experience ; go through ; undergo ; encounter ¶ 거래에서 이익을 보다 make a profit on the transaction // 큰 손해를 보다 suffer great losses ; suffer serious damage // 재미를 보다 have a good〔profitable〕 time ; have fun ; enjoy oneself ; enjoy prosperity // 욕을 보다 have a hard time of it ; have a bitter experience ; be put to shame ; be insulted ; be humiliated ; be disgraced ; be abused // 경사를 보다 have a happy occasion // 불상사를 보다 have an unhappy occasion

⑨ [기타] ¶ 장보러 가다 go to market ; go shopping ; go marketing // 소변을 보다 urinate ; ease nature // 손자를 보다 get a grandchild // 샛서방을 보다 have a lover ; have a secret love affair with // 관상을 보다 have one's face read 《by a fortuneteller》 // 손금을 보다 have one's fortune told 《by a palm reader》 // 사주를 보다 have one's fortune told 《by an astrologer》

보기 좋은 떡이 먹기도 좋다 속담 Names

and natures do often agree.

보기 좋다 [관용] be nice to look at

보다² ① [시험 삼아] try ; have a try《at》¶ 새옷을 입어 보다 try on a new suit//구두를 신어 보다 try shoes on//문을 열어 보다 try a door//재주 넘기를 해 보다 try at a somersault//신약을 써 보다 try a new remedy//해보겠다 I will try it.

② [경험] ¶ 영국에 가 보았느냐 Have you been to England? //다시 생각해 보겠습니다 Well, I'll think it over.

보다³ [추측·의향] seem ; it seems (to me)《that》; look like ; appear ¶ 비가 올려나 보다 It looks like〔is likely to〕rain. //참 그런가 보다 So it seems. //그는 아픈가 보다 He seems to be ill. /It seems (that) he is ill. //그는 친구가 많은가 보다 He appears to have a lot of friends. //죽어버릴까 보다 I wish I would die. /Shall I rather die at once?

*__보다⁴__ [비교의] than ; rather than ¶ 보다 (더) 나쁘다〔좋다〕 be worse〔better〕 than ; be inferior〔superior〕 to//차보다 커피를 즐기다 like coffee better than tea //그이는 내가 생각했던 것보다 키가 컸다 He was taller than I thought he would be. //백 번 듣는 것이 한번 보는 것보다 못하다 It is better to see a thing one time than to hear about it a hundred times.

보다못해 being unable to bear〔stand〕 the sight of《a happening》any more ; being more than one can bear to see《a happening》¶ 보다못해 그들의 싸움을 말렸다 Being unable to remain a mere spectator, I stopped their fighting.

⁑**보답 報答** recompense ; reward ; requital ; compensation **—하다** return ; repay ; reward ; recompense ; requite ; compensate ¶ 선에 대한 보답 the reward of virtue//보답으로 in return〔compensation〕《for》//우정에 보답하다 return friendship//수고에 보답하다 recompense 《a person》for his services ; recompense his services to《a person》; recompense 《a person》his services//악을 선으로 보답하다 repay〔requite〕 evil with good//은혜에 어떻게든 보답하고 싶습니다 I want to return your favor somehow.

보도 步度 pace ; step ; cadence

보도 步道 a footpath ; a sidewalk ; a footway ; a pavement

횡단 — a pedestrian crossing ; a zebra crossing〔zone〕《영》; crosswalk (for pedestrians)

보도 輔導 guidance ; direction ; lead ; protection and guidance **—하다** lead ; guide ; direct

—과 a guidance section **직업 —** vocational guidance

보도 寶刀 a treasured sword ¶ 전가의 보도를 빼다 have recourse to one's best (and rarely-used) weapon ; play one's trump card

보도 報道 news ; a report ; information ; intelligence **—하다** report ; inform〔notify〕《a person》of ; let《a person》know ; communicate《a matter》to ; cover《an accident》¶ 보도의 신속 promptness of information//신문 보도에 의하면 according to newspaper reports//보도에 접하다 receive the news of《a person's death》//잘못 보도하다 make a false report《of》; give out false news ; misreport//신문은 매일 일어나는 일들을 보도한다 The newspaper reports daily events.

— 가치 news value **—계 장교** a briefing officer **— 관제** a news blackout ; news censorship **— 기관** an information medium《*pl.* ~s -dia》; news media ; the press **—반** a press corps《*pl.* corps [kɔːz]》**—부** the press section **—부장** a news chief **— 사진** a news photo(graph)《*pl.* ~s》**— 사진사** a news〔newspaper〕 photographer〔cameraman〕 **—원** a reporter ; a newspaperman ; a newsman ; a newshound《속》**—전(戰)** a reportorial warfare ; a news competition **—진** a news front ; a press corps《미》; the pressmen《영》**—차** a news car

보도독거리다 creak ; grind ; grit ; grate ¶ 이를 보도독거리다 grind〔grate, grit〕 the teeth

보독 報毒 revenge ; vengeance ; vendetta ; retaliation **—하다** vent one's spite ; satisfy〔wreak〕 one's grudge ; revenge〔avenge〕 oneself《on a person》

보동보동 fleshy ; chubby ; plump **—하다** (be) fleshy ; chubby ; plump ; fat ; round and plump ¶ 보동보동 살찐 얼굴 a chubby face

보두다 保— endorse ; cosign ; give surety〔security〕 for ; find security for (보증인을 세우다)

보드기 a dwarf tree

보드랍다 (be) soft ⇨ 부드럽다 ¶ 보드라운 손〔천〕 a soft hand〔cloth〕//비단처럼 보드라운 살결 skin soft as silk

보드레하다 ⇨ 부드레하다

보드카 [술] vodka

보득솔 a dwarf pine tree

보들보들하다 (be) very soft ; tender ; supple ; flexible ¶ 보들보들한 살결 very soft skin

보듬다 embrace ; hug ; clasp《a person》in one's arms〔to one's bosom〕

보디 a body

—가드 a bodyguard **— 블로** a body blow (권투에서) **— 빌딩** body building

보따리 褓— a bundle ; a package ; a parcel

—장수 a packman ; a peddler ; a hawker **책〔빨래〕 —** a package of books〔laundry〕

보라¹ ⇨ 보랏빛

보라² [쐐기] an iron wedge used to split a tree ¶ 나무에 보라를 박다[치다] drive a wedge into a tree
보라매 a young hawk (tamed for hawking)
보라장기 —將棋 a slow-moving chess game
보라초 a kite that is all (light) purple except the top (tip)
*__보람¹__ worth ; effect ; result ¶ 보람있는 fruitful ; effective ; worthwhile // 보람없는 useless ; fruitless ; vain ; worthless ; futile // 보람도 없이 in vain ; to no purpose ; without result ; uselessly ; fruitlessly // 보람있는 수고 fruitful labors // 보람없는 인생 a fruitless life // 노력한 보람이 있어 시험에 합격했다 Thanks to his efforts[hard work], he passed the examination. // 수고한 보람이 있었다 I have not labored in vain. // 수고한 보람이 없었다 I have labored to no purpose[in vain]. // 그는 노력한 보람도 없이 시험에 실패했다 He failed in the examination in spite of[for all] his efforts. // 좋은 기회가 와도 노력하지 않으면 아무 보람이 없다 Good chance will avail you nothing without effort. // 그에게 말해도 아무 보람이 없다 It is mere waste of time[breath] to talk to him. // 이젠 그의 외아들이 죽었으니 인생은 그에게 아무 보람도 없다 Now his only son is dead, life is not worth living at all to him.
보람² a note ; a mark ; a sign —하다 mark ; sign
보랏빛 (royal) purple ; violet ¶ 보랏빛의 purple ; violet // 보랏빛이 도는 purplish
— 수정(水晶) amethyst 연— lilac 진— fluorite violet ; dark lilac
보령 寶齡 the age of the king
보로통하다, 뽀로통하다 ① (be) swollen [tumid] ¶ 보로통한 손 a swollen hand // 그의 다리는 수종으로 보로통하다 His legs swelled (up, out) with dropsy.
② [성이 나서] (be) sulky[sullen] ; morose[sour, glum] ; pout ¶ 보로통한 얼굴[표정] a sullen face[expression] // 뽀로통해지다 sulk ; become sulky ; get sour ; pout // 입을 뽀로통하고 있다 have the pouts ; be in the pouts // 그는 뽀로통해서 말이 없었다 He kept a sullen silence. // 무엇 때문에 뽀로통해 있느냐 What makes you so sulky ?
보료 a fancy mattress (used as cushion)
보루 堡壘 a fort ; a fortress ; a rampart ; a fortification ; a stronghold ; a battery ¶ 청교도의 보루 a stronghold of puritanism // 보루를 구축하다 fortify ; entrench ; construct a defense works
해안 — a seacoast fortification
*__보류__ 保留 reservation —하다 reserve ; defer (연기하다) ; hold back ¶ 결정은 다음 회의 때까지 보류되었다 The decision was deferred to the next meeting.
— 조건 a reservation ; a reserve — 조항 a reddendum 《*pl.* -da》
보름 ① [보름 동안] fifteen days ; half a month ¶ 보름 안에 within fifteen days [a fortnight] ② [보름날] the fifteenth day of a lunar month ¶ 정월 보름 the 15th of January // 보름께 around [towards] the middle of the month // 개 보름 쇠듯하다 miss[cannot afford] the good food appropriate to a feast day
—달 a full moon on the fifteenth night (of a lunar month) —밤 a fullmoon night — 차례 the ancestor-memorial service held on the fifteenth day of the month
보름보기 a one-eyed person ⇨ 애꾸눈이
보름사리 ① [조수] the high tide on the fifteenth of the lunar month ② [조기] a yellow corvina fish caught at the time of the high tide
*__보리__ barley ; Hordeum sativum (학명) ¶ 보리밥에는 고추장이 제격이다 Hotpepper sauce goes with boiled barley. /Put humble things with humble things.
—고추장 barley hot-pepper sauce — 깜부기 barley blight —논 a barley paddy-field —농사 barley raising[farming] ; barley crop (맥작) —누룩 barley malt —누름 the barley ripening (time) —밟기 treading[stepping on] barley plants —밥 boiled barley (and rice) —밭 a barley field — 베기 mowing[cutting] barley ; barley harvest — 수단(水鍛) barley flour mixed with honey —쌀 grain of barley ; barley corn —죽 barley gruel —차 barley tea — 타작 barley threshing ¶ 보리 타작하다 thresh barley — 파종 sowing barley —풀 《cut》 hay for barley-field fertilizer — 피리 a oaten pipe 보릿가을 the barley harvest (time) 보릿겨 barley bran 보릿재 ashes used to fertilize barley 보릿짚 barley straw
보리 菩提 [불교] Bodhi 《범》; the Supreme Enlightenment[Wisdom] 정각(正覺) ; (attainment of) Buddhahood 불과(佛果) ; the way of salvation
보리새우 a kind of small shrimp ; Acetes japonicus (학명)
보리수 菩提樹 a bo-tree ; a linden-tree ; a lime(-tree) ; Bodhendrum 《범》
보리심 菩提心 aspiration for Buddhahood ; a devout disposition
보린 保隣 mutual help among neighbors
—관 a settlement house — 사업 settlement work ; social (welfare) work —회 a neighborhood association
보릿고개 the farm hardship period ; spring cessation to the peasant ; the spring austerity ; the barley hump ¶ 보릿고개를 넘기다 get over the barley hump // 보릿고개가 지났다 The barley hump is over.
보링 [구멍을 뚫음] boring
보막이 洑— building a dammed pool (of

water) —하다 make〔build〕 a dammed pool

보매 apparently ; seemingly ; judging from appearances ¶ 얼핏 보매 at the first glance〔sight〕 // 보매 슬픈 것 같다 appear to be sad // 보매 바보 같다 look like a fool // 보매 그는 40쯤 되겠다 He looks about forty. // 보매 정직한 것 같지만 실은 그렇지 않다 He is not as honest as he looks〔as he apparently is〕.

보모 保姆 a nurse ; a nursery governess ; a kindergarten〔nursery-school〕 teacher

보무 步武 precise〔measured, marching〕 steps ¶ 보무 당당히 전진하다 march〔advance〕 in fine array ; go on proudly ; strut

보무라지 scraps ; bits ; lint ¶ 실 보무라지 waste pieces of thread // 네 옷의 보무라지를 털어라 Get the lint off your clothes.

보물 ⇨ 보무라지

†보물 寶物 a treasure ; [귀중한 것] a jewel ¶ 나라의 보물 a national treasure // 땅 속의 보물 a treasure-trove // 보물 찾기 treasure hunting ; a treasure hunt // 집의 보물 a family treasure ; an heirloom
—선 a ship loaded with treasures —섬 a treasure island

†보배 a treasure ; precious〔valuable〕 things ; valuables ; a jewel ¶ 숨은 보배 a buried〔hidden〕 treasure // 집안의〔나라의〕 보배 a family〔national〕 treasure // 어린이는 나라의 보배이다 Children are the treasure of our country. // 그는 우리 나라의 보배다 He is the pride of our nation.

보배롭다, 보배스럽다 (be) precious ; valuable

보법 dignity and the law〔rule〕

*보병 步兵 an infantryman ; a foot soldier ; infantry ; [보병목] rough cotton
—과 the infantry arm —교본 the Infantry Drill Regulation ; the Infantry Training Manual —전 an infantry action〔engagement〕 —중대〔대대, 연대〕 an infantry company〔battalion regiment〕 —총 a rifle —학교 an infantry school 경(輕)—대 light infantry 《L. I., Lt. Inf.》

*보복 報復 retaliation ; reprisal ; revenge ; requital —하다 retaliate ; revenge oneself on 《a person》 ¶ 보복적 retaliatory // 보복적 수단 a retaliatory measure〔step〕
—관세 a retaliative tariff —력 retaliatory power —정책 a policy of revanche ; a revanchist policy —폭격 《make》 a reprisal〔retaliatory〕 bombing 《on》 —행위〔수단〕 an act〔a measure〕 of retaliation ; a retaliatory act〔measure〕 대량— a massive retaliation

보부상 褓負商 a peddler ; a packman

보불 전쟁 普佛戰爭 the Franco-Prussian War (1870—71)

보비리 a miser ; a stingy〔close-fisted〕 fellow ; a scrape-penny ; a cheap skate

보비위 補脾胃 strengthening of one's stomach and spleen —하다 strengthen one's stomach ; [비위 맞추다] please 《a person's》 humor ; propitiate ; curry favor with 《a person》 ¶ 그는 상사에게 보비위한다 He toadies to his superior.

보사노바 [음악] bossa nova music

보살 菩薩 ① [불교] Bodhi-sattva 《범》 ; a Buddhist saint ; a Buddha elect ② [늙은 신령] an old She-Buddhist ③ [점쟁이] a fortuneteller
—탑 a pagoda under which is buried part of the remains of a Bodhisattva —할미 a Buddhist nun with an unshaved head

*보살피다 take care of ; look〔see〕 after ; watch over ; mind ; tend ¶ 환자를 보살피다 take care of〔for〕 a patient ; minister to the wants of a patient // 가사를 보살피다 look after〔mind〕 the household affairs // 우리가 없는 동안 아이들을 잘 보살펴 주시오 Please take good care of the children while we are away. // 그는 나를 친자식처럼 보살펴 준다 He takes quite a fatherly interest in me.

보상 報償 requital ; remuneration ; consideration ; compensation —하다 recompense ; requite ; remunerate ; reward ; repay ¶ …의 보상으로 in requital of〔for〕 ; in compensation for

*보상 補償 compensation ; indemnity ; indemnification ; reparation —하다 compensate for ; pay damages ; make good a loss ; indemnify 《a person》 against (for) ¶ 손해를 보상하다 indemnify 《a person》 for〔against〕 a loss ; compensate 《a person》 for a loss
—금 compensation (money) ; an indemnity ¶ 보상금을 받다 receive the compensation money from 《a person》 —링크제 [경제] compensation link —안 a compensation bill —작용 [정신 분석] compensation 수출— export compensation

보새 寶璽 the Royal〔Privy〕 Seal ; the king's seal

보색 補色 a complementary〔complement〕 color

보서다 保— go security for ; stand surety for

보석 步石 ① [디딤돌] a stepping-stone ② [돌층계] stone-steps ; a flight of stairs of stone

*보석 保釋 bail ; bond ; bailment —하다 bail 《a person》 out ¶ 보석을 허락하다 allow 《a person》 bail ; admit 《a person》 to bail // 보석이 되다 be released on bail // 보석 중이다 He is under bail〔free on bonds〕.
—보증인 a bail ; a bailsman 《*pl.* -men》 —원(願) an application for bail 병— sick bail

***보석 寶石** a jewel ; a gem ; a precious stone ; [총칭] jewellery 《영》 ; jewelry 《미》 ¶ 보석을 몸에 지니다 wear jewelry // 보석을 박다 set a stone 《in a ring》 ; jewel 《a ring》 with a stone
—공 a lapidary **—류** jewelry ; jewellery **— 반지** a ring set with jewels ; a jeweled ring **— 상자** a jewel case〔box〕 **— 세공** jewelry ; jewellery **— 조각(彫刻)** glyptography ; gem engraving
보석금 保釋金 bail (money) ¶ 보석금을 내다 give a bail 《for》 // 10 만원의 보석금으로 출감하다 be released〔liberated〕 on bail of 100,000 *won*.
보선 保線 maintenance of railway tracks
—공 a line(s)man 《*pl.* -men》 ; a track-layer 《미》 ; a platelayer 《영》 ; a section man (구간의) **— 공사** track (maintenance) work **—구** a (railway) maintenance office
보세 保稅 bond ¶ 보세의 bonded
— 가공(加工) bonded processing ¶ 보세 가공 수출〔무역〕 bonded processing exports〔trade〕 **— 공장(工場)** a bonded factory **— 지역(地域)** bonded area **— 화물(貨物)** bonded goods
보세 창고 保稅倉庫 a bonded warehouse ¶ 보세 창고에 맡기다〔넣다〕 bond ; store 《goods》 in bond // 보세 창고 유치의 in bond
— 예치 증권 a bonded warehouse warrant **— 인도** ex bond
보소 譜所 an office for compilation of genealogical tables〔family records〕
보송보송하다 (be) parched ; dried up 〔out〕 ; bone-dry ; be dry as a bone ¶ 보송보송한 빨래 the dried wash // 보송보송한 살결 soft and moistureless skin
보수 保守 conservation ¶ 보수적 conservative // 보수적 정신 a conservative spirit
— 반동주의 reactionary conservatism **— 세력〔파〕** the conservative force **—주의** conservatism **—주의자** a conservative ; a Tory 《영》 ; a standpatter 《미》 **— 진영** a conservative camp
***보수 報酬** remuneration ; recompense ; compensation ; pay ; a fee (의사·변호사의) ; a consideration ; a reward (상금) ; an honorarium ¶ 보수를 받지 않고 without consideration〔pay, fee, remuneration, recompense〕 ; for nothing // …의 보수로서 in consideration〔requital〕 《of》 ; in recompense〔reward, compensation, return〕 (for) // 보수를 주다 remunerate〔compensate, reward〕 《a person》 ; pay 《a person》 a fee // 보수를 받고 가르치다 teach for pay〔a consideration〕 // 무보수로 열심히 일하다 work hard without recompense〔pay, fee〕 // 성적에 따라 보수를 주다 reward〔pay〕 《a person》 according to his merits // 수고에 대한 보수를 드리겠습니다 I will pay you for your trouble〔for what you have done〕. // 발견한 사람에게는 1만원의 보수를 드리겠습니다 A reward of 10,000 *won* is offered to the finder. // 하인들은 보수를 받고 다 해고되었다 The servants were all paid off.
***보수 補修** mending ; repair **—하다** mend ; repair
— 공사(工事) repair works
보수계 步數計 a pedometer
보수당 保守黨 the conservative party ; the Conservatives ¶ 보수당의 conservative ; Tory 《영》
— 후보 a conservative〔Tory〕 candidate
보스 a boss ; a boss man 《미》
보스턴 Boston
보스턴백 a Boston bag ; an overnight
보슬보슬[1] gently ; softly ; drizzly ¶ 그날은 이슬비가 보슬보슬 내렸다 The day was drizzling.
보슬보슬[2] ⇨ 바슬바슬
보슬비 a drizzle ; a drizzling rain ¶ 보슬비가 내리고 있다 It is drizzling.
보습 補習 supplementary lessons ; refresher training 《미》 **—하다** supplement (education)
—과 a supplementary class〔course〕 ; a refresher course 《미》 **— 교육** supplementary education
보습살 beef rump
보시 布施 [불교에서] dana 《범》 ; Buddhist alms ; a temple offering **—하다** give alms ; give as a temple offering ¶ 보시를 청하다 ask for (an) alms
보싯돈 money collected from offerings at a Buddhist temple
보시기 a small bowl
보신 保身 self-preservation ; self-protection **—하다** preserve one's life〔oneself〕 ; protect one's life〔oneself〕
—술 the art of self-protection **—책** the means of self-protection
보신 補身 **—하다** build oneself up by taking tonics
—탕(湯) soup of dog's meat
보신 補腎 **—하다** invigorate oneself by taking tonics
—제(劑) a tonic ; a restorative ; an invigorant
보싸기 wrapping cherry bark around the grip of an archer's bow
보쌈김치 褓— Korean pickles wrapped in a large cabbage leaf like a bundle
보아 [···을 보아] for 《a person's》 sake ; out of consideration〔respect〕 for ; in deference to ¶ 너의 체면을 보아 out of consideration for your honor's sake〔for saving your face〕 ; for your sake ; on your account
보아란듯이 boastfully ; proudly ; ostentatiously ; for show ; showily ¶ 젊은 부부는 보아란듯이 손을 잡고 걸어간다 The young couple are walking hand in hand as if to attract other's attention〔to show

themselves off].

†**보아주다** take care of ; look after ; watch (over) ; see to ; attend to ¶ 아기를 보아주다 nurse the baby ; baby-sit 《미》 // 남의 일을 보아주다 attend to another's work // 그의 일을 보아주느라 고생했다 I had a hard time helping him. // 좀 봐주세요 Give me a break. /Have a heart, please ! /Give me a chance, please ?

보아한들 upon refection ; if one considers the matter carefully ; when you stop to think about it ¶ 보아한들 그럴 수가 있나 Thinking it through, how can it possibly be like that ?

보안 保安 the preservation of public peace — **경찰** peace preservation police **—관** a sheriff 《미》 **—등(燈)** a guard lamp **— 요원** the maintenance personnel (탄갱 따위의) **국가 —법** the National Security Law **육군 — 사령부** the Army Security Command

보암직하다 (be) attractive ; eye-catching ; appealing ; charming ; fine

보약 補藥 a restorative ; a tonic ; a bracer ; an adjuvant

보양 保養 a rest ; recreation ; relaxation ; recuperation (병후의) **—하다** recreate oneself ; have relaxation ; recuperate oneself (병후에) ¶ 눈의 보양 a feast to the eyes ; a sight for sore eyes // 보양하는 사람 a health seeker // 보양을 위하여 for (the good of) one's health ; for recreation // 보양하러 가다 go 《to a place》 for one's health // 형은 시골에서 병후의 보양을 하고 있다 My brother is now recuperating in the country.
—소 a convalescent hospital ; a rest home **—자** a health-seeker **—지** a health resort ; a healthy place

보양 補陽 —하다 aid〔strengthen〕 virility
—제(劑) medicine to aid〔strengthen〕 virility

보얗다, 뽀얗다 (be) milky ; creamy ; hazy ; misty ; heavy (in the air) ¶ 보얀 살결 a pearly skin // 숲에 안개가 보얗게 끼어 있다 The woods are veiled in mist. // 방안에 먼지가 보얗다 The air of the room is heavy with dust.

보어 補語 [문법] a complement
주격(主格)〔목적격(目的格)〕 — a subject〔an objective〕 complement

*__보여주다__ show ; let 《a person》 see ; display ¶ 신분증을 보여주십시오 Please show me your identification card. // 그 여자는 나에게 그림을 몇 장 보여 주었다 She showed me some pictures. // 그것 좀 보여 주십시오 Let me have a look at it. // 만년필을 보여주십시오 I'd like to see some fountain pens, please.

보옥 寶玉 a jewel ⇨ 보석

보온 保溫 keeping 《a thing》 warm **—하다** keep warm ¶ 보온을 위해서 for keeping warmth ; to keep 《a thing》 warm
—병(甁) a thermos (bottle, flask) ; a vacuum-bottle **—장치** a thermostat

보우 保佑 protection ; help ; assistance ; aid **—하다** protect ; help ; assist ; aid

보위 保衛 [보전] integrity ; preservation ; [방위] protection ; defense **—하다** preserve the integrity 《of》 ; preserve 《one's country》 intact ; defend

보위 寶位 the throne ; the crown ¶ 보위에 오르다 accede to the throne ; ascend〔come to, mount〕 the throne ; throne // 보위를 잇다 succeed to the throne
— 계승 succession to the throne

보유 補遺 a supplement 《to》 ; an addendum 《*pl.* -da》 ; an appendix 《*pl.* -dices》 **—하다** supplement ¶ 보유의 supplementary

†**보유 保有** possession ; (a) holding **—하다** hold ; possess ; keep ; retain
—물 〖법〗 tenement **—자** a possessor ; a holder **— 증권** security holdings **금 —고** gold holdings **적정 외환 —고** an adequate amount of foreign exchange holdings **정부 —미** the government's rice holdings ; rice held in stock by the government **핵 —국** a nuclear state

보유스름하다, 뽀유스름하다 (be) whitish ; milk ; frosty

보육 保育 nurture ; upbringing ; alimentation **—하다** bring up ; rear ; nurse
—기(器) an incubator **—원** a nursery school ; a crèche 《프》 ; a day nursery 《미》 **— 학교** a training school for kindergarten workers **아동 —** the bringing up〔care〕 of children

보은 報恩 gratitude ; requital〔repayment〕 of kindness〔a favor〕 ; repaying 《a person's》 kindness **—하다** requite 〔repay〕 another's kindness ¶ 보은을 위하여 in return for 《a person's》 kindness ; to show one's gratitude to〔for〕 《a person》 ; out of gratitude

보음 補陰 —하다 counterbalance one's virile powers
—제(劑) a medicine for counterbalancing one's virile powers

보응 報應 retribution ; nemesis **—하다** be requited〔repaid, rewarded〕

보이 [음식점 따위의] a boy ; a waiter ; [열차 따위의] a carriage boy ; [기선의] a steward〔cabin〕 boy ; [호텔·열차의] a porter 《미》 ; [호텔·극장 따위의] a page ; [호텔의] a bellboy 《미》
—장(長) a head waiter ; [호텔의] a bell captain

†**보이다¹** ① [눈에] see ; catch sight of ; [사물이 주어] be seen ; be visible ; show ; be in sight ; be open to the view ; appear ¶ 눈에 보이는 visible (to the naked eye) // 보이지 않다 be not seen ; be out of sight ; be invisible ; be closed

to the view ; cannot find 《a thing》 ; be missing // 보이지 않게 되다 go〔pass〕 out of sight ; be lost to sight 〔view〕 ; vanish ; disappear (from sight) ; [사람이 주어] lose sight of // 보이기 시작하다 [사물이 주어] come in sight〔into view〕 ; appear ; become visible ; [사람이 주어] come in sight of // 멀리 산이 보인다 We (can) see mountains in the distance. / Mountains can be〔are〕 seen in the distance. // 우리집에서 지리산이 잘 보인다 Our house commands a good view of Mt. *Chiri*. // 구름 한 점 보이지 않는다 Not a cloud is in sight. // 바다가 보이기 시작했다 The sea came into view. /We came in sight of the sea. // 사람이라고는 그림자도 보이지 않았다 Not a soul was to be seen〔in sight〕. // 그 여자가 웃자 옥같이 흰 이가 보였다 Her laugh revealed her pearl-white teeth. // 나는 학교가 보이는 곳에 산다 I live in sight of the school. // 유화는 좀 떨어져서 보면 더 잘 보인다 Oil paintings show to better advantage at a distance. // 내 시계가 안 보인다 I cannot find my watch. /My watch is missing. // 내가 그 곳에 갔을 때는 그 사람은 보이지 않았다 I found him gone when I arrived there. // 요새 K가 보이지 않는다 I have seen nothing of K lately. // 배가 뭍에서 멀리 떨어져 감에 따라 산이 보이지 않게 되었다 The mountain melted into the distance as the ship put out to sea.

② […인 것 같다] look ; seem ; appear ¶ 건강해〔행복해, 우울해〕 보이다 look well〔happy, blue〕 // 장사꾼같이 보이다 look like a merchant ; have the appearance of a merchant // 아픈 것같이 보이다 seem〔appear〕 to be ill // 이 계획은 잘된 것같이 보인다 This plan is likely to work well. // 그 사람은 정직한 사람같이 보였다 He struck〔impressed〕 me as honest. // 그는 나이보다 늙어 보인다 He looks older than his age.

보이다² [보게 하다] show ; let 《a person》 see〔look at〕 ; display ; exhibit ; evince ¶ 앨범을 보이다 show 《a person》 one's photo album // 실력을 보이다 show〔display〕 one's ability // 좋은 본을 보이다 set a good example // 의사에게 보이다 consult a doctor ; be examined by a doctor

보이 스카우트 [단체] the Boy Scouts ; [단원] a boy scout

— **대장(隊長)** a Scout Leader ; the Chief Scout — **대회(大會)** a boy scout rally ; [주로 국제적인] a jamboree

***보이콧** a boycott **—하다** boycott 《a shop, goods》

보이프렌드 a boyfriend

보익 輔翼 aid ; help ; assistance ; support **—하다** aid ; help ; assist ; support

보일락말락 —하다 be hardly seen ¶ 안개에 가려 해안이 보일락말락했다 The shore was barely visible through the fog.

***보일러** [기계] a boiler ¶ 석탄〔기름〕을 때는 보일러 a coal-〔an oil-〕fired boiler

보잇하다 (be) somewhat milky ; misty

보자기¹ a wrapping cloth ; a cloth-wrapper ¶ 보자기에 싸다 wrap 《a thing》 in a cloth

보자기² a diver (as for pearl or seaweed)

보잘것없다 (be) worthless ; valueless ; trifling ; insignificant ; useless ; be of no use ; be of no account ; be of little importance ¶ 보잘것없는 일 a matter of no importance ; a trifle // 보잘것없는 책 a worthless〔valueless, stupid〕 book // 보잘것없는 선물 a trifling gift // 보잘것없는 남자 a poor〔worthless, an insignificant〕 fellow // 보잘것없는 생각 a useless idea // 보잘것없는 일을 가지고 법석을 떨다 make a fuss about trifles // 그 파티는 보잘것없었다 The party was a dull affair. // 그 여자는 보잘것없는 사람과 결혼했다 She has married a nobody.

***보장 保障** guarantee ; security **—하다** guarantee ; secure ¶ 평화의 보장 security of peace ; peace guarantee // …의 보장에 의하여 by the guarantee of... // 강대국의 보장하에 under the guarantee of the powers // 언론의 자유를 보장하다 guarantee the freedom of speech

— **점령** guarantee occupation — **조약** a security pact **사회** — social security **집단** — collective security **상호 안전** — **조약** a mutual security treaty〔pact〕

보쟁기 a plow with a (plow) share ; [겨리] a plow pulled by two oxen

보쟁이다 commit adultery

****보전 保全** integrity ; preservation ; conservation ; maintenance **—하다** preserve〔safeguard〕 the integrity 《of》 ; preserve〔keep〕 《one's country》 intact ; keep 《a machine》 in good condition ; maintain 《a road》

— **처분** a preservative measure **국토** — conservation of national land **예방**— preventive maintenance

보전 寶典 a thesaurus 《*pl.* ~es, -ri》 ; a treasury ; a precious code ; a handbook (편람) ¶ 「영어 단어 숙어의 보전」 A Thesaurus〔Treasury〕 of English Words and Phrases

보정 補正 revision ; 〖수학·물리〗 correction ; 〖기계〗 compensation **—하다** revise ; correct

—**기(器)** a compensator — **예산** a revised〔supplementary〕 budget — **진자(振子)** a compensating pendulum

보제 補劑 [보약] a restorative ; a tonic ; [보조약] an adjuvant ; a synergist ; [염색의] an auxiliary agent

****보조 補助** assistance ; aid ; support **—하다** support ; aid ; assist ; subsidize ¶ 정부의 보조 a government grant // 남의 보조로 생활하다 live on the bounty of anoth-

er // 생활비를 보조하다 contribute to 《a person's》 support // 재정상의 보조를 받다 receive financial aid
— 기관 a subsidiary organ ; a subagency —부(簿) a supplementary account book — 어간(語幹) a "stem supplement" ; a nonfinal suffix added to an inflectional stem —원 a supplementary member — 의자 [예비의] a spare〔an extra〕 chair ; [버스 따위의] an auxiliary seat ; a supplementary folding seat ; a bracket seat —익(翼) an aileron —자 an assistant — 탱크 [비행기의] a belly tank — 함정 auxiliary vessels ; support ships — 화폐 subsidiary〔auxiliary〕 coins

보조 步調 step ; pace ¶ 경쾌한 보조 a light step // 빠른 보조로 at a fast〔good, great〕 pace // 보조가 맞지 않다 be〔walk〕 out of step ; break step // 보조를 맞추다 keep step〔pace〕 with, fall〔get〕 into step 《with》 ; act in concert with 《a person》 // 보조를 맞추어 행진하다 walk in step ; march keeping time // 보조를 빨리 하다〔늦추다〕 quicken〔slacken〕 one's pace

보조개 a dimple ¶ 그 여자는 양볼에 보조개가 있다 She has dimples on her cheeks. // 그 여자는 웃으면 보조개가 생긴다 Her face dimples with a smile.

보조금 補助金 a subsidy ; a bounty ; a subvention ; a grant-in-aid 《*pl.* grants-in-aid》 ; a grant of money ¶ 보조금을 주다 give a subsidy 《to》 ; subsidize // 보조금을 받다 be subsidized
정부 — a government subsidy〔protection〕

보조돛 補助— 〖해양〗 a studding sail ; a goosewing

보족 補足 a complement ; a supplement —하다 complement ; supplement ; make good 《a deficiency》 ; supply 《a want》 ¶ 보족적 complementary ; supplementary ; additional

***보존 保存** preservation ; storage ; conservation ; conservancy (산림, 하천의) —하다 preserve ; save ; keep (intact) ; conserve ; maintain

> 참고 **conserve**는 자유·이익·제도·특권·조건 따위를 「손상시키지 않고 현상대로 보존한다」의 뜻 **preserve**는 「위험·위해·부패 즉 파괴적인 힘으로부터 지키다」의 뜻

¶ 보존할 수 있는 식료품 nonperishable food-stuff // 영수증을 보존하다 keep〔preserve〕 a receipt // 잘 보존되어 있다 be well preserved ; be in fair preservation // 이 선로는 잘 보존되어 있다 This railway line is kept in good repair.
—림(林) a forest reserve〔preserve〕 —법 a method of preservation —비 the expense of preservation —운동 a conservation movement

보좌 補佐 assistance (보조) ; counsel (조언) ; an assistant (보좌역) ; a counsellor (고문) —하다 aid ; assist ; counsel ; help ; advise ; give advice ¶ 보좌의 구실을 하다 act as an adviser to 《a person》 // 어린 왕을 보좌하다 be adviser to a young king // 회장을 보좌하다 assist〔give counsel to〕 the president〔chairman〕
—관 an aide —인 an assistant ; a counselor ; an advisor 대통령 —관 a presidential aide

보좌 寶座 [왕의] a (royal) throne ; [부처의] the seat of Buddha's image ; the place where Buddha sits ¶ 보좌에 앉다 sit on the throne // 보좌에 앉히다 set 《a person》 on the throne

보주 補註 a supplementary note

보중 保重 conservation〔preservation〕 of one's health ; taking care of oneself —하다 conserve〔preserve〕 one's health ; take care of oneself

†보증 保證 guarantee ; assurance ; security —하다 guarantee ; assure ; give assurance for ; vouch for ; certify ; warrant ¶ 보증된 guaranteed ; secured // 그것이 사실이라는 것은 내가 보증한다 I assure you, it is true. // 그 사람은 보증할 수 없다 I cannot vouch for that man. // 그의 정직함은 내가 보증한다 I will answer for his honesty. // 원조를 보증하였다 He assured me of support. / He gave assurances that he would support me. // 완치를 보증합니다 I guarantee your cure. // 튼튼한 점은 보증합니다 I warrant you it is strong. // 위험을 무릅쓰고 자네 대부에 보증을 서겠네 I'll stick my neck out and cosign your loan. // 아직 보증 수리 기간 중이니까 무료로 고쳐 드리겠습니다 It's still under warranty, so we'll fix it free of charge.
— 계약 a contract of suretyship — 기간 the term of guarantee —서 a written〔letter of〕 guarantee ; [상품의] a warranty (card) — 수표 a certified check〔cheque 《영》〕 — 적립 준비금 a guarantee fund —주(株) a guaranteed stock — 채권 a guaranteed bond — 채무 surety obligations — 책임 the responsibility of a surety —품 an article certified genuine ; a warranted 〔guaranteed〕 article 신원 — fidelity guarantee (고용인의) 은행 — bank guarantee ; banker's guarantee

보증금 保證金 security (money) ; guaranty money ; deposit money ; a deposit ; key money (세든 사람 따위가 내는) 《영》 ¶ 보증금을 걸다 deposit security (money) 《with a person》 ; deposit 《ten thousand won》 as guaranty money

보증부 保證附 guaranteed ; warranted ; secured ; certified ¶ 5년간 보증부의 전기냉장고 an electric refrigerator guaranteed for five years // 10년간 보증부 [표시] With (a) 10-year warranty

⁑보증인 保證人 〖법〗 a guarantor ; a guaranty ; a bondsman ; a surety (연대의) ; a security (소송 따위의) ; [신원 따위의] a certifier ; a sponsor ; a reference (신원 조회처) ¶ 보증인이 되다 stand guarantee〔surety, security〕 《for》 ; go security 《for》 ; go 《a person's》 bond // 보증인을 세우다 give 〔find〕 surety〔security〕 《for》
부 — a collateral surety

보지 the vulva 《*pl.* ~s, -vae》

보지 保持 maintenance ; preservation **—하다** maintain ; preserve ; hold ; keep ¶ 선수권을 보지하다 hold the championship
—자 a holder **기록 —자** a record holder

보지 報知 information ; news ; a report **—하다** inform 《a person》 of 《a matter》 ; communicate 《a matter》 to 《a person》 ; let 《a person》 know ; report

보지락 enough rain to soak into the ground only the depth of a plow's furrow ; a light rain
—비 a light rain

보직 補職 assignment to a position ; appointment ¶ 보직되다 be assigned 〔appointed〕 《to the post of》

보짱 ① [담력] courage ; pluck ; heart ; nerve ; mettle ; grit (미) ; guts (속) ¶ 보짱 있는 사나이 a man of nerve ; a man with plenty of guts // 보짱이 있다 be bold〔brave, courageous, plucky, nervy, mettlesome〕 ; have pluck〔mettle〕 // 보짱이 없다 be timid〔nerveless, cowardly, white-livered, lily-livered, pigeon-hearted, faint-hearted〕 // 보짱이 크다 be generous〔magnanimous, large-minded, daring〕
② [마음속] heart ; mind ; intention ¶ 보짱이 검다 be black-hearted〔wicked, evilhearted, crafty, deep〕/검은 보짱을 품다 have some evil end in view ; have an ax to grind ; have an ulterior motive

보찜 만두 褓—饅頭 stuffed buns steamed together in cloth wrappings

보채 堡砦 a fort(ress) ; a fortification ; a stronghold ; a citadel ; a rampart

보채다 fret ; importune ; make a fuss ¶ 보채는 아기 a fretful baby // 보채는 말 a restive horse // 과자를 달라고 보채다 badger〔importune, tease〕 《a person》 for cookies // 돈을 달라고 보채다 importune 《a person》 for money // 보채는 아기를 달래다 soothe a hurt〔fretful〕 child // 아기들은 낯가림할 수 있는 무렵이 되면 잘 보챈다 Babies fret〔are fretful〕 when cutting their teeth.
보채는 아이 젖 준다 속담 The squeaking wheel gets the grease.

보철 補綴 supplement ; complement ; 〖치과〗 prosthetic dentistry ; dental prosthesis ; prosthetics ; prosthodontia **—하다** supplement ; complement
— 전문가 a prosthetic dentist ; a prosthetist ; a prosthodontist **부분〔전체〕 —** a partial〔full〕 denture

보첩 譜牒 a genealogy (book) ; a genealogical table ; a family record book

보청기 補聽器 a hearing aid ; [상표명] an Acousticon

***보초 步哨** a sentry ; a sentinel ; a guard ¶ 보초를 서다 stand sentry〔guard〕 ; be on sentry〔guard〕 // 보초를 세우다 post a sentry // 군인이 보초를 서고 있다 The soldier〔sentry〕 is on guard.
— 근무 sentry duty **—병** a guard ; a sentry **—선** a sentry-line

보추 [진취성] initiative ; aggressiveness ; gumption (구) ; ambition ; spirit ; drive
보추없다 관용 lack gumption〔drive, ambition〕

†보충 補充 supplement ; replacement ; replenishment **—하다** fill up ; replace ; replenish ; supplement ¶ 보충의 supplementary ; complementary // 결원을 보충하다 fill up a vacancy
—대 drafts ; reserves **— 문제** a supplementary question〔exercise〕 **— 선거인 명부** a supplementary voters' list **— 수업** supplementary lessons **—역** reservist duty **— 질문** 〖법〗 a supplementary question **— 증거** adminicle **— 판결** a supplementary judgment

보충병 補充兵 a reservist ; a recruit ; [총칭] reserve conscripts
—역 conscript reserve service **제1〔제2〕 —** a first〔second〕 class reservist

보칙 補則 supplementary rules

보크 [야구·당구] a ba(u)k

보크사이트 [광물] bauxite

보타이 a bow tie

***보태다** ① [보충] supplement ; make up (for) ; help out (비용을) ; supply (보급) ¶ 보탬이 되다 go toward ; do much to help ; be an aid〔a help〕 《to》 // 모자람을 보태다 supply〔make up〕 the deficiency ; replenish a shortage ; make up a deficit // 생활비에 보태쓰다 supplement〔help out〕 one's income 《by sidework》 // 이 돈을 빚갚는 데 보태겠다 This money goes toward the debts.
② [가산] add 《one number to another》 ; sum ¶ 여비를 보태서 including〔inclusive of〕 traveling expenses // 6에서 3을 보태다 add six to three // 2에서 3을 보태면 5이다 Two and three make 〔are〕 five. /Two added to three makes 〔is, equals〕 five. /Two plus three makes five. // 그는 늘 말을 보태서 한다 He always exaggerates.

†보통 普通 ¶ 보통의 [정상적인] normal ; regular ; [통상의] ordinary ; common ; usual ; everyday (일상의) ; conventional (인습적인) ; [일반적인] general ; universal ; average (평균의) ; commonplace (평범한) ; [중위의] medial ; mediocre (범용한) // 보통 사람 an average〔ordinary〕 man ; the man on〔in〕 the street ; a layman (전문가가 아닌) // 보통의 지식 common knowledge // 보통으로 usually ; commonly ; generally ; ordinarily ; normally ; in general // 보통이 아닌 unusual ; uncommon ; extraordinary ; abnormal // 보통 이상이다 be above the average〔mediocrity〕 // 보통 이하다 fall below the average〔mediocrity〕 // 보통 있을 수 있는 일로 생각하다 take 《a thing》 as a matter of course // 보통 3시간 걸린다 About three hours is the usual time required. // 그 사람은 확실히 보통 사람과 다르다 He is certainly out of the common run of men. // 금년 추위는 보통이 아니다 It is unusually〔exceptionally, abnormally〕 cold this year. // 그 나이에 아직 결혼을 못하는 것을 보면 보통 여자가 아니다 Something must be the matter with the woman, seeing that she is not yet married at that age. // 보통 무연 휘발유로 가득 채워 주시오 Fill her up with regular unleaded, please.

— 개념 [논리] an ordinary concept — 교육 a common education — 급행(열차) an ordinary express (train) — 명사(名詞) [문법] a common noun — 명사(名辭) [논리] a common term — 법 [법] common law —석 [특별석에 대하여] an ordinary seat ; [예약석에 대하여] an unreserved seat — 선객 a steerage passenger — 선거 popular〔universal〕 suffrage ; a popular vote — 열차 a slow〔a local, an accommodation〕 train — 예금 an ordinary deposit — 요금 the ordinary rate — 우편 ordinary mail〔post〕 — 은행 a commercial〔city〕 bank —주 [주식] a common stock 《미》 ; an ordinary (share) 《영》 —형(型) ordinary size ; standard

보통 고시 普通考試 the ordinary civil

보퉁이 褓— a bundle ; a package ; a packet ¶ 책 한 보퉁이 a package of books // 옷〔누더기〕 한 보퉁이 a bundle of clothes〔rags〕 // 보퉁이를 꾸리다 pack 《goods》 ; make a bundle // 보퉁이를 풀다 unpack 《a package》

보트 a (rowing) boat ; a rowboat ; a shell (1인승 경조용) ; a cutter(군함에 부속된) ; a gig (경조용 또는 선박에 부속된) ¶ 보트를 (배에서) 내리다 lower a boat // 보트를 띄우다 launch a boat // 보트를 젓다 row a boat ; have a pull 〔row〕 // 보트를 타러 가다 go for a row ; go boating

— 레이스 a boat race ¶ 보트 레이스를 하다 row a race — 선수 a boating man ; a rower ; a boatman ; an oarsman ; [전원] the (picked) crew ; the eight (에이트의) 고무 — a rubber raft

***보편 普遍** universality ; catholicity ; ubiquity ¶ 보편적인 universal ; omnipresent ; ubiquitous // 보편적으로 universally ; ubiquitously ; generally // 보편적인 진리 universal truth

— 개념 a universal〔general〕 concept —론 universalism —성 universality ; catholicity —주의 universalism — 타당성 universal validity —화 generalization

보폭 步幅 a stride ; a pace

보표 譜表 a (musical) staff ; a stave ; a score

— 기법(記法) staff notation

보푸라기 nap ⇨ 보풀

보풀 nap ; shag ; fluff ; pile ; fuzz ¶ 보풀이 선 nappy ; fluffy ; plushy ; cottony // 보풀이 서다 be nappy〔fluffy〕

— 명주 nubby〔rough〕 silk

보풀다 nap ; have a nap 《on cloth》 ; have fuzz 《on paper》

보풀리다 raise a nap 《on》 ; nap

보풀보풀 with a nap ; with fuzz —하다 have a nap ; (be) nappy ; downy

보필 輔弼 assistance (to the throne) —하다 assist ; advise ; counsel ; give advice 〔counsel〕 to

보하다 補— [몸을] strengthen 《a person's system》 ; tone up ; build up 《one's health》 ; [보직] appoint ; assign ; nominate ¶ 도지사에 보하다 appoint 《a person》 (to the post of) governor

보학 譜學 genealogy

—자 a genealogist

보합 步合 [율] rate ; ratio ; percentage

—고 (amount of) percentage —산(算) calculation of percentage

보합 保合 [경제] steadiness —하다 (keep) balance ; remain the same〔stationary, steady〕 ¶ 시세는 보합 상태이다 Prices are steady. /The market holds 〔remains〕 steady.

†보행 步行 walking —하다 walk ; go on foot ¶ 보행 곤란 difficulty in walking

—객〔군〕 a walker ; pedestrian ; a foot traveler〔passenger〕 —기(器) a baby-walker — 동물 a gressorial (animal) ; an ambulatory animal —실조(失調) ataxia — 연습 walking practice — 위반 traffic violation by a pedestrian — 위반자 a jaywalker 《미·구》 —인〔자〕 a pedestrian ; a walker ; a foot passenger —자 전용 교통 신호 pedestrian lights

***보험 保險** [보증] guarantee ; [생명·화재 따위의] insurance ; assurance ¶ 단체〔실업·종신·양로〕 보험 group〔unemployment, whole life, endowment〕 insurance // 보험에 들다 be insured // 보험을 계약하다 effect an insurance // 보험을 신청하다 apply for an insurance policy // 집에 100만원의 화재 보험을 걸다 have a house insured against fire for a million *won* // 100만원의 생명 보험에 들어 있다 I am insured for a million *won*. /I carry a million *won* life insurance. // 부업으로 보험 판매도 합니다 I also sell insurance on the side. // 보험 사기꾼들이 보험 회사와 보험

가입자 양쪽을 다 등쳐먹는다 Insurance con artists prey on both the insurance companies and policyholders.
— 가격 insurance〔insurable〕 value — 계약 an insurance contract — 계약자 a policyholder —금액 an insured〔insurance〕 amount — 기간 a term insured ; a period of insurance —료 a premium —률 insurance rates —업 insurance business —업자 an insurer ; an underwriter — 외교〔권유〕원 insurance canvasser ; an insurance agent〔salesman〕 — 증권 an insurance policy — 해약 the cancellation of an insurance contract ; surrender (적립금의 일부를 환불받고 하는) — 회사 an insurance company 간이 — [생명 보험] postal insurance ; postal life insurance ; post office life insurance 노동자 재해 보상 — workmen's compensation insurance 단체 — group insurance 대한 재—공사 the Korea Reinsurance Corporation 도난 — burglary insurance 생명 — life insurance ; life assurance 《영》 손해 — nonlife insurance 신용〔질병, 실업〕 — credit〔sickness, unemployment〕 insurance 양로 — endowment insurance 의료비 — medical expense〔payments〕 insurance 자동차 — automobile insurance 재(再)— reinsurance ; reassurance 《영》 재해 — casualty insurance 피—물 the property 〔the person〕 insured

보험금 保險金 insurance money ; [종신 보험의] a death benefit ¶ 가옥의 화재로 다액의 보험금을 받다 receive a large insurance payment for a house burnt
— 수취인 a beneficiary 사망 — a death benefit

보헤미아 Bohemia

보헤미안 a Bohemian ¶ 보헤미안의〔적인〕 Bohemian

보혈 寶血 〖기독교〗 the precious blood (of Jesus)

보혈 補血 nourishing of the blood **—하다** nourish the blood
—제 a hematic

†**보호 保護** protection ; shelter ; safeguard **—하다** protect ; shelter ; guard ; [옹호하다] safeguard ; [돌보다] look after ¶ 경찰의 보호 police protection // 생명과 재산의 보호를 위하여 for the protection of lives and property // …의 보호 아래 두다 place 《a person》 under the protection 《of》 // 국내 산업을 보호하다 protect home industries // 보호를 받다 be protected by ; receive protection // 보호를 주다 give protection to 《a person》 // 보호를 청하다 apply for police protection ; seek asylum 《in France》 (망명하여)
— 관세 protective tariff — 관세율 protective tariff —국 a protected state ; a protectorate —등(燈) a guard lamp —령 a protectorate —림 a reserved forest ; a forest reserve — 무역 protective trade — 무역주의자 a protectionist — 산업 a protected industry —색 protective coloring ; a protective color — 장치 a protective device ; a safeguard — 정책 a protective policy —조 a protected bird

보호 검속 保護檢束 arrest for protection **—하다** arrest 《a person》 for protection ; hold 《a person》 in protective custody

보호 관찰 保護觀察 〖법〗 probation ¶ 소년 범죄자의 보호 관찰 the probation of juvenile offenders
—관 a probation officer —소 a probation office — 제도 the probation system

보호 신청 保護申請 an application for protection ¶ 경찰에 (신변) 보호 신청을 하다 apply for police protection

⁑**보호자 保護者** a protector ; a guardian ; a patron ; a patroness (여자) ; a conservator (금치산자의)

보호 지역 保護地域 a reservation ; a sanctuary (야생 동물의) ¶ 인디언 보호 지역 a reservation for Indians ; an Indian reservation // 야생 동물 보호 지역 a sanctuary〔reservation〕 for wild animals ; a wild life sanctuary

보화 寶貨 a treasure ; precious〔valuable〕 things ; a highly-prized article ; valuables

복 〖물고기〗 a swellfish ; a globefish ; a puffer ¶ 복국 swellfish soup // 복 중독 swellfish poisoning

복 伏 the dog days ⇨ 복날
말— the end〔last〕 of the dog days ; the last period of the dog days 중— the middle (period) of the dog days 초— the beginning of the dog days ; the first period of the dog days

***복 福** (good) fortune ; blessing ; (good) luck ; bliss ; wealth (부) ; good (복리) ; mercy (은혜) ¶ 복된 happy ; blessed // 복이 많다 be fortunate ; be in luck // 복을 받다 be blessed // 복을 빌다 pray to God for mercy ; invoke a blessing 《upon a person》 // 신은 그에게 건강이라는 복을 주셨다 God blessed him with good health. // 그는 여러 가지로 복이 많은 사람이다 He has many felicities. // 마음이 가난한 자는 복이 있나니 Blessed are the poor in spirit. // 새해에 복 많이 받으십시오 Happy New Year !

복 蹼 a webfoot ; a web

복- 複 complex ; compound ; double ; compositive

복각 伏角 [물리] a dip (of the compass)
—계(計) an inclinometer ; a dip needle — 측원기(測遠機) a depression range finder 무—선 an aclinic line

복간 復刊 reissue ; revived publication ¶ 복간 잡지 제1호 the first number of a revived magazine

복강 腹腔 the abdominal〔peritoneal〕 cavity

— 임신 abdominal pregnancy
복걸 伏乞 —하다 prostate oneself and beg
복계 復啓 "Dear Sir : Thank you for your letter."
복고 復古 [정치상의] restoration ; revival (of the ancient regime) ; reaction ; [손실의 회복] recover —하다 restore ; recover ¶ 왕정 복고 the restoration of the Royal Regime ; the Restoration 《영》 —조(調) reactionary tendency ; a revival mood —주의 reactionism 왕정— the restoration of the monarchy ; the Restoration (영국)
복교 復校 reinstatement (at school) ; return to school —하다 be reinstated (at school) ; return to school ; be at school again ¶ 복교를 허락하다 allow 《a boy》 to return to school ; readmit 《a boy》 into school
*복구 復舊 restoration ; rehabilitation ; recovery —하다 be restored to normal (conditions) ; be brought back to the former state ¶ 철도는 곧 복구된다 The railway will be shortly reopened to traffic. / The trains will resume normal services.
— 공사 repair〔restoration〕 work —비 restoration expenditure〔expenses〕
복권 福券 a lottery ticket〔card〕 ¶ 복권이 맞았다 The lot fell on me. // 그는 복권에 당첨되어서 차를 사는 데 돈을 썼다 He won in the lottery and spent the money on a car.
복권 復權 rehabilitation ; reinstatement ; restoration of rights ¶ 복권시키다 rehabilitate ; reinstate
*복귀 復歸 return ; reversion —하다 return 《to》 ; revert 《to》 ; make a comeback ¶ 구제도로 복귀하다 return〔revert〕 to the old system // 직장에 복귀하다 return to work
복근 腹筋 an abdominal muscle
복날 伏— the dog day(s) ; the hottest period in (the) midsummer ¶ 복중에 in the period of the dog days ; in (the) midsummer
복놀이 伏— merrymaking on the dog day ; a midsummer outing —하다 hold〔keep〕 merrymaking on the dog day ¶ 복놀이 가다 go on a midsummer outing
복닥거리다 ⇨ 북적거리다
복달임 伏— ① [철] the hottest period during the dog days ; midsummer ② [복날의 관습] the custom of having hot soup to allay the summer heat —하다 have〔eat〕 hot soup to allay the summer heat
복당 復黨 rejoining the party —하다 rejoin the party ; be reinstated in the party
복대기 〖광물〗 the dross of gold ; slag ; residue left after gold is panned ¶ 복대기 삭히다 extract gold from slag
—금 gold extracts from slag —탕 a vat in which gold is extracted from slag 복대깃간 a factory where gold slag is resolved
복대기다 ① [법석] bustle ; be in a bustle ; be boisterous〔noisy〕 ¶ 복대기는 거리〔군중〕 a bustling street〔crowd〕 // 많은 사람들이 시장에서 복대기었다 Vast crowds bustled up in the market place.
② [정신을 못차리다] be pestered ; be pressed ¶ 일에 복대기다 be pressed with work // 어머니가 아이들에게 복대긴다 The mother is pestered with her children.
복대기치다 bustle ⇨ 복대기다
복더위 伏— a heat wave during the dog days ; a midsummer hot spell
복덕 福德 good luck and virtue ; 〖불교〗 the reward of virtue
—궁 one of the Twelve Zodiacal Divisions —성 Jupiter
복덕방 福德房 a real estate agency
*복도 複道 a corridor ; a passage ; a lobby ; a hallway 《미》
복되다 福— ⇨ 복스럽다
복류 複流 〖전기〗 a double current
복리 複利 compound interest ¶ 복리로 계산하다 compute at compound interest
—법 the compound interest method —표 a table of compound interest
*복리 福利 welfare ; well-being ; weal ; good ¶ 국민의 복리를 증진하다 promote the welfare of the people
— 사업 public welfare work — 시설 welfare facilities
복마 卜馬 a packhorse
복마전 伏魔殿 an enchanted hall ; an abode of demons ; a pandemonium ; a hotbed ¶ 정계의 복마전 a hotbed of political iniquity
복막 腹膜 〖해부〗 the peritoneum 《*pl.* -nea》
—염 peritonitis
복망 伏望 —하다 desire earnestly ; sincerely hope ; humbly beg ¶ 선처하시옵기 복망하나이다 I sincerely hope that you will take good care of it.
†복면 覆面 a mask ; disguise ; a veil —하다 mask oneself ; wear a mask ; muffle one's face ; have one's face masked ¶ 복면의 강도 a masked robber // 복면의 기사 a warrior in disguise
복명 復命 a report —하다 report (back) ; submit a report of 《a person》
—서 a report
복모음 複母音 〖음성〗 a diphthong
복무 服務 (public) service —하다 serve ; be in the service ¶ 군 복무를 하다 serve with colors ; perform military duties // 육군〔해군〕에 복무 중이다 be in the army〔navy〕 // 현역에 복무 중이다 be on active service
— 규정 the Public Service Regulations

(공무원의) ; the office (service) regulations ; 〖군사〗 standing orders — 기간 the period of (active) service ; a hitch 《미군·속》 — 시간 hours of service ; business〔service〕 hour — 연한 the term of service ; the tenure of office

복문 複文 〖문법〗 a compound sentence

복물 伏— heavy rains during the dog days〔midsummer〕 ¶ 복물지다 It rains heavily during the dog days〔midsummer〕.

복받치다 well up ⇨ 북받치다

복배 腹背 the back and front ; the front and rear ¶ 복배에 적을 맞다 be attacked both in front and rear

복백 伏白 Yours (very) truly ; Yours (very) faithfully 《영》 ; humbly presented by

복벗다 服— finish wearing〔put aside〕 one's mourning garb

복벽 復辟 the restoration of a dethroned king ; the restoration of the royal regime —하다 be restored to the throne ; 《a monarchy》 be restored
— 운동 a monarchist movement

복벽 腹壁 [해부] the abdominal walls ¶ 복벽의 abdominal
— 절개 (수술) laparotomy

복병 伏兵 an ambush ; an ambuscade ; men in ambush —하다 lie in ambush ; ambush ; ambuscade ¶ 복병을 만나다 fall into an ambush // 복병을 배치하다 make〔lay〕 ambush

복본위제 複本位制 〖경제〗 bimetallism ; the double-standard system
—론자 a bimetallist

*복부 腹部 〖해부〗 the abdomen ; the abdominal region ; the belly ¶ 복부의 abdominal
— 수술 an abdominal operation ; abdominal surgery ; ventrotomy — 임신 abdominal pregnancy

복분수 複分數 a compound〔complex〕 fraction

복비 複比 〖수학〗 compound ratio

복비례 複比例 compound proportion ; the double rule of three

복사 服事 ① service —하다 serve 〔minister〕 《to》 ② 〖카톨릭〗 an acolyte ; an altar boy ; a mass server

**복사 複寫 reproduction ; [복사물] a reproduction ; a duplicate ; a copy —하다 reproduce ; copy ; take a copy ; make a copy of 《the original》 ¶ 원고를 복사하다 copy a manuscript // 삽화는 사진을 복사한 것이다 The illustration is reproduced from the photograph.
—기 mimeograph ; a duplicator —대(臺) a copyboard — 사진 a photostat ; a photocopy — 사진기 a photostat ; a photocopier —용 잉크 copying ink —용 카메라 a reproduction camera —지 copying paper ; carbon paper ; transfer〔duplicating, tracing〕 paper —판(板) a copying press ; a duplicating apparatus ; a duplicator ; a mimeograph —필(筆) a copying pen

복사 輻射 radiation —하다 radiate ; be radiating ; be radiative
—광〔파〕 radiant light〔wave〕 — 난방 panel〔radiant〕 heating —선〔광〕 radiant light ; [광선] radiant rays — 에너지 radiant energy — 전력 radiation power — 전열기(電熱器) an electric radiator —체 a radiator

복사 伏射 firing from a prone position —하다 fire prone
— 자세 a prone firing position —호(壕) a sheltered trench

복사뼈 the anklebone ; the talus〔astragalus〕 (거골)

복사열 輻射熱 radiant heat ; radiation ¶ 복사열을 내다 emit〔give off〕 radiant heat
태양〔지구〕 — solar〔terrestrial〕 radiation

복사 화채 —花菜 a peach punch

복상 服喪 wearing mourning —하다 wear mourning ; go into mourning

복상 福相 a happy look ; a face with luck written on it

복색 服色 dress ; attire ; (personal) appearance ¶ 복색이 좋다〔나쁘다〕 be well〔ill〕-dressed // 복색에 무심〔세심〕하다 be indifferent〔careful〕 about one's personal appearance

복서 卜書 〖연극〗 stage directions

복서 卜筮 fortunetelling ; divination ; foretelling ; prognostication —하다 tell 《a person's》 fortune ; divine ; foretell ; prophesy

복서 a boxer

복선 複線 [겹줄] double lines ; [복선 궤도] a two-track line ; double-tracking ; a double track ¶ 복선으로 하다 double-track〔duplicate〕 a (railway) line // 그 철도는 복선이다 The railway is double-tracked.
— 공사 double tracking — 철도 a double track line 복— 〖철도〗 a four-track line ; a quadruple track〔line〕 가공(架空) —식 the double trolley system

복선 伏線 an underplot 《of a novel》 ; preparation ; ground work ¶ 복선을 펴다 forestall 《a person》 ; [소설에서] lay an underplot

복성 複星 〖천문〗 multiple stars

복성 福星 〖목성〗 Jupiter

복성 複姓 a family name composed of two Chinese characters ; a two-syllable family name

복성스럽다 (be) happy-looking ; full-faced ; plump ¶ 그녀의 얼굴은 복성스럽다 She has a cherubic face.

복소수 複素數 〖수학〗 a complex number

복속 服屬 subjection ; subjugation ; submission —하다 be subject(ed) 《to》 ; be subjugated ; submit 《to》 ; obey

복수 復水 condensed water
—실(室) a condensing chamber —판(瓣) a condensing valve
복수 覆水 spilt water
⁑복수 復讐 revenge ; avenge ; vengeance ; [보복] retaliation ; reprisal ; a vendetta

> 참고 일반적으로 **avenge**는 avenge a murder by bringing the criminal to trial (범인을 재판함으로써 살인에 보복하다)와 같이 부정 따위에 대한 「정의의 보복」을 의미하며 공식적인 복수를 뜻한다 **revenge**는 사람에 대한 (때로는 이유 없는) 「원한을 풀다」와 같은 개인적인 복수의 뜻으로 쓰인다

—하다 revenge 《oneself》 on ; be revenged〔avenged〕《on》; have〔take〕 one's revenge 《on》; pay off old scores ; retaliate ¶ 복수를 맹세하다 swear revenge // 그들에 대해서 복수할 작정이다 I will revenge myself on them. /I will be revenged on them. /I will retaliate on them. // 살해당한 주인을 위해서 복수했다 He avenged the death of his master. // 그 놈들에게 복수하고 말겠다 I'll get even with them !
— 수단 a retaliatory measure —심 retaliatory spirit —자 a revenger —전 a war〔battle〕 of revenge ; [경기의] a return game〔match〕
⁑복수 複數 the plural number ; compound numbers ¶ 복수의 plural
— 명사 a plural noun —형 〖문법〗 the plural form —제 환율 the plural〔multiple〕 exchange rate system
복수 腹水 〖의학〗 abdominal dropsy ; dropsy of the belly ; ascites
복수초 福壽草 〖식물〗 an Adonis ; a pheasant's-eye ; a garden pink ; Adonis amurensis (학명)
복술 卜術 the art of divination ; fortunetelling ; soothsaying
⁑복숭아 〖식물〗 a peach (tree) ; Pranus persica (학명)
—꽃 a peach blossom — 나무 a peach (tree) —빛 peach (color) ; pink —털 fuzz on a peach
복스럽다 福— (be) happy-looking ; fat and well-looking ; prosperous-looking
⁑복습 復習 review —하다 review ; go over ¶ 학과를 복습하다 review the lessons
— 시간 the review hour
복시 複視 〖의학〗 diplopia ; double vision ¶ 복시의 diploptic
복시합 複試合 〖정구〗 doubles ¶ 남녀 혼합 복시합 mixed doubles
복식 服飾 dress and its ornament
— 디자이너 a dress designer — 잡지 a fashion magazine —품 accessories (to a dress) ; [부인복의] the accessories of a woman's dress ; ladies' accessories 여성용 — ladies' trimmings
복식 複式 multiple forms〔formulae〕; [복식 부기] double-entry bookkeeping ; 〖수학〗 a compound expression〔formula〕
— 기관 a compound〔double-acting〕 engine — 기관차 a compound locomotive — 부기 bookkeeping by double entry ; the double entry system — 정구 tennis doubles — 투표 a plural vote — 학급 a combined class 《of more than one grade》
복식 호흡 腹式呼吸 abdominal breathing 〔respiration〕; the abdominal type of respiration
복신 福神 the God of Wealth ; Billiken ; a luck-bringer ; the mother of good luck
복심 腹心 ¶ 복심의 confidential ; trusted // 복심의 신하 a confidential retainer // 복심의 친구 a bosom friend ; [남자] a confidant ; [여자] a confidante
복심 覆審 〖법〗 trial de novo ; reexamination ; a renewal of procedure ; a review
—하다 try a second time ; hear again ; review ; retry
— 법원 a court of review
복싱 boxing ¶ 프로 복싱 professional boxing
복쌈 福— [민속] laver-wrapped rice eaten on the 15th of January of the lunar calender
복안 腹案 a plan〔scheme〕 in one's mind ; an idea ¶ 복안이 서 있다 have a plan ready
복약 服藥 taking medicine —하다 take medicine ¶ 복약시키다 administer 〔give〕 medicine
—량 dose —량 측정 dosimetry
복어 a globefish ; a swellfish ; a puffer ¶ 복어에 중독되다 be poisoned by swellfish
복역 服役 [병역] military service ; [징역] penal servitude —하다 [병역에] serve in the army〔navy〕; [징역에] serve time〔one's sentence〕 ¶ 복역중이다 [병역에] be in the service ; [징역에] be serving〔doing〕 one's sentence 〔time〕// 만기 복역하다 serve one's full time
— 기간 [병역의] a term of service ; [징역의] a term of sentence ; a prison term
복연 復緣 reconciliation (after separation) ; reinstatement —하다 be reinstated 《as a wife》
복염 伏炎 the heat of midsummer〔the dog days〕
복엽 複葉 a compound leaf ; [천엽] the reticulum of a ruminant
— 비행기 a biplane
복용 服用 [약의] internal use〔application〕; dosage ; taking medicine ; [옷의] wearing 《clothes》 —하다 take 《medicine》; use〔apply〕 internally ; [옷을] wear 《clothes》; put on ¶ 약을 복용하다 take medicine // 복용시키다 administer 《medicine》// 1일 3회 식후 복용 To be

taken three times a day after meals.
—량 dosage ; dose —자 a (medicine) taker
복원 復元 restoration 《to the original state》 —하다 be restored to the former state ; revert
— (모형)도 a reconstruction —력 dynamic stability ; force of restitution
복원 復員 demobilization ; disbanding ; deactivation —하다 be demobilized ; be discharged ; be disbanded ; be deactivated
— 군인 a demobilizd soldier ; a demob ; an ex-serviceman —령(令) a demobilization order
⁑복위 復位 restoration ; rehabilitation ; reinstatement ; reinstallment ; 〖의학〗 reduction —하다 be restored ; be rehabilitated ; be reinstated ; restore ; rehabilitate ; reinstate ; reinstall ; [탈골의] reduce
복음 複音 〖음성〗 a compound sound
*복음 福音 [반가운 소식] glad tidings ; good〔welcome〕 news ; a godsend ; [복음서] the Gospels ¶ 복음을 전하다 preach the gospel ; evangelize // 그것은 월급쟁이에게는 복음이다 It is good news for salaried men.
— 교회 the Evangelical Church — 전도 evangelism ; evangelization ; mission ; [설교] evangelical preaching ; [전도 사업] evangelical work — 전도자 an evangelist ; a minister (of the gospel) ; a missionary ; a gospel(l)er ; a fisher of men —주의 Evangelism (4) —서 〖성경〗 the (four) Gospels 공관(共觀) —서 the synoptic Gospels
복이나인 —內人 a servant to a lady-in-waiting at court
복입다 服— wear mourning
복자 a brass cup used for measuring oil
복자 卜者 a fortuneteller ; a diviner
복자 福者 a person who is beatified ; the Blessed
복자 覆字, 伏字 〖인쇄〗 a piece of printing type that is set wrong end to
복작거리다 ① [사람이] bustle ; throng ; crowd ; swam (벌떼처럼) ¶ 거리는 사람들로 복작거렸다 The street was thronged with people. // 해변은 해수욕객으로 복작거렸다 The beach was swarming with bathers.
② [끓어오르다] boil (over) ; seethe
⁑복잡 複雜 complication ; complexity ; intricacy ; involvedness ; a labyrinth ; a maze —하다 (be) complicated ; complex ; intricate ; tangled ; knotty ¶ 복잡기괴한 complicated and inscrutable // 복잡한 웃음 a mystic smile // 복잡한 표정 an expression of mixed feelings // 복잡한 문장 an involved style // 복잡한 일 complicated work // 복잡하게 되다 become complex ; be complicated // 이 소설의 줄거리는 복잡하다 The plot of this story is very intricate. // 인생은 매우 복잡하다 Life is exceedingly complex.
— 골절 〖의학〗 a compound fracture
복장 the center of the thorax〔chest〕
⁑복장 服裝, 服章 dress ; attire ; clothes ; costume ; a uniform ¶ 노동자의 복장을 하고 있다 be dressed as a workingman // 복장에 개의치 않다 be careless about one's dress ; do not care how one dresses // 복장은 수의로 (초대장에) Dress optional. // 훌륭한〔단정한〕 복장을 하고 있다 She is well〔neatly〕 dressed.
— 검사 dress inspection
복재 伏在 concealment ; latency —하다 lie concealed〔dormant, latent〕 ; lurk in 〔under〕 《a thing》 ¶ 이면에 복재하다 lie behind〔back of〕 《a thing》 ; lie at the bottom of 《an affair》
— 정맥 〖의학〗 a saphena 《*pl.* -nae》
복재기 服— a person wearing mourning
복쟁이 〖물고기〗 a globefish ; a swellfish ; a puffer
복적 復籍 —하다 be reinstated in one's original family ; return to one's original domicile
— 수속 《go through》 the formalities of one's return to the original domicile 〔family〕
복제 服制 dress regulation〔system〕 ; the traditional system of mourning attire (상복의) ; costume (복식) ¶ 복제를 정하다 adopt a definite〔special〕 uniform
*복제 複製 reproduction ; reprinting —하다 reproduce ; reprint ¶ 복제를 불허함 All Rights Reserved. /Reprinting prohibited.
— 사진 a photocopy —품 a reproduction ; a duplicate ; a replica —화 a reproduced picture
†복종 服從 obedience ; submission —하다 obey ; submit 《to》 ; yield 《to》 ; bow 《to》 ¶ 복종적 obedient ; submissive // 복종시키다 make 《a person》 obey 《an order》 ; make 《a person》 submissive // 부모에게 복종하다 obey one's parents // 명령에 복종하다 obey 《a person's》 orders
—심 obedience ; submissiveness ; a submissive spirit 절대 — absolute obedience ; complete submission
복죄 服罪 a plea of guilty —하다 plead guilty 《to》 ; enter a plea of guilty ; submit to a sentence
복주감투 a winter cap worn by monks or old people
복주머니 福— a lucky bag
복중 伏中 (the period of) the dog days ; the hottest period of summer ; midsummer
복중 服中 (in) mourning ; (during) the mourning period
복지 福地 a land of bliss ; a blessed land ; 〖성경〗 the Promised Land ; the

Land of Promise
복지 服地 cloth ; dress material
복지 福祉 (public) welfare ; well-being ; prosperity ¶ 국민의 복지를 증진하다 promote national prosperity〔the public good〕
— 국가 a welfare state — 사업 welfare work ; welfare — 시설 welfare facilities 아동 — 사업 child welfare work
*복직 復職 reinstatement ; rehabilitation
— 하다 resume office ; be reinstated 《in the service》 ; be rehabilitated ; be reappointed ; return to one's former position〔office〕 (스스로) ¶ 복직 발령이 났다 I was restored to my former position〔reinstated in the service〕.
복찜 well-seasoned steamed swellfish
복찻다리 a highway bridge over a small stream
복창 復唱 recital ; repetition ; rehearsal
— 하다 recite ; repeat 《an order》 ; rehearse
복채 卜債 a fortune-teller's fee
복처리 福— an unlucky〔unfortunate〕 person ; a person out of luck
복철근 複鐵筋 〖건축〗 double reinforcement
복첨 福籤 a lottery ¶ 복첨을 뽑다 hold a lottery
복통 腹痛 a stomachache ; a colic (급성의) ; a bellyache ; an abdominal pain
*복판 ① [한가운데] the middle ; the center ; the midst ; the heart ¶ 복판에〔으로〕 in the middle〔midst, heart〕 of // 도회지 복판에 in the midst〔middle, heart〕 of a big city // 길 복판에 서 있다 stand in the middle of the street // 그것은 그의 이마 한 복판에 맞았다 It struck him full in the forehead.
② [쇠갈비] beef attached to the ribs
복표 福票 a lottery ticket〔card〕
복합 複合 compositeness ; complex ; a compound
— 개념 a complex concept — 국가 a union of states ; a federation ; united states — 명사 〖문법〗 a compound noun
— 비료 composite〔compound, complex〕 fertilizer — 비타민B vitamin B complex
— 사회 a mixed society —어 〖문법〗 a compound (word) —체 a complex (body) —핵(核) 〖물리〗 a compound nucleus
복화술 腹話術 ventriloquism ; ventriloquy ; ventriloqual art ¶ 복화술을 사용하다 ventriloquize
—사(師) a ventriloquist
복회계법 複會計法 the double-account system
*볶다 ① [불에] parch〔roast〕 《beans》 ; fry (기름에) ; panbroil ¶ 볶은 콩 parched beans // 볶는 듯한 더위 parching heat // 고기를 볶다 roast (minced) meat // 차를 볶다 parch tea leaves // 콩이 덜 볶아졌다 The beans are not parched enough.
② [들볶다] tease ; pester ; annoy ; harass ; torment ¶ 과자를 사달라고 어머니를 볶다 tease〔pester〕 one's mother for candy // 빚을 갚으라고 볶다 dun 《a person》 for the payment of a debt // 나 좀 볶지 마라 You are a pest !
볶아대다 pester〔bother, annoy〕 《a person》 to death〔persistently〕 ; keep bothering〔pestering〕
볶아치다 rush 《the work》 ; rush about ; dash off
볶음 a roast ; a broil ; roasted〔pan broiled〕 food
—밥 frizzled〔fried〕 rice 닭— chopped roast chicken 떡— broiled rice-cake 미나리— broiled parsley
볶이다 ① [불에] be parched〔roasted〕 ; be fried ; be panbroiled ② [들볶이다] be teased ; be pestered ; be annoyed ; be harassed ; be tormented ¶ 빚쟁이에게 볶이다 be harassed by moneylenders // 아이들에게 볶이다 be pestered by one's kids
본 本 ① [본보기] an example ; a model ; a pattern (옷 따위의) ¶ 종이로 본을 뜨다 make a pattern out of paper 《for a dress》 ② [본관] family origin ¶ 본이 어디입니까 Where did your family originate ? ③ [본전] principal ; capital
본- 本 ① the main〔chief, principal〕 ¶ 본점 the main store // 본관 the main building ② the present〔current〕 ¶ 본년도 the current year 〔period〕 // 본회 the present meeting(s) ③ the real 〔regular, full-scale〕 ¶ 본명 real name // 본회의 a regular session ; a full-scale meeting
본가 本家 ① [본집] the main〔head〕 family ; the head house ; a main stock ② [친정] the maiden home of a married woman ; a wife's original〔maiden〕 family
본값 the original cost ¶ 본값에 팔다 sell at cost // 본값을 건지다 recover the cost
본거 本據 the headquarters ; a stronghold ; the base
—지 a stronghold ; headquarters ; the base of operation
본건 本件 this affair〔case, matter〕 ; the pending case ; the case in question
본건물 本建物 a main building
본격 本格 a genuine〔regular〕 style ¶ 본격적인 regular ; real ; full-scale // 본격적으로 되다 begin in earnest ; be regularized // 이제 본격적인 장마철이다 The rainy season has come in earnest.
— 소설 a serious novel
본견 本絹 pure silk
본계약 本契約 a formal contract〔agreement〕
본고 本稿 this manuscript〔article, piece of writing〕
본고장 本— ① [고향] one's native place ; one's home town ¶ 서울은 내가 난 본고장이다 *Seoul* is my birthplace. ② [원산

지] the home ; the place of origin ; the center (중심지) ; the habitat (동식물의 서식지) ¶ 사과의 본고장 the home of the apple // 입헌 정치의 본고장 the home of constitutional government // 파리는 유행의 본고장이다 Paris is the home of fashions.

본고향 本故鄕 one's native place ; one's (ancestral) home

본과 本科 a regular course ¶ 본과를 수료하다 finish the regular course
—생 a regular student ; an undergraduate (대학의)

본관 本官 [임시직에 대한] a regular official ; [겸직에 대한] the principal post ; [자칭] the present official ; I ; me ; this office

본관 本館, 本舘 the main building ; this building

†**본관 本管** a main (pipe) ; a water main

본관 本貫 one's ancestral home ; family origin

본교 本校 this〔our〕 school ; [분교에 대한] the principal school

†**본국 本國** one's home〔native〕 country ; one's own land ¶ 본국 정부 the home government // 본국으로 돌아가다 go 〔return〕 home
—법 〖법〗 lex domicilii ; the law of the domicile **— 송금액** home remittance **— 송환** repatriation **— 정부** the home government

본국 本局 [지국에 대한] the main office ; the head office ; [전화국] an exchange 《영》 ; a central office 《미》

본금 本金 the principal (sum)

본금새 本— the proper price

본기 本期 this〔the current〕 term ; this 〔the current〕 quarter

본남편 本— one's legal husband ; one's first husband ; one's ex-husband

본년 本年 this year ; the current〔present〕 year ¶ 본년도의 계획 the plan for the current year

본노루 an old deer

⁑**본능 本能** instinct ¶ 자기 보존의 본능 the instinct of self-preservation // 본능적(으로) instinctive(ly) // 아이들은 본능적으로 어두운 곳을 두려워한다 Children have an instinctive dread of the dark.
—주의 instinctivism **창조적 —** a creative instinct

*__본당 本堂__ the main〔inner〕 temple ; the main hall (of a temple)

본대 本隊 [군대의] the main body 〔force〕 ; [자기가 소속된] the detachment to which one belongs ; one's regular outfit

본댁 (your, his) esteemed home ; [정실] one's legal wife

본댁네 one's legal wife ; one's first wife

본데 good manners ; discipline ; experience ¶ 본데 있다 have good manners ; be experienced // 본데 없다 have no manners ; be inexperienced

본디 originally ; from the first ; by nature

본때 [본보기] a pattern ; a model ; an example ¶ 본때 없다 be unattractive ; be poor-looking ; be unshowy // 그녀는 그 옷을 입으면 한층 더 본때가 있다 She looks better in that suit. /That dress sets her figure off to better advantage. // 쓸데 없는 간섭을 하면 본때를 보여 줄 테야 I'll teach you to meddle in my affairs.
본때 있다 관용 be stylish ; be smart ; be impressive-looking ; be magnificent

본뜨다 model after a pattern ; make 《a thing》 after a pattern ; copy from a model ; imitate ¶ 파리의 유행을 본뜬 옷 a dress patterned on Paris fashion // 사람의 덕을 본뜨다 imitate the virtues of a man // 아버지를 본떠라 Follow your father's example.

본뜻 本— ① one's original purpose ; one's real intention ; one's will〔motive〕 ¶ 본뜻을 이루다 accomplish〔effect〕 one's purpose ; attain one's object // 그렇게 하는 것은 나의 본뜻이 아니다 It goes against my heart to do so. /It is far from me to do so. // 기분을 상하게 해드려 죄송합니다 그것은 결코 저의 본뜻이 아니었습니다 I'm sorry to hurt your feelings, I never meant to.
② [근본의 뜻] the original〔primary〕 meaning (원의) ; the true〔real〕 meaning (진의) ; the basic〔fundamental〕 meaning (근본의) ¶ 헌정의 본뜻 the basic principle of constitutional government

⁑**본래 本來** [원래] originally ; primarily ; essentially (본질적으로) ; naturally ; by nature ; inherently ¶ 본래의 original ; primary ; essential ; natural ; proper ; intrinsic // 본래의 뜻 one's original intention // 그는 본래 문학자이다 He is essentially a man of letters. // 본래는 절이었다 It was originally a temple.

본령 本令 this〔present〕 law〔ordinance〕 ¶ 본령은 공포한 날로부터 이를 시행한다 The present ordinance shall come into force as from the day of its promulgation.

본령 本領 [본분] one's province ; [특성] one's characteristic〔line, element〕 ¶ 본령을 발휘하다 show oneself at one's best ; come into one's own ; show one's real ability

본론 本論 the main subject ¶ 본론으로 들어가기 전에 before taking up the main subject // 본론에 들어가다 take up the main subject ; proceed to the main issue // 본론으로 돌아가다 return to the subject

본루 本壘 [본거] the base ; the main fort ; the stronghold ; 〖야구〗 the home base〔plate〕 ¶ 본루를 밟다 get home ; home in
—타 〖야구〗 a home run ; a homer ¶ 본

루타를 치다 hit a home run ; smack〔whack〕 out a homer
본류 本流 the main stream ; a main current
본리 本利 principal and interest
본말 本末 means and ends ; cause and effect ; the substance and the shadow ¶ 본말을 전도하다 put the cart before the horse ; reverse the right order of things
본맛 the original taste〔flavor〕
본망 本望 [염원] one's (long-cherished) desire〔dream〕; hope ; aim ; ambition ¶ 본망을 이루다 realize one's long-cherished desire
본명 本名 one's real name ¶ 본명으로 under one's real name // 본명을 대다 give one's real name
본무 本務 [본분] one's duty ; [본직] one's regular〔proper〕 work ; 〖윤리〗 moral duty〔obligation〕
—론 deontology
본무대 本舞臺 the main〔regular〕 stage
⁑본문 本文 the body《of a letter》; the text《of a letter》; [삽화에 대하여] letterpress《주로 영》; [이 문장] this sentence〔passage, article〕 ¶ 본문의 필자 the writer of this article ; [나] the (present) writer
— 비평 textual criticism
본문제 本問題 [본래의] the original problem〔question〕; [기본의] the fundamental〔main〕 problem ; [이 문제] this problem
본밑천 本— capital ; stock ; funds
본바닥 本— the home ; the place of origin ; a native place ; provenance ¶ 본바닥 사람 a native ; an indigene // 커피의 본바닥 the (original) home of the coffee plant // 서울 본바닥 사람 a native of *Seoul* ; an indigenous Seoulite // 영국은 대의 정치의 본바닥이다 England is the birthplace of representative government.
†본바탕 本— essence ; (real) substance ; essential quality ; one's disposition
본받다 本— model after a pattern ⇨ 본뜨다
본보기 本— an example ; a model ; a pattern (본) ¶ 애국심의 본보기 an example of patriotism // 본보기가 될 만한 행위 exemplary conduct // 스커트의 본보기 a paper pattern for a skirt // 본보기로 삼다 make a model〔an example〕 of《a person》; model oneself on〔upon〕《a person》// 본보기를 보이다 set〔give〕 an example to《a person》// 그를 본보기로 삼아라 Make him your model. // 그가 좋은 본보기이다 He is the perfect example of that.
본봉 本俸 one's regular salary ; a basic salary ; full pay
본부 本夫 one's legal husband ; one's first husband
본부 本部 headquarters ; the main〔head〕 office ; the administrative building (대학)
—중대 〖군사〗 headquarters company
본분 本分 one's position ; station in life ; one's duty〔part, function〕 ¶ 본분을 다하다 do〔discharge, fulfil〕 one's duty ; play one's part
본사 本社 [본점] the head office ; the main office ; [우리 회사] our company〔firm〕; we ¶ 본사의 통신원 our correspondent
본사 本寺 [불교에서] the temple where one first became a Buddhist priest ; [자기가 있는] this〔our〕 temple ; [본산] the main temple
본사내 本— ⇨ 본남편
본산 本山 [불교의] a head temple
본새 本— [생김새] the original looks〔features〕; [본바탕] the nature ; basic quality ¶ 본새가 곱다 be nice-looking ; look nice ; have good features // 본새가 사납다 have an ugly nature ; be ill-natured
본색 本色 one's real character ; one's true colors〔quality〕 ¶ 이 말에 그의 본색이 나타난다 This remark is very characteristic of him.
본서 本書 this book ; this volume ; the present book〔work〕; the book〔volume, work〕 in question ; the said book
본서 本署 [주된 관서] a principal office ; a chief police station ; [이 서] this office
본서방 ⇨ 본남편
본선 本線 [지선에 대한] the main line ; a trunk line ; the main track
본선 本船 this〔our〕 ship ; [주장이 되는] a mother〔depot〕 ship
— 인도 free on board《F. O. B., f. o. b.》(수출항에서) ; ex ship(수입항에서)
본성 本性 the original nature ; the real character ; one's true character
본성 本姓 one's original surname ; one's family name
본소 本訴 the original suit
본숭만숭하다 glance《over》; take a cursory view《of》; skim《over》 ¶ 그 편지를 본숭만숭했다 I glanced over the letter.
본시 本是 originally ; primarily ; essentially ; from the first ; by nature
본시험 本試驗 the final examination ; this examination
본식 本式 orthodox style〔fashion〕; proper form ¶ 본식으로 formally ; in due〔proper〕 form ; in orthodox style // 본식으로 신청하다 make a formal application
본실 本室 one's legal wife ; one's first wife
본심 本心 [진의] one's real intention ; one's heart ¶ 본심은 at heart // 본심으로 돌아가다 come to one's senses // 본심을 밝히다 unbosom oneself ; speak one's mind // 그것이 너의 본심이냐 Do you really mean it?
본안 本案 [원안] the original bill〔plan,

draft〕; [이 안건] this plan〔bill〕

본얼굴 本— one's original〔unchanged, unpainted〕 face

본업 本業 one's main business ; one's regular work〔trade〕 ¶ 본업 외의 일 a side work〔business, job〕; a sideline // 본업에 힘쓰다 attend to one's business

본연 本然 ¶ 본연의 natural ; inborn ; proper // 본연의 성질 one's true character

본영 本營 the headquarters

본원 本源 the origin ; the source ; the root (근원) ¶ 사물의 본원을 규명하다 study the origin of a thing ; trace a thing to its source

본원 本願 [숙원] a long-cherished desire〔wish〕; one's deepest wish ; one's heart's desire ; 〖불교〗 Purva-pravidhna 《범》; the Original Vow of Amida Buddha ¶ 본원을 달하다 realize〔accomplish〕 one's long-cherished wishes

본월 本月 this month ; the current month ; instant 《inst.》 ¶ 본월 5일 the 5th of this month ; the 5th inst.

본위 本位 ① a standard (기본) ; a principle (주의) ¶ 자기 본위의 사람 an egoist ; an ego(t)istic person ; a self-centered person // 고객 본위로 하다 make it a principle to serve customer's interests // 당사는 인물 본위로 채용합니다 In employing people we lay stress on their character. // 품질 본위가 폐점의 방침입니다 "Quality first" is our motto.
② [화폐의] standard
— 기호 〖음악〗 a natural — 화폐 a standard money〔coin, currency〕; legal tender 금〔은〕 — the gold〔silver〕 standard

본위제 本位制
단(單)〔복〕— monometallism〔bimetallism〕

본유 本有 ¶ 본유의 innate ; inborn ; natural
— 관념 innate ideas

*__본의__ 本意 one's will ; one's motives ; one's real intention ; one's original purpose ¶ 본의 아니다 be against one's will // 그것은 나의 본의가 아니었다 That was not my real intention. /I never meant to do so.

본의 本義 ⇨ 본지(本旨)

본이름 本— one's real〔original〕 name

*__본인__ 本人 [당자] the person in question ; the person himself〔herself〕; the principal (대리인에 대한) ¶ 본인 자신이 personally ; in person // 본인의 사진 one's own photograph // 본인을 만났다 I saw the man himself. // 본인이 그렇게 말했다 He said so himself.

본일 本日 today ; this day

본임자 本— the original owner〔master〕

본적 本籍 the domicile ; one's home address ; one's place of register

본전 本殿 the main temple 《of a shrine》; the inner shrine

본전 本錢 [원금] principal ; [밑천] capital ¶ 본전에 팔다 sell at cost // 재고 정리를 하느라고 TV를 본전에 판다고 하더군요 They said they were selling those TV sets at cost to get rid of an overstock. // 겨우 본전은 된다 We just break even. // 밑져야 본전이다 Trying wouldn't hurt. /Trying wouldn't do any harm.

본점 本店 [지점에 대한] the head〔main〕 office〔shop, store〕; [이 상점] this shop ¶ 본점 지배인 a general manager

본정 本情 [참된 심정] one's real intention ; one's mind〔heart, conscience〕 ¶ 본정으로 말하다 speak from one's heart

본제 本第 one's house back home〔in one's native place〕; one's home

본제 本題 the main subject〔topic, issue〕; the original subject ¶ 본제로 돌아가다 return to the subject

본존 本尊 〖불교〗 Sakyamuni the object of worship ; the principal icon

본종 本宗 relatives of the same clan

본죄 本罪 [이 죄] this sin〔guilt〕; [기본적 죄] a fundamental sin ; 〖카톨릭〗 an actual〔a personal〕 sin

본주 本主 [원주인] the original proprietor〔owner〕; [소유자] the owner〔proprietor, possessor〕

본줄거리 本— the main〔plot, point〕 《of a story》

본줄기 本— the main line

본지 本旨 the main〔principal〕 object〔purport〕; the object in view ¶ 본지에 합당하다 serve〔answer〕 the object in view // 교육의 본지에 어긋나다 go against〔be contrary to〕 the true aim of education

본지 本紙 this〔our〕 newspaper ¶ 본지의 독자 our readers // 본지에 기보한 바와 같이 as already reported in these columns

본지 本誌 this journal ; our magazine

본직 本職 [본업] one's main business〔occupation〕; [자신] I ; me ; myself ¶ 본직을 삼다 make 《it》 one's profession // 본직은 변호사이다 He is a lawyer by profession.

본진 本陣 military headquarters

**__본질__ 本質 true〔intrinsic〕 nature ; essence ; substance ¶ 본질적으로 essentially ; intrinsically ; in the nature of things ; in itself ; in essence
— 속성 an intrinsic attribute

본집 本— one's (own) home ; one's parents' home ⇨ 본가

본처 本妻 one's wedded wife ; a legal〔lawful〕 wife ; one's first wife

본체 本體 ① [본질] essence ; intrinsic nature ; [본형태] the true form ② 〖철학〗 substance ; entity ; the thing in itself ; noumenon ; 〖불교〗 reality
—론 ontology ; substantialism

본체만체 pretending not to have seen —

하다 neglect ; slight ; do not care for ; show indifference to ¶ 그는 길에서 나를 본체만체했다 He gave me the cold shoulder in the street. /He cut me cold in the street. // 이 아이들이 고생을 하고 있는데 너는 어떻게 본체만체 하느냐 How can you be so indifferent to the sufferings of these children ?

본초 本草 [한약재] medical〔medicinal〕 herbs ; [한약학] herbal medicine ; Chinese medical botany ¶ 본초 채집을 하다 herborize ; collect herbs
—가 a herbalist ; a botanist ; a phytologist ; a herb doctor — 강목(綱目) a botanical list ; a flora —학 botany ; phytology

본초 자오선 本初子午線 the prime〔standard〕 meridian

본촌 本村 [본 마을] the main village ; [이 마을] this〔our〕 village

본치 appearance ; figure

*본토 本土 the mainland ; one's native country ¶ 한국 본토 Korea proper
—박이 natives ; indigene ; aborigines —방위 home〔national〕 defense —인 natives ; mainlanders 중국 — the Chinese mainland ; China proper

본포 本鋪 the head〔main〕 office〔shop〕

본형 本形 the original form〔shape〕

본형 本刑 a regular penalty ; the appropriate punishment

본호 本號 this issue ; the current〔present〕 issue〔number〕

본회담 本會談 the full-dress talks ; the main conference

본회원 本會員 a regular member ¶ 본회원의 자격 full membership

본회의 本會議 a general meeting (총회) ; a plenary〔main〕 session 《of the National Assembly》

†볼¹ ① [뺨] a cheek ¶ 붉은 볼 a ruddy〔rosy〕 cheek // 볼이 핼쑥하다 have hollow〔sunken〕 cheeks ② [넓이] width ; breadth ¶ 버선 볼 the width of a Korean sock // 볼이 좁다〔넓다〕 be narrow〔wide〕 // 이 구두는 볼이 너무 좁다 These shoes are too tight for me. ③ [버선의] a patch (on Korean socks) ¶ 버선에 볼을 대다 put a patch on Korean socks

볼² ① [공] a ball ② 〖야구〗 a ball ¶ 볼에 손을 대다 swing at〔bat〕 a ball // 볼을 선언하다 declare "ball"

볼가심 a morsel of food ; a bite ; (a) bite and (a) sup —하다 have〔take, eat〕 a bite ¶ 볼가심할 것도 없다 do not have a bite to eat // 생쥐 볼가심할 것도 없다 haven't enough for a baby mouse to chew on ; haven't a crumb ; be utterly destitute ; be down and out

볼가지다 protrude ; project ; jut〔stick〕 out ; bulge out

볼강거리다 take a lot of chewing ; be chewy ; be leathery ; be lumpy

볼강볼강 chewy ; leathery ; lumpy ; hard to chew

볼거리 〖한의학〗 the mumps ¶ 볼거리가 나다 have (the) mumps

볼그대대하다, 볼그댕댕하다 (be) reddish

볼그레하다 (be) reddish ; rubicund ; be tinged with red ¶ 볼그레한 볼 rosy〔red〕 cheeks // 그는 술을 마셔서 얼굴이 볼그레하다 He is a little flushed with wine.

볼그무레하다 (be) reddish ; red-hued

볼그스름하다, 볼그족족하다 ⇨ 볼그대대하다

볼근거리다 chew on

볼긋볼긋 ⇨ 발긋발긋

볼긋하다, 뽈긋하다 be splashed with red

*볼기 the buttocks ; the hip ; the rump ¶ 볼기를 때리다 flog 《a person's》 buttocks〔hip〕 ; spank 《a person's buttocks》 // 볼기를 맞다 get spanked ; be flogged on the buttocks〔hip〕
—긴살 the rump

볼기짝 the buttocks ⇨ 볼기

볼기치다 spank

볼꼴 (outward) appearance ; show ; look

볼꼴사납다 (be) unsightly ; ungainly ; unseemly ; shabby ; ugly ; indecent ; improper ; mean ¶ 한길에서 그런 짓을 하는 것은 볼꼴사납다 It doesn't look good to do such a thing in the street. // 볼꼴사납게 굴지 마라 Don't behave disgracefully. // 참 볼꼴사납다 What a sight !

볼끈 all of a sudden (갑자기) ; tightly (꽉) ¶ 볼끈 성이 나서 in a burst of anger ; in a fit of anger ; in a miff〔huff〕 // 볼끈 성내다 fly into a rage〔passion, temper〕 ; flare〔flame〕 up // 주먹을 볼끈 쥐다 clench one's fist

볼끈거리다 fly into a rage easily ; get mad easily

볼끼 a kind of muff for protecting the cheeks and ears in cold weather

볼달다 reforge 《a blade》 ; patch up 《socks》

볼되다 ① [벅차다] be a strain on one ; (be) hard ② [억세다] (be) very tight

볼레로 [여자용 윗옷] a bolero 《*pl.* ～s》 ; [스페인 무용] bolero 《*pl.* ～s》

볼록거리다 palpitate ; swell and subside

볼록거울 〖물리〗 a convex mirror

볼록렌즈 〖물리〗 a convex lens

볼록면 —面 a convex surface

볼록하다 (be) swollen ; baggy ; bulging

볼륨 volume ¶ 볼륨이 있다 voluminous ; bulky

*볼링 bowling ¶ 볼링하러 가다 go bowling
—장(場) a bowling alley

볼만장만 looking on silently —하다 look on silently ; remain a spectator ; hold one's tongue

볼만하다¹ look on silently ; remain a spectator ; hold one's tongue

볼만하다² be worth seeing ; be worthy of

notice ¶ 비원은 가 볼만하다 The Secret Garden is well worth visiting.

볼맞다 ① [손발이 맞다] go cahoots ; make good partners ; be hand in glove 《with》 ② [걸맞다] fit like a glove ; go together nicely ; be well-matched ; make a good pair

볼멘소리 sullen〔sulky〕 words ; grouchy words 《미·구》 ¶ 볼멘소리로 대답하다 give a sullen answer // 그렇게 볼멘소리를 하지 않아도 좋을 텐데 You might speak more gently.

볼모 a pledge ; a security ; a hostage ¶ 볼모로 잡다 take〔hold〕 《a person》 as hostage // 볼모로 잡히다 be taken (as) hostage // 볼모로 앉아 있다 sit there doing nothing

볼받다 patch (up) ; put a patch on (Korean socks)

볼받이 patched socks

볼셰비즘 Bolshevism

볼셰비키 a Bolshevik 《*pl.* ~s, ~i》 ; a Bolshevist

볼썽 outward appearance ; show ; look ¶ 볼썽사납다 be ungainly〔unseemly, awkward, indecent〕

볼쑥거리다 keep sticking out abruptly

볼씨 the top piece on the main shaft of a treadmill〔water mill〕

***볼일** a business ; an engagement ; an errand (심부름) ; a job which must be done ¶ 볼일이 있어 on business ; on an errand (남의 부탁으로) // 아버지의 볼일로 on an errand for one's father // 볼일이 있다 have business on hand ; have something to do ; be engaged〔occupied〕 // 볼일이 없다 have nothing to do ; be free ; be disengaged // 나는 시내에 볼일이 있다 I have an errand to do in town. // 나는 지금 별로 볼일이 없다 I am not particularly engaged. // 내게 무슨 볼일이 있습니까 What do you want with me ? /What can I do for you ? // 지금부터 한 두 시간 볼일이 있다 I shall be engaged for about two hours from now on.

볼장 다 보다 be all up〔over, lost〕 《with》 ¶ 나는 인제 볼장 다 보았다 It is all up with me now.

볼칵거리다 squash something wet in one's hand

볼통거리다 speak bluntly〔surlily〕

볼통스럽다 (be) blunt ; brusque ; rough ¶ 볼통스러운 말투 a brusque way of speaking // 볼통스럽게 대답하다 give a blunt〔surly〕 reply ; reply snappishly // 그의 태도가 볼통스럽다 He has rough manners. /He is rough in manners.

볼통하다 (be) bulgy ; protruding

‡**볼트** ① 〖물리〗 a volt ; volts ; voltage ¶ 100볼트의 전류 a 100 volt current ② [나사못] a bolt ¶ 볼트로 죄다 bolt up ; fasten with a bolt

***볼펜** a ball(-point) pen

볼품 appearance ; show ; look(s) ¶ 볼품이 있다 make〔have〕 a good appearance 〔show, figure〕 ; be〔look〕 seemly〔decent, nice〕 ; be of good style // 볼품이 없다 make〔have〕 an ill appearance 〔show, figure〕 ; be unseemly〔indecent, awkward〕 // 방을 볼품있게 꾸미다 make a room look nice // 책이 볼품이 있다 This book is of elegant format.

볼호령 —號令 a howl of rage ; a roar of anger **—하다** give a howl of rage〔a roar of rage〕 ; howl ; roar ¶ 사장이 종업원에게 볼호령을 했다 The president roared at the employee.

†**봄** spring ; springtime ¶ 봄의 spring ; vernal ¶ 인생의 봄 the spring of life ; the flower〔prime, heyday〕 of youth // 이른〔늦은〕 봄에 in the early〔late〕 spring ; at the beginning 〔end〕 of spring // 봄날같다 look〔feel〕 like spring // 한국의 봄은 제주도에서 비롯한다 Spring enters Korea through *Cheju* Island.
—가물 spring drought **—갈이** spring plowing **—기운** a feel〔an air〕 of spring ; spring in the air **—날** a spring day ; spring weather **—농사** a spring crop **—누에** spring silkworms **—바람** a spring breeze **—베기** woodcut in the spring **—볕** spring sun(shine) **—보리** barley sown in the early spring **—비** spring rain **—빛** spring scene(ry) ; a spring view **—새** spring time **— 아지랑이** spring haze **—옷** spring wear **—추위** cold weather in the early spring ; a late frost

봄나물 spring greens〔herbs〕 ¶ 봄나물을 캐다 gather〔pick〕 spring herbs

봄낳이 cotton cloth (hand-)woven in spring

봄내 all through〔throughout〕 the spring ¶ 봄내 비 한 방울 오지 않았다 We have been without rain the whole spring long.

봄눈 spring snow ¶ 봄눈 녹듯하다 disappear〔vanish〕 into thin air ; [음식이] melt in one's mouth ; go down〔digest〕 smoothly ; make good eating

봄맞이꽃 〖식물〗 a rock jasmine ; Androsace saxifragaefolia (학명)

봄베 a gas cylinder
산소(酸素) — an oxygen cylinder

봄새 appearance ; show ; looks ⇨ 볼품

봄철 the spring season ; springtime

봄타다 lose one's appetite in the spring ; get spring fever ¶ 그는 봄을 탄다 He has no appetite with the spring weather.

봅슬레이 [경기용 썰매] a bobsleigh

봇논 洑— a paddy field watered by a reservoir〔dammed pool〕

봇도랑 洑— an irrigation ditch ; a ditch leading to a reservoir

봇돌 ① a support stone on either side of the fireplace ② a stone used to press down the wooden pieces over a roof

봇둑 洑— a dam ; a reservoir
봇물 洑— dam (water) ; water confined by dam ; water in a reservoir
봇일 洑— irrigation dam〔reservoir〕 work
봇줄 draw-cords on a draft animal
봇짐 褓— a bundle ; a package ¶ 봇짐을 짊어지다 carry a bundle on one's back ; shoulder a bundle
—장수 a peddler ; a packman
봉[1] dissipation ⇨ 난봉
봉[2] [낚시의] a sinker ⇨ 봉돌
봉[3] [땜질에서] a solder patch ¶ 봉박다 solder on a patch ; solder up a hole // 솥에 봉박다 solder up a hole in a kettle
봉 峰 a peak ; a top ; a summit
봉 封 a paper bag ¶ 약한 봉 a packet of medicinal herbs ; a dose of medicine
봉 鳳 a (male) phoenix
봉강 棒鋼 bar steel
봉건 封建 [제도] feudalism ; the feudal system ¶ 봉건적 feudal ; feudalistic ; [시대에 뒤떨어진] old-fashioned ; too conservative // 깊이 뿌리 박은 봉건 사상 deep-rooted feudalism // 그는 봉건적이다 He is too conservative.
— 군주 a feudal lord — 사상 a feudalistic idea — 시대 the feudal age〔times〕 — 제도 feudalism ; the feudal system 〔regime〕 ; feudality —주의 feudalism ; feudality
봉고도 棒高跳 a pole jump ; (a) pole vault《미》 ¶ 봉고도를 하다 pole-vault ; pole-jump
— 선수 a pole-vaulter ; a pole-jumper
†봉급 俸給 a salary ; wages ; pay ¶ 낮은 봉급의 underpaid ; low-salaried // 비싼 봉급의 high-salaried // 무봉급으로 without pay // 봉급을 받다 receive one's salary ; get paid // 봉급을 인상하다〔인하하다〕 raise〔lower〕《a person's》 salary // 그들에게 좀더 많은 봉급을 지불해야 한다 We must pay them more.
— 봉투 a pay envelope — 생활자 a salaried man ; a salary earner ; a white-collar worker ; the salaried class《총칭》 —일 pay day — 지불 대장 payroll 《미》 ; a pay sheet〔list〕《영》
봉기 蜂起 uprising ; insurrection ; revolt —하다 rise in revolt〔rebellion, arms〕 ; rise (up) against ¶ 농민 봉기 an uprising of the peasants ; an agrarian revolt
봉나다 ⇨ 난봉
*봉납 奉納 dedication ; offering ; presentation《to a deity》 —하다 dedicate ; offer ; make an offering ; present ; consecrate ; devote《a thing to god》
—물 an offering ; a votive offering 〔object〕 —액(額) a votive〔dedicated〕 tablet —자 an offerer ; a dedicator ; a consecrator
봉놋방 —房 a large guest room of an inn〔a tavern〕 ; an inn dormitory
봉당 封堂 the unfloored〔dirt-floored〕 area between two rooms ¶ 봉당을 빌려 주니 안방까지 달란다 Give him an inch and he'll take a yard.
— 마루 a dirt floor
봉대 烽臺 a signal fire post ; a beacon post
봉독 奉讀 reading reverentially〔deferentially〕 —하다 read with reverence
봉돌 a sinker ; a sink ; a bullet ¶ 줄에 봉돌을 달다 weight a line
봉두 峰頭 the peak ; the top ; the summit
봉두난발 蓬頭亂髮 shaggy〔unkempt〕 hair ; a rat's nest
봉랍 封蠟 sealing wax ¶ 봉랍으로 봉하다 seal《a letter》 with wax
봉랍 蜂蠟 propolis ; bee glue ; [밀랍] beewax
봉리 鳳梨 a pineapple
봉물 封物 a tribute ; a gift ; a present
봉밀 蜂蜜 honey ⇨ 꿀 ¶ 봉밀 저장용 항아리 a honeypot // 봉밀처럼 단 honey-sweet // 봉밀을 넣은 honeyed
—주(酒) mead
봉바리 a brass bowl for the use of women
봉박다 solder on a patch ; solder up a hole ; patch up a hole
봉박다 封— add something extra to a package
봉발 蓬髮 unkempt〔disheveled, tousled〕 hair
봉방 蜂房 a honeycomb ; a honey cell
봉변 逢變 ① [욕을 당함] receiving an insult ; having a bitter experience ; an insult ; humiliation ② [화를 당함] encountering a mishap ; a misfortune ; a calamity —하다 be insulted〔humiliated〕 ; have bitter experiences ; have a bad〔rough〕 time (of it) ; [화를 당함] meet with〔encounter〕 an unlucky accident〔a mishap〕 ; suffer an unexpected calamity
봉봉 [과자] a bonbon《프》
위스키 — a whisk(e)y bonbon
봉분 封墳 a (grave) mound —하다 mound《a grave》 ; build a mound over a grave
†봉사 奉仕 service ; attendance —하다 serve ; render service ; attend〔wait〕 on 《a person》 ¶ 사회 봉사를 하다 serve the community ; render public service // 궁중에 봉사하는 사람 a person in attendance on the royal family
— 가격 《sell at》 a sacrifice price ; 《offer at》 a reduced〔bargain〕 price — 사업 public welfare work —자 one who serves 《the public at large》 ; a servant 《of the people》 —품 a bargain 근로 — labor service 사회 — a service to the public ; a public service
봉사 奉祀 —하다 offer sacrifice to one's ancestors
—손(孫) a descendant offering sacrifice

to his ancestors
봉사 奉事 ① [장님] a blind man ② [섬김] service ; attendance —하다 serve ; attend ; wait on
뜨고도 못 보는 당달 봉사 [속담] There is no blindness like ignorance. /As blind as a bat. /Blind as a mole. /Blind as a owl.
봉살 封殺 『야구』 a force-out —하다 force 《a runner》 out 《at second base》
봉서 封書 a sealed letter
봉선화 鳳仙花 a (garden) balsam ; a touch-me-not
*봉쇄 封鎖 a blockade ; blocking up ; freezing —하다 blockade ; block up ; seal〔bottle〕 up ¶ 봉쇄를 깨뜨리다 break the blockade // 봉쇄를 풀다 lift the blockade
— 구역〔선〕 a blockade zone〔line〕 —선(船) a blocking ship ; a blockader — 정책 a blockade policy — 지불 restricted〔frozen〕 payment — 함대 a blockading squadron〔fleet〕 —항(港) a blockade port〔harbor〕 경제 — an economic blockade 직접〔간접〕 — a direct〔cruising〕 blockade 해상 — a naval〔sea〕 blockade
봉수 烽燧 a signal-fire ; a rocket ; a warning light ; a beacon ¶ 봉수를 올리다 fire a rocket as a signal ; light a signal-fire
봉술 棒術 the art of using a stick as a weapon
봉숭아 a (garden) balsam ; Impatiens balsamina (학명) ⇨ 봉선화
봉아술 蓬莪茂 『식물』 a zedoary ; Curcuma zedoaria (학명)
봉안 奉安 enshrinement —하다 enshrine ; lay in state
봉양 奉養 support ; maintenance —하다 support (one's parents) ; serve one's parents faithfully ¶ 그의 노모를 봉양할 사람은 그뿐이다 He is the sole support of his aged mother.
*봉오리 a bud ¶ 꽃봉오리 a (flower) bud // 피어나는 꽃봉오리 bursting buds // 봉오리를 맺다 bud ; put forth〔shoot out〕 (the) buds ; have buds
봉욕 逢辱 —하다 suffer an insult ; meet with shame〔humiliation〕 ; be put to shame ⇨ 욕보다
*봉우리 a peak ; a summit ; a top ¶ 산봉우리 a mountain top〔peak〕
봉인 鋒刃 [창·칼 따위의] a blade ; a spearhead
‡봉인 封印 sealing ; a seal —하다 put the seal upon 《a letter》 ; put 《a letter》 under seal ¶ 봉인을 뜯다 break〔take off〕 the seal
봉자채 逢子菜 『식물』 a (our Lady's) bedstraw ; Galium verum (학명)
봉작 封爵 investiture〔investment〕 with the titles of nobility —하다 invest with the titles of nobility
봉접 蜂蝶 bees and butterflies
봉접 鳳蝶 『곤충』 a swallow tail
봉정 奉呈 presentation ; dedication —하다 present ; dedicate ; offer
봉제 縫製 sewing ; needlework ; dressmaking —하다 sew ; do needlework ; sit at needlework
—공(사) a needleworker ; a dressmaker ; a worker in a sewing factory ; [바느질의] a seamster (남자) ; a seamstress (여자) — 공장 a sewing factory
봉제사 奉祭祀 ⇨ 봉사(奉祀)
봉조 棒組 『인쇄』 galley setting ¶ 봉조로 하다 set type〔set a manuscript〕 in a galley
봉족 奉足 help ; aid ; assistance —하다 help ; aid ; assist ; give 《a person》 assistance
—꾼 a helper ; an assistant ; an aide
봉지 封紙 a paperbag ¶ 약 한 봉지 a packet of medicinal herbs // 봉지에 넣어 주십시오 Put it in a paper bag for me.
봉직 奉職 government service —하다 serve 《at, in》 ; be in government service ; hold an appointment ¶ 학교에 봉직하다 be on the staff of a school
—처 a position ; a post
봉착 逢着 —하다 meet (with) ; encounter (with) ; be faced〔confronted〕 with ; chance〔happen〕 on ¶ 난관에 봉착하다 be faced with〔encounter〕 difficulties
봉창 封窓 [창을 봉함] sealing up the window ; [봉한 창] a sealed-up window ; [구멍창] a small blind window —하다 seal up a window
봉창질 hoarding things —하다 [물건을] hoard things ; [손해를] make up for 《a loss》 ; recover ; cover
봉축 奉祝 celebration of an occasion —하다 celebrate 《an occasion》 ¶ 그날을 봉축하기 위하여 in celebration of the occasion
봉치 wedding gifts sent by the bridegroom's family prior to the wedding
봉칫시루 rice cake to celebrate sending〔receiving〕 a wedding gift
봉친 奉親 the support of one's parents —하다 support one's parents
*봉토 封土 a fief ; a feud ; feudal territory
†봉투 封套 an envelope ¶ 봉투를 봉하다 seal an envelope
각— a side-opening envelope 반신용 — a return envelope 양(洋)— a side-opening envelope 편지 — a letter envelope
봉피 封皮 an envelope ; a cover ¶ 봉피를 뜯다 open〔unseal〕 an envelope
봉하다 封— ① seal 《an envelope, one's lips》 ; seal up 《a window》 ; stop up 《a hole》 ¶ 편지를 봉하다 seal a letter // 서랍을 봉하다 seal (up) drawers // 평론가의 입을 봉해라 Stop the mouths of critics. ② [제후를] invest 《a feudal lord》 with a feud〔fief〕 ; enfeoff ③ [작위 따위를] con-

fer《a peerage》; confer《a person》with a title

봉함 封緘 a seal ; sealing **—하다** seal《a letter》 ¶ 봉함하지 않고 loosely sealed // 봉함을 뜯다 break〔take off〕the seal
— 엽서 a letter card

봉합 封合 suture **—하다** suture ; stitch (together)

봉합 縫合 suture **—하다** suture ; stitch (together)

봉행 奉行 doing in obedience《to》; acting《upon》; carrying out《an order》 **—하다** do in obedience to《a superior's order》; carry out《an order》

봉헌 奉獻 dedication ; presentation ; consecration ; oblation **—하다** dedicate〔consecrate, offer〕《a thing》to《a superior, shrine》
—물 votive offerings **—자** a dedicator

봉화 烽火 a signal-fire ; a rocket ; a warning-light ; a beacon (fire) ¶ 봉홧둑 a height where a signal-fire was lighted // 봉홧대 a pole for bearing a beacon fire
—대(臺) a beacon lighthouse
봉화를 올리다 관용 light a signal-fire

봉화 鳳凰 a phoenix ; a fabulous bird

봐란듯이 ⇨ 보아란듯이

봐하니 so far as my observation goes ; so far as the appearances go ; to all appearance ¶ 봐하니 점잖은 분이 왜 이러시오 You look like a gentleman —You should behave yourself better.

뵈다 humbly see ⇨ 뵙다

뵘 filling up ; patching ; blocking off ; stopping up

뵙다 [웃어른을] see ; meet ; have an audience〔interview〕with ¶ 가 뵙겠습니다 I'll call on〔go and see〕you. // 참 뵙기 힘듭니다 I see very little of you. // 처음 뵙겠습니다 How do you do? // 어제 나는 대통령을 뵈었습니다 I was received by the President yesterday.

부 父 a father

부 否 no ; nay ¶ 가부 aye and no ; pro and con ; for and against // 부가 많았다 The noes had it.

부 負 ⇨ 음(陰)

†**부 部** ① [부문] a department ; a division ; a class ; a category ② [부수] a copy《of a book, a magazine》; a volume ¶ 부원 a member of the staff ; the staff《총칭》// 부장 the head〔chief〕of a department // 이 잡지 1부 a copy of this magazine // 3부로 된 소설 a novel in three parts

†**부 富** wealth ; riches ; a fortune ; opulence ¶ 부의 분배 distribution of wealth // 일국의 부 the wealth of a nation // 부를 이루다 grow rich〔wealthy〕; make〔amass〕a fortune // 백만 장자의 부도 하룻밤 사이에 없어지는 수가 있다 A millionaire's riches may vanish overnight.

부 賦 fu ; a chinese poetic genre ; an ode

부- 副 assistant ; deputy ; vice- ; sub-
—독본 a supplementary reader **—사령관** the deputy commander in chief **—심(審)**〖야구〗a sub-umpire〔-referee〕 **—의장** a vice-chairman **—주장**〖경기〗a subcaptain **—지배인** an assistant manager **—지사** a vice-governor **—총재** a vice-president **—통령** a vice-president

-부 附 ① [날짜] dated ; under the date of ¶ 이달 3일〔8월 15일〕부 편지 a letter dated 3rd inst.〔Aug. 15th〕 ② [부속] attached《to》; in attendance《upon》; belonging《to》; bearing ¶ 대사관부 육〔해〕군 무관 a military〔naval〕attaché to an embassy

‡**부가 附加** addition ; annexation ; supplement **—하다** add《to》; make addition(s) to ; supplement (보충) ; annex ; append (첨부) ; tack (첨가) ; subjoin (추가) ¶ 부가적 additional ; annexed ; supplementary ; extra (여분의)
— 가치〖경제〗value added **— 가치세** a tax on value added ; a value added tax
—물 an addition ; an annex ; an appendage ; an affix ;〖화학〗an adduct
—사(詞)〖문법〗an adjunct **—세** an additional〔a supplementary〕tax ; a surtax《미》; a supertax《영》 ¶ 부가세를 과하다 levy a supertax on《a person》 **— 소득세** an additional income tax **— 우편료** extra postage **— 저당** collateral (security) **— 형(刑)** an accessory〔an additional, a supplementary〕penalty

부각 fried kelp

부각 浮刻 relief **—하다** emboss ; raise ; [새기다] carve in relief ¶ 부각되다 be embossed ; stand out in bold relief《뚜렷이》// 부각시키다 bring《a thing》into relief // 새 무늬가 부각되어 있다 be embossed with a design of birds

부각 負角〖수학〗a negative angle

부각 俯角〖수학〗a dip ; an angle of depression〔declination〕

부각 腐刻 etching **—하다** etch

부감 俯瞰 **—하다** overlook ; look out upon ; command a bird's-eye〔an aerial〕view《of the city》
—도 a bird's-eye view《of》; a view from above **—도 촬영기** a kite camera **— 촬영** a crane shot

부갑상선 副甲狀腺〖해부〗the parathyroid (glands) ; the accessory thyroid glands
— 호르몬 parathormone

부강 富强 wealth and power **—하다** (be) rich and powerful ¶ 국가의 부강 the wealth and power of a nation

부개비잡히다 be badgered into《doing something》

부걱 with (a) foam〔bubbles〕; with barm (in fermenting)

부걱거리다 bubble up ; foam ; be barmy ; pop (in fermenting)

부검지 bits〔shreds〕 of straw
부결 否決 rejection **—하다** reject ; vote down〔against〕 ; kill ; veto ¶ 부결되다 be rejected〔voted down〕 // 의안을 부결하다 reject〔vote down〕 a bill // 제안은 30 대 22 로 부결되었다 The proposal was rejected by a vote of 30 to 22.
—권 a negative voice ; a right of veto ; a veto
부계 父系 the paternal〔male〕 line ; the spear side ¶ 부계의 paternal ; patrilineal ; on the paternal〔father's, spear〕 side ; 〖로마법〗 consanguinean
— 가족 a paternal〔patriarchal〕 family **— 사회** a patrilineal society **— 상속** patrilineal descent **— 친족** a relative on the father's〔paternal〕 side ; an agnate
부고 訃告 an obituary ; a report〔an announcement〕 of death ; the news of death ¶ 부고를 받다 receive the news of 《a person's》 death
부고환 副睾丸 〖해부〗 epididymis 《*pl.* -mides》
—염(炎) epididymitis
부과 賦課 levy ; imposition ; incidence **—하다** levy〔impose〕 《a tax》 on ¶ 소득세를 부과하다 levy an income tax 《on》 // 토지에 고정 자산세를 부과하다 impose a fixed assets tax on land
—금 dues ; taxes **—액** the amount imported ; assessment **자동 —(세)제** taxation-by-schedule system **재—** reimposition
부관 副官 an adjutant ; an aide ; an aide-de-camp 《프》
— 참모 an adjutant general **고급 —** a senior adjutant **전속 —** an aide-de-camp ; an aide
부관장 副館長 [박물관·도서관 등의] a deputy curator ; a vice-curator
부광 富鑛 [광석] a rich ore ; [광산] a rich mine
—(지)대 a bonanza
부교 浮橋 a pontoon〔floating〕 bridge
부교감 신경 副交感神經 〖해부〗 a parasympathetic (nerve)
부교재 副教材 an auxiliary textbook
부국 富國 a rich〔wealthy〕 country
— 강병(强兵) a wealthy country and a powerful army **—론** the Wealth of Nations **—책** a plan〔measure〕 for enriching one's country
부군 夫君 one's husband
부권 父權 paternal authority〔rights〕 ; 〖로마·법〗 patria potestas 《라》
— 사회 patriarchal society **— 시대** the age of patriarchy ; the patriarchal age **— 제도** patriarchy
부권 夫權 the husband's rights ; marital authority
부권 婦權 women's rights
부귀 富貴 riches and honors ; wealth and fame〔rank〕 ; prosperity ¶ 부귀를 타고나다 be born rich ; be born with a silver spoon in one's mouth
— 공명 wealth, rank and fame ¶ 부귀공명 속에 살다 live in honor and wealth **— 빈천** high and low ; men of all ranks **— 영화** wealth and prosperity ¶ 부귀 영화를 누리다 live in splendor〔wealth and honor〕 ; be at the height〔zenith〕 of one's prosperity
부그르르 simmering ; bubbling ¶ 물이 부그르르 끓다 The water simmers. // 비누 거품이 부그르르 일어난다 Suds bubble up.
****부근 附近** neighborhood ; vicinity ; environs ¶ 서울 부근 the vicinity〔environs〕 of *Seoul* // 부근의 neighboring ; adjacent ; nearby ; hard-by // 이 부근에 near〔around〕 here ; in this neighborhood〔vicinity〕 ; in and around this neighborhood // 부근에 아무도 없었다 There was no one about.
부근 副筋 〖해부〗 accessory muscle
부글거리다 boil ; seethe ; bubble up ; simmer ¶ 몹시 분해서 부글거리다 simmer with indignation
부글부글 [끓어서] on the simmer ; with a sizzling sound ; [거품이] boiling ; bubbling ; foamingly
부금 賦金 an instal(l)ment ; a premium (보험의)
부기 a stupid fool ; a simpleton ; a dolt ; a blockhead ; an idiot ; a ninny ; a nincompoop
부기 簿記 bookkeeping ¶ 부기를 달다 keep books〔accounts〕
—법 rules of bookkeeping **—봉(棒)** a ruler **—장** an account book **—학** (the art of) bookkeeping **가계 —** domestic bookkeeping **공장 —** factory bookkeeping **단식〔복식〕 —** bookkeeping by single〔double〕 entry **상업〔공업, 은행〕 —** commercial〔industrial, bank〕 bookkeeping
부기 附記 an addition ; an additional remark〔note〕 **—하다** add ; write〔mention〕 in addition
— 등기 a codicil to a registration
부기 浮氣 swelling ; dropsy (수종증) ¶ 부기가 가라앉다 The swelling subsides〔goes down〕.
부기우기 boogie-woogie
부꾸미 a kind of cake made by mixing various flours
부끄러움 shyness ⇨ 부끄럼
부끄러워하다 ① [창피해하다] feel shame 《at》 ; be〔feel〕 ashamed 《of》 ; be abashed ; consider something a shame〔shameful〕 ; blush ¶ 부끄러워하는 얼굴 an ashamed look // 가난을 부끄러워하다 be ashamed of being poor // 스스로를 부끄러워하다 be ashamed of oneself ② [수줍어하다] be〔feel〕 shy ; be coy ; be bashful ; be selfconscious ; be abashed ¶ 부끄러워하여 shyly ; coyly ;

selfconsciously // 부끄러워하지 말아라 Don't be shy〔bashful〕. // 그녀는 의사에게 진찰받는 것을 몹시 부끄러워했다 She was very shy of consulting a doctor.

*부끄럼 [수줍음] shyness ; bashfulness ; coyness ; [수치] shame ; humiliation ; disgrace ; dishonor ¶ 부끄럼을 모르다 be shameless ; have no sense of shame ; be lost to (the sense of) shame // 부끄럼을 알다 dread shame ; respect honor ; have a sense of shame // (나이들어) 부끄럼을 모르게 되다 outgrow one's bashfulness // 그녀는 부끄럼이라든가 분별 따위는 전혀 모른다 She has no sense of shyness or discretion. // 그녀는 전혀 부끄럼을 모른다 She is past all sense of shame. // 그녀는 무슨 일에나 부끄럼을 탄다 She is bashful in doing anything. // 비범한 재능이 있는 사람도 많은 사람 앞에서 이야기할 때에는 부끄럼을 타는 일이 흔히 있다 Men of great ability so often feel bashfulness in addressing a large assembly. // 나는 부끄럼을 무릅쓰고 질문을 했다 I bore shame to ask the question. // 부끄럼타지 말고 노래 하나 불러라 Don't be bashful, sing a song for us. // 청빈은 부끄럼이 아니다 Honest poverty is no disgrace.

부끄럼타다 [관용] be shy ; feel bashful

‡부끄럽다 ① [수치] (be) shameful ; disgraceful ¶ 신사로서 부끄러운 일 an act unworthy of a gentleman // 신사로서 부끄럽잖은 행동을 하다 act as a gentleman ; do 《a thing》 worthy of a gentleman // 부끄러워 낯을 가리다 hide one's face for shame // 부끄러워 얼굴을 붉히다 blush with shame // 부끄럽습니다 I am ashamed of myself. // 그들은 노동을 부끄러운 일로 알고 있다 They think it a shame to work. // 돈 없는 것이 부끄럽다 I am ashamed to be without money. // 그런 짓을 하고도 부끄럽지 않은가 Aren't you ashamed of having done such a thing? // 그 외에도 그는 차마 부끄러워서 말 못할 말을 했다 He said other things I cannot repeat for shame. // 남자라면 그것을 부끄럽게 여겨야 한다 A man must be ashamed of it. // 그 작품은 그의 명성에 부끄럽지 않다 That work is worthy of his reputation. // 부끄럽잖게 차려 입었다 They are in decent clothes. /They are respectably dressed.

② [수줍다] (be) shy ; bashful ; coy ¶ 그녀는 부끄러워 말도 못한다 She is too shy to speak. // 그녀는 부끄러운 듯이 보였다 She looked abashed〔shy〕. // 나는 여자가 부끄럽다 I am shy around women. // 나는 사진 찍히는 것이 부끄럽다 I am camera-shy.

부나방 〖곤충〗 a tiger moth

부낭 浮囊 ① [구명용] a life buoy ; a life belt ; a float (주머니) ; a life preserver 〔jacket〕; [수영용] a (tire) tube 《미》; a tyre ; water wings 《영》 ② [물고기의] an air bladder ; a swim(m)ing bladder ; a (gas) bladder ⇨부레

부내 部內 circles ; the department
정부(政府) — government circles

부넘기 〖건축〗 a raised kitchen fire entrance to an *ondol*〔hypocaust〕 flue

부녀 父女 father and daughter

부녀자 婦女子 ① [부인] a (married) woman ; a lady ② [부인과 여자] women and girls ; womenfolk ¶ 부녀자를 학대하다 bully the fair sex

부논문 副論文 a supplementary treatise

부농 富農 a rich〔wealthy〕 farmer

부닐다 act amiably〔friendly, affably〕 ¶ 착착 부닐다 stick close 《to a person》 eager to be helpful

부다듯하다 (be) feverish

부닥뜨리다 be confronted with ⇨ 부닥치다

*부닥치다 face ; confront ; encounter ; meet with ; come face to face with ; run up against ¶ 곤란〔적〕에 부닥치다 encounter〔be faced with〕 difficulties 〔the enemy〕 // 적의에 부닥치다 meet with hostility 《from》 // 그는 어려운 문제에 부닥쳤다 He is confronted with a hard problem.

부단 不斷 continuity ; ceaselessness ; constancy ; steadiness ; incessantness
—하다 (be) continual ; ceaseless ; constant ; steady ; incessant ¶ 부단한 노력 constant exertions ; a sustained〔perpetual〕 effort // 부단히 노력하다 make a ceaseless effort ; work tirelessly

†부담 負擔 a burden ; a charge ; responsibility (책임) ; an onus ; defrayment (경비의) ; [농짝] a pack hamper —하다 bear ; assume ; shoulder ; pay ; stand 《구》; defray ¶ 자기의 부담액 one's share (in the expenses) ; an allotment // 비용을 부담하다 bear〔defray〕 expenses // 국민에게 조세를 부담시키다 impose taxes on the people // 무거운 부담을 주다 impose a heavy burden on 《a person》 // 비용은 우리 회사에서 부담할 것이다 Our company will cover the expenses.
—금 one's share (in expenses) ; a share ; allotment 각자 — an equal split ; paying each for his own account ; a Dutch treat〔party〕 (회식 따위)

†부당 不當 injustice ; wrongfulness ; unreasonableness —하다 (be) unjust ; unfair ; unreasonable ; wrongful ; improper ; [과하다] undue ; excessive ¶ 부당한 요구 an excessive demand // 부당한 조치 an unfair dealing ; an injustice // 부당한 값 an unreasonable price // 부당하게 압박당하다 be unduly oppressed by 《a person》
— 거래 an unfair〔unconscionable〕 bargain — 과세 unreasonable taxation — 이득 excessive profits ; profiteering (행위)
— 지출 an unjust disbursement ; a mis-

appropriation of funds — 해고 『법』 unfair〔wrongful〕 dismissal
†부대 負袋 a (burlap) bag ; a (gunny) sack ; a bale ¶ 밀가루 한 부대 a sack of flour
부대 附帶 incidental ; accessory —하다 accompany ; be incidental〔accessory, appendant〕《to》; be attached〔annexed〕 to
— 결의(決議) an incidental vote ; a supplementary resolution —범(犯) a secondary〔an accessory〕 offense — 사건(事件) a side issue — 사업(事業) business incidental 《to》; a subsidiary enterprise — 사항(事項) a supplementary item — 상소(上訴) an incidental appeal (for revision) — 상황(狀況) collateral〔attendant〕 circumstances — 조건(條件) a collateral〔incidental〕 condition — 증서(證書) a collateral bond — 현상(現象) an epiphenomenon 《*pl.* ~s, -na》 — 현상설(說) 『철학』 epiphenomenalism
부대 部隊 a unit ; a corps ; a force ; a detachment (파견대) ; a squad (분대) ¶ 적의 대부대 a large enemy force
—기 a guidon ; a squad flag —장 a commander ; a leader 기갑 — an armored unit〔outfit〕 기계화 — a mechanized unit 기동 — a task force 외인 — a foreign legion 장갑 — an armored unit〔outfit〕 전투 — a fighting unit 후방 — rear-guard units
부대 富大 —하다 (be) fat ; plump ; corpulent ; stout
부대 浮帶, 浮袋 a life buoy ; a life belt ; a swimming tube ; a life preserver
부대끼다 be pestered 《by》; be troubled 《with》; be afflicted 《with》; suffer 《from》 ¶ 깡패들에게 부대끼다 be pestered by hoodlums // 더위에 몹시 부대끼다 suffer greatly from the heat // 기침에 부대끼다 be troubled〔afflicted〕 with a cough // 빚쟁이에게 부대끼다 be worried by creditors
부덕 不德 lack〔want〕 of virtue ; unworthiness ; vice —하다 (be) unworthy ; lack virtue ¶ 저의 부덕의 소치입니다 I have but myself to blame.
부덕 婦德 womanly〔female〕 virtues
부도 婦道 womanhood ; the duty of a woman ¶ 부도를 다하다 perform the duties of womanhood
부도 不渡 『경제』 dishonor ¶ 부도나다 be dishonored
— 수표 a dishonored〔bad〕 check ; a rubber check ¶ 부도 수표를 남발하다 pass a bad check — 어음 a dishonored〔bad〕 bill
부도 附圖 an appended〔attached〕 chart 〔map, diagram〕
부도덕 不道德 immorality ; lack of morality —하다 (be) immoral ; unvirtuous ; depraved ¶ 부도덕한 행위 immoral conduct
부도심 副都心 a subcenter of a metropolis
부도체 不導體 『물리』 a nonconductor of heat〔electricity〕; a nonconducting substance ¶ 유리는 전기의 부도체이다 Glass is a nonconductor of electricity.
부독본 副讀本 a supplementary reader
부동 不同 lack of uniformity ; inequality ; dissimilarity —하다 (be) unequal ; dissimilar ; uneven ¶ 부동이다 vary in size ; be uneven in quality // 표리가 부동한 double-dealing ; double-faced ; treacherous ; unfaithful ; dishonest // 요금은 계절에 따라 부동한다 The rent varies according to the season.
순서 — "No special order is observed." (게시)
부동 符同 —하다 collude 《with》; conspire 《with》; group〔gang〕 together ; go (in) cahoots
부동 浮動 —하다 float ; waft ; fluctuate ¶ 부동하는 floating ; fluctuating ; unsettled ; unsteady // 시황의 부동 an unsteady market
— 구매력 floating purchasing power — 성 instability ; unsteadiness — 시세 unsteady quotations — 인구 a floating population —주 floating stocks — 투표자 a floating〔unattached〕 voter ; a floater (특히 매수되기 쉬운) —표 a floating vote
부동 不凍 nonfreezing
—액 an antifreezing solution —제(劑) (an) antifreeze (agent) —항(港) an ice-free port ; a nonfreezing port —해 an ice-free sea
*부동 不動 immovability ; firmness ; stability ; immobility ¶ 한국의 민주주의 정책은 부동이다 Korea's democratic policy remains unshakeable.
—물 an immovable thing ; a fixed thing —성 immobility —심 an imperturbable mind — 자세 『군사』 the position at attention ¶ 부동 자세를 취하다 stand at〔to〕 attention
부동류항 不同類項 『수학』 dissimilar terms
부동명왕 不動明王 Acala 《범》; the God of Fire
*부동산 不動産 immovable property ; immovables ; realty ; real〔fixed〕 estate ¶ 부동산을 매매하다 deal in real estate // 백만 불의 부동산을 가지다 have a million dollars in realty ; have real estate worth a million dollars // 그는 많은 부동산을 소유하고 있다 He has extensive real estate holdings.
— 감정사 a real estate appraiser — 권리증 a title deed ; a land certificate ; muniments — 대부 a loan on real property — 등기 real-estate registration — 매매업자 a realty dealer ; a realtor 《미》 — 보험 property insurance — 소득 an income from immovables — 시가(時

價)〔과세〕 표준액 the standard value of real estate based on the current prices 〔computed for tax imposition〕 — 양도세 real estate sale〔transfer〕 tax — 취득세 real estate acquisition tax — 투자 investment in real estate

부동의 不同意 disagreement ; disapproval

***부두** 埠頭 a quay ; a wharf 《pl. wharves》 ; a pier ; a jetty
— 노동 조합 a stevedore union ; a longshoreman union — 사용료 quayage ; pierage ; wharfage —세 wharf dues ; jettage ; quayage — 인도 〚상업〛 ex〔free on〕 wharf ; ex quay — 인부 a stevedore ; a longshoreman ; a wharf man 전국 — 노동 조합 the National Docker's 〔Harbor Worker's〕 Union

부둑부둑하다 (be) damp-dry ; be dry enough for ironing ¶ 빨래가 부둑부둑하게 말랐다 The wash is dry enough to iron.

부둑하다 (be) damp-dry

부둣가 埠頭— a quay ; a pier ; the wharfside

부둥부둥 —하다 (be) chubby ; plump

부둥키다 clasp ; grasp ; clutch ; hold in one's arms ¶ 부둥켜안다 embrace ; hug ; give 《a person》 a hug // 인형을 부둥켜안다 clutch one's doll to one's breast // 두 소녀는 서로 부둥켜안고 울었다 The two girls embraced each other and wept.

부둥팥 ① [붉은] a fat redbean ② [덜 마른] a soft ripe bean

부드드하다 (be) grasping ; stingy ; niggardly

부드득, 뿌드득 with a grinding〔grating, creaking〕 sound —하다 grind ; grate ; grit ; creak ¶ 부드득거리는 구두 creaky shoes // 이를 부드득 갈다 grind〔grate, grit, gnash〕 one's teeth

†부드럽다 (be) soft ; tender ¶ 부드러운 손〔빛깔〕 a soft hand〔color〕 // 부드러운 살결 a tender skin // 부드러운 미소 a tender smile // 비단결처럼 부드럽다 be (as) soft as silk // 감촉이 부드럽다 feel soft ; be soft to the touch // 부드러운 목소리로 말하다 speak in a soft tone〔voice〕 // 마음씨가 부드럽다 have a soft〔tender〕 heart ; be tender-〔gentle-〕hearted // 이 담배는 맛이 부드럽다 This tobacco is mild.

부드레하다 (be) rather soft ; subdued ; mild

부득부득 persistently ; obstinately ; stubbornly ; doggedly ¶ 부득부득 고집을 부리다 stick doggedly to one's idea // 부득부득 가겠다고만 한다 He insists on going.

부득불 不得不 unavoidably ; under compulsion ; of necessity ; [싫지만] reluctantly ; against one's will ¶ 부득불 …하다 be compelled〔forced〕 to 《do》 // 부득불 그렇게 했다 I had no option but to do so. // 부득불 그렇게 하지 않으면 안 되었다 Necessity obliged him to that action.

부득이 不得已 unavoidably ; inevitably ; out of necessity —하다 (be) unavoidable ; necessary ; inevitable ; cannot be helped ¶ 부득이한 용무로 owing to〔on account of〕 an unavoidable engagement // 부득이 …하다 be obliged〔compelled, forced〕 to 《do》

부들 〚식물〛 a cattail ; a reed mace ; a bulrush ; Typha orientalis (학명)

부들부들 trembling ; quivering ; shivering ¶ 부들부들 떨다 [무서워서] tremble 《with fear》 ; shake 《with, for fear》 ; [격해서] quiver 《with emotion》 ; [추워서] shiver 《with, from cold》 // 부들부들 떨리는 손으로 with trembling hands // 그는 화가 나서 부들부들 떨었다 He trembled with rage.

부들부들하다 (be) soft ; tender ; supple ; flexible ¶ 부들부들한 가죽 a supple leather

부들자리 a cattail〔bulrush〕 mat

부듯하다, 뿌듯하다 (be) tight ; close-fitting ; full ¶ 부듯이 맞다 fit tightly ; suit to a T // 가슴이 뿌듯해서 말을 못했다 My heart was too full for words. // 배가 부듯해지도록 먹었다 He ate till he was full. // 사람으로 방이 부듯하다 The room was full of people.

부등 不等 inequality ; disparity —하다 (be) unequal ; incongruent
— 부호 a sign of inequality —식 〚수학〛 an inequality —호 〚수학〛 a sign of inequality

부등가리 a fire shovel

부등깃 down ; fluff ; pinfeathers

부등변 不等邊 ¶ 부등변의 scalene ; unequal-sided ; unequilateral ; 〚식물〛 oblique
— 사각형 an irregular quadrilateral ; a trapezium 《pl. ~s, -zia》 《미》 ; a trapezoid 《영》 — 삼각형 a scalene (triangle) ; an inequilateral triangle

부등속 운동 不等速運動 〚물리〛 ununiform motion

†부디 by all means ; without fail ; at any cost ; at all costs ¶ 부디 그러신다면 if you will have it so // 부디 와 주십시오 Be sure to come. /Come by all means. // 참 좋은 생각입니다 부디 그렇게 해 주십시오 An excellent idea! Do so by all means. // 그는 부디 가겠다고 한다 He insists on going. // 부디 몸조심 하십시오 Take good care of yourself. // 부디 만찬에 와 주십시오 Oblige us with your company at dinner. // 나를 보아 부디 그렇게 해 주십시오 Please do so to oblige me.

부딪다 bump into ⇨ 부딪치다

부딪뜨리다 knock against ; dash against ¶ 몸을 문에 부딪뜨리다 dash〔throw〕 oneself against the door // 자동차를 전신주에 부딪뜨리다 crash a car into a telephone pole // 그는 머리를 기둥에 부딪뜨렸다 He knocked〔bumped〕 his head against the post.

†**부딪치다** collide with ; bump against 〔into〕 ¶ 기둥에 부딪치다 run〔bump〕 against a post // 머리를 전신주에 부딪치다 knock one's head against a post // 곤란에 부딪치다 meet with difficulty // 서로 부딪치다 bump against each other ; run into one another // 자동차가 서로 부딪쳤다 The cars collided with each other. // 배가 바위에 부딪쳤다 The boat collided against a rock. // 장님이 내게 부딪쳤다 The blind man bumped into me. // 한번 부딪쳐 보겠다 I'll try. /I'll have a try.

부딪히다 be bumped〔crashed〕 into ; be bumped〔run〕 against ¶ 배가 바위에 부딪히었다 A boat was dashed against a rock. // 나는 어린아이한테 부딪히었다 I was run into by a boy.

부뚜 a straw mat for winnowing

—질 winnowing (with a mat) ¶ 부뚜질하다 winnow (with a mat)

부뚜막 a cooking fireplace ; a kitchen range ; a cooking-range

부뚜막의 소금도 집어 넣어야 짜다 〔속담〕 Everything demands some work. /No pains, no gains.

부라리다 glare ; look with glaring eyes ¶ 화가 나서 눈을 부라리며 with an angry glare // 그는 말하면서 무섭게 눈을 부라렸다 He glared fiercely as he spoke. // 그들은 서로 눈을 부라리며 서 있었다 They stood glaring at each other.

부라질 moving a baby's legs back and forth like a blacksmith's bellows **—하다** move a baby's legs like a bellows

부라퀴 a tough guy ; a shrewd fellow

부락 部落 a village ; a village community **—민** people of the (village) community ; village folk **— 회의** a village block association (상설 기구) ; a village meeting (회합) **농촌 —** a farming settlement

부란 腐爛 decomposition (시체의) ; ulceration (종기의) **—하다** decompose ; ulcerate ¶ 부란 시체 a decomposed〔putrefied〕 body

부란 孵卵 incubation ; hatching **—하다** hatch ; incubate

—기 (器) an incubator ; an incubator house ; a hatcher **— 기간** incubation time

부랑 浮浪 vagrancy ; vagabondage **—하다** wander about ; roam ; lead a vagrant life

—배 roughnecks ; toughs ; hoodlums ; hooligans **—아** a juvenile vagrant ; a street Arab〔arab〕 ; a guttersnipe **—자** a vagabond ; a loafer ; a tramp ; a hobo 《미》 ; a vag 《속》 ; a goldbrick 《미·속》 **—죄** vagrancy

***부랴부랴** hurriedly ¶ 부랴부랴 차에 타다 hurry into a car // 부랴부랴 기차에 타다〔내리다〕 hurry on〔off〕 a train // …을 가지러 부랴부랴 되돌아오다 hurry back for // 일을 부랴부랴 해치우다 hurry through one's work // 부랴부랴 현장으로 달려가다 rush to the scene // 늦을세라 부랴부랴 달려갔다 I hurried along for fear I should be late.

부러 on purpose ; intentionally ; deliberately ; knowingly ¶ 부러 웃다 force a laugh // 부러 거짓말하다 lie deliberately // 부러 그런 것이 아닙니다 I didn't do it intentionally〔on purpose〕. // 부러 하시는 말씀이시지요 You don't mean that, do you?

부러뜨리다 break ; snap (딱 하고) ¶ 지팡이를 부러뜨리다 break a stick 《in two》 // 나뭇가지를 부러뜨리다 break off a branch of a tree // 왼팔을 부러뜨리다 break one's left arm ; suffer a broken left arm // 막대기를 딱하고 부러뜨리다 snap a stick ; break a stick with a snap // 무릎에 대고 부러뜨리다 break 《a stick》 across one's knee

***부러워하다** envy ; be envious of ¶ 남의 것을 부러워하다 covet 《a person's》 things // 그들은 그의 행운을 부러워한다 They envy him his good luck. // 사람들이 그를 부러워한다 He is an object of envy. // 대체로 빈자는 부자를 부러워한다 The poor generally envy the rich. // 그는 결코 남의 재산을 부러워하지 않는다 He is never envious of others for their wealth.

***부러지다** break ; be〔get〕 broken ; give way ; snap (딱 소리내며) ; fracture (뼈가) ¶ 잘 부러지지 않는 막대기 a tough stick // 둘로 부러지다 break in two // 내 팔이 부러졌다 I have one of my arms broken. // 내 몸무게로 나뭇가지가 부러졌다 The branch gave way under me. // 의자 다리가 하나 부러졌다 One of the legs of the chair is broken.

부럼 nuts eaten on the 15th of the first month of the lunar calendar (to guard oneself against boils for a year)

****부럽다** (be) enviable ¶ 부러운 듯 enviously ; with envy ; with envious eyes // 부럽지 않다 feel no envy 《at》 // 네가 부럽다 I envy you. // 네 행운이 부럽다 I envy you your good fortune. // 그는 부러운 눈으로 그것을 보고 있었다 He was looking at it with envious eyes.

부레 an air bladder ; an air cell

—뜸 treating a kite-string with isinglass **—찜** a dish of steamed air bladder stuffed with beef and seasoning **—풀** fish glue ; isinglass

부레끓다 get mad ; be enraged

부레질 pasting something with isinglass **—하다** paste with isinglass

부려먹다 keep 《a person》 trotting〔on the trot, hard at work〕 ; drive 《a person》 hard ; work 《a person》 hard〔like a horse〕 ; sweat 《one's employees》 ; have 《a person》 at one's beck and call ; keep

〔have, hold, put〕《a person's》 nose 〔face〕 to the grindstone
부력 浮力 〖물리〗 buoyancy ; floatage ; [비행선의] lifting power ; lift ¶ 부력의 중심 the center of buoyancy
—계 a buoyancy gauge
부력 富力 wealth ; resources
부령 部令 a departmental ordinance 〔order〕 ¶ 교육부령 an Education Ministry ordinance
부로 父老 a village-elder ; an aged person (in a village)
⁑**부록 附錄** a supplement ; an appendix ¶ 타임지의 부록 a supplement〔magazine〕 to Time // 부록을 붙이다 add an appendix 《to a book》
부루나가다 last〔keep〕 longer than expected
부루말 a white horse
부루퉁이 a thing which bulges out
*__부루퉁하다, 뿌루퉁하다__ (be) swollen ; bloated ; [불만스러워서] sullen ; sulky ¶ 부루퉁한 손 a swollen hand // 뿌루퉁한 얼굴 a sullen〔sulky〕 look // 수종으로 다리가 부루퉁하다 His legs are swollen with dropsy. // 뿌루퉁하니 말이 없었다 He kept a sullen silence. // 무슨 일로 부루퉁하고 있나 What are you sulking about ?
부룩 catchcropping ; intercropping
부룩 박다 관용 plant in the space between the rows of another crop ; intercrop
부룩소 a young bull
부룩송아지 an unbroken calf
부룻 the bulk of a heap ; the amount in a heap
부룻동 the stem〔stalk〕 of lettuce
부류 部類 [종류] a class ; a kind ; [항목] a head ; [범주] a category ¶ 부류로 나누다 classify 《into, as, with》 ; catalogue // 부류에 들다 come under the head 《of》 // 다른〔같은〕 부류에 속하다 belong in a different〔the same〕 classification
부류 浮流 —하다 float about ; drift
— 기뢰 a floating〔drifting〕 mine
부르걷다 roll〔turn, pull〕 up 《one's sleeves》 ¶ 팔을 부르걷고 with one's sleeves rolled up
†**부르다**[1] ① 《the stomach》 (be) full ; have eaten one's fill ¶ 배부르게 먹다 eat heartily ; have a hearty meal ; eat one's fill ; eat to one's heart's content // 이제 배가 부르다 I have had plenty 〔enough〕.
② [임신해서] (be) pregnant ¶ 그 여자는 배가 부르다 She is big with child. / She is expecting. /She is pregnant.
③ [독·통 따위] (be) bulgy ; swollen ¶ 통이 배가 부르다 The barrel bulges in the middle.
*__부르다__[2] ① call 《a person》 ; call out to 《a person》 ; hail ; [불러오다] summon ¶ 부르면 들리는 곳에 within call // 불러도 안 들리는 곳에 out of hailing distance // 뒤에서 부르다 call after 《a person》 // 불러내다 call 《a person》 out // 큰소리로 부르다 shout out to 《a person》 // 이름을 부르다 call 《a person》 by name // 지나가는 택시를 부르다 hail a passing taxi // 의사를 부르다 send for a doctor // 서울에서 전문가를 부르다 send to *Seoul* for a specialist // 초인종을 눌러서 하인을 부르다 ring for a servant // 전화로 간호원을 부르다 telephone for a nurse // 병상에 근친을 부르다 summon immediate relatives to one's bedside // 잔치에 사람을 부르다 invite 〔ask〕 《a person》 to a banquet // 기생을 부르다 engage〔call in〕 a *kisaeng* // 만세를 부르다 cry "Hurruh !" // 어머님이 부르신다 Your mother is calling〔wants〕 you. // 사장님이 부르십니다 You are wanted at the president's office. // 부장님에게 불려갔었다며 You were called in by the boss ?
② [일컫다] call ; name ; style ; brand (악명) ¶ 그 아기를 조지라고 부르다 call the baby George // 그 아이를 조부의 이름을 따서 존이라고 부르다 name the boy John after his grandfather // 역적이라 부르다 brand 《a person》 as a traitor // 그는 이 가스를 아르곤이라고 불렀다. He termed this gas argon.
③ [값을] bid ; offer ¶ 부르는 값 the price asked〔offered〕 ; a bid // 값을 싸게 부르다 bid〔name〕 a low price // 얼마를 불렀습니까 How much did you bid for it ?
④ [노래를] sing ¶ 노래를 부르다 sing a song // 피아노에 맞추어 노래부르다 sing to piano accompaniment
부르대다 rant and rave ; vociferate ; bawl
부르르 ① [떠는 모양] trembling ; shivering ¶ 부르르 떨리는 손으로 with trembling hand // 부르르 떨다 tremble 《with fear》 ; shiver 《with cold》 ② [끓는 모양] seething ; boiling ¶ 물이 부르르 끓기 시작한다 The water comes to a bubbling boil. ③ [타오르는 모양] in a sudden burst of flame
부르릉 with a cough 《from a combustion engine》 **—하다, 거리다** splutter
부르심 a summons 《*pl.* -monses》 ¶ 신의 부르심 God's calling ; a divine summons 〔call〕 ; a vocation // 부르심을 받다 be summoned
부르주아 [개인] a bourgeois 《*pl.* ~》 ; [계급] the bourgeoisie ; the moneyed 〔propertied〕 class(es)
— 계급 the bourgeoisie **— 문학〔생활〕** bourgeois literature〔life〕 **— 취미** bourgeois taste
*__부르쥐다__ clench ¶ 주먹을 부르쥐고 with one's clenched〔closed〕 fist // 주먹을 부르쥐다 clench one's fist
†**부르짖다** shout ; cry ; utter〔give〕 a cry ; [감탄해서] exclaim ¶ 큰소리로 부르짖다 cry〔call〕 out // 성나서 부르짖다 shout 〔roar〕 with rage // 괴로워서 부르짖다 yell

with pain // 사람 살리라고 부르짖다 cry〔call out, scream〕 for help // 도둑이야 하고 부르짖다 cry "Thief !" // 불이야 하고 부르짖다 shout "Fire !" // 개혁을 부르짖다 cry (loudly) for a reform // 임금 인상을 부르짖다 clamor for a raise of pay // 산아 제한을 부르짖다 advocate birth control // 남북 통일을 부르짖다 cry out for the unification of Korea

부르짖음 [외침] a shout ; a cry ; an outcry ; an exclamation ; a yell ; a clamor ; [비명] a shriek ; a scream ; [노호] a roar ; a howl ¶ 개혁의 부르짖음 a cry〔clamor〕 for reform // 공창 반대의 부르짖음 a cry against licensed prostitution // 임금 인상의 부르짖음 a cry〔clamor〕 for a raise in pay // 민족의 부르짖음 the voice of the race

부르터나다 be discovered〔disclosed, detected〕 ; leak out

부르트다 blister ; rise in blister ¶ 데어서 부르트다 blister from a burn // 손이 부르텄다 My hand is blistered. // 발바닥이 부르텄다 I have got a soft corn on the sole of my foot. // 벌레에 물린 자리가 부르텄다 The sting of an insect has swollen up. // 새 구두를 신어서 발뒤축이 부르텄다 My new shoes have made blisters on my heels.

부름 a summons ; a call

부릅뜨다 glare fiercely ; make 《one's eyes》 glare ¶ 눈을 부릅뜨고 with glaring eyes // 눈을 부릅뜨고 보다 glare at 〔upon〕 《a person》 // 그는 호랑이처럼 나한테 눈을 부릅뜨고 서 있었다 He stood glaring at me like a tiger.

‡**부리**[1] ① [새의] a bill ; a beak ② [물건의] a pointed end〔head〕 ; a tip
발— the tips of the toes 총— muzzle (of a gun)

부리[2] 〖민속〗 a tutelary spirit ¶ 부리 세다 [한 집안이] be under strong influence from the guardian spirit

부리나케 in a great hurry ; in hot haste ; with all haste ; hurriedly ¶ 부리나케 일을 하다 rush one's work // 부리나케 식사를 하다 hurry over one's meal // 부리나케 계단을 올라〔내려〕가다 rush up〔down〕 the stairs // 부리나케 도망가다 flee in all haste // 부리나케 현장으로 달려가다 rush〔hurry〕to the spot〔scene〕

†**부리다**[1] ① [사람·말을] manage ; handle ; use ; keep ; employ ¶ 많은 사람을 부리다 employ many people // 하인을 부리다 keep a servant ; work a servant // 사람을 되게 부리다 overwork 《a person》 // 말을 부릴 줄 알다 know how to manage a horse // 사람을 잘 부리다 be clever in handing〔using〕 one's men // 그 부인은 남편을 잘 부린다 The wife manages her husband artfully. // 우리 과장은 사람 부리는 것이 거칠다 The boss of ours is a real slave driver.
② [기계·기구를] work 《a machine》 ; operate ¶ 기계를 부리다 operate a machine // 자동차를 부리다 drive a car
③ [재주·꾀를] play 《a trick》 ; start 《trouble》 ¶ 말썽을 부리다 start trouble ; start a quarrel 《with》 // 수단을 부리다 play a trick ; think up a ruse // 재주를 부리다 exercise one's talent ; perform a trick

***부리다**[2] unload ; discharge ¶ 배에서 짐을 부리다 unload〔discharge〕 cargoes from ships ; discharge a ship of her cargo

부리망 —網 a cow muzzle made of straw

부리부리하다 (be) big and bright ¶ 부리부리한 눈 big bright eyes

부리이다 get worked〔used〕 by someone else ; [고용되다] be employed 《in a bank》 ; be taken into 《a person's》 service

부리잡히다 《a tumor〔boil, swell〕》 come 〔draw, gather〕 to a head

부림꾼 a servant ; an employe(e)

부마 駙馬 a son-in-law of the king

부명 父命 one's father's order

***부모 父母** father and mother ; parents ¶ 부모의 사랑 parental love〔affection〕

부목 副木 〖의학〗 a splint ¶ 부목을 대다 splint ; apply splints 《to》

부묘 浮錨 a floating〔drift, drag〕 anchor

†**부문 部門** a section ; a department ; [분류] a class ; a group ; a category ¶ 세 부문으로 나누다 classify 《things》 into three sections // A부문에 넣다 classify 《things》 under A // A부문에 들다 come under A

부민 富民 wealthy〔rich〕 people ; the rich

부민 浮民 vagabonds ; tramps ; gypsies ; nomadic race

부박 浮薄 fickleness ; frivolity ; insincerity ; levity **—하다** (be) frivolous ; fickle ; insincere ; shallow ; flippant

부반장 副班長 a vice-president 《of a class》

부보 訃報 ⇨ 부고(訃告)

부보 附保 〖보험〗 covering (of) insurance ; insuring ⇨ 보험 **—하다** insure 《oneself》 ; assure 《one's life》 《영》 ; insure 《a goods, a house》 ¶ 위험〔손해〕에 (대하여) 부보하다 insure 《a thing》 against risk〔loss〕

부복 俯伏 prostration **—하다** lie prostrate 《before》 ; prostrate oneself 《before》 ; fall prostrate〔flat〕 《upon the ground》

***부본 副本** [복사] copy ; a duplicate ; a counterpart ; a reserve (여벌) ¶ 부본을 만들다 make〔take〕 a copy 《of》

†**부부 夫婦** man〔husband〕 and wife ; a married couple ¶ 젊은 부부 a young couple // 부부의 인연 the conjugal ties 〔knot〕 // 부부가 되다 be married ; become man and wife // 부부 사이가 좋다 He is happy with her.

— 관계〔사이〕 conjugal relations — 생활 married life ; wedlock ; cohabitation ¶ 부부 생활을 하다 live a married life ; live together ; share bed and board 《together》 — 싸움 a quarrel〔squabble〕 between husband and wife ; a husband-and-wife fight ; a family quarrel〔jar〕 ; a domestic scene ¶ 부부 싸움하다 quarrel with one's husband〔wife〕 ; make〔create〕 domestic scenes 맞벌이 — a couple working together for a living ; joint bread-winning 신혼 — a newly married couple ; the newlyweds 《미》

†**부분 部分** a part ; a portion ; a section ; a piece ; a fragment

> 참고 **a part**는 part와 거의 같은 의미로 사용되고 **section**은 잘라낸 부분 그리고 **portion**은 몫으로 맡겨진 부분 **piece**는 분리된 일부 **fragment**는 파편 단편 따위 불완전한 일부이다.

¶ 부분적으로 partially ; in part // 대부분 a large part ; the greater part 《of》 ; the majority

— 부정 〖문법〗 partial negation — 사회 a subgroup of society — 색맹 partial color blindness —식(蝕) a partial eclipse 《of the sun, of the moon》 —품 parts ; accessories

부빙 浮氷 floating ice

부사 副使 a vice envoy ; a deputy delegate

‡**부사 副詞** 〖문법〗 an adverb

—구〔절〕 an adverbial phrase〔clause〕

부사령관 副司令官 a deputy commander (in chief) 《*pl.* deputy commanders in chief》

부사리 a goring bull

부사장 副社長 a vice-president

***부산물 副産物** a by-product ; a residual 〔an accessory〕 product

부산하다 [바쁘다] (be) busy ; bustling ; [시끄럽다] noisy ; boisterous ; clamorous ; uproarious ¶ 부산히 busily ; noisily ; boisterously // 일로 부산하다 be busy with one's work // 할일없이 부산하다 be busy with nothing to mention in particular

부삽하다 浮澁— (be) crumbly

부상 父喪 the death of one's father ; mourning for one's father

‡**부상 負傷** a wound ; an injury ; a cut (벤 상처) —하다 be wounded ; get injured ; get hurt ¶ 왼쪽 팔에 부상하다 be wounded in the left arm ; have one's left arm wounded

—자〔병〕 a wounded〔an injured〕 person〔soldier〕 ; [총칭] the wounded 〔injured〕 ; casualties

부상 浮上 —하다 rise (to the surface) ; surface (잠수함이)

부상 副賞 an extra prize

부상 富商 a rich merchant

부생 浮生 transient〔ephemeral〕 life ; mutable life ; this fleeting life

부서 部署 one's post (of duty) ; one's place ¶ 부서로 가다 go to one's post ; take one's position〔place〕 // 부서를 지키다 keep〔remain at〕 one's post

부서 副署 countersignature —하다 countersign ; endorse ¶ 각 장관이 부서한 countersigned by the ministers

부서뜨리다 ⇨ 부스러뜨리다

†**부서지다** break ; be broken〔smashed〕 ; fall to pieces ; be wrecked ; [파손] break down ; get out of order ¶ 부서지기 쉽다 be easy to break ; be fragile〔frail〕 // 부서지지 않도록 하다 prevent〔protect〕 《a thing》 from breaking // 질그릇은 부서지기 쉽다 Crockery breaks easily. // 꽃병이 산산이 부서졌다 The vase has broken into pieces. // 두 차가 정면 충돌해서 모두 크게 부서졌어 Two cars collided head-on, totalling each other.

부선 艀船 a sampan ; a lighter ; a barge

—료(料) the sampan fare ; lighterage

부선거 浮船渠 a floating dock

— 사용료 the charge for transportation via floating dock

부설 附設 attachment ; annexation —하다 attach ; annex

— 도서관 an annex library ; a library attached 《to》

부설 浮說 a wild rumor ; a groundless report

부설 敷設 laying ; construction —하다 lay ; build ; construct ¶ 철도를 부설하다 build〔construct〕 a railway // 해저 전선을 부설하다 lay a submarine cable

—권 a right of construction — 기뢰 a submarine mine 기뢰 —함 a mine layer 철도 —권 a railway concession

부성분 副成分 an accessory ingredient

부성애 父性愛 father's〔paternal〕 love

부세 浮世 the (transient, transitory) world ; transient〔fleeting〕 life

부세 賦稅 taxation ; imposition of taxes —하다 tax ; impose a tax ; levy duties 《on》

‡**부속 附屬** attachment ; affiliation ; addendum —하다 be attached 《to》 ; belong 《to》 ¶ 서울 대학교 부속 병원 the Seoul University Hospital

— 건물 annex ; an accessory〔attached〕 building — 국민 학교 an attached elementary〔primary〕 school ; an elementary〔a primary〕 school affiliated to 《a university》 —물 adjuncts ; appendages ; belongings — 병원 a hospital in affiliation — 서류 annex ; annexed paper〔document〕 — 중〔고등〕학교 a middle〔senior high〕 school affiliated to 《a university》 —품 accessories ; fittings ; paraphernalia ; accoutrements ¶ 저는 자동차 부속품 장사를 하고 있습니다 I'm in the auto

parts business.
부속 部屬 being attached〔annexed〕 to a body〔department〕; a section ; a division
부속 기관 附屬器官 〖생물〗 an appendage ; 〖해부〗 an accessory organ
부손 a small fire shovel
부송 付送 sending ; forwarding ―하다 send ; forward
*부수 附隨 accompanying ―하다 accompany ; be annexed 《to》; be incidental 《to》 ¶ 부수적 accompanying ; incidental ; attendant // 부수적 비용 incidental expenses
―물 a concomitant ; an incident (권리·의무 따위) ; 〖해부〗 a collateral ― 사건 a dependent event ; incidents ― 사실 a collateral fact ― 서류 appended papers 〔documents〕; annexes ― 음악 incidental music ― 현상 a concomitant phenomenon
부수 負數 〖수학〗 a negative number ; a minus (quantity)
⁑부수 部數 the number of copies ; the circulation ; the edition ¶ 부수에 제한이 있다 The number of copies is limited. // 초판의 발행 부수는 3,000부였다 The first edition consisted of 3,000 copies.
발행 ― a circulation
⁑부수다 break ; smash ; destroy ; demolish ¶ 산산이 부수다 break to bits ; smash up // 접시를 부수다 break a dish // 집을 부수다 tear down〔demolish〕 a house // 자물쇠를 부수고 열다 force open a lock〔gate〕 // 도둑이 창을 부수고 들어갔다 The robber broke in through the window.
부수뜨리다 ⇨ 부스러뜨리다
부수상 副首相 a deputy prime minister ; a vice-premier
부수수 in disorder ; disheveled ; untidy ―하다 (be) disheveled ; disorderly ; untidy ; ill-kept
부수 식물 浮水植物 duckweeds ; floating weeds
부수입 副收入 an additional〔a side〕 income ; the income from a side job
부숭부숭하다 [마르다] (be) dry ; parched ; be dried up〔out〕; [곱다] fair ; refined ; clean
부스대다 fidget ; be never still ¶ 부스대는 아이 a restless child // 그는 항시 부스댄다 He is always in a fidget.
부스러기 small fragments ; scraps ; odds and ends ¶ 깎아낸 부스러기 shavings // 연필 깎은 부스러기 pencil shavings
고기 ― scraps of meat 금속 ― scrap 〔junk〕 metal 나무 ― chips of wood ; shavings (대팻밥) 빵 ― bread crumbs 종이 ― wastepaper
⁑부스러뜨리다 smash ; shatter into splinters ; break (down) ; destroy ; demolish ; crush ¶ 산산이 부스러뜨리다 break 《a thing》 to pieces ; smash 《a thing》 to bits // 그는 꽃병을 부스러뜨렸다 He smashed the flower vase to pieces.
부스러지다 break ; crumble ; fall〔come〕 to pieces ; collapse ; be destroyed ¶ 빵이 부스러지다 bread crumbles // 흙이 부스러지다 the earth breaks loose // 부스러지기 쉽다 be easy to break ; be fragile
부스럭거리다 rustle ; make a rustle 〔rustling sound〕 ¶ 낙엽이 바람에 부스럭거린다 The fallen leaves are rustling in the wind. // 거기서 무엇이 부스럭거리느냐 What is that rustling over there?
부스럼 a boil ; an ulcer ; an abscess ; a tumor ¶ 얼굴에 부스럼이 났다 I have got a boil on my face.
부스스 lightly ; gently ¶ 부스스 일어나다 《a person》 gently rise // 머리털이 부스스하다 one's hair is ruffled // 머리털이 부스스 일어서다 one's hair is lightly ruffled (by the wind)
부슬부슬[1] gently ; softly ¶ 부슬부슬 내리는 비 drizzling〔softly falling〕 rain // 비가 부슬부슬 내리고 있다 It drizzles. /The rain is drizzling down. /A gentle rain is falling. // 눈이 부슬부슬 내린다 It snows gently. /A light powdery snow falls.
부슬부슬[2] ⇨ 바슬바슬
부슬비 ⇨ 보슬비
부시 a metal striking piece used with flint to make fire ¶ 부시를 치다 make sparks with metal on flint ; get a light from a flint
―쌈지 a pouch for a flint fire-making set ―통 a tinderbox 부싯깃 tinder 부싯돌 a flint
부시다[1] (be) dazzling ; glaring ; blinding ¶ 눈이 부시도록 아름다운 여자 a lady of dazzling beauty ; a radiant beauty // 눈부신 헤드라이트 glaring headlights // 눈부시게 비추다 dazzle ; glare ; blind // 태양이 눈부시다 The sun is very dazzling. // 조명이 눈부시다 The light dazzles me. // 눈이 부셔서 뜰 수가 없다 My eyes are so dazzled that I cannot open them. // 광선이 세서 눈이 부셨다 The strong light dazzled my eyes.
부시다[2] [씻다] wash 《dishes》; rinse ; cleanse ; clean out
부시장 副市長 a deputy mayor
제 1〔제 2〕 ― a senior〔junior〕 deputy mayor
부시치다 strike fire ; strike a flint
부식 扶植 spread ; extension ; establishment (확립) ―하다 spread ; extend ; establish ; plant ; increase ¶ 자기의 세력을 부식하다 establish one's influence
부식 腐植 humus
― 산(酸) humic acid ― 토 humus soil ; mold
⁑부식 腐蝕 corrosion ; erosion ―하다 corrode ; rot ; erode (산에 의해) ; rust (녹슬다)
― 발염(拔染) 〖염색〗 an etching discharge ― 방지제 an anticorrosive

agent ; a corrosion inhibitor —성〔력〕 corrosiveness ; causticity — 시험 a corrosion〔an etch〕 test — 암석 saprolite — 작용 corrosive〔erosive〕 action ; corrosion ; erosion —제 (劑) a corrosive (agent) ; a corroder ; a caustic ; an eater ; 〖기계〗 an etching reagent ; 〖의학〗 a cauterant

부식물 副食物 a side dish ; food to eat with rice ; a subsidiary food

부신 副腎 〖해부〗 adrenal ; suprarenal (body)

부신경 副神經 accessory nerves

부신 피질 副腎皮質 〖해부〗 the adrenal cortex ¶ 부신 피질의 adrenocortical
— 호르몬 adrenocortical hormones

부실 副室 a concubine ⇨ 소실

부실 不實 —하다 ① [불성실] (be) unreliable ; insincere ; faithless ¶ 부실한 친구 a false friend // 부실한 아내 an undeserving wife // 부실한 남자 a faithless man〔lover〕 // 부실한 짓을 하다 act falsely ; break faith with 《a person》 ; do the dirty on 《a person》 // 그는 일을 부실하게 한다 He is not a conscientious worker. // 기업의 부실화를 막다 defend enterprises against insolvency ; protect enterprises from insolvency
② [내용이] (be) incomplete ; unsatisfactory ; poor ; short ¶ 결과가 부실한 회의 a conference poor in results ; an unfruitful conference // 연구가 부실하다 There is something yet to learn. // 조사가 부실하다 The investigation is not thoroughgoing enough. // 공급이 부실하다 The supply is restricted. // 고기 한 근이 부실하다 It is not a full pound of meat.
③ [몸이] (be) weak ; feeble ; delicate ¶ 몸이 부실하다 be weak ; be in delicate health // 그는 원래 몸이 부실하다 He is naturally delicate.
— 경영〔운영〕 insolvent operation — 공사 fraudulent work — 기업 an insolvent enterprise ; an improperly-run enterprise — 기장〔기재〕 false〔fake〕 entries

부심 副審 a subreferee

부심 腐心 —하다 take pains ; labor —하다 take pains ; be at pains 《to》 ; tax one's ingenuity ; rack one's brains ; be bent on

부싯깃고사리 〖식물〗 a lip fern

부썩 [갑자기] rapidly ; [우기는 모양] stubbornly ; obstinately ¶ 부썩 자라다 grow rapidly // 틀린 것을 맞다고 부썩 우긴다 He stands firm on his error.

부아 [폐] lungs ; [분개] exasperation ; anger ; rage ¶ 부아가 나다 be exasperated ; feel offended ; feel sore 《at》 // 부아통이 터지다 fly into a passion ; explode with anger ; get mad // 나는 그의 말에 부아가 났다 I was exasperated at his words. /His (imprudent) words stung 〔cut〕 me to the quick. // 부앗김에 in a fit of temper〔anger〕 ; borne away by anger

부앙 俯仰 —하다 look up and down ¶ 부앙하여 천지에 부끄러움이 없다 My conscience is quite clear. /God knows I am innocent.

부액 扶腋 —하다 support 《a person》 by the underarm ; help ; assist

†**부양 扶養** support ; maintenance —하다 support ; maintain ; sustain ¶ 양친을 부양할 의무가 있다 We are under obligations to support our parents.
— 가족 a dependent family — (가족) 공제 credit〔allowance, (tax) exemption〕 for dependents — (가족) 수당 a dependency allowance — 의무 the duty of supporting 《a person》 —자 a supporter ; a sustainer — 책임자 a person responsible for supporting 《the family》 ; a breadwinner

부양 浮揚 floating (up) ; floatage ; floatation ; refloating —하다 float ; be floated ; be buoyant ; be refloated (침몰선이) ¶ 기구를 부양하다 float a balloon
—기(器) a pontoon (침몰선 인양의) ; a raiser (잡은 고래를 인양하는) —력 buoyancy ; floatage —성 floatability — 작업 salvage operations

†**부언 附言** an additional remark ; a postscript —하다 add 《that》 ; add a remark ; remark parenthetically

부언유설 浮言流說 a wild rumor ; a groundless report

부얼부얼 —하다 [복스럽다] (be) plump ; chubby ; [털이] plump and hairy

⁑**부업 副業** a sideline ; a side job〔business〕 ; an avocation ; a subsidiary business〔occupation, work〕 ¶ 유리한 부업 a profitable〔remunerative〕 sideline // 부업으로 하다 do 《a thing》 on the side // 부업으로 보험판매도 합니다 I also sell insurance on the side. // 돈을 좀더 벌려고 부업으로 학원강의도 합니다 I also moonlight as an institute instructor to make some extra money. // 부업을 시작했다는 게 사실이냐 Is it true you're started moonlrghting ?

부엉부엉 (with a) hoot-hoot !

⁑**부엉이** 〖새〗 an owl ; a hoot owl ; a Chinese scops owl ; Otus scops stictonotus (학명) ¶ 부엉이가 운다 The owl hoots. // 부엉이 소리도 제가 듣기에는 좋다 We are apt to be blind to our own defects 〔faults〕.
—셈 a foolish〔stupid, silly〕 calculation

†**부엌** a kitchen ; a cuisine (호텔 따위의) ; a kitchenette (아파트의)
—데기 a kitchen〔scullery〕 maid —문 a kitchen door — 바닥 the kitchen floor — 설비 a kitchen unit 《영》 — 세간 kitchen utensils〔appliances〕 ; kitchenware — 심부름 scullery work —일 kitchen work ¶ 부엌일을 하다 do scullery work —칼 a kitchen knife

⁑**부여 附與** grant ; allowance ; bestowal

—하다 give ; grant ; vest ; invest 《a person》 with ¶ 칭호를 부여하다 invest 《a person》 with a title // 학위를 부여하다 confer a degree on 《a person》 // 그에게 이 권한을 부여한다 We vest this authority in him.

부여 賦與 endowment —하다 endow 《a person》 with ; bless 《a person》 with ¶ 우리들에게는 양심이 부여되어 있다 We are all endowed〔gifted〕 with a conscience.

*부여잡다 grab hard (with a twist)

부역 附逆 complicity〔taking part〕 in treason —하다 join〔take the side of〕 the enemy〔rebel army〕 ; take sides〔a side〕 with the enemy〔rebels〕 ; betray one's country to the enemy

—자 a traitor ; a betrayer ¶ 부역자가 되다 turn traitor to one's country — 행위 treachery ; treacherous〔treasonous, rebellious〕 act〔activities〕

부역 賦役, 夫役 compulsory〔statute〕 labor ; compulsory service ; slave labor ; a corvée 《프》 ¶ 부역을 과하다 put 《a person》 to slave labor ; exact statute labor from 《people》

부역 負役 statute labor ; drafted labor ; corvée 《프》

부연 附椽 〖건축〗 tilted eaves attached to the edges of rafters

부연 敷衍 amplification ; expatiation ; dilatation ; an elaborate comment —하다 expatiate〔dwell, elaborate〕 on ; expand ; develop ¶ 이 점은 더 이상 부연할 필요가 없다 We need not enlarge further upon this point.

부엽토 腐葉土 leaf mold

부영사 副領事 a vice-consul

부영이 [빛] a milky-white〔frosty, pearly〕 colo(u)r ; [짐승] a milky-white〔pearly〕 one

부옇다, 뿌옇다 (be) frosty ; misty ; hazy ; milky-white ¶ 살결이 부옇다 have a pearly skin // 안개가 부옇다 the fog is heavy // 안개 속에 송도가 부옇게 보였다 We could see the isle of *Songdo* dimly through the haze. // 먼지로 하늘이 부옇다 The sky is hazy with dust.

부예지다 get misty〔hazy〕 ; thicken ; blur ¶ 나는 지독한 근시이므로 안경을 벗으면 모든 것이 부예진다 As I am very nearsighted, everything becomes blurred when I take off my glasses.

부외 部外 outside 《a government service》 ¶ 부외로부터의 원조 aids from outside (the government service)

—자 an outsider ; people outside 《the government service》

부외 채무 簿外債務 off-the-book loans

부용 芙蓉 [연꽃] a lotus ; [목부용] a kind of rose mallow

부운 浮雲 a floating〔drifting〕 cloud

부원 部員 a member of the staff ; a staff member ; a staffman

편집— (a man on) the editorial staff

부원 富源 natural resources ; sources of wealth ¶ 무진장의 부원 an inexhaustible mine of wealth // 부원을 개발하다 exploit 〔develop〕 natural resources

부월 斧鉞 [도끼] battle-axes and halberds ; [정벌] conquest ; subjugation ; [중형] severe punishment ¶ 부월을 가하다 inflict〔impose〕 a punishment 《on》 ; punish (severely)

부위 部位 a region ; a part

심장 — the region of the heart

†**부유 富裕** wealth ; plenty ; affluence ; opulence ; prosperity —하다 (be) wealthy ; be well provided for ; have plenty ¶ 부유한 사람 a well-off person ; a person of easy means // 부유하게 살다 live〔be〕 in easy circumstances ; be well-off ; live in affluence // 부유하게 태어나다 be born rich ; be born of a rich family // 그 여자는 아주 부유하게 보였다 She had an air of great prosperity. // 이들 부유한 사람들에게는 높은 가격이 높은 품질을 의미한다 To these well-to-do people, higher prices mean better quality.

—층 the wealthy〔propertied〕 classes ; the rich ; the well-to-do ; the high-income bracket

***부유 浮遊** floating ; wafting —하다 float ; waft ; drift ¶ 공중에 부유하다 float in the air

— 기뢰 a floating mine —물 floating matters — 생물 a plankton — 식물 floating plants

부유 ⇨ 하루살이

부유 腐儒 a pedant ; a doctrinaire ; a vain〔musty〕 scholar

부유스름하다, 뿌유스름하다 (be) somewhat pearly〔milky, frosty, misty〕

부육 腐肉 tainted meat ; rotten〔putrid, putrefying〕 flesh ; carrion (동물 시체의) ¶ 부육을 먹는 동물 a scavenger // 부육을 먹는 새 a carrion bird

부음 訃音 a report of 《a person's》 death ; an announcement of death ; an obituary notice ¶ 부음에 접하다 hear〔be informed〕 of 《a person's》 death

부응하다 副應 meet ; conform to ; satisfy ; suit ¶ 목적에 부응하다 answer the purpose // …의 희망에 부응하다 meet 〔satisfy, gratify, carry out〕 a person's wishes // 기대에 부응토록 노력하겠습니다 I will do my best to act up to your expectation.

부의 賻儀 goods or gifts to aid in funeral —하다 give 《money, a gift》 toward funeral expenses

—금 donation for funeral expenses

부의 附議 submission for consideration ; presentation for discussion —하다 present〔submit〕 for consideration 〔discussion〕 ; refer 《a bill》 to 《a committee》

부의장 副議長 a vice-president ; a vice-

chairman ; a deputy speaker
부익 副翼 a (wing) flap
부익부 빈익빈 富益富貧益貧 The rich get richer and the poor get poorer.
*부인 夫人 Mrs. ; Madam ; wife ; lady ¶ 김씨 부인 Mrs. *Kim* // 부인께서 안녕하십니까 How is your wife ?
†부인 婦人 a woman ; a lady ; [총칭] the fair〔weaker, tender〕 sex ; womankind ; women ¶ 부인다운 womanly ; ladylike // 부인에게 자리를 양보하다 give up one's seat to a lady
—과 gynecology —과 의사 a gynecologist —병 women's diseases —복 a woman's dress —석 seats for ladies 중년 — a middle-aged〔an elderly, a matronly〕 woman ; a matron
†부인 否認 [부정] denial ; disapproval ; [거부] veto —하다 deny ; repudiate ; disclaim ; disapprove ; veto ; say no 《to》 ¶ 부인할 수 없다 be undeniable // 법안을 부인하다 veto a bill // 사실을 부인하다 deny a fact
—권 the veto power —자 a denier
부인회 婦人會 a women's society〔association〕
애국 — the Ladies Patriotic Society
부임 赴任 proceeding to one's new post —하다 leave〔start〕 for one's new post ¶ 새로 부임해 온 교장 a newly appointed principal〔superintendent〕
—지 one's new post
부자 夫子 a sage ; a master
공(孔)— Confucius ; Master *Kong* 촌(村)— a village〔country〕 scholar
부자 父子 father and son
부자 富者 a rich〔wealthy〕 man ; a man of wealth ; [부호] a millionaire ; a billionaire ¶ 부자가 되다 get〔become, grow〕 rich ; make a fortune
부자가 하나면 세 동네가 망한다 [속담] The dainties of the great are the tears of the poor. /The pleasures of the mighty are the tears of the poor.
부자상전 父子相傳 transmission from father to son
‡부자연 不自然 unnaturalness ; artificiality —하다 (be) unnatural ; artificial (인위적) ; strained ; affected ¶ 부자연스러운 웃음 a forced smile
부자유 不自由 inconvenience ; discomfort ; lack of freedom ; restriction —하다 be restricted〔limited〕 ; be not free ; (be) inconvenient ; uncomfortable ¶ 몸이 부자유한 사람들 disabled men // 부자유를 참다 put up with inconveniences〔discomforts〕 ; rough it // 오른손이 부자유스럽게 되다 lose the use of the right hand // 자신의 부자유를 참고 친구를 돕다 He puts himself to personal inconveniences to help a friend.
부자유친 父子有親 There should be affection between father and son.
부자재 副資材 subsidiary materials
부자지 the testicles and the penis ; male genitals〔genitalia〕
부작용 副作用 reaction ; a side effect ; an ill effect ¶ 부작용이 없는 harmless // 부작용을 일으키다 give rise to〔produce〕 ill effects ; cause harmful effects // 위에 부작용을 일으키지 않는다 do not act〔have no ill effect〕 on the stomach
부작위 不作爲 〖법〗 forbearance ; omission ; nonperformance
부잔교 浮棧橋 floating stage〔pier〕
부잣집 富者— a wealthy family ; a rich man's house ¶ 부잣집에 태어나다 be born rich ; be born with a silver spoon in one's mouth // 부잣집에 장가들다 marry a rich heiress
— 딸 a daughter of a rich man ; a bourgeois girl
부장 部長 the head〔chief, director〕 of a department ; a department manager
— 검사 a superintendent public prosecutor 경리 — the chief of the accountants' section〔department〕 인사 — the chief of the personnel department
부장 副長 〖해군〗 an executive (officer)
부장 副將 〖경기〗 subcaptain ; 〖군사〗 adjutant general ; the second in command of an army
부장품 副葬品 articles buried in a tomb ; burial accessories ; grave goods
†부재 不在 absence —하다 (be) absent ; be out ; be away from home ¶ 나의 부재중에 during〔in〕 my absence ; while I was away // 부재중이다 be absent 《from》 ; be away 《from home》 // 부재 증명이 되다 prove〔have〕 an alibi // A는 부재중이다 Mr. A is not at home〔not in, out〕.
—자 an absentee — 지주 an absentee landlord〔landowner〕 —(자) 투표 voting by mail ; [선원들의] absentee voting — 투표자 an absentee voter
부재 경영 不在經營 absentee management
부재 증명 不在證明 an alibi ¶ 부재 증명이 있다 have an alibi // 부재 증명을 내다 establish〔prove〕 an alibi
부저당 副抵當 collateral security
부적 符籍 a charm 《against ill luck》 ; a talisman 《against evil》 ; an amulet 《against calamity》
부적격 不適格 ¶ 부적격의 disqualified 《for the post》 // 부격적이 되다 be disqualified // 그는 그 일을 하기에는 부적격한 것 같다 He doesn't appear to be very capable of doing the work.
—자 a person disqualified〔unacceptable for〕 a position
‡부적당 不適當 unfitness ; unsuitableness ; inappropriateness —하다 (be) unfit 《for》 ; unsuited 《to》 ; inappropriate 《to》 ; inapt (성질상) ¶ 이번 자리는 저 사

람에게는 부적당하다 His new office is out of keeping with his character. // 그 일은 저 사람에게는 부적당하다 He is not the right man to undertake the task.

부적임 不適任 inadequacy ; unsuitableness ; unfitness ¶ 부적임의 inadequate ; unsuitable ; unfit ; unqualified
—자 an unqualified person ¶ 나는 이 지위에는 부적임자다 I am unfit for this post.

부적절 不適切 inappropriateness ; unsuitableness ; inadequacy **—하다** (be) inappropriate ; unsuitable ; inadequate ¶ 표현의 부적절 the infelicity of expressions

부적합 不適合 incongruity **—하다** (be) incongruent ; incongruous

부전 a colo(u)rful embroidered ribbon stuck on the front of a girl's dress

부전 附箋 a slip ; a tag ; a label ¶ 부전을 붙이다 tag ; label // 부전지를 붙여서 내다 forward 《a letter》 with an address tag attached ; readdress〔redirect〕《a letter》 // 그 편지는 부전이 붙어서 돌아왔다 The letter was mailed back with a tag explaining its nondelivery.

부전 不全 〖의학〗 imperfection ; incompletion ¶ 부전의 imperfect ; incomplete ; partial (부분적인)
발육 — underdevelopment ; undergrowth

부전 不戰 renunciation of war ; no war

부전나비 〖곤충〗 a hairstreak ; a gossamer-wing ; a lycaenid

부전승 不戰勝 an unearned win ¶ 부전승이 되다 get a win without playing〔fighting〕; [추첨으로] draw a bye

부전자전 父傳子傳 transmission from father to son **—하다** hand down from father to son ¶ 부전자전의 handed down from father to son // 그것은 부전자전해온 비법이다 The mysteries of the art have been handed from my ancestors.
부전자전 〔속담〕 Like father, like son.

부전 조약 不戰條約 《conclude》 an anti-war pact〔treaty〕; a peace〔no-war〕 pact ; a pact〔treaty〕 for the renunciation 〔outlawry〕 of war

부절 不絶 —하다 (be) incessant ; ceaseless ; continuous ¶ 부절히 all the time ; without interruption ; incessantly ; ceaselessly ; continuously

부절따말 a red〔sorrel〕 horse with a black mane

부절제 不節制 intemperance ; excess ; immoderation **—하다** (be) immoderate ; intemperate ; commit excesses ¶ 부절제한 생활을 하다 lead an intemperate life // 부절제로 인해 건강을 해치다 injure〔ruin〕 one's health by intemperance

부점 附點 having a dot ; dotted
— 음표 a dotted note **— 2분〔4분, 8분〕 음표** a dotted half〔quarter, eights〕 note
복— 음표 a double dotted note

부접 못 하다 ① be denied access to 《a person》; be kept from approaching ¶ 아들이 집에 부접 못 한다 The son cannot go to his family. // 어떤 방문객도 그에게는 부접 못 한다 He is always inaccessible to any visitor.
② cannot stand〔endure〕 ¶ 시어머니 구박에 며느리가 부접 못 했다 Harsh treatment by her mother-in-law was more than she could bear.

부접합 不接合 〖식물〗 asynapsis 《*pl.* -ses》

부젓가락 fire tongs

부정 不淨 ① uncleanliness ; dirtiness ; filthiness ; impurity ② an unclean event (that takes place in the family during the time of purification) ③ [첫거리] the first stage (of a shaman rite) **—하다** (be) unclean ; dirty ; filthy ; impure ; defiled ; have an unclean event take place in the family during the time of purification ¶ 부정한 재물 ill-gotten wealth ; filthy lucre // 부정치다 perform the first stage of a shaman rite ; perform shamanistic exorcisms // 부정보다 witness an unclean event during purification // 부정타다 be subject to〔suffer from〕 the evil resulting from breaking the taboo of uncleanness // 부정나다 have an unclean event occur
—풀이 exorcising the spirit of a dead out of his house

⁑**부정 不貞** infidelity ; unfaithfulness ; unchastity **—하다** (be) unfaithful ; faithless ; unchaste ; false 《to one's husband》

부정 不定 uncertainty ; indefiniteness **—하다** (be) uncertain ; unfixed ; unsettled ; indefinite ; irregular ¶ 주소 부정의 사람 a man of no fixed abode ; a vagabond ; a tramp
— 계수 〖수학〗 an indeterminate coefficient **— 관사** 〖문법〗 the indefinite article **— 대명사** 〖문법〗 the indefinite pronoun **— 방정식** 〖수학〗 an indeterminate equation **—법** 〖문법〗 the infinitive mood **—수** an indefinite number **—형** an indeterminate form

†**부정 不正** injustice ; unfairness ; dishonesty ; wrongfulness (불법) ; illegality (위법) ; unlawfulness (위법) ; vice (악덕) **—하다** (be) unjust ; unfair ; foul ; wrong ; unrighteous ; iniquitous ; illegal ¶ 부정한 수단으로 by a dishonest means ; wrongfully ; dishonestly ; unfairly ; out of square // 부정 승차를 하다 steal a ride on a train // 부정한 일을 하다 do a dishonest〔dishonorable〕 thing ; cheat 《in an examination》 // 금융 관계 회사들이 부정 거래에 깊이 관련되어 있는게 틀림없다 Financial companies must be pretty deeply involved in shaby dealings.

— 공무원 a corrupt〔venal〕 official — 공사 fraudulent work — 대부 a blackmarket loan — 명색 ill-gotten wealth — 부패 irregularities and corruption ; abuse of power and graft — 사건 a scandal ; [수회] a bribery〔corruption〕 case — 선거 a rigged election — 수단 《by》 a dishonest means — 이득 illicit 〔ill-gotten〕 gains —품 a fraudulent article ; an adulterated article ; a fraud — 행위 a dishonest act ; a dirty trick ; wrongdoing ; [시험 때의] cheating ; cribbing ; [경기 때의] foul play

*부정 否定 denial ; negation ; contradiction —하다 deny ; contradict ; disclaim ; gainsay ; say no ¶ 부정적 negative // 부정할 수 없는 undeniable ; indisputable ; incontestable // 부정하기 어려운 사실 an undeniable〔a stubborn〕 fact // 소문을 부정하다 deny the rumor // 편지의 필자임을 부정하다 deny having written the letter
— 명제 a negative (proposition) —문 〖문법〗 a negative sentence — 판단 a negation ; a negative assertion〔proposition〕 이중 — 〖문법〗 a double negative

부정규 不定規 ¶ 부정규의 irregular
—군 irregulars ; irregular troops —병 an irregular

부정기 不定期 irregularity ; (having) no schedule ¶ 부정기의 irregular ; unfixed ; nonscheduled
—선 a tramp(er) ; a nonregular liner — 열차 an extra train — 항(공)로 a tramp route — 항공 회사 a nonscheduled airline ; a nonsked 《미·속》 —편 nonregular service ; [항공편] an unscheduled (airplane) flight

부정당 不正當 injustice ; iniquity ; impropriety —하다 (be) unjust ; unrighteous ; iniquitous ; improper

부정맥 不整脈 〖의학〗 arrhythmia ; an irregular pulse

‡부정사 不定詞 〖문법〗 an infinitive
— 구문 an infinitival construction 분리 — a split infinitive

‡부정직 不正直 dishonesty ; untruthfulness —하다 (be) dishonest ; untruthful

부정 축재 不正蓄財 accumulation of wealth〔making a fortune〕 by illicit means —하다 accumulate〔amass〕 wealth by unlawful〔illicit〕 means ; make a fortune by illegal means
—자 an illicit fortune maker〔amasser〕

부정형시 不定形詩 free verse

‡부정확 不正確 inaccuracy ; incorrectness ; uncertainty ; incertitude —하다 (be) inaccurate ; incorrect ; uncertain ; inexact ; imprecise

*부제 副題 a subtitle ; a subheading

부조 父祖 ancestors ; forefathers ; forebears ; fathers ; father and grandfather ¶ 부조 전래의 ancestral

부조 不調 bad condition ; disorder ; slump ; unfavorableness ; irregularity —하다 be in a bad condition ; be in disorder ; be out of form (운동 선수가) ; be not one's usual self ; irregular ; (be) unfavorable

*부조 浮彫 relief ; relievo ; embossed carving
— 세공 raised〔relief〕 work

부조 扶助 support ; aid ; assistance ; help ; [잔치·상가에 보내는] a contribution —하다 support ; aid ; assist ; help ; sustain ; relieve ; render 《a person》 assistance ; give goods or money to aid ¶ 남의 생활을 부조하다 contribute to 《a person's》 support // 부조도 말고 제상다리도 치지 마라 Just keep your hands off my business.
—금 a relief fund ; an aid allowance ; a dole 상호 — mutual aid ; interdependence 잔치 — a contribution to the expenses of a banquet〔party, reception〕

부조리 不條理 irrationality ; absurdity ; unreasonableness ¶ 부조리한 irrational ; unreasonable

부조정실 副調整室 〖라디오·텔레비전〗 a control room

부조화 不調和 disharmony ; discord(-ance) ; incongruity ; lack of harmony —하다 (be) inharmonious ; disharmonious ; discordant ; incongruous

†부족 部族 a tribe

†부족 不足 [결핍] shortage ; lack ; want ; scarcity ; deficiency ; [금액] a deficit

> 참고 **want**는 필요한 것이 빠져 있다는 뜻 **lack**는 단순히 무엇인가가 빠져 있다는 뜻

—하다 be short 《of》 ; lack ¶ 자금 부족 때문에 owing to lack of funds // 백 원이 부족하다 be a hundred *won* short // 부족세를 물다 pay a fine 《on a letter》 // 부족을 보충하다 make good a deficiency ; supply a gap // 식량이 부족하다 《a person》 run short of provisions ; provisions run short // 아무런 부족 없는 생활을 하다 live in plenty〔comfort〕 // 이 사진은 노출 부족이다 This picture is underexposed. // 그는 사업을 너무 급속하게 확장시켜서 지금 일손이 부족하다 He expanded his business too rapidly, and now he's understaffed.
—액 shortage ; a difference ; wantage ; a deficit ; shortfall 《구》 ; shorts 수면 — want〔lack〕 of sleep 식량 — a scarcity 〔shortage〕 of food ; insufficiency of provisions

부존 賦存 —하다 be blessed〔favored〕 《with》
— 자원 natural resources ¶ 부존 자원이 많다 be blessed with natural resources

부종 浮腫 edema ; a (pathological) swelling ; dropsy (수종)

부주 ① [유전] a hereditary trait ; a family strain ② ⇨ 부조 (扶助)
부줏술 hereditary alcoholism〔drinking〕 (유전) ; liquor contributed by guests at a wedding〔funeral〕 (부조)
부주의 不注意 heedlessness ; carelessness ; inattention ; negligence ; neglect **—하다** (be) careless ; heedless ; inattentive ; negligent ¶ 부주의로 through one's carelessness // 운전사의 부주의로 인한 사고 an accident due to〔caused by〕 a careless driver // 부주의로 인하여 생기다 arise from carelessness // 나는 부주의하게도 그런 사람을 신용했다 I was imprudent enough to trust the man. // 그는 복장에 부주의하다 He is careless 〔slovenly〕 about his clothes. // 그런 사고는 부주의에서 일어난다 Such an accident happens through carelessness. // 내가 정말 부주의하였다 It was very careless of me.
운전 — careless driving
부주제 副主題 〖음악〗 the subsidiary theme
부주필 副主筆 an associate editor
부증 浮症 〖의학〗 a (pathological) swelling
부지 不知 ignorance ; not knowing **—하다** do not know ; be ignorant of ¶ 부지의 진술 a plea of ignorance ; a declaration of ignorance of a fact
부지 敷地 a (building) site ; a plot ; a lot ; ground ¶ 부지의 선정 the selection of a site 《for》 // 박람회의 부지 the exhibition grounds // 학교의 부지를 결정하다 decide the site for a school
— 면적 plottage **건축 —** a building site〔lot〕 **후보 —** the site proposed 《for》
부지 扶支 —하다 bear ; endure ; stick to ; stand ; hold out ¶ 부지 못하다 cannot stand ; be unable to remain // 그 녀석 여기서 부지 못하게 해놓겠다 I will make it too hot for him.
부지거처 不知去處 missing ; whereabouts unknown
부지군 an insincere and malicious person ; a perverse〔crabbed〕 person ; a cross-grained〔cross-tempered〕 person ; a faithless and ill-tempered person
부지기수 不知其數 (being) innumerable ; countless ; numberless
부지깽이 a poker
***부지런하다** (be) industrious ; diligent ; assiduous ; hardworking ¶ 부지런히 일하다 work hard ; be industrious in one's work // 부지런히 공부하다 work hard ; study with diligence ; be diligent in one's work // 부지런히 공부하다 work hard ; study with diligence ; be diligent in one's lessons // 그는 부지런한 사람이다 He is a hard worker〔hardworking man〕. // 그는 부지런한 사람으로 한시도 노는 일이 없다 He is too active to remain idle.
부지런한 물방아는 얼 새도 없다 속담 Standing pools gather filth. /The used key is always bright.
부지런히 diligently ; industriously ; assiduously ; earnestly
부지배인 副支配人 an assistant manager
부지불식간 不知不識間 ¶ 부지불식간에 unconsciously ; unwittingly ; unawares ; in spite of oneself ; without intention // 부지불식간에 나쁜 짓을 하게 되다 drift〔slip〕 into an evil course
부지사 副知事 a deputy〔lieutenant〕 governor
부지중 不知中 unconsciously ⇨ 부지불식간에
부지지, 부지직 ⇨ 바지지
부지하세월 不知何歲月 not knowing when something is going to be completed ¶ 그것은 언제 완성될지 부지하세월이다 Nobody can tell when it will be completed.
부직 副職 an additional post
부진 不振 dullness ; depression ; inactivity ; stagnation **—하다** (be) dull ; inactive ; stagnant ; slack ; flat ; backward ; be in a poor way ; be in bad condition ¶ 사업의 부진 business depression ; stagnation of trade ; a slump in business // 거래가 대단히 부진하다 Business is very dull〔slack〕. / Trade is at a very low ebb. // 그 팀의 성적이 매우 부진하다 The team made〔gave〕 a very poor showing.
거래 — 〖증권〗 lack of interest〔enthusiasm〕 **수출 —** inactivity〔a poor showing〕 of the export trade **식욕 —** lack 〔loss〕 of appetite ; inappetence ; anorexia
부진 不進 poor progress **—하다** make little〔poor, scant〕 progress ¶ 지지부진하다 make slow progress ; progress at a snail's pace
부진 不盡 inexhaustibleness ; endlessness **—하다** (be) inexhaustible ; endless ; unfailing
—근(수) 〖수학〗 a surd root **—수** 〖수학〗 an irrational number ; a surd
부질간 —間 a brassworker's furnace 〔smithery〕
부질없다 (be) vain ; futile ; useless ; idle ; trivial ¶ 부질없이 idly ; to no purpose ; in vain // 부질없이 시간을 보내다 idle away one's time // 부질없는 소리를 하다 talk nonsense ; utter an absurdity // 부질없는 짓을 하다 do a foolish thing
부집게 (flame) snuffers ; fire nippers ; a candle snuffer
부쩍 [우기는 모양] obstinately ; stubbornly ; persistently ; [갑자기] rapidly ; quickly ; remarkably ¶ 부쩍 우기다 persist stubbornly // 그는 산수 실력이 부쩍 늘었다 He has made a remarkable improvement in arithmetic.
부차적 副次的 (being) secondary ¶ 부차적인 원인 a secondary cause ; a bycause
***부착 附着** sticking ; adherence ; adhe-

sion ; cohesion **—하다** adhere〔stick, cling〕 to ; attach〔fasten〕 itself to
—력 adhesive power ; adhesion **—어** 〖언어〗 an agglutinative language

부창부수 夫唱婦隨 a way of life in which the wife follows the lead set by her husband ; conjugal harmony ; the wife concurring in the husband's ideas

‡**부채** a fan ; a folding fan ¶ 부채를 부치다 fan oneself ; use a fan
—꼭지 the pivot of a fan **—꼴** a fan-shape ; (the shape of) a fan ; sector form **—잡이** the (blindman's) left **—춤** a fan dance ; a dance with a fan **부챗살** the rib of a fan

*__부채 負債__ a debt ; liabilities ; dues ¶ 부채가 있다 be in debt ; be indebted to 《a person》 // 부채를 남기다 leave debts // 부채를 갚다 pay off debts // 부채를 지다 run〔get, fall〕 into debt // 100만원의 부채가 있다 be indebted to 《a person》 for 1,000,000 *won* ; owe 《a person》 1,000,000 *won*
—국 a debtor country **—상환** debt redemption **—액** the amount of debt(-s) ; indebtedness ; liabilities **—자** a debtor **고정〔미불, 미상환, 연불〕—** fixed 〔accrued, outstanding, deferred〕 liabilities **부동〔현금〕—** floating〔cash〕 liabilities **자본〔당좌〕—** capital〔current〕 liabilities **확정 —** 〖회계〗 a fixed charge

부채질 fanning **—하다** fan ; fan oneself (자신을) ; use a fan ; [선동하다] instigate ; incite ; stimulate ; stir〔work, key〕 up ; agitate ; [감정 따위를] enkindle ; kindle ; inflame ¶ 불에 부채질하다 fan the flames // 불붙는 데 부채질하다 fan the flames of 《a person's》 anger // 허영심을 부채질하다 inflate the vanity 《of a person》 // 그런 조치를 취하는 것은 불붙는 데 부채질하는 것과 같다 It is like adding oil to the fire to take such a step.

부처 [석가모니] Buddha ; [성인] a Buddhist saint ; [불상] an image of Buddha ¶ 부처님 가운데 토막같은 사람 a man too saintly to be true ; a tin Jesus // 그는 부처같은 사람이다 He is a saintly man.
부처 밑을 기울이면 삼거웃이 나온다 속담 The skeleton in the closet〔cupboard〕.

부처 夫妻 husband and wife ; a couple ¶ 윌슨씨 부처 Mr. and Mrs. Wilson ; the Wilsons

부처꽃 〖식물〗 a purple loosestrife

부처손 〖식물〗 a selsginella

부척 副尺 a vernier (scale)

부촌 富村 a rich〔wealthy〕 village

부총리 副總理 the Deputy Prime Minister

부총재 副總裁 a vice-president

부추 〖식물〗 a leek ; a scallion ; a shallot ; Allium odorum (학명)
—떡 rice cake stuffed with chopped pork and leeks **—장아찌** leeks seasoned with soysauce and condiments

‡**부추기다** incite ; urge ; stir up ; instigate ; agitate ¶ 부추기어서 싸움하게 하다 incite 《a person》 to a quarrel // 민중을 부추기어 난폭한 짓을 하게 하다 instigate people to violence // 그는 학생들을 부추기어 폭동을 일으켰다 He incited the students to riot. // 꼬마들을 부추겨서 싸움 시키지 말아라 Don't egg on little kids to fight.

부축 helping by holding a person's arms **—하다** help 《a person》 ; give one's arm to ¶ 노인을 자동차에까지 부축해 주다 help an old man to a car // 부인을 차에서 부축해 내리다 help a lady out of the car

부출 the four corner supports of a movable wardrobe closet (옷장의) ; toilet footboards (뒷간의)

부츠 [장화] boots ¶ 부츠를 신은 booted

부치다[1] [힘에] be beyond one's strength ¶ 힘에 부치다 be beyond one's power ; be beyond one // 그 일이 내 힘에 부친다 I find myself unequal to the task. // 힘에 부치는 일을 하려고 하지 마라 Attempt nothing beyond your strength.

부치다[2] [부채를] fan ¶ 부채를 부치다 fan oneself ; use a fan // 파리를 부쳐 쫓다 fan away flies // 손수건으로 부치다 fan oneself with a handkerchief // 석탄불을 부쳐 일으키다 fan the coals into a blaze

†**부치다**[3] [편지·물건을] send ; mail ; post ; remit (돈을) ; forward (짐을) ¶ 기차로 상품을 부치다 ship goods by rail // 돈을 부치다 remit money // 집에 가는 편지를 친구한테 부치다 send a letter home by a friend // 나는 트렁크를 기차로 서울까지 부쳤다 I have checked my trunk through to *Seoul*. // 이 편지를 항공편으로 부쳐 주시오 Please send this letter by airmail.

부치다[4] [논·밭을] till ; plow ; cultivate ; farm ; work a farm ¶ 논을 부치다 cultivate rice // 밭을 부치다 cultivate a field

부치다[5] [음식을] fry ; griddle ; cook on a griddle ¶ 달걀을 부치다 fry eggs

부치다[6] ① [회부하다] refer ; put ; commit ; submit ; hand over to (넘겨주다) ¶ 공판에 부쳐지다 be brought to trial ; come on before the judge 《for trial, for hearing》 ② [처리하다] ¶ 불문에 부치다 overlook ; pass over ③ [심정을 의탁하다] convey one's feelings in 《verse》 ; liken 〔compare〕 《one's feelings》 to 《flowers and birds》

부칙 附則 additional rules ; an additional clause ; a supplementary provision ; a subsidiary law

부친 父親 a father ; a paternal parent

부침 浮沈 ups and downs ; rise and fall ; vicissitudes ; [편지의] going astray en route ¶ 인생의 부침 ups and downs of life ; life's vicissitudes // 부침을 함께 하다 sink or swim〔stand or fall〕 together ; cast〔throw〕 in one's lot 《with》 // 국가 운

명의 부침에 관계되다 affect the future of a nation
부침개 a flat cake ; fried food
부침하다 sow〔seed〕 the field ; prepare fields for farming ; make a farm
†부탁 付託 a request ; a favor ; solicitation —하다 ask ; request ; make a request ; bet ; ask a favor of ¶ …의 부탁으로 at《a person's》request // 부탁하러 오다 come to《a person》for something // 부탁을 거절하다 refuse《a person's》request ; refuse《a person》a request〔favor〕// 부탁에 응하다 comply with《a person's》request // 부탁이 있습니다 I have a favor to ask of you. /I should like to make a request. /May I ask a favor of you? // 부탁 하나 들어줘 Do me a favor. ☞ ◖p. 1036◗
부탄 〖화학〗 butane
부터 ① [시간] from ; since ¶ 언제부터 since when // 아침부터 저녁까지 from morning till evening // 인생은 40부터이다 Life begins at 40. // 다음부터 더욱 조심해라 Be more careful from now on. // 그는 어렸을 때부터 영어를 배우고 있다 He has been studying English since childhood. ② [순서] beginning with ; first ; starting from ¶ …부터 시작하다 begin with〔at, by, on〕// 역사부터 공부하다 study history first // 15페이지 다섯째 줄부터 읽어라 Start reading from line five, page fifteen. // 너부터 시작해라 You begin first. // 무엇부터 시작할까 What shall I begin with? // 김씨 댁부터 방문하자 Let's make a round of visits, starting at Mr. *Kim*'s.
부통령 副統領 the vice-president
부패 —牌 〖광산〗 a joint exploiter〔operator〕 of a mine
*부패 腐敗 ① [물질적] rotting ; spoiling ; decomposition ; putrefaction —하다 [음식물 따위가] go bad ; rot ; be spoiled ; be decomposed ; [달걀이] addle ; [우유가] turn ¶ 부패한 rotten ; addled《eggs》// 부패하기 쉬운 perishable ; corruptible // 이 생선은 부패하기 쉽다 This fish is very apt to go bad〔be spoiled〕. ② [정신적] corruption ; decay ; depravity ; degeneration —하다 become corrupt ; decay ¶ 사회〔정치〕의 부패 the corruption of society〔politics〕// 부패한 spoiled ; corrupt // 부패한 정치가 a corrupt politician
—균 a saprogenous bacillus ; a saprophyte —물 decomposing matter ; septic (matter) —산(酸) a putrid acid —성 septicity —열 surgical〔septic〕 fever —중독 septic poisoning 사회적〔도덕적〕 — social〔moral〕 decay〔disintegration〕 ; dry rot
부평초 浮萍草 duckweed
부표 浮標 a buoy ; [낚시찌] a float ; a cork ; a quill
—등 a buoy light — 설치 buoyage 정박 — a mooring buoy
부표 否票 a negative vote ; a vote "no" ; a "nay" vote
부표 浮漂 floating ; floatage
— 식물 duckweed ; duckmeat
부표 付票 an attached tag ; attaching a tag —하다 attach a tag《to》
부푸러기 ⇨ 보풀, 보푸라기
부풀 fine nap (on the surface of cloth) ; fuzz (on the surface of paper)
†부풀다 ① [부푸러기가] have a fine nap (on the surface of cloth) ; have fuzz (on the surface of paper) ② [붓다·커지다] swell up ; get bulky ; expand ③ [성나다] get angry ; get sulky ④ [가슴이] be buoyant with ¶ 빵이 부풀다 The bread rises. // 살가죽이 부풀다 The flesh swells (up). // 그녀는 기대에 가슴이 부풀었다 She is buoyant with expectations. // 꽃봉오리가 부풀다 A bud swells.
부풀리다 swell out ; expand ; bulge ; inflate ; puff out ; [부푸러기를] raise a nap ¶ 풍선을 부풀리다 inflate a toy balloon // 공기 베개를 부풀리다 pump up a pillow // 가슴을 부풀리다 heave one's breast // 호주머니를 부풀리다 bulge〔swell out〕 one's pocket《with oranges》// 빵을 부풀리다 raise bread
부풀부풀 ⇨ 보풀보풀
부품 部品 parts ; [부속품] accessories ¶ 라디오와 부품 a radio set and parts // 부품을 조립하다 assemble parts into a complete whole
부프다 ① [부피가] (be) bulky ¶ 그것은 부프나 가볍다 It is bulky but light. ② [성급하다] (be) impatient ; hasty ; rash ¶ 그는 성미가 부픈 사람이다 He is a rash person.
부풋하다 ① (be) thick and bulky ② [말이] (be) exaggerated ; magnified
*부피 bulk ; size ; volume ¶ 부피가 큰 물건 an article of great bulk // 부피가 커지다 swell〔grow〕 bulk ; increase in volume
부하 負荷 ① [짐] carrying a burden ; a burden ; a load —하다 carry a load 〔burden〕 ; be loaded ② 〖전기〗 (carrying) an electrical load
— 시험 a load test —율 a load factor — 전동기 a loaded motor 안전〔활동, 경, 최대, 정지〕 — a safe〔live, light, breaking, dead〕 load
부하 部下 a subordinate ; a follower ; [전체] one's staff ; one's inferior ; one's men ¶ 부하 사병 the men under one's command // …의 부하로서 일하다 serve under《a person》// 그는 많은 유능한 부하를 거느리고 있다 He has many able men under him.
부하다 富— ① (be) rich ; wealthy ② [살찌다] (be) fat ; plump ; corpulent
부하다 附— attach ; affix ; laminate (금속판을) ; join (나무 따위)
부함장 副艦長 a commander (대형함의)

부탁

1 부탁의 표현

상대방에게 무엇을 해 주기를 부탁할 때 「~하여 주시겠습니까, 좀 … 해도 좋을까요?」라는 표현으로 Will[Would] you..., (please). / I'd like you to..., (please). / I must ask you to..., (please). / Would you be so kind as to.... / I have to ask you to ..., (I'm afraid). / Would you mind..., (please). 등을 쓸 수 있고, 또 May I ask you a favor? / Will [Would, Could] you do me a favor? 와 같은 표현을 쓸 수 있다.

¶ 뭣 좀 부탁할 것이 있는데요. There's something I'd like to ask of you. (★ 동년배나 그 아랫 사람에게는 I'd like you to do something for me.를 쓴다. I want you to do.... 처럼 want를 쓰면 약간 하대하는 표현이며 I'm sorry to bother[trouble] you, but could you...? / Can you give me a hand?는 구어적 표현.) // 문을 닫아주시겠습니까 — 네. 그러죠. Would you mind closing the window? — Certainly [Of course] not. (★ 형식상으로는 부정이지만 실제 뜻은 긍정임에 유의. Would [will] you (kindly) close the window? Certainly [Sure].와 비교가 된다. will보다 would가 정중한 표현.) // 창문 좀 닫아주십시오. — 그러죠. Please close the window. — All right. // 실례합니다. 시립병원 가는 길을 좀 가르쳐 주시겠습니까? Excuse me, but could you tell [show] me the way[how to get] to the Municipal Hospital?

2 응답

부탁의 응답으로 어떻게 할지를 모를 때는 No, I don't know how.... / I've no idea how.... / There's no way I can.... 등의 표현을 쓸 수 있고, 경험이 없어서 곤란할 경우는 I have no experience of.... / I don't think I have the qualifications [experience].... 등의 표현을 쓴다.

¶ 물론이지, 좋구말구. Yes, certainly. / Of course, I'll be glad to. / Yes, with [With] (great) pleasure. (★ 친한 사이에는 Sure! 또는 OK.를 쓴다.) // 힘 닿는 대로 해보겠습니다. I'll do my best for you. // 가능하면 해보겠습니다. I'll (do it) if I can. // 잠깐만 기다려 주십시오. Please wait a moment. // 유감입니다만 해드릴 수가 없습니다. I'm sorry, but I can't (do it). // 됐으면 좋겠습니다만 I wish I could, but.... // 달리 시간을 내어도 괜찮겠습니까? Could we make it some other time? // 노력은 해보겠지만 그것을 할 수 있을지 모르겠습니다. I'll try, but I don't know [I'm not sure] if I can (do it).

부합 符合 coincidence ; correspondence ; tally ; agreement ; conformity **—하다** coincide〔tally, agree〕 with ; fit in with ; correspond to ; answer ; accord ¶ (인상착의가) 그림과 부합하다 answer the description // 부합하지 않다 be discrepant ; be contradictory // 너의 견해가 나의 견해와 부합한다 Your view exactly corresponds to〔coincides with〕 mine.

부항항아리 附缸— a cupping glass

부형 父兄 parents and brothers
—회 a parents association

부호 符號 a sign ; a mark ; a cipher ; a symbol ; [전신의] a code ¶ 부호로 쓰다 jot down in cipher // 부호를 붙이다 mark
—표 a table of signs ; a list of symbols ; a code chart **—화(化)** 〖전산〗 encoding ; encodement

부호 富豪 a rich〔wealthy〕 man ; a man of wealth ; a millionaire ; a billionaire ¶ 부호가 되다 become rich ; amass a fortune // 그는 굉장한 부호다 He is as rich as Croesus. / He is rolling in gold.
— 계급 the wealthy class ; plutocracy ; plutes

부화 孵化 hatching ; incubation **—하다** hatch ; incubate ¶ 병아리를 부화하다 hatch out chickens
—기 an artificial incubator **—장** a hatchery **인공 —** artificial incubation

부화 浮華 ostentation ; vanity ; foppery ; frivolity ; levity **—하다** (be) ostentatious ; showy ; frivolous ; foppish

부화 附和 blind following **—하다** echo 《another's view》 ; chime in with ; follow 《another》 blindly ; follow suit without reflection

부화뇌동 附和雷同 blind following **—하다** echo 《another's view》 ; chime in with ; follow 《another》 blindly ; follow suit without reflection

†부활 復活 [갱생] resurrection ; rebirth ; [회복] revival ; [부흥] restoration **—하다** revive ; resurrect ; come to life again ; [부활시키다] revive ; restore ; bring to life ¶ 예수의 부활 the Resurrection // 오랜 관계를 부활시키다 revive old connections
—제〔절〕 Easter **—제 전야** the Easter vigil **— 주일** Easter Sunday

부회 附會, 傅會 a forced analogy ; a far-fetched interpretation ; sophistry ; distortion **—하다** make a forced analogy to ; give a farfetched interpretation to 〔of〕 ; distort ; twist

부회장 副會長 a vice-president ; a vice-chairman

부흥 復興 [재건] reconstruction : [부활] revival ; restoration ; [정신상의] renaissance ; renascence **—하다** reconstruct ; be reconstructed ; rebuild ; revive ; be revived ; restore ; make a comeback ¶ 인도의 부흥 the renaissance of India // 한국의 부흥은 현저하다 Remarkable is the rehabilitation of Korea.
— 목사 a revivalist (preacher) **— 사업** reconstruction〔rehabilitation〕 work **—회** a revival (service) **경제 —** economic rehabilitation ; an economic comeback **문예 —** 〖역사〗 the Renaissance ; the Revival

*__북__[1] a shuttle ; a spindle

⁑**북**[2] a drum ¶ 북소리 the sound of a drum // 북치는 사람 a drummer // 북을 치다 beat a drum

북

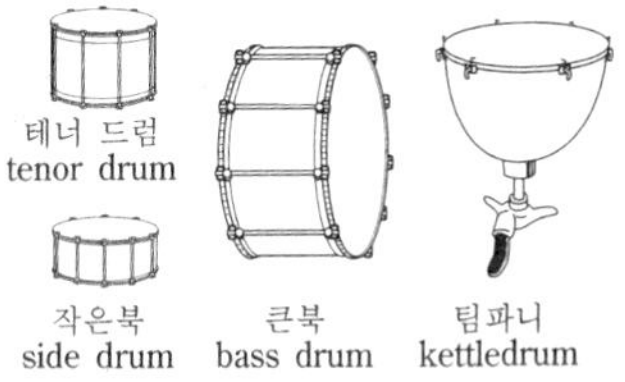

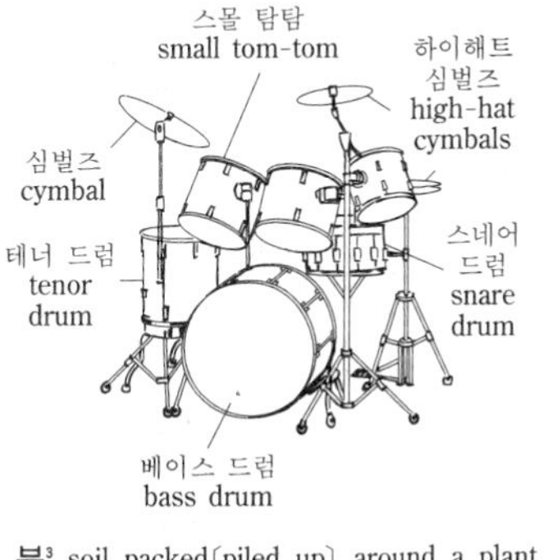

북[3] soil packed〔piled up〕 around a plant ¶ 나무에 북을 주다 heap soil around a plant

북[4] [소리가] with a scratch〔rasp, grate〕 ; with a rip ¶ 북 긁다 scratch // 헝겊을 북 찢다 rip a piece of cloth

†**북 北** the north ¶ 북의 north ; northern ; northerly // 북으로 to the north ; northward(s) // 북으로 가다 go north

북경 北京 Peking
— 원인(猿人) the Peking man (Sinanthropus pekinensis)

북광 北光 the aurora borealis ; the northern lights ; the polar lights

북구 北歐 Northern Europe ; Scandinavia ¶ 북구의 Scandinavian
— 사람 a Scandinavian **— 신화(神話)** the Norse mythology

북국 北國 the northern provinces ; the north ; a northern country ¶ 북국 사람 a northerner

⁑**북극 北極** the North Pole ¶ 북극의 arctic ; polar ; pole
—곰 a polar bear **—광** the aurora borealis ; the northern lights **—권** the Arctic circle〔zone〕 **—양〔해〕** the Arctic Ocean **— 지방** the Arctic〔polar〕 region **— 탐험대** a polar〔an Arctic〕 expedition (team)

*__북극성 北極星__ 〖천문〗 the polar star ; the polestar ; Polaris ; the North Star ; the lodestar〔loadstar〕 ; the Cynosure

북녘 北— the North ; the northern part

북단 北端 the northern end〔extremity〕

북대서양 北大西洋 the North Atlantic (Ocean)
— 조약 기구 the North Atlantic Treaty Organization 《NATO》

북더기 straw or grass refuse〔rubbish〕

북덕지 —紙 crumpled〔wrinkled〕 paper

북도 北道 [경기도 이북의] the northern provinces ; the provinces north of Gyŏnggi ; [남·북도의] the North (part of a split) province
경상(慶尙)— N. GyŎngsang

북돋다 ⇨ 북돋우다

⁑**북돋우다** ① [흙을] pile up earth around 《a plant, a flower》 ; hill up ② [고무하다] encourage ; invigorate ; strengthen ¶ 과수를 북돋우다 heap up soil around a fruit tree // 꽃을 북돋우다 grow flowers // 사기를 북돋우어 주다 stiffen〔stimulate〕 the morale 《of troops》 // 희망을 주어 용기를 북돋우다 encourage 《a person》 with hope

북동 北東 northeast
—풍 a northeasterly wind ; a northeaster

북두 a girth(-belt)〔bellyband〕 for a pack animal ; a cinch
—갈고리 a hook to tighten the girth

*__북두칠성 北斗七星__ 〖천문〗 the Great Bear ; the Plow ; the Ursa Major ; the Big Dipper 《미》

북등 —燈 a drum-shaped lamp

북류 北流 flowing north **—하다** flow north

북메우다 put on a drumhead〔drumskin〕

북면 北面 ① [북향] facing north **—하다**

face north ② [임금을 섬김] serving the king as a subject ; allegiance ━하다 serve as a subject〔retainer〕 ③ [면] the north side〔face〕
북미 北美 North America
남(南)— N. and S. America ; the two Americas
북바늘 a guard pin inside a shuttle
북반구 北半球 the Northern Hemisphere
북받자 getting a full *mal*-measure 〔bushel〕 of grain
북받치다 surge up ; gush forth ; well up ; be filled with 《emotion》 ; have a fit of 《anger》 ¶ 북받치는 기쁨 joy welling up in one's heart // 연민의 정이 북받치다 feel a gush of pity 《at the sight》 // 설움이 북받치다 sorrow wells up within one // 눈물이 북받치다 tears well up in one's eyes // 화가 북받친다 Indignation surges up within me. // 그 일을 생각하니 여러 가지 생각이 북받쳐 오른다 So many ideas spring up within me as I think of it.
북방 北方 [방향] the north ; northward ; the northern direction ; [지방] a northern district ; the northern section
— 민족 a northern race — 불교 the northern sects of Buddhism
북벌 北伐 an expedition to conquer the north ━하다 send an expedition to conquer the north
북부 北部 the north ; the northern part
북북 [갈다·긁다] hard ; roughly ; with a vengeance ; [찢다] to pieces ¶ 맷돌을 북북 갈다 grind a hand mill with a vengeance // 이를 북북 갈다 grind one's teeth furiously // 그는 편지를 북북 찢어 버렸다 He tore the letter to pieces.
북북동 北北東 north-northeast 《NNE》
북북서 北北西 north-northwest 《NNW》
북빙양 北氷洋 the Arctic Ocean
북상 北上 going north ; northing ━하다 go north ; proceed northward
북새 commotion ; hustle ; bustle ; hubbub ; [방해] disturbance ¶ 북새통에 in the confusion // 북새통에 잠입하다 sneak in during the confusion // 북새통에 아이를 잃다 lose one's child in the confusion of the crowd // 북새놓다 hustle and bustle ; be in confusion ; [방해놓다] cause disturbance
—판 a confusion ; a bustle ; a turmoil ; the scene of a commotion ¶ 북새판을 벌이다 make a row〔a tumult, an uproar〕
북서 北西 northwest
—풍 a northwesterly wind ; a northwester
북송 北送 repatriation to the north ━하다 repatriate to the north〔to North Korea〕
—선 a repatriation ship
북슬개 a big shaggy dog
북슬북슬 ━하다 (be) plump and hairy ; shaggy
북안 北岸 the north〔northern〕 shore 〔coast〕
북양 北洋 the northern ocean〔seas〕 ¶ 북양 어업 northern-seas fisheries
북어 北魚 a dried pollack
—보풀음 small slices of a dried pollack
—찜 (a seasoned and) steamed pollack
북위 北緯 north latitude ¶ 북위 30도 30 degrees〔30°〕 north latitude
—선 north parallel ; north latitude
북잡이 the drummer in a band of mendicant priests
북장지 a sliding door with paper on both sides
북적 北狄 〖역사〗 northern barbarians
북적거리다 bustle ; throng ; be crowded ; be congested ; be jammed up ¶ 북적거리는 거리 a crowded street ; a bustling street // 북적거리는 틈에 끼여들다 sneak in during the confusion
북적북적 in a bustle ; full of stir ; tumultuously ; bustling ; jostling ; in clamor ; in uproar
북쪽 北— the north ¶ 북쪽의 north ; northern ; northerly // 서울의 북쪽 20마일에 at 20 miles north of *Seoul* // 북쪽으로 가다 go north // 한국은 북쪽으로 만주와 접한다 To the north Korea borders on Manchuria.
북주다 ⇨ 북[3]
북지 北地 the northern region ; the north
북진 北進 going〔marching〕 north ━하다 go〔march〕 north ; sail north ; expand northward
북채 a drumstick
북천 北天 the northern sky ; 〖천문〗 the sky north of the zodiac
북춤 a drum dance
북치 a kind of small cucumber
북통 —筒 a drum frame ; a drum
—배 a fat belly
북틀 a drum stand
북편 北便 the northern part〔side〕 ; the north ¶ 북편에 on the north side 《of》
북풍 北風 the north wind ; the northerly wind
북한 北韓 North Korea
북해 北海 [영국 북쪽의] the North Sea ; [북쪽의] a northern sea
북행 北行 going north ; northing ━하다 go (up) north
북향 北向 facing north ; a northern aspect〔exposure〕 ━하다 face north ; have a northern exposure ¶ 북향집 a house facing the north
북회귀선 北回歸線 the Tropic of Cancer
분 ¶ 이분 this gentleman〔lady〕 // 여러분 ladies and gentlemen ; everybody ; all of you // 한두 분 a couple of poeple // 오늘 몇 분이나 오십니까 How many people are you expecting today ?
†분 分 ① [부분] a part ; a portion ¶ 4분의 1 a fourth (part) ; a quarter // 4분의 3

three quarters // 100분의 5 five-hundredths // 5만 분의 1의 지도 a map on the scale of 1 : 50,000
② [단위] a minute ¶ 15분 fifteen minutes ; a quarter (of an hour) // 4시 5분 five minutes past〔after 《미》〕 four ; four o five 《4 : 05》 // 5시 15분 전 a quarter to〔of, before 《미》〕 five ; four forty-five 《4 : 45》 // 6시 30분 half past six ; six thirty 《6 : 30》 // 북위 25도 15분 25 degrees 15 minutes north latitude 《25° 15' N. Lat.》
③ [몫·분량] a share ; a part ; a portion ¶ 이틀분의 음식 food for two days // 한달분의 연료 a month's supply of fuel // 3인분의 일을 하다 do the work of three men
④ [신분] social position ; standing ; [자력] means ; [상태] status ¶ 분에 넘치는 지위 an undeserved position // 분에 알맞게〔넘치게〕 생활하다 live within〔above〕 one's means // 분에 만족하다 be content with one's lot

분 粉 (face) powder ¶ 물분 liquid powder // 분내 scent of face powder // 분첩 a puff // 분을 바르다 powder one's face ; put powder 《on》 // 그 여자는 분을 짙게 바르고 있었다 Her face was thickly〔heavily〕 powdered.

분 盆 a pot
—받침 a flower stand

분 忿 indignation ; wrath ; anger ; rage ¶ 분이 나다 get indignant 《at》 ; be enraged 《at》 // 분을 돋우다 fan 《a person's》 anger // 분을 풀다 vent one's rage // 분을 참지 못하다 lose one's temper ; get angry ; get out of patience

분 糞 excrements ; feces ; dung ; droppings (새·짐승의)

분가 分家 a branch family **—하다** set up a branch〔separate〕 family

†**분간 分揀** discrimination ; distinction **—하다** distinguish (between two things, one from others) ; know ; tell 《from》 ; discriminate ¶ 분간하기 어려운 indistinguishable // 갑과 을을 분간하다 tell one thing from another // 그는 그 차이를 분간할 수 없었다 He was unable to see the difference. // 누구나 사과와 배는 분간할 수 있다 Anyone can tell apples from pears. // 음악가는 음향 중의 약간의 차이라도 분간할 수 있다 A musician can appreciate differences in sounds.

분갑 粉匣 a powder case ; a compact

*__분개 分介__ 〖부기〗 journalizing **—하다** journalize
—장(帳) a journal

분개 分概 judg(e)ment ; discernment ; understanding ¶ 분개없다 show poor judgment ; have little understanding

분개 憤慨 indignation ; resentment **—하다** (be) indignant 《about a thing, over a matter, at the word, with a person》 ; be enraged ; resent ¶ 분개하여 indignantly ; in a rage ; in resentment // 그는 너에 대해서 분개하고 있었다 He was mad〔very angry〕 at〔with〕 you. // 그의 행위는 국민들의 분개를 샀다 His conduct aroused great indignation among the people.

분격 憤激 exasperation ; indignation ; resentment **—하다** be exasperated ; be enraged ; be indignant

분견 分遣 detachment ; detail **—하다** detach ; detail
—대 a detachment —소 an outstation —함대 a detached squadron

분결같다 粉— (be) fair-skinned ; smooth and white ¶ 그 여자의 얼굴은 분결같다 She has a fair-skinned face.

분계 分界 a boundary ; demarcation ; a border **—하다** demarcate ; delimit

분계선 分界線 a boundary line ; a line of demarcation ¶ 분계선을 긋다 draw a line between 《the two》
군사 — the military demarcation line

분골쇄신 粉骨碎身 —하다 do one's (very) best ; exert oneself to the utmost ; do everything possible ; do as far as in one lies

분공장 分工場 a branch factory〔plant〕

분과 分課 a subdivision 《of a section》 ; a section of a bureau ; a section ; a branch **—하다** divide 《an office》 ; divide 《a bureau》 into sections

분과 分科 a department ; a section ; [부문] a branch ¶ 과학의 한 분과 a branch of science
— 위원회 a sectional〔subcommittee〕 meeting

분관 分館 an annex ; a detached building

분광 分光 spectrum 《*pl.* ~s, -ra》
— 감도 spectral sensitivity —계 a spectrometer — 분석 spectroscopic analysis —학 spectroscopy

분광기 分光器 a spectroscope ; a spectral apparatus
질량(質量) — a mass spectrograph

분광 사진 分光寫眞 a spectrogram ; a spectrograph
—기 a spectrograph —술 spectrography

분교 分校 a branch school

분교장 分教場 a branch of a school ; a detached classroom

분국 分局 a branch office〔bureau〕

분권 分權 decentralization of authority **—하다** decentralize power
—주의 decentralism 지방 — decentralization

*__분규 紛糾__ complication ; entanglement **—하다** become complicated〔entangled〕 ; be in a tangle ¶ 분규시키다 complicate 《matters》 ; aggravate 《the situation》 // 사건은 분규를 극하고 있었다 The affair was extremely complicated. /The affair was in a tangle.

분극 分極 〖전기〗 polarization

— 작용 polarizing action ; polarization — 전류 a polarizing current —제(劑) a polarizer

분근 分根 a split root ; splitting the root of a plant

분급 分給 distribution ; allocation ; apportionment —하다 distribute ; allocate ; apportion

‡분기 分岐 divergence ; ramification ; forking —하다 branch off ; diverge 《from》 ; ramify ¶ 큰길에서 분기되다 branch off from the main road

—선〔지선〕 a branch (line) ; a spur track ; [모선에서 갈라지는] a turnout track —역 a junction (station)

분기 憤氣 indignation ; wrath ; resentment

분기 奮起 rising ; rousing ; awakening —하다 rouse oneself 《to action》 ; bestir oneself ; be stirred up ; brace oneself up ¶ 분기시키다 rouse 《a person》 // 국가를 위하여 분기하다 rouse 〔bestir〕 oneself for the sake of the country

분기 噴氣 ejection ; spouting (가스·물 따위가)

—공 『기계』 a steam valve ; a gas escape ; [화산의] a fumarole ; a vent ; [고래의] a fistula 《*pl.* ～s, -lae》 ; a spout ; a spiracle

분기기 分岐器 『철도』 a turnout

분기점 分岐點 a diverging point ; a turning point ; [길의] a fork ; a crossroads ; [길·개울의] a crotch 《미》 ; [철도의] a division point ; a junction ; 『수학』 a branch〔ramification〕 point

분김 忿— (in) a fit of anger ¶ 분김에 in a moment〔fit〕 of anger // 그는 분김에 그 편지를 갈기갈기 찢었다 He tore the letter into pieces in a fit of anger.

분꽃 粉— 『식물』 a marvel-of-Peru ; a four-o'clock

분납 分納 installment paying〔delivery〕 —하다 pay in〔by〕 installments (돈을) ; deliver in parts〔installments〕 (물품을)

분내 粉— the smell(ing) of powder

분네 [분] a gentleman ; a lady ; [분들] gentlemen ; ladies

분노 憤怒, 忿怒 anger ; wrath ; rage ; indignation ; fury

> 참고 **anger**는 흔히 개인적 분노 **indignation**은 부정 불합리에 대한 공적 의분 **rage**는 자기를 잃어버릴 정도의 격노 **fury**는 광포한 분노 **wrath**는 문학적 용어

—하다 get angry ; get mad 《미》 ; get enraged ; get into rage ; flare up ¶ 분노에 찬 목소리 an angry voice ; an infuriated yell // 분노케 하다 enrage ; exasperate // 그 정도로는 국민의 분노를 달래기에 충분치 않다 That won't be enough to mollify the public's ire.

분뇨 糞尿 excretions ; night soil ; manure ; feces and urine ¶ 분뇨를 치다 remove〔dip up〕 night soil

—관 a soil pipe — 소각 장치 a night-soil incinerator — 수거인 a night-soil man — 운반차 a dung cart

분단 分團 a branch ; a (local) chapter ; a division

분단 分斷 dividing into sections ; cutting in halves〔pieces〕 —하다 divide into sections ; cut in halves〔pieces〕 ¶ 한반도의 분단 the partition of the Korean peninsula

—국 a divided〔partitioned〕 country 〔nation, state〕 영토 — division of territory

분담 分擔 assignment ; allotment ; share ; division of works (분업) —하다 share in ; share with 《another》 ; take partial charge 《of the work》 ¶ 분담된 일 an allotted task // 분담시키다 allot〔assign〕 a part of 《the work》 // 비용을 둘이 분담하다 share the expenses with each other // 지불을 분담하다 bear part of the expenses

—금 a share of expenses —액 an allotment ; 『법』 a contribution —자 a sharer 손해 — apportionment of a loss

분당 分黨 [나눔] splitting〔dividing〕 a political party ; [당] a party split ; a splinter party ; a wing of a split party —하다 split〔divide〕 a political party

—파(派) the seceders ; the separatists

분대 ⇨ 분대질

*분대 分隊 a squad (육군) ; a division (해군) ; a detachment (분견대) ; [대를 나눔] dividing into squads〔divisions〕 —하다 divide into squads〔divisions〕

—장 a squad leader (육군)

분대꾼 a troublemaker ; a meddler ; a nuisance

분대질 trouble ; complications ; meddling ; fuss —하다 bother〔disturb〕 《a person》 ; raise〔kick up〕 dust ; meddle

분도기 分度器 a protractor ; a graduator

분돋우다 忿— fan one's anger ; add insult to injury

분돋움 忿— fanning 《a person's》 anger —하다 fan〔stir up〕 《a person's》 anger

분동 分銅 a (balance) weight ; a counterweight ; a counterpoise

분등 分等 gradation〔grading〕 ; classification —하다 classify ; grade

분디나무 『식물』 Fagara schinfolia (학명)

분란 紛亂 disorder ; confusion ; chaos ; a trouble —하다 be in disorder ; fall into disorder

가정 — family trouble〔strife〕

†분량 分量 quantity ; measure ; a dose (약의) ¶ 적은 분량 a small quantity ; a small dose // 약의 분량을 잘못 주다 give a

wrong dose // 약의 분량이 지나치다 have an overdose

분력 分力 〖물리〗 a component (force)

분력 奮力 exercising one's strength ; doing one's best **—하다** put forth one's strength ; rally one's strength

분류 分流 a tributary〔branch〕 **—하다** branch from (a larger river)

†**분류 分類** classification ; grouping ; division ; assortment **—하다** classify 《as, into》 ; divide 《things》 into classes ; assort ; categorize ¶ 두 종류로 분류하다 divide into two classes // 색에 따라 분류하다 classify according to color

— 목록 a classified catalogue **— 번호** a class number (도서 따위의) **—법** a classification system ; classification **—표** a classified table

분류 奔流 a torrent ; rapids ; a rapid stream **—하다** rush ; flush ; run with rapidity

— 전기 〖전기〗 a jumping current

분류 分溜 fractional distillation ; fractionation **—하다** fractionate ; crack

—관 fractionating column **— 분해** fractional decomposition **— 장치** a fractionator **— 휘발유** cracked gasoline

분류학 分類學 taxology ; taxonomy ; the science of classification

—자 a taxonomist ; a systematist

†**분리 分離** separation ; segregation 〔detachment〕 (격리) ; secession (탈당) ; disjunction (분열) **—하다** seperate 《from》 ; divide ; part ; detach ; segregate ; secede 《from》 ; break away 《from》 ; branch off 《from》

> 참고 **separate** 함께 있는 사람이나 물건을 떼어놓다 **divide** 부분 부분으로 나누다 때때로 「할당하다」의 뜻을 갖는다 **part** 밀접하게 묶인 사람이나 물건을 분리하다 **sever** 전체로부터 그 일부를 확연히 떼어놓다

¶ 분리할 수 없는 inseparable ; indivisible // 본대에서 분리되다 detach oneself from the main body

— 계수법(係數法) 〖수학〗 a method of detached coefficients **—기** a separator ; [공기 청정기] an eliminator **—법** 〖화학〗 a method of chemical separation **— 운동** a separatist movement **—주의〔론〕** separatism ; secessionism **—주의자** a separatist ; a secessionist ; [흑인과 백인의] a segregationist **—파** seceders ; secessionists ; separatists ; 〖건축〗 the secession school **재산 —** separation of property **중앙 —대** a median strip (차도의)

분립 分立 separation ; independence **—하다** separate 《from》 ; secede 《from》 ; be independent 《from》 ¶ 군소 정당으로 분립되다 be divided into many small parties

분마 奔馬 a galloping horse

분만 分娩 childbirth ; delivery ; parturition **—하다** give birth to ; be delivered of ¶ 남아를 분만했다 She gave birth to〔was delivered of〕 a son.

—비 childbirth〔delivery〕 expenses **—(시)기** one's time ; period〔term〕 of delivery **—실** a delivery〔labor〕 room **—촉진제** an oxytocic **— 휴가** a maternity leave **무통(無痛)—** painless labor ; twilight sleep

분말 粉末 powder ¶ 분말로 만들다 reduce 《a thing》 to powder ; powder ; pulverize

—도(度) fineness **—차(茶)** powdered 〔ground〕 tea

분망 奔忙 pressure of work **—하다** (be) busily occupied〔engaged〕 ; very busy ¶ 회의 준비에 분망하다 be very busy preparing for a conference

분매 分賣 selling separately **—하다** sell 《things》 separately ; sell 《land》 in lots ¶ 각 권을 낱권으로 분매합니다 Separate volumes may be had singly.

분맥 分脈 a ramification 《of a nerve》

†**분명 分明** clearness ; obviousness **—하다** (be) clear ; plain ; obvious ; evident ; manifest ; distinct

> 참고 **clear**는 가장 일반적인 말로서 이해를 방해하는 애매함이 없는 것 **plain**도 보통 많이 사용되는 말로서 이해하기 쉽고 단순한 것 **obvious**는 뚜렷하여 바로 지각할 수 있는 것 **evident**는 외면적인 특징이 확연히 나타나 있는 것 **manifest**는 감각 특히 시각에 대하여 분명한 것을 가리킨다

¶ 분명한 구별 a sharp〔clear-cut〕 distinction // 분명히 plainly ; clearly ; distinctly ; obviously // 분명히 기억하다 remember clearly // 분명히 하다 make clear ; clear up ; clarify ; explicate // 자기의 입장을 분명히 하다 make one's position clear // 분명히 말해 둔다 I say this once for all. // 화재의 원인이 분명치 않다 The origin of the fire is unknown.

분모 分母 〖수학〗 a denominator

공— a common denominator **최소 공—** the least common denominator

분묘 墳墓 a tomb ; a grave ; a sepulchre

— 발굴 desecration of a tomb ; exhumation

분무기 噴霧器 a sprayer ; a vaporizer ¶ 과수에 분무기로 살충제를 뿌리다 spray fruit trees with insecticide

분문 噴門 〖생물〗 the cardia ; the esophageal orifice (of the stomach)

분바르다 粉— powder (one's face) ; put powder 《on》 ¶ 얼굴을 하얗게 분발랐다 Her face was thickly〔heavily〕 powdered.

분받침 盆— a pottery flowerpot holder

분발 奮發 (an) exertion ; (a) strenuous effort ; (an) endeavor **—하다** make an effort ; endeavor ; do one's best ; spurt —심 the spirit of exertion ; a strenuous spirit

분방 奔放 being wild〔free, unfettered〕 —하다 (be) wild ; extravagant ; free (-spirited) ; unrestrained

†**분배 分配** division ; distribution ; sharing ; allotment —하다 distribute 《among》 ; divide 《between, among》 ; share 《with, between》 ; give out

> 참고 **distribute, give out**는 「자기는 갖지 않고 타인에게 모든 것을 나누어 주다」의 뜻 **share**는 「자기도 일부를 차지하다」의 뜻 **divide**는 양쪽에 사용된다

¶ 부(富)의 분배 distribution of wealth // 종업원에게 이익을 분배해 주다 distribute the profits among one's employees // 그도 분배액을 받게 된다 He is to have a share.

—금 a dividend (in liquidation) (청산의) —론 a theory of distribution —액 a share —자 a portioner ; a distributor 이익 — division of profits ; profit sharing

분벽 粉壁 a whitewashed wall

†**분별 分別** [분류] classification ; assortment ; division ; [분변] distinction ; discrimination —하다 divide ; separate ; classify ; distinguish ; discriminate ¶ 분별 있는 사람 a man of sense // 분별할 수 없을 정도이다 be beyond〔out of〕 recognition // 방향을 분별할 수 없다 cannot tell the direction

—법 〖화학〗 fractionation

분복 分福 one's destined luck ; one's lot

분봉 分封 [제후의] enfeoffment —하다 enfeoff ; invest 《a person》 with a fief

분봉 分蜂 hiving off —하다 hive off ; split the hive

분부 分賦 allotment ; assignment ; allocation —하다 allot ; allocate

†**분부 吩咐, 分付** an order ; bidding ; a command ; directions〔instructions〕 (지령) —하다 bid ; tell ; give directions ¶ 분부를 내리다 give〔issue〕 orders // 분부에 따르다 obey 《a person's》 order ; toe the line // 분부대로 거행하렷다 Do as you are told.

분분하다 紛紛— [시끄럽다] (be) noisy ; tumultuous ; [어수선하다] confused〔pell-mell〕 ; [구구하다] divided 〔diverse, various〕 ; contradictory ; [말썽 많다] troublesome〔tangled〕 ¶ 분분한 소문 contradictory rumors // 의견이 분분하다 Their opinion is divided. / There is a diversity of opinion.

분비 分泌 〖생물〗 secretion —하다 secrete ¶ 분비성의 secretory

— 기관 a secretory organ ; a secernent —물 a secretion ; an exudate ; excreta (선(腺) 분비물) —선〔세포〕 a secreting gland〔cell〕 — 신경 a secreting nerve —액 secreting fluid ; juice —약 a secretive drug ; a secernent — 작용 secretion 내— internal secretion

분사 憤死 —하다 die of resentment 〔indignation〕 ; die in a fit of anger

‡**분사 噴射** jet ; spray ; injection

—관〔압축기〕 an injection pipe〔compressor〕 — 버너 a spraying burner — 성형(成形) [수지의] jet molding — 속도 jet velocity —수(水) injection water ; water jet —식 이륙 촉진 장치 a jato (unit) ; a jet-assisted take off —식 추진기 a jet propeller — 총 [우주 유영에 쓰는] a jet gun —판(瓣)〔송풍기, 구(口), 통, 펌프〕 a jet valve〔blower, orifice, pod, pump〕

‡**분사 分詞** 〖언어〗 a participle

—구〔절〕 a participle phrase〔clause〕 — 구문 a participial construction —형 a participle form 현재〔과거〕 — a present〔past〕 participle

분사 추진 噴射推進 〖항공〗 jet〔rocket〕 propulsion 《JP》

—기 a jet(-engined, -propelled, -powered) plane — 기관 a ram(jet) engine 〔motor〕 — 식 전투〔폭격〕기 a jet fighter 〔bomber〕

분산 分散 dispersion ; breakup ; decentralization ; bankruptcy (파산) —하다 disperse ; scatter ; diversify ; break up ; decentralize ¶ 광선의 분산 the dispersion of light // 그 집안은 분산되었다 The family has broken up.

— 가족 the sundered〔scattered, dispersed, broken up〕 family —도 degree of dispersion —성 dispersibility —율 the index of dispersion —주의 the principle of dispersal (함대의) — 투자 diversified investment 인구 —책 the population decentralization policies

분상 粉狀 ¶ 분상의 powdered ; pulverized

분서 焚書 book burning ; burning books —하다 burn books

—갱유(坑儒) 〖역사〗 burning books on the Chinese classics and burying Confucian scholars alive

‡**분석 分析** analysis 《*pl.* -ses》 ; assay (광석의) —하다 analyze 《a thing》 into ; assay ¶ 분석 결과 비타민 A가 대량 함유되어 있음이 밝혀졌다 Analysis showed that it contained much vitamin A.

— 비평 analytical criticism —소 an assay office — 시험 [금속의] assay ; assaying —실 an analytical laboratory ; a room for analysis —자 an analyst ; an assayer —표 an analysis table —학 analytics —학자 an analyst — 화학 analytical chemistry 소득〔가격〕 — income〔price〕 analysis 정량〔정성(定性), 원소〕 — quantitative〔qualitative, ultimate〕 analysis 정신 —(학) psychoanalysis 중량 — 〖화학〗 gravimetricanalysis

분선 分線 a branch line

분설 分設 establishment of a branch ;

separate installation —하다 establish 〔set up〕 a branch 《of》; install separately
분성 分性 〖물리〗 divisibility
분손 分損 〖경제〗 partial loss
분쇄 粉碎, 分碎 —하다 shatter 《a thing》 to pieces ; pulverize ; [목제품을] smash to splinters ; crush ; [적을] annihilate ; smash
—기 a pulverizer ; a grinder ; a crusher ; a mill (수동식)
분쇠 粉— lead used in making powder
분수 ① [분한] social standing〔status, position〕; means (자력) ; lot (상태) ¶ 분수에 넘치는 짓을 하다 get above oneself // 분수에 넘치게 살다 live above one's means // 분수에 알맞게 살다 live within one's means ; cut one's coat according to the cloth // 너는 네 분수를 모르냐 Don't you know your place? ② [분별] discretion ; good sense ; prudence ; judgment ¶ 분수없는 indiscreet ; imprudent ; thoughtless // 분수있는 sensible ; thoughtful ; discreet // 분수없는 짓 a rash act // 그는 분수없이 말을 한다 He doesn't know when to shut up.
‡**분수 分數** 〖수학〗 a fraction ; a fractional number ¶ 분수의 fractional // 분수로 나누다 fractionize
— 방정식 a fractional equation —식 a fractional expression 기약 — a fraction reduced to its lowest terms 부분 — partial fractions 진(眞)〔가〕— a proper 〔an improper〕 fraction
분수 噴水 a fountain ; a jet〔squirt〕 of water ¶ 분수를 만들다 set up a fountain // 분수가 솟고 있다 The fountain is playing.
—공(孔) a jet ; a spout ¶ 고래의 분수공 the blowhole〔spiracle, spout (hole)〕 of a whale —기(器) a waterspout —식 음료수 a drinking fountain —지(池) a spray pound
분수령 分水嶺 a watershed〔water parting〕; a divide ¶ 그 산맥이 그 나라의 분수령을 이루고 있다 The mountain range forms the backbone〔watershed〕 of the country.
분승 分乘 —하다 ride separately ¶ 3대의 버스에 분승하여 in three separate buses
분식 扮飾 dressing —하다 dress oneself
분식 粉食 flour ; flour-based meals ; powdered〔pulverized〕 food —하다 eat flour〔ground grain〕 ¶ 분식을 장려하다 encourage the use of flour for food
분식 粉飾 make-up ; toilet ; showy ornaments ; embellishment ; adornment —하다 make up 《one's face》; paint ; embellish ; decorate
분식 分蝕 〖천문〗 a partial eclipse 《of the sun, the moon》
분신 分身 the other self ; an incarnation of the Buddha
분신 焚身 burning oneself to death ; suicide by burning oneself ¶ 분신을 기도하다 make an attempt to burn oneself to death
— 자살 ⇨ 분신
분실 分室 [관청의] a branch〔detached〕 office ; [병원의] an isolated room
†**분실 紛失** loss —하다 lose ; miss ¶ 돈이 분실되다 The money is missing. // 반지가 분실되었다 A ring has disappeared 《from the dresser》.
—물 a missing〔lost〕 article ; lost property —물 신고 the report of the loss 《of an article》 —자 a loser ; the owner of a lost article
분압 分壓 〖기계〗 partial pressure
—기(器) a potentiometer ; a voltage divider
분야 分野 a sphere ; a field ; a realm ; a province ; a horizon ¶ 과학의 분야 the sphere〔field〕 of science // 산업의 각 분야 various fields of industry // 새로운 분야를 개척하다 open up a new field // 각 분야에 걸쳐 여자가 남자의 영역을 침범하고 있다 Women everywhere are invading the spheres of men.
연구 — a field〔an area〕 of study 전공 — a major field of study ; one's specialty
분양 分讓 —하다 sell 《land》 in lots ; distribute 《among》; parcel out
— 주택 a house for installment sale —지 (building) lots for sale ; subdivision 《미》
분업 分業 division of labor ; 〖경제〗 specialization —하다 divide work 《among》; specialize 《in》
— 시대 the age of specialization 국제 — international division of labor 의약 — separation of dispensary from medical practice
분여 分與 ⇨ 분급
분연 忿然 indignantly ; in anger ; in a rage —하다 (be) indignant〔wrathful〕; be in a rage ¶ 분연히 돌아섰다 He went away in indignation〔a huff〕. /He shook the dust off his feet.
분연 奮然 courageously ; resolutely ; boldly ; in a determined manner —하다 (be) resolute ; vigorous ; strenuous ¶ 분연 난국에 대처하다 face up to a crisis ; cope with a difficult situation unflinchingly
분열 分列 —하다 file off
—식 a march-past ; [항공기의] a fly-past ; an air review ¶ 분열식을 하다 march past ; have a march-past ; fly past (비행기의) — 행진 marching in file
분열 分裂 disruption ; disunion ; a split ; a division ; fission ; breakup ; disorganization —하다 be disrupted ; be split ; break up ¶ 정당의 분열 a disruption of〔a split in〕 a political party // 의식의 분열 dissociation of consciousness // 분열시키

다 split ; break up ; disrupt // 둘로 분열하다 split in half〔two〕// 분열시켜서 정복하다 divide and rule // 당은 그 문제로 3파로 분열되었다 The party split over the problem into three groups.
— 생식 (reproduction by) fission — 식물 a schizophyte — 조직 〖식물〗 meristematic tissue ; meristem —편(片) a segment 감수 — 〖생물〗 meiosis ; reduction division 다수 — multiple division (in reproduction) 사상적 — an ideological divsion 세포 — cell division ; segmentation 원자핵 — nuclear〔atomic〕 fission 핵— nuclear fission ; [식물의] nuclear division

분외 分外 ¶ 분외의 undeserved ; beyond one's lot ; undue ; unmerited // 분외의 지위 an undeserved position // 분외의 대망 an inordinate ambition

분요 紛擾 disorder ; confusion ⇨ 분란

분원 分院 a branch hospital〔institute〕; a detached building

분위기 雰圍氣 an atmosphere ; surroundings (환경) ; the air〔atmosphere〕 (대기) ¶ 종교적인 분위기 a religious atmosphere // 자유로운 분위기 속에서 in an atmosphere of freedom // 분위기를 깨뜨리다 destroy the atmosphere // 분위기를 조성하다 create〔produce〕 an atmosphere // 그 분위기가 싫다 The atmosphere is not to my liking.

분유 粉乳 powdered milk
탈지(脫脂)— nonfat dry milk

*__분자 分子__ 〖물리〗 a molecule ; 〖수학〗 a numerator ; [요소] an element ; a factor
— 구조 molecular structure —량 molecular weight —력 molecular force —설 a molecular theory —식 a molecular formula — 인력 molecular attraction — 전도도(傳導度) molecular conductivity 반동 — reactionary elements 부패 — corrupt elements 불온 — a disturbing element 불평 — malcontent elements

분잡 紛雜 confusion ; crowdedness ; congestion —하다 be in confusion 〔disorder〕; (be) crowded ¶ 아침의 분잡한 출근 시간 the morning rush hours // 분잡한 틈을 타서 in the confusion

분장 分掌 division〔allotment〕 of work load —하다 divide duties ; take partial charge of the work

분장 扮裝 make-up ; disguise ; impersonation —하다 make〔dress〕 up 《as》; be disguised 《as》; play〔act〕 the part〔role〕 《of》; impersonate 《a character》 ¶ 여자로 분장하다 dress oneself up as a woman ; be in the guise of a woman // 여주인공으로 분장하다 play a heroine ; play the role of a heroine
—실 [연극의] a dressing room ; a greenroom ; the backstage —자 an impersonator

분재 分財 distribution of property〔an estate, assets〕; apportionment of an inheritance —하다 distribute assets 《among》; apportion〔divide up〕 an inheritance
—깃 one's share of properties apportioned〔inherited〕

분재 盆栽 a potted plant ; pot-planting —하다 plant in a pot

분쟁 分爭 party strife〔struggle〕; factional rivalry〔feud, dissensions, conflict〕 —하다 have a factional fight〔dispute〕; have party strife〔struggle〕; be pitted against one another ¶ 분쟁에 끼어들지 않다 keep away〔stand aloof from〕 party strife // 분쟁을 일삼다 be given up to party squabbles

분쟁 紛爭 trouble ; a dispute ; dissension ; strife —하다 dispute ; get involved in troubles ; engage in controversy ; quarrel ¶ 분쟁을 일으키다 raise 〔kick up〕 dust // 분쟁을 해결하다 settle a dispute // 양자간에 분쟁이 일어났다 A dispute arose between the two.
— 조정 grievance mediation〔settlement〕 — 지역 troubled parts〔areas〕 (of the world) (세계의) — 처리 기관 grievance machinery 국제 — an international dispute 노사(勞使) — conflicts between labor and management

분전 奮戰 a desperate fight ; hard fighting ; a tight fight —하다 fight desperately〔heroically, hard〕 《against》 ¶ 끝까지 분전하다가 죽다 die in the last ditch ; fight to the death ; die gamely

분점 分店 a branch shop ; a branch office〔firm〕

분점 分點 〖천문〗 equinoctial points ; equinoxes
—월(月) a tropical month 평균〔진(眞)〕— the mean〔true〕 equinox

분젠등 —燈 a Bunsen burner

분종 盆種 pot-planting ; a potted plant —하다 grow〔plant〕 in a pot

†**분주 奔走** —하다 (be) busy ¶ 분주한 일정 a crowded〔heavy〕 schedule // 분주한 거리 a busy thoroughfare // 분주스럽다 be busily engaged ; be all busy // 분주다사하다 be busy and pressed with work // 눈코 뜰 사이 없이 분주하다 be (as) busy as a bee

‡**분지 盆地** 〖지리〗 a basin ; a valley

-**분지 分之** a part ; a fraction ¶ 3분지 1 a third (part) ; one third // 3분지 2 two thirds // 4분지 1 a quarter // 4분지 3 three quarters // 100분지 1 one hundredth ; one per cent // 백만분지 1 지도 a map on the scale of 1 : 1,000,000 ; a one-to-a-million map

분지르다 break ⇨ 부러뜨리다

분책 分册 a fascicle (of a book) ; a separate volume ; binding in fascicles —하다 bind〔issue〕 in fascicles ¶ 분책으로 출판하다 publish in parts // 분책으로 판매

하다 sell volumes singly
분첩 粉貼 a (powder) puff ; a kind of cardboard slate for children's writing practice
분초 分秒 a minute and a second ; an instant ; a moment ; the exact time ¶ 분초를 다투는 문제이다 It admits of no delay. /It is urgent.
‡**분출 噴出** gushing ; spouting ; eruption **—하다** [액체를] spout ; spurt ; gush out ; burst ; [연기·불을] belch up 《smoke》; shoot up : [방출하다] emit
—구(口) a jet ; an exhaust nozzle **—구(溝)** an eruptive canal **—물(物)** jet (구멍·파이프로부터의) ; ejecta ; eruptions (화산의) **—암(岩)** an effusive〔eruptive〕 rock ; an eruptive
분침 分針 a minute hand
분칭 分秤 a small balance beam
분탄 粉炭 powdered〔pulverized, dust〕 coal ; slack
분탕 焚蕩 dissipation ; squandering **—하다** squander ; dissipate
—질 squandering〔dissipating, going through, running through〕 one's fortune
분토 糞土 decayed soil ; rotten earth ; black earth
분통 憤痛 rage ; fury ; great indignation ¶ 분통이 터지다 get enraged〔infuriated〕 ; fly into a passion ; grow furious // 그 여자의 말에 그는 분통이 터졌다 He got furious at her remarks.
†**분투 奮鬪** a struggle ; a strenuous effort ; hard fighting **—하다** fight〔battle〕《against》; struggle (hard) ; make a strenuous effort ¶ 분투 노력하여 성공하다 fight one's way to success // 분투 선전하다 put up a good fight // 자유를 위하여 분투하다 fight for liberty
—가(家) a hard〔an energetic〕 worker **—노력** violent〔strenuous〕 efforts〔exertions〕 ; push **—정신** a fighting spirit ; an indomitable spirit ; gameness ; pluck
‡**분파 分派** a branch ; an offshoot ; a sect (종교의) **—하다** branch ; divide ; form a new sect
—주의 factionalism (파벌주의) ; fractionalism (공산당 따위의) **—행동** a factional action **—활동** factional activities
분패 憤敗 —하다 be defeated by a narrow margin
‡**분포 分布** distribution **—하다** be distributed ; range 《from one place to another》 ¶ 식물의 지리적 분포 the geographical distribution of plants
—도(圖) a distribution chart **—범위** (동·식물의) a range **인구—** the spread of population
분풀이 憤— giving vent to one's indignation ; retaliation **—하다** wreak one's wrath on 《a person》; blow off steam ; vent one's spite on 《a person》; retaliate ¶ 나는 그에게 분풀이할 일이 있다 I've got an old score to pay off on him. // 이봐 분풀이하려거든 내게 해라 Look, take it out on me.
분필 分筆 division of a lot
†**분필 粉筆** chalk ¶ 분필로 쓰다 write with〔in〕 chalk
분하다 扮— ⇨ 분장(扮裝)
분하다 憤— ① [원통하다] resent ; be exasperated〔provoked〕《by》; (be) indignant 《about a thing, over a matter, at the word, with a person》
¶ 분해서 이를 갈다 gnash〔grind〕 one's teeth in vexation // 그 소식을 듣고 분해서 어찌할 바를 몰랐다 He was hotly indignant upon hearing the news. // 그에게 그런 말을 들으니 분했다 I was resentful of what he had said. /I got sore about that remark of his. // 그의 처사가 분했다 I was exasperated by his proceeding. // 그 여자의 거만한 태도가 그를 분하게 했다 Her haughty attitude irked him.
② [아깝다] (be) sorry ; regrettable ¶ 분하게도 to my regret // 분하게 지다 be defeated by a narrow margin (경기에) // 실패한 것이 분했다 He was chagrined at his failure. // 그는 상을 못 탄 것을 분해했다 He was put out that he didn't win a prize.
분한 分限 ① [실용 한도] utility ; usefulness ; economical use ¶ 분한있게 돈을 써라 Spend your money wisely. /Put your money to good use. // 요새는 돈이 전보다 분한없다 Nowadays money is worthless than what it used to be.
② [분수] social status〔standing〕 ; social position ; means (재력) ¶ 분한을 지키다 cut one's coat according to the cloth // 자기의 분한을 지켜라 Remember who you are and what you are.
†**분할 分割** partition ; division **—하다** partition ; divide ; parcel ; dismember ¶ 토지를 분할하다 parcel (out) the land // 농장을 몇 개의 주택 단지로 분할하다 split a farm into housing lots // 그 강은 내 토지와 그의 토지를 분할해 준다 The river divides my land from his.
—매입 buying on the hire-purchase plan 《영》 : buying on the instalment〔easy-payment〕 plan 《미》 **—법** 〖논리〗 partition **—상속(제)** divided succession ; division of succession **—소유권** divided〔mixed〕 ownership **—인도** installment delivery **—주문** split order **—지배(책)** divide and rule ; divide et impera 《라》 **—지불** an easy payment plan ; payment in〔by〕 installments ; hire-purchase system
분할 分轄 separate control **—하다** control separately ; exercise separate control
분할불 分割拂 an easy payment plan ; payment in〔by〕 instal(l)ments ; hire-purchase system ¶ 분할불로 사다 buy on the installment〔hire-purchase, easy

payment〕 plan
분할 선적 分割船積 installment shipment **—하다** make installment shipment ; ship 《the goods》 in installments
분합 分閤 『건축』 windows〔sliding doors〕 used to shut the plank-floor room off from the court
‡**분해 分解** analysis : [용해] solution ; [물질의 분해] resolution ; decomposition **—하다** analyze ; dissolve ; decompose ; [기계를] take 《a thing》 to pieces 〔apart〕 ; break up ; dismantle ; [문장을] parse ¶ 기계를 분해하다 disassemble 〔break up〕 a machine // 물을 산소와 수소로 분해하다 resolve water into oxygen and hydrogen // 비행기를 분해해서 수송하다 ship an airplane in sections // 화합물을 원소로 분해하다 reduce〔dissolve, resolve〕 a compound into its elements // 이 총은 분해하기 쉽다 This gun disassembles〔takes to pieces〕 easily. // 이 시계를 분해해도 괜찮습니까 Is it okay if I take this clock apart ?
—도 『건축』 a deal drawing **— 사진** a photographic playback (텔레비전의) **—성** resolvability **— 세포** a clastic cell **— 수리** a thorough overhaul **— 작용** disintegration
분해하다 憤— feel indignation 《at》 ; be 〔feel〕 chagrined〔vexed, mortified〕 《at, by》 ; be sorry about ¶ 발을 구르며 분해하다 stamp on the ground〔stamp one's feet〕 with chagrin〔mortification〕 // 모욕을 당하고 분해하다 resent an insult // 실패를 분해하다 be chagrined by〔at〕 one's failure
분향 焚香 incense burning **—하다** burn 〔offer〕 incense
‡**분홍 粉紅** pink (color) ¶ 분홍 치마 a pink skirt
분화 分化 specialization ; differentiation **—하다** differentiate ; specialize ; branch 《into》
***분화 噴火** an eruption ; volcanic activity **—하다** erupt ; burst into eruption ; become active ¶ 화산이 맹렬히 분화했다 A volcano went〔burst〕 into violent eruption.
—구 a crater **—산** an active volcano
분회 分會 a branch ; a chapter
붇다 ① [물에 젖어서] swell ; get water-soaked〔bloated〕 ; grow〔become〕 sodden ¶ 쌀이 물에 불었다 Rice has swollen in the water. ② [늘어가다] increase ; swell ; rise ; grow ¶ 체중이 붇다 gain in weight ; put on weight // 눈이 녹아 강물이 불었다 The streams have swollen with melted snow. // 식구가 자꾸 붇는다 The family grows larger.
†**불**[1] ① [타는 현상] fire ; flame ; blaze ¶ 불이 붙은 lighted ; burning // 불이 잘 붙는 quick to catch fire ; inflammable // 담배에 불을 붙이다 light a cigarette // 불을 끄다 put out the fire // 불을 붙이다 light〔kindle〕 a fire // 불을 쬐다 warm oneself at the fire // 불이 붙다 catch fire ; burn // 불이 훨훨 타오르다 blaze fiercely // 성냥불을 붙이다 strike〔light〕 a match // 숯불을 피우다 make fire with charcoal // 불을 당기다 feed the fire // 불을 잘 피워놓다 keep up a good fire // 불 안땐 굴뚝에 연기 날까 Where there is smoke, there is fire. // 불 좀 빌려 주시겠습니까 May I have a light from your cigarette, please ? // 불 좀 있으세요 Got a light ?
② [등화] a light ; a lamp ¶ 불을 끄다 put out〔turn off〕 the light // 불을 켜다 turn on the light ; light a lamp // 방에 불이 켜 있다 The room is lighted. /The light is burning in the room. // 불이 나갔다 The light is out. // 불을 켜 놓은 채 잠들다 He goes to sleep with the light on.
③ [화재] a fire ; a blaze ; a conflagration (큰불) ¶ 불조심 precaution against fire // 불에 타다 be burnt down // 집에 불을 지르다 set fire to a house ; set a house on fire // 불이 났다 A fire breaks out. /There is a fire. // 집에 포탄이 맞아 불이 났다 A shell set fire to a house.
④ [비유적] ¶ 정열의 불 fire of passion // (아이가) 불이 나게 울다 break into a wild cry ; fall to crying aloud // 불을 보듯 환하다 be as plain as day ; be crystal-clear // 눈에 불이 났다 I saw stars. /There was an angry spark in my eyes.
불에 놀란 놈이 부지깽이만 보아도 놀란다 속담 A scalded cat〔dog〕 fears cold water. /The burnt child dreads the fire. /Once bitten twice shy.
불[2] [음낭] the scrotum 《*pl.* -ta》 ; [불알] the testicles ; the balls 《속》
불[3] 『농업』 a pannier ; the side flaps of a loading rack
불 弗 a dollar ¶ 미화 10불 ten U. S. dollars
불 佛 ① [불타] the Buddha ¶ 불구(佛具) altar fittings ② [프랑스] France
불 不 non- ; in- ; un-
불가 不可 —하다 be not right ; (be) wrong ; bad ; unadvisable ¶ 가도 아니고 불가도 아니다 It is neither good nor bad. // 가 20명 불가 10명 Twenty were in favor of it and ten against it. /The ayes were 20 and noes 10. // ABC는 가 D는 불가 A, B and C are passing grades, but D is a failure.
가— right or wrong ; good or bad
불가 佛家 [신도] a Buddhist ; a Buddhist family ; [절] Buddhist temple
‡**불가결 不可缺** indispensability ; absolute necessity **—하다** (be) indispensable 《to》 ; essential 《to》
†**불가능 不可能** impossibility ; unattainableness **—하다** (be) impossible〔unattainable〕 ¶ 불가능한 일 the impossible ; an impossible thing // 거의 불가능한

almost〔next to〕 impossible // 실현 불가능한 impossible of attainment〔realization〕 // 불가능한 일을 가능케 하다 turn an impossibility into a possibility
불가래 a wooden fire shovel
불가물 a severe drought
불가분 不可分 indivisibility ¶ 불가분의 indivisible ; undetachable ; inseparable // 불가분의 관계 an inseparable ralation ; an undetachable connection // 양자는 불가분의 관계에 있다 Both are inseparably related 《to each other》.
—체 an indivisible entity
불가불 不可不 inevitably ; really ought to ; unavoidably ; under compulsion ¶ 불가불 그렇게 했다 I had no option but to do so. /I had to do so. // 나는 불가불 내일 떠나야 한다. I really must leave tomorrow.
불가사리 〚동물〛 a starfish ; an asteroid ; [상상적 동물] an imaginary monster ; a mythical creature
불가사의 不可思議 a mystery ; a wonder ; a riddle ; a miracle **—하다** (be) mysterious 〔miraculous, inscrutable, strange〕
—론 〚철학〛 agnosticism
불가서 佛家書 the Buddhist scriptures ; Buddhist literature
불가시(광)선 不可視(光)線 〚물리〛 an invisible ray
불가역 不可逆 being irreversible
—성(性) irreversibility **— 현상** an irreversible phenomenon
불가입성 不可入性 〚물리〛 impenetrability
불가지 不可知 inscrutability ; unknowableness ¶ 불가지의 unknowable ; inscrutable ; inconceivable
—론 〚철학〛 agnosticism **—론자** 〚철학〛 an agnostic **—물** 〚철학〛 an unknowable ; the Unknowable
불가청 不可聽 inaudibility
—음 an inaudible sound
불가침 不可侵 inviolability ; nonaggression ¶ 불가침의 inviolable ; sacred
—권 an inviolable right ¶ 영토의 불가침권 the inviolability of territory **— 조약** a nonaggression pact〔treaty〕 ¶ 불가침 조약을 맺다 conclude a nonaggression pact 《with》
불가피 不可避 inevitability ; unavoidability **—하다** (be) inevitable ; unavoidable ¶ 불가피한 사정으로 인하여 owing to circumstances beyond control ; due to some unavoidable circumstances // 전쟁은 불가피한 것이 아니다 War is not inevitable. /We could avoid war.
불가항력 不可抗力 irresistible force ; force majeure ¶ 불가항력의 uncontrollable ; beyond control // 불가항력의 사고사 accidental death beyond human control〔through an act of God〕
불가해 不可解 an inscrutability ; a mystery ; a riddle **—하다** (be) mysterious ; incomprehensible ; inscrutable ; be hard to understand ¶ 인생은 불가해하다 Life is a mystery.
불각 佛閣 a Buddhist temple〔shrine〕 ⇨ 불당
불간섭 不干涉 nonintervention ; noninterference
—주의 nonintervention〔hands-off〕 policy
불감증 不感症 〚의학〛 frigidity ¶ 불감증의 여자 a frigid woman // 불감증이 되다 grow insensible 《to》
불강아지 a scrawny dog ; a lean puppy
불개 a mythical animal〔dog〕 thought to cause eclipses by eating the sun or the moon
불개미 〚곤충〛 a red ant ; Formica rufa (학명)
불개입 不介入 noninvolvement ; nonintervention ; neutrality ; holding〔keeping〕 the ring
— 정책〔방침〕 a noninvolvement〔nonintervention, hands-off〕 policy ¶ 전쟁 불개입 정책을 취하다 take a policy of noninvolvement in the war
불거지다 project ; protude ; bulge out ; jut out ; swell out
불걱거리다 [씹다] chew away ; [빨래를] scrub ; rub briskly
불걱불걱 chewing away 《on》 ; scrubbing away 《at》
불건강 不健康 unhealthiness ; bad〔ill〕 health **—하다** (be) unhealthy ; (be) unsanitary〔unwholesome〕 ; be in ill 〔bad〕 health
— 상태 〚의학〛 cachexia ; cachexy
불건전 不健全 unwholesomeness ; unsoundness ; morbidness **—하다** (be) unwholesome ; unsound ; morbid ; unhealthy ¶ 불건전한 사상 unwholesome ideas
불겅거리다 take a lot of chewing ; be chewy〔leathery, lumpy〕
불겅불겅 chewy ; leathery ; lumpy
불겅이 reddish cut〔pipe〕 tobacco
***불결 不潔** uncleanness ; an unsanitary condition **—하다** (be) dirty ; unsanitary ; unclean ; filthy ¶ 불결한 시장 a filthy market // 불결한 이야기 a filthy〔an indecent〕 talk // 불결하게 버려 두다 keep 《a room》 filthy // 부엌이 불결하다 The kitchen is very unsanitary.
불결과 不結果 a failure ; a negative〔an unfavorable〕 result ¶ 불결과로 끝나다 end in a failure ; fall through ; come to grief ; prove fruitless
***불경 不敬** disrespect ; irreverence ; blasphemy〔profanity〕 (신에 대한) **—하다** (be) disrespectful ; irreverent ; blasphemous
— 사건 a lèse-majesté affair 《프》 **—죄** 〚법〛 lése májesty **— 행위** an act of insulting and disrespectful nature
불경 佛經 the Buddhist scriptures ; Bud-

dhist classics ; the sutra ¶ 불경을 읽다〔외다〕 chant〔recite, read〕 a sutra ; intone the service

‡불경기 不景氣 [세상의] bad〔hard〕 times ; [상업의] (commercial, economic, financial, business, trade) depression ; recession (일시적인) ¶ 불경기를 타지 않는 사업은 당신 사업뿐인 모양이군 Your must be the only business not affected by the recession. // 불경기 때문에 죽을 지경이다 This recession is killing me. /This recession is murder. // 불경기가 계속돼서 실은 아슬아슬한 상황이다 With this prolonged slump, the situation is actually pretty touch-and-go.

불경작 不耕作 noncultivation

불경제 不經濟 poor〔bad〕 economy ; extravagance ; waste ━하다 (be) uneconomical〔unthrifty〕 ¶ 시간과 노력의 불경제 a waste of time and labor // 값싼 물건을 사는 것은 오히려 불경제다 It is poor economy〔uneconomical〕 to buy cheap goods.

불계승 不計勝 [바둑에서] a one-sided game ; a victory by a wide margin ¶ 불계승으로 이기다〔지다〕 win〔lose〕 (a game) by a wide margin

불고 不顧 ━하다 disregard ; take no notice of ; pay no heed〔attention〕 to ; ignore ; neglect ¶ 가사를 불고하다 neglect the home // 염치 불고하다 be shameless ; be dead to (the sense of) shame

불고기 roast meat

불고무래 a fire rake

불고문 ―拷問 an ordeal〔a torture〕 by fire ━하다 torture 《a person》 with fire ; subject 《a person》 to a fire ordeal

불공 不恭 disrespect ; impoliteness ━하다 (be) disrespectful〔rude, irreverent〕

불공 佛供 a Buddhist mass

불공 드리다 관용 hold〔offer〕 a Buddhist mass

불공대천 不共戴天 ¶ 불공대천의 원수 a mortal〔an irreconcilable〕 enemy ; a sworn〔dearest, deadly〕 foe

불공정 不公正 (be) unfair ⇨ 불공평

‡불공평 不公平 unfairness ; partiality ; injustice ━하다 (be) unfair ; partial ; unjust ; biased ; discriminate ¶ 불공평한 처사 an unfair dealing // 불공평하게 취급하다 discriminate against 《a person》 ; treat〔deal with〕 《a person》 unfairly

불과 不過 only ; merely ; no more than ━하다 be nothing but〔no more than, only〕 ¶ 불과 일주일 전에 but〔only〕 a week ago // 구실에 불과하다 That is only an excuse.

불과 佛果 Buddhahood ; Nirvana 《범》 ¶ 불과를 얻다 attain Buddhahood ; enter Nirvana ; achieve supreme enlightenment

불관 不關 indifference ; noninterference ━하다 do not mind ; be indifferent to ; do not concern oneself 《in》 ; do not care about ; have nothing to do with ; do not bother 《about》

*불교 佛敎 Buddhism ¶ 불교를 믿다 believe in Buddhism
―도 a Buddhist ― 문화 Buddhist civilization ― 미술 Buddhist art ― 음악 Buddhist music ― 청년회 the Young Men's Buddhist Association ― 회화 Buddhist paintings

*불구 不具 [기형] deformity ; malformation ; [얼굴의 손상] disfigurement ; [절름발이] a cripple ; [편지 끝에] Yours truly〔faithfully〕, ¶ 불구의 deformed ; crippled ; maimed ; disfigured ; lame
―자 a deformed person ; a cripple ; the handicapped〔disabled〕 《총칭》 ¶ 일생의 불구자가 되다 be crippled〔disabled〕 for life

불구 佛具 (Buddhist) altar fittings

†불구 不拘 ━하다 disregard ; be not deterred〔bothered, hindered〕 《by》 ¶ 불구하고 regardless of ; in spite of ; despite ; notwithstanding ; in the face〔teeth〕 of ; for all that // 그럼에도 불구하고 nevertheless ; none the less // 반대에도 불구하고 in the teeth of opposition // 비가 오는데도 불구하고 in spite of the rain

불구대천 不俱戴天 ⇨ 불공대천

불구속 不拘束 nonrestraint ¶ 불구속으로 without physical restraint

불굴 不屈 indomitability ; fortitude ━하다 (be) indomitable ; inflexible ¶ 불굴의 정신 an indomitable spirit

불귀객 不歸客 a dead〔deceased〕 person ¶ 불귀객이 되다 die ; pass away ; join the majority

‡불규칙 不規則 irregularity ; lack of system ━하다 (be) irregular〔unsystematic, unsteady〕 ¶ 불규칙하게 irregularly ; unsystematically ; by fits and starts ¶ 불규칙한 생활을 하다 live an irregular life
― 동사 〖문법〗 an irregular verb ― 변화 〖문법〗 an irregular conjugation

불균등 不均等 unevenness ; lack of uniformity ; inequality ; 〖화학〗 ununiformity ; nonhomogeneity

불균일 不均一 unevenness ; lack of uniformity ; inequality ; 〖화학〗 ununiformity ; nonhomogeneity

불균형 不均衡 disproportion ; want of balance ; inequality ; disparity ━하다 be out of balance ; (be) unequal ; ill-balanced ; disproportionate

불그데데하다 (be) reddish

불그뎅뎅하다 ⇨ 불그데데하다

불그레하다 (be) reddish ; be tinged with red

*불그스름하다 (be) reddish

불그죽죽하다 (be) somberly reddish

불근거리다 be touchy ; be easily offend-

ed ; be oversensitive
불근신 不謹愼 indiscretion ; imprudence **—하다** (be) indiscreet ; imprudent ¶ 불근신한 언동 indiscreet words or actions
불금 不禁 —하다 do not prohibit ; permit ; cannot bear〔help〕 doing ¶ 눈물을 불금하다 cannot help shedding〔cannot hold back〕 tears
불급 不及 —하다 (be) short (of) ; insufficient ; be no match 《for》 ; (be) unequal 《to》 ; fall behind
불급 不急 —하다 be not urgent〔pressing〕 ; be in no hurry
불긋불긋, 뿔긋뿔긋 —하다 (be) splashed〔dotted〕 with red
불긋하다, 뿔긋하다 (be) reddish ; ruddy
불기 —氣 fire ¶ 불기 없는 unheated ; fireless // 불기 없는 방 an unheated room // 화로에는 불기가 없다 There is no sign of fire in the brazier.
불기 佛紀 Buddha Era 《B. E.》 ¶ 불기 2천 5백 22년 2,522 B. E.
불기 不羈 freedom ; liberty ; independence **—하다** (be) independent ; free ; unrestrained ; unshackled
불기둥 a pilar of fire〔flames〕
불기소 不起訴 nonprosecution ¶ 불기소로 하다 drop 《a case》 ; do not prosecute 《a person》
— 처분 a disposition not to institute a public action
불기운 the heat of a fire ; [화세(火勢)] the force〔spread〕 of the fire ¶ 불기운이 더해가다〔떨어지다〕 The fire gains force〔goes down〕.
불긴 不緊 —하다 (be) not urgently needed〔necessary〕 《to》 ; not essential 《to》
불길 flames ; a blaze ¶ 불길에 싸이다 be enveloped in flames // 불길이 사납다 The flames are intense. // 불길이 약하다 The flames are weak.
†**불길 不吉** bad〔ill〕 luck **—하다** (be) unlucky ; ominous ; sinister ; inauspicious ¶ 불길한 날 an unlucky day // 불길한 예감 a gloomy foreboding ; an ominous presentiment // 불길한 징조 an ill〔evil〕 omen // 금요일은 불길한 날이라고 한다 Friday is believed to be an unlucky day.
불김 the heat〔warmth〕 from fire ¶ 젖은 옷이 불김에 말랐다 The wet clothes dried out by the fire.
불깃 a backfire ; a counterfire
불까다 castrate ; geld ; emasculate ¶ 불깐 닭 a capon // 불깐 말 a gelding // 불깐 소 a bullock // 말을 불까다 geld a horse
불깍정이 a real stinker
†**불꽃** a flame ; a blaze ; a spark ¶ 불꽃을 내뿜다 spark ; give off sparks ; sparkle // 불꽃이 굴뚝으로 날아오른다 Sparks fly up the chimney.
불꽃놀이 a display〔an exhibition〕 of fireworks ; a fireworks display ¶ 불꽃놀이를 하다 dispaly〔set off〕 fireworks ; do a fireworks display
불끈 [갑자기] suddenly ; casually ; [단단히] tightly ; fast ; hard ; forcibly ¶ 불끈 성을 내다 fly into a rage〔passion〕 ; flare〔flame〕 up // 주먹을 불끈 쥐다 clench one's fists // 남의 손을 불끈 쥐다 squeeze 《a person's》 hand // 불끈 동여매다 bind fast〔tight〕 // 생각이 불끈 떠오르다 an idea flashes upon 《a person》
불끈불끈 bursting into rages readily ; being quick to anger **—하다** burst into a rage readily ; get mad easily ; flare up
불나다 A fire breaks out〔starts, occurs〕. ¶ 불난 집 a house on fire // 어젯밤에 그 여관에 불났다 A fire broke out at the hotel last night. // 학교에 불났다 The school is on fire.
불나방 〖곤충〗 a garden tiger moth ; Arctia caja (학명)
불난리 —亂離 confusion〔disorder〕 at the scene of a fire
불내다 accidentally set fire 《to》
불놀이 a fireworks〔pyrotechnic〕 display ; [불장난] playing with fire **—하다** display〔set off〕 fireworks ; play with fire ¶ 오늘 밤에 불놀이가 있다 There will be a display of fireworks this evening.
불놓다 set fire to 《a house》 (방화) ; light a fuse (도화선에)
불놓이 shooting ; hunting **—하다** shoot (game) ; hunt
불능 不能 [무능력] incapacity ; inability ; incompetence ; [불가능] impossibility **—하다** (be) incapable ; incompetent ; impossible ; impotent (성적으로)
교접(交接) — impotence **지불 —** insolvency ; one's inability to pay
†**불다** ① [바람이] blow ¶ 바람이 모질게 불다 It〔The wind〕 blows hard. // 바람이 어느 쪽에서 불어오느냐 Where does the wind sit ?
② [입으로] blow ; breathe upon 《a thing》 ¶ 촛불을 불어 끄다 blow out a candle // 휘파람을 불다 whistle ; give a whistle // 불면 부풀어 오른다 It will be inflated if breathed upon.
③ [악기를] blow ; play 《on》 ¶ 나팔을 불다 blow a trumpet // 피리를 불다 play a flute // 다섯 시에 기상 나팔이 불었다 The reveille was sounded at five.
④ [고백하다] confess ; own up ; come clean ; make a clean breast 《of》 ¶ 죄상을 불다 confess to a crime // 그는 도둑질 하였다고 불었다 He owned up to the theft.
불단 佛壇 a Buddhist altar ; a family Buddhist altar〔shrine〕
불당 佛堂 a Buddhist temple〔sanctum〕
불당그래 a fire rake
불덩어리 a fireball ¶ 불덩어리가 되어 in a mass of flames

불도 佛道 Buddhism ; Buddhist doctrines ; the teachings of Buddha
불도 佛徒 a Buddhist
불도두개 a metal device for raising the wick of a lamp ; a wick-raiser
*불도저 a bulldozer ¶ 불도저로 땅을 밀다 bulldoze land
*불독 a bulldog
불돌 a flat stone cover placed on a brazier to keep a charcoal fire alive for a longer period of time ; a brazier stone
불되다 (be) extremely oppressive ; intolerably harsh〔cruel〕
불두덩 the pubic region
불등걸 pieces of glowing charcoal
불땀 heat ¶ 불땀이 세다 have strong caloric force ; be loaded with heat
—머리 the well-aired〔-sunned〕 end of a tree〔log〕
*불때다 make〔build〕 a fire ¶ 교실에 불때다 heat a classroom // 불땔 나무가 없다 have no wood to make a fire《with》// 난로에 불땔 연료가 없다 No fuel is left for the stove.
불땔감 firewood ; fuel
불땔꾼 a troublemaker
불똥 ① [탄 심지] the snuff《of a candle》; the charred portion《of a candlewick》
② [작은 불덩이] a spark
불똥이 튀기다 관용 spark ; give off sparks ; sparkle
불뚝 with a rude burst of anger ; flaring up
불뚝불뚝 with repeated rude bursts of anger ; flaring up again and again
불뚱거리다 get sulky ; scowl ; grouch《미·구》
불뚱불뚱 swelling up with anger ; quivering with rage
불뚱이 hot〔peevish〕 temper ; irritability ; irascibility ; spleen ; a choleric〔testy, touchy〕 person (사람)
불란서 佛蘭西 ⇨ 프랑스
*불량 不良 [행실이] wickedness ; delinquency ; [질이] badness ; inferiority —하다 (be) bad ; evil ; wicked ; delinquent ; poor ; inferior ; deleterious ¶ (사람이) 불량해지다 go to the bad ; become delinquent // 그의 학교 성적은 불량하다 He stands low in his school work.
— 도체 a nonconductor ; an insulator —배 the depraved ; a hoodlum ; a scoundrel ; a rowdy — 소녀〔소년〕 a bad〔delinquent〕 girl〔boy〕; a juvenile delinquent —품 inferior goods — 학생 a disorderly student —화(化) downfall ; degradation ¶ 불량화하다 become delinquent ; be degraded 발육 — poor development 성적 — poor〔unsatisfactory〕 results
†불러내다 call out ; call《a person》 to〔before〕; summon (법정에) ; call up (전화로) ¶ 문간으로 불러내다 call《a person》 to the door // 전화로 불러내다 call《a person》 up by telephone
불러들이다 call〔hail〕《a person》 in〔into〕; have《a person》 in
불러먹기 blackmail ; extortion —하다 blackmail《a person》; extort《a thing》 by intimidation
불러세우다 (call and) stop ; call《a person》 to stop
불러오다 summon ; call《a person》 to one ; [심부름꾼을 시켜서] send for《a person》; [불러모으다] call together ¶ 편지〔전화〕로 불러오다 write〔telephone〕 for a《person》; summon《a person》 by letter〔telephone〕// 의사를 불러오다 send《a man》 for a doctor
⁑불러일으키다 rouse〔gather〕 up ; stir up ; arouse ; excite ¶ 의분을 불러일으키다 give rise to a storm of one's indignation // 용기를 불러일으키다 muster〔recollect, summon (up), pluck up〕 one's courage
불려가다 be summoned to《the police》¶ 사장에게 불려가다 be called before the president // 법정에 불려가다 be summoned to the court
불력 佛力 the power〔influence〕 of Buddha
불령 佛領 a French possession〔territory〕
불로 不老 eternal youth —하다 (be) ever-young〔ageless〕; enjoy eternal youth ¶ 불로장생하다 live ever-young ; be ageless
—불사 eternal youth and immortality —불사약 the elixir of life —천(泉) a fountain of youth
불로 소득 不勞所得 unearned income ; a windfall income ; investment income
불로 장생 不老長生 eternal〔perennial, ageless〕 youth —하다 live ever-young ; enjoy eternal youth ; be ageless —약 an elixir of life
불로초 不老草 a herb of eternal youth
불룩거리다 quiver ; vibrate ¶ 좋아서 코를 불룩거리다 be puffed up with pride
*불룩하다 (be) swollen ; baggy ; bulging ¶ 과자로 불룩한 포켓 a bulging pocket with candies // 불룩한 지갑 a fat purse // 주머니를 불룩히 채우다 fill out a bag // 불룩해지다 swell《out》; expand ; bulk ; bulge《out》 (포켓이) ; be inflated (풍선이) ; rise (빵이) // 임신하여 배가 불룩하다 be big with child
불륜 不倫 immorality ; obliquity ; [행위] immoral conduct ; a liaison (이성간의)
*불리 不利 disadvantage ; a drawback ; a handicap —하다 (be) disadvantageous ; unfavorable ¶ 불리한 입장에 있다 be at a disadvantage ; be in a disadvantageous position // 그 결정은 우리에게 불리했다 The decision was unfavorable to〔against〕 us. // 형세가 우리에게 불리하다 The odds are against us. /The tide has

turned against us.

불리다¹ [배를] fill (one's stomach) ; [비유적] enrich oneself ; feather one's own net ¶ 공직을 이용하여 자기 배를 불리다 seek personal ends taking advantage of one's public office // 보리밥 한 그릇으로 주린 배를 불리다 gratify one's hunger on a bowl of boiled barley // 공금으로 자기 배를 불렸다 He enriched himself with public fund.

불리다² [쇠를] temper ; anneal ; [곡식을] winnow ; fan (away)

불리다³ [부름을 받다] be called ; be summoned ; be invited ¶ 법정에 불리다 be summoned to the court // 선생님에게 불리어 가다 be called before a teacher // 잔치에 불리다 be invited to a feast

불리다⁴ [바람에] be blown ¶ 먼지가 바람에 불리다 dust flies in the wind

불리다⁵ [액체에] soak ; steep ; [재물을] increase ; add to ; [과장하다] exaggerate ; magnify ; stretch 《the fact》 ¶ 쌀을 물에 불리다 soak rice in the water // 재산을 불리다 increase〔add to〕 one's fortune // 불려서 말하다 big ; exaggerate (a story)

불리다⁶ [악기를] make 《a porson》 blow ; [자백시키다] make 《a person》 admit himself guilty ; smoke 《a person》 out 《미·속》 ¶ 그에게 나팔을 불리다 have him blow a trumpet // 죄상을 강제로 불리다 force〔compel〕 a confession from 《a person》 ; force 《a person》 into confession

불림¹ tempering metal (쇠의)

불림² confession of〔informing on〕 one's accomplice (공범자의 자백) ; calling out (투전판의 정보 교환)

투전 — calling one's discards

*__불만 不滿__ dissatisfaction ; discontent — 하다, 스럽다 (be) discontented ; dissatisfied ; displeased ; disgruntled 《at》 ; unsatisfied 《desires》 ; unsatisfactory ¶ 불만스러운 결과 an unsatisfactory result // 불만스러운 표정 a dissatisfied look // 나로서는 조금도 불만이 없다 I have nothing to complain of. // 지위에 불만을 가지고 있다 I am discontented with my position.

성적 — sexual dissatisfaction

*__불만족 不滿足__ dissatisfaction ⇨ 불만

불망지은 不忘之恩 a favor〔benefit〕 never to be forgotten ; an unforgettable debt of gratitude

불매 동맹 不買同盟 a boycott (against purchasing) ; a buyers' strike

불매증 不寐症 insomnia

불면불휴 不眠不休 — 하다 work without sleeping or resting ; deny oneself sleep and rest ; work day and night

불면증 不眠症 〖의학〗 insomnia ; sleeplessness ¶ 불면증에 걸리다 suffer from insomnia

— 환자 an insomniac 피로성 — insomnia of exhaustion

불멸 不滅 [정신적] immortality ; [물질적] athanasia ; indestructibility ; imperishability — 하다 (be) immortal ; undying ; indestructible ¶ 영혼의 불멸 immortality of the soul // 물질 불멸의 원칙 the law of conservation of matter

불멸 佛滅 Buddha's death

불명 不明 [불분명] obscurity ; ambiguity ; [우둔] lack of perception〔brightness, wisdom〕 ; ignorance ; dullness — 하다 (be) obscure ; ambiguous ; indistinct ; unwise ; ignorant ; stupid ¶ 국적 불명의 선박 a vessel of unidentified nationality // 신원 불명의 시체 an unidentified body // 원인 불명의 화재 a fire of unknown origin // 자신의 불명을 사과하다 apologize for one's ignorance // 그의 죽음의 원인은 아직도 불명하다 The cause of his death still remains a mystery. // 이 모든 것이 내가 불명한 탓이다 It is entirely due to lack of insight on my part.

불명 佛名 [부처의] the name of Buddha ; [불호] the name of a Buddhist saint ; [신자의] one's Buddhist name

불명료 不明瞭 indistinctness ; obscurity ; ambiguity — 하다 (be) indistinct ; obscure ; be not clear

‡__불명예 不名譽__ dishonor ; disgrace ; shame — 하다 (be) disgraceful ; dishonorable ; inglorious ¶ 그것은 우리 가문에 불명예스러운 일이다 It brings disgrace upon our family.

— 제대 dishonorable discharge

불명확 不明確 indefiniteness ; indistinctness ; obscurity — 하다 (be) indefinite ; indistinct ; ill-defined ; vague ; obscure ; ambiguous

†__불모 不毛__ barrenness ; sterility ¶ 불모의 barren ; sterile ; waste // 불모의 땅 barren〔waste〕 land ; unproductive land ; a hungry soil

불목 the warmest part of the heated floor (above the fireplace) ¶ 불목에 앉다 sit on the warmest part of the heated room

불목 不睦 (family) discord ; disharmony ; trouble ; dissension — 하다 be in discord 《with》 ; be at enmity〔feud, strife, variance〕 《with》 ; be on bad terms 《with》

불목하니 a cook in a temple

불무하다 不無— be not lacking〔wanting〕 ; definitely exist

불문 佛文 a French sentence

—과 the Department of French Literature —학 French literature

불문 佛門 a Buddhist family

불문 不文 ① [무식] illiteracy ② [불성문] unwritten 《rule》

—율(律)〔법(法)〕 an unwritten law ; the common law — 헌법 an unwritten constitution

불문 不問 taking no notice ; giving no heed — 하다 take no notice of ;

ignore ; disregard ¶ 남녀노소를 불문하고 regardless of sex or age // 불문에 부치다 pass ⟪a matter⟫ over unnoticed ; shut one's eyes to ; take no notice ⟪of⟫ ; let ⟪a matter⟫ go unchallenged ; overlook

불문가지 不問可知 being easily understandable without asking ¶ 불문가지의 일이다 It goes without saying.

불문곡직 不問曲直 **—하다** do not inquire into the right or wrong ¶ 불문곡직하고 regardless of merits ; without inquiring into the right or wrong

불문율 不文律 an unwritten law〔rule〕; common law

불미 不美 **—하다** (be) ugly ; unsavory ; scandalous ; nasty ; disgraceful ¶ 불미스러운 일 a shameful thing ; a shame // 신사로서 불미스러운 행동 an act unworthy of a gentleman

불민 不敏 stupidity ; dullness ; incompetency **—하다** (be) dull ; dull-witted ; stupid ; incompetentl

불바다 a sea of flames ¶ 불바다를 이루었다 The flames have steadily spread.

불받다 suffer insult and〔or〕 injury

불발 不發 ① [떠나지 않음] **—하다** do not depart〔leave〕

② [안 터짐] misfire **—하다** misfire ; fail to be fired〔exploded〕

—탄 a blind shell ; a dud **—탄 처리** bomb disposal

불발 不拔 firmness ; steadfastness **—하다** (be) firm ; indomitable ; invincible ¶ 불발의 정신 an indomitable spirit

불밤송이 a chestnut which has dried up and fallen prematurely

불범 不犯 [침범 안 함] not trespassing 〔encroaching, intruding〕 **—하다** do not trespass〔encroach, intrude〕 upon

*‡***불법 不法** unlawfulness ; illegality ; injustice ; outrageousness **—하다** (be) unlawful ; illegal ; wrong ; unjust ¶ 분실된 카드를 다른 사람이 불법으로 사용하면 당신에게는 책임이 없습니다 You will not be liable for any unauthorized use of the lost card.

— 감금 illegal confinement〔detention〕 **— 몰수** ouster **— 소지** illegal possession ¶ 무기 불법 소지 illegal possession of weapon **— 입국** illegal entry **— 입국자** an illegal〔unlawful〕 entrant **—자** a lawless person **— 점거자** a squatter (건물·토지 따위의) **— 점유** unlawful occupation **— 처분〔조치〕** an illegal measure〔proceeding〕 **— 체포** an illegal arrest **— 출국** illegal exit **— 출판** illegal publication **— 침입** intrusion ; a forcible entry ; 〚법〛 (a) breach of close ¶ 불법 침입을 하다 intrude ⟪into⟫ ; trespass ⟪on, upon⟫ **— 침입자** an intruder ; a trespasser **— 침해** trespass **— 행위** an unlawful〔illegal〕 act

불법 佛法 [불교] Buddhism ; [부처의 교법] the law of Buddha

불벼락 ① [번갯불] a bolt of lightning

② [비유적] a tyrannical decree〔order〕 ¶ 불벼락을 내리다 issue a tyrannical decree

†**불변 不變** constancy ; unchangeability ; permanence **—하다** do not change ; be constant〔unchangeable, invariable, immutable〕 ¶ 불변의 법칙 an immutable law

— 가속도 uniform acceleration **—강(鋼)** invar **—색** a permanent〔fast〕 color **— 자본** a constant〔an invariable〕 capital **질량〔물질〕 —** 〚물리〛 conservation of mass 〔matter〕

불병풍 —屛風 a small folding screen set to protect a brazier fire from the wind

불볕 a broiling sun

불볕이 나다 관용 The sun comes out blazing.

불복 不服 insubordination ; disobedience ; [복죄하지 않음] pleading not guilty ; dissatisfaction **—하다** be insubordinate〔disobedient〕; plead not guilty ; deny one's guilt ; protest against ; object to ¶ 상관의 지시에 불복하다 do not respond to the instructions given by one's senior (officer)

— 신립 an appeal〔institution〕 of dissatisfaction **— 항소** an appeal of dissatisfaction ⟪to a higher office⟫

∗**불복종 不服從** insubordination ; disobedience ⟪to an order⟫ ⇨ 불복

불부채 a fan used in fanning the fire

∗**불분명 不分明** indistinctness ; obscurity **—하다** (be) indistinct ; obscure ; be not clear ; (be) ambiguous

*‡***불붙다** catch fire ¶ 불붙은 데 부채질하기 casting oil in the fire ; making matters worse // 불붙기 쉽다 be easy to catch fire ; be combustible

∗**불붙이다** light〔kindle〕 a fire ; light ¶ 담배에 불붙이다 light a cigarette // 램프에 불붙이다 light a lamp // 나무에 불붙이다 light the firewood

불비 不備 defect ; lack ; deficiency ; inadequacy ; [편지 끝에] 불비 상서(上書) Yours truly **—하다** (be) defective ; faulty ; deficient ¶ 교통 기관의 불비 defective means of communication // 불비한 점 a defect ; an imperfection // 위생 설비의 불비 lack of proper sanitation

불빛 [빛깔] flame color ; red ; [불의 빛] fire light ; light ¶ 시퍼런 불빛 a blue flame // 바다 위에 불빛이 가물거린다 The light glimmers on the waves.

불사 佛寺 a Buddhist temple

불사 佛事 a Buddhist service〔mass〕 ¶ 불사를 행하다 hold a Buddhist service

불사 不死 immortality ; eternal life **—하다** (be) immortal ; undying ; deathless

—약 an elixir of life

불사르다 burn ; commit ⟪a thing⟫ to the flames ; destroy ⟪a thing⟫ by fire ¶ 시체를 불사르다 cremate ; burn the body to ashes // 쓰레기를 불사르다 make a bonfire of rubbish ; burn garbage

불사신 不死身 an invulnerable body ; invulnerability ¶ 불사신의 invulnerable ; immortal // 나는 불사신이다 I am proof against death. / I have a charmed life.

***불사조 不死鳥** the secular〔undying〕 bird ; the phoenix

불사하다 不辭― do not decline ; act in an unreserved way ¶ …허가를 불사하다 be ready〔willing〕 to 《do》

불상 不祥 ―하다 (be) ill-omened ; ominous ; inauspicious ; sinister ; disgraceful ; scandalous

―사 a scandal ; a disgraceful affair ; an untoward incident

불상 不詳 ―하다 (be) unknown ; unidentified ⇨ 미상

불상 佛像 an image of Buddha ; a Buddhist image〔statue〕

불상놈 a very vulgar person ; a very lowborn〔humble〕 person

불상당 不相當 ―하다 (be) improper ; unsuitable ; unbecoming ; inappropriate

불상정안 不上程案 a deferment proposal 〔plan〕 of the discussion of the issue ; a plan to defer the discussion of the issue

불서 佛書 the Buddhist scriptures ; Buddhist literature

불선 不善 evil ; vice ; mischief ; [잘하지 못함] lack of skill ; clumsiness

불선명 不鮮明 indistinctness ; obscurity ―하다 (be) indistinct ; obscure ; dim ; blurred

불설 佛說 Buddha's teachings ; Buddhist doctrines

불섭생 不攝生 intemperance ; neglect of one's health ―하다 be careless of one's health ; neglect one's health ; be intemperate ¶ 불섭생의 careless of one's health ; intemperate

불성 佛性 the nature of Buddha ; innate 〔immanent〕 Buddhahood

불성공 不成功 failure ; ill success ―하다 be unsuccessful〔abortive〕 ; fail at ; meet with a failure ; prove abortive 〔fruitless〕 ; end in failure

불성립 不成立 failure ; miscarriage ; fiasco ―하다 fail ; fall through ; miscarry

불성설 不成說 unreasonableness ; impropriety

불성실 不誠實 insincerity ; dishonesty ; untruthfulness ―하다 (be) insincere 〔dishonest, unfaithful〕 ; lack sincerity ¶ 그녀는 그에게 불성실했다 She played fast and loose with him.

불성인사 不省人事 unconsciousness ; a coma ⇨ 인사불성 ―하다 lose consciousness ; become unconscious

불세지재 不世之才 an extraordinary talent〔gift〕 ; [사람] a man of rare talent ; a prodigy (with few parallels)

불세출 不世出 rarity ¶ 불세출의 extraordinary ; uncommon ; unparalleled ; unequaled ; matchless // 불세출의 영웅 the hero of the century

불소 不少 ―하다 be not a little〔few〕 ; be quite much ; be considerable

불소 弗素 〖화학〗 fluorine 《F, Fl》 ¶ 불소의 fluoric

―산 fluoric acid ―산염 fluorate 탄화(炭化)― fluorocarbon

불손 不遜 insolence ; haughtiness ; arrogance ―하다 (be) insolent ; arrogant ; haughty ¶ 불손하게 굴다 behave haughtily

불수 不隨 paralysis 《*pl.* -ses》 ¶ 불수가 되다 be paralyzed 《in an arm》 ; be partially paralyzed

반신― hemiplegia ; paralysis of one side ; partial paralysis 전신― total paralysis

불수의 不隨意 ¶ 불수의의 involuntary

―근 an involuntary muscle ―운동 an involuntary motion〔movement〕 ―작용 an involuntary action

불순 不純 impurity ―하다 (be) foul ; impure ¶ 불순한 마음 an impure heart // 불순한 사상 an undesirable idea // 당내의 불순 분자 rebellious elements of a party // 불순한 동기에서 from a dishonest motive

―분자 an impure element

***불순 不順** [성질] disobedience ; rudeness ; rebelliousness ; [날씨] unseasonableness ; changeableness ; [불규칙] irregularity ―하다 [성질이] (be) disobedient ; rude ; not gentle ; [일기가] unseasonable〔unfavorable〕 ¶ 불순한 일기 unseasonable weather

월경― menstrual irregularity

불순물 不純物 impurities ; 〖의학〗 foreign matter

***불순종 不順從** disobedience ; indocility ; recalcitrance ; insubordination ―하다 disobey ; be disobedient ; refuse to obey

불승인 不承認 disapproval ; refusal to consent ; veto ; non-recognition (정권의)

불시 不時 [제때 아님] being out of season ; [의외] unexpectedness ; suddenness ¶ 불시의 accidental ; unexpected ; unforeseen ; untimely ; emergent (긴급한) // 불시에 out of season (제때 아닌) ; unexpectedly ; incidentally // 도박장을 불시에 습격하다 make a surprise raid on a gambling den // 불시에 꽃이 피다 bloom out of season // 불시의 변에 대비하다 provide against emergencies〔a rainy day〕 // 검열관이 불시에 들이닥치다 The inspector drops in without advance notice.

불시착 不時着 an emergency landing ; a forced landing ―하다 make an emergency landing

―비행장 an emergency landing field ; a flight strip

불식 佛式 a Buddhist ritual〔rite, ceremony〕

불식 佛拭 wiping out ; sweeping off ; cleaning —하다 wipe out ; sweep off ; clean ¶ 불명예를 불식하다 wipe out a disgrace

불식 不息 —하다 do not take a rest 〔break〕; do not relax

*불신 不信 distrust ; disbelief ; discredit ; unbelief ; lack of confidence —하다 distrust ; mistrust ; discredit ; disbelieve ¶ 불신을 사다 lose one's credit
—감 (a) distrust ; (a) suspicion —자 an unbeliever ; an impious person

불신용 不信用 distrust ⇨ 불신

불신임 不信任 lack〔want〕 of confidence ; nonconfidence —하다 have no confidence 《in》; distrust
— 결의 nonconfidence resolution ; a vote of censure — 동의 nonconfidence motion — 투표 a vote of nonconfidence〔no-confidence〕; a nonconfidence〔noconfidence〕 vote 내각 — want of confidence in the Cabinet 내각 — 결의 a nonconfidence vote on the Cabinet

불신임안 不信任案 a nonconfidence〔no-confidence〕 motion ¶ 불신임안을 상정하다 call for a nonconfidence vote〔a vote of want of confidence〕 (in the Cabinet) ; place a nonconfidence vote on the order of the House // 정부 불신임안을 가결하다 pass a vote of nonconfidence in the Government

불신 풍조 不信風潮 a trend of mutual distrust ¶ 불신 풍조가 싹튼다〔만연한다〕 A trend of mutual distrust begins to develop〔is prevalent〕.

불신 행위 不信行爲 a breach of faith 〔confidence〕 ¶ 불신 행위를 하다 commit a breach of faith〔confidence〕; break faith 《with a person》; act in bad faith

불실 不實 ⇨ 부실(不實)

불심 佛心 [부처의 마음] the mercy 〔merciful heart〕 of Buddha ; [해탈] deliverance 《from worldly cares》; a mind free from evil passion

불심 不審 doubt ; suspicion ; unfamiliarity (알지 못함) —하다 (be) doubtful ; suspicious ; strange ; questionable

불심 검문 不審檢問 questioning (of a suspicious person by a patrolman) ¶ 불심 검문을 받다 be questioned 《by a patrolling policeman》

불심상관 不甚相關 —하다 affect slightly ; have little effect upon ; make little difference

불심상원 不甚相遠 —하다 be about right ; be not far from the truth ; make little difference

†불쌍하다 (be) poor ; pitiable ; pitiful ; sad ; pathetic ; touching ¶ 불쌍한 고아 poor orphan // 불쌍한 처지 a wretched 〔pitiful, miserable〕 plight〔lot〕 // 불쌍해서 out of pity〔sympathy〕 // 불쌍하게도 pitiful to tell ; I am sorry to say ; unfortunately // 불쌍한 생각이 들다 be touched with pity 《for》; touch one's heart ; feel pity for 《a person》 // 불쌍히 여기다 pity 《a person》; take pity〔compassion〕 on 《a person》 // 불쌍하기도 하지 What a pity ! /Poor thing〔girl, child〕 !

불쌍히 pitiably ; pitifully ; poorly ; miserably ¶ 불쌍히 지내다 live in misery // 불쌍히 여기다 feel pity for ; take〔have〕 pity on ; take compassion on ; pity 《a person》

불쏘다 [목적을] fail 《to reach one's goal》; [과녁을] miss a shot ; miss the target

불쏘시개 kindling wood ; kindlings ; a fire starter ; material for starting a fire ¶ 불쏘시개로 쓰기에 알맞다 be good to start a fire with

*불쑥 suddenly ; unexpectedly ; abruptly ¶ 머리를 불쑥 내밀다 pop one's head 《out of the window》 // 불쑥 말하다 speak bluntly ; blurt out a remark // 손을 불쑥 내밀다 thrust〔stretch〕 out one's hand // 불쑥 방문하다 pay a surprise visit // 큰 건물이 눈 앞에 불쑥 나타났다 An immense building rose before our eyes. // 어느 날 그가 난데없이 불쑥 나타났다 He barged〔popped〕 in one day.

불쑥거리다 protrude〔stick out, pop out, blurt out〕 repeatedly ¶ 주먹을 불쑥거리다 keep thrusting one's fist out

불쑥불쑥 popping out over and over again ; bulging out here and there —하다 bulge out here and there ; (be) full and bulging ¶ 사과 자루가 불쑥불쑥하다 The sack of apples bulges here and there.

불쑥하다 (be) protruding ; protrude ; stick out

불씨 a live coal ¶ 악성 인플레의 불씨 the tinderboxes of vicious inflation

‡불안 不安 uneasiness ; anxiety ; misgivings ; unrest ; insecurity ; uncertainty —하다 (be) uneasy ; anxious ; insecure ; uncertain ¶ 불안한 빛 an uneasy look // 정치적 불안 political unrest // 불안하게 느끼다 feel uneasy〔restless〕 《about》 // 혼자 사는 게 불안하지 않니 Don't you feel insecure living alone ?
—감 a feeling of uneasiness

*불안정 不安定 instability ; unrest —하다 (be) unstable〔unsettled, insecure〕 ¶ 불안정한 정부 an unstable government // 불안정한 지위 a precarious position
—감 unrest ; a sense of instability ; insecurity ; an unsettled feeling

불알 testicles ; a testis 《*pl.* -tes》; the balls 《속》 ¶ 불알을 까다 castrate ; emasculate
불알을 긁어 주다 관용 curry favor 《with a person》; get into 《a person's》 good grace

불야성 不夜城 nightless〔gay〕 quarters ; a nightless city ; an all-night city ; a place where night is like day ¶ 밤엔 전도시가 불야성을 이룬다 At night the whole city is brilliantly illuminated.

불어 佛語 French ; the French language ; 〖불교〗 Buddhist terms

*불어나다 increase ; gain ; grow ; breed (번식하다) ; multiply (배가하다) ¶ 10배로 불어나다 multiply ten times〔tenfold〕 // 살림이 불어나다 One's family fortune is prospering. // 가족이 불어난다 The family grows larger.

*불어넣다 [숨을] breathe into ; aspirate ; [사상 따위를] inspire ; infuse ; indoctrinate ; inoculate ; inform

불어리 a fire guard ; a screen device used to keep sparks from flying out of a brazier

불어세우다 exclude ; leave 《a person》 out 《in the cold》 ; boycott ; shun

불언가지 不言可知 —하다 be understandable without mentioning ; It goes without saying 《that》

불언실행 不言實行 deeds but not words ; work before talk ¶ 불언실행하는 사람 a man of few words but deeds ; a man of deeds but not words // 불언실행은 나의 생활 신조다 Deeds but not words is my principle in life.

불여귀 不如歸 〖새〗 a cuckoo ⇨ 소쩍새

불여우 〖동물〗 a red fox ; Vulpes kiyomasai (학명) ¶ 불여우 같은 계집 a shrew ; a vixen ; a spitfire

불여의 不如意 —하다 go wrong 〔amiss〕 ; go contrary to one's wishes ¶ 매사가 불여의하다 Things never turn out as I wish. /Everything goes wrong.

불역 不易 immutability ; unchangeableness ; constancy ¶ 불역의 immutable ; unchangeable ; invariable

—성 immutability

불연 不然 —하다 be not so〔the case〕 ; be far from it ; (be) untrue ¶ 불연이면 if it is not so ; or (else) ; otherwise

불연 佛緣 the providence of Buddha

불연성 不燃性 incombustibility ; noninflammability ¶ 불연성의 incombustible ; noninflammable

— 가스 inert gas(es) — 물질 incombustibles ; noninflammables — 필름 safety〔uninflammable〕 film

불연속 不連續 discontinuity ¶ 불연속의 discontinuous

—면 a surface of discontinuity ; frontal surface — 변이(變異) 〖생물〗 a discontinuous variation — 분포(分布) 〖생물〗 a discontinuous distribution —선(線) 〖기상〗 a line〔front〕 of discontinuity ; a gap in the isobaric line

불염포 不鹽脯 unsalted dried meat-slices

불온 不穩 unrest ; disquiet —하다 be disquieting ; threatening ; subversive ¶ 불온한 정세 a threatening situation ; the unrest ; the unsettled conditions // 불온한 행동 improper behavior // 불온한 언사를 쓰다 use improper words ; use〔indulge in〕 strong〔violent, sensational〕 language // 불온한 태도를 취하다 assume a threatening attitude

— 문서 seditious〔subversive〕 documents 〔literature〕 — 사상 a disquieting thought ; a threatening〔disturbing〕 idea

불온당 不穩當 inappropriateness ; impropriety —하다 (be) unfair ; unjust ; unreasonable ; improper ¶ 불온당한 처사 an unfair action〔dealing〕

불온 분자 不穩分子 a disturbing element ; a subversive

*불완전 不完全 imperfection ; incompleteness ; defectiveness —하다 (be) imperfect ; incomplete ; defective ; faulty ¶ 불완전한 점 a defect ; a fault ; an imperfection // 불완전하게 imperfectly ; incompletely ; defectively // 구조가 불완전하다 be defective in construction // 다소 불완전한 데가 있다 leave something to be desired

— 고용 underemployment — 독립(주권) incomplete independence〔sov- ereignty〕 — 독립(주권)국 a country which is still not quite independent〔sovereign〕 — 동사 〖문법〗 an incomplete verb — 연소 incomplete combustion — 타〔자〕동사 〖문법〗 an incomplete transitive〔intransitive〕 verb

불요불굴 不撓不屈 indomitableness ; tenacity ; inflexibility ; gameness ; dauntl essness ¶ 불요불굴의 indomitable ; indefatigable ; unyielding ; persevering ; inflexible ; unflinching ; resolute ; dauntl ess ; undaunted

불요불급 不要不急 —하다 be not urgent 〔pressing〕 ¶ 불요불급의 사업〔산업〕 nonessential enterprises〔industries〕

불용 不用 disuse ; inutility ; uselessness —하다 do not use ; make no use 《of》 ; discard ¶ 불용의 useless ; of no use ; unnecessary

— 기관 〖동물〗 a disused〔rudimentary, residual〕 organ —품〔물〕 a discarded 〔disused〕 article ; a useless thing ; junk ; lumber ; a discard ; castoffs

불용(해)성 不溶(解)性 insolubility ; insolubleness ; infusibility ¶ 불용성의 insoluble 《matter》 ; infusible

불우 不遇 misfortune ; adversity ; obscurity —하다 (be) adverse ; unfortunate ; ill-starred ¶ 불우한 작가 an unlucky 〔unsuccessful〕 writer // 불우한 일생을 보내다 live in obscurity all through one's life // 불우한 처지에 있다 be in adverse circumstances // 불우함을 한탄하다 complain of one's ill fate

— 아동〔청소년〕 unfortunate children 〔youths〕 — 이웃 돕기 운동 《launch》 a campaign to help unfortunate〔needy〕 neighbors

불우리 a flame guard to protect a lamp 〔brazier〕 from the wind

*불운 不運 misfortune ; ill luck ; adverse fortune ; a hapless fate —하다 (be) unfortunate ; ill-fated ; unlucky ¶ 불운하게도 unfortunately ; unluckily ; as ill luck would have it // 그 여자는 일평생 불운하였다 She led an ill-fated life. /She was hapless to the end of her life.

불원 不遠 —하다 ① [거리] be not far (off) ; be not distant
② [시간] be not far in the future ¶ 불원간 shortly ; before long ; in the near future // 불원천리하고 despite the long way // 불원한 장래에 국민이 각성해야 할 때가 올 것이다 The time will not be (far) distant when the nation will have to awaken.

*불유쾌 不愉快 unpleasantness ; disagreeableness ; discomfort —하다 (be) unpleasant ; disagreeable ; gloomy ; uncom fortable ¶ 아주 불유쾌한 광경 a sight too offensive to look at // 불유쾌하게 unpleasantly ; disagreeably ; uncomfortably // 남을 불유쾌하게 하다 make 《a person》 unhappy ; make 《a person》 feel unpleasant ; discomfort 《a person》 // 불유쾌하게 생각하다 feel 《another's behavior》 unpleasant ; be displeased 《with a person, at a thing》 // 아무리 불유쾌해도 진실을 이야기해 주어야 한다 They must be told the truth, however unpalatable it may be.

불은 佛恩 the grace〔mercy〕 of Buddha ; Buddha's blessings

불응 不應 nonacceptance ; declination ; disobedience ; [거절] refusal ; rejection —하다 do not accept〔grant, meet, comply with〕 ; ignore ; decline ; disobey ; refuse ; reject ; turn down ¶ 질문에 불응하다 do not answer〔respond to〕 a question // 호출에 불응하다 disobey a summons // 초대에 불응하다 decline an invitation

불의 不意 suddenness (돌연) ; unexpectedness (의외) ¶ 불의의 습격 a surprise attack // 불의의 내방 an unlooked-for〔a surprise〕 call // 불의의 상봉 an unexpected〔a chance〕 meeting // 불의에 unexpectedly ; suddenly ; abruptly ; all of a sudden ; without warning // 불의의 질문을 당해서 당황했다 I was embarrassed at his abrupt question. // 그 사람을 불의에 찾아가면 만나지 못할 것이다 You can not possibly see him without previous notice.

불의 不義 immorality ; impropriety ; infidelity ; perfidy ; injustice ; iniquity —하다 (be) immoral ; improper ; unjust ¶ 불의의 씨 a child out of wedlock ; a child born in sin ; a bastard

불이익 不利益 [불리] disadvantage ; a handicap ; a drawback ; [상책이 아님] inadvisability ; inexpediency —하다 (be) disadvantageous ; unprofitable ; unremunerative ; be against one's interests ; [상책 아니다] (be) inadvisable ; inexpedient ; impolitic ; [형편이 나쁘다] unfavorable ; adverse ; [해롭다] detrimental ; injurious ; prejudical ⇨ 불리(不利)

불이행 不履行 nonfulfilment ; breach ; nonobservance ¶ 상품 인도 불이행시는 in default of delivery // 선거 공약을 불이행하다 fail to implement one's campaign promises
—자 a defaulter 계약 — nonfulfilment of a contract ; breach of contract 약속 — failure to keep one's promise ; breach of (one's) promise 의무 — failure in duty ; nonperformance of an obligation ; 〚법〛 nonfeasance 조약 — a treaty violation ; nonobservance of a treaty 채무 — failure to pay one's financial debt ; 〚법〛 default

불인가 不認可 disapproval ; disapprobation ; disallowance ; [각하] rejection ; refusal —하다 reject ; refuse ; turn down ¶ 불인가되다 be turned down ; be rejected〔refused〕 ; be disapproved

불인견 不忍見 cannot bear witnessing〔to see〕 ; unable to bear〔stand〕 the sight of ; (being) too terrible to see ¶ 그녀의 비탄하는 모습은 불인견이었다 Her grief was painful to behold.

불일 不一 [불일치] disharmony ; disagreement ; discord ; [고르지 않음] irregularity ; unevenness ; lack of uniformity —하다 be in disharmony 《with》 ; (be) irregular ; uneven ; lack uniformity

불일간 不日間 ⇨ 불일내(不日內)

불일내 不日內 shortly ; before long ; soon ; in a few days

불일듯이 actively ; lively ; successfully ¶ 장사가 불일듯이 잘된다 One's business is thriving.

불일듯하다 (be) prosperous ; thriving ; flourishing ¶ 장사가 불일듯하다 One's business is spreading〔growing〕 like wildfire.

*불일치 不一致 discord ; discordance ; disagreement ; dissonance —하다 (be) discordant ; (be) disagreeing ; be in discord 《with》 ; inharmonious ; dissonant ¶ 불일치를 초래하다 lead to a discord
언행 — discordance between one's words and action ; inconsistency of one's words with one's action

불임 不妊 sterility ¶ 불임의 sterile ; barren
— 수술 sterilization

불임증 不妊症 sterility ; infertility ; infecundity ; 〚병리〛 acyesis ¶ 불임증에 걸리다 become sterile ; lose one's reproduc-

tive power // 불임증을 고치다 cure 《her》 sterility
— 치료약 a fertility drug

*불입 拂入 payment (into capital) ; subscription (구독 요금·기부금 따위의) ; (payment of) an instalment (월부 따위의) — 하다 pay in ; pay into 《a bank》 ; pay an instalment ; subscribe ¶ 구독 요금을 미리 불입하다 advance subscriptions to publications
—금 the sum of money (to be) paid — 자본 paid-up capital — 주식 a full-paid stock — 최고(催告) a call — 추징 assessment 분할 — payment by installments 일부 — partial payment ; payment on account 일시 — payment in lump sum 전액 — payment in full

불잉걸 burning charcoal

불자 佛者 [불제자] a Buddhist

불자동차 —自動車 a fire engine ; a fire truck

불잡다 ① [진화] check the fire ; put out 〔quench〕 a fire ② [켜들다] hold (up) a light〔lamp, candle〕

불장 佛葬 a Buddhist funeral ¶ 불장으로 하다 bury 《a person》 according to the Buddhist rites

불장난 playing with fire ; [남녀간의] playing with love ; an idle love affair — 하다 play with fire ; play with love

불전 佛殿 a Buddhist sanctum

불전 佛前 (before) the Buddhist altar

불전 佛典 Buddhist classics ; the Sutras (경전)

불제자 佛弟子 a Buddhist ; a believer in Buddhism

불조심 —操心 caution〔guarding〕 against fires — 하다 be careful not to start 〔have〕 a fire ; guard against fire

불종 —鍾 a fire bell ; a fire alarm

불종 佛鐘 a Buddhist temple bell

불좌 佛座 the seat of a Buddhist idol

불줄 [송전선] a power (transmission) line〔wire〕

†불지르다 set fire to 《a house》 ; set 《a house》 on fire ; fire 《a house》

불지피다 make〔build〕 a fire ¶ 아궁이에 불지피다 make a fire in the fireplace

불질 ① making a fire 《in the fireplace》 ② [총질] firing (a gun) ; shooting — 하다 make a fire ; [발사] fire ; shoot

불집 a fire hazard
불집을 건드리다 관용 bring a hornet's nest about one's ears

불집게 [심지 자르는] (fire) snuffers ; a candle snuffer ; [불 집는] fire nippers 〔pincers〕

불쩍거리다 rub and rub ; scrub away (at laundry)

불쩍불쩍 rubbing〔scrubbing〕 《clothes》 briskly ; rubbing and scrubbing ; scrubbing away

*불쬐다 warm oneself by the fire ; enjoy the fire ; warm 《a thing》 over a fire ¶ 손을 불쬐다 warm one's hands over a fire // 불쬐십시오 Please warm yourself by the fire.

불착 不着 nonarrival ; nondelivery ; [연착] overdue
— 우편 a lost letter

불찬성 不贊成 disapproval ; disapprobation ; dissension ; objection — 하다 disapprove 《of》 ; do not agree 《with, to》 ; dissent 《from》 ¶ 나는 그것에 불찬성이다 I am against it. // 당신은 가는 것에 찬성입니까 불찬성입니까 Are you for or against going? // 나는 그 혼담에는 절대 불찬성입니다 I am dead set against that match.
—자 a dissenter

불찰 不察 negligence ; carelessness ; lack of attention ; fault ; mistake ¶ 불찰로 owing to one's negligence // 그런 사람을 신용한 것은 내 불찰이었다 I made a mistake in trusting such a fellow. /I have only myself to blame for having trusted him.

불찰 佛刹 a Buddhist temple

불참 不參 absence ; nonattendance — 하다 be absent 《from》 ; absent oneself 《from》 ; fail to attend ¶ 부득이한 일로 모임에 불참했다 I was prevented by unavoidable business from attending the meeting.
—가 nonparticipation —계〔신고〕 a notice of absence —자 an absentee

불철저 不徹底 — 하다 be not thoroughgoing ; (be) halfway ; [논지가] inconsistent ; unconvincing ¶ 불철저한 처치 halfway measures // 불철저한 논의 an inconsistent〔inconclusive〕 argument // 불철저한 태도 a noncommittal〔dubious〕 attitude // 방법이 불철저하다 It is not a thoroughgoing〔drastic〕 method. // 나는 무엇이든 불철저하게 해 두는 것이 싫다 I hate leaving things half-done.

불철주야 不撤晝夜 day and night ; by day and by night ¶ 불철주야 일하다 work night and day ; work double tides 〔shifts〕

불청 不聽 — 하다 [듣지 않다] do not listen〔pay no attention〕 to 《a person》 ; do not lend one's ear to ; give no ear to ; [불승낙하다] do not consent to 《a proposal》 ; do not accept 〔admit, grant〕

불청객 不請客 an uninvited guest ; a gate crasher 《미》

불체포 특권 不逮捕特權 privilege of exemption from apprehension ; nonapprehension privilege

불초 不肖 an unworthy son ; your unworthy son ; I ; me ; myself ¶ 불초 자식 one unworthy of one's father

불출 不出 [못난이] a failure ; a good-for-nothing ; [나가지 않음] confining oneself at home ¶ 두문불출하다 keep〔stay〕

indoors ; confine oneself at home
불출장 〖경기〗 default
*불충 不忠 disloyalty ; unfaithfulness ; infidelity ; perfidy ―하다 (be) disloyal ; unfaithful ; fail in one's duty 《to the king》
―불효 disloyalty and filial impiety ; being a poor subject and a poor son
†불충분 不充分 insufficiency ; imperfection ; inadequacy ; shortage ―하다 (be) insufficient ; inadequate ; not enough ; unsatisfactory ; imperfect ; not up to the mark ¶ 자금이 불충분하다 be short of capital // 보수가 불충분하다고 생각하다 be dissatisfied with a remuneration // 조사가 불충분하다 An investigation is not thoroughgoing enough. // 그래도 아직 불충분하다 It is not yet up to the mark. // 아직 그 연구는 불충분하다 There is something yet to learn. // 공급이 불충분하다 The supply is restricted. // 증거 불충분으로 무죄가 되었다 He was acquitted for lack of evidence.
불충실 不忠實 ―하다 (be) disloyal ; unfaithful ¶ 직무에 불충실하다 be unfaithful to one's duty ; be neglectful of one's duties
불취동성 不娶同姓 not marrying with one of the same surname ; (extended) clan exogamy ―하다 do not marry with one of the same surname
불측지변 不測之變 an unforeseen disaster〔accident〕; an unexpected misfortune ; a sudden calamity
불측하다 不測― ① (be) bad ; wicked ; heinous ¶ 불측한 놈 a wicked 〔heinous〕 fellow ② (be) unforeseeable ; unfathomable ; inscrutable ; incomprehensible ¶ 그는 불측한 사람이다 He is very deep and one cannot fathom his designs.
불치 a hunted animal〔fowl〕; game ; a bag ; a catch ; a take
불치 不治 ① [병] incurability ② [정치] misgovernment ; maladministration ¶ 불치의 incurable ; fatal ; hopeless ; irrecoverable
―병 an incurable〔a fatal〕 disease ―환자 a hopeless case ; an incurable〔a confirmed〕 invalid ; an invalid for life
불친소 a bullock ; a steer
‡불친절 不親切 unkindness ; unfriendliness ―하다 (be) unkind ; unfriendly ; disobliging ; inhospitable ¶ 불친절한 상인 a disobliging merchant // 고객에 대해서 불친절하다 be inattentive to customers
불침략 不侵略 nonaggression
―조약 nonaggression pact〔treaty, agreement〕
*불침번 不寢番 night watch ; vigil ; a night watchman (사람) ¶ 불침번 서다 keep a night watch ; keep vigil
―병 a vigilant sentry
불컥거리다 squash something wet in one's hand
*불켜다 kindle ; light 《a lamp》 ; turn 〔switch〕 on 《an electric lamp》 ¶ 밤새도록 불을 켜놓고 있다 keep a light burning〔an electric light turned on〕 all night
‡불쾌 不快 ① unpleasantness ; displeasure ; discomfort ―하다 (be) unpleasant ; disagreeable ; uncomfortable ; cheerless ; displeased ; ill-humored ¶ 불쾌한 날씨 nasty weather // 불쾌한 냄새 an unpleasant〔offensive〕 smell ; stink // 불쾌하게 생각하다 feel unpleasant ; be displeased ; feel hurt // 불쾌한 얼굴을 하다 look offended〔hurt, displeased〕 // 불쾌하게 하다 hurt 《a person's》 feelings ; offend ② [편찮음] indisposition ―하다 be unwell ; be indisposed ; be out of sorts ¶ 다소 불쾌하다 feel rather poorly ; feel a bit out of sorts ; be not quite well
―지수 the Discomfort Index 《DI》 ; a temperature-humidity index 《THI》 (온습지수)
*불타 佛陀 Buddha
†불타다 burn ; blaze ; flame ; be in flames ¶ 불타는 사랑 a flaming love // 빨갛게 불타고 있는 난로 a red-glowing stove // 불타기 쉽다 be easy to burn ; be inflammable // 청춘의 정열에 불타다 burn with youthful ardor // 불타버리다 burn itself out // 배가 불타고 있다 The ship is on fire.
불탑 佛塔 a pagoda
불통 不通 ① interruption ; suspension ; tie-up ¶ 전신 불통 interruption of telegraphic communication ; lack of wire contact // 불통이 된 곳 a break 《on the line》 // 통신 불통이 된 지방 an isolated district // (교통) 불통이 되다 be interrupted〔held up, blocked, tied up〕
② [의사가] no understanding ; no communication ; ignorance (무지) ¶ 의사가 서로 불통이다 do not understand each other // 세상일에 불통이다 know little of the world
고집― having no understanding at all ; obduracy 전신(電信) ― interruption of telegraphic communication ; lack of wire contact
불통일 不統一 lack of unity ; [분열] disunion ; [부조화] disharmony
불퇴전 不退轉 determination ; a firm resolve ; an indomitable spirit ―하다 be determined ; be indomitable ; be steadfast ; be unswerving ; be unflagging ¶ 불퇴전의 결의 an indomitable resolve // 불퇴전의 노력을 하다 make unremitting exertions〔efforts〕
불투과성 不透過性 impermeableness
*불투명 不透明 opacity ; obscurity ―하다 (be) opaque ; obscure ; be not clear 〔lucid〕 ¶ 불투명한 태도 a questioning 〔an ambiguous, a vague〕 attitude

—도 opacity —색 an opaque color —액 〖사진〗 opaque — 유리 opaque glass —체 an opaque body〔substance〕

불퉁그러지다 bulge (out) ; protrude ; become protuberant

불퉁불퉁 with lots of knots〔bumps〕; [말씨] bluntly ; surlily —하다 (be) knotty ; rugged ; bumpy ¶ 불퉁불퉁한 길 a rough〔bumpy〕 road

불퉁스럽다 (be) rough ; rude ; gruff ; blunt ; curt ¶ 불퉁스럽고 때때로 반항적인 태도 one's abrupt and often antagonizing manner // 말버릇이 불퉁스럽다 talk bluntly ; be blunt of speech

불퉁하다 (be) protuberant ; bulgy ; protruding

불특정 不特定 unspecificness ¶ 불특정의 unspecific ; unspecified
— 기간 《for, over》 an unspecified term
— 다수인 many and unspecified persons
—물 an unspecified thing

*불티 sparks ; embers ; fire-flakes ¶ 불티 같다 be selling like hot cakes〔fun, wildfire〕 // 불티를 둘러쓰다 be covered with sparks // 불티가 튀어 오르다 sparks shoot up in the air

불패 不敗 invincibility —하다 do not suffer a defeat ; be unbeaten〔undefeated〕 ¶ 불패의 unbeaten ; unbeatable ; undefeated ; invincible // 불패의 기록을 자랑하다 have a proud record of all wins and no defeats

불펜 〖야구〗 a bull pen

⁑불편 不便 inconvenience ; inexpediency ; unhandiness ; [몸이] discomfort ; sickness —하다 (be) inconvenient ; incommodious ; unhandy ; [몸이] be feeling unwell ; be〔feel〕 uncomfortable ¶ 불편을 느끼다 feel〔be put to〕 inconvenience ; suffer inconvenience ; be inconvenienced // 불편을 느끼게 하다 cause 〔give〕 《a person》 inconvenience ; inconvenience〔incommode〕 《a person》 // 불편을 참다 endure〔put up with〕 inconvenience // 교통이 불편하다 lack traffic facilities ; be inconveniently located 《for the subway》 // 휴대하기 불편하다 be unhandy 〔unwieldy〕 to carry about // 부엌이 대단히 불편하게 되어 있다 This kitchen is very badly planned. // 나는 몸이 좀 불편하다 I feel a bit out of sorts. /I am not quite well. // 밤에 도착하면 불편할 것이다 You will be inconvenienced if you get there at night.

⁑불편부당 不偏不黨 impartiality ; nonpartisanship ; neutrality ; independence —하다 (be) impartial ; fair ; nonpartisan ; neutral ; independent (of prejudice) ¶ 불편부당의 신문 an independent newspaper // 불편부당의 태도를 취하다 remain neutral

⁑불평 不平 discontent ; dissatisfaction ; a complaint ; displeasure ; disaffection (정치상의) ; a grievance —하다 complain of〔about〕; grumble at〔about, over〕; make a complaint ¶ 불평의 소리 a voice of discontent // 불평을 품다 be discontented ; be disaffected 《toward the authorities》 ; have a grievance 《against》 // 불평을 억제하다 repress one's dissatisfaction // 불평이 가득하다 be extremely dissatisfied // 회사에 대해 불평이 있다 have a grievance against the company // 나는 아무 불평도 없다 I have nothing to complain of. // 그는 언제까지나 투덜투덜 불평을 하고 있었다 He kept on muttering and complaining. // 쌓인 불평이 드디어 폭발했다 The pent-up discontent at last found its vent. // 그는 밤낮 불평이다 He is a constant grumbler.
—가 a grumbler ; a crabber 《미·구》 ; a griper ; a grouser ; a (grumbling) malcontent (투덜거리는) — 거리 a comeback 《미·속》 — 분자 the malcontents ; a discontented〔disaffected〕 element

*불평등 不平等 inequality —하다 (be) unequal ; unfair ; discriminatory ¶ 불평등한 취급 a discriminatory〔an unfair〕 treatment ; unfair discrimination
— 동맹 a lopsided alliance — 조약 an unequal treaty

불포화 不飽和 being unsaturated
— 화합물 an unsaturated compound

불품행 不品行 misconduct ; immoral conduct ; loose morals ; profligacy (방탕)

불풍나게 busily ¶ 불풍나게 돌아다니다 bustle around busily

불피우다 make a fire

*불필요 不必要 —하다 (be) unnecessary ; needless ; unessential ¶ 불필요하게 unnecessarily ; needlessly // 이런 것은 불필요하다 This can be done very well without. /We can dispense with this. / We can go〔do〕 without this.

불하 拂下 disposal ; sale (of government property) ; transfer of state property to private ownership —하다 dispose of ; sell ; transfer
—품 articles (to be) disposed of by the government ; articles sold by the government

불학 佛學 Buddhist learning〔lore〕; Buddhology
—자 a Buddhist scholar

불학 무식 不學無識 utter ignorance ; illiteracy —하다 (be) utterly ignorant ; illiterate ; uneducated ; unlettered

불한당 不汗黨 a group of robbers ; brigands ; bandits

불합 不合 disagreement ; discord ; disharmony —하다 be in disagreement 《with》 ; be in discord 《with》

불합격 不合格 disqualification ; failure ; rejection ; elimination —하다 be disqualified ; come〔fall〕 short of the mark 〔standard〕 ; be found ineligible 《for》 ;

be rejected ; fail to pass〔be dropped in〕《an examination》 ¶ 시험에 불합격이 되다 fail in the examination // 신체 검사에 불합격이 되다 be rejected for physical reason // 이 방법은 실험 결과 불합격이 되었다 This method has been tried and found unsatisfactory.
—률 a failure rate —자 a disqualified〔rejected〕 person ; an unsuccessful applicant〔candidate〕 ; a failure —품 a rejected article ; off-grade goods ; a reject ; a throw-out

:불합리 不合理 irrationality ; absurdity ; unreasonableness **—하다** (be) irrational ; absurd ; preposterous ; unreasonable ¶ 불합리한 가격 an unreasonable〔outrageous〕 price // 그것은 너무 불합리하다 That is absurd〔unreasonable〕. // 13이라는 숫자를 두려워하는 것은 불합리하다 It is irrational to be afraid of number 13.

:불행 不幸 unhappiness ; misfortune ; ill〔bad〕 luck ; misery **—하다** (be) unhappy ; unfortunate ; unlucky ; miserable ¶ 잇따른 불행 a series〔succession〕 of misfortunes // 불행하게도 unfortunately ; as ill luck would have it // 불행을 당하다 suffer misfortune ; have〔meet with〕 a misfortune // 불행을 면하다 escape misfortune // 불행이 잇따르다 have a run of ill luck // 불행하게 태어나다 be born unlucky // 불행하게 지내다 lead〔live〕 an unhappy life // 불행히도 시험에 떨어지다 be so unfortunate as〔have the misfortune〕 to fail in the examination // 불행의 구렁텅이에 빠지다 sink into the depth of misery // 불행은 겹치기 마련이다 Misfortunes never come singly. // 나는 불행한 놈이다 Happiness and I are strangers.
불행중다행 〔관용〕 a stroke of good luck in the midst of misfortunes

불행사 不行使 nonuse ¶ 권리의 불행사 〖법〗 nonuser

불허 不許 nonpermission ; disapproval **—하다** do not permit ; do not allow ; do not approve 《of》 ¶ 사태는 일각의 유예를 불허한다 The situation does not allow〔permit〕 a moment's delay.
복제 — All rights reserved.

불허가 不許可 disapproval ; disapprobation ; disallowance ; rejection **—하다** disapprove ; disallow ; turn down ; do not permit ; refuse to authorize

불현듯이 suddenly ; all of a sudden ; abruptly ; unexpectedly ¶ 불현듯이 집 생각이 나다 be overcome with sudden homesickness // 불현듯이 약속이 생각났다 It suddenly dawned upon me that I had an appointment. // 그 여자는 불현듯이 그가 보고 싶었다 She had a sudden burning desire to see him.

불협화음 不協和音 〖음악〗 a dissonance ; a discord ¶ 불협화음의 dissonant ; discordant

불호 佛號 the name of Buddha ; the name of a Buddhist monk ; one's name as a Buddhist monk

불호령 —號令 an impetuous order **—하다** issue an impetuous〔a fiery〕 order ; give a strict command

불호박 —琥珀 red-amber

불혹 不惑 the age free from vacillation ; the age of forty ¶ 불혹을 지나다 be over forty years old

불화 弗貨 dollars ; American money ; an American dollar

***불화 佛畫** a Buddhist〔Buddhistic〕 painting〔picture〕

불화 弗化 〖화학〗 fluoride ; fluoridation
—물 a fluorid(e) —수소 hydrogen fluoride —수소산 hydrofluoric acid —암모늄〔칼슘, 칼륨〕 ammonium〔calcium, potassium〕 fluoride

불화 不和 disagreement ; discord ; dissension ; differences ; trouble ; disunion **—하다** be in discord 《with》 ; be at odds 《with》 ; be on bad terms 《with》 ¶ 불화의 discordant ; dissentious // 부부간의 불행 domestic differences // 불화의 원인 the seeds of discord
가정 — family troubles〔discord〕

불확대 不擴大 localization ; keeping an affair from spreading
— 방침 a nonexpansion〔nonaggravation〕 policy ; a localization policy (현지 해결) ¶ 불확대 방침을 취하다 adopt a policy of localizing a dispute〔an affair〕

:불확실 不確實 uncertainty ; unreliability ; unauthenticity ; dubiousness **—하다** (be) uncertain ; unreliable ; doubtful ; insecure ¶ 불확실한 보도 an unreliable〔unauthentic〕 report // 불확실한 장사 a shaky business

불확정 不確定 —하다 (be) indefinite ; indeterminate ; uncertain ; undecided ; unsettled
— 기간 〖법〗 a time uncertain — 명제 an indefinite proposition —성 원리 the uncertainty principle ; the principle of uncertainty — 신용장 an unconfirmed letter of credit — 자산 risky assets — 재산〔잔여〕권 〖법〗 contingent estate

불환 지폐 不換紙幣 an inconvertible note ; a fiat money 《미》 ; an irredeemable bank note

불활발 不活潑 inactivity ; dullness ; indolence ; 〔시장의〕 stagnation ; slackness ; depression **—하다** (be) dull ; inactive ; sluggish ; languid ; stagnant ; flat ; slow ; slack ¶ 시장 거래가 아주 불활발하다 The market is extremely dull〔stagnant〕.

:불황 不況 depression ; slump ; bad〔slack〕 business ; recession (일시적) ¶ 불황의 dull ; depressed ; slack ; stagnant

//세계적인 불황 a world-wide depression 〔slump〕 (in business) //불황이 점차 회복되어 가고 있다 Business is looking〔picking〕 up. /The dullness that has hung over the market is passing.
—기 a dull〔a dead, an off〕 season (in trade) ; a slack time〔season〕 — 대비 자금 "rainy-day" funds — 시대 lean years ; depression〔bad〕 days

불효 不孝 undutifulness〔impiety〕 to one's parents ; want of filial piety ; disobedience 《to parents》 —하다 (be) undutiful ; unfilial ; impious ; disobedient
—자 an undutiful〔unfilial, a thankless〕 son〔daughter〕

불효 佛曉 dawn ; daybreak ; early morning

*불후 不朽 immortality ; imperishability —하다 (be) immortal ; undying ; everlasting ; undecaying ; eternal ¶ 불후의 명성 immortal〔everlasting〕 fame //불후의 공 lasting merit ; imperishable service // 불후의 명예 an eternal honor //불후의 이름을 남기다 win eternal fame〔an imperishable memory〕 ; perpetuate〔immortalize〕 one's name

붉나무 〖식물〗 a sumac

†붉다 (be) red ; crimson (심홍) ; scarlet (진홍) ¶ 붉어지다 redden ; turn red //창피해서 얼굴이 붉어지다 blush with〔for〕 shame //화가 나서 얼굴이 붉어지다 be red with anger //흥분해서 얼굴이 붉어지다 flush (up) with excitement //서쪽 하늘이 저녁놀로 붉게 물들었다 The western sky is aglow with the setting sun. //그런 말씀 하시면 제 얼굴이 붉어집니다 You make me blush.

붉덩물 a muddy〔turbid〕 stream ¶ 붉덩물이 지다 a stream turns muddy

붉디붉다 (be) deep red ; crimson

붉으락푸르락 —하다 turn alternately pale and red

붉은가슴논종다리 〖새〗 a red-throated pipit ; Anthus spinoletta (학명)

붉은가시딸기 〖식물〗 a raspberry ; a wineberry

붉은거북 〖동물〗 a toggerhead (turtle)

붉은 광장 —廣場 the Red Square (모스크바의)

붉은발 a swollen vein at the site of an infection ; a varicose vein —서다 A swollen vein appears.

붉은배동고비 〖새〗 a Quelpart nuthatch

붉은배제비 〖새〗 a red-belly house swallow

붉은배지빠귀 〖새〗 a Korean brown thrush

붉은배티티 〖새〗 a Korean brown thrush

붉은배피리새 〖새〗 a Korean bullfinch

붉은뺨멧새 〖새〗 a grey-headed bunting

붉은토끼풀 〖식물〗 a red clover ; a trifolium ; Trifolium pratense (학명)

⁑붉히다 blush 《with shame》 ; color up ; turn red ; be shame-faced ¶ 얼굴을 붉히고 with a blush ; blushingly //성내어 얼굴을 붉히다 be red in the face with anger //그 여자는 얼굴을 붉혔다 A pink glow mounted to her cheeks.

붐 a boom ¶ 조선계의 붐 a boom in shipbuilding //붐이 일다 boom //지금 스테레오 붐이 일고 있다 The stereo is now booming.

⁑붐비다 (be) congested ; crowded ; packed ; thronged ; jammed ; jampacked ¶ 붐비는 시간 the rush hour // 극장이 붐비다 The theater is packed to capacity. //거리가 붐비다 The street is busy with traffic. /The street is jammed up. /The street is full of bustle. /The traffic is busy〔heavy〕. //정거장이 굉장히 붐볐다 The station was jammed inside. //굉장히 붐비는데요 What a crowd〔rush〕! /It is a hell of crowd. 《미·속》

붐하다 be dawn gray

*붓 a writing brush ; a brush ; any writing instrument ; a pen ¶ 붓을 들다 hold a pen ; put〔set〕 pen to paper ; write ; draw ; paint //그는 붓으로 먹고 산다 He lives by his pen〔depends upon his pen for his bread〕.
붓을 놓다 관용 lay down one's pen ; cease to write ; close (편지에서)

*붓꽃 〖식물〗 an iris ; a blue flag

붓끝 the tip of a (writing) brush ; the point of a pen ; [필봉] a stroke of the pen〔brush〕 ; manipulation of one's brush 〔pen〕 ; touch ¶ 붓끝이 닳았다 The tip of this brush has worn out. //그의 붓끝에 생사가 달렸다 Life and death hang upon his pen. //그의 붓끝에 걸리면 경친다 It is an awful thing to be made the target of his attack.

붓날다 be frivolous ; be light ; be flippant ¶언행이 붓날다 be flighty ; be giddy

붓날리다 speak〔act〕 flippantly ; do in a shallow way ; make one's words 〔deeds〕 superficial

붓다¹ ① [살가죽이] swell ; become swollen ; tumefy ; bloat ¶ 얼굴이 붓다 have a swollen〔bloated〕 face //각기로 인해서 다리가 부었다 My legs are swollen〔I have swollen legs〕 with beriberi. //다친 팔목이 몹시 부었다 The injured wrist swelled up badly. //눈이 부었구나 Your eyes are puffed up.
② [성나다] get sulky ; get angry ; sulk ; grow sullen ; fret ; get cross ; get peevish ¶ 부은 얼굴 a sulky face 〔look〕 ; a sullen looks ; sulks //부어 있다 be sulky ; be in the sulks //왜 그렇게 부었나 What makes you so sulky?

*붓다² ① [쏟다] pour 《into, out》 ; fill 《a cup》 with 《coffee》 ; put 《water in a bowl》 ; feed 《a lamp with oil》 ¶ 술을 붓

다 fill a glass with wine // 목욕탕에 물을 붓다 pour water into a bathtub
② [씨앗을] cast ; sow ; seed down ¶ 모판에 씨앗을 붓다 sow seed in a seedbed
③ [곗돈·월부금] pay by〔in〕 installment ¶ 재봉틀 값을 한달에 30,000원씩 붓다 pay for a sewing machine in installments of 30,000 *won* a month

붓다³ ⇨ 부수다

붓대 a brush handle ; the stem of a writing brush

붓두껍 a brush cap ; a metal cap for a brush tip

붓방아 fingering one's pen while searching ideas
붓방아 찧다 〔관용〕 finger one's pen ; chew on one's pencil

붓순나무 〖식물〗 a Japanese star anise ; a Japanese evergreen tree

붓장난 quill driving ; hack writing **—하다** drive a〔the〕 quill ; be a scribbler 〔hack writer〕

붓질 making a brush stroke **—하다** make strokes with a brush ; stroke

붓집 a brush-case

붓통 a brush-stand

붕 ① [방귀 소리] ¶ 방귀를 붕 뀌다 break wind ; let a fart ; fart ; poop 《비》
② [벌 따위의] humming ; buzzing ; droning
③ [엔진 소리 따위] whirring ; humming
④ [허망하게] in vain ; in smoke ; fleetingly ¶ (계획 따위) 붕 뜨다 end〔go up〕 in smoke

***붕괴 崩壞** collapse ; a breakdown ; a fall ; cave-in (함몰) ; 〖화학〗 disintegration ; 〖지질〗 degradation **—하다** collapse ; fall (down) ; give way ; break down ; crumble ; drop〔fall〕 to pieces ; cave〔fall〕 in (함몰하다) ¶ 광산의 갱도가 붕괴했다 The mine roof caved in.
—물 debris

붕궤 崩潰 ⇨ 붕괴

붕긋붕긋 《rising》 in little hills〔bumps〕 ; 《being》 loose〔bumpy, uneven〕 here and there **—하다** rise in little hills 〔bumps〕 ; be loose〔bumpy, uneven〕 here and there

붕긋하다 form a little hill〔bump〕 ; be a bit loose〔bumpy, uneven〕

붕당 朋黨 a faction ; a clique ; a coterie ¶ 붕당을 이루다 clique together
—심 a party〔cliquish〕 spirit ; cliquism

***붕대 繃帶** a bandage ; dressing ; bandaging ¶ 눈에 붕대를 한 사람 a person with a bandage over one's eye // 붕대를 감다 apply a bandage to 《the arm》 // 붕대를 풀다 unbandage ; undress 《a wound》 ; remove a bandage // 붕대를 바꾸다 change a bandage ; renew dressing // 그는 발에 붕대를 했다 He has his foot in bandages.
두루마리 — a roller (bandage) **멜빵 —** a sling ; a suspensory ¶ 팔에 멜빵 붕대를 하고 있다 have one's arm in a sling
압박 — a compression bandage

붕락 崩落 [붕괴] breaking ; a fall ; collapse ; crumbling ; [폭락] a slump in prices ; a sharp break ; a crash **—하다** collapse ; fall (down) ; break down ; crumble ; slump ; fall suddenly ¶ 일대 붕락을 초래하다 bring about a great break〔big fall〕

붕배 朋輩 a comrade ; a companion ; a friend ; a colleague ; an associate ; a mate ; a fellow ; a buddy

붕붕 《flatulating》 with a poop-poop-poop !

붕붕거리다 hum ; buzz ; make humming sounds ; [비행기 따위가] whirr ; buzz 《in the distance》 ¶ 벌이 붕붕거리며 날아다닌다 Wasps are buzzing about.

***붕사 硼砂** borax
—구(球) 시험 a borax bead test **—땜** plastering up with borax **천연 —** native borax ; tincal

붕산 硼酸 〖화학〗 boracic acid ; boric acid
—수 a boric acid solution **— 연고** boracic 〔boric〕 ointment **—염** a borate

붕소 硼素 〖화학〗 boron 《B》
수소화— boron hydride

붕어 〖물고기〗 a crucian (carp) ; a Prussian carp
— 사탕〔과자〕 a cookie in the shape of a crucian ; [사람] a person empty of substance ; an empty-headed〔-hearted〕 person **—찜** a steamed crucian carp stuffed with meat **—톱** a carp-backed saw

붕어 崩御 demise ; death ; passing away (of a king) **—하다** 《the king》 demise ; die ; pass away

붕어마름 〖식물〗 a hornwort ; Ceratophyllum demersum (학명)

붕우 朋友 a friend ; a companion
—유신(有信) Faith should reign over the relation between friends.

붕장어 —長魚 〖물고기〗 a conger ; a sea eel

붕정 鵬程 a long way ; a long distance
—만리(萬里) a long journey ; a long flight〔voyage, cruise〕

***붙다** ① [접착] stick 《to》 ; adhere 《to》 ; cling 《to》 ¶ 옷이 몸에 붙다 clothes cling to one's body // 집안에 붙어 있다 stick at home // 붙어 다니다 go about together // 풀이 잘 붙는다 A paste sticks well. // 손가락에 붙어 있다 It sticks to my fingers. // 책장이 붙어 있다 The leaves stick together. // 마당이 붙어 있다 Our gardens adjoin. // 굴이 바위에 붙어 있다 The oysters are stuck on the rock. // 꼭 붙어서 걸어간다 They walk keeping close to each other. // 벽마다 포스터가 붙어 있다 The posters are fixed on every wall. // 두 집이 서로 붙어 있다 Two houses stand close to each other. // 환자에게 간호원이

붙어 있다 The patient is attended by a nurse. // 두 부부가 늘 붙어 다닌다 The couple are inseparable. // 네 상의 뒤에 뭔가 붙어 있다 There's something stuck to the back of your Jacket. // 구두 밑창에 껌이 붙었는데 뗄 수가 없다 I've got some chewing gum stuck to the sole of my shoe and can't get it off. // 그 아이는 늘 텔레비전 앞에 붙어 있다 The boy is always glued to the television.
② [가담] join ; attach oneself to ; take the side of ; side with ; go over to 《the enemy》 ¶ 부자에게 붙다 attach oneself to the rich // 공산당에 붙다 join the Communist Party
③ [불이] catch fire ¶ 집〔옷〕에 불이 붙었다 The house〔His clothes〕 caught fire.
④ [시험에] pass ¶ 입학 시험에 붙다 pass an entrance examination
⑤ [교미하다] link〔lock〕 in copulation ; copulate ¶ 남의 여자를 붙어먹다 commit adultery with another's woman ; sleep with another man's wife

붙당기다 grab and pull ; yank 《on》 ; jerk 《along》

붙동이다 grab and tie

†**붙들다** ① [꽉 쥐다] catch ; seize ; take 〔get, catch, lay〕 hold of ; grasp〔grip, grab〕 ¶ 팔을 붙들다 seize 《a person》 by the arm // 머리채를 붙들고 끌어당기다 drag 《a woman》 by the hair // 붙들고 놓지 않다 keep one's hold on // 붙들고 있는 손을 늦추다 loosen〔release〕 one's hold on 《a person, a thing》 // 나는 그의 어깨를 붙들었다 I caught him by the shoulder.
② [잡다] catch ; arrest ; capture ; apprehend ; nab ¶ 도둑을 붙들다 arrest 〔catch, capture, nab〕 a thief // 말을 붙들다 pull up〔rein back〕 a horse // 범인은 아직 붙들리지 않고 있다 The culprit is still at large. // 경찰은 대부분을 붙들었으나 도망간 사람들이 수십명은 됐다 The police rounded up most of them, but scores escaped.
③ [만류하다] keep〔hold〕 《a person》 ; detain ; buttonhole 《a person》 ¶ 오래 붙들지 않겠습니다 I won't keep you long. // 떠나려 했으나 그는 자꾸만 붙들었다 I wanted to go, but he would buttonhole me. // 그는 나를 몇 시간씩 붙들고 이야기했다 He held me buttonholed for hours.
④ [돕다] help ; aid ¶ 일을 붙들어 주다 help 《a person》 in his work

***붙들리다** be caught ; be detained ; be arrested〔apprehended〕 ; be made to stay ¶ 붙들리지 않고 있다 remain at liberty〔large〕 // 붙들리지 않으려고 하다 keep out of 《a person's》 clutches // 그에게 두 시간 붙들렸다 I was detained for two hours by him. // 그는 백차(교통순경)에게 붙들렸다 He was pinched by a speed cop. // 도둑이 현장에서 붙들렸다 The thief was caught in the act. // 그 친구한테 붙들리면 도망갈 수가 없다 You can not get out of his clutches. // 일에 붙들려서 참가하지 못했다 I was unable to join in because I was detained from business.

붙따르다 stick to ; follow close behind ; dog 《someone's footsteps》

붙매이다 be caught ; be detained ; be subordinated ; be tied 《to》 ; be bound up 《with》

붙박아놓다 fasten 《a thing》 immovably ; fix firmly ; put aside 《in a corner, etc.》

붙박이 a fixture ; a built-in furniture ; fittings ¶ 붙박이로 as a fixture ; permanently ; immovably // 붙박이가 돼서 움직일 수 없다 It is stationary and not removable.
—장(欌)〔**책장, 서가, 캐비닛**〕 a built-in chest of drawers〔bookshelf, bookcase, cabinet〕 **—창**(窓) a fixture window ; a built-in〔an immovable, a blind〕 window

붙박이다 be fastened immovably ; be held in position ; be set up ¶ 기계가 붙박혀 있다 A machine is placed in position. // 그는 늘 집에 붙박혀 있다 He always sticks at home.

붙박이별 ⇨ 항성(恒星)

붙안다 hold 《a thing》 in one's arms

붙어다니다 follow 《a person》 about ; dangle about〔after, round〕 《a person》 ; shadow

붙어먹다 ① ⇨ 간통 ② ⇨ 기식(寄食)

붙어살다 ⇨ 기생(寄生)

붙어지내다 depend 《on a person》 for one's living ; be dependent

-붙이 things of 《a class, a group》 ; things of 《the same kind》 ; things made 《of》 ; things belonging 《to》
가루— bakery goods **뼈—** things made of bone **살—** kith and kin ; lineage **솜—** padded clothes **쇠—** articles of iron ; ironware **일가—** family relations ; relatives **제—** one's own people **털—** fur goods

†**붙이다** ① [부착·첨부] attach ; fix ; put on ; put up ; paste ; apply ¶ 우표를 붙이다 put a stamp on 《a letter》 // 광고를 붙이다 post a bill // 포스터를 붙이다 put up a poster // 꼬리표를 붙이다 attach a tag 《to a parcel》 // 고약을 붙이다 apply a plaster // 타일이 붙여져 있다 be lined with tiles // 책상을 벽에 붙여 놓다 place the table close to the wall // 우표 붙이는 것 좀 도와 줄까 Shall I help you put on the stamps ?
② [이름을] name ; give a name ; christen ¶ 별명을 붙이다 give a nickname 《to a person》 // 그 배에 아리랑호라는 이름을 붙였다 The ship was christened the *Arirang*.
③ [사람을] have 《a person》 in attendance ¶ 환자에게 간호원을 붙이다 have a nurse in attendance upon a patient ;

have a patient attended by a nurse // 피고에게 변호사를 붙여주다 provide the defendant with a lawyer
④ [불을] light ; kindle ; ignite ; apply ¶ 담배에 불을 붙이다 light a cigarette // 담뱃불 좀 붙입시다 Please give me a light. /May I trouble you for a light ? // 그는 파이프를 꺼내더니 불을 붙였다 He took out a pipe and lit up.
⑤ [중간에서] arrange ; bring two parties together for 《an enterprise, a negotiation》 ¶ 흥정을 붙이다 arrange a bargain ; get two parties to strike a bargain // 노름을 붙이다 arrange gambling // 싸움을 붙이다 make 《persons》 quarrel ; set 《dogs》 to fighting
⑥ [기식하다] live on ; sponge on ; hang on ; rely on 《someone》 for 《one's care》 ; put oneself under someone's care ¶ 나는 아저씨 집에 몸을 붙이고 있다 I live with my uncle's family. /I live on my uncle.
⑦ [첨가] give one's opinion ; make an additional comment ¶ 토의에 의견을 붙이다 give one's opinion in a debate // 조건을 붙이다 attach a condition
⑧ [때리다] ¶ 빰을 올려 붙이다 slap 《a person》 ; box 《a person's》 ears ; give 《a person》 a box on the ear(s)
⑨ [교미시키다] mate ; copulate ; pair ¶ 개를 붙이다 mate a dog
⑩ [가입] let 《a person》 in〔into〕 ; take 《a person》 in ; admit 《a person》 into ¶ 붙여주지 않다 keep 《a person》 out of 《a group》 // 저 아이는 붙이지 말자 Let's not let him in.
⑪ [내기에서] bet ; stake ; wager ¶ 십원을 붙이다 bet ten *won*

붙일성 一性 ⇨ 붙임성

붙임붙임 warmly ; amiably ; in a friendly way

*⁎***붙임성** 一性 sociability ; affability ; amiability ; friendliness ; openness ; outgoingness ¶ 붙임성이 있다 sociable〔affable, friendly, open, outgoing〕 ; be the sort who will come to you

붙임질 attaching ; gluing on〔together〕 **—하다** attach ; glue on〔together〕

붙임틀 a frame used in joining pieces of wood

붙임판 a metal vice for holding pieces of wood which are being joined

붙임풀 a kind of paste used in sewing

붙임혀 〖건축〗 an eave prop

†**붙잡다** seize ; grasp ; catch ; hold ; take 〔catch, hold〕 of ¶ 도둑을 붙잡다 seize a thief // 손을 붙잡다 grasp 《a person's》 hand // 일자리를 붙잡다 get a job // 붙잡아 주다 help〔aid〕 《a person》 // 자동차 손잡이를 붙잡다 hang〔hold〕 on to a strap 《in a car》 // 꼭 붙잡고 있어라 Don't release 〔let go〕 your hold〔grasp〕 on it.

붙잡히다 be caught ⇨ 붙들리다

붙장 一欌 a built-in cupboard ; a kitchen closet

붙좇다 follow (as a disciple or retainer) ; look up to ; respect ; revere ; admire ¶ 스승을 붙좇다 hold one's teacher in high esteem

붚달다 be hasty and rough ; be reckless ; be rough-and-ready

붚대다 treat in a quick and rough〔a rough-and-ready, an offhanded〕 manner

브라보 bravo

브라스 밴드 a brass band

브라운관 一管 a Braun tube ; a cathode-ray tube ; a picture tube
— 녹화(법) teletranscription

브라자빌 Brazzaville

브래지어 a brassière 《프》 ; a bra 《미·구》 ; falsies 《구》

*⁎***브랜디** brandy

브러시 a brush

⁑**브레이크**¹ a brake ; a brake device (장치) ¶ 브레이크를 걸고〔걸지 않고〕 with the brake on〔off〕 // 브레이크를 걸다 apply〔put on〕 the brake // 브레이크를 늦추다 take off the brake // 브레이크를 걸어 멈추다 brake 《a car》 to a stop // 브레이크가 듣지 않았다 The brake did not work.

브레이크² 〖권투〗 a break

브레인워싱 [세뇌] brainwashing

브레인 트러스트 a brain trust 《미》

브로마이드 [감광지] bromide paper ; [사진] a bromide photograph

*⁎***브로치** a brooch ; a breastpin 《미》

*⁎***브로커** a broker ¶ 브로커 노릇을 하다 act as a broker
부동산 — a realtor 《미》 ; an estate agent 《영》

브리지 ① [의치] ¶ 브리지를 하다 fix a bridge ② [카드놀이] ¶ 브리지를 하다 play bridge

브리핑 briefing

브이아이피 a V. I. P. ; a VIP 《*pl.* -s》 ; a very important person

브이티아르 a VTR ; a video tape recorder

*⁎***블라우스** a blouse

†**블라인드** a (window) blind 《영》 ; a shade 《미》 ¶ 블라인드를 올리다〔내리다〕 draw up〔pull down〕 a blind

블랙리스트 a blacklist〔book〕 ¶ 블랙리스트에 오르다 be put on a blacklist ; be black-listed // 블랙리스트에 올리다 put 《a person》 on a blacklist ; blacklist 《a person》

블레이저 코트 a blazer (coat)

블로킹 〖심리·경기〗 blocking

*⁎***블록** [권(圈)] bloc 《프》 ; [건축 재료] a block
— 건축 block building **— 경제** bloc economy **달러 —** the dollar bloc

블론드 blond(e) ¶ 블론드의 여자 a blonde // 블론드의 남자 a blond

블루머 bloomers

블루스 〖음악〗 blues
블루 진 (blue) jeans ¶ 블루 진을 입은 젊은이 a young man in blue jeans ; a jeaned teen-ager
†비[1] rain ; a rainfall ¶ 부슬비 a sprinkling rain // 억수같이 퍼붓는 비 a downpour ; a driving〔pouring〕 rain // 이슬비 a misty〔fine, drizzling〕 rain // 큰비 a heavy rain // 비를 맞으며 in the rain // 비가 와서 (시합을) 중지하다 be rained out // 비를 만나다 be caught in the rain // 비에 젖다 get wet // 눈물이 비오듯했다 Her eyes rained tears. // 비가 그친다 It stops raining. /The rain stops〔lets up〕. // 비가 억수같이 쏟아졌다 It rained cats and dogs. // 비가 오다 그치다 한다 It is raining on and off. // 비가 올 것 같다 It looks like rain. /It is going to rain.
비 온 뒤에 땅이 굳어진다 속담 After a storm comes a calm.
‡비[2] [쓰는] a broom ; a besom (마당비) ¶ 빗자루 a broomstick // 비로 쓸다 sweep with a broom ; besom
‡비 碑 a monument ¶ 비를 세우다 erect a monument
비 妣 one's deceased mother
비 妃 [왕비] a queen consort ; a princess ; [태자비] a crown princess
†비 比 [비율] ratio ; proportion ; [비교] comparison ; [대조] contrast ; [필적] an equal ─하다 compare 《a thing》 with 《another》 ; contrast 《a thing》 with 《another》 ; [필적] match ; equal ; [비유] compare 《to》 ; liken 《to》 ¶ 2와 3의 비 the ratio of two to three // …에 비하면 as compared 《with》 ; in comparison 《with》 // …에 비해 너무 크다 be out of proportion to 《a thing》 // A를 B에 비하다 compare A with B // 나이에 비해 젊다 be〔look〕 young for one's age // 지난해에 비해 감소되어 있다 It shows a decrease as compared with〔against〕 the preceding year. // 질적으로는 그것에 비할 만한 것이 없다 There is nothing equal to it in quality.
비 非 a mistake ; an error ; a fault
비- 非 [반] un- ; anti- ; non- ¶ 비과학적 unscientific // 비사교적 unsociable // 비사회주의자 an antisocialist // 비애국적 unpatriotic // 비예술적 inartistic // 비인도적 inhuman
─전투원 a noncombatant
-비 費 ⇨ 비용
건축〔생활〕─ the cost of construction 〔living〕
비가 悲歌 an elegy ; a dirge ; a song of lamentation
비각 incompatible ; opposite(s) ; (mutually) exclusive ; not going together ¶ 물과 불은 비각이다 Fire and water do not mix.
비각 碑閣 a monument〔tablet〕 house ; a building erected over a monument

비감 悲感 grief ; sorrow ; lamentation ; a sad feeling ─하다 feel sad ; grieve
비강 鼻腔 〖해부〗 the nasal cavity
─ 점막 the nasal mucous membrane 만성 ─염 〖의학〗 gleet
비거스렁이 the cool after a rain ─하다 cool off after a rain
비걱거리다, 삐걱거리다 creak ; squeak ¶ 삐걱거리는 소리 a creaking〔squeaking〕 sound // 의자가 비걱거린다 The chair creaks.
*비겁 卑怯 cowardice ; meanness ─하다 (be) cowardly ; [남자답지 못하다] unmanly ; [비열하다] mean ; [부정하다] foul ¶ 비겁한 자 a coward // 비겁하게도 …하다 be timid〔cowardly〕 enough to 《do》 // 비겁한 짓을 하다 hit below the belt // 비겁한 행동을 하다 play foul ; act cowardly
비게질 body scratching〔rubbing〕 《against a thing》 ─하다 scratch〔rub〕 its body against 《a thing》
비견 鄙見 one's humble opinion〔view〕 ¶ 비견으론 in my humble opinion ; to my thinking
비견 比肩 ─하다 rank with ; stand beside 《a person》 ; be comparable with 〔to〕 ¶ 그와 비견할 사람은 없다 No one can equal him. /He is unrivaled.
†비결 秘訣 a secret ; a key ; a knack ¶ 성공의 비결 the secret of success ; the key to success // 장사의 비결 the trick of a trade // 장수의 비결은 절제다 The secret of longevity is to be moderate in everything.
비결정론 非決定論 〖심리〗 indeterminism
비경 悲境 adversity ; adverse circumstances ; a sad〔miserable〕 condition ; distress ; a sad plight ¶ 비경에 빠지다 fall into adverse circumstances ; be reduced to distress
비경 秘境 unexplored〔untravel(l)ed〕 regions ; a mysterious land
비경이 a stretcher〔warp〕 beam
비계[1] 〖토목·건축〗 a scaffold ; scaffolding ; staging 《미》 ; a falsework ; a footing 〔foothold〕 ¶ 비계용의 기둥 a scaffolding pole // 비계를 설치하다 set up〔erect〕 a scaffold ; scaffold 《a house》
비계[2] the fat of meat ; lard
비계 秘計 a secret plan〔scheme, plot〕 ; one's best〔trump〕 card ¶ 비계를 쓰다 play one's best card
비고 備考 a note ; a remark
─란 a remarks〔reference〕 column ¶ 비고란에 기입하다 write in〔fill up〕 a remarks column ─ 부분 [법률 문서의] a recital
비곡 悲曲 a plaintive〔doleful〕 melody
비곡 秘曲 an esoteric〔a treasured〕 piece of music
비골 鼻骨 the nasal bone
비공 鼻孔 nostrils

비공개 非公開 (being) not open to the public ¶ 재판은 비공개가 될 것이다 The trial will be held in camera.
— 편지 a personal letter — 회의 a closed meeting ; a conclave
비공산국 非共産國 a non-Communist country
비공산화 非共産化 decommunization — 하다 decommunize
⁑비공식 非公式 informality ¶ 비공식적인 unofficial ; informal
— 견해 informal remarks ; unofficial comments ; a private〔personal〕 opinion — 보고 an unconfirmed report — 시합 an exhibition game〔match〕 — 회담 『외교』 conversation
비공인 非公認 ¶ 비공인의 unofficial ; unauthorized ; unrecognized
— 세계 기록 an as-yet-unratified〔a pending〕 world record
비과세 非課稅 tax exemption
—품〔品〕 a tax-free article
비과학적 非科學的 (being) unscientific
*비관 悲觀 pessimism ; a gloomy view ; [낙담] disappointment — 하다 be pessimistic of〔about〕 ; take a pessimistic view 《of》 ; [낙담하다] be discouraged ¶ 비관적 pessimistic ; gloomy ; discouraged // 전도를 비관하다 take a gloomy view of the future // 조금도 비관할 이유가 없다 There is no reason whatever for pessimism. // 비관하지 마라 Never say die.
비관론 悲觀論 a pessimistic view ; pessimism
—자 a pessimist ; a crapehanger〔crepehanger〕 《미·속》
†비교 比較 comparison ; [대조] contrast ; parallel — 하다 compare 《a thing》 with 《another》 ; draw a comparison 《between》 ¶ 비교적(으로) comparative(ly) ; relative(ly) // …과 비교하여 in comparison 《with》 ; as compared 《with》 ; as against ; in contrast 《with》 // 비교해서 말하자면 comparatively speaking // 비교 연구하다 make a comparative study 《of》 // 이것과 그것과는 비교가 안된다 There is no comparison between this and that. /This is no match for that. // 전년도에 비교해서 감소되고 있다 It shows a decrease as compared with〔against〕 the preceding year. // 한국 요리와 비교해 볼 때 미국 요리는 어떻습니까 How do American dishes compare with Korean ones? // 비싼 물건을 살 때는 여기저기 다니면서 가격을 비교해 보고 사라 Do comparison shopping when you buy big-ticket items.
— 문법〔언어학〕 comparative grammar 〔philology, linguistics 《미》〕 — 문학 comparative literature — 발생학〔생물학, 해부학〕 comparative embryology〔biology, anatomy〕 — 심리학 comparative psychology — 측정기 a comparator — 표 a comparative table
비교급 比較級 『문법』 the comparative degree
비교 연구 比較硏究 a comparative study — 하다 make a comparative study 《of》 ; study 《a subject》 by the comparative method
—법 the comparative method —자 [문학 또는 언어학의] a comparativist ; a comparatist
*비교적 比較的 comparative ; relative ¶ 비교적으로 comparatively ; relatively ; in 〔by〕 comparison
비구 飛球 『야구』 a fly (ball)
비구 比丘 a Buddhist priest〔monk〕 ; a *bigu*
비구니 比丘尼 a Buddhist nun ; a *biguni*
비구름 a rain cloud ; 『기상』 a nimbus 《*pl.* ～es, -bi》
비구승 比丘僧 a Buddhist monk ; a *bigu*
비국가적 非國家的 (being) unpatriotic
비국민 非國民 an unpatriotic person
비군사적 非軍事的 (being) nonmilitary
비군사화 非軍事化 demilitarization
비굴 卑屈 meanness, servility — 하다 (be) mean ; servile ; sneaking ; [사내답지 않다] unmanly ¶ 비굴한 자 an unmanly fellow ; a sneak
⁑비극 悲劇 a tragedy ¶ 가정의 비극 a domestic tragedy // 비극적 tragic // 비극적인 사건 a tragic affair ; a tragedy // 비극으로 끝나다 end tragically
— 배우 a tragedian ; [남자] a tragic actor ; [여자] a tragic actress — 작가 a tragic dramatist 가정 — a domestic tragedy
비근 卑近 — 하다 (be) familiar ; common ; plain ; simple ¶ 비근한 예를 들다 give a familiar example
비근거리다 be shaky〔rickety〕 ; wobble ; shake
비근비근 shaking ; wobbling ; loose (jointed)
비금 飛禽 flying creatures
비금비금하다 be much the same
비금속 卑金屬 a base metal
비금속 非金屬 nonmetal ¶ 비금속의 nonmetallic
— 광물 a nonmetallic mineral — 광택 nonmetallic luster — 원소 a nonmetallic element
비기 秘記 a writing of divination
†비기다¹ ① [승부를] end in a tie 〔draw〕 ; come out even ; tie 《with》 ¶ 비기기 a drawn game〔bout〕 ; a tie〔draw〕 // 시합에 비겼다 The game ended in a tie〔draw〕. ② [셈을] offset〔cancel〕 each other ; set off ; countervail ; counterbalance ; have losses offset by gains
비기다² [견줌·비유] compare to ; liken to ¶ 인생을 여행에 비기다 liken〔compare〕 life to a journey // 잠을 죽음에 비기다

compare sleep to death
비기다³ [때우다] patch up ; put a patch 《on》
비김수 —手 [장기 따위의] a tying move〔run, point〕; a draw ; a dead heat
비꼬다 ① [꼬다] twist ; twine ② [말을] give a sarcastic twist 《to one's words》 ¶ 비꼬아 말하다 say ironically ; make cynical remarks
비꼬이다 get〔be〕 twisted〔crooked〕; [심술궂다] be distorted〔perverse〕 ¶ 비꼬인 성질 a crooked disposition // 그는 마음이 비꼬여 있다 His heart is not in the right place. /He has a perverse mind. /He is prejudiced against 《a person》.
비꾸러지다 ① [비뚤어지다] be quite crooked ; be heavily tilted ; be at a very bad angle ② [빗나가다] go amiss ; go awry ; miss one's way〔one's road, time, goal, etc.〕
비끄러매다 tie ; bind ¶ 말을 비끄러매다 tie a horse
비끗거리다, 삐긋거리다 ① [잘 안되다] come〔fall〕 short of one's expectation ; go wrong〔amiss〕
② [어긋나다] do not fit in properly
비끗비끗, 삐긋삐긋 ① [어긋나다] not fitting properly ; not going in as it should ; not joining smoothly
② [일이] (going) amiss ; astray ; awry ; wrong ; (getting) out of line.
비끼다 ① [놓이다] lie aslant ; hang at an angle ② [비치다] shine at an angle ; light obliquely
비나리치다 flatter 《a person》; fawn upon 《a person》; curry favor with 《a person》
†비난 非難 criticism ; reproach ; blame ; condemnation ; denunciation (공공연한)
—하다 criticize ; reproach ; blame ; condemn ; denounce ; attack ; disapprove 《of》 ¶ 비난의 여지가 없는 irreproachable ; beyond〔above〕 reproach // 비난할 만한 reproachable ; blamable // 비난의 대상이 되다 be the target of criticism // 몹시 비난하다 criticize 《a person》 severely // 그 조치는 불공평하다는 비난을 면치 못한다 The step is open to the charge of unfairness. // 그 방침에 대한 비난의 소리가 높다 The policy is loudly attacked〔censured〕. // 내 견해로는 이 나라의 경제 침체에 대해서는 양당이 모두 비난받아야 한다고 생각한다 Well, in my opinion, both parties are to blame for this country's economic woes.
—자 a critic ; a censor ; an accuser
비너스 Venus
비녀 an ornamental hairpin ¶ 비녀를 꽂다 wear an ornamental hairpin
비녀 婢女 a woman slave
비녀장 a linchpin
비논리적 非論理的 (being) illogical ; irrational
비뇨 泌尿 〖의학〗 urination
— 생식기 the urinogenital〔urogenital〕 organs
비뇨기 泌尿器 the urinary organs
—과 urology —과 의사 a urologist —병 urinary diseases
‡비누 soap ¶ 세숫 비누 한 개 a cake of (toilet) soap // 세탁 비누 한 개 a bar of laundry soap // 비누로 손을 씻다 wash one's hands with soap and water // 얼굴에 비누칠을 하다 lather one's face
— 거품 soap bubbles〔froth〕; soapsuds ; suds ; lather — 공장 a soap works — 제조 soapmaking ; soap boiling — 제조자 a soap-boiler ; a soap manufacturer —질 soaping ¶ 비누질하다 soap 가루 — soap powder 물— liquid soap 바닷물용 — marine soap 빨랫〔세탁〕— 《a bar of》 washing〔laundry〕 soap 약용 — medicated soap 역성(逆性) — invert〔cationactive〕 soap 종이 — soap paper ; a soap leaf 칼리 — soft soap 화장〔세숫〕 — toilet soap 비눗갑 a soap case〔dish〕 비눗물 soapy water ; [거품이 인] soapsuds ; suds ; lather 비눗방울 a soap bubble ¶ 비눗방울을 불다 blow (soap) bubbles
‡비늘 scales ¶ 비늘 있는 scaled // 비늘을 벗기다 scale 《a fish》
비늘구름 〖기상〗 a cirrocumulus 《*pl.* cumuli》 ¶ 비늘구름으로 덮인 하늘 a mackerel sky
비늘김치 radish pickles stuffed with hot seasonings
비능률 非能率 inefficiency ¶ 비능률적 inefficient
*비닐 〖화학〗 vinyl
— 보자기 a vinyl cloth wrapper —선(線)〔튜브〕 a polyvinyl chloride wire〔tube〕 — 수지(樹脂) vinyl resin ; vinyl plastic —판(板) [레코드의] a vinyl disk 염화(鹽化)— vinyl chloride
비닐론 [상표명] Vinylon
†비다¹ be empty〔vacant〕; be free (손이) ; be hollow (속이) ¶ 빈 방 an empty room // 머리가 텅 빈 사람 an empty-headed man // 손이 비다 be free〔unoccupied〕; have one's hands free // 좌석이 비다 become less crowded // 이 열차는 비어 있다 The train is not crowded. // 너희 사무실에 자리가 하나 비었다며 I hear there's an opening in your office. // 또 다른 아파트는 한 달 후에 빕니다 Another Apartment will be vacated in a month. // 이번 주 화요일이나 수요일에 빈 좌석이 있나 좀 봐주세요 See if you have any open seats for this Tuesday or Wednesday, please. // 나는 주머니가 텅텅 비었다 I am broke. / I am in the red.
빈 수레가 더 요란하다 〔속담〕 Empty vessels make the greatest sound. /Shallow streams〔water〕 make most din.
비다² ⇨ 비우다
비다듬다 preen oneself ; arrange ; smooth 《down, out》

비단 非但 not only〔merely〕; as well as ¶ 비단 그뿐 아니라 not only that // 그는 비단 영어뿐만 아니라 불어도 안다 He understands not only English but French.

비단 緋緞 silk fabrics ; silks
—실 silk thread **—옷** silk dress **— 이불** silk bedding **— 장수** a silkman ; a silk trader〔merchant, mercer《영》〕

*__비단결 緋緞—__ the texture of silk ; a velvety texture ¶ 그녀의 피부는 비단결같다 Her skin is a velvety texture. // 그녀의 마음은 비단결같다 She is tenderhearted.
비단결 같다 관용 be soft as velvet

비단벌레 〖곤충〗 a buprestid (beetle)

비당파적 非黨派的 nonpartisan ; nonparty
— 외교 수행 the execution of nonpartisan diplomacy

비대 肥大 portliness ; corpulence ; 〖의학〗 hypertrophy **—하다** (be) fat ; portly ; corpulent ¶ 비대성의 〖의학〗 hypertrophic
심장 — hypertrophy of the heart ; an athlete's heart (과도한 운동에 의한)

비대다 assume another's name ¶ 남의 이름을 비대다 assume a false name ; give a wrong name

비대발괄 entreaty ; solicitation **—하다** beg ; entreat ; implore ; appeal 《to》; beseech

비도 匪徒 bandits ; outlaws ; insurgents ; rebels

비도 非道 [비행] injustice ; [잔인] cruelty ; [비인도] inhumanity ; atrocity ¶ 비도한 cruel ; inhuman ; unjust ; atrocious

비도덕적 非道德的 (being) unmoral ; immoral

비동맹 非同盟 nonalignment
— 외상 회의 the nonaligned foreign ministers conference **— 정책** a nonalignment policy **—주의** nonalignment **— 회의** Conference of Non-allied Countries

비둔 肥鈍 —하다 (be) corpulent ; fleshy ; fat ; [동작이] clumsy ; slow-moving ; [껴입어서] heavily clothed

‡**비둘기** a dove ; a pigeon (기르는) ¶ 비둘기 편으로 by a carrier pigeon // 비둘기를 날리다 toss〔fly, let loose〕 pigeons (into the air)
— 새끼 a fledgling pigeon ; a squab **—장** a dovecot(e) ; a dovehouse ; a pigeon house ; a pigeonry ; a columbary **군용 —** a military〔an army〕 carrier pigeon **통신용 —** a carrier〔homing〕 pigeon

비둘기파 —派 the doves ; a soft-liner ¶ 비둘기파의 dovish // 비둘기파의 정치가 a dove politician

비드득, 삐드득 grinding ; creaking

비듬 dandruff ; scurf ¶ 비듬 투성이의 dandruffy ; scurfy // 비듬을 없애다 remove dandruff
—약 a hair lotion〔tonic〕; a dandruff remover

비등 比等 —하다 be a match 《for》; be equal 《to》; be on a par 《with》; be about the same ¶ 그와 나의 영어 지식이 비등하다 His knowledge of English is on a par with mine. // 이것과 그것은 크기에 있어 비등하다 That is equal to this in size.

비등 沸騰 boiling ; effervescence ; seething **—하다** boil ; effervesce ; seethe ; [의논이] be agitated〔excited〕 ¶ 여론이 비등하다 Public opinion is agitated〔aroused〕.
— 곡선 〖물리〗 a boiling curve **—성 음료** a fizz 《미》; a fizzy〔an effervescent〕 drink **—수〔산(散)〕** an effervescent drink〔powder〕 **—천(泉)** a boiling spring

비등점 沸騰點 〖물리〗 the boiling point ¶ 비등점에 이르다 reach a boil ; come to the boil
— 기압계 a thermobarometer

비디오 video ¶ 비디오 좀 찍어 주시겠어요 Could you videotape, please ?
—테이프 videotape ¶ 비디오 테이프에 녹화하다 record on (a) videotape ; videotape // 이 비디오 테이프는 화상이 선명하지 못하다 This videotape has a grainy picture. **— 테이프 리코더** a video tape recorder 《VTR》

비딱, 삐딱 —하다 (be) rickety〔shaky〕

비딱거리다, 삐딱거리다 be shaky〔rickety〕; wobble

비뚜로, 삐뚜로 crooked ; obliquely ; aslant ; diagonally ¶ 그림이 삐뚜로 걸리었다 The picture hung askew〔wrong, crooked〕.

비뚜름하다, 삐뚜름하다 (be) crooked ; inclined ; slant ¶ 그림이 비뚜름하게 걸려 있다 The picture hung askew.

비뚜름히 at a rather bad angle ; somewhat crooked〔wrong, askew〕 ¶ 그는 모자를 비뚜름히 썼다 His hat is on somewhat askew.

비뚝거리다, 삐뚝거리다 ① [흔들거리다] be shaky〔rickety〕; wobble ¶ 비뚝거리는 의자 a rickety chair
② [걸음을] limp (along) ; walk with a limp ; walk lame ¶ 책상이 비뚝거리다 The table wobbles. // 그는 비뚝거리며 걷는다 He limps along.

비뚝비뚝, 삐뚝삐뚝 [흔들흔들] with a wobble ; shakily ; totteringly ; [절룩절룩] with a limp ; limping

비뚤거리다, 삐뚤거리다 ① [흔들거리다] stagger ; totter ; reel ; jolt (마차가) ¶ 비뚤거리는 마차 a ramshackle〔rickety〕 carriage // 무거운 짐으로 비뚤거리다 stagger with a heavy load // 노인이 지팡이를 짚고 삐뚤거리며 간다 An old man totters along with a cane.
② [구부러지다] wind ; curve ; meander

비뚤다, 삐뚤다 (be) crooked ; wrong ; tilted ; askew ; slanting ; be at the wrong angle ¶ 코가 비뚤다 have a crooked nose // 길이 비뚤어졌다 The road is crooked. // 그림이 비뚤어졌다 The picture is crooked.

비뚤비뚤, 삐뚤삐뚤 [흔들흔들] staggeringly ; totteringly ; [꼬불꼬불] meanderingly ; crookedly ¶ 비뚤비뚤한 길 a winding road // 비뚤비뚤 걷다 reel along ; walk zigzag

비뚤어지다, 삐뚤어지다 ① [기울다] get crooked ; slant ; tilt ; incline ¶ 비뚤어진 나무 a crooked〔gnarled〕tree ② [마음이] be perverse ; crooked ; twisted ; be dishonest ¶ 마음이 비뚤어지다 have a crooked mind // 어떻게 해서 그는 저렇게 성격이 비뚤어진 아이로 자랐을까 How did he ever grow up to be such a perverse child ? ③ [뒤틀어지다] be cross ; be in ill humor〔a bad temper〕; be displeased

비뚤이, 삐뚤이 a person with a twisted body〔limb〕; [비탈진 땅] the skirt of slope

비래 飛來 ―하다 fly ; come flying ; arrive at 《a place》 by air

비량 鼻梁 the ridge〔bridge〕of the nose

비럭질 begging ―하다 beg ; go begging

비렁뱅이 a beggar ⇨ 거지

비련 悲戀 tragic love ; disappointed love

*비례 非禮 discourtesy ; impoliteness ; rudeness

비례 比例 [비교] comparison ; [비율] ratio ; proportion ―하다 [비교하다] compare 《a thing》 with 《another》 ; [비하다] be proportionate 《to》 ; be in proportion 《to》 ¶ 성공에 비례하여 in proportion to one's success // 비례로 계산하다 do a sum in〔by〕proportion // 정〔반〕비례하다 be directly〔inversely〕proportional 《to》

― 계산 a sum in the rule of three ; a rule-of-three sum ― 배분 proportional allotment〔allocation〕―선 a proportional line ―세 regressive taxation ―수 a proportional number ―식 a proportional expression ― 중항〔중수〕a mean proportional ; the geometric mean ―차 proportional difference 단― simple proportion 반― inverse proportion 복― compound proportion 역(逆)― reciprocal proportion 정(正)― direct proportion 정(定)― definite〔constant〕proportion

비례 대표 比例代表 proportional representation

―제 the system of proportional representation ―주의 proportionalism

*비로소 for the first time ¶ 두 시간을 기다린 후에야 비로소 기차가 떠났다 I had to wait for two hours before the train started. // 죽은 후에야 비로소 그의 존재가치를 깨달았다 It was not until his death that I realized how much he meant to me. // 밤이 늦어서야 비로소 그가 왔다 He did not come until late in the evening.

†비록 if ; even if ; though ; even though ; supposing that ¶ 비록 그렇다 할지라도 even if it were so ; even so // 비록 나이는 젊지만 though he is young // 비록 농담이라 할지라도 even in joke // 비록 자네 말이 사실이라 할지라도 잘못이네 Granting it to be true, you are still in the wrong.

비록 秘錄 a secret memoir ; a confidential document

*비롯하다 begin ; start ; arise〔date〕《from》 (기원하다) ¶ …을 비롯하여 including ; headed by ; as well as // 담임 선생님을 비롯하여 많은 여학생이 식에 참석했다 A group of school girls headed by the teacher in charge attended the ceremony. // 시장을 비롯해서 20명이 출석했다 There were twenty present including the mayor.

*비료 肥料 a fertilizer ; manure ¶ 비료를 주다 fertilize ; manure

― 공업 the fertilizer industry ― 공장 a fertilizer plant 인조 ― artificial fertilizer 질소〔인산, 칼리〕― nitrogenous〔phosphatic, potash〕manure 합성 ― synthesized fertilizer 화학 ― chemical fertilizer〔manure〕

비루 〚의학〛 mange ¶ 비루먹다 catch〔get, suffer from, be affected by〕mange

비루먹은 강아지 대호를 건드린다 [속담] Fools rush in where angels fear to tread.

비루 鄙陋 meanness ; baseness ―하다 (be) mean〔base〕; contemptible

비류 比類 an equal ; a match ; a parallel ; a peer ; an example ¶ 비류가 없다 be unparalleled〔peerless, matchless, unique〕// 역사상 그 비류가 없다 It is without parallel in history. /It is unique in history.

비름 〚식물〛 amaranth ; pigweed

비릇다 go〔enter〕into labor (in the bearing of a child) ; start having labor pains

비리 非理 irrationality ; unreasonableness ; absurdity

*비리다 ① [냄새가] (be) fishy (생선이) ; bloody〔gory, sanguinary〕(피가) ¶ 비린내 a fishy smell〔taste〕// 피비린내 나는 싸움 a sanguinary struggle // 비린내가 나다 smell fishy // 물이 비리다 The water tastes fishy. ② [아니꼽다] (be) disgusting ; sickening ; loathsome

비리비리 ―하다 (be) thin〔skinny〕and dry ¶ 비리비리 여위다 be nothing but skin and bones

비리척지근하다, 비리치근하다 ⇨ 비릿하다

비린내 a fishy〔bloody〕smell

비린내 나다 [관용] smell fishy

비릿비릿 disgustingly ; sickeningly ―하다 (be) sickening ; disgusting

비릿하다 (be) somewhat fishy ; smell a little bloody

†비만 肥滿 fatness ; corpulence ; portliness ―하다 (be) fat ; plump ; fleshy ; corpulent ¶ 비만해지다 become fat〔portly,

plump, fleshy〕
—아 an overweight child ; an obese〔a fat〕 child〔boy, girl〕 —형(型) a pyknic〔pycnic〕 type
비말 飛沫 a spray ; a splash ¶ 비말을 일으키다 splash 《in the river》
— 감염 〖의학〗 droplet infection
*__비망록 備忘錄__ a memorandum 《*pl.* ~s, -da》 ; a memo 《*pl.* ~s》
비매 동맹 非賣同盟 combined refusal to sell ; a selling strike
비매품 非賣品 an article not for sale ; Not for sale. (게시)
비명 非命 an accidental〔unnatural, untimely〕 death ¶ 비명에 죽다 meet (with) a violent death ; die an unnatural death ; die with boots on
— 횡사 an unnatural〔untimely, accidental〕 death ; death by violence
*__비명 悲鳴__ a scream ; a shriek ; a cry of distress —하다 cry in distress ; shriek ; scream ¶ 비명을 지르며 도움을 청했다 She cried〔screamed〕 for help.
비명 碑銘 an epitaph ; an inscription
비명 秘命 a secret order
비목 費目 an item of expenditure
비목어 比木魚 〖물고기〗 a flatfish ; a halibut ; a turbot
비몽사몽 非夢似夢 a trance ; a half-conscious state ¶ 비몽사몽간에 between sleeping and waking ; half asleep
비무장 非武裝 demilitarization
— 도시 an open city — 조약 a nonfortification pact — 지대 a demilitarized zone 《DMZ》
비문 碑文 an epitaph ; an inscription
비문명 非文明 ¶ 비문명의 uncivilized ; barbarous
—국 an uncivilized nation
비문화적 非文化的 (being) uncivilized〔uncultured, unenlightened, preliterate〕
비물질적 非物質的 immaterial ; nonmaterial
비민주적 非民主的 undemocratic
†**비밀 秘密** a secret ; secrecy ; mystery ¶ 비밀의 secret ; confidential ; classified 《미》 ; private ; privy ; hidden // 공공연한 비밀 an open secret // 비밀히 secretly ; in secret ; confidentially ; privately // 비밀로 하다 keep 《a matter》 secret〔private, dark〕 // 비밀을 누설하다 reveal〔divulge, disclose〕 a secret ; let the cat out of the bag // 비밀을 알리다 confide a secret to 《a person》 ; let 《a person》 into a secret // 비밀을 지키다 observe secrecy ; keep a secret // 거기에 별다른 비밀은 없다 There is nothing secret about it. // 비밀이 누설되다 The secret leaks〔gets〕 out. // 약혼을 비밀로 해 두었다 Her engagement was kept secret. // 이것은 비밀인데 This is just between you and me. // 그는 비밀이 많다 He is so secretive.
— 결혼 a clandestine marriage — 경찰 secret police ; a G-man 《미》 — 교섭 secret〔sub rosa〕 negotiations — 누설 divulgence〔divulgation〕 of classified information ; leakage of a secret — 단체 a secret organization ; a sub rosa group — 명령 a secret〔sealed〕 order —문 a secret door ; a trap door — 문서〔서류〕 a secret〔confidential〕 document ; [급송 공문서] a secret despatch 〔dispatch〕 — 선거 secret ballot〔vote〕 — 외교 secret diplomacy — 정보 secret〔classified《미》〕 information ; an inside story ; [경마·투기에서 정보인이 주는] a tip-off 《미》 — 조사 private 〔secret〕 investigation ; a confidential inquiry — 조약 a secret treaty — 출판 a secret publication — 투표 secret ballot — 회담 a closed-door talk
비밀 결사 秘密結社 a secret society ; an underground organization ; a junto 《*pl.* -s》 ; a junta ; a cabal ¶ 비밀 결사에 가입시키다 initiate 《a person》 into a secret society
비밀 탐정 秘密探偵 a secret (service) agent ; a confidential〔an undercover〕 agent〔man〕
—사(社) a detective agency
비밀 통로 秘密通路 a secret〔concealed〕 passage〔path〕 ¶ 비밀 통로로 가다 go by a secret path
비밀 회의 秘密會議 a closed〔secret〕 meeting ; a secret〔closed-door〕 session ; a secret conference〔sitting〕 ¶ 비밀 회의를 하다 discuss 《a matter》 in camera〔behind closed doors〕 ; hold 〔have〕 a closed-door session ; go into a huddle 《미·구》
비바람 rain and wind ; a rainstorm ¶ 비바람을 무릅쓰다 brave a rainstorm ; go in the teeth of a rainstorm
비바리, 비발[1] a diving fisher-girl
비발[2] ⇨ 비용(費用)
비방 秘方 a secret recipe ; a secret medical prescription ; [비법] a secret method 〔process〕
비방 誹謗 abuse ; slander ; libel ; aspersion —하다 abuse ; slander ; libel ; revile ; cast aspersion on 《a person》 ; speak ill of ¶ 비방하는 자 a slanderer ; a vilifier
비번 非番 off duty ¶ 오늘은 비번이다 This is an off day for me. // 오늘 너 비번인 줄 알았는데 I thought this was your day off. // 톰이 오늘 비번이야 Tom is off today.
—날 a day off ; an off day — 순경 a policeman off duty
‡**비범 非凡** —하다 (be) remarkable ; uncommon ; extraordinary ; unique ¶ 비범한 사람 a remarkable man ; a man of unusual ability ; a prodigy // 비범한 재주 an unusual gift〔talent〕
비법 非法 unlawfulness ; illegality ⇨ 불법
*__비법 秘法__ a secret method〔process〕 ; a secret

비법인 非法人 ¶ 비법인의 unincorporated
비보 悲報 a sad news
비보 秘寶 treasure(s) ; a treasured article
비복 婢僕 female and male servants ; (domestic) servants
비본 秘本 a treasured book
비분 悲憤 indignation ; resentment ¶ 비분의 눈물 tears of indignation // 비분 강개하다 be full of righteous〔moral〕 indignation〔wrath〕 ; deplore《evils》
— 강개 sorrowful indignation ; deploring
비불이라 非不— truly ; really ; indeed ; forsooth
비브라토 〖음악〗 vibrato
비브라폰 a vibraphone
— 주자(奏者) a vibraphonist
비비꼬다 twist〔knot, braid〕 together tight〔over and over again〕 ¶ 실을 비비 꼬다 twist thread into string
비비꼬이다 be〔get〕 twisted〔braided, knotted〕 together tight
****비비다** ① [문지르다] rub ; chafe ¶ 눈을 비벼 졸음을 없애다 rub sleep out of one's eyes // 두 손을 비비다 chafe〔rub〕 one's hands // 비벼 지우다 rub out ; erase ② [송곳을] twist《a gimlet》; drill ; pierce《with a gimlet》 ③ [둥글게] make round ; roll ; make a roll ④ [뒤섞다] mix ¶ 양념을 넣고 밥을 비비다 mix rice food with seasonings
비비대기치다 shove and push ; hustle and jostle
비비대다 rub repeatedly
비비송곳 a long-handled gimlet
비비적거리다 rub repeatedly〔over and over again〕 ¶ 두 손을 비비적거리다 rub one's hands // 송곳을 비비적거리어 구멍을 뚫다 drill〔bore〕 a hole《in something》 with a gimlet
비비적비비적 rubbing and rubbing
비비틀다 twist〔wrench〕 tight
비비틀리다 get〔be〕 twisted tight〔hard〕
비빈 妃嬪 the queen and the royal concubine
비빔국수 a noodle hash
비빔밥 a rice hash ; rice food mixed with seasonings
비사 秘史 a secret history ; an inside history
비사 秘事 a secret ; private affairs
비사교적 非社交的 (being) unsociable ; uncompanionable
비사리 the bark of a bush clover
비사치다 inform gently (in an indirect way)
비사회적 非社會的 (being) antisocial
비산 飛散 —하다 fly away ; scatter ; disperse ¶ 사방으로 비산하다 fly in all directions
—성(性) 〖화학〗 fugacity —회(灰) [시멘트·벽돌에 혼입하는] fly ash
비산 砒酸 〖화학〗 arsenic acid
—연(鉛) lead arsenate —염(鹽) an arsenate — 칼슘 calcium arsenate
****비상 非常** ① [이상함] emergency ; contingency —하다 (be) emergent ; urgent ¶ 경관을 비상 소집하다 call out the police reserves // 비상 사태에 대비하다 be ready〔prepared〕 for emergencies ; provide against emergencies
② [비범] extraordinariness ; uncommonness —하다 (be) remarkable ; extraordinary ; uncommon ; exceptional ¶ 그는 비상한 머리를 가지고 있다 He has an unusual talent. // 그의 관찰력은 비상하다 He has a sharp eye《for》.
— 경계 an emergency guard — 경찰 emergency police — 계단 an emergency staircase — 계획《the Pentagon's》 contingency plans (미 국방성의) — 관제 emergency control —구 an emergency〔a fire〕 exit ; an escape shaft ; [게시] Emergency Exit ; Fire Exit —금 emergency funds ; a nest egg — 나팔 an alarm (call) — 대출 an emergency loan —등 an emergency light (선박 따위의) — 브레이크 an emergency brake — 사건 an unusual event〔case〕 ; an emergency — 사용 장치 stand-by equipment — 소집 an emergency call〔summons〕 ; an extraordinary summons to the colors (군대의) — 수단 exceptional measures ; emergency measures — 시국 an emergency situation — 신호 an alarm call — 전화 an emergency call ; a hurry call《미》 — 조치 an extraordinary step — 준비금 an emergency fund — 직통 전화 a hot line (미·러간의) — 훈련 an emergency drill
비상 砒霜 arsenic poison
비상 飛翔 flight ; soaring —하다 fly ; take a flight
비상 경보 非常警報 an alarm (signal) ; an emergency report
—기(器) an alarm
비상근 非常勤 (a) part-time service ¶ 비상근의 part-time
—직(職) a part-time position — 직원 수당 allowances to part-timers〔part-time service employe(e)s〕
비상 사태 非常事態 a state of emergency ¶ 비상 사태를 선포하다 declare〔proclaim〕 a (state of) emergency // 비상 사태에 있다 be under a state of emergency // 비상 사태에 대비하다 provide against emergencies ; be ready〔prepared〕 for emergencies
국가 — 선언 declaration of a state of national-emergency ; a state-of-national-emergency declaration
비상선 非常線 a cordon《of police》; a patrol line ; a fire line (화재의) ¶ 비상선을 돌파하다 break through the cordon〔a patrol line〕 // 비상선을 치다 draw a police cordon ; establish a fire line (화재의)

비상시 非常時 an emergency ; a crisis ¶ 국가의 비상시 a national emergency // 비상시에는 in case of emergency ; in an emergency // 비상시에 대비하다 be prepared〔ready〕 for emergencies
비상식 非常識 lack of common sense ; senselessness ¶ 비상식적 senseless ; eccentric ; thoughtless
비상용 非常用 for emergency ; [게시] For emergency use only.
— **사닥다리** an emergency ladder
비상장주 非上場株 unlisted shares
비색증 鼻塞症 〖의학〗 occlusion of the naris 《*pl.* -es》
비생산 非生産 unproductivity ; nonproductiveness ¶ 비생산적 unproductive ; nonproductive // 비생산적인 사업 a nonproductive enterprise
‡**비서 秘書** [책] a treasured book ; a secret document (문서) ; [비서직] a (private) secretary ¶ 비서의 일 secretarial work 〔duties〕 // 비서의 직 secretaryship (지위·임기)
— **정치** government by secretaries — **학교** a secretarial school **수석** — a chief secretary **장관** — a secretary to the Minister 《of》
비서실 秘書室 [사무실] a secretary's office ; the office of a secretary ; [비서과] a secretariat ; a secretarial section
비석 砒石 〖광물〗 arsenic
*__비석 碑石__ a tombstone ; a gravestone ; a stone monument ¶ 비석을 세우다 erect a stone monument〔tombstone〕
비설거지 getting 《a house》 in order for a rain **—하다** get everything ready for the rain ; protect〔shelter〕 《a thing》 from rain
비성 鼻聲 〖음성〗 a nasal (sound)
비소 砒素 〖화학〗 arsenic 《As》 ¶ 비소 중독 arsenical poisoning
—경(鏡) an arsenical mirror **—제(劑)** an arsenic compound ; an arsenide — **중독** arsenical poisoning ; arsenism
비소 鼻笑 sneering 《at》 ⇨ 코웃음
비소수 非素數 〖수학〗 composite number
비속 卑俗 vulgarity ; vulgarism **—하다** (be) vulgar ; coarse ; low
비속 卑屬 〖법〗 a descendant
직계〔방계〕 — a lineal〔collateral〕 descendant
비손 〖민속〗 rubbing hands (prayerfully) **—하다** rub hands prayerfully
비송 사건 非訟事件 a nonlitigation〔noncontentious〕 case
— **절차법** 〖법〗 the Voluntary Matters Proceedings Act
비수 匕首 a dagger ; a dirk ; a knife ¶ 비수로 찌르다 stab 《a person》 with a dagger
비수 悲愁 grief ; sorrow
비수리 〖식물〗 a kind of bush clover
비술 秘術 a secret art ; stratagem ; the mysteries ¶ 비술을 전수하다 initiate 《a person》 into the mysteries 《of》
‡**비스듬하다** (be) slightly tilted ; be a bit askew ¶ 모자를 비스듬히 쓰다 wear a hat tilted to one side // 탑이 한 쪽으로 비스듬하다 A tower leans on one side.
비스러지다 get out of shape ; be ill-shaped〔unshapely〕
비스름하다 (be) somewhat similar ; slightly resemble ¶ 그들은 성격이 비스름하다 They are somewhat alike in character.
비스코스 〖화학〗 viscose
—사(絲) viscose yarn — **수지(樹脂)** viscose resin
비스킷 a cracker 《미》 ; a biscuit 《영》
비스타비전 〖영화〗 [상표] Vista Vision
비슥거리다 dawdle ; beat about〔around〕 the bush ; hang back
비슬거리다 [비쓱거리다] reel ; totter ; stagger : [배돌다] dawdle ; hang back ¶ 무거운 짐을 지고 비슬거리다 stagger with a heavy load // 한 대 얻어맞고 비슬거리다 reel under a heavy blow
비슬비슬 reeling ; tottering ¶ 비슬비슬 걸어가다 walk with faltering steps // 비슬비슬 일어서다 stagger〔totter〕 to one's feet
비슷비슷하다 be much the same ; be all alike ; be of a sort ¶ 그들의 나이가 비슷비슷하다 They are about the same age. // 그들의 신장이 비슷비슷하다 They are all much the same in height.
비슷이[1] [유사하게] alike ; similarly ; likely ; nearly ¶ 비슷이 닮다 bear some resemblance to 《a person》
비슷이[2] [비스듬이] leaning a bit to one side ¶ 비슷이 기울어진 벽 a wall with a slight lean
‡**비슷하다**[1] be alike ; (be) similar ; like ; resemble ¶ 비슷한 사건 a similar case ; a case similar to 《a thing》 // 물과 비슷한 빛깔이다 It is similar in color to the water. // 비슷한 것을 본 적이 있다 I have seen the like. // 성격이 비슷하다 They are much alike in character.
비슷하다[2] [기울음] have a slight tilt to one side ; be a bit askew〔slanted〕 ¶ 비슷이 기울어진 벽 a wall with a slight lean
비시지 BCG (vaccine) 《Bacillus Calmette-Guérin》
— **접종(接種)** inoculation by BCG
비신 rain shoes
비신고 가산금 非申告加算金 an additional charge〔a fine〕 for the nonfiling of a (tax) return
비신사적 非紳士的 (being) ungentlemanly ¶ 비신사적 행위 conduct unbecoming to a gentleman
비실비실 ⇨ 비슬비슬 ¶ 비실비실 다가서다〔물러서다〕 sidle up to〔away from〕 《a person》
비실제적 非實際的 (being) unpractical ; unrealistic

†**비싸다** (be) expensive ; high ; costly ; dear ¶ 터무니 없이 비싼 가격 a ridiculously high price ; an exorbitant price // 기껏 비싸야 at most // 비싸게 먹히다 cost much ; come expensive // 비싸게 받다 charge too much ; overcharge // 비싸게 팔다〔사다〕 sell〔buy〕 at a high price // 값이 너무 비싸다 The price is too high. /It is too expensive.

비쌔다 [안 그런 체하다] decline reluctantly〔begrudgingly〕; pretend to decline 《an offer》; [어울리기를 싫어하다] avoid company ; keep〔hold〕 aloof

비쑥 〖식물〗 oriental wormwood

비쓱거리다 stagger ; reel ; totter ; walk with faltering steps ¶ 비쓱비쓱 staggeringly ; totteringly

비아냥거리다 make cynical remarks ; be sarcastic 《about》

비아냥스럽다 (be) sarcastic

비악, 삐악 ¶ 삐악삐악 울다 peep ; cheep ; pule

비애 悲哀 sorrow ; sadness ; grief ; pathos ¶ 비애에 가득찬 인생 a life full of sorrows // 인생의 비애 the sorrows of life ; the pathos of life // 비애를 느끼다 feel sad

—감 (a) sense〔feeling〕 of sorrow

비애국적 非愛國的 (being) unpatriotic

비약 飛躍 a leap ; a jump ; (a) flight ; [발전] rapid progress ; [활동] activity

—하다 leap ; jump ; [발전하다] make rapid progress ; [활동하다] be active ; play an active part ¶ 논리의 비약 a leap in argument ; a jump of logic // 비약적 발전을 이룩하다 make rapid progress ; take long strides

— 경기 a ski-jumping contest

비약 秘藥 a secret medicine〔remedy〕; a nostrum

비양 飛揚 [뽐냄] swaggering ; [뛰어오름] flying about **—하다** swagger ; throw one's weight around ; fly (in the air)

비어 飛魚 ⇨ 날치[2]

비어 飛語, 蜚語 a groundless〔wild〕 rumor ; a false report ; a canard 《프》 ¶ 비어를 퍼뜨리다 spread false rumors

유언— a (wild) rumor

비어 鄙語, 卑語 a slang (word) ; a vulgarism

비어지다 [밖으로 내밀다] jut out ; protrude ; project ; [드러나다] come to light ; be exposed〔disclosed, revealed〕 ¶ 셔츠 자락이 비어져 나와 있으니 바지 속에 집어 넣어라 Your shirt is hanging out. Tuck it in.

비어 홀 a beer hall 《미》; a beerhouse ; an alehouse 《영》

비엔날레 a biennale 《이》; a biennial exhibition

비역 sodomy ; unnatural sexual intercourse ; pederasty

비열 比熱 〖물리〗 specific heat

†**비열 卑劣** meanness ; baseness **—하다** (be) mean ; base ; cowardly ¶ 비열한 수단 a mean〔dirty〕 trick // 비열한 정신 a low spirit

—한(漢) a mean bastard ; a sneak ; a hound ; a cad

비염 鼻炎 〖의학〗 nasitis ; rhinitis

비영리 非營利 nonprofit-making

— 사업〔단체, 법인〕 a nonprofit(ing) 〔noncommercial〕 undertaking〔organization, corporation〕

비영비영하다 be weak and haggard from illness ; be wasted away

비예술적 非藝術的 (being) inartistic

비오리 〖새〗 a merganser ; a goosander

비옥 翡玉 green jade with red spots

‡**비옥 肥沃** **—하다** (be) fertile ; rich ; productive ¶ 비옥한 토지 fertile〔rich〕 soil

비올라 〖악기〗 a viola

‡**비옷** a raincoat ¶ 비옷을 입다 put on 〔wear〕 a raincoat

†**비용 費用** expense ; cost ; expenditure ¶ 여행 비용 traveling expenses // 지난달에 든 비용 expenses incurred during last month // 비용만 헛되게 쓰다 do not pay ; end in waste of money // 비용을 절약하다 cut down expenses // 비용이 들다 cost // 비용은 얼마든지 대어 주마 I will go to any expense. // 비용이 많이 든다 It costs a great deal. /The expense is very heavy. // 비용이 얼마나 듭니까 What will it cost ?

가변〔변동〕 — 〖경제〗 variable cost **간접 —** non-operation expenses **공공 —** public expense **제(諸)—** (sundry〔miscellaneous〕) expenses **제반 — 선불** charges forward **직접 —** direct expenses **한계〔평균, 주요, 추가〕 —** marginal〔average, prime, additional〕 cost

***비우다** empty ; vacate ; make empty ¶ 다락을 비우다 empty the closet of all its things // 잔을 비우다 empty a glass // 집을 비우다 (외출하여) leave a house empty ; stay away from home ; vacate a house (명도하다) // 월말까지 아파트를 비우겠습니다 I'm going to move out of the apartment by the end of the month.

비우호적 非友好的 (being) unfriendly

비운 非運 ill luck ; misfortune

비웃 〖물고기〗 a herring

— 백숙 boiled herring **—젓** salted herring

†**비웃다** laugh scornfully ; ridicule ; deride ; laugh〔sneer, jeer〕 《at》; mock 《at》

> 참고 **ridicule** 사람이나 물건을 업신여기다 악의에 의한 경우와 그렇지 않은 경우가 있다 **deride** 경멸하여 비웃다 **mock** 상대방의 특징을 풍자하고 경멸하면서 비웃다

¶ 남을 비웃다 sneer at others // 남의 성공을 비웃다 deride the success of others // (남을) 비겁하다고 비웃다 taunt 《a person》 with cowardice

‡비웃음 a sneer ; a jeer ; a gibe〔jibe〕; a derision ; a mock ; ridicule ; scorn ; a mocking laughter ; a scornful〔sardonic, cynical〕 smile〔laugh〕 ¶ 비웃음을 받다〔사다〕 be mocked〔derided, scorned〕; be jeered 《at》; excite ridicule ; be subjected to ridicule

비웃적거리다 tease ; bully ; make cynical remarks

비원 秘苑 the Secret Garden

비원 悲願 a merciful Buddhist prayer to save mankind ; one's earnest prayer〔wish〕 ¶ 비원을 이루다 attain〔achieve〕 one's earnest wish ; have one's earnest wish fulfilled〔answered〕

비위 脾胃 ① [비장과 위] spleen and stomach
② [기호·미각] taste ; palate ; liking ; choice ¶ 비위에 맞는 음식 a favorite food // 비위가 좋다 have a strong stomach // 비위가 까다롭다 have a pampered taste〔delicate palate〕 // 비위에 맞다 be to one's taste ; suit to one's taste〔palate〕 // 그 음식은 내 비위에 맞지 않는다 The food goes against my stomach. /My stomach revolts at the food.
③ [기분] humor ; temper ; a mood ¶ 상사의 비위를 맞추다 ingratiate oneself〔curry favor〕 with one's superior // 그런 짓은 내 비위에 안 맞다 It goes against the grain with me to do such things.
④ [뻔뻔스러움] impudence ; audacity ; cheekiness
비위가 좋다 관용 have a nerve to 《do》; be impudent〔cheeky〕; be brazen-faced
비위를 거스르다 관용 offend 《a person》; hurt 《a person's》 feelings ; get on 《a person's》 nerves ; rub 《a person》 the wrong way
비위를 맞추다 관용 please 《a person》; curry favor with 《a person》; get into 《a person》 good graces
비위가 상하다 관용 be offended ; feel hurt ; be disgusted〔displeased〕
비위가 틀리다 관용 get out of humor ; get cross ; be displeased

비위생 非衛生 poor sanitation ¶ 비위생적 unsanitary ; unhealthy ; unhygienic

†비유 比喩, 譬喩 a metaphor (은유) ; a simile (직유) ; a fable〔parable〕 (우화) ; a proverb (이언) ; an example 〔illustration〕 (예) ―하다 liken 《to》; compare 《to》; illustrate ; speak figuratively ¶ 비유적 figurative ; metaphorical // 그 광경이란 비유할 데가 없다 The scene baffles〔beggars〕 description. // 그는 미덕을 황금에 비유했다 He likened virtue to gold.

비육 肥育 fatting〔fattening〕 (up) ―하다 fat〔fatten〕 up 《cattle》; raise 《cattle》
―우(牛) cattle for fattening up ; beef cattle

비육지탄 髀肉之嘆 ¶ 비육지탄이 있다 be eager for the fray ; be all eagerness to do something ; get sick of staying behind the scenes

†비율 比率 ratio ; percentage ; rate ¶ 높은 비율로 at a high rate // 5대 2의 비율 the ratio of five to two // 비율을 내리다〔올리다〕 lower〔raise〕 the rate
구성 ― 〖통계〗 distribution ratio 남녀 ― the proportion of males to females

비음 鼻音 a nasal sound〔voice〕

비음악적 非音樂的 unmusical

비익 比翼 ① [두 새가 날개를 가지런히 함] flying side by side ; wings abreast ② [비익조] a legendary pair of male and female birds each with one eye and one wing and always flying together ③ [부부] a couple ; husband and wife

비익조 比翼鳥 ① a legendary pair of male and female birds each with one eye and one wing and always flying together ② [부부] a couple ; husband and wife

비익하다 裨益― benefit ; profit ; do 《a person》 good ; be beneficial 《to》; be instructive

비인 非人 an inhuman wretch ; a beast ; a brute

비인도 非人道 inhumanity ¶ 비인도적 inhumane

비인정 非人情 inhumanity ; heartlessness ; hardness

비인칭 非人稱 ¶ 비인칭의 〖문법〗 impersonal

비일비재 非一非再 frequent occurrence ; taking place time and again〔many times〕 ¶ 그런 일은 비일비재하다 It is just one of those common things. /It is of frequent occurrence.

비자 榧子 〖식물〗 a torreya nut
―나무 Torreya nucifera (학명)

비자 a visa ; visé ¶ 여권의 비자를 받다 have one's passport visaed〔visa'd, viséed, viséd〕
이민 ― an immigrant visa 입국〔출국〕 ― an entry〔exit〕 visa

비잔틴 ¶ 비잔틴식의 Byzantinesque
― 제국〔건축, 파〕 Byzantine Empire〔architecture, school〕

†비장 秘藏 treasuring ; storing in secrecy
―하다 treasure ; prize ; cherish ; store in secrecy
―품 a treasure ; a treasured article

비장 悲壯 ―하다 (be) tragic ; pathetic ; grim ; heroic ; plaintive (슬프다) ¶ 비장한 결의 a grim〔heroic〕 resolution // 비장한 죽음을 하다 die a tragic death
―미(美) tragic beauty

비장 脾臟 〖해부〗 the spleen
―병 a disease of the spleen ; splenopathy ―병 환자 a splenetic (patient) ―절제(술) splenectomy ; lienectomy ―학 splenopathy

비재 菲才 poor talent ; lack of ability ; incompetence
비적 匪賊 a bandit ; a rebel ; an outlaw
— 행위 banditry
비적비적 protruding〔coming out, jutting out〕 here and there
비적응 非適應 〖심리〗 maladjustment 《to one's social environment》 ¶ 비적응의 maladjusted
—아(兒) a maladjusted child
비적임 非適任 unfitness ; inadequacy ; incompetency ; incapacity ; inaptitude ¶ 비적임의 unfit 《for》 ; inadequate ; unqualified ; incompetent ; inapt
—자 an unqualified〔incompetent〕 person ; an incompetent
비전 vision ; foresight ¶ 비전이 있는 사람 foresighted person // 위대한 비전을 지닌 정치가 a statesman of great vision
비전 秘傳 a secret ; a mystery ; [비약] arcanum 《*pl.* -na》 ¶ 비전을 전수하다 initiate 《a person》 into the mysteries 〔secrets〕 of 《an art》
—서(書) a book of secrets
비전 非戰 renunciation of war
비전략 물자 非戰略物資 nonstrategic goods
— 무역 nonstrategic trade
비전론 非戰論 (an) antiwar argument ; pacifism (미) ; pacificism ; a pacific view 〔appeal, plea〕 ¶ 비전론을 제창하다 cry against war ; advocate peace
—자 a pacifist (미) ; a pacificist
비전투원 非戰鬪員 a noncombatant ; a civilian
비전하 妃殿下 [3인칭] Her Imperial 〔Royal〕 Highness 《H. I. H., H. R. H.》 ; [2인칭] Your Imperial Highness
비접 change of air〔scene〕
비접 나가다 관용 try change of air ; go 《to a place》 for a change of air
비정 非情 ¶ 비정의 cold-〔hard-, stone-〕 hearted ; heartless ; cruel ; hard ; fals ; faithless // 비정의 아버지 a cold-hearted father
비정 秕政 misgovernment ; misrule ; maladministration
비정규군 非正規軍 irregular troops
비정기선 非定期船 a tramp (steamer)
비정형시 非定型詩 free verse
비조 飛鳥 a flying bird ; a bird on the wing
비조 鼻祖 the founder ; the father
비조 悲調 a plaintive tone ; a mournful 〔pathetic〕 tone ¶ 비조를 띤 plaintive ; sad ; pathetic
비조합원 非組合員 a nonunionist ; a nonmember
비좁다 (be) narrow ; small ; [사람이 주어] be cramped〔confined〕 for room ¶ 비좁은 마을 a small hole of a town
비종교적 非宗敎的 (being) nonreligious
비주룩하다 stick〔thrust, jut〕 out a bit
비주류 非主流 [정당·파벌의] non(-) mainstreamers ; the non(-)mainstream faction〔group〕
비죽 poutingly
비죽거리다, 비쭉거리다 pout ; stick out one's lip ¶ 성이 나서 비죽거리다 pout in anger // 울려고 비죽거리다 pout〔sulk〕 almost in tears
비죽하다 ⇨ 비주룩하다
비준 比準 proportion (비율) ; a standard (표준) ; comparison (비교) ; contrast (대조) **—하다** compare ; contrast
*__비준 批准__ ratification **—하다** ratify ¶ 비준의 교환 the exchange of ratifications // 조약을 비준하다 ratify a treaty
—자 a ratifier
비준서 批准書 an instrument of ratification ; a ratification instrument ¶ 비준서의 기탁〔교환〕 the deposit〔exchange〕 of ratifications // 비준서를 교환하다 exchange ratifications 《of a treaty》
비중 比重 specific gravity ; [중요성의] relative importance ¶ 비중을 달다 find out the specific gravity 《of》
—계 a hydrometer ; a gravimeter ; an areometer (액체의) —표 a table of specific gravities
비지 residue in the preparation of bean curd
— 껍질 the outermost layer of skin ; the epidermis ; the cuticle —떡 dreg cake ; a cake made of bean-curd dregs and rice〔barley〕 flour — 찌개 a casserole of bean-curd dregs, salted shrimp, beef or pork, etc.
값싼 것이 비지떡 속담 You get what you pay for. /Buy cheap and waste your money.
비지에 부른 배가 연약과도 싫다 한다 속담 A full stomach is not interested in delicacies. /Provide enough bread and no one will ask for cake.
비지 鄙地 this place ; here ; my humble place of residence
비지땀 heavy sweat ¶ 비지땀을 흘리다 drip〔run〕 with sweat
비질 sweeping with a broom **—하다** sweep with a broom
비집다 [눈을] rub one's eyes open ; [틈을] push〔force〕 open ; spread apart
비쭈기나무 〖식물〗 Sakakia ochnacea (학명)
비쭉 poutingly ¶ 입술을 비쭉 내밀다 pout (one's lip) ; stick out one's lip // 창문 밖으로 머리를 비쭉 내밀다 pop one's head out of the window
⁑**비참 悲慘** misery ; distress ; wretchedness **—하다** (be) miserable ; wretched ; sad ; tragic ; pitiable ¶ 비참한 광경 a pitiable scene ; a pathetic sight // 비참한 사연 a tragic〔pathetic〕 story // 비참한 생활 a wretched〔miserable〕 life // 비참한 죽음을 하다 die a miserable death

비창 悲愴 sadness ; pathos ; sorrowfulness —하다 (be) sad ; sorrowful ; pathetic ; touching
— 교향곡 the "Pathetic" Symphony ; Tchaikovsky's sixth symphony
비책 秘策 a secret plan〔scheme〕; a subtle stratagem ; a secret 《of》
비척거리다 stagger ; totter ; reel
비척걸음 a staggering〔an unsteady〕 walk
비척비척 totteringly ; staggeringly ; unsteadily ¶ 비척비척 걷다 walk with faltering steps ; totter
비척지근하다 (be) slightly fishy ; smell 〔taste〕 somewhat fishy
‡비천 卑賤 humbleness ; lowliness ; lowly 〔humble〕 circumstances ; obscurity —하다 (be) lowly ; humble ; obscure ¶ 비천한 태생 a man of low birth
비철 非— off season ; out of season
비철 금속 非鐵金屬 nonferrous metals
비첩 婢妾 a concubine slave
비추 悲秋 [구슬픈 가을] a sad〔lonely〕 fall season ; [슬퍼함] grieving over the autumn
*비추다 ① [빛을] shed〔throw〕 light 《on》; light (up) ; flash 《on》; illuminate ¶ 얼굴을 비추다 throw a light on 《a person's》 face // 탐조등으로 해상을 비추다 sweep the sea with a searchlight // 회중 전등으로 어두운 구석을 비추다 shine a flashlight into the dark corner
② [그림자를] reflect ; mirror ; cast 《a shadow》 ¶ 거울에 몸을 비추어 보다 look at oneself in the glass // 얼굴을 물에 비추다 mirror one's face in the water // 자연을 거울에 비추다 hold the mirror up to nature // 산이 선명하게 그림자를 물위에 비추고 있다 The mountain casts its sharply defined reflection on the waters.
③ [비교·참조] compare 《with》; refer 《to》; check up on 《a matter》 ¶ 법에 비추어 according to the law // 사실에 비추어 in view〔the light〕 of facts // 현 물가 지수에 비추어 봉급이 인상되어야 한다 In view of the current price index, he should get an increase in pay.
④ [속이 드러나게] hold 《a thing》 up to〔against〕 the light ¶ 계란을 불빛에 비추어 보다 hold an egg against the light // 편지를 불빛에 비추어 보다 hold a letter closely to the light
비추이다, 비취다 have light shed 《on a thing》; get reflected
비축 備蓄 saving for emergency —하다 save for emergency
—미(米) reserved rice ; rice stored in the public granary
비취 翡翠 〖새〗 a kingfisher ; [보석] green jadeite ; jade
— 반지 a jade ring —색 jade green —옥 green jadeite ; jade —잠(簪) an ornamental jade hairpin
비치 備置 installment ; fitting ; equipment ; provision —하다 provide〔furnish, equip〕 with 《a thing》; install ; keep 《newspapers》 on file ¶ 비치된 잡지 periodicals kept on file // 무전 장치가 비치되어 있다 be equipped〔fitted〕 with a wireless apparatus // 난로가 비치되어 있다 It is provided with a stove.
비치근하다 ⇨ 비릿하다
‡비치다 ① [빛이] shine ¶ 햇빛이 찬란하게 비치다 The sun shines brightly. / The sun pours〔blazes〕 down powerfully.
② [그림자가] be reflected〔mirrored〕; fall upon ¶ 창문에 비친 사람의 그림자 the shadows of men falling on the window // 호수에 비친 옛성 an old castle mirrored in the lake
③ [드러나다] show 《through》; be seen 《through》 ¶ 인쇄가 뒷면에 비친다 The printing shows through on the other side.
④ [암시] hint 《at》; drive 《at》; feel 〔sound〕 《a person》 out on 《a thing》 ¶ 사의를 비치다 hint at resignation // 그 일에 관해서 말을 비쳐 봤다 I sounded him on the subject. /I felt him out on the matter.
비치파라솔 a beach umbrella
비칠거리다 totter ; dodder ; stagger ; reel
비칠비칠 unsteadily ; totteringly ; shakily —하다 totter ; dodder ; stagger ; reel ; be unsteady 《on one's feet》
비칭 卑稱 a humble name〔title〕
비커 〖화학〗 a beaker
비컨 a beacon
라디오 — a radio beacon
비켜나다 step back ; get out of the way ; keep clear 《of》
비켜서다 stand〔move〕 aside ; step〔stand〕 back ¶ 한두발 비켜서다 fall 〔draw〕 back a step or two
비키니 [수영복] a bikini ¶ 비키니 스타일의 bikinied
*비키다 get out of the way ; step aside 《from》; clear ; avoid ; dodge ¶ 길을 비키다 clear the road ; get out of the way // 소를 비켜서 가다 go around a cow // 자동차를 비키다 dodge a car ; get out of the way of a car // 비켜 비켜 Away ! /Get out of the way. // 잠깐만 자리를 비켜 주시겠습니다 Will you excuse us for a minute ?
‡비타민 vitamin(e) ¶ 비타민 A vitamin A // 비타민이 많다 contain〔be rich in〕 vitamin
— (B) 결핍증 avitaminosis (B) ; a vitamin (B) deficiency disease — 과다증 hypervitaminosis —정(錠) a vitamin tablet —제 a vitamin compound —학 vitaminology — 함유량 vitamin content 종합 — multivitamin 종합 —제 a multivitamin compound
비타협적 非妥協的 unyielding ; uncompromising ; intransigent ; hard-shell(ed)

《미·구》
— 태도 intransigence ; intransigency
비탄 飛彈 flying bullets
‡비탄 悲嘆 grief ; sorrow ; lamentation — 하다 grieve ; mourn ; sorrow 《over》 ; lament ; deplore ¶ 비탄에 잠기다 eat one's heart out // 아버지를 여의고 비탄에 잠겨 있다 She is greatly grieved〔heart-broken〕 over the death of her father.
†비탈 a slope ; an incline ¶ 비탈지다 be sloped〔graded〕
—길 a slope ; an uphill〔ascending〕 road
비통 悲痛 grief ; pathos ; bitterness ; deep sadness — 하다 (be) sad ; grievous ; pathetic ; touching ¶ 비통한 생각에 잠기다 be filled with deep sadness
비통제 非統制 ¶ 비통제의 noncontrolled 《goods》
비트적거리다 stagger ; totter ; reel
비트적비트적 totteringly ; staggeringly ; reelingly ; waddlingly ⇨ 비틀비틀
비트 제너레이션 —族 [총칭] the beat generation ; the beatniks ; [개인] a beat-nik
‡비틀거리다 stagger ; totter ; reel ¶ 비틀거리며 길을 걷다 reel〔walk staggering〕 along the street // 비틀거리며 일어서다 stagger to one's feet
비틀걸음 faltering steps ; reeling〔un-steady〕 steps ¶ 비틀걸음으로 걷다 reel along ; walk zigzag
‡비틀다 twist ; wrench ; screw ; contort ¶ 비틀어 끊다 wrench off 《a thing》 // 오른쪽으로 비틀다 turn to the right // 팔을 비틀다 twist 《a person's》 arm // 손을 비틀어 권총을 빼앗다 wrench〔wrest, twist〕 a pistol out of 《a person's》 hand
비틀리다 get〔be〕 twisted〔wrenched〕
비틀비틀 with faltering steps ; tottering-ly ; staggeringly ¶ 비틀비틀 일어서다 stagger to one's feet // 술에 취해 비틀비틀하다 reel under the influence of liquor
비틀어지다 get twisted ; get bent ; be dis-torted ¶ 열쇠가 비틀어지다 the key gets bent // 병마개가 비틀어지지 않는다 The bottle cap won't turn.
비틀하다 ⇨ 비릿하다
비틈하다 (be) oblique ; indirect ; allusive
비틈히 《say》 in a roundabout way ; vaguely ; by hinting ; indirectly
비파 琵琶 a lute ; a Korean mandolin
비파 枇杷 〖식물〗 a loquat ; a Japanese medlar
*비판 批判 criticism ; comment ; critique — 하다 criticize ; comment 《on》 ; judge ¶ 비판적 critical // 칸트의 순수 이성 비판 Kant's *Critique of Pure Reason* // 비판할 여지가 없다 be above criticism // 비판할 입장이 못 된다 I am not in a posi-tion to criticize.
—력 critical power〔ability〕 —론 criticism —자 a critic — 철학 critical philosophy 자기 — (a) self-criticism
†비평 批評 criticism ; comment ; critique (문예 작품의) ; review (신간 서적의) — 하다 criticize ; comment 《on》 ; review 《a book》 ¶ 그것에 관해서는 비평을 가하지 않았다 He made no comment on it. // 비평할 가치가 없다 It is beneath criti-cism.
—사 the history of criticism 문명 — crit-icism on civilization 문예 — a literary criticism 본문〔비교, 해석〕 — textual 〔comparative, interpretative〕 criticism
비평가 批評家 a critic ; a reviewer
미술〔문예〕 — an art〔a literary〕 critic
비평안 批評眼 a critical eye ¶ 비평안이 있다 have a critical〔discerning〕 eye // 비평안을 기르다 cultivate a critical sense
비폭력(주의) 非暴力(主義) (the doctrine of) ahimsa ; nonviolence ¶ 비폭력(주의)의 nonviolent
‡비품 備品 fixtures ; furnishings (집·방안의) ; equipment 《집합적》
— 목록 a list of 《office》 fixtures ; an inventory 부엌 — kitchen fixtures 사무용 — office equipment〔appointments〕
비프스테이크 (a) beefsteak
비하 卑下 [자신을 낮춤] abasement ; self-humbling ; [땅이 낮음] low level of ground ; [지위가 낮음] low standing 〔position〕 ; humbleness
†비하다 比— compare 《with, to》 ¶ 나는 키에 비해 체중이 모자란다 I'm underweight for my height. // 그는 나이에 비해 조금 늙어 보인다 He looks a bit old for his age. ⇨ 비교
비학술적 非學術的 (being) unacademic ; unscholarly ; unscientific
비합리 非合理 〖철학〗 irrational(ity) ; illogical(ity)
—주의 irrationalism
비합법 非合法 illegality ¶ 비합법적(인) illegal ; unlawful ; illicit // 비합법화하다 illegalize ; outlaw
비핵화 非核化 denuclearization
비행 非行 an irregularity ; a misdeed ; a misconduct ; a misdemeanor ; wrongdo-ing ¶ 남의 비행을 들추다〔폭로하다〕 bring〔put〕 a person's crime to light ; expose〔reveal〕 a person's mis-deeds〔misconduct〕
— 소년 a juvenile delinquent
†비행 飛行 flying ; a flight ; aviation (비행술) — 하다 fly ; make a flight
— 갑판 a flight〔flying〕 deck — 거리 fly ; a flight — 기록계 a flight recorder — 기지 an air base —대(隊) a flying corps — 대형(a) flight formation —모 an aviation cap〔flying helmet〕 —복 a flying dress〔suit, jacket〕 ; flying gear ; flight uniform〔suit〕 ; an aviation garment — 속도 (an) air speed ; (a) flying speed — 수당 a flight allowance — 시간 flying time ; flight hours —접시〔물체〕 a flying saucer〔object〕 — 학교 a flying〔flight, an

aviation] school 고〔저〕공 — a high〔low〕 flight 단독 — a solo flight 무사고 — accident-free flying ; flying without an accident 무착륙 — a nonstop flight 미확인 — 물체 an unidentified flying object ; a UFO 민간 — civil flying 세계 일주 — an around-the-world flight 시험 — a test flight ¶ 시험 비행을 하다 test 《an airplane》 in flight ; flighttest 《a plane》 야간 — a night flight 연습 — a training〔an exercise〕 flight 정기 — a regular air service 정찰 — a scouting flight 태평양 횡단 — a transpacific flight 편대 — a formation flight

†**비행기 飛行機** an aeroplane 《영》 ; an airplane 《미》 ; a plane ; aircraft 《총칭》 ¶ 비행기로 가다 fly〔go by air〕 《to Paris》 // 비행기 멀미가 나다 become airsick // 비행기에 타다 get aboard〔board〕 a plane
— 격납고(格納庫) an aviation shed ; an airdrome ; a hanger — 공장 an airplane 〔aircraft〕 factory — 사고 a plane〔an air〕 accident〔crash〕 ¶ 비행기 사고로 죽다 meet one's death in a plane accident — 수리공 an air mechanic — 시간표 an airline schedule — 여행 an air trip —표 an air ticket 《to London》 군용 — a military〔fighting〕 plane ; a warplane ; combat aircraft 《총칭》 단엽〔복엽〕 — a monoplane〔biplane〕 무인 — a pilotless plane 민간 — a commercial plane 수륙양용 — an amphibian (plane) 수상 — a seaplane〔hydro- plane〕 수송 — a transport plane 여객 — a passenger〔cabin〕 plane 연습 — a training plane 정기 — an airliner ; a clipper 《미》 정찰용 — a scout plane ; a reconnaissance machine 화물 — a goods〔cargo〕 plane ; a freighter

비행사 飛行士 an aviator ; a flier ; an airman ; a pilot ; an aeronaut ; a birdman 《속》
여류 — an aviatress ; an aviatrix ; a woman aviator ; a birdwoman 《속》

‡**비행선 飛行船** an airship ; a dirigible ; a blimp
— 격납고 an airship shed ; a (blimp) hanger — 계류탑 a mooring mast 경식〔연식, 반경식〕 — a rigid〔nonrigid, semirigid〕 dirigible

비행술 飛行術 aeronautics ; the art of flying ; aviation ; aerostatics ; air navigation ¶ 비행술의 aeronautic ; aeronautical

비행 시험 飛行試驗 a test flight ; an air trial ¶ 비행 시험을 하다 test 《a plane》 in flight ; flight-test 《a plane》

비행운 飛行雲 a vapo(u)r trail ; a condensation (vapor) trail ; a contrail ¶ 비행운이 길게 뻗쳐 있다 Vapor was trailing in the sky.

***비행장 飛行場** an airfield〔airport, airstrip〕 ; an aerodrome ; an airdrome 《미》

비행정 飛行艇 a floatplane ; a seaplane ⇨ 비행선

비행 중대 飛行中隊 a squadron
—장 a squadron leader

비현실성 非現實性 unreality

비현실적 非現實的 (being) unreal ; impractical ; fantastic ; impracticable (실행불가능한) ¶ 비현실적인 계획 an unfeasible plan

비협력 非協力 noncooperation ¶ 비협력적인 uncooperative

비호 飛虎 an agile tiger ¶ 비호같이 달리다 run as fast as lightning〔a tiger〕 ; run at a breakneck speed

†**비호 庇護** protection ; patronage —하다 protect ; shield ; take 《a person》 under one's wing ; harbor (범인을) ¶ 비호 하에 under the patronage 《of》 ; under the protection 《of》
—자 a guardian ; a protector ; a patron

비화 飛火 [불똥] flying sparks ; a leap of the fire ; [사건의] effect felt in unexpected quarters —하다 《flames, sparks》

비행기

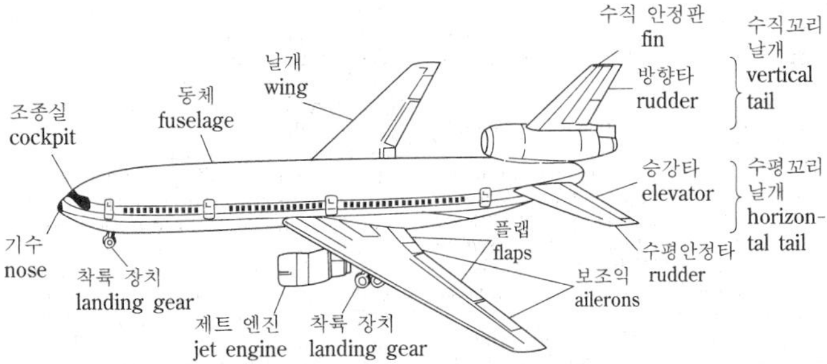

leap to《another house》; be drawn into《an affair》; be involved in (관련되다) ¶ 비화로 출화하다 Flying sparks start another fire. // 진전함에 따라 사건이 의외의 방면으로 비화했다 As the affair developed, its effect was felt in unexpected quarters.

비화 秘話 a secret story ; a secret history ; a behind-the-scenes story《of》

비화 悲話 a sad〔pathetic〕 story〔tale〕

비화 수소 砒化水素 〖화학〗 arseniuretted hydrogen

비효용 非效用 〖경제〗 disutility

비훼죄 誹毁罪 defamation ; slander ; libel

비희 悲喜 sorrow and joy ¶ 비희의 감이 교착하다 have a mingled feeling of joy and sorrow

빅수 ⇨ 비김수

빅토리아 호 —湖 Lake Victoria

빈가 貧家 a poor family ¶ 빈가에 태어나다 be born poor

빈개념 賓槪念 〖논리〗 the predicate ; an objective concept

빈객 賓客 a guest (of honor) ; an honored guest

빈고 貧苦 hardship of poverty〔destitution〕; pressure of poverty

‡빈곤 貧困 poverty ; indigence ; penury ; destitution ; need〔want〕 (궁핍)
— 하다 (be) poor ; needy ; destitute ; indigent ¶ 빈곤한 사람들 the poor ; poor folks // 빈곤에 빠지다 be reduced to poverty // 빈곤한 가정에 태어나다 be born poor // 빈곤하게 살다 live poorly〔in poverty〕; be badly off ; be in dire want

빈광 貧鑛 poor〔lean, low-grade〕 ore

빈국 貧國 a poor〔destitute, needy, have-not〕 country

빈궁 貧窮 destitution ; extreme poverty
— 하다 (be) destitute ; poverty-stricken

빈궁 嬪宮 the wife of the heir apparent

빈농 貧農 a poor farmer ; a needy peasant

빈대 a housebug ; a bedbug《미》
빈대 잡으려 초가삼간 태운다 〔속담〕 To burn one's house to get rid of the mice〔bedbugs〕. / Don't cut off your nose to spite your face.

빈대떡 a green-bean〔lentil〕 pancake

빈대코 a flat nose

빈도 頻度 frequency ¶ 빈도수가 높은 말 a word of high frequency // 용어의 빈도 frequency of the use of a word
—순 the order of frequency ¶ 사용빈도순으로 in the order of frequency of use

빈둥거리다, 뻔둥거리다 loaf around ; loiter about ; idle away one's time ; lead an idle life ¶ 집안에서 빈둥거리다 loaf at home // 일을 제대로 하지 않고 빈둥거리면 조만간에 해고당할 것이다 If you lie down on your job, you will be fired sooner or later.

†빈둥빈둥, 뻔둥뻔둥 idly ; lazily ; dawdlingly ; slothfully ; doing nothing ; on the bum《구》 ¶ 빈둥빈둥 세월을 보내다 loaf away one's days〔time〕; idle〔dawdle〕 one's time away ; lead an idle life

빈들거리다, 뻔들거리다 be idle ; loaf ; loiter ; lounge ; idle〔loaf, laze〕 one's time away ⇨ 빈둥거리다 ¶ 일정한 직업이 없이 빈들거리다 be at loose ends

빈들빈들, 뻔들뻔들 idly ; lazily ⇨ 빈둥빈둥 ¶ 빈들빈들 놀기만 하다 do nothing but idle about ; idle〔dawdle〕 one's time away

빈마 牝馬 a mare

빈말 idle〔empty〕 talk ; an empty promise ; empty words — 하다 have an idle chat ; gossip ; talk idly ¶ 빈말이 지나치다 carry the joke too far

빈미주룩하다 (be) slightly showing〔protruding, jutting out〕

빈민 貧民 the poor ; the needy ¶ 빈민을 구제하다 relieve the poor
— 구제 the relief of the poor (and needy) ; poor relief — 구호법 the poor law — 학교 a pauper school ; a charity〔ragged〕 school

*빈민굴 貧民窟 a slum ; a ghetto ; the slum〔poor〕 quarters ; the slums ¶ 빈민굴을 없애다 clear〔wipe out〕 slums
— 일소 clearance of slums ; slum clearance

빈발 頻發 frequent occurrence — 하다 occur frequently ; be frequent ¶ 교통 사고가 빈발한다 Traffic accidents occur very often. /A motor accident is a common occurrence.

빈방 —房 [가구가 없는] an empty room ; [사람이 쓰지 않는] a vacant room ¶ 빈방 있습니까 Do you have any vacancies?

*빈번 頻繁 frequency — 하다 (be) frequent ; incessant ¶ 빈번히 frequently ; repeatedly ; in rapid succession // 빈번히 일어나는 일 a matter of frequent occurrence // 왕래가 빈번한 거리 a busy〔bustling〕 street // 화재가 빈번히 일어난다 Fires are frequent.

빈병 —甁 an empty bottle ¶ 빈병 사는 사람 an empty-bottle gatherer

빈부 貧富 wealth and poverty ; (the) rich and (the) poor (사람) ¶ 빈부의 차별 없이 rich and poor alike // 빈부의 차가 두드러지게 나타나다 There is a noticeable distinction between (the) rich and (the) poor.

빈사 賓辭 〖논리〗 the predicate ; 〖언어〗 an object (word)

빈사 瀕死 a dying condition ¶ 빈사의 dying // 빈사의 환자 a dying patient // 빈사 상태에 있다 be in dying condition ; be on the verge of death ; lie at death's door

빈사과 一果 (a) hexagon-shaped candy
빈삭 頻數 ⇨ 빈번
빈상 貧相 a countenance that bespeaks poverty ; a meager〔haggard〕 look
빈소 殯所 a room where a coffin is placed until the funeral day
빈소리 useless〔pointless〕 words ⇨ 빈말
빈속 an empty stomach ¶ 빈속에 술을 마시다 have a drink on an empty stomach
빈손 an empty hand ¶ 빈손으로 with empty hands ; empty-handed ; without taking any present with one
*__빈약__ 貧弱 poorness ; scantiness **—하다** (be) poor ; scanty ; limited ¶ 내용이 빈약한 책 a book poor in substance // 빈약한 옷차림의 사람 a poorly-dressed person // 빈약한 지식 scanty〔smattering〕 knowledge
빈우 牝牛 a cow
빈자 貧者 a poor man ; the poor ; needy 〔indigent〕 people ¶ 빈자의 일등 the widow's mite
빈자떡 貧者— a kind of pancake made from lentil flour ¶ 빈자떡을 지지다 make lentil pancakes
빈자리 [공석] a vacant〔an unoccupied〕 seat ; [결원] a vacancy ; a vacant position ¶ 빈자리를 메우지 않고 그대로 두다 leave a position unfilled〔vacant〕 // 그녀의 빈자리를 메우려면 경험이 많은 사람이 필요할 것이다 It'll take someone with quite a lot of experience to fill her shoes.
‡__빈정거리다__ poke fun 《at》 ; banter ; make fun〔game, sport〕 《of》 ; make cynical remarks ¶ 빈정빈정 jokingly ; teasingly ; banteringly ; caustically ; sarcastically // 그 문제를 가지고 빈정거리다 banter on〔about〕 the subject // 빈정거리지 마라 Cut the sarcasm.
빈주먹 an empty hand ¶ 빈주먹으로 empty-handed〔barehanded〕 ; without funds // 빈주먹으로 장사를 시작하다 start a business without means ; go into business with almost nothing
빈지 〖건축〗 shutters ¶ 빈지를 닫다〔열다〕 put up〔take down〕 the shutters
빈집 a vacant house ; an empty〔unoccupied〕 house ¶ 그 집은 빈집이다 The house is unoccupied.
빈차 一車 an empty car
빈천 貧賤 poverty (and lowliness) **—하다** (be) poor and lowly ¶ 빈천한 가문에 태어나다 be born poor
부귀빈천이 물레바퀴 돌 듯한다 속담 The highest spoke in fortune's wheel, may soon turn lowest.
빈천지교 貧賤之交 a friend of one's needy 〔humble〕 days
빈촌 貧村 a poor village
빈총 一銃 an unloaded gun ¶ 빈총을 놓다 fire a blank
빈축 嚬蹙 a frown ; a grimace **—하다** frown〔scowl〕 ; 《at, on》 ; look on 《a thing》 with scorn〔disdain〕 ; be scandalized at ¶ 빈축할 만한 scandalous ; despicable ; objectionable // 남의 빈축을 사다 be frowned at〔on〕 // 그는 전번에 이쁘지 않은 여자는 여자가 아니라는 말을 했다가 여자 사원들의 빈축을 샀다 The other day he scandalized the female staff when he said that a woman who isn't pretty isn't a real woman.
빈칸 a blank column ; a blank (space) ¶ 빈칸을 메우다 fill in a blank ; fill up a space ; fill a vacancy // 빈칸을 남겨두다 leave a blank〔space, margin〕
빈탕 emptiness ; vacancy ; an empty nut (알이 없는) ; a blank 《in a lottery》
빈터 《공지》 vacant land ; an open space ; [건물이 없는] unoccupied ground ; a vacant lot
빈털터리 a penniless person ; a fellow without a penny ; a person destitute of money ¶ 빈털터리가 되다 go〔be〕 broke ; become penniless
‡__빈틈__ ① [간격] an opening ; a gap ; a crack ; a chink ¶ 빈틈없는〔없이〕 close (-ly) ; compact(ly) // 종이와 헝겊 조각으로 빈틈을 틀어막다 stuff the crevice with paper and rags
② [불비] unpreparedness ; a blind side ; an opening (for attack) ¶ 빈틈없이 경계하다 be on the alert ; be on 《one's》 guard // 빈틈없이 조사하다 make a thoroughgoing investigation // 옷차림이 빈틈없다 be irreproachably dressed // 일이 빈틈없이 잘 되어 있다 The work leaves nothing to be desired.
빈한 貧寒 poverty ; indigence ; penury ; pauperism **—하다** (be) poor ; needy ; indigent ¶ 빈한 막심하다 live〔be〕 in dire poverty ; be as poor as a church mouse ; be extremely poor // 빈한한 집에 태어나다 be born poor〔in a poor family〕 // 빈한해서 학교에 못 갔다 Want kept him from school.
빈혈 貧血 〖의학〗 an(a)emia
—성 an anemic constitution **—증** poverty of blood ; 〖의학〗 an(a)emia ; exsanguinity **악성〔외상성〕—** pernicious〔traumatic〕 anemia
†__빌다__¹ ① [구걸하다] ask ; beg ¶ 빌어 먹다 beg 《one's bread》 ; go begging
② [기원하다] pray ; supplicate ; wish ; entreat ¶ 병이 낫기를 하느님에게 빌다 pray to God for one's recovery // 빌다시피하여 부탁하다 beg on one's knees // 성공을 빕니다 I wish you (every) success. // 행운을 빕니다 I wish you good luck! / Best of luck! / Good luck! / I'll keep my fingers crossed for you.
③ [사죄하다] ask 《a person's》 pardon ; apologize 《to a person》 for ; beg〔make〕 an apology 《for》 ¶ 그는 자기의 잘못을 나에게 빌었다 He made me a humble apology for his misconduct.

빌다² ① [차용하다] borrow ; have〔get〕 the loan 《of》 ¶ 책을 빌다 borrow a book ② [힘을] have〔get〕 《a person's》 help ; enlist the help of ¶ 그의 말을 빌어 말하면 in his phrase ; to use his words ③ [방을] rent ; take ¶ 집을 빌다 rent〔take〕 a house

빌딩 an office building

빌레몬서 一書 〖성경〗 The Epistle of St. Paul to Philemon ; Philemon 《Philem.》

빌려주다 ⇨ 빌리다

†**빌리다** ① [대여하다] lend ; let 《a person》 have ; loan ¶ 빌려 준 돈을 거두다 collect debts ; call in the loans // 전화를 빌려주다 let 《a person》 use one's telephone // 지혜를 빌리다 give advice // 힘을 빌리다 help 《a person》 ; give helping hands 《to a person》
② [임대하다] hire (out) ; let (out) ; let on hire ; rent ; lease (부동산을) ¶ 말을 빌리다 hire horses out // 집을 빌리다 rent〔let〕 a house // 나는 한가할 때면 대부분 비디오를 빌려 보면서 시간을 보낸다 I spend most of my free time watching rented videos.

빌리어드 billiards ⇨ 당구

빌립보서 一書 〖성경〗 The Epistle of St. Paul (the Apostle) to the Philippians ; Philippians 《Phil.》

빌미 a curse ; an evil spell

빌미잡다 attribute 《a calamity》 to ; blame 《for a calamity》

빌붙다 flatter 《a person》 ; fawn upon 《a person》 ; play up to 《a person》

빌어먹다 beg (one's bread) ; go begging ; live as a beggar ¶ 빌어먹는 한이 있더라도 even if one would be reduced 〔brought〕 to beggary〔begging〕
빌어먹는 놈이 콩밥을 마다할까 속담 Beggars must〔should〕 be no choosers. /Never look a gift horse in the mouth.

빌어먹을 Damn... ! ; Damn it ! ¶ 빌어먹을 ! 비가 오네 Damn the rain !

빔¹ [끼움] inserting a piece of cloth 〔paper〕 to make 《a thing》 fit tighter

빔² ⇨ 비음

빕더서다 [비켜서다] stand out of the way ; step back ; [약속을] go back on one's word ; break one's word

*****빗** a comb ¶ 빗으로 머리를 빗다 comb (out) one's hair
一살 the teeth of a comb **얼레〔참〕一** a wide-tooth〔fine-tooth〕 comb

빗- mis- ; mistaken ; crooked ; sidewise ; aslant ; wrong ; astray

빗가다 go astray ; miss ⇨ 빗나가다

빗각 〖수학〗 an oblique angle
一기둥〔뿔〕 an oblique prism〔pyramid〕

빗금 a deviant crease〔fold, line〕

빗기다 comb 《a person's hair》 ; have someone comb 《a person's hair》 ¶ 하인을 시켜서 개의 털을 빗기다 have the servant comb the dog

†**빗나가다** turn away〔aside〕 ; wander 〔deviate〕 《from》 ; miss〔go astray〕 (총탄이) ¶ 과녁에서 빗나가다 go wide of the mark ; miss the target // 화제가 빗나가다 wander from the subject // 총탄이 빗나갔다 The shot went wild. /The bullet glanced off. // 종이를 벨 때 칼이 빗나갔다 The knife slipped while I was cutting the paper. // 그럴 듯하게 짐작은 했는데 정답에서 많이 빗나갔다 Pretty good guess, but wide of the mark. /Pretty good guess, but far off the mark.

빗다 comb 《the hair》

†**빗대다** perjure oneself ; make a false statement ; testify falsely ; misstate ¶ 이름을 빗대다 give a wrong〔false〕 name // 빗대지 마라 Stop fabricating a story. / Don't perjure yourself. // 빗대지 말고 바로 대라 Don't perjure yourself, tell the truth.

빗더서다 [방향을] stand a bit sidewise ; [비켜서다] stand out of the way ; step back

빗돌 碑一 a stone monument ; a monumental stone

빗듣다 be misinformed ; hear wrong ; mishear

빗디디다 miss one's step〔foot〕 ; lose one's footing 《on the stairs》 ; make a false step〔misstep〕 ¶ 발을 빗디디다 make a false step

빗뜨다 look sidewise ; look out of the corner of 《one's eye》 ¶ 눈을 빗뜨다 look out of the corner of one's eyes

*****빗맞다** ① [빗나가다] miss the mark ; go wide of the mark ; glance off ¶ 어뢰가 빗맞았다 The torpedo missed its mark 〔went wild〕.
② [뜻한 일이] go wrong ; backfire ; miscarry ¶ 계획이 빗맞다 be frustrated in one's design

빗먹다 saw diagonally ; veer off-line

빗물 rainwater

빗밑 clearing up (of the sky)

빗반자 an angled〔an inclined, a sloping〕 ceiling

빗발 a streak of rain ; rain ¶ 총알이 빗발처럼 쏟아지다 Bullets fall like rain.

빗발치듯 thick and fast (like streaks of rain) ; in (great) streaks ; in rain ¶ 빗발치듯 하는 탄알〔화살〕 a rain of bullets 〔arrows〕 // 빗발치듯 하는 질문 a volley of questions // 주문이 빗발치듯한다 We are flooded with offers. // 그들 주위에 총알이 빗발치듯 쏟아졌다 Bullets rained 〔streaked〕 thick and fast around them.

⁑**빗방울** raindrops ¶ 빗방울 소리 pattering of raindrops

빗변 〖수학〗 a hypotenuse ; an oblique side ¶ 직각 삼각형의 빗변 the hypotenuse of a right-angled triangle

빗보다 misjudge ¶ 사람을 빗보다 misjudge a person

빗살 the teeth of a comb
빗서다 ⇨ 빗더서다
빗소리 the sound of rain ; rain
빗속 《in》 the midst of rain
빗솔 a brush for cleaning combs
빗원기둥 『수학』 an oblique cylinder
‡빗장 a bolt ; a crossbar ; a bar ¶ 문에 빗장을 지르다〔벗기다〕 bolt〔unbolt〕 the gate
빗장고름 a bow-tied ribbon
빗장뼈 the collarbone ; the clavicle
빗접 a comb box ; an oilpaper comb holder
빗접고비 a comb cabinet
빗줄기 great streaks〔sheets〕 of rain ¶ 빗줄기가 세차다 It pours down./It rains cats and dogs.
‡빗질 combing 《one's hair》 ─하다 comb 《one's hair》
빗치개 a kind of pin for parting hair and cleaning combs
*빙, 삥 round ; in a circle ¶ 눈물이 빙 돌다 be moved to tears // 삥 둘러 앉다 sit in a circle // 섬을 한 바퀴 빙 돌다 go round the island ; make a tour of the island // 한 대 맞았더니 정신이 빙 돈다 My head swims〔spins〕 with a blow.
빙결 氷結 freezing ; congelation (of water) ─하다 freeze over ; be frozen over ; be ice-bound ; congeal
빙고 [놀이] bingo (game)
빙고 氷庫 an ice-house ; a store house for ice
빙고 憑考 [참조] reference ; consultation ; [고증] research ; investigation ; inquiry ─하다 refer to ; consult ; investigate ; study ; inquire into
빙과 氷菓 ices ; ice creams ; ice cakes
빙괴 氷塊 a lump〔chunk, piece〕 of ice
빙그레, 삥그레 with a beaming face ; beamingly ; smilingly ─하다 beam 《upon a person》 ; smile 《at a person》
빙그르르, 삥그르르 around smoothly ¶ 빙판을 한 바퀴 빙그르르 돌다 take a smooth turn around the ice
빙글거리다, 삥글거리다 smile 《at a person》 ; beam 《upon a person》
빙글빙글[1] 삥글삥글 around and around smoothly ¶ 빙글빙글 돌다 turn〔go〕 round and round ; spin ; twirl // 방이 빙글빙글 도는 것 같았다 The room seemed to spin round.
빙글빙글[2] smilingly ; beamingly ; with a smile ¶ 빙글빙글 웃는 얼굴 a beaming face ; a radiant look
빙긋거리다, 삥긋거리다, 삥끗거리다 beam ⇨ 빙글거리다
빙낭 氷囊 an ice bag〔pack〕
─ 걸이 an ice-bag suspender〔holder〕
빙당 氷糖 sugar candy ⇨ 빙사탕
빙모 聘母 the wife's mother ⇨ 장모
빙벽 氷壁 [산의] an ice ridge
빙부 聘父 the wife's father ⇨ 장인

빙빙, 삥삥 round and round ; repeatedly in a circle ¶ 빙빙 돌다 turn round and round
빙사탕 氷砂糖 sugar candy ; crystal sugar
*빙산 氷山 an iceberg ; an ice floe
빙상 氷上 ¶ 빙상에서 on the ice
─ 경기 ice sports
빙상 氷床 『지리』 an ice sheet
빙석 氷釋 ─하다 be cleared (의혹이) ; be dispelled
빙설 氷雪 ice and snow
빙수 氷水 ice water ; [음료] ice flakes with syrup
빙실 氷室 an icehouse ; a refrigeratory
빙실거리다, 삥실거리다 smile ; beam
빙어 ─魚 『물고기』 a smelt ; a pond smelt ; a sparling
빙원 氷原 an ice field
빙자 憑藉 ① [의지] reliance ; dependence ─하다 rely 《on》 ; depend 《upon》 ② [핑계] an excuse ; a pretext ; a plea ─하다 make〔find, invent〕 an excuse ; make a pretext ¶ …을 빙자하여 under color〔the cloak, the mask〕 《of》 ; on 〔under〕 the pretext〔plea, pretence〕 《of》 // 취직 알선을 빙자하여 사기하다 swindle 《a person》 out of money under the pretext of finding employment
*빙점 氷點 the freezing point ¶ 빙점 하 10 도 ten degrees of frost〔below zero〕
빙정석 氷晶石 『광물』 cryolite
빙초산 氷醋酸 『화학』 glacial acetic acid
빙충맞다 (be) clumsy ; dull-witted ; heavy ; stupid
빙충(맞)이 a thick-witted〔dull-headed〕 person ; a dolt
빙침 氷枕 an ice pillow ¶ 빙침을 베다 rest one's head on a pillow of ice
빙탄 氷炭 ice and charcoal ; [부조화] incompatibility ; discord ¶ 빙탄 불상용이다 be as incompatible as oil and water
빙퉁그러지다 ① [하는 일이] go wrong 〔amiss〕 ; backfire ② [성질이] have a crooked〔perverse〕 disposition
빙판 氷板 an icy road ; a frozen road
*빙하 氷河 [강] an icebound river ; 『지질』 a glacier ¶ 빙하 전기의 preglacial // 빙하 후기의 postglacial
─기(期) a glacial epoch ; the ice age ─ 성층 glacial sediment ─ 시대 the glacial age〔period〕 ─ 작용 the action of a glacier ; glacier operations ; glaciation ─ 퇴적물 glacial deposits ; a boulder drift
빙하다 be〔feel〕 dizzy from drinking ; be in drunken stupor
빙해 氷海 a frozen sea ; icy waters
빙해 氷解 clearance 《of doubt》 ─하다 be cleared〔dispelled〕
빙활 氷滑 ice skating
─장 an ice rink
삥땅 [버스 안내양의] pocketing ; pilfering (of the proceeds) ¶ 삥땅 누명을 씌우다 disgrace 《a bus conductress》 on charges

of having pocketed (part of the fares collected) // 그 안내양은 삥땅을 뜯었다 The bus conductress pocketed〔pilfered〕 some of the proceeds〔collected fares〕.

뻥등그리다 shake《one's head》to show a negative reaction ; show a reluctant gesture twirling one's head

삥삥매다 bustle about ; go about busily ; be at a loss《what to do》; be perplexed

†**빚** a debt ; a loan ; liabilities ¶ 빚이 1만원 있다 be indebted to《a person》for 10,000 *won* ; owe《a person》10,000 *won* // 빚을 갚다 pay〔clear〕 off debts ; get out of debt // 빚을 지다 run〔get, fall〕 into debt ; owe // 빚에 얽매이다 be deeply〔up to the ears〕 in debt // 빚이 없다 be free from debts // 빚 청산을 재촉하다 call up a debt ; dun《a person》for the payment of a debt // 우리정부가 그렇게 많은 빚을 지고 있는 줄 몰랐다 I didn't know our government was that much in the hole.

빚거간 —居間 [사람] an agent〔a broker〕 for money-lending ; a loan agent〔broker〕; [영업] agency〔brokerage〕 for money-lending ; a loan agency〔brokerage〕 **—하다** act as a loan agent ; act as an agent for moneylending

빚꾸러기 a person deeply in debt ; a debt-ridden person

***빚내다** borrow money《from》; obtain a loan《from》¶ 대지를 담보로 빚내다 get a loan on the lot

빚놀이 lending money

빚놓다 lend money ; loan (out) ¶ 고리로 빚놓다 lend money at a high rate of interest

빚다 ① [술을] brew ; distil ¶ 술을 빚다 brew rice wine ② [만두·송편 따위를] knead〔make〕 dough ③ [조성하다] come of〔from〕; foment ; cause ; arise《from》¶ 가난이 빚은 비극 a tragedy resulting from poverty

빚돈 a loan ; a debt ¶ 빚돈을 내다 make a loan // 빚돈은 한푼도 없다 I owe nothing to any one. /I owe no one.

빚두루마기 a debt-ridden person ; a person deeply in debt

빚물이 paying someone else's debts **—하다** pay debts for someone else ; clear off another's debt

빚받이 collecting debts **—하다** collect debts

빚어내다 bring about ; cause ; foment ; create ; produce

빚쟁이 a moneylender ; a usurer (고리 대금업자) ; a loan man

빚주다 lend out money ; make loans ; run a moneylending business ¶ 빚 주고 뺨 맞기 having good repayed with evil ; lending money and getting slapped

⁑**빚지다** run〔get〕 into debt ; incur〔contract〕 a debt ; owe ¶ 빚진 죄인이라 어찌할 수 없다 I am really in a fix—being, as they say, "a criminal in debt."

빚지시 loan agency〔brokerage〕; intermediation for money-lending〔a loan〕 **—하다** act as (a) loan broker〔agent〕; intermediate for a loan

†**빛** ① [광명] light ; [광선] a ray ; a beam ; [섬광] a flash ; a gleam (어둠 속의) ; [광휘] a luster ; radiance ; glow ; twinkle (별의) ; a sparkle (보석 따위의) ; a glitter ; [희미한] a glimmer ¶ 태양 빛 sunlight ; the sun's rays // 개똥벌레의 빛 the glow of a firefly // 빛이 잘 드는 방 a sunny room // 빛을 발하다 emit〔give out〕 light // 가로등 불빛으로 책을 읽다 read by the light of a street lamp // 어스레한 불빛에서 일하다 work in the faint light

② [빛깔] a color ; a shade ; a hue ; a tint ¶ 가을 빛 autumnal tints // 밝은 빛 a bright color // 어두운 빛 a dark color // 푸른 기 도는 붉은 빛 red of〔with〕 a blue tint

③ [안색 따위] a look ; an expression ¶ 피로한 빛이 보이다 look tired ; show signs of fatigue // 그 소식을 듣고 얼굴 빛이 달라졌다 He changed color at the news.

빛 좋은 개살구 [속담] Never judge from appearance. /Appearance is deceptive. / It is not the beard that makes the philosophers.

†**빛깔** a color ; a shade ; a hue ; a tint ¶ 밝은 빛깔로 그리다 paint in bright〔glowing〕 colors

빛 강도 —強度 the intensity〔strength〕 of light

†**빛나다** ① [빛이] shine ; be bright ; glitter ; gleam ; glimmer (까물까물) ; twinkle (별이) ; sparkle (반짝반짝) ; be lustrous〔glossy〕 (윤나다) ; be shiny (흰 옷이) ¶ 하늘에 빛나는 별 stars twinkling up in the sky // 기쁨으로 빛나는 눈 eyes sparkling with joy // 아침 햇빛에 빛나다 glitter in the rising sun // 눈이 빛나고 있었다 His eyes shone. // 빛난다고 반드시 금은 아니다 All is not gold that glitters. // 승리는 찬란하게 그의 머리 위에 빛났다 A brilliant victory fell〔went〕 to him. // 큰 희망에 얼굴이 빛난다 His face is radiant with a great hope.

② [출중하다] shine brilliantly ; cut a figure ¶ 빛나는 장래 a bright〔promising〕 future // 청사에 빛나다 remain long 〔immortal〕 in history // 형제 중에서 그가 가장 빛난다 He outshines all his brothers.

⁑**빛내다** light up ; make《a thing》shine ; brighten ¶ 국위를 빛내다 enhance national prestige ; bring glory to one's country // 이름을 해외에 빛내다 win international fame

빛살 rays of light

빛없다 be ashamed

빛접다 (be) shining ; glorious ¶ 그 사람이 한 일이 빛접다 He came through with flying colors. /He did himself proud.

빠개다 ① split ; cleave ② [어긋내다] spoil ; ruin ; wreck ¶ 장작을 빠개다 split firewood // 거진 다 된 일을 빠개다 spoil a plan which is almost accomplished

빠개지다 ① [조각나다] split apart ; cleave ¶ 이 나무는 잘 빠개진다 This wood splits nicely. // 머리가 빠개질 듯이 아프다 I have a splitting headache. ② [일이] get ruined ; be spoiled ; fail ; come to naught ¶ 우리 일이 빠개졌다 Our work came to naught.

빠그라지다 get broken

빠근하다 feel heavy ⇨ 뻐근하다

빠기다 boast ⇨ 뻐기다

빠끔하다 (be) open ⇨ 뻐끔하다

빠닥빠닥 **—하다** be dried out stiff ⇨ 뻐덕뻐덕하다

빠득빠득하다 ① (be) headstrong ; disobedient ; perverse ; hardheaded ② [떫다] (be) astringent ; puckery ; acrid ③ [눈이] (be) dry and tired ; burn ¶ 아이가 빠득빠득하다 be a perverse child // 감이 빠득빠득하다 The persimmon makes your mouth pucker. // 눈이 빠득빠득하다 My eyes are tired. /My eyes burn.

†**빠뜨리다** ① [빠지게 하다] throw into 《a river》 (물에) ; trap〔ensnare, entrap〕 (함정에) ; tempt〔entice, seduce, lure〕 (유혹에) ¶ 곤란한 입장에 빠뜨리다 land 《a person》 in difficulties // 유혹에 빠뜨리다 lead 《a person》 into temptation // 함정에 빠뜨리다 lure 《a person》 into a trap
② [빼어 놓다] omit ; leave out ; exclude ¶ 한 줄을 빠뜨리다 leave out a line // 소설 가운데 어려운 말은 빠뜨리고 읽는다 She skips hard words in a novel. // 그는 점호할 때 내 이름을 빠뜨렸다 He skipped over my name in the roll call.
③ [잃다] lose ; drop ; let it fall ¶ 지갑을 빠뜨렸다 I have dropped my purse. // 모자를 강에 빠뜨렸다 I let my hat fall into the water.

†**빠르다** ① [속도가] (be) fast ; swift ; rapid ; speedy ; quick〔agile, sharp, alert〕 (날쌔다) ¶ 빠른 기차 a fast train // 출세에의 빠른 길 a short cut to success // 빠른 냇물 a rapid stream // 계산이 빠르다 be quick at figures // 일이 빠르다 be quick about one's work ; be a quick worker // 눈치가 빠르다 be keen-eyed ; have sharp eyes // 동작이 빠르다 move quickly ; be quick in action // 병의 회복이 빠르다 recover quickly from illness // 이해가 빠르다 be quick to understand ; catch on fast ; be quick in the uptake // 진보가 빠르다 make rapid progress // 세월이 빠르다 (How) time flies ! // 빨라도 2주일 후에나 납품할 수 있습니다 We will be able to deliver in two weeks at the earliest.
② [이르다] (be) early ; soon ¶ 그 계획을 실행하기에는 아직 시기가 빠르다 It is premature to carry out the plan. // 그는 나보다 1년 빨리 졸업했다 He graduated from the school one year ahead of〔prior to〕 me. // 빠를수록 좋다 The sooner, the better. // 시기적으로 빠르다 The time is not mature yet. // 아직 시간이 빠르다 It is quite early yet. // 한 시간 빠르다 We are an hour too soon.

빠이빠이 Bye-bye !

†**빠지다** ① [떨어지다] fall〔get〕 into ; be drowned〔sunk into〕 (물에) ; fall〔be led, sink down〕 into (어떤 상태에) ¶ 개골창에 빠지다 be mired in a ditch // 곤경에 빠지다 get into trouble〔difficulties〕 ; run up against a snag // 물에 빠지다 fall into a river ; sink under the water // 물에 빠진 사람을 건져주다 save 《a person》 from drowning // 위험한 상태에 빠지다 be in danger ; run into danger // 진흙에 빠지다 stick〔be caught〕 in the mud // 혼수 상태에 빠지다 lapse〔fall〕 into a (state of) coma〔delirium, stupor〕 // 물에 빠진 사람은 지푸라기라도 붙잡는다 A drowning man will catch at a straw.
② [마음을 빼앗기다] indulge〔wallow〕 《in》 ; be given up 《to》 ; give oneself up 《to》 ; be addicted 《to》 ¶ 주색에 빠지다 give oneself up to women and wine ; wallow in sensual pleasure // 여자에 홈빡 빠지다 be dead gone on a girl ; be infatuated with a girl // 유혹에 빠지다 yield〔give in〕 to temptation // 우리 아들은 테니스에 빠져서 공부를 전혀 안 한다 Our son has gotten wrapped up in tennis and doesn't study at all.
③ [박힌 것이] come off〔out〕 ; fall out ; be taken off ; get removed ¶ 눈이 빠지게 기다리다 wait with a craned neck ; look forward to 《a matter, a person》 with impatience // 못이 빠져 있다 A nail is missing. // 이가 빠졌다 A tooth came out. // 털이 빠진다 The hair falls out.
④ [없다] be left out ; be omitted ; be missing〔wanting〕 ; be not included ; be dropped ¶ 두 페이지가 빠졌다 There are two pages missing. // 전문이 다 빠졌다 The whole passage is left out. // 명부에서 그의 이름이 빠졌다 His name is not (included) in the list.
⑤ [흘러나가다] drain ; flow off ¶ 그 땅은 물이 잘 빠진다 The ground is well drained. // 괸 물이 빠지기 시작한다 A pool of water begins to flow off. // 하수구 물이 잘 안 빠진다 It does not drain well.
⑥ [제외되다] be left out ; be excluded 〔exempted〕 《from》 ; be not included ¶ 초대에 빠지다 be left out of the invitation // 입선에서 빠진 것 중에도 가작이 있다 Some of those that have not been accepted are good.
⑦ [없어지다] come off ; be gone ; be got rid of ¶ 맥주 김이 빠졌다 The beer

tastes flat. // 빨아도 빛깔이 빠지지 않는다 The color stands the wash. // 얼룩이 잘 빠지지 않는다 The stains will not come off. // 힘이 빠졌다 All my strength is gone. // 이 얼룩은 빠질 것 같습니다 I think this stain will come off. // 줄어들지는 않지만 빨면 색이 빠질지도 모른다 It won't shrink but the color may run if washed. // 너는 도중에 힘이 빠져 버릴것이다 You'll run out of steam midway.

⑧ [살이] become〔grow〕 thin ; lose weight ; get lean ; become skinny〔peaked〕 ¶ 움푹 빠진 눈 sunken eyes // 살이 빠져 뼈와 가죽만 남다 be a mere bag of bones ; be nothing but skin and bones // 살이 빠진 것 같다 You appear to have lost weight.

⑨ [탈출하다] escape ; slip out ; get off ; avoid ; shun ; avert ; slip away 《from a meeting》 ¶ 좌석에서 빠져 나오다 leave one's seat ; slip out of the room // 집에서 빠져 나오다 slip〔steal〕 out of the house // 위험한 고비를 빠져 나가다 escape danger ; find one's way out of danger // 오늘 밤 송별회에는 빠질 수 없다 I can't excuse myself from the farewell party this evening. // 그는 겁을 먹고 같이 투자하기로 한 사업계획에서 빠지려고 했다 He got cold feet and wanted out of our joint investment project. // 이 일에서 빠져 주시오 Keep out of this.

⑩ [지나가다] go〔pass〕 through ; run ; lead 《into》 ¶ 빠져 나갈 수 없는 골목 a blind alley // 골목으로 빠지다 go through an alley // 이 길로 빠져 나가자 Let us go by this lane.

⑪ [못하다] be inferior 《to》 ; compare unfavorably 《with》 ; fall 《below》 ¶ 누구에게도 빠지지 않다 be second〔next〕 to none ; yield the palm to no one // 빠지지 않다 be as good as // 동생에 비해 용모가 빠지다 She compares unfavorably with her sister in beauty. // 문장은 그에게 빠지지 않는다 I can write as well as he. // 그 여자의 옷이 그중 빠졌다 Her dress was the least attractive one there.

⑫ [속다] be cheated ; be taken in ; be imposed upon ¶ 계략에 빠지다 fall into a trap // 그러한 속임수에 빠질 내가 아니다 That trick won't work with me. /I don't fall for such a trick. // 속임수에 빠졌다 I have been done〔taken〕 in.

⑬ [뽑히다] draw〔cast〕 《a winning number》 ; win 《in a lottery》

빠지지, 빠지직 ⇨ 바지지, 바지직

빠짐없이 thoroughly ; wholly ; in full ; to〔for〕 everybody ; without omission 〔exception〕

빡빡하다 ① [물기가 적다] (be) thick ; soupy ¶ 빡빡한 국 a thick soup // 빡빡해지다 thicken ; become thick

② [꽉 차다] (be) closely packed ; chock-full ; crammed 《with》 ¶ (승객이) 빡빡하게 들어차다 be jammed〔packed〕 like sardines

③ [기계 따위가] (be) stiff ; lack smoothness ; hard ; tight ; be not greasy ¶ 빡빡한 피스톤 a stiff piston

④ [고지식하다] (be) unadaptable ; hidebound ; straitlaced ; stuffed 《미·구》 ¶ 빡빡한 영감 a narrow-minded old man

빡작지근하다 feel heavy〔oppressed, strained〕 ¶ 가슴이 빡작지근하다 feel heavy in the chest // 몸이 빡작지근하다 feel exhausted ; be worn out

빤빤하다 (be) brazen-faced ; impudent ; audacious ; shameless ¶ 빤빤하게도 …하다 have the impudence〔face, cheek〕 to 《do》 ; be shameless enough to 《do》

빤히 ① [환히] bright(ly) ¶ 날이 빤히 트다 The day dawns bright and clear.

② [명백히] clearly ; plainly ; evidently ; obviously ; patently ¶ 빤히 알다 know for certain〔for sure〕 // 빤히 알면서 understanding clearly ; knowing full well ; with full knowledge ; in full possession of the facts // 너는 그렇게 속이 빤히 들여다보이는 칭찬을 할 필요가 없다 You don't have to make such transparent compliments.

③ [보다] fixedly ; hard ; intently ¶ 빤히 쳐다보다 stare at

†**빨강** red ; scarlet ; red colo(u)r ; red dye

빨갛다 (be) deep-red ; crimson ¶ 빨갛게 되다 redden ; turn red ; blush (얼굴이) ; be flushed 《with wine》 // 성이 나서 빨갛다 be red with anger // 빨갛게 칠하다 paint 《the wall》 red

‡**빨다**[1] [마시다] sip ; suck ; [피우다] smoke ; puff at ; [흡수하다] absorb ; suck in ¶ 젖을 빨다 suck the breast // 물기가 없어질 때까지 오렌지를 빨다 suck an orange dry // 담뱃대를 뻐금뻐금 빨다 suck at one's pipe // 압지가 잉크를 빨아들인다 Blotting paper absorbs ink.

빨다[2] [세탁하다] wash ; launder ; do washing ¶ 빨면 지워진다 It will come out in the wash. // 이 천은 빨아도 줄지 않는다 This cloth is unshrinkable.

빨다[3] [뾰족하다] (be) pointed ; sharp ¶ 끝이 빤 pointed ; sharp-pointed ; tapering

‡**빨대** a (drinking) straw ; a conduit pipe ; a pipette ¶ 빨대로 우유를 마시다 drink milk through a straw // 아무에게 빨대를 대다〔놓다〕 suck a person's substance ; drain a person dry ; take everything a person has

빨대대다 ① [빨대를] put in a straw ② [빨아 먹다] sponge〔fleece, prey on〕 《a person》

빨랑빨랑 hurriedly ; in a hurry ; in haste ; quickly ¶ 빨랑빨랑 해라 Hurry up ! 《미》 /Be quick ! /Sharp's the word !

†**빨래** wash ; washing ; laundry **—하다** wash ; launder ; do washing ¶ 빨래를 널어 말리다 hang out the wash〔washing〕

to dry // 빨래로 생계를 유지하다 She washes for a living.
—꾼 a launderer ; [여자] a washerwoman ; washwoman 《미》 —말미 a spell of dry weather during the wet season —질 washing 《clothes》 —집게 a clothespin 《미》 ; a clothespeg 《영》 —터 a wash place ; a laundry (near a well or stream) —통 a washtub —판 a washboard —품(삯) laundry charge 빨랫돌 a flat stone used as a washboard 빨랫방망이 a laundry paddle 빨랫비누 laundry soap 빨랫솔 scrub(bing) brush 빨랫줄 a clothesline ; a washline

*빨리 fast ; rapidly ; quickly ——하다 hasten ; quicken ; expedite ; accelerate ¶ 걸음을 빨리하다 quicken one's steps ; put on the pace // 속력을 빨리하다 get up speed ; speed up // 그렇게 빨리 말하지 마라 Don't speak so fast〔rapidly〕. // 빨리 해 Hurry up ! /Make haste ! /Be quick about it ! /On the double ! /Make it a quickie ! /Get the lead out ! // 택시 기사가 빨리 가 줘서 공항에 제때에 도착했다 My taxi driver made good time and I arrived at the airport just in time. // 좀 빨리 갑시다 Step on it, please. /Pick it up, please. /Speed it up, please. /Faster, please.

빨리다[1] [흡수당하다] be sucked 〔absorbed〕 ; [착취당하다] be fleeced 《of》 ; be squeezed out 《of》 ; [빨아 먹이다] suckle 《a baby》 ; nurse 《a baby》 ; give the breast 《to》

빨리다[2] [빨게 하다] let suck ; let suckle ; nurse with 《milk》 ¶ 어머니가 아기한테 젖을 빨리었다 The mother gave suck to〔nursed〕 her baby.

빨병 a canteen ; a water bottle ; a thermos (bottle)

빨빨 profusely ; dripping ; freely ¶ 땀을 빨빨 흘리다 be dripping with sweat

빨아내다 suck〔draw〕 out ; 〖의학〗 aspirate (고름 따위를)

*빨아들이다 [기체를] breathe〔draw〕 in ; inhale ; [액체를] suck in〔up〕 ; soak up ; absorb ; blot (압지로) ; sponge (해면으로) ¶ 담배 연기를 빨아들이다 inhale〔draw in〕 the smoke // 해면으로 빨아들이다 soak with a sponge ; sponge

빨아먹다 ① [음식을] suck ; imbibe ; sip ¶ 당과를 빨아먹다 suck a taffy // 한 모금 빨아먹다 take a suck 《at》 ② [우려내다] suck ; squeeze out ; sponge ¶ 백성의 피를 빨아먹다 squeeze the people

빨아올리다 suck up ¶ 나무는 땅에서 수분을 빨아올린다 Plants suck up moisture from the earth.

빨쪽이 ⇨ 발쪽이

빨치산 a partisan〔-zan〕 (fighter) ; a guerrilla

빨판 〖동물〗 a sucker ; a sucking-disk ; a acetabulum 《*pl.* -la》

빨펌프 a suction pump

빳빳이 ① [단단하고 곧게] straight(ly) ; stiffly ¶ 빳빳이 서다 stand straight // 셔츠에 풀을 너무 빳빳이 먹였다 They have put too much starch in my shirts.
② [완강히] headstrong ; firm ¶ 빳빳이 버티다 be unyielding ; stand firm

빳빳하다 ① (be) stiff ; straight ② [성질이] (be) headstrong ; firm ; unyielding ; willful ¶ 빳빳한 칼라 a stiff collar // 등이 빳빳하다 have a straight back // 목이 빳빳하다 have a stiff neck

†빵[1] bread ¶ 빵 문제 the question of bread and butter // 빵 부스러기 crumbs // 빵 한 조각 a slice of bread // 한 덩이의 빵 a loaf of bread // 빵에 버터를 바르다 spread butter on bread // 빵을 위해 일하다 work for bread // 인간은 빵만으로는 살 수 없다 Man shall not live by bread alone.

빵[2] [소리] pop ; bang ¶ 권총을 빵빵 쏘다 crack pistols // 병마개가 빵하고 튄다 The cork pops. // 빵하고 울리는 소리를 들었다 I heard it go pop.

빵가루 flour

빵꾸 a blowout ; a puncture ; a hole ¶ 빵꾸 나다 puncture ; blow out // 양말이 빵꾸 나다 a sock gets a hole in it ; get a hole in one's sock // 타이어가 빵꾸 나다 a tire is punctured

빵빵 ① [소리] with explosion after explosion ; popping and popping ② [모양] with hole after hole ; gaping and gaping

빵집 a bakery

빻다 grind ; powder ; pulverize ¶ 가루를 빻다 grind flour // 커피를 빻다 grind coffee

빼각거리다 squeak ; creak ; grate ¶ 그의 무게로 마루가 빼각거린다 The floor gives a creaking sound under his weight.

빼기 〖수학〗 subtraction

빼나다 excel 《a person》 in 《studies, sport》 ; surpass 《a person》 ¶ 빼난 eminent ; distinguished // 다른 사람보다 빼나다 stand out above the others ; have an advantage over others

†빼내다 ① [뽑다] pull〔draw〕 out ; extract ¶ 가시를 빼내다 draw〔pull〕 out a thorn // 못을 빼내다 pull out a nail // 총알을 빼내다 extract〔remove〕 a bullet
② [골라내다] select ; pick〔single〕 out ¶ 그 중에서 좋은 것을 하나 빼내다 pick a good one out of the lot // 지원자 50명 중 5명만 빼내다 select only five out of 50 applicants
③ [돌라내다] pilfer ; steal ¶ 짐을 빼내다 pilfer from loads
④ [꾀어내다] lure〔entice〕 《a person》 out ; hire 《a person》 away (고용인을)
⑤ [얽매인 몸을] ransom 《a person》 ; secure 《a person's》 liberty ¶ 몸값을 치르고 창녀를 빼내다 ransom a prostitute

빼놓다 ① [제쳐놓다] exclude ; leave 《a person》 out 《in the cold》 ; set aside ;

omit ; boycott 《a person》 ¶ 나만 빼놓고 모두 영화 구경하러 갔다 All went to the movies leaving me alone. // 일요일을 빼놓고는 매일 집에 있다 I am always at home except Sunday.
② [뽑아 놓다] draw〔pull〕 out ; extract ; uproot (뿌리를)
③ [골라 놓다] select ; pick〔single〕 out

†**빼다** ① [빼내다] pull out〔up〕 ; take out ; draw〔unsheathe〕 (칼을) ; extract〔pull out〕 (이를) ¶ 병마개를 빼다 open〔uncork〕 a bottle // 바람을 빼다 deflate // 이를 빼다 extract〔pull out〕 a tooth // 칼〔권총〕을 빼다 draw a sword 〔pistol〕
② [덜어내다] subtract〔deduct, take away〕 《from》 ¶ 열에서 둘을 빼다 subtract〔take〕 2 from 10
③ [삭제하다] remove ; cancel ; strike 〔cross〕 out ¶ 이자를 빼고 1만원 ten thousand *won*, exclusive of interest // 얼룩을 빼다 remove〔take out〕 a stain // 이름을 명부에서 빼다 strike 《a person's》 name off the list // 항목 하나를 빼다 strike out a clause // 일요일만 빼고 매일 학교에 간다 He goes to school every day except Sundays. // 이 얼룩을 빼려고 했지만 잘 안 빠진다 I tried to get this stain out, but it didn't come out. // 내 전화 번호를 전화 번호부에서 빼 주세요 I want my telephone number unlisted. /I want my telephone number taken off the telephone directory.
④ [꾸미다] affect ; assume ; put on airs ; pose 《as》 ¶ 점잔을 빼다 be prudish〔genteel〕 ; do the genteel
⑤ [회피하다] evade ; shirk ; avoid ¶ 꽁무니를 빼다 shirk one's responsibility // 발을 빼다 wash one's hands of 《an affair》 ; be through with ; sever connections 〔relations〕 with // 시간 중에 빼다 cut a class〔lesson〕
⑥ [차려 입다] dress〔doll〕 up ¶ 한 벌 쪽 빼 입었다 He is all dressed up. /He is dressed in his best.

빼닫이 a drawer ⇨ 서랍

빼돌리다 keep secret ; hide ; hoard secretly ; [선수 등을] hide 《a person》 away ; entice ¶ 빼돌려 둔 돈 pin money ; a secret hoard // 아무를 빼돌리다 hide 〔entice〕 a person away

빼뚝거리다 wobble ; limp ⇨ 비뚝거리다

빼뚤어지다 be tilted ; be perverse ⇨ 비뚤어지다

빼뜰다 ⇨ 빼앗다

빼먹다 ① [빠뜨리다] forget 《to mention》 ; leave out ¶ 말을 빼먹다 forget to mention // 시험 문제 하나를 빼먹다 forget to answer a question in the examination
② [훔치다] steal ; swipe ; pilfer ; ransack ¶ 짐을 빼먹다 pilfer baggage
③ [수업을] play truant ; cut a class 〔lesson〕 ¶ 학교를 빼먹다 play hooky 《미·속》

빼물다 [거만하게] pout one's lips in a lordly manner ; behave oneself haughtily ; [뻐물다] be intent on

빼빼 thin ; stringy ; skinny ; haggard ; gaunt ; emaciated ¶ 빼빼 마른 사람 a bag of bones ; a living skeleton // 빼빼 여위다 be worn to a shadow

빼쏘다 be exactly alike ; be as like as two peas〔eggs〕 ; be an exact counterpart 《of》 ; resemble closely ; be the picture 《of one's mother》 ¶ 그 아이는 아버지를 빼쏘았다 The boy is the very portrait of his father. /The boy is the (very) spit of his father.

빼앗기다 ① [탈취] 《a thing》 be taken away ; be robbed of 《a thing》 (도난) ; be plundered (약탈) ; be deprived of 《a thing》 (박탈) ¶ 권력을 빼앗기다 be deprived of one's power // 돈을 빼앗기다 be robbed of one's money // 시계를 빼앗기다 have one's watch stolen〔snatched away〕 // 주교의 직을 빼앗기다 be divested of one's bishopric // 그 사고로 많은 사람이 목숨을 빼앗겼다 The accident took a heavy toll of lives.
② [매혹] be fascinated ; be captivated ; be absorbed ¶ 독서에 정신을 빼앗기다 be absorbed〔engrossed〕 in reading // 여자에 얼을 빼앗기다 be captivated by a woman // 음악에 넋을 빼앗기다 be enraptured by music
③ [유린] be seduced〔dishonored〕 (정조를) ; be infringed (인권을)

‡**빼앗다** ① [탈취하다] snatch 《a thing》 from 《a person》 ; take 《a thing》 away from 《a person》 ; rob 《a person》 of 《a thing》 (훔치다) ; plunder (약탈하다) ; deprive 《a person》 of 《a thing》 (박탈하다) ¶ 권력을 빼앗다 deprive 《a person》 of his power // 남의 물건을 빼앗다 take another's property // 목숨을 빼앗다 take 《a person's》 life // 손에 쥔 핸드백을 빼앗다 snatch a handbag from her hand // 스페인의 영토를 빼앗다 wrest territory from Spain // 왕위를 빼앗다 usurp the throne
② [매혹하다] fascinate ; charm ; captivate ¶ 관객의 얼을 빼앗다 fascinate the audience // 넋을 빼앗다 captivate 《a person》
③ [짓밟다] seduce〔violate, dishonor〕 (정조를) ; infringe (인권을) ¶ 정조를 빼앗다 violate〔seduce, dishonor〕 a woman // 인권을 빼앗다 infringe〔trample on〕 personal rights

‡**빼어나다** excel 《in》 ⇨ 빼나다

빼치다 [빠져 나오게] let get away ; let go off ; [끝을 빨게] sharpen ; taper ; put a point on

빽 ① [소리] whistling ; piping ¶ 빽빽 울다 cheep ; peep ; chirp // 빽 소리내다 give forth a sharp sound // 기차가 기적을 빽 울린다 The train whistles.

② [빽빽하게] closely ; densely ; thickly ¶ 빽 차다 be jam-packed ⟪with⟫ ; be crowded ⟪with⟫ // 구경꾼이 집을 빽 둘러쌌다 The house is thickly surrounded by a crowd.

빽빽 [새소리] peep, peep ; [신호 소리] bleep, bleep ¶ 빽빽 울다 cheep ; peep ; chirp ; pipe (어린애가)

빽빽이 packed ; compact(ly) ; tight(ly) ; thick(ly) ; dense(ly) ¶ 소나무가 빽빽이 나다 Pine trees grow densely. // 집들이 빽빽이 들어서다 Houses stand close together. // 그 방에 사람들이 빽빽이 찼다 The room is packed with people.

빽빽하다 ① [촘촘하다] (be) close 〔dense, thick〕 ; closely packed (가득차다) ¶ 빽빽하게 closely ; thickly ; densely ; tightly〔to the full〕 (가득차게) // 빽빽하게 짜인 일정 closely-packed schedule // 빽빽하게 우거지다 grow thick 〔densely〕 // 빽빽하게 채워 넣다 cram ; pack closely ; fill to the full // 복도에 사람들이 빽빽하게 들어서 있다 The hall is crowded with people.
② (갑갑하다) ¶ 코가 빽빽하다 My nose is clogged〔stuffy〕.
③ [소견이 좁다] (be) fussy〔finical, narrow-minded〕 ¶ 그는 빽빽한 사람이다 He is a narrow-minded person.

뻐근하다 ① [몸이] feel heavy〔stiff〕 ; grow stiff ; have a dull pain ¶ 가슴이 뻐근하다 feel heavy in the chest // 어깨가 뻐근하다 feel stiff in the shoulders ; have a stiff shoulder ; one's shoulders grow stiff
② [일이] (be) hard ; tiring ; exhausting ; back-breaking

뻐끔하다 (be) cracked ; be split apart ¶ 입을 뻐끔히 벌리다 open one's mouth wide ; gape

뻐기다 [잘난 체하다] put on airs ; give oneself airs ; be haughty ; be overbearing ¶ 뻐기며 haughtily ; overbearingly // 동료에게 잘난 체하고 뻐기다 put on airs with one's equals // 몹시 뻐기다 throw one's weight around // 뻐기며 다니다 swagger ; strut // 그건 뻐길 일이 못된다 That's nothing to be proud of.

뻐덕뻐덕 —하다 be dried out stiff〔hard〕 ¶ 가죽이 뻐덕뻐덕하다 The leather is stiff. // 배를 저어서 손이 뻐덕뻐덕하다 My hands feel hard〔stiff〕 from rowing.

†뻔뻔하다 (be) brazen-faced〔shameless, impudent, cheeky, audacious〕 ¶ 뻔뻔하게 impudently ; audaciously ; shamelessly // 뻔뻔한 놈 a cheeky〔brazen-faced〕 fellow // 뻔뻔스럽게도 …하다 He has the face〔cheek, front〕 to ⟪do⟫ // 뻔뻔스러운 부탁입니다만 돈을 빌려 주실 수 없겠습니까 I am afraid it is asking too much, but would you mind lending me some money? // 뻔뻔하기 짝이 없군 Well, what cheek!

뻔하다 ① [분명] (be) clear ; evident ; obvious ; distinct ; unquestionable ; plain ¶ 뻔한 사실 an obvious fact ; the plain truth // 뻔한 거짓말 palpable lies // 그가 실패한다는 것은 뻔한 일이다 It is obvious that he will fail.
② [까딱하면 그렇게 될 형편이었으나 결국 그렇게 되지 않았음] be〔come, go〕 near ⟪doing⟫ ; almost ; nearly ; just barely escape ⟪doing⟫ ¶ 차에 부딪칠 뻔하다 almost hit a motor car ; come near being run over // 물에 빠질 뻔했다 I came near being drowned. /I was nearly drowned. // 죽을 뻔했다 I was nearly dead. /I was very close to death. /I had a close call〔shave〕. /I thought I'd die. // 그는 못 갈 뻔했다 He nearly didn't go. // 갈뻔했다 He almost went. // 하마터면 집사람 생일을 잊어먹을 뻔했다 I almost forgot my wife's birthday. /I came very close to forgetting my wife's birthday.

뻗장다리 ⇨ 벋장다리

뻗치다 [내밀다] stretch ; extend ; reach ; hold out ¶ 구조의 손을 뻗치다 give ⟪a person⟫ a helping hand // 손을 뻗쳐서 물건을 잡다 reach out for ⟪a thing⟫ ; hold〔stretch〕 out one's hand to take ⟪a thing⟫ // 세력을 뻗치다 extend one's power〔influence〕 // 세력이 해외로 뻗쳐 있다 His power extends beyond the seas.

뻣뻣하다 (be) straight ; stiff ⇨ 빳빳하다

뻣세다 (be) stiff and tough ; headstrong

뻥 ① [소리] bang ; pop ¶ 뻥하고 with a pop // 샴페인을 뻥뻥 터뜨리다 uncork one bottle of champagne after another // 병마개가 뻥 튀다 The cork pops. ② [구멍이] ¶ 뻥 뚫어지다 break open ③ [뻥짜] a flat failure ; a fiasco ④ [거짓] a lie ; an invention ; a falsehood

뻥그레 ⇨ 방그레

뻥나다 be disclosed〔exposed, divulged〕 ; be brought to light ; come out ; be ruined〔spoiled〕 ¶ 그 일이 뻥났다 Everybody got wind of the matter. / The thing was ruined.

뻥놓다 reveal ; divulge ; let out ; disclose ; expose ; lay bare ; ruin ; spoil ¶ 이 일을 아무한테도 뻥놓지 마라 This is secret. /Don't tell it to anybody.

뻥뻥 [소리] popping and popping ; with explosion after explosion ; [구멍] with hole after hole ; gaping and gaping

뻥뻥하다 be perplexed〔puzzled, bewildered〕 ; be at a loss ¶ 문제가 어려워서 뻥뻥했다 I was quite overwhelmed by the examination questions.

뻥뻥히 puzzled ; at a loss

뻥짜 a defective ; useless thing

†뼈 ① [골] a bone (동물의) ; a rib (갈비) ; ashes (유골) ¶ 뼈가 많은 고기 a bony fish // 뼈 속까지 to the bone (marrow) // 뼈까지 갉아먹다 [착취] exploit ⟪a per-

son》; bleed 《a person》 white // 뼈를 잇다 set the bone // 뼈를 바르다 bone 《a fish, a chicken》 // 이국 땅에 뼈를 묻다 die in a foreign land // 뼈와 가죽만 남았다 He is all skin and bone. /He is a mere skeleton〔bag of bones〕.
② [핵심] the gist; the substance 〔pith〕; main points; essential parts ¶ 뼈만 추려서 설명하다 give a gist 《of》; set forth the essential parts 《of》
③ [저의] an implication; a hidden meaning; the connotation ¶ 뼈 있는 말 words full of hidden〔latent〕 meaning; suggestive words
④ [기골] backbone; guts; mettle; spirit; grit 《미》 ¶ 뼈 있는 사람 a man of spirit // 뼈 없이 좋은 사람 a simple-minded〔credulous, good-natured〕 person; an easy mark 《미·속》

뼈고도리 a bone arrowhead

뼈끝 ① [끝] the tip of a joint (of a bone) ② [고기] flesh over the bone

뼈다귀 a bone ¶ 생선을 뼈다귀채 먹다 eat the fish, bone and all

†**뼈대** frame; build; physique ¶ 뼈대가 단단한 사람 a man of stout〔sturdy〕 build // 우산 뼈대 an umbrella rib; a frame of an umbrella // 뼈대가 굵은 bony; large-boned // 뼈대가 굵어지다 grow bony; [자라다] be brought up; be bred // 뼈대가 작다 one has a small frame

뼈들다 ① [일이] be hard and linger; be difficult and endless ② [손장난] play 〔fool, fiddle〕 around with a tool

뼈들어지다 do not cut well; become dull

뼈뜯이 tough meat torn from the bone

뼈마디 the joint of a bone; joints ¶ 뼈마디가 시다 have sore joints // 뼈마디가 아프다 I feel an ache in my joints.

뼈물다 [옷치장하다] dress up; be gaily dressed; [성내다] be touchy〔irritable〕; lose one's temper readily; [벼르다] plan; lay one's plan; intend; contemplate; be determined to

뼈붙이 things made of bone; boneware

뼈빠지다 (be) backbreaking; keep〔put〕 one's nose to the grindstone ¶ 가게가 전소되어 10년간 뼈빠지게 일한 것이 헛수고가 되었다 The fire gutted my store sending my 10 years' backbreaking work down the drain.

뼈저리다 cut to the heart; pierce deeply into one's mind ¶ 상호 협력의 필요성을 뼈저리게 느끼다 feel〔realize〕 keenly the necessity of mutual aid // 그의 비난은 뼈저린다 His reproach cuts me to the heart. // 7회말의 실수가 뼈저린 것이었다 That error in the bottom of the seventh really hurt. // 뼈저린 경험을 맛보지 않으면 깨닫지 못 할 것이다 He won't learn unless he has a few painful experiences.

뼈지다 [말이 여무지다] (be) sharp; pithy; piquant; [속이] solid ¶ 그 떡이 뼈지다 That rice cake is quite solid. // 그의 말은 뼈지다 His speech cuts to the quick.

뼘[1] stuffing material (such as cloth or paper used to tighten a loose stopper); a filler

⁑**뼘**[2] a span; the span of a hand ¶ 뼘으로 재다 span 《length》

뼘다 span 《length》; measure by the span ¶ 그 길이가 뼘어서 두자다 The length spans at two feet.

뼘들이로 one after another; in quick succession; consecutively

뼛성내다 get〔fall, fly〕 into a passion; flare up (in anger); fly into a rage; burn up

뽀뽀 Kiss-kiss! /Give us a kiss!

†**뽐내다** [체하다] affect; assume〔put on〕 airs; give oneself airs; pose 《as》; [자랑하다] boast; be proud 《of, that》; take pride 《in》; be overbearing〔haughty〕 ¶ 뽐내며 걷다 walk affectedly; swagger // 잘난 체하고 뽐내다 fancy oneself (a) something // 요리 솜씨를 뽐낸다 She prides herself on her cooking.

⁑**뽑다** ① [빼내다] pull out〔up〕; take out; draw (칼, 권총을); extract〔pull out〕 (이를) ¶ 권총을 뽑다 draw a pistol // 이를 뽑다 pull out〔extract〕 a tooth // 잡초를 뽑다 pull up weeds; weed 《a garden》 // 제비를 뽑다 cast〔draw〕 lots; draw // 탄환을 뽑아내다 remove〔extract〕 a bullet // 나는 사랑니를 뽑아서 부기가 가라앉을 때까지 외출하고 싶지 않다 I had my wisdom tooth pulled and don't want to go out until the swelling goes down.
② [가려내다] select; pick out; single out; elect (선거)
③ [모집하다] receive applicants for; book; recruit〔enlist〕 《troops》 (병사를)

-뽑이 a puller〔pincer, claw〕 for ¶ 못뽑이 a nail claw // 마개뽑이 a corkscrew

뽑히다 ① [빠지다] be taken out; be pulled out; come off ¶ 못이 쉽게 뽑힌다 The nail comes out easily. ② [선발] be singled out; be admitted; be allowed to enlist ¶ 축구 선수로 뽑히다 be singled out as a football player // 국회 의원으로 뽑히다 be elected to the National Assembly

뽕[1] 『식물』 a mulberry (leaf)

뽕[2] 《breaking wind; farting》 with a boo 〔poop〕 ⇨ 봉 ①

뽕나다 be disclosed〔divulged〕; be brought to light

***뽕나무** a mulberry tree
—**밭** a mulberry field〔plantation〕 — **열매** a mulberry

뽕놓다 disclose; reveal; divulge; expose

뽕빠지다 sustain〔suffer〕 a heavy loss; go into bankruptcy; fail; go bankrupt; be broke; have a hard time ¶ 결혼 잔치 차리기에 나는 뽕빠졌다 I am broke after giving the wedding reception. // 그 여자와 자주 교제하면 너 뽕빠진다 You will go broke if you date her so often. // 시험 치르기에 나는 뽕빠졌다 I'm done in from exams.

뽕뽕 ⇨ 붕붕

뽕잎 mulberry leaves ¶ 뽕잎을 따다 pick mulberry leaves

뾰로통하다 pout; (be) sulky ¶ 그 아이는 조금만 야단쳐도 뾰로통해진다 The boy gets sulky at the slightest scolding.

뾰롱뾰롱 **—하다** (be) ill-tempered; crossgrained

뾰루지 a pimple; a boil; a tumor ¶ 얼굴에 뾰루지가 나다 pimples break out on one's cheeks

뾰조록이 sticking out a bit

뾰조록하다 stick out a bit

뾰족구두 shoes with pointed toes

뾰족뾰족 **—하다** (be) all pointed

뾰족이 ⇨ 뾰조록이

뾰족집 a building which has a spire 〔steeple〕; a Catholic church

뾰족탑 —塔 a steeple; a spire; a pinnacle

†**뾰족하다** (be) pointed; sharp ¶ 뾰족한 머리 a peaked head // 뾰족한 코 a hawk 〔sharp〕 nose // 끝이 뾰족하다 be pointed at the end // 뾰족하게 하다 sharpen // 입을 뾰족하게 내밀다 purse up one's lips // 손가락이 뾰족하다 have tapered fingers

뿌그르르 ⇨ 바그르르

뿌다구니, 뿌다귀 [돌출부] a projecting part〔corner〕; a protrusion; a salient (part)

뿌두둑 ⇨ 부드득, 뿌드득

뿌드드하다 ⇨ 부드드하다

†**뿌리** ① [식물의] a root; [부스러기의] a nucleus; [밑동] the root〔base〕 ¶ 이 뿌리 the root of a tooth // 땅 속에 뿌리 내리다 take root in the ground // 뿌리째 파내다 dig 《a tree》 up roots and all // 뿌리 박고 싹이 터서 잎을 냈다 They took root, sprouted and sent forth leaves. // 그 개나리 가지는 벌써 뿌리가 붙었다 The forsythia branch has already struck root. ② [근본] the root; the cause〔origin, source〕; the bottom ¶ 질병의 뿌리 the cause of a disease // 뿌리 깊은 반일 감정 a deep-rooted anti-Japanese sentiment // 뿌리 뽑다 root up; eradicate; eliminate entirely // 사건의 뿌리를 캐다 probe a case to the bottom; dig into the bottom of a case

—등걸 a stump; a stub; a grub 《미》 **—접**(接) root-grafting **—혹** a (root) tubercle

뿌리 없는 나무에 잎이 필까 속담 No root, no fruit.

†**뿌리다** ① [비 따위가] drive; be driven 〔blown〕 into; blow〔sweep〕 in〔into〕 《the room》 ¶ 빗방울이 방안으로 뿌리었다 The rain swept into the room. // 지금 뿌린 향수는 뭐죠 What's that perfume you're wearing? ② [끼얹다] sprinkle; spray; scatter; throw about; strew 《with》 ¶ 돈을 뿌리다 spend money freely; make money fly // 모래를 뿌리다 sprinkle sands 《over》 // 씨를 뿌리다 sow seed // 그를 의과 대학에 입학시키기 위해 그의 부모가 많은 돈을 뿌렸다는 이야기를 들었다 I've heard it said that his parents spread around a lot of cash to get him into medical school.

뿌리치다 shake off; disengage oneself from 《a person's grasp》; [만류·권고를] turn a deaf ear 《to》; refuse; reject; turn down ¶ 뿌리치고 도망가다 tear oneself away 《from a person's grasp》 // 손목을 뿌리치다 shake off 《a person's》 hand // 유혹을 뿌리치다 thrust temptation away

뿌예지다 ⇨ 부예지다

뿌장구 a projecting piece; a projection; a sharp edge

뿌지지, 뿌지직 ⇨ 바지지

뿐 only; alone; merely ¶ 뿐만 아니라 besides; moreover; in addition; what is more // 갖고 있는 것이라고는 이것 뿐이다 This is all I have. // 그는 가난할 뿐만 아니라 몸도 허약하다 He is not only poor but sickly. // 아는 것이라고는 그것뿐이다 I know no more than that. // 나는 내 의무를 다했을 뿐이다 I have done nothing but my duty. // 그는 학자일 뿐만 아니라 시인이기도 하다 He is a poet as well as a scholar. // 믿을 사람은 너뿐이다 I have no one but you to rely upon.

-뿐더러 not only... but (also); as well as

뿐만 nothing but; only ⇨ 뿐

†**뿔** a horn; an antler (사슴의); a feeler (촉각) ¶ 뿔 세공 hornwork // 뿔로 받다 horn; gore

뿔이 돋다 관용 get angry

뿔관자 —貫子 a horn clasp for a chinstrap

뿔끈 ⇨ 불끈

뿔매 『새』 a Korean hawk-eagle

뿔뿔이 scattered; in all directions; separately ¶ 뿔뿔이 흩어지다 be scattered; disperse; break up // 가족이 뿔뿔이 헤어졌다 The family broke up. // 그들은 순경을 보자 뿔뿔이 흩어졌다 They scattered in all directions when they saw the policeman.

뿔싸움 horning each other (황소 따위)

뿔잔 —盞 a horn chalice

뿜다 [액체를] spout; spurt; gush out; burst; [연기·불을] belch 《smoke》; shoot up; [방출하다] emit ¶ 검은 연기를 뿜다 belch〔send〕 up black smoke // 고래가 물을 뿜다 The whale spouts (water). // 분수가 물을 뿜고 있다 The fountain is playing.

뿡 ⇨ 붕 ①

뿡뿡 with a poop-poop! ¶ 뿡뿡 소리내다 honk; hoot // 뿡뿡 경적을 울리며 달리다 run honking

뿌루퉁하다 ⇨ 뾰로통하다
뿌주룩이 ⇨ 뾰조록이
삐걱빼각 creaking and squeaking
삐걱삐걱 creaking ; squeaking
삐꾸러지다 ⇨ 비꾸러지다
삐다[1] [물이] subside ; drain 《away, off》 ; go down
***삐다**[2] [뼈를] break ; sprain ; dislocate ¶ 발목을 삐다 sprain one's ankle
삐대다 put 《a person》 to trouble ; bother ; annoy ; embarrass
†**삐라** a (hand) bill ; a leaflet ; a placard 〔poster〕 (벽보) ¶ 삐라를 뿌리다 distribute leaflets // 삐라를 붙이다 put up 〔stick〕 a bill ; post a placard
삐삐[1] gaunt ; haggard ¶ 삐삐 마른 사람 a living skeleton ; a mere shadow // 삐삐 마르다 be gaunt-looking ; be haggard ; be worn to a shadow
삐삐[2] screeching ; bawling ¶ 삐삐 울다 squall
삐삐[3] beeper ¶ 급하시면 삐삐로 불러 보시지요 If it's urgent, you may wish to call him through his beeper.
삐쭉 ⇨ 비쭉
삐치다[1] [삐침획을] draw a downward left-hand stroke
삐치다[2] ① [기운이 빠지다] become languid〔tired, weary, enervated〕 ② [토라지다] become〔turn〕 sulky
삑 [배게 들어선 모양] thickly ; densely ; [소리] with a whistle ; whistling
삑삑하다 (be) close ⇨ 빽빽하다
삑삑하다 (be) close ⇨ 빽빽하다
삘기살 beef shank
삥삥매다 bustle about ; go about busily ; be at a loss 《what to do》 ; be perplexed

사[1] stitching a buttonhole ; buttonhole stitching ; hem-stitching ¶ 사를 뜨다 stitch a buttonhole ; cross-stitch ; hem-stitch

사[2] 〖음악〗 sol ; G ¶ 올림 사조 G sharp《G#》∥내림 사조 G flat《G♭》∥사음 기호 a G clef

사 士 [사람] an officer ; a gentleman ; a figure ; [장기에서] a chessman in Korean chess

사 巳 [십이지의] the Sign of the Snake〔Serpent〕; [방향] the Direction of the Snake《Southeast-by-South》; [시간] the watch of the Snake《the period between 9 and 11 a. m.》

†**사 四** four ; [제4] the fourth ¶ 사분의 일 one quarter ; one fourth∥사 배 하 다 increase fourfold ; quadruple
—배 four times ; fourfold ; quadruple **—차원** 〖수학〗 the fourth dimension **제—종 우편물** fourth-class matter

사 死 death ⇨ 죽음

사 寺 a temple ; a shrine

사 私 [공에 대한] privateness ; self ; being personal ; [정실] favoritism ; partiality ; [비밀] secret ; privacy ¶ 사적인 private ; personal ; confidential∥사가 있는 selfish ; self-interested∥사를 두다 show favoritism ; play favorites
—경제 private〔individual〕 enterprise〔management〕

사 邪 [부정] wrong ; injustice ; unrighteousness ; [사악] evil ; vice ; heterodox ; [악의] malice ; spite ¶ 사는 정(正)을 이기지 못한다 Wrong cannot prevail over right.

사 社 [회사] a company ; a corporation《미》; [상회] a firm ; [사무소] an office ; [결사] an association ; a society ¶ 사의 일은 바쁩니까 Are you busy at your office ?

사 赦 pardon ; clemency ; leniency ; indulgence **—하다** pardon ; forgive ; absolve ; discharge ; grant clemency〔leniency〕 to《a person》

사 詞 [말] a written word ; a phrase ; a term ; a word ; a part of speech
명— a noun **형용—** an adjective

사 紗 thin silk ; gauze ; gossamer

사 辭 [인사] an address ; a speech ; a message
고별— a parting〔farewell〕 address **송별—** a farewell speech **취임—** an inauguration speech **환영—** a welcoming address

-사 史 history ; the annals ; chronicles (연대기)
한국— Korean history ; the history of Korea ; [서적] a history of Korea **현대〔근세, 상고〕—** contemporary〔modern, ancient〕 history

-사 事 fact
관심— a matter of interest ; a (matter of) concern

사가 史家 a(n) historian ; a chronicler

사가 私家 a private house〔residence〕; one's (private) home

사각 四角 a square ; a rectangular〔quadrangular〕 thing ; (having) four corners ¶ 사각이다 It is square〔four-cornered〕.
— 너트〔볼트〕 〖공학〗 a square nut〔square-headed bolt〕 **—주** a square pillar〔pole, column〕 **—추(錐)** 〖기하〗 a quadrangular pyramid **—형** a quadrangle ; a square ; a tetragon

사각

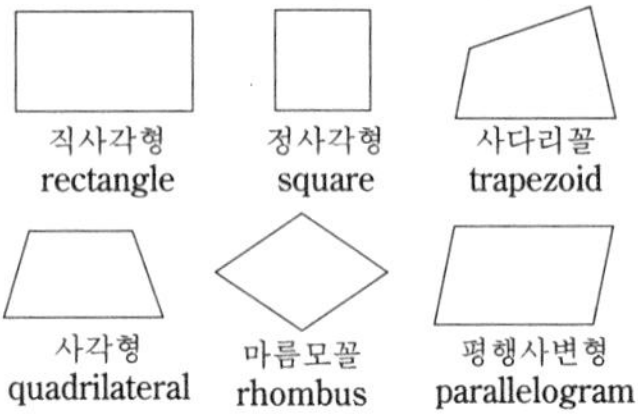

사각 死角 〖군사〗 the dead angle〔ground〕 of a gun

사각 射角 an angle of fire ; an elevation

사각 斜角 〖기하〗 an oblique angle ; a bevel

사각거리다 crunch ; be crisp〔crunchy〕 to the teeth ¶ 사과가 사각거린다 The apple munches with a crisp crunch.

사각 모자 四角帽子 a square-shaped cap ; a mortarboard ; a square college cap

사각사각 with a crunch ; crisply

사갈 spiked wooden shoes

사갈 蛇蝎 [뱀과 전갈] snakes and scorpions ; [사람] a malignant person

사감 私感 spite ; grudge ; resentment ; malice ; a bitter feeling ; rancor ¶ 사감을 갖다 bear〔owe〕《a person》 a spite ; have a spite against《a person》; harbor〔nurse〕 a grudge∥나는 자네에게는 아무런 사감도 없네 I don't bear any malice towards you.

사감 舍監 a dormitory dean ; a dormitory inspector〔superintendent〕; the supervisor of a dormitory ; [여자] a housemother ; a dormitory matron
사개 a dovetail (joint) ; 〖건축〗 pillar tenons ¶ 사개를 물리다 dovetail ; make a dovetail
— 다리 legs on the corners of a box **— 통** a dovetail at the top of a pillar
사거 死去 death ; decease ; demise ; passing (away) **—하다** die ; pass away ; decease ; expire ; breathe one's last
사거리 四— a crossroads ; four corners
†**사건 事件** [큰 사건] an event ; [사소한] an incident ; [일] an affair ; a matter ; a business ; [사고] an accident ; a mishap ; [우연의] a happening ; [법률상의] a case ; [음모] a plot ; a conspiracy ; [분규] a trouble ; a disturbance ; [추문] a scandal ¶ 역사상의 획기적 사건 the epoch-making events of history // 여행 중에 있었던 사건 an incident on〔of〕 the journey // 곧 잊혀지는 사건 a nine days' wonder // 이상한 사건 a mystery ; a wonderful occurrence // 극적 사건 a dramatic incident // 사회적 사건 a social event // (큰) 추문 사건 a (grave) scandal // 사건을 맡다 take an affair in one's hand // 일어난 사건에 대해서는 잠자코 있는 것이 좋다 You'd better be silent about what happened. // 그는 그 사건에 관련되어 있다 He is involved in the case. // 저 변호사는 많은 사건을 맡고 있다 The lawyer〔barrister〕 has plenty of briefs. // 그 사건은 미궁에 빠져 버렸다 The case has been wrapped in mystery. // 그 사건은 흐지부지되어 버렸다 The affair has been covered up. // 경관이 그 사건의 개략을 말했다 The policeman outlined the event.
사기 — a fraud case **살인 —** a murder case **소송 —** a lawsuit **수회 —** a bribery case **연애 —** a love affair
†**사격 射擊** firing ; shooting ; gunshot ; [사격술] marksmanship **—하다** shoot ; fire at 《a person》 ; fire on 《a fortress》 ¶ 사격의 명수 a crack shot // 소총 사격을 받다 be fired on by a rifle
— 경기회 a shooting match ; a rifle meeting **— 교련** rifle drill ; musketry instruction **— 대회** a rifle meeting **—술** marksmanship **— 신호** a shooting signal **— 연습** field firing ; battle practice **—장** a field〔ground〕 for shooting ; a shooting range〔gallery〕 **— 중지** firing halt **— 지휘** fire direction〔control〕 **각개 —** independent firing **간접 —** indirect fire **공격 준비 —** 〖군사〗 preparation ; preparatory fire **유효 —** effective fire **실탄 —** firing〔target practice〕 with live shells〔bullets〕 **일제 —** a volley (of bullets) **조총(弔銃) — 부대** a firing party〔squad〕 (군대 장례·사형 집행 때의)

사격전 射擊戰 an exchange of fire〔shots〕; a gun fight ¶ 사격전을 벌이다 fight a gun battle 《with》 ; exchange fire〔shots〕《with》
사견 私見 one's personal〔private〕 opinion〔view〕; one's personal point of view ¶ 저의 사견으로는 in my personal opinion ; it seems likely to me 《that》 // 그 사건에 대해서는 그는 사견을 제시했다 He presented his personal view of the affair. // 대통령은 군비 축소 문제에 대하여 사견을 털어 놓았다 The president outlined his personal views on the subject of disarmament.
사견 邪見 heretical views ; a wrong idea
사경 四更 the small〔wee〕 hours (of the morning) ; one to three o'clock in the morning
—추(니) an early cock (crowing)
사경 死境 the brink of death ; a deadly situation ; the gates of death ; miserable circumstances ; a piteous plight ; a deadly pass ¶ 사경에 처하다 be at the brink of death ; be placed in a miserable plight ; fall into great straits // 사경을 벗어나다 be saved from the jaws of death // 사경을 극복하다 overcome〔tide over〕 the deadly situation ; get over a deadly pass
사경제 私經濟 private〔individual〕 economy
사경회 查經會 a Bible class
사계 四季 ① [계절] the four seasons ; [각 계절의] the last month of each season ¶ 사계 지불 quarterly payment // 사계의 변화 changes of the seasons // 사계에 따라 변하는 경치 seasonal changes in scenery // 사계를 통하여 all the year round ; throughout the year ② 〖식물〗 the Chinese rose ; Rosa chinensis (학명)
사계 斯界 this field〔line, world〕; the specific field〔walk〕; the subject ; the profession ¶ 사계의 권위자 an authority on the subject // 그는 사계에 공헌한 바가 크다 He rendered great service to the cause.
사계 射界 a field〔zone〕 of fire
사고 四顧 —하다 look around〔round〕
사고 社告 an announcement of a firm ; a public notice made by a commercial establishment ; an advertisement
†**사고 事故** [예기치 않은] an accident ; a hitch ; a mishap ; trouble ; [원인] reasons ; circumstances ¶ 피할 수 없는 사고 때문에 owing to unavoidable circumstances // 사고를 일으키다 cause an accident // 사고 없이 도착하다 arrive without mishap // 장래의 사고에 대비하다 prepare for future contingencies // 사고의 원인은 부주의이다 The cause of every mishap comes from carelessness. // 그는 자동차 사고로 죽었다 He was killed in the auto〔car, motoring〕 accident. // 그는 불시의 사고로 죽었다 He was killed by a

ㅅ

sudden accident. // 무슨 사고로 못 왔습니까 What kept you from coming? // 나도 오늘 사고를 당했다 I was involved in an accident myself today. // 이제부터는 이런 사고가 다시 생기지 않도록 단단히 주의하겠습니다 I'll be very careful not to let this sort of slip-up happen again.
— 뭉치 a troublemaker; a troublebox; a jinx — 방지 운동 a "Safety First" movement; a movement for accident prevention —사(死) an accidental death 교통 — a traffic accident〔mishap〕 도난 — a robbery〔theft〕 case 여객기 — the crash of a passenger plane 자동차 — a car accident 철도 — a railroad mishap〔calamity〕

*사고 思考 thought; consideration; contemplation; speculation —하다 think; consider; speculate; conceive; reflect; cogitate
— 과정〔작용〕 a process of thinking; a thought process —력 thinking power; contemplative faculty — 방식 a way of thinking — 장애 〖의학〗 thinking disturbance — 중추 [뇌의] the ideation center 수평〔수직〕 — lateral〔vertical〕 thinking

사고 무친 四顧無親 —하다 have no one to turn〔look〕 to; be thrown upon the world

사곡 私穀 private grain; privately owned grains〔cereals〕

사곡 邪曲 crookedness; wickedness; craftiness; viciousness; evil-mindedness
—하다 (be) crooked; wicked; evil-minded; crafty; distorted

사골 四骨 the bones of the four legs of a cow〔bull〕

사공 沙工 a boatman; a rower; an oarsman; a ferryman
사공이 많으면 배가 산으로 올라간다 〔속담〕 Too many cooks spoil the broth.

†사과 沙果 an apple ¶ 속이 썩은 사과 an apple rotten at the core // 사과 파는 여자 an apple wife〔woman〕 // 새빨간 사과 a red-cheeked apple // 사과를 깎다 pare an apple
— 나무 an apple tree —산 malic acid —주 apple wine — 참외 a kind of cantaloup(e) — 화채 a punch made of chopped apple soaked in honey 인도 — a white winter pearmain

사과 絲瓜 〖식물〗 a sponge〔towel〕 gourd

‡사과 謝過 an apology —하다 apologize; make〔offer〕 an apology; beg 《a person's》 pardon ¶ 잘못을 사과하다 acknowledge oneself in the wrong; acknowledge one's fault // 실례를 사과하다 apologize to 《a person》 for one's rudeness // 사과를 받아들이다 accept 《a person's》 apology 《for his carelessness》 // 내가 한 일을 사과합니다 I apologize for what I did. // 당신에게 사과할 것이 있습니다 I owe you an apology. // 그가 사과함으로써 원만히 수습되었다 An apology on his part settled the quarrel amicably. // 이것은 사과한대서 끝나는 일이 아니다 This isn't something that can be written off with an apology. // 사과를 받을 사람은 나다 I'm the one who should receive an apology.
—장 a written apology — 편지 a letter of apology ☞ 《p. 1095》

사과탕 四—湯 beef soup made of lungs, tail, heel of round, and foreshank

사관 士官 an officer; a commissioned officer ¶ 육군〔해군, 공군〕 사관 학교 a military〔a naval, an air-force〕 academy
—실 the officers' quarters; [해군] a wardroom — 후보생〔생도〕 a cadet〔officer〕; a gentleman cadet 《영》; [육군] a military cadet; [해군] a midshipman; a naval cadet; [공군] an air-force〔aviation〕 cadet

사관 史觀 a historical view
유물 — the materialistic view of history
유심 — the idealistic view of history

사관 史官 a historiographer; a chronicler

사광 砂鑛 a placer mine; an alluvial gold mine

사교 司教 a bishop; a pontiff
—관(冠) a miter — 관구 a diocese; a bishopric; a see (대사교 관구에도 사용) — 교서 a pastorale — 대리 a commissary — 제도 episcopacy —주의 Episcopalianism

†사교 社交 social intercourse〔life〕; social gathering〔meeting, fellowship〕; society ¶ 사교적인 sociable; social // 그녀는 사교에 아주 능하다 She is quite a sociable woman.
—가 a sociable person; a good mixer 《미·속》 —계 society; social circles ¶ 사교계 사람들 society folk // 사교계에서 유명한 부인 a woman of social prominence; a woman of prominence in social circles // 사교계의 꽃 the queen of society // 사교계에서 성공하다 make〔be〕 a social success // 사교계에 나가다 make one's debut in society —란 a society column —복 party clothes; [여자용] an evening dress —성 sociality; sociability ¶ 그는 사교성이 아주 없다 He lacks sociability. /He has nothing of sociability in him. —술 the art of social intercourse —실 a social hall — 예의 social etiquette〔manners〕 —춤〔댄스〕 a social dance ¶ 사교춤을 배우다 take lessons in social dancing — 클럽 a social〔fashionable〕 club; a sorority (여학생의) 《미》

사교 私交 private intercourse

사교 邪教 heresy; a heretical〔perversive, false〕 creed; evil doctrines; heathenism; paganism; gentilism; a cult
—국 heathendom; pagandom; gentiledom —도 a heretic; a pagan; a gentile; a heathen

사 과

① 사과의 표현

상대방에게 몸을 부딪치거나 실수로 발을 밟았을 때 등의 평범한 실수를 했을 때 또는 남이 줄 서 있는 곳이나 앞을 지나 갈 때,「미안합니다, 용서하십시오, 실례합니다」를 표현할 때 Oh, I'm (very, really, terribly) sorry... ! / Sorry for[about].... / Excuse me (for....) / Pardon me (for...) / I beg your pardon (for....) 등의 표현을 쓴다.

미국에서는 Excuse me.쪽의 표현을 쓰는 것이 보통이고 영국에서는 I'm sorry.를 쓴다. (I'm을 생략하여 Sorry.라고 하기도 한다.) Pardon me.는 영·미 공통으로 많이 쓰이는데 다소 정중한 표현이다.

주체가 복수일 경우에는 Excuse us 로 한다. Please excuse my hat은 「모자 쓰고 있는 것을 양해하여 주십시오」의 뜻이 된다.

사과의 표현은 악센트의 위치에 따라서 의미가 틀려진다. Excúse me. / Párdon me.는 가벼운 사죄의 뜻이나 Excúse mé. / Párdon mé는 사죄의 뜻이 보다 강해진다. me만을 강조하면 「저야말로 죄송합니다」의 뜻이 된다.

¶ 잠깐 실례합니다 Excuse me for a moment. // 늦어서 죄송합니다. I'm sorry I'm late. / Sorry I'm a bit late. / I must apologize for being late // 기다리게 해서 죄송합니다. I'm sorry I've [to have] kept you waiting. // 장갑을 끼고 있는 것을 양해하여 주십시오. Please excuse my gloves. // (옷차림이) 이런 모습이어서 죄송합니다. Please excuse my appearance. // 미안하지만 역으로 가려면 어디로 가면 될까요? Excuse me, but how can I get to the station? // 대화도중에 미안합니다. I'm sorry to interrupt you. // 자주 방해를 끼쳐서 죄송합니다. I'm sorry to trouble you so often. // 정말 그럴 뜻은 없었습니다. I didn't really mean that at all. // 내가 그런 말을 하다니 대단히 경솔했습니다. It was utterly thoughtless of me to say a thing like that. // 지연된 데 대하여 심심한 사과의 뜻을 표합니다. We must express our deep [deep-felt] regret for the delay.

② 응답

상대방의 가벼운 실수에 대하여 「괜찮습니다, 천만에요, 관계없습니다」 등과 같이 사과에 대한 응답의 표현으로는 That's all right. / That's OK.가 가장 일반적인 표현이다. (★ Excuse me. / Pardon me. / I'm sorry. 에 대한 구어적인 답변) 이외에 Forget it. / Not at all. / Please don't worry. / It doesn't matter at all. / Not to worry.등의 표현을 쓸 수 있다. 또 Excuse me. / Pardon me.가 「실례합니다」의 뜻으로 쓰일 때의 답변은 Certainly. (★ 구어적인 대답은 All right. / OK.)

¶ 틀림없습니다. 염려마십시오. It's [That's] perfectly all right. Don't worry about it. // 사과하실 필요없습니다. 내 잘못입니다. Please don't apologize. It was my fault. [I was (the one) at fault.]

사구 砂丘 a (sand) dune ; a sand hill 〔pile〕; a down
—림 a forest on a sand dune
사구 四球 〖야구〗 four balls ; a walk ¶ 사구를 주다 give four balls // 연속 50회 무사구로 던지다 pitch 50 consecutive innings without issuing a base on balls // 사구로 리그 제 1위다 He leads the league in walks.
사구 死球 〖야구〗 a dead ball
사군자 士君子 a gentleman ; a man of honor ; a scholar ; a learned person ; a man of letters ; the literati
사군자 四君子 the Four Gracious plants 《plum, orchid, chrysanthemum and bamboo》; oriental painting of plum-blossoms, orchids, chrysanthemums and bamboos
사권 私權 〖법〗 a private right
사귀 邪鬼 a devil ; a demon ; an imp ; an evil spirit ; a fiend ; an evil genius ; a vampire
***사귀다** [친하게] make friends with ; strike up a friendship with ; go out with ; become a buddy with ; chum around with ; be one's pal ; [교제] cultivate 《a person》; associate with ; keep company with ; hang around〔about〕 with ; hold intercourse with ; mix〔mingle〕 with ¶ 사귀기 좋은 사람 a jolly fellow ; a congenial fellow ; a good mixer // 사귀기 어려운 사람 an odd ball ; an unattractive person ; a square // 좋은〔나쁜〕 사람들과 사귀다 keep good〔bad〕 company with // 남과 잘 사귀다 get acquainted with 《a person》 easily // 사귀기 어렵다 be hard to get acquainted with // 사귀고 보니 참 재미 있는 친구였다. I found him quite a jovial fellow. // 남편과는 얼마나 사귀다 결혼하셨습니까 How long did you go with your husband before you got married? // 너희 둘은 사귄 지 5년이 넘었다고 했지? You

ㅅ

two have been going together for over five years?

사귐 acquaintance; association; intercourse; relations; company

사귐성 sociability; affinity; affability; companionship ¶ 사귐성이 있다 be sociable; be congenial; be of congenial disposition // 사귐성이 없다 be uncongenial; be of incompatible temperament

사그라뜨리다 collapse; make 《a boil》 subside; let 《a thing》 wither

사그라지다 subside; recede; go down; wither; [썩어서] decompose; [녹아서] melt away; [종기 따위가] be resolved ¶ 뾰두라지가 사그라지다 A tumor collapses. // 불이 사그라지다 The fire burns low〔sinks〕. // 종기가 사그라지다 A swelling goes down.

사그랑이 a worn-out〔rotten〕 thing

사그랑주머니 a gimcrack; a trumpery; a gewgaw; a specious bargain

사극 史劇 a historical play〔drama〕

사근사근하다 ① [성질이] (be) amiable; agreeable; domicile; compliant; pleasant; sweet and gentle ¶ 사근사근하게 amiably; affably; pleasantly // 사근사근하게 대하다 make oneself agreeable to 《a person》 // 그 여자는 매우 사근사근한 사람이었다 I found his wife a hospitable woman. ② [먹기에] (be) fresh ¶ 이 배는 사근사근하다 The pear munches crisp.

ㅅ

사금 砂金 alluvial gold; gold dust ¶ 사금을 채집하다 wash for gold; pan〔gravel for〕 gold
— **지대** gold diggings — **채취** alluvial mining — **채취권** a placer mining right — **채취선** a placer (gold) mining boat

사금 賜金 a (government) grant of money in appreciation of one's services; a gift of money ¶ 일시 사금 5만원을 받다 be granted a sum of 50,000 *won*; be awarded with a grant of 50,000 *won* in appreciation of one's services

사금 謝金 remuneration; a fee; an honorarium; a tip

사금융 私金融 private loan ⇨ 사채(私債)

사금파리 broken pieces of chinaware; (porcelain) chips ¶ 사금파리에 손을 베다 cut one's hand on a broken piece of chinaware

***사기 士氣** morale; fighting〔martial〕 spirit ¶ 사기가 왕성하다 have high morale; be full of fighting spirit // 사기가 떨어지다 be〔become〕 demoralized // 사기를 고무하다 raise〔inspire〕 the morale // 사기에 영향을 끼치다 affect the morale // 군대는 사기와 전투력을 되찾았다 The army recovered its morale and fighting power. // 이 패전으로 사기가 완전히 떨어졌다 The defeat completely destroyed morale. // 전군의 사기는 매우 높다〔아주 떨어졌다〕 The morale of the whole army is very high〔low〕.

사기 史記 a history; a historical book〔work〕; a chronicle; the historical annals〔almanac〕

사기 死期 the hour〔time〕 of death; one's end〔time〕; the last hour ¶ 사기를 재촉하다 hurry〔hasten〕 one's death // 사기가 가깝다 His death〔end〕 is near. /His days are numbered.

사기 沙器 china; chinaware; earthenware; porcelain
— **그릇** ⇨ 사기(沙器) —**류** chinaware — **인형** a china doll —**전** a china store — **접시** a porcelain〔china〕 dish

사기 邪氣 [사심] malice; wickedness; an evil intention; [독기] pestilent〔noxious〕 vapor; malarial〔poisonous〕 air; miasma ¶ 사기가 있는 noxious; poisonous; malicious // 사기가 없는 innocent; harmless // 그는 사기가 없는 사람이다 He has no trace of malice in him.

사기 社旗 a flag with an emblem denoting a commercial firm

:사기 詐欺 swindle; cheat; deception; imposture; a confidence game —**하다** swindle; commit a fraud; defraud; impose ¶ 법률상의 사기 legal fraud // 대규모의 사기 an extensive swindle; a gigantic swindle // 교묘한 사기 very clever〔deliberate〕 fraud // 사기를 당하다 get swindled // 사기로 돈을 빼앗다 swindle 《a person》 out of his money; defraud 《a person》 of his money // 그는 작년에 나한테 100만원을 사기쳤다 He bilked me of one million *won* last year.
—**꾼** a swindler; a defrauder — **도박** fraudulent gambling — **수단** fraudulent means; jugglery; trickery —**죄** fraud; fake pretenses ¶ 사기죄에 걸리다 be accused of fraud — **취재** swindling — **투표** fraudulent voting — **행위** fraudulent practices **신용** — a confidence trick; a confidence game 《미》; a con game 《속》

사기업 私企業 〖경제〗 an individual〔a private〕 enterprise

사나나달 three or four〔four or five days〕; three〔four〕 days or so; the better part of a week

***사나이** [남자] a man; a male; the male sex; [남자다움] manhood; manliness; manly qualities ¶ 사나이 마음 man's heart // 사나이 중의 사나이 a man among men; a courageous man // 사나이의 a man's; masculine; male // 사나이다운 manly; manlike; manful // 사나이답게 manfully; in a manly way // 사나이답게 굴다 behave〔act〕 like a man; be a man; play the man // 네가 그보다 훨씬 사나이답다 You are much more of a man than he (is). // 사나이답잖은 짓이다 It is unworthy of a man.

사나토리움 a (T. B.) sanatorium; a sanitarium 《미》

사날[1] three or four days ; a few days ; several days

사날[2] one's own way ; willfulness ; selfishness ; having one's own way ; behaving as one pleases ¶ 무엇이든지 제 사날로 하다 have one's own way in everything // 그 여자는 사날이 너무 좋아서 못쓰겠다 She is no good—she always has to have her own way.

‡**사납다** (be) fierce ; rough ; violent ; wild ; ferocious ; run wild〔amuck〕; [운수가] (be) unlucky ; unfortunate ¶ 사나운 개 a fierce dog // 사나운 바다 a rough sea // 사나운 날씨 nasty weather // 사나운 짐승 a wild animal ; a fierce beast // 사나운 말 an unbroken horse // 사나운 사람 a rough ; a tough guy // 사나운 애 a rogue ; a rough child // 사나운 세상 the hard〔cruel〕 world // 사납게 fiercely ; roughly ; violently ; rudely ; wildly ; fero ciously // 성질이 사납다 have a violent temper // 마음씨가 사납다 be ungenerous〔harsh, bitter〕 // 운수가 사납다 have bad〔ill〕 luck ; be unlucky // 말버릇이 사납다 be rough in speech // 바다가 사납다 The sea is rough〔runs high〕.

사낭 砂囊 [모래의] a sandbag ; [날짐승의] a gizzard

사내 ① a man ⇨ 사나이 ② [남편] a husband

— **대장부** a man ; a great man (위인)

사내 社內 within〔in〕 the firm〔company, office〕

— **부채** internal liabilities — **유보** internal reserves — **일동** all the staff of a company

사내 寺內 the compound of a temple

사내아이 a boy〔child〕; a lad

사내 전화 社內電話 an (internal) office telephone system

— **번호** an extension number

사내종 a servant ; a manservant ; a retainer ; a follower ; a lackey ; a footman

†**사냥** hunting ; a hunt **—하다** hunt ¶ 사냥가다 go hunting ; go on a shooting expedition // 토끼 사냥가다 go on a hare hunt ; go rabbit-hunting // 여우 사냥하다 go fox-hunting // 코끼리 사냥가다 hunt ivory // 맹수를 사냥하다 hunt big game // 겨울에 말을 타고 사냥가다 hunt one's horse in winter

— **모자** a hunting cap ; a soft cap **—철** the hunting〔shooting〕 season ; an open season **—총** a hunting gun **맹수 —** big game hunting **총—** shooting ; hunting 《영》; a shoot **호랑이 —** tiger hunting 〔shooting〕

사냥감 game ; quarry ; a bag ; spoils 《of a chase》; winged game (새) ; big game (코끼리·호랑이 따위)

‡**사냥개** a hunting dog ; a hound

‡**사냥꾼** a hunter ; a huntsman

여우 — a fox-hunting man

사냥질 hunting ; shooting **—하다** hunt

여우 — fox-hunting

사냥터 a hunting ground〔field〕; a game preserve

사념 邪念 a vicious〔a depraved, an evil〕 mind ; a wicked intention ; evil thoughts ; [간계] a sinister design〔scheme〕 ¶ 사념 없는 마음 a heart innocent of evil ; godly thoughts ; a pious mind ; a noble heart // 사념에 빠지다 be wrapped in evil thoughts ; be seized〔possessed〕 with a vicious mind // 사념을 버리다 free oneself of evil thoughts

사념 思念 ⇨ 사려(思慮)

사농공상 士農工商 the traditional four classes of society 《scholars, farmers, artisans and tradesmen》

사느랗다, 싸느랗다 (be) chilly ⇨ 사늘하다

***사늘하다, 싸늘하다** [날씨가] (be) cool ; chilly ; icy ; [무섭다] be chilled ; feel a chill ; [태도가] (be) cool ; chilly ; distant

사니 沙泥 quicksand

†**사다** ① [구매] buy ; purchase ¶ 비싸게〔싸게〕 사다 buy dear〔cheap〕; make a good 〔bad〕 purchase // 물건을 외상으로 사다 buy a thing on credit // 물건을 월부로 사다 buy in monthly installments // 헐값에 사다 buy 《a thing》 at a dumping price ; buy 《a thing》 for a song // 잘 보지 않고 사다 buy a pig in a poke // 100원에 사다 buy 《a thing》 for 100 *won* // 현금으로 사다 buy for cash // 값이 너무 비싸서 못 사다 the price is beyond the reach of 《a person》 // 구두를 25,000원에 사다 buy a pair of shoes for 25,000 *won* // 그 여자는 오늘 새 모자를 샀다 She got a new hat today. // 자리를 확보하려거든 미리 표를 사두시오 If you want to be sure of a seat, you'd better get a ticket in advance. // 나로서 자동차는 도저히 살 수 없다 A car is beyond my purse. /I cannot afford to buy a car. // 지금 1,000원으로는 10년 전과 같은 것을 살 수 없다 A thousand *won* does not go so far today as it did ten years ago. // 행복은 돈으로 살 수 없다 Money cannot buy happiness. /Happiness cannot be bought with money. // 그는 월급을 책 사는 데 다 썼다 He spent all his salary on books. // 그것은 돈 주고도 못 산다 It cannot be bought for gold. // 그거 아주 싸게 샀다 It was a steal. /It was a read good buy. // 오늘은 제가 사겠습니다 I'm buying today. // 내가 술 한잔 사겠다 Have a drink on me. // 과장님이 모두에게 점심을 산다고 하신다 The boss says he's treating us all to lunch. // 정말 싸게 사셨네요 It was a real bargain. /It was a real good buy.

② [초래하다] incur ; invite ; bring 《a thing》 upon oneself ¶ 원한을 사다 incur

《a person's》 resentment〔hatred〕 // 분노를 사다 incur 《a person's》 anger ; offend 《a person》; lash 《a person》 into a fury // 환심을 사다 win〔gain〕 《a person's》 favor ; curry favor with 《a person》 // 아첨으로 환심을 사다 buy 《a person's》 patronage with flattery
③ [인정하다] appreciate ; give 《a person》 credit for ¶ 높이 사다 think highly of ; have a high opinion of 《a person》; have a high regard for 《a person》 // 그의 정직한 점을 사주다 appreciate his honesty ; give credit for his being honest // 우리는 그의 지력과 수완을 높이 산다 We have a high opinion of his intelligence and ability. // 그는 비서로서의 그 여자의 가치를 높이 사고 있다 He values her as a secretary.
④ [싸움을] ¶ 싸움을 사다 take up a quarrel ; accept a challenge
⑤ [여자를] ¶ 기생을 사다 engage〔call〕 a *kisaeng* girl

사다리 a ladder ⇨ 사닥다리
—차 [소방용] a (hook and) ladder truck ; an aerial ladder truck

사다리꼴 《기하》 a trapezoid ; [일반적으로] an echelon formation
— 회선망(回線網)〔굴착기, 준설기, 선〕 a ladder network〔excavator, dredge, track〕

ㅅ

사다새 《새》 a pelican

‡**사닥다리** a ladder ¶ 사닥다리를 올라가다 go up〔climb〕 a ladder // 사닥다리를 내려가다 go down〔step down〕 a ladder // 사닥다리를 놓다 set〔place〕 a ladder
비상 — an emergency ladder ; [화재용] a fire ladder ; a fire escape (비상계단) 줄 — a rope ladder — 층계 a staircase ; a flight of stairs

사단 社團 a corporation ; an association
— 법인 a corporate juridical person ; a corporation ; an incorporated body ; a corporation aggregate

사단 事端 the origin of an affair ; the cause of trouble ; beginning ; a trouble ; an incident ¶ 사단을 일으키다 stir up troubles ; give rise to complications

사단 師團 a (an army) division
—장 a division(al) commander — 사령부 the divisional headquarters 맹호 — the Tiger Division 백마 — the White Horse Division 상비 — a permanent division 수도 — the Capital Division

사담 史談 a historical tale〔story, narrative〕

사담 私談 a private talk〔conversation〕; a confidential talk —하다 talk privately ; have a private conversation with 《a person》

사답 私畓 a privately owned rice-field

사당 寺黨 a troupe of singing and dancing girls (in former days)

사당 私黨 a faction ; a cabal ; a sect

사당 祠堂 a (household) shrine ; an (ancestral) shrine ¶ 사당에 모시다 enshrine ; dedicate a shrine to 《a person》
— 치레 embellishment of a household shrine ; ostentation ; display

사대 collecting a suit ¶ 사대패를 모으다 collect in a suit // 사대로 모으다 collect in a suit

사대 私大 a private university〔college〕

사대 事大 submission〔subservience〕 to the stronger —하다 worship the powerful ; become a toady〔flunkey〕; serve the powerful
— 근성(根性) slavish submission to power —당 a toady〔flunkey〕 party ; trucklers — 사상 toadyism ; flunkeyism —주의 flunkeyism ; toadyism ; the worship of the powerful —주의자 a flunkey

사대문 四大門 the four main gates of old *Seoul*

사대 삭신 四大— ⇨ 사대 육신

사대 육신 四大六身 flesh and bones (of a human being) ; the whole body ; from head to foot ¶ 사대 육신이 아프다 I feel painful〔pain〕 in every joint. /My whole body aches.

사도 私道 a private road〔path〕

*****사도 使徒** an apostle ¶ 평화의 사도 an apostle of peace
— 신경 the apostolic creed ; the Apostles' Creed ; the Credo — 행전 the Acts of Apostles 십이 — the Twelve Apostles

사도 邪道 evil ways ; a wrong course ; vice ; heresy ; a heretical doctrine ¶ 사도에 빠지다 go astray〔wrong〕 // 그것은 사도이다 That's not a proper way of doing it.

사도 師道 the duty of teacher

사도 斯道 [유교 도덕] Confucian morality ; [이 분야] this subject ; this line ; this art ; this craft ; this profession ; this business

사도 士道 the code〔ideals〕 of a gentleman〔a Confucian scholar〕; gentlemanship

사돈 査頓 a relative〔relation〕 by marriage ; a matrimonial relation ; an inlaw 《미·구》 ¶ 사돈 관계를 맺다 get related by marriage 《to》; enter into matrimonial relation 《with》 // 너와 나는 이제 사돈간이야 You and I are now in-laws.
—댁 [사람] the wife of an in-law ; [집] an esteemed house〔family〕 of one's in-laws —집 a house〔family〕 of one's in-laws
사돈과 뒷간은 멀수록 좋다 [속담] Good fences make good neighbours.
사돈과 짐바리는 골라야 좋다 [속담] Like blood, like good, and like age, make the happiest marriage.
사돈의 팔촌 [관용] distant relatives

사동 使童 [사무실의] an errand〔office〕

boy ; a page ; a messenger (boy) ; [호텔의] a page (boy) ; a buttons 《영·속》 ; a bellboy 《미》 ; a bellhop 《미·구》

사동사 使動詞 〖문법〗 a causative verb

사동치마 四— a kite with four vertical color bands

사되다 私— (be) selfish ; self-interested ; partial

사두 마차 四頭馬車 a carriage〔coach〕 and four ; a carriage〔coach-〕and-four ; a four-horse coach〔carriage〕

사들이다 buy (in) ; purchase ; [상점이] store in ; stock in ; lay in ¶ 석탄을 대량으로 사들이다 lay in a large stock of coal

사등분 四等分 ¶ 사과를 사등분하다 divide an apple into four equal parts ; quarter an apple

사디스트 a sadist

사디즘 sadism

사또 [주장·원님에게] My lord !

사뜨다 buttonhole ; hemstitch ; cross-stitch

사뜻하다 (be) clean ⇨ 산뜻하다

사라사 cotton print ; calico
— **종이** fancy-figured paper

사라수 沙羅樹 〖식물〗 a sal (tree) ; a saul ; Shorea robusta (학명) ; 〖불교〗 ⇨ 사라 쌍수

사라쌍수 沙羅雙樹 the four pairs of sal trees that surrounded the Buddha when he went to Nirvana

사라지 a tobacco pouch

†**사라지다** disappear ; vanish ; be gone ; [시야에서] go out of sight ; be lost ; [마음에서] fade away ; [소리가] die away ; [숯불이] die out ; [죄·허물이] be wiped out ; [눈이] melt away ¶ 배가 수평선 너머로 사라졌다 The ship vanished beyond the horizon. // 그는 군중 속으로 사라졌다 He disappeared〔was lost〕 in the crowd. // 모든 희망이 사라져 버렸다 All our hopes are gone. // 그의 연설은 청중에게 영원히 사라지지 않은 감명을 주었다 His speech produced an everlasting impression on the audience.

†**사람** ① [인류] man ; mankind ; [개인] a man ; a person ; a (human) being ; one ; a soul ; [여러 개인] men ; people ¶ 사람의 목숨 human life // 사람의 일생 a man's life // 스미스라고 하는 사람 a Smith // 그는 마산 사람이다 He is〔comes〕 from *Masan*. // 거리에는 사람이라곤 하나도 보이지 않는다 There was not a soul to be seen in the street. // 하고 많은 사람 중에서 하필이면 그에게로 가다니 That you went to him of all people ! // 싫어하는 사람도 있다 Some people dislike it. // 그런 이름 가진 사람 여기 없는데요 There's no one here by that name. // 그같은 사람은 칭찬을 해주어야만 한다 His sort needs lots of praise. // 젊은 사람들을 위해서 길을 열어 줘야 한다는 생각이 든다 I just feel that I should make way for new blood.

② [세인] men ; people ; public ; [타인] others ; another man ; [아내] (my) wife ; [자신] I ; me ; [심부름꾼] a messenger ¶ 우리집 사람 my wife // 사람 앞에서 창피를 주다 humiliate 《a person》 in public〔the presence of others〕 // 사람을 보내다 send for 《a doctor》 ; send a messenger 《to》 // 사람을 깔보지 마라 Don't look down on me.

③ [인품] nature ; character ; personality ; [인재] an able man ; a competent 〔talented〕 man ¶ 사람이 좋다〔나쁘다〕 be good〔ill〕-natured // 그는 사람을 볼 줄 안다〔모른다〕 He is a good〔poor〕 judge of character. // 우리 교육계에는 사람이 없다 Our educational world is short of talent. // 그는 사람이 돼 있다 He has a fine〔firm〕 character. // 이 일을 모두 떠맡다니 너도 참 사람이 좋구나 You're really a pushover to let yourself get stuck with all this work.

④ [참다운 인간] a decent man ; a true man ; [성인] a grown-up ; an adult ¶ 역경이 그를 사람으로 만들었다 He is schooled in adversity. // 그들 세 고아는 다 훌륭한 사람이 되었다 The three orphans have grown up to be respectable persons.

사람에 버릴 사람 없으며 물건에 버틸 물건 없다 〔속담〕 Lay things by, they may come to use.

사람은 먹고 살기 마련이다 〔속담〕 Everyday brings its bread with it.

사람은 죽어서 이름을 남기고 호랑이는 죽어서 가죽을 남긴다. 〔속담〕 He who leaves the fame of good works after him does not die.

산 사람의 목구멍에 거미줄 치랴 〔속담〕 Every brings its bread with it.

사람구실 one's proper behavior ; bearing up ; living up to one's role **—하다** behave as a person should〔as befits one〕 ; live up to one's role〔name〕 ; do a proper job of it ; bear up〔nicely〕 ; be a man about it

사람답다 (be) humane ; truly human ; be worthy of the name of man ¶ 사람다운 사람 a man of decent character ; a true 〔decent〕 man

사람됨 [성질] (a) personal character ; (a) personality ; [타고난 성품] one's nature 〔disposition, temperament〕

사람 멀미 —하다 be〔get〕 sick of people

†**사랑** ① love 《for a person, of a thing》 ; [애정] affection 《for, towards a person》 ; [애착] attachment 《to, for》 ; [애욕] passion **—하다** love ; be fond of ; be attached to ; have a passion for ¶ 사랑하는 beloved ; dear // 사랑스러운 lovable ; lovely ; charming ; amiable // 사랑 없는 loveless // 부모〔형제, 부부〕의 사랑 parental〔fraternal, conjugal〕 love // 변함없는 사랑 steadfast love // 정신적인 사랑

platonic love // 사랑의 신 Cupid // 사랑의 여신 the goddess of love ; Venus // 사랑의 대상 the object of one's love〔affection〕// 사랑의 열매 the fruit of romance // 사랑의 표시 a love token ; a token of affection ; a pledge of love // 사랑의 속삭임 whispers of love ; soft nothings // 사랑에 빠지다 fall in love with // 사랑을 독점하다 monopolize《a person's》affection // 사랑의 노예가 되다 be enslaved by one's passion // 사랑의 보금자리를 꾸미다 build〔live in〕a love nest // 많이 사랑해 주십시오 Please honor me with your friendship. // 사랑과 나이가 무슨 상관이 있습니까 What's age got to do with love? / What does age have to do with love?
② [연인] one's love ; sweetheart ; darling ; beloved ¶ 어와 둥둥 내 사랑아 O, darling, my love!
— 노래 a love〔an amorous〕song — 매듭 a love-knot ; a nuptial〔marriage〕tie — 싸움 a matrimonial〔love〕quarrel
사랑에 빠지면 곰보도 미인으로 보인다 속담 Every lover sees a thousand graces in the beloved object.
갑작 사랑 영 이별 속담 Hot love is soon cold.

사랑 舍廊 a room ; a detached living room (partly available for entertaining male guests) ; the party room
— 놀이 entertaining male guests ; a party —문 the door of the party room —채 a detached house〔in front of the premises〕

사랑니 a wisdom tooth ¶ 사랑니가 나다 cut a wisdom tooth

†사랑스럽다 (be) lovable ; [매력이 있다] (be) lovely ; charming ¶ 사랑스러운 여자 a lovely girl ; a cute girl

사랑양반 舍廊兩班 one's husband ; the master of a house

사랑옵다 (be) lovely ; sweet ; attractive ; charming ; winning

사랑홉다 ⇨ 사랑옵다

사래¹ land allowed to a grave keeper〔a tenant-supervisor〕for his services
—논〔밭〕wet〔dry〕fields allowed to a grave keeper〔tenant-supervisor〕

사래² [서까래] a square rafter along the end of eaves

사래질 winnowing ; fanning —하다 winnow ; fan

사략 史略 an outlined history ; a short〔concise, condensed〕history

사량 思量 consideration ⇨ 사료(思料)

사레 a sneeze-like spasm of one's windpipe
사레 들리다 관용 get something caught in one's windpipe ; swallow the wrong way

***사려 思慮** thoughts ; consideration —하다 consider ; think over ; deliberate ¶ 사려 있는 thoughtful ; considerate ; deliberate ; well-considered ; prudent // 사려가 없는 thoughtless ; unthinking ; imprudent ; rash // 사려가 깊은 사람 a man of discretion〔prudence〕

사력 死力 a desperate〔frantic〕effort ¶ 사력을 다해 싸우다 fight to the death

사력 私力 private means ; personal authority

사력 社歷 the history of a company ; [책] a history of a company

사련 邪戀 illicit love ; wicked love ; guilty love

사령 司令 a (position of) command ; [일직·주번] a duty officer
—관 a commander ; an officer〔a general, an admiral〕in command ¶ 총사령관 the commander in chief // 최고 사령관 the supreme commander —부 the headquarters《HQ, H.Q.》¶ 총사령부 the General Headquarters《GHQ, G.H.Q.》—선 [우주선의] a command module —실 the commander's room —탑 [비행장의] a control tower ; [배의] a pilot-house ; [잠수함의] a conning tower

사령 死靈 a departed soul ; a ghost

사령 赦令 a decree of amnesty ; an act of grace〔oblivion〕

사령 辭令 ① [발령] an official order ; a government order ; [발령장] a writ〔warrant〕of appointment ¶ 임명(해임) 사령 a notice of appointment〔dismissal〕
② [언사] fair words ; address ; manner of speaking ¶ 사령에 능하다 be smooth tongued ; be a man of good address ; have a nice way of putting things
—장 a written appointment ; a writ of appointment 외교 — diplomatic language 임명 — a notice of appointment 해임 — a notice of dismissal

사례 事例 an instance ; an example ; a case ¶ 그러한 사례는 드물다 Those cases are rare.
— 연구 a case study — 연구법 〖교육〗 the case method

***사례 謝禮** [감사] thanks ; gratitude ; [보수] reward ; remuneration ; recompense
—하다 give thanks to ; reward ; remunerate ¶ 적으나마 사례의 표시로서 as a slight acknowledgement《of a person's services》// 깊이 사례하다 offer cordial thanks // 두둑히 사례하다 reward《a person》generously〔handsomely〕
—금 honorarium《*pl.* ~s, -is》

사로 仕路 ⇨ 벼슬길 ¶ 사로에 오르다 set out on one's official career

사로자다 sleep uneasily ; sleep a troubled sleep ; pass a restless night

사로잠그다 leave half unlocked ; lock halfway ; bolt《the door》loosely

‡사로잡다 [생포] catch alive ; capture ; take《a person》prisoner ¶ 범을 사로잡다 capture a tiger alive // 이 광고는 각처의 독자들을 사로잡을 것이다 This advertisement will capture the attention of readers everywhere.

사로잡히다 be taken alive ; be captured ; be taken prisoner ¶ 적군에게 사로잡히다 be captured by the enemy // 공포에 사로잡히다 be seized with terror // 인습에 사로잡히다 be a slave to convention

사록 史錄 historical records

사론 史論 a historical essay〔treatise, study〕

사론 私論 one's private opinion ; one's personal view

사뢰다 tell ; inform ⇨ 아뢰다

사료 史料 historical materials〔records, documents〕 ¶ 한국 동란의 사료를 수집하다 collect the materials for a history of the Korean War

— 편찬 historiography **— 편찬국** the Bureau of Compilation of Historical Materials

사료 思料 consideration ; considered judgment **—하다** think ; consider ; regard ; deem ; judge

사료 飼料 feed (stuff) ; forage ; fodder ; provender ¶ 돼지에게 사료를 주다 feed a pig

— 가게 a feedstore 《미》 **—용 곡류** feed grains **양계 —** feed for poultry

사류 홍수 射流洪水 a flash flood

사륙 배판 四六倍判 large octavo

사륙판 四六判 duodecimo ; crown octave ; 12mo ¶ 사륙판의 책 a duodecimo 《*pl.* ~s》

사르다¹ [태워버리다] commit to the flame ; throw into the fire ; burn ; [불을 지피다] make 《a fire in》 ¶ 묵은 서류를 불에 사르다 throw old documents into the fire // 아궁이에 불을 사르다 make a fire in the fireplace

사르다² [키질하다] winnow ¶ 쌀을 사르다 winnow the chaff from the grain

사르르 softly ; gently ¶ 눈을 사르르 감다 close one's eyes softly // 옷고름이 사르르 풀렸다 Her jacket-ties became quietly unlaced of themselves.

사름 the taking root of a transplanted riceplant ; the way a transplanted riceplant turns out

사릅 three years of age 《of a horse, an ox, a dog》

—잡이 a three-year-old horse〔ox, dog〕

***사리**¹ a coil ¶ 새끼〔국수〕 한 사리 a coil of rope〔noodles〕

사리² time of high tide

— 고기 fish caught at high tide

사리³ [인도 부인이 두르는] a sari

사리 私利 self-interest ; one's own interest ; self-profit ; personal profit〔gain〕 ; private advantage ¶ 사리를 도모하는 사람 a self-seeker ; a self-seeking person // 사리를 도모하다 have an eye to the main chance ; look to one's own interest ; feather one's own nest ; seek personal profit // 사리를 떠나다 put aside〔rise above〕 (one's) self-interest // 그는 사리사욕에 눈이 어두웠다 He was overruled〔blinded〕 by his self-interest.

사리 舍利 [유골] Buddha's bones ; a relic of the Buddha ; sarira ; [경전] Buddhist scriptures ; the Sutras

—탑 a pagoda preserving relics of the Buddha **—함** a reliquary

‡**사리 事理** facts ; reason ; propriety ¶ 사리에 밝은 사람 a man of sense ; a sensible person // 너의 말은 사리에 닿지 않는다 What you say is not reasonable.

사리 射利 unrestrained love of gain ; moneymaking by fair means or foul **—하다** seek (nothing) but profit ; aim for gain (unrestrainedly)

—심 a mercenary〔mercantile〕 spirit ; a speculative mind

사리다 [새끼를] wind up (in a coil) ; [국수를] wind (into a ball) ; [뱀이] coil (itself up) ; [몸을] spare oneself 〔pains〕 ; take it easy ; [못을] hammer back the protruding point of

사리사리 coil after coil ; in nice coils

사리풀 〖식물〗 henbane

사린 四隣 the whole neighborhood ; the surrounding countries ; (on) all sides ¶ 사린을 호령하다 lord it over the surrounding countries

사린교 a four-man palanquin ⇨ 사인교

†**사립 私立** private establishment ¶ 사립의 private ; privately-controlled // 그 병원〔학교〕은 사립이다 The hospital〔school〕 is a private institution.

— 대학 a private college〔university〕 **— 탐정** a private detective ; a private eye **— 학교** a private school 《미》 ; a voluntary〔a nongovernmental〕 school (관·공립에 대하여)

사립문 a gate made of twigs ; a twig gate

사립짝 one of the two doors of a twig gate

사마귀¹ a wart ; [무사마귀] a mole on the skin ¶ 사마귀가 많은 warty // 사마귀가 나다 get a wart // 뺨에 사마귀가 돋았다 A mole has formed on the cheek.

사마귀² 〖곤충〗 a praying mantis

†**사막 沙漠** a desert ¶ 끝없는 사막 a limitless desert // 황량한 사막 a bleak desert

— 동물 a desert animal **— 식물** desert plants **사하라 —** the Sahara Desert

†**사망 死亡** death ; decease ; passing (away) **—하다** die ; decease ; pass away ¶ 그는 자동차 사고로 사망했다 He was killed in an automobile accident. // 그녀는 암으로 사망했다 She died of cancer.

— 기사 an obituary (notice) ; a necrology **—란** an obit column ; death notices (in a paper) 《영》 **—률** a death rate ; mortality ¶ 사망률이 가장 높은 병 the most fatal〔murderous〕 disease **—수** the number of deaths **— 신고(서)** a notice of death **— 위험** mortality risks **— 진단**

서 a medical certificate of death ; a death certificate — 통계 statistics of mortality ; mortality returns — 통지 an announcement〔a notice〕 of (a person's) death ; a death notice —(자) 표 the death list ; 〖보험〗 [생명 보험] a mortality〔life〕 table
사망 보험 死亡保險 mortality life insurance
—금 a death benefit
사망자 the dead (person) ; the deceased ; [재난에 의한] the casualty ; victim ¶ 열차 사고로 많은 사망자가 났다 The railway accident caused many deaths. /Many lives were lost in the railway accident. / The train wreck took a heavy toll of lives.
— 명부 a death roll —수 the death toll — 통계 statistics of mortality returns
사매 私— a lynch ; illegal flogging ; private punishment
—질 lynching
사맥 事脈 the origin(s) of a matter ; the background ; the circumstances ; the details ¶ 사맥을 모르다 have no sense ; be ignorant 《of》
사면 四面 the four sides ; all sides ; all directions〔quarters〕 ¶ 사면이 바다로 둘러싸인 나라 a country surrounded by the seas ; a seagirt country ; an island country // 사면에서 공격을 받다 be attacked on every side
—체 a tetrahedron — 팔방 all sides ; every direction ¶ 사면 팔방으로 in every direction ; far and wide
사면 死面 a death mask ¶ 사면을 뜨다 take 《a person's》 death mask
사면 斜面 a slope ; a slant ; a slanting〔sloping〕 surface ; an inclined〔oblique〕 plane ; a tilted plane
—도 an oblique section — 묘사 an oblique description — 해머 a bevel-faced hammer 급— a steep incline〔slope〕 ; 〖축성〗 an escarpment 완— an easy incline〔slope〕
사면 赦免 pardon ; remission ; absolution ; amnesty —하다 pardon ; let off ; remit 《a punishment》 ; absolve 《a person from》 ; discharge 《the accused》 ; grant clemency〔leniency〕 to 《a prisoner》
—령 a decree〔an ordinance, an edict〕 of amnesty —장 a letter of pardon ; a pardon ; an absolution 일반 — a general pardon 특별 — a particular〔special〕 pardon
사면 辭免 resignation ; retirement from office —하다 resign 《one's office》 ; leave 《the services》 ; retire 《from office》
사면발이 〖곤충〗 [음슬] a crab louse ; [아첨꾼] a flatterer ; a toady ; a sycophant
사면 초가 四面楚歌 enemies on every side ; having the world against 《one》
사멸 死滅 extinction ; annihilation ; destruction ; death —하다 die out ; perish ; become extinct ; be annihilated ; be expired ¶ 사멸한 동물들 extinct animals
‡사명 使命 a mission ; an appointed task ; a commission ; an errand ¶ 사명을 다하다 fulfil〔discharge〕 one's mission // 사명을 띠다 be charged〔entrusted〕 with a mission // 그는 중대한 사명을 띠고 프랑스로 갔다 He was sent to France on an important mission. // 예술에는 숭고한 사명이 있다 Art has a lofty mission.
—감 a sense of duty
사명 社名 the name of a company〔firm, corporation〕
사명 社命 an order〔a directive〕 of the company〔firm, corporation〕
사모 思慕 [경모] longing ; yearning ; love ; deep attachment ; admiration ; adoration —하다 long for ; yearn after ; love dearly ; admire ; adore ; idolize ¶ 그녀는 그를 깊이 사모하고 있다 She is deeply attached to him. // 그들은 영리하게도 스승의 덕을 사모할 줄 안다 They are clever enough to adore their teacher for his virtue.
사모 師母 [스승의 아내] one's teacher's wife ¶ 사모님 [호칭] Madam ; Mrs ; your (good) lady ; Milady
사모아 [남태평양의 섬] Samoa ; the Samoan Islands ¶ 사모아의 Samoan
— 사람 a Samoan
사무 社務 the business〔affairs〕 of the company ; the company business〔affairs〕
*사무 事務 business ; office work ; clerical work ; affairs ¶ 사무적인 businesslike ; practical // 사무적으로 in a businesslike manner ; perfunctorily // 사무에 밝다 be quite familiar with the routine of the office ; be experienced in office work // 사무를 인계하다 hand〔pass〕 over business〔office work〕 // 사무를 인계받다 take over business 《from another》 // 사무에 바쁘다 be fully occupied with office work
—가 a talented office worker ; a man of business〔affairs〕 ; a practical man — 간소화 simplification of a business —관 a secretary ; an administrative official ; [정부직제의 3급 을류] the administrative official 3rd class junior — 관리 office management ; charge〔management〕 of business — 관장 management of local administration —국 a bureau〔secretariat〕 — 규정 regulations for business ; office regulations — 기계 a business machine ; an office machine — 능률 business efficiency — 당국 the authorities directly in charge ; the officials in charge —복 an office dress ; office wear ; an office uniform ; a working garment ; a duster 《미》 ; a dust〔covert〕 coat 《영》 —비 office expenses —소 an

office ; a business place —실 an office (room) —용품 office supplies ; stationery —원 a clerk ; an office clerk 〔worker〕 ¶ 여사무원 an office girl ; a business girl —인계 the taking over of an office 〔duties〕 ; succeeding to the duties of an office —장 a head official ; [배의] a purser —절차 business〔office〕 routine —직원 a clerical worker 〔employee〕 —차관 a permanent deputy-minister —착오 a clerical error ; an administrative mistake —총장 a secretary general

사무를 보다 관용 do office work ; be engaged in business ; be at one's desk

†**사무치다** touch the heart ; sink into the mind ; move ; pierce ; penetrate into ¶ 그 여자의 고생하는 모습이 가슴에 사무쳤다 My heart was touched by her sufferings. // 나는 그에 대한 원한이 뼈에 사무쳤다 I bear him an inveterate grudge. /I have deep-rooted rancor against him. // 그는 여자 친구에게 채인 것이 가슴에 사무친 것 같다 It really got to him when his girl friend broke off their relationship. // 우리 나이가 되면 그러한 점은 뼈에 사무치는 법이다 When you get to be our age, it cuts right to the bone.

사문 沙門 a Buddhist monk〔priest〕 ; a friar

사문 査問 inquiry ; inquest ; inquisition ; interrogation —하다 inquire 《into》 ; examine ; interrogate

— (위원)회 an inquiry〔a rogatory〕 commission ¶ 사문 위원회에 회부하다 commit for hearing by a court〔board〕 of inquiry

사문 死文 a dead letter ; a mere scrap of paper ¶ 사문화되다 prove (to be) a dead letter ; end up a mere scrap of paper

사문서 私文書 a private document ; private papers ¶ 사문서를 작성하다 draw up private papers

— 위조 the forgery of a private document

사문석 蛇紋石 〖광물〗 serpentine (rock)

사물 私物 a private〔personal〕 thing ; one's private property

†**사물 事物** objects ; things ; matters ; affairs

— 관할 material jurisdiction

사물 死物 a dead〔lifeless〕 thing ; an inanimate object〔matter〕

—계 inanimate nature — 기생 saprophytism — 기생식물 a saprophyte

사뭇 [멋대로] willfully ; foolhardily ; as one pleases ; at will ; [줄곧] without break ; all through ; [매우] very ; much ; a great deal ¶ 사뭇 들이키다 drink willfully // 1주일 내내 사뭇 바빴다 I was busy all through the week. // 생각했던 것과는 사뭇 다르다 It is quite different from what I thought.

사민 四民 the four classes 《the nobles, farmers, artisans, and merchants》 ; all〔four〕 estates of the nation

— 평등 the equality of the four classes in the country ; the equality of man

사바 娑婆 ⇨ 사바 세계

— 속심 earthly〔worldly〕 desires ¶ 사바 속심을 버리다 give up worldly ambitions

사바사바 paying a bribe 《속》 —하다 bribe an official ; buy off an official

사바 세계 娑婆世界 Sabha 《범》 ; the world of suffering ; this world ¶ 사바세계가 싫어졌다 I am sick of this world.

사박거리다 crunch softly ¶ 사박사박 with a crunch // 이 배는 사박사박하다 This pear is light and crisp. // 그는 모래밭을 사박사박 밟고 갔다 He walked across the sand with a soft crunch.

사박스럽다 (be) rambunctious (and obtrusive)

사반 死斑 a purple spot ; 〖의학〗 a liver

—병 〖의학〗 purpura

사반 四半 a quarter ; half a half

—기 a quarter ; a quarter term ¶ 사반기의 quarterly —분 a quarter (part) ; a fourth 《of it》 ; one-fourth

†**사발 沙鉢** a (porcelain) bowl ¶ 물 한사발 a bowl of water

—고의(袴衣) Korean underpants —밥 a bowlful of rice —시계 a bowl-shaped clock —잠방이 an unlined Korean undershirt (which reaches to the knee)

국〔밥〕— a soup〔rice〕 bowl

사발 四發 ¶ 사발의 [발동기의] four-engine ; four-motored〔-engined〕

— 폭격기 a four-motored bomber

사발농사 沙鉢農事 begging ; mendicancy —하다 beg food ; live as a beggar ; panhandle 《미·구》

사방 巳方 〖민속〗 the Direction of the Snake ; southeast-by-south

사방 四方 the four directions〔sides〕 ; all directions〔quarters〕 ; everywhere ¶ 사방이 고요하다 Everything is quiet. // 이 뜰은 사방 20미터이다 This garden is twenty meters square. // 폭발 소리가 10마일 사방에 들렸다 The explosion was heard within a radius of ten miles〔over a ten mile range〕. // 학생들이 사방에서 모여들었다 Students gathered from all quarters. // 그는 사방으로 그것을 찾아다녔다 He searched high and low〔every nook and corner〕 for it. // 적군은 사방으로 도망쳤다 The enemy soldiers fled away on all sides〔in every direction〕.

—등(燈) a square hand lantern

사방 砂防 erosion control ; protection against earth or sand slippage ; sand-bank fixing

— 공사 erosion control work ; anti-erosion work ; sand arrestation work —댐 〖토목〗 a debris barrier —림 an erosion control forest —법 〖법〗 the Sand Con-

ㅅ

trol Act — 조림 afforestation for erosion control
사방 斜方 ¶ 사방형의 rhombic
—면체 정계(面體晶系) a rhombohedral system — 사영(射影) 〖기하〗 trimetric projection — 십이면체 a rhombic dodecahedron — 육면체 a rhombohedron 《*pl.* ~s, -dra》 —주(柱) a rhombic prism — 추(錐) rhombic pyramid —형 a rhomb(us)
사방등 四方燈 a square hand-lantern
사방정 斜方晶 a prismatic crystal
—계(系) the rhombic〔orthorhombic, trimetric〕 system —계 유황 rhombic sulfur
사방침 四方枕 an armrest ; an elbow rest ¶ 사방침에 기대다 lean on an armrest
사방팔방 四方八方 [모든 방면] everywhere ; every direction ; all directions ; all sides ¶ 사방팔방에서 from every quarter〔direction〕 ; from all quarters
사배 四倍 four times ; quadruple —하다 multiply by four ; quadruple ; quadruplicate ¶ 사배의 임금 인상 a quadruple pay-raise
—체(體) 〖식물〗 tetraploid
사백 舍伯 my eldest brother
사백 詞伯 a man of letters ; a great poet ; a master poet
사백 四百 four hundred
사번 事煩 pressure of business ; being busy —하다 (be) busy ; be pressed with business
사범 師範 [모범] a model to others ; an exemplary person to others ; [스승] a master 《of judo》 ; a teacher ; a preceptor ; an instructor ; a coach
— 교육 teacher training ; normal education — 대학 the college of education — 학교 a normal school 권투 — a boxing instructor〔master〕
사범 事犯 a crime ; an offense ; an illegality
선거 — election illegalities 경제 — an economic offense
†**사법 司法** the administration of justice ; judicature ¶ 사법의 judicial ; judiciary
— 경찰 the judicial police — 경찰관 a judicial police officer —관 a judicial〔law〕 officer ; [총칭] judges and prosecutors ; the justice —관 시보 a probationary judicial officer — 관청 the Bureau of Judicial Affairs —권 judicial power ; the powers of jurisdiction — 기관 the machinery of law — 당국 the judicial authorities — 보호 사업 relief work for ex-convicts — 서사 a judicial scrivener — 시험 the judicial examination — 연도 a judicial year — 연수생 a judicial apprentice ; a student of the Legal Training and Research Institute — 연수원 the Judicial Research and Training Institute — 재판 a judicial trial — 재판관 a judge ; a judicial official — 재판소 a court of justice — 제도 the judicial system ; judicial system〔arrangements〕 — 행정 judicial administration 국제 — 위원회 the international committee of jurists 국제 — 재판소 the International Court of Justice
사법 死法 a dead law
사법 私法 〖법〗 private law ; private statute
—인 a private body corporate —학 the study of private law
사법 邪法 [사도] evil ways ; heresy ; [사술] black arts ; sorcery ; witchcraft
사변 四邊 the four sides ; all sides ¶ 사변에 all around ; on all sides
—형 〖수학〗 a quadrilateral ; a tetragon ; a quadrangle ; a trapezium 《*pl.* ~s, -zia》 《미》 ¶ 정사변형 a regular tetragon
사변 事變 [사고] an accident ; a disaster ; a calamity ; [변란] a trouble ; an incident ; a disturbance ; an uprising ; a conflict ; [급변] an emergency ; an exigency ¶ 국가에 사변이 일어났을 때 in case of a national emergency // 불의의 사변을 당하다 meet with an unexpected accident
만주(滿洲) — the Manchurian Incident
상해(上海) — the Shanghai Incident
6.25 — the June 25th Incident of Korea
사변 思辨 [구별] discrimination ; [사유] speculation ¶ 사변적 방법 speculative method
— 철학 speculative philosophy
사변 斜邊 〖기하〗 the hypotenuse ; an oblique side ¶ 3각형의 사변 the leg of a triangle // 직각 3각형의 사변 the hypotenuse of a right-angled triangle
사별 死別 separation by death ; bereavement —하다 be parted 《from a person》 by death ; be bereaved ¶ 부인과 사별하다 lose one's wife // 양친과 사별하다 be left an orphan
사병 士兵 a soldier ; a private ; an enlisted man ; the rank and file 《총칭》 ¶ 사병으로부터 대장까지 승진하다 rise from a private to be a four-star general
사보타주 sabotage —하다 sabotage ; go on〔stage〕 a sabotage〔go-slow strike〕 ; go slow
사보텐 a cactus 《*pl.* -ti, ~es》
사복 私服 civilian〔plain, ordinary〕 clothes ; mufti
— 경찰관 a plain-clothes policeman — 형사 a plainclothesman
사복 私腹 one's stomach ; one's self-interest ; one's selfish ends ; one's personal end
사복을 채우다 〔관용〕 enrich one's own pocket ; graft ; enrich oneself ; feather one's own nest
사복음 四福音 〖성경〗 the Four Gospels
†**사본 寫本** a manuscript ; a written copy ; [부본] a duplicate ; [등사물] a transcript

¶ 사본을 만들다 copy ; make a copy ; get a duplicate 《of》
사부 四部 [네 부분] four parts ; [사서] the traditional Four Classes of Chinese books《Classics, Histories, Philosophies and Anthologies》
—작 a tetralogy ; a four-part book —합주 a quartet —합창 a vocal quartet —합창곡 a four-part song
사부 師父 [스승과 부친] one's father and master ; [스승] a fathering master ; an esteemed teacher ; one's teacher
사부 師傅 [스승] a teacher ; a tutor ; a master ; [왕자의] a tutor to the prince
사부랑거리다 prattle ; chatter ⇨ 시부렁거리다
사부랑사부랑하다 (be) loosely stacked
사부랑삽작 with a light〔casual〕jump《across, up》¶ 돌 위에 사부랑삽작 올라서다 get on a stone with a light jump
사부랑하다 (be) bundled〔tied, piled up〕loosely ⇨ 서부렁하다
사부자기 with ease ; effortlessly ; stealthily
사부작사부작 easily〔effortlessly, without lifting a finger〕
사부주 the arrangements (for something) ¶ 사부주가 짜였다 the arrangements have been fixed〔made, set〕
사북 [부채·가위의] a pivot pin ; [요점] the pivotal〔vital〕point ; the point
사분 私憤 personal grudge〔resentment, spite〕《against》¶ 사분을 풀다 vent one's spite
사분 四分 dividing in four ; [시간] four minutes ; a quarter ; one-fourth ; [합금] an alloy of three parts of copper to one part of silver —하다 divide in four ; quarter ¶ 사분의 1 a quarter ; one-fourth // 사분의 3 three quarters ; three-fourths
—기 a quarter (of the year) ; a quarter term ¶ 제1사분기 the first quarter〔three months〕(of the year) —법 〖토목〗 the method of quartering ; 〖화학〗 quartation —위수(位數) 〖통계〗 a quartile —음 〖음악〗 a quarter tone〔step〕 —음부〔음표〕 〖음악〗 a crotchet《영》; a quarter note《미》 —의(儀) a quadrant —치(値) 〖수학〗 a quartile
사분거리다 ① [조르다] tease《a person for something》humorously ; importune half in fun ② [속삭이다] whisper ; talk in a low voice
사분사분, 사뿐사뿐 with soft〔muffled〕steps ; lightly ¶ 사뿐사뿐 걸어가다 walk lightly ; tread softly ; go with soft steps
사분사분하다 (be) good-natured ; amiable ⇨ 사근사근하다
사분 오열 四分五裂 utter disruption〔disunion, division, break-up, split, disorganization〕—하다 be utterly disrupted〔disunited, divided, disorganized〕; go to pieces ; be torn up〔asunder〕
사분하다 (be) somewhat〔a little〕loose〔slack〕; not quite tight
사불여의 事不如意 —하다《work》fall short of one's expectations
사붓사붓, 사뿟사뿟 with light-footed steps
사붙이 紗— (silk) gauze articles
사브르 〖펜싱〗 a saber ; a sabre
사비 私費 private expense ; one's own expense ¶ 사비로 at one's own expense〔cost〕; at private expense
—생 a private student
사비 社費 the company's expenses ; the upkeep〔outlays〕of a company ¶ 사비로 여행하다 travel at the company's expense
사뿐 with a soft〔muffled〕step ; softly ; lightly ¶ 사뿐사뿐 걸어가다 walk lightly ; tread softly ; go with soft steps
사사 私事 a private matter ; private affairs〔concerns〕; personal affairs ¶ 그는 남의 사사를 들추어 내기를 좋아한다 He has a nasty taste for exposing〔laying bare〕another's private affairs.
사사 事事 each〔every〕thing〔matter, affair〕; all things〔affairs, matters〕
—건건 (in) everything ; all cases ¶ 그는 사사건건 불평이다 He grumbles at everything. —물물(物物) everything ; all things ; every affair ; all matters
사사 師事 —하다 study under《a person》; become a pupil《of》; be a disciple《of》¶ 고명한 스승에게 사사하다 study under a renowned scholar ; receive instruction from one of the prominent professors // 나는 다년간 그에게 사사하였다 I sat at his feet for many years.
사사 謝辭 [사례] thanks ; an address of thanks ; [사죄] an apology ; [사양] humble refusal ; declining with thanks —하다 thank ; excuse oneself from ; refuse humbly ; decline with thanks ; apologize
사사기 士師記 〖성경〗 the Book of Judges
사사로이 私私— personally ; privately ; in private ; informally
사사롭다 私私— (be) personal ; private ; be of private business ¶ 사사로운 감정 personal feeling // 사사로운 청이 있어 왔습니다 I came to ask you a personal favor. // 이것은 사사로운 이야기인데요 This is something personal.
사사 오입 四捨五入 rounding off to the nearest integer —하다 round《a figure》off to the nearest whole number
사사일 私私— a private matter ⇨ 사사(私事)
사산 四散 scattering in all directions ; dispersion —하다 scatter〔disperse〕in all directions ; be dispersed
사산 死産 a stillbirth —하다 have a still-born child ; give birth to a dead child
—아 a stillborn child
사살 a scolding ; a rebuke ; a lecture ; a

ㅅ

nagging —하다 scold ; rebuke ; lecture ; nag ; give ⟪a person⟫ a scolding ¶ 사살을 듣다 be scolded ; be nagged at ; get a scolding
사살 射殺 killing by shooting ; shooting to death —하다 kill by shooting ; shoot ⟪a person⟫ dead〔to death〕 ¶ 탈영자는 무조건 사살한다 Any deserter shall be shot down without question.
사삼 沙蔘 a wild plant ⇨ 더덕
사삿집 私私— a private house〔home〕
사상 死相 a dead face ; a countenance presaging death ; a foreshadow of death ¶ 얼굴에 사상이 나타나 있다 We can read the shadow of death on his face.
사상 死傷 death and injury ; casualties ; losses
—병(兵) the killed and injured soldiers ; troop casualties
사상 事狀, 事相 a phase ; an aspect ; a phenomenon ⟪*pl.* -na⟫
사상 事象 a phenomenon ; phenomena ; an event ; an aspect ¶ 자연계에서 잇따라 일어나는 사상 the phenomena occurring consecutively in nature // 사회적 정치적 사상 social and political phenomena
†**사상 思想** thought ; an idea ; thinking ; ideology ; a notion ; a conception ¶ 건전한 사상 healthy〔sound〕 thoughts ; sane ideas // 사상이 풍부〔빈약〕하다 be rich〔poor〕 in ideas
—가 a thinker ; a philosopher ; a sage — 개조 thought-remolding — 경향 the trend of thought —계 the world of thought ; the realm of ideas ¶ 사상계의 지도자 a leader of public thought —극 a problem play — 내용 thought content — 문제 the thought problem —범(인) a political offense〔offender〕 — 선도 (judicious) guidance of public thought — 운동 an ideological movement —전 ideological warfare — 취체 thought control ; censorship of thought — 투쟁 ideological conflicts 과격 — radical〔Bolshevik〕 ideas 근대〔그리스, 과학, 정치〕 — modern〔Greek, scientific, political〕 thought 독립 — the integrity for independence 동양 — Oriental thought 사대 — flunkeyism ; toadyism 서양 — Western thought 신〔공산주의, 위험〕 — a new〔communist, dangerous〕 idea 자유 — liberal thought 중심 — the central thought 〔idea〕 진보 — progressive ideas 혁명 — revolutionary ideas
사상 捨象 〖철학〗 abstraction —하다 abstract
사상 絲狀 ¶ 사상의 thready ; threadlike ; filiform
—균 〖식물〗 a filamentous fungus —체 〖의학〗 a filament —충 〖동물〗 a filaria
사상 寫像 an image
—주의 imagism —파 the imagists
***사상 史上** in history ; on the pages of history ; in annals ¶ 사상의 인물 a historical character〔figure〕 // 사상 초유의 거사 an epoch-making event // 사상에 이름을 떨치다 immortalize one's fame in history ; abide in history
사상누각 沙上樓閣 a visionary project which soon collapses ; a house of cards
사상자 死傷者 the killed and injured 〔wounded〕 ; casualties ¶ 많은 사상자 heavy〔many, serious〕 casualties // 사상자의 수는 많았다 The toll of dead and injured was high. // 승객 중 20명의 사상자가 있었다 Twenty passengers were either killed or injured. // 열차가 탈선하여 많은 사상자를 내었다 The train was derailed, causing many casualties. // 다행히 사상자는 한 사람도 없었다 Fortunately there were no casualties.
— 명단〔명부〕 a casualty list ; a list of casualties —수 losses ; (the number of) casualties ; the toll of casualties ⟪미⟫ ; the killed and wounded ; the loss in killed and wounded — 총수 the total casualties
⁑**사색 思索** thinking ; speculation ; cogitation ; contemplation ; meditation —하다 speculate ⟪on⟫ ; think deeply ; muse ⟪on⟫ ; meditate on ; contemplate ; cogitate ; philosophize ¶ 사색적인 speculative ; meditative ; contemplative // 사색에 잠기다 be given to speculation ; do a great deal of thinking
—가 a thinker ; a philosopher ; a thinking person — 생활 a life of meditation — 파 the man of thought (행동파에 대응하는)
사색 四色 [네가지 빛깔] four colors ; [이조 때의 당파] the Four Factions (of the middle period of the *Yi* Dynasty)
— 당쟁 strife among the Four Factions
—판 four-color printing
사색 死色 deadly〔ghastly〕 pale look ; blanching complexion ; deathly paleness
사생 私生 illegitimate〔illegal〕 birth —하다 bear a child without formal marriage ; give birth to an illegitimate child
사생 死生 life and〔or〕 death ¶ 사생을 같이 하다 live and die together ; share each other's fate
— 결단 risking one's life ¶ 사생 결단하다 risk one's life ; be desperate // 사생 결단하고 싸우다 fight it out desperately〔at the risk of one's life〕 — 관두(關頭) ⟪at⟫ the brink of death — 동고(同苦) standing together in life and death
사생 寫生 sketching〔a sketch〕 from nature —하다 sketch ; make a sketch ⟪of⟫ ¶ 사생하러 가다 go sketching // 나는 기린을 사생하고 있다 I am doing a sketch of a giraffe.
—문 a nature sketch〔description〕 — 여행 a sketching trip〔tour〕 —첩 a sketchbook ; a sketch block —화 a sketch —

화가 a realistic painter
*사생아 私生兒 an illegitimate child〔son, daughter〕; a natural child ; a love-child ; a bastard ¶ 그는 사생아이다 He was born out of wedlock. /He is of illegitimate birth. // 그녀는 사생아를 낳았다 She was delivered of a love-child.
— 인지(認知) bastardization ; filiation — 출산 an out-of-wedlock birth
*사생활 私生活 private〔personal〕 life ¶ 남의 사생활에 간섭하지 마시오 You should not interfere in other's private concerns. // 당신은 남의 사생활에 너무 간섭하는 것 같소 I'm afraid you're getting too personal.
사서 司書 a librarian
—보(補) an assistant librarian
사서 四書 the Four Books (of Ancient China) ; the Analects of Confucius (논어), the Works of Mencius (맹자), the Doctrine of the Mean (중용), and the Great Learning (대학)
— 삼경 the Four Books and the Three Classics ; the Seven Chinese Classics — 오경 the Nine Chinese Classics
사서 史書 a history book ; writings by historians
사서 私書 a private document〔letter〕; a confidential letter
—함 a (private) mail box ; a post office box《P. O. B., POB》; a call box《미》 ¶ 중앙 우체국 사서함 제77호 CPO Box (No.) 77 // 국제 우체국 사서함 제123호 IPO Box (No.) 123
사서 辭書 a dictionary ⇨ 사전
사석 私席 an unofficial〔a private〕 occasion ¶ 사석에서 남의 욕을 하지 말아라 Don't speak ill of others at the unofficial occasion.
사석 沙石 sand and stone〔pebbles〕
사석 捨石 [바둑의] a sacrificed stone ; [비유적으로] a sacrifice ; 〖토목〗 a rubble mound ; riprap
—공 riprap work ; riprapping — 방파제 a riprap breakwater — 호안(護岸) a riprap foundation〔wall〕; a riprap
*사선 死線 [죽을 고비] the death line ; a crisis ; [포로 수용소의] the keep-off line for prisoners ¶ 사선을 넘어서 across the death line // 자유를 찾아 사선을 넘다 cross the death line seeking for liberty // 이때까지 몇번이나 사선을 넘었다 He has been threatened with death several times.
사선 私線 a private line ; a privately owned line ; a private railway line
사선 私船 a privately owned boat
사선 射線 a trajectory
사선 斜線 〖기하〗 an oblique line ; a slant line ; [지도 따위의] a shaded portion
사설 社說 an editorial ; a leading article ; a leader《영》 ¶ 사설에서 논하다 editorialize《on the subject》; discuss《the subject》 in an editorial article // 경제 문제에 관한 사설이 실렸다 There was an editorial on the economic subject in the paper.
— 기자 an editorialist ; an editorial〔a leader〕 writer —란 the editorial column —면 the leader〔editorial〕 page
사설 邪說 a heretical doctrine ; heterodoxy ; heresy ; perverse views
†사설 私設 a private establishment —하다 establish privately ¶ 사설의 privately established ; private
— 묘지 a private cemetery — 시장 a private market — 우편함 a mailbox《미》; a letter box《영》 — 철도 a privately owned railway ; a private〔nongovernmental〕 railroad (line) ; a railroad under private management — 학원 a proprietary school《미》 — 회사 a private-run company
사설 辭說 [노래 따위의] an account ; a telling ; a story ; [지껄여 대는] chattering ; prattling ; nagging —하다 chatter ; prattle ; nag ; talk for the sake of talking ¶ 웬 사설이 그리 기냐 You are talking too much !
— 시조 〖문학〗 a form of *sijo* with no restrictions on the length of the first two verses —쟁이 a chatterbox
사성 四聖 the Four Great Sages《Confucious, Buddha, Jesus and Socrates》
사성 四聲 the "Four Tones" of classical Chinese
사성 賜姓 bestowing a surname《on a subject》 —하다《the king》 bestow〔confer〕 a surname《on a subject》
사세 事勢 the way things are〔turn, shape up〕; the situation ; the development (of affairs) ¶ 사세 난처 (being) hard to cope with the situation // 지금 사세로서는 as matters stand ; judging by the current situation // 사세 부득이한 경우에는 in case there arise unavoidable circumstances // 사세가 어떤가 What is the situation〔state of affairs〕? /How do matters stand ? / How go things ? // 사세가 불리하다 The situation is unfavorable for me. /Things look bleak〔dismal〕. // 이것은 사세 부득이 한 일이다 This must be considered as an inevitable consequence of the circumstances.
사세 부득이 관용 driven by circumstances ; unavoidably ; out of sheer necessity
†사소 些少 —하다 (be) trifling ; trivial ; insignificant ; small ; little ; petty ; slight ; inconsiderable ¶ 사소한 일 a mere trifle ; a little thing // 사소한 돈 a trifling sum of money // 사소한 잘못 trivial mistakes // 사소한 과실 a minor error // 사소한 사건 an insignificant matter // 사소한 일에 구애하다 stick to trifles // 사소한 일을 걱정하다 worry about trifles // 그것은 사소한 일이다 It is nothing to speak

ㅅ

of. // 그는 사소한 일을 가지고 법석댔다 He made a mountain out of a molehill. // 사소한 물건이오나 받아 주십시오 This is my present for you, such (trifling) as it is. // 그런 사소한 일에 신경쓰지 마라 Don't worry over minor details like that.

사소 私訴 〖법〗 a civil action〔suit, proceeding〕

사소설 私小說 an autobiographical〔a private life〕 novel ; a novel based on the author's personal life ; an "I" story

사수 死守 a desperate〔stubborn, diehard〕 defense **—하다** defend to the last ; defend desperately ¶ 참호를 사수하다 defend a bunker to the last // 진지를 사수하다 defend a position desperately

사수 査收 receipt **—하다** receive ¶ 100 달러의 수표를 동봉했으니 사수하여 주시오 Enclosed please find a check for 100 dollars.

사수 射手 a shooter ; a marksman ; [포수] a gunner ; an archer
명— a crack shot

사수리살 an arrow (used in ancient archery)

사숙 私塾 a private school

사숙 私淑 —하다 emulate 《a person》 as a model ; pattern after ; admire 《a person》 and copy him ; model oneself on 《a person》 ¶ 이 교수를 사숙하다 be an admirer of Prof. *Lee*

사숙 舍叔 my uncle

사순재 四旬齋 [기독교의] Lent ¶ 사순재의 Lenten

사순절 四旬節 ⇨ 사순재

사술 邪術 witchcraft ; black arts ; sorcery ; black magic ; an evil trick

*__사슬__ chain ; chains ¶ 사슬로 매다 chain up 《a dog》 ; put 《a person》 in chains // 사슬을 풀다 unchain // 사슬에 매여〔묶여〕 있다 be in chains
— 고리 a link ; a tether **— 누르미〔누름적〕** unskewered〔unspitted〕 shish kebab **—돈** loose〔unstrung〕 coins **— 문고리** a chain doorlock **— 조교(吊橋)** a chain (suspension) bridge **— 톱니바퀴** 〖기계〗 a sprocket〔rag〕 wheel **금—** a gold chain

‡**사슴** a deer 《*pl.* deer》 ; [숫사슴] a stag ; a buck ; [5세 이상의 수컷] a hart ; [암사슴] a hind ; [새끼사슴] a fawn ¶ 한 떼의 사슴이 풀을 뜯고 있다 A herd of deer are feeding on grass. // 사슴 쫓는 포수 산을 못 본다 Scenery is lost on the keen sportsman.
— 가죽 deer skin **— 고기** venison **—뿔** an antler **— 사냥** deer-hunting ; deer stalking ¶ 사슴 사냥 가다 go deer-hunting **— 사냥꾼** a deer-hunter ; a deer stalker **— 사냥터** a deer park **— 사육장** a deer garden

사승 史乘 a history (book) ; annals ; chronicles

사승 四乘 〖수학〗 the fourth power

사시 巳時 〖민속〗 the Watch of the Snake ① the 6th of the 12 double-hours 《the period between 9 and 11 a. m.》 ② the 11th of the 24 hours 《9 : 30-10 : 30 a. m.》

사시 四時 ① the four seasons ⇨ 사철 ② [시각] four o'clock

사시 斜視 [눈] a squint ; strabismus ; [시선] looking askance **—하다** squint ; look askance ¶ 사시의 squint(-eyed) ; cross-eyed ; strabismal // 사시가 아주 심하다 have a fearful squint // 왼쪽 눈이 사시다 have a cast in the left eye
—계(計) a strabismometer **—도 측정** strabismometry **— 수술** 〖의학〗 strabotomy **—안** a squint-eye ; a cock-eye **내—** convergent〔cross-eyed〕 strabismus **외—** divergent〔wall-eyed〕 strabismus

사시 史詩 an epic〔a historical〕 poem

사시나무 〖식물〗 an aspen ; a poplar
사시나무 떨 듯하다 ⓔ관용 tremble like an aspen leaf ; shiver ; shudder

사시랑이 a frail person ; a fragile thing

사시장청 四時長青 —하다 (be) evergreen ; be verdant at all seasons ; be green all the year round

사시장춘 四時長春 [기후] everlasting spring ; [생활] an easy life ; a comfortable living ; a well-off life

사식 私食 food privately offered to a prisoner

사식 寫植 ⇨ 사진(—식자)

사신 死神 the god of death ; Death

사신 私信 a private message〔letter, telegram〕 ; a private communication ; a personal correspondence

사신 使臣 an envoy ; a (diplomatic) representative ¶ 사신을 파견하다 dispatch an envoy
각국 — foreign envoys ; foreign (diplomatic) representatives

사신 邪神 a demon ; a devil ; an evil spirit ; an evil deity ; a false god

사실 史實 a historical fact〔evidence〕

†**사실 事實** a fact ; a reality ; actuality ; truth ¶ 사실상 actually ; really ; as a matter of fact ; in (point of) fact // 사실인즉 to tell〔confess〕 the truth ; frankly 〔candidly〕 speaking // 사실 말이지 in truth ; truly // 사실상의 real ; actual ; virtual ; practical // 사실상의 사장 a virtual head of the company // 사실상의 정부 a de facto government // 물리학적 사실 a physical fact // 분명한 사실 an obvious 〔undeniable〕 fact ; a doubtless〔palpable〕 fact // 확고한〔기정의〕 사실 a fixed〔definite〕 fact ; an established 〔accomplished〕 fact // 엄연한 사실 a solemn fact // 주요한〔중심되는〕 사실 a main〔central〕 fact // 부수적인 사실 an accompanying〔additional〕 fact ; a dependent fact // 사실을 잘 조사해 보라 Inquire into the fact〔case〕 carefully. // 그것이 사실이냐 Is that the case ? //

그것은 사실이다 It is a fact〔true, real〕. //그것은 틀림없는 사실일 것이다 Really it must be so. //그것은 사실이 아니다 That is not the case. //그것은 사실과 반대이다 The opposite is true〔the case〕./It is contrary to the facts. //그것은 사실과 아주 다르다 It is far from the truth. //사실은 이렇다 The truth (of the matter) is this. //그의 예언〔꿈〕은 사실이 되었다 His prediction〔dream〕 has come true 〔been realized〕. //사실대로 말해라 Speak the truth./ State the facts as they are. //사실을 왜곡하지 말아라 Don't pervert the truth./Never falsify facts. //그의 보고는 사실에 근거하고 있다 His report is based on fact. //최근의 조사 결과 그는 뇌물을 받은 사실이 드러났다 A recent investigation disclosed the fact that he had taken a bribe. //사실을 알면서도 모르는 체하는 것은 좋지 않다 It's no good to shut one's eyes to the fact. //사실대로 말하는 게 뭐가 잘못됐냐 What's wrong with telling 〔saying〕 it like it is?
— 문제 a matter〔question〕 of fact ; [당면의] the (real) question at issue — 오인 『법』 a mistake of fact — 인정 fact finding 《미》 — 조사 fact-finding 기정(旣定) — an accomplished〔established〕 fact

사실 査實 an investigation〔a survey〕 of the facts ; an actual inspection ; a scrutiny of a case —하다 inspect ; make an investigation〔a survey〕 《of》 ¶ 사실한 결과 as a result of actual inspection

사실 寫實 a real picture ; realism ; representing things as they really are —하다 describe graphically ; give a graphic description〔representation〕 ; represent things as they really are ¶ 사실적인 realistic ; graphic //사실적으로 realistically ; graphically
— 소설 a realistic novel —주의 realism ; literalism 《미》 ; representationalism —주의자 a realist —파 the realistic〔representationalist〕 school

사실 私室 a private room ; [부인의] a boudoir 《프》

사실무근 事實無根 ¶ 사실무근의 absurd ; groundless ; unfounded // 그 소문은 사실무근이다 The rumor is groundless〔unfounded, fictitious〕.

***사심 私心** [사욕] selfishness ; a selfish motive ; self-interest ; [자기 생각] my (humble) mind ¶ 사심을 품다 harbor 〔bear〕 a selfish motive ; have an ax to grind //사심이 없다 be unselfish〔disinterested, impartial〕

사심 邪心 an evil mind ; an evil〔a sinister〕 design ; a wicked〔black〕 heart ; a malicious intention ¶ 사심에 찬 wicked ; malicious ; full of malice

†사십 四十 forty ¶ 제사십 the fortieth //사십에 첫 버선 (wearing) socks for the first time at forty ; doing something for the first time late in life //사십대의 남녀 a couple in their forties //그는 사십대이다 He is in his forties.

***사악 邪惡** wickedness ; viciousness ; evil ; vice —하다 (be) wicked ; vicious ; malicious ; sinister ; evil ; wrong ¶ 사악한 사람 a villain ; a wicked man

사안 私案 a private plan〔idea, design〕

사안 史眼 a historical view

사안 事案 a case

사암 砂岩 『지질』 sandstone

사약 死藥 poison ; a deadly drug

사약 賜藥 (the king's) bestowal of poison as a death penalty —하다 bestow poison 《on a person》 as a death penalty

사양 斜陽 the setting sun ; the evening sun〔light〕 ; slanting sunbeams
— 산업 the decaying〔declining〕 industry —족 the sunset class ; the fallen aristocracy ; the has-beens ; the declining upper-class families

사양 飼養 ⇨ 사육

사양 辭讓 [사절] declining (in favor of another) ; refusal (with appreciation) ; [겸양] reserve ; hesitancy ; holding back (with modesty) —하다 decline (with regrets) ; refuse courteously ; excuse oneself 《from》 ; hold back ; hesitate 《to do》 ¶ 그는 초대를 정중히 사양했다 He declined courteously the invitation with regret. //가는 것은 사양하겠습니다 I should like to be excused from going. //지금은 사양할 때가 아니다 This is no time for you to stand on ceremony. //사양 말고 말해라 Speak out freely. /Be outspoken. //무엇이든지 사양말고 요구해라 Don't scruple to ask anything. //맹목적인 사양은 미덕이 아니다 Hesitation without due reason is not a virtue. //그는 죽음도 사양치 않는다 He does not hesitate even to die. /He is ready〔willing〕 to die. //사양하지 마시고 많이 드십시오 Please go right ahead and help yourself.

사양머리 ⇨ 새앙머리

사어 私語 [은근한 얘기] private talk ; secret〔confidential〕 talk ; [속삭임] whisper(ing) ; mutter ; murmur —하다 have a private talk ; talk privately 〔secretly〕 ; whisper ; talk in whispers ; murmur

사어 死語 a dead language ; an obsolete word ¶ 고대 희랍어는 사어다 Ancient Greek is a dead language.

†사업 事業 [일·기업] a work ; an undertaking ; an enterprise ; a project ; activity ; operations ; [실업] a business ; an industry ; [직업] a vocation ; an occupation ; [업적] an achievement ; a deed ¶ 큰〔새로운〕 사업 a big〔new〕 undertaking〔enterprise〕 //매우 힘든 사업 a heavy 〔an arduous, an uphill〕 task //수지 맞는 〔유망한〕 사업 a paying〔promising〕 business //막중한 개발 사업 vital development venture //영구 불멸의 사업 an everlasting

ㅅ

achievement // 사업을 시작하다 undertake〔start〕 an enterprise // 사업을 완수하다 perform a deed // 사업을 하다 carry on business // 사업을 경영하다 run a business // 사업을 확장〔축소〕하다 extend〔reduce〕 business // 사업에 출자하다 finance an undertaking // 사업에 종사하다 engage in business // 사업에 성공〔실패〕하다 succeed〔fail〕 in business // 사업이 잘 되다 have〔do, enjoy〕 a thriving business // 사업이 잘 안되다 have a slump in business // 무슨 사업을 하십니까 What line〔kind〕 of business are you in? /What is your occupation? // 그는 큰 사업을 할 사나이다 He is a man to do big things. // 사업은 잘돼갑니까 How's your business coming? // 사업은 어디까지나 사업이다 Business is business. // 사업은 잘 됩니까 Is everything going well with your business?
—가 a man of enterprise ; an enterpriser ; a businessman ; an industrialist —계 the industrial〔business〕 world — 계획 a plan of operation ; a business program — 공채 an industrial bond —부 the promotion department —비 working expenses —세 an enterprise tax — 소득 an income from one's enterprise — 연도 a business year〔term〕 ; an accounting period — 자금 business funds —장(소) a place of business ; an establishment —주 a business proprietor 개척 — colonization〔reclamation〕 work 공공 — a public utility enterprise ; public utilities 교육〔사회, 자선〕 — educational〔social, charitable〕 work 문화 — a cultural enterprise ; cultural work 전기 — the electric(al) industry 정부〔민간〕 — a government〔private〕 enterprise

사업화 事業化 〔상업화〕 commercialization ; 〔공업화〕 industrialization —하다 industrialize ; commercialize

사역 使役 employment ; service ; work —하다 employ ; use 《a person》 ; press 《a person》 into service ; set 《a person》 to work
—견(犬) a working dog — 동사 〖문법〗 a causative verb

사연 事緣 the origin and circumstances of a matter〔case〕 ; the (full) story ; matters (as they stand) ¶ 어찌 된 사연이냐 What's the story? /What's it all about? // 그 사연을 말해 주시오 Tell me the whole story of it. // 사연은 이러하다 This is how it is. /The case stands thus.

사연 辭緣 contents (of a letter) ; what one intends to speak ; the gist ; the import ¶ 편지의 사연이 무엇이더냐 What was the letter about?

사열 四列 four lines〔rows〕 ¶ 사열로 정렬하다 be lined up four abreast // 사열로 행진하다 march〔go〕 by fours

사열 査閱 inspection ; examination —하다 inspect ; examine ¶ 사열을 받다 be inspected 《by》 ; undergo an inspection
—관 an inspector ; an examiner ; an inspecting officer (교련의) —대 a reviewing stand —식 a formal military inspection〔review〕 ; a parade 개선 —식 a triumphal military review

사염화 四鹽化 〖화학〗 tetrachloride
—물 〖화학〗 tetrachloride — 백금 platinumtetrachloride —연(鉛)〔티타늄〕 lead〔titanium〕 tetrachloride —탄소 carbon tetrachloride —탄소 소화기 a carbon tetrachloride fire extinguisher

사영 私營 private operation〔management〕 ¶ 사영의 private ; privately-operated 〔-run〕 // 그 철도는 사영이다 The railway is privately operated.
— 사업 a private enterprise

사영 射影 〖수학〗 projection
— 기하학 projective geometry —면 〖측량〗 a projecting plane — 평면 a projective plane 원주〔원추〕 — cylindrical〔conical〕 projection 정〔등각〕— orthogonal 〔isometric〕 projection

사영 斜影 a slanting shadow ¶ 거리에 사영을 던지다 cast a shadow obliquely down the street

사오 四五 four or five ¶ 사오일 four or five days ; several days // 사오회 four or five times

사옥 社屋 the building (of a company)

사외 社外 outside the company

사욕 沙浴, 砂浴 〔사람의〕 a sand bath ; 〔동물의〕 a dust bath ; dust bathing ; dusting —하다 have〔take〕 a sand bath ; bathe in dust

***사욕 私慾** a selfish desire ; selfishness ; self-interest ; a desire for personal gain ¶ 사욕의 selfish ; self-interested ; mercenary // 사욕이 없는 unselfish ; disinterested // 사욕에서 from a selfish motive // 사욕을 채우다 gratify〔satisfy〕 one's selfish desire // 사욕을 버리다 put aside self-interest // 사욕을 도모하다 have an eye to main chance ; feather one's own nest ; pursue one's self-interest

사욕 邪慾 an evil desire ; a selfish ambition ; an evil passion ; a sinful lust ; a carnal〔wicked〕 desire

사용 私用 〔쓰임〕 private〔personal〕 use ; appropriation ; misappropriation ; 〔볼일〕 private〔personal〕 business —하다 divert〔turn〕 to private use ; use for private purpose ; misappropriate ; embezzle 《public funds》 ¶ 공금을 사용하다 embezzle public funds ; divert public money to private use // 사용으로 인천에 가다 go down to *Inch'ŏn* on personal business // 사용의 전화는 삼가하십시오 Please refrain from using the telephone for private purposes. // 경리 계원이 그 회의 공금을 사용하였다 The treasurer misappropriated the society's funds.

†**사용 使用** use ; employment ; application (적용) ; consumption (소비) ; appropriation (충당) **—하다** use ; have the use of ; make use of ; put 《a thing》 to use ; employ ; apply ; consume ; appropriate ¶ 사용할 수 있는 usable ; fit for use // 사용할 수 없는 unfit for use // 유효 적절히 사용하다 make good use of // 여러번〔마음대로〕 사용하다 have the frequent〔free〕 use of // 사용되고 있다〔있지 않다〕 be in〔out of〕 use // 일반적으로〔일상〕 사용되고 있다 be in general〔everyday〕 use // 가스를 사용하다 use〔consume〕 gas // 시간을 독서에 사용하다 devote one's time to reading // 돈을 구제 사업에 사용하다 appropriate〔apply, devote〕 a sum of money to the relief of the poor // 알코올을 용해제로 사용하다 use alcohol as a solvent // 여가를 어떻게 사용합니까 How do you spend〔use〕 your spare time ? // 그들은 총기의 사용을 금했다〔허용했다〕 They banned〔allowed〕 the use of firearms. // 이 기계는 꽤 오래 사용한 것이다 This machine has been much of service. // 이 책상은 오래 사용할 수 있다 This desk stands long use. / This desk will give long service. // 이 번호는 고장이거나 현재 사용하지 않는 번호인 모양입니다 This number must be out of order or not in service at this time. // 혹시 그 번호가 사용되지 않고 있는 것은 아닌지 알아봐 줄 수 있습니까 Could you check and see if that number is out of service or something ?

— 가치 utility value ; the value in use **—권** the right of using ; the use **—량** the amount 《of a thing》 used ; the quantity 《of a thing》 consumed **—료** a rental fee ; the rental ; the rent ; the hire **—법** the way of using ; use ; how to use ; usage ; the directions (for use) 《on the medicine》 ; instructions ¶ 타이프라이터 사용법을 배우다 learn how to operate a typewriter // 장교가 신무기 사용법을 자세히 설명했다 The officer gave full and detailed instructions on the brand-new firearms. **—인** an employee (피고용인) ; a servant (하인) **—자** a user ; a consumer (소비자) ; an employer (고용자) **—중** "Be in Use" (게시) ; "Engaged" (방 따위) (게시)

사용 社用 firm〔company〕 business ; for the use of the firm ; for business use ¶ 사용으로 on (company) business // 사용으로 비품을 구입하다 purchase office stuffs〔facilities〕 for the use of a company

—족(族) expense-account plutocrats〔spenders, aristocrats〕 ; persons enjoying luxuries on the expense accounts (of their firms)

사우 祠宇 a shrine

사우 社友 [동료] a colleague (of a company) ; an office mate ; [관계자] a person connected with a firm〔company〕 ; a friend of a firm ¶ 사장 및 사우 일동 the president and his colleagues // 그는 신문사를 그만뒀으나 아직도 사우 격으로 관계하고 있다 He is no longer on the editorial staff, but is still connected with the paper as its "friend."

사운 社運 ¶ 사운을 걸다 risk〔stake, hazard〕 the future of the company 《on》

사우스 포 [야구·권투의 왼손잡이] a southpaw〔pitcher〕 ; a portsider 《미·속》

사운드 a sound

— 박스 a sound box **— 트랙** a sound track

사원 私怨 private〔personal〕 grudge〔spite, resentment〕 ¶ 사원을 품다 harbor a grudge 《against》 // 사원을 풀다 avenge one's grudge on 《a person》 ; wreak vengeance on

‡**사원 社員** an employee (of a company) ; the personnel ; (a member of) the staff ; [사무원] a clerk ; [회원] a member ; [조합원] a partner ¶ 사원 일동을 대표하여 on behalf of the staff // 사원이 되다 join the staff of (a company) // 사원을 줄이다〔늘이다〕 reduce〔increase〕 the staff // 정사원이 되다 be placed on the regular pay roll // 그는 출판사 사원이다 He is on the staff of a publishing company.

— 명부 the roster (of a company) **근무〔익명〕 —** an acting〔a dormant, a sleeping, a silent〕 partner **노무 출자 —** a working partner **신입〔퇴직〕 —** an incoming〔outgoing〕 partner〔employee〕 **업무 —** a managing partner **유한〔우선〕 —** a limited〔predominant〕 partner **정—** a regular member ; a staff member 《of a company》 **준—** a junior member **종신 —** a life member

사원 寺院 a monastery ; a (Buddhist) temple

†**사월 四月** April ; the fourth month of the year

사위[1] [꺼림] a taboo ; fear of something forbidden ; abhorrence ; loathing **—하다** shun〔avoid〕 《a thing》 as a sign of devil ; dislike superstitiously

사위[2] [윷의] one's desired point in a game of *yut*

***사위**[3] [서랑] a son-in-law ¶ 사위를 맞다 get a son-in-law // 사위가 되다 marry into a family

사윗감 a suitable person for a son-in-law **작은 —** a younger son-in-law **큰 —** the oldest son-in-law

사위 詐僞 deceit ; pretense ; dissemblance **—하다** pretend ; make false pretenses ; dissemble

사위 四圍 environment ; environs ; surroundings ; neighborhood ¶ 사위가 쥐죽은 듯 고요했다 The surroundings were deadly quiet〔silent〕 as the graveyard.

사위다 burn up ; burn to nothing ; 《a fire》

go out〔die〕; be reduced to ashes

사위스럽다 (be) taboo ; forbidden ; loathsome ; abhorrent ; ominous ; dreadful ¶ 사위스러운 행동 loathsome behavior // 그의 행동이 사위스럽다 I am appalled by his conduct.

사유 私有 private ownership〔possession, proprietorship〕 **—하다** possess oneself of ¶ 사유의 privately-owned ; private // 이 전답은 사유이다 These fields are private property.

—권 private ownership〔rights〕; the right of private property **—림** a private forest **—물** private possessions **— 재산** private〔individual〕 property **— 재산제** the private property system ; the private-ownership system **—지** private land **— 철도** a private railway

사유 思惟 thinking ; speculation ; cogitation **—하다** think〔speculate〕 about ; consider ; cogitate

— 기능 the thinking faculties **— 법칙** the law of thought **순수 —론** 〖철학〗 noetic(s)

사유 事由 a reason ; a cause ; a ground ¶ 사유 없이 without reason〔good cause〕 // 사유를 말하다 state the facts // 그가 지각한 사유는 이러하다 The reason why he is late is 《that, because》.

*__사육 飼育__ breeding ; raising ; rearing **—하다** breed ; raise ; rear ; keep

— 상자 a cage for insects (곤충 따위의) **—자** a breeder ; a 《bird》 fancier ; a raiser ; a rearer **—장** a farm ¶ 말의 사육장 a horse-breeding farm ; a stud **—학** thremmatology ; animal husbandry

‡**사육제 謝肉祭** the carnival

사은 謝恩 repaying a kindness ; expression of gratitude ; appreciation of favors **—하다** express gratitude ; repay a kindness

— (대)매출 thank-you sales **—회** a dinner〔party〕 given 《by graduates》 in honor of 《their teachers》; a thank-you party 《for the teachers》; a testimonial dinner

사은 師恩 a debt of gratitude one owes to one's teacher ; favors one receives from one's teacher

사음 —音 〖음악〗 G

— 기호 a G〔treble〕 clef

사음 舍音 a landowner's agent

사음 邪淫 lasciviousness ; lewdness ; licentiousness ; adultery **—하다** (be) lascivious ; immoral ; lewd ; licentious ; commit adultery

사음 문자 寫音文字 phonetic letters

사의 私意 self-will ; selfishness ; one's own will ; a bias ¶ 사의에서 selfishly ; from a selfish〔personal〕 motive // 사의를 개입시키다 act from a selfish motive ; be prejudiced

*__사의 謝意__ ① [감사의 뜻] gratitude ; thanks ¶ 사의를 표하기 위하여 선물을 하다 make a present in token of one's gratitude // 사의를 표하다 express one's gratitude ; tender one's thanks // 그는 머리를 숙여 정중하게 사의를 표하였다 He bowed his most profuse thanks (to her). ② (사과의 뜻) apology ¶ 사의를 표하다 express〔offer〕 one's apology

사의 辭意 [말뜻] the meaning of a word ; the import of a statement ; the drift of what one says ; [사퇴할 마음] one's resolution〔intention〕 to resign ¶ 사의를 표명하다 hint at resignation ; intimate〔make known〕 one's intention to resign ; announce one's resignation // 사의가 굳다 be firmly resolved to resign // 사의를 번복하다 reconsider one's resignation // 사의를 번복시키다 dissuade 《a person》 from resigning // 사의를 철회하다 withdraw one's resignation

사이¹ [목재량의 단위] a *sai* ; a unit of measure for timber 《=207.36 cubic inches》

†**사이²** ① [공간] a space (between two points) ; [간격] an interval ; [거리] distance apart ; [차이] a gap ¶ 사이에 between (둘의) ; among (셋 이상의) ; through (통하여) ; amidst (한가운데에) // 긴〔짧은〕 사이 for a long〔short〕 distance // 10킬로 사이를 for the distance of 10 kilometers // 서울과 부산 사이에 있는 정거장 a station between *Seoul* and *Pusan* // 일정한 사이를 두고 at regular intervals // 사이를 두다 leave a space 《for》 // 줄과 줄 사이를 떼다 leave space between the lines // 책 사이에 편지를 꽂다 put a letter between the leaves of a book // 나무 사이에 숨다 conceal oneself among the trees // 같은 사이를 두고 나무를 심다 plant trees at equal intervals // 두 집 사이가 좁다 There is not enough space between the two houses.

② [시간] an interval (between two points of time) ; a while ; a spell ; a pause ; a break ; time ; spare time ; leisure ¶ 잠깐 사이 for a little while // 한 시와 두 시 사이에 between one and two o'clock // 식사와 식사 사이에 between meals // 눈 깜짝하는 사이에 in a twinkle ; in an instant // 외출한 사이에 while one is out ; during one's absence // 어느 사이에 before one is aware of it ; without one's knowledge // 어느 사이에 봄이다 Here it is spring already. // 어느 사이에 비가 왔다 It rained before we knew it. // 공부할 사이가 없다 I have no time to study. // 그 사이에 줄곧 어디 있었니 Where have you been all this while? // 버스가 10분 사이를 두고 떠난다 Buses leave at 10 minute intervals. // 그는 말하는 사이에 자주 하품을 했다 He yawned frequently during a pause in the conversation. // 비가 쉴 사이 없이 내리고 있었다

There was no break in the rains.
③ [관계] relations ; terms ; connections ¶ 사이에 between ; among // 사이가 나쁘다 be on bad〔poor〕 terms ; do not get on well // 사이가 멀다〔가깝다〕 be on distant〔intimate〕 terms // 사이가 벌어지다 be estranged from each other // 사이를 조정하다 mediate between 《two persons》 ; act as a go-between // 저 분하고는 어떤 사이입니까 What is he to you ? /How is he related to you ? // 형제 사이입니다 We are brothers. / He is my brother. // 우리는 끊을래야 끊을 수 없는 사이이다 We are bound up with each other. // 그 여자와는 사돈이 되는 사이이다 She is a relation by marriage. // 너와 나 사이인데 사양할 필요가 뭐냐 You need not stand on ceremony with me.
사이가 좋다 관용 be on good terms

사이다¹ [음료] (a) clear soda pop ; clear carbonated drinks
—병 a pop bottle

사이다² [사게 하다] make〔let〕 buy ; sell

***사이렌** a siren ; a whistle ¶ 사이렌을 울리다 blow〔sound〕 a siren ; give〔blow〕 a whistle // 정오의 사이렌이 울린다 The noon siren blows.

사이버네틱스 [인공 두뇌학] cybernetics

사이비 似而非 pseudo- ; quasi ; manqué ; sham ; feigned ; pretended
— 군자〔신사〕 a hypocrite ; a would-be gentleman ; a snob — 기자 a quasi-reporter — 시인 a poet manqué — 신자 a pretended devotee — 언론인 a quasi-journalist — 예술가 a mock〔false〕 artist — 종교 false religion 〔teaching, cult〕 — 철학 pseudo-philosophy — 학자 a pretended scholar ; a charlatan

사이사이 ① [공간] spaces 《between》 ; intervals ; gaps ; distances ¶ 장미꽃 사이사이에 백합꽃을 심다 plant lilies among〔between 《미·구》〕 the roses
② [시간] (every) now and then ¶ 사이사이에 in the intervals 《of》 ; at intervals ; between whiles // 일하는 사이사이에 in the intervals of business ; in spare moments from one's work

사이좋게 on good〔friendly, cordial〕 terms 《with》 ; in peace〔harmony, concord〕 《with》 ; on even board 《with》 ; like good friends ¶ 당신 아내와 어머니는 사이좋게 지내고 있소 Are your wife and mother getting along all right together ?

†**사이즈** size ; [여성 신체의] vital statistics ¶ 사이즈를 재다 take the size 《of》 // 사이즈가 맞다〔안맞다〕 be〔not〕 one's size // 사이즈가 맞나 안맞나 입어보다 try one for size

사이참 [휴식] a break ; a brief-rest ; a respite ; an intermission ; recess ; [음식] a light meal between regular meals ; a snack ; refreshments

사이클 ① 〖전기〗 a cycle ¶ 매초 50 사이클 50 cycles per second ; 50Hz ② ⇨ 자전거
— 기관 a four(-stroke) cycle engine

사이클로이드 〖수학〗 a cycloid
내(內) — a hypocycloid

사이클로트론 〖물리〗 a cyclotron ¶ 사이클로트론의 cyclotronic

사이클링 cycling ; bicycling ¶ 사이클링을 가다 go on a cycling tour

***사이펀** a siphon
—병 a siphon bottle —식 기압계 a siphon barometer — 작용 siphonage — 주유기 a siphon lubricator

사익 私益 one's own interest ; self-interest ⇨ 사리(私利)

사인 ① [서명] a signature ; an autograph
— 하다 sign one's name ; put one's signature 《to》 ; autograph ¶ 사인이 든 브로마이드 an autographed still // 사인을 받다 get a person's autograph // 사인 좀 부탁합니다 Will you oblige me with your autograph ?
— 공세 storming for autographs ¶ 사인 공세를 받다 be besieged〔plagued〕 by autograph hunters —북〔첩〕 an autograph album — 수집가 an autograph hunter
② [신호] a signal ; a sign 《암호》 ¶ 투수에게 사인을 보내다 signal〔give signals〕 to the pitcher // 사인을 교환하다 exchange signals
③ 〖수학〗 sine 《sin》

사인 私人 a private person〔individual〕 ; a private citizen ¶ 사인으로서 말하다 speak in a private capacity // 사인으로서 행동하다 act as a private person

사인 死因 the cause of death ¶ 사인을 조사하다 investigate the cause of death // 사인이 불명하다 die from some unknown cause
— 통계 statistics of death causes

사인 私印 a private〔personal〕 seal ; a signet ¶ 사인을 찍다 stamp〔affix〕 one's personal seal
— 도용 theft and use of a private seal — 위조 forging〔forgery〕 of a private seal

사인교 四人轎 a sedan chair borne on poles by four men

사인조 四人組 a foursome ; a quartet(te)
— 강도 a band of four burglars

사일 巳日 〖민속〗 the Day of the Snake

사일런트 ① [무음자] a silent letter ② [무성 영화] a silent picture〔film〕

사일로 [농업] a silo 《*pl.* ~s》

⁑**사임 辭任** resignation ; retirement from office ; stepping〔going〕 out of office — 하다 resign ; leave the service ; quit〔go out of〕 office ¶ 사임을 권고하다 advise〔urge〕 《a person》 to resign // 클럽의 서기직을 사임하다 resign one's position as secretary of the club

사자 四者 ¶ 사자(간)의 quadripartite
— 협정〔회담〕 a quadripartite contract

ㅅ

〔conference〕

사자 死者 a dead person ; [총칭] the deceased ; the dead ; [사고로 인한] the fatalities ; loss of life ; [전쟁에 의한] the casualties

사자 私資 private funds ⇨ 사재(私財)

‡**사자 使者** an envoy ; a messenger ; a mission ¶ 사자를 보내다 send a messenger ; dispatch an envoy // 사자로서 가다 go on a mission // 낙엽은 겨울의 사자이다 The falling leaves are heralds of Jack Frost.

사잣밥 싸 가지고 다닌다 속담 Death keeps no calendar. /At every hour death is near.

사자 寫字 copying ; transcription
—료 a copying fee **—생** a copyist ; an amanuensis 《*pl.* -enses》 ; a scribe

†**사자 獅子** a lion
— 새끼 a lion cub **— 조련사(調練師)** a lion tamer〔trainer〕 **—코** a pug〔snub〕 nose ; a broad, squat nose ; an upturned nose **암—** a lioness

사자 없는 산에 토끼가 대장 노릇한다 속담 When the cat's way, the mice will play. /Well kens the mouse when the cat's out of mouse.

사자 嗣子 an heir ; an heiress (여자) ; a successor

사자후 獅子吼 the roaring of a lion ; [열변] harangue ; fulmination ; fiery eloquence ; a declamatory speech ; [불교의] the preaching of Buddha ; [질투의] the raging of a jealous woman ¶ 사자후를 토하다 harangue ; deliver a declamatory speech with eloquence

사장 沙場 a sandbank ; a sandy beach ; the sands ; a shoal

사장 社長 the president of a company
—직 presidency **무역 회사 —** the president of a trading company **부—** the vice-president **신문사 —** the president of a newspaper firm

사장 死藏 dead storage ; hoarding **—하다** hoard ; keep in dead storage ; keep 《a thing》 idle ¶ 다이아몬드를 사장하다 hoard diamonds

사장 査丈 senior relatives by marriage

사장 射場 a shooting〔firing〕 range ; a target practice range ; [활터] an archery ground〔plot〕 ; [실내의] a shooting gallery

사장 寫場 a photo(graphic) studio ; a photo atelier

사장 謝狀 a letter of appreciation 〔thanks〕

사장 社葬 a funeral (service) conducted by the company of the deceased

사장본 私藏本 a book belonging to〔in the library of〕 an individual

사재 私財 private funds〔property, means, assets, fortune, wealth, estate〕 ¶ 사재를 털어서 at one's own expense ; out of one's own pocket // 공공 사업에 사재를 바치다 contribute out of one's purse to public enterprises // 그 집과 가구는 나의 사재다 The house and furniture are my own assets.

사재 社財 property of a firm

사저 私邸 one's private residence 〔house, mansion〕

사적 史的 (being) historical ; historic ¶ 사적 연구 historical studies // 사적 사실 a historical fact // 사적 유물론 historical materialism

사적 史蹟 a historic(al) spot 〔place〕 ; historical relics〔remains, landmarks〕 ; a place of historical interest ¶ 사적을 찾다 visit places of historical interest // 사적이 풍부하다 be rich in historic associations // 사적을 보존하다 preserve historic remains
— 보존회 a society for the preservation of historic relics

사적 史籍 historical books〔works〕 ; history

†**사적 私的** (being) private ; personal ¶ 사적 감정 personal feeling // 사적 생활 one's private〔home〕 life // 그의 방문은 사적인 것이었다 His visit was of private character. // 무슨 사적인 감정이 있는 것으로 오해하지 마시오 Don't take it personally.

사적 事績 an achievement ; an accomplishment ; a deed ; services ; merits ; an exploit ¶ 위인의 사적 the deeds of a great man // 그의 사적은 역사에 오래 남을 것이다 His achievements will long remain in history. // 이 사적들은 역사에 전해지지 않고 있다 These deeds have passed out of history. // 그 분에게는 수많은 사적이 있다 He has numerous achievements〔exploits〕 to his credit. // 그는 문교부 장관으로서 많은 사적을 올렸다 He rendered considerable services as Minister of Education.

사적 事蹟 an evidence ; a vestige ; a trace

사적 射的 a target ; a mark

사전 私田 a private〔privately-owned〕 field

사전 私錢 counterfeit〔bogus, fake〕 money ; [경화] a counter〔false, bad〕 coin ; [지폐] a forged〔false〕 bank note
—꾼 [사용자] a user〔passer〕 of counterfeit money ; a smasher ; [제조자] a counterfeiter ; a coiner

사전 事前 ¶ 사전에 before a thing takes place〔materializes〕 ; before the fact ; in advance ; beforehand // 사전에 협의하다 have a prior consultation ; hold a preliminary consultation〔conference〕 // 사전에 강연의 준비를 하다 prepare one's lecture in advance
— 검사 a preliminary inspection〔examination〕 **— 검열** precensorship **— 공작** preparatory operations ; advancework **— 동의** prior consent ; consent before the fact **— 수회(收賄)** acceptance of a bribe before an act **— 승인** prior approval **—**

운동 [선거의] preelection campaigning ; precandidacy propaganda — 종범자 an accessory〔accessary〕 before the fact — 준비 advance preparations — 추정치 〖수학〗 an advance estimate — 통고 an advance notice ; a previous notice — 할당 the prearranged quota 《of rice delivery》 — 행위 an act before the fact — 협의 prior consultation — 확률 〖수학〗 a prior probability

†사전 辭典 a dictionary ; a lexicon ; a wordbook ¶ 사전을 찾다 look up 《a word》 in a dictionary ; consult〔refer to〕 a lexicon // 사전과 씨름하다 struggle〔wrestle〕 with a dictionary // 그는 살아있는 사전이다 He is a walking〔living〕 dictionary.

—식〔체〕 영어 dictionary English —체목록 [도서관 따위의] a dictionary catalog(ue) — 편집법〔학〕 lexicography — 편찬자 a lexicographer ; a compiler of a dictionary 불한 — a French-Korean dictionary

사절 四節 the four seasons ⇨ 사철

사절 四折 ¶ 사절의 folded in four ; fourfold // 사절로 하다 fold in four

—판 a quarto (edition)

*사절 使節 an emissary ; a delegate ; an envoy ¶ 사절로서 가다 go on a mission

—단 a mission ; a delegation 로마 교황 — a papal nuncio〔legate〕 교육 —단 an educational mission 군사 —(단) a military mission 친선 —단 a good will envoy〔mission〕

*사절 謝絶 refusal ; denial —하다 refuse ; decline ; deny ; turn down ¶ 면회를 사절하다 decline to see 《a person》 ; deny oneself to visitors ; be not at home to a visitor // 입장을 사절당하다 be denied admission 《to》

면회 — "No Visitors" (게시) ; [병원] "By appointment only" (게시) 외상 — "Cash Please" (게시) ; "No Credit" (게시) 입장 — "No Admission" ; [극장의 미성년 불가] "Adults Only" ; "No Children"

사절 死絶 extinction ; annihilation ; (a) death —하다 die out ; become extinct ; perish ; be annihilated

사정 私情 personal feelings〔regard, consideration, sentiment〕 ; bias ¶ 사정에 좌우되다 be swayed〔influenced〕 by personal feelings // 사정을 버리다 set aside personal sentiment // 법관은 사정을 초월해서 재판해야 한다 Judges should conduct the trial without personal feelings.

†사정 事情 ① [형편] circumstances ; the situation ; the state of things〔affairs〕 ¶ 부득이한 사정으로 owing to unavoidable circumstances // 가정 사정으로 for family reasons // 이런 사정으로 in〔under〕 these circumstances // 어떤 사정일지라도 under any circumstances // 사정이 허락하면 as far as circumstances permit // 미국 사정에 밝다 be conversant with American affairs // 사정이 참 딱하십니다 It's too bad ! // 사정이 있어 말할 수 없습니다 There is a certain reason why I cannot speak about it. // 한국에서는 사정이 다릅니다 Things are different in Korea. // 당신은 사정을 오해하고 있습니다 You have got the wrong end of the stick. // 무슨 사정이 있는 걸까 I wonder if there's some special reason. // 그래서 그가 정계 사정에 밝구나 So that's why he's so knowledgeable about me political world.

② [정상] consideration ; leniency ; indulgence —하다 ask leniency〔a favor〕 ¶ 사정이 있다 be considerate〔sympathetic〕 // 사정이 없다 have no consideration 《for》 ; be pitiless 《to》 // 아무리 사정해도 그는 모르는 체하였다 He remained deaf to our eager supplication.

동양 — conditions in the East 미국 — things American ; Americana 주택〔식량〕 — the housing〔food〕 situation 중국 — the state of affairs in China

사정 邪正 right and wrong ; good and bad ; just and evil ¶ 사정을 분별하다 know right from wrong ; have a clear sense of right and wrong

*사정 査定 [세금] assessment ; [예산] revision ; [자격] screening —하다 assess ; revise

— 가격 an assessed value〔price〕 — 기관 an assessing organ —액 an assessed amount —자 an assessor 세액 — the assessment of taxes 예산안 — a revised budget

사정 司正 audit and inspection

대통령 — 담당 특별 보좌관 the Special Presidential Assistant on Audit and Inspection

사정 射程 a range (of fire) ; a rifle range (소총의) ; a shooting range ¶ 사정 안〔밖〕에 within〔out of〕 range // 이 곡사포는 사정이 30마일이다 This howitzer ranges thirty miles.

원〔근〕거리 — a long〔short〕 range 유효 — the effective range

사정 射精 ejaculation ; a seminal emission ; an emission (of semen) —하다 ejaculate ; emit〔discharge〕 semen

—관 an ejaculatory duct

사정사정 pleadingly ; imploringly —하다 implore ; plead 《for》 ; beseech ; appeal 《to, for》 ¶ 도와달라고 사정사정하다 implore 《a person》 to help 《one》

사정없다 事情— (be) merciless ; ruthless ; unsparing ¶ 사정없이 mercilessly ; ruthlessly ; severely // 사정없이 처벌하다 show 《a person》 no mercy at all

ㅅ

사제 司祭 a priest ; a pastor ; a celebrant
사제 私弟 one's private home ; the private residence (of an official)
사제 私製 private〔illicit〕 manufacture ; privately made
— 담배 privately made cigarettes — 엽서 a private postcard ; a post card 《미》 —품 privately made goods
사제 舍弟 [아우] my younger brother ; [형에게] me ; I who am your younger brother
사제 師弟 teacher and student〔pupil〕 ; ·master and disciple ¶ 사제 관계가 밀접하다 There are intimate relations between masters and pupils.
사제 瀉劑 a laxative
사조 —調 〖음악〗 (the key of) G.
사 장〔단〕조 (a sonata in) G major〔minor〕
사조 査照 an investigation ; a survey ; a check up 《미》 ; examination **—하다** investigate ; survey ; check up ; examine
사조 思潮 the trend〔current〕 of thought ; the drift of public opinion
근대 — the current of modern thought 문예 — the trend of literature 시대 — the spirit〔thought〕 of the times ; the drift of public opinion at that time ; the *Zeitgeist* 현대 — contemporary thought
사조 詞藻 [문채] rhetorical flourishes ; flowery speech ; [시문] prose and poetry ; [재주] a talent for verse
사조 飼鳥 [가금] poultry ; a domestic fowl ; [기르는 새] a cage bird ; a pet bird
사족 士族 a noble〔distinguished〕 family (명문) ; a descendant of a gentleman (선비 자손) ¶ 그는 사족 출신이다 He comes of a good stock.
사족 四足 four legs ; limbs 《속》 ¶ 사족의 four-footed ; quadruped // 사족 성한 병신 an invalid with sound limbs ; an idler ; a wastrel
— 동물 a quadruped ; a four-footed animal **—류** the quadrupeds ; the four-footed species — 발이〔백이〕 a horse with white hooves
사족을 못 쓰다 관용 be unable to move one's limbs ; be spellbound ; be crazy about 《jewelry》 ; be a slave of 《money》 ; be addicted to 《alcohol》 ; be helplessly fond of 《women》
사족 蛇足 "a snake's foot" ; superfluity ; redundancy ; padding (문장의) ¶ 사족을 붙이다 make an unnecessary addition ; add a fifth wheel
사졸 士卒 a private ; the rank and file 《총칭》
사종 四從 a fourth cousin
사죄 死罪 a capital crime〔offense〕 ; a death penalty ; a crime punishable with death ; 〖가톨릭〗 a mortal〔deadly〕 sin
:**사죄 赦罪** pardon ; remission ; absolution ; [대사] amnesty **—하다** pardon ; remit 《a punishment》 ; absolve 《a person》 from
사죄 謝罪 an apology **—하다** apologize to 《a person》 for ; make〔beg, offer〕 an apology for ¶ 사죄를 요구하다 demand an apology // 그는 그 행동에 대하여 정중히 사죄했다 He made me 〔offered〕 a humble apology for his conduct.
— 광고 a notice of apology **—장** a written apology ; a letter of apology
사주 私鑄 counterfeit〔forged〕 coinage **—하다** counterfeit ; forge (coins)
—전 a counterfeit coin〔copper〕
사주 使嗾 instigation ; incitement **—하다** instigate ; incite ; provoke ; egg〔set〕 《a person》 on ¶ 친구의 사주로 instigated by one's friend ; at the instigation of a friend // 노동자들에게 파업을 사주하다 instigate workers to down tools ; instigate a strike // 그는 누구의 사주에 의해서 탈영했을 것이다 He must have deserted from his regiment on somebody's suggestion.
사주 砂洲 a sandbar ; a sandbank ; a reef
사주 四柱 the "Four Pillars" (the year, month, day and hour of one's birth) which are supposed to influence one's fortune ; fate
— 단자 a letter to the house of the fiancée (in which the Four Pillars of the bridegroom-to-be are written) **—쟁이** a fortuneteller ; a diviner **—점** one's fortune as determined by the Four Pillars
사주 보다 관용 have one's fortune told ; consult a fortuneteller
사주 社主 the head〔proprietor, owner〕 of a firm〔company〕
사주 四周 ⇨ 사위(四圍), 주위(周圍)
사주체 斜柱體 an oblique cylinder
사주 팔자 四柱八字 the Four Pillars and the Eight Characters (for the year, month, day, and hour of one's birth) ; [운수] fate ; destiny ; fortune ; one's lot ¶ 사주 팔자가 좋다〔세다〕 be born with good〔bad〕 destiny ; be born under a lucky〔an unlucky〕 star
사중 四重 [네겹] quadruple ; fourfold ; [불교의] the Four Major Prohibitions of Buddhism
—극(極) 〖물리〗 a quadrupole — 전신 quadplex telegraphy —주 a quartet —창 a vocal quartet —항(項) 〖물리〗 a quartet 현악 —주 a string quartet
***사증 査證** [증명] a certificate ; a license ; [입국 허가의] visa ; visé (프) **—하다** visa ; visé ; endorse ¶ 사증한 visaed ; visé'd // 여권의 사증을 받다 get

one's passport visé'd ; get a visa on one's passport
—료 a visa〔visé〕 fee 입국〔출국〕 — an entry〔exit〕 visa

‡사지 四肢 the limbs ; the legs and arms ; the members ¶ 사지를 자르다 cut off the limbs ; dismember a body // 사지가 떨렸다 My limbs trembled.
— 결손증 amelia — 골격 〖해부〗 the appendicular skeleton — 마비 diplegia ; quadriplegia

사지[1] [종이 오라기] paper streamers on ritual utensils

사지[2] [배의] a mooring pole (on a boat)

사지 死地 the place of death ; the jaws of death ; the point of death ; a fatal position ; deadly circumstances ¶ 사지에 빠지다 fall into the jaws of death ; be at death's doorstep ; be on the brink of death // 사지를 벗어나다 escape from the jaws of death ; come out of a fatal position // 그는 사지를 넘어 자유 세계로 귀순했다 He defected to the Free World across the point of death.

사지어금니 an indispensable thing〔person〕《for, to》; indispensables ; necessaries ; what one cannot do without ¶ 그는 사지어금니와도 같은 존재다 I cannot spare him. /His service can't be dispensed with.

사지춤 a dance performed with a lion's mask

사지코 a pug〔snub〕 nose ¶ 사지코의 pug〔snub〕-nosed

사직 司直 the judicial authorities ; a judge ; the bench 《총칭》 ¶ 그러한 비행은 사직 당국에 고발되어야 마땅하다 Such illegal conduct should be indicted to the judicial authorities.

사직 社稷 the guardian deities of the State ; sovereignty ; the State ; the genius loci ¶ 사직지신 a pillar of the State ; a leading statesman
—단 an altar to the State deities

‡사직 辭職 resignation —하다 resign (from) ; quit〔leave〕 office ¶ 사장직을 사직했다 He resigned as president of the company. // 그는 병 때문에 사직했다 He has resigned (his post) on grounds〔account〕 of ill health. // 사직한 것을 나중에 후회하지는 않겠지 Are you sure you won't be sorry you've quit?
— 승인〔청허〕 acceptance of a person's resignation —원 a request to resign ; a letter of resignation —자 a resigner 총— a general resignation ; a wholesale resignation

사진 沙塵 dust ¶ 사진을 일으키다 raise a cloud of dust // 지독한 사진이군 How dusty it is!

†사진 寫眞 a photograph ; a picture ; a photo ; a snapshot (스냅) ¶ 사진을 찍다 take a photograph of ; take a snapshot of // 사진을 찍게 하다 have one's photograph taken // 사진을 확대〔인화〕하다 enlarge〔print〕 a photograph // 사진을 찍히다〔찍히지 않다〕 pose〔refuse to pose〕 for a photograph〔photographer〕 // 사진을 현상하다 develop a film〔plate〕 // 사진을 찍기 싫어하다 be camera-shy ; suffer from cameraphobia // 사진반에 포위되다 face a battery of cameras ; be subjected to a barrage of cameramen // 사진이 잘 되었다 The picture turned out well. // 사진을 한장 보냅니다 I'll sending you a photograph of me. // 그 여자는 사진이 잘 나온다 She takes very good pictures. /She photographs very well. /She is very photogenic. // 이 사진은 실물보다 못하다 This picture does not do you justice. // 이 사진은 그 여자 실물보다 잘 나왔다 This picture flatters her.
—가 a photo artist ; a professional photographer〔cameraman〕; an artistic photographer — 결혼 marriage based on the exchange of photographs ; a photograph marriage ; a marriage arranged upon looking at each other's pictures only ¶ 사진 결혼하다 get married on the basis of pictures — 경기회 a photographic contest —관 a photo(graph) studio ; a photo atelier —광 a camera bug 《미·속》; a photo maniac ; a shutterbug —기 a camera ; a kodak — 기구 photographic apparatus〔equipment, supplies〕; camera apparatus〔gear〕 —기 상점 a camera shop — 기자 a cameraman — 대지 a photomount — 도락〔취미〕 a photo fad〔hobby〕 — 망원경 a phototelescope —반 the photo section ; [사람] a 《newspaper》 cameraman —부 the photo department — 분광기 a photospectroscope — 분석가 a photographic analyst —사 a photographer — 석판 a photolithograph —술 photography — 식자 photocomposition — 아연 철판 (凸板) [프린트] a photozincograph ; [술] photozincography ; photozincotypy — 전보 a phototelegram ; a telephotographic message ; a photoradiogram — 전송술 phototelegraphy ; wirephotography ¶ 사진 전송을 하다 phototelegraph ; telephotograph — 제판 a photoengraving ; phototype process — 지도 a photomap —첩 a photograph album —총 a camera gun — 촬영 대회 a photographic contest — 측량 photogrammetry ; surveying by photography —틀 a picture〔photo〕 frame —판 [凹판] a photogravure ; [凸판] a phototype ; a photostat — 판정 deciding by a photograph — 평판(平版) [술] photolithography ; [그림] a photolithograph ; a photolithoprint ; a photolitho — 화보 a

ㅅ

pictorial ; an illustrated magazine 광택 — a glazed photograph 몽타즈 — a photomontage 섬광(閃光)〔불투명, 전신(全身)〕 — a flashlight〔matted, full-length〕 photograph 전송 — phototelegraph 전신〔반신〕 — a full-〔half-〕length photograph 전자 — electrophotography 천연색 — a color photograph〔picture〕 항공 — an air〔aerial〕 photo 현미경 — a photomicrograph 흑백 — a black and white photograph〔picture〕

사질 舍姪 my nephew

사차 四次 ¶ 사차의 the fourth ; biquadratic ; quartic

— 방정식 a biquadratic〔quartic〕(equation) —식 a quartic —원 the fourth dimension

사찰 寺刹 a temple ⇨ 절

사찰 私札 a private〔personal〕 letter

사찰 査察 investigation ; inspection ; thought control (사상의) —하다 investigate ; inspect

— 계원 a special service man —관 an inspector — 비행 an inspection flight — 제도 an inspection system 공중 — an aerial inspection 세무 — tax investigation 지상 — a ground inspection 학원(정치) — (political) inspection on campus activities 현지 — an on-site inspection

사창 私娼 an unlicensed prostitute ; a streetwalker ; a woman of the street ; a whore ¶ 사창을 단속하다 clean out unlicensed prostitutes

—가(街) an unlicensed〔prostitute〕 quarters —굴 a brothel ; a bawdy house ; a house of ill fame — 박멸 운동 a crusade against streetwalkers

사창 紗窓 a gauze window

사채 私債 a personal debt〔loan, obligation〕 ; private liabilities ¶ 사채를 주다 make a private loan 《to》

— 동결 loan freeze 고금리 — 시장 an usurious private money market

사채 社債 a company bond ; a debenture ¶ 사채를 발행하다 issue bonds〔debentures〕

—권(券) a debenture ; a bond ¶ 사채권 양도〔신탁〕 debenture transfer〔trust〕 // 무기명 사채권 an unregistered〔a bearer〕 debenture ; a debenture (bond) payable to bearer // 무기한〔유기한〕 사채권 an irredeemable〔a redeemable〕 debenture —권자(權者) a debenture holder — 발행 flotation of debentures ; debenture issue〔flotation〕 ¶ 사채 발행고 the debentures issued ; the issue amount of debentures // 사채 발행 한도 the issue limit of debentures — 상환 debenture redemption — 유통 시장 debenture trading market — 이자 debenture interests — 인수자 a debenture underwriter 담보〔무담보〕 — a secured〔an unsecured〕 debenture 보증 — a guaranteed debenture bond 장기〔단기〕 — a long-〔short-〕 term debenture 전환(轉換) — a convertible debenture

사책 史冊 a history book

사천 〔몰래 모은〕 secret savings ; pin money ; 〔사삿돈〕 private funds

사천왕 四天王 the Four Devas ; the four heavenly guardians of Buddhism

*사철 四— the four seasons ; seasons of the year ; 〔부사적〕 all the year round ; in all seasons ; throughout the year ; always ¶ 사철 피는 꽃 a perennial flower // 사철 중에서 봄이 제일 기분 좋다 Spring is the most pleasant of all seasons. // 그는 사철 불평만 한다 He complains day in and day out.

사철 私鐵 〔사설 철도〕 a nongovernmental railroad line ; a railroad under private management ; 〔회사〕 a railway company ; a railroad corporation 《미》

사철 砂鐵 『광물』 iron sand ; magnetic sand

사철나무 『식물』 a spindle tree

사철쑥 perennial artemisia ; Artemisia capillaris (학명)

사체 四體 the limbs ; the extremities ; the members of the body

사체 死體 a corpse ; a dead body ; one's (last) remains ; 〔동물의〕 a carcass ; 〔미이라〕 a mummy

— 강직(强直) cadaveric stiffening〔rigidity〕 ; rigor mortis 《라》 — 검사 an inquest 《on the body of》 — 검안 a postmortem (examination) ; a coroner's inquest — 공포증 necrophobia — 안치소〔가치소(假置所)〕 a lich-house ; a mortuary ; a morgue ; a deadhouse — 유기〔발굴〕 abandonment〔exhumation〕 of a dead body — 해부 dissection of a dead body ; necrotomy ; 〔검시를 위한〕 an autopsy ; a postmortem (examination) ; necroscopy 타살 — the body of a murdered person〔of the victim of a murder〕 ; a corpus delicti 《*pl.* corpora delicti》 《라》

사체 斜體 (letters in) italics ; 〔필기의〕 an oblique hand ¶ 사체의 italicized

사초 莎草 ① 『식물』 a nut grass ② 〔잔디〕 lawn ; turf ; sod —하다 sod〔turf〕 a tomb〔grave〕

†사촌 四寸 a cousin

—간 〔사람〕 cousins ; 〔관계〕 cousinship ; cousinhood 외— a cousin on the mother's side 이웃 — a neighbor as good as a cousin

사촌이 땅을 샀나 배는 왜 앓아 〔속담〕 An envious man waxes with the fatness of his neighbour.

사춘기 思春期 adolescence ; puberty ; the awkward age ¶ 사춘기의 소년 an adolescent boy ; a boy at puberty // 사춘

기에 달하다 arrive at〔attain〕 puberty ; become adolescent ; reach the age of puberty

사출 射出 shooting out ; emission ; ejaculation ; catapulting ; radiation **—하다** shoot out ; emit ; project ; catapult
—각 〖기계〗 the angle of emergence **—근** 〖생리〗 an ejaculator **—기** a catapult **— 성형** 〖화학〗 injection molding **—수** 〖식물〗 medullary rays **— 좌석** 〖항공〗 an ejection〔ejector〕 seat

사춤 [틈] a gap ; a crack ; [흙 메우기] filling in a gap ; pointing ¶ 사춤치다 fill in 《a gap》 ; point 《a cleft》 ; plaster ; stuff clay into cracks of a wall

사취 砂嘴 〖지질〗 a sand spit

*__사취 詐取__ fraud ; deception ; swindle ; cheating **—하다** obtain by fraud ; swindle 《a thing》 from 《a person》 ; defraud 《a person》 of ¶ 금전을 사취하다 swindle money // 재산을 사취하다 defraud 《a person》 of his property // 그는 작년에 나한테 100만원을 사취했다 He bilked me of one million *won* last year.

⁑**사치 奢侈** luxury ; extravagance ; lavishness **—하다** indulge in luxury ; be extravagant〔lavish〕 ¶ 사치한 사람 an extravagant person ; a high liver // 사치한 생활 a life of luxury // 사치를 다한 방 a luxuriously appointed room // 사치를 다하다 be given to luxury ; roll in luxury // 사치를 삼가다 deny oneself luxury // 국민의 사치를 경고하다 warn the nation against extravagance in living // 그런 사치는 할 수 없다 I cannot afford such luxury. // 그는 봉급이 적기 때문에 사치라고는 모른다 His salary is low and he gets few luxuries. // 그는 매우 사치한 음식을 먹는다 He indulges in luxurious food.
— 관세 duty on luxury imports **—세** a luxury tax ; taxes on luxuries **—품** luxuries ; a luxury ; a luxurious article ; articles deluxe **— 풍조** sumptuous moods

*__사치스럽다 奢侈—__ (be) luxurious ; extravagant ; expensive ; fine ¶ 사치스럽게 luxuriously ; extravagantly ; in a luxurious〔grand〕 style // 옷이 사치스럽다 wear fine clothes // 그는 사치스러운 환경에서 살고 있다 He lives in luxurious surroundings. // 그는 사치스러운 취미와 습성에 젖어 있다 He indulges himself in extravagant tastes and habits.

사칙 四則 〖수학〗 the four arithmetical operations〔rules〕

사칙 社則 the company's〔firm's〕 regulations

사친회 師親會 a Parent-Teacher Association 《P. T. A.》

사침(대) [베틀의] a warp controller

사칭 詐稱 impersonation ; misrepresentation ; false assumption〔statements〕 **—하다** misrepresent oneself as ; falsely assume (another's name) ; sail under false colors ¶ A라고 사칭하고 under the feigned〔assumed〕 name of A // 관리라고 사칭하다 represent oneself (falsely) to be a government official
신분〔성명〕 — 〖법〗 false personation **학력 —** a false statement of one's academic career

사카린 〖화학〗 saccharin(e) ¶ 사카린의 saccharic

사커 soccer ; association football ⇨ 축구
— 선수 a soccer player ; a soccerite ; a booter

사타구니 the groin ; the crotch ⇨ 샅

사탄 Satan ⇨ 악마

사탑 斜塔 a leaning tower ¶ 피사의 사탑 the Leaning Tower of Pisa

*__사탕 砂糖__ ① [설탕] sugar ¶ 사탕에 절인 과일 candied fruits // 사탕을 치다 sugar ; sweeten 《food》 // 사탕을 정제하다 refine sugar
② [과자] candy 《미》 ; sweets 《영》 ; taffy ; comfit ; lollipop
—가루 granulated sugar **— 그릇** [식탁용의] a sugar bowl 《미》 ; a sugar basin **—단풍** 〖식물〗 a sugar maple ; a sugar tree **—무** a sugar〔white〕 beet **—밀(蜜)** treacle ; molasses **—선(腺)** 〖식물〗 a sugar gland **—수수** 〖식물〗 a sugar cane **—옥수수** 〖식물〗 a sorg(h)o 《*pl.* ~s》 ; a sweet〔sugar〕 sorghum **—집게** 《a pair of》 sugar tongs **가루 —** powdered sugar ; 《주로 영》 castor sugar **각—** cube〔cut, block〕 sugar **얼음 —** crystal sugar ; rock candy 《미》 ; sugar candy 《영》 **흑〔조제(粗製)〕—** raw〔unrefined〕 sugar ; muscovado **흰〔정제〕—** refined sugar

사탕 발림 砂糖— sugar-coated〔honeyed〕 words ; sweet talk ; flattery ; cajolery ; soft soap **—하다** sweet-talk ; sugar (up) ; butter (up) ; soft-soap ; say nice things to ; coax with honeyed words ¶ 나는 그에게 사탕 발림을 했다 I buttered him up. // 그는 사탕 발림으로 학생에게서 돈을 빼앗았다 He wheedled money from the pupil.

사태 the shank of beef

사태 死胎 a dead fetus
— 분만 a still-birth

*__사태 沙汰__ ① [산 따위의] a landslide ; a landslip ¶ 사태가 나서 교통이 마비되었다 The landslip blocked all the transportation facilities.
② [많음] a flood ; a deluge ; an avalanche ; lots ; a multitude ¶ 시장에 유리 그릇 사태가 났다 The market is glutted with glassware. // 불경기로 인하여 실업자 사태가 났다 Depression has brought forth a mass discharge of employees.

눈— an avalanche (of snow) 사람 — lots of people ; an avalanche of people 진흙 — a mud slide 편지 — an influx of letters

사태 事態 a situation ; the state of things〔affairs〕; the aspect〔look〕 of the situation ¶ 곤란한 사태 a plight ; a predicament ; a fix 《구》// 중동의 긴박 사태 the acute situation in the Middle East // 사태를 완화하다 ease the situation // 사태를 악화하다 aggravate the situation // 사태를 연구하다 take stock of a situation // 사태를 해결하다 settle a situation // 사태는 중대해지고 있다 Things are getting serious. // 사태는 호전되었다 Things had taken a favorable turn. // 사태는 험악일로를 걷고 있다 The matter threatens to assume serious proportions. // 나는 그 사태에 매우 당황했다 I was perplexed over the situation.

사택 私宅 one's home ; a private residence〔house〕

사택 社宅 a company house (for employees)

사토 沙土 sandy soil

사토장이 莎土— a gravedigger

사통 私通 ① [밀통] illicit intercourse ; an illicit liaison〔amour, love affair〕; intimacy ; fornication (미혼자와의) ; adultery (기혼자와의) **—하다** have an amour〔affair〕《with》; have improper relations 《with》; establish illicit liaisons 《with》 ② [편지의] private correspondence (about public affairs) ; [편지] a private letter〔note, message〕 **—하다** correspond〔keep a correspondence〕《with a person》 (about public affairs)

—자 a fornicator ; an adulterer ; an adulteress

사통 오달 四通五達 《roads》 running〔stretching〕 in all directions **—하다** run〔radiate, stretch〕 in all directions ¶ 철도가 사통 오달하고 있다 There is a network of railways. /The country is crisscrossed with railroads. // 파리의 개선문으로부터 수많은 도로가 사통 오달하고 있다 A number of avenues radiate from the Arc de Triomphe in Paris.

사통 팔달 四通八達 ⇨ 사통 오달(四通五達)

사퇴 辭退 ① [사양] (polite) refusal ; declining ; refusing to accept **—하다** decline (an offer) ; refuse to accept ; excuse oneself from ¶ 일부러 초대해 주셨는데 사정으로 사퇴합니다 I am sorry but I must decline your kind invitation. // 모처럼 직장을 주신 것은 감사하오나 사퇴하고자 합니다 Thank you for your kindness in offering the job, but I wish to be excused from it.

② [하직] excusing oneself from a senior's presence ; taking one's leave from elders **—하다** excuse oneself from a senior's presence ; take one's leave from elders

—서 〖법〗 a waiver **자진 —** voluntary resignation

사투 私鬪 personal strife ; a private fight **—하다** fight (privately) ; struggle personally

사투 死鬪 a (life-or-) death struggle ; a desperate〔die-hard〕 fight **—하다** struggle for life ; fight desperately ¶ 코끼리와 사자의 사투가 절정에 이르고 있다 A desperate fight between an elephant and a lion is on its crest.

⁑사투리 a dialect ; a brogue ; an accent ¶ 그는 전라도 사투리를 쓴다 He speaks with a *Chŏlla-do* accent. // 그 여자는 순전히 경상도 사투리를 쓴다 She speaks a broad *Kyŏngsang-do* dialect.

고향〔지방〕 — one's provincialism 시골〔지방〕 — a provincial dialect〔accent〕

사특 邪慝 wickedness ; viciousness ; villainy ; evil **—하다** (be) wicked ; vicious ; villainous ; evil

사파 娑婆 this world ⇨ 사바

사파리 (a) safari

—대(隊) a safari

***사파이어** 〖광물〗 sapphire

— 바늘 a sapphire stylus〔needle〕 (레코드 플래이어의)

***사팔눈** a squint (eye) ; cross-eyes ¶ 사팔눈의 squint〔cross〕-eyed ; cockeyed // 그는 심한 사팔눈이다 He has a fearful squint. // 그는 왼쪽이 약간 사팔눈이다 He has a cast in the left eye.

사팔뜨기 a cross-eyed〔squint-eyed〕 person ; a squinter

사포 砂布 sandpaper ; glass〔emery〕 paper

사표 師表 a model ; a pattern ; an example ; a paragon ¶ 세상의 사표로서 숭앙받다 be looked up to as a man of enlightenment and leadership // 그는 세상의 사표가 될 만한 사람이다 He is the salt of the earth.

***사표 辭表** a (written) resignation ; a letter of resignation ¶ 사표를 제출하다 hand〔send〕 in one's resignation // 사표를 철회하다 withdraw one's resignation // 사표를 수리〔반려〕하다 accept〔turn down〕《a person's》 resignation // 사표를 내든지 파면을 당하든지 양자 택일하라 Resign or be fired.

사푼 softly ; with a soft〔muffled〕 step ; lightly ¶ 사푼사푼 걸어가다 walk lightly ; go with soft steps ; tread softly

사품 the meanwhile ; the interim ; the leisure ; the time

사풋 with a light-footed step ; lightly

사풍 邪風 indecent〔outrageous〕 manners〔customs〕 ¶ 사풍스럽다〔맞다〕 (be) hasty ; rash ; imprudent ; outrageous

사풍 砂風 a sandstorm

사프란 〖식물〗 a saffron ¶ 사프란 색〔빛〕

ㅅ

의 saffron-colored ; saffrony ; saffron
— 나무 saffronwood (목재) — 꽃 a (saffron) crocus

사필귀정 事必歸正 [당연한 결과] a corollary ; a natural result ¶ 사필 귀정이다 Right will prevail in the end. /Wrong cannot last long. /Nothing goes uncorrected for long. /Truth will win out in the long run.

사하다 赦— pardon ; forgive ; excuse ; remit ; absolve

사하라 사막 —砂漠 the Sahara Desert

사학 史學 history ; historical science
—과 [학부] the history department ; [학과] a history course —자 a historian

사학 私學 [학교] a private school〔college, university〕; a private institution of learning ; [학설] a personal theory〔doctrine〕; one's own doctrine〔theory〕

사학 斯學 this study〔science, learning, subject, research〕 ¶ 사학의 대가〔권위〕 an authority on the subject ; an expert in research

사할린 Sakhalin

사항 事項 [일] a matter ; a subject ; [항목] an item ; an article ; particulars ; details ¶ 계획 사항에 대해서 in matters of the program // 모든 사항에 관하여 on all matters // 불만이 있는 사항에 대해서 upon the subject matter of the complaint // 자세한 사항을 생각해 내다 work out details
관련 — relevant〔related〕 facts 주요 — an essential particular ; a main point

사해 四海 the four seas ; the seven seas ; the whole world ¶ 사해가 평온하다 All the world is at peace.
— 동포 universal brotherhood〔fraternity〕; the brotherhood of mankind — 동포주의 cosmopolitanism

사해 死海 the Dead Sea

사해 死骸 a corpse ; a dead body ; 《a person's》 remains ; a cadaver

사행 私行 ① [생활·행위] a private life ; one's private conduct〔doings, affairs〕 ¶ 남의 사행을 들추어 내다 expose〔lay bare〕 another's private affairs
② [여행] a private〔personal〕 trip ; traveling incognito〔in disguise〕 (잠행)
— 하다 go out on one's personal business ; travel in disguise

사행 射倖 speculation ; taking a chance〔flyer〕; adventure — 하다 speculate ; take a chance〔flyer〕 《in》 ¶ 사행적인 speculative ; gambling
—심 a speculative〔gambling〕 spirit ¶ 사행심을 조장하다 stir up〔incite〕 the gambling spirit ; increase popular speculation

사행 蛇行 meandering — 하다 snake along ; go zigzag ; meander ; crawl meanderingly
— 운동 a serpentine motion

사향 思鄕 nostalgia ; homesickness ; thoughts of home ; yearning for one's home ; homecoming fever — 하다 think of one's home ; yearn for one's home ; be homesick〔nostalgic〕 ¶ 사향심이 일다 become homesick〔nostalgic〕; yearn〔long〕 for the sight of one's home
—병 homesickness ; nostalgia

***사향** 麝香 musk ¶ 사향이 든 musk scented // 사향내가 나다 smell like musk
—고양이 〖동물〗 a musk〔civet〕 cat —나무 〖식물〗 a musk tree —노루 〖동물〗 a musk deer ; a musk ; Moschus moschiferus —소 a musk-ox 《*pl.* -oxen》; a musk sheep —수 musk water〔scent〕 —쥐 〖동물〗 a muskrat ; a musk shrew ; Suncus murinus —초 〖식물〗 a wild thyme

사혈 死血 virulent〔impure〕 blood

사혈 瀉血 depletion (of blood) — 하다 deplete (blood)
—법 bloodletting ; bleeding ; depletion (of blood) —제 (a blood) depletive

사혐 私嫌 personal hatred〔disgust, aversion, repugnance, dislike〕

사형 私刑 lynch(ing) ; private punishment ¶ 사형을 가하다 lynch 《a person》; punish 《a person》 outside the law

사형 舍兄 [형] my elder brother ; [아우에게] I〔me〕 (who am your elder brother)

****사형** 死刑 capital punishment ; death penalty ; punishment by death ¶ 사형을 선고하다 sentence〔condemn〕 《a person》 to death ; give the death penalty // 사형을 집행하다 execute a death sentence ; execute a criminal // 사형에 처하다 put 《a person》 to death ; send 《a person》 to the scaffold // 사형을 폐지하다 abolish capital punishment // 그 살인범은 사형을 받았다 The murderer was sentenced to death. // 그런 짓을 하면 사형이다 It is punishable by death.
— 선고 a capital〔death〕 sentence ; a sentence of death —수 a condemned criminal ; a criminal under sentence of death ¶ 사형수 감방〔독방〕 a death〔condemned〕 cell ; [일련의] a condemned ward ; a death row —실 a death chamber —장 an execution ground ; [가스의] a gas chamber —죄 a capital offense〔crime〕 — 집행 execution ; [교수에 의한] hanging ; [전기에 의한] electrocution — 집행 영장 a death warrant ; an order for 《a person's》 execution — 집행 유예 a reprieve — 집행인 an executioner ; [교수형의] a hangman — 폐지 the abolition of capital punishment

ㅅ

사형 詞兄 you sir ; Mr. . . .

사화 士禍 a massacre of scholars ; the calamity〔purge〕 of literati

사화 史話 a historical story〔tale〕

사화 私和 ① [화해] reconciliation ② [송사의] a private settlement ; settlement out of court **—하다** reconcile ; become reconciled with ; make peace ; settle 《a matter》 privately〔out of court〕 ; settle amicably

사화 詞華 flowery language ; flowers of speech ; rhetorical flourishes

사화산 死火山 an extinct volcano

***사환 使喚** a messenger boy ; an errand boy ; a boy

사활 死活 life and〔or〕 death ¶ 이 사업은 회사의 사활을 좌우한다 The issue of this enterprise affects the very existence of the company.

— **문제** a matter of life or death ; a question of vital importance ; a vital question

‡**사회 司會** [진행을 맡아봄] direction of 〔directing〕 a meeting〔ceremony〕 ; chairmanship ; chairing 《a meeting》 ; emceeing ; [사회자] a chairman **—하다** preside at〔over〕 《a meeting》 ; chair a meeting ; take the chair 《at a convention》 ; conduct〔perform〕 the ceremony ; officiate at ; serve as chairman〔master of ceremonies〕 ; emcee ¶ A 교수의 사회로 with Prof. A in the chair ; under the presidency〔chairmanship〕 of Prof. A∥식은 시장이 사회했다 The ceremony was presided over by the mayor.∥우리 결혼식 사회 볼 사람 구했어요 Have you found someone willing go act as master of ceremonies at our wedding?

—봉 a gavel **—자** the chairman ; the president ; the master〔mistress〕 of ceremonies 《m. c., MC, M. C.》 ; (방송 따위의) a compère 《주로 영》 ; an emcee 《미·구》 ; the moderator (토론회 따위의) 《미》 ; the officiant (의식의) ; a quizmaster (퀴즈의) ; the toastmaster (연회의)

사회 死灰 ashes ; cinders

†**사회 社會** society ; the community ; [세계] the world ; [공중] the public ¶ 사회의 social ; public∥사회적인 social∥사회적으로 socially∥사회적 계급 social rank〔scale〕∥사회적 명사 a society personage ; a socialite∥사회적 의무 a public duty∥사회적 지위 one's social position〔standing〕∥사회적 차별 social discrimination∥사회적 감정 social feeling∥사회적 일원 a member of society∥사회의 이익 the public interest〔good〕∥사회의 풍조 the trend of public opinion ; the social trend∥사회의 적 a public enemy∥사회의 제재 social sanctions∥사회에 나아가다 go out into the world ; launch forth〔make a start〕 in life∥사회로부터 은퇴하다 retire from society〔active life〕∥사회에 공헌하다 contribute to public welfare∥사회에 해롭다 be harmful to society∥사회를 개선하다 reform〔reconstruct〕 society∥사회를 형성하다 form society∥사회를 알다 know the world∥사회를 위해 일하다 work for the public good∥그는 사회의 모든 사람들에게 인망이 있다 He is popular with all ranks of society.∥그것은 사회의 죄이다 Society is to blame for it.∥그는 사회에서 매장되었다 He has lost his social standing./He's ruined socially.∥요즈음 여성들은 결혼보다는 사회에 진출하기를 원한다 Newly-bred women prefer public life to marriage.

— 개량 social reform ¶ 사회 개량가 a social reformer∥사회 개량주의 reformism **— 개발** social development **— 경제** social economy **— 계약설** the theory of social contract **—과** social affairs division **— 과학** social science(s) **—관** one's outlook on the world(life) ; one's view of social life **— 관습〔환경〕** social usage〔environment〕 **— 교육** social education **— 교화 사업** a drive for social enlightenment **— 구조〔기구〕** the framework of society ; the social structure〔fabric〕 **—극** a drama of social problems **—당** the Socialists ; the Socialist Party ¶ 사회당원 a Socialist ; a member of the Socialist Party **— 대책〔통계학, 통제〕** social measures〔statistics, control〕 **— 도덕〔위생(학)〕** social morality〔hygiene〕 **— 도태** social selection ; the survival of the fittest (in a society) **—면** [신문의] the city news page ; the social page ; the local news page〔section〕 **— 문제** a social problem ¶ 사회 문제가 되다 become an object of public concern **— 민주당** The Social Democratic Party **— 민주주의** social democracy ¶ 사회 민주주의자 a social democrat **— 발전** social evolution **— 법칙** social law **— 보장** social security ¶ 사회 보장 제도 the social security system∥사회 보장법 The Social Security Act 《SSA, S. S. A.》 **— 보장 적립금** social security contributions **— 보험** social insurance ¶ 사회 보험 제도 social insurance programs **— 복지** social welfare ¶ 사회 복지 사업 social welfare service∥사회 복지 기관〔시설〕 social welfare organs 〔facilities〕 ; an organization for social welfare **—부** the local news section ; the city editor's section 《미》 ¶ 사회부장 the chief reporter ; the city (news) editor 《미》∥사회부 취재 기자 an assignment man ; a local- news reporter **— 불안** 《cause, breed, ferment》 social unrest〔disturbance〕 ¶ 사회 불안을 제거하다 dispel social unrest —사 social history — 사상 social thinking ; social ideas — 사업〔봉사〕 social〔welfare〕 work〔service〕 ¶ 사회 사업가 a social worker // 사회 사업 공동 모금 Community Chest // 사회 사업 단체 a social work organization —상 a social aspect ; phases〔aspects〕 of life — 상식 worldly knowledge — 생활 social〔community〕 life —성 sociality ; a social nature — 소설 a social novel — 심리학〔사상〕 social psychology〔thought〕 —악 a social evil ; social abuses〔ills〕 — 연대(連帶) social solidarity — 운동 a social movement ; a public campaign ; a socialist movement (사회주의의) ¶ 사회 운동가 a person engaged in a social movement ; a crusader // 사회 운동을 일으키다 start a social movement ; appeal to the mass of the people — 유기체 〖사회〗 a social organism — 윤리(학) social ethics ; social mode〔code〕 ; social morality — 의식 social consciousness —인 a social being ; a member of society — 인류학 social anthropology —장(葬) a public funeral ¶ 사회장을 지내다 give a public funeral ; bury at public expense — 정세 social conditions ¶ 사회 정세의 변화에 즉각 응하다 keep up with the trend of society — 정의 social justice — 정책 a social policy — 제도 the social system — 조사 a social survey — 조직 social structure〔fabric, organization〕 —주의 socialism ¶ 사회주의 국가 a socialist state // 길드 사회주의 guild socialism // 과학적〔공상적〕 사회주의 scientific〔Utopian〕 socialism // 수정 사회주의 revised socialism — 진화론 the theory of social evolution — 질서 public〔social〕 order — 집단 a social group〔community〕 —층 a social stratum 《*pl.* -ta》 — 풍조 the trend〔drift〕 of public opinion —학 [과학] sociology ¶ 사회학의 sociological ; sociologistic // 사회학자 a sociologist // 경제 사회학 economic sociology // 문화 사회학 cultural sociology // 형식 사회학 formal sociology ; [세속적 지식] worldly knowledge〔wisdom〕 ; knowledge of the world — 혁명 a social revolution — 현상 a social phenomenon — 형태 a social form ; the form of a society ; the type of social system — 형태론 social morphology — 화 socialization ¶ 사회화하다 socialize 《medicine》 문명 — a civilized community 봉건〔시민〕 — feudal〔civic〕 society 상류〔중류, 하류〕 — the higher〔middle, lower〕 class ; the high〔middle, low〕 society 외인 — the foreign community〔colony〕 원시〔혈연〕 — primitive〔blood〕 society 인간 — human society 일반 — the general public ; the public in general〔at large〕 학생 — student circles

사후 死後 ¶ 사후의 after death ; posthumous ; postmortem ; future // 사후에 after one's death ; posthumously // 사후의 명성 posthumous fame〔honors〕 ; fame after death // 사후의 생활 the life beyond the grave ; life after death ; [종교적] the incarnated life ; life after this life // 부친의 사후에 after the death of one's father // 사후의 일을 생각하다 look beyond the grave // 이 시체는 사후 1개월이 경과했다 The body had been dead a month.

— 강직 〖의학〗 cadaveric stiffening ; [상태] cadaveric rigidity ; rigor mortis — 공명 posthumous honors — 신탁 〖법〗 a legacy trust — 염색 〖생물〗 postmortal staining

사후 약방문 [관용] After death comes a doctor. /Prescription after death. /While men go after a leech, the body is buried.

사후 事後 ¶ 사후의 after the fact〔matter〕 ; ex post facto 《라》 // 사후에 after the fact ; post factum // 사후의 참고를 위해서 for further reference // 사후에 승낙을 구하다 ask for ex post facto approval〔consent〕 ; ask 《a person's》 approval after the fact

— 검열 post censorship — 보고 an ex post facto report — 보도(補導) aftercare — 승낙 an ex post facto approval〔consent〕 ; the later ratification of an accomplished act — 입법 an ex post facto〔a retrospective〕 law〔legislation〕

사후 伺候 [문안] making a courtesy call ; paying respect to ; [시중] attendance ; service ; waiting upon —하다 make a courtesy call 《on》 ; pay one's respects 《to》 ; wait upon 《a person》 ¶ 궁중에 사후하다 proceed〔go〕 to the Palace

사흗날 the third day of the month ⇨ 초사흗날 ¶ 7월 사흗날 the third of July

사흘 three days (3일) ; the third day of the month (사흗날) ¶ 사흘 동안 for three days // 사흘 걸러 every fourth day —돌이 every three days

사흘 굶어 도둑질 않는 사람 없다 [속담] Necessity knows no law.

사흘 굶은 개는 몽둥이 맞아도 좋아한다 [속담] A crust is better than no bread. /Poor folks are glad of porridge.

사흘 굶으면 양식 지고 오는 놈이 있다 [속담] Everyday brings its bread with it.

삭 朔 [달수] months ; [합삭] the conjunction of sun and moon ¶ 1, 2 삭 a couple of months

삭갈다 〖농업〗 plow〔plough 《영》〕 just once (before transplanting rice plants)

ㅅ

삭갈이 〖농업〗 plowing〔ploughing 《영》〕 just once (before transplanting rice plants) **—하다** ⇨ 삭갈다

*__삭감 削減__ reduction ; curtailment ; cut ; retrenchment **—하다** cut (down) ; curtail ; retrench ; reduce ; slash ; pare down ¶ 예산을 삭감하다 cut〔slash〕 the budget // 경비를 삭감하다 pare〔whittle〕 down expenses // 정부의 보조금이 대폭 삭감되었다 The Government subsidy has been drastically slashed. // 우리는 종업원들이 자진해서 봉급을 20% 삭감하기로 했기 때문에 아무도 해고하지 않았습니다 We have laid off no one, because our employees volunteered to cut their pay by 20 percent.
대— a drastic reduction〔cut〕 **정부 지출—** spending cut

삭과 蒴果 〖식물〗 a capsule (of a plant)

*__삭구 索具__ rigging

삭다 [옷 따위가] wear thin〔threadbare〕 ; [새끼 따위가] decay ; get rotten ; [죽 따위가] become sloppy ; [먹은 음식이] be digested ; digest ; [술 따위가] ferment ; [종기 따위가] get resolved ; [김치 따위가] acquire〔pick up, absorb〕 flavor ; [감정이] calm down ; be alleviated〔appeased〕 ¶ 화가 삭다 one's anger dies down ; one cools off

삭도 索道 a cableway ; a ropeway
—차 a cable car

삭막 索莫, 索漠 [기억이] dimness ; vagueness **—하다** (be) dim (in one's memory) ; [광야 따위가] dreary ; bleak ; desolate

삭망 朔望 〖천문〗 syzygy ; the first and the fifteenth days of the lunar month ; [제사] memorial rites held on the first and the fifteenth days of the lunar month

삭모 槊毛 decorative tassels

삭모 削毛 shearing **—하다** shear
—기(機) a shearing machine

삭발 削髮 haircutting ; [초목 따위의] random cutting〔felling〕 **—하다** have one's hair cut ; cut〔fell〕 at random

삭북 朔北 the north

삭빙기 削氷機 an ice-shaving machine

삭신 sinews and joints

삭심다 transplant (rice plants) after a single quick plowing of the field

삭연하다 索然— (be) dry〔desolate〕

삭월 朔月 the new moon

삭월세 朔月貰 monthly rent〔rental〕 ¶ 삭월셋방 a rented room // 삭월셋집 a rented house

삭은코 a nose that bleeds easily

삭이다 digest ; consume 《strength》 ¶ 음식을 삭이다 digest food // 분을 삭이다 swallow one's anger // 잘 먹고 잘 삭이다 eat well and digest well

삭일 朔日 the first day of the lunar month

삭정이 dead〔withered〕 branches on a tree ; dead twigs〔sprays〕

삭제 削除 elimination ; deletion ; striking out **—하다** eliminate ; remove ; cancel ; delete ; strike〔cross〕 out ¶ 두 자를 삭제하다 cross two words out // 명부에서 삭제하다 strike 《a person's name》 off the list // 서적의 잘못된 부분을 삭제하다 expurgate a book // 편지의 일부를 삭제하다 leave out a part of a letter // 제7조 1항을 삭제함 Art. VII, clause I is rescinded.
—판 an expurgated edition **무—판** a complete and unexpurgated edition ; an unabridged edition

삭조 索條 a cable ; a rope

삭직 削職 ⇨ 삭탈 관직

삭치다 [없애다] cancel ; erase ; cross〔mark〕 out ; void ; nullify ; [맞비기다] settle 《accounts》 ; balance 《books》

삭탈 관직 削奪官職 removing〔stripping〕 a government official from office **—하다** remove 《a person》 from office

삭풍 朔風 the north wind of winter ; a wind from the north

삭히다 [소화] digest ; make 《a thing》 ripe ; mellow ; [발효] cause 《a thing》 to ferment ; [종기 따위] resolve

삯 [품삯] wages ; pay ; [요금] fare ; charges ; [보수] remuneration ; a reward ¶ 하루에 30,000원씩 삯을 받고 일하다 work for a wage of 30,000 *won* a day
—군 a jobber ; a wage earner ; a hired man **—돈** ⇨ 임금 **—말** a horse for hire **—메기** a wage-paying farm job (that does not include meals) **—바느질** needle work for pay **—빨래** laundry done for pay ; taking in laundry **—일** job work **—전(錢)** ⇨ 임금 **—짐** a load〔luggage〕 to carry for hire **—팔이** wage earning ¶ 삯팔이꾼 a wage earner **—품** wage labor ¶ 삯품을 팔다 work for wages **기차—** a railway fare

†__산 山__ a mountain ; a hill (작은) ; the mountains ; the heights (고지) ; a peak (고봉) ; a mine (광산) ; a grave(yard) (산소)

> 참고 **mountain**은 보통 **hill**보다 높고 큰 것 그러나 이 구별은 절대적인 높이에 의한 것이 아니고 그 지방의 풍경에 현저한 변화를 주느냐 안 주느냐에 달려 있다 과히 높지 않은 산도 평지에 솟아 있으면 mountain이라 부르고 높은 산도 산악 지대에 있는 경우에는 hill이라고 부른다 영국의 경우에는 거의 모두 hill이라고 한다

¶ 설악산 *soraksan* // 금강산 *kumgangsan* // 산이 많은 mountainous ; hilly // 산같이 높은 mountainous 《waves》 ; mountain-

high // 산같이 쌓인 a mountain of ; lots of ; a heap〔pile〕 of // 산 넘어 골짜기 건너 up hill and down dale // 산을 올라가다〔내려가다〕 climb up〔down〕 a mountain // 산이 솟다 a mountain rises
산에 가야 범을 잡는다 속담 Rise all and gain all. /Nothing venture, nothing win.
산에서 물고기 찾기 속담 To seek a hare in a hen's nest. /You cannot get blood from a stone.
산 넘어 산 관용 mountain upon mountain
산 算 [계산] reckoning ; computation ; calculation ; [수자] number ── 하다 reckon ; compute ; count ; calculate ; number
산 酸 an acid ¶ 산의 acid
― 결핍(증) anacidity ― 과다(증) 『의학』 hyperacidity ―류 acids ― 적정(滴定) [정량법] acidimetry
-산 産 from 《where》; 《grown, produced, manufactured》 at〔in〕 ¶ 제주도산의 말 a horse from *Cheju* Island // 외국산의 foreign-made // 국산의 domestic
산가 山家 a cottage in the mountains ; a mountain house
산가 酸價 『화학』 acid value
산가지 算― a primitive counting stick ; a fortune-telling stick
산각 山脚 the foot of a mountain
산간 山間 among the mountains〔hills〕 ; a remote place
― 벽지 a remote and secluded place in〔among〕 the mountains ― 벽촌 a remote mountain village
산감독 山監督 [산림의] a forest ranger ; [광산의] a mine superintendent
산개 散開 (military) deployment ; extension ; development ── 하다 extend ; deploy ; spread out ; form an open 〔extended〕 order ¶ 산개해서 in extended order
― 대열 a loose order ; open order ― 성단 『천문』 an open cluster ―전 fighting in skirmish〔open, extended〕 order ; a skirmish
산견되다 散見― be seen here and there
산경 山景 mountain scenery
산계 山系 a mountain system ; a mountain chain〔range〕
알프스 ― the system of the Alps
산고 産故 childbirth ; delivery
***산고 産苦** birth pangs ; (labo(u)r) pains ; travail ; throes
산고양이 山― 『동물』 a wild cat
산곡 山谷 a mountain valley ⇨ 산골짜기
산골 山― a mountainous district ; a secluded place ¶ 산골 사람 hill〔mountain〕 folk ; a hillbilly // 산골에서 자라나다 be brought up in the hills
***산골짜기 山―** a mountain valley ; a gorge ; a ravine ; a glen
산과 産科 obstetrics
― 겸자(鉗子) obstetrical forceps ― 병동〔병상〕 a maternity ward〔bed〕 ― 병원 a maternity (clinic〔hospital〕) ; a lying-in clinic〔hospital〕 ― 의사 an obstetrician ; [남자] an accoucheur ; [여자] an accoucheuse ―학 obstetrics ; midwifery
산광 散光 『물리』 diffused〔scattered〕 light
산괴 山塊 a mass of mountains
산구 産具 obstetrical supplies
산국화 山菊花 a wild chrysanthemum
산굴 山窟 a mountain cave
산굽이 山― a mountain bend
산금 山禽 a mountain bird ⇨ 산새
산금 産金 gold mining ; gold producing ; gold digging (사금의) ── 하다 produce〔mine, dig〕 gold
―량〔고〕 gold output ―업 the gold-mining industry ―열 gold rush〔fever〕 ― 지대 a gold field
산기 産氣 travail ; labo(u)r ; [진통] pangs of childbirth
산기 産期 the time of delivery〔parturition〕 ; the period〔term〕 of delivery ; one's time ¶ 산기가 닥쳐온다 Her time is impending.
산기 酸基 『화학』 an acid radical
산기둥 『건축』 an unsupported column
산기슭 山― the foot〔base, bottom〕 of a mountain
산길 山― a mountain path〔road〕
산고대 山― the night chill from a mountain wind ── 하다 grow chill 〔cold〕 《at the mountain top》
산꼭대기 山― the mountain top ; the top〔summit〕 of a mountain ; peak ¶ 그 산꼭대기에는 사철 내내 눈이 있다 The mountain is crowned with snow all the year round.
산나물 山― wild edible greens ¶ 산나물을 캐다 pick wild greens
산놀이 山― a mountain excursion ; a picnic ; a hike
산놓다 算― calculate with sticks〔on an abacus〕
산다 山茶 『식물』 a camellia tree
산다리 『식물』 a kind of small white bean
산달 山― a hilly area ; a mountainous region
산달 産― the month of giving birth
산대 山臺 『민속』 medi(a)eval masked drama
―극 ⇨ 산디
***산더미 山―** a great mass ; a huge amount ; a mountain 《of》 ; a heap ; a pile ¶ 산더미 같은 축전 a mountain of congratulatory telegrams // 산더미 같다 be big as a mountain // 산더미같이 쌓다 pile 《things》 mountain high // 빚이 산더

미 같다 I have a pile of debts a mile high. //할일이 산더미 같다 I have lots of things to do. //접시가 설겆이대에 산더미처럼 쌓여 있다 Dishes are stacked up on the draining board.

산도 酸度 〖화학〗 acidity

— **측정** acidimetry

산도 産道 the parturient〔obstetric〕 canal

산독증 酸毒症 〖의학〗 acidosis

산돌림 a sporadic shower

산돌배 山— a wild pear

산동 散瞳 〖의학〗 mydriasis

산돼지 山— 〖동물〗 a wild boar〔hog〕

산드러지다 (be) vivacious ; lively ; sprightly ; gay ; buoyant ; light-hearted ¶ 산드러지게 걷다 walk buoyantly//산드러지게 웃다 laugh a gay〔coquettish〕 little laugh

산득, 산뜩 with a sudden chill ⇨ 선득

산들거리다 《the wind》 blow cool and gentle

산들다 go wrong〔amiss〕 ; fail ; be frustrated

⁑**산들바람** a gentle〔light〕 breeze

산들산들 gently ; softly ; in cool ripples ¶ 바람이 산들산들 불고 있었다 The breeze was blowing soft and fresh.

산등성마루 山— ⇨ 산마루

⁑**산등성이 山—** a (mountain) ridge

산디 〖민속〗 a makeshift stage for a Korean mask drama **—하다** put on a Korean mask drama

— **놀음** a mask drama — **도감** a *sandi* troupe **—탈** a *sandi* drama mask **—판** the scene of a *sandi* drama

산딸기 山— mountain〔wild〕 berries

산똥 undigested〔lienteric〕 excrement

⁑**산뜻하다** (be) clean ; clear ; fresh ; crisp ; bright ; vivid ; neat ; tidy ; trim ; smart ; nice ¶ 산뜻한 빛 a bright color//산뜻한 날씨 crisp weather //산뜻하게 색칠한 집 a neatly-painted house//산뜻한 음식 a kosher meal//산뜻한 옷 neat dress//산뜻한 공기 fresh air//산뜻한 맛이 없다 lack freshness//그 여자는 산뜻하게 치장했다 She is neatly dressed up. //소나무의 초록색이 산뜻하다 The green of the pine looks fresh. //그것은 뒷맛이 산뜻하다 It left a very pleasant aftertaste.

산란 産卵 laying eggs ; egg-laying ; spawning (물고기의) **—하다** lay eggs ; spawn (물고기가) ; blow (파리 따위가)

—관 an ovipositor **—기** the breeding time ; a spawning season (물고기의) **—장** a spawning ground (물고기의)

산란 散亂 dispersion ; discomposure ; diffusion (빛 따위의) **—하다** [장소가] be littered〔strewn〕 with ; be in (wild) disorder ; [마음이] (be) discomposed ; perturbed ; restless ¶ 산란한 마음을 가라앉히다 calm down the restless mind //종이가 흩어져 방안이 산란하다 The room is littered with scraps of paper.

산령 山靈 ⇨ 산신령

산로 山路 ⇨ 산길

산록 山麓 the foot〔base, bottom〕 of a mountain ¶ 기차가 태백산록을 지나간다 The railway skirts the base of the *Taebaek* Mountains.

— **지대** a piedmont district ; a piedmont

산류 酸類 〖화학〗 (the) acids

산릉 山陵 mountains and hills

산리 山里 a mountain village ; a village among mountains

⁑**산림 山林** a forest ; a woodland ¶ 산림을 보호하다 conserve forests//산림을 가꾸다〔벌채하다〕 afforest〔deforest〕 a mountain

— **남벌** reckless deforestation **—법** the Forest Law — **보호** forest conservancy **—업** the forestry industry — **조합** a forestry (owners) association **—청** the Office of Forestry **—학** forestry ; [수목학] dendrology **—학자** a dendrologist — **학회** the Forest Association — **행정** forest administration

산마루 山— the top of a mountain 〔ridge〕

—터기 the summit of a mountain

산마리노 San Marino

산막 山幕 a mountain lodge〔cottage〕 ; a hut

산만 散漫 diffuseness ; looseness ; vagueness ; desultoriness **—하다** (be) loose ; vague ; desultory ¶ 산만한 생각 a vague〔loose〕 idea//산만한 생각 a vague〔loose〕 idea//산만한 독서 desultory〔cursory〕 reading//주의가 산만한 inattentive//그는 정신이 산만하다 He is a scatterbrained person.

산말 a living language ; an adequate expression

산망스럽다 (be) flighty ; thoughtless ; imprudent ; flippant ¶ 산망스럽게 굴다 be flippant

산매 散賣 retail sale〔trade〕 ; retailing **—하다** retail ; sell by〔at〕 retail ; sell in small quantities

— **물가 지수** a retail price index **—상** a retailer ; a retail dealer **—업** retail trade ; small business **—점** a retail store〔shop〕 ¶ 산매점 주인 a storekeeper ; a shopkeeper 《영》 **—(상)품** retail goods

†**산맥 山脈** a mountain range〔chain〕 ; a range〔chain, group〕 of mountains ¶ 알프스 산맥 the Alps ; the Alpine range //우랄 산맥 the Ural Mountains

산머리 山— ⇨ 산꼭대기

산멱통 the throat of a living animal

산명 山鳴 a mountain rumbling

산명수려 山明水麗 scenic beauty ; picturesque scenery **—하다** be scenically〔naturally〕 beautiful

산모 産母 a woman delivered of a child ; a woman in childbed

— 보호 maternity protection

산모롱이 山— the spur of a hill〔mountain〕

산모퉁이 山— the spur of a hill〔mountain〕; the corner of a mountain foot

산목숨 one's life ¶ 산목숨을 겨우 이어가다 eke out one's living〔miserable existence〕

산무애뱀 〖동물〗 Elaphe quadrivirgata (학명)

산문 山門 [산의 어귀] the entrance of a mountain ; [절의 문] the entrance to〔the gate of〕 a Buddhist temple ; [절] a Buddhist temple

산문 産門 the vulva ; the vagina

*산문 散文 prose ; prose writings ¶ 산문적인 prosaic // 산문으로 쓰다 write (in) prose // 운문을 산문으로 고치다 turn a verse into prose

—극 a prose drama —시 a prose poem ; a poem in prose — 작가 a prose writer ; a prosaist ; a prosateur —체 prose style ; prosaism ; 《in》 prose

*산물 産物 [생산물] a product ; production ; produce 《총칭》; [성과] a product ; a result ; an outcome ¶ 주요 산물 staple products〔produce〕// 노력의 산물 the fruit〔harvest, product〕 of sheer labor〔hard work〕// 시대의 산물 creature of the times〔day〕// 두뇌의 산물 intellectual products // 그 지방의 산물은 이렇다 할 만한 것이 없다 The district produces nothing worth mentioning.

주요 — staple products〔produce〕

산미 産米 [쌀] rice products ; [해산쌀] rice for an expectant mother during her confinement〔childbirth〕

산미 酸味 acidity ; sourness ; a sour taste ¶ 산미가 있는 sour ; acid // 약간 산미를 띤 sourish ; subacid

산미끼 live bait

산밑 山— the foot〔base bottom〕 of a mountain

산바람 山— a mountain wind〔blast〕; a breeze from the mountain

산발 散發 sporadic occurrence ; scattered hits (야구의) —하다 occur〔break out〕 sporadically ¶ 산발적인 sporadic ; scattered // 산발적으로 sporadically // 우리팀은 상대방을 산발 안타로 눌렀다 Our team kept the rival hits well scattered.

—성 sporadic(al) — 안타 〖야구〗 scattered hits

산발 散髮 dishevelled〔loosened〕 hair —하다 have〔wear〕 one's hair loose〔dishevelled〕 ¶ 산발을 하고 with dishevelled〔disarranged〕 hair

산법 算法 arithmetic

십진 — decimal arithmetic

산벼락 a horrible experience ; living through a lightning strike ¶ 산벼락을 맞다 undergo a horrible experience

산벼랑 山— a mountain cliff〔precipice〕

산병 散兵 [사람] skirmishers ; scattered soldiers ; [상태] loose〔extended〕 order ; [작전] scattering〔dispersing〕 soldiers —하다 scatter (troops) ; deploy in loose order

— 교련 skirmish drill —선 a skirmish line —호 a fire〔firing, shelter〕 trench

산보 散步 a walk ; a stroll ⇨ 산책

산복 山腹 a mountainside ; the side of a mountain ; a hillside ¶ 공원은 산복에 있다 The park lies halfway up the hill.

산봉 山峰 a peak ; a summit

산봉우리 山— a mountain peak

산부 産婦 a woman in childbed ; a woman in her confinement

산부리 山— a mountain crag〔jutting out〕; a spur

산부인과 産婦人科 obstetrics and gynecology

— 의사 [산과] an obstetrician ; [부인과] a gynecologist ; a ladies' doctor

산부처 a living Buddha ; a virtuous person

산분 酸分 〖화학〗 an acid content

산불 山— a forest〔hill〕 fire

산붕 山崩 a landslide ; a landslip —하다 have a landslide ; 《a mountain》 collapse〔fall down〕

산비둘기 山— an Eastern ringdove ; Streptopelia orientalis (학명)

산비탈 山— a steep mountain slope

산뽕나무 山— a wild mulberry tree

산사 山寺 a temple on a mountain ; a mountain temple

산사(나무) 山査(—) 〖식물〗 a hawthorn ; a May tree〔thorn〕

산사람 山— a woodsman ; a mountaineer ; a wild man of the mountain

산사전 —辭典 a walking〔living〕 dictionary

*산사태 山沙汰 a landslide ; a land slip ; a landfall

산삭 産朔 the month of parturition〔giving birth〕

†산산이 散散— to〔in〕 pieces ; to atoms〔smithereens〕; scatteredly ¶ 그릇을 산산이 부수다 smash dishes to pieces // 비행기가 산에 부딪혀 산산이 부서졌다 A plane was crushed to fragments against the mountain. // 여객선이 암초에 부딪혀 산산이 부서졌다 A liner was dashed to pieces against the rocks. // 형사들은 범인을 잡기 위해서 산산이 흩어졌다 The detectives〔plainclothesmen〕 scattered to round up the culprit.

산산조각 散散— bits and pieces ; broken pieces ; fragments ; fractions ¶ 산산조각으로 부서지다 be broken in pieces ; fall asunder // 산산조각난 시체 a

dismembered corpse // 그 상자는 마루 위에 산산조각으로 흩어져 있었다 The box was on the floor in pieces. // 전구가 산산조각이 났다 The electric bulb was smashed to smithereens.
산산하다 (be) cool ; refreshing ⇨ 선선하다
산살바도르 San Salvador 《엘살바도르의 수도》
산삼 山蔘 wild ginseng
산상 山上 (on) top of a mountain〔hill〕
— **수훈(垂訓)** the Sermon on the Mount
산새 山— mountain birds
산색 山色 mountain scenery ; a hillscape
산설 山雪 snow which falls on the mountains ; mountain snow
산성 山城 a mountain fortress wall
산성 酸性 acidity ¶ 산성의 acid // 산성으로 만들다 acidify ; acidulate
—**도** acidity —**률** coefficient of acidity — **반응** acid reaction — **백토** acid clay —**비** acid rain — **산화물** an acid oxide — **소화 불량증** acid indigestion〔dyspepsia〕 — **시험** an acidity test —**염** acid chloride — **염료** an acid dyestuff — **유산염** a disulfate ; a bisulfate — **점토** acid clay —**증(症)** 〚의학〛 acidosis — **탄산 나트륨** sodium carbonate ; carbonate of soda — **토양** acid soil
산세 山勢 the physical aspect of a mountain ; geographical features of a mountain
산소 山所 a grave (yard) ; a tomb ; (an ancestral) burial ground
⁑**산소 酸素** 〚화학〛 oxygen ¶ 산소를 처리하다 oxygenate // 산소를 제거하다 deoxygenate
— **결핍** 〚의학〛 hypoxia ; anoxia (특히 강도의) ; anoxemia (특히 혈액의) — **압축기** an oxygen compressor — **요법** oxygen treatment ; oxypathy — **용접** oxyacetylene welding — **제거** deoxidization — **화합물** an oxygen compound ; an oxide — **흡입** oxygen inhalation — **흡입기** an oxygen breathing apparatus ; a lung motor **액체** — liquid oxygen ; lox **생물학적 — 수요** the biological oxygen demand 《BOD》
산소리 talking big ; bragging ; brave〔spunky〕 words —**하다** talk big ; do not give in
산소산 酸素酸 〚화학〛 oxyacid ; oxygen acid
산속 山— the heart〔recesses〕 of a mountain〔the mountains〕 ; deep in a mountain〔the mountains〕
산송장 a walking〔living〕 corpse ; the living dead ; a decrepit person
산수 山水 mountains and waters ; hills and streams ; [경치] landscape ; scenery ¶ 남원은 산수가 아름다운 곳이다 *Namwon* is a town noted for its beauties of nature〔scenic beauty〕.
—**도(圖)** a geographical picture of hills and waters —**미** natural beauty ; beauties of nature ; scenic beauty
⁑**산수 算數** reckoning ; calculation ; arithmetic ; mathematics ¶ 산수는 딱 질색이다 I have never been good at figures.
— **문제** an arithmetical problem ; a problem in arithmetic ; a sum (to do)
산수소 酸水素 〚화학〛 oxyhydrogen
—**염** an oxyhydrogen flame — **용접** oxyhydrogen welding — **취관** an oxyhydrogen blowpipe — **폭발 가스** oxyhydrogen detonating gas
산수화 山水畫 a landscape ; landscape painting (화법)
—**가** a landscape painter ; a landscapist
*＊**산술 算術** arithmetic ; the science of numbers ¶ 산술을 하다 do sums
—**가** an arithmetician — **급수(級數)** arithmetic progression —**장** a ciphering book — **평균** the arithmetic〔numerical〕 mean **상업** — commercial arithmetic
산스크리트 [범어] Sanskrit 《Skr., Skt., Sans.》
—**학자** a Sanskritist ; a Sanskrit scholar
산승 山僧 a Buddhist priest living in the mountains
산식 算式 an arithmetic expression ; a formula
산신 山神 a mountain god ; the god of a mountain
—**제(祭)** a religious service for the god of a mountain
산신령 山神靈 the guardian spirit of a mountain ; the god of mountains
산실 散失 get〔be〕 scattered and lost ; scatter and lose
산실 産室 a lying-in room ; a delivery room ; a maternity ward〔room〕
산아 産兒 a newborn baby ; childbirth
—**하다** give birth to a baby
산아 제한 産兒制限 birth〔conception〕 control ; birth〔family〕 limitation ; regulation of the number of births in a family ¶ 산아 제한을 하다 practice birth control // limit one's family〔offspring〕
—**론자** an advocate of birth control ; a birth control proponent —**법** Malthusian practices — **상담소** a birth control clinic
⁑**산악 山岳** mountain peaks ; mountains
—**기압계** an orometer —**병** mountain sickness —**부** a mountaineering〔an alpine〕 club — **비행** a flight over a mountainous district — **신앙** mountain worship —**전** mountain warfare — **지대** a mountainous area — **지방** a mountain〔mountainous〕 district〔country, region〕 — **터널** a mountain tunnel — **풍경화** a mountain-scape —**학** orogra-

phy ; orology —회 an alpine society ; an association of mountaineers ; an Alpine club

산안개구름 山— a stratus ⇨ 층운

산액 産額 the output ; (the amount of) productions ; the yield (농산물의)
총— the general output

산야 山野 fields and mountains ; moor and hill ¶ 산야의 초목 wild plants

산약 散藥 powder medicine ; a medicinal powder

산양 山羊 a goat (염소) ; an antelope (영양) ¶ 산양 가죽 장갑 kid gloves

산언덕 山— a hillock ; a hill ; a mound

산언저리 山— the edge〔brim〕 of a hill ; the ridge of a mountain

†**산업 産業** industry ¶ 산업의 industrial // 산업의 발달 industrial development // 산업의 합리화 the rationalization of industry // 산업의 지방화 localization of industries // 산업의 국영화 nationalization of industries // 산업을 장려하다 encourage industry
—가 an industrialist — 개발 industrial development〔exploitation〕 —계 the industrial world ; industrial circles — 공해 industrial pollution — 교육 industrial education — 구조 industrial structure —국 an industrial country〔nation〕 — 국유화 정책 a policy of industrial nationalization — 도로 an industrial road — 도시 an industrial city — 동원〔복원〕 industrial mobilization〔demobilization〕 — 박람회 an industrial exhibition —별 (노동) 조합 an industrial〔a vertical〕 union ; a labor〔trade 《영》〕 union ¶ 산업별 노동 조합 회의 [미국의] the Congress of Industrial Organizations 《C. I. O.》 — 분류 〖노동〗 industrial〔job〕 classification — 성장률 an industrial growth rate — 스파이 an industrial spy — 안전 industrial safety — 예비군 an industrial reserve army — 위생 industrial hygiene — 입국 a national economy based on industry — 자금 industrial funds — 자본 industrial capital — 재해 보상 보험 Workmen's Accident Compensation Insurance — 정책 an industrial policy — 조직 industrial organization — 조합 an industrial guild ; an industrial association —주의 industrialism — 지리학 industrial geography — 통제 the control of industry — 투자 industrial investment — 합리화 the rationalization of industry — 혁명 the Industrial Revolution —화 industrialization — 훈장 the Order of Industrial Merit 국방 — defense industry 성장 — a growth industry ; a incremental industry 수출 — the export industry 신흥 — the rising industry 영화 — the cinema industry 전시〔평화〕 — the war〔peace〕 industries 정보 — the communication〔information〕 industry 제1차 — the primary industries 주요〔기간〕 — the key〔chief〕 industries 철강 — the iron and steel industry 한국 — 은행 the Korea Development Bank

산역 山役 tomb work ; construction 〔repair〕 of a tomb —하다 construct 〔repair〕 a tomb ; dig a grave
—꾼 a graveyard worker ; a grave digger

산염화물 酸鹽化物 〖화학〗 an acid chloride

산욕 産褥 the quilt used at childbirth
—기 a lying-in〔confinement〕 period ; puerperium 《*pl.* -ria》 —부 a woman in childbed〔confinement〕 ; a lying-in woman —열 puerperal fever

산용 山容 the looks〔figure〕 of a mountain

산용 숫자 算用數字 Arabic figures 〔numerals〕

산울 ⇨ 산울타리

*__산울림__ 山— an echo ¶ 산울림이 울리다 an echo resounds

⁑**산울타리** a living〔growing〕 hedge ¶ 산울타리를 두르다 plant a growing hedge

산원 産院 a maternity hospital ; a lying-in hospital

산월 産月 month of parturition

산유 産油 oil producing
—국 an oil producing country

산육 産育 bearing and raising —하다 bear and raise ; bear and bring up

산은 産銀 [한국 산업 은행] the Korea Development Bank

산음 山陰 the shady side of a mountain

산읍 山邑 a mountain town

산인 山人 [산사람] mountain folks ; mountaineers ; [은사] a hermit ; a recluse ; a monk

산일 散佚 getting〔being〕 scattered and lost —하다 get〔be〕 scattered and lost ¶ 고전 작품의 산일을 방지하다 prevent the classics from being dispersed

산입 算入 inclusion ; calculating —하다 include in ; count〔reckon〕 in ; take into account

산자 橵子 〖건축〗 lattice sticks across roof rafters

산자수명 山紫水明 scenic beauty ; lovely scenery —하다 be scenically beautiful ¶ 산자수명한 곳 a scenic spot ; places of great scenic beauty

산장 山莊 a mountain villa

⁑**산재 散在** being scattered ; lying here and there —하다 be scattered about ; lie scattered ; lie here and there ; be found here and there ¶ 인가가 산재한 마을 a straggling village // 졸업생들이 전국에 산재해 있다 The graduates are scattered all over the country. // 들에 나무들이 산재해 있다

ㅅ

The plain is dotted with trees. // 근해에는 크고 작은 섬들이 산재해 있다 The neighboring sea is studded with islands, large and small.
산재 散財 waste of money ; a wasteful use of money ; dissipation ; extravagance **—하다** lavish money 《on》; waste (money) ; squander ; dissipate ; be extravagant
산쟁이 山— a mountaineer ; a woodsman
*__산적 山賊__ a bandit ; a brigand ¶ 산적의 소굴 a bandit's den
산적 山積 heaping〔piling〕 up ; accumulation **—하다** heap〔pile〕 up ; lie in a heap ; be piled mountain high ; have a lot of work on one's hand ¶ 할 일이 산적해 있다 have work cut out for 《one》 // 편지가 책상 위에 산적해 있다 Letters lie in a heap on the desk. // 역에 화물이 산적해 있다 Piles of goods lie undelivered〔awaiting delivery〕 at the station.
산적 散炙 shish kebab ; [사슬 산적] unskewered shish kebab
— 꼬챙이 a spit ; a skewer ¶ 산적 꼬챙이에 꿰다 spit〔skewer〕 《meat》
산적도둑 散炙— [미식가] an epicure ; a gourmet ; [시집간 딸] one's married daughter
산전 山田 a field in the mountains 〔hills〕 ; a field among hills
산전 産前 ¶ 산전에 before childbirth 〔delivery〕 // 산전 산후 before and after childbirth // 산전 산후의 휴가 maternity leave
산전수전 山戰水戰 fighting all sorts of hardships ¶ 산전수전을 다 겪은 사람 a person who has tasted the sweets and bitters of life ; a man of the world
산전수전 다 겪다 관용 go through hell and high water ; experience all sorts of difficulties
산정 山亭 an arbor in the mountains
산정 山頂 the top〔summit〕 of a mountain ; a mountaintop ⇨ 산꼭대기
산정 算定 computation ; calculation ; estimate ; assessment **—하다** compute ; calculate ; estimate ; work out ; assess ¶ 판매 가격을 산정하다 compute a selling price // 산정을 잘못하다 miscalculate ; make a mistake in calculation
— 가격 estimated value ; appraisal **—표** a plot ; a calculated graph (포병의) **— 환시세** a tal. qual.〔talis qualis〕 rate **상환액 —** assessment of the amount of redemption
산주 山主 the owner of a mountain
산줄기 山— a mountain range ; a chain of mountains ¶ 태백산줄기 the *Taebaek* range
산중 山中 a mountain recess ; the heart of a mountain ; the bosom of the hills ¶ 산중에 among〔in〕 the mountains
산중턱 山— ⇨ 산복(山腹)
산증 疝症 〖한의학〗 scrotal hernia
산지 山地 a mountainous district ; hilly country
산지 産地 a place〔an area〕 of production ; a producing center ; [동식물의] the home ; the habitat ; [말 따위의] a breeding center ; [식물의] a growing district ¶ 쌀의 산지 a rice-producing district // 유명한 말의 산지 a famous horse-breeding center // 담배의 산지 a tobacco-growing district // 한국은 세계 제일의 인삼의 산지이다 Korea is the greatest producer of ginseng in the world. // 바나나 산지가 격증 일로에 있다 The banana-producing areas are ever increasing.
산지기 山— a forest ranger ; [능지기] a grave keeper
산지니, 산진 山— a mountain hawk ; a wild〔an untrained〕 falcon
산질 散帙 having some volumes (of a set) missing ; an incomplete set **—하다** 《a set of books》 have some volumes missing ; be incomplete
산짐승 山— a mountain animal ; mountain beasts
산채 山菜 wild edible greens ; edible mountain herbs
산채 山寨 a mountain fastness〔stronghold〕 ; [산적의] a den of mountain bandits ; a mountain hangout
산채로 alive ¶ 산채로 잡다 catch〔capture〕 《a tiger》 alive
†**산책 散策** a walk ; a stroll ; a promenade ; an airing ; a constitutional (건강상의) **—하다** take a walk〔a stroll, a turn, the air〕 ; walk ; stroll ; have an outing ¶ 아침 산책 a morning walk // 한 시간 동안의 산책 an hour's walk // 운동을 위한 산책 a walk for exercise // 산책 나가다 go out for a walk // 정원을 산책하다 take a turn〔walk, stroll〕 in the garden // 멀리 산책가다 take a long walk // 잠깐 산책 나갈까요 How about a short walk? // 산책하다가 잠깐 들렀습니다 I have just dropped in while taking a walk. // 어제는 사장이 개 산책시키는 것까지 나를 시켰다 Yesterday the president even had me walk his dog!
—길 a promenade (포장된) ; a walk ; an esplanade (해안·호숫가 따위의) **아침 —** a morning walk
산천 山川 mountains and streams
— 초목 (all) nature ; natural scenery ; landscape ; plants and trees
산천어 山川魚 〖물고기〗 a trout 《단·복수 동형》
산초 山椒 〖식물〗 Chinese pepper
— 나무 a prickly ash ; Zanthoxylum piperitum (학명) **—어(魚)** a salaman-

der

산촌 山村 a mountain village

†산출 產出 production ; yield ; output ; yielding ; manufacturing —하다 produce ; yield ; bring forth ; manufacture ; turn out ¶ 금을 다량으로 산출하는 광산 a productive〔rich〕 gold mine

—고 the (amount of) production ; the yield 《of rice》 ; the output 《of gold》 —력 producing〔productive〕 power ; productivity —물 a product ; a production —지 a producing center ; a place of production〔origin〕

산출 算出 calculation ; computation ; reckoning —하다 calculate ; compute ; reckon ; figure out ¶ 산출된 세액 a calculated tax amount

산칠 山漆 〖식물〗 a wild lacquer tree

산코골다 pretend to snore

산타 마리아 Santa Maria

†산타 클로스 Santa Claus ; Father Christmas 《영》

산타페 Santa Fé

산탄 霰彈 case shot ; buckshot ; slugs ; shrapnel (유산탄)

—총 a shotgun —통 a canister — 효과 a shot effect

산태 山汰 a landslide ¶ 산태로 기차가 불통되었다 A landslide blocked the railway traffic.

산턱 山— the crest of a mountain

*산토끼 a hare ; a wild rabbit ; a jackrabbit

산토닌 〖약〗 santonin ; santonic acid

산토 도밍고 Santo Domingo

산통 算筒 a case for bamboo fortune slips〔counting-sticks〕

산통 깨뜨리다 관용 put a spoke in 《a person's》 wheel ; spoil〔ruin〕 《a plot》

산통 疝痛 〖의학〗 colic ; gripes

산티아고 Santiago

산파 產婆 a midwife ; a maternity nurse ¶ 산파 노릇을 맡다 assist at〔attend〕 a birth // 산파 역할을 하다 assist in the formation of 《a cabinet》 ; be instrumental in 《doing》

—술 midwifery ; obstetrics ; 〖철학〗 the maieutic(al) method —역 the job of a midwife ; [비유적] a sponsor

산판 山坂 a forest preserve

산패 酸敗 acidification —하다 acidify ; turn sour

—액 water-brash —유 sour milk

산포 山砲 a mountain gun〔howitzer〕 ; [산포수] a mountain hunter

—대 a battery of mountain artillery

산포 散布 distribution ; scattering ; sprinkling ; spreading ; diffusion —하다 scatter ; distribute ; sprinkle ; spread ; diffuse ¶ 마루 밑에 석회를 산포하다 sprinkle lime under the floor

—기(器) a sprinkler —도 〖통계〗 (measure of) dispersion —약 dusting powder — 오차 〖통계〗 a dispersion error

산포도 山葡萄 〖식물〗 wild grapes〔vines〕 ⇨ 머루

산표 散票 scattered votes ¶ 산표를 얻다 secure〔rake up〕 scattered votes

산하 山下 the foot〔bottom〕 of a mountain ¶ 산하의〔에〕 beneath〔under〕 a mountain

산하 山河 mountains and rivers

산하 傘下 under the influence〔protection〕 of ¶ 산하에 들어가다 be enlisted under the banner 《of》 ; respond to the summons 《of》

— 기관 an affiliated organization — 기업 affiliated enterprises — 노동 조합 affiliated〔subordinate〕 (labor) unions — 회사 subsidiary companies ; subsidiaries

산학 算學 arithmetic

산학 山學 orology ; orography

산학 공동체 產學共同體 an educational-industrial complex

산해 山海 mountains and seas ; land and sea

산해 진미 山海珍味 dainties〔delicacies〕 of all lands and seas ; dainties of many kinds ; a sumptuous feast ¶ 산해 진미를 먹고 살다 live on the fat of the land

*산허리 山— a mountainside ; a saddle of a mountain ; the waist of a mountain

산혈증 酸血症 〖의학〗 acidosis ; acidemia

산협 山峽 [계곡] a ravine ; a gorge ; [벽지] a remote and isolated place in the mountains

*산호 珊瑚 coral ¶ 산호 모양의 coralliform ; coralloid // 산호질의 coralline // 산호색의 coral // 산호를 채취하다 fish for coral

—도(島) a coral island〔atoll〕 — 목걸이 a coral necklace —석 corallite —수(樹) a coral —주(珠) a seed coral — 채취 coral fishing ¶ 산호 채취 어선 a coral boat —초 a coral reef ; an atoll (환초) ; a cay (해상에 일부만이 나와 있는 것) —충 a coral insect〔polyp〕 —충류 Anthozoa —해 the Coral Sea 석(石)— stony coral 알— a seed coral 적(赤)— red〔precious〕 coral

산화 山火 a forest fire ; a mountain〔hill〕 fire ⇨ 산불

*산화 酸化 oxidation ; oxidization ; oxygenation —하다 oxidize ; oxidate ; oxygenate ; be oxidized ¶ 산화하기 쉬운 금속 an easily oxidizable metal

—망간 manganese oxide —물 an oxide ; an oxidized substance ¶ 금속 산화물 a metallic oxide // 양성 산화물 an amphoteric oxide // 제1 산화물 a protoxide // 중성 산화물 a neutral oxide — 방지제 an anti-oxidant — 섬유소 oxycellulose —수소 oxide of hydrogen — 스

ㅅ

칸디움 scandia ; scandic oxide —아연 zinc oxide —안티몬 oxide of antimony —연(鉛) plumbic oxide —염 an oxidizing flame — 염료 oxidation dyestuffs — 적정(滴定) oxidimetry — 제(劑) an oxidizing agent an oxidizer — 제1금〔제2금〕 aurous〔auric〕 oxide — 제1동〔제2동〕 cuprous〔cupric〕 oxide — 제1철〔제2철〕 ferrous〔ferric〕 oxide —질소 nitric oxide ; laughing gas —철〔동〕 oxidized steel〔copper〕 —칼슘 calcium oxide — 효소 an oxidizing enzyme ; an oxidase 금속 —물 a metallic oxide 일〔이〕—탄소 carbon monoxide〔dioxide〕

산화 散華 ① 〖불교〗 a Buddhist rite of scattering〔strewing〕 flowers ② [장렬한 전사] a heroic death in battle ──하다 fall as flowers do ; die a glorious〔heroic〕 death

산황화물 酸黃化物 〖화학〗 oxysulphide

산회 散會 adjournment ; closing 《the meeting》 ; rising ──하다 break up ; adjourn ; disperse ; close ; rise ¶ 국회는 7시에 산회했다 The National Assembly rose〔adjourned〕 at 7 in the evening. ∥그 회의는 돌연 산회했다 The meeting came to an abrupt termination.

산후 産後 ¶ 산후의〔에〕 after childbirth〔parturition〕 ; after one's confinement∥산후의 회복 convalescence〔progress〕 after childbirth∥산후의 경과가 좋다〔나쁘다〕 The mother is doing well〔badly〕 after childbirth.

†**살**[1] [일반적] flesh ; [특히 식육] meat ; [근육] muscle ; [보충 설명] expatiation ¶ 살이 많은 과일 fleshy fruits∥살이 흰 여자 a woman of fair complexion∥이 호두는 살이 많다 This walnut has a lot of meat. ∥이 돼지는 살이 올랐다〔빠졌다〕 This pig has gained〔lost〕 weight. ∥이 대목에는 좀더 살을 붙여야겠다 This paragraph needs a little more expatiation.

—덩이 a lump〔piece〕 of flesh

살[2] [나무오리·대오리] a frame ; a rib ; lattice (strips) ; a spoke ; [빗의] a tooth ; [어살] a (fishing) weir ¶ 살 없는 창문 a window without a lattice support∥살에 잡힌 고기 fish caught in a weir∥자전거 바퀴의 살이 부러졌다 One of the spokes in my bicycle is broken.

—창 a lattice window 부채— the ribs of a fan 빗— teeth of a comb 우산— the frame〔spokes〕 of an umbrella 창— a lattice ; a lattice strip ; latticework

살[3] [화살] an arrow ; [빛살] a ray ; a beam ; [물살] a current ¶ 살같이 like an arrow∥살을 쏘다 shoot an arrow∥살이 빗맞았다 The arrow missed the target.

다림— the path of an iron ; the ease of ironing 햇— a sunbeam

살[4] [벌의] a sting ¶ 살에 쏘이다 get stung

†**살**[5] [나이] years of age ¶ 스무 살 twenty years of age∥일곱 살 난 아이 a child seven years old∥몇 살입니까 How old are you? /What is your age? ∥서른 살입니다 I am thirty (years old, years of age). /I am in my 30th year.

살[6] [노름의] increasing〔doubling〕 one's bet

살[7] [떡의] a cake-decoration pattern ¶ 떡에 살을 박다 press a pattern into the cake

살 煞 an evil spirit ; baleful〔evil〕 influence ; plague ; damnation ; the devil's work ; an ill-fated touch ¶ 그 여자는 살이 세다 She is plagued with the devil. /She is a femme fatale. ∥그는 살이 가서 병들었다 He has been plagued with illness.

살가다 煞— be damned〔plagued, beset〕 ; be under the influence of the devil

살가죽 the skin ⇨ 피부

살갈퀴 〖식물〗 a tare ; a vetch ; Vicia sativa (학명)

살갑다 [너르다] (be) broad-minded ; openminded ; receptive ; [다정하다] warm-hearted ; kind ; affable ; amiable ; genial

살강 a kitchen shelf ; a tableware shelf

살강거리다 ⇨ 설겅거리다

살갗 the skin surface ; the skin ; complexion ¶ 고운 살갗 smooth complexion ; a spotless skin

살거름 fertilizer〔manure〕 mixed with grain seeds before sowing

살거리 fleshiness ; fattiness ¶ 살거리가 좋은 fleshy ; corpulent ; fat

살결 the texture of the skin ; complexion ¶ 고운 살결 a lovely complexion ; a smooth skin∥부드러운〔거친〕 살결 a tender〔rough〕 skin∥그 여자의 살결은 거칠다 She has a rough complexion.

살결박 —結縛 stripping 《a person》 and tying 《him》 up

*__살구__ 〖식물〗 an apricot

—꽃 apricot blossoms —나무 an apricot tree ; Prunus armeniaca (학명) —빛 apricot (color) —씨 an almond —잼 apricot jam —편〔떡〕 an apricot honey-cake

살군두 a cord used to attach the blade of a plow to the handle

살균 殺菌 sterilization ; disinfection ; pasteurization ──하다 sterilize ; pasteurize ; disinfect ¶ 살균성의 disinfectant∥살균 우유 sterilized〔pasteurized〕 milk∥살균력이 있는 germicidal ; sterilizing∥D. D. T. 는 놀라운 살균력을 가지고 있다 D. D. T. has marvelous sterilizing

power.
—기(機) a sterilizer —력 sterilizing 〔germicidal〕 power —법 a germ-killing process ; pasteurism —소 alexin(-e) ; bacteri(o)cidin — 시험 a bactericidal test — 온도 a thermal death point — 우유 sterilized〔pasteurized〕 milk —제 a germicide ; a bactericide ; a sterilizer ; a disinfectant ; a germicidal agent ; a fungicide ; a microbicide

*살그머니 furtively ; stealthily ; by stealth ; in secret ; secretly ; on the sly ; quietly ¶ 살그머니 나가다〔들어오다〕 steal out 〔in〕// 살그머니 다가오다 steal near ; steal up to 《a person's》 side // 살그머니 쳐다보다 look furtively at 《a person》 ; steal a glance at 《a person》// 살그머니 돈을 손에 쥐어주다 slip a coin into 《a person's》 hands // 그 여자는 살그머니 자리를 일어섰다 She left her seat without a sound. // 나는 살그머니 화가 났다 I felt indignation well up in my heart.

살근거리다 rustle ; rub (together)

살근살근 rustling ; with a rustle

*살금살금 surreptitiously ; sneakingly ; furtively ; stealthily ; with stealthy steps ; behind 《a person's》 back ¶ 살금살금 가다 tiptoe to ; steal one's way to // 살금살금 나오다 crawl out // 살금살금 돌아다니다 skulk about // 나는 그 여자를 놀래 주려고 살금살금 뒷문으로 돌아갔다 I stole cautiously round to the back door to surprise her.

살긋하다 (be) tilted ; slanting ; be leaning to one side

살기 fleshiness ; fattiness ⇨ 살거리

살기 殺氣 a violent temper ; a murderous spirit ; excitement ; bloodthirstiness ¶ 살기 띤 threatening ; ferocious ; bloodthirsty // 살기등등하다 be bloodthirsty ; be out for blood ; one's blood is up // 그의 눈엔 살기가 등등했다 There was danger in his eyes. // 집회를 해산하라는 명령이 있자 장내에 살기가 감돌았다 A stormy atmosphere fell on the hall as the meeting was ordered to break up.

살기 충천 殺氣衝天 widespread bloodthirstiness〔excitement, ferocity〕 —하다 there is a widespread thirst for blood ; death is in the air

살길 a means to live ; a livelihood ¶ 살길을 찾다 seek a way to make a living // 살 길을 잃다 lose one's livelihood

살깃 the feather of an arrow ; an arrow feather

살깊다 (be) fleshy ; fat

살날 ⇨ 여명(餘命)

살내리다 get〔become〕 thin ; lose weight ; 《flesh》 fall away ¶ 살 내리는 약 a fat-reducer ; a flesh-reducer ; an antifat remedy // 너는 그전보다 살이 내린 것 같다 You have got much thinner than you were. /You appear to have lost weight.

†살다[1] ① [생존] live ; be〔stay〕 alive ; subsist ; exist ¶ 산 live ; animate ; living // 산 조개 a live shellfish // 산 모범 a living model〔pattern〕// 마치 산 사람에게 말하듯 하다 speak as if to the living // 사는 보람을 느끼다 find one's life worth living // 희망에 살다 live on hope // 백 살까지 살다 live to be a hundred // 쌀을 먹고 살다 live on rice // 살아서 돌아오다 return alive // 그는 오래 살지 못할 것이다 He will not live long. /His days are numbered. // 내가 살아 있는 동안에 네가 출세하는 것을 보고 싶다 I hope I live long enough to see you rise in the world. // 그는 지금 사느냐 죽느냐의 고비에 있다 He hovers〔hangs〕 between life and death.

② [생활] get along〔by〕 ; make a living ¶ 풍족하게〔어렵게〕 살다 be well-off 〔ill-off〕 ; make a good〔bad〕 living ; be in easy〔hard〕 circumstances // 월급으로 살다 live on one's salary // 붓으로 살다 live by one's pen // 서울에서 살다 live in *Seoul* // 그는 사는 데 걱정이 없다 He is free from bread and butter worry. // 나이 더 들어서 돈 걱정 없이 편히 살고 싶으면 열심히 일하라 Work hard if you want to get on Easy Street when you get older.

③ [거주] live ; dwell ; inhabit ; reside ¶ 사람이 살지 않는 uninhabited 《island》 ; untenanted 《house》 ; unoccupied // 살 수 있는 inhabitable ; good〔fit〕 to live in // 살 수 없는 uninhabitable // 살 집이 없다 be homeless // 시골에서 살다 live in the country // 살기 좋은 곳이다 It is a good place to live in. // 그 집에는 누가 사느냐 Who is the occupant of the house?

④ [생동] be enlivened ; have life given to 《it》 ¶ 그 초상은 마치 살아 있는 것 같다 The portrait is full of life〔lifelike〕. // 이 행 때문에 이 시는 살았다 This line gives piquancy〔life〕 to the poem.

⑤ [바둑에서] be freed from check ; escape from being captured ; be in play ; [야구에서] be safe ¶ 2루에 살다 be safe on second base

살다[2] [크기가] be more than ample ; be extra large ¶ 자수가 살다 be extra long

살다[3] serve 《one's term》 ¶ 3년간 징역을 살다 serve a sentence of three years' penal servitude

살다듬이 beating a nice shine into something —하다 beat a nice shine 《into》

살담배 cut tobacco

살닳다 suffer a loss on the original investment ¶ 100만원이나 살닳았다 I have lost up to a million *won* on the original investment.

살대¹ [화살대] the shaft of an arrow

살대² [버팀나무] a temporary support to keep a house upright ; a prop ; a stay ¶ 살대로 버티다 shore〔prop〕 up

살덩어리 a lump〔piece〕 of flesh

살돈 the outlay ; the money laid out ; the original funds

살똥스럽다 (be) defiant and daring ; blustering ; snappish

살뜰하다 [알뜰하다] (be) thrifty ; frugal ; saving ¶ 살뜰한 주부 a frugal housewife

살뜸 direct cauterization with nothing between the skin and the moxa

살랑거리다 [바람 따위가] blow gently ; [걸음걸이가] walk briskly ¶ 살랑살랑 gently ; briskly (걸음새) // 가을 바람이 살랑거린다 An autumn breeze blows softly. // 정원의 나뭇잎이 살랑살랑 봄바람에 나부꼈다 The leaves of the garden trees rustled in the spring breeze. // 그 여자는 살랑거리고 다닌다 She walks around briskly.

⁑**살랑살랑** ① [바람이] 《blow》 gently ; softly ② [걷는 꼴] 《walk》 with a mincing gait

살랑하다 (be) chilly ; cool ; be somewhat chilly〔cold〕

살래살래 wagging ; waving **—하다** wag ¶ 고개를 살래살래 흔들다 wag〔shake〕 one's head // 개가 꼬리를 살래살래 흔들며 왔다 The dog came wagging his tail.

살려내다 [위험·죽음에서] rescue 《a person》 from 《danger》 ; save 《a person》 from 《death》 ; [곤란·빈곤·고통에서] deliver 《a person》 out of

살려주다 save ; rescue ; spare ; make safe ¶ 목숨을 살려 주다 spare 《a person's》 life // 물에 빠진 사람을 살려 주다 rescue a drowning man // 제발 살려 주십시오 Spare me please. /Oh, have mercy on me.

살롱 a salon ; [파리의 미술전] the Salon

살륙 殺戮 slaughter ⇨ 살육

***살리다¹** ① [목숨을] save ; spare ; rescue ; bring round ; revive ; bring 《a person》 to life ¶ 목숨을 살리다 spare 《a person's》 life // 죽어가는 환자를 살렸다 The doctor saved the dying patient. // 그 잉어를 살려 둬라 Keep the carp alive. // 그 놈은 살려 둘 수 없다 He shall no longer live. /I will not allow him to live. // 살리든 죽이든 네 마음대로 해라 My life is in your hands〔at your mercy〕.
② [활용] make the most〔best use〕 of ; give life to ¶ 문장을 살리다 give life〔vividness〕 to one's writing // 돈을 살려 쓰다 make the best use of one's money ; spend one's money usefully // 사람을 살려 쓰다 employ a man efficiently

살리다² [크기·넓이·길이를] let out ; increase the size ; lengthen ¶ 옷의 접었던 것을 살리다 let out a garment // 소매끝을 살리다 let the sleeves out // 품을 살리다 let out the width

⁑**살림** [생계] living ; livelihood ; [살림살이] a household ; a household establishment ; housekeeping **—하다** keep house ; run a household ¶ 살림 비용 living〔housekeeping〕 expenses ; upkeep charges // 중류의 살림 a moderate scale of living // 집안 살림 domestic life // 살림이 넉넉하다 make〔earn〕 a good living ; be well〔comfortably〕 off ; be well-to-do ; be well-fixed 《미》 // 살림이 넉넉지 못하다 make a poor living ; be badly off ; be badly〔poorly〕 fixed 《미》 // 살림이 곤란하다 be hard up ; be unable to make a living // 이럭저럭 살림을 꾸려 나가다 manage to keep the pot boiling ; live from hand to mouth // 분에 맞는 살림을 하다 live within one's means ; cut one's coat according to one's cloth // 신분에 맞지 않는 살림을 하다 live beyond one's means // 살림을 꾸리다 set up a home // 살림을 나다 set up a separate household // 살림을 잘하다 be a good housekeeper // 시골 살림은 돈이 적게 든다 We can live cheaper in the country. /Living is easier in rural districts. // 그들은 적은 수입으로 근근히 살림을 꾸려 간다 They are just getting along on their small income. // 사는 방법에 달렸겠지만 하루에 만원으로 네 식구의 살림은 무리일거야 Ten thousand *won* a day is hardly enough for a family of four, though it may depend upon the style of living.
— 도구 household goods〔necessaries〕
—방 a living room

살림꾼 a housekeeper ; [알뜰한] a good housewife ¶ 그 여자는 살림꾼이다 She is an exemplary housewife.

살림 맡다 keep house ; take charge 〔care〕 of the household

***살림살이** housekeeping ; a household ; a household establishment ¶ 가난한 살림살이 a needy household ; a meager living // 살림살이의 고생 domestic cares // 물가고 때문에 살림살이가 어렵다 be rather badly off owing to the high cost of living

살림집 a (private) home ; a house for dwelling

살맛¹ the touch of skin

살맛² pleasure of living ¶ 살맛이 없다 have nothing to live for

살망살망 with a slender〔long-legged〕 gait

살망하다 (be) long-legged ; be slender from the waist down

살맞다 be struck by illness〔misfortune〕 (after attending a rite of another's family)
살며시 [살그머니] stealthily ; secretly ; furtively ; in secret ; [소리 없이] softly ; quietly ; gently ; lightly ; cautiously ¶ 살며시 집을 나가다 steal out of the house // 문을 살며시 열다 open the door cautiously // 살며시 자리를 뜨다 leave one's seat quietly // 살며시 미소하다 smile gently // 살며시 편지를 쥐어 주다 slip a letter into 《a person's》 hand // 그는 살며시 들어왔다 He came in without a sound. // 그는 살며시 가방을 들고 방을 나갔다 He smuggled a bag out of the room.
살몃살몃 with repeated stealth ; ever so furtively ; lightly ¶ 살몃살몃 걷다 walk lightly ; tread softly ; go with stealthy steps
살목 一木 a pillar-jack ; a support ; a brace ; a prop ¶ 살목으로 버티다 shore up ; prop up
살무사 a viper ; an adder ; an asp
살문 a lattice door〔window〕
살미 an elaborate curlicue ornamentation at the top of a pillar
살밀치 the crupper of a harness
살밑 an arrowhead ⇨ 살촉
살바람 [틈으로의] a draft (of air) ; [봄의] a chilly wind (of spring) ¶ 살바람이 들어온다 There is a draft here.
살박다 press a pattern into a cake ; decorate a cake
살받이 a target board ; the ground around a target
살방석 一方席 a device for polishing arrows
살벌 殺伐 **—하다** (be) bloody ; brutal ; savage ; warlike ¶ 살벌한 기풍 a combative〔wild〕 spirit // 살벌한 분위기 a warlike atmosphere // 계엄령이 선포되자 시가는 살벌한 기운이 감돌았다 As the martial law was proclaimed, the city was in a tense and violent atmosphere.
살별 〖천문〗 a comet
살보시 一布施 sexual relations with a Buddhist priest **—하다** have illicit sexual relations with a priest
살붙다 煞— ⇨ 살오르다(煞—)
살붙이 [친족] one's kith and kin ; a relative ; kinsfolk ; [살코기] meat
살빛 the color of the skin ; flesh color ; complexion ; cast ¶ 살빛이 희다 have fair skin〔complexion〕 // 살빛이 검다 have dark skin // 그 여자는 살빛이 좋다 She has a good complexion.
살사리 a sneak ; a wily〔tricky〕 man ; a schemer
*__살살__[1] gently ; softly ; slowly ; quietly ; lightly ; stealthily ¶ 살살 걷다 sneak about // 살살 피하다 evade furtively // 아이를 살살 달래다 comfort a child gently // 물이 살살 끓다 Water simmers. / Water boils up slowly. // 바람이 살살 분다 The wind blows softly. // 눈이 살살 녹는다 Snow melts imperceptively.
살살[2] [다리로] with a brisk crawl ; at a lively pace ; [머리로] with a gentle shake ; gently
살살[3] with a slight pain 《in the stomach》 **—하다** 《one's stomach》 aches
살살하다 [교활] (be) wily ; tricky ; cunning ; sly ; crafty ; scheming ; [섬세·우아] delicate ; fine ; dainty ; slim ; slender ; [위기] delicate ; precarious ; dangerous ¶ 살살한 고비 a delicate situation
살상 殺傷 killing and injuring ; bloodshed **—하다** kill and injure ; shed blood ¶ 수많은 살상 numerous casualties
살생 殺生 taking life ; killing animals **—하다** take life ; kill〔slaughter〕 animals ¶ 살생을 금하다 prohibit killing animals // 무익한 살생을 자행하다 kill animals needlessly〔without any reason〕
살생 금단 殺生禁斷 prohibition of shooting and fishing
살성 texture ; grain ; complexion ¶ 살성이 곱다 be of delicate〔fine〕 texture
살소매 the exposed part of the arm below the sleeve
살손 ① [맨손] one's bare〔empty〕 hands ¶ 살손으로 물고기를 잡다 catch a fish with one's bare hands ; [빈손으로] empty-handed ② [비유적] earnestness ; sincerity ; devotion ; wholeheartedness ¶ 일에 살손을 붙이다 devote oneself to a job ; put one's heart and soul into a job
살수 撒水 watering ; sprinkling water **—하다** water 《the street》 ; sprinkle 《the street》 with water
—차 a watering cart ; a sprinkler (truck) ; a water〔motor, street〕 sprinkler
살수건 一手巾 a piece of cloth used to polish arrows
살수세미 a scrubbing brush used in cleaning arrowheads
살신성인 殺身成仁 sacrificing oneself to preserve one's integrity **—하다** sacrifice oneself to preserve one's integrity ; make a martyr of oneself
살쐐기 〖한의학〗 a summer itch〔rash〕
살아가다 lead a life ; get along ; keep on living ¶ 그럭저럭 세상을 살아가다 manage to get along // 월 40만원으로 살아가다 live on 400,000 *won* a month
살아나다 ① [소생] revive ; be brought to life ; come to one's sense ; [꺼진 불이] flame up again ¶ 응급 치료를 받고 다시 살아나다 be resuscitated by first

aid // 숯불이 살아났다 The charcoal fire is burning brightly again. // 비가 오자 시든 초목이 다시 살아났다 After a rain the drooping grass and plants have come to life again. // 우리는 그가 살아나지 못할 것으로 단념했다 We gave up him for dead.
② [위기 모면] escape 《death, danger》; be relieved from hardship ¶ 구사일생으로 살아나다 have a narrow 〔hairbreadth〕 escape ; have a close shave ; escape by the skin of one's teeth // 인제 살아났구나 What a blessed relief!
③ [재기] regain ; recover ; rally ¶ 악의 세력이 다시 살아났다 The wicked have regained their strength.

살아 생전 —生前 (during) one's lifetime ¶ 살아 생전에 during〔in〕 one's lifetime ; while in life

살얼음 a thin coat〔sheet〕 of ice ; thin ice ¶ 그는 지금 살얼음을 밟는 기분이다 He is now on thin ice. // 강에 살얼음이 잡혔다 A thin layer of ice covered the river.
—판 a tricky〔delicate, touchy〕 situation
살얼음을 밟는 듯하다 관용 feel as if one were stepping on thin ice ; feel like treading on eggs

살오르다 grow〔become〕 fat ; put on weight

살오르다 煞— an evil influence〔spirit〕 ascends (within one) ; [띠앗] a household is torn with disharmony

살육 殺戮 killing ; slaughter ; massacre ; butchery —하다 kill ; massacre ; slaughter ; butcher ¶ 살육을 자행하다 kill mercilessly ; make a massacre 《of》

살의 殺意 murderous intent ; intent to murder〔kill〕 ¶ 살의를 품다 conceive a murderous design ; intend to kill 《a person》 // 그는 처음부터 살의가 있었던 것은 아니었다 It was not his original intention to kill the man.

-살이 living ; life
고생— leading a hard life 더부— parasitism ; dependence 머슴— working as a farmhand 시집— living with one's husband's parents 징역— serving one's term of imprisonment 처가— living with the family into which a man has married

†**살인** 殺人 homicide ; murder ; manslaughter

> 참고 **murder**는 살의가 있는 「모살」 **manslaughter**는 사전에 모의가 없었던 살인 **homicide**는 위 둘을 포함한 일반적인 말

—하다 commit murder〔homicide〕; murder〔kill〕 《a person》 ¶ 살인적인 terrible ; deadly ; death-dealing ; murderous ; cutthroat // 그런 일에 군대를 출동시키다니 바로 살인 행위이다 To send troops on such an errand is sheer murder.
— 가스 lethal gas —광(狂) homicidal insanity ; [사람] a homicidal mania ; phonomania — 광선 a death〔lethal〕 ray —귀(鬼)〔마〕 a devilish homicide ; a cutthroat ; a bloodthirsty felon ; a ghoul — 미수 an attempted〔a frustrated〕 murder ; a murder attempt — 미수자 an attempted murderer ; a would-be murderer —범〔자〕 a homicide ; a murderer ; [여자] a murderess ; a killer ; a slayer —사(砂) 〖군사〗 death sand (방사능을 함유한 모래·먼지 따위) — 사건 a case of murder ; a murder case —죄 homicide ; murder ; felonious homicide ¶ 여러번 살인죄를 범하다 commit several murders // 살인죄로 체포되다 be arrested on a charge of murder — 청부업자 a killer — 혐의자 a murderer suspect ; a suspect in a murder 과실 — involuntary homicide 대량 — mass〔multiple〕 murder

살잡다 prop〔shore〕 up ; jack up ; support ; buttress ¶ 쓰러져 가는 집을 살잡다 buttress a falling house

살잡이하다 ⇨ 살잡다

살잡히다 [구김살지다] be wrinkled 〔crumpled, rumpled, creased〕; wrinkle ; crumple ; [살얼음이 얼다] have a thin coat of ice ; be covered with thin ice

살점 —點 a piece of meat

살조개 〖조개〗 an ark shell ; Anadara granosa (학명)

살줄치다 let the line out on a kite ; give line to a kite

살지다 [몸이] (be) fat ; fleshy ; corpulent ; [땅이] rich ; fertile ¶ 살진 돼지 a fat pig // 살진 땅 fertile land

살집 fleshiness

살짝 [모르게] furtively ; by stealth ; in secret ; on the sly ; [쉽게] effortlessly ; easily ; [가볍게] softly ; lightly ; slightly ; gently ¶ 살짝 도망가다 sneak 〔slip〕 away〔out〕 // 살짝 해치우다 do it effortlessly // 살짝 두들기다 tap lightly

살짝곰보 a slightly pockmarked face 〔person〕

살쩍 the hair on one's temples ; sideburns

살쭈 a cattle broker ⇨ 쇠살쭈

살찌 the look of an arrow in flight ¶ 살찌가 곱다 an arrow flies nicely

†**살찌다** put on weight ; grow fat ; gain weight〔flesh〕; become corpulent 〔plump〕; [비옥] grow fertile〔rich, productive〕 ¶ 살찐 fat ; fleshy ; plump // 살찐 송아지 a fat calf // 그는 요새 살쪘다 He has been putting on weight

lately.
*살찌우다 make fat ; fatten 《it》 up
살차다 ① [혜성이] have a long tail ② [성질이] (be) cold and unapproachable ; be a cold fish
살창 —窓 a lattice window
살책박 a rice container made of twigs
살촉 —鏃 an arrowhead ; a barb of an arrow
살충 殺蟲 killing〔destroying〕 insects ; destroying worms ; insecticide ; fungicide
—등 an insecticidal lamp —제 an insecticide ; a vermicide ; a vermifuge ; a larvicide (유충의) ; an adulticide (성충의) ; an insect powder (가루의) ¶ 살충제 분무기 an insecticide sprayer ; a flit-gun ; an aerosol bomb 《미》
살치 the meat on short ribs
살치다 cross〔X, mark〕 out ; cancel ; void
살코기 lean〔red〕 meat
살쾡이 a wildcat
—자리 『궁술』 Lynx
살통 a jack ; a prop supporter
살팍지다 (be) sinewy ; muscular ; stout ; brawny ¶ 그는 살팍지다 He is built strong and lean.
살판[1] ① [판자] a heavy plank used to jack up the pillars of a house ; a handspike ② ⇨ 살판뜀 ③ ⇨ 살얼음판
살판[2] 『궁술』 making 20 hits in 50 shots or 10 rounds in archery
살판나다 become rich ; be lucky ; have a stroke of luck ; strike it rich ; come into a fortune ; one's ship comes in ¶ 그는 살판났다 His ship came in.
살판뜀 a somersault
살펴보다 look around〔about〕 ; watch for ; look into ; examine ¶ 사방을 살펴보다 look all around // 형세를 살펴보다 see how the wind blows〔things stand〕 // 그는 나의 행동을 살펴보고 있었다 He was spying on my movements.
살평상 —平床 a slat bed ; a bedstead with lattice flooring
살포 a spade for irrigation work
살포 撒布 ⇨ 산포
살풀이 煞— exorcism ; exorcising an evil spirit ; casting out devils —하다 exorcise ; have an exorcism ; drive out evil spirits
살품 the space between clothes and the chest ; the bosom ; the breast ¶ 어린 아이가 어머니의 살품에 손을 넣었다 The child thrusts the hand into its mother's bosom.
살풍경 殺風景 tastelessness ; inelegance ; bleakness ; dullness ; lack of refinement ; want of taste —하다 (be) tasteless ; inelegant ; bleak ; dull ; lacking in refinement ; dreary ; unrefined ¶ 살풍경한 정원 a garden lacking in taste ; a garden of bad taste // 살풍경한 경치 a dreary sight ; a bare landscape // 살풍경한 것 an eyesore // 광고 때문에 공원이 살풍경하다 The advertisements mar the beauty of the public park.
살피 [땅 사이의] a land mark ; a boundary marker ; [물건 사이의] a dividing mark ; a divider ; a place marker ¶ 살피를 꽂다 put dividers to mark one's place
‡살피다[1] ① [잘 보다] take a good look at ; watch ; look about〔out〕 ; inspect closely ¶ 사방을 살피다 keep a sharp look-out // 창밖을 살피다 peep〔look〕 out of the window // 방안을 살피다 peep 〔look〕 in at the room // 기회를 살피다 watch for an opportunity // 행동을 살피다 spy upon 《a person's》 movements // 형세를 살피다 see how things stand〔go on〕 ; wait and see ; see how the wind blows ; sit on the fence
② [판단] judge ; gather ; infer ; derive ¶ 이 사실로 살펴 보건대 judging from this fact // 심중을 살피다 read 《a person's》 mind ; enter into 《a person's》 feeling // 안색을 살피다 study 《a person's》 face
③ [주의하다] be careful ; look around ; watch out〔for〕 ; pay heed 《to》 ¶ 살펴 가시오 Take care of yourself. /Good-bye. // 차를 주차시키기 전에 주위에 수상한 사람(들)이 있나 살펴봐 Look around for a suspicious person or persons when you park your cars.
살피다[2] [천 따위가] (be) loose-woven ; gauze-like ; thin and coarse ⇨ 설피다
살핏살핏하다 (be) all rather loose woven ; gauze-like
살핏하다 (be) loose-woven ; gauze-like
‡살해 殺害 murder ; killing —하다 murder ; kill ; slay ; slaughter ; assassinate (암살) ¶ 살해를 꾀하다 make an attempt on 《a person's》 life ; attempt the life of ; compass 《a person's》 death ; plot the murder of 《a person》
— 사건 a murder case ; a case of murder —자 a murderer ; [여자] a murderess ; a slayer ; an assassin (암살자) — 현장 the scene〔spot〕 of murder 부친〔모친〕 — patricide〔matricide〕 유아 — infanticide
삵피 —皮 the skin of a wildcat
†삶 life ; living ; existence ¶ 삶의 투쟁 struggle for life // 삶에 지치다 get tired of living // 어렵게 삶을 이어가다 scrape a living ; earn a meager living
‡삶다 ① [물에] boil ; cook ; do 《meat》 ¶ 삶은 계란 boiled eggs // 고기를 푹 삶다 do meat well〔thoroughly〕 // 되 삶다 reboil ; cook over again // 너무 삶다 overboil ; overdo
② [사람을] appease ; tame ; coax ; win

over ; bribe ; corrupt ¶ 형사를 삶다 bribe〔buy, fix〕 a detective // 그를 삶아서 그것을 하게 할 수 있는지 알아보라 See if we can buy him over to do it.
③ [흙을] harrow ; till ¶ 흙을 삶다 harrow〔rake〕 the soil

삶아지다 be cooked ; cook ; be boiled ; boil ¶ 잘 삶아진 well-cooked〔-done〕 // 너무 삶아지다 be overboiled〔overdone〕

삶이 ① harrowing〔raking〕 tilled soil **—하다** harrow〔rake〕 (tilled soil)
② direct planting of rice seed on a harrowed paddy **—하다** plant rice seed directly on a harrowed paddy

*__삼__[1] hemp ; 〖식물〗 a hemp ¶ 삼으로 만든 hempen
—노 a hempen rope〔cord〕 **—실** twine

삼[2] [태아의] the amnion〔fetus membrane〕 and the placenta

삼[3] [눈동자의] a corneal ulcer ⇨ 삼눈

삼[4] [뱃바닥의] a bottom-plank on a boat

삼 三 three ¶ 제 3 the third〔3rd〕

삼 蔘 ginseng ⇨ 인삼

삼가 respectfully ; reverently ; humbly ; courteously ¶ 삼가 말씀드립니다 I beg to inform you. // 삼가 조의를 표합니다 I respectfully express my condolence. / Please accept my deepest condolence.

삼가 三價 〖화학〗 trivalence ; trivalency

‡__삼가다__ ① [조심] be discreet〔prudent, cautious, careful〕 ; take care of ¶ 말을 삼가다 be careful about one's words ; restrain one's tongue // 행동을 삼가다 be circumspect in behavior ; behave oneself prudently // 언행을 삼가다 use prudence〔be prudent〕 in speech and action ; be discreet〔circumspect〕 in word and deed // 말을 삼가라 Hold your impertinent tongue. /Keep a civil tongue in your head. // 앞으로 삼가겠습니다 I will be careful hereafter.
② [억제·절제] restrain oneself from 《doing》 ; abstain〔keep, refrain〕 from 《doing》 ; be moderate 《in》 ¶ 술을 삼가다 be temperate in drinking ; keep〔abstain〕 from drinking〔wine〕 // 욕정을 삼가다 abstain from sensual pleasure ; be continent // 음주 흡연을 삼가시오 You must be on your guard against wine and tobacco. // 남을 헐뜯는 짓은 삼가야 한다 You should refrain from faultfinding. // 회사를 사랑한다면 좀 더 지출을 삼가해 주세요 If you love your company, rein in your spending a bit more.

삼가르다 cut the umbilical cord on (a baby)

*__삼각 三角__ three angles ; (the) three-cornered ; triangularity ; a triangle (삼각형) ; trigonometry (삼각법) ¶ 삼각의 three-cornered ; triangular
—건(巾) a triangle (bandage) ; a cravat **— 관계** a three-cornered relation ; [남녀간의] a love triangle ; the eternal triangle ; a triangular〔triple〕 love affair ; a three-cornered romance **—근(筋)** 〖해부〗 a deltoid (muscle) **— 급수** a trigonometrical series **—기** a triangular pennant ; [요트의] a burgee ; a pennon (창기) **— 기둥** a trigonal〔triangular〕 prism **— 나선** a triangular screw thread **—돛** a jib ; a staysail ; a leg-of-mutton sail **—망** a triangular net **— 모자** a three-cornered hat **— 무역** triangular trade **— 방정식** a trigonometric equation **—법** 〖수학〗 trigonometry ; triangulation ¶ 평면〔구면〕 삼각법 plane〔spherical〕 trigonometry **—뿔(추)** a trigonal〔triangular〕 pyramid **—수** 〖수학〗 triangular numbers **—익(翼)** 〖항공〗 a delta wing **—자** a set square **— 자리** 〖천문〗 the Triangle ; Triangulum **—점** 〖측량〗 a triangulation point ; [푯돌] a stone marker of triangulation **— 좌표** triangular coordinates **—주** a delta **— 측량** triangular surveying ; triangulation ; a trigonometrical survey ¶ 2등 삼각 측량 〖토목〗 the second order triangulation **— 투쟁** a three-cornered 〔triangular〕 fight **—파(波)** a chopping wave **—(함수)표** a table of trigonometrical function **— 함수** 〖수학〗 trigonometrical function **— 항로** 〖항해〗 a triangular sea route

삼각 三脚 three legs ; a tripod ; [비경이] a warp beam ¶ 삼각의 three-legged ; tripodal // 2인 삼각 경기 a three-legged race
—가(架) a tripod (mounting) **— 걸상** a three-legged stool **— 기중기** a gin **— 분도기** a station pointer ; a three-armed protractor **이인 —** a three-legged race

*__삼각형 三角形__ a triangle ¶ 삼각형의 triangular ; trigonal ; three-cornered // 삼각형으로 만들다 triangulate // 삼각형으로 자르다 cut 《a thing》 into a triangular form // 대륙은 어느 것이나 삼각형이다 Each continent is of triangular shape.
구면 — a spherical triangle **등변〔부등변〕 —** an equilateral〔a scalene〕 triangle **역〔도(倒)〕—** an inverted triangle **예각〔둔각〕 —** an acute〔obtuse-〕 angled triangle **2등변 —** an isosceles triangle **정—** a regular triangle **직각 —** a right-angled triangle

삼간 초가 三間草家 a three-room thatched cottage ; a humble cottage

삼강 三綱 the three basic〔fundamental〕 principles in human relations ; the three bonds
— 오륜(五倫) the three bonds and the five moral rules in human relations

삼거리 三— an intersection of three streets〔roads〕 ; a three-way junction ; a three-forked road

삼거웃 waste bits of hemp (used to mix with sculpture clay)
삼겹실 three-ply thread
삼경 三更 (after) midnight ; the dead of night ; the small〔wee〕 hours
삼경 三景 the three famous views〔beauty spots〕 ¶ 한국 삼경(의 하나) (one of) the scenic-trio〔three noted views〕 of Korea
삼경 三經 the Three Classics (of Ancient China) 《the Book of Odes, the Canon of History and the Book of Changes》 ⇨ 사서(四書)
삼계 三界 ① 〖불교〗 the three worlds (of Heaven, Earth, and People) ② the past, present, and future existences
삼관왕 三冠王 〖경기〗 a triple crown ¶ 삼관왕이 되다 get〔win〕 a triple crown
삼광조 三光鳥 a Korean paradise flycatcher
삼교 三校 the third proof-reading
삼교 三敎 the three religions (Buddhism, Taoism, and Confucianism)
삼국 三國 three countries ; the Three States 《of》
— 시대 the period〔age, era〕 of the Three States **— 조약** a three-power 〔tripartite, triangular〕 treaty **— 통일** a unification of three nations **— 협상** a triple entente〔negotiation, talk〕 **— 회담〔협정〕** a tripartite conference〔agreement〕 **제—** the third power〔state〕 **제—인** a national of a third state
삼군 三軍 the entire armed forces (of a country) ; the whole army ; the three services 《the army, the navy and the air force》 ¶ 삼군을 질타〔호령〕하다 command a great army
— 열병식 a review of the whole army **— 의장대** the tri-service hono(u)r guard **— 합동 작전** a joint operation of the three armed services
삼굿 a hemp-steaming pit〔kiln, cauldron〕 **—하다** steam hemp to remove the outer covering
삼권 분립 三權分立 〖법〗 separation of the three powers 《administrative, legislative and judicial》 ; checks and balances
삼극 三極 ¶ 삼극의 tripolar
— (진공)관 a triode
삼꽃 ① 〖식물〗 hemp blossom (used as a medicinal herb) ② 〖한의학〗 a kind of feverish rash on a baby's skin
삼나무 杉— ⇨ 삼목(杉木)
삼남 三南 the three southern provinces (of Korea) ; the South ¶ 삼남은 풍작이다 The South enjoys a good harvest.
삼년 三年 three years ¶ 삼년마다의 triennial // 삼년마다 every three years // 삼년마다 한번씩 홍수가 난다 We have floods every three years.
—상(喪) mourning for three years ; a third year memorial service (for ancestors) **—생** [국민 학교의] a third-grade pupil〔boy, girl〕 《미》 : [대학·고교의] a third year student ; a junior 《미》
—생 식물 a triennial
삼노 [끈] a hempen twine ; a hemp cord〔rope〕
삼눈 a pupillary white〔red〕 speck
삼다 ① [무엇으로] make ; make 《a thing》 of ; have〔use, regard〕 《a thing》 as ¶ 그녀를 며느리로 삼다 make her one's daughter-in-law // 그의 효도를 거울로 삼다 make his filial piety one's mirror // 그는 그 고아를 양자로 삼았다 He adopted the orphan. // 그들은 석탄을 연료로 삼는다 They use coal as fuel. // 그 점은 문제 삼지 않아도 된다 That point may be left out of consideration. // 그는 오락 삼아 그림을 그린다 He practices painting for amusement.
② [신 따위를] make (a sandal) ; [섬유 실을] spin ¶ 짚신을 삼다 make a straw sandal // 삼을 삼다 spin hemp
삼단 a bunch of hemp
삼단 같은 머리 관용 long thick hair ; luxuriant hair
삼단계 三段階 three stage ; the third stage ¶ 삼단계의 계획 three stages planning // 삼단계 작전 a third stage operation
— 로켓 a three-stage rocket **— 방어** a three-way〔-fold〕 defence **— 확대** 〖사진〗 a triple extension frame
삼단 논법 三段論法 〖논리〗 a syllogism ¶ 삼단 논법으로 논하다 syllogize
사이비 — a false〔fallacious〕 syllogism **생략 —** an enthymeme **쌍지(雙肢)적 —** a dilemma **정언(定言)적〔가언(假言)적, 선언(選言)적〕 —** a categorical 〔hypothetical, disjunctive〕 syllogism
삼단도 三段跳 ⇨ 삼단뛰기
삼단뛰기 三段— 〖육상〗 hop, step 〔skip〕, and jump ; a triple jump
삼대 a hemp stalk
삼대 三代 three generations ¶ (제)삼대 대통령 the third president
삼대국 三大國 the Big Three
삼덕 三德 the three primary〔cardinal〕 virtues ① [서경의] wisdom, benevolence and valo(u)r ② [유교의] honesty, fortitude and meekness ③ [기독교의] faith, hope and charity
삼도내 三途— the River Styx ¶ 삼도내를 건너다 cross the (River) Styx
삼독 蔘毒 ginseng poisoning
삼독회 三讀會 〖법〗 the third reading (of a bill in the legislature)
삼동 三冬 the three winter months ; the three months of winter ¶ 삼동에 베옷을 입다 wear hemp clothes in winter
삼동 三同 having three parts joined together ; (being) in three sections

— 물림 a smoking pipe with a silver or copper band joining the two ends as a catch — 치마 a three-colo(u)r kite

삼동네 三洞— neighbors ; neighboring villages

삼두근 三頭筋 〖해부〗 the triceps

삼두 정치 三頭政治 a triumvirate ; a triarchy ¶ 삼두 정치의 triumviral

삼등 三等 the third class〔rate〕 ¶ 삼등 인생 the lowest life // 삼등으로 여행하다 travel (by) third class // 우리는 삼등을 타고 신혼 여행을 떠났다 We left for a honeymoon on the third-class train. // 부산행 삼등 두장을 주십시오 (Give me) Two third class singles (to) *Pusan*.

—국 a third-rate power〔nation〕; a minor country — 여객 a third-class passenger ; a steerage passenger (배의) — 열차 a third-class compartment〔carriage〕 —친 a relative in the third degree —표〔석〕 a third-class ticket〔seat〕 —품 a third-rate article

삼등분 三等分 trisection ; dividing into three equal parts —하다 divide〔cut〕 into three equal parts ; divide equally among the three

삼라 만상 森羅萬象 (all) creation ; (all) nature ; everything under the sun〔in nature〕; the universe

삼루 三壘 〖야구〗 the third base ¶ 삼루에 나아가다 go〔advance〕 to third ; take third // 삼루에 머무르다 be left on third base

—선 the third-base line —수 the third-base man —타 a three-base hit ; a three-baser ; a three-bagger ; a triple

삼류 三流 the third rate〔class〕 ¶ 삼류의 third rate〔class, grade, order〕; of the third order // 삼류의 인간 a third-rater 《속》

— 극장 a lower-class theater — 인물 a third-rater — 작가 a third-rate writer — 학교 a third-class school

삼륜차 三輪車 a tricycle ; a tandem ; [유아용] a velocipede ¶ 삼륜차를 타다 ride a tricycle

삼릉 三稜 a triangle

—경 a prism —근 〖해부〗 a deltoid (muscle) —석 〖광물〗 a dreikanter 《*pl.* ~(s)》

⁑**삼림** 森林 a wood ; a forest ¶ 삼림을 도벌하다 fell a forest tree in secret // 삼림을 초토화하다 burn a jungle to the ground

— 구획 a forest section —대(帶) a forest belt〔zone〕 — 동물 a forest animal —법 the Forest Law — 보호〔애호〕 forest conservation ; protection of forests — 자원 forest〔timber〕 resources — 조합 a forestry (owners') association — 지방〔지대〕 a forest area〔land〕; woodland ; a wooded region ; timberland 《미》 — 철도 a forest railway —학 forestry — 행정 forest administration

삼립 森立 —하다 bristle like a forest ; stand close together ; be dense〔thick〕 ¶ 삼립한 돛대 a forest of masts // 적진에는 군기가 삼립하고 있었다 The enemy camp bristled with hundreds of banners.

삼마누라 〖민속〗 the third of the twelve stages of an exorcism rite

삼막물 三幕物 a three-act play

삼매 三昧 absorption ; ecstasy ; concentration ; devotion

—경 a blissful state of self-forgetfulness ¶ 삼매경에 들어가다 attain the perfect state of spiritual concentration 독서 — absorption in reading

삼면 三面 ① three sides〔faces〕 ¶ 삼면에 on three sides // 삼면이 산으로 둘러싸이다 be surrounded by hills on three sides

② [신문의] the third page ; the human-interest page ¶ 범죄 사건으로 가득한 삼면 the third page full of crimes // 삼면을 장식하다 be printed in the social page〔column〕; go into the paper ; be featured by the paper

—각 〖기하〗 a trihedral angle —경 a dressing table surmounted by three mirrors ; a vanity〔dresser〕 with three mirrors — 기사 city news ; police news ; stories of human interest —체 〖기하〗 a trihedron 《*pl.* ~s, -dra》

삼모작 三毛作 three crops a year ; triple cropping for a year ¶ 월남에서는 삼모작을 하고 있다 They crop three times a year in Viet-Nam.

삼목 杉木 〖식물〗 a Japanese cedar ; a cryptomeria

삼문 三文 three farthings ; a very small sum of money ¶ 삼문의 가치도 없다 It is not worth a penny〔button, straw〕.

— 문사 a literary hack ; a penny-a-liner ; a hack writer ; a pulp writer ; a scribbler ; a wordmonger 《미》 — 문학 trash ; cheap reading — 소설 a cheap novel ; a dime novel 《미》; a penny dreadful (통속물의 싸구려 소설) ; a shilling shocker (선정적인 싸구려 소설) — 잡지 an obscure magazine

삼민주의 三民主義 Three Principles of the People (of Sun Yat-sen's China) ; the Threefold National Principle ; Sunwenism

삼바 〖음악〗 samba ¶ 삼바춤을 추다 dance the samba ; samba

삼박 with one stroke

삼박거리다 (one's eyes) blink lightly

삼박삼박 blinking (one's eyes) lightly

삼박자 三拍子 〖음악〗 triple time ; three counts ¶ 왈츠는 삼박자로 춘다 We dance the waltz in three counts.

삼반규관 三半規管 〖해부〗 the (three) semicircular canals
삼발 bloodshot veins of a corneal ulcer
삼발이 a tripod
***삼배 三倍** three times ; thrice ¶ 삼배의 three times as many〔much, large〕 as ; thrice ; treble // 수요는 공급의 삼배이다 The demand is three times as great as the supply. // 물가가 삼배나 뛰었다 Prices have trebled. // 3의 삼배는 9이다 Three times three is nine.
삼배 三拜 bowing thrice
삼백년제 三百年祭 the three hundredth anniversary ; a tercentenary
삼베 hemp cloth
삼별초 三別抄 a special capital defense unit
삼보 三寶 three treasures (ears, mouth and eyes)
삼복 三伏 the hottest period of summer ; midsummer ; dog days
— 더위 the sultry weather of the "dog days" ; the canicular heat ; the midsummer heat
삼봉낚시 三鋒— a three-prong fishhook
삼부 三部 three parts〔sections〕 ; three copies ; [부처] three departments ; [서적] three volumes ¶ 신곡(神曲)은 삼부로 되어 있다 Divina Commedia has three parts.
—곡 〖음악〗 a trilogy **—작** a trilogy **— 합주** 〖음악〗 an ensemble of three parts ; a trio ; a terzetto **— 합창** 〖음악〗 a chorus of three parts **— 형식** 〖음악〗 (a) ternary form
삼분 三分 dividing into three parts ; trisection ; [시간] three minutes **—하다** divide 《a thing》 into three (parts) ; trisect ¶ 삼분의 1 one-third ; a third // 삼분의 2 two-thirds
삼분오열 三分五裂 disruption ; breaking 〔tearing〕 asunder ; dispersion **—하다** break〔tear〕 asunder ; be broken〔torn〕 asunder ; be disrupted
삼불 [태를 사르는] the fire to burn an afterbirth
삼빛 三— the third degree of color saturation ; well〔heavily〕 saturated ; deep
삼사 三思 thinking over and over again ; speculation ; reflection 《on》 **—하다** think over and over again ; speculate〔reflect〕 《on》
삼사미 ① [세 갈래의] a point of trisection ; a triple prong ; a double notch ② [활의] a prong on an arrow
삼사 분기 三四分期 third quarter
삼사월 三四月 March or April ¶ 삼사월 긴긴해 the long (sunny) days of March and April (according to the lunar calendar)
삼삭 三朔 the three months of a season
삼산염기 三酸鹽基 a triacid base
삼산화물 三酸化物 〖화학〗 a trioxide
삼살방 三煞方 〖민속〗 an unlucky direction
***삼삼오오 三三五五** (by) twos and threes ; (in) groups (of two or three) ¶ 삼삼오오 떼지어 오다 come by twos and threes // 삼삼오오 이야기하며 가다 go in small conversing groups
삼삼하다 be not salty but tasty ¶ 이 시금치 나물은 너무 삼삼하다 This cooked spinach is seasoned very lightly.
삼삿반 蔘— a reed mat for drying ginseng
삼색 三色 three (primary) colors ; tricolor ¶ 삼색의 three-color ; tricolor ; tricolored
—관(管) tricolor tube **—기** a tricolor (flag) **— 무늬** a tricolored decorative pattern **— 사진** three-color〔trichromatic, trichromic〕 photography **—판** 〖인쇄〗 three-color〔tricolor, tricolored, trichromatic〕 printing **— 판법** three-color process **— 환등** a three-color magic lantern
삼색오랑캐꽃 三色— 〖식물〗 a pansy ; a heart's-ease
삼서다 get a corneal ulcer
삼선 三選 election for the third term ¶ 삼선되다 be elected for the third term // 삼선을 노리다 seek a third term // 대통령에 삼선되다 be elected president for the third term
삼성 三省 —하다 reflect upon oneself three times a day ; examine oneself over and over again ; introspect deeply
삼성 三聖 the three legendary founders of Korea ; the three holy sages (of the world, of old China) ; the three sages of Ancient Greece
삼성들리다 stuff oneself with food ; 《a shaman》 eat an exorcism feast greedily
삼세 三世 〖불교〗 the three divisions of the universe 《the regions of desire, form, formlessness》 ; the three states of existence 《the past, present, and future》 ; the three worlds 《Heaven, Earth, the world of the Mortals》 ; [삼대] three generations ; the third generation ; 《Richard》 the Third
삼세번 三—番 (exactly) three times ; thrice ¶ 나는 합격 증서를 삼세번 확인했다 I confirmed the letter of acceptance three times.
삼쇠 third gong (player) in a folk band
삼승 三乘 〖수학〗 cube **—하다** cube 《a number》 ; multiply 《a number》 by its square〔twice by itself〕 ¶ 3의 삼승은 27이다 The cube of 3 is 27.
—근 the cube root **—멱** the third power **—비** a triple〔triplicate〕 ratio
삼시 三時 [세끼] the three meal times (of breakfast, lunch and supper) ; three daily meals ; [세시] three o'clock
삼시욹 三— 3-ply cord〔rope〕

삼신 hemp sandals
삼신 三神 the legendary three founders of Korea (삼성) ; the three gods governing childbirth (삼신령)
삼실 hemp thread〔yarn〕
삼십 三十 thirty ¶ 삼십대의 청년 a young man of thirty // 그는 삼십대이다 He is in his thirties. // 일세대를 보통 삼십년으로 친다 One generation is denoted about every 30 years.
삼십육계 三十六計 escape ; flight ; running away ; decampment ¶ 삼십육계 줄행랑이 제일이다 A good runner is never caught. /Discretion is the better part of valor.
삼십육계를 놓다 관용 beat a retreat ; show one's heels
삼십팔도선 三十八度線 [남북한간의] the 38th Parallel ; 38 degrees north latitude ¶ 여기가 삼십팔도선입니다 This is on the 38th Parallel.
삼쌍둥이 三雙童— triplets
삼씨 hemp seed
— 기름 hempseed oil
-삼아(서) by way of ; for ; for the sake of ; as ¶ 모범 삼아(서) as a model ; as an example // 재미삼아(서) for amusement // 시험삼아(서) as a trial ; on a trial basis ; for a trial period // 일을 장난삼아(서) 하다 do a job for fun ; do a job half-heartedly // 산보삼아(서) for a walk // 동무 삼아(서) 같이 가다 go along for company's sake
삼엄 森嚴 solemnity **—하다** (be) solemn ; awe-inspiring ; grave ¶ 삼엄한 분위기 an awe-inspiring atmosphere // 삼엄한 경계망을 뚫고 도주하였다 He ran away〔disappeared〕 through tightly guarded police.
삼오야 三五夜 the fifteenth night by the lunar calendar ; the night of the full moon ¶ 삼오야 밝은 달 the shining full moon ; the moon shining at its full
삼옷 baby garment ⇨ 배내옷
삼용 蔘茸 ginseng and (deer) antler ¶ 삼용을 먹고 회복하였다 He recovered his health with the medication of ginseng and antler.
삼우 三友 pine, bamboo and plum blossom ; mountain and stream, pine and bamboo, lute and wine
삼원색 三原色 ⇨ 원색
†**삼월 三月** March ; Mar. ¶ 춘삼월 호시절 a rosy day of spring in March
***삼위 일체 三位一體** 〖기독교〗 the Trinity ; consubstantiality ¶ 삼위 일체가 되어 forming a Trinity
—론 Trinitarianism **—론자** a Trinitarian **—설** the doctrine of the Trinity
삼이웃 the surrounding neighborhood
삼인 三人 three persons〔men〕
—조 a triumvirate ; a trio 《of robbers》; a threesome ; triad ¶ 삼인조 강도 a trio of robbers ; a gang of three robbers
삼인칭 三人稱 the third person
— 단수〔복수〕 the third person singular〔plural〕
삼일 三日 the third day of the month ; three days ¶ 삼일 동안 for three days
—열 a tertian (fever) **— 예배** Wednesday evening church service
삼일 운동 三一運動 the 1919 Independence Movement
삼일장 三日葬 burial on the third day after death
삼일절 三一節 the anniversary of the Independence Movement of March lst, 1919
삼일천하 三日天下 a three-day reign ; a short-lived rule ¶ 그 정권은 삼일천하였다 The regime was in power for a very short period of time.
삼입 滲入 permeation ; infiltration ; percolation **—하다** permeate ; infiltrate ; percolate
삼잎 a hemp leaf
삼자 三者 ① ⇨ 제삼자(第三者) ② [삼인] three persons〔parties〕 ¶ 삼자간의 tripartite
— 범퇴 〖야구〗 ¶ 삼자 범퇴했다 All the three batters retired〔went out〕 in quiet order. **— 회담** a tripartite meeting 〔conference〕
삼잡이 excising a corneal ulcer
삼장 a hemp-rope net
삼재 三災 〖민속〗 one of the baleful stars ; 〖불교〗 the Three Disasters (of flood, fire and wind ; of war, pestilence and famine)
삼족 三族 the three sets of relatives 《of the father's side, the mother's side and the wife's side ; parents, brothers and sisters, and wife and children》 ¶ 삼족을 멸하다 annihilate the whole family and their closest kin
삼종 三從 a third cousin
삼종 三種 three kinds ; the third class
— 우편물 third-class mail matter
삼주기 三周忌 the second anniversary of 《a person's》 death
삼줄 umbilical cord ⇨ 탯줄
⁑**삼중 三重** triple ¶ 삼중의 threefold ; treble ; triple // 삼중으로 trebly ; triply // 삼중으로 하다 treble ; triple ; triplicate // 아군은 삼중으로 포위당했다 Our troops were surrounded trebly by the enemy.
— 결합 a triple bond **—고(苦)** a triple handicap 《of being blind, deaf, and unable to speak》; triple distress **— 도루(盜壘)** 〖야구〗 a triple steal **— 목적** a threefold purpose **—살(殺)** 〖야구〗 a triple play **—성** a triple star **—주(단)** 〖음악〗 a (musical) trio 《*pl.* ~s》 **—창(窓)** a triple window **—창곡(唱曲)** a terzetto 《*pl.* ~s, -ti》; a terzet **— 충**

돌 a three-way〔ternary〕 collision —탑 a three-storied pagoda — 포위군 a triple besieging army

삼지니 三— a three-year-old hawk〔falcon〕

삼지사방 —四方 all directions ¶ 삼지사방으로 둘러싸이다 be surrounded on all sides

삼지창 三枝槍 a three-pronged spear ; a trident ; [식탁의] a fork

삼진 三振 〖야구〗 a strike-out ; a fan ; three strikes ¶ 삼진당하다 be struck out ; fan (the air) // 삼진시키다 strike 《a batter》 out
— 탈취왕 the strike-out champion

삼짇날 the third day of the third lunar month

삼질 三— ⇨ 삼짇날

삼차 三次 the third time ; 〖수학〗 the third power ¶ 제삼차 5개년 계획 the third five-year plan
— 곡선 a cubic (curve) — 근수 a cubic root — 내각 the third cabinet — 방사선 a cubical parabola — 방정식 a cubic equation ; a cubic ; an equation of the third degree — 산업 the tertiary industry — 생산 tertiary production — 식 a cubic (expression) —원 three dimensions —원 세계 the three-dimensional world ; the world of three dimensions —원 영화〔입체 영화〕 a three-dimensional〔3-D〕 movie — 함수 a cubic 제—원 the third dimension

삼차 三叉
—로(路) a three-forked〔trifurcate(-d)〕 road ; a junction of three roads — 신경 the trigeminal〔trifacial〕 (nerve) — 신경통 trigeminal〔trifacial〕 neuralgia ; tic douloureux 《프》

삼창 三唱 reciting〔singing〕 three times ; [만세의] three cheers ¶ 만세를 삼창하다 give three cheers 《for a person》

삼척동자 三尺童子 a mere child ¶ 삼척동자라도 그것은 안다 Even a mere child knows it.

삼척 장검 三尺長劍 a long〔big〕 sword

삼천리 三千里
— 강산〔강토(疆土)〕 all Korea

삼천 세계 三千世界 the whole world ; the universe

삼첩기 三疊紀 〖지질〗 the Triassic period

삼촌 三寸 [길이] three inches ; [촌수] an uncle (on the father's side)
—댁 the wife of a paternal uncle ; an aunt 외— an uncle on the mother's side

삼촌설 三寸舌 the tongue

삼총사 三銃士 a triumvirate ; a trio ; three musketeers ¶ 회사의 삼총사 the triumvirate of the firm

삼추 三秋 the three months of autumn ; the three autumn months ; three years (3년) ¶ 일각이 여삼추(如三秋)이다 feel a moment as if it were three years ; be impatient of waiting ; be dying to see 《a person》

삼춘 三春 the three spring months ; three years (3년)

삼출 滲出 ooze ; exudation ; transudation
—하다 ooze out ; exude ; transude through
—물〔액〕 an exudation ; a percolate — 성 체질 exudative diathesis

삼층 三層 three stories〔floors, levels〕 ; the third floor 《미》 ; the second floor 《영》
— 갑판선 a three-decker —집 a three-storied〔-story〕 house

삼치 〖물고기〗 a kind of mackerel ; Scomberomorus niphonius (학명)

삼칠 三七 ① twenty-one ¶ 삼칠 나이에 at the age of twenty-one
② (the rate of) three to seven ¶ 성공할 가망은 삼칠이다 The chances of success are three to seven.

삼칠일 三七日 a baby's twenty-first day of life (celebrated with a party)

삼칼 a wooden knife used in trimming hemp leaves or scraping ginseng skin

⁑**삼키다** ① swallow ; gulp down ; engulf ¶ 음식을 너무 급히 삼키다 swallow one's food too quickly // 통째로 삼키다 swallow whole // 단숨에 삼키다 swallow at a gulp // 하품을 삼키다 suppress〔smother〕 a yawn // 파도가 배를 삼켰다 The waves engulfed〔swallowed〕 the ship.
② [남의 것을] make 《a thing》 one's own ; appropriate ; latch onto ¶ 남의 책을 슬그머니 삼켜버리다 take another's book for oneself by stealth

삼태 三胎 triplets

삼태기 a basket for carrying dirt〔rubbish〕 ; a carrier's basket

삼태봉 vegetables with many small roots

삼투 滲透 infiltration ; permeation ; osmosis ; permeance —하다 permeate ; infiltrate ; pass into
— 계수 an osmotic coefficient —성 osmosis ; permeability —압 osmotic pressure —압계 an osmometer — 작용 (an) osmotic action — 작전 infiltration operations 경제 — economic penetration

삼파전 三巴戰 a triangular contest ; a three-cornered fight ; a three-sided contest〔struggle, battle〕 ¶ 치열한 삼파전 a heated triangular contest // 삼파전을 벌이다 open〔start, begin〕 a three-cornered fight ; break out a three-sided battle

삼판선 三板船 a sampan

삼판 양승 三—兩勝 the best two out of three (games)

삼팔선 三八線 the 38th parallel
삼팔주 三八紬 a kind of Chinese silk
삼포 蔘圃 a field of ginseng
삼하 三夏 the three summer months ; three years (3년)
삼하다 《a child》 (be) annoying ; peevish ; fretful ; short-tempered
삼한 사온 三寒四溫 three days cold and four warm ; periodic freezes
삼할 三割 30 percent
— 타자 〖야구〗 a 300 hitter
삼할미 a midwife ; a maternity nurse ¶ 삼할미의 도움을 청하다 send for a midwife's help
삼합사 三合絲 three-ply thread
삼항식 三項式 〖수학〗 a trinomial expression
삼현 三絃 (the) three strings ; the Korean harp ¶ 삼현의 trichord ; three-stringed 《instruments》
***삽** a shovel ; a spade ; a scoop ¶ 삽으로 땅을 파다 spade the soil // 삽으로 모래를 푸다 shovel sand
—가래 a 2-man shovel with a rope attached to handle **—질** spade work ; shoveling ¶ 삽질하다 dig with a spade ; shovel **동력—** a power 〔mechanical〕 shovel **증기—** a steam shovel
삽괭이 a narrow-bladed hoe with a long shaft
삽사리, 삽살개 a shaggy dog ; a poodle
삽상하다 颯爽— (be) (cool and) crisp ; fresh ; refreshing ¶ 삽상한 가을바람 a crisp autumn breeze
삽시간 a twinkle ; a moment ; an instant ; a flash ¶ 삽시간에 in a moment ; in a flash ; in an instant ; in less than no time // 수술은 삽시간에 끝났다 The whole operation only lasted a moment.
⁑**삽입 插入** insertion ; interposition ; incorporation ; interpolation **—하다** insert ; put 《a thing》 in ; interpose ; interpolate ; incorporate ¶ 계약문에 한 마디를 삽입하다 insert a sentence in the contract
—구 a parenthesis 《*pl.* -ses》 ; an inserted comment **—물** an interposition ; an interpolation ; an insertion **—부** 〖음악〗 an episode **—사** 〖문법〗 an infix **—어** an interpolation **—음** an epenthetic sound ; epenthesis 《*pl.* -ses》
삽주 〖식물〗 Tractylis ovata (학명)
삽지 插紙 paper-feeding **—하다** feed paper (to a printing press)
—공 a (paper) feeder **—판** a feed board
삽화 插花 ⇨ 꽃꽂이
⁑**삽화 插話** an episode ¶ 삽화의 episodic ; episodical // 역사상의 삽화적 사건 an episode in history
⁑**삽화 插畫** an illustration (in a book) ; a plate ; a figure ; a cut ¶ 삽화가 들어 있는 잡지 an illustrated magazine // 삽화를 그리다 illustrate 《a book》 // 이 책에는 삽화가 많이 들어 있다 This book is profusely illustrated〔illustrated with pictures〕.
— 설명 a caption ; a cut line **— 화가** an illustrator 《to〔for〕 a book》 **색쇄(色刷)〔전채색(全彩色)〕—** a colored〔full-color〕 illustration **펜그림〔사진〕 —** a black-and-white〔photographic〕 illustration
삿갓 a bamboo hat ; a sedge hat ; a braided hat
—장이 [만드는 사람] a man who makes bamboo〔reed〕 hats **—쟁이** [쓴 사람] a man wearing a bamboo〔reed〕 hat
삿갓들이 sparsely planted rice plants
삿대 a (row) pole
삿반 —盤 a rush-tray ; a reed-tray
삿자리 a reed mat ¶ 삿자리를 펴다 spread a reed mat
상 上 [상부] the top ; the head ; the upper part ; [상등] the first 《class, grade》 ; the best ; the superior ; [상권] a first volume ; [접미] -ly ¶ 상반신 the upper part of 《a person's》 body // 상늙은이 the senior // 상팔자 the best lot // 상 이상 the very best ; extra fine // 상 중 하 3권(의 소설) a three-decker // 정의〔도덕〕상 in the cause of justice 〔morality〕 // 상업상 commercially // 이 물건은 상의 부류에 속한다 This article is one of the best. // 그의 학교 성적은 상이다 His school work〔record〕 is rather good.
***상 床** a table ; a small table ¶ 상을 놓다〔차리다〕 set the table ; lay〔spread〕 the table 《for dinner》 // 상을 치우다 clear the table // …을 상에 놓다 serve up 《a thing》 at 《a person's》 table // 상을 차려 놓았다 The table is ready.
⁑**상 相** [용모] look ; features ; countenance ; physiognomy ; [양상] appearance ; aspect ; phase ; 〖천문〗 a phase ; 〖문법〗 (verbal) aspect ; 〖지질〗 a facies 《단·복 동형》 ; 〖전기·화학〗 (a) phase ¶ 상을 찌푸리고 with a grimace ; with a wry face
단— the single phase **사회—** phases of social life **식(蝕)—** the phase of an eclipse **월(月)—** a phase of the moon **액—** liquid phase
상 商 [상업] trade ; commerce ; business ; [상인] a merchant ; a dealer ; 〖수학〗 the quotient
가구— a furniture dealer ; a dealer in furniture **도매—** [상인] a wholesale dealer〔merchant〕 ; a wholesaler ; [가게] a wholesale store〔house, firm〕 ; [일] a wholesale trade **소매—** [상인] a

retail dealer ; a retailer ; tradesman 《영》; [상점] a retail store〔shop〕; retail trade 포목— a draper

‡상 喪 mourning ¶ 상을 입다 go into〔be in〕 mourning for 《one's father》; observe mourning // 상을 알리다 announce 《a person's》 death // 상을 숨기다 withhold the announcement of 《a person's》 death // 상을 벗다 leave off〔go out of〕 mourning

상 想 an idea ; a conception ; a thought ¶ 좋은 상이 떠오르다 a bright idea crosses one's mind ; be struck with a bright idea // 상을 가다듬다 think deeply 《about》; meditate《on》; ponder 《over, on》

†상 像 a figure ; a statue ; an image ; [화상] a portrait ; a picture ¶ 사자의 상 a figure of a lion // 큐피드의 조상 a figure of Cupid // 성모 마리아의 상 an image of the Virgin Mary // 상을 만들다 make an image 《of》; [광선이] throw an image 《on a screen》

대리석〔동〕— a statue in marble〔bronze〕; a marble〔bronze〕 statue 목— a figure in wood ; a wooden statue〔image〕 실— a real image 자유의 여신— the Statue of Liberty 허— a virtual image

†상 賞 a prize ; [보수] a reward ¶ 금년도의 소파(小波)상 this year's *Sopa* prize // 노벨 의학상 the Nobel prize for medicine // 상을 타다 get〔gain, take, win〕 a prize // 상을 주다 give〔award〕 《a person》 a prize // 상을 내걸다 offer a prize // 너는 상을 탈 만하다 You deserve a reward.

우등— an honor prize 일등— the first prize ; first honors ; a blue ribbon

-상 相 a minister

외— the foreign minister ; the Minister of Foreign Affairs 재무— the Finance Minister

-상 上 [⋯의 관점에서] from the viewpoint〔standpoint〕 of 《morality》 // 교육상 from the educational point of view // 편의상 for convenience sake // 형편상 in view of circumstances

*상가 商街 the downtown ; the downtown〔shopping〕 area ; the business section〔quarters, center〕 ¶ 상가에 살다 live downtown // 상가에 가다 go downtown // 상가에서 주택 지구로 이사하다 move from downtown to uptown

상가 喪家 a mourner's house ; a family in mourning ¶ 상가집 개 같다 be as miserable as〔famished and lean like〕 a dog in a house of death

상가 商家 a store〔shop〕

상가 평균 相加平均 〘수학〙 an arithmetic mean

상각 償却 repayment ; refunding ; redemption ; [감가] depreciation —하다 repay ; refund ; redeem ; pay〔clear〕 off ; [고정 자산 따위를] write off ¶ 부채를 상각하다 pay one's debts // 100 만 원을 (감가) 상각에 충당하다 allocate one million *won* to depreciation // 선가를 상각하다 write off the cost of the vessels

— 수표 a cancelled check — 자금〔적립금〕 a depreciation fund ; a sinking fund — 자산 depreciable assets

상간 相姦 fornication

근친 — incest

상감 上監 His Majesty the King ; our sovereign Lord

상감 象嵌 inlaying ; damascening ; [세공물] inlaid work ; an inlay ¶ 상감박다 inlay 《a thing》 with 《gold》; damascene

— 세공 inlaid work —장(匠) an inlayer

상갑판 上甲板 an upper deck

상강 霜降 the 18th of the 24 seasonal divisions (⇨ c. 23 Oct.)

상객 上客 a good customer〔patron〕; a guest of honor ; a guest of high rank

상객 常客 a regular customer〔patron〕; a frequenter

상거 相距 the distance ; the space between

상거래 商去來 a commercial transaction ; a business deal ¶ 상거래가 활발하다 Business transactions are briskly carried on there.

상거지 上— the most wretched of beggars

상건 上件 ① an article of the highest quality ② the above(-stated) case〔matter〕

상격 相格 one's physiognomy ; one's physiognomical features

상격 相隔 being away from each other ; being separated —하다 be separated〔be away from〕 each other ; be apart

상견 相見 interview ; meeting 《a person》 —하다 interview ; meet 《a person》; face each other

상견 想見 imagination —하다 imagine ; picture〔figure〕 to oneself

상경 上京 coming〔going〕 up to the capital〔*Seoul*〕 —하다 come〔go〕 up to the capital〔*Seoul*〕 ¶ 목하 상경 중이다 He is up in *Seoul*. /He is now in *Seoul*.

상계 相計 a setoff ⇨ 상쇄

상계 商界 the business world ; the world of commerce ; business circles

상계 上計 the best policy ⇨ 상책(上策)

†상고 上古 ancient times ; antiquity ¶ 상고의 ancient ; antique ; time-honored

—사 ancient history

상고 上告 〘법〙 an appeal (to the supreme court) —하다 appeal 《to》; make an appeal ¶ 대법원에 상고하다

appeal to the Supreme Court // 상고를 기각하다 reject〔dismiss〕 the appeal
— 기각 dismissal of a final appeal — 기한 the appeal period ; the time limit for appeal — 법원 a court of final appeal ; a court of last resort ; a final appellate court — 신청서 a notice of〔a petition for〕 final criminal appeal — 신청인 an applicant for final criminal appeal —심 a court of appeal ; an appellate court ; a hearing of final appeal ; (a) trial of the Supreme Court — 이유서 a statement of the grounds of the final civil appeal —인 an appellant (of a final civil appeal) ; a demandant ; an applicant for revision — 취지서 a statement of the grounds of the final criminal appeal 피—인 a respondent of a final civil appeal

상고 尙古 worship of ancient civilization〔culture〕 —하다 worship ancient culture ; be devoted to past civilization
—벽(癖) addiction〔enthusiastic devotion〕 to things classical —주의 classicism ; classicalism ; conservatism

상고 詳考 a careful consideration〔examination ; scrutiny〕 —하다 consider〔examine〕 carefully ; think over ; scrutinize

상고대 hoarfrost on the tree〔grass〕

상고머리 square-cut hair ; a crew cut ¶ 상고머리로 깎다 dress〔cut〕 one's hair square

상공 上空 the upper air ; the skies《of *Seoul*》; high in the air〔sky〕 ¶ 1,000 미터의 상공에서 at an altitude〔a height〕 of 1,000 meters // 서울의 상공을 날다 fly over *Seoul*

상공 商工 commerce〔trade〕 and industry
—부 the Ministry of Commerce and Industry — 위원회 the Commerce and Industry Committee — 회의소 The Chamber of Commerce and Industry 대한 — 회의소 the Korea Chamber of Commerce and Industry《KCCI》

상공업 商工業 commerce and industry ¶ 상공업의 commercial and industrial // 상공업에 중점을 두다 lay〔place, put〕 (great) emphasis on〔upon〕 commerce and industry
—자 merchants and industrialists

상과 商科 a commercial course ; a department of business administration
— 대학 a college of commerce ; a commercial college ; a business college

상과 桑果 a sorosis

상관 上官 a higher officer ; a superior〔senior〕 official ; a chief ¶ 상관의 명령에 복종하다 obey one's chief's order // 그는 나의 상관이다 He is above me in rank.

상관 相關 [관여] concern ; relation ; participation ; correlation ; interrelation ; [간섭] interference ; [남녀 관계] relations ; connection —하다 [관련] be related〔correlated〕 to ; be connected with ; bear on ; [관여] participate《in》; be concerned《in》; concern oneself《in》; [간섭] interfere〔meddle〕 in ; [성관계] have a connection with ; have relations with ¶ 상관적 correlative ; interrelative ; mutually related〔connected〕 // 상관적으로 interrelatively ; correlatively // …에 상관하지 않고 regardless of ; without regard to ; irrespective of // 상관 없다 be not related ; have nothing to do with ; have no connection with ; be not concerned about ; don't mind ; don't care // 아무 것이나 상관 없다 Anything will do. // 남의 일에 상관 마라 Mind your own business.
— 개념 a correlative concept — 계수 『통계』 a coefficient of correlation ; a correlation coefficient ¶ 상관 계수표 a correlation coefficient table — 곡선 『수학』 a correlation curve ; a correlogram — 관계 correlation ; interrelation ; mutual relation —비 『통계』 (a) correlation ratio —성 interrelationship ; correlationship —어 『문법』 a correlative (word) — 작용 (a) correlation ; (an) interaction

상관 商館 a trading house ; a firm
외국 — a foreign firm

상관례 商慣例 ⇨ 상관습(商慣習)

상관습 商慣習 a commercial practice ; business usage〔custom〕

상괭이 『동물』 a porpoise

상궁 尙宮 a court lady

상권 上卷 volume one ; book one ; the first volume (of two or three)

상권 商權 [권력] commercial power〔supremacy〕; [권리] commercial rights

상궤 常軌 the proper bounds ; the normal course ; the beaten track ¶ 상궤를 벗어나다 break bounds ; go off the rails ; get off the beaten track ; go out of the common road〔ordinary groove〕 // 상궤를 벗어나지 않다 keep within bounds

상규 常規 established rules〔regulations〕; normal usages ¶ 상규에 따라 according to the normal usage

상그레 with a gentle smile ; with smiling eyes ¶ 상그레 웃다 smile gently〔blandly〕

상극 相剋 conflict ; incompatibility ¶ 상극이다 be incompatible with ; be discordant with // 물과 기름은 상극이다 Oil and water have an antipathy to each other. // 둘이는 서로 상극이다 They cannot hit it off together.

상근 常勤 ¶ 상근의 full time
—자 a full-timer ; a full-time〔whole-

time) employee
상글거리다 smile gently(blandly) ¶ 상글상글 with a gentle smile
상금 尙今 up to now ; until now ; still ; yet ¶ 상금 안 왔다 He has not come yet. //기린이 울지 못하는 동물인 줄을 상금 모르느냐 Haven't you learnt yet that giraffes are mute animals ?
***상금 賞金** prize money ; a prize ; an award ; [현상금] a reward ¶ 5천원의 상금 a prize of 5,000 *won*//상금을 걸다 offer a prize 《for》; offer a reward//상금을 타다 win(get) a prize ; [경기 따위에서] win a purse//범인 체포에 상금을 걸다 set (up) a prize on the arrest of the offender//상금을 기증하다 [경기·자선 따위에] put up(give) a purse
상급 上級 an upper class ; [국민학교의] a higher grade ; [과목] an advanced course ¶ 상급의 higher ; upper ; senior ; superior//상급 학년에 재학중이다 be in a higher grade of school
— 관리 a superior(senior) official ; a high-ranking (government) official **—관청** superior offices(authorities) ; a superior government office **— 법원** a higher(superior) tribunal(court) **—생** an upper-class student ; a senior student(boy, girl) ; an advanced student ; an upper-classman (대학·고등 학교의) 《미》 **— 장교** a higher ranking officer **— 학교** an advanced school ; a school of higher grade
상급 賞給 prizegiving **— 하다** award (present) a prize 《to》
상긋 with a (sudden) smile
상긋거리다 smile blandly
상긋방긋, 상긋상긋 smiling ; beaming
상긋하다 give a sudden smile
상기 上氣 a rush of blood to the head ; blush(ing) ; 〚한의〛 congestion of the head **— 하다** have a rush of blood to the head ; blush ¶ 상기한 볼 flushed cheeks
상기 上記 the above statements ⇨ 상술
상기 詳記 a minute description ; a full (detailed) account **— 하다** write(give) in detail ; set forth(describe) in full ; detail ; give a full account 《of》 ¶ 사정을 상기하다 detail the circumstances
상기 商機 a business opportunity (chance) ¶ 상기를 놓치다 miss(let slip) a business chance
†**상기 想起 — 하다** remember ; recollect ; call to mind ¶ 상기시키다 remind 《a person》 of ; put 《a person》 in mind 《of》//6·25를 상기하다 recall the memory of the Korean war
상기 喪期 the term(period) of mourning
상길 上— the highest(finest) quality ; the best quality ; top-grade(first class, first-rate) article ¶ 상길의 담배 the best quality cigarettes//상길의 종이 paper of the finest quality
상납 上納 tax payment to the government(authorities) **— 하다** pay to the authorities(government) ¶ 금전(물건)을 상납하다 pay to the authorities in money(kind)
—금 money paid as tax ; money paid to the state(Treasury) ; a fine (봉건 영주에게의) **—미** rice paid(delivered) as tax
†**상냥하다** [부드럽다] (be) gentle ; tender ; [정답다] sweet ; affectionate ; [싹싹하다] kind(ly) ; amiable ; nice ¶ 상냥함 gentleness ; kindness ; tenderness //상냥하게 생긴 gentle-looking//상냥하게 gently ; kindly ; nicely ; tenderly ; sweetly ; affectionately//마음이 상냥한 소녀 a kindhearted girl//…에게 상냥하다 be gentle(tender, kind, nice) to 《a person》//상냥한 목소리로 부르다 call in a gentle voice//그 여자는 누구에게나 상냥하다 She is nice to everyone./She treats everyone nicely.
상년, 쌍년 常— a vulgar(mean) woman ; a woman of low birth ; a lewd woman ; a bitch
상년 上年 last year
상년 祥年 a lucky(good) year
상념 想念 a notion ; a conception ; an idea ¶ 상념에 사로잡히다 be absorbed in meditation
상노 床奴 a boy servant ; a kitchen helper ; a bus boy
상놈 常— an ill-bred fellow ; a vulgar (humble) man ; a common person ¶ 그런 상놈은 혼을 내주어야 해 Such a bastard deserves a lesson.
상늙은이 上— the eldest(dean, senior) of a group of old men
상다리 床— table legs ¶ 상다리가 휘어지게 음식을 차리다 serve a full course dinner on the table
상단 上段 [인쇄면의] the upper portion (division) ; [상렬] the upper row ; [상좌] a place of honor ; [높은 자리] a dais
— 침대 [기차의] an upper berth
상단 上端 the top ; the upper end ¶ 안테나의 상단 the top end of an antenna
상달 上— October ; harvest month
상달 上達 a report (to a superior) **— 하다** report (to a superior)
***상담 相談** consultation ; counsel ; conference ; talk ; advice **— 하다** consult (with) 《a person》; confer ; take counsel 《with》; talk over 《a matter with a person》

> 참고 **consult** 조언을 줄 수 있는 사람과 중요한 일에 대해서 이야기하다 **confer** 동등한 사람과 의견이나 지식을 교환하다

¶ 상담 없이 without speaking to 《a person》; over 《a person's》 head // 상담한 후 after consultation with 《a person》; by agreement // 상담하러 가다〔오다〕 go〔come〕 to 《a person》 for advice // 상담에 응하다 give counsel〔advice〕 to 《a person》 // 모여서 상담하다 consult together; lay their heads together // 변호사에게 상담하다 consult a lawyer // 상담중이다 We are in consultation. // 그 일에 관하여 아버지와 상담하였다 I consulted with my father about the matter.

—란 [신문·잡지의] the advice column 《of a newspaper》; the advice department 《of a magazine》 **—소** an information bureau; a consultation office ¶ 결혼 상담소 a matrimonial advice office // 민원 상담소 the Civil Service Consultation Center // 무료 상담소 a free-advice office // 법률 상담소 a legal advice office // 직업 상담소 a vocational clinic // 아동 상담소 a child guidance clinic // 투자 상담소 an investment counsel office **—역** [회사 등의] a counsellor; a consultant (전문적인); [개인의] an adviser; a consultant; [총칭] an advisory board〔body〕

상담 商談 a business talk; bargaining; a deal; negotiations ¶ 상담을 결정하다 strike a bargain; close a deal // 우리 사장은 지금 A씨와 상담을 하고 있다 The head of our firm is talking with Mr. A for business. // 100만원으로 상담은 결정되었다 A bargain was struck at one million *won*. // 상담이 잘될 것 같다 The sales talks look like they're going to work out.

상답 trousseau makings; linen collected for the marriage of one's children

상답 上畓 a rich〔productive〕 rice field

상답 上答 an answer to one's superior **—하다** answer〔reply to〕 one's superior

*__상당 相當 —하다__ [적당하다] (be) proper; fit; suitable; [어울리다] becoming; befitting; appropriate; [지당하다] fair; reasonable; [훌륭하다] fair; tolerable; decent; [맞먹다] equivalent 《to》 ¶ 상당히 pretty; tolerably; fairly; considerably; decently // 사회적 지위가 상당한 of good social position // 상당한 집안 a respectable family // 상당한 금액 a good sum; a sizable sum (of money) // 상당한 인물 a respectable person; a person of consequence // 상당한 교육〔수입〕 a good education〔income〕 // 상당한 이유 a sufficient reason // 상당히 비싼 값 a pretty high price // 지위에 상당한 수입 an income befitting one's station // 상당한 생활을 하다 be comfortably off; live in respectable style // 상당한 책을 가지고 있다 have a good many books // 나이가 상당하다 He is well along in years. // 그의 재주는 상당하다 He is a man of considerable talent. // 1달러는 한국 돈으로 치면 약 800원에 상당한다 A dollar is equivalent to approximately 800 *won* in Korean money. // 나무의 뿌리는 사람의 위에 상당한다 What a root does for a tree is same as what a stomach does for a man. /What a root is to a tree is what a stomach is to a human body. // 돈을 상당히 모아두지 않으면 마음 놓고 나이를 먹을 수도 없다 Unless we put a tidy sum away, we won't even be able to get old safely. // 그의 영어 실력은 상당한 것이다 His ability in English is quite something.

상대 上代 ancient times; remote ages

상대 相對 ① [서로 대함] facing〔confronting〕 each other; seeing each other **—하다** face each other

② [짝패] a companion; a mate; a fellow; a partner; a date 《미·구》; a pal **—하다** keep company with; fall into company with; deal with 《a person》 ¶ 이야기 상대 a companion to talk to; a talking companion // 유쾌한 술 상대 a boon companion // 노는 상대 a playmate; a playfellow // 유쾌한〔싱거운〕 상대 an agreeable〔a poor〕 companion // 의논 상대 an adviser; a person to consult with; a confident; a counselor; [전문적] a consultant // 상대할 사람이 없어서 for lack of company // …을 상대로 하다 make a company of // 천한 사람과 상대하다 be addicted to low companions // 노름 상대를 하다 keep company in gambling // 상대하지 않다 take no notice of 《a person》; pay no attention to 《a person》; have nothing to do with 《a person》 // 아무도 나를 상대해 주지 않는다 Nobody takes (any) notice of me. // 상대할 사람이 못된다 He is no man to deal with. // 나는 말 상대도 없이 혼자 남게 되었다 I was left alone with no one to talk to.

③ [적수] an opponent; a rival; a match; [상대방] the other party **—하다** counter; act counterpart to; serve; contend with; play (against) 《a person》 ¶ 싸움의 상대 the other party to a quarrel // 만만찮은 상대 a tough customer 《구》 // 장기 상대를 하다 play (a game of) chess with // 좋은 상대를 만나다 meet 〔find〕 one's match // 그는 상대하기 어렵다 He is hard to deal with. // 우승 컵을 두고 상대하고 있는 것은 두 소년뿐이다 Only two boys are competing for the cup. // 나는 그를 상대로 소송을 제기했다 I brought an action against him. // 나는 도저히 그의 상대가 되지 못한다 He is more than a match for me. /I am no match for him. // 그는

그 여자의 훌륭한 결혼 상대이다 He is a good match with her.
④ relativity ; reciprocity ¶ 상대적인 relative // 상대적으로 relatively ; correlatively // 상대적 진리 a relative truth // 춥다는 말은 상대적 의미를 가진 말이다 Cold is a relative term.
— 개념〔오차〕 a relative concept〔error〕 — 분산도(分散度) 〚물리〛 relative dispersion — 빈도 〚통계〛 relative frequency —성 relativity —성 원리 〚물리〛 the theory of relativity — 습도〔점도〕 〚기상〛 relative humidity〔viscosity〕 —역 a coactor ; a partner (댄스 따위의) — 운동〔속도〕 〚물리〛 relative motion〔velocity〕 —주의 relativism

상대 商大 ⇨ 상과(—대학)

상대론 相對論 〚철학〛 relativism

상대자 相對者 the other〔opposite〕 party ; a counterpart ⇨ 상대

상대편 相對便 the other party ; one's opponent ; the other side

상도 常道 a normal course ; a proper〔regular〕 course ¶ 헌정의 상도 the normal course of a constitutional government // 학문의 상도 a regular course of learning // 상도로 복귀하다 restore to 《its》 normal course

상도 想到 anticipation ; thinking ahead to ; thought 《of》 —하다 anticipate ; think of ; think ahead to ; consider ; hit upon 《a plan》

상도덕 商道德 business〔trade〕 ethics
— 앙양 enhancement of business morality

상도의 商道義 ⇨ 상도덕

상동 相同 the same〔similar〕 relation ; 〚생물〛 homology
— 기관 a homologous organ ; a homologue — 염색체 homologous chromosome

상되다 常— (be) vulgar ; mean ; base ; ignoble ; humble ; low ¶ 상된 사람 a low〔mean〕 fellow // 상된 말 vulgar words ; coarse〔improper〕 language // 어쩌면 그렇게 상된 생각을 하느냐 How mean a thought !

상두 喪— a (funeral) bier ⇨ 상여

상두받잇집 〚민속〛 a house which faces the end of a street, disliked because funeral processions are liable to turn in front of it

상등 上騰 advance ; rise ; jump —하다 ascend ; rise ; jump

상등 常燈 ① a sanctuary lamp (in a temple) ② an all-night light

상등 上等 the first class ; the best grade ; top grade〔class〕 ; the first rate
—답 a first-rate paddy (field) — 모사 a fine quality of yarn —석 the first-class seat —품 a top grade article ; good stuff ; a first-class article

상등 相等 equality —하다 (be) equal

상등병 上等兵 a corporal

상란 上欄 [위] a top column ; [앞] the preceding column ¶ 상란에 서술한 바와 같이 as stated in the preceding column

상략 上略 omitting the preceding part ; omitted so far ; omitted to this point —하다 omit the preceding part

상략 商略 a commercial〔business〕 policy ¶ 상략상 그것은 부득이 하다 It is necessitated by our business policy.

상량 商量 deliberation ; consideration ; reflection ; speculation ; reasoning —하다 deliberate ; reflect〔speculate〕 on ; reason ; weigh

상량 爽涼 —하다 [날씨가] (be) cool and refreshing

상량 上樑 putting up the ridge beam ; completing the wooden framework of a house —하다 put up the ridge beam ; complete the wooden framework of a house ¶ 상량이 끝난 다음에 after the framing is complete
—식 the ceremony of putting up the ridge beam ; the celebration of the completion of the framework (of a house)

상량대 上樑— a ridge beam ; a ridgepole

상련 相連 connection ; contiguity ; linking

상련 相憐 mutual sympathy ¶ 동병상련하다 Fellow sufferers sympathize with each other. /Grief is best pleased with grief's company〔society〕.

상례 常例 a (common) usage ; an (established) custom ; a usual practice ; (a) convention ¶ 상례의 customary ; usual ; conventional ; common ; ordinary // 상례에 따라 in accordance with the custom〔usage〕 ; as usual // 상례를 따르다 follow〔observe〕 the conventional practice ; follow the usage〔custom〕 // 상례를 존중하다 respect customary practice // 상례를 무시하다 be contrary to〔defy〕 customary practice // 상례에 집착하다 stick to the custom ; move along the old groove

상례 喪禮 funeral rites ; the ceremonies of mourning

상례 上例 the above〔preceding〕 instance(s)〔example(s)〕

상로 商路 a business trip ; commercial traveling ; commercial pursuits

***상록 常綠** ¶ 상록의 evergreen ; indeciduous
—송 an evergreen pine —수 an evergreen〔indeciduous〕 ; evergreens 《총칭》

상록 詳錄 a full〔detailed〕 record —하다 make a full record ; record in detail

상론 詳論 a detailed explanation ; full discussion〔treatment〕 —하다 treat 《a subject》 in detail ; dwell〔expatiate, enlarge〕 upon ; deal with 《a subject》 in detail ; enter into detail

***상류 上流** [하천의] an upper stream〔course〕 ; the upper reaches〔waters〕 of a river ; [사회의] the upper〔higher〕

classes ; polite〔fashionable〕 society ; high society ¶ 상류의 upstream ; upper // 상류 사회에서 자란 사람 a high-bred person // 상류로 거슬러 올라가다 row upstream ; sail up a river // 그 강의 상류 3마일 지점에 작은 부락이 있다 There is a small village three miles up the river. // 그 고을의 상류급 인사들은 전부 참석했다 All the fashionable people of the town were present.

— 구배 〖토목〗 an upstream slope — 부인 a woman〔lady〕 of the upper〔higher〕 classes ; a society woman〔girl〕 ; a lady of fashion ; a fashionable〔high-born〕 lady — 사회 high〔polite〕 society — 생활 high life — 인사 (people of) gentility ; the gentry ; gentlefolk(s) ; men 〔people〕 of fashion〔quality, rank〕 ; the élite of society ; people of high birth ; 《a company of》 grand people ; persons high in the social scale ; society〔fashionable〕 people (사교계의) — 지방 an upright district

†**상륙 上陸** landing ; disembarkation ; going ashore — 하다 land 《in a country, at a port》 ; get to land ; beach at ; [군대가] disembark ; [선원이] go〔come〕 on shore ; [태풍이] strike ¶ 상륙을 허가하다 grant 《a person》 shore leave // 상륙을 금지하다 [선객의] forbid disembarkation ; [선원의] withhold shore leave // 상륙하여 있다 be ashore ; be on shore // 상륙시키다 put 《a person》 on shore 〔ashore〕 // 적전에 상륙하다 effect a landing in the face of the enemy // 무사히 상륙하다 come safe to land // 우리는 호주에 상륙하려 하고 있다 Australia is the country we are about to set foot in. // 태풍이 부산 해안에 상륙했다 The typhoon struck 〔hit〕 the shore of *Pusan*.

— 거점 a beachhead — 금지 stoppage of leave — 부대 a landing force —용 주정 (舟艇) a landing craft〔boat〕 ; a Landing Ship, Tanks 《LST》 —일 [수병의] liberty day — 작전 landing operations — 지점 a landing place〔area〕 ; a landing spot of disembarkation — 휴가〔허가〕 shore leave (수병·수부의) ¶ 상륙 휴가중의 수병 a sailor on shore leave

상리 商理 a proper way ; a matter of course ; the natural course to take

상마 —馬 a stallion

상막하다 (be) dim〔faint, vague, obscure〕 (in one's memory) ¶ 상막한 기억 a dim memory // 아잇적의 일은 기억이 상막하다 I have but a faint memory of my childhood.

상말 常— vulgar words ; a vulgarism ; indecent talk ; abusive language ; a slang expression ¶ 상말을 쓰다 use abusive language // 상말로는 …라고 한다 be commonly called... ; be called in a homely way ; be known colloquially 〔popularly〕 as

상망 想望 ① [사모] adoration ; yearning 《for》 — 하다 adore ; long for ② [기대] expectation ; anticipation — 하다 expect ; anticipate

상머리 床— the head of the table ¶ 상머리에 앉다 sit by〔at〕 the head of the table

상머슴 上— a heavy-duty farmhand

상면 上面 the upper side ; the top side ; the upside ; the surface

†**상면 相面** — 하다 meet 《with》 ; see each other ; interview ; have an interview 《with》 ; meet 《a person》 for the first time

상목 桑木 a mulberry tree ⇨ 뽕나무

상몽 祥夢 an auspicious dream ⇨ 길몽

상무 尙武 militarism ; warlike spirit ¶ 상무의 기상 militaristic〔martial〕 spirit ; martial ardor

상무 常務 regular business ; daily〔routine〕 work ; daily routine

— 위원 a member of a standing committee — 위원회 a standing committee — 이사 an executive〔managing〕 director

상무 商務 commercial〔business〕 affairs ; business operations

—관 a commercial attaché〔agent〕 —성 the Department of Commerce 《미》 ; the Board of Trade 《영》 — 참사관 a commercial councilor

상문 上文 the above (statement) ; the foregoing paragraphs ¶ 상문과 같이 as stated above

상문 喪問 〖민속〗 a baleful direction

—살(煞) the evil influence emanating from a place where someone has died — 풀이 an exorcism to ward off any evil influence that may have been acquired from visiting a house in mourning

상문 上聞 a royal hearing

상문 尙文 encouragement of learning

상미 上米 first-class〔grade A〕 rice ; best quality of rice ; rice of fine quality

상미 嘗味 taste sampling — 하다 sample the taste of

*__상미 賞味__ taste appreciation ; relish — 하다 appreciate the taste of ; eat with relish ; relish

상미 賞美 admiration ; praise ; adoration ; applause ; beauty appreciation — 하다 admire ; praise ; adore ; applaud ; appreciate the beauty of

상미 上味 relish ; flavor ; deliciousness

상민 常民 the common people ; the lower classes ; pleb 《속》 ¶ 상민으로 태어난 lowborn ; of humble birth〔origin〕

상밀 詳密 ⇨ 세밀(細密)

상박 上膊 the upper arm ; the brachium ¶ 상박의 brachial

—골 the humerus 《*pl.* -ri》 —근〔동맥〕 a brachial muscle〔artery〕 —부 the humeral region — 신경통 brachial

‡**상반 相反** being contrary to each other ;

conflicting with each other ; contradiction ; reciprocity **—하다** be contrary to each other ; conflict with each other ; disagree with each other ; be mutually contradictory ; run counter to each other ¶ 두 사람은 성격이 상반된다 Their natures are contrary to each other. // 서로의 이익이 상반한다 Our interests run counter to theirs. // 그는 도덕 진화는 자연적 진화와 절대적으로 상반한다고 말했다 Moral evolution, he said, is the absolute antithesis to natural evolution.
— 곡선 〖수학〗 a reciprocal curve **— 교배** 〖생물〗 reciprocal crossing **— 법칙** the law of reciprocity ; the reciprocity law **— 잡종** 〖생물〗 reciprocal hybrid

상반 上半 the first half 《of something》

상반기 上半期 the first〔upper〕 half of the year ; the first half of a term ¶ 상반기 무역 계획 the trade program for the first half of a year

*__상반신 上半身__ the upper half of the body ; the bust ¶ 상반신을 앞으로 굽히다 bend forward the upper part of the body
— 사진 a bust shot

상밥 床— a set dinner served at a restaurant
—집 a chop house ; an eating house

상방 上枋 the upper lintel ⇨ 상인방

상방 上方 the upper part ¶ 상방의 upper // 상방에 above ; upwards

상배 喪配 the death of one's wife **—하다** lose〔be bereaved of〕 one's wife ; meet the death of one's wife

상배 賞盃 a prize〔trophy, challenge〕 cup

상번 上番 guard mounting ; being on duty

상벌 賞罰 reward and punishment ; prizes and penalties ; praise and blame ; justice ¶ 상벌을 주다 mete out justice ; adjudicate praise and blame // 공정한 상벌을 주다 allot 《a person's》 praise and blame impartially ; decide rewards and punishments with fairness // 공죄에 따라 상벌을 주다 reward or punish according to 〔after〕 《a person's》 deserts // 상벌 없음 No reward and no punishment.

상법 商法 the commercial law〔code〕 ; business law

상변 上邊 the upside

상병 上兵 ⇨ 상등병(上等兵)

상병 傷病 the sick and wounded
—병(兵) the sick and wounded (soldiers) ; the invalid (soldiers) ¶ 상병병을 후송하다 send the invalids back (to the rear) **—병 수송기** an ambulance plane ; an air ambulance **—병 수송차** an ambulance (car) **— 포로** sick and wounded prisoners of war **— 포로 교환 협정** an agreement to exchange sick and wounded prisoners of war

상보 床褓 a tablecloth ; a table cover ; a meal cloth ¶ 상보를 덮다 put a cloth over a meal

상보 詳報 a detailed〔full〕 report ; full 〔detailed〕 information ; details ; particulars **—하다** report in full〔detail〕 ; give details ; give a full account〔particulars〕 of ; report at length ¶ 참사의 상보 a full report〔account〕 of the accident ; details of the disaster // 우리들은 아직 상보에 접하지 못했다 We are not as yet informed of the details.

상보 商報 a business〔shop〕 bulletin

상보다 床— set the table

상보다 相— read a person's physiognomy ; read the countenance of 《a person》

상보성 相補性 〖물리〗 complementarity

상복 喪服 a mourner's garb ; mourning clothes〔dress〕 ; sables ¶ 미망인의 상복 widow's weeds // 상복을 입다 be in black ; be clad in sables ; wear mourning〔a mourning dress〕
—감 mourning stuff

상복 常服 ordinary clothes ; everyday wear ; workaday clothing ; weekday clothes

상복부 上腹部 the epigastrium ; the upper part of the belly

상봉 相逢 meeting each other **—하다** meet each other ; meet with ¶ 그 삼형제는 17년 만에 상봉했다 The three brothers held their first reunion in seventeen years.

상부 上部 the upper part ; the top ; [위측] the upside ; [표면] the surface ; [윗관청] the superior office ; the office that rules 〔directs〕 ¶ 상부의 upper ; upside // 계단의 상부 the head of a staircase // 일람표의 상부에 at the top〔head〕 of the list // 상부의 명령 orders from the head office ; orders from higher-up // 신체의 상부를 앞으로 굽히다 bend the upper part of the body forward // 상부의 지시가 있을 때까지 pending instructions from the ruling office // 상부 지시가 있을 때까지 기다리다 wait for further instructions from the superior authority // 상부 지시에 따르다 follow the ruling office's directions
— 공사 〖토목〗 superstructure work **— 구조** a superstructure **— 명령** an order from above **— 장식 컷** [도서의] a headpiece

상부 上府 high-ranking officials ⇨ 상사(上司)

상부 喪夫 being widowed ; losing one's husband ; the death of one's husband **—하다** be widowed ; lose one's husband ; meet the death of one's husband
—살(煞) evil influence bringing about widowhood ; the misfortune of losing one's husband

상부 孀婦 a young widow

상부상조 相扶相助 mutual aid〔help〕 ; interdependence ¶ 어려울 때일수록 상부상조가 필요하다 It is keenly necessary to help each other in adversity.

상분수 常分數 a common fraction
***상비 常備** preparedness ; reservation **—하다** reserve (for) ; keep at hand ; have 《a thing》 always ready〔prepared〕; be provided with ¶ 상비의 standing ; permanent ; regular ; [예비의] reserve
—군〔함대〕 a standing〔stand-by, regular〕 army〔squadron〕; ready troops **—금** a reserve fund ; reserve funds ; reserves **—미(米)** reserve rice ; rice stored in a public granary **가정 —약** a household medicine
상빈 上賓 ⇨ 상객(上客)
상사 ① a rounded edge groove 《on a column》 ② a groover ③ the bamboo-encased lower part of an arrow shaft
상사 上士 a Master Sergeant
상사 上司 [관청] a higher office ; the authorities ; [사람] one's superiors ; a senior official ; higher-up 《미》 ¶ 상사의 허가를 얻어서 on the approval of superior authorities // 그는 나의 상사다 He is placed over me. /He is my senior. // 신입 사원과 상사의 사이에서 일한다는 것은 상당히 어렵다 It's quite difficult when your work puts you between your new employees and the higher-ups.
상사 相似 resemblance ; similarity ; similitude ; 〚생물〛 analogy ; pseudo-
—하다 be similar to ; be analogous 〔alike〕; resemble
— 기관 〚생물〛 analogous organs ; an analogue **—물** analog(ue)s ; an analogy ; a parallel **— 삼각형** 〚기하〛 a homologous triangle **—점** a point of likeness 《between》; a resemblance ; a similarity **—형** 〚기하〛 like figures ; similar figures
상사 相思 mutual〔reciprocal〕 love ; pining 〔longing〕 for each other
—하다 think of each other ; be in love with each other ; pine〔long, languish, swoon〕 for each other
—마(馬) a stud in heat
상사 商社 a firm ; a concern ; a trading house ; a commercial house
외국 — a foreign firm **종합 —** a general merchant
상사 商事 business affairs ; commercial matters
— 계약 a commercial contract〔agreement〕 **— 회사** a commercial firm〔company〕; a trading〔business〕 concern
상사 常事 an affair of common〔everyday〕 occurrence ; a common event ; the way of the world ¶ 나는 가난할 때 무시 당했습니다 그것은 인간 상사지요 I was ignored when I was poor, as is the way of the world.
상사 喪事 death ; mourning ¶ 상사가 나다 have mourning
상사람 常— the common people ; the populace ; a commoner ; a plebeian
상사병 相思病 lovesickness ¶ 상사병에 걸리다 be lovesick ; languish from love ; be lovelorn ; pine with love
상사치다 groove ; put a groove in
상사하다 die in one's teens ; die young
†상상 想像 imagination ; [공상] fancy ; [가정] supposition ; [추측] (a) conjecture ; speculation ; (a) surmise ; (a) guess
—하다 imagine ; fancy ; picture〔figure〕 to oneself ; suppose ; guess 《at》 ¶ 상상적 imaginative ; imaginary ; supposed // 상상할 수 있는 imaginable ; conceivable ; thinkable // 상상할 수 없는 unimaginable ; unthinkable ; inconceivable ; beyond (the bound of) conception // 아무리 상상해 보아도 by any stretch of the imagination // 상상이 맞다〔맞지 않다〕 guess right〔wrong〕 // 상상의 날개를 펴다 give full play to one's imagination // 쉽게 상상할 수 있다 You may easily imagine 《that》. / It can readily be imagined 《that》. // 상상할 수 없다 [사물이 주어] surpass all imagination ; be beyond conception〔imagination〕; [사람이 주어] can hardly〔cannot〕 imagine 《what it is》; be unable to form any idea〔notion〕 《of a thing》 // 상상력이 풍부하다 be imaginative ; have a lively imagination // 즐거운 미래를 상상하다 draw a fine picture of one's future // 나머지는 독자의 상상에 맡긴다 We leave the rest to our reader's imagination. // 언젠가는 인류가 화성에 도착한다는 것을 상상할 수 있다 It is conceivable that man will someday reach Mars.
—력 imagination ; imaginative power ¶ 그는 상상력이 풍부하다 He is imaginative. /He has a lively〔an active〕 imagination. // 그 여자는 상상력이 모자란다 She is unimaginative. /She has little〔small power of〕 imagination. /She lacks imagination. **—설** a hypothesis 《*pl.* hypotheses》 **— 세계** a dream world ; a Utopia ; an imaginary society **— 임신** an imaginary〔false〕 pregnancy ; pseudocyesis **—화(畵)** an imaginary〔a fancy〕 picture
상상봉 上上峰 the highest peak〔summit〕
상상치 上上— choice goods ; exclusive merchandise ; a top-quality article
상서 上書 writing〔sending〕 a letter to one's superior ; a letter to one's senior
—하다 write〔send〕 a letter to one's superior〔senior〕
상서 相書 a book of physiognomy ; a guide to phrenological interpretation ; a guide to reading people's faces
상서 祥瑞 a lucky〔good, propitious〕 omen ; a happy augury〔sign〕 ¶ 상서롭다 be of good omen ; be propitious 〔lucky, felicitous, auspicious〕
상석 上席 seniority ; precedence ; an upper〔a higher〕 seat ; the top seat ; the seat〔place〕 of honor ¶ 상석의 senior // …의 상석이다 outrank〔take precedence

over] of 《a person》; be placed over [above] // 식탁에서 상석을 차지하다 sit at the head of the table

상석 床石 the stone table in front of a tomb

상선 商船 a merchant ship ; a trading vessel ; a merchantman ; a vessel of commerce ; [총칭] the merchant marine ; merchant shipping ¶ 상선을 격침하다 sink ships of commerce [merchant vessels]

—기(旗) a merchant flag **—대(隊)** a merchant marine ; [회사의] a fleet **— 선원** a merchant sailor [seaman] **— 조례** the merchant shipping act

상설 常設 permanent establishment

—하다 establish permanently ¶ 상설의 standing ; regular ; permanent

— 국제 사법 재판소 the Permanent Court of International Justice **— 농업 위원회** the Permanent Agricultural Committee (국제 노동 기관의) **— 위원회** a standing committee ; a permanent commission

상설 詳說 a full [detailed] explanation ; expatiation ; enlargement **—하다** explain in detail ; give a full account of ; dwell on 《a subject》; expatiate ; enlarge upon ; enter fully into

상설 霜雪 frost and snow

†**상세 詳細** details ; particulars **—하다** (be) minute ; detailed ; particular ; full ; be in detail ¶ 상세히 in detail ; minutely ; at length ; at large ; fully // 상세한 보고 a detailed [full] report [statement] // 상세하게 언급하다 go [enter] into details ; descend to particulars // 상세히 보도하다 report in full [at length] ; give a full account 《of》 // 그의 설명은 극히 상세했다 He explained the matter down to the minutest details. // 상세한 것은 추후에 발표될 것이다 Full particulars will be announced later. // 상세한 것은 송씨에게 물어 보십시오 Apply to Mr. *Song* for further particulars [information].

상세 上世 [상고(上古)] ancient times ; remote ages ; [윗대] the previous age [generation]

상소 上疏 presenting a memorial to the king ; a memorial to the throne **—하다** appeal to 《a higher court》 ¶ 상소를 취하하다 withdraw an appeal

— 관할권 an appellate jurisdiction **—권** the right of appeal **— 신청서** a notice of criminal appeal **—심** an appellate trial **—인** an appellant **— 피고인** an appellee

상소리 vulgar words [language] ; indecent talk ; four-letter words ; abuse **—하다** use abusive language

⁑**상속 相續** succession ; inheritance ; descent **—하다** succeed 《to》; inherit ; fall heir to ¶ 아버지의 재산을 상속하다 inherit [succeed to] one's father's estate // 큰 재산을 상속하다 be heir to a large estate // 가산을 상속하다 succeed to a family property // 부친의 뒤를 상속하다 succeed one's father 《as》

—권 the right of succession [inheritance] ¶ 장자 상속권 primogeniture **— 동산** an heirloom **—법** the law of succession [inheritance] **— 분쟁** a dispute about [a quarrel over] the succession **—세** inheritance [succession] tax ; a death duty 《영》 **— 승인[포기]** acceptance [refusal] of succession **—인** a successor ; [남자] an heir ; [여자] an heiress **— 재산** an inheritance ; inherited property ; a heritage **— 제도** the inheritance system **공동 —인** a joint heir ; a coinheritor ; a parcener **법정 —인** an heir-at-law 《*pl.* heirs-at-law》; a legal heir **추정 —인** an heir presumptive 《*pl.* heirs presumptive》 **호주 —** succession to (the headship of) a house **호주 —인** the successor to a house ; the heir ; the heiress (여자)

상쇄 相殺 offsetting ; cancelling [balancing] each other ; a counterbalance ; a setoff **—하다** offset ; set off ; cancel each other ; cancel out ; counterbalance ¶ 득실이 상쇄된다 Advantages offset [counterbalance] disadvantages. // 통화 팽창은 생산 증대로 상쇄될 수 있다 Inflation can be offset by increased production.

— 계정 an offset account **— 관세** countervailing duties **—물** an offset **— 신용장** a back-to-back L/C [letter of credit] **—액** amount of the offset

상쇠 上— [농악] a first gong-player in a folk band

상수 上手 a better [good] hand ; a superior ; an expert ; an adept

상수 上壽 an age of one hundred years and over ; a man over a hundred years old

상수 常數 〖수학〗 a constant ; an invariable (number) ; [자연의 이치] the natural course of things ; destiny

마찰 — a constant of friction **절대 —** an absolute constant

상수도 上水道 waterworks ; water service [supply]

— 공사 waterworks **— 시설** water supply facilities

상수리 〖식물〗 an acorn

—밥 a dish of ground acorns steamed with redbeans and served with honey **—쌀** ground acorns

상수리나무 〖식물〗 an oak tree ; Quercus acutissima (학명)

상순 上脣 the upper lip

상순 上旬 the first ten days of a month ; the first part [third] of a month ¶ 6월 상순 early in June ; the beginning of June

상술 床— wine sold at tables with *anju* (=tidbits) on them

—집 an *anju* tavern

상술 上述 preceding descriptions〔explanations〕; the above statements〔discussion〕 ¶ 상술의 the above-stated ; the above-mentioned ; the aforesaid ; the said ; preceding ; foregoing // 상술의 금액 the said amount // 상술의 사실〔진술〕 the above facts〔statements〕// 상술한 바와 같이 as stated above ; as mentioned above ; as aforesaid

상술 商術 a trick〔knack〕 of the trade ; business ability〔talent, policy〕 ¶ 상술에 능하다 have a good sense for business // 악덕 상술에 넘어가지 않도록 주의하시오 You have to be careful not to be taken unscrupulous soles practices.

*상술 詳述 a detailed explanation ; a full account ; expatiation ; enlargement —하다 make〔give〕 a detailed explanation ; fully explain ; give a full account of ; enter fully into ; dwell〔enlarge〕 on ¶ 상술하면 to be more particular ; that is to say

상스럽다 常— (be) vulgar ; base ; low ; mean ; indecent ¶ 상스러운 사람 a vulgar〔mean〕 person ; a groveler // 상스러운 이야기 indecent talk ; a spicy story // 상스런 농담 a broad joke // 상스럽게 말하다 talk about indecent things ; use vulgar language // 그의 행동이 상스럽다 His behavior is in bad taste. // 그 사람은 약간 상스런 데가 있다 There is something sordid about him. // 그는 풍채나 태도에 있어서 결코 상스럽지 않았다 He was by no means unrefined either in looks or in manners.

상습 常習 [세상의] a common practice ; a regular〔an established〕 custom ; a convention ; a usage ; [개인의] a habit ; an inveterate habit ¶ 상습의 customary ; habitual ; regular // 상습적으로 habitually // 상습적 범죄 a habitual crime // 상습적 도박꾼 an inveterate〔a confirmed〕 gambler // 상습적 소매치기 a confirmed pickpocket // 상습적으로 …하다 be in the habit of ; make it a rule to // 그는 상습적인 거짓말쟁이이다 He is a habitual liar.

—범 a habitual〔confirmed〕 criminal ; an old〔a repeated〕 offender ; chronic offenders ; a jailbird ; a gaolbird 《영》; a recidivist ; an old lag 《속》 —범 가중죄 【법】 cumulative punishment —성 habitude ; recidivism —자 a habitual offender 마약 —자 a drug〔narcotic〕 addict

†상승 上昇 rise ; rising ; ascension ; ascent ; upward tendency ; rising trend —하다 rise ; ascend ; go up ; climb ; assume an upward curve ¶ 상승하는 ascending // 급히 상승하다 swing upward rapidly // 물가가 상승을 거듭하고 있다 Prices are rising steadily. /Prices are on the steady increase.

— 기류 《ride》 a rising current of air ; an ascending (atmospheric) current ; a bump ; an updraft —력 climbing power 《of an airplane》; the ascensional power 《of a balloon》 —선 a rising curve — 속도 rate of climb — 식물 a climber — 음계 【음악】 an ascending scale — 화서 【식물】 ascending inflorescence 절대〔실용〕 — 한도 【항공】 absolute〔service〕 ceiling

상승 常勝 ¶ 상승의 ever-victorious ; invincible ; undefeated

—군 an ever-victorious army〔-force, team〕 — 장군 an ever-victorious〔undefeated〕 general — 함대 an invincible fleet

상승 相乘 multiplication —하다 multiply ; involve

—법 a multiplication method —비(比) a geometrical ratio — 작용 synergism of 《penicillin and streptomycin》 —적(積) the product of a mass — 평균 geometrical average〔mean〕

상시 常時 [평상시] ordinary〔normal〕 times ; [언제나] at all times ; always ¶ 상시에 at ordinary〔normal〕 times

— 고용 regular employment — 고용인 a regular employee

상식 上食 sacrificial meals offered to the deceased ; offering of meals to a departed soul

상식 常食 staple〔daily〕 food ; normal diet —하다 usually eat ; live on ¶ 쌀을 상식으로 하다 live on rice // 과실을 상식으로 하다 make fruit one's staple food

‡상식 常識 common sense ; good sense ; basic knowledge practical sense 〔wisdom〕; mother wit ; horse sense 《미》 ¶ 상식적인 commonsense ; sensible // 건전한 상식 robust〔sound〕 common sense // 수출에 있어서의 상식 common sense in export management // 상식 있는 사람 a man of good〔common〕 sense // 상식 없는 사람 a senseless man // 상식적인 해결 방법 a very sensible settlement〔solution〕 // 상식적 견지에서 from a common sense standpoint // 상식적으로 생각해서 in the name of common sense ; from a common sense point of view // 상식이 있다〔없다〕 have〔lack〕 common sense // 상식이 풍부하다 have plenty〔a good deal〕 of sense ; be full of common sense // 상식에 벗어나다 be eccentric // 상식을 활용하다 exercise one's common sense ; use one's brains // 상식으로 판단하다 judge by 〔from〕 common sense // 그런 것은 상식이다 Everybody knows that. /It's a matter of common knowledge. // 그는 세련된 상식의 소유자이다 He has highly developed common sense. // 그는 교육은 받지 못했으나 상식은 풍부한 사람이다 He is illiterate, but a man of strong mother wit. // 국정 교과서에 오류가 있을 수 없다는 것은 상식적인 문제다 Our common sense tells us positively that the state textbooks are

free from errors. // 너의 거동은 상식에 어긋난다 Your actions are not in accordance with common sense.
— 시험 a general information test — 철학 common sense philosophy — 판단 common sense judgment 법률 — common sense in law

상신 上申 a report to one's superior — 하다 report〔state〕 to a superior official ; submit 《a written report》 to one's chief ; lay before the authorities
—서 a written report〔statement〕 —자 a reporter

*상실 喪失 loss ; forfeiture ; [인명의] bereavement — 하다 lose ; be deprived of ; forfeit ; divest oneself of ; be bereft of ¶ 기억을 상실하다 lose one's memory // 부모를 상실하다 be bereaved of one's parents // 그는 벌로서 권리를 상실했다 His right was forfeited of his crime.
권리 — the lapse due to a right (소멸에 의한) ; the loss of rights 기억 — loss of memory

상심 喪心 absent-mindedness ; abstraction ; stupor ; stupefaction — 하다 be absentminded ; be abstracted〔stupefied〕 ¶ 상심해서 with an abstracted air ; abstractedly // 비통해서 상심하다 be stupefied〔distracted〕 with grief // 상심해 있는 것 같다 look dazed ; be like a living corpse

상심 傷心 heartbreak ; grief ; sorrow ; distress — 하다 grieve ; be grieved ; sorrow ¶ 상심한 broken-hearted ; dejected // 아들을 잃고 상심하다 be grieved over the loss of one's son // 너무 상심하지마 Don't take it too hard.

상심 詳審 a detailed〔full〕 inspection — 하다 inspect fully ; make a detailed inspection ; investigate in detail

상씨름 上— the final match〔the finals〕 of wrestling

‡상아 象牙 ivory
— 세공 ivory-work ¶ 상아 세공사 an ivory worker〔turner〕 — 세관 a dentinal tubule(이의) — 야자 〖식물〗 an ivory palm — 제품 ivory manufactures ; ivories 《속》 — 조각 ivory carving ; [물건] a carving in ivory —질 dentine (이의) —(질) 섬유 dentinal fiber —탑 an ivory tower ¶ 상아탑주의 ivory-towerism // 상아탑주의자 an ivory-towerist ; an ivory-towerite // 상아탑의 생활을 하다 live in an ivory tower ; lead a scholastic life detached from the world ; shut oneself up in one's ivory tower — 해안 the Ivory Coast 모조〔인조〕 — imitation〔artificial〕 ivory 식물 — vegetable ivory

상악 上顎 the upper jaw ¶ 상악의 maxillary
—골 the upper jawbone ; the maxillary bone

상압 常壓 normal〔atmospheric〕 pressure
— 증류 〖화학〗 atmospheric distillation

상앗대 a boatman's pole ; a row pole ; a punting pole ¶ 상앗대로 배를 젓다 punt 〔pole〕 a boat ; propel a boat by poling
—질 poling ; pushing a boat with a pole ; propelling a boat with a pole ¶ 상앗대질하다 pole a boat

상애 相愛 mutual〔reciprocal〕 love — 하다 love〔be in love with〕 each other

상약 相約 an agreement ; an engagement ; a contract ; an appointment — 하다 agree ; make an engagement ; enter into a contract ; make an appointment

상약 常藥 a folk remedy〔medicine〕

‡상어 —魚 a shark
— 가죽 sharkskin ; shagreen ; sealeather ; fishskin — 기름 shark oil

†상업 商業 commerce ; trade ; commercial business — 하다 engage in commerce ; carry on business〔trade〕 ; conduct a business ¶ 상업의 commercial ; mercantile ; business // 상업상 commercially // 상업상의 용무로 on business // 상업을 영위하다 carry on commerce 〔trade, business〕 ; conduct a business // 상업에 종사하다 be engaged in commerce // 아버지는 상업에 종사한다 My father is a merchant.
—가(街) a business〔shopping〕 street — 거래 a commercial〔business, trade〕 transaction —계 the business world ; commercial circles — 고등 학교 a commercial high school — 광고 a commercial message (라디오의) — 교육 commercial education — 구〔지〕역 a business〔commercial〕 section〔district, center, quarter〕 —국 a mercantile nation — 금융 commercial finance — 대요〔통론〕 an introduction to commercial science — 도덕 commercial ethics〔morality〕 — 도시 a commercial〔merchant〕 town — 등기 commercial registration ; a commercial〔trade〕 register —란 [신문의] city articles ; a commercial〔financial〕 column 《미》 —문 commercial〔business〕 correspondence — 미술 commercial art — 방송 commercial broadcasting — 부기 commercial bookkeeping — 수학 commercial mathematics — 시대 a commercial era — 어음 a commercial bill 〔paper〕 ; a mercantile paper — 영어 business〔commercial〕 English — 용어 business terms ; commercial language — 은행 a commercial bank — 자본 a trading capital — 전쟁 commercial warfare ; business rivalry ; trade competition — 정책 commercial policy —주의 commercialism — 중심지 a commercial 〔business, shopping〕 center ; a center of commerce — 증권 a commercial instrument — 지리 commercial geography — 지리학 commercial geography —

화 commercialization ¶ 상업화하다 commercialize
상없다 常— (be) unreasonable ; irrational ; absurd
상여 喪輿 a (funeral) bier ¶ 상여를 메다 carry a bier
—꾼 a pallbearer ; a bier bearer **— 소리** a pallbearers' dirge **—집** a hut where a bier and accessories are kept
상여금 賞與金 a reward ; a bonus ; a premium ; a prize
연말 — a year-end bonus **특별 —** a special bonus
†**상연 上演** presentation (of a play) ; performance ; staging ; production **—하다** present ; play ; stage ; perform ; run ; put《a play》on the stage ¶ 신극을 상연하다 present a new play // 무단 상연을 금함 All rights reserved. /No performance may be given without written permission. // 그 연극은 상연을 금지당했다 The play has been interdicted. /A stage ban is placed on the play. // 그 연극은 지금 국립 극장에서 상연 중이다 The play is now being presented at the National Theater. // 학교극의 상연에 앞서 여러 번 연습했다 We held many rehearsals before presentation of our school play.
—권 performing〔acting〕 rights **—물** a play ; a piece ; [총괄적으로] a bill ; a program
상영 上映 showing ; projecting ; playing ; presenting《on the screen》 **—하다** show ; exhibit ; project ; screen ; put on the screen ¶ 영화를 상영하다 show a movie // 그 영화는 지금 단성사에서 상영 중이다 The film〔picture〕 is now on show at the *Dansungsa*.
상오 上午 the forenoon ; the morning ; a. m. ; A. M. ¶ 상오 5시에 at five in the morning ; at 5 a. m. // 상오 7시 30분 열차 the 7 : 30 a. m. train
상오리 常— 〖새〗 a greenwing ; a green-winged teal ; Anas crecca (학명)
상온 常溫 normal temperature
상옷 喪— a mourner's garb
상완 上腕 ⇨ 상박(上膊)
상완 賞玩 ⇨ 완상(玩賞)
상왕 上王 the abdicated king
상용 常用 common〔habitual, constant〕 use ; daily〔everyday, ordinary〕 use ; addiction **—하다** use commonly〔habitually〕 ; make regular use of ¶ 마약을 상용하다 be addicted to narcotics
— 대수(對數) common logarithms **—시** 〖천문〗 civil time **—어** common words 〔vocabulary〕 ; basic〔everyday〕 vocabulary **—일** 〖천문〗 a civil day **—자** a habitual user **— 한자** Chinese characters in common〔constant〕 use **아편 —자** an opium addict **자동차 —자** a motorist
상용 商用 commercial use ; business ; commercial business ; a business engagement ¶ 상용으로 on (commercial) business // 상용으로 방문하다 make a business call《on a person》// 상용으로 서울 여행 중이었다 I was on a business trip to *Seoul*.
—문 commercial correspondence ; a business letter **— 서식** a business form **—어** a commercial〔business〕 term
상용 常傭 keeping employed
— 운전 기사 one's regular chauffeur
상우다 harm ; hurt
상운 祥雲 propitious〔auspicious〕 clouds ¶ 상운이 감돌고 있다 Auspicious clouds hang over the place.
상운 祥運 good luck ; propitious〔auspicious〕 fortune
상원 上元 the fifteenth of the first month of the lunar calendar ; January fifteenth
†**상원 上院** the Upper House ; [영국] the House of Lords ; [미국·프랑스] the Senate
— 의원 a member of the Upper House ; [미국·프랑스] a senator ; [영국] a member of the House of Lords
상원 桑園 a mulberry plantation〔field〕
상위 相違 a difference ; dissimilarity ; divergence ; disagreement ; variation ; discrepancy ; a gap ; a gulf **—하다** differ《from》; disagree《with》; vary《from》; be different from ; be at variance《with》 ¶ 현격한 상위 wide〔diametrical〕 difference // 의견의 상위 a difference〔divergence〕 of opinion // 신분의 상위 disparity in social standing〔status〕 // 취미의 상위 disparity of tastes between A and B // 상위점 a point of difference // 둘 사이에는 상위점이 없다 There is no difference between the two. // 상기와 같이 상위 없음 I affirm the above to be true in every particular. /I hereby certify the above statement to be true and correct in every detail.
†**상위 上位** a high rank ; a superior position ; precedence ¶ 상위를 차지하다 rank high ; hold a high rank ; take precedence《in rank》// 대령은 중령의 상위다 Colonels outrank lieutenant colonels. // 미국 국무 장관은 다른 장관의 상위에 있다 The American Secretary of State outranks all other members of the Cabinet.
상유 上諭 a King's edict ; a mandate
****상응 相應** ① [호응] correspondence ; response ; respondence **—하다** correspond ; respond ; act in concert《with》 ¶ 육군과 공군이 상응하여 적을 공격했다 Ground troops and air squadrons attacked the enemy in concert.
② [상당] suitability ; fitness **—하다** (be) suitable〔due, proper, worthy〕 ; be suited to ; suit ; become ; befit ¶ 그에게 상응한 역할 a part fit for him // 신사에 상응한 행위 conduct becoming〔worthy of〕

a gentleman // 신분에 상응한 생활을 하다 live within one's means ; live in a style suitable to one's social status // 신분에 상응한 생활을 하라 Cut your coat according to your cloth. // 그는 그의 역량에 상응한 급료를 받고 있다 He gets the salary proportionate to his ability.

†**상의 上衣** a coat ; a jacket ; an upper garment ; [군대의] a blouse 《미》; a tunic 《영》; [특히 여자의] a blouse ; [여자·어린이의] a sack ; a sacque ¶ 상의를 벗고 in shirt sleeves // 상의를 입다〔벗다〕 put on 〔take off〕 one's coat // 상의를 입혀주다〔벗겨주다〕 help 《a person》 on〔off〕 with his coat

상의 上意 the wish〔will, intention〕 of the king〔one's superior〕 ¶ 상의 하달하다 convey the King's wishes to the people

‡**상의 相議** consultation ; conference ; discussion ; [담판] negotiation **—하다** consult with 《a person》; take counsel with ; confer with ; talk over 《a matter》; discuss 《a matter》; ask 《a person's》 advice ; negotiate ¶ 상의한 다음에 after consultation with 《a person》; after consulting 《a person》; by agreement // 미리 상의해 놓고 by advance arrangement // 상의 중이다 be in negotiation〔consultation〕 《with》 // 상의에 응하다 respond to consultation ; be a party to a consultation // 상의 하러 가다〔오다〕 go 〔come〕 to seek 《a person's》 advice ; go 〔come〕 to 《a person》 for advice // 상의를 받다 be consulted by 《a person》 about 《a matter》; be given counsel〔advice〕 // 변호사에게 상의하다 seek legal advice ; get the lawyer's opinion // 사장과 상의하겠다 I'll have a conference with the president. // 이 문제는 이 다음에 충분히 상의합시다 We shall talk the matter over some other day. // 나는 모든 일에 대해서 아버지와 상의한다 I ask my father's advice on every thing. // 그들은 지난밤 오래도록 상의했다 They conferred at great length last night. // 두 사람 사이에 상의가 원만히 이루어진 것 같다 It seems that an arrangement was duly made between them.

상의 上議 agenda **—하다** place 《an item》 on the agenda

상이 傷痍 wound ; injury
— 군인 a wounded soldier ; a disabled veteran〔ex-serviceman〕; the war disabled 《총칭》 **— 군인회** the Wounded Soldiers'〔Disabled Veterans'〕 Association

†**상인 商人** a merchant ; a trader ; a tradesman ; a dealer 《in》; a store keeper 《미》; a shopkeeper 《영》 ¶ 그는 상인티가 난다 He has something of the shopkeeper about him. /He smells of the shop.
— 근성 a tradesman's〔commercial, mercenary〕 spirit ; commercialism **— 도덕** a tradesman's morality **노점 —** a street trader **대—** a big merchant **도매〔소매〕 —** a wholesale〔retail〕 merchant ; a wholesaler〔retailer〕 **소—** a small tradesman **악덕 —** a wicked trader **행—** a traveling tradesman

상인 喪人 ⇨ 상제(喪制)

상인 常人 the common people ⇨ 상사람

상인방 上引枋 〖건축〗 the lintel ; the upper crosspiece (of a door, window)

상일 manual labor ; physical labor ¶ 상일을 하다 perform physical labor
—꾼 a manual laborer

상임 常任 a permanent post ¶ 상임의 standing ; permanent
— 서기 a permanent〔regular〕 secretary **— 위원** a member of a standing〔permanent〕 committee **— 위원회** a standing committee **— 이사** the executive secretary〔director〕 of a permanent committee **— 이사국** [유엔] a permanent member of the UN Security Council **— 지휘자** a permanent(musical) conductor

†**상자 箱子** a box ; a case ; a packing case ; a casket (귀중품용) ¶ 한 상자 (가득) a boxful // 상자에 든 cased // 나무 상자 a crate ; a wooden box // 사과 한 상자 a box of apples // 술 한 상자 a case of wine // 상자째로 사다 buy 《apples》 by the case 〔box〕 // 상자에 넣다 encase ; put 〔pack〕 《a thing》 in a box〔case〕 // 상자를 끄르다 unpack a case

상자성 常磁性 〖물리〗 paramagnetism

상작 上作 a good crop〔harvest〕; an abundant〔a plentiful〕 harvest

상잔 相殘 struggling with each other **—하다** struggle with each other
동족〔골육〕 — dog-eat-dog ; internal strife ; internecine feud

상장 喪杖 a mourner's walking stick

상장 喪章 a mourning band〔badge〕; a crape ¶ 상장을 달다 wear a crape 〔mourning band〕; [국기 따위에] drape the flags in mourning

상장 賞狀 a certificate of merit ; an honorary certificate ; a diploma of honor ; a testimonial

상장 上場 —하다 list 《stocks》
— 기준 〖주식〗 listing requirements **—주(株)** listed stocks〔shares〕

상장군 上將軍 the chief captain〔commander〕

상재 上— 〖불교〗 a monk who is first in line to succeed his master〔teacher〕

상재 上梓 publication ; printing **—하다** publish ; print

상재 霜災 frost damage ¶ 상재를 입다 suffer from frost

상재 商才 business ability〔capacity, acumen〕; a knack〔turn〕 for business ¶ 상재 있는 사람 a man of business ability

상쟁 相爭 strife ; struggle ; dispute ; conflict ; fight **—하다** be feuding with each other ; compete with one another ; have a dispute ; struggle against each other ; quarrel〔wrangle〕 with each other ; fight one another ¶ 골육상쟁하다 be engaged in an internecine feud

상적 相敵 [적을 상대함] antagonism ; contention ; [사람] an opponent ; an antagonist ; a rival ; a competitor ; a match ; an equal **—하다** contend ; be antagonized ; match ; equal ; rival ; compete with ; be a match for each other ¶ 상적할 수 없다 be peerless〔matchless, unrivaled, unparalleled, incomparable〕

상적 商敵 a commercial〔trade〕 rival ; a business competitor

상전 上典 one's lord ; one's master ; the employer ¶ 상전을 충실히 모시다 serve one's master faithfully // 상전처럼 행세하다 play〔act〕 the lord ; act like a lord

상전 相傳 [대대로] inheritance ; transmission from generation to generation ; [상호] handing down ; passing on
—하다 inherit ; transmit ; hand down ; pass on ¶ 상전의 hereditary ; inherited // 부자상전하다 be handed down from father to son

상전 桑田 a mulberry field
—벽해 convulsions of nature ; fickleness of things〔fate〕/Mulberry plantations have changed into a sea. /The world is a scene of changes, and to be constant in nature is inconstancy.

상전 詳傳 a full〔detailed〕 biography

상전 相戰 a fight ; fighting **—하다** conflict 《with》 ; fight 《with, against》

상점 商店 a shop ; a store 《미》 ¶ 대로변의 상점 stores and shops along the street // 상점을 벌이다 set up a store // 상점을 열다〔닫다〕 open〔close〕 a store // 그는 명동에 상점을 가지고 있다 He keeps a shop in *Myŏngdong*.
—가(街) a shopping street〔district, center〕 ; a shop-lined〔shopping〕 street **—장식** shop-dressing **—주인** a shopkeeper ; a shop owner ☞ ◖p. 1159◗

상접 相接 contact **—하다** come in contact 《with》 ; get in touch 《with》 ; get together ; meet

상정 上程 laying before the House ; presentation 《of a bill》 **—하다** lay 《a bill》 before the House ; present 《a bill》 ; introduce ; bring up 《a bill》 for discussion

상정 常情 ordinary human nature ; universal feelings ¶ 그렇게 생각하는 것은 인지 상정이겠지 It is quite natural that one should think so. // 쾌락을 추구하는 것이 인간의 상정이다 The desire to pursue pleasure is but too natural to the human nature.

상정 想定 a hypothesis ; a supposition ; assumption **—하다** suppose ; imagine ; assume
—량 an estimated volume

상정 傷情 injuring one's feeling **—하다** injure〔impair, violate〕 one's feeling 〔friendship〕

상제 上帝 God ⇨ 하느님

상제 喪制 ① [사람] a man who is in mourning for his parents or grandparents ; a mourner ¶ 상제가 되다 be bereaved of one's parents ; wear mourning ; be in mourning ② [제도] the ritual of mourning
맏— a chief mourner

상조 尙早 prematurity ; prematureness ¶ 상조의 premature ; too early〔soon〕 // 시기상조이다 Time is not mature yet. // 그 계획을 실행하기에는 시기상조이다 It is premature to carry out the plan. // 네가 결혼하기에는 시기상조이다 You are not old enough to get married.

상조 相助 mutual aid〔assist, help〕 ; interdependence **—하다** help each other ; aid〔assist, help〕 one another ; cooperate ; (be) interdependent
—회 a friendly〔benefit〕 society

상존 尙存 —하다 there is〔are〕 still ; still exist ; be still in existence〔being〕 ; [잔존] remain

상종 相從 association ; company ; friendly relations ; intercourse ; acquaintanceship ; fraternization **—하다** associate 《with》 ; hold intercourse 《with》 ; keep company 《with》 ¶ 오랜 상종 long acquaintance // 그와는 언제 상종해도 재미있다 I always enjoy his company. // 그 패거리들과는 상종 않는 것이 좋다 Avoid company with that set. // 그와 상종 못하게 된 것이 유감이다 I am sorry to have lost his society〔company〕.

상좌 上座 the top seat ; an upper seat ; [주빈의] the seat〔place〕 of honor ; [식탁의] the head (of a table) ¶ 그는 상좌에 앉았다 He sat at the top〔head〕 of the table.

상주 上奏 a report〔an address〕 to the throne **—하다** report to the throne ; submit 《a matter》 to the throne
—문(文)〔서(書)〕 a memorial to the throne

상주 常住 residence ; residing ; 〖불교〗 everlasting existence ; constancy ; eternity **—하다** reside 《at, in》 ¶ 일본에 상주하는 교포들 fellow countrymen who reside in Japan ; Korean residents in Japan // …에 상주한 자 those who were habitually resident 《in》 ; habitual residents 《in》
—불멸 〖불교〗 immortality and indestructibility ¶ 상주불멸하다 live forever ; be immortal and indestructible ; be eternal **—인구** a settled population

상주 喪主 the chief〔principal〕 mourner

상주 詳註 detailed notes

상주 常駐 —하다 station permanently

상 점

일반적으로 상점은 미국에서는 store, 영국에서는 shop이라고 하는 것이 보통이지만 대규모 가게에는 store를 쓴다. 영국에서 shop은 주로 소매점, 상점 및 물품을 제조 수리 판매하는 상점 등에 모두 쓰지만 미국에서는 이발소 (barber shop), 커피 숍 (coffee shop), 구두 수선집 (shoe repair shop) (★ 보통 양화점은 shoe store라고 한다) 등, 상품을 쌓아두고 파는 곳이 아닌 경우에는 shop이라 한다. 그러나 아직도 관용적으로 shop을 사용하는 경우가 있으므로 주의가 필요하다.

① store를 사용하는 경우

의류품점 clothing store / 문방구점 stationery store / 전기기구점 electrical appliance store / 백화점 department store (★ 영국은 그냥 stores라고도 함) / 가구점 furniture store / 카메라점 camera store (★ 촬영을 주로 하는 사진관은 photo studio) / 철물점 hardware store / 귀금속상 jewelry store / 주류 판매점 liquor store / 식료품점 grocery store / 전문점 specialty store / 일용잡화점 convenience store (★ 시골의 구멍가게는 general store, 자질구레한 잡화를 취급하는 곳은 variety store) / 야채가게 vegetable store (★ 영국에서는 greengrocer's (shop), greengrocery라고도 함) / 드럭스토어 drugstore (★ 미국에서는 약품류 이외에 일용잡화·화장품·담배·책과 소다수·커피 등 가벼운 음료도 취급; chemist's shop 《영》)

② shop을 사용하는 경우

신사 양품점 men's shop / (주문)신사복점 tailor shop; tailor's shop 《영》 / 장난감 가게 toyshop / 전당포 pawnshop / 빵집 bakeshop; baker's shop / 모자가게 hat shop / 만화가게 print shop / 화장품점 cosmetic(s) shop / 꽃가게 flower shop / 쌀가게 rice shop / 골동품점 curio [antique] shop / 토산품점 gift shop / 레코드점 record shop / 생선가게 fish shop (★ 영국에서는 fishmonger) / 도자기점 china shop / 스포츠용품점 sporting goods shop / 담배가게 tobacco shop / 안경점 optical shop / 커피전문점 coffee shop / 이발소 barbershop 《미》 (★ 영국에서는 barber's (shop)라고도 함) / 미용실 beauty shop; beauty parlor[salon]

③ shop, store의 생략

정육점의 경우 butcher's shop의 shop이 생략되어 butcher's로 쓰는 것이 있다. 집·상점·사원·병원 등 장소나 건물을 나타내는 경우 관용적으로 생략하기도 한다.

제과점 confectioner's (★ 빵·과자·케이크류 취급은 baker's) / 양화점 shoemaker's / 세탁소 dry cleaner's / 모피상 furrier's / 전당포 pawnbroker's / 담배가게 tobacconist's / 시계점 watchmaker's / 꽃가게 florist's / 문방구점 stationer's / 여성모자점 milliner's / 양장점 dressmaker's / 양복점 tailor's

④ 기타

제과점 confectionery (★ 과자·아이스크림·케이크 등을 만들어 파는 곳) / 유제품 판매점 dairy (★ 우유·크림·버터·치즈 등을 파는 곳) / 식료품 잡화점 grocery / 신문 판매대 newsstand / 슈퍼마켓 supermarket / 세탁소 laundry / 빵집 bakery / 신사양품점 men's outfitter; (men's) outfitter 《영》; haberdashery 《미》 (★ 와이셔츠·넥타이·혁대 등을 파는 곳. 영국에서는 잡화점(바늘, 실 등을 취급)을 가리킴) / 식당 restaurant / 다방 tearoom / 부티크 boutique (★ 소규모의 고급 여성복 판매점)

⑤ 설명식으로 나타내는 경우

운동구점 store for sporting, 양장점 store for ladies' accessories의 경우처럼 뒤에 전치사 for를 붙여서 표현하는 경우와, store selling bags and hats처럼 현재분사를 사용하는 경우가 있다.

⑥ 상점 간판

간판에 상호를 쓸 경우에는 Hank's나 Brown's처럼 소유격의 상호를 크게 쓰고 그 뒤에 beer hall이나 confectionery 등 점포의 종류를 작게 쓰는 경우가 많다. 또한 유명 백화점의 경우 department store를 굳이 써넣지 않는다 (Macy's, Harrod's 등). 외견상 명확하지 않을 때는 restaurant, drugstore 등 점포의 종류를 크게 쓰는 경우가 많다.

— 특파원 a permanently stationed correspondent

상중 喪中 the period of mourning; in mourning ¶ 상중에 during the period of mourning // 상중이다 be in mourning 《for》

상중하 上中下 top, middle, and bottom ; the first, the second, and the third ; the three grades of good, fair and poor ; [품질] fine, medium, and poor ¶ 상중하 한질 a set of three volumes ; [소설] a trilogy
상지 上肢 the upper limbs ; the arms
상지 常紙 paper of poor quality ; low-grade paper
상지상 上之上 the very best ; the top ; the best of the best
—품 an article of the very best quality
상질 上秩 ⇨ 상길
*‡***상징 象徵** a symbol ; an emblem ¶ 상징적인 symbolical ; emblematic **—하다** symbolize ; be symbolic of ; stand as a symbol 《for》; represent ¶ 대통령은 그 나라의 상징이다 The president is the symbol of the State. // 비둘기는 평화의 상징이다 The dove is an emblem of peace.
—극 a symbolic play〔drama〕 **—시** symbolical poetry **—어(語)** symbolic words **—주의** symbolism **—주의자** a symbolist **—주의자 운동** the symbolist movement **—파** the symbolic school ; the symbolists
상찬 賞讚 praise ; admiration ⇨ 찬상(讚賞)
상찰 詳察 full〔detailed〕 consideration ; careful observation **—하다** consider fully〔in detail〕; observe carefully
상창 傷創 a wound ; an injury ; a cut
상채 償債 payment ; repayment ; reimbursement ; refundment ; redemption **—하다** pay back ; return ; repay
상책 上策 a good〔capital〕 plan ; the best policy〔thing〕 ¶ 그 이상 상책이 없다 It's the best thing we can do. // 그것은 상책이 아니다 It is impolitic〔not advisable〕 to do so. // 고생하고 싶지 않거든 실수하지 않는 것이 상책이다 If you want to stay out of trouble, you'd best not make any mistakes.
상책 商策 a business policy
상처 喪妻 the death〔loss〕 of one's wife ; bereavement of one's wife **—하다** be bereaved of〔lose〕 one's wife ; (one's wife) die〔pass away〕
†**상처 傷處** a wound ; a wounded part ; an injury ; a hurt ; a cut ; [타박상] a bruise ; [깊은] a gash ; slash ¶ 깊은 상처 a deep〔serious〕 wound ; a deep gash〔slash〕// 상처를 입다 get〔receive〕 a wound // 상처가 아물다 The wound closes. // 상처를 꿰매다 sew up a wound // 상처가 남는다 It leaves a scar. // 상처는 몹시 아팠다 The wound hurt me badly.
옛— an old wound〔sore〕; a scar
상천 上天 ① [하늘] the sky ; the heavens ② [하느님] God ; the Lord ③ [겨울 하늘] the winter sky
상체 上體 〖해부〗 the upper part of the body〔trunk〕
— 운동 exercise of the upper part of the body
상초 上草 cut tobacco of the finest quality ; top-grade leaf〔tobacco〕
상초 上焦 the upper chest
***상추** lettuce
—쌈 lettuce-wrapped rice
상춘 賞春 enjoying spring ; admiring the spring scenery
—객 admirers of the spring scenery
상춘 常春 an everlasting spring
상충 相衝 contradiction
상층 上層 [건물의] the upper stories ; [지층의] the upper layer ; the upper stratum 《*pl.* -ta, ～s》; [사회의] the upper classes ; [공중의] the upper region
— 계급 the upper classes ; a higher stratum of society **— 공기〔기류〕** the upper air〔current〕 **— 대기〔선교〕** the upper atmosphere〔bridge〕 **—운(雲)** the upper clouds ; altostratus (clouds)
상치 上— top-quality stuff ; an article of superior quality
상치 相値 a conflict ; a collision ; discord **—하다** be in discord 《with》; collide 《with》; clash 《with》; run counter 《to》; (be) contrary 《to》 ¶ 영어 시간과 역사 시간이 상치한다 English class conflicts with history class.
상침 上針 ① [바늘] a good needle ② [바느질] decorative saddle stitching 《on clothes》
상칭 相稱 symmetry ¶ 상칭적인 symmetric(al)
좌우 — bilateral symmetry ⇨ 대칭
*‡***상쾌 爽快** refreshingness ; exhilaration **—하다** (be) refreshing ; exhilarating ¶ 상쾌한 공기 exhilarating〔bracing〕 air // 기분이 상쾌하다 feel refreshed // 심신을 상쾌하게 하다 refresh 《a person》 in mind and body // 오늘 같은 날에는 정말 기분이 상쾌해진다 A day like today really lifts your spirits.
상큼상큼 with light steps ; briskly ; lightfootedly ; lightly ¶ 상큼상큼 걷다 walk briskly
상큼하다 (be) slender-legged ; long-legged ; lanky
상타다 賞— win〔get〕 a prize ; be awarded a prize ¶ 그는 최고 득점으로 상탔다 He won the prize with the highest marks. // 전시회에서 처음으로 상탔다 He obtained his first victory at the show.
상탄 賞嘆 admiration ; high praise ; applause ; laudation **—하다** admire ; praise highly ; applaud ; extol ; speak highly of ¶ 상탄할 만하다 be admirable ; be praiseworthy ; be worthy of admiration // 보는 사람마다 상탄하지 않을 수 없었다 All those who saw it were filled with〔lost in〕 admiration.
*‡***상태 狀態** a condition ; a state ; a situa-

tion ; the state of things〔affairs〕

> 참고 **state** 사람이나 물건이 그 당시 놓여진 일반적 상황 **condition** 주위의 상황이나 기타 원인에 의해서 만들어진 사람 또는 물건의 상태 **situation** 사람이 놓여진 환경 (이 양자의 관계가 중시된다)

¶ 현 상태로서는 as matters〔things〕 stand (now) ; under〔in〕 the present condition // 위험한 상태 a critical condition ; a dangerous state // 환자는 위험 상태를 벗어났다 The patient is out of danger now. // 현 상태로서는 난동이 일어날 가능성이 있다 The present indication of affairs points to the possibility of disturbances. // 브레이크 상태가 아주 나쁘다 Your brakes are in bad shape. // 이 상태대로라면 콘서트의 성공은 틀림없다 At this rate, the concert's sure to be a success. // 이 상태 같아서는 이번주 내내 바쁠거다 If things keep up like this, we'll be busy all week.

건강 — the state of health ¶ 건강 상태가 좋다〔나쁘다〕 be in good〔bad〕 health **경제〔기후〕** — economical〔climatic〕 conditions **생활** — living conditions ; a condition of life ¶ 빈민의 생활 상태를 개선하다 improve the condition of the poor **실의** — a state of dejection **위험** — a critical〔dangerous〕 condition ; a crisis **재정** — a financial condition **정신** — a mental state ; one's state of mind **혼수** — (에 빠지다) (fall into) a comatose〔lethargic〕 condition

상태 常態 a normal state〔condition〕 ; an ordinary〔a usual〕 state ¶ 상태로 복귀하다 return〔get back〕 to normal〔the normal condition〕

상통 相— face ; countenance ; phiz 《속》 ; ugly mug 《속》 ¶ 상통을 찌푸리고 with a grimace

상통 相通 mutual understanding ; communication ; community **—하다** understand each other ; be in touch with one another ; communicate ; 《 there》 be something in common between ¶ 의사가 상통하다 understand each other ; come to a mutual good understanding ; be of the same opinion // 유무를 상통하다 minister to each other's wants ; fill each other's needs // 기맥이 상통하다 keep〔be〕 in touch with ; have a tacit understanding with // 정을 상통하다 form a connection

상투 a topknot (of hair) ¶ 상투를 올리다 tie a topknot

—관 a topknot(cover) piece ; a skullcap **— 기둥** 〖건축〗 a pillar with a topknot-shaped tenon at the top **— 꼬부랑이〔쟁이〕** a person with a topknot **상툿고** the coil of a topknot **상툿바람** a bare topknot ; bareheaded ; hatless

상투 常套 conventionality ; commonplaceness ; triteness ; a stereotype ; a platitude ¶ 상투의 conventional ; commonplace ; trite ; hackneyed

— 수단 an old trick ; a well-worn device ; stereotyped〔worn-out〕 measures ; familiar ways ; one's usual〔routine, hackneyed〕 practice ¶ 상투 수단을 쓰다 use one's old trick ; rely on familiar steps **—어** a hackneyed〔trite〕 expression ; a platitude ; a trite saying

상투 相鬪 fighting with each other ; an exchange of blows **—하다** fight with each other ; exchange〔trade〕 blows

상판(대기) face ; ugly mug ⇨ 상통

상팔자 上— good fortune ; a happy〔the best〕 lot ; high living ¶ 상팔자를 타고나다 be born under a lucky star // 자신의 상팔자를 감사하다 thank one's lucky stars

상패 賞牌 a medal ; a medallion (큰 것) ¶ 상패를 수여받다 win〔be awarded〕 a medal

— 수령자 a medalist **— 수여식** a medal-awarding ceremony

상편 上篇 the first volume (of a book in two or three volumes)

상포 喪布 cloth for funeral use

—계 a mutual-aid society to cover funeral costs

†**상표 商標** a trademark ; a brand ¶ 상표를 등록하다 register a trademark ; trademark // …의 상표가 붙어 있다 It bears the trademark 《of》 // 상품에 상표를 붙이다 brand a product ; put a trademark on a product // 상표를 침해하다 pirate〔infringe upon〕 a trademark

—권 trademark right **— 도용** trademark piracy **— 등록법** the trademark registration law **— 등록필** [표시] Registered **—법** the Trademarks Law **— 침해** a trademark infringement ; piracy of a trademark **등록 —** a registered trademark

상품 上品 ① [품질] a high-grade 〔first-rate〕 article ; a superior article ¶ 최상품의 of the highest〔finest〕 quality ; of extra superior quality // 이 물건은 상품이다 This article is superior in quality. ② 〖불교〗 the Land of Supreme Happiness

⁑**상품 商品** an article of commerce 〔trade〕 ; a commodity ; goods 《총칭》 ; merchandise ; wares ; commodities ; stock (재고)

> 참고 **goods**는 소매상이 취급하는 상품 (일상어) **merchandise**는 도매상 따위가 취급하는 상품(전문어)

¶ 각종 상품을 취급하다 deal in various lines of merchandise // 상품화하다 produce 《an article》 on a commercial scale // 상품을 팔아치우다 clear goods // 상품을 사들이다 lay in a stock (상점이) // 상품을 분류하다 assort goods // 이 물건은 상품이

되지 않는다 The article is unmarketable 〔unsalable〕. // 벌꿀은 중요한 상품이다 Honey is an important article of commerce. // 이 상품을 팔 전략을 세우자 Let's try to map out a strategy for selling this product.

— 견본 a commercial sample —권 a merchandise bond〔coupon〕; an exchange ticket; a gift certificate — 매매대장 a merchandise book — 매입〔매출〕대장 a purchase〔sales〕 book — 목록 a catalog(ue); [재고의] an inventory — 시장 the commodity market — 재고 the amount of stock — 중개인 a commodity broker — 진열관 a commercial〔commodity〕 museum — 진열실 a showroom — 진열장 a showcase — 진열창 a show window — 차관 commodity loans —학 the study of merchandise — 회전율 merchandise turnover 중요 — staple 〔major〕 goods; staple commodities

상품 賞品 a prize ¶ 상품을 타다 get〔win, gain, obtain〕 a prize // 상품을 수여하다 award 《a person》 a prize; bestow a prize 《on》; present a prize 《to》

— 수여식 a ceremony for awarding prizes

상품 거래소 商品去來所 a commodity exchange

—법 the Commodity Exchange Law

상풍증 傷風症 〖의학〗 a stuffed-up nose; a nose cold; coryza

상피 上皮 〖생물〗 the epithelium; [표피] the epidermis

—선(腺) an epidermal gland — 세포 an epithelial cell — 세포막 a hypoderm(a) — 종 〖병리〗 an epithelioma 《*pl.* ～s, -mata》

상피 象皮 elephant skin

—병 elephantiasis

상피 相避 incest ¶ 상피붙다 commit incest

상피리 〖물고기〗 Scombrops boops (학명)

상하 上下 ① [위아래] top and bottom; the upper and lower sides〔parts〕; up and down ¶ 상하로 above and below; upward and downward; [높고 낮게] high and low

② [신분] the upper and lower classes; high and low; superiors and inferiors; all classes of people; [치자와 피치자] ruler and ruled ¶ 상하 합심 단결하여 all classes of people being in perfect union // 상하 구별 없이 irrespective of rank; without distinction of social standing; both high and low // 사랑에는 상하 차별없다 Love is a leveler.

③ [책] the first and second volumes ¶ 상하 2권으로 된 책 a book in two volumes; a double-decker

—동(動) an up-and-down motion; [지진] a vertical shock —수도 water supply and drainage

상하 常夏 (an) everlasting summer ¶ 상하의 나라 a land of everlasting summer

상하다 傷— ① [훼손] damage〔be damaged〕; injure〔be injured〕; hurt〔get hurt〕; spoil〔be spoiled〕 ¶ 심한 서리로 곡식이 상했다 The crop was damaged by a heavy frost. // 트렁크가 운반 도중에 상했다 My trunk was damaged in transit. // 고기가 상했다 The meat is spoiled. / The meat has gone bad. // 이것 때문에 그는 건강이 상했다 This impaired his health. // 고기를 이처럼 내버려두면 상한다 If you just leave the meat out like this, it'll go bad.

② [상심] hurt〔be hurt〕; offend; worry; wound〔be wounded〕 ¶ 감정을 상하다 hurt 《a person's》 feelings // 어머니의 속을 상하다 worry one's mother // 속상하게 굴지마라 Must you be such a worry to me?

③ [여위다] become〔grow〕 thin; grow haggard ¶ 얼굴이 상하다 have a face all pinched and drawn // 몸이 상했다 He got skinny.

상학 上學 the opening〔beginning〕 of school —하다 《school》 begin ¶ 우리 학교는 오전 9시에 상학하고 오후 5시에 하학한다 Our school begins at 9 a. m. and finishes at 5 p. m.

— 시간 the hour at which school begins —종 the beginning bell

상학 相學 the science of physiognomy; phrenology

골—자 a phrenologist 인—자 a physiognomist (관상가)

상학 商學 commercial science

—부〔과〕 the department〔course〕 of commercial science —사〔박사〕 a Bachelor〔Doctor〕 of Commercial Science 《B.〔D.〕C. S.》; a Bachelor of Commerce

상한 上限 maximum; the upper limit ¶ 상한선을 두다〔정하다〕 fix the limits; set a limit // 상한선을 넘다 pass the limit; go beyond the limit

상한 象限 〖기하〗 a quadrant

—의(儀) 〖천문〗 a quadrant — 전위계 a quadrant electrometer

상합 相合 coincidence; agreement; correspondence; congruence —하다 coincide; agree; correspond

상항 上項 the above item〔provision〕

상항 商港 a commercial port〔harbor〕

***상해 傷害** wound; injury; harm; lesion; casualty —하다 injure; do 《a person》 an injury; inflict an injury upon ¶ 상해를 입은 것 같다 He seems to have been wounded.

— 보상 accident compensation — 보험 accident〔casualty〕 insurance —죄 a crime against person ¶ 상해죄로 고발되다 be prosecuted on a charge of injuring 《a person》 — 치사(죄) bodily injury resulting in death

상해 詳解 a detailed explanation ; a full commentary **—하다** explain minutely 〔in detail〕; give a detailed explanation 《of》

상해 霜害 frost damage ; damage by 〔from〕 frost ¶ 상해를 입다 be frosted ; be injured〔spoiled〕 by frost

상행 上行 going up ; going toward *Seoul* **—하다** go up ; go toward *Seoul* ¶ 상행 막차는 5시에 도착합니다 The last train up arrives at five.

—선(船) an upward-bound boat — 열차〔선(線)〕 an up train〔line〕

상행위 商行爲 a commercial〔business〕 transaction

상향 上向 an upward tendency〔movement〕; an upturn ; an uptrend

—선(線) an upswing

상현 上弦 〚천문〛 the first quarter 《of the moon》

—달 a waxing moon ; a young moon

상혈 上血 hemoptysis ⇨ 토혈

상형 常衡 avoirdupois (weight) ¶ 상형 5파운드 5 pounds avoirdupois

상형 문자 象形文字 a hieroglyphic character ; a hieroglyphic ; a pictograph

— 학자 a hieroglyphist

***상호 相互** mutual(ity) ; reciprocal(ity) ¶ 상호의 mutual ; reciprocal // 상호간의 이익을 위하여 for mutual benefit // 상호 동의에 의하여 by mutual consent // 상호 돕다 help〔aid〕 each other

— 감응〔유도〕 〚전기〛 mutual induction — 견제 mutual control — 계약 a mutual contract — 관계 mutual〔reciprocal〕 relation ; interrelation(-ship) ; reciprocity ; correlation — 무역 fair trade — 방위 원조 계획 the mutual defense assistance program — 보험 mutual insurance — 부조 mutual aid〔assistance〕 — 부조론 〚윤리〛 mutualism — 안전 보장 mutual security ¶ 상호 안전 보장 조약 a Mutual Security Pact〔Treaty〕 — 원조 mutual assistance〔aid〕 — 원조 조약 a mutual assistance pact〔treaty, agreement〕 — 의존 interdependence ; mutual dependence — 이익〔편의〕 mutual interests〔convenience〕 — 작용 reciprocal action ; (an) interaction ; (an) interplay — 조약 a reciprocal〔bilateral〕 treaty — 조직 a co-operative〔mutual aid〕 system — 조합 a co-operative society ; a mutual aid association — 참조 cross〔reciprocal〕 reference — 통신 mutual〔two-way〕 communication ; intercommunication — 협조 bilateral agreement

상호 商號 a firm〔trade〕 name

상혼 商魂 a commercial spirit ; commercialism

상환 相換 interchange ; exchange 《for》 **—하다** interchange ; exchange

—권 an exchange ticket ; a coupon — 준비금 a reserve for exchange —증 a receipt ; an exchange ; a bond 대금 — collect (on delivery) 《미》; cash on delivery 《C. O. D》

상환 償還 repayment ; refund(ment) ; redemption (공채의) ; amortization (연부의) **—하다** repay ; refund ; redeem ; amortize ¶ 외국 차관을 상환하다 redeem 〔refund, retire〕 a foreign loan // 공채를 상환하다 redeem a loan // 국채를 상환하다 sink a national debt // 공채의 상환기는 2010년이다 The bond is to mature in 2010.

— 계산서 recourse account —금 repayments — 기금 the sinking fund for redemption — 기한 the term of redemption ; maturity (만기) ¶ 상환 기한은 10년이다 The term of redemption is ten years. / The bond is redeemable in ten years. — 의무자 a recourse debtor — 청구 recourse — 청구권 (the right of) recourse 국채 —액 the amount of the national loan redeemed 만기전 — prior redemption 추첨 — redemption by drawing

†**상황 狀況** the state of things〔affairs〕; conditions ; a situation ; circumstances ¶ 현 상황으로는 under〔in〕 the present condition〔circumstances〕; as things are〔stand〕; as matters stand ; as things go // 상황에 따라 판단을 하다 judge from〔by〕 the existing state of things // 그곳 상황을 알려 주십시오 Please let me know how matters stand in your town.

— 증거 circumstantial evidence — 판단 circumstantial judgement 부대 — attendant condition

상황 上皇 the abdicated emperor

상황 商況 commercial〔trade〕 conditions ; the business situation ; the market situation〔trend〕 ¶ 상황이 여전히 부진하다 The business situation continues (to be) depressed. /Trade is dull as before. // 상황이 활발하다 Trade is brisk〔active〕.

— 보고 a market report〔bulletin〕 — 부진 dull〔inactive, slack, depressed〕 market — 시찰 a market survey 해외 — commercial conditions abroad

***상회 商會** a company ; a firm

상회 上廻 **—하다** top ; be more than ; exceed

상훈 賞勳 citation of merit ; a prize and a decoration

—과 the Decorations Section

상흔 傷痕 a scar ¶ 상흔이 없어지다 The scar dies away〔disappears〕. /The scar leaves no trace. // 상흔이 남아 있다 The scar still remains.

샅 the crotch ; a fork(ing) ; the inside of the thigh

샅바 a thigh band (of a wrestler) ; loincloth ¶ 샅바 지르다 bind the legs of

— 씨름 wrestling with a thigh band

살살이 (in) every nook and cranny〔corner〕; everywhere ; all over ¶ 살살이 뒤지다 look in〔search〕 every nook and cranny ; rummage // 집안을 살살이 뒤지다 ransack the house 《for》; search the whole house ; look around 《for it》 all the length of the house // 나는 이 근처를 살살이 알고 있다 I know every inch of this neighborhood.

샅폭 —幅 the crotch piece (of a cloth pattern)

새[1] [띠] sod ; turf ; [억새] purple eulalia ; [이엉] straw thatch

새[2] 〖광물〗 auriferous ore (s) ; gold content

새[3] ⇨ 샛바람

†**새**[4] 〖새〗 a bird ¶ 새발의 피 practically nothing ; a mere midget // 새의 깃 a feather ; down (부드러운) // 새의 지저귀는 소리 chirping ; twittering ; a chirp ; a twitter ; the song of a bird ; [숲속의] wood notes // 장속의 새 a caged bird // 새를 기르다 keep a cage bird // 새를 길들이다 train a bird // 새가 운다 A bird chirps. // 일찍 일어나는 새가 벌레를 잡는다 The early bird catches the worm. // 손에 있는 새 한마리가 숲에 있는 새 두 마리보다 낫다 A bird in the hand is worth two in the bush.

—장 a bird cage **—집** a bird('s) nest

새

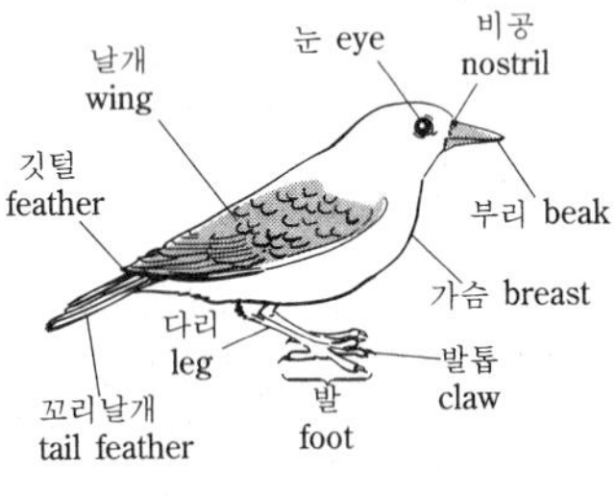

새[5] [피륙의] a unit measuring the density of warp threads in cloth (by 20 strands) ¶ 석새 60-strand warp

새[6] new ; fresh ; novel ; recent ; up-to-date

— 말 a new word **— 발명** a new invention **— 사상** up-to-date ideas **— 생활** a new life **— 신** a new pair of shoes

새[7] interval ⇨ 사이

새- deep ; dark ; intense ¶ 새빨간 거짓말 a downright lie ; a pure fabrication // 새까맣다 be deep〔jet-〕black // 새까맣게 타다 be burned black // 새맑다 be limpid // 새하얗다 be snow〔pure〕 white // 무서워서 새파래졌다 She turned pale with fear.

새 璽 the Great Seal ⇨ 국새

새가슴 a pigeon〔chicken〕 breast ¶ 새가슴의 pigeon-breasted ; chicken-breasted

새겨듣다 listen carefully to ⇨ 새기어듣다

새경 the annual salary given to a farm servant

새고막 〖조개〗 an ark shell ; a bloody clam

새곰하다 (be) sourish ⇨ 새금하다

새그물 a fowler's〔fowling〕 net ; a sparrow net

새근거리다 ① [숨을] breathe hard ; gasp ; pant ¶ 새근거리며 gasping (ly) ; panting (ly) ; out of breath // 새근거리며 말하다 gasp out ; speak panting (out of breath) // 숨이 차서 새근거리다 gasp for breath // 성이 나서 새근거리다 breathe hard with anger // 새근거리며 달려 왔다 He arrived panting.

② [뼈마디가] feel a slight pain ; feel a slight twitch of arthritis ¶ 뼈마디가 새근거리다 feel a dull pain in one's joints

새근새근, 쌔근쌔근 quietly ; peacefully ¶ 아기가 새근새근 잘 잔다 The baby is sleeping peacefully.

새근하다 have a slight pain

새금새금하다 (be) all sourish

새금하다 (be) sourish ¶ 이 사과는 새금하다 This apple tastes a bit sour.

새기다[1] ① [조각하다] sculpture ; carve (나무에) ; engrave (금속·돌 따위에) ; model (진흙 따위로) ¶ 나무에 초상을 새기다 carve an image in wood // 금판에 초상을 새기다 engrave figures upon a plate // 나무〔돌〕에 이름을 새기다 carve one's name on a tree〔in a stone〕

② [간직하다] engrave 《an image》 on one's memory ; print 《a thing》 on one's mind ; [사물이 주어] impress on 《a person》 ¶ 그것은 나의 마음에 깊이 새겨져 있다 It is written indelibly on my heart. // 그의 말은 나의 기억에 강하게 새겨져 있다 His words are strongly impressed on my memory.

새기다[2] interpret ; explain ; construe ; accept ; take ¶ 바르게 새기다 interpret rightly // 여러 가지로 새기다 interpret variously // 그가 말한 것은 틀리게 새겨졌다 His remarks were wrongly construed.

새기다[3] ruminate ; chew the cud ⇨ 되새기다

새기어 듣다 listen carefully to ; pay attention to

새김 ① [뜻의] interpretation ; paraphrase ; explanation ; translation (번역) ¶ 이 법조문은 사람에 따라 새김이 다르다 This provision is interpreted variously by different persons.

② [조각] carving ; engraving ; sculpture

새김질 ① [조각] carving ; engraving ; sculpture **—하다** carve ; engrave ; chisel ; sculpture

② [반추] ruminating ; chewing the cud **—하다** ruminate ; chew the cud

새김칼 a graver ; a burin ; a chisel

새꽤기 an unsheathed stalk ⦅of a straw⦆

***새끼**[1] a straw rope ¶ 새끼를 꼬다 make 〔twist, strand〕 a rope // 새끼로 짐짝을 묶다 rope a bale // 새끼를 쳐서 교통을 차단하다 rope off traffic

— 발 a straw-rope blind ; a rope curtain **—틀** a straw rope making machine **— 한사리** a fold of rope

새끼[2] ① [새의] a chicken ; a chick ; a young bird ; a brood (한배의) ; [동물의] the young ⦅총칭⦆ ; a cub ; [말의] a foal ; a colt ; [개의] a pup ; a puppy ; [괭이의] a kitten ; a kitty ; [양의] a lamb ; [염소의] a kid ; [물고기의] a fry ¶ 새끼를 배다 be with young // 새끼를 낳다〔치다〕 bring forth (its) young ; propagate // 쥐는 해마다 5, 6회 새끼를 낳는다 A female rat may have five or six litters yearly.

② [욕] a guy ; a brat (경멸) a chap ; a rogue ¶ 저 새끼 that fellow ; that ; swine〔brute〕 // 요놈의 새끼야 You rascal ! // 이 바보 새끼야 You fool ! // 건방진 새끼로군 You shameless scoundrel !

③ [자식] [구어] a kid ; a tot ; a toddler ; a son (사내) ; a daughter (딸) ; a child

④ [이자] interest ¶ 새끼를 치다 yield 〔bear〕 interest // 새끼를 쳐서 돈을 갚다 pay a debt with interest

—집 the womb of an animal

고슴도치도 제 새끼는 함함하다고 한다 [속담] The owl thinks her own young fairest. /The crow thinks her own birds fairest.

새끼발가락 a little toe

새끼발톱 a little toenail

새끼벌레 larva ⦅*pl.* -vae⦆ ⇨ 애벌레

새끼손가락 a little finger

새끼손톱 a little fingernail

새끼줄 a straw rope ¶ 새끼줄을 쳐서 막은 곳 a roped-off place

새나다 leak out ; get〔slip〕 out ; be disclosed ⇨ 새다 ¶ 세상(밖)으로 새나다 leak out to the world // 비밀이 새났다 The secret got out.

새나무 brushwood〔reeds, straw, etc.〕 for making a fire

새날 a new day

새남 a shaman's exorcism for the dead **—하다** pray for the souls of the dead

***새다** ① [날이] dawn ; ⦅day⦆ break ¶ 날이 샌다 The day breaks〔dawns〕. // 날이 새니 맑고 고요한 아침이었다 The morning broke fair and calm.

② [기체·액체가] leak (out) ; escape ⦅from⦆ ; [광선이] come〔shine〕 through ; [말소리가] be heard outside ¶ 지붕에서 비가 샌다 The roof leaks rain. // 가스〔공기〕가 샌다 Gas〔Air〕 escapes. // 통에서 물이 샌다 The water leaks out of the cask. // 문틈으로 불빛이 새어 나왔다 The light shone〔streamed〕 through the chinks of the doors. // 석양빛이 나무 사이로 새어 왔다 The rays of the late sun slanted in streams through the trees. // 이야기 소리가 가끔 창 밖으로 새어 나왔다 Their voices were sometimes heard outside the window.

③ [비밀이] get〔slip〕 out ; leak out ; be disclosed ¶ 비밀이 적에게 샌다 The secret leaks through to the enemy. // 비밀이 샜다 The secret got out.

새달 next month ; the coming month ¶ 새달의 오늘 this day (next) month // 새달 초하루 the first of next month

새댁 [새집] a new house ; [신부] a bride

⁑**새되다** (be) shrill voiced ; sharp ¶ 새된 소리로 in a shrill voice ; with a shriek // 새된 소리를 내다 give a shriek

새둥주리 a bird's nest ; a cage

새득새득 slightly dry ; withered **—하다** (be) somewhat dry ; withered ; wizened ¶ 새득한 소나무 a blighted pine (tree)

새들다 act as go-between〔matchmaker〕

새들새들 slightly wilted ⇨ 시들시들

새디즘 sadism

새때 between meals

새뜨다 (be) separated ; be at a distance ; be spaced (at intervals) ; (be) slow ¶ 사람 그림자가 새뜬 거리 a street with few passengers // 두 집이 새뜨다 The two houses stand some distance from one another. // 버스는 5분간씩 새뜬다 The buses leave at five-minute intervals.

새뜻하다 (be) fresh and bright ¶ 새뜻한 빛깔 bright color // 새뜻한 옷을 입고 있다 be neatly dressed

***새로** newly ; anew ; afresh ¶ 새로 오신 선생님 the new teacher // 새로 들어온 사람 a newcomer ; a freshman ; a person new to the service // 새로 지은 집 a newly built house // 새로 한 시 one o'clock in the morning // 새로 시작하다 begin afresh ; make a fresh start // 영어를 새로 배우다 learn English from the ABCs // 새로 지은 고층 건물이 관광 명소가 되었다고 들었습니다 I heard a newly-built high rise building has become a tourist attraction.

새로에 far from ⦅doing⦆ ; instead of ⦅doing⦆ ; on the contrary ¶ 실망하기는 새로에 far from being disappointed // 그는 저축은 새로에 그날 그날의 생활에도 곤란하다 Far from saving money, he can hardly make his living. // 만족하기는 새로에 성냈다 Far from being satisfied, he was angry.

⁑**새로이** newly ; anew ; afresh ⇨ 새로 **—하다** renew ; make new ; refresh ¶ 결의를 새로이 하다 make a fresh determination

새록새록 with a new〔one〕 thing popping up after another ; in succession ¶ 불행이 새록새록 일어났다 One misfortune followed on the heels of another.

†**새롭다** (be) new ; fresh ; vivid ; novel ;

recent ¶ 새로운 것 a novelty // 새로운 집 a new house // 새로운 말 a new word ; a newly coined term // 새로운 사상 an up-to-date idea ; new ideas ; a new thought // 새로운 소식 fresh news // 아직도 기억에 새롭다 be still fresh in one's memory // 새롭게 하다 renew ; renovate ; bring 《a thing》 up to date // 노력을 새롭게 하다 renew one's effort 《for》 // 무슨 새로운 소식이라도 있습니까 (Is there) Any news? // 별로 새로운 일이 없습니다 Nothing fresh〔new〕 has happened.

새롱거리다 flirt ; dally ; chatter ; talk glibly

새롱새롱 flirting ; dallying ; glibly

새마을 금고 —金庫 The *Saemaŭl Kumgo* ; a village savings body ; a village-level banking institution for mutual savings and loans

새마을 운동 —運動 *Saemaŭl* Movement ; the new community〔village〕 movement

농촌〔도시〕 — the rural〔urban〕 new community movement

새막 —幕 a shed built in a field to ward off sparrows

새맛 freshness ; novelty ¶ 새맛을 내다 display originality 《in》

새매 〖새〗 the Asiatic sparrow hawk ; Accipiter nisus nisosimilis (학명)

새머루 〖식물〗 a kind of wild vine ; Vitis flexuosa (학명)

새머리 spare ribs

새모이 bird feed

새무룩하다 (be) sulky ; sullen ; peevish ; glum ; moody ⇨ 시무룩하다

새물 ① [과실·생선] the first (product) of the season ② [옷] fresh-washed clothes ¶ 새물 셔츠를 입다 wear a fresh shirt

— 사과〔오이, 포도〕 early apples 〔cucumbers, grapes〕

새물내 a fresh-washed smell (of clothes)

새물 청어 —青魚 ① 〖물고기〗 the first herring on the market ② [무경험자] a new〔green〕 hand ; a novice ; a tenderfoot ; a freshman

새박 milkweed seeds

— 덩굴 ⇨ 박주가리

새발심지 a 3-tongued wick

새발장식 —裝飾 a bird's foot decoration

새밭 a field (full) of eulalia

†**새벽**[1] dawn ; daybreak ¶ 새벽에 at dawn 〔daybreak〕 ; at the peep of day // 새벽부터 저녁까지 from dawn till dusk // 새벽이다 Morning dawns. /It dawns. // 새벽 호랑이다 be shorn of one's power // 새벽길을 떠나다 start 《on one's journey》 early in the morning

—녘 the time of dawning ; toward daybreak ¶ 새벽녘에 at break of day ; at dawn ; early in the morning **—달** the waning moon〔crescent〕 (at dawn) **— 바람** a morning breeze **—밥** breakfast at dawn **—일** early-morning chores **—잠** a sound〔deep, fast〕 sleep at dawn

새벽달 보려고 초저녁부터 나 앉으랴 속담 Don't build the sty before the litter comes. /Boil not pap before the child is born.

새벽[2] 〖건축〗 plaster ; wall mud ¶ 벽에 새벽을 바르다 plaster a wall

—질 plastering

새벽같이 early in the morning ; before sunrise ¶ 새벽같이 일어나다 rise with the sun

새벽동자 cooking at dawn **—하다** cook (rice) at dawn

새보다 shoo away sparrows from crops

새봄 early springtime ; early in spring

새부랑거리다 gabble ; wag one's tongue ; talk garrulously

새빨갛다 be a vivid red ; (be) crimson ; brazen ¶ 새빨갛게 달다 be red-hot // 부끄러워서 얼굴이 새빨갛다 blush (up) to the roots of one's hair ; blush for shame

새빨간 거짓말 관용 a downright〔plumb〕 lie ; a pure fabrication

새빨개지다 turn〔become〕 red ; flush deeply ¶ 나는 술을 조금만 마셔도 얼굴이 새빨개진다 A little drink makes me deeply flushed.

새사냥 bird shooting ; fowling **—하다** go shooting birds ; go fowling

—꾼 a fowler

새사람 ① [신인] a new man〔face〕 ; a new-comer ② [신부] a (recent) bride ③ [회복자] a convalescent ④ [갱생자] a reborn man ; a reformed man ¶ 그는 전연 새사람이 되었다 He is quite another man now.

새살 granulation tissue ; proud flesh ¶ 새살이 나오다 granulate

새살거리다 carry on〔behave〕 flippantly ; chatter merrily

새살궂다 (be) very light and talkative ; (be) dreadfully flippant〔frivolous〕

새살 떨다 ⇨ 새살거리다

새살새살 talkatively ; flippantly

새살스럽다 (be) flippant ; frivolous ; shallow ¶ 새살스런 여자 a shallow woman

새삼 〖식물〗 dodder ; love vine ; Cuscuta japonica (학명)

새삼스럽다 ¶ 새삼스럽게 again ; anew ; [이제 와서] now ; after so long a time ; at this belated time〔hour〕 ; when it is too late // 새삼스럽게 말할 것도 없지만 it is hardly necessary to say 《that》 // 새삼스럽게 잊은 일을 꺼내다 go out of his way to bring up a matter long forgotten // 새삼스럽게 뭘 걱정하고 있나 You needn't make yourself so uneasy now. // 새삼스럽게 말할 것도 없는 일이다 It needs no repetition here. // 새삼스럽게 그런 말 해봐야 아무 소용없다 It is (of) no use to say such a thing now when it is too late. // 상식의 필요성을 새삼스럽게 느꼈다 I felt all the more keenly the importance of common sense. // 새삼스럽게 말할 필요도 없지만 음주 운전만은 하지 마시오 I don't think I have to tell you that I don't have you drinking and driving.

새새 ① ⇨ 새실새실 ② ⇨ 사이사이

새새틈틈 ① [공간] every nook and cranny〔corner〕 ¶ 새새틈틈 찾다 look in every nook and cranny〔corner〕 ② [시간] at intervals ; at one's odd moments

새색시 a bride

새서방 ─書房 a bridegroom

새수못하다 dare not put one's hand to

새실새실 grinningly ── 하다 be grinning ; grin

새싹 a sprout ; a bud ; a shoot ¶ 새싹이 나다 bud ; sprout ; shoot forth ; put forth buds〔shoots〕

새아기 one's new daughter-in-law

새아기씨 a bride

새아주머니 one's new sister-in-law

새알 a sparrow egg ¶ 새알 꼽재기만하다 be a mere particle ; be small or worthless

새알심 a small dumpling in red-bean gruel

새암 jealousy ; envy ── 하다 be jealous 《of》 ; be envious 《of》 ¶ 새암이 나다 feel〔become〕 jealous // 남의 성공을 새암하다 be jealous of another's success // 그 여자는 새암이 많다 She is apt to be jealous (of others).

─바리 a jealous〔an envious〕 person

새앙 〖식물〗 ginger

─나무 a ginger plant ─뿔 [생각] ginger-root stumps ; [소의] stumps of horns 《on cattle》 ─손이 a person with stumps for fingers (because of amputation) ─엿 taffy made of wheat gluten mixed with ginger juice ─즙 ginger juice ─차 ginger tea ─초(醋) vinegar boiled with ginger juice ─편 rice cake made with honey, ginger juice, and black wheat gluten

새앙머리 a kind of hairdo worn by palace maidens ; hair done up to two locks

새앙쥐 〖동물〗 a mouse ; [사향뒤쥐] muskrat

새옹 a small brass kettle

새옹지마 塞翁之馬 ¶ 인간 만사 새옹지마 An evil may sometimes turn out a blessing in disguise. /Inscrutable are the ways of Heaven.

새완두 ─豌豆 〖식물〗 a vetch (plant) ; Vicia hirsuta (학명)

*새우¹ 〖동물〗 [큰 새우] a lobster ; [보리 새우] a prawn ; [작은 새우] a shrimp ¶ 새우로 잉어를 낚다 throw a sprat to catch a whale〔mackerel〕 ; give an egg to gain an ox

새우² mud under roofing tiles

새우나무 〖식물〗 a hop hornbeam ; Ostrya japonica (학명)

*새우다¹ sit〔stay〕 up all night ; keep vigil ¶ 공부로 밤을 새우다 study all night long // 울음으로 밤을 새우다 pass a whole night in tears ; weep all night // 이야기로 밤을 새우다 talk the night away // 밤을 새워 간호하다 sit up with an invalid all night ; keep an all-night vigil // 하룻밤 새우기 위하여 닻을 내리다 cast anchor for the night

새우다² be jealous 《of》 ⇨ 새암하다

새우등 a bent back ; a stoop ¶ 나이가 들어 새우등이 되었다 His back is bent with age.

새우잠 sleeping all curled up

새우잠을 자다 관용 sleep curled up

새우젓 salted shrimps ; tiny shrimps pickled with salt

‡새장 ─欌 a (bird) cage ¶ 새를 새장에서 기르다 keep a bird in a cage

새전 賽錢 a money offering ; an offertory ── 하다 make a money offering to 《a deity》

─함(函) an offertory box〔chest〕

새조개 〖조개〗 a cockle ; Fulvia mutica (학명)

새중간 right in the middle〔midst〕 《of》

새집¹ ① [집] a new house ; a newly built house ¶ 새집을 짓다 build a new house ② [사돈집] the house of a new relative by marriage ③ [신부] a bride

새집² a bird's nest ; a sparrow's nest

새짬 ① [공간의] an opening ; an aperture ; a crack ; a chink ; a gap ② [시간의] ⇨ 짬¹

새쪽 〖해양〗 the east ; the eastward

새창 the lower intestine of an ox

새척지근하다 (be) sourish (by being spoiled)

새초(미역) dried brown seaweed of high quality

새총 ─銃 ① an air rifle ; a fowling piece ② a slingshot ; a catapult 《영》

새출발 ─出發 a fresh start〔departure〕 ── 하다 make a fresh start〔a new beginning〕 ; set out anew ¶ 새출발해 보다 try a new start

새치 premature gray hair ¶ 그는 새치가 많다 Though young, he has much gray hair.

새치근하다 ⇨ 새척지근하다

새치기 [끼어듦] cutting in ; [빼앗음] snatching ── 하다 cut in 《a line》 ; break into ; snatch 《another's portion》 ¶ 저 여자 새치기하는 것 봤니 Did you see that lady cut in the line ?

새치름하다 [체하다] (be) cold ; aloof ; reserved ; [모른 체하다] play the innocent ; wear an innocent look ; pretend not to know〔be moved〕 ¶ 그 여자의 새치름한 태도 her cold attitude // 내 말에 그 여자는 새치름했다 She bridled at my remarks.

새치부리다 behave oneself with reserve ;

be too polite
새침데기 a reserved person ; an indifferent person ; an ostensibly modest person
새침하다 (be) cold ⇨ 새치름하다
새카맣다 (be) pitch-dark ; jet-black ; raven
새콤하다 (be) sour ; acid
새큰거리다 ache (in a joint)
새큰하다 (be) aching ((in a joint))
새털 a feather (깃털) ; down (솜털)
새털구름 〖천문〗 a cirrus ((*pl.* cirri))
새퉁스럽다 (be) flippant ; silly
새퉁이 a flippant〔silly〕 person〔act〕 ¶ 새퉁이 부리다 act silly
*새파랗다 ① (be) deep blue ; indigo ; [얼굴이] pale ; pallid ② [젊다] (be) young ; rising ¶ 새파란 하늘 the deep blue sky // 무서워서 얼굴이 새파랗게 질렸다 She turned pale〔white〕 with fear.
새하얗다 (be) dazzling white ; snow-white ; pure white ¶ 새하얀 셔츠 an immaculate shirt
‡새해 a new year ¶ 새해를 맞이하다 greet〔hail〕 the New Year // 새해를 축하하다 celebrate the New Year // 새해에 복 많이 받으십시오 (I wish you) a Happy New Year ! /A Happy New Year (to you) !
— 문안 sending New Year's greetings through a messenger to one's relatives
— 전갈 sending New Year's greetings through a messenger ((to one's relatives))
— 차례 a New Year's ancestor-memorial ceremony
새호리기 〖새〗 a hobby ; a falcon
색¹ [소리] with a hiss
색² [자루] a sack ; [통·집 따위] a case ((for glasses)) ; [피임구] a condom ((프)) ; a rubber ((속)) ; a (contraceptive) sheath ; [손가락용] a thumbstall (엄지손가락의) ; a fingerstall (기타 손가락의) ¶ 색 드레스〔코트〕 a sack dress〔coat〕 // 손가락에 색을 끼다 wear a fingerstall
†색 色 ① [빛] color ⇨ 빛깔 ¶ 색칠하다 color // 줄어들지는 않지만 빨면 색이 빠질지도 모른다 It won't shrink but the color may run if washed.
② the same sort ¶ 구색을 잘 갖춘 물건 well-sorted articles // 좀 색다른 것 something that is out of the ordinary // 색다른 것을 좋아하다 be fond of novelty ; care for anything new
③ [색사] lust ; carnal desire ; sensual pleasure ; sex ¶ 색쓰다 have sex ; have sexual relations // 색에 빠지다 be addicted to lust〔sensual pleasure〕 // 색을 좋아하다 be amorous ; be lustful ; be licentious
④ [용모] womanly beauty ; feminine charms ¶ 여자의 미색에 홀딱 반하다 be smitten with a woman's beauty
☞ ⦅p. 1169⦆
색각 色覺 the sense of color ; color discrimination
색갈다 change ; make a change ; diversify ¶ 음식을 색갈다 get some variety into one's diet // 이번에는 색갈아 붉은 타이를 사겠다 I'll buy a red tie for a change.
색감 色感 the color sense ; color sensation
색감도 色感度 〖물리〗 color sensitivity
색골 色骨 a sensual〔lewd〕 person ; an over-sexed person ; a lecher ; a Don Juan
색광 色狂 a sex-crazed person ; sexual mania ; [남자] a sex mania ; erotomania ; [여자] a nymphomaniac ; a sexual maniac
—증 [남자] satyriasis ; [여자] nymphomania
색구 索具 ⇨ 삭구
색깔 色— color ⇨ 빛깔
색다르다 色— (be) different ; novel ; unusual ; uncommon ¶ 색다른 것 something different // 색다른 모자 a fancy〔new-look〕 hat // 색다른 사나이 a queer fellow // 색다른 일 an unusual thing // 그는 좀 색다르다 He is a little peculiar. // 그에게는 아무런 색다른 데가 없다 There is nothing unusual about him.
색대 a sharp-pointed bamboo or metal instrument for checking the quality of rice in a bag
색덕 色德 (a lady's) beauty and virtue ¶ 색덕을 겸비하다 combine〔have both〕 beauty and virtue // 그 여자의 색덕에 반하다 fall in love with her for her beauty and virtue
색도 索道 a cableway ; a ropeway
색도 色度 chromaticity
색동 色— (cloth with) stripes of many colors
— 마고자 a child's jumper with sleeves of many-colored stripes —옷 a rainbow-striped garment for children — 저고리 a girl's jacket with sleeves of multicolored stripes
색등 色燈 a colored lantern〔light〕
색떡 色— a colored rice-cake
색마 色魔 a sex maniac ⇨ 색광
색맹 色盲 color blindness ; daltonism ¶ 색맹의 color-blind
— 검사 a color-blindness test 적〔녹〕— red〔green〕 blindness 전(全)— total color blindness ; achromatopsia ; achromatic vision
색미투리 色— brightly decorated hemp sandals for children
색사 色事 a love affair ; an amour
색사진 色寫眞 a color picture
색상 色傷 illness resulting from sexual excess
색상 色相 the tone of color ; a color tone
색색 ((breathe)) calmly ; quietly ; peacefully ¶ 색색 잠을 자다 sleep sweetly〔calmly, peacefully〕
색색거리다 [부드럽게] breathe lightly

색

일상생활에서 사용되는 색의 표현은 어떤 색을 어떻게 느끼는가에 따라 동·서양이 서로 다를 수가 있다. 같은 색의 명칭도 동·서양의 문화·관습 등에서 오는 차이가 있다. 「푸른 신호등」은 영어로는 green light로 표현하는 것과 같이 실생활에서의 실제의 색과 다른 표현들이 있다.

① 색의 종류

검은색 black / 칠흑 jet black, coal black
흰색 white / 유백색 milk white / 상아색 ivory white
적색 red / 주홍색 scarlet / 진홍색 crimson / 주색 vermilion / 연자색 dark red / 밤색 maroon / 적자색 claret / 붉은 벽돌색 brick (red) / 버찌색 cerise / 암적색 wine red / 핑크 pink
청색 blue / 하늘색 sky blue, azure / 짙은 남색 navy blue / 코발트 블루 cobalt blue [ultra marine] / 군청색 ultra marine / 연두색 olive / 청록색 sea green / 선록색 emerald green / 남색 indigo
황색 yellow / 레몬색 lemon yellow / 담황색 pale yellow / 황토색 yellow ocher, ocher (yellow) / 호박색 amber (yellow) / 다갈색 drab / 암갈색 chocolate, umber, dun, dark brown / 황갈색 tan / 밤색 chestnut brown / 적갈색(팥색) russet / 브론즈 bronze / 금색 gold / 베이지색 beige
회색 gray / 진주색 pearl / 은색 silver / 은백색 silver gray
자색 purple, violet / 연어살색 salmon pink / 장미색 rose / 연한 자주색 mauve / 담자색 lavender

② 합성된 색의 표현

「…의 색을 띤」을 다음과 같이 표현한다. blackish, whitish, reddish, bluish, greenish, yellowish, brownish, pinkish, purplish, grayish.

황색의 예를 들면 황색과 녹색을 합성했을 경우, 황색 yellow / 푸른 빛이 도는 황색 greenish yellow / 황록색 yellow green / 누른 빛이 도는 녹색 yellowish green / 녹색 green의 순서로 표현할 수 있다.

색의 농담, 명암, 강약 정도에 따라 적당한 수식어를 붙여 사용한다.

선명한 핑크색 vivid pink / 밝은 황색 bright yellow / 짙은 적색 strong red / 심록색 deep green / 담청색 light blue / 암청색 dark blue / 옅은 자색 pale purple

이외에 느낌에 따라 연한 tender / 수수한 soft / 부드러운 subdued / 우중충한 dull / 진한 rich / 화려한 showy 등을 사용한다.

③ 색깔의 상징적 표현

black (옷차림의) 정장, (경영의) 흑자(黑字), 죽음, 비애, 실망, 험악한, 흉악한
¶ 요주의 인물 리스트 black book [list] / 약탈, 공갈 blackmail / 암시장 black market / 상복을 입고 있다. be in black / 장사가 잘된다[흑자이다]. The business is in the black.

white 청순, 고결함, 공정, 순결, 진실, 결백, 청결, 신성함, 공포, 죽음, 유령, 겁이 많음, 항복.
¶ 길일 a white day / 선의의 거짓말 a white lie / 백기, 항복 a white flag / (공포 등으로) 안색이 창백해지다 turn white / 꽁무니 빼다 show the white feather

blue 희망, 성실, 명랑, 경건, 영원, 불안, 냉철, 심려, 최우수, 우울, 음침함, 새침함, 쌀쌀 맞음
¶ 맑은 하늘 blue sky / 최우수상 blue ribbon / 마음이 우울하다 feel blue / 울적해 보이다 look blue / (음악의) 블루스 the blues

green 진심, 기쁨, 청춘, 원기, 호조, 안전, 포근함, 미숙, 불길함, 공포, 병색, 요괴스러운, 질투
¶ 눈이 내리지 않은 포근한 성탄절 a green Christmas / 생선(활어) green fish / 덜 익은 과일 green fruit / 숙성되지 않은 술 green liquor / 막 나온 치즈 green cheese / 그는 풋내기이다. He is a green hand. / 청신호 a green light[signal] / 매우 부러워하는 green with envy

yellow 겁쟁이, 음침함, 선정적(煽情的), 주의, 검역(檢疫), 질투가 심한
¶ 망나니 a yellow dog / 황색기, 검역기 a yellow flag / 선정적 저널리즘 yellow journalism / 겁 많은 성격 yellow streak / 노란 표지본 (19세기 중엽의 선정소설) yellow back

gray 현명, 원숙, 노련함, 백발, 비관, 고난, 부정, 불쾌, 외로움, 노년.
¶ (머리가) 백발이 되다 grow gray / 어두운 장래 the gray future / 외로운 인생 a gray life / 먼 옛날 the gray past / 원숙한 지혜 gray wisdom / 백발의, 연로한, 노련한 gray headed

pink 젊음, 활력, 신선함, 희망, 완벽, 홍분, 격노, 좌익적 성향, 몹시 취함.
¶ 유행의 진수 the pink of fashion / 그들은 모두 건강하다. They are all in the pink of health. / 해고 통지 a pink slip

purple 정의, 왕후, 귀족, 화려함, 미사여구(美辭麗句), 고상함, 격노, 비속함
¶ 왕후 귀족 가문에 태어나다 be born in (the) purple / 황제의 지위에 오르다 be raised to the purple / 격노하여 안색이 새빨개지다 turn purple with rage

red 정열, 열렬, 사랑, 자선, 순교, 용기, 축하, 격노, 위험, 과격, 유혈, 전쟁, 화재, 범죄, 적자, 좌익의, 혁명의
¶ 격노하여 얼굴이 빨개지다 become red with rage / 적자이다 be in the red / 적군, 공산군 the Reds / 정중한, 성대한 red-carpet 《미》 / 위험 신호 a red flag / 적자, 손실 red ink

④ 색에 관한 표현

¶ 그녀는 당황해서 얼굴이 빨개졌다. She became red [flushed] with embarrassment. // 그 소년은 꽃은 빨갛게 하늘은 파랗게 칠했다. The child colored the flower red and the sky blue. // 그녀는 그 광경을 보자 안색이 창백해졌다. She turned pale at the sight. // 그의 얼굴에 핏기가 없다. 그가 아픈 것 같다. He was colorless, we thought he was ill. // 햇빛으로 빨간 커튼의 색이 바랬다. Sunlight had discolored the red curtains. // 해가 지면서 하늘이 붉게 물들었다. Sunset dyed the sky red.

〔softly〕 ¶ 애기가 색색거리며 잠을 잔다 The baby sleeps sweetly.

색색이 **色色**— in〔with〕 various〔divers〕 colors

색소 **色素** coloring matter ; a pigment ; 〖생물〗 a pigmentary
— **결핍증** 〖의학〗 albinism — **세균** pigment bacteria — **세포** a pigment cell ; a chromatophore —**암** melanotic cancer —**액** a staining solution —**체** 〖동물〗 chromatophore ; chromatogen —**층** 〖해부〗 a pigment layer — **형성** 〖생물〗 pigmentation **식용** — food colors

색소폰 〖악기〗 a saxophone
— **주자** a saxophonist ; a saxophone player

색수차 **色收差** chromatic aberration ; chromatism

색스혼 〖악기〗 a saxhorn

색시 [신부] a bride ; [처녀] a maiden ; a girl ; [아내] a wife ; [접대부] a waitress ; a barmaid ¶ 색시를 얻다 take 〔get〕 a wife ; get married
색싯감 a likely (prospect for a) bride **색싯집** [처가] one's wife's home〔family〕 ; [갈보집] a brothel

색신 검사 **色神檢査** an examination of the color sense ; a color test

색실 **色**— dyed〔colored〕 thread

색심 **色心** [색욕] lustful mind ; sensual desire ; 〖불교〗 Matter and Mind

색쓰다 **色**— have〔practice〕 sexual relations〔intercourse〕

색안경 **色眼鏡** tinted glasses ; colored spectacles ; sunglasses ¶ 색안경을 쓰고 있다 wear colored glasses ; have sunglasses on

색약 **色弱** 〖의학〗 color weakness ; dyschromatopsia ; color blindness

색연필 **色鉛筆** a colored pencil

색옷 **色**— colored〔dyed〕 clothes ⇨ 무색옷

색욕 **色慾** sexual desire ; sexual〔carnal〕 appetite ; lust ; a craving for sex ¶ 색욕의 만족 sexual gratification ; gratification of sexual desire // 색욕이 강한 strongly-sexed

색유리 **色琉璃** colored glass ; stained glass

색의 **色衣** dyed cloths ; colored garments ⇨ 색옷

***색인** **索引** an index ¶ 색인이 없는 indexless 《book》 // 색인을 달다 index 《a book》 ; provide 《a book》 with an index ; append an index to 《a book》
자구(字句) — index verborum

색정 **色情** sexual urge(s) ; sexual desire 〔passion〕 ; carnal desire ; lust ¶ 색정을 일으키는 소설 a suggestive novel // 색정을 일으키다 excite〔stimulate〕 sexual desire
—**광** sexual insanity ⇨ 색광 — **도착증(倒錯症)** erotopathy

***색조** **色調** the color tone ; shade

색종이 **色**— colored paper ; a square piece of colored paper

색주가 **色酒家** [사람] a loose barmaid ; a prostitute bar ; [집] a bar of ill fame ; a shady bar ; a combination bar-whorehouse

***색채** **色彩** [빛깔] a color ; a hue ; tints ; coloring ; coloration ; [기미] a color ; coloring ; a tinge ; a tincture ¶ 지방적 색채 local color // 색채의 배합 color scheme // 색채가 풍부한 문체 a colorful 〔florid〕 style // 정당 색채가 강한 사람 a man with a strong political coloring // 색채가 풍부하다 be colorful ; be full of colors ; abound in color
— **감각** color sensation —**파** the colorists — **팔면체** a color pyramid — **환각** 〖의학〗 chromatism — **효과** a color effect

색채움 **色**— [구색] assorting all varieties
—**하다** assort all varieties needed ; fill in ; round out ; replace missing parts 〔items〕

색체 **色滯** a pale〔pallid〕 face

색출 **索出** —**하다** search〔seek, ferret〕 out ; hunt〔round〕 up ; track down ¶ 경찰이 간첩을 색출했다 The police ferreted out the spies.

색칠 **色漆** [칠] colored lacquer ; [칠하기] coloring ; painting —**하다** apply col-

ored lacquer ; color ; paint
색탐 色貪 lust ; lewd〔lecherous〕 desire **—하다** lust 《for sex》 ; have lecherous desires
색향 色香 ① beauty ; charm ; attractions ② color and scent 《of a flower》
색황 色荒 lechery ; sexual dissipation
샌님 ① [생원님] a gentleman scholar ; a gentleman
② [의뭉한] a prudish fellow ; an indecisive person
샌드 sand
—백 a sandbag **—페이퍼** sandpaper
‡**샌드위치** a sandwich
—맨 a sandwich man **햄—** ham sandwiches
‡**샌들** sandals ; sandal shoes
샌퍼라이즈 ¶ 샌퍼라이즈의 [상표명] Sanforized
샌프란시스코 San Francisco 《Frisco》
샐그러지다 ⇨ 실그러지다
샐녘 dawn ; daybreak
샐닢 half a copper coin
‡**샐러드** salad ¶ 샐러드를 만들다 mix 〔dress〕 a salad
—유〔기름〕 salad oil **야채 —** a vegetable salad **캐비지〔양배추〕 —** a cabbage salad ; coleslaw 《미》 **프루트〔과일〕 —** a fruit salad **햄—** ham salad
샐러리 a salary ¶ 한 달 100만원의 샐러리를 받고 있다 draw a salary of 1,000,000 *won* a month 《from the firm》
—맨 a salaried man ; an office worker ; a white-collar worker 《미》 ; the salariat(e) 《총칭》 ; wage earner ; the salaried class
샐비어 〖식물〗 a salvia
*__샐쭉 —하다__ (be) distorted ⇨ 실쭉
샐쭉경 —鏡 ovalshaped glasses〔spectacles〕
*__샘__[1] a spring ; a fountain ¶ 콸콸 솟는 샘 a gushing spring // 청춘의 샘 the Fountain of Youth // 샘이 솟는다 A fountain gushes out.
샘[2] jealousy ⇨ 새암
샘구멍 a fountainhead ; a headspring ; a source
샘물 spring〔fountain〕 water ¶ 샘물 줄기 a stream of spring water
샘바르다 (be) (acutely) jealous
샘받이 a paddy field which has a spring in it
샘솟다 gush〔spring〕 out〔forth〕 ; well up ¶ 샘솟듯 흘러 나오다 gush out like a spring // 눈물이 샘솟다 tears well up in one's eyes ; tears gush out
샘터 ① a fountain(site) ② a washing place watered by a spring ¶ 샘터에서 빨래하다 do the laundry at a fountain
샘터지다 a (dried-up) well revives
샘플 a sample ¶ 샘플을 보여주시오 Show me a sample. ⇨ 견본
— 오더 a sample order (견본 주문) **— 케이스** a sample case (견본 상자)
샛- [빛깔이] vivid ; deep ; intense ; pure ; genuine ¶ 샛맑다〔샛말갛다〕 be limpid
샛강 —江 a large river which divides to pass around an islet
샛거리 work-break snacks
샛검불 fireweeds
샛길 a byway ; a side road ; a lane ; a narrow path ¶ 샛길로 빠져가다 take a byway
샛노랗다 be a vivid〔golden, bright〕 yellow
샛문 —門 a side gate
샛바람 the east wind ; an easterly wind
샛밥 [곁두리] snacks for farmhands ; [끼니외] a meal taken at an irregular time
샛별 the morning star ; Venus ; Lucifer
샛서방 —書房 a paramour ; a secret lover
생 ⇨ 새앙
생[1] **生** ① [생명] life ¶ 생의 철학 philosophy of life ; life philosophy // 생을 받다 receive the gift of life ; come into existence // 생자필멸 All living beings are bound to die. /Man is mortal.
② [삶] living ; existence ; life (생활) ¶ 생의 충동 the will to live // 생의 투쟁 fighting〔struggle〕 for life // 생을 누리다 enjoy life // 생과 사(死) life and death
생[2] **生** I ; me ¶ 생이 전에 말씀 드린 바와 같이 as I have informed you before
생- 生 ① [익지 않은] raw ; unripe ; green ¶ 생것 raw food ; unripe fruit ② [가공하지 않은] raw ; fresh ; uncooked ; crude ; unprocessed ; natural ¶ 생고무 crude rubber // 생굴 a raw oyster ③ [살아 있는·마르지 않은] live ; living ; green ¶ 생나무 a live tree ④ [공연한] unreasonable ; irrational ; arbitrary ¶ 생벼락 unreasonable scolding // 생트집 an unreasonable dispute // 생돈 money spent to no purpose // 생사람 잡다 inflict injury upon an innocent person
-생 生 ① [성에 붙여 청년의 뜻] young ¶ 강생 young Mr. *Kang* ② [학생] a student of... ¶ 장학생 a scholarship student ③ [생년의] ¶ 10월생의 아이 a child born in October // 당신은 몇년생입니까 When were you born ? ④ [식물의] ¶ 일년생의 annual // 이년생의 biennial // 다년생의 perennial
생가 生家 one's parents' home ; the house of one's birth ; one's birth-home
생가슴 borrowing care ; anticipation of trouble ; a needlessly troubled breast 〔soul〕 ¶ 생가슴 태우다 be needlessly troubled〔upset〕 // 생가슴 태우지 말라 Let the future take care of itself.
생가죽 生— rawhide
생가지 生— a live (tree) branch
†**생각** ① [사고] thinking ; [사상] a thought ; an idea ; [관념] a notion ; a concept ; a conception **—하다** think 《of, about》 ;

give thought 《to》; conceive ; reflect ; meditate

> 참고 **think** 널리 쓰이는 일반어로서 머리를 써 어떤 일을 이해하고 해결하려고 하다 **reflect** 지난 일을 천천히 그리고 진지하게 생각하다 **meditate** 어떤 일을 모든 각도에서 검토하고 집중적으로 생각하다

¶ 좋은 생각 a happy〔good〕 idea ; a capital〔splendid〕 idea // 묘한 생각 a queer notion // 새롭고 진보적인 생각을 가진 사람 a man of new and progressive ideas // 사회 교육에 관한 잘못된 생각 a wrong conception of social education // 내 생각에는 to my (way of) thinking // 생각을 전하다 convey thoughts // 생각에 잠기다 be lost in thought ; be in reverie // 혼자 생각하다 think to oneself // 많이 생각하다 think hard // 생각하지 않도록 하다 try not to think 《of》; try to forget 《a matter》 // 생각이 다르다 have a different way of thinking 《from》 // 생각하지 않을 수 없다 I cannot get 《the problem》 off my mind. // 좋은 생각이 떠올랐다 A good idea occurred to me. // 진보적 생각을 가지고 있다 He has progressive〔advanced〕 ideas〔views〕. // 생각하면 할수록 모르게 된다 The more I think about it, the more confused I get. // 생각하기도 싫다 I dislike the very thought of it.

② [의도] an intention ; a plan ; an idea ; a view ; a purpose **—하다** intend 《to do》; have in mind ; think of 《doing》; plan to ; be going to 《do》 ¶ 의사가 될 생각 the idea of becoming a doctor // …할 생각으로 with a view to ; for the purpose of // 아무 생각 없이 with no definite idea // 생각을 품다 cherish an intention // 법률가가 될 생각으로 공부하다 study with the intention of becoming a lawyer // 가고 싶은 생각이 있다〔없다〕 have a〔have no〕 mind to go // 결혼할 생각은 없다 I have no intention of getting married. // 나는 선생이 될 생각이었다 I intended to become a teacher. // 나는 그 애를 기사를 만들 생각이다 I am going to make him an engineer.

③ [추억·숙고] recollection ; remembrance **—하다** ponder ; reflect ; think over ¶ 생각한 끝에 on reflection // 어렸을 때의 생각 childhood memories // 생각이 나다 remember ; recall ; have the recollection // 장래를 생각하다 ponder upon the future // 내 말을 잘 생각해보라 Think over what I told you. // 내일까지 생각하게 해주시오 Let me think it over till tomorrow. // 생각해 보니 내가 잘못했다 I found on reflection that I had been wrong. // 그 말을 한 생각이 나지 않는다 I have no recollection of having said that.

④ [상상] imagination ; supposition **—하다** think ; believe ; imagine ; suppose ¶ 생각할 수 없는 unimaginable ; unthinkable // 생각 좀 해봐 Just imagine ! // 우리가 북극에 있다고 생각하자 Let us imagine that we are at the north pole.

⑤ [바람] desire ; longing ; wish **—하다** desire ; long ; pine ¶ 사과 생각이 나다 feel like (having) an apple // 생각과 틀리다 be contrary to one's expectations // 임 생각이 나다 long for one's sweetheart // 만사가 생각과 같이 되지 않는다 Things don't go as we wish. /Everything goes wrong with me. // 집 생각이 난다 I began to think of home.

⑥ [기대] expectation ; supposition ; hope **—하다** expect ; hope ¶ 생각이 어긋나다 be disappointed in one's expectations // 일이 생각대로 되다〔안되다〕 things go according to〔contrary to〕 one's expectations // 결과가 생각대로 되다 the results turn out just as one expects // 만사가 생각대로 되어간다 Everything is going on as expected. // 만사가 생각대로 되지 않는다 Everything goes wrong 〔amiss〕 with me. /Things don't go as we wish. // 생각했던 것보다 일이 쉬웠다 I found the work easier than I had expected.

⑦ [분별] discretion ; prudence ; (good) judgment **—하다** consider ; take into consideration ; care for ; think of ; pay attention to ¶ 생각이 있는 prudent ; discreet ; thoughtful // 생각 없이 thoughtlessly ; imprudently ; rashly // 내 생각으로는 in my judgment ; to my thinking // 생각이 부족하다 be wanting in judgment // 남을 생각하다 consider others // 건강을 생각하다 take one's health into consideration // 내일을 생각하다 take thought for tomorrow // 어머니를 생각하다 think of one's mother // 일을 생각없이 하다 do a thing thoughtlessly // 생각을 잘해서 행동하다 act with judgment ; look before one leaps // 그것은 생각할 문제다 It is a matter for consideration. // 당신 생각대로 하십시오 I leave this matter to your discretion〔good judgment〕. // 네가 그러한 짓을 한다는 것은 생각이 부족하다 It is indiscreet of you to do such a thing. // 그 여자는 남편을 조금도 생각하지 않는다 She never gives her husband a thought〔a second thought〕. // 이웃 사람들 생각도 좀 해 줘야지. Don't you have any consideration for your neighbors ? // 그들은 다른 사람들에게 폐를 끼치는 것 따위는 생각하지 않는다 They never stop to think they might be bothering other people. // 우리 나라의 세금 제도는 좀더 생각해 볼 필요가 있다 More thought should be put into our country's tax system.

⑧ [의견] opinion ; views ; [제안] a suggestion **—하다** ponder ; reflect ; think over ¶ 정해진 생각 a settled〔definite〕

opinion // 흔들리는 생각 an irresolute mind // 내 생각으로는 in my opinion ; to my mind〔thinking〕// 내 생각은 My idea is 《that》; I am of (the) opinion 《that》// 자기 생각을 말하다 speak one's mind ; give 《a person》 one's opinion ; make a suggestion // 너의 생각은 어떠냐 What is your opinion ? /What do you say to that ? // 나는 네 생각과 다르다 I have a different opinion from yours. // 그 문제에 관한 생각들이 다 달랐다 There was a great diversity of opinion on that question. // 잘 생각하셨습니다 Good thinking.
⑨ [각오] a resolution ¶ 네가 그 기분이면 이쪽도 생각이 있다 Two can play at that game. // 네가 싫다면 나도 생각이 있다 I'll have to see about if you don't want to.

생각건대 come to think of it ; I think〔believe〕; It seems〔appears〕 to me that ¶ 생각건대 인생은 꿈에 지나지 않다 When we think of it, life is nothing but a dream. // 생각건대 유감스런 짓을 하고 말았다 On reflection I find I have done a regrettable thing.

†**생각나다** come to mind ; occur to one ; flash upon 《one》 (갑자기) ; dawn upon 《one》 (서서히) ; be reminded of ; remember ¶ 소년 시대가 생각나다 be reminded of one's childhood // 생각나는 온갖 수단을 다 쓰다 employ〔use〕 all possible measures one can think of // 좋은 아이디어가 생각났다 He hit upon a good idea. /A good idea occurred to him. // 그의 이름이 생각나지 않는다 His name does not come to mind. // 너를 보니 내 동생이 생각난다 You remind me〔put me in mind〕 of my brother.

생각다못해 at wit's end ; after much thinking

생각되다 look ; appear ; be regarded (as) ; be thought of (as) ; seem to be ¶ 좋게〔나쁘게〕 생각되다 be well〔ill〕 thought of // 재미 있게 생각되었다 It looked like fun. // 눈이 올 것 같이 생각된다 It looks as though it might snow.

생각해내다 [안출] think out 《a plan》; think up ; work out 《a scheme》; think of ; devise ; invent ; [상기] recall ; remember ; recollect ; be reminded of ¶ 계획을 생각해내다 think〔work〕 out a plan // 그의 이름을 생각해내다 recall〔remember〕 his name

***생강 生薑** ginger

생거름 生— raw manure ; fertilizer unmixed

생것 raw stuff ; uncooked food ⇨ 날것

생게망게하다 be hard to think of〔to figure out, to make out, to conceive〕 ¶ 생게망게하니 이해가 안 간다 I am not convinced yet.

생견 生絹 raw silk

생경 生硬 crudeness ; immaturity
—하다 (be) crude ; raw ; stiff : unrefined ¶ 생경한 문장 a crude style // 생경한 번역 an unreadable translation

생경 生梗 discord between two persons

†**생계 生計** livelihood ; living ¶ 생계를 돕다 contribute to 《a person's》 support // 생계가 넉넉〔곤란〕하다 be well〔badly〕 off ; be in easy〔straitened〕 circumstances // 문필로 생계를 세우다 make a living by literary work ; live by one's pen
—비 living cost(s) ; the cost of living ; living expense(s) **—비 지수** an index of living costs ; a cost-of-living index **— 수단** a means of living **— 유지자** a family supporter

생고무 生— crude rubber

생과 生果 green fruits

생과부 生寡婦 a divorced〔separated〕 wife ; a grass widow

생과실 生果實 ⇨ 생과

생과자 生菓子 (a) cake ; (a) pastry

생굴 a raw〔fresh〕 oyster

생글거리다 smile ¶ 생글거리며 with a smile ; smilingly

생금 生金 unrefined gold ; native〔rude〕 gold ¶ 생금덩이 a nugget (of gold)

생금 生擒 capture **—하다** capture 《a tiger》 alive ; take 《a person》 prisoner

생급스럽다 [뜻밖] (be) abrupt ; unexpected ; [터무니 없다] absurd ; irrelevant ; nonsensical ; impertinent

생긋 smiling gently ; sweetly

생긋거리다 ⇨ 생글거리다

⁑**생기 生氣** animation ; life ; vitality ; spirit ; soul ¶ 생기 있는 animated ; vital ; lively // 생기 없는 lifeless ; spiritless ; dull ; inanimate // 생기가 발랄하다 be quick with life ; be vigorous〔energetic, vivacious〕; be full of life // 생기를 불어넣다 infuse〔put〕 life into ; enliven // 생기를 없애다 sap the vitality of ; deprive 《a person》 of his spirit

†**생기다** ① [손에 들어오다] get ; obtain ; come by ¶ 직업이 생기다 get〔find〕 a job // 비싼 차가 한대 생기다 come by an expensive car // 우연히 이 책이 생겼다 I happened to get possession of this book.
② [발생] arise ; occur ; happen ; take place ; come to pass ; break out ; chance ; transpire ¶ 화제로 인하여 생긴 손해 the damage caused by fire // 좋은 결과가 생기다 produce good results // 선원중에 페스트가 생겼다 Plague has broken out among the crew. // 불면증은 여러 가지 원인에서 생긴다 Sleeplessness arises from many causes. // 그것은 지난달 생긴 일이다 It took place〔occurred〕 last month. // 내 신변에 큰일이 생겼다 A serious matter happened to me. // 화재는 흔히 부주의에서 생긴다 Carelessness is often the cause of fires. // 이 병은 무절제에서 생긴다 This disease originates from〔has its origin in〕 intemperance.

③ [존재하게 되다] come into being ; form ; be born (어린애가) ¶ 아들이 생겼다 A son has been born to us. // 섭씨 0도에서 얼음이 생긴다 Ice forms at the temperature of 0℃. // 비가 와서 곳곳에 웅덩이가 생겼다 Pools formed at places owing to the rain. // 이리하여 미합중국이 생기게 된 것이다 This is how the United States of America came into being.
④ [보이다] look (like) ; seem ; appear ¶ 정직하게 생기다 look honest // 이상하게 생기다 look funny // 잘〔못〕생기다 have good〔bad〕 looks // 상인같이 생기다 look like a merchant ; have the appearance of a merchant // 시골내기같이 생기다 have 〔bear〕 a rural air // 그 여자 어떻게 생겼는데 What did she look like ?

생김새 personal appearance ; looks ; features ¶ 생김새가 단정하다 have a handsome face ; be good-looking // 그 여자는 생김새가 예쁘다 She has good features. // 나는 그의 생김새가 싫었다 I didn't like his looks.

생김생김 looks ⇨ 생김새

생나무¹ a ginger plant ⇨ 새앙나무

생나무² **生—** [수목] a live tree ; [생목] green〔unseasoned〕 wood ¶ 생나무를 찍어 넘어뜨리다 cut down a live tree // 생나무는 마른 나무보다 쪼개기 쉽다 Green wood cleaves more easily than dry.

생남 生男 the birth〔begetting〕 of a son **—하다** give birth to a son ; get a son ; beget a son ; be delivered of a son

생남례 生男禮 celebration of the birth of one's son **—하다** treat those who congratulate one on the birth of one's son

생녀 生女 the birth〔begetting〕 of a daughter **—하다** give birth to a daughter ; get a daughter ; beget a daughter ; be delivered of a daughter

생년 生年 the year of one's birth
— 월일 the date of (one's) birth

생니 a healthy tooth

생담배 a cigarette burning of itself in the ash tray

생도 生徒 a pupil ⇨ 학생
—대 a cadet corps **사관 —** a cadet ; a midshipman (해군의)

생돈 生— money spent to no purpose ¶ 생돈을 쓰다 waste〔throw away, fritter away〕 one's money ; spend money purposelessly

생동 〖광물〗 unexploited mineral vein ; a virgin vein

생동 生動 being full of life ; animation **—하다** be full of life ; be animated

생동 生銅 〖광물〗 unrefined copper ; native copper

생동생동하다 be still lively〔vigorous〕 ; be as vigorous〔lively〕 as ever ¶ 고된 일을 하고도 생동생동하다 He is as fresh as a daisy even after such a hard work.

생동찰 a kind of glutinous millet

생되다 (be) crude ; be new to《a work》; be unfamiliar with《a job》; be a greenhorn ¶ 생된 말 crude speech

생득 生得 (being) innate ; inborn
— 관념 〖철학〗 an innate idea **—권** one's birth right **—설** the theory of innate ideas ; nativism

생딱지 生— a scab ; a crust

생딴전 生— irrelevant remarks ; an impertinent act

생땅 untouched soil〔ground〕

생때같다 (be) healthy ; robust ; sound ; fine and dandy

생떼 生— ⇨ 떼

생떼거리 perverse asking ; dunning
생떼거리를 쓰다 관용 badger ; dun ; demand perversely

생래 生來 by nature ; naturally ; by birth ¶ 생래의 natural ; innate ; (in) born ; inbred ; constitutional // 생래 몸이 약하다 be constitutionally weak

‡**생략 省略** [뺌] omission ; [줄임] abbreviation ; abridgment **—하다** omit ; abbreviate ; abridge ; shorten ¶ 생략한 omitted ; abridged // 생략하지 않고 without abridgment ; in full
—문 an abridged〔elliptical〕 sentence **—법** ellipsis **— 부호** apostrophe ; 〖음악〗 an abbreviation **—어** a clipped word ; an abbreviation

생량 生涼 coolness in autumn **—하다** become cool
— 머리 early autumn ; the beginning of the cool season

생력군 生力軍 a vigorous〔strong〕 person ; an energetic fellow

생력화 省力化 elimination〔reduction〕 of labor

생령 生靈 people ; lives ; souls

생로 生路 living ; a livelihood ⇨ 생계

***생리 生理** physiology ¶ 생리적 physiological // 생리적 결함 a physiological defect // 생리적 변화기 [여자의] change of life ; menopause // 생리적 요구 a physiological requirement〔necessity, impulse〕 // 생리적 현상 physiological phenomena
—대 a hygienic band ; a sanitary napkin〔towel, belt〕 **— 위생** physiology and hygienics **—일** a monthly period ; one's menstrual〔catemenial〕 period ; one's monthly days **— 작용** a physiological function **—학** physiology **— 휴가** a menstruation holiday ; a monthly physiological leave ; a special monthly leave for women **정신 —학** psychophysiology

생마 生馬 an unbroken〔untamed〕 horse
— 새끼 an untamed pony ; [비유적] a rude〔boorish〕 person ; a boor ; a cad ; a churl

생매 生埋 ⇨ 생매장

생매장 生埋葬 burying alive **—하다** bury《a person》alive ¶ 생매장되다 be buried alive

생맥주 生麥酒 draught〔draft〕 beer ; beer on draught〔draft〕
생먹다 [말을 안듣다] do not take〔follow〕《a person's advice》; do not obey ; [모른 체하다] ignore ; disregard ¶ 남의 말을 생먹다 ignore another's remarks
생멧소 生— borrowing money up to the value of a cow and paying it back by installments from the yearly crop
생면 生面 ① one's first meeting〔interview〕 ② a person whom one met for the first time ━하다 meet〔interview, be introduced to〕《a person》 for the first time
—목 a stranger —부지 an utter stranger
생면주 生綿紬 raw silk cloth
생멸 生滅 birth and death ; appearance and disappearance
†생명 生命 [목숨] life ; [중요한 것] the soul ¶ 군함의 생명 the life of a warship // 생명과 재산의 안전 safety of life and property // 생명을 걸고 at the risk of one's life // 허다한 생명을 희생하고 at the cost of many lives // 외국인의 생명과 재산을 보호하다 protect the lives and property of foreigners // 생명에는 지장이 없다 be out of danger // 그의 시의 생명은 서정성에 있다 The soul of his poetry is its lyricism.
—감 liveliness — 보험 life insurance〔assurance 《영》〕 — 보험 회사 a life insurance〔assurance 《영》〕 company —표 〖확률〗 a life table — 확률 life probability
생명선 生命線 [중요 지역] a lifeline ; [손금의] the line of Life ; the Lifeline ¶ 생명선을 지키다 guard one's lifeline // 지중해는 영국의 생명선을 이루고 있다고 한다 The Mediterranean is said to constitute Britain's lifeline.
생명수 生命水 life-giving〔life-saving〕 water
생모 生母 one's own〔real, natural〕 mother
생모시 unbleached ramie cloth
생목 生— [안삭은 음식] regurgitated food ¶ 생목이 오르다 have food regurgitate
생목¹ 生木 [직물] unbleached cotton cloth
생목² 生木 green wood ⇨ 생나무
생목숨 ① [목숨] life ; body and soul ¶ 겨우 생목숨을 이어가다 barely keep body and soul together ② [죄없는 목숨] an innocent 《person's》 life
생무지 a greenhorn ; a raw novice ; a tenderfoot ; a rank amateur ¶ 장사에는 생무지다 He is a greenhorn in the business.
†생물 生物 a living〔an animate〕 thing ; an organism ; a creature ; life 《총칭》
—계 the biological world ; animate creation ; life — 공학 bionics —권 the biosphere — 물리학 biophysics — 분포학 chorology — 생태학 bioecology — 숭배 animal worship — 시대 a geological era which includes the Paleozoic ; the Mesozoic and the Cenozoic —암 〖광물〗 a biogenetic rock ; biolith — 자생 spontaneous generation — 지리학 biological geography ; biogeography — 진화 biological evolution —체 an organism — 통계학 biostatics — 평형 biotic balance 〔equilibrium〕 — 화학 biochemistry — 화학자 a biochemist
*생물학 生物學 biology ¶ 생물학적 biological // 생물학적 요인 biological factor
—자 a biologist —주의 biologism
생민 生民 the people ; the public ; the populace
생밤 生— raw chestnuts
‡생방송 生放送 [라디오] live broadcasting ; [텔레비전] live〔television〕 coverage 《of an event》; a live broadcast ; a live telecast (텔레비전의) ; a live program
━하다 cover〔carry〕《an event》 live 《by radio, television》; broadcast〔televise〕《an event》 live (and unedited) ¶ 텔레비전으로〔라디오로〕 생방송되다 be televised〔broadcast〕 live
생배 生— ¶ 생배를 앓다 be sick with envy
생베 生— unbleached linen〔flax〕
생벼락 an unreasonable scolding ; an undeserved misfortune
생벼락을 맞다 관용 get an unreasonable scolding ; meet sudden misfortune
생병 生病 a breakdown ; sickness caused by overwork〔anxiety〕 ¶ 생병이 날 지경이다 be on the point of a nervous breakdown
생복 生鰒 raw〔fresh〕 abalone
생부 生父 one's own〔real, natural〕 father
생부모 生父母 one's own〔real〕 parents
생불 生佛 a living Buddha ; an incarnation of Buddha
*생사 生死 life and〔or〕 death ; living and dying ¶ 생사에 관한 문제 a matter of life and death ; a vital question // 생사가 불명한 사람들 missing persons ; persons whose fate is unknown // 생사를 같이하다 share one's fate 《with》; throw in one's lot with 《another》
—관두(關頭) a crisis ; a critical situation
생사 生絲 raw silk ¶ 고치에서 생사를 잣다 reel off raw silk from cocoons
— 검사기 a serigraphe — 검사소 a silk conditioning house — 시장〔상인〕 a raw-silk market〔merchant〕
생사 —紗 ⇨ 서양사
생사람 ① [죄없는] an innocent person 〔party〕 ¶ 생사람 잡다 [살해] kill an innocent person ; [모해] inflict injury upon an innocent person ② [관계없는] an unconnected〔unrelated〕 person ③ [생때 같은] a vigorous〔robust〕 person
†생산 生産 ① production ② birth
━하다 produce ; make ; turn out ¶ 생산적 노동 productive labor // 생산적 사업

productive industry // 생산을 제한〔증가〕하다 curtail〔increase〕 the production // 석탄 생산이 활발치 못하다 Coal production is lagging.
— 가격〔비〕 production cost ; cost of production — 가치 productive value — 계수 coefficient of production —고〔액〕 an output ; a yield ; production — 공장 the production line ; a manufacturing plant — 과잉〔과잉 —〕 overproduction — 관계 relative production — 관리 production management by workers ; production control — 기간 period of production — 기관 the production line(s) ; instruments of production — 기술 manufacturing technique〔know-how〕 — 능률 《increase》 production efficiency — 도시 a producing city —력 productive capacity ; production power ; productivity — 목표 a goal of production ¶ 생산 목표에 달하다 attain the goal of production —물 a product ; [집합적] produce — 방식 production method — 부족〔과소 —〕 underproduction — 설비 production〔productive〕 facilities ; plants and equipment — 성(性) productivity ¶ 한국 생산성 본부 the Korea Productivity Center // 아시아 생산성 기구 the Asia Productivity Organization 《APO》 — 수단 means of production — 실적 actual production〔output, yield〕 —업 the manufacturing business — 연도 a production year —율 rate of production ; production rate — 의욕 the will to produce ; a zeal〔an enthusiasm〕 for industrial production —자 a producer ; a maker —자 가격 a producer('s) price — 자본 capital for production ; productive capital —재 producer('s) goods ; production〔productive〕 goods — 제한 curtailment of production ; restriction of output — 조합 a producers'〔an industrial〕 guild〔association〕 ; a producers' cooperation —지 a producing center〔district〕 ¶ 사과의 생산지 an apple-producing center — 지수〔함수, 곡선〕 production index〔function, curve〕 —지 증명서 a certificate of origin — 카르텔 a producer's cartel — 확장〔증가〕 expansion〔increase〕 of production 국민 총—(고) the gross national product(ion) 《GNP》 대규모 — large scale production 대량 — mass production 1인당 —량 production per person 지정 —자 a designated〔an approved〕 maker 총 —비 the total cost of production

생살 生殺 sparing life and〔or〕 taking it ; letting live and〔or〕 killing
—권 the power of life and death

생살 生— healthy flesh ; new skin

생살여탈 生殺與奪 sparing life and killing ; giving and taking life away —하다 hold the power of life and death 《over》

생색 生色 a favorable impression ¶ 생색을 내다 make a good impression // 에어컨디셔너에서는 겨우 생색낼 정도의 바람만 나온다 The air-conditioner only gives out a token breeze.

생생이 taking a person's money by cheating in gambling
—판 a scene of crooked gambling ; a crooked game

†생생하다 生生— (be) lively ; fresh ; be full of life ¶ 생생한 채소 fresh vegetables // 생생한 기억 a fresh memory // 꽃이 생생하다 The flowers are fresh. // 그 광경은 지금도 내 마음속에 생생하게 남아 있다 The sight is still vivid in my mind.

생석회 生石灰 limestone ; quicklime

***생선 生鮮** (a) fish ; fresh〔raw〕 fish ¶ 생선을 요리하다 dress fish // 바다에서 생선을 잡다 fish in the sea // 고양이한테 생선 가게를 맡길 꼴이 되었다 It's like having the fox guard the henhouse.
— 가게 a fish shop — 구이 roast fish — 묵 fish cake — 시장 a fish market — 안주 a relish 《taken with wine》 ; a (side) dish — 장수 a fishmonger 《영》 ; a fish dealer 《미》 ; a fish peddler (행상) —회 sliced raw fish ; slices of raw fish

생성 生成 creation ; formation ; coming into being ; 〖철학〗 becoming ; generation —하다 [이루어지다] be created ; be formed ; [이루다] create ; form ; generate
—계 〖화학〗 the formation system — 문법 generative grammar —물 〖화학〗 a product

생소 生疎 [친하지 못함] unfamiliarity ; [미지] ignorance ; [무경험] inexperience —하다 (be) unfamiliar ; unacquainted 《with》 ; strange ; unpracticed ; inexperienced ¶ 생소한 땅 a strange land // 생소한 사람 an unacquainted man // 생소한 일 unaccustomed〔unfamiliar〕 work // 나는 이런 일에는 생소하다 I am unaccustomed〔new〕 to this kind of business.

생소리 unreasonable talk ; an unreasonable remark ; an absurdity ; a lie ; a fabrication —하다 talk nonsense ; make an unreasonable remark〔demand〕

생손 a sore finger ⇨ 생인손

생수 生水 spring water
—받이 a rice field irrigated with spring water

생시 生時 ① [출생] the time〔hour〕 of one's birth ② [생활] one's waking hours ③ [인생] one's lifetime ¶ 꿈이냐 생시냐 Am I dreaming or awake ?

***생식 生食** eating uncooked food ; eating〔taking〕 《it》 raw —하다 eat uncooked food ; eat 《the fish》 raw

생식 生殖 reproduction ; procreation ; generation —하다 reproduce ; generate ; procreate ¶ 생식력이 있는 generative ; reproductive ; progenitive // 생식 불

능의 neuter
—기(期) a period of reproduction — 기능〔작용〕 generative〔reproductive〕 function ; reproduction —력 generative〔sexual, procreative〕 power ; seminal power ; fecundity (여성의) ; virility (남성의) —모세포 a gonocyte ; gametocyte — 불능 impotence ; sterility — 불능자 an impotent (person) ; 〖법〗 a spado 《pl. spadones》 —선〔샘〕 the genital〔sex, sexual〕 gland ; gonad — 세포 a gamete ; a sex cell ; a generative〔reproductive, germ〕 cell —소(素) germ plasm —욕 the reproductive urge — 원세포 a gonium 《pl. -nia》 — 작용 a generative process 단성〔무성〕 — monogeny ; asexual reproduction 분열 — reproduction by division

생식기 生殖器 the genital〔sexual〕 organs ; genitals ; the reproductive〔generative〕 organs ; the organs of generation 〔reproduction〕
— 숭배 phallicism ; phallic worship — 장애 genital troubles〔disorders〕

생신 生辰 a birthday ⇨ 생일

생쌀 生— raw〔uncooked〕 rice

생아버지 生— ⇨ 생부

‡**생애 生涯** ① [일생] a life ; a career ; lifetime ② [생활] living ¶ 행복한〔비참한〕 생애 a happy〔miserable〕 life // 학자로서의 생애 one's career as a scholar // 생애의 가장 자랑스러운 때 the proudest moment of one's life // 생애를 마치다 end one's life〔days〕

생약 生藥 a herb medicine
—학 pharmacognosy ; pharmacognosia

생양목 生洋木 unbleached calico〔cotton〕

생어 生魚 a fish ; a live fish

생어머니 生— ⇨ 생모

생억지 irrational insistence on having one's own way ; stubbornness ; perversity ¶ 생억지를 쓰다 demand one's own way ; stick to one's unreasonable opinion

생업 生業 an occupation ; a calling ; a trade ¶ 고기잡이를 생업으로 삼다 make one's livelihood by fishing ; be a fisher by trade
— 자금 a rehabilitation fund ; a fund for operating business

생옥양목 生玉洋木 unbleached calico

생왁진 生— live vaccine

생우유 生牛乳 raw milk

생울타리 a hedge ; a quickset 《영》

생원 生員 a person who passed the lower civil examination ; Mr. ; esquire

생월 生月 the month of one's birth

생유 生乳 ⇨ 생우유

생육 生肉 raw meat

생육 生育 rearing ; bringing up — 하다 bring up ; rear ; raise

생으로 生— ① [날로] raw ② [무리하게] unreasonably ; forcibly ; irrationally ; wrongfully ; [까닭 없이] without any reason ; causelessly ¶ 굴을 생으로 먹다 eat oysters raw

생이 〖동물〗 a kind of shrimp

생이별 生離別 a lifelong separation〔parting〕 ; separation by circumstances — 하다 part 《from a person》 forever〔for life〕 ; part 《from one's spouse》 never to meet again ¶ 그것이 생이별이 될 줄을 그는 꿈에도 생각지 못했다 Little did he think that it would be a lifelong parting. // 그 부부는 전쟁으로 생이별했다 The couple were separated by the war.

생이지지 生而知之 knowing it when born — 하다 know it to the manner born 〔from birth〕 ; know it intuitively

생인발 a sore toe ; a boil on the tip of a toe

생인손 a sore finger ; a boil on the tip of a finger

†**생일 生日** a birthday ; one's natal day ¶ 생일을 축하하다 celebrate 《a person's》 birthday // 그녀의 생일은 10월 24일이다 Her birthday is October 24. // 생일을 축하합니다 Happy birthday to you ! // 그녀의 생일이 올해는 토요일이다 Her birthday falls on Saturday this year.
—빠낙 the time one has a birthday party — 선물 a birthday present〔gift〕 — 잔치 a birthday party ; the celebration of a birth ; a birthday celebration

생자 生子 delivery of a boy ⇨ 생남

생자 生者 a living person ; 〖불교〗 living beings〔things〕 ; animated nature
—필멸 Man is mortal. /All living things must die. /No birth without death. ¶ 생자 필멸의 이치 the mortality of life

생장 生長 growth ; growing — 하다 grow (up) ; thrive ¶ 생장을 돕다 foster〔help〕 (the) growth // 생장을 방해하다 check 〔hinder, hamper〕 (the) growth // 충분히 생장하다 reach 《its》 full growth ; complete 《its》 growth ⇨ 성장(成長)
— 곡선〔식, 구배〕 a growth curve〔formula, gradient〕 — 기간〔과정〕 a growth period〔process〕 —량 growth —률 growth〔increment〕 percentage ; the rate of growth

생장작 生長斫 unseasoned firewood

생재 生財 the increase of one's fortune 〔property〕 — 하다 increase in one's fortune

생재기 生— ① [종이·피륙의] undamaged cloth〔paper〕 ② ⇨ 생무지

생전 生前 lifetime ¶ 생전에 during〔in〕 one's lifetime ; during one's life // 서울은 이번이 생전 처음이다 This is my first visit to *Seoul*. // 생전 해봐 되는가 However hard you may try, you will not be able to do it.

†**생존 生存** existence ; being ; life ; survival — 하다 exist ; live ; survive ; outlive ¶ 생존을 유지하다 maintain one's existence
—권 the right to live ¶ 생존권을 위협하

다 menace ⟪a person's⟫ right to live —능력 viability — 목적 the aim of life —욕 a desire for existence ; the will to live —자 a survivor ¶ 난파선의 유일한 생존자 the sole survivor from the shipwreck 적자 — the survival of the fittest

생존 경쟁 生存競爭 the struggle for existence ¶ 격심한 생존 경쟁 a hard 〔fierce〕 struggle for existence

생죽음 生— a violent〔an unnatural〕 death —하다 die a violent〔an unnatural〕 death

*생쥐 mouse ; musk rat ⇨ 새앙쥐

생지 生地 untouched soil〔place〕 ; one's birthplace

생지옥 生地獄 a living hell ; a hell on earth

생질 甥姪 one's sister's son ; a nephew —녀 one's sister's daughter ; a niece

생짜 生— unripe〔green〕 fruits ; uncooked stuff ; raw fish〔meat〕

*생채 生菜 a salad ; raw〔uncooked〕 vegetable

무— a radish salad 오이 — a cucumber salad

생채 生彩 [광채] brilliance ; luster ; [생기] vividness ; life ; vitality

생채기 a (nail) scratch

생철 —鐵 zinc ; sheet zinc ; tin-plate ; a galvanized iron sheet

— 땜장이 a tinsmith ; a tinner — 세공 tinwork〔tinware〕 — 지붕 a zinc〔tin〕 roof —통 a zinc bucket

생청 生淸 unrefined〔raw〕 honey

생청붙이다 say unreasonable things ; make a contradictory statement

생청스럽다 (be) preposterous ; contradictory ; far-fetched ; unreasonable

생체 生體 a living body

— 염색(법) vital staining —학 〖인류〗 somatology — 학자 a somatologist — 해부 vivisection

생치 生雉 an uncooked pheasant

생칠 生漆 unrefined sap of the lacquer tree ; unboiled lacquer

생탈 deliberately caused trouble ; intentional disturbance

생태 生態 mode of life ; ecology ¶ 현대 여성의 생태 the mode of life of today's women

—계 an ecosystem — 변화 ecological adaptation —종 an ecospecies ⟪단·복수 동형⟫ —학 (the study of) ecology ¶ 각개 생태학 autecology // 고생태학 paleoecology // 군집 생태학 synecology —형 an ecotype

생트집 picking fault ; a false charge ; unreasonable〔malicious〕 fault-finding ; purposeful fault-finding ¶ 생트집을 잡다〔하다〕 provoke ; pick fault ⟪with⟫ ; make false charges ; find fault with ⟪a person⟫ purposefully // 생트집을 잡지 마라 Stop riding me !

생파리 a cool and distant person ; "a cold fish" ¶ 생파리를 떼다 give〔turn〕 ⟪a person⟫ the cold shoulder

생판 生板 ① [백지] blank ; groundless ; unfounded ; false ; empty ; complete ignorance〔unfamiliarity〕 ; [사람] an ignoramus ; a greenhorn

② [부사] groundlessly ; unjustly ; unreasonably ; outrageously ¶ 생판 속이다 cheat ⟪a person⟫ callously〔outrageously〕

생포 生捕 capture ; catching alive

—하다 capture ; take ⟪a person⟫ prisoner ; catch ⟪an animal⟫ alive ¶ 곰〔호랑이〕을 생포하다 catch〔capture〕 a bear 〔tiger〕 alive

생풀 生— [풀] raw starch ; [품질] starching a whole bale of cloth —하다 starch a whole bale of cloth

생피 生— ⇨ 생혈

생피 生皮 rawhide ; a raw skin

생핀잔 undeserved reproaches ¶ 생핀잔을 주다 have no call to put ⟪a person⟫ to such shame

생필름 生— raw film

생필품 生必品 ⇨ 생활(—필수품)

생혈 生血 fresh blood ; warm blood ; lifeblood ; vital blood ¶ 생혈을 빨아 먹다 suck the lifeblood ⟪of⟫

생호령 生號令 a wrong reprimand ; an unjust〔unreasonable〕 scolding —하다 scold ⟪a person⟫ unreasonably

생화 profession ; vocation ; career ; business ; [벌이] earnings ¶ 의술을 생화로 삼다 make medicine one's career

생화 生花 a natural flower ; a real flower

생화학 生化學 biochemistry ; chemicobiology

생환 生還 returning alive —하다 return alive ¶ 중대에서 생환자는 불과 세명이었다 Only three survived〔were left alive out〕 of their wholly destroyed company. —자 a survivor

†생활 生活 life ; living ; existence ; livelihood ; subsistence —하다 live ; exist ; make a living ; subsist ¶ 의의 있는 생활 a life worth living // 간소한 생활 a plain living // 규칙적〔불규칙적〕 생활 a regular〔desultory〕 life // 불안정한 생활 a precarious life // 충실한 생활 a rich〔full〕 life // 편안한 생활을 하다 live free from care ; live in comfort // 행복한 생활을 보내다 lead a happy existence ; live happily ; live a happy life // 생활을 보증하다 guarantee ⟪a person's⟫ living ; secure ⟪a person's⟫ livelihood // 겨우 생활해 나가다 barely manage to eke out a living // 가난한 생활을 하다 make a poor living // 비참한 생활을 하다 lead a miserable life 〔existence〕 // 분에 맞는 생활을 하다 live within one's means // 신분에 맞지 않는 생활을 하다 live beyond〔above〕 one's means // 월급으로 생활하다 live on one's

salary // 고독한 생활을 보내다 lead〔live〕 a lonely life // 그에게는 생활 걱정이 전혀 없다 He is quite free from bread and butter worries. // 그 소녀는 생활 때문에 낮에는 일을 하고 밤에는 학교에 다닌다 The girl works for her living〔keep〕 by day and goes to school by night. // 그의 양친은 시골에서 평화스러운 생활을 하고 있다 His parents lead a peaceful life in the country. // 그 여자는 이웃 아이들에게 영어를 가르치며 생활하고 있다 She lives by teaching English to the children in the neighborhood. // 연금만으로는 생활해가는 데에 불충분하다 Social security doesn't provide enough to live on.

— 간소화 the simplification of life — 개선 (운동) (a movement for) the improvement of living conditions —고 the grim realities of life — 과학 domestic science — 교육 education for living ; practical education —권(權) living rights —권(圈) a zone〔sphere〕 of life — 기능 a vital function — 기록 human document —난 the difficulty of living〔earning a livelihood〕 ; living difficulties ; economic distress ; 《struggle against》 hard living —력 vitality ; vital energies〔power〕 ; resourcefulness ¶ 생활력이 강한 사람 a person (full) of vitality — 보호 livelihood protection〔assistance〕 ; [빈민 구제] relief of the poor (and needy) — 보호법 the Livelihood Protection Law — 불안 economic insecurity —비 living expenses ; the cost of living — 상태 living conditions — 수준 the standard of living ¶ 생활 수준이 높다〔낮다〕 have a high 〔low〕 standard of living〔life〕 — 안정 stabilization of livelihood — 양식 the mode〔style, manner〕 of living ; a way of life ; a life-style ; a modus vivendi 《*pl.* modi vivendi》 《라》 — 임금〔급〕 living wages ; subsistence pay — 전선 the battle of life — 조건 the living condition ; the condition〔terms〕 of life — 필수품 necessities〔essentials, essential goods〕 of life ; daily〔living〕 necessaries — 현상 vital phenomena — 환경 life environment 도시 — city〔urban, town〕 life 문화〔사치〕 — civilized〔lavish〕 living 사회〔일상, 정신, 결혼〕 — social〔everyday, spiritual, married〕 life 원시 — a primitive life 이중 — a double〔dual〕 life 전원 — rural life ; living in the country 절약 — thrifty living 최저 — a minimum standard of living〔life〕

생황 笙簧 a reed instrument (consisting of a number of pipes of different lengths)

생회 生灰 limestone ; quicklime

생획 省畫 omission〔dropping〕 of strokes in writing a Chinese character

—하다 omit〔drop〕 (strokes) ; abbreviate one's characters

생후 生後 after〔since〕 one's birth ¶ 생후 5개월이 되는 유아 a five-month-old baby

생흙 uncultivated soil

샤머니즘 shamanism

샤워 a shower bath ¶ 샤워를 하다 take a shower

샤프 ① [날카로운] sharp —하다 (be) sharp ② [음악] a sharp 《기호 : #》

— 펜슬 an automatic 《미》〔a mechanical 《영》〕 pencil

—실 a shower stall

샤프롱 a chaperon(e)

샤프트 〖기계〗 a shaft

— 크랭크 a crankshaft

샴 Siam ; Thailand (1949년부터의 정식 국명) ¶ 샴 말 Siamese // 샴 사람 a Siamese 《*pl.* ～》 // 샴 쌍둥이 Siamese twins (몸이 붙은 쌍둥이)

*샴페인 champagne ¶ 샴페인 잔을 들어 축하하다 drink champagne in honor of 《the event》 // 샴페인을 너무 일찍 터뜨리다 Pop champagne too soon

— 글라스 a champagne glass — 사이다 champagne cider

*샴푸 shampoo ¶ 샴푸로 머리를 감다 shampoo one's hair ; have a shampoo

*샹들리에 a chandelier ; a pendant

샹송 a chanson 《프》

— 가수 a chanson singer

섀도우 캐비닛 [야당 내각] a shadow cabinet

섀미가죽 chamois (leather) ; shammy ; shamoy

서 [셋] three ¶ 서 돈 three (Korean) ounces // 서 되 three (Korean) quarts

†서 西 west 《W》

서 序 a narrative style ; [머리말] a preface ; a foreword ; an introduction

서 書 [서적] a book ; writings ; [서간] a letter ; an epistle ; [서류] a document ; [필적] handwriting ; [서도] calligraphy

†서 署 an office ; a station

서- 庶 half-blood ¶ 서동생 a younger half brother

서가 書架 a book shelf ; a stack ; a bookstand

서가 書家 a calligrapher ; a calligraphist ; a master of the writing brush ; a penman

서각 犀角 a rhinoceros' horn

*서간 書簡 a letter ; an epistle ; a note ; correspondence 《총칭》 ; [외교 문서] a note

—문 letter writing — 문학 epistolary literature —전 letter〔writing〕 paper ; [묶은 것] a writing pad —집 a collection of letters ; the Collected Letters 《of Lawrence》 —체 epistolary〔letter writing〕 style —체 소설 an epistolary novel

서거 逝去 death ; decease ; demise ; passing away —하다 die ; decease ; pass away

서걱거리다 crunch ⇨ 사각거리다

서경 西經 the west longitude ¶ 서경 50도

longitude 50 degrees west ; fifty degrees west longitude

서경 敍景 description of scenery ; a scenery sketch
—문 descriptive writing **—시** a poem describing scenery ; descriptive poems

서경 書經 Book of History ; the Canon of History

서고 書庫 a library ; a bookroom

서곡 序曲 a prelude ; an overture ; a prologue

서관 書館 [서점] a bookstore ; a bookshop ; [출판사] a book〔publishing〕 company

서광 曙光 dawn ; aurora ; [희망] hope ; prospects ¶ 성공의 서광 a gleam of success // 희망적인 서광 a flash of hope // 아직도 평화의 서광은 보이지 않는다 There is as yet no prospect of the return of peace.

서교증 鼠咬症 rat-bite fever〔disease〕

서구 西歐 Western Europe
— 문명 Western civilization〔culture〕 **— 연합** the Western Eurpopean Union 《WEU, W. E. U.》 **—인(人)** a Westerner ; a European **— 제국** [유럽의] European countries ; [서유럽의] countries in Western Europe **—풍** European ; Western **—화** Europeanization ; Westernization

서그러지다 (be) broad-minded ; magnanimous ; generous ; open-hearted

서근서근하다 ⇨ 사근사근하다

서글서글하다 ① [눈이] 《eyes》 (be) round and large ; have large round eyes ② [마음이] (be) free and easy ; be not easily bothered by little things ; (be) open-hearted ; magnanimous

***서글프다** ① (be) lonesome ; lonely ; forlorn ¶ 서글픈 노래 a touching〔plaintive〕 song // 어쩐지 서글프다 I cannot discover the reason I feel so sad today.
② be moved〔touched〕 to tears

서기 西紀 Anno Domini 《A. D.》 ¶ 서기 1995년 A. D. 1995 ; the year of our Lord 1995

†**서기 書記** a clerk ; a secretary ; a writer ; a clerical staff 《총칭》
—관 a secretary **—관보(補)** an assistant secretary **—국** a secretariat **—장** a chief clerk〔secretary〕 ; a secretary-general 《*pl.* secretaries-》 (정당의) **삼등 —관** a third secretary ¶ 주한 미대사관 삼등 서기관 a third secretary at the U. S. Embassy in *Seoul* **재판소 —** a law clerk ; a clerk of a law court

서기 暑氣 the heat ; hot weather

서기 瑞氣 auspicious signs ; a good omen

***서까래** a (house) rafter
—감 raftering (material)

서껀 and so on ; and the like ; and others

서남 西南 southwest
—서 southwest by west

서남풍 西南風 a southwester ; a southwesterly wind

서남향 西南向 facing southwest ; (having) a southwest aspect ¶ 서남향의 창 a southwest window // 이 집은 서남향이다 This house faces southwest.

서낭 ① a tutelar(y) deity ; a local god ② the tree where a tutelar deity dwells
—단(壇) an altar for a tutelary deity **—신(神)** a tutelary deity ; a genius loci 《라》 ; a local god **—제(祭)** the festival of the local god

서낭당 the shrine of a tutelary deity

서너 about three ; three or four ; a few (of) ¶ 백묵 서너 개 a few pieces of chalk

서너너덧 about three or four ; from three to five ; a few (of)

서넛 about three ; three or four ; a few (of)

서녀 庶女 a daughter born of a concubine ; an illegimate daughter

서녘 the west ; westward

서느렇다 (be) cool ⇨ 서늘하다

***서늘하다** ① [선선하다] (be) cool ; refreshing ¶ 서늘한 바람 a cool breeze // 서늘 해진다 It gets〔becomes〕 cool.
② [놀라서] have a chill ; be chilled ; feel a chill ¶ 놀라서 가슴이 서늘했다 I was chilled with fright.

†**서다** ① [서 있다·기립] stand (up) ; rise ; rise to one's feet ; get on〔to〕 one's feet ¶ 자리에서 (일어)서다 rise from one's seat // 종일 서 있다 be on one's feet all day // 그는 창 옆에 서 있었다 He was standing beside the window. // 버스 안이 혼잡해서 죽 서 있었다 The bus was so crowded that I had to stand〔keep standing〕 all the way.
② [멈추다] stop ; halt ; make a halt ; come to a stop ; come to a standstill ¶ 시계가 서다 a watch stops // 이 기차는 수원에서 선다 This train will stop at *Suwon.* // 엔진이 섰다 The engine went dead. // 행렬이 갑자기 섰다 The procession was suddenly brought to a halt. // 게 섰거라 Halt ! /Stop ! // 어디를 가나 서로 부딪칠 정도로 차가 많고 조금 가다가 서고 조금 가다간 서고 한다 It's bumper-to-bumper and stop-and-go everywhere.
③ [건립·창립] be built ; be erected ; be established ¶ 새 정부가 서다 a new government is established // 이 거리에도 집이 많이 섰다 A lot of houses have been built along this road. // 이 학교는 100년 전에 섰다 This school was founded a hundred years ago. // 병원이 동네 한복판에 서 있다 The hospital stands〔is situated〕 in the center of the town.
④ [조리가] hold good ; hold water ¶ 이론이 서다 one's theory stands to reason ; one's reasoning holds good // 이론이 서지 않는다 Your theory does not hold

good. /Your argument does not hold water. /Your argument has no leg to stand upon.
⑤ [남을 위해서] stand (as) ; serve (as) ¶ 보증 서다 stand surety // 중매 서다 act as go-between // 신부의 들러리를 서다 stand up with the bride (as bridesmaid) // 보초 서다 stand sentry ; stand sentinel
⑥ [면목이] save one's honor〔face〕 ¶ 그렇게 하면 내 낯이 선다 That will save my face. // 그렇게 하면 내 면목이 서지 않는다 That will put me out of countenance.
⑦ [칼날 따위가] stand out (sharply) ¶ 날이 서다 have a keen〔sharp〕 edge // 이 칼은 날이 잘 선다 This knife takes a nice edge. // 이마에 핏줄이 서다 a vein stands out on one's forehead
⑧ [장이] be held〔opened〕 ¶ 장이 서다 a fair is held〔opened〕 // 오늘은 장이 서는 날이다 This is the day for the fair. /It is market-day today.
⑨ [잉태] ¶ 아이가 서다 become pregnant ; get with child
⑩ [만들어지다] be formed ; be laid ; be established ¶ 계획이 섰다 My plan is formed〔laid〕. // 새로운 외교 정책이 섰다 A new foreign policy has been worked out. // 우리는 정책이 아직 서지 않았다 Our policy has not been established yet.
⑪ [결심이] make up one's mind ; make a resolve〔resolution〕 ¶ 결심이 안 서다 be irresolute ; hesitate to 《do》

서당 書堂 a village schoolhouse ; a private school
서당 개 삼년에 풍월 읊는다 속담 Practice makes perfect.

서대기 〚어류〛 a sole ; Rhinoplagusia japonica (학명)

서덜 ① [강변] a stony riverside
② [생선의 뼈] the bones of a fish

서도 西道 the northwestern provinces of Korea
— 잡가 folk songs of the northwestern provinces

서도 書道 calligraphy ; penmanship ¶ 서도의 대가 a master〔great〕 calligrapher

서독 西獨 West Germany

서두 書頭 ① [글의 첫머리] the introduction〔opening〕 of a book〔paragraph〕 ② [책의 윗부분] the margin at the top of a page
③ [책의 가장자리] page margins of a book ; page edges of an uncut book
— 하다 cut the pages of 《a book》

서두 序頭 the beginning ; a prolog(ue) ¶ 서두를 떼다 make introductory remarks

†**서두르다** hurry (up) ; hasten ; be in a hurry ; make haste 《with》 ; be impatient (조급하게) ¶ 서둘러 hurriedly ; in haste ; in a hurry // 서두르는 바람에 그것을 잊어버렸다 I forgot it in my hurry. // 왜 그런지 모르지만 그는 아주 서두르고 있었다 He was in a feverish hurry, (though) I do not know why. // 너무 서두르지 말라 Don't be so impatient. / What's the hurry〔your hurry〕? // 서두르면 손해다 Haste makes waste. /Haste spoils the work. 서둘러 Make it a quickie. 《라》 // 승리를 조급히 서두르면 저렇게 실패하기 쉽다 When people get impatient to win, they tend to make mistakes like that. // 일을 좀 더 서둘러서 해줘 Do it with a little more hustle.

서두어 鼠頭魚 〚물고기〛 a sillago

서둘다 ⇨ 서두르다

서라말 a white horse with black spots ; a piebald horse

*__서랍__ a drawer

서랑 壻郞 your〔his〕 esteemed son-in-law

서러움 sorrow ; grief ⇨ 설움

서러워하다 sorrow〔grieve〕 《at, over》 ; feel sad〔sorrowful〕 《at》 ; be distressed 《over》 ¶ 서러워서 in sorrow ; sorrowfully // 아버지의 죽음을 서러워하다 grieve 〔mourn〕 over one's father's death // 서러워하고 있을 때가 아니다 This is no time to give way to sorrow.

*__서럽다__ (be) sad ; sorrowful ; doleful ; rueful ; unhappy ¶ 서러운 이야기 a sad 〔pathetic〕 story // 서러운 목소리로 in a sad〔sorrowful〕 voice // 서럽게도 Sad 〔Sorry〕 to say... /It is a pity that... // 서러워지다 become sad〔grievous, sorrowful〕 // 그 말을 들으니 서럽다 His remarks make me sad. // 나의 일생은 서러운 일뿐이었다 My life has been a series of sorrows.

서력 西曆 the Christian era ; Anno Domini
— 기원 Anno Domini 《A. D.》

‡**서로** mutually ; each other ; one another ¶ 서로 돕다 help each other〔one another〕 // 그들은 서로 집을 방문하고 지낸다 They visit each other's〔one another's〕 house. // 그들은 서로 좋아한다 They are fond each other.

서로치기 doing the same thing for each other **—하다** each does for the other

‡**서론 序論** an introduction ; introductory 〔prefatory〕 remarks ; a prolegomenon

서론 緖論 an introduction ; prefatory remarks

†**서류 書類** documents ; papers ; instruments ¶ 모든 필요한 서류 절차는 이미 마쳤다 I've already finished all the necessary paperwork.
— 송청 〚법〛 sending papers of a case to the prosecutor's office **— 양식** paper forms **— 전형** selection of candidates by examining their personal histories ¶ 서류 전형하다 select candidates by examining their career papers **—철** a file ; a folder **—함** a filing cabinet ; a cabinet for record files **관계 —** related papers **기밀〔비밀〕 —** confidential papers ; 〚군사〛 classified papers 《미》 ; secret documents

선적 — shipping documents 인가 — a document of permission 일건 — papers bearing on the affair 증거 — documentary evidence ; papers〔documents〕 which prove 《a fact》

서른 thirty ¶ 서른살 thirty years of age // 서른번째 thirtieth

서름서름하다 ① [소원하다] (be) distant ; estranged 《from》 ; alienated 《from》 ¶ 두 사람 사이가 점점 서름서름해졌다 The two have gradually become estranged〔drifted apart〕.
② [일에] know little of ; be unacquainted with ; be uninformed〔ignorant〕 of ; be inconversant with ¶ 세상사에 서름서름하다 know but little of the world ; be out of touch with the world

서름하다 [사람에게] (be) estranged 《from》 ; (be) distant〔stand-offish〕 toward 《a person》 ; [태도가] be unfamiliar with 《a thing》 ¶ 둘 사이는 차츰 서름해졌다 The two have gradually became estranged.

서릊다 ① [쓸다] throw out ; sweep
② [설겆다] do dishes

‡서리[1] frost ; white frost ¶ 서리가 내리고 있다 Frost falls. // 마당에 서리가 내렸다 There is frost on the ground.
— 병아리 a chicken born in late autumn ; [비유적] a weakling ; a runt 된— a heavy frost ; a sharp frost 무— an early frost

서리[2] a group raid 《on another's property》 (out of a mischievous motive) —하다 make a raid 《on another's property》 닭 — a raid on a person's chickens 참외 — a raid on a melon patch

서리[3] [무더기] a mass ; a group
나무 — a lot of wood 사람 — a crowd 〔throng〕 of people

서리 署理 [사람] a chargé d'affaires 《프》 ; a deputy official ; an acting director ; [일] administering as an acting director ; procuration ; proxy ; attorneyship —하다 administer 《affairs》 as an acting director ¶ 서리를 보다 act for ; act in place〔behalf〕 of ; stand proxy for
교장 — an acting principal ; the acting director 《of the school》 국무 총리 — the acting premier

서리 犀利 keenness ; acuteness —하다 (be) keen ; acute ; penetrating

서리다[1] ① [김이] steam up ; get steamed ¶ 안경에 김이 서렸다 My glasses steamed up. // 유리창에 김이 서렸다 The window is steamed up. ② 《an expression, color, blood》 suffuse 《the eyes, the face》 ; 《an emotion》 fill one's breast ③ [기가 꺾이다] have the starch taken out of one ; be taken down a peg〔notch〕

서리다[2] coil ⇨ 사리다

서리막이 a protective cover against frost ; a frost protector —하다 shelter 《a tree》 from the frost

서리맞다 be touched with frost ; be frosted 《over》 ; [비유적] be frustrated ; be nipped in the bud ¶ 꽃이 서리맞았다 The flower is nipped by frost. // 장사에서 서리맞다 fail in one's business

서리서리 coil after coil ; in a coil ; round and round ; in a circle ¶ 줄을 서리서리 감다 wind a rope round 《a thing》

서림 書林 a bookstore ; a bookshop ⇨ 서점

서릿바람 a frosty wind ; a chilly wind

‡서릿발 ① frost columns ; ice needles ② rigor ; sternness ; relentlessness ¶ 서릿발 같은 논고 a most relentless argument

서막 序幕 ① [극의] an opening act 〔scene〕 ; a curtain raiser ② [일의] a prelude 《to an entertainment, event》 ; a beginning ¶ 이것이 학교 분규의 서막이 됐다 This proved a prelude to the complications at the school.

서머 summer
— 스쿨 a summer school (하기 학교) — 타임 daylight-saving time 《DST》 《미》 ; summer time 《S. T.》 (하기〔태양 절약〕 시간) 《영》 — 하우스 a summer house (피서용 별장)

서머하다 feel ashamed ¶ 서머한 표정이다 be shamefaced // 서머해서 그런 말을 할 수가 없었다 I was ashamed to say such things.

서먹하다 feel awkward〔embarrassed〕 ; be ill at ease ; (be) unfamiliar ¶ 서먹하게 침묵을 지키다 keep awkward silence // 그들 사이가 서먹해졌다 They don't get on so well as before. /They are on bad terms now.

서면 書面 [편지] a letter ; [문서] writings ; a document ; [내용] contents ¶ 서면으로 by letter ; in writing ; in a written statement // 서면 또는 구두로 in writing or orally
— 결의 a documentary resolution — 심리 a documentary examination — 주문 a written order

†서명 署名 signing ; autographing ; a signature ; an autograph —하다 sign one's name ; affix〔attach〕 one's signature 《to a document》 ; write one's autograph ¶ 조약에 서명하다 sign a treaty // 협약에 서명하다 put an agreement under one's signature // 타이프한 편지에 서명하다 affix one's signature to a typewritten letter
—국 a signatory — 날인 signing and sealing —부 an autograph album — 운동 a signature-seeking campaign〔drive〕 ; a campaign to obtain signatures —자 a signer 《to》 ; a signatory 하기〔상기〕 —자 the undersigned〔abovesigned〕

서명 書名 the title〔name〕 of a book ¶ 그 신간의 서명은 「인간의 행위」이다 The new book is entitled "Human Behavior".

서모 庶母 one's father's concubine
서목 書目 [서류의] the list of contents (attached to a document) ; [책자의] a catalogue of books
참고 — a list of reference books ; a bibliography
서몽 瑞夢 a lucky〔an auspicious, a propitious〕 dream
서무 庶務 general affairs
—과 the general affairs section — 규정 regulations concerning office routine
⁑서문 序文 a preface ; a foreword ; an introduction

> 참고 **introduction**은 본문 중의 「서론」 **preface**는 본문과는 별도로 저자 또는 저자 이외의 사람이 쓴 「서문」 **foreword**는 짧고 간결한 「머리말」

¶ 서문을 쓰다 preface 《a book》 ; write a preface to 《a book》
서민 庶民 common people ; populace ; commoners ; the commons ; the masses (대중)
— 계급 the humble classes ; the working classes — 금고〔은행〕 the People's Bank — 금융 petty loans for the working classes ; small loan finance — 문학 popular literature — 사회 democratic 〔demotic〕 society
서반구 西半球 the Western hemisphere
서발 序跋 a preface and a postscript 《to a book》 ; prolog(ue) and epilog(ue)
서방 西方 [서쪽] the west ; [서양] the West ; Western countries
— 정토 〖불교〗 the Western Paradise ; the Buddhist Elysium —측 (the side of) the West ; the Western Powers
서방 書房 [남편] one's husband ; one's master ; [호칭] Mr.
서방맞다 get a husband ; be married 《to》
서방 정토 西方淨土 the Western Paradise ; the Buddhist Elysium
서방질 (a married woman's) adultery ; cuckolding —하다 cuckold ; commit adultery
서배 鼠輩 worthless fellows
서벅거리다 crunch softly
서벅돌 a fragile〔crumbly〕 stone
서법 書法 calligraphy ; penmanship
서법 敍法 〖문법〗 the mood
서변 西邊 the westward ; the western part
†서부 西部 the western part ; the west ; the West (미국의)
—극 a western drama〔film〕 ; cowboy pictures ; a horse opera 《미·속》 — 음악 western music — 전선 the Western Front — 지방 the West (미국의)
서부렁섭적 with a light〔casual〕 jump across〔up〕
서부렁하다 (be) slightly loose
*서북 西北 the northwest ; the northwestward ; [한국의] the western and northern provinces of Korea ¶ 서북의 northwestern ; northwesterly // 서북으로 northwestward
—서 (西) the north-west-by-west ; west-northwest 《WNW》 —풍 a northwestern wind ; a northwesterly — 항로 the northwest passage — 해안 the northwestern coast
서북향 西北向 facing the northwest ; a northwestern exposure〔aspect〕
서분서분하다 (be) docile ⇨ 사분사분하다
서분하다 (be) slightly loose ⇨ 서부렁하다
서브 a serve ; 〖경기〗 a service ¶ 서브(를) 넣다 serve 《a ball》 // 서브를 받다 receive the service // 서브가 훌륭하다〔서투르다〕 be a good〔poor〕 server
서브권 —權 〖배구〗 《one's》 serve ¶ 서브권을 얻다 get the serve // 서브권을 되찾다 get back the serve
서브타이틀 a subtitle ¶ 서브타이틀을 붙이다 subtitle 《a book》
서비스 ① [친절·봉사] a service 《종종 *pl.*》 —하다 give one's service ; attend on 《a customer》 ¶ 서비스가 좋다〔나쁘다〕 They give good〔poor〕 service 《in that hotel》. // 이것은 서비스입니다 This is on the house. ② 〖정구·탁구〗 a service ⇨ 서브
—료(料) a tip ; [요정 따위의] the cover charge ¶ 서비스료로 셈의 1할을 청구하다 charge ten percent of the bill for service // 서비스료를 포함시키다 include service charges in the bill — 스테이션 a service station — 코트 〖정구〗 a service court
서뿐 ⇨ 사뿐
서뿟서뿟 with a light-footed step ⇨ 사뿟사뿟
서사 序詞 (a) prologue ; (a) foreword ; (a) preface
서사 敍事 narration ; description —하다 narrate ; describe ¶ 서사적 descriptive ; narrative
—문 a description ; a narrative —시 an epic (poem) ; descriptive poetry ; [총칭] epos ; epic poetry —시 시대 the age of epos〔the epic〕 — 시인 an epic poet ; an epicist
서사 書肆 a bookstore
서사 書寫 transcription ; copying
—료 a copying fee
서산 西山 a western mountain
서상 瑞相 a good omen ; an auspicious 〔happy〕 sign
서생 書生 [유생] a student of Chinese classics ; a young Confucianist ; [남의 집 일을 돕는] a student dependent ; a student houseboy
서서히 徐徐— slowly ⇨ 천천히
서설 序說 an introduction ; introductory remarks ; prolegomenon 《*pl.* -na》
서설 瑞雪 propitious〔auspicious〕 snow ; snow of good omen

서성거리다 walk up and down restlessly ; go back and forth disquietly ¶ 서성거리지 말 것 No Loitering. // 그는 어찌할 줄 몰라 서성거렸다 He walked back and forth, uncertain what to do. // 요즈음 수상한 남자가 집 밖에서 서성거리고 있다 There's been a suspicious-looking man hanging around outside my house lately.

서성서성 pacing back and forth uncertainly

서속 黍粟 millet

서수 序數 〖수학〗 an ordinal (number)
—사(詞) ordinal numerals

⁑서술 敍述 description ; depiction ; narration ; 〖논리〗 predication **—하다** describe ; depict ; narrate ¶ 서술적 descriptive ; narrative // 서술의 형식 a form of description〔narration〕
—문〔어〕 the predicate (of a sentence) **—자** a narrator ; a depictor **— 형용사** 〖문법〗 a predicative adjective

서스펜디드 게임 〖야구〗 a suspended game

***서스펜스** suspense ¶ 서스펜스가 넘치는 suspenseful
— 소설 a novel of suspense

서슬 ① [칼날] the sharpness〔edge〕 of a blade ¶ 서슬이 시퍼런 칼 a sharp〔glittering〕 sword
② [기세] one's mettle〔spirit〕 ¶ 서슬이 시퍼렇다 be mettlesome ; be sharp

서슴거리다 hesitate ⇨ 서슴다

서슴다 hesitate ; waver ; falter ¶ 서슴지 않고 without hesitation〔flinching〕 // 죽음도 서슴지 않다 do not hesitate even to die

서슴서슴 hesitatingly ; shilly-shally ; falteringly ; irresolutely

서슴없다 (be) unhesitant ¶ 서슴없이 without hesitation ; unhesitatingly // 그는 무엇이든 서슴없이 할 사람이다 He will go to any extreme.

서식 書式 a (fixed) form ; a formula ¶ 제 3 호 서식 Form No. 3 // 일정한 서식 a prescribed〔due〕 form // 서식대로 in due form ; according to〔in accordance with〕 the form prescribed // 서식대로 기입하다 fill up〔in〕 a blank〔form〕
—집(集) a collection of forms ; a formulary

서식 棲息 habitation ; inhabitation **—하다** inhabit ; live ¶ 서식할 수 있다 be inhabitable // 수중에 서식하다 live in water // 숲에 서식하다 inhabit a forest
— 동물 an inhabitant 《of the wood》 **—지** a habitat ; a haunt ; a home

서신 書信 [편지] a letter ; a message ; an epistle ; [편지 왕래] correspondence ; communication

서악 序樂 an overture ; a prelude

서안 西岸 the west coast

서안 書案 a writing table ; a desk ; a draft

†서약 誓約 an oath ; a vow ; a pledge **—하다** swear ; vow ; pledge ; take〔swear, make〕 an oath ; give one's pledge 《that》 ; pledge oneself 《to do》 ; give one's word ¶ 서약을 지켜서 faithful to one's vow ; in conformity with one's pledge // 서약시키다 administer an oath to // 비밀을 지키겠다고 서약하다 take an oath of secrecy // 서약을 실행하다 put one's pledge into effect // 서약을 지키다〔깨뜨리다〕 keep〔break〕 one's pledge
—서 a written oath〔pledge〕 ; a written promise〔pact〕 ; a covenant **—자** a pledger ; a party to a covenant ; a recognizor

†서양 西洋 Western countries ; the West ; the Occident
—목(木) cotton cloth **— 문명** Western civilization **— 문학** Western literature ; European literature **—사(紗)** loosewoven cotton cloth ; imported silk muslin **—식** Western style ; Occidental〔European〕 manner **—인** a Westerner ; an Occidental ; a European **— 제국** the Western countries **—풍** ⇨ 양풍 **—화(化)** Westernization ; Europeanization **—화** ⇨ 양화(洋畫)

서어하다 齟齬— ① (be) inconsistent〔contradictory〕 ② (be) frustrated

***서언 序言, 緖言** a foreword ; a preface ⇨ 머리말

서역 西域 the countries bordering on Western China

서열 暑熱 the (summer) heat

서열 序列 order ; grade ; rank

서염 暑炎 extremely hot weather ; the intense heat (of summer)

서예 書藝 calligraphy ; penmanship ¶ 서예의 대가 a master〔great〕 calligrapher

서운 瑞雲 propitious〔auspicious〕 clouds ; clouds of good omen

서운하다 [주로 1인칭 주어] (be) sorry ; regrettable ; unsatisfied ; feel somewhat unsatisfied ; miss ¶ 서운한 대우 unfair treatment // 당신이 거기에 오지 않아서 서운했소 I missed you there very much. // 어쩐지 서운한 점이 있소 It leaves something to be desired.

서운해하다 [주로 2·3인칭 주어] be sorry ; be saddened by ; miss ¶ 그 처사를 서운해하고 있다 He considers that treatment unfair.

서울 *Seoul*〔the capital of Korea〕 ; [수도] a capital ¶ 영국의 서울 런던 London, the capital of England
— 깍쟁이 the shrewd Seoulite ; a Seoulite **—내기** *Seoul*-born ; a Seoulite **— 시민** a citizen of *Seoul* ; a Seoulite 《구》 **— 시장(市長)** the Mayor〔Governor〕 of *Seoul* (Metropolis) **— 시청** the City Hall of *Seoul* ; the *Seoul* Metropolitan Government (Office) **—역** *Seoul* Station **— 장안** 《in》 all *Seoul* **— 특별시** the Metropolis of *Seoul* ; the *Seoul* Metropo-

lis
서울 소식은 시골 가서 들어라 속담 You must go into the country to hear what news at London./Go abroad and you'll hear news of home./If you will learn news, you must go to the oven or the mill.
서울에 가야 과거를 급제하지 속담 Nothing venture, nothing win.
서원 書院 [글방] a lecture hall ; an auditorium ; [제사하는 곳] a memorial hall for Confucianist services to honor distinguished scholars and statesmen
서원 署員 ① [경찰서] a member of the police staff〔force〕 ② [세무·소방서] a member《of the tax office, the fire station》
서원 誓願 a vow ; a pledge ; an oath ―하다 vow〔make a vow〕 to ; swear (an oath) ; pledge oneself to ; pronounce a vow
―서(書) a written oath〔pledge〕 공식 ― a public vow
서유럽 西― West(ern) Europe ; the West
서이 [세 사람] three persons ; [셋] three ¶ 아이가 서이 있는 아버지 a father of three children
서인도 西印度 West(ern) India
― 제도(諸島) the West Indies
서임 敍任 appointment ; investiture ; installation ―하다 appoint ; install
서자 庶子 [첩자식] a child born of a concubine ; [사생아] an illegitimate child ; a natural child ; a bastard ; a child born out of wedlock
서작 敍爵 conferment of a peerage ; ennoblement ―하다 confer a peerage on ; ennoble ; knight ; raise to the peerage ¶ 그들은 서작되었다 They earned their peerages.
서장 西藏 ⇨ 티벳
서장 書狀 a letter ; a note ⇨ 편지
서장 署長 the head of a government office 경찰 ― a police superintendent ; the chief constable ; the chief of a police station
†서재 書齋 ① a study ; a library ② a village school
―인(人) a scholar ; an academic person
서적 書籍 books ; publications
― 목록 a catalog(ue) of books ― (수집)광 [일] bibliomania ; [사람] a bibliomaniac ―상 [가게] a bookshop《영》; a bookstore《미》; [사람] a bookseller ― 애호가 a lover of books ; a bibliophilist ; bibliophile ― 출판업 the publishing business ― 해제 a bibliography
서전 緖戰 the beginning〔an early stage〕 of a war
서절 暑節 the hot season ; midsummer
서점 書店 a bookshop ; a bookstore ¶ 그것은 어느 서점에서나 구할 수 있다 You can get it through any bookseller〔at any bookseller's〕.
서점 西漸 a westward advance〔movement, penetration〕; a drive to〔pressure on〕 the west
서정 庶政 general administrative affairs (of a state)
― 쇄신(刷新) purification〔renovation〕 of officialdom ; enforcement of official discipline
*서정 敍情, 抒情 delineation〔description〕 of feeling ; lyricism ―하다 delineate〔describe〕《one's》 feeling ¶ 서정적 lyrical // 이 작가는 서경(敍景)보다는 서정에 능숙하다 This writer is a delineator of passions rather than of scenery.
―문 lyric writing ―시 a lyric (poem) ; an ode ; [총칭] lyric poetry ; lyric verse
― 시인 a lyric poet
서조 瑞兆 a good〔an auspicious〕 omen
서족 庶族 descendants from a concubine ; a concubine line of the family
서주 序奏 an introduction
―곡 an entree〔overture〕; a prelude
서중 暑中 during the hot weather ; the hot season ; midsummer
*서지 書誌 a bibliography
―학 the (science of) bibliography ―학자 a bibliographer
서지 serge (cloth) ¶ 남색의 서지 blue serge // 얇은 서지 sergette
―옷 a serge suit 면― cotton serge 순모― woolen serge
서진 書鎭 a (paper) weight ⇨ 문진(文鎭)
⁑서쪽 西― the west ; the westward ¶ 서쪽의 west ; western ; westerly // 서쪽으로 west ; westward ; toward the west // 서쪽으로 가다 go west〔westward〕; proceed west // 저 멀리 서쪽에 삼각산이 솟아 있다 Mt. *Samgak* soars to the west.
서차 序次 order ⇨ 차례
서창 西窓 a west(ward) window
서책 書冊 books ; publications
서천 西天 the western sky ; the sky in the west
서철 西哲 [사람] a Western philosopher ; [철학] Western〔European, Occidental〕 philosophy
서첩 書帖 a scrapbook (of writings and pictures)
서체 書體 handwriting
서체 暑滯 indigestion due to the heat
서출 庶出 an offspring of a concubine ¶ 서출의 born out of wedlock
서취 書取 ⇨ 받아쓰기
서치라이트 a searchlight ¶ 서치라이트로 비추다 turn〔play〕 a searchlight《on, about》
서커스 a circus (show) ; a bigtop《미·구》 ¶ 서커스 단장〔곡예사〕 a circus master〔performer〕// 서커스를 흥행하다 run a circus
서캐 nits ¶ 서캐 훑듯 하다 leave no stone unturned《in a search》

— 조롱 〖민속〗 a girl's wooden tag — 훑이 a fine-tooth comb

서클 a circle
독서 — a reading circle 정치〔사회〕 문제 연구 — a study circle for political 〔social〕 problems

서털구털 clumsily — 하다 (be) clumsy ; churlish ¶ 서털구털한 품행 boorish manners ; rustic manners // 서털구털한 대답을 하다 give a random answer

서퇴 暑退 abatement〔easing〕 of the hot weather ; cooling down — 하다 The hot weather abates. /It cools down〔off〕.

‡서투르다 ① [소원하다] (be) unfamiliar ; strange ② [미숙하다] (be) unpracticed ; unskilled ; awkward ; clumsy ; poor ¶ 서투른 동작 stiff manners // 계산이 서투르다 He is bad at figures. /He is a bad〔poor〕 hand at accounts. // 한국 사정에 서투르다 be unfamiliar with things Korean // 서투른 영어로 말하다 speak in poor〔broken〕 English // 젓가락질이 아직 서투르다 He is still awkward with chopsticks. // 옷을 서투르게 입었다 She dressed awkwardly.
서투른 과방 안반 타박 〔속담〕 A bad workman always blames his tools.

서편 西便 the west ¶ 서편의 west ; western // 교회의 서편에 (to the) west of the church

서평 書評 a book review
—가 a book reviewer —난 the book-review columns

서표 書標 a book mark(er)

서푼 —分 three *pun* ; of little worth ¶ 서푼어치도 못 된다 It is not worth a farthing〔penny, button〕.

서푼서푼 with soft (muffled) step(s) ; lightly

서품 敍品 ordination
—식(式) the ceremony of ordination

서풋(서풋) with a light-footed step

서풍 西風 [서쪽에서 부는 바람] a west 〔westerly〕 wind ; 〖시〗 zephyr (의인화하여) ; [추풍 (⇨ 갈바람)] an autumn wind 〔breeze〕

서풍 書風 a kind〔style〕 of writing ; handwriting

서핑 surfing

서학 西學 Western Learning

서한 書翰 a letter ; an epistle

서해 西海 the west(ern) sea ; [황해] the Yellow Sea

‡서행 徐行 going slow(ly) ; "Slow (down)" (게시) — 하다 go slow(ly) ; crawl ; slow down
— 속도 (a) slow speed — 신호기 a slow speed signal

서향 西向 (having) a west exposure ; facing west
—집 a house facing west ; a house with a western exposure ; a house open to the west

서향나무 瑞向— 〖식물〗 daphne

서혜 鼠蹊 〖해부〗 the groin
—부 the groin〔inguinal〕 region —선(腺) 〖해부〗 the inguinal glands —선종(腫) 〖의학〗 a bubo 《*pl.* -es》

서화 書畫 paintings〔pictures〕 and writings
— 골동 《deal in》 objects of art and curios —상 a dealer in pictures and writings — 전람회 an exhibition of pictures and writings —첩 a scrapbook of pictures and writings

서훈 敍勳 conferment of a decoration ; bestowal of an order — 하다 confer a decoration ; invest 《a person》 with a decoration ; decorate

석 three ¶ 석달 three months

석 石 ⇨ 섬[1]

석 錫 tin

-석 席 a seat ; a place
부인— the ladies' seat 일반— a general admission seat

석가 釋迦 Sakyamuni ; Buddha ¶ 석가에게 설법하기 Teach your grandmother to suck eggs.
—모니, —여래(如來) ⇨ 석가

석가산 石假山 an artificial hill 《in a garden》 ; a rock garden

석각 石刻 stone carving — 하다 carve in stone

석간 夕刊 an evening paper ; the evening edition
— 신문〔지〕 an evening paper

석경 夕景 evening scenery

석경 石鏡 a mirror ; a looking glass

석계 石階 stone steps

‡석고 石膏 gyps(um) ; plaster of Paris (소석고) ; gesso (미술용)
— 모형 〖의학〗 a plaster cast — 붕대 plaster bandage —상 a plaster bust〔figure, statue〕 — 세공 plaster work ¶ 석고 세공인 a plasterer — 조각 gypsography —틀 a gypsum〔plaster〕 mold 분말 — land plaster 섬유 — satin spar〔stone〕

‡석공 石工 [석수] a stonecutter ; a stonemason ; [석공업] masonry

석관 石棺 a stone coffin ; a sarcophagus

석광 錫鑛 a tin mine ; stannary

석괴 石塊 a (piece of) stone ; a pebble
— 포장(鋪裝) stone block pavement

석교 石橋 a stone bridge

석구 石臼 a stone mill〔mortar〕

석굴 石窟 a stone cave ; a rocky cavern
—암 *Sogguram* cave〔grotto〕

석권 席卷 — 하다 make a conquest of ; sweep 《over a place》 ¶ 전아시아를 석권하다 sweep over the whole of Asia

석기 石器 a stone implement ; [석조물] stone work
— 시대 〖고고〗 the Stone Age ¶ 구석기 시대 the pal(a)eolithic age ; the Old Stone Age // 신석기 시대 the neolithic age ; the New Stone Age 박편(剝片)〔핵〕 — a flake〔core〕 tool

석남 石南 〖식물〗 a rhododendron ; Andromeda polifolia (학명)
석녀 石女 a sterile〔barren〕 woman
석년 昔年 [옛날] ancient times ; [작년] last year
석뇌유 石腦油 〖화학〗 naphtha
석다 [눈이] melt ; thaw ; [양조물이] mellow ¶ 술이 석다 rice wine mellows
석다치다 drive a horse with a bit in its mouth
석단 石壇 a stone platform〔stage〕
석대 石臺 a stone embankment
석도 石刀 a stone blade
석돌 ⇨ 푸석돌
석동 〖민속〗 ① [말] the third of the four markers to be taken around the board in a game of *yut* ② [판] one's third round in a game of *yut*
— 무늬 letting three markers pile up at one point on the *yut* board
석두 石頭 a foolish〔stupid〕 man
석등 石燈 ⇨ 장명등(長明燈)
석랍 石蠟 〖화학〗 coal oil ; paraffin (wax)
석류 石榴 〖식물〗 a pomegranate (tree)
석류석 石榴石 〖광물〗 garnet
석마 石磨 ⇨ 맷돌
석면 石綿 〖광물〗 asbestos ; chrysotile
석명 釋明 explanation ; elucidation ; explication —하다 explain ; give an explanation of ; make clear ; clear up ; elucidate ; explicate ; vindicate
석묵 石墨 black lead ; graphite ; plumbago
석문 石門 a stone gate
석물 石物 stone figures (of men and animals) placed before a tomb
석박 錫箔 tinfoil
석반 夕飯 supper
*석방 釋放 release ; liberation ; discharge ; acquittal —하다 set 《a person》 free〔at liberty〕 ; release ; liberate ; acquit ; let off ¶ 그는 재판을 받고 무죄 석방됐다 He was tried and acquitted.
석벌의 집 石— [벌집] a beehive built in between the rocks ; [사물] a thing which looks like a beehive in the rocks
석벽 石壁 a stone wall ; a cliff (낭떠러지)
석별 惜別 parting with regrets ; regretful parting ; reluctance to leave —하다 part with regrets ; regret parting ¶ 석별의 눈물 tears at parting // 석별의 정 a heartbreaking sentiment at parting
—연 a farewell party〔banquet〕
석부 石斧 a stone axe
석불 石佛 a stone (statue of) Buddha
석비 石碑 a stone monument
석비레 clay mixed with soft〔crumbly〕 stones
—담 a wall built of clay mixed with soft stones
석사 碩士 [선비] a worthy scholar (though holding no office) ; [학위] Master
— 과정 the master's course — 논문 a master's thesis — 학위 a master's degree 문학 — Master of Arts (M. A.) 이학 — Master of Science (M. S(c).)
석산 石山 a stony mountain ; a rock(y) mountain
석산 石蒜 〖식물〗 *Manjusaka* 《범》 ; *Lycoris radiata* (학명)
석삼년 —三年 nine years ; a long time
석상 石像 a stone image〔statue〕
석상 席上 during the meeting ; in company ¶ 회의 석상에서 발언하다 speak at a conference
석새 60-strand warp
— 삼베 60-strand (coarse) hemp cloth
— 짚신 coarse straw-sandals
*석쇠 gridiron ; grill
석수 石手 a stonemason ¶ 석수질 masonry (work)
석수 石獸 a stone image of an animal (set before a tomb)
석수 汐水 the evening tide
석수어 石首魚 a yellow corvina fish ⇨ 조기
석순 石筍 〖광물〗 a stalagmite
석순 席順 ⇨ 석차
석양 夕陽 the setting sun ; the evening sun ¶ 석양녘 toward sunset // 석양빛 the splendor〔glow〕 of the setting sun
석얼음 [수정 속의] flaws in a crystal ; [유리창의] frostwork on a window(-pane) ; [뜬얼음] floating ice ; an ice floe ¶ 창에 석얼음이 끼었다 The windows have iced up.
석연하다 釋然— be relieved from doubt ; free from doubt ; be satisfied 《with the explanation》 ¶ 석연히 with sudden relief from doubt ; with sudden illumination // 석연치 않다 be not quite satisfied 《with the explanation》 // 석연치 않은 인물 a doubtful character
석염 石鹽 〖광물〗 rock salt
—갱 a salt mine — 채굴 salt-mining
*석영 石英 〖광물〗 quartz
— 반암(斑岩) quartz porphyry —사 quartz sand —암 quartzite — 유리 quartz glass — 조면암(粗面岩) quartz trachyte — 편암(片岩)〔규장암(珪長岩)〕 quartz schist〔felsite〕 녹(綠)— prase
*석유 石油 petroleum ; kerosene (등불용)
— 가스 petroleum gas ¶ 액화 석유 가스 liquefied petroleum gas 《LPG》 —갱(坑) a petroleum well ; an oil well — 공업 the petroleum〔oil〕 industry — 난로 a kerosene stove —등 an oil〔kerosene〕 lamp — 발동기〔엔진〕 a petroleum〔an oil〕 engine〔motor〕 — 수출국 기구 the Organization of Petroleum Exporting Countries 《OPEC》 — 업자 an oilman — 유제 petroleum emulsion —왕 an oil baron〔king〕 — 탱크 an oil tank — 회사 an oil company 대한 — 공사 the Korea Oil Corporation 《KOCO》

석유 자원 石油資源 petroleum resources ; oil riches ¶ 석유 자원을 개발하다 develop〔exploit〕 petroleum resources
석유 화학 石油化學 petrochemistry
— 공업 the petrochemical industry — 공장 a petrochemical plant — 제품 petrochemicals
석유황 石硫黃 〖광물〗 orpiment arsenic trisulfide ; gold pigment
석의 釋義 a commentary ; an exposition
석이 石耳 〖식물〗 a manna lichen ; Gyrophora esculenta (학명)
석이다 [녹게 하다] cause《snow》 to thaw ; thaw ; [양조물이] cause《a brew》 to mellow ; ferment
석인 石人 a stone statue ; a stone image
석인 石印 a stone seal
석일 昔日 old days ⇨ 옛날
석임 fermenting ; fermentation —하다 ferment ; undergo fermentation
석자 a ladle with meshes《for dipping up fried food》
석장 錫杖 a monk's staff
석장 石匠 ⇨ 석공, 석수
석재 石材 stone ; building stone
—상 a stone dealer
석전 石田 a stony field
석전 石戰 [놀이] a mock fight with stone missiles
석전 釋典 Buddhist scriptures
석전 釋奠 the (semiannual) festival in honor of Confucius
석조 夕照 the evening glow
석조 石造 (being) stone built ; (of) stone ¶ 석조집 a stone house
— 가옥〔집〕 stone〔stone-built〕 house〔building〕
석존 釋尊 Sakyamuni ; Buddha
석종유 石鍾乳 〖광물〗 a stalactite
석주 石柱 a stone pillar〔column〕 ; a pillar of stone
석죽 石竹 〖식물〗 a pink ; a China pink ; Dianthus sinensis (학명)
석차 席次 the order of seats〔places〕 ; a seating order ; precedence ; standing ; ranking ¶ 졸업 석차 graduation standing // 석차가 떨어지다〔올라가다〕 lose〔gain〕 one's place in the class
— 다툼 a quarrel over precedence (회장(會場) 따위에서의) ; a competition for higher class standing (학교에서의)
석찬 夕餐 dinner ; supper ; the evening meal
석창포 石菖蒲 〖식물〗 a sweet flag ; sweet rush ; Acorus gramineus (학명)
석천 石泉 a spring coming out of the stones
석청 石淸 wild honey ; honey found in the crevices of rocks
석촉 石鏃 a flint arrowhead
석총 石塚 ⇨ 돌무덤
석축 石築 a stone wall for reinforcement
석출 析出 eduction ; extraction —하다 educe ; extract
†**석탄 石炭** coal ¶ 불타는 석탄 덩이 a hot coal // 석탄을 때다 burn coal // 석탄을 싣다 take in coal ; coal // 석탄을 파다 dig (out) coal // 석탄을 연료로 쓰다 use coal for fuel // 동력 자원으로서 석유와 전력이 석탄과 대치되었다 As the source of power, petroleum and electricity have now replaced coal.
— 가루 coal dust — 가스 coal gas —갱 a coal mine〔pit〕 — 갱부 a (coal) miner ; a collier — 건류(乾溜) coal carbonization —계(系) 〖지질〗 the Carboniferous System —광 a coal mine — 광업권 the coal mining right — 그릇, —궤 a coal scuttle —기(紀) the Carboniferous (period) — 도매상 a coal factor — 매장량 coal deposits — 보급지 a coal base — 산 carbolic acid ; phenol — 산지 a coal field —선 [운반용의] a collier《영》; a coal ship — 액화(液化) coal liquefaction ; liquefaction of coal — 운반 인부 a coal heaver ; a coalwhipper — 저장소 a coalbin — 조절 장치 a coal economizer — 찌끼 (coal) cinders —차 a coal truck〔lorry〕 —층 a coal seam ; a coal bed —통 a coal-box — 포대 a coalsack — 화학 coal chemistry 기관용 — steam coal 대한 — 공사 the Korea Coal Corporation
석탑 石塔 a stone pagoda〔tower〕
석태 石苔 〖식물〗 lichens ; moss
석판 石板 a slate ; a slab of stone
*__석판 石版__ lithography (기술) ; a lithograph (그림)
— 용지 lithographic paper — 인쇄 lithography ; lithographic printing —화 a lithograph ¶ 착색 석판화 a chromolithograph 사진 —술 photolithography
석패 惜敗 defeat by a narrow margin ; a regrettable defeat —하다 lose〔be defeated〕 by a narrow margin ; suffer a regrettable defeat
석편 石片 a piece of stone
석필 石筆 a slate pencil
석하 夕霞 an evening mist〔haze〕
석학 碩學 a great scholar ; a distinguished scholar ; a man of deep learning
석함 石函 a stone case〔box〕
석화 石花 an oyster
석화 石火 [돌을 쳐서 일어난 불] flint fire ; [순간] a flash ¶ 전광석화같이 like a flash of lightning ; in a flash
—광음 fleeting time
석화채 石花菜 〖식물〗 agar-agar
석황 石黃 orpiment
⁑**석회 石灰** ① lime ② calcium carbonate (탄산칼슘) ¶ 석회가 되다 calcify ; calcine
— 가루 lime powder —동(洞) a lime grotto —분(分) lime percentage〔ratio〕 —석 limestone —수 limewater ; lime and water —유 milk〔cream〕 of lime —질

compounds of calcium ¶ 석회질의 calcareous ; calcic — 질소 calcium cyanamide ; lime nitrogen —토(土) lime mortar — 해면류 calcarea —화(化) calcification —화(華) calcareous ; sinter ; calcsinter ; travertin(e) ; (calcareous) tufa ; calc-tufa〔tuff〕; flowers of lime 생 — quick〔caustic, unslaked〕 lime 소 — slaked〔slack, dead, hydrated〕 lime 탄화 — (calcium) carbide

섞갈리다 be confusing ; be confused 〔mixed up〕; get tangled〔complicated〕 ¶ 이 사건은 여러 문제가 섞갈려 있다 Various circumstances are involved in this event.

† **섞다** mix ; blend ; mingle ; adulterate (with)

> 참고 **mix**는 「섞다」의 가장 일반적인 말 **blend**는 복합 성질의 것을 얻기 위하여 두 세 가지를 「섞다」 혼합물에 각 성질이 다소 남음 **mingle**은 식별할 수 있는 각 요소를 「섞다」 **adulterate**는 나쁜 성질의 것을 섞어서 열등 불순한 것으로 만듦

¶ 사실과 허구를 섞은 소설 a novel blending fact and fiction // 물감을 섞다 mix paints // 빨강에다 흰색을 섞다 blend red with some white // 우유에다 물을 섞다 adulterate milk with some water // 과실을 몇 종류 섞어서 주시오 Mix (up) several kinds of fruits, please. // 이 술은 물을 섞었다 This drink is adulterated with water. (나쁜 술)/This drink is diluted with water. (먹기 좋게 하기 위해서)

섞바꾸다 take the wrong one ; mistake one for the other ; mistake 《a person》 for another ; mix 《things》 up

섞바뀌다 be mixed up ; be mistaken for

섞사귀다 mix〔associate〕 with 《a person of different social standing》

섞음질 adulteration —하다 mix 《a thing》 with ; adulterate ¶ 섞음질하지 않은 pure // 섞음질한 물건 a mixture ; a compound ; impurities

†**섞이다** be mixed〔mingled, blended〕 ¶ 물과 기름은 섞이지 않는다 Oil and water will not mix.

섟[1] [노염] a fit of anger ; a sudden feeling of anger ; [의심] a sudden feeling of doubt ; a (passing) doubt ; a (moment of) suspicion

섟[2] [물가의] a good place to moor a boat

섟삭다 [의심이] be resolved〔dispelled〕; [노염이] 《anger toward a person》 relent ; fade

선 a meeting〔an interview〕 with a view to marriage ; an interview between the prospective bride and groom ; a marriage meeting ¶ 선 보고 하는 결혼 an arranged〔a prearranged〕 marriage // 두 사람은 선도 안 보고 결혼했다 They were married without even going through the formality of a preliminary interview 〔without even a previous chance of seeing each other〕.

선 보다 관용 see each other with a view to marriage ; have an interview with a prospective bride〔bridegroom〕

선 先 ① [장기·바둑에서] the first move ② [죽은] deceased ¶ 선대인 your late father
③ [먼저] ahead ; first (of all)

†**선 善** good ; goodness ; virtue ¶ 선과 악 good and evil ; virtue and vice // 선한 일 good〔virtuous〕 deeds

†**선 線** a line ; a route (교통의) ; a cable 〔wire〕 (전신·전화의)
교통— the lines of transportation 3번— [철도 선로] Track Three ; the third track 38— the 38th parallel 송전 — a power-transmission line〔wire〕 자오 — the meridian line 전(電)— an electric line〔wire〕; a power cable (고압선) 전신 〔전화〕— a telegraph〔telephone〕 wire 평행〔교차〕— a parallel〔cross〕 line〔cable〕 호남— the *Honam* line
선을 긋다 관용 draw a line

*__선 腺__ a gland
—세포 조직 parenchyma 내분비— a ductless gland ; an endocrine (gland) 임파— a lymphatic gland

선 [옷·방석의] an edge ; edging ; a frill ; a border ; trim(ming) ¶ 선을 두르다〔치다〕 sew on a frill〔a border, some edging, some trimming〕

선 禪 Zen ; Dhyana ; Buddhist meditation

선 選 selection ; choice
명작— a selection of masterpieces

선- [덜됨] untrained ; unskil(l)ed ; immature ; green ; new ; novice ; clumsy ; green and fresh
—머슴 a wild〔mischievous〕 boy —무당 a new shaman —밥 half-cooked rice —잠 a light sleep ; a catnap

-선 船 a ship ; a vessel
수송— a transport ship

선가 船價 [배삯] boat〔passage〕 fare ; passage ; freight (rates) ; freightage ; shipping charges ; [배 가격] the cost of a ship (조선비) ; the price of a ship

선가 禪家 the Zen sect ; a Zen temple (집) ; a Zen priest (사람)

선가 船架 a slipway

선각 先覺 foresight ; seeing〔perceiving〕 in advance
—자 a man of foresight ; a pioneer ; a forerunner ; a precursor ; a pathfinder

선감 善感 an effectual vaccination

선개교 旋開橋 a swing〔swivel, turn〕 bridge

선객 先客 a preceding visitor

선객 船客 a (ship) passenger
— 명부 a passenger list〔manifest〕 —실 the passenger quarters 삼등 — a third-

class passenger ; a steerage passenger ; [집합적] the steerage 일등 — a first-class passenger

선거 船渠 a dock

—문 a dock gate — 사용료 dockage ; dock charge〔dues〕 건— a dry dock ; a graving dock

†**선거 選擧** election —하다 elect ; vote for ; return ¶ 선거전의 pre-election《campaign》// 선거에 이기다〔지다〕 win〔be defeated〕 in an election // 선거를 참관하다 witness〔observe〕 polling〔the polls〕// 선거는 3월에 실시된다 The election will take place in March.

— 간섭 《the government》 interference in an election — 공보 the official gazette for election ; a campaign bulletin — 대책 위원회 the election polling committee —민 the voters ; the electorate 《총칭》 — 방송 a 《radio, TV》 broadcast for election campaigning — 방해 election obstruction —법 the election law(s) —법 위반 violation of election laws — 비용 expenses for an election campaign — 사무 election campaign business — 사무소 an electioneering〔a campaign〕 office — 사무장 a campaign manager — 사범 election irregularities — 소송 an election case〔lawsuit〕 — 속보 a prompt report of election returns — 연설 a campaign speech ; an election address (정견 발표의) ; a vote-getting speech (응원의) — 운동 an election campaign ; electioneering ; campaigning — 운동원 an election campaigner ; an election worker ; a participant in the election campaign — 운동비 campaign〔electioneering〕 expenditures — 위원 an election committeeman — 위원장 a campaign chairman ; the chairman of an election committee 《영》 — 위원회 an election committee — 유세 an electioneering〔a stumping〕 tour —인 an elector ; an electress (여자) ; a constituent ; a voter ; the electorate 《총칭》 —인단 the electoral college —인 명부 a poll book ; the voter's list —인 자격 electorship ; the qualifications of an elector ; voting qualifications〔requirements〕 —일 the day of election ; the election〔polling〕 day — 자금 an election campaign fund — 자금 규제법 the election campaign fund regulation law —전(戰) (an) election campaign〔fight〕 — 제도 an election system — 참관인 a witness at an election — 참모 a campaign manager —후(候) 〖역사〗 [신성 로마 제국의] an Elector ; an electoral prince 국회의원 — the election of the Assemblymen 공명〔무효〕 — a fair〔an invalid〕 election 대통령 — a presidential election 보궐 — a by-election ; a special election 《미》 중간 — an off-year〔an interim〕 election 지명 — a nomination (미국 대통령의) 총— a general election 대통령 —인 the presidential electoral college deputies 대통령 —인단 the electoral college (=선거인단) 대통령 —단 선거 the presidential electoral college balloting〔vote〕 ; the election by the presidential electoral college (=선거인 선거)

☞ ◖p. 1191◗

선거 강령 選擧綱領 an election platform

선거 관리 選擧管理 election administration

— 내각 a caretaker government — 위원회 an election administration commission —인 an election judge ; a returning officer 중앙 — 위원회 the Central Election Management Committee 《CEMC》

선거구 選擧區 an election〔electoral, a voting〕 district ; a constituency ; a precinct

대〔중, 소〕 —제 the major〔medium, minor〕 constituency〔electorate〕 system

†**선거권 選擧權** suffrage ; the franchise ; the right to vote ; voting rights ¶ 선거권을 주다 enfranchise ; give the franchise 《to》// 선거권을 행사하다 exercise one's franchise ; exercise the ballot // 선거권을 박탈하다 deprive 《a person》 of the right of casting a ballot ; disfranchise ; disenfranchise

—자 an electorate ; an elector ; a (qualified) voter 보통 — universal〔popular〕 suffrage ; the universal franchise 부인 — the women's〔female〕 suffrage

선겁다 [놀랍다] (be) astonishing ; surprising ; startling ; [재미없다] uninteresting

***선견 先見** foresight ; prescience ; divination —하다 foresee ; see beforehand ¶ 선견 지명이 있는 foresighted ; farseeing ; farsighted ; long-sighted // 선견지명이 없는 lacking foresight ; short-sighted // 선견지명이 있다 have foresight ; be far-sighted

선견 부대 先遣部隊 advance troops ; the first contingent ; the vanguard

선견지명 先見之明 foresightedness ; the gift of foresight ; farseeing wisdom〔intelligence〕 ; vision ¶ 선견지명이 있는 사람 a man of foresight ; a foreseer // 선견지명이 있다 possess the gift of foresight ; have farseeing wisdom

선결 先決 prior〔previous〕 decision —하다 decide〔settle〕 beforehand ; decide〔come〕 first

— 문제 a previous〔prior〕 question ; a matter claiming〔calling for〕 prior settlement ¶ 돈 마련이 선결 문제이다 How to raise money is the first consideration.

선경 仙境 a fairyland ; an elfland ; an enchanted land〔garden〕 (경치가 좋은 곳)

선고 先考 one's deceased father ; one's late father

†**선고 宣告** ① 〖법〗 sentence (판결) ; judg-

선 거

▶**보통선거** popular [universal] election **직접선거** direct election **간접선거** indirect election

▶**총선거** general election **지방선거** local election **지방자치 단체장선거** election of the heads of local autonomies **시장선거** election of a mayor; mayoral election

▶**선거제도** election system **국민 참정권** universal suffrage **선거관리위원회** the Election Administration Committee

▶**보궐선거** election to fill a vacancy; by-election 《영》; special election 《미》 **예비선거** primary [preliminary] (election) 《미》 **대통령 예비 선거** Presidential primary (election) 《미》 **중간선거** off-year election 《미》

▶**신임[불신임]투표** vote of confidence [nonconfidence, censure] **국민투표에 호소하다** go to the people 《정치지도자가》

▶**선거구** election [electoral] district; constituency **유권자** (eligible) voter; elector **선거구민** constituent; electorate **대[소]선거구제** large [small] constituency **전국구** national [nationwide] constituency; Korea-at-large constituency **1인 구(區)** single-seat constituency **2인구(區)** two-seat constituency **선거구 개정** redrawing of electoral zone [districts]; rezoning; redistricting; gerrymander 《당리 당략을 위한》 **비례대표제** election by [under] a proportional representation system

▶**입후보** candidacy; candidature 《영》 **입후보하다** run [stand] in an election; be [become] a candidate; announce one's candidacy; file one's candidacy **입후보 공탁금** deposit for filing candidacy **입후보자** candidate ¶ 입후보자를 내세우다 field [ticket] a candidate; put on the (party) ticket **현역 후보** incumbent (candidate) **후보자의 난립** crowded field of candidates; proliferation of candidates

▶**유력 후보** major candidate [contender]; hopeful ¶ 그는 민주당의 유력한 대통령 후보다. He is a Democratic presidential hopeful. **열세 후보** underdog candidate ¶ 그는 열세 후보지만 선거운동에 열심이다. Although an underdog, he is running hard.

▶**선거의 공시(公示)** official announcement of an election; public notice of an election **선거를 실시하다** hold [call] an election

▶**선거 작전** campaign strategy **선거운동을 하다** stage [deploy, mount, push] a campaign; engage in electioneering **선거자금** campaign spending [expenditure, fund, money, cost] **선거 참모** (chief) campaign strategist

▶**선거운동** election campaign **선거 운동원** campaign worker[staffer]; campaigner; campaign volunteer; electioneer **사전 준비자** advance agent [man 《미》] **선거운동차** campaign car [truck] **선거포스터** campaign poster **선거용 우편물** campaign mail [letter] **정견발표, 선거연설** campaign speech **공개토론** public debate **TV토론** TV debate

▶**선거 유세하다** stump; go on the hustings; hit the campaign trail [road] **선거용 정견(政見)** voting intention (후보자) **연호(連呼)** repetitive shouting of a candidate's name **악수작전** handshake tactic **투표를 부탁하다** ask one to vote for ...; solicit votes for; canvass for... **후보지지 부탁을 위해 돌아다니다** declare support for...; come out in support of...; throw one's support behind...; line up behind ...; jump [hop, get, climb] on a person's bandwagon **선거 초반전[종반전]** early [final, last] stage of a campaign **선전(善戰)하다** put up a good fight **고전(苦戰)** difficult [uphill] campaign ¶ 이번에는 그는 고전하고 있다 This time he is campaigning uphill.

▶**표밭** grass roots **조직표(組織票)** organized votes ¶ 후보자는 보통 조직표 획득에 가장 큰 노력을 기울인다. Candidates usually spend their efforts in winning organized votes **부동표(浮動票)** floating [shifting, uncommitted] votes **개인표** individual votes; unorganized votes **고정표** solid votes; loyal votes **지지표(支持票)** (votes cast in) support **동정표(同情票)** sympathy votes **여성표** women's votes **노조표(勞組票)** labor vote(s) **농촌표** farm vote(s) **노인표** votes of the old people

▶**부정선거** vote rigging **선거법 위반** election law violation; violation of the election law **선거 방해** campaign obstruction **사전 운동(事前運動)** campaigning outside the official campaign period **매수(買收), 매표(賣票)** vote buying **금권선거** bankrolled [moneyed] election **기업동원의 선거**

election campaign with all-out corporate support 향응하다 wine and dine; treat 호별 방문 door-to-door [house-to-house] canvassing (for voters)
▶투표용지 voting paper 《영》; ballot 투표용지 기입소 voting booth ; polling booth 《영》 투표함 ballot box 투표일 election day; voting day 투표소 polling place [station 《영》] 《건물전체를 말함》 ⇨ polling booth 선거인 명부 electoral roll [register]; poll book; poll 투표소에 가다 go to the polls 선거권 취득 연령 voting age
▶투표율 voter turnout 높은 투표율 heavy poll 낮은 투표율 light poll 투표 직후 조사 exit poll 《미》 투표결과를 발표하다 declare the poll 투표입회인 official observer at a polling place [station 《영》] 부재투표 absentee vote [ballot] 기권 abstention 기명[무기명]투표 open [secret] vote 무효투표 spoiled vote
▶개표 counting of votes; vote count (-ing) 투표가 종료하다 The voting ends. The polls close. 투표예측 vote projection 《방송이나 신문에서 다수득표자를 예상 하는 것》 개표결과 election returns 다수표를 얻다 head the polls 개표 속보 up-to-the-minute returns 최종(개표)결과 final returns 선거 개표 보고 election returns 당선을 확정하다 call [declare] a winner 차점이 되다 be [become] the runner- up; end up as runner-up 당선〔낙선〕하다 win [lose] an election; be [fail to be] elected

ment (심판) ; verdict (배심원의) ② [의사 따위의] pronouncement ━하다 sentence ; pass〔pronounce〕 a sentence upon 《a person》 ; condemn ; adjudge ; pronounce ¶ 사형의 선고 a sentence of death // 불치의 병임을 선고받다 be pronounced incurable // 무죄를 선고하다 acquit 《a prisoner》 of a charge // 피고는 무기형의 선고를 받았다 The accused was sentenced to life imprisonment. // 5년형의 선고를 받았다 He was sentenced to five years' imprisonment〔penal servitude〕.
━문 a written sentence ━ 유예 probation 파산 ━ a decree of bankruptcy
선고 選考 ⇨ 전형(銓衡)
선곡 選曲 selection of music
선공 先攻 batting first 《in baseball》 ━하다 (go to) bat first
선과 善果 good fruit ; a good result〔outcome〕 ¶ 선과를 맺다 bear〔bring forth〕 good fruit
선과 選科 an elective〔a special〕 course
━생 an elective〔a special, a nonregular〕 student ; a special 《미》
선관위 選管委 ⇨ 선거 관리(━위원회)
선광 選鑛 concentration〔dressing, separation〕 of ores ; dressing ━하다 dress 《the ores》 ; concentrate
━기 an ore separator ━대(臺) a cradle ; a rocker ━부(夫) an ore dresser ; a jigger ━소 a dressing plant 부유 ━ ore dressing by flotation
선교 宣敎 missionary work ; gospel preaching ━하다 evangelize ; propagandize ; preach the gospel
━사 a missionary ━원(院) (the Congregation for) the Propagation of the Faith (바티칸의)
선교 禪敎 〖불교〗 the Seon〔zen〕〔Dhyāna〕 and the various non-Seon〔Doctrinal〕 Sects of Buddhism
선교 船橋 [배를 잇댄 다리] a pontoon 〔floating, bateau〕 (bridge) ; [배의 다리] a bridge
━ 갑판실 a bridge house
선구 船具 ship's fittings ; rigging ; gearing (색구) ; tackle (조종 도구)
━상 a ship chandler ; a tackle store
선구 先驅 a pioneer ⇨ 선구자
선구안 選球眼 〖야구〗 (a) batting eye ¶ 선구안이 좋다〔나쁘다〕 have a sharp 〔poor〕 batting eye
⁑**선구자 先驅者** a forerunner ; a pioneer ; a herald ; a precursor ; an outrider (마차의 선도자) ¶ 뻐꾸기는 봄의 선구자이다 The cuckoo is a harbinger of spring.
선군 先君 ① ⇨ 선왕(先王) ② one's late father
선굿 an exorcism rite performed by a shaman in the standing position
선근 善根 〖불교〗 good〔charitable〕 deeds ; deeds of Buddhist merit
선글라스 (a pair of) sunglasses ; 《wear》 dark glasses
선금 先金 a prepayment ; payment in advance ; an advance ; the money prepaid〔paid in advance〕 ¶ 선금치르다 pay in advance ; prepay
선급 船級 (ship's) classification〔class〕
선남 선녀 善男善女 good men and women ; pious〔devout, religious〕 people ; votaries ; the faithful
선납 先納 prepayment ; payment in advance
회신료 ━ 전보 a collect telegram
선내 船內 (the inside of) the ship ¶ 선내를 수색하다 search the ship
━ 측면도 an inboard profile
선녀 仙女 a fairy ; a nymph
선다형 選多型 a multiple choice system
선단 a vertical〔an up-and-down〕 hem

선단 船團 a fleet of vessels
수송 — [호위함이 딸린] a convoy of transport ships 출어 — a fishing fleet 포경 — a fleet of whalers
선달 〖건축〗 a piece of wood set over a handspike〔house-jack, pillar-jack〕
선대 先代 the previous age〔generation〕; the predecessor (선조)
선대 船隊 a fleet of ships ⇨ 선단
선대 先貸 payment in advance ; advance payment
· †선도 先導 guidance ; leadership —하다 guide ; lead ; take the lead ; precede ¶ 교장의 선도로 학교를 시찰하다 inspect the school under the guidance of the principal
—자 a guide ; a leader ¶ 문명의 선도자이다 be in the vanguard of civilization —차 [경찰 등의] a (police) pilot car —함 a guide ship
선도 鮮度 (the degree of) freshness ¶ 선도가 높은〔낮은〕 very fresh〔not very fresh〕 // 선도가 떨어지다 lose (some of) 《its》 freshness
선도 善導 proper〔judicious〕 guidance —하다 lead〔guide〕 properly ; guide aright ; instruct ; lead 《a person》 to the path of virtue ; lead 《a person》 into the right path ¶ 국민 사상의 선도 proper guidance of public thought // 선도 받다 be influenced for good 《by》
—책 measures for proper guidance ¶ 청소년의 선도책이 시급히 요청된다 Establishment of measures for proper juvenile guidance is urgently called for.
선도 禪道 〖불교〗 the Way of Seon 〔Dhyāna〕; Seon (sect of) Buddhism
선도 先渡 forward〔future〕 delivery
선돌 〖역사〗 a menhir ; a monolith
⁑선동 煽動 instigation ; abetment ; incitement ; agitation ; stirring up —하다 instigate ; abet ; incite ; stir up ; agitate ; set on ; fan

> 참고 **incite**는 다른 사람에게 자극을 주어 행동이나 행위에까지 이르게 하나 그 행동의 선악 시비를 묻지 않는다 **instigate**는 그 결과적 행동이 나쁘든가 나쁘게 될 경우에 한한다

¶ 선동적 inflammatory ; seditious ; incendiary // 선동적 정치가 a demagogic politician ; a seditious demagogue // 선동의 목적으로 for agitative〔demagogic〕 purpose // 파업을 선동하다 instigate workers to go out on strike // 국민을 선동하여 국가의 분열을 꾀하는 자는 위험 분자이다 Agitators who stir up divisions in a nation are dangerous.
— 연설 an inflammatory〔seditious〕 speech〔harangue〕 — 연설가 a stump orator ; an agitator ; a demagogue —자 an instigator ; an agitator ; an abetter ; 〖법〗 an abettor — 정치가 a demagogic politician ; a political demagog —죄 sedition 대중 —가 a rabble-rouser
선동이 先童— the firstborn of twins
*선두 先頭 the head ; the top ; the lead ; the van(guard) ; the first ¶ 국기를 선두로 with the national flag at the head // 선두에 서다 be at the head ; take the lead ; take the van ; head // 행렬의 선두에 서다 clear the way at〔for〕 a procession // 노동 운동의 선두에 서다 lead the van in the labor movement ; be in the van of the labor movement
— 부대 the van ; the leading troop — 주자 a front-running man ; a front-runner —차 the lead car — 타자 〖야구〗 a lead-off man (멤버 중의) ; the first batter (그 회(回)의)
선두 船頭 the prow (of a boat) ; the bow ; the stem ¶ 선두에서 선미까지 from stem to stern
선두르다 fringe ; border ; margin ; frill ; trim ; sew on a frill ¶ 상보에 선두르다 trim a tablecloth with frills
선두리 〖곤충〗 a water beetle
선드러지다 (be) buoyant ; gay ; lighthearted ¶ 선드러지게 웃다 laugh lightheartedly
선드리다 禪— 〖불교〗 engage in Buddhist meditation
선득, 선뜩 —하다 [추워서] (be) chilled ; feel chilly ; feel a chill〔cold〕; [놀라서] shudder 《at》; have a thrill of horror ¶ 나는 가슴이 선득했다 My blood ran cold〔chill〕. /A cold shiver ran through me.
선득거리다 ① [추워서] feel chilly ② [놀라서] shudder 《at, to see》 ⇨ 섬뜩하다
선득선득, 선뜩선뜩 [추워서] chilly ; [놀라는 느낌] shudderingly ; with a thrill of horror
선들거리다 blow gently〔softly〕 ¶ 선들거리는 바람 a gentle〔cool〕 breeze
선들다 禪— 〖불교〗 go into a Buddhist sanctuary to meditate
선들바람 a cool〔gentle〕 breeze
선등 船燈 a ship's lamp
선떡 a half-done rice cake
선똥 half-digested excrement
⁑선뜻 ① [빨리] quickly ; nimbly ② [쾌히] gladly ; readily ; willingly ; with (good) grace ; with pleasure ¶ 선뜻 요구를 받아들이다 willingly comply with〔consent willingly to〕 another's request // 선뜻 승낙하다 readily〔willingly〕 consent 《to》 // 선뜻 돈을 빌려 주다 lend money with good grace
선뜻하다 [선명하다] (be) clear ; fresh ; [보기 좋다] neat ; tidy ; clean
†선량 善良 goodness —하다 (be) good ; virtuous ; right ¶ 선량한 민중 good people ; law-abiding people
선량 選良 a representative of the people ;

a member of Parliament
선려 鮮麗 resplendent〔brilliant〕 beauty
—하다 (be) gorgeous ; vivid ¶ 선려한 색깔 a bright〔vivid〕 color
선령 船齡 a ship's age ; the age of a ship〔vessel〕
선례 先例 a precedent ⇨ 전례
선로 船路 a ship's route〔course〕; a sea route ; a seaway ⇨ 뱃길
†선로 線路 a railway line ; a railroad track ; a railroad line 《미》 ¶ 선로를 놓다 lay a railroad line〔track〕// 선로를 횡단하다 cross a railroad track
— 건설 line construction —공 a line(s)-man ; a trackman — 공사 railroad〔line〕 construction —반 a trackmaintenance gang — 순회 a route inspection — 청소부 a fluffer — 표지 a track indicator
선류 蘚類 『식물』 mosses
선륜 線輪 ⇨ 코일
선린 善隣 (being) good neighbors ; neighborly friendship ; a good-neighbor relationship ¶ 선린의 정의를 유지하다 maintain a good-neighbor relationship
— 관계 good neighborly relations 《with》
— 정책 a good neighbor policy
‡선망 羨望 envy —하다 envy ; feel envy 《toward》; be envious of ; regard 《a person》 with envy ; look enviously 《at》 ¶ 선망의 대상이 되다 become an object of envy 《among》
선망후실 先忘後失 forgetfulness ; a poor〔short〕 memory —하다 be forgetful ; forget easily
선매 先賣 selling in advance ; advance〔prior〕 sale —하다 sell in advance ; sell beforehand
입도(立稻) — pre-harvest sale of a rice crop
선매권 先買權 right of pre-emption〔prior purchase〕 ¶ 선매권을 얻다 pre-empt
선머리 先— the head ; the lead ; the van ¶ 행렬의 선머리 the van of a procession〔parade〕// 선머리에 서다 take the lead ; be at the head
선머슴 a wild〔naughty〕 boy
선명 宣明 proclamation ; announcement ; declaration ; promulgation ; enunciation
—하다 announce ; proclaim ; declare
†선명 鮮明 clearness ; distinctness ; lucidity ; vividness —하다 (be) clear ; sharp-cut ; distinct ; vivid ¶ 선명치 않다 lack clearness (태도가) ; be dim (색채가) // 기치를 선명히 하다 assume a definite attitude ; define〔clarify〕 one's position // 이 비디오테이프는 화상이 (거칠고) 선명하지 못하다 This videotape has a grainy picture.
—도(度) (degree of) definition ; visibility ; resolution (사진의) ; distinction (텔레비전의) — 야당 a clear-cut opposition party
선명 船名 a ship's name
선모 旋毛 ⇨ 가마[1]
선모 腺毛 a tentacle ; glandular hair(s)
선모충 旋毛蟲 a trichina
—병 trichinosis
선무 宣撫 placation ; pacification
— 공작 pacification work〔activity〕 —반(班) a pacification〔win-over〕 squad ; authorized placators ; a pacification unit
선무당 a new〔novice〕 shaman
선무당이 장구 나무란다 A bad workman quarrels with his tools. /He is not a mason who refuses a stone.
†선물 先物 ① ⇨ 맏물, 현물 ② 『경제』 futures ¶ 선물을 사다 deal in futures ; buy futures
— 거래〔가격, 매매〕 advance business〔price, bargain〕 — 시장〔시세〕 futures market〔quotation〕
선물 膳物 a present ; a gift

> 참고 **gift**는 다액의 돈 귀중품의 경우에 쓰이는 일이 많다 **present**는 가까운 친지 사이에 많이 쓰인다

—하다 give〔make, send〕 《a person》 a present ; make a gift 《to》 ¶ 선물을 받다 take〔accept〕 a gift // 하느님의 선물 a gift〔blessing〕 of Heaven ; a godsend // 그녀 선물로 이것이 어떨까 How would this do as a present for her ? // 그녀의 결혼선물로 우리가 무엇을 주면 좋을까 What do you think we should give her as a wedding gift ?
크리스마스〔신년〕 — a Christmas〔New Year〕 gift 생일 — a birthday remembrance〔present, gift〕
선미 船尾 the stern (of a ship) ; the buttock(s) ; the poop ¶ 선미에 astern ; aft
—재 a sternpost
선미 鮮美 freshness and beauty ; fresh beauty —하다 (be) fresh〔vivid〕 and beautiful
선민 選民 the chosen〔privileged〕 people ; the elect (신의)
— 의식 elitism
선바람 (one's) present attire ; the outfit one has on ¶ 선바람으로 just as one is
‡선박 船舶 a vessel ; a ship ; a bottom ; [집합적] shipping ; craft ; fleet
— 검사 증서 a ship inspection certificate
—과(課) the marine section — 관리료 husbandage — 관리 위원회 the shipping controllers' committee — 국적 증서 the certificate of a ship's nationality — 등기부 the shipping register —법 『법』 the Ships Act — 보증 ship's warrant — 사용료 charterage —세 the shipping tax — 서류 the ship's papers — 소유자 a shipowner — 안전법 the Ships Safety Act —업 the shipping industry —용품 ship's stores — 임대료 (사용료) charterage — 입항〔출항〕 신고 a ship's clearance inward〔outward〕; a ship's entry〔clear-

ance〕 ― 적재량 ship's burden ― 직원법 〖법〗 the Ships' Officers Act ― 채권자 a ship's creditor ― 회사 a shipping company

‡선반 ―盤 a shelf ; a rack ¶ 선반에 얹다 put 《a thing》 on a shelf ; shelve

선반 旋盤 a lathe
―공 a lathe operator ; a turner ; a latheman ― 공장 a turnery ; a lathe shop ― 대(臺) a lathe bed ― 세공 lathe work ; turnery 동력 ― a power lathe 자동 ― an automatic lathe

†선발 先發 starting〔going〕 in advance ; getting〔taking〕 a head start ―하다 start〔go〕 in advance ; go ahead 《of》 ; get〔take〕 a head start
―대 an advance party〔force, element, contingent〕 ― 투수 a starting pitcher ; a starter

선발 選拔 selection ; choice ―하다 select ; choose ; pick〔single〕 out ¶ 선발된 selected ; chosen ; picked // 선발에서 빠지다 be left out in the select list
― 경기 an elimination match ; tryout ― 대 the pick of the troops ; a corps d'élite ― 시험 a selective examination ; a selection examination ― 야구 시합 elimination baseball games ― 위원회 a selection committee ―팀 a picked team ; 《all-star》 selection

*선배 先輩 a senior ; a superior ; an elder ; an old timer 《미》 ; predecessor ¶ 대선배 a big senior // 선배 연하다 make much of one's seniority ; pose as a senior ; assume a patronizing attitude // 2년 선배이다 be one's senior by two years ; be two years one's senior // 선배를 돋보이게 하려고 그 점은 양보했다 I decided to concede the point to make a senior colleague look good.

선번 先番 precedence ; one's turn to make the first move

선변 ―邊 interest paid monthly

선변 先邊 interest paid in advance 《on loan》

선별 選別 sorting ; assortment ―하다 assort ; sort

선병 腺病 a glandular〔lymphatic〕 disorder ; lymphadenitis ; scrofula ¶ 선병의 lymphatic ; scrofulous
―질 scrofulousness ; the scrofulous tendency (of a body)

선보다 ⇨ 선

선보름 先― the first half of a month

선복 船卜 (ship's) cargo ; freight

선복 船腹 [배의 내부] bottoms ; 〔freight〕 space ; [수송 능력] (shipping) tonnage
― 과잉 an excess of bottoms ― 부족 the scarcity〔shortage〕 of bottoms〔tonnage〕

선봉 先鋒 the van ; the vanguard ; the advance guard ; the scouting line ¶ 선봉이 되다 lead the van ; become the spearhead of an advance〔attack〕

선부 先父 one's deceased〔late〕 father

선부 先夫 one's deceased〔late〕 husband

선분 線分 〖수학〗 a segment (of a line)

선불 a stray bullet
선불 맞은 호랑이 뛰듯 (속담) hopping mad ; furious

*선불 先拂 advance payment ; payment in advance ; prepayment ―하다 pay in advance ; prepay ¶ 이 사람에게는 선불로 받으세요 Have this man pay in advance.
운임 ― [철도의] freight to collect 《미》 ; carriage forward 《영》 ; [배의] freight payable at destination 요금 ― 전보 a collect telegram

선불선 善不善 good and〔or〕 evil

선비[1] a scholar ; a classical scholar ; a student of Chinese classics ; a gentleman

선비[2] [청소 도구] a long-handled broom

선비 先妣 one's deceased〔late〕 mother

선비 鮮卑 〖중국사〗 the Sien-pei (people)

선사 ① [선물] presentation ② [신불에게 공양] offering ¶ 친구에게 선사하다 send a gift to a friend // 신불에게 선사하다 make offerings to a god

선사 先史 ¶ 선사의 prehistoric(al)
― 시대 the prehistoric age ― 인류학 prehistoric anthropology ―학 prehistory

선사 先師 one's deceased〔late〕 teacher

선사 禪師 a Zen master〔priest〕 ; an esteemed priest ¶ 달마 선사 Saint *Dalma*

선산 先山 an ancestral〔a family〕 burial ground ; a mountain where one's ancestors are buried

선상 船上 on the ship ¶ 선상에(서) on board (a ship) ; aboard
― 생활 life on board〔shipboard〕

선상 扇狀 a fan form〔shape〕 ⇨ 선형(扇形)
― 삼각주(洲) a fan delta ―지(地) a fan ; an alluvial fan

†선생 先生 a teacher (학교 따위의) ; instructor (교수자) ; a (school) master ; a (school) mistress (여자) ; a doctor (의사) ; [호칭] sir ; ma'am ¶ 영어 선생 a teacher of English ; an English teacher

선서 宣誓 an oath ; parole ―하다 swear to ; take an oath ; pledge one's word of honor ¶ 취임 선서를 하다 administer the oath of office // 선서시키다 administer an oath 《to a person》 ; attest ; swear (an oath) ; put an oath // 선서를 파기하다 break one's parole〔oath〕
―문 a deposition ; an affidavit ―식 a swearing-in〔oath-taking〕 ceremony ― 증서 a deposition ― 증언 deposition ; sworn testimony ― 증인 a deponent

선선하다 ① [시원하다] (be) cool ; refreshing ¶ 선선한 눈매 clear eyes // 선선해지다 become〔get〕 cool ② [성질이] (be) candid ; frank ; free and easy ;

openhearted ¶ 사람이 선선하다 be openhearted // 선선히 대답하다 answer frankly // 선선히 승낙하다 give in with good grace

선선히 candidly ; frankly ; openly ; with (good) grace ; cheerfully ; vivaciously ¶ 선선히 대답하다 answer frankly // 선선히 승낙하다 give in〔acquiesce〕 with good grace // 선선히 자기 잘못을 인정하다 acknowledge one's fault with good grace // 선선히 자백하다 make a manly confession

선세 先貰 advance payment of rent ; prepaid rent ── 하다 pay rent in advance ; repay the rent

선셈 先― prepayment ; settling an account in advance ── 하다 prepay ; settle an account in advance

선소리 foolish〔silly〕 talk ; an absurd remark ; nonsense ¶ 선소리를 하다 talk nonsense ; make an absurd remark

선소리 先― a shout〔cry, yell〕 from the front ¶ 선소리치다 shout〔call out〕 from the front

선손 先― ① [먼저 착수함] forestalling ; the initiative ; the lead ¶ 선손을 쓰다 take〔seize〕 the initiative ; forestall 《another》 ; get the start of ; steal a march on ② [선손질] the first blow ¶ 선손을 걸다 strike the first blow

선손질 先― the first blow ; starting a fight

선수 先手 [선손] forestalling ; the initiative ; [바둑·장기에서] the first move ; an opener 《in a chess game》 ¶ 선수를 놓다 make the first move ; take the initiative

선수 船首 the stem ; the prow (of a ship) ⇨ 이물 ¶ 선수에서 선미까지 from stem to stern

*선수 選手 a player ; an athlete ; a champion (선수권 보유자) ; a team (전체) ¶ 야구 선수 a baseball player ; the nine (전체) // 선수가 되다 become a player // 올림픽 선수로 뽑히다 be chosen an Olympic player

─단 a team ; a squad 정구 ─ a tennis player 초대 ─ a guest player 후보 ─ a substitute ; a bench polisher (야구의)

선수권 選手權 a championship ; a title ; the crown ¶ 선수권을 차지하다 win〔gain, capture〕 the championship // 선수권을 보유하다 hold〔retain〕 the championship // 선수권을 방어하다 defend the title (권투 등에서) // 선수권을 빼앗다 wrest the championship 《from》 // 선수권을 잃다 lose the championship〔title〕 // 선수권을 다투다 contend〔play〕 for the championship ; play for the title

─ 대회 a championship series ; the championships ─ 보유자 a champion ; a championship holder ; a titleholder ; a defender ─ 시합 a title match ; a title bout 세계 ─ a world〔an international〕 championship〔title〕 전국 ─ a national championship〔title〕

선술 仙術 Taoist (occult) magic ; magic arts ; wizardry

*선술집 a (stand) bar ; a (drinking) tavern

선승 先勝 ── 하다 win the first game ; score the first point

선승 禪僧 『불교』 a Zen priest〔monk〕

선시선종 善始善終 ── 하다 start well and finish well ; do a consistently good job ; do well consistently

선신세 鮮新世 『지질』 the Pliocene (epoch)

†선실 船室 a cabin ; a stateroom (1등의) ; the passenger's quarters ¶ 1〔2〕등 선실 a first〔second〕-class cabin // 3등 선실 the steerage // 선실 배당표 a berth list // 선실 겸 요리실 a cuddy // 선실을 예약하다 reserve a passage〔berth〕 ; book a berth

선심 善心 ① [착한 마음] virtuous mind ; kind heart

② [남을 돕는 마음] generosity ; kindness ; benevolence ¶ 선심을 쓰다 do a kindness 《for a person》 ; do something nice 《for a person》

─ 공세 pork-barrelling ; the use of patronage for political advantage ; favoritism

선심 線審 a linesman ; a line umpire

선악 善惡 good and evil〔bad〕 ; virtue and vice ; goodness and badness ; right and wrong (정과 사) ¶ 동기의 선악을 불문하고 regardless of whether the motive is good or bad〔innocent or not〕 // 선악을 분별하다 know good from bad ; discern good from bad ; distinguish right from wrong

─과(果) 『성경』 the fruit of the Tree of Knowledge

선약 仙藥 a wonderful remedy〔medicine〕 ; a panacea ; the elixir of life

선약 先約 a previous engagement〔appointment, date〕 ¶ 선약이 있다 have a previous engagement // 선약 때문에 초대에 응할 수 없어 유감입니다 I regret that a previous engagement prevents me (from) accepting your kind invitation.

선양 宣揚 enhancement ; exaltation ── 하다 enhance ; raise ; exalt ¶ 국위를 선양하다 enhance the prestige of one's country ; promote the national prestige

국위 ─ enhancement of national prestige

선양 禪讓 abdication (of the throne)

선어 鮮魚 fresh fish ⇨ 생선

†선언 宣言 declaration ; proclamation ; profession ; statement ; pronouncement ; announcement ── 하다 declare ; make a declaration ; pronounce ; profess ; proclaim ; announce ¶ 개회를 선언하다 call (a meeting) to order // 입후보를 선언하다 announce one's candidacy

─ 판결 a declaratory judgment 공산당 ─

the communist manifesto 독립 — the declaration of independence 포츠담 — the Potsdam Declaration (of 1945) 폭탄 — a thunderbolt-like declaration

선언 명제 選言命題 〖논리〗 a disjunctive (proposition) ; a disjunction

선언서 宣言書 a (written) declaration ; a manifesto ; a statement

선업 善業 a good (charitable) deed ; good works

선열 先烈 the patriot of old
순국 — the martyred patriots

선영 先塋 ⇨ 선산(先山)

선왕 先王 the late〔preceding〕 king

선외 選外 being left out of the selection〔choice〕 ¶ 선외가 되다 be left out of the selection ; be rejected ; fail to be accepted∥그의 소설은 선외에도 못 들었다 His story was not even mentioned.

선외 가작 選外佳作 a work of which honorable mention is made ¶ 선외 가작에 들다 receive honorable mention ; win an honorable mention

선용 善用 good use **—하다** make good use of ; make the most of ; put (money) to (a) good use ; employ time well ¶ 여가의 선용 making good use of spare time〔hours〕

선운산 〖광산〗 the left side of a mine pit

선웃음 a forced〔feigned, mock〕 laugh ¶ 선웃음을 웃다 force a laugh ; pretend to smile

†**선원 船員** [집합적] the crew ; a ship's company ; [개인] one〔a member〕 of the crew〔the ship's company〕 ; a seaman ; a mariner ; a crewman
—법 the Seamen's Law — 생활 a sailor's life ; a seafaring life — 수첩 a seaman's pocket ledger —실 the crew's quarters ; the crew space — 위생 the hygiene of seafarers 고급 — a (ship's) officer ; the quarter-deck 보통 — ratings 하급 — the forecastle 《총칭》 ; a sailor ; a jack tar 《속》 ; a jacky 《속》 ; a stoker (화부)

선위 禪位 abdication (of the throne) **—하다** abdicate ; vacate the throne

선유 船遊 boating ⇨ 뱃놀이

선율 旋律 melody ¶ 선율적인 melodious ; of a harmonized melody
—법 melodics —학 〖음악〗 melodics 중복 —법 double counterpoint

***선의 善意** a favorable sense (좋은 의미) ; good intentions (좋은 의도) ; 〖법〗 good faith ; bona fides ¶ 선의의 well-intended ; bona-fide ; innocent∥선의의 제3자 a third party in good faith ; the bona-fide third party∥선의로 in good part〔faith〕 ; bona-fide∥선의로 해석하다 take 《it》 in a favorable sense ; put a good construction on 《a person's remarks》

선의 船醫 the ship's doctor〔surgeon〕

선의권 先議權 the right to prior consideration

선인 仙人 a hermit ; an ascetic ; a Taoist Immortal ; a genie

선인 先人 [선친] my deceased〔late〕 father ; [옛사람] predecessors ; forerunners ; precursors

선인 船人 a sailor ⇨ 뱃사람

선인 善人 a virtuous person ; a good man

선인선과 善因善果 the results〔fruits〕 of good deeds ; the rewards of virtue

선인장 仙人掌 〖식물〗 a cactus ; a prickly pear ; Opuntia Tuna (학명)

선일 a job which requires one to stand ; a stand-up task ; working on one's feet

선일 先日 the other day ; some〔a few〕 days ago

선일부 先日附 postdating ; dating forward ¶ 선일부로 하다 postdate 《a letter, check》 ; date forward
— 수표 a postdated check

***선임 先任** seniority ; [선임자] a predecessor ¶ 선임순으로 in the order of seniority ; by seniority
—권 the seniority right — 장교 a senior officer

선임 選任 election ; assignment ; nomination (지명) **—하다** select and appoint ; elect ; assign 《a person to a post》 ; nominate ¶ 변호인의 선임 designation of counsels (by the government)∥소송 대리인 선임 procuration

선임 船賃 ⇨ 뱃삯

선입 先入 prior entry **—하다** enter first ; preoccupy ; prepossess
—관 a preconception ; a prejudice ; a prepossession ; a bias ; a prepossessed idea ; preconceived opinions ¶ 선입관을 가지다 have a preconceived idea

선입감 先入感 a preconception ; a prejudice ; a bias

선입견 先入見 a preconception ; a prepossession ; a preoccupation ; a prejudice ; a preconceived idea ¶ 선입견을 가지다 have a preconceived idea〔opinion〕∥…한 선입견을 품게 되다 be prepossessed with the impression 《that...》∥선입견을 버리다 divest oneself of a preconceived idea〔of prejudice〕 ; get rid of one's prejudice 《against》∥난 그 나라가 싫다는 선입견이 있어 I have a prejudice against the country.

선입 선출법 先入先出法 〖회계〗 first in, first out 《FIFO, fifo》

선자 選者 a selector ; an elector ; a judge

선자귀[1] [나무 깎는] a large hatchet

선자귀[2] [분합문] a two-piece latticed door at the side veranda in a house

***선잠** a light sleep ; a broken sleep ; a catnap ; drowsing ; a doze ¶ 선잠을 자다 catnap ; sleep with one eye open ; drowse ; take a little nap ; fall into a doze ; take forty winks

선장 船匠 a ship carpenter ; a shipwright
*선장 船長 a (ship's, sea) captain ; a commander ; a master (of a ship) ; a master mariner ; a skipper (소상선의)
— 면허장 a master's certificate of competence ; a master's license — 선교 the captain's bridge — 수입 신고서 a master's entry —실 a captain's cabin —직 captaincy ; mastership — 해난 증명서 captain's protest
선재 船材 (ship-building) timber〔lumber〕
선저 船底 a (ship's) bottom
— 검사 bottom inspection — 굽기 breaming — 도료 bottom paint — 저당 대차 〖해사법〗 bottomry
선적 船籍 ① [국적] the country of registry of a ship ¶ 미국의 선적을 가진 배 a ship of American registry ② [등기부] the registry of a ship
— 기호 a nationality mark — 불명선 a vessel of unknown nationality〔identity〕 — 증서 a certificate of (a ship's) nationality —항 the port of registry
*선적 船積 [발송] shipping ; shipment ; [적재] loading ; lading
— 가격 a free on board price ; an F. O. B. price — 계약 a shipment〔loading〕 contract —불 cash on shipment — 비용 shipping charges〔expenses〕 — 서류 shipping documents — 송장 a shipping invoice — 안내서 a shipping advice — 지시서 a shipping order — 취급인 a shipping clerk〔agent〕 — 통지서 a shipping note — 하물 cargo ; shipping goods —항 a port of shipment
⁑선전 宣傳 propaganda ; propagandism ; propagation (보급) ; publicity ; advertisement (광고) —하다 propagate ; propagandize ; advertise ; make propaganda《for》; give publicity《to》¶ 자기 선전 self-advertising // 사상을 선전하다 propagate an idea〔ideology〕// 자동차 판매 사원은 새 모델에 관해 장황한 선전을 늘어놓기 시작했다 The car salesman started a song and dance about the new model. // 우리 제품의 우수성을 선전하는 것이 중요하다 It's important to make a pitch for our products.
— 공세 a propaganda offensive ; a propaganda onslaught〔attack〕 — 공작 propaganda maneuvers —극 a propaganda drama — 기관 propaganda machinery ; organs of propaganda — 노선 a propaganda line —문 a broadside — 방송 an advertisement broadcast ; a commercial —부 a publicity department — 부원 a publicity man ; a public relations man — 비용 advertising expenses — 삐라 a leaflet ; a handbill ; a propaganda bill — 업자 a publicity agent — 영화 a propaganda film —용 사진 a promotion picture — 운동 a propaganda〔publicity, promotion〕 campaign —전 propaganda war ; propaganda warfare —차(車) a sound car〔truck〕 — 활동 propaganda activity ; a publicity build-up — 효과 propaganda effect(s) 가두 —원 a town crier ; an advertisement man
선전 宣戰 a declaration〔proclamation〕 of war —하다 declare〔proclaim〕 war《upon, against》
— 포고 a proclamation〔declaration〕 of war
선전 善戰 fighting a good fight ; fighting admirably〔well〕 —하다 fight a good fight ; fight admirably〔well〕
선점 先占 〖법〗 prior occupation —하다 preoccupy ; acquire by occupancy
—권자 an occupant — 취득 acquisition by occupancy
선정 善政 good government〔administration〕 ; just rule ¶ 선정을 베풀다 govern well ; rule wisely
선정 選定 selection ; choice —하다 select ; choose ; make a selection〔choice〕《of》
— 도서 목록 a reading list ; a reference (reading) list
선정적 煽情的 (being) sensational ; suggestive ; lascivious ; sex-appealing ¶ 선정적 소설 a lascivious novel ; a suggestive story
선제 先帝 the late Emperor ; an ex-Emperor
선제 先制 a head start ¶ 선제점을 따다 score first runs〔points〕
선제 공격 先制攻擊 a containment offensive ; [핵 공격] a preemptive strike ¶ 선제 공격을 가하다 strike《the enemy》 first〔before he goes into action〕 ; carry out a preemptive strike against《the enemy's nuclear installations》
⁑선조 先祖 an ancestor ; a forefather ; a progenitor ; a predecessor
선조 線條 a streak ; a line ; filament
가스 —등 a gas filled filament lamp — 세공 [금은의] filigree work
선조총 旋條銃 a rifle
선종 禪宗 the Zen〔Dhyāna〕 sect of Buddhism ; Zen Buddhism
선주 船主 a ship's owner
—기(旗) a house flag — 협회 a shipowners' association
선주자 先住者 a former occupant《of a house》
선줄 a vertical〔lengthwise〕 vein of ore ; a lengthwise mineral vein
선지 clotted blood of cattle
—피 fresh blood ¶ 코에서 선지피가 흐르다 blood gushes from the nose 선짓국《make》 ox-blood soup 선짓덩이 clotted blood ; a lump of coagulated ox-blood
선지자 先知者 a prophet (who knows the future) ; a seer ; a predictor
선진 先進 seniority ; advance ; leadership
—국 an advanced country ; a highly developed country ; a forward country

선진 先陣 〖군사〗 the van (of an army) ; the advance guard ; the vanguard ; a scouting line (전초선) ¶ 선진이 되다 lead the van

선집 選集 a selection ; an anthology ¶ 영시 선집 a selection of English poems

선착 先着 ① first arrival ¶ 선착순으로 by order of arrival ; in the order of receipt ; on a first-come-first-served basis // 선착 5명까지 입상 Prizes given to the first five persons.
② [선착순] undertaking first ; prior 〔first〕 start〔commencement〕

선창 先唱 ① [노래] chorus leading ② [주장] advocacy ; introducing ; advancing (the cause of) ━하다 [노래] lead the chorus ; [주장] advocate ; introduce ; lead ; advance the cause of
━자 a chorus leader ; [주장자] a ring leader

선창 船窓 a porthole

⁑선창 船艙 a wharf ; a quay ; a pier ; [배의] a hatch ; the hold
━내 화물 under-deck cargo ━ 사용료 wharfage ; pierage ; pier dues ; quayage

선채 先綵 betrothal presents ; engagement gifts

선책 善策 a good plan ; a fine scheme

선처 善處 adequate management ; proper dealing〔step〕 ━하다 make the best 《of》 ; tide over 《difficulties》 ; act with prudence ; use discretion 《in》 ; deal adequately with ; deal with 《something》 as one thinks fit ¶ 시국에 선처하다 meet 〔cope with〕 the situation properly ; take a proper step to meet the situation

선천 先天 apriority ; innateness ; inbornness ; inherence ¶ 선천적 native ; inborn ; innate ; inherent ; congenital // 선천적으로 by nature ; naturally ; innately ; intuitively ; congenitally ; inherently // 선천적 불구 a congenital deformity
━론 nativism ; apriorism ━ 변이 〖동물〗 congenital variation ━병 a congenital 〔hereditary, connate〕 disease ━성 apriority

선철 先哲 an ancient sage ; wise men of the past ¶ 선철의 교훈 the teaching of an ancient sage

선철 銑鐵 pig iron ⇨ 무쇠

선체 船體 the body of a ship ; the hull

선출 選出 election ━하다 elect ; return 《영》 ¶ 부산에서 선출되다 be elected for *Pusan*

선충 線蟲 an eelworm ; a nematode
━류 Nematoda (학명)

*선취 先取 ━하다 preoccupy ; take first ¶ 한 점을 선취하다 score a first run ; score the first point of the game
━(득)점 runs scored first ━ 유치권 〖법〗 a prior lien

선취 船醉 ⇨ 뱃멀미

선취 특권 先取特權 the right of priority ; a prior right ; a priority ; a preferential right ¶ 선취 특권이 있다 hold prior rights

선측 船側 the ship's side ; the side of a ship
━ 인도 free alongside (ship) 《F. A. S.》

선치 善治 ⇨ 선정(善政)

선친 先親 my deceased〔late〕 father

선키 one's height when standing

선탁 宣託 an inspiration ; a revelation ; an oracle

선탄 選炭 coal dressing〔washing〕 ; concentration of coal ━하다 concentrate 〔dress〕 coal
━기(機) a coal washer ; a coal-dressing machine

선태 蘚苔 a moss ; a bryophyte
━류 Bryophyta (학명) ━학 bryology

†선택 選擇 selection ; choice ; option ━하다 select ; choose ; pick (out) ; make one's choice

> 참고 **choose**는 가장 일반적인 말 **select**는 선악·양 불량·호 불호의 차이를 결정하여 신중히 선택하는 경우에 쓰인다

¶ 직업의 선택 choosing one's occupation // 선택을 잘못하다 make a bad choice ; choose the wrong one // 선택의 여지가 없다 You have no choice in this matter. // 내게는 선택의 여지가 없다 I have no alternative.
━ 과목 an optional course ; an elective subject ; a minor ━법 a method of selection ━ 투표 preferential voting ━ 항로 an alternative route

선택권 選擇權 option ; the right of choice ¶ 선택권을 포기하다 waive an option

선팽창 線膨脹 〖물리〗 linear expansion
━ 계수 the coefficient of linear expansion

선편 船便 shipping service ¶ 선편으로 by ship〔water〕 // 선편으로 목포까지 가다 take a ship to *Mokp'o*

선편 先鞭 the initiative ; leading

선평 選評 selection and criticism ━하다 select and criticize

선포 宣布 proclamation ; promulgation ━하다 proclaim ; promulgate

선표 船票 a (ship) passenger ticket ; a boat ticket

*선풍 旋風 a whirlwind ; a cyclone ; a tornado 《*pl.* ~es, ~s》 ¶ 선풍 같은 cyclonic // 선풍을 일으키다 create a great sensation (비유적) // 선풍에 휩쓸리다 be caught up in a cyclone // 선풍이 일어나다 a whirlwind takes place〔springs up〕
검거 ━ a sweeping roundup ; a wholesale arrest 역━ an anticyclone

⁑선풍기 扇風機 an electric fan ; a motor fan ¶ 선풍기를 돌리다 set an electric fan going〔in motion〕 ; start〔turn on〕 an electric fan // 선풍기를 끄다 turn〔switch〕

off an electric fan
천장 — a ceiling fan 탁상 — a desk fan 회전 — an oscillating fan

선하 船荷 freight ; cargo ; lading ¶ 선하를 적재하다 load cargo // 선하를 내리다 discharge cargo

선하다 (be) vivid ; fresh ; distinct ¶ 선히 vividly ; freshly // 그 광경이 눈에 선하다 I have a vivid recollection of it. /The scene is still lingering in my eyes.

선하 증권 船荷證券 a bill of lading 《B/L》 ¶ 선하 증권을 발행하다 issue a bill of lading (covering the shipment)
— 원본 an original B/L 선적〔선적항〕 — a shipped〔port〕 B/L 수입〔수출〕 — an import〔export〕 B/L 양도 불능 — non-negotiable B/L

선하품 [억지의] a forced yawn ; a feigned yawn ; [소화 불량시의] a yawn caused by indigestion —하다 force a yawn ; feign a yawn

선학 先學 scholars in the past ; one's senior scholars

선학 禪學 the doctrine of the *Seon* sect

선함 船艦 ships ; vessels

*선행 善行 a good deed ; good conduct ¶ 선행을 표창하다 officially recognize 《a person's》 good deed

선행 先行 preceding —하다 precede ; be ahead of
—권 (도로 교통의) the right of way —사 〖문법〗 an antecedent — 조건 a condition precedent ; an essential prerequisite

선향 先鄕 one's ancestral home

선향 仙鄕 a fairyland ; an enchanted land ; an elysium

선향 線香 a joss stick ; an incense-stick ¶ 선향을 피우다 burn incense-sticks

선험 先驗 a priori 《라》 ; transcendental
—론 transcendentalism —적 인식 transcendental cognition —적 확률 a priori probability — 철학 metempirics ; transcendental philosophy ; transcendentalism

선헤엄 treading water ; a standing stroke ¶ 선헤엄을 치다 tread water

선현 先賢 ancient sages

선혈 鮮血 (fresh) blood ; life blood

선형 扇形 a fan shape ; 〖기하〗 a sector

선형 船型 the type〔class〕 of ship〔vessel〕 ; [모형] a model of a ship

†선호 船號 a ship's name ; the name of a vessel

선호 選好 preference

선홍색 鮮紅色 scarlet

선화 仙化 natural death —하다 die a natural death

선화 線畫 line〔lineal〕 drawing〔engraving〕

선화지 仙花紙 reclaimed paper

선황 先皇 the late Emperor

†선회 旋回 turning ; circling ; revolution ; rotation —하다 circle ; turn〔revolve〕 round ; rotate ; encircle ¶ 비행기가 배의 상공을 선회했다 An airplane circled round above the ship.
— 무도 a pirouette — 비행 circuitous flying ; circling ; a circle — 운동 a turning movement —축 a pivot — 포탑 a (revolving) turret 수직 — 〖항공〗 a vertical turn

선후 先後 [앞뒤] front and rear ; beginning and end ; [순서] order ; sequence ¶ 말의 선후가 뒤바뀌다 get confused in one's talk // 선후가 전도되어 있다 The order is inverted. /That's an instance of putting the cart before the horse.
— 도착(倒錯) reversing the proper order ; putting the cart before the horse —획(劃) the order of strokes in a Chinese character

선후책 先後策 a remedial〔relief〕 measure ; a countermeasure ; remedies ¶ 선후책을 강구하다 consider the remedies ; consider how to cope with the situation ; take remedial measures

선훈 船暈 seasickness

섣달 December ; the last month of the year ¶ 섣달 그믐 New Year's Eve

섣부르다 (be) clumsy ; awkward ; tactless

섣불리 awkwardly ; carelessly ¶ 섣불리 하다가는 if one is not careful ; if not properly handled // 이것은 섣불리 손댈 수 없는 일이다 This is certainly a matter not to be lightly handled. /The matter requires careful handing.

설 New Year's day ; the New Year ¶ 설 음식 festive dishes for the New Year // 설을 쇠다 celebrate the New Year

설 說 ① [의견] an opinion ; a view ; [종교상의] a doxy 《속》 ¶ 설을 같이하다〔달리하다〕 agree〔disagree〕 《with a person》 on an opinion // 설을 굽히다〔굽히지 않다〕 change〔stick to〕 one's views // 그 기원에 관해서는 여러 가지 설이 있다 There are a variety of views about its origin. // …라는 설을 주장하는 사람도 있다 Some say〔are of the opinion〕 that... // 타살설이 유력하다 The dominant view〔majority opinion〕 is that the man was murdered.
② [학설·신조] a theory ; a doctrine ¶ 말더스의 설 the Malthusian theory〔doctrine〕 // 플라톤의 설을 따르다 follow Plato // 새로운 설을 확립하다 establish〔put forward〕 a new theory
③ [풍설] a rumo(u)r ; talk ¶ …라는 설이 있다 There is a rumor that... // 일설에는 …라고 한다 One version says that... // 그런 설이 세상에 나돌고 있다 Rumors to that effect are in the air.

설- ¶ 설삶다 parboil // 설익은〔삶은〕 [음식] underdone ; half-boiled ; half-cooked ; rare ; [과일] unripe ; half-ripe

설거지 dishwashing —하다 do the dishes ; wash dishes

설겅거리다 chew hard ; taste lumpy ; be not thoroughly cooked ; be half-done

설겅설겅 hard-chewing ; lumpy-tasting

설겆다 wash ; do 《the dishes》 ¶ 그릇을 설겆다 do the dishes

설경 雪景 a snow-covered scene〔landscape〕 ; a landscape of snow ; a snowscape

†**설계 設計** a plan ; a design **—하다** draw (up) a plan 《for》 ; plan ; design ; lay out ¶ 설계가 잘된 집 a well-planned house // 생활의 설계 life planning // A씨의 설계로 upon the design of Mr. A // 정원을 설계하다 lay out a garden design // 건물을 설계하다 design a building

—도 a plan ; a design drawing ; [청사진] a blueprint **—서** specifications **— 약도** an outline plan **—자** a designer ; a planner ; a drafter ; projector **도시 —** city planning ; a city plan **생활 —** life planning

설계 雪溪 a snow valley〔gorge, ravine〕

설골 舌骨 hyoid bone

‡**설교 說敎** preaching ; a sermon **—하다** preach ; preach a sermon 《on》 ; occupy the pulpit (단상에서) ¶ 설교를 듣다 hear a sermon ; hear 《a person》 preach ; be given a scolding // 설교를 들려주다 preach to 《a person》 ; read 《a person》 a lecture // 선생님한테 단단히 설교를 들었다 I had a long lecture from my teacher. // 설교는 그만둬 Stop sermonizing ! /None of your moralizing.

—단 a pulpit **—소** a preaching station ; a mission hall **—자** a preacher ; a pulpitarian **순회 —** a preaching tour

설기[1] [떡] steamed rice cake

설기[2] [상자] a wicker trunk

설깃 rump (of beef)

설날 New Year's Day

설늙은이 [겉늙은이] a man old for his years ; a man prematurely aged

설다 ① [덜 익다] be unripe ; green ; immature ; half-done (음식이) ¶ 선 과일 green〔unripe〕 fruit // 그 사과는 설었다 The apple is unripe〔green〕. // 나는 선고기가 좋다 I like my meat rare. // 술이 설었다 The wine is not thoroughly fermented. ② [생소하다] (be) strange ; unfamiliar ; [서투르다] green ; inexperienced ¶ 낯이 선 사람 a stranger ③ sad ⇨ 서럽다

설다듬이 a rough job of cloth fulling

설다루다 mismanage ; handle wrongly 〔carelessly〕 ; do a poor job (of it) ; do a halfway job

설대 〖식물〗 an arrow bamboo ; Arundaria japonica (학명) ; a bamboo pipe-stem

‡**설득 說得** persuasion **—하다** persuade ; prevail on ; talk 《a person》 over ; bring 《a person》 over ¶ 설득하여 못하게 하다 dissuade 《a person》 from doing ; reason〔argue〕 《a person》 out of doing // 아무리 설득해도 귀국하려 들지 않았다 Nothing would induce him to go home. // 그 여자를 설득하는 건 문제가 아니다 She is easy to prevail upon. // 제발 그 여자와 결혼하지 못하게 설득할 생각일랑 마라 Please don't try to talk me out of marrying her. // 대통령이 의료제도 개혁안에 대해서 납세자들을 설득시키기는 쉬운 일이 아닐 것이다 The president will have a hard time selling the taxpayers on his health care reform plan. // 그것에 대해 네가 나를 설득시켰다 You talked me into it. /You sold me on it.

— 대표 an explainer ; an explaining representative **—술** (one's) persuasive art

†**설득력 說得力** persuasive〔reasoning〕 power ; 《one's》 powers of persuasion ¶ 설득력이 있다 (be) persuasive ; (be) forceful // 자기의 견해를 설득력있게 표현하다 give one's view in a way that carries conviction ; speak convincingly // 그의 발언에는 설득력이 없다 There is no persuasion〔force〕 in his remarks.

설듣다 half-hear ; hear amiss ; mishear ; [못듣다] fail to hear ; miss 《words》 ; fail to catch 《words》

설라마 雪羅馬 a white horse with black spots ⇨ 서라말

설량계 a snow gauge

설렁 a call bell ; a doorbell

—줄 a bell rope ; a bellpull

설렁거리다 [바람이] blow gently ; [걷다] walk briskly ⇨ 살랑거리다

설렁설렁 [바람이] 《blow》 gently ; softly ; [걸음을] 《walk》 with brisk steps ¶ 설렁설렁 부는 바람 a gentle breeze ; a soft breath of air

설렁탕 —湯 a kind of beef soup with rice

설렁하다 be somewhat chilly〔cold〕 ; (be) chilly ; cool

설레다 ① [가슴이] flutter ; feel uneasy ; fidget ; pit-a-pat ; palpitate ¶ 놀라서 가슴이 설레다 one's heart flutters〔goes pit-a-pat〕 with fright ② [서성거리다] move about uneasily ; be restless ¶ 설레지 말고 한 자리에 앉아 있어라 Don't be so restless. Keep your seat.

설레설레 waving ; wagging ¶ 아니라고 머리를 설레설레 흔들다 shake one's head in denial

설령 設令 if ; even if ; (even) though ; although ; admitting〔granting, supposing〕 that ; however… may ; whatever… may ; what if ¶ 설령 그것이 사실이라 할지라도 네가 역시 나쁘다 Granted it is true 〔Granting it to be true〕, you are still in the wrong.

†**설립 設立** foundation ; establishment ; organization ; institution

> 참고 **foundation**은 기초를 놓는 것 **establishment**는 foundation보다 뜻이 강하고 영속적인 존재로 하는 것 **institution**은 foundation이나 establishment보다 범위가 넓고 영속적이 아닌 것에도 사용된다

—하다 found ; establish ; institute ; set up ; organize ¶ 새 학교를 설립하다 found a new school // 새 상사를 설립하다 float a new business company

— 등기 registration of incorporation **— 발기인** a promoter **— 위원** an establishment committee **—자** a founder **— 취지서** a prospectus **법인 단체 — 허가서** a charter **회사 — 자금** fund for the establishment of a company

설마 impossible ; that cannot be ; by no means ; on no account ; [회화에서] You don't say (so) ! /Really ? ¶ 미친 사람 아닐까—설마 (그러리라고) Isn't he mad ? That cannot be. /Isn't he mad ? Impossible ! / Isn't he mad ? You don't say so ! /Isn't he mad ? Surely not. // 설마 그런 일은 없으리라고 생각했다 I never thought it possible. // 설마 그렇게 되지는 않겠지 It is not at all likely. // 설마 그렇게 되리라고는 생각지 않았다 I little suspected that things would turn out that way. // 설마 그가 그런 짓이야 안 하겠지 He is the last man to do such a thing. /It is not at all likely that he will do such a thing.

설맞다 receive a flesh wound ; be nicked by (a bullet) ¶ 총알에 설맞았다 I received a flesh wound. // 너 매를 아직 설맞았구나 You have just had a taste of the beating you deserve.

설맞이 welcoming the New Year

설맹 雪盲 snow blindness ; 〖의학〗 niphablepsia

설멍설멍 with a slender〔long-legged〕 gait

설멍하다 ⇨ 살망하다

설면하다 be estranged ; be alienated ; (be) distant

†**설명 說明** explanation ; description ; illustration (도해) ; elucidation **—하다** explain ; illustrate (예시) ; account for (이유를) ; make plain〔clear〕 ; describe ¶ 사건의 윤곽을 설명하다 outline the event // 좀더 잘 설명해 주시오 Please explain it more clearly. // 왜 그러한 행동을 했는지 설명해 보시오 Please account for your conduct. /Please explain why you acted like that. // 영어의 철자에 관한 법칙을 설명하겠다 I will illustrate the spelling rules of English. // 자동차 판매원은 새 모델에 관해 장황한 설명을 늘어놓기 시작했다 The car salesman started a song and dance about the new mode.

—도 a diagram **—서** an explanation ; an explanatory (note) ; an exposition ; a description (물품의) **—자** an explainer ; an expositor ; an elucidator ; an interpreter

설문 設問 making up a question ; a question ; a questionnaire ¶ 다음 문장을 읽고 아래의 설문에 답하라 Read the following and answer the questions given below.

설밥 snow falling on New Year's day

설백 雪白 snow-white ; pure white

설법 說法 a Buddhist sermon ; preaching **—하다** preach (a sermon)

설보다 mistake (in seeing) ; see unclearly or wrongly ; fail to see ¶ 그는 나를 형〔동생〕으로 설보았다 He mistook me for my brother.

‡**설복 說服** persuasion ⇨ 설득 **—하다** persuade ; prevail on ; convince 《a person》 of (his error) ; argue down

설봉 舌鋒 the tongue ¶ 설봉이 날카롭다 have an incisive〔trenchant〕 tongue // 날카로운 설봉으로 with an incisive tongue ; 《criticize》 sharply

설분 雪憤 venting one's rage ⇨ 분풀이

‡**설비 設備** equipment(s) ; facilities ; conveniences ; accommodation(s) (내용 설비) **—하다** equip〔fit, provide, furnish〕 with ; accommodate ¶ 설비가 되어 있다 be equipped〔fitted, provided, furnished〕 with // 그 공장은 자가 발전의 설비를 갖추고 있다 The factory has its own lighting plant. // 그 호텔은 모든 근대적 설비가 갖추어져 있다 The hotel is equipped〔fitted〕 with all modern comforts and conveniences. // 그 호텔은 설비가 좋다〔잘 되어 있다〕 The hotel is admirably accommodated〔well- equipped〕.

설비 수출 設備輸出 ⇨ 플랜트(— 수출)

설빔 New Year's garb **—하다** dress up for the New Year

—옷 a new year's garment

설사 泄瀉 loose bowels ; diarrhea〔diarrhoea〕 **—하다** have loose bowels ; suffer from diarrhea ¶ 설사를 막다 bind the bowels ; stop diarrhea

—약 a diarrhea remedy ; a binding medicine

설사 設使 even if ¶ 설사 그것을 제공한다 해도 그는 받지 않을 것이다 Even if you offer it to him, he won't accept it.

설산 雪山 a snow(-covered) mountain ; a mountain covered with snow

설상 舌狀 ¶ 설상의 tongue-shaped ; linguiform

— 기관 a lingua ; a tongue-like organ **—화** 〖식물〗 a lingulate flower ; a ray flower (국화과 식물의)

설상 雪上 (on) top of the snow

—가상(加霜) misfortune on top of misfortune ; out of the frying-pan into the fire ; misfortunes never come singly ¶ 설상가상으로 비까지 오기 시작했다 To make us more miserable, it began to rain. // 설상가상으로 그녀는 아들까지 잃었다 To complete the sum of her miseries, she lost her son. **—차(車)** a snowmobile ; a snow car〔vehicle〕

설상골 楔狀骨 cuneiform bone ; sphenoid (bone)

설선 雪線 〖지리〗 the snow line

설설¹ gently heating ¶ 물이 설설 끓다

water simmers // 방이 설설 끓다 a room is comfortably warm

설설² ① [기는 모양] crawl ; cringe ; cower ¶ 비서가 그의 무서운 눈초리 앞에 설설 긴다 The secretary cowers before his stern gaze.
② [고개를] with a gentle shake of the head
설설 기다 관용 cringe 《before》

설소차 雪搔車 a snow-plow

설쇠다 celebrate the New Year ; hold a New Year celebration ¶ 설쇠고 찾아 보겠다 I will call on you after the New Year celebrations are over.

설술 wine to celebrate the New Year

설신경 舌神經 a lingual〔gustatory〕 nerve

설암 舌癌 〖의학〗 tongue cancer ; cancer of the tongue

설야 雪夜 a snowy night

설연 設宴 holding〔giving〕 a banquet〔dinner〕 **—하다** hold a banquet ; give a dinner〔feast〕

설염 舌炎 〖의학〗 glossitis

설영하다 設營— [세우다] construct ; [준비하다] prepare ; arrange

설왕설래 說往說來 arguing back and forth **—하다** argue back and forth ; bandy words 《with》

설욕 雪辱 vindication of one's honor **—하다** clear oneself of a disgrace ; vindicate one's honor ; wipe out one's shame ; exonerate oneself 《of》 ; get revenge for one's defeat ¶ 이전의 실패를 설욕하다 wipe out the stain〔disgrace〕 of a former defeat
—전 a return match〔game〕 ; a fight for vindication ; a campaign to recover one's credit〔honor〕

설움 sorrow ; grief ; lamentation ; sadness ; distress ¶ 설움을 못 이기다 be overcome with sorrow // 가슴에 설움이 가득 차다 one's heart is filled with grief // 그 여자는 설움 속에 세월을 보낸다 She is living in sorrow.

설원 雪冤 exoneration ; vindication ; clearing oneself of a false charge **—하다** clear oneself (of a false charge) ; exonerate oneself (from guilt) ; prove〔establish〕 one's innocence

설원 雪原 a snowfield ; the frozen waste

설유 說諭 admonition ; exhortation ; reprimand **—하다** admonish ; exhort ; reprove ; reprimand ; warn ; advise ; caution ¶ 설유로 방면된다 be released with a reprimand

설음 舌音 〖음성〗 a lingual sound

설음질 dishwashing ⇨ 설거지

설익다 get〔be〕 half-done〔half-cooked〕

설인 雪人 [히말라야의] a〔an abominable〕 snowman ; a yeti

설자다 sleep fitfully〔poorly〕

설잡다 hold 《a thing》 loosely ; half-hold ¶ 개를 설잡으면 도망간다 If you do not hold the dog's leash tight enough, he will get away.

설전 舌戰 a verbal〔wordy〕 battle ; a war of words ; an argument **—하다** engage in a wordy〔verbal〕 battle 《with》 ; fight verbally ; argue

설정 設定 establishment ; creation ; institution ; fixing ; setting up **—하다** establish ; create ; institute ; set up ; fix ¶ 자금을 설정하다 set up a fund // 권리를 설정하다 create a right // 다만 자네가 나한테 돈을 빌리려면 담보를 하나 설정하라는 것뿐이야 I just want you to put up collateral for the loan.
—치(値) 〖전기〗 a set point **— 행위** an action of creation〔establishment〕

설정 雪程 a snow-covered road

설주 —柱 a side post ; a support (pillar)

설죽다 be half-alive

설중 雪中 the midst of snow ; in the snow ; through the (midst of) snow ¶ 설중 행군 a march in the snow

설차림 preparing the New Year's festive dishes

설천 雪天 a snow sky ; a snowy day

설철 屑鐵 scrap iron

설측음 舌側音 〖음성〗 a lateral (sound)

설치 設置 establishment ; foundation ; institution **—하다** establish ; institute ; set up ; found ; create ¶ 학교를 설치하다 establish〔found〕 a school // 영사관을 설치하다 set up a consulate // 위원회를 설치하다 organize〔set up〕 a committee // 그 가격에 배달료와 설치비도 포함돼 있습니까 Does the price include delivery and installation charges ?

설치다¹ leave 《it》 half-done ; stop 《work》 halfway ; do 《a thing》 by halves ¶ 간밤에는 잠을 설쳤다 I slept badly last night.

설치다² run wild ; riot ; be unruly ¶ 도대체 누가 이 방에서 설쳤느냐 Whoever has been running riot in this room ?

설치류 齧齒類 〖동물〗 rodents

설컹 hard chewing ; lumpy-tasting

***설탕 雪糖** sugar ¶ 설탕을 넣다 sugar ; sweeten 《food》 with sugar // 커피에 설탕을 넣을까요 Do you have sugar in your coffee ?
— 가루 powdered〔granulated〕 sugar ; castor sugar 《영》 **— 그릇** [식탁용의] a sugar bowl 《미》 ; a sugar basin 《영》 **—물** sugared water **— 조림** food preserved in sugar **— 집게** (a pair of) sugar tongs **각—** lump〔cube〕 sugar **모래 —** granulated〔crystallized〕 sugar **백〔정제〕—** white〔refined〕 sugar **빙(氷)—** crystal sugar ; rock candy 《미》 ; sugar candy 《영》 **흑—** raw sugar ; muscovado **과일 — 조림** succades ; candied fruit

설태 舌苔 the coat on one's tongue ; a coated tongue ; tongue fur〔fuzz〕 ¶ 혀에 설태가 끼었다 The tongue has become furred.

설통발 a fish trap ; a fishweir ; a fish garth
설파 說破 ① [밝힘] exposure ② [깨뜨림] confutation ; refutation —하다 expose ; confute ; refute ¶ 사실과 조리로써 상대방을 설파하다 confute one's opponent by facts and logic
설파제 —劑 a sulfa drug ; sulfas
설편 雪片 a snowflake ⇨ 눈송이
설피다 (be) loose-woven ; gauze-like
설피창이 loose-woven stuff ; gauze
설핏설핏 —하다 (be) all rather loose-woven ; gauze-like
설핏하다 (be) rather loose-woven ; gauze-like
설하선 舌下腺 a sublingual gland
설하 신경 舌下神經 the hypoglossal (nerve)
설한 雪寒 cold weather following snow fall ¶ 엄동 설한 the cold of winter
설해 雪害 snow damage
설형 楔形 cuneiform (writing) ; wedge-shape(d)
— 문자 a cuneiform character ; cuneiform letters ; cuneiform (writing)
설혹 設或 even if
설화 舌禍 trouble brought on by a slip of the tongue ; an unfortunate〔a disastrous〕 slip of the tongue
— 사건 trouble caused by one's incriminating utterance (in public) ¶ 설화 사건을 초래하다 be indicted〔criticized〕 for what one (has) said
설화 雪花 ① [눈송이] snowflakes ② [나뭇가지의] snow on the branches
— 석고 alabaster
설화 說話 a tale ; a story ; a narration
— 문학 narrative〔legendary〕 literature
설화체 說話體 a narrative style
— 소설 a novel in narrative form
섧다 ⇨ 서럽다
섬[1] ① a straw sack ¶ 쌀 섬 a rice bag ② [단위] a unit of volume 《5.12 U.S. bushels, 47.6 U.S. gallons》 ; a *sŏm*
섬[2] [층계] a flight of stairs〔steps〕
†섬[3] an island ; an isle ; [작은 섬] an islet ¶ 섬 사람 an islander // 섬에 살다 live in an island // 섬을 돌아보다 make a tour of islands
섬 纖 small ; fine ; delicate
섬거적 a straw mat ; straw matting ; a mat made from straw bags
섬게 〖동물〗 a sea urchin
*섬광 閃光 a flash
— 경보기 a flashing crossing signal — 계수기 〖물리〗 a scintillometer —기 a flashing apparatus —등 a flash lamp —분 〖사진〗 flash powder — 사진 flashlight photography — 신호 a flashing light signal — 전구 a flash lamp〔bulb, tube〕 ; a photoflash lamp

섬교 纖巧 delicacy ; exquisiteness
†섬기다 serve 《one's master》 ; take service 《with, under》 ; render service to 《one's country》 ; work under another ; work for 《a firm》 ; [모시다] minister to ; attend on ; page ¶ 남편을 섬기다 be devoted〔attentive〕 to one's husband // 스승을 섬기다 obey one's teacher // 신을 섬기다 serve God // 두 주인을 섬기다 serve two masters // 어버이를 잘 섬기다 be filial to one's parents
섬나라 an island〔insular〕 country
— 근성 insularity ; insularism
섬놈 an islander ; a native of an island
섬누룩 coarse〔inferior〕 malt
섬돌 stone steps ; a flight of steps
섬뜩하다 have a fright ; be taken by surprise ; (be) frightened ; startled ; shocked ; feel a shock ¶ 섬뜩하여 in astonishment ; struck with terror ; frightened 《at》 ; aghast // 인형이 너무 잘 만들어지면 뭔가 섬뜩한 느낌이 든다 When dolls are too well-made, there's something eerie about them.
섬망 譫妄 delirium ; allophasis
섬멸 殲滅 annihilation ; total〔complete〕 destruction ; a crushing defeat —하다 annihilate ; destroy totally ; wipe out ; stamp out
—전 an annihilation operation ; an exterminatory war
섬모 纖毛 ① 〖동물〗 a cilium 《*pl.* cilia, ~s》 ; [집합적] ciliation ¶ 섬모의 ciliary ② ⇨ 섬유(纖維)
—반(盤) 〖동물〗 a ciliary disc — 운동 ciliary movement —충 a ciliate —충류 Ciliata
섬벅, 섬뻑, 썸벅, 썸뻑 cutting with light stroke 《with knife》
섬벅거리다 wink ; blink
섬서하다 (be) unkindly ; cool ; curt
섬섬 纖纖 being delicate —하다 (be) slender ; delicately formed
—옥수(玉水) slender〔soft, delicate〕 hands
섬섬하다 閃閃— (be) flashing ; sparking ; gleaming ; glittering
*섬세 纖細 delicacy ; fineness —하다 (be) delicate ; fine ; subtle ; exquisite

> 참고 **delicate**는 가냘픔 미묘함 정밀함의 뜻이 함축되어 있고 **fine**도 이에 가깝다 **exquisite**는 특정한 사람 즉 전문적인 안식을 갖추고 있는 사람에게만 이해될 수 있는 오묘한 섬세함을 나타낸다

¶ 섬세한 감정 delicate feeling〔sentiment〕
섬약 纖弱 frailty ; delicacy —하다 (be) frail ; fragile ; delicate
섬어 譫語 [헛소리] a delirium ; nonsense ; [잠꼬대] talking in one's sleep
*섬유 纖維 a fiber ; a strand ; textiles ¶ 섬

유성(性)의 fibrous // 섬유상(狀)의 fibriform
— 공업 the fiber〔textile〕 industry — 공장 a textile mill — 구조 fiber structure — 기계 textile machinery —상 물질 a fibrous material — 석고 satin gypsum — 세포 〖식물〗 a fibrous cell —소 〖화학〗 cellulose ; 〖생화학〗 fibrin —속 〖해부〗 a fascicle ; fascicular fibers —업자 a textile industrialist — 유리 fiber〔fibrous, spun〕 glass — 작물 a fiber crop — 제품 textile goods — 조직 a fibrous tissue —증(症) 〖의학〗 fibrosis —질 fibroid material —층 〖해부〗 a fibrous layer — 형성질 fibrino-plastin 경질〔인피〕 — a hard 〔cordage〕 fiber 단— filament 동물〔식물〕성 — an animal〔a vegetable〕 fiber 인조〔합성, 화학〕 — an artificial〔a synthetic, chemical〕 fiber 천연〔목〕 — a natural〔wood〕 fiber

섬지기 〖농업〗 a rice-field requiring a *sŏm* of seed

섬질 planing off〔away〕 the side of a board —하다 plane off the side 《of》

섬쩍지근하다 《fear, nervousness, uneasiness》 be haunting and persistent

섬참새 〖새〗 a russet sparrow

섬화 閃火 a flash ; a spark
— 방전(放電) spark discharge

섭금류 涉禽類 〖새〗 the wading birds ; Grallatores (학명)

섭동 攝動 〖천문〗 (gravitational) perturbation

섭력 涉歷 versatile experience ; wide experience —하다 gain〔have〕 versatile experience ; become〔be〕 widely experienced

섭렵 涉獵 extensive reading —하다 read extensively ; range over ¶ 널리 문헌을 섭렵하다 range over an extensive literature // 여러 학자의 저술을 섭렵하다 dip into the works of great authors ; survey〔study〕 authorities

*섭리 攝理 (Divine) Providence ¶ 신의 섭리에 맡기다 trust in Divine Providence // 자연의 섭리에 의해서 by provision of nature

섭새기다 emboss ; carve in relief

섭새김(질) embossed carving ; relief —하다 ⇨ 섭새기다

섭생 攝生 care of health ; preservation of one's health ; 〖의학〗 regimen —하다 take care of one's health ¶ 섭생을 게을리하다 disregard hygienic rules ; neglect one's health ; be careless about one's health
—가 a person careful of his health ; a valetudinarian —법 the rules of health ; hygiene

섭섭하게 to one's regret ; regretfully ; unfortunately ¶ 섭섭하게도 그는 오지 않았다 To my disappointment, he did not come.

†섭섭하다 [1인칭이 주어] (be) sorry ; sad ; disappointed ; regret ; [가주어 it를 주어로] regrettable ; sad ; disappointing ; to be regretted ; vexing (유감) ¶ 섭섭해 하다 [2·3 인칭이 주어] be sorry about ; be sad over ; be disappointed over ; regret ; be vexed (유감) // 그가 못 와서 섭섭하다 I regret〔It is regrettable, It is too bad〕 that he can't come. // 그는 실패한 것이 섭섭하기 짝이 없었다 He was chagrined at〔mortified by〕 his failure.

섭씨 攝氏 Celsius 《C》
— 온도계 a centigrade thermometer ; a Celsius

섭양 攝養 care of health ⇨ 섭생

섭외 涉外 negotiation ; liaison
— 계원 a public relations man ; a liaison clerk〔officer〕 —과〔부〕 the liaison〔public relations〕 section〔division〕 — 관계 public relations — 사무 public relations 〔P. R.〕 work ; liaison business

*섭정 攝政 regency ; a regent (사람) —하다 rule as regent
— 황태자 the Prince Regent — 황후 the Queen〔Empress〕 Regent

섭조개 〖조개〗 a mussel

섭집게 pincers〔a pair of tongs〕 used in catching mussels

섭취 攝取 intake ; ingestion ; adoption —하다 take ingest ; take in ; swallow ; assimilate ¶ 타국의 문명을 섭취하다 adopt a foreign civilization
—물 ingesta 칼로리 —량 caloric intake

섭치 a useless〔poor, worthless〕 one among many things

섭호선 攝護腺 the prostate (gland)
—염 prostatitis ; inflammation of the prostate

섯등 a seawater-filtering implement making salt

섯밑 the flesh at the bottom of an ox tongue

섰다 a kind of Korean card game

*성 anger ; indignation ; rage ; wrath ¶ 성이〔을〕 나다〔내다〕 grow angry ; be offended〔indignant〕 ; get mad 《미》 // 성이나게 하다 offend ; anger ; outrage // 성을 잘내다 be quick to take offense // 그녀는 아무 것도 아닌 일에 성을 곧 잘 낸다 She easily loses her temper for nothing. // 나는 그녀가 성을 내고 있는 것을 본적이 없다 I have never seen her out of temper.

*성 姓 a family name ; a surname ¶ 성과 이름 one's full name

*성 性 ① [본성] nature ; disposition (기질) ② [문법] gender ③ [남녀의] a sex ¶ 성의〔적〕 sexual // 성에 눈뜨다 wake up sexually ; be awakened of sexual instinct // 성적으로 조숙하다 sexually precocious
—관계 sexual relations —기 a genital 〔reproductive〕 organ —문제 a sex problem —범죄 sex crimes —병 venereal

disease —본능 the sex instinct〔urge〕 —억제 sex control —연구 sexology —자각 sexual awareness ; the awakening of sex〔sexual instinct〕 —전환 sex change〔reversal〕; sex transformation —지식 knowledge of sexual matters —행위 sexual intercourse —호르몬 a sex hormone —희롱 sexual harassment 남〔여, 중〕— masculine〔feminine, neuter〕 gender

†성 城 a castle ; a fortress ; a citadel ; a city wall ¶ 성을 함락시키다 take〔capture〕 a castle // 성을 내놓다 surrender a castle (to the enemy)

†성 省 [행정부] a ministry ; a department (of the government) ; [중국의 행정 구역] a province

교육— the Department of Education 국방— the Department of Defense 《미》; the Ministry of Defence 《영》 내무— the Department of the Interior 《미》; the Home Office《영》 노동— the Department of Labor《미》; the Ministry of Labour and National Service 《영》 농무— the Department of Agriculture 《미》; the Ministry of Agriculture and Fisheries 《영》 미국 국무 — the U. S. Department of State 법무— the Department of Justice 《미》; the Chancery 《영》 산동— Santung Province 상무— the Department of Commerce 《미》; the Board of Trade 《영》 외무— the Foreign Office 우정— the Post Office Department 《미》; the Post Office 《영》 재무— the Treasury Department 《미》; the Exchequer 《영》 후생— the Welfare Ministry ; the Ministry of Public Welfare

‡성 聖 [성인] a sage ; a saint ; [한 학문에 도통한 사람] a great master ¶ 성 베드로 St. Peter // 성 간디 the sage Gandhi // 악성 베토벤 Beethoven, a supreme musical composer ; the great composer Beethoven

성가 成家 ① [학문·기술을] establishing oneself as a master〔an authority〕; developing a style of one's own
② [집을] establishment of one's own household ; success in life —하다 [학문·기술을] establish oneself as a master ; develop a style of one's own ; make a name for oneself ; [집을] establish one's own household ; succeed in life ; make a fortune of one's own ¶ 자수 성가하다 make one's own efforts

성가 聲價 reputation ; repute ; fame ; popularity ¶ 성가를 높이다 enhance one's reputation // 성가를 유지하다 maintain〔keep up〕 one's reputation ; retain〔keep〕 one's prestige

‡성가 聖歌 a sacred song ; a hymn
—대 a choir —대장 a choirmaster —집 a hymnal ; a hymnbook

성가 聖架 the Cross ; the Holy Rood

성가 聖駕 the royal carriage〔chariot, coach〕

‡성가시다 (be) annoying ; troublesome ; bothering ; harassing ; pesky 《미》; persistent ; importunate ; inquisitive ¶ 파리가 성가시다 the flies are annoying // 성가시게 질문하다 trouble 《a person》 with questions ; be inquisitive // 성가시게 굴지 마라 Don't bother me ! (방해마라) /What a nuisance ! (귀찮다) /Leave me alone ! (상관마라) // 그 남자가 자꾸 찾아와서 성가시다 I am annoyed〔bothered, troubled〕 by his frequent visits.

성가퀴 城— a battlement (atop a wall)

성각 城閣 the watchtower of a castle

성감 性感 sexual feeling
—대(帶) erotogenic zones

성게 a sea urchin

†성격 性格 character ; personality ¶ 성격적인 characteristic // 성격의 차이 dissimilarity〔disparity〕 in character // 성격상의 결점 a flaw in one's character // 좋은 성격을 갖추다 bear〔possess, have〕 a good character // 그의 성격은 나하고는 전혀 반대다 His character is diametrically opposed to mine. // 형제간이지만 성격은 아주 딴판이다 They are brothers, but quite dissimilar in character. // 주인공의 성격이 잘 묘사되어 있다 The character of the hero is well described. // 그의 성격이 거기에 잘 나타나 있다 His personality asserts itself there strongly.
—극 a character drama — 묘사 character drawing〔delineation〕 — 배우 a character actor〔actress〕 — 파탄〔이상〕자 an abnormal character ; a screwball 《속어》 — 형성 character formation — 희극 a comedy of character 선천〔후천〕적 — inherited〔acquired〕 character

성결 nature ; disposition ; personality ; character ; individuality ; temper ¶ 성결이 곱다〔사납다〕 have a lovely〔nasty〕 disposition

성결 聖潔 holiness and purity
— 교회 the Holiness Church

*성경 聖經 the Bible ; the Book ; the Scriptures ; sacred books ; a holy book ¶ 성경의 Biblical ; scriptural // 성경의 귀절 a biblical expression ; a scriptural phrase
— 낭독 a scripture reading ; a Bible lesson — 문학 Biblical literature — 연구회 a Bible class ; a Bible-study group — 용어 Biblical language — 이야기 a Bible story — 인용구 a Biblical quotation — 학자 a Biblical〔Bible〕 scholar ; a Biblicist — 해석학 hermeneutics — 협회 a Bible society 개역 — the Revised Version 《of the Bible》 《R. V.》 신〔구〕약 — the New〔Old〕 Testament 흠정역 — the Authorized Version 《of the Bible》 《A. V.》

성경현전 聖經賢傳 the works left us by

the sages of the past
†성공 成功 success ; accomplishment ; achievement (성취) ──하다 [사물이 주어] succeed ; be〔prove〕 successful ; [사람이 주어] succeed 《in》 ; win〔achieve〕 success 《in》 ¶ 성공의 가망이 있다 have a chance of success // 그는 사업에 대성공을 했다 He was a great success〔very successful〕 in the enterprise. /He made a great coup in the enterprise. // 성공을 빕니다 I wish you success. / May you succeed ! // 그 실험은 성공하지 못했다 The experiment did not come off.
—자 a successful man ; a success
성공회 聖公會 the Anglican Church 《영》 ; the Protestant Episcopal Church 《미》
—원 an Anglican 《영》 ; an Episcopalian 《미》
성과 成果 a result ; a product ; fruit ; an outcome ¶ 노력의 성과 the fruit of one's labor ; the result of one's efforts // 성과 있는 productive // 훌륭한 성과를 거두다 obtain excellent results
성과학 性科學 sexology
성곽 城廓 a castle ; a citadel ; a fortress ; a stronghold ; castle walls ; an enclosure
성관 盛觀 a grand spectacle〔sight〕
‡성교 性交 sexual intercourse ; coitus —하다 have sexual intercourse
— 불능 impotence ; impotency — 불능자 an impotent person — 연령 a copulation age — 중단 coitus interruptus〔reservatus〕 《라》
성교 聖敎 ① the sacred teachings ; royal instruction ② Catholicism
—회(會) the holy Catholic Church
성교육 性敎育 sex education ; sex information
성구 聖具 a sacred utensil
— 보관실〔인〕 a sacristy〔sacristan〕
성군 星群 a cluster〔group〕 of stars ; an asterism
성군 聖君 a good and wise king
성군작당 成群作黨 forming a gang 〔cabal, faction〕 ──하다 form a gang ; gang〔band〕 together ; cabal
성귀 聖句 〖종교〗 a reading ; a lesson ; a lection
—집 a lectionary
성귀 成句 a set phrase ; an idiomatic phrase〔expression〕
—어 an idiom
성규 成規 rules ; regulations
성극 聖劇 a biblical drama
성글벙글 smilingly ; beamingly ; with a bland smile ¶ 성글벙글 웃는 얼굴 a beaming face ; a radiant look
성금 result ; consequence ; outcome ; effect ; avail ; use ; worth
성금 誠金 a donation ; a contribution ; a gift of money ; a subscription ¶ 성금을 내다 contribute ; donate
방위 — a contribution to the national defense fund 원호 — a donation for the needy
‡성급하다 性急— (be) hasty ; impatient ; quick-tempered ; impetuous ; rash ¶ 성급한 사람 a man of quick temper ; a hotspur // 너무 성급히 굴지 마라 Easy does it.
성기 星期 a wedding date
성기 性器 genitalia ; genitals ; sexual 〔genital, productive, generative〕 organs ⇨ 생식기
성기 聖器 〖기독교〗 a consecrated〔sacred〕 vessel
성기다 ① [거리·간격이] be sparsely〔thinly, scatteredly〕 spaced ; be far apart ; have a gap〔gaps〕 between ¶ 머리털이 성기다 be thinly haired ; one's hair is thin // 언덕에 나무가 성기게 서 있다 The hill is sparsely wooded. // 집들이 성기다 There are scattered houses there. / The place is sparsely dotted with houses.
② [관계가] (be) estranged ; alienated ; be not on good terms ⇨ 소원하다
성깃성깃 thinly ; sparsely ; scatteredly ; sporadically ; here and there ¶ 벌판에는 나무가 성깃성깃 서 있었다 The field was sparsely dotted with trees.
성깃하다 be rather sparsely〔thinly〕 spaced ; have something of a gap between
성깔 a sharp temper ; an irritable disposition
†성나다 get〔grow〕 angry〔offended〕 with 《a person》〔at a thing〕 ; lose one's temper ; take offense ; get mad 《미》 ; be out of temper ¶ 그는 곧잘 성을 낸다 He is easily offended. // 그 여자는 내 말에 성이 나 있다 She is offended at what I said.
성내 城內 inside a fortress〔a city wall, a castle〕 ; within the city ; the city
‡성내다 get angry ⇨ 성나다
†성냥 matches ; a light (불) ¶ 성냥 한 갑 a box of matches // 성냥을 켜다 light 〔strike〕 a match
—갑 a matchbox ¶ 성냥갑 같은 집 a house like a matchbox ; a matchbox of a house —개비 a matchstick —불 the light of a match 안전 — a safety match 종이 — a matchfolder ; a matchbook
성냥노리 a blacksmith's year-end collection of bills
성냥일 blacksmithing ; smith work
성냥하다 forge ; anneal ; temper
성녀 聖女 〖카톨릭〗 a woman saint
‡성년 成年 full〔adult, legal, lawful〕 age ; one's majority ; a man's〔woman's〕 state ¶ 성년이 되다 come of age ; attain one's majority ; arrive at manhood〔womanhood〕
—식 the celebration of one's coming of

age ; a coming-of-age ceremony —자 an adult ; a major ; a person of legal〔full〕 age
성년 盛年 the prime of life〔manhood〕
성년 聖年 〖카톨릭〗 a holy year
성능 性能 performance ; efficiency ; ability ; capability ; capacity ; power (of airplanes, arms)
— 검사〔시험〕 an efficiency〔a performance〕 test — 계수 quality factor — 곡선 a performance curve
성단 星團 a group〔cluster〕 of stars
성단 聖壇 a pulpit ; an altar ; a shrine
성단 聖斷 Royal decision
성담곡 聖譚曲 〖음악〗 oratorio
‡성당 聖堂 a church ; a Catholic Church ; a sanctuary
성대 〖물고기〗 a gurnard
성대 聖代 an age of sage rulers ; a glorious reign
성대 盛大 —하다 [번영] (be) prosperous ; flourishing ; thriving ; [훌륭하다] splendid ; grand ; magnificent ; successful ¶ 성대한 회합 a successful meeting // 성대하게 splendidly ; successfully ; on a large scale (대규모로)
성대 聲帶 the vocal cords〔bands〕
— 모사〔모방〕 vocal mimicry 가— a false vocal cord
성덕 盛德 flourishing virtue(s)
성덕 聖德 [성인의] saints' virtues ; saintly virtues ; [임금의] royal virtues〔favor〕
성도 星圖 〖천문〗 a celestial map
성도 成道 [석가의] Buddha's attainment of Great Wisdom ; [예술의] attainment of perfection
성도 聖徒 a (Christian) saint ; an apostle ; a disciple of Christ ¶ 성도 베드로 Saint Peter
—전 hagiology ; the lives of the saints
성도 聖都 the Holy City ; Jerusalem
성도덕 性道德 sexual morality
성도착증 性倒錯症 sexual perversion
성랑 城廊 a castle tower
성량 聲量 the volume of one's voice ¶ 성량이 풍부하다 have a full〔resonant, powerful〕 voice
성려 聖慮 the King's wish〔thought, pleasure〕
성력 誠力 wholehearted devotion ; sincerity and energy ¶ 성력을 다하다 devote oneself whole-heartedly
성령 聖靈 the Holy Ghost ; the Holy Spirit
— 강림 the descent of the Holy Spirit 《on the apostles》 — 강림절 Whitsuntide ; the season of Pentecost
성례 成禮 completion of the ceremonies of marriage —하다 complete the ceremonies of marriage.
성례 聖禮 [예식] a sacred ceremony ; 〖기독교〗 Christian ceremonies
성루 城壘 a fort ; a fortress ; ramparts ¶ 성루를 지키다 take one's stand in a fortress ; guard the ramparts
성루 城樓 a castle turret
성리 性理 human nature and natural laws
—학 philosophy ; metaphysics
성립 成立 existence (존립) ; completion (완성) ; realization (실현) ; materialization ; formation (조직) ; conclusion (체결) —하다 [존립하다] exist ; come into being〔existence〕 ; [조직] be formed ; [실현되다] be realized〔effected〕 ; materialize ; [체결하다] be concluded ; […으로 이루어지다] be made up of〔composed of〕 ; consist of ¶ 금년도 예산이 어제 성립됐다 The budget for the current fiscal year was given the Assembly's final approval yesterday. // 두 사람 사이에 타협이 성립됐다 A compromise has been effected between the two. // 그의 동의가 15표 대 30표로 성립됐다 The motion introduced by him was carried by 30 votes to 15. // 그 회사는 성립될지 안될지 의심스럽다 It is doubtful whether the proposed company will be formed. // 조약이 성립됐다 The treaty was concluded.
— 예산 the approved budget
성마르다 be narrow-minded and hot-tempered
성막 聖幕 〖카톨릭〗 a tabernacle
성만찬 聖晩餐 Holy Communion ; the Sacrament of the Lord's Supper ; the Eucharist
성망 聲望 reputation ; fame ; popularity ¶ 성망이 높다 be highly reputed ; be very popular
†성명 姓名 one's family name and given name ; a full name ; a name ¶ 성명 불상의 unidentified ; unknown
—부 a name list ; a register (of names)
— 점호(點呼) a roll call — 판단 onomancy
성명 盛名 fame ; renown ; honor ; glory ; reputation ; an illustrious name
성명 聖名 〖카톨릭〗 a holy name
성명 聲名 reputation ; fame ; popularity
성명 聲明 (a) declaration ; (a) statement ; (an) announcement —하다 declare ; announce ; make a statement ¶ 반대〔찬성〕를 성명하다 declare oneself against〔for〕
—서 a (public) statement ; a communiqué 《프》 ; a manifesto (정부·정당의) ¶ 성명서를 발표하다 issue a statement 《on》
—전 an exchange of charges and countercharges 공동 — a joint statement 공식 — an official statement
성명없다 姓名— (be) nameless ; unknown ; unrecognized ; insignificant
성모 聖母 the Holy Mother ; our Lady ; the Virgin Mary
— 마리아 the Virgin Mary ; Blessed Mary — 숭경(崇敬) hyperdulia — 잉태

the Immaculate Conception
성묘 省墓 ―하다 visit one's ancestral graves
―객 a visitor to his ancestral tomb
성묘 聖廟 ⇨ 문묘
성무 星霧 ⇨ 성운(星雲)
성문 成文 reducing to writing
― 계약 a written contract ―권 a deed ―법(률) a statute ; a law ; a written 〔positive〕 law ; a lex scripta 《라》 ; a jus scriptum 《라》 ―화 codification ; legalization ¶ 성문화하다 codify ; put in statutory form
성문 城門 a castle〔city〕 gate
성문 聲門 〚해부〛 the glottis
성문 聲紋 a voiceprint
성미 性味 nature ; disposition ; temperament ; character ¶ 성미가 좋은〔나쁜〕 사람 a good-natured〔ill-natured〕 person∥성미에 맞다 [사람이] be congenial in temperament with 《a person》 ; be born under the same star ; [음식이나 일 따위가] be congenial to one's tastes ; agree with 《a person》∥그들은 서로 성미가 안 맞는다 They are not congenial in temperament with each other. /They are not suited to each other. ∥말은 잘못 다루면 성미가 사나와진다 Badly treated, horses become vicious. ∥그 사람 하고는 전혀 성미가 안 맞는다 He is an individual totally different in cast from me. ∥그런 거친 방법은 내 성미에 맞지 않는다 Rough measures like that go against my grain.
성미 誠米 ritual rice
성배 聖杯 〚카톨릭〛 the (Holy) Grail
성벽 性癖 disposition ; predisposition ; propensity ; a characteristic ; a mental habit
성벽 城壁 a castle wall ; a rampart
성별 性別 sex distinction
성병 性病 a venereal disease 《V. D.》 ¶ 성병 감염 venereal infection∥성병의 예방 prevention of venereal diseases
― 치료소 a V. D. clinic ―학 venereology ― 환자 a person venereally infected
성보 城堡 a fortress ; a rampart ; a citadel
성복 成服 ⇨ 성불성(成不成)
성부 聖父 〚기독교〛 God the Fàther ; the Father
성부 城府 town (walls) ; a (town) boundary
성분 成分 an ingredient ; a component ; an element ; a constituent ¶ 주요 성분 the chief〔principal〕 ingredient
― 시험〔검사〕 a chemical experiment 〔test〕 공기〔약〕 ― the composition of air〔a medicine〕 부― an accessory ingredient 중요 ― the chief〔main, principal〕 ingredients 《of》
성불 成佛 attaining Buddhahood ; entering Nirvana ―하다 attain Buddhahood ; enter Nirvana ; become a Buddha
성불성 成不成 success and〔or〕 failure ; the outcome
성사 成事 accomplishment ; achievement ; success ―하다 succeed ; accomplish ; achieve ; be successful ¶ 모사 재인(在人)이요 성사 재천(在天)이라 Man proposes, God disposes.
성사 盛事 a splendid enterprise ; a great event
성사 聖事 [성스러운 일] divine service ; 〚카톨릭〛 a sacrament
혼배(婚配) ― the sacrament of matrimony
성산 成算 confidence of success ; prospects of sure success ; chances of success ¶ 성산이 있다〔없다〕 be confident〔have little hope〕 of success∥성산이 있느냐 Are you quite sure of success ? ∥성산이 없는 사업은 찬성할 수 없다 I cannot approve (of) an undertaking that offers scanty hope of success.
성상 星霜 years ; time ¶ 십년의 성상 ten years' time
성상 聖上 His Majesty ; the King ; the Emperor
성상 聖像 an icon ; a sacred image〔portrait〕
― 연구 iconography ; iconology ― 연구가 an iconologist ; an iconographer ― 예배 iconolatry
성상학 性相學 physiognomy ¶ 성상학의 physiognomical
―자 a physiognomist
성색 聲色 voice and countenance ; demeanor
성생활 性生活 sex life ; sexual life
***성서 聖書** the (Holy) Bible ; the Scriptures ; the Book (of books) ; the sacred volume
― 협회 a Bible society
성선 性腺 〚해부〛 a sex gland ; a gonad ⇨ 생식(―선)
성선설 性善說 the ethical doctrine of innate goodness ; the view that man is born good ; the view of human nature as fundamentally good
성성이 猩猩― 〚동물〛 an orang-outang
성성하다 星星― (be) grizzled ; gray (streaked) ¶ 백발이 성성한 노인 a gray-haired old man
성세 聖世 an age of sage rulers ; an era of wise rule ; a prosperous〔glorious〕 age
성세 盛世 a prosperous〔glorious〕 age ; an era of prosperity
성세포 性細胞 ⇨ 생식(―세포)
성소 性巢 a gonad
성소 聖所 〚성경〛 the holy place ; sanctum
성쇠 盛衰 ups and downs ; rise and decline ; prosperity and decline ; vicissitudes ¶ 로마의 성쇠 the rise and fall of Rome∥국가의 성쇠가 걸리다 affect the

destiny〔welfare〕 of the country
성수 聖壽 the King's age ¶ 성수 만세 Long live the King!
성수 星宿 〖천문〗 the stars; the constellations
성수 星數 one's fortune; one's star
성수 聖水 holy water
성수기 盛需期 high-demand season ¶ 성수기를 맞이한 상품 things most in demand
‡**성숙 成熟** ① [과실의] ripening **―하다** ripen; be ripe ¶ 성숙한 감 ripe persimmon
② [발육] full〔complete〕 growth; maturation **―하다** attain full growth; mature ¶ 성숙한 처녀 a mature〔marriageable〕 girl
③ [숙성] maturity; ripeness **―하다** mature; ripen; attain〔come to〕 maturity ¶ 기운(機運)이 성숙하다 An opportunity ripens〔matures〕.
성숙기 成熟期 puberty; adolescence; (the age of) maturity ¶ 성숙기에 달하다 arrive at puberty; become adolescent; attain (to) maturity
***성스럽다 聖―** (be) holy; sacred; august; divine
성시 成市 opening a fair〔market〕 **―하다** open a fair ¶ 문전 성시하다 have a constant stream of visitors; be thronged with callers
성시 盛時 the prime of life; a prosperous age
성시 城市 a walled city
성신 星辰 the stars; heavenly bodies
― 숭배 astrolatry
성신 聖神 the Holy Spirit
― 강림 the descent〔advent〕 of the Holy Spirit
†**성실 誠實** sincerity; fidelity; honesty; integrity **―하다** (be) sincere; faithful; truthful; honest; single-hearted
―성(性) sincerity; faithfulness
성심 誠心 sincerity; good faith ¶ 성심성의로 sincerely; heartily; wholeheartedly; devotedly; from one's heart; from the bottom of one's heart // 성심 성의를 다하다 deal with 《a matter》 in all sincerity; devote oneself heart and soul 《to a thing》
성싶다 [ㄴ·은·는·ㄹ·을 뒤에서] seem (to be); appear (to be); I guess (that)... ¶ 재미 있을 성싶다 It sounds like fun. // 비가 그칠 성싶지 않다 There is no sign of the rain ceasing. // 눈이 올 성싶다 It seems likely to snow. /It looks as though it were going to snow. // 그를 한 번 본 성싶다 It seems to me that I have met him before. // 그 계획은 좋을 성싶다 The plan appears to be a good one. // 그녀는 회복될 성싶지 않았다 It seemed as if she would not recover. // 그가 있을 성싶은 곳은 다 찾아 보았다 I looked for him in every likely place.
성씨 姓氏 a family name; a surname; one's last name
성악 聲樂 vocal music
―가 a vocalist **―과** a vocal music course
― 연습 training of one's voice; voice culture
성악 聖樂 sacred music
성악설 性惡說 the ethical view that human nature is evil; the doctrine of original sin
성안 成案 a definite plan〔draft〕; a concrete program **―하다** form a definite plan; draft
성안 城― ⇨ 성내(城內)
성애 ① [대접함] an after-bargain treat ② [덤받음] receiving an extra goods when shopping
성애 性愛 sexual love
성야 星夜 a starry〔starlit〕 night
성야 聖夜 Christmas Eve
성어 成語 [어귀] a (set) phrase; [말을 이룸] forming a word〔set phrase〕
성어 成魚 an adult fish
성업 成業 the completion of one's work; the completion of one's studies〔a school course〕 **―하다** complete one's work〔studies〕 ¶ 자식의 성업을 기다리다 wait for one's son to complete his school course
― 공사 the Adjustment Corporation
성업 盛業 a thriving business ¶ 성업중이다 drive a thriving〔booming, prosperous〕 trade
성업 聖業 a sacred〔holy〕 work〔enterprise〕
성에[1] (a layer of) frost ¶ 냉장고의 성에를 제거하다 defrost a refrigerator
성에[2] the handle of a Korean plow (쟁기의)
성엣장 ice drifts; drifting ice
성역 聖域 sacred precincts; holy grounds
성역 聲域 a range of voice; 〖음악〗 a register ¶ 그녀의 성역은 놀랍게 넓다 The range of her voice is astonishing.
성연 盛宴 a magnificient banquet; a grand feast
성염 盛炎 intense heat; the hottest weather〔season〕
성영 〖카톨릭〗 the Holy Child; the Infant Christ
성왕 聖王 a sage king
성외 城外 outside the walls (of a castle); beyond the wall
성욕 性慾 sexual desire; sexual〔carnal〕 appetite ¶ 성욕이 강한 strongly sexed // 성욕을 만족시키다 gratify one's carnal appetite // 성욕을 자극하다 stimulate sexual feeling
― 결핍 sexual disinclination〔apathy〕 **― 과도** aphrodisia; morbid sexual excitement **― 도착** sexual perversion〔inversion〕 **― 도착자** a sexual pervert **― 앙진**

sexual incitement〔impulse〕; erotomania
변태 — abnormal sexuality
성우 聲優 a radio performer〔actor, actress〕
*성운 星雲 a nebula《*pl.* neblae》
—상 nebulosity —설 the nebular hypothesis〔theory〕 와상〔가스〕 — a spiral〔gaseous〕 nebula 환상 — an annular nebula ; a ring nebula
성운 盛運 good fortune ; good luck ; prosperity
성원 成員 [정족수] a quorum ; [구성원] a constituent (member) ¶ 성원을 이루다 constitute〔form〕 a quorum ; [영국 하원에서] make a House
— 미달 lack of a quorum ¶ 성원이 미달되다 fail to meet the quorum《required for the session》; do not come up to〔be short of〕 the quorum
성원 聲援 (a shout of) encouragement ; support ; cheering (경기의) —하다 shout encouragement ; encourage ; cheer ; root (for a team)《미》¶ 맹렬히 성원하다 root wildly (for a team) ; give a college yell for a team
—자 a cheerer ; a rooter
성월 星月 the moon and stars
성위 星位 〖천문〗 the position of a fixed star ; the configuration
성유 聖油 consecrated oil ; chrism
성은 聖恩 royal favor (왕의) ; divine favor (신의)
성음 聲音 a vocal sound
— 문자 a phonogram ; phonetic letters〔script〕 —학 phonetics
성읍 城邑 a castle town
‡성의 誠意 sincerity ; good faith ¶ 성의 있는 sincere ; earnest // 성의 없는 insincere // 성의로써 sincerely ; earnestly // 성의를 피력하다 show one's good faith ; lay〔bare〕 one's heart
*성인 成人 an adult ; a grown-up person ; a grown-up ¶ 성인이 되다 attain adulthood〔manhood, womanhood〕; come of age
— 교육 adult education —병 diseases of adult people ; geriatric diseases —부(部) an adult division —식 a coming-of-age ceremony — 학교 an adult school
†성인 聖人 a sage ; a saint ; a holy man
성인도 시속(時俗)을 따른다 〔속담〕 When in Rome, do as the Romans do.
성자 姓字 a surname ; the surname character
성자 聖者 a saint ; a holy man
성자 聖子 the Son of God ; the (Holy) Son
성자 盛者 a prosperous person
성작 聖爵 〖가톨릭〗 a communion cup ; a chalice
†성장 成長 growth —하다 grow (up) ; be brought up ¶ 성장한 grown-up ; full grown ; adult ; matured // 성장이 빠르다 grow quickly〔rapidly〕; be fast growing // 성장하여 훌륭한 청년이 되다 grow into a fine young man // 성장할수록 더 한층 예뻐졌다 As she grew older, she became more and more beautiful. /The older she grew, the more beautiful she became.
— 곡선 a growth curve — 기간〔과정〕 a growth period〔process〕 — 반응 〖화학〗 growth reaction — 산업 a growth industry — 요인 a growth factor —주(식) a growth stock — 호르몬 growth hormone
경제 — economic growth 고도 — rapid growth
성장 盛裝 full dress〔uniform〕; a gala dress ; beautiful attire —하다 be dressed in one's best ; dress oneself handsomely ; be finely〔richly〕 dressed ; be in gala dress〔costume〕 ¶ 성장한 여인들 richly gowned ladies // 성장을 하고서 in gala dress ; in full feather〔fig〕 // 성장시키다 dress up《one's daughter》
성장률 成長率 a rate of growth ; a growth rate
경제 — a rate of economic growth
*성적 成績 (a) result ; (a) record ; score ; grade ; merit ¶ 학교에서 좋은 성적을 내다 make〔get〕 good marks at school ; do well at school // 사업의 성적을 올리다 obtain a satisfactory result in business // 성적이 좋다〔나쁘다〕 have〔make〕 a good〔bad〕 record // 이번 학기에 영어 성적이 올랐다〔떨어졌다〕 I have got a better〔worse〕 grade in English this semester. // 이번 달의 영업 성적은 어떻습니까 How are the business results this month?
—제 a merit system — 지수 achievement quotient《A. Q.》 —표 a list of students' records ; a report card ; an academic record ; a grade sheet ; a transcript (of academic record) (사본) 시험 — the result(s) of an examination 영업 — business results〔showings〕 학교 —《one's》 school record〔work, credits〕 학업 — scholarly attainment
성적 性的 sexual
— 매력 sex appeal ; sexual attractiveness — 욕망 sexual appetite〔desire〕 — 지식 knowledge of sexual matters — 충동 a sex urge〔drive〕; a sexual impulse — 흥분 sexual excitement〔arousal〕
성적 聖蹟 a sacred〔holy〕 place with historic associations
성적순 成績順 the order of merit ¶ 성적순으로 앉다 sit in the order of merit〔the achieved performance records〕
성전 聖典 the Bible ⇨ 성경
성전 盛典 a grand〔an imposing〕 ceremony
성전 聖殿 a sacred hall ; a sanctuary ; a temple
성전 聖戰 a holy war
성전 成典 a code of statute law
성전 性典 a book on sex
성전환 性轉換 the change of sex ; a sex

change
— 수술 a sex exchange operation —자 a transsexual
성정 性情 nature ; temper ; temperament
성조 性燥 — 하다 (be) quick-tempered ; hot-headed
성조 聲調 a tone of voice
성조기 星條旗 the Stars and Stripes ; the Star-Spangled Banner 《the U. S. flag》
성좌 星座 a constellation ; an asterism ¶ 오리온 성좌 the constellation of Orion
— 조견도(早見圖) a star chart ; a planisphere —표 a table〔catalog〕 of constellations
성주 〖민속〗 the home-site guardian god ; a hearth god ; a tutelary deity ¶ 성주받이 a shaman rite to induce the home-site god to enter〔reenter〕 the house
성주 聖主 a good and wise king
성주 城主 the castle owner ; the lord of a castle
성주간 聖週間 〖카톨릭〗 Holy Week
성중 城中 inside (of) a castle〔city〕
성지 城址 the ruins〔remains〕 of a castle〔fortress〕
성지 聖旨 the royal will〔wish〕
*성지 聖地 sacred ground ; the Holy Land ; Palestine
— 순례 a pilgrimage to the Holy Land
— 순례자 a pilgrim to sacred places〔the Holy Land〕
성지 城池 a moat
성직 聖職 holy orders ; the clergy ; the ministry
— 서임 ordination —자 a churchman ; a minister ; a clergyman ; a cleric ; a man of the cloth ¶ 성직자가 되다 take〔be admitted to〕 (holy) orders ; join〔go into〕 the church ; be ordained (to the priesthood)
†성질 性質 ① [기질] nature ; disposition ; temperament ; temper ¶ 성질이 좋은〔나쁜〕 사람 a man of good〔bad〕 character ; a good〔an ill〕-natured man
② [고유한 특성] property ; qualities ; attribute ¶ 석탄의 성질 the properties of coal // 그는 시인으로서의 성질을 다분히 가지고 있다 He has the qualities〔making〕 of a poet in a high degree.
③ [사물의 성질] character ; nature ; make-up

> 참고 **nature**는 인간·동물 따위의 「타고난 성질」 **disposition**은 반드시 타고 난 것만은 아닌 「개인의 성질」 **temper**는 감정적으로 본 성질인 「기질」 **character**는 정신적·도덕적으로 본 「성격」 **property**는 본래의 성질인 「특성」의 뜻 **quality**는 가장 일반적인 말로서 좋은 의미로 많이 쓰인다 **attribute**는 고유의 성질인 「속성」 **temperament**는 「체질」 **make-up**은 「체질과 성격」의 뜻

¶ 일의 성질 the character of the business // 그 문제의 성질상 from the nature of the matter // 이 두 문제는 성질이 다르다 The two questions are of different character. // 이런 성질의 돈은 받을 수가 없다 I cannot accept money of that nature.
성징 性徵 〖생물〗 a sex〔sexual〕 character **1차** — a primary sex character **2차** — a secondary sex character
성찬 盛饌 a sumptuous〔capital〕 dinner ; a feast ; a good table ; a plentiful supply of food ¶ 성찬을 베풀다 give a feast ; set a good table ; entertain ; give 《a person》 hospitality
성찬 聖餐 Holy Communion ; the Lord's Supper ; the Sacrament
—배(盃) a communion cup —식 the Communion〔Lord's Supper〕 service —탁자 a communion table
성찰 省察 self-examination ; self-reflection ; introspection
*성채 城砦 a fortress and a stockade ; a fortified and garrisoned city
성책 城柵 a fortress and a palisade
성천자 聖天子 a wise and virtuous king
성철 聖哲 a sage ; the wise
성체 成體 〖생물〗 an adult (animal)
성체 聖體 [왕의] the person of the king 〖카톨릭〗 the Eucharist ; the Blessed Sacrament
— 강복 Benediction of the Blessed Sacrament — 거동 a sacramental procession — 공존 consubstantiation — 배수(拜受) (Holy) Communion — 봉헌 Oblation — 성사 Sacrament ; the Holy Communion
성총 聖寵 [왕의] royal grace〔favo(u)r〕 ; 〖카톨릭〗 divine grace〔favor〕
성충 成蟲 〖동물〗 an imago 《*pl.* imagos, imagines》 ; an adult insect
—기 the imaginal stage
성충 誠忠 true〔devoted〕 loyalty
*성취 成娶 taking a wife ; marrying a woman — 하다 marry (a woman) ; take to wife
성취 成就 completion ; accomplishment ; attainment ; achievement ; fulfilment ; realization — 하다 accomplish ; attain ; achieve ; fulfil ; realize

> 참고 **accomplish**는 계획의 처음부터 끝까지를 포함한 「성취」 **achieve**는 곤란하거나 또는 중대한 일을 「성취하다」의 뜻 **attain**은 「노력해서 목적에 도달한다」는 것 **fulfil**은 「약속 명령 의무 따위를 다한다」는 뜻 즉 complete

¶ 소원 성취를 신명께 빌었다 I fervently prayed to God for the realization of my wishes.
성층 成層 〖지질〗 bedding ; stratification
—암 (a) sedimentary rock ; (a) stratified rock — 화산 a stratovolcano

성층권 成層圈 the stratosphere ¶ 성층권의 stratospheric // 성층권을 비행하다 fly through the stratosphere
— **비행** a stratosphere flight — **비행기** a stratoliner ; a stratoplane — **연구자** a stratospherist **아(亞)—** the sub-stratosphere
성칙 聖勅 a Royal rescript
성큼성큼 with big strides ¶ 성큼성큼 걷다 stalk ; stride ; take〔walk〕 long〔big, great〕 steps // 성큼성큼 앞으로 나서다 stride ahead
성큼하다 (be) slender-legged ; long-legged ; tall ; slim ¶ 그 여자는 몸이 성큼하다 She has a slim figure.
성탄 聖誕 the sacred birth 《of a saint or king》
성탄목 聖誕木 a Christmas tree
성탄절 聖誕節 Christmas (day)
성터 城— the ruins〔remains〕 of a castle ; a ruined castle ; the site of an ancient castle
성토 聲討 censure ; debate
— **대회** 《stage》 a rally
성패 成敗 success and〔or〕 failure ; hit and〔or〕 miss ; victory or defeat ¶ 성패에 관계 없이 (whether) successful or not // 성패는 천운에 달려 있다 Success or failure depends on chance.
성풀이 —하다 vent one's anger〔rage〕 ¶ 아내에게 성풀이하다 vent one's rage on his wife
성품 性品 nature ; disposition ; temper ; temperament
성하 城下 under the castle wall(s) ¶ 성하지맹 surrender ; capitulation
성하 盛夏 high summer ; midsummer
— **염열** the extreme heat of midsummer
성하 聖下 His〔Your〕 Holiness 《교황에 대한 존칭》
성하다 ① [온전하다] (be) intact ; undamaged ; good ¶ 성한 생선 fresh fish // 물건을 성하게 두다 leave〔keep〕 a thing intact
② [건강하다] (be) healthy〔sound〕 ; be in good condition ¶ 몸성히 잘 있다 be as sound as a horse〔roach〕 ; be as fit as a fiddle ; be doing quite well
성하다 盛— [초목이] (be) dense ; rampant ; thick ; [기운·세력이] prosperous ; flourishing ; active ; lively ; vigorous ¶ 상업이 성하다 Trade is flourishing. // 불이 성하다 The fire is leaping〔burns lively〕. // 정원에 풀이 성하게 자라고 있다 The garden is overgrown with grass. /The grass grows thick in the garden.
성하지맹 城下之盟 capitulation ; surrender
성학 星學 〖천문〗 astronomy
—가 an astronomer
성함 姓銜 (your, his) esteemed name ¶ 성함이 어떻게 되시지요 May I have your name ?
성해 聖骸 sacred bones
—함(函) a reliquary
성행 性行 character and conduct
성행 盛行 prevalence ; vogue **—하다** prevail ; be prevalent〔rampant, fashionable〕 ¶ 도박이 성행하다 gambling is prevalent // 그 노래는 한 때 크게 성행했다 The song had〔acquired〕 a great vogue at one time.
성행위 性行爲 a sex〔sexual〕 act ¶ 성행위를 하다 perform a sexual act ; have sex 《with》
***성향 性向** disposition ; propensity ; inclination
소비〔저축〕 — propensity to consume〔save〕
성현 聖賢 saints ; sages ¶ 성현의 가르침 the teachings〔instructions〕 of the sages ; the words of the wise
성혈 聖血 the sacred blood (of Jesus)
성형 成形 ① [형체를 만듦] forming ; shaping ; modeling ② 〖생물〗 an adult form ③ 〖의학〗 correction of deformities ; [얼굴의] face-lifting
—력(力) plasticity — **병원** a plastic hospital — **봉합술** plastic suture — **수술** 《undergo》 a plastic operation ¶ 내 얼굴 성형 수술하는데 얼마나 들까요 What will it cost to lift my face ? — **외과** plastic surgery ; restorative surgery — **외과의(醫)** a plastic surgeon **미용 — 외과** cosmetic surgery
성형 星形 a star shape
성호 聖號 a cross ¶ 성호를 긋다 (bless) cross oneself ; make the sign of the cross on one's breast // 이마에 성호를 긋다 cross one's brow ; pass one's hand across one's forehead
성호르몬 性— a sex hormone
성혼 成婚 a wedding ; a marriage
성홍열 猩紅熱 〖의학〗 scarlet fever ; scarlatina
단순〔악성〕 — scarlatina simplex〔maligna〕
성화 成火 annoyance ; irritation ; vexation ; a bother ; a trouble ; a torment ¶ 성화나다 be irritated ; be vexed ; be nettled ; become impatient // 없는 돈을 자꾸 달라니 성화로다 You are a pest, the way you keep asking for money I don't have.
—거리 a source of irritation ; a bother ; a nuisance
성화 星火 ① [운석] meteor
② [불빛] the light of a shooting star
③ [급한 일] an urgent matter ; an emergency ¶ 성화처럼 재촉하다 make an urgent request 《for》 ; press hard 《for》
성화 聖化 sanctification **—하다** sanctify
성화 聖火 sacred fire(s)
—대 a flame-holder — **릴레이** a sacred-fire〔-torch〕 relay — **주자** a

flame-bearer 올림픽 — the Olympic Flame〔Torch〕 올림픽 — 최종 주자 the anchor〔last runner〕 of the Olympic Flame relay

성화 聖畫 a holy〔sacred, religious〕 picture

성화 聲華 worldwide fame ; great fame 〔renown, honor, glory〕

성화같다 星火— ⇨ 성화(星火) ③

성황 盛況 prosperity ; prosperous condition ; success ¶ 성황을 이루다 be a great success ; be in a prosperous condition // 그 상점은 대성황을 이루고 있다 The shop is doing a roaring business.

성황당 城隍堂 a village shrine ⇨ 서낭당

성훈 聖訓 the teachings〔instructions〕 of a wise man〔saint〕 ; the instructions of a king

성히 in good condition ; healthy ⇨ 성하다

섶[1] [나무] kindling ; brushwood

섶[2] [지탱] a support ; a prop ¶ 섶으로 나무를 받치다 support a plant with a stick

섶[3] [옷의] the outer collar of a coat
—안 an inturned collar

세 three ¶ 세 사람 three men

†**세 稅** a tax ; a duty (물품세) ; taxes ; taxation (과세) ¶ 과세(課稅)하다 impose 〔levy〕 a tax 《on》// 납세하다 pay a tax // 징세하다 collect taxes // 과세되다 be taxable〔dutiable〕; be subject to duty // 중세(重稅)에 허덕이다 groan under heavy taxation
개인〔법인〕 소득— an individual〔a corporate〕 income tax 교통— a road traffic tax 국— a national tax 근로〔종합〕 소 득 — an earned〔a consolidated〕 income tax 상속— a death〔a succession〕 tax 영업〔소비, 증여〕— a business〔consumption, gift〕 tax 입항〔운하 통행〕— harbor〔canal〕 dues 지방— a local tax 《미》; the rates 《영》 직접〔간접〕— a direct〔an indirect〕 tax 증여— a gift tax 통행— a toll

세 世 a generation ; an age ; an epoch ¶ 루이 14세 Louis XIV

*****세 貰** rent ; hire (사용세) ; loan ¶ 세들어 살다 rent a house // 세가 비싼〔싼〕 집 a high-〔low-〕rent house // 세를 올리다〔내리다〕 raise〔lower〕 the rent
집〔방〕— house〔room〕 rent

세 勢 influence ; power ; might ; strength

-세 let's ; let 《me, him》 ¶ 가세 Let's go. // 그의 말도 좀 들어 보세 Let him have his say.

세가 世家 a distinguished〔noble〕 family

세가 勢家 a powerful family ; an influential person

세가락 three digits ; three-toed
— 딱따구리 a Korean three-toed woodpecker — 도요 〚새〛 a sanderling — 메추라기 a Burmese button-quail

†**세간** household furniture〔utensils〕 ¶ 세간이 많다 be well furnished // 세간나다 set up housekeeping of one's own // 세간내다 set up a separate home for 《one's son》
부엌 — kitchen utensils ; kitchenware

세간 世間 the world ; society ; life ; 〚불교〛 the mundane world

세간나다 establish〔set up〕 a branch〔separate〕 family ; create a new family ; establish oneself in a new〔branch〕 family ¶ 장가들어 세간나다 get married and set up a branch family

세간차지 a house〔household〕 caretaker ; a house manager

세간 치장 —治粧 interior decorating ; furnishing **—하다** do the interior decoration of a house

세거 世居 residing 《in a place》 for generations **—하다** reside〔settle down〕 《in a place》 for generations

세거리 a three-way junction〔intersection〕

세경 細徑 a path ; a lane

†**세계 世界** ① [지구] the world ; the earth ¶ 세계적 international ; worldwide ; all over the world // 세계적 문제 a worldwide question ; an international problem 〔issue〕 // 온 세계에서 in all the world ; all over〔throughout〕 the world // 세계 일주 여행을 하다 make a round-the-world trip
② [우주] the universe ; the cosmos
③ [세상] the world ¶ 저따위 바보는 전 세계에서도 없을 것이다 He is the biggest fool on earth.
④ [특수한 사회] a world ; a society ; circles ; a realm ; sphere ¶ 꿈의 세계 the realm of dreams ; dreamland // 이상의 세계 an ideal world // 어린이의 세계 the world of children // 그들은 우리와는 다른 세계에서 살고 있다 They live in a world different from ours.
— 각지 all parts of the world ; the four corners of the world — 경제 world 〔international〕 economy —관 an outlook on the world ; a world view — 국가 the world state — (신)기록 a (new) world record ¶ 세계 기록 보유자 a world-record holder — 대전 the World War ¶ 제1〔2〕차 세계 대전 the First〔Second〕 World War ; World War Ⅰ〔Ⅱ〕 — 만유 a world tour — 박람회 an international exposition ; a world's fair — 보건 기구 the World Health Organization 《WHO》 —사 world history ; the history of the world — 사조 the current thoughts of the world —상 a picture of the world ; a world picture — 선수권 대회 the world championship meet〔series〕 —어 a universal〔world〕 language — 연방 the World Federation of Nations — 은행 the World Bank ; the International Bank for Reconstruction and Development 《IBRD》 —인 a citizen of the world ; a cosmopolitan — 인권 선언 the Universal Declaration of Human Rights — 일주 a tour round the world ; a round-the-

world trip ; globetrotting ; [배로] circumnavigation of the earth — 일주 비행 a round-the-world〔world-circling〕 flight — 전쟁 a global〔world〕 war — 정부 the World Government — 정세 the situation of the world ; the drift of affairs in the world — 정신 the world spirit〔soul〕 — 정책 a world〔global〕 policy — 제일 the greatest〔best〕 in the world ¶ 세계 제일을 자랑하다 beat the world 《in》 —주의 cosmopolitanism ; internationalism — 지도 a map of the world — 평화 world peace ; the peace of the world

세계 歲計 an annual budget〔account〕

세계 기상 기구 世界氣象機構 the World Meteorological Organization

세계 노동 조합 연맹 世界勞動組合聯盟 the World Federation of Trade Unions 《WFTU》

세계 산업 노동자 동맹 世界産業勞動者同盟 the Industrial Workers of the World 《IWW》

세곡 稅穀 grain paid as a tax

*__세공 細工__ craftsmanship ; ware ; handiwork ; work ; workmanship —하다 work ; craft

—물 a (piece of) work ; a handiwork ; ware —인 a worker ; a craftsman ; an artisan —장(場) a workshop 그물 — netting ; network 금속 — metalware 조가비 — shellwork 종이 — paper work 금속 —사 a metal worker ; a smith 미술 —품 an art object ; ornamental ware ; an objet d'art 《프》

세공 細孔 a slit

세관 細管 a small tube〔pipe〕

세관 稅關 a custom(s) house ; the customs ¶ 세관에서 소지품을 신고하다 declare something // 세관에서 관세를 지불하다 clear goods // 세관 검사대로 가십시오 Proceed to customs, please.

— 감시선 a customs inspection boat ; a revenue cutter — 검사관 a customs examiner ; an inspector — 구내 customs compounds —리(吏) a customhouse officer ; a customs officer〔inspector〕 ; a customs agent — 명세서 a customs specification — 법규 customs regulations — 송장 a customs invoice — 수속 customs formalities ; entry procedure — 수수료 an entry fee ; a customs fee — 신고서 a bill of entry ; a customs declaration — 압수품 custom house seizures —장 the director〔superintendent〕 of a customhouse ; a customs director ; the collector of customs — 절차 customs formalities 《미》 서울 — the Seoul Customs

세광 洗鑛 〚광산〛 ore washing —하다 wash ore

—반(盤) a frame —조(槽) a buddle ; a hutch

세교 世交 a long-standing〔traditional〕 friendship between families

세궁민 細窮民 the indigent ; the poor〔needy〕 ; paupers

세궁역진 勢窮力盡 —하다 be pushed to the wall ; be driven to the last log 〔extremity〕

*__세균 細菌__ a bacillus 《*pl.* bacilli》 ; a bacterium 《*pl.* bacteria》 ; a germ ; a microbe ¶ 세균의 bacterial ; microbial // 세균 검사를 행하다 examine bacteriologically

— 검사 a bacteriological examination ; bacilloscopy — 배양 germiculture ; bacterial culture ; bacilliculture — 요법 bacteriotherapy ; bacillotherapy —전(戰) bacteriological〔germ〕 warfare — 집단 a colony of bacteria ; a bacterial colony ; zoogloea —탄 a germ bomb —학 bacteriology ; microbiology —학자 bacteriologist — 현미경 검사 bacterioscopy

*__세금 稅金__ a tax ; a duty ; a charge ; dues ¶ 세금을 체납하다 fail to pay a tax on the date due ; let taxes fall in arrears // 담배에는 어느 정도 세금이 붙어 있습니까 What is the duty on tobacco ? // 나는 세금 공제 후〔전〕의 순〔총〕수입이 한 달에 5000달러쯤 된다 I make about five thousand dollars after〔before〕 taxes a month. /I net〔gross〕 about five thousand dollars a month.

— 감면 tax cut — 공제 deduction of tax — 부담 a tax burden〔load〕 — 인상 tax hike — 체납 tax arrearage ; tax delinquency — 포탈 tax evasion

*__세기 世紀__ a century ¶ 19세기 후기 the late 19th century

세기 貰器 dishes for rent ; rented dishes

세기말 世紀末 the end〔turn〕 of a century ; fin de siècle 《프》 ¶ 세기말의 대사건 the salient event of the century // 세기말적 불안 fin-de-siècle mood〔unrest〕

세끼 three (daily) meals 《a day》

세나다¹ 《a wound or swelling》 get worse ⇨ 덧나다

세나다² sell well ; enjoy a good demand ; be much sought after ; be rare〔precious〕 ¶ 요사이 달걀이 세난다 Eggs are selling well these days.

세나절 taking entirely too long 《to do something》

세납 稅納 tax payment ⇨ 납세

세내다 貰— rent ; take on hire ; pay to use ¶ 집을 세내다 rent a house

세네갈 Senegal ¶ 세네갈의 Senegalese —말 Senegalese

세농 細農 small farming ; a poor farmer ; a needy peasant

†**세놓다 貰—** let out on hire ; hire out 《a car》 ; rent (to) ; lease

세뇌 洗腦 brainwashing ; indoctrination —하다 brainwash ; indoctrinate

— 공작 brainwashing

†**세다¹** ① [강력] (be) strong ; powerful ;

mighty ; hardy ; muscular (힘이) ¶ 힘이 센 사람 a strong-armed man ; a brawny man. ② [강렬] (be) violent ; strong ; hard ; severe ; fierce ; intense ; heavy ; keen ¶ 센 바람 a strong〔severe, violent〕 wind // 터가 세다 《a site》 be ill-omened〔unlucky, ill- fated〕// 그는 술이 세다 He is a heavy drinker. // 물결이 세다 The sea is rough.

세다² [머리털이] become white〔gray〕; whiten ; [안색이] turn pale ¶ 머리가 많이 세어졌네 그려 Your hair is rapidly turning gray, isn't it? // 걱정으로 머리가 하얗게 세었다 Anxiety has turned her hair gray.

센 개 꼬리 시궁창에 삼년 묻었다 보아도 센 개 꼬리다 속담 A crow is never the white for washing herself.

†세다³ count ; reckon ; enumerate ; number ; take a count of ; calculate (산출) ¶ 돈을 세다 count the money // 잘못 세다 miscalculate ; count wrong ; miscount // 빠짐없이 세다 keep count of // 1에서 100까지 세다 count from one to one hundred // 이러한 예는 이루 다 셀 수 없을만큼 많다 Such examples are too many to enumerate〔innumerable〕.

알 까기 전에 병아리 세지 마라 속담 To count one's chickens before they are hatched.

세단 [자동차] a sedan

***세대 世代** a generation ¶ 젊은 세대 the rising〔younger〕 generation

— 교번(交番) 〖생물〗 alternation of generations **— 교체** a shift in generations ¶ 세대 교체를 부르짖다 call for a shift in generations **유성〔무성〕 —** 〖생물〗 the sexual〔asexual〕 generation

‡세대 世帶 a household ; housekeeping

—수 the number of households **—주** a householder ; the head of a household 〔family〕

세도 世道 public morals

— 인심 public morals and popular attitudes

세도 勢道 (political) power〔influence, authority〕

—길 a way to power **—꾼** a man of power〔influence〕 **—집** a family in power

세도를 부리다 관용 wield〔exercise〕 power 《over》; have a hold 《on, over》

세뚜리 ① [세 겸상] three persons dining together at one table ② [나눔] dividing into three portions

***세레나데** 〖음악〗 a serenade

‡세력 勢力 influence ; power ; strength ; force ; energy ¶ 세력이 있다 be influential〔powerful, mighty〕// 세력이 없다 be powerless // 세력을 얻다 have power 《over》; come to〔into〕 power ; gain ground // 세력을 잃다 lose power〔influence〕// 세력을 미치다 influence ; exercise〔have〕 influence 《with, over》// 세력을 회복〔확대〕하다 regain〔extend〕 one's power〔influence〕// 세력을 떨치다 wield power // 이 고을에서 제일가는 세력가가 누구입니까 Who is the most influential (man) in this town?

—가 a man of influence〔weight〕; an influential man ; a powerful man ; a power (사업계에서) **— 균형** the balance of power ; the power balance ¶ 세력 균형을 유지하다〔깨뜨리다〕 maintain〔break〕 the balance of power **— 다툼** a struggle〔contest, grab, scramble〕 for power **— 범위〔권〕** a sphere〔scope〕 of influence〔power〕; [깡패 등의] one's range 〔domain〕 ¶ 세력권을 침범하다 break into a person's domain〔territory〕// 세력권을 다투다 quarrel over one's sphere of interest // 세력권을 넓히다 widen〔enlarge, expand〕 one's sphere of influence **— 보존** conservation of energy **안정 —** a stabilizing force〔factor〕 ¶ 극동의 안정 세력 the main prop and stay of the Far East **평화〔호전〕 —** the forces-of-peace 〔-war〕 **현유 —** [군비의] effective strength

***세련 洗練, 洗鍊** polishing ; refinement

—하다 polish up ; refine ¶ 세련된 신사 a polished〔refined〕 gentleman // 세련된 문장 a polished style // 세련된 말씨 refined phraseology // 세련되다 be polished〔refined, finished, elegant〕// 오늘은 세련되어 보이는데 You look sharp today.

‡세례 洗禮 baptism ; palingenesis ¶ 포화의 세례 volley of fire // 세례를 받다 be baptized ; receive baptism // 세례를 베풀다 administer baptism 《to》; baptize // 세례를 받고 신자가 되다 be baptized into the Christian faith // 근대 사상은 전부 과학의 세례를 받고 있다 The whole of modern thought is steeped in science. /Modern thought has been baptized with science.

—명 a baptismal〔christian〕 name ; a name of baptism **—식** baptism ; a baptismal ceremony〔service〕 **— 요한** John the Baptist **—자** a baptist **유아 —** infant baptism **재(再)—** re-baptism **침수 —** baptism by immersion

***세로** [명사] length ; [부사] perpendicularly ; vertically ; lengthwise ; endwise ¶ 세로 2피트 가로 3피트 two feet by three ; two feet long and three feet wide // 세로 두자다 be two feet long ; measure two feet in length // 세로 베다 cut lengthwise ; sliver

—줄 a vertical〔perpendicular〕 line ; a stripe

세로 世路 the path of life

세로 細路 a narrow lane〔path〕

세로지 —紙 [종이결] paper grain that runs lengthwise ; [긴 조각] slip of paper 〔cloth〕

세론 世論 public opinion ⇨ 여론(輿論)
세론 細論 a detailed discussion ⇨ 상론(詳論)
세루 serge ¶ 세루옷 a serge suit
세루 世累 troubles of the world ; worldly cares
세류 細流 a streamlet ; a small stream ; a brooklet ; a rivulet
세류 細柳 a weeping willow
세륨 〖화학〗 cerium 《Ce》
세리 稅吏 a tax collector ; a revenue officer
세립 細粒 a granule ; an infinitesimal grain
—철 〖광물〗 fine-grained iron
세마 貰馬 a horse for hire ; a hired horse ; a hackney
세마치 a large (3-man) blacksmith's hammer
세말 細末 (fine) powder —하다 pulverize ; grind to powder
세말 歲末 the close of the year ; the year-end
*세면 洗面 washing up (one's face)
—기〔대야〕 a washbowl 《미》; a (wash-hand) basin 《영》; a washbasin —대 a washstand ; a washing stand ; a wash-hand stand 《영》 —소 a washroom ; a lavatory ; a toilet room
세모 (a) triangular (thing) ¶ 세모나다 have three corners ; be triangular
— 기둥 a trigonal prism —꼴 a triangle ; a trilateral —본 a set square ; a triangle —뿔 a trigonal pyramid — 송곳 a triangle drill —줄 a triangular file
세모 歲暮 the close of the year
세모 細毛 a cilium
세모래 細— fine sand
세모시 細— ramie cloth of fine texture
세목 細目 details ; particulars ; items ¶ 세목으로 나누다 itemize
교수 — a detailed plan for instruction ; a (teaching) syllabus
세목 稅目 items〔headings〕 of a tariff ; items of taxation ; tax items
세무 稅務 taxation business ; tax affairs
—관 a revenue officer〔official〕 —사 a licensed tax accountant — 사찰 tax investigation — 상담소 a tax information office —서 a tax office ; a revenue office —서원 a tax-office clerk ; a tax collector —서장 the superintendent of a tax〔revenue〕 office — 행정 tax administration — 회계 tax accounting
세무 細務 trifling affairs ; sundry duties 〔tasks〕
세물 貰物 rented objects ; objects for rent
—전 a renter's store
세미 細微 minuteness ; diminutiveness ; fineness ; delicacy
‡세미나 a seminar
세미다큐멘터리 〖영화〗 semidocumentary film
‡세미콜론 a semicolon ¶ 세미콜론을 치다 put a semicolon
세미파이널 [준결승] semifinals
세미프로 [사람] a semiprofessional ; a semipro 《속》 ¶ 세미프로의 semiprofessional ; semipro 《속》
세민 細民 the indigent ; the poor ; the needy ; paupers ; the poverty-stricken ; the poverty-ridden
*세밀 細密 minuteness ; elaborateness
—하다 (be) minute ; detailed ; fine ; close ; elaborate ¶ 세밀하게 minutely ; in detail ; closely // 세밀한 검사 minute 〔close〕 examination // 그것은 세밀한 분석이 필요하다 It requires a detailed analysis.
세밑 歲— the end of the year ; the year-end
세발 洗髮 (a) shampoo ; washing of the hair ; hair wash(ing) —하다 wash the hair ¶ (이발소 같은 데서) 세발 해받다 have one's hair shampooed
—제(劑) a hair wash ; a shampoo
세발뛰기 hop-step-and-jump ; hop-skip-and-jump
*세배 歲拜 [인사] the New Year's greetings〔call〕; [절] a formal bow of respect to one's elders on New Year's Day ¶ 세배를 가다 pay a visit (of respect) on New Year's Day // 세배를 하다 wish each other a happy New Year ; exchange New Year's greetings ; perform a New Year's bow (절을 하다)
—꾼 a New Year's caller〔visitor〕; visitors who come to pay respect on New Year's Day —상 《prepare》 the New Year's feast (served to visitors) 세뱃돈 the New Year's gift of money given to one's juniors ; a handsel
세버들 細— a weeping willow
세법 稅法 [법률] the tax law ; [과세 방법] a system〔scheme〕 of taxation
세별 細別 subdivision ; breaking down
—하다 subdivide ; itemize ; break down 〔into parts〕
세보 世譜 a genealogy
†세부 細部 details ; the fine parts ; the minutiae
세부득이 勢不得已 by force of circumstances ; by an unavoidable circumstance —하다 (be) unavoidable ¶ 세부득이한 경우에는 in situations〔cases〕 that demand〔compel〕 it ; when unavoidable
세분 洗粉 washing powder
세분 細分 subdivision ; breaking down
—하다 subdivide ; break down
세비 歲費 an annual allowance (수당) ; yearly expenditure (비용)
세비제 洗鼻劑 〖의학〗 a collunarium 《*pl.* -ria》
세빌랴 Sevilla ; Seville
세사 世事 worldly affairs ; mundane mat-

ters ; the ways of life ¶ 세사에 능한 사람 a worldly-wise man ; a man of the world // 세사에 어둡다 know little of the world〔the ways of the world〕; be wanting in worldly wisdom
세사 細沙 fine sand
세사 細事 trifles ; a trivial affair ; a matter of no consequence ; a frivolity
세살 three years of age
세살 때 버릇이 여든까지 간다 속담 The child is (the) father of〔to〕 the man.
세살 細― [문살 따위] slender ribs〔frames〕
―문 a crude window with a small frame
세살 歲煞 〖민속〗 bad timing ; choosing a poor year for going a certain direction ; a year when the direction is deemed unlucky
세살부채 細― a narrow-ribbed fan ; a fan with fine ribs
*세상 世上 ① [세계·사회] the world ; society ; the times ; an age (시대) ¶ 세상이 싫어지다 be〔get〕 sick of the world // 세상(일)을 잘 알다〔모르다〕 know much〔nothing〕 of the world // 세상이란 본래 그런거야 So has the way of the world always been. /Take the world as it is. // 지금은 원자력의 세상이다 This is an atomic age. // 세상사란 변하는거야 You know things〔times〕 are constantly changing. // 세상은 넓은 것 같아도 좁다 The world is not so wide as it appears. /The world is a small place after all.
② [사람들] people ; the world ; the public ¶ 세상에 알려지다 be made public ; come to light ; become public ; get abroad // 세상이 다 안다 All the world knows it. /It is a matter of common knowledge. // 세상이 뭐라고 할까 What will people〔the world, Mrs. Grundy〕 say ?
③ [인생] life ; one's lifetime ¶ 세상에 별일 다봤다 Never in my life have I seen anything like that ! /Of all things ! // 세상 오래 살다 보니 별것을〔별소리를〕 다 보게 되는군〔듣겠군〕 Now I've seen〔heard of〕 everything.
④ [독무대] without rivals ¶ 그가 없어졌으니 이제 우리들의 세상이다 Now that he is gone, we are our own masters.
세상을 떠나다 관용 depart this life ; pass away ; leave this world
세상 世相 social conditions ; the world ⇨ 세태
세상맛 世上― 《taste》 the sweets and bitters of life ¶ 세상맛을 알다 know what the world is like
세상 물정 世上物情 ¶ 세상 물정에 밝은 worldly-wise ; [이해심 있는] sensible // 세상 물정에 밝은 사람 a man of the world ; a sensible man // 세상 물정을 모르는 사람 a person who is ignorant〔knows but little〕 of the world
세상사 世上事 ⇨ 세사(世事)
세상살이 世上― the way of living ; the mode of life ; living ―하다 lead a life ¶ 세상살이의 법 the art of living ; how to live // 가련하게 세상살이하다 live a wretched〔dog's〕 life
세상없어도 世上― for all the world ; at any cost ; at all costs〔risks〕; by all means ¶ 세상없어도 그따위 짓은 못하겠다 I wouldn't do that on any account.
*세상에 世上― in the world ; on earth ¶ 세상에 이게 무슨 일이람 What on earth is it ? // 원 세상에 별꼴이야 Well now I've seen everything.
세석 細石 gravel ; pebbles
세설 細雪 a light snow〔snowfall〕; powder(y) snow ; powder
세설 細說 ① [설명] a detailed〔full〕 account ; a minute explanation ; expatiation ―하다 explain fully ; give a detailed account of ; expatiate
② [잔소리] faultfinding
세세 世世 generation after generation ⇨ 대대
세세하다 細細― (be) minute ; fully detailed ¶ 세세히 기록하다 write down the full particulars // 세세히 말하다 give full details ; tell all the details
세소 細小 minuteness
*세속 世俗 ① [풍습] common〔popular, vulgar〕 customs ② [속세] the mundane world ¶ 세속의 worldly ; mundane
―주의 secularism ―화(化) secularization
†세수 洗手 ―하다 wash (one's hands and face) ; wash up
―수건 a hand towel
세숫대야 a washbasin
세숫물 water for washing up
세숫비누 toilet soap
세수 稅收 the yield of taxes ; tax revenues〔yields〕 ¶ 세수의 증가〔감소〕 an increase〔a drop〕 in revenue
세슘 〖화학〗 cesium 《Cs》
세습 世習 the way〔customs〕 of the world
*세습 世襲 transmission by heredity ; descent ―하다 transmit from generation to generation
―군주 a hereditary monarch ―권 a hereditary right 《to》 ―재산 hereditary property〔estate〕; freehold ; patrimony ; heritage
세시 歲時 ① the New Year ⇨ 설 ② times and seasons
―기(記) an almanac
세심 細心 carefulness ; prudence ; scrupulosity ; circumspection ¶ 세심한 주의를 하고서 with the greatest possible care ; most carefully // 세심한 주의를 하다 pay close〔scrupulous〕 attention 《to》

세쌍둥이 —雙— triplets ¶ 세쌍둥이를 낳다 have three at a birth
세안 歲— before the current year is out ; within the present year
세안 洗眼 eyewashing **—하다** wash one's eyes ¶ 세안 치료를 받다 have one's eyes-washed
—병(甁) an undine **—약** an eyewash ; an eye lotion ; a collyrium 《*pl.* ~s, -ria》
세액 稅額 tax amount ; tax liability ; an assessment
— 산정 the assessment of a tax **— 조정** settlement of a tax **결정 —** the settled tax-amount
세업 世業 hereditary occupation
세우 細雨 a drizzle ; a fine〔misty〕 rain ¶ 아직 세우가 내리고 있다 It's still drizzling.
†**세우다** ① [서게 하다] stand 《a candle》 ; make stand ; (put) erect ; raise ; set up ; put up 《a notice-board》 ; set 《a book》 on edge〔end〕 ; stand 《a long thing》 on end ; hoist 《a flag》 ; plant 《a pillar》 ; prick up (one's ears) ; stop〔park〕 《a car》
② [건조하다] build ; construct ; erect 《a statue, monument》 ; set〔put〕 up ; raise (an edifice) ; rear ¶ 새로 집을 세우다 have a new house built ; build oneself a new house
③ [설립·조직하다] establish 《a school, firm》 ; found ; set up ; organize 《a union》 ; institute
④ [정하다] institute 《a system》 ; lay down 《rules》 ; establish 《regulations》 ; enact 《a law》
⑤ [계획을] form〔make, lay〕 《a plan》 ; shape ; lay (down) 《one's course》 ; map out 《a program》
⑥ [학설 따위를] set up ; frame ; bring ; set forth ; put 《forward》 《an argument》 ; lay down 《a proposition》 ; make one's case ; develop ; formulate 《a theory》
⑦ [공훈을] render 《distinguished services》 ; perform 《meritorious deeds》
⑧ [뜻을] have 《an object》 in view ; establish in one's mind ; set 《an object before one》 ; be inspired by ambition
⑨ [사람을 어느 위치에] put up ; appoint ; nominate ¶ 후보자로 세우다 put up a candidate ; have 《a person》 stand for 《the Assembly》 // 보증인을 세우다 find〔appoint〕 surety
⑩ [칼날 따위를] sharpen ; put an edge 《on a knife》 ¶ 톱날을 세우다 set (the teeth of) a saw
⑪ [체면을] save one's face〔honor〕
세운 世運 the luck of the times〔age〕
세워총 —銃 ¶ 세워총을 하다 order arms
세원 稅源 a source of revenue ; tax sources

***세월 歲月** ① [시간] time and tide ¶ 세월은 사람을 기다리지 않는다 Time and tide wait for no man. // 세월이 유수같다 Time flies like an arrow. // 세월은 정말 유수 같구나 How time flies !
② [시세] (the) times ; things ; business ; conditions ¶ 세월이 좋다〔나쁘다〕 Times are good〔bad〕. // 요새 세월이 어떻습니까 How goes it with you ? /How is business these days ? // 세월이 별로 없습니다 Business is kind of slow.
가는 세월 오는 백발 [속담] Time end tide wait for no man.
세월이 약 [속담] Time cures all things. /Time is a healer.
세위 勢威 power ; authority ; influence
세율 稅率 tax rates ; a tariff
—표 tax rate scales ; a table of tax rates
국정 — a statutory tariff **협정〔보복, 특혜〕 —** conventional〔retaliatory, preferential〕 tariff
세의 世誼 generations of family friendship ⇨ 세교
세의 歲儀 a year-end gift
세이레 the 21st day of a baby's life (celebrated with a party)
세이프 〖야구〗 safe ¶ 3루에서 간신히 세이프되다 be narrowly safe on the third base // 세이프를 선언하다 declare safe
세이프티번트 〖야구〗 a safety bunt
세인 世人 people ; the world ; the public ¶ 일반 세인 people in general ; the public at large ; the populace // 세인의 이목을 피하다 avoid public notice ; slip from the sight of the world
세인트 헬레나 Saint Helena
세일 a sale ¶ 세일은 오늘 끝나지만 나중에 그 물건을 세일가격으로 사실 수 있습니다 The sale ends today but you can buy it at the sale price later. // 그 품목이 언제 다시 세일하는지 아십니까 Do you know when the item will go on sale again ?
바겐 — a bargain sale
세일러복 —服 a sailor〔middy〕 blouse ; a school uniform for girl students ¶ 세일러복을 입은 아이 a child in a sailor suit
‡**세일즈맨** a salesman ; [지방을 순회하는] a travel(l)ing salesman ; a commercial travel(l)er ; [호별 방문하는] a house-to-house salesman ¶ 도서의 세일즈맨 a salesman in books
‡**세입 歲入** [국가의] an annual revenue ; [개인의] an annual income
— 관세 revenue duties **— 세출(歲出)** revenue and expenditure **— 예산액** estimated (amount of) revenues **— 위원회** [미국 상원] the Finance Committee ; [영·미국 하원] the Ways and Means Committee **— 징수액** a collected amount of revenue
세입 稅入 revenue ; tax income〔yield, intake〕 ; income from taxes
***세자 世子** the Crown Prince

세자 洗者 a baptist ; one who baptizes
세자 細字 small type ; small〔fine〕 characters〔letters〕
세장 a crosspiece on an A-frame
세장 洗腸 〖의학〗 an irrigation of the colon
세저 細苧 ⇨ 세모시
세전 世傳 handing down from generation to generation ¶ 세전지물(世傳之物) things handed down from generation to generation
세전 歲前 before the New Year
세절목 細節目 minor details ¶ 세절목에 구애받다 stick to minor details
세정 世情 the affairs of the world ⇨ 세상(世上)
세정 洗淨 washing ; cleaning **—하다** wash ; rinse 《a bottle》 ; clean
세정 稅政 tax administration
세제 稅制 a system of taxation ; a tax system
— 개혁 a tax reform〔revision〕 ; a reform〔revision〕 of the taxation system **— 정리** readjustment〔overhaul〕 of the tax system
세제 洗劑 cleaning material ; a detergent ; a detersive ; a cleanser ¶ 이 스커트를 보통 세제로 세탁해도 좋습니까 Are you sure it's all right to wash this skirt with regular detergent?
중성〔합성〕 — a neutral〔synthetic〕 detergent
세제곱 〖수학〗 cubing ; cube **—하다** cube ; multiply 《a number》 by its square ¶ 2의 세제곱은 8이다 The cube of 2 is 8.
—근(根) a cube root ¶ 세제곱근 풀이 extraction of the cubic root // 세제곱근 풀이하다 extract the cube root 《of》 ; cube-root **—비(比)** a triple〔triplicate〕 ratio
세족 洗足 footbath ; 〖종교〗 foot washing **—하다** take a footbath ; wash a foot
세존 世尊 Buddha ; Sakya
세주 細註 detailed notes
†**세주다 貰—** lease ; let (for rent) ; rent ¶ 집을 세주다 rent a house to 《a person》
세째 the third
세차 洗車 car washing **—하다** wash down a car
—장 a car wash
세차 (운동) 歲差(運動) 〖천문〗 precession (of the equinoxes)
세차다 (be) violent ; intense ; furious ; powerful ; mighty ; vigorous ; energetic ; lively ¶ 세찬 토론 a hot debate // 비가 세차게 뿌리고 있다 It is raining heavily〔hard〕.
세찬 歲饌 [음식] food for treating New Year's guests ; [선물] New Year's gifts
세책 貰冊 a book for lending ; a book to loan out ; a book for hire ; a rental book ; a book from a rental library
—업 the book-lending business **—집** a rental library
***세척 洗滌** washing ; lavation ; lavage ; rinsing ; toilet (분만·수술 후의) **—하다** wash ; rinse ; swill ; rinse out 《impurities》 ; absterge ¶ 위를 세척하다 carry out a lavage of the stomach
—기 a washer ; a washing〔cleansing〕 device ; a syringe **—약** a cleansing lotion〔solution〕 ; a wash ; an abstergent ; a detergent **—유(油)** treated oil
세초 歲初 the beginning of the year
세출 歲出 annual expenditure(s)
— 예산액 estimated expenditures **—외 자금** non-appropriated funds **—위원회** [미국 의회의] the House Appropriation Committee
세치 three inches
— 각목 a square lumber three inches wide
세치 細緻 —하다 (be) minute ; close ; delicate
세칙 細則 detailed rules ; bylaws ; minor regulations
시행 — rules for operation ; regulations relative to the application of the law
세칭 世稱 what is known as ; what is called ; what people〔we〕 call ; the so-called ¶ 세칭 6월 사건 the so-called "the June Incident"
세컨드 〖야구〗 the second base ; [2루수] the second baseman ; 〖권투〗 a second ; [둘째 아내] a second (wife)
세컨드핸드 ⇨ 중고품(中古品) ¶ 세컨드핸드의 secondhand
‡**세탁 洗濯** laundry ⇨ 빨래
—기 a washing machine ; a washer ¶ 전기 세탁기 an electric washing machine ; an automatic washer **—물** the laundry ; the wash(ing) **— 비누** laundry soap **—소** a laundry (establishment) ; a cleaner's ¶ 그것은 세탁소에 보내는 것이 안전할 것 같군요 I think you'd be safer sending it to the cleaner's. **—업자** a laundryman ; a washerman ; a (dry) cleaner **—장** a wash place ; a washhouse
세태 世態 the prevailing state of society ; social conditions ; the way〔order〕 of the world
— 인정 the way(s) of the world ; life and men ¶ 이 소설은 세태 인정을 잘 묘사하고 있다 This novel is a perfect picture of (our private and social) life.
세터 [개] a setter (dog)
세톨박이 a bur which has three chestnuts in it
세톱 細— a fine-tooth saw
세트 ① [한 벌] a set ¶ 이 컵들 한 세트죠 These cups form a set, don't they? ② 〖연극〗 a (stage) set ; a (movie) setting ③ [라디오·텔레비전의] a receiving set ; a radio set ; a television set ④ [퍼머넌트의] a wave set **—하다** get〔give〕 a permanent wave ⑤ [경기의] a set ¶ 3세트

의 시합 a three-set match // 테니스를 1세트하다 play a set of tennis
세트 포지션 〖야구〗 the 《pitcher's》 set position
세파 世波 ups and downs〔vicissitudes〕 of life ¶ 세파에 시달리다 be tossed about in the storms of life ; go through the whirlpools of life
세파 細波 ripples ; wavelets ; tiny waves
세판 승부 —勝負 a three-game match ; 〖레슬링〗 a two-out-of-three-fall match
세편 細片 a small piece ; splinters ; flinders
세평 世評 [평판] public opinion ; popular judgment〔verdict〕; [인기] popularity ; [소문] hearsay ; rumor ¶ 세평에 의하면 people〔they〕 say 《that》; it is said〔reported〕《that》; a rumor has it 《that》 // 세평을 두려워하다 be afraid of what people say ; be shy of popular〔public〕 judgment // 세평에 오르다 be talked about ; be the talk of the town ; become common talk // 그는 청렴한 인사라는 세평이다 He is reputed to be a man of strict integrity.
세평 細評 minute criticism ; detailed comments **—하다** criticize minutely ; make a detailed criticizm 《on, of》
세폐 細幣 an annual〔a yearly〕 tribute
— 겨냥 the very thing (wanted) ; the right thing 《for》
***세포 細布** fine-textured hemp cloth
세포 細胞 〖생물〗 a cell ¶ 세포의 cellular // 공산당 세포 a communist cell
—막 the cell wall〔membrane〕 **— 분열** cell division ; (a) cell-cleavage ; segmentation **— 유전학** cytogenetics **— 조직** cellular tissue **—질** protoplasm ; cytoplasm ¶ 세포질의 cytoplasmic ; cellular **—체** a cell body **—학** cytology **—핵** a (cell) nucleus ; a mesoplast ; a karyon **— 형성** cytogenesis **— 호르몬** biodyne **생식 —** a reproductive〔generative〕 cell **원생 —** bioplasm
세피리 細— 〖악기〗 a kind of narrow flute
세필 細筆 ① [가는 붓] a slender-writing brush ; a hair pencil (수채화용) ② [가늘게 쓰기] writing in small characters
세하 細蝦 a shrimp
세후 歲後 after the New Year
섹션 a section
섹셔널리즘 sectionalism
섹스 sex
— 어필 sex appeal ; sexual attractiveness ¶ 섹스 어필하다 be sexually attractive
섹시하다 (be) sexy ; sexually attractive〔appealing〕; glamorous ¶ 섹시한 여자 a sexy〔glamour〕 girl
섹트 a sect
센둥이 a white puppy
센말 〖언어〗 an intensive〔emphatic〕 variant of a word
센머리 gray hair ; white hair
센물 [경수(硬水)] hard water
센서스 a census
‡**센세이션** (a) sensation ¶ 센세이션을 일으키다 create〔cause〕 a sensation ; make a stir ; create a furor
센스 a sense ¶ 센스가 있다〔없다〕 have good〔no〕 sense // 센스가 있는 sensible // 센스가 있는〔없는〕 사람 a person with a〔no〕 sense of ...
센터 ① 〖야구〗 the center field ; [사람] a center fielder ② [중심지] a center 《of trade, business, etc.》
— 플라이 a center fly ¶ 센터 플라이를 치다〔쳐서 잡히다〕 fly〔fly out〕 to center
쇼핑 — a shopping center
센터링 〖공학·축구〗 centering
센털 gray〔grey 《영》〕 fur ; white fur
센텐스 a sentence
센토 CENTO 《the Central Treaty Organization》
†**센트** a cent ¶ 1달러 4센트의 one dollar and four cents
센트로렌스 강 —江 [캐나다의] the Saint Lawrence River
‡**센티** [미터법의] centi- ; [센티미터] a centimeter〔-re〕《cm》
—그램 a centigram **—리터** a centiliter **—미터** a centimeter
센티멘틀 sentimental ; gooey 《속》; heart-tugging ¶ 센티멘틀한 이야기 a sticky tale // 센티멘틀해지다 become sentimental
—리즘 sentimentalism
***셀러리** [야채의 일종] celery
셀로판 cellophane
—지(紙) cellophane paper **— 테이프** cellophane tape
***셀룰로우스** 〖화학〗 cellulose
***셀룰로이드** 〖화학〗 celluloid
셀프서비스 self-service
셀프타이머 a self-timer ; an autotimer ¶ 셀프타이머가 장치된 카메라 a camera with a built-in self-timer
†**셈¹** ① [계산] count(ing) **—하다** count ; reckon ; calculate ¶ 셈이 틀리다 make a mistake in numbers ; miscalculate // 이곳에서는 내가 셈을 치르겠소 I'll pick up the tab here.
② [회계] account **—하다** keep accounts ¶ 셈에 넣다 take 《a thing》 into account // 셈을 치르다 settle accounts
③ [분별] sense ; discretion ; judgment ¶ 셈이 없다 have no sense
셈² [의도] an intention ; a design ; [생각] an idea ; [목적] a purpose ; [동기] a motive ; [예측] an expectation ; hope ; [계획] a design ; an idea ; [예산] an estimate ; [계산] a calculation ¶ …할 셈으로 with the intention〔object, idea〕 of ... ; with a view to ... ; with the view of ... ; for the purpose of ... ; in the hope of ... ; in the expectation of ... //

…할 셈이다 intend to ((do)) ; will ((do)) ; have a mind to ((do)) ; mean to ((do)) ; think of ((doing)) ; expect to ((do)) ; be going to ((do)) ; figure on ((doing)) (미) // 그는 도대체 어쩔 셈인지 알 수가 없다 I cannot quite see〔understand〕 his motive〔idea〕. // 어쩔 셈으로 그런 말을 했지 In〔With〕 what spirit did you say so ? // 이 도시에는 얼마나 머무르실 셈입니까 How long are you going to stay in this city ? // 나는 그를 만날 셈이었다 I expected to see him. // 그는 사과하는 셈으로 뭐라고 했다 He said something by way of apology. // 나는 농담을 할 셈이었다 I intended it to be a joke. // I meant it as〔for〕 a joke.

셈나다 grow sensible (in intelligence) ; acquire common sense ; mature ; get some sense ; become possessed of discretion ; begin to understand what is going on around one ¶ 셈나기도 전에 아버지가 돌아가시다 lose one's father before one can remember〔while still a little child〕 // 이제 셈나는구나 You are a man〔young lady〕 now.

셈들다 grow in intelligence ⇨ 셈나다

셈본 arithmetic ¶ 셈본의 arithmetic(al)
—문제 a problem in arithmetic ; an arithmetic problem

셈속 ① [내막] the inside details〔story〕 ; the real state of things ¶ 그 사건의 셈속 the inside of the event
② [맘속] a hidden intention ; an ulterior motive ; one's intention〔bosom〕 ¶ 무슨 셈속이 있겠지 He must have an ulterior object in view. // 그의 셈속을 모르겠다 It is impossible to fathom his real intention. /I cannot quite see〔understand〕 his motive〔idea〕.

셈치다 suppose ; assume ; grant ((that)) ¶ 셈치고서 on the supposition ((that)) // 그것을 잃어버린 셈치자 Let us suppose that we lost it.

셈판 ① [사정] the state of things ; the circumstances (of the affair) ; the matter ; the reason〔cause〕 (원인) ¶ 무슨 셈판인지 모르겠다 I don't know how the matter stands. /I cannot make head or tail of it. ② [주판] an abacus

셈펴이다 ⇨ 셈평 펴이다

셈평 ⇨ 셈평 펴이다

셈평 펴이다 become better off ; see easier days ; have one's prospects improve

†**셋** three ¶ 셋째로 third(ly)

셋갖춤 a suit of clothes ; a three-piece lounge suit

셋돈 貰— rent (money)

셋말 貰— a horse for hire

***셋방 貰房** a room for rent (미) ; a room〔an apartment〕 to let (영) ; [관광객을 위한] a tourist apartment ; [세든 방] a rented room ¶ 셋방 있음 [광고] Rooms for rent. (미) ; Rooms to let. (영) // 셋방 구함 [광고] Room Wanted.
—살이 living in a rented room

셋붙이 a three-piece suit〔jacket, vest, trousers〕

셋소 貰— an ox for hire

셋줄 a way〔means, method〕 of exercising one's influence〔authority, power〕

셋집 貰— a house for rent (미) ; a house to let (영) ; a rental house ; [게시] To let. / For rent. ¶ 셋집을 구하다 seek〔look for〕 a house to let // 셋집을 구하러 돌아다니다 hunt for a house for rent

셍기다 ① [말을] enumerate ; rattle on〔away〕 ; say in rapid-fire order ; talk volubly
② [일거리를] provide ; supply (continuously) ; feed ((work, jobs, tasks)) to ((a person)) ; keep ((a person)) hopping with one ((job)) after another ¶ 살림(을) 셍기다 take care of one's living expenses

셔츠 [속옷] an undershirt ; an undervest (영) ; a vest (영) ; a singlet (영) ; [와이셔츠] a shirt ¶ 셔츠 바람으로 in one's shirt sleeves // 셔츠 바람이 되다 be stripped to the undershirt
— 제조업자 a shirtmaker **털〔비단〕 —** a wool(l)en shirt〔silk singlet〕

‡**셔터** ① [사진기의] a shutter ¶ 셔터를 누르다 release〔press, click, snap〕 the shutter ; trigger a camera // 셔터만 누르면 됩니다 You just press the shutter. ② [문의] a shutter ¶ 셔터를 내리다 pull down〔put over〕 a shutter
자동 — an automatic shutter

셔틀콕 a shuttlecock

셧 아웃 〖야구〗 a shut-out ((game)) ¶ 셧 아웃 시키다 shut out ((the opposing team)) // 셧 아웃 당하다 get a shut-out

셰르파 a Sherpa

셰리 [술] sherry

셰어 〖상업〗 [시장 점유율] a (market) share ¶ 셰어 20%의 시장을 점유하고 있다 have a 20% market share ((in agricultural machines))

셰이커 a (cocktail) shaker

셰퍼드 a German shepherd dog

†**소**[1] a cow (암소) ; a bull (황소·종우) ; an ox ((*pl.* oxen)) (거세된) ; cattle ((총칭)) ¶ 소 두마리 two head of cattle // 소걸음으로 at a snail's pace // 소를 치다 keep a cow // 소같이 먹다 eat like a horse
—가죽 cowhide **—떼** a herd of cattle
소 같이 일하고 쥐같이 먹어라 속담 Scatter with one hand, gather with two.
소 귀에 경 읽기 속담 To sing psalms to a dead horse. /To whistle psalms to the taffrail. /Knock at a deaf man's door.
소 꼬리보다 닭 대가리가 낫다 속담 Better be the head of a dog〔fox, mouse, lizard〕 than the tail of a lion. /Better be the head of a pike than the tail of sturgeon. /Better be the head of an ass than

the tail of a lion. /Better be first in a village than second at Rome. /Better be the head of the yeomanry than the tail of the gentry.

소 발에 쥐잡기 속담 The net of the sleeper catches fish.

소 잃고 외양간 고친다 속담 To lock the stable door after the horse is stolen. /After death, the doctor. /To cover the well after the child has been drowned in it. /It is too late to shut the stable door when the steed is stolen.

소² a seasoned mixture used as a stuffing for bun ; stuffing ; dressing ; filling ¶ 만두에 소를 넣다 stuff a bun〔dumpling〕

만두— bun stuffing **팥—** bean jam

소 小 smallness ; littleness ; small ; little ; minor ; lesser ; miniature

—규모 small scale **—도시** a small town **—문제** a minor problem **—아시아** Asia Minor **—위원회** a subcommittee

소 少 [적은] little ; few ; scarce ; young (젊은)

—량 a little ; some **—수** a few ; some

소 沼 a swamp ; a marsh ; a bog ; a pond

—택지 a marshy place

소 簫 a Korean wind instrument resembling a panpipe

소가 小暇 a bit of leisure ; a short break〔respite〕; a brief moment of spare time ¶ 소가를 틈타 독서하다 read in the short intervals of business ; read at odd moments

소가 小家 one's concubine

소가요곡 小歌謠曲 〚음악〛 a canzonet

소가족 小家族 a small family

— 제도 the small-family system

소가지 nature ; disposition ; temperament ¶ 소가지가 나쁘다 be ill-natured ; be wicked

소각 燒却 destruction by fire ; incineration **—하다** destroy by fire ; burn up ; reduce to ashes ¶ 쓰레기를 소각하다 burn up the rubbish ; make a bonfire of the refuse

—기〔로〕 an incinerator ; a trash burner

소간사 所幹事 one's business〔affair〕; matters related to one's office

일상 — the daily routine ; everyday business

소갈머리 nature ; temper ; disposition ; [생각] intention ¶ 소갈머리 없는 사람 a thoughtless〔inconsiderate〕 person ; an insensible man

소갈증 消渴症 〚한의학〛 a disease symptomized by thirst

*__소감 所感__ one's impressions ; thoughts ; [의견] an opinion ¶ 소감을 말하다 give one's impression《of something》; express one's impressions〔thoughts〕// 소감을 한마디 말하겠다 Let me say a few words about it. // 어제 저녁 회의에 대한 소감을 듣고 싶소 Please tell me how the meeting last night struck you.

소강 小康 a lull ; a respite ¶ 전투〔시장〕는 일시 소강 상태에 있다 There is a momentary lull in the fighting〔market〕. // 그의 병이 소강 상태에 있다 There is a slight improvement in his condition.

†**소개 紹介** introduction ; presentation ; [추천] recommendation **—하다** introduce《to, into》; present《to》; recommend ¶ 정식 소개를 하다 make a formal introduction // 자기 소개를 하다 introduce oneself《as》// 김군의 소개로 입회하다 join the society through Mr. *Kim's* introduction // 한국의 풍물을 미국에 소개하다 introduce things Korean to the American public // 나의 친구 김군을 소개합니다 Allow me to introduce〔present〕 to you my friend Mr. *Kim*. /May I introduce my friend Mr. *Kim* to you? /"Introducing Mr. *Kim*" (명함에서) // 방금 소개받은 김입니다 My name is *Kim* as has been mentioned in my introduction. // 그분의 얼굴은 알지만 정식으로 소개는 받지 않았습니다 I know him by sight, but have never met him formally. // 너에게 소개시켜 줄 수 있을 만한 시공업자를 알고 있다 I know a good contractor I can put you in touch with.

—료 brokerage ; commission **—업** brokerage ; commission agency ; go-between business **—자** an introducer **—장** a letter of introduction **자기 —** self-introduction **직업 —소** a public employment agency〔exchange〕 ☞ 《p1224》

소개 疏開 [산개] decongestion ; dispersion ; dispersal ; deployment (군대의) ; [철거] removal ; evacuation **—하다** disperse ; thin out ; remove ; evacuate 《*Seoul*》; move《to a place》for safety ¶ 공장을 소개하다 dismantle a plant〔mill〕 // 부산으로 소개하다 evacuate to *Pusan*

—자 an evacuee **—지** one's place of refuge **강제 —** forced〔compulsory〕 removal〔evacuation〕

소개념 小槪念 minor (term)

소거 a spinning wheel

소거 消去 elimination **—하다** eliminate

—법 〚수학〛 elimination

소건 訴件 〚법〛 a case

소격 疏隔 estrangement ; alienation

—하다 estrange ; alienate ¶ 두 사람 사이를 소격시키다 estrange one from the other

소견 所見 one's views〔opinions〕; idea(s) ; impressions ¶ 얕은 소견 a shallow view ; a superficial idea // 나의 소견으로는 in my opinion // 소견을 말하다 state〔give〕 one's views ; express〔state〕《oneself》

—표 a written opinion (about a pupil from the school where he has studied)

소결 燒結 〚야금〛 sintering **—하다** sinter

*__소경__ a blindman ; a sightless person ; the

소 개

영국과 미국에서는 사람을 소개할 때 다음과 같은 사항에 주의할 필요가 있다. 남자들끼리, 여자들끼리 있을 때 원칙적으로 연하의 사람을 연상의 사람에게 먼저 소개한다. 남성과 여성의 경우에는 먼저 남성을 여성에게 소개한다. 또 처음 만나서 자기를 소개할 때는 보통 여성이나 연배가 높은 사람부터 한다. 「How do you do? My name is …. / Excuse me, my name is ….」와 같이 먼저 인사를 하고 자기 이름을 밝히는 것이 보통이다. 많은 사람 앞에서 자기를 소개할 때는 May I[Let me] introduce myself. (Lee Chungmin., marketing manager. East-south Trade.) / Allow me to introduce myself. 등과 같이 소개말을 하고 이름과 직책, 회사명 순으로 밝히는 것이 보통이다. 소개의 말이 끝나면 서로간에 How do you do? / I'm glad to meet you. / I've been looking forward to meeting you. 등으로 인사를 주고 받는다.

① 처음 만났을 때

¶ 제 소개를 하겠습니다. 제이름은 김입니다. 예일대학 4학년입니다. (Excuse me, but) May I [Let me] introduce myself. My name is Kim. I am a senior at Yale university. (★ 파티석상 등의 개방적인 분위기에서는 곧바로 My name is… 라고 소개하기도 한다.) // 안녕하세요.(처음 뵙겠습니다.) 한국출판사 편집부장 김 민수입니다. How do you do? (I don't think we've met before.) I'm Kim Minsoo. chief editor in Hankook publishing company. // 안녕하십니까. Bill의 친구 John Davis입니다. How do you do? I'm John Davis, a friend of Bill's.

② 소개 받았을 때

¶ 안녕하세요. 존씨. 저는 샐리 메이슨이라고 합니다. How do you do? [Hello?] Mr. John? I'm Sally Mason. // 안녕하세요. 만나서 반갑습니다. 존 스미스입니다. (How do you do?) I'm glad to meet you. I'm [My name is] John Smith.

③ 두사람을 소개할 때

¶ 존, 이 사람은 내 친구 김입니다. 김, 이 사람은 내 친구 존입니다. John, this is my friend Kim. Kim, this is my friend John. (★ full name을 쓰면 정중한 표현이 된다. 첫번째 말만으로 양측 소개를 끝낼 수도 있다.) // 아, 이쪽은 피터야. 피터 이쪽은 제니야. Oh, Look, here's Peter. Peter, meet Jenny. 처럼 간단하게 소개할 수도 있다. 같은 또래에서 잘 쓰인다. // 화이트 양, 김군을 소개합니다. Miss White, May I introduce Mr. Kim? (★ 상대방에게 허가를 구하는 듯한 정중한 어조. 대답은 Yes, please. 또는 Certainly.로 한다. 소개자는 다시 This is Mr. Kim.을 덧붙이면 된다.) // 그린양, 이군을 소개해 드리겠습니다. Miss Green, I'd like to introduce Mr. Lee. / Please let me [allow me to] introduce Mr. Lee. (★ 마찬가지로 정중한 표현. 답변은 Yes, please.)

④ 다수를 소개할 때

¶ 여러분, 노스웨스트 항공사 서울 지점의 모간씨, 존즈씨, 그리고 쥬디양을 소개합니다. Gentlemen[Everybody], I want you to meet Mr. Morgan, Mr. Jones, and Miss Judy of the Seoul office of Northwest Airlines. // 여러분, 영어선생님으로 새로 오신 스미스 선생님을 소개합니다. Students, this is Mr. Smith, your new English teacher.

⑤ 헤어질 때의 인사

처음 만나서 소개받고 알게된 사람과 헤어질 때의 인사는 다음과 같다.

¶ 만나게 된 것을 기쁘게 생각합니다. I'm very glad to have met you. / It was really nice meeting you. // 또 뵈었으면 좋겠습니다. I hope to see you, again.

---

blind 《총칭》 ¶ 소경이자 귀머거리인 blind and deaf // 소경이 되다 become〔go〕 blind ; lose one's sight // 날 때부터의 소경이다 be born blind // 사람을 소경 취급하는군 He apparently thinks I know nothing at all.

— 막대 a blindman's stick

소경 문고리 잡기 〔속담〕 A blind man may sometimes catch〔hit〕 the hare〔crow, mark〕.

소계 小計 a sub-total ; a total ¶ 소계 만 원이다 It totals 10,000 *won*.

소고 小鼓 a tabor

소고 溯考 **—하다** look〔trace〕 back 《on

the past》; look over 《past records》
소고의 a short jacket (worn by ladies)
소곡 小曲 a short piece of music〔poetry〕; an arietta
*소곤거리다 whisper; murmur; speak under one's breath; talk in whispers ¶ 서로 소곤거리다 exchange whispers; whisper to each other // 상대방의 귀에 대고 한두마디 소곤거리다 whisper a word or two into another's ear
*소곤소곤 in whispers; in an undertone; secretly; softly ¶ 소곤소곤 이야기하다 talk in whispers // 그 둘이는 무엇인지 소곤소곤하고 있었다 Those two were whispering about something.
소곳이 ⇨ 다소곳이
소곳하다 be drooping〔hanging〕 low; be bowed〔lowered〕
소공업 小工業 a small industry
—국〔도시〕 a small industrial nation〔city〕
소관 所管 jurisdiction; [권능] competency ¶ 소관에 속하다 be under the jurisdiction 《of》; fall within the jurisdiction 《of》 // 소관 밖이다 be beyond the jurisdiction 《of》 // 그 일은 우리 소관이라고 생각합니다 I think that job belongs in our jurisdiction.
— 다툼 jurisdictional rivalry —청 the competent authorities; the authorities concerned 외무부 — 사항 matters under the jurisdiction of Ministry of the Foreign Affairs
소관 所關 relation; relationship; matters concerned
—사 one's business; one's concern; one's affairs — 서류 all the documents related to 《the matter》; documents relative to the case
소구 〖악기〗 a tabor; a small drum
소구 小球 a small ball〔globe〕; [혈구] a globule
소구 小丘 a small hill; a hillock
소구잡이 a tabor〔small-drum〕 player
소구치 小臼齒 〖해부〗 a premolar〔bicuspid〕 (tooth)
소국 素— vegetable soup
소국 小局 [도량의] narrow-mindedness; a short-sighted〔circumscribed〕 view; [판국의] a small situation
소국 小國 a small〔minor〕 country; a weak nation; a minor〔lesser〕 power ¶ 약소 국가 a minor〔lesser〕 power
소굴 巢窟 a den; a haunt; a nest; a lair; [범죄의] a breeding-place; a hotbed; a hangout ¶ 갱의 소굴 a hangout for gangsters // 거지의 소굴 a haunt for beggars // 도둑의 소굴 a den of robbers〔thieves〕; a robber's hideout // 범죄의 소굴 a breeding-place〔hotbed〕 of crime // 이 지대는 부랑자의 소굴로 되어 있다 These districts are infested with vagabonds.
소권 訴權 〖법〗 the right of action
소규모 小規模 a small scale ¶ 소규모의 small-scale // 소규모로 on a small scale; in a small way
소극 消極 the negative pole; the negative; the cathode; [작용] depolarization ¶ 소극적 negative; passive; conservative; nonresisting // 소극적 전법 passive tactics // 소극적 정책 negative policy // 소극적 태도를 취하다 take a negative attitude; act passively // 소극적으로 일을 하다 do things on negative lines
— 명제 a negative proposition —성 passivity; passiveness —제 〖전기〗 a depolarizer —주의 negativism —주의자 a negativist
*소극 笑劇 a farce
소극장 小劇場 a little theater
†소금 salt ¶ 소금에 절인 salted; pickled〔preserved〕 with salt // 소금에 절이다 salt 《fish》; preserve in salt // 10시간 소금에 절여 두다 let 《it》 remain in salt for ten hours // 생선에 소금을 뿌리다 sprinkle salt on fish; sprinkle fish with salt // 소금을 찍어서 먹다 eat 《a thing》 with salt // 소금으로 간을 맞추다 season with salt
—장사 a salt merchant
소금구이 ¶ 소금구이로 하다 broil 《fish》 with salt
소금기 saltiness; a salty taste ¶ 소금기 있는〔없는〕 salty〔saltless〕 // 소금기 있는 물 brackish water
소금물 salt water ¶ 소금물에 담그다 soak〔steep〕 in brine
소금버케 salt that has lumped〔hardened〕; coagulation of salt
소금엣밥 plain food〔fare〕; a poor meal
소금쟁이 〖곤충〗 a water strider; a pond skater
소금정 小金井 a papered wooden〔bamboo〕 cover for a coffin or a corpse
소금쩍 lumps of salt in a substance; a precipitation of salt
소급 遡及 going back to the past; retroactivity; retroaction; 〖법〗 relation 《to》 —하다 go back to the past; retrace the past; be retroactive ¶ 5월 1일로 소급하여 retroactive to May 1
—력 retroactive〔retrospective〕 power; retroactivity —법 a retroactive〔retrospective〕 law; ex post facto law
소기 小朞 the first anniversary of a death ⇨ 소상(小祥)
소기 所期 one's expectation; anticipation ¶ 소기한 바와 같이 as one expected〔hoped for〕; as was expected; as might have been expected // 소기의 목적을 달성하다 achieve the desired end; realize the object one had in mind // 소기의 성과를 올리다 achieve the expected results
소기 笑氣 〖화학〗 laughing gas; nitrous oxide
소기 沼氣 marsh gas; 〖화학〗 methane

소꼽 toy flatware〔kitchenware〕; toy goods used in playing house
—놀이〔장난〕 ⇨ 소꼽질
‡소꼽동무 a childhood friend ; a friend 〔playmate〕 of one's childhood ; a friend from one's childhood ¶ 두 사람은 소꼽동무다 They have known each other since they were boys〔girls〕 together 〔from childhood〕.
소꼽질 playing with a doll house ; playing house ; playing at housekeeping —하다 play house ; play at housekeeping ; play with a doll house ¶ 신접살이라 생활이 마치 소꼽질하는 것 같다 Being quite a young couple, their life is a sort of playing at housekeeping.
‡소나기 a (sudden) shower ; a passing rain ¶ 소나기가 오다 it showers // 소나기를 만나다 be caught in a shower // 소나기가 올 것 같다 It looks like a shower. /It is going to shower.
—구름 cumulo-nimbus (cloud) ; a shower-cloud —밥 sudden overeating (by someone of a usually modest appetite) —술 sudden overdrinking of liquor (by an unlikely person)
소나무 a pine (tree) ¶ 소나무 잎 pine needles // 소나무 숲 a pine-grove
소나무겨우살이 〖식물〗 a species of Spanish〔Florida〕 moss ; Usnea longissima (학명)
소나타 〖음악〗 a sonata
—형식 a sonata form
소납 necessaries ; (pre) requisites
*소네트 a sonnet ¶ 소네트 시인 a sonneteer
†소녀 少女 a young〔little〕 girl ; a maid (-en) ¶ 소녀다운 girlish
—가극 a girls' opera —단 the Girl Scouts —소설 a story for girls —시절 (young) girlhood —취미 (school) girlish tastes
†소년 少年 a boy ; a lad ; a youth
—노동 child labor ; minor〔juvenile〕 labor —단 the Boy Scouts —단원 a boy scout —문학 juvenile literature —범죄 juvenile delinquencies〔offenses〕 —법 the juvenile law —보호 juvenile protection —부 [법원의] a Juvenile Court —시대 one's boyhood ; one's early days —원 a (juvenile) reformatory (school) ; a training school ; an approved school 《영》 —잡지 a children's magazine ; a juvenile journal 불량— a bad〔delinquent〕 boy 비행— a juvenile delinquent
소농 小農 a small〔petty〕 farmer ; a peasant proprietor〔landholder〕
—가 a small farmer's household ; a small farmer —계급 peasantry —조직 the peasant-proprietor〔small-farm〕 system —지(地) small holdings
소뇌 小腦 〖해부〗 the cerebellum 《*pl.* ~s, -bella》
소다 soda
—공업 the alkali manufacture —비누〔석회, 펄프〕 soda soap〔lime, pulp〕 —수 soda water〔pop〕 —크래커 a soda cracker —회(灰) soda ash 무수〔가성〕— anhydrous〔caustic〕 soda
소달구지 an oxcart
소담 小膽 timidity ; cowardice —하다 (be) cowardly ; timid ; faint-hearted ¶ 소담한 짓을 하다 act cowardly
—자 a coward
소담 笑談 a funny〔humorous〕 story —하다 tell a funny story
소담스럽다 (be) delicious ; juicy〔tasty〕 looking ; look nice and ripe
소담하다 (be) pleasantly plump ; full ; juicy〔tasty〕; nice and ripe ¶ 소담한 꽃송이 a full-petaled flower // 소담한 색시 a buxom girl
소당 小黨 a small〔minor〕 (political) party
소대 小隊 a platoon
—장 a platoon leader〔commander〕 —훈련 close-order drill 《미》 비행— an element 선두— a leading section
소대상 小大祥 the first and second anniversaries of a death
소댕 the lid〔cover〕 of a kettle
—꼭지 the handle of a kettle cover〔key〕
소도 小島 an islet ; a small island ; a cay
소도구 小道具 stage property ; props
소도둑놈 ① [도둑] a cattle thief ; a cattle rustler ② [욕심쟁이] a greedy and bad-tempered person
소도록하다 ⇨ 수북하다
소도리 a small hammer
소도시 小都市 a small〔smaller〕 town
소독 消毒 disinfection ; sterilization ; pasteurization (우유 따위의) ; [훈증] fumigation ; [정화] decontamination —하다 disinfect ; subject 《something》 to disinfection ; sterilize ; pasteurize ; fumigate ; decontaminate ¶ 증기로 소독하다 sterilize by steam // 끓는 물로 소독하다 sterilize in boiling water // 화염으로 칼을 소독하다 sterilize a knife in a flame // 일광으로 소독하다 disinfect by the sun's rays 〔by sunning〕 // 소독이 완전하다 be properly disinfected
—기 a sterilizer ; a disinfector —력 the disinfective〔sterilizing〕 power 《of sunshine》 —면 sterile cotton —붕대 sterilized bandages —수 an antiseptic solution —실 a disinfecting room —액 an antiseptic solution —약〔제〕 a disinfectant —의(衣) a disinfected garment〔overall〕 —저(箸) sanitary chopsticks ; sterilized chopsticks 일광— disinfection by sunning 증기〔유황〕— sterilization by steam 〔sulphur〕
소동 小童 a kid ; a little boy ; a boy servant
소동 騷動 [소란] disturbance ; agitation ; [다툼] strife ; a dispute ; [혼란] confusion ; disorder ; a row ; a tumult ; a

commotion ; [폭동] a riot ; a rising ¶ 소동을 일으키다 raise〔create〕 a disturbance ; stir up troubles // 소동을 진압시키다 put down a riot // 쓸데 없는 일로 큰 소동이다 make a great disturbance about a trifle // 소동이 일어나다 a riot arises // 소동이 일어날 것 같다 Trouble is brewing. // 아침 일찍부터 웬 소동이냐 What a racket for so early in the morning? // 뭣 때문에 이 소동이야 What's the big deal?

소동맥 小動脈 〖해부〗 an arteriole ; a small arterial branch ¶ 소동맥의 arteriolar

소두 《birthday》 gifts exchanged between the families of newly-weds

소두 小斗 a half-*mal* measure

소두 小豆 a redbean

소두 小頭 a small head ¶ 소두의 microcephalic ; microcephalous

—증 〖의학〗 microcephalia ; microcephaly

소두엄 barn manure

소듐 〖화학〗 sodium

소드락질 robbery ; plunder ; pillage —하다 rob ; ravage ; plunder

*__소득 所得__ an income ; earnings ¶ 월 100만원의 소득이 있다 have a monthly income of a million *won*

— 배증 계획 the income-doubling program — 수준 an income level —액 the amount of (one's) income ¶ 소득액의 사정(査定) the assessment of one's income // 소득액 80만원이라고 신고하다 return one's income at 800,000 *won* —자 an income earner —층 an income group 국민 — the national income 근로 — earned income 불로 — unearned income 순〔총〕— net〔gross〕 income 실질 — real income 종합 — the consolidated income 현물 — an income in kind 저〔고〕—자 a small 〔large〕 income earner〔obtainer〕 ; people in the lower〔upper〕 brackets of income

소득밤 an unshelled dried chestnut

소득세 所得稅 an income tax

—법 the Income Tax Law 종합〔개인, 법인〕 — the composite〔individual, corporate〕 income tax 특별 — the special income tax

소득소득 —하다 (be) withered ; dry

소들소들 —하다 (be) withered ; dry

소들하다 (be) not enough〔sufficient〕

소등 消燈 putting out lights ; blackout —하다 put out the lights ¶ 소등 나팔을 불다 sound "lights out" // 소등 시간은 11시다 All lights have to be put out at eleven.

— 나팔 《sound》 taps 《미》 — 시간 the hour for putting out lights ; lights-out

소띠 the characteristics of (one born under the sigh of) the Ox

소라 ① [조개] a conch ; a wreath shell ; a top shell ; a trochoid ; Turbo cornutus (학명) ② [악기] a shell trumpet ; a trumpet shell ¶ 소라를 불다 blow a trumpet shell

—딱지 the shell of a conch —젓 salted conch

소라게 hermit crab

소라고둥 a conch ; a trumpet shell ; a triton

소락 小落 〖경제〗 a slight fall 《in prices》

소락소락 —하다 (be) frivolous ; light ; thoughtless

소란 小欄 a railing ; a reinforcing or protecting strip ¶ 소란을 치다 attach the broider pieces 《to a panel》

‡__소란 騷亂__ disturbance ; commotion ; a riot —하다 (be) noisy ; disturbing ; troubled ¶ 소란한 세상 troubled times // 소란을 일으키다 raise〔create〕 a disturbance // 소란은 멎었다 The disturbance has been quieted. // 손님 접대로 대소란이었다 They made much ado to entertain their guests.

소란반자 小欄— a panelled ceiling ; a coffering

소란죄 騷亂罪 ¶ 소란죄를 발동하다〔적용하다〕 invoke〔apply〕 the anti-riot law 《against extremist demonstrators》

소래기 a kind of saucer

소략 疎略 carelessness ; roughness ; negligence ; inattentiveness —하다 (be) rough ; careless ; negligent ; rude ; inatt entive

†__소량 少量__ a small quantity〔amount〕 ; a small portion ; a small dose ; a little ; a touch ; a dash ¶ 소량의 물 a little water ; a small quantity of water // 소량의 모르핀 a small dose of morphine

소련 蘇聯 the Soviet Union ; Soviet Russia ; the U.S.S.R 《the Union of Soviet Socialist Republics》 ; Russia

— 국기 the hammer and sickle ; the sickle and hammer —군 the Soviet〔Russian〕 army —인 the Soviets — 정부 the Soviet Government ; the Kremlin — 최고회의 the Supreme Council of the Soviet Union

소렴 小殮 shrouding〔covering〕 a corpse —하다 shroud (a corpse)

소렴포 小殮布 a shroud ; a winding sheet

소령 少領 [육군] a major ; [해군] a lieutenant commander ; [공군] a squadron leader 《영》

소로 小路 a narrow path ; a lane ; an alley

소론 所論 one's view ; one's opinion ¶ 나의 소론은 in my opinion ; I am of the opinion 《that》

소롱하다 消— squander ; waste

소루 疎漏 [부주의] carelessness ; inadvertence ; [빠뜨림] an oversight —하다 [부주의하다] (be) careless ; inadvertent ; [되는대로 하다] cursory ; negligent

소르르 ① [풀어지는 모양] smoothly ; easily ¶ (허리띠가) 소르르 풀리다 slip off ② [바람이] gently ; softly ¶ 바람이 소르

르 분다 There is a gentle breeze. /The wind blows gently.
③ [졸음이] drowsily ¶ 잠이 소르르 오다 sleep steals upon one // 소르르 조는 사이에 잠이 들어버렸다 Doziness〔A drowsy feeling〕 coming over me, I soon feel asleep.

소르본느 대학 一大學 the Sorbonne

*__소름__ gooseflesh ; goose pimples〔bumps〕 ¶ 소름끼치는 공포 a thrill of horror // 온 몸에 소름이 끼치다 be gooseflesh all over // 그 말을 들으니 온 몸에 소름이 끼친다 The news sent a chill to the marrow of my bones. // 그 말에 그는 소름이 끼쳤다 At the word every drop of his blood was chilled. // 생각만하여도 소름이 끼친다 The mere thought makes me shudder.

†**소리** ① [음향] (a) sound ; (a) noise ¶ 나팔〔장구〕 소리 the sound of a trumpet〔drum〕 // 대포 소리 the roar of a cannon // 소리를 내다 make a sound〔noise〕 // 자동차 소리에 잠을 못 자다 cannot sleep for the traffic // 아무 소리도 들리지 않았다 Not a sound was heard.
② [음성] a voice ; a call ; a cry (외침) ; a talk ; a word ; a note (새·벌레의) ¶ 소리를 지르다 yell out // 그게 무슨 소리냐 What do you mean ? // 별 소리 다 한다 The things you say !
③ [노래] a folk song ; a ballad **—하다** sing a folk song ¶ 소리를 잘하다 sing well // 소리가 좋다 have a fine voice
소리 없는 고양이 쥐 잡듯 속담 Silence catches a mouse.
소리 없는 벌레가 벽을 뚫는다 속담 He that is silent, gathers stones.

소리 小利 a small profit ; little gain ¶ 목전의 소리에 눈이 어두워지다 be blinded by a small immediate profit

소리 小吏 a petty official

소리개 〖새〗 a (black) kite

소리결 a sound wave

소리굽쇠 a tuning fork

소리글자 〖언어〗 a phonetic symbol ⇨ 표음문자(表音文字)

소리마디 a syllable

소리맵시 tone color〔quality〕

소리소리 yelling ; roaring ¶ 소리소리 지르다 yell ; roar

소리쟁이 a (ballad) singer

소리지르다 shout ; yell ; roar ⇨ 소리치다

*__소리치다__ shout ; bawl ; utter〔give〕 a cry ; cry〔call〕 out ; yell ; raise one's voice ¶ 정지하라고 소리치다 call out to《a person》 to stop // 나오라고 소리치다 shout to《a person》 to come out // 소리쳐 도움을 구하다 yell for help // 소리칠 것 없다 You needn't shout.

소리판 a disk ; a phonograph record

소림 疎林 a thin〔sparse〕 wood〔grove〕

소립 小粒 a small grain ; a fine particle

소립자 素粒子 〖물리〗 an elementary particle

소릿값 phonetic value

소마 urine
소마 보다 관용 urinate

소마걷이 〖건축〗 a kind of rounded trimming on the wooden block which sits on top of a square pillar

소마소마 timidly ; in fear and trembling ; cautiously ; nervously **—하다** (be) timid ; nervous ; cautious ; be in fear and trembling

소만 蘇滿 Russia and Manchuria
— 국경 the Soviet-Manchurian border(s)〔frontier〕

소말리아 Somalia

소망 所望 desire ; wish ; hope ; request ; expectation **—하다** desire ; wish for ; hope for ; expect ¶ 소망이라면 if one wishes〔desires〕 // 소망에 따라 at〔by〕《a person's》 request ; complying with《a person's》 request // 너의 소망은 이루어질 것이다 You will have your wish. /Your desire will be satisfied〔realized〕. // 소망이시라면 드리겠습니다 You shall have it if you want it. // 나의 소망은 마침내 이루어졌다 My hopes have at last been realized.

소망 素望 one's long cherished desire〔wish〕

‡**소매** a sleeve ¶ 소매가 긴〔짧은〕 long〔short〕-sleeve // 소매에 매달리다 cling to《a person's》 sleeve ; [애원] implore《a person to do》 ; appeal to《a person》 for mercy // 눈물로 소매를 적시다 wet one's sleeve with tears // 소매를 잡다 hold《a person》 by the sleeve
소맷길 the sleeve part of cloth **소맷동** the lower part of a sleeve **소맷부리** [겉옷의] the edge〔lower part〕 of a sleeve ; [셔츠의] a cuff ; a wristband **소맷자락** the lower edges〔the ends〕 of a sleeve ; the hem of a sleeve
소매를 걷다 관용 roll up one's sleeve

*__소매 小賣__ retail sale **—하다** retail ; sell by retail《영》 ; sell at retail《미》 ¶ 1킬로그램에 소매로 1,000원이다 be a thousand *won* a kilogram at retail // 그는 도매로 가져와서 소매로 판다 He buys wholesale and sells at retail.
— 가격 a retail price **— 물가 지수** a retail price index **— 물가 통계 조사** the Retail Price Survey **—부** a retail department **—상** retail trade ; small business **— 상인** a retail dealer ; a retailer ; a storekeeper ; a shopkeeper **— 시장** a retail market **—점** a retail store〔shop〕 **— (상)품** retail goods

*__소매치기__ [사람] a pickpocket ; a cutpurse ; a dip《미·속》 ; [행위] pocket-picking ; dipping《미·속》 ¶ 소매치기 두목 a master pickpocket ; a Fagin // 소매치기를 당하다 have one's pocket picked // 소매치기 주의 Beware of〔Look out for〕 pickpockets. (게시)

소매통 the width〔breadth〕 of a sleeve ¶ 소매통이 넓은 저고리 a wide-sleeved coat
소맥 小麥 wheat ⇨ 밀
소면 素麵 plain noodles (without meat)
소면 素面 [화장않은 얼굴] an unpainted face ¶ 소면을 보이다 let one's unpainted face be seen《by》; [비유적] lift one's visor
소면기 梳綿機 a carding machine ; a card
소멸 消滅 [절멸] extinction ; extinguishment ; [소실] disappearance ; [실효] nullification ; termination
—하다 become extinct ; cease to exist ; disappear ; vanish ; lapse ; be nullified ; become null〔void〕; be extinguished ; terminate ; be expiated (죄가) ¶ 권리의 소멸 lapse of one's rights // 계약의 소멸 the discharge of contract // 죄상의 소멸 expiation // 자연 소멸하다 become extinct automatically ; work itself out ; wear off // 본 조약은 오는 7월 5일로 소멸한다 This treaty shall terminate on the 5th of July. // 그의 죄는 모두 소멸해 버렸다 His sins are all blotted out.
— 시효 extinctive〔negative〕 prescription 공유권 — extinguishment of common property 권리 — extinguishment〔lapse〕 of one's rights 자기 — self-effacement 자연 — natural extinction〔death〕 ¶ 자연 소멸하다 die out〔go out of existence〕 in the course of time ; cease to exist as a matter of course
소멸 燒滅 destruction by fire —하다 destroy by fire ; reduce〔be reduced〕 to ashes
소멸 掃滅 a (clean) sweep ; extermination —하다 sweep away〔off〕; drive off ; clear away〔off〕; make a clean sweep of ; deterge (상처 따위를) ; [근절] make an end of ; stamp〔root〕 out ; exterminate ; eradicate ¶ 해적을 소멸하다 sweep〔scour, clear〕《the sea》 of pirates // 폐풍을 소멸하다 sweep away abuses ; eradicate〔root out〕 evil customs
소명 昭明 brightness ; cleverness —하다 (be) bright ; clever
소명 召命 a royal summons ¶ 소명을 받들어 in response to a royal summons
*소모 消耗 consumption ; exhaustion ; dissipation ; waste ; decrement ; wear and tear ; 〖의학〗 contabescence ; phthisis ; marasmus —하다 consume ; exhaust ; dissipate ; waste ; use up ¶ 정력을 소모하다 dissipate〔waste〕 one's energy
—비 wear and tear expenses —열 〖병리〗 hectic fever —율 the attrition rate — 자산 current〔liquid, wasting〕 assets —전 a war of attrition —증 〖의학〗 a wasting disease ; marasmus —품 consumption goods ; articles of consumption ; supplies ; expendables 《미》 사무용 —품 office supplies
소모 梳毛 carded wool
—기 a carding machine —사(絲) worsted ; combed yarn
소목 小木 a joiner ; a cabinetmaker
소목장이 小木— a cabinetmaker ; a joiner
소몰이 a cattle drover ; cattle droving
소묘 素描 rough drawing ; a rough sketch
소문 小門 ① a small gate ② [보지] vulva 《속》
†소문 所聞 a rumor ; a report ; hearsay ; gossip ; common talk ¶ 헛소문 an idle rumor // 소문난 very famous // 소문이 나다 a rumor gets started〔stirred up〕; a rumor circulates // 소문을 내다 start〔stir up〕 a rumor ; put a rumor in circulation // 소문을 퍼뜨리다 spread〔air〕 a rumor ; shout it about // 소문이 자자하다 Word has been spreading〔getting around〕. // 당신이 부인과 이혼할 거라는 소문이 퍼지고 있다 Rumors are flying that you will divorce your wife. // 그에 관한 어떤 소문을 우연히 들었다 I happened to hear a certain rumor about him.
나쁜 소문은 빨리 퍼진다 속담 Bad news travels fast.
소문난 잔치가 비지떡이 두레반이다(소문난 잔치에 먹을 것 없다. 소문난 물산이 더 안된다) 속담 Great boast and small roast.
소문만복래 笑門萬福來 Fortune comes to a merry home. /Laugh and be〔grow〕 fat.
소문자 小文字 a small letter ; minuscule
소밀 疏密 density ; thickness ; compactness
소바리 loading an ox ; an ox load
*소박 素朴 simplicity ; naivety ; artlessness —하다 (be) simple ; artless ; naive ; plain ¶ 소박한 사람 a simple man
소박 疏薄 maltreatment ; ill treatment ; mistreatment ; abuse ; desertion —하다 maltreat〔ill-treat〕《one's wife》; desert ; abandon ¶ 소박 맞다 be mistreated〔abused〕; get deserted
소박데기 疏薄— a mistreated〔an abused, a deserted〕 wife
소박이 stuffed cucumber pickles
소반 小盤 a small dining table ; a tray
소반 素飯 a plain meal ; plain fare
소반응 素反應 〖화학〗 (an) elementary reaction
소밥 素— a plain meal〔dinner〕; meatless food
‡소방 消防 fire fighting ; fire service ; the prevention and extinction of fires ¶ 소방에 진력하다 fight the fire ; arrest the spread of a fire ; get a fire under control ; extinguish a fire
—관 a fire fighter ; a fire officer ; a fireman — 기구 fire-fighting equipment〔apparatus〕 —대 a fire brigade ; a fire company ; a fire-fighting team〔unit〕 (공

(공장이나 군대의) —대장 a fire marshal〔chief〕 —모(帽) a smoke helmet ; a fire hat —법 the Fire Services Act —본부 the fire defense headquarters ; a fire department — 비상선 a fire line —사(士) a fireman ; a fire fighter — 사닥다리 a fire ladder ; [신축식] an extension ladder —서 a fire(-brigade) station ; a fire department ; a firehouse 《미》 — 연습 a fire drill —원(員) a fireman 《*pl.* -men》 ; a fire fighter —정 a fireboat —차 a fire engine〔truck〕 — 펌프 a fire(-engine) pump

소변 小便 (human) urine ; piss ; [마소의] stale ¶ 소변을 보다 urinate ; pass urine〔water〕 // 소변을 참다 contain〔retain〕 one's urine ; neglect calls of nature
— 검사 urine examination — 금지 [게시] Decency forbids. /No nuisance here. / Commit no nuisance. 《영》/No Urinating. —기 a urinal (receptacle) —소 a urinal ; a toilet (room) ; a lavatory

소복 素服 white〔mourning〕 clothes —하다 wear white clothes

소복하다 be heaped up ⇨ 수북하다

소분 小分 a subdivision ⇨ 세분

†**소비 消費** consumption ; spending ; expenditures —하다 consume ; spend ; expend ¶ 일인당 쌀의 소비량 the per capita consumption of rice // 시간을 소비하다 spend〔waste〕 time ; put in time 《구》 // 돈을 소비하다 spend money // 의복에 다액의 돈을 소비하다 expend〔spend〕 much money on one's clothes // 이 차는 휘발유를 참 많이 소비합니다 This car is a gas guzzler.
— 감퇴 decrease of consumption ; underconsumption — 경제 consumer economy —고 (the amount of) consumption — 단위 a consumption unit — 도시 a consuming〔consumer〕 city — 물자 consumer goods ; consumables — 생활 one's daily life as a consumer — 성향 the propensity to consume —세 the consumption tax ; excise tax〔duty〕 —액 the amount of consumption —자 a consumer ; [소비 대중] the consuming public —자 가격 the consumers' price —재 consumer(s') goods ; consumer products —재 공업 consumer industry — 절약 economy in consumption — 제한 restriction on consumption — 조합 a consumers' cooperative society ¶ 소비 조합의 매점 a cooperative store ; a co-op 《구》

소사 小史 a short history

소사 小使 an errand boy ; a servant ; a janitor ; a messenger ; an office boy

소사 小事 a trifle ; a trivial〔small, trifling, minor〕 matter ¶ 소사에 구애하다 bother〔worry〕 about trifles ; strain at a gnat

소사 小辭 〖논리〗 a minor term

소사 掃射 [기관총의] volley (of small arms) ; machine-gunning —하다 machine-gun ; sweep with fire ; mow

소사 燒死 death by fire —하다 burn〔be burned〕 to death ; perish in a fire〔in flames〕
—자 a person burnt to death ; [총칭] the dead in a fire —체 a charred body

소사나무 〖식물〗 the Korean hornbeam

소사스럽다 (be) crafty ; cunning ; tricky ; sly ¶ 소사스러운 짓을 하다 do a tricky thing ; be dishonest

†**소산 所産** a product ; an outcome ; an outgrowth ; fruit ; a result ¶ 노동의 소산 the products of labor
—물 products ; [농산물] produce

소산 消散 dissipation ; dispersion ; disappearance ; vanishing —하다 dissipate ; disappear ; disperse ; vanish ; [증발] evaporate ; [안개 따위가] lift ¶ 시계에서 소산하다 vanish out of sight // 운무와 같이 소산하다 vanish into the thin air

소살 燒殺 destruction〔killing〕 by fire ; incineration 《미》 —하다 burn to death ; burn alive ; incinerate 《미》

소삼 蕭森 ① [쓸쓸함] loneliness ; desolation ; desolateness ; bleakness —하다 (be) lonely ; desolate ; bleak ; deserted ② [울창] thickness ; denseness ; luxuriance —하다 (be) thick ; dense ; luxuriant ¶ 소삼하게 자라다 grow thick(ly)〔dense(ly)〕

소삽하다 蕭颯 — 《wind》 (be) sobbing ; wailing ¶ 가을 바람소리가 소삽하다 The autumn wind is sobbing.

소상 小祥 the first anniversary of the death of a person

소상 小像 a statuette ; a figurine

소상 塑像 a plastic〔plaster〕 image ; a clay figure

소상 昭詳 —하다 (be) full ; detailed ; minute ¶ …에 소상하다 know well about 《America》 ; be at home in〔on〕 《French history》

소상인 小商人 a small trader〔shopkeeper, tradesman, businessman〕 a retail dealer〔merchant〕 ; a retailer

소생 小生 I ; me ; myself

소생 所生 one's children〔offspring〕 ; progeny ¶ 소생이 없다 be childless ; be without issue // 소생이 많다 He has many children. /He has a large family.

***소생 蘇生** revival ; resuscitation ; reanimation —하다 revive ; resuscitate 《from death》 ; be restored〔brought back〕 to life ; come back to life ; return to life ; recover consciousness ¶ 마치 소생한 것 같은 느낌이었다 I felt as if I had risen from the dead. // 그를 소생시킬 수는 없었다 We could not resuscitate him. /We could not bring him back to life. // 비가 오자 초목은 소생했다 The grass and plants were freshened after a rainfall.

소서 小署 11th of the 24 seasonal divisions 《c. 7 July》

-소서 please do ; I beg you to do ; pray ¶ 백세 천세 누리소서 Long may you live ! /Long live the king ! (왕에게) // 용서하소서 I beg you to forgive me.

소석고 燒石膏 plaster of Paris ; burnt 〔oxidized〕 plaster

소석회 消石灰 slaked lime ; calcium hydroxide

소선거구 小選擧區 a small electoral district ; [1구 1인의] a single-member constituency
—**제** the single-member electorate〔constituency〕 system

‡**소설 小說** a novel ; a story ; fiction 《총칭》

> 참고 **novel**은 18세기 이후의 신소설 **story**는 novel과 같은 뜻 또는 이야기

¶ 소설 같은 이야기 a romantic〔fiction-like〕 story // 소설을 쓰다 write a novel // 소설을 써서 살아가다 live by one's novels // 소설을 각색하다 dramatize a novel ; adapt a novel to the stage // 이것은 동아일보에 연재된 소설이다 This is a story published serially in the *Dong-A Ilbo*.
—**가** a novelist ; a fiction〔story〕 writer —**문학** novel literature ; fiction —**적** romantic ; fictitious —**책** a novel ; a storybook —**형식** the novelistic form ; the form of fiction **교양** — an educational novel **단편** — a short story ; a novelette ; a storiette **모험** — a story of adventures ; an adventurous story **문제** — a problem novel **반**— anti-roman 《프》 **사실** — a realistic novel **신문** — a newspaper novel **심리** — a psychological novel **역사** — a historical novel **연애** — a love story **연재** — a serial story ; story in daily installments **장편** — a (full-length) novel **추리** — a detective story ; a mystery story **통속** — a popular novel **현상** — a prize novel〔story〕

소설 小雪 20th of the 24 seasonal divisions 《c. 22 Nov.》

소설 所說 one's opinion〔view, argument, theory〕

소성 小成 a small success ; a humble lot in life ¶ 소성에 만족하다 be contented with a small success

소성 素性 nature ; character ; temperament ; disposition ; personality

소성 塑性 〖물리〗 plasticity ¶ 소성이 있다 be plastic
—**변형** plastic deformation —**유동** plastic flow

소세 梳洗 washing one's face and combing one's hair ; dressing —**하다** wash one's face and comb one's hair ; dress oneself

소세계 小世界 a little world ; a microcosm(os)

소세포 小細胞 〖동물·식물〗 a cellule

소소리바람 a chilly bleak wind ; a desolate wind ; a whirlwind ; a cyclone

소소리패 frivolous youngsters

소소하다 小小— (be) trivial ; small ; insignificant

소소하다 昭昭— (be) clear ; plain ; distinct ; obvious ; evident

소소하다 蕭蕭— (be) dreary ; bleak ; sobbing ; whining (바람) ; desolate (황량)

†**소속 所屬** one's position〔post, place〕 —**하다** belong to ; be attached to ; be under the command〔control〕 of ¶ 공화당 소속의 국회 의원 an Assemblyman belonging to the Republican Party ; a parliamentary member of the Republican Party // 소속시키다 attach ; assign ; put under the command〔control〕 of // 나의 소속은 아직 미정이다 I am not yet assigned any post. /I am still free from any affiliation
—**부대** one's regiment〔unit〕 ; one's home post

소손 燒損 damage by〔from〕 a fire —**하다** be damaged by a fire ; be partially burned in the flames
—**품** articles saved from burning

†**소송 訴訟** a lawsuit ; a suit ; an action (at law) ; litigation ; legal proceedings 〔steps〕 —**하다** sue 《a person for damages》 ; institute〔file〕 suit 《for》 ; prosecute 《a person for defamation》 ; litigate ; go to law 《with》 ; take〔institute〕 legal proceedings 《against》 ¶ 소송에 이기다〔지다〕 win〔lose〕 a suit // 소송을 제기하다 institute〔start, raise〕 a suit 《against》 ; enter〔bring, take〕 an action 《against》 // 소송을 취하하다 drop〔discontinue〕 a suit // 소송 수속을 하다 take legal proceedings 《against a person, for one's right》 ; proceed 《against a person》 // 소송 중이다 be at law ; be pending in the court ; be in litigation // 이 사건은 소송이 된다 The case is actionable〔will lie〕. // 수년 간에 걸친 소송 후 원고측에 유리한 판결이 있었다 After several years of legal proceedings judgment has at last been given〔passed〕 in favor of the plaintiff.
—**각하** dismissal of a case —**관계인** a litigant ; [전원] the litigants —**능력** litigation capacity —**당사자** the parties to〔in〕 a lawsuit ; the litigants —**대리인** a counsel ; a process attorney ; an attorney —**법** the code〔law〕 of legal procedure —**비용** the costs (of a lawsuit) ; court costs —**사건** a case in litigation ; a judicial〔legal〕 case ; a lawsuit ; a cause —**위임장** a warrant of attorney —**의뢰인** a client ; a brief 《구》 ; a plaintiff ; a suitor —**절차** judicial〔legal〕 procedure ; (legal) proceedings ; practice ¶ 소송 절차를 취하다 take〔institute〕 legal pro-

ceedings 《against a person》 — 행위 acts of procedure 민사〔형사〕 — a civil〔criminal〕 suit 반대 — a cross-suit ; a cross action 이혼 — a suit〔an action〕 for divorce 행정 — administrative litigation

소송 감정 訴訟鑑定 legal advice〔consultation〕

소수 a bit over ; a bit upward of ; plus some (extra) ¶ 세 말 소수 three *mal* and a bit over // 넉 달 소수 little over 〔more than〕 four months

소수 小數 〖수학〗 a decimal (fraction) ¶ 소수점 이하 3위까지 계산하다 calculate down to three decimal places

—위 a decimal place —점 a (decimal) point 유한〔무한〕 — a terminating〔an interminating〕 decimal

⁑**소수 少數** a small number ; a minority ; a few ¶ 회의의 참석자는 소수였다 There were a small number of people present at the meeting. /There was a small 〔poor〕 attendance at the meeting. /The meeting was poorly attended. // 우리는 소수파다 We are in the minority. /We are a minority group. // 그 정당은 국회에서 소수당이다 The party forms a small minority in the National Assembly. /The party is represented in the National Assembly by a minority.

—당 the minority ; a minor (political) party — 독점 〖경제〗 oligopoly — 민족 a minority race — 의견 the opinion of the minority ; a minority opinion ; the minority views — 정예주의 the principle 〔policy〕 of having affairs run by a select few〔fewer people of superior ability〕

소수 素數 〖수학〗 a prime number

소수 疏水 drainage ; 〔수로〕 a canal

소수나다 《land》 increase its crop yield

소수성 疎水性 hydrophobic property

소스 sauce ¶ 소스를 치다 put sauce 《on》 ; sauce 《meat》 ; pour sauce 《over》

—병 a sauce pot ; 〔배 모양의〕 a sauceboat

소스라뜨리다 ⇨ 소스라치다

⁑**소스라치다** be frightened ; be taken aback ; start 《with fright》 ¶ 그 광경을 보고 소스라치다 be frightened〔startled〕 at the sight ; start up at the sight // 문이 꽝하고 닫히자 그 여자는 소스라치게 놀랐다 The slamming of the door made her start.

소슬하다 蕭瑟— (be) lonely and desolate ; bleak ; chilly ; sobbing ¶ 소슬한 가을 바람 a bleak autumnal wind

소승 小乘 〖불교〗 Hinayana ; the Lesser Vehicle ¶ 소승적 견지 a narrow point of view

— 불교 Hinayana〔Southern〕 Buddhism ¶ 소승 불교 신자 a Hinayanist ; a Theravadin

소승 少僧 a young priest〔monk〕

소승 小僧 this humble servant of Buddha ; I

소시 少時 one's youth ; one's boyhood ¶ 소싯적에 in one's earliest day〔childhood〕

소시민 小市民 a petit bourgeois

⁑**소시지** (a) sausage

햄— ham sausage

소식 小食 light eating —하다 eat little〔sparingly〕

—가 a light〔small〕 eater

소식 素食 a meatless meal

소식 蔬食 vegetable food ; a vegetable diet

***소식 消息** news ; tidings ; information ; a report ; a letter ¶ 기쁜〔나쁜〕 소식 a piece of good〔bad〕 news ; good〔evil〕 news〔tidings〕 // 소식을 듣다 hear〔learn〕 the news of 《a person》 ; hear of 《person》 // 소식이 있다 hear from 《a person》 // 소식이 없다 hear nothing〔none〕 from 《a person》 // 소식을 가져오다 bear 〔bring〕 the news 《of》 // 그는 우리에게 가족의 소식을 가져왔다 He brought us tidings of our family. // 무소식이 희소식 No news is good news. // 그 사람의 소식을 들었느냐 Have you heard anything of him? // 등반대는 19일에 출발한 후 소식이 전혀 없다 Nothing has been heard of the mountaineering party since its departure on the 19th. // 가끔 소식 주게 Drop me a line once in a while.

—통 〔개인〕 a well-informed person ; a person in the know ; an insider ; 〔집단〕 well-informed quarters〔circles, sources〕 ¶ 외교계의 소식통 the well-informed diplomatic sources

소식자 消息子 〖의학〗 a (surgical) probe ; a sound

소신 所信 one's belief〔conviction〕 ; one's opinion〔view〕 ¶ 소신을 피력하다 give 〔express〕 《one's》 opinion ; express one's belief ; voice one's conviction // 소신대로 단행하다 act according to one's conviction // 소신을 굽히지 않다 be unshakable〔firm〕 in one's convictions

소실 小室 a concubine

— 자식 a child by a concubine ; an illegitimate child

***소실 消失** disappearance ; vanishing ; loss —하다 disappear ; vanish ; die away ; lose

소실 燒失 destruction〔loss〕 by fire —하다 be destroyed〔consumed〕 by fire ; be burnt down ; be razed to the ground ; be reduced to ashes ¶ 모든 가재를 소실하다 lose all one's household goods in the fire // 소실을 면하다 be saved from the fire ; escape (destruction by) fire〔the flames〕

— 가옥 burnt houses ; houses destroyed by fire — 구역 the burnt district ; the area devastated〔ravaged, laid waste〕 by the fire ; the area swept by the flames

소심 小心 —하다 〔담이 작다〕 (be)

timid ; cowardly ; fainthearted ; [조심 깊다] prudent ; cautious ; scrupulous ; circumspect
—자 a coward ; a timid person ; a chicken-hearted person
소아 小兒 a young〔little〕 child ; an infant ; a baby
—병 a child's disease ; infantilism ¶ 소아병적 infantilistic —시절 infancy ; childhood —어 a nursery word ; baby talk 《총칭》
소아 小我 〖철학〗 the relative〔empirical〕 ego
소아과 小兒科 pediatrics ; pediatry ¶ 그 의사는 소아과 전문이다 The doctor specializes in pediatrics.
—병원 a children's hospital —의사 a children's doctor ; a child specialist ; a pediatrist〔pediatrician〕
*소아마비 少兒麻痺 infantile paralysis ; (acute anterior) poliomyelitis ; polio 《구》 ¶ 소아마비에 걸리다 suffer from〔be affected with〕 poliomyelitis ; be stricken with polio
—바이러스 a polio virus —예방 주사 a preventive injection against poliomyelitis ; 《get》 a polio shot 뇌성— cerebral palsy
소아시아 小— Asia Minor
소안 笑顔 a smiling〔beaming〕 face
소액 少額 a small〔petty〕 sum〔amount〕 (of money)
—국채 a small government bond ; a baby bond —대부금 a small loan —보험 petty-sum insurance —지폐 small notes〔bills〕 ; notes of small〔low〕 denominations ; shinplasters 《미》 —채권 a small bond —환(換) a postal order 《P. O.》 ; a postal note 《미》 ¶ 3천원의 소액환 a postal order for 3,000 *won*
소액 현금 少額現金 petty cash
—출납부 a petty cashbook
소야곡 小夜曲 〖음악〗 a serenade
—가수 a serenader
소양 小恙 a minor illness ; complaint
소양 素養 [소지] a grounding 《in》 ; an elementary knowledge 《of》 ; [조예] acquirements ; attainments ; [수련] training ¶ 소양이 있는 cultured ; trained ; cultivated // 문학의 소양 literary attainments // 소양이 있다 be well-grounded 《in music》 // 외국어의 소양이 없다 have no knowledge of foreign language ; do not know any foreign language // 거기에는 영어의 소양이 필요하다 It demands a knowledge of English.
소양배양하다 (be) thoughtless ; childish and frivolous ; injudicious ; immature ; naive
소양증 搔痒症 〖한의〗 pruritus ; itching
소업 所業 one's occupation〔profession, calling, job〕
소여 所與 datum ; what is given ; the given ...
소연 小宴 a small feast ; an informal dinner (party) ; a dinnerette ¶ 소연을 베풀다 hold a small (dinner) party
소연기 消煙機 a smoke consumer
소연하다 昭然— (be) clear ; plain ; obvious
소연하다 蕭然— (be) lonely ; lonesome ; desolate ; bleak ; solitary ¶ 소연한 장소 a lonely〔desolate〕 spot
소연하다 騷然— (be) noisy ; uproarious ; turbulent ; clamorous ¶ 장내가 소연해졌다 The hall was thrown into an uproar.
소염제 消炎劑 〖약〗 an antiphlogistic (agent)
소엽 小葉 a small leaf ; 〖식물〗 a leaflet ; 〖해부〗 a lobule
소영사 所營事 one's undertakings ; one's business
소옥 小屋 a shed ; a shack ; a hut ; a cabin ; a cottage ; a small house
소옥 엔진 燒玉— a hot-bulb engine
소외 疎外 (an) estrangement ; alienation ; neglect —하다 estrange ; alienate ; neglect ; slight ; avoid〔shun〕 《a person's》 company ¶ 소외 당하다 be shunned〔neglected〕 ; be out of favor 《with》 // 친구에게 소외 당하다 be treated distantly by one's friend
—감 a sense of alienation
소요 所要 need ; requirement ; what is needed〔required〕
—금액 the necessary〔required〕 sum —시간 the time required ; the necessary time —조건 required conditions ; requirements ; requisites
소요 逍遙 a ramble ; a saunter ; a walk —하다 walk leisurely ; stroll〔ramble, saunter〕 about ; take a stroll ¶ 뜰을 소요하다 take a turn〔stroll〕 in the garden ; stroll〔wander〕 about the garden
—학파 〖철학〗 the Peripatetic school ¶ 소요학파의 철학 Peripatetism
소요 騷擾 a disturbance ; a commotion ; a riot ¶ 소요를 일으키다 cause〔create〕 a disturbance〔riot〕
—죄 (the crime of) sedition ¶ 소요죄로 검거되다 be arrested on the charge of sedition
†소용 所用 use ; usefulness ; service ; [물건] what is used ; necessaries ; expenses ¶ 소용되다 be used ; be needed // 크게 소용되다 be of (great) use〔service〕 // 소용없다 be useless ; be of no use〔avail〕 ; be no use 《구》 // 소용에 닿다 serve the purpose ; be useful〔serviceable〕 // 이 도시에서는 전화는 크게 소용없다 The telephone is of little use in this town. // 그에게 충고해 봤자 소용없다 Advice is no use to him. // 네가 부정해도 소용없다 It is no use your trying to deny it. // 말해 봤자 무슨 소용이냐 What is the

use of talking?/Of what use is it to talk?/There is no use (in) talking./It is of no use to talk〔talking〕. // 당신과 얘기해 보았자 소용이 없을 거야 I won't be able to get anywhere with you. // 학교에 말하는 것은 소용이 없었다 Talking to school got us nowhere.

*소용돌이 a whirlpool; a swirl; an eddy; vortex 《*pl.* ~es, -tices》
—꼴 a volution; a volute; a swirl —무늬 a scroll

*소용돌이치다 whirl; eddy ¶ 소용돌이치는 급류 swirling torrents // 소용돌이 속에 말려 들다 be drawn into a whirlpool〔vortex〕

소우 小雨 a light〔drizzling〕 rain; a drizzle; a thin〔fine〕 rain

소우주 小宇宙 〖철학〗 a microcosm

소웅성 小熊星 ⇨ 소웅좌

소웅좌 小熊座 〖천문〗 the Little Bear 〔Ursa Minor〕; the Little Dipper

†소원 所願 one's desire〔wish〕 ¶ 이루지 못한 소원 an unfulfilled desire // 소원대로 as one wished; according to one's desire // 소원을 들어 주다 comply with one's wishes // 소원 성취하다 realize one's cherished wishes // 자네 소원이라면 무엇이든지 들어 주겠네 I can refuse you nothing.

소원 素願 one's long-cherished desire; one's heart's desire

소원 疏遠 estrangement; alienation —하다 (be) estranged〔alienated〕 ¶ 소원하여지다 become estranged〔alienated〕 《from》 // 그 두 사람은 왜 소원하여 졌느냐 What has estranged the two from each other?

소원 訴願 a petition; an appeal —하다 petition; appeal; make petition; hand 〔send〕 in one's petition ¶ 소원을 제기하다 present a petition // 추방 해제를 소원하다 petition 《the authorities》 for one's repatriation
—법 the Administrative Appeal Law —위원회 the Petition Committee —인 an appellant; a petitioner

소원 溯源 investigation of the origin 《of a matter》 —하다 trace 《it》 back; trace 《a thing》 to its origin

‡소위 所謂 what is called; what you〔we, they〕 call; the so-called; as it is called; quote-unquote ¶ 그는 소위 귀공자다 He is what is called a young prince. // 그 여자는 소위 X세대 여성이다 She is what we call a X generation girl. // 그들의 소위 자유주의 견해라는 것도 보수적 태도의 반향에 지나지 않았다 Their so-called liberal views were merely an echo of the conservative attitude. // 소위 운명이란 것은 사람이 스스로 친 거미줄이다 What a man calls fate is a web of his own weaving. // 그것은 소위 우리들의 일부 정치 지도자라는 사람들의 입으로부터 나오는 매우 무책임한 말장난이다 It's very thoughtless rhetoric that is coming out of some of our quote-unquote leaders in the political arena.

소위 少尉 〔육군〕 a second lieutenant; 〔해군〕 an ensign 《미》; an acting sublieutenant 《영》

소위 所爲 one's conduct; act; behavior; deed; doing; work ¶ 두통을 날씨의 소위로 돌리다 put one's headache down to the weather // 그의 소위임에 틀림 없다 It must be his doing. // 누구의 소위냐 Who has done it?

소위원회 小委員會 a subcommittee

†소유 所有 possession; ownership; property —하다 have; own; possess; hold; be in〔hold〕 possession of; be possessed of ¶ 김씨 소유의 owned by 〔belonging to〕 Mr. *Kim* // 이 토지〔집〕는 나의 소유이다 This land〔house〕 belongs to me. // 소유가 되다 come〔pass〕 into 《a person's》 possession // 소유자가 바뀌다 《it》 change ownership〔hands〕 // 많은 집을 소유하고 있다 He owns a large number of houses.
—격 〖문법〗 the possessive〔genitive〕 case —권 (the right of) ownership; proprietorship; proprietary〔proprietorial〕 rights; a right〔title〕 《to a thing》; dominium —권 보호 protection of property —권 이전 transfer of ownership —권 침해 infringement of ownership —물 one's possessions; one's property —본능 acquisitive instinct —욕 a desire to possess 《a thing》; possessiveness ¶ 소유욕이 강한 possessive; grasping; acquisitive; covetous —자〔주〕 an owner; a proprietor; a possessor ¶ 소유자가 없는 ownerless —지 land owned by〔belonging to〕 《a person》; one's land; one's estate; one's landed property ¶ 김씨의 소유지 Mr. *Kim*'s land 공동 —자 a joint〔common〕 owner; a co-owner 일부 —자 a part owner

소유성 小遊星 〖천문〗 an asteroid; minor〔lesser〕 planets

†소음 騷音 a noise; cacophony ¶ 거리의 소음 street noise; noises in the street // 요란한 소음 ear-splitting noise; the din 《of a factory》
—방지 prevention〔suppression〕 of noise; arrest of noise ¶ 소음 방지 운동 an anti- noise movement〔campaign〕 // 소음 방지 조례 a noise control regulation

소음기 消音器 a silencer; a damper; a muffler; a noise suppresser

소읍 小邑 a small town

소이 小異 slight difference; minor〔petty〕 differences —하다 (be) slightly different ¶ 대동소이하다 There is little to choose between them./They are practically the same./It's six of one and half-a-dozen of the other.

소이 所以 the reason; (the reason) why

¶ 가난한 소이로 나를 경멸한다 He despises me because I am poor. // 내가 사직한 소이는 바로 여기 있다 This is the reason why I have resigned my office. // 그는 다만 연장자라는 소이로 그 자리를 유지하고 있는데 불과하다 He holds the post merely in〔by〕 virtue of his seniority.

소이연 所以然 a reason ; (the reason) why

소이탄 燒夷彈 an incendiary ; an incendiary bomb〔shell〕 ; a fire bomb

소인 小人 [나이 어린] a child ; a little one ; a minor ; a runt ; [키가] a little man ; a dwarf ; a pigmy ; a hop-o'-my-thumb 《영》 ; [사람됨이] a mean〔stingy〕 person ; an insignificant〔a worthless〕 person ; a small mind ; a man of small character ; a mind of no caliber ; [신분] I ; me ; myself ¶ 소인은 노하기 쉽다 A little pot is soon hot.
—국 a land of pigmies ; Lilliput **—배** small fry

소인 消印 a postmark ; a cancellation stamp **—하다** postmark ; cancel with a stamp ¶ 보스턴의 소인이 찍혀 있는 편지 a letter bearing the Boston postmark // 이 봉투의 소인으로 봐서 judging from the postmark on this envelope

소인 素人 an amateur ; a non-professional
—극 amateur theatricals ; an amateur dramatic performance

소인 素因 a factor ; a basic〔primary〕 cause〔factor〕 ; a principle ; a fundamental ; a disposition ; 〖의학〗 predisposition ¶ 폐병의 소인 a predisposition to consumption // 그의 오늘의 성공은 청렴 결백이 소인이다 His present success is due mainly to his spotless integrity.

소인 訴因 〖법〗 a charge

소인 燒印 a brand ; a branding iron ; a stigma 《*pl.* ～s, -mata》 (형벌용) ¶ 소인을 찍다 brand 《cattle, goods》 ; mark 《cattle, goods》 with a brand

소인수 素因數 〖수학〗 a prime factor

소일 消日 whiling away〔killing, passing〕 time **—하다** while away〔kill〕 time ¶ 독서로 소일하다 spend one's time in reading // 하는 일 없이 빈둥거리고 소일하다 idle one's time away ; loaf // 어떻게 소일하고 계십니까 How are you getting on ? // 어제는 재미있게 소일했다 I had a mighty good time yesterday.
—거리 a diversion ; a time killer ; a pastime

소임 所任 one's duty〔task〕 ; one's office ; one's mission ¶ 중대한 소임 an important duty ; a great task〔mission〕 // 소임을 다하다 do〔discharge〕 one's duty ; accomplish one's mission // 특별한 소임을 띠고 on a special mission // 나는 나의 소임을 다했을 뿐이다 I have only done what it was my duty to do.

소자 小子 [부모에게] I ; me

소자 小字 a small letter〔character〕

소자 素子 〖전기〗 an element ; 〖천문〗 an element ; data
반도체 — a magnetodiode **발광 —** a light emitting display 《LED》

소자본 小資本 little capital ¶ 소자본으로 장사를 시작하다 start one's business with little capital〔on a shoestring 《미》〕

소작 小作 tenancy ; tenant farming ; share cropping 《미》 **—하다** tenant (a farm)
—권 a tenant right ¶ 소작권을 확립하다 secure one's tenant right **—농** tenant farming ; [사람] a tenant (farmer) **—료** farm rent ; rent for tenancy **—인** a tenant (farmer) ; a sharecropper 《미》 ; a cottage farmer ; tenantry 《총칭》 **— 쟁의** a tenancy dispute〔trouble〕 ; an agrarian dispute **— 제도** the tenant(-farming) system ¶ 소작 제도를 폐지하다 abolish〔discontinue〕 the tenant system

소작 燒灼 〖의학〗 cauterization ; cautery **—하다** cauterize
—기(器) a cautery ; a cauter **—제(劑)** a cauterant ; a caustic

소장 少壯 vigorous youth ; the young
—파 younger members〔set〕 ; the younger group〔faction〕 **— 학파** the young school

소장 小腸 〖해부〗 the small intestines ; chitterlings (돼지 따위)
— 간막(間膜) mesentery **—선(腺)** glands of the small intestines **—염** enteritis

소장 少將 [육군] a major general ; [해군] a rear admiral ; [공군] an air vice-marshal 《영》

소장 所長 the head 《of an office, a factory》

소장 所掌 one's task〔duty, office〕

소장 所藏 one's possession〔collection〕 ¶ 김씨 소장의 owned by〔in the possession of〕 Mr. *Kim* // 그 도서관의 소장 도서는 20만 권이다 The library has a collection of 200,000 volumes.
— 골동 one's collection of curios ; curios in one's possession **— 서화** one's collection of writings and paintings

소장 消長 prosperity and decay ; rise and fall ; ups and downs ; ebb and flow ; the vicissitudes of fortune ¶ 일국의 소장 the rise and fall of a nation ; the welfare〔destiny〕 of a nation

소장 訴狀 a petition ; a written complaint ; a bill (of complaint) ; pleadings ; a brief ¶ 소장을 제출하다 present a petition

소재 所在 [사람의] one's whereabouts ; where a person is ; [물건의] the place where a thing is ; [건물 따위의] the site ; [위치] the position ; the situation ; the location ¶ 소재가 불명이다 be

missing ; 《someone's》 whereabouts are unknown // 소재를 발견하다 discover 《a person's》 whereabouts ; locate 《an enemy》 // 소재를 감추다 conceal one's whereabouts ; cover one's traces ; disappear ; hide 《oneself》 // 책임 소재를 명확히 하다 clarify where the responsibility lies
—지 the location ; the site ; the seat 《of an office》 —처 one's whereabouts ; one's dwelling place

소재 素材 matter ; material ; [작품의] the subject matter

소재 所載 ¶ 소재의 printed ; published ; reported // 전호에 소재된 바와 같이 as reported〔stated〕 in the previous number〔issue〕

소저 小姐 a young lady ; a young mistress

소전 小傳 a short〔brief〕 biography ; a biographical sketch〔profile〕 ; biographical notes

소전 所傳 a legend ; a〔an oral〕 tradition ; a record (기록)

소전제 小前提 〖논리〗 a minor premise

소절 小節 [예절] minor matter of etiquette or protocol ; [절조] minor points of honor ; trifles ; 〖음악〗 a bar

소정 所定 ¶ 소정의 fixed ; prescribed ; designated ; established // 소정의 양식 a prescribed form // 소정의 시간〔장소〕 the fixed〔appointed〕 hour〔place〕 // 소정의 학과 the prescribed course of study // 소정의 시간을 초과하다 outrun〔exceed〕 the time allotted // 소정의 위치에 자리잡다 take one's place

소정 小艇 a small boat

소제 小題 a subtitle ; a subhead

소제 掃除 cleaning ⇨ 청소(淸掃)
— 도구 dusting〔scrubbing〕 things —부(夫) a cleaner ; a sweeper ; a scavenger —부(婦) a cleaning woman ; a charwoman ; a scrubwoman 《미》

소조 小潮 the neap ; the neap-tide

소조 小鳥 a little〔small〕 bird

소조 塑造 modeling ; molding
— 예술 plastic arts

소조 蕭條 —하다 (be) dreary ; desolate ; bleak

소주 小註 detailed notes ; minute notes ¶ 소주를 달다 add detailed notes〔comments, remarks〕 to

소주 燒酒 distilled liquor ; hard liquor ; ardent spirits
막— crude〔low-grade〕 spirits

소죽 —粥 boiled fodder
—통 a boiled-fodder tub〔bucket〕

‡소중 所重 importance ; significance ; valuableness —하다 (be) important ; weighty ; significant ; valuable ; dear ; precious ¶ 소중히 seriously ; with care〔caution〕 ; carefully // 소중한 물품 a valuable〔treasured〕 article ; a treasure ; valuables // 소중한 일 the main〔important〕 thing // 소중한 자식 a precious〔beloved, dear〕 child // 소중한 친구 a valued friend // 생명 다음 갈 정도로 소중한 물건 a thing next〔near〕 to one's heart ; a thing as dear as life itself // 무엇을 하든지 건강이 제일 소중하다 In everything health should be the first consideration. // 영어를 배우는 데 제일 소중한 것은 끊임없는 연습이다 The first requisite in the study of English is constant practice. // 나는 돈보다 시간을 소중히 여긴다 I consider time more important than money.

소증 素症 ① [고기가 먹고 싶음] a craving for meat ¶ 소증이 나다 crave meat ; have a craving for meat ② 〖의학〗 protein deficiency

소증기선 小蒸氣船 a steam launch

소증사납다 (be) evilly motivated

소지 沼地 bogland ; marshland ; swampland ; a marshy〔swampy〕 place

†소지 所持 possession —하다 possess ; have ; bear ; carry ¶ 여권을 소지하다 have a passport // 그 여행자는 다액의 돈을 소지하고 있었다 The traveler carried a large sum of money.
—금 funds〔money〕 in hand〔in one's pocket〕 —자 a possessor ; a holder ; a bearer —품 one's things〔belongings, havings〕 ; one's personal effects ¶ 소지품을 조사하다 examine〔check up on〕 one's things (at hand)

소지 素地 a foundation ; a basis ; ground

소지 小指 [손의] the little finger ; [발의] a little toe

소지 素志 one's original intention ; one's initial purpose〔aim, object〕

소지 燒紙 sacrificial paper (burned to a departed spirit)

소진 消盡 vanishing completely ; total disappearance ; exhaustion —하다 totally vanish ; disappear altogether ; exhaust

소진 燒盡 reduction to ashes ; total destruction by fire —하다 be reduced to ashes ; be totally destroyed by fire ; burn to nothing ; be burnt away〔out〕

†소질 素質 [자질] temperament ; character ; nature ; composition ; a turn ; fiber ; stuff ; quality ; [체질] constitution ; diathesis ; predisposition (병의) ¶ 시적 소질 poetical temperament // 암에 걸릴 소질 a predisposition to cancer // 유전적 범죄 소질 inherited criminal tendencies // 정치가의 소질이 있는 사람 man of political fiber〔caliber〕 // 문학적 소질이 있는 사람 a person of a literary turn (of mind) // 소질의 향상 improvement of the quality // 학생들의 소질이 저하되고 있다 The quality of the students is declining. // 저는 음악에는 별로 소질이 없습니다 I don't have a very good ear for music.

*소집 召集 a call ; a summons ; [동원] mobilization ; [의회 따위의] convoca-

tion ; [징집] a levy —하다 call 《a meeting》 ; convene 《an assembly》 ; convoke ; summon 《a session》 ; call up 《reserves》 ; call up for service ; draft into the army ¶ 국회의 소집 the convocation of the Assembly // 소집에 응하여 at the call // 임시 국회를 소집하다 convene〔summon〕 a special session of the Assembly // 예비병을 소집하다 call up the reserves // 비번 경찰을 소집하다 call out police reserves // 소집되어 전선으로 가다 be called away to the front〔war〕 // 소집에 응하다 arise at the summons

— 기일 the date of induction — 나팔 a bugle call —령 a draft call — 영장 a call-up paper〔card〕 ; a draft notice 《미》 ; a summons to the colors — 해제 discharge from military service ; an honorable discharge — 해제자 a separatee 연습 — a maneuver levy 임시 — partial mobilization

소쩍새 a cuckoo

소차 小差 a small〔slight, little〕 difference

소찬 素饌 plain side dishes (without meat or fish)

소창 消暢 (a) recreation ; (a) diversion ; a pastime —하다 refresh oneself 《with a song》 ; divert oneself〔one's mind〕 ; recreate〔unbend, amuse〕 oneself ; find one's recreation 《in a pastime》

소채 蔬菜 vegetables ; greens ; garden products ; garden truck 《미》 ¶ 소채의 vegetable // 소채를 가꾸다 grow〔raise〕 vegetables

—밭 a kitchen〔vegetable〕 garden ; a market garden ; a truck farm〔garden〕 《미》 — 재배 농가 a kitchen gardener

소책 小策 a petty artifice〔trick〕 ¶ 소책을 부리다 resort to petty tricks〔artifices〕

*소책자 小冊子 a pamphlet ; a booklet ; a leaflet ; a brochure

소천지 小天地 a small world

소철 蘇鐵 〖식물〗 a cycad (plant)

소철광 沼鐵鑛 〖광물〗 bog iron (ore)

소청 所請 a request ; an entreaty ¶ 소청에 의하여 at the request 《of a person》 ; at 《a person's》 request // 소청이 있다 have a favor to ask 《of a person》 // 소청을 들어 주다 comply with〔grant〕 a request // 한 가지 소청이 있습니다 There is something I want to ask you. /I have a request to make of you.

*소총 小銃 a rifle ; small arms 《총칭》

— 사정 거리 a rifle range ; the range of rifleshot —탄 a bullet ; a rifleshot 엠원 — an M-1 rifle 카빈 — a carbine

소추 訴追 legal action ; prosecution ; proceedings ; charges ; accusation ; impeachment —하다 file〔institute〕 charges 《against》 ; take〔start〕 proceedings ; prosecute ¶ 파면의 소추 removal proceedings 《against a judge》

— 위원회 the Impeachment Committee

—자 a prosecutor

소춘 小春 October of the lunar calendar ; Indian summer

소출 所出 crops ; yield(s) ; products

소치 小齒 〖의학〗 a denticle ¶ 소치상〔소치 모양〕의 denticular ; denticulate(d)

—상(狀) 돌기 a small toothlike process ; a denticle

소치 所致 result ; reason ¶ 나이의 소치로 because of〔owing to〕 age // 과실을 타인의 소치로 돌리다 lay the fault at another's door ; put the blame on 《another》 // 우리가 늦은 것은 오직 너의 소치였다 It was all through you that we were late.

소침 消沈 depression ; gloom ; feeling blue ; melancholy —하다 feel blue ; feel melancholy ; get depressed ; sink into gloom ¶ 소침하여 with a dejected air ; pulling a long face

소켓 a socket ; a receptacle 《미》 ¶ 소켓을 달다 fix a socket // 소켓에 끼우다 fit〔screw〕 《a light bulb》 into the socket ; socket

쌍— a two-way socket

소쿠라지다 [물결이] leap up

소쿠리 a bamboo basket ; a crate

소크 백신 the Salk (polio) vaccine

소탈 疎脫 informality ; unceremoniousness ; unconventionality —하다 (be) informal ; free and easy ; unceremonious ; offhand ; unconventional

소탐대실 小貪大失 incurring a great loss by pursuing a small profit —하다 suffer a big loss in going after a small gain

소탕 掃蕩 sweeping ; clearing ; mopping up ; mop-up ; a clean-up (operation) —하다 sweep ; drive ; clear ; scour ; stamp〔wipe〕 out ; get rid of ; mop〔clear〕 up ¶ 해적을 소탕하다 sweep the pirates from the seas ; suppress〔wipe out〕 pirates // 잔적을 소탕하다 mop up the remnants of the enemy

—전 a mopping-up operation ; a clean-up operation

소태 〖식물〗 [나무] a kind of sumac ; Picrasma ailanthoides (학명) ; [껍질] sumac bark ¶ 소태 같다 be very bitter

소택 沼澤 a swamp ; a marsh ; a bog ; a pond

—지 marshland ; bogland ; a marshy〔swampy〕 place

소톱 a small saw

소통 疏通 [의사의] mutual understanding ; communication ; [물 따위의] drainage —하다 [의사가] have〔enjoy〕 mutual understanding ; [물 따위가] drain off ¶ 의사가 소통하다 understand each other ; come to a mutual understanding // 양자간의 의사 소통이 결핍되어 있다 There is lack〔want〕 of understanding between the two.

*소파 a sofa

소파 小波 ripples ; small waves ; wavelets

소파 搔爬 〖의학〗 curettage ; scooping out ; curettement **—하다** curet(te) ; scrape〔remove〕《a growth from a cavity》 with a curette ¶ 소파 수술을 하다 perform curettage《on》// 소파 수술을 받다 undergo curettage

소편 小片 a bit ; a small piece ; a fragment ; a splinter

소편 小篇 ⇨ 단편(短篇)

†**소포 小包** a parcel ; a package

> 참고 **parcel**은 우편 소포 정도의 꾸러미 **package**는 소하물 정도로 포장된 짐 꾸러미

¶ 소포로 보내다 send《a thing》 by parcel post ; send《books》 as a postal package

— **우편** parcel post — **우편료** parcel post postage〔charge, rates〕 — **우편물** a postal parcel〔package〕

소포자 小胞子 〖식물〗 a microspore

—낭(囊) a microsporangium《*pl.* -gia》 **—엽(葉)** a microsporophyll

소폭 小幅 [폭의] single breadth ; [범위의] a narrow range ; narrow limits ¶ 소폭의 변동을 보이다 move within narrow limits ; move narrowly ; be narrowly mixed

— **등락** fluctuations of a narrow range (주식 따위의)

소표제 小標題, 小表題 a subtitle ; a subhead(ing)

소품 小品 [문예의] a literary sketch ; a pastel ; a short composition ; [제 작품의] a small painting〔sculpture〕; [물건의] a trifling article ; [연극·영화의] property

—곡 a short piece of music ; a musical sketch — **담당** a property man〔master〕 **—문** a short piece ; an essay ; a (literary) sketch ; a vignette

†**소풍 逍風** an outing ; airing oneself ; an excursion ; a picnic **—하다** go for an outing ; take a walk ; go on〔for〕 an excursion ; make〔take〕 an excursion《to, into》 ¶ 교외로 소풍가다 take a walk in the suburbs ; go for an outing to the suburbs

—객 an excursionist ; a holidaymaker

***소프라노** 〖음악〗 soprano ; [가수] a soprano《*pl.* ～s, -ni》; a soprano singer ¶ 소프라노로 노래하다 sing in soprano

소프트 soft

소프트볼 (a) softball ; playground ball

소프트(아이스)크림 (a) soft ice cream

***소프트웨어** 〖전자 공학〗 software

소피 所避 going to the toilet ; relieving oneself **—하다** go to the toilet ; relieve oneself

소피스트 [고대 그리스의] a sophist

소피아 Sofia

소하 消夏 summering ; spending〔passing〕 the summer **—하다** avoid the heat of summer ; summer

소하다 素— abstain from fish and meat ; stick to a vegetarian diet

소하물 小荷物 a parcel ; a packet ; package《미》 ¶ 소하물로 as a parcel // 소하물을 보내다 send〔forward〕 a packet ; express a package《미》

— **계원** 〖철도〗 a checkman — **임시 보관소** a parcels room《미》 **—차** a parcels〔luggage〕 van ; an express car《미》 — **취급소** a parcels office

소학교 小學校 a primary school ; an elementary school ⇨ 국민 학교

소한 小寒 the 23rd of the 24 seasonal divisions ; the period of lesser cold

소한 小閑 a bit of leisure ; a little〔spare〕 time ; a short break

소할 所轄 jurisdiction ; sphere of influence〔authority〕; competency ⇨ 관할(管轄) ¶ 소할 외〔내〕다 be beyond〔within〕 the jurisdiction《of》

소해 掃海 sweeping of the sea ; mine sweeping〔dragging〕; dragging《for mines》 **—하다** sweep the sea《for mines》; drag〔dragnet〕 the sea《for drowned bodies》

—대 a sea-clearing party — **작업** sea-clearing operations ; mine sweeping〔dragging〕 **—정(선)** a mine sweeper

소핵 小核 〖동물·식물〗 [세포] a micronucleus《*pl.* ～es, -clei》

소행 所行 one's act〔deed, doing, conduct, behavior〕 ¶ 소행이 사납다 be ill-behaved // 소행머리가 못마땅하다 I don't like the way he acted. // 그는 지금까지 이러한 소행을 저지른 일은 없었다 He has never acted like this before. // 이것은 그 놈의 소행이 틀림없다 It must be his doing.

소행 素行 conduct ; behavior ; one's natural character ¶ 소행이 나쁜 사람 a man of bad conduct〔loose morals〕// 소행이 좋아지다 improve in one's conduct // 소행을 삼가다 be prudent in one's conduct

소향 所向 one's designation ; the end of one's journey ; the place where one is to go〔is going〕

소향 燒香 burning incense ⇨ 분향

소허 少許 a small quantity

소협주곡 小協奏曲 〖음악〗 a concertino《*pl.* ～s》

‡**소형 小形, 小型** a small size ; pocketsize ¶ 소형의 small-sized ; under-sized ; small ; midget ; baby // 소형화하다 miniaturize

— **권총** a pocket pistol — **미사일** a bantam missile — **비행기** a moth〔tiny, midget〕 plane ; a light plane〔aircraft〕 — **자동차** small-sized〔baby〕 car — **전구** a miniature lamp — **전함** a pocket battleship — **카메라** a miniature camera ; a minicam — **트럭** a light (delivery) truck **—판** a miniature〔pocket〕 edition — **필름** a microfilm **—화(化)** miniaturization

소형 素馨 〖식물〗 a jasmine
소호 小毫 the least thing ⇨ 추호(秋毫)
소호 沼湖 marshes and lakes
소홀 疎忽 carelessness ; negligence ; indifference ━하다 (be) distant ; cool (towards); indifferent ; careless ; negligent ; inattentive ¶ 소홀히 carelessly ; roughly ; indifferently ; negligently ; inattentively // 소홀함을 사죄하다 beg 《another's》 pardon for one's carelessness // 공부를 소홀히 하다 neglect one's studies〔lessons〕// 근무를 소홀히 하다 be remiss in the discharge of one's duties // 소홀한 짓을 하다 act carelessly〔thoughtlessly〕
소화 小話 a short story〔tale〕; an anecdote ; a vignette
소화 笑話 a funny〔humorous〕 story ; a joke
*소화 消化 digestion ; absorption ; consumption ━하다 digest ; absorb ¶ 공채 소화 absorption of government bonds // 소화하기 쉬운〔힘든〕 digestible〔indigestible〕; easy〔hard〕 of digestion〔to digest〕// 소화하기 힘든 음식 foods that are hard to digest // 충분히 소화되지 않은 지식 ill-digested〔half-baked〕 knowledge // 소화가 빠르다〔느리다〕 be quick〔slow〕 of digestion // 소화를 돕다 promote〔help, aid〕 digestion // 소화를 방해하다 disturb digestion // 이것은 소화가 잘 된다〔안 된다〕 This digests well〔poorly〕. // 야채는 소화가 잘된다 Vegetables digest well.
—관 an alimentary〔a digestive〕 canal〔tract〕 —기 a digestive organ ; [계통] the digestive system —기 질환 (a) digestive trouble —력 digestive power —불량 indigestion ; dyspepsia ; digestive disorder ¶ 소화 불량에 걸리다 have an attack of indigestion // 그는 소화 불량이다 He suffers from indigestion〔dyspepsia〕. —선(腺) a peptic〔digestive〕 gland —액 digestive fluid〔juice〕 — 작용 the digestive process —제 a digestive ; a peptic ; an aid to digestion — 효소 digestive enzymes
*소화 消火 fire extinguishing ; fire fighting ━하다 extinguish〔put out〕 a fire ¶ 소화용의 for fire-extinguishing purposes // 소화에 힘쓰다 fight a fire
—기 a fire extinguisher — 용수 water (available) for fire-fighting —전 a (fire) hydrant ; a fireplug — 호스 a fire hose
*소환 召喚 a summons ; a subpoena ; a call ; 〖법〗 monition ; citation ━하다 summon ; call ; cite ; subpoena ; demand with a summons ; serve a subpoena on 《a person》 ¶ 소환에 응하다 answer the summons // 법정〔위원회〕에 소환되다 be summoned before the court〔committee〕
—장 a summons ; a subpoena ; a writ of summons ; a citation ¶ 증인에 대한 소환장 a subpoena to testify // 소환장을 내다 issue a summons 《against a person》; serve 《a person》 with a summons
*소환 召還 recall ━하다 recall ; call back ; summon to return ¶ 본국에 소환되다 be recalled ; be summoned home // 전보로 본사에 소환되다 be recalled to the home〔head〕 office by telegraph
소활 疎闊 ① [태만·부주의] carelessness ; negligence ; inadvertency
② [소원] estrangement ━하다 (be) careless ; negligent ; inadvertent ; be〔become〕 estranged 《from each other》
소회 所懷 one's cherished intentions ; one's intimate impressions〔opinions, thoughts〕 ¶ 소회를 말하다 give〔express〕 one's intimate impressions〔opinions, thoughts〕// 어젯밤의 모임에 대한 소회를 말해보시오 Please tell me how the meeting last night struck you.
소회하다 sail upstream
소휴지 小休止 〖음악〗 a short halt〔rest〕; a pause
*속 ① [깊숙한 안] the inside ; the interior ; the inner part ¶ 속에 amid(st) ; in // 봉투 속 the inside of an envelope // 깊은 산속 the heart of a mountain // 물 속 깊이 deep in the water ; at the bottom of the sea // 어둠 속에 in the dark // 속속들이 to the back ; (know) inside out // 땅 속에서 파내다 dig out (of the ground) ; dig up // 숲 속을 지나다 pass through a forest // 뱃속이 아프다 I have a pain in my insides. // 연못 속에 물고기가 많다 There are many fish in the pond. // 사과가 속까지 썩었다 This apple is rotten to the core.
② [마음의] the heart ¶ 마음 속 the bottom of one's heart // 어리석은 속 one's foolish heart // 마음 속의 목적 an ulterior object ; one's hidden object // 속이 검은 black-hearted ; sinister-minded // 속이 두근거리다 one's heart beats fast // 마음 속이 빤히 들여다 보인다 can see through 《a person's》 intentions // 속을 썩히다 worry oneself about 《a matter》; be worried〔worrisome〕; be exasperating ; feel anxious about // 그는 속 넓은 사람이다 He is large-hearted〔broad-minded〕. // 키가 크면 속이 없다 If a man is too tall, he lacks "sense". // 그의 말이 속에 사무쳤다 His words went home to my heart. // 그는 장사 속을 잘 안다 He knows business inside out.
③ [속에 든 것] contents ; (the) substance ; the filling ; stuff ⇨ 소 ¶ 속을 넣다 (이불·떡 따위의) stuff // 지갑 속을 털다 empty one's purse
속 屬 a family ; a tribe ; a series ; 〖생물〗 a genus
속 續 continuation ; a sequel ; an installment ; a continuation 《of》; a follow-up 《of》; a sequel 《to》; a supplement 《to》; [부분의] a series

—편 a supplement〔second〕 volume ; a follow-up 《미》 ; a sequel 《of, to》 ; a continuation 《of》 ¶ 본서와 그 속편 this book and its sequel〔successor〕
속 贖 [속죄] atonement ; expiation ; [속전] ransom ; [배상] indemnity ; indemnification —하다 atone〔expiate〕 for ; indemnify
속 束 bind ⇨ 뭇, 단
속가 俗家 a layman's house
속가 俗歌 a popular song ; a folksong ; a ditty ; a ballad
속가량 —假量 a rough estimate (based on one's feelings)
속가루 the finest powder〔flour〕
속가죽 inner part of hide〔leather〕
속간 俗間 the world ; the public at large ; people (in general)
속간 續刊 continuation of publication —하다 continue to publish ; publish consecutively ; continue (its) publication
속개 續開 continuation ; resumption —하다 continue ; resume 《a meeting》 ¶ 국회는 내일 속개한다 The Assembly will resume its session tomorrow.
속객 俗客 a worldling ; [불가에 대해] the laity ; a layman
속건성 速乾性 ¶ 속건성의 잉크〔바니시〕 quick-drying ink〔varnish〕
속겨 inner chaff〔bran〕
속격 屬格 〖문법〗 the genitive (case) 목적격 — the objective genitive 부사적 — the adverbial genitive
속결 速決 a prompt〔immediate, quick〕 decision ; snap judgment —하다 decide promptly〔immediately, on the spot〕 — 속행 prompt decision and execution
속계 俗界 the mundane world ; the earthly〔secular, everyday〕 world ¶ 속계의 일 worldly things ; mundane affairs // 속계의 고뇌 worldly cares and worries // 속계를 버리다 renounce the world // 속계에 초연하다 stand〔keep, hold〕 aloof from the world
속고갱이 the heart ; the very heart〔core〕
속곡 俗曲 a folk song ; a ballad ; a folk melody
속곳 a slip ; a petticoat ; underwear worn by women ¶ 속곳 바람에 with nothing on but a slip
속공 速攻 a swift attack —하다 launch a swift attack against 《the enemy》 ; lose no time in attacking 《the enemy》
속관 屬官 a subordinate government official ; a government clerk
속구 速球 〖야구〗 a fast〔speed〕 ball ; a speeder ; a sweeper — 투수 a fast-ball pitcher ; a sharpshooter ; a speedballer 《미·속》
속국 屬國 a subject state〔country〕 ; a tributary (state) ; a dependency ¶ 속국이 되다 become a tributary 《to》 ; 《a country》 be subject 《to》 ; come〔pass〕 under the sway 《of》
속궁리 —窮理 reflecting to oneself ; considering —하다 mull over
속긋 a tracing (on translucent paper, of a design or written character beneath) 속긋 넣다 관용 trace calligraphy〔designs〕
*속기 速記 ① [속필] quick〔prompt, rapid〕 writing ② [속기법] shorthand ; stenography —하다 note down fast ; take rapid notes 《of》 ; write〔take down〕 in shorthand ; write〔take〕 shorthand ¶ 속기한 연설 a steno-graphed address 〔speech〕 // 속기로 in shorthand ; stenographically // 속기를 배우다 learn shorthand ; take lessons in stenography // 연설을 속기하다 take down a speech in shorthand ; take stenographic notes of a speech // 속기도 할 줄 압니까 Do you take shorthand also ?
—록 stenographic records ; shorthand 〔stenographic〕 notes ; a shorthand report ¶ 의회의 속기록 parliamentary records // 속기록을 참조하다 refer to the stenographic records 《of》 — 문자 a stenographic character ; a logogram ; a stenograph —법 stenography —사 a shorthand writer〔reporter〕 ; a stenographer ; a stenog 《구》 —술 stenography ; shorthand (writing)
속기 俗氣 vulgarity ; worldliness ; worldly ambition ¶ 속기가 있다 be vulgar ; be worldly // 속기가 없다 be above the world
속꺼풀 the inner layer of the outer cover
속껍데기 an inner shell ; an inner layer of skin ; the derma
속껍질 the inner layer of skin or cover ; the derma
속끓이다 suffer anxiety ; be overanxious ; worry
속나깨 fine bran of buckwheat
속내 mind ; intention ¶ 속내를 모르겠다 be unable to read 《a person's》 inner thought
속내다 sharpen 《the blade of a plane 〔drill〕》 ; put an edge〔point〕 on
속내평 the real state 《of affairs》 ; the internal conditions ; the inside 《of a matter》 ; the inside story ¶ 속내평을 떠보다 inquire into the real state ; fathom 《a person's》 mind
속념 俗念 worldly considerations〔thoughts, ambitions〕 ; vulgar〔commonplace〕 thoughts ; earthly desires ; worldliness ¶ 속념을 떠나다 free 《oneself》 from earthly desires
속눈 [곱자의] the inside scale (of a carpenter's square)
속눈뜨다 peer〔peek〕 through halfclosed eyes
속눈썹 the eyelashes ¶ 긴 속눈썹 long lashes
인조 — a false eyelash
속눈치 (an inkling of) one's real attitude

*속다 be cheated ; get deceived ; be defrauded ; be fooled ; be imposed upon ; be taken in ; be duped ¶ 속기 쉬운 credulous // 속기 쉬운 사람 a person easily deceived ; a dupe ; a gull // 물건을 속아 사다 get gypped 《in buying something》 《미·속》 ; get stung ; buy a lemon // 감쪽같이 속았다 I was fairly taken in. // 그 여자는 속아서 그 남자와 결혼했다 She was tricked into a marriage with that man. // 사람을 속이려다 도리어 속다 The biter bit. // 그는 여자의 엉큼한 농간에 속지 않는다 He is able to withstand the wiles of women. // 놈들에게 속지는 않겠다 They shan't outsmart me. /They can't fool me. // 아 속았구나 I was taken (for a ride). /I got taken. /I was had. /I have been done. // 속지 않고 중고차를 사기란 쉬운 일이 아니다 It's not easy to buy a used car without being taken for a ride. // 그의 감언이설에 속아서 저금한 걸 전부 건네줬니 You fell for sweet talk and handed over all your savings?

속닥거리다 whisper ⇨ 숙덕거리다

속단 速斷 a hasty conclusion ; an immediate judgment ; a prompt decision —하다 make〔draw〕 a hasty conclusion ; jump to a conclusion ; decide hastily ; be hasty in conclusion ; give an immediate judgment ; be prompt in decision ¶ 이제는 성공이 확실하다고 속단하다 jump to〔at〕 the conclusion that this will ensure one's success // 속단하지 말고 내 말 좀 끝까지 들어 봐 Don't jump to conclusions. Hear me out.

*속달 速達 special delivery ; express delivery —하다 deliver by express ¶ 속달로 by express // 편지를 속달로 보내다 send a letter by express〔special delivery〕 // 소포를 속달로 보내다 express a parcel 《to》 —료 an express-delivery charge ; a special-delivery fee — 우편 [제도] express-〔special-〕delivery postal service ; [우편물] special delivery mail 《미》 ; express delivery mail 《영》 — 편지 a special-delivery letter

속달거리다 whisper

속달다 be anxious〔eager〕 to ; be impatient to ; be worried ¶ 시험 결과를 알지 못해 속이 단다 I am anxious about the result of the examination. // 그까짓 일을 가지고 속달아 할 것 없다 Don't worry yourself about such a thing.

속달뱅이 a small scale

‡속담 俗談 a proverb ; a saying ¶ 속담에 있듯이 as the proverb says〔runs, goes〕

속답 速答 a quick answer ; a prompt reply —하다 answer〔reply〕 quickly ; make a prompt reply ; answer promptly

속대¹ the heart 《of vegetables, of bamboo》 ¶ 배추의 속대 the heart of a cabbage

—국 cabbage-heart soup —쌈 rice wrapped in cabbage hearts

속대² [댓개비의] heart of bamboo

속대중 one's personal estimate ; a rough guess based on one's feelings ¶ 남의 말만 듣고 속대중하다 make a rough guess from what others have said

속더께 scum below the surface

†속도 速度 speed ; velocity ; pace ; rate ; 〖음악〗 tempo ; time ¶ 가감 속도 variable speed // 속도 제한 시속 20마일 speed limit 20 M. P. H. // 1초 15미터의 속도로 at the rate〔a speed〕 of 15 meters a second // 속도가 늘다〔줄다〕 gain〔lose〕 in speed // 속도가 빠르다〔느리다〕 be high〔low〕 speed ; be rapid〔slow〕 // 속도를 올리다 increase speed ; speed up ; step on the gas (자동차의) // 속도를 줄이다 decrease the speed ; slow down // 속도를 조절하다 regulate the speed // 속도를 재다 measure the speed 《of》

—계 a speedometer ; a speed indicator ; autometer (자동차의) ; tachometer (유속·회전의) —비 velocity ratio — 위반 going over〔exceeding〕 the speed limit ; violation〔infringement〕 of the speed regulations ¶ 속도 위반자 a speeder ; a violator of the speed regulations // 속도 위반을 하다 break〔violate〕 the speed regulations — 제한 speed regulation ; a speed limit ¶ 속도 제한 표지 an overspeed limit sign // 속도 제한 장치 a speed-limiting device ; an overspeed limiter // 속도 제한을 하다 set〔place〕 a speed limit 《on》 ; enforce〔lay down〕 speed regulations — 조절기 a speeder ; a speed regulator 제한 — 《at》 regulation speed ; 《within》 the speed limit 초(初)— initial velocity

속독 速讀 rapid〔fast〕 reading —하다 read rapidly〔fast〕 ; speed-read

—가(家) a fast〔rapid〕 reader

속돌 〖광물〗 a pumice stone

*속되다 俗— (be) vulgar ; low ; base ; common ; popular ; worldly ; earthly ; [성직에 대하여] secular ; lay ¶ 속된 취미〔말〕 vulgar tastes〔words〕 // 속된 마음 worldliness ; worldly ambition // 속된 사람들 worldly people // 속되게 commonly ; popularly // 속된 말로 하자면 to use a common word〔phrase〕 ; as is commonly said // 속되지 않다 be above the world

속등 續騰 a continued rise ; a further advance —하다 continue to rise ; advance further

속뚜껑 [시계의] a cap ; [그릇의] an inner lid

속뜻 ① [참뜻] the inner〔true〕 meaning〔sense, significance〕 ② [본심] one's real intention ; one's true motive ¶ 그의 속뜻을 알 수 없다 I can't see what he really means. /I can't make out what he is driving at.

속락 續落 a continued fall〔drop〕 ; a further decline ; sagging ; sliding **—하다** keep falling〔dropping〕; keep sagging〔sliding〕 ¶ 화폐 가치의 속락 a continued fall of the value in money

속량 贖良 ① emancipation of slaves ; freeing slaves ② freeing《a person》of a burden ; taking on《someone's》burden〔misfortune〕 **—하다** emancipate ; free《a slave》; free《a person》of a burden

†**속력 速力** speed ; rate ; velocity ¶ 속력이 빠른 fast ; speedy ; fast-going // 꽤 빠른 속력 a good speed // 속력이 느린 slow ; slow-going // 아슬아슬한 속력 a breakneck speed // 속력 23노트의 순양함 a cruiser of 23 knots speed // 한 시간 60마일의 속력으로 at a speed〔the rate〕of 60 miles per hour // 전속력으로 (at) full speed ; with all speed ; with the throttle wide open // 속력을 가하다 accelerate (the) speed ; increase (the) speed ; speed up // 이 자동차는 최대 150 마일까지의 속력을 낼 수 있다 This motorcar develops a maximum speed of 150 miles. // 자동차는 굉장한 속력으로 달렸다 The motorcar ran at a tremendous rate.
— **범위** a speed range — **시험** a speed trial〔test〕 — **제한** speed regulation ; a speed limit **경제** — an economical speed **대**— a great〔headlong〕speed **상승** — a climbing speed **제한** — a regulation speed **최대** — the greatest〔maximum〕speed **통상**〔**반**〕 — a normal〔half〕speed

속령 屬領 a subject〔vassal〕state ; a dependency ; a territory ; a possession

속례 俗禮 conventional etiquette ; ceremonial customs

속례 俗例 a popular custom ; a common usage ; a common way ; convention

속론 俗論 conventional views ; vulgar〔popular〕opinion

속류 俗流 the common crowd ; the ordinary run of men ; the masses

속리 俗吏 a bumble ; a Jack-in-office
— **근성** bumbledom

속립 결핵 粟粒結核〖의학〗miliary tuberculosis

속마음 one's innermost feelings ; the bottom of one's heart ¶ 속마음은 at bottom ; in one's heart of hearts // 속마음을 터놓다 unbosom oneself ; open one's heart ; confess // 속마음은 좋은 사람이다 He is a good man at heart. // 그의 태도는 거칠지만 속마음은 착하다 He has a rough manner, but deep down he's quite nice.

속말 a confidential talk ; a private talk ; a little talk〔chat〕 ¶ 친구에게 속말을 하다 confide a secret to a friend ; take a friend into one's confidence ; have a little talk with a friend // 낯선 사람에게 속말을 털어놓다 have a confidential talk with a stranger

속명 俗名 ①［본명 이외의］a popular name ; a common name
②［속된 명성］worldly fame〔reputation〕
③［법명에 대한］a secular name

속명 屬名〖생물〗a generic name

속무 俗務 mundane affairs〔business〕; worldly〔earthly〕cares ; down-to-earth matters ; daily routine

속문학 俗文學 vulgar literature

***속물 俗物** ①［사람］a vulgar person ; a snob ; a Philistine ; a worldling ②［물건］mean〔vulgar〕stuff
— **근성** snobbery ; Philistinism

속바람 a shuddering gasp

속바지 underpants ; drawers

속바치다 贖— pay (as) ransom

†**속박 束縛** restraint ; restriction ; fetters ; a yoke **—하다** restrict ; bind ; fetter ; restrain ; shackle ¶ 자유를 속박하다 restrict《a person's》freedom // 속박을 받다 be restricted ; be placed under restraint ; be subject to restraint // 행동을 속박당하다 be restricted in one's movements // 시간에 속박되다 be restricted by time // 속박을 벗어나다 free oneself from restraint ; get rid of restraints ; throw off the yoke
—**력**〖물리〗constraining force — **운동**〖물리〗constrained motion — **전자**〖물리〗a bound electron — **하전**〖전기〗bound charge

속발 束髮 **—하다** dress one's hair ; do up one's hair ; arrange one's hair ;［상투를］wear a topknot

‡**속발 續發** successive〔frequent〕occurrence **—하다** occur frequently〔in succession〕; follow (closely one upon another) ¶ 사고의 속발 a series of accidents // 최근 화재가 속발한다 Fires are frequent these days. // 재난이 속발했다 One misfortune followed on the heels of another.

속발톱 the half-moon of a toenail ; a lunula

속밤 a chestnut

속방 屬邦 a subject〔vassal〕state

속배 俗輩 the common crowd

속배포 —**排布** one's inmost bosom ; intentions ; one's heart〔design〕; an ulterior motive ¶ 속배포가 있는 사람 a man of intrigue // 무슨 속배포가 있는 모양이다 He is up to something more than meets the eye.

속버선 double-layer inner socks (worn under heavy cotton-padded outer socks)

속벌 a set of underwear

속병 —**病** internal〔intestinal〕sickness〔disease〕
—**쟁이** a stomach sufferer

속보 速步 a quick step ; a quick march ;〖마술(馬術)〗a trot

속보 速報 a newsflash ; a prompt report ; a quick announcement **—하다** report

promptly ; announce quickly
—판 a flash board ; a bulletin board ; a newsboard 선거 — prompt〔hour-by-hour〕 reports of the election returns
속보 續報 further news ; additional〔further〕 particulars
속보이다 reveal one's heart ; give oneself away ; disclose one's intention ; wear one's heart on one's sleeve
속부피 the capacity《of a vessel》; the volume《of a cask》
속빼다 〚농업〛 plow (a rice field) for the second time
속뽑다 sound《a person》out ; read《a person's》mind
속뽑히다 be made to reveal one's heart ¶ 속뽑히는 말 remarks which betray oneself
속사 俗事 worldly affairs〔matters〕; daily routine〔affairs〕; business ¶ 속사에 쫓기다 be engrossed in〔busy with〕 daily affairs
속사 速射 quick〔fast〕 firing ; quick fire ; rapid fire —하다 fire quickly
—포 a quick-firing〔quick-fire〕 gun ; a rapid-fire gun〔cannon〕; a quick-firer
속사 速寫 quick copying ; [사진의] a snapshot —하다 copy quickly ; snapshot ; take a snapshot
— 카메라 a snapshot〔candid (소형)〕 camera
속사랑 inner〔hidden〕 love
속사정 —事情 the inside〔unrevealed〕 circumstances
속삭거리다 ⇨ 속삭이다
속삭속삭 in whispers ; under one's breath
†속삭이다 whisper ; murmur ; speak under one's breath ; talk in whispers ¶ 속삭임 a whisper ; a murmur // 사랑의 속삭임 soft nothings ; whispers of love // 귀에 대고 속삭이다 whisper in《a person's》ear // 서로 속삭이다 exchange whispers ; whisper to each other
속산 速算 rapid calculation
속살 ① [옷속의] parts of the body ordinarily covered by clothing ; the skin under clothes ¶ 속살이 희다 have a fair skin ② the inner meat of《a lobster》
속살거리다 whisper ; murmur
속살다 have inner strength ; (be) unbending ; undaunted ; proud ¶ 그는 가난하지만 속살다 He is poor but proud.
속살찌다 ① [살찌다] (be) fat ② [실속있다] (be) substantial ; solid ; rich
⁑속상하다 —傷— ① be distressing〔worrisome, annoying, exasperating〕; get on one's nerves ② be distressed〔worried, annoyed, exasperated, vexed, troubled〕 ¶ 기차를 놓쳐서 속상하다 I am mad at missing the train. // 이런 사소한 일이 때로는 속상하게 한다 Such trifles occasionally ruffle my temper. // 뭐가 그렇게 속상하냐 What are you sore〔mad〕 at ? /What hurt your feelings ?
속상해하다《you, he》be distressed〔troubled, annoyed, exasperated, worried, harassed〕; be annoyed at〔worried over, vexed by〕
속새 ① 〚식물〛 the scouring rush ; a horsetail (plant) ② [사포] sandpaper
속새질 rubbing with sandpaper ; sandpapering down —하다 rub with sandpaper ; sandpaper
속생각 inward thoughts ; thinking to oneself —하다 think〔figure〕 to oneself
속생설 續生說 〚생물〛 biogenesis ; biogeny
속서 俗書 ① [책] a worthless〔trifling〕 book ② [필적] unrefined handwriting ; a hand lacking in grace
속설 俗說 a common〔popular〕 saying ; common talk ; a popular version《of an incident》; folklore ; a proverb
속성 俗姓 [중의] one's secular surname
속성 速成 quick mastery ; rapid completion ; short-course training —하다 train quickly ; give a quick training ; complete rapidly ¶ 속성으로 as quickly as possible ; quickly // 영어를 속성으로 배우다 learn English in a quick way
—과 a short course ; an intensive course
— 교수 short-course instruction —법 a quick method〔way〕; a shortcut ; a royal road
속성 屬性 〚논리〛 an attribute ; a property
⁑속세 俗世 the mundane world ; this world ¶ 속세를 떠난 unworldly ; supermundane // 속세를 버리다 renounce the world
속세간 俗世間 this world ; the earthly world ¶ 속세간의 worldly ; earthly ; mundane // 속세간을 버리다 forsake〔retire from〕 the world // 속세간이 싫어지다 be weary〔sick〕 of life
속셈 ① an intention ; inner thoughts ; a design ; a purpose
② [암산] mental arithmetic〔calculation〕 ¶ …할 속셈으로 with the intention《of》; with a view to《doing》// 나의 속셈으로는 in my estimation // …할 속셈이다 intend《to do, doing》; mean to《do》; have the intention of《doing》// …할 속셈이 없다 have no mind〔intention〕 to《do》; have no intention of // 어떤 속셈인지 전혀 모르겠다 I cannot quite see〔understand〕 his motive〔idea〕.
속셔츠 an undershirt ; underwear
속소위 俗所謂 what is commonly called〔said〕; to use a common word ; put《something》in layman's terms
속속 續續 one after another ; in a steady〔constant〕 stream ; in close〔rapid, quick〕 succession ¶ 보도가 속속 들어온다 Reports pour in. // 주문이 속속 밀려든다 Orders pour in. // 새 집들이 속속 들어선다 New houses spring up like mush-

rooms.

속속곳 women's underwear ; lingerie

속속들이 to the core ; thoroughly ; inside out ; wholly ¶ 속속들이 썩다 be rotten to the core // 사람의 마음을 속속들이 알다 know a man through and through // 비밀을 속속들이 캐내다 root out a secret // 그렇게 속속들이 캐묻지 마라 Don't be so inquisitive.

속속이풀 〖식물〗 a marsh cress ; Rorippa palustris (학명)

속속히 速速— rapidly ; fast

속손톱 the lunula of a fingernail

속수 무책 束手無策 resourcelessness ; helplessness ; being at one's wit's end ¶ 어떻게 처리해야 할지 속수 무책이다 I am at a loss how to do it. /I am at my wit's end.

속습 俗習 (a) convention ; a (popular) custom ; common usage ; a vulgar practice

속 심 俗心 a worldly mind ; worldly thoughts ; worldliness

속쌀뜨물 clear rice water (from rinsing well-washed rice)

속썩다 be depressed ; feel sick at heart ; be disheartened ; be dejected ; feel blue〔gloomy〕 ¶ 속썩어하지 마라 Cheer up ! /Don't be discouraged !

속씨식물 —植物 angiosperm

속아넘어가다 be deceived ⇨ 속다

속악 俗惡 vulgarity ; inelegance ; coarseness ¶ 속악한 취미 vulgar〔low, Philistine〕 taste

속악 俗樂 popular〔folk〕 music ; vulgar music

속 안 俗眼 the layman's eye〔opinion, view〕 ; the common eye ; the popular view

속앓이 ⇨ 속병

*속어 俗語 a slang word〔expression〕 ; slang (집합적) ; [일상 회화 용법] a colloquialism ; a colloquial expression ¶ 속어로는 in common speech // 속어를 쓰다 use vulgar speech

속어림 one's personal〔mental〕 estimation ; guess ¶ 속어림으로 in one's estimation〔thought〕

속 언 俗言 a vulgar saying ; common talk ; slangy speech ; slanguage 《속》

속언 俗諺 a common〔popular〕 saying ; a household word ; a saw ; an old saw ; a proverb

속없다 lack prudence〔discretion〕 ; have no definite opinion〔views〕 of one's own ; have no fixed views of one's own ¶ 속없는 사람 a man without settled convictions ; a shallow person

속여먹다, 속여넘기다 swindle ; cheat

속연 續演 the continuation of a show ¶ 60일간의 속연 60 day's run —하다 continue to stage〔put on〕 《a play》 ; 《a show》 runs consecutively 《for two months》

속연 俗緣 worldly〔secular〕 connections 〔ties〕 《with》

속열매껍질 〖식물〗 an endocarp

속영 續映 a continued run 《of a film》 —하다 continue to show 《a movie》 ; run (consecutively) 《for three weeks》

속 옷 underwear ; underclothes ; undergarments

속요 俗謠 a popular song ; a folk song

속요량 —料量 conjecturing to oneself ; making a private estimate —하다 conjecture to oneself ; privately estimate

속음 俗音 a popular pronunciation of a Chinese character

†속이다 deceive ; cheat ; take in ; trick ; swindle ; defraud ; play a trick 《on a person》 ; impose on

> 참고 **cheat** 가장 일반적인 말로서 부정 수단에 의하여 갖고 싶은 것을 손에 넣는 것 **deceive** 진실을 감추기 위하여 또는 갖고 싶은 것을 얻기 위하여 다른 사람에게 거짓말을 믿게 하는 것 **trick** 교활한 수단을 써 상대방을 속이고 갖고 싶은 것을 손에 넣는 것 **swindle** 상대방에게 파고 들어 금품을 앗아 내는 것 **defraud** 주로 법률 용어 사기에 의하여 남의 권리나 재산을 빼앗는 것

¶ 속기 쉬운 credulous // 속이기 쉬운 사람 a dupe ; a gull ; a gullible person // 사람을 속이다 cheat 《a person》 ; serve 《a person》 a trick // 이름을 속이다 give a false name // 적을 속이다 mislead an enemy // 자기 자신을 속이다 deceive oneself // 사람을 속여 돈을 빼앗다 cheat 《a person》 out of his money ; swindle 《a person》 out of money ; swindle money out of 《a person》 // 속여서 …시키다 cheat 〔deceive, trick〕 《a person》 into doing 《something》 // 속여서 결혼시키다 cheat 《a person》 into marrying // 겉모양을 보고 속다 be deceived by appearance // 속여서 승낙시키다 trick 《a person》 into consent // 너를 속여서 여기에 데리고 온 것이다 I have brought you here by a ruse. // 그는 나를 속였다 He pulled the wool over my eyes. // 속이지 마라 Don't fool me !

*속인 俗人 ① [속물] a worldling ; a vulgar person ② [불문에 대한] a layman ; the laity

속인 屬人 ¶ 속인의 individual ; personal —주의 〖법〗 the personal〔nationality〕 principle ; the principle of personal (privilege for) jurisdiction — 특권 personal privileges〔rights〕

속 임 수 a trick ; trickery ; deception ; cheat (-ing) ; fraud ; swindle ¶ 속임수를 쓰다 play a trick on 《a person》 ; trick 《a person》 ; cheat 《a person》 // 속임수에 넘어가다 fall victim to fraud ; be cheated // 속임수로 돈을 빼앗다 obtain money by

fraud // 여자의 속임수에 걸리다 be caught in a woman's toils
속잎 the inner leaves
속자 俗字 the popular〔simplified〕 form of a Chinese character
속잠방이 short underpants
속장 the inside pages
속장 束裝 preparations for a journey **—하다** make preparations〔equip oneself, fit oneself out〕 for a journey ; prepare for a trip〔journey〕
속장 屬長 [감리교의] the leader of a sectional prayer meeting
속적삼 an undershirt ; underwear
속전 贖錢 a ransom
속전속결 速戰速決 an intensive〔all-out〕 surprise offensive〔attack〕
— 전법 blitz tactics
속절 俗節 ancestor-memorial days
속절없다 (be) hopeless ; futile ; vain ; unavailing ¶ 속절없이 futilely ; in vain ; to no good purpose // 속절없는 세상 a futile world
속정 俗情 [생각] earthly〔lay〕 opinion ; [인정] popular sentiment
속종 one's inmost thoughts ; one's opinion〔view〕
속죄 贖罪 atonement ; expiation ; redemption **—하다** atone for a《crime》; make atonement for《one's sin》; expiate《one's sin》; expiate oneself ; redeem《oneself》 from sin ¶ 속죄의 기도 purgatorial prayers // 죽음으로써 속죄하다 expiate a crime with death ; pay with death for a crime
—금 ransom **—론** the doctrine of atonement **—자** a penitent
속주다 speak one's mind ; open one's heart《to a person》; take《a person》 into one's confidence
속중 俗衆 people ; the masses ; the public ; the common
속지 屬地 a possession ; a dependency ; a territory ; a dominion
—주의 the territorial principle ; the principle of territorial privilege for jurisdiction
속진 俗塵 the world ; earthly〔mundane〕 affairs ¶ 속진을 멀리 하다 keep aloof from the madding crowd ; be free〔isolated〕 from the hustle and bustle of everyday life ; live secluded from the world
속짐작 one's personal〔mental〕 estimation
속창 a shoe liner ; an inner sole ¶ 속창을 깔다 put liners《in shoes》
속체 俗體 ① [속인의 풍채] the laity ② [체제] vulgarity ; Philistinism ; vulgar style
속출 續出 continuous〔successive〕 occurrence〔appearance〕 **—하다** occur〔appear〕 in succession ; crop up《one after another》 ¶ 사고의 속출 a series of accidents // 사건이 속출했다 I had a crop of troubles. // 재난이 속출했다 One misfortune followed on the heels of another.
속취 俗臭 vulgarity ; low〔vulgar〕 taste ; earthiness ; worldliness ¶ 속취가 나는 of low taste ; vulgar ; worldly-minded // 속취 분분하다 be extremely vulgar
속취 俗趣 vulgar〔bourgeois〕 taste ; Philistinism
속치레 interior decoration ¶ 속치레를 하다 decorate the interior
속치마 an underskirt ; a chemise ; a slip ; a petticoat
속치부하다 —置簿— record in one's mind〔memory〕; make a mental note《of》; keep in mind
속치장 —治粧 interior decoration〔design〕
속칭 俗稱 a popular designation ; a familiar name ; a common name **—하다** call〔name〕 popularly ; be popularly known as ¶ 속칭 …이라 하다 be popularly known《as》; be commonly called ...
‡**속타다** be distressed ; be vexed ; be harassed ; be annoyed ; be worried《about》; fret ¶ 속타게 하다 irritate ; vex ; fret // 어머니가 보고 싶어 속타다 be consumed with a desire to see one's mother // 시험 결과가 걱정이 되어 속탄다 I am anxious about the result of the examination.
속타점 —打點 a decision in one's heart **—하다** decide in one's heart
속탈 a stomach upset〔disorder〕
속태 俗態 vulgar〔low, unrefined〕 appearance
속태우다 [스스로] worry (oneself) ; be worried《about》; be distressed ; be nervous ; [남을] worry ; cause worry〔anxiety〕 to ; bother ; make nervous ¶ 친구를 속태우다 cause anxiety to friends // 몹시 속태우다 fret oneself to death // 하찮은 일에 속태우다 worry over trifles // 그 일로 그를 속태우다 bother him with the matter // 속태우다 병이 나다 worry oneself into illness ; fret oneself ill // 그런 일로 속태우지 마라 Don't worry yourself about such a thing. /Don't let that worry you. // 그녀는 매사에 너무 속을 태운다 She bothers too much about everything. // 무엇을 그렇게 속태우느냐 What are you so nervous〔worried〕 about?
속투 續投 continued pitching **—하다** continue to pitch
속티 俗— vulgar〔unrefined, low〕 appearance
속판 ① [목차] a table of contents ② [속마음] one's inmost heart ; one's innermost feelings ; one's inward thoughts
속편 續篇 a sequel《to》; a second volume《of》; a continuation《of》; a follow-up《미》; [영화] a serial film
속표지 —表紙 the title page ; the front page ; the title leaf

속필 速筆 quick〔rapid〕 writing ; a hasty scribble ; a fast hand 《with pen》 ¶ 그는 속필이다 He writes fast.

속하다 速— (be) fast ; quick ; rapid ; swift ¶ 속히 fast ; quickly ; promptly ; in haste // 대답을 속히 해라 Answer promptly. /Give me a prompt answer. // 속히 해라 Be quick about it. /Make haste. / Hurry up !

속히 더운 방 쉬 식는다 〔속담〕 Soon hot soon cold.

†**속하다 屬—** [소속하다] belong 《to》 ; appertain 《to》 ; [가입하다] be affiliated with ; join ¶ 고래는 동물에 속한다 A whale belongs to the animal life. // 대나무는 풀의 종류에 속한다 The bamboo belongs to the grass family. // 그것은 나의 직무에 속한다 That is among my duties. // 거부권은 대통령의 권한에 속한다 The veto power is invested in the president. // 그는 공화당에 속해 있다 He is affiliated with the Republican Party. / He is a Republican.

속하다 贖— ⇨ 속죄 (贖罪)

속학 俗學 popular learning ; secular learning〔studies〕

속한 俗漢 a layman ; a worldling

속항 續航 the continuation of a voyage **—하다** continue the voyage ; keep the sea (배가)

‡**속행 速行** [걸음] walking fast ; [행동] prompt action **—하다** go〔walk〕 quickly ; carry out speedily ; take prompt action

†**속행 續行** continuation ; continuance **—하다** proceed〔go ahead〕 with ; continue ; resume ; go on 《with》 ; carry on ; keep on 《doing》 ¶ 토의를 속행하다 continue〔proceed with〕 debates // 경기를 속행하다 proceed with the game // 교섭을 속행하다 continue negotiations

속현 續絃 remarriage 《by a man》 **—하다** 《a man》 remarry ; marry again ; take another wife

속화 俗化 vulgarization ; popularization ; secularization **—하다** vulgarize ; popularize ; secularize ; [속화되다] be vulgarized〔popularized〕 ; become vulgar〔degenerated〕 ; be secularized

속화 俗畫 a commonplace painting ; an uninspired picture

속화 俗話 gossip ; town talk

속환이 俗還— one who has returned to secular life (from the priesthood)

속회 續會 resumption of a meeting **—하다** 《a meeting》 resume ; resume 《a meeting》

속회 屬會 [감리교의] a divisional prayer meeting

속효 速效 immediate effect ; instant results ¶ 속효가 있다 have〔produce〕 immediate effect ; 〖의학〗 be active

—약 a quick remedy 《for》 ; a miraculous cure 《for》

솎다 thin out ; weed out ¶ 무〔배추〕를 솎다 thin out the rows of radish〔cabbage〕

솎음 thinning out ; weeding out **—하다** thin〔weed〕 out

†**손¹** ① hand ¶ 오른〔왼〕 손 the right〔left〕 hand // 손을 들다 raise one's hand ; [찬성하여] show one's hand ; [때리려고] lift one's hand against 《a person》 // 손을 내밀다 hold out one's hands // 손으로 만들다 make by hand // 손이 맞아 일하다 work hand in hand ; work in cahoots // 손이 닿는 곳에 있다 be within one's reach ; be within one's grasp // 손이 닿지 않는 곳에 있다 be beyond one's reach ; be out of one's grasp // 손에 손을 잡고 걷다 walk hand in hand // 손을 쥐다 [주먹] clench one's fists ; close one's hands ; [남의 손을] grasp another's hand ; [악수하다] shake hands ; clasp hands 《with》 ; shake 《a person》 by the hand // 사람의 손을 끌다〔잡다〕 lead〔take〕 a person by the hand // 손을 흔들다 wave one's hand // 손대지 마시오 Hands off. 《미》 (게시) // 손들어 [강도가] Stick'em up ! /[찬성의] Hands up ! /[항복의] Throw up your hand ! // 전시품에 손대지 마시오 Visitors are requested not to touch the exhibits. // 길을 건널 때 아이들의 손을 잡고 인솔하지 않으면 걱정이 된다 When we're crossing the street, I worry unless I'm leading kids by the hand.

② [일손·도움] a hand ; a helping hand ¶ 여러 사람의 손으로 된 번역 a translation by various hands // 손을 빌려주다 give 《a person》 a hand // 자기 손으로 목숨을 끊다 die by one's own hands // 가난한 사람에게 구조의 손을 뻗치다 extend help〔a helping hand〕 to the poor // 이 일은 여러 사람의 손이 필요하다 This work calls for many hands.

③ [소유] the hands 《of》 ; possession ; power ¶ 물건이 손에 들어오다 a thing comes into one's hands ; one gets ; obtain ; come by ; put one's hands on 《a thing》 // 남의 손에 넘어가다 fall into another's hands // 미인을 손에 넣다 win (the heart of) a belle // 서울은 적군의 손에 들어갔다 *Seoul* fell into the enemy's hands. // 그 편지가 그들의 손에 들어갔다 The letter fell into their hands. // 그의 생사는 내 손에 달렸다 His life is in my hands. // 새로운 정보를 손에 넣었다 I am in possession of new information. // 그 상품은 어디에 가도 손에 넣을 수 없다 The article is nowhere to be handed.

④ [수고] trouble ; care ¶ 손이 드는 일 laborious〔troublesome〕 work // 손이 가다 take〔need〕 a lot of care ; require attention ; be troublesome // 손을 덜다 save trouble // 이 일은 손이 많이 간다 This is painstaking work. // 이 세공은 퍽 손이 많이 갔다 This work is pretty elaborate. //

이 집은 여기저기 손볼 데가 많다 There is a lot of slapdash (work) about this house.

⑤ [때림] a blow ; strike ¶ 누가 먼저 손을 댔느냐 Who started the fight? / Who struck the first blow?

⑥ [관계] connection ; meddling ¶ 정부와 손을 끊다 break with one's mistress// 여러 가지 일에 손을 대다 try one's hand at everything// 개혁에 손을 대다 try one's hand at reform// 투기에 손을 대다 dabble in speculation// 남의 일에 손을 대다 meddle in other people's affairs// 그 여자에게 손대지 마라 Keep away from her. // 만일 당신이 그것을 주장한다면 당신과 손을 끊겠다 If you insist upon it, I wash my hands of you. // 그 회사와는 손을 끊었다 We have severed our connection with the company. // 그 회사는 전국에 손을 뻗치고 있다 The firm is branching out〔has branches〕 all over the country.

⑦ [관대] liberality ; generosity ¶ 손 큰 사람 a generous giver

손이 많으면 일도 쉽다 속담 Many hands make light work. /Many a little makes a mickle. /Many a mickle makes a mackle.

손을 끊다 관용 wash one's hands of 《one's business》

손을 대다 관용 have relations 《with》 ; set one's hand to ; start ; strike ; hit ; give a blow to

손을 뻗치다 관용 concern oneself in〔with〕 《a matter》

손이 맞다 관용 be hand in glove ; be in cahoots

손이 모자라다 관용 be short of hands

손이 크다 관용 be generous〔liberal, openhanded〕

손

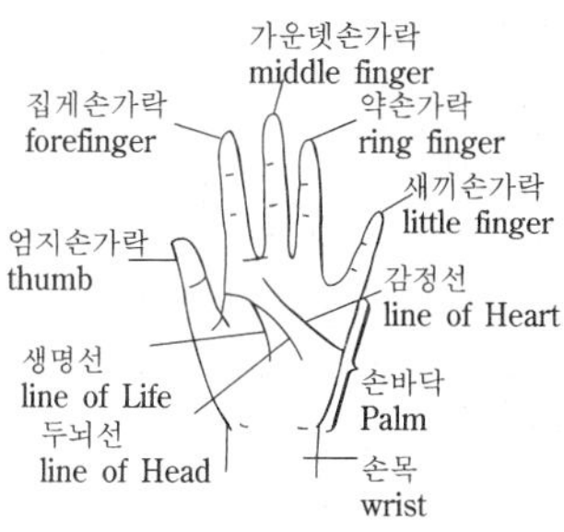

손² a guest ; a customer ⇨ 손님

손은 갈수록 좋고 비는 올수록 좋다 속담 Fresh fish and newcome guests smell in three days. /A constant guest is never welcome. /Do not wear out your welcome.

손³ [귀신] a wandering evil spirit

손⁴ ⇨ -다손 치더라도

손 孫 descendants ; posterity ; offspring ; sons and grandsons ⇨ 후손

손 損 loss ; damage ; disadvantage ; a handicap ⇨ 손해 ¶ 손보다 suffer a loss

†**손가락** a finger ¶ 다섯개의 손가락 the five fingers ; the thumb and fingers// 손가락 마디 a finger joint ; a knuckle// 손가락에 끼다 put 《a ring》 on a finger// 손가락을 꼽아 세다 count on one's fingers// 손가락을 퉁기다 crack fingers ; snap one's fingers// 그런 사람들은 손가락으로 셀 수 있을 정도 밖에 안된다 Such men may be counted on the fingers.

가운뎃— the middle〔long〕 finger ; the second finger **새끼—** the little finger **약—** the ring〔third〕 finger **엄지—** the thumb **집게—** the index finger ; the forefinger ; the first finger

손가락싸개 a fingerstall ; a thumbstall (엄지손가락의) ¶ 손가락싸개를 끼고 with a stall on a forefinger

손가락자국 a 《dirty》 finger mark 〔print〕 ; a thumb mark (엄지손가락의)

손가락질 pointing 《at, to》 ; shunning ; scorning **—하다** point 《at》 ; shun ; scorn ¶ 사람을 손가락질하다 point a finger at 《a person》 ; point at 《a person》// 동네 사람에게 손가락질 받다 be shunned by the villagers// 손가락질하는 것은 실례이다 It is impolite to point.

손가방 a briefcase ; a portfolio ; a valise ; a handbag

손거스러미 a hangnail

손거울 a hand mirror

손거칠다 (be) light-fingered ; have thievish habits ; be a kleptomaniac ; have light fingers ¶ 손거친 사람 a kleptomaniac ; a person given to pilfering ; a thievish man// 저 친구는 손이 거칠다 His fingers are light〔lime-twigs〕. /He has sticky fingers.

손겪다 entertain a guest

손겪이 entertaining a guest ; a reception

손결 the texture of the skin of the hand

손곱다 one's hands are numb with cold ; be benumbed (with cold) ; have numb hands ¶ 추워서 손이 곱았다 The cold benumbed our fingers. // 손곱아서 펜을 쥘 수가 없다 My fingers are so contracted by cold that I cannot hold a pen.

손공 —功 handicraft ; fine hand-work ¶ 이 책꽂이는 손공이 많이 들었다 The bookcase took a lot of fine work.

손구루마 a handcart

손궤 —櫃 a (portable) case〔box〕 ; a casket

손그릇 everyday household utensils

손금 the lines in the palm of one's hand ¶ 손금을 보이다 have one's palm read// 손금이 좋다〔나쁘다〕 have lucky〔omi-

nous〕 lines in one's hand
―쟁이 a palmist ; a palm reader
손금을 보다 관용 read one's palm ; tell fortunes by the lines of the hand
손금 損金 losing money ; a loss of money ; pecuniary loss
손기 ―旗 a handflag
손기계 ―機械 a hand(-operated) machine
손길 an outstretched hand ¶ 손길 잡다 join〔clasp〕 hands
손꼽다 count on one's fingers ¶ 손꼽는 leading ; principal ; prominent // 손꼽는 사업가 a leading businessman // 손꼽아 기다리다 look forward to ; anticipate // 그는 이 마을에서는 손꼽는 재산가이다 He is one of the wealthiest citizens of the town. // 아버지의 귀가를 손꼽아 기다렸다 We waited for father's return, counting the days (on our fingers).
손꼽이치다 rank 《among》 ; count ¶ 손꼽이치는 leading ; ranking ; prominent ; outstanding ; distinguished // 한국에서 손꼽이치는 절 one of Korea's outstanding temples
손끝 fingertips
손끝 맵다 have an evil hand ; have a contaminating touch ¶ 그는 모든 일에 손끝이 맵다 He fouls up everything he touches.
손끝 맺다 remain idle ; look on with folded arms ; stand by with one's hands folded ¶ 손끝 맺고 있을 때가 아니다 This is no time for us to remain idle〔twiddle our thumb〕.
손넘기다 ① [잘못 세다] skip numbers in counting ; miscount ; short-count ; short ② [시기를 잃다] miss an opportunity ; lose one's chance
손녀 孫女 a granddaughter
손놀림 a way of using one's hand ¶ 어색한〔서투른〕 손놀림으로 with clumsy hands ; clumsily ; awkwardly
손놓다 give up 《doing one's work》 ; stop 《doing》 ; lay off ¶ 그 사건에서 손놓았다 I washed my hands of that affair.
손누비 quilting by hand
― 버선 hand-quilted socks
†**손님** ① [방문객] a caller ; a visitor ; company (두사람 이상) ; a guest (초대한) ¶ 불의의 손님 an unexpected caller ; an uninvited guest (불청객) // 손님을 맞다 receive a caller // 손님을 초대하다 invite company 《to tea》 // 손님을 대접하다 entertain company 《with music》 // 시골에서 손님이 와 있다 have a country visitor
② [고객] a customer ; custom 《총칭》 ; a client (변호사 따위의) ; clientele ; a guest (호텔 따위의) ¶ 손님이 없다 have no custom // 저 가게는 손님이 많다 That shop has many customers. // 손님들의 기분을 상하지 않도록 주의하시오 Be careful not to offend the customers.
③ [승객] a passenger ; a fare (택시 따위의)
④ [관중] an audience ¶ 손님이 적은 계절 a dull season // 입장 손님이 많다〔적다〕 have a large〔poor〕 house (극장 따위)
가는 손님은 뒤꼭지가 예쁘다 속담 Fresh fish and newcome guests smell in three days. /A constant guest is never welcome. /Do not wear out your welcome.
손대 a hand rod ; a shaman's wand
손대기 an errand boy
†**손대다** ① [만지다] touch ; lay one's hands on ¶ 손대지 않고 두다 leave 《something》 untouched〔alone〕 // 저금을 손대지 않고 두다 leave the savings intact // 주인의 돈에 손대다 make free with one's master's money // 손대지 마라 Do not touch it. / Hands off. (게시)
② [착수하다] begin ; start ; set about ; set one's hand to ¶ 일에 손대다 set about one's work // 새로 손대다 begin afresh ; make a new start // 연구에 손대다 start on a course of study // 무엇부터 손댈까요 Which shall I begin with ? // 이것부터 손댑시다 Let's begin with this one.
③ [때리다] strike ; hit ; give 《a person》 a blow ; take a fist 《to》 ; give a blow 《to》 ¶ 얼굴에 손대다 strike 《a person》 in the face // 누가 먼저 손댔느냐 Who started the fight ? /Who struck the first blow ?
④ [관계하다] take a hand 《in the matter》 ; try one's hand 《at a thing》 ; make a pass 《at a woman》 ; meddle 《in a person's affairs》
손대야 a hand basin
손대중 measuring〔weighing〕 by hand ; hand-measurement ¶ 그의 손대중이 과히 틀림없다 He measures things by hand fairly accurately.
손더듬이 groping ; fumbling ; feeling for ¶ 맹인은 손더듬이로 문께로 갔다 The blind man groped his way to the door.
손덕 ―德 a lucky hand 《in gambling》
손도끼 a hand ax ; a hatchet
손도장 ―圖章 sealing 《a document》 with a thumbprint ¶ 문서에 손도장을 찍다 seal a document with one's thumb
손독 ―毒 a hand-borne infection ; hand poisoning
손독이 오르다 관용 be infected by touching with one's hands
손동작 ―動作 hand movement(s) ; manual activity
손득 損得 ⇨ 손익
손들다 ① [거수] raise〔hold up〕 one's hand ; [공격] lift one's hand 《against》 ¶ 손들어 Hands up ! /Put your hands up ! /Stick'em up. 《속》
② [지다] be beaten〔defeated〕 ; [항복하다] yield 《to》 ; surrender ; give in ; throw up one's hands ¶ 손들었다 I'm beaten 〔done for〕. /You win. // 손들기 직

전이다 I'm about to throw in a towel.
③ [애먹음] be floored ; be annoyed 《by》 ¶ 그 더위에는 손들었다 I can't stand the heat.

손등 the back of the hand

손때 dirt from the hands ; finger marks ¶ 손때가 묻은 finger-marked ; soiled by the hand // 손때가 묻은 책 a thumb-marked〔well-thumbed〕 book // 손때가 묻다 become hand-stained ; be well thumbed // 손때를 묻히다 soil 《anything》 with the hand // 그 교과서는 몹시 손때가 묻어 있었다 The school-books were badly thumbed.

손떠퀴 a touch ¶ 손떠퀴가 좋다 have the touch of luck〔the golden touch〕; have luck on one's side // 손떠퀴가 나쁘다 have the touch of misfortune

*__손떼다__ [끝내다] finish ; complete ; get 《a thing》 off one's hands ; [관계를 끊다] finish with ; break 《one's connection》 with ; wash one's hands of ; be through with ¶ 그와는 손뗐다 I am through with him. // 이 일을 내일까지 손떼지 않으면 안 된다 I must get this work finished by tomorrow. // 그들은 서로 손뗄 수 없는 사이다 They are closely〔inseparably〕 connected. /They are inseparably bound up with each other. // 우리는 지금 손뗄 수 없다 We can't back out now.

손료 損料 rent (fee) ; hire ¶ 손료를 받고 빌려주다 let out 《a thing》 on hire ; rent〔hire〕 out ; take rent for

손말명 〖민속〗 the spirit of a (dead) virgin

손맑다 ① [생기는 것이 없다] (be) poor ; be inept at moneymaking ② [인색하다] (be) stingy ; miserly

손맵다 have an evil hand ⇨ 손끝 맵다

손맺다 fold one's arms ⇨ 손끝 맺다

손모 損耗 wear and tear

손모가지 ① ⇨ 손 ② ⇨ 손목

⁑**손목** the wrist ¶ 손목을 잡다 take 《a person》 by the wrist ; catch 《a person's》 wrist

— **시계** a wristwatch

손바구니 a hand basket

손바느질 needlework ; sewing by hand

⁑**손바닥** the palm of the hand ¶ 네 기분은 손바닥 보듯이 알 수 있다. I can read your feelings like a book.

손바람 the swish〔swing〕 of a hand ¶ 일에 손바람이 나다 get into the swing of one's work

손발 hand and foot ; the limbs (사지) ¶ 손발이 큰 사람 a person large of limbs // 손발이 큰 big-limbed // 손발을 묶다 bind 《a person》 hand and foot // 손발이 되어 일하다 serve 《a person》 like a tool // 그의 손발이 차가워졌다 His extremities grew cold. // 이것은 손발에 좋은 운동이 됩니다 This will form a good exercise for the limbs.

손발이 맞다 관용 be hand in glove 《with》 ; be in cahoots 《with》

손방 inexperience ; green hand(edness)

손방 巽方 〖민속〗 southeast ; the southeastern quarter

손버릇 a habitual action of the hands ; a habit of stealing (도벽) ¶ 손버릇이 사납다 be light-fingered // 수업중에 손버릇으로 연필을 가지고 장난한다 The boy has a habit of toying with a pencil in class.

손보기 prostitution

손보다 see to it that there are no defects ; touch up ; take care of ; repair ; fix ; put one's hand to 《it》 ¶ 그녀가 도와주는 것은 고맙지만 하는 일마다 잘못하니 모두 다시 손보아야만 한다 It was nice of her to help, but she did everything wrong and it all has to be done over again.

손봐 주다 give 《a person》 a helping hand ; help in ; assist in ¶ 일을 손봐 주다 help 《a person》 to do his work ; assist 《a person》 in his work ; lend a hand with 《a person's》 work

손부 孫婦 the wife of one's grandson

손부끄럽다 be〔feel〕 embarrassed (by nonfulfil(l)ment of a request for which one has extended one's hand)

손붙이다 begin ; start ; set one's hand 《to》 ; set about 《to》

손비비다 rub one's hands

손빌다 receive help

손뺌 〖바둑〗 intentional negligence

손뼉 the flat of one's hand

손뼉 치다 관용 clap one's hands ; applaud

손사래 waving one's hand **—하다** wave one's hand

손살 the fork of the hand ; the space 〔web〕 between fingers

⁑**손상 損傷** damage ; injury ; 〖법〗 damnification **—하다** damage ; injure ; impair ; damnify ; ruin ; spoil

> 참고 **spoil** 가치·힘·아름다움·효용성을 감손하다 **ruin** 가치·효용성·아름다움·행복·건강 따위를 해치다 **injure** 외관·건강 따위를 해치다 **damage** 가치·효용성을 상실하다 **impair** 가치·힘을 손상시키다

¶ 손상되다 get damaged ; be injured ; sustain an injury ; suffer a loss // 광고 방송에 유명 인사를 쓰면 광고의 메시지에 손상을 준다 Using a popular celebrity detracts from its message as a commercial.

명예 — libel ; defamation ; slander (구두의)

손샅 the space between fingers

손색 遜色 inferiority ¶ 손색이 있다 be inferior 《to》 ; suffer by comparison 《with》 // 손색이 없다 bear〔stand〕 comparison 《with》 ; compare favorably 《with》; be by no means inferior 《to》// 이 점에서는 한국은 결코 서양에 손색이 없다 In this regard Korea can stand comparison with Europe and America.

손서 孫壻 the husband of one's granddaughter

손서투르다 be a poor hand 《at》; be all thumbs ¶ 손서투르게 with a clumsy hand // 하는 짓이 손서투르다 All his fingers are thumbs. /He has two left hands.

손설다 ⇨ 손서투르다

손속 [손안] in (one's) hand ; [도박 용어] gambler's luck ; the golden touch ¶ 손속이 좋다 be a lucky gambler

†**손수** with one's own hands ; personally ; in person ¶ 손수 검사하다 make a personal inspection // 손수보다 observe personally ; see 《a thing》 with one's own eyes

손수건 —手巾 a handkerchief

손수레 a handcart ; a hand truck ; a push car ; a barrow ; a handbarrow ; a wheelbarrow (외바퀴의) ; a go-cart 《미》; a trolley (행상이 끌고 다니는) 《영》 ¶ 손수레로 나르다 convey〔carry〕《a thing》 in a handcart ; wheelbarrow

손숫물 water for washing hands

*__손쉽다__ (be) easy ; simple ; light ¶ 손쉬운 문제 a simple question ; an easy problem // 손쉬운 일 an easy〔a light〕 task ; a soft job // 손쉽게 easily ; with ease ; without difficulty ; readily (바로) // 손쉽게 돈을 벌다 make an easy gain // 그가 있는 곳을 손쉽게 찾아냈다 I found out his whereabouts easily. /I had no difficulty in discovering where he was. // 그렇게 손쉽게 인수할 수는 없다 I can't undertake it so readily.

손시 巽時 〖민속〗 the 10th of the 24 hour periods 《8 : 30-9 : 30 a. m.》

손시늉 a gesture ; (a) gesticulation ; signs ; a hand signal ; dumb-show —**하다** gesture ; gesticulate ; make〔use〕 gestures〔signs〕; motion 《for a person to do》; give a hand signal ¶ 손시늉으로 부르다 motion a person toward 《one》; beckon to a person // 손시늉으로 가라고 하다 motion 《a person》 away // 손시늉으로 말하다 speak〔talk〕 by signs〔gesture〕; gesticulate ; talk in signs〔sign language〕 // 농아자는 얘기를 손시늉으로 한다 The deaf and dumb talk in sign language.

†**손실 損失** loss ¶ 가벼운 손실 a small 〔trifling〕 loss // 큰 손실 a great 〔heavy, serious, severe〕 loss // 손실을 입다 suffer 〔sustain〕 a loss // 손실을 초래하다 incur a loss ; bring a loss on oneself // 손실을 주다 inflict a loss 《on》 // 손실을 회복하다 retrieve〔recover〕 one's loss // 손실을 보상하다 balance up〔make up, compensate for, recoup〕 a loss // 그의 죽음은 학계의 큰 손실이라 하겠다 His death means a serious loss to the world of science. —**각(角)** 〖물리〗 a loss angle —**액** the amount of loss ; the loss

손심부름 a petty errand

손싸다 (be) deft ; dexterous ; nimble-fingered ; quick-handed

손쓰다 [수배하다] arrange for ; make arrangements〔preparation〕 for ; [조치하다] take a step〔measure〕; make a move ; take action ; [애쓰다] endeavor 〔try〕 to 《do》 ¶ 교묘히 손쓰다 make a clever action // 미리 손쓰다 make preparations in advance // 여러모로 손쓰다 try every possible means

손씻이 a small gift (for a service) ; a gratuity ; tips —**하다** give a small gift ; tip

손아귀 the space between the thumb and the fingers ; [수중] 《in》 the hands ¶ 손아귀에 있다 be in one's hand // 나라를 손아귀에 쥐다 hold the state in the hollow of one's hand

손아귀에 넣다 관용 capture ; take possession of ; come by

†**손아래** juniority ; being subordinate ¶ 손아랫사람 one's inferior ; a junior ; a subordinate ; a person of lesser rank // 손아래 뻘 younger〔subordinate〕 relationship // 나보다 세살 손아래이다 He is my junior by three years.

손어림 measuring roughly with one's hands ; hand measurement —**하다** use one's hands to make a rough estimate 《of》

‡**손위** seniority ¶ 그는 나보다 세살 손위다 He is my senior by three years.

손윗사람 one's senior ; one's superior ¶ 그는 손윗사람에게 공손하다 He is deferential toward his superiors.

손익 損益 profit and loss ; loss and gain ; advantage and disadvantage —**감정〔보고〕** the profit-and-loss account〔report〕 —**계산서** a statement of profit and loss —**계정** the profit-and-loss account

손익다 get accustomed 《to》; be 〔become〕 a good〔practiced〕 hand 《at》 ¶ 손익은 사람 an old hand 《at》 // 그는 초년병을 다루는 데 손익었다 He is an old hand at handling a new conscript.

손일 manual work ; handiwork ; handicraft

*__손자 孫子__ a grandson

손자귀 a hand adz(e)

손잡기다 have one's hands full ; have one's time fully engaged ; be pressed with business ; be busy ; be engaged ¶ 일에 손잡겨서 나갈 수 없다 My hands are too full to go out.

손잡다 ① [손을 붙잡다] take 《a person》 by the hand ; grasp another's hand ; [악수하다] shake hands ; clasp hands 《with》 ② [화해하다] make peace 《with》 [제휴·합작하다] join〔clasp〕 hands 《with》;

cooperate 《with》; join together; tie up 《with》; go into partnership 《with》; be aligned 《with》; fall in line 《with》; go hand in hand 《with》; [동맹하다] combine 《with》; ally oneself 《with》; join forces 《with》 ¶ …과 기술면에서 손잡고 있다 be technically tied up with 《another company》

†**손잡이** a handle; a knob (문 따위의); a grip(e) (기구의); a pull (잡아당기는); a catch; an ear (조끼 따위의) ¶ 문의 손잡이 a door knob // 손잡이를 달다 fix a handle // 손잡이를 돌리다 turn a knob // 손잡이가 떨어졌다 The handle〔knob〕 is off. **—끈** [버스 따위의] a (hand) strap; 〖해양〗 a becket

손장난 fingering; trifling; toying with one's hands; fidgeting; fiddling; fumbling **—하다** trifle; fumble; fidget; fiddle 《with》 ¶ 공기돌을 가지고 손장난하다 toy with a pebble

손장단 beating time with the hand

손재간 —才幹 ⇨ 손재주

손재수 損財數 the doom to lose one's possession

***손재주** hand skill; deftness; adroitness ¶ 손재주 있는 사람 a nimble〔deft〕-fingered person // 손재주 없는 사람 a butterfingers // 그녀는 손재주가 있다 She is smart with her fingers. // 그는 손재주가 전혀 없다 His fingers are all thumbs.

손전등 —電燈 a flashlight; an electric torch

손주다 stake 《a plant》; use a stick as support 《for a vine》 ¶ 박덩굴에 손주다 stake a gourd vine

손질 handling; care; [수선] repair; mending **—하다** handle with care; care for; repair ¶ 손질이 잘된 정원 a well-kept garden // 손질이 잘 되어 있다 be in a good state of repair; be (kept) in a good repair // 손질이 안 되어 있다 be out of order // 손질을 잘하다 take good care of // 나무를 손질하다 trim the trees // 구두를 손질하다 have one's shoes mended // 배가 손질이 잘 되어〔잘 안되어〕 있다 The boat is in good〔bad〕 repair. // 정원은 손질이 안되어 있었다 The garden was left neglected〔uncared for〕.

***손짓** a motion〔signal〕 of the hand; a gesture; signs; signals **—하다** gesture; gesticulate; make a gesture; sign; use signs; motion 《for a person to do》 ¶ 앉으라고 손짓하다 motion 《a person》 to sit down // 손짓으로 가라고 하다 motion 《a person》 away // 손짓으로 사람을 부르다 motion 《a person》 to come toward 《one》; beckon 《a person》 // 손짓으로 말하다 speak by signs; talk in sign language // 손짓으로 나타내다 make a dumb show // 벙어리는 손짓으로 말한다 The deaf and dumb talk in sign language.

손찌검 striking; hitting; beating **—하다** strike 《a person》; beat; hit

손치다[1] take in lodgers

손치다[2] ① [매만져 바로잡다] smooth; put in order ② [흐트러지다] get out of order; get messed up; get scattered

손치르다 entertain one's guests; give a party; play host 《to》

손크다 ① [후하다] (be) generous; liberalhanded ¶ 손큰 사람 a liberal giver; a person with a big〔generous〕 hand // 손크게 돈을 쓰다 be free with one's money; dip into one's pocket ② [수단이 좋다] (be) resourceful

손타다 be stolen; be sensitive to handling; be lost〔damaged〕 through handling

†**손톱** a fingernail ¶ 손톱을 길게 기르다 have one's nail grow long // 손톱을 깎다 trim〔cut〕 one's nails // 손톱을 닦다 manicure one's nails // 손톱으로 할퀴다 scratch with one's nail // 양심이라고는 손톱만치도 없다 He has not an atom of〔not the slightest〕 conscience in him. // 손톱이 길다 Your fingernail is unkempt. **—깎이** a nail clipper〔nipper〕 **—눈** the quick; the flesh around the fingernail **—묶음** 〖인쇄〗 parentheses; round brackets **— 자국** a nail mark; a scratch; a crescent spot (made by pinching) ¶ 손톱 자국을 내다 mark with one's nails

손틀 a hand-operated sewing machine

손티 slight pockmarks; blemished skin ¶ 얼굴에 손티가 있다 be slightly pockmarked

손표 —標 an index (mark); 〖인쇄〗 a fist

손풀무 a pair of hand(-operated) bellows

손풍금 —風琴 an accordion; a concertina; a hand organ

†**손해** 損害 [손상] damage; injury; harm; [손실] a loss; [사상] casualties

> 참고 **damage**는 무생물에 **injury**는 생물에 관해서 흔히 쓰인다

¶ 물적 손해 property damage // 인적 물적 손해 loss of life and property // 경미한 손해 slight〔trifling〕 damage // 막대한 손해 dire〔serious, heavy〕 damage // 홍수〔폭풍〕에 따른 손해 damage from a flood〔storm〕 // 30만 원의 손해 300,000 *won* worth of damage // 손해를 입히다 damage; injure; do harm 《to》; work damage 《on》; inflict a loss〔injury〕 《on》 // 손해를 입다 suffer〔sustain〕 damage〔a loss〕; receive injuries // 손해를 메꾸다 cover a loss; balance〔offset〕 a loss // 손해에 대한 책임이 있다 be liable for damage // 화재로 인한 손해는 보험금으로 충분히 보상되었다 The loss caused by the fire was amply covered by the insurance. // 손해는 약 5천만원으로 추산되고 있다 The damage〔loss〕 is estimated〔put down〕 at about fifty million *won*. // 그녀는 사람은

좋은데 숫기가 없어서 손해를 본다 She's a nice person, but she loses out because of her bashfulness.

— 보험 insurance against loss ; nonlife insurance —액 the amount of damages —율 loss ratio — 증명 certificate of damage

손해 배상 損害賠償 compensation for damages ; reparation for damages ; indemnity (배상금) ¶ 손해 배상을 하다 pay for damage ; indemnify 《a person》 for damage // 손해 배상을 청구하다 demand〔claim〕 damages 《against a person》

—금 damages — 청구권 a claim for damages 자동차 — 보장법 〖법〗 the Automobile Accident Compensation Security Act

손회목 (the most slender part of) a wrist

손훅치기 [씨름] a knee-grab chest-shove

†**솔**¹ a pine ; a pine tree

†**솔**² a brush ¶ 먼지를 솔로 털다 brush off dust

솔³ [표적] an archery target

솔⁴ ⇨ 솔기

솔⁵ 〖의학〗 skin pustules

솔가 率家 —하다 take one's family along ¶ 솔가하여 만주로 이주하다 emigrate to Manchuria with one's family

솔가리 fallen pine needles ; pine straw ¶ 솔가리를 긁다 rake pine needles

솔가지 pine twigs〔branches〕

솔개 ⇨ 소리개

솔권 率眷 taking〔leading〕 away one's family **—하다** take〔lead〕 one's family away

‡**솔기** a seam (in clothing) ¶ 솔기가 있는〔없는〕 seamy〔seamless〕 // 솔기가 터지다 a seam opens〔runs〕 // 솔기를 2중으로 하다 sew extra seams // 솔기가 나오지 않도록 꿰매다 sew so that the seams do not show

솔깃하다 take an interest in ; be interested in ; be enthusiastic about ¶ 솔깃해서 with enthusiasm ; with interest // 솔깃해서 귀를 기울이다 listen to 《a person》 with interest〔intently〕 // 그다지 솔깃하지 않았다 I did not feel half so positive as I ought. // 솔깃해서 말을 듣다 listen to 《a person》 intently〔with interest〕

솔나무 ⇨ 소나무

솔나방 〖곤충〗 ⇨ 송충나방

솔다¹ ① [가렵다] (be) itchy and sore ; irritating

② [좁다] (be) narrow ; small ; cramped ¶ 칼라에 쓸려서 목이 솔다 one's neck is sore from the chafing of one's collar // 이 옷은 품이 솔다 This coat is tight // 저고리 품이 솔다 The jacket is skimpy.

솔다² ① [귀가] 《one's ears》 ache ; get sore ; have sore ears ¶ 잔소리에 귀가 솔다 My ears ache with her constant nagging. /I am sick〔tired〕 of her complaining.

② [말라 죄어들다] dry up ; tighten up with dryness

③ [무솔다] 《a vegetable》 decay from the damp

솔대 a lath ; a thin slat

솔따비 a weeder-plow〔-plough 《영》〕 used to dig out pine roots

솔딱새 〖새〗 a Siberian flycatcher

솔래솔래 ¶ 솔래솔래 빠져나가다 steal out of〔slip away from〕 《a room》 one by one // 곶감이 솔래솔래 적어지더니 다없어지고 말았다 Dried persimmons became fewer, till (at last) they were quite gone.

솔로 〖음악〗 a solo 《*pl.* ~s, -li》 ¶ 솔로로 노래하다 sing a solo // 솔로를 하다 [악기로] play solo

— 가수 a soloist 피아노 — a piano solo

솔로몬 제도 —諸島 [남태평양의] the Solomon Islands

솔바탕 an archery field ; a shooting range

솔방울 a pine cone

솔밭 a pine grove〔forest〕

솔보굿 pine bark

솔봉이 a young rustic ; a boorish young man

솔부엉이 〖새〗 a brown hawk-owl

솔불 a fire set to pine knots

솔뿌리 a pine root

솔새 ① 〖새〗 Swinhoe's willow-warbler ② 〖식물〗 a kind of pampas grass ; Themeda japonica (학명)

솔선 率先 taking the lead〔initiative〕 **—하다** lead ; take the lead〔initiative〕 《in》 ; be a pioneer〔leader〕 ; make〔take up〕 the running ¶ 솔선하여 on one's own initiative // 솔선하여 …하다 be the first to 《do》 ; take the lead〔initiative〕 in 《doing》 ; set an example of ; act as pioneer 《in》 // 그는 솔선하여 그 운동을 일으켰다 He took the initiative〔lead〕 in the movement. // 그는 솔선하여 외래종의 식물을 재배했다 He took the lead in cultivation of the foreign plants. // 교장부터 솔선하여 금주했다 The principal set an example of abstinence for the whole school.

솔솔 softly ; gently ; smoothly ; easily ; readily ; nicely ¶ 문제가 솔솔 풀리다 solve the hard question without effort // 바람이 솔솔 분다 The wind blows softly〔gently〕. /There is a gentle breeze. // 실이 솔솔 잘 풀린다 The tangled thread straightens out nicely.

솔송나무 〖식물〗 a hemlock spruce

솔수펑이, 솔숲 a pine forest ; a pine copse

솔이끼 〖식물〗 hair〔haircap〕 moss ; Polytricum juniperinum (학명)

솔잎 pine needles

— 상투 a topknot braided out of short hair

솔잎란 —蘭 〖식물〗 a whisk fern ; Psilo-

tum nudum (학명)
솔잣새 〖새〗 a Korean crossbill
†솔직 率直 frankness ; candidness ; outspokenness ; plainness —하다 (be) frank ; candid ; plain ; straight ; outspoken ; open ; openhearted

> 참고 **frank** 생각이나 감정 따위를 기탄없이 얼굴이나 행동에 나타내는 것 **open** 감추지 않고 천진스럽다 **outspoken** 감추지 않고 전부를 말하다 **candid** 정직하여 조금도 거짓이 없기 때문에 듣는 상대방이 곤란한 때도 있다

¶ 솔직한 비평 outspoken comments // 솔직한 고백 a frank confession // 솔직한 질문〔답변〕 a straight question〔answer〕// 솔직한 사람 a down-right man ; an openhearted person ; a straightforward person // 솔직히 frankly ; candidly ; plainly ; straight-out // 솔직히 말하자면 frankly speaking ; to speak honestly ; in plain words ; to be frank〔candid〕 with you // 서로 솔직히 말하다 have a heart-to-heart talk with 《a person》// 일어난 일을 솔직히 말하다 give an unvarnished account of what happened // 솔직히 의견을 말하여 주시오 Give your honest views. // 솔직하게 논평을 했다 She was outspoken in her remarks. /She gave outspoken comments. // 솔직히 말하면 네 잘못이다 To be plain with you, you are to blame. // 왜 솔직히 말하지 않지 Why don't you give it to me straight ? // 솔직히 말할게요 I'll level with you // 그가 그것을 솔직히 말하기만 하면 좋을텐데 If only he could come right out and say it.
†솔질 brushing —하다 brush ¶ 옷에 솔질하다 give one's clothes a brushing
솔트 SALT 《Strategic Arms Limitation Talks》
솔포기, 솔폭 a thick-branched small pine tree
†솜 cotton ; cottonwool ¶ 옷에 솜을 넣다 pad〔wad〕 clothing ; stuff a gown with cotton // 솜을 틀다 gin cotton ; fluff cotton // 귀를 솜으로 막다 stop one's ears with cotton ; cottonwool one's ears
—덩이 a ball of cotton —뭉치 a wad of cotton
솜대 〖식물〗 a black bamboo
솜덩이 a ball of cotton
솜돗 a willowing mat (for cotton)
솜두루마기 a padded outer coat
솜먼지 bits of cotton
솜몽둥이 a cotton-tipped stick (used as a dauber)
솜뭉치 a wad of cotton
솜바지 cotton-padded trousers
솜반 a thin layer of cotton ; a thin slice of cotton
솜버선 cotton-padded socks
솜붙이 (cotton-)padded clothes ; wadded 〔padded〕 garments
솜사탕 cotton candy ; spun sugar ; candy fluff
솜솜 —하다 (be) pockmarked
†솜씨 skill ; ability ; deftness ; dexterity ; tact ¶ 훌륭한 솜씨 a splendid〔creditable〕 performance // 솜씨 좋은 skillful ; clever ; dexterous ; tactful // 솜씨 좋게 skillfully ; cleverly // 솜씨가 있다〔없다〕 be clever 〔clumsy〕 at 《a thing》 ; be skillful〔awkward〕 《in doing a thing》// 솜씨를 보이다 show〔exhibit, display〕 one's skill ; show much tact // 요리 솜씨가 좋다 be a clever cook ; be handy in the kitchen // 사건을 솜씨 있게 처리하다 manage the matter skillfully〔with skill〕// 그는 연장을 쓰는 데 솜씨가 있다 He is handy with a tool.
솜옷 padded clothes
솜저고리 a padded jacket
솜채 a cotton-beating stick
솜털 down ; fluff ; [새의] pinfeathers ¶ 솜털이 돋은 downy // 복숭아의 솜털 peach fuzz
— 방석 a downy cushion
솜틀 a willow(er) ; a willowing machine ; a cotton gin
솜화약 —火藥 gun cotton ; cotton powder
솟고라지다 ① [끓다] boil up ② [용솟다] leap up
솟구다 raise ; make rise ¶ 몸을 솟구다 rise on one's toes
솟구치다 raise quickly ; make a quick rise ; soar
솟나다 ⇨ 소수나다
†솟다 ① [높이] rise〔soar, tower〕 high ¶ 구름 위에 솟다 rise〔tower〕 above the cloud ; rise to the sky // 종달새가 하늘 높이 솟는다 A skylark soars to the sky. ② [샘 따위가] gush〔spring〕 out〔forth〕 ; flow out ; well out ¶ 눈물이 솟다 tears well (up) in one's eyes // 샘물이 솟는다 A well flows.
솟대 ① 〖고제도〗 a pole erected to honor a successful civil service examinee ② 〖민속〗 a pole signifying prayer for a good harvest ③ an acrobat's pole
솟대쟁이 a masked acrobat who performs his feats on the top of a pole
솟보다 buy dear ; pay too much ; make a bad bargain
솟아나다 gush〔spring〕 out〔forth〕 ; flow 〔stream〕 out〔forth〕 ; well up〔out, forth〕 ¶ 눈물이 솟아나다 tears well (up) in one's eyes ; one's eyes are filled with tears // 노여움이 가슴속에 솟아났다 A violent anger surged up in his heart.
솟을대문 a tall〔lofty〕 gate
솟을무늬 embossed pattern on a cloth ; embossment ; brocade
솟치다 raise ; set higher ; lift up ¶ 몸을 솟치다 jump up ; stand on tiptoes
송 頌 a eulogy ; a panegyric ; an encomi-

um
송가 頌歌 a hymn ; a doxology ¶ 송가를 부르다 chant hymns of praise
송경 誦經 reciting〔chanting〕 a sutra ―하다 recite〔chant〕 a sutra
송골매 a Siberian peregrine falcon ; a duck hawk
송골송골 [땀·소름이] 《appear》 in profuse beads
*송곳 a gimlet (나사·송곳) ; an awl (작은 송곳) ; auger (큰 송곳) ; a drill (광석용) ¶ 송곳으로 구멍을 뚫다 bore a hole with a gimlet // 송곳을 돌려서 구멍을 뚫다 drive a gimlet 《into》 // 송곳으로 허벅다리를 찌르다 pierce 《a person's》 thigh with an awl
송곳니 a canine tooth ; a cuspid
송곳칼 a combination knife-drill
송구 送球 handball
송구 悚懼 ―하다 be filled with awe ; be overwhelmed (with shame or gratitude) ¶ 친히 돌봐주시니 송구스럽습니다 To be helped by you, sir, is too great an honor for me. /I am overwhelmed by your assistance, sir. // 나는 송구스러워 머리가 올라가지 않는다 I am too much awed to raise my head. // 부인께서 친히 술을 따라주시니 송구스럽습니다 You are too kind, Ma'am. /Your condescension really overpowers me, Ma'am.
송구 영신 送舊迎新 ―하다 see the old year out and the new year in ; ring out the old ring in the new
송근유 松根油 pine oil ; oil of turpentine
송금 送金 remittance ―하다 send 《a person》 money ; remit money 《to》 ¶ 우편환으로 5천원 송금하다 remit〔make a remittance of〕 5,000 *won* by postal money order // 송금을 약속하다 promise a remittance // 고향에서 송금이 끊어졌다 I have no more remittances from home. // 즉시 송금해 주시면 감사하겠습니다 A prompt remittance would be appreciated. // 귀하의 송금은 정히 입수하였습니다 Your remittance has come to hand〔been duly received〕.
― 수수료 a remittance charge ; a charge for remittance ― 수취인 the remittee ― 수표 a remittance check 〔draft〕 ―액 the amount of remittance ― 은행 a remittance bank ―인 the remitter 예정 ― covering remittance
송기 松肌 pine endodermis
―떡 a cake flavored with pine endodermis
송기관 送機管 an airpipe
송낙 a Buddhist nun's hat (made of Wisteria chinensis)
송낙뿔 outcurved horns (of an ox)
송년 送年 bidding the old year out (and the new year in)
*송달 送達 delivery ; dispatch ; forwarding ―하다 send ; deliver ; forward ; dispatch ; [교부하다] serve ¶ 영장을 송달하다 serve a writ on 《a person》 ; serve 《a person》 with a writ
―부 a chitbook ; a delivery book 대리 ― delivery by an agent
송당송당 with hasty〔random〕 whacks ¶ 무를 송당송당 썰다 whack away at a radish // 송당송당 바느질하다 sew hastily〔roughly〕
송덕 頌德 eulogy ―하다 eulogize
―문 a eulogy ; an encomium ; a laudatory address ; a tribute ; a panegyric ; a memorial ―비(碑) a monument(erected) in honor of 《a person, a person's distinguished services to the country》 ; a monument in eulogy of a person's virtuous deeds
송독 誦讀 recitation ; recitation from memory ―하다 recite ; recite from memory
*송두리째 root and branch ; all ; completely ; thoroughly ¶ 송두리째 가져 가다 take away everything (one can lay hands on) // 도박으로 재산을 송두리째 없애다 gamble away all one's property // 뼈까지 송두리째 먹다 eat bone and all // 고양이가 쥐를 송두리째 먹어 버렸다 The cat ate up the rat, neck and crop. // 빚을 송두리째 갚다 repay all one's debts // 송두리째 근절됐다 It was exterminated root and branch. // 지갑에서 만년필까지 송두리째 떼었다 I was stripped of all I had in my pockets from purse to fountain pen.
송로 松露 ① [이슬] dew on pine needles ② [버섯] a truffle ; a mushroom
*송료 送料 carriage (fee) ; postage (우편의) ; shipping charge ¶ 책의 송료 the postage for a book
― 선불 carriage prepaid
송림 松林 a pine forest〔grove〕
송목 松木 a pine tree ⇨ 소나무
송백 松柏 the pine and the nut pine
―과 coniferae ―과 식물 a conifer ; a coniferous plant
송별 送別 a farewell ; a send-off ―하다 bid 《a person》 a farewell ; give 《a person》 a send-off
―사 a farewell speech ; a parting address ―회 a farewell party〔meeting〕 ; a send-off dinner ; a good-bye party ¶ 송별회를 열다 give a farewell reception ; throw a send-off party 《속》 // 그를 위해서 송별회를 열었다 A farewell dinner was given in his honor〔for him〕.
송별연 送別宴 a farewell dinner〔party〕 given for 《a person》 before his departure
송부 送付 sending ; forwarding ; remittance (돈의) ―하다 send ; forward ; remit (돈을)
송사 訟事 a lawsuit ; a suit ; litigation ―하다 sue ; file suit ; go to law 《with》 ; take legal proceedings 《against》 ; litigate
송사 頌辭 a laudatory address ; a eulo-

gy ; a memorial ; a panegyric
송사리 〖물고기〗 a minnow ; a killifish
송상 送像 ―하다 send〔transmit〕 a (television) picture 《to》
송송 ① [잘게] into small pieces ; finely ; mincing ② [구멍 따위가] full of small holes ; perforated ¶ 파를 송송 썰다 chop scallion into small pieces // 솥에 구멍이 송송 뚫려 있다 The oven has holes all over the bottom.
송수 送水 water supply ; supplying with water ―하다 supply water
―관 a water pipe ; a water main (본관)
송수신기 送受信機 〖통신〗 a transmitter-receiver
송수화기 送受話器 [탁상 전화 따위의] a handset ; a French telephone
송신 送信 transmission 《of a message》 ―하다 transmit〔dispatch〕 a message
―국 a transmitting station ―기 a transmitter ; a transmitting set ―자 the sender ; the transmitter ; the person sending ―탑 a transmitting tower 무전―기 a wireless〔radio〕 transmitter
송아리 a small bunch〔cluster〕 《of flowers, fruit》
*송아지 a calf
송악 〖식물〗 an ivy
송알송알 ① [땀이] in profuse drops ② [술이 괴어서] fermenting ; bubbling ¶ 땀이 송알송알 나다 perspire profusely
송액 松液 rosin ; pine resin
송어 松魚 a trout ; a salmon trout
송연하다 悚然― be horror-struck ; be terrified〔horrified〕 《at》 ; shudder with fright
송영 送迎 welcome and send-off ; greeting and farewell ―하다 welcome and send off ; receive 《a person》 and send 《another》 off
―사 greeting and farewell addresses ―위원회 a reception committee
송영 誦詠 recitation 《of a poem》 ―하다 recite 《a poem》
송유 松油 turpentine
송유 送油 oil supply ; sending oil ―하다 supply oil
―관 an oil pipeline
*송이 a cluster〔bunch〕 《of a fruit》 ; a blossom 《of a flower》 ; a flake 《of snow》 ¶ 포도 한 송이 a bunch of grapes // 바나나 한 송이 a cluster of bananas
송이밤 a chestnut with the bur on it
송이송이 in clusters ; in bunches
송이술 undiluted liquor ; unwatered wine
송이재강 lees ; grains
송자 松子 ⇨ 솔방울
송장 a dead body ; a corpse ; a cadaver ; one's remains (유해) ¶ 송장을 파내다 exhume a corpse // 그는 산 송장이다 He is a living corpse.
*송장 送狀 an invoice ; a dispatch note ¶ 송장의 변경 reconsignment // 송장을 작성하다 invoice ; make out an invoice // 상품의 송장을 적다 invoice goods
― 금액 invoice value ― 변경 reconsignment 내지〔외국〕 ― an inland〔a foreign, a shipping〕 invoice 약식 ― an abstract invoice 정정 ― a corrected invoice 확정 ― definite bills
송장개구리 a brown frog ; Rana japonica (학명)
송장메뚜기 a kind of grasshopper ; Patanga succinta (학명)
송장벌레 〖곤충〗 a burying beetle ; a gravedigger ; Nicrophorus japonicus (학명)
―과 Silphidae
송장헤엄 the backstroke ¶ 송장헤엄을 치다 do the backstroke ; (swim) backstroke
송장헤엄치개 〖곤충〗 a backswimmer ; Notonecta triguttata (학명)
송적 送籍 a transfer of domicile ―하다 transfer 《a person's》 domicile 《to》
송전 送電 power〔electric〕 transmission ; transmission of electricity ; electric supply ―하다 transmit power ; supply the (electric) current ¶ 송전을 끊다 cut 〔shut〕 off the current
―력〔용량〕 (power-) carrying〔transmission〕 capacity ―선 a power transmission line〔wire〕 ; a power cable (고압선) ―전차선 a live trolley wire ―탑〔소〕 a (power-) transmission tower 〔site〕
송정 送呈 ―하다 send 《a book》 as a present ; present 《a book》
송죽 松竹 pine and bamboo
송지 松脂 pine resin ; rosin
송진 松津 pine resin
송채 送綵 sending red and blue silk from the bridegroom's family to the bride's (after setting the date for the wedding)
송청 送廳 sending to the prosecutor's office ; committal for trial ―하다 send to the prosecutor's office ; commit 《a person》 for trial
송축 頌祝 blessing ; a eulogy ; commendation and benediction ―하다 bless ; praise and bless ; eulogize
송충나방 松蟲― a pinecaterpillar moth ; Dendrolimus spectabilis (학명)
송충목 松蟲木 caterpillar-eaten pine
송충이 松蟲― a pine-eating caterpillar ¶ 송충이를 대하듯 싫어하다 hate 《a person》 like a serpent〔viper〕 // 송충이가 갈잎을 먹으면 떨어진다 The cobbler should stick to his last.
인간 ― a human caterpillar
송치 an unborn calf
송치 送致 sending ; dispatching ; commitment ―하다 send ; forward ; dispatch ; make a commitment ¶ 불량 소년의 송치를 받다 (소년원이) receive juvenile delinquents
송판 松板 a pine board ; a deal

송편 a rice cake steamed on a layer of pine needles
송풍 松風 [바람] a wind passing through the pine trees ; a breeze in the pine trees ; [바람 소리] the whispering 〔soughing〕 of wind among the pines
송풍 送風 ventilation ; [바람] an air blast ; a forced draft ─하다 send air 《to》 ; ventilate 《a room》
─관 a blastpipe ─기(機) an air blower ; a ventilator ─기관 a blowing〔fan〕 engine
송화 松花 pine pollen
송화 送話 transmission (of speech) ─하다 transmit
─구 a mouthpiece ─기 a (voice) transmitter ; a sender ─료 telephone charges ─선 a transmitting line
송환 送還 repatriation ; sending back (home) ─하다 send back ; send home ; repatriate ¶ 군인이 병으로 송환되다 be invalided home
─자 a repatriate ; a deportee ; a returnee 《미》
‡솥 an iron pot ; a kettle (물끓이는) ; a cauldron (가마솥) ¶ 솥을 걸다 install a kettle in a fireplace
─뚜껑 the lid〔cover〕 of a kettle 밥─ a rice kettle 증기─ a steam cooker
솥은 검어도 밥은 검지 않다 (속담) A black hen lays a white egg.
같은 솥 밥을 먹다 (관용) break bread with ; live under the same roof 《with》 ; eat at the same mess
솥귀 the ears〔handles〕 of a kettle
솥땜장이 a tinker
솥물 rust spots in a new kettle
솥발 the tripod base of a kettle ; kettle legs
솥발이 a litter of three puppies
솥솔 a kettle〔pot〕 brush ; a scouring brush
솥전 the rim of a kettle〔pot〕
솥전 ─廛 a kitchen-hardware shop
솥젖 the three side pieces on the rim of an iron pot to suspend the pot on the hearth
솨, 쏴 with a cool gust ; briskly ; whistling ¶ 바람이 쏴 분다 The wind whistles〔hisses, pipes〕. // 비가 쏴 내린다 The rain pours down in a torrent 〔hard, in showers, cats and dogs〕.
솰솰 with a great flow ; in torrents ; briskly ¶ 솰솰 흐르다 rustle along // 물을 솰솰 뿌리다 shower〔water over〕 《the grass》 // 머리를 솰솰 빗다 comb one's hair briskly
쇄골 鎖骨 〖해부〗 the collarbone ; the clavicle
쇄광 碎鑛 〖광물〗 rock crushing
─기 a crusher ; a crushing machine
쇄국 鎖國 national isolation ; seclusion ; exclusion of foreigners ─하다 close a country ; close the door 《to foreigners》 ; exclude foreigners 《from a country》
─주의〔정책〕 a policy of seclusion ; a national isolation policy ; seclusionism ─주의자 a seclusionist
*쇄도 殺到 rush ; a flood ─하다 rush 〔sweep, pour〕 in ; rush to ; throng to 《a place》 ¶ 주문이 쇄도하다 have a rush 〔pressure〕 of orders // 신청이 쇄도하다 be flooded〔deluged〕 with applications 〔offers〕 // 감사장이 사방에서 쇄도했다 Letters of thanks poured in from all quarters. // 항의가 쇄도했다 Complaints came snowing in. // 아침부터 손님이 쇄도했다 The shop was crowded with customers from the morning on. // 진정자들이 의사당에 쇄도했다 Petitioners thronged to the Assembly.
쇄목 碎木 timber grinding
─기 a grinder ─펄프 ground pulp
쇄빙 碎氷 [일] breaking the ice ; [물건] rubble〔fragmentary〕 ice ─하다 break 〔smash〕 ice
쇄빙선 碎氷船 an icebreaker ; an iceboat
쇄상 鎖狀 ¶ 쇄상의 chain-like
쇄석 碎石 rubble ; broken stone ; debris ; smashed rock ; 〖토목〗 macadam ─하다 break stone ; smash〔crush〕 rock ¶ 쇄석을 깔다 macadamize 《a road》
─기 〖의학〗 a lithotrite ; a lithotritor ─술 〖의학〗 lithotrity (방광 결석의) ─포도(鋪道) a macadam〔macadamized〕 road
쇄신 刷新 reform ; renovation ; innovation ; a clean-up ─하다 reform ; introduce〔make〕 a reform ; renovate ; innovate ; clean up ¶ 생활 양식의 쇄신 a reform of the mode of living // 정계의 쇄신 political reform〔clean-up〕 // 시정의 쇄신 innovation of municipal administration // 대쇄신을 행하다 carry out a radical reform ; cleanse the Augean stables
쇄신 碎身 ¶ 분골쇄신하다 exert oneself to the utmost ; do everything one can〔in one's power〕 ; do as much as in one lies
쇄암기 碎岩機 a stone crusher
쇄전 鎖電 chain lightning
쇄탄기 碎炭機 a coal crusher
쇄토기 碎土機 a break barrow
쇄편 碎片 a fragment ; a splinter ; a broken piece
쇄항 鎖港 closing the ports ─하다 close the ports ; exclude foreigners from the ports
†쇠 iron (철) ; metal (금속) ; a compass (지남철) ; a key (열쇠) ; a lock (자물쇠) ; brass (놋쇠) ¶ 쇠 같은 의지 an iron will // 그는 쇠같이 굳은 의지를 가진 사람이다 He is a man of iron will.
쇠-[1] [작은 종류] a small one ¶ 쇠고래 a small whale ; a gray whale
쇠-[2] [소의] of cattle ¶ 쇠고기 beef
쇠가죽 oxhide ; cowhide

쇠갈고리 an iron hook
⁑쇠고기 beef
쇠고둥 〖조개〗 a whelk ; Buccinum striatissimun (학명)
쇠고랑 handcuffs ; manacles ; darbies 《속》 ¶ 쇠고랑을 채우다 handcuff ; manacle ; put 《a person》 in irons ; slip 〔place〕 handcuffs on 《a person》 ; shackle the hands // 쇠고랑을 채워서 호송하다 escort 《a criminal》 in handcuffs
쇠고래 〖동물〗 a gray whale ; Rhachionectes glaucus (학명)
쇠고리 an iron ring ; a clasp ; a detent ¶ 쇠고리를 걸다 clasp // 쇠고리를 끄르다 unclasp
쇠곤 衰困 fatigue ; exhaustion
쇠골 cow's brains
쇠공이 an iron pestle〔pounder〕
쇠구들 a floor〔room〕 which will not warm up ; a cold floor
쇠귀 a cow's ears ¶ 쇠귀에 경읽기 preaching to deaf ears ⇨ 우이독경
쇠귀나물 〖식물〗 an arrowhead
쇠귀신 ―鬼神 [사람] a stubborn person
쇠기름 beef tallow
쇠기침 a chronic cough
쇠꼬리[1] [베틀신의] the treadle-line of a loom (that attaches to the *sin dae*)
쇠꼬리[2] [소의] a cow's tail ; oxtail
쇠꼬챙이 an iron〔brass〕 skewer ; a steel spit
쇠끄트러기, 쇠끝 scraps of iron
쇠뇌 a catapult
쇠다[1] ① [채소가] 《vegetables》 become tough (and stringy)
② [병이 덧나다] get worse ; grow chronic ; take a bad turn ; take a turn for the worse ¶ 윗병이 쇠다 one's stomach trouble becomes worse
*쇠다[2] [명절을] celebrate ; observe ; keep 《one's birthday》 ¶ 성탄절을 쇠다 keep 〔commemorate〕 Christmas // 한국에선 설을 쉽니다 New Year's Day is kept as a festival in Korea.
쇠다리 a cow's leg ; an ; [고기] a leg 〔shank〕 of beef
쇠달구 the iron head of a piledriver 〔groundleveler〕
쇠닻 an iron anchor
쇠도리깨 [무기] an iron club ; a bludgeon
쇠두겁 a metal cap〔lid〕
쇠딱지 dirt on children's heads
쇠똥[1] [쇠부스러기] iron slag ; dross ; scoria
쇠똥[2] ① cattle dung ② [쇠딱지] dirt on children's heads
쇠똥찜 fomenting a tumor with heated cow dung
쇠뜨기 〖식물〗 a horsetail ; joint grass
쇠로 衰老 getting old and infirm ⇨ 노쇠
쇠막대기 an iron bar〔rod〕 ; a metal rod
쇠망 衰亡 ruin ; decline ; fall ; downfall
―하다 decline ; decay ; fall into ruin ; collapse ¶ 로마 제국의 쇠망 the decline and fall of the Roman Empire
쇠망치 an iron hammer
쇠머리 a cow's head
쇠먹이 cattle food ; fodder
쇠메 a〔an iron〕 hammer ; [큰 것] a sledge ; a sledgehammer ; a maul
쇠멸 衰滅 ⇨ 쇠망(衰亡)
쇠목 ―木 the center〔-re〕 board in the front of a chest of drawers
쇠못 an iron nail ; a nail
쇠몽둥이 an iron bar ; an iron rod
쇠몽치 a small metal bar
쇠문 ―門 an iron gate〔door〕
쇠물푸레나무 an ash tree
쇠뭉치 a mass of iron ; pig iron
†쇠미 衰微 decline ; decay ; wane ; decadence ; ebb tide ―하다 decline ; decay ; wane ; go into decay ; sink in decay ; fall into decay ; be at a low ebb ¶ 쇠미의 극에 이르다 fall into the extreme of decadence // 쇠미해 가고 있다 be on the wane〔decline〕 // 그 당시에는 상업은 쇠미했다 Trade was in decadence〔at a low ebb〕 at that time.
쇠밀화부리 ⇨ 고지새
쇠발고무래 〖농업〗 an iron rake
쇠백장 a butcher
쇠버즘 a kind of ringworm
쇠부스러기 iron waste〔scraps〕
쇠북 a bell ⇨ 종(鐘)
쇠불알 the testicles〔testes〕 of a bull ; bull's testicles
쇠붙이 metal things ; ironware ; hardware
쇠비름 〖식물〗 a purslane ; Portulaca oleracea (학명)
―나물 purslane greens
쇠뼈 cow〔bullock〕 bones
쇠뿔 an oxhorn
― 참외 a horn-shaped melon
쇠뿔도 단김에 빼랬다 [속담] Strike the iron while it is hot. /Hoist your sail when the wind is fair. /What's worth doing is worth doing promptly.
쇠사다리 a metal ladder
†쇠사슬 chains ; irons ; fetters ¶ 쇠사슬에 매인 죄수 a prisoner in chains // 쇠사슬로 매다 enchain ; chain up ; put 《a person》 in chains // 쇠사슬을 풀다 unchain ; unlink ; undo the chain ; put out of chain // 개가 쇠사슬에 매여 있다 The dog is on the chain〔is kept chained up, is enchained〕.
쇠살쭈 a cattle broker〔buyer, dealer〕
쇠새 the common Indian kingfisher ⇨ 물총새
쇠서 ① 〖요리〗 (an) oxtongue ② 〖건축〗 ⇨ 쇠서받침
쇠서받침 〖건축〗 ornamental cow's tongues (at the top of a column)
쇠숟가락, 쇠술 a brass spoon
쇠스랑 a rake ; a forked rake
쇠시리 〖건축〗 grooving the sides of a lat-

ticed door or the sharp edges of a pillar (for decoration)
쇠심 beef〔ox〕 tendon
—떠개 sinewy beef
†**쇠약 衰弱** weakness ; sinking ; debility ; breakdown ; enervation ; emaciation ; 〖의학〗 asthenia **—하다** weaken ; grow weak ; sink ; be debilitated ; be enervated ; be emaciated ; (be) worn out ¶ 쇠약한 weak ; weakened ; emaciated // 병후 아직도 몸이 쇠약하다 He is still weak after his illness. // 환자가 마구 쇠약해간다 The patient is sinking fast. // 몸이 쇠약해져서 수술할 수가 없다 She is too weak to be operated upon. // 너무 걱정을 해서 신경이 쇠약해져 버렸다 I worried so much I was a nervous wreck.
—증 a wasting〔consumptive〕 disease **전신 —** general prostration〔weakening, debility〕
쇠양배양하다 (be) thoughtless ; heedless ; imprudent ; indiscreet ¶ 무엇이든지 쇠양배양해서는 안된다 Use prudence in whatever you do.
쇠운 衰運 declining fortune ; one's waning star ; decline ; decadence ¶ 쇠운의 극에 달하다 be at the nadir of one's fortunes ; reach 《its》 lowest ebb // 쇠운을 만회하다 retrieve one's fortunes ; regain one's former prosperity
쇠자루 a metal handle
—칼 a metal-handled knife ; a metal-haft sword
쇠잔 衰殘 failing ; decaying **—하다** fail ; decay ; [쇠약] be debilitated ; be enfeebled
쇠잡이 a gong beater
쇠장식 —裝飾 metal fittings〔fixtures〕 ; metallic parts ¶ 쇠장식을 박다〔달다〕 nail〔fix〕 metal fittings 《on》
가구용 — furniture fittings **건축용 —** builder's hardware
쇠족 —足 ox-hoof
쇠죽 a gruel of beans and straw for cattle
— 가마 a large kettle to cook cattle feed in **—물** water used in boiling cattle feed **— 바가지** a cattle-feed dipper **—통** a boiled-fodder tub〔bucket〕
쇠줄 metal〔iron〕 wire ; a cable ; a chain
쇠지랑물 stored cattle urine
쇠지랑탕 a urinarium
쇠지레 a crowbar
쇠진 衰盡 decay ; exhaustion **—하다** decay ; exhaust
쇠짚신 straw hoof-wrappings for cattle
쇠창살 —窓— an iron window bar ; a grating
쇠천 a small copper coin
쇠코뚜레 a cow's nose-ring
쇠테 an iron〔a metal〕 frame〔rim〕
쇠톱 a hack saw
쇠통 an iron tank〔tub〕
†**쇠퇴 衰退** decline ; decadence ; deterioration (퇴화) ; decay ; wane
쇠파리 a cow fly ; a warble fly
쇠팥 〖식물〗 a kind of hard bean
쇠폐 衰弊 decay ; collapse ; ruin **—하다** decay ; collapse ; go to ruin
쇠푼 a small〔petty〕 sum of money
‡**쇠하다 衰—** [쇠약] become weak ; lose vigor ; be enfeebled ; [시들다] wither ; fade ; [쇠망] decline ; go into decay ; [쇠퇴] fall off ; fail ; dwindle ; fall away ¶ 명성이 쇠하다 fall into the shade ; be on the wane // 건강이 쇠하다 decline〔be broken〕 in health ; fail in one's health // 기억력이 쇠하여 가다 one's memory is failing // 나의 몸은 나날이 쇠하여 가고 있다 I am wasting away (in body) day after day.
쇠혀 [소의 혀] a cow's tongue ; [쇠서] beef tongue
쇠호두 a kind of hard walnut
쇤네 I ; me ; your servant
쇳내 smelling of rust ; a metallic taste ¶ 쇳내가 나다 give a taste of iron
쇳냥 ⇨ 돈냥
쇳덩이 a lump of metal
쇳독 —毒 metallic poison(ing)
쇳돌 ore
쇳물 a metallic stain ; a rust spot ; rusty water ¶ 셔츠에 쇳물이 묻었다 You have a rust spot in your shirt.
쇳밥 iron chips
쇳소리 a metallic sound
쇳조각 an iron piece ; a scrap of iron
쇳줄 a mineral vein ; a vein of ore
쇼 a show
— 걸 a show girl **— 윈도** a show window ¶ 쇼 윈도를 장식하다 dress a show window // 쇼 윈도를 구경하고 다니다 windowshop ; go window-shopping **— 케이스** a showcase
쇼맨 a showman
—쉽〔기질〕 showmanship ¶ 쇼맨쉽이 농후하다 be quite a showman ; be affected in one's manner
쇼크 a shock ¶ 쇼크를 받다 be shocked // 쇼크를 주다 give 《a person》 a shock
—사(死) death from shock ¶ 페니실린 주사에 의한 쇼크사 death due to shock from a penicillin injection
쇼킹 ¶ 쇼킹한 shocking // 쇼킹한 사건 a shocking accident
†**쇼핑** shopping **—하다** shop ; do one's 〔the〕 shopping ¶ 어디에서 주로 쇼핑하십니까 Where do you usually shop ?
—백 a shopping bag **— 센터** a shopping center
†**쇼트** ① 〖야구〗 a shortstop ¶ 쇼트를 보다 play shortstop ② [단편] a short (소설·영화의) ③ 〖전기〗 a short circuit
쇼트케이크 a shortcake
쇼트팬츠 《a pair of》 shorts
숄 a shawl ¶ 숄을 두르다 wear〔put on〕 a shawl

수 [수컷] a male ; a cock (새의) ; a bull (소·고래 따위의) ; [접두어] male ; bull ; he ; cock ; tom ¶ 수컷 a male // 수캐 a male dog // 수코양이 a tomcat ; a he-cat ; a male cat // 수탉 a rooster ; a cock // 수퇘지 a boar (pig)

수 手 ① [손] a hand
② [수단] a means〔way〕; a hand ; [꾀] a trick ; a game ; [장기 따위의] a move ¶ 어떻게 할 수가 없다 be in a deadlock ; have no control 《over》; be utterly beyond control ; there is no help for it // 수를 바꾸다 resort to other means ; try some other means ; change one's plan ; sing another tune (태도를 바꾸다) // 수에 넘어가다 be fooled by a trick ; be taken in ; play into the hands of 《the enemy》// 백방으로 수를 다하다 try all possible means〔every means in one's power〕// 할 수 밖에 없다 cannot help doing ; have no choice but to do // 그런 수에는 안 넘어 간다 None of your games ! /That trick won't do with me. / You can't use that excuse again. // 그것 좋은 순데 That's a wise course to take 〔follow〕. // 참 그런 수도 있어 I see that's another course open. // 두서너 수면 이길 수 있었는데 Another two or three moves and I should have won the match. // 또 그 수로군 The same old game ! // 수를 바꾸어 보자 We shall try it some other way 〔another means〕. // 역시 당신은 나보다 한 수 위〔아래〕다 After all, you are a cut above〔below〕me.
③ [가능성·능력] possibility ; ability ; capacity ¶ 세계 대전이 일어날 수도 있다 There is the possibility of another world war happening. // 그는 영어를 가르칠 수 있다 He is able to teach English. /He is capable of teaching English. // 우리들이 이길 수는 없다 There is no possibility of our victory. // 새 극장은 1,200명을 수용할 수 있다 The new theater has a (seating) capacity of 1,200. / The new theater has seating accommodation for〔can seat〕1,200 people.

수 水 〖민속〗 (the essence of) Water (regarded as representing North, Winter, and Black)

수 秀 [학업 성적의] Excellent ; A 《미》 ¶ 전과목 수 straight A's // 전과목 수의 학생 a straight A student // 전과목 수로 졸업하다 graduate 《from a school》 with an all-A record〔with straight A's〕// 사회과에서 수를 받다 get "A" for social studies

†**수 數** ① [운수] luck ; fortune ¶ 수가 좋다〔나쁘다〕 have good〔bad〕fortune // 수가 나다 run into a piece of good luck
② [수효] a number ; a figure ¶ 수 많은 many ; numerous ; a great many ; a large number of // 수를 세다 count ; take count of // 수를 맞추다 make up the count // 수없이 많다 be innumerable ; be without number // 수가 한정되어 있다 be limited in number // 수가 많다 be many ; be large in number // 수가 적다 be few ; be small in number // 학생수가 600에 가깝다 The number of students is close to six hundred. /The students number nearly 600. // 수로 압도당했다 They were overwhelmed by numbers. // 수로써는 당할 수가 없다 They exceed us in number. /We are outnumbered by them.
③ [몇] a few ; several ¶ 수년 후에 after several〔a few〕years

수 壽 ① [장수] long life ; longevity
② [연령] one's age ¶ 수하다 enjoy a long life ; live long // 수가 짧다 be short-lived

수 繡 embroidery ¶ 수놓다 embroider // 금실로 화조(花鳥)를 수놓다 embroider figures of birds and flowers in gold thread
—틀 a taboret ; an embroidery frame

수 首 a piece ; a poem ; a selection ¶ 시 한 수를 짓다 compose a poem

수간 樹幹 a tree trunk ; a shaft

수간 數間 ¶ 수간 두옥 a small hut

수간 獸姦 bestiality ; zooerastia

수감 收監 confinement ; commitment ; imprisonment **—하다** confine〔put〕in prison ; imprison ; commit 《a person》 to prison ¶ 수감중이다 be in confinement
— 영장 a warrant for imprisonment 〔confinement〕; a commitment

수감 隨感 occasional thoughts〔impressions〕; random thoughts
—록 stray notes ; essays ; impressions 《of Korea》

수갑 手匣 handcuffs ; manacles ⇨ 쇠고랑 ¶ 수갑을 채우다 put handcuffs on 《a person》; handcuff 《a person》

수갑 水閘 a lock 《of a canal, river》
— 고저도(高低度) a lockage **—세** toll paid for a lock ; lockage

수강 受講 attending a lecture **—하다** attend a lecture ; take a course
—생 a trainee ; a person present at a lecture class (강습회의) ; a participant (참가자)

수개 修改 repair ; improvement **—하다** repair ; improve ; mend

수개 數箇 several 《items》; a few 《pieces》

수갱 竪坑 a shaft ; a pit

***수건 手巾** a towel ; a handkerchief (손수건) ¶ 수건으로 닦다 wipe〔rub〕with a towel ; dry 《one's hand》 on a towel // 수건을 짜다 wring a towel (out, dry) // 수건을 축이다 moisten a towel
—걸이 a towel-hanger **— 돌리기** (a game of) drop-the-handkerchief **세수 —** a face towel

수검 受檢 —하다 be inspected ; be subjected to inspection ; undergo〔go through〕an examination
—자 an examinee ; a subject of inspec-

tion
수검 搜檢 inspection ; check(ing) ; examination —하다 inspect ; check ; examine
수결 手決 one's signature
수결을 두다 [관용] sign
수경 水景 a water view ; a waterscape
—화 a waterscape (painting)
수경법 水耕(法) hydroponics ; water culture ; tank farming
— 농장 a hydroponic farm
수경성 水硬性 〖화학〗 hydraulicity ; hydraulic property
— 시멘트 hydraulic cement〔lime, mortar〕
수계 水系 water system
수계 水界 [지구 표면의] the hydrosphere
수계 授戒 giving commandments (of Buddhism) ; Buddhist initiation〔ceremony〕
—회 a ceremony of Buddhist confirmation
수계 受戒 receiving the commandments of Buddhism ; becoming a disciple of Buddha ; receiving Buddhist confirmation
수계수 數係數 〖수학〗 a numerical coefficient
†수고 toil ; labor ; pains ; an effort ; efforts ; trouble ; [진력] good offices ; service —하다 work〔labor〕 hard ; take pains ; suffer troubles ¶ 수고한 보람 없이 for all one's pains // 수고가 들다 require much trouble // 수고를 덜어 주다 save 《a person》 trouble // 수고에 보답하다 reward 《a person》 for his trouble // 수고를 끼치다 give〔cause〕 《a person》 trouble ; put 《a person》 to trouble ; trouble 《a person》 // 수고를 아끼지 않다 spare no pains 《to do》 ; take the trouble 《to do》 // 많은 수고를 하여 그림을 그렸다 He went to great pains to draw this picture. // 수고를 끼쳐 미안합니다 I am sorry you've been put to all this〔that〕 trouble. /I am sorry for the trouble I have caused you. // 수고하셨습니다 Many thanks for your trouble. /I appreciate what you have done. /Thanks for a job well done ! // 수고한 보람이 있었다 It was worth it. // 원로에 오시느라고 수고하셨습니다 Thanks a lot for coming down here. /You are kind enough to come (and see me) all the way. // 수고한 보람이 없었다 All the efforts were in vain. // 일부러 그런수고 할 필요 없어요 Don't go to that trouble. / Don't bother.
수고롭다 (be) troublesome ; toilsome ; laborious ; tiresome ; painstaking ¶ 수고로운 일 a laborious task〔job, work〕 // 수고롭지만 이 편지를 좀 부쳐 주시겠습니까 May I trouble you to post this letter for me ? /Do you mind posting this letter ?
수고스럽다 (be) troublesome ⇨ 수고롭다
수곡선 垂曲線 ⇨ 현수선(懸垂線)
*수공 手工 handiwork ; handicraft ; manual work ; manual arts ¶ 수공이 들다 take much trouble ; involve much labor
— 교육 manual training —업 manual trade〔labor〕 ; handicraft —업자 a handicraftsman —업품 handiworks —품 a piece of handiwork
수공 水攻 flooding ; attacking an enemy citadel by flooding it〔by cutting off its water supply〕 ¶ 성을 수공하다 flood〔inundate〕 a castle ; [물을 끊다] cut off the water-supply to a castle
수공 殊功 ⇨ 수훈(殊勳)
수공예 手工藝 handicraft ; manual arts and crafts
—품 a piece of handicraft〔handiwork〕
수관 樹冠 〖식물〗 the crown (of a tree)
수관 水管 a water pipe
수괴 首魁 a ringleader
수괴 羞愧 shame ; disgrace
†수교 手交 handing (over) —하다 hand over ; deliver ; place 《a thing》 in another's hand ¶ 편지를 그에게 수교해 주시오 Please give this letter into his own hands.
수교 修交 amity ⇨ 수호(修好)
수교위 dumplings stuffed with beef and cucumber
수구 水球 〖운동〗 water polo
수구 壽具 a shroud and its accessories ; cerements ; graveclothes
수구 守舊 conservatism ; adherence to traditional customs —하다 be conservative ; adhere to traditional customs
— 세력 conservative force —파 the conservatives
수구레 tough beef directly under the skin
수구막이 the land obstructing the view of the mouth of a river
수국 水菊 〖식물〗 a hydrangea
수군 水軍 the naval forces
수군거리다 talk in whispers ; speak under one's breath ¶ 수군수군 in a undertone ; in whispers // 그들은 서로 몇번이나 수군거렸다 Many whispers passed between them. // 귀에다 대고 수군거리다 whisper in 《a person's》 ear
수굿이 drooping〔hanging〕 low
수굿하다 be drooping〔hanging〕 low ; be bowed〔lowered〕
수궁 守宮 〖동물〗 a gecko ; a wall lizard
수권 水圈 the hydrosphere
수권 授權 authorization ; delegation of legal power
— 대리인 an authorized agent — 자본 authorized capital
수그러지다 ① [머리가] hang down ; droop ; drop ; dangle ; be bowed ¶ 졸려서 머리가 수그러지다 one's head hangs heavy with sleep // 그의 업적에는 머리가 수그러진다 I bow down in admiration before his achievement. // 저 사람의 인내력에는 머리가 수그러진다 I take off my hat to his perseverance.

② [기세·정도] fall ; sink ; go down ; drop ; abate ¶ 몸의 열이 수그러지다 The fever abates. // 그의 분노가 수그러졌다 His anger was appeased. // 시세가 수그러졌다 The market price is on the wane. // 폭풍이 수그러졌다 The storm has abated〔died down〕.

⁑수그리다 lower (one's head) ; hang ; droop ; drop ; bow ⇨ 숙이다

수금 水禽 a waterfowl ; a water bird ; an aquatic bird
—류 swimmers ; Natatores

수금 囚禁 imprisonment ; confinement

⁑수금 收金 bill collecting ; collection of money —하다 collect money ; collect bills ¶ 수금하러 다니다 go round bill collecting
—원 a debt collector ; a bill collector

수금 竪琴 a harp ; a lyre (고대 그리스의)

수급 需給 supply and demand ; demand and supply ¶ 수급을 조정하다 keep the balance of demand and supply
— 계기(計器) a utility meter — 계획 a supply and demand program — 관계 supply-demand relation ; relations between supply and demand — 조정 adjustment of demand and supply

수급 收給 income and outgo ; [국가의] revenue and expenditure

수급 首級 a decapitated head

수급자 受給者 a recipient 《of a pension》

수긍 首肯 assent ; consent ; a nod (in approval) —하다 assent to ; consent to ; nod in approval of ; [납득하다] be convinced 《of, that》 ; be persuaded 《of, that》 ¶ 수긍시키다 win 《a person's》 consent ; convince 《a person》 of〔that〕 ; persuade 《a person》 of // 이렇게 설명하면 쉽게 수긍이 갈 것입니다 I think this explanation is sufficiently convincing. // 그의 의견에는 수긍할 수가 없다 I cannot endorse his opinion.

수기 手技 the manual arts ; handicraft(s)

수기 手記 a note ; a memo(randum) 《*pl.* ~s, -da》 ; a memoir ¶ 수기를 적다 note down ; take note of

수기 手旗 a flag ; a general's flag (장군기)
— 신호 flag signaling〔semaphore〕 ; flag-wagging (속) ¶ 수기 신호를 하다 signal with flags〔by flagging〕 ; flag-signal

수기목 〖식물〗 a Japanese cedar ; a cryptomeria

수기 응변 隨機應變 ⇨ 임기 응변(臨機應變)

수꽃 〖식물〗 a male flower

수꽃술 〖식물〗 a stamen

수꿀하다 a (be) horrible ; horrifying ; shuddering

수나다 數— hit a jackpot ; have unexpected luck

수나사 a male screw

수나이 weaving fabrics on halves

수낙 受諾 acceptance ⇨ 수락

수난 水難 ① [해난] a disaster by water ; sea casualties ¶ 수난을 당하다 be drowned (익사하다) ; be shipwrecked (난파하다) // 수난으로 아들을 잃다 lose one's son by drowning
② [수해] flood-disaster ⇨ 수해
— 구조 rescue at sea

†수난 受難 suffering ; a severe trial ; ordeals ; crucifixion —하다 suffer ¶ 예수의 수난 the sufferings of Christ on the cross ; the (Saviour's) Passion
—극 a Passion play —상 a crucifix —악 Passion music —일 Good Friday —주 Passion Week

*수납 收納 [농산물의] purchase ; collection ; [금전의] receipt —하다 [농산물을] purchase ; crop ; reap ; [금전을] receive
—계(원) a receiver ; [은행의] a receiving teller —액 the amount received —장 an account book — 전표 a receipt (voucher) ; a receiving slip 국고 —금 money taken into the (National) Treasury

수냇소 a calf reared by a future borrower

수냉식 水冷式 water-cooling system ¶ 수냉식의 water-cooled // 수냉식 엔진 a water-cooled engine

*수녀 修女 a nun ; a sister 《of the Catholic Church》 ; a sister of charity ¶ 수녀가 되다 enter〔go into〕 a convent ; take the veil ; take the vows of a nun
—원 a nunnery ; a convent ¶ 수녀원장 a mother superiors ; an abbess

수년 數年 several years ; some〔a few〕 years ; a number of years ¶ 수년간 for several years ; for some years // 수년 전 some years ago // 앞으로 수년간 for some years ahead〔to come〕

수놈 a male ¶ 그 개 수놈입니까 암놈입니까 Is that dog a he or a she? ⇨ 수컷

수뇌 首腦 the brains ; the heads〔chiefs〕 ; the leaders ¶ 정당의 수뇌 the soul of a party // 참모 본부의 수뇌 the brains of the General Staff // 3수뇌 회담 the big-three talks〔conference〕 // 혁명의 수뇌자가 되다 play the leading part in a revolution
—부 the chief〔top-level〕 executives 《of a company》 ; the governing body —자 the head ; the leader ; the leading role ¶ 미국 정부의 수뇌자 the heads of the American Government — 회담 a summit〔top-level〕 conference〔meeting〕 ; a talk〔conference〕 at the top〔summit〕

수뇌 髓腦 〖해부〗 the myelencephalon

수뇨관 輸尿管 〖해부〗 the urethra
—염 urethritis

수눅 the seam of a stocking patch
— 버선 a kind of baby socks〔bootees〕

수다 數多 ① [다수] a great many ⇨ 다수
② [말이 많음] talkativeness ; loquaci-

ty ; garrulity ; gab ¶ 수다쟁이 a talkative person ; a prattler ; a chatterbox (여자) // 수다쟁이 할머니 an old gossip // 쓸데 없이 수다를 떠는 여자 a woman garrulous about trifles // 수다를 떨지 마라 Shut your big mouth. // 수다는 웅변이 아니다 A wealth of words is not eloquence. // 그는 수다쟁이다 He has a big〔loud〕 mouth./ He is a big〔loud〕 mouth./He is big 〔loud〕-mouthed. // 나는 수다쟁이라서 그것을 비밀로 할 수 있을는지 모르겠다 I'm such a blabbermouth. I don't know if I can keep that a secret.

수다를 부리다 관용 chatter verbosely ; talk a blue streak ; wag one's chin 〔tongue〕

수다스럽다 數多— (be) talkative ; garrulous ; loquacious ; wordy ; prattling ; chattering ¶ 수다스러운 여자 a lady gossip // 그 여자는 여간 수다스럽지 않다 She is a confirmed gossip.

수다하다 [많다] (be) many ; numerous

수단 Sudan 《아프리카 북동부의 독립국》 ¶ 수단의 Sudanese

— 사람 a Sudanese

†**수단** 手段 a means ; a measure ; a way ; a step ; [궁리] device ; [방편] an expedient ; a shift ¶ 정당한 수단 a justifiable means〔step〕 // 수단과 방법 ways and means // 부정한 수단 a foul means ; an unjust step // 효과적인 수단 (an) effective 〔effectual〕 means ; an efficient step // 평화적 수단 a peaceful means // 외교적 수단 diplomatic means〔steps, moves〕 // 단호한 수단 a decisive〔drastic〕 measure 〔step〕 // 비열한 수단 a dirty trick // 일시적 수단 makeshift ; an expedient // 최후의 수단 the last measure〔shift, resort〕 // 목적을 달성하기 위한 수단 a means to an end // 최후의 수단으로서 as a last resort // 수단을 취하다 take a measure〔step〕 ; adopt a means〔measure〕 ; resort to a means ; make〔take〕 a move 《on a case》 // 수단을 강구하다 devise a means ; find a measure 《for》 // 갖은 수단을 다 쓰다 exhaust every means ; leave no means untried ; leave no stone unturned // 할 수 있는 수단을 다하다 take all possible steps ; adopt all the means in one's power // 그 외에는 수단이 없다 No other means〔No alternative〕 is left./This is the only remaining alternative. // 내빼는 것 밖에 수단이 없었다 Flight was my only resource. // 그는 목적을 달성키 위해선 수단을 가리지 않는다 He will accomplish his purpose by fair means or foul〔by hook or by crook〕.

수단 繡緞 a kind of brocade

수단추 a male snap〔fastener〕 ; a stud ; a button

*__수달__ 水獺 〖동물〗 an otter

—피 an otter skin〔fur〕

수답 水畓 a paddy field ; a wet field

‡**수당** 手當 an allowance ; a bonus (상여) ¶ 매달의 수당 a monthly allowance // 수당이 많다 have a good allowance // 수당을 주다 give an allowance // 1만원의 수당을 지급하다 allow 《a person》 10,000 *won* ; give an allowance of 10,000 *won* to 《a person》 // 시간외 근무에는 초과 수당을 받는다 You are paid extra for overtime. // 그는 2만원의 수당을 받고 있다 He is allowed twenty thousand *won* a month.

—금 a pecuniary aid 가족 — a family allowance 근무지 — a worksite allowance 연말 — a year-end bonus 전시〔피복〕 — a war〔clothing〕 allowance 초과 근무 — an overtime allowance 통근〔부양, 지역〕 — a commutation〔dependent, regional〕 allowance 퇴직 — a retirement〔severance〕 allowance 특별〔임시〕— a special〔temporary〕 allowance

수대 手帶 〖카톨릭〗 a maniple

수대 獸帶 〖천문〗 the zodiac ; the girdle

수더분하다 (be) simple and honest ; artless ; unsophisticated ; naive ; simple-hearted〔-minded〕 ¶ 수더분한 사람 an easygoing person // 수더분한 시골 노인 an old countryman, simple and honest by nature

†**수도** 水道 [설비] water works ; water service〔supply〕 ; [수로] an aqueduct ; a water duct ; a water course ; [용수] city water ; service water ; service pipes ¶ 수도가 없는 가정 a home with no service pipes // 수도를 놓다 have water pipes laid ; have water supplied // 수도를 틀다 〔잠그다〕 turn on〔off〕 water // 댁에선 수도를 쓰십니까 우물을 쓰십니까 Do you use city or well water ?

—꼭지 a tap ; a hydrant ¶ 수도꼭지를 틀어 놓다 leave a tap open — 공사 water (-supply) works —관 a water〔service〕 pipe ; a water main (본관) —교 an aqueduct (bridge) —국(局) the Waterworks Bureau —료 water rates 〔charges〕 —물 city〔service〕 water — 수원지 a catchment area

수도 水稻 a waterfield〔moist-land〕 rice plant ; aquatic rice

수도 囚徒 a prisoner ; a (criminal) convict ; a jailbird (미·구)

수도 受渡 receipt and delivery —하다 receive 《payment》 and deliver 《goods》

수도 首都 a capital (city) ; a metropolis

‡**수도** 修道 cultivation of oneself ; asceticism ; spiritual discipline

—사 a monk ; a friar (탁발승) — 서원 monastic vows —승 a monk —원 a religious house ; a monastery ; a cloister ; an abbey (대수도원) ; [수녀원] a convent ; a nunnery —원 생활 monasticism ; a monastic life —원장 a superior ; an abbot ; an archimandrite ; the Father Superior —회 a religious〔monastic〕 order ; an order (of religious regu-

lations) ; a congregation
수도 隧道 a tunnel
수도권 首都圈 the National Capital region ; the Metropolitan area
수동 受動 passivity ; passiveness ¶ 수동의 passive // 수동적으로 passively // 그는 활동적인 사람이지 수동적인 사람은 아니다 He is a man of active, not of passive, nature. // 그는 수동적인 기질의 소유자다 He is a man of passive disposition.
—성 범죄 〖법〗 a passive crime —태 〖문법〗 the passive voice
수동 手動 ¶ 수동의 hand-operated 〔worked〕 ; manual
— 브레이크 a hand brake — 펌프 a hand pump
수동 樹洞 a hollow in an old tree trunk
수두 水痘 〖의학〗 chicken pox ; varicella
수두룩하다 (be) abundant ; plentiful ; overflowing ¶ 달걀을 그릇에 수두룩하게 담다 fill a vessel full of eggs // 시장에는 물건이 수두룩하다 The market is glutted with commodities. // 돈이 수두룩하다 have plenty〔lots〕 of money // 할 일이 수두룩하다 We have a plenty of work to do. // 이 강에는 고기가 수두룩하다 This river abounds with fish. // 이런 종류는 세상에 수두룩하다 This is quite an ordinary type.
수득수득 dried up hard〔severely〕 —하다 be all dried up
수들수들 dried up partially —하다 be partially dried up ; be (a bit) withered
수때우다 數— forestall predicted bad luck by deliberately undergoing a lesser hardship beforehand ; exorcise
수땜 數— forestalling predicted bad luck by deliberately undergoing a lesser hardship beforehand
수떨다 make a fuss ; bustle
수라 水剌 a royal meal ; the king's dinner ¶ 수랏간 a royal kitchen // 수랏상 a royal table
수라장 修羅場 a scene of utter confusion ; a pandemonium ; a scene of violence ¶ 수라장화하다 become a scene of carnage // 회장은 수라장이 되었다 The meeting-hall was thrown into great confusion.
†수락 受諾 acceptance ; agreement —하다 accept ; agree to
수란 水卵 a poached egg
—자 an egg poacher
수란을 뜨다 관용 poach an egg
수란관 輸卵管 〖해부〗 an oviduct ; the Fallopian tubes
수람 收攬 grasping —하다 win ; grasp ; take hold of ¶ 인심을 수람하다 win the hearts of the people ; win the people over
수량 水量 the quantity〔volume〕 of water ; water volume ¶ 수량이 는다 The water increases in volume.
—계 a water gauge〔meter〕
수량 數量 quantity ; volume ¶ 수량이 늘다〔줄다〕 increase〔decrease〕 in quantity // 수량에 있어서 능가하다 exceed in quantity
수럭수럭 lively ; vivacious —하다 ⇨ 수럭스럽다
수럭스럽다 (be) vivacious ; lively ; cheerful ; gay ; sprightly
수렁 a slough ; a quagmire ; a bog ; a mire ¶ 수렁에 빠지다 fall in the mire ; be〔get〕 bogged
—논〔배미〕 a marshy〔swampy〕 rice field
†수레 a wagon ; a cart ; a carriage ; a vehicle
—바퀴 a wagon wheel —홈 a rut
수려 秀麗 grace ; beauty —하다 (be) graceful ; beautiful ; handsome ; fine ; comely ¶ 수려한 금강산의 모습 the graceful figure of Mt. *Kumkang* // 수려한 산모습이 보인다 We see the graceful figure of the mountain.
*수력 水力 water power ; hydraulic power ¶ 수력을 이용하다 make use of hydraulic 〔water〕 power
— 공학 hydraulic engineering — 기계 a hydraulic machine — 발동기〔기중기〕 a hydraulic motor〔crane〕 — 발전 water-power generation ; generation of hydroelectric power — 발전소 a water-〔hydroelectric-〕power station〔plant〕 ; a hydropower plant〔station〕 — 승강기 a hydraulic lift ; a hydraulic elevator 《미》 — 자원 water-power resources — 전기 hydroelectricity —학 hydraulics
수련 修鍊 training ; practice ; culture ; discipline ; drill —하다 train ; practice ; cultivate ; discipline
—생 novice —원 novitiate —의(醫) an apprentice doctor 정신 — training of the mind
수련 睡蓮 〖식물〗 a water lily ; a pond lily
수련하다 (be) gentle ; kind ; sweet ; tender ; meek
수렴 收斂 ① [가혹한 세금] levying and collecting of heavy taxes ; exaction ② [수축] astriction ; contraction ; 〖수학·생리·물리〗 convergence ③ [추렴] joint contribution ④ [금욕] continence —하다 exact ; collect strictly〔mercilessly〕 ; (be) astringent ; astrictive ; contract ; converge
— 광속(光速) a convergent pencil of light〔rays〕 — 급수 〖수학〗 a convergent series (of numbers) —성(性) astringency — 적용 astriction —제 an astringent ; an astrictive —현상 〖생물〗 convergence
수렴청정 垂簾聽政 regency by the queen mother (from behind the veil)
*수렵 狩獵 shooting 《영》 ; hunting 《미》 ¶ 수렵하러 가다 go shooting〔hunting〕
—가 a hunter ; a huntress (여자) ; a

sportsman ; a Nimrod — 금지기 the close season —기 the hunting season ; the open season —법 the game law〔acts〕—장 a (game) preserve —조 a game fowl〔bird〕—지 a hunting ground — 허가증 a shooting license ; a hunting license —회〔여행〕a hunting〔shooting〕party〔trip〕

수령 守令 a magistrate ; a local governor

수령 首領 a leader ; the head ; the chief ; a boss ; a chieftain (산적의) ; a ringleader ¶ 보수당의 수령 Y씨 Mr. Y, leader of the Conservatives // 수령이 되다 assume the leadership《of a party》; lead a party

수령 受領 receipt ; acceptance —하다 receive ; accept ; be in receipt《of》; be (the) recipient of ; [사물이 주어] be placed in one's hand ¶ 금패를 수령하다 receive〔obtain, be awarded, take〕a gold medal // 1등상 금패를 수령하다 carry off the first-class gold medal // 정히 수령하였습니다 Received with thanks.

—국 a recipient country —자 a receiver ; a recipient ¶ 명예 학위 수령자 an honorary degree recipient // 금패 수령자 a gold medalist —증 a receipt

수령 樹齡 the age of a tree

†수로 水路 a waterway ; a watercourse ; [항해로] a lane

— 관측소 a hydrographic observatory —교 an aqueduct (bridge) —도(圖) a hydrographic map —지(誌) sailing directions ; a pilot — 측량 a hydrographical survey — 측량술 hydrography — 표지 a beacon —학 hydrography —학자 a hydrographer

수로 안내 水路案內 [안내하는 일] pilotage ; piloting ; [사람] a pilot ¶ 수로 안내를 하다 pilot《a boat》// 수로 안내를 요청하다 take on a pilot

—료 pilotage (dues) —선 a pilot boat 공인 —인 a licensed pilot 입항〔출항〕—료 inward〔toward〕pilotage

수록 收錄 gathering ; collection ; [기재] recording ; mention —하다 gather ; collect ; [기재하다] record ; write down ; mention ¶ 사전에 수록되어 있다 find their places in dictionary pages ; find room in the dictionary // 이 단어는 사전에 수록되어 있지 않다 This word finds no recognition in the dictionary. /The dictionary gives no mention of this word.

*수뢰 水雷 a torpedo ; a (naval) mine (기뢰) ¶ 수뢰를 부설하다 lay〔place〕a mine ; mine // 수뢰를 발사하다 fire〔discharge〕a torpedo ; torpedo // 수뢰에 걸리다 strike〔hit〕a mine // 수뢰로 공격하다 torpedo《a vessel》

— 구축함 a torpedo-boat destroyer — 발사관 a torpedo tube — 방어망 torpedo netting — 부설 구역 the mine field — 부설함 a mine layer —정 a torpedo boat — 함대 a torpedo-boat flotilla 부유 — a buoyant mine 촉발 — a contact mine

수뢰 受賂 accepting a bribe —하다 accept〔receive〕a bribe ; be bribed

수료 修了 completion《of a course》—하다 complete ; finish《courses of study》¶ 전과정을 수료하다 complete the regular course of study // 4학년 과정을 수료하다 finish the four-year course

수류 水流 a (water) current ; a stream (of water)

— 펌프 a water-jet pump

수류 獸類 beasts ; animals ; brutes

수류탄 手榴彈 a hand grenade〔bomb〕; a pineapple《속》¶ 수류탄을 던지다 throw a hand grenade at《a person》

—병 grenadier a grenade-thrower

수륙 水陸 land and water

— 공동 작전 amphibious operations — 양서 동물 an amphibian ; an amphibious animal — 양용 부대 an amphibious corps — 양용 비행기〔전차〕an amphibious plane〔tank〕; an amphibian — 양용차 Landing Vehicle Tractor《LVT》

수르르 smoothly ; gently

수리 〖새〗 an eagle

— 둥지 an aerie —부엉이 an eagle-owl

수리 水利 utilization of water ; water supply (급수) ; irrigation (관개) ; water transportation (수운) ¶ 그 지방은 수리의 편의가 있다 The locality has facilities for water transport. // 수로 공사 덕택으로 그 지방은 수리의 편의가 좋아졌다 The land is under better irrigation as a result of the construction of the canal.

— 공사 irrigation works —권 water rights ; a water concession — 사업 irrigation works〔projects〕— 조합 an irrigation association —학 hydrography

수리 受理 acceptance ; receipt —하다 accept ; receive ; take up ¶ 원서를 수리하다 receive an application // 사표를 수리하다 accept a resignation // (재판소가) 사건을 수리하다 take cognizance of a case // 10월 10일 이후의 원서는 수리하지 않는다 No application later than October 10th will be received.

†수리 修理 repair ; mending —하다 repair ; make repairs ; mend ; fix (미·구) ¶ 수리중이다 be under repair ; be undergoing repairs // 지붕을 수리하다 fix the roof // (시계점에서) 시계를 수리하다 have a watch mended // 수리하러 보내다 send《a thing》for repairs // 수리가 잘 되어 있다 be in good repair // 수리가 잘 안 되어 있다 be out of order // 네 차는 지금쯤 수리가 불가능할지도 모르겠다 I'm afraid your car may be beyond repair by now.

—공 a repairman — 공장 a repair shop ¶ 자동차 수리 공장 an auto repair shop —비 repairing charges ; the cost of

repairing
수리 數理 [수학 이론] a mathematical principle ; [계산법] mathematics ¶ 수리적(으로) mathematical(ly) // 수리적 두뇌가 있다 have a head for mathematics
— 경제학〔**통계학, 물리학**〕 mathematical economics〔statistics, physics〕
수리검 手裏劍 a throwing-knife《*pl.* knives》 ¶ 수리검을 던지다 throw a knife 《at a person》
수리딸기 a kind of wild strawberry
수리먹다 《a chestnut ; an acorn》 become〔go〕 soft
수리수리 —하다 have one's sight dimmed with fever ; (be) feverish
수리치 〖식물〗 a kind of marsh plant ; Serratula deltoides (학명)
수리학 水理學 〖토목〗 hydraulics
수림 樹林 a wood(s) ; a forest
—길 a forest path
수립 樹立 establishment **—하다** establish ; set up ; found ¶ 계획을 수립하다 devise〔work out, formulate〕 a plan // 신정부를 수립하다 form a new government // 국책을 수립하다 establish〔formulate〕 a national policy
수마 睡魔 drowsiness ; sleepiness ; somnolence ; (the arms of) Morpheus ; [의인적] the sandman ; the dustman ¶ 수마에 붙들리다 become drowsy〔sleepy〕; be overpowered by drowsiness ; go to the land of Nod // 수마와 싸우다 try not to fall asleep
수마 水魔 a flood ; an inundation
수만 數萬 tens〔scores〕 of thousands ; myriads ¶ 수만의 관객 scores of thousands of spectators
수말 a male horse
수말 水沫 ① [거품] a bubble ; a foam ; a froth ② [물보라] spray ; a splash
수매 收買 (a) purchase ; buying ; [정부의] procurement **—하다** purchase ; buy (out) ¶ 정부의 미곡 수매 가격 the Government's purchasing price of rice
수맥 水脈 a water vein ; a water stratum 《*pl.* -ta》
⁑**수면 水面** the surface of the water ¶ 수면에서 한자 위〔밑〕(에) one foot above 〔below〕 the surface (of the water) // 수면에 떠오르다 come up〔rise〕 to the surface (of the water) ; surface (잠수함이)
†**수면 睡眠** sleep ; slumber **—하다** sleep ; slumber ; have a sleep ¶ 수면중 in one's sleep // 수면중에 사망하다 die in one's sleep // 수면을 방해하다 disturb 《a person's》 sleep // 충분한 수면을 취하다 have enough〔sufficient, a good〕 sleep // 수면중이다 He is sleeping〔asleep〕.
—병 sleeping sickness **— 부족** want 〔lack〕 of sleep ; curtailed sleep ; ¶ 그의 신경 쇠약은 수면 부족이 원인이다 His nervous prostration is due to want of sleep.
— 시간 sleeping hours ; hours of sleep ¶ 수면 시간을 줄이다 curtail〔cut down〕 sleep ; rob oneself of sleep **—제** a sleeping drug〔tablet, pill〕; sleeping powder (분말) ; a narcotic (마취제) ; a soporific
⁑**수명 壽命** the length〔span〕 of life ; life span ; life ¶ 인간의 평균 수명 the average span of a man's life // 자동차의 수명 the expected life span of a motor car // 수명이 길다〔짧다〕 be long-〔short-〕 lived ; have a long〔short〕 life // 수명이 연장되다 take a new lease of life // 한국 사람의 평균 수명은 70이다 The average life span of Korean people is seventy. // 내각의 평균 수명은 2년이다 The average life span of the cabinet is two years. // 그 내각은 수명이 짧았다 That cabinet was short-lived. // 그녀는 수명을 다했다 She died a natural death.
평균 — the average span of (human) life ; the average life expectancy (생명 보험의) ¶ 자동차의 평균 수명은 얼마나 됩니까 What's the average life span of a car ?
수명 受命 commission
— 법관〔**판사**〕 a commissioned judge
수모 手母 a bridesmaid
수모 受侮 scorn ; disdain ; slight **—하다** be insulted ; be humiliated ; suffer insult〔humiliation〕
수모 首謀 ⇨ 주모(主謀)
수모 誰某 certain ones ; so and so
수모자 首謀者 a ringleader ; a prime mover ; the chief plotter
수목 cloth made of used〔secondhand〕 cotton
*__수목 樹木__ a tree ; an arbor 《*pl.* arbores》; [총칭] trees (and shrubs) ¶ 수목이 없는 woodless ; naked ; bare (of trees) // 수목이 울창한 woody ; wooded ; arboreous // 수목으로 덮인 tree-covered 《hills》 // 수목으로 둘러 싸인 embowered 《house》
— 숭배 dendrolatry **—원** an arboretum ; a tree garden **—학** dendrology **—한계선** the timberline
수무지개 the brighter arch of a twin rainbow
수묵 水墨 India ink ; [수묵화] a painting in India ink
—화(畫) a painting in India ink ; an Indian ink painting ; a black-and-white drawing
수묵 지다 관용 get smudged
수묵 치다 관용 cover up ; gloss over 《a mistake》
수문 手紋 the lines in the palm of the hand
수문 水門 a floodgate ; a lock ; a sluice
수문 水紋 a water ring ; [무늬] water 〔wavy〕 patterns in silk
수문 守門 keeping〔guarding〕 a gate
—군 sentries ; guards
수문수답 隨問隨答 —하다 follow questions with answers ; answer readily ;

have ready answers
수미 首尾 beginning and end ; alpha and omega ¶ 수미 일관하여 consistently ; all of a piece // 수미 상접하다 be continuous ; run in unbroken succession
수미 愁眉 knitted eyebrows ; a worried look
수밀도 水密桃 (a kind of) peach
수박 【식물】 a watermelon
수박 겉핥기 superficiality ; shallowness ¶ 수박 겉핥기의 지식 a superficial〔half〕 knowledge
수반 首班 a head ; [내각 수반] the premier ¶ 내각의 수반 the head of a cabinet ; the chief executive 《미》// 수반이 되다 occupy the first place ; stand at the head ; head 《the Cabinet》// 수반으로 지명하다 designate 《a person》 the premier 《of a new administration》
**수반 隨伴 accompaniment ; concomitance ──하다 accompany ; go〔come〕 with ; be concomitant with
─자 an attendant ; a follower ; a suite 《총칭》
수반 水盤 a basin ; [꽃꽂이용의] a flower bowl〔basin〕
수발 鬚髮 beard and hair
수방 水防 flood control ; prevention of floods ; defense against floods
─ 대책 a measure to prevent floods ─ 본부 the flood defense headquarters ─ 훈련 a flood-fighting drill
수방석 繡方席 an embroidered cushion
수배 手配 arrangements ; preparations ; [배치] disposition of men ──하다 arrange ; prepare ; make arrangements 〔preparations〕 ; make dispositions ¶ 경찰에서 수배중인 사람 a man wanted by the police // 수배가 잘되다 be well arranged 《for》// 요소마다 수배하다 make dispositions at important points // 사방으로 수배하여 찾다 send men in all directions in search of 《a person》// 환영회의 수배를 하다 make arrangements for the reception
─ 사진 a photograph of a wanted criminal ; an art 《미·속》 ─자 [경찰의] a criminal wanted by the police ; a fugitive from justice ; a wanted man
수배 受配 ──하다 draw one's rations
─자 a recipient of rations〔distribution, a dividend〕
수배 數倍 several times ¶ 수배로 늘어나다 increase several times // 높이가 이것의 수배다 It is several times as high as this.
수백 數百 hundreds ¶ 수백명 several hundred people ; hundreds of people
수백만 數百萬 millions ¶ 수백만명 millions of people
수범 首犯 the principal (offender) ⇨ 주범(主犯)
수범 垂範 setting an example ──하다 set an example ¶ 솔선수범하다 take the initiative and set an example 《for others》
수법 手法 technique ; technical skill ; mechanism ; style ; mannerism (틀에 박힌)
수변 水邊 the water's edge ; the edge of the water ; the waterside
수병 水兵 a sailor ; a seaman ; a blue jacket ; a (Jack) tar 《속》 ; a devil dog 《미·속》
─모 a sailor('s) hat ─복 a sailor suit 〔uniform〕 1등〔2등〕 ─ a first-〔second-〕 class seaman
수병 水甁 a (water) jar〔jug〕
수병 守兵 a guard ; a garrison 《총칭》 ; guards
수병 繡屛 an embroidered folding screen
수보다 數─ tell〔read〕 one's fortune ; have one's fortune told
수복 收復 reclamation ; recovery ──하다 reclaim ; recover ; repatriate
─민 repatriated people ─ 지구 a reclaimed area
수복 修復 ──하다 repair ; mend ; [답장하다] reply
수복 壽福 long life and happiness ¶ 수복강녕 long life, happiness and peace
수부 水夫 a sailor ; a seaman ; a mariner ; a seafarer ; a Jack tar 《속》 ¶ 노련한 수부 an old salt ; a shellback ; a veteran seaman // 수부가 되다 become a sailor ; go to sea
─장(長) a boatswain
수부 首府 a capital ; a metropolis ⇨ 수도
수부 首部 [미사일의 원추부] a nose cone
수부종 planting seed directly in a paddy (without transplanting) ──하다 plant seed directly in a paddy
수북수북 so that all are heaped up ──하다 all are heaped up ¶ 밥을 수북수북 담다 fill a bowl heaping full of rice
수북이 heap up (mountain-high) ; fill 《a vessel》 to overflowing〔heaping〕 ; full to the brim // 접시에 먹을 것을 수북이 담다 fill a plate with food // 밥을 수북이 대접하다 serve ricebowls brimful ; fill 《the bowl》 heaping full of rice
수북하다 be heaped up ; be heaping full ¶ 할 일이 수북하다 have a heap of work to do // 쟁반에 과자가 수북하다 Cakes are heaped up on the tray.
수분 水分 moisture ; water ; juice (즙) ¶ 수분이 많은 moist ; watery ; juicy 《fruit》 ; succulent 《plant》// 수분이 많은 야채 juicy vegetables // 수분을 제거하다 dehydrate
수분 守分 ──하다 be content with one's lot ; keep to one's status in life
수분 受粉 pollination ──하다 pollinate
인공 ─ artificial pollination
수분 授粉 【식물】 fertilization ──하다 pollinate ; fertilize
수불 受拂 receipts and disbursements ; collections and payments ──하다 receive and pay ; collect and pay

—금 incomes and outgoes
수비 水肥 liquid manure
수비 守備 defense ; garrison ; 〖야구〗 the fielding ; the field **—하다** defend ; guard ; garrison ¶ 수비하고 있다 be in garrison // 수비를 맡다 be on garrison duty ; go〔be sent〕 into garrison (파견되어) ; [야구] take the field // 수비를 엄중히 하다 strengthen the defenses // 수비가 강하다〔약하다〕 They are strong〔weak〕 on defense. // 그 도시는 엄중히 수비되어 있다 The city is heavily garrisoned.
—대 a garrison ; guards ¶ 국경 수비대 the border guards ; a frontier garrison // 철도 수비대 the railway guards —병 a garrison ; a guard —율 〖야구〗 a fielding average —전 a defensive war〔fight〕 —측(側) 〖야구〗 the team in the field ; the defensive team
수빙 樹氷 silver thaw
수사 修史 compilation of a history ; historiography
***수사 修辭** rhetoric ; a figure of speech ; a rhetorical flourish ¶ 수사적 기교 a rhetorical device
—학 rhetoric ¶ 수사학상의 rhetorical —학자 a rhetorician
수사 數詞 〖문법〗 numerals
수사 修士 a monk ; a friar ; a brother ⇨ 수도승
수사 手寫 copying by hand ; a hand copy
—본 a copybook ; a book copied by hand
수사 搜査 (criminal) investigation ; search ; detection **—하다** investigate 《a case》 ; conduct an investigation ; search for ; look for ¶ 수사 방침을 바꾸다 change the plan of investigation // 범인이 수사선상에 나타나다 the criminal appears on the line of police investigation
—계 a (police) detective —과 the criminal investigation section —과원 an investigator ; an investigation agent —망 the police dragnet ¶ 수사망에 걸리다 be caught in the police dragnet // 수사망을 펴다 spread〔drop〕 the dragnet —반 a crime〔criminal investigation〕 squad —본부 the investigation headquarters —선 the line of police investigation ¶ 수사선상에 오르다 appear on the line of police investigation — 주임 the chief investigator — 카드 a 'wanted' card 과학(적) — scientific crime detection ; criminalistics 범죄 — criminal investigation 국립 과학 — 연구소 the National Scientific, Criminal & Investigation Laboratory 합동 — 반 the joint investigation team
수사납다 (be) unlucky ; unfortunate
수사돈 —査頓 the father of one's son-in-law
수산 水産 [수산물] marine〔aquatic〕 products ¶ 수산물이 풍부하다 abound〔be rich〕 in marine products
— 가공품 processed marine products — 국 the Fisheries Bureau — 기사 a marine product expert — 대학 a fisheries college —물 marine products — 시험장 a fisheries experiment station — 식(료)품 sea food —업 fisheries ; the marine products industry — 조합 a marine products association —청 the Fisheries Agency —학 fishery science ; the science of fisheries — 학교 a fisheries school — 협동 조합 the fisheries cooperative union
수산 蓚酸 〖화학〗 oxalic acid
—염 oxalate
수산 授産 providing 《people》 with work ; giving employment
수산화 水酸化 〖화학〗 hydration
—나트륨 sodium hydroxide —물 a hydroxide —바륨 barium hydroxide —아연 zinc hydroxide —암모늄 ammonium hydroxide —제이금 auric acid —제일철 ferrous hydroxide —철 hydrated iron —칼륨 potassium hydroxide —칼슘 calcium hydroxide
수삼 水蔘 fresh〔green, undried〕 ginseng
수삼차 數三次 several times
수상 水上 [수면] the water surface ; [상류] the upper reaches of a river ¶ 수상에 on the water // 수상에 뜨다 float on the water ; come up to the surface of the water (가라앉았던 것이)
— 가옥 a house built on stilts over the water — 경기 aquatic〔water〕 sports ; aquatics ¶ 수상 경기 대회 a swim meet ; an aquatic competition — 경찰 the water 〔harbor, marine〕 police — 교통 waterborne traffic —목 timber carried down river on floats —(비행)기 a water plane ; a seaplane ; a hydro- airplane ; a hydro 《구》 — 생활 aquatic life ; life on the water — 생활자 a waterfarer — 선수권 the swimming〔aquatic〕 championship — 스키 water skiing ; [도구] water skis ¶ 수상 스키를 하다 water-ski — 운동 aquatic sports〔exercise〕 — 운송 transportation by water ; water transportation
***수상 首相** the prime minister ; the premier ¶ 수상의 직 premiership // 러시아의 제 1 부수상 the first deputy premier of Russia
— 대리〔서리〕 the acting prime minister —직 premiership ; prime ministry 전— an ex-premier ; a former prime minister 제 1 부— [러시아의] a first deputy premier 영연방 — 회의 the Prime Ministers' Conference
수상 受像 television reception ; (received) image **—하다** receive the image
—관(管) a picture〔an image-receiving〕 tube —기 a television receiver〔set〕 ; a TV set 《속》 —력 [텔레비전의] reception —면 the television screen ; the tele-

screen
수상 受賞 winning a prize **—하다** receive〔win〕 a prize ; be awarded a prize ¶ 전람회에서 처음으로 수상했다 He obtained his first victory at the show.
— 소설 a prize novel **—자** a prize winner〔awardee〕 ¶ 노벨상 수상자 a winner of the Nobel Prize ; a Nobel laureate **— 작품** a prize winner
수상 授賞 awarding a prize ; prize giving **—하다** award〔give〕 a prize
수상 殊常 suspiciousness **—하다** (be) suspicious ; doubtful ; dubious ; shady ; fishy 《속》 ¶ 수상한 여자 a woman of suspicious character // 수상한 회사 a bogus company // 수상히 여기다 suspect ; feel suspicious about // 저놈이 수상하다 I suspect his guilt. // 나는 수상한 사람이 아니올시다 You must not regard me with suspicion. // 저 두 남녀의 사이가 수상하다 I suspect an undue familiarity between the two. // 그는 자선이란 이름으로 여러가지 수상한 짓을 한다 He does many questionable things in the name of charity. // 어쩐지 수상한 여자라고 생각했었다 She struck me as suspicious. // 여기 뭔가 좀 수상한데 I smell something fishy around here. /I smell a rat around here.
수상 手相 ⇨ 손금
수상 隨想 occasional〔random, stray, desultory〕 thoughts
—록 essays ; stray notes
수상 穗狀 the shape of an ear〔a spike〕 ¶ 수상의 ear-shaped
— 화서(花序) 〖식물〗 spike
수상스럽다 殊常— (be) suspicious
수색 羞色 a blush of shame ; an ashamed〔abashed〕 look ; a bashful flush
수색 愁色 a worried〔an anxious〕 look ; a gloomy〔melancholy〕 air ; the traces of sorrow ¶ 수색을 띠다 wear a worried look
†**수색 搜索** (a) search ; searching ; a hunt **—하다** search〔hunt, look〕 for ; make a search for ¶ 수색중이다 be searching for 《a person》 ; be after 《a person》 ; be in quest of ; be being searched for ; be wanted (범인을) // 수색원을 내다 ask the police to search (for a son) ; apply to the police for a search // 하천을 뒤지고 시체를 수색하다 drag a river for a dead body // 경찰에서는 범인을 수색중이다 The police are on the trail〔track〕 of the culprit. /The offender is wanted by the police.
— 구역 a search area **—권** the right of search **—대〔기, 정〕** a search(-ing) party〔plane, boat〕 **— 영장** a search warrant
수생 水生 aquatic ; living〔growing〕 in water
수서 水棲 aquatic ; living in water
— 동물 an aquatic (animal)
수서 手書 one's own handwriting ; a holograph ; an autographic letter **—하다** write for oneself ; write in one's own hand ; autograph
†**수석 首席** the top seat ; the head seat ; [사람] the head ; the chief
— 전권〔대표〕 the chief delegate ; the head of the delegation **— 판사** the chief judge **외교단 —** the doyen of the diplomatic corps
수선 fuss ; ado ; bustle ; stir ¶ 수선을 떨면서 with much ado // 수선스럽다 be tumultuous ; be noisy ; be boisterous // 밖이 수선스럽다 there is a hubbub outside // 손님을 맞느라고 수선을 피우다 make much ado to receive a guest // 하찮은 일에 수선을 피우다 make a great fuss about trifles ; raise a storm in a teacup ; make much ado about nothing
—쟁이 a fuss budget ; a chatterbox
수선을 피우다 관용 make〔raise〕 a fuss 《over》
‡**수선 修繕** repair ; mending **—하다** repair 《a house》 ; mend 《a watch, shoes》 ; refit 《ships》 ; make repairs 《on》 ; fix 《미·구》 ; [수선시키다] get 《a thing》 mended〔repaired〕

> 유의어 **mend**는 일반적인 말로서 의복 완구 따위 **repair**는 비교적 복잡한 기계나 신 따위의 수선을 의미하며 미국에서는 mend, repair 대신에 fix가 흔히 사용된다

¶ 수선중이다 be being repaired ; be under repair ; be undergoing repairs // 수선이 잘 되어 있다 be in good repair // 수선이 잘 되어 있지 않다 be in disrepair // 수선이 불가능하다 be beyond repair // 시계를 수선시키다 have a watch mended // 수선하러 보내다 send 《a thing》 for repair
—공 a repairer ; a repairman ; a mender **— 공구** repair tools **— 공장** a repair shop **—비** repairing expenses ; the cost of repairs **응급〔가(假), 대〕—** emergency 〔temporary, major〕 repairs
수선 垂線 a perpendicular (line)
수선거리다 make noise ; make〔raise〕 a fuss ; stir
수선떨다 make〔raise〕 a fuss ; fuss 《about》 ; bustle 《about》 ¶ 하찮은 일로 수선떨다 make a (great) fuss about trifles ; make much ado about nothing
수선스럽다 (be) noisy ; clamorous ; bustling ¶ 수선스러운 여자 a woman easily flurried ; a bustling woman〔girl〕
수선피우다 ⇨ 수선떨다
수선화 水仙花 〖식물〗 a daffodil (나팔 수선) ; a jonquil (노랑 수선) ; a narcissus
수성 水成 ¶ 바위가 수성인 hydrogenous
— 광상 a sedimentary deposit **—론** 〖지질〗 neptunism **—암** aqueous rocks ; sedimentary rocks

수성 水星 〖천문〗 Mercury
수성 獸性 bestiality ; beastliness ; brutality ; animality ¶ 수성의 bestial ; brutal ; carnal // 수성을 나타내다 expose brutality
수성 가스 水性— water gas
수성 도료 水性塗料 water paint
수성 유제 水性乳劑 an aqueous emulsion
수세 水勢 the force of water〔a current〕
수세 水洗 flushing ; washing
—식 변소 a flush toilet ; a water closet 《W. C.》 ¶ 수세식 변소로 개조하다 convert the lavatory into a flush toilet
수세 收稅 tax gathering〔collection〕; collection of taxes —하다 collect taxes
—리 a tax collector ; a revenue official ; a publican (고대 로마의)
수세 守勢 a defensive attitude ; the defensive ; [검술에서] parade ; guard ¶ 수세의 defensive ; passive // 수세를 취하다 assume〔take〕 the defensive ; stand on the defensive ; [야구] take the field
수세 受洗 receiving〔taking〕 baptism —하다 be baptized
수세공 手細工 handiwork ; handwork ; handicraft
수세다 手— be a good player ; be a skilled hand 《at a game》; be strong
수세미 a scrubber made from a sponge gourd
—외 a sponge gourd ; a snake gourd
수소 a bull ; a steer ; an ox
*수소 水素 〖화학〗 hydrogen ¶ 수소의 hydrogenous ; hydric
— 가스 hydrogen gas —산 hydracid — 첨가 hydrogenation — 폭탄 a hydrogen bomb ; an H-bomb ; a fusion bomb —화물 a hydride 중— heavy hydrogen
수소문 搜所聞 inquiring into rumors —하다 inquire into rumors ¶ 수소문하여 잃은 아이를 찾다 search for a lost child by tracing rumors
수속 手續 process ; procedure ; proceedings (소송의) ; formalities ; steps ; red tape —하다 go through (due) formalities ; take proceedings ; take steps 《in a matter》 ¶ 입학 수속 entrance formalities // 소송 수속 legal procedure // 법률상의 수속 legal formalities // 수속을 게을리하다 neglect the procedure ; fail to take steps // 이혼 수속을 하다 take proceedings for divorce // 수출〔수입〕 수속에 정통하다 be familiar with export〔import〕 procedure // 정식 수속을 밟다 go through due formalities // 입회 수속을 가르쳐 주십시오 tell me how to join the association. // 그것은 다만 수속상의 문제입니다 It is just a matter of procedure. // 입국 수속을 다 마쳤다 I have gone through the entry procedure. // 앞으로 귀찮은 수속은 없을 것입니다 There will be no annoying red tape to go through.
*수송 輸送 transportation ; conveyance ; traffic ; deportation ; carriage —하다 convey ; transport ; deport ; carry ¶ 수송중이다 be in transit // 군대를 수송하다 transport〔convey〕 troops // 그 생선은 원거리로 수송할 수 없다 The fish will not bear transportation to any great distance.
— 계획 a schedule of transport —기 a transport plane ¶ 군대 수송기 a troop transport plane ; a troop carrier // 화물 수송기 a cargo craft ; a sky-freighter // 대형 수송기 a sky truck —난 transport difficulties —대 〖군사〗 a transportation unit —량 the volume of traffic ; carloadings —력 transport〔transportation, carrying〕 capacity ; carrying〔transit〕 power —로 a transport route — 보험 transport insurance —선(線) a line of transportation —선(船) a transport ship — 시설 transportation facilities — 열차 a transport train — 증권 a consignment note 군사 — military transport 육상〔해상〕 — transport by land〔sea〕 항공 — air transport ; airlift
수쇄 手刷 hand-printing ¶ 수쇄의 hand-printed
— 롤러 a brayer — 인쇄기 a hand printing-press ; a handpress
수쇠 the male〔protruding〕 part of a hinge
수수 〖식물〗 Indian millet
—깡 kaoliang stalk —개떡 a coarse cake made of glutinous kaoliang —경단 a kind of honey cake made of glutinous kaoliang —쌀 grains of kaoliang
수수 收受 receipt —하다 receive
수수 授受 giving and receiving ; delivery ; transfer —하다 give and receive ; transfer
*수수께끼 a riddle ; an enigma ; a conundrum ; a puzzle ; a mystery ; a nut to crack ; a quiz ¶ 우주의 수수께끼 the riddle of the universe // 수수께끼의 인물 an enigmatic person ; a mystery man ; a sphinx ; a riddle // 수수께끼 같은 enigmatic ; mysterious ; puzzling // 수수께끼 같은 이야기 a puzzling story // 수수께끼 같은 말 a sphinx-like remark // 수수께끼를 내다 give〔ask〕 《a person》 a puzzle〔riddle〕 to guess〔make out〕 // 수수께끼 놀이를 하다 play riddles // 수수께끼를 풀다 solve〔interpret, guess, find out〕 a riddle ; puzzle out 《a matter》 // 자네 이야기는 꼭 수수께끼 같네 You talk in riddles. // 중국은 커다란 수수께끼다 China is a great enigma. // 그의 사인은 아직도 수수께끼로 되어 있다 The cause of his death is cloaked in mystery. // 그것은 영원히 풀 수 없는 과학자들의 수수께끼이다 It is a standing puzzle of the scientists.
수수돌 calcite which contains gold dust
수수료 手數料 a commission ; a fee ; service charge ; a percentage ¶ 수수료를 받다 charge a fee ; make a charge // 3퍼센트의 판매 수수료를 지불하다 pay a

three percent commission on a sale

수수방관 袖手傍觀 indifferent observation **—하다** look on with folded arms ; stand idle ¶ 수수방관하고 있을 때가 아니다 This is no time for us to remain idle. // 수수방관만 하는 대신에 한번 시도도 해보지 뭐 Let's give it a go too, instead of just sitting around on our hands.

수수하다[1] [맵시가] (be) ordinary looking ; be of average appearance ; (be) plain ; unpretentious ; [질이] moderate ; average ¶ 수수하게 옷을 차리다 be dressed unpretentiously // 물건 값이 수수하다 The price of the article is moderate. // 이런 수수한 무늬의 셔츠에는 그런 화려한 넥타이가 어울리지 않는다 A loud necktie like that doesn't go with the quiet pattern of this shirt.

수수하다[2] [시끄럽다] (be) distracting ; noisy

수술 〖식물〗 a stamen

†**수술 手術** an operation ; a surgical operation **—하다** operate on 《a person》 for ; perform a surgical operation for ¶ 수술을 받다 undergo a surgical operation ; be operated on // 수술중에 죽다 die under the knife // 외과 의사가 환자를 수술했다 The surgeon performed an operation on〔upon〕 the patient. // 수술후의 회복이 극히 양호하다 His postoperative recovery is good and speedy. // 수술하기에는 때가 늦었다 It is too late to perform an operation on him. // 나는 맹장을 수술했다 I had my appendix out.

— 담당 의사 an operating surgeon **—료** charges for operation ; operation charges **—복** an operating gown〔dress〕 **—비** charges for operation **—실(대)** an operating room〔table〕 **대—** a major operation **복부 —** an operation on the abdomen

수슬수슬하다 《smallpox》 be somewhat dried up

수습 收拾 controlling ; coping 《with》 **—하다** deal〔cope〕 《with》 ; control ; have in hand ¶ 시국을 수습하다 save〔cope with〕 the situation ; have the situation in hand // 수습할 수 없게 되다 get out of control〔hand〕 ; become uncontrollable 〔unmanageable〕 // 인심을 수습하다 win the hearts of the people ; gain public opinion // 분규가 심하니 수습할 길이 없다 The affair has become too complicated for us to manage.

수습 修習 apprenticeship ; probation **—하다** receive training 《in》 ; practise oneself 《in a trade》 ; learn 《the business routine of an office》 ¶ 수습중이다 be on probation ; be in training

— 간호원 a probationer nurse **—공(생)** an apprentice ; a probationer ; a trainee ; a student **— 기간** the probationary period ; the period of apprenticeship **— 기자** a cub reporter ; a junior reporter **— 제도** apprenticeship scheme ; a learner's training system

수시 收屍 laying out a body for burial **—하다** lay out (a body) ; prepare a corpse for burial

수시 隨時 [부사적] at any time ; [필요에 응해서] on demand ; as occasion calls ¶ 수시 응변으로 as occasion arises〔demands, calls〕 // 수시 변통하여 accommodating oneself to circumstances

수식 水蝕 erosion (by the action of water)

⁑**수식 修飾** ornamentation ; embellishment ; 〖문법〗 modification **—하다** ornament ; embellish ; 〖문법〗 modify ; qualify ¶ 수식하지 않고 without embellishment // 그 이야기는 꽤 수식되어 있다 The story is considerably embroidered〔embellished〕.

—어 〖문법〗 a modifier ; a qualifier

수식 數式 a numerical formula〔expression〕

수신 水神 a water god ; a naiad

수신 受信 the receipt of a message ; reception **—하다** receive a (telegraphic, wireless, cable) message ; receive ¶ 라디오로 수신한 연설문 a speech monitored by radio

—국 a receiving office〔station〕 ; an office of receipt **—기** a receiver ; a receiving set〔apparatus〕 ; a recorder **—료** a (radio, television) receiving fee **—부(簿)** a letter and telegram register **—상황** reception conditions **— 안테나** a receiving antenna **—인** an addressee ; a recipient **— 장치** a receiving apparatus〔set〕 **단파 —** short-wave reception

수신 修身 moral training (수양) ; [학과] morals ; moral science ; ethics **—하다** practice〔cultivate〕 morals ¶ 수신 제가하다 cultivate one's morals and then rule the family

— 강화(講話) a lecture on morals **— 제가(齊家)** moral training and home management

수심 水深 the depth of water ¶ 수심을 재다 sound the depth ; take soundings

수심 愁心 melancholy ; distress ; grief ; sadness ; apprehension ¶ 수심에 잠기다 be lost in apprehension ; be grief-stricken ; be heavy-hearted

수심 獸心 a brutal heart ; a bestial mind **인면(人面) —** man in face, brute in mind ; a beast with a human face

수심 垂心 〖수학〗 an orthocenter

수십 數十 several tens ; scores ; dozens ¶ 수십명 scores of men // 수십년 several decades ; scores of years // 수십명씩 떼지어 오다 people come in〔by〕 scores

수아주 a kind of fine〔good〕 silk

수알치새 〖새〗 an eagle owl

수압 手押 ⇨ 수결(手決)

수압 水壓 water〔hydraulic〕 pressure ¶ 수

압이 약하다 The water pressure is low.
—계 a water-pressure gauge ; a piezometer —관 a hydraulic pipe ; a penstock —기 a hydraulic press — 기관 a hydromotor —력 hydraulic power — 시험 a hydraulic test

수액 水厄 a flood disaster ; a deluge

*수액 樹液 (tree) sap ; milk

수약자 受約者 〖법〗 a promisee

수양 收養 fostering ; adoption 《of children》 —하다 foster ; adopt 《children》 —딸〔아들〕 an adopted〔a foster〕 daughter〔son〕 — 아버지〔어머니〕 a foster father〔mother〕

수양 修養 culture ; cultivation ; self-culture —하다 improve oneself〔one's mind〕 ; cultivate ; train ¶ 수양 있는 사람 a cultured person〔mind〕 // 정신을 수양하다 improve〔cultivate〕 one's mind〔character〕 // 수양을 쌓다 do a great deal in self-culture // 수양을 게을리 하지 않다 make a constant effort to improve oneself // 너는 아직 수양이 부족하다 You still have room for moral training.
—법 a method of moral culture ; how to cultivate one's mind —서 a book on self-culture —회 a conference to promote moral living 정신 — moral〔spiritual〕 culture

수양골 the ox brain

수양버들 垂楊— a weeping willow

수양액 水樣液 〖해부〗 aqueous〔vitreous〕 humor ; eyewater

수어 守禦 defense —하다 defend

수업 受業 taking lessons〔a course〕 —하다 take lessons〔a course〕 in ; study

†수업 授業 school (work) ; teaching ; instruction —하다 teach〔give〕 lessons 《to》 ¶ 수업 시간 school hours // 수업 일수 the number of school days // 수업 중에 during school hours ; at school // 수업이 끝난 후 after school // 주에 20 시간의 수업을 맡다 have twenty classes a week // 수업을 까먹다 dodge〔skip ; cut〕 a lesson // 수업 시간은 8시부터 3시까지이다 School hours are from eight to three. // 학생들은 수업중이다 The boys are now at school〔in class〕. // 오늘은 이것으로 수업을 끝마치겠습니다 So far for today. / Class (is) dismissed. // 김선생은 수업중이다 Mr. *Kim* is now teaching (his class). // 수업은 8시에 시작한다 School begins at eight. // 내일은 수업이 없다 There will be no school〔class〕 tomorrow.
—료 school〔tuition〕 fee — 시간 school hours ¶ 수업 시간 중에 during school hours〔the lesson〕 ; in class — 일수 the number of school days 과외 — extra classes 하계 — 〔대학의〕 the summer session

수업 修業 〔면학〕 pursuit of knowledge ; study ; 〔수료〕 completion of a course —하다 prosecute one's studies ; pursue knowledge ; study ; get an education ; complete a course (수료하다) ¶ 의학을 수업하다 study medicine // 중 2학년을 수업하다 finish the second year course of middle school // 수업 연한은 3년이다 The course of study covers three years.
— 연한 the years required for graduation from a school ; the years required for completing a course of study ¶ 본교의 수업 연한은 4년이다 The course of study in our school extends over four years.

수없다 ① 〔도리 없다〕 be unable to do ; (be) impossible ; helpless ② 〔재수 없다〕 (be) unlucky ; unfortunate ¶ 이제는 수 없다 Now it cannot be helped. // 폭풍우로 출발할 수 없다 The storm prevents us from starting. // 나는 그 문제를 풀 수 없었다 The problem was utterly beyond me. // 나는 그런 사치는 할 수 없다 I cannot afford such luxury. // 그건 도저히 참을 수 없다 It is more than I can bear. // 그 회답은 연기할 수 없다 The answer admits no delay. // 할 수 없는 것은 아니다 It is not impossible. // 인간의 힘으로 할 수 없는 것은 없다 Human power is equal to anything.

수없다 數— 〔무수하다〕 (be) innumerable ; countless ; numberless ¶ 수없이 innumerably ; countlessly ; without number

수에즈 운하 —運河 the Suez Canal

*수여 授與 〔증서 따위의〕 conferment ; presentation ; 〔상품의〕 awarding —하다 confer 《a degree on a person》 ; award 《a medal》 ; give ; grant ; present 《a thing to a person, a person with a thing》 ; decorate 《a person with an order》 ¶ 학위를 수여하다 confer a degree on 《a person》 // 금메달을 수여받다 be awarded a gold medal // 졸업 증서를 수여하다 present a diploma // 면허장을 수여하다 grant 《a person》 a license

수여리 〖곤충〗 a queen bee

수여식 授與式 a conferment ceremony
군기 — presentation of the colors 상품 — distribution〔awarding〕 of prizes 졸업 증서 — a graduation ceremony ; commencement exercises 《미》

수역 水域 waters
공동 규제 — jointly controlled fishing zone〔waters〕 ; a joint fishing waters 중립 — neutral waters

수역 囚役 labor forced upon prisoners

수역 獸疫 a livestock disease ; an epizootic

수연 水鉛 wulfenite ; molybdenum

수연 水煙 water spray〔mist〕
—통(筒) a hooka(h) ; a water pipe

수연 壽宴 a birthday feast for an old man

수연이나 雖然— however ; nevertheless ; notwithstanding

수열 數列 〖수학〗 a series ; (a) progression
등비〔기하〕 — geometrical progression
등차 — arithmetical progression
수염 鬚髥 [턱수염] a beard ; a goatee ; [콧수염] a mustache ; [구레나룻] whiskers ¶ 수염이 텁수룩한 bushy-bearded ; heavily bearded ; hairy // 수염이 없는 beardless // 수염을 기르다 grow〔raise〕 a mustache // 수염을 기르고 있다 wear〔have〕 a mustache〔beard〕 // 수염을 깎지 않았다 He is unshaven. /He has an unshaven face. /He needs a shave (badly). // 아침마다 수염을 깎는다 I shave myself〔my face〕 every morning. // (이발소에서) 수염을 깎았다 I had my mustache trimmed. // 수염만 밀어주시오 [이발소에서] I want only a shave.
— 수세 a heavy beard — 자리 (whisker) fuzz 가짜 — a false mustache〔beard〕 보리 — barley beard 옥수수 — corn silk

수염

턱수염 beard　구레나룻 whiskers　코밑수염 mustache

수염 手染 hand dying ¶ 수염한 hand-dyed
수염수리 鬚髥— 〖새〗 an Altai bearded vulture
수영 〖식물〗 a sour sorrel ; a dock
†**수영 水泳** swimming ; a swim ; bathing **—하다** swim ; bathe ; have a swim ¶ 수영을 배우다 learn (how) to swim // 수영하러 가다 go swimming 《in the river》 ; go for a swim // 수영을 잘한다 He swims well. /He is a good swimmer. /He is good at swimming.
— 경기 (the sport of) swimming — 대회 a swimming meet — 모자 a swimming cap —복 a swimming〔bathing〕 suit ; a swimsuit — 선수 a swimmer ; [남자] a merman 《미》 ; [여자] a mermaid 《미》 —술 the art of swimming ; natation —장 a swimming〔bathing〕 place ; a swimming pool〔tank〕 — 팬츠 bathing drawers ; swim〔swimming〕 trunks 《미》 한국 — 연맹 the Korea Swimming Federation
수예 手藝 handicraft ; the manual arts
—품 handicraft articles ; a fancy article
수온 水溫 water temperature
수완 手腕 ability ; skill ; capability ; capacity ¶ 정치적 수완 a political capacity // 수완이 있는 able ; capable ; talented ; skillful // 수완을 발휘하다 show〔display〕 one's ability〔skill〕 // 그는 행정적 수완이 없다 He lacks (in) administrative ability. // 현 위치에서는 충분히 수완을 발휘할 수가 없다 His present position gives little scope to his ability.
—가 a man of ability ; an able〔a capable〕 man ; [특히 돈벌이의] a go-getter 《미·속》 ¶ 그는 정말 수완가이다 He is a real wheeler-dealer. // 그 회사 사장은 대단한 수완가이다 The president of the company is quite a wheeler-dealer. 외교 — diplomatic ability
수요 壽夭 longevity and〔or〕 premature death
†**수요 需要** demand ; requirement ¶ 수요의 탄력성 elasticity of demand // 꾸준한 수요 steady demand 《for goods》 // 공급과 수요의 법칙 the law of supply and demand // 수요가 있다 be in demand ; be wanted // 수요가 적다 be unmarketable // 수요를 충족시키다 supply〔meet〕 a demand // 국내 수요에 응하다 meet domestic needs // 이 상품은 수요가 아주 많다 There is a great demand〔rush〕 for these articles. // 수요가 많고 공급이 적다 The demand exceeds the supply. // 수요가 감퇴하고 있다 The demand is lagging〔diminishing〕.
— 가격 a demand price — 감소 reduced〔decreased, decreasing, lesser〕 demand — 곡선 a demand curve — 과다 excessive〔excess in〕 demand —자 a user — 증가 increased〔increasing, greater〕 demand 가 — disguised demand ; [투기성] speculative demand ; [일시적] temporary demand 유효 — effective demand
†**수요일 水曜日** Wednesday
수욕 水浴 bathing ; a bathe (수영) ; [냉수욕] a cold〔water〕 bath **—하다** bathe in water ; have〔take, get〕 a bathe 《in a river》 ; take a cold〔water〕 bath
수욕 羞辱 humiliation ; shame ; disgrace ; mortification ; ignominy
수욕 受辱 —하다 be〔get〕 humiliated ; be insulted ; be disgraced
수욕 獸慾 a bestial desire ; carnal desires ; lust ; sexual appetite〔instinct〕 ¶ 수욕을 채우다 satisfy one's carnal desires
수용 收用 expropriation **—하다** expropriate ¶ 토지를 수용하다 expropriate 《a person》 from the land〔estate〕
토지 — expropriation of land ; eminent domain 토지 —권 (the right of) eminent domain 토지 —법 the law of expropriation of land ; the Compulsory Purchase of Land Act
†**수용 收容** accommodation ; admission ; reception ; [불량소년 따위의] consignment ; custody **—하다** take in ; accommodate ; admit ; hold ; seat ; [형무소에] commit 《a person》 to jail ¶ 피난민을 수용하다 house the refugees // 병

원에 수용되다 be admitted to a hospital // 형무소에 수용되다 be committed to jail // 이 극장은 2,000명을 수용할 수 있다 The theater seats〔admits〕 two thousand persons. // 부상자들은 근처의 병원에 수용되었다 The wounded persons were taken to a neighboring hospital.
— 기간 a period of consignment (비행 소년의) — 능력 capacity ; accommodation ; a seating capacity —소 a home ; an asylum ; a concentration camp (포로의) ; a repatriate reception center (귀환자의) — 인원 the number of persons to be admitted〔accommodated〕 —자 inmates (양로원 따위의) ; inpatients (병원의) ; prisoners (형무소의)

**수용 受容 acceptance ; reception — 하다 accept ; receive
—성〔력〕 receptive capacity ; receptiveness ; receptivity ; recipience ; recipiency — 태세 preparations to receive ¶ 수용 태세를 취하다 get ready to receive

수용 需用 consumption — 하다 consume —자 a consumer

수용 瘦容 a lean〔thin, skinny〕 face〔look〕 ; a worn face

수용성 水溶性 solubility in water ¶ 수용성 비료 watersoluble fertilizer

수용액 水溶液 an aqueous solution

수우 殊遇 special〔high〕 favor ; cordial〔warm〕 treatment

수우 水牛 ⇨ 물소

수운 水運 water traffic ; water transport ; transportation by water ¶ 수운이 좋은 구역에 위치하다 be located within easy reach of water transport // 수운의 편이 좋다 There are waterways available here.

수원 水源 the source〔head〕 of a river ; a river-head ; [수도의] a source of water supply ; a fountainhead ¶ 수원에서 하구까지 from source to mouth // 수원으로 거슬러 올라가다 trace a river to its source // 이 강의 수원은 어딥니까 Where does this river rise ? // 이 강의 수원은 …이다 the river rises〔takes its rise〕 among《hills》
—지 a gathering ground ; a catchment area〔basin〕 ; a reservoir (수도의)

수원 受援 receipt of (foreign) assistance —국 a recipient country — 태세 arrangements necessary for receipt of foreign assistance

수원 隨員 a member of《a person's》 suite ; an attendant ⇨ 수행원(隨行員)

수월 數月 several months ; a number of months

수월내기 (a man who is) a pushover ; a namby-pamby

수월래놀이 ⇨ 강강수월래

수월스럽다 (be) easy ⇨ 수월하다

수월찮다 be no pushover ; be some trouble ¶ 수월찮이 무겁다 be heavier than it looks

수월하다 (be) easy ; be no trouble ; be a pushover ; be a snap〔cinch〕《미·속》 ¶ 하기가 수월하다 it is no trouble to do ; have no difficulty to do

수월히 easily ; with ease ; readily ; without difficulty ¶ 수월하게 번 돈 easily gained money // 수월하게 돈을 벌다 make an easy gain // 수월하게 번 돈은 쉽게 없어진다 Easy come, easy go.

수위 首位 the premier〔leading〕 position ; the first〔head〕 place ¶ 수위를 차지하다 lead〔rank first, hold (the) first place〕《in》 // 수위에서 전락하다 forfeit one's primacy // 부산은 한국의 무역 항구로서 수위를 차지한다 *Pusan* stands first on the list of Korean trade ports.
— 타자 〖야구〗 the leading hitter ¶ 수위 타자가 되다 win the batting title

수위 水位 the water level ¶ 수위가 높다〔낮다〕 be of a high〔low〕 water level // 수위가 높아진다 The water rises.
—계 a water gauge ; a hydrograph —표 a water mark 위험 — the dangerous water level

수위 守衛 a guard ; a door-keeper ; a janitor ; 〔왕실·회의장 따위의〕 a sergeant-at-arms
—실 a guard office ; a (porter's) lodge —장 the chief guard

수위 秀偉 — 하다 (be) excellent ; superior《to》 ; outstanding ; great and excellent

수유 須臾 a little while ⇨ 잠시

수유 授乳 nursing ; suckling ; lactation — 하다 nurse ; feed ; suckle ; give the breast (to a baby)
—기 a period of lactation ; the lactation —열(熱) milk fever

수유관 輸乳管 〖해부〗 the lactiferous duct

수유자 受遺者 〖법〗 a devisee (부동산의) ; a legatee (동산의)

수육 cooked beef

수육 獸肉 flesh of animals ; meat

**수은 水銀 mercury《Hg》 ; quicksilver ; hydrargyrum ¶ 수은의 mercurial ; mercuric // 수은으로 처리하다 mercurialize ; mercurate // 수은(주)가 오른다 The mercury rises. // 내륙 분지에서는 수은주가 90도 이상까지 올라갔었지요 The mercury hit upper 90's in the valley. // 일기 예보에 따르면 오후에는 수은주가 영하 6도로 내려갈 거래요 The weatherman says the mercury will drop to 6 degrees below zero in the afternoon. // 서울에서는 수은주가 영하 15도까지 떨어진다 The mercury dips as low as 15 degrees below zero in *Seoul*.
—광 mercurial ore —구 a mercury bulb — 기압계 a mercurial gauge —등 a mercury lamp — 연고 mercurial ointment — 온도계 a mercury thermometer —제(劑) a mercurial preparation ; a mercurial —

주 a mercurial column — 중독증 mercurialism ; mercury poisoning

수은 受恩 reception of benefits〔favors〕 —하다 receive benefits〔favors, kindness〕

수음 手淫 self-abuse〔-pollution〕; masturbation ; onanism —하다 commit self-abuse ; masturbate ; practice masturbation

수음 樹陰 the shade of a tree

수응 酬應 —하다 meet the demand of others ; give as requested

수의 遂意 fulfilment of a wish ; realization of a hope —하다 fulfil one's wish ; realize a hope ; have《a thing》as one wishes

수의 壽衣 a shroud ; garments for the dead

수의 隨意 voluntariness ; option ¶ 수의의 voluntary ; optional ; free // 수의로 voluntarily ; at will ; as one pleases ; at one's pleasure // 그 돈은 수의로 사용하시오 The money is entirely at your disposal.
— 계약 a private〔free〕 contract ; a contract ad libitum — 과목 an optional〔elective〕 subject ; an elective —근(筋) a voluntary muscle — 선택 one's free〔optional〕 choice — 판단 discretion

수의 獸醫 a veterinary surgeon ; a veterinarian ; a vet《속》
—사법 〖법〗 the Veterinary License Act —업 veterinary (surgeon's) business —학 veterinary medicine〔science〕 — 학교〔과 대학〕 a veterinary school〔college〕

수이 ⇨ 쉬이

수이 殊異 peculiarity —하다 (be) markedly〔peculiarly〕 different《from》; remarkably distinctive《from》

수익 收益 earnings (총수익) ; gains (이익) ; proceeds (매상고) ; returns (투자에 대한) ¶ 수익이 있는 profitable ; lucrative // 수익이 있는 회사 a going concern // 수익을 올리다 make profits ; realize a profit ; realize《one million *won*》; make《a million *won*》
—금 earnings ; gains ; proceeds —력 earning power —률 an earning rate —세 the profit tax — 잉여 earned surplus —자 a beneficiary ; a person enriched (이익자) — 자산 live assets — 체감 diminishing returns 순— net earnings 총— gross earnings

수익다 手— get used to ⇨ 익숙하다

수인 囚人 a prisoner ; a convict ; a jailbird《미·속》
— 호송자 a prison van

수인 數人 several persons ; a few people

수인성 질병 水因性疾病 waterborne diseases

수일 秀逸 superexcellence ; supreme excellence —하다 (be) superexcellent ; supremely excellent ; superb

수일 數日 a few days ; several days ¶ 수일 전에 a few days ago // 수일 후에 after〔in〕 several days ; several days later〔afterwards〕

수일 隨一 ⇨ 첫째 ¶ 수일의 the best〔first〕; number one《No. 1》// 북국 수일의 명승지 the most picturesque place in the Northern provinces

수임 受任 acceptance of an appointment —하다 be named ; accept an appointment〔office〕; take office《as》
—자 a nominee ; an appointee ; a mandatory ; a committee

⁑수입 收入 an income (개인의) ; a revenue (법인·국가의) ; [수취금] receipts ; [매상금] proceeds ; turnover ¶ 회사의 수입 company's revenue // 상당한 수입이 있는 사람 a man with a good〔comfortable〕 income // 수입의 범위 내의〔이상의〕 생활을 하다 live within〔beyond〕 one's income // 월 백만원의 수입이 있다 He has an income of one hundred *won* a month. // 수입이 많다〔적다〕 He has a large〔small〕 income. // 이 달에는 뜻밖의 수입이 좀 생겼기 때문에 경기가 좋아 I can afford to be generous because I had a little windfall this month. // 나는 좀더 수입이 좋은 일을 찾고 있다 I'm looking for a job that pays better. // 수입에 맞는 생활이라고는 할 수 없다 It would be hard to say that he's living within his means.
— 인지 a revenue〔fiscal〕 stamp ; a tax stamp 고정 — a fixed income 국가 — national revenues 실제 — one's net receipts ; an actual income 임시 — perquisite 입장료 — the gate (money) ; the total admission receipts 잡— miscellaneous receipts 조세 — internal revenue 총— a total〔gross〕 income 평균 — an average income

†수입 輸入 importation ; import ; introduction (문명의) —하다 import ; introduce ¶ 서양 문명의 수입 the introduction of Western civilization // 수입을 금지하다 prohibit the import(ation)《of》// 수입이 수출을 초과하고 있다 The imports exceed the exports. /There is an adverse〔unfavorable〕 balance of trade. // 한국은 호주에서 양모를 수입한다 Korea imports wool from Australia.
—국 an importing country — 금지 an import prohibition — 담보율 the import deposit〔mortgage〕 rate — 면장 an import license — 무역 import trade ¶ 수입 무역 통제법 the Import Control Law —상 an importer — 성향 the propensity of import —세 import duties〔tariffs〕 — 수속 the process of import ; import formalities — 신고서 an import declaration — 신용장 an import credit memorandum — 어음 an import bill — 억제〔금지〕 품목 an import- restricted〔-banned〕 item —업 the importing business — 의존도 the rate of dependence on imports — 제한

import restrictions — 초과 excess of imports (over exports) —품 (overseas) imports ; imported articles〔goods〕; an import item — 할당 import allocation — 할당 제도 the import quota system —항 a port of entry — 허가제 an import licensing system 무환(無換) — an import without credit 밀— smuggling ¶ 밀수입품 smuggled〔contraband〕 goods 〔articles〕 외자 — the introduction of foreign capital

수 있다 ① [사람이 주어] can 《do》; be able to 《do》; be capable 《of doing》; be equal to 《the task》; [사물이 주어] (be) possible ¶ 할 수 있으면 if possible // 내가 할 수 있는 일이면 무엇이든지 하겠다 I will do anything in my power. // 수입으로 훌륭히 생활할 수 있다 His income enables him to live a decent life. // 누구나 이 문제에 대하여 의견을 말할 수 있다 Every one is entitled to his opinion on this subject. // 오늘은 학교 갈 수 있겠니 Do you feel up to going to school today? ② (be) lucky ; have luck

수자리 戍— guarding the frontier (경비); frontier guards (경비원) —하다 guard the frontier

수자원 水資源 water resources
— 개발 the development of water resources 한국 — 개발 공사 the Korea Water Resources Development Corporation

수작 酬酌 ① [술잔의] exchanging wine cups ② [말의] exchanging words ; talk ; a remark ; a comment —하다 exchange wine cups ; exchange words ; talk ; say ; remark ; comment ¶ 헛된 수작을 하다 talk nonsense ; say silly things ; talk rot

수작 秀作 an excellent〔outstanding〕 work 《of art》

수작 授爵 conferment of titular distinction〔a peerage〕; elevation to the peerage —하다 confer a peerage 《on》; ennoble ; elevate to the peerage ; make 《a person》 a peer ¶ 수작식을 행하다 hold an investiture

수잠 a light sleep ¶ 수잠들다 doze off

수장 水葬 burial at sea〔in the sea〕; water burial —하다 bury at sea ; consign 《the body》 to a watery grave ¶ 수장되다 be buried at sea

수장 收藏 garnering 《agricultural produce》; collection —하다 garner ; store up ; collect

수장 修粧 remodeling ; embellishment —하다 remodel ; repair ; embellish
— 기둥 a temporary pillar for remodeling purposes — 도리 a wall beam

수장 袖章 a sleeve badge ; sleeve stripes ; [갈매기 모양의] a chevron ¶ 수장을 달다 put on a chevron

수재 水災 a flood disaster
— 대책 anti-flood measures —민 flood sufferers〔victims〕

수재 手才 skill of hand ; handicraft

수재 秀才 a genius ; a prodigy ; a talented man ; a brilliant man ¶ 그는 학교에서 제일 가는 수재다 He is the brightest boy in the whole school. // 저 집안 사람들은 모두가 수재다 That family boasts of a galaxy of talent. /All the children are talented in one way or another. // 그 학교에서는 많은 수재를 배출했다 The school has produced〔turned out〕 many brilliant men.
— 교육 education of〔for〕 gifted children〔bright young intellectuals〕

수저 ① a spoon ② spoon and chopsticks
—집 a spoon bag

수저 水底 the bottom of the water〔sea, river〕

수적 手迹 handwriting ; a holograph ; an autograph

수적 水賊 a robber on the water ; [해적] a pirate ; a sea robber〔rover〕

수적 水滴 a drop of water ; a waterdrop

수전 水田 a paddy field ; a rice paddy ; a wet field ⇨ 논

수전 水戰 a sea battle ; a naval battle 〔engagement〕; a naval encounter ; naval warfare 《총칭》 ¶ 산전수전 다 겪은 사람 an old stager〔campaigner〕

수전 水電 hydroelectricity

수전 守戰 a defensive war
— 동맹 a defensive alliance

수전노 守錢奴 a miser ; a niggard ; a skinflint ; a screw ; a tightwad 《미·속》

수전증 手顫症 〚한의〛 tremor of the hands

수절 守節 maintaining one's integrity ; faithfulness —하다 maintain one's integrity ; remain faithful〔chaste, true〕 to one's husband

‡**수정 水晶** (rock) crystal ¶ 수정같이 맑은 물 crystal-clear water
—궁(宮) the Crystal Palace —석 cryolite — 세공 crystal ware — 시계 a crystal 〔quartz〕 clock〔chronometer〕 —체 〚해부〛 crystalline lens〔humor〕; the eye lens —판 〚전기〛 a quartz plate 연(煙) — veined〔smoky〕 quartz 자(紫)— amethyst

수정 受精 〚생물〛 fecundation ; fertilization ; 〚식물〛 pollination —하다 be fertilized ; be pollinated
— 능력 fertility ; fertilizing power —란 a fertilized egg 인공 — artificial insemination 체외 — external fertilization

‡**수정 修正** [의안·조문 따위의] amendment ; revision ; modification ; [사진의] retouching —하다 amend ; modify ; revise ; retouch ; correct ¶ 헌법의 수정 an amendment of the Constitution // 수정하여 as amended ; in an amended〔a modified〕 form // 수정하지 않고 without amendment〔modification〕 // 의안을 수정하

다 amend a bill // 자귀를 수정하다 alter〔modify〕 the wording ; modify the phraseology // 일부를 수정하다 make a partial amendment〔revision〕 《of》 // 사진을 수정하다 retouch a negative // 그 법안은 수정된 것이다 The bill has undergone revision. // 이 사진은 수정된 것 같다 This photograph appears to have been retouched.
— 신고 a revised return〔report〕 —안 an amended〔a revised〕 bill ; an amendment — 예산 a revised budget —자 an amender ; a retoucher (사진의) — 자본주의 revised〔modified〕 capitalism —주의 revisionism ¶ 수정주의 노선을 걷다 take 〔follow〕 the revisionist course〔line〕 —주의자 a revisionist

수정 修整 adjustment ; regulation —하다 adjust ; regulate

수정과 水正果 a fruit punch (made of honey, dried persimmons, pine nuts and cinnamon)

수정관 輸精管 〖해부〗 a seminal vesicle ; the vas deferens 《*pl.* vasa deferentia》

수제 手製 (being) handmade ; [자가제의] homemade ; of domestic make ; [수제품] handiwork —하다 make by hand ¶ 옛날의 수제품이 지금의 기계품보다 튼튼하다 Old handmade work will outwear new machine goods.

수제비 a clear soup with wheat flakes in it
—태견 unseemly behavior toward one's elders 나깨 — clear soup with buckwheat flour siftings in it

수제자 首弟子 the best pupil ; the most able student (of a teacher)

수조 水槽 a cistern ; a water tank
—차 a tank car〔truck〕

수조 水藻 an aquatic plant

수족 水族 aquatic animals ; the finny race 〔tribe〕 ; sea creatures ; water life
—관 an aquarium

수족 手足 hands and feet ; hand and foot ; the limbs (사지) ¶ 수족을 결박하다 bind 《a person》 hand and foot // 수족을 묶이다 be bound hand and foot // 수족이 되어 일하다 serve 《a person》 like a tool ; serve 《a person》 as his man Friday ; be at another's beck and call

수족 곡선 垂足曲線 〖수학〗 a pedal curve

수종 水腫 〖의학〗 dropsy
— 다리 dropsical legs

수종 隨從 [시중] attendance 《on》 ; service ; [사람] an attendant ; a servant —하다 attend ; serve ; wait upon

수좌 首座 [수석] the top seat ; the seat of honor ; the head ; 〖불교〗 the Most Reverend Priest

수죄 首罪 the capital sin ; the most serious offense〔crime〕

수죄 數罪 accusation of crimes —하다 accuse 《a person》 of crimes

수주 受注 —하다 receive〔accept〕 an order
—고(高) the amount of orders received

수주머니 繡— an embroidered purse

†수준 水準 water level ; [표준] a level ; a standard ¶ 지적 수준이 높은 사람 a people on〔at〕 a high intellectual level // 수준에 달하다 reach the level ; be up to par // 수준에 못 미치다 be below the level ; fall short of the standard // 그는 대기업의 부장 수준의 월급을 받고 있다 I hear he's making as much as a department head in a major company.
—기(器) a (spirit) level —선 a horizontal line —점 a bench mark 《BM》 — 측량 leveling ; plane survey 문화 — the cultural level ¶ 그 나라는 문화 수준이 높다 The nation has a high level of culture. 생활 — the standard of living ; the living standard ¶ 생활 수준을 높이다〔낮추다〕 raise〔lower〕 the standard of living 최고 — the highest level

‡수줍다 (be) shy ; bashful ; timid ¶ 그 여자는 수줍어 말도 못한다 She is too shy to speak. // 그 여자는 나를 만나면 수줍어했다 She was shy about seeing me. // 그 여자는 사람들 앞에 나서면 수줍어한다 She is bashful in company. // 수줍어하지 말고 갖고 싶은 것이 있으면 말해라 Don't be shy about telling me what you want. // 수줍어 하지 마라 Don't be bashful.

*수줍음 shyness ; bashfulness ; timidity

†수중 水中 underwater ; submarine ¶ 수중에 under water ; in the water // 수중에서 작업하다 work under water // 수중으로 사라지다 disappear〔sink〕 in the water ; go under // 수중에 살다 live in water // 수중으로 뛰어들다 jump〔plunge〕 into the water ; take to the water
— 발사관 a submerged tube — 속력 an underwater〔a submerged〕 speed — 안경 [관측용] a hydroscope ; water glasses ; [수영용] goggles —전 subsurface warfare — 전파 탐지기 a sonar — 청음기 a hydrophone ; a subaqueous sound locator — 폭발 an underwater explosion 〔detonation〕 — 폭탄〔폭뢰〕 a submarine bomb ; a depth charge

수중 手中 in the hands ; within one's power (세력 안에) ¶ 수중에 넣다 secure ; capture ; possess oneself of ; take possession of ; come by // 수중에 들어오다 fall into one's hand // …의 수중에 있다 be in the possession 《of》 ; be at the mercy 《of》 // 죽이든 살리든 그는 당신 수중에 있다 He is at your mercy. / You can make or break him. // 지금 수중에 돈 가진 것 있니 Do you have money on〔with〕 you ?

수중다리 〖의학〗 dropsical legs ⇨ 수종

수중익 水中翼 a hydrofoil
—선(船) a hydrofoil (craft)

수증 受贈 receipt 《of a gift》; acceptance —하다 receive ; accept ; be favored with ; be given
수증기 水蒸氣 steam ; vapor
수지 —紙 scraps of paper ; waste paper ; [변소의] toilet paper ; facial tissue paper ¶ 그따위 증서는 수지나 마찬가지다 Such a bond is a mere scrap of paper. // 수지 좀 다오 Give me some tissues.
—통 a wastepaper basket 《영》; a waste-basket 《미》
수지 手指 fingers
수지 樹脂 resin ; rosin ; vegetable tallow-plastic ¶ 수지가 많은 resinous
— 가공 plasticization — 광택 resinous luster — 비누 resin soap —성 물질 resinoid —화 resinification 고형(固型) — galipot 합성 — plastics
수지 收支 income and expenditure ; receipts and expenditure〔disbursement〕 ¶ 수지의 균형을 유지하다 maintain equilibrium between incomings and outgoings ; balance receipts and disbursement // 수지 결산을 하다 settle the accounts ; strike the balance // 국제 수지를 결산하다 balance international payments // 수지를 맞추다 make both〔two〕 ends meet // 수지가 안 맞는다 We can't make both ends meet. /It does not pay.
— 결산 settlement of accounts — 계산 calculation ; reckoning ; accounts ; balancing — 균형 equilibrium between incomings and outgoings — 일람표 a statement of income and expenditure ; a balance sheet
수지 獸脂 animal fat ; grease ; tallow
수지니 手— a trained falcon
수지맞다 [사물이 주어] pay ; be profitable ; [사람이 주어] find one's account in ¶ 수지맞는 장사 a paying business ; a good bargain // 수지 안 맞는다 It doesn't pay. /Not a paying business. // 이 사업은 수지가 맞는다 This business pays. /This business is on a paying basis.
수지상 樹枝狀 [결정(結晶) 따위] arborization ; arborescence ¶ 수지상의 arborescent
*수직 垂直 perpendicular(ity) ¶ 수직의 perpendicular ; vertical // 수직으로 perpendicularly ; vertically ; at right angles 《to》 // 수직으로 교차하는 두 직선 two lines crossing at right angles // 수직이 아니다 be out of plumb
— 강하 〖항공〗 a vertical descent ; a nose-dive — 경사 [광산] underlay (of ore) —선〔면〕 a perpendicular〔vertical〕 line〔plane〕; a perpendicular ; a vertical — 안전판 a vertical stabilizer (of an airplane) — 이착륙기 a vertical take-off and landing craft 《VTOL》
수직 手織 handweaving ¶ 수직의 woven by hand ; handwoven ; homespun
—기 a handloom — 무명 homespun cotton cloth —물 a handwoven fabric ; homespun ; domestics 《미》
수진 手陳 ⇨ 수지니
수질 水蛭 〖동물〗 a leech
수질 水疾 seasickness ⇨ 배멀미
수질 水質 the quality of water ¶ 수질이 좋은〔나쁜〕 샘 a well whose water is good〔bad〕 for drinking
— 검사 water analysis〔examination〕 ¶ 수질을 검사하다 analyze〔examine〕 water
수집 收集 collection ; gathering —하다 collect ; gather
*수집 蒐集 the collection 《of data, materials》; the compilation 《of data, materials》 —하다 collect ; compile
—가 a collector —벽 a collecting mania ; a mania for (stamp) collecting 우표 — stamp collecting ; philately
수짠지 a delicacy of sliced pheasant meat or chicken mixed with pickles in soup
수쪽 the right half of a contract〔an IOU, a check〕
수차 水車 [물레방아] a water mill〔wheel〕; [터빈] a water〔hydraulic〕 turbine
수차 收差 〖물리〗 aberration
구면(球面) — spherical aberration
수차 數次 several times ; time and again ¶ 수차의 방문 several visits
수찬 修撰 editing 《a book》; redaction ; compilation —하다 edit ; redact ; compile
수찰 手札 [자필 서한] an autographic letter ; [자필의 편지] my letter
수창 首唱 advocacy ; pioneering ; originating —하다 advocate ; promote ; be first to 《do》; pioneer 《in》; advance
—자 an advocate ; a pioneer
수채 a sewer ; a drain ; a ditch ¶ 수채를 만들다 lay out a drain // 수채를 쳐내다 clean〔scour〕 a drain // 수채가 막혔다 The drain is obstructed〔clogged up〕
—통 a drain pipe ; a sewer pipe 수챗구멍 an outfall ; a gully hole ; a drainage vent〔outlet〕
수채움 filling up〔rounding up〕 the number —하다 fill up〔round up〕 the number
수채화 水彩畫 a watercolor (painting) ; a painting in watercolors ¶ 수채화를 잘 그리다 paint well in watercolors
—가 a watercolor painter ; a watercolorist ; an aquarellist — 물감 water color —법 watercolor painting ; water colors ; an aquarelle 《프》
수처 數處 several places
*수척 瘦瘠 emaciation —하다 (be) thin ; haggard ; gaunt ; emaciated ¶ 수척한 얼굴〔모습〕 a haggard face〔figure〕 // 수척하여 옛 모습을 찾을 수 없다 be a mere shadow of one's former self ; be worn to a shadow // 슬픈 나머지 얼굴이 수척해졌다 Sorrow has left its traces on her face.

수천 數千 thousands ; several thousands ¶ 수천의 사람 thousands of people
수철 水鐵 〖광물〗 pig iron
수첩 手帖 a note book ; a reminder 〔memorandum〕 book ; a pocket book
수청 守廳 bed service
수청 들다 관용 give 《a person》 bed service ; attend〔wait〕 on 《a man》 at night as 《his》 mistress
†수초 水草 [수생 식물] a water〔an aquatic〕 plant ; [물과 풀] water and grass ; [물풀] a water grass ; a waterweed
수촉 手燭 a (portable) candlestick ¶ 수촉에 불을 붙이다〔켜다〕 light a candlestick
수축 收縮 contraction ; shrinking ; constriction ―하다 contract ; shrink ; be constricted ¶ (팽창한 화폐를) 수축시키다 deflate // 추위는 액체를 수축시킨다 Cold causes the contraction of liquids.
― 계수 a coefficient of contraction ―근 〖해부〗 a contractile muscle ; a contractor ; a constrictor ―력 contractile force 〔power〕 ―성 contractibility ; contractility
수축 修築 repair (of a building) ; improvement ; mending ; restoration ―하다 repair ; renovate ; make improvements 《in》 ; mend ; restore ¶ 집을 약간 수축하다 put some improvements into a house // 수축중이다 It is under repair. /It is being repaired.
⁑수출 輸出 export ; exportation ―하다 export ; ship abroad ¶ 철을 수출하다 ship iron abroad // 소맥의 수출을 금지하다 prohibit the export of wheat // 무기의 수출을 금지하다〔해금하다〕 place〔lift〕 an embargo on the exportation of arms // 우리 나라의 수출은 증대일로에 있다 Our exports are increasing.
― 가격 an export price ― 공단 the export industrial corporation〔park〕 ― 금융 export financing ― 금지 an export ban ; an embargo ― 면장 an export license ― 목표 export target〔goal〕 ― 무역 the an export trade ― 산업 an export industry ¶ 한국 수출 산업 공단 the Korea Export Industrial Corporation ―세 export duties ― 수속 export formalities ― 승인제 the export licensing system ― 시장 다변화 the diversification of export markets ― 신용장 an export letter of credit ―액 the amount of export ― 어음 an export bill ―업 the export business ― 업자 an exporter ; an export trader ― 장려 encouragement of exportation ― 장려금 an export subsidy ; a bounty on exports ― 진흥 정책 export promotion policy ― 초과 an excess of exports ; a favorable balance of trade ― 할당 an export quota (system) ―항 an export port ― 허가장 an export permit ―환 export exchange 기아(飢餓) ― hunger export 마산 ― 자유 지역 관리청 the *Masan* Free Export Zone Administration
수출 경기 輸出景氣 an export boom
수출 실적 輸出實績 the actual exports 〔amount exported〕
수출입 輸出入 exportation and importation ; imports and exports ¶ 수출입의 차액 the balance of trade
― 금지품 contraband goods ―업 export and import trade〔business〕 ―업자 exporters and importers ― 은행 an export-import bank ―품 the imports and exports ; import-export goods ― 회전 기금 an import and export revolving fund
수출품 輸出品 exports ; export(ed) goods ; an exportation ; export articles
― 명세서 a shipping list〔bill〕 ― 전시회 an exports exhibition 중요 ― important 〔principal, staple, chief〕 export items 〔exports〕
수취 收取 〖법〗 collection ; acquisition ―하다 acquire 《products from》 ; collect 《fruits》
수취 受取 receipt ; receiving ―하다 receive ; accept ; take
― 어음 a bill payable to the bearer ―인 a recipient ; a receiver ; a remittee (송금의) ; a beneficiary (연금·보험금 따위의) ; a consignee (하물의)
*수치 羞恥 shame ; disgrace ; dishonor ; infamy ¶ 수치스럽다 be dishonorable ; be disgraceful ; be shameful // 수치를 알다 respect oneself ; have a sense of shame // …을 수치로 알다 think it a shame to 《do》 // 수치를 모르다 be shameless ; be lost〔dead〕 to (the sense of) shame // 가난은 수치가 아니다 Poverty is no disgrace. // 그것은 사나이의 수치다 A man must be ashamed of it. // 그는 그의 집안의 수치다 He is a shame to his family. // 저 따위는 우리 학교의 수치다 He is a disgrace to our school.
수치 數値 numerical value ¶ …의 수치를 구하다 evaluate
수치질 ―痔疾 external〔protruding〕 hemorrhoids
수침 水沈 a water pillow〔cushion〕
수캉아지 a male pup
수캐 a male dog
수커미 a male spider
수컷 a male
수케 a male crab
수코양이 a tom cat
수콤 a male bear
수구렁이 a male serpent
수꿩 a male pheasant ; a cock-pheasant
수클 [써먹는 글] productive or practical scholarship ; knowledge that can be put to some good use ; useful studies
수키와 a convex roofing tile ¶ 수키와와 암키와 convex and concave roofing tiles
수탁 受託 trust ; [상품 판매의] consignment ―하다 be given in trust ; be

entrusted with 《a thing》; take charge of 《a thing》 ¶ 수탁자의 자격으로 in a fiduciary capacity〔character〕
—금 money given in trust〔charge〕; trust money —료 a depository —물 a thing put under〔in〕 one's custody 〔charge〕; a thing entrusted; a charge — 법원 a court of requisition —자 a trustee; a consignee; an assignee; a fiduciary; a bailee — 판매 sales on consignment — 판사 a commissioned judge 공동 —인 a cotrustee
수탄 愁嘆 lamentation; grief; sorrow —하다 grieve 《for, over》; lament (over) 《a person's death》
수탄 獸炭 animal charcoal
수탈 收奪 [착취] exploitation —하다 exploit 《one's workers》
†수탉 a rooster; a cock
수탐 搜探 investigation; search —하다 investigate; search
수태 受胎 conception; impregnation; 〖생물〗 fecundation; fertilization —하다 conceive; be impregnated; become pregnant; be fecundated ¶ 수태한 fertile; fertilized // 성모 마리아의 수태 the Immaculate Conception
— 고지(告知) 〖기독교〗 the Annunciation — 능력 〖생물〗 fertility —력 conceiving power — 조절 conception control — 현상 〖생물〗 fertilization; fecundation; impregnation 인공 — artificial conception〔fertilization〕
수토 水土 water and soil; climate (풍토)
수톨쩌귀 the pintle of a hinge
수통 水桶 a water pail〔bucket〕 ⇨ 물통
수통 水筒 a water bottle〔flask〕; a canteen
수통 水筩 ① [관] a water pipe ② [수도전] a hydrant
—박이 a street hydrant
*수퇘지 a (male) hog; a boar
수틀 繡— an embroidery frame〔hoop〕; a tambour (for embroidering)
수판 數板 ⇨ 주판(籌板)
수펄 a (male) bee; a drone
수펌 a (male) tiger
수평이 a forest
수편물 手編物 knitting by hand ¶ 수편물의 hand-knit(ted); knit by hand // 이 양말은 수편물이다 These stockings are hand-knitted.
†수평 水平 the water level; the horizon ¶ 수평의 level; even; horizontal // 수평으로 horizontally; at a level with 《a thing》 // 수평으로 하다 level // 물과 지붕이 수평이다 The water is level with the roof.
—각 a horizontal angle — 거리 a horizontal distance —기(器) a level —력 horizontal force —면 a horizontal plane; water level; a level surface —봉 a horizontal bar — 비행 a level flight —선 the sea line; the horizon ¶ 수평선에 나타나다 appear on the horizon // 수평선 아래로 가라앉다 sink〔disappear〕 below the horizon — 운동 a horizontal movement; [계급적] the social equality movement — 이동〔분포〕 〖생물〗 horizontal migration〔distribution〕 —적 사고 lateral thinking — 폭격 horizontal bombing
수평(아리) a male chick
수포 水泡 [거품] foam; bubble; [헛수고] naught; nothing ¶ 수포로 돌아가다 come to naught〔nothing〕; prove〔result in〕 a failure; be brought to naught; end in smoke
수포(진) 水泡(疹) 〖의학〗 a blister; a tetter
수폭 水爆 a hydrogen bomb; an H-bomb ¶ 원수폭 금지 세계 대회 the World Conference for the Prohibition of Atom and Hydrogen Bombs
— 실험 an H-bomb test; a thermonuclear test — 탄두 a hydrogen〔an H-bomb〕 warhead
†수표 手票 a check ¶ 10만원 짜리 수표 a check for 100,000 *won* // 김씨앞 수표 a check in favor of Mr. *Kim* (on the Bank of Korea) // 수표로 지불하다 pay by check // 수표를 현금으로 바꾸다 cash a check // 귀하의 수표를 서울 무역 회사 앞으로 발행해 주시기 바랍니다 Please make your check payable〔out〕 to *Seoul* Trading corporation.
— 발행인 the issuer of a check —법 the Checks Act —책 a checkbook 무기명 — a check to bearer; a bearer check 보통 — an open check 부도 — a dishonored check 분실〔위조, 변조〕 — a lost 〔forged, raised〕 check 은행 — a bank check 지불 보증 — a certified check 횡선 — a crossed check
수표 水標 a watermark
수표 數表 a table; [책] a table book
수풀 a wood; a grove; a thicket; [큰] a forest
수프 soup; dishwater 《미·속》 (특히 맛이 없는) ¶ 짙은〔맑은〕 수프 thick〔clear〕 soup; potage〔consommé〕 // 수프를 마시다 eat soup // 수프를 뜨다 dip up soup 《with a ladle》
— 고기 soup meat — 냄비 a stockpot — 접시 a soup plate; a soup tureen (뚜껑이 있는) 고체 — a soup square 야채 — vegetable soup
수피 樹皮 the bark of a tree
수피 獸皮 the skin of an animal; a fur; a pelt
수피둘기 a male pigeon
‡수필 隨筆 an essay; stray〔random〕 notes; jottings; a miscellaneous writings
—가 an〔a light〕 essayist; a miscellaneous writer; a miscellanist —란 a miscellany column; a column for literary jottings — 문학 essay literature —집 a collection of essays〔literary jottings〕

수하 手下 a subordinate ; a retainer ; a henchman ; an underling ; a follower ; [총칭] a following ; men under one's order ; staff ¶ 수하에 under one's command ; under the power〔control〕of // 수하를 데리고 with one's men
— 친병 soldiers under one's command ; one's men

수하 水下 the lower reaches of a stream

수하 誰何 ① [불심 수하] a challenge ② [누구] anyone ; who ; what —하다 challenge ; question ¶ 수하받지 않고 통과하다 pass unchallenged // 수하를 막론하고 regardless of who it may be

수하다 壽— enjoy a long life ; live long ; live to a great age

⁑**수하물 手荷物** luggage《영》; baggage《미》; [휴대할 수 있는] hand luggage〔baggage〕; personal effects ¶ 수하물 한 개 a piece of luggage // 많은 수하물 much〔a lot of〕luggage // 수하물을 맡기다 have one's luggage checked // 수하물을 안다 carry personal effects in one's arms
—계 a luggage clerk《영》; a baggage master《미》— 운반인 a luggageman ; a baggageman《미》— 일시 보관소 a check-room《미》; a cloak-room —차 a luggage van《영》; a baggage car《미》— 취급소 a luggage office《영》; a baggage room〔office〕《미》—표 a baggage check《미》; a luggage ticket《영》 무임 — free luggage ; free baggage《미》

†**수학 數學** mathematics ; math(s)《구》¶ 수학의 mathematical // 수학 숙제를 끝내고 싶다 I want to get my math assignments finished.
— 문제 a mathematical problem — 시간 a mathematics lesson —자 a mathematician 고등 — higher mathematics 응용〔순수〕— applied〔pure〕mathematics

수학 受學 receiving an education ; being taught〔given lessons〕—하다 receive〔get, obtain〕an education ; learn ; study ; be taught

수학 修學 pursuit of knowledge ; study ; learning —하다 study ; learn ; pursue knowledge
— 여행 a school excursion〔trip〕; a study tour ; a trip for educational purposes ¶ 수학 여행을 가다 make〔go on〕a school excursion to《*Kyŏngju*》

수할치 a falconer

*****수해 水害** [손해] flood damage ; a flood disaster ; [홍수] a flood ; an inundation ¶ 수해를 입다 suffer from a flood ; be damaged by a flood // 이 지방은 해마다 다소의 수해를 입는다 This district suffers to some extent from floods every year.
— 구제 flood relief — 대책 [방지] a flood control measure ; anti-flood measures ; [구제] a relief measure for flood sufferers — 방지 prevention of flood ; flood control ; river control — 이재민 flood sufferers〔victims〕; sufferers from a flood — 지구 a flooded〔flood-stricken〕district

수해 樹海 a wavy sea of emerald leaves ; a sea of leafage〔foliage, trees〕

수행 修行 [불교의] ascetic exercises ; practice of austerities ; discipline ; [훈련] training —하다 study ; practice ; train oneself in ; practice austerities〔asceticism〕¶ 수행을 쌓다 undergo discipline〔training〕; go through the mill // 그는 아직 수행중인 몸이다 He is still an apprentice.
—자 a disciplinant

†**수행 遂行** accomplishment ; achievement ; execution ; performance ; discharge ; effectuation —하다 achieve ; accomplish ; carry out〔through〕; execute ; perform ; discharge

> 참고 **perform** 보통 시간·노력·주의·숙련을 요하는 일을 하다 **execute** 계획·명령을 실행하다 **discharge** 의무를 수행하다

¶ 직무의 수행 the performance〔discharge〕of one's duties // 계획을 수행하다 carry out a plan // 업무를 수행하다 conduct business // 임무를 수행하다 perform one's duty

⁑**수행 隨行** attendance —하다 accompany ; follow ; attend《on》; accompany《a person》; be in《a person's》suite ¶ 수행하여 in attendance upon《a person》; accompanying《a person》; in the suite of // …를 수행하여 내한하다 accompany《a person》to Korea
—원 a member of the suite〔retinue〕; an attendant ; [총칭] a suite ; an entourage ; a retinue ; (a train of) attendants ¶ A씨와 그 수행원 Mr. A and his suite

수행 獸行 a bestial act ; bestiality ; [폭행] an assault ; an outrage ; an attack

수향 水鄕 a waterside〔riverside, lakeside〕village

*****수험 受驗** sitting for an examination ; taking〔undergoing〕an examination —하다 take〔undergo, sit for, go through〕an examination ¶ 수험 자격이 있다 be qualified for examination // 수험 준비를 하다 prepare oneself for an examination
— 과목 subjects of examination —교 a school〔college, university〕of one's choice —료 the examination fee ; the expense for the examination — 번호 an examinee's seat number —생 a student preparing himself for an examination —자 a candidate for an examination ; an examinee — 자격 qualifications of candidacy for examination — 지옥 the ordeal of examination —표 an admission ticket for an examination ; a certificate for an

examination
*수혈 輸血 blood transfusion **—하다** transfuse (blood) ; give a blood transfusion 《to》 ¶ 수혈의 제공자 a donor of blood for transfusion // 수혈로 살아났다 A blood transfusion saved his life.
수형 受刑 being under sentence **—하다** serve time (in prison)
— 성적 a prison-service record **—자** a convict ; a convicted person ; a prisoner under sentence
수형 手形 ⇨ 어음
†**수호 守護** protection ; guard ; safeguard **—하다** protect ; guard ; safeguard ; watch over 《a person》 ¶ 신의 수호 divine protection // 수도 수호의 임무를 맡다 undertake to safeguard the capital city **—신** a guardian〔protecting〕 deity ; a tutelary god〔spirit〕 ; a patron saint
수호 修好 amity ; friendship ; friendly relations **—하다** get along amicably
— 조약 a friendship pact〔treaty〕 ; a treaty of amity〔friendship〕 ¶ 수호 조약을 체결하다 conclude〔sign〕 a treaty of amity〔friendship〕 《with》
수호이 [소련의 전투기] Sukhoi
수화 水火 water and fire ¶ 수화 불통하다 be at enmity ; be like cats and dogs
— 불통 enmity **— 상극** mutual aversion ; incompatibility
수화 繡畫 an embroidered picture
수화 水化 hydration
—물 a hydrate **— 석회** calcium hydroxid(e) ; hydrated lime
수화 受貨 receipt of goods
—인 a consignee ¶ 아무를 수화인으로 하여 to the consignation of a person
수화 手話 [손짓으로 말함] talking with the hands〔fingers〕 ; [그 말] the finger language
—법 chirology ; dactylology
‡**수화기 受話器** a (telephone) receiver ; an earphone ¶ 수화기를 들다 pick up the receiver // 수화기를 놓다 hang up the receiver // 수화기를 귀에 대다 put the earphone to the ear
‡**수확 收穫** [거둠] harvest ; harvesting ; [농작물] a harvest ; a crop ; a yield

> 참고 **crop** 일반적인 말이며 성장 도중의 것에도 수확 이후의 것에도 쓰인다 **yield** 작물의 양과 액수를 말한다 **harvest** 다소 딱딱한 말이며 수확 작업이나 수확 따위 주로 수확을 생각하고 쓰는 말

—하다 gather a harvest〔crop〕 ; reap ; harvest ; gather〔take〕 in ¶ 수확이 많다〔적다〕 have a good〔bad, poor〕 harvest〔crop〕 // 노력은 했으나 수확이 별로 없었다 The effort yielded but a sorry crop.
—고 the yield ; the crop **—기(機)** a harvester ; a reaping machine **—기(期)** the harvesting season ; the harvest (time)
— 연도 a crop year **— 예상** harvest prospects ; the harvest〔crop〕 estimate
— 체감 〖경제〗 diminishing return **— 체증** 〖경제〗 increasing return
수황증 手荒症 kleptomania
수회 收賄 acceptance of a bribe ; corruption ; corrupt practices ; graft 《미》 **—하다** take〔receive, accept〕 a bribe ; graft ¶ 그는 수회 혐의로 구속되었다 He was arrested on the suspicion〔charge〕 of having taken a bribe.
— 사건 a bribery affair〔case〕 ; a graft scandal 《미》 **—자** a recipient of a bribe ; a bribee ; a corrupt official (공무원) ; a grafter 《미》 ; a boodler 《미·속》
수회 數回 several times ; on several occasions ¶ 수회 시도하다 make several attempts // 수회에 걸쳐 강연하다 give a series〔course〕 of lectures // 수회 경고했으나 그는 듣지 않았다 My repeated warnings were lost upon him.
수효 數爻 a number ; a figure ; an amount ¶ 수효를 세다 count ; take account of ⇨ 수(數)
수훈 垂訓 —하다 teach ; instruct
산상— the Sermon on the Mount
수훈 殊勳 distinguished〔meritorious〕 services ¶ 수훈 타자 〖야구〗 a winning hitter // 수훈을 세우다 distinguish oneself ; render distinguished service ; win one's spurs (전쟁에서)
—상 [운동 경기 등의] a prize for a distinguished performance **—자** a person who has rendered distinguished services
—타 〖야구〗 a winning hit
수희 隨喜 heartfelt〔deep〕 gratitude ; overwhelming joy ; adoration **—하다** feel heavenly joy ; adore
숙감 宿憾 ⇨ 숙원(宿怨)
†**숙고 熟考** mature consideration〔reflection〕 ; deliberation **—·하다** think 《a matter》 over ; give 《a matter》 careful consideration ; consider 《a matter》 carefully ; ponder on〔over〕 《a matter》 ¶ 숙고한 끝에 after careful consideration ; after mature reflection // 그 문제는 숙고를 요한다 The subject demands〔requires〕 careful consideration. /We must give careful consideration to the subject. /We must give the matter careful consideration. // 우리는 지금 그 문제를 숙고 중이다 We now have the matter under consideration. /The matter is now under consideration. // 살까말까 숙고 중이다 I am just considering whether to buy or not.
숙군 肅軍 a purge in the army ; restoration of military discipline
숙근 宿根 an old root
—초 a perennial plant
†**숙녀 淑女** a lady
숙다 ① [앞으로] droop ; bow ; be bent ② [기운이] go〔die〕 down ; subside ¶ 익

은 벼 이삭이 숙다 The rice stalks are bent with grain.

†**숙달 熟達** proficiency **—하다** become skilled 《in》; become proficient 《in》; master; be well up 《in》 ¶ 숙달한 adept 《in, at》; skilled 《in》; versed 《in》 // 영어에 숙달하다 master English; attain proficiency in English; become proficient in English // 전자 계산기의 조작에 숙달하다 become skillful〔expert, an expert〕 in the operation of the electronic computer

숙당 肅黨 a purge in the party

숙덕 淑德 womanly graces; a feminine virtue

숙덕거리다 whisper; talk in whispers; exchange whispers ¶ 그들은 자꾸만 숙덕거렸다 Many whispers passed between them.

숙덕숙덕 in whispers; under one's breath

숙덕이다 whisper ⇨ 숙덕거리다

숙덜거리다 ⇨ 숙덕거리다

*__숙독 熟讀__ careful reading; perusal **—하다** read carefully; peruse ¶ 숙독 음미하다 read with appreciation // 숙독할 만한 가치 있는 책 a work which will repay a careful perusal; a book worth careful reading

숙람 熟覽 careful inspection; scrutiny **—하다** inspect carefully; go over 《every page of a book》; scrutinize; review

숙려 熟慮 careful〔mature〕 deliberation ⇨ 숙고

‡**숙련 熟練** skill; expertness; dexterity ¶ 숙련된 skilled; skillful; expert; experienced // 이런 일은 대단한 숙련이 필요하다 This kind of work requires great〔much〕 skill.

—공 a skilled worker〔workman, hand, 〔craftsman〕; a master mechanic; skilled 〔trained〕 labor 《총칭》 **—자** an expert; a man of experience; a practiced〔skilled〕 hand; an old stager

숙망 宿望 a long-cherished desire; ambition; one's heart's desire ¶ 숙망이 있다 have a long-cherished desire // 숙망을 이루다 attain one's long-cherished desire

숙맥 菽麥 beans and barley

숙면 熟眠 a sound〔heavy, deep〕 sleep **—하다** sleep well〔soundly, heavily〕; have a good sleep ¶ 숙면하고 있다 He is fast asleep. // 나는 숙면을 못한다 I am a bad〔light〕 sleeper.

숙명 宿命 fate; destiny; fatality; predestination; one's fated lot

> 참고 **destiny**는 「애당초 정해진 운명」이라는 뜻이며 **fate**가 destiny 보다 엄숙한 말 **lot**는 심지를 뽑아 「우연히 얻어 걸린 운명」의 뜻

¶ 숙명적인 fatalistic; predestined // 이렇게 되는 것도 내 숙명이다 This is my destiny. /I am destined to come to this pass. // 그들은 다시 만날 수 없는 숙명이었다 They were destined never to meet again.

—론 fatalism ¶ 숙명론적 fatalistic **—론자** a fatalist

*__숙모 叔母__ an aunt

‡**숙박 宿泊** lodging; stopping; staying; [군대의] billeting **—하다** stop〔stay, put up〕 at 《a hotel》; lodge 《at, in》; take up one's lodgings〔quarters〕; [군대가] be billeted〔quartered〕 ¶ 숙박시키다 accommodate; lodge; billet (군대를) // 친구 집에 숙박하다 put up〔stay〕 at a friend's; stop with a friend // A호텔에 숙박 중이다 He is a guest at A Hotel. /He is staying at A Hotel.

—료 lodging charge; board and lodging; hotel rate〔expenses, charges〕; a hotel bill ¶ 호텔 숙박료에 가산시키세요 Put it on my hotel bill, please. **—부** a hotel register **— 설비** sleeping〔overnight〕 accommodations **—소** one's lodgings〔quarters〕 **—인** [하숙인] a lodger; a boarder; a paying guest **간이 —소** a common lodging house 《영》; a municipal lodging house (시영의); a flophouse (노동자의)

숙변 宿便 [변] feces contained long in the intestines; [증상] coprostasis; fecal 〔stercoral〕 stasis

숙병 宿病 a chronic〔an inveterate〕 disease; an old complaint ⇨ 숙환(宿患)

*__숙부 叔父__ an uncle

숙부드럽다 (be) gentle; meek; modest; reserved

숙사 宿舍 lodgings; quarters; a hotel; a billet (군대의)

— 할당 allocation〔allotting〕 of quarters

숙사 熟絲 boiled silk thread

숙상 肅霜 a heavy frost

숙설거리다 talk in whispers ⇨ 속살거리다

숙성 夙成 precocity **—하다** (be) precocious; be wise beyond one's age; be big for one's age (몸집이) ¶ 숙성한 아이 a precocious child // 그녀석 나이에 비해서 숙성한데 He is too smart for his age, that little fellow.

숙성 熟成 〖전기·화학〗 ag(e)ing; 〖화학〗 ripening; maturing; maturation; 〖사진〗 digestion

— 온도 the ripening temperature

숙세 宿世 one's previous life; one's former (state of) existence

*__숙소 宿所__ one's address; one's place of abode; one's quarters ¶ 숙소를 옮기다 change one's lodgings〔quarters, hotel〕; remove // 그의 숙소를 알고 있다 I know where he stays. /I have his address.

숙수 熟手 a fancy cook; a caterer

숙수 熟睡 a sound sleep ⇨ 숙면

숙숙하다 肅肅— [고요하다] (be) silent; hushed; [엄숙하다] solemn

숙시 熟柿 a ripe (and soft) persimmon ; a mellow persimmon ⇨ 홍시(紅柿)
숙시 熟視 steady gaze ; stare ; scrutiny ── 하다 gaze 《at, on》 ; stare 《at》 ; look hard〔steadily, intently〕 ; scrutinize ; examine ; inspect ¶ 얼굴을 숙시하다 gaze 《a person》 in the face ; gaze into 《a person's》 face // 사람을 숙시하다 gaze at 《a person》 intently
숙시주의 熟柿主義 a waiting policy
숙식 宿食 board and lodging ; bed and board ── 하다 board and lodge ¶ 숙식비를 지불하다 pay for one's board and lodging
숙씨 叔氏 (your, his) esteemed third brother (elder or younger)
숙야 夙夜 morning and evening ; day and night ; always
‡숙어 熟語 an idiom ; an idiomatic phrase ; a (set) phrase ¶ 신숙어 a new-coined phrase // 숙어집 a phrase book ; a dictionary of phrases
숙어지다 hang down ; droop ; be bowed ⇨ 수그러지다
숙연 宿緣 destiny ; fate ; 〖불교〗 a karma 《범》
숙연하다 肅然— (be) solemn ; reverential ; silent ¶ 숙연히 silently ; quietly ; solemnly // 숙연히 옷깃을 여미다 be struck with reverence
숙영 宿營 billeting ; quartering ; [숙사] military quarters ; billets ── 하다 be billeted〔quartered〕 《on a town》 ; bivouac ; camp
—지 a billeting place
숙우 宿雨 a long rain ; a long spell of rainy weather
숙원 宿怨 an old grudge〔score, rancor〕 ; deep-rooted enmity ; an old feud ¶ 숙원을 갚다 satisfy one's old grudge ; work off an old grudge ; pay off old scores // 숙원을 품다 have an old grudge against 《a person》 ; be rancorous against 《a person》
숙원 宿願 ⇨ 숙망(宿望)
숙의 熟議 deliberation ; careful consultation ; careful consideration ── 하다 deliberate on 《a matter》 ; consider carefully ; discuss fully ; talk 《a matter》 over ¶ 숙의한 끝에 after careful consideration // 그와 숙의했다 I went over the matter thoroughly with him.
*숙이다 lower 《one's head》 ; hang ; drop ; bow ; droop ¶ 공손히 머리를 숙이고 with a humble〔deep, low〕 bow // 머리를 숙이고 부탁하다 stoop to ask ; beg // 부끄러워서 고개를 숙였다 He hung his head in shame.
숙적 宿敵 an old enemy ; a mortal enemy ; an ancient foe
숙정 肅正 regulation ; enforcement ¶ 관기를 숙정하다 enforce official discipline
†숙제 宿題 homework ; a home task ; home lessons ; an assignment 《미》 ; [미결 문제] an open〔a moot, a pending, an unsettled〕 question ¶ 방학 숙제 a holiday task // 다년간의 숙제 a question of long standing // 숙제를 내다 set 《a person》 a home task〔homework〕 // 숙제를 하다 do one's home lessons〔task〕 // 숙제로 하다 leave 《a matter》 in abeyance // 숙제를 도와주다 help a boy with his homework // 숙제를 해결하다 settle a pending question
—장 a workbook 방학 — a holiday task
숙죄 宿罪 original sin ; sin from an earlier life
숙주 宿主 〖생물〗 a host (to parasites)
숙주(나물) green bean sprouts
숙지 熟知 full knowledge ; familiarity ── 하다 know well〔thoroughly〕 ; be fully aware 《of》 ; have thorough knowledge 《of》 ; be familiar with ¶ 그것은 숙지하고 있다 I am fully aware of it. // 이것은 여러분이 숙지하는 사실이겠습니다 I think you are all aware of this.
숙지근하다 (be) abating
숙직 宿直 night duty ; night watch ── 하다 be on night duty ; keep night watch
— 교대 a shift of night duty — 교사 a night-duty teacher —비 a night watch allowance —실 a night duty room —원 a person on night duty ; a night watchman
숙질 叔姪 an uncle and his nephew 〔niece〕
숙채 宿債 long standing〔old〕 debts
숙철 熟鐵 pig iron
숙청 肅淸 a purge ; a cleanup ; liquidation (살해) ── 하다 stage a purge ; clean up ; liquidate ¶ 숙청 공작을 시작하다 begin a house cleaning
— 운동 a purge campaign 《against》 ; a crusade 《against》
숙체 宿滯 chronic indigestion〔dyspepsia〕
숙취 宿醉 a hangover ; a sickhead ; the morning-after ── 하다 have a hangover ; suffer from the aftereffects of the previous night's drink ¶ 너무 마시면 내일 숙취로 고생할 것입니다 Beware of drinking too much, or you will have a "head" tomorrow morning.
— 치료법 hangover cures
숙친 熟親 intimacy ; a very close relationship ── 하다 (be) intimate ; close
숙폐 宿弊 an evil of long standing ; a deep-rooted evil ; an inveterate abuse ¶ 숙폐를 일소하다 sweep away all the old evils
숙혐 宿嫌 [오래된 혐의] suspicion of long standing ; [오래된 혐오] a long-harbored〔deep-rooted〕 dislike〔distaste, hatred, aversion〕
숙환 宿患 a chronic〔an inveterate〕 disease ¶ 숙환으로 쓰러졌다 He succumbed to the inveterate disease at length.
숙흥야매 夙興夜寐 rising early in the

morning and going to bed late at night
순 旬 ① [10일간] a period of ten days ② [10년] a decade ¶ 상〔중, 하〕 순 the first〔middle, last〕 part of a month // 7순이 넘다 be over seven decades old ; be over seventy years old
순 筍 a sprout ; a shoot ; a bud ¶ 순이나다 bud out ; sprout
죽— a bamboo shoot
순 巡 ① [활쏘기의] a round (of a shooting 5 arrows) ② ⇨ 순행(巡行) ③ [차례] order of rounds
순 純 pure ; genuine ; unalloyed ¶ 순 한국식 purely Korean style ; orthodox Korean fashion // 순수입 net income // 순거짓말 a pure fabrication
-순 順 [순서] order ; [차례] turn ¶ 날짜순으로 in sequence of date // 크기 순으로 according to size // 번호순 numerical order // 가나다순으로 in alphabetical order // 선착순으로 by order of receipt // 성적순 《in》 the order of merit ; the scholastic rank of a student // 연령순으로 in order of age ; by priority of age ; according to seniority // 신청순으로 in the order of application // 키순으로 서다 stand in order of height
순간 旬刊 ¶ 순간의 《a magazine》 published〔issued〕 every ten days
†순간 瞬間 a moment ; a second ; an instant ¶ 순간적 momentary ; instantaneous // 순간적으로 in a moment ; in an instant // 순간적 쾌락 the mere pleasure of the moment // 일순간도 지체할 수 없다 There is not a moment to lose. // 그 말을 들은 순간 그의 얼굴이 창백해졌다 The moment〔instant, minute〕 he heard it, he turned dead white.
— 촬영 a snapshot ; snapshooting — 최대 풍속 the maximum instantaneous wind speed
순강 巡講 a lecturing tour — 하다 make a lecturing tour
—자 an itinerant lecturer
순검 巡檢 a tour of inspection ⇨ 순찰(巡察)
순견 純絹 pure silk ; all-silk
— 양말 sheer silk stockings
†순결 純潔 purity ; cleanliness ; chastity ; virginal purity (동정) — 하다 (be) pure ; clean ; unspotted ¶ 마음이 순결한 사람 a pure-hearted person ; a person pure in heart // 순결한 처녀 a chaste maiden ; a virgin // 순결한 사랑 platonic〔pure〕 love
— 교육 education in sexual morality
*순경 巡警 a policeman ; a patrolman
교통 — a traffic policeman 기마 — a mounted policeman 사복 — a policeman in plain clothes
순경 順境 a favorable condition ; favorable circumstances ¶ 순경에 처하다 be in favorable circumstances ; be in a fair way ; be in prosperity
순계 純系 『생물』 pure line
순교 殉教 religious martyrdom ; baptism of blood — 하다 die a martyr
—사(史) a martyrology —자 a martyr ¶ 순교자가 되다 die a martyr for one's faith ; die for one's belief〔faith〕 —(적) 정신 the spirit of martyrdom
순국 殉國 dying for one's country — 하다 die for one's country
— 선열 a (patriotic) martyr — 정신 the spirit of martyrdom ; patriotism
순국산 純國產 ¶ 순국산의 of entirely Korean make ; all-Korean (production) ; genuinely home-produced〔-manufactured〕
—품 an all-Korean product ; purely Korean-goods
순금 純金 pure gold ; solid gold ¶ 순금의 all-gold ; pure-gold // 순금 반지 a solid gold ring
순난 殉難 dying for society〔one's country, one's cause〕 ; martyrdom — 하다 die for society〔one's country, one's cause〕
순당 順當 — 하다 (be) proper ; right ; natural ; reasonable ¶ 순당한 이치이다 stand to reason ; be in the nature of the case
순대 a sausage made of beef and bean-curd stuffed in pig intestine
—국 pork soup mixed with sliced *sundae* sausage
순도 純度 degree of purity
순되다 純— (be) simple(-hearted) ; sincere
순두부 uncurdled bean curd
순라 巡邏 a patrol ; a round ; a patrolman
—군 a patrolman (in former days)
순량 純良 being pure〔genuine, good〕 — 하다 (be) pure ; pure and good ; genuine ; wholesome
— 포도주 genuine wine —품 a genuine article
순량 純量 net weight
순량 馴良 being well tamed — 하다 (be) tame ; gentle ; meek
순량 順良 being good and obedient — 하다 (be) good and obedient ; meek ; law-abiding
순력 巡歷 a tour ; an inspection tour (in former days) — 하다 tour ; make a tour of
*순례 巡禮 a pilgrimage — 하다 make a pilgrimage 《to》
—자 a pilgrim ; a palmer —지 a place of pilgrimage ; a pilgrimage resort
순로 順路 the usual〔regular〕 route
*순록 馴鹿 a reindeer
순리 純利 net profit
순리 純理 pure reason ; scientific principles
—론 rationalism ¶ 순리론적 rationalistic

—론자 a rationalist
순리 順理 submission to reason ; reasonableness —하다 be reasonable ; accord with reason ¶ 그렇게 하는 것이 순리다 That is the proper means to take.
순막 瞬膜 〖생리〗 a nictitating membrane ; a haw
순만 順娩 easy delivery ⇨ 순산(順產)
순망간 旬望間 between the 10th and the 15th of a lunar month
순면 純綿 pure cotton ; all-cotton
— 제품 all-cotton material〔fabrics〕
순모 純毛 pure wool ; all wool
— 제품 all-wool goods〔fabrics〕
순무 〖식물〗 a turnip ; Brassica rapa (학명)
—채 a salad of finely sliced turnip
순무소속 純無所屬 ¶ 순무소속의 purely independent〔unattached〕; 〖정치〗 completely neutral ; purely nonpartisan 《members of the National Assembly》 ⇨ 무소속(無所屬)
— 의원 a pure independent
순문학 純文學 pure〔polite〕 literature ; belles-lettres 《프》 ¶ 순문학의 belletristic
—가 a belletrist — 소설 a purely literary novel
순물 water strained off coagulating beancurd
순미 純味 unalloyed taste ; pure flavo(u)r
순미 純美 pure beauty ; absolute〔unalloyed〕 beauty —하다 be of absolute beauty
*순박 純朴, 淳朴 simplicity ; homeliness ; Arcadianism —하다 [성질이] (be) simple and honest ; unsophisticated ; naive ; simple-hearted ; [풍속이] homely ; simple-mannered 《people》 ; Arcadian 《life》 ¶ 순박한 시골 노인 an old country man simple and honest by nature
*순방 巡訪 a round of calls〔visits〕 —하다 make a round of calls ; visit one after another ¶ 각국을 순방하다 make a tour of various countries
순배 巡杯 passing the wine cup around
순백 純白 a pure〔snowy〕 white ; sheer〔virginal〕 white —하다 (be) snow-white ; immaculate
†순번 順番 order ; sequence (순서) ; turn (교대) ¶ 순번으로 in order ; in turn ; by turns (교대로) // 순번으로 서다 stand in a queue // 순번을 기다리다 await one's turn // 순번이 오다 one's turn comes round
순보 旬報 a ten-day report ; a report〔periodical〕 issued every ten days
순복 順服 submission ; obedience
순분 純分 fineness ; [금·은·보석의 중량 단위] carat ; [순도 표시] karat
순분도 純分度 fineness (of gold and silver) ; carat (금의)
순뽕 筍— a newly sprouted mulberry leaf
순사 殉死 ① suicide committed for one's country
② self-immolation (of an attendant on the death of his lord) ; suttee (과부의) —하다 die for one's country ; immolate〔kill〕 oneself on the death of one's lord〔master〕; die a martyr's death ; follow one's lord to the grave
순산 順產 an easy delivery〔labor, birth〕 —하다 have an easy delivery ; give an easy birth to ¶ 처가 순산했습니다 My wife was fortunate in her confinement.
순색 純色 unmixed color ; solid color ; (of) one color
†순서 順序 [차례] order ; sequence ; [방법] system ; method ; [수속] procedure ; formalities ¶ 순서 있는 orderly ; systematic // 순서 있게 in good order ; in regular sequence ; systematically // 순서를 어기다 follow the wrong order // 순서를 밟다 go through due formalities // 순서가 틀렸다 be in wrong order ; be out of order
—표 a list ; a (written) program
순석 巡錫 a preaching tour of a Buddhist priest —하다 make a preaching tour
순성 順成 satisfactory〔easy, unimpeded〕 achievement —하다 succeed 《in attempts》 satisfactorily ; be well along ; be accomplished〔attained〕 without any difficulty
순성 馴性 tameness ; meekness
순소득 純所得 net income
순손 純損 dead loss ; a net loss
†순수 純粹 purity ; genuineness —하다 (be) pure ; genuine ; full-blooded ; trueborn ¶ 순수한 포인터 a pointer of pure stock ; a pedigreed pointer // 순수한 에스키모인 a full-blooded Eskimo
— 논리학 pure logic — 문학 pure literature — 소설 pure fiction —시 pure poetry — 예술 pure art — 이성 pure reason ¶ 순수 이성 비판 [칸트의] the Critique of Pure Reason —주의 purism — 철학 metaphysics
순수 巡狩 a royal tour〔trip, progress〕 —하다 make a royal tour
순수입 純收入 net income ¶ 세금 공제 후의 순수입이 한 달에 5000달러쯤 된다 I make about five thousand dollars after taxes a month. /I net about five thousand dollars a month.
순순하다 淳淳— (be) kind and gentle 《in admonishing》 ; earnest ; patient ¶ 순순히 earnestly ; patiently ; gently // 순순히 타이르다 inculcate 《a fact》 upon 《a person》 // 순순히 타일러서 그녀의 잘못을 깨닫게 하려 했다 He tried to talk her out of her silly ideas. /He tried patiently to convince her of her error.
순순하다 順順— ① [태도가] (be) obedient ; docile ; submissive ¶ 순순히 quietly ; without trouble ; obediently // 순순히 자백하다 confess frankly // 순순히 충고를 듣다 accept 《a person's》 advice with

good grace
② [음식이] (be) light ; plain
순시 巡視 a tour〔round〕 of inspection ; an inspection ; a round of visits —하다 make a tour〔go on a round〕 of inspection ; inspect ; [일터를] patrol ; walk one's beat ¶ 공장 내를 순시하다 inspect〔go over〕 a factory // 피난민 수용소를 순시하다 make a tour of refugee camps
—선 a patrol boat —인 a patrolman ; a supervisor ; a floorwalker (백화점의)
순시 瞬時 a moment ; an instant ¶ 순시에 in a moment ; in a twinkling
‡순식간 瞬息間 a brief instant ¶ 순식간에 in the twinkling of an eye
순실 純實 honesty ; guilelessness ; earnestness —하다 (be) honest ; unsophisticated ; guileless ; earnest ; serious ; sober
순실 淳實 simplicity and sincerity —하다 (be) simple and sincere
순애 純愛 pure〔genuine〕 love ; chaste〔Platonic〕 love
*순양 巡洋 a cruise ; cruising —하다 cruise ; sail about
— 전함 a battle cruiser —함 a cruiser 경—함 a light cruiser 보조 —함 an auxiliary cruiser 중—함 a heavy cruiser
순양 馴養 domestication ⇨ 순육(馴育)
순업 巡業 a provincial tour (by a theatrical company) ; a tour of the country 《미》 —하다 tour (the country) ; take a show on the road ; hit the road (지방을) 《미》
순여 旬餘 more than ten days ; ten days or so
순역 順逆 obedience and disobedience ; loyalty and treason ; right and〔or〕 wrong ¶ 순역을 분별하다 discriminate between right and wrong
순연 順延 postponement ; deferment —하다 postpone ; defer ; put off ¶ 우천시 순연 in case of rain, to be postponed 《till the next fine〔fair〕 day》
순연 純然 —하다 (be) pure ; absolute ; perfect ; outright ; out-and-out ; veritable
순열 順列 〖수학〗 permutation ; linear arrangement
— 조합 permutations and combinations
순위 順位 order ; ranking ; precedence ¶ 테니스의 순위 tennis ranking // 순위를 다투다 contend for precedence // 순위를 결정하다 decide the ranking
— 결정전 a play-off
순위표 順位表 a graded〔ranking〕 list ¶ 순위표를 만들다 make a graded list 《of》 ; rank 《them》 in a hierarchical order
순유 巡遊 a (pleasure) tour —하다 make a tour ; go on a tour ; travel about ¶ 구라파를 순유하다 make a tour of Europe
순육 馴育 taming —하다 tame ; domesticate
순은 純銀 pure〔sterling〕 silver ; solid silver
— 숟가락 a sterling spoon
순음 脣音 〖음성〗 a labial (sound)
순응 順應 adaptation ; accommodation ; adjustment —하다 adapt〔accommodate〕 oneself 《to circumstances》 ; adjust oneself 《to》 ¶ …에 순응하여 in sympathy with // 환경에 순응하다 adapt〔accommodate, acclimate〕 oneself to circumstances // 시대에 순응하다 go with the tide〔times〕 // 대세에 순응하다 accept the logic of events
—성 adaptability ; adaptableness ¶ 그는 사태의 변화에 대한 순응성이 풍부하다 He has a high degree of adaptability to altered conditions.
순이익 純利益 net〔clear〕 profit ¶ 순이익 100만원을 얻다 net〔clear, gross, realize〕 a profit of one million *won* // 이 거래로 상당한 순이익을 보았다 The transaction netted me a good profit.
순익 純益 net profit ⇨ 순이익
—금 net〔clear〕 profit
순일 旬日 [초열흘] the tenth day of the month
순일 純一 purity ; genuineness ; homogeneity ; uniformity —하다 (be) unmixed ; pure ; genuine ; uniform
순잎 sprouted leaves
순장 殉葬 〖옛제도〗 burial of the living with the dead (as an attendant on the death of his lord) —하다 bury alive with the dead
순적백성 舜一百姓 a man of pure and simple heart
순전 純全 purity ; spotlessness ¶ 순전한 [순수한] pure ; sheer ; [전적인] absolute ; utter ; perfect ; outright ; downright ; out-and-out ; thorough // 순전히 wholly ; purely ; completely ; utterly ; perfectly // 순전한 개인 문제 a purely personal matter // 순전한 오해 sheer misunderstanding // 그건 순전한 사기다 It's a downright swindle.
순절 殉節 dying in defense of one's chastity〔integrity, loyalty〕 —하다 die for one's chastity
순정 純正 simplicity ; purity ; honesty —하다 (be) honest ; upright ; pure ; genuine
— 과학 pure science — 수학 pure mathematics — 철학 pure philosophy ; metaphysics
순정 純情 pure (and simple) heart〔mind〕 ; naivety ; self-sacrificing devotion ¶ 순정의 소녀 a simple-hearted girl
— 소설 a boy-meets-girl story
*순조 順調 a favorable〔normal〕 condition ; favorableness ; smoothness ; [날씨의] seasonableness ¶ 순조로이 favorably ;

satisfactorily ; smoothly ; swimmingly ; normally ; without a hitch // 순조롭다 be favorable〔well, satisfactory, smooth, seasonable (날씨가)〕// 순조로운 날씨 seasonable〔favorable〕 weather // 순조로이 진행되다 progress satisfactorily ; go well ; be well along ; proceed favorably (담판 따위가) ; go smoothly // 환자의 경과가 순조롭다 The patient is progressing favorably. // 무역이 순조로와졌다 The trade has recovered its normal condition. // 순조롭게 이야기가 진행되어 나도 깜짝 놀랐다 I'm amazed myself. Everything went one, two, three.

*순종 純種 a full〔pure〕 blood ; a thoroughbred ¶ 순종의 full〔pure〕-blooded ; thoroughbred ; pure-bred ; of unmixed breed

‡순종 順從 docility ; obedience ; submissiveness ; acquiescence —하다 obey ; submit ; acquiesce ; yield 《to》 ¶ 양친에게 순종하다 obey one's parents

순주 醇酒 choice wine

순지르다 筍— ⇨ 순치다(筍—)

순직 純直 simplicity and uprightness —하다 (be) simple(-minded) and upright ; honest ; straight

순직 殉職 dying at one's post of duty ; death in harness —하다 die at one's post of duty ; be killed in the performance of one's duties ; die in harness
— 경관 a policeman who died on duty —자 a victim to his post of duty ; a martyr to duty

†순진 純眞 naivety ; purity ; naiveté (프) —하다 (be) naive ; pure ; genuine ; sincere ¶ 순진한 처녀 a maiden pure in heart // 순진한 마음 a pure and simple heart // 순진한 사랑 pure love ; Platonic love ; devoted love (부부간의)

순차 順次 order ; turn ¶ 순차적으로 [점점] gradually ; [차례로] in order ; successively ; in regular sequence

*순찰 巡察 a patrol ; a round of inspection —하다 patrol ; make〔go on〕 a round of inspection
—대 a patrol party — 대원 a patrolman — 장교 an officer on patrol —차 a (police) patrol car ; a squad car

순채 蓴菜 a watershield plant ; Brassenia purpurea (학명)

순치 馴致 ① [길들임] domestication ; taming ② [초래] bringing about ; giving rise to —하다 tame ; domesticate ; naturalize ; habituate ; lead to ; bring about〔forth, on〕 ; give rise to

순치다 筍— cut off sprouts〔buds, shoots〕 ; trim 《a plant》 ; cut 《a plant》 back

순치음 脣齒音 〖음성〗 a labiodental〔dentilabial〕 sound

순탄 順坦, 純坦 —하다 [길이] (be) even ; level ; smooth ; [성질이] gentle ; mild ; not fastidious

순풍 淳風 a good custom
—미속 good morals and manners

순풍 順風 a favorable wind ; a fair wind ¶ 인생은 순풍에 돛을 단 듯이 언제나 순조로운 것은 아니다 Life is by no means a smooth〔plain〕 sailing.
순풍에 돛을 달다 관용 sail before the wind ; be under easy sail

‡순하다 順— ① [성질이] (be) gentle ; docile ; obedient ; amiable ; meek ; tender ¶ 성질이 순하다 be meek in temper ② [맛이] (be) mild ; smooth ¶ 그 담배는 순하다 The cigarettes are mild.
③ [일이] (be) smooth ; go well

순하다 殉— sacrifice〔immolate〕 oneself 《for the country》 ; die 《for the cause》 ; die a martyr to〔for〕 《one's faith》

*순항 巡航 a cruise ; cruising —하다 go on a cruise ; cruise
—권(圈) a cruising zone —선 a cruiser ; a cruise boat — 속도 《at full》 cruising speed

순행 巡行 a patrol ; a tour ; a round —하다 make a tour〔round〕 ; go on a patrol

순행 巡幸 a royal tour —하다 《a king》 make a tour

순행 順行 going〔doing〕 in order ; 〖천문〗 direct motion

순혈 純血 pure blood ¶ 순혈의 pure-blooded ; pure-bred ; thoroughbred (말 따위)

순화 醇化 refinement ; sublimation ; idealization —하다 refine ; purify ; sublimate ; chasten ; idealize

순화 純化 purification —하다 purify

순화 馴化 acclimatization ; naturalization ; acclimation (미) —하다 acclimatize〔acclimate〕 《oneself to a country》 ¶ 그 식물은 아직 한국의 풍토에 순화되지 않았다 The plant is not yet acclimated in Korea〔has not yet acclimatized itself to Korea〕.

‡순환 循環 circulation ; rotation ; cycle —하다 circulate 《through》 ; rotate ; cycle ; recur ; revolve ¶ 낮과 밤의 순환 alternation of day with night // 계절은 순환한다 The seasons rotate. // 경기와 불경기는 순환한다 Prosperity and depression move in a cycle.
— 계통 the circulating system (of the blood) — 곡선 a recurring curve — 급수 recurring series —기 a cycle — 논법 〖논리〗 arguing in a circle —론 circular reasoning ; a vicious circle — 반응 circular reaction —선(線) a loop〔belt〕 line ; a circular railway — 소수 circulating〔recurring〕 decimals 경기 — a business cycle ; a trade cycle (영) ¶ 경기 순환설 the cycle theory

‡순회 巡廻 a round ; a tour ; a trip —하다 go (on) one's round ; make a tour

— 강연 a lecturing〔lecture〕 tour ; barnstorming — 공연 a provincial〔local〕 performance ; a show on tour ; a road show — 구역 one's beat〔round〕 — 극단 a touring company — 대사 a roving ambassador ; an ambassador-at-large — 비행 a surveillance flight — 재판 a court of assize — 재판소 a circuit court — 진료반〔도서관〕 a traveling clinic〔library〕 — 판매인〔상인〕 a traveling salesman ; a commercial traveler ; a drummer 《미·속》 지방 — provincial tour 《of professional wrestlers》

순후 醇厚, 淳厚 pure-mindedness ; warmheartedness —하다 (be) pure-minded ; warm-hearted

‡숟가락 a spoon ¶ 설탕 한 숟가락 a spoonful of sugar // 숟가락으로 뜨다 spoon up 〔out〕
밥— a table spoon 찻— a teaspoon

숟갈 a spoon ⇨ 숟가락

*술[1] rice wine ; wine ; liquor ; alcoholic drinks ; spirits ; intoxicant ¶ 술 탓으로 under the influence of wine // 술을 마시다 drink // 술을 빚다 brew〔make〕 rice wine ; distil alcoholic liquors // 술이 약하다 get easily drunk ; be easily overcome by drink ; be a poor drinker // 술에 취하다 get drunk ; become intoxicated ; be dazed by liquor // 술에 취하여 자다 drink oneself asleep // 술을 삼가다 refrain 〔abstain〕 from liquor // 술을 끊다 cut out wine ; give up〔quit〕 drinking // 술을 따르다 pour out wine // 술은 입에도 대지 않습니다 I don't touch alcohol. // 내가 술 한잔 사겠다 Have a drink on me. // 벌써 술이 오르기 시작한다 I'm already beginning to feel high. // 술 마시면서 얘기하자 Let's talk over the cups. // 술버릇이 좋다 He is merry in his cups. // 술이 취해도 까딱없다 He carries his liquor well. // 술 한 잔 안 하시겠소 Won't you have a drink? // 술이 취한 손님은 구내에 더 있을 수 없습니다 Customers who had one too many are not allowed to stay on the premises. // 그는 술이 일단 몇 잔 들어가면 입을 다물게 할 길이 없다 Once he's had a few, there's no shutting him up.
술과 안주를 보면 맹세도 잊는다 속담 When wine is in, the wit is out.
술은 괼 때 걸러야 한다 속담 Make hay while the sun shines.

*술[2] [분량] a spoonful ; [술대] a plectrum ; a pick

술[3] [쟁기의] the blade-guard of a Korean plow〔plough 《영》〕

술[4] [장식용] a tassel ; a tuft ; a fringe ¶ 술 달린 기 a tasseled flag

술[5] 〖식물〗 the pistils and stamens of a flower
수— a stamen 암— a pistil

술[6] [부피] the thickness of a book or paper

술 戌 the Sign of the Dog 《11th of the 12 Earth's Branches》 ¶ 술시 the Watch of the Dog 《the 11th of the 12 double-hours, the period between 7 and 9 p. m.》

술가 術家 a conjurer ; a witch ; a magician

술값 drink money ¶ 번 돈은 모두 술값으로 날아가고 만다 All the money earned goes for drink.

술객 術客 a conjurer ⇨ 술가

술계 術計 an artifice ; a trick ; craft ; a stratagem

*술고래 a strong〔heavy〕 drinker ; a tippler ; a soaker

술구더기 unwanted grains of rice on fermenting wine

술국 broth prepared to be taken with liquor
—밥 barroom broth mixed with rice

술기 —氣 [술기] the smell〔odor〕 of liquor ; an alcoholic smell ; [취기] intoxication ; tipsiness

술기운 the influence of wine〔liquor〕

술김 the influence of liquor ¶ 술김에 under the influence of liquor ; in a drunken fit ; emboldened by wine ; in one's cups // 술김에 하는 싸움 a drunken brawl // 술김에 부리는 객기 Dutch courage // 술김에 다투다 quarrel under the influence of liquor

*술꾼 a drinker ¶ 큰 술꾼 a drunkard ; a sot ; a tippler ; a heavy drinker ; a boozer 《미·속》

술내 the smell〔odor〕 of liquor ; an alcoholic smell

술년 戌年 〖민속〗 the Year of the Dog

술대 〖음악〗 a plectrum〔pick〕 used in playing a Korean harp

술도가 —都家 a brewery ; a distillery

술독 [항아리] a liquor jug ; [주정뱅이] a sot〔drunkard〕

술독 —毒 ⇨ 주독(酒毒)

술래 a tagger ; a hoodman (눈가리고 하는) ¶ 네가 술래다 You are it.

술래잡기 tag ; prisoner's base ; [눈감고 하는] blindman's buff ; hide and seek —하다 play tag ; play hide-and-seek

술렁거리다 be perturbed ; be disturbed ; be unsettled ; be agitated ¶ 그 소식을 듣고 학생들은 술렁거렸다 The students were agitated by〔with〕 the news.

술렁술렁 disturbed ; in a commotion ; upset ; perturbed ; uneasy ; all abuzz

술레 〖식물〗 a kind of pear tree

술맛 the taste〔flavor〕 of wine〔liquor〕

술망나니 a drunkard ; a sot ; a lush

술 먹은 개 a drunkard ; a drunken person

술명하다 (be) modest ; inconspicuous

술밑 yeast ; ferment

술바닥 the bottom part of the bladeguard of a plow

술밥 steamed rice for making wine
술방 戌方 〖민속〗 the Direction of the Dog 《northwest-by-west》
술버릇 ¶ 술버릇이 나쁘다 be quarrelsome in one's cups ; be a bad drunk // 술버릇이 좋다 be a good drunk
술법 術法 magical tricks ; conjury ; magic ; mysteries ¶ 술법을 쓰다 practice magic ; lay a spell 《upon》
술병 —甁 a liquor bottle
술병 —病 an alcoholic disorder〔disease〕 ¶ 술병나다 drink oneself ill ; drink too much and fall ill
술부대 —負袋 a drunkard ; a heavy drinker ; a tippler ; a boozer 《미·속》
술살 fat put on by habitual drinking ¶ 술살이 오르다 get fat from alcohol
술상 —床 a drinking table ; a bar table ¶ 술상을 차리다 prepare dishes to accompany drink ; set the drinking table
술서 術書 a book of conjury ; a book of magic
술수 術數 conjury ⇨ 술법
술술 ① [막힘 없이] fluently ; facilely ; [순조롭게] smoothly ; without a hitch ; swimmingly ; [쉽게] easily ; readily ; [솔직하게] frankly ; unreservedly ¶ 술술 말하다 speak fluently〔with fluency〕 // 어려운 문제를 술술 풀다 solve a hard question easily〔without an effort〕 // 술술 자백하다 confess frankly ; confess with good grace // 일이 술술 잘 되어 나갔다 The matters went on swimmingly.
② [물 따위가] leaking badly ; softflowing ¶ 주전자에서 물이 술술 샌다 The kettle leaks badly. /Water is leaking from the kettle in a steady stream.
③ [비바람이] gently ; softly ; drizzling (비가) ¶ 비가 술술 내린다 The rain is drizzling down. /It drizzles. // 바람이 술술 분다 The wind blows gently. /There is a gentle breeze.
술시 戌時 〖민속〗 the Watch of the Dog ① the 11th of the 12 doublehours 《the period between 7 and 9 p. m.》
② the 21st of the 24 hours 《7 : 30-8 : 30 p. m.》
술안주 —按酒 a relish (taken with wine) ; a side dish ; an accompaniment of〔for, to〕 wine ; a snack eaten with drinks ¶ 술과 술안주 wine and some eatables // 술안주로서는 최고다 It is a capital accompaniment of drinks.
*＊**술어 述語** 〖문법〗 a predicate ¶ 술어적인 predicative
— **동사** a predicate verb
†**술어 術語** a technical term ; [총칭] technics ; professional language ; (scientific) terminology ; nomenclature ¶ 법의학의 술어 medicolegal terms
술일 戌日 the Day of the Dog
술자리 a banquet ; a feast ; a drinking party ¶ 술자리에서 시비를 하다 have a quarrel while drinking
＊**술잔** a wine cup ; a liquor glass ; a goblet ¶ 술잔을 돌리다 pass the wine cup round ; circulate the wine cup // 술잔을 비우다 drain〔drink off〕 the cup ; drink the cup dry
술잔치 a drinking party ; a feast
술장사 the liquor-selling business
술장수 a liquor dealer ; a wine seller
술주자 a liquor cask〔straining tub〕
†**술집** a drink shop ; a tavern ; a grogshop ; a bar ; a pub
— **여급** a barmaid — **주인** a barkeeper
술찌끼 wine lees ; (brewer's) grains ; draff
술책 術策 an artifice ; a stratagem ; a trick ; wiles ; tactics ; a policy ¶ 술책을 부리다 resort to tricks
술청 the counter of a stand-up bar ; the bar (술집)
술추렴 collecting money for a drinking bout **—하다** have everyone chip in for a drinking party
술친구 a boon〔convivial, bottle〕 companion ; a drinking companion〔pal〕 ; a companion in one's revels ; a fellow toper
술타령 —打令 ① [술에 빠짐] abandoning oneself to drinking ② [술을 청함] suggesting〔asking for〕 a drink **—하다** abandon oneself to drinking ; be steeped in liquor ; be soaked in drink ; be boozy 《미·속》 ; suggest〔ask for〕 a drink
술탈 an upset〔accident, sickness〕 due to drinking
술통 a wine barrel ; a wine keg
술파리 a fly in a wine jug ; a kind of summer fly
술판 a drinking bout〔party〕 ¶ 술판을 벌이다 hold〔give, have〕 a drinking bout
술회 述懷 [털어 놓음] an effusion of one's thoughts (and feelings) ; [회상] recollection ; reminiscence **—하다** relate〔express〕 one's thoughts〔reminiscence〕 ; speak reminiscently ¶ 과거를 술회하다 recall the past
—**담** one's memoirs〔reminiscences〕
*＊**숨**¹ a breath ; breathing ; respiration ¶ 단숨에 all in a breath // 숨막히는 stuffy ; suffocating ; close ; oppressive // 숨가쁘게 out of breath ; panting ; breathlessly // 숨을 죽이고 with bated breath ; in breathless suspense〔expectation〕 ; with breathless anxiety〔interest〕 // 숨이 가쁘다 breathe hard ; be short of breath (병자가) // 숨막히다 be choky〔stifling, stuffy, suffocating〕 // 숨을 내쉬다 breathe out ; exhale // 숨을 들이쉬다 breathe in ; inhale // 숨을 돌리다 take〔gather〕 breath ; recover one's breath ; take a pause〔short rest〕 (쉬다) // 경기의 마지막은 숨막히는 열전이었다 There was a thrilling finish to the race. // 더워서 숨이

막힐 지경이었다 We were stifled by the heat. // 한 5천원만 더 있으면 한숨 돌리겠네만 If I just had five thousand *won* more, I could tide over this difficulty. // 자주 숨이 차고 현기증이 납니다 I get easily short of breath and dizzy.

숨² [채소 따위의] the crispness of fresh vegetables ¶ 배추가 숨이 죽었다 The cabbage has lost its crispness.

숨결 breathing ; respiration ¶ 숨결이 거칠다 breathe hard ; be short of breath (병자가)

숨고다 pant ; be choked ; be suffocated

숨골 ⇨ 연수(延髓)

숨구멍 〖해부〗 the trachea ; the windpipe

숨기 一氣 signs of breathing ; the breath ¶ 숨기가 없다 show no sign of life

†**숨기다** [안 보이게] hide 《away》 ; conceal ; [몰래] harbor ; shelter ; [비밀로 하다] keep〔hide, conceal〕 《a matter》 from 《a person》 ; keep secret〔back〕 ; [덮어서] cover 《a fact》 ; veil ; screen ; disguise 《one's nationality》 ¶ 숨김 없이 straightforwardly ; frankly ; openly // 숨김 없이 말하자면 to be frank with you ; to tell the truth // 몸을 숨기다 hide (oneself) behind〔in, under〕 // 잘못을 숨기다 cover one's mistake // 이 일을 오랫동안 숨겨왔다 I have long kept it to myself. // 숨기지 말고 말해 봐 Speak it out. /Tell me everything about it. /Spit it out. 《속》

숨기척 ⇨ 숨기

숨넘어가다 breathe one's last ; expire ; die

†**숨다** ① [몸을 숨기다] hide ; hide〔conceal〕 oneself ; take cover ; be〔lie〕 in hiding ; seek〔take〕 refuge〔shelter〕 《in, under, behind》 ; [안 보이게 되다] disappear (from sight) ; be lost sight of ; be hidden from sight ¶ 숨어서 out of sight ; in secret (남 모르게) // 책상 뒤에 숨다 take shelter behind the desk // 숨어 있어 Lie close ! // 달이 구름 뒤에 숨었다 The moon went〔disappeared〕 behind the clouds. // 조용해질 때까지 숨어 계시는 게 날 거요 You had better keep out of sight till the excitement is over.
② [은둔하다] retire from the world ¶ 산야에 숨다 retire from public service ; live in seclusion
③ [알려져 있지 않다] be unknown ; be lurking in ¶ 숨은 자선가 an unknown〔anonymous〕 philanthropist // 숨은 천재 a hidden genius

숨대 ⇨ 숨구멍

*__숨바꼭질__ hide and seek ── **하다** play hide and seek

숨박질 ⇨ 숨바꼭질

숨뿌리 〖식물〗 an aerial root

숨소리 the sound of breathing ¶ 숨소리를 죽이다 hold one's breath ; catch one's breath

숨숨하다 (be) pockmarked

†**숨쉬다** breathe ; respire ; draw one's breath ; take breath ¶ 숨쉴 사이도 안주다 give 《a person》 not a moment's respite

숨어들다 steal in〔into〕 ; get in by stealth

숨은장 〖건축〗 a hidden〔an invisible〕 peg

숨죽다 lose strength and freshness ; be 'killed'

숨지다 breathe one's last ; expire ; gasp one's life away ; die ; give up one's breath

⁑**숨차다** be out of breath ; (be) breathless ; panting ; be short of breath ¶ 숨찬 목소리로 말하다 gasp〔puff, pant〕 out 〔forth, away〕

숨탄것 animals ; creatures that breathe

숨통 一筒 the windpipe ⇨ 숨구멍

숨틀 the breathing apparatus ; the respiratory organs

숫- pure ; unspoiled ; spotless ; undefiled ; innocent ¶ 숫처녀 a virgin ; an innocent 〔unsophisticated〕 girl

숫간 一間 a low room added to the back of a house for storage or for guests

숫구멍 〖해부〗 the fontanel

숫국 ① [사람] a simple〔an innocent〕 person ② [물건] a virgin thing ; an unused article

숫기 一氣 innocence ; openness ¶ 숫기 좋다 be unashamed〔unabashed, bold, outgoing〕

숫돌 a whetstone ; a rubstone ; a grindstone ; a hone (면도용) ¶ 숫돌에 갈다 sharpen 《a knife》 on a whetstone

숫되다 (be) naive ; artless ; unaffected ; unsophisticated ; rustic ; homely ; simple

숫보기 a naive〔simple, guileless〕 person

숫사람 ⇨ 숫국 ①

숫색시 an innocent young girl ; a virgin

숫실 繡— embroidery thread

*__숫자__ 數字 a figure ; a numeral ¶ 숫자상의 numerical // 숫자상의 잘못 numerical errors // 정확한 숫자 precise figures // 숫자를 들다 give〔cite〕 figures // 숫자로 나타내다 state〔express〕 in figures // 대단한 숫자가 되다 amount to big figures
☞ ◖ p. 1291 ◗

숫잔대 〖식물〗 a lobelia ; Lobelia sessilifolia (학명)

숫접다 (be) pure ; innocent ; chaste ¶ 숫저운 색시 an innocent girl

숫제 ① [차라리] rather ; preferable ¶ 그 따위 짓을 해야 한다면 숫제 죽는 편이 낫겠다 If I had to do such a thing, I would (rather) die first. // 수모를 당할 바엔 숫제 죽는 편이 낫겠다 Death is preferable to dishonor.
② [진심으로] sincerely ; whole-heartedly ¶ 숫제 마음을 바치다 completely devote oneself to 《one's husband》
③ [전적으로] (not) at all ; from the first 〔beginning〕 ¶ 장사가 숫제 안 됩니다 My

숫 자

수를 나타내는 말은 **수사**(numeral)라고 하며, 이것에는 one, two, three... 처럼 수를 세는 **기수**(cardinal number)와 first, second, third...등과 같이 순서를 나타내는 **서수**(ordinal number)와의 두가지가 있다.

1 기수 (cardinal numbers)

(1) 보통 문장 내에서 12까지의 수는 문자(文字)로 표기하는 경우가 많은데 시각·날짜·계산 등은 아라비아 숫자를 쓰기도 한다. 문어체의 문장에서는 1에서 100까지의 수와 100 이상의 수 중에서도 정수(整數) (round numbers)가 아닌 수는 문자로 표기한다. 그러나 문장 앞머리에서는 어떠한 경우에도 문자를 쓴다. 또한 같은 문장에서 두 번 이상 수가 반복될 때는 숫자나 문자 어느 쪽이든 통일시켜야 한다.

(2) 기수(基數)에는 대명사·명사·형용사의 용법이 있다.

① 형용사

세 아이 three children / 다섯 가족 five families / 책 2권 two books

② (대)명사

1에서 10까지 세시오. Count from one to ten. / 3은 작은 수다. Three is a small number. / 그들중 5명이 결석하였다. Five of them were absent.

(3) 4자리 이상의 수는 읽기 쉽게 하기 위하여 (,)를 찍는다. 첫번째 comma는 thousand, 두번째는 million, 세번째는 milliard의 단위이고 《미》에서는 hundred 다음의 and는 종종 생략한다.

¶ 9,837,006 nine million eight hundred (and) thirty-seven thousand (and) six.

(4) 수사 또는 수를 나타내는 형용사를 동반해도 단위명인 hundred, thousand, million, billion에는 -s를 붙이지 않는다.

¶ 10만권의 책 one hundred thousand books

(5) 정수(round number)를 나타낼 때는 후미에 -odd나 or so를 붙인다.

¶ 약 90 90-odd / 90 or so.

(6) 12를 나타내는 dozen이나 20을 나타내는 score, 2를 나타내는 couple로 표시하는 방법도 있다.

¶ 6 a half dozen / half a dozen // 18 a dozen and a half // 70년 three score years and ten (★ 사람의 수명을 나타낼 때) 는 a couple of days 2, 3일)

(7) 불특정 다수를 나타낼 때는 어림수에 따라 다음과 같이 표기한다.

¶ 몇 백의 hundreds (of…) // 몇 천의 thousands (of…) // 몇 만의 tens of thousands (of…)

(8) 로마자는 연호, 왕·여왕의 계승 순위, 논문의 장, 페이지, 시계의 문자판 등에 쓰인다. 로마자의 소문자는 논문 등에서 서문의 페이지나 설명문의 소구분을 나타낼 때에 한정되어 쓰인다. 기본 수의 기호는 I(1), V(5), X(10), L(50), C(100), D(500), M(1000)으로 나타내며 로마 숫자의 원칙으로서는

① 병렬(竝列)은 덧셈을 나타낸다.

VI = V+I = 6 / XXIV = XX+IV = 24

② 작은 수의 기호 오른쪽에 큰 수의 기호가 오면 큰 수에서 작은 수를 뺀다.

IV = V − I = 4 / IX = X − I = 9 / XC = C − X = 90

¶ 제2장 chapter II (★ chapter two 또는 the second chapter라고 읽는다.) // 제2차 세계대전 World War II (★ World war two 또는 the second World War로 읽는다.) // 엘리자베드 2세 Elizabeth II (★ Elizabeth the Second로 읽는다.)

2 서수 (ordinal numbers)

(1) 서수는 first, second, third를 제외하고는 기수에 -th를 붙여 만들지만, five → fifth, twelve → twelfth, eight → eighth, nine → ninth 등과 같은 예외도 있다. (★ eighth와 ninth의 철자에 주의.)

(2) 서수(序數)에는 (대)명사·형용사·부사의 용법이 있으며 보통은 the를 붙여 쓴다.

① 형용사

첫번째 사람 the first man / 둘째 해 the second year / 100분의 1 the (one) hundredth part (★ one은 보통 붙이지 않는다.)

② (대)명사

그가 제일 먼저 왔다. He was the first to come. / 5월 5일 the fifth of May, May the fifth (★ 흔히 May 5 또는 May 5th로 쓰고 위와 같이 읽는다.)

③ 부사

2등(칸)으로 여행하다. travel second / 그는 반에서 첫째이다. He stands first in his class.

3 분수 (fractions)

(1) 분수를 읽을 때는 분자(numerator)를 기수로, 분모(denominator)를 서수로 읽는다. 문자로 나타낼 때도 마찬가지이다. 분자가 2 이상의 수일 때 분모를 복수형으로 한다.

¶ 1/9 a [one] ninth // 2/9 two ninths

(2) 1/2, 1/4의 읽는 방법과 쓰는 방법에 유의.

¶ 1/2 a half / one half // 1/4 a quarter / one[a] fourth / a[the] fourth part //

3/4 three-quarters/three-fourths // 4/7 four-sevenths // 63/100 sixty-three hundredths

(3) 123/456같은 복잡한 분수는 over를 사용하여 one hundred (and) twenty-three over four hundred (and) fifty-six와 같이 분자·분모 모두 기수로 표기. 15/5과 같은 가분수는 fifteen over five와 같이 읽는다.

(4) 분수를 명사로 쓸 때는 보통 둘로 분리하여 표기하여 쓰지만 형용사로 쓸 때는 하이픈을 붙인다.

¶ 나는 일을 3/5 끝냈다. I've finished three fifths of the job. // 하루는 1년의 1/365이다. A day is one three hundred (and) sixty-fifth of a year. // 그는 2/3의 다수를 얻었다. He got a two-thirds majority.

(5) $1\frac{3}{4}$ 와 같은 대분수(mixed number)는 보통수와 분수를 구분하여 one and three quarters로 읽는다.

④ 소수 (decimal fractions)

0.123은 (zero) point one two three, 4.025는 four point zero two five, 19.87는 nineteen point eight seven으로 읽는다. (★ 소숫점 위 「0」은 보통 생략.)

¶ 1미터는 39.37인치이다. A meter is thirty-nine point three seven inches.

⑤ 횟수·돗수

반 half / 단일 single / 2배[중,겹]double / 3배[중,겹] treble[triple] / 4배 quadruple / 1회 [번] once / 2회 [번] twice / 3회 [번] three times (★thrice는 문어적) / 2중[겹] two-folds / 3중[겹] three-folds

⑥ 그 밖의 수

3^2…three squared; the square of three

3^3…three cubed; the cube of three

3^4…three to the fourth (power)

3^5…three to the fifth (power)

$\sqrt{9}$…the square root of nine

$\sqrt[3]{1000}$…the cube root of a thousand

¶ 5의 2제곱은 25이다. Five squared is twenty-five. // 36의 2평방근은 6이다. The square root of thirty-six is six.

⑦ 계산

문자로 표현하는 것은 수식을 그대로 읽는 것과 같다.

¶ 5 더하기 2는 7(5+2=7)이다. Five plus two is [equals] seven. / Five and two are [is, make(s)] seven. // 7 빼기 2는 5(7−2=5)이다. Seven minus two is [equals] five. / Two from seven leaves five. // 3곱하기 4는 12(3×4=12)이다. Three times four is [are, makes, equals] twelve. (★ 원래 three times four는 영어에서 4의 3배란 뜻. two times 대신에 twice를 쓰기도 한다.) // 15 나누기 3(15÷3=5)은 5이다. Fifteen divided by three is [give, makes, equals] five. // 4대 8은 6대 12와 같다. Four is to eight, as six is to twelve.

⑧ 주소·방번호

번지·방번호 등의 경우는 3행 이상의 숫자는 기수(基數)로 읽는 것이 보통이다.

종로구 관철동 25의 16 25-16 Kwanchol-dong, Chongno-gu (★숫자는 twenty-five[two five] sixteen으로 읽는다.) // 하야트호텔 915호실 Room 915, Hyatt Hotel (★ Room nine fifteen[nine one five], Hyatt Hotel로 읽는다.)

⑨ 전화번호

¶ 긴급을 요할 때에는 112를 돌리십시오. In emergency dial 112. (★ one-one-two로 읽는다.) // 내 사무실 전화번호는 02-866-8800, 구내전화 329번입니다. My office phone number is 02-866-8800, extension 329. (★ o-two, eight-six-six, eight-eight-0-0, extension three-two-nine으로 읽는다.)

⑩ 연호 · 날짜 · 시각

3자리 이상의 연호는 보통 두자리씩 끊어서 읽는다. 1995년은 nineteen ninety-five, 1900년은 nineteen hundred, 1905년은 nineteen (hundred and) five 또는 nineteen o[óu] five로도 읽는다.

「기원…」을 뜻하는 A.D., 「기원전…」 B.C.는 《미》에서는 숫자 뒤에 《영》에서는 숫자 앞에 위치한다.

¶ 아우구스투스 황제는 기원전 63년에 태어나 서기 14년에 죽었다. Emperor Augustus was born in (the year) 63 B.C. and died in (the year) 14 A.D. // 곧 2000년대에 들어서게 된다. We will soon go into [are moving towards] the 2000s. (★ 2000s는 two thousand로 읽는다.) // 5월 5일에 상경하겠습니다. I will come up to Seoul on May 5 [the fifth of May]. // 부산행 8시 50분발 기차가 10분 늦게 출발합니다. The 8: 50 Pusan train will leave ten minutes late. (★8: 50는 eight fifty로 읽는다.)

⑪ 연령 · 학년

¶ 나는 17세 고등학교 2학년생입니다. I'm seventeen (years old) and a second-year student [sophomore 《미》] at a high school. // 내 형은 대학 3년생이다. My brother is in the third year [a junior 《미》] in college. // 그녀는 40대 초반[중반, 후반]이다. She is in her early [mid, late] forties. // 그는 20세 전후이다. He's twenty or so [or thereabouts].

⑫ 페이지 · 장

¶ 그것은 이 책의 제3장에 들어 있습니다. It is described in chapter three of this book. // 교과서 10페이지를 여십시오. Open your textbook(s) to[at 《영》] page 10. (★ page ten으로 읽는다.) // 이것은 마태복음 4장 12절에서 인용한 것입니다. This is a quotation from Matthew 4: 12. (★ (chapter) four, (verse) twelve로 읽는다.) // 셰익스피어는 햄릿(3막 1장 56행)에서 이렇게 썼다 '죽느냐 사느냐 그것이 문제로다'. Shakespeare writes in Hamlet: 'To be, or not to be: that is the question.' (3. 1. 56). (★ act three, scene one, line fifty-six로 읽는다.) // 25페이지의 10행부터 20행까지를 영역하시오. Put into English lines 10-20 on page 25. (★ lines ten to [through] twenty on page twenty-five로 읽는다.)

⑬ 금액

¶ 집 임대료는 10만원입니다. The (house) rent is 100,000 won. // 5달러 2센트를 지불했다. I paid $ 5.20. (★ five dollars and twenty cents로 읽는데 구어에서는 five twenty로도 가능하다.)

⑭ 기타

¶ 나는 기어를 2단에 놓고나서 3단으로 바꾸었다. I put the car in [into] second (gear) and then changed to[into] third. // 부산행 열차는 5번홈에서 출발합니다. The Pusan train leaves from platform 5. (★ platform (number) five로 읽는다.)

business is no good at all. // 숫제 안 가는 게 좋다 You better not go at all. // 이건 숫제 모르겠는데요 I can't make head or tail of this.

숫지다 (be) simple ; simple-hearted ; naive ; homely ¶ 숫진 사람 a simple-hearted person

숫처녀 —處女 an immaculate〔undefiled〕 virgin

숫총각 —總角 an innocent bachelor

숫하다 (be) naive ⇨ 숫되다

숭경 崇敬 reverence ; veneration **—하다** venerate ; revere

†**숭고** 崇高 sublimity ; loftiness ; the sublime **—하다** (be) sublime ; lofty ; noble

—미 sublime beauty ; the sublime

숭굴숭굴 plump ; amiable (태도가) **—하다** (be) chubby ; plump ; happylooking ; [태도가] affable ; amiable ; easygoing ; be easy to get along with ¶ 숭굴숭굴 살이 찐 어린이 a chubby child // 누구에게나 숭굴숭굴하다 He makes himself agreeable to everybody.

숭늉 drinking water boiled in a kettle where rice has been steamed ; scorched rice-tea

숭덩숭덩 ⇨ 송당송당

†**숭배** 崇拜 worship ; adoration ; admiration **—하다** worship ; adore ; admire ; idolize ; make an idol of ¶ 나는 톨스토이를 진심으로 숭배하고 있다 I have a sincere admiration for Tolstoy.

—자 an admirer ; a worshipper ; an adorer ; an idolater ; a votary **개인 —** the cult of personality **아폴로 —** the cult of Apollo **영웅〔조상〕 —** hero〔ancestor〕 worship **우상 —** idol worship ; idolatry **자연 —** the cult of nature ; nature worship ; naturism

***숭상** 崇尙 respect 《for learning》

—하다 respect ; revere ; esteem

숭숭 minced ; perforated ⇨ 송송

숭어 〖물고기〗 a mullet

— 국수 noodles in mullet soup **—찜** batter-coated sliced mullet cooked with seasoning

숭어뜀 a handspring **—하다** turn handsprings

숭엄 崇嚴 solemnity ; sublimity ; majesty

—하다 (be) solemn ; sublime ; majestic

***숯** charcoal ¶ 숯을 굽다 make charcoal 《in a kiln》 // 화로에 숯을 지피다 feed 《the fire》 with charcoal ; put more charcoal on the fire

—덩이 a lump of charcoal **—막** a charcoal burner's shed **—불** a charcoal fire **—섬** a charcoal sack **—쟁이** a charcoal burner〔maker〕

숯이 검정 나무란다 속담 The kettle calls the pot black-brows.

숯가마 a charcoal kiln〔pit〕

숯검정 charcoal soot

숯내 smell of burning charcoal ; charcoal smoke ¶ 숯내가 나다 smell burning charcoal // 숯내를 맡다 be poisoned by charcoal fumes

숯등걸 charcoal cinders ; half-burned charcoal

숯머리 a headache from inhaling charcoal fumes ¶ 숯머리를 앓다 be poisoned by charcoal fumes

숯장수 ① [숯 파는] a charcoal dealer
② [얼굴 검은] a man of dark complexion

숱 thickness ; density ; richness ; quantity (수량) **—하다** (be) plentiful ; thick ; rich ¶ 숱이 많은 머리 tufty〔flowing〕 hair ; a profusion〔wealth〕 of hair ; thick hair

†숲 a wood ; a grove ; a forest

> 참고 **forest** 넓은 면적을 덮는 잔풀 욱어진 자연 상태의 산림 **grove** 보통 소면적의 잔풀이 없는 숲으로서 인공적으로 과일 나무 따위를 심는 것을 말한다 **wood (s)** forest 보다 자연 상태가 아닌 보다 인간 생활과 가까운 것을 말한다

¶ 숲 속을 헤매다 wander about in the woods

숲길 a path〔trail〕 through a forest〔wood〕; a woodland path

숲정이 a wood near a village

쉬[1] Shoo! (새 쫓는 소리)

쉬[2] the eggs of the fly ; flyblow

쉬[3] [조용히] Hush ! /Sh ! /Hist ! /Whist ! ¶ 쉬 조용히 해라 Hush ! Be quiet !

쉬[4] [어린이 오줌 뉠 때] Psss ! ; Tinkle-tinkle !

쉬[5] ① [곧] soon ; presently ; before long ; shortly ¶ 쉬 돌아오겠습니다 I will be back soon.
② [쉽게] easily ; readily ⇨ 쉽다

쉬다[1] [음식이] go bad ; turn sour ; spoil ¶ 쉰 밥 spoiled rice

†쉬다[2] [목소리가] get〔grow〕 hoarse〔husky〕 ¶ 쉰 목소리 a husky〔hoarse〕 voice // 목이 쉬도록 지껄이다 talk oneself husky // 그 여자는 목이 쉬었었다 Her voice sounded husky.

쉬다[3] ① [휴식하다] rest ; take〔have〕 a rest ; relax ¶ 쉬지 않고 일하다 keep at work // 다방에서 쉬다 rest at a tea room // 쉴 사이도 없다 have no time to take a rest // 조용히 쉬다 rest quietly // 쉬엇 [호령] Stand at ease ! // 쉬어 가면서 일해라 Take it easy. ② [일을] rest 《from one's work》; rest on the oars ; lay off 《미》; [휴가를 얻다] take a holiday ; take〔have〕 a day off ; [결석·결근하다] stay away 《from》; be absent 《from》 ¶ 일을 쉬다 rest on one's oars ; knock off 《구》 // 병으로 하루 쉬다 take a day off on account of illness // 한 시간 쉬고 두 시간 일하다 lay off an hour and work two // 3일간 일을 쉬다 stay away from work for three days // 1주일간 쉬다 take a week's holiday ; lay off a week // 학교를 쉬다 stay away from school ; absent oneself from school ; miss school // 회사를 쉬다 be absent from one's office // 하루 푹 쉬고 나면 내일은 다시 일하러 나올 수 있을 겁니다 A good day's rest should bring him back to work tomorrow. // 너는 내일부터 쉬느냐 Are you taking off from tomorrow ? ③ [중지하다] lie idle ; be at a standstill ¶ 쉬지 않고 continuously ; on end ; without a break // 기계가 현재 쉬고 있다 The machine is standing idle. // 여름에는 장사를 쉽니다 We do not keep on this business in summer. ④ [잠자다] sleep ; go to sleep ; [자리에 들다] go to bed ; retire ; turn in ¶ 잘 쉬다 sleep well ; have a good night's rest

쉬다[4] [숨을] breathe ; respire ; draw one's breath ; take breath ¶ 숨을 들이쉬다〔내쉬다〕 breathe in〔out〕 // 한숨을 쉬다 sigh ; heave a sigh

쉬다[5] [피륙을] soak cloth in the water in which rice has been washed so as to gloss the cloth

쉬르리얼리스트 a surrealist

쉬르리얼리즘 surrealism ; superrealism ¶ 쉬르리얼리즘의 surrealistic

쉬쉬하다 hush up 《a matter》; suppress ; keep 《a matter》 secret ¶ 그 일에 대하여 쉬쉬하고 있다 Their lips are all strictly sealed. /They are gagged about it.

쉬슬다 《a fly》 lay eggs 《upon meat》; 《a fly》 blow 《meat》 ¶ 쉬슨 고기 blown〔fly-blown〕 meat

쉬엄쉬엄 with frequent rests ; intermittently ; in easy stages ; off and on ¶ 쉬엄쉬엄 일하다 work taking frequent breaks ; do a job in easy stages

쉬이 easily ; readily ; soon ; before long ⇨ 쉬[5]

쉬지근하다 (be) rather stale-smelling ; musty ; sourish

쉬척지근하다 (be) quite stale-smelling ; musty ; sourish

쉬파리 a blowfly ; a bluebottle fly

쉬하다 《a child》 "tinkle" ; urinate

쉰 fifty ¶ 쉰 살 fifty years of age

쉰내 a sour〔sourish smell〕; a stale smell

쉰둥이 a child that a person gets at the age of fifty ; a child born to a person fifty years of age

쉼표 〖음악〗 a rest ; a pause ¶ 온〔2분, 8분〕 쉼표 a whole〔a half, an eighth〕 rest // 4분 쉼표 a quarter〔crotchet 《영》〕 rest

쉽게 easily ; without difficulty ; with ease ; plainly ; simply ¶ 쉽게 번 돈은 쉽게 나간다 Easy come, easy go. // 너는 언제나 사물을 지나치게 쉽게 생각한다 You always take an overly optimistic views of things. // 그는 이 문제를 쉽게 풀었다 He solved this problem in no time at all.

†쉽다 ① [용이하다] (be) easy ; simple ; light ¶ 쉬운 일 an easy〔a light〕 task ; a soft job // 알기 쉽다 be easy to understand // 이 소설은 읽기 쉽다 This story is easy to read〔understand〕. // 이 상자는 부서지기 쉽다 This box is easy to break〔easily broken〕. // 노력은 하고 있지만 그게 어디 말처럼 쉬워야지 I try to, but it's easier said than done. ② [경향] be apt to ; be prone to ; be liable to ; be ready to ¶ 잘못을 저지르기 쉽다 be liable to err // 감기 들기 쉽다 be susceptible to a cold // 그렇게 생각하기 쉽다 We are apt to think so. // 오후에는 비가 오기 쉽겠다 It is likely to rain this afternoon.

‡쉽사리 easily ; readily ; with ease ; without difficulty ; with little trouble ¶ 쉽사

리 접근할 수 없다 be difficult of access // 돈을 쉽사리 벌다 make an easy gain // 그의 병은 쉽사리 낫지 않았다 It was long before he got well. // 쉽사리 돈을 갚아 줄 것 같지 않다 He seems in no hurry to pay me the money. // 쉽사리 승낙할까 I'm afraid he will not give a ready consent.
슈미즈 a chemise ; [메리야스제] a vest
슈샤인 shoeshine
— 보이 a shoeshine boy
슈즈 [구두] shoes
슈크림 chou à la crème 《프》 ; a cream puff
슈트 a suit
—케이스 a suitcase
슈퍼 super(-)
—맨 a superman **— 수신기** a super-heterodyne receiver
*__슈퍼마켓__ a supermarket
슛 〖스포츠〗 shooting ; a shoot **—하다** 〖농구·축구〗 kick〔throw〕 《a ball》 ; ¶ 롱슛 a long shoot // 슛을 날리다 release a shoot // 슛시키다 〖농구〗 sink a shot ; make〔shoot〕 a basket ; 〖축구〗 shoot a goal
스가랴서 —書 〖성경〗 The Book of Zechariah ; Zechariah
스내치 〖역도〗 [인상] the snatch (lift)
스낵 바 a snack bar
⁑**스냅** [사진] a snap shot ¶ 스냅 사진을 찍다 snapshot ; snap 《a person》 // 너의 스냅 사진을 찍어 줄게 I will take a snapshot of you.
스님 [중] a priest ; [스승중] master 〔teacher〕 of a Buddhist priest
*__스라소니__ 〖동물〗 a lynx ; [사람] a gaunt person ; weakling
스란치마 a long skirt (that hides the feet)
스러지다 ⇨ 사라지다
-스럽다 be ; be like ; seem ; suggest ¶ 변덕스럽다 be capricious // 사랑스럽다 be lovely // 신비스럽다 be mysterious
스르르 gently ; softly ¶ 눈을 스르르 감다 softly close one's eyes // 고통이 스르르 가셨다 The pain suddenly decreased in severity.
-스름하다 ① [빛깔] (be) tinged with... ; somewhat ; -ish ¶ 불그스름하다 be tinged with red ; be reddish // 푸르스름하다 be somewhat blue ; be bluish ② [형상] (be) tending to ; somewhat ; -ish ¶ 동그스름하다 be roundish // 가느스름하다 be thinnish
스리 a tiny blood blister in the mouth ; a wound from chewing on the inside of one's cheek (while eating)
스리랑카 Sri Lanka
⁑**스릴** [전율] a thrill ¶ 스릴을 느끼다 have a kick〔thrill〕 《from》
스릴러 [연극·영화·소설의] a thriller ; a chiller ; a hair-raiser
†**스마트하다** (be) smart ; stylish ; handsome ; posh 《영·속》 ; clever ; [옷차림이] (be) smartly dressed ; look sharp 《미·속》 ; [풍채가] have a smart appearance ¶ 그는 정말 스마트한 옷차림을 하고 있었다 He looked as if he had just come out of a bandbox.
스매시 〖정구〗 smashing ; a smash **—하다** smash
스멀거리다 itch ; feel creepy ; feel crawly ¶ 등이 스멀거리다 one's back itches
스멀스멀 itchy ; crawly ; creepy
⁑**스모그** [연무(煙霧)] smog ¶ 스모그가 낀 smoggy // 스모그가 심한 도시 a town full of hanging smog
—주의보 《issue》 a smog warning
스모킹 smoking
— 룸 a smoking room
스무 twenty ; a score ¶ 스무 번째 the twentieth
스무나무 〖식물〗 Zelkova
스무드하다 (be) smooth ¶ 만사가 스무드하게 진행된다 Everything goes smoothly.
*__스물__ twenty ; a score ¶ 그 여자는 스물 한두 살쯤 되어 보인다 She is apparently in her early twenties.
⁑**스미다** soak〔sink〕 into ; permeate ; penetrate ; spread (잉크 따위가) ¶ (빗물이) 지붕으로 스며들다 soak through a roof // (교훈이) 마음에 스미다 sink into one's mind // 물이 땅 속으로 스며든다 The water sinks into the ground. /The water permeates through the soil. // 물이 바위틈에 스민다 Water infiltrates through a rock. // 그의 충고가 가슴에 스며들었다 His advice was well imprinted on our minds. // 땀이 셔츠에 스며들었다 The perspiration soaked through my shirt. // 물이 지하실에 스며들었다 Water has seeped into the basement.
스바냐서 —書 〖성경〗 The Book of Zephaniah ; Zephaniah
스스럼없다 [친하다] (be) intimate ; friendly ; familiar ⇨ 스스럽다 ¶ …과 스스럼없는 사이다 be familiar〔friendly〕 with... ; be on friendly〔intimate〕 terms with... ; be friends with... // 스스럼없어지다 become intimate with... ; get acquainted with... // 스스럼없이 intimately ; closely
스스럽다 feel constrained ; feel ill at ease ; have scruples 《about doing》 ; be shy of 《doing》 ¶ 스스럼없이 without constraint ; without reserve ; freely // 어른 앞에서 스스럽다 feel constrained around older people // 그는 자네 앞에서는 어쩐지 스스러워한다 He somewhat feels constraint in your presence. // 필요한 것이 있으면 스스러워하지 말고 말해라 Don't scruple to ask for anything you want.
스스로¹ [자기 자신] oneself ; by oneself ; in person ¶ 스스로 지휘하다 take personal command of ; be in personal command of // 너 스스로 가 봐라 Go yourself. // 자기 일은 자기 스스로 해라 Look after yourself. // 당신이 스스로 가보는 게 좋겠다 You had better go in person.

*스스로² ① [저절로] of itself ; of its own accord ; automatically (자동적으로) ¶ 문이 스스로 열렸다 The door opened of itself. // 그것은 스스로 명백해질 것이다 It will become clear of itself.
② [자진해서] of one's own accord ; of one's free will ; of one's own initiative ¶ 그것은 그가 스스로 한 짓이다 He did it of his own accord. // 그는 스스로 사임했다 He resigned voluntarily.

스승 a teacher ; a master ¶ 스승과 제자 master and disciple ; teacher and pupil

스와질랜드 Swaziland

스웨덴 Sweden ¶ 스웨덴의 Swedish
— 말 Swedish — 사람 a Swede — 체조 Swedish gymnastics

‡스웨터 a sweater ; a pull-over ¶ 스웨터를 짜다 knit a sweater

스위스 Switzerland ¶ 스위스의 Swiss // 스위스제의 《a watch》 of Swiss make ; Swiss-made
— 사람 a Swiss

스위트 홈 a sweet home

‡스위치 a switch ; [전등의] a light switch ¶ 스위치를 넣다〔끄다〕 switch〔turn〕 on〔off〕 // 전등 스위치를 끄다 switch off the light // 그것은 자동으로 스위치가 꺼진다 It switches itself off.

스윙 〖음악〗 swing (music) ; 〖경기〗 a 《long》 swing

스쳐보다 [슬쩍] glance at ; take a glance at ; [대강대강] take a cursory〔hasty〕 glance at ¶ 사람을 스쳐보다 steal a glance at a person // 일람표를 스쳐보다 take a cursory glance at a list

‡스치다 graze past〔by〕 《a person》 ; go past by 《a person》 ; glance off ; skim (수면을) ¶ 새가 수면을 스쳐 날아갔다 A bird skimmed over the water. // 총알이 벽을 스쳐갔다 The bullet grazed the wall. /The bullet glanced off the wall. // 그 여자는 나의 옆을 스쳐갔다 She went past〔brushed〕 by me. // 공상이 나의 머리속을 스쳐갔다 A fancy flitted through my mind.

‡스카프 a scarf 《*pl.* ~s, scarves》

‡스카우트 a scout —하다 scout (for) 《young talent》 ¶ 스카우트하고 다니다 scout about〔round〕 // 스카우트의 눈을 끌다 attract the attention of a scout // 이럴 때 유일한 방법은 타사의 인재를 스카우트해 오는 일이다 At a time like this, the only thing left is to do headhunting.

스카이 다이빙 sky diving ¶ 스카이 다이빙을 하다 sky-dive // 스카이 다이빙을 하는 사람 a sky diver

스카이 라운지 a sky lounge

스카이라인 [지평선] the horizon ; [산이나 건물이 하늘에 그리는 윤곽] a skyline ; [산의 유람 코스] a (scenic) mountain highway

스카이 사인 [공중 광고] an advertising sign erected in a high place ; a sky sign

스카이웨이 [고가도로] a skyway ; [산의 유람 코스] a (scenic) mountain highway
북악 — the *Bugak* Mountain Highway

스카치 [위스키] Scotch (whisky) ; [테이프] Scotch tape ; cellophane tape

스칸디나비아 Scandinavia ¶ 스칸디나비아의 Scandinavian
— 반도 the Scandinavian Peninsula — 사람 a Scandinavian

스캔들 a scandal ¶ 세상을 떠들썩하게 하는 스캔들 a sensational scandal // 그 스캔들은 그가 차기 사장으로 승진하는 것을 위태롭게 할 수도 있다 The scandal could jeopardize his chances of becoming the next president.

†스커트 a skirt ¶ 스커트를 입다〔벗다〕 put on〔take off〕 one's skirt
롱〔타이트, 플레어, 플리이트〕 — a long〔tight, flared, pleated〕 skirt

*스컹크 〖동물〗 a skunk

스케르초 〖음악〗 a scherzo 《*pl.* ~s, scherzi》 《이》

†스케이트 [활주] skating ; [기구] 《a pair of》 skates ¶ 스케이트 타러 가다 go skating // 스케이트를 타다 skate 《on the ice》 ; do skating
— 구두 a pair of skates —장 a (skating) rink 롤러 — roller skates ; roller-skating
피겨〔스피이드〕 — figure〔speed〕 skating

스케일 ① [규모] a scale ¶ 스케일이 큰〔작은〕 large-〔small-〕scale ; on a large〔small〕 scale ② [인물] a caliber ¶ 스케일이 큰〔작은〕 사람 a man of large〔small〕 caliber

스케줄 a schedule ; a program ¶ 꽉 찬 스케줄 a crowded〔crammed, tight〕 schedule // 일의 스케줄 a work schedule // 스케줄대로 as scheduled ; on〔according to, up to〕 schedule // 스케줄에 없는 unscheduled 《flight》 // 스케줄을 짜다 make〔map, lay〕 out a schedule // 여름 방학의 스케줄을 짜다 make a schedule for the summer vacation // 스케줄을 새로 짜다 reschedule // 일은 스케줄 대로 진행되고 있다 The work is all right and according to schedule.

‡스케치 a sketch —하다 make〔take〕 a sketch 《of a thing》 ; sketch ¶ 스케치 풍의 sketchy // 스케치하러 가다 go sketching
—북 a sketchbook

스코어 [구기] a score ; 〖음악〗 a music score ¶ 5대 3의 스코어로 by a score of 5 to 3 // 20대 5라는 큰 스코어 차로 by a lopsided score of 20 to 5 // 스코어를 따다 score up ; record the score // 스코어를 기록하다 keep (the) score // 2대 2의 타이 스코어를 이루고 있다 The score is tied at 2 to 2.
—보드 a scoreboard —북 a scorebook —시트 a score sheet 타이 — a tie score ; an even stephen

스코치 [양복감] (Scotch) tweed
— 테리어 a Scotch terrier

스코틀랜드 Scotland ¶ 스코틀랜드의 Scot-

tish ; Scotch
—말 Scotch — 사람 a Scotchman ; a Scot ; the Scotch 《총칭》
스콜 a squall
스콜라 철학 —哲學 Scholasticism ; Scholastic philosophy
—자 a Scholastic ; a Schoolman
스쿠너 a schooner
스쿠터 a motor scooter ¶ 스쿠터를 타다 take a ride in a motor scooter
스쿠프 [특종] a scoop ; a beat 《미》 —하다 scoop 《news, a rival paper》
스쿨 a school
— 버스 a school bus
스쿼시 [음료] 《lemon》 squash
스퀘어 댄스 a square dance ¶ 스퀘어 댄스를 추다 have a square dance
스퀴즈 (플레이) 〖야구〗 a squeeze (play) —하다 run〔try〕 a squeeze ¶ 스퀴즈로 결승의 1점을 올리다 score the winning run on a squeeze play
‡스크랩 (a) scrap ¶ 스크랩을 만들다 paste 《newspaper clippings》 into a scrapbook
—북 a scrapbook
스크럼 [럭비] a scrum ; a scrimmage 《주로 미》 ; a scrummage 《영》 ¶ 스크럼을 짜다 form a scrummage ; scrimmage ; [비유적] join forces〔hands〕 《to do》 // 스크럼을 풀다 break up a scrummage
스크루 a screw (propeller)
‡스크린 [영사막] a screen ; [영화계] the screen
— 테스트 a screen test
스크립터 a scripter ; a scriptwriter
‡스크립트 a 《TV》 script
— 걸 a script girl
스키어 a skier ; a ski runner
†스키 《a pair of》 ski(s) ; skiing ¶ 스키타러 가다 go skiing // 스키를 타다 ski // 스키를 타고 가다 go on skis // 스키를 신다 put on skis
— 경기 a skiing match — 구두 ski boots — 대회 a grand skiing match —복 a ski suit —장 a skiing ground — 점프 ski jump

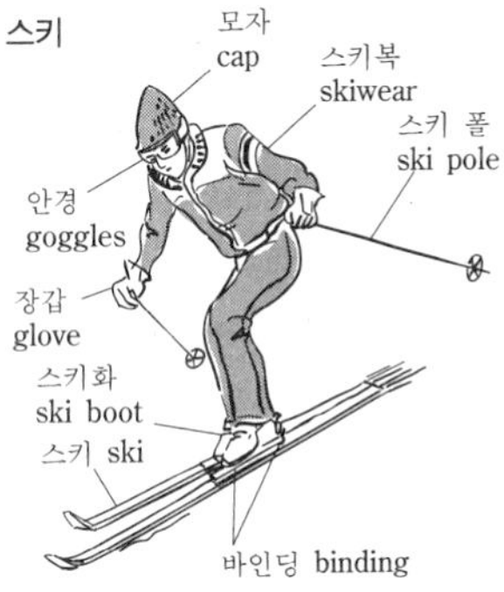

†스타 a star ; a star actor〔actress〕 ¶ 일류 스타 a star of the first class〔magnitude〕 // 스타가 되다 become a star ; be starred ; rise to stardom
— 시스템 the star system — 플레이어 a star player 영화 — a film〔movie〕 star
스타덤 stardom
‡스타디움 stadium 《*pl.* ~s, -dia》
스타터 [경기의] a starter ; [자동차의] a (self-) starter
스타트 start(ing) ; point of departure ; [경마·자동차 등의] a getaway —하다 start ; make a start ¶ 스타트에서 골까지 《lead》 from start to finish // 스타트가 좋다〔나쁘다〕 start well〔poorly〕 ; start quick〔slow〕 ; make a good〔poor〕 start // 스타트를 끊다 (make a) start
— 계원 a starter — 라인 a starting line
— 신호 a starting signal
스타팅 starting
— 멤버 a starting member
스타우트 [흑맥주] stout
†스타일 [몸매] one's form ; one's figure ; [양복 따위의] a style ; a mode of fashion ; a cut ; [양식] a style ; a fashion ; a mode ; [문체] one's style ; one's manner of writing ¶ 최신 유행의 스타일 the latest style〔pattern〕 // 그녀는 스타일이 좋다〔나쁘다〕 She has a good〔poor〕 figure. / She's got a〔no〕 figure. // 그의 문장은 특수한 스타일이다 His writings have a peculiar style.
—북 a stylebook 스타일리스트 [문장의] a stylist ; [복장의] a dandy
스타카토 〖음악〗 staccato 《이》
†스타킹 《a pair of》 stockings
심리스 — seamless stockings
스탈린그라드 Stalingrad 《현 Bolgograd》
스태그플레이션 〖경제〗 stagflation
스태미나 stamina ; staying power ; capacity for standing fatigue ¶ 스태미나가 있다〔없다〕 have〔lack〕 stamina // 스태미나를 강화하다 develop〔build up〕 one's stamina
스태프 a staff 《총칭》 ¶ 스태프 일동 all the members of the staff // 스태프의 일원이다 be on the staff 《of》 // 스태프가 모자라다 be insufficiently staffed ; be short of hands
스탠더드 a standard
†스탠드 ① [관람석] stands ; [지붕 없는] the bleachers 《미》 ¶ 스탠드가 꽉 찼었다 The stands were filled solidly to the capacity. ② [대] a stand ¶ 잉크 스탠드 an inkstand ③ [탁상 전등] a desk lamp ; a floor lamp (마루에 놓는) ④ [간이 식당] a food stand ; [매점] a stand ; a booth ⑤ [주유소] a gas〔filling〕 station
— 플레이 a grandstand play ¶ 스탠드 플레이를 하다 play to the grandstands ; grandstand 《구》 커피 — a coffee stand
스탠스 〖야구·골프〗 a stance

스탬프 a stamp ; [날짜 도장] a datemark ¶ 스탬프를 찍다 stamp 《a card》; [소인] post stamp
— **잉크** stamp ink **기념** — a commemoration stamp
스테레오(-) [음향 장치] a stereo 《*pl*. ~s》; a stereo set ; [방식] the stereophonic sound (reproduction) system
— **녹음** stereophonic〔stereo〕 recording — **레코드** a stereophonic record〔disk〕 — **방송** stereophonic broadcasting — **음향** stereo-phony — **재생 장치** a stereophonic sound reproduction system — **전축** a stereo (phonograph) — **카메라** a stereo(scopic) camera — **테이프** a stereo tape —**판(板)** a stereotype ; a stereo
스테이션 a (railway) station
— **왜건** a station wagon
†**스테이지** the stage ⇨ 무대 ¶ 스테이지를 밟다〔떠나다〕 go on〔off〕 the stage
— **댄스** a stage dance — **매니저** a stage manager
‡**스테이크** a steak
비프 — a (beef) steak **햄버그** — a Hamburg steak
스테이터스 심벌 a status symbol
스테이플 a staple
스테이플 파이버 staple fiber
스테인드 글라스 stained glass
스테인레스 stainless steel ¶ 스테인레스제의 《a gas range》 of stainless steel ; stainless steel 《knife》
스텐실 페이퍼 stencil paper
스텝 a step ¶ 스텝을 밟다 step ; dance // 왈츠의 스텝을 밟다 dance a waltz ; execute waltz steps // 가볍게 스텝을 밟다 step airily
스토리 story
스토아학파 —學派 the Stoic school
스토어 a store ; a shop 《영》
지하철 — a subway station store
‡**스토브** a stove ; a heater ¶ 스토브를 피우다 make a fire in the stove ; light a stove〔heater〕
가스 — a gas heater〔stove〕 **석유〔전기〕** — an oil〔electric〕 heater **석탄〔나무〕** — a coal〔wood〕 stove
스톡 ① [재고] a stock ¶ 스톡이 많다 have a large stock 《of》// 스톡이 없다 be out of stock // 스톡이 부족하다 The stock runs short. ② [스키의] a ski stick
스톡홀름 Stockholm
스톱 stop **—하다** stop ¶ (트럼프에서) 스톱을 걸다 call a halt
— **워치** a stop watch ¶ 스톱 워치를 누르다 start a stop watch
***스튜** stew
— **남비** a stewpan ; a saucepan **쇠고기** — stewed beef ; beef stew
스튜던트 파워 student power
스튜디오 a studio 《*pl*. ~s》
***스튜어디스** a stewardess ; an air hostess 〔stewardess〕

스트라이크[1] [파업] a strike ; a walkout **—하다** strike ; go on (a) strike ; walk out ¶ 스트라이크를 중지하다 halt〔call off〕 a strike // 스트라이크 중지 명령 a stop-strike order // 스트라이크 중이다 be on strike ; a strike is on // 임금 인상을 요구하여 스트라이크로 들어가다 go on strike for higher wages〔pay〕
— **배신자** a strikebreaker ; a scab ; a rat 《속》 — **존** the strike zone — **활동** strike activities
스트라이크[2] [야구·볼링] a strike ¶ 스트라이크가 되다 score a strike ; [볼링] get a strike // 카운트는 원 스트라이크 투 볼 The (batter's) count is two balls, one strike.
스트럭 아웃 〖야구〗 struck out ¶ 스트럭 아웃이 되다 be〔get〕 struck out // 스트럭 아웃을 먹이다 strike a batter out
스트레스 〖의학〗 《dispel》 stress ¶ 스포츠로 스트레스를 해소하다 get rid of stress by engaging in sports // 그는 스트레스가 쌓이면 신경질이 된다 He becomes irritable when stress builds up.
—**병** a stress disease — **학설** the stress theory
스트레이트 ① [운동 경기의] a straight (victory) ; 〖야구〗 a straight ball〔pitch〕; 〖권투〗 《give》 a straight 《punch on》 ¶ 스트레이트로 이기다 win a straight victory 《over》; win in straight sets // 스트레이트로 지다 suffer a straight defeat 《from》; lose in straight sets ② [술 따위] straight (미) ; neat (영) ¶ 위스키를 스트레이트로 마시다 drink whisky straight
스트렙토마이신 〖약〗 streptomycin
스트로 a straw ; [종이로 만든] a sipper ¶ 스트로로 우유를 마시다 suck milk through a straw
스트로보 〖사진〗 [상표명] a Strobo ; an electric flash
스트로크 a stroke ¶ 원 스트로크의 차로 이기다〔지다〕 win〔lose〕 《the race》 by a stroke
스트론튬 〖화학〗 strontium 《Sr》
스트리키니네 〖약〗 strychnin(e) ; strychnia
스트리퍼 a strip teaser ; a stripper
스트립 쇼 a strip show ; a strip tease ; a burlesque (미)
스틸[1] 〖야구〗 [도루] a steal ¶ 홈 틸을 하다 steal home
스틸[2] [영화의] a still (photograph)
스틸[3] [강철] steel
스팀 steam ; [난방] steam heating ; [난방 장치] a steam heater ¶ 스팀이 들어오다 be steam-heated 《in the room》// 스팀으로 방을 덥게 하다 heat a room by steam
스틱 a (walking) stick (영) ; a cane (미) ⇨ 지팡이
스파게티 spaghetti
스파르타 Sparta ¶ 스파르타식의 Spartan

— 사람 a Spartan —(식) 교육 Spartan training〔education〕
스파링 『권투』 sparring
— 파트너 one's sparring partner ¶ 아무의 스파링 파트너로서 링에 오르다 meet a person in the ring as his sparring partner
‡스파이 a spy ; a secret agent ; a undercover man ; an informer ¶ 스파이 임무를 띠고 on a spy mission // 스파이 노릇을 하다 engage in espionage ; act as spy
—단 a spy ring —망 a network of spies ; espionage — 비행 a spy〔an espionage〕 flight ; an intelligence flight — 비행기 a spy plane — 영화 a cloak-and-dagger film — 활동 espionage (activities) 산업 — an industrial spy ; an undercover man 이중 — a double agent
스파이크 [구두의] a spike ; [배구의] a spike ; spiking —하다 spike 《the first baseman, a volley ball》 ¶ (신에) 스파이크를 박다 spike 《shoes》
— 구두 spiked shoes
스파크 『전기』 a spark —하다 spark
스패너 a wrench (미) ; a spanner (영)
스퍼트 a spurt —하다 put on a spurt
라스트 — the last spurt
‡스펀지 sponge ⇨ 해면(海綿)
— 고무 sponge rubber — 볼 a sponge ball — 케이크 a sponge cake
스페어 a spare ; spare parts
— 타이어 a spare tire
*스페이드 a spade ¶ 스페이드의 에이스 an ace of spades
스페이스 (a) space ; room ¶ 스페이스를 떼어 놓다 space out ; make room 《for》
스페인 Spain ¶ 스페인의 Spanish
—말 Spanish ; the Spanish language — 사람 a Spaniard ; the Spanish 《총칭》
스펙타클 a spectacle
— 영화 a spectacular film
*스펙트럼 a spectrum 《*pl.* ~s, -tra》
— 분석 spectrum analysis — 사진 a spectrogram
스펠링 spelling ¶ 그 단어의 스펠링을 가르쳐 주십시오 Please tell me how to spell that word.
스포이트 [만년필에 잉크를 넣는] fountain pen filler
스포일 [망침] spoiling
†스포츠 sports ; a sport ¶ 보는〔손수하는〕 스포츠 spectator〔participant〕 sports // 스포츠를 하다 take part in〔participate in, practice, go in for〕 a sport
—계 the sportsdom (미) ; the sporting world — 기자 a sports writer — 뉴스 (a piece of) sporting news — 방송 sportscast — 센터 a sports center — 신문 a sporting newspaper〔journal〕 — 아나운서 a sports announcer ; a sportscaster — 용어 sporting terms ; sports jargon — 용품 sports equipment ; sporting goods — 용품점 a sports shop — 잡지 a sports magazine — 카 a sports car
— 하이라이트 sports highlights
‡스포츠맨 a sportsman 《*pl.* -men》 ; an athlete ¶ 스포츠맨다운 sportsmanlike // 스포츠맨답지 않은 unsportsmanlike ; unsporting
—쉽〔정신〕 sportsmanship
스포크 [바퀴살] a radius ; spoke
스포크스맨 a spokesman ¶ 외무부의 스포크스맨 a Foreign Office spokesman ; a spokesman of the Foreign Ministry
스폰서 [상업 방송의] a sponsor ¶ 라디오〔TV〕프로의 스폰서 a radio〔TV〕 program sponsor // 스폰서가 되다 sponsor 《a concert》 // 스폰서가 있는 sponsored〔sponsor-financed〕 《TV program》
‡스폿 a spot
— 뉴스 spot news — 라이트 《focus》 a spotlight 《on》 — 방송 spot broadcast — 아나운스 a spot announcement
스푸트니크 the sputnik
‡스푼 a spoon ¶ 스푼으로 하나 a spoonful 《of salt》 // 스푼으로 뜨다 spoon up〔out〕 《soup》
— 레이스 an egg-and-spoon race
스프 staple fiber ¶ 스프가 섞인 mixed with staple fiber
스프레이 [분무기] a spray
스프린터 [단거리 선수] a sprinter
스프링 ① [용수철] a (metal) spring ¶ 스프링 침대 a spring bed ② [봄] spring (time)
— 보드 a spring board — 코트 a spring coat ; a topcoat ; a light overcoat
스프링클러 a (water) sprinkler
— 장치 a sprinkler system
스피드 speed ⇨ 속도(速度) ¶ 스피드를 내다 speed up ; gather〔get up, put on〕 speed ; step on it〔the gas〕 (구) // 시속 60 킬로의 스피드를 내다 get〔develop〕 a speed of 60 kilometers an hour // 스피드를 떨어뜨리다 decrease〔reduce〕 the speed ; slow down // 스피드를 내서 at high speed ; at speed
—광 a speed maniac ; a speed-fiend (미) — 레이스 a speed race — 볼 『야구』 a speedball — 시대 the age of speed —업 speedup ¶ 스피드업하다 speed up — 제한 speed regulation ; a speed limit
스피디하다 (be) speedy
스피로헤타 [파상균] a spiroch(a)ete
스피츠 『동물』 a spitz (dog)
스피치 a speech ; an address ¶ 스피치하다 make〔deliver〕 a speech
테이블 — an after-dinner speech
스피커 [확성기] a (loud) speaker ; [라디오의] a radio speaker ¶ 스피커로 방송하다 announce through a loudspeaker
고음용 — a tweeter 저음용 — a woofer
스피트볼 『야구』 a spitball ; a spitter
‡스핑크스 the sphinx ; a sphinx 《*pl.* ~es, sphinges》 ; an enigmatic person
슬개건 반사 膝蓋腱反射 『의학』 a knee

jerk
슬개골 膝蓋骨 〖해부〗 the kneepan ; the kneecap ; the patella 《*pl.* -lae》
슬겁다 (be) broad-minded ; open ; receptive ; warm-hearted ; kind (친절) ¶ 마음 쓰는 것이 슬겁다 He is quite broad-minded.
슬관절 膝關節 〖해부〗 the knee joint
―염 gonarthritis
슬그머니 furtively ; by stealth ; secretly ; in secret ; on the sly ¶ 슬그머니 가 버리다 steal along 《one's way》 // 슬그머니 들어오다〔나가다〕 steal〔slip〕 into〔out of〕 《a room》 // 슬그머니 돈을 쥐어 주다 slip a coin into 《a person's》 hand // 슬그머니 쳐다보다 watch 《a person》 furtively ; steal a glance at 《a person》 // 그의 말에 슬그머니 화가 났다 At his words I felt indignation swell up in my heart. // 나는 슬그머니 무서워졌다 Fear stole into my heart.
슬금슬금 stealthily ; sneakingly ; furtively ; covertly ; by stealth ; on the sly ¶ 슬금슬금 내빼다 sneak off〔away〕 ; slip away // 슬금슬금 쳐다보다 cast covert glances at 《a person》
슬금하다 (be) wise and broad-minded ; clever and generous
슬기 wisdom ; sagacity ; prudence ; intelligence ; good sense ¶ 슬기가 있다 have good sense ; be intelligent〔wise〕
†**슬기롭다** (be) wise ; sagacious ; prudent ; intelligent ; sensible ¶ 슬기로운 소년 a sensible〔an intelligent〕 boy
슬다[1] ① [알을] lay ; blow (파리가) ; spawn (물고기가) ¶ 물고기가 알을 슬다 a fish lays eggs // 파리가 쉬를 슬다 a fly blows eggs // 어떤 파리는 과일에 쉬를 슨다 Some flies blow fruit.
② [녹이] rust ; become〔get〕 rusty ¶ 녹이 슨 칼 a rusty knife
슬다[2] ① [푸성귀가] wither ; wilt
② [사라지다] 《the boil》 disappear ; vanish ; be gone
③ [풀죽이다] soften 《starched cloth》
슬라브 Slav
―말 Slavic ¶ 슬라브말의 Slavic **― 민족** the Slavs ¶ 슬라브 민족의 Slavic **― 사람** a Slav
슬라이더 〖야구〗 a slider
슬라이드 ① 〖야구〗 a slide ② [환등] a (lantern) slide ; a transparency ¶ 컬러 슬라이드 color slides〔transparency〕 // 슬라이드를 끼우다 slide down a slide ③ [현미경의] a slide
―제 〖노동〗 ⇨ 슬라이딩 스케일
슬라이딩 〖야구〗 sliding
― 스케일 〖노동〗 a sliding scale (system)
슬랄롬 〖스키〗 slalom
슬랙스 slacks ¶ 슬랙스를 입은 여인 a girl in slacks
슬랭 a slang word〔expression〕 ; a word of slang ; [총칭] slang
슬러거 〖야구〗 a slugger
슬럼가 ―街 a slum ; slums ; a back alley ¶ 대도시의 슬럼가 the slums of a large city
슬럼프 a slump ¶ 슬럼프에 빠지다 hit〔fall into〕 a slump // 슬럼프에서 벗어나다 get out of a slump // 슬럼프에 빠져 있는 야구팀 a slump-ridden baseball team
‡**슬레이트** a slate ¶ 슬레이트 지붕 a slate roof // 슬레이트 지붕의 slate-roofed // 슬레이트로 지붕을 이다 cover a roof with slates ; slate a house
‡**슬로건** a slogan ; a motto 《*pl.* ~es, ~s》 ¶ …라는 슬로건을 내걸고 under the slogan of ... // 슬로건을 내세우다 publish a slogan
슬로 모션 slow motion ¶ 슬로모션으로 《shoot the motions of a swimmer》 in slow motion
― 영화 a slow-motion picture
슬로바키아 Slovakia
슬로 볼 〖야구〗 a slow ball ; a ball thrown for a change of pace
슬로프 a slope
‡**슬리퍼** 《a pair of》 slippers ; backless slippers ; scuffs ; mules ¶ 슬리퍼로 바꿔 신다 change into slippers
슬립 ① [속옷] a slip ; an underdress ¶ 슬립이 보인다 Your slip is showing. ② [미끄러짐] a slip **―하다** slip ; skid ¶ 슬립 방지가 된 타이어 a skidproof tire // 슬립 다운되다 slip down ③ [전표] a slip
슬며시 [드러나지 않게] stealthily ; furtively ; [가만히] gently ; softly ; quietly ; lightly ; tenderly ¶ 슬며시 자리를 뜨다 leave one's seat quietly〔stealthily〕 // 슬며시 집을 나가다 steal out of the house // 애기를 슬며시 안다 pick up a baby cautiously // 조금 전에 슬며시 영업부를 들여다 보았다 I took a casual peek into the sales department a short while ago.
슬미지근하다 (be) lukewarmish ; barely warm ¶ 그를 다루는 방법이 너무 슬미지근하다 That's too mild a way of dealing with him.
슬반사 膝反射 〖의학〗 a patellar reflex ; a knee jerk
슬슬 slowly ; gently ; lightly ; nicely ¶ 슬슬 걷다 walk leisurely // 사람을 슬슬 속이다 swindle a person nicely // 우는 아이를 슬슬 달래다 soothe a crying baby gently // 상처를 슬슬 문지르다 rub the wound lightly // 바람이 슬슬 불다 the wind blows gently
슬쩍 ① [몰래] secretly ; in secret ; furtively ; stealthily ; by stealth ; sneakingly ; on the sly ¶ 슬쩍 보다 steal a glance at 《a person》 ; cast a furtive glance at // 슬쩍슬쩍 훔치다 pick and steal ; sneak ; pilfer ; filch // 슬쩍 집을 나가다 steal out of the house // 그는 방에서 슬쩍 빠져 나갔다 He sneaked〔slipped〕 away out of the room.
② [능숙하게] deftly ; skillfully ; adroit-

ly ; easily ; lightly (가볍게) ¶ 일을 슬쩍 슬쩍 처리하다 manage ⟪a matter⟫ skillfully // 질문을 슬쩍 피하다 diplomatically ignore a question ; cleverly parry a question // 주먹을 슬쩍 피하다 lightly parry a blow

슬치 a whitebait that has spawned

*‡**슬퍼하다** sorrow〔grieve〕⟪at, over⟫ ; feel sad〔sorrowful〕⟪at⟫ ; be distressed ⟪over⟫ ; [애석히 여기다] mourn ⟪for, over⟫ ; regret ¶ 슬퍼해야 할 sad ; regrettable ; deplorable // 슬프게 하다 make ⟪a person⟫ sad ; grieve ⟪a person⟫ // 아버지의 죽음을 슬퍼하다 grieve〔mourn〕over one's father's death // 남의 불행을 슬퍼하다 feel sorry for ⟪a person's⟫ misfortune ; mourn for ⟪a person's⟫ misfortune // 쓸데 없이 슬퍼할 때가 아니다 This is no time to give way to sorrow.

†**슬프다** (be) sad ; sorrowful ; mournful ; doleful ; rueful ; unhappy ¶ 슬픈 일 a sad event // 슬픈 이야기 a sad〔pathetic〕story // 슬픈 듯한 sorrowful ; sad-looking // 슬픈 얼굴 a sad face // 슬픈 표정 a sorrowful countenance // 슬픈 곡조 a plaintive melody // 슬픈 듯 sadly ; sorrowfully ; dolefully // 슬프게도 Sad to say . . . /It is a pity ⟪that⟫ // 슬프도다 Alas ! /Woe is me ! // 그녀는 이 이야기를 듣고 슬펐다 She felt sad at this talk. // 그 여자가 고생하는 것을 보니 슬프다 Her troubles sadden me. /I am〔feel〕sad at her troubles. // 고양이가 죽었을 때 메리는 몹시 슬펐다 It was a sad day for Mary when her cat died.

†**슬픔** sorrow ; sadness ; grief ; lamentation (비탄) ¶ 남 모르는 슬픔 a hidden sorrow // 슬픈 나머지 in one's grief // 슬픔에 잠기다 be in deep grief〔sorrow〕; be buried in grief ; yield to sorrow // 기쁨과 슬픔이 엇갈리다 have a mingled feeling of joy and sorrow

슬피 sadly ; sorrowfully ; mournfully ; plaintively ¶ 슬피 울다 cry sorrowfully〔in a mournful manner〕

슬하 膝下 the care of one's parents ¶ 부모 슬하에서 지내다 live under the parental roof // 부모 슬하를 떠나다 leave (one's parental) home

슴베 the handle end of a knife ; a tang

***습격 襲擊** an attack ; an assault ; a raid ; a storm ; a charge **—하다** attack ; raid ; charge ; assault ; swoop down upon ; fall〔set〕upon ¶ 불의에 습격하다 make a surprise attack // 적진을 습격하다 attack〔storm〕an enemy position // 습격하여 고을을 점령하다 take a town by assault〔storm〕

—대 an attacking force ; a storming party ; an assault troop

습곡 〖지질〗 a fold〔bend〕⟪in a stratum⟫ ; [요곡(撓曲)] a flexure **—하다** bend repeatedly so as to form folds ⟪in⟫ ; flex **— 산맥** a fold-mountain range ; folded mountains

†**습관 習慣** a habit ; a way ; a custom ; a practice

> 참고 **custom**은 다소나마 영속성 있는 사회적 또는 개인적 습관 **habit**은 개인이 무의식적으로 몸에 익힌 버릇이나 습관

¶ 습관적 habitual ; customary // 습관적으로 habitually ; form habit // 습관성의 habit-forming ⟪drug⟫ // 습관을 기르다 form a habit ; accustom oneself to ⟪a task, do⟫ // 습관이 붙다 get into〔acquire〕a habit ; take to ⟪idling, drinking⟫ // 습관을 지키다 keep〔adhere to〕old custom ; toe the line // 습관을 고치다 break ⟪a person, oneself⟫ of a habit ; get rid of a bad habit // 습관은 제2의 천성이다 Habit is a second nature. // 그 습관은 버리는 것이 좋다 You had better give up〔break off〕the habit. // 그것은 그의 습관이 되어 있다 It is a habit with him. // 그는 코를 긁는 습관이 있다 He has a habit of scratching his nose. // 그 습관은 어느 지방에서는 아직도 지켜지고 있다 The custom still obtains in some district. // 7시에 일어나는 것이 그 여자의 습관이다 It is her custom〔the custom with her〕to get up at seven.

*‡**습기 濕氣** moisture ; dampness ; humidity ¶ 습기가 있다 be moist〔damp, humid, soggy〕// 습기가 끼다 get damp〔humidified〕; moisten // 오늘은 습기가 많다 It is so humid today. // 김에 습기가 스며들었다 The laver has become damp.

-습디까 ⇨ -ㅂ디까 ¶ 그거 괜찮습디까 Was it all right ? // 책이 얼마나 있습디까 How many books were there ? // 그 방 쓸만큼 큽디까 Was the room large enough ?

-습디다 ⇨ -ㅂ디다 ¶ 그 영화 퍽 재미있습디다 I enjoyed the movie very much. // 그 사람 가고 없습디다 (When I got there) He was gone. // 창문이 열려 있습디다 I found the window was open.

-습시다 let's ⇨ -ㅂ시다

†**-습니까** be ? ; do ? ¶ 춥습니까 Is it cold ? // 먹습니까 Does he eat ?

-습니다 be ; do ¶ 춥습니다 It is cold.

습도 濕度 humidity ¶ 습도가 높다〔낮다〕show a high〔low〕percentage of humidity // 습도를 재다 determine the humidity **—계** a hygrometer ; a hygroscope **— 측정** hygrometry **상대〔절대〕—** relative〔absolute〕humidity

습득 拾得 picking up **—하다** pick up ; find ⟪lost property⟫

—물 a find ; a found article ; a thing〔an article〕found **—자** a finder

습득 習得 learning ; acquirement **—하다** learn ⟪English⟫ ; acquire ⟪an art⟫ ; master ¶ 습득할 수 있는 acquirable // 지식의

습득 acquisition〔acquirement〕 of knowledge // 3년간 영어를 습득하다 master English in three years
습래 襲來 an attack ⇨ 내습
습랭 濕冷 〖한의학〗 rheumatism in the lower part of one's body
습성 習性 a habit ; habitude ; a second nature
습성 濕性 wetness
— 늑막염 wet〔moist〕 pleurisy ; pleurisy with effusion
습속 習俗 convention ; usage
습습하다 (be) brisk ; lively ; manly
습용 襲用 using〔employing〕 hereditarily —하다 follow ; adopt ; inherit
습유 拾遺 an addendum ; a supplement ; gleanings (낙수) —하다 add a supplement〔an addendum〕
습윤 濕潤 dampness ; humidity ; moistness —하다 (be) damp ; humid ; moist
습의 襲衣 a shroud ; the dress for a dead body for burial
습자 習字 calligraphy ; penmanship
— 선생 a writing master —지 writing paper —책 a writing book ; a copy book 영어 — English penmanship
습자배기 襲— a bowl containing perfumed water for washing a corpse
습작 習作 an essay ; a study ; an étude 《프》
습작 襲爵 succession to the peerage —하다 succeed to the peerage
습전지 濕電池 a galvanic battery
습종 濕腫 abscesses and ulcers 《on the leg》
습증 濕症 a disease caused by damp
*습지 濕地 swampy land ; boggy〔damp〕 ground ; marsh ; wet land
습지 濕紙 damp〔moistened〕 paper
습진 濕疹 〖의학〗 eczema
습포 濕布 a wet compress〔pack, pad cloth〕 ; 〖의학〗 a poultice (약을 바른) ; a cataplasm —하다 apply a poultice 《to》 ; put a wet compress 《on》
—제 poultice (medicine) 냉— a cold compress〔pad〕 온— a stupe ; a hot compress
습하다 濕— (be) damp ; dampish ; humid ; moist ; soppy ; wet ¶ 습한 공기〔기후〕 damp〔muggy〕 air〔weather〕
습하다 襲— wash a dead body ; cleanse the corpse
승 勝 a victory ; a win ¶ 3승 1패 three victories〔wins〕 and〔against〕 one defeat // 3승하다 win three games
승 升 a measure of capacity 《1.588 quart, 0.48 gallon》
승 乘 〖수학〗 multiplication —하다 multiply ¶ 2승〔3승, 4승〕하다 raise to second〔third, fourth〕 power // 5에다 3을 승하다 multiply 5 by 3
-승 乘 [탈것의] riding ; a ride 2인〔1인〕— 비행기 a two-〔single-〕 seater (plane) 5인— 자동차 a five passenger car ; a five-seater (automobile)
승 僧 a monk ⇨ 중
승가 僧家 [신분] the Buddhist Priesthood ; [중] a monk
*승강 昇降 going up and coming down ; ascent and descent ; rise and fall —하다 ascend and descend ; go up and come down ; rise and fall ; fluctuate
—구 an entrance ; [배의] a hatch(way) —기 an elevator 《미》 ; a lift 《영》 —타 〖항공〗 an elevator
*승강 乘降 getting on and off 《a car》 ; boarding and alighting
—객 passengers getting on and off 《a train》 —장(場) a (station) platform
승강이 a petty quarrel ; wrangling ; altercating —하다 have a petty quarrel ; wrangle 《with》 ¶ 서로 승강이를 벌이다 wrangle against each other
승개교 昇開橋 a lift bridge
†승객 乘客 a passenger ; a fare (택시 따위의)
— 명부 the passenger list —수 the number of passengers carried — 안내소 an inquiry〔information〕 office for passengers 갑판 — a deck passenger 기차 — a train passenger 일등 — first-class passengers
승검초 a kind of angelica plant
승격 昇格 elevation of the status ; the raising of status ; promotion in status —하다 raise in status ; be promoted〔elevated〕 in status ¶ 대학으로 승격하다 grow to university status ; be raised to the status of university // 승격시키다 raise to the status 《of》 ; elevate 《a school》 to a higher status // 공사관을 대사관으로 승격시키다 raise a legation to the rank〔status〕 of an embassy
승경 勝景 a fine view ; beautiful scenery ; a beauty〔scenic〕 spot
승계 承繼 succession ; continuation ⇨ 계승
승교 乘轎 a sedan chair ; a palanquin
승교점 昇交點 〖천문〗 an ascending node
승근 乘根 〖수학〗 the root
승급 昇級 promotion ; rise ; advancement ; preferment —하다 obtain〔get, win, receive, attain〕 promotion ; be promoted〔advanced〕 ; rise (in rank) ¶ 마구 승급하다 win speedy promotion // 과장에서 국장으로 승급하다 be promoted from sectional chief to bureau director // 승급할 가망이 없다 There is little chance of advancement.
승급 昇給 an increase in pay ; a rise〔raise〕 in salary ; a pay hike —하다 have one's pay〔salary〕 increased〔raised〕 ; get an increase in pay ¶ 승급이 빠르다 have frequent raises in salary // 6호봉에서 5호봉으로 승급하다 have one's

salary raised from the 6th grade to the 5th
—률 the rate of increase in salary
승기 勝機 a winning chance ; a chance of victory ¶ 승기를 놓치다 miss a chance of victory
승낙 承諾 consent ; assent ; agreement ; acceptance ; approval —하다 consent 〔agree, assent〕 to ; give one's consent to ; comply with ; acquiesce in ¶ 승낙을 얻고 with 《a person's》 consent // 승낙 없이 without 《a person's》 consent ; without leave // 승낙을 구하다 ask 《a person's》 consent // 쾌히 승낙하다 give a willing consent ; consent with a ready answer (즉석에서) // 억지로 승낙시키다 enforce 〔compel〕 assent 《to a matter》 // 승낙해 주시겠습니까 Have I your consent ?
—서 a written consent〔acceptance〕 — 연령 〚법〛 the age of consent
승냥이 a jackal
승니 僧尼 Buddhist priests and nuns
승단 昇段 promotion —하다 be promoted 《to a higher grade》
승당 僧堂 a Buddhist monastery
승도 僧徒 priests ; monks
승도복숭아 僧桃— 〚식물〛 a nectarine
승려 僧侶 a Buddhist monk ; a priest ¶ 승려가 되다 be ordained a priest ; enter the priesthood
— 계급 the clergy ; the priesthood
승률 勝率 the percentage of victories (to the total number of matches)
†승리 勝利 victory ; triumph ; conquest ; a win (경기의) ¶ 사랑의 승리자 a successful lover // 정의의 승리 the triumph of justice // 승리를 얻다 win〔gain, achieve〕 a victory ; score〔achieve〕 a triumph ; win 〔carry〕 the day ; come off victorious // 최후의 승리를 얻다 gain the final victory ; win in the long run // 승리의 영관을 얻다 win laurels〔the laurel〕 // 승리는 우리의 것이다 The day is ours. /The victory is on our side. /The game has ended in favor of our side. // 나는 이번 승리에 취할 시간이 없다 I don't have the time to savor this win.
—자 a victor ; a conqueror ; a winner (경기의) — 투수 the winning pitcher 대— a great〔signal, landslide〕 victory 완전— a complete victory ; a perfect triumph
승마 乘馬 horse riding ; riding —하다 ride a horse ; mount〔get on〕 a horse ; take horse ¶ 승마 연습을 하다 take riding lesson // 승마 [구령] Mount ! /To horse !
— 구락부 a riding club —길 a riding road —대 a mounted corps ; a cavalcade — 바지 riding breeches ; jodhpurs —복 a riding dress ; a riding habit (여자용) —상(像) an equestrian statue〔figure〕 —술 (the art of) riding ; horsemanship — 연습 riding exercises —화(靴) a riding boots
승멱 乘冪 〚수학〛 a power
승무 僧舞 a dance in Buddhist attire ; a Buddhist dance
*승무원 乘務員 [열차] a trainman 《미》 ; a train crew 《총칭》 ; [전차 따위의] a carman ; men on car service 《총칭》 ; [비행기의] a crewman ; a stewardess (여자) ; a crew 《총칭》
승문 僧門 the Buddhist priesthood
승방 僧房 a Buddhist nunnery
승법 乘法 〚수학〛 multiplication
—표 a multiplication table — 함수 a multiplicative function
승벽 勝癖 an unyielding spirit ; a competitive spirit ¶ 승벽이 강해서 지기를 싫어하다 have too high a spirit to submit to another
승병 僧兵 a monk soldier ; a warriormonk
승보 勝報 ⇨ 첩보(捷報)
승복 承服 ① [자백] confession of a crime ② [따름] submission —하다 confess a crime ; submit ; yield to 《 another's view》
승복 僧服 a priest's robe ; clerical garb
승부 勝負 [승패] victory or defeat ; the outcome ; the issue (결과) ; [시합] a contest ; a game ; a match ; a bout ¶ 승부없는 시합 a drawn game ; a tie (game) ; a draw ; a dead heat (경주에서 동시착) // 승부를 다투다 contend for victory // 승부를 짓다 try conclusion 《with》 ; fight to the finish ; fight it out ; break the ties (동점인 경우) ; play out
승산 乘算 〚수학〛 multiplication
승산 勝算 a chance〔prospect〕 of victory ; chances of success ; odds ¶ 승산이 있다 have〔stand〕 a chance of success // 전혀 승산이 없다 The chances are dead against us. // 우리 편에 승산이 있다 The odds〔chances〕 are in our favor. // 처음부터 승산이 없었다 It was the lost cause from the start. // 이번 선거에서는 거의 승산이 없다 He has but a small chance in the election. // 아무래도 승산이 바뀌기 시작한 것 같다 Apparently the odds have started to shift.
승상 承相 a prime minister ⇨ 정승
승서 陞敍 promotion ; advancement —하다 promote ; advance
*승선 乘船 embarkation ; boarding —하다 embark 《in a ship》 ; go〔get〕 on board 《a ship》 ; board 《a ship》 ; take ship ¶ 급히 승선하다 bustle on board // 승객 여러분께서는 9시까지 승선해 주시기 바랍니다 The passengers are requested to be on board by 9 o'clock.
—권 a passage ticket —료 passage money〔fare〕 —항 a port of embarkation
승세 乘勢 taking advantage of the circumstances ; seizing the right moment —하다 take advantage of the circumstances ; seize the right moment

승세 勝勢 ⇨ 승산(勝算) ¶ 승세에 있다 stand a good〔fair〕 chance of winning the game〔play〕; the chances are in one's favor
승소 勝訴 winning a lawsuit **—하다** win a lawsuit ¶ 피고가 승소했다 Judgment was given for the defendant.
승수 乘數 〖수학〗 the multiplier
피— the multiplicand
승승 장구 乘勝長驅 pressing hard on the heels of enemy; making a long drive taking advantage of victory **—하다** make a long drive taking advantage of victory; press hard on the heels of enemy; seize〔avail oneself of〕 an opportunity
승아 〖식물〗 dock; sorrel; Rumex acetosa (학명)
승압 昇壓 —하다 boost〔raise〕 the voltage 《of》
—기 〖전기〗 a step-up〔boosting〕 transformer; a booster
승야 乘夜 [밤을 타서] under the cover〔favor〕 of night〔darkness〕
— 도주 escaping in the night **— 월장** scaling a wall under cover of darkness
승용마 乘用馬 a riding horse; a saddle horse; a mount
승용차 乘用車 a passenger car; a motorcar〔an automobile〕 for riding ¶ 고급 승용차 a de luxe car // 승용차의 운전수 a chauffeur
승운 勝運 (good) luck ⇨ 운(運)
승원 僧院 a monastery; a cloister
승인 勝因 the cause of the victory
†**승인 承認** [용인] recognition; acknowledgment; admission; [동의] consent; agreement; [인가] approval **—하다** recognize; acknowledge; approve; admit; give consent to; hold with ¶ 승인을 얻어 with 《a person's》 approval // 승인을 바라다 seek〔ask for〕 the approval of 《a person》 // 독립을 승인하다 recognize the independence of 《a country》 // 그는 고인의 법적 상속인으로 승인받았다 He was recognized〔acknowledged〕 as a lawful heir to the deceased. // 법안이 법률화하기 전에 주지사의 승인이 필요하다 The governor's assent〔approval〕 is needed before the bill becomes law.
승임 陞任 receiving promotion
*‡**승자 勝者** a victor; a winner
승적 僧籍 the priesthood; the holy orders ¶ 승적에 들다 enter the priesthood; become a priest
승전 承前 continuation 《from》; "continued from" **—하다** continue; be continued from
승전 勝戰 victory; a successful war; triumph **—하다** win a war〔battle〕
—고 the drum of victory
승점 勝點 [점수] a win; [표시] a victory mark
승정 僧正 a bishop
승제 乘除 〖수학〗 multiplication and division
가감 — the four operations〔rules〕 of arithmetic
승지 勝地 a beautiful place; a place noted for beautiful scenery; a scenic spot
승직 僧職 the priesthood ¶ 승직에 취임하다 enter〔be in〕 the priesthood
†**승진 昇進** promotion; advancement; rise **—하다** be promoted〔advanced〕 《to》; rise 《to》; get〔obtain〕 promotion ¶ 승진시키다 raise〔promote, advance〕 《a person》 to // 승진의 길을 막다 block the way〔avenue〕 of promotion // 승진의 길을 열다 open up the way of promotion // 승진의 기회가 있다 have a chance of advancement〔promotion〕 // 육군 대위로 승진하다 be promoted to captain // 승진이 빨랐다 His promotion has been rapid. // 다음 사장 승진은 우리 부장이 될지도 모르겠다 Just maybe our division chief will turn out to be the next president.
승차 乘車 taking a train〔car〕 **—하다** take〔board〕 a train; get on a car; get aboard 《a train》; [군대가] entrain 《for some place》
—구 an entrance to a platform; [게시] Way In **—권** a (railway, railroad, tramcar) ticket; a passenger ticket **—권 매표구** a ticket window; a booking office 《영》 **— 규정** rules for passengers **—역** the〔one's〕 entraining point〔station〕 **—장** [정류장] a car〔bus〕 stop; a 《bus》 depot; a platform **— 제한** restriction on railway travel **무임 —권** a free pass **택시 —장** a taxi stand; a cabstand
승차 陞差 advancement to a higher position **—하다** be promoted〔advanced〕 to a higher position
승창 a stool
승척 繩尺 a measuring rope〔cord〕
승천 昇天, 陞天 ascension; death (죽음) **—하다** ascend to〔into〕 heaven〔glory〕; die (죽다) ¶ 성모의 승천 the Assumption
—일 Ascension day; Holy Thursday
승통 承統 succession to a lineage ⇨ 계승(繼承) **—하다** succeed〔accede〕 to the lineage 《of》
승패 勝敗 victory and defeat; the issue 《of a battle》; the final consequence ¶ 승패를 결하다 try conclusions〔the issue〕 with 《a person》; fight to the finish; decide the issue 《of the battle》 // 아직 승패를 헤아릴 수 없다 The issue is in doubt. /The issue is uncertain. // 이것이 승패의 분기점이다 The issue hangs on this point. // 승패에 구애하지 않는다 I do not worry about the issue of a contest.
승하 昇遐 the death〔demise〕 of a king **—하다** 《a king》 die〔demise〕
승하다 乘— multiply
승함하다 乘艦— go on board a war-

ship ; embark ; [승무원이] join one's ship
승합 乘合 riding together ; sharing a vehicle ⇨ 합승
승홍 昇汞 corrosive sublimate ; mercuriochloride
—수 a solution of corrosive sublimate
승화 昇華 〚화학〛 sublimation —하다 sublimate ; sublime
—물 a sublimate —암 sublimation
시[1] [감탄사] Pshaw ! ; Huh ! ; Hmph ! Damn !
시[2] 〚음악〛 si
⁑시 市 a city ; a town ; a municipality ; [시장] a market ; a fair ¶ 시의 municipal ; city
— 당국 the municipal〔city〕 authorities ¶ 시 당국은 거리에 침 뱉는 사람들을 단속하기로 결정했다 The city government has decided to crack down on people who spit on the street. —청 a city hall
시 是 (what is) right ; righteousness ; justice
†시 時 o'clock ; time ; hour ¶ 3시 three o'clock // 지금 몇 시입니까 What is the time ? /What time is it now ? // 몇 시에 일어나십니까 What time do you get up ?
†시 詩 poetry《총칭》; [한 편의] a poem ; lines ; verse ; an ode ¶ 시와 산문 poetry and prose // 밀튼의 시 the poems of Milton // 시를 짓다 compose〔write〕 a poem // 이 경치는 바로 한 편의 시다 These views are a poem.
—어 poetic diction 교훈— didactic poetry 극— dramatic poetry 산문— prose poetry ; a prose poem 서사— epic poetry 서정— lyric poetry 풍자— satirical poetry
시- vivid ; deep ; intense ¶ 시꺼멓다 be jet-black
시- 媤 of the husband ;《an in-law》 on the husband's side
시가 市價 market price ¶ 시가의 변동 market fluctuations // 시가로 팔다 sell at the market price
시가 市街 the streets《of a city, town》
—전 street fighting〔battling, warfare〕; street-to-street fighting —지 a town ; a city (area) ; an urban district —행진 a street march〔parade〕 ¶ 시가 행진을 하다 march〔parade〕 along〔down〕 the street 신〔구〕— new〔old〕 town
시가 時價 the current price ; the market price ¶ 시가로 in current prices // 그 꽃병은 시가로 100만원이다 The vase is valued at a million *won* today.
시가 媤家 the family of one's husband
시가 詩歌 poems and songs ; poetry
— 선집 an anthology
시가렛 a cigarette
— 케이스 a cigarette case — 페이퍼 cigarette paper
시가 a cigar
시각 時角 〚물리〛 an hour angle
—환(環) an hour circle
시각 時刻 the time of day ; time ; hour ; a short time ¶ 약속한 시각 the appointed time // 출입하는 시각 time out and in // 폐점 시각에 at closing time // 시각을 놓치지 않고 without losing a moment ; without delay ; instantly ; immediately ; at once // 이런 시각에 어디를 쏘다니고 있었느냐 Where have you been fooling around at this time of night ? // 바로 그 시각에 도착할게 I'll be there right on time.
*시각 視角 〚물리〛 the visual〔optic〕 angle ; an angle of vision〔view〕 ; [견지] a point of view ; an angle
†시각 視覺 the sense of sight ; vision ; eyesight ; sight ¶ 시각을 잃다 lose one's eyesight〔sight〕
— 교육 visual education〔instruction〕 ¶ 시각 교육 자료 visual aids — 기관 an organ of vision ; the visual organ — 중추 the visual center
시간 屍姦 necrophilia ; necrophily
†시간 時間 ① time ; [한 시간] an hour ② [학교의] a class hour ; a lesson ; a class ¶ 경과된 시간 elapsed time // 정확한 시간 correct〔right〕 time // 영어 시간 an English lesson // 한 시간의 산책〔일, 독서〕 an hour's walk〔work, reading〕 // 반 시간 half an hour ; a half hour《미》 // 시간과의 경쟁 a battle against time // 한 두 시간마다 every hour or two // 시간에 맞추어서 punctually ; on time ; at the appointed〔fixed〕 time ; as regular as a clock // 한가한 시간에 during one's leisure hours // 몇 시간이고 일하다 work for hours (and hours) // 시간제로 일하다 work by the hour // 시간제로 고용하다 engage《a person》 by the hour // 시간가는 줄도 모르다 by unaware〔unconscious〕 of the passage of time // 시간을 낭비하다 waste one's time // 시간이 모자라다 have not enough time《for, to do》 // 시간을 지키다 be punctual // 시간을 묻다 ask the hour // 시간에 늦다 be late for ; be behind time for // 시간 외로 일하다 work overtime〔extra hours〕 // 시간을 절약하다 save time // 생각할 시간을 달라고 말하다 ask for time to consider // 회합 시간을 지정하다 appoint the time for a meeting // 시간이 경과하다 Time passes. // 그것은 시간이 걸린다 That takes time. // 수업 시간은 50분이다 The hour lasts fifty minutes. // 아침 식사 시간은 7시이다 Our breakfast hour is at seven o'clock. // 시간이 없다 We are pressed for time. // 이제 곧 끝날 시간입니다 The time is nearly up. // 독서할 시간이 없다 I have no time for reading. // 이제 잘 시간이다 It is about time to go to bed. // 시간의 여유를 다오 Give me time. // 시간은 충분히 있습니다 We have plenty of time. // 그것을 바로잡을 시간은 아직

있다 There is still time to set it right. // 몇 시간 걸립니까 How long〔How many hours〕 does it take? // 시간 전에 도착했다 I was there before the time set〔appointed〕. // 그곳은 서울에서 3시간 걸린다 The town is three hours distant from *Seoul*. // 뉴욕에서 필라델피아까지는 기차로 2시간 걸린다 It is two hours from New York to Philadelphia by rail. // 사무실을 찾는 데 꽤 시간이 걸렸다 I had quite a time locating your office. // 그는 시간을 지키지 않는다는 이유로 해고됐다 He was dismissed on the ground that he was found unpunctual. // 사고가 일어난 시간은 오후 4시 45분이었다 The time of the accident was 4 : 45 P. M. // 누가 옳은지 시간이 지나면 알게 될 것이다 Time will show which of us is in the right. // 오후에는 시간이 좀 있습니다 I have some time to spare in the afternoon. // 시간은 돈이다 Time is money. // 오늘은 시간이 지독히도 안 간다 Time is really dragging today. // 이렇게 늦은 시간에 전화를 걸어서 죄송합니다 I'm sorry to call you at this hour // 그는 퇴직한 후로 시간이 남아돌아 주체를 못하시고 있다 He has got too much free time on his hands since he retired. // 그는 시간만 나면 기타를 친다 He plays the guitar every free second he's got. // 이번 주에 시간을 내서 그를 방문하자 Let's find some time this week to pay him a visit there.

— 강사 a part-time lecturer〔instructor〕 — 관념 an idea of time —급(給) payment by the hour ; time wages — 급수 water rationing ; an hour-restricted supply of water — 기록기 a time clock〔recorder〕 — 문제 a question〔matter〕 of time — 엄수 punctuality — 예술 arts based on tempo —외 근무 overtime work ¶ 시간외 근무를 하다 work overtime〔extra hours〕 —외 수당 overtime pay —외 전보 a late message —외 전보 요금 a late fee —외 취급료 extra charges after office hours —제 가정 교사 a visiting tutor〔governess〕 —제 임금제 the pay-by-the-hours fare system — 제한 a time limit —차(差) a time lag —표 a timetable ; a schedule 《미》 경과 — elapsed time 규정 — regular〔prescribed〕 hours 배당 — time assigned 소요 — the time required 《for a task》 수업 — school hours 식사〔점심〕 — meal〔lunch〕 time 영업〔집무〕 — business〔office〕 hours 취침 — bedtime 통행 금지 — curfew hours 휴식 — recess ; a break

☞ ◀ p. 1307 ▶

시객 詩客 a poet

시거에 [우선 당장에] for the moment ; hastily ; [곧] at once ; immediately

시건드러지다 (be) saucy and impudent

시건방지다 (be) saucy ; pert ; impudent ⇨ 건방지다 ¶ 시건방진 행동 a high-flown behavior

시게 grain sold in the market place

—전 market stalls that deal in grain

시겟금 the market〔selling〕 price of grain

시겟바리 a horseload of grain bound for market

시경 詩經 the Book of Odes ; the Book of Songs

시 경찰국 市警察局 [서울의] the Metropolitan Police Board〔Bureau, Headquarters〕

—장 Metropolitan Police Director ¶ 서울시 경찰국장 the Seoul City Police Director

†**시계** 時計 a clock (괘종) ; a watch ; a pocket watch (회중) ; a wristwatch (손목) ; a timepiece ; a timekeeper ¶ 시계의 제꺽제꺽하는 소리 the ticking of a clock // 시계의 태엽을 감다 wind a watch〔clock〕 // 시계를 고치다 mend〔repair〕 a watch (자기가) ; have〔get〕 one's watch mended〔repaired〕 (시계포에서) // 시계를 시보에 맞추다 set one's watch by the time signal // 시계가 빠르다 The watch gains. // 시계가 늦다 The watch loses. // 저 시계는 정확하다 That watch is right〔correct〕. // 시계가 잘 맞는다 The watch keeps good time. // 시계가 섰다 The watch has stopped. // 시계가 1시를 친다 The clock strikes one. // 시계가 30분 빨랐다 The watch was half an hour fast. // 시계 바늘을 한 시간 앞당겨 놓았니 Did you set your watch one hour ahead? // 시계 바늘을 한 시간 뒤로 돌려놓는 것을 깜빡 잊어 버렸다 I forgot to set my watch one hour backward.

—공 a watchmaker ; a clockmaker — 딱지 a watchcase — 바늘 the hands of a clock〔watch〕 — 방향 clockwise rotation ; a right-handed screw — 소리 ticking of a clock — 수리공 a watch mender — 장치 clock work — 제조 watchmaking ; clock making —줄 a watch chain〔guard〕 ; a fob (chain) —탑 a clock tower —포 a jeweler's ; a jewelry store 《미》 ; a watchmaker's 《영》 — 폭탄 a time〔delayed action〕 bomb —학 horology 뻐꾹 — a cuckoo clock 야광 — a luminous watch 자동 — a self-winding watch 전자 — an electric clock 진자 — a pendulum clock 추— a pendulum clock 탁상 — a table clock 팔목 — a wrist watch 8일 태엽 — an eight-day clock

†**시계** 視界 the field of vision ; visibility ⇨ 시야

시고 詩稿 a draft poem

시고모 媤姑母 an aunt on one's husband's side

—부 the husband of an aunt on one's husband's side

†**시골** the country ; a rural district ; the provinces ; [고향] one's home〔coun-

시간 · 날짜 · 요일

1 시간의 표현

① 일반적인 표현

「몇시 몇분」이라고 표현할 때 보통의 회화에서는 대개 시간만 나타내어 「8시 25분이다」는 「It's eight twenty-five.」(★ 하이픈에 주의)와 같이 간단히 표현한다. 그러나 「3시 4분입니다.」와 같이 1분에서 9분까지의 표현은 「It's three o[ou] four.」와 같이 표현하는 것이 보통이다.

② 정시 표현

7시, 8시와 같이 정시를 표현할 때는 o'clock을 쓴다. 오전은 in the morning, 오후는 in the afternoon, 저녁(5시 이후)은 in the evening을 사용한다. 정오 12시는 (twelve o'clock [twelve]) noon, 자정은 (twelve o'clock [twelve]) midnight를 쓴다.

¶ 정각 7시입니다. It's seven sharp. / It's exactly seven 오전 10시입니다. It's ten (o'clock) in the morning. // 정각 12시입니다. It's twelve (o'clock) noon. (★ 시각을 표현할 때는 보통 숫자를 쓰지 않고 문자로 쓴다.) // 우리집은 7시에 저녁을 먹는다. We have dinner at seven (o'clock). (★ in the evening이 생략된 것. o'clock도 보통 생략.) // 나는 매일 아침 6시에 일어나 7시경에 집을 나선다. I get up at six every morning and leave home (at) about [around] seven. (★ at은 보통 생략.)

③ 「…시…분」의 표현

30분까지는 past 또는 after (미), 30분을 지나 「…분전」이라고 표현할 때는 to 또는 before (미)를 쓴다. 15분은 quarter (a quarter (영)), 30분은 half를 쓴다. 그러나 30분이 지나도 past나 after를, 15분은 quarter 대신 fifteen minutes, 30분은 half대신 thirty minutes로 표현해도 틀린 것은 아니다.

¶ 오전 9시 10분입니다. It's nine ten in the morning[a.m.]. / It's ten (minutes) past [after] nine in the morning. // 학교는 8시 15분에 시작합니다. School starts [begins] at (a) quarter past [after] eight. // 그는 8시 15분 전에 출발했다. He started at (a) quarter to[before (미)] eight. // 그는 오후 3시 30분경에 돌아올 것이다. He will be back (at) about [around] half past three in the afternoon.

④ 약식 표현

시간을 표현하는 데는 일반적으로는 약식 표현을 많이 쓴다. 10시 20분은 10: 20 (10. 20 (영))로 숫자로 표기하고 읽을 때는 ten twenty로 한다. 오전은 a.m. (ante meridian의 약자), 오후는 p.m. (post meridian의 약자)을 사용한다. 보통은 소문자이지만 대문자를 쓰는 경우도 있다. o'clock은 생략한다.

¶ 오전 9시입니다. It's 9: 00 a.m. (★ nine a.m. [éiem]이라고 읽고 00은 읽지 않는다.) // 현재 오후 9시 5분입니다. It's 9: 05 p.m. (★ nine-o[ou]-five라고 읽는다.) // 이 수업은 2시 45분에 끝난다. This period ends at 2: 45 (p.m.).

⑤ 시간에 대한 문의와 대답

「몇시」인가를 물을 때는 What time is it (now)? (★ be동사에 현재의 의미가 있으므로 now는 생략해도 된다.) / What's the time? / What time do you have? / Have you got the time? (★시계를 갖고 있습니까? Do you have the time?) 등으로 표현한다. 또 정중한 표현으로는 Please tell me the time. / Could you tell me the time? 등과 같이 표현한다. 정확한 시간을 물을 때는 Do you have the correct time?이라고 한다.

당신은 몇시에 일어납니까? What time do you get up?는 At what time do you....에서 at이 생략된 것이다. 그러나 정확한 시간을 물어볼 경우에는 at을 생략하지 않는다.

¶ 비행기는 몇시에 이륙합니까? At what time does the plane take off? // 당신 시계는 몇시입니까? What time is it by your watch? // 내 시계는 9시 15분을 가리키고 있다. My watch says 9: 15. / I have nine fifteen. // 9시 17분입니다. It's nine seventeen by my watch. / 그렇다면 내 시계가 2분 느리군요. Then I'm afraid my watch is two minutes slow. // 5시가 가까와 옵니다. It's close to five. // 6시 30분이 다되 갑니다. It's going to be six thirty.

⑥ 기타

간결·정확을 필요로 하는 경찰이나 군대, 교통기관 또는 교통표지판이나 시간표 등에는 24시간 개념으로 나타내기 때문에 a.m. 혹은 p.m.을 붙이지 않는다. 오후 1시를 13: 00로 표기하고 thirteen hundred hours로 읽는다.

¶ 현재 15시 30분입니다. It's 15: 30. (★ fifteen (hundred) thirty로 읽는다.) // 17시 25분발 기차는 취소되었다. The 17: 25

train has been canceled.(★ seventeen twenty-five로 읽는다.)

2 날짜 표현 방식

① 표현 방식

1995년 8월 15일이라고 표현할 때는 미국식으로는 월, 일, 년도의 순으로 August 15, 1995로 표기하고 August (the) fifteenth, nineteen ninety-five 또는 날짜를 fifteen으로 기수로 읽는 경우도 많다. 영국식은 일, 월, 년도의 순으로 15th August, 1995로 표기하고 the fifteenth of August, nineteen ninety-five로 읽는다. 1900년일 경우는 nineteen hundred로 읽는다. 서력(西曆) 794년 seven (hundred) ninety-four A.D..

월을 표기할 때는 August를 Aug.로 생략형을 쓴다. 날짜를 말하는 문장의 주어는 시간의 경우와 마찬가지로 it를 사용하거나 today, the date, today's date 등을 사용한다.

¶ 오늘은 9월 1일이다. It's Sept.[Sep.] 1 today. (★ Today is Sept.[Sep.] 1.로 할 수도 있다.)//1학기는 4월 8일에 시작한다. The first term starts [begins] on Apr. 8.

② 날짜에 대한 질문과 대답

날짜를 물을 때는 date를 쓰는 것이 가장 좋지만 day of the month를 쓰기도 한다.

¶ 오늘은 며칠입니까? What's today's date? / What day of the month (is it) today? // 오늘은 10월 29일입니다. It's Oct. 29 today. / Today is Oct. 29. // 당신 생일은 며칠입니까? When is your birthday? // 바로 오늘입니다. That's today!

3 요일 표기방식

① 표기방식

보통 It이나 Today를 주어로 하여 표기한다. it을 주어로 하는 구문에서는 today를 생략하기도 한다.

¶ 오늘은 금요일이다 It's Friday (today). / Today's Friday. // 내일은 일요일이다. Tomorrow is Sunday. / It's Sunday tomorrow.

② 요일에 대한 질문과 대답

요일을 물을 때는 보통 What day is it today?로 한다. 좀 더 명확하게 요일을 물어볼 경우에는 day of the week를 써서 What day of the week is it today?로 쓰기도 한다. 또한 허물없는 사이에는 다소 애매하기는 하나 What's today?를 쓰기도 하고 Today's Monday.처럼 대답하기도 한다.

¶ 다음 일요일에 무엇을 할 예정입니까? What are you going to do next Sunday?(★요일이 부사적으로 쓰일 때 next, last 등이 앞에 붙으면 전치사는 생략한다. He will leave here Sunday. 처럼 구어에서는 요일 앞의 전치사를 생략하기도 하지만 일반적으로는 on Sunday로 on을 붙이는 것이 맞다.)// 토요일에는 수업이 몇 시간 입니까? How many class do you have on Saturdays?(★특정한 요일에 반복되는 것이 있을 때는 복수형을 쓴다.)

try) ; one's home town 《미》

> 참고 전원적인 풍토 그것 자체의 경우에는 **rural** 그것이 인간과 관계되어 「시골티나는 세련되지 못한 소박한」 따위 선악의 감정을 포함할 경우에는 일반적으로 **rustic**을 사용한다

¶ 시골의 country ; rural (전원적) ; rustic (촌스런) ; provincial // 시골 사투리 country brogue ; a provincial accent // 시골의 풍경 rural scenery 《총칭》; a rural scene // 시골의 풍습 rural manners ; country fashion // 시골의 생활 rural〔country〕 life // 시골에서 자라난 country-bred ; brought up in the country // 시골티 나는 countrified ; provincial // 시골에 가다 go into the country // 시골에서 살다 live in the country // 시골로 은퇴하다 retire into the country // 도회지에서 사는 것보다 시골에서 사는 것이 건강에 좋다 It is better for the health to live in the country than in town. // 시골 사람은 의리가 있다 Country people have a strong sense of duty. // 시골은 추색이 짙었다 The country-side glowed with color in the fall.

—길 a country lane〔road〕 **— 색시** a country girl **—집** a country house ; a cottage

시골고라리 a stupid countryman ; a bumpkin ; an awkward clumsy yokel

시골구석 a remote place〔corner〕 ; a remote village ; an out-of-the-way place 〔corner〕 ; the black country ; the backwoods 《미》 ¶ 시골 구석에서 살다 live in a remote country place ; live in an out-of-the-way place // 시골 구석에서 자라나다 be brought up in some little country village

시골나기 a country person ; a farmer ; a rustic ; rural folk ; a backwoods-man

*__시골뜨기__ a country bumpkin ; a hick ; a yokel ; a hillbilly

시골말 a country dialect ; backwoods talk ; a local expression ; a localism

시골티 the rural〔rustic, country〕 air ⇨ 촌티 ¶ 시골티 나는 rusticated ; rustic ; countrified ; boorish

시공 施工 carrying out 《construction work》 ; construction ━하다 carry out 《construction work》

━도(圖) a contract drawing

시공 時空 〖물리〗 space time ¶ 시공의 spatio temporal

시구 市區 a municipal district ; streets

━ 개정 street improvement

시구 始球 opening of a ball game ¶ 시구식을 행하다 throw〔pitch〕 the first ball ; throw out the first ball 《from the grandstand》 // 지사의 시구로 시합이 개시되었다 The game was opened〔started〕 with the first ball tossed by the governor.

*시구 詩句 a verse ; a stanza ; a stave

시구식 始球式 opening ceremony of a ball game ¶ 시구식을 하다 throw〔pitch out, kick〕 the first〔commencement〕 ball // A씨의 시구로 시합이 시작되다 start〔begin〕 a game with the first ball tossed by Mr. A

시국 時局 the situation ; the state of things ; an emergency (비상시) ¶ 시국의 추이 changes in〔development of〕 the situation // 시국에 관한 의견 one's view on the situation // 시국에 비추어 in view of 〔considering〕 the (current) situation // 시국에 대처하다 meet〔deal with, cope with〕 a situation // 시국을 수습하다 save 〔improve〕 the situation // 시국을 타개하다 tide over a critical situation // 시국을 논하다 discuss the present〔existing, current〕 situation

━ 강연회 a lecture〔meeting〕 on the situation ━ 편승자 an opportunist 중대 ━ a critical juncture

시군 市郡 cities〔towns〕 and countries

시굴 試掘 prospecting ; trial digging ; a prospect (1 회의) ━하다 prospect for 《gold》 ; bore for 《oil》 ¶ 시굴원을 제출하다 send in an application for permission to prospect 《a mine》

━갱 a test〔trial〕 pit ━권 prospecting rights ━원 an application for prospecting ━자 a (mining) prospector

시굼하다 (be) sourish ; acidulous

시궁 a cesspool ; a ditch ⇨ 시궁창

━ 구멍 the opening of the cesspool ━쥐 a brown rat ; a gutter〔water〕 rat

시궁창 a cesspool ; a sink ; a ditch ; a drain ¶ 시궁창에 빠지다 fall into a ditch

시그널 a (traffic) signal

시그러지다 fade ; vanish

시극 詩劇 a poetical drama ; a drama in verse ; a verse play

시근거리다[1], 씨근거리다 [숨을] breathe hard ; gasp ; pant ; heave ; puff (and blow) hard ¶ 시근거리며 말하다 speak while panting ; puff〔gasp〕 out

시근거리다[2] [관절이] feel a slight twitch of arthritis

시근시근[1] [숨을] short of breath ; with heavy gasps

시근시근[2] ━하다 《a joint》 be very sore

시근하다 have a twinging ache (in one's joints) ; be painful〔sore〕 (뼈마디가)

시글시글 swarming ; wiggling ; writhing ━하다 (be) swarming ; wiggling

시금 試金 assaying ━하다 assay ; make an assay of

━석 a touchstone ; a Lydian stone ; [시험] a test ; a touch ; a test case ¶ 중대한 시금석 an important〔a critical〕 test // 이 일은 그의 수완의 시금석이다 This work is the touchstone〔test case〕 of his ability. ━술 the art of assaying ━자 an assayer

시금떨떨하다 (be) sour and puckery ; sourish and astringent

시금시금하다 (be) all rather sour

시금씁쓸하다 (be) rather sour and bitter

*시금치 〖식물〗 spinach ; spinage

시금하다 (be) a bit sour ; acidulous

시급 時急 emergency ; urgency ; imminence ━하다 (be) urgent ; pressing ; imminent ; immediate ¶ 시급히 at once ; immediately ; as soon as possible ; urgently // 이것은 시급히 해결을 요하는 문제이다 The matter must be settled without delay.

시기 時期 time ; the times ; [계절] season ; the time of the year ; [경우] an occasion ¶ 등산의 시기 a good time 〔season〕 for mountaineering // 시기가 오면 when the time comes // 매년 이 시기에는 at this time every year // 시기가 절박하다 Time presses. // 지금이 공부하기 가장 좋은 시기이다 This is the best season for study. /Now is the best time for study. // 그 계획을 실행하기에는 아직 시기가 이르다 It is premature to carry out the plan.

†시기 時機 an opportunity ; a chance ; the time ; the (proper) moment ¶ 시기를 놓치지 않고 losing no time // 시기가 적합하다 be opportune ; be timely ; be appropriate ; be well-timed // 시기를 기다리다 wait for a favorable time〔ripe opportunity〕 ; wait for the right moment // 시기를 엿보다 watch for a chance〔good opportunity〕 // 시기를 잡다 seize〔take〕 the opportunity // 시기를 놓치다 miss〔let slip〕 an opportunity ; lose one's chance // 시기가 나쁘다 The time is not opportune 〔ripe〕. // 시기를 보아서 그에게 충고하시오 You may take occasion to give him a warning. // 그렇게 생각하기에는 시기 상조다 It would be premature〔rash〕 to think so. // 투자하기에는 시기 상조다 The time is not yet ripe for investment.

시기 猜忌 jealousy ; green envy ; envy ━하다 be jealous of ; be envious of ; regard with jealous of ; be envious of ; regard with jealousy ¶ 시기심을 못 이겨

driven by jealousy ; out of jealousy // 시기심이 많다 be extremely jealous 《of》
—심 jealousy ; envy ¶ 시기심을 일으키다 feel〔become〕 jealous 《of》
시꺼멓다 (be) deep black ; jet-black ; coal-black ¶ 시꺼멓게 타다 be scorched black
†시끄럽다 [소란하다] (be) noisy ; boisterous ; clamorous ; uproarious ¶ 시끄럽게 noisily ; clamorously ; uproariously ; boisterously // 시끄러운 소리 a tumult of noise // 시끄러운 거리〔교실〕 a noisy street〔classroom〕 // 시끄러운 음악 noisy music // 시끄러운 세상 a troubled world // 시끄러운 문제 a troublesome problem // 시끄러워서 owing to the noise ; because of the noise // 시끄럽게 떠들다 make much noise〔clamor〕 ; make clamor // 시끄러운 사회 문제가 되다 become a serious social problem // 바깥이 시끄럽다 There is a commotion outside. // 그 문제에 대해 세론이 시끄럽다 The matter aroused keen public controversy. // 시끄러워 Be quiet ! /Silence !
시끈가오리 〖물고기〗 an electric ray ; a numbfish
시나리오 a scenario 《*pl.* ～s》 ; a screenplay
— 라이터 a scenario writer ; a scenarist ; a screenwriter
시나브로 [틈틈이] at odd moments ; in between other jobs
시나이 반도 Sinai Peninsula
시난고난 gradually getting worse ¶ 병이 시난고난하다 His sickness grows worse.
†시내 a brook(let) ; a rivulet ; a stream(let)
시냇가 the bank of a stream
시내 市內 the city ; the area within the city limits ¶ 시내에 in the city ; within the city limits // 시내에 살다 live in the city // 시내 구경하다 go sightseeing the city ; see〔do〕 the city
— 거주자 city residents — 전차 a (city) streetcar 《미》 ; an urban tramcar 《영》 — 전화 local phones —판 the city edition
시냇물 the water of a brook〔stream〕
시너 (a) thinner
시네라마 [상표] a Cinerama
시네마 a cinema ; a kinema
시네마스코프 [상표] a Cinema Scope
시녀 侍女 a waiting woman〔maid〕 ; a lady in waiting ; a lady attendant ; a lady's maid
시누렇다 (be) a vivid〔bright, golden〕 yellow
시누이 a sister-in-law for a married woman ; a sister of one's husband
시뉘 올케 the sister of one's husband and the wife of one's brother
†시늉 [흉내] imitation ; mimicry ; [거짓으로 하는] pretense ; simulation —하다 pretend ; feign ; sham ; imitate ¶ (원숭이가) 사람 시늉을 하다 mimic man // 우는 시늉을 하다 pretend to cry // 미친 시늉을 하다 pretend to be mad ; feign oneself to be mad // 바보 시늉을 하다 play〔act〕 the fool // 죽은 시늉을 하다 feign〔sham, simulate〕 death // 그저 먹는 시늉만 하다 merely make a pretense of eating
시니컬하다 (be) cynical ; cynic
‡시다[1] [맛이] (be) sour ; acid ; tart ¶ 신 사과 a sour apple // 신 우유 sour milk // 신맛이 나다 taste sour
시다[2] [뼈가] (be) stinging ; painful 《in the joints》 ¶ 발목이 시다 feel a dull pain in one's ankle
시다[3] [행동이] (be) unseemly and unpleasant ; intolerable ¶ 눈꼴이 시다 hate to see
시닥나무 〖식물〗 a kind of maple
시단 詩壇 the world of poetry ; poetical circles
시달 示達 written instructions ; directions ; a directive ; an order —하다 instruct ; direct
시달리다 be afflicted〔troubled〕 with ; be annoyed〔harassed〕 by ; be agonized ; suffer from ; be molested ¶ 가난에 시달리는 사람 a poverty-stricken person // 병에 시달리다 suffer from〔be afflicted with〕 disease // 남편에게 시달리다 be mistreated by one's husband // 빚에 시달리다 be harassed with debts // 생활에 시달리다 be harassed by the problem of living // 그들은 이 문제에 시달리고 있다 The question is giving them trouble. // 방문객에 시달리다 I am troubled with visitors. /I am annoyed by many visitors.
시당숙 媤堂叔 an uncle (who is a cousin of one's husband's father)
†시대 時代 ① [시기] an age ; a period ; an era ; a time ; an epoch ¶ 조선 시대 the *Chosŏn* Dynasty period〔era〕 // 원자력 시대 an age of atomic power ; the atomic age // 다음 시대의 사람들 the next generation // 아버지 시대에는 in my father's days // 옛날 같은 좋은 시대가 돌아오기 바라다 sigh for the good old times to return // 아인슈타인의 이론은 물리학에 신시대를 이룩했다 Einstein's theory marked a new epoch in physics.
② [시세] the times ¶ 시대의 요구 the needs〔demands〕 of the times // 시대에 뒤떨어진 사람 a back number ; a mossback // 시대에 앞서다 be ahead of the times // 시대에 뒤떨어지다 be behind the times // 시대에 역행하다 put〔set〕 back the clock // 시대와 보조를 맞추다 keep pace with the times ; keep abreast with the times
— 감각 the sense of the times — 구분 the division 《of history》 into periods ; periodization —극 a historical play〔drama〕 ; a period adventure drama〔film〕 —병 a morbid idea of the times〔age〕 — 사상 current thoughts〔ideas, sentiments〕 — 사조 the trend

〔current〕 of the times —상 the phases of the times — 소설 a period novel — 정신 the spirit of the times — 착오 (an) anachronism — 풍조 the fashion of the day 빙하 — the Ice Age 삼국 — the era of the Three Kingdoms 석기 — the Stone Age 암흑 — the Dark Ages 우주 — the space age 원자력 — the atomic age

시댁 媤宅 [집] the house of one's husband ; [식구] the family of one's husband

시도 示度 a reading ; indication ; registered〔recorded〕 degrees ¶ 태풍 24호의 중심 시도는 895밀리바였다 The registered central atmospheric pressure of Typhoon No. 24 was 895 millibars. // 온도계의 시도는 영하 12도이다 The thermometer shows a reading of 12 degrees below zero.

시도 市道 [시와 도] cities and provinces ; [시의 도로] a city〔municipal〕 road

†**시도 試圖** an attempt ; testing ; a tryout ; a venture ; an experiment —하다 attempt ; make an attempt ; try out ; test ; have a trial ¶ 그 방법을 시도하다 give the method a trial // 그의 최초의 시도는 실패로 돌아갔다 His first attempt came to a failure.

시도식 始渡式 opening ceremony of a new bridge

시동 始動 starting ¶ 시동을 거십시오 Start your car, please. // 아침에는 특히 시동이 잘 안 걸린다 It doesn't start very well, especially in the morning.
—기(機) a starter ; a starting engine — 장치 a starting device〔system〕
시동을 걸다 관용 set〔start〕 a machine

시동 侍童 a page ¶ 시동의 신분 pagehood ; pageship

시동생 媤同生 one's husband's younger brother

시드 —하다 〖경기〗 seed 《a player》
—선수 a seeded player

시드니 Sydney

‡**시들다** [초목이] wither ; die ; fade (away) ; be shriveled ; wilt ; droop ; [기세가] be dejected ; be dispirited ¶ 시든 손 a withered hand // 시들어 가는 잎 yellowing leaves // 서리에 꽃이 시들어 버렸다 The frost killed the flowers. // 젊음의 의기가 시들었다 The youthfulness has faded 〔died out〕. // 그의 인기도 시들었다 His popularity is off color〔on the wane〕.

시들방귀 dull〔disagreeable〕 stuff

시들병 —病 marasmus

시들부들, 시들시들 slightly wilted〔withered〕 —하다 (be) slightly wilted ; have withered a little ¶ 꽃이 시들시들 시들었다 The flower withered somewhat.

시들이 unconcernedly ; halfheartedly ; lightly ; belittlingly ¶ 시들이 여기다 make light of ; take lightly ; hold 《a thing》 in low esteem ; slight ; neglect ; disdain // 시들이 대답하다 give a dry answer ; answer in a halfhearted manner

시들하다 ① be disinclined〔indisposed〕 to 《do》 ; be reluctant to 《do》
② (be) unsatisfactory ; unsavory ; insipid
③ be dissatisfied ; be discontented ¶ 시들한 이야기 a dull story // …의 말을 시들하게 듣다 listen to 《a person》 apathetically // 일하기가 시들하다 be indisposed to the work〔to do the work〕 // 그는 그 제안을 받고도 시들했다 He was not interested in the proposal. // 그것은 어쩐지 시들하다 It leaves something to be desired.

시디시다 be sour as sour can be ; (be) very sour

시뜻하다 ① ⇨ 시들하다 ② [싫증나다] (be) fed up 《with》 ; sick〔weary〕 《of》 ; feel a repugnance 《to, for》

시래기 dried radish leaves

시량 柴糧 fuel and food

시러베아들 an unreliable person ; a silly person

‡**시럽** sirup 《미》 ; syrup 《영》

시렁 a wall shelf ; a rack ¶ 시렁 가래 crosspoles used as a shelf // 시렁에 얹다 put 《a thing》 on a shelf

†**시력 視力** sight ; eyesight ; vision ; visual power ¶ 불완전한 시력 defective vision // 시력의 결함 an optical defect // 시력이 약하다 have bad sight ; be weak-sighted ; be weak in sight // 시력을 잃다 lose one's sight〔eyesight〕 ; be deprived of one's eyesight // 시력을 회복하다 recover one's sight ; have one's sight restored // 시력이 감퇴하다 My eyes are dimmed. / My eyesight is failing.
— 감퇴 amblyopia — 검사 a test of vision〔visual power〕 ; an eyesight test ; optometry — 검사표 an eyesight test chart ; an eye chart

†**시련 試鍊** a trial ; a test ; an ordeal —하다 try ; make a trial ; give an ordeal ¶ 신의 시련 a divine test // 시련을 이겨낸 우정 well-proven〔old and tried〕 friendship // 가혹한 시련 bitter〔severe, sore〕 trials〔ordeals〕 // 시련을 겪은 well-tried ; weather-beaten ; seasoned // 시련을 당하다 be tried ; undergo a trail ; be put to the test ; go through the mill // 시련을 견디다 stand the test〔trail〕 // 국민은 이 국가적 시련을 이겨낼 각오이다 People are determined to go through this national trial.

시론 時論 a current view〔opinion〕 ; [일반의 여론] public opinion ; public sentiment ; [시사평] comments on current events

시론 詩論 poetics ; a criticism of poems ; an essay on poetry

시론 試論 an essay 《in, on》

시료 施療 free〔gratuitous〕 medical treat-

ment —하다 treat《a person》gratuitously ; give《a person》free medical treatment ¶ 시료를 받다 be treated free of charge ; be treated for nothing
— 병원 a charity hospital ; a dispensary ; a public〔free〕clinic
시료 試料 [광석의] a sample ore
시루 an earthenware steamer
—떡 steamed rice cake 시룻밑 a mat placed in the bottom of a steamer 시룻방석 a steamer mat-cover 시룻번 dough used to fill the gap between a steamer and a cauldron
시룽거리다 chat flippantly〔frivolously〕; fiddle-faddle ; romp about ; play joke ¶ 시룽시룽 romping about ; joking
시류 時流 [풍조] the current of the times ; the trend of the world ; the fashion of the day ¶ 시류를 따르다 follow the fashion ; swim with the tide〔stream〕; go with the current of the times // 시류에 앞서다 be in advance〔ahead〕of the times
시르죽다 be disheartened ; be dispirited ; be depressed〔dejected〕; be in a low spirit
시름 anxiety ; worry ; trouble ; grief ¶ 시름이 많다 be full of troubles〔cares〕; be care-laden // 시름을 놓다 feel relieved ; be relieved of worry // 그것을 듣고 한시름 놓았다 The news took a weight off my mind. // 그 소식을 들으니 한 시름 놓인다 It's a relief to hear that news.
시름겹다 be full of worries〔troubles, anxieties, cares〕
시름시름 ¶ 시름시름 앓는 병 a lingering illness // 그는 시름시름 앓았다 He was long in recovering from his illness.
시름없다 (be) worried ; anxious ; absent-minded ¶ 시름없이 absent-mindedly ; vacantly ; blankly ; listlessly // 시름없이 창밖을 내다보다 look out the window absent-mindedly
시리다《a body part》(be) cold ¶ 귀가 시리다 My ears are cold.
시리아 Syria ¶ 시리아의 Syrian
— 사람 a Syrian
시리즈 a series ¶ 시리즈로 출판하다 publish《a novel》in a serial form ; serialize《a story》
—물 a serial 월드 — the World Series
시립 市立 ¶ 시립의 municipal ; city // 그 병원은 시립이다 The hospital is maintained at municipal expense.
— 도서관 a city library — 병원 a municipal hospital — 학교〔대학〕a municipal school〔college, university〕; a school〔university〕under city management
시마력 時馬力 a horse-power hour
시말 始末 the beginning and the end ; the fact of the matter ; the circumstances ; the particulars
—서 a written explanation〔apology〕¶ 시말서를 써내다 be asked〔required〕to give〔send in〕a written explanation〔account〕; be called to account
시망스럽다 (be) harsh ; cruel ; merciless
시매기다 時— set the fixed time《for doing something》; set limits to time
시맥 翅脈 〖곤충〗 nerve ; nervure
시먹 〖미술〗 black projection lines
시먹다 (be) contrary
시멘트 cement ¶ 시멘트를 바르다 cement
— 공사 cement work — 공장 a cement plant〔factory〕— 기와 a cement tile — 방수제 a waterproofer of cement — 운반선 a cement carrier〔tanker〕— 접합(接合)〔도포(塗布)〕cementation — 혼합기〔시험기〕a cement mixer〔tester〕수경(水硬) — hydraulic cement 칼러 — color cement 특수 — special cement
시모 媤母 the mother of one's husband ; a woman's mother-in-law
시묘 侍墓 mourning at the graves of one's parents —하다 mourn at the graves of one's parents during the mourning period
시무 始務 the opening of government offices for the year ; reopening of office business after the New Year holidays
—식(式) the opening ceremony
시무 時務 current affairs ; the requirements of the time
— 시간 business hours
시무 視務 attending to business ; execution of one's business ; business —하다 attend to business〔duty〕; execute one's business ; work
시무룩하다 (be) sulky ; sullen ; displeased ; ill-humored ; glum ; touchy ; [날씨가] cloudy ¶ 시무룩하여 with a displeased look ; with a sulky face // 시무룩하니 말이 없다 keep a sulky silence // 날씨가 시무룩하다 The sky is sulky. // 그는 시무룩하니 말도 않고 앉아 있었다 He sat sullen and silent. // 시무룩한 얼굴을 왜 하고있지 Why the long face? // 그런 시무룩한 얼굴은 보이지 말아라 Don't put on such a long face.
시문 時文 current literature ; contemporary writings
—체 current style of writing
시문 詩文 poetry and prose
—선(選) a selection of prose and poetry
시문 試問 a question ; an examination ; an interview —하다 interview《a person》; question《a person》; put a question《to a person》
시물 施物 an alms ; a handout《미》
†시민 市民 a citizen ; the townsmen ; the townsfolk ; citizenry《총칭》¶ 서울 시민 the citizens of *Seoul* // 선량한 소시민 a good petit bourgeois
— 계급 bourgeoisie《프》— 교육 civic education —권 (the right of) citizenship ; civil〔civic, citizens'〕rights ¶ 시민

권을 주다 grant citizenship to 《a person》; naturalize 《미》// 미국의 시민권을 획득하다 acquire citizenship in the United States — 대회 a citizens's rally〔mass meeting〕 — 사회 civil society — 생활 the civic life —세 a municipal tax

시반 屍斑 〖의학〗 a purple spot

시발 始發 the start ; the first departure —하다 start ; depart the terminal ¶ 시발 오전 6시 the first train〔car〕 starts at 6 a. m. // 서울 시발 부산행 열차 a train bound for *Pusan* from *Seoul*

—역 the terminal ; the starting〔commencing〕 station ; the station of origin — 전차 the first streetcar

시방 時方 now ⇨ 지금

시방서 示方書 specifications

⁑시범 示範 setting〔showing〕 an example ; a model for others —하다 set an example ; show〔give〕 a good example ¶ 시범적으로 by way of showing an example

— 경기 an exhibition game〔match〕 — 농장〔학교〕 a model farm〔school〕

시법 詩法 prosody

시베리아 Siberia ¶ 시베리아의 Siberian — 사람 a Siberian — 철도 the Siberian Railway

시변 市邊 ① 〔변두리〕 the suburbs〔outskirts〕 of a city〔town〕 ② 〔장변리〕 interest carried on a loan in the market

시보 時報 ① 〔평론〕 a review ; a bulletin ; current news ② 〔시간을 알림〕 a time signal〔siren〕 ; announcement of the time

시보 試補 a probationer

사법관 — a probationary judicial officer ; a judicial officer on probation

시복 諡福 beatification —하다 beatify 《a person》

—식 beatification

시볼레 a Chevrolet (car) ¶ 77년형 시볼레 a '77 Chevrolet

시봉 侍奉 serving〔waiting on〕 one's parents —하다 serve one's parents filially

시부 媤父 the father of one's husband ; a woman's father-in-law

시부 詩賦 poem and improvisational poetic writing ; Chinese poetry

시부렁거리다, 씨부렁거리다 prattle ; chatter ; jabber ; talk nonsense ; talk useless things

시부모 媤父母 the parents of one's husband ; a woman's parents-in-law

시부저기 effortlessly ; easily ; "without lifting a finger"

시부적시부적 ⇨ 시부저기

시분 —粉 a line drawn with powder

시비 市費 municipal〔city〕 expenses ; 〔경비〕 city expenditure ¶ 시비로 at municipal expense

시비 侍婢 a lady〔maid〕 in waiting ; a waiting woman ; a maidservant

시비 是非 〔잘 잘못〕 right and wrong ; the propriety ; 〔싸움〕 a dispute ; a quarrel ; a fight ; an argument ¶ 남녀 공학의 시비 the propriety of coeducation // 시비의 판단 discrimination of right and wrong // 시비를 가리다 discriminate〔distinguish〕 between right and wrong ; tell right from wrong // 시비를 걸다 provoke〔pick〕 a quarrel 《with a person》 ; make〔kick up〕 a row // 하찮은 일로 시비하다 quarrel〔argue〕 about trifles // 그와 시비를 해도 소용없다 There is nothing to be gained by arguing with him.

— 곡직 the right and the wrong ; the crooked〔twisted〕 and the straight —조(調) a fighting〔defiant〕 attitude ; an aggressive attitude ¶ 시비조의 aggressive ; bellicose

시비 詩碑 a monument inscribed with a poem

시비 施肥 fertilization ; manuring —하다 manure ; apply manure ; fertilize

시비주비 是非— a fight-picker ; a quarrel-seeker ; 〔흠잡이〕 a faultfinder

시뻘겋다 (be) crimson ; deep red ¶ 시뻘겋게 되다 turn red〔crimson〕 ; flush deeply // 성이 나서 얼굴이 시뻘겋게 되다 be black〔crimson, purple〕 with anger

시쁘다 (be) unsatisfying ; be not contented with ⇨ 시들하다

시사 時事 the events of the day ; current〔present〕 events〔affairs, issues, questions〕 ¶ 시사를 논하다 discuss〔talk of〕 current events〔topics of the day〕 // 시사에 밝다 be well posted in current affairs ; be well-informed of current events // 시사에 어둡다 be ignorant of the times ; be out of touch with the current events // 시사를 해설하다 comment on the issues of the day

— 문제 a current question ; issues of the day ; current topics — 사진 a news photo — 소설 a current-affair novel — 영어 current English — 주간지 a newsweekly — 평론 comments on contemporary〔current〕 topics ; a contemporary — 해설 comments on current topics ; news commentary ; an interpretation of current events — 해설자 a news commentator ; a commentator on current events ; a lecturer on world affairs

시사 時祀 ⇨ 시향

시사 試寫 a preview ; a private show(-ing) —하다 preview ¶ 시사회를 하다 give a preview 《of a film》

—실 a projection room —회 a (cinema, movie) preview ; a trade show

시사 詩史 a history of 《Chinese》 poetry

시사 試射 trial〔test〕 firing —하다 try out ; test 《a weapon》 ¶ 권총을 시사하다 try out a pistol

—장 a firing range —탄 a trial-shot

시사 示唆 suggestion —하다 hint ; suggest ; be suggestive of ; give suggestions ¶ 매우 시사적이다 be 《very》 suggestive ; be full of suggestions

시사 侍史 ① [비서] a private secretary ② [편지 겉봉에] Esquire 《Esq.》; respectfully

시산 試算 a trial (calculation) ━하다 calculate ; try

━표 a trial balance (sheet)

시살 弑殺 a regicide ; murdering one's lord〔parents, king〕 ━하다 murder 《one's master, parents》; commit regicide ; assassinate 《a King》

시삼촌 媤三寸 an uncle of one's husband

━댁 the wife of an uncle of one's husband

⁑시상 施賞 awarding (a prize) ━하다 award 《a person》 a prize ; bestow a prize 《on》

━식 a ceremony of awarding prizes

시상 時相 〖문법〗 the tense

시상 視床 〖해부〗 a thalamus 《*pl.* -mi》; an optic thalamus

시상 詩想 a poetical idea〔sentiment〕

시새 fine sand

시새우다 be terribly jealous 《of》; be green with envy 《of》; be green with jealousy ; be envious 《of》; envy ¶ 시새워서 그렇게 말하는 것이겠지 He must be saying such things out of jealousy. // 그들은 서로 시새운다 They are jealous of each other.

시생 侍生 I ; me ; your humble servant

시생대 始生代 〖지질〗 the Archeozoic Era

시서 詩書 [시경과 서경] the Odes and the Histories ; [시와 서예] poetry and calligraphy

시서느렇다 be quite cold ; have grown cold

시서늘하다 [음식이] (be) quite cold

시석 矢石 arrows and stones ; archery and slinging

시선 視線 one's eye(s) ; the line of vision〔sight, collimation〕; the level of vision ¶ 시선을 던지다 turn one's eyes〔gaze〕 upon 《a person》; throw one's eyes 《upon》 // 시선을 피하다 avoid 《a person's》 eye ; escape 《another's》 gaze // 시선을 돌리다 avert〔turn away〕 one's eyes // 시선을 모으다 attract public gaze ; be the cynosure of all eyes // 시선이 맞았다 Their eyes met. // 모든 사람의 시선이 그에게 쏠렸다 All eyes were turned upon him.

시선 詩仙 a great〔master〕 poet

시선 詩選 selected poems ; an anthology ; a selection of poems

당(唐)━ A Selection of Poems of the Tang Dynasty

시설 施設 establishment ; institution ; equipment ; [시설물] facilities ; establishments ━하다 establish ; equip ; institute ¶ 환자의 치료 시설이 있다 have facilities for the treatment of patients // 우리 시에는 오락 시설이 부족하다 Our city needs more facilities for recreation.

━비 the cost of equipment ━ 투자 investment in equipment 공공 ━ public services ; a public institution 공군 ━ air installations 교육 ━ educational facilities 군사 ━ military establishments 방화 ━ fire prevention equipment 산업 ━ industrial facilities 상점 ━ the fittings of a store 세탁 ━ arrangements for washing 조리〔취사〕 ━ arrangements for cooking 하수 ━ sewerage arrangements ; a sewer system 호텔 ━ hotel facilities〔accommodations〕

시설 柹雪 bloom ¶ 곶감에 시설이 앉았다 The dried persimmons have bloom on them.

시성 詩聖 a great poet

시성 諡聖 canonization ━하다 canonize 《a person》 as a saint

시성식 示性式 〖화학〗 a rational formula

시세 市稅 a municipal tax〔duty, rate〕

시세 市勢 ① [시장의] market conditions ② [도시의] the conditions of municipal life ; the state of city affairs

━ 조사 municipal census-taking ¶ 시세 조사를 하다 take a municipal census

시세 時世 the times ; the age ; the trend of the age ; the tendency of the times ¶ 시세에 뒤지다 fall behind the times // 시세를 따르다 swim with the current // 시세에 역행하다 swim against the current // 그는 시세에 앞서가고 있다 He is far ahead of his times.

시세 時勢 ① the current〔situation, signs〕 of the times ; the drift of the times ; the spirit of the age ; the condition of life ② [시가] the current price ; the market price ; business conditions ¶ 험한 시세 disturbed〔unsettled, turbulent〕 times // 쌀 시세 the (current) price of rice // 요즘 시세 the current quotation // 거래소의 시세 exchange quotation // 오르는〔내리는〕 시세 a rising〔sagging〕 tendency // 시세를 한탄하다 blame 《it》 on the times // 시세가 오르다 rise〔advance〕 in price // 시세가 내리다 fall〔decline〕 in price // 시세를 올리다 be a bull market // 시세를 타고나다 be born under a lucky star // 시세가 이롭다 The times are favorable. /The situation is opportune.

━폭(幅) a price range ; price changes〔fluctuations〕 ━폭 제한 〖증권〗 curbing of excessive fluctuations

시세닿다 時勢━ come up with a fair price ; get one's price ; be reasonable in price

시소 a seesaw ¶ 시소를 타고 놀다 (play on a) seesaw

━ 게임 a seesaw game

시속 時速 speed per hour ; velocity per hour (바람의) ¶ 시속 30마일 30 miles

per hour 《30 m. p. h.》
시속 時俗 the customs of the age 〔times〕; the manners and ways of the age
시솔 侍率 serving superiors while looking after subordinates
시숙 媤叔 brothers of one's husband
시술 施術 a surgical operation —하다 operate ; perform an operation
시스템 (a) system
시습 時習 frequent〔repeated〕 review 《of lessons》 —하다 review 《one's lessons》 frequently ; go through〔over〕 《one's lessons》 occasionally
시승 試乘 a trial ride —하다 have a trial ride 《in》; test 《a vehicle》
—차 a demonstrator
시시 각각 時時刻刻 hourly ; every hour 〔moment, minute〕; moment by moment ; constantly ; from moment to moment ¶ 시시 각각으로 변화하다 change every moment // 날씨가 시시 각각으로 변한다 The weather varies from hour to hour. // 형세는 시시 각각으로 변해 간다 The situation is changing every hour〔moment〕. // 물은 시시 각각으로 불어 갔다 The water became higher and higher every moment.
*시시덕거리다 laugh and talk over nothing ; laugh sillily ; talk nonsense
시시덕이 a nonsensical character ; a silly fool
시시때때로 時時— ⇨ 시시로
시시로 時時— from time to time ; now and then ; occasionally ; frequently
시시부지 —하다 be buried in oblivion ; drift into obscurity ; come to nothing ; end in smoke ; vanish ¶ 시시부지하게 일하다 go halfway with one's work // 돈이 시시부지하게 없어졌다 My money seemed to have evaporated. // 그들의 계획이 시시부지하게 끝났다 Their plans went up in smoke. // 그 사건이 시시부지하게 끝났다 The affair ended in nothing. /The affair has faded into oblivion. // 그 소문은 시시부지하게 없어졌다 The rumor blew over. // 무슨 일이든지 시시부지하게 하기는 싫다 I hate leaving things half done.
시시비비 是是非非 —하다 argue about what is wrong and what is right ; quarrel over right and wrong ; call a spade a spade ¶ 시시비비주의 a free and unbiased policy ; a fair attitude
⁑시시하다 (be) dull and flat ; uninteresting ; trifling ; trivial ; petty ; insignificant ; worthless ; silly ; be of little importance ; be of no account ¶ 시시한 것 a matter of no importance ; a trifle // 시시한 강연 a tedious〔dull〕 speech // 시시한 책 an uninteresting〔a worthless〕 book // 시시한 일 a thing of no value ; a trifle // 시시한 배우 a poor actor // 시시하다는 듯이 with a disappointed〔bored〕 look // 시시한 말을 하다 talk nonsense〔rot〕; say silly things // 시시한 일에 화를 내다 get angry over a trifling thing
시식 時食 seasonable foods ; food in season
시식 試植 trial planting —하다 plant for trial
시식 試食 tasting ; sampling —하다 sample ; taste ; try ; obtain a foretaste 《of》
—회 a sampling party
시식돌 施食— 〖불교〗 a stone on which to offer food to demons while reading Buddhist scriptures after a ceremony for a dead soul
시신 侍臣 an official in attendance ; a courtier
시신 屍身 a dead body ; a corpse
시신경 視神經 the visual〔optic〕 nerve
—상 〖생리〗 the optic thalamus —염 〖의학〗 optic neuritis
시신세 始新世 〖지질〗 the Eocene (epoch)
시신통 始新統 〖지질〗 the Eocene (series)
시심 詩心 poetic sentiment〔instinct〕
시아버님 媤— 《your, my, her》 esteemed father-in-law
시아버지 a woman's father-in-law ; one's husband's father
시아이디 CID 《Criminal Investigation Detachment》
시아이시 CIC 《Counter Intelligence Corps》
시아이에이 C. I. A. 《Central Intelligence Agency》
시아주버니 one's husband's brother ; a woman's brother-in-law
시안 〖화학〗 cyanogen
—화물(化物) a cyanide
시안 試案 a tentative plan
시앗 a concubine of one's husband
시애틀 Seattle
*시야 視野 a field〔range〕 of vision 〔view〕; a visual field ; [시계] visibility ; purview ; horizon ¶ 시야가 넓은〔좁은〕 사람 a man of a broad〔narrow〕 outlook on life // 시야에 들어오다 come in sight of ; come within the field of vision // 시야에서 사라지다 go out of sight // 시야를 막다 obstruct 《a person's》 field of vision ; obstruct 《a person's》 view (전망을) // 시야를 넓히다 widen〔broaden〕 one's mental vision // 그는 시야가 넓다〔좁다〕 His mental vision is broad〔narrow〕.
시야비야 是也非也 arguing right and wrong ⇨ 시시비비
시약 試藥 a reagent ; a test ¶ 시약병 a reagent bottle
시약 施藥 gratuitous dispensation of medicine〔medicine dispensed free〕 —하다 dispense medicine 《free》
시약불견 視若不見 —하다 pretend not to have seen〔noticed〕; blink 《a fact》; wink at 《a thing》; cut

시어 詩語 poetic diction〔language, word〕
***시어머니** one's husband's mother ; a woman's mother-in-law
시어머님 媤— 《your, my, her》 esteemed mother-in-law
시업 始業 commencement of work ; opening ; inauguration **—하다** commence〔begin, start〕 work ; open
—식 the opening ceremony〔exercises〕; an inaugural ceremony **—시간** the opening hour 《of a school, of a firm》
시에라리온 Sierra Leone
시엠 CM ; [라디오·텔레비전의 광고] a commercial (message)
시여 施與 a donation ; a contribution ; an offering **—하다** give ; dispense ; donate ; contribute ; give free ; give《money, things》 in charity
시역 a difficult〔demanding〕 task
시역 市域 the city limit(s) ; the municipal area
시역 始役 starting construction work **—하다** begin〔start〕 (a construction job)
시역 時疫 ⇨ 유행병(流行病)
시역 弑逆 regicide ; the murder of one's lord ⇨ 시살
시역 視域 〖물리〗 the field of vision〔view〕; the visual field ¶ 망원경의 시역 the field of a telescope
—렌즈 field lens〔glass〕
시연 試演 a demonstration ; a trial performance 《of a play》; a rehearsal ; a preview **—하다** give a trial performance ; rehearse 《a play》
공개 — a public rehearsal〔demonstration〕
시영 市營 municipalization ; municipal management〔operation, ownership〕 ¶ 시영의 municipalized ; city-operated〔-run〕// 시영의 가스와 수도 사업 municipal trading〔enterprise〕 in gas and water ; municipal supply of gas and water service // 시영으로 하다 municipalize
—버스 a city〔municipal〕 bus **—주택** a municipal dwelling house **—화** municipalization ¶ 시영화하다 municipalize
시오니즘 Zionism
시온 〖지리〗 Zion
시왕가르다 perform a shamanist service for the repose of 《a person's》 soul
시왕 가름 a shamanist requiem
시외 市外 the outskirts of a city ; outside the city limits ; the suburbs ¶ 시외의 suburban // 시외에 out of town ; outside the city in the suburbs 《of》; on〔at〕 the outskirts 《of》// 시외 2마일 two miles outside (of) the city limits // 시외에서 살다 live in a suburb〔in the suburbs〕 《of *Seoul*》
—거주자 an out-of-towner **—선** [전화의] a long-distance line ; a trunk line 《영》 **—전차** a suburban streetcar **—주택** a suburban house **—통화** an out-of-town〔a long-distance〕 call ; a toll call ; a trunk call 《영》 **—통화 교환수** a toll operator ; a trunk operator 《영》
시외가 媤外家 one's husband's mother's house〔family〕
시외 버스 a cross-country bus
시외삼촌 媤外三寸 one's husband's maternal uncle ; the brother of the mother of a woman's husband
시외 전화 市外電話 [선] a toll line ; a trunk line 《영》; [통화] a toll〔a long-distance, an out-of-town〕 call
—감사 a toll service inspection **—교환대** a toll (switch) board
시용 試用 a trial ; a test **—하다** try ; make a trial of ; use as a trial
시우 時雨 a seasonable rain
시우 詩友 a poetical friend ; friends in poetry
시우쇠 pig iron
시운 時運 luck ; fortune ; the tide ; propitiousness of the times ¶ 시운이 변하여 at the turn of the wheel // 시운이 불리하다 The condition is unfavorable to us. // 시운이 형통하다 The luck is good for us.
시운전 試運轉 [기차 따위] a trial trip〔run, voyage〕; [기계 따위] a test (working) **—하다** make〔conduct〕 a trial run 《of a car》; try out 《a machine》 ¶ 엔진의 시운전 a test run of an engine // 전차의 시운전을 하다 conduct〔have〕 a trial run of the electric train
시울 ⇨ 가장자리
시원섭섭하다 feel relieved but sorry ; feel mixed emotions of joy and sorrow ¶ 학교를 졸업하니 시원섭섭하다 be graduating 《a school》 with mixed emotions
시원스럽다 [태도가] (be) brisk ; quick ; active ; [성질이] frank ; forthright ; unreserved ¶ 시원스러운 사람 a man of frank disposition ; a man of free and frank nature // 시원스럽지 못한 사람 a self-contained〔reserved〕 man // 시원스럽게 일을 하다 do one's work in a brisk way ; do one's job with alacrity // 시원스럽게 말하다 speak briskly ; give a satisfactory account ; get right down to the point // 그녀는 시원한 성격 덕분에 여자들에게도 인기가 있다 Her straight forward personality also makes her popular with other girls
시원시원하다 (be) clear and brisk ; bright ; lively ; animated ¶ 시원시원하게 대답하다 give a straightforward〔an unhesitating〕 answer // 말을 시원시원하게 하다 talk brightly ; be a sparkling conversationalist // 일을 시원시원하게 하다 be a brisk worker ; do one's work in a brisk way
시원찮다 (be) unsatisfactory ; dull ; lack liveliness〔briskness〕 ¶ 시원찮은 태도 a lukewarm attitude // 시원찮은 대답 an

indefinite and unsatisfactory answer // 먹은 것이 시원찮다 have one's appetite still unsatisfied // 시원찮은 사람이다 He does not know his own mind. /He never gives a direct yes or no.

†**시원하다** ① (be) cool ; refreshing ; [기분이] feel refreshed ; feel relieved ② [태도가] (be) bright ; brisk ; active ; smart ; outspoken (언어가) ¶ 시원한 바람 a cool〔refreshing〕 breeze // 시원한 아침 공기 the fresh air of the morning // 시원한 눈 bright〔clear〕 eyes // 시원한 데에 두다 keep 《a thing》 in a cool place // 날로 시원해진다 It is getting cooler day by day. // 할말을 다 하고 나니 속이 시원하다 Now that I have had my say, I feel better. // 빚을 다 갚고 나니 속이 시원하다 Now that I have paid all my debts, a load is off my mind. // 그 일을 끝내고 나니 중책을 벗은 것 같아 속이 시원하다 I feel relieved of a heavy burden by the completion of that work. // 반응이 시원치 않았다 The reaction's been zip.

†**시월 十月** October 《Oct.》
— **막사리** around the end of October — **상달** October the Harvest Month

시위[1] a bowstring

시위[2] [홍수] a flood ; an inundation.
시위가 나다 관용 be flooded ; be inundated

시위 示威 demonstration ; display ; showing **—하다** demonstrate ; display ; show off ¶ 전쟁 반대 시위 an anti-war demonstration // 학생 시위 a student demonstration
— **운동** a demonstration (against the government) ; an intimidatory action — **운동자** a demonstrator ; a demonstrant — **행진** a parade **가두** — a street demonstration

시위 侍衛 the Royal Guards **—하다** guard〔escort〕 the king ; serve as an attendant to the king

시위 소찬 尸位素餐 sinecurism ; sinecureship ; [지위] a sinecure ¶ 시위 소찬의 몸 a sinecurist ; the holder of a sinecure

시위적거리다 do in an easygoing manner

시유 市有 city〔municipal〕 ownership ¶ 시유의 city-owned // 시유로 하다 municipalize
— **재산** municipal property **—지** city land

시율 詩律 rules of meter (for poems) ; metrics

시은 施恩 doing 《a person》 a favor **—하다** do 《a person》 a favor ; bestow favors on 《a person》 ; confer (a) favor

시음 試飮 sampling 《a drink》 **—하다** sample〔try out〕 《a drink》

시읍면 市邑面 cities, towns, and villages ; municipalities
—장 the mayor of a city or town ; the headman of a village

시의 侍醫 a court physician ; a physician to the king

시의 時宜 circumstances ; the occasion ¶ 시의를 얻은 timely ; well-timed ; opportune ; expedient // 시의에 맞지 않은 untimely ; ill-timed ; inopportune // 시의에 따라 according to circumstances

시의 猜疑 suspicion (의혹) ; distrust (불신) ; jealousy (시기) **—하다** suspect ; doubt ; distrust ; be jealous ¶ 시의심이 강하다 be of suspicious〔distrustful〕 nature // 시의의 눈으로 보다 look upon 《a person》 with suspicious eyes ; eye 《a person》 with suspicion

시의회 市議會 a city〔municipal〕 assembly
— **의사당** a municipal assembly hall — **의원** a municipal assemblyman ; a member of the municipal assembly ; a (city) councilman 《미》 ; a city councillor 《영》
— **의원 선거** a municipal election — **의장** the president of a city assembly

시인 是認 approval ; acknowledgment ; endorsement ; admission **—하다** approve 《of》 ; acknowledge ; endorse ; admit ¶ 시인할 수 있는 admissible // 잘못을 시인하다 admit one's mistake // 진술이 사실임을 시인하다 admit the statement to be true // 패배를 시인하다 admit oneself beaten // 그는 그것을 자기가 썼음을 시인한다 He admits having written it. // 나는 내가 잘못했다는 것을 시인한다 I admit that I was wrong.

†**시인 詩人** a poet ; a poetess (여류)

시일 a seal ¶ 시일을 붙이다 seal up ; put a seal 《upon》

시일 侍日 『천도교』 the day of divine service for the *Cheondo* religion ; Sunday

시일 時日 [때] time ; days ; hours ; [날짜] the date ; the date and hour ; the time ¶ 시일의 경과 the elapse of time // 시일과 장소 time and place // 시일이 없어서 for the lack of time // 시일이 걸리다 take〔require〕 time // 시일을 정하다 appoint the day ; fix the date ; choose the day // 약속 시일을 엄밀히 지키다 keep the date punctually // 회의 시일을 연기하다 postpone〔put off〕 the meeting 《until》

시자 侍者 an attendant ; (a member of) a retinue

시작 試作 trial manufacture (기계·상품) ; trial growing (재배) ; a study (예술품) ; an essay (문장·그림 따위) **—하다** manufacture for trial ; cultivate〔grow, raise〕 for trial ; compose〔write, sculpt〕 as an experiment
— **전시회** a study exhibition **—품** a trial product

시작 詩作 composing〔writing〕 (of) poems ; versification ; versemaking **—하다** write〔compose〕 poems ; versify ¶ 시작에 열중하다 devote oneself to the composition of poems

†**시작 始作** the beginning ; the commence-

ment ; the start ; the outset ; the opening ; the origin (기원) ―하다 begin ; commence ; start ; go into ; launch

참고 **begin** 가장 일반적인 말 **commence** 의식이나 재판 따위를 시작할 때 쓰이며 딱딱한 말 **start** begin과 비슷하여 어느 쪽을 사용해도 무방하지만 start는 첫 출발점을 강조하는 말이다

¶ 시작부터 from the first〔beginning〕// 시작부터 끝까지 from start to finish ; from beginning to end // 이야기를 처음부터 시작하다 begin the story at the beginning // 다시 시작하다 start all over again // 운동을 시작하다 start〔launch〕 a movement // 회의를 시작하다 open the meeting // 장사를 시작하다 start business ; go into business // 영어를 배우기 시작하다 take up English // 사업을 시작하다 embark on an enterprise // 일을 시작하다 set about one's work ; go to work // 새 생활을 시작하다 enter upon a new life // 겨울철이 시작됐다 The winter has set in. // 학교는 3월에 시작한다 School will begin in March. // 이 풍습은 조선 시대부터 시작된 것이다 The practice dates from the *Choseon* Dynasty period. // 영화가 시작됐다 The movie is (going) on. // 전쟁이 시작됐다 A war broke out. // 지금 새삼스럽게 시작된 것이 아니다 That is an old story. // 이 사건은 질투에서 시작됐다 This case originated in jealousy. // 일은 시작이 어려운 것이다 Beginnings are always hard. // 무엇부터 시작할까 What shall I begin with? // 아이들이 싸우기 시작했다 The children fell to quarreling. // 나는 이야기를 중단한 곳으로부터 다시 시작했다 I took up the story where I left off.

시작이 나쁘면 끝이 나쁘다 속담 An ill〔bad〕 beginning, an ill〔bad〕 ending. /A good〔hard〕 beginning makes a good ending.

총올치로 그물 시작이라 속담 By one and one the spindles are maid. /The goose is plucked feather by feather.

시작이 중요하다〔반이다〕 속담 A good beginning is half the battle. /Well begun is half done.

시장 hunger ; an empty stomach ―하다 be hungry ; feel empty ¶ 몹시 시장하다 be savagely〔ravenously〕 hungry ; have a wolf in one's stomach // 시장해 하다 complain of hunger // 시장기를 달래다 appease〔alleviate〕 one's hunger

시장이 감식 속담 Hunger makes hard beans sweet.

시장이 반찬이다 속담 Hunger is the best sauce. /Nothing comes amiss to a hungry man.

***시장 市場** a market ; a fair ; a mart ; a trading center ¶ 시장에 가다 go to market // 시장에 내놓다 put〔place〕《a thing》 on the market // 시장에 나와 있다 come to〔be on〕 the market // 시장을 개척하다 find a market for 《goods》 ; cultivate 〔open up〕 a market // 시장을 확장하다 extend a market // 사실 이것은 가장 최근에 시장에 나온 최신 제품입니다 As a matter of fact, this is a state-of-the-art product just out of on the market.

― 가격 a market price〔rate〕 ― 가치 market value ― 경제 the market economy ― 분석 a market analysis ― 생산 production for markets ―성 marketability ¶ 시장성이 있는 marketable // 시장성이 없는 유가 증권 unmarketable securities ― 점유율 a (market) share ― 조작 market operations 공설 ― a public market 국내 ― a home market 금융 ― the financial market 노동 ― the labo(u)r market 도매 ― a wholesale market 선물 ― a future(s) market 암― a black market 외국 ― a foreign market 자본 ― the capital market 주식 ― stock exchange〔market〕 중앙 ― a central market 증권 ― the stock〔exchange〕 market 지방 ― a local market 투기 ― a speculative market 투자 ― an investment market 국제 ― 쟁탈 the international scramble for markets

☞ ❰ p. 1319 ❱

***시장 市長** a mayor ; [직위] mayoralty ¶ 서울 시장 the Mayor of *Seoul* // 런던 시장 the Lord Mayor of London

― 관사 a mayor's mansion ― 부인 a mayoress ― 선거 a mayoral(ty) election ―직〔임기〕 mayoralty

시장기 hunger ¶ 시장기가 심하다 be terribly hungry // 시장기를 느끼다 feel hungry // 대포 한 잔으로 시장기를 덜다 allay hunger with a glass of wine

시장 조사 market research (시장 자체에 대한) ; marketing research (시장 활동 전반에 걸친)

― 전문가 a market researcher

시재 時在 ① [갖고 있는 것] supplies 〔cash〕 on hand ② [현재] the present (time)

―액(額) [금액의] (actual) amount in 〔on〕 hand ; [물품의] the goods in stock

시재 試才 selecting talented persons through examination ―하다 test (out) 《a person's》 talent ; examine and select as a talented person

시재 詩材 material for poetry ; a subject for a poem

***시적 詩的** poetic ; poetical ¶ 시적 미 poetic beauty // 시적 공상 poetic fancies // 시적 정서 poetic feeling // 시적 풍경 poetic scenery // 시적 정의 poetic justice // 시적 허용 poetic license

― 감흥 a poetic inspiration ― 생활 a poetic life

시적거리다 do reluctantly〔unwillingly〕 ¶ 시적시적 without enthusiasm ; with

시 장

marketing은 그 내용으로서 「상품 개발」(product development = merchandising), 「매입」(buying), 이를 위한 「시장 조사」(market research[study]), 「유통 정책」(distribution channel policy), 「판매,영업」(sales or selling), 「판매 촉진」(sales promotions), 「광고·선전」(commercial and advertising) 등의 모든 것을 포함하는 개념이다. 이 중에서 시장 조사(market research)는 극히 일부의 기능이다. 따라서 「광고 연구」(ad research)나 「유통 경로 조사」(distribution channel survey), 「소비자 분석」(consumer analysis)이나 「제품 연구」(product study) 등도 모두 마케팅 연구의 한 분야라고 할 수 있다. 그러나 이 광의의 marketing을 협의의 market study로 오인하거나 관용적으로 market study와 동일시하는 입장도 있기 때문에 주의해서 전후 관계, 문맥에 따라 정확하게 판단하는 것이 중요하다.

시장 조사는 크게 「인구 통계적 특성」(demographic characteristics)의 조사(★시장이나 소비자의 수, 장소, 인종, 지역별 등 주로 (정)량적(quantitative)인 조사를 하는 것)와 「심리 동태 측정」(psychographics) (★ 소비자의 취미, 기호, 성향, 정신 구조 등 주로 질적, 성질상으로 조사하는 것)의 시장 분류 측정방법을 쓴다. 이외에 시장의 큰 움직임을 조사하는「추세 분석·동향 분석」(trend analysis)도 있다.

little spirit ; listlessly ; reluctantly

시전지 詩箋紙 paper for writing poems and letters ; writing paper

시절 時節 time ; occasion ; season ¶ 시절에 맞지 않는 out of season ; unseasonable // 젊은 시절에 in one's youth ; while young // 학교 시절에 in one's school days // 이런 시절에 in these times ; at this time of year // 시절이 오면 when the (right) time comes // 시절이 오기를 기다리다 wait for a chance ; bide one's time // 그 시절에는 우리들은 텔레비전을 몰랐다 In those days, television was still unknown to us. // 그 시절에는 미니스커트가 유행했었지 Mini skirts were in style in those days〔back then, at that time, then〕. // 우리가 군에 있었던 시절 생각나니—그 시절이 좋았지 Do you remember the old days when we were in the army ? Those were the days ! // 그 시절 정말 고생스러웠다 Those were hard〔awful, terrible〕 times !

시점 時點 a point of〔in〕 time ¶ 이 시점에〔에서〕 at〔from〕 this point of time // 오늘의 시점에서 as of today

시점 視點 a visual point ; [관점] a point of view

시접 an inseam

시정 市井 [거리] the town ; the street ; [사람] a tradesman ; a merchant ; townsmen

—인(人) a man in〔on〕 the street

시정 是正 correction ; readjustment ; reform **—하다** correct ; rectify ; revise ; reform ¶ 잘못을 시정하다 correct a mistake ; correct errors // 사회의 악습을 시정하다 uproot〔stamp out〕 social evils

시정 施政 administration ; government **—하다** administer ; govern

— 방침 an administrative policy ; a ministerial program ¶ 시정 방침을 정하다 decide upon the administrative policy **— 연설** a speech on one's administrative policies〔program〕 ; an administrative policy speech

시정 市政 municipal〔city〕 government〔administration〕 ; civic affairs ¶ 시정의 civic ; municipal // 시정을 개혁하다 reform municipal government〔administration〕

— 개선 civic betterment〔improvement〕

— 조사회 a committee of inquiry into municipal administration

***시정 詩情** poetic feeling〔sentiment〕

***시제 時制** 〖문법〗 the tense ¶ 현재〔과거, 미래〕 시제 the present〔past, future〕 tense

시제 時祭 ancestor-memorial services performed in each season of the year

시제 市制 municipal system〔organization〕 ; municipality ¶ 시제를 실시하다 municipalize ; organize as a municipality

시제 詩題 a poetic theme ; a subject for a poem

시조 始祖 the founder ; the originator ; the father ; the progenitor ¶ 노동 운동의 시조 the father of the labor movement // 이씨 조선의 시조 the founder of the *choseon* Dynasty

—새 〖새〗 an archaeopteryx

시조 時調 a Korean verse〔ode〕 ; *shijo* ¶ 시조를 읊다 recite a poem // 시조를 짓다 compose a poem

시조하다 loaf〔dawdle〕 on one's job ; do a half-hearted job ; work slowly

시종 始終 the beginning and the end ; [부사적] from start to finish ; throughout ; all the way ¶ 시종 여일하게 consistently // 시종 일관하다 be the same

from beginning to end
*시종 侍從 a lord in waiting ; a chamberlain
— 무관 a military aide-de-camp to His〔Her〕 Majesty ; an aide to His〔Her〕 Majesty ; an officer in attendance on the King〔Queen〕; an equerry —장 the Grand Chamberlain
*시주 施主 [사람] an offerer ; a benefactor ; a donator ; [행위] offering ; oblation —하다 offer ; donate ; make an offering 《to a temple》
시주 詩酒 verses and wine
시준 視準 collimation —하다 collimate
—기 a mercury collimator
‡시중 attendance ; waiting on ; care ; service —하다 attend ; wait on ; look after ; take care of ; serve ¶ 시중들고 있다 be in attendance 《on a person》// 남편의 시중을 들다 take care of one's husband // 부모를 시중하다 take care of one's parents // 어린애의 시중을 들다 look after a child ; take care of children // 환자를 시중하다 attend〔care for〕a patient // 빨래하는 어머니를 시중들다 help mother with washing
시중 市中 (in) the city ; (in) the street
— 금리 the open market (interest) rate ; the commercial (interest) rate — 시세 the open market price — 은행 a commercial〔city〕bank
시즌 a season ¶ 야구〔수영, 사냥〕 시즌 the baseball〔bathing, hunting〕 season
시즙 屍汁 water from a corpse
시지에스 단위 —單位 the C. G. S.〔c. g. s., cgs〕 units
시지근하다 (be) somewhat sour ; sourish
시지르다 doze ; drowse ⇨ 졸다
시집 媤— one's husband's home〔family〕 ¶ 시집 보내다 marry off 《one's daughter》
시집도 아니 가서 기저귀감 장만한다 [속담] Don't build the sty before the litter comes. /Boil not pap before the child is born.
시집 詩集 a collection of poems ; an anthology
시집가다 媤— marry ; get〔be〕 married to ; take a husband ¶ 그 여자는 시집갈 나이가 지났다 She is past marriageable age. // 이름 없는 여자도 명문의 집에 시집갈 수 있다 A woman of no birth may marry into the purple.
시집 보내다 媤— give 《one's daughter》 (away) in marriage ; marry 《one's daughter》 off ; marry one's daughter 《to》; give 《a man》 the hand of 《one's daughter》
시집살이 married life〔housekeeping〕 in the home of the husband's parents ¶ 시집살이를 잘하다 keep house well // 시집살이에 고생하다 lead a hard married life
시차 時差 a time difference ; the equation of time ¶ 서울과 런던은 9시간의 시차가 있다 There is a nine hour's difference between *Seoul* and London time.
—계 an equation timepiece —제 staggered work-hour system ¶ 시차제 출근 differentiation of office attendance hours ; staggered office〔commuting〕 hours
시차 視差 〖천문〗 parallax
‡시찰 視察 inspection ; observation —하다 inspect ; observe ; make an inspection 《of》; visit ¶ 여러 학교를 시찰하다 inspect various schools // 현장을 시찰하다 take a view of the scene // 미국에 상업 시찰을 가다 go to America to observe commercial affairs
—관 an inspector —단 an inspection party ; a group of inspectors ; an observation group〔party〕 — 여행 an inspection〔observation〕 tour ; a tour of inspection ¶ 시찰 여행을 하다 make an observation trip ; make a tour of inspection —원 an observer ; an inspector
시창 the poop deck 《of a ship》
시찾다 be on the verge of death ; be at death's door
시채 市債 a municipal bond〔loan, obligation〕 ¶ 시채를 발행하다 issue a municipal loan
시책 施策 a policy ; a measure —하다 enforce〔execute〕 a policy
시척지근하다 (be) sourish
시청 市廳 the city hall ; the municipal building
시청 視聽 seeing and hearing ¶ 시청을 집중시키다 concentrate one's attention 《on》
텔레비전 —료 television subscription fee
시청 試聽 an audition —하다 audition
—실 an audition room
시청각 視聽覺 (the senses of) sight and hearing ; the visual and auditory senses
— 교실 an audiovisual classroom ; a language laboratory — 교육 audiovisual education — 교재 audiovisual materials 〔aids〕
시청률 視聽率 a program〔an audience〕 rating ; a (popularity) rating
— 조사 audience measurement〔research〕 ; an audience rating survey
시청자 視聽者 a (TV) viewer ; a televiewer ; [총칭] the TV audience
— 여론 조사 the audience response rating — 참가 프로 a participation show
시체 詩體 a form〔style〕 of verse ; a verse form〔style〕
*시체 屍體 a corpse ; a dead body ; a carcass (동물의) ¶ 시체를 인수하다 claim the body // 시체를 발견하다 find〔recover〕 a body // 시체로 발견되다 be found dead // 시체를 인도하다 hand 《a person's》 body over 《to》
— 검사 an inquest — 검사관 a coroner

— 안치소 a morgue ; a mortuary ; a dead house — 유기 criminal disposal of a dead body — 해부 dissection of a dead body ; necrotomy ; an autopsy
시체 時體 the customs of the times ; the fashion of the day
시초 始初 the beginning ; the start ; the origin ; the outset ¶ 시초의 first ; initial ; original // 시초에 at the beginning〔start〕// 시초부터 from the first〔beginning〕// 시초부터 끝까지 from start to finish ; from beginning to end // 시초부터 이야기하다 begin the story from the beginning // 시초부터 다시 시작하다 start all over again // 일은 언제나 시초가 어려운 것이다 Beginnings are always hard.
시초 柴草 dry grass used for fuel
시초 詩抄 a selection of poems ; selected poems — 하다 select poems
시추 試錐 drilling ; boring
—기(機) a drill ; a drilling machine —선 an oil prospecting rig 해저 석유 — offshore oil(-well) drilling
시축 詩軸 a verse scroll ; a scroll of poems
시취 屍臭 the smell of a dead body ; a putrid smell
시취 詩趣 poetical interest〔sentiment, feeling〕¶ 시취가 풍부하다 be full of poetical interest
시치근하다 ⇨ 시척지근하다
시치다 baste ; tack ¶ 시침질 basting ; tacking
시치름하다 ⇨ 새치름하다, 새침하다
시치미[1] feigned innocence〔ignorance〕; feigned indifference ; dissimulation ¶ 시치미를 떼고 with an air of innocence ; with a straight face // 시치미를 떼고 물어보다 ask《a person》pretending ignorance // 시치미떼도 소용이 없다 It's no use acting dumb.
시치미떼다 관용 pretend not to know ; play the innocent ; put on a poker face ; feign indifference
시치미[2] [매의] an identification tag attached to a falcon's tail ; a falcon tag
시칠리아 Sicily ; Sicilia《이》
시침 ① ⇨ 시침질 ② ⇨ 시치미
시침 時針 the hour hand《of a watch》
시침질 tacking ; basting
시카고 Chicago
시커멓다 (be) jet-black ; deep-black ; be as black as coal
시큰거리다 feel a dull pain《in one's joints》; tingle ; twinge
시큰둥하다 (be) impudent ; fresh ; impertinent ; pert ; cheeky
시큰하다 ⇨ 새큰하다
시클라멘 〖식물〗 a cyclamen
⁑시큼하다 (be) sourish
†시키다 [강제] make《a person do》; cause《a person to do》; [허가] allow《a person to do》; [방임] let《a person do》; leave《a person to do》; [의뢰] have《a person do》; get《a person to do》; order ¶ 식사를 시키다 order dinner // 일을 시키다 make《a person》work ; put《a person》to work // 사직시키다 force《a person》to resign ; dismiss《a person》// 구두를 수선시키다 have one's shoes mended // 진화시키다 get the fire under control // 임신 시키다 get a woman with child // 극장 구경을 시키다 treat《a person》to the theater // 서울 구경 시키다 show《a person》around *Seoul* // 시키는 대로 하다 do as one is told // 그것은 일반에게 구경시키지 않는다 They do not let the public see it. // 그에게 시키겠다 I will make him do it. // 그에게 자백시켜야 한다 He must be made to confess.
시타이크아이젠《Steigeisen《도》》〖등산〗 climbing irons ; crampons
시탄 柴炭 firewood and charcoal ; fuel
—상 a fuel〔wood-and-coal〕dealer
시탕하다 侍湯— administer medicine to one's sick parent ; attend〔wait on, serve〕one's sick parent
시태 an ox load〔pack〕
시태 時態 the current situation ; the times ; a sign of the times
시토 SEATO《the Southeast Asia Treaty Organization》
시퉁머리터지다 (be) fresh ; sassy ; smart-alecky ; cheeky
시퉁스럽다 (be) impertinent ; impudent ; pert
†시트 [자리] a seat ; [종이의] a sheet ; [침대의] a (bed) sheet ¶ 침대의 시트를 갈다 change the sheets on one's bed
— 노킹 〖야구〗 seat knocking
시트론 citron
—수(水) citron water
시틋하다 [싫증나다] be fed up with ; be sick of ; be tired of ; [시들하다] (be) unsatisfactory ; reluctant
시파 柴杷 〖농업〗 a small rake for covering up seeds after planting them
시판 市販 marketing ; sale at a market
—하다 market ; put〔place〕on the market ; place on sale ; sell at a market ¶ 시판되다 come into the market
— 가능성 marketability — 가능품 marketable goods — 기관 a marketing organization — 방법〔과정〕 marketing methods〔process〕 —본(本)〔판(版)〕 a trade book〔edition〕 —품 an article〔goods〕 on the market 공동 — joint marketing
시퍼렇다 (be) deep blue ; deadly pale (창백하다) ; [권세가] powerful ; influential
시편 詩篇 〖성경〗 the Book of Psalms
시평 時評 comments on current events〔topics〕
—가 a commentator —란 editorial columns 문예 — comments on current literature
시폐 時弊 the evils of the times ; existing

evils〔abuses〕 ¶ 시폐를 고치다 remedy〔correct〕 the evils of the times // 시폐를 통탄하다 be indignant with the corruptness of the times
시풍 詩風 a style of poetry ; a poetical style
시프레히코르 Sprechchor 《그》; choral speaking
시필 試筆 the first writing of the year ── 하다 do the first writing of the year
신년 ─ the New Year's writing
시하 侍下 a person with both parents living ; being under one's parental roof
─인(人) (to...) Esquire
시하 時下 at present ; at this time (of the year) ; now ¶ 시하 엄동지절에 in this season of cold winter
-시하다 視─ regard as ; consider 《to be》 ¶ 위험시하다 regard 《a thing》 as dangerous
시학 詩學 poetics ; poetry ; prosody
시한 時限 a time limit ; limit of time ; lock-up (문 닫는 시간) ; curfew (통금 시간)
─ 폭탄 a time bomb
시할머니 one's husband's grandmother
시할아버지 one's husband's grandfather
†시합 試合 a game ; a match ; a contest ; a bout (권투 따위) ; a fight ; a tournament ; a meet ── 하다 play 《against》 ; have a game〔match, bout〕 《with》 ; meet ¶ 시합 개시 the start of ; a match ; a kick-off (축구) // 시합에 나가다 take part in a game // 시합에 이기다〔지다〕 win〔lose〕 a game // 시합을 신청하다 challenge 《a person》 to a game〔bout〕 // 농구 시합을 하다 have a basketball game 《with》
─장 a court (정구) ; a (ball) park (야구) ; a diamond (야구) ; a ring (권투) ; a field (축구) 단식〔복식, 혼합〕 ─ a singles〔doubles, mixed〕 match
시해 弑害 ⇨ 시살(弑殺)
*시행 施行 operation ; enforcement ; carrying out ── 하다 put 《law》 in operation 〔force, effect〕 ; carry into effect ; enforce ¶ 시행되다 take effect ; go into effect ; become effective〔operative〕 // 시행되고 있다 be in force〔operation〕
─ 규칙 enforcement regulations ; regulations relative to the application of a law ─ 기간 a period of effectiveness ─ 기일 a date of enforcement ─령 an Enforcement Ordinance ─ 세칙 detailed enforcement regulations ; detailed regulations for the application of a law ─지 an enforcement area
시행 착오 試行錯誤 〖심리〗 trial and error
─법 the rule〔method〕 of trial and error
시향 時享 ① 〔가묘에서의〕 the seasonal ancestor-memorial rites ② 〔산소에서의〕 a rite performed in October before the grave of distant ancestors

시허옇다 (be) pure white ; snow-white
†시험 試驗 ① an examination ; a test ; an exam 《속》 ── 하다 examine 《a person》; test ¶ 시험을 치르다 take〔sit for〕 an examination ; undergo an examination ; go up for an examination // 시험을 시행하다 hold〔give〕 an examination ; examine // 시험 준비를 하다 prepare〔read, study〕 for an examination // 시험 감독하다 preside over an examination // 시험에 합격〔낙제〕하다 pass〔fail in〕 an examination // 영어 시험을 보다 have an examination in English ; examine 《a class》 in English // 시험 공부를 하다 cram for an examination // 그 문제가 시험에 나왔다 The subject is asked in an examination.
② 〔실험〕 an experiment ; a test ; a trial ── 하다 test ; try ; put to the test ; experiment 《on》 ¶ 시험적 experimental ; tentative // 시험적으로 on trial ; tentatively ; experimentally // 시험을 해보다 put 《a thing》 to the test // 시험적으로 써보다 give 《a person》 a trial ; take 《a person》 on trial // 슬롯 머신으로 내 운을 한번 시험해 봐야겠다 I think I'll try my luck at the slot machine.
─ 감독 proctoring of an examination ; invigilation 《영》 ; 〔사람〕 a proctor ; an invigilator 《영》 ─ 공부 preparation 〔cramming〕 for an examination ─ 과목 the subjects for examination ; an examination subject ─관(官) an examiner ─관(管) a test tube ─기(器) a tester ; a testing machine ─ 기간 a probation ; a term of trial ─ 기일 the date of an examination ─ 답안지 an examination 〔exam〕 paper ; a test paper 《미》 ─대 a test board〔desk〕 ; a testing stand ; 〖전화〗 a wire chief desk ─로(爐) 〔화학 실험용〕 a test kiln〔furnace〕 ; 〔원자로〕 a testing reactor ─료 an examination fee ─ 문제 a question (for examination) ; an examination question (한 문제) ─ 발사 a test fire ; test firing ─ 방법 the method of examination ─ 비행 a test〔a trial, an experimental〕 flight ; a flying test ─ 비행사 a test pilot ─ 생산 pilot production ─ 성적 통지 a report of one's score on a test ─소 an experimental station ─실 a laboratory ─ 위원 an examiner ; an examination board 《총칭》 ─장 an examination room〔hall〕 ─ 제도 an examination system ─ 준비 preparation for an examination ─ 지옥 an ordeal of (entrance) examinations ─ 채용 기간 a probationary period ─필 〔게시〕 Tried 경쟁 ─ a competitive〔screening〕 examination 구두 ─ an oral examination 국가 ─ a state examination 본〔예비〕 ─ a final 〔preliminary〕 examination 인물 ─ a character test ; a personal interview 입사 ─ a test〔an examination〕 for service in a business company ; an entrance〔employ-

ment) examination 입학 — an entrance examination 자격〔검정〕 — a qualifying examination 중간 — a mid-term examination 필기 — a written ex-amination 학기말 — a term examination

시험지 試驗紙 ① test〔examination〕 paper ② 〚화학〛 litmus paper

시현 示現 revelation (by a divinity) ; manifestation ——하다 reveal ; manifest ; show

시형 詩形 a poetic form ; a meter —학 prosody

시호 諡號 a posthumous epithet〔title, name〕 ¶ 시호를 추증하다 grant 《a person》 a posthumous epithet

시호 試毫 ⇨ 시필

시호 時好 the current fashion ; the vogue 〔mode〕

시호 詩號 a poet's pen name

시홍 視紅 〚생리〛 visual purple

시화 視話 [벙어리의] lip language —법 visible speech

시화 詩化 poetization ——하다 poetize 〔reading〕

시화 詩話 a talk on poetry

시화 詩畫 [시와 그림] a poem and a picture ; [그림을 곁들인 시] an illustrated〔a pictorial〕 poem —전 an exhibition of illustrated poems 《by》

†시황 市況 the market ; market conditions ¶ 활발한 시황 a brisk market // 시황이 한산하다 The market is quiet. — 보고 a market report 주식 — the stock market ; stock exchange quotations

시회 詩會 a poetry club〔party〕

시효 時效 〚법〛 prescription ¶ 형의 소멸 시효 extinctive prescription of punishment〔prosecution〕 // 시효에 걸리다 be barred by prescription ; prescribe — 기간 the period of prescription — 정지 suspension of prescription — 중단 interruption of prescription 소멸〔취득〕 — negative〔positive〕 prescription ; extinctive〔acquisitive〕 prescription

시후 時候 [계절] season ; [기후] climate ; weather ¶ 불순한 시후 unseasonable weather — 문안 compliments of the season

시흥 詩興 poetic inspiration ¶ 시흥이 일다 be inspired to compose a poem // 그 경치를 보고 시흥이 솟았다 The poet in me moved at the view.

†식 式 ① [양식] form ; [형] style ; type ; model ; fashion ; plan ; [방법] a method ; a system ¶ 독일식 교수법 a German method of teaching // 고딕식 건물 an architecture of Gothic style // 한국식 호텔 a Korean-style hotel // 서양식으로 in European〔Western〕 style ; on the European plan // 저런 식으로 in that way〔manner〕 // 서양식으로 경영하다 operate on European〔Western〕 lines ② [의식] a ceremony ; exercises ; rites ; rituals ¶ 식을 올리다 hold a ceremony ; have a ceremony performed ③ [수학·화학의] an (algebraic) expression ; a (chemical) formula ¶ 식으로 표시하다 formularize 《a theory》 // H_2O는 물의 화학식이다 H_2O is the formula for water. 결혼— a wedding (ceremony) 구조— a structural formula

식 蝕 〚천문〛 an eclipse ; occultation

식각 蝕刻 〚인쇄〛 etching — 요판(凹版) 〚조판〛 aquatint — 요판화(畫) an aquatint

식간 食間 ¶ 식간에 between meals // 식간에 약을 먹다 take medicine between meals

식객 食客 a dependent ; a hanger-on ; a parasite ¶ 식객 노릇을 하다 live on 《a person》 ; eat 《a person's》 salt

식견 識見 knowledge ; insight ; discernment ; vision ; knowledge and judgment ¶ 식견 있는 사람 a man of broad view and understanding

식경 食頃 [부사적] for the period of having a single meal ; for a while

식곤증 食困症 languor (after a meal) ; drowsiness ; the stupor induced by a full stomach

식구 食口 members of a family ; a family ; mouths to feed ¶ 식구가 많다〔적다〕 have a large〔small〕 family to support ; have many〔few〕 mouths to feed // 식구가 늘다 have new mouths to feed // 식구가 줄다 have less mouths to feed // 다섯 식구 a family of five // 한 식구처럼 대하다 treat 《a person》 just like〔as〕 a member of the family

식권 食券 a meal〔food〕-ticket

식균 작용 食菌作用 phagocytosis

식기 食器 tableware ; a dinner set ; [주발] a bowl —장 a pantry ; a cupboard (찬장)

식나무 〚식물〛 a Japanese aucuba

식다 get cold ; cool (off) ; [열의가] cool down ; get cool ; abate ; subside ; flag ; be chilled ¶ 저녁을 식기 전에 먹다 eat before dinner gets cold // 식지 않게 하다 keep 《food》 from getting cold // 열의가 식다 lose interest 《in》 // 달기 쉽고 식기 쉽다 be of a changeable mind ; be fickle 〔capricious〕 // 그녀에 대한 애정이 식다 one's love for her cools down // 그의 영어에 대한 열도 곧 식어 버렸다 His enthusiasm for English died down soon.

*식단 食單 a menu ; a bill of fare

‡식당 食堂 a dining room〔hall〕 ; a restaurant ; a cafeteria (간이 식당) ; a mess hall (군대의) —차 a dining car 《미》 ; a dining coach 《영》 ; a restaurant car 《영》 ; a diner ; a buffet car 《영》 ☞ 《 p. 1324 》

식 당

영국이나 미국에서는 주 1회 내지 2회는 밖에서 식사하는 것이 습관화되어 있다. 우리와 달리 영·미나 유럽에서의 외식은 식당 예약을 미리 해두거나 웨이터가 안내하기 전에 임의로 자리에 앉지 않는다거나 정장차림만 허용되는 등 약간의 형식이나 절차를 익혀 두지 않으면 실수를 하게 되거나 실례가 되는 경우가 종종 있다.

1 주문 (order)

① 영·미에서는 일반적으로 식당 입구에서 손님(guest)의 코트나 주요 소지품 등을 맡겨두는 보관소(cloakroom)가 있다. 보관소에 코트나 소지품을 맡기는 것을 check라고 한다. 비교적 규모가 큰 식당에서는 손님이 올 경우 즉시 웨이터장(headwaiter)이 나타나 손님의 수에 따라 앉을 자리(seat)를 안내한다.

② headwaiter의 안내로 자리에 앉게 되면 웨이터가 메뉴(menu)를 가지고 하나하나 주문을 받게 된다 (return to the table to take one's order). (★ 이때 보관소에 맡기지 않은 핸드백이나 지갑 등을 빈 좌석이나 테이블 위에 놓아서는 안된다.) 주문할 때는 메뉴 중에서 그 식당이 가장 잘하는 요리(specialty)를 청하여도 좋고 웨이터에게 "What would[do] you recommend (today)?" 라고 추천을 받아도 좋다. 주문을 할 때는 계산을 각자 부담할 때 (go Dutch; pay separately; split the bill) 또는 전표를 각각 요구할 때(We want separate checks.) 등으로 의사 표시를 미리 하여야 한다.

2 메뉴 (menu) 와 식사 코스 (dinner course)

① 메뉴는 크게 두 가지로 나누어 정식(table d'hôte[tɑ́:bldóut])과 취향대로 즐길 수 있는 요리(a la carte[æ̀ləkɑ́rt] dish)가 있다.

정식은 요리의 순서가 있다. 우선 맨 처음 입맛을 돋우기 위해 와인(wine)이나 맥주 등과 함께 오르되브르(hors d'oeuvre)가 나오게 된다. 카나페(canapé)도 같은 일종이다.

② 그 다음에는 수프(soup)가 나온다. 수프는 두 종류가 있는데 콩소메(consommé =clear soup)와 포타지(potage =thick [cream] soup)로 나뉘며 주문할 때 선택한다.

③ 다음에는 빵(bread)이 나온다. 빵은 white bread, brown bread, roll이 있는데 마찬가지로 웨이터에게 선택 주문한다. 버터는 보통 식탁 위에 놓여있으며 멀리 있으면 "Will you pass (me) the butter, please?"라고 옆사람에게 부탁한다.

④ 다음에는 본격적인 요리(main dish, main course)가 나오게 되는데 요리 용어로 entrée(=entry)라고 한다. 보통 생선이나 고기 요리가 나오게 된다. 고기 요리(steak)를 주문할 때는 완전히 익힌 것(well-done)인지, 살짝 익힌 것(medium)인지, 겉만 익힌 것(rare)인지 의사 표시를 해야 한다. 지방질을 뺀 고기는 fillet라고 한다.

⑤ 마지막으로 디저트(desert)가 있다. 디저트로는 케이크(cake)나, 아이스크림(ice cream) 등이 나온다. ice cream은 바닐라(vanilla), 초콜릿(chocolate) 등의 맛과 향이 서로 다른 것들이 많다. 커피는 식사중에 마실지(with one's[the] meal), 식사 후에 마실지(after the meal) 의사 표시를 하여야 한다.

3 지불 (payment)

영국이나 미국에서는 대금 지불이 보통 식탁에서 이루어진다. 계산서를 요구할 때는 "May we have the check[bill], please?" 라고 한다. 팁은 보통 계산 금액의 15%로 한다.

식대 食代 [식당의] the charge for food ; [하숙의] (the charge for) board ; [가정의] table expenses ⇨ 식비(食費)

식도 食刀 a kitchen knife

식도 食道 〖해부〗 the gullet ; the esophagus
—경(鏡) an esophagoscope **—암** cancer of the esophagus **—염** 〖의학〗 esophagitis **— 절개** esophagotomy **— 협착** stricture of esophagus ; esophagostenosis

식도락 食道樂 epicurism ; gourmandism
—가 an epicure ; a gourmet ; a gourmand ; a free liver ¶ 저 사람은 식도락가이다 He is an epicure. /He is addicted to the pleasures of the table.

식되 a kitchen measure ; a measuring cup

식량 食量 capacity for eating

†**식량 食糧** food ; provisions ; foodstuffs ¶ 1일분의 식량 a day's provisions〔ration〕// 식량의 결핍 a shortage of food // 식량을 공급하다 supply with provisions // 식량이 떨어지다 run out of food
— 관리 food control **—난** the difficulty of obtaining food **— 문제** the food problem **— 부족** a shortage of provisions ; a food shortage **— 사정** the food situation ¶ 식량 사정이 악화되었다〔좋아졌다〕 The food situation has taken an unfavorable〔a

favorable〕 turn. — 위기 a food crisis — 정책 the food policy 비상 — emergency rations 예비 — a reserve of provisions

*식료 食料 food ; provisions ; ration ; foodstuffs ¶ 좋은 식료가 되다 be edible ; be good to eat ; be fit for food // 3일분의 식료를 가지고 있다 be provisioned for three days

—품 articles for food ; provisions ; food stuff ; groceries —품상 a grocer 《미》 ; a provisions dealer ; a groceryman —품점 a grocery (store) ; a provisions shop ; a food store

식리 殖利 bringing in interest〔profit〕 —하다 bring〔bear〕 interest ; bring in return ; contribute profit ; earn (profits)

식림 植林 afforestation ; tree planting —하다 afforest 《a mountain》 ; plant trees ; reforest 《land》 with trees

— 계획 a reforestation plan — 사업 a reforestation project —지 a plantation

식모 食母 a kitchenmaid ; a cook ; a maidservant ; a (house) maid ; a domestic (help) ¶ 식모살이하다 be in domestic service // 식모를 두다 keep a kitchenmaid

식목 植木 planting trees ; forestation ; tree planting —하다 plant trees ; transplant trees

— 운동 a tree-planting campaign〔drive〕 —일 Arbor Day 《미》

식물 食物 food ; provisions ; foodstuff ¶ 영양분 있는 식물 nourishing food // 쌀을 식물로 하다 live on rice

†식물 植物 a plant ; vegetation 《총칭》 ; plant〔vegetable〕 life 《총칭》 ¶ 식물의 vegetable ; plant ; botanical // 식물의 표본 a botanical specimen // 식물의 분포 the geographical distribution of plants // 식물성 기름 vegetable oils // 이 구내에는 600종의 식물이 있다 The ground contains 600 different kinds of plants.

—계 the vegetable kingdom — 관찰〔도감〕 핸드북 a field guide to plants —구계(區界) flora — 군락(群落) a plant community — 기재학(記載學) descriptive botany —대(帶) a floral zone — 병리학 vegetable〔plant〕 pathology — 분류학 systematic botany — 분포 a geographical distribution of plants — 사회학 plant sociology — 생리학 vegetable〔plant〕 physiology — 생태학〔조직학〕 plant ecology〔histology〕 ; ecological〔structural〕 botany —성 vegetability ; vegetable property —성 버터 vegetable butter — 세포〔섬유〕 a vegetable cell〔fiber〕 — 세포학 plant cytology — 염기 a plant〔vegetable〕 base —원 a botanical garden — 지(誌) a flora ; a herbal — 지리학 geographical botany ; plant geography —질 vegetable matter — 채집 《go》 plant collecting — 표본 a botanical specimen — 플랑크톤 phytoplankton —학 botany — 학자 a botanist — 해부학 vegetable〔plant〕 anatomy ; phytotomy — 형태학 morphological botany — 호르몬 plant hormone ; phyto-hormone — 화학 plant chemistry ; phytochemistry 고산〔열대〕 — alpine〔tropical〕 plants 기생 — a parasitic plant ; a phyto-parasite 다년생 — a perennial plant 양성 — a sun plant 음생〔음지〕 — a shade plant 현화〔은화〕 — a flowering〔flowerless〕 plant ; a phanerogam〔cryptogam〕 한국 — 도감 a pictorial〔an illustrated〕 book of the Korean flora

식물 인간 植物人間 a human vegetable

*식민 植民 colonization ; settlement ; [사람] a colonist ; a settler —하다 colonize ; settle ; plant a colony ¶ 미국에 식민하다 colonize America ; plant settlers in America

— 사업 colonization — 시대 the colonial period — 업무 colonial affairs — 정책 a colonial policy —주의 colonialism —지 a colony ; a settlement —지 무역 a colonial trade —지주의자 a colonialist —지풍(地風) a colonialism —지화(地化) colonialization 구(舊)—지 an ex-colony 반(反)—지 운동 an anti-colonial movement 반—지주의 anticolonialism 반—지주의자 an anticolonialist 비(非)—지화(地化) decolonialization

식반 食盤 a small dining table

*식별 識別 discernment ; identification ; discrimination —하다 distinguish 《between, from》 ; discriminate ; discern ; tell 《things》 apart ¶ 식별할 수 있는 distinguishable // 차이점을 식별하다 discern difference 《between》 // 선악을 식별하다 discern good from evil // 매와 까마귀를 식별하다 distinguish a hawk from a crow // A와 B를 식별하다 distinguish〔discriminate〕 A from B ; distinguish〔discern〕 between A and B

—력 power of discernment ; discrimination —역 『심리·생리』 the threshold of〔for〕 discrimination —종(種) 『식물』 a differential species 색(色)— color vision 개인 —법 the method of identification 야외(野外) —점(點) [새의] a field mark

식보 食補 —하다 invigorate〔build up〕 one's body through diet ; diet on nourishment

식복 食福 ¶ 식복이 있다 be blessed with things to eat

식부 植付 planting —하다 plant 《a section with corn》 ; do the planting

— 면적 the acreage〔area〕 under crop ; the planted area〔acreage〕 — 토지 a planted land

식분 食分 『천문』 a phase of an eclipse

식비 食費 food expenses〔cost〕 ; the charge for board (하숙의) ¶ 식비를 포함하다 include board // 매월 80,000원의 식비를 내다 pay 80,000 *won* for one's board every month // 방세와 식비를 합해서 한달에 얼마입니까 What do you charge a month for lodging and food ?

식빵 食— bread ¶ 식빵 한 덩어리 a loaf of bread

식사 式辭 a formal address ; a congratulatory address (축사)

†**식사 食事** a meal ; fare ; dinner ; diet ; cuisine (호텔의) ; board (하숙의) **—하다** take a meal ; dine ; eat ¶ 간단한 식사 a simple repast // 식사 준비를 하다 prepare a meal ; set the table (식탁을) // 식사를 같이하다 dine〔take dinner〕 with 《a person》 ; dine together // 하루에 세 번 식사하다 take three meals a day // 식사중이다 be at table〔dinner〕 // 급히 식사하다 make a hasty meal ; snatch a hurried meal // 밖에서 식사하다 dine〔eat〕 out // 식사하면서 이야기하다 talk at table // 체격에 비해서 식사량이 적구나 You have a small appetite for someone your size.
— 시간 mealtime ; dinnertime **— 예법** table manners

식사

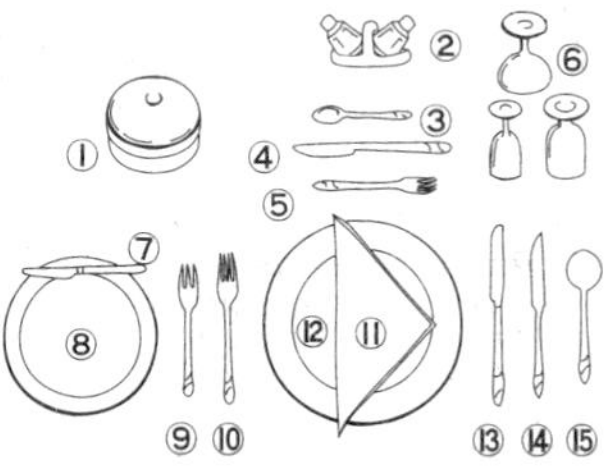

① 버터 접시 butter container〔dish〕
② 양념병 cruet
③ 티스푼 teaspoon
④ 과도 fruit knife
⑤ 과일 포크 fruit fork
⑥ 글라스 glasses
⑦ 버터 나이프 butter knife
⑧ 빵 접시 bread plate
⑨ 생선용 포크 fish fork
⑩ 고기용 포크 fork
⑪ 냅킨 napkin
⑫ 접시 plate
⑬ 나이프 knife
⑭ 생선용 나이프 fish knife
⑮ 수프스푼 soupspoon

식산 殖産 increase of production ; industry ; production **—하다** increase production ; foster (national) industry
— 공업 the productive〔production〕 industry

식상 食傷 food poisoning (중독) ; indigestion (소화 불량) ; surfeit (물림) ; disagreement of food **—하다** be surfeited ; be poisoned by food ¶ 생선먹은 것이 식상했다 The fish I ate upset〔disagreed with〕 me.

식생활 食生活 dietary life ; eating habits ¶ 식생활을 보다 즐겁게 하다 increase the pleasure of the table // 식생활조차 어렵다 find it hard to earn one's daily bread ; be badly pressed for living

식성 食性 taste ; preference ; palate ¶ 식성에 맞는 음식 agreeable〔favorite〕 food // 식성에 맞다 suit〔please〕 one's taste〔palate〕 // 식성이 까다롭다 be fastidious about food

식세포 食細胞 〖동물〗 a phagocyte

식솔 食率 ⇨ 식구

식수 植樹 planting trees ; tree planting **—하다** plant trees

식수 食水 drinking water ; potable water

식순 式順 the order〔program〕 of a ceremony

식식, 씩씩 ¶ 식식거리다 breathe heavily ; gasp ; pant // 그는 식식거리며 뛰어왔다 He came running out of breath.

식언 食言 retracting〔breaking〕 one's promise ; eating one's words **—하다** eat one's words ; retract〔break〕 one's words

식염 食鹽 table〔common, culinary〕 salt
— 그릇 a saltcellar **—수** a solution of salt ; a saline solution **— 주사** salt injection

*****식욕 食慾** appetite ; desire to eat ¶ 식욕이 없다 have no appetite // 식욕이 없어지다 lose one's appetite // 식욕이 왕성하다 have a hearty〔wolfish, keen〕 appetite // 식욕을 채우다 satisfy one's appetite // 식욕을 자극하다 stimulate〔sharpen, whet〕 one's appetite // 식욕이 난다 His appetite improves. // 식욕이 감퇴한다 My appetite decreases. // 이것은 당신 식욕을 없앨 겁니다 This will spoil your appetite. // 그다지 식욕이 없는 것 같구나 You don't seem to have much of an appetite.
— 감퇴 a decrease〔falling-off〕 of appetite ; a poor〔dull, feeble〕 appetite ; loss of appetite **— 부진** lack〔loss〕 of appetite ; inappetence ; anorexia **— 증진** improvement〔promotion〕 of appetite

식용 食用 edibility ; table use ¶ 식용의 edible ; eatable // 식용에 적합하다 be edible ; be good〔suitable〕 to eat
— 개구리 an edible frog ; a bullfrog **—근(根)** edible roots **— 기름** edible oil〔fat〕 **— 버섯** edible mushrooms **— 색소** food coloring **— 식물** esculent plants ; plants for food **—어** an edible fish ; a food fish **— 유지(油脂)** edible oil and fat **—품** articles of food ; eatables ; food

식육 食肉 meat ; meat-eating **—하다** eat meat ; be carnivorous
— 가공업자 a meat processor **— 동물〔조(鳥)〕** a predatory〔carnivorous〕 ani-

mal〔bird〕; a predator ; a carnivore ―류 the carnivorous〔meat-eating〕 animal ; carnivores ; predators ; Carnivora (학명) ―우 beef cattle ― 중독 meat poisoning ; kreotoxism ; creotoxism

식은땀 a cold sweat ¶ 식은땀을 흘리다 be in a cold sweat ; sweat with fear (무서워서) // 이마에 구슬 같은 식은땀이 솟아났다 A cold perspiration stood in beads upon his forehead.

식은죽 cold gruel〔porridge〕 ¶ 그런 것은 식은죽 먹기다 That's nothing. /Nothing is easier. /That's (as) easy as pie. 《미·속》 /I could do it before breakfast. 《영·속》 // 시간이 이렇게 많은데 그건 식은 죽 먹기야 With this much time, it's a cinch.

식은죽 먹기 (속담) an easy task〔job〕; a piece of cake 《구》 //

식음 食飮 eating and drinking

식음을 전폐하다 (관용) give up eating and drinking ; fast

‡식이 食餌 food ; a diet

― 요법 a dietary treatment

*식인 食人 cannibalism ¶ 식인의 maneating ; cannibal ; cannibalistic

―귀 a cannibal demon ―종 a cannibal race ; cannibals ; man-eaters

식일 式日 ① a ceremonial day ② [날마다] every day

식자 植字 〚인쇄〛 typesetting ; typography ―하다 set (in) type ; compose ¶ 식자의 a typographical error

―공 typesetter ; typo 《*pl.* -s》; a compositor ―기(機) a typesetting〔composing〕 machine ; a typesetter ; a linotype ―대 a composing stand〔frame〕 ―오류 a typographical〔printer's〕 error ; a misprint ―판 a galley 사진 ― photo-letter composition ; photographic lettering 사진 ―기 a photocomposer 자동 ―기 a composing machine

식자 識者 a learned man ; intelligent 〔informed〕 people ; men of intelligence ; a person with good sense

― 우환 Ignorance is bliss. /A little learning is a dangerous thing.

식장 式場 the hall〔place〕 of ceremony ; the place where a ceremony is held

식적 食積 indigestion ; dyspepsia

‡식전 食前 ¶ 식전에 before a meal ; before breakfast // 식전에 목욕하다 take a (morning) bath before breakfast

― 바람 before breakfast (time) ; on an empty〔unbreakfasted〕 stomach ―술 appetizer wine ; an appetizer ―참(站) the early morning (before breakfast) ; a stopping place reached before breakfast

식전 式典 a ceremony ; rites ; rituals

식중독 食中毒 food poisoning ; sitotoxism ¶ 식중독을 일으키다 (식중독에 걸리다) be poisoned by food ; [음식이 주어] disagree with 《a person》

식지 食指 the index finger ; the forefinger

식지 食紙 oiled paper for covering food

식체 食滯 indigestion ; dyspepsia

‡식초 食醋 vinegar

―산 〚화학〛 acetic acid

식충 食蟲 〚생물〛 insect-eating ; an insect-eater ; an insectivore

― 동물 an insectivore ; an insectivorous animal ―류 Insectivora ― 식물 an insectivorous plant ; a carnivore 《*pl.* -ra》

식충이 食蟲― [탐식자] a glutton ; a gourmand ; a gorger ; a belly-slave ; [밥벌레] a good-for-nothing

식칼 食― a kitchen knife ; a cleaver ; a butcher knife

†식탁 食卓 a (dinner) table ; the board ¶ 식탁용의 for table use // 식탁에 앉다 sit (down) at (the) table // 식탁을 보다 lay the cloth ; set the table // 식탁에 오르다 be served at table

―보 a cloth ; a tablecloth ―염 table salt ― 예의(범절)〔매너〕 table manners

식탈 a stomach upset caused by overeating ; food poisoning ; indigestion

식탐 食貪 gluttony ―하다 be greedy ; be gluttonous ; be voracious ⇨ 탐식

식품 食品 food ; articles of food ; groceries ⇨ 식료품

― 가공 food processing ― 가공업자 a food processor ― 공업 the food industry ― 위생 food hygiene ¶ 식품 위생법 the Food Sanitation Act〔Hygiene Law〕 ―점 a grocer's (shop) 《영》; a grocery (store) 《미》 ― 중독 foodstuff poisoning ―학 sitology ― 화학 food chemistry ― 회사 a food company 불량 ― illegal 〔unsanitary〕 foodstuff ; substandard food 인스턴트 ― convenience food ; precooked food ; instant 《속》 주요 ― staple foods ; staples

식품 관리 食品管理 food control

―법 the Staple Food Control Law ― 제도 the food control system 《skin》

식피 植皮 skin grafting ―하다 graft

― 수술 a skin-grafting operation ; dermatoplasty ; dermoplasty

식혜 食醯 a sweet drink made from fermented rice

― 가루 dried malt used for fermenting rice

식후 食後 ¶ 식후에 after dinner〔a meal〕 // 식후 30분에 복용하다 take 《a pill》 30 minutes after each meal

식히다 cool ; let 《a thing》 cool ¶ 더운 물을 식히다 cool hot water ; let hot water cool ; blow hot water to cool it (불어서) // 열을 식히다 reduce a fever // 조금 머리를 식힌 다음에 와라 Come back when you've cooled down a little.

신¹ footgear ; footwear ; shoes ¶ 신을 신다 put on one's shoes // 신을 벗다 take off one's shoes // 신을 신은 채 들어가다 enter〔go in〕 with one's shoes on

갖― Korean leather shoes 고무― rubber

shoes 나막― wooden clogs 에나멜― patent-leather shoes 짚― straw sandals

신² joy ; delight ; amusement ; enthusiasm ; excitement ¶ 신이 나다 get excited ; be keyed up ; become enthusiastic ; warm up // 신이 나서 설교하다 preach with great fervor // 혼자 신이 나서 낄낄거리다 chuckle with delight to oneself // 신이 나서 혼자 멋대로 지껄이다 give reins to one's tongue // 관중들은 아주 신이 났다 The audience was〔were〕 frantic with joy.

신 辛 〖민속〗 ① the 8th of the 10 celestial stems ② ⇨ 신방(辛方) ③ ⇨ 신시(辛時)

신 申 〖민속〗 ① the sign of the Monkey ② ⇨ 신방(申方) ③ ⇨ 신시(申時)

신 臣 [신민] a subject ; [가신] a retainer ; a vassal ; [자기] Your Majesty's servant ; I ; me

신 信 faith ; fidelity ; belief ; trust ; reliance ; credit

†신 神 God ; the Almighty ; [주] the Lord ; the〔our〕 Father ; [조물주의] the Creator ; [신령] a spirit ; [귀신] a demon ; [다신교의] a god ; a deity ; [여신] a goddess ¶ 전능의 신 the Almighty God // 사랑의 신 the god of love ; the blind god // 신의 은총 divine blessing ; a blessing of God ; the grace of God // 신의 조화 divine work ; an act of God // 신의 가호 divine protection ; providence // 신의 뜻 the divine will // 신의 심판 divine judgment // 신에게 기도드리다 pray to God // 신을 믿다 believe in God

신 腎 ① [신장] the kidney ② [음경] the penis

신- 新― new ; modern ; latest ; novel ; up-to-date ¶ 신유행 the latest fashion // 신내각 the new Cabinet // 신무기 a new weapon // 신여성 the modern woman

신 a scene ¶ 라스트 신 the last scene // 러브신 a romantic〔love〕 scene // 극적 신을 전개하다 develop a dramatic scene

신가정 新家庭 a home of newlyweds ; a new home

신간 身幹 stature ¶ 신간순으로 in order of stature

신간 新刊 a new publication ; a newly published book ; a recent release ―하다 publish 《a new book》
― 목록 a list of new publications ― 비평 a book review ―서 안내 [신문 등의] a book notice ― 서적 a new book〔publication〕 ― 소개 a book review ― 소개자 a book reviewer ― 예고 a notice of forthcoming publications ; an advertisement〔announcement〕 of forthcoming books

신간 新墾 ⇨ 개간(開墾) ―하다 reclaim fresh land ¶ 신간의 newly reclaimed〔tilled〕
―지 newly developed〔reclaimed〕 land

신갈나무 〖식물〗 a Mongolian oak

신감각파 新感覺派 a neo-sensualist

신개지 新開地 [개발 지역] a new〔newly-opened〕 land ; a newly-peopled district〔suburb〕 ; [개간지] newly developed〔reclaimed〕 land ; a newly cultivated area

신건이 a dull person ; a bore ; an insipid person ; a silly fool

신격 神格 divinity ; godhead
―화 deification ¶ 신격화하다 deify ; apotheosize

‡신경 神經 nerves ¶ 신경의 nervous ; nerve // 신경이 둔한 사람 a dull-nerved man // 신경을 건드리다 get〔jar〕 on one's nerve // 신경을 빼다 extract a nerve ; have a nerve out (의사가) // 신경이 날카롭다 be sensitive ; be nervous // 신경이 둔하다 be dull ; be insensible ; be thick-skinned // 신경을 세심하게 쓰다 pay careful attention 《to》 // 그의 신경을 건드리지 않도록 조심하라 Be careful not to get on his nerves. /Give him lots of room. // 나는 운동 신경이 그리 발달하지 않았다 I'm so uncoordinated. // 너는 병 낫는 데에만 신경 써라 You're just to concentrate on getting well. // 나한테 신경 쓰지 마 Don't mind me.
―계 〖해부학·동물〗 a nervous system ―계통 the nerve system ―공(孔) a neuropore ― 과민 hypersensitivity ; nervousness ; oversensitiveness ¶ 그는 신경과민이다 He is thin-skinned. /He is all nerves. ― 과로〔피로〕 nerve strain ―과의(사) a neurologist ―병 a nervous disease ; neurosis ¶ 신경병의 nervous ―병리학 neuropathology ― 병리학자 a neuropathologist ―병 전문가 a neuropathist ; a nerve specialist ; a psychiatrist ―병학 neurology ―병 환자 a neuropath ; a neurotic ― 섬유 a nerve fiber ― 세포 a nerve cell ; a neuron ― 쇠약 nervous breakdown〔prostration, debility〕 ; neurasthenia ¶ 과로로 신경 쇠약에 걸리다 have a nervous breakdown from overwork ― 쇠약자 a neurasthenic ―염 neuritis ― 외과(학) neurosurgery ― 외과의 a neurosurgeon ―원(原) a brain cell ―원 섬유 neurofibril ― 이상 nerves ― 자극 〖해부학〗 innervation ―전 psychological warfare ; a white〔nerve〕 war ―절 〖해부학〗 a (nerve) ganglion 《*pl.* ~s, -glia》 ; a nerve knot ― 절제 neurotomy ; 〖수의학〗 nerving ― 정신병(증) neuropsychosis ― 정신 의학 neuropsychiatry ― 정신 의학자 a neuropsychiatrist ― 조직 nervous〔nerve〕 tissue ― 조직 붕괴 neurolysis ― 조직학 neurohistology ―증 a nervous disease ; neurosis ; neuropathy ― 지배 〖생리〗 innervation ― 지배계 the neuromotor system ― 진정제 a nervous sedative ; a nervine ―질 nervousness ; nervous temperament ―통 neuralgia ¶ 신경통을 앓

다 suffer from neuralgia —통 약 an antineuralgic —학 neurology — 해부학 neuroanatomy — 해부학자 a neuroanatomist —핵 a nerve nucleus —형질 neuroplasm 반사 — 《develop good》 reflexes 감각〔운동〕 — 세포 a sensory〔motor〕 neuron 뇌척수(腦脊髓) —계 the cerebrospinal nervous system 중추〔자율, 말초〕 —계 the central〔autonomic, peripheral〕 nervous system

신경지 新境地 a new land ; a new stage ; new ground ¶ 신경지를 개척하다 break new ground ; carve out a new career // 자유를 누릴 수 있는 신경지를 찾다 seek a new land where one can enjoy freedom

*신경질 神經質 nervousness ; a nervous temperament ¶ 신경질의 nervous ; high-strung ; (highly) sensitive ; delicate // 아주 신경질적인 사람 a man of highly nervous temperament // 신경질을 부리다 show nervousness // 신경질이 나게 하다 make 《a person》 nervous ; get on 《a person's》 nerves

신경향 新傾向 a new tendency〔trend〕
—파 the Anti-Conventional School

신고 申告 a statement (신립) ; a report (보고) ; a declaration (세관에서) —하다 state ; report ; declare ; make〔file〕 a return ¶ 고용인의 비행을 신고하다 report an employee for misconduct // 소득세의 신고를 하다 make〔file〕 an income tax return // 세관에 신고하다 make a declaration at the custom house // 경찰과 보험회사에 도난 신고를 했다 I filed a theft report to the police and to my insurance company.
— 납부 payment by self-assessment — 마감 날짜 the final day for filing —서 a statement ; a return ; a declaration ; a report ¶ 주소 변경 신고서 하나 얻을 수 있을까요 Could I have a change of address form ? —세 a self-assessed tax — 용지 a return blank〔form〕 —자 an applicant ; a reporter —제 the report system 녹색 — a green-paper report 《on business income》 ; green return 세관 — a customs declaration 소득세 —서 an income tax return 예정 — a provisional return 확정 — a final return

신고 辛苦 hardships ; trials ; tribulations ; adversity ; [고심] labor ; pains ; trouble ; toil —하다 go through hardships ; toil (and moil) ; take pains ¶ 신고를 겪다 suffer hardships ; undergo privations ; have bitter experience

신고안 新考案 a new device ; a novel contrivance ; a new gadget ¶ 신고안의 newly-devised〔-contrived, -designed, -invented〕

신곡 新曲 a new musical composition ; a new tune

신곡 新穀 new grain ; a new crop of rice (햅쌀)
—머리 a harvest time

신곡 神曲 The Divine Comedy (by Dante)

신골 the (shoe) last ; shoetrees ; shoe〔boot〕 stretchers ¶ 신골에 맞추다 put〔set〕 《one's shoes》 on the last
— 방망이 a shoemaker's hammer

신공 神功 divine help ; god's grace

신관 (a) complexion ; a look ; a countenance ¶ 신관이 좋으십니다 You look well.

신관 信管 a fuse (of an explosive charge) ¶ 신관을 끊다 cut a fuse // 신관이 타고 있다 The fuse is sputtering.
격발(擊發)〔근접(近接)〕 — a percussion〔proximity〕 fuse 시한 — a time fuse

신관 新官 a newly-appointed official ; a new appointee
— 사또 the newly-appointed governor〔administrator〕

신관 a new building ; [별관·증축건물] an annex ; an extension 《미》

신교 信敎 religious belief ; religion ; faith ¶ 신교의 자유 religious freedom

*신교 新敎 Protestantism ; the Reformed Faith
—도 a Protestant — 이론 Protestant theology

신구 新舊 the new and the old ¶ 신구의 old and new // 신구 사상의 충돌 a collision between old and new ideas
— 관리 incoming and outgoing officials
— 장관 the incoming and outgoing ministers

신국면 新局面 a new aspect〔phase, situation〕 ¶ 신국면을 전개하다 develop a new phase ; assume〔take on〕 a new aspect

신권 神權 divine right
— 정치 theocracy 제왕 —설 the doctrine〔theory〕 of the divine right of kings

신권 新券 [새로 발행된 은행권] a new (bank) note

신규 新規 a new regulation ; a new project ¶ 신규의 new ; fresh // 신규로 anew ; afresh ; newly // 신규로 채용하다 hire〔employ〕 a new hand
— 계정 a new account — 사업 a new enterprise〔undertaking, business, project〕 — 예금 new deposits

신극 新劇 a new play〔drama〕 ; a new school of acting (파)
— 여배우 a new-drama actress — 운동 a theatrical reform movement ; a new-drama movement in the theatrical world

신금 宸襟 the King's mind〔heart〕 ¶ 신금을 괴롭히다 give great anxiety to His Majesty

신기 神技 superhuman skill ; unsurpassed abilities ¶ 신기에 가깝다 That is beyond human power.

신기 神奇 being marvelous〔miraculous, wonderful〕 —하다 (be) marvelous ;

miraculous ; wonderful ¶ 신기한 소문 a strange rumor // 약이 신기하게 잘 듣는다 The medicine works like magic. /The medicine has a marvelous efficacy〔curative power〕.
신기 神氣 vigor ; vitality ; spirit ; the mind ¶ 신기가 차 있다 be full of energy 〔vigor〕; be in high spirits // 신기가 쇠하다 become less energetic ; fall into low spirits
‡신기 新奇 novelty ; originality —하다 (be) novel ; new ; original ¶ 신기한 방법으로 in a novel way // 신기한 것을 좋아하다 be fond of novelties〔novelty〕
신기 神祇 the deities of heaven and earth
신기 神機 ① [계기] a marvelous opportunity ; a golden chance ② [기략] divine resources〔expedients, tact〕
신기다 put《footwear》on《a person》; get《a person》to put on《footwear》¶ 아이에게 양말을 신기다 put socks on a child ; have a child put his socks on
신기록 新記錄 a new record〔mark〕 ¶ 신기록을 세우다 make〔create, establish〕a new record // 물가 앙등이 신기록을 이루고 있다 The prices are on all-time high.
세계 — a new world record
신기료 장수 a shoe repairer ; a cobbler
신기루 蜃氣樓 a mirage ¶ 신기루가 나타나다 a mirage appears
‡신기원 新紀元 a new epoch〔era, stage〕 ¶ 신기원을 이루는 사건 an epoch-making〔epochal〕 event // 신기원을 이루다 make an epoch
신기축 新機軸 a new departure ; a novel contrivance ; a novelty ; a dodge ; a wrinkle (구) ¶ 신기축을 이루다 make a new departure ; strike out a new line〔a line for oneself〕// 종전의 작풍에 비해서 신기축을 이루는 것이라 하겠다 This is the new departure from the conventional art of story writing.
신나다 get in high spirits ; be〔get〕elated ; feel triumphant《over》¶ 신나는 시합 an exciting〔interesting〕game // 그 영화 참 신나더라 The picture thrilled〔excited〕me a great deal. /I've got a much of fun out of the picture. // 그는 아들의 성공에 신이 났다 He is highly elated over his son's success. // 신이 난다고 너무 속도를 내지 마라 Don't get carried away and go too fast.
신나무 〖식물〗 the Amur maple
신날 the four main ropes on which the sole of a straw sandal is woven
신남 信男 a male believer in Buddhism
신낭 腎囊 〖해부〗 the scrotum《*pl.* -ta》
신낭만주의 新浪漫主義 neo-Romanticism
신내기 新— a newcomer《in, to》; an incomer (영)
신내리다 神—《a medium》fall into trance ; be possessed by a spirit
신녀 信女 a female believer in Buddhism
신년 申年 the Year of the Ape
‡신년 新年 a new year ; New Year's Day ¶ 신년초에 at the beginning of the New Year // 신년을 축하하다 celebrate the New Year // 신년을 맞이하다 greet the New Year // 근하 신년 Happy New Year ! /I offer you my hearty wishes for your happiness in the New Year.
†신념 信念 belief ; faith ; conviction (확신) ¶ 신념이 강한 사람 a man of conviction ; a man of strong〔steadfast, sturdy〕faith // 신념에 살다 act up to one's conviction // 강한 신념을 가지고 있다 have a strong〔firm〕conviction《that》
신다 put on ; have on ; wear ¶ 오늘은 이 신을 신으세요 Put on these shoes today. // 빨리 양말을 신어라 Pull your socks on quickly. // 그는 비신을 신고 나갔다 He went out in rain shoes. // 그녀는 초록색의 신을 신고 있었다 She was in〔wore, was wearing〕her green shoes. /She had her green shoes on. // 저 신을 신어 보시죠 Try those shoes on. // 이 신은 꽤 오래 신었다 These shoes have been a lot of wear. // 이 신은 아직도 신을 수 있다 These shoes are still good to wear. // 이 신은 이제 못 신겠다 These shoes are worn out. // 추워질 테니까 스타킹을 신은 위에 양말을 신지 그래 It'll be cold, so why don't you wear socks over your stockings ?
신당 神堂 a shrine ; a joss house
신당 新黨 a new political party ¶ 신당을 결성하다 organize a new political party
신대륙 新大陸 the New Continent ; the New World ; Americas
신덕 神德 divine virtue〔help〕; divinity
‡신도 信徒 a believer ; a devotee ; a follower ; an adherent ; the faithful《총칭》
—회 [프로테스탄트의] a bebe 그리스도교 — a believer in〔an adherent of〕Christianity ; a Christian 불교 — a Buddhist
신돌이 ornamental ridge of a shoe
신동 神童 a〔an infant〕prodigy ; a wonder boy〔child〕; a boy wonder
신둥부러지다 (be) presumptuous ; forward ; obtrusive ; impertinent ; impudent ; uppish (구)
신뒤축 a shoe heel ¶ 신뒤축이 높은 신 high-heeled shoes // 신뒤축이 닳았다 The heels are worn (down).
*신디케이트 〖경제〗 a syndicate ¶ 신디케이트를 조직하다 form a syndicate
신딸 神— the young successor to an aging *mudang*
신랄 辛辣 —하다 (be) sharp ; severe ; bitter ; cutting ; biting ; poignant ; pungent ¶ 신랄한 비평 a scathing〔caustic, severe〕criticism // 신랄한 필치 an acrimonious pen // 신랄한 풍자 biting〔bitter, cutting〕sarcasm // 신랄한 어조로 in acrid tones〔language〕// 신랄한 언사를 쓰다 make caustic〔cutting〕remarks ; have a biting tongue

*신랑 新郞 a bridegroom
—감 a suitable〔likely〕 bridegroom — 들러리 the best man — 신부 the bride and the (bride) groom ; the bridal pair ; the newlyweds 《미·속》 ; the contracting parties (결혼식 등에서 쓰이는 말) ; a new 〔newly-married〕 couple

신래 新來 ¶ 신래의 newly-arrived ; newcome
— 환자 a new patient

신력 神力 divine power ; superhuman strength

신력 新曆 the solar calendar

신령 神靈 a divine spirit ; the soul ¶ 신령의 가호 divine protection
—계 the spiritual world 산— the god of a mountain ; the guardian spirit of a mountain

신례 新例 a new example〔precedent〕 ¶ 신례를 만들다 set〔establish〕 a new example

신록 新綠 fresh verdure ; tender〔fresh〕 green ¶ 신록의 계절 the season of fresh green // 신록으로 덮이다 be mantled 〔robed〕 in fresh verdure

†신뢰 信賴 confidence〔trust〕 (신임) ; faith ; reliance —하다 trust ; put trust 〔faith〕 in ; believe〔confide〕 in ; place confidence in ; rely〔depend〕 on ¶ 세인의 신뢰를 받다 win public confidence // 그는 신뢰할 수 없다 He is not to be trusted.

신망 信望 confidence and popularity ¶ 신망을 얻다 gain〔obtain, win〕 the confidence 《of》 // 신망을 잃다 lose〔forfeit〕 the confidence 《of》 // 세인의 신망을 얻다 win public confidence // 신망이 두텁다 enjoy 〔possess〕 the confidence 《of》

신면목 新面目 a new aspect〔phase, side〕 ¶ 신면목을 나타내다 present a new aspect

신명 身命 body and life ¶ 신명을 걸고 at the risk of one's life // 나라를 위해 신명을 바치다 lay down one's life for one's country

신명 神明 a deity ; a divinity ; God ¶ 신명의 가호로 by the protection of God ; by God's protection // 천지신명께 맹세하다 swear before Heaven

신명기 申命記 〖성경〗 Deuteronomy

신명나다 get〔become〕 light-hearted 〔cheerful, gay (-spirited), convivial, enthusiastic〕 ; be exhilarated ; be captivated ; get excited ¶ 신명나서 in the excess of mirth ; in a merry mood ; enthusiastically

신명지다 (be) merry ; cheerful ; joyous ; enthusiastic ; convivial ; thrilled

신묘 辛卯 〖민속〗 the 28th year of the sexagenary cycle ; the Year of the Hare

신묘 神妙 being mysterious and marvelous —하다 (be) mysterious ; marvelous ; wondrous

신문 訊問 questioning ; an examination 《of a witness》 ; a query ; an inquest —하다 question ; examine ; interrogate ; cross-examine
—실 an interrogation room —자 an examiner — 조서 an interrogatory ; a protocol of examination 유도 — a leading question 직접 — examination in chief

†신문 新聞 a newspaper ; a paper ; a journal ; the press 《총칭》 ¶ 신문의 journalistic ; press ; newspaper // 3일전의 신문 a three-day-old paper // 오늘 신문에 in today's paper // 신문에 나다 appear〔be reported〕 in the paper(s) // 신문에 나지 않게 하다 keep out of the newspapers // 신문을 배달하다 deliver newspapers // 신문을 발행하다 publish〔issue〕 a newspaper // 신문에서 보다 read〔see〕 《an item》 in the newspaper // 신문에서 호평을 받다 have〔rejoice〕 a good〔favorable〕 notice in the press // 신문에서 얻어맞다 be attacked〔pounded〕 in the press ; be traduced by a newspaper // 댁에서는 무슨 신문을 보십니까 What newspaper do you read〔take in, subscribe to〕?
—값 the 《monthly》 charge for the newspaper —계 the newspaperdom ; the newspaper world ¶ 신문계에 투신하다 enter the field of journalism — 광고 newspaper advertising ; a newspaper advertisement — 구독료 the subscription for〔of〕 a paper — 구독자 a newspaper reader〔subscriber〕 — 기사 a newspaper account〔article〕 ; news — 기자 a pressman ; a reporter ; a journalist ; a newsman 《미》 — 기자단 a press corps — 기자석 the press gallery〔box〕 ; the reporters' gallery — 기자 신분증(명서) a press card〔pass〕 — 기자 클럽 a press club — 논조 press comments 《on the foreign policy》 —대(代) ⇨ 신문 구독료 — 매점 a newsstand — 발표 a press release — 발행인 a newspaper publisher 《미》 ; a newspaper proprietor 《영》 — 배달 〔사람〕 a newsman ; a newsboy ; a newspaper delivery man ; a (news) paper boy — 보급소 a newspaper agency — 보도 a press report ; press reporting 《총칭》 —사 a newspaper office〔company〕 ¶ 신문사를 경영하다 run a newspaper — 사업 the newspaper industry — 소설 a serial story (in a newspaper) — 스크랩 newspaper clippings 《미》 ; newspaper cuttings 《영》 —업(무) journalism — 열람대 a newspaper stand — 열람실 a newspaper room — 용지 newsprint (paper) — 윤리 강령〔규정〕 the Press Moral Code —전(戰) a press campaign ; newspaper propaganda —지 a newspaper ; the newspaper itself —체(體)〔조(調)〕 a journalistic style ; journalese — 통신사 a press 〔news〕 agency — 판매점 a newsstand — 팔이 a newsboy ; a newsman ; a news

vendor ― 편집국 the editorial office ―학 (the study of) journalism ―학과 [대학의] a journalism course ―학 교수 a professor of journalism ―학부 a school of journalism ― 협회 press association 대― a major〔larger〕 newspaper 석간 ― an evening paper 소형 ― a tabloid paper 신참 ― 기자 a junior reporter ; a cub reporter 영자 ― an English (-language) (news) paper 일간 ― a daily (newspaper) 조간〔석간〕 ― a morning〔an evening〕 paper 주간 ― a weekly newspaper 한국 ― 회관 the Press Center of Korea

신물 bile vomited up

신물이 나다 (관용) get sick and tired of

신미 辛味 a hot〔spicy〕 taste

신미 新米 new rice ⇨ 햅쌀

신미 新味 freshness ; something fresh ; novelty

신민 臣民 subjects ; a subject

신바닥 a shoe sole ; the bottom of one's shoes

신바람 excitement ⇨ 신[2]

신발 footwear ⇨ 신[1]

― 가게 a footwear shop ― 장수 a footwear dealer

신발명 新發明 a new〔recent〕 invention ¶ 신발명의 newly invented ; of recent invention

신발족 新發足 a new〔fresh〕 start ―하다 make a new〔fresh〕 start ; start a fresh

신방 申方 〖민속〗 the direction of the Monkey ; southwest by west

신방 辛方 〖민속〗 west by north

신방 新房 bridal room ; a bridal bed ¶ 신방에 들다 go〔get〕 into bridal bed

신벌 神罰 divine punishment〔judgment〕 ; divine retribution ; visitation ; a judgment of God ; Heaven's vengeance ¶ 신벌을 받다 be punished by God ; be visited with divine punishment

신법 新法 [방법] a new method ; new techniques ; [법률] a new law ; new regulations

신볘나 a shoe seam

신변 身邊 (by) the side of 《a person》 ; on the person ¶ 신변의 위험 one's personal danger // 신변을 경계하다 protect 《a person》 from danger ; watch over 《a person》 // 신변을 돌보다 attend on 《a person》 ; look after 《a person》 // 그의 신변은 언제나 경찰 호위 하에 있다 He is always under police escort.

신병 身柄 one's person ¶ 신병 불구속으로 without physical restraint ; in one's own custody // 신병을 인수하러 가다 go to claim〔receive〕 《a person》 // 신병을 넘겨주다 hand 《an offender》 over 《to》

신병 身病 illness ; sickness (미) ; a disease ; a malady (만성의) ¶ 신병으로 사직하다 resign on account of ill health // 신병으로 쓰러지다 succumb to disease

*신병 新兵 a new〔fresh, raw〕 recruit ; a new conscript ; a rookie 《속》

― 훈련 boot〔recruit〕 training

신복 信服 submission ―하다 be convinced ; submit to // 신복할 만한 주장 convincing argument // 신복시키다 convince 《a person》

신볼 the width of a shoe

‡신봉 信奉 belief ; faith ―하다 believe in ; adhere to ; have faith in

―자 an adherent ; a devotee ; a believer

신부 神父 a (holy) father ¶ 신부가 되다 be ordained a priest〔to the priesthood〕

‡신부 新婦 a bride ; a newlywed wife

― 들러리 a maid-of-honor ; a bridesmaid ― 의상 bridal costume〔dress〕 ― 학교 a finishing school

‡신분 身分 [지위] a social position〔standing, status〕 ; a station〔situation〕 in life ; [신원] identity ; origin ; birth ¶ 신분이 높은 사람 a man of position ; a person of high standing // 신분이 낮은 사람 a lowly person ; a man humble〔low〕 in social standing // 신분을 밝히다 disclose one's identity // 신분을 증명하다 identify oneself

신분 증명 身分證明 identification

―서 an identification card ¶ 신분 증명서의 제시를 요구하다 demand identification 《from》 // 신분 증명서를 보이다 show identification 《to》

신불 神佛 gods and Buddhas ¶ 신불의 가호 divine protection

‡신비 神秘 mystery ¶ 자연계의 신비 the mysteries of nature // 신비스럽다 be mystic ; mysterious ; miraculous ; occult ; esoteric // 저 산은 어딘지 신비스럽다 There is something mysterious about that mountain. // 그 여배우는 아직 10대인데도 신비한 매력을 갖고 있다 That actress is still in her teens, but she has a mysterious appeal.

―경 a land of mystery ―극 a mystery drama ― 소설 a mystery story ― 요법 a miraculous cure ―주의 mysticism ―주의자 a mystic ― 철학 esoterics ; mystic philosophy ―파 a mystic school

신빙 信憑 credence ; credit ; trust ―하다 credit ; place confidence 《in》 ; give credence 《to》 ; put trust 《in》

―성 authenticity ; credibility

신사 辛巳 〖민속〗 the 18th year of the sexagenary cycle ; the Year of the Serpent

†신사 紳士 a gentleman ; a man of honor ; a fine-looking man (단정한 사람) ¶ 신사다운 gentlemanlike ; gentlemanly // 비신사적 ungentlemanly ; unworthy of a gentleman // 신사적으로 in a gentlemanly way〔manner〕 // 신사인 체하다 play a gen-

tleman // 신사의 체면에 관한 문제다 That would be beneath your dignity as a gentleman.
—도 the code〔ideals〕 of a gentleman —록 a Who's Who ; a directory — 협정 a gentleman's〔gentlemen's〕 agreement —화 men's shoes 시골 — a rustic gentleman

신사 神祠 a shrine

신사복 紳士服 a lounge suit 《영》; a sack coat ; a business suit 《미》

신사업 新事業 a fresh〔new〕 enterprise ; a new undertaking〔project〕

신산 辛酸 hardships ; privations ; trials ¶ 신산을 맛보다 go through hardships ; have reverses of fortune

신상 神像 an image〔idol〕 of a deity〔god〕

신상 身上 [몸] one's body ; [형편] one's lot〔condition, circumstances〕; [경력] one's history〔career, life〕 ¶ 신상 문제 one's personal affairs // 신상을 걱정하다 be anxious for another's welfare // 신상에 관한 질문은 하지 마라 Don't ask personal questions.
— 문제 one's personal affairs ¶ 신상 문제를 의논하다 consult with 《a person》 〔seek a person's advice〕 about one's personal affairs — 상담 consultation 〔advice sought〕 about 《a person's》 affairs — 상담란 an agony column 《미》; a home-council column ; the human relations column — 조사서 a report card on one's family

신상 紳商 a great〔wealthy, rich〕 merchant ; a merchant prince

신상필벌 信賞必罰 dispensation of justice both to services and crimes ; never fail to reward a merit or let a fault go unpunished

신색 神色 complexion ; color ; a look ; countenance ; an expression ¶ 신색이 좋습니다 You look well.

***신생 新生** new birth ; rebirth ; newborn ; renascence ¶ 신생 대한 민국 the new Republic of Korea
—국 newly emerging nation —대 〚지질〛 the Cenozoic〔Cainozoic〕 era〔period〕 —아(兒) a new-born baby〔infant〕; 〚의학〛 a neonate

신생명 新生命 new〔changed, reformed, regenerated〕 life

신생애 新生涯 a new (stage of) life ; a new career
— 운동 a new-life〔life-reform〕 movement

신생활 新生活 a new life ¶ 신생활에 들어가다 start a new life ; start one's life anew〔afresh〕; start one's life all over ; make a fresh start in life ; turn over a new leaf

신서 新書 a newly published book ; a new book

신서 信書 a letter ; (personal) correspondence 《총칭》 ¶ 신서의 비밀을 침범하다 violate the privacy of (personal) correspondence

신석 腎石 (a) renal calculus
—병 nephrolithiasis

신석기 新石器 〚고고〛 a neolith
— 시대 the Neolithic Age〔age〕; the New Stone Age

신선 神仙 a Taoist hermit with supernatural powers ; a wizard
—경 a fairly land —담(譚) a fairy tale

†**신선 新鮮** freshness —하다 (be) fresh ¶ 신선한 과실〔야채〕 fresh fruits〔vegetables〕 // 신선하게 하다 freshen ; refresh // 신선미가 부족하다 lack freshness // 창문을 열고 신선한 공기를 방안에 넣어라 Open the window and let in fresh air.
—도(度) (the degree of) freshness —미(味) freshness

신선 新選 new selection (책) ; a new anthology —하다 newly select ; newly elect (선출하다)
— 의원 a newly-elected〔returned〕 member of the National Assembly

신선로 神仙爐 a brass chafing dish

신설 伸雪 vindication of one's honor —하다 vindicate one's honor ; clear oneself of a disgrace

신설 新設 new establishment〔organization〕; creation —하다 establish〔organize〕 newly ; create ; found ¶ 신설의 newly organized ; newly established // 학교를 신설하다 establish〔found〕 a school
— 공장 a new factory — 회사 a newly-established〔-organized, -formed〕 company ; a new company

신설 新說 a new theory〔doctrine〕 (학설) ; a new view〔light, version〕 (견해) ¶ 신설을 내세우다 propound〔advance〕 a new theory // 이 문제에 대해서 신설이 나왔다 A new light has been thrown upon the problem.

신성 新星 〚천문〛 a nova 《*pl.* ~s, -vae》 ¶ 영화계의 신성 a new film star ; a new star in 《Korea's》 filmdom

†**신성 神聖** sacredness ; sanctity ; holiness ; inviolability —하다 (be) sacred ; holy ; sanctified ; hallowed ; consecrated ; divine

> 참고 **holy**는 근본적으로 종교에 관련되고 종교적으로 깊이 존경받는 정신적인 순수함을 의미한다 **sacred**는 성스러운 것으로서 다른 것들과 떨어져 고매한 목적에 바쳐지는 것과 범할 수 없는 것을 의미한다 **divine**은 「신성을 가지는 신으로부터 나오는 신에 관계되는」의 뜻으로 최고의 위대함을 나타낸다

¶ 신성한 교제 a spiritual friendship // 신성화하다 make holy ; consecrate ; sanctify ; hallow // 신성시하다 hold 《a thing》 sacred // 신성하다 hold 《a thing》 sacred

// 신성 불가침이다 be sacred and inviolable // 결혼은 신성한 것이다 Marriage is sacred〔a holy thing〕.
— 동맹 『역사』 the Holy Alliance — 로마 제국 the Holy Roman Empire
*신성 神性 divine nature ; divinity ; godhood ; godhead
신세 indebtedness ; a debt of gratitude ; an obligation ¶ 신세를 갚다 repay 《a person's》 kindness // 신세를 많이 졌습니다 Thank you for your kind help. /I am much indebted〔obliged〕 to you. /I owe you much for your kindness. // 나는 부모의 신세를 지고 싶지 않다 I don't want sponge off my parents.
신세를 지다 관용 be under indebtedness to ; be indebted to ; be obliged to
신세 身世 one's lot〔condition, circumstances〕 ¶ 딱한 신세 adverse circumstances ; a sad lot // 신세타령하다 tell the story of one's own poor life ; bewail one's lot
‡신세계 新世界 a new world ; the New World (미대륙)
신세대 新世代 the new generation〔era〕 ¶ 신세대의 젊은이 the coming〔young〕 generation
신소리[1] fresh talk ; a saucy reply ; a pert answer —하다 talk saucy ; have a saucy tongue ; give cheek ¶ 신소리 마라 None of your lip〔cheeks, impudence〕. / Don't say such silly things.
신소리[2] [신발의] the scuff of one's footsteps ; sound of walking shoes
신소설 新小說 the new-style fiction 《총칭》 ; a new-style novel〔story〕
†신속 迅速 quickness ; rapidity ; swiftness ; promptitude ; speediness ; celerity —하다 (be) quick ; rapid ; swift ; speedy ; prompt ¶ 신속히 quickly ; swiftly ; promptly // 이 명령을 신속히 수행해라 Be prompt to carry out this order.
신수 身手 one's appearance ; one's air ; one's mien ; one's bearing ¶ 신수가 훤한 사람 a person of good bearing〔fine presence〕 // 신수가 환하다 have a fine appearance ; have a good bearing // 신수가 훤하십니다 You look like a million.
신수 身數 one's luck〔fortune〕 ¶ 신수 좋은 사람 a fortunate person // 신수가 피다 be in luck's way ; one's fortune changes for the better ; fortune turns in one's favor
신승 辛勝 —하다 win 《a game》 by a narrow〔small〕 margin ; nose〔edge〕 out 《미·속》
신시 辛時 『민속』 the 20th of the 24hour periods 《6 : 30～7 : 30 p. m.》
신시 新詩 modern poem
신시대 新時代 a new age〔era, epoch〕
신식 新式 a new style〔type〕 ; a new method (방법) ¶ 신식의 new-style ; new-type ; new ; [현대적] up-to-date ; modern ; new-fashioned // 신식화 modernization
— 무기 a new-type weapon — 생활 a new mode of living ; modern living —총 a new-type gun
신신부탁 申申付託 —하다 request earnestly ; repeatedly request ; beg ; entreat ¶ 신신부탁합니다 I entreat this favor of you.
신실 信實 sincerity ; honesty ; truth ; faithfulness ; good faith —하다 (be) sincere ; steady and honest ; faithful
신심 信心 faith ; piety ; devotion ¶ 신심이 깊다 be devout ; be pious // 신심이 생기다 become pious
신안 新案 a new idea〔design, plan〕 ¶ 특허국에 신안 특허를 신청하다 apply to the Patent Office for a patent on a new design
—물 『상업』 novelties ; a gimmick 《미·속》 — 특허 a patent on a new device 실용 — a utility model 실용 — 특허(를 신청하다) (apply for) a utility model patent
†신앙 信仰 faith ; belief —하다 believe 〔have faith〕 in ¶ 신앙의 자유 freedom of faith // 신앙을 버리다 forsake〔renounce〕 a faith // 신앙 생활을 하다 lead a religious life
— 개조(個條) the articles of faith ; a creed ; the apostles' creed — 고백 a confession of faith ; profession — 고백자 a professant of religion — 무차별론 indifferentism — 생활 a life of faith ; a religious〔pious〕 life — 요법 faith cure ; divine healing ; Christian science —인 a believer ; a devotee
신약 信約 a covenant ; a pledge
신약 神藥 a wonder〔miracle〕 drug ; a wonder-working remedy
신약 新約 『성경』 the New Testament
— 시대 New Testament times — 전서 the Complete New Testament
신어 新語 a new word ; a newly coined 〔newfangled〕 word ; a new coinage ; neologism ¶ 신어를 만들다 coin new words ; neologize
— 사용 neologism — 사용자 a neologist
신어미 神— 『민속』 an aging *mudang* (=spiritualistic medium) who passes her craft on to her successor
신여성 新女性 the modern girl ; the new woman
신역 身役 physical labor
신역 新譯 a new translation〔version〕
신열 身熱 fever ; (body) temperature ¶ 높은〔낮은〕 신열 high〔low〕 fever // 신열이 나다 have a fever ; become feverish // 신열이 오르다〔내리다〕 one's fever〔temperature〕 rises〔falls〕
신염 腎炎 『의학』 nephritis ; Bright's disease
신예 新銳 new and superior ¶ 신예의 new

and powerful 《weapon》
—기(機) a newly produced war plane **— 병기** new (powerful) weapons **— 부대** fresh troops

†**신용 信用** confidence ; trust ; credit ; faith ; dependence ; reliance **—하다** trust ; confide in ; place confidence in ; give credence to ¶ 신용할 수 있는 trustworthy ; reliable ; reputable ; creditable // 신용할 수 없는 unreliable ; incredible // 언제나 신용할 수 있는 친구 an unfailing friend // 회사의 신용 상태 the credit standing of a firm // 신용할 수 있는 피고용인 a reliable employee // 신용을 얻다 win〔gain〕 a confidence of // 신용을 잃다 lose credit with // 신용을 손상하다〔유지하다〕 impair〔maintain〕 one's reputation 〔credit〕 // 그를 신용하지 않는다 I have lost faith in him. // 1년 보장이란 말을 신용하고 이 차를 샀다 I bought this car on the strength of a one-year guarantee. // 내 말을 신용 못하겠다는 말인가 Don't you believe me〔my word〕? /Do you doubt my word? // 그들은 어느 정도 신용할 수 있다 They deserve some degree of credit. // 그는 신용할 수 있는 사람이 못 된다 He is not the sort of man to be trusted. // 당신의 신용 상태를 조사해 봐야겠습니다 We have to check out your credit. // 당신의 신용 카드 한도액 50만 원이 초과 사용되었다 Your credit limit of 500,000 *won* has been exceeded. // 신용도가 좋지 않은 사람과는 거래를 하지 않는 게 우리의 방침이다 Our policy is not to do business with anyone who has bad credit. // 저 회사의 사장은 어딘가 신용할 수 없다 There's something about the president of that company I just don't trust.
— 거래 dealings〔sales〕 on credit **— 기관** an organ of credit **— 대부** a credit loan ; a loan on credit ; a charter loan ¶ 신용 대부해 주다 give〔grant〕 《a person》 a credit 《for three million *won*》 **— 보증기금** the trust guarantee **— 상태** one's financial〔credit〕 status〔standing〕 ¶ 회사의 신용 상태 the credit status of a firm // 신용 상태를 조사하다 inquire into〔make sure of〕 a person's financial status **—장(狀)** a credit ; a letter of credit 《L/C》 ; a bill of credit **— 조사** a credit research **— 조사인** a credit man **— 조합〔금고〕** a credit association〔union〕 **— 조회** a credit〔confidential〕 inquiry **— 증권** credit paper ; an instrument of credit **— 화폐** (fiduciary) fiat money **무담보 —** clean credit **상업 —** commercial〔trade〕 credit

신우 腎盂 〖해부〗 the pelvis of the kidney
—염 〖의학〗 pyelitis

신울 the outer rim of shoes

⁑**신원 身元** one's identity (성명 따위) ; one's origin ; one's antecedents (경력) ¶ 신원 불명의 unidentified // 신원이 확실한 사람 a person with good antecedents // 신원이 판명되다 be identified // 신원을 조사하다 look〔inquire〕 into 《a person's》 antecedents // 신원을 증명하다 prove one's identity ; identify oneself // 신원을 조회하다 refer to 《a company》 for 《a person's》 character // 신원을 보증하다 stand guarantee 《for》 ; vouch for 《a person's》 character
— 보증서 a reference ; a character **— 보증인** a reference ; a safety **— 인수인(引受人)** a surety ; a guarantor ; a guarantee (for fidelity) **— 조회** referring to 《a company》 for 《a person's》 character **— 조회처(照會處)** a reference **— 증명서** an identification card

신원 新元 the New Year ⇨ 새해

신원 伸寃 —하다 redress a grievance ; clear oneself of a false charge ; vindicate oneself

신월 新月 a new〔young〕 moon ; the prime of the moon ; a crescent (초승달)

신위 神位 an ancestral tablet

신유 辛酉 〖민속〗 the 58th year of the sexagenary cycle ; the Year of the Fowl

⁑**신음 呻吟** moaning ; groaning ; a groan ; pining (고민) **—하다** moan ; groan ; be harassed 《by poverty》 ; pine ¶ 독재의 압제 밑에서 신음하다 groan under the tyranny 《of》 // 중과세에 신음하다 groan under the heavy tax // 병상에서 신음하다 be confined to bed suffering severely

신의 信疑 belief or disbelief〔doubt〕 ; credit or discredit ¶ 신의가 반반이다 I can't tell whether it is credible or not. /I am half in doubt.

신의 神醫 a wonderful physician

신의 神意 the divine will ; God's will ; Providence

⁑**신의 信義** faith ; fidelity ; truthfulness ¶ 신의가 있다 be faithful ; be true // 신의가 없다 be perfidious ; be truthless ; be faithless ; be insincere // 신의를 지키다〔깨뜨리다〕 keep〔break〕 faith 《with a friend》
국제 — international faith

신이상주의 新理想主義 neo-idealism

신인 神人 ① a man of god ; a godlike person ; a prophet ② god and man ¶ 그의 죄는 신인 공히 용서치 않으리라 He has sinned against God and man.
— 동형 anthropomorphism **— 상통** communication between god(s) and men

신인 新人 a new man ; a new figure ; a rising man ; a man of advanced ideas ¶ 문단의 신인 a new figure〔face〕 in the literary world // 이제야 기대하고 있던 신인을 구한 것 같다 Looks like we finally got a newcomer with some promise.

신일 申日 〖민속〗 the Day of the Monkey

†**신임 信任** confidence ; trust ; credence **—하다** confide in ; trust ; put confi-

dence in ¶ 내각에 대한 신임 the confidence in Ministry // 신임 받는 사람 a trusted man // 신임을 얻다 win〔obtain, gain〕 the confidence of ; find the confidence with ; be trusted by // 신임을 받고 있다 enjoy the confidence of // 신임을 배반하다 betray 《a person's》 confidence

—장(狀) credentials ; a letter of credence ¶ 신임장을 제출하다 present one's credentials — 투표 a vote of confidence

신임 新任 a new appointment —하다 newly appoint to office ¶ 신임의 newly-appointed // 신임 인사를 하다 make an inaugural address

— 교수 a newly appointed professor — 교장 the new principal — 대사 a newly accredited ambassador — 인사 《make》 an inaugural address —자 a new appointee —지 a new post of duty

***신입 新入** (newly) entering ; incoming ; new ¶ 여기서 일하게 된 신입 사원입니다 I'm the new recruit here.

—생 a new student〔pupil〕; a freshman —자 a newcomer ; a novice

신자 信者 a believer ; a devotee ; an adherent ; the faithful 《총칭》 ¶ 기독교 신자가 되다 become a Christian ; turn Christian ; be converted to Christianity (개종) ; embrace Christianity

불교 — a believer in Buddhism ; an adherent of Buddhism

신자 新字 a newly made letter〔character〕

신작 新作 a new work ; a new production ; a new composition (작곡) ¶ 신작을 발표하다 publish a new (piece of) work ; give the first public performance of a new piece 《of music》

신작로 新作路 a newly constructed road ; a highway

신장 —欌 the shoe chest

‡**신장 伸張** extension ; expansion ; elongation —하다 extend ; expand ; elongate ¶ 세력의 신장 extension of one's influence // 국위를 해외에 신장하다 extend national prestige overseas // 외국 무역을 신장하다 expand〔increase〕 foreign trade

—계(計) an extensometer ; an extensimeter —근 the extensor (muscle) —기(器) 〖화학〗 a stretcher —률 the coefficient of expansion — 분자(分子) 〖화학〗 an extended molecule —성 expansibility ; elongation 세력 — extension of one's influence

†**신장 身長** height ; stature ¶ 신장이 5척이다 stand five feet ; be five feet in stature〔height〕// 신장이 자라다 grow 〔advance, increase〕 in stature // 신장을 재다 take〔measure〕 one's height // 신장 부족으로 불합격이 되다 be rejected because one is under height // 당신은 신장이 얼마나 됩니까 How tall are you? / What's your height?

신장 神將 ① [장수] a general of superhuman ability ② [귀신] a powerful spirit

—대 a shaman's (spirit-invoking) wand

신장 腎臟 〖해부〗 the kidneys

— 결석 a kidney stone ; a nephrolith — 병 kidney trouble —염 nephritis ; Bright's disease

신장 新裝 [복장] a new dress ; a new attire ; a new garb ; [장비] a new equipment ; [장정] a new binding —하다 give a new look to ; furnish up ; [개축하다] remodel ¶ 신장된 서울역 newly furnished〔constructed〕 *Seoul* station

신장 新粧 refurnishment ; redecoration —하다 give a new look 《to》 ; refurnish ; redecorate

신저 新著 a new work 《of an author》 ; [신간서] a new publication ; books newly published ¶ 신저 한권을 증정합니다 Kindly accept a copy of my work just out.

신전 —廛 a shoe store〔shop 《영》〕

신전 神前 before God〔gods〕

†**신전 神殿** a shrine ; a sanctuary

신절 臣節 loyalty (to one's lord) ¶ 신절을 다하다 remain loyal to one's lord to the end

신접살이 新接— life in a new home ; starting housekeeping

신정 神政 theocracy

신정 新正 the New Year ; the first month of the new year (정월)

신정 新政 a new government (정부) ; a reformed administration

신정 新訂 a new revision —하다 newly revise

—판 a newly revised edition

신정 新情 newly developed affection ; a new love ; young love

신정권 新政權 a new regime

신정책 新政策 a new policy

신제 新制 a new system

신제 新製 new manufacture —하다 newly make ¶ 신제의 newly-made ; newly-fangled

—품 a new product

신조 神助 the help of Heaven ; divine grace〔aid, intervention〕

신조 信條 a creed ; an article of faith ; [신념] a principle ; a belief ¶ 신조를 지키다 keep〔follow, be true to〕 one's creed

생활 — one's principles of life

신조 新造 new construction〔building〕 —하다 construct〔build〕 anew ; [말따위를] mint ; coin

—어(語) a (newly-)coined word

신조소주의 新彫塑主義 〖미술〗 neoplasticism

신종 信從 ―하다 follow with confidence ; believe and follow ; rely on

신종 新種 [씨] a new species ; [모양] a new type ; [변종] a new variety ¶ 신종의 벼 a new variety of rice // 신종을 만들어 내다 cultivate a new variety 《of》

― 사기 a new type of swindling

신주 神主 an ancestral tablet ¶ 신주를 모시다 enshrine one's ancestral tablet

신주 新株 a new stock〔share 《영》〕 ¶ 신주를 공모하다 collect new stocks publicly

― 공모 invitation of public to new stocks

― 인수권 preemptive rights

‡신중 愼重 prudence ; discretion ; circumspection ; caution ; care ―하다 (be) prudent ; cautious ; careful ; circumspect ; discreet ; judicious ; deliberate ¶ 신중하게 carefully ; cautiously ; prudently ; circumspectly ; discreetly ; with prudence // 신중히 심의하다 give careful consideration to 《a matter》 ; deliberate on 《a matter》 // 신중한 태도를 취하다 take 〔assume〕 a cautious〔prudent〕 attitude 《in》 ; use prudence // 신중하게 행동하다 act with prudence ; move with circumspection ; watch one's step

신중절 a Buddhist nunnery〔convent〕

신지식 新知識 up-to-date knowledge 〔information〕 ; advanced ideas

신지피다 神― be divinely inspired ; be possessed by a spirit

신진 新進 rising ; coming forth

― 작가 a rising〔coming〕 writer ; a young writer

신진 대사 新陳代謝 [신구 대체] renewal ; replacement ; regeneration ; change ; 〖생리〗 metabolism ; metastasis ―하다 be renewed ; be replaced ; be regenerated ; replace the old with the new ; the new takes the place of the old ¶ 신진 대사의 metabolic // 신진 대사 시키다 metabolize ; change by metabolism // 저 회사에서는 사원들의 신진 대사가 심하다 The staff of the company is constantly changing. // 인체는 항상 신진 대사를 행한다 The human body is subject to metabolism.

신짝 a shoe ; an odd shoe (of a pair) ¶ 헌 신짝처럼 버리다 reject 《a thing》 as worthless ; cast 《a thing》 away like a dirt

신착 新着 a new〔fresh〕 arrival ―하다 newly arrive ; be a new arrival

― 양서(洋書) newly-imported foreign books ; a fresh arrival of foreign books ―품 new arrivals ; newly arrived 〔imported, received〕 goods

신찬 新撰 new compilation ―하다 newly compile〔select, edit〕 ¶ 신찬의 newly compiled〔edited〕

― 국어 독본 The New Language Readers

신참 新參 a newcomer ; a freshman ; a Johnny-come-lately ; [미숙자] a green hand ; a novice ¶ 신참의 new ; newappointed (신임의) ; green (미숙한)

신창 a shoe sole ¶ 신창을 갈다 resole shoes

신천옹 信天翁 〖새〗 an albatross

신천지 新天地 a new world ¶ 신천지를 개척하다 open up a new field of activity ; break fresh ground

†신청 申請 application ; request ; petition ; filing ; 〖법〗 motion ―하다 apply 《for》 ; make an application ; petition 《for》 ; file 《for a license》 ; move ¶ 정부에 허가를 신청하다 apply to the Government for permission // 전매 특허를 신청하다 apply for a patent 《to the Patent Bureau》 // (변호사가) 증인 소환을 신청하다 move that the witnesses be summoned // 면허장은 신청하면 얻을 수 있다 A license may be obtained upon application. // 특허 신청 중이다 Application for a patent is pending. // 낸시에게 데이트 신청을 했다가 거절당했어 I asked Nancy out, but she turned me down. // 필요한 게 있으면 신청하세요 Please put in a request for anything you need.

― 기한〔마감〕 the deadline for making application 《for》 ; a time limit for application ―서 a written application ¶ 신청서를 제출하다 send in a written application ; apply 《to the office for》 // 이 신청서를 작성하신 후 다시 오십시오 Fill this application form out and come back, please. ―순 the order of application received ¶ 신청순으로 in the order of application ―인 an applicant ; a petitioner ; a claimant (배상의) ; a proposer ; [신문 따위의] a subscriber ― 접수처 a place for application 여권 ― an application for a passport〔license〕

신청부같다 [걱정이 많다] be beset with worries ; (be) harassed ; [불만족] dissatisfied ; disappointed

†신체 身體 the body ¶ 신체의 bodily ; physical ; corporal ; personal // 신체의 결함 a physical defect // 신체의 자유 personal liberty // 신체가 건전하다 be sound in body // 신체의 자유를 잃다 be disabled ; be crippled // 신체를 단련하다 build up a healthy body // 올해는 거의 전사원이 신체 검사를 받은 것 같다 It seems that almost all the staff took their physicals this year.

― 검사 a physical examination ; a physical check-up 《미》 ¶ 신체 검사를 하다 [건강의] check up〔examine〕 one's health ― 결함 a physical defect ― 발부(髮膚) our body and all its members ― 장애자 a physically handicapped person ― 장애자 복지법 the Disabled Persons Welfare Law ― 조직 (a) bodily tissue ☞ ⟪ p. 1339 ⟫

신체

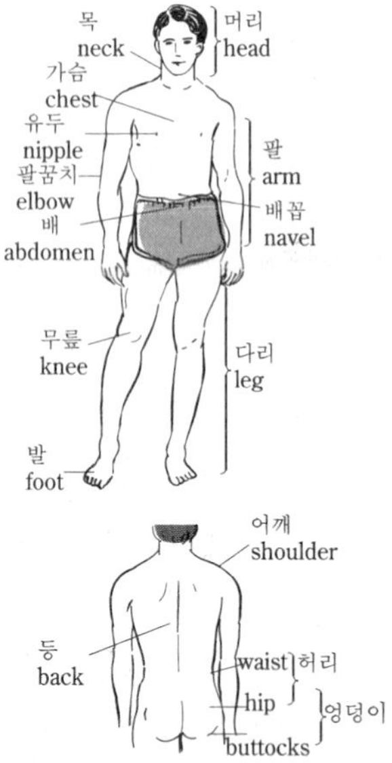

신체시 新體詩 the new style poetry ; a new style poem

신체제 新體制 a new structure〔system, set-up〕

신축 辛丑 〖민속〗 the 38th year of the sexagenary cycle ; the Year of the Ox

신축 新築 building ; constructing ; a new building (건물) **—하다** newly build〔construct〕 ¶ 신축 중의 집 a house under construction

— **가옥** a new(ly)-built〔new〕 house — **건물** a new building — **계획** a building program — **낙성식** the celebration of the completion of a new building

신축 伸縮 expansion and contraction **—하다** expand and contract

—계(計) an extensometer — **관세** a flexible tariff ⟪미⟫ — **사닥다리** an extension ladder **—성** elasticity — **세율** a flexible tariff ; a sliding scale of rates — **조항** a flexible〔an escalator〕 provision

신축 자재 伸縮自在 elasticity ¶ 신축 자재의 elastic ; flexible ; telescopic ; capable of expansion and contraction // 이것은 신축 자재입니다 This may be expanded or contracted as one pleases.

신춘 新春 early spring (이른 봄) ; the New Year (신년)

신춘 문예 新春文藝 a literary contest in spring ¶ 신춘 문예 소설 부문 당선작 a prize-winning entry in the department of novels of a spring literary contest

신출 新出 the first product of the season ; [사람] a new comer ; a new figure〔face, man〕

신출귀몰 神出鬼沒 elusiveness ; preternatural swiftness ; sudden appearance and disappearance **—하다** suddenly appear and suddenly disappear ; be elusive ¶ 신출귀몰의 phantomlike ; elusive ; protean // 신출귀몰의 행동 elusive movements // 신출귀몰한 도적 a protean〔an elusive〕 burglar

신출내기 新出— a newcomer ; a green hand ; a novice

신코 the top〔tip〕 of a shoe ; a toe-cap

***신탁 信託** trust **—하다** trust ⟪a person⟫ with ⟪a thing⟫ ; leave ⟪a thing⟫ in trust with ⟪a person⟫ ¶ 신탁을 받다 hold ⟪a thing⟫ in trust // 재산을 신탁하다 leave one's property in trust

— **계약** a trust agreement — **계정(計定)** a trust account — **관리인** a trust executor〔administrator〕 — **기금** trust funds ¶ 신탁 기금을 설정하다 provide〔create〕 the trust fund **—료** a trust fee **—물** a trust **—법** the Trust Act **—부** [은행의] a trust department — **수익자** a beneficiary **—업** trust business — **예금** a trust deposit — **은행** a trust bank **—자** a truster ¶ 피신탁자 a trustee — **재산** an estate〔a property〕 in trust ; a trust estate ; trust property — **증권** a trust instrument — **증서** a trust deed〔certificate〕 — **통치** trusteeship ¶ 신탁 통치 이사회 the Trusteeship Council // 신탁 통치 지역 a trust territory // 유엔의 신탁 통치하에 두다 put under a UN trusteeship — **투자** trust investment — **해제** cancellation of trust **공익** — a charitable trust **금전〔대부〕** — money〔loan〕 trust **명목** — a nominal trust **법인(法人)〔개인〕** — a corporate〔personal〕 trust **보험** — an insurance trust **수익** — a beneficial trust **유기(有期)〔영속〕** — a limited〔perpetual〕 trust **유언(遺言)〔생존〕** — a testamentary〔living〕 trust **투자** — investment trust

***신탁 神託** an oracle ; a divine message〔revelation〕 ¶ 꿈에 신탁을 받다 receive a divine revelation in a dream

신탄 薪炭 firewood and charcoal ; fuel

—비 fuel〔firing〕 expenses **—상** a fuel dealer ; a firewood and charcoal dealer

신통 神通 —하다 (be) wonderful ; marvelous ; extraordinary ; admirable ¶ 신통한 아이 an extraordinary child // 거참 잘 그렸다 신통한데 What a nice picture ! It's a wonder !

—력 an occult〔a supernatural〕 power ; divine power

신통치 않다 神通— (be) not good ;

신 체

인체(the human body)는 크게 머리(head), 사지(the limbs), 몸(body)과 몸통(trunk; torso)의 네 부분으로 나누어 진다. 이러한 신체의 각 부위명칭은 해부학적 호칭과 문학적 호칭이 있으며 chest와 breast가 bust와 bosom으로 navel과 umbilicus가 bellybutton 등으로 달리 표현되기도 하므로 유의할 필요가 있다.

① 기관(器官)의 명칭

뇌(腦) brain / 목젖 pharynx / 후두(喉頭) larynx / 식도(食道) gullet; esophagus / 척수(脊髓) spinal cord / 혀 tongue / 구강(口腔) oral cavity / 위(胃) stomach / 장(腸) intestines / 십이지장(十二指腸) duodenum / 췌장(膵臟) pancreas / 신장(腎臟) kidney / 간장(肝臟) liver / 담낭(膽囊) gall-bladder / 직장(直腸) rectum / 기관지(氣管支) bronchus / 폐 lung / 심장(心臟) heart / 혈관(血管) blood vessel / 동맥(動脈) artery / 정맥 vein(靜脈) / 고환(睾丸) testicles / 음경(陰莖) penis / 난소(卵巢) ovary / 자궁(子宮) uterus; womb / 질(膣) vagina / 항문(肛門) anus / 방광(膀胱) bladder / 요도(尿道) urethra / 근육(筋肉) muscles / 신경(神經) nerve / 뼈 bone / 두개골(頭蓋骨) skull / 골반(骨盤) pelvis / 관절(關節) joint

② 신체에 관한 표현

▶머리가 큰 top-heavy / 직모(直毛) straight hair / 곱슬머리 kinky hair / 고수머리 curly hair / 빳빳한 [부드러운] 머리 bristly [soft] hair / 칠흑같은 머리 jet-black hair / 갈색[금발] 머리 blond(e) hair

▶둥근 얼굴의 moon-faced; round-faced / 네모진 얼굴의 square-faced / 긴 얼굴의 oval-faced (★ long face는 시무룩한 얼굴)

▶짙은 눈썹 heavy [bushy] brows; thick[abundant] brows / 반달 눈썹 arched [crescent-shaped] eyebrows / 수북한 눈썹 shaggy eyebrows / 긴 속눈썹 long eyelashes

▶푸른 눈 blue eyes / 갈색 눈 brown eyes / 엷은 갈색 눈 hazel eyes / 쌍꺼풀 double-edged eyelid / 검은 눈동자 dark eyes (★ black eyes는 얻어맞아서 생긴 검은 멍이 든 눈.) / 눈이 튀어나온 bug-eyed / (동양계의) 가늘게 치켜올라간 눈 almond-eyed; slant-eyed / 길고 가느다란 눈 slit-eyed / 튀어나온 눈 protuberant eyes / 말똥말똥한 눈 beady eyes / 움푹 들어간 눈 sunken eyes / (놀라서) 휘둥그래진 눈 saucer eyes (★ 눈이 휘둥그래진 saucer-eyed) / 눈 꼬리의 주름 crow's-foot

▶높은 코 long nose (★ high nose라고 하지 않음.) / 콧날이 선 with a long shapely nose / 낮은 코 short nose / 큰 코 large [big] nose / 납작코 flat nose / 매부리코 Roman nose; aquiline nose; hawk nose / 뾰죽코 Grecian nose; Greek nose / 주먹코 bulbous nose; bottle nose; potato nose / 들창코 snub nose; upturned nose; turned-up nose; pug nose / (어린이의) 작고 둥근 코 button nose / 딸기코 strawberry nose; rosedrop / grog blossom / 코의 미용 성형 nose job(★ 정식 명칭은 rhinoplasty)

▶뻐드렁 입술 protruding lower lip / 야무진 입술 fight lips / 입술이 두툼한 lippy / 뻐드렁니의 buck-teethed; projecting [protruding]-teethed

▶턱이 뾰족한 lantern-jawed / 주걱턱 a jutting chin; spoon chin / 뾰죽턱 pointed chin

▶하얀 피부 fair skin / 거무스름한 피부의 dark-skinned / 매끈한 피부 milky-soft skin / 거친 피부 coarse[rough] skin / 주름이 많은 wrinkly

▶민틋한 어깨 sloping shoulders / 딱 벌어진 어깨 square shoulders; broad shoulders / 등이 굽은 round-shouldered

▶풍만한 젖가슴 large breasts / 큰 가슴 thick chest / 새가슴의 pigeon-[chicken-] breasted

▶올챙이배 pot-belly; bay window 《미》

▶엉덩이가 작은 narrow-hipped / 펑퍼짐한 엉덩이 a flat butt

▶마디가 굵고 억센 손 rough and bony hands / 다리가 긴 [짧은] long [short]-legged / 다리가 날씬한 leggy / 무 다리 piano legs / 다리가 굵은 thick-legged / 안짱다리의 bow-legged; bandy-legged; pigeon-toed / 밭장다리의 knock-kneed / 평발의 flat-footed; splayfooted

▶살찐 《경멸조》 fat; 《완곡》 stout; robust / 통통한 plump; chubby / 여윈 thin / 깡마른 skinny / 뼈만 앙상한 bony / 홀쭉이 skeleton / 날씬한 slim; slender

▶키다리 beanpole / 키가 큰 tall / 키가 작은 사람 shorty; shortie / 우람한 heavy-built; heavyset / 땅딸막한 dumpy / 아담한 체격의 of medium build / 체격이 좋은 well-built

unsatisfactory ; uninteresting ; dull (활발치 못함) ¶ 신통치 않은 용모 plain〔homely〕 feature // 신통치 않게 여기다 think poorly of

신트림 belching up a bit of sour vomit

신틀 a wooden frame for weaving Korean sandals

신파 新派 a new school ; a new-school drama (신파극)

— **배우** an actor of the new school ; a new-school (play) actor — **연극** a new-school play〔drama〕 ; the new drama

신판 新版 a new publication ; a new edition ¶ 신판의 newly-edited〔published〕 최— the newest edition

신편 新編 a new edition

신품 新品 a new article ¶ 신품이나 다름없다 look brand-new ; be only slightly used

신품 성사 神品聖事 〖카톨릭〗 holy orders

신풍 新風 a new phase ¶ 신풍을 불어 넣다 usher in a new phase 《in》

신필 宸筆 the king's autograph

*****신하 臣下** a subject ; a retainer ; a vassal ; a minister

*****신학 神學** theology

—**교** a theological school〔seminary〕 — **박사** a Doctor of Divinity 《D. D.》 —**생** a theological student —**자** theologian **목회(牧會)**〔**평화, 교조**〕 — pastoral〔irenic, dogmatic〕 theology **사변(思辨)**〔**자연, 천계(天啓)**〕 — speculative〔natural, revealed〕 theology

신학기 新學期 a new (school) term ; the new semester

신학문 新學問 modern sciences

신한 宸翰 a royal letter

신해 辛亥 〖민속〗 the 48th year of the sexagenary cycle ; the Year of the Swine

신허 腎虛 〖한의〗 loss of virility ; impotence

신형 新型 a new〔the latest〕 style〔fashion, model〕 ; a novelty

— **자동차** a new model〔style〕 car

†**신호 信號** a signal ; signaling —**하다** signal 《a person to do》 ; make〔give〕 a signal ¶ 신호를 무시하다 disregard a signal // 신호를 무시하고 횡단하다 jaywalk 《미·구》 // 발차의 신호를 하다 give a starting signal ; raise a hand as a signal for starting // 파란 신호가 켜졌다 The signal showed 'Proceed'. // 한 노파가 빨간 신호를 무시하고 건널목을 횡단하려고 했다 An old woman was about to cross the street against a red traffic light. // 신호음이 들리지 않는다 I don't get a dial tone.

—**기(旗)** a signal〔code〕 flag —**기(機)** a signal (apparatus) ; a semaphore ; a railroad signal — **뇌관(雷管)** a signal detonator —**등** a signal lamp〔light〕 ; a blinker (명멸 방향 지시등 따위) ¶ 빨간 신호등마다 다 설 작정이오 Are you going to make all the red lights ? // 복잡한 교차로에서 빨간 신호등을 무시하고 달렸다 I ran a red light at a busy intersection. —**로켓** a signal rocket —**법** signal code —**소** a signal station —**수** a signalman ; a flagman 《미》 ; a signaler — **전파** a (radio) beam —**탑** a signal tower —**포(砲)** a signal gun **경계** — a caution signal **교통** — a traffic signal **기상(氣象)** — a weather signal **농무** — a fog signal **무선** — a wireless signal **수기** — a flag signal(ing) ; 〔군대의〕 semaphore **시각(視覺)** — an optical〔a visible, a visual〕 signal **위험** — a danger signal ; a signal of danger **음향** — an audible signal **자동** — an automatic signal **자동 폐색(自動閉塞)** — 〖철도〗 an automatic block signal **적(赤)**— a red〔danger〕 signal ; a red (traffic) light ; a stoplight **정지** — a signal of "Stop" ; a red light **조난** — a distress signal ; an SOS ¶ 조난 신호를 띄우다 send off an SOS ; signal the distress // 배에서 조난 신호를 보냈다 The ship signaled its distress〔sent an SOS〕. **주의** — a precaution signal ; a signal of "Caution" **진행** — a clear signal ; a signal of "Proceed" **철도** — a railroad signal〔semaphore〕 **출발** — a signal for starting ; a starting signal **"통화중"** — 〖전화〗 a busy〔an engaged 《영》〕 signal **폭풍우** — a storm signal **해상** — a marine〔nautical〕 signal **호출** — a call signal〔sign〕

*****신혼 新婚** a new marriage —**하다** be newly married ; become a newlywed ¶ 신혼의 newly-married ; newly-wedded

— **부부** newly-married〔wedded〕 couple ; newlyweds — **생활** newly-married life ; newlywed life — **여행** a honeymoon ; a wedding trip〔tour, journey〕 ¶ 신혼 여행을 떠나다 go (off) on a honeymoon — **여행자** honeymooners

신화 神化 deification —**하다** deify ; get deified

‡**신화 神話** a myth ; a mythological story ; mythology 《총칭》

—**극** a mythological play — **세계** a mythic(al) world — **시대** the legendary 〔mythological〕 age ; the mythical〔fabulous〕 age ; the age of fables —**학** mythology —**학자** a mythologist **건국** — the birthmyth of a nation **그리스** — Greek mythology

신환자 新患者 a new patient

신효 神效 wonderful efficacy —**하다** (be) wonderfully efficacious

신흥 新興 newly rising ; up-and-coming —**하다** newly rise

—**국** a rising nation — **계급** a newly-risen〔-rising〕 class ; a newly-awakened class — **도시** a boom〔new, mushroom〕 town — **문학** new literature — **부유 계급** the new-rich class — **산업** a rising〔burgeoning〕 industry — **세력** the growing power ; the new emerging forces 《NEFOS》 — 소득층 a new income stratum — 아프리카 제국 the emergent African countries — 재벌 a newly-rising business tycoon — 종교 a newly-risen 〔new〕 religion

신희 新禧 New Year congratulations 〔greetings, good wishes〕

†**싣다** ① [적재하다] load 《a cart with vegetables》 ; take 《passengers》 on board (배가) ; carry ; take in 《passengers》 ¶ 야채를 실은 수레 a wagon loaded with vegetables // 군인들을 실은 열차 a train carrying soldiers // 경관을 실은 자동차 a motor-car bearing policemen // 도중에서 승객을 싣다 pick up passengers // 그 버스는 손님을 너무 많이 실었다 The bus was overloaded. // 그 기선은 천 명의 승객을 실을 수 있다 That steamer can accommodate 1,000 passengers.
② [기재하다] record ; put in ; carry ; publish ¶ 신문에 소설을 싣다 publish 〔print〕 a novel in a newspaper // 잡지에 논설을 싣다 put an article in a magazine // 신문에 광고를 싣다 put〔insert〕 an ad in a paper
③ [물을] water〔store water〕 (in a paddy, reservoir)

†**실** thread (바느질 실) ; yarn (방적사) ; a string ; a line ; twine

> 참고 **thread**는 바느질실·목면·합성 섬유·금속 따위의 실 **yarn**은 자은실이며 직물 따위에 쓰이는 말 **string**은 thread보다는 굵고 cord보다는 가는 끈이며 꾸러미를 묶든가 진주 따위를 꿰는 것 그리고 악기의 현 **line**은 낚시줄 등임 가는 순서대로 나열하면 thread <string <cord <cable 또한 **cord**는 악기의 현 전용의 말

¶ 실 같은 stringy ; threadlike ; linear // 실을 꼬다 twist thread // 실을 감다 reel thread ; spool // 실을 뽑다 take out the stitches (수술 후에) // 실을 잣다 spin yarn〔thread〕 // 바늘에 실을 꿰다 thread a needle // 바늘 귀가 작아서 실이 잘 꿰지지 않는다 The needle-eye is too small to hold the thread.
—바늘 [실을 꿴 바늘] a needle and thread —밥 waste thread ; silk waste —패 a spool ; a reel

실 室 a room ; a chamber ; an apartment ; a compartment (기차의) ¶ 기차의 1등실 the first-class compartment
갱의— a changing room

실 失 [과실] an error ; [불리] disadvantage ; [손실] loss

실 實 the truth〔reality〕 (진실) ; actuality (현실) ; sincerity (성실) ; substance (실질)

실가 實家 the family in which one was born ; one's parents' home ; 〖법〗 one's original house

실가 實價 ① [진가] intrinsic〔true〕 value ; sterling worth ¶ 이것은 500원에 샀지만 실가는 적어도 800원이 된다 I bought this for 500 *won*, but its intrinsic value is at least 800 *won*. ② [가격] actual〔real〕 price ③ [원가] cost price ¶ 실가로 at actual cost ; at cost price

실각 失脚 —하다 lose one's position ; fall ; be overthrown ¶ 실각한 정치가 a knock-out politician

†**실감** 實感 actual feeling〔sensation〕 ; solid sense —하다 feel actually ; realize ; experience ¶ 실감나는 lifelike ; true to nature // 실감이 나다 be true to nature // 실감나게 말하다 say feelingly // 이 그림은 실감이 안 난다 This picture is not true to nature〔realistic enough〕.
— 온도 〖의학〗 an effective temperature

***실감개** a spool ; a reel ; a bobbin

실개천 a streamlet ; a small brook ; a brooklet

실격 失格 disqualification ; elimination ; 〖법〗 incapacity —하다 be disqualified 《for a post, from doing something》 ; be unseated from 《the Diet》 (의원이) ; [경기에서] be eliminated 《from, out of》 ; be put out of the race〔running〕
— 경기자 a suspended player —자 a disqualified person

실경 實景 the actual view〔scene〕 ; nature ¶ 이 그림은 실경을 그린 것이다 This picture is drawn from nature.

실고추 shredded〔threaded〕 red pepper

실골목 a narrow back-street ; an alley

실과 實科 a practical course ¶ 이론을 먼저 공부하고 다음에 실과를 가르칩니다 We teach the theory of the subject first and then its application.

실과 實果 fruit ⇨ 과실(果實)

실국수 thin〔thread-like〕 noodles

실국화 —菊花 a daisy

실군 實軍 a competent worker ; a good hand

실굽 the base of a porcelain dish
— 달이 a porcelain dish with a base attached

실권 失權 [권리] loss of one's rights ; disfranchisement ; [권력] loss of power 〔authority〕 —하다 lose one's rights ; be disfranchised ; lost one's power

실권 實權 real〔actual〕 power ¶ 실권을 쥐다 hold real power // 정치의 실권을 쥐다 assume the helm of the State ; hold the reins of government // 정치의 실권이 군인들 손에 들어갔다 The reins of government passed into the hands of military caste. // 실권자가 누구냐 Who's calling the shots ?

실그러지다, 씰그러지다 get distorted ; get out of shape〔balance〕 ; be pushed out of shape ; wobble

실금 a fine crack ; a thread-like fissure

실긋거리다, 씰긋거리다 shift from side to side ; wobble ; be unsteady〔shaky〕 ¶ 실긋거리는 책상 a shaky desk
실긋실긋 shifting from side to side ; wobbling(ly) ; unsteadily
실기 實技 practical technique〔skill〕; practical〔physical〕 training (체육의)
— 시험 practical (talent) examination ; [운전의] driving test 미술 — 시험 fine arts talent test
실기 失期 missing an appointed time ; failing in one's promise —하다 fail to keep an appointed time ; fail in one's agreement〔promise〕
실기 失機 missing an opportunity —하다 lose the chance ; miss an opportunity ; fail
실기 實記 a true record ; an authentic record〔account〕; a history
한국 동란 — a history of Korean war
실기죽거리다 wobbling a bit ; rather unsteadily
실꾸리 a ball of thread〔yarn〕
실낱 a strand ; a ply ; a single thread ¶ 실낱 같은 목숨 a life hanging by a thread // 실낱 같은 목소리 a feeble voice
*실내 室內 the (interior of a) room ¶ 실내의 indoor // 실내에서 indoors ; in〔inside〕 a room ; within the house ¶ 실내를 장식하다 upholster a room
— 노동자 an indoor worker — 안테나 an indoor antenna — 운동 indoor exercise — 유희 an indoor game〔amusement (오락)〕 —(음)악 chamber music — 음향학 room acoustics — 장식 interior decoration — 체육관 a gymnasium 《*pl.* ~s, -sia》; a gym (구) — 체조 indoor gymnastics — 풀 an indoor swimmng pool〔bath〕
실내복 室內服 a house dress ; [화장복] a dressing gown ; a negligee (여자의)
실내화 室內靴 slippers ; scuffles
실념 失念 a lapse of memory ; oblivion
—하다 forget ; lose the remembrance〔memory〕 of ; [사물이 주어] escape〔slip from〕 one's memory
실농 失農 missing the season for farming
—하다 miss the season for farming
실농군 實農軍 a solid〔steady, worthy〕 farmer
실눈 narrow eyes ¶ 실눈을 뜨고 보다 narrow one's eyes ; look through half-closed eyes
실담 實談 a true story ; an authentic account
실답다 實— (be) sincere ; trustworthy ; faithful
실답지 않다 實— (be) untrustworthy ; unreliable ; untrue ; insincere ; not to be depended upon
실덕 失德 loss of virtue —하다 meet dishonor ; lose one's virtue
실뒤 〖건축〗 the narrow space of ground left behind a house
실떡거리다 prattle ; chatter ; say silly things
실뚱머룩하다 (be) disinclined ; unwilling ; uninterested ; reluctant
실뜨기 cat's-cradle
실락원 失樂園 [밀튼의] Paradise Lost
실랑이질 bothering〔pestering〕《a person》
—하다 bother〔pester〕《a person》
실량 實量 real quantity
*실력 實力 one's (real) ability〔talent〕; [진가] worth ; merit ; [무력] force ; arms ¶ 실력 있는 사람 a man of ability〔worth, merit〕; an able〔a capable, an efficient〕 man // 실력 있는 교사 a competent〔an able〕 teacher // 실력이 있다 be able ; be capable ; be talented // 실력에 호소하다 appeal to arms ; go on a strike // 수학의 실력을 기르다 make oneself proficient in mathematics // 숨은 실력을 보이다 display one's hidden talent // 시험에서 실력을 충분히 발휘하다 do oneself justice in the examination // 학력보다는 실력을 중시한다 I esteem real ability more than academic titles. // 그는 영어 실력이 좋다 He is proficient in English.
—자 an influential person ; a power ; a potentate — 제도〔주의〕 the merit system — 테스트 an achievement test — 행사 use of force 정계 —자 a strong man〔one of the prominent figures〕 in politics ; an influential leader of a political party
실력 實歷 actual experiences ; one's career〔life〕
실련 失戀 a broken heart ⇨ 실연(失戀)
*실례 失禮 rudeness ; impoliteness ; discourtesy ; impudence ; disrespect ; bad manners ; a breach of etiquette ¶ 실례를 저지르다 act rudely ; commit a breach of etiquette // 실례되는 말을 하다 say rude things ; make rude remarks ; use rude language // 실례를 불구하고 …하다 take the liberty of 《doing》; make bold to 《do》 // 좌중에 하품하는 것은 실례다 It is bad manners to yawn in company. // 식사 중에 담배 피우는 것은 실례다 It is against etiquette to smoke at table. // 실례지만 A씨 아니십니까 Excuse me, sir, but are you not Mr. A? // 실례했습니다 I beg your pardon. // 잠깐 실례합니다 Excuse me a moment. // 먼저 실례하겠습니다 Please excuse my leaving earlier. // 이만 실례합니다 I must be going now. /I must say goodbye. /Now I must excuse myself.
*실례 實例 an example ; an instance ; an illustration ¶ 실례를 두서넛 들자면 to give a few examples // 실례를 들다 give an example〔illustration〕
†실로 實— really ; indeed ; in fact ; in truth ; truly ¶ 실로 아름답다 How fine it is! // 이것은 실로 인생의 비극이다 This is

in truth one of life's tragedies.
*실로폰 ⇨ 목금(木琴)
실록 實錄 an authentic〔a true, a faithful〕 record〔history, story, account〕; chronicles
—물 a factual〔true〕 story — 소설 a historical novel 조선 — a true record of the *Chosŏn* Dynasty
실론 Ceylon (지금은 스리랑카 공화국) ¶ 실론의 Ceylonese
—말 Cingalese ; Sin(g)halese — 사람 a Ceylonese ; a Sin(g)halese
*실루엣 a silhouette ¶ 실루엣으로 나타낸 옆모습 a profile in silhouette
실룩거리다, 씰룩거리다 twitch ; quiver ¶ 얼굴〔눈시울〕이 실룩거리다 one's face 〔eyelids〕 twitches
실룩실룩, 씰룩씰룩 with repeated twitching〔jerking, quivering〕; in a jerky way
실리 失利 (a) loss —하다 lose (money) 《over》; suffer a loss
실리 實利 utility ; an actual profit ; material gai〔interest〕; benefit ¶ 실리적 utilitarian ; practical ; pragmatic ; mercenary
— 실익(實益) utility ; usefulness —주의 utilitarianism ; materialism
실리다 ① [기재되다] be printed〔reported〕; be recorded ; be given 《in a dictionary》; be mentioned ; be put 《on the list》 ¶ 기록에 실리다 put 《a matter》 on record // 광고가 실리다 put〔insert〕 an advertisement in 《a paper》 // 신문〔잡지〕에 소설이 실리다 publish a novel in a newspaper〔magazine〕 // 기사가 신문에 실렸다 An account of the incident is reported〔appears, is carried〕 on the newspapers. // 그 단어는 사전에 실려 있다 The word is given 〔found〕 in the dictionary. // 그녀는 앰뷸런스에 실려 갔다 She was taken away in an ambulance.
② [실어서 보냄] get 《a thing》 loaded ; load ¶ 쌀을 짐차에 실리다 load a wagon with rice // 애를 서울행 기차에 실리다 place a child on a train for *Seoul* // 그녀는 앰뷸런스에 실려 갔다 She was taken away in an ambulance.
실리카 『화학』 silica (규토)
실리코운 『화학』 [규소 수지] silicone
실리콘 『화학』 ① [규소] silicon ② [규소 수지] ⇨ 실리코운
실린더 『기계』 a cylinder
⁑실링 [영국의 옛 화폐] a shilling 《*s.*, /》
*실마리 ① [실끝] the end of a thread ② [단서] a beginning ; the first step ; a clue (사건 해결의) ¶ 문제 해결의 실마리 the first step toward the solution of the question // 실마리를 얻다 find a clue // 출세의 실마리가 되다 lead to success in life ; become the first step to one's success in life // 그 비밀은 탐색할 실마리가 없다 The mystery has no clue to it.
⁑실망 失望 disappointment ; discouragement ; despair —하다 be disappointed 《at, in, of》; be discouraged ; be disheartened ; despair ¶ 실망적인 결과 a disappointing result // 실망시키다 disappoint ; dash 《a person's》 hopes ; discourage // 실망하지 말라 Keep your heart up. /Never say die. // 실망의 빛을 띠었다 He looks disappointed. // 우리는 그 소식을 듣고 실망했다 We were disappointed at the news. // 그가 너를 실망시키는 일은 없을 것이다 He will never let you down. // 그 여자는 실망한 나머지 자살하고 말았다 She killed herself out of despair. // 자네가 나를 실망시키지 않을 줄 알기 때문에 위험을 무릅쓰고 결심한 거야 I decided to risk my neck because I know you will not let me down. // 나를 실망시키지 마 Don't let me down.
실머리동이 a kite with a colored paper band across the head
실머슴 實— a hardworking〔diligent〕 farmhand
실명 失名 name unknown ⇨ 무명
—씨 an unknown〔an anonymous, a nameless〕 person ; an unknown
실명 失明 loss of eyesight〔sight〕 —하다 lose one's sight ; become sightless ; become〔go〕 blind ¶ 두 눈 다 실명하다 lose the sight of both eyes
—자 a blind〔sightless〕 person ; the blind 《총칭》
실명 失命 losing one's life —하다 lose one's life
실명 實名 one's real name
실모 實母 one's real mother
실무 實務 practical affairs〔business〕; service ; administrative work ; business practice ¶ 실무의 재능이 있다 have a talent for business ; be possessed of business talent // 실무에 밝다 be experienced〔versed〕 in business/실무에 어둡다 be not familiar with office routine ; be out of touch with the world // 실무를 배우다 train oneself in practical business
—가 a businessman ; a man of business (affairs) — 연수 in-service training —자(급) 회담 working-level talks
실물 失物 loss of goods〔things〕 —하다 lose one's goods〔things〕
실물 實物 the real thing ; an actual〔a natural〕 object ; [진짜] a genuine thing ; the original ¶ 실물의 real ; genuine // 실물대의 사진 a life-size〔full-size〕 photograph // 실물 이상의 크기로 『미술』 on a heroic scale // 이 사진은 실물보다 훌륭하다 This picture is better than the original. // 이 초상은 실물을 그린 것이다 This portrait was painted from life. // 너는 실물이 훨씬 더 잘생겼어 You look much better in real life. // 그 사람 실물은 어떻게 보이든 How did he look in real life? // 나는 실물을 보고 싶었다 I wanted to get a look at the real thing.

— 거래 spot transaction — 경비 expenses in kind — 경제 object-economy — 광고 an object-advertisement — 교수 an object lesson ; object teaching — 묘사 model drawing —세(稅) a tax in kind — 주의 〖미학〗 materialism — 크기 《painting》 actual size ; the size of the original ¶ 실물 크기의 as large as life ; full-size(d) ; life-size(d) // 실물 크기로 확대한 사진 a life-size enlargement of a photograph

실미적지근하다 (be) lukewarm ; tepid

실바람 a light breeze ; a wisp of breeze

실반대 a coil of cocoon silk

실밥 ① [실보무라지] waste (pieces of) thread〔yarn〕 ② [솔기] a seam ¶ 실밥이 터지다 a seam opens〔runs〕

실백 實栢 a pine-nut kernel

실뱀 〖동물〗 a small stringy snake

실뱀 한 마리가 온 바닷물을 흐린다 (속담) One scabbed sheep will mar a whole flock.

실뱀장어 —長魚 an elver ; a small eel

실버들 a (slender) weeping willow

실보무라지 waste (pieces of) thread〔yarn〕

실부 實父 one's real father

실비 實費 [비용] actual expense ; (real) cost ¶ 실비로 팔다 sell 《a thing》 at cost — 제공 service at actual expense — 진료소 a clinic operated at cost ; a "cost" clinic — 판매 cost sale

실사 實査 an actual inspection〔survey〕 ; a working survey ; a survey on the spot —하다 inspect actually ¶ 실사를 거쳐 through an actual inspection

실사 實寫 a real picture ; a picture〔photograph〕 taken from life ; 〖영화〗 an actuality film —하다 take a picture〔photograph〕 on the spot ; film〔make a film of〕 《an event》

실사회 實社會 the actual〔real〕 world ; the everyday〔sober, workaday〕 world ¶ 실사회에 나가다 enter active life ; go out〔launch out〕 into the world ; get a start in life

실산 實算 〖수학〗 practice

실살 實— invisible〔hidden〕 profit ¶ 실살스럽다 have inner〔real〕 substance

실상 實相 real facts 《of a case》 ; actual circumstances ; the actual condition ; the real state of affairs ; reality ¶ 사회의 실상 the true picture of life

실상 實狀 [실제의 사정] actual〔true〕 circumstances〔conditions〕 ; [실제의 상태] the actual〔real〕 state of affairs ; a real situation ¶ 러시아의 실상 the real state of affairs in Russia // 실상을 알다 know the actual circumstances // 실상을 털어놓다 take 《a person》 into one's confidence // 이러한 실상이기 때문에 such being the case

실상 實像 〖물리〗 a real image

실색 失色 changing countenance ; losing color —하다 lose color ; turn pale〔white〕 ; change countenance ¶ 그 소식을 듣고 실색했다 Color left his face when he heard it.

실생활 實生活 real〔actual〕 life ; realities of life

실선 實線 a solid〔full〕 line

실성 失性 —하다 become insane ; go mad ; lose one's mind〔reason, wit〕 ; be out of one's mind〔head〕

실세 失勢 loss of power —하다 lose power〔influence〕

실소 失笑 sudden uncontrollable laughter —하다 burst out laughing ; break〔burst〕 into laughter ¶ 실소를 금치 못하다 cannot help laughing 《at something》 ; cannot repress laughter ; cannot hold one's laughing

실속 實— content ; substance ; material gain〔interest〕 ¶ 실속 없는 겉치레 a mere show without reality // 실속이 있다 be substantial ; be full of matter ; be rich in contents (내용) // 실속 없다 be nominal ; be hollow ; be poor in contents

실속 失速 〖항공〗 a stall —하다 stall

†**실수 失手** ① [실책] a blunder ; a slip ; a mistake ; a bungle ; a miscarriage ; a stumble ; an error ② discourtesy ⇨ 실례(失禮) —하다 commit a blunder ; make a slip〔mistake〕 ¶ 1루수의 실수 the first baseman's error // 어마어마한 실수를 저지르다 make〔commit〕 a grave blunder // 말을 실수하다 make a slip of the tongue // 그런 사람을 믿은 것이 나의 실수였다 I made a mistake in trusting such a man. // 7회말의 실수가 뼈아픈 것이었다 That error in the bottom of the seventh really hurt. // 내가 그렇게까지 말을 했는데도 여전히 실수를 하다니 After all my warning, you still did it wrong. // 그는 처음부터 실수를 했는데 나중에도 만회를 하지 못했다 He tripped up at the beginning and never recovered after that. // 김 선생은 실수없이 거래를 매듭지어 주었다 Mr. *Kim* put together the deal without a hitch.

실수 實收 real〔actual, net〕 income ; one's take-home pay (세금, 보험 따위를 공제한) 《미》 ; the net profits〔proceeds〕 ¶ 실수령액 take-home pay // 10 만원의 실수를 올리다 realize 100,000 *won* 《from》

실수 實數 ① [실제의 수] an actual number ② 〖수학〗 a real number〔quantity〕 ; a multiplicand (피승수)

실수 實需 〖증권〗 actual demand

실수요 實需要 actual consumption ; consumption requirement

실수입 實收入 ⇨ 실수(實收)

†**실습 實習** actual training ; practice 《in》 ; (practical) exercise —하다 practice ; have (practical) training ¶ 공장에서 실습하다 have practical training at a factory

//법관 실습을 하다 serve a practical apprenticeship at the bench
—생 a student apprentice ; an apprentice ; [병원의] an intern — 시간 practice hours 교육 — teaching practice 교육 —생 a student teacher

실시 實施 execution ; operation ; enforcement —하다 put in operation〔force, practice〕; put in effect ; enforce 《a law》; give effect to ; carry into effect ¶ 실시되다 take effect ; come into force 〔operation〕; become effective // 이 계획은 실시되지 않았다 This plan was not carried out. // 그 법률이 실시되었다 The law was put in force. // 이력서를 심사한 후에 면접을 실시할 겁니다 Only after screening the resumes, we will conduct persond interviews.
— 계획〔안〕 an enforcement〔a working〕 plan — 설계도 〖건축〗 the execution drawing

†실신 失神 a swoon ; a faint ; fainting ; a coma —하다 swoon ; faint ; fall into a swoon ; lose consciousness ; fall unconscious〔senseless〕 ¶ 실신한 사람처럼 like a man in a trance // 실신 상태에 있다 be in a swoon〔faint〕 // 피를 보고 실신하다 swoon at the sight of blood // 굶주려서 실신하다 faint with hunger // 놀라서 실신할 뻔하다 be frightened out of one's wits

실실 with a silly snicker〔snigger〕 ¶ 실실 웃다 snicker ; snigger ; giggle

실심 失心 —하다 lose heart ; be dispirited〔disheartened〕

실쌈스럽다 ① [언행이] (be) sincere ; faithful ; reliable ② be always excited 〔hot-headed〕 and noisy

실안개 a thin mist

실액 實額 actual amount of money

실어증 失語症 〖의학〗 aphasia
— 환자 an aphasi(a)c

실언 失言 a slip of the tongue ; an improper remark ; an impropriety in speech ; misstatement ; lapsus linguae 《라》 —하다 make a slip of the tongue ; make an improper remark ; use improper language ¶ 실언을 사과하다 apologize for one's slip of the tongue // 실언을 규탄하다 blame 《a person》 for his improper language // 실언을 취소하다 retract one's misstatement // …라고 말 한 것은 그의 실언이다 He made a mistake in saying 《that》. . .

실업 失業 unemployment —하다 lose one's job〔work, place〕; be thrown out of work ; be fired ; be unemployed ; be at a loose end ¶ 거리를 헤매는 실업자들 out-of-work men mooching about the streets // 실업자를 구제하다 relieve unemployed people // 실업 수당을 받고 있다 be on the dole ; be on (unemployment) relief // 실업시키다 throw 《a person》 out of employment // 실업자가 많다 There is much unemployment. // 실업자가 증가한다 Unemployment increases. // 나는 실업자이다 I'm out of work.
— 노동자 a jobless laborer ; an unemployed worker — 대책 a relief measure for the unemployed ; unemployment policy —률(率) an unemployment rate — 문제 an unemployment problem — 보상 unemployment compensation — 보험 unemployment insurance — 상태 the state of being out of work ; joblessness — 수당 allowance ; unemployment a dole 《영》 —자 an unemployed person ; a jobless person ; a person out of work 〔employment〕; [총칭] the unemployed ; the workless ; the jobless — 조사 an unemployment census ; an investigation of the unemployment situation
계절적 — seasonal unemployment 잠재 — latent unemployment

*실업 實業 industry (생산업) ; business (상업·실무) ¶ 실업에 종사하다 be engaged in business
—가 a businessman ; an industrialist ; a city man 《영》 —계 the industrial〔business〕 world ; business〔industrial〕 circles ¶ 실업계에 들어가다 enter〔go into〕 business — 교육 industrial〔technical〕 education ; vocational education — 전문학교 a technical college — 학교 a vocational〔technical, business〕 school ; a trade school 《미》 대 —가 a captain of industry

실없다 (be) untrustworthy ; unreliable ; insincere ; idle ; vain ; silly ¶ 실없이 nonsensically ; senselessly ; uselessly ; frivolously ; idly // 실없는 소리 idle talk ; silly talk // 그 여자가 하는 말은 모두 실없는 소리다 What she says is all nonsense.

실없쟁이 a silly〔senseless〕 person ; an unreliable〔untrustworthy〕 person

실연 失戀 a disappointed〔an unreturned〕 love ; a disappointment in love ; a broken heart ; [짝사랑] an unrequited〔a oneside〕 love —하다 be crossed〔disappointed〕 in one's love ; have a disappointment in love ; have one's heart broken ¶ 그 여자는 실연했다 She had a disappointment in love 《for a person》. // 그 여자한테 실연당했다 He was disappointed in love for the girl. /His love for the girl was not requited〔returned〕. // 나는 최근에 남자 친구에게 실연을 당해 우울하다 My boyfriend just broke up with we and I feel depressed
—자 a disappointed lover ; a lovelorn person

실연 實演 stage performance ; [공연] an exhibition ; a demonstration ; a live show ; a presentation in the flesh —하다 give a stage performance ; give an exhibition〔a demonstration〕; demonstrate

실오리 a piece of thread〔string〕 ¶ 실오리 같은 희망 a ray〔shadow〕 of hope ; the sole remaining hope // 몸에 실오리 하나 걸치지 않고 without a stitch (shred) of clothing
실온 **室溫** room temperature
실외 **室外** outdoor(s) ¶ 실외에서 outside (of) a room ; outside ; out of doors
†**실용** **實用** practical use ; utility **—하다** put 《a thing》 to practical use ¶ 실용적인 practical ; pragmatic ; serviceable ; utilitarian // 실용 본위의 (intended) for practical use // 실용적인 물건 articles for practical use ; serviceable articles // 실용적이다 be of practical use // 실용성이 없다 have no practical use // 실용과 장식을 겸하다 answer the purpose of both utility and decoration // 그의 별명은 최근에 실용화되었다 His invention has lately been put to practical use.
— 가구 utility furniture **— 단위** a practical unit **—성** practicality ; utility **— 수명** 〚전기〛 working〔service〕 life **— 신안** a utility model **— 영어** practical English **— 주의** utilitarianism ; 〚철학〛 pragmatism **—주의자** a utilitarian **—품** a useful〔utility〕 article ; [필수품] necessaries
실은 **實—** really ; in reality〔fact, truth〕 ; as a matter of fact ; the fact〔truth〕 is... ; to tell the truth ; to speak honestly ; to be frank with you ¶ 실은 이렇다 The truth is this. /I'll tell you what. // 실은 내 잘못이었어 The truth is that I was mistaken.
실의 **失意** disappointment ; despair ; dejection **—하다** be disappointed ; be disheartened ; despair ¶ 실의에 잠긴 사람 a disappointed man ; a person living in obscurity // 깊은 실의 속에 빠져 있다 be at the nadir of one's fortune // 그는 말년을 실의 속에서 지냈다 He spent the evening of his life in obscurity.
실익 **實益** an actual〔a net〕 profit ; practical benefit ; practical use ¶ 실익이 있다 be useful ; be profitable〔lucrative〕 // 취미와 실익을 겸하고 있다 It is useful as well as beautiful. /It is profitable as well as interesting. // 그런 것이 과연 실익이 있을지 의심스럽다 I doubt if such a thing is of any practical use.
실인 **實印** a registered seal ; a legal seal
실인심 **失人心** **—하다** become unpopular ; lose the hearts of the people
실인증 **失認症** 〚의학〛 agnosia
실자 **實子** one's real son
실장 **室長** [부·국의] a section chief ; [연구실의] the head of a laboratory
†**실재** **實在** actual〔real〕 existence ; reality **—하다** exist ¶ 실재의 actual ; real ; existent // 실재하지 않다 be unreal ; be non-existing
—론 〚철학〛 realism ; externalism **—론자** a realist

실적 **實績** actual results ; [업적] accomplishment ; [영업의] business showings ¶ 실적을 올리다 give〔get, attain〕 actual〔satisfactory〕 results ; produce results ; bear fruit ; bring results // 아직 실적이 오르지 않고 있다 The work has not yet born fruit. // 그 조합은 실적을 올리고 있다 The cooperative is a working reality〔making a good showing〕.
— 제도 the merit system
실전 **實戰** actual fight(ing) ; an actual battle ; action ; real warfare ¶ 실전에 참가하다 engage in actual fighting ; see active service ; be in action // 그 군함은 실전에 참가했다 The warship has seen war service. // 그는 몇차례 실전에 참가했다 He has been in several wars.
실점 **失點** a mark obtained by the opponent
실정 **失政** misgovernment ; maladministration ; misrule **—하다** misgovern ; misrule ¶ 거듭하는 실정으로 내각은 부득이 총사직을 했다 The Cabinet was forced to resign in a body owing to a series of maladministration cases.
실정 **實情** actual〔true〕 circumstances ; the real state of things〔affairs〕 ; a real〔an actual〕 condition ; a real situation ¶ 소련의 실정 the real state of affairs in Russia // 실정을 알다 know the actual circumstances // 실정을 토로하다 take 《a person》 into one's confidence // 실정에 어둡다 be out of touch with things as they are // 그는 실정을 말하지 않는다 He keeps me in the dark about〔as to〕 how the matter stands.
실정법 **實定法** 〚법〛 the positive law
실제 **實弟** one's real (younger) brother
†**실제** **實際** [사실] the truth ; a fact ; [이론이 아닌] practice ; [현실] reality ; actuality ; [실정] an actual condition ¶ 실제의 real ; true ; actual ; concrete (구체적인) ; practical ; effective // 실제의 가치 real〔actual〕 value // 이론과 실제 theory and practice // 실제의 이야기 a true story // 실제로는 행해질 수 없는 제안 impracticable suggestion // 실제로 있었던 일 an actual occurrence // 실제적인 지식이 있다 have a practical〔working〕 knowledge 《of English》 // 실제로 응용하다 put a theory in practice
—가 a practical man **— 경험** practical〔actual〕 experience ; practical knowledge **— 교육** practical instruction **— 문제** a practical question **— 생활** a practical life **— 소득** a real income **— 조사** an actual〔on-the-spot〕 survey ; the field work〔firsthand〕 investigation 《of social conditions》
실조 **失調** (a) malfunction ; disharmony
영양 — malnutrition ; malnourishment
실족 **失足** missing one's foot〔step〕 **—하다** miss one's foot〔step〕 ; lose one's

footing ; make a false step ; slip ; trip ¶ 계단에서 실족하다 miss one's footing on the stairs // 실족하면 목숨을 잃을 판이었다 One misstep meant certain death.

실존 實存 existence
—주의 existentialism —주의자 an existentialist — 철학 existential philosophy

실종 失踪 disappearance ; missing ; abscondence —하다 disappear 《from one's home》; abscond ; be missing ¶ A 씨의 실종 사건 the disappearance of Mr A // 돈을 가지고 실종하다 abscond with the money // 그는 지난달부터 실종중이다 He has been missing since last month.
—계 a report of disappearance — 선고 adjudication of disappearance —자 a missing person ; an absconder

실주 實株 a real stock ; a spot share

실증 實證 an actual proof —하다 prove ; demonstrate ; verify ; establish by evidence ; substantiate ¶ 실증적 positive // 실증을 잡다〔들다〕 hold〔give〕 the actual proof of ; have the goods on 《a person》 《미》
—주의 positivism —주의자 a positivist — 철학 positive philosophy

실지 失地 a lost territory ¶ 실지를 회복하다 recover lost territory

†**실지 實地** practice ; actuality ; reality ¶ 실지로 in practice ; practically ; actually // 실지로 행하다 carry 《a theory》 into practice ; practice 《a theory》 // 실지로 탐험하다 explore personally // 저는 실지로 경험한 바를 말씀드리는 것입니다 I speak from experience. // 그는 장사의 실지 경험이 부족하다 He lacks practical experience in business. // 상상과 실지와는 딴판이었다 I found the reality quite different from what I had imagined.
— 검사(檢査) personal inspection ; 《take》 a firsthand look — 검증 an inspection on the scene ; an on-the-spot inspection〔investigation〕 — 견학 firsthand study — 견학 여행 a field trip — 경험 practical〔actual〕 experience — 관찰 actual observation — 답사 an actual survey — 시험 a practical test — 연구 a field study 《of modern war》 — 연습 practical exercises ; practice — 응용 (practical) application — 조사 an actual〔on-the-spot〕 survey

실지렁이 〖동물〗 a tubificid

‡**실직 失職** unemployment —하다 lose one's employment〔job, place〕; be out of work
—자 a jobless person ; the unemployed

‡**실질 實質** substance (물질) ; essence (본질) ; quality (성질) ; contents (내용) ; worth (진가) ¶ 실질적 substantial ; essential ; material // 실질상 in quality ; in substance〔essence〕; substantially // 실질적 원조 substantial aid // 실질적 차이 material difference // 외관보다는 실질을 택하라 In all things you must prefer substance to appearance〔shadow〕. // 실질에 있어서는 큰 차이가 없다 They are little different in essence.
— 임금 real〔substantial〕 wages

실쭉 —하다 ① [물건의 꼴이] (be) distorted ; misshapen ¶ 공이 실쭉하다 The ball is out of shape.
② [얼굴이] look sullen ; (be) sulky ; be in the sulks〔pouts〕 ¶ 실쭉해서 말도 않다 keep a sulky silence // 조금만 꾸짖어도 실쭉해진다 He gets sulky at the slightest scolding.

실쭉거리다 [모양이] move in a misshapen way ; [얼굴이] pout ; sulk

실쭉실쭉 [물건의 모양이] distorting ; distorted ; [얼굴이] sullen ; sulky ⇨ 실쭉하다

실책 失策 a faulty policy ; an error ; a mistake ; a slip ; a blunder ¶ 실책을 저지르다 make a mistake ; commit a blunder ; fall into an error // 그 훌륭한 아내와 이혼한 것은 그의 일생의 대실책이었다 He committed the greatest imprudence〔folly〕 in his life in divorcing his wise wife.

실천 實踐 practice —하다 practice ; put 《a theory》 in practice ; live up to action ; reduce 《a doctrine》 to practice ; translate 《a theory》 into action〔practice〕 ¶ 실천적인 practical // 실천적으로 practically // 실천 궁행하다 act up to one's principles ; live up to one's faith〔profession〕 // 그 교훈을 실천하라 Carry those precepts into practice. // 그는 단지 종교를 설교하는 것 뿐만 아니라 스스로 실천한다 He does not merely preach religion but lives it as well. // 과거에 한번도 새해 결심을 실천한 적이 없었어 I have never lived up to my New Year's resolutions in the past.
— 도덕〔이성, 철학〕 practical morality〔reason, philosophy〕 — 윤리(학) practical ethics —주의 activism

실첩 a sewing basket (for thread and bits of cloth) made of paper

‡**실체 實體** 〖철학〗 substance ; subject ; noumenon ; entity ; essence ¶ 실체가 없는 inessential 《figure》; unsubstantial ; incorporeal // 실체화 하다 substantiate
—경(鏡) a stereoscope — 관측 〖토목〗 stereoscopic measurement —론 substantialism ; ontology ; noumenalism —론자 a noumenalist ; a substantialist —법 a substantial law ; the substantive law — 사진 a stereoscopic photograph —설(說) the substantiality theory ; substantialism —성 substantiality — 촬영 〖토목〗 stereophotographing —화(畫) a stereograph —화(化) substantialization

실총 失寵 the loss of (royal) favor —하다 lose (royal) favor

실추 失墜 loss ; fall —하다 lose ; fall ;

forfeit ; sink ¶ 권력의 실추 one's fall from power // 신용을 실추하다 lose one's credit ; sink in people's estimation
실측 實測 survey ; actual measurement **—하다** survey ; make a survey of 《a forest》 ; measure ¶ 실측 위치 the position by observation〔actual measurement〕 // 산림을 실측하다 survey a forest
—도 an ordnance map **— 효율** 〖전기〗 efficience by input-output test
실컷 to one's heart's content ; to one's satisfaction ; heartily ; to the top of one's bent ; as much as one likes〔wishes〕 ; to the full ; to the fullest measure ; to the utmost ; to the hilt ¶ 실컷 울다 cry 〔weep〕 one's fill ; have good cry ; have one's cry out // 실컷 웃다 laugh heartily ; have a good hearty laugh ; laugh one's head off // 실컷 먹다 eat one's fill // 실컷 마시게 하다 let 《a person》 drink his fill // 인생을 실컷 즐기다 enjoy life to the full // 실컷 먹었습니다 I have done ample justice to the meal.
실켜다 reel off silk threads
실크햇 a silk hat ; a top〔high〕 hat ; a stovepipe hat 《미·구》 ; a chimney-pot hat 《영·구》
실큼하다 be somewhat disliked〔disinclined〕 《to do》 ; rather unpleasant 〔unpleasing〕
실탄 實彈 [소총의] a ball〔live, loaded〕 cartridge ; [대포의] shell ; a loaded shell ; a live shell ; a solid〔round〕 shot **— 사격** ball firing (소총의) ; target practice with live shells (대포의)
실태 失態 ① [실책] a blunder ; indiscretion ; a fault ; an error ¶ 실태를 부리다 commit a blunder ; disgrace oneself ② [창피] (a) disgrace ; (an) ignominy
실태 實態 the actual condition〔state〕 ; the realities
— 조사 research on the actual condition **— 조사 위원회** a fact-finding committee
실터 the narrow empty area between two houses
실테 a skein of thread
실토 實吐 a true confession ; telling the whole truth ; speaking with sincerity **—하다** confess ; spit out the truth ; tell the whole truth ; disclose one's real intention ¶ 실토하게 하다 get the truth out of 《a person》
실톱 〖기계〗 a fret saw ; a jigsaw 《미》
실톳 a spool(ful) of thread
실퇴 〖건축〗 a narrow veranda(h)
실투 失投 〖야구〗 a careless pitch〔throw〕 **—하다** deliver〔throw〕 a ball carelessly ; make a careless pitch
실파 a small green onion
실팍지다 (be) substantial ; massive ; stout ; sturdy ; stalwart ¶ 실팍지게 생긴 사내 a man of sturdy physique〔substantial built〕 ; a strongly built man // 실팍지게 지은 집 a solidly built house
실팍하다 ⇨ 실팍지다
실패 a spool ; a bobbin ¶ 실패에 실을 감다 wind thread on a spool
†**실패 失敗** a failure ; a blunder ; miscarriage ; a reverse ; a fiasco ; a miss ; an error ; a mistake **—하다** fail ; end in a failure ; go wrong ; be unsuccessful ; fall through ; miscarry ; come a cropper (크게) ¶ 사업에 실패하다 fail in one's business // 역사 시험에 실패하다 fail in a history examination ; flunk in a history exam 《미·속》 // 실패로 끝나다 end in a failure〔fiasco〕 // 계획이 실패하다 one's plan fails〔goes wrong〕 ; [사람이 주어] fail in one's attempt ; be balked〔frustrated〕 in one's plan // 사사 건건 실패하다 fail at every step ; everything goes wrong with 《one》 // 실패하고서 비로소 깨닫다 learn a lesson by failure // 그는 결혼에 실패했다 His marriage was a failure. // 그 계획은 실패하기 마련이다 The scheme is doomed to failure. // 실패는 성공의 어머니이다 Failure is but the threshold of〔a stepping stone to〕 success. /Failure teaches success.
—자 a failure ; a social failure (낙오자) **대—** a glaring〔complete〕 failure ; a fiasco 《*pl.* ~(e)s》
실패작 失敗作 [솜씨] bad make〔workmanship〕 ; poor work〔execution〕 ; [제품·작품] a failure ; a poorly-made article
실하다¹ 實— [깨를] soak (sesame seeds) to remove the skins
실하다² 實— ① [건강] (be) healthy ; strong ; robust ; strongly-built
② [내용이] (be) full ; substantial ; rich in content ; solid
③ [풍유] (be) wealthy ; well-to-do ; solid ¶ 장사 밑천이 실하다 have enough business funds
④ [믿을 만하다] (be) trustworthy ; reliable ; solid ; substantial ¶ 실한 친구 a stanch〔solid〕 friend
실학 實學 practical science ; realism
—주의자 a realist **—파** a positive school
실함 失陷 a fall ⇨ 함락
실행 失行 a misdeed ; misconduct ; an immoral〔a wrong〕 act **—하다** misbehave (oneself) ; act immorally
†**실행 實行** [이행] fulfilment ; [실시] execution ; operation ; [실천] practice ; deed ; action ; [수행] execution ; performance **—하다** fulfil ; execute ; practice ; act ; carry out ; live up to ; put into operation〔effect, practice〕 ¶ 실행할 수 있는 practicable ; workable ; feasible // 실행 불가능한 impracticable ; infeasible // 계약을 실행하다 execute a contract // 계획을 실행하다 carry out a plan // 의논은 그만두고 실행할 때가 왔다 It's time to leave talking begin doing. // 그는 말뿐이지 실행이 없는 친구다 He is a man of

words, and not of deeds. / He is all talk and no action. // 그대가 주장하는 바를 언제나 실행하라 Always practice what you preach. // 우리의 계획은 실행에 옮겨지지 않았다 Our plans did not materialize. // 실행상 practically ; in practice // 실행상의 practical ; executive
—가 a man of deeds〔action〕; practical minds — 기관 an executive organ —난(難) impracticability ; infeasibility —력 power of execution ; executive ability 〔faculty〕 ¶ 실행력이 있다 have executive talent // 실행력이 있는 사람 a person of action — 예산 the working budget — 위원 an executive committee

†실험 實驗 [개개의] an experiment ; a test ; [실험을 하는 일] experimentation —하다 experiment 《on》; make〔conduct〕 an experiment 《on, with》 ¶ 실험적 experimental // 실험적으로 experimentally ; as an experiment // 과학상〔교육상〕 실험 a scientific〔an educational〕 experiment // 핵실험의 금지 a ban on nuclear test // 실험 단계에 있다 be in the experimental stage // 동물 실험을 하다 experiment on animals // 화학 실험을 하다 make〔carry out〕 an experiment in chemistry ; make a chemical experiment — 과학 an empirical science — 극장 an experimental theater — 농장 an experimental farm — 단계 the mock-up stage —대 a testing bench —론 〖철학〗 positivism — 물리학 experimental physics —소 an experimental station ; a laboratory — 소설 an experimental romance —식(式) an empirical formula 《*pl.* ~s, -lae》 —실 a laboratory — 심리학 experimental psychology — 자료 [비유적] a guinea pig ; a laboratory rabbit —장〔지역〕 [신무기 등의] a testing ground〔area〕 —주의 〖철학〗 experimentalism ¶ 실험주의자 an experimentalist — 철학 empirical philosophy 핵— a nuclear (explosion) test

실험 대학 實驗大學 (a college for) a pilot program of higher education

†실현 實現 realization ; materialization ; actualization ; fruition ; attainment —하다 realize 《one's ideal》; actualize ; materialize ; bring to fruition〔realization〕; come true (희망 따위가) ¶ 실현할 수 있는 realizable ; possible of realization // 실현되다 be realized ; be materialized ; come to pass ; become a reality // 다년간의 꿈을 실현하다 make a dream of many years an actuality〔a reality〕 // 그의 꿈이 실현됐다 His dream has come true.

실형 實兄 one's own elder brother

실형 實刑 actual punishment ; imprisonment

실화 失火 an accidental fire —하다 start a fire accidentally ; take fire by accident ; have a (accidental) fire ¶ 실화의 원인 the origin〔cause〕 of an accidental fire // 실화가 아니라 방화였다 The fire was not accidental, but incendiary. // 화재 원인은 실화였다 The fire was of accidental origin.

실화 實話 a true story ; an authentic account
— 기사 fact articles 《of a magazine》 범죄 — a factual account of crime

실황 實況 the real〔actual〕 condition ; the actual state of things ; the actual scene ¶ 실황을 시찰하다 inspect the real condition // 지금부터 행진 실황을 방송해 드리겠습니다 I am now going to bring you a word picture of the parade.
— 방송 broadcasting on the spot ; minute-to-minute broadcasting ; a running commentary — 방송자 a play-by-play announcer ; an on-the-scene commentator ; a commentator

실효 失效 a lapse ; losing effect ; abatement ; becoming null and void ; invalidation —하다 lapse ; lose effect ; become null and void ¶ 조약의 실효 the lapsing of a treaty

실효 實效 effectiveness ; [약의] efficacy ; efficiency (능률) ¶ 실효가 있다 be effective ; be efficacious
— 가격 an effective price —성 effectiveness —치 virtual〔effective〕 value

싫건좋건 whether one will〔like it〕 or not ¶ 싫건좋건 가야 한다 I have no choice but to go. /I have to go whether I like it or not.

‡싫다 ① [사물이 주어] (be) disagreeable ; unpleasant ; hateful ; disgusting ; repulsive ; loathsome ; detestable ; offensive ② [사람이 주어] do not like ; dislike ; be unwilling 《to do》; hate ; be loath 〔reluctant〕 《to do》 ¶ 싫은 일 a distasteful〔an unpleasant〕 work ; an irksome 〔ungrateful〕 business // (보기) 싫은 녀석 a disgusting〔disagreeable〕 fellow // 싫어지다 be disgusted 《with》; be sick 《of》; be weary〔tired〕 《of》 // 싫은 기색을 하다 look displeased // 이런 책은 싫다 I don't like this sort of book. // 나는 뱀이 싫다 I have a strong dislike for snakes. /I hate snakes. // 세상이 싫어진다 I grow sick of the world〔life〕. // 그 사람이 싫어졌다 I've grown tired of him. /I've grown out of love with him. // 나는 도시에서 살기가 싫다 I do not like living in the city. // 그 녀석 보기도 싫다 I hate the very sight of him. /The very sight of him makes me sick〔is quite disgusting〕. // 너는 보기 싫다 You make me sick. // 싫으면 그만두어라 You need not do so if you don't want to. // 그렇게 하는 것이 나는 싫다 It goes against me to do it. // 나는 그를 도와 주기 싫다 I am reluctant to help him. /I hate to help him. // 그의 거동이 어쩐지 싫다 His manners are abhorrent to our feelings. // 거저 주어도 싫다 I would not

have it even as a gift. ∥당신은 나를 만나는 것이 싫어졌지요 You have lost interest in me, I suppose? ∥그 날은 사람 만나기가 싫었다 I was in no mood to see any caller that day.

‡싫어하다 dislike; have a dislike to〔for〕; hate; abhor; detest; grudge《doing》; be loath《to do》; be unwilling; be reluctant《to do》

> 참고 **hate** 일반적으로 몹시 싫어하여 적의라든가 해치고자 하는 마음이 포함되어 있다 **detest** 마음 속으로부터 싫어하여 때로는 경멸의 기분이 포함되어 있다 **abhor** 몸서리 나도록 싫어하다 **loathe** 메스꺼우리만큼 싫어하다

¶ 교제를 싫어하다 shun society∥그 결혼을 싫어하다 frown upon the match∥싫어하지 않고 일하다 work without grudge∥그는 싫어하는 것 같았다 He seemed unwilling. ∥그는 어디에 가나 사람들이 싫어한다 He makes himself disagreeable wherever he is. ∥싫어하는 딸을 억지로 시집보냈다 They married off his daughter against her will. ∥투수들이 그를 싫어하는 거나 아닌지 I wonder if the pitchers have it in for him.

†싫증 ―症 dislike; disgust; repulsion; aversion; repugnance ¶ 싫증이 나다 be tired of; get sick of; be fed up with; be bored with; feel a repugnance to∥그는 일에 싫증이 났다 He grew tired〔sick〕 of his work. /He was fed up with the work. ∥나는 그 일에 싫증이 나기 시작했다 I was about tired of that business. ∥그 여자에게 싫증이 났다 He has fallen out of love with his girl. ∥그 남자의 촌스러운 데에 싫증이 났다 She was repelled by his rustic manners.

심 [심줄] sinew; tendon

심 心 ① [마음] mind; heart; feeling; emotion ¶ 심적 mental; psychological∥애국심 patriotism ② [핵심] the core (과실의); the heart (목재의) ¶ 심까지 썩다 be rotten to the core ③ [심지] a wick ④ [연필의] lead ⑤ [옷의] a pad; padding ¶ 심을 넣다 pad《a sash》 ⑥ [줄기] a string ⑦ [새알심] a dumpling

심 審 a trial; a hearing ¶ 제 1심에서 at the first trial

심각 深刻 seriousness; gravity; acuteness; poignancy **―하다** (be) serious; grave; keen; acute; poignant ¶ 심각한 인생 문제 a serious〔deep, profound〕 problem of life∥심각해지다 worsen; become intensified〔aggravated, acute〕; [문제·정세가] assume serious aspect〔an acute phase〕; become more critical〔urgent, strained〕∥생활난이 점점 심각해진다 The difficulty of living is felt more and more keenly. ∥그의 작품은 어딘가 심각한 데가 있다 His novels are somehow incisive. /His novels are characterized by unsparing sincerity. ∥쟁의가 점점 심각해가고 있다 The dispute threatens to be aggravated.

―화 intensification; aggravation

심간 心肝 the heart (and liver)

심검 審檢 ⇨ 심사(審査)

심경 心境 a state〔frame〕 of mind; a mind; a mental state ¶ 심경의 변화 a change of mind; a change in one's mental attitude∥심경을 피력하다 open〔speak〕 one's mind∥그것이 지금 나의 심경이다 That is how I feel now.

― 소설 a psychological novel

심경 深更 the dead of night; midnight

심경 深耕 deep plowing **―하다** plow deep

심계 항진 心悸亢進 〖의학〗 palpitation (of the heart)

심고 a bowstring loop

심규 深閨 women's apartments〔quarters〕; boudoir (프)

심근 心筋 〖해부〗 the heart muscle; a myocardium《*pl.* -dia》

― 경색 myocardial infarction **―염** myocarditis **― 운동도(圖)** a myocardiogram

심금 心琴 heartstrings; the deepest emotions

심금을 울리다 관용 touch a string in《a person's》 heart

심기 心氣 the mind; mood; sentiment ¶ 심기 전환 the diversion of one's mind

심기 心機 the mind; a mental attitude ¶ 심기 일전(一轉)하다 one's mind takes a new turn; [사람이 주어] change one's mind; turn over a new leaf

심기다 ① [심어지다] get〔be〕 planted ② [심게 하다] have《a person》 plant; cause to plant

심난 甚難 extreme difficulty **―하다** (be) extremely difficult

심낭 心囊 〖해부〗 the pericardium

심내막 心內膜 〖해부〗 an endocardium《*pl.* -dia》

―염 endocarditis

심뇌 心惱 anguish《of heart》; sufferings; mental affliction

†심다 plant《a tree》; set《a plant》; sow (씨를) ¶ 정원에 나무를 심다 plant trees in a garden; plant a garden with trees

심대 甚大 ―하다 (be) very great; enormous; immense; tremendous; heavy; serious ¶ 그들은 심대한 피해를 입었다 They suffered heavy damage. / Serious harm was done to the district.

심떠깨 ⇨ 쇠심떠깨

심덕 心德 virtue; uprightness of heart ¶ 심덕이 좋은 사람 a man of virtue; a kind-hearted man

심도 深度 depth ¶ 심도를 재다 measure the depth; sound (the sea); fathom

―계 a sea gauge; a deep sea indicator

위험〔안전 잠항〕 — a critical〔safe submarine〕 depth

심돋우개 a wick-raiser ; a wick control

심드렁하다 linger (on) ; hang (on) ; drag (on) ¶ 심드렁한 신병 a protracted〔lingering〕 disease ; a long illness // 교섭이 심드렁하다 The negotiations dragged on〔along〕.

심란 心亂 disturbance〔confusion〕 of mind —하다 be disturbed in mind ; get confused in mind ¶ 심란한 하룻밤을 지내다 pass the night in anxiety // 심란한 마음을 가라앉히다 compose oneself ; gather one's scattered wits

심려 心慮 worry ; care ; anxiety ; concerns —하다 fear ; apprehend ¶ 심려를 끼치다 give 《a person》 occasion to feel anxiety ; give 《a person》 a trouble // 여러 가지로 심려를 끼쳐 죄송합니다 I am sorry to have occasioned you so much anxiety.

심력 心力 mental power〔faculty〕

심령 心靈 the spirit ; the soul ¶ 심령의 spiritual ; spiritualistic
—계 the spiritual world —술 [강신술(降神術)] spiritualism — 연구 psychical research ; psychicism —학 psychics ; spiritism —학자 a psychicist — 현상 a spiritual〔psychic〕 phenomenon

심로 心勞 cares ; anxieties ; worries ; strain —하다 be worried ; suffer from a nervous strain ¶ 심로의 빛 a care-worn look ; concerned〔worried〕 air

심록 深綠 dark〔deep〕 green

†심리 心理 a mental state ; mentality ; the mind ; psychology ¶ 한국인의 심리를 이해하다 understand Korean mentality〔psychology〕 // 그의 심리를 모르겠다 I have no idea of his real state of mind. /I cannot understand his psychology. // 그녀는 남편의 심리를 잘 알고 있었다 She knew her husband's psychology.
—극 [정신 요법] psychodrama — 묘사 (a) psychological description — 상태 a mental state ; mentality ; psychology —설 psychologism — 소설 a psychological novel — 요법 psychotherapy — 작용 psychosis ; mental process — 작전 psychological tactics — 전쟁 psychological warfare —주의 psychologism ; mentalism — 테스트 a psychological test — 현상 a psychological phenomenon

*심리 審理 trial ; examination ; inquiry ; [형사 사건의] hearing —하다 try 《a case》 ; examine ; inquire into 《a case》 ; handle ¶ 심리를 받다 be tried at the bar // 심리에 부치다 place 《a person》 on trial ; try 《a person》 // 심리 중이다 The case is pending 《in the court》. /The case is on trial.
—서 a document of trial 재— (a) retrial ; (a) rehearing ; reexamination ; 〖법〗 a review

‡심리학 心理學 psychology ; mental psychology〔science〕 ¶ 심리학상(으로) psychological(ly)
—자 a psychologist 교육 — educational〔pedagogical〕 psychology 군중 — mass〔mob〕 psychology 게시탈트 — Gestalt psychology 기술 — psychography 동물 — animal psychology 물리 — physical psychology 민족〔종족, 인종, 사회〕 — folk〔race, ethnical, social〕 psychology 발달 — development psychology 범죄 — criminal psychology 산업 — industrial psychology 실험 — experimental psychology 심층 — depth psychology 이상〔사회〕 — abnormal〔social〕 psychology 아동 — child psychology 일반〔변태, 비교, 문화, 응용, 고등〕 — general〔abnormal, comparative, cultural, applied, advanced〕 psychology 임상(臨床) — clinical psychology 행동 — behavioristic psychology 형태 — Gestalt psychology ; form psychology ; psychology of figure

심마니 ginseng-diggers

심메 going to dig wild ginseng
심메 보다 〔관용〕 pick〔find〕 a ginseng in the mountains

†심문 審問 a trial ; a hearing ; an examination ; an inquiry ; an inquest —하다 hear 《a case》 ; examine ; try ¶ 이 사건의 심문 the hearing of the case // 심문을 받다 be given a hearing ; be examined ; be tried // 수회 사건의 심문이 10일에 열린다 The hearing of the bribery case will be held on the 10th.

심미 審美 appreciation of the beautiful ¶ 심미적 aesthetic // 심미적 견지 aesthetic point of view
—가 an aesthete —안 an eye for the beautiful ; an aesthetic sense ; an aesthetic appreciation ; aesthetic discernment —주의 aestheticism —파 an aesthetic school —학 aesthetics

심박동 心搏動 〖의학〗 a heart beat
—수 heart rate

심방 〖건축〗 the cross beam of a roofed gate

심방 心房 〖해부〗 an atrium 《*pl.* -ia》

심방 尋訪 a visit ; a call —하다 visit ; make a call

*심벌즈 [악기] cymbals
— 연주자 a cymbalist

심병 心病 ① [근심] anxiety ; worry ② [졸도] syncope ; a fainting fit

심보 disposition ; nature ; mind ¶ 심보가 고약한 사람 an ill-natured man // 심보가 비뚤어지다 have a crooked〔wicked〕 mind

심복 心服 admiration and devotion ; honest〔hearty〕 submission〔obedience〕 —하다 be implicitly obedient ; be devoted ; serve faithfully ¶ 심복받고 있다 enjoy the esteem of ; win the admiration and devotion of // 학생들은 교장에게 심복

하고 있다 The students are devoted to their principal.

*심복 心腹 ① [가슴과 배] the heart and the stomach ② [긴요한 것] the indispensable ③ [믿는 사람] one's confidant ¶ 심복지인 a bosom friend // 심복 부하 a devoted retainer ; a confidential follower

심볼 a symbol ; an emblem ¶ 청춘의 심볼 a symbol of youth // 올리브 가지는 평화의 심볼이다 The olive branch is symbolic of peace.

—리즘 symbolism

‡심부름 an errand ; a message —하다 go on an errand for 《a person》 ; run 〔do〕 errands for 《a person》 ; take a message // 심부름 보내다 send 《a person》 on an errand〔a message〕 // 그는 나의 심부름을 갔다 He has gone on an errand for me. // 심부름 좀 해다오 Can you do a little errand for me ? // 댁의 따님을 심부름 좀 보낼 수 있습니까 Can your daughter do a little errand for me ?

—군 an errand boy ; a messenger ; [편지 등의] the bearer ; [특허 밀사] an emissary ; [신(神)의 사자] a familiar spirit ; a familiar ; a servant ¶ 심부름꾼 편에 편지를 보내다 send a letter 《to the office》 by messenger〔hand〕 // 심부름꾼 편에 답장을 주십시오 Send back word by the bearer.

심부전 心不全 〖의학〗 cardiac insufficiency ; heart failure

심사 心事 the thoughts of the heart ; cares ; concerns ¶ 심사가 복잡하다 be disturbed〔confused〕 in mind

심사 心思 ill nature ; cross temper ; malice ; perverseness ; cantankerousness ; crabbedness ¶ 비열한 심사 a mean spirit〔motive〕 // 심사가 나다 get cross ; bear malice // 심사가 나서 험담하다 disparage 《a person》 out of spite

심사가 사납다 관용 be malicious ; ill-natured ; ill-tempered ; crooked ; spiteful

심사 부리다 관용 do 《a person》 something mean ; treat 《a person》 unfair ; disturb another's pleasure》 ; frustrate ; get in the way

심사 審査 judgment ; examination ; inspection ; investigation ; screening 《미》 —하다 judge ; examine ; investigate ; screen ; inspect ¶ 심사에 합격하다 be accepted ; pass inspection ; be found eligible // 심사중이다 be under examination // 심사의 결과를 보고하다 report on one's finding // 이력서를 심하한 후에 면접을 실시할 겁니다 Only after screening the resumes, we will conduct personal interviews.

—관 a judge ; an examiner ; a juror ; a jury 《총칭》 —부 the inspection department (전매청 따위의) ; the examination division (교통·상공 따위의) —(위)원 a judge ; an examiner ; [콩쿠르의] a juror — 위원장 the foreman of a jury ; the president of the board of examiners ; the chairman of the screening〔awarding〕 committee — 위원회 a judging committee — 제도 the screening system ; the review system 재— (a) reexamination ; 〖법〗 a review

심사 深謝 hearty〔sincere, cordial〕 thanks ; deep gratitude —하다 thank 《a person》 heartily ; express one's sincere gratitude

†심사 숙고 深思熟考 meditation ; contemplation ; deliberation ; deep thought —하다 meditate 《on》 ; contemplate ; consider 《a matter》 carefully ; ponder 《on, over》 ; give a deep thought ¶ 심사 숙고하는 deep-thinking ; thoughtful ; prudent // 심사 숙고한 끝에 after careful consideration

심산 心算 intention ; purpose ; calculation ; a design ¶ …할 심산으로 with the intention of ; with a view to 《doing》 // …할 심산이다 intend ; have the intention of 《doing》 ; think of 《doing》 ; mean // 아들을 군인을 만들 심산이다 design one's son to be a soldier // 어떻게 할 심산이냐 What do you intend to do ? // 그렇게 할 심산입니다 I intend to do so. /I am thinking of doing so. // 케이크는 파티에 쓸 심산이었다 The cake was intended for the party. // 그 이야기로 너를 불안하게 만들 심산이었다 The story was calculated to keep you in suspense. // 그 말로 그의 감정을 상하게 할 심산이었다 That remark was calculated to hurt his feelings.

심산 深山 a high mountain ; mountain recesses ; remote mountains

— 유곡 high mountains and secluded valleys ; steep mountains and dark valleys

심살내리다 have something to worry about all the time

심상 心像 〖심리〗 an image ; a mental image

심상 尋常 —하다 (be) ordinary ; common ; usual ¶ 심상치 않다 be uncommon ; be unusual ; be extraordinary ; [병세·사태가] be serious ; be critical // 그의 병세가 심상치 않다 His illness has taken a serious turn (for the worse). // 사태가 심상치 않다 The affair has taken on a bad〔an ugly〕 look. // 그는 어딘가 심상치 않은 데가 있다 He has something out of the common in him. // 하늘이 어째 심상치 않다 한차례 비가 올 것 같은 모양새다 The sky has become threatening. I'd say we're in for a shower.

*심성 心性 nature ; disposition ; mind ; mentality

심성암 深成岩 〖지질〗 plutonic〔abyssal〕 rocks

*심술 心術 cross temper ; ill nature ; per-

verseness ; cantankerousness ; crabbedness ¶ 심술궂다 be ill-tempered ; be cross ; be bad-tempered ; be mean // 심술스럽다 be screwy ; be somewhat ill-natured // 심술부리지 말고 어서 비켜라 Don't be so cross, but get out of the way.

—꾸러기 an ill-natured person ; a cross-grained person ; a crosspatch (여자·어린이) —패기 a cross child ; a perverse youngster ; a crosspatch ; a naughty boy

심술내다 관용 get〔become, grow〕 cross 〔perverse〕 ; behave perversely

심술부리다 관용 be cross with 《a person》 ; be unkind to 《a person》

심신 心身 body and mind〔soul〕 ; body and spirit ¶ 심신의 건강 both physical and mental health // 심신의 피로〔휴양〕 mental and physical exhaustion〔rest〕 // 심신 공히 건전하다 be sound in mind and body ; be sound physically and mentally // 심신을 바치다 give oneself body and soul to 《one's work》 ; devote oneself entirely 《to a cause》 // 청년의 심신을 단련하다 train both bodies and spirits of the young

—증(症) 〖의학〗 a psychosomatic disorder —증 환자 a psychosomatic (patient)

심신 心神 mind ; mentality ¶ 심신 상실 상태에 있다 〖법〗 *be non compos* (*mentis*) 《라》 ; be not of sound mind

심실 心室 〖해부〗 the ventricles of the heart ¶ 우〔좌〕 심실 the right〔left〕 ventricle

심심 深甚 —하다 (be) deep and profound ¶ 심심한 사의를 표하다 [감사] express〔extend〕 one's deepest gratitude〔thanks〕 《to》 ; [사과] offer one's sincerest〔deepest〕 apologies ; apologize most humbly

심심소일 —消日 killing time

심심파적 —破寂 ⇨ 심심풀이

심심풀이 [소일] killing time ; whiling away the hours ; beguiling one's hours ; pastime —하다 kill〔waste〕 time ; while away the time〔the hours〕 ; beguile one's hours ¶ 심심풀이로 꽃을 가꾸다 grow flowers as a hobby // 심심풀이로 정구를 치다 play tennis to kill time // 심심풀이로 책을 읽다 read a book to pass the time // 낚시질은 좋은 심심풀이다 Fishing is a good time-killer.

심심하다[1] feel ennui ; be bored ; find time hanging heavily〔heavy〕 on one's hands ¶ 심심하여 죽을 지경이다 be bored to death ; be oppressed with tedium ; suffer from ennui ; be busy with nothing to do // 심심하지 않으신지요 I am afraid you find it a bore.

심심하다[2] [맛이] taste flat

심쌀 心— rice used in making gruel

심악하다 甚惡— (be) harsh ; cruel ; merciless ; devilish ; inhuman

심안 心眼 the mind's eye ; inward eyes ¶ 심안을 뜨다 open one's spiritual eyes

심야 深夜 the dead of night ; midnight ; small hours (새벽 2·3 시경) ¶ 심야에 at midnight ; in the dead of night // 심야까지 far into the night ; till late at night // 심야까지 공부하다 burn the midnight oil

— 방송 midnight broadcasting — 흥행 a midnight show

심약 心弱 feeble-mindedness ; weak-mindedness —하다 (be) feeble-minded ; weak-minded ; irresolute

***심연** 深淵 an abyss ; a gulf ; an abysmal chasm ¶ 절망의 심연 an abyss of despair

심오 深奧 profundity ; abstruseness —하다 (be) profound ; abstruse ; esoteric ¶ 심오한 원리 an esoteric〔abstruse〕 principle // 심오한 연구 recondite studies // 심오한 학문 profound learning // 심오한 의미 a deep meaning

심원 心願 one's heart's desire ; one's heartfelt wish ; one's dearest wish

심원 深遠 profundity ; depth —하다 (be) profound 《theory》 ; deep 《meaning》 ; abstruse 《idea》 ; recondite 《doctrine》 ; unfathomable ; esoteric

심원 深怨 a deep-rooted grudge ; intense resentment —하다 have〔bear〕 a deep grudge 《against》

심의 審議 deliberation ; consideration ; discussion ; review —하다 deliberate on 《a matter, subject》 ; consider ; discuss ¶ 심의를 거듭한 끝에 after due deliberation // 심의 중이다 [사물이 주어] be under discussion〔consideration〕 // 심의에 부치다 refer 《a matter》 to discussion // 심의가 보류되다 be shelved ; be pigeonholed ; be burked // 문제를 심의하다 deliberate on the question // 법안을 계속 심의하다 carry the deliberation on a bill into the next session

—권 the right to deliberate — 기관 an organ of consultation — 미결 사항 unfinished business — 미결 의안 a pending bill ; a bill shelved〔tabled 《미》〕 —회 a deliberate council ; an inquiry commission 교육〔경제〕 —회 an educational 〔economic〕 council

심이 心耳 〖해부〗 the auricles of the heart 우〔좌〕— the right〔left〕 auricle

심인 尋人 a missing person ; a person who is sought for

—란(欄) the agony columns

†**심장** 心臟 the heart ¶ 심장의 고동 the beating〔throbbing, palpitation〕 of the heart // 심장이 약하다 suffer from a weak heart // 심장이 약한〔강한〕 사나이이다 He is weak-〔strong-〕hearted. // (놀라서) 심장이 멈추었다 My heart stood still. // 심장이 두근두근했다 My heart went pit-a-pat.

— 거대증 megalocardia —경(鏡) a cardioscope — 기능 부전 cardiac insufficiency ; insufficiency of the heart ; heart failure — 마비 a heart attack ; paralysis of the heart — 발작 heart failure ; cardiac paralysis ; a heart attack — 병 a heart disease〔trouble〕 —부 the heart 《of a city》 — 비대(증) hypertrophy of the heart ; cardiac hypertrophy ; cardiomegaly — 수축 systole —염 inflammation of the heart ; carditis — 운동 검사 cardiography — 운동표 cardiogram — 이식(수술) a heart transplant 〔graft〕 (operation) — 이완〔개장(開張)〕 dilatation of the heart — 절개술 cardiotomy — 파열〔멸〕 rupture of the heart ; cardioclasis — 판막 valves of the heart — 판막증 a valvular disease of the heart — 팽창 dilation of the heart —형 a heart shape ; a heart

심장 深長 —하다 (be) profound ; deep ¶ 의미 심장하다 It is full of significance. /It is pregnant〔fraught〕 with meaning.

심재 心材 〖건축〗 heartwood ; duramen

심적 心的 mental ; psychological ; psychical
— 기제(機制) 〖심리〗 mechanism — 상태 a mental state ; a state of mind ; mentality — 작용 a mental〔psychical〕 action — 태도 a mental attitude — 포화 mental saturation — 현상 a mental phenomenon

심전계 心電計 〖의학〗 an electrocardiograph

심전도 心電圖 〖의학〗 an electrocardiogram 《ECG》

심정 心情 one's heart ; one's feelings ; affection ¶ 그의 심정을 이해하다 appreciate how he feels // 당신의 심정은 잘 알겠습니다 Of course I understand your feeling. /I can understand that psychology.

심줄 a sinew ; a tendon

심중 心中 one's mind ; one's intention ; one's inmost thoughts ; one's true motive ¶ 심중의 비밀 the secrets of one's breast // 심중에 품다 keep 《a secret》 in one's bosom ; cherish 《a hope》 in one's heart // 남의 심중을 알아차리다 read another's thoughts // 심중을 털어놓다 take 《a person》 into one's confidence ; unburden〔unbosom〕 oneself to 《a person》 ; lay bare one's heart

심중 深重 prudence ; discretion ; carefulness ; circumspection —하다 (be) prudent ; discreet ; cautious

심증 心證 ① 〔인상〕 an impression ¶ 심증을 해치다 give 《a person》 an unfavorable impression ; hurt 《a person's》 feelings ② 〖법〗 〔판사의 확신〕 a conviction ; a strong belief ¶ 심증을 갖다 have a firm belief 《that》 // 심증을 얻다 gain a confident belief

***심지 心—** a wick ¶ 심지를 끊다 snuff the candle (초의) ; crick〔trim〕 a wick (남포의) // 남포의 심지를 너무 돋우다 turn (up) a wick too high // 남포의 심지를 낮추다 lower〔turn down〕 a wick

심지 心地 nature ; temper ; disposition ; character ¶ 심지 바른 사람 a right-minded person // 심지가 사납다 be perverse ; be crooked

심지 心志 mind ; intention ; the will ; purpose

심지어 甚之於 even ; not so much as ; so far as ; what is worse ¶ 그는 심지어 그녀가 거짓말장이라고 까지 했다 He went so far as to say that she was a liar. // 그는 심지어 자기의 먹을 것까지도 주어 버렸다 He even gave away his own food. // 심지어는 건강마저 잃었다 What is worse, he lost his health. // 그는 심지어 제 이름도 못 쓴다 He cannot so much as write his own name. // 그는 심지어 결혼 반지까지 팔았다 He went so far as to sell his wedding ring.

심천 深淺 the relative depth (깊이) ; deep and shallow

심청 沈淸 dark〔deep, navy〕 blue

심축 心祝 hearty blessing ; earnest congratulations〔wishes〕 —하다 bless 《a person》 in one's heart ; celebrate ; pray 〔wish〕 for 《a person's happiness》 from one's heart

심취 心醉 〔도취〕 fascination ; infatuation ; 〔감복〕 admiration ; devotion —하다 be fascinated〔charmed〕 《with》 ; come under the spell of 《a person》 ; be infatuated 《with》 ; adore ; worship ¶ 서구 문명에 심취하다 be infatuated with Occidental civilization // 춘원에 심취하고 있다 He is an enthusiastic admirer of *Chunwon*.
—자 an enthusiastic admirer ; an enthusiast ; a fan ; a devotee

심층 深層 the depths 《of one's consciousness》
— 심리학 depth psychology

심통 心統 (bad) disposition ⇨ 심지(心地) ¶ 심통이 사납다 be crooked ; be perverse

심통 心痛 mental suffering〔agony, anguish〕 ; heartache ; agony of mind ; worry ; distress —하다 (be) troubled 〔worried〕 《about》 ; painful

⁑심판 審判 〔경기의〕 refereeing ; umpireship ; 〔하느님의〕 judgment ; trial ; 〔재판〕 adjudgment ; 〔심판하는 사람〕 an umpire ; a referee —하다 referee 《a game》 ; act as umpire ; judge ; adjudge (재판하다) ¶ 심판의 판정 an umpire's decision // 최후 심판의 날 the Judgment Day ; the Last Judgment ; the doomsday // K씨의 심판 아래 with Mr. K as umpire ; Mr. K acting as umpire // 심판을 보다 act as referee〔umpire〕 // 심판에게 불평하다 object to〔kick at〕 an umpire's

decision
—관〔원〕 a judge ; an umpire ; a referee ; a ref. —부 [특허 따위의] the Judgment Division 제 1위〔제 2위〕 — a first〔second〕 place judge 최후 — the Last Judgment ; the Great Assize
심포니 a symphony
— 오케스트라 a symphony orchestra
심포지엄 a symposium 《*pl.* -sia》
심피 心皮 〖식물〗 a carpel
심하게 甚— terribly ; awfully ; severely ; violently ; outrageously
†심하다 甚— [격렬하다] (be) extreme ; great ; gross ; intense ; hard ; terrible ; excessive ¶ 심한 폭풍우 a violent storm // 심한 눈 a heavy snow // 심한 통증 an acute〔a severe, a violent〕 pain // 심한 감기 a nasty cold // 심한 손실 a heavy loss // 심한 차이 a wide〔great〕 difference // 심한 경쟁 keen〔fierce, vehement, hot〕 competition // 심한 오해 serious misunderstanding // 심한 잘못 a gross mistake // 심한 더위〔추위〕 intense〔bitter, severe〕 heat〔cold〕 // 기침이 심하다 I have a bad cough. // 두 사람 사이에 경쟁이 심하다 There is a keen competition between the two. // 심한 상처를 입었다 He was terribly〔seriously〕 wounded. // 그는 심히 실망했다 He was greatly〔very much〕 disappointed. // 네 농담이 너무 심하다 You carry your joke too far. // 돈이 심히 궁하다 He is badly hard up〔in want of money〕. // 심한 말을 했다 He used abusive〔violent, bad, strong〕 language.
심해 深海 the deep sea ; deep waters ¶ 심해의 abysmal
— 구조 작업 deep-sea salvage (work) — 서식 동물 abyssal fauna —어 a deep-sea〔an abyssal〕 fish — 어업 deep-sea fishing ; fishing〔fishery〕 for abyssal fish ; ocean fishery —용 측심기 a bathymeter — 측정〔측심(測深)〕 deep-sea sounding ; bathymetry — 측정기〔측심기〕 a bathymeter ; a depthsounder — 탐험선 a bathyscaphe
심혈 心血 heart's blood ¶ 심혈을 기울인 작품 a book embodying the author's whole mental energy ; one's most laborious work // 심혈을 기울여서 heart and soul ; with one's heart's blood // 심혈을 기울이다 put one's heart and soul into 《one's work》 ; put forth all one's energy
심호흡 深呼吸 deep respiration〔breathing〕 ; a deep breath —하다 breathe deeply ; do deep breathing ; draw a deep breath ; practice breathing
심혼 心魂 one's heart〔soul〕 ¶ 심혼을 기울이다 put one's heart and soul into 《one's work》
심홍 深紅 crimson ; scarlet ¶ 심홍의 crimson ; cardinal
심화 心火 anger ; passion ; heart-burning ¶ 심화가 솟다 burn with wrath〔jealousy〕
심화 深化 deepening —하다 deepen
심황 〖식물〗 turmeric
심황 深黃 deep yellow ; saffron (color)
심회 心懷 thoughts of the heart ; the mind ; the heart
심후 深厚 ¶ 심후롭다 [감사·우정이] (be) profound ; deep
심히 甚— very ; very much ; most ; greatly ; exceedingly ; highly ; badly ; excessively ; awfully ; terribly ¶ 심히 취하다 be heavily〔hopelessly, dead〕 drunk // 심히 피곤하다 I am very tired. // 그는 돈에 심히 곤란을 받고 있다 He is badly hard up〔in want of money〕. // 이러한 사고가 빈발한다는 것은 심히 유감이다 It is a matter of sincere regret that such accidents should happen so frequently.
†십 十 ten ; the tenth ¶ 십분의 1 one tenth // 십인 십색 So many men, so many minds. / No man is alike.
십각형 十角形 a decagon ¶ 십각형의 decagonal
십간 十干 the ten calendar signs ; the ten celestial stems
십계명 十誡命 〖성경〗 the Ten Commandments ; the Decalogue
십구 十九 nineteen ¶ 제십구 the nineteenth // 십구분의 일 one-nineteenth
—공탄 a nineteen-holed briquet(te)
십년 十年 ten years ; a decade ¶ 십년 마다 every ten years ; decennially // 십년을 하루같이 ten years as one day ; tirelessly ; without a break for ten years // 십년 감수하다 cut ten years from one's life ; be scared to death ; have a hard time of it // 십년이면 강산도 변한다 Ten years is an epoch.
— 일득 one success in ten years ; a success once in a blue moon —제 the tenth anniversary —지계(之計) a farsighted policy — 지기(知己) an old friend ; a friend of long standing
*십대 十代 the teens ¶ 십대의 사랑 a teenage romance // 십대의 사람들 teenagers // 나는 나의 십대를 시골에서 지냈다 I spent my teens in the country.
십륙 十六 sixteen ¶ 제십륙 the sixteenth
십만 十萬 a hundred thousand ¶ 수 십만 hundreds of thousands 《of people》
— 억토 〖불교〗 eternity ; paradise ; a region one trillion miles from the earth
십면체 十面體 〖수학〗 a decahedron ¶ 십면체의 decahedral
십분 十分 [시간] ten minutes ; 〖수학〗 division in ten ; [충분히] enough ; sufficiently ¶ 십분의 tenth ; decimal // 십분의 일 a tenth // 십분하다 divide into ten // 자기 실력을 십분 발휘하다 make the most what one has
십배 十倍 ten times ; tenfold ¶ 십배로 하다 multiply 《the number》 ten times
십사 十四 fourteen ¶ 제십사 the fourteenth

—행시 a fourteen-line verse ; a sonnet
십삼 十三 thirteen ¶ 제십삼 the thirteenth
십상 [어울림] just right ; just the (right) thing ; the thing wanted ; admirable ; perfect ¶ 하이킹 날씨로는 십상이다 This is an ideal day for hiking. // 네게는 그 모자가 십상이다 That hat was "made" for you. // 재떨이로 쓰기 십상 좋다 It makes an admirable ash tray.
십상 팔구 ⇨ 십중 팔구
십생 구사 十生九死 a narrow escape ⇨ 구사 일생
십억 十億 a thousand million ; a billion 《미》
십오 十五 fifteen ¶ 제십오 the fifteenth // 십오분 fifteen minutes ; a quarter 《of an hour》
—야 a full moon night
십육 十六 sixteen ¶ 제십육 the sixteenth
—밀리 영화〔촬영기〕 a 16mm film〔camera〕 —분 음표 a semiquaver ; a sixteenth note
십이 十二 twelve ; a dozen ¶ 제십이 the twelfth
—각형 a dodecagon —궁 the Twelve Houses ; zodiacal constellations —면체 a dodecahedron — 사도 〖기독교〗 the (Twelve) Apostles —지 〖민속〗 the 12 Earth's Branches ; the twelve horary signs —진법 〖수학〗 duodecimals ; the duodecimal system (of notation)
십이궁도 十二宮圖 the horoscope
†십이월 十二月 December
십이지장 十二指腸 〖해부〗 the duodenum
— 궤양 duodenal ulcer —염 duodenitis ; inflammation of the duodenum — 절개술 duodenotomy —충 a hookworm ; a Dochmius duodenalis ; an ancylostome — 충병 hookworm disease ; ancylostomiasis ; uncinariasis
십인 십색 十人十色 So many men, so many minds. /No man is alike. /So many herds, so many wits/Many lords, many laws.
십일 十一 eleven ¶ 제십일 the eleventh
†십일월 十一月 November
*십자 十字 a cross ¶ 십자의 crossed ; crucial ; cruciate ; cruciform // 십자로 crosswise // 십자를 긋다 [기도] cross oneself ; make the sign of cross on one's breast〔forehead〕
—군 the crusades ; the crusaders —군 전사 a crusader ; a soldier〔warrior〕 of the Cross —로(路) a crossroads 《보통 단수 취급》 ; X-roads ¶ 십자로에 서다 be〔stand〕 at the crossroads — 말풀이 a cross-word puzzle — 절개 〖수술〗 a crucial incision — 포화 a cross fire ¶ 십자포화를 퍼붓다 cross-fire 《the enemy》 —형 a cross (shape) ; curciform ¶ 십자형의 cross-shaped // 십자형으로 crosswise —형 무늬 a crisscross pattern —화 〖식물〗 a cruciferous〔cruciate〕 flower ¶ 십자화과의 cruciferous —화과 식물 a crucifer — 화관(花冠) a cruciform corolla 적— the Red Cross
†십자가 十字架 a cross ; [예수의] the Holy Cross ¶ 십자가에서 죽다 die upon the cross
—상 a crucifix ¶ 십자가상의 cruciform 성— the holy〔real, true〕 cross 성 — 발견절 [5월 3일] Invention of the Cross
십자가를 지다 관용 bear one's cross
십자매 十姉妹 〖새〗 a society finch ; a lovebird
*십장 什長 ① the chief workman ; a foreman ; a boss of a construction crew ② [옛날 병제에서] the corporal of a file of ten
십전 구도 十顚九倒 —하다 suffer many hardships ; go through ups and downs of life
십종 경기 十種競技 decathlon
— 참가자 a decathlon contestant
†십중 팔구 十中八九 in nine cases out of ten ; ten to one ; most likely ; almost ¶ 그는 십중 팔구 실패할 것이다 Ten to one, he will fail.
*십진 十進 progressing by ten ¶ 십진의 decimal ; denary
— 급수 decimal scale —법〔제〕 the decimal system ; the denary scale〔notation〕 ¶ 십진법화하다 decimalize // 십진법으로 decimally — 분류법 the decimal classification (도서의) ; the Dewey〔decimal〕 system —산(算) decimal arithmetic 〔numeration〕 ¶ 십진산의 decimal ; denary
십철 十哲 ten sages ¶ 공문(孔門)의 십철 the ten leading disciples of Confucius
십칠 十七 seventeen ¶ 제십칠 the seventeenth
십팔 十八 eighteen ¶ 제십팔 the eighteenth
—금 18-carat gold
십팔기 十八技 18 martial arts
십팔번 十八番 the eighteenth ; [장기(長技)] one's forte〔speciality〕 ; one's favorite performance〔song〕
싯누렇다 (be) vivid yellow
싯뻘겋다 (be) vivid red
싯퍼렇다 (be) deep blue ; deadly pale (안색이) ⇨ 시퍼렇다
싯허옇다 be extremely white
싱가포르 Singapore ¶ 싱가포르의 Singaporean
— 사람 a Singaporean
싱건지 lightly-salted〔-spiced〕 *kimchi*
싱겁다 ① be not properly salted ; taste flat ; (be) insipid ¶ 음식이 싱겁다 The dishes taste flat. // 이 국물은 싱겁다 This soup needs a bit of salt.
② [하는 짓이] (be) flat ; dull ; boring ; pointless ; tedious ¶ 싱거운 사람 a boring person ; a wishy-washy person // 싱거운 이야기 a dull story

싱겅싱겅하다 《a room》 be chilly
싱그레, 씽그레 gently smiling
싱글 ① [양복] a single-breasted coat ② [탁구 등의] a singles (match) ③ [야구의] a single (hit)
— 베드 a single bed **— 코트** a single court
싱글거리다 beam with a smile ; smile sweetly〔gently〕 ¶ 싱글거리면서 with a (sweet) smile on one's face
싱글벙글 smilingly ; with a broad smile ; with a smiling face **—하다** be all smiles ; smile happily ; beam 《upon》
싱글싱글 ⇨ 싱글벙글
싱둥싱둥하다 (be) still lively ; hale and hearty ; be full of life〔energy〕; be in high spirits ¶ 그 노인은 아직도 싱둥싱둥하다 The old man still remains hale and hearty.
싱숭생숭 —하다 feel restless〔nervous, fidgety〕; be in a fidget ; have a birdlike restlessness ; have one's attention distracted ¶ 봄에는 마음이 싱숭생숭하다 My mind wanders during the springtime.
*__싱싱하다__ (be) fresh ; new ; lively ; full of life ¶ 싱싱한 야채〔과일〕 fresh vegetables〔fruit〕// 이슬이 내린 아침엔 풀잎이 모두 싱싱하다 On a dewy morning the leaves of the grass are all fresh.
싱커 〖야구〗 a sinker (ball)
싱크탱크 [두뇌 집단] a think tank〔factory〕《미·속》
싱크로트론 〖물리〗 a synchrotron
싶다 ① [하고 싶다] I want ; I wish ; I hope ; I should〔would〕 like to 《do》; I am〔feel〕 inclined to 《do》; I feel like 《doing》 ¶ 함께 가고 싶다 I should like to go with you. // 내일은 날씨가 좋았으면 싶다 I hope it will be fine tomorrow. // 이렇게도 하고 싶고 저렇게도 하고 싶지만 무엇 하나 한 것이 없다 I want to do this and that, but so far have done nothing. // 그녀가 보고 싶어 죽겠어 I'm dying to see her. // 한국에 어서 가 보고 싶군요 I can't wait to go to Korea. // 여보 간식 좀 먹고 싶은데 I feel like some snacks, honey.
② […같이 보이다] look like ; seem ; appear ; be likely to ¶ 그가 올 성 싶다 He is likely to come. // 비가 올 성 싶다 It looks like rain. // 그들의 목소리를 들은 성 싶다 I seem to hear their voices.
싶어하다 [2·3인칭이 주어] want to ; feel like 《doing》; be desirous of 《doing》 ⇨ 싶다 ¶ …을 하고 싶어하다 be eager〔anxious〕 to 《do》// 그는 가고 싶어한다 He wants to go. // 그 여자하고 몹시 결혼하고 싶어한다 He is mad to marry her.
싸각거리다 ⇨ 사각거리다
‡**싸개**¹ a wrapper ; cover material ; a slip cover ; wrapping paper
—쟁이 an upholster **—질** upholstering **—통** a scramble ; a crowded struggle
싸개² one who urinate or defecate
똥— a pants-wetter **오줌—** a bed wetter
싸고돌다 ① [위요] form a small clique〔an inside group, an intimate circle〕 around ② [비호] shield ; protect ; stand by ; cover up for ¶ 아들을 싸고돌다 shield one's son
싸구려 cheap (stuff, things) ; a (good) bargain ; an inferior article ; a flivver 《미·속》
— 시장 a cheap market **— 식당** an eating house ; a cheap restaurant **— 자동차** a flivver
†**싸다**¹ wrap up〔in〕; do up ; bundle 《clothes》; [짐싸다] pack up 《goods》; [가리다] cover 《things with》; mantle 《in》; envelop 《in》 ¶ 보자기에 싸다 wrap up in a cloth-wrapper // 담요로 몸을 싸다 wrap oneself in a blanket // 그 문제는 신비에 싸여 있다 The subject is enveloped〔veiled〕 in mystery. // 접시는 짚으로 싸였다 The dishes were packed in straw. // 시 전체가 안개에 싸여 있었다 The whole town was shrouded in mist. // 그것을 종이로 싸 주시오 Wrap it up in paper. // 선물용으로 곱게 싸 주십시오 Please gift-wrap it. // 매일 점심을 싸 가지고 다니기로 했다 I decided to brown-bag it every-day.
싸다² ① [똥·오줌을] excrete 《urine or feces》; void ; discharge ¶ 똥을 싸다 have a bowel movement ; ease oneself // 오줌을 싸다 pee ; urinate ; pass water〔urine〕; piss 《속》
② [혼나다] be put to it ; have a hard time of it ¶ 빚 갚기에 똥쌌다 I was hard put to it to pay off my debts.
싸다³ ① [빠르다] (be) swift ; fast ¶ 입이 싼 사람 a glib talker // 싸게 briskly ; at a brisk pace // 입이 싸다 be flippant // 걸음이 싸다 be swift of foot // 싸게 다녀오너라 Go and come back quickly.
② [불이] burn fast ; [불기운이] intense ¶ 불이 싸다 The fire burns briskly.
†**싸다**⁴ ① [값이] (be) inexpensive ; cheap ; low-priced ; low ; economical ¶ 싼 가게 a cheap store ; a cheaper store (딴 가게보다 싸게 파는 집) // 싼 집세 a low rent // 싸게 cheaply ; inexpensively ; economically // 싸지다 become cheap ; fall〔go down〕《in price》// 싸게 하다 make 《a thing》 cheaper ; reduce〔cut〕 the price 《of》// 싸게 손에 넣다〔사다, 팔다〕 get〔buy, sell〕《a thing》 cheap // 물건을 싸게 사다 buy things cheaply // 싸게 사서 비싸게 팔다 buy low and sell high // 싸게 보다 value at a low price ; hold a thing cheap ; underrate // 이것을 싸게 샀다 I got this at a bargain. // 그거 아주 싸게 샀다 It was a steal. /It was a real good buy. // 바나나가 그전에는 한국에서 매우 비쌌었지만 요즘은 매우 싸다 Bananas used to be very expensive in Korea, but nowadays

they are a dime a dozen. // 어디가도 우리보다 더 싼 데는 없습니다 This is the lowest price anywhere. // 사과가 싸졌다 Apples have gone down (in price) 〔become cheaper〕. // 싸게 휴가를 즐기고 싶으면 화물선으로 여행할 일이다 If you want a cheap vacation, travel on a freight boat. // 값이 싸졌다 The price has come down〔fallen〕. // 그 여자는 혼례 의상을 될 수 있는 대로 싸게 빌렸다 She borrowed a wedding dress as cheaply as possible. // 그것은 싼 목걸이였다 It was an inexpensive necklace. // 계란은 지금 놀랄 정도로 싸다 Eggs are wonderfully cheap now. // 겨울보다 여름이 생활비가 싸다 Living is cheaper in summer than in winter. // 나는 이 차를 매우 싸게 샀다 I bought this car for a song.

② [처벌이] be well deserved ; be none too little ; be due ¶ 죽어도 싸다 deserve death ; need to be killed

싸다니다 run〔bustle〕《about》 ¶ 사방으로 싸다니다 bustle in and out ; hang about 〔around〕; bum around 《미·속》 // 하루 종일 싸다니다 bustle about all day long

싸대다 ⇨ 싸다니다

싸데려가다 The groom side provides all the wedding expenses.

싸라기 [쌀] half-crushed rice ; [눈] tiny pellets of hail

‡싸락눈 snow grains ; snow pellets ; soft hail

싸리 〖식물〗 a bush clover

싸리버섯 an edible mushroom ; Clavaria botrytis (학명)

싸매다 (wrap and) tie up

†싸우다 [적과] fight 《with, for, against》; combat 《with》; [곤란과] struggle 《with, against》; [사람과] quarrel 《with a person, about a matter》; [겨루다] fight ; play ¶ (적과) 잘 싸우다 fight a good battle // 우승을 걸고 싸우다 challenge for championship ; play for the title // 정정당당하게 싸우다 play a fair game // 운명과 싸우다 strive against fate // 빈곤과 싸우다 battle with〔against〕 poverty // 추위와 싸우다 struggle against the cold // 죽음과 싸우다 fight off death // 끝까지 싸우다 fight to the end // 자유〔정의〕를 위해 싸우다 fight for liberty〔in the cause of justice〕 // 우리는 2배나 되는 병력과 싸웠다 We fought with a force twice our number. // 그들은 한 여자를 두고 싸운다 They fight over a woman. // 그들은 하찮은 일로 늘 싸운다 They always quarrel with each other about trifles. /They are always at odds about little things. // 그 사람 간밤에 부인하고 대판 싸웠다고 하던데요 He said he had a big fight with his wife last night. // 상사하고 싸웠어 I had a run-in with a boss. // 그들은 바로 전날 공급업자들 중 하나와 싸웠다 They had a run-in with one of their suppliers just the other day.

†싸움 ① [투쟁] a struggle ; [전투] a fight ; a battle ; a combat ; [교전] an engagement ; [전쟁] a war ; warfare ; a conflict ; [논전] a contest ; [접전] a scuffle ; a skirmish ; a bout **—하다** fight (a battle) ; engage in a battle ; wage a war 《on》; struggle ; strive ¶ 치열한 싸움 a severe〔die-hard〕 battle // 인생의 싸움 the battle of life // 싸움을 좋아하는 warlike ; belligerent // 싸움에 지다 lose a battle〔the day〕 // 싸움에 이기다 win〔gain〕 a battle〔the day〕 // 싸움을 걸다 challenge (to battle) ; provoke war // 싸움을 선언하다 declare war // 싸움을 시작하다 go to war 《against》 // 장기간에 걸친 노사간의 싸움이 원만하게 해결되었다 A long-drawn-out conflict between employers and workers came to the end with a full agreement. // 강자가 반드시 싸움에서 이기는 것은 아니다 The battle is not always to the strong.

② [언쟁·불화] a quarrel ; a fight ; a dispute ; [분쟁] a trouble ; a conflict **—하다** have a quarrel〔dispute〕; quarrel ¶ 법률상의 싸움 a judicial dispute // 학술상의 싸움 academic controversies // 싸움을 시작하다 begin a dispute ; open hostilities // 싸움을 말리다 make 《persons》 stop quarreling ; smooth over a quarrel // 싸움을 걸다 provoke a quarrel ; pick a fight

—꾼 a man of combative spirit ; a fire-eater 《미·속》 **부부 —** a matrimonial quarrel ; a quarrel between husband and wife ; a domestic scene (squabble) **집안 —** an internal〔a domestic〕 trouble〔dissension〕; a family quarrel〔dispute〕

***싸움터** a battleground ; a battlefield ¶ 싸움터의 이슬로 사라지다 be killed on the battlefield // 싸움터에 나가다 go to war ; go to the front

싸움판 the scene of a quarrel〔fight〕 ¶ 싸움판이 벌어지다 A fight takes place.

싸움패 —牌 a gang of roughs〔hooligans, hoodlums〕

싸이다 be〔get〕 wrapped ; be covered ; be enveloped ¶ 종이에 싸인 책 a book wrapped in paper // 눈에 싸인 산정 a peak covered with snow // 화염에 싸인 집 a house enveloped in flames // 안개에 싸인 마을 a village shrouded in mist

싸잡다 put〔lump〕 together ; sum up ; cover up ; round up ; include

싸전 —廛 a rice store

—장이 a rice dealer

싸전에 가서 밥 달라 한다 속담 To seek hot water under cold ice.

싸하다 [박하 맛처럼] (be) minty ; peppermint ; mentholated ; cool ; [아리듯이] piquant ; pungent ; spicy ; tongue-biting ; tingling ; tingly ; sharp ; [샴페인처럼] fizzy

‡싹¹ [씨앗의] a bud ; [가지의] a sprout ; a shoot ; [근원·시초] germ ; [싹수] good omen ¶ 싹이 트다 bud ; shoot ; sprout ; germinate ; put forth shoots ; begin to develop // 봄이 되면 식물은 새싹이 나온다 Plants push out new shoots in spring. // 범죄의 싹은 미리 잘라 버려야 한다 We must nip a crime in the bud. // 그의 사업은 이제 싹이 보인다 His business is now in luck's way.

싹² ① [베는 소리나 모양] 《cut off》 with a clean stroke ¶ 천을 싹 자르다 cut a cloth with a snip ② [모두] with a clean sweep ; completely ; entirely ; thoroughly ¶ 도둑이 집안의 물건을 싹 쓸어 갔다 The thief swept the house clean. // 돈을 벌자 그의 태도가 싹 달라졌다 Ever since he grabbed a fortune, all of a sudden, he became a different man.

싹독거리다 snip ; slice ; mince ; chop ¶ 싹독싹독 snip-snip ; chop-chop ; slice-slice // 무를 싹독싹독 자르다 cut radish up chop-chop-chop

싹독싹독하다 [문장이] (be) choppy ; abrupt ; disconnected

싹수 a good omen ; promise ; hope 싹수가 있다 be promising ; show promise of success

싹수가 없다〔노랗다, 틀렸다〕 관용 be hopeless ; show no promise of success ; have no prospect 《of》

싹싹¹ imploringly ; humbly ; entreatingly ¶ 잘못했다고 싹싹 빌다 humbly beg 《a person's》 pardon ; beg for forgiveness with tears in one's eyes // 살려 달라고 싹싹 빌다 beg for one's life wringing one's hands

싹싹² ① [베다] with clean strokes ¶ 싹싹 베다 cut off with clean strokes ② [쓸다] with clean sweeps

싹싹하다 (be) affable ; amiable ; suave ; kind ; docile ¶ 그 여자는 누구에게나 싹싹하다 She is affable to everybody.

*****싹트다** bud ; sprout ; put forth shoot ; germinate ; 《a matter》 begin to develop ¶ 그들 사이에는 사랑이 싹텄다 Love budded 《between》 them.

싼값 cheap price ¶ 싼값으로 물건을 사다 buy a thing cheap ; make a good bargain

싼흥정 (a great) bargain ; a good buy

†**쌀** (raw, uncooked) rice ; (any) hulled grain (곡류) ¶ 쌀을 생산하는 농민 farmers who grow〔raise, cultivate〕 rice // 쌀을 씻다 wash rice // 쌀을 빻다 pound rice // 쌀을 안치다 prepare rice for boiling
—가게 a rice store **—가루** rice flour **—가마니** a straw rice bag〔sack〕 **—겨** rice bran **—궤** a rice chest **—농사** [재배] cultivation of rice ; rice growing ; [수확] rice crop〔harvest〕 **—누룩** malted rice **—눈** an embryo bud (of rice) **—알** [쌀의 알] a grain of rice ; [모든 알곡의] a grain of any hulled cereal **—책박** a rice container made of twigs

쌀강아지 a short-haired pup

쌀개¹ [방아의] the main shaft〔pivot〕 of a mill

쌀개² a short-haired dog

쌀고치 a fine white cocoon

쌀골집 a kind of sausage

쌀광 a storeroom for rice

쌀농사 —**農事** [재배] cultivation of rice ; rice culture ; [수확] the rice crop〔harvest〕 ¶ 쌀농사가 잘〔잘 안〕되다 have a good〔poor〕 crop of rice

쌀눈 an embryo bud (of rice)

쌀되 ① [되] a measure (used in measuring rice) ② [쌀] one *doe* worth of rice

쌀뜨물 the waste water left over from washing rice ; rice water

쌀랑거리다 ⇨ 살랑거리다

쌀랑쌀랑 ⇨ 살랑살랑 ①

쌀랑하다 ⇨ 살랑하다

쌀래쌀래 ⇨ 살래살래

쌀밥 boiled〔cooked〕 rice

쌀벌레 a rice weevil

쌀보리 《식물》 rye

쌀부대 —**負袋** a rice bag

쌀쌀¹ ⇨ 살살²

쌀쌀² ¶ 배가 쌀쌀 아프다 have a little stomachache

*****쌀쌀하다** (be) chilly ; (rather) cold ; distant ¶ 쌀쌀하게 coldly ; chillingly ; indifferently // 쌀쌀한 바람 a chilly wind // 쌀쌀한 태도 a distant air〔manner〕 ; a cold attitude // 쌀쌀한 사람 a cold-hearted person // 쌀쌀한 대답 a cold reply // 쌀쌀하게 대하다 treat 《a person》 indifferently ; give a cold shoulder to 《a person》 // 그녀는 나에게 몹시 쌀쌀했다 She was very short〔curt〕 with me. // 그는 요새 나에게 쌀쌀해졌다 He grew cold towards me of late. // 그녀는 애인이 있다며 쌀쌀하게 나의 제안을 거절했다 She said she had a boyfriend and turned me down cold.

쌀알 ① [쌀의 알] a grain of rice ② [모든 알곡의] a grain of any hulled cereal

쌀장사 dealing in rice

쌀장수 a rice dealer

쌀풀 rice starch〔paste〕

쌈¹ ① rice wrapped in leaves (of lettuce, etc.) ¶ 상치〔김〕쌈 lettuce-〔seaweed-〕 wrapped rice ② a pack (of 24 needles)

쌈² ⇨ 싸움

쌈지 a (tobacco) pouch

쌈질 fighting ; quarrel(l)ing **—하다** fight ; quarrel

쌉사래하다 (be) a bit bitter

쌉살하다 (be) slightly bitter ; bitterish

쌍 雙 a pair ; a couple ; a brace ; twin ¶ 꿩 한 쌍 a brace of pheasants // 한 쌍의 젊은 부부 a young married couple

쌍가마 雙— a double vortex of hair on the crown of one's head

쌍가마 雙駕馬 a sedan-chair carried by two horses, one fore and the other aft

쌍가마 속에도 설움은 있다 [속담] Crowns have cares.
쌍가지 소켓 雙— a two-way socket
쌍각류 雙殼類 〖동물〗 bivalves
쌍갈 〖건축〗 cornice mo(u)lding
쌍갈랫길 雙— a crossroad(s)
쌍갈지다 divide〔fall〕 into two parts ¶ 쌍갈진 가지 twin branches
쌍견 雙肩 both shoulders ; one's shoulders ¶ 국가의 운명을 쌍견에 짊어지다 bear the destiny of the nation on one's shoulders // 한국의 장래는 제군의 쌍견에 달려 있다 Korea's future rests on your shoulders.
쌍겹눈 雙— an eye with a double eyelid
쌍고치 雙— a double cocoon ; a dupion (cocoon)
—실 dupion silk
쌍곡선 雙曲線 a hyperbola
— 공간 hyperbolic space **—면** a hyperboloid **— 함수** a hyperbolic function
쌍구균 雙球菌 a diplococcus 《*pl.* -ci》
쌍그렇다 look cold and forlorn ¶ 그는 쌍그렇게 옷을 입었다 He looks pitifully ill-clad for the weather.
쌍극 雙極
— 안테나 a dipole antenna **—자(子)** 〖물리〗 a dipole
쌍꺼풀 雙— a double-edged eyelid
쌍꺼풀 지다 [관용] acquire〔have〕 a double-edged eyelid
쌍날 雙— a double blade ; a double edge
—칼 a double-edged sword
쌍동기 雙胴機 a twin-fuselage plane
쌍두 雙頭 a pair (of animals) ; two head(s) ¶ 쌍두의 뱀 a double-headed snake
— 마차 a carriage and pair
***쌍둥이 雙童—** twins ; twin children ; twin sons〔daughters〕 ; twin brothers 〔sisters〕 ; [그 중의 한 사람] a twin ¶ 쌍둥이를 낳다 give birth to twins
—자리 〖천문〗 the Twins ; Gemini **남자〔여자〕 —** boy〔girl〕 twins ; twin brothers 〔sisters〕 **세—** triplets
쌍떡잎 雙— 〖식물〗 a double seed-leaf 〔-cotyledon〕 ; [형용사적] dicotyledonous
쌍맹이 雙— 〖광산〗 a sledge hammer (used with pick in mining)
쌍무 雙務 ¶ 쌍무적 bilateral ; reciprocal
— 계약〔협정〕 a bilateral〔reciprocal〕 contract ; a two-way agreement **—주의** bilateralism
쌍무지개 雙— a double rainbow
쌍바라지 雙— a French window
쌍반점 雙半點 a semicolon 《 ; 》
쌍발 雙發 [엔진의] (having) twin engines 〔motors〕 ; [총] (having) double-barrels ¶ 쌍발의 〖항공〗 bimotor(ed) ; twin-engine(d) 〔-motor(ed)〕
— 비행기 a twin-motor plane ; a twin-engine(d) plane ; a bimotored airplane **—총** a double-barrel(ed gun)
쌍방 雙方 both parties ; both sides ; either party ¶ 쌍방의 both ; either ; mutual // 쌍방의 이익〔의무〕 mutual interest〔obligation〕 // 쌍방의 행위 bilateral action // 쌍방의 동의로 by mutual agreement // 그것은 쌍방을 모두 만족시킬 것이다 That will satisfy both parties.
쌍벽 雙璧 [옥] a pair of jewels ; [사람] the two great masters〔authorities〕 ; the matchless twin stars ¶ 한국 문단의 쌍벽 the two great writers of Korea ; the two giant figures in the field of Korean literature
쌍봉낙타 雙峰駱駝 〖동물〗 a Bactrian (two-humped) camel
쌍분 雙墳 twin graves
쌍생 雙生 gemination **—하다** grow in pairs〔couples〕
쌍생아 雙生兒 ⇨ 쌍동이(雙童—)
1〔2〕란성 — identical〔fraternal〕 twins
쌍성화 雙— ① [양난] an annoyance〔a trouble〕 at every turn ; an awkward situation ; a dilemma ② [겹친 성화] one annoyance〔trouble〕 on top of another
쌍수 雙手 both hands ¶ 쌍수를 들어 찬성하다 give one's hearty support 《to》 ; approve whole-heartedly
쌍수 雙袖 both sleeves
쌍시류 雙翅類 Diptera (학명)
쌍심지 雙— a double wick
쌍십절 雙十節 [중국의] the Double Tenth (Anniversary)
쌍쌍이 雙雙— by twos ; in pairs ; in couples ; two by two ¶ 젊은 연인들이 쌍쌍이 공원을 거닐고 있다 Young lovers are seen taking a walk in the park arm in arm.
쌍안 雙眼 two eyes ; both eyes ; a pair of eyes ; binoculars
—경 (a pair of) binoculars ; [야외·육군용] a field glass ; [해군용] a marine glass ; [극장용] an opera glass ¶ 쌍안경으로 보다 look through a field glass **—망원〔현미〕경** a binocular telescope 〔microscope〕 **— 사진기** a stereo(scopic) camera
쌍알 雙— an egg with a double yolk
쌍어궁 雙魚宮 ⇨ 물고기자리
쌍열박이 雙列— a double-barreled gun
쌍엽 雙葉 ¶ 쌍엽의 bifoliate
— 식물 a bifoliate plant
쌍자엽 雙子葉 ⇨ 쌍떡잎(雙—)
—류 Dicotyledones **— 식물** 〖식물〗 a dicotyledon ; a dicotyledonous plant
쌍장부 雙— twin tenons ¶ 쌍장부끌 a kind of double-bladed chisel
쌍정 雙晶 〖광물〗 a twin (crystal)
쌍제 雙蹄 〖동물〗 a cloven foot〔hoof〕 ¶ 쌍제의 cloven-footed〔-hoofed〕
—수(獸) a cloven-hoofed animal
쌍지팡이 (a pair of) crutches
쌍창 雙窓 a window consisting of two panes

— 미닫이 a double sliding door
쌍촉 雙— twin tenon ends
쌍칼 two swords
—잡이 a two-sword fencer ; a two sworded man
쌍코 雙— a shoe toe decorated with two stripes
쌍태 雙胎 a double〔twin〕 fetus
— 임신 twin〔bigeminal〕 pregnancy
쌍해사전 雙解辭典 a bilingual dictionary
쌍홍장 雙—欌 a kitchen cupboard〔sideboard〕
*쌓다 ① [겹겹이 포갬] pile up ; heap《up》; stack ; lay ¶ 산같이 쌓다 heap up《things》(mountain-) high // 벽돌을 쌓다 lay bricks // 건초를 쌓다 stack hay // 책상에 책을 쌓다 heap a desk with books // 돈을 산같이 쌓아도 행복은 살 수 없다 No amount of wealth〔money〕 can buy happiness.
② [구축] build ; erect ; raise ; construct ¶ 둑을 쌓다 build〔lay〕 an embankment // 벽〔담〕을 쌓다 build a wall // 탑을 쌓다 erect a tower
③ [축적] accumulate ; gain ; acquire ; store up ; amass ¶ 거액의 재산을 쌓다 amass〔make〕 a big fortune // 경험을 쌓다 acquire〔accumulate〕 experience // 덕을 쌓다 strive after virtue
쌓이다 be piled up ; be heaped ; get accumulated ; [눈 따위가] lie《on》 ¶ 쌓이고 쌓인 결과 the cumulative effects // 눈이 땅 위에 쌓이다 Snow piles up on the ground. // 눈이 100밀리나 쌓였다 The snow lay 100 millimeter deep. // 책상 위에 먼지가 많이 쌓여 있었다 Thick dust lay〔settled〕 on the desk. // 할 일이 태산같이 쌓였다 I have stacks of work to do. // 일을 지나치게 하면 스트레스가 쌓여 몸에 좋지 않다 If you work too hard, you'll build up stress and ruin your health.
쌔고쌨다 (be) superabundant ; superfluous
쌔다 ① ⇨ 싸이다 ② ⇨ 쌓이다
쌔비다 [훔치다] swipe ; steal
쌕쌕이 a jet (plane)
쌜그러지다 ⇨ 씰그러지다
쌨다 [흔하다] (be) plentiful ; abundant ; commonplace ¶ 한국에는 박사 학위를 가진 사람들이 쌔고 쌨다 Ph D's are a dime a dozen in Korea.
쌩 ⇨ 씽
쌩쌩날다 flit
쌩이질 a sudden〔an unexpected〕 disturbance〔interruption, obstacle, hindrance〕
써걱거리다 ⇨ 사각거리다
써내다 write and submit〔present, hand in, turn in〕
써넣다 write in ; make an entry《into》; [용지에] fill out the bland《미》; fill up〔in〕 the form《with one's name》《영》; insert (by writing)
써늘하다 ⇨ 서늘하다
써다 ebb ; flow back ; [감수] subside
써레 〖농업〗 a harrow
—질 harrowing a field ¶ 써레질하다 harrow a field ; harrow
써렛발 the prongs〔pegs, spikes, tines, teeth〕 of a harrow
써리다 〖농업〗 harrow ¶ 밭을 써리다 harrow a field
써먹다 use ; make use of ¶ 써먹을 만하다 be useful ; be of use // 써먹을 데가 없다 be useless ; be of no use ; be of no avail ; be unfit for any employment
썩¹ ① [아주] very much ; greatly ; exceedingly ; awfully ¶ 노래를 썩 잘 부른다 He sings very well. // 썩 재미있었다 I have had such a good time.
② [곧] right away ; immediately ¶ 썩 물러가거라 Get away immediately !
썩² ⇨ 싹²
*썩다 ① [부패] go bad ; rot (물건이) ; spoil (음식이) ; turn sour (우유 따위가) ; decompose ; corrode ; stale ; decay ; corrupt ¶ 썩은 bad ; rotten ; spoiled ; stale // 썩은 달걀 an addled〔rotten, bad〕 egg // 썩은 생선 rotten〔stale〕 fish // 썩은 버터 rancid butter // 썩은 과실 spoiled〔rotten〕 fruit // 썩는〔썩지 않는〕 쓰레기 biodegradable〔nonbiodegradable〕 garbage // 달걀은 썩기 쉽다 Eggs are apt to addle〔rot, go bad〕. // 무더운 날씨에는 고기가 썩기 쉽다 Meat readily taints in close weather. // 넌 정신이 썩었구나 Your mind is tainted.
② [속이]《one's heart》 become heavy ; break ¶ 실패로 말미암아 속이 썩는다 He is blue over his failure. // 망나니 아들로 어머니의 속이 썩는다 The mother's heart is heavy because of her wayward son.
③ [재주가]《one's knowledge》 gather dust〔rust〕; get〔become〕 rusty ¶ 도서관에서 책이 썩는다 The books are gathering dust on the library shelves.
썩은 새끼도 쓸 데가 있다 (속담) All's fish that comes to the net. /All's grist that comes to the mill.
썩둑- ⇨ 싹둑-
썩썩¹ imploringly ⇨ 싹싹
썩썩² [피륙 따위를 베다] with one clean stroke after another ¶ 썩썩거리다 cut without a stop
썩썩하다 (be) frank ; open-hearted ⇨ 싹싹하다
썩어빠지다 rot completely ; be utterly rotten
썩은새 rotten thatch
*썩이다 ① [부패] let《a thing》 rot〔decay〕; corrupt ; spoil ¶ 달걀을 썩이다 spoil an egg
② [방치] leave unemployed ; let go to waste ¶ 돈을 썩이다 let one's money stay unemployed // 지식을 썩이다 do not use〔waste〕 one's knowledge // 그 좋은 재주를 썩이고 있다 His great talents are left

to rust.
③ [속을] eat one's heart out 《with》; make one sick at heart; make one's heart break ¶ 걱정으로 속을 썩이다 eat one's heart out with anxiety // 그는 취직을 못해 속을 썩이고 있다 He worrys much about his failure to find work.

썩정이 something rotten〔spoiled, decayed〕

썩초 一草 black tobacco of poor quality

썩히다 let 《a thing》 rot ⇨ 썩이다

‡**썰다**[1] chop; mince; dice; slice; cut up; spin off (키다); harrow (써리다) ¶ 잘게 썰다 cut into small pieces

썰다[2] ebb; fall; go out ¶ 조수가 썰고 있다 The tide is ebbing.

썰레놓다 manage to accomplish a hard job

‡**썰매** a sled; a sleigh; a sledge ¶ 썰매를 타다 sled; drive in a sledge (말로) // 눈 위에서 썰매를 타다 slide over the snow in a sleigh
— **놀이** sledding; sleighing; sleigh riding **자동** — a motor sledge

*__썰물__ an ebb; ebb tide ¶ 썰물 때에 at low tide // 지금은 썰물이다 The tide is ebbing〔on the ebb〕.

썰썰하다 feel hungry ¶ 배가 썰썰하다 I feel hungry.

쏘개질 taletelling — **하다** tell〔carry〕 tales

†**쏘다** ① shoot; fire; discharge ¶ 적을 쏘다 shoot the enemy // 서로 쏘다 exchange shots // 총〔화살〕을 쏘다 shoot a rifle〔an arrow〕 // 권총으로 쏘다 shoot 《a person》 with a revolver; fire a revolver at 《a person》 // 새를 단 한발로 쏘아 잡다 kill a bird with a single shot // 쏘아붙이다 shoot back // 쏘앗 Fire! (구령) ② [벌레가] sting; bite ¶ 벌이 쏘다 A bee stings. // 벌에 쏘이다 get stung by a bee ③ [말로] blow 《a person》 up; storm at 《a person》

쏘다니다 run around; roam; wander; gad 《about, out》 ¶ 여기저기 쏘다니다 wander〔roam〕 《about》 from place to place // 일자리를 구하러 쏘다니다 pound the pavement〔sidewalks〕 looking for a job // 쏘다니지 마라 Stop running around so much!

쏘대다 ⇨ 쏘다니다

쏘삭거리다 incite; instigate; induce; stir up ¶ 군중을 쏘삭거려 반대케 하다 stir up people against 《the government》

쏘시개 tinder
불— tinder; kindling wood

쏘아보다 glare 《at》; scowl 《at》; frown 《at》; look angrily〔fiercely, menacingly〕 《at》; look sharply in the face; throw 《a person》 a furious look; give 《a person》 a fierce stare ¶ 쏘아보아 입을 다물게 하다 stare 《a person》 into silence // 그녀는 무서운 얼굴로 나를 쏘아보았다 She gave me a fierce scowl. /She scowled at me terribly.

쏘아올리다 [하늘에] shoot up; send up; set off; let off; launch 《인공 위성을》 ¶ 불꽃을 쏘아 올리다 display〔set off〕 fireworks // 인공 위성을 쏘아 올리다 put〔get, fire〕 an artificial satellite into the sky

쏘이다 ① [벌레에] be stung ¶ 벌에 쏘이다 get stung by a bee // 나는 이쪽저쪽에서 벌레에게 쏘였다 I have insect bites all over. ② [볕에] expose to sun ⇨ 쐬다

쏘지르다 ⇨ 쏘다니다

쏙 〚동물〛 a kind of crab; Upogebia major (학명)

쏙대기 [해초] a kind of laver

쏙독새 〚새〛 the Korean goatsucker〔jungle nightjar〕

쏙소그레하다 be all of a nice size ¶ 달걀들이 쏙소그레하다 The eggs are all of a nice size.

쏙쏙 ⇨ 쑥쑥

쏜살 a shot arrow ¶ 쏜살같다 be swift as an arrow // 쏜살같이 날다 shoot like an arrow; fly with lightning speed // 쏜살같이 닫다 run like a bullet shot out of a gun

쏟다 pour out; spill; drop; empty; [마음을] be bent on; devote oneself; be devoted to; concentrate ¶ 병속의 것을 쏟다 empty a bottle // 땅 위에 물을 쏟다 dash water over the ground // 연구에 정력을 쏟다 concentrate one's energies on the research // 통의 물을 쏟다 empty out the water from a pail // 물을 조금씩 쏟아라 Pour out water little by little. // 누가 잉크를 쏟아 놓았다 Someone has upset the inkstand. // 그는 그 여자에게 정신을 쏟고 있다 He is infatuated with the woman.

쏟뜨리다 pour out; spill ⇨ 쏟다

쏟아넣다 ① [액체·곡물 따위를] pour in〔into〕 ¶ 자루에 보리를 쏟아넣다 pour barley in a sack ② [돈 따위를] lay out 《money》 in; put 《money》 into; invest 《capital》 in; sink 《money》 in ¶ 사업에 전재산을 쏟아넣다 put all one's fortune in an enterprise

†**쏟아지다** pour 《out, in, down》; get〔be〕 spilt ¶ 비가 쏟아진다 The rain is pouring down. // 선물이 쏟아져 들어왔다 Gifts poured in from all quarters.

쏠 a small waterfall; a cascade

쏠다 [쥐 따위가] gnaw; chew; bite ¶ 줄을 쏠아 끊다 gnaw through a rope // 벽을 쏠아 구멍을 내다 gnaw a hole through a wall

쏠리다 [기울다] incline 《to》; lean 《to, toward》 ¶ (집이) 한쪽으로 쏠려있다 be leaning to one side; be out of the perpendicular // 탑이 한쪽으로 쏠려 있다 The tower leans from the perpendicular. // 그 여자한테 마음이 쏠린다 I am attracted by her. // 그는 공산주의에 쏠리고 있다 He has a leaning towards〔falls for, goes for〕 communism.

쏠쏠하다 (be) so-so

*__쐐기__¹ [V자형의] a wedge ; a chock (바퀴나 통을 못 움직이게 하는) ; linchpin (차바퀴를 멈추는) ¶ 쐐기 모양의 wedge-shaped ; cuneiform // 쐐기를 치다 drive a wedge in // 쐐기로 멈추다 wedge ; chock **─ 문자(文字)** a cuneiform (character) ; a sphenogram

쐐기² 〖곤충〗 a caterpillar

쐐기풀 〖식물〗 a nettle

쑤다 cook 《hot cereal, porridge》; boil ; prepare ; make ¶ 죽을 쑤다 cook gruel // 풀을 쑤다 prepare paste

쑤석거리다 ① [뒤져 찾느라고] ransack ; rummage 《in》; stir up ; [막대기 따위로] poke〔stir〕 about 《with a stick》; rake 〔poke up〕 《the fire》 ¶ (찾느라고) 서랍 속을 쑤석거리다 ransack〔rummage (in)〕 a drawer 《for a thing》
② [꼬드기다] instigate ; incite ; prod ; needle ; set〔spur, egg〕 《a person》 on ¶ 아무를 쑤석거려 …시키다〔하게 하다〕 set 〔needle〕 a person to 《do》

쑤셔넣다 thrust〔shove, tuck〕 in〔into〕; stuff〔cram, pack〕 into ; poke〔strike〕 into ; ram〔bump〕 into

쑤시개 a poke ; a pick
굴뚝 ─ a chimney poke 이─ a toothpick

†**쑤시다** ① [아프다] twinge ; tingle ; smart ; prickle ; feel prickly ; feel sharp pains ; throb with pain ¶ 머리가 쑤시다 have a splitting headache // 다리가 쑤시다 have a twinge in one's leg // 옆구리가 쑤시다 have a smart pain in the side // 이가 쑤신다 I have a toothache. /My teeth ache. // 온 몸이 쑤신다 I feel sharp pains all over my body. // 얻어 맞은 뺨이 몹시 쑤셨다 His cheeks tingled from the slap.
② [찌르다] pick ; poke ¶ 이를 쑤시다 pick one's teeth // 핀으로 쑤셔서 구멍을 내다 pick holes with a pin // 양탄자를 쑤셔 구멍을 내다 poke a hole in a carpet

쑥¹ wormwood ; mugwort ; artemisia ; sagebrush

쑥² shame ; impropriety ; indecency ¶ 너도 쑥이다 Shame on you!

쑥³ ① [내민 모양] way out ; [들어간 모양] way in ¶ 쑥 내민 눈썹 projecting eyebrows // 쑥 나온 눈 projecting eyes // 쑥 들어간 눈 hollow〔sunken〕 eyes // 혀를 쑥 내밀다 stick one's tongue out.
② [힘차게] with a jerk ¶ 쑥 잡아당기다 〔밀어넣다〕 pull〔push〕 with a (sudden) jerk ; give 《it》 a vigorous pull〔push〕 // 말뚝을 땅에서 쑥 뽑다 jerk a stake out of the ground // 칼을 쑥 뽑다 draw one's sword in flash ; whip out one's sword

쑥갓 a crown daisy ; Chrysanthemum coronarium (학명)

쑥국화 ─菊花 〖식물〗 a tansy ; Tanacetum boreale (학명)

쑥대 a wormwood〔mugwort〕 stalk
─밭 a plot〔patch〕 of wormwood ; a field overgrown with mugwort

쑥대강이 disheveled〔unkempt〕 hair ¶ 네 머리는 쑥대강이구나 Your hair is a mess.

쑥덕공론 ─公論 secret talks ; a secret conference ; a caucus **─하다** discuss 《things》 under one's breath ; hold secret discussions ¶ 쑥덕공론으로 계획을 세우다 plan 《a thing》 through secret talk

쑥떡 a cake made of rice flour and artemisia〔wormwood〕 paste

쑥밭 ¶ 쑥밭이 되다 be completely devastated ; be reduced to complete ruin // 쑥밭을 만들다 turn 《a place》 into ruins ⇨ 쑥대밭

쑥버무리 steamed rice cake mixed with mugwort

쑥새 〖새〗 a rustic bunting

쑥수그레하다 ⇨ 쑥소그레하다

쑥스럽다 (be) unbecoming ; unseemly ; indecent ; improper ¶ 신사로서 쑥스러운 짓 conduct unbecoming to a gentleman // 쑥스럽게 굴다 cut an awkward〔a ridiculous〕 figure ; expose oneself to ridicule

쑥쑥 ① [들어감·내밂] ¶ 쑥쑥 내밀다 protrude all way out // 쑥쑥 들어가다 sink all way in ② [뽑는 모양] ¶ 쑥쑥 뽑다 jerk out〔yank (구)〕 repeatedly ③ [쑤심] ¶ 쑥쑥 쑤시다 prick ; tingle ; hurt

쑬쑬하다 (be) tolerable ; passable ; fairly good ; so-so ¶ 쑬쑬히 so-so ; passably ; tolerably ; moderately // 생김생김이 쑬쑬하다 be fairly good-looking ; be fair to middling 《미·구》

쓰개 headgear ; head-dress (여자의) ; hat

†**쓰다**¹ [글씨를] write ; [글을] compose 《a poem》; write ; pen 《a story》; [적다] put〔write, note〕 down ¶ 영어로 쓰다 write in English // 잉크로 쓰다 write in ink // 연필로 쓰다 write in〔with a〕 pencil // 글씨를 잘 쓰다 write a good hand // 편지를 쓰다 write a letter ; write to 《a person》 // 잡지에 글을 쓰다 write for a magazine // 과학에 관하여 쓴 책이다 It is a book on science. // 카드에는 뭐라고 써 드릴까요 What would you like written on the greeting card?

†**쓰다**² ① [사용] use ; employ ; make use of ; put to use ¶ 튀김에 기름을 쓰다 use oil for frying // 함부로 쓰다 put 《a thing》 to a bad use // 벽돌을 쓰다 employ bricks 《in building》 // 젓가락을 쓰다 employ chopsticks 《in eating》 // 머리를 쓰다 use one's brain ; do brain work // 연장 쓰는 법을 배우다 learn the use of a tool // 이것은 무엇에 씁니까 What is this used for? // 이 솔은 오래 써서 닳았다 This brush has been worn out by long use. // 우리는 냄비 만드는 데 알루미늄을 쓰고 있다 Aluminum is employed for our cooking pots. // 내 사전을 쓰고 있니 Are you using my dictionary? // 내 차를 쓰십시오 My car is at

your service. // 타자기를 얼마든지 쓰셔도 좋습니다 You are welcome to the use of my typewriter. // 외출 중에는 내 방을 마음대로 쓰시오 I will give〔allow〕 you the run of my room while I am out. // 사전은 쓰기 위해서 산 거지 장식용으로 산 것이 아니다 The dictionary was bought for use, not for ornament. // 그는 눈을 못 쓰게 되었다 He has lost the use of his eyes.

② [사람을] employ ; hire ; use ; take 《a person》 into one's service ; keep 《a servant》 ¶ 많은 사람을 쓰다 employ many people // 하인을 열 사람 쓰고 있다 keep ten servants // 시험삼아 써 보다 take 《a person》 on trial // 그 공장에서는 직공을 천 명 이상 쓰고 있다 The factory employs more than a thousand hands. // 그들은 내가 쓰고 있는 사람들이다 They are in my employ〔service, pay〕. // 본인을 영어 교사로 써 주십시오 I beg to offer my services as a teacher of English.

③ [소비하다] use ; spend ¶ 석탄을 많이 쓰다 use much coal // 돈을 물같이 쓰다 spend money like water // 옷에 돈을 쓰다 spend money on clothes // 다 써 버리다 use up ; run〔go〕 through 《money》 ; consume ; exhaust // 돈을 함부로 쓰다 put money to bad use // 번 돈을 모두 술값으로 써 버린다 All his money earned goes on drinking. // 버는 대로 다 써 버린다 He spends all he earns. // 한 달에 설탕을 얼마나 쓰십니까 How much sugar do you consume a month ?

④ [말을] use ; speak ¶ 훌륭한 영어를 쓰다 speak good English ; express oneself in good English // 건방진 말을 쓰다 use haughty language // 브라질에서는 무슨 말을 씁니까 What language is spoken in Brazil ?

⑤ [술법을] practice ; do ; deal in ¶ 마술을 쓰다 do conjuring tricks ; deal with the devil ; practice magic

⑥ [약을] administer 《medicine》 ; dose ; use ; apply ¶ 약을 쓰다 administer a medicine 《to a patient》 ; [바르다] apply a medicament 《to a diseased part》 // 이 약을 쓰면 병이 낫습니다 This medicine will cure you of your disease.

⑦ [색을] have sex ; copulate

⑧ [힘을] exert oneself (노력하다) ; apply〔use〕 force (폭력을) ; use one's strength〔energy〕 (정력을)

쓰다³ put on ; wear ; cover ¶ 모자를 쓰다 put on〔wear〕 a hat ; have a hat on // 모자를 쓰고 있지 않다 have no hat on ; be bareheaded // 안경을 쓰다 put on glasses ; have spectacles on ; wear spectacles // 우산을 쓰다 hold up an umbrella ; have an umbrella up // 이불을 쓰다 pull the bedclothes over one's head // 먼지를 쓰다 be covered with dust // 물을 뒤집어 쓰다 pour water on oneself // 남의 죄를 쓰다 take upon oneself another's fault

쓰다⁴ [뫼를] choose the site of a grave (by geomancy) ¶ 뫼를 쓰다 set up a grave

†**쓰다⁵** [맛이] taste〔be〕 bitter ¶ 쓴 맛 a bitter taste // 쓴 약 bitter medicine // 쓴맛을 보다 taste a bitter〔hard〕 experience // 그 소식에 입맛이 썼다 I was bitter about the news.

쓰다듬다 stroke 《one's beard》 ; pat 《a child on the head》 ; pass one's hand over 《one's face》 ; smooth down 《one's hair》 ; rub 《a person's chin》 ¶ 턱을 쓰다듬다 touch〔rub〕 one's chin // 어린이의 턱을 쓰다듬어 어르다 chuck a child under the chin // 대머리를 쓰다듬다 pass one's hand over one's bald head

쓰디쓰다 (be) extremely bitter

‡**쓰라리다** ① [상처가] (be) sore ; smart ; burning ② [괴롭다] (be) painful ; sore ; bitter ; distressing ; grievous ¶ 쓰라린 경험 a bitter experience // 가슴이 쓰라리다 《it》 wring one's heart // 할퀸 상처가 아직도 쓰라리다 The scratch still smarts. // 연기때문에 눈이 쓰라리다 The smoke makes my eyes smart. // 가난한 사람들이 헐벗고 있는 것을 보면 가슴이 쓰라린다 It wrings my heart to see the poor in ragged clothes.

쓰라림 [상처] soreness ; smart(ness) ; [괴로움] pain ; painfulness ; bitterness

쓰러뜨리다 throw down ; knock〔bring〕 down ; trip up (발을 걸어서) ; fell ; blow down (바람이) ¶ 사람을 때려서 쓰러뜨리다 knock 《a person》 down // 나무를 쓰러뜨리다 fell a tree ; blow down a tree (바람이) // 집을 쓰러뜨리다 demolish〔pull down〕 a house // 정부를 쓰러뜨리다 overthrow〔topple〕 a government

†**쓰러지다** ① [서 있던 것이] fall〔come〕 down ; collapse (도괴하다) ; go〔roll〕 over ¶ 쓰러질 것 같은 집 a tumble-down house // 마루 위에 쓰러지다 fall down on the floor // 바람으로 쓰러지다 be blown down // 앞으로〔뒤로〕 쓰러지다 fall forward〔backward〕 // 쓰러져 가고 있다 be on the point of falling ; be tottering to its fall ; be ready to collapse // 지진으로 많은 집이 쓰러졌다 Many houses were destroyed by the earthquake. // 바람으로 나무가 쓰러졌다 The wind brought〔blew〕 down the trees.

② [병고·피로 따위로] break down 《from exhaustion》 ; go〔be〕 down 《with an illness》 ; fall in faint (기절하여) ; be laid up 《with cold》 ¶ 기진하여 쓰러지다 sink down on〔to〕 the ground // 배가 고파서 쓰러질 지경이다 be faint with hunger

③ [몰락하다] be ruined ; be overthrown ; [파산하다] fail ; go〔be〕 bankrupt ¶ 쓰러져 가는 정부 a tottering government // 은행이 쓰러지다 A bank fails. // 이 회사는 쓰러져 가고 있다 This company is on the verge of bankruptcy.

④ [죽다] die ; fall down dead ; fall a victim to ; succumb to《cancer》¶ 암으로 쓰러지다 die of cancer ; be carried off by cancer // …의 손에 쓰러지다 fall〔meet one's end〕at the hand of

쓰렁쓰렁하다 (be) estranged and lonely

*__쓰레기__ waste ; sweepings ; garbage ; refuse ; rubbish ; scraps ; trash《미》¶ 종이 쓰레기 waste paper // 나무 쓰레기 chips of wood // 인간 쓰레기 dregs of humanity ; a bum《미》; the scum of society // 그는 쓰레기 같은 인간이다 He is dirt. // 쓰레기 버리면 벌금 20,000원 20,000 *won* Fine for Littering. // 쓰레기를 버리지 마시오 Don't be a litterbug.

—꾼 a rubbish gatherer ; a garbage man **—차** a garbage wagon ; a disposal truck ; a dust cart《영》**—처리** refuse disposal **—통** a dustbin ; a garbage can ; a litter box〔pail〕; trash can **부엌—** kitchen refuse ; garbage《미》

쓰레받기 a dustpan

쓰레질 sweeping

쓰레하다 (be) leaning ; tottering

쓰르라미〖곤충〗a species of cicada ; Tonna japonensis (학명)

쓰르람쓰르람 chirping (of a cicada)

쓰리다 ache ; smart ; tingle ; burn ¶ 가슴이 쓰리다 have heartburn // 피부가 쓰리다 The skin smarts. // 눈이 쓰리다 My eyes are smarting.

쓰이다¹ [글씨가] write ; be written ; [쓰게 하다] let《a person》write ¶ 이 펜은 글씨가 잘 쓰인다 The pen writes well. // 이 소설은 쉽게 쓰여 있다 This story is written in plain language. // 그 일에 대하여 신문에 뭐라고 쓰여 있느냐 What do the papers say about it ? // 그는 아들에게 편지를 쓰게 하였다 He had his son write a letter.

쓰이다² ① [들다·소용되다] be spent ; be consumed ; take ; cost ¶ 이 엔진에는 석탄이 많이 쓰인다 This engine consumes much coal. // 그 일에는 사람 손이 많이 쓰인다 The work takes〔requires〕quite a number of hands.

② [사용되다] be used ; be made use of ; be employed ; serve ¶ 일상 생활에 쓰이는 물건 articles in daily use // 흔히 쓰이다 be in common use // 널리 쓰이게 되다 come into general use // 안 쓰이게 되다 get〔go〕out of use // 이 방은 서재로 쓰인다 This room now serves as my study. // 알코올은 때로는 용제로도 쓰인다 Alcohol is sometimes employed〔used〕as a solvent.

쓰적거리다 ① [비비어지다] rub〔chafe〕against each other ② [대강대강 쓸다] sweep slovenly

쓰적쓰적 [비벼짐] rubbing ; chafing ; [쓰레질] sweeping roughly

쏙 [슬쩍]《slip away》quickly and quietly ; [척]《bolt》abruptly ; [빨리]《pass by》rapidly ; [슬슬]《rub》deftly〔lightly〕

쓱싹 —하다 ① [돈 따위를] pocket ; peculate ; embezzle ; sneak《미·속》¶ 남의 돈을 쓱싹하다 embezzle money from《a person》// 그 돈의 대부분을 쓱싹했다 He pocketed most of the money.

② [상쇄하다] offset〔cancel〕each other ; wipe off《a debt》; square up《속》

③ [얼버무리다] cover up

쓱싹거리다 emit a rasping sound ; make a grating sound ; rasp ; grate ¶ 쓱싹쓱싹 with a (continuous) sawing sound

쓱쓱《rubbing, stroking》with deft strokes ¶ 두 손을 쓱쓱 비비다 rub one's hands // 머리를 쓱쓱 쓰다듬다 smooth (down) one's hair

쓴맛 단맛 the bitters and the sweets ; prosperity and adversity ¶ 인생의 쓴맛 단맛을 다 보다 taste the sweets and bitters of life

쓴술 liquor made from nonglutinous rice

쓴웃음 a bitter〔wry, grim〕smile ¶ 쓴웃음을 짓다 smile a bitter smile // 나는 그저 쓴웃음 지으며 참을게 I'll just grin and bear it.

쓸개〖해부〗the gall-bladder ; the gall ¶ 쓸개 빠진 놈 a spiritless person

—머리 beef from the top of the gall-bladder **—즙** bile ; gall

쓸까스르다 rub《a person》the wrong way ; irk ; irritate ; nettle

*__쓸다¹__ sweep ¶ 마루를 쓸다 sweep the floor // 먼지를 쓸어내다 sweep the dirt out〔away〕// 쓸어 모으다 sweep up together ; sweep into a heap // 판돈을 쓸다 sweep the (gambling) board ; win all the money // 유행병이 한 고을을 쓸었다 The epidemic swept〔prevailed throughout〕the town.

쓸다² [줄로] rasp ; file ¶ 줄로 쓸어서 매끈하게 하다 file《a thing》smooth ; file away roughness

쓸데 (a) use ; service ; usefulness ; [필요] necessity ; need

*__쓸데없다__ be of no use〔value〕; (be) useless ; worthless ¶ 쓸데없이 unnecessarily ; to no purpose ; in vain // 쓸데없는 놈 a useless〔good-for-nothing〕fellow // 쓸데없는 책 a book of no value ; a worthless book ; a stupid book // 쓸데없이 돈을 쓰다 waste money ; spend money wastefully // 쓸데없이 애썼다 I have labored in vain. // 울어도 쓸데 없다 It is no use crying. /It is of no use to cry. /There is no use in crying.

쓸리다¹ ① [쓸게 하다] let〔make〕sweep ¶ 하인에게 방을 쓸리다 have a servant sweep the room

② [피동] be swept ; get swept ¶ 홍수에 다리가 쓸려 나갔다 The bridge was washed away by the swollen river.

쓸리다² [줄·톱으로] get rasped〔filed〕

†**쓸모** use ; usefulness ; utility ¶ 쓸모가 있다 be of use ; be useful〔serviceable〕// 쓸모가 없다 be useless〔of no use〕; be good-for-nothing ; be no good // 쓸모가 많다 be of wide〔extensive〕 use // 무엇이든지 쓸모가 다 있는 법이다 Everything has its use. // 아무 짝에도 쓸모가 없는 놈이다 He is a good-for-nothing (fellow). // 인간은 무엇인가 한 가지 점은 쓸모가 있다 Everyone's got to have at least one thing going for him.

‡**쓸쓸하다** [적적하다] (be) lonely ; lonesome ; [날씨가] dreary ; gloomy ; dismal ¶ 쓸쓸한 얼굴 a cheerless look ; lonely〔cheerless〕 countenance // 쓸쓸한 웃음 a wan〔melancholy, sad〕 smile // 쓸쓸한 곳 a lonely〔desolate〕 spot // 쓸쓸하게 느끼다 feel lonely // 쓸쓸하게 지내다 lead a lonely life // 이국에서 쓸쓸히 죽다 go to die forlorn in a foreign land // 네가 없어 매우 쓸쓸했다 We missed you badly. // 말벗이 없으니 쓸쓸하다 I feel lonely having no one to talk to.

쓸어들이다 sweep in ; rake in

쓸어버리다 sweep out〔away〕; brush up

쓸음질 filing

쓿다 polish 《grain》

쓿은쌀 cleaned〔polished〕 rice

씀바귀 a sowthistle ; Lactuca dendata (학명)

씀씀이 expense ; expenditure ¶ 씀씀이가 많다 have large expenditures ; spend money liberally // 씀씀이가 적다 be modest in expenditure ; spend little // 씀씀이가 헤프다 spend money wastefully ; throw money around (like a drunken tailor) // 너는 돈 씀씀이가 너무 헤프다 You're too much of a spendthrift.

씁쓰레하다 be〔taste〕 a bit bitter

씁쓸하다 (be) somewhat bitter ; bitterish

씌다 ① [귀신이] be possessed by some evil spirit ; be obsessed by〔with〕 a demon ② ⇨ 쓰이다[1,2] ③ ⇨ 씌우다

씌우다 [모자 따위를] put 《a hat》 on 《a person's head》; cover 《a thing》 with ; [죄 따위를] impute 《a fault》 to 《a person》; lay〔put, fix〕 《a fault》 on 《a person》; fix 《a blame》 on 《a person》; charge 《a person》 with 《a blame》; shift 《responsibility》 on to 《a person》; lay 《a crime》 at 《a person's》 door

†**씨**[1] ① [종자] a seed ; a stone ; [사과 따위의] a pip ; [핵 속의] a kernel ¶ 씨 없는 포도 seedless grapes // 씨가 많은 seedy // 씨를 뿌리다 sow seed ; sow // 밭에 씨를 뿌리다 sow the fields ; plant the field // 씨를 받다 gather the seeds
② [동물의] a breed ; [혈통] a stock ; a lineage ; [아이] a child ¶ 불의의 씨 a child born in sin // 씨가 좋다 be of〔bred from〕 a good〔fine〕 stock // 씨는 같지만 배가 다르다 They are of the same father but of different mothers. // 그의 씨를 배다 She is with child by him.
③ [원인·재료] cause ; source ; a subject ¶ 불화의 씨를 뿌리다 sow the seed of trouble ; sow discord ; give rise to a quarrel
씨도둑은 못한다 속담 Of evil grain no good seed can come. /The litter is like to the sire and dam.

씨[2] [피륙의] woof ; weft ; the widthwise threads ¶ 씨와 날 woof and warp

씨[3] [품사] a part of speech ; a grammatical category of words

†**씨 氏** [경칭] Mister 《Mr.》; Missis 《Mrs.》; Miss ; [가계·혈통] a lineage ; birth ; a clan ; a family ; [성] a family name ; a surname ¶ 김씨 Mr. *Kim* // 안동 김씨 the *Kims* of *Andong*

씨감자 seed potatoes

씨그둥하다 (be) unpleasant to hear ; offensive〔harsh, inconsonant〕 to the ear

씨근벌떡거리다 gasp and gulp ; pant

씨금 ⇨ 위선(緯線)

씨눈 〖식물〗 the germinal disk ; an embryo ; 〖동물〗 a fetus

씨다리 a nugget of alluvial gold

씨닭 a chicken raised for breeding

씨도 一度 degree of latitude

씨도리(배추) a cabbage left in the field for seed

씨돼지 a breeding pig

씨름 wrestling ; a wrestling match (승부)
—하다 wrestle ¶ 씨름의 수 a wrestling trick ; chip // 영어와 씨름하다 wrestle with English // 씨름을 한판 하다 have a wrestling bout 《with》; try a fall 《with》
—꾼 a wrestler **—판** a wrestling match **발—** ankle〔shin〕 wrestling **팔—** wrist wrestling

씨름잠방이 wrestling trunks

씨말 a breeding horse ; a stud(horse) ; a stallion

씨명 氏名 family name and personal name ; names ; a full name

씨무룩하다 ⇨ 시무룩하다

씨뿌리다 sow〔plant〕 seed ; seed

씨소 a breeding ox ; a seed bull

씨식잖다 (be) wanting ; inferior ; be somewhat weak in the head

씨아 a cotton gin ¶ 씨아로 목화의 씨를 빼다 gin cotton
—손 the handle of a cotton gin

씨알 ① [종란] an egg for breeding ② 〖광산〗 a tiny nugget

씨알머리 a bad seed ; a rogue ; a nasty fellow ¶ 씨알머리 없다 be nasty

씨암탉 a brood hen ; a breeder
— 걸음 mincing steps

씨앗 a seed ¶ 씨앗을 뿌리다 sow seed ; sow

씨양이질 —하다 bother a busy person

씨억씨억 firmly and briskly ; energetically
—하다 (be) energetic

씨우적거리다 grumble ; complain

씨우적씨우적 grumbling ; complaining
씨젖 〖식물〗 endosperm ; [배유] albumen
†**씨족 氏族** a family ; a clan
— **사회** a clan society — **제도** the family〔clan〕 system
씨종 a hereditary slave
씨주머니 a seed bag ; an ascus
씨줄 (a line of) latitude
씩씩하다 (be) manly ; valiant ; brave ; courageous ; gallant ; vigorous ¶ 씩씩하게 bravely ; valiantly ; gallantly ; vigorously // 씩씩한 남자 a fine strapping fellow ; a dashing fellow // 씩씩한 기상 a brave heart // 씩씩하게 싸움터로 나가다 go out to war most gallantly
씰그러뜨리다 misshape ; swerve ; distort
씹 ① [음부] the vulva ; the vagina ② [성교] sexual intercourse ; coitus 《라》 — **하다** have sexual intercourse 《with》 ; copulate
씹거웃 a woman's pubic hair ; pubes
‡**씹다** chew ; masticate ¶ 음식을 잘 씹다 chew one's food well // 씹어뱉듯이 말하다 speak disgustedly
씹히다 be chewed〔masticated〕 ; [씹게 하다] let 《a person》 chew ¶ 잘 씹히지 않다 be hard to chew // 밥에 돌이 씹히다 bite on a grit in the rice
씻가시다 wash and rinse
씻기다 wash ; be washed ; be carried away (풍랑에) ; have 《a person》 wash (씻게 하다) ¶ 큰 비에 길이 씻기다 A road is washed〔carried away〕 with heavy rains. // 그릇이 잘 씻기지 않다 This dish does not wash well. // 남편에게 그릇을 씻기다 have one's husband wash dishes // 이렇게 좋은 날씨에는 마음에 있던 근심까지도 말끔히 씻겨 나간다 Nice weather like this wipes every care from your mind.
†**씻다** ① wash ; cleanse ; rinse ¶ 얼굴을 씻다 wash one's face // 물로 손을 씻다 wash one's hands with water // 병을 씻다 cleanse a bottle // 몸을 씻다 wash oneself // 상처를 씻다 bathe a cut // 눈을 씻다 bathe one's eyes 《in water》 // 마음을 씻어 주는 좋은 음악을 듣고 싶다 I'd like to hear some good music-something to refresh the spirit.
② [누명을] wipe out ; clear oneself of ¶ 씻을 수 없는 치욕 indelible〔ineffaceable, lasting〕 disgrace // 누명을 씻다 wipe off a dishonor ; wipe out a stain on one's name ; clear oneself of a (false) charge
③ [닦아내다] wipe off ; mop ¶ 이마의 땀을 씻다 wipe the sweat off the brow ; mop one's brow // 눈물을 씻다 dry one's eyes ; wipe one's tears away // 입을 씻다 wipe one's mouth
씻부시다 wash 《dishes》 clean ; cleanse ; clean
씻어내다 wash off〔out〕 ; wipe out ; clear away
씻은듯이 clean ; bright ; completely ; thoroughly ¶ 종기가 씻은 듯이 낫다 A boil is all healed up. // 하늘이 씻은 듯이 맑다 The sky is as clear as can be.
씽 whistling ; hissing ; whizzing ¶ '씽'하는 소리 a whistling sound ; a sough (바람의) // 바람이 온종일 씽씽 불었다 The wind whistled all day long.
씽씽하다 ⇨ 싱싱하다

ㅇ

*아[1] Ah ! /Oh ! /O ! /Alas ! /Dear me ! / Good gracious ! /(Good) Heaven ! / Why ! /Well ! / Hey ! /[말을 걸 때] I say ; Say ; Look here. ¶ 아 귀찮다 Oh, bother ! // 아 그는 죽었다 Alas ! He is no more ! // 아 그렇습니까 Is that so 〔right〕? /Really ? // 아 덥다 How hot ! // 아 아름답다 Oh ! How beautiful ! // 아 야 단났군 Ah ! That's the trouble. // 어제 그 여자를 만났지—아 그래요 I saw her yesterday. Oh ! Did you ? // 아 아버님이 살아계신다면 O that my father were living ! /How I wish my father were alive. // 아 졸립다 I'm (very) sleepy. // 아 지금 곧 갈게 Yes, I'm coming. // 아 이 사람아 Say〔I say〕, you ! / Hey, you !

아[2] ¶ 수길아 이리 오너라 Come here, *Sugil* !

아 亞 [아시아] Asia ; Asian ¶ 구아(歐亞) 대륙 the Eurasian Continent

아 阿 Africa ; African ¶ 아아(阿亞) 블록 the Afro-Asian bloc

아- 亞 sub- ; near-
—과(科) a subfamily —류(流) an adherent ; an epigone ; a bad second ; a follower 《of》 —성(聖) a sage of second rank —열대 the subtropical zones 〔regions〕; the subtropics —종(種) a subspecies —황산 sulphurous acid

아가 a baby ; a babe ⇨ 아기 ; [호칭] My darling ! /Baby ! /Daughter ! / Daughter-in-law !

아가 雅歌 〖성경〗 The Song of Solomon (솔로몬의 아가)

아가리 a mouth ; a muzzle ; a snout ¶ 아가리를 벌리다 open one's trap ; bawl ; talk // 아가리 다물어라 Shut up ! /Knock it off !

*아가미 the gills of a fish ; the branchia
— 호흡 branchial respiration

아가사창 我歌査唱 attributing one's failure to another ; taking another's place in remonstration

아가씨 a young lady ; a young girl ; an unmarried lady ; a maid(en) ; [호칭] Miss ; you ; Young lady ! ¶ 촌〔도시〕 아가씨 a country〔town〕 girl // 어여쁜 아가씨 a lovely〔charming〕 little girl // 아가씨 어디서 오셨어요 Where are you from, Miss ? // 송 장군댁의 아가씨다 She is the daughter of General *Song*.

아가위 the fruit of the hawthorn ; the haw
—나무 the Chinese hawthorn

아감 gills
— 구멍 a gill slit〔cleft〕; a branchial cleft
—딱지〔뚜껑〕 a gill cover ; an operculum
—뼈 branchial bones ; a branchial skeleton —젓 salted fishgills

아강 亞綱 〖동물〗 (biological) subclass

아객 雅客 [아취있는 사람] a man of taste ; [문인] a writer ; a knight of the pen

아고산대 亞高山帶 the subalpine zone

아교 阿嬌 a charming〔an attractive〕 girl 〔woman〕

*아교 阿膠 glue (made from oxhide) ¶ 아교질의 gluey ; glutinous ; gelatinoid ; gelatiniform // 아교를 붙이다 glue 《to》 ; fasten 《a thing》 with glue

아구 亞區 〖생물〗 a subregion

아구맞추다 round out the number ; make it come out even〔as it should〕 ; bring it up to the proper amount

아국 我國 our country〔land, nation〕 ; this country (of ours)

아군 我軍 our forces〔troops, army〕 ; friendly forces

*아궁이 a fuel hole ; a fireplace

아귀[1] ① [갈라진 곳] a crotch ; a fork ¶ 손아귀 the space between the thumb and the index finger // 입아귀 the corner of the mouth
② [두루마기·속곳의] side slit on an overcoat〔a petticoat〕 (like slash pocket) ¶ 두루마기에 아귀트다 provide an overcoat with side slit
③ [씨의] that part of a seed through which it sprouts ¶ 씨가 아귀트다 A seed sprouts open.

아귀[2] 〖어류〗 an angler-fish ; a sea devil

아귀 餓鬼 〖불교〗 a hungry ghost ; a famished devil〔demon〕 ; Preta 《범》 ; [비유적] a greedy person ; a person of voracious appetite ¶ 아귀 같은 greedy ; voracious // 아귀같이 먹다 gobble〔wolf〕 one's food

아귀다툼 argument ; a spat ⇨ 말다툼

아귀세다 (be) tough ; firm ; strong-minded ; have a strong grip ¶ 아귀센 아이 a tough boy

아귀아귀 greedily ; ravenously ; with avidity ¶ 아귀아귀 먹다 gobble〔wolf, devour〕 one's food ; shovel 《food》 into one's mouth

아귀토 —土 the weatherproofing of mud cement seen at the ends of eaves tiles

아그레망 agrément 《프》 ; approval ; acceptance ; agreement 《by a government》 ¶ 아그레망을 요청하다 ask for an agrément // A씨를 대사로 영국 정부의 아

그레망을 요청하다 request〔ask for〕 the British Government's agreement to the appointment of Mr. A as an ambassador // 아그레망을 주다 give agrément 《to》

아그배 『식물』 a Toringo crab-apple
—나무 Malus sieboldii (학명)

아긋하다 (be) a bit open〔ajar, apart〕; do not quite fit; be not quite fitting together

‡아기 ① a baby; an infant; a child; a babe (시어) ¶ 사내〔여자〕 아기 a baby boy〔girl〕 // 아기를 낳다 give birth to a child; have a baby // 내가 아기인 줄 알아 I was not born yesterday. ② [딸·며느리] dear; darling; pet

아기 고사리 bracken〔fern〕 sprouts

아기똥거리다 toddle; totter; waddle ¶ 아기똥거리며 걸어가다 toddle one's way

아기똥아기똥 waddlingly; in a waddling manner; toddlingly; totteringly

아기똥하다 (be) haughty; be puffed up

아기서다 be〔become〕 pregnant; be with child; conceive

아기자기 —하다 (be) sweet; charming; be tingling with pleasure; (be) very happy; be full of interest ¶ 아기자기한 이야기 a juicy story // 아기자기한 분위기 congenial〔homely〕 atmosphere // 아기자기하게 살다 live happily together // 이 군은 아기자기한 결혼 생활을 하고 있다 Mr. *Lee* is leading a very happy married life.

아기작- ⇨ 아기똥-

아기작거리다 toddle; walk with a toddling gait

아기집 [자궁] the womb; the uterus 《*pl.* -ri》

‡아까 (a little while) ago; some time ago; a moment ago ¶ 아까부터 for some time; since a while ago // 아까 말씀 올린 그분 the man of whom I spoke a little while ago // 그는 조금 아까 출발했다 He started just now.

아깝다 (be) regrettable; pitiful; [귀중하다] precious; valuable; be of great value; (be) too good (너무 좋다) ¶ 아깝게도 regrettably; lamentably; sad to say // 아까운듯이 reluctantly; grudgingly; unwillingly // 아깝게도 패하다 be defeated by a narrow margin // 아까운 일이군 What a pity it is! // 서둘러라 일각이 아깝다 Hurry up, there is no time to lose. // 아깝게도 그는 젊어서 죽었다 It's too bad that he died young. // 그의 죽음은 국가를 위해 아까운 일이다 His death is a great loss to the country. // 목숨이 아깝거든 거기서 움직이지 마라 Stay where you are, if you want to stay alive. / Do not, for your life, stir from the spot. // 그것을 버리는 것은 매우 아깝다 It is too good to throw it away. // 그것을 내놓기가 아깝다 I can ill spare it. // 그런 일에 시간을 낭비하는 것은 아깝다 Time is too precious to spend for such a thing.

*아끼다 grudge; spare; be sparing of; value ¶ 아끼는 stingy; close-fisted; miserly // 아끼지 않다 be liberal; lavish 《with》 // 돈을 아끼다 begrudge〔grudge〕 money; be frugal of one's money // 돈보다 명예를 아끼다 value honor above riches // 목숨을 아끼다 hold one's life dear; be reluctant to lose one's life // 비용을 아끼다 spare expense // 사람을 아끼다 make much of 《a person》 // 수고를 아끼지 않다 spare no effort〔pain〕; do not spare oneself; lavish labor 《on》 // 시간을 아껴 쓰다 use one's time sparingly; value time

아끼다 똥 된다 [속담] He who saves for tomorrow saves for the cat.

있을 때 아껴야지 없으면 아낄 것도 없다 [속담] Better sapare at brim than at bottom. /It is too late to spare when the bottom is bare.

*아낌없이 unsparingly; ungrudgingly; generously; freely; unstintedly; without stint ¶ 돈을 아낌없이 낭비하다 lavish money on; be liberal with one's purse // 자선을 위해서 돈을 아낌없이 내다 give money freely to charities // 시간과 노력을 아낌없이 쓰다 give time and effort unsparingly 《to a thing》

아나 ① [아이들에게] there; look here; hey (there); say; listen ¶ 아나 네 이름이 뭐지 You, there, what's your name? // 아나 이것 받아 Here you are! ② [고양이에게] Here kitty 〔puss〕!; Kittykitty!

아나나스 『식물』 an ananas; a pineapple

‡아나운서 a (radio, TV) announcer
여자 — a lady announcer; a woman announcer (미)

아나크로니즘 anachronism

아나키 anarchy
—스트 an anarchist —즘 anarchism

아낙 [내간] a woman's room; woman's quarters; a boudoir; [아낙네] a woman
—군수 a stay-at-home; a person who stays at home all the time

아낙네 a woman; a wife ¶ 아낙네들 the womenfolk

아날로그 analog(ue)
— 계산기〔컴퓨터〕 an analog(ue) computer

†아내 a wife; one's better-half; a spouse (배우자) ¶ 남의 아내 another's wife // 아내를 얻다 take a wife; take 《a woman》 to wife // 아내로 맞이하다 make 《her》 one's wife // 그 여자는 훌륭한 아내가 될 것이다 She will make a good wife. // 좋은 아내는 집안의 보배다 A good wife is a household treasure.

아내가 귀여우면 처갓집 말뚝 보고 절한다 [속담] Love me, move my dog.

아네로이드 aneroid
— 고도계 an aneroid altimeter — 기압계 an aneroid (barometer)

아네모네 〖식물〗 an anemone
아녀자 兒女子 children and women ; a young girl ; a skirt
아노락 〖방한용 외투〗 an anorak
아뇨 [대답이 부정일 때] no ; nay 《문》; [대답이 긍정일 때] yes ⇨ 아니
*__아늑하다__ (be) cozy ; snug ; comfortable ¶ 아늑한 방 a snug〔cozy〕 room
아는체하다 feign knowledge ; pretend as if one knew ; have a knowing look ; pretend to know ¶ 아는 체하는 놈 a knowing fellow ; a know-all 《구》
†**아니** ① [부사] not ¶ 조금도 …아니다 not . . . at all ; not in the least // 아니 가다〔오다〕 do not go〔come〕 // 이것은 내것이 아니다 This is not mine. // 갈 기분이 없는 것도 아니다 He is not entirely unwilling to go.
② [대답] no ¶ 하나 더 드시겠어요—아니 이제 충분합니다 Won't you have another (one)? No, thank you. // 아니 괜찮아 I don't care ! /Never mind ! // 과자는 싫어합니까—아니 좋아합니다 Don't you care for〔like〕 sweets? Yes, I do. // 편지를 썼니—아니 나중에 쓸테다 Have you written the letter? No, I am going to write it later.
③ [놀람] Why ! ; What ! ; Good Heavens ¶ 아니 이게 웬일이냐 Why, what happened? // 아니 그것을 어디서 구했니 Why, where did you find it? // 아니 동생이 죽었다고 What ! Brother dead? // 아니 그 전부를 그에게 주었다고 What, did you give him all of it?
아니땐 굴뚝에 연기날까 〔속담〕 Does smoke rise from a chimney where a fire has not been lit? /No smoke without some fire.
아니꼬와하다 be sick of ; be disgusted at ; be nauseated at〔by〕; be revolted by
아니꼽다 ① [사물이 주어] (be) disgusting ; sickening ; nauseating ¶ 아니꼬운 냄새 nauseating odor // 하는 짓이 아니꼽다 《A person's》 behavior is disgusting.
② [사람이 주어] be nauseated ; be sick ¶ 보기만 해도 아니꼽다 The sight sickens me. /My gorge rises at it.
아니나다를까 just as was expected ; as one expected ; as might have been expected ; sure enough ¶ 아니나 다를까 언짢아하였다 As might have been expected, he was disgusted by the news. // 아니나 다를까 그는 거기에 있었다 Sure enough, I found him there. // 아니나 다를까 그는 얼굴을 나타내지 않았다 As might have been expected, he failed to turn up.
†**아니다** be not ; no ¶ 그것을 본 것은 내가 아니고 내 동생이었다 Not I, but my brother saw it. // 죄지은 사람은 내가 아니라 그 남자이다 It is not I who am guilty, but he. // 그는 헌신적이 아니다 He is not unselfish. // 이것은 불가능한 일이 아니다 가능하다 It is not impossible. It's possible. // 그것은 결코 쉬운일이 아니다 It is no picnic. // 가겠니—아니 안간다 Will you go? No, I won't
아니라고 《say》 that it is not ; saying that it is not ¶ 그는 그것이 자기 것이 아니라고 주지 않았다 He wouldn't give it saying that it was not his.
아니라도 even if〔though〕 (it is) not
아니라면 if (you say) it is not
아니면 either 《you》 or 《I》 ¶ 너 아니면 내가 가야만 한다 Either you or I am to go.
아니스 〖식물〗 anise
아니오 [대답이 부정일 때] no ; [대답이 긍정일 때] yes ¶ 맥주 좋아하지 않습니까—아니오, 좋아합니다 Don't you like beer? Yes, I do. // 죄송합니다—아니오 별 말씀을 Excuse me. Not at all〔Don't mention it〕.
아니참 Oh ; Uh ; Oh my ; That reminds me ; That's it ¶ 아니참 내 모자 Dear me ! I've left my hat behind.
아니하다 ⇨ 않다
아닌게아니라 sure enough ; really ¶ 아닌게아니라 네말이 옳다 Indeed you are right. // 아닌게아니라 그녀는 매력이 있었다 Sure enough, she was charming. // 아닌게아니라 좋은 방법이지만 실행하기 어렵다 A good plan, to be sure, but it is hard of practice.
아닌밤중 —中 ¶ 아닌밤중에 홍두깨격으로 abruptly ; unexpectedly ; out of the blue ; all of a sudden ; all at once // 아닌밤중에 총소리가 났다 A shot rang out through the night.
아닌밤중에 홍두깨 〔관용〕 a great surprise ; a bolt from the blue
아닐린 〖화학〗 aniline
— 염료 aniline dyes
아다지오 〖음악〗 an adagio 《이》
아닥치듯 arguing violently
아담 〖성경〗 Adam
아담 雅淡 —하다 (be) nice ; refined ; elegant ; neat ; tidy ¶ 아담한 집 a nice〔refined〕 house // 아담한 문체 an elegant style
아데노이드 〖의학〗 adenoids
-아도 but ; yet ¶ 그는 작아도 튼튼하다 He is small, but strong.
아도니스 [신화] Adonis
아동 兒童 a child 《*pl.* children》; a juvenile ; [생도] a pupil ; boys and girls 《총칭》 ¶ 아동의 juvenile // 취학전의 아동 preschool children // 아동의 복장을 하고 있다 be dressed in a juvenile manner
— 건강 상담소 a clinical consultation office for children **— 교육** juvenile education ; the education of children **—극** juvenile drama ; a play for children **—기** childhood **— 도서관** a juvenile 〔children's〕 library **— 문학** juvenile〔children's〕 literature **— 문학자** a writer of juvenile stories **— 보호** child welfare —

보호 사업 juvenile protection work — 복지(법) the Child Welfare (Law) — 복지 시설 a child welfare institution — 상담소 a child consultation center ; child-guidance clinics — 소설 juvenile novels — 수당 a children's allowance — 심리학 juvenile〔child〕 psychology — 연구 the study of children 초등 학교 — elementary school children ; school boys and girls 학령 — children of school age

아둔패기 a stupid person〔dummy〕 ; a dolt ; a screw ball ; nut 《미·속》

아둔하다 (be) dull ; stupid ; dense ; thick ; dim〔slow〕-witted ; scatter-brained ; thickheaded ¶ 아둔하기도 하다 How stupid can you get ! // 술을 마시면 머리가 아둔해진다 Wine dulls the senses. / Wine muddles one's brain.

아드님 Your〔his〕 esteemed son

아드득아드득 with a crunching sound ¶ 아드득아드득 씹다 munch ; crunch // 아드득아드득 이를 갈다 grind〔grate〕 one's teeth

아드등거리다 bicker ; quarrel ; [불화하다] feud〔be at feud〕 《with》 ¶ 사소한 일로 아드등거리다 bicker over trifles

아드레날린 『의학·화학』 adrenalin(e)

아드롱이 mottled spots〔pattern〕 ; mottling

아드리아 해 —海 the Adriatic Sea

*아득하다 (be) far away ; far off ; remote ; be a good〔long〕 way off ; be afar ; be in the distance ¶ 아득한 옛날 remote antiquity ; dim past // 아득한 훗날에 in the remote〔far-off〕 future // 가도가도 아득한 천리길 a long, long way to go // 갈 길이 아득하다 have a long way to go // 아득하게 보이다 I see it a long way off. // 그 날이 오는 것도 그리 아득하지는 않다 The day will not be far distant.

†아들 a son ; a boy ¶ 좋은〔나쁜〕 아들을 가지고 있다 be blessed with a good son〔be cursed with a bad son〕 // 그것을 한 것은 우리집 아들 놈이 아닙니다 My boy is innocent of it. /It was not my boy who did it.

—딸 son(s) and daughter(s) —자식〔놈〕 my son〔boy〕

아들이삭 a side ear (of grain)

아등그러지다 get warped ; get twisted out of shape

아디스 아바바 Adis Ababa (이디오피아의 수도)

아디유 an adieu 《프》 《*pl.* ~s, -x》 ; goodby(e)

아딧줄 a sail line〔rope〕

아따 (oh) boy ; gee ; well ¶ 아따 말도 많이 한다 Oh boy, you really talk, don't you ! // 아따 네 맘대로 해라 Well, do as you like.

아뜩하다 (be) suddenly dizzy ; giddy ¶ 그 소식에 정신이 아뜩하다 be stunned by the news

아라베스크 arabesque

아라비아 Arabia ¶ 아라비아의 Arabian ; Arabic

— 고무 gum arabic — 낙타 Arabian camel —말 an Arab (horse) — 문자 Arab characters — 반도 the Arabian Peninsular — 사람 an Arabian ; an Arab — 사막 the Arabian Desert — 숫자 Arabic numerals〔figures〕 —어 Arabic — 풀 glue ; mucilage —해 the Arabian Sea

아랄해 —海 Aral Sea〔Lake〕

아람 [밤·상수리 따위] (being) fully ripened on the tree

밤— tree-ripened chestnuts

아람치 one's share ; one's own

⁑아랍 Arab

— 세계 the Arab world ; Arabdom — 연맹 the Arab League — 연합 the United Arab States — 제국 the Arab States 범— 주의 Pan-Arabism 통일 — 공화국 the United Arab Republic 《U. A. R.》

아랍 석유 수출국 기구 —石油輸出國機構 the Organization of Arab Petroleum Exporting Countries 《OAPEC》 ⇨ 석유(— 수출국 기구)

아랑 the sediment〔dregs〕 left from brewing liquor

아랑곳 concern ; interest —하다 concern oneself 《with》 ; take an interest 《in》 ¶ 그 일에 네가 아랑곳할 것 있느냐 What concern is it of yours ? // 내가 아랑곳할 것 없다 I don't care about it. // 내 일에 아랑곳 하지 마라 Leave me alone. / Hands off my business. // 그녀는 무엇에나 아랑곳하는 여자다 She meddles with everything.

아랑곳없다 have nothing to do 《with》 ; be no concern of 《one's》 ; have no interest 《in》 ¶ 그것은 네가 아랑곳 할 바 아니다 That's none of your business.

아랑주 —紬 silk stuff with cotton blended

†아래 the bottom ; the foot ; the base ; the lower part ¶ 아래의 lower ; under ; [하위의] subordinate // 아래쪽 the underside // 아래에 down ; under ; beneath ; below ; [하층에] downstairs // 책상 아래에 under a desk // …의 보호 아래 under the protection 《of》 // 이러한 정세 아래에서 under such a situation // 계단 아래에 at the foot of the stairs // 아래에서 세째 번 the third from the bottom // 언덕 아래 the bottom〔foot〕 of a hill // 이 아래 정거장 the next station down // 30세보다 아래 사람들 persons under thirty (years of age) // 위에서 아래까지 (주인에서 하인에 이르기까지) from the master downwards〔down to the servants〕 // 아래에 내려놓다 put〔set, lay〕 down // 아래를 보다 look down // 아래에서 기다리다 wait downstairs // 아래로 내려오다 come down ; come downstairs // 아래에서 받치다 support 《a thing》 from below // 아래와 같다 as follows // 달이 지평선 아래로 졌다 The moon sank below the

ㅇ

horizon. // 대위는 소령의 아래다 The captain is beneath the major. // 그는 나보다 두 살 아래다 He is two years younger than I. /He is younger than I by two years. // 무릎 아래를 다쳤다 I got hurt below the knee. // 하늘 아래 새로운 것 없다 There is nothing new under the sun.

아래옷 lower garment ; bottom piece ; the bottom(s) of a garment

아래위 up and down ; above and below ; [신분의] the upper and lower classes ; high and low ¶ 아래위 한 벌 a suit ; an ensemble // 아래위 사람 one's juniors and seniors // 아래위 구별없이 both high〔great〕 and low〔small〕// 아래위로 움직이다 move up and down ; bob // 사람의 아래 위를 훑어보다 look a person up and down

—턱 classification into seniors and juniors〔superiors and inferiors〕

아래윗막이 ① [막은 부분] end pieces ; top and bottom pieces ② [옷] upper and lower (garments) ; top(s) and bottom(s)

아래윗벌 a suit 《of clothes》; an outfit ; an ensemble 《프》

아래짝 the lower one 《of a pair set》; the lower piece 《of a 2-part object》; the bottom member

아래쪽 down ; lower position〔direction〕; the south ¶ 아래쪽을 보다 look down

아래채 the outer-wing building

아래층 —層 the downstairs ¶ 아래층에서〔으로〕 downstairs // 아래층으로 가다 go downstairs // 아래층으로 떨어지다 fall downstairs // 아래층에서 기다리다 wait downstairs

아래턱 the lower〔under〕 jaw〔chin〕

아래통 the lower part (of the body)

아랫것 [하인·고용인] servants ; employees ; [손 아랫사람] one's inferiors

아랫길 ① [길] the low(er) road ; the way below ② [품질] inferior quality ; poorer〔lower〕 grade

아랫녘 the southern part 《of Korea》; the south

아랫녘장수 a prostitute ; a street-girl

아랫눈썹 the lower eyelashes

아랫니 the lower teeth

아랫대 —代 the future〔later, coming〕 generation

아랫도리 the lower part (of the body) ; [옷의] lower garment(s)

아랫동 the lower part (of a thing) ¶ 나무의 아랫동 the base of a tree

아랫막이 ① [막은 부분] bottom endpiece ; bottom piece ② [옷] bottom (garment) ; bottoms ; lower garment

아랫머리 the bottom end ; the bottom (of two similar ends)

아랫목 the place on the *ondol* floor nearest the fireplace ; the seat of honor ¶ 아랫목에 앉히다 give 《a person》 a seat of honor

아랫물 downstream

아랫반 —班 a lower class〔grade〕; the lower form

아랫방 —房 an outer wing room

아랫배 the belly ; the abdomen ¶ 아랫배가 아프다 have a bellyache

아랫벌 the lower garment ; the lower suit

아랫사람 [연령이] one's junior ; [지위가] one's inferior ; a subordinate

아랫사랑 —舍廊 a guest room in the outer wing of a house

아랫수염 —鬚髥 a beard ; chin-whiskers

아랫입술 the lower lip ¶ 아랫입술을 깨물다 bite one's lower lip

아랫잇몸 the lower gum(s)

아랫자리 ① [자리] the seat of a junior 〔an inferior〕; the lower position ② 〖수학〗 one position down ; the next decimal position ; the second position

아랫집 the house just below ; a nextdoor house

아량 雅量 generosity ; liberality ; tolerance ; magnanimity ; broad〔large〕-mindedness ¶ 아량 있는 generous ; liberal ; magnanimous // 아량 없는 intolerant ; ungenerous ; illiberal ; narrow-minded // 아량을 베풀다 make allowance for ; show oneself to be magnanimous // 나의 우위를 인정할 만한 아량이 그에게 있었다 He had the grace to acknowledge my superiority.

아련하다 (be) dim ; vague ; faint ; obscure ; hazy ; misty ¶ 아련한 달빛 a vague moonlight // 마음에 아련하다 have a dim recollection 《of》

아령 啞鈴 a callisthenic iron dumbbell

— 체조 exercise with dumbbells ; dumbbell exercise ¶ 아령 체조를 2, 3회 하다 practice a few exercises with dumbbells

아로새기다 engrave〔carve〕 elaborately ; make an elaborate bas-relief ; chisel ; cut ; notch ¶ 마음에 아로새기다 engrave upon one's mind ; bear in mind // 나무에 이름을 아로새기다 cut one's name on a tree // 그것은 나의 마음에 깊이 아로새겨져 있다 It is written indelibly on my heart.

아롱다롱하다 (be) spotted〔spotty〕; dotted ; speckled ; mottled ; blotched ¶ 무늬가 아롱다롱한 천 cloth speckled with designs // 아롱다롱한 양복감 mottled material

아롱아롱하다 (be) variegated ; mottled

아롱(이) a mottled one〔thing〕; a mottled animal ; mottling

아롱지다 (be) variegated ; mottled ; blotched

아뢰다 tell〔inform〕 a superior ; say ; mention ¶ 지난날 아뢴 바와 같이 as I told you the other day // 아뢸 말씀은… I beg your pardon, sir, but // 아뢰옵니다 손님이 오셨습니다 Please, sir, someone wants to see you.

아류 亞流 an adherent ; a follower ; an epigone ; a (bad) second《to》

아르 an are (=100 sq. meters)

아르곤 〖화학〗 argon

아르롱이 a mottled pattern〔spot〕; mottles ; specks

아르바이트 Arbeit (도) ; a side job ; a sideline ; a part-time job ; a self-help job ; a side employment ; a student job
—하다 do a side job ; work for school expenses ¶ 아르바이트를 찾다 seek (for) a side job // 그는 아르바이트를 하여 대학을 마쳤다 He has worked his way through college.
—학생 a working student ; a student worker ¶ 아르바이트 학생을 채용하다 employ a student worker

아르에스시 R. S. C《Referee Stop Contest》(아마추어 권투에서의 T. K. O.)

아르에이치 Rh ¶ 아르에이치식 혈액형 an Rh blood group
—마이너스 Rh negative《Rh—》 **—인자** 〖의학〗 an Rh〔a rhesus〕 factor **—플러스** Rh positive《Rh ＋》

아르오티시 R. O. T. C《Reserve Officers' Training Corps》

아르키메데스 Archimedes (그 287 ? -212 B. C.) ¶ 아르키메데스의 원리 the Archimedean〔Archimedes'〕 principle

아르페지오 〖음악〗 an arpeggio《*pl.* ~s, -peggi》《이》

아르헨티나 Argentina ; the Argentine ¶ 아르헨티나의 Argentine

아른거리다 flicker ; flit ; glisten ; blink ; [마음에] haunt《one》; swim in one's head ¶ 램프불이 아른거린다 The lamp flickers. // 창에 햇빛이 아른거린다 The window glitters in the sun. // 나무 사이로 햇빛이 아른거린다 The light is gleaming through the trees. // 그 여자의 모습이 아른거리다 Her figure still haunts me.

아름 the span of both arms ; an arm-stretch ¶ 한아름의 장작〔책〕 an armful of firewood〔books〕 // 몇 아름이나 되는 나무 a tree measuring several arms' stretches around

아름다움 ⇨ 미(美) ¶ …의 아름다움에 매혹되다 be struck by the beauty of... ; fall under the spell of《a person's》charm // 자연의 아름다움을 느끼다 appreciate the beauties of nature

†**아름답다** (be) beautiful ; pretty ; lovely ; fine ; picturesque ; [얼굴이] good-looking ; handsome ¶ 아름다운 여자 a beautiful woman ; a beauty // 아름다운 경치 a lovely〔picturesque〕 scenery ; a fine view // 아름다운 목소리 a sweet voice // 아름다운 소녀 a pretty girl // 아름다운 이야기 a beauty story ; a beauty episode // 아름다운 행실 exemplary conduct // 아름답게 beautifully ; finely ; nicely // 아름답게 하다 make《a thing》beautiful ; beautify ; add beauty《to》// 아름답게 꾸미다 decorate beautifully // 마음씨가 아름답다 be noble-minded ; have a heart of gold // 그 여자는 아름답게 꾸며 입고 있었다 She dressed herself beautifully. /She is finely dressed. // 이만큼 아름다운 경치를 본 적이 없다 I have never seen such a fine view as this.

아름드리 an armful
—나무 a tree measuring more than the both arms' span around

아름차다 be beyond one's power〔capacity〕; be too much for《one》; be beyond one's control ¶ 이 일은 내게는 아름차다 I find myself unequal to the task. /This work is beyond my capacity. // 이 애는 나에게는 아름차다 This child is beyond my control.

†**아리다** [맛이] (be) biting ; tingling ; [상처가] tingling ; smarting ; smart ; [수족이] numbed ; asleep ; benumbed ¶ 맛이 아리다 taste sharp ; be pungent ; have a biting〔burning〕 taste // 눈이 아리다 one's eyes smart《from the smoke》// 찰상이 아리다 The scratch still smarts. // 목이 아리다 My throat smarts. // 추워서 손가락이 아리다 My fingers are asleep with cold.

아리땁다 (be) lovely ; charming ; coquettish ¶ 아리따운 처녀 a charming young lady

아리송하다 (be) ambiguous

아리스토텔레스 Aristotle (그 384-322 B. C.)

아리아 〖음악〗 aria

아리안 〖인종〗 Aryan
—족〔인종〕 Aryan races

아리잠직하다 [작고 얌전하다] (be) small, soft and gentle ; [솔직하다] (be) candid ; frank ; outspoken ; [천진하다] (be) unsophisticated ; childlike ; innocent

아린산 亞燐酸 〖화학〗 phosphorous acid
—염(鹽) phosphite

아릿하다 sting the tip of one's tongue ; (be) biting ; tingling ; sharp-tasting ; acrid ; numbed ; taste acrid

†**아마** probably ; perhaps ; maybe (미) ; likely ; in all probability〔likelihood〕; in nine cases out of ten ¶ 아마 …일 것이다 The chances〔odds〕 are《that》// 아마 그는 올 것이다 He will probably come. / He is likely to come. /It is likely that he will come. // 아마 그 여자는 오지 않을 것이다 Perhaps she will not come. /The chances〔odds〕 are that she will not come. // 아마 그를 만나지 못할 것이다 I am not likely to see him. // 그는 아마 지금쯤은 집에 닿았을 것이다 He must have arrived home by now. // 아마 날씨가 좋아질 것이다 I hope it will be fine. // 아마 비가 올 것이다 I am afraid (that) it will rain. // 했더라면 아마 성공했을 것이다 If he had tried, he would probably have succeeded. /If he had tried his hand at

it, he would have been successful.

아마 亞麻 flax hemp

—사(絲) flax yarn〔line〕; hemp thread —씨〔인〕 linseed ; flaxseed —유 linseed oil —천〔포〕 linen

아마도 perhaps ; indeed ; quite probably ; presumably ; likely ; like as not ⇨ 아마

아마릴리스 〖식물〗 an amaryllis

아마존¹ 〖식물〗 [백미꽃] a kind of mosquito-trap

아마존² Amazon ¶ 아마존의 Amazonian 《woman》

—강 the Amazon (River)

‡아마추어 an amateur ; a dabbler ; a non-professional ; the inexperienced ¶ 아마추어다운 amateurish

— 규정 requirements for amateurship — 노래 자랑(대회) an amateur singing contest ; Amateur Singers on the Air — 무선가 an amateur radio operator ; a (radio) ham — 연극 클럽 an amateur dramatic club 《A. D. C.》

아말감 〖화학〗 amalgam

—은(銀) silver amalgam

아망 a child's pride〔cockiness〕

아망부리다 〔관용〕 show one's pride 〔cockiness〕; be cocky

†아메리카 America ; the United States (of America) 《U. S. A》 ⇨ 미국

— 인디언 an (American) Indian a Native American ; [줄여서] an Amerind ; a Red Indian ; an Injun 《속》 —주〔대륙〕 the American continent 남북 — North and South America ; the Americas ; two Americas 중앙 — Central America

아메리칸 리그 the American League

아메리칸 풋볼 American football

— 선수 an American footballer ; a gridder 《구》

아메바 〖동물〗 an amoeba 《*pl.* ~s, -bae》 ¶ 아메바의〔같은〕 amoebic ; amoeboid

—성 이질 amoebic dysentery — 운동 amoebic movement

아멘 〖기독교〗 Amen !

아명 兒名 one's baby〔childhood〕 name

아목 亞目 〖동물〗 (biological) suborder

†아무 ① [사람] anyone ; anybody ; everybody ; [부정] nobody ; none ; no one ¶ 아무나 구별 없이 irrespective of persons // 아무나 every man Jack ; every mother's son of them // 그것은 아무나 할 수 있다 Anybody can do that. // 아무도 모른다 No one can tell. /Nobody knows that. // 아무도 없었다 There was no one present. /None were present. /None were present. // 아무에게나 약점은 있다 We all have weak points.

② [사물] any ; any old ; [부정] no ; not at all ¶ 아무것이나 좋아하는 것 anything one likes // 아무 곤란없이 without any difficulty ; with perfect ease // 아무 관계도 없다 have no relation〔connection〕 whatever 《with》; have nothing to do 《with》; be through 《with》 《미》 // 아무때나 오시오 Come and see me any time. // 아무 말도 하지 않았다 He said nothing. /He kept his mouth shut. // 아무 이상 없다 Nothing is wrong with it. /Everything's O. K. // 양자 사이에는 아무 상위도 없다 There is no differnce between them. // 아무 가치도 없다 It is of no value whatever. // 아무 소용도 없다 It is no use learning such a thing. // 도움이 된다면 아무 일이라도 하겠다 I shall do anything to help you. // 아무것도 모른다 I know nothing 《of》/I don't know at all〔in the least〕 《what》/I haven't the slightest 〔remotest〕 idea 《what》/I am completely in the dark 《as to》.

*아무개 Mr.〔Mrs., Miss〕 so and so ; a certain person ¶ 아무개씨 Mr. so-and-so // 김 아무개 one〔a certain〕 Mr. *Kim* // 김 아무개라는 사람 a man called something-or-other *Kim* // 영어에서는 아무(개)한테도 지지 않는다 He is second to none in English.

†아무것 anything ; something ; [부정] nothing ; none (사람) ¶ 아무것이나 좋아하는 것 anything one likes // 아무것도 아닌 일 [쉬운 일] an easy thing ; [사소한 일] a small〔trifling〕 matter ; nothing serious ; a trifle // 그런 일은 아무것도 아니다 It is quite easy to do so. /It is of no consequence. /It matters nothing to me. /That's nothing. // 그는 학자도 아무것도 아니다 He is nothing of a scholar. // 아무것도 아닙니다 Nothing is the problem // 아무것도 아닌 걸 가지고 야단치지 마세요 Don't chew me out for nothing. // 이것은 아무것도 아니야 You haven't seen anything yet.

*아무데 any place ; anywhere ¶ 아무데나 가도 좋다 You may go anywhere (you like). /You may go wherever you like. // 아무데도 안 간다 I am not going anywhere. // 아무데라도 좋다 Any place will do. // 당신이 간다면 아무데라도 나는 따라가겠다 I will follow you wherever you go. // 그것은 아무데나 있다 Everywhere you go, you will find it.

‡아무때 any time ; any day ; whenever ; always ; all the time ¶ 아무때나 좋다 Any time will do. // 아무때라도 좋을 때 오시오 Please come (at) any time 〔whenever〕 you like. /You are welcome at any time. // 그는 아무때라도 당신을 만날 겁니다 He will see you any time 〔at any time 《영》〕. // 그가 오고 싶을 때 아무때나 만나겠다 I will see him whenever he likes to come.

‡아무래도 ① anyway ; anyhow ; no matter what one may do ; for anything ; for all the world ; come what may ; for the life of one ; by any means ¶ 아무래도 그것을 할 수 없다 I can't do it anyway. // 아무래

도 그것을 벗어날 수 없었다 I couldn't get out of it anyhow.
② [결코 …이 아닌] by no means ; on no account ; never ¶ 이런 계획은 아무래도 허가할 수 없다 I will on no account〔by no means, never〕 approve of such a plan. // 이 문은 아무래도 열리지 않는다 This door will not open. // 그는 아무래도 들어주지 않았다 He would not〔refused to〕 listen to me. // 아무래도 그의 이름이 생각나지 않는다 I cannot, for the life of me, remember his name.
③ [무관심] ¶ 아무래도 좋다는 태도를 취하거라 Take an indifferent attitude 《toward》. // 그까짓 일은 아무래도 좋다 That does not matter. // 아무래도 좋다 네 뜻대로 해라 It doesn't matter, you may do as you please. /Have it your own way.

아무러면 《no matter, it makes no difference》 whatever〔however〕 it is ; whoever says it ¶ 모양이 아무러면 어떠냐 I do not care a button〔a straw, a bit, a damn〕 how I look. // 사람들이 아무러면 어쩌냐 Don't mind what people say. // 그거야 아무러면 어떤가 What does it matter? /Let that go. /What of that?

아무런 [부정] any sort of ; no ¶ 아무런 사고 없이 without any accident // 아무런 생각도 없이 unintentionally ; without intention ; unsuspectingly // 아무런 까닭도 없이 for naught // 아무런 위험도 없이 without the least danger // 아무런 소용도 없다 be good for nothing ; be utterly useless

아무런들 ⇨ 아무러면

아무렇거나 anyhow ; anyway ; in any case ; at any rate ¶ 아무렇거나 꼭 오겠소 I will come at any rate. // 아무렇거나 출발하자 Let's start anyway. // 아무렇거나 시험은 쳐보겠소 I'm going to take the examination whether I'll succeed in it or not.

아무렇게 in whatever way ; however

아무렇게나 in any manner one pleases ; indifferently ; half-heartedly ; carelessly ¶ 아무렇게나 일하다 do a slapdash job // 아무렇게나 대답하다 give a random answer // 아무렇게나 말하다 talk at random ; talk wild ; say anything〔the first thing〕 that comes into one's head // 아무렇게나 하시오 Do as you please. /You shall do it anyway.

아무렇게도 ¶ 아무렇게도 생각 안하다 make little〔nothing〕 of ; do not care at all ; do not care a straw〔fig, pin〕 《about》 // 아무렇게도 말할 수 없다 I cannot say anything definite 《on the matter》.

아무렇든지 anyhow ; no matter what ; in any event〔case〕 ; at any rate ; at all events ¶ 아무렇든지 방법을 강구해보겠습니다 I will find some means to do so. // 아무렇든지 출발 전에 알려주겠다 In any event, I will let you know before I start.

아무렇지(도) 않다 [태연하다] (be) indifferent ; unconcerned ; [무사하다] safe ; sound ; all right ¶ 아무렇지도 않은 듯이 lightly ; casually ; in an indifferent way // 아무렇지도 않게 여기다 make〔think〕 nothing of ; care nothing for // 아무렇지 않게 말하다 speak lightly 《of》

아무려니 Impossible! /You don't say so. /You're telling me! 《미·구》 ¶ 아무려니 그가 그런 짓을 했을라구 He is the last man to do such a thing.

아무려면 ① [설마] by no〔any〕 means ; under any circumstances ; in any way〔case〕 ¶ 아무려면 그럴까 How could it possibly be? /I can't believe it. /It can't be so. ② ⇨ 아무렴

아무렴 Of course! /Certainly! ¶ 그에게 답장했니—아무렴 Did you answer 〔give a reply to〕 his letter? Naturally!〔Of course! / Sure!〕 // 가느냐고—아무렴 Will I go, you say? Sure, I will.

아무르강 一江 [흑룡강] the Amur River

***아무리** however (much)... (may) ; no matter how... (may) ¶ 아무리 일해도 however hard one may work ; no matter how hard one may work // 아무리 부자라도 however rich a man may be ; no matter how rich a man may be // 아무리 급히 굴어도 however much one may hurry // 아무리 봐도 장군 같다 He looks exactly like a general. // 아무리 많은 법률을 만들어도 이런 범죄는 없어지지 않는다 No number of laws will check such crimes. // 아무리 바람이 불어도 오늘은 꼭 출항한다 Let the wind blow as hard as it will, we must set sail today. // 아무리 해도 그의 이름이 생각안난다 For the life of me, I can't remeber his name.

아무말 (not) any word ¶ 아무말도 없이 without (saying) a (single) word ; not uttering a single word ; in perfect silence ; without 《a person's》 permission (허가 없이) // 아무말도 할 것이 없다 I have nothing to say. // 아무말도 없이 그는 나가 버렸다 He went out without saying anything〔a word〕.

아무아무 ⇨ 아무개

아무일 something ; anything ; nothing (부정) ¶ 아무일 없이 without accident 〔mishap, a hitch〕 ; quietly // 종일 아무일도 없었다 Nothing happened all day. / The day passed quietly. // 그 여자와 나 사이에는 아무일도 없다 Nothing's cooking between her and me.

아무짝 any use ¶ 아무짝에도 쓸모가 없다 It is of no use whatever.

아무쪼록 by all means ; as much as one can ; to the best of one's ability ; I beg ; If you please ¶ 아무쪼록 빨리 as quickly as possible // 아무쪼록 노력해 보겠소 I'll try my best to do so. // 아무쪼록

내 말을 들어주시오 I beg you to listen to me. // 아무쪼록 결정을 번의해 주십시오 I beg of you to change your decision. // 아무쪼록 몸조심하십시오 Take the best possible care of yourself. // 아무쪼록 안부 전해주십시오 Give 《her》 my best regards 〔wishes〕.

아문 衙門 [옛 제도] public offices

아물거리다 ① [물체가] be glimpsed now and then ; (be) dim〔hazy〕; [마음에] haunt 《a person》 ¶ 먼데서 아물거리다 come in and out in the distance // 등불이 아물거린다 The lamp flickers. // 그의 모습이 아물거린다 The image of his visage still haunts me.
② [똑똑찮게] talk〔act〕 ambiguously ; equivocate ¶ 대답을 아물거리다 give a vague answer

아물다 heal 《up》; be healed 《of a wound》 ¶ 상처가 아물었다 The wound has healed up. /He has been healed of his wound.

아물리다 [상처를] treat 《a wound》; make 《a wound》 heal ; [일을] finish up ; complete ¶ 고약으로 아물리다 help heal 《a wound》 with an ointment

아물아물 flickeringly ; glimmeringly ; dimly ; vaguely ; dazzlingly ―하다 flicker ⇨ 아물거리다 ¶ 아물아물 보이다 come in and out of sight

아뭏든 ⇨ 아무렇든

아미 蛾眉 eyebrows of a beautiful woman ; arched eyebrows ; shapely eyebrows

아미노 〖화학〗 amino
―산 amino acids

아미타불 阿彌陀佛 〖불교〗 Amitabha

아바나 Havana

아바단 Abadan

아방가르드 avant-garde 《프》; the vanguard

아방게르 avant-guerre 《프》; prewar ; before the war

아방튀르 aventure 《프》; an amorous adventure ; a love affair

아버님 one's father

†아버지 a father ; [어린이말] papa ; dad ; daddy ¶ 근대 음악의 아버지 the father of modern music // 아버지의 사랑 paternal affection // 아버지 없는 fatherless // 아버지답다 be fatherly ; be fatherlike ; be paternal // 아버지답지 않다 be unfatherly // 아버지를 닮다 take after one's father // 아버지를 잃다 be left fatherless // 아 하늘에 계신 우리 아버지 O, Father in heaven, we pray thee... (기도문)
―날 Father's Day 《미》
아버지 종도 내 종만 못하다 〔속담〕 A bird in the hand is worth two in the bush. /Better a sparrow in the hand than a pigeon on the roof.

아범 father ; [하인] an elderly manservant

아베마리아 Ave Maria ; Hail Mary

아베크 avec 《프》: [남녀 한쌍] a young man with his girl friend ; a girl with her boy friend ; a (young) couple ; [데이트하는 남녀] a rendezvousing couple ; a pair of young lovers ; boys and girls on a date ―하다 have a date 《with》; go on a date ; rendezvous ¶ 이 공원은 젊은 남녀들의 아베크 장소로서 안성맞춤이다 This park is a favorite rendezvous for young men and women.

*아부 阿附 flattery ; sycophancy ; adulation ―하다 flatter 《a person》; fawn 《upon》; curry favor with 《a person》; play up to 《a person》 ¶ 상사에게 아부하다 ingratiate oneself〔curry favor〕 with one's superiors // 그에게는 아부가 통하지 않는다 He is proof against flattery.

아브라함 〖성경〗 Abraham

*아비 father ¶ 아비없는 자식 a fatherless child ; an illegitimate〔a natural, a love〕 child (사생아)

아비 阿比 〖새〗 the red-throated diver

아비규환 阿鼻叫喚 agonizing cries ; appalling confusion ¶ 아비규환의 참상 an agonizing〔a heartrending〕 scene ; a babel ; a scene of dire confusion

아비산 亞砒酸 〖화학〗 arsenious acid
―염 arsenite

아비시니아 Abyssinia

아비잔 Abidjan

아비지옥 阿鼻地獄 Avici 《범》; the lowest hell of Buddhism ; the veriest hell

‡아빠 papa ; daddy ; dad ; pop 《미·속》

아뿔싸 Dear me! /O my! /Darn it! /Gosh! /Damn! ¶ 아뿔싸 이렇게 하는 것이 아닌데 Well, I have made a mess of it. // 아뿔싸 또 졌구나 Gosh! I lose 〔You win〕 again. // 아뿔싸 이 일을 어쩐담 O my! What shall I do? // 아뿔싸 우산을 잊어 먹었구나 Gosh! I forgot to bring my umbrella with me.

*아사 餓死 death from hunger ; death by starvation ―하다 die of starvation 〔hunger〕; starve〔be starved〕 to death ; perish by〔with〕 famine ¶ 아사시키다 starve 《a person》 to death ; starve out 《a person》 // 아사선상을 헤매다 be on the verge of starvation

아삭 [씹는 소리] with a crunch ―하다 crunch ¶ 아삭 베어 물다 bite at with a crunching sound

아삭거리다 be crispy ¶ 이 사과는 아삭거린다 This apple is crisp.

아삭아삭 crunching ; crisping ―하다 be crisp〔crispy, crunchy〕 ¶ 아삭아삭한 사과 a crispy apple // 과자를 아삭아삭 먹다 crunch a biscuit up

아샘 Assam

아성 牙城 the inner citadel ; the stronghold ; [본부] the headquarters ¶ 국제 공산주의의 아성 the stronghold of international communism // 보수의 아성 the stronghold of conservatism

아성 亞聖 sage〔saint〕 of second rank
아성층권 亞成層圈 the substratosphere ¶ 아성층권을 날다 fly in the substratosphere
— **비행** a substratospheric flight — **비행기** a substratospheric plane
아세아 亞細亞 ⇨ 아시아
아세안 ASEAN 《the Association of Southeast Asian Nations》
— **각료 회의** the ministerial meeting of the ASEAN
아세테이트 〖화학〗 acetate
— **견사(絹絲)** acetate rayon〔silk〕; cellulose acetate fiber
아세톤 acetone
아세틸렌 〖화학〗 acetylene
— **가스** acetylene gas — **램프** an acetylene torch — **발생기** an acetylene (gas) generator — **용접 장치** acetylene welding equipment
아소모열 亞消耗熱 a sub-hectic fever
아속 亞屬 〖생물〗 a subgenus 《*pl.* -genera》
아속 雅俗 culture and vulgarism; the stylish and the common; [사람의] the refined and the vulgar; [언어의] the classical and the colloquial ¶ 아속 혼합의 문체 a colloquo-literary style
아손 兒孫 children and grandchildren
아수라 阿修羅 Asura 《범》 ¶ 아수라처럼 싸우다 fight like a demon; fight like Kilkenny cats
—**왕** the King of the Asuras
아순시온 Asuncion
아쉬워하다 miss; feel the lack of; be inconvenienced by not having ¶ 아쉬운 감이 들다 feel something wanting 〔lacking〕; have an unsatisfied feeling // 그는 10,000원쯤 잃어도 아쉬워하지 않을 거야 He wouldn't miss 10,000 *won* if he lost it. // 그가 떠나면 친구들이 매우 아쉬워할 것이다 He will be sorely missed by a circle of personal friends.
아쉰대로 lacking anything better; inconvenient though it is; by way of a makeshift; such as it is; making do with what one has ¶ 아쉰대로 이것을 쓰시오 Use this as a makeshift. // 그때는 매우 바빠서 아쉰대로 그것을 했다 I did at some inconvenience to myself as I was exceedingly busy at that time.
†**아쉽다** miss; feel at a loss; (be) inconvenient; lacking ¶ 아쉬움을 느끼다 be put to〔feel〕 inconvenience; be inconvenienced // 없어서 아쉽다 feel the lack of; be inconvenienced by not having // 아쉬움을 참다 put up with inconvenience // 아쉴 것 없다 suffer no inconvenience // 이 집에 응접실이 없어서 아쉽다 It is inconvenient not to have a reception room here.
아스라이 [아득히] far (off, away); in the distance; [희미하게] dimly; vaguely; faintly ¶ 아스라이 보이다 be seen dimly 〔a long way off〕
아스라하다 be far off〔up〕
아스러뜨리다 ⇨ 바스러뜨리다
아스러지다 ① [덩어리가] be broken into pieces; crumble ② [살이] be abraded; get rubbed raw
아스스 ⇨ 으스스
아스트린젠트 [화장수] astringent
아스파라거스 〖식물〗 an asparagus
아스팍 ASPAC 《Asian and Pacific Council》
아스팔트 asphalt ¶ 아스팔트 포장의 asphalt-paved // 아스팔트를 깔다 asphalt 《streets》; pave〔lay〕 《streets》 with asphalt
—**길** an asphalt(ed) 〔a blacktop〕 road — **도료** asphalt japan — **시멘트** asphalt cement — **혼합기** an asphalt mixer
아스피린 〖약〗 (an) aspirin
아슬아슬 —**하다** ① (be) dangerous; risky; critical; perilous ¶ 아슬아슬한 승부 a close game; a tight match // 아슬아슬한 고비 a fateful〔critical〕 moment // 아슬아슬하게 narrowly; at the critical moment; in the nick of time; at the eleventh hour; by the skin of one's teeth // 아슬아슬하게 구조되다 escape narrowly; have a narrow escape // 아슬아슬한 고비에서 이기다 win by a narrow margin // 아슬아슬하게 기차를 잡았다 I caught the train at the eleventh hour. // 불경기가 계속돼서 실은 아슬아슬한 상황입니다 With this prolonged slump, the situation is actually pretty touch-and-go.
② [춥다] be〔feel〕 chilly; be shivery 《with cold》
아슴푸레하다 ⇨ 어슴푸레하다
아습 a nine-year-old 《ox, horse》
‡**아시아** Asia ¶ 아시아 (사람)의 Asian; Asiatic
— **개발 은행** the Asian Development Bank 《ADB》 — **경기 대회** the Asian Games; the Asiad — **경제 협력 기구** the Organization for Asian Economic Cooperation 《OAEC》 — **극동 경제 위원회** the Economic Commission for Asia and the Far East 《ECAFE》 — **대륙** the Asiatic Continent; the continent of Asia — **민족** an Asian nation — **반공 연맹** the Asian People's Anti-Communist League 《APACL》 — **사람** an Asian〔Asiatic〕 — **생산성 기구** the Asian Productivity Organization —**성** Asianness 《of the Asians》 — **영화제** the Asian Film Festival — **유행성 독감** Asian influenza〔flu〕; the Asiatic flu — **인종** Asian races — **콜레라** [진성 콜레라] Asiatic cholera — **태평양 각료 이사회** the Asian and Pacific Council 《ASPAC》 **동남** — **국가 연맹** the Association of Southeast Asian States 《ASAS》 **소**— Asia Minor **중앙** — Central Asia
아시아 아프리카 ¶ 아시아 아프리카의 Afro-Asian
— **그룹** the Afro-Asian〔African-Asian,

Asian-African〕 Group ― 블록 the Afro-Asian〔African-Asian〕 bloc ― 회의 the Asian-African Conference
아식 축구 ―式蹴球 Association football ; soccer
‡아씨 [호칭] a married lady ; your lady ; Mrs. ; madam
아아 [일이 잘못된 때] Oh-oh !
아아 阿亞 Africa and Asia ; Afro-Asian ; Afro-Asiatic
― 블록 the Afro-Asian bloc ― 어족 the Afro-Asiatic〔Hamito-Semitic〕 language family ― 회의 the Afro-Asian Conference
아악 雅樂 (classical) court〔ceremonial〕 music ¶ 아악을 연주하다 play ceremonial music
―기 instruments for court music
아야 Ouch ! ¶ 아야 아프다 Ouch, it hurts.
아얌 a fur cap worn by women in winter ¶ 아얌드림 the long silk tail attached to an *a-yam*
아양 coquetry ; winsomeness ; flattery ¶ 아양스럽다 be coquettish ; coy ; winsome // 그 여자는 만나는 사람에게마다 아양을 떤다 She coquets with every fellow she sees.
아양을 부리다 관용 play the coquette ; flatter ; make up to 《구》
아어 雅語 refined diction〔speech〕 ; a polite expression ; an elegant word ; a genteelism
아역 兒役 [역] 《play》 a child's part 《in a play》 ; juvenile part ; [사람] a child actor
‡아연 亞鉛 『화학』 zinc 《Zn》 ¶ 아연을 씌운 galvanized ; coated with zinc // 아연을 씌우다 zinc 《iron》
―광 zinc ore ― 도금 zinc galvanizing ― 연고 zinc ointment ― 제판(製版) zincography ―철(판) galvanized iron ―판 a zinc sheet〔plate〕 ―판(版) 『인쇄』 a zinc plate ; a zincograph (돌판) ―화 zinc flowers ; zinc oxide ―화 연고 zinc (oxide) ointment
*아연 俄然 suddenly ; all of a sudden ; abruptly ¶ 아연 활기를 띠다 perk up 《in business》 ; begin to show sign of activity suddenly // 아연 긴장하다 become suddenly tense〔strained〕
아연 啞然 ¶ 아연하여 agape (with wonder) ; aghast ; speechless ; in blank amazement // 아연해 하다 be amazed 《at》 ; stand aghast 《at》 ; be struck dumb 《by》 ; be taken aback // 아연케 하다 strike 《a person》 dumb ; dumbfound // 그들은 이 뜻밖의 재난에 아연할 뿐이었다 They stood aghast at this unforeseen disaster.
아연 실색 啞然失色 ―하다 turn pale with surprise〔fright〕 ¶ 그 소식을 듣고 그는 아연 실색했다 Color drained from his face when he heard the news. /At the news he changed color.
아열대 亞熱帶 the subtropics ; the subtropical zone ¶ 아열대의 subtropic(al) ; near-tropical
― 기후 a subtropical climate ― 식물 a subtropical plant
아열성열 亞熱性熱 subfebrile temperature
*아예 from the very first〔the beginning〕 ; (not) by any means ; altogether ; never ¶ 아예 그런 생각은 없었다 I never intended to do so. // 아예 그런 짓은 말아라 Never do such a thing.
아옹 a miaow ―하다 miaow ; mew
아옹거리다 gripe ; bicker ; squabble
아옹하다 ① [어옹하다] (be) sunken ; hollow-looking ② [속이 좁아] (be) disgruntled ; griped ; be complaining 〔griping〕 to oneself
아우 a man's younger brother ; a woman's younger sister
아우거리 『농업』 hacking up the soil to get rid of weeds
아우러지다 get joined together ; harmonize ; unite
아우르다 put together ; merge〔add〕 《one thing》 to ¶ 아울러 (joining) together ; in addition // 아울러 말하다 make an additional remark
*아우성 shouting ; a yell ; a clamor ; a scream ; a shriek ¶ 아우성치다 raise a hubbub ; utter〔give〕 a scream ; clamor ; cry ; scream
아우타다 [젖먹이가] suffer a younger sibling ; (a child) get thin from premature weaning as a result of the mother's new pregnancy
아우타르키 autarchy ; autarky
아욱 『식물』 the marsh mallow
아울러 and ; both ; together 《with》 ; along with ; in addition ; also ; at the same time ; as well as ; besides
아울리다 join ; mix ; (be) becoming ⇨ 어울리다
아웃 ① [구기에서] out ; a put out 《PO》 ¶ 아웃시키다 get 《a player》 out ; put out 《a player》 // 아웃되다 be (put) out ; be out 《of play》 ② out(side)
―도어 outdoor(s) ―드롭 『야구』 an outdrop ―라인 an outline ―사이더 an outsider ―오브포커스 [영화에서] out of focus ―커브 『야구』 an outcurve ―코너 『야구』 the outside(corner) ―파이팅 『권투』 outfighting
아위 阿魏 『식물』 asafetida
아유 阿諛 flattery ⇨ 아첨(阿諂)
아유구용 阿諛苟容 flattery ; adulation ; toadyism ―하다 flatter ; toady ; fawn 《on, upon》
아음 牙音 『언어』 ¶ velar sounds ; a velar
아음속 亞音速 subsonic speed〔velocity〕 ¶ 아음속의 subsonic
†아이 a child ; a kid 《속》 ; a boy ; a boy-child (사내아이) ; a girl ; a girl-child (계

집아이) ; a (preschool) child ; a baby ; [자기의] (one's own) son〔daughter〕 ¶ 큰 아이 a big boy // 아이들 시간 the Children Hour (TV · 라디오의) // 아이다운 childlike (좋은 의미에서) ; childish (유치한) // 아이 때부터 from one's childhood 〔boyhood〕 ; from a child // 아이가 많다 have lots of kids (in one's family) // 아이가 없다 be childless ; be without issue // 아이를 배다 get〔be〕 with child ; conceive a child // 아이를 보다 tend a baby ; baby-sit 《미》 // 아이 취급하다 treat 《a person》 as a child ; baby 《a person》 // 결혼해도 아이가 없다 Their married life is blessed with no children. // 그는 이제 아이가 아니다 He is no longer a child. // 아이를 울리지 마라 Don't make〔let〕 the child cry.

—방 a nursery — 아버지 the father of (the) children ; one's husband — 어머니 the mother of (the) children

아이 낳기 전에 기저귀감 장만하다 속담 Don't build the sty before the litter comes. /Boil not pap before the child is born.

아이 자라 어른 된다 속담 The child is the father of the man.

아이고(머니) Oh ! /Ah ! /Oh my ! /My goodness ! /Ouch ! ¶ 아이고 다 틀렸다 Heavens ! /By Jove ! // 아이고머니나 Dear me ! // 아이고 너무 하는데 Oh, how unkind you are ! // 아이고 가엾어라 What a pity ! /Poor thing〔girl, child〕 ! // 아이고 아파라 Ouch ! How it hurts. // 아이고 좋아라 My, what a pleasant surprise. // 아이고 죽겠다 Oh, I am dying. // 아이고 이 일을 어쩌나 Well, what am I to do now !

아이누 [사람] an Ainu ; [종족] the Ainus ; [말] Ainu

아이다호 Idaho 《I., Id., Ida.》

†**아이디어** an idea ¶ 아이디어가 풍부한 사람 a man of ideas // 정말 좋은 아이디어다 It is really a good idea.

아이러니 (an) irony

아이론 [다리미] an iron ; a flatiron ; a smoothing iron ; [머리용] a curling iron ¶ 아이론을 켠 채로 두다 leave an iron heated // 아이론으로 다리다 iron out 《clothes》 ; press 《the trousers》

—대 an iron board〔stand〕 전기〔증기〕 — an electric〔a steam〕 iron

아이모 〖상표명〗 [소형 촬영기] an Eyemo (camera)

아이보리 코스트 [공화국] Ivory Coast

아이비엠 [펀치 카드 방식] I. B. M. 《International Business Machines》 ; an IBM computer (기계)

아이 섀도 eye shadow ¶ 아이 섀도를 하다 put on〔wear〕 eye shadow

아이소토프 〖화학·물리〗 an isotope

아이스 ice

— 링크 an ice-rink —박스 [냉장고] an icebox ; ice chest 《미》 — 쇼 an ice show — 캔디 ice candy ; flavored shaved ice — 커피 iced coffee — 케이크 a popsicle 《미·속》 — 큐브 an ice cube — 티 iced tea — 픽 an ice pick — 하키 ice hockey

†**아이스크림** (an) ice cream ; an ice 《영》

— 선디 《eat》 an ice-cream sundae ; a sundae — 소다 ice-cream soda — 제조기계 an ice-cream freezer — 콘 an ice-cream cone

아이슬란드 Iceland ¶ 아이슬란드(사람·말)의 Icelandic

—말 Icelandic — 사람 an Icelander

아이시비엠 I. C. B. M. 《an Intercontinental Ballistic Missile》

아이시에이 I. C. A. 《the International Cooperation Administration》

아이아르비엠 I. R. B. M 《an Intermediate Range Ballistic Missile》

아이엔에스 I. N. S. 《the International News Service》 (1958년 U. P.와 합병, U. P. I로 됨)

아이엘오 I. L. O. 《the International Labor Organization》

아이엠에프 IMF 《the International Monetary Fund》

— 8 조국(條國) an IMF Article 8 nation

아이오와 Iowa 《Ia.》

아이오시 IOC 《the International Olympic Committee》

아이오유 〖경제〗 I. O. U. 《I owe you》

아이젠 Steigeisen 《도》 ; [등산용] climbing irons ; a climber ; crampons ¶ 신에 아이젠을 대다 attach climbing irons to one's boots

아이지다 have a stillbirth〔stillborn baby〕

아이쿠 Oh ! ; Ouch ! Gee Whiz ! ; Wow !

아이큐 an IQ〔I. Q.〕 《intelligence quotient》 ¶ 그 소년의 아이큐는 109이다 The boy has an IQ of 109.

아이티 Haiti ¶ 아이티의 Haitian

—말 Haitian — 사람 a Haitian

아이피아이 I. P. I. 《the International Press Institute》

아인산 亞燐酸 Phosphorous acid

아일랜드 Ireland

— 공화국 the Republic of Ireland

아잇적 one's childhood〔boyhood〕 ¶ 아잇적에 when a child ; in one's childhood 〔boyhood, infancy〕

아작아작 ¶ 아작아작 먹다 crunch ; munch 《crackers》

아장거리다 toddle ; totter ; shamble ¶ 아장거리는 아기 a toddler

아장걸음 toddling step〔gait〕 ; mincing steps

아장바장 ⇨ 어정버정

아장아장 toddlingly ; with toddling steps ¶ 아장아장 걷다 toddle〔waddle〕 along 〔about〕 // 아장아장 걷는 아이 a toddler ; a toddling child

아재 [아저씨] an uncle ; [아주버니] one's husband's brother
아쟁 牙箏 a seven-stringed fiddle (used in court music)
†**아저씨** an uncle ; a man of one's parent's age
아전 衙前 a petty official of provincial town
아전인수 我田引水 drawing water to one's own mill ; seeking〔promoting〕 one's own interest ; arguing from a self-centered angle ¶ 아전인수격인 selfish ; self-seeking // 아전인수격인 견해 a selfish view // 그것이 바로 아전인수다 That is drawing water to one's own mill. /That's too self-centered.
아제 [아저씨] an uncle ; [자매의 남편] the husband of a girl's sister
아종 亞種 〖생물〗 a subspecies
‡**아주** ① [전혀] very ; quite ; really ; perfect(ly) ; altogether ; exceedingly ; utterly ; entirely ; (not) at all ¶ 아주 조금 a very little // 아주 기분이 좋다 feel quite well // 아주 피곤하다 be dead tired // 아주 곤란하다 be hard pressed // 아주 불쾌하다 feel very unpleasant // 아주 춥다 It is extremely〔terribly〕 cold. // 아주 영리하다 He is remarkably clever. // 거기 아주 오래 머물고 있었다 He stayed there quite a long time. // 그는 아주 가버렸다 He has gone for good. // 아주 재미있었다 I have had such a good time. // 여기는 아주 시끄럽다 It is so noisy here.
② [감탄사] Oh really ? ! (약간 조롱조로) /Damn it ! /Hang it ! /Dash it ! ¶ 아주—너에게 질까봐 Damn it ! See who is the stronger !
아주 亞洲 the Continent of Asia
아주 阿洲 the Continent of Africa
아주까리 〖식물〗 a castor-bean (plant) ; a castor-oil plant ; Ricinus communis ; a Palma Christi 《*pl.* Palmae Christi》 (학명)
— 기름 castor oil
†**아주머니** an aunt ; an auntie 《아》 ; an aunty 《아》 ; [부인] a (middle-aged) lady **옆집 —** the lady next door **주인 —** a landlady ; a mistress ; a hostess ; a madam
아주먹이 ① [정미] polished rice ; refined rice ② [솜옷] clothes with permanently stitched cotton padding
아주버니 one's husband's elder brother
아줌마 auntie ; aunty ¶ 샐리 아줌마 Auntie Sally
***아지랑이** heat haze〔wave〕 ; shimmering (air) ¶ 아지랑이가 끼었다 Heat waves are shimmering. /The air is shimmering. /The heat is waving the air.
— 현상 〖물리〗 schlieren **— (현상)법** 〖사진〗 schlieren method〔process〕
아지작 with a crunch ; with a crunchy sound **—하다** crunch ; munch ; champ
아지작거리다 crunch 《biscuit》 ; crush noisily ¶ 아지작아지작 crunching ; crushing // 사과를 아지작거리다 munch an apple
아지직 with a crack〔crash, creak〕
아지트 an agitating point ; a hideout 《미·속》
†**아직** yet ; as yet ; still ¶ 아직 9시가 안되었다 It is not yet nine (o'clock). // 아직 도착안했다 It has not arrived (as) yet. // 아직 미해결이다 It is yet to be solved. // 아직 불완전하다 It is still far from perfect. // 사랑을 하기에는 아직 어리다 You are too young to be in love. // 아직(도) 더 있다 I have still more. // 아직(도) 5마일 남았다 We have still five more miles to go. // 아직 살아 있다 He's still alive. // 아직 비가 오고 있다 It is still raining. // 아버님이 미국 가신 지 아직 석달밖에 안되었다 It is only three months since my father went to America.
아직까지 so〔thus〕 far ; up to now ; till now ; up to the present ¶ 이 규칙은 아직까지 유효하다 This rule holds good so far. // 아직까지는 일이 수월했다 So far the work has been easy. // 아직까지 코끼리를 본 일이 없다 I have never seen an elephant. // 아직까지 그것은 꿈에 지나지 않는다 So far, it is only a dream.
아질산 亞窒酸 〖화학〗 nitrous acid
—염 nitrate
아질하다, 아찔하다 be〔feel〕 dizzy〔giddy〕 ; feel faint ; have vertigo ¶ 머리가 아찔하다 My head swims〔spins〕. / I feel dizzy.
아집 我執 egoistic attachment ; egotism ; tenacity ; obstinacy ¶ 아집이 있다 be self-assertive ; be self-willed ; be obstinate ; be (self-) opinionated
***아차** Heavens ! /By Jove ! /My goodness ! /Dear me ! /Oh my ! (여성어) / Hang it ! /Darn it ! /Damn ! ¶ 아차 책을 잊고 왔군 Shucks, I left my book behind. // 아차 또 졌구나 Gosh, I lose〔you win〕 again.
‡**아첨 阿諂** flattery ; adulation **—하다** flatter 《a person》 ; fawn upon 《a person》 ; curry favor with 《a person》 ; play up to 《a person》 ¶ 윗사람〔권세가〕에게 아첨하다 cringe to one's superiors〔the powerful〕 // 그에게는 아첨이 통하지 않는다 He is proof agaist flattery.
—쟁이 a flatterer ; a sycophant ; a toady
아취 雅趣 elegance ; tastefulness ; charm ; artistry ; refinement ¶ 아취 있는 사람 a man of (refined) taste // 아취 있게 tastefully ; with taste ; in good taste // 아취 있다 be tasteful ; be elegant ; be graceful // 아취가 없다 be tasteless ; be commonplace // 아취 있는 생활을 하다 lead a tasteful life
-아치 ¶ 동냥아치 a beggar // 벼슬아치 a

petty official // 장사아치 a peddler ; a trader

아치 雅致 good taste ; elegance ; grace ; artistry ; gusto ¶ 아치 있는 elegant ; graceful ; refined ; tasteful ; artistic // 아치 있는 별장 a tasteful cottage // 그 정원은 자못 아치 있게 꾸며져 있다 The garden is very tastefully laid out.

‡아치 an arch ; a green arch 《of welcome》 ¶ 아치형의 arch-shaped ; arched

†아침 morning ; morn 《시》 ; [아침 밥] breakfast ¶ 아침에 in the morning // 아침 내 all (the) morning // 아침 일찍이 early in the morning // 아침부터 저녁까지 from morning till night〔evening〕; all day (long) // 10일 아침에 on the morning of the 10th // 일요일 아침에 on Sunday morning // 어느 겨울 아침에 one winter morning // 그는 아침 일찍〔늦게〕 일어난다 He is an early〔a late〕 riser. // 일요일 아침에 만납시다 I'll see you on Sunday morning. // 그는 아침 나절에는 공부하고 오후에는 논다 He works in the morning and plays in the afternoon. // 그는 10일 아침에 올 것이다 He will come on the morning of the 10th.

—거리 breakfast makings ; foodstuff for breakfast —결 the forenoon — 기도 a morning prayer ; matins 《교회의》 —나절 the forenoon —놀 the morning glow ; the glow of sunrise in the sky —먹이 food for breakfast — 바람 the morning breeze —밥 breakfast ¶ 푸짐한 아침(밥) a big〔solid, substantial〕 breakfast // 아침(밥)을 먹다 take〔have〕 breakfast ; breakfast // 아침(밥) 잡수셨습니까 Have you had your breakfast? / Good morning. (아침 인사) —상 a breakfast table〔tray〕 —선반 time off for breakfast and a rest 《on the job》 —술 wine drunk early in the morning — 안개 the morning mist — 이슬 the morning dew —잠 a morning nap —참 a breakfast break (in work) —해 the morning sun ¶ 아침해를 온 몸에 받다 be bathed in the morning sun

아침저녁 morning and evening ; [조반과 석반] breakfast and supper ¶ 아침저녁으로 제법 쌀쌀하다 We have cooler mornings and evenings now.

아카데미 an academy

—상 [영화] an Academy Award ; the Oscar ¶ 아카데미상 수상 배우〔여배우〕 the Oscar actor〔actress〕 —즘 academism — 학파 the Platonists

아카시아 〖식물〗 an acacia

*아케이드 an arcade

‡아코디언 an accordion

아퀴 [끝매듭] the final touches ; finishing ; settlement ¶ 일의 아퀴를 짓다 wind up one's work ; finish one's work ; bring a matter to a conclusion ; give the final touches to the job ; finish up

아크등 —燈 an arc light〔lamp〕

아크라 Accra

아크로바트 [재주] acrobatics ; [사람] an acrobat

— 댄스〔댄서〕 an acrobatic dance〔dancer〕

아크릴 〖화학〗 acryl ; acryloyl

—계 섬유 acrylic fibers

아킬레스 Achilles

—건(腱) Achilles tendon

아타세 an attaché

아탄 亞炭 〖광물〗 lignite ; brown coal

아테네 Athens

아토니 〖의학〗 atony

아톰 an atom

아트지 —紙 art paper ; slick〔glossy〕 paper

아틀라스 [신화] Atals

아틀리에 an atelier 《프》 ; a studio 《*pl.* ~s》 ; [일터] a workshop

아파치 an Apache

‡아파트 an apartment house〔building〕 《미》 ; a block of flats 《영》 ; [방] an apartment 《미》 ; a flat 《영》 ¶ 작은 아파트 a rooming house // 아파트 살림을 하는 flat-dwelling 《people》 // 아파트에 살다 live in rooms in an apartment 《미》 ; live in a flat 《영》

—군(群) an apartment block 고급 — a luxury apartment〔flat 《영》〕 분양 — an apartment offered for sale ; condominium 서민 — apartment house〔building〕 for the low incomer〔income bracket〕 임대 — a rental apartment

*아파하다 feel a pain ; feel sore ; hurt ; complain of pain

*아편 阿片 opium ; an opiate (제품) ¶ 아편을 피우다 smoke opium

—굴 an opium den〔joint〕 — 매매 opium traffic —상 an opium peddler — 상용 the opium habit —연(煙) opium tobacco ; opium smoke — 전쟁 the Opium War — 중독 opiumism ; opium poisoning ; opium addiction — 중독자 an opium addict ; a dopester ; a hophead ; an opium fiend

아포스테리오리 〖철학〗 a posteriori 《라》

아포스트로피 an apostrophe

아폴론 〖신화〗 Apollon

—형 apollonian type

‡아프다 ① [신체·상처 따위가] feel〔have〕 a pain 《in》 ; [신체가 주어] pain ; ache ; smart ; hurt ; sting

> 참고 **pain**은 심히 아픈 것 **ache**는 머리 배 이 따위가 욱신욱신 아픈 것 **smart**는 쑥쑥 쑤시듯 아픈 것 **hurt**는 외부의 상처가 아픈 것 **sting**은 눈 따위가 찌르는 듯 아픈 것

¶ 아파서 울다 cry with pain // 아파하다 complain of pain ; be in pain // 아픈 데를 건드리다 touch 《a person》 on a sore place ; [비유적] touch 《a person》 on a

ㅇ

sore〔tender〕 spot〔point〕 // 등허리의 아픈 곳에 고약을 바르다 apply a plaster to a sore place on one's back // 머리가 (깨질 듯이) 아프다 I have a (splitting) headache. // 배가 아프다 I feel〔have〕 a pain in my stomach. // 아이고 아프다 Ouch! How it hurts me. // 어디가 아프냐 Where's the pain? // 무릎의 찰과상이 아프다 My cut knee pains me. // 목〔발〕이 아프다 I have a sore throat〔foot〕. // 손가락의 화상이 많이 나았지만 아직 아프다 My burnt finger is much better, but it still smarts. // 팔이 쑤시고 아프다 The pain shoots up my arm. // 연기로 눈이 아프다 The smoke makes my eye smart./The smoke irritates my eye. // 등산 후 온몸이 쑤시고 아팠다 After climbing the mountain, I ached all over. // 열 때문에 그녀는 온몸이 아팠다 The fever caused her body to ache. // 상처가 아파서 잠이 오지 않았다 The smart of his wound kept him awake. // 충치가 아파서 야단났다 I have a bad tooth that is worrying me.
② [마음이] ache; have a pang; (be) painful; trying; be hard to bear ¶ 잃어버린 개를 생각하면 그녀는 가슴이 아팠다 She had a pang of sorrow when she remembered her lost dog.

아프레 aprés 《프》
—**게르** aprés-guerre 《프》; postwar

아프로디테 [신화] Aphrodite

아프리오리 a priori 《라》

*__아프리카__ Africa ¶ 아프리카의 African // …을 아프리카화하다 Africanize // 남아프리카 태생의 백인 an Afrikander; an Afrikaner; a Boer
— **단결 기구** the Organization of African Unity 《OAU》 — **사람** an African —**주** the African Continent

아프트 Abt
—**식 철로** an Abt system rairoad; a cog〔rack〕 railway

아플리케 〖자수〗 appliqué 《프》

아픔 [고통] a pain; an ache; [쑤시는] a smart; [눈·목의] sore; [마음의] (mental) pain; [슬픔] grief; sorrow; sore; pain; [짓궂게 괴롭히는 것] a pain in the neck ¶ 가슴〔위〕의 아픔 a pain in the breast〔stomach〕 // 이별의 아픔 the sorrow of parting // 격심한 아픔 a severe〔sharp, an acute〕 pain // 아픔을 느끼다 feel〔have, suffer〕 a pain // 아픔을 가라앉히다 allay〔alleviate, mitigate, ease〕 the pain // 아픔이 멎다 the pain stops // 아픔을 참다 stand〔bear, endure〕 the pain // 아픔이 가셨다 The pain has left me〔has gone〕./I no longer feel any pain.

아피아 Apia

아하 Dear me!; My goodness!; Well!; What-do-you-know! ¶ 아하 그것을 깜박 잊었구나 Oh my goodness! It slipped right out of my mind!

아하하 Ha-ha!/Hmmph! ¶ 아하하 웃다 laugh aloud; [일부러] force〔feign〕 a laugh

아한대 亞寒帶 the subarctic (zone); the sub-frigid zone

아해 兒孩 a child ⇨ 아이

아형 雅兄 Sir; You sir

아호 雅號 a pen name; a nom de plume 《프》; a pseudonym; a literary name ¶ 그는 다산이라는 아호를 썼다 He wrote under the pen name of *Dasan*.

아혹 訝惑 uncanny suspicion; doubt; a distrust; misgivings

†**아홉** nine ¶ 아홉째 the ninth; No. 9
—**무날** the 3rd and 18th days of the tide cycle —**수** years of age ending in 9, considered climacteric
아홉 섬 추수한 자가 한 섬 추수한 자더러 그 한 섬 채워 열 섬으로 달라고 한다 관용 Riches have made more covetous men, than covetousness hath made rich men.

아황산 亞黃酸 〖화학〗 sulfurous〔sulphureous 《영》〕 acid
—**가스** sulfurous acid gas —**나트륨** sodium sulfite〔sulphite 《영》〕 —**소다** ⇨ 아황산나트륨 —**염** sulfite

아흐레 the ninth day of the month; 〔아홉 날〕 nine days

아흐렛날 [제 9 일] the ninth day

아흔 ninety ¶ 아흔째 the ninetieth

아희 兒戲 (mere) child's play; a playgame; childishness ¶ 아희 같다 be childish; be puerile; be like child's play // 너의 일은 내것과 비교하면 아희와 같다 Your work is a playgame compared with mine.

악[1] Oh!/Dear me! ¶ 악 뱀이 있다 Oh! There's a snake.

악[2] desperation; anger; exploding〔pent-up〕 feelings ¶ 악이 받치어 desperately; frantically; with the fury of desperation; like mad 《구》 // 악이 받치다 become〔grow〕 desperate; get mad

†**악 惡** evil; wrong (부정); vice (악덕); wickedness (사악) —**하다** (be) bad; evil; wrong; wicked; vicious; malicious; ill-natured ¶ 선과 악 good and evil // 악한 사람 a wicked〔bad〕 man; a villain; a scoundrel // 악을 선으로 갚다 return good for evil // 악에 빠지다 fall into evil ways // 악으로 유인하다 tempt 《a person》 to vice〔wrong〕 // 도시의 저 근처는 악의 소굴이다 That part of the town is a hotbed of vices. // 그는 선에도 악에도 강하다 He has a great capacity for either good or evil.
사회— social vices〔ills〕
악으로 모은 살림 악으로 망한다 속담 Ill〔Evil〕 gotten, ill〔evil〕 spent./Ill-gotten goods never prosper./Stolen goods never thrive.

악감정 惡感情 ill feeling〔will〕; ill blood; animosity; an unfavorable impression; a grudge ¶ 국제간의 악감정 international animosities // 악감정을 품다 bear 《a person》 an ill will〔a grudge〕; have an ill feeling towards〔against〕《a person》// 악감정을 주다 impress 《a person》 unfavorably ; make an unfavorable impression 《on a person's mind》// 그는 가끔 악감정을 사람에게 주곤한다 He often impresses others unfavorably.

악곡 樂曲 a musical piece〔composition〕; a piece of music ; a tune

악골 顎骨 〖해부〗 a jawbone ; a maxillary bone
상〔하〕— the upper〔lower〕 jawbone

악공 樂工 a court musician

악구 惡球 〖야구〗《throw, hit》 a wild ball

악구 樂句 〖음악〗 a clause ; a phrase ; a section
모방 — a repetition

*악귀 惡鬼 an evil spirit ; a devil ; a demon ; the Evil One ¶ 악귀가 들리다 be possessed by〔with〕 a devil

악극 樂劇 an opera ; a musical〔music〕 drama〔play〕
—단 a musical troupe ; an opera company〔group〕

‡악기 樂器 a musical instrument ¶ 악기를 연주하다 play on a musical instrument
— 반주 instrumental accompaniments —점 a music shop ; a shop for musical instruments 건반 — a keyboard instrument ; a key〔keyed〕 instrument 관〔취주〕— a wind instrument 금관 — (a) brass 목관 — a woodwind (instrument) 타— a percussion instrument 현— a string instrument ; the strings

악기류 惡氣流 a treacherous〔dangerous〕 air current ; air turbulence ; turbulent air

악녀 惡女 a wicked woman ; a virago ; a witch

악념 惡念 an evil intention〔thought〕; malicious intent ; a sinister motive ¶ 악념이 있는 evil-minded ; evil-disposed ; malicious ; malignant

악다구니 a name-calling quarrel ; bickerings ; mud-flinging〔-slinging〕; a brawl ; an altercation ; [반목] enmity ; an ill will ; an antagonism ; a hostility
—하다 brawl ; engage in mud-flinging at each other ; fling〔throw〕 mud 《at》; wrangle

악단 樂壇 the musical world ; musical circles

†악단 樂團 an orchestra
— 연주 a band concert —원 a member of an orchestra 교향— a symphony orchestra

악담 惡談 abuse ; slander ; abusive〔foul〕 language ; vituperation —하다 abuse ; speak ill of ; call 《a person》 names ¶ 악담을 늘어놓다 curse 《a person》; slander ; abuse // 그 녀석은 악담을 잘한다 He is a scandalmonger〔scandalbearer〕.

*악당 惡黨 a villain ; a ruffian ; scoundrel ; [깡패] a hooligan ; a hoodlum 《미·구》

악대 樂隊 a (musical) band ; a brass band (취주) ¶ 악대의 연주회 a band concert // 악대를 선두로 with a brass band at the head // 악대가 연주하고 있다 A band is playing.
—원 a bandsman ; a bandman — 음악 band music —장 a bandmaster 육군〔해군, 공군〕 군— a military〔naval, air force〕 band

악대소 [거세한 소] a castrated bull ; a bullock ; an ox

‡악덕 惡德 vice ; immorality ; corruption ; evil conduct ¶ 악덕을 쌓다 commit a series of vicious acts ; commit one vice after another
— 기업주 vicious enterpriser〔entrepreneurs〕 — 기자 a corrupt newspaperman — 변호사 a fixer 《미·속》; a shyster 《미·구》 — 상인 wicked〔dishonest〕 dealers ; unscrupulous traders — 신문 a yellow paper ; the corrupt press 《총칭》 — 증권 회사 a bucket 《속》

악도리 a tough guy ; a roughneck ; a ruffian ; a brawler ; a bad egg 《구》

악독 惡毒 viciousness ; perversity ; harshness —하다 (be) vicious ; naughty ; venomous ; perverse ; harsh ¶ 악독한 짓 vicious practices

악동 惡童 a bad〔naughty, mischievous〕 boy〔child〕; a street Arab (도회지의)

악랄 惡辣 viciousness ; knavishness ; craftiness —하다 (be) vicious ; mean ; nasty ; crafty ; villainous ; unscrupulous ¶ 악랄한 수단 knavish tricks ; villainous measures ; foul play // 악랄한 짓을 하다 do a nasty thing ; play a mean trick ; be given to sharp practices (상습적으로)

악력 握力 grip ; grasping power ¶ 악력이 세다 have a strong grip
—계 a hand-dynamometer

악령 惡靈 an evil spirit ; a black angel

악례 惡例 an evil precedent ; a bad example

악리 樂理 theory of music ; music theory

†악마 惡魔 an evil spirit ; a devil ; a demon ; a fiend ; [마왕] Satan ; the Evil One ¶ 악마 같은 devilish ; fiendish // 악마를 물리치다 drive out evil spirits
—주의 Satanism ; diabolism —파 the Diabolists ; the Satanic school

악머구리 a croaker ; a frog
악머구리 끓듯 하다 〔속담〕 make a lot of noise ; sound like a bunch of frogs croaking away

악명 惡名 an evil reputation ; a bad name ¶ 악명이 자자하다 become notorious // 반역자의 악명이 씌워지다 be branded as a traitor

악모 岳母 one's mother-in-law ; the

ㅇ

mother of one's wife
*악몽 惡夢 a bad〔an evil〕 dream ; a hideous〔terrible〕 dream ; a nightmare ¶ 악몽에서 깨어나다 start from a nightmare // 제정신으로 돌아오다 come to one's senses // 악몽에 시달리다 be troubled by 〔with〕 nightmares ; suffer from nightmares
*악물다 clench《one's teeth》; set《one's jaws》; shut one's teeth hard ; take a firm bite of ; hang on to ; will not let go (놓지 않다) ¶ 이를 악물고 with one's teeth set ; with clenched teeth // 이를 악물고 일하다 clench one's teeth and dig into the job ; work with firm determination // 이를 악물고 싸우다 fight bitterly 〔fiercely〕 // 이를 악물고 하면 안되는 것이 없다 Nothing is impossible to a determined mind.
악바리 a tough fellow ; a hard〔shrewd〕 man
악법 惡法 a bad law ; evil laws
악벽 惡癖 a bad〔vicious, ill〕 habit ; a vice ¶ 음주의 악벽 the vice of intemperance // 악벽이 붙다 contract a vice // 악벽을 교정하다 overcome a bad habit ; cure 〔break〕《a person, oneself》of bad habit
악병 惡病 a malignant〔bad, virulent〕 disease ¶ 악병에 걸리다 be seized with a malignant disease
악보 樂譜 a musical note ; music ; a score ¶ 악보를 읽다 read music // 악보를 달다 set《a song》to music // 악보를 만들다 compose music // 악보를 보고〔안 보고〕 연주하다 play at sight〔by ear, from memory〕
—대 a music-rack〔-stand〕 —집 a music book 관현 — a full〔an orchestral〕 score 단행(單行) — sheet music 피아노 — a piano score
악부 岳父 one's father-in-law ; the father of one's wife
악사 樂士 a bandsman ; a musician
—석 [무대의] the orchestra ; the musicians' box —장 a chief music master ; a bandmaster
악사 惡事 evil ; evil-doing ; an evil thing 〔deed〕 ; a wrong ; villainy ; a crime (죄악) ¶ 악사를 저지르다 do evil 〔wrong〕 ; play the knave ; commit a crime // 악사를 꾀하다 plot evil // 악사를 쌓다 commit one crime after another // 가난 때문에 악사를 저질렀다 Poverty drove him to evil-doing. // 악사 천리 An evil deed will become known a thousand miles off. /Ill news runs 〔spreads〕 fast〔apace〕.
악상 樂想 〖음악〗 a theme ; a motif ; a melodic subject
악서 惡書 a harmful book ; undesirable publications ; a bad book ¶ 악서를 추방하다 put harmful books out of circulation
악선전 惡宣傳 vile〔pernicious〕 propaganda ; false propaganda ; a sinister rumor
악설 惡說 abusive〔foul〕 language ; abuse ; slander ; curse ; malediction — 하다 speak ill of《a person》; abuse ; slander ; curse ; backbite
악성 惡聲 a bad voice ; [욕] evil-speaking ; scandal ; abuse ; [악평판] evil reputation ; ugly rumors
악성 樂聖 a celebrated musician ¶ 악성 베토벤 Beethoven, the master (of music)
악성 惡性 malignancy ; viciousness ¶ 악성의 bad ; malignant ; vicious ; virulent
— 감기 a malignant influenza ; a nasty 〔bad〕 cold — 빈혈 pernicious anemia — 인플레 vicious inflation — 종양 〖의학〗 a malignant tumor
‡악센트 ① [강세] an accent ; a stress ; [어조] a tone ; [악센트를 붙임] accentuation ¶ 악센트의 accentual // 악센트가 있는 accented ; accentuated ; stressed // 악센트가 없는 unaccented ; unaccentuated ; unstressed ; stressless // 첫 음절에 악센트가 있는 단어 a word stressed on the first syllable // 악센트를 붙이다 accent《a word on the second syllable》; place an accent on《a syllable》; accentuate《a word》; stress《the first syllable》// 둘째 음절에 악센트가 있다 The accent is〔falls〕 on the second syllable. ② [양재] an accent ¶ 악센트를 주다 accent《coat pockets》
악속 惡俗 ⇨ 악풍(惡風)
악송구 惡送球 〖야구〗 a wild ball — 하다 throw a wild ball
악수 —水 ⇨ 억수
*악수 握手 a handshake ; [화해] reconciliation ; [제휴] a union — 하다 shake hands《with》; [제휴] join hands《with》; [화해] make peace《with》¶ 굳은 악수 a vigorous handshaking // 악수를 나누다 shake hands with each other // 악수를 청하다 offer〔hold out〕 one's hand // 그는 진심으로 악수하면서 나를 맞아 주었다 He greeted me with a hearty handshake.
악수 惡手 [바둑·장기 따위의]《make》a bad move ; a wrong move
악순환 惡循環 a vicious circle《of wages and prices》¶ 악순환을 야기하다 cause 〔start〕 a vicious circle // 악순환이 일어난다 A vicious circle arises.
악습 惡習 a bad habit (버릇) ; an evil〔a corrupt〕 practice (풍습) ; abuses (악폐) ¶ 악습을 타파하다 do away with abuses // 악습을 일소하다 extirpate evil practices // 악습에 물들다 contract〔get into〕 a bad habit // 나는 이 악습을 버려야겠다 I will get rid〔break myself〕 of the bad habit. /I'll overcome this bad habit.
악식 惡食 [음식] coarse〔gross〕 food ; plain food ; a poor〔frugal〕 meal ; coarse 〔plain〕 fare ; [먹기] gross feeding ; [불교에서] eating meat《despite Buddhist

teachings》 —하다 eat repulsive things ; be a gross feeder ; be eccentric in matters of food ¶ 악식이 몸에 배다 become accustomed〔get used〕 to plain fare
—가 a gross〔foul〕 feeder

악심 惡心 an evil mind〔intention〕; a malicious intent ; an evil thought 〔impulse〕; a sinister motive ¶ 악심 있는 evil-minded ; evil-disposed ; malicious ; malignant // 악심을 일으키다 be tempted 《to do》; yield to temptation // 그는 악심을 일으키어 그 돈을 훔쳤다 He was tempted to steal the money.

악쓰다 惡— yell (in anger, in protest) ; bawl out ; [힘쓰다] struggle desperately ¶ 악쓰며 desperately ; in 〔with〕 desperation // 악쓰며 덤벼들다 bawl at 《a person》 furiously

악아 [아들·딸·며느리에게] My dear! ; My pretty! ; Say! 《미》 ; Look (here) ; [아들에게] Sonny! ; My boy!

*악어 鰐魚 a crocodile ; an alligator (북미산의) ; a gavial (인도산의)
— 가죽 crocodile skin〔hide〕; alligator skin〔leather〕 —류 the crocodilians — 핸드백 an alligator handbag

악언 惡言 ⇨ 악설(惡說)

악업 惡業 a misdeed ; a wrongdoing ; an evil deed ; a wicked act ; 〖불교〗 karma 《범》 ¶ 전세의 악업 evil doings in one's former existence

악역 惡疫 a plague (역병) ; a pestilence (페스트, 악역) ; an epidemic (전염병) ¶ 악역이 만연하고 있다 A pestilence rages 〔is prevalent〕.
— 유행지 a plague spot〔region〕; a plague-stricken district ; an infected district — 유행지 발항(發港) 증명서 a foul bill (of health)

악역 惡役 a villain's part ; a villain ; a heavy ¶ 그는 악역을 잘한다 He plays a villain's part very well.

악연 惡緣 evil destiny ; an unfortunate affinity〔connection, relation〕

악연 愕然 aghast ; appalled ; shocked ; in surprise ; amazedly —하다 be amazed〔astonished〕; be shocked〔startled〕; be thunderstruck ; be appalled ; stand aghast ¶ 악연하여 빛을 잃다 turn pale with consternation ; be terror-stricken // 악연하여 어찌할 바를 모르다 be frightened out of one's wits

악영향 惡影響 a bad effect ; an evil influence ; harm ¶ 악영향을 미치다 have〔exert〕 a bad influence 《upon》; infect // 청년의 정신에 악영향을 미치다 have a demoralizing influence upon the minds of youths

악용 惡用 abuse ; misuse ; improper use —하다 abuse ; misuse ; put to a bad use ; make bad use 《of》; turn 《a thing》 to evil account ¶ 금력을 악용하다 make ill use of one's wealth // 권력〔지위, 무력〕을 악용하다 abuse one's authority〔position, power〕 // 타인의 이름을 악용하다 use another's name for evil purposes ; make illicit use of another's name

악우 惡友 a bad〔an evil〕 companion 〔friend〕; bad company 《총칭》 ¶ 악우와 사귀다〔를 피하다〕 keep〔keep out of〕 bad company // 악우가 생기다 get 〔fall〕 into bad company // 악우 때문에 악에 빠지다 be led astray by a bad friend // 악우와 사귀지 마라 Don't keep company with bad friends.

악운 惡運 ill luck ; bad fortune ; an evil fate ¶ 악운이 세다 have the devil's own luck ; prosper〔thrive〕 in spite of one's evil courses // 악운이 다하다 come to the end of one's ill luck // 그에게는 악운이 따른다 An evil fate pursues him.

악음 樂音 a musical tone〔sound〕

**악의 惡意 ill will ; malice ; spite ; ill feeling ; a sinister motive ; an evil intention ; a malicious intent ¶ 악의 있는 ill-intentioned ; evil-minded ; malicious ; spiteful // 악의 없는 innocent ; harmless ; with no harm // 악의에서 out of spite ; from malice // 악의를 품다 bear ill will against 《a person》; bear 《a person》 malice // 악의로 받아들이다 take 《a thing》 ill〔amiss〕; take 《a thing》 in bad part // 악의로 말한 것이 아니다 I meant no harm. /I meant well. // 그는 나에게 악의를 품고 있다 He bears me ill will. /He bears ill will to〔toward〕 me. /He means ill towards me. // 그의 말에 악의는 조금도 없었다 There was no malice whatever in what he said.

악의 악식 惡衣惡食 poor clothing and poor food ; a plain dress and a simple meal —하다 be ill-clad and poorly fed ¶ 악의 악식에 만족하다 be content with coarse clothing and poor food ; lead a simple life

악인 惡人 a bad〔wicked〕 man ; a knave ; a villain ; a scoundrel ¶ 악인은 망하고 선인은 성한다 The wicked are punished, the good come into their own.

악인 惡因 a cause of evil
— 악과(惡果) 〖불교〗 An evil cause produces an evil effect. /Sow evil and reap evil.

악장 樂長 a conductor ; a music director ; a bandmaster ; an orchestra leader

악장 樂章 a movement (of music) ; a chapter ¶ 제 1악장 the first movement

악장치다 brawl ; wrangle ; quarrel noisily〔angrily〕

악전 惡錢 ill-gotten money ; [악화] a bad coin ; crooked money

악전 樂典 the rules for writing music ; musical grammar

악전고투 惡戰苦鬪 a desperate fight ; a hard battle ; [경기] a close game ; a tight match ; [경쟁] a close contest —하다 fight hard ; fight desperately 《against great odds》 ; fight with one's back to the wall ; struggle hard 《against》 ¶ 역경에서 악전고투하다 struggle〔grapple〕 with adverse circumstances // 선거에서 악전고투하다 have a close contest in the election

악절 樂節 『음악』 a passage

악정 惡政 misgovernment ; misrule (국왕의) ; maladministration (실정) ¶ 악정에 시달리다 suffer from bad government〔misgovernment〕 // 악정으로 다스리다 misgovern〔misrule〕 a country

악조 樂調 musical tone

악조건 惡條件 adverse〔unfavorable〕 conditions〔factors, circumstances〕 ; bad conditions

악조증 惡阻症 nausea accompanying pregnancy ; morning sickness

악종 惡種 a bad seed ; a hoodlum ; a villain ; a scoundrel ; a wicked fellow ; a rascal

악증 惡症 [병] (the condition of) a malignant disease ; a violent disorder ; [못된 짓] a bad habit ; bad conduct ; evil ways

악지 ⇨ 억지

악질 惡疾 a malignant〔virulent〕 disease ¶ 악질에 걸리다 be seized with a malignant disease

악질 惡質 evil nature ; inferior〔bad〕 quality ; malignancy ; wickedness
— 범죄 a flagrant offense — 분자 bad elements ; undesirables — 선전 pernicious propaganda —업자 a wicked dealer〔trader〕

악착 齷齪 narrow-mindedness ; wickedness ; stubbornness ; tenacity (끈기) ¶ 악착 같다 be unyielding〔stouthearted〕 ; be tough〔stubborn〕 // 악착같은 여자 a tough woman // 악착같이 일하다 grub along ; toil and moil // 돈벌이에 악착 같다 be engrossed in money making ; be overly anxious to get rich

악착스럽다 be unyielding ⇨ 악착

악처 惡妻 a bad〔wicked〕 wife ¶ 악처는 일생의 환난(患難)이다 A bad wife is a lifelong dearth〔the shipwreck of her husband〕.

악천후 惡天候 foul〔bad, poor〕 weather ; unfavorable〔execrable, indifferent〕 weather ; [거친] rough〔stormy, inclement〕 weather ¶ 악천후를 무릅쓰고 in spite of bad weather // 악천후로 인해 우리는 출발할 수가 없었다 Due to nasty weather, we couldn't leave.

‡악취 惡臭 a bad〔nasty〕 smell ; an offensive odor ; stench ; stink ¶ 악취 나는 ill-smelling ; foul〔bad〕-smelling ; stinking // 악취를 풍기다 have〔give out〕 a bad smell ; smell bad ; stink // 악취가 코를 찔렀다 An offensive smell greeted my nose. // 도랑에서 심한 악취가 났다 There was a terrible stench from the ditch. // 이 가죽은 악취를 풍긴다 This leather smells bad. /This leather gives out a bad smell. // 악취가 가득 차 있었다 The air was impregnated with filthy odors. // 썩은 생선의 악취로 가슴이 답답해졌다 The stink of the spoiled fish made me sick.

악취미 惡趣味 bad〔vulgar〕 taste

악티늄 『화학』 actinium 《Ac》

악패듯 harshly ; relentlessly ; ruthlessly

‡악평 惡評 [평판] a bad reputation ; ill repute ; [비난] unfavorable〔adverse〕 criticism —하다 speak ill of 《a person》 ; make a malicious remark 《about》 ; criticize adversely (신문에서) ¶ 악평을 퍼뜨리다 circulate scandal about 《a person》 // 악평이 자자하다 be notorious 《for》 // 그는 세상의 악평을 받고 있다 He is ill spoken of. // 그에게는 악평이 끊이지 않는다 He is a constant subject of scandal.
—가 a poor penman ; a bad penman ; a scrawler〔scribbler〕

악평등 惡平等 perverted〔blind〕 equality ¶ 악평등에 시달리다 suffer from perverted equality

악폐 惡弊 an evil ; a vice ; evil〔corrupt〕 practices ; abuses ¶ 악폐를 일소하다 do away with abuses〔evils〕 ; sweep away abuses ; clear society of its evils // 그들은 사회의 악폐를 바로 잡으려고 했다 They tried to reform social abuses. /They tried to clear society of its evils.

악풍 惡風 bad〔evil〕 manners ; evil ways ; an evil ; a bad custom〔practice〕 ¶ 세상의 악풍에 물들다 be infected with the evil ways of the world // 소년은 사회의 악풍에 물들기 쉽다 Boys are easily infected with the evil ways of the world.

악필 惡筆 bad (hand) writing ; a bad 〔poor〕 hand ; a villainous scrawl ; illegibility ¶ 그는 악필이다 He is a bad〔poor〕 penman. /He writes a bad 〔poor〕 hand. // 악필은 일생의 손이다 Bad writing is a lifelong disadvantage 〔loss, curse〕.

악하다 惡— (be) bad ⇨ 악(惡)

악학 궤범 樂學軌範 An Illustrated Text on Traditional Music (책 이름)

‡악한 惡漢 a wicked fellow ; a villain ; a scoundrel ; a rascal ; a rogue ; a knave

악행 惡行 evil conduct ; wrongdoing ; an evil deed ; a wicked act ; misdoings ¶ 악행에 빠지다 be given to evil ways ; take to an evil course

악형 惡刑 a severe〔cruel〕 punishment ¶ 악형을 과하다 punish cruelly〔severely〕 ; inflict a severe punishment 《on》

†악화 惡化 [정세 따위의] a change for the worse ; aggravation ; [품질] deterioration ; debasement ; [심정 따위] degeneration ; corruption —하다 become 〔grow〕 worse ; worsen ; go from bad to

worse ; aggravate ; deteriorate ; be deteriorated ¶ 정세가 악화한다 The situation grows worse. /The situation takes a bad turn. // 병세가 악화한다 One's condition grows worse 〔takes a turn for the worse〕. // 양국간의 관계가 나날이 악화하고 있다 The relations between the two countries are growing worse. // 파업 정세가 악화될 듯하다 The strike situation threatens to become serious.

악화 惡貨 a bad coin〔money〕 ¶ 악화는 양화를 구축한다 Bad money drives out good money.

악희 惡戱 a naughty act ; a practical joke ; roguery ; mischief

†**안**¹ ① [내] the interior ; the inside ¶ 안으로부터 from within ; from the inside // 안에만 있다 stay indoors all the time // 안에 없다 be〔stay〕 away from home ; be out // (집) 안에서 뛰어나오다 run out of the house // 안으로 모시다 show (a person) to the guest room // 내가 외출중에는 안에서 쇠를 채워 주십시오 Lock the door from within〔on the inside〕 while I am out. // 안에 머물러 있기에는 너무나 아까운 날씨다 This is too fine a day to be indoors. // 이 안이 덥지 않니 It's a little hot in here, isn't it?
② [이내] within ; inside of ; less than ¶ 2,000원 안 less than〔not exceeding〕 2,000 *won* // 역에서 100미터 안 within a hundred meters of the station // 수일 안에 within a few days ; in the course of a few days // 1주일 안에 within〔inside of 《속》〕 a week // 기한 안에 within the time limit // 수입 안에서 생활하다 live〔keep〕 within one's income // 1시간 안에 거기에 가겠습니다 I will be there within an hour.
③ [이면] the back ; the wrong side ; the reverse side ; the other side ; inside ¶ 옷의 안쪽 the inside of the clothes // 동전의 안 the reverse〔tail〕 side of a coin ; tails // 안을 뒤집다 turn inside out
④ [옷의] a lining ¶ 안을 대지 않은 unlined // 안을 대다 line 《clothes》 // 그 옷은 안이 비단이다 The dress has a silk lining.
⑤ [내실] the woman's quarters ; the inner room ; a boudoir ¶ 어머니는 안에 계십니다 Mother is in back.
⑥ [아내] one's wife ; [여자] females ; womenfolk

안² not ⇨ 아니

안 案 [제안] a proposal ; a proposition 《미》 ; a suggestion ; [고안] an idea ; a device ; a design ; [계획] a plan ; a scheme ; a program ; a project ; [의안] a bill ; a measure ¶ 안을 내다 make a proposal〔suggestion〕 ; propose // 안을 철회하다 withdraw the proposal // 안을 제출하다 present〔submit〕 a bill // 안을 세우다 make〔elaborate〕 a plan // 안을 짜다 make a draft ; draw up a plan
명— a good idea **예산—** a budget bill **정부—** a Government bill

안간힘 holding back〔containing〕 an urge ; restraining 《indignation》 ; sitting on ¶ 참으려고 안간힘 쓰다 try hard to restrain one's indignation
안간힘을 쓰다 관용 hold back an urge ; restrain 《one's indignation》 ; strain to

*****안감** lining (material) ; a cloth for lining

안강 安康 peace and good health ; comfortable circumstances **—하다** be well〔healthy〕 ; be safe and sound

안강 鮟鱇 〖물고기〗 an angler fish ; a devilfish ⇨ 아귀

안갚음 repaying one's indebtedness to one's parents **—하다** repay one's parents for taking care of one as a child

‡**안개** (a) fog ; (a) mist ; haze

> 참고 **mist**는 미세한 수증기로 되어 있고 **fog**는 mist보다도 훨씬 짙은 것이다

¶ 안개가 짙은 foggy // 안개 낀 아침 a misty〔foggy〕 morning // 짙은 안개 a dense〔thick, heavy〕 fog // 안개에 쌓인 fog-bound // 안개에 싸이다 be enveloped in fog // 안개가 짙어진다 The fog thickens. // 산 꼭대기가 안개에 싸였다 The mountaintop is wrapped in mist. // 안개가 낀다 A fog sets in. // 안개가 걷힌다 The fog lifts〔clears up〕. /The mist clears away. // 안개가 끼어 있다 It is foggy 〔misty〕.
— 구름 stratus clouds **— 상자** 〖물리〗 a cloud chamber **—속** [미궁] mystery ; a maze ; a labyrinth ¶ 사건이 안개속에 묻혔다 The case has been shrouded in mystery.

안거 安居 a quiet〔peaceful, tranquil〕 life **—하다** live quietly ; lead a peaceful life

안건 案件 a case ; an item ; a matter ¶ 중요한 안건 an important matter

안걸이 [씨름에서] an inside foot-trip

안검 眼瞼 〖해부〗 an eyelid ; a palpebra 《*pl.* -rae》
— 경련 spasmodic winking **—염** 〖의학〗 blepharitis ; inflammation of the eyelid

‡**안경 眼鏡** glasses ; [귀에 거는] (a pair of) spectacles ; [코안경] eyeglasses ; a pince-nez 《프》 ; [방진·비행사용] goggles ¶ 돗수 높은 안경 powerful spectacles ; glasses with heavy lenses // 안경을 낀 사람 a man in spectacles // 안경을 쓰다〔벗다〕 put on〔take off〕 one's glasses // 안경너머로 보다 look over (the edge of) one's glasses // 안경을 닦다 wipe 〔polish〕 one's glasses // 안경 없이는 책을 읽을 수 없다 He can't read (books) without glasses. // 당신의 안경은 몇도입니까 —7도입니다 What is the strength of your glasses? It is 7 (degrees). / How strong are your glasses? It is 7

(degrees). //제 눈에 안경이지 안 그래 Love sure makes people blind, doesn't it?

— 가게 an optician('s) —다리 the bow 〔earpiece〕 on a pair of spectacles —알 a spectacle lens — 자국 imprints (on the skin) from wearing glasses —쟁이 a bespectacled person; a glasses-wearer; Four eyes 《속》 —집 a spectacles case —테 a spectacles〔glasses〕 frame; a rim 금테 — gold-rimmed spectacles 두초점 — bifocals 볼록렌즈 — bull's-eye glasses 색— colored〔smoked〕 glasses; sunglasses 외알 — an eyeglass; a monocle

안계 眼界 the range〔field〕 of vision; sight; view; the visual field; prospect ¶ 안계가 넓은〔좁은〕 having a wide〔narrow〕 field of view//안계 내〔외〕에 있다 be within〔beyond〕 the field of vision//안계에 들어오다 come in sight〔view〕//안계에서 벗어나다 go out of sight//과학은 인간 정신의 안계를 넓힌다 Science enlarges the mental horizon〔vision〕. //갑자기 안계가 넓어졌다 A wide prospect burst upon my view. //저 사람은 안계가 넓다 His mental horizon is wide.

안고나다 take 《a person's fault, responsibility》 upon oneself; be charged with 《a duty》 ¶ 네가 손해보면 내가 안고나겠다 I'll answer for your possible losses. //그는 책임을 안고나서 사직했다 He took the responsibility〔blame〕 upon himself and resigned.

안고름 the inside tie-string (on a Korean coat)

안고 수비 眼高手卑 a good critical eye with no executive skill; wishful thinking

안고 지고 with arms full and back laden; heavily loaded 《with》

안고지다 be entrapped by one's own trick; fall into the pit one dug for another; get boomeranged

안공 a kind of vise to hold boards together

안공 眼孔 an eyehole; an eye socket

안과 眼科 〖의학〗 ophthalmology

— 병원 an ophthalmic hospital —의 an ophthalmologist; an oculist; an eye-doctor〔-surgeon〕; an eye-specialist —학 (the study of) ophthalmology

안과하다 安過— get along comfortably without any trouble; live in peace; pass (time) peacefully〔tranquilly〕

안광 眼光 the brightness of the eye; the glitter of one's eyes; insight; vision ¶ 안광이 날카롭다 He has piercing〔penetrating〕 eyes. /He is eagle-eyed.

안구 眼球 an eyeball; the globe of an eye

— 건조증 xerophthalmia — 결막 ocular conjunctiva —염 ophthalmitis — 은행 an eye bank

안구 鞍具 saddlery; saddle gear; horse gear; harness

안기다[1] ① [품에] throw oneself in a person's arms; cuddle; nestle in a person's arms ¶ 안기어 있다 be embraced; be in a person's arms//자연의 품에 안기다 be (nestled) in the bosom of nature//아이는 어머니 품 속에 안겨 있었다 The baby was in her〔his〕 mother's arms.

② [알을] set; make 《a hen》 sit on 《eggs》 ¶ 알을 안기다 set 《a hen》 on 《eggs》

③ [죄·책임 따위를] fix on 《a person》; charge 《a person》; lay 《the blame》 on 《a person》; put 《responsibility》 on someone's shoulders ¶ 가짜를 안기다 pass a false article for a genuine one//비용을 안기다 charge the expenses to 《a person》//책임을 안기다 shift the responsibility on (to) 《a person》; pass the buck 《to》//죄를 안기다 fix the guilt on 《a person》//대임을 안기다 entrust 《a person》 with a great task; charge 《a person》 with an important duty

④ [때리다] strike 《a person》 hard ¶ 한 대 안기다 give 《a person》 a sound blow; beat 《a person》 soundly

안기다[2] ① [안게하다] make 《a person》 hold〔take〕 《someone》 in his arms; make 《a person》 embrace〔hug〕 ¶ 어머니에게 아기를 안기다 put the baby in its mother's breast〔bosom〕

안남 安南 Annam ¶ 안남(사람)의 Annamese

—말 Annamese —미(米) Annam rice —사람 an Annamese; an Annamite

†안내 案內 [인도] guidance; conducting; [초대] invitation; [통지] advice; a notice **—하다** show 《a person》 over 〔into〕; conduct 《a person》 to 〔over〕; [좌석에] usher; lead the way 《to》; [길을 가리키다] show the way 《to》 ¶ A씨의 안내로 under the guidance of Mr. A//좌석에 안내하다 usher to a seat//거리를 안내하다 show 《a person》 around the town//방에 안내해 드리시오 Show him into the room. //안내해 주시겠습니까 Would you kindly act as my guide?

—계 a clerk at the information desk; a desk clerk; [극장 따위의] an usher (-ette) —도 a guide map; a road-map —서 a guidebook; a roadbook; a hand book —소 an information bureau; an inquiry office —인 a guide; [좌석의] an usher; an usherette (여자) —장 a letter〔note〕 of invitation; an invitation (card, note); [상업용] an advice; an advice note —표 a directional sign 오락〔연예〕 — [신문의] the entertainment guide

†안녕 安寧 ① (public) peace; tranquility; good health; [복지] well-being; welfare **—하다** be well; be all right; be in good health ¶ 안녕과 질서를 유지하다〔교

란하다) maintain〔disturb〕 peace and order (in the country)
② [인사] ¶ 안녕하십니까 How are you?/Good morning〔day〕. (오전에)/ Good afternoon. (오후에)/Good evening. (저녁에) // 안녕하셨습니까 How have you been? // 안녕히 가십시오 Good-bye./ Bye-bye./Adieu. (멀리 갈 때) // 안녕히 계십시오 Good-bye ; [밤에] Good night. // 아버님께선 안녕하시냐? — 네 안녕하십니다 How is your father? Thank you, he is fine. // 자 그럼 안녕히 계십시오 Bye now.

안노인 —老人 an old woman〔lady〕《of the household》

†**안다** ① [팔에] hold〔take, carry〕《a baby》 in one's arm(s) ; embrace ; hug ¶ 안고 있다 have 《a baby》 in one's arms // 안아 일으키다 lift up 《a person》; help 《a person》 get to his feet ; [자고 있는 사람을] help 《a person》 sit up in bed // 안아 올리다 take up〔raise, lift, pick up〕《a child》 in one's arms // 끌어 안다 draw 《a person》 closer to one's breast ; clasp 《a person》 in one's arms // 바람을 안고 가다 go against the wind // 애기는 내 팔에 안기어 무심히 웃었다 The baby smiled an innocent smile in my arms.
② [새가 알을] sit on 《eggs》; brood on 《eggs》; hatch ¶ 암탉이 알을 안고 있다 The hen is sitting〔brooding〕 on eggs.
③ [책임·의무 따위를] take upon〔on〕 oneself 《a person's responsibility》; shoulder ; undertake ; assume ¶ 남의 빚을 안다 shoulder 《a person's》 debt // 우리 청년들은 무거운 책임을 안고 있다 A great responsibility rests upon us young men.

안다리후리기 〖레슬링·씨름〗 a chip

안단테 〖음악〗 andante 《이》

안단티노 〖음악〗 andantino 《이》

안달 fretting, impatience **—하다** fret 《over》; fret oneself ; worry oneself about ; be over-anxious 《to》; be impatient ; be on tenterhooks ; be nervous ¶ 가지 못해 안달하다 be anxious to go ; be champing at the bit // 나가고 싶어 안달하다 cannot bear to stay any longer // 안달하여 병이 나다 fret〔worry〕 oneself sick // 그렇게 안달하지 마라 Don't fuss about it so much. /Don't be so impatient. // 그 여자는 심하게 안달을 했는데 그게 다 그 여자의 남편을 위해서라고 하니까 겨우 납득을 하더군 She put up quite a fuss but finally came around when I told her it was all for her husband's
—뱅이 a fretful person ; a worrywart〔-bug〕; a hasty-pants

안대 眼帶 an eye bandage ¶ 안대를 하다 have one's eyes bandaged

안댁 —宅 your〔his〕 wife ; Madam

안데스 산맥 —山脈 the Andes Mountains

****안도** 安堵 relief ; reassurance **—하다** be〔feel〕 relieved ; feel at ease ; breathe again ¶ 안도의 숨을 내쉬다 heave a sigh of relief ; be〔feel〕 quite relieved
—감 a relieved feeling ; a feeling of relief

안도라 Andorra

안돌이 a narrow precipitous place in a mountain pass where one has to hug the rocks **—하다** hug 《the road, pass, curve》

***안되다** ① [금지] must not ; should not 《do》; ought not to 《do》 (해서는 안되다) ; shall not (안시키다) ; don't (하지마라) ; be forbidden〔prohibited〕 (금지되어 있다) ; be not allowed (허가되지 아니 하다) ; be not supposed to (안되게 되어 있다) ¶ 그것에 손대면 안된다 Don't touch it. /You must not touch it. /You are not allowed〔forbidden〕 to touch it. // 이 방에서 담배를 피워서는 안된다 You are forbidden〔not allowed〕 to smoke in this room. /You are prohibited from smoking in this room. /Smoking is prohibited 〔forbidden〕 in this room. // 거짓말을 해서는 안된다 You should not〔ought not to〕 tell a lie. // 들어가면 안됩니까 May I not come in? // 네 안됩니다 No, you must 〔may〕 not. // 다섯시 이후에는 학교에 남아 있어서는 안되게 되어 있습니다 We are not supposed to stay in school after five. // 오랫동안 운전을 안했더니 잘 안된다 I am a little rusty at driving.
② [필요·의무] must ; have (got) to (않으면 안된다) ; need (필요가 있다) ; be required to (요구되고 있다) ¶ 거기에 안 가면 안됩니까 Must I〔Do I have to〕 go there? // 오늘은 치과 의사에게 안가면 안된다 I have (got) to go to the dentist's today. // 대학에 추천되려면 80점 이상 따지 않으면 안된다 You are required to get more than 80 points (if you want) to be recommended to the college. // 나는 늦어도 8시 20분까지 학교에 도착하지 않으면 안된다 I must〔have to, have got to〕 be in school at the latest at 8 : 20. // 거기에 가지 않으면 안될 것이다 I shall have to go there. /It will be necessary for me to go there. // 어제 거기에 가지 않으면 안되었다 I had to go there yesterday. // 유감스럽게도 초대를 거절하지 않으면 안되겠습니다 I am sorry to decline your invitation. // 뜰의 잡초를 뽑지 않으면 안된다 The garden needs weeding. // 싫거나 좋거나 그의 지시를 따르지 않으면 안된다 It is imperative that we should obey his instruction. // 우리들은 좋든 싫든 간에 규칙을 지키지 않으면 안된다 We ought to〔should〕 observe the rule whether we like it or not.
③ [예방] ¶ …하면 안되니까 lest... should ; (so) that... may not ; so as not to ; for fear that // 비가 오면 안되니까 lest〔for fear〕 it should rain // 젖으면 안되니까 in case you should get wet // 선생님

께 꾸지람 들으면 안되니까 가만히 있자 Let's not tell our teacher, (so) that he may not scold us〔so as not to be scolded by him〕. //비가 오면 안되니까 우산을 가지고 가거라 Take your umbrella with you lest〔for fear〕 it (should) rain. //지각하면 안되니까 서두르자 Let us hurry up, so that we may not be too late 〔behind time〕.
④ [유감] (be) sorry《for》; regrettable ; have pity《on》 ¶ 참 안됐군요 I'm sorry
안되는 놈은 두부에도 뼈라 속담 The bread never falls but on its buttered side.
안되는 놈은 자빠져도 코가 깨진다 속담 The bread never falls but on its buttered side.
안뒤곁 the backyard of the main building (of a house)
안드로메다 Andromeda
— **성운(星雲)** the Andromeda nebula — **좌** 〖천문〗 Andromeda
안뜰 the inner court〔courtyard〕
†**안락 安樂** ease ; comfort —**하다** (be) easy ; comfortable ¶ 안락한 생활 an easy〔carefree〕 life //안락하게 지내다 live in comfort〔easy circumstances〕; live at ease ; live comfortably ; live on a bed of down〔roses, flowers〕; be comfortably off ; be sitting pretty《미·속》
—**사(死)** mercy killing ; (artificial) euthanasia ; an easy death — **의자** an easy chair ; a club chair ; an armchair ; a grandfather('s) chair
안력 眼力 strength of vision ; power of observation ; perception ; discernment 〔discerning power〕; [감식력] insight ; penetration ; [천리안] second sight ; clairvoyance ¶ 안력 있는 discerning ; penetrative ; penetrating // 안력을 잃다 lose one's sight //안력이 쇠퇴하다 one's eyesight is falling ; one's eyes are dimmed //대단한 안력을 갖고 있다 He has a keen discernment. /He is a man of acute insight〔observation〕.
안료 顔料 [화장용] cosmetics ; face-paints ; [도료] paints ; colors ; [색소] a pigment
안마 按摩 massage ; shampoo(ing) ; [운동 중 또는 운동 후의] rubdown —**하다** massage《a person, a person's back》 ¶ 어깨〔목〕를 안마하게 하다 have one's stiff shoulder〔neck〕 massaged
—**기** a kneader —**사** a massagist ; a masseur (남)《프》; a masseuse (여)《프》 — **요법** a massage treatment ; osteopathy ; chiropractice — **치료** a massage treatment ; osteopathy
안마 鞍馬 a saddled horse ; [체조용] a side horse
†**안마당** ⇨ 안뜰
안면 安眠 peaceful〔quiet, good〕 sleep ; a calm rest ; a comfortable sleep —**하다** sleep well ; sleep peacefully〔quietly〕; have a quiet sleep ; have a good night's rest ; sleep in peace ¶ 안면 못하는 사람 an uneasy sleeper //안면이 안되다 cannot get a quiet〔good〕 sleep ; have a troubled〔unquiet〕 sleep //안면을 방해하다 disturb《a person's》 sleep 〔rest〕//나는 안면을 못했다 I was wakeful. /I had a bad night. /I had a troubled sleep. /Something kept me from a quiet sleep. //열 때문에 안면을 못했다 The fever kept me from a quiet sleep. //바람 소리 때문에 안면을 못했다 My sleep was disturbed by the noise of the wind.
— **방해** disturbance of sleep ; nuisance at night ¶ 안면 방해이니 라디오를 꺼라 Put out the radio as it disturbs my sleep.
‡**안면 顔面** ① [얼굴] the face ¶ 안면의 facial //안면의 표정 facial expression //안면에 부상을 입다 get hurt〔injured〕 in the face ② [지면] an acquaintance ¶ 안면이 있다 be acquainted《with a person》; know《a person》//그와는 안면이 있다 I am acquainted with him. //전혀 안면이 없다 He is quite a stranger to me.
—**각** the facial angle〔index〕 — **경련** a histrionic spasm ; a facial tic〔spasm〕 — **골** facial bone —**근** facial muscle — **동맥** a facial artery — **박대** treating an acquaintance meanly — **부지** having no personal acquaintance《with a person》— **신경** a facial nerve — **신경 마비** facial paralysis — **신경통** face-ache ; facial neuralgia — **표정** facial expression
안목 inside〔interior〕 dimensions ; inside measurements (of a room〔bowl〕)
안목 眼目 an appreciative eye ; a good eye《for》; an eye《for》; a sense of discrimination ⇨ 안식 ¶ 안목 있는 사람 a man of insight〔discrimination〕; a discerning person //안목이 있다 have an eye 《for》//안목에 틀림이 없다 have an unerring critical eye
안무 按撫 placation ; pacification ; quelling popular discontent —**하다** pacify《the people》; appease ; calm
— **공작** pacification work〔activity〕
안무 按舞 dance composition ; posture ; [사람] a choreographer ; a dance composer —**하다** choreograph compose《a ballet》; arrange dance
—**가** a choreographer ; a dance director
안문 —門 the inner door ; the inner gate
안민 安民 —**하다** appease〔calm〕 the people ; restore order and confidence
안반(짝) a dough board ; a board for rice-cake making
안받다 [부모가] enjoy a son's devotion in their old age ; [까마귀가] be fed by《its》 grown-up young
안받음 repayment〔recompense〕 to one's

parents
안받침 inner〔inside〕 support
안방 —房 the inner room ; the main 〔the women's〕 living room ; the women's quarters ; a boudoir ; the back 〔inside〕 part of the house
안배 按排, 按配 [배치] arrangement ; disposition ; [배분] distribution ; assignment —하다 arrange ; distribute ; assign ; set in order ¶ 역할을 안배하다 assign duties 《to》
안번지기 [씨름에서] a defensive stance with the wrestler's right foot forward
안벽 —壁 the inner wall
안벽 岸壁 a quay(-wall) ; a pier ; a wharf ¶ 안벽에 대다 bring〔moor〕《a steamer》 alongside a pier
안보 安保 security ¶ 국가의 안보 문제 national security problems
— 외교 diplomacy for national security
— 이사회 [유엔의] the Security Council
총력〔집단〕 — all-out〔collective〕 security 한미 — 조약 the Korea-U. S. Security Pact〔Treaty〕
*안부 安否 safety ; welfare ; health ; well-being ; [소식] news ; tidings ; a letter ¶ 안부를 묻다 inquire〔ask〕 after 《a person, a person's health》 // 안부를 염려하다 worry〔be concerned〕 about 《a person's》 safety (조난을 당했을 때) // 친구의 안부를 묻다 ask after a friend // 안부를 알리다 let 《a person》 know how one is (getting along) // 가끔 편지로 안부를 알려 다오 Write to me once in a while and let me know how you are. // 일행의 안부가 염려되고 있다 We are apprehensive about the safety of the party. // 댁내 여러분에게 안부 전해 주십시오 Give my best regards to your family. / Remember me kindly to your family. // 아내도 당신께 안부 전한답니다 My wife wishes to be remembered to you. /My wife joins with me in sending kind regards to you. (편지에서)
안부 眼部 the eye region ¶ 안부의 통증 a pain in the eye region
안부모 —父母 one's female parent ; one's mother
안부인 —夫人 (your, his) esteemed wife ; madam
안분 安分 content ; satisfaction with one's lot —하다 be content (with one's lot)
안분 按分 proportional division —하다 divide〔distribute〕 proportionally 《among》
— 비례 proportional distribution ¶ 안분 비례로 proportionally ; in proportion ; pro rate
안빈낙도 安貧樂道 being content amid poverty and taking pleasure in acting in an honest way
안사돈 —査頓 a daughter's mother-in-law ; a daughter-in-law's (real) mother
안사람 (my) wife
안산 案山 a hill on the opposite side ; a mountain on the opposite side of a house or a grave
안산 安產 an easy delivery〔birth, labor〕 ⇨ 순산(順產)
안산암 安山岩 〖광물〗 andesite
안살림 housekeeping ; home life
안상 관절 鞍狀關節 a saddle joint
†안색 顏色 ① [혈색] the color of one's face ; complexion ¶ 안색이 좋다〔나쁘다〕 look fine〔bad〕 ; look well〔unwell, pale〕 ; have a good color〔have no color〕 // 안색이 희다〔검다〕 have a fair 〔dark〕 complexion // 안색이 좋아지다〔나빠지다〕 look better〔worse〕 ; gain〔lose〕 color // 안색이 변하다 turn pale ; turn livid ; change color〔countenance〕 // 무서워서 안색이 변하다 turn pale with fear
② [표정] a look ; a countenance ; an expression ¶ 안색에 나타나다 show ; betray 《one's feeling》 // 불안한 안색이다 look uneasy // 사람의 안색을 살피다 study the pleasure of 《a person》 ; hang on 《a person's》 smiles // 너의 안색으로 알 수 있다 I can see it in your face.
안성맞춤 安城— the right thing ; the thing wanted (wanted) ; just the thing ; the very best thing (like the brassware of *Anseng*) ; the very thing desired 〔wanted〕 ¶ 안성맞춤의 fit ; ideal ; suit 〔adapted〕 for ; made to order // 안성맞춤의 날씨 ideal weather 《for an outing》 // 그 일에는 그가 안성맞춤이다 He is just the man for the position. /He is the right man in the right place. /He is cut out for the job. /He is admirably adapted for the work.
안섶 an in-turned *jeogori* collar
안손님 a lady visitor ; a woman caller ; a guest of one's wife
안수 按手 the laying on of hands (in prayer) —하다 impose hands 《on a person》 ; confirm 《a person》
—례 the order of confirmation ; the ordination
안스럽다 ⇨ 안슬프다
안슬프다 be sorry for troubling someone who is worse off than oneself ¶ 자네에게 돈을 치르게 하다니 안슬프기 짝이 없네 It wouldn't be proper to have you pay the bill.
안식 安息 rest ; repose ; relaxation ; sabbatical —하다 rest ; take a rest ; repose
—교 The Seventh-Day Adventist Church
—년 a sabbatical year —일 the Sabbath ; a Sabbath day ; the Lord's day ; Sunday ¶ 안식일을 지키다 keep〔observe〕 the Sabbath
안식 眼識 insight ; discernment ; discrimination ; penetration ; a critical〔discerning〕 eye ¶ 전문가의 안식 an expert's eye // 안식이 있는 사람 a discerning〔keen-eyed〕 person ; a man of insight // 안식이

ㅇ

있다 have an eye 《for》 // 예술적 안식을 기르다 train〔develop〕 artistic discrimination〔judgment〕 // 그것을 감별하려면 전문가의 안식이 필요하다 It needs an expert's eye to distinguish it from the real thing.

안식구 —食口 female members of a family

안식처 安息處 a place to find peace ; a refuge ¶ 종교에서 안식처를 구하다 find relief in religion ; seek refuge〔solace, peace〕 in religion

안식향 安息香 benzoin

안신 雁信 a letter ; news ; tidings

안심 [쇠고기의] lean meat of short ribs

†**안심 安心** relief ; peace of mind ; assurance ; reassurance ; security **—하다** be〔feel〕 relieved ; be at ease〔peace〕 ; feel safe〔confident〕 ; rest assured ¶ 안심하고 with an easy mind ; without fear ; without anxiety ; with confidence // 안심하고 맡겨 둘 수 있는〔없는〕 사람 a reliable〔an unreliable〕 person // 안심 안되는 병세 a serious〔critical〕 condition // 안심시키다 set 《a person》 at ease ; ease 《a person's》 mind ; relieve 《a person's》 anxiety ; put 《a person》 at ease // 그것을 듣고 안심했다 I was relieved at the news. // 그가 혼자 강에 가서 안심이 안된다 I am a little worried about his having gone to the river all alone. // 마침내 그가 와서 모두 다 안심했다 At last he arrived to the great relief of everybody. // 그 점은 안심하십시오 Put your mind at rest on that score. /Set your mind at rest about that. /You may take it easy on that score. // 환자는 이제 안심입니다 The patient is out of danger. // 나는 그렇게 안심이 안되오 I'm not so sure 《about it》. // 고비를 넘겼으니 안심하오 I can assure you that the worst is over. // 발견될 염려가 없어서 안심입니다 I feel safe from discovery. // 절대로 대부금 지불을 못하는 일은 없을 테니까 안심하게나 Rest assured. I'll never fall behind in my loan payments. // 그 소식을 들으니 안심이 된다 It's a relief to hear that news. // 안심하고 나에게 맡겨 주세요 Please set your mind at ease and leave it to me.

안심부름 errands around the house ; household chores ; a woman's errand

안심입명 安心立命 spiritual peace and enlightment ; calm resignation (to fate) ; philosophy

안심찮다 安心— ① (be) uneasy ; be ill at ease ; (be) anxious ; uncertain ¶ 안심찮게 여기다 feel uneasy 《about》 ; be anxious〔worried〕 《about》 ; be uncertain 《over》 // 나에게는 안심찮은 일이 많다 I am worried about many things. /Many things weigh on my mind.
② feel sorry ¶ 자네의 폐를 끼치다니 안심찮네 It pains me to think of all the trouble I am causing you.

안아맡다 bear〔shoulder, undertake〕 《a person's》 responsibility ; take 《a responsibility》 for ; take upon oneself ; assume 《responsibility》 ¶ 빚을 안아맡다 shoulder 《person's》 debt

안아맹이 〖광산〗 a hole for dynamite, drilled over one's shoulder with one's back to to the wall

안아 일으키다 raise〔lift up〕 《a person》 in one's arms ; help 《a person》 to sit up

안압 眼壓 〖의학〗 intraocular pressure

안약 眼藥 eye-water〔lotion〕 ; eye-drops ; medicine for the eyes ¶ 안약을 넣다 apply eyelotion ; drop some eye-lotion into one's eyes
—병 a dropper ; an eyedropper

안양반 —兩班 the lady of the house ; the mistress ; the wife ; the Mrs. ; madam

안어버이 the mother ; the female parent

안염 眼炎 inflammation of the eyes ; ophthalmia

안온 安穩 peace ; quiet ; tranquility ; calmness **—하다** (be) peaceful ; quiet ; tranquil ; calm ¶ 안온하게 peacefully ; in peace ; quietly ; tranquilly // 안온한 세상 peaceful〔tranquil〕 times // 안온하게 살다 live in peace

안올리다 color the inside of ¶ 그릇을 안올리다 paint the inside of a bowl

안옷 [속옷] the undergarments ; [여자옷] garments for the womenfolk

안와 安臥 lying quiet ; a quiet rest **—하다** lie quiet in bed

안위 安危 safety and danger ; security ; welfare ; fate ¶ 국가의 안위 a national crisis // 이것은 국가의 안위에 관한 중대한 문제다 This is a matter of vital importance to the welfare of the State. /This vital question affects our national welfare.

***안이 安易** easiness ; ease **—하다** (be) easy ; easygoing ¶ 안이한 easy ; easygoing // 안이한 생활 an easy life // 안이한 생각 an easygoing〔happy-go-lucky〕 way of thinking // 안이하게 easily ; at ease ; at one's ease // 안이하게 생각하다 take things easy

안일 housework ; woman's work ¶ 안일을 하다 do housework

안일 安逸 ease ; idleness ; indolence ; lotus-eating **—하다** (be) easy ; be at ease ; (be) idle ; indolent ¶ 안일한 생활 a life of ease // 안일에 빠지다 live in ease〔idleness〕 ; lead an indolent life
무사 **—주의** a peace-at-any-price principle

안잠자기 a (sleeping-in) housemaid ¶ 안잠자기를 두다 keep a housemaid

안잠자다 live in 《a house》 as a housemaid

안장 安葬 burial ; interment **—하다** bury ; inter ; entomb ; commit to the earth

—지 a burial ground
‡안장 鞍裝 a saddle ¶ 안장을 얹다 saddle 《a horse》; put on a saddle // 안장을 풀다 unsaddle 《a horse》
안장코 鞍裝— a flat nose ; a nose with a sunken bridge ; a bulldog nose
안저지 a nurse(ry) maid
안저 출혈 眼底出血 〖의학〗 cerebral hemorrhage in one's eyes
안전 the inside rim 《of a jar》
안전 —殿 the inner palace ; the king's residence
†안전 安全 safety ; security ; freedom from danger ——하다 (be) safe ; secure ; be free from danger ¶ 안전한 장소 a place 〔zone〕 of safety // 안전하게 safely ; securely ; in safety // 안전을 도모하다 make 《a thing》 secure // 교통의 안전을 위협하다 endanger traffic safety // 자신의 안전을 도모하다 look to〔seek〕 one's own safety // 가내 안전을 빌다 offer prayers for peace and prosperity to the family // 여기는 안전하다 You are safe from all dangers here. /This place is safe〔secure〕.
—감 a sense of security — 계획 a safety program — 교육 safety education — 권(圈) a safety zone —기 a safety bolt〔catch, guard〕; a cut-out switch (전기) — 기준 safety standards —등 a safety lamp 《in mines》 —띠 a safety belt — 면도 a safety razor — 보장 security — 보장 이사회 [UN의] the Security Council — 보장 조약 a security treaty 〔pact〕 —성 safety — 신호 a clear〔safety〕 signal — 운전 careful driving —율 safety rate〔efficiency〕; degree of safety — 장치 a safety device 〔appliance, catch〕 — 제일주의 the safety-first principle — 주간 Safety Week — 지대 a safety zone ; a street refuge —책 a safety measure ¶ 안전책을 강구하다 take a safety measure // 안전책을 취하는 편이 좋다고 생각한다 I think you should adopt a plan that's fail-safe. — 통신 전술 safety communication tactics —판 a safety valve — 핀 a safety pin 집단 — 보장 collective security
안전 眼前 ¶ 안전의 immediate ; imminent ; impending // 안전의 광경 a view (spreading) before one // 안전의 적 the enemy in sight // 안전에 before one's eyes ; under one's nose ; in one's presence ; on the spot // 바로 안전에서 under one's very nose // 안전에 벌어지다 spread out before one〔one's eyes〕 // 넓은 전망이 안전에 전개되다 A wide panorama spreads〔opens〕 out before us.
안전 관리 安全管理 〖노동〗 safety supervision
—자 a safety supervisor
안전모 安全帽 a safety〔crash〕 helmet ; a hard〔crash〕 hat
안전 지도 安全指導 〖노동〗 safety direction
—관 a safety director
*안절부절못하다 be restless〔nervous, anxious, fidgety, irritated〕; be on pins and needles ¶ 안절부절못하는 사람 a restless person ; a scatterbrain // 안절부절못하여 irritatingly ; impatiently ; uneasily ; nervously ; restlessly ; in a fidget // 나는 그 사람 앞에서는 안절부절못한다 I get quite embarrassed〔nervous〕 in his presence. // 그 여자는 시간이 지나가는 것을 안절부절못하며 기다리고 있었다 She was greatly impatient with the slow passage of time. // 그 소식을 들을 때까지 우리는 안절부절못했다 Until we heard the news, we were all on edge. // 그는 안절부절못하여 의자에 앉아 있을 수가 없었다 He was very nervous and couldn't sit still in the chair. // 그는 아침부터 안절부절못하였다 He's been acting fidgety since morning. // 왜 그렇게 안절부절못하나 Why are you fidgeting so?
안정 安靜 rest ; repose ; quiet ; peace ——하다 (be) tranquil〔peaceful, quiet〕; be at ease ¶ 안정시키다 set at ease ; quiet ; relieve // 안정을 유지하다 lie quietly ; keep quiet // 의사는 절대 안정을 명했다 The doctor prescribed a complete rest for him.
— 요법 a rest cure 절대 — absolute 〔complete〕 rest〔quiet〕
†안정 安定 stability ; [평형] equilibrium ; [안정화] stabilization ; [침착] settlement ; composure ——하다 be〔become〕 stabilized ; be settled ; settle ¶ 통화의 안정 currency stabilization ; stabilization of the currency // 물가의 안정 price stabilization // 생활의 안정 security ; the security of living // 경제의 안정 economic stabilization // 안정되어 있다 be stable〔settled〕 // 안정되어 있지 않다 be unstable ; be unsettled ; lack stability // 안정시키다 stabilize // 국민 생활을 안정시키다 stabilize national life // 안정을 유지하다〔잃다〕 keep〔lose〕 equilibrium〔balance〕 // 생활이 안정되어 있다 have a sure means of livelihood // 그 여자는 감정이 안정되어 있지 않다 She is emotionally unstable. // 물가가 점차로 안정되어 가고 있다 Prices (of commodities) are gradually getting stabilized. // 그는 아직도 안정된 직업을 찾지 못했다 He still hasn't found a steady job.
—감 a sense of stability ¶ 안정감이 있는 stable ; secure ; well-balanced // 안정감이 없는 unstable ; shaky ; unsettled — 공황 a stabilization crisis —도 stability — 세력 a stabilizing power〔force〕 ¶ 극동의 안정 세력 the main prop and stay〔backbone〕 of the Far East —의(儀) a ship stabilizer — 인구 a stable population — 자금 a stabilization fund — 장치 a stabilizer ; an equilibrator — 정권 a stabilizing government —책 stabilization measures — 통화 stabilized currency —판

ㅇ

(板) a stabilizing fin 자동 ― 장치 〖경제〗 a built-in stabilizer
안정 眼睛 the pupil〔apple〕 of the eye
안존하다 安存― [성질이] (be) quiet and gentle ; be at ease ; be calm and well-behaved genial ; [상태] be at peace
안좌 安坐 [편안한 앉음새] quiet sitting ⇨ 책상다리
안주 安住 living in peace ; peaceful living ; a serene life ; a comfortable life ―하다 live peacefully ; lead a comfortable life ; lead a peaceful living ¶ 안주할 땅을 찾다 seek a place for peaceful living // 종교에 안주를 찾다 find relief in religion
안주 按酒 appetizers served with drinks ; cocktail appetizers ; appetizer dishes ; a relish 《taken with wine》 ; garnish ; garnishings ; a condiment ; garniture ¶ 술과 안주 wine and some eatables // 이것은 술안주에 좋다 This goes very well with wine. // 안주는 무엇이 있느냐 What are the cocktail dishes ? /What is the appetizer ? // 술안주가 아무것도 없다 I have nothing to take with wine.
―감 hors d'oeuvres makings
안주머니 an inside pocket 《of the coat》 ¶ 안주머니에 넣다 keep 《it》 in one's inner pocket
안주인 the lady of the house ; a landlady ; the hostess
안중 眼中 ¶ 안중에 두지 않다 think nothing of ; set at naught ; pay no attention to ; take no notice of // 이 점을 안중에 두다 take it into account // 자기 밖에는 안중에 없다 He thinks of nothing〔no one〕 but himself. // 그러한 녀석은 내 안중에 없다 Such a man is beneath my notice. // 그의 안중에는 정부도 여론도 없다 He sets both the Government and public opinion at naught. // 그의 안중에는 다만 돈 뿐이다 He thinks of nothing but money.
안중문 ―中門 a mid-gate (leading to the inner court)
안질 眼疾 an eye disease〔trouble, disorder〕 ; sore eyes ¶ 안질에 고춧가루 red pepper in a sick eye ; a very annoying thing // 그는 안질을 앓고 있다 He is suffering from an affection of the eyes. /He is afflicted with an eye disease.
안집 the inner building〔wing〕 ; the main building〔wing〕
안짝 ① inside a limit ; within ; less than ; not more than ; not exceeding ¶ 1,000원 안짝의 금액 a sum not exceeding 1,000 *won* // 일주일 안짝에 within〔inside of〕 a week // 역에서 100미터 안짝에 within a hundred meters of the station // 수입 안짝에서 생활하다 live within one's income // 기부금은 100만원 안짝이었다 The subscriptions amounted to little short of a million *won*.
② the first line (of a couplet)
안짱다리 a bow-legged person ¶ 안짱다리로 걷다 walk intoed
†안쪽 the inside ; the inner part ¶ 안쪽의 inside ; inner // 안쪽에 inside ; within // 안쪽에서 from the inside ; from within // 트랙의 안쪽 코스 the inside track ; the lanes on the inside of a track // 안쪽에서 열다 open from within // 통의 안쪽을 깨끗이 해라 Clean the inside of the tub. // 이 코트는 털을 안쪽으로 입느냐 아니면 바깥쪽으로 입느냐 Is this coat worn with the fur inside or outside ? // 이 문은 안쪽으로 여느냐 아니면 바깥쪽으로 여느냐 Does this door open inwards or outwards ? // 그 여자는 문의 바로 안쪽에 서 있었다 She was standing just inside the gate. // 문의 안쪽에서 열쇠가 잠겨 있다 The door hooks on the inside.
안쫑잡다 bear in mind ; lay 《a matter》 to heart ; keep in mind ; [헤아림] estimate 《at》 ; grasp the general idea of
안찝 [안감] lining material ; [내장] the viscera of an animal ; the guts
안차다 (be) bold ; fearless ; dauntless
안착 安着 safe arrival ; [물품의] safe receipt ―하다 arrive safe(ly)〔in safety〕 ; reach 《a place》 safe and sound ; [물건이] reach in good condition ; duly reach ¶ 그가 목적지에 안착했다는 말을 들었다 I heard that he had got to his destination safe and sound.
안창 [구두의] an inner sole ; a shoe liner ¶ 안창을 깔다 put liners in shoes
안채 the main building〔wing〕 (of a house)
안채 眼彩 the brightness of the eyes ⇨ 안광(眼光)
안총 眼聽 ⇨ 안력(眼力)
안출 案出 contrivance ; invention (발명) ―하다 contrive ; devise ; originate ; invent ; study out ; strike out ; work out ; think out ¶ 일책(一策)을 안출하다 think〔work〕 out a plan
―자 a contriver ; a projector ; an inventor ; an originator
안치 安置 placing ; laying down ; installation ; [격리 감금] keeping an exile in his place of exile ―하다 install 《an image in a shrine》 ; enshrine ¶ 유해를 안치하다 lay 《a person's》 body in state // 절에 불상을 안치하다 install a Buddhist image in a temple // 그 동상은 받침대 위에 안치되어 있다 The statue rests on a pedestal.
안치다[1] get 《rice》 ready to cook ; prepare for cooking
안치다[2] press upon one ; threaten ; bear down ; be imminent ; impend
안치수 ―數 inside〔interior〕 measure〔measurement〕 ; interior width ¶ 안치수가 10센티미터이다 be 10 centimeters in the clear〔on the inside〕
안타 安打 〖야구〗 a (safe) hit ; a safety ; a base hit ¶ 훌륭한 안타 a clean hit // 3루

ㅇ

타를 넘는 안타 a hit through third // 안타를 치다 hit ; make a hit // 좌〔우〕익으로 안타를 치다 hit to left 〔right〕 field // 적을 3 안타로 봉쇄하다 hold the opponents to three hits

내야 — an infield hit **산발** — scattered hits **우익〔좌익, 중견〕** — a hit to right 〔left, center〕 **적시** — a timely hit **집중** — bunched hits ; fireworks ; a swat parade〔streak〕 ; a volley of hits **무— 시합** a no-hit game ; a no-hitter 《구》

안타까워하다 ① [애태우다] be nervous 〔upset, agitated〕 about ; be impatient ; be all hot and bothered ; be anxious about〔over〕 ; be frustrated by ; be tantalized at ; be annoyed by ; be vexed at ¶ 알고 싶어 무척 안타까워하다 be pretty anxious to know about // 모든 것이 잘 될 것이니 그리 안타까워하지 말게 Don't be so nervous, everything will turn out all right.

② [애처로워하다] be heartbroken at ; be distressed〔devastated〕 by

안타깝다 [사물이] (be) heartbreaking ; distressing ; [사람이] frustrating ; tantalizing ; annoying ; make one feel sorry ; get on one's nerves ¶ 방학을 안타깝게 기다리다 await〔wait for〕 the vacation impatiently // 어린애가 저렇게 우는 것을 보니 안타깝다 It makes my heart hurt to see the baby crying so bitterly. // 그는 안타까울 정도로 무능하다 He is lamentably 〔sadly〕 incompetent. // 볼 수 있을 뿐 만지지 못하니 정말 안타깝다 It is tantalizing to see it but not be allowed to touch it. // 우물우물하고 있어 정말 안타깝다 I am impatient at your slowness. // 참으로 안타깝구나 How vexing〔provoking〕! /You try〔tax〕 my patience !

안타깝이 an impatient person ; a nervous person ; an eager-beaver

안타깨비 a coarse silk woven from broken threads

안타다 ride in front of 《a person》 (on a horse) ; ride double

안태우다 be worried〔annoyed〕 ; be anxious 《about》 ; worry oneself ; [남을] give 《a person》 trouble ; keep 《a person》 in suspense ; bother ; worry

안택 安宅 a shaman rite to appease the household god **—하다** hold a rite for the household god

—경(經) incantation read to appease the household god **—굿** the shaman rite for the household god

‡안테나 an antenna 《*pl.* ~s》 ; aerial ¶ 안테나를 세우다 set up〔put up〕 an antenna // 안테나를 치다 stretch〔support, prop〕 an antenna

— 반사기〔개폐기, 회로, 지주, 지향 성도〕 an antenna reflector〔switch, circuit, support, pattern〕 **— 축전지〔전류, 애자〕** an antenna condenser〔current, insulator〕 **래빗 —** a rabbit-eared aerial **쌍극 —** a dipole aerial **자동차용 —** an auto antenna **접지 —** an grounded antenna

안틀다 be within a certain price〔quantity〕 ; be less than

안티고네 [신화] Antigone

안티모니, 안티몬 〖화학〗 antimony 《Sb》

안티피린 〖약〗 antipyrine

안팎 ① [안과 밖] the interior and exterior ; the inside and outside ; the ins and outs ¶ 인생의 안팎 the ins and outs of life // 안팎으로〔에〕 within and without ; inside and outside 《the house》 ; in and out ; at home and abroad (국내외의) // 문 안팎으로 both inside and outside the gate // 학교는 안팎이 깨끗하다 The school house is spick-and-span inside and out. // 그 이야기는 안팎이 있다 There are two sides to the story. // 이 옷감은 안팎을 구별할 수가 없다 I cannot tell which is the face of this cloth.

② [표리] two sides ; both sides ; the right and the wrong sides ¶ 안팎이 있는 double-faced〔-dealing〕 // 안팎이 없는 single-hearted // 안팎이 있는 사람 a double-dealer ; a double-faced man ; a hypocrite (위선자) // 행동에 안팎이 있다 carry two faces under one hood ; play a double game // 그는 안팎이 있는 사나이다 He has two faces. /He plays a double game. // 사람이 안팎이 있어선 못쓴다 You must not be one thing in 《a person's》 presence and another behind his back.

③ [내외] more or less ; around ; some ; almost ¶ 일주일 안팎 about a week // 연령은 50 안팎이다 He is about 50. /He is fifty or thereabouts〔so〕. // 비용은 1,000원 안팎일 것이다 The expenses will be in the neighborhood of 1,000 *won*.

안팎곱사등이 a person with a humpback and a protruding chest

안팎 노자 —路資 the round-trip fare ; (traveling) expenses for a round trip ¶ 전주까지 안팎 노자가 얼마입니까 How much is it round-trip to *Chŏnju* ?

안팎벽 —壁 inner and outer walls

안팎심부름 inside and outside chores

안팎일 inside and outside work

안팎채 inner and outer buildings

안편지 —便紙 [내간] a letter from a woman to a woman

안표 眼標 a sign ; a mark ; an earmark ; a landmark ; a pylon ; a guide **—하다** make〔leave, put〕 a mark 《on》 ; (ear-) mark ¶ 언덕을 안표로 하여 길을 잡다 follow the road with the hill as a guide

안피지 雁皮紙 rice paper

안하 眼下 ¶ 안하에 right beneath the eyes ; under one's eyes ; just〔right〕 below one's eyes // 안하에 내려다 보다 overlook ; command 《a view of》 // 전시를 안하에 내려다 보다 overlook the whole

ㅇ

city ; command a whole view of the city below
안하무인 眼下無人 leaving《a person, a thing》 out of account〔consideration〕; taking no account〔consideration〕; taking no account〔notice, thought〕 of《a person》; set at naught ; make naught《of》 ¶ 안하무인이다 be audacious ; be haughty ; be supercilious ; think of none but oneself // 천하의 영웅도 그에게는 안하무인이다 Not a hero in the land but sinks into insignificance in his eyes.
안한 安閑 **—하다** be at peace ; be at leisure ¶ 안한히 있을 수 없다 I can't bear sitting idle. /This is no time for idling.
안항 雁行 your〔his〕 esteemed brother
안해 [지난 해] the immediately preceding year ; last year
안형제 —兄弟 a girl's sister
안호주머니 an inner pocket ; an inside《breast》 pocket《of the coat》
†**앉다** ① [자리에] sit ; take a seat ; sit down ; squat down ; be seated ; set oneself ¶ 앉아서 하는 일 a sedentary occupation // 요 위에 앉다 sit up in bed // 책상에 앉다 sit at a desk // 바로 앉다 sit straight《up》// 편하게 앉다 sit at one's ease // 무릎을 꿇고 앉다 sit on one's knees // 자 앉으시오 Please take a seat. // 앉아서 당하고만 있을 건가요 Are you going to take it lying down?
② [지위에] take up ; hold《a position》 ¶ 좋은 자리에 앉다 occupy a good position // 왕위에 앉다 ascend〔accede to〕 the throne // 책상에 먼지가 앉았다 Dust gathered on the table. // 그가 회사에서 좋은 자리에 앉아있는 것은 아버지 덕택이다 His high position in the company is due to his father.
③ [새 따위가] perch〔alight, sit, settle〕 on ; roost (보금자리에) ¶ 새가 나뭇가지에 앉아 있다 A bird perched on one of the branches. // 나무에 몇 마리의 참새가 앉아 있다 There are some sparrows in the tree. // 천장에 파리가 앉아 있다 There is a fly on the ceiling.
④ [건물 따위가] be located〔situated〕《in, on》; face《on》 ¶ 너의 집은 잘 앉았다 Your house is nicely situated. // 이 건물은 잘못 앉았다 This building has a bad〔poor〕 aspect.
⑤ [딱지 따위가] be covered《with a scab》; [종두가] take ¶ 종기에 딱지가 앉았다 A scab formed over the boil.
앉은검정 the soot on the bottom of a kettle ; kettle-black (used medicinally)
앉은뱅이 a cripple (who is wholly deprived of the use of his legs)
— 저울 a platform scale
앉은부채 〖식물〗 a skunk cabbage
앉은일 a sedentary job〔work, occupation〕
앉은자리 a seat which has been taken ; one's seat〔sitting〕 ¶ 앉은자리의 immediate ; impromptu ; ready ; instant ; prompt ; extemporaneous ; extempore (즉흥의) // 앉은자리에서 then and there ; on the spot ; extempore ; offhand ; at a sitting // 앉은자리에서 거절하다 decline then and there // 앉은자리에서 연설하다 make an offhand speech // 앉은자리에서 맥주 6병을 마시다 finish up half a dozen bottles of beer at a stretch // 앉은자리에서 시를 짓다 compose a poem extempore // 그는 앉은자리에서 몇마디의 소견을 말했다 He made a few offhand remarks.
앉은장사 a sedentary trade〔business〕 ¶ 앉은장사를 하다 keep a shop
앉은차례 —次例 seating order ; order of seats
앉은키 one's height when seated ; sitting height
앉을깨 the seat of a loom (베틀의) ; a straddle seat ; the kickboard on a swing
앉을자리 a place to sit ; a seat ¶ 앉을자리를 가리키다 motion to a seat
앉음새 the way one sits ; one's seated posture
앉히다 ① [앉게 하다] place《a person》 in a seat ; seat《a person》 ¶ 상좌에 앉히다 seat《a person》 at the head of the table ; give《a guest》 the place of honor // 손님을 작은 식탁에 앉히다 seat the guests at small tables // 어린애를 방석 위에 앉히다 put a baby on a cushion
② [자리에] put in a position of authority ; appoint《a person to》
③ [버릇을] discipline ; teach (manners)
④ [장부에] set down〔enter〕 as an item
†**않다** be not ; do not ¶ 그는 정직하지 않다 He is not honest. // 나는 그런 짓은 하지 않는다 I will not do such a thing. // 금주에는 그다지 물건을 사지 않았다 I have bought few things this week. // 그것은 좋지도 나쁘지도 않다 It is neither good nor bad. // 키가 크지도 작지도 않다 He is neither tall nor small.
않을 수 없다 be compelled〔forced, obliged〕 to《do》; be〔find oneself〕 under the necessity〔compulsion〕 of《doing》; be hard put to it to《do》; be driven by dire〔sheer〕 necessity to《do》 ¶ 좋아서가 아니라 하지 않을 수 없었다 I did it of necessity, not of choice.
†**알¹** ① [새·닭의] an egg ; [물고기·조개류의] spawn ¶ 갓 낳은 알 a new-laid egg // 삶은 알 a (hard-) boiled egg // 알을 낳다 lay eggs ; spawn (물고기가) // 알을 까다 hatch an egg // 알을 품다 sit on an egg ; brood // 알을 품게 하다 set《a hen》 on eggs // 알을 깨다 break〔crack〕 an egg // 알을 풀다 beat (up) an egg // 닭들이 알을 잘 낳는가 How are the chickens laying?
② [작고 둥근 것] a ball ; a bead ; a bulb ¶ 콩알만하다 be as small as a bean // 알이 고른 달걀이 있다 There are even-sized

eggs.
③ [작은 열매·낟알] a nut ; a grain ; a berry ¶ 알이 들다 go〔run〕 to seed ; grow ripe ; ripen
④ [양배추 따위의] a head ; a bulb ¶ 알이 잘 밴 양배추 a cabbage with a good head
날〔생〕— a raw egg 쌀〔모래〕— a grain of rice〔sand〕 생선 — fish eggs ; spawn ; roe ; caviar 오리— a duck egg 유리— a glass bead

알² ⇨ 아래 ¶ 알로 down ; under ; below // 알로 떨어지다 fall down ; go to the ground

알- bare ; naked ; stripped ¶ 알밤 a shelled chestnut // 알몸 a naked body

알갱이 a kernel ; a grain ; a berry ; a granule (작은)

알거지 a man with no property at all ; a person as poor as a crow〔church mouse〕 ; a real beggar

알게 하다 ⇨ 알리다

알겨먹다 swindle (money) out of 《a person》 ; trick a weaker 《person》 out of 《a thing》 ¶ 당신의 돈을 알겨먹으려는 광고 advertising designed to trick your purse // 그는 불쌍한 소녀의 돈을 알겨먹었다 He tricked the poor girl out of her money.

알겯다 《a hen》 cluck for a rooster (to mate with)

알곡 —穀 cereals ; pure grain ; husked 〔thrashed〕 grain

알과녁 a (target) bull's-eye

알구지 the crotch of the supporting stick of an A-frame

알궁둥이 bare buttocks〔bottom〕

알기 쉽다 (be) easy to understand ; intelligible ; comprehensible ; plain ; easy ; [글씨체가] legible ¶ 알기 쉽게 intelligibly ; simply // 알기 쉽게 말하면 to speak in plain language // 알기 쉽게 하다 simplify // 그의 영어는 알기 쉽다 His English is easy to understand. /He speaks plain English.

알깍쟁이 ① [지독한 인색군] a real tightwad ; a real stinker ; a real miser ; a penny pincher ② [땅군] a true-to-life snake-catcher ; [부랑자] an ill-natured boy ; a tramp

알껍질 an egg shell

†알다 ① [일반적으로] know ; have〔get〕 a knowledge 《of》 ; be well aware 《of》 ; learn ; be familiar 《with》 ; be acquainted 《with》 ¶ 널리 알려진 widely known // 알려지지 않도록 secretly ; stealthily // 알지 못하는 사이에 before one knows // 내가 알고 있는 바로는 so far as I know ; to (the best of) my knowledge // 아는 체하다 pretend to know // 알지 못하는 체하다 pretend〔feign〕 ignorance // 속속들이 알다 know〔understand〕 thoroughly // 이름〔얼굴〕을 알고 있다 know 《a person》 by name〔sight〕 // 자기의 결점을 알고 있다 be aware of one's shortcomings // 전혀 알지 못하다 have not the least〔slightest〕 idea of ; be utterly〔completely〕 ignorant of // 거의 알지 못하다 know very little ; have little knowledge of // 그가 지금 어디에 살고 있는지 아느냐 Have you got any idea where he lives now ? // 나는 지난 주에 그것을 알았다 I knew about it last week. /I heard〔was informed〕 of it last week. // 어째서 그가 오지 않는지 알지 못한다 I don't see why he doesn't come. // 어떠한 사태가 일어날지 알지 못한다 There is no telling〔knowing〕 what may happen. // 신문으로 너의 해외 여행을 알았다 I have learned through the papers that you are going abroad. // 그 여자는 양친이 알지 못하는 사이에 운전 면허를 땄다 She got a driving license without the knowledge of her parents. // 그를 알지 못하는 사람이 없다 He is known to everybody. // 아는 것이 병이다 Ignorance is bliss. // 때가 지나면 알게 될 것이다 Time will tell. // 이 책이 재미있다는 것을 알았다 This book proved interesting. // 정확히는 알지 못한다 I don't know for certain. // 그는 프랑스어도 약간 알고 있다 He has some knowledge of French, too. // 그 일이 그에게 적합하지 않다는 것을 알았다 It turned out he was not the man for the job. // 그가 겁쟁이라는 것을 알았다 He proved to be a coward. // 그 여자가 부지런하다는 것을 알았다 She proved to be industrious. // 이 근처는 잘 알지 못한다 I am a stranger here. // 이 근처는 잘 안다 I am well acquainted with the neighborhood. /I know every inch of this neighborhood. // 진상이 알려졌다 The truth has come out. // 너 이것 알아 You know what ? // 이사할 경우에는 며칠 전에 알려야 되느냐 How many days' notice am I supposed to give in case I intend to move ? // 이제 대강은 알겠다 Now I think I get the picture.
② [이해하다] understand ; comprehend ; see ; get ; [의미 따위를] grasp ; [어려운 것을] make out ; [설명·강의 따위를] follow ; [음악 따위를] appreciate ¶ 건강의 고마움을 알다 appreciate the bliss of health // 알았습니다 I see. /Sure, I get you. 《미》 // 그 계획이 현명하지 못함을 알았다 We saw that the plan was unwise. // 나를 진정으로 알아주는 것은 너뿐이다 You're the only one that really understands me. // 아 이제 알았다 Ah, that accounts for 〔explains〕 it ! // 너의 기분을 잘 안다 I am sensible of your feeling. // 이 책을 읽으면 고대 희랍의 생활을 알게 된다 This book will give you a good idea of life in ancient Greece. // 좋은 음악은 들으면 안다 I know good music when I hear it. // 그녀는 그림을 볼줄 안다 She has an eye for pictures. // 내 말을 알아 듣겠습니까 Do you understand〔get〕 me ? /

ㅇ

Do you see what I mean? //내 설명을 알아듣겠습니까 Can you follow my explanation? //저 사람이 무엇을 말하고자 하는지 알겠습니까 Have you any idea what he is driving at? //이 작가가 말하고자 하는 바를 알겠습니까 Can you make sense of what this author says? //당신이 하는 말은 알 수 없다 I don't understand you〔what you say〕./I don't get you〔your meaning〕. //그렇게 어려운 것은 나는 알 수 없다 That's too difficult for me to understand. //네 말은 도무지 알 수 없다 I haven't a remote〔the remotest〕 idea of what you mean. //그것은 희미하게 밖에 알지 못한다 I have only a misty idea of it. //이 경치의 아름다움을 알지 못합니까 Don't you feel the beauty of this landscape? //그는 음악을 안다〔알지 못한다〕 He has an〔no〕 ear for music. //네 말은 알겠다 I know what you mean. //그 뜻을 아직도 알 수 없습니까 Is the meaning still obscure〔dark〕 to you? //우리가 얼마나 걱정하고 있었는지 너는 알지 못한다 You have no idea (of) how anxious we have been. //누가 그것을 했는지 전혀 알지 못한다 I have not the least idea who did it. //함부로 갈겨 써 놓은 이 글씨를 나는 도무지 알 수가 없다 I can make nothing of all this scribble. //그는 자연의 아름다움에 대해서 잘 알지 못한다 He hasn't much feeling for natural beauty. //그 책은 전문가 밖에 알지 못한다 The book is comprehensible only to specialists. //당신이 나에게 기대하고 있는 바를 나는 잘 알지 못한다 I am not clear as to what you expect me to do. //그의 편지는 무엇을 말하고 있는지 알 수 없다 I can't make sense of his letter. //나는 그림의 좋고 나쁨을 알 수 없다 I am no judge of pictures. //그는 농담을 알지 못한다 He can't see a joke. //그녀는 그 농담의 요점을 알지 못하였다 She missed the point of the joke. //강의를 잘 알아들을 수 없었다 I didn't make much of that lecture. //경찰관은 그 제복으로 알 수 있다 You can tell a policeman by his uniform. //아무도 알 수 없어요 God〔The devil〕 knows. //그는 옛 친구의 목소리를 대번에 알았다 He recognized his old friend's voice. //마침내 그가 옛 학우라는 것을 알았다 I finally placed him as an old schoolfellow. //그가 어떤 인물인지 알았다 I saw through him. //자기의 잘못임을 알았다 He found that he was mistaken. //장래 일은 알 수 없다 The future is hidden from us. //이렇게 떨어져 있어서는 누군지 알 수 없다 I can't tell at this distance who it is. //무어가 무엇인지 알 수 없다 I can't tell which is which. //익사자가 누군지 알 수 없다 The drowned man is not identified. //어떻게 했으면 좋을지 알 수 없다 I am〔feel〕 doubtful (about) what I ought to do. //그는 다음에 무엇을 했으면 좋을지 알지 못했다 He felt dubious (about, as to) what to do next. //나는 어떻게 했으면 좋을지 전혀 알 수 없었다 I was at a loss what to do. //한동안 너를 알아보지 못했다 I didn't recognize you for the moment. //알겠습니다 Got it. //똑바로 알아 두었으면 한다 I wish you'd start getting things straight.

③ [아는 사이] be acquainted with; know; [아는 사이가 되다] become〔get〕 acquainted with; make 《a person's》 acquaintance ¶ 내가 잘 아는 부인 a woman of my acquaintance //알지 못하는 얼굴 strange〔unfamiliar〕 faces; strangers //그를 잘 알고 있다 I know him well. //내가 알고 있는 사람 중에는 그런 사람이 없다 There is no such person that I know of. //대개는 내가 알지 못하는 사람들이었다 Most of them were strangers to me. //그녀를 어느 파티에서 우연히 알게 되었다 I picked her up at a party. //너희 둘은 어떻게 알게 되었니 How did you two meet?

④ [인정하다·깨닫다] recognize; realize; find; see; notice; be convinced of ¶ 위험을 알다 sense〔realize〕 danger; be awake to danger //자기의 잘못을 알다 be convinced of one's error //잘못을 알다 find out one's mistake //음모가 있으리라고는 알지 못했다 I little suspected a plot. //그의 결점을 잘 알고 있다 I am wide awake to his weak points. //조 박사는 현대의 저명한 건축가로서 동서에 알려져 있다 Dr. *Cho* is known all over the world as one of the leading architects of the day.

⑤ [발견] find; notice; perceive; sense; realize ¶ 물정을 아는 사람 a sensible man; a man of sense; a person of understanding //가난의 고통을 알다 go through〔know〕 poverty //그 여자는 남자를 안다 The girl has been around. //그의 사무실을 금방 알았다 I soon found his office./I had no difficulty (in) finding his office. //그 집은 길 모퉁이에 있기 때문에 금방 알 수 있다 The house stands at the corner of the street, so you can't miss it. //어떻게 말하면 좋을지 알 수 없었다 He could not find words to express his feeling. //성적을 언제 알 수 있는지 그에게 물었다 I asked him when the result will be announced.

⑥ [관지(關知)하다] have to do with; be concerned with ¶ 네가 알 바 아니다 It is none of your business./That is my lookout. //그 자식이 죽는대도 내 알 바 아니다 He may die for all I care. //하나를 들으면 열을 안다 A word to the wise is sufficient.

⑦ [느끼다] feel; be sensible of〔to〕; be conscious of; be alive to ¶ 수치를 알다 be alive to a sense of honor; be sensible to shame //은혜를 알다 be sensible of kindness

⑧ [간주하다] regard (as); look upon

ㅇ

(as) ; consider ; think of (as) ; take 《for》 ¶ 그것을 명예로 안다 We regard it as an honor. // 그들은 그를 바보인 줄 알았다 They considered him (to be) a fool. // 그녀는 그를 스미드로 알았다 She took him for Smith. // 나를 무엇으로 알아 What do you take me for? // 그들은 계약이 파기된 것으로 알았다 They considered that the contract was canceled. // 세상은 그를 그 운동의 주모자로 알고 있다 The public regard〔think of〕 him as the leader of the movement.

아는 것이 힘이다 속담 Knowledge is power.

아는 길도 물어 가라 속담 Be prudent to a fault. /Be overcautious. /Make assurance doubly sure. /Better ask the way than go astray.

알돌 a round stone ; a cobble (stone)

알땅 naked〔unvegetated〕 land

알뚝배기 a small earthen bowl ; an unglazed pottery bowl

알뜯이 a crab with spawn removed

알뜰살뜰 ―하다 (be) extremely frugal 〔thrifty〕 ; prudently saving ⇨ 알뜰하다 ¶ 아무리 알뜰살뜰히 해도 한달에 5만원 가지고는 못산다 I cannot keep body and soul together on less than 50,000 *won* a month, even if I practice severe economy.

알뜰하다 (be) prudent ; thrifty ; frugal ; assiduous ¶ 알뜰한 농가 a frugal farm family // 알뜰한 살림 a frugal life // 알뜰한 살림꾼 a prudent housekeeper // 자원의 알뜰한 개발과 사용 the prudent use and development of resources // 알뜰히 frugally ; thriftily ; economically // 알뜰하게 살다 live close〔frugally〕 ; lead a frugal life // 알뜰하게 공부하다 be assiduous in one's work ; devote oneself to study ; study wholeheartedly // 알뜰히 하다 use 〔practice〕 economy // 알뜰히 돈을 모으다 save money frugally

알라 〖종교〗 Allah

알락 ⇨ 얼룩

―나방 〖곤충〗 a leaf skeletonizer moth ―도요 〖새〗 a wood-sandpiper ―뜸부기 〖새〗 a swinhoe's crake ―오리 〖새〗 a gad wall ―할미새 〖새〗 a white-faced wagtail ―해오라기 〖새〗 a bittern

알랑거리다 seek to gain favor by flattery ; curry favor with 《a person》 ; fawn upon 《a patron》 ; flatter ; cringe ; [여자가] coquet ; play the coquette ¶ 웃사람〔권력자〕에게 알랑거리다 cringe to〔fawn upon〕 one's superiors〔the powerful〕

알랑쇠 a flatterer ; a sycophant ; an apple polisher 《미》 ; a door mat 《속》

알랑수 resort to flattery

알랑알랑 cunningly ; with flattery ¶ 알랑알랑 여자를 꾀다 seduce a girl with flattery

알래스카 Alaska 《Alas.》 ¶ 알래스카의 Alaskan

― 공로 the Alaskan Highway ; [별칭] Alean Highway ― 사람 Alaskan

알량하다 [반의적] (be) just fine〔dandy, ducky, grand〕 ¶ 알량한 놈 Oh, a fine fellow! // 알량한 소리를 하다 make grand talk indeed ; talk nonsense 〔rot〕 ; say silly things // 넌 참 알량한 친구다 A fine friend you have been! // 알량한 소리 작작해라 Nonsense!

알레고리 an allegory

알레그레토 〖음악〗 allegretto 《이》

알레그로 〖음악〗 allegro

***알레르기** allergie 《도》 ; 〖의학〗 allergy ¶ 알레르기성의 allergic // 나는 꽃가루에 알레르기 반응을 일으켜 I'm allergic to pollen.

―성 질환 allergic diseases

알렉산드리아 Alexandria

알려지다 ⇨ 알리어지다

알력 軋轢 friction ; discord ; feud ; strife ; quarrel ¶ 알력이 생기다 produce friction ; cause discord // 알력을 피하다 avoid friction // 당원간에 언제나 알력이 있다 There is constant discord among the members of the party. // 그들 사이에 알력이 생겼다 Friction has developed among them. /They are now in discord.

알로까다 (be) shrewd ; astute ; sharp ¶ 알로깐 녀석 a sharp customer // 저렇게 알로깐 놈을 뜯다니 어림없다 It's hopeless to try to get money out of such a sharp customer.

알로하 셔츠 an aloha shirt

알록달록 mottled ⇨ 얼룩덜룩

알록점 ―點 mottles ; dapples ; spots ; dots ; speckles ; polka dots

알롱이 a mottled〔dotted〕 effect〔pattern〕 ; dots

알루마이트 alumite

― 제품 alumite ware ― 주전자〔냄비〕 an alumite kettle〔pan〕

‡**알루미늄** alumin(i)um 《Al》 ¶ 알루미늄으로 처리하다〔입히다〕 aluminize

―선〔조각〕 aluminum wire〔scrap〕 ― 제품 aluminum ware ― 합금 aluminum alloy ― 합판 alclad

알른거리다 glisten ; glitter ; sparkle ; flicker ; shine ; blink (빛이) ⇨ 어른거리다

알른알른 sparkling ; glittering ; glistening ; shining

†**알리다** let 《a person》 know ; tell 《a person》 ; inform 《a person》 ; notify 《a person》 of ; acquaint 《a person》 with ; give 《a person》 to understand 《that》 ; communicate 《a fact》 to 《a person》 ; [흉보따위를] break the news to 《a person》 ¶ 전화로 알리다 telephone 《a person》 ; send a message by the telephone // 편지로 알리다 write to 《a person》 // 출발 날짜를 알리다 let 《a person》 know when one leaves // 알리지 않고 그냥 두다 keep 《a matter》 secret 《from a person》 ; keep 《a

ㅇ

person》 in the dark ; keep 《a matter》 from 《a person》 ; keep 《a person》 ignorant 《of》 // 미리 알리다 give notice beforehand ; forewarn 《a person》 of 《a matter》 // 경찰에 알리다 communicate with the police ; report 《a fact》 to the police // 계속 알리다 keep 《a person》 informed 《of》 ; keep 《a person》 in close touch 《with》 // 내일 알려드리겠소 I'll let you know tomorrow. // 그것을 널리 세상에 알려야 한다 The matter must be given wider publicity. // 병자가 위독하니 알릴 사람에게 알려야 한다 Considering the patient's critical condition, all closely related with him ought at once to be informed about it. // 안착을 알렸다 I informed him of my safe arrival. // 그에게는 알리지 않으면 안된다 We must let him know it. /It must be made known to him. // 그녀에게 너의 과거 실패담을 알려야 할지 어떨지 잘 모르겠다 I wonder if I should let her in on your past fiascos. // 내가 결혼한다는 이야기를 여자 직원들에게는 알리지 마라 Don't let on to any of the female staff that I'm getting married. // 그는 친구에게도 알리지 않고 파리로 여행을 떠났다 He left for Paris without the knowledge of his friends.

알리바이 an alibi ; an excuse 《미·구》 ¶ 완전한 알리바이 a watertight alibi // 알리바이를 조작하다 frame〔create〕 an alibi // 알리바이를 세우다 make〔fix〕 an alibi ; set up〔establish〕 an alibi // 알리바이를 속이다 fake the alibi // 알리바이를 입증하다 prove an alibi // 그의 알리바이는 여간해 깨지지 않았다 His alibi took some breaking.

†**알리어지다** ① [남이 알게 되다] be〔get, become〕 known 《to》 ; come to 《a person's》 knowledge ¶ 알려지지 않도록 in secret ; secretly ; by stealth // 세상에 알리어지다 become generally known ; be known to the general public ; spread widely
② [판명되다] turn out (to be) ; prove (to be) ; be revealed ; be found ; be disclosed ; be identified (신원 따위) ¶ 소문은 거짓임이 알려졌다 The rumor turned out false.
③ [유명해지다] become famous〔well known〕 ; win〔earn, come to〕 fame ¶ 알려진 famous ; noted ; well-known // 알려지지 않은 unknown ; obscure ; nameless

†**알맞다** (be) fit ; becoming ; fitting ; suitable ; appropriate ; adequate ¶ 알맞는 값 moderate price // 알맞는 말 a happy 〔fitting〕 remark // 알맞는 운동 a proper amount of exercise ; moderate exercise // 알맞는 음주 drinking in moderation // 알맞는 직업 a suitable job // 알맞는 집 a suitable house // 알맞는 예 an apt instance // 경우에 알맞는 suitable to〔proper for〕 the occasion // 귤 재배에 알맞는 suitable for the growing of oranges // 아이들에게 꼭 알맞는 책 books right〔fit〕 for children // 알맞게 suitably ; adequately ; reasonably ; moderately ; in moderation ; properly // 알맞는 때에 at a proper time ; just at the right moment ; just in time 《for》 // 알맞게 먹다 eat and drink moderately ; be moderate in eating and drinking // 알맞게 오다 come just in time ; come in the nick of time // 기질에 알맞다〔알맞지 않다〕 be〔be not〕 agreeable to one's temperament // 그는 그 지위에 알맞다〔알맞지 않다〕 He is well fitted〔unfitted〕 for the position. // 그 운동은 여자에게 알맞다 The sport is suited to girls. // 그는 선생이 알맞다 He is suited to be〔for〕 a teacher. // 운동도 알맞게 하면 약이 된다 Exercise taken in moderation will do you good. // 끽연은 그의 건강에 알맞지 않다 Smoking doesn't agree with him. // 이 물은 음용에 알맞다 This water is good to drink. // 그는 결원 후임으로 알맞다 He is fit for the vacancy.

*‡**알맹이** [과실] a stone ; a kernel ; [실질] substance ; matter ; contents ¶ 알맹이 없는 unsubstantial ; empty ; poor // 알맹이 있는 substantial ; solid // 알맹이 있는 일 solid work // 알맹이 없는 강의 a lecture of little substance ; a poor lecture // 그의 연설은 알맹이가 있다 His speech is instructive〔edifying〕. // 이 책은 너무나 알맹이가 없다 This book is poor in content. // 외형보다도 알맹이 있는 것을 택해야 한다 In everything you must prefer substance to appearance.

알몸 ① [나체] a naked〔nude〕 body ; nudity ; stark-nakedness ¶ 알몸의 naked ; nude ; stark-naked // 알몸으로 in the nude ; with nothing on ; in one's bare skin ; in the altogether 《구》 // 알몸이 되다 strip oneself bare〔naked, stark-naked〕 ; take off all one's clothes ; strip off one's clothes // 알몸으로 있다 be without a shred of clothing ; have nothing〔not a stitch〕 on // 알몸으로 만들다 strip 《a person》 of all 《his》 clothes ; strip〔make〕 《a person》 naked〔to the skin〕
② [빈털털이] pennilessness ¶ 알몸뿐인 사람 a penniless man ; a man with no property but his own body // 알몸으로 with an empty pocket // 알몸이 되다 be stripped of all one's possessions ; go broke 《속》 ; become penniless ; lose the shirt off one's back // 알몸으로 시작하다 start business with nothing // 딸을 알몸으로 시집보내다 marry off one's daughter with no dowry provided

알몸뚱이 ⇨ 알몸

알바늘 a needle without its thread ; a naked needle

알바니아 Albania
—인(人) an Albanian — **공화국** the People's Republic of Albania

알반대기 [지짐이] a kind of fried-egg dish
알밤 a (shelled) chestnut
알배기 a fish full of roe
알부랑자 —浮浪者 a brazen-faced rascal 〔scoundrel〕; a professional tramp
알부민 〖화학〗 albumin
알부피 net bulk
알뿌리 〖식물〗 ⇨ 구근(球根)
알사스로렌 Alsace-Lorraine
알선 斡旋 good〔kind〕 offices; mediation (중개); intercession; arbitration; recommendation (추천) **—하다** intercede; recommend; put in a good word 《for a person》; say a good thing 《for》; use one's good offices; conciliate; assist ¶ 송씨의 알선으로 through the good offices of Mr. *Song*∥취직을 알선하다 help 《a person》 (to) find employment∥알선을 부탁하다 request 《a person's》 services; ask for 《a person's》 mediation∥교원 물색에는 내가 알선의 수고를 하지요 My services are at your disposal in finding teachers. ∥그는 나를 위해서 여러 가지 알선을 해 주었다 He did many good offices for me. ∥A씨는 나를 위해서 B씨에 대하여 알선의 수고를 해주었다 Mr. A exercised his good offices with Mr. B in my behalf. ∥노동청의 알선으로 쟁의가 해결되었다 Through the Labour Office's mediation the strike came to an end.
—업자 an (employment) agent **—자** a mediator; an intermediary **직업 — 계획** a placement plan **직업 —소** an employment agency
알선 —線 〖전기〗 a naked electric wire
알섬 a small uninhabited〔deserted〕 island
알속 the substance of a secret; the actual content; the real〔net〕 amount 〔weight, distance, bulk〕
알송편 a folded fried egg
알슬다 spawn; shoot spawn (물고기가); lay〔deposit〕 eggs; blow (곤충이); oviposit (산란관으로) ¶ 땅속에 알을 스는 곤충도 있다 Some insects deposit their eggs in the soil.
알심 hidden sympathy (동정); hidden strength (힘); [고갱이] core; kernel
알싸하다 taste hot〔sharp〕; bite; be irritatingly strong to the taste; (be) pungent; have a burning taste ¶ 알싸한 소스 a piquant sauce∥알싸한 고추 a hot pepper∥낙엽이 타는 알싸한 냄새 the autumn's pungent smell of burning leaves
알쌈 [계란포] an eggroll stuffed with chopped meat ⇨ 알송편
알쏭달쏭하다 ① [무늬가] (be) motley; jumbled; intricated ¶ 알쏭달쏭한 광대옷 a motley costume∥알쏭달쏭한 무늬 a bewildering〔puzzling, jumbled, mixed〕 pattern
② [뜻이] (be) vague 《idea》; obscure; ambiguous 《meaning》; hazy 《notion》; dim 《memory》 doubtful; evasive; equivocal ¶ 알쏭달쏭한 물음 a puzzling question∥알쏭달쏭하게 말하다 speak ambiguously〔vaguely〕; equivocate∥알쏭달쏭한 대답을 하다 give a vague answer ∥알쏭달쏭한 말을 하다 speak 《of a matter》 in general terms∥알쏭달쏭한 태도를 취하다 maintain an ambiguous〔uncertain〕 attitude 《toward》; take〔assume〕 a noncommittal〔dubious〕 attitude 《toward》 ∥알쏭달쏭한 진술을 하다 make an ambiguous statement∥그의 대답은 짧고 알쏭달쏭하였다 His answers were brief and evasive. ∥너의 설명은 너무나도 알쏭달쏭하다 Your explanation is too vague. ∥무어가 무언지 알쏭달쏭하다 I cannot make any sense of it. /I cannot make neither head nor tail. ∥그 법률에는 알쏭달쏭한 점이 많다 The law is full of ambiguities.
알쏭하다 ⇨ 어리숭하다
알씬거리다 hang〔fool〕 around in a person's presence (to curry his favor); flatter; fawn 《upon a person》
*****알아내다** find out; make out; detect; discover; locate (장소를) ¶ 비밀을 알아내다 find out 《a person's》 secret∥그의 거처를 알아냈다 I found out〔located〕 his whereabouts.
*****알아듣다** hear; catch〔get〕 《the meaning》; [도리를] listen to reason; be reasonable; [납득하다] understand; comprehend; appreciate; realize; [구별하다] tell 《the difference》 by hearing ¶ 목소리를 알아듣다 recognize 《a person's》 voice∥말을 알아듣다 catch 《a person's》 words〔what a person says〕; catch 《a person's》 meaning 〔point〕∥알아듣게 설명하다 explain convincingly〔to a person's satisfaction〕∥나는 너의 말을 못 알아듣겠다 I don't understand. /I don't understand what you are talking about. /I don't dig it. /You are talking over my head.
†**알아맞히다** guess right; be right in one's conjecture; make a good guess ¶ 알아맞힌〔못 알아맞힌〕 추측 a happy〔wrong〕 guess∥주머니에 무엇이 들어 있는지 알아맞혀 봐라 Guess what I have in my pocket. ∥알아맞혔다 You have guessed it!
알아방이다 be put on the alert; be alerted and take countersteps; find out and forestall
‡**알아보다** [문의] inquire 《at a place, of a person》; refer 《to》; [조사] investigate; examine; search ¶ 사무실에 알아보다 inquire at an office about 《a matter》∥마음을 알아보다 search 《a person's》 heart∥김씨에게 알아보다 inquire of Mr. *Kim* about 《a matter》∥원인을 알아보다 inquire into the cause∥취직 자리를 알아보다 look out for a job∥옛친구를 알아볼

ㅇ

수 없었다 I could scarcely recognize my old friend. // 알아보니 그것은 오보였다 On inquiry, it turned out to be a false report. // 나에 관해선 전 고용주한테 알아보시기 바랍니다 I refer you to my former employer as to my character. // 혹시 그 번호가 사용되지 않고 있는 것은 아닌지 알아봐 줄 수 있습니까 Could you check and see if that number is out of service or something?

†**알아주다** acknowledge ; recognize ¶ 어려운 사정을〔진가를〕 알아주다 appreciate 《a person's》 difficulties〔real worth〕 // 능력을 알아주다 recognize 《a person's》 ability // 저 여자 알아줘야 해 You've got to hand it to her. /You've got to hand it to her.

‡**알아차리다** ① provide 《for》 ; prepare 《for》 ; take precaution 《against》
② sense ; become aware of ⇨ 알아채다

†**알아채다** become aware〔conscious〕 of ; sense 《danger》 ; suspect ; perceive ; get wind〔scent〕 of ; [눈으로] notice ; take notice of ; [사물이 주어] come under one's notice ; come to one's knowledge ¶ 누구에게도 알아채이지 않고 without attracting any attention ; with no one the wiser // 사람의 눈치를 알아채다 read 《a person's》 mind // 남이 싫어하는 것을 알아채다 sense 《a person's》 dislike // 알아채이지 않게 들어가다〔나오다〕 slip in〔out〕 ; steal in〔out〕 // 그것을 알아채지 못하였다 It did not come under my notice. // 그는 감시당하고 있는 것을 알아챘다 He perceived that he was being watched. // 그는 자기의 제안이 환영받지 못하는 것을 알아챘다 He sensed that his proposals were unwelcome.

알아하다 do at one's discretion ; do as one thinks fit ; act for oneself ; do with care ¶ 알아해라 Do as you please. /Do it your own way. /You may do it as you think fit. // 그 일은 네가 알아해라 I leave the matter to your discretion.

알알이 grain〔berry〕 after grain〔berry〕 ¶ 알알이 세다 count one by one

알알하다 (be) prickly ; smart ; tingle ¶ 눈이 알알하다 My eyes are smarting. // 연기가 알알하다 The smoke makes my eyes smart. // 맞은 뺨이 알알했다 His cheeks tingled from the slap. // 긁힌 데가 아직도 알알하다 The scratch still smarts.

알약 a tablet ; a tabloid ; a pill

알은체 ―하다 ① show concern〔interest〕 ; interfere 《in a matter, with a person〕 ; meddle in〔with〕 ; step in ¶ 그 일에는 알은체하지 않는다 He won't have anything to do with it. /He shows no interest 《in it》. // 내 일이 아니면 알은체하고 싶지 않다 I don't want to interfere in what is not my business.
② [인사] recognize ; notice ; greet ¶ 그는 길에서 나를 보고도 알은체하지 않았다 He cut〔snubbed〕 me on the street. // 그는 지나가면서 알은체했다 He gave me passing recognition.

알음 [안면] an acquaintance(ship) ; [이해] understanding ; comprehension ; appreciation ¶ 알음 있는 미국인 an American of my acquaintance // 사업상의 알음 a business acquaintance // 알음이 있다〔없다〕 have〔have no〕 acquaintance with // 조금 알음이 있다 have a slight acquaintance // 알음이 많다 have a large〔wide〕 acquaintance // 그와는 알음이 없다 I have no personal acquaintance with him. /He is quite a stranger to me. // 저분하고 알음이 있습니까 Are you acquainted with him? // 조금 알음이 있습니다 I know him very slightly.

알음알음 [아는 관계] mutual acquaintance ; [친분] shared intimacy ; friendship ¶ 알음알음이 있다 have a nodding acquaintanceship 《with》 ; know each other by sight

알음알이 ① [친지] an acquaintance ; acquaintanceship (관계) ¶ 알음알이가 많다 have a wide acquaintance ; have a wide circle of acquaintance // 그 여자는 거기에 많은 알음알이가 있다 She has many acquaintances in the place.
② [재능] cleverness ; knowledge ; knowhow ; the gradually growing knowledge〔talent〕 of a child

알음장 letting one know with a look〔wink〕 **―하다** give a significant look〔wink〕

알자리 the setting place 《of a hen or bird》

알장 ―欌 the smallest chest of drawers ; a clothes-chest

알전구 ―電球 a naked electric〔light〕 bulb

알젓 salted roe ; salted caviar(e)

알제기다 have〔get〕 a white speck on the pupil of one's eye

알제리 Algeria

알제이 Algiers ; Alger

알조판 ―組版 〘인쇄〙 [행간을 떼지 않는 조판] solid〔close〕 printing (인쇄) ; soild typesetting (조판) ¶ 알조판으로 하다 set solid ; close up

알주머니 the spawn sac of a fish ; [가오리·상어 등의] a sea purse

알짜 the cream ; the essence ; quintessence ; the best thing〔part〕 ; the choice ¶ 알짜를 고르다 take the essence 〔best〕 of ; cream off // 도적이 알짜만 골라 갔다 The thief took the best of everything〔all the best ones〕.
― **물건** an article of superfine〔the highest〕 quality ; an A one〔1〕〔a choice〕 article ; the best (of its kind) ; the finest〔choicest〕 stuff

알짝지근하다 (be) rather hot〔spicy, peppery〕 ; taste a bit sharp

알짬 the most important〔the best〕 of the contents ; the essential〔vital, critical〕

material ; the core ; the essence ; the cream ; the most significant matter 〔substance〕

알짱거리다 [알랑거리다] curry favor with ; fawn upon ; [할일없이] loaf around idly ; hang about 《a person》 ¶ 집 부근을 알짱거리다 lurk〔prowl〕 about the house

알짱알짱 [속이는 모양] going around hoodwinking people with flattery ; [돌아다니는 꼴] loafing around idly ; loiteringly

알천 the core of one's fortune ; one's most precious thing

알칼로이드 〖화학〗 an alkaloid ¶ 알칼로이드의 alkaloidal

*** 알칼리** 〖화학〗 alkali

—계(計) an alkalimeter **— 금속** alkali metals **—액(液)** lye **— 재생 고무** alkali reclaimed rubber **— 정량법(定量法)** alkalimetry **— 중화물** an alkali ; an alkaline (agent) **— 토류(土類)** alkaline earths **— 혈증(血症)** 〖의학〗 alkalosis

알칼리성 —性 alkalinity ¶ 알칼리성의 alkaline

— 결핍 alkaline deficiency **— 반응** alkaline reaction **— 염료** alkaline dyes **— 토양** alkali soil

알칼리화 —化 alkalization **—하다** alkalize ; alkalify ¶ 알칼리화할 수 있는 alkalifiable

*** 알코올** 〖화학〗 alcohol ; spirits ¶ 알코올(성)의 alcoholic // 알코올에 담그다 preserve 《a thing》 in spirits ; alcoholize // 그는 알코올을 입에 대지도 않는다 He does not touch alcohol.

— 램프 an alcohol〔a spirit〕 lamp **—분(分)** alcoholic content〔strength〕 ¶ 알코올분이 많은 술 hard liquor // 알코올분이 적은 술 drinks with low alcoholic content **— 온도계(計)** an alcohol thermometer **— 음료** alcoholic beverages〔drinks〕 **— 중독(中毒)** alcoholism ; alcoholic poisoning ¶ 알코올 중독에 걸리다 suffer from alcoholism **— 중독자** an alcoholic **공업용 —** industrial alcohol **무수 —** absolute alcohol **변질 —** denatured alcohol **제3 —** tertiary alcohol

알타이 Altai(c) ¶ 알타이의 Altaic

—말 Altaic **— 산맥** the Altai Mountains **— 어족** the Altaic language family

알탄 —炭 an oval〔egg-shaped〕 briquet(te)

알토 alto

— 가수 an alto (singer)

알통 muscles ; muscular development of the biceps ¶ 알통을 내다 flex one's muscles ; show one's biceps

알파 alpha 《α》 ¶ 플러스 알파 《10,000 *won*》 plus something // 알파와 오메가 alpha and omega // 알파이자 오메가이다 be the alpha and omega 《of》 ; be the first and the last

—선 α-rays ; alpha rays **— 입자** α〔alpha〕 particles

†**알파벳** the alphabet ¶ 알파벳 순으로 in alphabetical order // 알파벳 순으로 늘어놓다 arrange alphabetically〔in alphabetical order〕

알파카 〖동물〗 an alpaca

알팔 —八 《hold the two cards of》 one and eight 《in one's hand》

알프스 Alps ¶ 알프스의 Alpine

— 산맥 the Alps

알피니스트 an Alpinist

알합 —盒 a small wooden bowl with a lid

알항아리 a small jar

알현 謁見 an (imperial) audience **—하다** have an audience 《with》 ; be received in audience 《by the king》 ; be presented 《to》 ¶ 알현을 허락하다 grant an audience to

*** 앎** knowledge ; wisdom ¶ 앎이 많다 be well-informed ; know a lot (of things) ; have seen much of life

앓는소리 moaning ; groaning ; complaints **—하다** moan ; groan ; complain 《of illness》 ; make complaints ¶ 그의 앓는소리를 들어주었다 I perseveringly listened to his tale of woes.

*** 앓다** be ill 《with》 ; be sick ; be afflicted 〔troubled〕 with ; suffer from (illness) ¶ 눈을 앓다 have eye trouble ; suffer from an eye disease // 신경통을 앓다 be troubled with neuralgia // 폐를 앓다 suffer from consumption ; have a lung〔chest〕 trouble // 이를 앓다 have a toothache // 몹시 병을 앓다 be seriously ill ; suffer from a grave illness // 열병을 앓고 누워 있다 be laid up with a fever

앓던 이 빠진 것 같다 속담 be like having a sore tooth fall out ; feel sudden relief

-앓이 ache ; sickness ¶ 가슴앓이 a pain in the chest // 배앓이 a stomachache // 이앓이 a toothache

암[1] [암컷] a female ; a she ; a hen-bird (새의) ¶ 암캐 a bitch〔she-dog〕 // 암코양이 a female cat // 암탉 a hen // 그것은 암컷이냐 수컷이냐 Is it a she〔female〕 or a he〔male〕 ? /What is the sex ?

암[2] [감탄사] Of course ! /Naturally ! /To be sure ! /Surely ! /Certainly ! /Why not ? ¶ 너 가느냐—암 가지 Are you coming ? Sure ! // 가느냐고—암 가고 말고 Will I go, you say ? Sure, I will. // 암 그렇게 하는 것이 우리의 의무이지 Needless to say, it is our duty to do so. // 학교가 재미 있느냐—암 그렇고 말고 Do you enjoy school ? Why, certainly. 〔Why not ? 〕

*** 암** 癌 〖의학〗 cancer ; a cancerous growth ; [화근] a gangrenous evil ; a stumbling block ¶ 시정의 암 a cancer to〔a curse in〕 the municipal administration // 암에 걸리다 get〔suffer from〕 can-

ㅇ

cer // 암이 생기다 develop a cancer 《of, on》 // 암으로 죽다 die of cancer // 혀에 암이 생겼다 A cancer grew on his tongue.
—세포 cancerous cells —퇴치 운동 an anticancer campaign〔drive〕 국제 —퇴치 연합 the International Union against Cancer 발— 물질 a carcinogenic〔cancerogeni〕 substance ; a carcinogen 설(舌)— cancer of the tongue 식도— cancer of the esophagus 위— stomach〔gastric〕 cancer 유— mammary cancer ; cancer of the breast 직장— a cancer of the rectum 폐— cancer of the lung ; lung cancer 피부— skin cancer

암 庵 a monk's cell ; a small Buddhist temple

암갈색 暗褐色 dark brown ; dun ¶ 암갈색의 dark brown

암거 暗渠 a culvert ; an underdrain
— 배수 drainage by a culvert ; underdraining ; underdrainage

암거래 闇去來 black marketeering ; blackmarket〔underground〕 dealings ; underhand〔undercover〕 transactions ; an off-the-book deal ; transaction on the black market ; shady trading —하다 sell〔buy〕 《goods》 on the black market ; black-market ; black-marketeer ; handle〔engage in〕 a black-market business
— 근절〔퇴치〕 an uprooting of black marketeers — 루트 a black-marketeering channel ; an illegal channel —상 ⇨ 암매상 —품 black-market〔bootleg〕 goods — 행위 an illegal act ; a black-market deal

암구다 set animals to copulating ; couple ; mate

암굴 岩窟 a cave ; a (rocky) cavern ; grot(to)

***암기 暗記** memorizing ; learning by heart ; memory work —하다 learn 〔get〕 by heart ; commit to memory ; memorize 《미》 ¶ 암기하고 있다 know 《a poem》 by heart ; have 《a thing》 at one's finger tips〔fingers' end〕 // 암기를 잘하다 excel in memory work // 되풀이 읽어서 암기하다 commit to memory by repeated reading ; con // 교과서를 암기하다 learn one's text by heart // 나는 그 시를 암기하고 있다 I know the poem by heart. // 그는 무엇이든지 암기하고 있다 He commits everything to memory. /He learns everything by heart.
— 과목 memory subjects ; memory work —력 (one's powers of) memory ; retentive power ¶ 암기력이 좋다〔나쁘다〕 have a good〔poor, bad〕 memory ; be strong 〔weak〕 in memory

암꽃 a pistillate flower ; a female flower

암꽃술 〖식물〗 a pistil

암나사 —螺絲 a female〔an internal〕 screw

암내 ① the (offensive) smell of armpits ; underarm odor ; body odor 《미》
② [암컷의] the odor of a female animal in heat〔estrus〕 ¶ 그에게서는 암내가 난다 His body smells bad.
암내 내다 관용 be in rut ; go on heat ; be in heat ; rut

암단추 a female button〔snap〕

암달러 暗— a black-market dollar
— 거래 a black-market dollar transaction — 상인 an illegal dollar dealer — 시장 the dollar black market

암담 暗澹 —하다 (be) dark ; gloomy ; dismal ¶ 암담한 전도 gloomy prospects ; a black〔dark〕 outlook // 지저분하고 암담한 이야기 a sordid, gloomy story // 장래가 암담하다 The future looks dark〔gloomy, black〕. /The outlook is black.

암당나귀 —唐— a jenny donkey ; a jennet

암둔 闇鈍 imbecility ; feeble-mindedness —하다 (be) imbecile ; feeble-minded ¶ 암둔한 사람들 dark souls

암띠다 ① be a person who loves secrets ② be easily embarrassed

암록색 暗綠色 dark green

암루 暗淚 silent tears ¶ 암루를 흘리다 be moved to silent tears

암류 暗流 an undercurrent ¶ 그의 농담에는 우울한 암류가 흐르고 있었다 There was an undercurrent of melancholy beneath his jokes.

암만[1] [값·수량] a certain amount ; such and such amount

암만[2] Amman

암만해도 by all means ; at all costs ; at any cost ; by hook or crook ; to all appearance(s) ; in every respect〔way〕 ; all things considered ¶ 암만해도 생각나지 않는다 I cannot, for the life of me, remember it. // 암만해도 문이 안 열린다 The door will not open. // 암만해도 그를 보낼 수가 없었다 Nothing could induce him to go. // 이러한 계획은 암만해도 허가 못한다 I will on no account〔by no means, never〕 approve of such a plan. // 그는 암만해도 들어 주지 않았다 He would not〔refused to〕 listen to me. // 그는 암만해도 40세로는 보이지 않는다 He does not look forty by any manner of means. // 암만해도 그 여자를 설득할 수 없었다 I could not persuade her after all my efforts. // 나는 암만해도 못하겠다 I just can't do it. // 저 둘은 암만해도 부부로밖에 보이지 않는다 They are more like man and wife than anything else.

암말 a mare ; a female horse

암매 暗賣 a black-market sale ; an illicit sale —하다 sell on〔in〕 the black market

암매 暗買 a black-market purchase ; an illegal〔unauthorized〕 purchase —하다 buy in the black market

암매매 暗賣買 black-market dealings —하다 black-market ; black-marketeer
암매상 暗賣商 a black-market dealer ; a black-marketeer ; a secret〔an illegal, an illicit〕dealer ; [주류의] a smuggler ; a bootlegger ; [밀양조자] an illicit distiller
암매장 暗埋葬 ⇨ 암장(暗葬)
암맥 岩脈 〖지질〗 a dyke ; a dike
암모늄 〖화학〗 ammonium
황산〔탄산, 초산, 염화〕— ammonium sulfate〔carbonate, nitrate chloride〕
암모니아 ammonia《NH_3》¶ 암모니아(성)의 ammonia(cal) // 암모니아와 화합하다 ammoniate
— 가스 ammonia gas — 고무 gum〔Persian〕ammonia — 냉동법 ammonia refrigeration — 비료 ammonite —수(水) ammonia (water) ; aqueous〔aqua〕ammonia ; an ammonia solution ; ammonia(cal) liquor ; spirit of hartshorn — 합성법 a synthetic ammonia process —화성(化成) ammonification 고체 — rock ammonia 액체 — liquid ammonia
암무지개 the fainter of a double rainbow
암묵 暗默 silence ; tacitness ¶ 암묵의 silent ; tacit // 암묵의 양해 tacit understanding // 암묵리에 tacitly ; by a tacit consent ; by implication ; in silence // 암묵리에 허락하다 give a tacit〔an implicit〕permission
— 계약 an implied contract
암물 [샘물] clear milk-white spring water
암반 岩盤 a base rock ; a rock floor ; a solid foundation
암벽 岩壁 a rock wall ; a rock face
암사 지도 暗射地圖 a blank map
암산 岩山 a rocky mountain
암산 暗算 mental arithmetic ; mental calculation —하다 do《a sum》in mental arithmetic ¶ 암산으로 in mental arithmetic // 519에 곱하기 38을 암산으로 하다 multiply 519 by 38 mentally
*암살 暗殺 assassination —하다 assassinate ; murder ¶ 암살을 기도하다 make an attempt on《a person's》life ; attempt《a person's》life ; plot the death of《a person》// 암살을 당하다 be〔get〕assassinated
— 기도〔계획〕an assassination plot against《a person》; a plot against the life of《a person》— 미수 an attempted assassination ; an unsuccessful attempt at assassination —자 an assassin
암상 jealousy ; envy
—꾸러기 a jealous person
암상 岩床 〖지질〗 a rock floor ; a sheet
암상 暗箱 〖사진〗 a camera (obscura) ; bellows (주름상자) ; [전자 공학에서] a black box
암상부리다, 암상피우다 nurse jealousy ; have〔feel〕envy ; [일부러] pretend to be jealous
암상인 暗商人 ⇨ 암매상(暗賣商)
암새 a female bird
암생 식물 岩生植物 〖식물〗 a rock plant ; a lithophyte
암석 岩石 a rock ; a crag ; a boulder ¶ 암석이 많은 rocky ; craggy
—권 the lithosphere — 분류학 petrography — 조각 a petroglyph —학 lithology ; petrology ; the study of rocks
암선 暗線 〖물리〗 obscure rays
암설 岩屑 〖지질〗 debris ; detritus
암소 a cow
암송 暗誦 recitation ; memorization —하다 recite ; recite from memory ; say by rote ¶ 시를 암송하다 recite a poem // 영어를 암송하다 give an English recitation
암쇠 ① [열쇠·자물쇠] a keyhole plate ② [맷돌의] the bottom〔pounding〕plate of a mill ; the gudgeon〔rynd〕of a millstone ③ [돌쩌귀의] the catch part of a hinge
암수 female and male
암수 暗數 a foul play ; a trick ; a means of deception ⇨ 속임수 ¶ 암수를 쓰다 play《a person》foul ; play a trick《on a person》
—거리 fraud ; deception ; trickery ; double-dealing
암순응 暗順應 dark adaptation〔accommodation〕
암술 〖식물〗 a pistil
암술대 〖식물〗 the style (of a flower)
암스테르담 Amsterdam
†암시 暗示 a hint ; a suggestion ; an allusion ; an intimation —하다 hint《at》; suggest ; allude《to》; intimate ; imply ; insinuate

> 참고 **hint** 멀리 돌려서 말하다 **suggest** 그럴 심산으로 또는 모르는 사이에 눈치채게 하다 **imply** 말 속에 포함시켜 이야기하다 **intimate** 상대방이 눈치채지 않도록 교묘히 말하다 **insinuate** 상대방이 싫어하는 말을 자기도 모르게 하다

¶ 암시적인 suggestive // 암시적 태도〔거동〕a suggestive air〔manner〕; mystification // 어떤 어려운 집안 사정을 암시하는 편지 a letter alluding to some unspeakable family difficulties // 암시를 주다 give《a person》a hint // 암시를 얻다 get〔receive〕a hint《from》// 그에게 암시는 소용 없다 He can't take a hint. // 이 사실에서 암시를 얻어 그는 소설을 썼다 He wrote a novel suggested by this fact.
—력 suggestive power — 요법 suggestive therapy 자기 — autosuggestion 피—성 suggestibility
암시세 暗市勢 a black-market price ; off-the-books quotations
암시장 闇市場 a black market
암실 暗室 a dark room ; a darkroom
— 램프 a darkroom lamp

ㅇ

암암리 暗暗裡 ¶ 암암리에 tacitly ; obscurely ; implicitly ; secretly // 암암리에 승낙하다 give a tacit consent // 암암리에 풍자하다 hint at 《a person's folly》 ; insinuate 《that》 // 암암리에 처리하다 dispose of 《a thing》 in secrecy
암야 暗夜 a dark night ¶ 암야를 틈타서 under (the) cover of night〔darkness〕 ; taking advantage of the darkness of night // 암야에 등불을 얻은 기분이었다 I felt as if I found a light on a moonless night.
암약 暗躍 secret〔behind-the-scene〕 action〔maneuvers〕 **—하다** act secretly〔behind-the-scene〕 ; engage in secret maneuvers ; be active behind-the-scene
암약 闇弱 —하다 (be) ignorant and weak
암염 岩鹽 〖광물〗 rock-salt ; halite
—갱 a salt mine **— 채굴** salt-mining
암영 暗影 a (dark) shadow ; gloom ¶ 암영을 던지다 cast a shadow〔gloom〕 over〔on〕 // 암영이 감돌다 A gloom hangs 《over the house》.
암운 暗雲 dark〔murky〕 clouds ¶ 암운으로 덮이다 be shrouded in dark clouds
암유 暗喩 〖수사〗 a metaphor ⇨ 은유 ¶ 암유적 metaphorical
암자 庵子 a monk's cell ; a small Buddhist temple ¶ 암자를 짓다 build a hermitage
암자색 暗紫色 a dark purple color ; a dark mauve
암장 岩漿 〖지질〗 (rock) magma
암장 暗葬 secret burial **—하다** bury secretly (in another's lot)
암적색 暗赤色 a dark red color ; garnet
암전 暗轉 a dark change 《of scenery》 ; changing sets during a stage black-out
암종 癌腫 〖의학〗 a cancer ; a cancerous growth〔tumor〕
암죽 —粥 thin rice soup (as baby food) ; thin rice gruel ; water gruel ; hot cereal ; pap
암중 暗中 (in) the dark ; (in) darkness
—모색 groping in the dark ¶ 암중모색하다 grope (blindly) in the dark **— 비약** secret maneuvers ; a still hunt 《구》 ¶ 암중 비약을 꾀하다 be active behind the scenes ; engage in secret maneuvers ; move stealthily
암지르다 put〔weld, fix, join〕 in to make a whole ; make up the parts of ; complete ; integrate ; amalgamate
암쪽 a counter-foil ; a stub ; a left half of a transaction book ¶ 수표장의 암쪽 the stubs of a check〔receipt〕-book
⁑암초 暗礁 a reef ; a submerged〔sunken〕 rock ¶ 암초에 걸리다 strike rock ; go〔run〕 on a reef ; come to〔reach〕 a deadlock (회의 따위가) // 암초를 피해가다 steer clear of a rock // 배가 암초에 걸려 부서졌다 The ship was wrecked on a rock〔reef〕.
—맥 a ledge
암치 a dried (and salted) female seaperch
암치질 —痔疾 〖의학〗 internal hemorrhoids
암캉아지 a female puppy
암캐 a she-dog ; a bitch
⁑암컷 a female (animal) ; a she ¶ 새의 암컷 a she-bird // 그것은 암컷이냐 수컷이냐 Is it a she〔female〕 or a he〔male〕? / What is the sex?
암코양이 a female cat
암꿩 a hen pheasant
암클 ① [활용 못하는 지식] impractical〔useless〕 knowledge ; (mere) book learning ② [낮춤말] *Hangul* script
암키와 a female roof-tile
암탈개비 〖곤충〗 a butterfly larva
†암탉 a hen ; a pullet (병아리의)
암탉이 울면 집안이 망한다 속담 It is a sad house where the hen crows louder than the cock. /It is a sorry flock where the ewe bears the bell.
암탉 울어 날 새는 일 없다 속담 It is a sad house where the hen crows louder than the cock. /It is a sorry flock where the ewe bears the bell.
암톨쩌귀 the female joint of a hinge ; a gudgeon
암톹 a sow ⇨ 암퇘지
암퇘지 a sow
암투 暗鬪 a secret strife〔feud〕 ; an undercover struggle ; veiled enmity ; discord ¶ 그들 사이에는 끊임없는 암투가 벌어지고 있다 There is constantly veiled enmity among them. // 두 집안은 수세대에 걸쳐 암투를 계속하고 있었다 The two families had been feuding with each other for generations.
암팡스럽다 be strong〔plucky, active〕 for one's size ; (be) bold ; intrepid ; dauntless ; fierce ; daring ; energetic ¶ 암팡스러운 얼굴 생김새 a dauntless face // 암팡스럽게 싸우다 fight ferociously〔stubbornly〕 (like a wildcat)
암팡지다 (be) bold ⇨ 암팡스럽다
암펄 [수여리] a female bee ; a queen (bee)
암펌 a tigress
암페어 〖물리〗 an ampere(s)
암평아리 a female chick ; a pullet
암표 闇票 an illegal ticket ; a scalper's ticket
암표 暗標 winking ; a secret mark〔sign〕
암표상 闇票商 [행위] ticket-scalping ; [사람] a ticket broker ; a (ticket) scalper 《구》
암피둘기 a she-dove ; a she-pigeon
암하다 (be) jealous
암행 暗行 traveling in secret〔disguise〕 ; incognito traveling **—하다** travel incognito〔in secret, in disguise〕
— 어사 a royal secret commissioner ;

an undercover emissary〔agent〕 of the king ; the *Choseon* Dynasty's powerful royal secret investigator

†**암호 暗號** [주로 상업용] a code ; [군호] a password ; a watchword ; a sign ; [비밀 암호] a cipher ¶ 암호를 풀다 decode〔decipher〕 a message in code // 암호를 쓰다 write《a message》in code〔cipher〕 // 암호를 대다〔말하다〕 give a password // 암호로 전보를 치다 send a telegram in code〔cipher〕; wire cryptographically
—계 a communications code clerk **— 글씨〔문자〕** a cipher ; a code word **—문** a cryptogram ; a cryptograph **—법** cryptography **—장** a code book **— 전보** a telegram in cipher〔code〕; a cipher〔code〕 telegram **— 통신** a signal ; cryptography **— 풀이** a cipher-key **— 해독** code-breaking ; cryptanalysis ; cryptography **— 해독관** a cipher officer **문자 —** a letter code **숫자 —** a figure code **전신 —** a telegraphic code ; a cable code **해외 — 전보** a cablegram in code ; a code(d) cable

암호명 暗號名 a code name ; code designation

암회색 暗灰色 a dark gray color ; taupe

*__암흑 暗黑__ darkness ; blackness **—하다** (be) dark ; black ; gloomy
—가 the dark quarters ; the underworld ; a gangland **— 대륙** the Dark Continent **—면** the dark〔gloomy〕 side《of society》; the seamy side《of life》¶ 세상의 암흑면을 보다 look upon the dark side of life **—색** a pitch dark color **— 시대** [중세의] the Dark Ages ; [일반의] a dark age

암흑계 暗黑界 the underworld

압각 壓覺 〖심리〗 pressure sensation

압권 壓卷 the (very) best (one) ; the masterpiece ; the highlight 《미》 ; the acme ; the best part《of a book》¶ 현대 소설 중의 압권 the best modern novel // 그것은 그날밤 행사의 압권이었다 It was the highlight of the evening.

압도 壓度 《degree of》 pressure

⁑**압도 壓倒 —하다** overwhelm ; overcome ; overpower ; weigh down ; surpass ; crush ; excel ; outrival ¶ 압도적으로 overwhelmingly ; overpoweringly // 압도적 승리 an overwhelming〔a sweeping〕 victory ; [선거에서의] a landslide (victory) // 반대당을 압도하다 mow down the opposition // 압도적 다수로 당선되다 be elected by a sweeping〔an overwhelming〕 majority of votes // 인구가 타시를 압도하다 exceed〔surpass〕 any other city in population // 외국품을 압도하다 drive foreign goods out of the market // 품질에서 단연 압도하다 lead the world in quality // 한국산은 당지에서는 외국산에 압도당하고 있다 Foreign manufactures drive Korean goods out of the market here.

압려기 壓濾器 a filter press

⁑**압력 壓力** pressure ; stress ¶ 대기의 압력 atmospheric pressure // 압력이 높다〔낮다〕 the pressure is high〔low〕 // 압력을 가하다 give〔apply〕 pressure《to》; pressure〔put pressure upon〕《a person》; press《on》// 이 타이어에는 인치당 10파운드의 압력이 가해진다 There is a pressure of ten pounds to the inch on this tire.
— 가감기 a pressure governor **—계** a manometer ; a pressure gauge ¶ 압축 압력계 a compression pressure gauge // 자기 압력계 a pressure recorder // 진공 압력계 a vacuum manometer **— 단체** a pressure group **—솥** a pressure cooker **— 시험** a pressure test **— 저항** pressure resistance **대기 —** atmospheric pressure **절대〔최대〕 —** absolute〔maximum〕 pressure

압록강 鴨綠江 the Yalu River

압류 押留 attachment ; seizure ; distraint ; distress **—하다** attach ; seize ; distrain《upon a person's property》¶ 재산을 압류당하다 have one's property attached // 물품을 압류하다 seize〔distrain upon〕《a person's》goods // 압류표를 붙이다 paste distraint-paper《on goods》// 저금의 압류를 신청하다 file an attachment on《a person's》bank account // 압류를 해제하다 release《property》from attachment // 세무서 직원들이 압류하러 왔다 The taxation officers came to levy on the property.
— 명령 an order of attachment **— 영장** a warrant〔writ〕 of attachment ; a seizure note ; a distress warrant **—인** a seizor ; a distrainer **— 재산** property under distraint ; attached〔seized〕 property **— 집행** service〔execution〕 of attachment **— 채권자** an execution creditor **—품** seized〔attached〕 goods **— 해제** release from attachment **가—** provisional attachment〔seizure〕; sequestration **부동산〔동산〕 —** real〔personal〕 distress **저당물 —** foreclosure of a mortgage **전재산 —** grand distress **피—인** a distrainee

†**압박 壓迫** pressure ; oppression ; tyranny ; coercion ; persecution **—하다** exert pressure upon《a person》; oppress ; suppress ; coerce ; be oppressive to ; use pressure ; press ¶ 생활의 압박 the stress〔pressure〕 of life // 관헌의 압박 official pressure ; the pressure of the authorities // 압박을 받고 under pressure ; under (the) pressure of // 압박을 받다 be pressed ; be subjected to pressure // 언론의 자유를 압박하다 suppress the freedom of speech // 압박을 강화하다 intensify one's pressure on // 적을 압박하다 press the enemy hard // 가난하고 약한 사람을 압박하다 oppress the poor and weak // 학교 당국의 압박으로 계획은 중지됐다 The plan was given up under

ㅇ

〔because of〕 the pressure of the school authorities.
—감 a sense of oppression ; an oppressive sensation — 민족 an oppressing race — 붕대 a compress —자 an oppressor 정신적 — moral pressure 피— 민족 an oppressed people
압복 壓伏 subjection by force ; subduing ; overwhelming ; overpowering ; overcoming —하다 overwhelm ; overpower ; overcome ; hold in subjection
압사 壓死 death from pressure —하다 be crushed〔pressed, squeezed〕 to death ¶ 기계에 깔려 압사하다 be crushed to death under a machine
압살 壓殺 killing by pressing〔squeezing〕 —하다 crush 《a person》 to death ¶ 곤충을 압살하다 crush a worm under (the feet)∥기계에 깔려 압살되다 be crushed to death under a machine
압설기 壓舌器 〖의학〗 a depressor
압송 押送 sending 《a criminal》 in custody —하다 escort 《a criminal》 ; send 《a person》 in custody 《to》
압수 押收 confiscation ; seizure ; attachment —하다 seize ; take over ; confiscate ; take legal possession of 《a person's property》 ¶ 서류를 압수하다 capture〔retain〕 papers
— 수색 영장 a seizure and search warrant — 영장 a confiscation warrant —품 a confiscated article ; seized property ; confiscated goods
압수물 押收物 ⇨ (압수(—품))
압수 펌프 壓水— a force pump
압승 壓勝 an overwhelming victory〔triumph, win〕 [선거] ; a landslide (victory) —하다 win an overwhelming victory 《over》 ; defeat decisively ; overwhelm ; swamp
압연 壓延 rolling —하다 roll
—강 rolled steel — 공장 a rolling mill ; a roll-mill —관 a rolled tube —기 a rolling machine〔mill〕 ; a roller — 알루미늄 합금 rolled aluminium alloy 열간〔냉간〕 — hot〔cold〕 rolling
압운 押韻 〖시〗 rhyme ; rime —하다 rhyme ; rime
—시 a rhyme ; a rhymed verse — 형식 a rhymed scheme
압인 押印 sealing —하다 seal ; affix a seal 《to》
—기 a stamper ; a stamp machine ; a punch —자 a sealer 자동 —기 an autostamper
압점 壓點 [지혈시의] a pressure point
압정 押釘 a (thumb) tack ; a fastener ; a push-pin
압정 壓政 tyranny ; despotism —하다 tyrannize 《over a country》 ¶ 압정에 신음하다 groan under tyranny〔oppression〕 ; suffer from tyranny
*압제 壓制 [압박] oppression ; [폭정] tyranny ; [강제] despotism ; [압제] coercion —하다 oppress ; tyrannize over ; rule with a rod of iron ¶ 압제적 oppressive ; tyrannical ; despotic ; high-handed ∥압제적으로 in an oppressive manner ; oppressively ; tyrannically ; with a high hand∥압제적인 처사 a high-handed piece of work∥압제에 신음하다 groan under tyranny ; suffer from tyranny∥압제를 가하다 oppress ; tyrannize over 《people》∥압제를 벗어나다 be freed from tyranny〔oppression〕∥그 선생은 우리한테 너무 압제적이었다 The teacher was very oppressive〔tyrannical〕 to us.
—력 despotic power —자 an oppressor ; a despot ; a tyrant — 정부 a despotic government — 정치 despotism
‡압지 壓紙 blotting paper ; a (paper) blotter
‡압착 壓搾 pressure ; compression ; pressing —하다 compress ; press
— 가스 compressed gas — 공기 compressed air — 공기관 a compression tube — 공기판 a compression tap〔valve〕 —기 a compressor ; a press — 여과기 a filter press — 펌프 a compression pump ; a compressor — 효모 pressed yeast
‡압축 壓縮 compression ; constriction ; condensation —하다 (com)press ; condense ; constrict
— 가스 compressed gas —계 a piezometer — 공기 compressed air —기〔펌프〕 a compressor — 기관 a compression〔compressed air〕 engine — 냉동기 a compression refrigeration machine —력 a compressive force —성〔률〕 compressibility — 시험기 a compression tester — 압력계 a compression pressure gauge — 응력 compressive stress — 화약 compressed guncotton
압출 壓出 pressing〔squeezing〕 out
—기 an extruding machine
앗 Oh ! /O dear ! /O my ! /Heaven ! ¶ 앗 큰일이다 Good Heavens ! /Dear me ! ∥앗 지갑이 없어졌다 My God ! My purse is gone ! ∥앗 모자를 잊고 왔다 Dear me ! I've left my hat behind.
앗기다 have something taken〔stolen〕 ⇨ 빼앗기다
*앗다 ① [빼앗다] take 《a thing》 away from 《a person》 ; snatch 《a thing》 from 《a person》 ; rob 《a person》 of 《a thing》 ; deprive 《a person》 of 《a thing》 ; plunder ; [마음을] fascinate ; charm ; captivate ⇨ 빼앗다
② [씨빼다] gin 《cotton》
③ pay for labor in kind ¶ 품을 앗다 exchange labor
앗아가다 snatch 《a thing》 away 《from a person》
앗아넣다 force in ; twist in
앗아라 Oh no ! /Stop ! ¶ 앗아라 싸우지

마라 Oh no! Stop fighting!

앙 ① [어린아이의 울음] ¶ 앙하고 울다 cry loudly; burst out crying ② [놀라게 하는 소리] bo(h)! ; boo!

앙가발이 a short bowlegged person; [달라붙는 사람] a person hard to get rid of〔to shake off〕 ¶ 앙가발이의 bowlegged

앙가슴 the part of the chest between the two breasts; the middle of the chest〔bosom〕

앙가주망 engagement 《프》

앙각 仰角 an angle of elevation; (gun) elevation

앙감질 hopping (on one leg) **—하다** hop

앙갚음 revenge; retaliation; repayment; blow for blow; measure for measure; reprisal **—하다** revenge oneself on 《a person》; be revenged〔avenged〕 on; retaliate 《on》; repay; get even〔square〕 with 《a person》; get back on 《a person》 ¶ 앙갚음을 결심하다 resolve to be even 《with》// 앙갚음으로 사람을 죽이다 kill 《a person》 for revenge// 앙갚음 당하다 be retaliated 《by》; receive measure for measure// 그에게 앙갚음 하겠다 I will pay him out. /I'll fix him for that. // 그는 너에게 앙갚음한다고 맹세하고 있다 He swears that he will revenge himself on you.

앙고라 Angora
— 고양이 an Angora (cat) **—직(織)** angora **— 토끼** an Angora (rabbit) ¶ 앙고라 토끼털 angora wool

앙골라 Angola ¶ 앙골라의 Angolan// 앙골라의 원주민 an Angolan

앙괭이 〖민속〗 a witch who is supposed to visit houses on New Year's night in search of children's shoes to fit her feet; [얼굴] a shape of one's face stained randomly with ink
앙괭이 그리다 관용 blacken one's face; daub black on one's face

앙구다 [식지 않게] keep 《food》 warm; [여러 가지 음식을] put 《several kinds of food》 on the same plate; [사람을] accompany or see 《a person》 on his way

앙그러지다 ① [음식이] (be) well prepared; nicely〔well〕 seasoned; [먹음직스럽다] (be) delicious-looking; appetizing; tempting ② [어울리다] (be) becoming; suitable; nice; shapely; good looking; orderly ¶ 앙그러지게 일하다 do a job nicely

앙글방글 ① 《a child smiles》 sweetly; beamingly ② [선웃음] with a smirk; with a phony smile; with an insincere〔a deceptive〕 smile

앙금 deposit; grounds (커피 따위의); dregs; lees (술찌꺼기); sediment; settlings (밑바닥의) ¶ 앙금이 가라앉다 settle 《at the bottom》// 앙금을 가라앉히다 settle 《the contents of a barrel》

앙금앙금 crawlingly; sprawlingly ⇨ 엉금엉금

앙달머리 a person swollen with inordinate〔audacious〕 ambition ¶ 앙달머리스럽다 be inordinate; be ambitious; be pert; be cheeky; be forward

앙당그러지다 ① [뒤틀리다] warp; be warped〔distorted〕; curve; be curved ② [옴츠러지다] shrink 《with fear》; curl〔huddle〕 oneself up

앙당그리다 ⇨ 앙당그러지다 ②

앙등 昂騰 a sudden rise; an advance; jump; appreciation (화폐 가치의) **—하다** rise suddenly; advance 《in price》; go up; shoot; skyrocket; jump; soar; appreciate (화폐가) ¶ 집세의 앙등 the rise of〔in〕 house rent// 원료값의 앙등 the advance of the raw material// 생활비의 앙등 the rising cost of living// 갑자기 앙등하다 jump; boom; shoot up// 앙등 경향이 있다 show an upward tendency; be looking up// 물가가 놀랄 만큼 앙등하고 있다 The prices are skyrocketing. /The prices are staggeringly high. // 쌀값은 끊임없이 앙등하고 있다 The price of rice shows a steady advance.

앙망 仰望 look up to with hope; beg; entreat; hope; desire; request; wish ¶ …하시기 앙망하나이다 We earnestly desire 《that》; It is my earnest hope 《that》; I pray 《that》// 오래 사귀어 주시기를 앙망합니다 I hope to enjoy your long acquaintance. // 곧 답장해 주시기를 앙망합니다 Kindly favor me with an early answer. // 고람을 앙망하나이다 I beg to submit it to〔for〕 your inspection. // 목록을 송부해 주시기 앙망합니다 Please oblige〔favor〕 us with your catalog. // 참석해 주시기를 앙망하나이다 A cordial invitation is extended to you. /You are cordially invited. /Your presence〔attendance〕 is respectfully requested.

앙모 仰慕 —하다 look up to with respect; regard 《a person》 with love and respect; admire; adore ¶ 그는 부하의 앙모를 한몸에 받고 있었다 He was held in high esteem by his men. // 그는 그들의 은인으로서 앙모를 받고 있다 He is looked up to as their benefactor.

앙바틈하다 (be) short and broad; fat and short; stocky; squabby; stumpy ¶ 앙바틈하고 당찬 포수 a stocky hard-hitting catcher// 앙바틈한 남자 a stocky man; a chunky fellow

앙버티다 stick; cling; hold on to; be tenacious; resist to bitter end; bear down ¶ 끝까지 앙버티다 hold out to the last; keep at it; stand out〔firm〕

앙살 —하다 fuss〔grumble〕 in opposition; be balky ¶ 앙살부리는 증인에게 출두를 명하다 order reluctant witnesses to appear// 일에 관해 앙살부리다 grumble over one's task// 그 여자는 늘 앙살부린다 She is always fussing about something

or other.
앙상궂다 (be) terribly gaunt
앙상블 an ensemble 《프》 ¶ 스포티한 앙상블 [부인복의] a sports ensemble
앙상하다 (be) haggard ; gaunt ; thin ; spare ¶ 앙상한 사람 a skinny person ; a skeleton // 뼈만 앙상하다 be nothing but skin and bones ; be a mere bag of bones // 잎이 떨어진 나무가 앙상하다 The trees look thin with most of their leaves fallen.
앙세다 staunch ; be weak-looking but have hidden strength
앙숙 怏宿 ¶ 앙숙이다 be on bad terms 《with》 ; bear a grudge against each other ; [부부가] lead a cat-and-dog life
앙시 仰視 —하다 look up 《at, to》
앙심 怏心 grudge ; enmity ; malice ; spite ; ill feeling ; a bitter feeling ¶ 앙심 깊은 revengeful ; vindictive ; spiteful ; bitter // 앙심 깊은 여자 a vindictive woman // 앙심 품다 bear〔nurse〕 a grudge against 《a person》 ; have a grudge 〔spite〕 against 《a person》 // 앙심을 사다 incur 《a person's》 enmity ; earn 《a person's》 spite // 앙심을 갚다 take revenge on 《a person》 revenge ; oneself 《upon a person》 ; settle〔pay off〕 old scores 《with a person》 // 앙심을 잊다 forget one's grudge 《against》 // 우리는 그들에게 앙심이 없다 We have no rancor (at heart) against them.
앙알거리다 ⇨ 웅얼거리다
앙앙 怏怏 —하다 be discontented〔dissatisfied〕 ; be despondent ; be unhappy ; be disconsolate ; be heartsick ¶ 마음이 앙앙하다 be low-spirited ; be disconsolate ; be in the blues〔doldrums〕
앙양 昂揚 elevation ; exaltation ; enhancement **—하다** exalt ; enhance ; promote ; uplift ; raise ; whip up 《war spirit》 ¶ 국민 정신의 앙양 the upsurging〔enhancement〕 of national sentiment // 사회 도의의 앙양 uplifting of the standard of public morals // 국위를 앙양하다 heighten〔raise, enhance〕 national prestige // 자유민권 사상을 앙양하다 promote the ideal of civil liberties
앙와 仰臥 lying on one's back **—하다** lie on one's back
앙증하다, 앙증스럽다 (be) disproportionately small ; tiny ; little ¶ 앙증한 계집애 a chit of a girl ; a pert girl
앙진 昂進 rise ; 〖의학〗 acceleration ; exasperation **—하다** rise ; grow ; accelerate ; exasperate ¶ 병세가 앙진하다 one's condition grows worse〔takes a turn for the worse〕
 심계 — heart acceleration
앙짜 an irritatingly jealous man ; [점잔 뺌] putting on airs ; giving oneself airs ; assuming an air of importance
앙천 대소 仰天大笑 a great〔hearty〕 laugh ; a roar〔burst〕 of laughter **—하다** laugh loudly ; burst out laughing ; have a hearty laugh ¶ 농담을 듣고 앙천대소하다 have a good〔hearty〕 laugh about a joke
앙칼스럽다 (be) fierce ; vehement ; stubborn ; unyielding ; dauntless ¶ 앙칼스러운 여자 an aggressive woman // 그 여자는 앙칼스럽게 말대답했다 She gave a sharp retort.
앙칼지다 (be) fierce ; sharp ; tenacious ; pertinacious ; persistent ; unyielding
앙케트 enquête 《프》 ; a public opinion poll 〔survey〕 ; a questionnaire ¶ …에 관한 앙케트 a questionnaire on . . . // 앙케트에 대한 회답 replies submitted to a questionnaire
앙코르 an encore ¶ 세 번 앙코르를 받아 노래하다 sing three encores // 앙코르를 청하다 demand〔call for〕 an encore ; call 《a singer》 before the curtain ; encore 《a singer》 // 앙코르를 받다 receive〔get〕 an encore ; be encored // 앙코르를 받고 "…"을 노래하다 sing "…" as an encore
앙큼상큼 with short steps ; toddling ; stealthily ¶ 앙큼상큼 걷다 walk with short steps
앙큼스럽다 (be) audacious ⇨ 앙큼하다
앙큼하다 (be) overambitious ; audacious ; presumptuous ⇨ 엉큼하다
앙탈 —하다 scheme to evade ; try to be delivered from 《a burden》 ; fuss ; nag ; whine ; grumble ¶ 앙탈 부리는 여자 a nagging woman // 공연히 앙탈하다 make a big fuss over nothing ; grumble at nothing // 그는 그 일을 하지 않으려고 앙탈했다 He tried frantically to get out of the work.
앙토 仰土 plaster between rafters
앙티로망 anti-roman 《프》
앙혼 仰婚 marriage with 《a person》 of higher standing ; a morganatic marriage **—하다** marry above one ; marry into a higher status
앙화 殃禍 calamities ; disaster ; woe ; misfortune ¶ 앙화 받다 be cursed 《by》 // 앙화를 자초하다 view the wrath of heaven ; bring a calamity upon oneself // 앙화를 피하다 keep out of harm's way
†**앞** ① [미래] the future ; the time to come ; a prospect ¶ 앞으로 in (the) future ; from now on ; here after // 앞으로의 future ; coming ; to come // 앞으로 10년 후 ten years from now // 앞을 내다보다 look into the future ; look ahead // 앞(일)을 생각하다 think of the future // 앞으로 그런 일은 다시 안하겠다 I won't ever do it again. // 이 장사는 앞으로 장래성이 없다 This business has no future. // 너희들은 앞(날)이 요원하다 You have a long way to go. // 그는 앞(날)이 길지 않다 He cannot live much longer. /He has not long (but a short time) to live.

② [전방·전면] the front ; the fore (part) ¶ 앞으로〔에〕 in front of ; before ; forward ; ahead ; away ; off ; farther ; beyond ; opposite (맞은 편) // 앞 현관 the vestibule // 앞 줄 the front row // 앞 바퀴 the front wheel // 앞 페이지에 on the opposite page // 10마일 앞에 ten miles ahead〔away〕 // 집 앞에 in front of the house // 곧장 앞으로 가다 go straight ahead // 앞으로 가 [구령] Forward march ! // 버스 앞쪽은 비어 있었다 The front of the bus was empty. // 열차 앞쪽에 자리를 발견했다 I found a seat in the front part of the train. // 1등 차는 앞에서 세번째 차량이다 The first-class coach is the third one from the head of the train. // 배는 앞이 가라앉아 있었다 The ship was down by the head. // 저 앞에서 왼쪽으로 돌아주세요 Please turn left up ahead there.

③ [면전] presence ¶ 앞에서 in 《a person's》 presence ; in the face of 《a person》 // 사람들 앞에서 in the presence of others ; in company ; in public // 사고는 내 눈 앞에서 일어났다 The accident happened in my presence〔before my eyes, in front of my eyes, under our nose(s)〕. // 나는 사람들 앞에서 이야기하는 데에 익숙하지 않다 I'm not accustomed to making a speech in public. // 그는 사람들 앞에 나가는 것을 싫어한다 He doesn't like to be seen in company. // 그 여자는 우리들 앞에서 감정을 억제하려고 했다 She tried to restrain her feelings in our presence. // 사람들 앞에서 그런 말을 하는 것이 아니다 You should not say such things in company. // 신 앞에 모든 인간은 평등하다 In the sight of God all men are equal.

④ [순위] the former ; [이전] previous ¶ 앞서 before ; ahead of ; in advance of ; first ; previously ; earlier ; formerly // 앞서 말한 above-mentioned ; before-mentioned ; aforementioned // 일행보다도 3일 앞서 three days ahead〔in advance〕 of the party // 악대를 앞세우고 headed by a brassband // 앞서 말한 바와 같이 as previously stated // 앞을 달리다 get ahead of 《a person》 ; get〔have〕 the lead // 앞서 가다 go ahead〔first〕 ; go before 《a person》 // 앞서 걷다 lead the way // 앞을 다투어 …하다 struggle to 《do》

⑤ [몫] a share ; a portion ¶ 그는 한 사람 앞에 1달러씩 주었다 He gave us a dollar apiece〔each〕. /He gave a dollar to each (one) of us. // 그의 재산의 대부분이 맏아들 앞으로 갔다 Most of his estate went to the eldest son. // 그는 제 앞만 차린다 He is out for his own interest only. /He is out to feather his own nest.

⑥ [편지의] addressed〔directed〕 to 《a person》 ; [어음의] drawn in one's favor ¶ …앞으로의 편지 a letter addressed to 《a person》 // 남궁씨〔H은행〕 앞으로 어음을 발행하다 draw a check in favor of Mr. *Namgung*〔upon H Bank〕 // 송씨의 사무실〔자택〕 앞으로 편지를 쓰다 write Mr. *Song* at his office〔home〕 // 여기 당신 앞으로 온 편지가 있소 Here's a letter for you. // 귀하의 수표를 서울 무역회사 앞으로 발행해 주시기 바랍니다 Please make your check payable〔out〕 to Seoul Trading Corporation.

앞가림 having just enough education to get by **—하다** have just enough education to get by

앞가슴 the breast ; the chest (part) 《of a body, garment》

앞갈이 〖농업〗 ① [애벌갈이] the first tillage〔plowing, ploughing 《영》〕 of a rice field ② [보리갈이] the first crop

앞길 the road ahead ; the distance one has to travel over ; the way yet to go ; the future ; prospects ; outlook ; hope ; promise ; possibilities ¶ 앞길이 유망한 청년 a promising young man ; a young man of great promise ; a young man with a bright〔rosy〕 future // 앞길이 멀다 have a long way to go // 앞길이 유망하다 have a bright future〔prospects〕 《before one》 // 앞길을 걱정하다 be anxious about one's future // 앞길을 축복하다 wish 《a person》 success // 그의 앞길이 창창하다 He has the world before him. // 앞길의 행복을 빕니다 I hope you have a happy future before you. // 앞길이 암담하다 The prospects are quite gloomy〔bleak〕. // 우리는 앞길이 아직 멀다 We are yet far from our object〔goal〕. /The end is still far to see.

***앞날** ① the future ; the days ahead〔to come〕 ; the remainder of one's life〔days〕 ; the rest of one's life ¶ 앞날을 염려하다 feel anxious about one's future // 앞날을 위해 저축하다 save money for the future // 앞날의 계획을 세우다 make plans for the future ; map out one's future course // 그의 앞날이 멀지 않다 His days are numbered. // 너의 앞날은 길다 You have your long life ahead of you. // 앞날의 일은 걱정해도 소용없다 It's pointless to worry about what lies ahead.
② [전날] the other day ; a few days ago

앞날개 [곤충의] a fore wing

앞니 a front tooth ; a fore-tooth ¶ 앞니가 나다 cut one's front teeth

앞다리 ① [짐승의] the forelegs〔forepaws〕 ¶ 앞다리 들고 서다 [개가] sit erect on the haunches with the forepaws raised ; beg
② [이사할 집] one's new residence〔house〕 ¶ 앞다리를 얻어 놓고 집을 팔다 sell one's house after one has procured a new one
③ [앞잡이] an intermediary ; an agent

앞단추 a front button ; a (trouser-) fly

button ¶ 바지의 앞단추를 채우다 do up a fly button
앞닫이 a vamp ; a toe cap
앞당기다 move 《a date》 up ; advance 《a date》 ; make 《anything》 earlier ¶ 기일을 앞당기다 advance the date // 2일 앞당기다 shift two days ahead ; advance 《the date》 by two days // 여섯째 시간의 국어를 셋째 시간으로 앞당기다 move up the Korean language lesson from the sixth hour to the third // 날짜는 8월 10일에서 8월 3일로 앞당겨졌다 The date was advanced from Aug. 10 to Aug. 3. // 시계 바늘을 한 시간 앞당겨 놓았니 Did you set your watch one hour ahead? // 너 결혼식 날짜를 앞당기려고 하지 You're pushing up the date of the wedding?
앞대 the southern section〔region〕《of a country, a province》
앞대문 一大門 the front gate
앞두다 have 《a distance》 ahead ¶ 1주일 앞두다 have a week to go // 40마일 앞두다 have forty miles ahead to cover
앞뒤 [전후] before and behind ; the front and the rear ; [순서] order ; sequence ; [결과] consequences ¶ 앞뒤 생각없이 without thought ; regardless of the consequences ; recklessly // 앞뒤가 맞지 않다 be inconsistent〔incoherent〕// 앞뒤를 생각않다 be impetuous 〔thoughtless, reckless, rash〕// 앞뒤를 잘 생각하다 be prudent ; look before and after ; be circumspect // 앞뒤를 둘러보다 look before and after ; look around one // 앞뒤가 전도되어 있다 The order is inverted 〔reversed〕. // 그가 방금 말한 것은 앞뒤가 맞지 않는다 What he says just isn't logical.
앞뒤가 맞다 [관용] be consistent〔coherent, relevant〕
앞뒷집 the neighboring houses ; the neighbors ; houses in front and in the rear
앞뜰 a front yard〔garden〕
앞머리 the forehead ; the sinciput ; the front end
앞멧군 a hammerman ; a hammersmith
앞못보다 be blind ; can't see what is going on ; be ignorant ; be not farsighted
앞무대 一舞臺 an apron stage ; a proscenium 《*pl.* -nia》
앞문 一門 a〔the〕front gate〔door〕
앞바다 the offing ; the open sea ¶ 앞바다에 있는 섬 an off-lying island // 앞바다에 in the offing ; off the shore 〔coast〕; offshore ; out at sea // 인천 앞바다에서 off (the coast of) *Inchŏn* // 앞바다로 나가다 get〔take, gain〕an offing ; stand out to sea // 앞바다까지 요트로 나갔으면 한다 I'd like to take my sailboat out in the offing.
앞바닥 the foresole of a shoe
앞바람 a south〔southerly〕wind ; a head wind ⇨ 마파람
앞바퀴 a fore wheel
앞발 a paw ; a forefoot (of a quadruped) **一질** kicking (with) the forefeet
앞배 the belly ; the abdomen ¶ 앞배가 나온 potbellied
앞볼 a toe patch for Korean socks
앞산 一山 the mountain in front (of a house)
***앞서** ① [이전에] before ; already ; previously ¶ 앞서부터 for some days〔time〕past // 이에 앞서 prior to this ; before this // 앞서 말한 바와 같이 as previously stated // 앞서 들은 바와 같이 as I have heard it before // 어머니는 누구보다도 앞서 일어난다 Mother gets up earliest of all.
② [미리] beforehand ; in advance ; previously ; in anticipation ; formerly ; the other day ; some time〔a few days〕ago ¶ 정한 시간에 앞서 before〔prior to〕a designated hour // 남보다 앞서 가다 go ahead of others // 앞서 준비하다 have 〔get〕《a thing》 ready beforehand 〔in advance〕; make preparation in advance // 앞서 승인을 얻다 obtain 《a person's》 prior approval // 출발에 앞서 알리겠다 I'll let you know before I leave. // 앞서부터 병으로 누워 있다 He has been sick in bed for several days. // 그는 앞서 정해 놓은 장소에서 기다리고 있었다 He was waiting at the prearranged spot.
앞서거니 뒤서거니 alternating in the lead ; neck and neck ; nip and tuck 《미·구》 **一하다** alternate in the lead ; run neck and neck ; be nip and tuck ¶ 앞서거니 뒤서거니 하는 경주 a ding-dong race // 두 선수가 앞서거니 뒤서거니 들어왔다 The two runners came in, the one following on the heels of the other.
***앞서다** [선행] go before〔ahead of〕; precede ; go in advance of ; take the lead ; leave 《a person》 behind ; [탁월] excel ; outdo ; surpass 《a person》 ¶ 부모에 앞서 죽다 die before one's parents // 경기에서 앞서다 get the lead in a race // 세상보다 50년 앞서다 be fifty years ahead of the world ; be fifty years ahead of the times // 남보다 앞서서 …하다 take the initiative in 《doing》 // 부모에 앞서 가는 불효를 사죄하다 apologize for preceding one's parents to the grave // 무엇보다 앞서는 것은 돈이다 Money is the first consideration〔requisite〕. // 공익은 사리에 앞선다 Public interest takes precedence over private interest. /Consideration is given to public interest before private interest.
앞서서 prior to ; earlier than ¶ 출발에 앞서서 before one leaves ; before〔prior to〕one's departure // 남보다 앞서서 가다 go ahead of others // 어머니는 누구보다 앞서서 일어난다 Mother gets up earliest of all. // 그는 누구보다도 앞서서 왔다 He

came earlier than any other. /He was the first to come.

앞세우다 make 《a person》 go ahead ; let 《a person》 lead〔precede〕 ¶ …을 앞세우고 led〔headed〕 by ; be preceded by // 아내〔부모〕를 앞세우다 survive one's wife 〔parents〕 // 행렬에 악대를 앞세우다 place a band at the head of a procession // 정치 문제보다 경제를 앞세워야 한다 We must give priority to economic problems over political ones.

앞수표 一手票 a postdated check〔bill〕

앞앞이 for each one ; in front of each person ; each ; apiece ; respectively ¶ 앞앞이 하나씩 one piece each ; one apiece // 앞앞이 방이 있다 Each one of us has a room to himself. /We each have our own room. // 앞앞이 그 책을 한 권씩 가지고 있다 We have each a copy of the book. // 그들은 앞앞이 사과 세 개씩을 받았다 They were given three apples each. /Each of them was given three apples.

앞에총 一銃 [구령] Port arms ! ¶ 앞에 총을 하다 port

— 자세 the port

앞이마 the front forehead

앞일 the future ; the time to come ¶ 앞일을 생각하다 think of〔look to〕 the future ; have the future in mind // 앞일을 걱정하다 worry about one's future // 앞일에 대비하다 prepare for the future // 앞일에 대해서 희망에 가득 차 있다 be full of hope for the future // 앞일을 예언하다 foretell the future ; predict what future has in store for 《a person》 ; make predictions of coming events // 앞일을 누가 아랴 Who knows what the future has in store for us ? /No one can tell〔There is no knowing〕 what will happen in (the) future. // 앞일을 생각하니 한심하다 It is discouraging to think of my future.

앞자락 the front part 《of a skirt, coat》

앞잡이 ① [안내] a guide ; a cicerone (관광객의) ; a leader ¶ 앞잡이가 되다 lead 《a party》 ; act as a guide

② [주구] an agent ; a tool ; a cat's-paw ¶ 경찰의 앞잡이 a stool pigeon ; a police spy〔agent〕 // 앞잡이가 되다 act as an agent 《for》 ; make oneself a cat's-paw of 《a person》 // 앞잡이로 쓰다 use 《a person》 // 자본가의 앞잡이가 되다 act as the running dog of a capitalist // 그는 독재자의 앞잡이에 불과했다 He was a mere tool of the dictator. /He was merely an instrument of the dictator.

†**앞장** [일] the lead ; the head ; [사람] a leader ; a pioneer ; the vanguard ¶ 앞장서서 at the head of // …을 앞장세우고 led by 《a person》 ; with 《a person》 in the lead // 앞장서다 lead ; head ; be at the head ; be the first 《to do》 ; take the lead〔initiative〕 // 행렬에 앞장서 가다 walk at the head of a parade ; lead a procession // …하는 데 앞장서다 take the initiative in 《doing》 // 유행에 앞장서다 lead 〔set〕 the fashion // 교육 개혁에 앞장서다 take the lead in education reform // 그는 이 운동에 앞장서 있다 He leads the van in this great movement.

앞정강이 the (fore-) shin ; the (fore-) shank

앞지느러미 a forefin

***앞지르다** pass 《a person in race》 ; get ahead of 《a person》 ; leave 《a person》 behind ; outdo ; steal a march upon ; be beforehand with ; get〔have〕 the start of ¶ 앞차를 앞지르다 pass a car ahead〔in front〕 // 훨씬 앞지르다 get far ahead of 《a person》 ; outdistance // 남의 말을 앞질러 말하다 take the word out of another's mouth // 앞지르지 마시오 No (by-) passing. (게시) // 내가 그것을 2년 앞서 배우기 시작했는데 지금은 그가 앞질러 버렸다 I began to learn it two years earlier, but have already been outstripped by him. // 경기를 동시에 시작했는데 당신은 나를 앞질렀다 We started playing at the same time, but you're pulled ahead of me. // 우리 회사가 경쟁사를 앞지르게 되었다 At last we're been able to outsmart our competitor.

앞집 the house in front

†**앞쪽** [방향] the front ; [앞부분] the fore (part) ; [화폐 따위의] the head ; the obverse ¶ 앞쪽의 front ; fore ; forward ; frontward // 앞쪽에 in front 《of》 ; ahead ; forward ; in the forward direction // 한걸음 앞쪽으로 나오다 take a step forward // 앞쪽을 보라 Look to your front !

앞차 an earlier departing car〔train〕 ¶ (기차의) 맨 앞차 the foremost car // (자기 차의) 바로 앞차 the car〔train〕 next ahead

앞차다 (be) reliable ; dependable ; reassuring ; encouraging

앞참 (be) reliable ; dependable ; reassuring ; encouraging

앞참 一站 the next stage〔stop〕

앞창 一窓 the front window

앞채 the front building〔wing〕 (of a house) ; [가마채] the front carrying-pole (of a sedan chair) ; [앞마구리] the front end-board of a saddle-rack

***앞치마** an apron ; a slip ; a lap ; a pinafore (어린애의) ¶ 앞치마를 두른 소녀 a girl wearing an apron // 앞치마를 두르다 put on an apron

애¹ [수고] troubles ; efforts ; [걱정] worry ; solicitude ; annoyance ; impatience ; anxiety ¶ 생활 문제로 애타다 be harassed by the question of life // 그는 그 문제로 애태우고 있다 He is troubled〔worried〕 about〔over〕 the matter.

애쓰다 관용 make efforts ; take pains (수고)

애타다 관용 be worried ; be troubled ;

be nervous

애태우다 관용 be anxious ; worry oneself (스스로) ; worry (남을)

애² a child ⇨ 아이 ¶ 애를 밴 여인 a woman with child ; a pregnant woman // 애어머니가 되다 become a mother ; attain motherhood // 애를 업다 carry〔have〕 a child on one's back // 애가 없다 be childless // 애가 많다 have many children 《to feed and clothe》 ; have a large family 《to provide for》 // 애를 기르다 rear〔bring up〕 a child ; raise a child 《미》 // 애 취급하다 treat 《a person》 like a child ; baby a child

애- [처음] the very first ; [어린] little ; tiny ; the very young (미숙한) ; green ; immature ; raw ; inexperienced —벌 the first time〔round〕 —송아지 a newborn calf —순 a fresh sprout

*애가 哀歌 an elegy ; a dirge ; a sad〔plaintive〕 song

애걔 Why ! /My ! /How poor〔little, paltry〕 ! ¶ 애걔 이것뿐이냐 My, is that all ?

애걸 哀乞 begging ; pleading ; supplication ; entreaty ; an appeal —하다 implore ; beg〔plead〕 for ; appeal ¶ 그 여자는 그에게 가지 말라고 애걸했다 She implored him not to go.

애걸복걸 哀乞伏乞 —하다 beg earnestly ; implore ; supplicate

애견 愛犬 one's pet〔favorite〕 dog —가 a dog-lover ; a lover of dogs ; a dog-fancier

애경 愛敬 affection and respect ; love and esteem ; loving respect —하다 venerate ; love with respect ; hold 《a person》 in high esteem

애고 愛顧 favor ; patronage ; love ; custom ; care —하다 patronize ; favor ¶ 애고를 받고 under the patronage of // 애고를 받다 be patronized 《by》 ; receive favors 《from》 // 애고를 바랍니다 I solicit〔request〕 your patronage.

애고 Oh ! /Dear me ! ⇨ 아이고

애고대고 crying and wailing —하다 cry and wail

애고머니 [감탄사] Heavens ! /By Jove ! /O my ! /Dear me ! /Good God ! ⇨ 아이고

애곡 哀哭 wailing ; mourning ; lamentation ; grief ; plaint —하다 mourn 《for, over》 ; lament 《for》 ; grieve 《at, over》 ; wail

†애교 愛嬌 (personal) charms ; winsomeness ; attractiveness ; courtesy (장사치들의) ¶ 애교 있는 charming ; winning ; winsome ; lovely ; attractive ; amorous // 애교 있는 눈 charming〔winsome〕 eyes // 애교 없는 unattractive ; sour (용모) ; blunt (태도) ; curt (대답 따위가) // 애교를 부리다 be profuse of one's smile (for everybody) ; be all smiles (for everybody) ; display one's charm // 그 여자는 애교가 넘쳐 흐른다 She is overflowing with smiles.
— 머리 a kiss-curl ; a lovelock ; a kiss-me-quick

애교심 愛校心 love of one's school ; attachment〔affection〕 to one's Alma Mater

애구 Oh ! ; Oh, my goodness !

*애국 愛國 love of〔for〕 one's country ; patriotism ; nationalism ¶ 애국적인 patriotic // 비애국적인 unpatriotic
— 단체 a patriotic society〔organization〕
— 부인회 the Women's Patriotic Association — 선열 deceased patriots — 운동 a patriotic movement —자 a patriot — 정신 patriotism

애국가 愛國歌 a patriotic song ; the national anthem (국가)

*애국심 愛國心 patriotic sentiment〔feeling, spirit〕 ; patriotism ; nationalism ; chauvinism (배타적인) ¶ 애국심에 불타는 마음 one's heart burning〔glowing〕 with patriotism // 애국심이 있다 be patriotic ; have a love for one's country // 애국심을 고취하다 infuse〔instil〕 patriotism into the heart of 《people》

애금가 愛禽家 a bird-lover ; a bird-fancier ; a lover of birds

애긍 哀矜 compassion ; pity —하다 (be) pitiable ; piteous ; pathetic

애기 ⇨ 아기

애기 愛機 one's favorite〔own〕 plane

애기 愛妓 one's favorite *kisaeng*

애기나리 〖식물〗 fairy-bells

애기씨름 wrestling by beginners〔novices〕

애기잠 the first dormant period of the silkworm

애꾸눈이 a one-eyed person ¶ 애꾸눈이의 one-eyed ; blind of one eye // 애꾸눈이가 되다 lose (the sight of) one eye

애꿎다 be to be pitied ; (be) innocent ; guiltless ¶ 애꿎은 사람 a blameless〔innocent〕 person

애끊다 feel one's heart rent〔torn to pieces〕 ; feel as if one's heart were breaking ; feel as if one's heart would break ; one's heart bleeds ¶ 애끊는 슬픔 heartbreaking grief // 그 말을 들으니 애끊는 듯했다 I felt my heart would break to hear that. /My heart was fit to break when I heard it. /It was heartrending news to me.

애끌 a big chisel

애끓다 fret 《about》 ; worry (oneself) 《about》 ; be overanxious ; be all roiled up ; go〔get〕 into a stew 《about》 ¶ 애끓어 병이 나다 fret〔worry〕 oneself ill

애늙은이 a young person who behaves like an old person

애달다 (be) impatient 《at》 ; overanxious ; be anxious 《to》 ¶ 너를 다시 만나려고 애달고 있다 She is impatient to see you again.

애달프다 (be) heartbreaking ; aching ; sorrowful ; pathetic ; painful ; distressing ¶ 애달픈 소식 heartbreaking news // 애달픈 마음을 털어놓다 confess a heartrending sorrow

애닯다 ⇨ 애달프다

애당심 愛黨心 party loyalty ; party〔partisan〕 spirit

***애당초** (from) the very first time ; the start ; the outset ; the beginning ; the commencement ; in the first place ¶ 애당초의 first ; original ; initial // 애당초의 계획〔생각〕 one's〔the〕 original plan〔intention〕// 애당초에 at first ; at the start〔outset, beginning〕; [원래] primarily ; originally // 애당초부터 from the first // 그것은 애당초부터 성공적이었다 It was successful〔a success〕 from the start. // 애당초에는 회원이 불과 3명이었다 We had only three members to start with. // 애당초에 서울에 왔을 때는 여기에 공원이 없었다 The first time I came up to *Seoul* I found no parks here.

***애도 哀悼** grief ; condolence ; mourning ; sorrow ; regret ; lamentation **—하다** mourn 《for, over》; grieve 《over, at》; regret ¶ 애도의 뜻을 표하여 in token of respect to the memory of a 《person》// 애도의 뜻을 표하다 express one's regret〔sorrow〕 at 《a person's》 death ; express one's regret〔sorrow〕 over the death of 《a person》; [유족에게] express one's condolence〔sympathy〕《in a person's bereavement》

—가(歌) a lamentation ; an elegy **—사** a funeral oration ; a condolatory address **—자** a condoler ; a mourner

애독 愛讀 love of reading ; reading (for pleasure) ; bibliophilia **—하다** read 《a book》 with pleasure ; read and enjoy ; read 《a magazine》 usually〔regularly〕; like to read ; be fond of reading ; enjoy reading ¶ 그는 로렌스를 애독한다 Lawrence is his favorite author. /He is devoted to〔a devotee of〕 Lawrence. // 이 책은 중학생들이 애독하고 있다 This book is popular〔a favorite〕 with middle-school boys. // 나는 셰익스피어를 애독하고 있다 I am a lover of Shakespeare. /Shakespeare is my favorite author.

—서 one's favorite book **—자** a devoted〔an appreciative〕 reader ; an audience 《총칭》; a subscriber (구독자) ¶ (저작이) 애독자가 많다 have a large circle of readers

애동대동하다 (be) very young ; be still a boy〔kid〕

애돝 a yearling pig

애드 an ad(vertisement) ; advertising

—맨 an ad-man **—벌룬** an advertising balloon ; an ad-balloon 《구》 ¶ 애드벌룬을 올리다〔내리다〕 send up〔pull down〕 an advertising balloon

애디슨(씨)병 —(氏)病 [부신 장해] Addison's disease

애락 哀樂 grief and joy ; grief and pleasure

애련 哀憐 pity ; compassion **—하다** (be) piteous ; pitiable ; pathetic ; touching ¶ 애련의 정을 금치 못하다 be overwhelmed with pity 《for》; have〔take〕 great compassion ; be greatly moved with compassion 《for》

애로 隘路 a narrow path ; a defile (산중의) ; a bottleneck (일의) ¶ 애로를 타개하다 break〔uncork〕 the bottleneck ; push through an impasse // 이 계획에는 많은 애로가 있다 There are a series of bottlenecks in the way of this program. // 정부는 생산의 애로를 타개하고자 하고 있다 The Government is trying to break the bottleneck of production.

애리조나 Arizona 《Ariz.》

애림 愛林 forest conservation〔protection〕; loving〔cherishing〕 the forests

— 녹화 Keep the Trees Green. /Save the Trees. **— 사상** interest in forest conservation **— 주간** Arbor Week

애마 愛馬 one's favorite〔pet〕 horse

***애매 曖昧** vagueness ; obscurity ; ambiguity (말뜻의) ; equivocation (용어의) **—하다** (be) vague ; obscure ; ambiguous ; dubious ; evasive ; equivocal

> 참고 **obscure** 명확하게 표현되지 않았든지 그렇지 않으면 독자의 이해력 부족 때문에 의미가 확실하지 않다 **vague** 막연하여 명확하지 않다 **ambiguous** 여러 가지 의미로 해석될 수 있다 **equivocal** 고의로 여러 가지 의미로 해석될 수 있도록 되어 있다

¶ 애매한 풍설 a vague rumor // 애매한 기사 news of doubtful authority ; news from unreliable sources // 애매한 대답을 하다 give a vague〔an equivocal〕 answer // 애매한 진술을 하다 make an ambiguous statement // 애매한 태도를 취하다 maintain an uncertain〔a dubious〕 attitude 《toward》; assume a non-committal attitude 《toward》// 그 문장은 뜻이 애매하다 The meaning of that sentence is ambiguous〔obscure〕. // 그 법률에는 애매한 점이 많다 The law is full of ambiguities. // 나는 그 여자로부터 애매한 대답을 받았다 I received an equivocal reply from her.

애매미 〖곤충〗 a kind of cicada

애매하다 be falsely charged ; be wrongly accused 《of stealing》; be unjustly convicted 《of a forgery charge》; be unjustly suspected 《of》; get an unwarranted scolding ; (be) innocent ¶ 애매한 사람을 죽이다 kill an innocent person // 그는 애

매하게 죄를 썼다 He was falsely charged 〔accused〕.
애먹다 have bitter experience ; have a hard time of it ; be troubled ; be worried 《about》 ; be anxious 《about》 ; be in distress ; be harassed ¶ 돈이 없어 애먹고 있다 He is hard up for money. //그것을 얻는데 애먹었을 것이다 He must have had a hard time getting it.
애먹이다 harass ; annoy ; bewilder ; embarrass ; give 《a person》 trouble ; bother ; cause annoyance to 《a person》 ; put 《a person》 in a fix 〔dilemma〕 ¶ 어려운 질문으로 선생님을 애먹이다 annoy one's teacher with hard questions // 마을 사람들은 다리가 떠내려가서 애먹고 있다 The bridge was washed away much to the inconvenience of the villagers.
애먼 ① [엉뚱한] irrelevant ; wrong ; far-fetched ; unlikely
② [죄 없는] innocent ; uninvolved ; wrongly accused ¶ 애먼 사람 죄인 만들지 마라 Don't get the wrong man for your culprit.
애면글면 struggling with all one's might ; doing one's feeble best **―하다** do one's feeble best
애모 哀慕 lamentation ; wail **―하다** grieve ; lament ; mourn
애모 愛慕 affection 《for, toward》 ; attachment 《to, for》 ; love ; yearning **―하다** love ; be attached to ; yearn after〔for〕 ¶ 애모의 정 a feeling of affection // 애모를 받다 be (dearly) beloved by 〔of〕 // 학생들에게 애모를 받고 있다 be the idol of one's pupils
*__애무 愛撫__ love ; endearment ; caress ; petting **―하다** love ; pet ; fondle ; caress ; cherish
애물 ① [애태움] a (cause of) worry ¶ 우리 딸이 이제 애물 노릇을 하지 않게 됐으니 기쁘다 We're delighted she's finally going to be out of our hair. ② [죽은 자식] a son who died young
애바르다 be alive to one's interests ; be money-mad ; be keen on〔about〕 money-making ¶ 어떻게 저렇게 애바를 수가 있나 How on earth can he be so money-mad !
애바리 a shrewd man of business ; a greedy person ; a miser
애벌 the first time〔round〕 ; a rough job of it ¶ 애벌 찌다 steam for the first time // 일을 애벌하다 make short work of it ; dispose of it lightly ; make a rough job of it
―갈이 a first〔rough, preliminary〕 plowing〔ploughing 《영》, tilling〕 **―김** rough weeding **―빨래** a first laundering ; rough washing **―일** a rough job ; a lick and a promise
*__애벌레__ a larva ; a newborn insect
애벌칠 ―漆 a first〔ground〕 coat ; a primary〔rough〕 coat ; (a) priming
애별 哀別 a sad parting ; a grievous separation
애브노멀 abnormal ; unnatural
애사 哀史 a sad〔pathetic〕 story〔history〕 ; a tragedy
애살스럽다 (be) miserly〔mean〕 and stingy ; penny-pinching ; tight-fisted
애상 哀傷 grief ; sorrow ; lamentation **―하다** grieve ; lament ¶ 애상의 곡 a song of sorrow ; elegy
애서 愛書 fondness for books ; love of books ; one's favorite books
―가 a book-lover ; a bibliophile **―광** bibliomania ; craze〔madness〕 for books ; a bibliomaniac
애서다 get with child ; become pregnant
*__애석 哀惜__ grief ; lamentation ; sorrow **―하다** grieve ; lament ; mourn ; be regrettable ; sorrow over 《a person's death》 ¶ 애석한 마음 (a) regret ; (a) pity // 애석해 하다 regret // 애석한 일이다 It is a pity 《that》 // 정말 애석하구나 What a pity it is !
애석 愛惜 ―하다 be loath to 《part》 ; hold precious ; be reluctant to part with ; miss ¶ 떠나게 되어 애석한 마음 금할 길 없습니다 I can't stand parting from you. /I am very loath to part from you.
―상 a consolation prize
애성이 anger ; indignation ; resentment
애소 哀訴 an appeal ; a petition ; supplication ; entreaty ; pleading **―하다** appeal 《to》 ; make an appeal 《to》 ; implore ; plead ; petition 《to》 ; entreat ¶ 애소에 굴복하다 yield to 《a person's》 solicitations // 구원을 애소하다 appeal 《to a person》 for help // 그 여자는 그에게 가지 말라고 애소했다 She implored him not to go.
애솔 a young pine tree
―밭 a grove of young pines
애송 愛誦 love of reciting 《a poem》 ; recitation of one's favorite poem(s) **―하다** love to recite ; sing 〔read〕 with pleasure
―시 one's favorite poems **―집** one's favorite anthology ; a collection〔an anthology〕 of one's favorite poems
애송아지 a (young) calf ; a newborn calf
애송이 a very young person ; a greenhorn ; a novice ¶ 그는 너무 애송이다 He is as green as grass. /He is a greenhorn.
애수 哀愁 sorrow ; sadness ; grief ; pathos ¶ 애수를 자아내다 make 《a person》 feel sad // 애수를 느끼다 feel sad 〔sorrowful〕
애순 young buds ; fresh sprouts ; sprouts ; shoots
애시 哀詩 an elegy
애식 愛息 one's beloved〔dear, darling〕

child

애써 as much〔far〕 as possible ; as much as one can ; diligently ; assiduously **—하다** endeavor〔make efforts〕 to 《do》 ; take good care to 《do》 ¶ 나는 애써 눈물을 삼키었다 I made an effort to gulp down tears.

***애쓰다** exert〔strain〕 oneself ; work hard ; endeavor ; do one's best ; take pain〔trouble〕 ; make an effort ; make efforts ; strive 《for》 ¶ 몹시 애쓰다 make a great effort ; strive hard // 애써 공부하다 study hard // 나라를 위해 애쓰다 serve one's country // 명성을 얻으려고 애쓰다 strive for fame // 애쓴 보람이 없었다 All my efforts went for nothing. // 마침내 애쓴 보람이 있었다 Efforts were finally rewarded. /My efforts bore fruit finally. // 애쓰지 않으면 얻는 것이 없다 Nothing can be obtained without effort. // 애써주셔서 감사합니다 Thank you for your trouble.

애애 靄靄 —하다 (be) hazy ; misty ; cloudy ; dark ; [화기] peaceful ¶ 화기 애애한 가정 a home in peace and harmony〔happiness〕 // 화기가 애애하다 be peaceful and harmonious ; be comfortable〔relaxed〕 ; be cozy

애연가 愛煙家 a habitual〔regular〕 smoker

애오라지 somehow ; somewhat ; in one way or another ¶ 애오라지 답장을 하다 give an answer one way or the other // 애오라지 해놓고 볼 일이다 It must be done somehow or other〔in one way or another〕. /At any rate I will try.

애옥살림 a poor〔miserable〕 life〔home〕 ; needy circumstances ; narrow〔reduced, straitened〕 circumstances **—하다** live in poverty〔want〕 ; live in a small way ; eke out a scanty living

애옥하다 (be) poor ; shabby ; needy ; be in want ; (be) destitute

애완 愛玩 —하다 be fond of ; fondle ; make a pet of ; prize ; treasure

—가 a lover ; a fancier (동식물의) **—동물** a pet (animal) **—물** one's prized〔cherished〕 article〔possession〕

애욕 愛慾 love and lust ; passion ¶ 애욕의 노예가 되다 be enslaved by one's passions ; fall a prey to passion ; become a slave of passion

애용 愛用 one's favorite use ; habitual use **—하다** use regularly〔habitually〕 ; make habitual use of ; patronize ¶ 애용하는 favorite // 애용하는 카메라 a camera for one's personal use // 국산품을 애용하다 patronize home products

—가 a habitual〔regular〕 user ; a patron **—약** the medicine one regularly takes ; one's favorite medicine

†애원 哀願 an appeal ; supplication ; pleading ; an entreaty **—하다** entreat ; implore ; plead〔beg〕 《for》 ; appeal 《to, for》 ¶ 애원하듯이 imploringly // 구조를 애원하다 appeal〔implore〕 《a person》 to help 《one》

—자 an implorer ; a suppliant

애육 愛育 tender nurture **—하다** bring up 《a child》 with tender care ; nurse〔foster〕 with tender care ; coddle

애음 愛飮 fondness of drinking **—하다** be fond of drinking ; love to drink ; drink〔take〕 regularly

—가 a regular drinker

‡애인 愛人 a〔her〕 lover (남자) ; a〔his〕 love (여자) ; a dear heart ; a sweetheart (남녀 공통이나 주로 여자) ¶ 두 애인 a pair of lovers // 애인 역을 맡은 배우 an actor for a lover's role // 애인이 생기다 get her man (여자의)

애잇닦기 rough wiping ; giving a first polish 《to》

애자 愛子 one's (beloved) child ; one's darling ; one's dear child

애자 哀子 I who am the chief mourner (부고에서)

애자 碍子 〖전기〗 an insulator

애잔하다 (be) very weak ; delicate ; infirm ; frail ; childish ; naive ; sorrowful ¶ 애잔한 얼굴 a childish face // 수심에 잠긴 애잔한 모습 a sorrowful appearance ; a pitiful sight ; the pitiable spectacle of a human being in distress

애장서 愛藏書 one's treasured book

애저 —猪 a suckling pig

—구이 roast suckling pig **—찜** steamed suckling pig

***애절하다 哀切—** (be) sad ; touching ; pathetic ¶ 애절한 이야기 a sad〔pathetic〕 story

애젊다 look younger than one's age ; be still a bit boyish〔girlish〕 ¶ 애젊은이 a youngster ; a lad

애정 哀情 sadness ; (a feeling of) sorrow ; grief

†애정 愛情 love 《for a person, of a thing》 ; affection 《for, towards a person》 ; a tender feeling ; attachment ; devotion ¶ 애정이 넘치는 affectionate ; loving ; warmhearted // 애정 없는 결혼 a loveless marriage // 애정이 넘치는 편지 an affectionate letter // 아이에 대한 부모의 애정 the affection of a parent for a child // 애정을 차지하다 win 《a person's》 heart // 애정을 가지다 have an affection 《for, toward》 // 애정을 표시하다 show one's love 《for》 // 그녀는 동생에 대한 애정이 깊다 She is gentle and affectionate toward her younger sister. // 아내에 대한 애정은 조금도 변함이 없다 His affection for his wife remains unabated. // 나에 대한 그 여자의 애정은 사라졌다 Her love for me was dead.

애제자 愛弟子 one's favorite disciple〔pupil〕

애조 哀調 a plaintive〔sorrowful〕 tone ; a mournful〔sad〕 melody ; 〚음악〛 a minor key ¶ 애조를 띤 sad ; mournful ; plaintive

애조 愛鳥 one's pet bird
—가(家) a lover of birds ; a bird fancier
— 주간 Bird Week

애족 愛族 loving one's people **—하다** love one's people
애국— devotion to one's country and to one's people

애주 愛酒 love of wine **—하다** be fond of liquor ; love wine ; drink habitually
—가 a habitual drinker ; a lover of wine

애중 愛重 —하다 love and prize ; make〔think〕 much of ⇨ 애지중지하다

애증 愛憎 love and hatred ; likes and dislikes ¶ 애증의 염(念)이 강하다 have a strong partiality 《for a person》 // 부하에 대하여 애증이 있다 be partial toward one's subordinates // 애증은 근본을 따져보면 같은 것이다 Love and hatred are one and the same thing. /Love and hate spring from the same source.

애지중지 愛之重之 —하다 value highly ; prize ; treasure ; dote 《upon》 ¶ 내가 애지중지하는 물건 my most prized possessions // 그는 아버지가 주신 시계를 애지중지하다 He treasures the watch his father gave him. // 그 여자는 손자를 애지중지한다 She dotes on〔upon〕 her grandson.

애착 愛着 attachment ; affection ; love ¶ 집에 대한 애착 attachment to one's home // 애착을 느끼다 become attached 《to》 // 애착을 느끼지 않다 be not attached 《to》 // 그는 고아들에게 깊은 애착을 느끼고 있다 He feels a passionate love for the orphans. // 그는 학문에 강한 애착을 갖고 있다 He has a strong love of learning.

애창 愛唱 —하다 love to sing 《a song》
—곡(曲) one's favorite song ; a song one likes to sing

애채 a newly sprouted branch of a tree ; a shoot ; a sprout ¶ 애채가 나다 《a tree》 put out new shoots

애처 愛妻 one's (beloved) wife ¶ 애처가 a devoted husband // 그는 애처가다 He is devoted to his wife.

***애처롭다** [슬프다] (be) pitiful ; pitiable ; pathetic ; touching ; sorrowful ¶ 애처로운 광경 a pitiable scene ; a pathetic sight // 애처로운 이야기 a sad〔pitiful, pathetic〕 story ; a heart-rending episode ; a sob story 《미》 // 애처로운 생활 a miserable life〔existence〕 // 애처롭게 생각하다 pity 《a person》 ; take pity 〔compassion〕 on 《a person》 ; feel〔be〕 sorry for 《a person》 // 버림받은 아이들이 애처로왔다 The deserted children were pitiful. // 정말 애처로운 광경이었다 The sight touched 〔appealed to〕 my heart. // 그 광경은 차마 볼 수 없을 만큼 애처로운 것이었다 The sight was too harrowing to look at. // 굶주린 아이들은 보기에도 애처로왔다 The starving children were a piteous sight.

애첩 愛妾 one's (favorite) concubine ; one's mistress

애초 the first ; the beginning ; the commencement ¶ 애초에 at first ; at the start〔outset〕 ; primarily ; originally // 애초의 계획 one's〔the〕 original intention 〔plan〕 // 애초부터 from the first〔outset, start〕 // 애초에는 실패했다 I failed (in it) at first. // 애초의 계획에는 그가 가기로 되어 있었다 According to the original plan, he was to go.

애칭 愛稱 a pet name ; a term of endearment ¶ 애칭으로 부르다 call 《a person》 by his pet name // 윌리엄의 애칭은 빌이다 "Bill" is the nickname for William. // 바니는 토끼의 애칭이다 "Bunny" is a pet name for a rabbit.

애타 愛他 loving others ; altruism ¶ 애타적 altruistic
—심 an altruistic spirit **—주의** altruism
—주의자 an altruist

***애타다** be much worried ; worry oneself sick ; be overanxious ; be quite uneasy 《about》 ¶ 아이가 아프면 어머니는 여러가지로 애가 탄다 A mother of a sick child has many worries. // 그의 주소를 몰라 애가 탄다 It fidgets me not to know where he is. // 지각하지 않나 하고 애가 탔다 She was anxious lest she should be late for school.

애태우다 ① [자기] worry oneself 《about》 ; feel anxiety ; concern oneself 《about》 ¶ 그런 것에 애태우지 마라 Don't let that trouble〔worry〕 you. // 그 여자는 하찮은 일에 애태운다 She worries about little things.
② [남을] worry ; annoy ; vex ; tantalize ; cause 《a person》 anxiety ; give 《a person》 much trouble ¶ 부모를 애태우다 worry〔grieve〕 one's parents

애통 哀痛 grief ; lamentation ; sorrow ; distress ; mourning **—하다** grieve ; lament ; mourn 《for, over》 ; deplore 《for》 ¶ 애통할 일 deplorable〔lamentable〕 incident // 애통한 나머지 in the fullness of one's grief〔sorrow〕 // 애통 터지다 be quite worried ; be very anxious 《about》 ; deplore deeply // 사람의 불행을 애통하다 feel sorry for 《a person's》 misfortune

애통터지다 ⇨ 애타다

애틀랜타 Atlanta

애틋하다 (be) heart-rending ; painful ; distressing ; deplorable ¶ 애틋한 사랑을 고백하다 confess one's ardent love

애티 childishness ; puerility ¶ 애티나다 be childish // 애티를 벗다 grow up ; leave childhood behind

애팔래치아 산맥 —山脈 the Appalachian Mountains

애프터서비스 after-sale service ; (repair)

service ; servicing (on the goods sold to customers) **—하다** service 《a motorcar》; provide maintenance 《for》 ¶ 조그마한 가게 쪽이 애프터서비스가 낫다 Small shopkeepers offer better after-sale service. // 이 기계에 대해서는 회사에서 애프터서비스를 합니다 We will provide after-sale service on this machine.

애프터케어 [의학] aftercare

애해 [기막히거나 가소로울때] Oh yeah ! ; Well ! ; Ha(h) ! ; Eh !

애햄 hem ; ahem

애향 愛鄕 love of one's home

—심 local patriotism ; love of one's home〔native place〕 ¶ 그는 애향심이 있다 He loves his home town.

애호 哀號 wailing ; a moan **—하다** wail ; moan

†애호 愛好 love 《for, of》; a liking 《for》 **—하다** be fond of ; like ; love ; have a liking for ; care for 《movies》; be devoted 《addicted》 to ; take much delight in ¶ 평화 애호의 peace-loving // 술을 애호하다 be addicted to drink // 우리는 평화를 애호하는 국민이다 We are a peace-loving nation.

—자 a lover 《of music》; [동물 따위의] a 《bird》 fancier ; [예술 따위의] a devotee ; a dilettante ; an amateur ; [열심가] an enthusiast ; a fan ; an aficionado ; a votary **평화 — 국민** a peace-loving nation

애호 愛護 [보호] protection ; preservation ; loving〔tender〕 care ; kindly treatment ; [보존] conservation **—하다** keep safely ; cherish ; protect 《a person》; preserve ; treat 《an animal》 with tender care ; be kind to 《an animal》

동물 — 협회 the Society for the Prevention of Cruelty to Animals 《S. P. C. A.》

애호가 愛好家 a lover 《of music》; [동물 따위의] a 《bird》 fancier ; [예술 따위의] a devotee ; a dilettante ; an amateur ; [열심인 사람] an enthusiast ; a fan ; an aficionado ; a maniac ; a votary

문학 — a literary enthusiast **야구 —** a baseball fan **연극 —** a theatergoer ; a playgoer **영화 —** a movie fan **평화 —** a lover of peace ; a peace lover

애호박 a green〔young〕 pumpkin

애화 哀話 a sad〔pathetic〕 story ; a tragic tale

애환 哀歡 joys and sorrows 《of life》

애휼 愛恤 charity ; compassion

— 운동 a charity campaign

애희 愛戱 love play

액 厄 misfortune ; mishap ; disaster ; ill-luck ¶ 액을 막다 prevent〔forestall〕 misfortune ; keep〔ward〕 off evil fortune ; drive away evil // 액을 당하다 have an accident ; meet with a misfortune // 무서운 액이 그들에게 닥쳤다 A frightful calamity befell them.

액 額 [금액] an amount ; a quantity ; a sum ; [채권의 액면] a denomination ¶ 거액에 달하다 amount to big figures ; reach a vast amount

생산— the volume of manufacture ; the amount of production **소— 지폐** a note of a small denomination **소비 —** the amount consumed **예정 —** the budget sum〔figure〕 ; the estimate

액 液 [액체] liquid ; fluid ; [용액] solution ; [즙] juice (과실의) ; sap (나무의) ¶ 액을 짜내다 squeeze out juice ; tap 《a tree》; juice

—랭식(冷式) 엔진 a liquid-cooled engine **—성(性)** liquidity **—압(壓)** fluid pressure **—제(劑)** liquid medicine

액기 腋氣 the offensive smell of the armpit

액날 厄— an unlucky〔evil, a bad〕 day ; a critical day 《for the crops》 ¶ 13일은 액날이라고 한다 The thirteenth day of a month is believed to be an unlucky day.

액년 厄年 an unlucky〔evil, ill-fated〕 year〔age〕 ; a critical age ¶ 작년은 나에게는 액년이었다 Last year was an ill-fated year for me. // 한국에서는 39세가 남자의 액년이다 In Korea thirty-nine is the critical age for a man.

액달 厄— an unlucky〔evil, ill-fated, a critical〕 month ¶ 이 달은 액달이었다 This month was an unlucky month〔one〕 for me.

액때우다 厄— escape〔prevent〕 a misfortune by undergoing beforehand one of lesser degree

액땜 厄— an escape from misfortune by undergoing beforehand one of lesser degree ; [액막이] driving away〔getting rid of〕 devils ; exorcism ¶ 액땜으로 알다 bear a mishap rather willingly as the price for forestalling a misfortune of greater degree

액량 液量 liquid measure

액막이 厄— preventing〔forestalling〕 misfortune ; warding off evil ; exorcism ; protecting 《a person》 from〔against〕 evils **—하다** prevent〔ward off, take steps against〕 misfortune ; drive away evils ; protect 《a person》 from evils

—굿 a yearly exorcism by a shaman **—부적** a charm〔talisman〕 against misfortune〔evil〕

액면 液面 the surface (of a liquid)

액면 額面 face-value ; par value ; a denomination ¶ 1,000원과 5,000원의 액면 denomination of 1,000 *won* and 5,000 *won* // 액면 이하로〔이상으로〕 below〔above〕 par ; at a discount〔premium〕 // 액면 그대로 1,000주 사다 buy one thousand shares at par // 액면에서 200원 하락하다 fall 200 *won* below par // 그 소문은 액면대로 받아들일 수 없다 We cannot take the rumor at its face value. // 네 말

을 액면대로 받아들이겠다 I will take you at your word. // 국민은 그 공동 성명을 액면 그대로 받아 들였다 The people took the communique at its facevalue.
— 금액 nominal value — 상환 redemption at par value
액모 腋毛 underarm〔armpit, axillary〕 hair ; hair of the armpit
액비 液肥 a liquefied fertilizer ; liquefied manure
액사 縊死 death by hanging —하다 die by hanging ; hang〔strangle〕 oneself
액살 縊殺 murder by strangling —하다 strangle 《a person》 to death
액상 液狀 ¶ 액상의 liquefied // 액상을 유지하다 keep〔remain〕 liquefied
액세서리 accessories ; accessaries ¶ (양재에서) 액세서리를 달다 wear accessaries ; wear trimmings 《on the suit, coat》
액셀러레이터 an accelerator (pedal) ¶ 액셀러레이터를 밟다 step〔press〕 on the accelerator〔gas pedal〕 ; push〔shove〕 one's foot down on the accelerator ; push down〔press on〕 the gas
액션 action
— 드라마 an action drama
액수 額數 a sum ; an amount ; a volume ; a number ¶ 큰〔적은〕 액수 a large〔small〕 amount of money // 상당한 액수 a good sum of money ; a good round sum ; a sizable amount of money ; a considerable sum of money 《미》 // 액수로 해서 100만원 정도 about a million *won* in value // 엄청난 액수에 달하다 reach a colossal amount ; amount 〔come up, run up〕 to big figures // 손해를 본 액수는 500만원에 달한다 The damage amounts to five million *won*.
액아 腋芽 〖식물〗 axillary buds
액운 厄運 calamity ; misfortune ; disaster ; adverse fortune ; ill luck ; bad (luck) ¶ 액운을 당하다 have a misfortune ; meet (with) a disaster ; come to grief // 액운을 면하다 escape a disaster 〔calamity〕
액월 厄月 ⇨ 액달(厄—)
액자 額子 a (picture) frame ¶ 액자에 끼운 결혼 사진 a framed wedding picture // 액자에 끼우다 set〔put〕 《a picture》 in frame ; frame 《a picture》
액자 額字 letters written on a signboard 〔tablet〕
액즙 液汁 juice ; sap ⇨ 즙(汁)
‡액체 液體 a liquid ; a fluid ¶ 액체의 liquid ; fluid
— 공기〔암모니아〕 liquid air〔ammonia〕 — 동력학 hydrodynamics — 비중계 a hydrometer ; an aerometer ; a spindle — 비중 측정법 hydrometry ; aerometry — 압력 hydraulic pressure — 연료 liquid fuel — 온도계〔열량계〕 a liquid thermometer〔calorimeter〕 — 정력학 hydrostatics — 탄산 liquid carbon dioxide
액취 腋臭 underarm〔armpit〕 odor ; the (offensive) smell of an armpit
액화 液化 liquefaction —하다 liquefy 《coal》 ; be liquefied ; become〔turn to〕 liquid ¶ 액화하기 쉬운 liquescent
— 가스 liquefied gas —기 a liquefier — 온도 the temperature of liquefaction 석탄 — liquefaction of coal
액화 厄禍 [재앙] a calamity ; a disaster ; [불행] a misfortune ; an evil ; [사고] an accident
앤생이 a weak person〔thing〕 ; a weakling ; a fragile thing
앤저스 ANZUS 《Australia, New Zealand, the United States of America (Security Treaty)》
†앨범 an album ¶ 붙이는 앨범 a paste-in album // 끼워넣는 앨범 a slip-in album // 앨범에 붙이다〔끼우다〕 paste〔slip〕 《a picture》 in an album
앰풀 an ampoule ; an ampule
앰프 [증폭기] an amplifier ¶ 앰프를 단 기타 an amplified guitar
앳되다 look young ; (be) childlike
앵[1] [소리] 《with》 a buzz ; a hum ; a drone ; a whiz ; a zoom ¶ 모기가 귓가에서 앵앵댔다 The mosquitoes buzzed about my ears. // 앵 달리다 hum along
앵[2] [불쾌할 때] Oof ! ; Oh ! ; Hmph !
앵글로색슨 Anglo-Saxon
— 민족 the Anglo-Saxon race ; the Anglo-Saxons
앵돌아지다 make an abrupt turn ; turn one's back ; turn sulky ; get cross ; be angry with 《a person》 ¶ 그 여자는 조금만 야단쳐도 앵돌아진다 She gets sulky at the slightest scolding.
앵두 〖식물〗 a cherry ¶ 앵두 같은 입술 lips as red as a cherry
—나무 Prunus tomentosa (학명)
‡앵무새 鸚鵡— a parrot ; a parakeet ¶ 앵무새처럼 남의 말을 외다 repeat〔echo〕 《a person's》 words
—병 psittacosis ; parrot fever〔disease〕
— 조개 a (pearly) nautilus
앵미 rice of an inferior quality ; poor rice
앵속 罌粟 〖식물〗 a poppy
—화 a poppy (flower)
앵앵 humming ; buzzing ; droning ¶ 앵앵거리다 hum ; buzz ; whig ; zoom // 모기가 앵앵거리는 소리를 들었다 I heard the faint hum of a mosquito. // 탈곡기가 딱정벌레들처럼 앵앵 돌아갔다 The threshing machine was droning like a gigantic swarm of beetles. // 먼 곳에서 비행기의 앵앵하는 소리가 들려왔다 There came a drone from a distant plane.
앵커리지 Anchorage
앵하다 (be) resentful〔remorseful〕 ; feel bitter〔offended〕 ; be in the blues ¶ 손해를 봐서 앵하다 feel bitter〔remorseful〕 about one's loss

야 ① [놀라서] Oh!/Oh dear!/Good heavens!/Dear me!/O my!/My eye!/Good gracious! ¶ 야 큰일 저질렀구나 O my! Now you've done it! // 야 모자를 놓고 왔다 Dear me! I've left my hat behind.
② [부를 때] Hey (you)!/Hey there! ¶ 야 너는 누구냐 Hey there, who are you?

야 野 ① [들] a field; a plain; a farm ② [야당] an opposition party; [민간] being outside the government ¶ 야에 있다 be in opposition (야당에); be in private life; remain out of office // 그는 야에 있는 지 벌써 9년이다 He has been nine years out of government service.

*야간 夜間 night; the night time ¶ 야간의 night; nocturnal // 야간에 at〔by〕 night
— 개장 opening at night — 경기 a night game〔match〕 — 근무 night duty; night work〔shift〕 — 당직 a night watch〔duty〕 — 도주 flight by night —부 the evening section of a school — 비행 a night flight; night flying — 연습 a night practice〔exercise〕 — 외출 금지 a curfew — 촬영 photographing at night; night photography — 통행 금지 a curfew — 통화 a night telephone call — 폭격 night bombing — 학생 an evening〔a night〕 school student

야거리 a one-mast boat

야견 野犬 a stray dog; a homeless 〔ownerless〕 dog ¶ 야견 몰이를 하다 round 〔hunt〕 up stray dogs

야경 夜景 a night view〔scene〕 ¶ 서울의 야경 a night view of *Seoul*
—화(畫) a night piece; a nocturne

야경 夜警 night watch; a night watchman (사람); a fire-watcher ¶ 야경하다 be on 〔stand〕 night watch; make the round 《of a district》 at night
—꾼 a night watchman〔watcher〕 —단 a vigilance corps〔committee〕

야경스럽다 夜警— (be) noisy〔clamorous, disturbing〕 in the night

야고보 〖성경〗 Jacob
—서 the Book of Jacob

야곡 夜曲 〖음악〗 a nocturne

야광 夜光 noctilucence ¶ 야광의 noctilucent
— 도료 a luminous paint — 시계 a luminous〔glow〕 watch; a watch with a luminous〔an illuminated〕 dial —주(珠) a gem that emits light at night〔in the dark〕 —충(蟲) a noctiluca 《*pl.* -cae》; a phosphorescent animalcule

†야구 野球 baseball; ball (game) ¶ 고려대학과 연세대학의 야구 시합 a baseball game between *Korea* University and *Yonsei* University // 야구를 하다 play baseball // 야구 시합을 하다 have〔hold〕 a baseball game〔match〕 《with》; play a baseball game 《with》; cross bats 《with》
—계 baseball circles; the baseball world —공 a baseball —부 a baseball club ¶ 야구부장 the president of a baseball club // 야구부 주장 the captain of a baseball team — 선수 a baseball player; a ballplayer; the nine 《선수 전원》 —열 a baseball fever; a mania for baseball —장 a ball park; a diamond; a baseball field 〔ground〕 —팀 a baseball team —팬 a baseball fan 직업 —단 a professional baseball team 직업 — 선수 a professional baseball player; a pro ballplayer 《미·구》 ☞ ◖p. 1422◗

야근 夜勤 night duty; night work; nightshift —하다 take night duty; be on night work〔night-shift〕 ¶ 야근 중이다 be on night duty
— 수당 night-work〔overtime〕 allowance — 시간 night-shift〔-work hours〕 —자 a night worker; a night clerk (사무원); night shift 《총칭》

야금 冶金 metallurgy
— 공장 a metallurgical works — 기사 a metallurgical engineer —술 (technique, art of) metallurgy —업 metallurgical industry〔enterprise〕 —학 (the science of) metallurgy —학자 a metallurgist 건식 —법 pyrometal-lurgy 습식 —법 hydrometallurgy

야금 野禽 a wild bird〔fowl〕

야금거리다 eat by bites

야금야금 bit by bit; bite by bite —하다 take repeated little bites ⇨ 야금거리다 ¶ 야금야금 먹다 eat by bits; eat a little bit at a time // 야금야금 먹어 들어가다 eat into little by little; invade gradually; encroach

야긋야긋하다 (be) notched; jagged; have teeth

야기 夜氣 [밤공기] night air; [냉기] the cool of the night

†야기 惹起 —하다 bring about〔on〕; cause; arouse; create; give rise〔birth〕 to; provoke; lead to ¶ 문제를 야기하다 raise a problem // 전쟁을 야기하다 bring about〔on〕 a war; provoke a war // 물의를 야기하다 lead to controversy // 그의 연설이 대소동을 야기했다 His speech gave rise to great commotions. // 무엇이 세계대전을 야기했느냐 What was the cause of〔caused, brought about〕 the World War? // 압제가 국민의 반란을 야기했다 Oppression provoked the people to rebellion. // 그것이 이 전쟁을 야기한 직접적 원인의 하나였다 It was one of the immediate causes of the war. // 그의 연설은 교육계에 문제를 야기했다 His speech occasioned a stir in educational circles.

야기부리다 scold 《at》; rate 《a person》 roundly; grumble 《at》; murmur 《at》; chide; grouse 《속》 ¶ 그는 골이 나면 누구에게나 야기부린다 He works off his anger〔bad temper〕 on everybody around

야 구

1 야구 용어

① 투수 및 투구

▶투수 pitcher / 우완 투수 right-handed pitcher; right-hander / 좌완 투수 left-handed pitcher; left-hander; southpaw; lefty 《속》/ 선발 투수 starting pitcher; starter / 구원 투수 relief pitcher; reliever; fire fighter 《속》; fireman / 승리[패배] 투수 winning [losing] pitcher / 속구 투수 fastball pitcher; fastballer / 주전 투수 ace pitcher

▶투구 pitching; delivery; serving / 마운드 mound; hill / 투구판 pitcher's plate / 속구 fastball / 커브 curve / 보크 balk / 변화구 breaking ball / 스크루 볼 screw ball; odd-ball / 슬라이더 slider / 싱커 sinker / 땅 볼 grounder / 체인지 업 change-up; change of pace / 포크 볼 fork ball / 피치아웃 pitchout / 스트라이크 strike / 볼 ball / 폭투(爆投) wild throw; wild pitch / 사구(死球) hit-batter; hit by pitch / (고의) 사구(四球) (an intentional) base on balls; pass; walk / 견제 pick-off / 삼진(三振) strikeout / 자책점 earned run / 방어율 earned run average / 세이브 save / 파울 foul

② 야수 및 수비

▶포수 catcher / 내야수 infielder / 1 [2, 3] 루수 first [second, third] baseman / 외야수 outfielder; fly-chaser; fly-hawk / 좌[우]익수 left [right] fielder / 중견수 center fielder / 유격수 shortstop / 수비 fielding / 수비 연습 fielding practice / 시합전의 연습 pre-game drill / 중간 수비 halfway position / 병살 double play / 중계플레이 cut-off play / 에러 error / 야수 선택 fielder's choice / 수비[타격] 방해 interference / 주루(走壘) 방해 obstruction (★ 공을 놓치다 drop; fumble; flub; fluff)

③ 타자 및 타구

▶타자 batter; hitter / 1번 타자 lead-off (batter) / 강타자 slugger; power [long] hitter; power house / 수위 타자 leading hitter; batting crown / 3관왕 triple crown / 지명 타자 designated hitter / 대타자 pinch hitter / 스위치 히터 switch-hitter / 4번 타자 cleanup / 대주자(代走者) pinch runner / 주자 runner / 안타 base hit; single / 연속 안타 barrage / 집중타 rally / 내야 안타 infield hit / 2루타 double; two-base hit; two-bagger / 3루타 triple; three-base hit; three-bagger / 적시 안타 timely hit / 단타(單打) single; one-base hit; one bagger / 홈런 home run; homer; four-bagger / 만루의 bases loaded / 만루 홈런 grand slam (homer); bases-loaded homer / 선제 홈런 lead off home run / 경기 종료 홈런 game-ending home run / 필드 홈런 inside-the-park home run; field home run / 결승 홈런 game-winning home run / 세이프 safe / 플라이 fly / 라이너 liner / 도루(盜壘) steal / 스퀴즈플레이 squeeze play / 내야 뜬공 infield pop; pop-up / 드래그 번트 drag bunt / 희생 번트 sacrifice bunt / 희생 플라이 sacrifice fly / 타율 batting average

④ 야구장

▶구장(球場) stadium; ballpark / 내야 diamond; the infield / 외야 the outfield / 더그아웃 dugout / 본루(本壘) home (plate) / 1루(一壘) first (base) / 2루(二壘) second (base) / 3루(三壘) third (base) / 벤치 bench / 불펜 bullpen / 펜스 fence / 타자석 batter's box / 코치 박스 coach's box / 관람석 stands / 내야석 infield bleachers / 외야석 outfield bleachers / 파울라인 foul line / 점수판 scoreboard / 백네트 backstop

⑤ 심판·감독

▶구심 plate umpire / 주심 umpire-in-chief; chief umpire / 누심(壘審) base umpire / 감독 manager; pilot / 코치 coach / 구단(球團) (ball) club

⑥ 경기

▶득점 runs / 낙승 romp / 연승 [패] winning[losing] streak / 접전 clinched game; clincher / 일방적인 경기 one-sided game / 역전승 come-from-behind game / 투수전 pitcher's game; pitching duel / 무안타 경기 no-hitter / 무안타 무득점 경기 no-no / 타격전 batting duel; slugfest / 완전 시합 perfect game / 연장전 extrainning game / 타율 batting average / 타점 RBI(runs batted in) / 타점왕 RBI king / 승리 타점 game winning runs batted in / 홈런왕 home run king / 아웃 out; away / 오픈 경기 exhibition game / 자유 계약 선수 free agent/주간(晝間) 경기 day game / 야간(夜間) 경기 night game / 무승부 tied game; drawn game / 몰수(沒收) 경기 forfeited game / 더블헤더 double-header; twin bill (★제1 시합은 opener, 제2 시합은 nightcap) / 게임차(差) games behind; deficiency / 리그 승패 성적 game [league] standing / 회(回) inning; stanza / 회 초(初) first half; top / 회 말(末) second half; bottom / 공격측 팀 team at bat / 수비측 팀 fielding team; team in the field; field / 협살(挾殺) rundown / 동네 야구 sandlot baseball (★홈 그라운드에서 시합하다 playing at home (ground); playing as host[franchise team] / 상대 구장에서 시합하다 playing as visitors)

② 야구의 표현

① 승패에 관한 표현

¶ 시합은 비겼다. The game was tied. / The game ended in a tie. // 타이거스가 자이언츠와의 더블헤더에서 승리했다. The Tigers swept the double-header with the Giants. / The Tigers took both ends of the twin bill with the Giants. // 오비 베어스팀이 롯데 자이언츠팀을 5대 0으로 이겼다. The OB Bears beat[defeated, downed] the Lotte Giants by the score of five to zero. // 타이거스팀이 3연승 후에 처음으로 패했다. The Tigers suffered their first loss after three straight wins. // 지난해 내셔널리그 챔피언인 타이거스팀이 시즌 첫 경기에서 패했다. Last year's National League champion Tigers lost their first game of the season.

② 타구에 관한 표현

¶ 그는 좌측 관람석에 홈런을 날렸다. He hitted a home run into the left field stands. // 그는 좌익에 안타를 쳤다. He singled to left. // 그는 3회초[3회말] 좌중간[우중간]에 3루타를 날렸다. He hit [blasted] a triple into left center [right center] (field) in the top[bottom] of the 3rd inning. // 그의 내야 뜬공으로 투아웃이 되었다. He popped out for second out. // 그는 세번째 타석에서 2타점을 올렸다. He drove in two runs in his three at bats. // 그의 2루타로 두점을 얻었다. He drove in two runs with a double. // 그의 타율은 3할 1푼 1리이다. He has a hitting average of .311. // 그는 희생타로 3루 주자를 홈으로 불러들였다. He lofted a sacrifice fly to call in the runner from third. // 그는 9회에 만루 필드 홈런을 날렸다. He slammed a bases-loaded inside-the-park homer in the ninth inning. // 존의 1루타로 스미스가 홈인했다. Smith scored on John's single. // 그는 3루측 땅볼로 아웃되었다. He grounded out to third.

③ 투구에 관한 표현

¶ 그는 15게임에 출장하고 있다. He has pitched[hurled] 15 games. // 그는 투구에 난조를 보이고 있다. He is having control trouble. / He is having trouble with his control. // 그의 역투로 양키스가 레드삭스를 2 대 1로 제압했다. He pitched the Red Sox to 2-1 victory over the Yankees. // 그는 15경기에 등판해서 3승 2패의 성적을 거두었다. He appeared in fifteen games with a three(-to-)two [3-2] record. / He was three (to) two [3-2] in fifteen appearances. // 그는 52경기에 출전해서 3.14의 방어율을 기록하고 있다. He appeared in 52 games and had a 3.14 earned-run average. // 자이언츠팀에서 출전한 3명의 피처는 단 1개의 안타만을 허용하였다. Three Giants pitchers allowed only one hit. // 베어스팀은 강력한 투수진을 확보하고 있다. The Bears have a strong[great] pitching staff. // 그의 완투로 금년 시즌의 첫 개가를 올렸다. He went the distance [route] for his first victory of the season. // 그는 윌슨을 3구 3진으로 물리쳤다. He struck out Wilson on three pitches. // 톰슨은 빌리를 사구로 내보냈다. Tomson walked Billy to load the bases. // 투수가 1루 주자를 연달아 견제했다. The pitcher threw to first again and again to hold the runner close [check the runner]. // 원아웃 풀카운트에서 존은 사구를 얻었다. With one out, John walked[drew a walk] on a full count[3-2 pitch]. // 구원투수 화이트가 승리를 움켜쥐었다. The win[victory] went to reliever White. / Reliever White got[gained] credit for the win[victory]. // 신인 존슨에게 패배를 안겨주었다. Rookie Johnson was charged with the loss. / The loss went [was charged] to rookie Johnson. // 양키스는 단타로 2명의 주자를 내보냈다. The Yankees put two runners on with singles.

④ 수비에 관한 표현

¶ 이번에는 양키스가 수비이다. The Yankees are fielding now. // 그는 내야 외야 모두 능하다. He can play outfield as well as infield. // 그는 1루를 맡았다. He played first base. // 레즈팀의 내야 수비는 강하다. The Reds have a sure-handed infield. // 다저스팀의 1루수가 6회 말[초]에 중대한 실책를 범했다. The Dodger's first baseman committed a costly error in the bottom[top] of the sixth inning.

⑤ 주자에 관한 표현

¶ 그는 2루 도루에 완벽하게 성공했다. He made a clean steal of [to] second base. / He cleanly stole second. // 그는 한 게임에서 세 번의 도루에 성공했다. He stole three bases in a single game. // 그는 이번 시즌에서 여덟번째 도루를 했다.

He stole his eighth base of the season. // 그는 도루왕이다. He leads in the number of bases stolen. / He holds the record in the number of bases stolen. // 그는 3루로[홈으로] 슬라이딩을 했으나 터치아웃되었다. He was touched out sliding into third[home (plate)]. // 그는 2루에 머리부터 슬라이딩을 하여 세이프되었다. He slid head-first into second safely.

him.

야뇨증 夜尿症 bed-wetting ; enuresis

야다하면 if there is no help for it ; if compelled〔forced〕 ¶ 야다하면 그만두어라 If you are in a fix, don't trouble yourself further.

야단 惹端 ① [소란] a clamor ; an uproar ; a row ; a commotion ; [곤란] a trouble ; a plight ; a fix **―하다** be uproarious〔in commotion〕 ¶ 급료를 올리라고 야단이다 clamor for a higher wage ; clamor for a pay raise // 참 야단났다 Well, what a fine fix this is ! / Things have come to a pretty pass ! // 비가 곧 안 온다면 야단나겠는데 If it doesn't rain soon, we'll be in a hell of a fix.
② [호령·호통] scolding ; giving 《a person》 a scolding ; chiding ; rebuke ¶ 야단치다 give a good scolding〔talking〕 《to》 ; bawl 《a person》 out ; scold violently ; rebuke ; dress down // 야단맞다 be scolded roundly ; get a sharp scolding // 장난하는 아이를 야단치다 scold a boy for his mischief // 들키면 야단맞는다 If you are found out, you will catch it. // 그 여자는 말을 듣지 않아서 어머니한테 야단맞았다 She was reproved by her mother for disobedience. // 그는 회사에 늦어서 야단맞았다 He got into a row for being late at the office. // 아무것도 아닌 걸 가지고 야단치지 마세요 Don't chew me out for nothing. // 시험 점수가 나빠 부모님한테 야단맞을 게 걱정이다 I get a bad grade, and I'm afraid of getting a dressing down from my parents. // 그는 상사한테 심하게 야단을 맞았다 The boss fairly tore into him.

*****야단법석 野壇法席** a boisterous merry-making ; a spree ; a racket
―하다 have high jinks ; go〔be〕 on the spree ¶ 이웃집에서 왜 야단법석인지 모르겠구나 I wonder what all the racket's about next door. // 아이들의 짓궂은 장난에 야단법석 떨지 마시요 Don't make such a fuss all the time about kids' pranks.

야단스럽다 惹端― (be) noisy ; clamorous ; uproarious ; tumultuous ; vociferous

야담 野談 a historical romance ; an unofficial historical story〔tale〕
―가 a (professional) historical story-teller ; a historical romancer **―책** a story book

*****야당 野黨** a party out of〔not in〕 power ; a nongovernment party ; an opposition party ; [2대 정당의 경우] the opposition ; the outs ¶ 야당의 영수 the Opposition leader ; the leader of the Opposition // 그의 당은 야당이다 His party is in opposition〔out〕.
― 공세 an offensive (move) taken by the outs against the government **― 당수〔기관지〕** an Opposition leader〔organ〕 **― 연합** a combination of parties out of power ; coalition between nongovernment parties **― 의석** the Opposition benches **― 통합** merger of the opposition parties **제1 ―** the leading opposition

야당스럽다 ⇨ 매몰스럽다

야도 夜盜 [도둑] a night thief ; a burglar ; [도둑질] burglary ¶ 야도짓을 하다 commit burglary

야도충 夜盜蟲 a night crawler ; an army worm ; a nightwalker 《영》

야독 夜讀 reading at night ; night study **―하다** read in the night ; study till late at night

야드 a yard 《yd.》 ¶ 1 야드에 얼마로 팔다 sell by the yard
―자 a yard ; a yardstick **― 줄자** a yard tape **―파운드법** the yard-pound system of measurement

야드르하다, 야드를하다 ⇨ 야들야들하다

야들야들하다 (be) soft and delicate ; soft ; shiny ¶ 야들야들한 손 soft and delicate hands // 야들야들한 가죽 supple leather // 감촉이 야들야들하다 feel soft ; be soft to the touch // 야들야들하게 하다 soften ; tenderize

야료 惹鬧 heckling ; catcalling ; jeering ; hooting ; denouncing
―하다 disturb ; hoot 《at》 ; heckle ; catcall 《at》 ; jeer ; interrupt〔heckle〕 《a speaker》 ; hiss〔shout, hoot〕 down 《a person》 ¶ 그는 청중들로부터 야료를 당했다 He was jeered (at) by his audience. // 그는 연설을 하려고 일어섰으나 청중의 야료로 물러났다 He stood up to speak but his audience cried 〔hissed〕 him down.
―꾼 an interrupter ; a hooter

야릇하다 (be) queer ; strange ; odd ; peculiar ; curious ¶ 야릇한 꿈 a strange dream // 야릇한 사람 a queer person ; an oddity // 야릇한 기분이다 feel strange // 야릇한 얼굴을 하다 make a queer face ; look puzzled // 야릇하게 굴다 behave oddly // 운명이란 야릇하다 Fate plays strange tricks.

야리다 ① [여리다] (be) soft ; tender ; frail ; fragile ⇨ 여리다 ¶ 야린 빛깔 a soft〔light〕 color ② [조금 모자라다] be not enough ⟪for⟫ ; be insufficient ⟪for⟫ ; be short ⟪of⟫ ¶ 옷감이 야리다 The material is a little short to make a suit of clothes.

야마 野馬 a wild horse

†**야만 野蠻** savagery ; savageness ; barbarity ; barbarism **—하다** (be) savage ; barbarous ; barbarian ; barbaric ; uncivilized

> 참고 **barbarian** 「문명적」「문화가 있는」 civilized에 반대되는 말로서 「미개의」 「문화의 영역에 이르지 못한」 상태를 뜻함 **barbarous** barbarian의 나쁜 면 (흉악 난폭 무지 잔인 따위)을 강조한 말로서 때로는 문명인 문명사회의 야만적 면을 나타내는 데에도 쓰인다 **barbaric** 주로 취미 기호 따위의 조악함을 나타낸다

¶ 야만적 풍습 uncivilized manners ; a barbaric custom // 야만적 행위 a barbarous act ; (act of) barbarity // 이 습관은 야만 시대의 유물이다 This custom is a relic of the barbaric times. // 세계의 어느 지방에서는 주민들이 아직도 야만적 생활을 하고 있다 People are still living in barbarism in some parts of the world.

—국 an uncivilized land〔country, nation〕 **— 시대** the barbaric times 〔age〕 ; barbarous days **—인** a savage ; a barbarian ; an uncivilized man ; a wild man ; savage〔barbarous〕 people

야말로 indeed ; just ; only ; exactly ¶ 너야말로 잘못이다 It is you that are in the wrong. // 이것이야말로 내가 찾고 있던 책이다 This is the very book (that) I have been looking for. // 나야말로 용서를 빌어야 하겠습니다 It is I who must apologize. // 이번에야말로 찾아가 뵙겠소 I shall call on you without fail this time. // 그거야말로 우리가 구하던 것이다 That's the very thing. // 그야말로 적임자다 He's the right man ⟪for it⟫.

야망 野望 personal ambition ; aspiration ¶ 만만한 야망 a devouring〔consuming〕 ambition // 야망 있는 ambitious // 야망을 품다 have〔entertain, harbor〕 an ambition ; be ambitious // 야망을 실현하다 have one's ambition realized // 그는 사장이 되려는 야망을 가지고 있다 He has ambitions to become the president. // 미국은 쿠바에 대해서 조금도 영토적 야망이 없다고 그가 언명했다 He declared that the U.S. has no territorial design upon Cuba.

야맹 夜盲 〖의학〗 nyctalopia ; night blindness

야멸스럽다 (be) cold-hearted ; unfeeling ; heartless ; stone-hearted ; callous ; inconsiderate ; insensible ¶ 야멸스러운 행동 an inconsiderate action // 남의 기분을 몰라주는 야멸스러움 a callous disregard for the feelings of others // 그는 야멸스러운 사나이다 He has a heart of stone. /He has no feelings. // 나는 그러한 야멸스러운 짓을 못한다 I have not the heart to do such a cruel thing. // 나를 야멸스럽다고 그 여자는 말한다 She says my heart is a stone.

야멸치다 (be) cold-hearted ⇨ 야멸스럽다 ¶ 야멸치게 뿌리치다 reject〔refuse〕 flatly // 너는 정말 야멸치구나 How inconsiderate you are ! /How unkind of you !

야무지다 (be) stout ; sturdy ; hard-headed ; staunch ¶ 야무지게 firmly ; securely ; steadily // 야무진 사람 a man of firm character // 야무진 성품 a stout-minded〔hard-headed〕 man ; a staunch character // 야무지게 한 일 dependable work // 야무지게 묶다 tie tightly〔fast〕 ; fasten tight // 야무지게 붙들다 hold ⟪a thing⟫ tightly〔fast〕 ; hold on fast to a strap // 저 집은 야무지게 지어져 있다 The house is substantially built. // 저 남자에게는 야무진 데가 없다 He lacks firmness of character. /He has no backbone.

야물거리다 mumble

야물다 ① [익다] ripen ; get ripe ; mature ② (be) stout ⇨ 야무지다

야바위 trickery ; swindle ; fraud ; imposture ; deception ¶ 5만원을 야바위당하다 be swindled out off 50,000 *won*

야바위치다 관용 play a trick upon ⟪a person⟫ ; cheat〔swindle〕 ⟪a person⟫ ; pull the wool over ⟪a person's eyes⟫ ; sell ⟪a person⟫ a bill of goods

야박 野薄 heartlessness ; stinginess **—하다** (be) hard-hearted ; cool-hearted ; unkind ; unfeeling ; stingy ¶ 야박한 세상 this barren world ; this cold hearted 〔heartless, cruel〕 world // 야박한 짓을 하다 behave in a heartless manner // 그들은 야박한 인간들이다 They are people without feelings.

야반 夜半 midnight ; the middle of the night ¶ 야반의 midnight // 야반에 at midnight ; at dead of night ; in the middle of the night // 야반의 달 a midnight moon // 야반까지 공부하다 work till late in the night ; burn the midnight oil ; study far into the night

— 도주 flight by night ¶ 야반 도주하다 run away under cover of night ; flee by night ; give ⟪a person⟫ the slip **— 도주자** a fly-by-night(er) ⟪미·속⟫

야발 ⇨ 야살

야밤중 夜— the middle of the night

야번 夜番 night watch ; duty at night ; night guard ; [사람] a night watchman ; a night watcher ¶ 야번을 하다 keep night watch ; be on duty at night ; be on night duty

*⁎***야비 野卑** vulgarity ; coarseness ; meanness ; bad taste **—하다** (be) vulgar ;

coarse ; mean ¶ 야비한 사람 a vulgar〔contemptible〕 fellow // 야비한 말 a vulgar expression ; vulgarism ; coarse language // 야비한 태도 a coarse manner // 야비한 취미〔풍습〕 unrefined〔boorish, vulgar〕 taste〔customs〕 // 그런 일을 하는 것은 야비하다 It is bad taste to do such a thing. // 그 사람의 이야기는 너무 야비해서 들을 수가 없다 His talk is too low to listen to.

야비다리치다 feign〔affect〕 humility ; pretend modesty

야사 野史 an unofficial〔unauthorized〕 history〔chronicle〕

야산 野山 a hill (on a plain) ; a hillock

야살 peevishness ; perverseness ; crabbedness ¶ 야살스럽다 be perverse ; be peevish ; be impertinent ; be saucy ; be crabbed ; be cross-grained // 야살 떨다 behave in a saucy manner ; be cross ; do something impudent

—쟁이 a peevish〔cross〕 person ; an impertinent〔saucy〕 fellow ; a crab

야살부리다 behave impudently〔impertinently, insolently〕

야상곡 夜想曲 〖음악〗 a nocturne

†**야생 野生** ¶ 야생의 wild ; uncultivated **—하다** grow wild ; grow without cultivation ¶ 벼는 야생하지 않는다 Rice does not grow wild. // 이 식물은 야생이다 These plants grow wild.

— 과일 wild fruit **— 생물** [총칭] wildlife ; wilding **— 식물〔동물〕** wild plants〔animals〕 **—화(化)** going wild

야성 野性 wild〔savage, unpolished〕 nature ; brutal nature ; rusticity ; uncouthness ; boorishness ¶ 야성적 wild〔boorish〕 // 야성을 나타내다 [동물이] run wild ; [사람이] give vent to one's savage instinct ; commit barbarity

—미(美) unpolished beauty **—미(味)** an air of roughness〔being untamed〕 ¶ 그에게는 야성미가 있다 There is something rough about him. **—아(兒)** a wild boy

야성화 野性化 going wild **—하다** go wild ; become feral ¶ 야성화한 《cattle》 gone wild ; turned feral

야소 耶蘇 ⇨ 예수

—교 ⇨ 기독교

야속 野俗 —하다 (be) cold-hearted ; heartless ; unfeeling ; unfriendly ; unkind ; cruel ; inconsiderate ¶ 야속한 마음 a cold〔an unfeeling〕 heart ; a heart of stone // 야속한 말을 하다 speak cruelly〔heartlessly〕 ; say a harsh〔mean〕 thing // 야속하게 굴다 be hard on 《a person》 ; behave coldly 《towards》 // 야속하게 거절하다 give 《a person》 a point-blank 〔flat〕 refusal // 나는 그런 야속한 짓은 못하겠다 It is not in my nature to do such a thing. /I have not the heart to do such a thing.

***야수 野獸** a wild beast〔animal〕 ¶ 야수같은 beastly ; beastlike ; brutal

—성 brutality ; bestiality ; brutal〔bestial〕 nature **—파** 〖미술〗 [화가] a Fauvist ; a Fauve ; [주의] Fauvism

야수 野手 〖야구〗 a fielder

— 선택 《be safe on》 a fielder's choice

내— an infielder **외—** an outfielder

야수다 watch for a chance ; wait for an opportunity

야숙 野宿 ⇨ 노숙(露宿)

야순 夜巡 night watch ; night patrol **—하다** beat the round at night ; go on one's rounds at night ; be on night patrol

야스락거리다, 야슬거리다 chatter ; talk profusely ; be verbose ; be prolix ; perorate

야스락야스락, 야슬야슬 in a profuse〔wordy〕 way ; profusely

야습 夜襲 a night attack〔raid, assault〕 ; a surprise by night ; a nocturnal sortie **—하다** make〔attempt〕 a night attack 《on the enemy》 ; [비행기로] make a night raid 《on *Tokyo*》

야시 夜市 a night market ; a market open in the evening

—점 a night stall ¶ 야시점을 내다 open〔set up〕 a night stall

야식 夜食 [저녁밥] supper ; [밤참] a late snack ; a midnight meal ¶ 야식을 먹다 have a midnight snack

야심 夜深 being late at night **—하다** be late at night ¶ 야심토록 일하다 work far into the night // 야심토록 책을 읽다 sit far into the night reading // 우리는 야심토록 서로 이야기했다 We talked far into the night.

‡**야심 野心** [야망] ambition ; aspiration (포부) ; [음모] a sinister design ; an intrigue ¶ 야심적 ambitious ; [음모적] designing ; treacherous // 야심 없는 unambitious ; disinterested // 만만한 야심 a devouring〔consuming〕 ambition // 엉뚱한 야심 an inordinate ambition // 야심을 품다 have〔entertain, harbor〕 an ambition ; be ambitious // 야심 만만하다 burn with〔be full of〕 ambition ; be highly ambitious // 영토적 야심을 갖지 않다 have no territorial ambition // 야심을 실현하다 have one's ambition realized // 그는 야심이 전혀 없는 남자다 He is quite without ambition. /He is too tame. // 회장이 되고자 하는 야심이 있다 He has ambitions to become the president.

—가 an ambitious〔enterprising〕 person ; a man of ambition ; a highflyer ; a schemer

야업 夜業 night work ; evening work ; [야근] a night shift **—하다** work at night ; [공장이] operate at night ; do a night shift ; do night work

— 수당 an allowance for night work ; a nightwork allowance ; overtime〔O/T〕 allowance

야연 夜宴 an evening party〔banquet〕 ¶ 야연을 베풀다 give〔hold〕 an evening party

＊**야영 野營** a camp ; camping ; military encampment in the country〔in the open air〕; bivouac **—하다** camp (out) ; make camp ; encamp ; bivouac
— 연습 camping exercises **—자** a camper **—지** a camping ground ; a campsite ; a bivouac **— 행군** a camping trip

야옹 mewing ¶ 야옹하고 울다 mew

⁑**야외 野外** [들판] the fields ; [옥외] the open air ; [교외] the outskirts《of a town》; the suburbs《of a city》 ¶ 야외의 field ; open-air ; outdoor ; out-of-door // 야외에서 in the open air ; out of door // 야외로 산보나가다 take a stroll out of town // 당시 인간은 야외에서 난폭한 생활을 보냈다 In those days men lived a rough-and-ready life in the open air.
— 강연 a field〔an open-air〕 lecture **— 경기** field games **— 교련** field training ; field military drill **—극** an outdoor play ; a pageant ¶ 야외극을 상연하다 give a play on an open-air stage ; give a pageant **— 극장** an outdoor theater **— 사생** outdoor sketching **— 승마** cross-country riding **— 연설** an open-air〔outdoor〕 speech **— 연습** field exercises ; field work **— 연습일** a field day **— 연주회** an open-air concert **— 요리** a cookout **— 운동** outdoor〔field〕 exercises〔sports〕 **— 작업** field work ; field study **— 촬영** location

야우 夜雨 rainfall at night

야운데 Yaoundé (카메룬의 수도)

⁑**야위다** become〔get〕 thin〔lean〕; lose《one's》 weight ; grow gaunt ; lose flesh (병으로) ⇨ 여위다

＊**야유 揶揄** banter ; tease ; raillery ; chaff ; ridicule **—하다** make fun〔sport〕 of ; poke fun at ; banter《a person》 on〔about〕《a thing》; ridicule ¶ 야유하는 사람 a heckler // 여자를 야유하다 banter with a girl // 야유하여 연단에서 끌어내다 boo《a person》 off of the platform // 너를 야유하고 있는 거야 He's fooling〔making fun of〕 you. /He is pulling your leg, isn't he ?

야유 野遊 a picnic ; an outing ¶ 야유하러 가다 go on a picnic ; go picnicking
—회 a picnic party〔group〕

야유 夜遊 evening amusement ; night amusement〔pleasure〕 **—하다** go out in the evening for pleasure ; amuse oneself by night ¶ 야유에 나가다 go out pleasure-seeking at night
—객 a night-bird

야음 夜陰 the dark of night ; the dead of night ¶ 야음을 타고 under cover of darkness〔the night〕; taking advantage〔availing oneself〕 of darkness

야인 野人 [촌사람] a rustic ; a boor ; a bumpkin ; a countryman ; a farmer ; [재야인] a person out of official position

＊**야자 椰子** 〖식물〗 a coconut palm ; a coconut tree
— 열매 a coconut **—유** palm〔coconut〕 oil ; coconut milk

야장 冶匠 a (black) smith ; a metal worker ; a hammerman

야전 野戰 field operation ; field warfare ; a plain〔an open〕 battle
—군 the field army **— 병원** a field hospital **— 우체국** a field post-office **— 우편** the field-post ; mail〔post〕 for the field **— 잠바** a field jacket **— 장비** field equipment **— 전화** field telephone **— 통신** field communications **—포** a field gun ; a fieldpiece **— 포병** field artillery **— 포병 중대** a field battery

야전 夜戰 night operation **—하다** engage in night warfare

야조 夜鳥 a night-bird ; a nocturnal bird

야조 野鳥 a wild fowl ; wild birds
— 포획자 a fowler

야죽거리다 wag one's tongue in a flattering manner ; gabble flatteries

야지 野地 open fields ; the plains

야지랑 떨다 act〔behave〕 unabashfully and cunningly

야지랑스럽다 (be) unabashedly deceitful ; tricky ; sly ; provokingly cool

야지러지다 wane ; chip ⇨ 이지러지다

야짓 without skipping ; all ; thoroughly ; wholly ; entirely

야차 夜叉 a female demon ; a yaksa《범》

야찬 夜餐 a midnight snack

＊**야채 野菜** vegetables ; greens ; greenstuff ; garden truck (시판용의)《미》 ¶ 야채의 vegetable // 야채를 가꾸다 raise〔grow〕 vegetables ; grow garden truck
—밭 [가정의] a kitchen〔vegetable〕 garden ; [대규모의] a truck farm《미》; a market garden《영》 **—상** a vegetable peddler (행상) ; a greengrocer ; a greengrocery (가게) **— 샐러드** vegetable salad **— 수프** vegetable soup **— 요리** a vegetable〔vegetarian〕 dish ; greens ; dish of cooked green vegetables **— 프라이** fried vegetables

야청 —青 a dark blue color

야초 野草 wild grass〔herbs〕

야취 野趣 rural beauty ; rural scenery ; rusticity ¶ 야취 있는 rustic ; rural ; pastoral ; idyllic // 야취가 풍부하다 be rich in rustic beauty

야코죽다 feel small ; be overawed《by》

야코죽이다 overawe ; score off ; wipe the eye《of a shooter》

야크 〖동물〗 a yak《*pl.* ～s, [총칭] yak》
—털 yak hair

야트막하다 ⇨ 야틈하다

야틈하다 be somewhat〔rather〕 shallow〔light〕《in hue》

야포 野砲 a field-gun ; a fieldpiece ; field artillery 《총칭》
—대〔중대〕 a field-artillery corps〔battery〕
*__야하다 冶—__ [빛깔이] (be) gaudy ; too gay〔gaudy〕 《for a person》 ; flashy ; garish ¶ 야한 옷 gaudy clothes // 야하게 차려 입다 be gaudily〔loudly, flashily, conspicuously〕 dressed // 그 옷은 그 여자에게 야한 것 같다 The clothes look too gay〔young〕 for a woman of her age.
야학 夜學 an evening〔a night〕 class 《of a night school》 ¶ 동교의 야학부 the evening session of the school // 야학에 다니다 attend〔go to〕 night school ; attend an evening class // 야학에서 가르치다 teach an evening〔a night〕 school 〔class〕 // 야학에서 독일어를 배우다 learn German in an evening〔a night〕 class
—생 a night〔an evening〕 school pupil 〔student〕
야합 野合 an illicit union〔connection〕 ; [공모] collusion ; conspiracy **—하다** form an illicit connection ; have illicit intercourse ; [공모] plot together ; conspire 《with》 ; be in with 《a person》 ¶ 야합한 부부 a common-law couple // 야합으로 생긴 아이 a child born of an illicit connection // 야합하여 in collusion 〔conspiracy, league〕 《with》 // 야합하여 부부가 되다 marry〔jump〕 over the broomstick
*__야행 夜行__ night-traveling ; a night trip ; nocturnal travel ; travel by night **—하다** go〔travel〕 by night
— 동물 a nocturnal animal **—성** the nocturnal habit 《of an animal》
야화 野花 wild flowers
야화 野火 a field〔bush〕 fire ; a prairie fire
야화 夜話 a folk tale〔story〕
야회 夜會 an evening party ; a soirée 《프》 ; [무도회] a ball ¶ 야회를 개최하다 give〔hold〕 an evening party
—복 an evening dress ; evening clothes ; an evening suit ; [남자의] a dress coat
약 略 [축소] abbreviation ; curtailment ; [생략] omission ; [약자] an abbreviation
약 葯 〖식물〗 the anther (of a flower)
*__약 約__ [대략] about ; some ; round ; nearly around ; approximately ; more or less ¶ 약 50세 about fifty years old // 약 20마일 some 20 miles ; 20 miles or so // 약 500명 about〔around, some〕 500 people // 수출 총액은 약 백억불이다 The total export value is in round figures 10 billion dollars. // 그 모자는 약 5천원입니다 The hat costs around 5,000 *won*. // 그것은 약 100만원 정도의 것이다 It is in the neighborhood of one million *won*. // 손해는 약 50만원으로 추산된다 The damage was roughly estimated at 500,000 *won*.
⁑**약 藥** ① medicine ; a drug ; a pill (알약) ; a specific (특효약) ; a tonic (강장제) ; a remedy (치료제) ¶ 약의 medical // 약 1회분 a dose of medicine // 약을 먹다 take medicine // 약을 처방하다 prescribe medicine 《for a patient》 // 약을 먹이다 administer medicine 《to》 // 이 약은 잘 낫는다 This medicine acts 〔works, operates〕 well. /This medicine does me good. // 이 약은 잘 들었다 This medicine has taken effect. // 이 약은 어디에 잘 듣느냐 What is this medicine good for ? // 이 약은 쓰다 This medicine is bitter to the taste 〔tastes bitter〕. // 이것은 감기에 잘 듣는 약이다 This is a good medicine for a cold. // 좋은 약은 입에 쓰나 몸에 이롭다 A good medicine is bitter to the mouth but of value for the body. // 이 약 좀 지어주세요 (처방전대로) Will you fill this prescription, please ?
② [화학 약품] chemicals ; chemical preparations〔pastes, powder, pills〕 ; pharmaceuticals ¶ 구두약을 칠하다 shine shoes
③ [이익] good ; benefit ¶ 그것은 약이 된다 It is good for the health. /It does 《a person》 good. // 모르는 게 약이다 Ignorance is bliss. // 그들에겐 친절 같은 것은 약에 쓰려도 없다 They have no spark of kindness in them. // 매일 적당한 운동을 하는 것은 건강에 약이 된다 It will do you good〔It is good for the health〕 to take a moderate amount of exercise every day.
—병 a medicine bottle ; a bottle of medicine ; a phial ; a vial 《미》 ¶ 약병을 흔들다 shake up a bottle of medicine **—상자** a medicine chest〔cabinet, case〕 **—장수** a travelling patent-medicine salesman ; a medicine peddler **가루—** powdered medicine ; a powder **감기—** medicine for a cold **구두—** shoe polish **내복—** an internal medicine **두통—** a headache remedy **모기—** a mosquito stick **물—** liquid medicine **알—** a pill **특효—** a specific medicine **파리—** fly spray〔paste〕 **화상—** a remedy for burns
-약 弱 [모자라다] a little less than ; a little short of ; a little under ¶ 1할약 a little less than 10 per cent // 7마일약 a little less than 7 miles // 40 약 a little under forty
약가 藥價 ⇨ 약값
약가심 藥— chasing the after-taste 《of a medicine》 **—하다** cut the after-taste 《of a medicine》 ¶ 약가심으로 사과를 먹다 eat an apple to chase the bitter taste of the medicine
약값 藥— the price of medicine ; the charge for a medicine ; a medical fee ; a doctor's bill ¶ 약값을 치르다 pay for medicine ; pay a doctor's bill
†**약간 若干** some ; a little ; a bit ; a few ; somewhat ¶ 약간의 [수·양] some ; [수] a few ; a number of ; [양] a little ; some quantity of // 약간의 돈 some money // (군

인) 약간명 a number of (soldiers) // 약간 비슷한 somewhat similar // 오늘은 기분이 약간 좋은 편이다 I feel a little better today. // 약간 자르는 게 훨씬 보기가 낫겠어요 A little trim would make it look much better. // 저 그림은 약간〔조금〕 오른쪽으로 기울어져 있는 것 같다 That picture looks like it's tilted slightly to the right.

약고추장 藥─醬 sautéed red pepper sauce

약골 弱骨 being poor〔delicate〕 in health ; a weak〔feeble, delicate〕 constitution ; a weakling (사람) ¶ 그는 약골이다 He has a weak〔delicate〕 constitution. /He is delicately built.

약과 藥果 ① [과줄] a cake made from wheatflour, oil, and honey ② [쉬운 일] an easy thing ; a sure thing ; a cinch ¶ 그것은 약과다 That's easy. / That's as simple as A B C. /That's a cinch. 《미·속》 // 저런 녀석을 이기는 것은 약과다 It's child's play to beat him. // 이건 약과야 You haven't seen anything yet. /This is nothing.

약관 弱冠 ① twenty years of age (20세) ; a youth of twenty ; a young man ; an early age ; youthfulness ¶ 약관에 at the age of twenty ; while (one is) in one's youth ; at an early age // 그는 약관으로 등과했다 He passed the higher civil service at an early age〔the age of twenty〕.
② youth ; an early age ¶ 그는 약관 30세에 그 직에 임명되었다 He was appointed to the post at the young age of 30.

약관 約款 a stipulation ; an agreement ; a provision ; a contract ; an article ; a clause

약국 藥局 a pharmacy ; a chemist's shop ; an apothecary ; a drugstore 《미》 ; [병원의] a dispensary ; a pharmacist office ¶ 한국 약국방 the *Korea* Pharmacopoeia

약국 弱國 ⇨ 약소 (─ 국가)

약기 略記 a brief〔short, rough〕 sketch ; an outline ; a quick write-up **─하다** make a short sketch 《of》 ; give a rough sketch 《of》 ; outline ; jot down ¶ 제2차 세계 대전에 대하여 약기하라 Give an outline of World War Ⅱ. // 이름은 약기하지 말 것 Your name should be written in full.
─법(法) abridged notation

약꿀 藥─ honey prepared as a medicine

약농 藥籠 a medical chest〔cabinet〕

*__약다__ (be) shrewd ; clever ; smart ; sharp ; cunning ; crafty ¶ 약게 smartly ; agilely ; cleverly // 약은 녀석 a shrewd man ; an old fox ; a smart guy ; a cute chap // 약은 수작 a shrewd way (of handling business) // 약게 굴다 behave shrewdly ; be tactful

약대 〖동물〗 a camel ⇨ 낙타

약대 藥大 a college of pharmacy

약대접 藥─ [한약의] a medicine bowl

⁑**약도** 略圖 a rough sketch ; [지도] an outline map ; a sketch map ; [계획] a rough plan ¶ 서울의 약도를 그리시오 Draw an outline of *Seoul*. // 여기에서 댁까지의 약도를 그려주시오 Please make a sketch map showing the way to your house from here.

약동 躍動 a lively motion ; a stir ; a throb ; a palpitation ; a movement **─하다** move lively ; be quick with life ; be full of life ; stir ; throb ¶ 가슴이 약동함을 느끼다 feel a stir in one's heart

약동이 ─童─ a shrewd〔clever〕 boy ; a smart boy

약되다 藥─ 《medicine》 be effective as medicine ; be good for the health

약량 藥量 dosage

약력 略歷 a brief (personal) history ; a brief (personal) record ; a sketch of one's life ; a brief survey of one's career ; a memoir (고인의)

약력학 藥力學 pharmacodynamics

약령 藥令 a drug market held each spring and fall in former times
약령 보다 관용 shop for drugs at the drug market
약령 서다 관용 hold a drug market

약리 藥理
─ 작용 a medical action **─학** pharmacology

약막대기 藥─ a stick on each side of the medicine-straining cloth

약명 略名 an abbreviated form of one's name

약모 略帽 an ordinary〔everyday〕 cap

약문 略文 an abridged sentence

약물 藥─ medicinal waters ; mineral waters ⇨ 약수

약물 藥物 drugstuffs ; drugs ; medicines ; materia medica 《라》
─ 소독 disinfection (by disinfectant) **─ 알레르기** drug allergy **─ 요법** medication ; medicinal therapy ; pharmacotherapy **─ 중독** medicinal poisoning **─학자** a pharmacologist

약물군 a spa visitor

약물터 藥─ a mineral spring ; a spa

약밥 藥─ flavored glutinous rice mixed with honey ; dates, chestnuts

⁑**약방** 藥房 a pharmacy 《영》 ; a drug store 《미》
약방에 감초 속담 a Jack-of-all-trades

약방문 藥方文 a prescription (slip) ; a recipe ¶ 약방문을 쓰다 write (out) 〔give〕 a prescription ; prescribe // 약방문을 받다 have a prescription filled 〔made up〕
사후 약방문 관용 the doctor after death

약변화 弱變化 〖문법〗 weak conjugation (동사의)
─ 동사 weak verbs

약병 藥瓶 a medicine bottle ; a vial ; a phial
약보 a shrewd〔cunning, smart〕 person
약복 略服 an ordinary dress ; an abbreviated clothes ; informal attire ; undress ¶ 그는 약복을 입고 있다 He is in undress. / He wears easy dress. // 약복도 괜찮습니다 Undress will do.
약봉지 藥封紙 a paper-bundle of medicine ; a medicine packet
약분 約分 〖수학〗 reduction of a fraction (to its lowest terms) **—하다** reduce a fraction ; abbreviate ; cancel ¶ 약분할 수 없는 irreducible // 약분할 수 있는 reducible
약빠르다 (be) shrewd ; sharp ; clever ; smart ; cunning ¶ 약빠르게 shrewdly ; smartly ; tactfully ; cleverly ; cunningly // 약빠른 사람 a shrewd fellow ; a sharp 〔cunning, smart〕 person // 약빠르게 굴다 act tactfully ; move smartly // 거래에 있어서 약빠르다 be smart in one's dealings // 그는 약빠르게도 그 기회를 놓치지 않았다 It was very smart of him not to miss the chance.
약빠리 a shrewd〔sharp, cunning, smart〕 one ; a quick-witted person ; a smart guy
약사 略史 a short〔brief〕 history ; a historical sketch ; an outline history ¶ 한국의 약사 an outline〔a shortened〕 history of Korea
약사 藥師 ⇨ 약제(—사)
— 국가 시험 a state examination for pharmaceutical chemists〔pharmacists〕
약사발 藥沙鉢 a cup of poison offered by the king as an honorable execution ¶ 약사발을 내리다 offer 《a person》 a cup of death ; put 《a person》 to death
약사법 藥事法 the pharmaceutical affairs law
약삭빠르다 be full of shifts and devices ; be ready〔quick〕-witted ; be shrewd 〔clever, witty, forward〕 ¶ 약삭빠른 사람 a smart man ; a quick-witted person // 약삭빠르게 굴다 behave alertly〔cunningly〕 // 그는 약삭빠르게 마음먹은 대로 하는 것 같지 않니 He's clever at getting his own way, isn't he ?
약석 藥石 medicine ¶ 약석의 효과 없이 《die》 in spite of every medical treatment
약설 略說 a summary ; a brief explanation ; a résumé 《프》 **—하다** give an outline of ; summarize ; sum up ; resume
약설 略設 informal establishment ; simple〔limited〕 fittings **—하다** set up 〔establish〕 simply ¶ 소연(小宴)을 약설하오니 왕림을 바라나이다 You are cordially requested to attend a small party held 《at》.
약성 藥性 the nature〔properties〕 of a drug〔medicine〕
약세 弱勢 〖증권〗 a slack ; bearish trend ¶ 시장은 강세에서 약세로 변했다 The market's gone from bullish to bearish.
약소 略少 (being) little ; scanty ; few **—하다** (be) scanty ; insignificant ; few ; little ¶ 약소한 돈 a little money // 약소하지만 이것 좀 받아 주십시오 This is little something for you.
약소 弱小 the weak and small ; the weak ; the minor ; the lesser **—하다** (be) small and weak
— 국가 a lesser power ; a minor power ; a small and weak nation **— 민족** the people of a small and weak power
†**약속 約束** an engagement ; an agreement ; an appointment ; a promise ; a convention (관습) ; a date 《미》 **—하다** promise ; make a promise ; make an appointment〔engagement〕 ¶ 약속의 promised ; appointed ; agreed // 구두 약속 a verbal promise // 거짓 약속 a false promise // 약속대로 according to one's promise ; true to one's word〔promise〕 ; as promised〔appointed〕 // 약속한 날에 on the appointed day // 약속한 시간에 at the appointed time // 약속을 지키다 keep one's promise〔word〕 ; keep one's appointment〔engagement〕 // 약속을 이행하다 carry out〔fulfil〕 one's promise // 약속을 지키게 하다 hold 《a person》 to his promise // 약속을 깨뜨리다 break one's promise〔word〕 ; go back on one's word // 만날 약속을 하다 make an appointment〔a date〕 《with a person》 ; date 《a girl》 // 약속을 취소하다 call off one's engagement ; withdraw one's promise // 그가 오겠다고 (나에게) 약속했다 He promised (me) to come. / He promised (me) that he would come. // 내주는 약속이 많다 I have numerous engagements for next week. // 나는 그 여자에게 약속했다 I've given her my word. // 그는 결혼한다는 약속으로 그 여자를 속였다 He seduced her under a promise of marriage. // 아저씨는 내게 그 시계를 주겠다고 약속했다 My uncle promised me the watch〔the watch to me〕. // 누구에게나 비밀을 지키겠다고 약속해 주시오 Please promise (me) not to tell the secret to anyone. // 내일 무슨 약속이 있느냐 Have you any appointment tomorrow ? // 나는 세 시에 변호사와 만날 약속이 있다 I have a three o'clock engagement with my lawyer. // 나는 그 여자와 데이트 약속을 했다 I made a date with her. // 그녀에게 데이트의 약속을 받을 수가 없었다 I couldn't pin her down to a date. // 그는 약속을 지킨다 He keeps his promise. / He is a man of his word. /He is as good as his word. // 그는 열심히 공부하겠다는 약속을 지켰다〔깨뜨렸다〕 He kept〔broke〕 his promise to work hard. // 그는 약속을 안 지킬 사람이 아니다 He's not the sort of man who would go back on his word. //

그 여자의 오늘 약속 상대는 A이다 Her date today is A. // 나는 약속의 이행을 요구한다 I urge you to keep your promise. // 급하게 일에 열중하다 보니 하마터면 약속을 잊을 뻔했다 I got caught up in a rush job and almost forgot my appointment.

약속 어음 約束— a promissory note ; an advance note ; a note of hand ¶ 약속 어음을 발행하다 issue a promissory note
— 발행인 a promisor

약속 우편 約束郵便 contract mail matter ; second-class postal matter 《미》 ; promissory post

약손 藥— a soothing touch of the hand ; a comforting hand

약손가락 藥— the third finger ; the ring finger

약솜 藥— surgical cotton ; absorbent 〔sanitary〕 cotton

약수 藥水 medicinal water ; mineral water

약수 約數 〖수학〗 a divisor (of a number) ; measure

약수 略授 ⇨ 약장(略章)

약수건 藥手巾 a hemp cloth for straining herb medicine

약수터 藥水— a mineral spring resort ; a spa

약술 略述 a brief account ; an outline ; a summary ; a brief〔short, rough〕 sketch **—하다** summarize ; give a rough sketch 《of》 ; make a short sketch 《of》 ; sketch ; outline ; give an outline 《of》 ¶ 십자군에 대하여 약술하라 Give an outline of the Crusades.

약술 藥— medicinal wine〔liquor〕

약시 弱視 〖의학〗 amblyopia ; weak sight ; weakness of sight ¶ 약시의 weak-eyed 〔-sighted〕 ; amblyopic

약시시 藥— administering medicine 《to a patient》 **—하다** administer〔prescribe, compound, give〕 medicine 《 to a patient》 ; dispense medicine ¶ 환자에게 약시시하다 prescribe for a patient ; dose a patient

약시중 藥— administering medicine 《to a patient》 **—하다** administer medicine

*****약식 略式** informality ¶ 약식의 informal ; unceremonious ; summary // 약식으로 informally ; without formality ; in an informal way // 혼례는 약식으로 거행되었다 The marriage ceremony was gone through without due formality.
— 명령 a summary order — 복장 ordinary〔informal, everyday〕 dress 〔clothes〕 ; abbreviated clothes — 재판 a summary trial ; summary proceedings — 절차 informal proceedings ; 〖법〗 summary procedure — 처분 summary disposition

약식 藥食 flavored glutinous rice ⇨ 약밥

약실 藥室 [약국] a pharmacist's office ; a pharmacy ; a druggist's ; a drugstore ; a doctor's medicine room ; [총의] a powder〔cartridge〕 chamber

약쑥 a wormwood

약액 藥液 a medicinal fluid ; a liquid medicine

약약하다 (be) reluctant ; unwilling

약어 略語 an abbreviated〔a shortened〕 word ; an abbreviation ; a contraction ¶ bldg.는 building의 약어이다 Bldg. is an abbreviation for building.
— 풀이 a key to abbreviations

약언 略言 a brief statement ; a summary ; an outline **—하다** state briefly ; summarize ; outline ; sum up ¶ 약언한다면 in short ; in a word ; to put it briefly〔in a nutshell〕 ; to make a long story short

약여하다 躍如— (be) vivid〔lifelike, graphic〕 ; be true to life

약오르다 [사람이 주어] get angry 〔mad〕 ; be offended ; take offense ; get irritated ; be vexed〔exasperated〕 ; be stung to the quick ¶ 그 여자는 그들의 행동에 약이 올랐다 Her temper was ruffled up by their behavior. // 참 약오른다 How vexatious ! // 그가 성공하다니 약이 오른다 His success is a sore point with me. // 저 녀석의 말투에 약이 올랐다 I got sore about that remark of his. // 30초로 기차를 놓치다니 약오른다 It is exasperating to miss the train by half a minute. // 그에게 지다니 약오른다 I cannot stand being beaten by a man like that.

약올리다 make 《a person》 angry ; vex ; anger 《a person》 ; provoke 《a person》 to anger ; offend〔give offense to〕 《a person》 ; make 《a person》 mad 《미》 ¶ 약올리는 말 provoking words // 그 여자의 말이 그를 약올렸다 Her remarks stung him to the quick. // 무엇이 그토록 약올리느냐 What are you sore〔mad〕 at ? /What hurts your feelings ? // 이런 사소한 일이 약을 올린다 Such trifles occasionally ruffle tempers. // 자식 약올리네 How he irritates me !

약용 藥用 medicinal use **—하다** use 《a thing》 for medicinal purposes ¶ 그것은 약용이 된다 It is used for〔is applied to〕 medicinal purposes. /It has healing qualities.
— 비누 a medicated soap — 식물 a medicinal plant〔herb〕 — 크림 a medicated cream — 포도주 medicinal wine — 학 medical botany — 효모 medicinal yeast

약육강식 弱肉强食 the law of the jungle ; The weak are the prey of the strong. /The weak fall prey to the strong. /The stronger prey upon the weaker. /The weak become the victims of the strong.

약은꾀 shrewd tricks〔wiles〕 ; cunning 〔cunningness〕

약음기 弱音器 a mute ; [관현악기의] a

sordine ; a sordino ; [피아노·취주악기의] a damper ¶ 현(弦)에 약음기를 달고 with muted strings

약자 略字 [한자의] a simplified character ; a simpler form 《of》 ; [약어] an abbreviated word ; an abbreviation ¶ 약자로 쓰다 write a character in simplified form // F.는 무엇의 약자입니까 What does F. stand for? // F.는 Fahrenheit의 약자이다 F. stands for〔is short for〕 Fahrenheit.

약자 弱者 the weak ; the loser ; a weak person ; the underdog ¶ 약자의 편을 들다 side with〔stand by〕 the weak // 강자에 대해 약자를 돕다 champion the weak against the strong

약장 略章 a miniature medal〔decoration〕 ; a miniature

약장 藥欌 a medicine-chest

약장 略裝 ⇨ 약복

약재 藥材 medicines ; drugs ; drugstuffs ; pharmaceuticals ; medica

약저울 藥— pharmacy scales

약전 藥典 the pharmacopoeia ¶ 약전에 따라 조제한 약 an officinal medicine 〔drug〕 // 약전에 따른 처방전 an officinal prescription

— 주해 a dispensatory 대한 — the Korean Pharmacopoeia

약전 略傳 a biographical sketch ; a sketch of one's life ; a short biography ; a memoir (고인의)

약전 弱電 a weak (electric) current

—기기(器機) a light electrical appliance

약전기 弱電機 light electric appliances

*약점 弱點 a vulnerable point ; a weak point〔spot, side〕 ; a defect ; a weakness ; a flaw ; [불리한 점] a disadvantage ; one's blind side ¶ 약점을 폭로하다 betray one's weak point // 남의 약점을 이용하다 avail oneself of another's disadvantage ; take advantage of another's weak point(s) // 적에게 약점을 잡히다 give a handle to the enemy // 남의 약점을 건드리다 touch 《a person》 on a sore spot // 사람의 약점을 꿰뚫어 보다 perceive 〔know, get〕 the length of another's foot // 약점을 가지다 have a weakness ; have a weak point〔spot〕 // 그는 너의 약점을 이용하여 자기의 욕망을 만족시켰다 He played on your weakness for the satisfaction of his own desires. // 그는 나의 약점을 알고 있다 He has got my sore spot. /He has a hold on〔upon〕 me. // 사람에게는 누구나 약점이 있다 We all have weak points〔spots〕.

약정 約定 an agreement ; a contract ; a promise ; an engagement —하다 agree ; contract ; make a contract〔an agreement〕 ; promise ¶ 약정한 agreed ; contracted ; stipulated // 약정에 의해서 by agreement ; by arrangement // 우리들은 하루 여덟시간 일하기로 약정되어 있다 We are under an agreement to work eight hours a day.

— 기간 the stipulated time —서 an agreement ; a (written) contract ; a deed of contract ; a bond ; a pact — 이율 the rate of interest agreed upon ; the agreed rate of interest —자 a promiser ; a promisor ; a stipulator 가— a provisional contract〔agreement〕 ; a conditional contract ; a convention 구두 — a verbal promise ; a spoken agreement

*약제 藥劑 drugs ; chemicals ; medicine

—사 a pharmacist ; a pharmaceutist ; a druggist ; a (pharmaceutical) chemist —학 pharmacology ; pharmaceutics

약조 約條 [언약] a promise ; a pledge ; [규정] rule ; an agreement ; a condition —하다 promise ; pledge ¶ 약조한 바에 따라 according to the agreement // 약조를 지키다 keep one's pledge〔engagement〕 ; keep faith with a man

—금 a contract deposit

약졸 弱卒 a cowardly〔weak〕 soldier

약종 藥種 pharmaceutical supplies ; pharmacopoeia

—상 a seller of materia medica ; a drug merchant ; an apothecary ; a chemist

약주 藥酒 [약술] a medicinal wine ; [술] rice wine

약지 藥指 the ring finger ; the third finger ⇨ 약손가락, 무명지

약진 弱震 a minor shock of earthquake ¶ 약진이 있었다 A slight earthquake was felt.

약진 藥疹 〖의학〗 a medicinal exanthema

약진 躍進 advance by rushes ; rush ; dash —하다 [돌진] dash 《for, on》 ; rush 《for》 ; advance 《on》 ; leap forward ; [진보] make rapid advance 〔progress〕 ¶ 한국 경제의 약진 Korea's economic advance // 일대 약진을 하다 make a great advance ; make rapid strides // 약진에 약진을 거듭하다 advance by leaps and bounds // 제5위에서 제1위로 약진하다 jump from the fifth place to the top // 한국의 화학 공업은 최근 일대 약진을 이루었다 Chemical industries in Korea have recently made a remarkable development.

약질 弱質 a weak〔delicate〕 constitution ; a person of feeble strength ; a weakling

약차약차 若此若此 such and such

약체 弱體 a weak body ¶ 약체의 weak-bodied ; weak ; effete // 약체화하다 weaken ; become weak // 현 정부는 다소 약체다 The present Government is making rather a poor show.

— 내각 an effete〔a frail〕 Cabinet — 보험 substandard (life) insurance — 정부〔회사〕 a weak government〔concern〕

약초 藥草 medicinal herbs ; a medical plant

—상 a herbalist —원 a herb garden ; a herbary — 채집가 a herbalist —학 medical botany —학자 a herbalist ; a medical botanist

약취 掠取 capture ; occupation ; plunder —하다 capture ; occupy ; plunder ; seize ; take

약칭 略稱 an abbreviation ; an abbreviated name ; a short designation ¶ MSA는 상호 안전 보장법의 약칭이다 MSA is short〔stands〕 for the Mutual Security Act.

†약탈 掠奪 plunder ; pillage ; looting ; sack —하다 plunder ; pillage ; loot ; sack ; strip 《a person》 of 《a thing》 ¶ 도시를 약탈하다 plunder〔sack〕 a town // 그들은 시민의 의류와 보석류를 약탈하였다 They plundered〔looted〕 the citizens of clothes and jewelry.

— 농법 plunder farming ; a slash-and-burn method of agriculture —물 looted goods ; booty ; spoil ; plunder —자 a plunderer ; a looter ; a marauder —주의 a policy of spoliation

약탕관 藥湯罐 a clay pot for preparing medicines

약통 the body of a round carrot ; ginseng root

약포 藥圃 a herb garden

약포 藥脯 beef slices dried and flavored with spices

약포 藥包 ① a chartula ② a cartridge

약포 葯胞 an anther cell ; a theca

약품 藥品 medicines ; medical supplies ; [매약] drugs ; [화학 약품] chemicals —명 drug names — 회사 a pharmaceutical company 불량 — illegal〔fraudulent〕 medicines〔drugs〕

약하 若何 How then ? /What if ? /How about ? ⇨ 여하

†약하다 弱— [연약] (be) weak ; feeble ; [섬약] frail ; [허약] infirm ; [미약] faint [섬세] delicate ; [술 따위가] light ; mild ; weak ; small ; thin ¶ 약한 사람 a weak person ; the weak 《총칭》 // 약한 술 weak〔mild〕 wine // 약한 담배 mild tobacco // 마음이 약한 faint-hearted ; soft-hearted ; chicken-hearted ; timid // 의지가 약한 weak-willed // 약하게 weakly ; feebly ; faintly // 몸이 약하다 have a weak〔delicate〕 constitution ; be delicately built ; be weak in body // 약하게 하다 weaken ; enfeeble // 약해지다 become 〔grow〕 weak // 그는 점점 약해졌다 He grew weaker. // 병으로 그 여자는 약해졌다 Sickness has weakened her. // 일본제 구두는 약하다 Shoes made in Japan do not wear well. // 그의 체력이 약해졌다 His strength grew faint 〔declined〕. // 심장이 약하다 He has a weak heart. // 시력이 약하다 He has bad sight. /He is weak in sight. /He is weak-sighted. // 그는 의지가 약하다 He is infirm of purpose. // 그는 술이 약하다 He is a poor drinker. /He is easily drunk. // 그는 배멀미에 약하다 He is a poor sailor. /He easily gets seasick. // 그는 수학이 약하다 He is weak in mathematics. // 그의 맥박은 아주 약했다 His pulse was very feeble. // 강자는 약한 자를 보호해야 한다 The strong should protect the weak. // 약한 자를 괴롭히지 마라 Don't bully〔tyrannize over〕 the weak. // 이 세균은 일광에 약하다 This germ has a very low degree of sunlight tolerance. // 모든 남자들은 젊은 여자에게 약하다 Everyman has a soft spot for young women.

약하다 略— abbreviate ; abridge ; shorten ; contract ; [생략하다] cut out ; omit ; leave out ¶ 약하여 for short ; for shortness' 〔brevity's〕 sake // 약하지 않고 in full ; fully // (이름 따위를) 약하지 않고 쓰다 write in full // 의식을 약하다 dispense with formalities // 약하여 그를 고바우라고 부른다 He is called *Kobau* for short. / We call him *Kobau* for short. // cannot를 약하여 can't라고 쓴다 "Can't" is an contraction for "cannot". // 인사는 일체 약합시다 Let us do without formal greetings. // 미합중국을 약하여 the U. S. 라고 부른다 The United States of America is called the U. S. for short. // 여기에는 조동사 will이 약해져 있다 Here an auxiliary verb "will" is understood. // 이하 약한다 The rest is omitted 《from this . . . 》.

약하다 ⇨ 약분(—하다)

약학 藥學 pharmacy ; pharmacology —과 the pharmaceutical department —대학 the college of pharmacy —부 the department of pharmacy —사〔박사〕 a bachelor〔doctor〕 of pharmacology ; Phar. B. 〔D. 〕 —자 a pharmacologist

약해 略解 a rough〔brief〕 explanation —하다 give a brief explanation of outlines

약해 藥害 harmful effects of a medicine

약협 藥莢 a cartridge case

약호 略號 a code address ; an abbreviation ; a short designation

전신 — a telegraphic code address

*약혼 約婚 an engagement (to be married) ; betrothal ; a promise of marriage ; affiance —하다 engage oneself 《to a person》 ; be engaged〔betrothed〕 《to a person, to marry a person》 ; give one's hand to (여자가) ; make an engagement ¶ 약혼한 남녀 an engaged pair〔couple〕 // A양과 B씨의 약혼 the engagement of Miss A to Mr. B // …와 약혼한 사이다 be engaged〔betrothed〕 to marry 《a person》 // 약혼을 피로〔파기〕하다 announce〔break off〕 the engagement 《of one's daughter to a man》

— 기간 the term of engagement ; the engagement period — 반지 an engagement〔a betrothal〕 ring — 선물 a betrothal〔an engagement〕 present —식 an engagement ceremony〔party〕 —자 an engaged person ; a fiancé (남) 《프》 ; a

fiancée (여) 《프》; the betrothed; one's intended husband 〔wife〕 **— 잔치** a feast of betrothal **— 파기** a breach of promise of marriage
약화 略畫 a (rough) sketch ¶ 약화를 그리다 make a rough sketch 《of》; sketch
⁑**약화 弱化** weakening **— 하다** weaken; be weakened; become weakened; enfeeble; attenuate ¶ 약화된 시력 weakened eyesight
약화학 藥化學 pharmaceutical chemistry
약효 藥效 the effect〔virtue, power〕 of a medicine; remedial result ¶ 이 약은 곧 약효를 나타냅니다 The drug will soon work upon〔on〕 you. // 그 약은 즉각 약효를 나타냈다 The medicine had an immediate effect on me.
얄궂다 (be) treacherous; perverse; nasty; ill-tempered; quaint; queer; curious ¶ 얄궂은 운명 queer fate // 얄궂은 날씨 nasty weather // 얄궂은 심사 a perverse state of mind // 얄궂게 들리다 sound strange // 얄궂은 얼굴을 하다 make a queer face; look puzzled // 얄궂게 웃으며 말하다 talk with a nasty smirk
얄긋거리다 quiver; be quivery; be unsteady〔shaky, rickety〕 ¶ 얄긋거리는 의자 a rickety〔shaky, rocky〕 chair
얄긋얄긋 in a rickety manner
얄긋하다 (be) distorted; contorted; twisted; sagged
얄기죽거리다 sway one's hips to and fro
얄따랗다 (be) rather〔somewhat〕 thin
얄라차 [감탄사] Why! /O my! /Hang it! /[젠장] Gee! /Gosh!
얄망궂다 (be) imprudent; frivolous; uncompliant; crossgrained ¶ 얄망궂게 imprudently; frivolously; crossgrainedly // 얄망궂은 짓 an unmannerly act // 얄망궂게 굴다 act imprudently; behave erratically; be cross with 《a person》
얄망스럽다 (be) imprudent ⇨ 얄망궂다
얄밉다 (be) offensive; mean and nasty; saucy; cheeky; pert; hateful; detestable ¶ 얄밉게 provokingly; detestably // 얄미운 놈 a nasty〔saucy〕 fellow // 얄미운 태도 an impudent manner // 얄밉게도 …하다 be impudent enough to 《do》; have the cheek〔brass, face〕 to 《do》 // 얄미운 소리를 하다 say spiteful〔cheeky〕 things // 참말 얄미운 놈이다 What a repulsive 〔an odious〕 wretch he is! // 그 놈은 얄미울 정도로 침착했다 He remained provokingly cool〔calm〕.
얄밉상스럽다 (be) rather hateful
얄브스름하다 (be) rather thin
얄찍하다 ⇨ 얄팍하다
얄타 Yalta
— 협정〔회담〕 the Yalta Pact〔Conference〕
얄팍얄팍 — 하다 be rather thin
얄팍하다 (be) rather thin ¶ 얄팍한 책 a thin book
†**얇다** (be) thin ¶ 얇은 옷〔종이〕 thin clothes〔paper〕 ⇨ 엷다
얇다랗다 (be) rather thin ⇨ 얇다
얌냠하다, 얌냠거리다 smack one's lips; lick one's chops
얌심 jealousy; spite; green envy; malice ¶ 얌심스럽다 be mean and jealous; be spiteful
—꾸러기〔데기〕 a spiteful person; a mean and jealous person
얌심 부리다 [관용] display〔show〕 jealousy
얌전떨다, 얌전부리다 be prudish; behave nicely
*****얌전하다** ① [행동] (be) gentle; well-behaved; graceful; modest; decent; nice ¶ 얌전하게 gently; modestly; nicely // 얌전한 처녀 a modest〔well-behaved〕 girl // 얌전한 아이 a real nice boy // 얌전하게 굴다 behave nicely; behave oneself; bear oneself gracefully; be modest〔graceful〕 in manner // 얌전하게 듣다 listen to 《a person》 with patience // 얌전하게 앉다 sit properly // 나이와 함께 얌전해지다 sober down with age // 얌전하게 걷다 walk gracefully // 얌전하게 굴지 않으면 아무데도 안 데리고 간다 If you don't behave yourself, I won't take you anywhere. // 저 놈은 얌전하게 말하면 더욱 뻔뻔스러워지는 놈이다 The fellow is apt to get bold when I show reserve in what I say. // 제임스는 반에서 얌전한가요 Is James a good boy in class?
② [일·작품] (be) good; fine; excellent; nice; neat ¶ 글을 얌전하게 쓰다 write neatly // 일을 얌전하게 하다 do a nice job // 옷을 얌전하게 입다 dress neatly〔nicely〕
얌체 a selfish person; a shameless fellow ¶ 저런 얌체 봤나 That really takes the cake!
얌치 a sense of honor ⇨ 염치
양 胖 tripe; the cud pouch; the wall of ox stomach
†**양 羊** a sheep; a ram (수컷); a ewe (암컷); a wether (거세한); a lamb (새끼양) ¶ 양치는 사람 a shepherd // 길잃은 양 a stray lamb // 양털을 깎다 shear a sheep // 양같이 순하다 be as gentle as a lamb
—가죽 sheepskin; roan **—고기** mutton **—떼** a flock of sheep **—우리** a sheepfold; a sheepcote **—털** wool
양 陽 the positive ¶ 음과 양 *Yin* and *Yang*; the positive and the negative; the male and female principles
†**양 量** ① [분량] quantity; amount; volume ¶ 양의 증가 an increase in quantity // 양적(으로) quantitative(ly) // 양이 줄다〔붇다〕 diminish〔gain〕 in quantity // 술〔담배〕의 양을 줄이다 reduce drinking 〔smoking〕 // 양이 적다〔많다〕 be small〔large〕 in quantity // 양이 많아지면 질이 떨어진다 What we gain in quantity we lose in

quality. // 이 음식점은 양이 많다 The portions at this restaurant are generous.
② [식량] one's capacity for food〔wine〕 ¶ 양껏 to one's fill ; to one's heart's content ; stomachful // 양이 큰 사람 a great eater ; a heavy feeder // 양껏 먹다〔마시다〕 eat〔drink〕 one's fill ; eat〔drink〕 to one's heart's content // 술은 양을 넘으면 해롭다 Excessive drinking does one harm. // 양보다도 질을 취한다 I prefer quality to quantity.
교통— traffic volume 주량 one's capacity for wine

양 良 fine ; good ; [등급] "B" ¶ 양민 the good people // 양서 a good book

양- 洋 things from overseas ; foreign ; in foreign style ; Western ; European ¶ 양품 imported〔foreign-made〕 goods // 양풍 European style // 양춤 a Western dance

양- 兩 both ; two ; a pair ; a couple ¶ 양면 two faces ; both sides // 양용 (for) double use // 양인 both persons

양- 養 adopted ; foster
—아들 an adopted〔a foster〕 son —아버지 a foster father

-양 洋 an ocean ; the sea ¶ 대서양 the Atlantic (Ocean) // 인도양 the Indian Ocean

†**-양 孃** Miss ¶ 김 양 Miss *Kim*

양가 良家 a good〔respectable〕 family ¶ 양가의 처녀 a daughter of a good family〔parentage〕 // 양가집 태생이다 come of a respectable family ; be wellborn

양가 兩家 two〔both〕 houses〔families〕

양가 養家 an adoptive family ; the adopting household ¶ 양가의 어버이 one's adoptive parents

양가구 洋家具 Western-style furniture

양각 陽刻 engraving in relief ; embossed carving ; (bas-) relief ; raised carving ¶ 양각으로 하다 emboss ; carve in relief // 반양각하다 bring into harsh relief
— 세공 relief〔raised〕 work ; embossment ; chasing

양각 兩脚 both legs
—기(器) 《a pair of》 compasses

양간하다 陽乾— dry in the sun

양갈보 洋— a foreigners' whore ; a prostitute who is patronized by foreigners

양감 量感 ¶ 양감이 있는 massive ; voluminous

양갱 羊羹 sweet jelly of red beans

양견 兩肩 one's (both) shoulders

***양계 養鷄** poultry farming〔keeping〕 ; chicken raising ; egg-raising —하다 raise poultry〔chickens〕 ; keep chickens ¶ 양계가 하고 싶다 I want to raise poultry〔chickens〕. // 이 마을은 양계가 성하다 Poultry keeping thrives in this village.
—가 a poultryman ; a chicken-farmer ; an egg-man —업 poultry raising〔farming〕 ; the poultry industry —장 a poultry farm〔yard〕 ; a chicken farm〔run〕

양곡 糧穀 corn 《영》 ; grain 《미》 ; cereals ; provisions ¶ 양곡을 나르다 carry corn ; haul grain 《미》
— 거래소 the grain exchange center — 도매상 a corn-factor ; a grain broker 《미》 — 도입 imports〔importation〕 of grains —상 a grain〔corn〕 merchant — 수급 계획 a plan for demand and supply of grains — 시장 the grain 〔corn〕 market — 증산 increased grain production〔output〕 — 창고 a granary ; a corn reserve ; a grain elevator 《미》

양공주 洋公主 ⇨ 양갈보(洋—)

양과자 洋菓子 Western-style cakes〔confections〕

양관 洋館 a European-〔Western-〕style building ; [공관] legations of the foreign countries

양광 陽光 (spring) sunlight ; sunshine ; sunbeams

양광 佯狂 feigned insanity ; pretending to be mad

양구에 良久— after a while ; later on

양국 兩國 both〔two〕 countries ¶ 양국간의 유대 (friendly) ties between the two countries

양군 兩軍 both armies ; both teams (야구·축구 따위의) ¶ 양군간에 치열한 싸움이 벌어졌다 A fierce fight broke out between the two armies.

양궁 洋弓 Western-style archery (궁술) ; a Western-style bow (도구)

***양귀비 楊貴妃** 『식물』 a (opium) poppy
—씨 a poppy-seed

양극 陽極 『전기』 the positive pole ; the anode
—광(선) an anode glow〔ray〕 —판(板) a positive (plate)

양극 兩極 both extremities ; the two poles ; the north and south poles ; the positive and negative poles ¶ 양극의 bipolar
—성 polarity — 지방 the polar circles〔areas〕 음양 — the positive and negative poles

양극단 兩極端 both〔the two〕 extremes ¶ 양극단은 일치한다 Extremes meet. // 그들의 의견은 양극단을 달리고 있다 They are poles apart in opinion〔their opinions〕.

양근 陽根 『화학』 a positive radical ; [음경] the penis

양글 ① [소의] plowing and load-carrying by an ox ② [두번 수확] getting a crop from a rice field twice a year

양금 洋琴 a kind of zither
—채 a zither stick ; a stick with which one strikes the strings of a Korean zither ¶ 양금채 같다 be fine and frail ; be sweet (목소리가) // 양금채 같은 몸이다 be of delicate health

양기 養氣 nursing one's energy ; cultivating one's mental strength —하다 cultivate〔develop〕 courage ; build oneself up

양기 陽氣 ① [볕] sunlight ; sunshine ② [남자의] the male〔positive〕 element in nature ; vigor ; vitality ; virility ; energy ¶ 양기 좋은 사람 a great sexual debauchee // 양기를 보호하다 nurse one's energy // 양기가 왕성하다 be full of energy ; have great vigor
양기 涼氣 coolness
양기와 洋— an Occidental-type roofing tile
양끝 兩— both ends
양끼 兩— two meals ; breakfast and supper
양난 兩難 a dilemma ¶ (진퇴)양난이다 be in dilemma ; be in a fix **—하다** be in dilemma ; be in a (pretty) fix ; be on the horns of a dilemma
양날 兩— ¶ 양날의 double-bladed ; two-edged // 양날의 칼 a double-edged sword
양날톱 兩— a double-bladed saw
양냥고자 the end of an archery bow where the string is attached
양녀 洋女 Western〔European, American〕 women
양녀 養女 a foster daughter ; an adopted daughter ¶ 양녀가 되다 be adopted a〔as〕 daughter 《by a person》 // 양녀로 기르다 foster a girl as one's daughter
*__양념__ spices and condiments ; dressing materials ¶ 양념이 든 spicy ; seasoned // 양념을 너무 치다 season 《a dish》 too highly // 이 수프는 양념이 적다 There's not enough seasoning in this soup.
—병 a cruet ; a caster
양념을 치다 관용 season 《meat, food》 with spices ; put spices 《into soup》
양다리 兩—
양다리 걸치다 관용 try to have 《it》 both ways ; [기회주의] sit on the fence ; play double
양단 洋緞 foreign satin
양단 兩端 both ends ; both extremes ; either end
양단 兩斷 —하다 cut〔break〕 in two ; bisect ¶ 양단되다 get split in two // 일도양단하다 resort to a drastic measure ; cut the Gordian knot // 선체는 양단되어 버렸다 The ship has broken in half〔twain〕.
양단간 兩端間 anyway ; anyhow ; at any rate ; somehow or other ¶ 양단간 해야 할 일이다 I must do it anyhow. /It must be done somehow or other. // 양단간에 손해는 없다 Whatever may be the issue, he has nothing to lose. /He has nothing to lose either way. /This is safe against all possibilities. // 양단간에 그것은 정말이다 Believe it or not, it's a fact. // 양단간 그렇게 하겠습니다 I will do so, anyway. // 양단간 떠납시다 Let's start, anyway. // 합격하든지 못하든지 양단간에 시험은 치러야겠다 I'm going to take the examination whether I'll succeed in it or not.
양단자 陽端子 the positive terminal
양달 陽— a sunny place〔spot〕 ¶ 양달의 sunny // 양달 쪽 the sunny side // 양달에서 볕을 쬐다 bask〔sit〕 in the sun ; sun oneself // 양달에서 말리다 dry 《a thing》 in a sunny spot // 양달에 내놓다 keep 《a thing》 in the sun
—쪽 the sunny side
양담배 洋— imported tobacco ; American cigarettes〔tobacco〕
양당 兩堂 (both) parents
양당 兩黨 the two political parties
— 외교 bipartisan diplomacy **— 제도〔정치〕** the two-party system〔politics〕 《미》
양도 糧道 supply of provisions ¶ 적의 양도를 끊었다 We cut off the enemy's supply of provisions.
양도 兩刀 two swords ; a sword in either hand
— 논법 a (logical) dilemma
양도 洋刀 foreign cutlery
양도 讓渡 transfer ; conveyance ; assignment (권리의) ; cession (영토의) ; negotiation (어음의) **—하다** transfer 《to》 ; hand 《a thing》 over 《to》 ; convey 《a thing》 to 《a person》 by deed 《영》 ; deed 《a thing》 to 《미》 ; alienate ¶ 양도할 수 있는 transferable ; assignable ; negotiable (어음) // 양도 불능의 untransferable ; unassignable ; unnegotiable (어음) // 소유권을 양도하다 yield possession // 그는 사업을 아들에게 양도했다 He handed over his business to his son. // 저희 영업을 O 상사에 양도하였습니다 We have ceded our business to 〔turned our business over to〕 Messrs. O & Co.
— 가격 a transfer〔sale〕 price **—물** premises **— 소득** capital gains **— 소득세** a transfer income tax ¶ 양도 소득세를 부과하다 impose a transfer income tax **—인** a transferer ; an assigner ; an alien (at)or **— 증서** a (deed of) transfer ; a conveyance ; an assignment **이서 —** transfer by endorsement **재산 —인** a settlor **피—인** a transferee ; an assignée 《프》
양도체 良導體 〖전기〗 a good conductor 《of heat, electricity》 ¶ 구리는 전기의 양도체다 Copper is a good conductor of electricity.
*__양돈 養豚__ hog〔pig〕 raising〔breeding〕 ; hog farming ; pig keeping ; swine keeping **—하다** raise〔rear〕 hogs ; breed hogs ; hog-farm
—가 a pig breeder〔farmer〕 ; a swineherd ; a hog raiser 《미》 **—업** the hog raising industry **—장** a hog farm ; a hog yard ; a swinery ; a piggery
양동이 洋— a metal tub ; a metal bucket ¶ 양동이에 물을 붓다 pour water into a (metal) bucket
양동 작전 陽動作戰 a feint operation ; diversionary activities ¶ 양동 작전을 하

다 make a feint ; feint
양돼지 洋— a pig of a foreign〔Occidental〕 breed ; a fat〔greedy〕 person
양두 兩頭 ¶ 양두의 double-headed ; bicephalous
—사 (蛇) an amphisbaena — 정치 diarchy ; duumvirate
양두 구육 羊頭狗肉 crying out wine and selling vinegar ; using a better name to sell inferior goods ; all outside show ; making an extravagant advertisement
양두 마차 兩頭馬車 ⇨ 쌍두 마차
양딸 養— ⇨ 양녀(養女)
양딸기 洋— the Alpine strawberry
양떼구름 〖기상〗 a cumulocirrus (cloud)
양력 揚力 〖물리〗 upward force ; lift (on the wing of an airplane)
양력 陽曆 the solar calendar ; Julian calendar ¶ 양력 5월 5일 May 5 of the solar calendar
양로 養老 taking care of the aged ; provision for old age ; living at ease in one's old age
— 보험 old-age insurance〔assurance〕 ¶ 양로 보험에 들다 be insured against old age — 시설 an institution for the aged — 연금 an old-age pension ¶ 양로 연금을 받다 draw an old-age pension —원 an old people's〔folk's〕 home ; an asylum for the aged — 자금 an endowment
양론 兩論 two opposite opinions
양류 楊柳 〖식물〗 a willow
양륙 揚陸 landing ; unloading ; disembarkation —하다 land ; unload ; disembark
—기 an unloader — 기간 days for landing —비 landing charges —선 a lighter ; a barge — 수속 landing formalities — 인부 a dock hand ; a docker ; a stevedore —장 a landing place〔platform〕 —지 a designated landing place —항 a port of discharge ; an unloading port
†양립 兩立 coexistence ; compatibility —하다 be compatible 《with》 ; coexist 《with》 ; stand together ¶ 양립할 수 있다〔없다〕 be compatible〔incompatible〕 《with》 // 자본주의와 사회주의는 양립 못한다 Capitalism is incompatible with socialism. // 이 사상은 우리 나라의 전통과 양립하지 못한다 This idea is inconsistent with the tradition of our country.
양마 良馬 a fine horse
양막 羊膜 the amnion 《*pl.* -nia》
*양말 洋襪 socks (짧은) ; stockings (긴) ; hose 《미》 ¶ 양말 한 켤레 a pair of socks〔stockings〕 // 양말을 신지 않은 stockingless ; no-stocking
— 대님 sock-suspenders ; garters —류 hosiery 나일론 — nylon stockings 순모 — all-wool hosiery〔socks〕
양머리 洋— hair dressed in European 〔Western〕 style
양면 兩面 both〔two〕 faces〔sides〕 ¶ 양면의 double-faced ; both-sided // 인생의 양면 both bright and seamy sides of life
— 가치 〖심리〗 ambivalence — 날염(捺染) duplex printing — 레코드 a double-sided〔-faced〕 record — 인쇄 printing on both sides of the paper — 인쇄 기계 a perfecting machine〔press〕 — 정책 a two-pronged policy
양명 揚名 gaining fame〔renown〕 —하다 make a name ; rise to fame ⇨ 입신 양명
양명학 陽明學 the doctrines〔philosophy, teaching〕 of *Wang Yangming*
—자 a scholar of the *Wang Yangming* school —파 the *Wang Yangming* school (of learning)
양모 養母 a foster mother ; an adoptive mother
†양모 羊毛 wool ; pile ¶ 양모의 woolen // 양모 같은 wool-like ; woolly ; floccose // 양모를 깎다 fleece〔shear〕 sheep
— 거래소 a wool exchange ; a wool hall 《영》 — 공업 the woolen and worsted industry — 공장 a woolmill —상 a wool merchant ; a woolman ; a wool stapler — 제품 woolen goods —직 woolen fabric 〔textiles〕
양모제 養毛劑 a hair tonic
양목 洋木 (fine) cotton cloth
양묘 養苗 cultivating the saplings〔young trees〕 —하다 nurse the saplings
—장 a tree nursery
양묘기 揚錨機 a capstan ; a windlass
양물 陽物 ⇨ 음경
양미 糧米 rice ; provisions ; food
양미간 兩眉間 the space between the eyebrows ; the brow ¶ 양미간을 찌푸리다 knit〔bend〕 one's brows ; frown 《at, on, upon》 // 양미간이 넓다〔좁다〕 have wide-set〔close-set〕 eyebrows〔eyes〕
양민 良民 good citizens〔people〕 ; peaceable people ; law-abiding citizens
— 학살 slaughter〔massacre〕 of the innocent people
양반 兩班 the two upper classes of old Korea ; the nobility ; a nobleman ; a gentleman ; an aristocrat ¶ 양반으로 태어나다 be of noble birth〔blood〕 // 사장님은 바쁘신 양반입니다 Our boss is a busy man.
양방 兩方 both ; the two ; either ; each of the two ; [부정] neither ¶ 양방의 both ; either // 양방이 모두 both ; the two // A, B 양방 both A and B
*양배추 洋— cabbage
—밭 a cabbage patch
양버들 洋— 〖식물〗 a poplar
양법 良法 [법] a good law ; [방법] a good method〔plan, measure〕
양변 兩邊 both sides ; either side ¶ 양변에 on both sides // 길의 양변엔 구경꾼들이 인산을 이루고 있었다 The street was lined with spectators on either side.
양병 養兵 building up〔raising〕 military

forces **—하다** build up〔train〕 military forces ; maintain an army

양병 養病 curing a disease ; nursing one's health ; tending 《a sick person》 ; [악화] aggravating a disease **—하다** cure a disease ; improve one's health ; [악화] aggravate a disease ¶ 그는 해변으로 양병하러 갔다 He has gone to the seaside to recuperate.

양병 佯病 ⇨ 꾀병

†**양보 讓步** concession ; conciliation ; compromise **—하다** concede ; make a concession ; recede 《from》 ; yield (굴하다) ¶ 양보적 concessive ; conciliatory // 양보시키다 persuade 《a person》 into submission ; bring 《a person》 round // …을 위하여 양보하다 concede 《the point》 in 《a person's》 favor // 요구 앞에 양보하다 make a concession to a demand // 조금도 양보 않다 make no concession ; do not yield a single point // 어느 편도 양보 않다 neither would give in // 공을 남에게 양보하다 disclaim one's own merit in favor of others // 본의는 아니지만 양보하여 너에게 동의하마 I'll stretch a point and agree with you. // 양보적인 태도를 취했다 We took a conciliatory attitude. // 사건은 쌍방의 양보로 결말이 났다 The case was settled by mutual concessions. // 서로 조금씩 양보합시다 Let's meet halfway. / Let's go for a golden mean. /Let's go for the happy meduim. // 나는 타협도 양보도 않겠다 I'll not compromise or make any concession. // 지금껏 노동자측에서도 경영자측에서도 한 발짝도 양보를 하지 않았다 So far, neither labor nor management has given an inch.

—절(節) 〖문법〗 a concessive clause

양복 洋服 Western〔European〕 style clothes〔clothing〕 ; Occidental dress ; a Western〔European〕 dress ¶ 주문한 양복 a suit made to order // 양복 차림의 in Western clothes // 양복을 입다 put on Western〔European〕 clothes ; wear Western〔European〕 (style) clothes // 양복 한 벌을 맞추다 have〔get〕 a suit of clothes made

—감 cloth ; yardage〔material〕 for foreign clothes **—걸이** a coat hanger ; a coatrack **—장** a wardrobe **—장이** [만드는] a tailor ; a dress-maker (양재사) ; [입은] a man in Western clothes **—점** a tailor's (shop) ; a clothing store **—지** cloth ; stuff ; suiting ; material

***양봉 養蜂** bee-keeping ; bee-culture ; apiculture **—하다** keep bees ; engage in apiculture ¶ 양봉에 종사하다 engage in apiculture ; keep bees

—가 a bee-keeper ; an apiarist ; an apiarian ; an apiculturist **— 상자** a wooden beehive ; a movable comb hive **— 식물** a bee plant **—업** bee-farming **—장** a bee-farm〔-yard〕 ; an apiary ; a bee garden

양부 良否 good or bad ; quality ¶ 승진은 성적의 양부에 따른다 Promotion depends upon one's service. // 물건의 양부를 조사한 후 확답을 드리겠습니다 I shall give a definite answer after examining the quality of the goods.

양부 養父 a foster father ; an adoptive father

양부모 養父母 foster parents

양부인 洋婦人 a foreign lady ; [창녀] a foreigner's whore

양분 兩分 bisection ; dividing〔cutting〕 into two **—하다** bisect ; halve ; cut 〔divide〕 《a thing》 into two

양분 養分 nourishment ; nutrient ; nutritious substance〔matter〕 ; nutritional elements ; sustenance ¶ 양분이 있다 be nourishing ; contain nourishment // 양분을 흡수하다 take nourishment 《from》 // 적당히 양분을 취하는 것이 건강상 중요하다 Proper nutrition is important for good health.

— 비율 nutrient ratio

양비둘기 a rock dove〔pigeon〕

양사 羊舍 a sheep shed

양사 洋絲 ⇨ 양실(洋—)

양사자 養嗣子 an adopted heir

양산 洋傘 an umbrella ⇨ 우산

***양산 陽傘** a parasol ; a sunshade ¶ 양산을 펴다 open〔spread, unfold〕 a parasol // 양산을 접다 close〔shut, fold〕 a parasol

양산 量産 mass production **—하다** mass-produce

***양상 樣相** an aspect ; a phase ; appearance ; looks ; a condition ; 〖논리〗 a modality ¶ …의 양상을 이루다 assume an aspect 《of》 // 심상치 않은 양상을 이루다 look unusual ; assume an extraordinary aspect // 양상을 일변시키다 change the whole appearance

양상 군자 梁上君子 a thief〔robber〕 ; a rat

양상치 洋— lettuce

양생 養生 [보건] care of health ; preservation of one's health ; [보양] recuperation **—하다** take care of one's health ; nurse one's health ; improve〔promote〕 one's health ; [병후에] recuperate oneself ¶ 양생에 좋다 be hygienic ; be good for the health ; be beneficial to health // 치료 보다는 양생이 낫다 Prevention is better than cure. // 나는 양생으로서 매일 뱀장어를 먹는다 I eat eel every day to preserve my health.

—법 a regimen ; rules for one's health ; sanitation ; hygiene

양서 洋書 a foreign〔Western〕 book ; European and American books

양서 良書 a good book ; a valuable work ¶ 양서를 구하다 seek〔choose〕 good books

양서 兩棲 ¶ 양서의 〖동물〗 amphibious

— 동물 an amphibian (animal) ; an amphibious animal ; a batrachian (ani-

mal) —류 Amphibia ; Batrachia
양성 兩性 both sexes ; the (two) sexes ¶ 양성의 bisexual
— 구유(具有) hermaphroditism ; androgyny — 구유자 a hermaphrodite ; an androgyne — 생식 amphigony ; gamogenesis ; digenesis —체 〖생물〗 a bisexual — 혼합 amphimixis —화(花) 〖식물〗 a bisexual〔an androgynous〕 flower
양성 陽性 positivity ¶ 양성의 positive ; active
— 반응 positive reaction ¶ 투베르쿨린 반응은 양성 반응이었다 The tuberculin test proved positive. — 원소 a positive element — 전환 [투베르쿨린의] change to positive —화(化) bringing〔coming〕 into the open ¶ 정치 자금을 양성화하다 bring out into the open sources of political funds ; make public the sources of political funds
†양성 養成 training ; education ; [함양] cultivation ; nurture —하다 train ; educate ; cultivate ; bring up ; nurse ¶ 교원을 양성하다 train teachers // 실업에 종사하고자 하는 자를 양성하다 equip men for business // 체력을 양성하다 cultivate〔develop〕 one's physical strength // 인재를 양성하다 cultivate men of talent〔ability〕 // 독립 정신을 양성하다 foster〔cultivate〕 the spirit of independence
— 기간 a training period ; the period of apprenticeship —소 a training school 〔center〕 ¶ 그 대학은 사실상 관리의 양성소였다 The University was in practice the〔a〕 nursery of government officials. 교원〔간호원〕 —소 a training school for teachers〔nurses〕 ; teachers'〔nurses'〕 training school
양성 良性 〖의학〗 ¶ 양성의 benign 〔benignant〕 《disease》
— 종양 benign tumor
양성하다 釀成— brew ; forment ; breed ; foster ; create ; produce
양소매 책상 兩—册床 a kneehole desk
양속 良俗 good customs and manners
미풍 — a good and beautiful custom
양손 兩— both〔the two〕 hands ¶ 양손에 꽃 be doubly blessed ; [비유적] sit between two beauties
양손 養孫 an adopted grandchild ; the adopted child of one's son
양수 讓受 acquisition by transfer ; inheritance ; taking over —하다 obtain by transfer ; take over ; receive ; inherit
—인 a grantee ; a transferee ; an assignee —증 a certificate of receipt ; a receipt form
양수 兩手 both hands ; [장기·바둑] a double point〔check〕 in a game ¶ 양수로 들다 hold 《a thing》 with both hands
—잡이 [사람] an ambidexter ; an ambidextrous person ; [장기·바둑에서] scoring a double point〔check〕 with a single move
양수 羊水 amniotic fluid ¶ 양수가 나오다 the water breaks
양수 揚水 water pumping ; pumping water
양수기 量水器 a water meter
양수기 揚水機 a water pump
양순 良順 —하다 (be) good and obedient ; meek ; docile ; peaceable ¶ 양순한 백성 law-abiding〔obedient〕 people // 양순한 어린이 a docile〔well-behaved〕 child // 양순한 성질 a gentle nature ; a yielding disposition // 양순하게 말을 듣다 do as one is told without objection ; listen to 《a person's》 suggestion〔advice〕 // 서커스의 동물은 대개 양순하다 Most circus animals are tame.
양순음 兩脣音 〖음성〗 a bilabial
양식 洋式 Western〔European, American, Occidental〕 style ¶ 양식의〔으로〕 in Western fashion〔style〕
— 가옥〔건축〕 a Western-style house 〔building〕
양식 洋食 Western food ; foreign cookery 〔dishes〕 ¶ 양식 먹는 법 Western table manners
— 식사법 Western table manners — 요리법 Western cooking —점 a restaurant (serving foreign dishes)
*양식 良識 good sense ¶ 양식 있는 사람 a sensible〔intellectual〕 person ; a person of sense ; a person of sound judgment // 그의 양식을 의심하다 doubt if he is really sound in judgment〔if his judgment is sound〕 // 나는 네가 그런 바보짓을 하지 않을 양식은 있는 줄 알았다 I thought you had more sense than to do such a foolish thing.
양식 養殖 raising ; farming ; culture ; breeding ; rearing —하다 raise ; rear ; cultivate ; plant (굴 따위)
—장 a nursery ; a farm ; a breeding ground —지(池) a culture pond — 진주 a culture(d) pearl ; an artificially induced pearl —학 thremmatology 굴— oyster farming 진주 — pearl culture
†양식 樣式 a mode ; form ; modality ; 〖건축〗 a style ; an order ¶ 일정한 양식 a fixed form // 양식화하다 conventionalize
— 기입 blank filling 생활 — one's style 〔mode〕 of living ; a way of life ¶ 생활양식을 바꾸다 change one's mode〔style〕 of living
양식 糧食 provisions ; food ; bread ; supplies ; rations ; victuals ¶ 마음의 양식 mental〔spiritual〕 food ; [책 따위] mental pabulum // 그날 그날의 양식을 벌다 earn one's daily bread // 양식이 충분하다 have an ample supply of food ; be well provisioned // 양식이 부족하다 provisions fall 〔run〕 short ; [사람이 주어] run short of provisions // 양식이 떨어지다 provisions give out ; [사람이 주어] run out of pro-

visions // 양식의 공급을 끊다 cut off the supply of food // 양식을 지급하다 provision ; provide 《a person》 with food // 양식을 저장하다 lay in provisions // 5일분의 양식을 휴대하다 take a 5-day supply of food // 빵은 생명의 양식이다 Bread is the staff of life.

양식기 洋食器 foreign-style tableware ; dinnerware ¶ 양식기 한 벌 a set of dinnerware ; a dinner set〔service〕

양신 良辰 a lucky〔propitious〕 day

양실 洋— foreign〔imported〕 thread ; Western sewing cotton ; machine cotton

양실 洋室 a Western-style room ; a room furnished in foreign style

양실 兩失 a double loss ; a double failure **—하다** lose both ; suffer〔have〕 a double loss

****양심 良心** conscience ; conscientiousness ; the still small voice (양심의 속삭임) ; the inner voice ¶ 한조각의 양심 a scrap of conscience // 양심의 가책 the pang〔pricks, stings〕 of conscience // 학자적 양심 academic〔scientific〕 honesty ; a scholarly conscience // 양심적(으로) conscientious (ly) // 양심적인 재판장 a conscientious judge // 양심적인 상인 an honest trader // 양심이 없는 conscienceless // 양심을 만족시키기 위해 for conscience(') sake // 양심을 등지다 go against〔run counter to〕 (the dictates of) one's own conscience // 양심에 부끄럽지 않다 have a clear〔good〕 conscience // 양심에 부끄럽다 have a bad〔guilty〕 conscience // 양심(의 명)을 좇아서 행하다 act according to (the dictates of) one's conscience // 양심의 가책을 받다 be conscience-stricken ; be stung by conscience ; feel the qualms 〔pricks, stings〕 of conscience // 사람의 양심에 호소하다 appeal to〔address〕 another's conscience // 그것은 양심의 문제다 It is a point of conscience. // 그것은 그의 양심을 괴롭혔다 It weighed upon his conscience. // 그는 양심의 가책을 받는다 His conscience smites him. /He has qualms 〔pricks〕 of conscience. // 그는 양심이라곤 손톱만큼도 없다 He has not an ounce of conscience. // 누구에게나 양심은 있다 Everyone has a conscience. // 그런 짓은 나의 양심이 허락치 않는다 I cannot, in conscience, do such a thing. // 너의 양심에 물어 봐라 Listen to what the still small voice tells you ! // 그는 그러한 짓을 하고 양심의 가책을 받았다 His conscience smote 〔reproached〕 him for the deed. // 너의 양심에 맡긴다 I leave you to your conscience.

양심 兩心 duplicity ; a double heart

양심 養心 mental〔moral〕 culture ; cultivation of the mind **—하다** improve oneself ; cultivate one's mind

양쌀 洋— foreign rice

양아들 養— an adopted son ; a foster son

양아버지 養— an adoptive father ; a foster father

양아욱 洋— 〖식물〗 a geranium

양아치 a ragpicker ⇨ 넝마(—주이)

양악 洋樂 Western〔European〕 music **—가** a player〔musician〕 of Western 〔European〕 music (instrument)

양안 兩岸 both banks〔sides〕 ; either bank ¶ 강의 양안 both banks of the river

양안 兩眼 both eyes
양안이 모두 안 보이다 〔속담〕 be blind of 〔in〕 both eyes

양안 良案 a good〔capital〕 idea〔plan〕

양약 良藥 a good medicine ; an efficacious medicine〔remedy〕
양약은 입에 쓰다 〔속담〕 A good medicine tastes bitter. / Unpleasant advice is a good medicine.

양약 洋藥 Western drugs〔medicine〕 ; foreign〔imported〕 drugs
—국 a foreign-medicine〔-drug〕 shop 〔store〕

양양 洋洋 —하다 (be) vast ; broad ; boundless ; wide ; [전도가] bright ; great ¶ 양양한 대하 a lordly〔mighty〕 river // 양양한 대해 a vast expanse of sea ; the boundless ocean // 그에게는 양양한 전도가 있다 He has a great〔rosy〕 future before him. /He has an unlimited future.

양양하다 揚揚— (be) triumphant ; exultant ; conceited ; self-satisfied ¶ 의기 양양한 triumphant ; exultant // 의기 양양하게 exulted ; exultantly ; elated ; proudly ; triumphantly ; in triumph ; with flying colors ; in high feather

양어 養魚 fish-breeding〔-farming〕 ; fish culture ; pisciculture **—하다** breed 〔raise〕 fish
—가 a fish-farmer〔-breeder〕 ; a pisciculturist **—장** a fish-farm **—지** a fish-pond ; a breeding pond ; a piscina

양어깨 ⇨ 쌍견(雙肩)

양어머니 養— a foster-mother

양어버이 養— foster parents ⇨ 양부모

양언 揚言 speaking publicly ; announcement ; declaration **—하다** say publicly ; announce ; declare ; assert

양여 讓與 transfer ; cession (영토의) ; concession (이권의) ; surrender (포기) ; alienation ⇨ 양도 **—하다** transfer ; assign ; concede 《a privilege to a person》 ; make over 《one's rights to another》 ¶ 권리를 양여하다 transfer one's rights to 《a person》

양염 陽炎 heat waves〔haze〕

양옥 洋屋 a Western-〔European-, American-〕 style house

양요 兩凹 double-concave
— 렌즈 a double-concave lens

양요리 洋料理 foreign〔Western-style〕 food〔dishes, cooking, cookery〕 ; Euro-

pean dishes〔food〕
양용 兩用 《for》 double use ; combined use
수륙 — 비행기〔전차〕 an amphibian plane〔tank〕
양우 良友 a good friend
양우리 羊— a sheep pen〔fold〕
양웅 兩雄 two heroes〔great men〕
양원 兩院 both Houses〔Chambers〕 ; the two Houses ¶ 양원일치의 의견 a concurrent vote of both Houses // 양원을 통과하다 pass both Houses
— 의원 members of both Houses — 제도 a bicameral system — 협의회 a joint conference of the two Houses 상하 — the Houses of Representatives and Councilors ; the Houses of Commons and Lords 《영》 ; the House and Senate 《미》
양위 讓位 abdication (of the throne) ; demise of the Crown — 하다 abdicate the throne 《in favor of the Crown Prince》 ; demise〔vacate〕 the throne
양유 羊乳 goat('s) milk
*양육 養育 bringing up ; rearing ; breeding ; fostering ; care 《of babies》 — 하다 bring up ; rear ; nurse ; raise ; foster ¶ 자녀의 양육 the rearing〔bringing up〕 of children // 검소하게 양육되다 be reared〔brought up〕 in simplicity // 아기를 우유로 양육하다 bring up〔raise〕 a child on cow's milk // 너는 여아의 양육에는 부적당하다 You are not fit to bring up girls. // 그 여자는 네 아이를 맡아 양육했다 She took four children and brought them up.
— 법 the way〔method〕 of bringing up children ; the care and feeding of children — 비 the expense〔cost〕 of bringing up a child — 원 a poorhouse 《영》 ; a workhouse 《미》 ; [고아의] an orphanage ¶ 양육원에 수용하다 take 《an orphan》 into an orphanage — 자 a fosterer ; a rearer ; a breeder ; a supporter
양육 羊肉 mutton
양으로 陽— [드러나게] openly ; publicly ; frankly
양은 洋銀 German〔nickel〕 silver ; albata
양의 洋醫 a physician who practices Western medical science ; a Western (medical) doctor ; a Western physician
양의 良醫 a good〔skillful〕 physician
양의 兩儀 yim and yang ; heaven and earth
양이 攘夷 exclusion〔expulsion〕 of foreigners
— 론 exclusionism ; anti-alienism ¶ 양이론자 an anti-alienist
양이 洋夷 Western barbarians
양이온 陽— 〖물리〗 a positive ion ; a cation
양익 兩翼 both wings ; [대열의] both flanks

양인 兩人 two persons ; both parties ; a pair ; a couple ¶ 양인이 모두 both (of them) ; either (of the two)
양인 洋人 a Westerner ; a foreigner ; an Occidental
양인 良人 a good-hearted person
양일 兩日 two days ; a couple of days
— 간 for〔in〕 two days〔a couple of days〕 ; within two days
양입 계출 量入計出 measuring one's spending by one's means
†양자 兩者 both (persons, parties, events, things) together ¶ 양자 합의하에 under joint〔bilateral〕 agreement
— 택일 selecting one alternative
양자 量子 〖물리〗 quantum
— 론 the quantum theory — 물리학 quantum physics — 역학 quantum mechanics
양자 陽子 〖물리·화학〗 a proton
†양자 養子 a foster child〔son, daughter〕 ; an adopted son〔daughter〕 ; one's son by adoption ; a son-in-law ; [행위] adoption ¶ 양자로 가는 집 the adoptive family ; one's family of adoption // 양자로 삼다 make an adopted child 《of》 ; adopt 《a person》 as one's child〔son〕 // 양자로 가다 be〔get〕 adopted into 《a person's》 family ; become 《a person's》 adopted child // 양자로 주다 give one's child 《to a person》 // 나의 셋째 아들은 작년에 어느분에게 양자로 갔다 A certain person adopted my third son last year as his legal heir. // 그는 지체 있는 집에 양자로 들어갔다 He was adopted into a respectable family.
양자강 揚子江 the Yangtse River
양잠 養蠶 raising silkworms ; silk raising ; silk culture ; sericulture — 하다 raise〔rear〕 silkworms ¶ 금년의 양잠 수확 this year's crop of silk
— 가 a silk raiser〔grower〕 ; a sericulturist — 농가 a silk-raising farmer ; a silk-farmer — 소 a cocoonery — 실 a silkworm nursery〔house〕 — 업 the silk-raising 〔sericultural〕 industry — 지 a silk〔silkworm〕-raising district
*양장 洋裝 ① [양복] foreign〔European, American〕 clothes ; foreign-〔Western-〕 style dress — 하다 be dressed in Western-style〔after Western fashion〕 ; wear Western-style clothes ; dress in foreign〔Western-style〕 clothes ¶ 그녀는 양장이 어울린다 She looks better in Western dress.
② [제본] binding a book in Western style ¶ 양장한 책 a book bound in foreign〔Western〕 style
— 부인 a lady in foreign〔Western〕 dress
— 점 a dressmaking shop ; a couture house
양장 羊腸 ① the entrails of a goat ② a winding〔twisting, tortuous〕 path ; a

narrow meandering road ¶ 양장의 winding ; zigzag ; meandering // 양장 같은 산길 a winding〔twisting〕 mountain path ; a narrow meandering mountain road

양장 良將 a good〔an able〕 general

*__양재 洋裁__ foreign (style) dressmaking
—사 a dressmaker ; a seamstress **—학원** a (foreign style) dressmaking school

양재 良才 [재목] good timber ; good material ; [인재] a man of ability ; a competent person

양재기 洋— enamelware

양잿물 caustic soda (used as a cleansing material)

양적 量的 quantitative ¶ 양적으로 quantitatively

양전 兩全 —하다 be satisfactory〔advantageous〕 to both sides〔parties〕
—지책 a plan advantageous〔satisfactory〕 to both sides

양전 陽轉 『의학』 positive conversion **—하다** change to〔turn〕 positive

양전기 陽電氣 『물리』 positive〔plus, vitreous〕 electricity
—선 positive rays

양전자 陽電子 『물리』 a positron

양정 糧政 food administration〔policy〕

양젖 羊— goat('s) milk

*__양조 釀造__ brewing ; distillation ; brewage **—하다** brew 《beer》; distil 《whisky》 ¶ 맥주를 양조하다 brew beer // 위스키를 양조하다 distil(l) whisky // 맥주는 보리로 양조한다 Beer is brewed from barley.
—량 the quantity brewed **—법** the method of brewing **—세** tax on brewage **— 시험소** a brewing laboratory **—업** the brewery business **—(업)자** a brewer ; a distiller **—장** a brewery ; a distillery **—학** zymology ; zymurgy

양조모 養祖母 one's adoptive grandmother

양조부 養祖父 one's adoptive grandfather

양종 良種 a good〔fine〕 breed

양종 洋種 a foreign breed ; Western kind〔seeds〕 ¶ 양종의 foreign origin 〔breed〕
—닭 a chicken of foreign stock

양주 洋酒 foreign wine〔liquors〕
—류 liquors and drinks **—상** a wine merchant ; a dealer in foreign liquors

양주 兩主 husband and wife ; man and wife ; a (married) couple ; a (wedded) pair ¶ 양주 싸움은 칼로 물베기 The quarrel of a married couple is (like) cutting water with a knife./Domestic quarrels are soon forgotten./Domestic scenes are not to make a fuss about./ Domestic quarrels are soon healed.

양즙 胖汁 (ox-)tripe broth

양지 良知 intuitive knowledge ; intuition

양지 洋紙 (machine-made) paper

*__양지 陽地__ a sunny place〔spot〕 ; the sun ; sunshine ¶ 양지의 sunny ; in the sun // 양지에 in the sun // 양지에서 말리다 dry in the sun // 양지에 내놓지 않다 keep 《a thing》 out of the sun
—쪽 the sunny side ; a sunny place
양지가 음지되고 음지가 양지된다 속담 Sunny spots get darkened and dark spots get sunny./Life has many ups and downs./Life is full of ups and downs./ Sadness and gladness succeed each other./Joy and sorrow are next-door neighbours./Bad luck often brings good luck./The worse luck now, the better another time.

양지 諒知 understanding ; appreciation **—하다** understand ; appreciate ; know ¶ 양지하시기 바랍니다 This is to give notice 《that》; This is to inform you 《of》; I beg to inform you 《that》

양지 羊脂 mutton-tallow

양지꽃 陽地— 『식물』 cinquefoil

양지머리 the bricket of beef
—뼈 the ribs of an ox〔a beef〕

⁑**양지바르다 陽地—** 《a place》 be sunny ; be full of sunshine ¶ 양지바른 곳에 묻히다 be buried on a sunny slope of a mountain // 양지바른 곳에 집을 짓다 build a house in a sunny place

양진 痒疹 『의학』 prurigo

양진영 兩陣營 both camps〔parties〕 ; the two opposing sides ¶ 동서 양진영 the camps of the East and West ; the East and West camps ; the two power blocks of the world // 동서 양진영에 속하지 않은 나라들 unaligned〔nonaligned〕 countries

양질 良質 good quality ; superior quality ¶ 양질의 of good quality ; superior ; good (in quality)

양짝 兩— both counterparts ; two pairs 〔couples〕

*__양쪽 兩—__ both sides ; either side ; [사람] both ; the two ; either ; each of the two ; neither ⇨ 두 사람 ¶ 양쪽의 both ; either // 길의 양쪽에 on either side of the street ; on both sides of the street // 나는 양쪽 말고삐를 끌어 당겼다 I pulled both (the) reins. // 그것은 양쪽 모두 내것이다 They are both mine. // 양쪽 모두 내것이 아니다 Neither (of them) is〔are〕 mine. // 양쪽 모두 가지고 싶지 않다 I want neither (of them)./I don't want either (of them). // 길의 양쪽은 구경꾼으로 가득했다 The street was lined with spectators on either side. // 길을 건널 때는 양쪽을 잘 살펴라 Look carefully in both directions 〔Look both ways carefully〕 before crossing the street. // 양쪽이 모두 일리가 있다 Much may be said on both sides. // 양쪽 다 알고 있다 I know both of them./I know them both. // 양쪽 다 모른다 I know neither of them. // 그들은 양쪽이 다 행복했다 They were both happy. // 양쪽 다 결석이다 Both are absent./They are both absent. // 그 학생들은 양쪽 모두 숙제를 끝마쳤다 The pupils have both

done their home work.
양차 兩次 two times ; twice
양차렵 light cotton padding worn in spring and fall
양찰 諒察 sympathy ; sympathetic understanding〔consideration〕 ―하다 take into consideration〔account〕; sympathize with ; consider ; understand ¶ 사정을 양찰하다 make allowances for the circumstances // 양찰을 바라다 seek an understanding with《a person》about《a matter》// 이와 같은 사정이오니 아무쪼록 양찰하여 주시기 바랍니다 Such being the case, I pray you will kindly excuse me〔sympathize with my situation〕.
양책 良策 a good plan〔scheme〕; a good〔fine〕 idea ; a good policy ; a capital plan ¶ 그것 양책이군 That's a good idea.
양처 兩處 two〔both〕 places
양처 良妻 a good wife ¶ 현모양처 a good wife and wise mother // 현모양처주의 교육 an education for making good wives and wise mothers
양철 兩凸 double convex
― 렌즈 a biconvex lens
양철 洋鐵 galvanized iron ; tinned iron ; tin-plate ; zinc
― 가위 (a pair of) snips ― 깡통 a tin ; a can《미》 ―공 a tinman ; a tinner ; a tinsmith ― 공장 a tinplate shop ― 제품 tinware ― 지붕 a tin roof ―집 a tin-roof house ―통 a tin pail ; a metal bucket ―판 a tinplate sheet ; tinned sheet
양청 洋靑 deep〔Prussian〕 blue ; ultramarine
양초 糧草 provisions and fodder
†양초 洋― a (wax) candle ; a taper (가는 것) ¶ 양초를 켜다 burn〔light〕 a candle // 양초를 불어 끄다 blow out a candle // 양초가 다 닳아져 간다 The candle is burning low.
―대 a candlestick ; a candleholder ― 동강 a candle end ― 심지 the wick (of a candle) ; a candlewick
양촉 諒燭 ⇨ 양찰
양추 涼秋 cool autumn ; September of the lunar calendar
양춘 陽春 spring ; the springtime ; January (of the lunar calendar) ¶ 양춘 3월에 in March, when spring comes round with its warm sunshine
― 가절 the pleasant springtime
양춤 洋― a Western dance
양취 佯醉 feigned〔sham〕 drunkenness ; pretending to be drunken
양측 兩側 both sides ; either side ¶ 길의 양측에 on either side of the street ; on both sides of the street // 길의 양측에 늘어서다 be lined on either side of the street
양치 養齒 brushing one's teeth ; rinsing the mouth ―하다 brush one's teeth ; rinse (out) one's mouth ; gargle (the throat)
― 그릇 a gargling bowl ―물 gargling water ― 물약 a gargle ; a mouth wash ― 소금 dentifrice salt ; tooth powder ―질 brushing one's teeth ; rinsing the mouth ¶ 소금물로 양치질하다 rinse one's mouth with salt and water
‡양치기 羊― sheep-raising
*양치류 羊齒類― 〖식물〗 the ferns
양치질 ⇨ 양치(養齒)
†양친 兩親 parents ; one's father and mother ¶ 양친의 parental // 양친이 없는 아이 an orphaned child ; an orphan // 양친 슬하에 under one's parental roof // 양친을 잃다 lose〔be deprived of, be bereft of〕 one's parents ; become orphaned // 그 여자는 양친이 없는 아들 둘을 인수했다 She took in two orphaned children.
양친 養親 ① [양부모] foster〔adoptive〕 parents ② [봉양] supporting one's parents
양코 洋― a foreigner's nose ; a large protruding nose ; a foreigner
―배기 a Yankee
양키 a Yankee ; a Yank《속》
― 기질 Yankeeism
‡양탄자 洋― a carpet ; a rug ; [감] rugcloth ; carpeting ¶ 양탄자를 깔다 spread a carpet ; carpet《a room》// 마루에 두꺼운 양탄자가 깔려 있다 The floor is thickly carpeted.
양태 ① the brim of a Korean hat ② 〖물고기〗 a flathead ; a dragonet
양태 樣態 a mode ⇨ 양상(樣相)
*양털 羊― wool ; sheep's hair ⇨ 양모(羊毛)
양토 壤土 ① ⇨ 토양 ② loamy soil
양토 養兎 rabbit raising〔farming〕; rabbit rearing ―하다 raise〔breed〕 rabbit
―장 a (rabbit) warren ; a rabbitry ¶ 양토장 주인 a warrener
‡양파 洋― an onion
양팔 兩― two〔both〕 arms
*양편 兩便 both sides ; either side ¶ 길 양편에 on either side〔both sides〕 of the street // 그렇게 하면 양편에서 만족할 것이다 That will satisfy both parties. // 양편 다 싫소 I don't like either (of them). // 양편이 상대방의 속셈을 알고 있었다 Either knew what was on the other's mind. // 양편에 은행나무가 줄지어 있다 On either side of the road grows a long line of gingko trees.
양푼 a large brass basin〔bowl〕
양품 洋品 foreign articles〔goods〕
―점 haberdashery ; a foreign-goods shop〔store〕; a fancy (goods) shop〔store〕; a haberdasher's (store)
양풍 良風 a good custom
― 미속 a good and beautiful custom
양풍 洋風 foreign〔European, Western〕 style ; Occidental custom(s) ; foreign manner ¶ 양풍의 foreign-style ; of for-

eign style // 양풍의 건물 a building in foreign style ; a foreign style building // 양풍의 생활 Western style living // 양풍 장식의 방 a room furnished in European style // 양풍으로 머리를 손질하다 dress one's hair in Western style

양피 羊皮 sheep skin ; goat skin ; a roan (무두질하지 않은)
— 구두 sheepskin〔goatskin〕 shoes —지 parchment ; sheepskin ; membrane

양학 洋學 Western〔European〕 learning ¶ 양학을 배우다 study Western science

양항 良港 a good harbor

양항라 洋亢羅 sheer cotton ; batiste ; muslin

양해 諒解 [이해] understanding ; comprehension ; consent ; agreement ; approval ; approbation —하다 understand ; comprehend ; consent to ; agree with ; approve of ; appreciate ¶ 상호의 양해 mutual understanding // 상호 양해하에 by mutual agreement // 양해할 수 있는 comprehensible ; understandable // 양해하기 어려운 incomprehensible ; beyond one's comprehension // 양해가 되다 come to 〔arrive at〕 an agreement〔understanding〕 // 양해를 구하다 seek an understanding with 《a person》 about 《a matter》 // 그것은 나에게는 양해가 안된다 It is beyond 〔above〕 my comprehension. /It is incomprehensible to me. /It is double Dutch to me. // 이웃에 양해를 먼저 구해두는 편이 좋을 것이다 We'd better give the neighbors advance notice.
— 사항 agreed items

양해 羊— 〖민속〗 the Year of the Sheep

양행 洋行 ① [외국행] foreign travel ; going〔traveling〕 abroad ; travel abroad ; a visit abroad 《to a foreign country》 —하다 go abroad ; travel abroad ; go on a foreign tour ¶ 양행에서 돌아온 사람 a person who has been abroad // 양행 중에 during one's stay abroad // 양행중이다 be abroad // 양행을 명령받다 be ordered abroad // 양행한 일은 없다 I have never been abroad. // 그는 회사 일로 양행하였다 He has been sent abroad by his firm.
② [점포] a foreign business firm ; a hong (중국의)

양향성 兩向性 〖심리〗 ambiversion ¶ 양향성인 사람 an ambivert

양형 量刑 weighing of offense ¶ 양형상의 정상 참작 extenuating circumstances in the examination of an offense

양호 養護 protective care 《of children》 ; protection ; nursing —하다 protect ; take 《a child》 under one's protection ; give protective care ¶ 아동의 양호 child protection
— 교사 a nurse-teacher — 시설 a protective institution ; a home for dependent, neglected and abused children

양호 良好 (being) good ; satisfactory —하다 (be) good ; fine ; excellent ; favorable ; satisfactory ¶ 극히 양호한 성적 an excellent record // 경과가 양호하다 make satisfactory progress

양호 兩虎 two tigers ; two heroes
— 상투(相鬪) a Titanic struggle

양호 유환 養虎遺患 Keeping a tiger will only bring trouble upon oneself.

양호필 羊毫筆 a writing-brush made of wool

양홍 洋紅 foreign red dyes ; carmine ; crimson

양화 洋畫 ① [그림] a Western (style) painting〔picture〕 ; an oil painting
② [영화] a foreign movie〔film〕
—가 an oil painter ; an artist of Western painting — 전문(영화)관 a foreign-film theater ; a movie-theater that shows foreign films only

양화 洋靴 leather shoes ; shoes (단화) ; boots (반장화)
—점 a shoe store —점 주인 a shoe maker ; a shoe dealer — (직)공 a shoemaker

양화 陽畫 〖사진〗 a positive (picture print)

양화 良貨 good valid money ; good money〔coin〕 ¶ 악화는 양화를 구축한다 Bad money drives out good money.

양회 洋灰 cement

***얕다** ① [깊이가] (be) shallow ¶ 얕은 물 a shoal ; a shallow // 얕은 해안 a shoaling beach // 얕은 못 a shallow pond ; a pond of small depth // 얕은 항구 a harbor with shallow water close in shore // 얕은 물을 건너다 wade // 개울이 얕아서 걸어서 건널 수 있었다 The stream was shallow and we could walk across it. // 물이 얕은 곳에서 헤엄쳐라 You should swim in shallow water.
② [천박] (be) shallow ; superficial ¶ 얕은 꾀 transparent subterfuge〔guile〕 // 꾀가 얕은 사람 a shallow person // 생각이 얕은 사람 a short-brained person // 얕은 지식〔소견〕 a superficial knowledge〔view〕 // 여자의 얕은 생각에서 through her shallow thinking // 그의 영문학 실력은 얕다 He has a smattering knowledge of English literature. // 의사와 결혼하면 잘 살겠거니 하는 얕은 생각에서 그 여자는 그와 결혼했다 She married him with the shallow notion that marriage with a doctor would bring her an easy living. // 자기가 없어지면 남편도 정신을 차릴 것이라는 얕은 생각에서 집을 뛰쳐 나갔다 She ran away from home prompted by the shallow idea that her disappearance would bring her husband to his senses.
③ [빛깔] (be) light ; pale ¶ 얕은 초록빛 light green
④ [관계] (be) slight ; be not close ¶ 나와 그이는 교제가 얕다 I am only slightly acquainted with him. /I have but slight acquaintance with him. // A와 B는 관계가

얕다 A is only slightly related with B. /A has only slight relations with B.
⑤ [높이] (be) low ; [키] short ¶ 천장이 얕은 방 a room with a low ceiling // 지붕이 얕은 집 a house with a low roof
⑥ [지위] (be) low ; humble ; lowly ¶ 지위가 얕다 be low in position // 그는 신분이 얕다 He is of low birth [social position].
얕은 내도 깊게 건너라 [속담] Look before you leap.

얕디얕다 (be) ever so shallow [light, low, superficial]

***얕보다** look down upon ; make light of ; despise ; hold 《a person》 in contempt ; belittle ¶ 얕볼 수 없는 적 a formidable enemy // 약한 적이라도 얕보지 마라 Don't belittle [underrate] even a weak enemy [rival]. // 이것들은 얕보아서는 안된다 These things are not to be despised. // 그는 우리를 가난한 친척이라고 얕보고 있다 He looks down upon us as poor relations. // 사람들은 그를 어린애라고 얕보고 있다 They make light of him as a mere boy. // 그가 가난하다고 해서 얕보아서는 안 된다 You should not despise him because he is poor. /You should not look down upon him because he is poor.

***얕잡다** make a low estimate of ; underrate ; despise ; neglect ; make light of ¶ 병을 얕잡다 make light of one's illness // 그것은 교육을 얕잡은 생각이다 Your opinion does an injustice to education. // 사람을 얕잡아보면 안된다 You ought not to hold people cheap.

얕추 in a shallow fashion ; shallowly

얘 [호칭] sonny ; you ; there ; hey ; [이 애] this child [boy, girl] ¶ 얘야 Hey, you ! // 얘 잠깐 기다려 Hey, just a minute ! // 얘 넌 무엇을 하고 있는 거야 Hey, old boy ! What's that you're doing there ? // 얘야 이리 오너라 Hey you, come here !

어 [감탄] oh ; well ; why ; [대답] yes ; yea ¶ 어 내 연필이 없네 Well, what happened to my pencil ? // 어 지금 나가네 Yes, I'm coming.

†**-어 語** a word ; a term (전문어) ; a language (언어, 국어) ¶ 라틴계어 a word of Latin origin
법률— legal terms ¶ 법률어로 말하면 in legal [law] parlence [terminology] **비속—** a slang ; a vulgarism **상업 용—** terms of business **속—** colloquial language ; colloquial expression (낱낱의) **외국—** a foreign language **전문—** technical terms ; a nomenclature

어가 御駕 a royal carriage

어가 漁歌 fishermen's song

어간 an interval (of a time, space) ; a gap ; a space

어간 語幹 the stem of a word

어간유 魚肝油 cod-liver oil ⇨ 간유

어감 語感 a feel(ing) for words ; a linguistic sense ; sensitivity to language ; Sprachgefühl 《도》 ¶ 어감이 예민하다 have a keen sense of language // 어감이 좋다 sound well ; be euphonic [euphonious] // 어감이 나쁘다 do not sound well ; lack euphony ; sound jarring
—받이 a shoulder-pad

어개 魚介 [어류와 조개] fish(es) and shellfish(es) ; [해산물] marine products

어거리 풍년 —豊年 a bumper(-crop) year

어거하다 馭車— [미소를] drive 《ox or horse》 ; urge 《a horse》 ; [제어] manage ; control ; bring under control ; lead ¶ 어거하기 쉬운 easy to manage [control] ; controllable ; easily manageable // 어거하기 어려운 hard to control ; intractable ; unmanageable ; hard to manage // 부하를 잘 어거하다 manage one's men well ; control one's subordinates well

어격 語格 ⇨ 어법(語法)

어겹 a mess ; a jumble

어구 漁具 fishing gear ; fishing implements ; fishing tackle 《총칭》

어구 漁區 a fishing place [area] ; a fishing-ground [district] ; a fishing-bank

어구 語句 ⇨ 어귀(語句)

어군 魚群 a shoal [school] of fish
— 탐지기 a fish-finder

어군 語群 〖문법〗 a word group

어굴 語屈 being argued down to silence ; being silenced in an argument **—하다** be at a loss for an answer ; be put to silence ; be argued down

어귀 an entrance ; an entry 《미》 ; a way in ; an ingress ; the mouth ; an approach 《to a tunnel》 ¶ 강의 어귀 an entry to a river ; an estuary // 항구의 어귀 mouth of a harbor // 방의 어귀 the door of a room // 마을의 어귀 an entrance to a village // 옛날은 관촌이 전주의 어귀였다 In former times *Kwanch'on* was the gateway to *Chŏnju*.

어귀 語句 words and phrases ¶ 어귀의 용법 phraseology ; wording

어귀어귀 ravenously ; voraciously ; greedily ¶ 어귀어귀 먹다 eat ravenously ; eat away with a savage appetite // 어귀어귀 씹다 chew on food ; eat with a stuffed mouth

어귀차다 (be) strong ; firm ; strongminded ; unyielding

어그러지다 [빗나가다] be put out of joint ; be twisted ; deviate [swerve] from ; [불일치] be contrary to ; conflict with ; go wrong 《with》 ; go 《against》 ; [사이가] become estranged from ; go badly ¶ 기대가 어그러지다 [어그러지지 않다] be contrary to [meet, live up to] one's expectation // 법에 어그러지다 be against law // 예의에 어그러지다 violate propriety ; be a lapse of etiquette // 목적에 어그러지지 않다 answer one's purpose // 사이가 어그러지다 be estranged 《from》; be on bad terms 《with》// 책상 다리 하나가 어그러졌다 One of the legs of the table slipped out of joint. // 기대에 어그러지지 않게 노력하겠습니다 I will do my best to live up to your expectation. // 그것은 약속과 어그러지는 일이다 That runs counter to what was promised. // 오해가 생겨 둘 사이가 어그러졌다 Mutual misunderstanding led to their estrangement. // 만사가 어그러지고 말았다 Everything went against me. /Nothing came up to my expectation.

어근 語根 the root〔radical〕 of a word ; an etymon 《*pl.* ~s, -ma》; a radix 《*pl.* ~es, -dices》

어근버근 not fitting into each other properly ; not dovetailing ; not meshing ; [사람이] not getting along smoothly ; on bad terms 《with》 **—하다** do not dovetail 〔fit together, mesh〕; do not get along 〔harmonize〕 ¶ 어근버근해지다 fall out 《with》; disagree 《with》; become estranged from

어금니 a molar (tooth) ; a grinder ; a back tooth

어금막히다 lie crisscross〔crosswise〕

어금지금하다 be rather even ; be much alike ; be of little difference ; be much the same ¶ 모두 어금지금하다 They are much the same. /There is little difference between them. /There is little to choose between them. /They are six of one and half a dozen of the other. // 그 점에 있어서 양자가 어금지금하다 There is little to choose between the two in that respect.

***어긋나다** ① [엇갈리다] cross〔pass〕 each other ; miss each other on the road 〔way〕; [빗나가다] go amiss ; go crisscross ; go wrong with ¶ 길이 어긋나서 그를 못 만났다 We took different paths, so I missed (seeing) him. // 계획이 어긋나다 be baffled in one's design // 예상이 어긋나다 guess wrong // 기대에 어긋나다 fall short of〔fail to come up to〕 one's expectations // 우리 기대에 어긋나지 않기를 바란다 Please see that you prove yourself worthy of the confidence we repose in you. /See to it that you do not betray our confidence (in you). /Try hard not to disappoint us in our hope. // 모든 것이 계획과는 어긋난다 Everything goes wrong with me. /Everything runs counter to my expectations. // 이음매의 나사가 낡아 문이 어긋나 있다 The screws on the hinge are loose, so the door's out of line.

② [틀리다·위반되다] depart〔deviate〕 from ; run counter to ; be contrary to ; be at variance with ¶ 의견이 서로 어긋나다 hold contrary〔different〕 opinions // 행동이 어긋나다 be at cross-purposes with ; go crisscross with // 규칙에 어긋나다 be against〔contrary to〕 the rule // 인도에 어긋나다 be against humanity // 가르침에 어긋나다 deviate from 《a person's》 teachings // 명령에 어긋나다 act against orders ; run counter to orders // 견본과 조금도 어긋나지 않다 correspond exactly to the sample

어긋놓다 lay crosswise ; stack them crisscross〔at angles〕

어긋맞다 face each other crosswise ; be at odd angles from each other ; be crisscross

어긋매끼다 alternate 《with》; stack〔insert〕 in alternation ¶ 검은 줄과 흰 줄을 어긋매끼다 alternate white lines with black

어긋물리다 fit securely ; put in gear ; dovetail ¶ 사개를 어긋물리다 join a tenon and mortise ; dovetail // 톱니바퀴를 어긋물리다 engage〔enmesh〕 gears ; put it in gear

어긋버긋하다 be out of joint with each other ; (be) loose ; uneven

어긋하다 be a bit out of joint

어기 漁期 fishing season

어기다 go against ; act〔offend〕 against ; run counter 《to》; [위반하다] break ; violate ; transgress ¶ 시간을 어기지 않고 punctually ; on time 《미》// 1초도 어기지 않고 punctually to the second // 기대를 어기다 be contrary to 《a person's》 expectations ; fall short of 《a person's》 expectations // 법을 어기다 infringe the law ; offend against the law // 명령을 어기다 disobey 《a person's》 orders // 규칙을 어기다 violate the regulations // 약속을 어기다 break one's promise // 문법을 어기다 break the rules of grammar ; make a grammatical mistake // 맹세를 어기다 break a vow // 뜻을 어기다 fail to meet 〔comply with〕 《a person's》 wishes ; act against 《a person's》 wishes // 약속을 어기지 않다 be true to one's word ; be as good as one's word ; keep one's promise // 충고를 어기다 act against 《a person's》 advice // 시간을 어기지 않다 be punctual〔on time〕 to the minute // 법률을 어기면 벌을 받는다 There is a punishment for infringing the law. /If you offend against the law, you will earn punishment. /The violation of the law will bring you punishment. // 규칙을 어기지 말라 Don't act contrary to the rules. // 신임을 어기지 않도록 하겠다 I will try to be worthy of your trust. // 말씀을 어기는 것 같지만 그는 나쁘지 않다고 생각합니다 I venture to disagree with your opinion that he is to blame. // 그의 처신은 선례를 어기는 것이다 What he has done is against all precedents. // 그는 약속을 어긴 일이 없다 He has never failed to keep his word. // 그것은 헌정 정신을 어기는 것이다 It runs counter to the spirit of constitutionalism 〔constitutional government〕.

어기대다 disobey ; oppose ; go against ; be insubordinate to ; kick against 《authority》; run counter to ¶ 부모한테 어기대다 disobey one's parents // 어기대지 말고 하라는 대로 해라 Don't talk back, just do what you are told.

어기뚱거리다 shuffle along ; waddle ; totter ; swagger

어기뚱하다 (be) haughty and insolent ; audacious ; inordinate ; impertinent ; pert ; saucy ; [허순하다] be a bit loose

어기적거리다 totter ; waddle ; walk listlessly ; trudge along ; shuffle along

어기적어기적 listlessly ; totteringly

어기중하다 於其中— be in the middle ; (be) middling ¶ 어기중하게 좋다 be middling good

어기차다 (be) obstinate ; stubborn ; headstrong ; determined ; resolute ; pers istent ¶ 어기찬 아이 a headstrong child // 어기차게 obstinately ; stubbornly ; persistently // 어기차게 자설을 주장하다 persist in〔hold tenaciously to〕 one's own view

어김 a breach ; a failure ; violation ¶ 어김 없는 unerring ; infallible // 어김 없이 without fail ; surely // 어김 없이 와 주십시오 Come without fail. /Don't fail to come. / Be sure to come. // 월말까지는 어김 없이 그 돈을 주겠다 You shall have the money without fail by the end of the month.

***어깨** ① the shoulder ¶ 처진〔둥근, 벌어진〕 어깨 sloping〔round, square〕 shoulders // 어깨에 메다 shoulder ; bear 〔carry〕 on one's shoulder // 총을 어깨에 메고 with a gun on one's shoulder // 어깨를 두드리다 tap〔pat, clap, slap〕 《a person》 on the shoulder // 어깨를 펴다〔움추리다〕 square〔shrug〕 one's shoulders // 어깨가 뻐근하다 have stiff shoulders ; feel stiff in one's shoulders // 어깨로 숨쉬다 breathe hard〔laboriously〕; gasp for breath ; pant // 어깨를 나란히 하고 걷다 walk shoulder to shoulder〔abreast, side by side〕 《with a person》 // 군중 속을 어깨로 밀어헤치며 나아가다 shoulder one's way through the crowd // 그는 어깨에 총을 메고 있었다 He had a rifle slung across the shoulder. // 이 상의는 어깨 폭이 당긴다 This coat is narrow across the shoulders.
② [비유적] ¶ 어깨가 가벼워지다 feel relieved (of responsibility) // 어깨를 나란히 하다 can compare with〔stand beside〕 《a person》; rank with ; take rank with ; be on a par with // 전자 공학계에서 그와 어깨를 나란히 할 자는 없다 He is unrivaled〔unequaled, matchless〕 in the world of electronics. /He has no equal 〔rival〕 in the field of electronics. // 경치에 있어서 한국과 어깨를 나란히 할 수 있는 나라는 적다 There are few countries that can compare with Korea in scenery 〔scenic beauty〕.

어깨걸이 a shawl

어깨 글자 〖인쇄〗 a superscript ; a superior letter

어깨넘엇글 odd pieces of information acquired by overhearing other persons learning their lessons ; picked up knowledge ¶ 어깨넘엇글로 알고 있다 have picked up bits of knowledge ; have a smattering knowledge of various things

어깨동무 [동무] an old playmate ; a bosom friend from childhood ; a childhood friend ; [동작] putting arms around each other's shoulders **—하다** put arms around each other's shoulders ¶ 어깨동무하고서 걷다 walk arm in arm

어깨 번호 —番號 a superior〔superscript〕 number

어깨뼈 the shoulder blade ¶ 어깨뼈가 부러지다 get one's blade bone broken

어깨차례 —次例 the order of turns ; [키] order of height

어깨총 —銃 [총을 멤] shouldering one's rifle ; [구령] Shoulder arms ! **—하다** shoulder〔slope〕 arms ¶ 어깨총의 자세를 취하다 come to the shoulder〔slope〕 // 우로〔좌로〕 어깨총 [구령] Right〔Left〕 shoulder arms !

어깨춤 a shoulder dance ; moving one's shoulders up and down ¶ 어깨춤을 추다 dance with one's shoulders moving up and down ; dance for joy

어깨통 the circumference of one's shoulders ; one's shoulder measurements

어깻바대 a shoulder pad

어깻바람 wiggling one's shoulders with delight ; swaggering ¶ 어깻바람이 나서 swaggeringly ; in high spirits

어깻숨 a shoulder-heaving breath

어깻죽지 the shoulder joint

어깻짓 moving one's shoulders

어꾸수하다 (be) tasty ; juicy ; palatable ; dainty ; good ; [말씨] pleasing ; delightful ¶ 어꾸수한 음식 a tasty dish // 그의 말투는 어꾸수하다 He speaks in a tactful〔pleasing〕 manner.

어눌 語訥 **—하다** be slow of speech ; have an impediment in one's speech ; (be) in articulate ; stammer ; falter

†**어느** ① [의문] which ; what ¶ 어느 누구 who // 오늘은 어느 모자를 쓰십니까 Which hat are you going to wear today ? // 시내의 어느 곳에 살고 계십니까 In what part of the town do you live ? // 이번에 오시는 것은 금주의 어느 날입니까 What〔On what〕 day of the week will you be here next ? // 어느 소년이 수상했습니까 Which boy won the prize ? // 어느 차를 타시겠습니까 Which car will you take ? // 어느 길

을 가면 됩니까 Which way shall I go〔do it〕? // 배운 선생 중 어느 분이 제일 좋았느냐 Which teacher of all those you were under did you like best? // 어느 김씨 말이냐 큰 김씨냐 작은 김씨냐 Which Mr. *Kim* do you mean, the older or the younger?

② [어느 …이나] any; every (모든 것의); [부정문에서] none ¶ 어느 것이나 whichever; any one // 어느 학교에서도 영어를 가르치고 있다 English is taught at any school. // 어느 책도 재미 없다 None of the books are interesting. // 어느 점에서 보든지 그것은 잘못이다 It is wrong from every point of view〔in every respect, to all appearance(s)〕. // 어느 길로 가든 역에 도착할 것이다 Whichever way you (may) take, you will get to the station. // 어느 신문이나 그 사건을 보도하고 있다 Every newspaper reports the event.

③ [한] a; one; a certain; some; unnamed ¶ 어느 날 one day (과거); some day (미래) // 어느 날 아침〔저녁〕 one morning〔evening〕 // 어느 사람 a certain person; an unnamed person // 어느 때 once // 어느 곳에서 at a certain place // 어느 의미로 in a sense // 어느 경우에서는 in some cases; sometimes // 어느 한가지 일에 전념해라 Devote yourself to some one subject. // 그녀는 프랑스의 어느 곳에 갔다 She went to some place in France. // 나는 그것을 어느 책에서 읽었다 I read it in some book or other. // 어느 바보가 그 꽃병을 깨버렸다 Some fool or other has broken the vase.

*어느 것 which ¶ 어느 것인가 any; some; either (둘 중의) // 어느 것이나 any; all; every; either; [부정의 경우] none; no; neither // 어느 것이든지 any; any one; whichever; either // 어느 것이 제일 좋습니까 Which do you like best? // 어느 것인가 마음에 드셨습니까 Do you like any of them? / [둘의 경우] Do you like either of them? // 어느 것이나 굉장히 멋있다 All of them are splendid. // 어느 것도 마음에 안 든다 I like none〔do not like any〕 of them. // 어느 것을 원하느냐 Which do you want? // 어느 것이 어느 것인지 모르겠다 I can not tell which is which. // 어느 것부터 시작할까 Which shall I begin with〔take up first〕? // 차와 커피 가운데 어느 것을 좋아합니까 Which do you like better, tea or coffee?

*어느 겨를에 in what spare moments; when with so little time to spare ¶ 일하면서 어느 겨를에 시험 준비를 했느냐 How did you ever find time to prepare for examination in the midst of your work? // 어느 겨를에 그런 짓을 하고 있겠니 Where can I find the time to do such things?

어느 누구 anyone; who(ever) ¶ 그는 영어에 있어서 어느 누구에게도 뒤지지 않는다 He is second to none in English.

*어느덧 before one knows〔is aware〕; while one is not aware of it; unawares; unnoticed; without one's knowledge ¶ 세월이 어느덧 지나갔다 The years stole by. // 어느덧 가을이 왔다 Autumn has stolen up on us. / Autumn slipped up on us unawares. // 겨울 방학도 어느덧 지나가 버렸다 The winter vacation has passed all too soon. // 우리들은 어느덧 서울에 도착했다 We reached *Seoul* before we knew it. // 백합이 어느덧 피었다 A lily bloomed before I was aware of it.

어느 때 what time; when ¶ 어느 때든지 any time; whenever; always; all the time; at all times; ever; [부정] never // 어느 때고 any time; some time (or other); some day // 어느 때든지 좋다 Any time will do. // 어느 때고 출발할 준비가 되어 있다 We are ready to start at moment's notice. // 어느 때든지 좋을 때 오십시오 Come (at) anytime〔whenever〕 you like〔please〕. // 어느 때고 후회할 때가 있을 것이다 You will be sorry for it sooner or later.

어느새 in no time; so soon; quickly; without one's knowledge; already ¶ 그는 어느새 가버렸다 He has slipped away. // 어느새 영어를 그렇게 배웠니 How did you ever learn English so well so fast? // 지금 막 꾸지람을 듣고 또 어느새 그런 장난을 해 You got scolded a moment ago, and now you are again up to mischief!

어느 세월에 —歲月— when on earth; when(ever) ¶ 어느 세월에 그가 올지 아무도 모른다 No one can tell when he will come.

*어느 정도 —程度 to some degree; to a certain extent; somewhat; more or less ¶ 어느 정도의 성공을 거두다 attain a measure of success // 어느 정도 영어를 말하다 speak English a little // 어느 정도 병이 낫다 get somewhat better // 과학에 대하여 어느 정도 알고 있다 know something about science; have some knowledge of science // 너는 어느 정도 관계하고 있느냐 To what extent are you concerned? // 대부분의 사람은 어느 정도 이기적이다 Most people are more or less selfish. // 어느 정도 그를 좋아했다 I rather liked him. // 어느 정도 가망이 있느냐 Is there any chance at all? // 너도 그것에 대해서는 어느 정도 책임이 있다 You are also more or less responsible for the matter. // 어느 정도 사실인것 같다 It seems to be true in a way. // 이 보고는 어느 정도 사실과 다르다는 것이 판명됐다 The report proved to be some way from the truth. // 어느 정도의 가격을 생각하고 계십니까 What price range do you have in mind?

†어느 쪽 ① [의문] which side ¶ 어느 쪽이

냐 하면 if anything ; if I have to say ; rather // 어느 쪽이 이겼느냐 Which side won? // 종로의 어느 쪽에 삽니까 What part of *Chong-no* do you live in? // 어느 쪽이라고 말할 수 없다 It is hard to say which. // 광선과 음향은 어느 쪽이 더 빠르냐 Which travels faster, light or sound?
② [무엇이든] whichever ¶ 어느 쪽이든 좋아하는 것을 가지게 할 것이다 They will let you have whichever you like. // 어느 쪽으로 가도 한곳에 나온다 Whichever road you may take, you will come to the same place. // 어느 쪽이 필요한가 Which do you want? // 어느 쪽이 어느 쪽인지 알 수 없다 I cannot tell which is which. // 어느 쪽부터 시작할까 Which shall I begin with〔take up first〕?
③ [선택] either... or ; neither... nor (부정) ¶ 어느 쪽이든 좋으니 하나 주시오 Give me one, please ; either will do. // 두 형제 중에서 어느 쪽도 모른다 I know neither of his two brothers. // 어느 쪽이든 상관 없다 It makes no great difference either way. // 너는 영어나 불어나 어느 쪽인가를 필수과목으로 배워야 한다 You must learn either English or French as a compulsory subject. // 어느 쪽도 소용 없다 Neither will answer my purpose.
④ both ¶ 이 책들은 어느 쪽이나 다 재미있다 These books are both interesting. // 어느 쪽이나 다 알고 있다 I know both of them. /I know them both. // 어느 쪽이나 다 결석이다 Both are absent. /They are both absent. // 어느 쪽이나 다 나의 것이 아니다 Neither (of them) is〔are〕 mine. // 길을 건너기 전에 어느 쪽이나 잘 보시오 Look carefully in both directions before crossing the street. /Look both way carefully before crossing the street.

어느 천년에 —千年— ⇨ 어느 세월에

어느 틈 in so little time ; in no time (at all) ; so soon ; quickly ; already ¶ 어느 틈엔가 그는 빠져 나가버렸다 He went〔slipped away unnoticed.

어는 점 freezing point ⇨ 빙점

어도 魚道 the regular course for fish ; a fishway

어두움 darkness ⇨ 어둠

어두워지다 become〔get〕 dark

어두육미 魚頭肉尾 fish-heads and animal-tails

어두커니 in the morning twilight

어두컴컴하다 (be) very dark ¶ 어두컴컴한 밤 a dark night // 어두컴컴한 데서 부딛치다 run into 《a person》 in the dark : collide against 《a post》 in the dark // 이 방은 어두컴컴하다 This room is poorly lighted.

어둑새벽 the dusk at dawn ; the dark before the dawn ⇨ 여명

어둑어둑하다 《the day》 be rather dark ; (be) dusky ¶ 날이 어둑어둑하다 It gets dark. // 어둑어둑해진다 It is getting dark.

어둑하다 be a bit dark ; get dark

어둔 語鈍 slowness〔thickness〕 of speech **—하다** be slow of speech ; (be) tongue-tied

†**어둠** darkness ; (the) dark ; dimness ; [저녁] dusk ; twilight ¶ 밤의 어둠 the shadows of night // 어둠의 세상 the dark world // 어둠 속에(서) in the dark ; in darkness // 어둠을 타고 under cover of darkness〔night〕 // 어둠 속을 더듬어 가다 grope one's way in the dark ; go along a dark road // 어둠을 타고 도망가다 make one's escape in the darkness ; beat off in the dark 《미》 // 어둠을 뚫고 보다 peer into the darkness // 어둠 속에 어린애를 혼자 두지 말라 Don't leave the child alone in the dark. // 부엉이는 어둠 속에서도 잘 본다 The owl can see well in the dark.
—별 [금성] the evening star ; Venus **—상자** a dark box

‡**어둠침침하다** (be) dark and dismal ; dusky ; somber ; dim ; obscure ¶ 어둠침침한 방 a dim room // 어둠침침한 빛 dim〔feeble〕 light // 어둠침침한 데서 독서하다 read in a poor light // 전등이 어둠침침하다 The lamp is dim〔not bright〕.

†**어둡다** ① (be) dark ; dim ; dusky ; murky ; gloomy

> 참고 **dark** 일반적으로 쓰이는 말 빛이라고는 전연 또는 거의 없는 상태 **dim** 빛이 충분하지 않고 물건이 또렷이 보이지 않는 상태 **dusky** 새벽이나 저녁 같은 때의 박명 상태 **murky** 짙은 안개처럼 무거운 느낌을 주는 어둠 **gloomy** 구름 낀 음산한 어둠

¶ 어두운 방 a dark room ; a dimly lighted〔lit〕 room // 어두워지기 전에 while it is light ; before (it gets) dark // 어두워진 뒤에 after dark // 어두워지다 become dark〔dim〕 ; darken ; [하늘이] be overcast // 등불을 어둡게 하다 dim〔turn down〕 a light ; shade a light // 그에게는 어두운 일면이 있다 He has a gloomy turn of mind. // 매일 어두운 새벽에 일어난다 I rise before daybreak〔dawn, it is light〕 everyday. // 고양이는 어두운 데서도 눈이 보인다 A cat can see even in the dark (place). // 사방이 어두워졌다 Darkness fell. // 점점 어두워진다 It's getting〔growing〕 darker. // 하늘이 어두워졌다 The sky darkened〔became overcast〕.
② [무지] be ignorant〔badly informed, ill-informed〕 of ; know but little of ; be not well acquainted with ; be a stranger to 《the circumstances》 ¶ 세상 일에 어둡다 know but little of the world // 시국에 어둡다 be ignorant of current events ; be less informed of the current affairs of the world // 저 사람은 법률에 어둡다 His knowledge of law is very limited. // 나는 이 근처의 지리에는 어둡다 I am a strange

here〔around here, to this place, in this neighborhood〕. /I am not well acquainted with this locality〔neighborhood〕. // 나는 그 문제에 어둡다 I know but little〔very little, practically nothing, nothing〕 of the subject. /I am not familiar with the subject.
③ [정신·마음이] (be) dark ; shady ; underhand ¶ 어두운 과거를 가진 사람 a man with a shadowy past // 그의 행동에는 어두운 데가 없다 He is above board. /His conduct is above board. // 그는 어두운 짓을 했다 He did something shady. /He did crooked business. /He played foul.
④ [감각이] (be) weak ; dull ; slow ¶ 눈이 어둡다 have bad eyes〔weak vision, failing sight〕 // 귀가 어둡다 be hard〔slow, dull〕 of hearing // 수학에 어둡다 be slow at mathematics // 나이를 먹으면 눈이 어두워진다 Our sight grows dim〔misty〕 with age.

어드레스 address ⇨ 주소

어드밴티지 〖정구〗 advantage
— **룰** an advantage rule — **리시버** an advantage receiver — **서버** an advantage server

†어디[1] ① where ; what place ¶ 여기가 어딥니까 Where are we now? // 내일 피크닉은 어디로 가면 좋겠습니까 Where shall we go on a picnic tomorrow? // 당신은 어디에 사십니까 Where do you live? // 그는 어디 갔을까 Where has he gone, I wonder? // 어디가 아프니 Where do you feel the pain? // 어디로 모실까요 Where to? // 따님 대학은 어디로 갈 건가요 Where is your daughter going to college? // 어디 가서 한잔 하자 Let's go someplace and have a drink.
② ¶ 어디에도 anywhere ; [부정] (not) anywhere ; nowhere // 어디에 가도 wherever〔no matter where〕 you (may) go // 어디든지 가도 좋다 You may go anywhere (you like). /You may go wherever you like. // 어디든지 마찬가지다 Everywhere you go, you will find the same thing. // 나는 어디에도 안 갑니다 I'm not going anywhere. // 어디나 휴일을 즐기는 사람들로 붐볐다 There were lots of holidaymakers everywhere.
③ ¶ 어디에서 from where // 어디에서인지 모르게 나타나다 appear from nowhere // 어디에서 왔습니까 Where have you come from? /Where do you come〔are you〕 from? (출신지) // 오늘(의 수업)은 어디서 부터입니까 Where are we to begin today?
④ ¶ 어디엔가 somewhere ; anywhere (의문문에) // 그는 어디엔가로 사라져 버렸다 He vanished I know not where. // 주말에 어디엔가 가셨습니까 Did you go anywhere over the weekend? // 어디엔가에서 본 사람이다 I remember seeing him somewhere. // 어디엔가에서 우산을 놓고 왔다 I have left my umbrella somewhere. // 그는 이 근처 어디엔가에 살고 있다 He lives somewhere near〔about〕 here. // 어딘지 수상한 데가 있다 There's something shady about him.
⑤ ¶ 어딘가(의) some ; any (의문문에서) // 그는 어딘가 미국의 대학에서 공부한 사람이다 He went to school at some university in America. // 대회중에는 호텔은 어디나 만원이었다 Any〔Every〕 hotel was full during the convention. // 어디 학교에 다니고 있습니까 What school do you go to〔attend〕? /Where do you go to school?
⑥ ¶ 어디까지 how far ; to what extent (어느 정도) // 요전번에는 어디까지 했습니까 [수업에서] How far did we go last time? /Where were we last time? // 저 사람은 어디까지 신용할 수 있을지 모르겠어 I wonder how far I can trust him. // 어디까지 고집을 부리면 속이 시원하겠니 How persistent must you be?
⑦ ¶ 어디나〔어디든지〕 anywhere at all // 부산 같으면 어디라도 알고 있다 I know every inch of *Pusan*.
⑧ ¶ 어디까지나 endlessly (끝없이) ; to the end〔last〕 (최후까지) ; completely ; thoroughly (완전히) ; stubbornly ; persistently (고집 세게) // 그는 어디까지나 제 의견을 고집했다 He persisted in his opinion to the bitter end. // 논쟁은 어디까지나 계속되었다 The dispute lasted endlessly. // There was no end to the dispute. // 가로수가 어디까지나 계속되고 있다 There is an endless〔interminable〕 avenue of trees. // 그 여자는 어디까지나 숙녀이다 She is every inch a lady. // 나는 어디까지나 당신을 돕겠소 I will stand by you to the last〔through thick and thin〕.

어디[2] well ; now ; well now ; let me see ¶ 어디 한번 해 보죠 Well, I will try. // 어디 무엇인가 보자 Let's see what you have got. // 어디 영어 한번 해보아라 Well now, let me hear you speak some English.

어디까지 how far ; to what extent ¶ 그의 이야기는 어디까지가 사실인지 알 수 없다 I can't say how far his story is true.

어디까지나 anywhere ; to the end of world ¶ 어디까지나 네 편이다 I'm with you all the way.

어딘가, 어딘지 somehow ; in some respects ; in some way〔wise〕 ; without knowing why ⇨ 어쩐지 ¶ 그는 어딘지 세련된 데가 있다 There is something refined about him.

어따 Here! /Hey! ⇨ 아따 ¶ 어따 이것 먹어라 Here, eat this!

어떠하다 (be) how ⇨ 어떻다

어떠한 what kind of ⇨ 어떤

†어떤 ① [여하한·어떠한] what kind〔sort〕 of ; what... like ¶ 어떤 이유로 why ; for what reason ; what for // 어떤 용무로 on what business ; what for // 어떤 까닭인지

somehow ; for some reason or other // 어떤 것이든지 anything // 어떤 투로 how ; in what way // 어떤 일이 있더라도 whatever may happen ; under any circumstances // 어떤 사람인가 What is he like ? /What sort of a man is he ? // 잠수함이란 어떤 겁니까 What is a submarine like ? // 빚을 진다는 것이 어떤 것인가를 알고 있다 I know what it is to be in debt. // 어떤 사람이라도 그것을 알고 있다 Anybody knows that. // 어떤 사태가 벌어지는지 보고 있거라 See how things will shape up. // 최근 어떤 영화를 보았습니까 What movie have you seen lately ?

② [어떤 …라도] any ; every ; no... ¶ 어떤 사람이라도 anybody ; everybody ; any〔every〕 person ; nobody (부정) // 어떤 짓을 해서라도 at all costs ; at any cost ; by any means ; at all hazards // 어떤 일을 당하더라도 however hard〔ill〕 one is treated〔handled〕 // 어떤 일이 있더라도 whatever may happen ; by all means ; [어떤 사정 아래서도] under〔in〕 any circumstances ; [결코 (…않다)] 《not》 for all the world ; on no account ; under no condition // 너 때문이라면 어떤 일이라도 한다 I will do anything I can for you〔your sake〕. // 나는 어떤 일이라도 개의치 않는다 I don't mind any work. // 어떤 사정이 있더라도 약속은 지키지 않으면 안된다 You must keep your promise under any circumstances. // 돈만 있다면 어떤 일이라도 할 수 있다 Money will enable you to do anything and everything. // 어떤 짓을 해서라도 그것은 이룰 결심이다 I am determined to accomplish it at all costs. // 어떤 담배도 일체 피우지 않는다 He never uses tobacco in any form. // 어떤 적은 빚이라도 갚지 않으면 안된다 A debt no matter how small must be paid. /The least debt must be paid.

③ a certain ; some ¶ 어떤 날 one day // 어떤 아침〔저녁〕 one morning 〔evening〕 // 어떤 사람 a certain person ; someone ; a Mr. So-and-so (모씨) // 어떤 때 once ; once upon a time (옛날 옛적) // 어떤 곳에서 at a certain place ; somewhere (어디선가) // 어떤 경우에는 on some occasion(s) ; in some cases ; sometimes // 어떤 의미로는 in a sense ; in a way ; in a manner // 어떤 사람이 나에게 10만원을 빌려 주었다 A certain person lent me 100,000 *won*. // 어떤 것은 좋지만 어떤 것은 나쁘다 또한 어떤 것은 좋지도 나쁘지도 않다 Some are good, some are bad, and others are neither good nor bad. // 어떤 사람이 나에게 …해 달라고 한다 A certain person〔party〕 wants me to 《do》 // 어떤 한 가지 일에 전심하십시오 Devote yourself to some subject.

***어떻게** ① how ; in what manner〔way〕 ; by what means ¶ 어떻게 보아도 to all appearance ; in every respect // 어떻게 해서라도 by all〔any〕 means ; at any cost // 어떻게 그것을 요리해 먹습니까 How do you cook it ? // 어떻게 거기 갔느냐 How did he get there ? // 어떻게 그렇게 됐느냐 How did it happen ? /How comes〔came〕 it ? 《미·구》 // (이 편지를) 어떻게 할까요 What shall I do (with this letter) ? // 요즈음 어떻게 지내십니까 How are you getting along these days ? // 자네는 그가 어떻게 할 것으로 생각하나 What do you suppose he will do ? // 어떻게 이 문제를 풀었습니까 How did you solve this problem ? // 어떻게 여기 왔느냐 How is it that you are here ? // 나는 어떻게 하면 좋을지 모른다 I am at a loss what to do. // 그 여자 어떻게 생겼는데 What did she look like ? // 자네 어떻게 여기 혼자 왔나 How come you are here alone ? // 어떻게 깎아 드릴까요 How would you like your hair done ? // 다른 사람이 벌써 내 신용 카드를 사용했으면 어떻게 하지요 What if someone has already used my credit card ?

② [어느 정도] how ; how much ; to what extent ¶ 그가 어떻게 고마운지 He was so kind ! // 어떻게나 바람이 부는지 How it blows ! // 어떻게 말했기에 그가 그렇게 슬퍼합니까 What did you ever say to make him so sad ?

어떻게 되다 turn out somehow or other ; be managed ¶ 그이가 어떻게 되었을까 I wonder what has become of him. // 어떻게 (잘) 되겠지 Somehow it will come out all right. // 그 정도의 돈이라면 어떻게 되겠지 If that is all the money required, I think I can manage (to raise) it for you. // 걱정 마라 어떻게 될 터이니 Take it easy, I think I can manage it somehow.

어떻게든 ⇨ 어떻든지

어떻게 하다 take some measure ; do somehow ; manage somehow ; manage to do ¶ 어떻게 하여(서든지) somehow (or other) ; one way or another ; by some means or other ; by all means ; at any risk〔cost, sacrifice〕 // 어떻게 해나가다 muddle on ; rub on〔along〕 ; [생활을] eke out one's livelihood // 어떻게 해봐야 한다 Something must be done. // (너를 위하여) 어떻게 해보겠다 I will see what I can do for you. /I will fix you up. // 어떻게 해서든지 도와주어야 한다 Something must be done to help him. // 내가 어떻게 하여 드리겠습니다 I will manage〔fix〕 it for you. // 어떻게 하여 보겠습니다 I will see to it somehow or other. // 그는 어떻게 해서든지 그 일을 해낼 겁니다 I think he will manage to accomplish the task.

어떻다 ① how ; what ¶ 재미가 어떻습니까 How is business (going on) ? // 의견은 어떠합니까 What is opinion ? /Do you have〔Have you〕 anything to say ? // 어떠하십니까 How are you ? // 날씨가 어떻습니까 How does the sky look like ? // 요

새는 어떻습니까 How are things with you? // 결과는 어떻습니까 How about the result? // 제주도 여행은 어떠했습니까 How did you like your tour of〔trip to〕 *Cheju-do*? // 자네의 새 사업은 어떤가 How's your new business coming? // 한국 요리와 비교해 볼 때 미국 요리는 어떻습니까 How do American dishes compare with Korean ones? // 새로 온 너의 부장님 어때 How do you like your new boss? // 이곳 미국의 주유소에서 일하는 심정이 어떻습니까 How do you feel working at a gas station here in the us?
② [권하면서] ¶ 차 한잔 어떻습니까 How do you like tea? /May I offer you a cup of tea? // 어떻습니까 거기에 가는 것은 What do you say to our going there? // 어떻습니까 산책이나 할까요 What do you say to a walk? / How about going for a walk?
③ somehow ¶ 어떻다고 말할 수 없는 이상한 소리 a strange, unearthly sound // 요즘 날씨는 어떻다고 말할 수 없다 There is no telling about the weather nowadays. // 이 약을 마셔보는 것이 어떻겠습니까 What do you say to trying this medicine? /what〔How〕 about trying this medicine? /Suppose you try this medicine? /Why don't you try this medicine?

⁂어떻든지 at any rate; in any case; anyhow; regardless; whether or not ¶ 무엇이 어떻든지 간에 anyway; be that as it may // 어떻든지 빨리 as soon〔quickly〕 as possible〔one can〕 // 비용은 어떻든지 to say nothing of expenses; apart from the question of expense // 어떻든지 해봐라 Do it as best you can. /Try and do it somehow or other. // 성공하든지 실패하든지 어떻든지 좋다 Success or failure makes no difference to me. /Success and failure are alike indifferent to me. // 10시까지는 어떻든지 거기 가겠소 I will contrive to be there by ten o'clock. // 돈은 있고 없고 간에 어떻든지 사람이 진실해야 한다 A man should be sincere regardless whether he is rich or poor. // 어떻든지 이 연구를 금년 안으로 완성하고자 한다 I earnestly desire to complete these researches by the end of this year at any cost.

어떻씨 adjective ⇨ 형용사

어뜩 suddenly in passing; by chance 〔accident〕 ¶ 어뜩 듣다 hear by chance; overhear // 어뜩 보다 glance at 《a thing》; take a quick glance at 《a thing》

어뜩비뜩 ① [불손] improperly; imprudently **—하다** (be) improper; imprudent ¶ 어뜩비뜩한 행동 imprudent〔fidgety〕 behavior // 어뜩비뜩한 태도로 나오다 behave in a disorderly manner
② [줄이] sinuously; zigzagging **—하다** (be) sinuous; zigzag ¶ 어뜩비뜩한 줄 a sinuous〔uneven〕 line

어뜩하다 feel dizzy〔giddy, faint〕 ¶ 정신이 어뜩하다 feel dizzy〔faint〕; one's head swims〔reels〕 // 피로해서 정신이 어뜩하다 I'm so tired I think I'll faint.

-어라 ① [명령] Do! ¶ 그것을 입어라 Put it on. // 여기 있어라 Stay here. ② [감탄] How... !; what... ! ¶ 아이구 가엾어라 What a pity!

어란 魚卵 fish eggs; spawn

어람 御覽 his majesty's inspection; royal inspection

어량 魚梁 a (fish) weir; a fish trap

어런더런 hustling and bustling; people going and coming

어럽쇼 Oh; Why; Good gracious; Dear me; My, My! ¶ 어럽쇼, 여기서 널 만나다니 Hell! you here? /Imagine 〔Fancy〕 meeting you here! // 어럽쇼, 내 우산이 어디 갔나 Where is my umbrella, I wonder?

어레미 a coarse sieve; a riddle; a bolter ¶ 어레미질을 하다 sieve

어려움 difficulty; hardship ¶ 어려움을 극복하다 get over a difficulty // 그는 어려움을 모르고 자라서 다른 사람의 괴로움을 이해 못한다 He grew up without knowing any hardships, so he just doesn't understand other people's pain.

어려워하다 feel constrained; be〔feel〕 ill at ease; have scruples about 《doing》; scruple 《to do》; show deference; pay deference to; act in deference to; be afraid〔shy〕 《of》 ¶ 어려워하지 않고 unreservedly; without reserve; without scruple; without hesitation // 어려워하여 in deference to; in diffidence to // 어려워하지 않다 be free before other people; make oneself free and easy〔at home, at ease〕 // 어려워하지 않고 큰 소리로 말하다 speak loudly without scruple // 어려워하는 태도로 인사하다 bow stiffly // 어려워하지 말고 편히 앉으시오 Make yourself at home and sit comfortably. // 이양은 어딘가 그를 어려워하는 기색이 있다 There is something reserved in Miss *Lee's* manner toward him. // 나는 누구 앞에서도 어려워하지 않고 나의 의견을 말한다 I give my opinion in anybody's presence. // 나를 어려워하지 마십시오 Please don't stand on ceremony with me.

어련무던하다 (be) quite satisfactory; nice

어련하다 (be) certain; proper; natural; reasonable; it stands to reason ¶ 나는 이 일 때문에 무척 애를 썼지 — 어련하셨겠습니까 I took much pain to do this. I can easily imagine. // 부모가 자식을 사랑하는 것도 어련한 일이다 It is only natural that parents should love their children.

어련히 naturally; surely; certainly; as a natural consequence; in the natural course of events ; as a matter of course ¶ 내버려 둬 어련히 잘 알아서 할라구 Let him alone, he will take care of himself. ∥그도 이젠 어린애가 아니야 어련히 잘 알아서 할라구 He is no longer a chicken. We can rely upon his discretion. ∥그는 어련히 성공할까 He is sure to succeed. /It is certain that he will succeed.

어렴성 reserve ; restraint ; constraint ; deference (경의) ; diffidence ; a scruple ¶ 어렴성 없는 unreserved ; free from constraint ; unconstrained ; rude ; obtrusive ; pushing ; forward (주제넘은) ∥어렴성 없는 놈 a fellow with no scruples ∥어렴성 없는 친구 a candid friend ; a friend on frank terms ∥어렴성 없이 boldly ; pertly ; forwardly ; without reserve ; without ceremony ∥어렴성 없이 말하다 speak out ; speak without reserve ∥어렴성 없이 굴다 make free with 《a person》 ; take liberties with 《a person》 ∥어렴성 없이 말하는 편이 좋다 You had better speak out〔freely〕. ∥그의 태도와 말은 어렴성이 너무 없다 His manners and speech are too free. ∥술 때문에 완전히 어렴성이 없어졌다 Wine broke down〔banished〕 all reserve.

어렴풋이 dimly ; faintly ; vaguely ; indistinctly ¶ 어렴풋이 보이는 광경 a dim〔an obscure〕 view ∥어렴풋이 기억하고 있다 have a dim recollection 《of》 ; remember dimly ∥어렴풋이 보이다 be seen dimly〔at a dim distance〕 ∥피리 소리가 어렴풋이 들렸다 There came to my ears the distant music of a flute. ∥종 소리가 어렴풋이 들린다 A sound of a bell is faintly heard.

⁑**어렴풋하다** (be) faint ; dim ; vague ; hazy ; misty ¶ 어렴풋한 빛 a glimmer ; a faint gleam of light ∥어렴풋한 소리 a faint sound ∥어렴풋한 기억을 더듬다 trace back a vague memory ∥창에 어렴풋한 빛이 보였다 We perceived a glimmer of light in the window. ∥그에게는 어렴풋한 희망마저 없었다 He had not the faintest gleam of hope.

어렵 魚獵 fishing ; fishery **—하다** fish **—선** a fishing boat〔vessel〕 ; a fisherboat **— 시대** the fishing age **—학** piscatology

†**어렵다** ① [곤란] (be) hard ; difficult ; [복잡하다] ¶ 어렵게 in a hard〔difficult〕 way ; with difficulty ∥어렵지 않은 easy ; simple ∥어려운 일 a laborious task ; a difficult matter ∥어려운 문제 a hard 〔tough〕 question ; a hard nut to crack ∥어려운 수술 a delicate operation ∥어려운 시험 a hard〔stiff, severe〕 examination ∥비위를 맞추기 어려운 사람 a person hard to please ∥어려운 입장에 있다 be in a difficult〔delicate〕 situation ∥너무 어렵게 생각하다 take 《a matter》 too seriously ∥첫째 문제가 어려웠다 The first question puzzled〔beat〕 me. ∥설명하기 어렵다 It is hard to explain〔of explanation〕. ∥어려운 문제다 That's a hard nut (for me) to crack. ∥이것은 참기 어렵다 This is intolerable. /This is unbearable. ∥그것은 말하기 어렵다 It is hard to say. ∥이 이론은 내게는 어렵다 The theory is way over my head. ∥그의 회복은 어렵다 His recovery is doubtful. ∥일이 어렵게 되었다 Things have come to a pretty〔nice〕 pass. ∥이 문제는 내게는 너무 어렵다 This problem is above me〔too hard for me〕. ∥독일어는 그리 어렵지 않다 German is not so difficult to learn. ∥이 구절이 어려워서 알 수 없다 This passage is too difficult for me to understand. ∥이 영화는 어려워서 모르겠다 This movie is over my head. /This movie is beyond me. ∥좀 어려운 주문입니다만 한번 해보겠습니다 That's a tall order, but I'll try. ∥그들은 우리가 어려울 때 등을 돌린다 Whenever we hit on hard times, they turn their backs on us.
② [조심스럽다] feel awkward〔constrained〕 ; be〔feel〕 ill at ease ; have scruples about 《doing》 ¶ 그 사람 앞에서는 어렵다 I feel constrained〔ill at ease〕 in his presence. /I feel uneasy around him. ∥어렵지만 창문을 좀 닫아 주십시오 Would you mind shutting the window?
③ [생활이] (be) poor ; needy ; indigent ; destitute ¶ 어려운 살림 narrow 〔straitened, needy〕 circumstances ∥어려운 사람들 poor people ; the poor (and needy) ∥어려운 살림을 하다 be in narrow circumstances ; live in poverty ; lead an indigent life ; be badly off ∥어려운 집안에 태어나다 be born poor ; be born of〔in〕 a poor family ∥그는 어렵게 자랐다 He grew up〔was brought up〕 in a poor family.

어렴칙하다 (be) faint ; dim ; vague

어로 漁撈 fishing ; fishery
—과 [수산 학교의] the fishery course **— 금지 구역** a restrictive fisheries zone **—선** a fishing boat **—술** the art of fishing ; halieutics **—작업** ⇨ 어로 **—장** a fishing ground **— 저지선** the fishing restriction line **— 협정** a fisheries agreement

어로불변 魚魯不辨 ignorance ; illiteracy

어록 語錄 analects ; sayings
카알라일— a Carlyle Calendar

어뢰 魚雷 a torpedo ¶ 어뢰를 발사하다 discharge〔fire〕 a torpedo
— 발사관 a torpedo tube ; a launching tube **— 방어망** a torpedo net **—정(대)** a torpedo speedboat ; a motor torpedo boat ; a PT boat 《미》 **공중 —** an aerial torpedo

어룡 魚龍 〖고생물〗 an ichthyosaur

어루꾀다 wheedle ; coax ; lure〔seduce〕 with flattery ¶ 사람을 어루꾀어 돈을 빼앗다 wheedle 《a person》 out of his money ; lie 《a person》 out of his money

//그녀는 노인을 어루꾀어 갖고 싶은 것을 울거냈다 She wheedled round the old man till she got what she wanted.

어루더듬다 grope ; fumble ⟪in the darkness⟫ for ; feel about for ; feel after ⟪the handle⟫ ¶ 주머니속의 열쇠를 어루더듬다 feel〔fumble〕 about in one's pocket for a key // 어루더듬어 문을 열다 fumble a door open // 어둠속을 어루더듬어 가다 feel〔grope〕 one's way in the dark // 나는 어둠속에서 성냥을 어루더듬어 찾아야 했다 I had to grope〔fumble, feel〕 for the matches in the utter darkness.

어루러기 〚의학〛 leucoderma ; vitiligo ; a piebald skin ; white macula (in the skin) ; albinism ¶ 팔에 어루러기가 났다 My arm broke out.

어루룽더루룽, 어루룽어루룽 variegated ; mottled ; blotched **—하다** (be) variegated ; spotted ; mottled

어루만지다 ① [가볍게 문지르다] pass one's hand〔one's fingers〕 over ; stroke ; touch ; rub ¶ 어린애의 머리를 어루만지다 pat a child on the head // 개를 어루만지다 pat a dog // 턱을 어루만지다 rub one's chin // 자기 대머리를 어루만지다 pass one's hand over one's bald head // 머리털을 어루만지다 smooth〔comb〕 down one's hair // 산들바람이 얼굴을 어루만졌다 The breeze fanned our cheeks.
② [위로하다] pacify ; comfort ; stroke ⟪a person⟫ down ; mollify ; soothe ¶ 앓던 아이는 어머니가 손으로 어루만지자 조용해졌다 The sick child was comforted by the gentle stroke of his mother's hand.

어루쇠 a mirror of polished metal ; an iron mirror

어룽 spots ; dapples ; mottles
—이 a mottled thing〔animal〕 ; mottling

어룽거리다 be dappled〔spotted, variegated〕 ¶ 길은 나무 사이로 비치는 햇빛에 어룽거렸다 The lane was mottled with the sunbeams filtering through the leaves.

어룽더룽 ⇨ 어루룽더루룽

어룽더룽하다 (be) dappled ; spotted ; variegated

어룽지다 (get, be) variegated ; mottled

어류 魚類 fishes ; the finny tribe ; pisces ¶ 이 호수에는 많은 어류가 산다 There are many fish〔fishes〕 in the lake.
—지(誌) ichthyography **—학** ichthyology **—학자** an ichthyologist

어르다 dandle ⟪a baby⟫ (무릎에 앉히고) ; nurse ; humor ; fondle ; try to please ; play with ; pet ¶ 어린아이를 어르다 dandle a baby // 우는 아이를 어르다 humor a crying baby // 어린아이를 얼러서 웃기다 provoke〔persuade〕 a baby to smile // 그 여자는 아이를 팔에 안고 얼렀다 She humored a little child by dancing it in her arms.
어르고 뺨 치기 속담 To give one〔a dog〕 roast meat, and beat him with the spit.

어르룽이 mottled spots ; mottled pattern ; mottling

어르신네 [남의 아버지] your esteemed father ; your〔his〕 father ; [존칭] an esteemed elder ; sir ; you ¶ 어르신네께서 집에 계신지요 Is your father at home?

어른 ① [성인] a man ; an adult ; a grown-up person ; a full-grown man ; a grownup ¶ 어른의 adult ; grown-up // 어른의 세계 the adult world // 어른의 생각 an adult's idea ; what a grown-up person thinks // 어른답지 않다 be childish〔puerile〕 ; [남자답지 않다] be unmanly ; be unbecoming for a grown person ; be unworthy of a man (of discretion) (도량 없다) // 어른티 나다 look like a grown-up person // 어른티 내다 assume an air of a grown-up person ; act〔behave〕 like a man // 어른이 되다 grow up (to be a man) ; become a man〔woman〕 ; grow into a man〔woman〕 ; reach〔arrive at〕 manhood〔womanhood〕 ; reach adult life ; come of age // 어른처럼 말하다 talk like a man // 어른 취급하다 treat ⟪a person⟫ like a grown-up // 어른의 품삯을 받다 receive a full-rate pay // 입장료 어른 1,000원 Admission 1,000 *won* per adult. // 그는 어른이 되면 비행사가 된다고 한다 He says he wants to be a pilot when he grows up.
② [웃사람] one's seniors ; one's elders ; one's superiors ; one's betters ¶ 집안의 어른 the head of a family ; the eldest man in the family // 어른 앞에서 그런말을 하면 못 쓴다 You shouldn't talk like that in the presence of your elders.

어른거리다 flicker ; glimmer ; waver before the eyes ¶ 어른거리는 빛 a glimmering light // 물결 위에 어른거리는 햇빛 sunlight playing on the wave // 아들의 영상이 눈앞에 어른거린다 The image of my son keeps coming and fading in front of my eyes. // 촛불이 어른거리다가 꺼졌다 The candle flickered and then went out. // 그 사람의 모습이 아직도 눈앞에 어른거린다 The memory of his visage still haunts me.

어른스럽다 [온순하다] (be) gentle ; mild ; meek ; [의젓하다] (be) well-behaved〔-mannered〕 ; modest ; look like a grown-up ; [깜찍함] (be) precocious ¶ 어른스럽게 굴다 behave like a grown-up (person) // 그 아이는 어른스럽게 말한다 The child talks like a man.

어른어른 flickering(ly) ; glimmering(ly) ; wavering(ly)

어름 [가운데] right in the middle ; right in between ; halfway ; [끝과 끝이 닿은 데] an intersection ; an intersection point ¶ 길 어름 a junction // 어름에 midway ; halfway

어름거리다 ① [말을] say ambiguously ;

equivocate ; mumble ; prevaricate ¶ 말을 어름거리다 make a vague remark ; equivocate // 대답을 어름거리다 mumble the answer ; equivocate in replying
② [일을] scamp ; fudge ; skimp ¶ 일을 어름거리다 scamp one's work ; slur over one's work ; fudge one's work // 계산서를 어름거려 꾸미다 fudge up an account // 그는 절대로 일을 어름거리지 않는다 He never goes halfway with his work. /He never scamps his work. // 저 선생님은 때때로 번역에서 어름거린다 That teacher fakes up his translation from time to time.

어름어름 equivocally ; ambiguously ; sloppily

어리¹ 〖건축〗 a door-frame〔-case〕; a frame

어리² [병아리의] a hen-coop ; a wicker cage for chickens
— 장사 poultry peddling — 장수 a poultry peddler —전 a poultry store〔dealer〕

어리광 playing the baby ; a child's coquetry ¶ 어리광부리다〔떨다, 피우다〕 play the baby 《to》; display winning ways ; presume upon another's love ; behave like a spoilt child // 어리광조로 말하다 speak in coquettish tone ; coo 《at》; purr 《at》 // 이 애는 어리광만 부려 야단이다 This is quite a spoilt child. // 소녀는 어머님께 어리광부려 인형을 샀다 The girl coaxed〔wheedled〕 her mother into buying a doll for her. // 또 아빠한테 어리광부리는군 You are again making up to your papa.

어리굴젓 salted oyster with hot pepper

어리눅다 pretend to be foolish〔stupid〕

*****어리다**¹ [유소하다] (be) very young ; juvenile ; youthful ; [유치하다] childish ; infant ; [미숙하다] green ; infantile ; crude ; inexperienced ¶ 어린 나뭇잎 young leaves // 어린 마음 a child's mind ; one's innocent heart // 어릴 때에 in one's earliest days〔childhood〕 // 어릴 때의 동무 an old playfellow ; a playmate in one's childhood ; a childhood friend // 어릴 때부터 알다 know 《a person》 from his infancy // 생각이 어리다 have immature ideas // 나이는 어리지만 생각하는 것은 어른이다 have an old head on young shoulders // 그는 어렸을 때 미국에 건너갔다 He went over to the United States at an early age. // 그에겐 어딘지 어릴 때의 모습이 남아 있다 He still retains some traces of his infant features. // 끔찍한 광경을 보고 어린 마음에 대단히 놀랐다 The fearful sight made a deep impression on my childish mind. // 어린 마음에도 아주 슬펐다 Child as I was, I felt very sad. // 어릴 때 어떤 아이였습니까 What were you like as a child?
어릴 때 굽은 길맛가지 [속담] As the twig is bent, so is the tree inclined.

*****어리다**² [눈물이] 《one's eyes》 dim〔glisten〕 with tears ; 《one's eyes》 swim with tears ; be suffused with tears ; be moved to tears (사람이 주어) ¶ 눈물 어린 눈 moist〔dewy〕 eyes ; eyes suffused with tears ; eyes moist with tears // 눈물 어린 얼굴 a tearful face // 눈물 어린 눈으로 with one's eyes swimming with tears // 그 슬픈 이야기는 우리 눈에 눈물을 어리게 했다 The pathetic story moved us to tears〔drew tears from us〕. // 슬픈 소식을 읽고 그 여자의 눈에 눈물이 어렸다 Her eyes moistened as she read the sad news.

어리다³ [눈이] be dazzled ; be glared ; be blinded ¶ 눈이 어릴 정도로 희다〔아름답다〕 be dazzlingly white〔beautiful〕 // 눈물이 어리어서 눈을 뜰 수가 없다 My eyes are so dazzled that I cannot open them. // 강한 빛 때문에 눈이 어린다 The strong light dazzles my eyes. // 번쩍이는 헤드라이트 때문에 눈이 어리었다 The glaring headlights dazzled〔blinded〕 our eyes〔us〕.

어리다⁴ ① [기억하다] haunt ¶ 그의 얼굴이 아직도 눈에 어린다 The memory of his visage still haunts me. ② [깃든] be filled 《with》 ③ [엉기다] congeal ; coagulate ; clot ; curdle

어리대다 hang〔loaf〕 around ; wander 《about》; loiter〔shuttle〕 along ¶ 그는 이 근처를 어리대었다 He loitered about this place.

*****어리둥절하다** become〔feel〕 confused ; be stunned〔stupefied〕; be bewildered ; be at a loss ; lose one's presence of mind (당황) ¶ 어리둥절하여 in confusion // 어리둥절케 하다 bewilder ; stun 《a person》; baffle ; take 《a person》 aback // 어리둥절해서 어찌 할 바를 모르다 be quite at a loss what to do // 그는 그 소식을 듣고 잠시 어리둥절했다 He was stunned by the news for a while. /The news struck him speechless〔dumb〕 for a while. // 그의 갑작스런 방문에 우리는 어리둥절하였다 His surprise visit upset〔embarrassed〕 us. // 그는 어리둥절하여 답이 틀렸다 He gave a wrong answer in confusion. // 처음으로 연단에서면 어리둥절해진다 The inexperienced feel nervous on the platform.

어리마리 drowsing —하다 (be) drowsy

어리벙벙하다 (be) confounded ; disconcerted ; bewildered ; overwhelmed ¶ 어리벙벙한 얼굴을 하다 look perplexed〔worried〕 // 어리벙벙해서 어찌할 바를 모르다 be so bewildered that one does not know what to do // 그 여자가 갑자기 울음을 터뜨려서 어리벙벙했다 Her sudden outburst of tears discomposed me. // 그는 어리벙벙한 듯 잠시 나를 바라보았다 He surveyed me a moment in a dazed sort of fashion. // 일이 바뀌어 어리벙벙하다 I feel out of myself in this new line of business.

어리보기 a stupid person ; a blockhead ; a fool ; a coward

어리뻥뻥하다 ⇨ 어리벙벙하다

†어리석다 (be) foolish ; silly ; stupid ; simple ; half-witted ; slow-witted ; dull-headed ¶ 어리석게도 foolishly // 어리석은 사람 a foolish person ; a fool ; a dunce // 어리석은 짓 a foolish act ; a folly // 어리석은 이야기 an absurd〔a fabulous〕 story // 어리석은 생각 a foolish 〔preposterous〕 idea // 그런 짓을 할 만큼 어리석지는 않다 I am not such a fool〔so foolish〕 as to do so. /I know better (than to do so). // 어리석은 짓일랑 하지 마라 Don't make yourself ridiculous. // 어리석게도 그것을 믿었다 I was fool enough to believe that. // 그 여자와 결혼하다니 어리석기 짝이 없다. It would be the height of folly to marry her.

어리숭하다 ① [사람이] be a bit foolish ; look a little foolish〔stupid〕 ¶ 그 아이는 보기에 어리숭하지만 꽤 재주가 있다 The boy looks foolish but he has quite a bit of talent.
② [사물이] (be) dim ; hazy ; vague ; indistinct ; obscure ¶ 어리숭한 기억 a dim memory // 기억이 어리숭하다 have a dim memory

어리어리하다 be all misty ; (be) all dim 〔hazy, indistinct, vague〕 ; be all a little foolish (-looking)

어리전 —廛 a poultry shop

어리치다 swoon ; faint

어리칙칙하다 be pretending to be stupid ; be so impudent as to pretend to be a fool

어리호박벌 a hornet

어린 魚鱗 fishscales

어린것 a little one ; a young one ; a youngster ; a kid ¶ 집에 어린것이 많다 have a lot of kids (in one's family)

어린녀석 a little chap ; a brat ; an urchin

어린년 a little girl ; a little wench

어린애 ⇨ 어린이

*어린이 a child ; a youngster ; [남아] a boy ; [여아] a girl ; [영아] a baby ; an infant ; little ones《총칭》 ¶ 어린이를 위한 책 juvenile reading ; a book for children // 어린이 같은 childlike ; childish

> 참고 **childlike**는 「순진하고 귀여운」 「철없는」 따위의 좋은 뜻에 사용하고 **childish**는 「어른답지 않다」라는 나쁜 뜻에서 사용한다

// 어린이가 없는 childless ; having no children of one's own // 어린이 장난 같은 childish ; puerile ; like a child's play // 어린이 시절에 in one's childhood 〔boyhood, girlhood, infancy〕 // 어린이 취급하다 treat《a person》 like a child // 어린이 시절에 익힌 것은 평생 잊혀지지 않는다 What is learned in the cradle is carried to the grave. // 나는 이제 어린이가 아니란 말야 I'm no longer a chicken〔child〕. // 그를 어린이 때부터 알고 있다 I have known him from my childhood〔from a child〕. // 우리 할머니는 나이가 드시니 다시 어린이가 되었다 Our grandmother, getting very old, has entered her second childhood. // 곧 그들은 어린이를 가질 것이다 They will soon have a baby 〔child〕. /A child will be born to them before long. // 그런 것은 어린이도 안다 A mere child knows it. // 그는 텔레비전을 갖게 되어 어린이처럼 좋아한다 He is as pleased as a boy with a television set. // 나도 너와 같이 어린 시절이 있었다 I was once a child〔boy, girl〕 like you. // 어린이를 교육시키는 데는 많은 돈이 든다 The education of children is a great expense.
— 교육 child education —날 Children's Day —방 a nursery — 백서 a White Paper on Children ; a Juvenile White Paper — 속임수〔장난〕 mere child's play ; a puerile〔childish〕 trick ; kid stuff — 시간 [라디오·텔레비전의] the Children's Hour — 시절〔시대〕 childhood ; boyhood ; girlhood ; infancy — (연)극 juvenile theatricals — 은행 a children's bank — 헌장 the Children's Charter — 회관 a children's hall

*어림 a rough guess ; an estimate ¶ 어림잡다 guess ; estimate《at》 ; make an estimate《of》 // 지나치게 어림잡다 overestimate // 적게 어림잡다 underestimate // 기부금의 총액을 적게 어림잡아도 100만원은 된다 The total sum of the contributions is conservatively estimated at a million *won*. // 관광객은 어림잡아 10만 정도다 The number of visitors is roughly estimated at 100, 000. // 이렇게 되면 당초의 어림과는 크게 틀린다 This is very much different from the original estimate.
—셈 a rough calculation〔estimate〕 ; a rough sum ¶ 어림셈으로 at a rough estimate ; roughly ; approximately —수 a rough number〔figure〕 ; round numbers ; approximate figures ¶ 어림수로 천은 된다 The number approximates to 1, 000. /It comes to 1, 000 in round numbers.

어림없다 be far from ; be beyond《one》 (능력이) ; be nonsensical ; be beyond the stretch of《imagination》 (상상도 못하다) ; impossible ¶ 어림없는 수작 preposterous remarks // 어림없는 요구 a preposterous demand // 어림없는 이야기 an impossible story // 내가 빌다니 어림없는 이야기다 Apology on my part is too absurd〔out of the question〕. // 그것은 내 힘으로는 어림없다 That is far beyond my capacity〔power〕. // 영어 실력으로는 우리는 그에게 어림도 없다 He is far beyond us in English. // 내가 그런 거짓말을 믿다

니 어림없는 일이다 It is ridiculous to expect me to believe such a lie. // 어림없는 소리 하지 마라 What a thing to say! / Absurd! /That's all eye! // 어림도 없다 That's way off the mark.

어림쟁이 a weak-minded person ; a spineless fellow

*어림짐작 a rough-and-ready guess ; guesswork ¶ 어림짐작으로 by guesswork ; by feel // 어림짐작으로 말하다 make〔give〕 a random guess ; talk at random // 어림짐작으로 잘 맞추다 make a good shot《at》// 어림짐작으로 시계를 2시 30분에 맞추었다 I set my watch by guess at half past two.

어릿거리다 be in a daze ; be dull 〔absent-minded〕 ¶ 어릿거리지 마라 Look alive! /Wake up!

*어릿광대 a clown ; a buffoon

어릿하다 ⇨ 아릿하다

어마 [놀람] My! /Oh! /Good heaven(s)! /O dear! ¶ 어마 이게 누구냐 Oh, my! It is certainly a surprise to see you! // 어마 무슨 소리일까 O dear! What can that noise be? // 어마 참 많이 컸구나 Oh my! What a big boy you've grown to be!

어마어마하다 [당당하다] (be) grand ; magnificent ; solemn ; majestic ; [과장적] ostentatious ; pompous ; [대단하다] tremendous ; colossal ¶ 어마어마한 고층건물 an imposing skyscraper // 어마어마한 부자 a man of colossal wealth // 어마어마한 행렬 a stately procession // 어마어마한 직함 an ostentatious title ; a long handle to one's name // 어마어마한 광경 an awesome sight // 어마어마하게 힘센 장사 a man of enormous strength // 어마어마한 큰 저택에 살다 live in a grand mansion〔palace〕// 그는 그 어마어마한 경치에 경탄했다 He was awe-stricken by the grandeur of the scene. // 그는 어마어마한 돈을 남겨 놓고 죽었다 He died with a mint of money.

어망 漁網 a fish(ing) net ; a dragnet (끄는 것) ; a casting-net (투망)

어맹증 語盲症 alexia ; word blindness

어머나 [놀람] Oh! /Why! /Dear me! /O my! /Good gracious! ¶ 어머나 너무해요 Oh, how mean of you! // 어머나 저것 봐 Look! What is that? // 어머나 참 예쁘네 O my, how nice! // 어머나 가엾어라 What a pity!

†어머니 ① a mother ¶ 어머니의 mother's ; maternal // 친 어머니 one's real mother // 어머니의 사랑 mother's love 〔affection〕; maternal love // 어머니다운 motherly ; maternal // 어머니가 없는 motherless // 저 형제는 어머니가 틀린다 They are brothers by different mother. // 그 여자는 이제 3남매의 어머니가 됐다 She is now the mother of three children. // 그 여자는 빈민의 어머니였다 She was a mother to〔the mother of〕 the poor.
② [사물의 근본] origin ; source ; cause ; motive ¶ 필요는 발명의 어머니 Necessity is the mother of invention.
—날 Mother's Day — 사랑 maternal affection〔love〕; the mothers' love —회 mother's meeting

어머님 (my) dear mother

어멈 [하인] a housemaid ; an amah ; a maidservant

어명 御名 the personal name of a king ; the royal name

어명 御命 a royal command〔mandate〕; an order from the king ¶ 어명을 내리다 issue a royal order

어물 魚物 dried fish ; stockfish
—전 a dried-fish shop

어물 御物 Royal properties

어물거리다 equivocate ; prevaricate ¶ 대답을 어물거리다 evade any definite answer ; give a vague answer // 일을 어물거리다 do a sloppy job ; scamp one's work

어물다 (be) feeble〔feeble-minded, weak〕

어물어물 equivocally ; evasively ; carelessly ; slowly ; lazily ; hesitatingly ¶ 어물어물하지 말고 promptly ; without delay 〔hesitation〕// 일을 어물어물하다 scamp one's work ; do evasive work // 어물어물하다가 기회를 잃다 dally away one's opportunity // 어물어물 소일하다 dawdle away one's time // 어물어물하지 말라 Look sharp. /Be quick. // 의외의 사건이 터져 교섭이 어물어물되어 버렸다 Owing to the unforeseen incident, the negotiations were allowed to drop. // 어물어물할 때가 아니다 This is no time for sitting idle. // 어물어물하지 말고 네 생각을 말해봐라 Out with it! Never stand shilly-shally. // 도대체 무얼 그렇게 어물어물하고 있는거냐 Why on earth have you been so long? // 어물어물하다가는 음악회에 늦겠다 Hurry up or you'll be late for the concert.

어물쩍 equivocally ; quibblingly ; evasively
—하다 equivocate ; quibble ; evade ; dodge

어물쩍거리다 equivocate ; skimp ; do slapdash ¶ 말을 어물쩍거리다 equivocate // 그는 어물쩍거리며 찬성하지 않았다 He did not give his consent to the proposal on one pretext or other. // 농담으로 생각하고 어물쩍거려 넘기려고 했다 He tried to turn it off as a joke.

어미 a mother
— 고양이 a mother cat — 나무 [접목의] the stool ; the stock —새 a parent 〔mother〕 bird

어미 語尾 the ending of a word ; a suffix (접미어) ¶ 어미에 붙이다 suffix // 어미를 흐리다 equivocate ; quibble ; do not commit oneself // 너의 말은 어미가 똑똑하

지 않다 You slur your words' ending.
— 변화 inflection ; declension ; conjugation ¶ 라틴말은 어미 변화가 많다 Latin is a highly inflected language. — 탈락 apocope

어민 魚民 fishermen
— 조합 fishermen's cooperative society

어백 魚白 milt《of fish》; soft roe

†어버이 parents ; father and mother ¶ 어버이의 parental // 친 어버이 one's true parents // 어버이와 자식 parent and child // 어버이다운 parentlike ; parental // 어버이를 여의다 lose one's parents ; be deprived of one's parents ; become orphaned // 어버이에 불효하다 be unkind to one's parents ; ill-treat one's parents // 어버이 슬하에 있다 be under one's parental roof ; be dependent on one's parents ; be living at one's parents expense // 어버이를 공경하라 You ought to respect〔be respectful towards〕 your parents. // 자식은 어버이를 본받는다 As the old birds sing, so the young ones twitter.

어벌쩡하다 (be) evasive ; mystify ; hoodwink

어법 語法 diction ; wording ; expression ; phraseology ; 〖문법〗 syntax ; grammar ; usage ¶ 어법에 어긋나다 violate grammar ; make a grammar slip
— 위반 solecism ; a breach of syntax ; a slip in grammar 셰익스피어 — Shakespeare's〔Shakespearian〕 language〔idiom〕 아메리카 — American usage in English ; Americanism

어별 魚鼈 fish and snapping turtles ; sea creatures

어보 魚譜 an atlas of fish

어복 魚腹 the belly of fish

*어부 漁夫 a fisher(man) ¶ 어부지리를 얻다 fish in troubled water ; play off one person against another ; win advantages for oneself from a disturbed state of affairs ; make profit out of two contestants

어부바 Up we go ! — 하다 ⇨ 업다

어부슴 魚— 《hold》 a (shamanic) fish-feeding service (on the 15th of lunar January)

어분 魚粉 fish meal

어불성설 語不成說 lack of logic ; illogicalness ¶ 어불성설이다 be illogical ; do not hold water ; lack logic // 그것은 전혀 어불성설이다 That's against all reason. / That doesn't stand to reason at all.

어비 魚肥 fish manure ; fish fertilizer

어빡자빡 irregularly ; disorderly

어뿔싸 Gosh ! /Alas ! ⇨ 아뿔싸

어사 語辭 words ; language ; speech

어사 御史 a royal secret inspector ; a royal emissary who travels incognito to check on local governments

어사리 fishing with a moored net — 하다 fish with a moored net

어살 a weir ; a wooden fence in the water to trap fish

어상 —商 a cattle dealer

어상 魚商 a fish dealer ; a fishmonger

어상반 於相半 likeness ; similarity ; resemblance — 하다 be much like ; be almost similar ; be nearly alike ; there is little if any difference ¶ 빛깔이 어상반하다 be similar in color // 어상반하게 보이다 look alike // 그의 월급이나 내 월급이나 어상반하다 His salary is almost the same as mine. // 그들의 성격은 어상반하다 They are alike in character.

어새 御璽 the royal seal ; the Privy Seal

‡어색 語塞 — 하다 [말의 막힘] be at a loss for word ; [기분] feel awkward〔embarrassed〕 ; (be) bashful ; be〔feel〕 abashed ; feel ill at ease ; (be) clumsy ; crude ¶ 어색한 문장 crude style ; clumsy wording // 어색한 핑계 a clumsy excuse // 어색한 몸가짐 awkward〔stiff〕 manners // 영어로서는 아주 어색한 표제 a title which is extremely awkward in English // 어색한 느낌을 주다 It makes us feel constrained〔ill at ease〕. // 어젯밤의 연주회에서 그는 꼴이 매우 어색하였다 He cut a very miserable figure at last night's concert. // 나는 아무 말도 않고 앉아 있었으나 매우 어색했다 I, sitting in silence, felt awkward. // 돈이 부족해서 어색했다 I felt awkward to find myself short of cash. // 사람 앞에 나서기가 좀 어색하다 I feel kind of shy to be seen in public. // 그 말을 들으니 나는 어색했다 The remark embarrassed me.

어서 ① [빨리] quick(ly) ; fast ; promptly ; rapidly ; without delay ; in haste (급히) ¶ 어서 오너라 Come quick ! / Hurry up ! / Make haste ! /Make it snappy ! // 어서 계속 해라 Go ahead ! // 어서 대답해 Answer promptly. /Give me a prompt answer. // 어서 많이 드십시오 Please help yourself.
② [환영] (if you) please ; kindly ¶ 어서 오십시오 Come right in, please. / Welcome ! // 어서 들어오십시오 Please walk in.

-어서 (and) so ; and then ; so... that ; because (of) ; on account of ; for ; as ; from ¶ 이렇게 늦어서 미안합니다 I am sorry to be so late.

-어서가 not that... (but that...) ; not because... (but because) ¶ 그것은 돈이 없어서가 아니다 It is not that〔because〕 I haven't got money.

-어서도 too ; also ; either ; as well ¶ 품질뿐 아니라 크기에 있어서도 이것이 제일이다 This comes the first in size as well as quality.

-어서야 not till〔until〕 ; (only) if ; when ¶ 어른이 되어서야 건강의 고마움을 알았다 I did not know the blessing of health till I grew up.

어석거리다 crunch ; crush with one's teeth ; chew with a crushing sound
어석소, 어석송아지 ⇨ 어스럭송아지
어선 漁船 a fishing boat〔vessel, craft〕; a fisher boat ¶ 어선은 대개 저녁에 나가서 아침에 들어온다 Fishing smacks, as a rule, go out in the evening and return in the morning.
—대(隊) a fishing fleet **소—** a cog
어설프다 ① [성기다] (be) coarse ; rough ; slovenly loose ¶ 어설프게 뜬 그물 a net with large meshes
② [탐탁찮다] (be) sloppy ; [부주의] careless ; negligent ¶ 어설피 in a slovenly way ; carelessly ; clumsily // 어설피 하다가는 if one is not careful ; if one is unlucky ; if not properly handled // 일하는 것이 어설프다 be a sloppy worker ; do a slovenly job // 어설프게 하는 일이 잘될리 없다 A half measure is always a failure. // 그들은 모두 어설프게 알고 있다 They all have a smattering of knowledge. // 그의 영어는 아직도 조금은 어설프다 His English is still a little bit shaky.
어섯 a bit ; part ; [모자라는] less than completely ¶ 어섯 눈뜨다 get a rough idea of it ; become dimly aware of it
어성 語聲 a voice ; a tone (of voice)
어세 語勢 stress 《on a word》; emphasis ; (dynamic, stress) accent ; a tone 《of voice》 ¶ 어세를 높이다 emphasize ; lay〔put, place〕 stress 《on a word》 // 어세를 높이어 말하다 speak emphatically〔with emphasis〕
어소 御所 the Royal palace
어수룩하다 (be) naive ; simple ; simple-hearted ; unsophisticated ¶ 어수룩한 사람 a simple person // 어수룩한 생각 a simple〔an unsophisticated〕 idea // 사물을 어수룩하게 생각하다 take things simple and easy // 그는 좀 어수룩한 데가 있다 He is something of a simpleton. // 그 여자는 어수룩하지 않다고 생각한다 I suppose she is sophisticated. // 어수룩하게 그런 얘기에 속지 마라 Don't be so naive as to be taken in by such a story. // 그의 눈앞에 어수룩한 표정의 식모가 서 있었다 He saw before him a young servant girl of somewhat vacant countenance. // 너는 참 어수룩하구나 You ought to know much of the world. // 내가 그것을 믿을 만큼 어수룩해 보이냐 Do you think I am so naive as to believe it ?
어수선산란하다 —散亂— be in utter confusion
어수선하다 (be) chaotic ; be out of order ; be in disorder〔confusion〕; be in a muddle〔mess〕 ¶ 어수선한 머리를 한 채로 with one's disheveled hair // 어수선해지다 fall into disorder〔confusion〕; get confused // 어수선한 세상 troubled times // 마음이 어수선하다 be distracted // 방이 아주 어수선했다 The room was in a terrible mess. // 아버지가 갑자기 아프셔서 집안이 어수선합니다 We are in confusion at home owing to the sudden illness of father. // 그 소식을 듣고 마음이 어수선했다 My mind was disturbed at the news. // 그 나라의 정계는 어수선하다 The political world of the country is in a chaotic condition. // 연회석이 어수선해지기 시작했다 Ceremony began to give way to merry-making in the banquet(ing) hall. // 아직 모든 것이 어수선하다 Everything's still a mess.
어순 語順 〖문법〗 word order
어숭그러하다 turn out pretty good〔favorable, satisfactory, smooth〕; [사람이 주어] be easy to get along with ¶ 어숭그러하게 진행되다 progress pretty satisfactorily ; go pretty well // 의외로 일은 어숭그러하게 진척됐다 Contrary to our expectation, the matter went on smoothly.
어스 〖전기〗 ground 《영》; earth 《미》 ¶ 어드 되어 있다 be (electrically) grounded
—선 a ground wire ; an earthed line **—판(板)** a ground〔an earth〕 plate
어스러기 a worn spot of a seam ; a fraying
어스러지다 ① [말·행동이] become〔get〕 abnormal〔queer, erratic〕
② [닳다] get torn〔broken, worn〕 off at the edge ¶ 칼날이 어스러졌다 The cutting edge of the knife was chipped off. // 그 사람은 좀 어스러진 성품이다 He is a queer sort of fellow.
어스럭송아지 a big〔hefty〕 calf
***어스레하다** (be) dusky ; dim ¶ 어스레한 빛 dim〔feeble, faint〕 light ; glimmer // 어스레한 방 a dimly-lit room // 어스레한 빛에 in the dim〔feeble〕 light // 어스레한 저녁에 in the dusk of evening // 어스레해지다 become rather dark // 전등이 어스레하다 The electric light is dim.
***어스름** dusk ; dim〔feeble, faint〕 light ¶ 어스름 속에서 읽다 read in the twilight〔dusk〕
—달 a clouded〔dim, hazy〕 moon **— 달밤** a misty moonlight night **— 저녁** a dusky evening
어슬렁거리다 hang about〔around〕; hover about〔in〕; wander about ; prowl ; loiter ¶ 어슬렁어슬렁 prowling ; roving // 어슬렁어슬렁 걷다 walk at a leisurely pace ; shuffle along // 바닷가를 어슬렁거리다 take a stroll on the beach // 정원을 어슬렁거리다 take a turn in a garden // 그는 몇 시간이고 거리를 어슬렁거렸다 He prowled〔roamed about〕 the street for hours. // 수상한 두 사람이 그 집 부근을 어슬렁거리는 것이 보였다 Two suspicious-looking men were seen prowling about the house. // 호랑이가 먹을 것을 찾아 어슬렁거리고 있다 A tiger is prowling after its prey. // 이 밤중에 어디를 어슬렁거리고 있느냐 Where have you been hanging

around at this time of night?

*어슬렁어슬렁 slowly; lazily; idly; sluggishly ¶ 어슬렁어슬렁 걷다 walk lazily〔idly〕; lounge《about》// 그 곰은 어슬렁어슬렁 가버렸다 The bear lumbered away.

어슬하다 (be) dusky ⇨ 어스레하다

어슴새벽 early dawn; daybreak ¶ 어슴 새벽에 towards morning〔daybreak〕; at peep of dawn // 어슴새벽부터 일하다 work from early dawn

어슴푸레 dimly; faintly; hazily ¶ 어슴푸레 알고 있다 be slightly acquainted with《a matter》// 날이 어슴푸레 밝기 시작했다 Day was beginning to break〔dawn〕.

어슴푸레하다 (be) dim; vague ⇨ 어렴풋하다

어슷거리다 drag one's feet listlessly

어슷비슷하다 be much〔almost, nearly〕the same; be almost similar; be of a sort; be much of a muchness; be six of one and half a dozen of the other ¶ 그들은 모두 어슷비슷하다 They are both of a sort. // 두 사람의 경력은 어슷비슷하다 There is a parallel point in their lives. /We can trace a parallel between their careers. // 두 사람의 처지는 어슷비슷하다 There is little〔not much〕to choose between the two persons in their circumstances. /There is little difference between the two persons in their circumstances. // 그 점에 있어서는 양자가 어슷비슷하다 There is little to choose between the two in that respect.

어슷하다 (be) slant; oblique; diagonal; skew ¶ 어슷하게 aslant; slopewise; obliquely; diagonally // 어슷하게 하다 incline // 어슷하게 기울다 slant // 어슷하게 자르다 cut diagonally // 어슷하게 나아가다 advance obliquely // 어른쪽으로 어슷하게 기울다 slant to the right

어시장 魚市場 a fish market

어시호 於是乎 hereupon; thereupon; at this (point); with regard to this

어안 魚眼 fish eyes
—석(石) a fisheye stone

어안 렌즈 魚眼— a fisheye lens

어안이 벙벙하다 be dumbfounded; be amazed; be struck dumb; be dazed; be taken aback ¶ 어안이 벙벙한 얼굴 an amazed look // 어안이 벙벙하여 어찌할 바를 모르다 be quite at a loss what to do // 그는 어안이 벙벙하여 말문이 막혔다 He was dumbfounded. /He was openmouthed with surprise. /He was (struck) dumb〔speechless〕with astonishment. // 그 소식에 어안이 벙벙해졌다 The news struck me dumb. // 그 대답에 어안이 벙벙했다 I was dumbfounded by the answer. /The answer beat me. // 그는 어안이 벙벙한 얼굴로 서 있었다 He was standing with an amazed look.

-어야 should〔ought to〕《do》; must〔have to〕《do》 ¶ 너는 좀 더 일찍 일어났어야 했다 You should have got up earlier.

-어야지 be going to; would ¶ 그녀에게 이 책을 주어야지 I am going to give her this book.

어어 Oh-oh! ⇨ 아아

어어이 [부르는 소리] Say!; Hey!; Hello!; Yoo-hoo!

어언간 於焉間 before one knows〔is aware〕; while one was not aware of; so soon; in no time at all; unawares; unnoticed ¶ 어언간 세월이 흘렀다 Years came and out. // 그해는 어언간 지나갔다 The year sped on. // 어언간 3년이 지났다 So three years glided away. // 겨울 방학도 어언간 지나가버렸다 The winter vacation has passed all too soon.

*어업 漁業 fishery; the fishing industry
—권 a fishery〔fishing〕right —기상 weather forecasting for fishermen —법 the Act〔Law〕of fisheries —전관 수역 (exclusive) fishing waters〔fishery zone〕; a fishing zone —조약 a fishery agreement —조합 a fishermen's union〔association〕 —허가증 a fishing license —협동 조합 a fishermen's cooperative association —회사 a fishing establishment; a fishery company; fishery interests 근해— coast〔offshore〕fishery 연안— inshore〔coastal〕fishery 원양— pelagic〔deep-sea, ocean〕fishery 하천〔담수〕— river fishery 공동 —권 common of fishery〔piscary〕 한일 —회담 the Korean-Japanese fishery talks

어여머리 a large plait of false hair worn by a woman in ceremonial dress

어여차 Heave-ho! /Yo-heave-ho! ¶ 어여차 어여차 끌다 drag《a load》with 'heave-ho'

어연간하다 (be) considerable; moderate; tolerable ⇨ 엔간하다

어연번듯하다 be honest and respectable to all appearances

어염 魚鹽 fish and salt
—시수(柴水) daily necessities

어엿하다 (be) respectable; decent; unblamable ¶ 어엿한 신사 an honorable〔a decent〕gentleman // 어엿한 집안 a respectable family // 그는 이제 어엿한 가장이다 He is now master of his own house. /He is now providing for his own family.

어영 대장 御營大將 the Director of the Royal Palace Keeper's Bureau

어영청 御營廳 the Royal Palace Keeper's Bureau

어옹 漁翁 an old fisherman

어용 御用 official business; government service
—기자 a journalist in government pay —노동 조합 a company(-kept) union —신문 a government〔mouthpiece〕organ; a

subsidized organ of the government ; a government mouthpiece ; the kept press — 의원 a government-controlled national assemblyman — 학자 a government-patronized scholar ; an unprincipled scholar

*어우러지다 be〔get〕 joined together ; harmonize ; unite ¶ 들에는 백화가 어우러져 피어있다 The field is alive〔bright〕 with all sorts of flowers blooming.

어우렁더우렁 loafing around with a group —하다 loaf around with a group

어우르다 put together ; unite ; combine ; connect ; join together ¶ 힘을 어우르다 join efforts ; cooperate // 힘을 어울러서 회사를 만들었다 They got together and started a firm.

†어울리다 ① [조화되다] (be) becoming 〔suitable〕 ; become ; suit ; match ¶ 어울리는 모자 a hat that becomes 《one》 ; a becoming hat // 잘 어울리는 짝 a good pair〔match〕 // 옷에 어울리는 모자 a hat which goes with one's suit // 어울리는 말〔행동〕 remarks〔behavior〕 proper to the occasion // 어울리지 않는 ill-matched ; unworthy 《of》 ; out of place ; improper ; unreasonable // 어울리지 않는 부부 an ill-matched couple // 신사〔교육자〕에게 안 어울리는 행동 a conduct〔an act〕 unbecoming to〔unworthy of〕 a gentleman〔an educator〕 // 어울리지 않는 결혼 an ill-assorted marriage // 옷이 어울리다 become 《a person》 ; sit well on 《a person》 // 그 옷은 당신에게 어울립니다 That dress becomes you. /You look nice〔well〕 in that suit. // 이것이 더 잘 어울릴 것이오 This would be more becoming to you. /This would suit you better still. // 그는 학생 신분에 어울리지 않는 말을 한다 He talks unlike a student. // 수수한 검은 옷은 그 여자에게 어울리지 않는다 The plain black dress does not suit her. // 양탄자와 커튼이 잘 어울린다 The carpet and curtain are a good match. // 그 그림은 방에 어울리지 않는다 The picture does not suit the room. // 선생 노릇은 너에게 어울리지 않는다 Your being a teacher doesn't seem right to me somehow. // 정말 예쁘고 어울리는 부부였어요 Yes, they were indeed a handsome, well-matched pair. // 그런 일은 나에게 안 어울린다 I am not fit for such work. // 저 청년은 우리 딸에게는 어울리지 않는다 That young man is not a good match for our daughter. // 그 드레스가 그 여자에게 매우 잘 어울린다고 생각한다 I think the dress is very becoming on her. // 나는 그들이 어울리지 않는 부부라고 생각했었어 I thought they were a mismatch. // 이 색은 당신 나이에 어울리지 않아요 This color doesn't go with your age. // 그 헤어 스타일은 너한테 아주 잘 어울린다 That hairdo is very becoming on you. // 나는 네가 좀더 영업사원에 어울리는 옷을 입었으면 한다 I want you to dress in a manner more befitting a sales representative.

② [교제하다] join ; mix 《with》 ; associate 《with》 ; mingle 《with》 ; keep company 《with》 ¶ 외국 사람과 어울리다 mix with foreigners // 귀족들과 어울리다 mix with the aristocracy // 잘 어울리(지 않)는 사람 a good〔bad〕 mixer // 불량 소년의 무리와 어울리다 join a band of bad boys // 저 사람과는 어울리지 말아라 You should keep clear of that fellow. // 그는 어울리기 쉬운 사람이다 He is easy to get on with. /He is a good mixer. // 그는 그 여자와 어울리고 있다 He keeps company with her. // 대체로 예술가끼리 어울린다 Artists usually associate〔consort〕 with artists. // 부정직한 사람과는 어울리지 않는 편이 좋다 You had better not associate〔mix, mingle〕 with dishonest people. /You had better avoid the company of dishonest people. // 어울리는 친구를 보면 어떤 사람인가를 안다 A man is known by the company he keeps. /We know a man by his company. // 아드님이 동네 아이들과 잘 어울려 놉니까 Does your son get along with the neighborhood kids?

어웅하다 (be) hollow ; sunken ¶ 어웅한 눈 hollow eyes

*어원 語源 the etymology (of a word) ¶ 어원적으로 연구하다 make an etymological study 《of words》 // 어원을 조사하다 trace a word to its origin ; study the etymology of a word ; etymologize 《a word》 // 빵의 어원은 포르투갈어이다 The word "pan" is derived from Portuguese. // 이 말들은 어원이 같다 These words have the same pedigree〔origin〕.
—학 etymology —학자 an etymologist

어유 魚油 fish oil

어육 魚肉 [생선] fish ; [생선과 수육] fish and meat

어음 『상업』 a bill ; a draft ; a note ¶ 어음을 인수하다 accept a bill // 어음을 거절하다 dishonor a bill // 어음을 현금과 바꾸어 받다 get a draft cashed // 어음을 발행하다 draw a credit〔bill〕 《for 5,000 *won*》 on 《a person》 // 어음을 할인하다 discount a bill // 어음이 만기가 된다 The bill falls due.
— 계원 a note-teller ; a bill clerk — 계정 a bills account — 교환 clearing — 교환소 a clearing house — 금액 the sum due on a bill — 기일 the date of a bill — 발행〔수취〕인 the drawer 〔payee〕 of a bill —법 the Bills of Exchange and Promissory Notes Act — 사기 bill fraud — 소지인 a bill holder — 유통 기간 the currency of a bill — 인수 acceptance of a bill — 인수인 the acceptor of a bill — 재할인 rediscounting of a bill — 중매인 a bill broker — 지불〔부도〕 payment by 〔nonpayment of〕 a bill — 지불인 the payer〔drawee〕 of a bill 개인 — a private

bill 공(空)— a kite 기일 경과〔만기〕 — an overdue〔a matured〕 bill 기한부 — a term bill ; usance (bill) 단독(환) — a sole〔sola〕 bill 무자금 — a bill unprovided for 백지식 — a blank bill〔note〕 부도 — a dishonored bill ; a bill of dishonor 삼개월 지불 — a bill due in three months 상업 — a (trade) bill ; a commercial〔mercantile〕 paper〔bill〕 십만원짜리 — a draft〔bill〕 for 100,000 *won* 약속 — a promissory note ; a bill of debt 요구불 — a note on demand ; a cash order 《영》 우량 — a fine〔gilt-edged〕 bill 위조 — a forged bill 유통 — a negotiable bill 융통 — an accommodation bill 은행 — a bank draft〔bill〕 《영》 ; an addressed bill 일람불 — a note at sight ; a sight〔presentation〕 bill ; a demand draft 일부후불(日附後拂) — a bill payable after date 일부후정기불 — bills payable 《so many》 months〔days〕 after sight 장기〔단기〕 — a long〔short〕(-dated) bill 정기불 — a bill payable on fixed date ; a time bill 즉시불 — a prompt note 지불 — a bill payable 지정식 — a bill to order 지참인〔지정인〕 지급 — a bill payable to bearer〔order〕 할인 — a discount bill 환— a bill of exchange

어음 語音 the pronunciation ; the sound of a words ; a tone〔note〕

어의 語義 the meaning of a word ¶ 일반적인 어의로는 in the common acceptation of the word ; in a sense in which the word is generally understood // 어의를 밝히다 define〔clarify the meaning of〕 a word

어의 御醫 a court〔royal〕 physician

어의 御衣 King's clothes ⇨ 어복(御服)

어이¹ [짐승의 어미] a mother animal — 새끼 mother and litter ; a mother animal and her cubs〔puppies〕

어이² [어찌] why ; how ⇨ 어찌 ¶ 어이 알았으리오 그 사람이 바로 그가 찾고 있던 그의 아저씨인 줄이야 How should we know that the man was his very uncle he was looking for? // 당신이 모르는데 내가 어이 알겠소 How should I know if you do not?

어이³ [부르는 소리] hello ; hey ; say ; hello

어이구 Oh! /Ouch! ⇨ 아이고

어이어이 Alas! /Woe! ¶ 어이어이 울다 wail〔cry〕 one's heart out

***어이없다** be struck dumb ; be dumbfounded ; be amazed〔aghast〕 《at》 ¶ 어이없는 요구 exorbitant demands // 어이없는 값 a fabulous〔frightful〕 price ; an exorbitant〔extravagant〕 price // 어이없는 말을 하다 make absurd remarks ; talk wild // 그것은 어이 없는 짓이다 That is out of all reason. /That is quite outrageous. // 어이없어 말이 안 나왔다 I was speechless〔struck dumb〕 with amazement // 그녀석의 뻔뻔스러움에는 어이가 없었다 I was amazed at his audacity. // 내 건망증에 나 자신 어이가 없다 I am disgusted with myself for my short〔poor〕 memory. // 어이가 없어 서로 얼굴만 쳐다볼 뿐이었다 We all gazed at each other in blank dismay.

어이없이 easily ; without difficulty ; helplessly ¶ 어이없이 지다 be easily beaten // 어이없이 죽다 die a sudden death // 그는 정말 어이없이 죽었다 His death came so suddenly.

어이쿠 [감탄사] Oh! ; Ouch!

어일싸 [경멸] Hum! /Hah! /Well!

-어 있다 be in a state resulting from ; be done ¶ …으로 되어 있다 consist of ; be made (up) of

어장 漁場 fishing grounds ; a fishing place

어저귀 〖식물〗 an Indian mallow

어저께 yesterday ⇨ 어제

어적거리다 munch ; crunch ; chew ¶ 어적어적 with a munching〔crunching〕 // 사과를 어적거리다 munch (at) an apple

어적어적 with a munching sound **— 하다** ⇨ 어적거리다

어전 魚箭 a (fish) weir ; a fish trap ⇨ 어살

어전 御殿 a palace

어전 御前 the Royal presence ¶ 어전에서 in the presence of the King // 어전에 나가다〔을 물러나다〕 come into〔leave〕 the Royal presence

— 회의 a council in the Royal〔Imperial〕 presence ; an Imperial conference

어정 carelessness ; negligence ; slovenliness ; looseness ¶ 일을 어정으로 하다 do a slapdash job

어정거리다 walk leisurely along ; walk at leisurely pace ; stroll ; saunter ¶ 공원을 어정거리다 saunter about a park // 이 밤중에 어디를 어정거리고 있었나 Where have you been hanging〔fooling〕 around at this time of night?

어정뜨다 (be) careless ; negligent ; slovenly ; loose ¶ 어정뜨게 carelessly ; negligently ; in a slovenly way

어정뱅이 ① a person suddenly elevated (to wealth or position) ② a negligent〔sloppy〕 person

어정버정 walking leisurely ; sauntering ; rambling ¶ 어정버정 걷다 stroll ; ramble about // 어정버정하지 말고 어서 가라 What are you all loitering about over there for? Be off this moment.

어정어정 ⇨ 어정버정

어정잡이 a man of a mere show ⇨ 어정뱅이

어정쩡하다 (be) suspicious ; doubtful ; dubious ; questionable ; disputable ; evasive ; [애매하다] vague ; ambiguous ¶ 어정쩡한 태도 a dubious attitude // 어정쩡한 인물 a questionable character // 어

정쩡한 신사 a gentleman of a kind // 어정쩡한 여자 a demirep // 어정쩡한 대답 an evasive answer // 어정쩡한 영어로 in faulty English

†**어제** yesterday ¶ 그를 만난 것은 바로 어제다 It was only yesterday that I met him. // K양을 처음 만난 것을 어제 일처럼 기억하고 있다 I remember, as though it were yesterday, the first sight of Miss K. // 그 여자를 만난 지가 바로 어제 같다 It seems only yesterday since I saw her. **— 신문** yesterday's paper **— 아침** yesterday morning **어젯밤** last night 〔evening〕 **어젯저녁** last evening 〔night〕; yesterday evening

어제 御製 a poem or prose-piece of Royal composition ¶ 세종의 어제 a work written by King *Sejong*

†**어조 語調** the tone of the voice ; euphony ; accent ; [표현] a turn of expression ¶ 진지한〔흥분한〕 어조로 in an earnest 〔excited〕 tone // 슬픈 어조로 in accents of grief ; in a sad tone // 어조를 낮추다 tone down ; soften one's voice ; speak in a gentle voice // 어조를 높이다 raise one's voice // 그는 아주 진지한 어조로 말했다 His tone was very earnest. // 미국 사람은 어조로 알 수 있다 I can tell an American by his accent. // 그는 연설 어조로 내게 그렇게 말했다 He said so to me as if he were making a speech.

어조사 語助辭 a particle in classical Chinese

어족 語族 a language family ; a family of language ; related languages **우랄알타이 —** the Ural-Altaic language family **인도 유럽 —** the Indo-European language family

어족 魚族 fishes ; the finny tribe ; Pisces

어좌 御座 the royal throne ; the king's chair ¶ 어좌에 앉다 sit on the throne ; take the royal seat

어줍다 (be) dull ; indecisive ; lukewarm ; inanimate ; [저리다] become numb ; be numbed ; be asleep ¶ 어줍은 대답 a noncommittal reply ; a vague reply // 어줍은 사람 a dolt ; a dull〔stupid〕 fellow

어중간 於中間 halfway ; the middle **—하다** be about halfway ; be about midway ¶ 어중간히 half ; partially // 일을 어중간히 하다 do things by halves // 어중간히 끝났다 It is half finished. // 어중간히 그만두려거든 처음부터 하지 마라 You leave it undone than leave it half-done〔-way〕. // 그는 일을 어중간하게 하지 않는다 He goes the whole hog. /There are no half measures about him. // 어중간한 것은 무엇이나 잘 되지 않는다 A half measure is always failure. /Things done by halves are never done right. // 나는 어중간한 것을 싫어한다 I don't like to do things by halves. /I want all or nothing. // 어중간한 학문을 할 바에는 차라리 하지 않는 편이 낫다 One may as well know nothing than know things by halves. // 지금부터 출발해도 시간이 어중간하다 If we start now, we shall arrive there at an awkward hour. /It will be too early〔late〕 if we go now. // 어중간하나 위치에 있다는 것은 힘든 일이다 It's tough to be in a position without any real authority.

어중되다 be either too small〔little, short〕 or too big〔much, long〕; be unsuitable either way ; be insufficient either way ; be not perfectly fit

어중이떠중이 (anybody and) everybody ; all sorts and conditions of men ; the ruck ; the rabble ; every Tom, Dick and Harry ¶ 병정이 된답시고 시골에서 모여든 어중이떠중이 a mere rabble of field hands pretending to be soldier // 어중이떠중이 할 것 없이 재판정에 모여 들었다 A swarm of people gathered around the court.

어지간하다 ① [상당하다] (be) passable ; tolerable ; considerable ② [무던하다] (be) enough ; sufficient ; decent ¶ 어지간히 fairly ; tolerably ; passably ; pretty well〔much〕; considerably ; quite (대단히) // 어지간히 잘 pretty well // 어지간한 성공 a tolerable success ; a fair (measure of) success // 어지간한 수입 a handsome income // 어지간한 학교 성적 a pretty good record at school // 어지간히 춥다 be quite cold // 어지간히 지내다 be fairly well off ; make a decent living ; live in respectable style // 그는 불어를 어지간히 잘한다 He speaks French pretty well. // 그는 어지간한 사람이다 He is a man of competent ability. /He is not a man to be despised. // 하루 일로는 어지간하다 It is a good day's work. // 여기서부터 어지간히 멀다 It is a good distance from here. // 그는 어지간히 이해력이 좋다 He has a fair amount of sense. // 병자가 어지간히 좋아졌다 The patient has improved considerably. // 그 여자는 정구도 어지간히 한다 She is not half bad at tennis. // 이 그림은 어지간히 잘 돼있다 This picture is done pretty well.

어지간히 ⇨ 어지간하다

-어지다 ① [되다] become ; get to be ¶ 흐려지다 get cloudy ② [수동·자동] get〔be〕 done ¶ 찢어지다 tear ; get torn // 떨어지다 fall ; drop

어지러뜨리다 ① ⇨ 어지르다 ② [어지럽게 하다] make a person dizzy〔giddy〕

어지러이 ⇨ 어지럽다

어지럼 dizziness ; giddiness ; loss of equilibrium ; vertigo 《*pl.* ～s, -tiginess》 ¶ 어지럼을 타다 be subject to dizziness ; feel dizzy

‡**어지럽다** ① [눈·머리가] (be) dizzy ; get〔feel〕 giddy ; feel strange〔queer〕; have a sensation of giddiness ; one's

head turns〔swims〕 ¶ 어지러울 정도로 높은 곳〔속도〕 a dizzying height〔speed〕// 어지럽게 변천하는 세상 the giddy whirl of modern life ; the dizzy ; dazing〕 bustle of life ; the bustling world // 머리가 어지럽다 one's brain reels ; one's head swims // 이따금 어지럽다 often get dizzy spells ; have frequent dizzy spells
② [무질서] be in disorder ; (be) troubled ; chaotic ; turbulent ; disturbed ; disorganized (나라가) ¶ 어지러운 세상 troubled〔troublous〕 times ; unsettled times // 어지러운 방 a disorderly room // 방이 어지럽다 The room is in wild disorder. // 이렇게 어지러운 세상에서 그곳만은 안전하다 In these troubled times it is the safe place. // 그 회사는 재정 사정이 아주 어지럽다 The finances of the company are badly disorganized. // 의혹 사건으로 전국이 어지럽다 The whole country is agitated over the scandal. // 이 문제로 세상이 몹시 어지럽다 Excitement runs high in the country about this question.

*어지르다 scatter (about) ; put in〔throw into〕 disorder ; disarrange ; litter 《with》 ¶ 어질러져 있다 [물건이] be scattered about ; be in an untidy state ; [방 따위가] be in disorder ; out of order〕 ; be littered 《with things》 // 방을 어지르다 litter a room 《with odds and ends》 // 어질러 놓다 leave 《things》 lying about // 책상 위에 종이를 어질러 놓다 litter a desk with papers // 방바닥에 땅콩을 어지르다 litter peanuts over the floor // 어질러진 방을 치우다 tidy (up) a room in disorder // 이 방은 몹시 어질러져 있다 This room is in wild disorder. // 어지르지 마시오 No Litter. (게시) // 너 또 네 방을 어질러 놓았구나 당장 깨끗이 치워라 You messed up your room, again ! Clean it up immediately.

어지빠르다 be too big or little to be right ; be not what is wanted

-어지이다 wish ¶ 속히 회복되어지이다 I wish you a speedy recovery (to health).

어지자지 a hermaphrodite

어진 御眞 the portrait of a king

어진혼 —魂 the soul〔spirit〕 of a good-natured man ¶ 어진혼 나가다 be taken aback ; be frightened out of one's senses 《with》 ; be shocked off one's feet

어질다 (be) gentle ; kind-hearted ; merciful ; generous ; benevolent ; wise ¶ 어진 마음 a compassionate heart ; benevolence // 어진 임금 a benevolent ruler ; a gracious lord // 아이들에게 어질다 be gentle with children

어질더분하다 (be) disorderly〔untidy〕 ; topsyturvy ; be messed〔jumbled〕 up

†어질어질, 어찔어찔 giddily ; dizzily ; in a whirl —하다 feel dizzy〔giddy〕 ¶ 어질어질한 느낌 a swimming sensation // 수면부족 때문인지 어질어질하다 My head swims, perhaps from lack of sleep.

*어째(서) why ; for what reason ; how is it that ⇨ 어찌하여 ¶ 어째 늦었느냐 Why were you late ? // 어째서 그러냐 How so ? // 어째 왔느냐 How is it that you are here ? 그는 어째 그러냐 How can he be like that ? // 어째서 그런지 모르겠습니다 I cannot tell you why. // 그가 어째 늦는지 모르겠다 I wonder why he is late. // 어째서 나를 쳐다보느냐 What are you looking at me for ? // 어째서 웃느냐 What makes you laugh ? // 어째서 그가 자살했을까 Why did he kill himself ? // 어째서 그렇게 생각합니까 Why do you think so ? /What makes you think so ? // 그가 어째 안 왔다고 생각하느냐 Why do you think he did not come ?

*어쨌든 anyhow ; anyway ; at any rate ; in any case ; somehow or other ; setting aside ; apart〕 ¶ 그것은 어쨌든 however that may be ; be that as it may // 비용은 어쨌든 setting aside〔apart from〕 the question of expense // 어쨌든 나가자 Let's start, anyway. // 어쨌든 그것은 해야 한다 It must be done somehow or other. // 선악은 어쨌든 사실이다 It may be right or wrong, but it is a fact. // 비가 올지도 모르지만 어쨌든 떠나겠다 It may rain, but anyhow I shall go out. // 어쨌든 오정까지 그를 기다려 보자 Well, at any rate, I will wait for him till noon. // 어쨌든 저 친구는 좋은 인물이다 Altogether he is a very nice fellow. // 어쨌든 그의 일은 끝났다 He has finished the work somehow or other. // 어쨌든 준비만은 해야겠다 In any case〔At all events〕, I will make preparation for it. // 돈은 어쨌든 그는 남편감으로 훌륭하다 Setting money aside, he will make a suitable husband. // 합격할지 안 할지 모르지만 어쨌든 시험은 쳐보겠습니다 I'm going to take the examination whether I'll succeed in it or not.

*어쩌다가 by chance ; by accident ; by haphazard ; incidentally ; casually ; unexpectedly ; [이따금] once in a while ; from time to time ; now and then ¶ 어쩌다가 오는 손님 a casual visitor // 어쩌다가 있는 일 a rare occurrence ; instance〕 // 나는 어쩌다가 그 사람의 집 옆을 지났다 I happened to pass by his house. // 어쩌다가 그 소리가 내 귀에 들려왔다 It came to my ears by chance. // 어쩌다가 그는 거기 있게 되었다 He happened ; chanced〕 to be there. /It happened that he was present. // 어쩌다가 그를 길에서 만났다 I met him by accident on the street. // 그는 어쩌다가 놀러 온다 He comes and sees us once in a while. // 어쩌다가 그를 찾아갔는데 그는 집에 없었다 I could not find him at house, a rare thing as it is to make a call on him. // 손님은 어쩌다가 있을 뿐입니다 We rarely have visitors.

*어쩌면 ① [추측] possibly ; maybe ; perhaps ; likely ¶ 어쩌면 그럴는지도 모른다 It may perhaps be so. //어쩌면 그는 외출했을 것이다 He may possibly have gone out. //어쩌면 그는 안 갈 것이다 Probably he will not go. //어쩌면 그 소식은 사실일지 모른다 The report may be true, though I am not sure. //어쩌면 그 여자가 방문해 달라고 그에게 말했을지도 모른다 She might have asked him to call upon her perhaps. //어쩌면 그가 옳을지도 모른다 He is perhaps [probably] right. /He may be right. /Maybe he is right. //어쩌면 그는 안 올 게다 I am afraid he will not come. /There is no probability of his coming. //어쩌면 그는 2, 3일 중에는 돌아올 게다 The chances are [It may well be] that he will come back within a few days.
② [감탄] how ; what ¶ 어쩌면 색시가 그렇게 이쁠까 How beautiful she is ! //어쩌면 이렇게 경치가 좋을까 What a fine prospect ! //어쩌면 사람이 저럴까 How can he be like that ? //어쩌면 저렇게 뻔뻔할까 What an impudence !

어쩌자고 for what reason [purpose]

어쩐지 ① [웬일인지] for some reason or other ; somehow ; without knowing-why ; in some way ; indefinably ¶ 어쩐지 두렵다 have an unaccountable fear //어쩐지 슬프다 Somehow I feel sad. //저 사람은 어쩐지 무섭다 I have a vague fear of him. /I fear him without knowing why. //어쩐지 울고 싶은 기분이다 Somehow I feel like crying. //그 여자는 어쩐지 슬퍼졌다 A melancholy feeling stole [crept] over her. //어쩐지 중대한 일이 일어날 것만 같다 Something tells me [I have a presentiment] that a serious matter would happen.
② [그래서] so it is why ; it is no wonder that ¶ 어쩐지 기쁜 얼굴을 하고 있더라 That explains his happy look. //어쩐지 그 여자가 오전중 무척 좋아하더라 No wonder that she was the happiest girl all that long morning.

어쩔 수 없다 (be) unavoidable ; urgent ; inevitable ; necessary ; pressing ¶ 어쩔 수 없이 unavoidably ; inevitably ; reluctantly ; unwillingly //어쩔 수 없이 …하다 be obliged [compelled] to 《do》 //나이는 어쩔 수 없다 Age will tell. //안된 일이긴 하지만 어쩔 수 없는 일이지 뭐 Too bad, but it's just one of those things.

어쭙지않다 (be) ridiculous ; conceited ; contemptible ; pert ; frisky ¶ 어쭙잖은 놈 a perky [saucy] fellow //그가 우주인이 되겠다니 어쭙잖은 이야기다 He wishes to become a spaceman. What a joke !

*어찌 ① [방법] how ; in what way ; by what means ⇨ 어떻게 ¶ 어찌 해서든지 by all means ; in any way ; at any cost ; at all costs //어찌 할 수 없는 unavoidable ; inevitable //어찌 할 수 없이 unavoidably ; at the end of one's tether //어찌 할 수 없는 경우엔 at a pinch ; in case of emergency //어찌 할 수 없게 되다 be in for it ; be at a pinch ; find oneself in a fix //그는 어찌 해야 좋을지 모를 만큼 기뻤다 He could not contain himself for joy. //어찌 그와 알게 되었느냐 How did you come to know him ? //그가 어찌 되었을까 What has become of him ? //어찌 해야 좋을지 모르겠다 I am at a loss what to do. /I don't know what to do with myself. //어찌할 바를 모르다 be puzzled ; perplexed] 《what to do》 ; be quite embarrassed ; be at a loss ; do not know 《what to do》 //어찌할 바를 모르게 하다 puzzle ; perplex ; bewilder
② [왜] ¶ 어찌 해서 why ; for what reason ⇨ 어째
③ [반문] how ; why ¶ 어찌 내가 화내겠소 Why should I get angry ? //어찌 그가 불평하지 않겠소 No wonder that he makes complaints.
④ [감탄] how ; what ⇨ 어찌나

어찌나 too ; so ; very ; awfully ; quite ¶ 어찌나 슬픈지 in (the excess of) one's grief //어제는 날씨가 어찌나 좋은지 산책에 나섰다 It was so fine yesterday (that) I went out for a walk. /It was such a fine day yesterday (that) I went out for a walk. //이 책은 어찌나 어려운지 내게는 이해하기 곤란하다 This book is too difficult for me to understand. //당신이 어찌나 보고 싶었던지 몰라 I'm so glad to see you. //어찌나 더운지 잠이 오지 않았다 I couldn't sleep, it was so hot. //어찌나 우스운지 대답을 못했다 I could not answer him at all for a while, I was laughing so.

어찌씨 an adverb ⇨ 부사(副詞)

어찔하다 become giddy ; have vertigo ; be subject to an attack of vertigo ¶ 두 비행기가 어찔한 높이에서 서로 스쳐갔다 The planes flushed past each other at that dizzy height. //그 여자는 어찔하여 철길 위에 넘어졌다 She was seized with faintness and fell on to the railway track.

어차피 於此彼 anyhow ; anyway ; in any [either] case ; at any rate ; after all (결국) ¶ 어차피 인간은 죽어야 한다 Man will die after all. //어차피 그러리라고 생각했었다 I thought as much. //어차피 해보았자 소용 없다 Do what you will, it will avail nothing at all. //어차피 그것은 해야 한다 I must [am bound to] do it anyhow. //자네는 어차피 실망할 걸세 Whatever you may choose, you will be disappointed. //어차피 하려면 큰 일을 해라 If you do anything at all, do something great. //어차피 살아날 수 없다면 먹고 싶은 것이나 먹도록 해라 Let him eat what he likes, if there is no hope for his life. //어차피

나는 그 방면으로 가는 길입니다 I'm going that way anyhow. // 어차피 지불해야 한다면 지금 지불해라 If you are going to pay it at all, you had better do it now. // 어차피 할 바에는 똑똑히 해라 If you do it at all, do it well.

어채 魚菜 boiled fish sticks and vegetables

어처구니 a very big person〔thing〕; a real; regular〕 monster; a giant〔whale〕

어처구니없다 be dumbfounded; be taken aback; (be) monstrous; fabulous; absurd; egregious ¶ 어처구니없이 큰 벌 a monster of a bee // 어처구니없는 계획 a wild〔an absurd〕 project; a wild-cat scheme // 어처구니없는 값 an exorbitant〔a fancy, a fabulous〕 price // 어처구니없는 거짓말 a whopping lie // 어처구니없이 값싼 ridiculously cheap // 어처구니없는 말을 하다 say extraordinary 〔absurd〕 things; talk wild // 어처구니없어 말을 못하다 be speechless with amazement; be dumbfounded // 일동은 어처구니없어 서로 얼굴을 마주 보았다 We all gazed at each other in blank dismay. // 그는 어처구니없는 값을 요구했다 He asked an out-of-the-way price. // 그 녀석 어처구니없는 말을 지껄이고 있구나 What he says is enough to make a cat laugh. // 그 덕분에 우리는 어처구니없는 일을 당했다 He landed us in one big mess.

어촌 漁村 a fishing village〔hamlet, settlement〕; a sea village

*어치 〖새〗 a jay; Garrulus glandarius (학명)

-어치 worth; value ¶ 1000원어치의 달걀 one thousand *won*'s worth of eggs // 사과를 2,000원어치 주시오 Give me two thousand *won*'s worth of apples.

값— worth ¶ 사람의 값어치 a man's worth // 그것은 아무 값어치도 없다 It is not worth anything at all.

어치렁거리다 toddle; stagger; trudge along

어치렁어치렁 trudgingly; totteringly —하다 ⇨ 어치렁거리다

어칠거리다 ⇨ 어치렁거리다

어칠비칠 totteringly; staggeringly; unsteadily —하다 stagger ¶ 어칠비칠 걷다 walk with unsteady steps; be unsteady in one's gait // 어칠비칠 일어서다 stagger to one's feet

어탁 魚拓 a fish print

어투 語套 one's way〔habit〕 of speaking; one's manner of speech; one's way 〔manner〕 of talking ¶ 그의 어투로는 그는 무엇이든지 알고 있는 것 같다 By the way he talks, he seems to know everything about it. // 그의 힘찬 어투때문에 연설은 효과적이었다 His forceful delivery made the speech effective.

어퍼컷 〖권투〗 an uppercut ¶ 어퍼컷을 먹이다 deal〔land〕 《a person》 an uppercut; deliver an uppercut 《to the jaw》

어폐 語弊 a faulty〔misleading〕 expression; defects in expression; unfitness of expression; misuse of words ¶ 어폐가 있다 be misleading; be liable to be misunderstood; be not proper language 〔words〕 // 어폐가 있는지는 모르지만… It may not be a proper; right〕 word to express, 《but》/It may be wrong in saying, 《but》 // 그것은 어폐가 있는 말이다 It is not the proper word./The word is misleading.

어포 魚脯 dried slices of fish

어피 魚皮 fishskin

어필 an appeal —하다 appeal 《to》

어필 御筆 a king's handwriting〔autograph〕; the writing of a king

어하다 (over)indulge 《one's child》; make much of; pamper; pet; fondle ¶ 어하며 키우다 bring up 《a child》 indulgently

어학 語學 language study; philology; linguistics ¶ 어학의 linguistic // 어학의 천재 a born linguist; a genius in language // 어학의 재능 a linguistic talent // 어학을 잘하다 be a good linguist; be a clever linguist; be strong〔proficient〕 in languages // 어학을 잘 못하다 be a poor linguist // 어학에 소질이 있다 have a talent for learning languages

— 교사 a language master〔teacher〕 — 교수 language instruction — 교육 language teaching〔instruction〕; linguistic education — 레코드 a language record —력 linguistic ability〔attainments〕 —자 a linguist — 지식 linguistic knowledge — 천재 a born linguist; a genius in language〔for languages〕

어항 魚缸 a fish globe; a glass fish bowl

어항 漁港 a fishing port

어허 oh; well; indeed; I see ¶ 어허 11시다 Why! It is eleven. // 어허 그러냐 Well, is that so? // 어허 너 잘했다 Indeed, you did well. // 어허 그랬구나 I see, that's the reason. // 어허 참 잘못했군 Bless my soul!

어험 hem; ahem; hum

어혈 瘀血 〖한의학〗 extravasated blood

어협 漁協 ⇨ 어업(— 협동조합)

어형 語形 〖언어〗 the form〔shape〕 of a word; a (language) form

— 변화 conjugation; inflection

어형 魚形 ¶ 어형의 ichthyoid; fishlike

— 수뢰 a torpedo; a tinfish 《속》

어화 漁火 a fishing fire; a fisherman's fire (to lure fishes)

어회 魚膾 slices of raw fish; sliced 〔minced〕 raw fish; sashimi ¶ 다랑어의 어회 slices of raw tuna; sliced tuna // 어회를 만들다 slice raw fish; prepare sliced raw fish

어획 漁獲 a catch of fish; a fish catch; fishery ¶ 어획이 많다 get a good catch

// 이 근해에서는 고등어의 어획이 많다 Large quantities of mackerel are caught off this coast.
—고 the (amount of) catch ; the haul —기 fishing season —물 fish ; catch —장 a fishery ; a fishing place〔bank, shoal〕 ¶ 굴 어획장 oyster fisheries — 할당 《salmon》 fishing〔catch〕 quota

⁑**어휘 語彙** a vocabulary ; a glossary ; one's stock of words ¶ 풍부한 어휘 an abundant ; extensive〕 vocabulary ; a copious vocabulary // 충분한 어휘 a sufficient vocabulary // 빈약한 어휘 a meager〔small〕 vocabulary // 어휘가 풍부〔빈약〕하다 be rich〔poor〕 in vocabulary // 어휘를 풍부하게 하다 enrich〔increase, enlarge, widen〕 one's vocabulary // 이 사전은 어휘가 풍부〔빈약〕하다 This dictionary contains a rich〔meager〕 vocabulary. // 그는 영어의 어휘가 풍부하다 He has an extensive vocabulary of English. / His English vocabulary shows a wide range. // 나의 한정된 어휘로는 내 생각을 충분히 말할 수 없었다 I could not express myself fully with my limited vocabulary. // 셰익스피어의 어휘는 18,000어였다 Shakespeare's vocabulary was 18,000 words.
—집 a word-book ; a vocabulary — 통계 lexical〔vocabulary〕 statistics

억 億 a〔one〕 hundred million ¶ 10억 a milliard 《영》 ; a billion 《미》

억겁 億劫 〖불교〗 eternity ; perpetuity

†**억누르다** hold〔force〕 《a person》 down ; pin down ; press down with force ; suppress ; oppress ; restrain ; control ; check ; keep under ¶ 억누를 수 있는 controllable // 억누를 수 없는 uncontrollable ; irrepressible // 억눌리다 be overpowered ; get forced down // 격정을 억누르다 hold one's passion in check ; contain oneself // 노여움을 억누르다 contain one's anger ; hold in one's temper ; repress〔keep down〕 one's anger // 눈물을 억누르다 repress〔keep back, force back〕 one's tears // 웃음을 억누르다 stifle a laugh ; repress a smile // 그는 웃음을 억누를 수 없었다 He did badly at trying to suppress a smile. // 그는 나의 이의를 모두 억눌러버렸다 He overbore all my objections. // 억눌려 있던 그의 분노가 폭발했다 His smothered anger suddenly broke out. // 그는 일평생 형제 자매에게 억눌려 왔다 He has been sat upon by his brothers and sisters all his life. // 그는 부인한테 완전히 억눌려 있다 He is quite under the thumb of his wife.

억눌리다 get forced down ; be overpowered ; repressed〕 ; get pressed down

억단 臆斷 a conjecture ; a surmise ; a guess (work) ; a hasty conclusion —하다 conjecture ; guess ; jump〔leap〕 to a conclusion ¶ 실정을 살펴보지도 않고 억단하다 pass judgment without careful inquiry into the circumstances

억대 億臺 the mark〔level〕 of a〔one〕 hundred million ¶ 억대에 달하다 touch 〔rise to〕 the level of a hundred million (*won*) ; touch〔hit〕 the one hundred million mark ; level〕

억류 抑留 detention ; detainment ; internment —하다 detain ; keep by force ; seize ¶ 억류 중의 under detention
—국 a detaining country —선 an interned ship —소 a detention〔an internment〕 camp (피)—자 a detainee ; an internee

억만 億萬 [억] a hundred million ; [무수] myriads ; countless numbers ¶ 억만의 countless ; numberless
— 년 countless years —장자 a billionaire ; a multimillionaire

억매 抑買 ⇨ 강매(強買) ¶ 억매 흥정으로 사다 be forced to buy 《a thing》

억매 抑賣 ⇨ 강매(強賣)
— 흥정 a forced trade〔transaction〕

억병 億甁 a large drinking capacity ¶ 억병으로 마시다 drink like a fish ; drink hard〔deep〕 ; guzzle // 그는 억병이다 He has an enormous capacity for liquor.

억보 an obstinate person ; a headstrong person ; a bullhead ; a bigot ; a stubborn person

억새 〖식물〗 purple eulalia ; a kind of reed

억설 臆說 [억측] a notion without foundation ; a conjecture ; a surmise ; speculation ; [가정] an assumption ; a supposition ; a hypothesis (가설) ; [학리적 가설] a theory —하다 make a conjecture ; surmise ; speculate 《about》 ; presume ¶ 그것은 억설에 지나지 않는다 That is a mere conjecture. // 언어의 기원에 관한 억설은 여러 가지 있다 Several theories have been postulated in regard to the origin of speech. // 내각 갱질에 대한 여러 가지 억설이 나돌고 있다 Speculation is rife as to the resignation of the cabinet.

*****억세다** ① [세차다] (be) strong ; tough ; firm ; tenacious ; resolute ¶ 억센 기질 a violent temper // 억센 경상도 사투리 broad *Kyŏngsang-do* dialect // 억세게 stubbornly ; doggedly ; stiffly ; stoutly ; unbendingly // 흔히들 해방 후에 억세진 것은 여자와 양말이라고 한다 It is often said that in Korea it is "women and stockings" that have grown much stronger since the liberation. // 그는 나의 약점을 이용하여 억세게 나오고 있다 Taking advantage of my weakness, he shows a bold front with me.
② [뻣뻣하다] (be) stiff ; tough ; rigid ¶ 억센 수염 a tough beard // 억센 머리털 wiry hair // 이 배추는 억세다 This is a tough cabbage. // 쇠고기가 억세다 This beef is tough.

‡**억수** a pouring〔heavy, torrential, drenching, downpour of〕 rain ; down pour ; cloudburst 《미》 ¶ 비가 억수같이 내린다 It rains cats and dogs. /The rain is pouring down (in torrents). /It rains a solid sheet. // 비가 올 때는 의례히 억수로 퍼붓는다 It never rains but it pours.

억수장마 a long spell of heavy rain ¶ 억수장마 들다 a steady heavy rain sets in

‡**억압 抑壓** restraint ; suppression ; check ; pressure ; repression **—하다** suppress ; check ; restrain ; oppress ; hold 《a person》 down ¶ 개성을 억압하는 경향이 있는 교육 education that tends to repress individuality // 억압당하다 be suppressed〔oppressed, repressed〕 // 언론의 자유를 억압하다 repress freedom of speech ; lay an embargo on〔upon〕 free speech

*__억양 抑揚__ [음조의] intonation ; modulation ; pitch ; accent ; inflection (of the voice) ¶ 억양 있는 modulated ; intoned // 억양 없는 목소리 a monotonous voice ; a singsong voice // 억양을 붙이다 modulate ; intonate ; intone

—격(格) [영시] an iamb ; an iambic ; an iambus 《*pl.* ~es, -bi》 ¶ 억양격의 iambic **— 음부** 〖음악〗 a circumflex

억울 抑鬱 ① [답답함] suffering distress ; being in distress ; depression ; mortification **—하다** (be) regrettable ; depressing ; be vexed 《at》 ; be mortified 《by》

② [원통·누명] being mistreated ; suffering undue treatment ; being falsely charged ; being unjustly suspected of a guilt **—하다** suffer unfairness ; feel victimized ¶ 억울하게 under a false accusation ; on a false charge // 억울한 책망을 듣다 get an undeserved scolding // 억울한 죄를 입다 be falsely charged 《with》 ; be falsely〔wrongly〕 accused 《of》 // 억울해서 눈물을 흘리다 shed tears in one's mortification〔chagrin〕 // 억울해 죽겠다 I am mortified at being mistreated. // 억울한 사정이 있어 왔습니다 I came to see you to talk about my grievance. // 그건 억울합니다 You do me wrong〔an injustice〕. /I am innocent of the charge.

—병증 melancholia **—증** depression

†**억제 抑制** suppression ; repression ; control ; restraint ; holdback ; constraint **—하다** repress ; suppress ; control ; restrain ; put a curb 《on》 ; hold in check ; keep within bounds ; [절제] moderate ¶ 억제할 수 없는 uncontrollable ; unmanageable // 감정을 억제하다 suppress〔smother〕 one's feelings ; keep one's feelings under control // 인플레를 억제하다 hold back inflation // 경찰은 그들 힘으로는 폭도를 억제할 수 없다는 것을 알았다 The police found the mob uncontrollable〔beyond the control〕.

—력 restraint ; control **— 작용** inhibitory ; inhibitive〕 action **— 재배** late raising 《of plants》 (현상) **—제〔액〕** 〖사진〗 a restrainer

억조 億兆 a hundred million and a billion〔a trillion 《미》〕 ; [다수] myriads

— 창생 the people ; myriads of people ; the masses ; the million(s) ; the multitude ; the common people

억지 unreasonableness ; stubbornness ; obstinacy ¶ 억지가 아닌 reasonable ; fair ; natural // 억지로 일 시키다 force 《a person》 to work // 억지로 결혼시키다 make 《a person》 marry against his〔her〕 will ; force 《a person》 into marriage // 억지 부리지 마라 Be reasonable. /Don't be obstinate, you know. // 그는 그것을 하겠다고 억지 썼다 He doggedly persisted in doing it. // 알지도 못하면서 억지 쓰지 마라 Don't be so positive when you are not sure〔certain〕.

— 웃음 a forced〔feigned, strained, set〕 smile **— 핑계** a lame〔forced〕 excuse **— 해석** forced interpretation

억지 부리다 관용 insist on having one's own way ; persist stubbornly ; insist doggedly ; uphold

억지 세다 관용 be stubborn〔obstinate, headstrong, self-opinionated〕

억지 抑止 ⇨ 억제(抑制)

—력 a deterrent 《to an all-out war》 **핵—력** a nuclear deterrent

*__억지로__ by force ; forcibly ; compulsorily ; by violence ; against 《a person's》 will ; whether willing or not ; willy-nilly ; in a high-handed way ¶ 억지로 …하게 하다 force 《a person》 to 《do》 ; compel // 억지로 웃다 force a smile // 억지로 들어가다 enter a room by force // 억지로 복종시키다 enforce obedience on 《a person》 // 그는 졸렸지만 억지로 눈을 뜨고 있었다 Though he was sleepy, he willed〔forced〕 himself to stay awake. // 부모는 딸을 억지로 그 남자한테 시집 보냈다 The parents forced their daughter into marrying the man. // 병자에게 억지로 음식을 먹여서는 안된다 Food should not be forced on the patient. // 3, 4백명의 군중이 몰려들어 억지로 입장하려고 했다 Between 300 and 400 persons crowded about, trying to force an entrance. // 그는 내가 싫다고 해도 억지로 술을 마시게 했다 He made me drink against my will.

억지손 a strong measure ; high-handedness ¶ 억지손 쓰다 take a strong〔drastic〕 measure ; be high-handed 《with a person》

억지스럽다 (be) high-handed ; obstinate ; wilful ; demanding ; stubborn ; insistent

억지 춘향이 doing against one's will ; compelling ; compulsion ; coercion ; forcing ¶ 억지 춘향이로 by force ;

against one's will ; under compulsion ; under forced pressure // 그건 억지 춘향이다 That's a forced thing.

억척 being unyielding ; toughness ; stiffness ; stubbornness ¶ 억척 같은 여자 a tough woman // 억척스럽다 be unyielding ; be stout-hearted ; be stubborn ; be unrelenting ; be dogged // 저렇게 억척스러운 사람은 처음이다 His obstinacy really beats me.

—꾸러기 a dogged〔an obstinate〕 person ; a tough〔hard-headed〕 person **—배기** a tough〔stubborn〕 child

억척 부리다 관용 show toughness 〔stubbornness〕 ; be dogged

*** 억측 臆測** a guess ; a conjecture ; speculation ; a surmise ; a supposition **—하다** guess ; suppose ; conjecture ; surmise ; speculate 《upon》 ¶ 당찮은 억측 a wrong guess // 억측할 수 없는 beyond all conjectures ; inscrutable // 억측에 지나지 않다 be a mere conjecture〔guess work〕 // 너의 억측이 들어맞았구나 Your guess was right.

억판 extremely strained circumstances ; dire poverty ; a bare living ¶ 사는 것이 억판이다 live in dire poverty

억패듯 harshly ; ruthlessly ; relentlessly ; violently ; without mercy ¶ 사람을 억패듯 부리다 drive 《a person》 hard

억하심정 抑何心情 It is hard to understand why... ; I don't know why... ; How comes〔is〕 it that... ? ¶ 억하심정으로 …하느냐 Why〔How〕 in the world... ? // 억하심정으로 그런 짓을 했을까 What made him do such a thing, I wonder ?

언감생심 焉敢生心 How dare you... ? ¶ 언감생심 여기 돌아왔느냐 How dare you come here again ? // 언감생심 내 앞에서 그런 말을 하느냐 How dare you say such a thing in spite of my presence ?

언감히 焉敢— how dare ; daringly ; impudently ; audaciously ; boldly ¶ 언감히 그런 말을 내게 하느냐 How dare you say such a thing to me ?

언거번거하다 (be) talkative ; garrulous ; long-winded ; long-tongued ¶ 너무 언거번거하지 마라 Don't talk too much.

언걸 undeserved affliction〔loss, blame〕 incurred on another's account

언걸 입다 관용 suffer undeservedly in place of another ; be the (scape) goat

언구럭 a slick manner (in wheedling) ¶ 언구럭 부려 빼앗다 wheedle 《a person》 out of 《a thing》

언구럭 부리다 관용 act slick ; wheedle

† 언급 言及 reference ; allusion ; comment **—하다** refer〔allude〕 to 《a matter》 ; touch on ; make mention of ; make reference 《to》 ¶ 이미 언급한 above-mentioned ; as stated above // 역사는 그 문제에 대하여 언급 않고 있다 History is silent on the subject. // 기록은 그 사건에 언급이 없다 The records contain no mention of the incident. // 그 일에 관해서 언급을 회피하였다 He evaded making his comment on it.

언니 an elder〔older〕 brother of a boy ; an elder〔older〕 sister of a girl ¶ 큰〔가운데, 작은〕 언니 a boy's oldest〔next oldest, third oldest〕 big brother

언더라인 an underline ; an underscore **—하다** underline 《a word》 ; underscore ¶ 그 말은 언더라인쳐졌다 The words were underlined.

언더셔츠 an undershirt ; underwear

언더웨어 underwear

† 언덕 a hill ; a hillock ; a height ; a rising ground ; a slope ¶ 가파른 언덕 a steep ascent〔slope〕 // 언덕 위〔아래〕에 at the head ; foot〕 of a slope // 언덕진 hilly ; sloping // 언덕을 올라〔내려〕가다 go up 〔down〕 a hill

—길 a slope ; a sloping road **—밑** 《at》 the foot of a slope **—밥** rice cooked part soft hard by sloping the raw rice in the pot **—배기** the top of a hill ; a hilltop **—위** 《at》 the head of a slope

언도 言渡 a sentence ; a judgment ; a verdict ; a pronouncement **—하다** sentence ; condemn ; pass a sentence upon 〔on〕 ; pronounce ¶ 판결을 언도하다 give〔render, deliver, pronounce〕 judgment 《upon》 ; pass ; pronounce, give〕 sentence 《upon》 // 사형을 언도하다 sentence〔condemn〕 《a person》 to death // 사형을 언도받다 be sentenced to death // 무죄를 언도하다 acquit 《a person》 of the charge // 무죄를 언도받다 be acquitted

—서 a written sentence **무죄 —** a pronouncement of "not guilty" **사형 —** a sentence of death

언동 言動 one's speech and behavior ; words and actions ¶ 언동을 삼가다 be careful〔discreet〕 in one's speech and conduct ; action〕

언뜻 in an instant ; in a flash ; suddenly ; [우연히] by chance ; by accident ¶ 언뜻 보면 at first sight〔glance〕 // 언뜻 보다 glance〔blink〕 at 《a thing》 ; take a quick look at 《a thing》 // 언뜻 듣다 overhear ; hear by chance // 언뜻 보이다 get〔catch〕 a glimpse of // 언뜻 눈에 띄다 catch sight of // 언뜻 머리에 떠오르다 flash across one's mind ; occur to 《a person》 // 그는 언뜻하면 그 소리를 한다 He is in the habit of saying 《that》. // 그의 이름이 언뜻 생각나지 않는다 His name does not occur to me right offhand. // 그 말이 언뜻 내 귀에 들려 왔다 It came to my ears by chance. // 나는 그 회사에 공석이 있다는 것을 언뜻 들었다 I happened to hear there was a vacancy〔an opening〕 in that firm. // 울타리 사이로 그의 뒷모습이 언뜻 보였다 The opening in the fence gave a glimpse of his back view.

*언론 言論 speech ; discussion ¶ 언론의 자유 freedom of speech ; liberty of speech ; [신문·잡지의] the freedom of the press // 언론의 억압 pressure on discussion〔public opinion〕 // 언론의 자유를 침해하다 infringe on the freedom of the press

—계 the press — 기관 an organ of expression〔public opinion〕 — 압박〔탄압〕 pressure on discussion〔public opinion〕; a gag upon freedom of speech〔the press〕 — 자유 the freedom of the press ; freedom of speech ; the right of free discussion —전 wordy warfare ; a verbal battle ; a war of words ; discussion 한국 — 연구원 the Korean Journalism Research Institute

언리학 言理學 glossematics

언막이 an irrigation dam〔barrage〕

언명 言明 declaration ; announcement ; statement ; assertion —하다 declare ; state ; announce ; make a statement ; proclaim ; assert ; make an assertion ¶ 정부가 앞서 언명한 바와 같이 as was recently declared by the Government // 대통령이 언명한 바에 의하면 according to the President's declaration // 언명을 피하다 be wary of explicit statements // 사직을 언명하다 make definite statement of one's intended resignation ; pledge oneself to resign // 그것은 언명할 수 없다 I can't make any statement about it.

언문 諺文 the Korean script ; the Korean letters ⇨ 한글

언문 言文 the written and spoken language ; the colloquial and the literary

— 일치 the identity〔unification〕 of the written and spoken language ; unity of speech and writing ¶ 언문 일치체로 쓰다 write in colloquial style

언밸런스 unbalance

언변 言辯 eloquence ; oratorical talent ; oratorical power ; speaking ; the gift of the gab 《속》 ¶ 언변이 있는 having the gift of the gab ; eloquent ; fluent // 언변이 있는 사람 an eloquent speaker ; a gifted speaker // 언변이 좋다 be eloquent〔fluent〕; have a fluent〔ready, glib〕 tongue // 언변이 없다 be slow of speech ; be awkward in speaking ; be a poor speaker

언비천리 言飛千里 A word〔rumor〕 flies〔spreads, travels〕 far and fast.

언사 言辭 words ; speech ; language ; expression (표현) ¶ 외교적 언사 diplomatic language // 언사를 조심하다 be careful〔discreet〕 in speech // 불손한 언사를 쓰다 use improper language ; be careless in speech ; talk insolently

언색호 堰塞湖 a damned lake

언설 言說 a remark ; an opinion ; a statement

언성 言聲 a voice ; a tone (of voice) ¶ 화난 언성 an angry voice // 맑은 언성 a clear〔silvery, ringing〕 voice // 굵은 언성 a deep〔full〕 voice // 가냘픈 언성 a faint voice // 언성을 높여 loudly ; aloud ; in a rough〔hard〕 voice ; in a harsh tone // 언성을 높이다 raise〔lift〕 one's voice ; raise one's pitch // 언성이 점점 높아졌다 They were coming〔getting〕 to high words. // 사소한 일에 언성을 높일 필요 없다 You need not shout at such a trifle. /You ought to be more quiet about so small a matter. // 그는 언성을 낮추어서 속삭였다 He sank his voice to a whisper. // 그는 감정이 치밀어 언성이 높아졌다 His voice was getting thick with emotion.

언약 言約 a verbal promise ; one's word ; an oral agreement ; a pledge ; a vow —하다 (make a verbal) promise ; give one's word ; pledge 《oneself》; agree to ¶ 굳게 언약한 두 애인 plighted lovers // 부부의 언약을 맺다 plight one's troth ; plight oneself to 《a person》; be pledged to 《a person》 // 굳게 언약하다 make a solemn promise ; give one's word of honor // 그의 언약은 어김이 없다 His word is as good as his bond. /He is a man of his word.

†언어 言語 language ; speech ; words ¶ 언어로 in words〔speech〕 // 언어가 통하다 a language is understood // 언어로 표현할 수 없다 be beyond words〔description〕; be indescribable ; baffle〔beggar〕 description // 언어 거동에 주의하다 be careful in speech〔words〕 and behavior〔actions〕; mind one's p's and q's // 그는 언어가 명석하다 His words are articulate. /He speaks very clearly. // 그의 언어 거동은 꼭 상스러운 사람 같다 He speaks and behaves just like a churl. // 그 풍경의 아름다움은 언어로 표현키 어렵다 The beauty of the scenery beggars description. /The scenery is beautiful beyond description.

— 교정 speech clinic ; logopedics — 능력 (the faculty of) speech —도(島) 〖언어〗 a speech island — 불통 difficulty of communication ; difficulty in making oneself understood ; language difficulty — 상통 facility of communication — 실조 aphasia ; speech impediment — 실조자 an aphasic ; a person who has difficulty in speaking — 심리학 linguistic psychology — 심상(心象) verbal image — 장애 〖의학〗 aphasia ; speech impediment ; disorders of speech ¶ 그는 언어 장애 때문에 변호사 되기를 단념했다 He gave up becoming a lawyer on account of speech defect. — 중추 the speech center ; the speech-control centers of the brain — 지도 a linguistic atlas — 지리학 dialect 〔linguistic〕 geography — 철학 philosophy of language —학 philology ; linguistics ; the science of language

—학과 the linguistic〔philological〕 department —학자 a philologist ; a linguist —학회 a linguistic〔philological〕 society —형태학 morphology ; accidence —활동 speech function

언어 감각 言語感覺 a linguistic sense

언어도단 言語道斷 ¶ 언어도단의[말할 수 없는] undescribable ; beyond expression ; description〕; [당찮은] outrageous ; abominable ; [어리석은] absurd ; ridiculous ; preposterous // 언어도단의 행위 a scandalous conduct // 언어도단의 처치 an outrageous measure // 언어도단이다 be beyond expression ; be unspeakable〔outrageous, absurd〕 // 불결하기가 언어도단이다 be unspeakably 〔indescribably〕 filthy // 그의 행동은 언어도단이다 His conduct cannot be too severely criticized. // 그런 요구를 하다니 언어도단이다 It is unreasonable of him to demand such a thing. // 자기 아이를 버리다니 언어도단이다 It is outrageous to desert one's own child. // 그들의 죄악은 언어도단이다 Their crime is beyond all power of language. // 빈민굴의 참상은 언어도단이다 The condition in the slum areas 〔quarters〕 are perfectly scandalous.

언어 행동 言語行動 ⇨ 언동(言動)

언언사사 言言事事 all words and things ¶ 언언사사에 간섭하다 meddle in everything

언외 言外 ¶ 언외의 unexpressed ; implied ; unspoken // 언외의 의미 implications // 언외의 의미를 읽다 read between the lines // 언외에 암시하다 hint at ; allude to

언월 偃月 a crescent (moon) ; the sickle ; horned〕 moon
—도(刀) a scimitar ; a falchion

언재 言才 oratorical talent〔skill〕; eloquence ; gift of gab 《속》

***언쟁 言爭** a quarrel ; a dispute ; an argument ; a wrangle ; an altercation ; bickering ; a brawl —하다 quarrel ; dispute ; have words 《with a person》 ¶ 둘은 심한 언쟁을 했다 High words exchanged between them. // 언쟁이 싸움으로 번졌다 They proceeded from words to blows. /The quarrel came to hard blows.

언저리 the edge ; the brim ; the rim ; bounds ; limits ¶ 강의 언저리 the brink of a river // 도시의 언저리 the edge of a city ; the city limits

†언제 ① [의문] when ; (at) what time ; how soon ; what date〔day〕; whenever ¶ 언제 출발합니까 When are you going to start? // 언제쯤 졸업합니까 When will you be graduated? // 너는 언제 시계를 잃어버렸느냐 When did you lose your watch? // 그가 언제 올지 모르겠다 I don't know when he will come. // 그이는 언제 오리라고 생각합니까 When do you think he will come? // 그를 만난 것이 언제였는지 잊어버렸다 I don't remember〔have forgotten〕 when I saw him. // 언제 전화하면 좋을지 말해 주십시오 Tell me when I should phone. // 아침마다 언제쯤 일어납니까 What time do you wake up every morning? // 그는 언제인지 모르게 없어져 버렸다 He disappeared nobody knew when. // 언제 준비가 끝납니까 How soon can you be ready?
② [미래] someday ; some time ; sometime ; some other day〔time〕 (언제 한번) ; in the near future ; out of these days (언제 한번 가까운 장래에) ; sooner or later ; sometime or other (조만간) ¶ 언제 한번 전화하겠습니다 I'll call you one day soon. // 언제 한번 와 주십시오 I hope you will come sometime soon. // 그것에 대해 언제 한번 상의해보자 We'll talk about it some other time. // 언제 한번 만납시다 I should like to see more of you some time. // 여름 방학중에 언제 한번 제주도에 갈는지 모르겠다 I may go to *Cheju-do* some time during the summer vacation. // 언제 한번 뉴욕을 방문하시거든 내 딸을 만나 주십시오 If you visit New York, please visit my daughter there.
③ [과거] once ; the other day ¶ 언제 한번 그를 만난 기억이 난다 I remember seeing him once. // 언제 한번 만난 사람이 누구냐 Who is the man I met the other day?

언제고 some day ; some time (or other) ; in time ¶ 내주 중 언제고 sometime next week // 언제고 형편 좋은 때에 at some convenient time // 언제고 그 일이 생각날 것이다 Some day you will remember it.

언제까지 ① how long ; till when ¶ 언제까지 이 전쟁이 계속될 것인지 How long will this war last? /When will this war end? // 언제까지 문을 엽니까 How late are you open? // 이 예약을 취소하려면 언제까지 통고해야 합니까 Until when do I have to cancel this reservation? ② by what time ; how soon ¶ 언제까지 이 일을 끝내지 않으면 안됩니까 By what time 〔How soon〕 must I finish this task? ③ as long as one likes ; forever 《미》; for ever 《영》 ¶ 언제까지나 좋으실 대로 계십시오 You may stay as long as you like. // 이 행복이 언제까지나 계속되기를 빕니다 I wish this blessing would last forever 〔for ever〕.

†언제나 always (항상) ; usually (평소에) ; habitually (습관적으로) ; whenever... ; every time (…할 때마다) ¶ 언제나 거짓말을 하는 사람 a habitual liar // 아버지는 언제나 후하다 My father is always generous. // 그는 언제나 담배를 피우고 있다 He is smoking all the time. // 둘은 만나면 언제나 싸웠다 The two were always quarreling. /Whenever〔Everytime〕 the two met, they quarreled. /The two never met without quarreling. //그는 언제나 부모에게 걱정만 끼친다 He is a constant source of anxiety to his parents. //그는 언제나 아침 산책을 한다 He is in the habit of going for a walk in the morning. //그는 언제나 지각한다 It is usual with him to be late. /He is a habitual late-comer. //일요일에는 언제나 무엇으로 소일하십니까 What do you usually do on Sundays?

†**언제든지** (at) any time ; whenever ; [항상] always ; all the time ; at all times ¶ 언제든지 좋으실 때 오시오 Come (at) any time〔whenever〕 you like 〔please〕. //언제든지 좋다 Any time will do. //그는 일요일에는 언제든지 집에 있다 He is always at home on Sunday. //언제든지 돕겠습니다 I'm ready to help you. //언제든지 출발할 수 있게 되어 있다 We are ready to start at a moment's notice. //언제든지 이런 좋은 일이 있다고 생각하면 안된다 Such good things cannot be expected to occur everyday.

언제부터 from what time ; since when ; how long ¶ 언제부터 몸이 아팠습니까 How long have you been sick?

언제 어느때 (at) any moment〔time〕 ; every moment ¶ 그는 언제 어느때 올지 모른다 He may come〔turn up〕 at any moment.

언제쯤 about what time ; when ; how soon ¶ 그가 언제쯤 올지 모르겠다 I wonder when he will come.

*__언젠가__ [미래의] some time ; some day ; one day ; one of these days ; [과거의] once ; at one time ; before ; the other day ¶ 언젠가는 some time or other //언젠가 또 찾아 뵙겠습니다 I shall see you some time again. //언젠가 너에게 말한 책이 이것이다 This is the book I spoke of to you some time ago. //언젠가 후회할 때가 올 걸 The time will come when you will repent it.

언죽번죽 audaciously ; shamelessly ; brazenly ; cheekily ; impudently ; unblushingly

언중유골 言中有骨 the implied meaning ; veiled intention〕 in a remark ¶ 언중유골이다 More is meant than said. /He speaks up with implicit bitterness.

언중유언 言中有言 implications in 〔behind〕 a direct statement ¶ 언중유언이다 The word implies some other meaning. /What he says is very suggestive.

언질 言質 a pledge ; a promise ; a commitment ¶ 언질을 잡히지 않게 말하다 make a noncommittal statement //그는 언질을 주지 않았다 He did not commit himself. /He was noncommittal. //결코 도망가지 않겠다는 언질을 주었다 He gave his parole not to try to escape. //언질을 주었으니 이제는 돌이킬 수 없다 I have committed myself and cannot draw back now.

언질을 잡다 관용 take 《a person's》 pledge

언질을 주다 관용 give a pledge ; give 〔pledge〕 one's word ; make a promise ; commit〔pledge〕 oneself 《to》 ; go on record 《미》

언짢다 (be) bad ; feel bad ¶ 언짢은 꿈 a bad dream //언짢은 날씨 a foul weather //언짢은 소식 bad news //속이 언짢다 be sick to one's stomach ; one's stomach feel uneasy //사람의 마음을 언짢게 하다 make 《a person》 unhappy //언짢게 말하다 speak ill of 《a person》 //내 말을 언짢게 여기지 마라 Don't feel bad about what I said. /Don't take what I said too hard.

언책 言責 [책임] responsibility for one's words ; [책망] a verbal reprimand ¶ 언책을 지다 be responsible〔bear the responsibility〕 for a statement //언책을 지우다 hold 《a person》 responsible for his words //언책을 어기다 break one's promise〔word〕

언청이 (a person with) a harelip ; (a person with) a cleft palate ; a hare-lip ¶ 언청이의 hare-lipped

쌍언청이가 외언청이 타령한다 속담 The kettle calls the pot black-brows.

언치 ① [마소의] a pad ② 《새》 a jay

언탁 言託 verbal request〔trust, commission〕 **—하다** request〔ask〕 verbally ; entrust verbally

언턱 a raised part ; a ridge ¶ 언턱지다 be bumpy ; be uneven

문— a doorsill ; a threshold

언턱거리 the cause (of a dispute, of a quarrel) ; pretense ; excuse ; pretext ; grounds ¶ 싸움의 언턱거리를 만들다 sow the seeds of strife ; give 《a person》 an excuse (to accuse) //아무 언턱거리없이 나는 해고를 당했다 I was fired without good cause.

언필칭 言必稱 every time one opens one's mouth (it is invariably to say...) ; always ; habitually ; invariably ; ever ¶ 그는 언필칭 자식 자랑이다 He never opens his mouth without boasting of his son. //그는 언필칭 옛날 자랑이다 He is always harping on the glories of his former days. //그는 언필칭 "틀림 없어" 라고 한다 He has a way〔habit〕 of saying, "There is no doubt about it."

언하 言下 ¶ 언하에 promptly ; readily ; directly ; at a word //언하에 물리치다 reject 《a proposal》 flatly

언해 諺解 Korean annotation〔translation〕 of Chinese classics **—하다** annotate 〔translate〕 《a Chinese classic》 in Korean

*__언행 言行__ words〔speech〕 and behavior ; actions, deeds〕 ; sayings and doings ¶ 언행 공히 in word and deed //언행을 삼가다 be careful in one's speech and behav-

ior〔words and deeds〕// 언행이 일치하다 act up to what one says ; be as good as one's words // 그는 언행이 일치하지 않다 He says one thing and does another. /What he says does not correspond with what he does. /He is a hypocrite. // 언행이란 흔히 상반하기 마련이다 Saying is one thing and doing another. /Saying and doing are liable to disagree.
—록 a chronicle of one's sayings and doings〔actions〕; memoirs — 불일치 discordance between one's words and actions — 일치 consistency of speech and action ; acting up to one's words — 일치자 a man of his word ; a man who acts up to what he says

*얹다 put on ; place〔lay, set〕《a thing》 on ; load (짐을) ¶ 어깨에 손을 얹다 put one's hand on 《a person's》 shoulder // 수레에 짐을 얹다 load a cart // 라디오 위에 책을 얹다 put a book on the top of the radio // 지붕에 기와를 얹다 tile a roof // 머리를 얹다 marry〔get married to〕《a man》; marry into 《a family》 // 그녀는 그것을 손바닥 위에 얹어서 그에게 내보였다 She held it out to him upon her open palm.

얹어주다 give an extra ; throw 《a thing》 in (for good measure) ¶ 돈을 조금 얹어주다 pay a little extra 《to a person》

얹은활 a stringed bow

얹히다 ① [놓이다] be placed ; be put ; be set ; be laid ¶ 그릇이 선반에 얹혀있다 The dishes are put on the shelf.
② [음식이] sit〔lie〕 heavy (on the stomach) ; get〔be〕 poisoned by food ¶ 음식이 얹히다 food lies heavy on the stomach // 생선을 먹고 얹힌 것 같다 I'm afraid the fish disagreed with me.
③ [붙어살다] be a dependant on 《a person》; depend upon 《a person》 for support ; live〔hang, sponge〕 on 《one's relations》 ¶ 딸에게 얹혀 살다 live off one's daughter // 그의 삼촌은 그에게 얹혀 살고자 했다 His uncle wanted to come and live off him.
④ [좌초하다] run aground ; be stranded ; be driven on a rock ¶ 암초에 얹히다 run on a sunken rock ; be driven on to the rock // 배가 목포 해안에서 얹혔다 The ship ran aground on the coast of *Mokpo*.

†얻다 ① [획득] get (일반적으로) ; [능력·노력 따위로] acquire ; obtain ; procure (훌륭한 교육 따위를) ; [자리나 집 따위를] secure ; [서적 따위] derive 《from》 ; [일해서] earn ; [승리·이익·신용 따위를] win ; gain ; [부귀·권력·명성 따위를] acquire ; gain ; [지식을] gain ; acquire ; [받다] receive ; be given ; draw 《a salary》 ¶ 얻을 수 있다 be obtainable ; can be got ; be within one's reach // 얻을 수 없다 be unobtainable ; be beyond one's reach // 지위를 얻다 obtain〔secure〕 a position // 명예를 얻다 gain〔win〕 a reputation // 신용을 얻다 win another's confidence // 직업을 얻다 find an employment ; get a position〔job〕 // 대량으로 얻을 수 있다 be available in large quantities // 얻는 것이 많다 much benefit ; learn a great deal 《from this book》 // 그렇게 함으로써 얻는 것이라곤 없다 gain nothing by doing so // 과반수의 투표를 얻다 gain a majority vote // 이 책에서 얻는 것이 많다 learn a great deal from this book // 나는 그의 승낙을 얻었다 I have obtained his consent. // 나는 자네에게 휴가를 얻도록 권한다 I recommend you to take a holiday. // 그의 말에서 아무 것도 얻은 것이 없다 I could gather nothing from his statements. // 자네는 마치 얻지 못할 것을 탐내는 어린애 같다 You are just like a child crying for the moon. // 그렇게 말을 하면 성과를 얻지 못할 결세 You will get nowhere if you speak like that. // 그렇게 해도 얻는 것은 하나도 없다 There is nothing to be gained by doing so. // 담배 한 개비 얻을 수 있습니다 Can I bum a cigarette ?
② [결혼] marry〔take〕《a woman》 in marriage ¶ 아내를 얻다 take a wife // 사내를 얻다 take up〔carry on〕 with a man (바람을 피우다) // 첩을 얻다 keep a mistress〔concubine〕

얻어내다 drive in 《the tying run》; bang out 《a hit》

얻어듣다 learn by hearsay ; pick up 《information》 by hearsay ; get wind of ; [사물이 주어] come to one's ears ¶ 얻어들은 지식 knowledge acquired along the way (without any special effort) ; picked-up knowledge // 얻어들은 지식이 많다 have a smattering knowledge of many things // 친구로부터 얻어듣다 get 《it》 out of a friend // 비밀을 얼핏 얻어듣다 have an inkling of the secret // 상대방에 대해서 뭐 얻어들은 바가 있나요 Have you heard anything about the other party ?

얻어맞다 get〔receive〕 a blow ; get licked ; be struck ; be〔get〕 thrashed ¶ 뺨을 얻어맞다 get slapped // 머리를 얻어맞다 be struck on the head // 호되게 얻어맞다 be struck hard ; receive a hard blow ; get a sound thrashing // 머리를 호되게 얻어맞았다 I received hard blow on the head. /I got a good lick over the head. // 얼굴을 호되게 얻어맞았다 He was beaten badly in the face. // 그런 짓을 하면 얻어맞는다 If you do such a thing, you will get licked. // 또 얻어맞고 싶으냐 Are you begging for another punch〔thrash〕? /Do you want another thrashing ? // 그는 턱을 한대 얻어맞고 넘어졌다 He was knocked down by a blow on the chin.

얻어먹다 ① go (about) begging ; beg

one's bread ; beg food ; live as a beggar ¶ 밥을 얻어먹다 beg one's food // 얻어먹는 신세가 되다 be reduced〔brought〕 to beggary〔begging〕 // 얻어먹으며 가다 beg one's way (to a place)
② [욕 따위를] ¶ 욕을 얻어먹다 get called names ; be slandered ; be spoken ill of // 그는 친구로부터 잔뜩 욕을 얻어먹었다 He was basely slandered by his friends.

얼[1] [흠] a scratch ; a bruise (과일의) ; a flaw ; a fault ¶ 얼이 있는 cracked ; bruised // 얼이 가다 get scratched // 이 사과는 거의가 얼이 있다 These apples are much bruised. // 얼이 있으니까 좀 싸게 하겠습니다 It has some flaws, so I will lower it a little in price.

얼[2] [정신] spirit ; mind ; [혼] soul ; [의지] will ¶ 한국의 얼 the spirit of Korea // 애국의 얼 patriotic spirit ; patriotism // 얼 빠진 abstracted ; stupefied // 얼이 빠져 vacantly ; blankly ; absent-mindedly ; in a daze // 얼이 빠지다 become absent-minded ; lack sense // 얼이 빠져 쳐다보다 gaze at 《a thing》 vacantly ; look dazedly at 《a thing》 // 얼을 빼다 captivate 《a person》 // 얼빠진 초상이다 This portrait has no soul〔life〕. // 그 여자의 아름다움에 얼이 빠졌다 He was captivated by the girl's beauty.

얼간 salting lightly ; saucing slightly ; pickling slightly with salt ¶ 얼간한 slightly salted
— 고등어 lightly salted mackerel **—구이** broiled salted fish **—쌈** cabbage heart that is preserved in salt to be eaten in the winter

얼간망둥이 a simpleton ; a blockhead ⇨ 얼간이

얼간이 a fool ; a half-wit ; an ass ; a dunce ¶ 얼간이 같은 놈 You stupid donkey ; blockhead〕! // (지갑을) 소매치기 당하다니 얼간이로군 Got your pocket picked ! What an ass you are !

***얼갈이** ① [논 따위] winter plowing ② [채소 따위] growing vegetables in the wintertime ; winter-grown vegetables ; winter-sown greens ; early vegetables of the year grown in the winter time

얼개 structure ; framework ; make-up

얼거리 the general〔overall, schematic〕 structure ; an outline ; the layout ¶ 사건의 얼거리를 말하다 give outlines of the affair

얼결 the confusion of the moment ⇨ 얼떨결

†얼굴 ① [낯] a face ; features ¶ 아름다운 얼굴 a handsome〔fair〕 face // 표정이 풍부한 얼굴 expressive features // 말라빠진 얼굴 a meager face // 얼굴 생김새 features ; looks // 얼굴을 씻다 wash one's face ; wash oneself // 얼굴을 붉히다 blush ; color (up) // 두 손으로 얼굴을 가리다 bury one's face in one's hands // 얼굴을 맞대다 meet face to face 《with a person》 // 얼굴을 보이다 show one's face〔nose〕 ; make one's appearance ; show〔turn〕 up (나타나다) ; visit (방문) // 창너머로 얼굴을 내밀다 stick〔put〕 one's head out of the window // 얼굴을 들여다보다 look into 《a person's》 face // 얼굴을 보다 look 《a person》 in the face // 얼굴을 서로 쳐다보다 look at each other〔one another〕 // 어린애가 얼굴을 새빨갛게 하고 울어댔다 The child screamed itself red in the face. // 그는 내 얼굴을 똑바로 바라봤다 He looked me in the face. // 그 소식을 듣자 그녀의 얼굴이 새파래졌다 Her face went white at the news. / Hearing the news, she turned pale. // 그의 얼굴은 알고 있다 I know him by sight. // 요새 그의 얼굴을 볼 수 없다 I don't see much of him these days. // 그 여자는 얼굴 값을 한다 She is full of her own beauty. /She makes you pay for her beauty. /She exploits her beauty.
② [얼굴 표정] a look ; looks ; a countenance ; an expression ; a visage ¶ 기쁜〔슬픈〕 얼굴 a happy〔sad〕 look〔countenance, expression〕 // 성난 얼굴 an angry look // 뽐내는 듯한 얼굴 a proud look // 웃는 얼굴 a face wreathed in smiles // 불만스런〔슬픈 듯한, 실망한〕 얼굴을 하다 make〔pull〕 a long face // 얼굴을 찡그리다 make〔pull〕 a face〔faces〕 《at a person》 ; make a wry face ; mop and mow // 그녀는 아파서 얼굴을 찡그렸다 Pain lined her forehead. // 자 눈물을 닦고 얼굴을 고치세요 Wipe your tears away and make up your face, will you ? // 그 여자는 비웃는 얼굴로 나를 보았다 She threw a look of contempt at me. // 그는 얼굴로 사람됨을 판단하기에 능하다 He is a good judge of faces. // 그의 걱정이 얼굴에 나타나기 시작한다 His troubles are beginning to show in his face.

얼굴

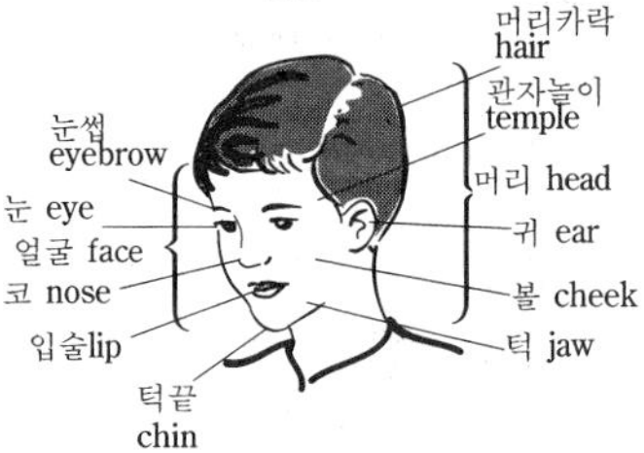

얼굴빛 ① [안색] complexion ; color ¶ 좋은〔나쁜〕 얼굴빛 a good〔bad〕 complexion // 얼굴빛이 좋다〔나쁘다〕 look well〔pale〕 // 얼굴빛이 변하다 change color〔countenance〕 ; [창백하게] turn pale (as white as a sheet) // 무서워서 얼굴빛이 변

하다 turn yellow with fear
② [표정] a face ; a look ; a countenance ; an expression ¶ 불안한 얼굴빛을 하다 look uneasy // 얼굴빛을 살피다 read 《a person's》 face〔countenance〕; study the pleasure of 《a person》; hang on 《a person's》 smiles // 너의 얼굴빛으로 알 수 있다 I can see it in your face. /Your face speaks (for itself).

얼근덜근 ① [맛이] rather hot ; peppery ; heavily seasoned ② [술이] somewhat ; rather] intoxicated ¶ 얼근덜근 취하다 be rather tipsy

얼근하다 ① [맵다] taste rather hot ; (be) rather hot-tasting ; peppery ; pungent ; heavily seasoned ¶ 얼근하게 양념하다 season food rather heavily
② [취하다] (be) rather tipsy ; rather intoxicated ¶ 그는 얼근한 기분이다 He looks gay (with drink).

얼금뱅이 a pockmarked person ; a person with a pitted face ⇨ 곰보

얼금숨숨 lightly pockmarked

얼기설기 entangled ; in complete disorder ¶ 얼기설기 얽힌 entangled ; complicated ; complex ; intricate // 얼기설기 얽힌 사정 a perplexed state of things // 얼기설기 얽힌 사건 a complicated〔tangled〕 affair // 일이 얼기설기 얽혀졌다 The matter has become quite complicated. /The affair is getting entangled. // 이것에는 여러 가지 사정이 얼기설기하다 This is a very complicated matter.

얼김 flurry ; confusion ; bustle ; turmoil ; hustle and bustle ¶ 얼김에 on the spur〔in the heat〕 of the moment ; in the confusion // 얼김에 기차를 잘못 탔다 In my hurry I took a wrong train. // 자전거를 피하다가 얼김에 넘어졌다 I stumbled down in trying to dodge a bicycle. // 싸우다가 얼김에 그를 죽였다 I was quarreling with a man and killed him in the heat of the moment. // 그는 급히 도랑을 뛰어 넘다가 얼김에 지갑을 떨어뜨렸다 He dropped his purse at the instant of jumping over a ditch.

얼낌덜낌에 in the confusion of the moment

얼넘기다 skimp〔scamp〕 《one's work》

얼넘어가다 scamp over〔off〕

얼녹이다 alternately freeze and melt

****얼다** freeze ; be frozen ; be benumbed with cold (몸이) ; 〔기가 꺾이다〕 get〔feel〕 self-conscious ; get nervous ; lost one's composure ; get〔have〕 stage fright ¶ 언 frozen // 언 손 numbed hands // 얼어붙은 연못〔강〕 a pond〔river〕 frozen all over // 꽁꽁 얼다 be frozen hard ; stiff〕 // 꽁꽁 얼어붙다 be frozen fast // 추워서 손이 얼다 one's hands are benumbed with cold // 얼어죽다 freeze to death // 추워서 몸이 얼었다 I felt as cold as ice. // 호수가 약 한자의 두께로 얼었다 The lake is frozen (over) about a foot thick. // 수도가 얼었다 The water pipe has frozen (up). // 고기가 꽁꽁 얼어 얼음 덩어리 같다 The meat is frozen to a block of ice. // 처음으로 내가 TV에 출연했을 때 나는 얼었었다 The first time I appeared on TV, I got self-conscious〔stage fright〕. // 연못에 얼음이 얼었다 Ice has formed on the pond.

***얼떨결** the confusion of the moment ¶ 얼떨결에 in the confusion of the moment ; in a moment of bewilderment // 얼떨결에 그렇게 말해버렸다 He said so in his bewilderment. // 얼떨결에 기차를 잘못 탔다 In my hurry I took a wrong train.

***얼떨떨하다** (be) confused ; upset ; confounded ; puzzled ; dazed ; bewildered ; lose one's head ; be at a loss ¶ 얼떨떨한 표정 a puzzled look〔expression〕 // 얼떨떨하여 in confusion ; confusedly // 얼떨떨해지다 get confused ; be upset ; lose one's head ; be bewildered // 얼떨떨하게 하다 confuse ; disconcert ; bewilder ; upset ; take 《a person》 aback // 어떻게 대답해야 할지 얼떨떨하다 be at a loss how to reply // 나는 매우 얼떨떨하였다 I was all adrift. // 돌연한 질문에 얼떨떨했다 I was put out〔confused, embarrassed〕 at his abrupt question. // 그는 점잖은 말을 늘어놓아 나를 얼떨떨하게 만들었다 He confused me with a deluge of polite words. // 그 여자는 처녀 출연이라 얼떨떨했다 She was in a flutter of excitement over her debut on the stage. // 돌연 영어로 말을 걸어 왔기 때문에 매우 얼떨떨했다 Being abruptly spoken to in English, I was quite flurried. // 그는 위험에 직면해서도 얼떨떨해 하지 않았다 He showed presence of mind in the face of the danger.

얼떨하다 ① (be) confused ; disconcerted ; ⇨ 얼떨떨하다 ¶ 얼떨해 하다 be all in a flurry ; be confused ; be disconcerted
② [머리가] (be) dizzy ; giddy ; groggy ¶ 머리가 얼떨하다 My head buzzes. /My head aches. /My head swims. // 잠을 못 자서 정신이 얼떨하다 I feel groggy〔stupefied〕 from lack of sleep.

얼뜨기 a stupid person ; a half-wit ; a blockhead ; a half-witted fellow ¶ 그에게 그런 말을 하다니 얼마나 얼뜨기 같은 짓이냐 How stupid〔silly〕 of you to tell him such a thing !

얼뜨다 (be) stupid ; slow-witted ; dull-headed ; silly ¶ 얼뜬 짓을 하다 do a stupid thing ; make a fool of oneself // 얼뜬 녀석아 You stupid donkey ! /Blockhead ! // 그는 좀 얼뜨다 He is a bit soft (in the head). /He has a soft place in his head.

얼락녹을락 freezing and thawing by turns ; now freezing and then melting ¶

금년 겨울에는 얼음이 얼락녹을락 하여 스케이팅의 재미를 못 봤다 We could not enjoy skating this winter because it was frozen and melted by turns. // 그는 얼락녹을락 여러 해를 두고 그 여자를 농락했다 For years, he had played with her affections.

얼락배락 fluctuating ; waving and waning ; rising and falling

얼러기 a spotted〔pied〕 animal

얼러맞추다 play up to ; flatter ; humor ; please another's humor ; pay court to ((another)) ; lick another's boots ; curry favor with (아첨) ¶ 얼러맞추기 힘들다 be hard to please // 남편을 잘 얼러맞추다 contrive to get to the soft side of her husband // 얼러맞추면 그는 다루기가 쉬운 사람이다 Properly treated, he is perfectly easy to handle〔manage〕.

얼러먹다 eat together ; share ((in))

얼러방망이 a threat ; a scare
—짓 threatening with one's fists

얼러붙다 grapple with ; wrestle with ; come to a fist fight ¶ 얼러붙어 싸우다 fight hand to hand ; fight a close fight ; grapple with ((a person))

얼러치다 ① [때리다] strike〔hit, score〕 two or more at one time ; lump ((things)) together ② [셈을] count in the lump ; make a combined price ((for the pair, for the lot))

얼럭 a stain ; a blot ; a mottle ⇨ 얼룩

얼럭광대 a regular entertainer〔performer〕

얼럭덜럭 —하다 (be) stained ; mottled ; variegated ⇨ 얼룩덜룩

얼럭지다 become stained〔blotted〕 ⇨ 얼룩지다

얼럭집 a house built in mixed styles ; a house with part tile-roofing, part grass-roofing

얼렁뚱땅 cunningly ; trickily ; flatteringly ; playing false ¶ 얼렁뚱땅 빼앗다 wheedle ((a person)) out of ((a thing)) ; deprive ((a person)) of ((a thing)) trickily // 일을 얼렁뚱땅 해치우다 do a slapdash job ; scamp one's work // 그녀는 노인을 얼렁뚱땅 속여서 필요한 것을 얻어냈다 She wheedled round the old man till she got what she wanted.

얼렁뚱땅하다 [엉너리로] mystify ; befuddle ; behave evasively ; beat around the bush ¶ 얼렁뚱땅하여 돈을 빼앗다 juggle ((a person)) out of his money // 얼렁뚱땅하지 말고 정신 차려 일해라 Don't be so sloppy, pay more attention to your work.

얼렁장사 joint business ; partnership —하다 run business in partnership with ((a person)) ; enter〔go〕 into partnership with ((a person))

⁑얼레 a reel ; a spool ; a kitestring ; a bobbin ¶ 얼레에 감다 spool ; reel ; wind ((thread)) on a bobbin // 얼레에서 실을 풀다 unwind from a reel

얼레빗 a coarse comb

얼레살 a reel spoke ¶ 얼레살 풀다 start on the path of ruin ; dissipate one's fortune ; indulge in ((wine, gambling))

얼레지 〖식물〗 an adder's tongue lily ; a dogtooth violet
— 가루 dogtooth violet starch

⁑얼룩 [오점] a stain ; a spot ; a blot ; [반점] a blotch ; a speckle ; dapples ; mottles ; variegation ¶ 잉크의 얼룩 an ink spot // 얼룩 빼는 약 a spot remover // 얼룩진 spotted ; stained ; dappled ; patched // 얼룩을 빼다 remove〔take out〕 stains〔blurs, patches〕 ((on one's clothes)) // 옷에 얼룩이 지지 않도록 하다 save〔keep〕 clothes from spots and stains // 그것은 흰색과 갈색의 얼룩개였다 It was a white and brown dog. /It was a dog spotted with white and brown. // 그의 개는 갈색 바탕에 흰 얼룩이 있었다 His dog was brown with white splashes.
— 고양이 a tabby (cat) ; a brindled cat
— 말 a piebald (horse) ; a zebra —뱀 a speckled snake —소 a brindled cow〔ox〕

얼룩덜룩 —하다 (be) mottled ; dappled ; variegated ; parti-colored ; spotted ; stained

얼룩얼룩 —하다 (be) spotted ; dappled ; mottled ; motley ; speckled ; variegated ; brin-dled (호랑이, 고양이 따위가) ; piebald (희고 검게) ¶ 얼룩얼룩한 옷감 variegated cloth // 볕과 그늘로 얼룩얼룩한 잔디밭 a lawn checkered with sunlight and shade // 피에로는 얼룩얼룩한 옷을 입고 있었다 The pierrot was in a mottled〔parti-colored〕 dress.

얼룩이 ① [동물] a dappled〔spotted〕 animal ; a brindled dog ② [점] a spotted〔mottled〕 effect ; dots

***얼룩지다** become stained〔blotted〕 ¶ 얼룩진 stained ; spotted ; smeared ; [무늬진] mottled ; variegated // 옷에 얼룩지지 않도록 주의하다 be careful so as not to get one's clothes stained with spots and stains // 이 옷감은 얼룩지기 쉽다 This material spots easily. // 나무 사이로 비치는 햇빛으로 길이 얼룩져 있었다 The lane was mottled with the sunbeams filtering through the leaves.

얼룽덜룽하다 (be) variegated ; mottled ; dotted

얼룽이 ⇨ 얼룩이

***얼른** [빨리] fast ; quickly ; rapidly ; promptly ; speedily ; hastily ; at once ; immediately ¶ 얼른 해라 Hurry up ! / Make haste ! /Don't be long about it. / Make it snappy ! // 얼른 대답하라 Answer promptly. /Give me a prompt answer. // 그녀는 얼른 우리에게 알려 줬다 She hastened〔ran〕 to tell us the news. // 얼른 자라서 훌륭한 사람이 돼라 Make haste and grow up to be a great man. // 얼른 시험

의 결과를 알고 싶다 I am anxious to know the result of the examination.

얼른거리다 ⇨ 어른거리다

얼리다[1] freeze ; make ice ; refrigerate ; [얼게 되다] get frozen ¶ 얼린 채소 frozen vegetables // 생선을 얼리다 freeze〔refrigerate〕 fish

얼리다[2] join ; club〔hand〕 together ; associate with ; mix with ; mingle with ⇨ 어울리다 ¶ 군중과 얼리다 mingle in the crowds // 나쁜 친구와 얼리지 마라 Avoid〔Don't keep〕 bad company. // 그는 우리와 얼려서 그 모험을 할 것이다 He will join in with us and take the risk.

얼마 ① [수량] how many (수) ; how much (양) ¶ 이 호박의 무게는 얼마냐 How much does this pumpkin weigh ? / How heavy is this pumpkin ? /What is the weight of this pumpkin ? // 여기서 서울까지는 거리가 얼마나 되느냐 How far is it from here to *Seoul* ?
② [금액] how much ; what ¶ 저 모자는 얼마입니까 How much is that hat ? / What will you charge for that hat ? // 그 쇠고기는 1파운드에 얼마 합니까 How much a pound is that beef ? // 얼마야 What does it come to ?
③ [비율] by ; so much ¶ 하루 얼마로 by the day ; at so much a day // 하루 얼마로 일하다 work〔be hired〕 by the day // 쌀은 지금 1킬로당 얼마에 팔리고 있다 Rice is now sold at so much 〔such and such price〕 a kilogram.
④ [정도] to some extent ; in some degree ; in a way〔manner〕 ¶ 얼마 있다가 a little later ; after a while〔time〕 // 얼마 있으면 before long ; shortly ; in a little while ; soon ; presently // 얼마 멀지 않은 곳에 not far off〔away〕 ; at a short distance

†**얼마간** —間 some ; somewhat ; more or less ; to some extent ¶ 돈을 달라기에 얼마간 주었다 He asked for money, so I gave him some. // 그것은 얼마간은 사실이다 To some extent it is true.

†**얼마나** ① [의문] [수] how many ; [양] how much ; [정도] how ; how far ; [시간] how long ; [거리] how far ; [크기] how large ; [높이] how high ; [무게] how heavy ; [금액] how much ; what ¶ 책이 얼마나 있습니까 How many books do you have ? /How large is your library ? // 돈이 얼마나 필요합니까 How much money do you need ? // 시간은 얼마나 걸립니까 How many hours〔How long〕 does it take ? // 그는 지금 얼마나 갔을까 How far has he gone, I wonder ? // 한국에 와서 얼마나 되십니까 How long have you been in Korea ? // 여기서 역까지의 거리는 얼마나 됩니까 How far is it from here to the station ? // 그 집의 넓이는 얼마나 됩니까 How large is the house ? // 한라산의 높이는 얼마나 됩니까 How high is Mt. *Halla* ? / What is the height of Mt. *Halla* ? // 이 돌의 무게는 얼마나 됩니까 How heavy is this stone ? /What is the weight of this stone ? // 당신의 체중은 얼마나 됩니까 How much do you weigh ? // 출퇴근 시간이 얼마나 걸립니까 How long is your commute ? // 그가 결혼하기 전까지 얼마나 더 많은 여자들과 헤어질 지 궁금하다 I wonder how many more girls he is going to break up with before he gets married.
② [감탄] what ; how ¶ 얼마나 아름다운 경치냐 What a fine scene (it is) ! // 얼마나 기쁠까 How glad your people must be ! // 그 얼마나 아름다운 소리로 저 새는 지저귀고 있는가 How sweetly the bird is singing ! // 이 얼마나 좋은 날씨인가 What a fine day it is !

얼마든지 any ; any amount ; without limit (한없이) ; as much〔many〕 as one wants〔likes〕 ; [부정문에] 《not》 many〔much〕 ¶ 얼마든지 원하는 대로 as many〔much〕 as one wants // 얼마든지 가져도 좋다 You may take as much〔many〕 as you like. // 얼마든지 가지고 싶은 대로 가지시오 You shall have as much〔many〕 as you want. // 그것을 사기 위해서라면 돈을 얼마든지 내놓겠다 I will pay any price for that. // 그는 돈이라면 얼마든지 갖고 있다 He has no end of money. // 네가 원하면 얼마든지 우리 집에 있어도 좋다 You can stay with us as long as you want.

얼마르다 freeze-dry

얼마만큼 ⇨ 얼마큼

얼마쯤 ⇨ 얼마큼

얼마큼 ① [의문] (＝얼마만큼) ⇨ 얼마나 ② [정도] some ; something ; somewhat ; a little ; partly ; partially ; more or less ; in a way ¶ 그는 소지금의 얼마큼을 그 부인에게 주었다 He gave the woman some of the money he had with him. // 환자는 오늘은 얼마큼 기분이 좋다 The patient is slightly〔a little, somewhat, some 《구》〕 better today. // 얼마큼이라도 있는 것은 없는 것보다 낫다 Something is better than nothing. // 그는 얼마큼 음악가 기질이 있다 He has something of the musician in him. /He is somewhat of a musician. // 술을 마시니까 얼마큼 기분이 좋아졌다 As I had a drink of wine, I felt a little better. // 마음 착한 아가씨는 불쌍한 노인에게 얼마큼의 돈을 주었다 The kind girl gave some money to the poor old man.

얼마르다[1] freeze up hard ; freeze dry ; be frozen into drying

얼마르다[2] be not quite dry ; be only half dry

얼멍덜멍 —하다 (be) lumpy ; bumpy ; be full of lumps ; (be) rough ; coarse ¶ 죽이 얼멍덜멍하다 The gruel has lumps in it.

얼밋얼밋 hesitantly ; falteringly —하다

hesitate ; be hesitant ; falter ¶ 얼밋얼밋 하지 않고 without hesitation〔flinching〕// 얼밋얼밋 말하다 falter ; stammer

얼바람둥이 a crazy person ; a crackpot

얼바람맞다 act〔behave〕 absurdly〔silly〕

얼버무리다 ① [말을] speak ambiguously ; equivocate ; cover up talking ; shuffle ¶ 적당히 얼버무리다 give an evasive answer ; talk oneself out of trouble somehow for the time being // 얼버무리지 말고 똑똑히 대답하라 Don't shuffle, give a clear answer. // 그는 말뜻을 적당히 얼버무렸다 He quibbled about the meaning of the word. // 너는 항상 웃으며 얼버무린다 You always laugh and evade the question.
② [섞어 버무리다] mix〔jumble〕 up ; mix 《ingredients》 well ¶ 얼버무려 샐러드를 만들다 mix up salad dressing
③ [삼키다] swallow without chewing well ; swallow 《food》 quickly ; swallow in lumps

얼보다 can not see straight〔clearly〕 ; see blurred〔incorrectly〕

얼보이다 be seen dimly〔blurred〕 ; be seen distortedly ¶ 글자가 얼보여서 읽기 어렵다 The writing is blurred and difficult to read.

얼부풀다 be frozen and swell up ; swell up from freezing

얼빠지다 lose one's senses ; be out of one's senses ; be absent-minded ; be half-witted ; be dull-headed ; be stupefied ¶ 얼빠진 사람 a stupid person ; a half-wit ; a simp // 얼빠진 짓을 하다 do a silly〔stupid〕 thing ; make a fool of oneself // 얼빠진 사람같이 보이다 have a vacant〔stupid〕 look ; look blank〔stupefied〕 ; look like a (dying) duck in a thunderstorm // 소매치기 당했다고—얼빠진 녀석 같으니 Got your pocket picked ! What an ass you are ! // 그렇게 얼빠진 얼굴을 하고 서 있지 마라 Don't stand there looking like a fool. // 나는 얼빠진 짓을 해 버렸다 I really blew it.

얼빼다 drive 《a person》 out of his mind ; strike 《a person》 dumb ; captivate 《a person》 ; take 《a person》 aback : stun ¶ 구경꾼을 얼빼다 shock the spectators off their feet

얼빰붙이다 slap 《a person's face》 in the heat of the moment〔in spite of oneself〕

얼싸 Bravo ! /Hurray ! ¶ 얼싸 좋다 Hurray, isn't it fun ?

얼싸안다 hug ; embrace 《a person》 ; give 《a person》 a tight hug ; clasp 《a person》 in one's arms ; hold〔take〕 《a person》 in one's arms ¶ 서로 얼싸안다 embrace each other ; be in each other's arms // 목을 얼싸안다 throw〔lock, fold〕 one's arms around〔about〕 《a person's》 neck // 어머니는 기뻐서 그를 얼싸안았다 The mother hugged him for joy. // 둘은 얼싸안고 울었다 The two threw themselves into each other's arms and wept. // 두 사람은 기뻐서 얼싸안고 춤을 추었다 The two danced with joy in each other's arms.

얼쑹덜쑹 **—하다** (be) motley ; jumbled ; mixed-up ; confusing

얼씨구 Hurrah ! /Oh, boy ! /Whoopee ! /What a delight ! /What a pleasure ! ¶ 얼씨구 좋구나 Hurrah ! /Whoopee ! /That's a boy !

얼씬거리다 [오다] come around ; show up ; hang around ; loiter ; [어른거리다] flicker ; glisten

얼씬못하다 dare not come around〔show up〕 ; do not appear before 《a person's》 eyes at all ¶ 다시는 감히 내 집에 얼씬 못할 것이다 He will never dare to enter my house again.

얼씬얼씬 loiteringly ; loafing around **—하다** ⇨ 얼씬거리다

얼씬없다 be entirely out of sight ; do not show up for even a moment

얼씬하다 appear briefly ; make one's appearance ; show oneself ; show〔turn〕 up ¶ 얼씬하지 않다 do not appear at all

얼어붙다 freeze up〔over〕 ; be frozen hard ; be frozen fast to ¶ 강이 꽁꽁 얼어붙었다 The river is frozen over. // 얼어붙을 것 같은 추위다 It is freezing (cold). // 문이 문지방에 얼어붙어서 열리지 않는다 The door has frozen to the groove and will not open. // 그 길은 아침 나절을 얼어붙어 있다 The road is frozen hard all morning. // 북극해에서는 배가 때때로 얼어붙을 때가 있다 Sometimes ships are icebound in the Arctic Ocean.

얼얼하다 [상처가] smart 《with pain》 ; [맛이] taste hot ; (be) pungent ¶ 맛이 얼얼하다 have a burning〔biting〕 taste // 얼얼하게 아프다 have a tingling pain ; smart // 생채기가 아직 얼얼하다 The scratch still smarts.

얼없다 be just the same ; (be) quite correct ; certain〕

얼요기 a mere morsel 《of food》 ; a frugal meal **—하다** eat just a bite 《of food》

†**얼음** ice ¶ 살얼음 thin ice // 얼음덩이 a cake of ice ; [큰] a block of ice ; [작은] a small ice // 얼음장 a layer〔coat〕 of ice ; a piece of ice ; a sheet of ice // 얼음에 채운 생선 fish packed in ice // 얼음 같은 icy ; ice-cold // 얼음이 되다 turn〔be frozen〕 into ice // 얼음을 지치다 skate 〔slide〕 on the ice // 얼음을 먹다 take〔eat〕 ice // 얼음을 녹이다 melt ice // 얼음 속에 재다 pack 《fish》 in ice // 얼음이 갈라졌다 The ice cracked. // 연못에 얼음이 얼었다 The pond is frozen over. // 얼음이 언다 Ice forms 《in a pond》. // 맥주는 얼음에 채워져 있습니다 The beer is on the ice. // 오늘 밤엔 얼음이 얼겠다 We shall have ice tonight. // 스카치 위스키를 얼음에 타 주세요 Scotch on the rocks, please.

— 가게 an ice shop — 과자 ices ; ice candy — 사탕 sugar candy 《영》; rock candy 《미》 — 상자 an icebox — 위스키 whisky on ice (cubes) — 주머니 an ice bag —집 ice shop —찜 relieving fever with an ice bag — 창고 an icehouse — 판 an icy ground ; an iced ground 인조 — artificial ice

얼음박이다 [국부가 주어] become〔be〕 frostbitten ; be affected with chilblains ; [사람이 주어] have chilblains ¶ 발에 얼음이 박이다 get 〔have〕 one's feet frostbitten

얼음장같다 be (as) cold as ice ¶ 방바닥이 얼음장 같다 The floor is as cold as ice.

얼음지치기 sliding on the ice ; skating —하다 slide on the ice ; skate

†얼음지치다 ⇨ 얼음

얼음판 ice-covered〔icy〕 ground ; an iced ground ; the ice ¶ 얼음판에서 얼음 지치다 skate on an ice rink

얼입다 suffer a loss from another's fault ; suffer undeservedly due to another's failure

얼젓국지 slightly pickled vegetables

얼쩍지근하다 ① [맛이] (be) a bit spicy ; hot-tasting ¶ 맛이 얼쩍지근하다 have a hot ; spicy, peppery〕 taste ② [상처가] (be) smarting ; prickling ③ [취하다] (be) slightly drunk ; rather tipsy

얼쭝거리다 cajole ; coax ; wheedle ; get around 《a person》 ¶ 얼쭝거리며 사람을 속이다 impose upon 《a person》 by flattery

얼쭝얼쭝 by honeyed tongue ; flatteringly ; coaxingly ; cajolingly ¶ 얼쭝얼쭝 사람을 속이다 impose upon a person by flattery

얼쯤얼쯤 hesitant(ly) ; reluctant(ly) — 하다 hesitate ; waver

얼찐거리다 flatter ; beguile ; play up to

얼추 [거의] nearly ; almost ; about ; roughly ; approximately ¶ 얼추 말하자면 roughly speaking ; in brief〔short〕// 얼추 다 되었다 It is practically finished. /I have as good as finished my work. // 일이 얼추 끝났다 I am nearly through with my work. // 얼추 맞췄다 That's about right. // 얼추 보아 거리는 5마일쯤이라 생각한다 I roughly estimate the distance at about five miles. // 그 편지를 얼추 훑어봤다 I glanced (my eyes) over the letter. /I ran my eyes over the letter. /I gave the letter the once-over. // 그 책을 얼추 읽어 봤다 I have run through the book. // 신문을 얼추 훑어본다 I skim (through) the newspaper. // 그 수는 얼추보아 60～70을 넘지 않았다 The number did not exceed, roughly speaking, 60 or 70.

얼추잡다 make a rough estimate ; make a draft 《of》; outline ¶ 계획을 얼추잡다 outline a plan // 방문객 수는 얼추잡아 1,000명 가량이다 The number of visitors is roughly estimated at 1,000. // 손해는 얼추잡아 50만원입니다 The (amount of) damage is roughly estimated at half a million *won*.

얼치기 something half-and-half ; a thing of double aspect ; a half-and-half person ; a fool (사람) ; things half-done (일) ¶ 얼치기의 halfway ; half-done // 얼치기로 일을 하다 do 《a thing》 by halves ; leave 《a thing》 half-done // 그는 일을 얼치기로는 하지 않는다 He goes the whole hog. /There are no half measures about him. // 얼치기 공부라면 안 하는 것이 낫다 One may as well know nothing than know things by halves.

얼크러지다 get entangled〔involved, complicated, messed up〕 ¶ 얼크러진 실을 풀다 untie entangled knots ; unravel a thread // 실이 얼크러졌다 The thread has got entangled. /The thread is raveled.

얼큰하다 ⇨ 얼근하다

얼키설키 complicatedly ⇨ 얼기설기

얼토당토아니하다 (be) irrelevant ; have nothing to do with ; bear no relation to ; extravagant ; wrong ; absurd ¶ 얼토당토않은 사람 a rank outsider to the job ; a most unlikely man for the job // 얼토당토않은 잘못 a fatal mistake // 얼토당토않은 요구 a preposterous demand // 얼토당토않은 말을 하다 say something quite beside the point ; say incoherent things // 얼토당토않은 말을 하지 말라 Don't talk nonsense. /That is absurd. // 얼토당토않은 이야기다 Nothing could be farther from the truth. /Now this is a tremendous mistake. // 그는 때때로 얼토당토않은 일을 한다 He does often most absurd things.

얽다[1] ① [엮다] bind ; weave ; interwind ¶ 얽어 매다 tie (up) ; join〔fasten〕 together // 얽어서 꾸러미로 하다 tie up in a bundle ; bundle up 《books》// 가지를 얽어 고리짝을 만들다 weave twigs into a basket ② [꾸며대다] coin ; fabricate ; frame up ; make up ; forge ¶ 이야기를 얽다 make up a story

얽다[2] ① [마마자국] be pitted with smallpox ; be pockmarked ; become marked with pits ¶ 얽은 자리 smallpox marks ; pockmarks // 얼굴이 얽은 남자 a pockmarked man ; a man with a pitted face // 그의 얼굴은 얽었다 His face is pitted 〔scarred〕 with smallpox. /His face is pockmarked.
② [흠] be pitted〔scarred〕; have many flaws ¶ 얽은 rough ; uneven ; pitted ; bruised // 이 사과는 얽었다 This apple is bruised. // 이 물건이 좀 얽었으므로 싸게 해드리지요 It has some flaws, so I will lower it a little in price.

얽동이다 [짐짝] tie up ; bind〔up〕; chain (사슬로) ¶ 물건을 한데 얽동이다 bind

〔up〕 things into a bundle // 단단히 얽동이다 tie fast〔hard〕 // 범인을 얽동여매다 tie a criminal with cords

얽둑빼기 a pockmarked person ; a person with a pockmarked〔pitted〕 face

얽둑얽둑 with deep pocks **—하다** (be) pockmarked ; pitted ; pocky ¶ 얽둑얽둑 얽은 사람 a person with a pitted face ; a person with a pocky face // 얼굴이 얽둑얽둑 얽다 one's face is pitted〔pockmarked〕

얽매다 [결속] bind〔tie〕 up tight ; fasten ; restrict ¶ 상자를 끈으로 얽매다 bind (up) a box with a cord // 사람을 얽매다 tie 《a person》 up // 규칙으로 얽매다 restrict 《a person》 by rule

얽매이다 [속박] be bound ; be tied〔fettered〕 ; be restricted ; [분주하다] be busy with ; be occupied with ; be engrossed in ¶ 습관에 얽매이는 사람 a man bound to custom // 습관에 얽매이지 않는 사람 a man unbound to custom // 아이들 일에 얽매이다 be taken up with the care of children // 가사에 얽매이다 be occupied with household duties // 규칙에 얽매이다 be bound by a rule ; be screwed down to a rule // 인정에 얽매이다 be overcome by one's affection ; be prompted by human motives // 인습에 얽매이다 be fettered by tradition ; be a slave to tradition // 시간에 얽매이다 be restricted by time ; have little time to call one's own

얽빼기 ⇨ 얽둑빼기

얽어매다 bind up ; tie up ¶ 개를 사슬로 얽어매다 chain up a dog // 그는 톰의 두 발을 얽어매지 못했다 He failed to tie Tom's feet together.

얽이 [얽는 일] tying〔trussing, binding〕 up securely ; [일의 순서·배치] (getting) an overall picture〔an outline, a rough idea〕 of things

얽이 치다 tie crisscross〔crosswise〕 ; outline〔sketch out〕 《a plan》

얽적빼기 ⇨ 얽둑빼기

얽적얽적 heavily pockmarked **—하다** (be) heavily pockmarked

얽죽빼기 ⇨ 얽둑빼기

얽죽얽죽 ⇨ 얽적얽적

* **얽히다** be〔become, get〕 entangled ; get caught in ; be involved ; get complicated ; twine round ¶ 얽힌 것을 풀다 disentangle ; unravel ; untie // 얽혀 들다 be〔become〕 entangled〔involved〕 // 실이 얽혔다 The thread has got entangled. // 담쟁이가 나무에 얽혀 있다 The ivy twined the tree. // 이 사건에는 여러 사정이 얽혀 있다 Various circumstances are involved in this event. /This is a very complicated matter.

엄개 掩蓋 a cover ; a covering ; [대포의] a gun apron

⁑ **엄격 嚴格** severity ; sternness ; rigor ; strictness **—하다** (be) strict ; stern ; rigorous ; severe ; austere

> 참고 **severe** 사람 언동 법률 처벌 따위가 엄격하고 때로는 무정하다 **stern** 간청 따위에 움직이지 않고 절대로 심약함 관대함을 나타내지 않는다 **austere** 엄격한 극기를 나타내며 정열 장식 따위를 피하여 간소를 신조로 한다

¶ 엄격한(히) strict(ly) ; stern(ly) ; severe(ly) ; rigorous(ly) // 엄격한 규칙 rigid regulation // 엄격한 가정 a strict home ; a sternly moral family ; a well-ordered home // 엄격한 가훈 strict home discipline // 엄격한 선생 a strict〔severe〕 teacher // 엄격한 아버지 a stern〔strict, hard〕 father // 엄격히 말하자면 strictly speaking ; in the strict sense of the word // 엄격하게 구별하다 make a sharp distinction 《between》 // 엄격히 기르다 bring up 《a child》 rigorously // 그는 부하에 대해서 엄격하다 He is strict with his men. // 우리 아버지는 엄격하지만 자애로운 분이었다 Stern as he was, our father was full of affection to us. // 그는 엄격한 가정에서 자랐다 He was brought up in a stern family.

엄계 嚴戒 strict watch **—하다** keep strict guard〔watch〕 《against over》

엄교 嚴敎 stern〔rigorous〕 teaching

* **엄금 嚴禁** strict prohibition ; a ban ; an interdict **—하다** prohibit〔forbid〕 strictly ; ban ; place 《a thing》 under a ban ¶ 외출을 엄금하다 strictly forbid 《a person》 to go out // 강당에서는 끽연을 엄금하고 있다 Smoking is strictly prohibited in the auditorium. // 아버지는 그런 책을 읽는 것을 엄금했다 Father has strictly forbidden us to read such books.
개방 — Close the door after you. 끽연 — No Smoking. 무용자 출입 — No admission except on business. 소변 — Commit no nuisance. 화기 — Inflammable. /Use of fire strictly prohibited.

엄나무 〖식물〗 the thorny ash (tree) ; Kalopanax pictum (학명)

엄니 the fangs of a carnivorous animal ¶ 엄니를 드러내다 snarl ; growl 《at》

엄닉 掩匿 concealment ; hiding **—하다** hide ; conceal ; cover 《up》

엄달 嚴達 giving strict orders **—하다** give〔issue〕 strict orders〔instructions〕

엄대 a tally stick with notches ¶ 엄대질하다 sell on credit with a notched pole

엄동 嚴冬 a severe〔hard〕 winter ¶ 엄동(설한)에 in the cold of winter ; in the depth〔dead〕 of winter

엄두 the very thought 《of doing something》 ¶ 엄두도 못내다 cannot even conceive the idea of 《doing》 ; be hardly thinkable ; be beyond one's power // 이야

기한다는 것은 아무도 엄두를 못 냈다 No one dared to speak with him. // 그러한 일은 엄두도 못냈다 Such a thing never entered my head〔mind〕. // 저항 따위는 엄두도 못낼 일이다 Resistance is inconceivable〔out of the question〕. // 그들은 올 엄두도 못냈다 They did not dare to come.

‡**엄마** [어린이말] ma ; mama ; mammy ; mummy

엄매 a bleat ; a moo ¶ 엄매하고 울다 bleat ; moo

엄명 嚴命 a strict order〔command〕; stringent directions ; rigid instructions **—하다** give strict orders〔directions, instructions〕 ¶ 엄명에 따라 under〔by〕 strict order 《of a commanding officer》

‡**엄밀 嚴密** strictness ; exactness ; rigidity **—하다** (be) exact ; close ; strict ¶ 엄밀한 검사 a close examination ; a rigid inspection // 엄밀히 strictly ; exactly ; closely // 엄밀한 의미에서 in the strict sense // 엄밀히 말하면 strictly speaking // 엄밀히 조사하다 investigate 《a matter》 closely ; make a close examination of 《a thing》 // 교정을 엄밀히 보다 read the proof with religious care // 법을 엄밀히 집행하다 enforce a law to the letter

엄발나다 be likely to deviate〔go away〕 《from》; behave in an aberrant manner

엄벌 嚴罰 a severe〔heavy〕 punishment **—하다** punish 《a person》 severely ; deal severely with 《a person》 ¶ 그는 엄벌을 받아 마땅하다 He deserves a severe punishment.

—주의 enforcement of severe punishment ; a severe punishment policy ; martinetism

엄범부렁하다 ⇨ 엄부렁하다

엄벙덤벙 rashly ; recklessly ; carelessly ; frivolously ; blindly ; thoughtlessly ; at random ; sloppily **—하다** act thoughtlessly〔rashly〕; go at it half-heartedly ; be frivolous〔not serious〕 ¶ 그는 일을 엄벙덤벙한다 He does a sloppy job.

엄벙뗑 ⇨ 얼렁뚱땅

엄벙하다 (be) sloppy ; be not serious ; (be) frivolous ; ambiguous ; evasive ¶ 엄벙한 문장 a loose style

엄봉 嚴封 a hermetic seal **—하다** seal hermetically ; seal up

엄부 嚴父 [엄한 아버지] a stern〔strict〕 father ; [아버지] one's father

엄부럭 ⇨ 엄살, 심술(心術)

엄부렁하다 (be) bulky but empty ; slovenly ; loose ; sloppy ; trumpery ; showy but worthless ¶ 엄부렁한 위인 a sloven // 그는 엄부렁하다 He wants screwing up〔needs winding up〕. // 그것은 엄부렁하다 It is not so good as it looks.

엄비 嚴秘 strict secrecy ¶ 엄비에 붙이다 keep 《a matter》 a strict secret

엄살 exaggeration of pain〔hardship〕; a big fuss ¶ 엄살부리다 exaggerate〔pretend〕 pain〔hardship〕; make a big fuss // 도와 달라고 부탁했더니 그는 바쁘다고 엄살부리며 거절했다 When I asked him for some help he turned me down giving me some song and dance how busy he was

—꾸러기 a fussy person ; a fusser ; a crybaby

엄선 嚴選 careful selection **—하다** select carefully ; be very strict〔most rigorous〕 in selecting

‡**엄수 嚴守** strict observance〔observation〕; rigid adherence 《to rules》 **—하다** observe strictly〔scrupulously〕; rigidly adhere 《to》 ¶ 시간의 엄수 punctuality // 시간을 엄수하다 be punctual (to the minute) ; be (always) in time // 규칙을 엄수하다 observe the rules 《to the letter》 // 약속〔비밀〕을 엄수하다 keep one's promise〔a secret〕 strictly

엄수 嚴修 conducting 《a funeral service》 with solemnity **—하다** conduct〔hold〕 《a funeral service》 solemnly ; duly perform 《a funeral service》 ¶ 희생자들의 추도식이 어제 엄수되었다 The funeral service for the victims was conducted yesterday with solemn ceremony.

‡**엄숙 嚴肅** seriousness ; solemnity ; gravity ; dignity **—하다** (be) grave ; serious ; solemn ¶ 엄숙히 gravely ; seriously ; solemnly // 엄숙한 어조 a solemn tone // 엄숙한 의식 a solemn ceremony ; an impressive ceremony // 엄숙한 얼굴 a grave countenance // 엄숙히 말하다 speak gravely // 엄숙해지다 be awestruck ; be inspired with awe // 식은 아주 엄숙히 거행됐다 The ceremony was conducted with the utmost solemnity.

‡**엄습 掩襲** a surprise〔sudden〕 attack **—하다** make a sudden〔surprise〕 attack ; take 《the enemy》 by surprise ¶ 추위가 엄습해 왔다 The cold weather took the people by surprise. // 독수리가 토끼를 엄습했다 The eagle swooped down a hare. // 졸음이〔공포가〕 그들을 엄습했다 Sleep〔Fear〕 fell suddenly upon them. // 커다란 위험이 시가를 엄습했다 A great peril overtook the town.

엄시하 嚴侍下 having only one's father alive to serve〔look after〕

엄엄하다 奄奄— be short of breath ; be gasping (for breath)

엄연 儼然 —하다 (be) solemn ; grave ; stern ; majestic ; authoritative ¶ 엄연히 solemnly ; gravely ; with severity 〔dignity〕; authoritatively // 엄연한 사실 a grim〔stern〕 reality ; the stark fact ; the stern realities of life // 이 도덕률은 아직도 엄연히 존재하고 있다 This moral law is still in full force.

엄전스럽다 嚴全— ⇨ 엄전하다

엄전하다 嚴全— (be) decent ; modest ; well〔mild〕-mannered ; well-conducted ¶ 엄전한 부인 a lady with good manners ; a well-bred woman ¶ 말씨가〔처신이〕 엄전하다 be refined〔decent, modest〕 in speech〔manner〕

엄정 嚴正 exactness ; rigidity ; strictness ; rigor ; fairness **—하다** (be) exact ; strict ; fair ; impartial ; unprejudiced ¶ 엄정한 비판 an impartial criticism // 엄정한 의미에서 in the strict sense of the word // 엄정하게 다루다 deal with 《an affair》 in strict fairness 엄정히 행하다 deal with 《an affair》 in strict fairness

— 과학 an exact science **—주의** puritanism (종교·도덕상의) **— 중립** 《observe, keep》 strict neutrality

엄존 儼存 real existence **—하다** [사실이] (really) exist ; [법률이] be in full force

***엄중** 嚴重 strictness ; severity ; rigorousness ; closeness **—하다** (be) strict ; severe ; stringent ; stern ; rigorous ¶ 엄중히 strictly ; severely // 엄중한 규칙 a strict〔stringent〕 rule // 엄중한 조사 a close examination // 경찰의 엄중한 단속 strict police supervision // 엄중히 처벌하다 punish 《a person》 severely // 문단속을 엄중히 하다 secure the doors ; fasten the doors tightly // 엄중히 감시하다 guard strictly ; keep a strict watch 《over》 // 엄중히 금지하다 prohibit strictly // 엄중히 단속하다 enforce strict control 《on, over》

***엄지** [손의] the thumb ; the big finger ; [발의] the big toe

엄지 —紙 paper used for a check〔transaction memorandum〕

엄지머리 총각 —總角 a lifelong bachelor

엄지발가락 the big〔great〕 toe

엄지발톱 the nail of the big toe ; the big toe nail

****엄지손가락** the thumb ; a pollex

엄지손톱 the nail of the thumb ; the thumb nail

엄징 嚴懲 a severe〔heavy〕 punishment 〔chastisement〕 **—하다** punish〔chastise〕 《a person》 severely ; inflict a severe punishment 《on a person》

엄쪽 the counterfoil of a bill ; the stub of a check

엄책 嚴責 a severe reproof〔reprimand〕 ; a bitter〔harsh〕 criticism **—하다** scold 〔reprimand〕 severely〔harshly〕 ; give 《a person》 a sharp punishment

엄처시하 嚴妻侍下 petticoat government ¶ 엄처시하의 남편 a henpecked〔submissive〕 husband ; a man tied to his wife's apron strings // 엄처시하이다 be tied to one's wife's apron strings ; be wife-ridden ; be a henpecked husband ; be dominated by one's wife

***엄청나다** (be) absurd ; wild ; terrible ; ridiculous ; exorbitant ; surprising ; frightful ¶ 엄청나게 awfully ; terribly ; absurdly // 엄청나게 큰 very big ; huge ; monstrous ; gigantic // 엄청난 값 an exorbitant〔extravagant〕 price ; a ridiculously high price // 엄청난 생각 a wild〔fantastic, rash〕 idea // 엄청난 숫자 enormous 〔colossal, stupendous〕 number // 엄청나게 싸다 be dog-cheap ; be dirt-cheap // 엄청나게 춥지 It is jolly cold, isn't it? // 참 엄청나게 큰 개구리인데 What a monster of a frog this is! // 비도 엄청나게 오는데 What beastly rain! /How it rains! // 그렇게 엄청난 이야기가 있단 말인가 How can that be? /That's quite absurd. // 그의 성공은 참으로 엄청나다 His success is really surprising. // 그는 무슨 엄청난 짓을 할 게다 He is sure to set the Thames on fire. // 엄청난 이야기라 믿어지지 않았다 The extravagance of his story made us doubt him.

엄칙 嚴飭 severe admonition ; strict expostulation ; rigid warning〔caution〕 **—하다** admonish 《a person》 severely ; expostulate 《with a person》 strictly

엄친 嚴親 a stern〔strict〕 father ; [자기의] one's own father

엄탐 嚴探 a strict investigation ; a close search **—하다** search〔investigate〕 strictly〔closely〕 《for》 ; be on a sharp lookout 《for》 ¶ 범인을 엄탐중이다 A strict search is being made for the offender. /The police are hot on the trail of the culprit.

엄파이어 an umpire ¶ 엄파이어를 보다 act as umpire 《in a game》 ; umpire 《a game》

엄펑소니 a trick ; a swindle

엄펑스럽다 (be) swinding ; crooked ; deceitful ; cheating

엄폐 掩蔽 hiding ; concealment **—하다** cover up ; mask ; conceal ; suppress ; cover 《a fact》 dark ¶ 범죄의 흔적을 엄폐하다 cover up the traces of a crime

—물 a cover ; a shelter **—호(壕)** a covered trench ; an entrenchment ; a dugout ; a bunker ; a shelter

엄포 a bluff ; bluffing ; threat ; intimidation ; a menace ¶ 엄포 놓아 쫓아내다 scare 《a person》 away // 엄포 놓아 따르게 했다 We frightened him into submission. // 해고시킨다고 엄포 놓았다 He threatened to dismiss me.

****엄하다** 嚴— (be) severe ; strict ; stern ; rigid ; rigorous ; harsh ; stringent ; bitter ¶ 엄하게 severely ; strictly ; rigorously // 엄한 심문 a searching question // 엄하게 벌주다 punish severely // 엄하게 꾸짖다 scold severely // 법을 엄하게 시행하다 enforce a law with rigor // 자식에게 엄하다 be stern〔strict〕 to one's children // 저 선생님은 학생에게 엄하다 That teacher is severe with his pupils. // 규칙이 최근에 엄하게 됐다 The regulation have been tightened up recently. // 타인에게 관대하

고 자신에겐 엄할지어다 Be lenient to others, and severe with yourself.

엄한 嚴寒 the intense〔severe〕 cold ; the rigor of winter ¶ 엄한지절에 in the depth〔dead〕 of winter ; in the coldest season

엄형 嚴刑 severe〔heavy, harsh〕 punishment ¶ 엄형에 처해지다 be sentenced to severe punishment

엄호 掩護 cover(ing) ; protection ―하다 cover ; protect ; shelter 《from》 ¶ 엄호하에 under cover 《of》 ; backed up 《by》 // 작전을 엄호하다 cover an operation // 측면을 엄호하다 cover the flank // 해병대의 상륙을 엄호하다 cover the marines' landing // 포병대의 엄호하에 싸우다 fight under cover of the artillery

―대 a covering force ― 사격 a covering fire ; curtain fire ― 진지 a covering position ― 포화 a wall〔cover〕 of fire ; a barrage

엄혹 嚴酷 severity ; rigor ; harshness ―하다 (be) severe〔rigorous, harsh, hard, stringent〕

업 〖민속〗 a household mascot ; a luck animal〔person〕

업¹ 業 [직업] work ; an occupation ; a calling ; a profession (전문의) ; a (line of) business ; a trade ¶ …을 업으로 하다 be a . . . by profession ; make a profession〔business〕 《of》 // 부친의 업을 계승하다 succeed one's father in his occupation

업² 業 〖불교〗 Karma 《범》

업계 業界 business circles〔quarters, world〕 ; the industry ; the trade ¶ 업계의 거물 a big shot in the world of business // 업계의 화제가 되어 있다 be the talk of the trade // 업계를 재편성하다 reorganize the industry

―지 a trade paper〔magazine〕

업구렁이 〖민속〗 a luck snake ; 〖동물〗 a bluegreen snake

*업다 carry on one's back ; shoulder ¶ 아이를 업은 여자 a woman with her baby on her back ; a woman with baby on back

업두꺼비 a luck toad

업둥이 a foundling foster child

업무 業務 business ; business matters ; service ; duty ; operations ; affairs ¶ 업무의 확장 extension of business // 업무상의 질병이나 부상 sickness or injuries due to occupational cases // 업무에 진력하다 attend to one's business with diligence // 업무를 태만히 하다 neglect one's business // 이렇게 바쁜 시간에 농담이나 하고 다니면 업무량을 늘려 주겠다 Joke around at a busy time like this and I'll increase your work load.

― 관리 business management〔control〕 ― 담당 사원 an active〔a managing〕 partner ― 보고 a report on operation(s) ; a business〔an operational〕 report ―부 the Operation Department ; the Business Department ― 분담표 a work responsibility schedule 《미》 ― 사원 a member of management department ―상 과실 치사죄 an accidental〔involuntary〕 homicide arising out of duty ―상 보관 현금 cash in one's custody in the conduct of business ―상 질병〔부상〕 sickness〔injuries〕 due to occupational cases〔arising out of duty〕 ― 시간 office 〔business〕 hours ―용 for business use 〔purposes〕 ― 집행 the management of business ; the execution of one's duty ― 집행 방해 interference in the execution of one's duty 철도 수송 ― railroad transportation service

업보 業報 〖불교〗 retribution for the deeds of a former world

업숭이 a dull〔stupid〕 fellow ; a dunce ; a blockhead

업신여기다 despise ; scorn ; disdain ; look down upon ; make〔set〕 light of ; hold 《a person》 cheap ; slight ; treat〔regard〕 《a person》 with contempt ¶ 업신여기는 태도〔얼굴〕 a contemptuous air〔look〕 // 업신여김을 받다 be slighted ; be held in contempt // 부모를 업신여기다 slight one's parents // 업신여기는 눈으로 보다 eye 《a person》 with contempt ; look at 《a person》 contemptuously // 그는 너를 업신여긴다 He looks down upon you. // 사람을 업신여기지 마라 Do not hold me cheap. // 가난하다고 그를 업신여기지 마라 Do not disdain him because he is poor.

업왕 業王 the household deity of luck ; the God of Wealth

업원 業寃 〖불교〗 a retribution in this world for the sins of a previous life ; Karma effects

⁑업자 業者 businessman ; the trade ; traders 〔dealers, businessmen〕 concerned ; makers〔manufacturers〕 concerned ¶ 업자를 모으다 call in traders concerned

― 단체 a trade association

업저버 an observer ; [총칭] an observer delegation ¶ 업저버로서 참석하다 attend 《a conference》 as an observer〔in the capacity of observer〕

업저지 a girl baby-watcher〔-sitter〕

⁑업적 業績 [개인의] work ; achievements ; results ; contributions ; [회사 따위의] business result ¶ 물리학상의 업적 one's achievements in physics // 금년도의 업적 [회사 따위의] the results for this year // 업적을 올리다 produce achievements ; make a better showing

― 보고 a business report

업종 業種 types of industry〔enterprise〕 ; a category of business

―별 industrial classification ; classification by industry ¶ 업종별로 하다 classify by industry ―별 임금 prevailing wages by industry

업태 業態 business conditions〔status〕 ― **보고** [회사의] a business report ― **조사** a business conditions survey **금년도** ― [회사의] the results for this year

업히다 ① [등에] ride on ⦅a person's⦆ back ; be carried on ⦅a person's⦆ back ¶ 아이가 등에 업히다 a child gets on ⦅a person's⦆ back ② […위에] lie upon another ; be piled on ¶ 주전자 위에 찻잔이 업혀 있다 A teacup is placed on top of the teapot.

†**없다** ① [존재하지 않다] do not exist ; there is no... ¶ 없는 것보다는 낫다 be better than nothing // 없는 말을 퍼뜨리다 spread a false rumor // 병에 잉크가 조금 밖에 없다 There is little ink in the bottle. // 전송하는 사람이 없었다 No one came to see me off. // 이 백화점에는 없는 것이 없다 This department store carries everything. // 그는 우리 사무실에서 없어서는 안될 사람이다 He is a jewel〔gem〕 in our office. // 어제 전화했더니 넌 집에 없더라 I called you yesterday, but you weren't in.

② [소유하지 않다] have not〔no〕; do not have ¶ 돈 없이 without money // 없는 사람들 the poor (and needy) ; poor people // 있는 사람과 없는 사람 a have and a have-not // 그는 없는 집에 태어났다 He was born poor. /He was born of〔in〕 a poor family. // 저 사람은 자식이 없다 He has no children.

③ [결여] want ; lack ; be wanting〔lacking〕 ⦅in⦆ ; [다하다] be out ⦅of⦆ ; run short ⦅of⦆ ¶ 흥미 없는 uninteresting // 세간이 없는 방 a room empty of furniture // 재수 없다 be unlucky // 없어진 것으로 치고 단념하다 give up for lost // 자금이 없다 We lack〔are out of〕 funds. // 그는 용기가 없다 He is wanting in courage. / He lacks courage. // 이 강에는 수초가 없다 This river is clear of weeds. // 우물에 물이 없다 The well has run dry.

④ [눈에 띄지 않다] be gone〔missing〕; be lost ¶ 방금 책상 위에 두었던 책이 없다 I cannot find the book that I just put on the table. // 어디를 찾아도 지갑이 없다 I cannot find my purse anywhere. /My purse is nowhere to be found.

⑤ [결점 따위가] be free ⦅from⦆ ; be clear ⦅of⦆ ¶ 결점〔아픔, 잘못, 걱정〕이 없다 be free from faults〔pain, error, anxiety〕

⑥ [없다면] if there were not ; but for ; without ; except for ; if it were not for ¶ …이 없었더라면 but for ; except for ; without ; if it were not for // 너의 도움이 없었더라면 나는 성공 못했을 것이다 But for your help, I could not have succeeded. /If it had not been for your help, I should have failed.

⑦ [죽고 싶다] be deceased ; be defunct ¶ 부모 없는 아이 an orphan // 아버지가 없다 one's father is deceased ; have no father

⑧ [기타] ¶ 나는 웃을 수 밖에 없었다 I could not help laughing. // 어찌할 수 없다 I can't help it.

***없애다** [제거] remove ; get rid of ; do away with ; leave out ; [낭비] waste ; spend ; squander ; lose ¶ 해충을 없애다 exterminate harmful insects // 빈민굴을 없애다 clear slums // 사람을 죽여 없애다 kill〔slay, murder〕 a man // 장애물을 없애다 remove obstacles ; clear the way of obstacles // 이름을 명부에서 없애다 strike ⦅a person's⦆ name off a list // 돈을 다 써 없애다 throw one's money away ; run through one's fortune // 어떻게 하면 전쟁을 없앨 수 있을까 How can we abolish war?

없어지다 ① [분실하다] lose ; be〔get〕 lost ; be missing ; be gone ¶ 없어진 책 a lost〔missing〕 book // 면목이 없어지다 lose one's face // 고통이 이제 없어졌다 The pain has now passed. // 금고 속의 돈이 없어졌다 The money in the safes is gone. // 내 열쇠가 없어졌다 I've lost my key. /My key is missing.

② [다하다] [사물이 주어] run out〔low, short〕; be exhausted ; be used up ; be gone ; [사람이 주어] run out〔short〕 of ¶ 돈이 자꾸 없어진다 My money is going fast. /My money is rapidly running out. /I am running out of my money. // 식량이 없어졌다 Our food supplies have failed〔run out〕.

③ [소멸하다] disappear ; vanish ; be gone ; go away ¶ 희망이 없어지다 become hopeless // 열이 없어졌다 The fever has left〔broken〕. /I am free from fever. // 비가 오기 시작하니까 사람의 그림자가 없어졌다 The streets emptied 〔were emptied〕 in no time when it began to rain. // 이른 봄을 기다리는 마음도 눈이 오므로 없어졌다 Our hope for an early spring vanished when the snow fell. // 그 약은 외기에 쐬면 약효가 없어진다 The medicine loses its effect if exposed to the air.

없이 without ¶ 틀림〔의심〕없이 without fail〔doubt〕 // 할 수 없이 unavoidably // 그지없이 endlessly ; infinitely // 맥 없이 listlessly ; dejectedly // 휴일도 없이 without holidays // 정신 없이 absent-mindedly // 뜻없이 senselessly // 한푼 없이 되다 become penniless // …없이는 못한다 I cannot do without ⦅that⦆. /I cannot dispense with ⦅that⦆. // 공기 없이는 하루도 살아갈 수가 없다 Without〔But for, If there were no, Were it not for〕 air, we could not live even a single day. // 신문 없이는 세계 정세를 모른다 But for newspapers, we could not know what is going on in the

world.
없이살다 live in poverty〔want〕; be badly 〔poorly〕 off ; make a poor living ; lead an indigent life
엇- obliquely ; aslant ; diagonally
엇가다 go awry ; deviate ; turn aside ; diverge 《from》; be perverse (언동이) ¶ 줄이 엇가다 a line gets off ; tilt ; slant ; be out of line // 엇가는 말을 하다 make perverse remarks
엇갈리다 cross (each other) ; miss each other on the road ¶ 가슴에 희비가 엇갈리다 joy and grief alternate in one's breast // 우리 편지가 서로 엇갈렸다 Our letters have crossed. // 그와 나는 엇갈렸다 He came just after I had left.
엇걸다 make a diagonal loop ; stack ¶ 소총을 엇걸다 stack rifles // 상자를 끈으로 엇걸어 매다 put the ribbon around the box in a diagonal loop
엇걸리다 be made in a diagonal loop ; be stacked
엇겯다 weave〔loop〕 at an angle
엇결 cross-grain (of wood)
엇구뜰하다 (be) rather tasty
엇구수하다 [음식이] (be) rather tasty ; [이야기가] rather humorous〔amusing〕
엇그루 a tree stump that has been cut off diagonally
엇깎다 cut obliquely ; cut slantwise
엇나가다 ⇨ 엇가다
엇대다 ① [어긋나게] fix〔put〕 askew 〔obliquely〕 ¶ 옷에 헝겊을 엇대다 put a patch on one's clothes cockeyed // 책상을 고칠 때 다리를 엇댔다 In repairing the table I put the leg on crooked.
② [비꼬아] insinuate ; make innuendo ; satirize ¶ 말을 엇대고 하다 make an insinuating remark
엇되다 (be) snobbish ; self-important ¶ 엇된 놈 a snob
엇뜨기 a squinter
엇뜨다 squint (one's eyes)
엇먹다 [날이] cut at an angle〔askew〕; [비꼬다] distort 《remarks》; twist 《words》
엇메다 strap under one arm and over the other shoulder (across one's chest) ¶ 가방을 엇메다 sling a satchel from the shoulder across one's chest
엇바꾸다 exchange (with each other) ; interchange ¶ 책을 엇바꾸다 exchange books with each other
엇베다 cut diagonally〔at an angle〕 ¶ 종이를 엇베다 cut paper diagonally
엇보 一保 mutual surety〔security, guarantee〕 ¶ 두 사람이 엇보를 서다 Two persons stand surety for each other.
엇부루기 a young ox ; a male calf
엇붙다 《a thing》 touch at an angle
엇비뚜름하다 be a bit crooked on one side
엇비슷하다 be about alike ; be almost similar ; be nearly the same ¶ 높이가 엇비슷한 두 책상 two tables of almost even height // 그와 나는 키가 엇비슷하다 He is about as tall as I am.
엇서다 be perverse ; be cross-grained ; be self-centered ¶ 엇선 놈 a curmudgeon ; a selfish person
엇섞다 mix in alternation
엇셈 an offset ; settlement〔balancing〕 of accounts **—하다** settle〔balance〕 accounts
엇송아지 a young ox ; a male calf
-었겠다 [추측] probably did ; I should think ¶ 그는 스물은 못 되었겠다 He is under twenty, I should think
-었느냐 [의문] whether it was〔did〕 ¶ 너 어디 있었느냐 하루 종일 보이지 않으니 Where have you been that I haven't seen you all day long?
-었는지 [불확실] whether it was〔did〕 ¶ 누구였는지 아는가 Do you know who it was? // 갔었는지도 모른다 Maybe he went. // 그가 정말 그런 말을 했는지 기억하는가 Do you remember whether he really said that?
-었었다 did (at an earlier time) ; had done ¶ 갔었었다 went (and back) // 왔었었다 came (and left again) ; was here (but isn't now) // 먹었었다 ate (but is hungry again)
-었었으나 ¶ 처음엔 꽤 문제되었었으나 이젠 순조로이 진행된다 At first it was quite a problem, but now it's going smoothly.
엉거능측하다 (be) crafty ; wily ; full of sly ways
엉거주춤하다 hover ; hesitate ; waver 《between》 ¶ 엉거주춤하지 말고 결정해라 Get off the fence and make up your mind. // 엉거주춤하지 말고 서든지 앉든지 해라 Either stand up or sit down stop hovering about! // 그는 갈까 말까 잠시 엉거주춤했다 He hovered for a while unable to make up his mind whether he should go or not.
엉겁 stickiness ; a sticky covering 《of something》 ¶ 손에 엿이 엉겁을 했다 The hands were all sticky with taffy.
엉겁결에 unexpectedly ; all of a sudden ; suddenly ; at lightning speed ; before one knows it
*엉겅퀴** the wild thistle ; Cirsium japonicum (학명)
엉구다 firm 《a plan》 up ; get 《a plan》 accomplished ; arrange
엉그름 a crack that has spread as a mud floor dries ; a mud crack
엉글벙글 bubbling ; gurgling ¶ 아기가 엉글벙글 웃다 a baby chortles
엉금엉금 crawling ; creeping ; on all fours ¶ 엉금엉금 기어가다 go on all fours
엉기다 ① [응축] congeal ; curdle (우유 따위) ; clot (피가) ; coagulate ; thicken ¶ 엉긴 피 clotted blood // 우유가 엉기다 milk

curdles // 국이 잘 엉기었다 The soup has thickened nicely.
② [뒤얽히다] be all tangled up
엉기정기 pell-mell ; in a jumble ; in confusion ¶ 엉기정기 벌여 놓다 place 《things》 in disorder
엉너리 bamboozlements to ingratiate oneself ; deceitful ingratiation ¶ 엉너리치다 try all sorts of tricks to win favor // 상사에게 엉너리치다 ingratiate oneself〔curry favor〕 with one's superiors
엉너릿손 the skill of ingratiating oneself
엉덩방아 a fall on one's backside〔behind, buttocks〕 ; a pratfall 《미·구》 ¶ 의자에 잘못 앉아 마루바닥에 엉덩방아를 찧었다 I missed the chair and sat right down on the floor.
엉덩방아를 찧다 관용 fall on one's backside〔buttocks〕 ; land on one's rear ; have〔take〕 a pratfall 《미·구》 ; do a half-split
***엉덩이** the buttocks ; the rump ; the hips ¶ 엉덩이가 큰 여자 a woman with full hips // 엉덩이를 때리다 (벌로서) spank a child // 여자의 엉덩이를 쫓아다니다 hang about〔dangle after〕 a girl ; chase after a girl's skirt // 어떤 남자가 나한테 음란한 말을 하고 엉덩이를 만졌단 말이야 A man said dirty words and touched my behind. // 나는 엉덩이가 무거워 못한다 I just can't seem to bring myself to do it. // 이 남자는 엉덩이가 무겁다 This guy's got lead in his pants.
엉덩이가 무겁다〔느리다〕 관용 be sluggish ; be slow ; be lazy ; [오래 머무르다] stay too long ; outstay 《a person's》 welcome
엉덩잇바람 swaying walks
엉덩잇짓 swaying〔swinging〕 one's hips ; hip movements **—하다** sway〔swing〕 one's hips ; make hip movements
엉덩춤 a hip dance ; a hula ¶ 엉덩춤 추는 사람 a hip dancer ; a hip twister // 엉덩춤을 추다 dance a hula
엉덩판 the hips ; the buttocks ; the rump ¶ 엉덩판이 크다 have big hips
엉두덜거리다 be muttering and grumbling ; be bitching and griping
엉두덜엉두덜 muttering and grumbling ; bitching and griping
†**엉뚱하다** (be) extraordinary ; extravagant ; fantastic ; unreasonable ; outrageous ; preposterous ¶ 엉뚱한 생각 a bold idea ; an extravagant notion // 엉뚱한 사람 a wild-eyed person ; a wild-eyed visionary ; a crazy fool // 엉뚱한 소리를 하다 say extravagant things // 그는 21세기에 이상국을 건설하겠다는 엉뚱한 생각을 가지고 있다 He has some wild-eyed scheme to build a Utopia in the twenty-first century. // 그의 덕택으로 나도 엉뚱하게 협의를 받고 있다 Thanks to him, I've come under suspicion too. // 그는 매우 조용해 보이지만 가끔 엉뚱한 짓을 한다 He seems very quiet, but sometimes he does something really off the wall.
엉망 a mess ; (in) bad shape ; a muddle ; a wreck ¶ 엉망이 되다 get out of shape ; be spoiled // 방안이 엉망이었다 The whole room was in utter disorder. // 내 모자가 엉망이다 My hat is in bad shape. /My hat was crushed out of shape. /My hat is a mess.
엉버틈하다 (be) spread-out widely
엉성하다 ① [마르다] (be) gaunt ; raw-boned ; thin ; sparse ; be skin and bones ¶ 말라서 뼈만 엉성하다 be wasted to a skeleton // 뜰에 풀이 엉성하게 났다 The garden is thinly covered with grass. // 잎이 떨어져서 나무가 엉성하게 보인다 The trees look thin with most of their leaves fallen.
② [안째이다] (be) thin ; sparse ; loose ; coarse ¶ 엉성하게 자란 나무가지 loosely-grown twigs // 엉성하게 짜다 knit with large stitches
③ [눈에 서툴다] (be) unfamiliar ; [탐탁치 않다] (be) unsatisfactory
엉세판 penury ; destitution ; utter poverty
엉엉 bawling ; squalling ¶ 엉엉 울다 cry bitterly ; cry one's heart out ; bawl one's head off
엉엉거리다 cry bitterly ; cry one's heart out ; [하소연하다] complain of one's hard lot ; deplore one's misfortune
엉정벙정 with superfluous things scattered about **—하다** be all cluttered up
엉클다 tangle ; make a tangle of ; mix up
엉클샘 [미국 정부·미국인] Uncle Sam 《속》
***엉클어지다** [실·머리털이] get tangled ; [일이] be〔become〕 entangled ; be complicated ¶ 엉클어진 머리털 tangled〔matted〕 hair ; hair in tangles // 엉클어진 것을 풀다 disentangle ; unravel 《the tangles》 // 실이 엉클어졌다 The thread is tangled. // 일이 엉클어졌다 The matter became complicated. /The affair is in a tangle.
엉큼대왕 —大王 a man of wild〔grandiose〕 ambition ; a deep one
엉큼성큼 with long strides〔steps〕 ¶ 엉큼성큼 걷다 walk with long steps ; stride ; stalk
엉큼스럽다 be full of deep-seated ambition ; (be) preposterous ; inwardly bold 〔audacious, presumptuous〕 ¶ 엉큼한 사람 a deep one ; a man swollen with suppressed ambition // 엉큼한 생각 a wild ambition〔scheme〕 ; an inordinate desire
엉큼엉큼 with long strides ⇨ 엉큼성큼
엉큼하다 be full of deep-seated ambition
엉키다 get tangled ⇨ 엉클어지다
엉터리 ① a fake ; a sham ; a gyp ; a clip ¶ 이 타자기는 엉터리다 This typewriter is a piece of junk. // 그는 일을 엉터리로 한다 He does a slapdash job.

② [근거] ground ; foundation ¶ 엉터리없는 수작 groundless remarks // 그 값이 엉터리없다 The prices are outrageous.
③ [윤곽] framework ; layout ; general plan ¶ 일의 엉터리가 잡히다 the general plan of a job is drawn up〔laid out〕; the framework of a project is set up

엊그저께, 엊그제 a few days ago (수일 전) ; the day before yesterday (그저께)

엊빠르다 ⇨ 어지빠르다

엊저녁 last evening ; yesterday evening ; last night

*****엎다** upset ; overturn ; overthrow ; turn 〔tip〕 over ; turn upside〔face〕 down ; capsize (배를) ¶ 우유잔을 엎다 upset a glass of milk // 책을 엎어 놓다 put a book face down // 책상을 엎다 overturn a desk // 현 정부를 엎다 overthrow the present government // 성난 파도가 배를 엎다 raging waves capsize a boat

엎드러뜨리다 make a person fall on his face

엎드러지다 fall down ; fall on one's face ¶ 문지방에 걸려서 엎드러지다 tip over the threshold // 엎드러지면 코 닿을 데 right in front of your nose ; just around the corner

엎드려쏴 〖군사〗 firing from a prone 〔lying-down〕 position ; prone fire
— 자세 prone position

엎드려팔굽혀펴기 〖체조〗 push-up

***엎드리다** prostrate oneself ; lie on the ground ; throw oneself down on the knees ¶ 제단 앞에 엎드리다 prostrate oneself before an altar // 엎드려 자다 sleep on one's stomach

엎디다 ⇨ 엎드리다

엎어놓다 put 《a thing》 face〔top〕 down 〔upside-down〕

엎어누르다 press down ; oppress ; suppress ; overwhelm

*****엎어지다** be upset ; be turned over ; be overthrown ; be turned upside down ; fall on one's face ; fall down ; capsize (배가) ¶ 엎어지면 코 닿을 데 right in front of your nose ; a stone's-throw away ; just around the corner // 얼음판에 엎어지다 fall down on the ice // 계획이 엎어지다 one's plan is upset // 배가 엎어지다 a boat capsizes // 현 정부가 엎어지다 the present government is overthrown

***엎지르다** spill ; slop ¶ 마루에 물을 엎지르다 spill〔slop〕 water on the floor ; slop the floor // 그릇에서 물을 엎지르다 spill water from a vessel

엎쳐뵈다 humble oneself ; kowtow ; bow

엎치다 ⇨ 엎다

엎치락뒤치락 up-and-down ; turning over and over **—하다** toss about ; turn over and over ¶ 잠이 안와서 엎치락뒤치락하다 toss about on the bed unable to get to sleep // 마음이 엎치락뒤치락하다 be capricious ; be fickle ; be inconstant

엎친 데 덮치다 add to one's troubles ; make things worse ; Ill comes often on the back of worse. ¶ 엎친 데 덮치기로 what is worse ; to add to one's miseries ; to make things worse // 불행이 엎친 데 덮치다 have one misfortune on top of another // 엎친 데 덮치기로 비까지 왔다 To make matters worse, it started to rain.

에¹ [감탄사] well ; well now ; let me see ; uh ¶ 에 어디로 갈까 Well, where shall we go ?

†에² ① [시간] at ; in ; on ¶ 2시에 at two // 아침〔저녁〕에 in the morning 〔evening〕 // 제 시간에 in time // 일요일에 on Sunday
② [나이] at ¶ 일곱살에 학교에 가다 go to school at the age of seven
③ [장소] at ; in ; on ¶ 방에 in the room // 오른편에 on the right hand // 서울에 도착하다 arrive in *Seoul*
④ [방향] to ; in ¶ 학교에 가다 go to school // 땅에 떨어지다 fall to the ground // 전쟁에 나가다 go to war
⑤ [간접 목적] to ¶ 은행에 보내다 send 《it》 to the bank // 도서관에 책을 기증하다 donate a book to the library
⑥ [비례] at ; in ; for ; by ; per ¶ 하루에 두번 twice a day // 10년에 한번 once in ten years // 1,000원에 팔다 sell for a thousand *won* // 설탕은 1파운드에 얼마냐 How much is sugar a pound ?
⑦ [관련] for ; to ; in ; of ¶ 그 사람에 관해서 concerning that person // 건강에 좋다 be good for health // 감기에 걸리다 catch a cold // 취미에 맞다 be to one's taste // 공부하기에 바쁘다 be busy studying
⑧ [동작주] by ; with ¶ 총알에 맞다 be hit by a bullet // 그의 박학에 놀랐다 I marveled at his profound scholarship.
⑨ [원인] for ; because ; since ¶ 추위에 감각을 잃었다 I was numb from 〔with, because of〕 the cold. // 덤비는 바람에 책을 가지고 갈 것을 잊어버렸다 In my hurry I forgot to bring the book.
⑩ [열거] and ; and all that ; and what not ; and the like ¶ 술에 고기에 잘 먹었다 I have had enough drinks, meat and the like.
⑪ [대조] against ; on ; with ; and ; in contrast (with) ¶ 흰 바탕에 금 무늬 a gold figure on〔against〕 a white background // 그 여자는 노란 저고리에 다홍치마를 입었다 She wore a yellow coat and a pink skirt.

*****에게** to ; at ; for ; by 《a person》 ¶ 우리에게 돈을 주다 give us money // 어머님에게 편지를 쓰다 write to one's mother // 남에게 일을 해주다 do the work for someone else // 아이에게 밥을 먹이다 feed the child // 남에게 돈을 먹히다 have one's money swindled away by 《a person》 // 영국 사람에게 배우다 be taught by an Englishman

에게도 to〔at, for, by〕《a person》 also〔even〕 ¶ 한씨에게도 홍씨에게도 편지를 쓰다 write letters both to Mr. *Han* and to Mr. *Hong*∥병난 사람에게도 일을 하게 하다 make even the sick people work

*__에게로__ toward〔to〕《a person》 ¶ 어머니에게로 가거라 Go to your mother.∥그 허물이 누구에게로 돌아갈까 Who(m) does that mistake go back to?∥그녀의 사랑이 그에게로 옮겨 갔다 Her love drifted to him.

에게서 from《a person》 ¶ 어머님에게서 편지가 오다 receive a letter from one's mother∥그 말은 친구에게서 들었다 I heard that from a friend of mine.∥이 돈이 누구에게서 나왔느냐 Who(m) did this money come from?

에게 해 一海 the Aegean Sea

에고 ego
—이스트 an egoist **—이즘** egoism **—티즘** egotism

에구구 Oh oh! ; Oh dear! ¶ 에구구 이거 웬일이야 Oh, dear, what's the matter?

에구데구 [우는 꼴] (crying and) wailing

에구(머니) ⇨ 아이고(머니)

에굽다 be curved at a slight angle

에그그 ⇨ 에끄

에끄 Oh! ; Oh my goodness! ; good heavens! ¶ 에끄 바위 밑에 뱀이 있네 Goodness, there is a snake under the rock!

에끼 How could you! /Ugh! /Oh, no! /Fie! /Damn it! ¶ 에끼 나쁜 놈 Ugh! What a dreadful person you are!∥에끼 그런 말 하지 마라 Oh, no! Don't say such a thing.

에끼다 [상쇄하다] cancel out ; nullify ; cross off《accounts》; write off《debts》; strike off《a balance》; offset each other ¶ 이것으로 그 손실을 에낄 수 있다 This will offset the loss.

*__에나멜__ enamel ¶ 에나멜을 바르다 enamel
— 구두 enameled shoes ; patent〔enameled〕 leather shoes **—선** enamel wire **—질(質)** enamel **— 페인트** enamel paint

에너지 〖물리〗 energy ¶ 일에 에너지를 쏟다 direct one's energies to one's task
—량 energy content of (cosmic rays) **—론(論)** energetics **— 보존 법칙** the principle〔law〕 of the conservation of energy **— 혁명** a revolutionary change in the form of energy used ; a revolution in energy ; an energy revolution **— 효율〔양자〕** energy efficiency〔quantum〕 **결합 —** binding energy **열〔전기〕 —** heat〔electrical〕 energy **운동 —** kinetic〔actual, motive〕 energy **잠재 —** latent〔potential〕 energy **화학 —** chemical energy

에넘느레하다 lie scattered about

에누리 [비싸게] overcharge ; [감가] reduction of〔in〕 price ; discount ; [과장] exaggeration **—하다** [비싸게] overcharge ; [깎다] bid low ; beat down the price ; haggle ; [과장] exaggerate ; overstate ¶ 에누리하지 않고 without haggling∥마구 에누리하다 drive the hardest bargain《with the dealer》∥좀 에누리해서 말하면 If I may be allowed a little exaggeration∥에누리 없이 얼마요 Tell me your lowest price.∥저 가게에서는 늘 에누리해서 부른다 That store always overcharges.∥그렇게 에누리하지 마십시오 Don't bid so low.∥에누리는 없다 We have no second price.

에는 as for ; to ; at ; in ¶ 내 생각에는 in my opinion〔view〕∥일기가 좋은 날에는 on a fine day∥그래 미국에는 언제 떠나실 예정입니까 Well, when are you leaving for the States?∥연극에는 두 가지 종류가 있다 There are two kinds of drama.

*__에다__[1] ⇨ 에이다

에다[2] into ; onto ; upon ; for ; to ¶ 종이에다 쓰다 write it (down) on paper∥책상 위에다 책을 놓다 put a book on the desk∥벽에다 지도를 걸다 hang a map on〔to〕 the wall∥5에다 6을 보태다 add 6 to 5∥무엇에다 쓰느냐 What is it used for?

*__에덴__ 〖성경〗 Eden
— 동산 the garden of Eden

에델바이스 〖식물〗 an edelweiss

에도 to ; at ; in ; also ; either ; even ¶ 가는 데에도 오는 데에도 both in going and coming back∥밤에도 못자다 can't〔don't〕 sleep at night either〔even at night〕∥일요일에도 극장에 가다 go to the theater on Sundays too (as well as other days)∥그것은 서울에도 부산에도 없다 They have it neither in *Seoul* nor in *Pusan*.∥무슨 일에도 시기와 장소가 있는 법이다 There is a time and a place for everything.

에돌다 hover around shy ; linger hesitantly ; hang around without doing anything ; make a detour ¶ 암초를 에돌다 steer clear of the rocks∥에돌지 말고 일 좀 해라 Stop hanging around empty-handed, do something!

에두르다 ① encircle ; surround ; enclose ¶ 집을 돌담으로 에두르다 enclose a house with a stone wall
② [말을] make a roundabout statement ; resort to circumlocution ; get around〔skirt〕 a subject ¶ 말을 에둘러 하다 talk in a roundabout way

에뜨거라 Oh my! ; Oh (I thought I'd jump out of my skin)!

에라 ① [체념] oh well ; all right ; oh my ¶ 에라 그럼 극장에 가자 All right then, let's go to the show.∥에라 일이 다 틀렸다 Oh my! Everything went wrong.
② [주의·환기] hey ; hey there ; you there ¶ 에라 비켜라 Hey there, move aside.
③ [금지] Don't! /Stop!

에러 an error ; a bungle ; a fumble (공을

헛잡음) ¶ 야수(野手)의 에러 a fielder's error // 투수〔포수〕의 에러 a battery error // 에러를 범하다 make an error ; fumble
에로 [에로티시즘] eroticism ; [형용사적] erotic ; obscene ; sexual ; sensual
— 문학 pornography — 사진 a pornographic〔an obscene〕 photograph〔picture〕 ; an erotic photograph — 소설 a sexy novel — 영화 a purple film — 잡지 an obscene magazine of sexy stories
에로스 [사랑의 신] Eros
에루화 Oh what fun !
에만 ① [장소] just〔only〕 to〔at, in〕 ¶ 다방에만 드나든다 He does nothing but visit tea rooms. ② [사물] only ; simply ; ... alone ¶ 그는 한 가지 일에만 열중하고 있다 He is absorbed in only one thing.
*에메랄드 〖광물〗 an emerald
에멜무지로 ① [시험삼아] on trial ; tentatively ; as an experiment ; to see 《how it is》 ¶ 에멜무지로 해보다 have a trial ; have a try ; give 《a thing》 a trial ② [느슨히] 《tie it》 loosely
에베레스트 [히말라야의] Mt. Everest
에보나이트 [경화 고무] ebonite ; hard rubber
에부수수하다 ⇨ 부수수(—하다)
에비 Look out ! /Mustn't touch ! / Naughty-naughty !
*에서 ① [장소] at ; in ¶ 집에서 일하다 work at home // 공원에서 산보하다 take a walk in the park
② [출발점] from ¶ 2시에서 3시 사이에 between two and three // 학교에서 돌아오다 come back from school // 기차에서 내리다 get off〔down from〕 the train // 5페이지에서 시작하다 begin at page 5 // 말에서 떨어지다 be thrown off a horse // 창문에서 뛰어내리다 jump out of a window // 대학에서 쫓겨나다 be expelled from the university // 해는 동쪽에서 뜬다 The sun rises in the east. // 열에서 둘을 빼면 여덟이 남는다 When you take two from ten, it leaves eight. // 초봉은 70만원에서 75만원이다 The commencing〔starting〕 salary ranges from 700,000 to 750,000 *won*.
③ [주격] ¶ 우리 학교에서 이겼다 Our school won. // 회사에서 나한테 시계를 주었다 The company gave me a watch.
④ [동기·원인] from ; out of ¶ 책임감에서 from a sense of duty〔responsibility〕 // 호기심에서 out of curiosity // 모두가 시기심에서 저지른 일이었다 That was all done out of envy.
⑤ [견지] from ; by ; according to ¶ 교육적 견지에서 보면 from an educational point of view
⑥ [보다] ¶ 이에서 더 큰 사랑이 없나니 There is no greater love than this.
에서도 at〔from〕 《a person》 also 〔either〕 ; even at〔from〕 ¶ 회의에는 일본에서도 사람이 왔다 People came to this conference from Japan too.
에서만 only〔just〕 at〔in, from〕 ¶ 우리의 기백은 오로지 시단에서만 찾아 볼 수 있다 The spirit of Korea can be (truly) seen only in the field of poetry.
에세이 an essay
에센스 [정수] essence
에스 ① [알파벳] the letter "S" ② [여학생간의 동성애인] one's sis〔sister〕 ; one's pet ③ [의복의 사이즈] S ; small (size)
에스겔서 —書 〖성경〗 The Book of Ezekiel ; Ezekiel 《Ezek.》
에스더서 —書 〖성경〗 The Book of Esther ; Esther 《Esth.》
에스라서 —書 〖성경〗 The Book of Ezra ; Ezra
에스오에스 [조난 신호] an SOS (call) ¶ 에스오에스를 발하다〔수신하다〕 send out〔pick up〕 an SOS (call)
⁑에스컬레이션 〖군사〗 escalation ¶ 투쟁의 에스컬레이션에 의한 전면 전쟁의 야기 further escalation of conflict into an all-out war
에스컬레이터 an escalator ; a moving staircase
— 조항(條項) an escalator clause
에스컬레이트 —하다 escalate ¶ 분쟁이 에스컬레이트하여 전면 전쟁이 되었다 The conflict escalated into an all-out war.
에스코트 [행위] escort ; [사람] an escort
⁑에스키모 an Eskimo 《*pl.* ~, ~(e)s》 ; an Esquimau 《*pl.* ~x》 ¶ 에스키모의 Eskimo
에스페란토 〖언어〗 Esperanto
—주의자(사용자) an Esperantist
에스프리 esprit 《프》
에야디야 Yo-ho ! ; Yo-heave-ho !
에어 air
—메일(포스트) air mail〔post〕 — 브레이크 an air brake — 컨디셔너 an air conditioner — 포켓 an air pocket —포트 an airport
에우다 ① [에워싸다] encircle ; surround ② [지우다] cross out〔off〕 ; strike off 〔out〕 ; eliminate ¶ 계약서에서 한 조목을 에우다 cross an item off a written contract
에우로페 [신화] Europe
*에움길 a roundabout way ; a long way round ¶ 에움길을 가다 go a roundabout way ; take the long way around
†에워가다 ① [우회] go a long way around ¶ 길을 에워가다 go a long way around ; take the roundabout way ; make a detour ② [지우다] strike out 《an entry in a ledger》
*에워싸다 surround ; enclose ; encircle ; hem in ¶ 집을 담으로 에워싸다 enclose a house with a wall // 적을 에워싸다 surround the enemy // 삼면이 산으로 에워싸이다 be surrounded on three sides by hills // 사람들이 영화 배우를 에워싼다 People crowd round a movie actor.

에의 《the invitation》 to ; at ; in ¶ 성공에의 길 the road to success
에이다 [도려내다] gouge 《out》 ; hollow out ; scrape out ¶ 바가지 속을 에이다 hollow out a gourd // 통나무를 에이어서 함지박을 만들다 hollow a log into a large bowl // 살을 에이는 듯이 춥다 be cutting 〔piercing, biting〕 cold ; be nippy ; the cold cuts right through you
에이레 Eire
에이스 ① the ace ; the leading player ② [카드놀이] an ace
에이에프피 AFP 《Agence France Presse》
에이커 an acre
‡에이프런 [앞치마] an apron ; [비행장의] an apron ¶ 에이프런을 걸치다 wear an apron
— 스테이지 an apron stage
에이 피 AP ; A. P. 《Associated Press》
에인절피시 〖물고기〗 an angelfish
에잇 〖불쾌〗 Darn 《it, me, you》 ! / Damn ! ¶ 에잇 빌어먹을 Damn it ! / Hang it ! // 에잇 맘대로 해라 O, you may do as you please ! // 에잇 될대로 되어라 Go to hell〔the devil〕 !
에참 Shuck ! ; Damn ! ; Darn !
에칭 [작품] an etching ; [기술] etching
에카페 ECAFE 《the Economic Commission for Asia and the Far East》
에쿠아도르 Ecuador
— 사람 an Ecuadorian
에크 Oh ! /Oh my goodness ! /Heavens ! Dear me !
*에테르 〖물리·화학〗 ether
에토스 ethos
에튀드 an étude 《프》 ; a study
에트랑제 an étranger 《프》 ; a stranger
에티켓 etiquette ; good manners ¶ 식사의 에티켓 table manners // 에티켓을 지키다 observe the rules of etiquette // 에티켓에 어긋나다 be against etiquette ; be not proper
에틸 〖화학〗 ethyl ¶ 에틸의 ethylic
—알코올 ethyl〔grain〕 alcohol
에틸렌 〖화학〗 ethylene
— 가스 ethylene gas 염화 — ethylene chloride
에페 〖펜싱〗 an épée
에펠 탑 —塔 the Eiffel Tower
에폭 an epoch
— 메이커 an epoch maker
에프엠 FM 《Frequency Modulation》 ; F. M. ; f-m ; f. m.
—국 an FM station — 방송 an FM broadcast
‡에피소드 [삽화] an episode〔incident〕 ; [일화] an anecdote ¶ 그에게는 많은 에피소드가 있다 There are many episodes told of him.
에필로그 [끝맺음말] an epilogue
에헤 [가소로움·기막힐 때] Oh ! ; Oh my ! ; Good lord !
에헴 ahem —하다 hem ; clear one's throat
‡엑스 ① [미지·미정의 것] X ; an unknown quantity〔factor, entity〕 ② [약] an extract〔essence〕 《of beef》
—(광)선 X-ray(s) — 세대 X Generation (전체) ; a GenXer (개인)
엑스트라 an extra (hand) ; a super ¶ 엑스트라 노릇을 하다 play an extra part 《in a picture》 // 엑스트라를 고용하다 hire extra hands 《for a movie》
— 여배우 extra girls〔ladies〕
엑스퍼트 an expert
엑스형 —形 X-shape
엑조틱 exotic —하다 be exotic〔foreign〕
엔 [일본의 화폐 단위] yen 《¥》
엔간하다 (be) considerable ; fair ; decent ; tolerable ; passable ; [구어] extraordinary ; terrible ; terrific ¶ 엔간히 fairly ; pretty ; tolerably ; considerably ; decently // 엔간한 교육 a good education // 엔간한 수입 a handsome income // 엔간한 거리 a good distance // 엔간한 미인 an awfully beautiful girl ; a terrific looker // 이익을 엔간히 올리다 make a good profit // 영어를 엔간히 한다 He speaks English fairly well. // 그는 엔간히 개를 무서워 한다 He is terribly afraid of dogs.
엔굽이치다 [강이] bend ; wind ; meander ¶ 강이 평야를 엔굽이쳐 흐른다 A river winds〔meanders〕 through open field.
엔담 an enclosure ; an encircling wall
엔들 even though ; even ; also ; too ¶ 그만한 것이 우리 집엔들 없으랴 What makes you think we wouldn't have such a thing at our house too ? // 명공엔들 실수가 없으랴 Even Homer sometimes nods.
엔조이 —하다 enjoy 《life》
엔지 〖영화〗 N. G. 《No good》
엔지니어 an engineer
엔진 an engine ¶ 엔진을 걸다 start an engine ; [크랭크를 돌려] crank up an engine // 엔진을 멈추다 stop an engine // 엔진이 고장나다 have some engine trouble ; an engine is out of order // 엔진이 걸렸다 The engine caught. // 엔진이 이상해졌다 Something went wrong with the engine. // 엔진을 점검해야 할 것 같습니다 Maybe you need a turn-up.
가스 터빈 — a gasturbine engine 선박용 — a marine engine 항공 — an aero-engine
엔테베 Entebbe
엔트로피 〖물리〗 an entropy
엔트리 [참가 등록] an entry ¶ 엔트리를 마치다 enter oneself 《for a contest》
엘레지 an elegy
엘렉트라 콤플렉스 Electra complex
엘렉트로닉스 electronics
엘렉트론 〖전자〗 an electron
†엘리베이터 an elevator 《미》 ; a lift 《영》 ; [화물용] a hoist ; a freight elevator 《미》 ¶ 엘리베이터의 버튼 the up〔down〕 button // 엘리베이터를 타고 올라가다〔내려가다〕 go up〔down〕 in an elevator

— 운전원 an elevator operator〔boy, girl〕
*엘리트 [총칭] the elite 《of society》; the chosen (few)
— 의식 elitism ; elite consciousness
엘바 섬 Elba Island
엘베 강 —江 the Elbe River
엘에스디 LSD 《lysergic acid diethylamide》
엘피(레코드) an L.P. record 《a long playing record》
엘피지 LPG 《liquefied petroleum gas》
엠 ① [글자] the letter "M" ② [돈] money ③ [음경] penis ④ [경도] menses ; menstruation ⑤ [의복의 사이즈] M ; medium (size)
엠피 [헌병] an M.P. ; the military police
엥 [짜증나고·성나고·딱할 때] Oof! ; Oh! ; Hmph!
엥겔 [독일 통계학자] Engel, Loreng Ernest (도 1821—96)
— 계수 Engel's Coefficient — 법칙 Engel's law
여 [물속의 바위] a sunken rock in the sea ; a reef
여 女 a woman ; a girl ⇨ 여자
-여 餘 more than ; over ; above ; and more ; in excess of ¶ 백여 명 a hundred odd men // 20여 년 more than twenty years ; twenty odd years
‡여가 餘暇 leisure ; spare time ; off hours ¶ 여가가 없다 have no time to spare // 여가에 독서하다 read in one's leisure hours ; pass one's spare time in reading // 여가를 이용하다 make use of one's spare time // 일의 여가를 타서 in the intervals of one's work // 가르치랴 책을 쓰랴 여가가 없다 Between teaching and writing, I have little time to spare.
여가수 女歌手 a female〔woman〕singer ; a songstress
여각 餘角 『기하』 the complementary angle
여간 如干 some ; a little ¶ 그는 여간한 일에는 성내지 않는다 He hardly gets angry over trifles. // 그를 거기서 보고 나는 여간 놀라지 않았다 I was not a little surprised to see him there. // 그는 여간 영리하지 않다 He is remarkably clever. // 아이를 기르기란 여간 어려운 일이 아니다 It is no easy thing to bring up a child. // 그는 여간해서 살아날 것 같지 않다 His recovery is beyond hope.
여간내기 如干— a man of mediocre abilities ; a mediocrity ¶ 그는 여간내기가 아니다 He is not an ordinary kind of man.
여간 아니다 (be) uncommon ; unusual ; extraordinary ; remarkable ¶ 여간 아닌 미인 a rare beauty // 여간 아닌 노력을 하다 make great efforts // 고집이 여간 아니다 be as obstinate as a mule // 오늘 추위가 여간 아니다 It is terribly cold today. // 그의 재주가 여간 아니다 He has a rare talent.
여감 女監 a prison ward〔cell〕for females
†여객 旅客 a passenger ; a traveler ; a tourist ; the traveling public 《총칭》
— 계원 a passenger agent —기 a passenger (air)plane ; an airliner — 명부 a list of passengers —선 a passenger ship — 수입 passenger traffic receipts — 수하물(手荷物) traveler's baggage 《미》〔luggage 《영》〕— 수하물 보관소 a luggage room ; a cloakroom 《영》 — 안내소 a travel bureau ; an inquiry office 《영》 —업 passenger〔tourist〕trade — 열차 a passenger train — 운송 passenger transport — 운송업 the business of carrying passengers〔passenger transit〕 — 운수 passenger traffic — 운임 passengers' fares — 전무 a train master ; a passenger guard ; a conductor 《미》 —차〔열차〕 a passenger car〔train〕
여건 與件 a postulate ; a given condition ; 『논리』 a datum
‡여걸 女傑 a heroine ; a brave〔heroic〕 woman ; an Amazon
여겨듣다 listen carefully〔intently, attentively〕《to》 ¶ 여겨들을 가치가 있다 be worth listening to // 선생님의 말을 여겨듣다 listen attentively to what the teacher has to say
여겨보다 see closely ; look hard at
여격 與格 『문법』 the dative (case)
— 동사 a dative verb
여경 女警 a policewoman
여경 餘慶 recompense〔reward〕for one's charities ; guerdon ¶ 적선지가 필유여경이라 Virtue brings its own reward.
여계 女系 the female line〔lineage〕
여공 女工 a factory girl ; a woman worker ; a workwoman
*여과 濾過 filtration ; percolation —하다 filter ; filtrate ; percolate ¶ 불순물을 여과해내다 filter out the impurities
—기 a filter —독 a filterable virus ; an ultravirus —성 filterability —성 균 『생물』 a virus —성 병원체 『의학』 a filterable virus —액 filtrate —지(紙) filter paper —지(池) a filter bed〔basin〕—층(層) a filter layer —함〔낭〕 a filter box〔bag〕 원심〔흡인, 열〕 — centrifugal〔sucking, heat〕 filtration
여관 女官 [나인] a court lady ; a lady-in-waiting ; a maid of honor
*여관 旅館 a hotel ; an inn ¶ 여관에 들다 put up〔stop〕at a hotel
—겸 요리점 a hotel-cum-restaurant —비 lodging expenses ; hotel bills —업 the hotel business — 주인〔경영자〕 a hotel keeper ; an innkeeper ; the proprietor of a hotel〔an inn〕; a hotelier 상인용 — a commercial hotel 피서객용 — a summer hotel
여광 餘光 afterglow ; lingering light
여광 濾光 filtering light
—기〔관〕 a lightfilter
여교사 女教師 a schoolmistress (초등 학교

의) ; a lady teacher ; a woman school-teacher

여교원 女教員 ⇨ 여교사

여구 如舊 being as of old ; being unchanged by time **—하다** be as of old ; remain unchanged

여국 女國 a (legendary) land of women ; a manless land

여국 與國 an ally ; an allied nation

여군 女軍 a woman soldier ; Women's Army Corps ; WAC

*여권 旅券 a passport ¶ 영사의 증명이 있는 여권 a passport viséd〔visaed〕 by the consul // 여권을 신청하다 apply for a passport // 여권을 내주다 issue a passport // 여권에 사증을 받다 have one's passport visaed

—법 the Passport Act **— 사증** a (passport) visa ¶ 여권을 사증하다 visa a passport // 여권의 사증을 받다〔해 받다〕 have〔get〕 one's passport visaed **가짜 —** a false passport **관용(官用) —** an official passport **외교관 —** a diplomat's passport **프랑스행 —** a passport for France

여권 女權 women's〔woman's〕 right ; woman〔women's, female〕 suffrage (참정권)

— 신장 extension〔expansion〕 of women's rights **— 신장론** feminism **— 신장론자** a feminist ; [참정권 획득 운동가] a suffragist ; a suffragette〔woman suffragist〕 (여자)

여급 女給 a waitress ; a barmaid (바의) ; a maid

†여기 this place ; here ¶ 여기에〔로〕 here // 여기까지 (up) to this place ; so far ; thus far // 여기 어디에 in this neighborhood ; about here // 여기 있거라 Stay right where you are ! // 여기가 어디냐 What place is this ? // 오늘은 여기까지 합시다 So much for today.

여기 餘技 a hobby

여기다 think ; consider 《as》 ; regard 《as》 ; take 《as》 ¶ 그것을 귀찮게 여기다 regard it as a bother // 사람을 어린애로 여기다 treat 《a person》 as a child // 제안을 우스꽝스럽게 여기다 regard the offer as absurd // 돈을 천하게 여기다 treat money cheap // 그 돈은 없어진 것으로 여기자 Let us regard the money as gone. // 그는 자기 자신을 훌륭하다고 여기고 있다 He considers himself very important. // 그의 말은 농담으로 여기는게 좋겠다 You had better treat his words as a joke. // 나는 그의 말이 사실이라고 여기고 있다 I hold his statement to be true.

여기자 女記者 a woman reporter

†여기저기 here and there ; from place to place ; in places ¶ 여기저기를 보다 look this way and that // 여기저기서 문의가 오다 receive inquiries from various quarters〔far and near〕

여뀌 a kind of water-pepper

여낙낙하다 (be) gentle ; nice ; sweet

여난 女難 misfortunes〔troubles〕 through women

여남은 some ten odd ; somewhat over 〔more than〕 ten ¶ 여남은 사람 a dozen men // 여남은 날 ten odd days

여년 餘年 the rest〔remainder〕 of one's life ⇨ 여생

여년묵다 age ; be time-honored ¶ 여년묵은 고목 a venerable old tree

여념 餘念 wandering thoughts ; straying attention ¶ 여념이 없다 be absorbed in 《one's study》 ; be intent on ; be engrossed in ; be bent on ; be deeply occupied with // 공부에 여념이 없다 devote oneself to one's studies // 그는 독서에 여념이 없었다 He was absorbed in his book.

여느 [보통의] ordinary ; commonplace ; [그 밖의] other ; different

여느 때 ordinary times ¶ 여느 때처럼 as usual // 빨간 옷을 입다니 여느 때와는 다르군요 It's unusual for you to be wearing red, isn't it ?

*여단 旅團 a brigade ¶ 여단으로 편성하다 form into a brigade

— 부관(副官) a brigade major 《영》 **— 사령부** the brigade headquarters **—장** a brigade commander ; a brigadier **— 편성** forming into a brigade ; brigade **보병 —** an infantry brigade **혼성 —** a mixed 〔composite〕 brigade

여닫다 open and shut 《a gate, a door》

*여닫이 opening and shutting〔closing〕 ; [미닫이] sliding doors and windows

여담 餘談 a digression ¶ 여담이지만 incidentally ; by the bye〔way〕 ; in this connection I may add that // 여담은 그만하고 to return to the main subject ; enough (of) digression // 여담을 하다 make a digression ; wander away from the main subject〔topic〕

여당 餘黨 the remnants of (a defeated) party ; the rest of the bandits ; stragglers (낙오자)

*여당 與黨 the government party ; the administration party 《미》 ; an "in" party ; a party in power ; the ministerial party ¶ 여당(측)의 ministerial // 여당측 의원 the ministerialists

여대 女大 a women's college

—생 a student at a women's college ; a woman college student ; a coed (남녀 공학 대학의) 《미·구》

여덕 餘德 the lingering influence of a great virtue ¶ 조상의 여덕 the influence of one's ancestors

여덟 eight ¶ 여덟 번 eight times // 여덟째 the eighth // 여덟 시 eight o'clock

여덟팔자 ¶ 여덟팔자 걸음 a splay-footed walk // 이마에 여덟팔자를 그리다 knit one's brows ; frown

여독 旅毒 ⇨ 노독(路毒)

여독 餘毒 the aftereffect 《of a poison, a sickness》 ¶ 한숨 자고 여행의 여독이나 푸시오 Sleep off your fatigue of the journey.
여동 putting aside a small spoonful of rice before eating
—대 a container of a small spoonful of the boiled rice put aside for ghosts before eating —밥 the rice put aside
여동 女童 ⇨ 계집아이
여동생 女同生 a younger sister
여드레 [8일간] eight days ; ⇨ 여드렛날
여드렛날 the eighth day (of the month)
*여드름 a pimple ; an acne ¶ 여드름 난 얼굴 a pimpled face // 여드름이 나다 have acne ; pimples break out on one's face // 여드름을 짜다 squeeze open a pimple // 또 얼굴에 여드름이 나버렸어 My face has broken out again. // 여드름을 짜지 않는 것이 좋다 그것은 상처 자국을 남길거야 You had better not pop the pimple. I'll leave a scar.
여든 eighty ¶ 여든이 넘다 be over eighty
여든대다 over-assert oneself ; be willful 〔obstinate〕
여들 없다 (be) clumsy ; ungainly
여듭 an eight-year-old horse〔ox〕
여등 余等 [우리들] we ; us
여등 汝等 [너희들] ye ; you
여래 如來 Buddha
*여러 many ; several ; various ; diverse ¶ 여러 사람 several people // 여러 학교 many schools ; various schools
‡여러 가지 various ; all kinds〔sorts〕 of ; several ; diverse ¶ 여러 가지 꽃 all kinds of flowers ; flowers of all kinds // 여러 가지 물건 all sorts of things // 여러 가지 취미를 가진 사람 a person of diverse interests // 여러 가지 의견 diverse views ; various opinions // 여러 가지로 variously ; in various〔many〕 ways // 여러 가지 사정으로 owing to various circumstances // 여러 가지 할 일이 있다 have much〔many things〕 to do // 여러 가지로 위로 하다 console 《a person》 in every way // 여러 가지로 방법을 써보다 try every means possible // 여러 가지로 힘쓰다 do all one can ; exert oneself in various ways // 소설도 여러 가지다 There are novels and novels. // 장미꽃에는 여러 가지가 있다 There are many varieties of roses. // 자동차에는 여러 가지 종류가 있다 There are several kinds of motorcars.
여러 날 many days ; several days ¶ 여러 날 걸리다 it takes many days
여러 달 many months ; several months ¶ 여러 달째 앓다 have been sick for months
여러대 —代 many generations ¶ 여러대째 서울서 살다 have lived in *Seoul* for many generations
여러모로 in various〔many〕 ways ; in more ways than one ; one way or another
*여러 번 often ; frequently ; several times ; many times ; many a time ; [되풀이해서] again and again ; over and over again ; repeatedly ¶ 여러 번 해서 실패하다 He repeatedly tried in vain. /Every time he tried, he failed. /All his endeavours ended in failure. // 그에게 여러 번 말했다 I told him over and over again. // 여러 번 미국에 가본 일이 있다 I have been to America a number of times.
*여러분 gentlemen ; ladies and gentlemen ; my friends ; you ; all of you ; everybody ¶ 여러분 안녕하십니까 Good morning, everybody.
여러 해 (for) many〔several〕 years
—살이(풀) a perennial (plant)
여럿 many ; many people ; a large number ¶ 여럿이 왔었나 Did many come ? // 파티에 여럿이 와 있다 There are many at the party. // 여럿이 그 시험에 낙제했다 Many failed in the examination.
여력 餘力 reserve〔surplus〕 power〔energy, strength〕 ¶ 여력이 충분히 있다 have a great〔plenty of〕 reserve energy 〔strength〕 // 시간으로나 돈으로나 그를 고용할 여력이 없다 I have neither time nor money to spare for hiring him.
여례 女禮 (the rules of) etiquette for ladies
여로 旅路 a travel ; a journey ¶ 여로에 오르다 start on a journey
여록 餘祿 an additional profit
여록 餘錄 a record of the rest ; a follow-up story
*여론 輿論 public opinion ; public sentiment ; the prevailing view ; the popular voice ¶ 여론을 일으키다 arouse〔stir up〕 public opinion // 여론을 조사하다 poll the public // 여론에 귀를 기울이다 give careful attention to the trends of public opinion // 여론에 호소하다 appeal to public opinion // 여론을 따르다 obey the dictates of public opinion ; act in accordance with public opinion // 여론에 대항하다 defy public opinion // 여론이 반대하고 있다 Public opinion is against it.
— 비판 the forum of public opinion — 조사 a public-opinion poll〔census〕 ; a straw poll ; a survey of public opinion — 조사원 a polltaker ; a pollster ; a public-opinion sampler
여론 餘論 complementary discussion
여류 女流 a lady ; a woman
— 가수 a woman〔girl〕 singer ; a songstress ; a songbird — 문학자 a lady of letters ; a literary woman ; a bluestocking — 비행가 a woman aviator 《*pl.* women aviators》 ; an aviatrix — 수영가 a woman swimmer ; a mermaid — 시인 a poetess — 작가 a lady〔woman, female, fair〕 writer ; an authoress
†여름 summer ; summertime ¶ 여름날 a summer day // 여름옷 summer clothes 〔clothing〕 // 올〔지난〕 여름 this〔last〕

summer // 초여름에 early in summer // 여름내 through (out) the summer // 여름용의 for summer use ; [옷] for summer wear // 한여름에 in the height of summer ; at midsummer // 여름을 지내다 summer ; spend the summer 《at *Taejŏn*》 — 모자 a summer hat ; [밀짚 모자] a straw hat — 방학 the summer vacation 〔holidays〕 —옷〔살이〕 summer clothes 〔wear〕 ; a summer suit —철 the summer season ; summertime 한— 《in》 midsummer ; 《in》 high〔the height of〕 summer

여름에 하루 놀면 겨울에 열흘 굶는다 속담 They must hunger in frost that will not work in heat. /An idle youth, a needy age.

여름밀감 —蜜柑 a Chinese citron ; a summer orange

여름타다 be susceptible to summer heat ; take hot weather hard ¶ 그는 여름타지 않는다 The hot weather never bothers him.

여리꾼 a tout ; a shill 《for a shop》 ; a decoy ; a customer-baiter

*여리다 (be) soft ; tender ; frail ; fragile ; [모자라다] be insufficient ; short ¶ 여린 빛깔 a soft color ; a light color // 여린 꽈리 a soft ground-cherry // 한 벌 짓기에는 옷감이 좀 여리다 The material is a little short to make a suit of clothes.

여린뼈 cartilage ; gristle

여립켜다 lure customers with a shill

여마리꾼 a spy

여망 餘望 the remaining hope

여망 輿望 popularity ; confidence ; esteem ¶ 국민의 여망을 받다 enjoy the confidence of the nation

여맥 餘脈 what (little) pulse〔strength〕 is left

여명 餘命 one's remaining days ; the remainder of one's life ¶ 그는 여명이 얼마 남지 않았다 His days are numbered. /He has but a few years left. /He is not long for this world.

여명 黎明 dawn ; daybreak —기 the dawning ¶ 문예 부흥의 여명기 the dawning of the Renaissance —(기) 문학 literature at the dawn of a new era〔age〕

여모 女帽 women's headgear ; [베] a hempcloth to cover a dead woman's head when the corpse is shrouded

여무 女巫 a female shaman

여무지다 (be) hard ; strong ; ripe ; mature ¶ 여무진 나무 hard wood // 여무진 사람 a man of spirit

여물[1] cattle feed ; fodder ; forage — 곳간 a hayloft — 작두 a chaffcutter ; a haycutter —죽 boiled cattle feed ; boiled fodder — 중독 forage poisoning —통 a manger ; a crib

여물[2] saltish well water

여물다 ① [익다] ripen ; get ripe ; mature ② [사람이] (be) tough ; firm ; full-spirited ; vigorous ¶ 일이 잘 여물었다 Plans are well matured.

여미다 adjust ; arrange ¶ 옷깃을 여미다 adjust one's dress ; straighten oneself // 옷깃을 여미고 듣다 listen with attention ; listen with sincerity

여반장 如反掌 (being) very easy ; as easy as falling off a log ¶ 그러한 일은 여반장이다 It is as easy as falling off a log. / That's an easy task〔job〕. /That's a very easy matter for me. /It is as easy as shelling peas.

여배우 女俳優 an actress — 양성소 an actresses' training school — 지망자 a would-be actress 주역 — [무언극·쇼 등의] the principal〔leading〕 actress 최우수 —상 the Best Actress award

*여백 餘白 blank ; space ; margin (난외의) ¶ 여백이 많은 페이지 a short page // 여백이 있으면 if space permits // 여백을 남기다 leave space ; leave a margin // 여백을 메우다 fill in space ; fill in〔up〕 the blank // 여백에다 쓰다 write in a blank space // 이 책은 여백이 많아 써 넣기에 아주 편리하다 This book is very convenient as it has a broad margin to write on.

여벌 餘— leftovers ; remnants ; remains ; extra ; surplus ; spare ¶ 여벌 옷 a spare suit // 긴급시에 쓸 여벌 타이어 an extra tire for emergency use // 여벌로 남겨 두다 save 《things》 for later use // 여벌이 하나 있다 There is an extra. // 여벌로 남은 것이라고는 하나뿐이다 There is only one left.

여법 如法 〖불교〗 observance of Buddha's teachings

여병 餘病 a complication ; a secondary disease ¶ 여병이 병발하지 않는 한 unless complications arise // 여병을 병발하다 have a complication arise〔set in〕 ; produce a complication ⇨ 합병증

‡여보 hello ; say 《미》 ; I say ; hey (there) ; excuse me ; listen ; [부부 간에] my dear ; honey ; darling ¶ 여보 여보 이게 뭐요 Look here ! What is this ? // 여보 봉급 타면 곧장 돌아와요 Hello dear ! Come straight back to home as soon as you get paid.

여보게 [남을 부를 때] ⇨ 여보

여보시오 I say ; say 《미》 ; excuse me ; please ; [전화에서] Are you there ? 《영》 /Hello ! 《미》 ¶ 여보시오 김선생이십니까 Hello ! Is that you, Mr. *Kim* ? // 여보시오 여기가 무슨 동입니까 Excuse me but what is the name of this street ?

여복 女服 a female〔woman's〕 dress ; ladies' clothes ; female attire

여봐란듯이 demonstratively ; ostentatiously ; showily ; for〔out of〕 display 〔show, parade〕 ; to attract attention ; to show off ¶ 여봐란듯이 행동하다 act demonstratively // 화려하게 차려 입은 여성들이 여봐란듯이 거리를 누비고 다닌다 Overdressed women flaunt down the streets.

*여부 與否 yes or no ; whether or not ; if ¶ 성공 여부 success or failure // 그 일의 가능 여부를 알 수 없다 I don't know whether it is feasible or not. // 여부를 똑똑히 대답하시오 Answer with a plain "yes" or "no".

여부없다 (be) sure ; certain ; definite ; unquestionable ; unmistakable ¶ 한 시간 내에 갈 수 있을까—여부없지 Can we get there in an hour? Of course! 〔Certainly! /There is no question about it.〕

여북 how (much) ; very ; greatly ; much ; to a considerable degree ¶ 여북 원통하랴 He must be awfully grievous. /I can well imagine his grief. // 여북해서 그것을 훔쳤겠니 He must have stolen it of perforce. // 이 소식을 들으면 여북이나 좋아할까 How glad he will be to hear the news. // 여북해서 남자가 울겠나 What miserable circumstances a man must be in to make him cry!

⁑여분 餘分 an extra ; an excess ; a surplus ; leftovers ¶ 여분이 없다 have no surplus〔extra〕 // 돈의 여분이 있다 carry some extra money ; have some money to spare // 여분의 옷은 한 벌도 없다 I have no spare suit of clothes.

여불비(례) 餘不備(禮) [편지의 맺음말] Yours truly ; Sincerely yours

*여비 旅費 traveling expenses ; travel cost ; mileage (공무원의) 《미》 ¶ 여비를 절약하다 save travel expenses // 여비를 지급하다 allow traveling expenses // 미국까지의 여비는 왕복 얼마입니까 What will it cost for a journey to America and back? /How much will it cost to travel to America and back?

여사 如斯 ―하다 be like this ⇨ 여차

여사 女史 [기혼자] Lady ; Madame ; Mrs ; [미혼자] Miss ¶ 박여사 Lady 〔Miss, Mrs, Madame〕 *Pak*

여사무원 女事務員 an office girl ; a female clerk

여상 女相 a womanlike〔girlish〕 face 〔countenance〕 ; womanish features

여상하다 如上― be as above

여색 女色 [미색] feminine〔a woman's〕 beauty ; a woman's charms ; [미인] a beautiful woman ; [성교] sexual intercourse with a woman ; coition ; [색욕] lust ; sexual〔carnal〕 desire〔passion〕 ¶ 여색을 좋아하는 lewd ; lascivious ; licentious // 여색에 사로잡히다 be infatuated with a woman ; be captivated by the charms of a woman // 여색을 쫓다 run after woman ; seek carnal pleasures // 여색에 빠지다 indulge in carnal pleasures

여생 餘生 the rest〔remainder〕 of one's life ; one's remaining years ¶ 여생을 조용히 보내다 live a quiet life for the rest of one's days // 여생을 자선 사업에 바치다 devote one's remaining years 〔the rest of one's days〕 to charity // 그는 여생을 안락하게 보냈다 He lived in comfort for the rest of his days.

여서 女壻 a son-in-law ; the husband of one's daughter

†여섯 six ¶ 여섯째 the sixth
— 쌍둥이 sextuplets

†여성 女性 women in general ; a woman ; womanhood 《총칭》 ; femininity 《총칭》 ; womankind 《총칭》 ; the fair 〔feminine, gentle, soft, softer, weaker〕 sex ; [문법] the feminine gender ¶ 여성적인 feminine ; womanly ; [유약한] effeminate // 저 남자는 다분히 여성적인 데가 있다 He has much of the woman in composition.
—관 a view of womanhood — 교육 the education of women〔girls〕 —난 the ladies' columns — 명사〔어미〕 〖문법〗 a feminine noun〔ending〕 — 문제 the women's problem —미 the womanly 〔feminine〕 beauty — 반액 [게시] Half-price admission for ladies. (영화관에서) —복 a woman's dress —어(語) feminine expressions〔words〕 ; female language — 운〔휴지〕 〖시〗 a feminine rhyme 〔caesura〕 — 잡지 a women('s)〔the ladies'〕 magazine — 중심설 〖철학〗 the gyneco-centric theory — 찬미자 an admirer of the fair sex — 참정권 woman suffrage — 합창 a female chorus — 해방론 feminism ; the theory〔principle〕 of the emancipation of women — 호르몬 〖의학·동물〗 the female (sex) hormone

여성 女聲 a woman's〔female〕 voice
— 합창 a woman's〔female〕 chorus

여세 餘勢 surplus power〔energy〕 ; reserve energy ; momentum ; 〖물리〗 impetus ; inertia ¶ 여세를 몰아 driving on without a stop ; availing oneself of the gathered momentum

⁑여송연 呂宋煙 a cigar 《from Luzon》 ¶ 여송연을 피우다 smoke a cigar

여수 女囚 a female prisoner〔convict〕

여수 旅愁 ennui〔tedium〕 of a journey ; loneliness on a journey ; a traveler's melancholy〔sadness〕 ; the nostalgia of a trip ; traveler's nostalgia〔homesickness〕 ¶ 여수를 느끼다 feel homesick〔melancholy〕 on a journey // 여수를 술로 달래다 beguile the loneliness〔tedium〕 of a journey in drink ; relieve one's loneliness on a journey in drink

여수 與受 giving and receiving ―하다 give and receive ; transfer

여수 餘數 remainder ; surplus ; excess

여술 女― a woman's spoon

여습 餘習 traces of old customs ; surviving customs ¶ 봉건 시대의 여습 customs still existing since from the feudal age

여승 女僧 a Buddhist nun ¶ 여승이 되다 become a Buddhist nun ; take the veil
여식 女息 a daughter
‡여신 女神 a goddess ; a female god 〔deity〕 ¶ 자유의 여신 the Goddess of Liberty
여신 餘燼 embers ; smouldering ruin (불난 자리의)
여신 與信 credit
— 업무 a loan business — 한도(액) a credit line〔limit〕 ; a line of credit
여실 如實 being in accord with reality ; vividness ; reality — 하다 (be) lively ; vivid ; be true to life ¶ 여실히 vividly ; graphically ; realistically ; true to life ; as things really are // 인생을 여실히 그리다 depict〔describe〕 life just as it is // 소련의 실정을 여실히 보여주다 hold up a true mirror to the existing state of affairs in the Soviet Union // 전투 묘사가 여실하다 The account of the battle is strikingly vivid. // 걸음걸이가 그의 성격을 여실히 나타냈다 The very way he walked bespoke the man.
여심 女心 《win》 woman's heart ; [처녀의] maidenly feelings
여아 女兒 a girl ; one's daughter
여암 〖건축〗 a bar along the edge of eaves
여압복 與壓服 a pressurized〔pressure〕 suit
여앙 餘殃 retribution ; calamity
여액 餘厄 remains of ill luck ; lingering misfortune ; remaining disaster
여액 餘額 the balance ; the remainder
여야 與野 the Government party and the Opposition party
여열 餘熱 remaining〔lingering〕 heat 〔fever〕
여염 餘炎 [불] lingering flames ; burning cinders ; [더위] lingering summer heat
여염 閭閻 residential districts ; [계층] a middle-class community ; respectable citizenry
—집 private residence (예사 살림집) ; commoner's house ¶ 여염집의 부녀 wives and daughters of respectable citizens〔middle-class community〕 — 하숙 a private boarding house
†여왕 女王 a queen ¶ 여왕 같은 queenly ; queenlike // 사교계의 여왕 a belle 〔queen〕 of society // 여왕답게 군림하다 queen it 《over》
—개미 a queen (ant) —국 a queendom —벌 a queen (bee〔wasp〕) 빅토리아 영국 — Victoria, Queen of England 엘리자베스 — Queen Elizabeth
†여우 〖동물〗 a fox ; a vixen (암컷) ; a cub (새끼) ; [사람] a cunning fellow ; a fox ¶ 여우 같은 foxlike ; foxy // 여우 같은 놈 a sly fellow ; a fox // 여우 같은 늙은이 a foxy old man // 여우 같다 be cunning ; be as cunning as a fox // 여우에 홀리다 be possessed〔bewitched〕 by a fox // 여우에 홀린 것 같다 feel bewildered〔mystified〕 // 여우처럼 간사하게 굴다 behave like a fox ; act cunningly 〔craftily〕 // 여우같이 얄밉다 be hateful as a cunning〔sneaky〕 fox // 여우가 여자로 둔갑했다 A fox transformed himself into〔took the shape of〕 a woman. // 여우가 운다 A fox barks 〔yelps〕.
— 가죽 a fox fur ; a fox skin — 가죽 제품 a fox piece —굴 a fox earth — 꼬리 a fox's tail ; a foxtail ; a fox brush ; a bush — 목도리 a fox-fur muffler —볕 short spell of sunshine on a rainy day ; fitful〔intermittent〕 sunshine ¶ 여우볕이 나다 the sun comes out for a few minutes on a rainy day —비 a fitful rain ; intermittent showers ; short spell of rain with the sunshine ; a sun-shower ; a light rain while the sun shines — 사냥 fox hunting —털 fox fur —털 목도리 a fox-fur muffler
여우를 만나려다 호랑이를 만난다 〔속담〕 Out of the frying pan into the fire.
‡여우 女優 ⇨ 여배우
여우 如右 being as on the right ; as the preceding ; as stated above — 하다 be as on the right ; be as the preceding 〔as stated above〕
여우오줌풀 〖식물〗 Carpesium maci macrocepalum ocepalum (학명)
여우원숭이 a lemur a macaco 《*pl.* ~s》 ; a galago 《*pl.* ~s》
여운 餘韻 a trailing note ; aftertaste ; [여음] lingering sound ; reverberations ; [여덕] the (good) influence of the deceased or predecessors ¶ 여운이 있는 trailing ; lingering ; suggestive // 그것은 여운이 있는 시다 The verse is laden with suggestions. /The poem is pregnant and suggestive. // 음악의 여운이 한동안 감돌았다 The music was lingering a while in my ear.
*여울 rapids ; a shoal ; the shallows ; swift (strong) current ¶ 여울을 건너다 ford rapids
—목 the neck of the rapids
*여위다 get〔become〕 lean〔thin〕 ; grow 〔become〕 gaunt ; lose (one's) weight ; get emaciated ; lose flesh (병으로) ¶ 여윈 thin ; lean ; skinny ; emaciated ; scrawny 《미》 // 여윈 얼굴 a haggard face // 여위어 피골이 상접하다 be worn to a shadow ; be wasted to a skeleton // 전보다 여위었다 You have got thinner than you were. / You appear to have lost flesh. // 그 여자는 여위어 빠졌었다 She was thin and drawn.
여윈잠 a light〔poor〕 sleep ¶ 여윈잠을 자다 pass〔have〕 a poor〔bad〕 night ; sleep badly
여유 餘裕 ① [여력] reserve ; [잉여] a surplus ; margin ; [여지] room ; [시일의] time (to spare) ; [견적] allowance

《for》; [활동의] scope ¶ 마음의 여유 inner resources ; latitude of mind // 여유가 있다〔없다〕 have〔have no〕《time, money》 to spare ; can(not) afford 《to do, a thing》 // 여유가 충분하다 have plenty in reserve ; have more than enough ; have full〔large〕 scope // 시간 여유가 없다 be pressed for time ; have limited time // 살 여유가 없다 cannot afford to buy 《a thing》 // 여유를 남기다 leave a margin ; leave something in reserve // 일곱 사람이 들어갈 여유가 있다 There is enough room for seven persons. // 그들은 여유있는 생활을 하고 있다 They live in comfort 〔comfortably〕. / They are well〔comfortably〕 off. // 이제 10원의 여유도 없다 Now I can't really spare ten *won*. // 기차로는 아직 한 시간의 여유가 있습니다 You have an hour's leeway to catch the train. // 일단 만형이 일을 얻으면 금전적인 여유가 좀 생길거야 Once our oldest gets a job, we should have a little more financial leeway. // 7시에 출발해서 여유를 갖는 게 낫지 않아 Wouldn't it be better to leave at seven and give yourself some leeway ? ② [침착] composure ; placidity ¶ 여유작작한 태도 an easy and graceful attitude // 여유를 잃다 lose composure 〔one's presence of mind〕 // 그는 여유만만하다 He has much〔enough strength〕 in reserve. /He is calm and at ease.

여의 女醫 ⇨ 여의사

여의 如意 ―하다 turn out as one wishes ; be to one's desire〔expectations〕 ¶ 여의하게 되다 go〔work〕 well ; come up to one's expectations // 여의치 않다 go wrong ; fall short of one's expectations // 매사가 여의치 않았다 Everything has gone wrong with me.

―주(珠) 《범》 cintāmani

여의다 lose 《one's parents》; be bereaved of 《a child》; marry off 《one's daughter》 ¶ 자식〔양친〕을 여의다 lose 〔survive〕 one's child〔parents〕 // 아버지를 여의다 have one's father die // 남편을 여의다 be left a widow ; be widowed ; lose one's husband ; be bereaved of one's husband // 딸을 멀리 여의다 marry off one's daughter to someone far away

여의사 女醫師 a lady〔female〕 doctor ; a woman doctor〔physician〕

여인 女人 a woman ; a married woman **―극** a performance given by actresses only **―금제(禁制)** [게시] No admittance to woman. /No woman admitted. /Off limits to women. **― 천하** petticoat government

여인 麗人 a beauty ; a belle ¶ 남장의 여인 a young woman in male attire

***여인숙 旅人宿** an inn ; a cheap inn 〔hotel〕 ; a lodging house

싸구려 ― a flophouse 《미》 ; a doss house 《영·속》

여일 如一 ―하다 (be) consistent ; changeless ; just the same ¶ 시종 여일하게 consistently ; invariably ; from first to last // 시종 여일 충성을 다하다 remain faithful 《to a person》 to the last

†여자 女子 a woman ; a female ; a lady ; [여아] a daughter ; a baby girl ; woman 《총칭》 ; the female〔fair〕 sex ¶ 여자의 female ; woman's ; feminine ; lady('s) ; girl('s) // 여자용의 lady's ; for ladies' use // 여자 같은 womanish ; effeminate ; unmanly (나쁜 뜻에서) // 여자다운 womanlike ; ladylike ; womanly (좋은 뜻에서) // 여자답지 않은 unwomanly ; unladylike // 허영심이 강한 여자 a woman full of〔thirsty after〕 vanity // 그는 여자가 잘 따른다 He is a ladies' man. // 그것은 여자가 할 일이다 That's sissy stuff. // 그애는 자라서 여자다워졌다 She has now grown to womanhood. // 그 여자는 여자다운 데가 없다 There is little of the woman in her. // 범죄 뒤에는 여자가 있다 There is a woman in it. // 약한 자여 그대 이름은 여자로다 Frailty, thy name is woman ! // 거의 모든 대학이 여자의 입학을 허가한다 Almost all the universities are open to woman.

― 감독 [공원(工員)의] a forewoman ; [영화의] a female director **― 고등학교** a girls' (senior) high school ; a girls' upper secondary school **― 교육** women's education ; education of girls **― 급사** a waitress **― 대학** a women's college **― 마음** a woman's heart **― 사무원** an office girl **― 손님** a lady visitor **― 주인** ⇨ 여주인 **― 중학교** a girls' junior high〔lower secondary〕 school **― 차장** ⇨ 여차장 **― 친구** a girl 〔woman〕 friend **― 학생** a girl student ; a co-ed (남녀 공학 대학의) 《미·구》 **― 호주** the female head of a house

여자는 돌면 버리고 그릇은 돌리면 깨진다 속담 A woman and a glass are ever in danger. /He that lets his horse drink at every lake, and his wife go to every wake, shall never be without a whore and a jade

여자는 사흘을 안 때리면 여우가 된다 속담 A spaniel, a woman, and a walnut tree, the more they're beaten the better they be.

여자 셋이 모이면 새 접시를 뒤집어 놓는다 속담 Three women (and a goose) makes a market. /Three women and a goose makes a market.

여자의 말은 들어도 패가하고 안 들어도 망신한다 속담 A woman's is no great thing, but he who won't take it is a fool.

여자가 아니 걸린 살인 없다 속담 No war without a woman. /No mischief but a woman or a priest is at the bottom of it.

여장 旅裝 traveling outfit〔suit〕 ; a traveler's equipment ¶ 여장을 차린 사람 a person equipped for a journey // 여장을 차리다 prepare for a journey ; equip oneself for a travel // 여장을 풀다 take a rest after a travel

여장 女裝 a female dress ; female attire 〔costume〕 —하다 be dressed〔disguised〕 in female attire ; be dressed as a woman ¶ 여장한 남자 a man in woman's dress

여장부 女丈夫 a heroine ; a brave〔manly〕 woman ; Amazon ⇨ 여걸(女傑)

여재 餘財 remaining fortune ; money 〔funds〕 to spare ; one's available funds

여적 女賊 a woman robber ; a pirate in petticoats ; a gun moll 《속》

여적 餘滴 drippings
문단 — literary jottings

*여전 如前 —하다 (be) unchanged ; the same ; be as before ; be as usual ; be as of old ¶ 여전히 as it used to be ; as ever ; as before ; still // 여전히 아름답다 be as beautiful as ever // 그는 여전히 원기왕성하다 He is as strong as ever. // 그는 의사가 경고해도 여전히 술을 마신다 He keeps on drinking in defiance of his doctor's warning. // 요새 어떻게 지내십니까—여전합니다 How are you getting along these days? The same as usual. // 여전히 바쁜 것 같구나 You look as busy as ever.

여점원 女店員 a saleswoman ; a sales girl ; a saleslady ; a shop girl

여정 旅程 a journey ; an itinerary ; a distance (to be covered) (거리) ¶ 하루의 여정 a day's journey // 일행의 여정을 짜다 arrange the itinerary of the party

여정 旅情 the weary thoughts of a traveler ; the tedium of a journey ¶ 여정을 위로하다 beguile the monotony of the journey ; console the weary thoughts〔heart〕 of a traveler

여정하다 be much〔nearly〕 the same

여제 女弟 a (younger, little) sister

여제 女帝 an empress ; a queen

여존 女尊 respect for woman
—남비 respect for women and scorn for men —주의 petticoatism

여종 女— a female slave〔servant〕

여좌 如左 —하다 be as on the left

여죄 餘罪 other crimes〔charges〕 ; further crimes ; additional charges ¶ 여죄를 추궁하다 inquire into further crimes // 그에게는 여죄도 있을 것 같다 He is suspected of other crimes.

여주 〖식물〗 the balsam-pear ; Momordica charantia (학명)

여주인 女主人 [여관 따위의] a landlady ; [요정 따위의] a mistress ; a proprietress

여주인공 女主人公 a heroine

여줄가리 bits and pieces ; minor matters ; incidentals ; odds and ends

여중 女中 ⇨ 여자 (—중학교)

여중군자 女中君子 a woman of virtue ; a lady of high virtue ; a real lady

여중호걸 女中豪傑 a heroic woman ; a manly〔masterly〕 woman

여증 餘症 the remaining symptom of a disease ; a complication

여지 〖식물〗 a litch ; a lichi ; a litch nut (열매)

†여지 餘地 room ; space ; margin ; scope ; leeway ¶ 개량〔발전〕의 여지 room〔margin〕 for improvement〔development〕 // 말할 여지가 없다 admit of no argument 〔comment〕 ; be evident ; it goes without saying // 변명할 여지가 없다 have not a leg to stand on 《구》 // 여지 없이 거절당하다 be flatly refused // 여지 없이 패배하다 be defeated〔beaten〕 all hollow // 논의할 여지가 없다 It is out of the question. / There is no room for argument〔discussion〕. / It admits of no dispute. // 타협할 여지가 없다 It admits of no compromise. // 논의할 여지가 있다 It is open to discussion. // 개선할 여지가 많다 There is much room for improvement. / It leaves much to be desired.

여지껏 ⇨ 여태까지

여진 餘震 an aftershock ; a secondary shock ; an after tremor〔quake〕

여질 女姪 a niece

여짓거리다 keep hesitating 《to speak》 ; be hesitant ; hesitate ¶ 여짓거리며 hesitatingly ; nervously ; hesitantly // 여짓거리지 마라 Don't be so fidgety. / Stop fidgeting. // 여짓거리지 말고 가부를 말해라 Don't hesitate to say yes or no. / Say yes or no without hesitation.

여짓여짓 hesitating to speak

여쭈다 ① [아뢰다] tell 《to a superior》 ; inform ; say ② [알아보다] ask 《a person about a thing》 ; inquire 《of a person about a thing》 ¶ 인사를 여쭈다 greet 《a superior》 // 또 한가지 여쭈어 볼 말이 있습니다 I have one more question to ask you.

여쭙다 tell 《to a superior》 ; say ; inform ; explain ; state ; mention ¶ 전날 여쭌 대로 as I told you the other day // 잠깐 여쭤보겠습니다 Excuse me, 《but》

여차 a trifle ; an easy thing

여차 如此 —하다 be like this ; be such way ¶ 여차하면 in case of emergency ; in time of need ; if need be ; when the moment arrives ; if compelled〔forced〕 ; when occasion demands // 여차여차하다 be so and so ; be such and such // 여차여차한 이유로 for such and such reasons ; such being the case ; under these circumstances // 여차여차한 말을 하다 say so and so // 여차여차한 경우에는 여차여차하게 하라고 가르쳐주었다 He gave me advice to do so and so on such and such occasions. // 우리는 여차하면 싸울 준비가 되어 있다 We are prepared for war at a moment's notice. // 그 여자는 여차할 때 대

처할 수 있는 그런 사람이었다 She was of a sort that could rise to an emergency.

여차장 女車掌 a girl conductor ; a conductress

여창 女唱 the female parts of a song ; [사람] a male soprano

여창 旅窓 a hotel room

여청 女― ① [여자 소리] a womanish voice ¶ 여청으로 말하다 talk in a womanish voice ② ⇨ 여창(女唱)

여체 女體 the body of (a) woman

여축 餘蓄 [저금] savings ; [저장] a store ; a stock ; [예비] reserve ; supplies **―하다** save (up) ; put by ; put 〔lay〕 aside ; reserve ; store ¶ 한 푼의 여축도 없다 have not a penny saved 〔laid by〕 // 수입 중에서 얼마를 여축해 두다 save something from〔out of〕 one's income // 다소의 여축이 있다 have some savings ; have some money saved

여치 a katydid ; a kind of grasshopper ; Gampsocleis ussuriensis (학명)

여타 餘他 the others ; the rest ; the remainder

여탈 與奪 giving and depriving ¶ 생살여탈지권을 쥐다 have〔hold〕 the right 〔power〕 of life and death over 《a person》; have 《a person》 at one's mercy **―(지)권** the power to give and to take away **생살―권** the power of life and death 《over》 ; life-and-death power 〔authority〕 《over》

여탐 consulting 《one's elders》 before acting **―하다** consult 《one's elders》 **―굿** a shaman dance ritual dedicated to the spirits of one's ancestors on some happy family occasion

여탕 女湯 a bathroom for woman ; the ladies' compartment of a public bath

여태 till now ; until〔up to〕 now ⇨ 여태까지 ¶ 그는 여태 병상에 누워 있다 He is still bed-ridden after all these years.

여태까지 till now ; until now ; up to the present ; by this time ; so far ; hitherto ; yet ; as yet ¶ 여태까지 없었던 사건 an unprecedented event // 여태까지 사람에게 알려지지 않은 비밀 a secret hitherto unknown to people // 여태까지 무엇을 하고 있었느냐—편지를 쓰고 있었습니다 What have you been doing all this while? I have been writing a letter. // 여태까지 이렇게 어려운 고비를 당한 적이 없다 I have never had such a trying time in my life.

여택 餘澤 blessings which remain behind ¶ 근대 문명의 여택 the benefits 〔blessings〕 of modern civilization

여투다 put aside ; hoard up ; save 《money》; keep ; store ; preserve ¶ 집세를 주기 위하여 돈을 여투어 두다 put the money aside towards the rent

여트막하다 ⇨ 야틈하다

*__여파 餘波__ an aftermath ; an aftereffect ; [폭풍의] a trail ¶ 전쟁의 여파 the aftermath of the war // 경제 공황의 여파 a secondary effect〔an aftermath〕 of an economic panic // 여파를 받다 be under the influence 《of》; be affected by the sequel 《of》 // 태풍의 여파로 파도가 높다 Waves are high, because of a typhoon passing near. / The sea is running high on account of a typhoon passing near.

여편네 [아내] one's wife ; [결혼한 여자] a (married) woman ¶ 여편네를 얻다 take 〔get〕 a wife ; be married to a woman **여편네 셋만 모이면 쇠접시도 녹는다** (속담) Three women (and a goose) makes a market. / Three women and a goose makes a market.

여폐 餘弊 a surviving evil

여풍 餘風 surviving custom ; a relic 《of》 ¶ 거기에는 아직도 봉건 시대의 여풍이 있다 Some customs of the feudal age still survive there.

여필 女筆 a woman's handwriting ¶ 이 편지는 여필 같다 This letter seems to be written by a woman.

여필종부 女必從夫 a wife should follow her husband ; wives should be submissive

여하 如何 what 《about》; how 《about》; how things are ; state ; condition(s) ¶ 여하한 what ; what kind〔sort〕 of ; what ... like // 여하히 how ; in what way // 여하한 이유로 why ; for what reason // 여하한 희생을 내더라도 at any cost〔price, sacrifice〕 // 여하한 일이 있더라도 whatever may happen ; under any circumstances // 수입 여하에 따라 지출을 조절하다 adjust one's expenses to one's income // 그는 여하한 위협도 두렵지 않다고 한다 He says he fears no danger whatever. // 여하한 일이 있더라도 내 할 일은 한다 Nothing shall prevent me from doing my duty. // 여하한 부자도 그런 짓은 할 수 없다 The richest man cannot afford such a thing. // 조건 여하에 따라서는 해보겠다 I will do it if proposed conditions are acceptable. // 성공은 노력 여하에 달려 있다 Success depends upon your efforts. // 여하한 일이 있더라도 내일은 결석해서는 안된다 You must on no account be absent tomorrow. // 결과 여하는 아직 불명이다 We don't know yet what the outcome will be.

*__여하간 如何間__ anyway ; at any rate ; anyhow ; in any case ; at all events ; be that as it may ¶ 오고 안 오고는 여하간 whether you come or not // 그것은 여하간 however that may be ; be that as it may // 비용의 문제는 여하간 setting aside 〔apart from〕 the question of expense // 여하간 떠나자 Let's start, anyway. // 여하간 해보는 것이 좋을 것이다 At all events you had better try. // 여하간 그렇게 하겠습니다 I will do so anyway. // 여하간 나로서는 전혀 모르는 일이다 But in any

case, I know nothing about it. // 여하간 정오까지 그를 기다려 보자 Well, at any rate, we will wait for him till noon.

‡여하튼 如何 — anyway ; in any case ; at any rate ; at all events ¶ 여하튼 그는 위대한 인물이다 He is a great man, at all events. // 여하튼 전쟁은 이겨야 한다 A war must be won at any cost. // 합격 여부는 여하튼 시험은 치러볼 생각입니다 I am going to take the examination whether I'll succeed in it or not.

여학교 女學校 a girl's school

여학생 女學生 a girl student ; a schoolgirl ; [공학의] a co-ed 《미·구》; a bobby soxer

여한 餘恨 a smouldering〔surviving〕 grudge ; one's unsatisfied grudge〔spite〕

여한 餘寒 the lingering cold〔winter〕; the after-winter cold ¶ 여한이 아직 가시지 않는다 The cold still lingers.

†여행 旅行 a travel ; traveling ; a journey ; a tour ; an excursion ; a trip ; a voyage

> 참고 **travel**은 일반적인 여행 **trip**은 짧은 여행 **tour**는 유람여행 **excursion**은 「소풍」에 해당되고 사람이 많은 경우에 주로 쓰인다 **voyage** 「항해」 **journey** 는 「수일간의 여행」을 말하며 원래는 프랑스말로 「하루의 여행」에서 나온 말

—하다 travel ; journey ; make〔go on〕 a journey〔trip, tour〕; take a trip 《to a place》 ¶ 여행의 계절 a tourist season // 기차〔배〕로 여행하다 travel rail〔water〕// 도보로 여행하다 travel on foot // 미국을 두루 여행하다 travel throughout〔to all parts of〕 America // 세계를 무전 여행하다 work one's way round the world // 수학 여행담을 하다 give an account of one's school journey〔excursion〕// 그들은 쉬며 놀며 여행하였다 They traveled by easy〔short〕 stages. // 그는 프랑스를 구석구석까지 여행하였다 He traveled France from end to end. // 그는 볼일이 있어 부산에 여행하였다 He made a journey to *Pusan* on business. // 그는 유럽을 널리 여행하였다 He traveled extensively〔widely〕 in Europe. // 작년 여름 우리들은 유럽을 여행하며 다녔다 Last summer we traveled around〔made a tour of〕 Europe. // 그는 해외 여행의 준비를 하고 있다 He is preparing for a trip abroad. // 여행의 계획을 짜는 것은 즐겁다 It is fun to plan a journey〔to map out a trip〕. // 그는 여행을 떠나고 부재중이다 He is away on a journey 〔trip〕. // 그는 여행을 떠났다 He started 〔set out〕 on a trip〔journey〕. // 그를 여행에 떠나 보냈다 I sent him on a journey. // 그는 세계 일주 여행을 했다 He made a journey round the world. // 그는 여행에서 돌아왔다 He returned〔came back〕 from his travels〔journey〕.

—가 a (great) traveler **— 가방** a traveling bag ; a suitcase ; [대형의] a trunk **— 권** a passport **—기** travels ; a diary of one's trip ; a travel book ¶ 미국 여행기 a book of travel in America // 나는 여행기를 쓰고 있다 I am writing a book about my travels. **—담** an account of one's travel(s) ; a travelog(ue) **—법** a mode of travel **—사** a travel〔tourist〕 agency **— 상해 보험** travel accident insurance **— 수표** a traveler's check **— 안내** a travelers' handbook ; a guidebook (for travelers) **— 안내서** a guidebook ; a Baedeker **— 안내소** a tourist bureau **— 일기** a travel diary ; a traveler's journal ; an itinerary **— 일정** an itinerary **—자** a traveler ; a tourist ¶ 여행자용 수표 a travelers〔traveler's〕 check **—중** during one's journey ; on one's travels **—지** [목적지] the destination : [체재지] the place of one's sojourn **강연〔시찰〕 —** a lecture〔an inspection〕 tour **기차 —** a journey by rail **도보 —** a walking tour ; a hike **무전 —** traveling without money **세계 일주 —** a round-the-world trip ; globe-trotting **수학 —** a school excursion **신혼 —** a honeymoon ; a wedding tour **유람 —** a jaunt ; an excursion **해외 —** overseas travel **대한 —사** the Korea Tourist Bureau **세계 —가** a tourist going round the world〔on a world tour〕; a globe-trotter **우주 — 시대** space travel age ☞ ◖p. 1502◗

여행 勵行 strict enforcement〔observance〕; rigorous execution **—하다** carry out strictly ; enforce rigidly ; execute rigorously ; observe strictly ; put into force〔operation〕 ¶ 법률의 여행 the enforcement of laws // 규칙이 전혀 여행되지 않고 있다 Discipline is not maintained at all.

규칙 — strict enforcement of the regulations **금주 —** strict〔rigid〕 enforcement of prohibition ; prohibition enforcement **대청소〔소독법〕 —** a general cleaning〔disinfection〕

여향 餘香 a lingering fragrance〔odor〕; a faint scent

여향 餘響 an echo ; a lingering sound ; reverberation

여호수아서 —書 〖성경〗 The Book of Joshua ; Joshua 《Josh》

***여호와** 〖성경〗 Jehovah

여혼 女婚 the wedding of one's daughter ; one's daughter's marriage

여황 女皇 an empress

여흥 餘興 unexhausted fun〔mirth〕; an entertainment ; a sideshow ¶ 여흥으로 by way of entertainment ; as a sideshow // 파티는 끝났으나 여흥은 가시지 않았다 The party is over, but the fun is not. // 여흥으로 일류 유행 가수들의 노래가 있었다 For entertainment, the leading popular singers' songs were presented.

여히 如— as like ¶ 하기와 여히 as follows ; as in the following // 상기와 여히 as above ; as in the preceding

***역** 譯 translation ; rendering ⇨ 번역 ¶ 오역 a mistranslation // 그 책은 햄릿의 한국어 역입니다 The book is a Korean translation of Hamlet.

역 驛 a (railway, railroad) station ; a train depot 《미》 ; [옛날의] a government-run post-stage ¶ 역에서 사람을 전송〔배웅〕하다 see off〔meet〕 《a person》 at the station **—건물** a railway station building **—부** a station porter ; a navvy ; a laborer 《미》 ; a coolie 《중국 따위의》 ; a station handworker (잡부) **—사(舍)** a station house **—원** a station-employee〔-clerk〕 ; the station staff 《총칭》 **—장** a stationmaster ; a station agent 《미》 **—장실** the stationmaster's〔station agent's〕 office **—전 광장** the station front ; a station plaza **—(전)길** a station road ; a depot street 《미》 **소(小)—** a whistle stop (급행이 특정 신호를 받은 때만 정차하는 시골역)

역 亦 [역시] too ; also ; as well ; likewise

역 役 [연극의] a part ; a role ¶ 어린이 역 a juvenile part // 알맞은 역 a part well suited to 《a person》 // 춘향의 역을 하다 play the role〔part〕 of *Chunhyang* // 햄릿 역을 맡기다 cast 《a person》 for Hamlet // 1인 2역을 하다 play a double role

⁑**역** 逆 an opposite ; inverse (거꾸로) ; reverse (반대) ; 〖수학〗 converse ¶ 역의 contrary ; reverse ; inverse ; opposite // 역으로 in opposition ; contrariwise // 역은 반드시 진(眞)이 아니다 Converses are not always true.

—기뢰(機雷) a countermine **—대여(貸與)** a reverse lend-lease **—동 기어** a reversing gear **—로켓** a retro-rocket **—류 차단기** 〖전기〗 a reverse-current circuit breaker **—립(立)** a handstand ; a headstand **—명(命)** disobedience **—발(發)** [총·포의] backfire **—법칙** 〖물리〗 the law of reciprocity **—변** an adverse change ¶ 역변의 〖수학〗 contra variant **—분사** retro-firing 《of a rocket》 **—분사 장치** a retro-rocket〔retro-fire〕 system〔device〕 **—비** 〖수학〗 an inverse ratio **—산(算)** inverse〔reverse〕 operation **—상(上)** a rush of blood to the head ; dizziness ; vertigo ; frenzy ; madness ; distraction ; nympholepsy **—상(像)** a reverse image **—성(成)** 〖언어〗 back-formation **—성어(成語)** a back-formation **—송(送)** sending back **—수(手)** a

역

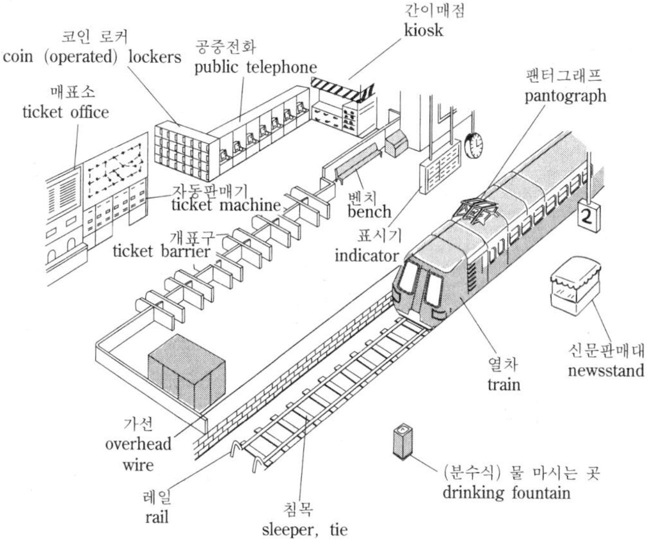

여 행

「여행」의 가장 일반적인 표현은 **travel**을 쓴다. 관광을 목적으로 어느 장소를 찾아 보통 1일 이상으로 갈 때는 **tour**, 어느 특정의 장소를 방문할 목적으로 하는 짧은 여행은 **trip**, 또 어느 정도 이상의 거리를, 특히 육상(陸上)에서 비교적 오랜 기간 동안 하는 여행은 **journey**, 비교적 장기간 배로 하는 여행은 **voyage**, 작은 규모의 소풍이나 1일의 단체 여행 등은 **excursion**으로 표현한다.

① 일정·여행의 종류

▶여행 일정 itinerary / 여행사 대리점 travel agency / 여행 안내소 touist[travel] information office / 예약 reservation / 예약 상황 reservation status / 예약 변경 reservation chage / 예약 재확인 reconfirmation (of a reservation) / 예약계 reservations clerk[agent] / 안내 책자 guidebook ; brochure / 시간표 timetable / 숙박시설 accommodations / 시내 관광 city sightseeing / 관광 버스 sightseeing bus / 여행지[행선지] destination / 민박 guest house ; tourist home

▶비행기 여행 air travel ; plane trip ; flight / 기차 여행 train travel ; train trip / 1박여행 overnight trip / 3박4일의 여행 trip of 4 days and 3 nights / 일주일간의 사막여행 one-week trip in the desert / 개인 여행 individual trip ; independent tour / 해외 여행 overseas travel ; trip[travels] abroad / 국내 여행 domestic tour / 단체 여행 package ; guided[conducted, group] tour[trip] / 관광 여행 sightseeing trip / 위락 여행 pleasure trip / 휴가 여행 vacation trip / 10일간의 유럽 여행 10-day trip to Europe / 80일간의 세계 일주 여행 80-day tour around the world ; 80-day around- the-world tour / 출장 여행 business trip (★ 출장비 traveling expenses) / 시찰 여행 study [inspection] tour / 수학 여행 school excursion / 실지 견학 여행 field trip / (항공 회사의) 초대 여행 invitation tour (★ 초청자측 비용 부담 여행은 all expenses-paid trip)

② 공항과 역

▶대합실 waiting lounge / 편도 승차권 one-way ticket / 왕복 승차권 round-trip ticket, return ticket 《영》 / 급행권 express ticket / 침대권 berth ticket / 탑승권 boarding pass / 보통 열차 local train / 급행열차 express (train) / 창옆 좌석 window (seat) / 통로쪽 좌석 aisle (seat) // 수하물 보관소 a left baggage office // 분실물 보관소 a lost-and-found office

③ 해외 여행

▶여권 passport / 일반 여권 ordinary passport / 공용 여권 official passport / 외교여권 diplomatic passport / 1회 여권single passport / 복수 여권 multiple passport / 사증(査證) visa / 예방 접종 증명서 vaccination certificate [book] ; yellow card / 여행자 수표 traveler's check / 수하물상환증 claim tag / 세관 신고서 customs declaration form / 세관 the customs / 출국 수속 embarkation procedure, departure formalities / 면세품점 duty-free shop

④ 표현

¶ 매표소[안내소]가 어디에 있습니까? Where is the ticket office [information desk]? // 부산행 1장 주십시오. I'd like a ticket to Pusan, please. // 제주까지 요금은 얼마입니까? How much is the fare to Cheju? // 특별열차를 타시려면 추가 요금을 내셔야 합니다. You have to pay extra for the specially reserved coach. // 다음 열차는 몇번선에서 출발합니까? What track[What number platform] does the next train leave from? // 천안에서 보통열차로 갈아타십시오. Change to a local train at Chŏnan. // 대구행 다음 열차는 몇시에 출발합니까? — 잠깐 기다리십시오. 시간표를 봐드리겠습니다. What time does the next train for Taegu leave? — Wait a minute. Let me check the train schedule[timetable 《영》]. // 이 열차에 식당차가 있습니까? Is there a dining car on this train? // 미안합니다. 이 자리에 앉아도 될까요? Excuse me, Is this seat taken? // 나는 뉴욕의 관광 여행을 계획하고 있다. I am planning a sightseeing trip to New York. // 나는 부산에서 1박할 예정이다. I am planning to stay overnight in *Pusan*. / I am planning an overnight stay in *Pusan*. // 나는 북경으로 2박 3일 여행을 떠나려고 합니다. I am going to make a three-day trip to Peking. (★ 1박 여행은 an overnight trip) // 여기서 비행기[기차] 예약을 할 수 있습니까? Can I reserve an airplane [a train] seat here? / Can I make a reservation for a flight[a train trip] here?

¶ 1인실로 예약을 하려고 합니다. I'd like to make a reservation for [reserve] a single room. // 1박 2식 요금이 얼마입니까? What's the rate with breakfast and dinner? // 여행 계획은 이미 세워놓았겠지요? — 아뇨, 그냥 떠나고 볼

참입니다. Have you made the plans for your trip yet? — No, I'm (just) going to play it by ear. // 여권을 보여주십시오. May I see your passport, please? // (세관에) 신고하실 물건 있습니까? Do you have anything to declare? // 알려드립니다. 대한항공 샌프란시스코행 75편 탑승객은 5번 탑승구로 탑승하시기 바랍니다. Attention please! Korea Air Lines flight 75 for San Francisco is now boarding at gate no. 5. / Attention please! All passengers boarding flight 75 for San Francisco will please proceed through gate no. 5. // 75편 항공기는 정시에 출발[도착]할 예정입니다. Flight 75 will leave[arrive] on time. // 좌석은 어디로 할까요? — 금연석에 창 옆 좌석으로 주십시오. (공항 카운터에서) Where would you like to sit? — I'd like (to have) a window seat in the non-smoking section. // 출국 수속은 마치셨습니까? Have you gone through the departure procedure? // 뉴욕 현지 시간은 몇 시 입니까? What's the local time in New York?

foul〔dirty〕 trick ¶ 역수를 쓰다 use a foul trick ; [유도에서] dislocate a joint ; [권투에서] hit below the belt **—수단〔방법〕** a topsy-turvy proceeding **—수식(數式)〔방정식〕** 〖수학〗 a reciprocal expression 〔equation〕 **—신(臣)** a rebellious subject〔retainer〕 ; a rebel ; a traitor ; an insurgent **—심(心)** a traitorous mind ; a rebellious design ; treasonous intent ; treachery ; perfidy **—아(兒)** an agrippa 《*pl.* -pae》 **—운** a reverse of fortune ; adverse〔bad〕 fortune **—일(日)** an evil day 《for fishermen》 **—자기(磁氣)** 〖물리〗 diamagnetism **—작용** an adverse effect ; a reaction **—장치** a reverse gear **—전 장치** a reversing gear〔device〕 ; a reverse **—전 핸들〔레버〕** a reversing handle 〔lever〕 **—제공** 〖상업〗 a counter-offer **—증거** evidence to the contrary **—진** retrogression ; backward movement ; countermarch **—코스** the reverse course ; retrogression **—타** a backhander ; a backhand stroke **—탐지** ¶ [전화를] 역탐지하다 trace the call ; detect 〔trace back〕 the telephonic source **—함수** a reversed function **—행 운동** 〖천문〗 [혹성의] retrograde motion **—화(火)** a backfire **—환 어음** a redraft **—회전** 〖기계〗 backlashing ; 〖정구·탁구〗 a backspin ; 〖스키〗 a counter **—효과** a counter result ; a contrary〔reverse, boomerang〕 effect ; an adverse reaction

역결 逆— [나무의] reverse grain ; interlocked grain

역겹다 逆— (be) disgusting ; revolting ; sickening ; nauseating ; nauseous ; intolerable ; detestable ; offensive ; [서술적] be disgusted 《at, by, with》 ; be sick (to one's stomach) 《from》 ¶ 역겨운 냄새 a sickening〔an offensive〕 smell // 역겨운 아첨 fulsome flattery // 역겹도록 to a sickening degree ; revoltingly ; disgustingly ; fulsomely // 역겹게 생각하다 have a dislike 《for》

***역경 逆境** an adverse〔unfavorable〕 situation〔circumstances〕 ; adversity ; adverse fortune ¶ 역경의 사람 a man in adversity ; a man with whom the world has not gone well // 역경에 처하다 be in〔fall into〕 adversity // 역경과 싸우다 struggle with adversity // 역경을 극복하다 tide over a difficult situation // 역경에서 시련을 쌓다 be schooled in adversity // 역경에 잘 대처하다 make the best of a bad bargain ; make the best of one's ill fortune // 역경이 사람을 만든다 Adversity is a training for man. // 그는 역경에서나 순경에서나 나의 좋은 친구였다 He has been a good friend to me in adversity or in prosperity.

역경 易經 the Book of Changes ; the Yi-king

역광선 逆光線 counter light ¶ 역광선으로 사진을 찍다 take a picture against the light
— 사진 a shadowgraph 《미》 ; a back-lighted shot

역군 役軍 a coolie ; a manual laborer 《on construction site》 ; [일꾼] a worker ¶ 개혁 운동의 역군 an active worker for the reform ; an ardent worker in the movement

역기 力器 a barbell ; the weight ¶ 역기를 들다 lift the weight 《in the press》 ; exercise a barbell

역기 力技 ⇨ 역도(力道)

역내 域內 ¶ 역내의 within the area
— 무역 intra-trade

역년 曆年 a calendar〔civil〕 year

역년 歷年 year after〔by〕 year ; lapse of years ; [왕조의] the ruling period of a dynasty ; a dynastic era **—하다** elapse ; pass ; go by

역단층 逆斷層 〖지질〗 an overthrust

역담보 逆擔保 counter-security

역대 歷代 successive generations ; generation after generation ; many generations
—기 chronicle **—내각** all successive cabinets **—왕** kings of many generations

역대여 逆貸與 reverse lend-lease

역도 力道 weight lifting
— 선수 a weight lifter

역도 役徒 (a group of) rebels ; insurgents ; traitors

역독 譯讀 oral translation **—하다** read and translate 《an English reader》

역두 驛頭 the front of the station

역들다 take sides with ; support ⇨ 역성

역량 力量 ability ; capacity ; capability ¶ 역량 있는 able ; capable ; competent // 역량 있는 정치가 an able〔a capable〕 statesman // 역량에 따라 according to one's ability // 역량이 있다 have the ability to 《do》 // 역량을 시험하다 try one's talent // 역량을 나타내다 display one's ability // 이 일을 감당할 역량이 없다 You are not equal to this work.
— 검사 a power test **—껏** with full force ; with all one's strength ; [전력을 다하여] with all one's might ; with might and main ; to the utmost of one's power
어학 — one's linguistic ability **영어 —** one's command of English
역력 歷歷 —하다 (be) clear ; plain ; obvious ; vivid ¶ 역력한 증거 a manifest evidence // 역력히 plainly ; vividly ; clearly // 감사하는 빛이 그의 얼굴에 역력히 나타난다 A feeling of gratitude can be plainly seen on his face.
역로켓 逆— a retro rocket
역류 逆流 [흐름] flowing backward ; [조류] an inverse〔upstream〕 current ; a counter-current ; a back current ; an adverse tide ; [혈액] regurgitation **—하다** flow backward ; go against〔up〕 the stream〔current〕
역리 逆理 irrationality ; absurdity ; unnaturalness ; a paradox ¶ 역리의 irrational ; contrary to reason ; absurd ; illogical
역리 疫痢 dysentery
역링크제 逆—制 〚경제〛 counter link
역마 驛馬 a post horse
역마을, 역말 驛— a post town
역마차 驛馬車 a stagecoach
역모 逆謀 a conspiracy ; a plot〔scheme〕 of treason ; a design to revolt **—하다** conspire to rise in revolt ; plot〔conspire〕 together ; plot treason 《against》
역무 役務 (labor) service
— 배상 reparation in service
역문 譯文 a translation
역반응 逆反應 inverse reaction
역방 歷訪 a round of visits〔calls〕 **—하다** make a round of calls〔visits〕 《to》 ¶ 각국을 역방하다 make a tour of various countries // 명사를 역방하다 make a round of calls on men of note
역법 曆法 the 《Roman》 calendar
‡**역병 疫病** an epidemic ; a plague ; a pestilence ¶ 역병이 유행하다 the plague is prevalent // 역병이 발생하다 an epidemic breaks out
역부족 力不足 want of ability ¶ 역부족이다 be wanting in ability ; be incapable ; be beyond one's capacity // 그로써는 그 일에 역부족이다 He is not equal to the task〔doing it〕. /He is not competent enough for the task. /The task is beyond his capacity.
역불급 力不及 (being) beyond one's capacity〔ability〕 **—하다** be beyond one's ability〔compass, reach〕 ; be above one's ability
역비 逆比 〚수학〛 an inverse ratio
—례 an inverse proportion ¶ 역비례하다 be inversely proportional 《to》 ; be in inverse proportion 《to》
역빠르다 (be) shrewd ; clever ; smart ; cunning
역사 力士 a strong man ; a man of great physical strength ; a Hercules
역사 役事 construction work ; engineering〔architectural〕 work **—하다** do construction work
역사 驛舍 a station building
‡**역사 歷史** ① history ; [기록] annals ; a history ; a chronicle ¶ 역사의 historic ; historical

> 참고 **historical**은 「역사상」의 뜻이지만 **historic**은 「역사상 찬연히 빛나는」의 뜻으로서 감정적 요소를 포함함

¶ 역사적 사건 a(n) historic event // 한국의 역사 Korean history ; the history of Korea // 역사상의 사건〔사실, 인물〕 a(n) historical event〔fact, figure〕 // 역사상 유명한 곳 a(n) historic spot ; a place of historic interest // 역사 이전의 prehistoric // 역사에 남다 find a place in history ; go down in history // 역사를 장식하다 adorn the history 《of》 // 역사상 유래가 없다 be unparalleled in history // 역사를 더듬다 trace the history 《of》 // 역사에 영향을 끼치다 affect history ; have an important role in history // 역사는 되풀이한다 History repeats itself. / History runs its cycle. // 역사는 매일 이루어지고 있다 History is being made every day. // 그 사건에 대해서 역사는 말이 없다 History is silent on the event. /The event is not mentioned in history. // 그는 대정치가로서 역사에 남을 것이다 He will go down in history as a great statesman. // 그의 이름은 역사에 남을 것이다 His name will stay put in history. // 역사에 의하면 그는 독살되었다는 것이다 History shows〔tells〕 that he was poisoned. // 그는 권투 역사에 남을 일을 했다 He made boxing history. // 그 도시는 빛나는 역사를 가지고 있다 The city has a glorious history.
② [내력] history ; tradition (전통) ¶ 역사 있는 학교 a school with a long history // 역사 깊은 대학 an old〔ancient〕 university
③ [개인의] a personal history ; a life history ; one's career
—가 a historian ; a historiographer **—관** historical view **—극** a historical play〔drama〕 ¶ 셰익스피어의 역사극 Shakespeare's histories **—(상) 명소** a historic spot〔scene〕 ; a place of historic interest
—(상) 사실〔인물〕 a historical fact〔per-

son〕 — 소설 historical (novel) — 연표 a history chart — 이래 since the dawn 〔beginning〕 of history — 이야기 a historical story — 정신 the historical mind —주의 historicism — 지리 historical geography — 철학 historical philosophy —학 a(n) historical study —학파 〖경제·법〗 the historical school —화 a history painting〔picture〕 동양〔서양, 세계〕 — Oriental〔Occidental, world〕 history

역사 轢死 death from a vehicular〔car, train〕 accident ; being killed by a train 〔an automobile〕 —하다 be run over and killed ; be killed by a vehicle 〔train, car〕
—자 a person run over and killed.

역산 逆産 ① [도산] 〖의학〗 cross birth ; breech birth ② [재산] a property of a traitor〔rebel〕

역산 逆算 inverse〔reverse〕 operation —하다 reckon backward ; calculate back 《to》

역살 轢殺 —하다 run over and kill ; kill by running over ¶ 역살되다〔당하다〕 be run over and killed // 열차에 역살되다 be killed by a train

역서 易書 a fortune book

역서 譯書 translated books ; translations

역서 曆書 an almanac ; a calendar

역선전 逆宣傳 counter-propaganda ; false propaganda —하다 carry out counterpropaganda

역설 力說 assertion —하다 emphasize ; accentuate ; lay stress on ; put emphasis on ; assert emphatically ¶ 필요성을 역설하다 emphasize〔be emphatic about〕 the necessity 《of》 // 그 점은 역설할 필요가 있다 It deserves special emphasis. // 나는 장래에 대해서는 두렵지 않다고 역설했다 I had no fear for the future, I said and I laid great emphasis on that.

*역설 逆說 a paradox ¶ 역설적 paradoxical // 역설적으로 말하면 paradoxically speaking
—가 a paradoxer ; a paradoxist

역성 partiality ; favoritism —하다, —들다 take sides with ; stand up for ; support ; give partial favor to ¶ 그는 그 학생에게 역성들었다 He showed undue favor to the student. // 나는 그 여자가 남편의 역성을 드는 것을 좋게 보았다 I liked her for standing up for her husband.

역성 逆成 〖언어〗 back-formation
—어(語) a back-formation

역세 歷世 many generations ; successive generations ; generation after generation ⇨ 역대(歷代)

역수 易數 the art of divination〔fortunetelling〕

역수 逆水 backwater ; a backset ; a countercurrent ⇨ 역류(逆流)

역수 逆數 〖수학〗 a reciprocal (number)

역수입 逆輸入 reimportation ; reimport —하다 reimport

역수출 逆輸出 reexportation ; reexport —하다 reexport

역술 譯述 translation —하다 translate —자 a translator

역습 逆襲 a counterattack ; a counteroffensive ; a retort (반박) —하다 make a counterattack 《against》 ; counterattack ¶ 적의 역습을 격퇴하다 repulse an enemy counterattack // 적군의 역습은 적어도 한 동안은 성공했다 The enemy counteroffensive has met at least temporary success.

*역시 亦是 [또한] too ; also ; as well ; likewise ; [아직도] still ; all ; (just) the same ; [결국] after all ; [예상대로] as was expected ; as one expected ¶ 그러나 역시 그는 벌을 받았다 He was punished all the same. // 나 역시 그렇소 So am I. /Me too. 《구》 // 두번째 시도도 역시 실패로 돌아갔다 The second attempt was likewise a failure. // 역시 그 친구는 내가 예상한 대로 성공을 거두고 있어 You see? He's coming through just as I expected. // 역시 결혼 상대는 성격을 보고 골라야 한다 When all is said and done, one's choice of a marriage partner should be based on character.

역시 譯詩 a translated poem ; a poem in translation ¶ 엘리어트의 역시를 읽다 read Eliot's poems in translation

역신 疫神 the spirit of smallpox

역암 礫岩 〖지질〗 a conglomerate

역어 譯語 translated words〔terms〕 ; words 〔terms〕 used in a translation ¶ 이 말에 대한 적당한 우리말의 역어가 없다 There is no appropriate〔proper, adequate〕 Korean equivalent to this word.

역연 歷然 —하다 (be) clear ; manifest ; evident ; obvious ; plain ; distinct ; vivid ¶ 역연히 clearly ; manifestly ; evidently ; obviously ; distinctly // 교살당한 흔적이 역연하다 There is a clear evidence of his having been strangled.

역연하다 亦然— be (also) the same

역영 力泳 —하다 swim with powerful strokes

역외 域外 ¶ 역외에서 out of the area
— 구매 an offshore purchase — 조달 offshore procurement

역용 逆用 a reverse〔perverse〕 use —하다 make a reverse use 《of》

역우 役牛 a work cow

역원 驛員 a station employee ; the station staff 《총칭》

역원 役員 an official ; an officer ; (a member of) the board
—석 officers' seats — 선거 the election of officers —실 an executive office —주(株) management shares —회 an officers' meeting ; [단체] the board of directors ; [회의] an executives'〔a directors'〕 meeting ; a meeting of (the board

of) directors
역일 歷日 a calendar〔civil〕 day
역임 歷任 successive〔consecutive〕 service in various posts —하다 hold various posts in succession ¶ 그는 여러 관직을 역임했다 He has consecutively filled various government posts.
*역자 譯者 a translator
역작 力作 a great〔an elaborate〕 work ; a tour de force (경멸조로) 《프》 —하다 work elaborately〔strenuously〕 《on》 ¶ 이것이 그의 최근의 역작이다 This is one of his latest works which cost him painstaking efforts.
—품 a masterpiece ; a fine literary effort
역작용 逆作用 (a) reaction ; counteraction ; (a) reverse action
역장 驛長 a stationmaster ; a station agent 《미》
—실 a stationmaster's office
역저 力著 a labored work ; a fine literary work
역적 力積 〖물리〗 an impulse
역적 逆賊 a rebel ; a traitor ; an insurgent ¶ 역적 모의하다 conspire to rise in revolt 《against》// 역적의 누명을 쓰다 be branded as a traitor〔rebel〕
—질 rebellion ; treason
역전 力戰 a hard〔desperate〕 fight —하다 put up a good fight ; fight desperately
역전 歷戰 long record of active service ¶ 역전의 veteran ; battle-tested // 역전의 용사 a veteran ; a hero of many battles
역전 逆轉 reversal ; reversion ; retrogression —하다 reverse 《itself》 ; be reversed ; [비행기가] loop the loop ¶ 형세가 역전했다 The situation reversed itself. /The tables were turned. // 안타 한 개만 나면 역전한다 (야구에서) A hit will turn the tide in the game.
역전 驛前 the front of the station
— 광장 a station square〔front, plaza〕 —(대)로 a station road ; a depot street 《미》
역전 경주 驛傳競走 a long-distance relay race ¶ 경부간 역전 경주에는 8개 팀이 참가했다 Eight teams participated in the long-distance relay race between *Seoul* and *Pusan*.
역전승 逆轉勝 a come-from-behind victory —하다 win 《a game》 after defeat seems certain ; win a come from-behind victory 《over》 《미·구》
역점 力點 (the point of) emphasis〔stress〕
역점 易占 divination ; fortunetelling ⇨ 점(占)
역정 逆情 anger ; displeasure
역정 나다 관용 be angry ; be out of temper
역정 내다 관용 get〔become, grow〕 angry 《with a person, at a matter》 ; lose one's temper
역조 力漕 rowing with all one's might —하다 row with all one's might〔with powerful strokes〕 ; pull hard on the oars
역조 歷朝 successive dynasties〔reigns〕
역조 逆調 an adverse〔unfavorable〕 condition ¶ 무역의 역조 (현상) an adverse balance of trade ; an unfavorable trade balance
역조 逆潮 [바람과의] a head-tide ; [조수와의] a cross-tide
역종 役種 the classification of service status
역주 譯註 translation and annotation ; translation with notes ¶ C교수 역주의 햄릿 Hamlet translated and annotated by Prof. C
—서 a copy of translation with notes
역주하다 力走— sprint ; run as fast 〔hard〕 as one can ; [경주에서] make a spurt ; sprint
역진 力盡 exhaustion (of strength) —하다 be exhausted ; use up one's strength
역질 疫疾 ⇨ 천연두
역청 瀝靑 bitumen ; asphalt
—암 pitchstone —탄 bituminous coal
역코스 逆— the road back ; the reverse course ; things opposing to the right principle ¶ 역코스를 취하다 take the reverse course // 그가 하는 일은 어쩐지 역코스를 밟고 있다 His doing is somewhat contrary to the right principle.
역투 力鬪 a mighty struggle ; a hard fight ; a fight with all one's strength —하다 fight hard
역투 力投 all-out pitching —하다 〖야구〗 pitch hard
역풍 逆風 a contrary〔cross〕 wind ; a headwind —하다 make headway against the wind
역하다 逆— ① [비위가] feel nausea ; feel sick ; be sick at the stomach 《미》 ② [마음에 거슬리다] be repelled 《by》 ; feel offended ; be irritated ③ [거역] go〔act〕 against ; disobey ¶ 남의 뜻을 역하다 act against 《a person's》 wishes
*역학 力學 dynamics ; mechanics ¶ 역학의 dynamic (al)
—자 a dynamist 동— kinetics 생체(生體) — vital dynamics 응용 — applied mechanics 정— statics
역학 易學 the science of divination ; fortune-telling lore
역학 疫學 epidemiology
—자 an epidemiologist
†역할 役割 a part ; a role ; a cast (of characters) (배역 전체) ¶ 역할을 정하다 assign a part ; allot duties // 중대한〔주동적〕 역할을 하다 play an important 〔a leading〕 role〔part〕 《in a matter》 // 형용사의 역할을 하다 function as an adjective // 그녀는 여러 가지 역할을 할 것이다 She will wear many hats.
역해 譯解 an annotated translation ;

translation with (explanatory, commentary) notes ―하다 translate with (commentary) notes ; translate and annotate ; decode
역행 力行 strenuous efforts ; endeavor ; exertion ―하다 make an energetic〔a strenuous〕 effort ; exert oneself 《for a thing》
역행 逆行 retrogression ; retrogressive motion ; reverse〔backward〕 movement ; countermarch ; retrogradation ―하다 go〔move〕 backward ; retrogress ; retrograde ; countermarch ; [상반하다] run counter to ; be contrary to ; recede ; reverse ¶ 시대에 역행하다 row〔swim〕 against the stream ; go against the times // 민주주의에 역행하다 run counter to democracy // 그만큼 세상사에 역행하고 있는 사람도 드물다 It's rare for someone to run against the current of the times as much as he does.
역혼 逆婚 marriage in reverse order
역회전 逆回轉 〖기계〗 backlashing
역효과 逆效果 a counter result〔outcome〕 ; an adverse reaction ; a boomerang〔reverse〕 effect ¶ 역효과를 내다 produce a quite contrary result ; have a reverse〔an adverse〕 effect 《on》
엮다 ① [얽어만들다] plait ; knit together ; weave ¶ 짚을 엮다 plait straw // 돗자리를 엮다 plait a straw mat ② [편찬] compile ; edit ; write ; weave ¶ 역사를 엮다 compile〔write〕 a history // 이야기를 엮다 weave a story
엮음 ① [엮는 일] weaving ; [엮은 물건] a piece of weaving ; a woven thing ② [편찬] compiling 《일》 ; a compilation 《책》 ; [형용사적] compiled by
연 鉛 lead ⇨ 납
연 鳶 a kite ¶ 연을 날리다 fly a kite // (실을 당기어) 연을 내리다 draw in a kite
*연 蓮 〖식물〗 a lotus
―근(根) a lotus root ―꽃 a lotus flower ―못 a lotus pond ; a pond ―사(絲) a lotus thread〔fiver〕 ―실(實) a lotus pip
연 年 a year ¶ 연 1회 once a year // 연 1회의 yearly ; annual // 연 2회의 half-yearly ; biannual // 연 4회의 quarterly // 연 1할의 이자 10 per cent interest per annum // 연 2회 상여금을 받다 receive bonuses biannually
―년(세세) every year ; yearly ; annually ; year by〔after〕 year ; year in and year out ―로자 the aged ; an elder ―말 the year-end ―상자 elders ; seniors ―수입 a yearly income ― 오푼 이자 interest of five percent per annum〔a year〕 ; annual interest of five percent ―운 the luck attending one's age ―월 years ; time ― 1회〔2회〕 once〔twice〕 a year ; annually〔biannually〕 ― 평균 yearly mean〔average〕 ―하자(下者) a junior 최―상자 the oldest ; the most aged
연 輦 a royal sedan-chair〔palanquin〕
연 延 [총계] the total ; the aggregate
― 근로 시간 the total number of working hours ; the total man-hours
연 連 ① [종이의] a ream ② [계속] consecutively ; continuously ¶ 양지 2 연 two reams of paper // 연사흘 동안 for three consecutive days ; three days in succession〔in a row〕
연가 戀歌 a love song ; an amatory poem
연간 年刊 [간행물] an annual publication ; a yearly ¶ 연간의 yearly ; annual
연간 年間 during the course of a year ; for a year ¶ 10년간 during〔for〕 a period of ten years
― 계획 the program for the year ― 생산고 yearly output
연감 軟― ripe〔soft, mellow〕 persimmon
연감 年鑑 a yearbook ; an annual ; an almanac
경제 ― an economic yearbook 정치 ― the political yearbook 통계 ― the statistics yearbook
연갑 年甲 a contemporary ; a person of about the same age ¶ 그는 내 연갑이다 He is about my age.
연강 軟鋼 mild〔soft〕 steel
연강 鍊鋼 wrought steel
연거푸 continuously ; successively ; consecutively ; in succession ; one after another ¶ 연거푸 세 번 이기다 win three consecutive〔straight〕 games // 그는 연거푸 담배를 피운다 He is a chain smoker. // 총소리가 세 번 연거푸 났다 There were three gun shots in rapid succession. // 화재가 세 군데서 연거푸 일어났다 Fires broke out at three different places in a row // 베이커 씨 방에 전화 좀 연결시켜 주십시오 Please connect me with the room of Mr. Baker.
연건평 延建坪 the total floor space
†연결 連結 connection ; linking ; coupling ―하다 connect ; attach ; couple ; interlink ; join ¶ 섬과 육지를 연결하는 다리 a bridge linking an island to land // 객차를 연결하다 couple cars // 열차에 식당차를 연결하다 attach a dining car to a train
―기 a coupler ; a connector ; a connecter ―봉(棒) a coupling rod ―수 a coupler hand ― 장치 a coupling device ―침 a coupling pin〔link〕 5대 ― 전차 five-carriage〔-car, -coach〕 train
연계 連鷄 a chicken ⇨ 영계
연계 連繫 complicity in a crime ; connection with other person's crime ; contact ; liaison ¶ 연계가 있다 be closely connected 《with》 ; be linked 《with》
*연고 軟膏 a salve ; an ointment ; an unguent
붕산(硼酸) ― boric ointment 수은 ― mercurial ointment
연고 緣故 ① [까닭] a reason ; a cause ; a ground ② [관계] relation(ship) ; con-

nection ; a tie ; pull 《속》 ¶ 연고가 없다 have no connection 《with》 ; have nothing to do 《with》
—권 preemptive rights ¶ 연고권을 인정하다 give 《a person》 preemptive rights **— 자** a relative **— 채용** employment of workers through personal connection ¶ 연고 채용으로 입사하다 get a post in a company through one's personal connection

연고로 然故— therefore ; accordingly ; consequently ; hence ; because of that ; so that

연골 軟骨 ① a cartilage ; gristle ② [어린 사람] a young〔an immature〕 person ; a greenhorn
— 두개(頭蓋) chondrocranium **—막** the perichondrium 《*pl.* -ria》 **— 봉합(縫合)** synchondrosis **—성 경골** a cartilage bone **— 세포** a cartilage cell ; a chondrocyte **— 어(魚)** a cartilaginous fish ; a selachian **— 어류(魚類)** chondrichthyes **—염** 〖병리〗 chondritis **— 조직** cartilaginous〔cartilage〕 tissue **—질(質)〔소(素)〕** 〖생화학〗 chondrin **—판** a cartilaginous plate **—한** a weak character ; a backboneless fellow **갑상(甲狀) —** the thyroid cartilage

연공 年貢 an annual tribute ¶ 연공을 바치다 pay an annual tribute 《to》

연공 年功 [근속] long service ; [공로] long and meritorious service ; [경험] long (years') experience ¶ 연공에 의하여 through long continuous service ; owing to long service // 연공을 쌓다 have long experience // 승진은 연공 위주로 한다 Promotion goes by seniority.
— 가봉 a long service allowance ; a longevity pay ; an additional salary for long service **— 규정** seniority provisions **—자** a veteran 《of》 ; an old hand 《at》 ; an old-timer **— 제도** the seniority rule 〔system〕

연관 聯關 ⇨ 관련(關聯)

연관 鉛管 a lead pipe ; a lead tube ; plumbing 《총칭》
—공 a plumber **— 공사** plumbing (work) **— 장치** plumbing fixture

†**연구 硏究** study ; research (전문적) ; [조사] investigation ; inquiry **—하다** study ; make a study 《of》 ; conduct researches 《in》 ; [조사] investigate ; inquire into ¶ 연구적 태도 a studentlike attitude // 과학적 연구 scientific researches〔study〕 // 전문으로 연구하다 make a special study of ; specialize 《in》 // 연구를 발표하다 publish one's research work // 연구를 지도하다 direct study // 법률 연구를 시작하다 take up 〔begin〕 the study of law // A씨 밑에서 연구하다 study with〔under〕 Mr. A // 그는 중국 역사를 연구하고 있다 He is making researches in Chinese history. // 그 문제는 신중히 연구하고 있는 중이다 The problem is receiving careful study. // 음악 연구차 프랑스 유학을 명 받았다 She was sent to France to study music.
—가 a student ; an investigator ; a research worker ¶ 김군은 카알라일의 연구가다 Mr. *Kim* is a student of Carlyle **—과** a postgraduate course ; a seminar **—과생** a postgraduate (student) **— 기관** a research institution **— 논문** a (research) treatise ; a dissertation (학위 논문) ; a monograph (전공 논문) **— 단체** a research organization **— 문제** a subject of study **—반** a research team **— 발표** [출판물에 의한] the publication of the results of one's research work ; [학회에서의] presenting one's report 《on》 ; [구두에 의한] reading one's paper **— 발표회** a meeting for reading research papers **— (방)법** a method of study〔research, inquiry〕 ; methodology (방법론) **— 보고** a report of research ; a research paper 《보고서》 **—비** research funds〔expenses〕 **—생〔원〕** a research assistant ; a researcher ; a laboratory work ; a labman 《미·속》 **—소** a research institute 〔laboratory〕 **— 소원(所員)** a research worker **— 수당** the research allowances **— 시설** a research installation **—실** a study (room) ; an office ; [세미나의] a seminar(y) ; [화학 따위의] a laboratory ; a lab **—심** the spirit of study 〔inquiry〕 ; 《have》 an inquiring mind **— 여행** 《go on》 a study tour **— 자료** research materials〔data〕 **— 제목** a subject for study 〔inquiry〕 ; a laboratory subject **— 조사** research and investigation **— 조성금** a research-aid fund **— 좌담회** a symposium ; a forum 《on a given subject》 **—회** [단체] a society for the research〔study〕 《of》 **기초 —** basic research **문법 —** studies in〔a study of〕 grammar **문학 —** literary researches **위탁 —** researches commissioned 《by a corporation》 **개인 —실** [교수의] a professor's office **김 교수 —실** Professor *Kim*'s office **문학 —회** a literature society **수리(水理) —실** a hydraulic laboratory **영문학 —실** an office of English literature **영어 —회** an English circle〔society〕 **전염병 —소** the Infectious Diseases Institute **한국 고전 —가** a student of old Korean classics

연구 軟球 a soft ball ; a sponge ball 《for tennis, baseball》

연구 聯句 a couplet

연구개 軟口蓋 〖생물〗 the soft palate ; the velum ; palatum molle ¶ 연구개의 velar

연구 활동 硏究活動 research activities

†**연극 演劇** a dramatic performance ; a play ; a drama ; theatricals (아마추어의) ¶ 연극조의 theatrical ; stagy // 연극에 미친 stage-struck〔-mad〕 // 연극을 상연하다

put〔present〕 a play on the stage // 연극을 보러 가다 attend〔go to〕 the theater // 소설을 연극화하다 dramatize a novel // 연극이 끝나다 a play comes to an end // 그는 정말 울고 있는 것이 아니라 연극을 하고 있을 뿐이다 He is not really crying he is just acting (the part). // 그 연극은 지금 국도 극장에서 상연 중이다 The play is now being presented at the *Gukdo* Theater.

—계 the theatrical world ¶ 연극계에 등장하다 go on the stage —계 인사들 the theatrical people〔world〕; theatrical circles — 구경 theater-going ; playgoing — 광 a crazy for playgoing —부 a theatrical club — 비평 dramatic criticism — 애호가 a playgoer ; a theatergoer —인 theater play people —팬 a playgoer ; a theatergoer — 프로그램 a playbill ; a program of a play —학 dramatics — 학교 a dramatic school

연근 蓮根 a lotus root

‡연금 年金 an annuity ; a pension ¶ 연금을 타다 receive a pension ; draw one's pension // 연금이 붙다 become entitled to a pension // 퇴직하여 연금으로 생활하다 retire to live on a pension

— 수령자 an annuitant — 제도 the pension system — 증서〔공채〕 an annuity certificate〔bond〕 국민 — a national pension〔annuity〕 단체〔생잔(生殘)〕 — a group〔reversionary〕 annuity 무기〔유기, 정기〕 — a perpetual〔terminable, term〕 annuity 종신 — a life annuity 즉시〔불시(不時)〕불 — an immediate〔a contingent〕 annuity 질병〔양로〕 — an invalidity〔old-age〕 pension 국민 —법 the National Pensions Act

연금 軟禁 informal confinement ; house arrest —하다 confine informally ; put under house arrest ¶ 연금 상태에 놓이다 be placed under the state of house arrest // 아버지는 연사흘 동안 딸을 방안에 연금했다 The father confined〔restricted〕 his daughter to her room for three days in a row.

***연금술 鍊金術** alchemy

—사 an alchemist

연급 年級 a year ; a form 《영》; a grade

연급 年給 an annual〔a yearly〕 salary

연기 年期 a term ; a fixed period (of years)

‡연기 延期 postponement ; deferment ; [연장] prolongation ; adjournment (회의) ; respite (집행의) ; 〖법〗 stay ; continuance —하다 postpone ; put off ; defer ; delay

> 참고 **delay** 무엇인가 방해하는 것이 있어 연기한다 **defer** 더 좋은 시기까지 연기하다 **postpone** 어떤 이유로 해서 확정된 어느 기일까지 연기하다

¶ 8일간의 연기 a postponement of eight days // 처형의 연기 a stay of execution // 연기되다 be postponed ; be put off〔over〕 // 무기 연기되다 be postponed indefinitely // 우천으로 연기되다 be postponed 《till the first fine day》 on account of rain // 출발을 다음 날까지 연기하다 postpone〔put off〕 one's departure until the next day // 복무 기한 연기 신청을 내다 turn in a request for the extension of service // 재판소는 판결을 연기할 것이다 The court will stay judgment.

(사형) 집행 — reprieve 지불 — postponement of payment

†연기 煙氣 smoke ; fume ¶ 검은 연기 black〔murky〕 smoke // 담배 연기를 뿜다 blow a cloud of smoke // 연기로 숨이 막히다 be suffocated〔choked〕 by smoke // 연기처럼 사라지다 vanish into thin air ; end in smoke // (기차가) 연기를 뿜으면서 역을 떠나다 puff out of a station // 굴뚝에서 연기가 난다 Smoke is coiling〔rising〕 up from a chimney. /The chimney is giving off coils of smoke. // 방 안에 연기가 자욱하다 The air in the room is thick with smoke.

담배 — cigarette smoke

아니땐 굴뚝에 연기날까 속담 There is no smoke without fire. /Out of nothing, nothing comes. /Where there's smoke, there's fire.

†연기 演技 performance ; acting ; playing ¶ 좋은 연기를 보여주다 show no mean dramatic power ; put in splendid acting // 연기가 자연스럽다〔딱딱하다〕 acting is natural〔stiff〕

—자 a performer ; an actor —장 an entertainment hall ; a variety hall — 종목 a repertoire〔repertory〕; a program of entertainment

연기 連記 —하다 list ; write down together ; catalogue ; write in series ; enter in a list

—제 [투표의] the plural ballot system — 투표 cumulative voting ; vote with plural entry 무기명 — 투표 a secret vote with plural entry

연기 年期 a term ; a period

연내 年內 ¶ 연내에 before the end of the year ; before the year is out ; within the year // 이 다리는 연내에 준공을 보게 된다 The bridge will be built before the end of the year.

연년 年年 every year ; year after year ; from year to year ; yearly ; annually

연년 連年 successive years ; one year after another ; for a series of years

연년생 年年生 a child born within a year of another ¶ 그들은 연년생이다 They are brothers born within a year of each other. // 아이가 연년생으로 태어났다 Each child was born one year after another.

연년익수 延年益壽 longevity ; prolonging

life — 하다 prolong life ; live long
연놈 (nasty) man and woman ; Jack and Jill
연단 演壇 a platform ; a rostrum ; [설교단] a pulpit ¶ 연단에 서다 take〔appear on〕 the platform ; appear before the audience
연달 鳶— a bamboo-frame of a kite ; a kite ; a kite-frame
연달 練達 skill ; dexterity — 하다 be skilled ; be experienced 《in》 ; be versed 《in》 ¶ 연달한 사람 an expert ; a veteran ; an old hand
연달다 continue ; keep on ; go on ; keep going ; be continuous ; keep on after ; be succeeded by ; follow ; ensue ¶ 연달아 one after another ; without a break ; continuously ; continually ; successively ; consecutively // 연달아 손님이 있다 have relays〔a constant stream〕 of visitors〔callers〕 // 연달아 이야기하다 keep up a conversation ; go〔keep〕 on talking // 불행한 일이 연달아 있다 have a run of ill luck〔a series of misfortunes〕 ; misfortune comes one after another // 전화가 연달아 걸려 오다 have telephone calls almost without a break // 연달아 세 번 이기다 win three games consecutively〔in succession, on end, in a row〕 // 그들은 세 게임을 연달아 졌다 They have lost three games in a row〔straight, back to back, on end, running〕. /They have lost three straight games.
연달리다 連— ⇨ 연달다
연달아 連— ⇨ 연달다
연당 蓮堂 a pavilion〔shrine〕 standing beside a lotus pond
연당 蓮塘 a lotus pond
*연대 年代 [시대] an age ; an epoch ; a period ¶ 역사상의 연대 historical dates // 1990년 대 the nineteen-nineties ; the 1990's // 연대순으로 in chronological order
—기 chronology ; a chronicle ; annals — 기극(記劇) a chronicle play —기 편자 an annalist ; a chronicler —순 chronological order ; order of date —순 카드 배열법 〖도서〗 the chronologic filing system — 표 a chronological table —학 chronology ; (the study of) scientific dating —학자 a chronologist ; a chronologer
연대 連帶 solidarity ; collective〔joint〕 responsibility — 하다 be jointly and severally liable to ; be collectively responsible 《to a person for a thing》 ¶ 연대로 돈을 꾸다 borrow money jointly〔on joint responsibility〕 // 연대로 책임을 지다 be collectively responsible 《to a person for a thing》
— 보증 joint liability on guarantee — 보증인 a joint surety — 약속 어음 a joint and several note — 증서 a joint and several bond — 채무 joint obligation〔debt〕 — 채무자 a joint and several debtor — 채무 증서 a joint bond — 책임 joint liability〔responsibility〕 ; solidarity ¶ 연대 책임으로 on joint responsibility
*연대 聯隊 a regiment ¶ 전방 연대로 배속되다 be assigned to a line regiment
—기 the regimental colors〔standard〕 — 병력 a regimental force〔strength〕 — 본부 the regimental headquarters — 부관 a regimental adjutant —장 the regimental commander 기병 — a cavalry regiment 보병 — an infantry regiment
연도 年度 a year ; a term ; a calendar year (달력의) ; a fiscal〔financial〕 year (회계 연도) ; a school year (학교의) ; a business year (사업 연도) ¶ 1994년도 회계 fiscal year 1994 ; FY 1994 // 1995년도 예산 the budget of the fiscal year 〔FY〕 1995 // 1980년도 졸업생 graduates in the class of 1980 // 연도초〔말〕에 at the beginning〔end〕 of the fiscal year // 회계 연도가 바뀔 때 at the end 〔change〕 of the fiscal year // 내년도로 이월하다 carry over 《an account》 to the next fiscal year
— 보고 an annual report — 예산 the budget for the 《1995》 fiscal year —초〔말〕 《at》 the beginning〔end〕 of the fiscal year 금— the current year 사업 — the business year 영업 — a business year 회계 — the fiscal year
연도 連禱 litany ; rogations
연도 沿道 a route ; a course ; the roadside ; the wayside ¶ 연도에 along the road ; by the roadside // 서울에 이르는 연도에는 군중이 꽉 차 있었다 The route leading to *Seoul* was lined with crowds of people〔spectators〕.
연도 the passage into a tomb ; a dromos
연독 鉛毒 lead-poisoning ; plumbism ; saturnism
연돌 煙突 [굴뚝] a chimney ; a smokestack ; a funnel (기관·배의) ; a stovepipe (난로의)
연동 peristalsis ; vermiculation ; peristaltic movement — 하다 creep ; worm
연동 聯動 gear(ing) — 하다 be connected〔linked, coupled〕 《with》 ; be geared 《with》
—기(機) a clutch — 장치 a gear 《of a machine》 — 전환 장치 a gearshift
연두 [빛깔] light green
연두 年頭 the beginning〔start〕 of the year ; New Year's Day (설날)
— 교서 the President's annual State of the Union Message to Congress 《미국의》 ; the President's annual State of the National Message 《한국의》 —사 New Year's address〔message〕
연두 軟豆 light green ; limecolor
—빛〔색〕 ⇨ 연두
연락 宴樂 merrymaking ; festivities ; gaieties ; revelry ; jollity
*연락 連絡 connection ; contact ; liaison ; communication ; relation — 하다 make

contact with ; get in touch with ; connect with ; form a connection〔liaison〕 with ; communicate ¶ 연락을 유지하다 keep in communication with ; keep in touch with // 연락이 끊어지다 lose contact with // 기지와의 연락이 끊어졌다 We have been cut off from the base. /We have lost contact with the base. // 이 기차는 부산에서 제주도행의 배와 연락된다 This train connects at *Pusan* with a boat for *Chejudo*. // 연락만 주시면 즉시 갈 수 있습니다 I can come on instant's notice. // 연락바람 R. S. V. P. /Please reply. // 지금 어디로 전화를 걸면 그와 연락이 되는지 혹시 아십니까 Do you have any idea where he can be reached right now ? // 오늘 휴가 내서 쉬겠다고 본인이 직접 연락했습니까 Did he call in himself to say he'd be taking the day off today ?

—계 a liaison〔contact〕 man **—기** a liaison aircraft **—기관** a liaison organ **—망** a network of communication **—부** a liaison department〔section〕 **— 사무** liaison business **—선** a ferryboat ; a ferry steamer ; a railway ferry **—소** a liaison office **— 승차권** a connection〔an interline〕 ticket **—역(驛)** a connecting station ; a junction ; a joint station 《영》 ; a union station 《미》 **— 운전** combination service **— 장교** a liaison officer **—점** a junction **—처** where to make contact **— 회의〔협의회〕** a liaison conference〔council, committee〕 **긴밀 —** a close contact

연락 부절 連絡不絶 ceaseless traffic ¶ 인마가 연락 부절이다 The street is thick〔heavy〕 with human and vehicular traffic.

연래 年來 for years ; (for) some years ; these years ¶ 연래의 희망 a long-cherished desire // 연래의 현안 an outstanding〔a long-pending〕 problem〔issue〕 // 10년래의 벗 a friend of 10 year's standing // 이번 눈보라는 20년래 가장 심한 것이다 This is the biggest snowstorm we have had in the past 20 years. /We have the biggest snowstorm in 20 years.

†**연령 年齡** age ; years (of age) ¶ 연령의 차 disparity of age // 연령에 불구하고 regardless of age ; with no age limit // 연령순으로 in order of age ; according to seniority // 연령보다 젊게 보이다 look much younger than one's age // 이 병은 연령에 관계 없이 생긴다 The malady occurs at all ages.

— 감정 the determination〔estimation〕 of age **— 구성** an age structure **—별** an age bracket **—별 사망자 수** number of deaths by age group **— 불문(不問)** irrespective of age ; with no age limits **— 제한** the age limit **—차(差)** disparity〔discrepancy〕 of age **— 총계** the combined years 《of a group》 **—층** an age group〔bracket〕 ¶ 그와 같은 연령층의 사람들 people in his age bracket **결혼 —** the marriage〔marriageable〕 age ; the age of marriage **평균 —** the average〔mean〕 age

연례 年例 ¶ 연례의 yearly ; annual

— 보고 an annual report **— 총회** annual general meeting **— 행사** annual events ; conventional events (of long standing) **—회** annual meeting

연로 年老 old〔advanced〕 age **—하다** (be) old ; aged ; elderly ¶ 연로하여 허리가 굽다 be bent with the weight of years

⁑**연료 燃料** fuel ¶ 연료 부족 때문에 owing to the lack of fuel // 연료가 떨어지다 run out of fuel // 연료를 보급하다 refuel 《a plane》 // 연료를 절약하다 save fuel // 연료가 부족하다 Fuel is badly needed (for the winter).

— 가스 fuel gas **— 공학** fuel engineering **— 보급** supply of fuel ; refueling **— 보급소** a fueling station〔depot〕 **— 부족** lack〔dearth〕 of fuel ; fuel shortage **—비** cost of fuel ; fuel expenses 〔charge〕 **— 소비량** the amount of fuel consumed ; fuel consumption **—유** fuel oil **— 탱크** a fuel tank **액체〔고체, 기체〕 —** liquid 〔solid, gaseous〕 fuel **항공 —** aviation fuel

연루 連累 [연좌] implication ; complicity ; involvement **—하다** be implicated 〔involved〕 《in》 ; be connected with

—자 an accomplice ; a confederate ; a partner ; a person involved〔concerned〕 ¶ 연루자가 더 있을 성 싶다 Some other persons may possibly be involved in the crime. **범죄 —** complicity with another in a crime

연륜 年輪 an annual ring〔layer〕 ; the ring of a tree ; age

연리 年利 an annual〔a yearly〕 interest 〔rate〕 ¶ 연리 1할로 at an annual interest of ten percent ; at 10 percent per annum

연립 聯立 alliance ; union ; coalition **—하다** be allied ; be united〔combined〕 ; unite

— 내각 a coalition cabinet **— 방정식** simultaneous equations **— 정부** a coalition government ; a fusion administration **— 주택** a tenement house 〔residence〕

연마 硏磨 ① [기계] grinding ; polishing **—하다** (give a) polish ; grind ; brush up ② [연구] study ; research **—하다** study hard ; research ; make a study 《of》

—기 a grinder ; a grinding machine ; an abrasive machine ; polisher (렌즈 따위의) **—분** polishing powder **—제** an abradant ; an abrasive **—지** sandpaper ; emery paper

연마 鍊磨 training ; drilling ; practice ; improvement ; cultivation **—하다** train ; drill ; improve ; cultivate ; practice constantly ; exercise ¶ 다년간 연마한 보람이 있어 by virtue of many years' training // 기술을 연마하다 improve one's skill // 신체를 연마하다 improve one's physical fitness // 정신을 연마하다 cultivate〔train〕 one's mind

연막 煙幕 a smoke screen ¶ 연막으로 가리다 cover 《a ship》 with a smoke screen
— 전술 smoke-screen tactics —탄 a smoke shell
연막을 치다 관용 lay down a smoke screen ; [속이다] hide behind a smoke screen ; camouflage ; beguile

연만 年滿 old〔advanced〕 age ; senility —하다 (be) old enough ; aged ; senile

연말 年末 the end〔close〕 of the year ; the year-end
— 대매출 the year-end bargain sale — 상여금 the year-end bonus〔allowance〕

연맥 燕麥 [귀리] oates

†연맹 聯盟 a league ; a federation ; a union ; a confederation ; an alliance ¶ …와 연맹하여 in league 《with》 // 연맹을 조직하다 form a league〔federation〕 // 연맹에 가입하다 join a league // 연맹을 이탈하다 resign〔secede〕 from a league // 연맹을 맺다 conclude〔form〕 an alliance with
—국 allied countries — 이사회 the League Council 경제 — an economic league 국제 — the League of Nations 육상 경기 — the Federation of Athletic Associations 학생 — the students' league

연면 連綿 —하다 (be) continuous uninterrupted ; unbroken ; consecutive ¶ 연면히 continuously ; consecutively ; in an unbroken line

연명 延命 —하다 barely manage to live ; eke out an existence ; survive ¶ 간신히 연명하다 make a bare living ; eke out a precarious living // 박봉으로 겨우 연명하다 eke out a livelihood on one's meager pay

연명 連名 joint signature —하다 sign jointly ¶ 50명의 연명 청원서 a petition signed by 50 persons // 연명으로 안내장을 내다 send an invitation under joint signature
— 상소 a joint petition to the ruler — 진정서〔초대장〕 a joint petition〔invitation〕 — 투표 a joint ballot

연모 [도구] an instrument ; an implement ; a tool ; [재료] material ; stuff

연모 戀慕 love ; attachment ; yearning 《after》 —하다 (fall in) love ; be charmed 《with》 ; become attached 《to》 ; conceive love 《for》 ; long〔pine〕 《for》 ; yearn 《after》 ¶ 연모를 받다 be loved ; be yearned for

연목 椽木 a rafter

연목구어 椽木求魚 —하다 seek a fish on a tree ; fish in the air ; attempt〔seek〕 the impossible

연목구어 속담 It is very hard to shave an egg.

연못 蓮— a lotus pond ; a pond

*연무 煙霧 mist ; haze ; smog (도시의)

연무 演武 military drill〔exercise〕 —하다 have military drill ; engage in military exercise
—장 a military exercise hall ; a drill hall

연무 鍊武 military exercise —하다 practice military exercise

연문 戀文 a love letter ; a billet-doux 《프》

연문 衍文 pleonasm ; a redundant word〔sentence〕

연문학 軟文學 sentimental literature ; erotic〔amorous, light〕 literature

연미복 燕尾服 an evening coat ; a swallow-tailed coat ; a tail coat ; a dress coat ; a full-dress coat

연민 憐憫 compassion ; pity ; mercy ; commiseration —하다 (be) poor ; pitiful ; touching ¶ 연민의 정을 느끼다 take pity〔compassion〕 on 《a person》 ; be touched〔moved〕 with pity 《for》

연발 延發 the postponement of one's departure ; delayed departure —하다 start late ; postpone one's departure ¶ 기차가 한 시간 연발했다 The train started an hour late.

연발 連發 ① [사격] firing in succession ; running fire ; a volley —하다 fire in rapid succession ; fire in volleys
② [발생] occurrence in succession ; successive occurrence —하다 occur〔happen〕 one after another ; take place in succession ¶ 사고가 연발하다 accidents occur one after another // 질문을 연발하다 ask one question after another
—총 a revolver ; a magazine rifle〔gun, pistol〕 ; a repeating firearm〔rifle〕 ; a repeater 6 —총 a six-shooter ; a six-chambered〔six-shot〕 revolver

연방 continuously ⇨ 연해연방

연방 蓮— a lotus pip

*연방 聯邦 a (federal) union ; a confederation ; a federation ; a confederacy ; a federal state ; a commonwealth

> 참고 **federation**은 각주가 제각기 권력을 보유하면서 결합된 것을 말하며 **confederation, confederacy**는 외부의 사정에 응해서 주권국이 공동 행동을 취할 때의 영속적 또는 일시적인 결합을 말한다 federation은 더욱 밀접한 결합을 나타낸다

— 수사국 the Federal Bureau of Investigation 《FBI》 — 재판소 a federal court — 정부 a federal government —제 a federal system ; federalism —주의 federalism —주의자 a federalist — 준비 은행 the Federal Reserve Bank 말레이지아 — ⇨ 말레이지아 소비에트 — ⇨ 소비에트 영(국)— ⇨ 영국

연배 年輩 [동년배] a person of the same age ; a contemporary ¶ 자네 연배의 청년 young men of your age
연백 鉛白 white lead ; lead foil
연번호 連番號 a serial number
연변 年邊 an annual〔a yearly〕 interest〔rate〕 ¶ 연변 6부로 at an annual interest of six percent ; at 6 percent perannum
연변 沿邊 the area along a river〔railroad, route, border〕 ¶ 철도 연변의 집들 houses on〔along〕 a railway〔railroad〕 line
연별 예산 年別豫算 an annual budget
연병 練兵 military drill ; troop training ; military exercise **—하다** drill ; parade **—장** a parade〔drill〕 ground〔field〕
연보 年報 an annual report〔bulletin〕
연보 年譜 a chronological personal history ; a life story in chronological order
연보 捐補 church offerings ; alms ; almsgiving ; charity ; donation **—하다** make contributions ; give donations ; give alms〔charity〕
—금〔돈〕 money contributed〔offered〕 **—함** an offertory box
연보라 軟— light purple ; lilac
연봉 年俸 an annual〔a yearly〕 salary ; a yearly stipend ¶ 연봉 1만불로 at $10,000 a year ; at an annual salary of $10,000 // 저 사람은 연봉 800만원이다 He draws an annual salary of 8,000,000 *won*. /His salary is eight million *won* a year.
연봉 蓮— a lotus bud
연봉 連峰 a chain of mountains ; a mountain range〔chain〕
알프스 — the Alps range
연봉잠 蓮—簪 a hairpin shaped like a lotus bud
연부 年賦 a yearly〔an annual〕 installment ¶ 연부로 사다 buy《a thing》 by〔in〕 yearly installments
— 상환 redemption by〔in〕 yearly installments
연분 緣分 a preordained〔predestined〕 tie〔bond〕 ; fate ; connection ; relation ¶ 연분이 있어 as fate would have it // 연분이 두텁다 have a close tie《with a person》 ; be closely bound up together // 연분을 끊다 break off《with a person》 ; have done with《a person, a matter》// 부부의 연분을 맺다 contract a marriage ; tie the marriage knot // 그들 부부는 천생연분이다 They are made for man and wife. /They are a well matched couple.
연분수 連分數 〚수학〛 a continued fraction
연분홍 軟粉紅 light pink
연불 延拂 deferred payment
— 방식《on》 deferred payment basis ;《under》 the deferred payment formula **— 수출** export on easy-payment〔deferred-payment〕 term ; export by deferred account
연불 年拂 ⇨ 연부(年賦)
연비 聯臂 [소개] indirect introduction ; [지면] indirect acquaintance **—하다** introduce indirectly ; form〔have, make〕 acquaintance with《a person》 in one way or another
연비 連比 〚수학〛 a continued ratio
연비례 連比例 〚수학〛 continued proportion
연뿌리 ⇨ 연근(蓮根)
연사 演士 a speaker ; an orator ; a lecturer
연사 練絲 scoured thread〔yarn〕
연사 撚絲 twisted thread〔yarn〕 ; twine
연사 장치 連射裝置 a draft gear
연사질 beguiling《a person》 into revealing himself
연산 連山 a range〔chain, group〕 of mountains ; a mountain range ¶ 남북으로 걸친 연산 a range of mountains running north and south
연산 年産 annual〔yearly〕 production ; a yearly〔an annual〕 output
— 능력 annual capacity of production
연산 演算 〚수학〛 operation
—자(子) an operator **역—** an inverse operation
연상 年上 [사람] elders ; seniors ¶ 연상의 older ; senior ; major // 연상의 처 a wife older than one // 3년 연상이다 be one's senior by three years ; be three years older than one // 누가 연상이냐 Which is older〔elder〕?
†**연상 聯想** association (of ideas) **—하다** associate《A with B》 ; be reminded《of》 ¶ 연상시키다 remind《a person》 of ; bring up the image of ; be suggestive of ; suggest // 그를 보면 죽은 동생이 연상된다 He reminds me of my dead brother. // 그의 기술은 오랜 훈련을 연상시킨다 His skill suggests a long training. // 아인슈타인 하면 곧 상대성 원리를 연상한다 We associate Einstein with the theory of relativity.
— 관념 an associate **—설** 〚철학〛 associationalism **— 심리학** associationism **유사〔대비, 근접〕 —** association by similarity〔contrast, contiguity〕
연서 連署 joint signature ; countersignature **—하다** sign jointly ; countersign ; sign《a document》 with another ¶ 연서로 under joint signature // 선거인 30인 이상의 연서로 under the joint signature of thirty or more electors
—국 a cosignatory ; the Cosignatory Powers **—인** a joint signer ; a cosignatory
연서 戀書 a love letter ; a billet-doux《프》
연석 緣石 a curbstone ; a curb ; a kerb《영》
연석 宴席 (one's seat in) a banquet hall ¶ 연석에 참석하다 attend a banquet

〔feast, dinner〕 // 연석을 베풀다 give a dinner party ; hold a banquet

연석 硯石 a Chinese inkstone〔ink-slab〕

연석 連席 sitting together ; attendance ; presence **—하다** attend ; be present at ; sit at ; be in attendance at ¶ …의 연석하에 with... in attendance at // 회의에 연석하다 attend a meeting ; sit as a member at the meeting

—자 attendants **— 회의** a joint meeting

연선 沿線 the area along the line ¶ 철도 연선에 on〔along〕 a railway line // 철도 연선에 있다 be on a railroad line // 철도 연선을 따라 북으로 행군하다 march north along a railway line

†**연설 演說** a (public) speech ; an address ; an oration ; a lecture ; speech-making **—하다** deliver a speech〔an address〕 ; address 《an audience》 ; speak 《to an audience, on a subject》 ; make an oration ; [즉흥적으로] give a talk 《on》 ¶ 영어 연설 an English speech ; a speech in English // 연설조로 in an oratorical tone // 연설을 잘〔못〕하다 be a good〔poor〕 speaker // 연설을 시작하다 open a speech // 연설을 방해하다 interrupt 《a person》 in his speech ; heckle (선거에서) // 연설을 속기하다 take down a speech in shorthand // 연설을 중지시키다 order the speaker to sit down ; cut short the speaker // 원고를 보면서 연설하다 make a speech from notes // 그의 연설을 들었느냐 Have you heard him speak in public ? // 그는 어떤 제목으로 연설을 했느냐 What did he speak on ?

—법 elocution ; oratory ; oration **— 어조** an oratorical〔a declamatory〕 tone **—자** a (public) speaker ; an orator **—집** a collection of one's speeches **—투** the style of speaking **—회** an oratorical〔a speech〕 meeting **—회장** a meeting hall **기조 —** ⇨ 기조 **대통령 후보 수락 —** the acceptance speech **명—** an eloquent speech **영어 —** an English speech ; a speech in English **즉석 —** an impromptu speech **추도 —** a memorial address **탁상 —** an after-dinner speech ; a table speech

연성 延性 〖물리〗 ductility ; malleability ¶ 연성의 malleable

연성 軟性 soft(ness) ; mild(ness)

— 하감 〖의학〗 a chancroid ; a soft chancre ¶ 연성 하감의 chancroidal

연세 年歲 age ; years of age ¶ 연세가 많다 be advanced〔well up〕 in years〔age〕 ; be old ; be an old man // 연세가 70이다 be seventy years old〔of age〕

연소 年少 tender age〔years〕 ; juvenility ; youth **—하다** (be) young ; young in years ¶ 연소한 탓으로 석방되다 be freed on account of minority〔one's being too young〕 // 왕이 연소하여 섭정을 두어 정사를 다스렸다 A regent was appointed to administer state affairs for the young king.

— 근로자 a minor worker ; a child laborer

연소 延燒 the spread of the fire **—하다** [불이] spread ; [건물이] catch fire ; burn down under the spreading fire ¶ 연소를 면하다 escape the fire〔the spreading flames〕 // 연소를 방지하다 check the spread of the flames // 불은 바람 부는 쪽으로 연소했다 The fire spread leeward. // 불이 이웃집으로 연소했다 The fire spread to the neighboring houses.

***연소 燃燒** combustion **—하다** burn ; ignite ; catch〔take〕 fire ¶ 연소성의 combustible ; inflammable

—기(器) a (gas) burner **—물** combustibles ; inflammable articles **—성** combustibility ; inflammability **— 시간** burning time **—실** a combustor ; a combustion chamber **— 장치** a burner ; a combustion apparatus **완전 —** perfect〔complete〕 combustion **자연 —** spontaneous combustion **완전 — 장치** a smoke consumer

연소 燃素 〖화학〗 phlogiston

—설 the phlogiston theory

†**연소자 年少者** a youth ; young people ; youngers ; those of few years ; minors ; people under age ¶ 연소자의 실업 unemployment among young people // 연소자의 보도 counselling for minors

— 범죄 juvenile delinquency

‡**연속 連續** continuity ; continuation ; continuance ; succession ; sequence ; a series ; a chain (연쇄) **—하다** continue ; be continuous ; last ; follow one after another

> 참고 **consecutive**는 1 2 3… 처럼 일관하여 끊어지지 않고 그 순서가 정해져 「연속하다」의 뜻 **successive**는 단순히 상호의 관계 위치를 나타내어 「연속하다」의 뜻으로서 consecutive만큼 직접적인 일관성이나 정해진 순서를 나타내지 않는다

¶ 연속적 consecutive ; successive // 3회 연속 강연 a series of three lectures // 불행의 연속 a series of misfortunes // 6개월 연속 흥행 a six months' run // 연속적인 살인 사건 a chain〔series〕 of murder cases // 연속 3안타 a barrage of three singles // 20일간 연속해서 for 20 consecutive days ; for 20 days without a break〔on end〕 // 연속적으로 쏘다 fire in rapid succession // 학교를 연속 2개월간 결석하다 absent oneself from school for two months on end // 영화가 연속 상연되다 The film runs continuously. // 요즈음 나는 액운의 연속이다 It never rains but it pours for me these days. // 그의 인생은 불행의 연속이었으나 His life was an endless chain of misfortunes.

—군(群) 〖수학〗 a continuous group —만화 a comic strip ; a strip of comics ; funnies 《미·구》 —물 a sequel ; a serial — 방송극 broadcast of dramatic series — 번호 consecutive〔running〕 numbers — 변이 〖생물〗 continuous variation — 비행 a nonstop〔sustained, continuous〕 flight — 상연 consecutive presentation〔performance〕 of a play〔drama〕 — 상영 consecutive〔continuative〕 showing of a film — 소설 a serial story — (3)안타〔호머〕 (three) back-to-back〔consecutive〕 hits 〔homers〕 —체 〖철학·수학〗 a continuum 《*pl.* -tinua》

연송 連誦 —하다 recite 《a whole book》 from first to last

연쇄 連鎖 a chain ; a link ; a series ; a connection

—군 〖유전〗 a linkage group —극 a play combined with moving picture ; a screen-and-stage play ; a combination play — 반응 〖물리〗 (a) chain reaction — 법 〖논리〗 sorites ; 〖수학〗 the chain rule — 비례 〖수학〗 chain proportion —상(狀) 구균 〖의학〗 a streptococcus 《*pl.* -cocci》 —식 〖논리〗 sorites ; [철도 신호] the interlocking system —점 a chain store 《미》 ; a multiple shop 《영》 — 지수 a chain index number — 추리 a chain of reasoning

연수 年數 the number of years ¶ 연수가 늘어감에 따라 as years go by ; with lapse of time // 이것은 연수가 상당히 되는 나무다 The tree is many years old. /This is an old tree.

연수 年收 an annual〔yearly〕 income ¶ 그의 연수는 8백만원이다 He has an annual income of eight million *won*. /He earns 〔makes〕 eight million *won* a year.

연수 延髓 〖해부〗 the medulla oblongata ; the afterbrain

연수 研修 study and training —하다 study 《science》 ; master 《English》 ; take〔go through〕 a training 《in》 ; pursue the study 《of history》

—생 a trainee —소〔원〕 an in-service training institute — 여행 a study tour 〔trip〕 — 제도 the (in-)service training system 사법 —원 the Judicial Training Institute 외무 공무원 —원 the Foreign Service Training Institute

연수 軟水 soft water

연수정 煙水晶 smoky quartz ; morion

연숙 鍊熟 dexterity〔mastery〕 through practice〔drill, training〕 —하다 be skilled〔practiced〕 in ; be a good hand at ; be at home in

†**연습 鍊習** practice ; exercise ; training ; a drill ; warming-up (경기 전의) ; a rehearsal (연극의) —하다 practice ; (have) exercise ; train ; drill ; rehearse ¶ 영어 문법 연습 a drill〔an exercise〕 in English grammar // 연습용 총 a training gun // 연습이 부족하다 lack training 〔practice〕 // 경기에 대비해서 연습하다 train for the race // 체육관에 가서 연습하다 go to the gymnasium for a workout〔training exercise〕 // 외국인을 상대로 영어 회화를 연습하다 practice speaking English on a foreigner // 학생에게 영작문을 연습시키다 drill students in English composition // 바이올린 켜는〔타자기 치는〕 연습을 하다 practice on the violin〔typewriter〕 ; take lessons in violin〔typewriter〕 // 연습을 하면 잘하게 된다 You will improve by exercise〔practice〕.

— 경기 a practice game〔match〕 —곡 〖음악〗 a study ; an étude —기 a trainer ; a training plane — 문제 exercises ; questions for study ; [제목] for study — 비행 a practice〔training〕 flight ; school flying —생 a trainee ; a student —선 a training ship — 시간 rehearsal time —실 a practice room —장 an exercise〔a drill〕 book ; a workbook —함〔함대〕 a training ship〔squadron〕 무대 — a stage rehearsal 사격 — gunnery exercise ; target practice 총— [무대 연습의] a dress rehearsal

†**연습 演習** [익힘] practice ; an exercise ; [기동 훈련] maneuvers ; [모의전] a sham battle ; mock〔mimic〕 warfare ; a seminar (대학의) —하다 practice ; carry out exercies ; hold〔carry out〕 maneuvers ¶ 영문법 연습 a seminar in English grammar

—림 an experimental plantation 기동 — maneuvers 반공 — an antiair raid drill ; air defense exercises 사격 — rifle practice 예행 — a rehearsal ; a preliminary exercise〔training〕 ; dry run 《미》

연습 부족 練習不足 lack of training ¶ 연습 부족이다 be out of practice ; be not sufficiently trained // 그것은 연습 부족 때문이다 It comes from insufficient practice.

연승 連勝 straight〔consecutive, successive〕 victories ; a series of victories ; victory after victory —하다 win〔gain〕 consecutive〔successive〕 victories ; win victory after victory ; win every battle ¶ 3연승하다 win three consecutive games ; win three games〔victories〕 consecutively〔in a row〕 // 연전 연승하다 win every battle // 자이언트 팀은 그해 두번이나 13연승을 했다 The Giants ripped off twice a winning streak of thirteen straight that year. // A팀은 B팀에 연승했다 The A team chalked their consecutive victory over the B team.

연승 連乘 〖수학〗 continual multiplication —하다 multiply continually

—적(積) continued product

연시 年始 the beginning of the year

연시 軟柿 〖식물〗 a mellowed〔ripe〕 persimmon

연시간 延時間 the total number of hours ;

the total man-hours
연식 軟式 nonrigid〔soft〕 type
— 비행선 a non-rigid airship ; a dirigible balloon — 야구 kittenball ; kitty ball ; softball 《미》 rubber-ball baseball
— 정구 softball tennis
연실 鳶— a kite-string ¶ 연실을 풀다 let out the string of a kite // 연실을 감다 haul in the string of a kite
연실 蓮實 [연밥] a lotus pip
†연안 沿岸 the coast ; the shore ¶ 연안에 on〔along〕 the coast〔shore〕 ; coastwise // 연안을 항해하다 sail along the coast
—류 a littoral current — 무역 coastal〔coastwise〕 trade — 방어 coast(al) defense — 수로 안내인 a coasting〔coastal〕 pilot — 어업 coastal〔inshore〕 fishery —항 a coastal port — 항로 coastwise〔coastal〕 service — 항로선 a coasting〔coastal〕 vessel ; a coaster — 항행 coastal〔coastwise〕 navigation 태평양 — 도시 cities on the Pacific
†연애 戀愛 love ; tender passion〔emotin, sentiment〕 ; affections ; amour ; love making —하다 fall in love 《with》 ¶ 순결한 연애 pure love // 정신적 연애 Platonic love // 연애에 탐닉하다 indulge in love affairs // 연애는 신성하다 Love is sacred. // 그는 평생토록 연애를 해본 적이 없다 His whole life has been loveless.
— 결혼 a love marriage ; a love match ¶ 연애 결혼을 하다 marry for love —관 a view〔theory, philosophy〕 of love — 대장 a Don Juan ; a libertine — 문제 a love problem — 문학 erotic literature — 사건 a love affair ; an amour ; a romance — 생활 a life devoted to love ; a love life — 소설 a romance〔love story〕 —술 the art of love ; erotic art —시〔시인〕 a love poem〔poet〕 — 지상주의 love for love's sake — 철학 philosophy of love — 편지 love letter 동성 — homosexual〔unisexual〕 love ; [남자간의] unnatural love ; sodomy ; [여자간의] Lesbian love ; sapphism 삼각 — a trangular 〔triple〕 love affair ; a (love) triangle 자유 — free love
연액 年額 an annual sum ; a yearly amount ¶ 연액 800만원의 이익 an annual profit of〔amounting to〕 eight million *won* // 그의 수입은 연액 600만원 이상이다 He earns〔draws〕 more than 6,000,000 *won* a year.
— 보장 임금제(도) guaranteed annual wage system
연야 連夜 night after night ; every night ¶ 연야의 nightly // 사흘 동안 연야 계속 작업하다 work for three consecutive nights
*연약 軟弱 tenderness ; weakness ; effeminacy ; [근육 따위의] flabbiness ; flaccidity —하다 (be) tender ; weak ; weak-hearted ; effeminat ; feeble ; frail ¶ 연약한 아이 a frail child // 연약한 나무 a tender plant // 연약해지다 weaken ; (grow) effeminate // 연약한 여성에게는 힘겨운 일이다 The work is too heavy for a tender woman.
— 외교 weak-kneed diplomacy
연어 連語 [복합어] a compound ; [구] a phrase
*연어 鰱魚 〖물고기〗 a salmon 《단복수 동형》 ; Onchorhynchus pets (학명) ¶ 얼간 연어 salted salmon
— 새끼 a young salmon ; a pink 《영》 — 통조림 canned salmon 《미》 ; tinned salmon 《영》
*연역 演繹 deduction ; deductive reasoning —하다 deduce 《from》 ; evolve ¶ 연역적(으로) deductive(ly) ; a priori ; syllogistic(ally) // 연역적 추리 deductive inference〔reasoning〕 // 연역적 의론 an a priori argument // 연역적 허위 a deductive fallacy
—법 the deductive method〔logic〕 ; deduction ; apriorism ; syllogism
연연 娟娟 a light color ; being light houed and beautiful being pretty and beautiful —하다 (be) light colored ; light and beautiful ; pretty and beautiful
연연 戀戀 strong attachment〔affection〕 —하다 be ardently attached 《to》 ; be fond 《of》 ; be unwilling to let go ; cling 《to》 ; long〔yearn, pine〕 《for》 ¶ 지위에 연연하다 be reluctant to give up one's position // 그 여자는 그에게 아직도 연연한 정을 품고 있다 She still retains a lingering love for the man. // 연연한 사연을 담은 긴 편지를 그녀에게 보냈다 He wrote a long letter to her saying how crazy he was about her.
연염 beef rump
*연예 演藝 a performance ; (musical, dramatic) entertainments —하다 perform ; entertain ; put on entertainment ¶ 연예계의 사람 men in the entertainment world〔business〕 // 연예인 일행은 노래와 춤으로 장병들을 위문했다. A company of entertainers entertained troops with songs and dances. // 그 여자는 연예계에서 아직도 활동하고 있지 She's still active in the showbiz.
—계 the entertainment world〔business〕 —기자 an entertainments reporter —란 the entertainments column〔section〕 — 방송 theatrical broadcasts ; an amusement (radio) program —업 show business —인 a performer ; an entertainer ; an artiste —장 an entertainment hall ; a variety theater ; a vaudeville house〔theater〕 《미》 ; a music hall ; a place of entertainment
연옥 煉獄 purgatory ; hell ¶ 연옥 같은 고통 purgatorial sufferings // 연옥의 고통을 겪다 go through purgatory〔hell〕
연옥색 軟玉色 light bluish green
연와 煉瓦 (a) brick ⇨ 벽돌
—조(造) 건물 a brick building ; a build-

ing in brick

연용 連用 continuous use **—하다** take 《medicine》 continuously

연우 煙雨 [가랑비] a misty〔fine, drizzling〕 rain ; drizzle

연운 年運 the fortune〔luck〕 of the year

연원 淵源 an origin ; a source ; a beginning ; an inception ; a fountainhead **—하다** come from ; originate in ; take rise in ; issue out of ¶ 연원을 더듬다 trace the origin of ; trace 《a thing》 to its source

연월 煙月, 烟月 [달빛] misty moonlight ; [시절] peaceful times

연월일 年月日 the date ¶ 연월일을 기입하다 date 《a letter》; give the date ; affix〔attach, out〕 a date 《to a paper》// 연월일이 없는 편지 an undated letter // 연월일 순으로 철하다 file in close chronological order

연유 緣由 [유래] origin ; derivation ; source ; [사유] a reason ; a cause ; a ground **—하다** originate 《in》; be derived 《from》; derive itself〔its origin〕 from

연유 煉乳 condensed milk

연유 燃油 fuel oil

—선 an oil-burning ship

연음 延音 a prolonged〔held, lengthened〕 sound ; a long vowel〔syllable〕

— 기호 〖음악〗 a long mark ; a length mark

연의 演義 [늘여 설명함] expansion ; amplification ; [주해] an exposition ; a commentary ; [통속적 개작] a popular version ; an adaptation for popular reading **—하다** explain ; comment 《on the text》; elcidate

삼국지 — a popular version of the historical novel *Samkukchi*

연이나 然— however ; but ; and yet ; still ; nevertheless

연이율 年利率 annual rate of interest ⇨ 연리

연익 年益 an annual profit ; the profit per annum

†**연인 戀人** a sweetheart (남녀) ; a lover (주로 남자) ; a love (주로 여자) ; a best girl 《미》; a ladylove ; one's mistress (정부) ¶ 한쌍의 연인 a pair of lovers // 옛날의 연인 one's old flame // 연인이 생기다 get her man (여자에게) // 그녀는 나의 연인이다 She is my girl.

연인 連印 joint affixing of signature seals **—하다** affix one's seal jointly 《to a document》

연인원 延人員 the total man-days ; the total number of persons〔workers〕 ¶ 승객 연인원 the total number of passengers carried // 연인원 2,500명 2,500 man-days // 그 공사는 연인원 5,000명을 요했다 The work required 5,000 mandays.

연일 連日 every day ; day after〔by〕 day ; day in and out ; consecutive days ; several days in succession ¶ 연일 계속되는 가뭄〔비〕 a long spell of dry〔rainy〕 weather // 연일 비가 내린다 It rains day in and day out. // 극장은 연일 대만원이다 The theater is drawing a full house every day. // 그 상점은 연일 성황을 이루고 있다 The shop is doing a roaring business every day. // 출근 시간에는 버스마다 연일 만원이다 Every bus is loaded to its full capacity every day at rush hour.

— 연야(連夜) day(s) and night(s)

연일수 延日數 the total number of days ; a man-day 《미》

연임 連任 reappointment ; reelection (재선) **—하다** be reappointed ; be reelected ; resume the office ¶ A 은행장에는 김씨가 연임되었다 Mr. *Kim* has been reappointed President of the A bank.

연잇다 連— [연속하다] continue ; follow one after another ; [연결하다] join one after another ; conect〔link, piece〕 together ¶ 연이어 continuously ; successively ; in succession ; without intermission〔a break〕; at a stretch ; one after another // 세번을 연이어 three consecutive times ; three times running // 연이어 3일간 for three consecutive〔successive〕 days ; for three days running〔on end〕 // 연이은 불행 a train〔series, chapter, succession〕 of misfortunes ; the consecutive misfortune // 연이어 손해를 보다 suffer series of losses ; suffer loss upon loss // 면장의 종이를 연잇다 put some pieces of paper together // 교통 사고가 연이어 일어났다 Traffic accidents occurred in succession. // 한달 동안 연이어 비가 왔다 It has rained for a month running〔in a row〕. // 연이어 김씨의 강연이 있었다 It was followed by Mr. *Kim's* lecture.

연잎 蓮— a lotus leaf

연자매 硏子— a millstone worked by horse or ox

연자맷간 a beastworked mill

연자방아 硏子— ⇨ 연자매(硏子—)

연작 連作 —하다 plant consecutively ; make a repeated cultivation

†**연장** a tool ; an implement ; a utensil (특수용) ; an instrument (계기) ¶ 농사에 쓰는 연장 a farming tool〔utensil〕; farm implements // 연장 한벌 kit ; an outfit

—궤 a tool-boox〔-chest〕; a (workman's) kit **—주머니** a tool-bag

‡**연장 年長** seniority ¶ 연장의 older ; elder ; senior // 마을의 최고 연장자 the oldest man in the village // 그는 나보다 2년 연장 입니다 He is two years older than I. /He is my senior by two years. /He is two years my senior. // 진급은 연장 여부에 구애됨이 없이 능력에 따라 실시할 것임 Promotion will be made on the basis of demonstrated abilities regardless of

seniority.
—자 an elder (원로) ; a senior (연상) ; a superior in age

연장 延長 extension ; continuation (지속) ; prolongation ; 〖수학〗 production **—하다** extend ; lengthen ; prolong ; renew (계약 기한 따위) ; produce ⟪a line to the point⟫ ¶ 선의 연장 the production of a line // …의 연장이다 be an extension of // 철도를 연장하다 extend a railway // 수명을 연장하다 lengthen one's span of life // 회기를 연장하다 prolong the session // 기간을 2년으로 연장하다 increase the term to two years // 군 복무기간이 3년으로 연장되었다 The term of military service was extended to three years. // 그 회합은 밤까지 연장되었다 The meeting was prolonged into the night. // 요즈음 연장 근무가 많군요 Lately you've been putting in a lot of overtime, dear.
— 구역 the reach —기호 〖음악〗 a hold ; a pause ; a fermata ⟪이⟫ —선 an extension (line) ; a prolongation —성 〖심리〗 extensity —전 〖야구〗 extra innings ¶ 연장전 끝에 지다 lose in overtime ⟪to the Giants⟫ // 시합은 연장전으로 접어 들었다 The match went into extra innings. (야구에서)

연재 連載 serial publication **—하다** publish serially ; give〔present〕 in serial form ; serialize ⟪미⟫ ¶ 소설을 연재하다 publish a novel serially〔in installments〕 // 그것은 모 일간 신문에 연재되었다 It was published serially in a daily newspaper.
— 만화 comic strips —물 a serial (story) ; a story given in installments ¶ 신문의 연재물 a serial story in a newspaper ; a newspaper serial — 소설 a serial novel

연적 硯滴 a Chinese ink water container ; a container for Chinese ink slab water

연적 戀敵 a rival in love ; a rival lover ; a rival suitor

연전 年前 some〔a few, a couple of〕 years ago ; a few years back〔before〕

연전 連戰 a series of〔successive〕 battles ; battle after battle ; every battle **—하다** fight a series of battles ; participate in successive battles

연전 揀箭 retrieving arrows
—동(童) a boy who retrieves arrows

연전연승 連戰連勝 a succession〔series〕 of victories **—하다** win consecutive victories ; gain a series of victories ; win every battle one fights ; win battle after battle ; win victory after victory ¶ 우리 육해군은 연전연승했다 There was an unbroken series of victories for our army and navy. // 5회나 (연전)연승하다 with five straight games〔battles〕

연전연패 連戰連敗 a succession〔series〕 of defeats **—하다** lose every battle that one fights ; be defeated〔suffer defeat〕 in every battle ; lose one battle after another〔battle after battle〕

연접 連接 connection ; junction ; combination **—하다** connect ; combine ; interlock (열차를) ; switch (전화를)
—봉(棒) 〖기계〗 a connecting rod ; a pitman —부 〖생물〗 a synapse

연정 戀情 (a feeling of) love ; attachment ; tender passion〔feeling〕 ¶ 불타는 연정 burning passion ; passionate love // 연정에 불타다 burn with love ⟪for a person⟫ ; languish in love ⟪for⟫ // 연정을 느끼다 feel attached to ⟪a girl⟫ // 연정을 고백하다 confess one's love // 연정은 이성과 합치하지 않는다 Love and reason do not go together.

연제 演題 the subject (of a lecture) ; the theme ¶ 문명이란 연제로 강연하다 speak〔lecture〕 on the subject of civilization // 연제는 미정이다 The subject of a lecture is undecided.

연좌 連坐 ① [관련] implication ; involvement ; complicity **—하다** be implicated〔involved〕 in ⟪an affair⟫ ¶ 의혹 사건에 연좌되다 be involved〔implicated〕 in a scandal ; link one's name with a scandal ② [앉음] sitting down in a group **—하다** sit down in a group
— 데모 a sit-in〔-down〕 demonstration ¶ 연좌 데모하다 stage a sit-down demonstration — 스트라이크 a sit-down strike — 전술 sit-down tactics ¶ 연좌 전술을 취하다 resort to sit-down tactics — 제도 the guilt-by-association system ; the involvement system

†**연주 演奏** a musical performance **—하다** perform ; play ; render ; give a performance ¶ 기타를 연주하다 play the guitar // (악대가) 국가를 연주하다 strike up the national anthem // 군악대의 연주가 있을 것이다 A military band will render 〔play〕 selections.
— 곡목 a repertoire ; a (musical) program —기술 technical skill ; technique —법 execution ; technique ; interpretation — 여행 a recitel〔concert〕 tour —자 a player ; a performer 처녀 — one's maiden recital

연주창 連珠瘡 〖의학〗 scrofula ; struma ; the king's evil

연주회 演奏會 a concert ; a recital (독주회) ; a joint recital (합동 연주회) ¶ 연주회를 개최하다 give a concert〔recital〕 // 그것이 그녀가 연주회에 나온 최후였다 It was her last concert appearance.
피아노 — a piano recital

연죽 煙竹 a tobacco pipe

연줄 緣— a relation ; a connection ; pull ; interest ; good offices (알선) ; medium (중개) ; influence (세력) ¶ 연줄이 좋은 사람 a well-connected person // …의 연줄로 through the influence

〔medium, good offices〕《of》// 연줄을 구하다 make interest ; hunt up connections // 좋은 연줄이 있다 have a strong pull // 연줄을 맺다 form〔establish〕 one's connections 《with》// 연줄을 끊다 sever〔cut off〕 one's connections with ; be through with // 좋은 연줄을 타서 출세하다 rise to prominence taking advantage of a strong pull // 그는 동창생 연줄로 취직했다 He got a position through the influence of his schoolmate. // 그는 실력보다 연줄 덕분으로 현 지위를 차지했다 He owed his present position to influence, not merit. // 연줄이 있었어 I have a few connections. // 이제 나는 연줄에 의지하는 수밖에 없다 All I can do now is rely on my connections. // 아버지 친구의 연줄로 일을 얻었다 I got a job though the connections of a friend of my father's.

연줄 鳶— [연실] the string of a kite

연줄연줄 緣—緣— through one's connections ; through one connection after another ; on the strength of some connection ¶ 친지를 찾아 그의 거처를 연줄연줄 알아보았다 I inquired into his whereabouts through my acquaintances.

연중 年中 the whole year ; all the year round ; throughout the year ; every day of the year ¶ 연중 무휴간 a year-round publication // 농부들은 연중 내내 열심히 일하지 않으면 안된다 Farmers must work very hard all through the year. // 큰 거리는 연중 내내 번잡하다 The main street is busy all the times〔seasons〕 of the year. // 박물관은 연중 공개된다 The museum remains〔is〕 open all the year round.
— 무휴 open year round ; Open Throughout The Year. (게시)

연중 행사 年中行事 (regular) annual 〔yearly〕 events〔affairs, features, tunctions〕 ¶ 그 경기는 학교의 연중 행사가 되었다 The match became a part of the annual school routine. // 이 지방에서는 홍수가 연중 행사처럼 일어난다 Flood is practically an annual occurrence in this district.

연지 蓮池 a lotus pond

*****연직 鉛直** perpendicular(ity) ; vertical (-ity) ; (being) plumb
—각 a vertical angle ; an angle of elevation —면 a vertical plane —선 a vertical〔plumb〕 line

연질 軟質 soft(ness)
— 고무 soft rubber — 유리 soft glass

연차 年次 ① [나이 차례] order by age ; seniority order ¶ 연차로 in order of age ② [해수 차례] order by year ; chronological order ¶ 연차의 annual ; yearly // 연차적으로 chronologically
— 계획 a (long-term) yearly plan〔program〕 — 대회〔총회〕 an annual general meeting —보고〔예산〕 an annual report 〔budget〕 — 휴가 an annual vacation 〔holiday, leave〕

연차 年差 〖천문〗 an annual〔a yearly〕 variation

연착 延着 late〔belated, delayed〕 arrival ; delay 《in deliver》 —하다 arrive late〔behind time〕 ; be delayed ; be overdue ¶ 연착한 우편물 belated mail // 그 열차는 한시간 연착했다 The train arrived an hour late. /The train was an hour overdue〔behind time〕.

연착 連着 soft landing ¶ 달에 연착하다 make a soft landing on the moon

연찬 研鑽 study ; prosecution of one's studies〔research〕 —하다 study ; prosecute 《one's studies》 ; accomplish oneself ¶ 다년간의 연찬의 결과 after years of study

연창 —窓 a storm window

연천 年淺 —하다 be short〔brief〕 in years ; be not long ¶ 그 회사는 창립한지 아직 연천하다 It is only a short time since the company was founded.

연철 鍊鐵 〖야금〗 wrought iron
—로(爐) a puddling furnace ; a puddler
—법 puddling

연체 延滯 delay ; arrear ; procrastination —하다 be delayed ; be overdue ; be remiss ; be in arrears (지불 따위) ¶ 지불이 연체되다 become remiss in one's payment // 집세가 3개월이나 연체되었다 The rent is three months overdue.
—금 arrears ; arrearages — 대출(貸出) overdue bank loans —세(금) taxes in arrears — 이자 interest for〔on〕 delay 〔arrears〕 ; overdue interest —인 a person who is in arrears ; a delinquent —일변(日邊) daily interest for arrearages — 일수 days in arrears — 집세 arrears of rent — 통지 overdue notice

연체동물 軟體動物 a mollusc ; Mollucca 《총칭》
—학 malacology —학자 a malacologist

연초 年初 the bebinning of the year ⇨ 연시(年始) ¶ 연초에 at the beginning of the year ; in the fresh of the year

연초 煙草 tobacco ⇨ 담배

연초록 軟草綠 light green

*****연출 演出** production ; presentation —하다 produce 《a play》 ; present ; stage ; perform ¶ 거기서 일장의 희극이 연출되었다 A comic scene was enacted on the spot.
—가〔자〕 a producer ; a dirctor 《미》 —대본 an action copy〔script〕 —법 execution ; the manner of performance ; interpreation ; dramaturgy — 효과 stage effect

연춧대 輦— [연의] a side board attached to the yoke of a royal sedan chair

연치 年齒 age ; years ; time of life

연타 軟打 〖야구〗 a bunt ; bunting ⇨ 번트

연타하다 連打— [종 따위를] clang 《a bell》 repeatedly ; [구타] deliver a shower of blows 《on a person》

*연탄 煉炭 a briquet
— 가스 coal gas — 가스 중독 anthracite coal gas poisoning — 공장 a briquet manufactory — 난로 a briquet stove — 제조기 a briquet pressing machine 십구공 — a 19-hole briquet

연통 煙筒 a smoke pipe ; a stove pipe ; a smokestack ; a funnel (기선의) ; a chimney (굴뚝) ¶ 두개의 연통을 가진 기선 a two-funneled steamer // 연통을 소제하다 sweep a chimney // 연통이 잘 통한다 This smoke pipe draws freely. // 연통이 메었다 The chimney is choked up.
— 소제부 a chimney sweeper〔cleaner〕

연투하다 連投— 〖야구〗 take the mound in 《three》 successive games

연파 軟派 the moderate party ; the moderates ¶ 연파의 의원 a moderate member ; a trimmer ; a timeserver // 연파 학생 a romantic group of students // 저 친구는 연파에 속한다 He is rather on the softer side.
— 문학 erotic literature

연판 鉛版 a stereotype ; a plate ¶ 연판을 뜨다 stereotype ; make a stereotype of // 연판으로 인쇄하다 stereotype
—공 a stereotyper — 인쇄 stereotypography — 인쇄공 a stereotypographer — 제조〔제조법, 인쇄술〕 stereotypy ; stereotype

연판 連判 a joint signature〔seal〕 —하다 sign〔seal〕 jointly ¶ 연판에 가맹하다 add one's name to joint signatures // 연판에서 이탈하다 disavow one's signature
—자 a cosignatory —장 a list of signers to the compact ; a compact〔covenant〕 under joint signature

연패 連敗 defeats in succession ; successive defeats —하다 suffer successive defeats〔reverses〕 ¶ 연패의 장군 a general with no victory to his credit // 연전연패하다 lose every battle ; be a constant loser // 3회 연패하다 lose three consecutive games〔battles〕 // 선거에서 연패하다 suffer successive defeats in the elections

연패 連覇 ⇨ 연승(連勝)

연평수 延坪數 the total floorage ; the total floor space 《of a building》

연포 練布 glossed〔boiled-off〕 cloth

연폭 連幅 joining 《paper》 ; piecing together —하다 join〔piece〕 together

연표 年表 a chronological table ; [연대기] chronology
세계사〔한국사〕 — a chronological table of world〔Korean〕 history

연풍 軟風 a gentle breeze ; a light〔soft, mild〕 wind ; a zephyr 《시》

†연필 鉛筆 a (lead) pencil ¶ 연필 끝 a pencil point // 연필 심 a pencil lead // 연필을 깎다 sharpen a pencil // 연필로 쓰다 write in pencil ; write with a pencil // 벽지에 연필의 낙서자국이 있다 There are pencilings〔pencil marks〕 on the wallpaper.
— 깎개 a pencil sharpener —화 a picture in pencil ; a pencil sketch 색— a color pencil 제도 — a drawing pencil

연하 嚥下 swallowing ; deglutition —하다 swallow ; gukp down ; gorge

연하 煙霞 haze ; fog and mist

연하 年賀 the New Year's greetings ; the compliments of the season
—객 a New Year's caller〔visitor〕 — 우편 New Year's mail

연하 年下 juniority ¶ 연하의 younger ; junior

†연하다 軟— ① [무르다] (be) tender ; soft ; mild ¶ 연한 고기 tender meat // 연하게 하다 soften ; make soft ; tenderize ② [빛이] (be) light ; soft ¶ 연한 빛깔 a light color // 연한 광선 a soft〔subdued〕 light // 연한 태양빛 soft rays of the sun // 연한 차 weak tea // 연한 우유 watery milk // 빛깔을 연하게 하다 lighten the color ; make the color light

연하다 連— connect ; link ; join ; adjoin ¶ 두 집이 서로 연해 있다 The two houses adjoin each other. // 작은 나라를 사이에 두고 두 강대국이 연해 있다 The small country is sandwiched in between two great powers.

-연하다 然— pretend to be ; act as if 《one were》 ; have〔put on〕 the airs of ¶ 학자연하다 put on the airs of a scholar // 왕자연한 생활을 하다 live like a prince

연하장 年賀狀 a New Year's card ¶ 연하장을 보내다 send 《a person》 a New Year's card〔the New Year's greetings〕

연학 硏學 the pursuit of one's studies ; study —하다 pursue one's studies ; study (hard) ¶ 연학기(期) time for study // 연학차 도미하다 go to America for study

연한 年限 a term ; a period ; length of time ¶ 연한을 채우다 serve one's term // 연한이 찼다 The term has expired〔is up〕.
복무 — a term of service〔office〕 수업 — a term of study 의무 — an obligatory〔a compulsory〕 term of service ; the term of obligation 재직 — a tenure of office

†연합 聯合 combination (연결) ; union (조합) ; league ; alliance (동맹) ; concert (일치) ; amalgamation (합동) ; incoporation ; confederacy ; coalition (정당의) —하다 combine 《with》 ; ally ; unite 《with》 ; join ; league 《with》 ; amalgamate 《with》 ; confederate 《with》 ¶ 연합하여 in league〔combination, concert〕 with // 연합하여 적에 대항하다 unite in the struggle against an enemy // 여러 교회가 연합해서 예배를 보았다 Many of the churches held joint services. // 잉글랜드와 스코틀랜드는 연합하여 하나의 왕국을 이루었다 England and Scotland were unit-

ed into one kingdom.
— 고사 joint examination〔test〕 — 단체 a federation — 작전 combined〔joint〕 operations — 전선 the united front — 함대 a combined fleet〔squadron〕

연합국 聯合國 the Allied Powers〔Nations〕; the Allies
— 관리 위원회 the Allied Control Committee —인 Allied nationals — 점령군 the Allied Occupation Firces — 총〔최고〕사령관 the Supreme Commander for the Allied Powers《SCAP》 — 총사령부 the General Headquarters of the Allied Powers《GHQ》

연합군 聯合軍 the allied forces ; the Allies ; the combined forces

연해 沿海 coastal waters ; the coast ; the inshore ¶ 연해의 coastal ; inshore ; littoral ; longshore // 연해안을 항해하다 sail coastwise ; sail along the coast
— 경비 coastal defense〔guard〕 —도시 coast cities — 무역 coastal〔coastion〕 trade —선(船) a coastion vessel ; a coastal trader — 어업 inshore〔coastal〕 fishery ; longshore fishing — 지방 the littoral zone — 항로 a coastal line — 항해 a coastal voyage

연해 連— successively ; incessantly ; continuously ; unceasingly ; without a break ¶ 전화가 연해 걸려 오다 have telephone calls almost without a break // 불행이 연해 생기다 have a run of ill luck ; one misfortune follows another // 연해 눈이 온다 It continues snowing. /It keeps on snowing.

연해 煙害 smoke pollution

연해안 沿海岸 the coast ; the shore
— 지대 coastland

연해연방 successively ; contnuously ; one after another ¶ 연해연방 손님이 오다 have a constant stream of visitors ; visitors come one after another // 자동차가 연해연방 지나간다 There is a constant〔continuous〕 stream of cars.

연해주 沿海州 〖지리〗 the Maritime Provinces (of Siberia)

연행 連行 —하다 walk〔take, escort〕《a suspect to a police station》 ¶ 그는 취조를 받기 위해 경찰서에 연행되었다 He was taken to the police station for interrogation. // 순경이 그를 연행해 갔다 The policeman walked him off〔away〕.

연혁 沿革 history ; origin and development ¶ 방문자에게 학교의 연혁을 설명하다 brief visitors on the school history
—지(誌) a historical record ; a history

연호 年號 the name of ans era ; a chronological era

연화 軟化 softening ; mollification ; weakening —하다 soften ; mollify ; tone down ; go soft ; 〖경제〗 weaken
— 경향〔시세(時勢)〕 a weakening tendency —도(度) a softening degree — 요인 a weakening〔discouraging〕 factor —제 a softener 식육(食肉) —제 a tenderizer

연화 軟貨 soft money〔currency〕

연환 連環 a chain

‡연회 宴會 a feast ; a dinner party ; a banquet ; an entertainment ¶ 연회를 열다 give a dinner party ; hold〔give〕 a banquet // 연회에 참석하다 attend a party
—장 a banquet(ing) hall — 정치 politicking by wining and dining 신년 — a New Year's feast〔banquet, (dinner) party〕

연회 年會 an annal convention〔meeting〕

연후 然後 after that ; afterwards ¶ 연후에 after that ; thereafter ; afterwards ; thenceforth

연휴 連休 consecutive holidays ¶ 연휴를 즐기다 enjoy straight holidays // 이번 3일 연휴에 특별한 계획이라도 있니 Do you have any plans for this 3-day weekend ?

연희 演戲 a play ; theatricals ; dramatics ; dramatic performances —하다 give a play ; perform a play on the stage

*열[1] ten ; half a score ¶ 열번째 the tenth // 열시 ten o'clock // 열살 가량의 계집아이 a girl about ten years odd // 열 남짓한 ten odd《people》 // 열겹의〔으로〕 tenfold // 그 사람의 명령을 하나에서 열까지 다 복종할 수는 없다 I cannot obey him in every particular. // 지자는 하나를 듣고 열을 깨닫는다 A word to the wise is enough.
열 길 물 속은 알아도 한 길 사람의 속은 모른다 〔속담〕 You can sound water ten fathoms deep, but you cannot sound the human heart a single fathom.
열 번 찍어 안 넘어가는 나무 없다 〔속담〕 Little strokes fell oaks.

열[2] ① [챗열] a whiplash ② [총열] a gun barrel

†열 列 a line ; a row ; a file ; a column (종렬) ; a rank (횡렬) ; procession (행렬) ; a queue ¶ 열을 지어 in line〔row, file, queue〕 // 열 밖에 out of the ranks // 2열로 in a double line ; in two rows〔ranks〕; in double file〔column〕 // 4열로 줄선 군인 soldiers four rows deep // 열을 짓다 from a line〔row, file〕 // 1열로 서다 line up〔be drawn up〕 in single file // 열지어 행진하다 march in files ; parade in columns // 열을 이탈하다 drop out of line // 많은 사람들이 극장 앞에 열지어 서 있었다 A large number of people queued up before the theater. // 저 열은 덜 붐빈다 Those lines over there are less crowded.

‡열 熱 ① [열기] heat ; warmth ¶ 열의 caloric ; thermic ; thermal // 열을 발생하다 generate heat // 열을 가하다 heat ; apply heat // 열을 발산하다 radiate〔give off〕 heat
② [체온] temperatue ; [병원] fever ¶ 높은〔낮은〕 열 a high〔low〕 fever // 열을 재다 take one's temperature // 열이 나다

develop fever ; become feverish // 열을 식히다 bring down fever // 감기로 열이 났다 My cold has brought on a fever.
③ [열광·유행] enthusiasm ; fever ; mania ; craze ; fad ¶ 열을 내다 become hot ; become enthusiastic 《over》 ; have a craze 《for》 // 미국열이 한창이다 Things American have recently become all the rage. /There is a mania〔fad〕 for things American. // 열을 식히다 cool down one's enthusiasm // 일반의 야구열을 돋우다 fire the interest of the public in baseball // 공부에 열을 안내다 do one's lessons in a half-hearted way ; take little interest in one's school work
④ [격정·노함] passion ; anger ; heat ; vehemence ; fury ¶ 열이 나다 be heated (with passion) ; be vehement ; get angry ; get hot under the collar // 열이 나서 아무를 때리다 strike a person in passion
—기관 a heat engine ; a thermomoter —단위 ⇨ 열량 단위 —복(방)사 heat 〔thermal〕 radiation —에너지 thermal energy —용량 thermal〔heat〕 capacity —전달 heat transfer〔transmission〕 —효율 『물리』 thermal efficiency 문학— a craze 〔mania〕 for literature 미국— the America boom 야구— baseball fever ; enthusiasm for baseball 우표 수집— a stamp-collecting craze ; a rage for stamp collecting 태양(복사)— solar 〔radiant〕 heat 투기— speculation fever

열- young ; new ¶ 열무 a young radish

열각 劣角 『기하』 a minor angle

열간 가공 熱間加工 hot working

열간 압연 熱間壓延 hot rolling

열강 列强 the Great Powers ¶ 세계의 열강 the Word Powers

*__열거 列擧__ enumeration —하다 enumerate ; list ; go〔run〕 through the list 〔catalog〕 of ¶ 이루 다 열거할 수 없다 be too many to enumerate

열검파기 熱檢波器 a thermo-detector

열고 나다 busy oneself in ; be bent〔intent〕 on ; be in a hurry 《to do》 ¶ 돈벌기에 열고 나다 be intent on〔be absorbed in〕 making money // 방을 정돈하느라고 열고 났다 She busied herself in keeping the room in order.

열관리 熱管理 control of heat ; heat control
—자(사) a heat controller

†**열광 熱狂** wild enthusiasm ; a fever of enthusiasm ; excitement ; passion ; fanaticism ; frenzy —하다 go wild with enthusiasm ; be wildly excited ; go crazy over ; run mad after ¶ 열광적인 wild ; frantic ; fanatic (광신적) ; hectic // 열광하여 wildly ; enthusiastically ; frantically // 열광적 환영을 받다 be receive with wild enthusiasm ; be given an enthusiastic welcome // 청중을 열광시키다 make the audience wild with enthusiasm // 모두 열광하고 있다 They are wild with excitement. // 그는 야구에 열광하고 있다 He is crazy over baseball.

열구름 floating〔drifting〕 clouds ; moving 〔passing〕 clouds

열국 列國 the Powers ; the nations of the world ; all countries ¶ 열국 회의 a conference of the Powers ; an international conference // 열국의 간섭 foreign intervention // 구라파 열국 the European Powers // 지금 세계의 열국은 2대 진영으로 대별할 수 있다 Now the world may be divided into two major camps.

⁑**열기 熱氣** ① [더운 공기] heat ; hot air ; heated atmosphere ¶ 열기를 뿜다 radiate〔give off〕 heat
② [열정] ardor ; enthusiasm ¶ 열기 있게 일하다 work ardently // 열기에 사람을 욕하다 call 《a person》 names in a fury
③ [신열] fever ¶ 열기가 좀 있군요 You have a slight fever.
— 기관 a hot-air engine — 난방 hot-air heating — 소독 hot-air sterilization

열기 列記 enumeration ; listing —하다 enumerate ⇨ 열거

열김 熱— ① [열정] ardor ; enthusiasm ; fervor ; passion ; heat ; excitement
② [홧김] anger ; indignation ; fury ; a fit of anger〔temper, rage〕 ¶ 열김에 in (one's) anger ; in a fury ; in indignation ; in a fit of anger〔rage〕 // 그는 열김에 자리에서 벌떡 일어났다 He started his seat in indignation.

열끼 dauntless spirit

열나다 熱— ① [몸에] have (a) fever ; become feverish ; develop fever ; come to have fever ¶ 저녁이면 열이 난다 I have a fever every evening.
② [열중] become enthusiastic 《about》 ; have a craze 《for》 ; be mad 《for》 ; be keen〔intent〕 《on》 ¶ 열이 나서 춤추다 be mad on dancing // 돈 모으기에 열나다 be intent on making money
③ [화나다] become hot 《with anger》 ; get〔become〕 angry ; get excited ; flate up 《with anger》 ; be furious ; be heated with passion ; get heated up ¶ 열이 나서 이야기하다 speak with great heat // 사소한 일에 열나다 get mad on the slightest provocation // 그 여자 열나게 하네 She burns me up. /She gets me fired up.

열나절 a very long time

열넷 fourteen ¶ 열넷째 the fourteenth

열녀 烈女 a heroine ; a heroic woman ; a woman of chaste reputa tion ; an exemplary woman ; an exceptionally virtuous woman ¶ 열녀는 불사 이부 A woman of virtue marries but once.

⁑**열다¹** ① open ; lift (뚜껑을) ; unfold (펴다) ; undo (꾸러미를) ; unlock (자물쇠를) ¶ 비틀어 열다 wrench open // 부숴 열다 break open // 억지로 열다 force open //

문을 열어 놓다 keep〔leave〕 the door open // 5페이지를 열다 turn to page 5 ; open the book at page 5 // 문을 열면 복도로 나선다 The door open into the passage. // 그는 자물쇠를 비틀어 열었다 He picked a lock. // 창문을 열어 놓고 자거라 Sleep with the windows open.

② [개시] open ; set up ¶ 가게를 열다 open a hop〔store〕 ; set up in business

③ [개최] hold ; give open ¶ 운동회를 열다 hold an athletic meeting // 잔치를 열다 give〔hold〕 a banquet // 회의를 열다 hold a meeting // 전람회를 열다 hold an exhibit 《of》

④ [길을] ¶ 길을 열다 clear the way 《for》 ; make way 《for a person》 // 후진을 위하여 길을 열어주다 give the young fellows a chance ; make way for one's juniors // 젊은 사람들을 위해서 길을 열어줘야 한다는 생각이 든다 I just feel that I should make way for new blood.

†**열다²** [열매가] bear 《fruit》 ; grow (열매가 주어) ¶ 열매가 잔뜩 열린 나무 a tree laden with fruits // 열매가 열다 bear fruits // 이 나무에 열매가 잘 열린다 This tree bears well. // 돈이 열리는 나무는 없소 I've got no bush money grows on.

열다섯 fifteen ¶ 열다섯째 the fifteeth

열단위 熱單位 〖물리〗 a heat〔thermal〕 unit

***열대 熱帶** the tropics ; the torrid zone ¶ 열대의 tropical

—병 a tropical disease **—성 저기압** tropical atmospheric pressure **— 식물** a tropical plant ; tropical flora 《총칭》 **—어** a tropical fish **— 의학** tropical medicine **— 조(鳥)** a tropic bird **— 지방** the tropics ; the torrid zone

열댓 about〔around〕 fifteen ¶ 열댓살 가량의 나이 somewhere about fifteen years of age // 열댓명이 떼를 지어 in a group of fifteen or so

열도 列島 a chain〔group〕 of islands ; an archipelago

유구 — the Ryukyu Islands

열도 熱度 [열] (degree of) heat ; temperature ; [열심의 정도] degree of enthusiasm

—계 a calorimeter

열독 閱讀 peruse ; reading over **— 하다** peruse ; read ; examine 《a book》 ; run through

열둘 twelve ¶ 열두째 the twelfth

****열등 劣等** inferiority ; low grade **— 하다** (be) inferior ; poor ¶ 그는 반에서 성적이 가장 열등하다 He is the poorest student in the class.

—국 a backward country ; a weak country **—생** a backward〔slow〕 student **—아** a feeble-headed〔-minded〕 child ; a subnormal〔an inferior〕 child **— 인종** an inferior race **—재** 〖경제〗 inferior goods **—품** low-grade articles〔goods〕 ; an article of inferior quality

열등감 劣等感 a sense of inferiority ; (an) inferiority complex ¶ 열등감을 갖다 have a sense of inferiority ; be possessed by inferiority complex // 열등감을 갖게 하다 give 《a person》 an inferiority complex // 그는 열등감에 사로잡혀 있다 He is swayed by a feeling of inferiority.

열락 悅樂 joy ; pleasure ; delight ; mirth ; gaiety **— 하다** be pleased 《about》 ; take pleasure〔delight〕 in ; delight〔rejoice〕 《in, at, over》

열람 閱覽 perusal ; reading ; inspection **— 하다** peruse ; read ; inspect ¶ 그는 비장했던 서적을 일반이 열람토록 제공했다 He offered the treasured books for public reading.

—권 a library admission ticket **—인** a reader ; a visitor **—표** a call slip **도서 —료** an admission fee (of a library) **무료 —** free admission (to a library)

열람실 閱覽室 a reading room

— 직원 a reading room attendant

열량 熱量 heat capacity ; calorid (단위) ¶ 열량이 많다〔적다〕 be high〔low〕 in calories // 이 음식물은 2,000칼로리의 열량이 있다 The diet represents a heat value of 2,000 calories.

— 가치 calorific value **—계** a calorimeter **— 단위** a unit of heat ; a thermal unit **— 측정(법)** calorimetry **—학** calorifics

열력 閱歷 [경력] a career ; a personal history

†**열렬 熱烈 — 하다** (be) ardent ; fervent ; passionate ; fiery ; glowing ¶ 열렬히 ardently ; fervently ; passionately // 열렬한 어조로 in fiery tone ; in an impassioned tone ; in glowing terms // 열렬한 애국자 an ardent〔a glowing〕 patriot // 열렬한 사랑 passionate〔ardent〕 love // 열렬히 사랑하다 love 《a person》 passionately ; be madly in love 《with》 // 열렬한 사랑이 식어지다 passionate love begins to cool down // 열렬한 기독교 신자가 되다 become a devout Christian // 이렇게 열렬한 환영을 받을 줄은 몰랐다 Little did I think of being so warmly welcomed.

열루 熱淚 hot〔burning, feverish〕 tears ¶ 열루를 흘리며 with burning tears in one's eyes ; shedding hot tears // 감사하여 열루를 흘리다 drop firey tears of gratitude

열릅 the age of ten (of a horse〔row〕)

†**열리다** ① open ; be opened ; be unlocked (자물쇠 따위) ¶ 좌우로 활짝 열리다 swing open right and left // 누르니까 문이 열렸다 The door yiedded to the pressure. // 이 열쇠라면 모든 문이 열린다 This key opens every door. // 창문이 모두 열려 있다 All the windows are open. // 9시에 막이 열린다 The curtain rises at 9 p.m. // 당신 등 뒤의 지퍼가 열렸습니다 The zipper is open on your back. /Your back is unzipped.

② [개최] be held ; be given ; take place

¶ 체육 대회는 5월 5일에 열린다 The athletic meeting will be held on the fifth of May. //전국 낚시 대회가 내일 수원 교외에서 열린다 A nationwide fishing contest will take place tomorrow somewhere around *Suwon*. //그 회의는 목하 서울에서 열리고 있다 The conference is now meeting〔sitting, in session〕 in *Seoul*.
③ [개발] become civilized ; be modernized ; be enlightened ¶ 그 나라는 1차 대전 후 크게 열렸다 The nation has been greatly enlightened since World War I.
④ [열매가] bear fruit ; fruit ; grow 《열매가 주어》 ¶ 열매가 많이 열린 나무 a tree laden with fruits//이 나무는 열매가 잘 열린다 This tree bears well. //나무에 열매가 그득히 열려 있다 The trees are thickly hung with fruits.
⑤ [귀가] hear ; catch ¶ 귀가 열렸어 I can hear !
⑥ [길이] be opened ; open ¶ 출세할 길이 열리다 be given a chance of success in life//다음 마을로 연결되는 길이 수일 내에 열린다 A road leading to the next town will be opened to traffic in a few days.

⁑열망 熱望 an ardent wish ; a fervent hope ; a burning〔an eager〕 desire ; a longing **—하다** desire earnestly〔eagerly〕 ; be anxious 《for》 ; be eager 《for, to do》 ; thirst 《for》 ; aspire after ; be keen on ; be dying for 《a girl》 ¶ 평화를 열망한다 We are eager for peace. //실업계에 진출하기를 열망한다 I have a great desire to enter business. //그 여자는 여배우 되기를 열망하고 있다 She has aspiration to be an actress.

†열매 fruit ; a nut (견과) ; a berry (장과) ¶ 열매를 맺다 bear fruit ; produce a result (비유적) //그의 꿈이 열매를 맺었다 His dream bore fruit〔came true〕. //두 사람의 사랑이 열매를 맺었다 Their love matured into marriage. //마침내 우리의 노력이 열매를 맺었다 At last our efforts have come to fruition.
열매될 꽃은 첫 3월부터 알아본다 [속담] First impressions are the most lasting. / The first blow is halfly the battle.

열무 a young radish
— 김치 young radish *kimchi*

열바가지, 열박 a gourd bowl made by splitting the gourd before steaming

열반 涅槃 〖불교〗 Nirvana ¶ 열반에 가다 enter〔pass〕 into Nirvana

열변 熱辯 impassioned〔fervent, fiery, eloquent〕 speech ; passiontate eloqunce ¶ 열변을 토하다 make an impas-sioned 〔fiery〕 speech ; deliver a fervent speech ; speak with fervor〔heat〕 ; harangue

열병 熱病 a fever ; a febrile disease ; [장티프스] typhoid fever ¶ 열병에 걸리다 catch〔suffer from〕 a fever〔feverish complaint〕

⁑열병 閱兵 troop review〔inspection〕 **—하다** inspect〔review〕 troops ; pass troops in review ; inspect soldiers at a parade
—식 a formal military inspection〔reviewing〕 ; a review (of troops)

열복 悅服 willing submission **—하다** submit willingly

열부 烈婦 a heroing ; a heroic woman

열분해 熱分解 〖화학〗 pyrolysis

열브스름하다 (be) rather thin

열비 劣比 a minor ratio ; a ratio of lesser inequality

열사 烈士 a patriot ; a man of fervid loyalty ; a hero
순국 — a martyr

열사병 熱射病 heatstroke ; heat prostration ; heat apoplexy ¶ 열사병에 걸리다 suffer from〔be affected by〕 heatstroke

열사욕 熱砂浴 〖의학〗 arenation ; ammotherapy

열살 ten years of age ¶ 열살난 소녀 a ten-year-old girl ; a girl of ten ; a girl ten years old

열상 裂傷 a laceration ; a lacerated wound

열생학 劣生學 dysgenics

열석 列席 attendance ; presence **—하다** attend ; be present at ; sit at ¶ 열석하에 in the presence 《of persons》 ; with 《persons》 in attendance//회의에 열석하다 attend〔be persent at〕 a meeting ; sit as a member at a meeting//많은 사람들이 식에 열석했다 Many people were present at the ceremony. /The ceremony was attended by many people.
—자 those pressent ; attendants ; an attendance 《총칭》 ¶ 다〔소〕수의 열석자 a large〔small〕 attendance

열선 熱線 〖물리〗 thermic〔heat〕 rays ; infrared waves〔rays〕 (적외선)
— 전류계〔풍속계, 마이크로폰〕 a hot wire ammeter〔anemometer, microphone〕

⁑열성 熱誠 earnestness ; ardor ; enthusiasm ; zeal ; devotion (헌신) ; sincerity (성심) ¶ 열성적 warm ; earnest ; enthusiastic ; devoted ; hearty ; ardent ; zealous//열성을 다하여 with zeal〔devotion〕 ; heart and soul ; warmly ; enthusiastically//열성적인 교육가 an earnest educationist//열성스럽다 be ardent ; be earnest ; be zealous//열성이 넘치다 be overflowing with enthusiasm//열성껏 나라에 봉사하다 serve one's country with one's whole heart ; devote oneself to one's country//열성적으로 일에 착수하다 set to work with great eagerness//열성어린 환영을 받았다 I was warmly welcomed. /I received a warm reception. //그의 한마디 한마디에 열성이 서려 있었다 Every word of his speech reflected his earnestness.
—가 an enthusiast ; a zealot (열광자)

열성 劣性 〚생물〛 inferiority ; recessiveness
—감 inferiority complex **— 인자** a recessive factor **— 형질** a recessive (character)

열세 劣勢 numerical inferiority ; inferiority in numbers **—하다** be inferior in numbers〔strength〕 ¶ 열세를 만회하다 turn the tables〔tide〕

열셋 thirteen ¶ 열셋째 the thirteenth

†열쇠 a key ¶ 문의 열쇠 the key to a door // 고리에 낀 열쇠 keys on a ring // 열쇠로 자물쇠를 열다 unlock〔open a lock〕 with a key // 열쇠로 문을 잠그다 lock the door with a key // 열쇠를 돌리다 turn the key 《in a lock》 ; give the key a turn // 분명히 문에 열쇠를 채웠느냐 Are you sure you locked the door ? // 열쇠를 자물쇠에 끼워 놓지 말라 Don't leave the key in the lock. // 그는 문제 해결의 열쇠를 쥐고 있다 He holds the key to the solution of the problem. // 유머는 사람의 마음을 여는 열쇠다 Humor is the key to the hearts of men. // 차 안에 열쇠를 놔 두고 문을 잠갔습니다 I'm locked out of my car.
— 구멍 a keyhole **— 묶음** a buch of keys (on a ring) **현관 —** a key to the front door

‡열심 熱心 enthusiasm ; zeal ; ardor ; eagerness ; earnestness ; keenness ¶ 열심이다 be enthusiastic〔eager, assiduous, earnest, ardent, zealous, keen〕 // 열심히 zealously ; enthusiastically ; ardently ; earnestly ; warmly ; passionately ; wholeheartedly ; in an earnest manner // 열심이 지나쳐 in the excess of one's zeal // 열심히 공부하는 학생 an eager〔earnest〕 student // 열심히 노력하는 사람 a strenuous worker // 열심히 …하게 되다 become〔get〕 enthusiastic 《about, over》 ; come to be intent on ; enthuse 《미·속》 // 열심히 듣다 listen intently 《to》 ; lend an attentive ear 《to》 ; be all ears // 열심히 공부하다 study〔work〕 hard ; apply oneself closely to one's studies // 부〔명성, 명예〕를 얻으려고 열심이다 be eager for wealth 〔fame, honor〕 // 그는 아주 열심이다 He is in good〔real, dead〕 earnest. // 그 여자는 춤에 열심이다 She is mad on dancing. // 그는 영어 공부에 대단히 열심이다 He is bent upon learning English. // 그는 이제 아버지가 되었기 때문에 아마도 열심히 일하기로 결심했나 보다 Since he's a father now, he probably decided to buckle down.

열십자 —十字 a cross ; the Chinese character "ten" ¶ 열십자의 crossed ; cross-shaped ; cruciform // 열십자로 crosswise // 열십자의 창 a coss-shaped〔cruciform〕 spear // (가슴에) 열십자를 긋다 cross oneself ; make the sign of the cross on one's breast // 열십자로 매다 tie in a cross

열쌔다 (be) quick ; prompt ; active ; nimble ; smart ; agile ¶ 열쌔게 quickly ; promptly ; nimbly ; with alacrity // 행동이 열쌔다 be quick〔prompt〕 in acting // 열쌔게 해내다 make a smart job of it // 열쌔게 기회를 잡다 be prompt〔quick〕 to seize an opportunity

열씨 列氏 Réaumur ¶ 열씨 12도 12 degress〔12〕 R
— 한란계 a Réaumur thermometer

열아홉 nineteen ¶ 열아홉째 the nineteenth

열악 劣惡 —하다 (be) inferior ; coarse ; poor ; deteriorated 《article》

†열애 熱愛 ardent〔passionate〕 love ; a strong attachment 《for》 ; devotion **—하다** love 《a person》 passionately〔fervently〕 ; be madly in love 《with》 ; be passionately devoted 《to》

열어젖뜨리다 push open (밀어서) ; fling open ; force open (무리하게) ¶ 그는 창문을 열어젖뜨렸다 He flung the window open. // 그는 잠긴 문을 열어젖뜨렸다 He forced the locked door open.

열없다 ① [겸연쩍다] (be) shy ; bashful ; feel awkward ; feel abashed ; feel ill at ease ; feel like a cat in a strange attic ¶ 열없게 bashfully ; awkwardly // 열없게 웃으며 grinning sheepishly ② [겁많다] (be) timid ; cowardly ; chicken-hearted ; whit〔lily〕-livered ; effeminate

열없쟁이 a shy person ; an unassertive person ; a softy ; a stick 《속》

열여덟 eighteen ¶ 열여덟째 the eighteenth

열여섯 sixteen ¶ 열여섯째 the sixteenth

열역학 熱力學 〚물리〛 thermodynamics

열연 熱演 an impassioned〔ardent, enthusiastic〕 performance ; a superb play **—하다** play〔perform〕 《a part》 enthusiastically ; put spirit into one's part

열왕기 列王記 〚성경〛 the Book of Kings

열원 熱源 heat-source ; heating sources

열위 列位 [연설·편지에서] ladies and gentlemen ; gentlemen ; sirs

＊열의 熱意 zeal ; ardor ; enthusiasm ; eagerness ¶ 열의 있는 zealous ; ardent ; enthusiastic ; eager // 열의를 표시하다 show〔manifest〕 zeal 《for》 // 열의가 없다 be not enthusiastic 《about》 ; have no enthusiasm 《for》

열이온 熱— thermion
—관 a thermionic valve〔tube〕 **— 검파기** a thermionic detector **— 방사** thermionic emission **— 전류** a thermionic current

열일곱 seventeen ¶ 열일곱째 the seventeenth

열자 劣者 an inferior ; the weak

열자기 熱磁氣 〚물리〛 thermomagnetism
— 효과 thermomagnetic effect

열자석 발전기 熱磁石發電機 a pyromagnetic generator

열장이음 〚건축〛 [잇기] dovetailing ; [이은 것] a dovetail (joint) ; a fantail **—하다** dovetail

열적다 (be) shy ; timid ⇨ 열없다

열전 熱戰 a fast fight ; [경기] a close game ; a hot contest ; fast going (권투) ; a hot war (냉전에 대하여) ¶ 열전이 벌어지고 있다 A close game is going on. / The game is very close.

열전 熱電 ⇨ 열전기
—대(對) a thermocouple ; thermoelectric couple **— 온도계** a thermoelectric thermometer **— 전류계** a thermoammeter **—지(池)** a thermoelectric battery **—퇴(堆)** a thermoelectric pile ; a thermopile

열전 列傳 a series of biographies ; lives ¶ 여러 고승의 열전 the biographies of the saints of all sects

열전기 熱電氣 〖물리〗 thermoelectricity ; thermal electricity ¶ 열전(기)의 thermoelectric
— 온도계 ⇨ 열전 온도계

열전도 熱傳導 thermal conduction
—율 thermal conductivity

열전류 熱電流 a thermoelectric current ; a thermocurrent

열전자 熱電子 〖전기〗 thermion ; 〖물리〗 a thermoelectron
—관 a thermionic tube **— 전도(傳導)** thermionie conduction **— 전류** a thermionic current

†**열정 熱情** ardor ; fevor ; passion ; warmth ; ardent〔passionate〕 love ¶ 열정적 passionate ; ardent ; fervent // 애국의 열정 patriotic ardor // 청년의 열정 youthful zest // 열정 어린 편지를 쓰다 write a passionate〔impassioned〕 letter // 애국의 열정이 넘치다 be full of patriotic ardor
—가 an ardent〔a passionate〕 person ; a hot-blooded (열렬한)

열정 劣情 low passion ; passions ; carnal desires〔appetite〕 ; licentious impulses ; lust ¶ 열정을 자극하는 소설 a suggestive〔lascivious〕 novel // 열정을 자극하다 excite〔imflame〕 the base passion ; be suggestive ; pander to one's lust

열좌 列座 presence ; attendance **—하다** (be) present 《at》 ; attend ; sit at ¶ 열좌한 사람들 those present ; the company ; the assemblage

†**열중 熱中** enthusiasm ; zeal ; mania ; craze **—하다** devote oneself 《to》 ; give oneself up 《to》 ; be bent〔intent〕 on 《doing》 ; be absorbed〔immersed, engrossed〕 《in》 ; be enthusiastic 《about, for, over》 ; be crazy〔mad〕 《about, on, over》 ¶ 테니스에 열중하다 be much given to tennis // 독서에〔공부에〕 열중하다 be absorbed〔immersed〕 in reading〔one's studies〕 // 경기에 열중하다 be engrossed in one's game // 우표 수집에 열중하다 have a craze for stamp collecting // 정치에 열중하다 go in for politics // 춤에 열중하다 be mad〔crazy〕 about dancing // 그는 사업에 열중하고 있다 He is engrossed in business. // 그는 돈벌이에 열중한 나머지 딴 일을 돌보지 않는다 He is too intent thing〔bent〕 on money making to think any thing else. // 그는 그 여자에 열중해 있다 He is infatuated with the woman. // 그는 토론에 열중한 나머지 그렇게 말했다 He spoke like that in the heat of discussion. // 그는 매사에 열중하는 기질이다 He goes heart and soul into anything. // 나는 오랫동안 테니스에 열중했다 I've had a passion for tennis for years. // 공부에 열중하지 않으면 입학 시험에 떨어질 거다 You'd better put your heart into your studies, or you're going to fail your entrance exams.

열증 熱症 (a) fever ; a fever case ; pyrexia

열진 烈震 a violent〔disastrous〕 earthquake

열쭝이 a newly hatched bird ; a chick out of its shell ; [사람] a small weak person

†**열차 列車** a train ¶ 열차편으로 by train // 열차를 운전하다 run〔operate〕 a train // 오후 4시 15분 열차로 출발하다 leave 《*Seoul*》 by the 4 : 15 p. m. train // 열차의 전복을 꾀하다 attempt to wreck a train // 그 열차는 여섯시 반에 도착한다 The train is due at six-thirty.
— 사고 a train accident **— 시간표** a train timetable〔schedule〕 **—장** a conductor 《미》 ; a passenger guard ; a train master **— 전화** a train telephone ; a railophone 《미》 **급행 —** an express (train) **병원 —** an ambulance train **보통〔완행〕 —** a slow train ; an accommodation train 《미》 ; a local train **상행〔하행〕 —** an up〔a down〕 train **야간 —** a night train **임시 —** an extra train **장갑 —** an armored train **직행 —** a throuht train **특급 —** a limited express (train) **특별 —** a special train **화물 —** a freight train 《미》 ; a goods train 《영》

열창 —窓 a window that opens

열채 a whip with a last ; a cat-o'-nine-tails

열처리 熱處理 heat treatment
—공 a heat treatment worker **—장치** a heat treatment equipment

열탕 熱湯 boiling water〔broth〕 ¶ 열탕을 끼얹다 dash boiling water 《over》 ; pour hot water 《over》 // 열탕 소독하다 scald (out) 《a vessel》 ; clean〔disinfect〕 in boiling water // 열탕에 데다 scald oneself ; be〔get〕 scalded with boiling water

열퉁적다 (be) awkward ; clumsy ; gawky ; coarse ¶ 열퉁적은 말 coarse speech // 열퉁적은 사람 a gawk ; an awkward fellow

열파 熱波 a heat wave

열패 劣敗 defeat (through one's inferiority) **—하다** be defeated (through inferiority) ; be bested ; be beaten ; suffer a defeat ; get the worst of it ; be worsted

¶ 우승 열패 the survival of the fittest ; the weakest goes to the wall
열팽창 熱膨脹 thermal expansion
—률 the coefficient of thermal expansion
열품 劣品 low-grade goods ; an article of inferior〔poor〕 quality
열풍 烈風 a strong〔heavy, violent, severe〕 wind ; a hurricane ; a gale ¶ 열풍이 불다 It blows a gale.
열풍 熱風 a hot wind ; a sirocco 〔simoon〕 (사하라 사막의) ; a hot blast (용광로의)
열하나 eleven ¶ 열하나째 the eleventh
열하다 熱— heat ; make hot ; [고도로] ignite ; heat intensely ¶ 그것은 열하면 빨개진다 When heated, it turns red.
열하루 eleven day ; [제11일] the eleventh day ¶ 열하룻날 the eleventh day of the month // 5월 열하루 the eleventh of May ; May 11(th)
열학 熱學 〖물리〗 thermotics ; calorifics
열핵 熱核 thermonuclear
— 무기〔탄두〕 thermonuclear weapon 〔warhead〕 **— 반응〔동력, 융합〕** thermonuclear reaction〔power, fusion〕 **— 폭발〔실험〕** a thermonuclear explosion 〔test〕
열혈 熱血 hot blood ; fervent zeal ; ardor ; ardent blood ; fieriness
— 남아 a hot-blooded man **— 시인** a fiery〔passionate〕 poet **— 청년** a passionate〔sanguine〕 youth **—한(漢)** a hot-blooded〔-headed〕 man ; an arduous〔a fervent〕 soul
열호 劣弧 〖수학〗 a minor arc
열화 烈火 a blazing〔raging〕 fire ; furious 〔devastating〕 flames ¶ 열화같이 노하다 fire〔flame, flare〕 up ; fly into a fury 〔rage〕 ; burn with anger ; be mad with rage ; be infurated ; be red with anger // 모욕을 받고 열화같이 노하다 be terribly enraged at an insult
열화 熱火 furious flames ; a blazing fire ¶ 열화 같은 더위 fiery heat // 열화 같은 연설 a fiery speech
열화 劣化 〖화학〗 deterioration
열화학 熱化學 thermochemistry
열확산 熱擴散 thermal diffusion ; thermodiffusion
—율 thermal diffusivity
열흘 [10일] ten days ; [열흘째] the tenth day ¶ 열흘도 못되어 in less than ten days // 매월 열흘날에 봉급을 타다 get paid on the tenth of every month
—날 the tenth day 《of the month》
열흡수 熱吸收 absorption of heat
†엷다 ① [두께가] (be) thim ⇨ 얇다 ¶ 입술이 엷다 have thin lips ; be thin-lipped ② [빛깔이] (be) light ; pale ; faint ; thin ¶ 엷은 빛 a light color ③ [천박하다] (be) shallow ; shallowminded ; superficial 《learning》 ¶ 속이 엷은 사람 a shallow person ; a short sighted person // 정이 엷다 be not close 〔intimate〕 ; be rather cool
엷붉다 be light red
염 a small stony ishand ; a rocky islet
염 炎 an inflammation
늑막— pleuris ; pleurisy ; pleuritis **폐—** pneumonia ; inglammations of the lungs
염 殮 shrouding ⇨ 염습(殮襲)
염가 廉價 a moderate〔cheap, low〕 price ¶ 염가의 cheap ; moderate〔low〕 priced ; inexpensive // 고본 염가 판매 "Second-hand books sold cheap." /"Bargain-priced used books." // 염가로 사다 buy cheap〔at a bargain price〕 // 염가로 팔다 sell cheap〔at a reduced price, at a bargain-price〕 ; clear off (재고품 정리로) ; undersell (경쟁자 보다) // 다른 상점에서 더 염가로 입수할 수 있다 We can get them cheaper〔on better terms〕 elsewhere.
—판 a cheap〔popular〕 edition 《of a book》 **— 판매〔대매출〕** a bargain sale **—품** low〔popular〕 priced goods
염갱 a bine pit ; a salt pit〔pan〕
염결 廉潔 integrity ; uprightness ; probity ; honesty **—하다** (be) upright ; honest ; high-minded ; clean-handed ¶ 염결한 사람 a man of probity〔integrity〕 ; a man of upright character
염광 a salt mine
염교 〖식물〗 a scallion ; a shallot ; Allium Bakeri (학명)
염글리다 bring to success〔pass〕 ; bring 《a plan》 off ; accomplish ; earry out
염기 厭忌 dislike ; repugnance ; abhorrence **—하다** dislike ; loathe ; detest ; abhor ; feel〔have〕 a repugnance 《for》
염기 〖화학〗 a base ¶ 염기성의 basic ; positive ; electropositive // 염기화하다 basify
—도(度) basicity **—류** the bases ; the basic group **—성 반응** basic reaction **—성 산화물** a basic oxide **—성 염〔암(岩)〕** a basic salt〔rock〕 **—성 염료** basic dyestuffs〔dyes〕 **—성 탄산염** ceruse **—소(素)** a basyl(e) **유기 —** an organic base
염낭 —囊 a money pouch ; a purse ; a small moneybag
염담 恬淡 unselfishness **—하다** (be) unselfish ; undemanding
†염두 念頭 mind ¶ 염두에 두다 bear 〔keep, have〕 《a thing》 in mind ; keep 《a thing》 in view ; have 《a matter》 at heart ; give thought〔heed〕 to // 염두에 두지 않다 do not care 《about》 ; give no thought〔heed〕 to ; take no thought of // 염두에 떠오르다 occur to one〔one's mind〕 ; come into one's head ; come across one's mind ; call〔come〕 to mind // 그런 일은 염두에 두지 말라 Don't think〔care〕 about it. /Dismiss it from your mind. /You had better forget about it. // 그것은 수년간 내내 염두에서 사라지지 않았다 It has haunted me 〔never been

off my mind〕 for years. // 어느 회사 제품을 염두에 두고 계십니까 What make do you have in mind?

염라 閻羅 ⇨ 염마(閻魔)

염라국 閻羅國 〖불교〗 Hades; the nether world; the land〔kingdom〕 of the dead; hell; the infernal〔regions〕

염라 대왕 閻羅大王 Yama 《범》; Pluto 《라》; the King〔Judge〕 of Hades; the King〔Ruler, Judge〕 of Hell; the lord of the dead〔lower world〕

염량 炎凉 ① [한서] heat and cold ② [분별] discernment; discretion; good sense; prudence ③ [성쇠] rise and fall; ups and downs; vicissitudes

†**염려 念慮** [걱정] anxiety; concernsolicitude; worry; care; [불안] fear; uneasiness; apprehendion; misgivings; a weight on one's mind **—하다** worry 《about》; be〔feel〕 anxious〔uneasy〕 《about》; be concerned 《about》; apperehend; fee〔have〕 misgivings; be afraid 〔have fear〕 《for》; fear ¶ 염려하는 빛으로 with a worried air // 염려한 나머지 being overcome with anxiety // 염려를 끼치다 give〔cause〕 《a person》 anxiety 〔worry〕; give〔put〕 《a person》 trouble; trouble 《a person》 // 염려말게 Don't worry. /Never mind. / Take it easy. 《미·구》 // 그점에 대해서는 염려할 것 없다 Make your mind easy on that score. / You have nothing to worry about on that point. // 그의 건강이 염려된다 I feel uneasy〔am anxious〕 about his health. // 염려할 정도의 병은 아니다 There is nothing to worry about this disease. // 네가 운전을 하면 염려스럽다 I'm not so sure about your driving. // 지금부터 그런 상태니 앞날이 염려된다 If that's the way it is now, I shudder to think about what lies ahead.

염려 艶麗 (voluptuous) beauty; charm **—하다** (be) charming; enchanting; beautiful; fascination; coquettish ¶ 염려한 여자 a voluptuous beauty〔woman〕; a glamor girl

⁑**염료 染料** dyes; dyestuffs ¶ 염료가 좋다〔나쁘다〕 The dye is fast〔weak〕.
— 공업 the dye industry **— 제조** dye making〔manugacture〕 **무기 —** mineral dyes **인조〔합성〕 —** artificial〔synthetic〕 dyes **천연 —** natural dyes

염류 salts
—천(泉) a saline spring; a mineral salt spring

염마 閻魔 [염라대왕] Yama 《범》; Pluto 《라》; the King〔Judge〕 of Hades 《그》

염매 廉賣 a bargain〔cheep〕 sale; dumping; selling at small profits **—하다** sell cheap; sell at low prices; sell at a bargain; sell at a discount ¶ 저 제과점에서는 과자를 염매하고 있다 That bakery is having a sale of sweets.
— 경쟁 a price war〔competition〕; dumping **— 시장** a bargain〔cheap〕 market **—품** bargain〔low〕 priced goods

염모 染毛 hair-dyeing
—제(劑) a hairdye

염문 艶文 a love letter; a billet-doux 《*pl.* billets-doux》 《프》

염문 艶聞 (rumor of) a love-affair; one's episode of love; a petticoat affair; a romance ¶ 염문이 있다 have a romance; be associated with a love affair // 그는 염문이 자자하다 His romance is much gossiped about. /His love affair is in everyboy's mouth.

염발제 染髮劑 a hairdye

염밭 a salt farm〔field, pond〕; a saltern; a salina

염백 廉白 uprightness; integrity; honesty; purity **—하다** (be) upright; clean-handed; incorruptible; be above corruption

염병 染病 ① [장티푸스] enteric fever; typhoed (fever); abdominal typhus ¶ 염병을 치르다 get over〔recover from, be cured of〕 typhoid fever // 염병할 놈아 Devil take you!
② [전염병] a contagious disease; an epidemic

염복 艶福 good fortune in love; much romance ¶ 그는 염복이 있다 He lacks no beauty〔beautiful girl〕. /He is a favorite with the ladies.
—가 a ladies' pet〔man〕; a gallant; a beau; a man dogged after by many beauties

염분 salt; salt content; salimity ¶ 염분있는 saltish; saline; salty // 바닷물에는 다량의 염분이 있다 Sea-water contains much salt. // 그것은 염분이 주성분이다 It has salt for its main ingredients.

염불 念佛 a Buddhist invocation〔prayer〕; a prayer to Buddha; the repetition of sacred name of Amida **—하다** pray to Amida Buddha; tell 〔say, recite〕 one's beads; offer〔chant〕 a prayer
산까마귀 염불한다 속담 Practice makes perfect. /All things in their being are good for something.

염사 艶事 a love affair; a romance

염산 〖화학〗 hydrochloric acid; muriatic acid (상품명으로)
— 가리 potassium〔kalium〕 chlorate; chlorate of potash **— 가스** hydrochloric acid gas **— 아연** butter of zinc **—염** hydrochloride

***염색 染色** dyeing **—하다** dye
—공 a dyer **— 공장** a dye works; a dye house **—기(機)** a dyeing machine 〔range〕 **—물** dyed goods **—법** a process of dyeing **— 분체(分體)** 〖생물〗 a chromatid **—사(絲)** 〖식물·동물〗 a chromonema 《*pl.* -mata》; a genonema **— 시험** a dyeing test **—질** chromatin; karyotin 머

리 —약 a hairdye

염색체 染色體 a chromosome

— 입자(粒子) a chromiole 성— a sex chromosome X〔Y〕 — an X〔a Y〕 chromosome 이상 — a hetero chromosome

염생 식물 鹽生植物 a salt plant ; a halophyte

염서 炎暑 intense〔extreme〕 heat ; a heat wave

—지절(之節) the hot weather ; (at) this time of hot summer days

염서 艶書 a love-letter ; a billet-dous 《*pl.* billets-doux》 《프》

염세 厭世 pessimism ; weariness of life 〔the world〕 ¶ 염세적인 passimistic ; world-weary

—가 a pessimist ; [사람을 싫어하는] a misanthrope ; a misanthropist —관 a pessimistic〔misanthropic〕 view of life ; pessimism — 자살 a suicide from being sick of life〔from taedium vitae〕 ¶ 그는 염세 자살하였다 He committed suicide from a disgust for existence. —주의 pessimism — 철학 pessimistic philosophy

†염소 a goat ¶ 염소가 운다 A goat bleats.

— 가죽 goatskin — 가죽 장갑 kid gloves — 수염 a goatee —털 goat hair 새끼 — a kid ; a goatling 수〔암〕— a he-〔she-〕 goat ; a billy-〔nanny-〕goat

염소 chlorine ¶ 염소와 화합하다 chlorinate ; chloridate ; chlaridize

—법 a chlorine method —산 chloric acid — 산염 chlorate —산 칼륨 potassium chlorate — 살균 chlorination —수 chlorine water — 처리 chlorination

염수 salt water ; brine

—선(選) brine assortment —호(湖) a saline lake

염습 殮襲 shrouding —하다 wrap 〔clothe〕 dead body in a shroud ; dress the deceased ; shroud

염연 恬然 —하다 (be) tranquil ; carefree

염열 炎熱 intense〔extreme〕 heat ; sultriness ; broiling weather ¶ 염열이 찌는 듯한 날 a scorching〔sweltering, burning hot〕 day

*염오 厭惡 dislike ; hatred ; aversion ; repugnance ; abhorrence ; disgust ; loathing —하다 dislike ; hate ; loathe ; be averse 《to》 ; abhor ¶ 염오할 사건 an abominable incident ; a scandal // 몹시 염오하다 regard 《a person》 with great aversion ; hate 《a person》 like a viper

‡염원 念願 one's (heart's) desire ; one's dearest wish ; one's cherished desire —하다 desire ; wish ¶ 오랜 염원 one's long-cherished desire // 나의 염원이 이루어졌다 My prayer has been answered. / I have had my desire fulfilled. / My long-cherished desire has been fulfilled.

염의없다 (be) shameless

염장 〖의학〗 salt plasma

염장 [조미료] seasonings ; condiments ; spices ; [소금과 장] salt and soy sauce

염장 —하다 preserve with salt ; salt (away)

염장이 殮— an undertaker in washing and dressing the dead ; a mortician

염전 a salt farm〔field, garden〕 ; a salina ; a saltern

염전화 salterization —하다 salterize

염접 —하다 tuck in the edge ; even up the edges of 《cloth》 by folding

염정 a salt well

염좌 捻挫 a sprain —하다 sprain 《one's ankle》

염주 念珠 a rosary ; (a string of) beads ; a chaplet ¶ 염주를 세다 tell 〔count, recite, finger〕 one's beads (of a rosary)

—나무 a kind of linden —알 [한개] a bead ; [한 묶음] the beads of a rosary

염증 厭症 dislike ; disgust ; an aversion ; repugnance ¶ …에 염증이 나다 get sick of ; grow weary of ; be disgusted with ; feel a repugance to // 일에 염증이 났다 He grew sick (and tired) of his work. / He was fed up with the work.

염증 炎症 an inflammation ¶ 염증을 일으키다 be〔become〕 inflamed ; start inflammation

—열 an inflammatory fever

염직 染織 [물들임] dyeing 《colth》 ; [염색과 직조] dyeing and weaving —하다 dye cloth〔textile fabrics〕 ; dye and weave

— 공장 a dye works

염직 廉直 integrity ; honesty ; probity ; uprightness —하다 (be) honest ; upright ; clean-handed ; straightforward ¶ 염직한 사람 a man of integrity ; an upright man

염천 炎天 hot weather ; the hot〔blazing, broiling〕 sun ; the heat of the sun ; [남쪽 하늘] the southern sky ¶ 염천 아래 under the burning sun // 염천 하에서 행군하다 march under〔in〕 the burning〔blazing〕 sun

염천 a brine〔saline〕 spring

염출 捻出 —하다 ① [안출] contrive ; devise ¶ 채무 변상의 방법을 염출하다 work out a plan for financing one's obligations

② [비용 따위를] contrive to raise ; manage to make ¶ 자금을 염출하다 contive to raise funds ; hit on a new source of revenue // 백만원을 염출하다 devise to raise a million *won*

염치 廉恥 a sense of honor ; a sense of shame ¶ 염치가 있다 have a sense of honor // 염치가 없다 have no sense of honor ; be shameless

염탐 廉探 spy ; secret observation ; espionage —하다 spy 《upon》 ; pry 《upon》 ; make secret observations ;

smell〔scent〕 out 《one's movements》 ¶ 적정을 염탐하다 spy on the enemy
— 꾼 a spy ; a scout ; a secret agent
염통 the heart
염통머리 ⇨ 염치(廉恥)
염포 殮布 shroud
염하다 廉— ① [싸다] (be) inexpensive ; cheap ② [청렴하다] incorruptible ; upright ; clean-handed ; have integrity
염하다 殮— ⇨ 염습(殮襲)하다
염해 damage from sea wind
염호 a salt〔saline〕 lake
염화 chloridation —하다 chloridize
— 가리 potassium chloride —금〔백금〕 gol〔platinum〕 chloride —물 a chloride —수소 hydrogen chloride —연〔철〕 lead〔iron〕 chloride —은〔비닐〕 silver 〔vinyl〕 chloride — 칼슘〔나트륨〕 calcium〔sodium〕 chloride
엽견 獵犬 a hunting dog ; a hound ; a gun dog 《미》
엽관 운동 獵官運動 office-hunting〔-seeking〕 ; place-hunting ¶ 엽관 운동을 하다 run〔hunt〕 hot office
엽궐련 葉— a cigar ¶ 엽궐련을 물다 put〔hold〕 a cigar in one's mouth ; have〔hold〕 a cigar between one's teeth 〔lips〕 // 엽궐련을 피우다 smoke a cigar ; puff at one's cigar
엽기 獵奇 bizarrerie hunting ; hunting after grotesqueries —하다 seek〔hunt〕 the bizarre ¶ 엽기적 curiosity-seeking // 엽기심에서 out of curiosity
— 문학 bizarre literature — 소설 abizarre story —심 (wicked) curiosity —취미 a taste for〔love of〕 the bizarre
엽기 獵期 the hunting〔shooting, open〕 season ¶ 엽기가 되었다 The shooting season has opened〔set in〕 .
엽렵하다 獵獵— (be) clever ; smart ; thoughtful
엽록색 葉錄色 leaf green
엽록소 葉綠素 『식물』 chlorophll
엽록체 葉綠體 a chloroplast
엽맥 葉脈 『식물』 a vein (지맥) ; a nerrve (맥리) ; a nervure (주맥)
엽병 獵柄 『식물』 a leafstalk ; a stipe ; a stalk ; a sterm
엽사 獵師 a hunter ; a huntsman ; a huntress (여자)
엽색 獵色 philandering ; lewdness ; lechery ; debauchery
—꾼 a philanderer ; a libertine ; a lewd person ; a debauchee ; a lecher
*엽서 葉書 a postcard ; a postal card 《미》 ¶ 엽서를 내다 send a postcard 《to》
관제〔사제〕 — an official〔a private〕 postcard 그림 — a picture postcard ; a postcard 《미》 반신용 — a reply (postal) card 봉함 — a letter card 왕복 — a postcard with reply paid ; a reply-paid postcard ; a return postcard
엽액 葉腋 『식물』 an axil ; an axilla
엽우 獵友 a huntin companion
엽전 葉錢 a Korean brass coin
엽조 獵鳥 a game bird〔fowl〕 ; [총칭] game
엽차 葉茶 coarse tea ; [재창] the second brew of tea
엽채류 葉菜類 green vegetables ; edible herbs
엽초 葉草 leaf tobacco
엽초 葉鞘 『식물』 a vagina 《*pl.* -nae》 ; a sheath ; an ocrea 《*pl.* -ae》
*엽총 獵銃 a hunting〔sporting〕 gun ; [조총] a fowling piece ; a shot-gun ; [맹수용] a hunting rifle
엽치다 hull (barley) roughly
엽침 葉針 a leaf spine
엿 wheat-gluten ; glutinous rice jelly ; taffy ; candy ¶ 엿을 빨다 suck wheatgluten
—장수 a wheat-gluten〔candy, taffy〕 vendor〕
엿- six ¶ 엿새 six days
엿가락 a stick of taffy ; a piece of taffy
엿가래 ⇨ 엿가락
*엿기름 malt ; germ〔germinated〕 barley ; a dry sprout ¶ 엿기름을 만들다 malt
— 가루 powdered malt
*엿듣다 overhear ; listen secretly to ; eavesdrop ; play the eavesdropper ¶ 엿듣는 사람 an eavesdropper // 전화를 엿듣다 tap the wires ; listen in on a 《person's》 telephone conversation // 문에 서서 엿듣다 esdrop at the door // 엿보거나 엿들어서는 안된다 You must not peep or eavesdrop.
엿물 taffy liquid (to be boiled)
엿밥 lees left after taffy water has been strained
*엿보다 watch〔wait〕 for 《an opportunity》 ; look (out) for 《a chance》 ; spy out 〔on〕 ; steal a glance at ; look furtively at ¶ 기회를 엿보다 watch for a chance // 형세를 엿보다 see how the wind blows ; see how things stand〔go on〕 ; wait and see ; sit on the fence // 남의 눈치를 엿보다 study 《a person's》 face on the sly // 틈새를 통해서 엿보다 peep through a crack 〔crevice〕
엿살피다 spy on〔into〕 ; observe furtively 〔secretly〕
엿새 [엿샛날] the sixth day (of a month) ; [6일] six days
엿죽(방망이) [방망이] a taffee-stirring stick ; [쉬운 일] an easy task〔job〕
엿치기 a taffy-breaking game —하다 play a taffy-breaking game
영[1] [산뜻한 기운] a clean bright atmosphere 《in a house, room》
영이 돌다 관용 have a clean bright atmosphere about it
영[2] ⇨ 이엉
영 令 [명령] an order ; a command ; [법령] an ordinance ; a law ; a decree ; an

act ¶ 문교부령 an education ministry ordinance // 영을 내리다 order ; command ; dictate ; issue 《a decree》 ; promulgate 《a law》 // 영을 거역하다 disobey 〔protest against〕 《a person's》 order

영 永 forever ⇨ 영영

‡영 零 zero 《*pl.* ~s, ~es》 ; nought ; nothing ; a cipher ¶ 영하 10도 ten degrees below zero // 1대 0으로 by score of one to zero // 시험에 영점 맞다 get zero in an examination ; get no marks // 그 팀은 영패했다 〖야구〗 That team lost the game without scoring a single run.
—도 ⇨ 영도 —봉(封) 〖정구〗 a love game ; 〖야구〗 a shutout

영 領 a territory ; a possession ; a domination ; a protectorate ; a mandate ; a fief

영 嶺 a ridge ; a (mountain) pass ; a high hill

영 靈 [신령] a divine spirit ; the spirit ; the soul ; [망령] the ghost ; a shade ¶ 영의 세계 a world of spirits // 영과 육 body and soul ; the spirit and flesh // 영육의 조화 harmony of body and soul

영가 靈歌 a spiritual
흑인 — negro spirituals

영각 [황소 울음] mooing ; lowing ; moo

영감 令監 an old man ; an elderly man ; a patriarch ; one's husband (남편) ; [존칭] lord ; sir

‡영감 靈感 inspiration ; intellectual intuition ; afflatus ; 〖심리〗 extrasensory perception ¶ 영감을 받다 be inspired // 시인은 영감을 얻었다 The poet was inspired. /An inspiration burst upon the poet.

영걸 英傑 ① [인물] a great man ; a hero ; a mastermind ② [기상] heroic qualities〔character〕

영검 靈— a miracle ; God's response

영겁 永劫 eternity ⇨ 영원

영결 永訣 separation by death ; the last 〔final〕 parting〔farewell〕 —하다 be separated by death ; part forever ; bid one's last farewell 《to》
—식 a funeral ceremony〔services, rites〕

영경 英京 the capital of England ; London

영계 —鷄 a spring chicken
— 백숙 boiled chicken with rice

영계 靈界 [영적인 세계] the spirit(ual) world ; [종교계] the religious world ¶ 영계의 현상 spiritual〔psychic〕 phenomena

영고 榮枯 prosperity and decline ; ups and downs ; rise and fall ; vicissitudes ¶ 인생의 영고 성쇠 the ups and downs of life ; the vicissitudes of life

영공 領空 territorial air〔sky〕 ; sovereign airspace ¶ 중국의 영공을 침범하다 violate the Chinese airspace〔the territorial sky of China〕
—권 aerial domain — 침범 violation of (another country's) territorial airspace

영관 領官 a field-officer ¶ 영관급 장교 field grade officers

영관 榮冠 the crown (of glory) ; the laurels ; the palm ¶ 승리의 영관을 쓰다 win laurels ; be crowned with victory ; bear〔carry away〕 the palm // 노력한 보람이 있어 성공의 영관을 얻었다 His efforts were crowned〔rewarded〕 with success. /Success crowned〔attended〕 his efforts.

†영광 榮光 honor ; glory ¶ 영광스러운 역사 a glorious history // 영광스럽다 be glorious ; be honorable ; be an honor 《to》 // 영광으로 여기다 esteem 《it》 an honor 《to do》 // …의 영광을 가지다 have the honor 《to do, of doing》 ; be honored with // 분에 넘치는 영광이올시다 The honor is more than I deserve. // 참석해 주셔서 영광스럽습니다 We feel highly honored by your presence. // 나도 환영회에 초대의 영광을 받았다 I was also honored with an invitation to the welcome party. // 그와 몇 마디 이야기만 해도 영광스러운 일이다 To exchange few words with him is in itself a privilege.

영교 靈交 spiritual communion 《with》 —하다 hold communion with ¶ 사람과 자연의 영교 an intercommunication of man with nature
—술 spiritualism ; spiritism

‡영구 永久 permanence ; eternity ; perpetuity —하다 (be) lasting ; permanent ; eternal ¶ 영구히 eternally ; permanently ; forever ; for good // 반영구적인 semi-permanent // 영구 불변하다 remain unchanged forever
— 공채(公債) permanent debt — 운동 a perpetual motion — 자석 a permanent magnet

영구 靈柩 a coffin ; a hearse ; a casket
— 열차 a funeral train —차 a (motor) hearse ; a funeral carriage ; an obituary 〔a mortuary〕 car

영구성 永久性 permanency ¶ 영구성 있는 permanent

영구치 永久齒 a permanent tooth ; the second teeth

영국 英國 Britain ; England ; Great Britain (영본토 즉 England, Wales, Scotland) ; the United Kingdom (of Great Britain and Northern Ireland) ; the British Empire ; Greater Britain (식민지를 합친 대영국) ; the British Commonwealth of Nations (영연방) ¶ 영국의 English ; British ; Britannic ; Anglican // 영국제의 made in England ; English-make ; of English make
— 공군 the Royal Air Force 《R. A. F》 — 국교회 the Church of England ; the Anglican — 국기 the British flag ; the Union Jack —국민 a British subject ; a British national —국왕〔여왕〕 the King

〔Queen〕 of England ─군함 His〔Her〕 Majesty's Ship ; H. M's ship ─ 사투리 Britishism ; Anglicism ; British accent ─ 정부 the British Government ; H. M.'s Gevernment ; Whitehall ; Downing Street ─풍 Anglicism ; Britishism ─ 황태자 the Prince of Wales

영국인 英國人 an Englishman ; an Englishwoman (여) ; a Britisher ; a Briton ; John Bull (별명) ; [총칭] the British ; the English
─ 기질〔식〕 John-Bullism

영금 a bitter experience〔humiliation〕 ¶ 영금을 보다 undergo a bitter humiliation ; have a bitter exprience

영남 嶺南 *Yeongnam* ; southeastern Korea

영내 營內 inside barracks ; on compound ¶ 영내의 within〔in〕 barracks ; in the compound
─ 거주 living in barracks ; bcing stationed in the compound area ─ 근무 service in barracks ; duties within the compound ─ 생활 a barrack life

영내 領內 the domains ; the territory ¶ 영내(에서) within the territory

영년 永年 a long period〔lapse〕 of years ; a long time ; many〔long〕 years ; [부사적] for many years ; for a long time

영농 營農 farming ─하다 engage in farming〔agriculture〕
─가 an agriculturist ; a farmer

영농 자금 營農資金 farming fund

영단 英斷 a decisive〔drastic〕 measure ; a resolute step ; prompt decision ¶ 영단을 내리다 take a decisive measure ; take a drastic step ; act decisively ; deal 《with a matter》 in a decisive way ; cut the Gordian knot // 이 일은 일대 영단이 필요하다 The case calls for a drastic〔decisive〕 measure.

영단 營團 a corporation ; a management foundation〔group〕
주택 ─ a housing corporation

영달 令達 an instruction ─하다 instruct

영달 榮達 distinction ; worldly fame ; advancement ¶ 영달을 바라다 hanker after〔aim at〕 distinction ; aspire to 〔after〕 high honors // 재능이 있으면 영달의 길도 있다 All honors are open to talent.

영당 影堂 〖불교〗 a shrine〔hall〕 where the portrait of an illustrious person is enshrined

영대 永代 eternity ⇨ 영세
─ 소유권 a perpetual ownership ─ 재산 perpetuity ─ 차지(借地) a perpetual leasehold ; a fee farm 《영》 ─ 차지권 a perpetual lease ; a lease in perpetuity ─ 차지인 a perpetual leaseer

영도 零度 zero degree ; the freezing 〔zero〕 point ¶ 영하 10도 ten degrees below zero ; 10° of frost // 영도 이하의 온도 the degrees of frost 《영》 // 영도 이상으로 오르다〔이하로 내리다〕 rise above 〔fall down below〕 zero
절대 ─ absolute zero ; zero degree Kelvin 《0° K, −273.7℃》

영도 領導 leading ; lead ; leadership ; direction ; guidance ─하다 lead ; take the lead ; guide ; direct ¶ 김씨의 영도하에 under Mr. *Kim's* leadership // 정당을 영도하다 lead〔steer〕 a political party
─자 a leader

영독 英獨 England〔Britain〕 and Germany ¶ 영독의 English〔British〕 and German ; Anglo-German

영독 獰毒 fierceness ; ferocity ─하다 (be) fierce ; ferocious ; savage ; truculent ¶ 영독한 얼굴을 하고 있다 look fierce

영동 嶺東 *Yŏngdong* ; the region of *kangwon* Province

영락 零落 ruin ; downfall ; reduced circumstances ─하다 be ruined (financially) ; go to ruin ; go to the bad ; fall on bad days ; sink〔come down〕 in the world ; fall low ; be in distress ; be busted 《미·속》 ; go broke 《미·속》 ¶ 그가 영락하는 것도 당연하다 He deserves to go under.
─ 생활 a wretched life

영락없다 (be) unfailing ; infallible ; certain ¶ 영락없이 infallibly ; without fail ; for sure ; certainly // 내 계산이 영락없다 There could be no mistake in my account. // 그는 영락없이 과녁을 맞힌다 He never misses the target.

영랑 令郞 your〔his〕 son

영령 英領 [영지(領地)] British territory ; a British dominion ; [영유(領有)] British possession ; [직할 식민지] a Crown Colony ; [자치령] a British Dominion ¶ 영령이다 belong to England ; be a British possession

영령 英靈 the spirit〔soul〕 of the dead 〔departed〕 ; [군인의] the war dead ; [애국 지사의] the fallen patriots ¶ 영령이여 고이 잠드소서 May your noble soul rest in peace !

영롱 玲瓏 ─하다 (be) brilliant ; clear and bright ; lucid ; translucent ¶ 영롱한 구슬 bright gems // 영롱한 문체 a crystal clear style

영륜 映倫 [영화 윤리 위원회] the Motion Picture Ethics Commission

영리 營利 profit(-making) ; money-making ; gain ¶ 영리적인 commercial ; money making ; lucrative ; mercenary // 영리에 급급하다 be bent solely upon profit ; be engrossed in money-making // 이것은 영리적인 계획이 아니다 This is not a money-making scheme. // 저 학교는 영리주의다 That school is run for profit.
─ 단체 a profit-making organization ─ 법인 a profit-making corporation ; a

juridical person established for profit —자본 lucrative capital —주의 commercialism — 회사 a company established for profit 비— 단체 a nonprofit organization

†영리 怜利 —하다 (be) clever ; bright ; intelligent ; smart ; sagacious ; wise ; brainy

> 참고 **clever**는 나면서부터 머리가 좋고 손과 두뇌가 잘 움직인다는 뜻 **bright**는 마음의 움직임이나 태도의 활발함을 말하며 어린이나 손아랫사람에 대해서 사용한다 **wise**는 총명하여 지식도 지능도 있다는 뜻

¶ 영리하게 보이는 intelligent-looking // 영리한 아이 a bright child // 영리한 말을 하다 say smart things // 그는 영리하게 생겼다 He looks intelligent. // 그는 영리한 사람이다 He has lots of brains. /He is a sensible man. // 그는 영리해서 그런 짓은 안한다 He knows better than that. /He is too clever to do such a thing. // 그는 때로는 너무 영리해서 탈이야 His cleverness often overshoots itself.

영리 사업 營利事業 a profit-making enterprise ; an undertaking for profit ; a commercial enterprise ; lucrative business

영림 營林 forest management〔administration〕; afforestation ; forestry
—국 a forestry bureau〔office〕 —서 a local forestry office

영마루 嶺— the top of a mountain pass

영망 令望 good reputation ; high repute ; renown

영매 令妹 your〔his〕 younger sister

영매 靈媒 a spirit medium ; a (psychic) medium

영매 英邁 —하다 (be) wise and masterful ; brave and sagacious ¶ 영매한 사람 a mastermind ; a man of parts // 영매한 군주 an illustrious sovereign〔lord〕

영면 永眠 eternal sleep〔rest〕; death ; passing away ; quietus —하다 pass away ; die ; sleep the long sleep

영명 英明 —하다 (be) clear-sighted〔headed〕; perspicacious ; sagacious ; wise ; bright

영명 英名 fame ; glory ; reputation

영명 令名 a fair name ; fame ; reputation ; good repute ¶ 영명이 높다 be highly renowned ; enjoy an excellent reputation ; be famed // 영명을 더럽히다 compromise〔tarnish, defile〕《one's》 fair name // 그는 학자로서 영명이 높다 He is distinguished〔well-known〕 as a scholar.

영몽 靈夢 an inspired dream〔vision〕; a prophetic vision ; a divine revelation in a dream ¶ 영몽을 꾸다 have〔dream〕 an inspired dream

영묘 靈廟 an ancestral shrine ; a mausoleum

영묘 靈妙 —하다 (be) ethereal ; inexplicable ; unutterable ; exquisite ; subtle ; inscrutable ; mysterious ¶ 영묘한 미 ethereal beauty // 영묘〔불가사의〕한 일 an inscrutable fact

*영문 ① [까닭] a reason ; a cause ; a ground ; why ¶ 무슨 영문인지 모르지만 for some unknown reason ; for some reason or other ; somehow (or other) // 영문을 모르겠다 I don't know why. // 어떻게 된 셈인지 영문을 모르겠다 There is neither rhyme nor reason about it. // 왜 화를 내고 있는지 영문을 모르겠다 I don't see any reason for his anger.
② [형편] circumstances ; the matter ; the case ¶ 영문을 캐묻다 inquire into the circumstances // 저 사람이 안 오는 것은 무슨 영문일까 What's the matter with him that he doesn't come? // 나보다 네가 그것을 먼저 알고 있다니 무슨 영문이냐 How comes it that you know it before me?

*영문 英文 English ; English composition〔writing〕; an English sentence ¶ 영문으로 쓰다 write《a letter》 in English // 영문을 한글로 번역하다 translate〔change〕 English into Korean
—과 [학과목] the English literature course ; [학부] the English department ; the department of English language and literature — 기자 a writer in English — 소설 an English novel ; a novel〔story〕 in English — 타이피스트 a typist in English — 편지 a letter in English ; an English letter

영문 營門 a barrack gate

영문 국역 英文國譯 English-Korean translation ; translation from English into Korean

영문법 英文法 English grammar

영문학 英文學 English literature ¶ 영문학을 전공하다 specialize〔major《미》〕 in English literature
—과 ⇨ 영문(—과) —자〔사〕 a scholar〔an history〕 of English literature 한국—회 the English Literary Society of Korea

영문 해석 英文解釋 ① [이해] construing an English text ; understanding English ; the understanding of English ② [국역(國譯)] ⇨ 영문 국역

영물 靈物 a spiritual〔holy, sacred, divine〕 being
—학 pneumatology

영미 英美 England〔Britain〕 and America ; Britain and the United States ; [형용사적] English〔British〕 and American ; Anglo-〔English and〕 American
—인 the English (men) and Americans

영민 英敏 cleverness ; sharpness ; keenness ; (mental) acuteness ; acumen —하다 (be) quick witted ; keen ; sharp ; bright ; clever ; sagacious ; acute ¶ 영민한 두뇌 a clear head ; a keen intellect //

머리가 영민한 사람 a nimble-witted person

영바람 high spirits ; exhilaration ; elation ¶ 영바람이 나서 exultantly ; triumphantly ; proudly ; in fine〔good〕 feather ; with flying colors // 영바람이 나다 be in high spirits ; be elated〔exhilarated〕

영법 泳法 a swimming style〔form, stroke〕

영법 英法 〖법〗 (the) English law

영별 永別 the last parting ; the final farewell **—하다** part forever ; be separated by death ¶ 영별을 고하다 bid one's last farewell 《to》

영봉 靈峰 a sacred〔hallowed〕 mountain 〔peak〕

영부인 令夫人 your〔his〕 (esteemed) wife ; Mrs... ; Madame 《프》 ¶ 김박사와 영부인 Dr. and Mrs. *Kim*

영불 英佛 England and France ¶ 영불의 Anglo-French

영빈관 迎賓館 a reception hall ; a guest house

영사 映射 reflection **—하다** shine 《upon》 ; reflect

영사 映寫 projection **—하다** project 〔throw〕 《a picture》 on the screen

—기 a (movie) projector ; a cineprojector ; a cinematograph **—기사** an operator ; a projectionist 《미》 **—막** a (cinema) screen **—시간** the running time for a film **—실** a projection room〔booth〕 ; the booth

*__영사 領事__ a consul ; a consular representative

—관 a consulate **—관원** a consular attaché〔official〕 ; the staff of a consulate 《총칭》 **—단** the consular body〔corps〕 **—보** a consular assistant **—재판(권)** consular jurisdiction **—재판소** a consular court **—조약** a consular agreement **—증명료** consular fee ; consulage **—(증명) 송장** 〖상업〗 a consular invoice **명예—** an honorary consul **부—** a vice-consul **총—** a consul general **카이로 주재 한국—** the Korean Consul at Cairo **한국 주재 미국—** an American consul stationed in Korea

영사 影寫 a tracing **—하다** trace 《a drawing》

영사 營舍 barracks ; cantonments

영상 領相 the Premier ; the Prime Minister

영상 映像 an image ; a reflection ; a reflex

영상 零上 above zero ¶ 영상 2도 two degrees above zero

영상 影像 [영정] a (painted) picture of a person ; a portrait ; [그림자] a shadow ; phantom

영생 永生 eternal life ; immortality **—하다** live eternally ; enjoy immortality

영생이 〖식물〗 peppermint ⇨ 박하(薄荷)

영서 令壻 your〔his〕 (esteemed) son in law

영서 永逝 death ; eternal sleep ⇨ 영면

영서 英書 an English book ; English literature (영문)

영선 營繕 building and repairs ; repair works ; maintenance (정비) **—하다** build and repair

—과 building and repairs section **—비** building and repairing expenses

영성 靈性 divine nature ; divinity ; spirituality

영성체 領聖體 〖카톨릭〗 Holy Communion

영세 永世 eternity ; permanence ; everlasting generations ¶ 영세의 eternal ; permanent ; perpetual // 영세토록 forever ; eternally ; permanently ; perpetually

영세 零細 being paltry〔petty〕 **—하다** (be) paltry ; petty ; trifling ; insignificant ; scant ; fragmentary

—농(가) a petty〔an ultra-small〕 farmer ; a poor-landed peasant **—어민** a poorly equipped〔destitute〕 fisherman **—업자** a small-scale businessman **—자금** small〔petty〕 funds

영세 領洗 〖카톨릭〗 baptism ¶ 영세를 베풀다 baptize

—명 one's baptismal〔Christian〕 name

영세민 the indigent ; the poor ; the poverty-stricken ; the poverty-ridden ; paupers ; the needy people ¶ 영세민을 돕다 relieve the poor

영세 불망 永世不忘 **—하다** remember forever ; bear in mind forever ; be ever in one's mind

영세 중립 永世中立 permanent neutrality

—국 a permanently neutral country 〔state〕

⁑**영속 永續** everlastingness ; permanency ; perpetuity ; long continuance **—하다** last long ; remain permanently ; have a long life ; continue ; stand forever ¶ 영속적인 lasting ; permanent ; perpetual ; continual // 영속하지 않다 be of short duration ; be short-lived // 이것은 영속할 것 같지 않다 It does not bid fair to last long.

—성 perpetuity

영손 令孫 your〔his〕 (esteemed) grand child〔grandson, granddaughter〕

영솔 領率 command ; supervision ; direction ; direct ; take the lead of ¶ A 장군이 영솔하는 군대 the army under the command of General A // 군대를 영솔하여 진군하다 march at the head of an army

영송 迎送 welcome and send-off ; greeting and farewell **—하다** meet and see off ; welcome and send off ; greet and bid

영송 詠誦 ⇨ 낭송(朗誦)

영수 領水 ⇨ 영해(領海)

⁑**영수 領收, 領受** receipt **—하다** be in receipt of 《a letter》 acknowledge ; receive ; receipt 《of》 ¶ 영수증을 쓰다

make (out) a receipt〔voucher〕// 영수필 "paid"; "received"// 정히 영수함 Received with thanks. // 일금 5만원 정히 영수함 I acknowledge receipt of the sum of 50,000 *won*. (서한) / Received 《of Mr. A》 the sum of 50,000 *won*. (증서)
—인 a receiver; a recipient **—필(畢)** Paid. /Received.

영수 領袖 a leader; a chief; a boss 《미》; a protagonist ¶ 정당의 영수 a leader of a political party; a political leader

영수증 領收證 a receipt 《for》; a voucher 《for》; an acknowledgment 《for》 ¶ 영수증을 쓰다 make out a receipt 《for》// 영수증을 주다 give 《a person》 a receipt 《for》
가— an interim receipt

영습자 英習字 English penmanship
—장 an English copybook

영시 零時 twelve o'clock; the zero hour; noon (정오); midnight ¶ 영시 30분 half past〔after〕 twelve; twelve thirty

영시 英詩 [전체] English poetry〔verse〕; [시편] an English poem; a poem in English

영식 令息 your〔his〕 (esteemed) son

영아 嬰兒 a suckling; a nursling; an infant; a baby; a new-born child ¶ 아직 못 걷는 영아 an infant in arms
— 사망률 infant mortality; the death rate of infants **— 살인범** an infanticide **— 살인죄** infanticide **— 위탁소** a baby farm; a day nursery; a crèche 《프》

영악 獰惡 savage; fierceness; ferocity; cruelty **—하다** (be) fierce; ferocious; savage; cruel ¶ 영악한 사람 a fierce fellow; a Tartar

영악하다 (be) clever; smart; sharp; shrewd; have gumption ¶ 영악한 아이 a smart child

영애 令愛 your〔his〕 (esteemed) daughter

영약 靈藥 a miraculous〔wonderful〕 medicine; a marvelous〔sovereign〕 remedy; a royal elixir; a wonder〔miracle〕 drug 《미》

영양 羚羊 〖동물〗 an antelope

***영양 營養, 榮養** nourishment; nutrition; alimentation ¶ 영양이 좋은 well-nourished〔-fed〕// 영양부족의 ill-fed〔-nourished〕; underfed; undernourished // 이 아이는 영양을 더 많이 섭취해야 한다 This child needs feeding up.
— 과다 supernutrition **—률** caloric percentage **—물** nutriments; nutritious〔nourishing〕 food **—분** nutritive substance〔elements〕; a nutriment; a nutrient **— 상태** nutritive conditions **— 생리학** nutritional physiology **— 섭취량** (a) caloric intake **—식** a nourishing meal **— 연구소** a dietetic laboratory **— 요법** a dietary cure **— 장애** nutrition lesion〔disorder〕 **—제** a medicine for promoting nutrition; a tonic

영양 令孃 your〔his〕 (esteemed) daughter

영양가 營養價 nutritive〔food〕 value〔power〕; nutritive qualities ¶ 영양가가 높은 of high nutritive value; highly nutritious

영양 부족 營養不足 undernourishment; insufficient〔want of〕 nutrition; malnutrition; innutrition; low〔imperfect〕 nutrition ¶ 영양 부족 때문에 through lack of nourishment

영양사 營養士 a dietitian; a dietician; a nutritionist

영양 실조 營養失調 unbalanced nutrition; malnutrition; dystrophy; dystrophia ¶ 영양 실조에 빠지다 suffer from malnutrition

영양학 營養學 the science of nutrition; dietetics; sitology
—자 a nutritionist; a dietitan; a dietician

†**영어 英語** English; the English language〔tongue〕 ¶ 영어의 English // 영어로 쓴 편지 a letter (written) in English // 영어를 사용하는 국민 an English speaking people // 정확한〔바른〕 영어 correct〔proper〕 English // 세련된〔저속한〕 영어 polished〔vulgar〕 English // 산 영어 living English // 순수한 영어 the King's〔Queen's〕 English // 영어로 말하다〔쓰다〕 speak〔write〕 in English // 영어로 번역하다 translate〔put, render〕 into English // 영어를 쓰다 speak English; write English // 영어를 유창하게 하다 speak fluent English // 영어를 잘하다〔영어가 서툴다〕 be good〔not good〕 at English; have a good〔poor〕 knowledge of English; have a wonderful〔poor〕 command of English // 영어가 늘다 improve〔make progress〕 in one's English // 사랑을 영어로 무엇이라고 합니까 What is the English for *sarang*? // 이 나라에서는 영어를 쓰지 않는다 English is not spoken in this country. // 그는 영어로 의사 소통이 가능하다 He can make himself understood in English.
— 강습회 an English class **—계** the English speaking world **— 교사〔선생〕** a teacher of English; an English teacher (영어 선생은 an Énglish teacher이고, an English téacher는 영국인 선생의 뜻) **— 교육** the teaching of English; English language teaching **—극** a theatrical performance given in English **— (사용) 국민** an English speaking people **— 소설** an English novel; a novel in English **— 시험** an examination in English **— 연설** an English speech **— 웅변 대회** an English oratorical〔speech〕 contest **—책〔잡지〕** an English book〔magazine〕 **— 편지** a letter (written) in English **—학** English philology〔linguistics〕 **— 회화** English conversation **고대〔중세, 근세〕—** old〔middle, modern〕 English **구어 —**

colloquial English 미국〔영국〕 — American〔British〕 English 상업 — commercial〔business〕 English 순수 — [영국의] the King's〔Queen's〕 English 시사 — current English 신문 — journalistic〔newspaper〕 English 실용 — practical〔living〕 English 일상 — everyday English 표준 — standard English 현대 — current〔present-day〕 English

영어 囹圄 a prison ; a jail 《미》 ¶ 영어의 몸이 되다 be put in prison〔jail〕; be imprisoned〔incarcerated〕

영어 營漁 fishing ; fishery
— 자금 a fishery fund ¶ 영어 자금을 방출하다 release the fishery funds 《for》

영업 營業 business ; trade ; commercial pursuits **—하다** do〔conduct〕 business ; engage in business ; carry on〔run, operate〕 a business ; trade in ¶ 영업용의 for business use〔purposes〕 // 영업 중이다 be in operation // 영업을 시작하다 open〔commence〕 business // 영업을 방해하다 obstruct〔interfere with〕 one's business // 영업을 쉬다 suspend business ; close one's shop // 영업을 허가하다 authorize 《a person》 to carry on the business // 영업 시간은 오전 9시부터 오후 5시까지 Open from 9 a. m. to 5 p. m. /Office〔Business〕 hours ; from 9 a. m. to 5 p. m.
— 감찰 a business〔trade〕 license —권 right of trade〔business〕; good will — 금지〔정지〕 prohibition〔suspension, discontinuance〕 of business — 방침 a business policy — 방해 obstruction of business — 보고 a business report —부 the business department —비 operating〔working, running, business〕 expenses ; overhead charges — 성적 the results of operations 《for 1994》 —소〔장소〕 a business office ; a place of business — 시간 business〔office〕 hours — 안내 a business guide ; a catalog(ue) — 연도 a business year — 이익 trading profits —일 a business day ; week days —자 a business manager ; a trader — 자본〔자금〕 a working capital — 종목 the category〔kind, line〕 of business

영업세 營業稅 business tax

영업주 a business proprietor

영업 허가 營業許可 business license ¶ 영업 허가를 받다 secure a license to operate

⁑**영역 英譯** an English translation〔version〕 **—하다** translate〔render, put, turn〕 into English ¶ 톨스토이의 작품을 영역본으로 읽다 read Tolstoy's works in English version〔translation〕 // 다음 문장을 영역하라 Put the following sentences into English.
국문 — translation from Korean into English ; Korean-English translation

영역 靈域 sacred precincts〔ground〕; holy precincts〔ground〕

영역 領域 [영토] a territory ; a domain ; a possession ; [분야] a province ; one's line ; a field ; a sphere ¶ 영역을 확장하다 expand〔extend〕 one's territory // 정신병학의 영역 the field〔domain, sphere〕 of psychiatry // …의 영역이다 be in one's line〔province〕 // 자기 영역을 벗어나다 move in another's sphere

영영 永永 forever ; eternally ; perpetually ; for good (and all) ¶ 조국을 영영 떠나다 leave one's homeland permanently〔for good, never to return〕 // 그후 그로부터 영영 소식이 없다 Nothing whatever has been heard of him ever since.

영영 무궁 永永無窮 eternity ; perpetuity ; infinitude ; immortality **—하다** (be) eternal ; perpetual ; everlasting ; infinite ; immortal ¶ 영영 무궁토록 forever ; eternally ; perpetually ; immortally

영예 榮譽 honor ; distinction ; glory ; fame (명성) ¶ 영예로운 honorable ; glorious // 영예로운 날 a glorious〔splendid〕 day // 국가의 영예 the glory of a nation // 영예를 지니다 have the honor of 《a player》; be loaded with honors ; be covered with glory // 영예로 여기다 feel〔consider, esteem〕 《it》 an honor // 이 영예를 돌아가신 어머님과 나누고 싶다 I wish I could share this honor with my deceased mother. // 임금은 영예의 근원 The sovereign is the foundation of honor.

영외 營外 outside barracks ¶ 영외 거주하다 live outside〔out of〕 barracks ; take one's lodgings outside barracks

영요 榮耀 honor (영예) ; glory (영광) ; distinction

영욕 榮辱 glory and shame ; honor and contempt ; reputation and disgrace

영용 英勇 —하다 (be) intelligent and doughty〔valiant〕; be a bold warrior

†**영웅 英雄** a hero ; a great man ¶ 영웅적 행위 a heroic deed // 영웅심에 불타다 burn with ambition // 국민적 영웅이 되다 become a national hero // 그는 영웅다운 기질이 있다 He is cast in heroic mold. / Heroic blood runs in his veins. // 그는 참말로 영웅이다 The man is a veritable hero.
— 숭배 hero worship —주의 heroism

⁑**영원 永遠** eternity ; permanence ; perpetuity ; immortality **—하다** (be) eternal ; perpetual ; everlasting ; permanent ; immortal ; imperishable ¶ 영원히 eternally ; forever ; permanently ; for good (and all) ; perpetually ; for keeps 《미·구》 // 영원한 잠 eternal sleep // 영원한 진리〔생명〕 an eternal truth〔life〕 // 영원한 평화 a lasting〔everlasting, permanent〕 peace // 영원히 떠나버리다 leave 《a place》 never to return // 이름을 영원히 남기다 immortalize one's fame〔name〕 // 신은 영

원히 존재한다 God is eternal.
—성 eternal nature ; eternity ; perpetuity
영위 營爲 [관리] management ; administration ; running ; operation 《미》 **—하다** carry on ; operate〔run〕《a hotel》; manage ; conduct
영위법 零位法 the zero method
영유 領有 possession **—하다** possess ; take〔get, be in〕possession of ¶ …의 영유로 되다 be annexed to ; fall into 《a person's》 hands ; come into 《a person's》 way
—권 dominium —지〔물〕 a possession
영육 靈肉 body and soul〔mind, spirit〕; spirit and flesh
— 일치 the unity〔oneness〕 of body and soul ; the union of body and soul
영윤 令胤 your〔his〕 (esteemed) son
영의정 領議政 a prime minister ; the chief minister
영이별 永離別 a last parting ; a lifelong separation〔parting〕 **—하다** part for life〔forever〕; part〔separate〕《from a person》 never to meet again ¶ 그것이 그와의 영이별이 되리라고는 꿈에도 생각 못했다 I did not even imagine that I was not to see him again in life.
영인 英人 ⇨ 영국인
영인 影印 photoprinting ; [인쇄술] phototypography **—하다** photoprint ; print〔reproduce〕 by phototypography
—본 a photoprint ; a photographic print
영일 寧日 a peaceful〔quiet〕 day ; rest ¶ 영일이 없다 be kept busy all the time ; not a single day passes quietly // 다망하여 영일없다 I am so busy that I have hardly a minute to call my own〔a day to idle away〕.
영자 英字 an English letter ¶ 영자의 English
— 신문 an English (-language) newspaper ; a newspaper in English
영자 英姿 an impressive〔a gallant〕 figure ; a majestic〔dignified〕 appearance ; a noble mien ¶ 그가 늠름한 영자를 나타냈다 He made his majestic appearance.
영자 影子 a shadow ; a silhouette an image
영작 榮爵 peerage ; a title
***영장 令狀** a warrant ; a writ ; a written order ¶ 영장에 의한 체포 arrest with a warrant // 영장을 발부하다 issue a warrant 《for a person's arrest》 // 영장을 집행하다 execute a warrant ; serve a writ on 《a person》
— 송달인 〖법〗 a process server — 집행 the execution of a warrant (가택) 수색 — a search warrant 구속〔체포〕 — a warrant of arrest 소환 — a (writ of) summons ; a subpoena 압류〔차압〕 — a writ of attachment
영장 靈長 a supreme creature ¶ 사람은 만물의 영장이다 Man is the lord of (all) creation.
—류 〖동물〗 Primates (학명)
영재 英才 [재주] talent ; sagacity ; genius ; high intelligence ; [사람] a brilliant〔gifted〕 person ; a man of talent ; a genius ; a talent ¶ 저 학교는 허다한 영재를 배출했다 The school has turned out a lot of talented men.
— 교육 specific education for brilliant children ; special education for the gifted children〔the precocious〕
영적 靈的 spiritual ; incorporeal ¶ 역사상의 대인물과 영적으로 교제하다 associate in spirit with great historical characters
— 교류 spiritual sympathy — 생활 spiritual〔inner〕 life
영전 榮轉 transfer on promotion ; promotion **—하다** be promoted (and transferred) to 《a higher post》; be transferred on promotion ¶ 그는 본사로 영전됐다 He was transferred to the head office on promotion. // 그의 부산 전임은 영전이다 His transfer to Pusan is a change for the better.
영전 影殿 a hall where the royal portraits are kept
영전 靈前 ¶ 영전에 before the spirit of the departed〔deceased〕 // 고인의 영전에 바치다 offer 《a thing》 to the spirit of the departed
영절스럽다 (be) plausible ; specious ; likely ; verisimilar ; appear to be true ¶ 영절스러운 아기 an admirable child ; a likely lad
영점 零點 zero ; the zero point ; no marks ; no point ; [경기에서] a duck ; a duck's egg ; a goose egg 《미》; [빙점] the freezing point ¶ 영점을 맞다 get no marks ; get zero ; get a duck (경기에서) // 야구 시합에서 영점으로 지다 lose a game without scoring a single run // 그는 교사로서 영점이다 As a teacher he is a failure.
영접 迎接 reception ; welcome ; meeting (출영) **—하다** welcome ; receive ; meet ; go out to meet (출영)
— 위원회 a reception committee
영정 影幀 a portrait (scroll)
영제 令弟 your〔his〕 (esteemed) younger brother
영조 營造 building ; erection **—하다** build ; construct ; erect
—물 an establishment ; a building ; a structure ; [총칭] public works
영조 靈鳥 a sacred bird
영존 永存 durability ; permanence ; perpetuity **—하다** remain〔exist〕 forever〔perpetually〕
—성 perpetuity
영주 英主 a wise ruler〔king〕; an illustrious sovereign〔monarch〕; a heroic king
영주 永住 a permanent residence **—하다** reside permanently 《in》; settle down 《in

a place》; make one's home 《at, in》 ¶ 이 곳에 영주하고 싶다 I should like to settle here permanently.
—민 permanent residents ; denizens ; settlers —자 permanent resident ; a denizen ; a settler —지 a permanent domicile ; one's permanent home
영주 領主 a feudal lord ; the lord of the manor
영주권 永住權 denizenship ¶ 영주권을 얻다 be denizened
영중 英中 England〔Britain〕 and China ¶ 영중의 Anglo-Chinese
영지 領地 ① [영토] a territory ; a possession ; a dominion ; a domain ; a demesne ② [봉토] a fief ; feudal tenure ; a feud ; a vassalage
영지 靈地 a holy ground〔land〕 ; a sacred place
영지 英智 wisdom ; sagacity ; intelligence
영진 榮進 promotion ; advancement ; preferment ; rise —하다 be promoted 〔advanced〕 《to a higher position》 ; get promotion
영질 令姪 your〔his〕 (esteemed) nephew 〔niece〕
영차 Yo-ho ! /Yo-heave-ho !
영창 映窓 a paper window ; window slides (for admitting light)
영창 營窓 a guardhouse ; detention barracks ; a military jail〔lockup〕 ¶ 영창에 갇히다 be confined in the guardhouse
중— detention in the guardroom for a serious offense
영채 映彩 brilliant〔radiant〕 color ; brilliancy ; splendor
영천 靈泉 a magical〔wonder-working〕 fountain ; a hot spring (온천) ¶ 불로 불사의 영천 a fountain of eternal youth
영철 英哲 great discernment ; wisdom ; perspicacity ; [사람] a man of great discernment —하다 (be) sagacious ; perspicacious ; be of great discernment
영치 領置 provisional holding ; keeping in custody —하다 detain ; place in the custody 《of the prison officer》
—물 personal belongings kept in custody
영탄 詠嘆 [읊음] recital of a poem ; [감탄] exclamation ; [찬탄] admiration —하다 recite a poem ; exclaim ; admire
*영토 領土 a territory ; a possession ; a dominion ; a domain ¶ 영토를 확장하다 extend one's territory // 영토적 야심을 품다 harbor territorial ambitions // 타국의 영토를 침입하다 encroach upon the territory of another country
—권 territorial rights — 문제 a territorial problem — 보전 territorial integrity — 분쟁 a territorial dispute — 주권 territorial sovereignty ; sovereignty upon land — 침범 encroachment upon the territory of another country — 획득 acquisition of territory
영토 확장 領土擴張 expansion of territory ; territorial expansion〔aggrandizement〕 —론자 an expansionist —열 land hunger ; a territorial ambition — 정책 expansionism ; a policy of territorial expansion
영특하다 英特— (be) wise ; sagacious ; perspicacious ; intelligent
영판 just like ; [아주] very ; awfully ¶ 그들 두 형제의 얼굴이 영판 다르다 I see no likeness whatever between those two brothers.
영패 零敗 a shutout ; a whitewash ; a skunk 《미》 —하다 be nosed out ; fail to score ; be skunked ; 〖정구〗 be defeated in a love game ; 〖야구〗 be shut out ¶ 영패시키다 whitewash ; skunk ; shut 〔nose〕 out // 간신히 영패를 면하다 barely miss being shutout
영피다 put out〔forth〕 one's strength 〔energy〕 ; show spark〔life〕
*영하 零下 below zero ; sub-zero ¶ 영하의 기온 sub-zero temperature // 영하 16도로 내리다 fall to 16 degrees below zero
영하다 靈— [영험이] be marvelously responsive to prayers ; [효험이] (be) wonder-working ; wonderfully efficacious ; be magical in its effect ¶ 영한 의사 a wonderful doctor ; an excellent physician
영학 英學 the study of English ; English studies
—자 an English scholar
*영한 英韓 England〔Britain〕 and Korea ; English-Korean ; Anglo-Korean
— 대역 an English-Korean translation — 대역본 an English book with Korean translation — 사전 an English-Korean dictionary
영합 迎合 flattery ; adulation ; ingratiation —하다 flatter ; curry favor 《with》 ; fawn 《upon》 ; chime in 《a person's mood》 ¶ 악취미에 영합하다 cater to corrupt taste // 영합적 태도를 취하다 assume an ingratiatory attitude // 남의 설에 영합하다 echo〔compromise with〕 《another's》 opinion // 여론에 영합하다 go with the current of the time
—주의 opportunism ; timeserving
영해 領海 territorial waters ; a closed sea ¶ 영해 내〔외〕에서 within〔outside of〕 territorial waters
—선 a territorial water line 외국 — foreign waters
*영향 影響 influence ; consequence(s) ; effect (결과) ; affection (일시적) —하다 influence ; have an effect on ; exert influence on ; affect ; tell on ¶ 전쟁의 영향 the effect of a war // 불교의 영향으로 under the influence of Buddhism // 악영향을 미치다 have〔exert, exercise〕 a bad effect〔an evil influence〕 《upon》 ; affect adversely // 영향을 받다 be influenced

〔affected〕 by // 여러가지 영향을 받다 undergo various influences // 환경이 주는 영향은 크다 Environment is a potent influence. // 우량은 농작물의 성장에 영향을 준다 The amount of rain affects the growth of crops. // 수면 부족이 점차 건강에 영향을 미친다 Lack of sleep gradually tells on the health. // 그 사건은 그의 전생애에 영향을 주었다 The incident colored his entire life.

*영향력 影響力 influence ; the influencing power ; the power of influence ¶ 영향력을 행사하다 exercise one's influence 《over》 // 영향력이 있다 be influential ; be powerful

영험 靈驗 a miracle ⇨ 영검

영현 英顯 the spirit of the departed ; [전사자의] the souls of the departed war heroes ; the spirits of the war dead

영형 令兄 your〔his〕 (esteemed) elder brother

†영혼 靈魂 a soul ; a spirit
— 불멸(설) (the doctrine of) the immortality of the soul ; immortality — 창조설 creationism

†영화 榮華 [번영] glory ; prosperity ; splendor ; pomp ; [호화] luxury ; extravagance ¶ 영화로운 glorious ; prosperous ; luxurious // 속세의 영화 the pomps and glories of the world ; vain glories // 잠깐 동안의 영화 a brief span of prosperity // 영화를 극하다 be at the height of one's prosperity ; live in splendor // 영화롭게 살다 live in luxury ; live sumptuously

영화 靈化 spiritualization ; etherealization
—하다 spiritualize ; etherealize

†영화 映畫 a motion picture ; a movie 《미》 ; a cinema ; a moving picture ; a picture ; a film ; [총칭] the movies ; the cinema ; the screen ¶ 영화화하다 cinematize〔film, make a movie of〕 《a novel》 ; picturize 《영》 ; make 《a novel》 into a movie // 영화를 만들다 produce a film // 영화를 상영하다 show a movie 〔film〕 ; put a film on the screen // 영화를 찍다 film ; take a motion picture 《of》 ; shoot pictures // 영화 구경가다 go to the movies〔pictures, cinema 《영》〕 // 영화에 출연하다 play in a movie〔film〕 ; appear on the screen // 그 영화는 명보 극장에서 상영 중이다 The picture is on at the *Myungbo* Theater.
—가(街) the cinema quarters — 각본 a scenario — 감독 a (film) director ; a producer 《영》 — 검열 film censorship — 극 a film play〔drama〕 ; a photoplay ; a screen drama — 대본 a (dialogue) script ; a continuity — 배급 회사 a film〔movie〕 distributing agency 〔company〕 — 사업 the movie〔motion picture〕 industry — 상영권 film rights — 스타 a movie〔film〕 star —인 a movieman —제 a film festival — 제작 film production — 제작〔촬영〕소 a movie〔cinema〕 studio ; a lot 《미》 ¶ 국립 영화 제작소 the National Film Production Center — 제작자 a film producer — 제작 회사 a film producing company — 조감독 an assistant director — 편집 film editing〔cutting〕 — 편집자 a movie editor —평 a film review ; a movie criticism —팬 a film 〔movie〕 fan ; a filmgoer ; a moviegoer 《구》 개봉 — a first-run film ; a newly released film 교육 — an educational film 뉴스 — a newsreel ; a news film 단편 — a short motion picture ; a shorty 《미》 ; a short subject ; a short 《속》 무성 — a silent film〔picture〕 문화〔극, 기록, 만화〕 — a cultural〔feature, documentary, cartoon〕 film 발성 — a sound film〔picture〕 ; a talkie ; a talking picture〔film〕 입체 — a three-dimensional motion picture ; a 3-D picture 전쟁 — a war picture 천연색〔흑백〕 — a (techni) color 〔black and white〕 film 아시아 —제 the Asian Film Festival

영화 英貨 British currency〔money〕 ; sterling ; the pound ¶ 영화 100파운드 100 pounds sterling ; 100 sterling // 영화의 하락〔등귀〕 a fall〔rise〕 of the pound // 영화로 환산하다 covert into English currency

영화계 映畫界 the cinema〔film, screen〕 world ; screendom 《미》 ; filmdom ; picturedom ; movie land

영화관 映畫館 a cinema 《영》 ; a cinema house〔palace〕 ; a cinematograph theater ; a movie house〔theater〕 ; a moving 〔motion〕 picture theater ; a picture hall
—주 a cinema house proprietor ; a film exhibitor

영화 배우 映畫俳優 a cinema〔film, movie, screen〕 actor〔actress〕 ; a photoplayer ; [여우(女優)] a cinema actress ¶ 영화 배우가 되다 appear on the screen

영화 윤리 위원회 映畫倫理委員會 the Motion Picture Code of Ethics Committee

영화화 映畫化 cinematization ; filming ; picturization —하다 cinematize ; cinematograph ; film 《a novel》 ; picturize

옅다 ① [깊이 따위가] ⇨ 얕다
② [빛이] (be) light ; pale ¶ 옅은 푸른빛 a light blue

†옆 the side ; the flank (측면) ¶ 옆에(서) by the side 《of》 ; aside ; by ; beside ; near ; close by〔to〕 ; next 《to》 // 옆으로 on〔to〕 one side ; aside ; sidewards ; sideways ; crosswise ; crossly ; horizontally ; transversely // 옆길 a by-road ; a byway ; a pass ; a sideway // 옆을 본 사진 a portrait〔photograph〕 in profile // 내 옆의 학생 a student next to me // 옆에 앉은 사람 a person sitting next (to) one // 옆을 지나가다 pass by // 옆에 놓다 put 《a

thing》 aside // 옆으로 눕다 lie on one's side ; lay oneself down sideways // 옆으로 밀다 push 《a thing》 aside // 옆으로 비키다 step aside ; give way to 《a person》 // 옆으로 줄을 긋다 draw a line horizontally ; draw a horizontal line // 옆을 보다 look aside // 옆에서 덤벼들다 attack 《a person》 from the side // 모자를 옆으로 비켜 쓰다 wear one's hat aslant〔on one side〕; cock one's hat // 옆에서 말참견을 하다 poke one's nose in 《a matter》; meddle in 《another's affair》 // 윗머리는 그냥 놔 두고 옆만 좀 쳐 주세요 Leave the top alone and just trim the sides.

—문 a side entrance ; a side door —방 an adjoining room —얼굴 the side face ; a profile —자리 the next seat ; a side seat (버스 따위의) —줄 a side line

옆갈비 side ribs

†**옆구리** the side ; the flank ¶ 왼편 옆구리 the left side // 옆구리가 아프다 have a pain (stitch) in one's side ; one's side aches // 옆구리를 쿡쿡 찌르다 give a poke in 《a person's》 ribs // 옆구리를 차다 kick 《a person》 in the side // 책을 옆구리에 끼다 carry a book under one's arm

옆길 a side road〔way〕 ¶ 옆길로 가다 take a side road

옆널 a side board ; a sidepiece

옆들다 help ; lend a helping hand ; take sides〔part〕 with 《a person》; side with 《a person》; support

옆막이 a horizontal side-block

옆머리 the side of the head ¶ 옆머리에 상처를 입다 get hurt on the side of one's head

옆면 —面 a side ; sides ⇨ 측면(側面)

옆모습 a profile ; a side face ; a face in profile ¶ 옆모습을 그린 초상화 a portrait drawn in profile // 옆모습을 그리다 draw a profile 《a person》 // 옆모습이 아름답다 have a good〔fine〕 profile

옆바람 a side wind

옆발치 at〔close to〕 the feet of 《a person》 lying down

옆옆이 on this side and that ; on all sides

옆질 [배의] rock(ing) ; rolling —하다 《a boat》 rock ; roll (from side to side)

*__옆집__ a next door〔house〕; a neighboring house ; an adjacent house ¶ 옆집의 next ; next door ; adjoining ; neighboring // 왼쪽 옆집 the next door on the left side // 그 여자는 우리 옆집에 산다 She lives in the house next to ours. /She lives next door to me.

— 사람 a (next door) neighbor

옆쪽 the side ; the flank ¶ 옆쪽의 side ; flank // 옆쪽에 앉다 sit by 《a person》; sit by 《a person's》 side

옆찌르다 nudge 《a person》 in the ribs ; give a nudge ¶ 옆찌르고 귓속말을 하다 nudge 《a person》 and whisper in his ear

옆폭 a side board ; a sidepiece

옆훑이 a side grooving〔fluting〕 plane 〔chisel〕

예[1] old days ; the past ; days gone by ; ancient〔old〕 times ; former years ¶ 예로부터 from old〔ancient〕 times // 예나 지금이나 같다 It is the same now as in old times.

*__예__[2] ① [대답] yes ; certainly ; all right ; very well ; [출석의 대답] here ; present ; yes 《sir, madam》 ¶ 예 알았습니다 Yes, certainly. /All right, sir. /Very well, sir.

② [반문] Eh? /What? ¶ 예 그러세요 Is it? /Is that so? /Really?

*__예__ 例 ① [실례] an example ; an instance ; a case ; an illustration

> 참고 **instance** 일반적인 진술을 증명하는 것으로서 예거되는 사람 또는 사례 **example** 한 종류의 대표적인 예로서 예거되는 것 **illustration** 어떤 일을 증명하는 데 도움이 되는 예

¶ 유사한 예 a similar case // 예를 들면 for instance〔example〕 《e. g.》 // 예를 들다 cite〔give, draw, take〕 an instance 〔example〕 // 남의 예를 좇다 follow 《a person's》 example ; follow suit ; follow the example of ; follow in 《a person》 footsteps // 그는 곤충의 예로 파리를 들었다 He instanced the fly as an insect. // 이것이 좋은 예다 This is a good example. /This is a case in point. // 한국도 예외가 아니다 Korea is no exception to the rule. // 링컨이 가난한 아이로서 출세한 한 예이다 Lincoln is an instance of a poor boy who rose to fame.

② [전례] a precedent ; a parallel (유례) ¶ 예 없는 일 an unheard-of affair ; an unprecedented matter // 예가 되다 become a precedent // 선례를 따르다 follow a precedent // 여태 그런 예가 없다 There is no precedent〔parallel〕 for this. /It is without (a) precedent.

예 禮 ① [절] a salutation ; a salute ; an obeisance ; a bow —하다 bow ; salute ; make a bow〔an obeisance〕 to drop〔make〕 a curtsy (부인이)

② [예의] etiquette ; courtesy ; civility ; propriety ; decorum ¶ 예를 잃다 be impolite〔uncivil〕; be rude〔ill-mannered〕; be wanting in courtesy // 예를 다하다 extend 《a person》 every courtesy ; show 《a person》 every civility // 그렇게 하면 예에 벗어난다 It is not 〔against〕 etiquette to do so.

예각 銳角 〖기하〗 an acute angle

예각 豫覺 ⇨ 예감

*__예감__ 豫感 a presentiment ; a premonition ; a hunch ; a presage ; foreboding —하다 have〔experience〕 a presentiment〔foreboding〕 《of》 ¶ 불길한 예감 a gloomy foreboding // 죽음을 예감하다

have a premonition of death // 어쩐지 네가 오늘 올 것 같은 예감이 들었다 I had a hunch that you would come today. / Something told me that you would come today. // 그의 예감이 들어맞았다 His presentiment came true. // 독살당할 것 같은 예감을 하고 있다 He has a presentiment that his life will be taken by poison. // 내가 뭐라고 했냐 내 예감을 늘 딱 들어맞는다 What did I tell you ? My hunches are always right on the money.

*예견 豫見 foreknowledge ; prescience ; precognition **—하다** foresee ; foreknow ¶ …을 예견하고 in anticipation of...

예결 위원 豫決委員 a member of the budget committee

—회 the budget committee ; [국회] the Standing Committee on Budget ; the Appropriations Committee (세출) 《미》

†**예고 豫告** an advance〔a previous〕notice ; a notice ; a previous〔preliminary〕announcement ; a warning (경고) **—하다** give〔advance〕notice ; warn 《a person》 of ; notify ; announce〔inform〕in advance〔previously, beforehand〕 ¶ 예고 없이 without (previous) warning〔notice〕; at a moment's notice (즉석에서) // 예고한 대로 as previously〔already〕announced // 가격 인상을 소비자에게 예고하다 warn consumers of an increase in price // 한달 전에 (해고를) 예고하다 give a month's notice〔warning〕// 그는 사전 예고 없이 방문했다 There was no advance notice of his coming. /He made a surprise visit. // 예고한 것보다 못하다 It does not come up to what we expected from the preliminary announcement.

—편 a preview ; a prevue ; a trailer **신간 —** the announcement〔notice〕of new〔forthcoming〕books ; book notices

예과 豫科 preparatory course (과정) ; a preparatory department (부) ¶ 2년제 예과 a two years' preparatory course // 예과를 수료하다 complete the preparatory course

—생 a preparatory course student ; a prep student 《미·구》 **대학 —** the preparatory course of〔for〕a college

예광탄 曳光彈 a tracer shell〔bullet〕; a light〔flame〕tracer

예궐 詣闕 ⇨ 입궐(入闕)

예규 例規 an established rule〔regulation〕 ¶ 관계 예규에 따라 처리하다 dispose 《a matter》 as prescribed by the regulation concerned

*예금 預金 a deposit ; money on deposit ; a bank account ; credit **—하다** deposit (in the bank) ; place money on deposit ¶ 예금을 찾다 draw〔withdraw〕one's money〔one's deposit〕from the bank // 3만원 예금이 있다 have 30,000 *won* in (the) bank〔on deposit〕; have a bank account of 30,000 *won* // 아직 예금이 남아 있다 I still have a balance at my bank. // 당좌 예금으로 하시겠습니까 정기 예금으로 하시겠습니까 Will you deposit as a current account or as a fixed one ?

—계〔과〕 the deposit department〔section〕(of a bank) ; [사람] a deposit teller **— 계정** deposit account **— 대부** a deposit loan **—액** the deposited amount 《in a bank》 **— 원장** a deposit ledger **— 이율** a deposit rate **— 이자** interest on〔of〕deposits **—자** a depositor **— 준비금** a reserve for deposit **— 준비율** a deposit reserve rate **— 증서** a certificate of deposit ; a deposit certificate〔note, receipt〕 **— 채무** deposit liabilities **— 통장** a (deposit) passbook ; a bankbook **—표** a deposit slip **당좌〔저축, 정기, 보통〕—** a current〔a savings, a fixed, an ordinary〕deposit〔account〕 **신탁 —** a deposit in trust **은행 —** a bank deposit〔account〕; a deposit in a bank **통지 —** a deposit at notice〔call〕 **특별〔별단〕—** a special deposit

예금주 預金主 a depositor

소액 — a small depositor

예기 [나무랄 때] Damn it ! ; Damn you ! ¶ 예기 나쁜 놈 You rascal !

예기 銳氣 [기세] spirit ; dash ; ardor ; [원기] vigor ; energy ¶ 예기 있는 젊은이 young〔fresh〕blood // 예기를 꺾다 break 《a person's》 spirits

예기를 기르다 관용 conserve one's energy ; foster high spirits ; store up one's energy

*예기 豫期 [기대] expectation ; anticipation ; [희망] hope ; [선견] foresight ; forecast **—하다** expect ; anticipate ; hope for ; look forward to ; have in prospect ; calculate on ; foresee ; forecast ¶ 예기치 않은 unexpected ; unlooked-for // 예기했던 대답 the hoped for answer // …을 예기하고 in expectation〔anticipation〕《of》 // 예기한 대로 as (was) expected // 자네를 여기서 만날 줄은 전혀 예기치 않았다 I did not in the least expect to see you here. // 그것은 예기한 대로였다 It was just as I expected. /It proved to be up to my expectations. // 그것은 예기한 것 이상이었다 It was far better than was anticipated. /It exceeded all our expectations.

예기 藝妓 a *kisaeng* (-girl) ; a professional beauty and entertainer

예끼 [나무라는 소리] Damn it〔you〕! ; Confound it〔you〕! ¶ 예끼 나쁜놈 You rascal !

예납 豫納 payment in advance ; advance payment ; prepayment **—하다** pay in advance ; prepay

반신료 — 전보 a reply-paid telegram

예년 例年 a normal〔an ordinary〕year ; the average year (평년) ; every year (매년) ¶ 예년의 행사 an annual function

〔event〕// 예년의 2할 감 20 percent below normal // 예년대로 as usual ; as in other years // 예년에 비해 compared with other years // 예년과 달리 unusually // 금년 겨울 날씨는 예년보다 추웠다 This winter has been severer than usual. /The weather has been unusually cold this winter.

예능 藝能 (artistic) accomplishments ; art ; public entertainments ; theatricals (연극)

—계 the artiste〔entertainment〕 world ; the world of show business ; the entertainment business〔field〕 **—과** the art course **—인** an artiste《프》; a public 〔professional〕 entertainer ; a performing artist ; showfolk《총칭》

예니레 six or seven days ; about a week

예니세이 강 —江 the Yenisei River

예닐곱 six seven ; about half a dozen

예단 豫斷 prediction ; presupposition **—하다** predict ; presuppose

예답다 禮— (be) courteous ; ceremonious ; polite ; civil ¶ 그는 언행이 예답다 He has good manners. /He is well-mannered.

예대 禮待 an honorable treatment ; a cordial〔warm〕 reception **—하다** receive《a person》 courteously〔cordially〕 ; treat《a person》 with respect

예도 藝道 an art ; accomplishments ; artistry

예둔 銳鈍 sharpness and dullness ; keenness and bluntness ; shrewdness and stupidity

예라 [비켜라] Get away ! /Be gone ! /[그리 말라] Stop ! /Cut it out ! /[시도·포기] all right ; good ; well ¶ 예라 저리가라 Be off with you ! // 예라 울지마라 There, there ! Don't cry ! // 예라 그런 말 마라 Stop talking like that ! // 예라 내가 해보지 All right, I'll take it on. // 예라 집어 치워라 Well then, I'll quit〔knock off〕.

예레미야 〖성경〗 Jeremiah

—서 (the Book of) Jeremiah

예령 豫鈴 the first bell

예로부터 from old〔ancient〕 times ; from very remote〔early〕 ages ; from the time immemorial ; since the days of antiquity

예루살렘 Jerusalem

*‡**예리 銳利** sharpness ; keenness **—하다** [연장이] (be) sharp ; cutting ; sharp edged ; [두뇌·판단이] keen ; acute ; shrewd ¶ 예리한 연장 a sharp instrument ; a sharp edged tool // 예리한 필봉 pungent style // 예리한 논법 a keen argument // 예리한 비평 sharp〔cutting〕 criticism // 머리가 아주 예리하다 be (as) keen as a razor // 그곳의 면접은 예리하게 파고드는 것으로 잘 알려져 있으니까 침착해라 The interview is famous for sharp, in-depth question, so play it cool.

예림 藝林 artists' circles

예망 曳網 a seine ; a draught ; a draw 〔towing〕 net

예매 豫買 advance purchase ; purchase in advance ; subscription **—하다** buy 〔purchase〕 in advance ; subscribe for

예매 豫賣 advance sale〔subscription〕 ; sale in advance **—하다** sell (tickets) in advance

—권 a ticket sold in advance ; an advance ticket

예멘 Yemen ¶ 예멘의 Yemeni

— 사람 a Yemeni

예명 藝名 a professional name ; a stage 〔screen〕 name ¶ 그의 예명은 김운학이다 He is professionally known as *Kim Un-hak*. /He is known on the stage as *Kim Un-hak*.

예모 禮帽 a ceremonial hat ; a silk hat ; a top hat

예모 禮貌 decorum ; (good) manners ; etiquette ¶ 예모 바른 사람 a well-bred person // 예모 없는 ill-mannered ; ill-bred ; discourteous // 예모답다 be well-mannered ; be courteous ; be civil ; be polite

예문 例文 an illustrative sentence〔example〕 ; an example (sentence)

예문 藝文 art and literature ; science and literature

예물 禮物 a gift ; a present ¶ 신랑 신부가 예물을 교환했다 The bride and bridegroom exchanged wedding presents.

†**예민 銳敏** keenness ; sharpness ; acuteness ; sensitiveness **—하다** (be) sharp ; keen ; acute ; clever ; shrewd ; quick-witted ; penetrating ¶ 예민한 관찰 a keen〔acute〕 observation // 예민한 코 a keen nose // 예민한 감각 a keen〔quick〕 sense // 머리가 아주 예민하다 be as sharp as a needle // 귀가 예민하다 be keen of hearing ; have sharp ears // 개는 후각이 예민하다 Dogs have an acute sense of smell. // 그는 예민한 성격이다 He's very careful about details.

예바르다 禮— (be) courteous ; decorous ; polite ; civil ¶ 예바르지 않다 be discourteous ; be rude ; be ill-bred ; be ill-mannered

예방 禮訪 a courtesy call **—하다** pay 〔make〕 a courtesy call on《a person》

†**예방 豫防** [방지] prevention ; protection 《against》 **—하다** prevent ; keep off ; protect oneself《against》; take preventive measures〔steps〕《against》; take precautions《against》¶ 예방할 수 있는 preventable // 악역을 예방하다 prevent the plague from spreading // 전염병을 예방하다 prevent infectious disease // 배멀미 예방으로 레몬을 먹다 take lemons for a preventive against seasickness // 치료보다 예방 Prevention is better than cure.

—법 a precautionary〔preventive〕 measure〔step〕 ; a method of prevention ; a precaution **—약** a preventive medicine 《of, for, against》; a prophylactic (medicine) 《against fever》 — 위생 preventive hygiene〔sanitation〕 — 의학 preventive medicine — 전쟁 a preventive war — 접종 a vaccination 《against, for》 — 정신 의학 orthopsychiatry — 주사 a preventive injection〔inoculation〕 ¶ 예방 주사를 맞다 be inoculated against 《typhoid》 —책 a precautionary measure ¶ 예방책을 강구하다 take precautionary measures〔steps〕 // 병에는 청결이 최상의 예방책이 다 Keeping clean is a safeguard against disease.

†**예배 禮拜** worship ; (divine) service (교회의) ; adoration —**하다** worship ; adore ¶ 예배에 참석하다 attend (divine) service ; attend chapel (학교 따위의) ; attend mass (천주교의) // 천주를 예배하다 worship God // 엎드려 예배하다 worship on one's knees // 매 일요일 오전 10시에 예배가 있다 Service is held every Sunday at ten.
—**당** a chapel ; a place of worship —**자** a worshipper **가정** — family worship **아침**〔**저녁**〕 — morning〔evening〕 service **약식** — plain service

예법 禮法 courtesy ; manners ; decorum ; etiquette ; form ¶ 예법에 맞다 be good form ; conform to etiquette // 예법에 어긋나다 go〔be〕 against etiquette // 예법을 배우다 learn good manners ; take lessons in manners
식탁 — table manners

예병 銳兵 picked troops〔men〕 ; the pick〔flower〕 of an army ; the effectives ⇨ 정예(精銳)

‡**예보 豫報** forecast(ing) ; prediction —**하다** forecast ; predict ¶ 예보한 바와 같이 as (was) previously reported 〔announced〕 // 일기를 예보하다 forecast the weather // 예보가 틀린다〔맞다〕 A forecast goes wrong〔proves right, comes true〕.
일기 — a weather forecast ¶ 일기 예보에 의하면 이따금 소나기가 내릴 것이라 한다 The weather forecast predicts occasional showers.

예복 禮服 a full dress ; a dress suit ; a ceremonial dress ; an evening dress (야회의) ¶ 예복을 입다 be in full dress // 이번에는 예복 착용이 필요치 않다 This is not a dress affair.
궁중 — a court suit ; a full court dress **평상** — a frock coat ; a morning coat ; a dress coat

*__예봉 銳鋒__ [칼끝] a sharp point ; [논봉·필봉] the brunt of an attack〔argument〕 ; a vigorous attack ¶ 예봉을 꺾다 blunt〔take off〕 the edge of ; break the brunt of 《the enemy's attack》 // 예봉을 꺾을 수 없다 They carry everything before them. /I find the force of his argument irresistible.

예불 禮佛 [불교] worship before the image of Buddha —**하다** hold worship in front of Buddha

†**예비 豫備** [준비] preparation ; [마련] reserve ; spare —**하다** prepare〔provide〕 for ; reserve ¶ 예비의 preparatory ; introductory ; preliminary ; reserve ; spare // 예비로 가지고 있다 have 《a thing》 in reserve // 예비 조사를 하다 make a preliminary inquiry ; inquire 《into a matter》 beforehand // 예비역으로 편입되다 go〔be converted〕 into reserve (status)
— **검사** a preliminary inspection — **고사** a preliminary examination — **공작** spadework ; preliminaries —**교** a preparatory school — **교섭** preliminary negotiations —**군** reserve troops ; armed reserve —**금** reserve funds —**병** a reservist — **부품** spare parts — **사단** a reserve division — **선거** a preliminary election — **선수** a reserve (player) — **수단** a preliminary step — **시험**〔**회의**〕 a preliminary examination〔conference〕 — **실** a spare room —**역(役)** service in the (first) reserve ¶ 예비역 장교 a reserve officer // 제2예비역 the second reserve // 예비역에 편입되다 be placed on the reserve list ; be transferred to the (first) reserve — **자금 부족** reserve shortage — **점검** (a) preliminary inspection〔examination〕 — **조사** a preliminary examination〔investigation, inquiry〕 — **조판(組版)** 〖인쇄〗 preliminary typesetting — **지식** a preliminary〔previous, background〕 knowledge (of a subject) —**품** reserve stocks ; spare parts (자동차 따위의) — **함대**〔**선대**〕 a reserve fleet **대학 입학 자격 — 고사** the state-run qualifying tests for the entrance to colleges **향토 —군** the Homeland Reserve Forces

†**예쁘다** (be) pretty ; lovely ; sweet ; beautiful ; nice ; charming ; good looking ; attractive ; shapely (모양이) ¶ 예쁜 인형 a pretty doll // 예쁜 꽃 a beautiful flower // 예쁜 여자 a lovely girl ; a nice looking girl // 예쁘게 차려 입다 dress up ; dress oneself beautifully // 참 예쁜 개지요 What a love of a dog!

예쁘장스럽다 (be) lovely ⇨ 예쁘장하다

*__예쁘장하다__ (be) rather pretty ; comely ; good-looking ; be on the pretty side

예사 例事 a common practice ; an everyday occurrence〔affair〕 ; a matter of common〔everyday〕 occurrence ; an ordinary affair ¶ 예사가 아닌 unusual ; extraordinary ; uncommon // 분위기로 보아 예사가 아닌 걸 The atmosphere is charged. // 그는 실패해도 예사다 He is none the worse for his failure. // 이 노선에서는 열차가 연착하는 것이 예사다 Delayed arrival of trains on this line is a matter of almost daily occurrence. // 당신에게는 예삿일일지는 모르지만 나에게는 그

렇지 않다 It might not make any difference to you, but it bothers me.

예사롭다 例事— (be) common ; ordinary ; usual ; run-of-the-mill ; commonplace ; humdrum ; be of no consequence ; be as usual ; ¶ 예사로운 일 an everyday occurrence // 그는 어딘가 예사롭지 않은 데가 있다 There is something uncommon〔peculiar〕 about him. /He has something out of the common.

‡**예산** 豫算 an estimate ; a budget **—하다** estimate ; budget 《for》 ¶ 3천만원의 예산으로 at an estimated cost of 30 million *won* // …할 예산으로 in anticipation of… // 예산의 범위 내에서 within the limit of budgetary appropriation // 예산을 세우다 make an estimate // 예산을 짜다 make a budget ; draw up an estimate // 예산의 수지를 맞추다 balance the budget // 예산을 초과하다 exceed the estimates // 내 예산대로 안되었다 My estimates have gone wrong〔amiss〕. // 예산이 없다 The budget does not allow it. /It has no budgetary appropriation. // 건축비의 예산은 2천만원이다 The cost of building is estimated at 20 million *won*.

— **결손** a budgetary deficit — **삭감** reduction of appropriation ; a curtailment in the budget — **생활** a life accoroding to planned budget — **연도** a budget year — **제도** a budget(ary) system — **조치** a budgetary measure — **초과** an excess over the estimates — **편성** compilation of the budget **내년도** — the budget for the coming (fiscal) year **본(本)**— a principal〔an original〕 budget **수정** — a revised budget **잠정** — a provisional budget **지불** — the payment estimates **총**— the total〔general〕 budget〔estimates〕 **추가** — a supplementary budget **평시〔전시〕** — a peacetime〔wartime〕 budget

예산안 豫算案 a draft budget ; [의안(議案)] a budget bill ; a bill of budget ¶ 예산안을 국회〔의회〕에 제출하다 submit a budget to the National Assembly ; present the estimates for the budget to the National Assembly

— **심의** deliberation on the budget **추가경정** — the budget supplement bill

예산외 豫算外 [비목에 안든 것] (being) outside the budget ; [예상 밖] unexpected ; unforeseen ¶ 건축이 예산외 공사가 되었다 The construction has got into extras.

— **국고 부담** national treasury charge out of budget — **수입** receipts outside of budget — **지출** extraordinary disbursements ; defrayment unprovided for in the budget

‡**예상** 豫想 [예기] expectation ; anticipation ; [예측] forecast ; presumption ; an estimate **—하다** expect ; anticipate ; forecast ; presume ; estimate ¶ 예상외의 unexpected ; unlooked-for // 예상외로 unexpectedly ; beyond one's expectations // …을 예상하고 in expectation〔anticipation〕 of // 예상외로 좋다 be better than (was) expected // 예상을 뒤엎다 go (be) against one's expectation ; upset one's expectation // 장래를 예상하다 forecast〔anticipate〕 the future // 예상대로 되다 come up to one's expectations ; answer〔meet〕 one's expectations // 정치적인 반동이 일어날 것으로 예상하다 anticipate a political reaction // 예상에 어그러졌다 It was contrary to my expectations. // 그 결과는 나의 예상 밖이었다 The result exceeded my expectations. // 예상했던 정도는 아니었다 It did not come up to〔fell short of〕 my expectations. // 예상외로 빨리 돌아왔다 He came back much earlier than I had expected. // 이 숫자들은 한달간의 예상 매출을 나타낸 것이다 These figures are monthly sales projections in a month.

— **생산고〔수확고〕** estimated production 〔crop, yield〕 — **수입** a prospective income **—액** estimates — **이익** an imaginary〔estimated, anticipated〕 profit ; paper profit **경기(景氣)** — a business forecast **장기** — a long range forecast

예상사 例常事 an ordinary affair ; a matter of common〔everyday〕 occurrence

예상외 豫想外 being outside anticipation 〔expectation〕 ; being unlooked-for ¶ 예상외의 unexpected ; unforeseen ; unlooked-for // 예상외로 (in a manner) beyond one's expectations // 예상외로 성적이 나빴다 The results did not come up to my expectations.

예새 a wooden potter's knife

예서 隸書 ornamental "seal" characters

예선 曳船 [끄는 배] a tugboat : [배를 끌기] towing

—로(路) a towpath **—료** towage

예선 豫選 [경기] a preliminary match 〔contest〕 ; an elimination contest ; a tryout ; [선거] a preliminary〔primary〕 election ; a primary 《미》 **—하다** hold a preliminary contest ; preelect ¶ 100미터 예선 a 100 meter preliminary ; the trial heat of the 100 meters // 예선에서 통과〔탈락〕되다 be qualified〔dropped off, disqualified〕 at a preliminary contest

***예속** 隸屬 subordination **—하다** be under the control〔authority〕 《of》 ; be subordinate〔subject〕 《to》 ; subordinate oneself 《to》 ; belong 《to》 ¶ 예속시키다 subjugate ; bring under complete control // 예속을 요구하다 demand vassalage

—국 a subject nation ; a dependency — **적 지위** a subordinate position

‡**예수** Jesus (Christ)

—교 ⇨ 기독교 **—교인〔도〕** a Christian — **그리스도** ⇨ 예수

예순 sixty

†**예술 藝術** art ; an art (특정의) ; fine arts (미술) ¶ 예술적 가치가 있는 작품 a work of great artistic value // 예술을 감상하다 appreciate art

—가 an artist ¶ 예술가 기질 artiness // 예술가 기질의 사람 a person of an artistic turn〔bent〕 of mind ; a person of artistic temperament〔nature〕 **—계** the world of art ; the art world ; artistic circles **— 교육** art education **— 대학** a university of arts **—미** beauty of art **— 본능** art instinct **— 비평** criticism of art **— 사진** an artistic photograph **— 사진가** an art photographer **—원** the Art Academy **— 작품** a work of art **—적 양심〔가치〕** artistic conscience〔merit〕 **—적 충동** an art impulse **—제** an art festival **— 지상주의** art for art's sake **— 지상파** the art for art school **—학** science of arts **—학부** the department of arts **— 형식** an art form **동양〔서양〕 —** Oriental〔Western〕 art **청각〔시각〕 —** aural〔visual〕 art

예술은 길고 인생은 짧다 [관용] Art is long, life is short.

예스럽다 look old ; (be) antiquated ; archaic ¶ 예스런 말투 an archaic expression // 예스런 습관 old customs

예습 豫習 preparations of lessons ; rehearsal (극·음악 따위) **—하다** prepare lessons ; rehearse ¶ 내일 학과의 예습을 하다 prepare tomorrow's lessons // 예습하지 않고 학교에 가다 go to school without doing one's preparation

‡**예시 例示** illustration ; exemplification **—하다** illustrate ⟪by example⟫ ; exemplify

예시 豫示 indication ; foreshadowing **—하다** indicate ; show a sign of ; foreshadow ; prefigure ; portend

예식 例式 an established form ; a form ¶ 예식에 따라서 in due form

예식 禮式 [예법] etiquette ; manners ; form ; [의식] a ceremony ; a rite

—장 a ceremony〔wedding〕 hall ; a marriage ceremony hall

예심 豫審 a preliminary hearing〔trial, examination〕 ¶ 예심 중이다 be sub judice ; be under a preliminary hearing〔examination〕

— 결정서 the decision in writing of a preliminary examination **— 수속** preliminary proceedings **— 조서** the protocol〔minutes〕 of the preliminary examination **— 종결〔결정〕** the conclusion〔decision〕 of a preliminary trial **— 판사** an examining judge ; a preliminary court judge

†**예약 豫約** preengagement ; precontract ; booking (좌석 따위) ; reservation ; subscription (출판물) ; a pledge (기부금 따위) ; an advance sale (제품) **—하다** preengage ; make a reservation ⟪at a hotel, on a steamer⟫ ; book ⟪in advance⟫ ; reserve ; sell in advance ; subscribe ⟪for⟫ ; [기부금] promise ; pledge ¶ 좌석을 예약하다 book a seat ⟪in advance⟫ ; reserve a seat ⟪at a theater⟫ // 방을 예약하다 engage a room beforehand // 예약을 취소하다 cancel〔call off〕 a reservation〔an advance order, subscription〕 // 예약 주문에 응하다 accept an order in advance // 예약에 주문을 받으러 다니다 canvass for subscriptions ⟪for books⟫ // 이 방은 예약되어 있습니다 This room is reserved. // 우리는 몇 종류의 잡지를 예약했다 We have subscribed for several magazines. // 화요일 2시로 예약해 두겠습니다 We'll put you down for Tuesday 2 P. M. // 베이커씨께서 오늘 날짜로 예약은 하셨는데 아직 들어 오시지 않았습니다 Mr. Baker made a reservation for today, but he hasn't checked in yet. // 토요일 비행기 예약은 가능합니다만 We can book you for Saturday, though. // 서울행 비행기 예약을 하려고 합니다 I'd like to book a flight to *Seoul*. // 수요일 오후 1시 30분 로스엔젤레스를 출발해서 목요일 6시 30분 서울에 도착하는 012편에 예약이 되셨습니다 Your reservation is confirmed for flight 012 departing from Los Angeles at 1 : 30 p. m. Wednesday and arriving in *Seoul* at 6 : 30 p. m. Thursday.

—금 the subscription price ; a deposit **— 도서** a subscription book **— 독자** a registered reader ; a subscriber **— 모집** invitation for subscriptions **—석** a reserved seat **—자** a subscriber **— 주문** an advance order **— 출판〔판매〕** publication〔sale〕 by subscription

예언 例言 a preface ; a foreword ; introductory remarks ; an introduction

‡**예언 豫言** a prophecy ; a prediction ; a forecast **—하다** prophesy ; foretell ; predict ; make a prediction ¶ 예언할 수 있는 predictable ; foreseeable // 앞일을 예언하다 make predictions of coming events // 전쟁이 언제 끝날 것인가를 예언하다 predict〔prophesy〕 when the war will end // 예언이 틀리다 a prophecy fails // 예언이 적중했다 The prediction was fulfilled〔came true, proved correct〕.

—자 a prophet〔prophetess(여자)〕 ; a predictor ; a prognosticator ; a soothsayer

예열 豫熱 〚기계〛 preheating

—기 a preheater **—로** a preheating furnace〔oven〕

예예 yes, sir ; all right, sir **—하다** [굽실대다] cringe ⟪to⟫ ; fawn ⟪upon⟫ ; be servile〔obsequious〕 ⟪to⟫

‡**예외 例外** an exception ¶ 예외의 exceptional // 예외적인 용법 an exceptional use // 예외 없이 without exception // …은 예외로 하고 except ; excepting ; with the exception of // 자네와 같은 경우는 예외로 한다 We will make an exception in〔of〕

your case. // 이 규칙에는 한가지 예외가 있다 There is one exception to this rule. // 예외 없는 규칙은 없다 Every rule has its exceptions. /There is no rule without exceptions.

예우 禮遇 honorable treatment ; cordial reception **—하다** receive 《a person》 courteously〔warmly, cordially〕; treat 《a person》 with respect
— 정지 [의원·외교관 등의] suspension of the privileges

예원 藝苑 the world of artists and men of letters ; artistic and literary circles ; an athen(a)eum

예의 銳意 zealously ; energetically ; assiduously ; earnestly ; eagerly ; ardently ¶ 예의 전심하다 devote oneself to ; apply oneself closely to // 예의 검토하다 inquire into 《a matter》 assiduously ; make a close study 《on》 // 예의 노력하다 do one's best ; exert all possible efforts // 예의 사회 개량에 힘쓰다 concentrate〔focus〕 one's efforts〔energies〕 on social reform

†**예의 禮儀** courtesy ; politeness ; civility ; [예절] manners ; etiquette ; decorum ; good form ¶ 외교상의 예의 diplomatic etiquette // 예의 바른 courteous ; polite ; civil // 예의 바르게 in a civil way ; politely ; courteously // 예의를 모르는 discourteous ; rude ; ill-mannered〔-bred〕 // 예의상 as a matter of courtesy ; out of courtesy〔politeness〕 // 예의를 무시하고 in disregard of etiquette // 예의를 지키다 observe the proprieties // 그는 예의 바르다 He has good manners. /He is well-mannered. // 그는 예의를 모른다 He has no manners. /He is ill-mannered. // 친한 사이에도 예의가 있어야 한다 Intimacy does not justify lack of courtesy among friends. /There should be courtesy even among intimates. // 연필로 편지를 쓰는 것은 예의에서 벗어난 짓이다 It is bad form to write a letter in pencil.
— 범절 the rules of etiquette **형식적 —** sham courtesy ; outward decorum

예인 藝人 an artiste ; a player ; a (public〔professional〕) performer ; an entertainer ; talent 《총칭》

예인망 曳引網 a seine ; a dragnet

예인선 曳引船 a tug (boat) ; a towboat ; a towing vessel ¶ 그 좌초된 배는 저 예인선에 의해 예인되어 왔다 The stranded ship was towed〔pulled, dragged, hauled, drawn〕 by that tugboat.

예입 預入 —하다 make a deposit 《in a bank》
—금 a deposit ; money on deposit ; [은행 계정] deposit with other banks

예장 禮狀 a letter of thanks〔appreciation〕 ¶ 예장을 보내다 send a letter of thanks ; write to 《a person》 in acknowledgment of his kindness

예장 禮裝 a ceremonial dress ; a full dress **—하다** wear a ceremonial dress ; be in full dress ¶ 예장을 하고 in full dress // 그는 예장으로 점잖게 차렸다 He looked imposing in full dress.

예전 old days〔times〕; former days ; the past ¶ 예전 사람들 men of old times // 예전부터 from old times // 예전에 in old〔ancient〕 times ; in the old days ; once ; in former days // 예전대로 as of old ; as usual ; unchanged ; as it was before // 그녀는 예전의 그녀가 아니다 She is not her former self. // 그것은 예전부터 행해지고 있다 It's an old practice. // 예전에 여기 절이 있었다 A temple was〔stood〕 here in the old days. /Formerly there was a temple here.

예절 禮節 propriety ; decorum ; etiquette ; manners ¶ 예절을 지키다 observe the proprieties // 예절을 모르다 have no sense of propriety ; have no manners

†**예정 豫定** prearrangement ; previous arrangement ; a program(me) ; a schedule ; a plan **—하다** arrange beforehand ; prearrange ; plan ; predetermine ; make a program ; map out ; [시일을] set ; schedule ¶ 예정된 prearranged ; appointed ; intended ; expected ; predeterminate // 예정한 행동 a planned act ; a prearranged course of action // 예정대로 according to program ; as arranged ; as scheduled // 19일로 예정된 결혼식 the wedding set for the 19th // …할 예정이다 expect 《to do》 ; plan 《to do》 ; be expected ; be due ; be scheduled ; be designed 《for》 // 예정한 시간에 on the scheduled time ; at the appointed time // 예정보다 일찍 ahead of time ; before (the scheduled) time // 예정보다 하루 늦게 one day behind time〔schedule〕 // 예정을 변경하다 change the program〔plan〕 // 예정이 어긋나다 have a hitch in the program ; have the plan frustrated // 그는 내일 서울에 도착할 예정이다 He is expected to be in *Seoul* tomorrow. // 배는 예정 시간보다 몇시간 앞당겨서 출범했다 The steamer sailed some hours ahead of schedule. // 모든 일이 예정대로 되었다 Everything turned out as arranged beforehand. // 출산 예정일이 언제입니까 When is your baby due ?
— 기일 a prearranged date **—설** a doctrine of predestination **—수** the prescribed number **—안** a program ; a prospectus **—액** the estimated amount **— 정가** the probable price **—표** a schedule **출발〔도착〕 — 시간** the expected time of departure〔arrival〕 **출범 —일** the scheduled date of sailing **출산 —일** one's expected date of confinement

예제 [여기저기] here and there ; everywhere

예제 例祭 a regular〔an annual〕 rite
예제 例題 [보기] an example ; [연습 문제] an exercise
예조 禮曹 [육조의] the Ceremonies〔Protocol〕 Board
*예증 例證 illustration ; exemplification ; an example ; an instance ; a proof —하다 illustrate ; exemplify ¶ 예증으로서 by way of illustration ; as an example 〔instance〕// …의 예증이 되다 illustrate ; be illustrative of ; serve as an example of // 이론을 예증하는 여러가지 사실을 들다 enumerate facts in illustration of one's theory
예지 叡智 supreme intelligence ; wisdom ; intellect
예지 豫知 foreknowledge ; foresight ; foreboding —하다 foresee ; know beforehand ; forebode ; foresee
예진 豫診 a preliminary medical examination —하다 make a diagnosis in advance
예진 豫震 a foreshock ; a preliminary tremor
*예찬 禮讚 admiration ; praise ; glorification ; eulogy ; worship ; adoration —하다 admire ; glorify ; worship ; praise ; sing the praises of ; adore ; idealize ¶ 모성 예찬 the glorification of motherhood // 미의 예찬 a beauty cult ; glorification of beauty // 자연의 예찬 the cult of nature
—자 a worshipper ; an admirer ; an adorer
예찰 豫察 —하다 guess〔surmise〕 beforehand ; conjecture in advance
*예측 豫測 a prediction ; a forecast ; presupposition ; estimation (어림) ; prediction —하다 predict ; foretell ; forecast ; estimate ; presuppose ¶ 대풍작이 될 것으로 예측하다 forecast a bumper crop // 예측이 어긋났다 The prediction didn't come true. // 승패는 예측할 수 없다 The fate of a battle cannot be foreseen. // 내년의 일을 예측할 수 없다 I can't make a prediction about next year. // 예측이 불가능하다 It's anyboy's guess. /Your guess is as good as mine // 예측을 불허한다 It's a tossup. // 그들의 예측은 아주 빗나갔다 Their projections were way off.
예치물 預置物 an article left on deposit ; an article given in trust ; a charge
예탁 預託 depositing ; deposition —하다 deposit 《money with a bank》
—금 deposit money (특히 은행의) —자 a depositor — 은행 a depositing bank 미국 — 증권 an American depositary receipt
예탐 豫探 detection ; spying ; preliminary investigation —하다 spy on〔into〕 ; investigate secretly ; sound 《a person》 ; feel out ; throw out〔put up〕 a feeler ¶ 적정을 예탐하다 spy upon the enemy's movements
—꾼 a spy ; a secret agent
예편 豫編 —하다 transfer 《a person》 to the first reserve ; place〔register〕 《a person》 on the reserve list ¶ 예편되다 go into the first reserve ; be placed 〔registered〕 on the reserve list
예포 禮砲 a (gun) salute ¶ 21발의 예포를 쏘다 fire a salute of 21 guns
예풍 藝風 one's artistic taste ; acting (연극) ; one's personal technique (음악)
예하 隷下 ⇨ 휘하(麾下)
예항 曳航 towing —하다 take 《a ship》 in tow ; tow
예해 例解 an example ; an illustration ; an exemplification —하다 exemplify ; illustrate ; give example ; explain by examples
예행 豫行 a rehearsal ; a preliminary run through〔performance〕 —하다 give a rehearsal ; rehearse ; try out ¶ 졸업식의 예행을 하다 have a rehearsal of a graduation ceremony
— 연습 a rehearsal ; a preliminary drill 〔training〕 ; preliminary exercises
예화 預話 a fable ; an apologue ; an allegory ; a parable (그리스도 등의)
예회 例會 a regular meeting ¶ 예회를 열다 hold a regular meeting
월— a monthly meeting
예후 豫後 prognosis ; convalescence ; aftereffects ¶ 그는 예후가 좋다 He is convalescing favorably.
옌장 Darn ! /Damn ! /Pshaw ! /Goodness ! /O my gosh !
옛 old(en) ; ancient
옛글 ancient writings
옛길 an old road
†옛날 ancient times ; antiquity ; old days ; the past ; former years〔times〕 ¶ 옛날 이야기 an old story // 옛날 풍속 old customs // 그리운 옛날 the good old days // 옛날 사람들 men of old times // 옛날 일 a thing of the past ; a past issue ; an old story // 옛날에 in old〔ancient〕 times ; in former days ; formerly ; once // 옛날 옛적에 once upon a time ; long, long ago // 옛날부터 from old times // 그녀는 옛날의 그녀가 아니다 She is not her former self. // 옛날에 한 할아버지가 살고 있었다 Once upon a time there lived an old man. // 옛날 그곳에 절이 있었다고들 한다 They say that a temple stood there in the old days. // 아주 옛날 사진이구나 These pictures are from ages ago. // 그는 내가 옛날부터 사귄 친구이기 때문에 그의 인격은 내가 보증할 수 있다 He's a close friend from way back, so I can vouch for his character.
옛말 an archaic word ; an old saying 〔proverb〕 ; an old story
옛모습 [얼굴 모습] 《a person's》 face〔visage, looks, image, figure〕 ; [흔히] traces ; vestiges ; shadow ; flavor ¶ 그에게는 옛모습이 없다 He is a mere ghost

of his former self. // 그 거리에 가도 번화했던 옛모습은 이제 조금도 볼 수 없다 If you visit the town, you will find that there remains no longer any vestige of its former glory.

옛사람 the ancients ; men of old ; the deceased ; the departed ; the dead ¶ 옛사람이 되다 die ; pass away

옛사랑 a bygone love ; an old love

옛상처 —傷處 an old wound ; a scar ¶ 옛상처를 건드리다 [비유적] rake up unpleasant old stories

옛식—式 an old〔an ancient, a time-honored〕 rite〔custom, style〕 ¶ 옛식을 따라 in accordance with the old rite〔custom〕

옛싸움터 an ancient battlefield ; an old battleground ; the scene of an ancient battle

옛이야기 an old story ¶ 이젠 그것도 다 옛이야기가 되었다 It is now an old story. // 그것은 옛이야기에 불과하다 It is nothing more than an old story.

옛일 a thing of the past ; bygones ; the past ; a past event ¶ 옛일을 생각하다 think of the past // 옛일은 옛일이다 Let bygones be bygones. // 이제는 그것이 옛일이 되었다 It is now a thing of the past.

옛적 old days ⇨ 옛날

옛정 —情 the sentiment〔affection〕 of bygone days

옛집 an old nest〔haunt〕 ; one's old home〔house〕 ; one's former haunt ; one's late residence ¶ 옛집이 그립다 have a longing for one's old haunt // 옛집으로 돌아가다 return to one's old haunt〔place of work〕 ; make a comeback

옛추억 —追憶 the memory of old days ; old memories ¶ 옛추억을 더듬다 think of the good old days

옛친구 —親舊 an old friend ; an old buddy 《미·속》

옜네 ⇨ 옜다

옜다 [물건을 줄 때 쓰는 말] Here it is ! ; Here you are ! ; This〔it〕 is for you ! ; Here yours is ! ¶ 옜다 이것 가져라 Here, take this.

옜소 ⇨ 옜다

†**오** oh ; ah ; [아랫사람에게] yes ; [옳지] right ¶ 오 이제 알겠다. Oh, now I understand ! // 오 가엾은 사람 Ah, poor fellow ! // 오 슬프다 Alas, woe is me ! // 오 그렇고 말고요 Oh, indeed !

오 午 ① the horse ; the seventh of the 12 horary signs ② the direction of the horse 《south》 ③ the hour of the horse 《noontime》 **—년** the year of the horse **—시** noontime

†**오 五** five ¶ 제 5 the fifth // 5배(의) fivefold ; quintuple // 5분의 일 one-fifth // 제5장 the fifth chapter

오 伍 [대오] file ; a line ; [조(組)] a five-man〔-men〕 squad ¶ 선두의 오 a leading file

오가다 come and go ; keep coming and going

오가리 ① dried slices of pumpkin ② all dried-up (잎이) ; shriveled ¶ 오가리들다 dry up ; shrivel ; wither ; curl up // 가뭄으로 모가 오라리들다 the drought withers the young rice plant

오가리솥 a cooking pot with the mouth narrower than the body

오각 五角 five angles ; [형용사적] pentagonal

오각형 五角形 a pentagon ¶ 오각형의 pentagonal ; five-cornered

오갈들다 ① [오글쪼글해진다] wither ; shrivel ; be shriveled up ② [주눅이 들다] be in a funk ; lose courage ; get〔have〕 cold feet 《구》

오갈피 〖한의〗 the root bark of various araliaceous shrubs

오감 五感 the (five) senses

오감스럽다 (be) flippant ; frivolous ; be odd and rash

오감하다 (be) (quite) satisfactory ; enough

오거리 五— a five-way crossing

오경 五經 the Five Classics (of Ancient China) ; the Five Books of Confucianism

오계 五戒 the five Buddhist commandments (against murder, theft, adultery, falsehood and intemperance)

오계 誤計 a wrong plan〔scheme〕 ; miscalculation ; a mistaken step ; blunder

오고가다 come and go ; keep coming and going ; go back and forth ¶ 오고 가는 사람들 streams of people going and coming

오곡 五穀 the five grains 《rice, millet, beans, wheat and barnyard millet》 **—밥** a dish made with all five grains

오공이 悟空— a short stocky person ; a spunky runt

오관 五官 the five sensory organs 《of hearing, seeing, tasting, smelling and feeling》

오구 [어구] a kind of fish-trap basket

오구 烏口 a drafting〔draftsman's〕 pen

오귀발 〖동물〗 a starfish (불가사리)

****오그라들다** curl up ; contract ; wither ; shrink ; shrivel ¶ 구두가 오그라들다 shoes become〔get〕 tight // 몸이 오그라들 정도로 춥다 It is cold enough to shrivel one up. // 목재는 마르면 오그라든다 Wood contracts as it dries.

오그라뜨리다 dent ⇨ 오그리다

***오그라지다** be crushed ; be battered ; become warped ; get curled〔rolled〕 up ; be broken ; be wrecked ¶ 오그라진 남비 a dented pan // 오그라진 차 a dented car // 사람이 오그라지다 a person gets withered // 나뭇잎이 오그라진다 The leaves curl up.

오그랑오그랑하다 be wrinkled and withered all over ; (be) wizened

오그랑이 ① a shrunk object ; a thing pushed in or shriveled up ② a crooked〔perverse〕 person ; a cranky person

오그랑장사 a failing business ; an unprofitable〔a losing〕 business

오그랑하다 be pushed in ; be shriveled up ; become indented ; be battered

오그르르 [물이] simmering ; boiling ; [벌레 가] swarming **—하다** simmer ; boil ; swarm

오그리다 ① [몸을] curl (one's body) up ; crouch ; huddle ; cower ¶ 몸을 오그리고 자다 sleep curled up ; sleep in a ball // 그는 방 한 구석에 몸을 오그리고 앉았다 He crouched in a corner of the room. ② [물건을] bend 《something》 out of shape ; batter ; crush ; break ¶ 남비를 오그리다 batter a pan

오글거리다 ① [물이] boil in bubble ; simmer ; sizzle ② [벌레가] squirm in a swarm ; swarm ⇨ 우글거리다 ¶ 꿀벌이 오글거리는 마당 a garden swarming with bees // 산에 산적이 오글거린다 Brigands swarm in the mountain.

오글보글 [물·찌개] bubbling ; simmering **—하다** bubble ; simmer

오글오글 ¶ 물이 오글오글 끓다 water simmers // 벌레가 오글오글 끓다 worms wriggle about in a swarm

오글쪼글 —하다 (be) wrinkled and withered ; shriveled ; wilted ¶ 오글쪼글한 노파 an old withered woman ; a crone ; a hag // 오글쪼글 마른 손 a shriveled hand // 배가 오글쪼글 말랐다 The pear is all shriveled up.

오금 the crook〔hollow, inside curve〕 of the knee〔elbow〕 ; the popliteal region ; ham ¶ 그는 마누라 앞에서 오금을 못 쓴다 He is under his wife's thumb.

오금을 못 쓰다 관용 be unable to move around ; [비유적] be intimidated ; be under 《a person's》 thumb

오금뜨다 be always on the move ; gad about

오금박다 catch 《a person》 in his contradiction ; trap〔corner〕 《a person》 with his own words ; squelch ; discomfit ; silence ¶ 오금박히다 be caught in one's contradiction

오금팽이 the inner angle of a bend 〔curve〕

오긋오긋 —하다 (be) widely dented ¶ 들통 밑이 오긋오긋 욱었다 The bucket has dents on its bottom.

오긋이 pressed in ; pushed in ; dented ; dimpled

오긋하다 be pressed in ; be dented ; be pushed in ; be crushed a little out of shape ; be sunk ; be nicely curved ¶ 찻주전자 밑이 오긋하게 들어갔다 The teakettle has a dent on its bottom.

오기 傲氣 an unyielding〔indomitable〕 spirit ; obstinacy ; a proud temper ; pride ¶ 오기부리다 stick to one's own opinion ; have one's own way

오기 誤記 an error〔a mistake〕 in writing ; a miswriting ; a slip of the pen ; a clerical error ; amisentry **—하다** make an error in writing ; miswrite ; write wrong ; make a pen slip

오나가나 always ; all the time ; wherever one goes ; everywhere you turn ; making no difference ¶ 그는 오나가나 사람을 골탕먹인다 He always takes people in.

오냐 yes ; yea ; well ; all right ¶ 오냐 알았다 Yes, I see. // 오냐 그 일은 내가 맡았다 All right. I will undertake the work. // 오냐 그렇게 해라 You can do so. // 오냐 오냐 울지 마라 There, there ! Don't cry ! // 오냐 쏠테면 쏘아봐라 Go ahead and shoot, if you are going to. // 오냐 두고 보자 You shall soon smart for this.

오년 午年 〖민속〗 the Year of the Horse

오뇌 懊惱 agony ; mental anguish ; mortification **—하다** be agonized ; be in agony〔anguish〕 ; have a mental struggle ; be sick at heart

오누이 brother and sister ; siblings

오뉘죽 rice gruel mixed with mashed red bean

오뉴월 五六月 May and June〔The fifth and sixth months〕 of the lunar calendar ¶ 오뉴월 긴긴 해 the livelong summer day

— 염천 the hot weather of midsummer

오는 [다음의] next ; coming ; to come ; forthcoming ¶ 오는 일요일(에) (on) next Sunday ; on Sunday next // 오는 20일에 on the 20th (of this month)

†**오늘** today ; this day ¶ 오늘부터 앞으로 from this day forth ; on and after today // 오늘 중에 in the course of today ; before the day is out // 오늘까지도 up to today ; to this day // 오늘밤 tonight // 오늘 아침〔오후〕 this morning 〔afternoon〕 // 전주〔내주의〕의 오늘 this day week ; this day last〔next〕 week ; a week ago〔from〕 today // 작년〔내년〕의 오늘 this day year ; a year ago〔after〕 today // 오늘은 며칠입니까 What day of the month is this ? // 오늘은 11월 3일입니다 It is the third of November today.

⁑**오늘날** these days ; the present time ; nowadays ; today ¶ 오늘날의 of the day ; of the present time ; contemporary // 오늘날의 한국 the Korea of today ; Korea today // 생존 경쟁이 심한 오늘날 in these days of severe struggle for existence // 오늘날 그런 일을 생각하는 사람은 아무도 없을 게다 No one would think of such things nowadays. // 오늘날의 나는 2, 3년 전의 내가 아니다 I am not what I was two or three years ago.

오늘밤 this evening ; tonight ¶ 오늘밤 중

에 in the course of the night// 오늘밤은 이 집에서 묵자 Let us stay here for the night.

오늬 the notch of an arrow ; the nock ¶ 오늬 무늬 a herringbone (pattern) // 화살에 오늬를 붙이다 notch an arrow // 오늬를 시위에 걸다 fit an arrow on the string ; nock an arrow

†**오다** ① [도착] comereach ; arrive 《at》; [나타나다] show up ; turn up ; appear ¶ 미국에서 온 사람 a person from America // 기차가 올 때까지 till the train comes in // 모임에 안 오다 fail to show up at the meeting // 왔다 be here ; have arrived 〔come〕; have come // 가지러 오다 come for 《a thing》// 올라 가다 come up // 이리 오너라 Come here. /Come this way. // 그는 오늘은 안 올 것이다 He isn't coming today. /He won't be here today. // 무슨 일인지 보고 와라 Go and see what is the matter. // 역에까지 갔다 왔다 I have been to the station. // 무슨 일로 왔느냐 What has brought you here? // 좋은 기회가 온다 A good opportunity occurs〔presents itself〕. // 편지가 왔느냐 Has the mail come yet? // 자동차가 오는 것이 보였다 I saw a motorcar coming. // 너한테 전화가 왔다 You are wanted on the phone. // 버스가 온다 Here comes our bus! // 선생이 아직 안 왔다 The teacher hasn't shown up yet. // 자 누구든지 오라 내가 상대해 주지 Let any one come, I am his man. // 서울에 다 왔군요 We're approaching *Seoul*. // 내가 다시 여기 오나 봐라 This is the last time I'll ever come here.
② [계절·시일이] come (round) ; draw near ; set in ; be due (기한이) ¶ 겨울이 온다 Winter comes〔sets in〕. // 어느새 봄이 왔다 Spring has come before I knew it. // 곧 여름 방학이 온다 The summer vacation is just around the corner.
③ [비·눈이] ¶ 비가 온다 Rain's coming on! /It begins to rain. // 서리가 온다 It frosts. // 소나기가 온다 It showers. // 전깃불이 온다. The light comes on.
④ [유래] come 《from》; be brought 〔introduced〕《from》¶ 영어에서 온 말 a word of English origin ; a word derived from English // 미국에서 온 춤 a dance of American origin // 그 사상은 구라파에서 왔다 Those ideas were introduced into Korea from Europe.
⑤ [기인] come of ; be due to ; arise from ; originate in ¶ 과식에서 오는 병 sickness arising from overeating // 그것은 과식에서 온 것이다 It comes of overeating. // 가난은 전쟁에서 온다 Poverty stems from war.
⑥ [되다] get ; become ; grow ¶ 따뜻해 오다 It is getting warmer.

오다가다 occasionally ; at times ; now and then ; once in a while ; on rare occasions ; sometimes ; by chance ; casually ¶ 오다가다 만나다 meet by chance // 오다가다 찾아와 주어도 괜찮을 텐데 You might come and see us once in a while. // 그에게서 오다가다 소식이 있다 I hear from him once in a while. // 비행기는 안전하지만 오다가다 떨어지는 수도 있다 Planes are safe but once in a while they crash.

오달지다 [물건이] (be) solid ; compact ; [짜임새가] tight and strong ; have a fine weave ; [사람이] be solidly built ; (be) firm ; smartish

오답 誤答 an incorrect〔a wrong〕answer ; an error

오대양 五大洋 the Five Oceans

오대주 五大洲 the Five Continents

오데르 강 —江 the Oder River

오도 悟道 apprehension of the truth ; spiritual awakening ; enlightenment ; the attainment of supreme wisdom **—하다** attain enlightenment ; be awakened ; attain supreme wisdom ; be spiritually enlightened ; form one's philosophy of life

오도깝스럽다 (be) abrupt and frivolous ; flippant ; rash ; imprudent ¶ 오도깝스런 수작 flippant remarks // 오도깝스럽게 굴다 act rashly ; commit a rash act

오도독 with a crunching sound **—거리다** crunch ¶ 오도독오도독 crunching ; munching ; champing // 오도독오도독 먹다 champ ; crunch 《food》
—뼈 cartilage ; gristle

오도미 〖물고기〗 a (sweet red) sea bream

오도방정 a rash act ; flightiness ; giddiness ; frivolity ; carelessness ¶ 오도방정을 떨다 act frivolously ; behave in a giddy way

오도카니 blankly ; vacantly ; idly ; absent-mindedly ⇨ 우두커니

오독 誤讀 misreading **—하다** misread ; read wrong ¶ 암호 전보를 오독하다 misread a code〔cipher〕telegram

오독도기 ① 〖식물〗 the arbor monkshood ② [불꽃] a string of firecrackers

오돌오돌 hard and lumpy ; gristly ; fibrous ; tough **—하다** (be) hard and lumpy ; gristly ; fibrous ; tough

오동 烏銅 oxidized〔blackened〕copper

오동 梧桐 a paulownia tree
오동씨만 보아도 춤춘다 〖속담〗 Don't build the sty before the litter comes. / Boil not pap before the child is born.

오동보동하다 be a bit pudgy

오동지 五冬至 the 5th and 11th lunar months

오동철갑 all black with dirt〔stain〕

오동통하다 (be) short and fat ; dumpy ; pudgy ; plump ; corpulent ¶ 오동통한 계집애 a plump girl // 오동통한 얼굴 a bonny face ; a buxom face

오동포동하다 ⇨ 오동보동하다

⁑**오두막 —幕** a hut ; a shed ; a hovel ; a

shanty ¶ 오두막을 짓다 put up a shanty **—집** a hut ; a shanty ; a hovel ; a shed

오두미 五斗米 a small salary ¶ 오두미를 (벌기) 위해 굽실거리다 bend the knee for small pay

오둠지 ① [옷의] collar ; the back part of the neckband of a Korean jacket ② [그릇의] the upper part of a vessel〔bowl, dish〕

오들오들 shivering ; trembling ¶ 오들오들 떨다 quiver《with emotion》; shiver《with cold》; tremble《with fear》; shake《for fear》; quake // 전신이 오들오들 떨리다 be all of a tremble〔shake〕// 무서워서 오들오들 떨리다 tremble with fear // 손이 오들오들 떨려서 쓸 수 없었다 I could not write as my hand shook.

오등 吾等 we ; us

***오디** a mulberry

오디션 [영화·라디오] an audition

오똑 high ; aloft ⇨ 우뚝

오뚝이 a tumbling doll ; a tumbler

오라[1] [오랏줄] a red rope formerly used for binding a criminal ; a rope to bind a criminal with ¶ 오라로 묶다 bind〔tie up〕a criminal ; seize〔arrest, take up〕a culprit

오라[2] right ; true ; correct ; yes ¶ 오라 네가 옳다 Yes, you are right.

오라기 bits of thread〔cloth, paper〕¶ 실오라기 a scrap of thread // 헝겊 오라기 a piece〔scrap〕of cloth // 옷에 실오라기가 묻다 have bits of thread on one's clothes

오라버니 a girl's older brother

오라범댁 the wife of a girl's older brother

오라비 ① ⇨오라버니 ② [남동생] a girl's younger brother

오라지다 be trussed up

오라토리오 〖음악〗 an oratorio

***오락 娛樂** amusement ; recreation ; entertainment ; pastime ; pleasure ; a hobby (도락) ¶ 오락으로 for pleasure ; for one's pastime ; as a pastime // 독서는 좋은 오락이다 Reading is a good pastime. // 그 도시에는 오락 시설이 없다 The town lacks amusement facilities.

— 기사 entertainment accounts **—물** a plaything ; [영화의] a film for amusement **— 시설** recreation facilities ; facilities for public amusement **—실** an amusement hall ; a recreation room **— 잡지** a magazine for amusements **—장** a place of amusement〔entertainment〕; a casino **실내 —** indoor amusements ☞《 p. 1552 》

오락가락 —하다 come and go ; go back and forth ; wander ; mill around ¶ 비가 오락가락 하다 rain off and on ; rain by fits and starts // 구름이 오락가락 하다 the clouds come and go // 정신이 오락가락하다 one's mind wanders〔strays〕

오랏줄 ⇨ 오라[1]

오랑캐 a barbarian ; a savage ; a foreigner

오랑캐꽃 a violet

오래[1] a neighbo(u)rhood unit within a village

***오래**[2] long ; for a long time ¶ 오래 된 old ; ancient ; antique ; time-honored ; oldfashioned ; stale (음식이) ; time-worn ; aged // 오래 사귄 친구 a friend of long standing // 오래 전 long time ago ; long ago // 오래 살다 live long ; live to a ripe old age ; enjoy longevity // 오래 끌다 be prolonged // 오래 걸리다 take a long time // 오래 걸려 하다 be slow in doing ; take one's time in doing // 오래 머무르다 stay long ; make a long stay // 이 이상 오래 머물 수 없습니다 I can't stay any longer. /I can stay no longer. // 오래 못 뵈었습니다 I haven't seen you for a long time.

***오래가다** stand long use ; last long ; wear long ; stay long ; live long (병자가) ¶ 오래가는 durable ; enduring ; lasting // 오래 못 가다 be short-lived ; never keep〔last〕long ; wear ill // 그 유행은 오래가지 않는다 That fashion will not prevail〔continue〕long. // 그 가방은 오래가지 못한다 That bag will not last for a long time.

오래간만 after a long time〔interval, silence, absence, separation〕; a long time since ; for the first time in many days〔years〕 ¶ 오래간만입니다 We haven't met for ages. /I haven't seen you for a long time. /It is an age〔ages, a long time〕since I saw you last〔I last saw you〕. /Long time no see. // 오래간만에 자네 목소리 듣는군 Long time no talk. // 오래 간만에 집에 돌아왔다 I went home after a long absence. // 그들은 오래간만에 만나 매우 기뻐했다 They were very pleased to see each other after a long separation. // 오래간만에 그에게서 편지를 받았다 I heard from him after a long silence. /I received a letter from him after a long silence. // 오래간만에 날씨가 좋다 It's a long time since we had such a fine day. /This is the first fine weather we've had in many days.

오래다 be a long time since〔ago〕; be of long standing ; be long continued ; (be) long ; extended ¶ 오랜 습관 a custom of long standing ; an old custom // 오랜 교제 an intercourse of long standing // 오래된 이야기 an old story // 오랜 옛날 great antiquity ; time immemorial // 오래지 않아 before long ; not long after ; shortly // 그를 본지 오래다 It has been a long time since I saw him last.

***오래도록** for long ; till late ; a long while ; forever ; eternally ; for ever and ever ¶ 그는 오래도록 아내로부터 소식을 듣지 못했다 He hasn't heard from his wife for a long time.

오 락·취 미

1 오락

① 실내

▶트럼프 playing cards (★ trump는 「으뜸패」란 뜻. 카드 한 벌은 pack. 주요 놀이로는 브리지(bridge), 컨트랙트 브리지(contract bridge), 블랙잭(blackjack), 캐나스타(canasta), 피노클(pinoc(h)le), 포커(poker), 러미(rummy), 혼자서 하는 카드놀이(solitaire, patience 《영》) 등이 있다)

▶당구 billiards / 주사위 dice / TV 게임 TV game; home video game; jocktronics

② 야외

▶하이킹 hiking / 피크닉 picnic (★hiking은 주로 야외를 산보하는 것을 가리키고 picnic은 야외 또는 실내에서 하는 식사에 비중을 둠. 배낭(backpack)을 지고 하는 산보는 backpacking.) / 산보 walking / 스케이트보드 타기 skateboard / 롤러스케이트 타기 roller-skating / 후리스비 frisbee / 요트 타기 yachting / 파도 타기 surfing / 수상 스키 water-skiing / 스카이다이빙 sky-diving

▶낚시 fishing (★특히 취미로서의 낚시는 angling) / 강 낚시 river fishing / 바다 낚시 sea fishing

▶사냥 hunting (★영국에서는 사냥개(hound)를 이용하여 사냥감(game)을 쫓는 것을 주로 가리키며 (여우 사냥 fox hunting, 토끼 사냥 hare hunting), 총을 쏘아서 새를 사냥하는 것은 shooting이라 한다. 미국에서는 구별없이 쓰기도 한다.) / 승마 horse riding

③ 영화 · 연극 · 음악회

▶영화관 movie theater; cinema 《영》 / (영화 간판의) 상영중 Now playing.; Now showing. / 다음주 상영 Next attraction. / 개봉박두 Coming soon. / 예고편 preview / 자율 규제 film ratings (★미국과 영국에서는 영화 내용에 따라 관객의 입장을 제한하고 있다. 미국－G (For General Audience; 어린이 입장가), PG (Parental Guidance Needed; 부모의 지도 필요), R(Restricted; 17세 이하는 성인 동반 필요), X(X-rated; 성인용), 영국－U(Universal; 어린이 입장가), A(13세 이하 부적), AA(13세 이하 불가), X(성인용, 17세 이하 불가)) / 음악회장 concert hall / 매표소 box office; booking office 《영》 / 입장료 admission (fee) / 입장권 admission ticket / 당일권 today's ticket / 예매권 advance ticket / 무료 초대권 complimentary ticket; freebie; freebee 《미》 / 장내 안내원 usher / 통로 aisle / 2층석 mezzanine / 휴게실 foyer; crushroom 《영》 / 무대 stage; board / 특별석 box; loge

④ 파티

▶크리스마스 파티 Christmas party / 신년회 New Year party / 생일 파티 birthday party / 결혼 기념일 파티 wedding anniversary party / 만찬회 dinner party / 오찬회 lunch party / 칵테일 파티 cocktail party / 송별회 farewell party / 티 파티 tea party (★ 주로 차, 케이크, 스낵 등의 간단한 다과회, 오후 2~3시 경) / 환영회 welcome party / 서프라이즈 파티 surprise party (★ 본인 모르게 준비하여 놀라게 해 주는 파티) / 파자마 파티 pajama party (★ 주로 어린이들이 모여서 함께 밤을 지냄) / 하우스 워밍(＝집들이) house warming / 포틀럭 파티 potluck party (★ 초대받은 손님들이 술과 음식을 가지고 오기로 되어 있는 파티) / 초대장 invitation card (★ 초대장에 R.S.V.P. (Répondez s'il vous plaît. = Please answer. 《프》) 라고 적혀 있으면 참석여부를 알려주는 것이 예의. 초대장에 "black tie"라고 적혀 있으면 「정장 차림 요망」이란 뜻으로 남성은 턱시도(tuxedo)에 검은 나비 넥타이(black tie)를 착용하여야 한다.)

⑤ 어린이 놀이

▶숨바꼭질 hide-and-seek / 돌차기 놀이 hopscotch / 등짚고 넘기 leapfrog / 공기놀이 bean-bags (★헝겊 주머니에 콩·팥 등을 넣어 던지며 노는 놀이) / 구슬 치기 marble / 3목 놀이 tick-tac-toe; nought-and-crosses 《영》

2 취미

취미에 해당하는 영어에는 hobby와 pastime이 있는데 음악 감상이나 우표 수집 같은 정적인 것에 사용하고 스포츠처럼 동적인 활동에는 쓰지 않는다. recreation은 스포츠, 오락 등을 포함하는 일반적인 뜻을 지니고 있고 avocation은 딱딱한 표현이다.

▶독서 reading / 음악 감상 listening to music / 우표 수집 collecting stamps / 화폐 수집 collecting coins / 서예 calligraphy / 뜨개질 knitting / 자수 embroidering / 유화 그리기 oilpainting / 수채화 그리기 watercolor painting / 서양 쌍육 backgammon / 다트 놀이 darts / 장기 go game / (일요일의) 집꾸미기 home carpentry[do-it-yourself] / 원예 gardening / 사진 촬영 photography

오래뜰 the yard〔court〕 in front of the gate ; the front yard ; an outdoor court
오래오래 for a long long time ; forever ; eternally ¶ 오래오래 병을 앓다 suffer from a lengthy illness // 이름을 오래오래 전하다 immortalize one's fame // 오래오래 살다 live long ; live on
*오랫동안 for a long time ; for a long while ¶ 오랫동안 소식이 없다 hear nothing 《from a person》 for long // 오랫동안 편지 못드려 죄송합니다 I must apologize for my long silence. /I apologize to you for having not written to you for so long. // 얼마나 오랫동안 나가 있었느냐 How long have you gone ?
오량 五樑 five beam construction
—집 a house with 5 main beams ; a large house
오레오마이신 〖약〗 aureomycin
오렌지 an orange ¶ 오렌지색의 orange ; orange colored
— 주스 orange juice
오려내다 cut〔clip〕 (out) 《from》 ⇨ 오리다 ¶ 오려내기 cutting ; clipping 《미》 // 둥글게 오려내다 cut a round piece 《out of paper》 ; cut out round // 참조용으로 기사를 오려내다 cut out〔clip〕 an article for reference
오련하다 (be) dim ; faint ; pale and lovely ; vague ; diaphanous ¶ 오련히 dimly ; vaguely ; diaphanously
오로라 an aurora
*오로지 only ; solely ; exclusively ; wholly ; entirely ; devotedly ¶ 그는 오로지 돈벌이만을 생각하고 있다 He is solely bent on making money. // 그는 오로지 돈을 위해 일한다 He works solely for money. // 어학의 습득은 오로지 연습에 있다 Practice is the only way of mastering a language. // 친구라고는 오로지 너뿐이다 You are the only friend I have.
오롯하다 (be) perfect ; full ; complete
오롱이조롱이 a group of small things〔persons〕 ¶ 그녀는 아이들을 오롱이조롱이 다 데리고 내 집에 왔다 She came to my house with the whole bunch of her children.
오롱조롱 in groups 《of small things》 ; in bunches ; in clusters ¶ 토마토가 오롱조롱 열리다 tomatoes grow in bunches
*오류 誤謬 a mistake ; an error ; a fallacy ¶ 오류를 범하다 commit a fault ; make an error // 오류를 시정하다 mend one's ways ; correct an error ; rectify a mistake // 오류를 깨닫다 see the error of one's ways
오륜 五倫 moral rules to govern the Five Human Relations (of master and servant, of father and son, of husband and wife, of brothers, of friends)
오륜 대회 五輪大會 the Olympiad ; the Olympic Games
오르가슴 orgasm
†오르간 〖악기〗 an organ
— 주자 an organist 리드 — a reed organ ; a cabinet organ ; a harmonium ; an American organ 파이프 — a pipe organ
오르내리 ascent and descent ; fluctuations ; ups and downs
오르내리다 ① go up and down ; rise and fall ; fluctuate ; [먹은 것이] do not settle ¶ 층계를 오르내리다 go up and down stairs // 먹은 것이 오르내리다 suffer from indigestion // 물가가 오르내리다 The market shows fluctuation.
② [입에] be talked about ; be gossiped about ; be in everybody's mouth ¶ 그녀는 행실이 좋지 않아 남의 입에 오르내렸다 Her conduct gave rise to scandals. /Her conduct was on everybody's lips.
†오르다 ① go up ; climb ; ascend ; rise ; [타다] mount

> 참고 **climb** 노력해서 서서히 오르다 **ascend** 다소 딱딱한 말이며 climb에 비해서 곧 바로 편하게 오르는 뜻 **mount** ascend에 가까우나 정상까지 오른다는 뜻이 포함되어 있다

¶ 산〔나무〕에 오르다 climb a mountain〔tree〕 // 말에 오르다 mount a horse // 기차에 오르다 board a train // 왕위에 오르다 come to the throne // 지위에 오르다 be promoted〔raised〕 to a higher position // 계급이 오르다 rise in rank // 월급이 오르다 get a salary raise // 물가가 오르다 prices go up // 굴뚝에서 연기가 오르다 smoke rises〔coils up〕 from a chimney // 법안이 의회에 오른다 A bill is brought before the Assembly. // 봄 미나리가 상에 오르다 Spring parsley is served on the table.
② [게재] be registered ; be recorded ; be included ; be entered ¶ 그의 딸이름이 전화 번호부에 올랐다 His daughter's name is put in the telephone directory. // 그녀의 추문이 신문에 올랐다 Her scandal is reported in a newspaper. // 그의 공적이 역사에 올랐다 His achievement is recorded in history.
③ [전염] be infected ; be contracted ; [때가] be soiled ; get dirty ¶ 옴이 오르다 be infected with the itch〔scabies〕
④ [입에] be talked about ; become the talk of ; be gossiped about ; be on people's lips ¶ 그녀의 행실이 마을 사람들의 입에 올랐다 Her conduct became the talk of the town.
⑤ [기타] ¶ 약이 오르다 get angry // 얼굴에 술이 오르다 one's face is flushed with liquor // 불이 오르다 catch fire // 살이 오르다 put on weight // 벌써 술이 오르기 시작한다 I'm already beginning to feel high.
오르되브르 *hors d'oeuvre* 《프》
오르락내리락 rising and falling ; going up

and down
오르르 all in a rush ; rumbling ; simmering ⇨ 우르르
오르막 an uprise ; an upward slope ; uphill
—길 an uphill road
*오른 the right
오른손 the right hand ; the whip hand
오른손잡이 [일] right handedness ; dexterality ; [사람] a righthanded person ; a right hander ; a dextral ¶ 오른 손잡이의 right handed 《pitcher》
†오른쪽 the right side ¶ 오른쪽에 on the right side 《of》 // 오른쪽으로 가다 keep to the right // 첫째 모퉁이에서 오른쪽으로 돌아가라 Take the first turning to the right. // 이 길을 곧장 걸어가면 오른쪽에 학교가 있다 Go down the road straight and you will see a school on your right // 내 차의 오른쪽 여기저기가 쭈그러지고 긁히고 했어 The passenger side of my car got dents and scratches all over. // 책장을 오른쪽 벽에 대고 놓을까요 Shall I put the bookshelf against the right-hand wall ?
오른팔 ① [오른쪽의 팔] the right arm ② [심복] one's right-hand man ; one's right hand ¶ 그는 나의 오른팔로서 일해왔다 He has worked as my right-hand man.
오른편 the right side ⇨ 오른쪽
오름새 an upward tendency 《of the market》 ; a rising market
오름차 〖수학〗 an ascending series
*오리[1] a duck ; a drake (숫오리)
새끼 — a teal ; a duckling
오리[2] a strip ¶ 대오리 a strip of bamboo // 나무오리 a strip of wood
오리 五厘 half a *jun*
오리 五里 five *ri* (Korean miles)
오리 汚吏 a corrupt official
*오리나무 〖식물〗 the alder tree
오리너구리 〖동물〗 a duck bill
오리다 cut off〔away〕 ; cut out ; carve out ¶ 신문에서 광고〔기사〕를 오려내다 cut 〔clip〕 an advertisement〔article〕 from a newspaper // 잡지에서 그림을 오려내다 cut pictures from magazines
오리목 a lath ; a strip of board
오리무중 五里霧中 utter bewilderment ; (being) quite in the dark〔fog〕 ; all at sea ; all up in the air ; at large ¶ 오리무중에서 헤매다 be befogged ; be in a fog ; lose〔be out of〕 one's bearings // 우리들은 이 문제에 대해서는 오리무중이다 We are all at sea on this subject. // 나는 오리무중이다 I have my mind in a fog. // 그 강도는 살인한 후 오리무중이다 The burglar has been at large after he had committed the murder.
오리발 ① a webfoot ; a web-fingered hand ② [단짝] a chum ; a side kick
오리엔테이션 orientation
오리엔트 [동양] the Orient
오리온자리 〖천문〗 Orion
오리지낼리티 《have》 originality
오리지널 original
오림장이 a lath cutter ; a lumber cutter
오막 ⇨ 오두막
오막살이 (living in) a grass hut〔humble cottage〕 ; a hovel life —하다 lead a hut life ; be a hut dweller
‡오만 傲慢 arrogance ; haughtiness ; insolence ; pompousness —하다 (be) arrogant ; haughty ; overbearing ; insolent ; pompous ¶ 오만하게 arrogantly ; haughtily ; proudly // 손아랫사람에게 오만하게 굴다 be haughty to one's inferiors // 오만부리다 give oneself airs ; bear oneself haughtily ; assume a haughty attitude ; hold one's head high ; act in a lordly manner
오만 五萬 ever so much ; innumerable ; thousands ; millions ¶ 오만 가지 일 ever so many things to do // 오만 가지 수단을 다 쓰다 leave no stone unturned ; try every possible means // 오만 가지 물건을 팔다 sell things of every sort and kind
오만상 五萬相 a distorted〔frowning, wry, puckered〕 face ; a grimace ; a scowl ¶ 오만상을 하다〔찌푸리다〕 distort one's face ; make〔pull〕 a face ; make grimaces ; pucker up one's face ; screw one's face into wrinkles
오망 迂妄 —하다 (be) cranky ; cantankerous ; flighty
오망떨다 迂妄— do cranky〔whimsical, flighty〕 things ; be harebrained ; be flighty
오망부리 a partly defective〔crushed, warped〕 shape ; bad shape ; a disproportionate〔deformed〕 figure
오망하다 ⇨ 우멍하다
오매불망 寤寐不忘 —하다 remember when awake or asleep ; bear in mind all the time
오면체 五面體 〖수학〗 a pentahedron
오명 汚名 disgrace ; dishonor ; infamy ; a stigma (누명) ¶ 오명을 씻다 wipe off a dishonor ; clear one's name of the disgrace ; clear one's name
†오목 sunken-in ; depressed ; concave
—거울 a concave mirror〔reflector〕 —누비 a kind of deep quilt stitching —다리 quilt-stitched baby socks
오목 五目 a game of *Badook* with five checkers placed in a row
오목눈이 〖새〗 the long-tailed tit
오목오목 —하다 be dented all over 《the bottom》 ; be sunk here and there ¶ 비에 마당이 오목오목 패었다 The ground is washed out in little hollows all over from the rain.
오목하다 be pressed〔pushed〕 in ; (be) depressed ; dented ; sunk ¶ 눈이 오목하다 have deep-set〔recessed〕 eyes ; be hollow-eyed

오묘 奧妙 profundity ; abstruseness ―하다 (be) profound ; abstruse ; recondite
오무래미 a toothless old person ; a shrivel-gummed old person
오문 誤聞 mishearing ―하다 hear amiss ; mishear
*오물 汚物 filth ; dirt ; dust ; muck ; sewage (하수도의) ; garbage (부엌의) ¶ 오물의 처분 disposal of garbage
― 처리 공장 a sewage purification plant
― 처리 시설 sanitation facilities ; filth treating equipment
오물거리다 ① [벌레 따위가] swarm ; teem with ; be alive with ¶ 벌집에 벌들이 오물거린다 The hive is alive with bees.
② [음식을] mumble ; chew on ¶ 빵 껍질을 오물거리다 mumble on a crust // 잇몸으로 오물거리다 chew on one's gums
③ [말을] mumble ¶ 말을 오물거리다 mumble one's words
오물오물 ① [벌레 따위가] wrigglingly ; in swarms ; in a swarm ¶ 지렁이가 오물오물 기어가다 an earthworm wriggles along
② [입 속에서] mumbling ; munching ; mouthing ; chewing on ¶ 사과를 오물오물 씹다 munch an apple
③ [말을] mumblingly ¶ 오물오물 말하다 mumble〔mouth〕 one's words
오므라들다 close ; curl〔shrink, shrivel〕 up ; wither ¶ 오므라든 입 a puckered〔pursed〕 mouth // 상처가 오므라들었다 The wound has closed.
오므라지다 ⇨ 오므라들다
오므리다 pucker ; purse ; close up ; shut ¶ 입을 오므리다 pucker up one's mouth〔lips〕; purse up one's lips // 우산을 오므리다 shut〔close, fold〕 an umbrella // 몸을 오므리다 make oneself small ; huddle up
*오믈렛 an omelet
오미 a (land) sink
오미 五味 the Five Tastes (of sour, bitter, pungent, sweet and salty)
오미자나무 〖식물〗 Maximowiczia chinensis (학명)
오밀조밀 奧密稠密 ① [면밀] (be) very meticulous ; scrupulous ; circumspect ¶ 오밀조밀한 필치 a meticulous bit of writing ② [솜씨가] (be) elaborate ; exquisite ; fine-wrought ¶ 오밀조밀한 세공품 elaborate handiwork // 오밀조밀하게 꾸민 정원 an exquisite garden
오바다서 ―書 〖성경〗 The Book of Obadiah ; Obadiah 《Obad》
오발 誤發 accidental firing ; firing by accident ―하다 fire by accident
오방 午方 〖민속〗 the Direction of the Horse〔South〕
오배 五倍 quintuple ; five times 《as many as》; fivefold ―하다 multiply 《a number》 by five ; quintuplicate
오버코트 an overcoat
오버타임 overtime ¶ 오버타임을 하다 work overtime
― 수당 overtime pay〔allowance〕
*오벨리스크 [기념탑] an obelisk
오변형 五邊形 a pentagon
오보 誤報 an incorrect〔erroneous〕 report ; a false report ; misinformation ; wrong information ―하다 give a false report ; misreport ; misinform about〔on〕 ¶ 그것은 오보였다 The report proved false〔incorrect〕. // 그 신문은 가끔 오보를 낸다 That paper often gives wrong information.
오보록하다 (be) dense ; thick ; be thick with
오보에 〖악기〗 an oboe
오복 五福 the Five Blessings〔longevity, wealth, health, love of virtue, peaceful death〕
오분 五分 ① [나누기] ¶ 오분의 3 three-fifths ―하다 divide 《a thing》 into five parts ② [시간] five minutes
오불관언 吾不關焉 a detached〔an unconcerned, a nonchalant〕 air ―하다 disregard ; be indifferent 《to》; assume an unconcerned air ; take a nonchalant air 《toward》
오붓이 amply ; abundantly ; cozily ; snugly
오붓하다 ① (be) enough ; ample ; substantial ; sufficient ¶ 오붓하게 살다 lead a comfortable living ; be well〔comfortably〕 off ② (be) comfortable ; cozy ; snug ¶ 오붓한 자리 a cozy corner
오븐 an oven ; a quick oven
오비 an old boy 《O. B.》; alumnus 《*pl.* -ni》
오비다 poke ; scrape out ; pick ⇨ 우비다
오비이락 烏飛梨落 A pear drops as (soon as) a crow flies from the tree. / One inadvertently gets suspected by others.
오빠 a girl's elder brother
오사리 the early catch of fish at high tide ; unseasonably harvested crops
오사리잡놈 a reprobate ; a debauchee ; a depraved person
오사바사하다 be likable but capricious ; (be) affable but fickle
오산 誤算 miscalculation ; wrong estimate ―하다 make a miscalculation〔wrong estimate〕; miscalculate ; miscount ¶ 전략상의 오산 a strategic miscalculation
오살 誤殺 manslaughter by mistake ―하다 kill 《a person》 by mistake
오색 五色 the five cardinal colors 《blue, yellow, red, white, black》; variegated colors
오색이 영롱하다 관용 shine brilliantly in various colors ; be very colorful ; be resplendent
오색잡놈 五色雜― a reprobate ; a rogue ; a scamp
오서 誤書 an error in writing ; a clerical error ; a slip of the pen ―하다 make

an error in writing ; write wrong〔incorrectly〕
오선 五線 〖음악〗 the staff ; the stave
—보(譜) staff notation —지 music paper ; a music sheet
오세아니아 [대양주] Oceania
*오소리 〖동물〗 a badger
오손 汚損 stain ; soil ; damage —하다 stain ; soil ; damage ; be spoiled〔stained〕
†오솔길 a (narrow) path ; a (lonely) lane ; a trail ¶ 숲속의 오솔길 a path through a forest
오송 誤送 miscarriage ; misdelivery —하다 miscarry ; misdeliver
오수 午睡 a nap ; siesta
오수 汚水 sewage ; foul〔filthy〕 water ; slops ¶ 오수처리 sewage disposal〔treatment〕
—관 a soil pipe
오순도순 harmoniously ; on good terms ; in amity ¶ 오순도순 잘 놀다 play together well // 오순도순 잘 지내다 live happily together
오스카상 —賞 〖영화〗 an Oscar
— 수상배우〔여배우〕 an Oscar actor〔actress〕
오스트레일리아 Australia ¶ 오스트레일리아의 Australian
— 사람 an Australian
오스트리아 Austria ¶ 오스트리아의 Austrian
— 사람 an Austrian
오슬오슬 shivering —하다 feel〔be〕 chilly ; (be) shivery ¶ 오슬오슬한 날씨 chilly weather // 오슬오슬 떨다 shiver with cold // 오슬오슬 춥다 feel chills // 열로 오슬오슬 떨리다 have chills with the fever
오시 午時 the Hour of the Horse
오식 誤植 a typographical error ; a misprint ; a printer's error ; a literal error ; an erratum 《*pl.* -ta》 —하다 misprint ¶ 오식이 수두룩하다 be full of misprints // 오식을 교정하다 correct errors in proof
— 정정표 (table of) errata ; a list of corrigenda
오신 誤信 a misbelief ; a fallacy —하다 misbelieve ; hold an erroneous belief
오심 誤審 (a) misjudg(e)ment ; [경기의] wrong refereeing ; 〖법〗 a miscarriage of justice ; mistrial —하다 misjudge ; judge wrongly ; referee wrongly
*오십 五十 fifty ¶ 오십보 백보이다 be six of one and half a dozen of the other
—년제 a semicentennial
‡오싹 —하다 feel〔have〕 a chill ; shudder 《with horror》 ; shiver ; feel a thrill 《of horror》 ¶ 몸이 오싹하다 feel a chill creep over one ; a shudder passes over one〔runs through one's frame〕 // 오싹하게 하다 make one's blood cold ; send a cold shiver〔shudders〕 down one's spine // 생각만 해도 등골이 오싹하다 shudder〔be horrified〕 at the bare 〔mere〕 thought〔idea〕 《of》 // 잠시 비행기가 고장난 줄 알고 오싹했다 For a second I thought something was wrong with the plane, and my blood ran cold.
오싹오싹 chilling ; shivering
*오아시스 an oasis 《*pl.* -ses》
오얏 a plum
—나무 a plum (tree)
오언절구 五言絶句 a quatrain with five Chinese characters in each line
오엑스 true-false ¶ 그 선생님의 시험은 오엑스 시험이 아니니까 열심히 공부하지 않으면 안될 것이다 We'll have to study hard for the teacher's exam, since it isn't a true false test.
— 문제 true-false questions — 시험 a true-false test
오역 誤譯 mistranslation ; wrong〔erroneous〕 translation —하다 mistranslate ; translate incorrectly〔erroneously〕 ¶ 오역이 없다 be free from errors of translation // 오역을 지적하다 point out mistakes in a translation
오연 傲然 arrogance ; haughtiness —하다 (be) proud ; arrogant ; haughty ¶ 오연히 arrogantly ; haughtly ; overbearingly ; proudly // 오연하게 굴다 show the attitude of haughtiness〔arrogance〕 ; behave arrogantly〔haughtily, overbearingly〕
오열 嗚咽 choking with sobs ; sobbing ; weeping —하다 sob ; weep
오열 五列 the Fifth Column ; the Fifth Columnists ; secret agents
‡오염 汚染 contamination ; pollution —하다 be contaminated〔polluted〕 ; be soiled〔stained〕 ; be imbued
— 대책 an antipollution measure —도 a pollution level — 물질 a pollutant ; a contaminant — 제거 decontamination 공기 — air pollution 방사능 — radioactive contamination 환경 — environmental pollution
오욕 汚辱 disgrace ; dishonor ; ignominy —하다 disgrace ; dishonor ; stain ; sling mud at ; bring disgrace upon 《a person》 ¶ 오욕을 입다 suffer disgrace ; be disgraced ; incur disgrace // 오욕을 참다 endure obloquy ; eat dirt 〔humble pie〕
*오용 誤用 misuse ; wrong use ; misapplication —하다 misuse ; misapply ; use 《a thing》 for a wrong purpose
오월 五月 May ¶ 오월의 여왕 a May queen
— 단오(端午) *Tano* ; the festival on the fifth day of the fifth month of the lunar calendar
오월동주 吳越同舟 bitter〔implacable〕 enemies in the same boat
오유 烏有 reverting to nothing ; vanishing away ¶ 오유로 돌아가다 be reduced to nothing ; be burnt down ; fall to the

ground
오의 奧義 the secrets ; the mysteries ; profound meaning ; recondite principles ¶ 오의를 터득하다 master the art of ; dive into the secrets of
*오이 a cucumber
—지 cucumbers pickled in salt —채 chopped cucumbers seasoned with vinegar and other seasonings
오인 吾人 [나] I ; me ; [우리] we ; us ; [인류] mankind ; human being
오인 誤認 misconception ; a mistaken acknowledgment〔recognition〕 ; misunderstanding —하다 misconceive ; mistake 《for》 ; misrecognize
오일 oil ; gasoline
— 스토브 an oil stove
오일 五日 five days ; the fifth day of the month
오일 午日 〖민속〗 the Day of the Horse
오입 誤入 whoring —하다 visit a brothel ; consort with a whore ; whore
—쟁이 a man who frequents a brothel ; a libertine ; a debauchee ; a rake —판 the demimonde 《프》
오입쟁이 제 욕심 채우듯 〔속담〕 Lechery and covetousness go together.
오자 誤字 a wrong word ; an erratum ; a misprint (인쇄의) ; a clerical error ¶ 이 판은 오자투성이다 This edition is full of errors.
오작 烏鵲 crow and magpie
오장 五臟 the five viscera (of heart, liver, spleen, lungs and kidneys)
오장육부 五臟六腑 the five viscera and the six entrails (of gall bladder, stomach, small and large intestines, the paunch, the bladder and the bowels)
오쟁이 a small straw bag
‡오전 午前 the forenoon ; the morning ; ante meridiem 《a. m., A. M.》 ¶ 오전 9시에 at nine in the morning ; at 9 a. m. // 오전 6시 차 the 6 a. m. train // 그는 오전에는 집에 있다 He is at home in the morning.
*오전 誤傳 a false report ; misinformation
오점 汚點 a blot ; a blotch ; a (dirty) spot ; a blur ; a stain ; a smear ; [결점] a flaw ; a blemish ¶ 오점이 없는 stainless ; spotless // 씻을 수 없는 오점 an indelible stain〔a blot〕 《on one's name》 // 오점을 찍다 stain ; spot ; leave a stain
오젓 salted shrimps (made of the year's early catch)
오정 午正 noon ; midday ; the meridian hour ¶ 오정에 at noon // 오정 12시 twelve noon ; high noon
오조 early-ripening variety of millet
오존 〖화학〗 ozone ¶ 오존의 ozonic
— 발생 장치 an ozone apparatus ; an ozonier
오졸거리다 keep dancing〔swaying〕 ; move rhythmically

오종 경기 五種競技 pentathlon ; five events
— 선수 a pentathlete ; a pentathlonist 근대 — modern pentathlon
오종종하다 ① [빽빽하다] (be) dense ; thick ; compact ; [서술적] be packed 〔studded〕 《with》
② [얼굴이] (be) meager 《face》 ; seedy 《look》 ; unprepossessing ; petty ; mean
오죽 very ; indeed ; how ¶ 그것을 보면 네 아버지가 오죽 좋아 하시겠니 How glad your father will be to see it ! // 그것을 보고 오죽이나 놀랐겠니 What was his surprise to see that ! // 오죽이나 낙담했을까 I can well imagine your disappointment. // 오죽 배가 고프겠니 You must be very hungry.
오죽잖다 be not up to par ; be below the average
*오줌 urine ; piss 《속》 ; stale (소·말) ¶ 오줌을 재리다 be incontinent // 이 골목은 오줌 냄새가 난다 This lane has a smell of stale urine.
—버캐 crust of urine stains —소태 〖의학〗 frequency of urination ; having a weak bladder —장군 a container for urine
오줌 누다 〔관용〕 urinate ; pass water ; piss 《속》
오줌이 마렵다 〔관용〕 feel nature's call ; feel the urge to urinate
오줌똥 feces and urine ; human waste ; excreta
오줌싸개 a bed-wetter
오줌통 ① a urinal tub ② [방광] the urinary bladder
오중 五重 fivefold ; [다섯겹] five layers
—주〔창〕 a quintet(te) —탑 five-storied pagoda
‡오지 奧地 the interior ; up-country ; the back region ; the back country 《미》 ; the back land ¶ 오지의 inland 《town》 ; back country 《미》
오지그릇 earthenware ; pottery (with a dark brown glaze)
오지다 ⇨ 오달지다
오지랖 the front of an outer garment
오지랖 넓다 (be) interfering ; meddlesome ; intrusive ; obtrusive ¶ 오지랖 넓게 굴다 interfere ; intermeddle ; intrude ; obtrude ; thrust〔poke〕 one's nose into ; horn in 《구》
오지직거리다 crackle ; crack ; pop ; seethe (물이) ¶ 오지직거리며 타다 burn with a crackle
†오직 only ; merely ; solely ; but ¶ 오직 한 가지 이유 the only〔sole〕 reason // 오직 울기만 하다 do nothing but cry // 친구라고는 오직 너 하나뿐이다 You are the only friend I have.
오직 汚職 ⇨ 독직 (瀆職)
오진 誤診 an erroneous〔a wrong, mistaken〕 diagnosis —하다 make a wrong

diagnosis ; diagnose erroneously
오짓물 glaze (in pottery)
오징어 a cuttlefish ; a squid
—포 a dried cuttlefish **뼈—** a cuttlefish
오차 誤差 〖수학〗 an (accidental) error
—론 the theory of error **개인 —** a personal error〔equation〕 **관측 —** an observational error **평균 —** an average error
오착 誤錯 a mistake ; an error **—하다** err ; make an error〔a mistake〕
오찬 午餐 a luncheon ; a lunch ¶ 오찬을 들다 take lunch ; lunch // 오찬에 초대하다 invite 《a person》 to a luncheon // 오찬을 같이하다 lunch〔take lunch〕 with 《a person》
—회 a luncheon party ¶ 오찬회를 개최하다 give a luncheon (party)
오채 五彩 the five colors
오체 五體 the (whole) body ; the whole frame ; the limbs ¶ 오체가 멀쩡하다 He is without any physical defect.
오촌 五寸 one's cousin's son〔daughter〕; one's father's cousin
— 아저씨 a great-uncle's son ; uncle **— 조카** a cousin's son〔daughter〕
오층 五層 five stories〔floors, levels〕; the fifth floor
오칭 誤稱 a misnomer **—하다** call by a wrong name ; call wrongly〔erroneously〕
*__오케스트라__ an orchestra
오케이 (an) O.K. ; an okay ; All right. ¶ 오케이하다 O.K.〔okay〕《a plan》; give an O.K. 《to》
오키나와 〖지리〗 Okinawa ¶ 오키나와의 Okinawan
— 사람 on Okinawan

오탁 汚濁 being filthy and turbid ; corruption ; impurity **—하다** (be) filthy and turbid ; impure ¶ 오탁지세 a corrupt age ; the corrupt〔depraved, degen-erated〕 world
오토메이션 automation ¶ 오토메이션으로 생산 원가 절감 bring down the cost of production by automation // 오토메이션화하다 automate ; automatize
— 공장 an automated plant〔factory〕
오토바이 a motorcycle ; an autocycle

> 참고 오토바이는 **autobike**의 와전

오토자이로 an autogiro 《*pl*, ~s》; a gyroplane
오톨도톨 —하다 (be) rugged ; knotty ⇨ 우툴우툴
오트밀 oatmeal ; porridge
오트 볼타 Haute Volta ; Upper Volta
오판 誤判 misjudgment ; a mistrial ; miscarriage of justice〔law〕 ¶ 오판으로 전쟁을 도발하다 provoke a war by miscalculation
— 사건 a misjudgment case
오팔 〖광물〗 opal
오퍼 〖무역〗 an offer **—하다** make an offer
구매 — a buying〔buyer's〕 offer ; a bid **반대 —** a counter offer **원(原)—** an original offer **판매 —** a selling offer ; an offer **확정(기한부) —** a firm offer
⁑__오페라__ an opera
— 가수 an opera(tic) singer **그랜드 —** grand opera
오페레타 an operetta

오토바이

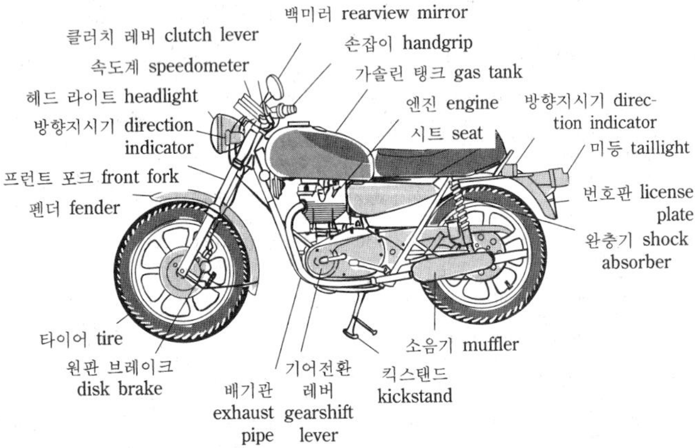

오포 午砲 the midday〔noon〕 gun ¶ 오포를 쏘다 fire the noon gun
오프셋 〖인쇄〗 offset ; set off 《영》 ¶ 오프셋 판으로 하다 offset
오프셋 인쇄 offset printing〔lithography〕; offset ¶ 오프셋 인쇄로 하다 offset
—기 an offset (printing) press **사진 —** photo offset printing
오픈 게임 an open game
오픈 카 an open car ; a convertible (car)
오피스 an office
— 걸 an office girl
오한 惡寒 a chill ; a cold fit ; 〖의학〗 rigor ¶ 오한이 나다 feel a chill ; catch a chill
오할 五割 50 per cent
오합무지기 五合— five underskirts of different lengths
오합지졸 烏合之卒 (an undisciplined) mob ; a disorderly crowd ; rabble ; ruck
†**오해 誤解** misunderstanding ; misconception ; misapprehension **—하다** misunderstand ; misapprehend ; misconceive ; misconstrue (어귀를) ¶ 오해를 받다 be misunderstood // 오해를 사다 cause〔invite〕 misunderstanding // 오해를 풀다 clear〔remove〕 misunderstanding // 오해를 초래하기 쉽다 be liable to lead to misunderstanding // 문귀가 명료해서 오해의 여지가 없다 The words are clear and unmistakable. // 그것은 너의 오해다 That's a misunderstanding on your part. /You are wrong in your judgment. // 너는 오해하고 있다 You labor under a misunderstanding. // 너는 나를 오해하고 있다 You do me an injustice〔wrong〕 with your misunderstanding. // 이 점에 대해서 너의 오해를 풀어야만 되겠다 I must undeceive you on this point. // 입싸움은 오해에서 일어났다 The quarrel originated in a misunderstanding. // 나를 오해하지 마라 Don't misunderstand me. /Don't get me wrong. /Don't take it the wrong way.
오행 五行 〖민속〗 the Five Elements ; the Five primary substance 《metal, wood, water, fire, earth》
오현 五絃 [5개의 줄] five strings ; [악기] a five stringed musical instrument
—금(琴) a pentachord
오호 嗚呼 Alas ! ¶ 오호 그녀는 가고 없구나 Alas ! She is no more.
오호츠크 해 —海 the Sea of Okhotsk
오호호 Ha ha ! /Tee hee !
오활 迂闊 thoughtlessness ; carelessness ; heedlessness ; stupidity ; ignorance ; unfamiliarity **—하다** (be) careless ; thoughtless ; heedless ; inattentive ; stupid ; unfamiliar ; ignorant
†**오후 午後** afternoon ; p. m. ¶ 오후 5시에 at 5 p. m. ; at five in the afternoon // 어제 오후 yesterday afternoon // 일요일 오후에 on Sunday afternoon ; in the afternoon on Sunday
†**오히려** rather (than) ; sooner (than) ; preferably ¶ 치욕을 받느니보다 오히려 죽는 게 낫다 I would rather〔sooner〕 die than suffer disgrace. // 나는 오히려 집에 있는 편이 낫다 I would just as soon stay at home. // 그는 학자라기보다 오히려 작가다 He is not so much a scholar as a writer. /He is not a scholar so much as a writer. /He is rather a writer than a scholar. // 너는 오히려 가지 않는 편이 낫다 You had better not go there.
옥 玉 ① jade ; jadeite (경옥) ; nephrite (연옥)
② [구슬보석] a precious stone ; a gem ; a jewel ; a bijou ¶ 옥에 티 a flaw in a gem ; a fly in the ointment ; a flaw in one's otherwise perfect character // 옥 같은 사내 아이 a bouncing boy ; a gem of a boy // 옥을 굴리는 듯한 목소리(로) (in) a silvery voice // 금이야 옥이야 하고 사랑하다 love one's child like the apple of one's eye
—가락지 a jade ring
옥에도 티가 있다 속담 No silver〔gold〕 without its dross. /There are spots even in the sun. /The best cloth may have a moth in it.
옥 獄 a prison ; a jail ; a gaol 《영》; a lockup ¶ 옥에서 나오다 be released from prison // 옥에 가두다 imprison 《a person》; throw〔put〕 《a person》 into prison // 옥을 뚫다 break jail〔prison〕 // 옥에 들어가다 be sent to prison
옥고 獄苦 the hardships of prison life ¶ 옥고를 견디다 endure the hardships of prison life // 옥고를 치르다 groan〔languish〕 in prison ; serve one's term of imprisonment
옥고 玉稿 (your, his) esteemed manuscript
옥내 屋內 the inside〔interior〕 of a house ¶ 옥내의 indoor ; covered // 옥내에서 indoors ; within doors
— 경기장 a gymnasium **— 공기** the indoor air **— 노동** indoor labor **— 배선** interior wiring ; house wiring **— 온도** the indoor temperature **— 장면** 〖연극〗 an interior
옥니 ① an inturned tooth ② [옥치] a jade tooth
—박이 a person with inturned teeth
옥다 get bent inward ; turn inward ; get〔be〕 misshapen
옥답 沃畓 rich〔fertile, fat〕 paddyfields
옥당목 玉唐木 calico of inferior quality ; inferior calico
옥도 沃度 iodine
—정기 tincture of iodine ; iodine tincture **—제** an iodine preparation **—칼리** iodide of potassium **— 포름** iodoform
옥돌 玉— a precious stone ; a gem
옥동자 玉童子 a precious son ; an angel〔a gem〕 of a boy
옥란 玉蘭 〖식물〗 Chinese〔white〕 magno-

lia ; a yulan ; Magnolia denudata (학명)
옥리 獄吏 ⇨ 옥사쟁이
옥문 獄門 a prison gate ; the gate of a jail
옥밀이 a kind of gimlet with turned-in bit
옥바라지 獄— —하다 supply a prisoner with clothes and food from outside the prison
옥사 獄舍 a jail ; a prison
옥사 獄事 administration of the major criminal cases such as murder and high treason
옥사 獄死 death in prison —하다 die in prison
옥사쟁이 獄鎖匠— a jailer ; a gaoler 《영》; a turnkey ; a prison keeper〔warden〕; a guard
옥살이 獄— prison life ; life behind bars
옥상 屋上 (on) the roof ; the rooftop ; the housetop
— 정원 the roof garden — 주택 a penthouse
옥새 a defective roof-tile with a bent-in end
옥새 玉璽 the Royal Seal ; the privy seal
—관 the Lord Keeper of the Privy Seal ; Lord Privy Seal
옥색 玉色 light blue ; jade green
옥생각 perversion ; distortion ; a biased interpretation ; a distorted view —하다 distort ; pervert ¶ 남의 말을 옥생각하다 pervert another's words
옥석 玉石 ① [옥돌] precious stones ; jade ② [옥과 돌] precious stones and pebble stones ; jades〔gems〕 and stones ③ [좋은 것과 나쁜 것] wheat and tares
경주 돌이면 다 옥석인가 속담 All is not gold that glitters.
옥석구분 玉石俱焚 gems〔jades〕 and stones burned together ; indiscriminate destruction of good and bad alike
옥석혼효 玉石混淆 a mixture of wheat and chaff ; a jumble of wheat and tares ; thread and thrum
옥셈 miscalculation ; short-changing oneself —하다 miscalculate〔miscount〕 to one's own disadvantage ¶ 돈을 옥셈하다 short-change oneself
옥소 沃素 iodine ⇨ 옥도
옥쇄 玉碎 a death for honor —하다 die honorably ; die but never surrender ; prefer death to dishonor ; suffer honorable death ¶ 대장부는 옥쇄할지언정 와전(瓦全)을 부끄럽게 여긴다 Better to die in the attempt than seek an ignominious safety.
옥수 玉水 clear water ; crystal water
옥수 玉手 [왕의] the king's hand ; [미인의] a beautiful (woman's) hand
†옥수수 corn 《미》; Indian corn ; maize
옥시풀 『약』 Oxyful 《상표명》; oxydol ; oxygenated water
옥신각신 —하다 wrangle ; altercate ; squabble ; argue ¶ 서로 옥신각신 말다툼하다 wrangle with each other
옥신거리다 ① [북작거리다] swarm ; crowd ; throng ¶ 벌이 수없이 옥신거리다 bees swarm by the thousands // 사람들이 옥신거리다 be thronged with people ② [환부가] tingle ; ache ; smart ; rankle ; throb with pain ¶ 어제 베인 상처가 자꾸 옥신거린다 The wound keeps smarting from a cut I got yesterday.
옥안 玉顔 [왕의] the king's face ; the royal visage ; [미인의] a beautiful (woman's) face
옥야 沃野 a fertile〔rich〕 field〔plain〕 ¶ 옥야 천리 a vast stretch of fertile plain
*옥양목 玉洋木 calico
옥양사 玉洋紗 fine calico
*옥외 屋外 outside the house ; the outdoors ; the open (air) ¶ 옥외의 outdoor ; open-air ; outside
— 노동자 an outdoor〔open-air〕 laborer — 배관〔배선〕 outdoor piping〔wiring〕 — 연설 an outdoor〔open-air, a stump〕 speech — 유희〔운동〕 outdoor〔open-air, field〕 exercise〔sports〕 — 장면 『연극』 an exterior — 조명 exterior illumination — 집회 an open-air meeting ; an out-of-door gathering
옥음 玉音 [임금의] the king's voice ; [미인의] a beautiful (woman's) voice ; [편지] your letter
옥이다 ⇨ 욱이다
옥자강이 an early-ripening (variety of) rice plant
옥자귀 an adz(e) with a turned-in end
옥잠화 玉簪花 a plantain lily ; Hosta undulata (학명)
옥장사 ⇨ 오그랑 장사
옥장이 玉匠— a lapidary ; a jewel cutter
옥졸 獄卒 a jailer ; a gaoler 《영》; a warden 《미》
옥좌 玉座 the Royal seat ; the throne ¶ 옥좌에 앉다 sit on the throne ; take the Royal seat
옥죄이다 feel cramped ; be tight ; be fitting too closely ¶ 옥죄이는 옷 tight clothes // 웃옷의 겨드랑이가 옥죄인다 The coat cuts me under the arm.
옥중 獄中 the inside of a jail ; in jail〔prison〕 (옥중에서)
—기 a diary written in prison
옥창 獄窓 ① [창] the window of a jail〔prison house〕
② ⇨ 옥중(獄中) ¶ 옥창에 있는 사람 a prisoner behind bars
옥체 玉體 ① [임금의] the person of the king ; His Majesty's person〔health〕 ② [미인의] the body of a beautiful woman ③ [존체] the noble body ; your body ; you
†옥타브 『음악』 an octave ; eighth
옥탄가 —價 『화학』 an octane number〔rating〕 ¶ 높은〔낮은〕 옥탄가 a high〔low〕 octane number // 옥탄가가 높은 가

옥토 沃土 fertile〔rich, fat〕 soil〔land〕 ¶ 황무지를 옥토화하다 make barren soil fertile

옥토끼 [흰 토끼] a white rabbit ; [전설의] the rabbit in the moon

옥편 玉篇 a Chinese-Korean dictionary ; a dictionary of Chinese characters ; [사전] a dictionary

옥호 屋號 a shop〔store〕 name

옥황상제 玉皇上帝 the highest of the heavenly gods of Taoism ; the Lord ; Heaven ; the Supreme Being ; the king of kings

온 all ; whole ; entire ; complete ; perfect ; full ; total ¶ 온 백성 the whole nation // 온 세상 all the world ; all over the world // 온 누리 the whole universe // 온 몸에 all over the body ; from head to foot // 온 힘을 다하여 with all one's might // 온 나라에 알려지다 be known all over〔throughout〕 the country

온각 溫覺 the sense of heat〔warmth〕 ; temperature sensation

온감 溫感 the sense of heat〔warmth〕 ; sensory experience of temperature

*__온갖__ all kinds〔sorts〕 of ; every kind of ; all manner of ; all ; every ; every possible ; whatever... all ; various ¶ 온갖 것 all ; everything // 온갖 기회 every and any occasion // 온갖 사람 all sorts of people // 온갖 수단을 다하다 try every means available // 온갖 고생을 다하다 go through all kinds of hardship imaginable // 온갖 준비를 갖추다 make every preparation // 광산 종업원들을 사고로부터 보호하기 위하여 온갖 수단을 다해야 할 것이다 Everything possible〔All possible things〕 should be done to protect the miners from accident.

*__온건 穩健__ moderateness ; moderation ; soundness **—하다** (be) moderate ; sensible ; sound ; slow and steady ¶ 온건한 생각 moderate views // 온건한 의론 a sound argument // 그의 사상은 온건하다 He has a sound mind.

—론자 a moderate **—주의** moderatism **—주의자** a moderatist **—파** the moderate party〔wing〕 ; the moderates

온고지신 溫故知新 **—하다** review the old and learn the new ; carry the knowledge gained into a new field ; take a leaf out of a wise man's book

온골 a whole width of cloth〔paper〕

온기 溫氣 warmth ; warm air ¶ 온기가 있다 be warm // 온기가 없다 be not warm ; have no warmth

— 난방 hot-air heating

온난 溫暖 warmth ; being warm〔mild〕 **—하다** (be) warm ; mild

— 전선(前線) 〖기상〗 a warm front

온달 a full moon

‡**온당 穩當** reasonableness ; being just and proper ; appropriateness ; fittingness **—하다** (be) just and proper ; reasonable ; right ¶ 온당한 요구 a reasonable claim // 온당한 언사 proper language // 온당한 조치 a just and proper measure // 이와 같은 행동은 신사로서 온당하지 않다 Such conduct is not proper for a gentleman. // 그 해석은 온당하다 That is a sensible interpretation of the passage.

온대 溫帶 the temperate〔variable〕 zone ; the warm latitudes〔belt〕

— 식물 the flora of the temperate zone **—어(魚)** the Temperate Zone fishes **—지방** the temperate regions〔latitudes〕 **아(亞)—** the subtemperate zone

온데간데없다 suddenly disappear ; vanish (in smoke)

온도 溫度 temperature ¶ 높은〔낮은〕 온도 a high〔low〕 temperature // 온도를 재다〔조정하다〕 take〔adjust〕 the temperature // 온도가 올라가다〔내려가다〕 the temperature rises〔falls〕 《to 30 degrees》 // 오늘밤의 최저 온도는 영하 5도쯤 될 것이다 The lowest temperature tonight will be about 5 degrees below zero.

— 조절 thermostatic control **— 조절 장치** a thermostat **실내 —** the shade〔room〕 temperature **연간 평균 —** the annual mean temperature **절대〔표준〕 —** the absolute〔standard〕 temperature

‡**온도계 溫度計** a thermometer ; the mercury ¶ 온도계가 섭씨 19도를 가리키고 있다 The thermometer〔mercury〕 stands at 19℃. // 온도계가 영도로 내리면 물이 언다 When thermometer is below zero, water will freeze.

섭씨〔화씨〕 — a centigrade〔Fahrenheit〕 thermometer **최고〔최저〕 —** a maximum〔minimum〕 thermometer

온돌 溫突 the Korean under-floor heating system ; a hypocaust

온두라스 Honduras

온디콩 a kind of yellow bean with a gray pod

온라인 방식 〖전산기〗 the on-line information processing system

온면 溫麵 noodles served in hot soup ; warm noodles

온몸 ⇨ 전신(全身)

온밤 the whole night ¶ 간밤엔 온밤을 꼬빡 뜬눈으로 새웠다 I stayed awake all night yesterday.

온상 溫床 a hotbed ; a warm nursery ¶ 악의 온상 a hotbed of vice〔social evils〕 // 자유의 온상 the cradle of liberty // 이 학원은 이상적 평화주의 온상으로서 유명했다 This academy was well-known as a hotbed of idealistic pacifism.

온새미로 intact ; whole (just as it was made) ; unbroken

온색 溫色 a warm color

온수 溫水 warm water ; hot water

— 공급 hot-water supply **— 난방** hot-water heating **— 방열기** a hot-water radiator — 시설 a hot-water supply system

온순 溫順 gentleness ; geniality ; docility ; obedience **—하다** (be) gentle ; genial ; docile ; meek ; obedient ; compliant ¶ 나는 그를 온순한 녀석으로 생각해 왔으나 그에 대한 평가를 바꿨다 I'd thought of him as just a mild-mannered guy, but I've revised my opinion of him.

온쉼표 —標 〖음악〗 a whole rest

‡**온스** [단위] an ounce 《oz.》

***온실 溫室** a greenhouse ; a hothouse ; a glasshouse 《영》 ; a greenery ¶ 온실 성장 hothouse growth // 온실에서 피게 하다 force 《a plant》 to bloom in a hothouse // 온실 재배하다 grow 《plants》 under glass
— 식물 a hothouse〔greenhouse〕 plant 〔flower〕 **— 재배** glass culture

온아 溫雅 —하다 (be) graceful ; bland ; amiable ; affable ; suave ; kindly ¶ 온아한 말 graceful language // 온아한 사람 a graceful〔gentle〕 person

온열 요법 溫熱療法 thermotherapy

온욕 溫浴 a hot〔warm〕 bath **—하다** take a hot〔warm〕 bath
— 요법 the hot-water cure ; treatment by warm water

온유 溫柔 gentleness ; mildness ; tenderness ; docility ; clemency ; warmth **—하다** (be) gentle ; meek ; mild ; tender ; sweet ; docile ; warm

온음 —音 〖음악〗 a whole tone ⇨ 전음
—계 the diatonic scale **— 음계** the whole-note scale **—표** a whole note 《미》 ; a semibreve 《영》

온이로 entirely ; altogether ; in its entirety ; wholly

온장 —張 the entire sheet ; a whole piece of paper ; uncut paper

온장고 溫藏庫 a heating cabinet

온전 穩全 soundness ; intactness **—하다** (be) sound ; whole ; intact ; unimpaired ; perfect ¶ 집안에 온전한 접시라고는 하나도 없다 There isn't a whole plate in the house.

온정 溫井 a hot spring

†**온정 溫情** warm-heartedness ; a warm feeling ; kindliness ; warmth ; heartiness ; geniality ; cordiality ¶ 온정 있는 warm-hearted ; cordial ; kindly ; genial ; hearty ; warm
—주의 paternalism ; the kind-feeling policy

온존 溫存 —하다 keep ; preserve ; retain ¶ 옛 전통을 온존하다 cherish old traditions

***온종일** —終日 all day (long) ; the whole day ; all through the day ; throughout the day ; from morning to〔till〕 night ¶ 온종일 책을 읽다 read books all day long // 어제는 온종일 비가 왔었다 It rained yesterday from morning till night. // 온종일 기다리고 있었다 I was kept waiting all the day.

온집안 the whole family ; all the family ; all over the house ¶ 온집안을 찾다 search all over the house

온채 the whole〔entire〕 house ¶ 온채를 새로 짓다 build a whole new house ; rebuild the entire house

***온천 溫泉** a hot spring ; a medical〔thermal〕 spring ; a spa (광천) ¶ 온천에 가다 take the baths〔waters〕 ; visit〔go to〕 a spa
—수 thermal waters ; mineral waters **—여관** a hotel at a hot spring resort ; a hot spring hotel ; a bath hotel **— 요법** a hot spring cure **—장** a hot spring ; a hot-bath resort ; a watering place **온양 —** the *Onyang* springs

온천하다 ① [온전하다] ⇨ 온전(—하다) ② [상당히 많다] (be) quite a lot of ; a good many 《books》 ; not a few 《books》

온축 蘊蓄 a stock of knowledge ; profound〔extensive〕 knowledge ; erudition

온탕 溫湯 [온천] a hot spring ; thermal waters ; [욕탕] hot〔warm〕 water 〔bath〕 ; [국] hot soup

온통 all ; wholly ; entirely ; altogether ; completely

온폭 —幅 the overall〔whole〕 width of cloth〔paper〕

온혈 溫血 warm blood
— 동물 a warm-blooded animal ; a homoiothermic〔homeothermic, homoiothermal〕 animal

†**온화 溫和** mildness ; gentleness ; benignancy ; geniality ; clemency **—하다** (be) mild ; gentle ; quiet ; benign ; genial ; clement ; temperate (기후가) ¶ 온화한 기후 a mild〔temperate, clement, benign〕 climate ; agreeable weather // 온화한 사람〔미소〕 a gentle person〔smile〕 // 온화한 성질 good〔sweet〕 temper // 성질이 온화하다 be of a gentle character

‡**온후 溫厚** gentleness ; mildness ; suavity **—하다** (be) gentle ; mild ; suave ; affable ¶ 온후한 신사 a courteous gentleman // 그는 온후한 사람이다 His personality is gentle and sincere.

올[1] ① [가닥] ply ; texture ; strand ¶ 세 올 실 three-ply thread // 올이 고운〔거친, 성긴〕 천 cloth of fine〔coarse, loose〕 texture ② [직물의 날] warp

올[2] this year ⇨ 올해 ¶ 올 안에 in the course of this year ; before the year-end // 올 여름 휴가 the coming summer vacation ; the last summer vacation // 올에는 비가 많이 왔다 We have had a lot of rain this year.

올- early ripening ¶ 올벼 early ripening rice // 올콩 early beans

올가미 a noose ; a snare ; a trap ; a lasso ; a hook ; [꾀] a trick ; a cheat ¶ 올가미로 잡다 (en)trap ; (en)snare ; catch 《an animal》 in a trap // 올가미를 놓

다 lay a snare ; set〔lay〕 a trap 《for an animal》// 올가미에 걸리다 be caught in a trap ; fall into a snare ; be ensnared ; be entrapped // 보기 좋게 올가미에 걸렸는 걸 I was clean taken in.

올가미를 씌우다 관용 put the rope on 《a person》

올강거리다 ① [⋯을] chew on 《sinewy stuff》; mumble ¶ 질긴 고기를 올강거리다 chew on a piece of tough beef ② [⋯이] be hard to chew ; be tough ¶ 고기가 올강거려 잘 씹히지 않는다 This beef is tough to chew.

올강올강 chewing ; mumbling (ly) ; mouthing ¶ 올강올강 씹다 chew on 《a thing》; mumble

올곧다 [사람이] (be) upright ; straight ; honest ; right-minded ; [줄이] straight ; direct ¶ 올곧은 사람 an upright person // 올곧은 줄 a straight〔direct〕 line

올나이트 all-night
— **흥행** an all-night show

올내년 一來年 this and next year ; this year and the next

올되다 ① [직물의 올이] (be) fine ; close ; [지능이] be precocious ; be wise above one's age ; be advanced for one's age ② [곡물이] rareripe ; ripening early ¶ 올된 아이 a precocious child

올드 미스 an old maid ; a spinster

올딱 vomit up what one has just eaten

***올라가다** ① [높이] go up ; ascend ; mount ; climb ; rise ; soar (솟다) ¶ 나무에 올라가다 climb a tree // 산에 올라가다 climb (up)〔go up〕 a mountain ; ascend a mountain // 강을 올라가다 go up a river // 2층에 올라가다 go upstairs // 지붕에 올라가다 get〔go up〕 on the roof // 연단에 올라가다 step on〔mount〕 the platform // 하늘 높이 올라가다 soar〔go up〕 in the air ; soar skyward // 서울에 올라가다 go〔come〕 up to *Seoul*〔town〕// 무더운 7·8월에는 섭씨 35도까지 기온이 올라갑니다 The temperature climbs as high as 35 degrees Celsius during the sizzling months of July and August.
② [승진·승급] rise ; be promoted ; be raised ; be advanced ¶ 신용이 올라가다 rise in 《a person's》 opinion // 지위가 올라가다 rise in rank ; be promoted 《to a higher position》// 이름이 올라가다 rise to fame ; win fame // 월급이 올라가다 one's salary is raised ; get a raise in one's salary ; get one's salary increased〔raised〕 // 3학년으로 올라가다 get one's promotion to the third year〔grade〕
③ [물가가] go up ; rise ; advance ; soar (폭등하다) ; shoot up (급등하다) ¶ 물가가 올라간다 Prices rise〔go up〕. // 물가가 급히 올라갔다 Prices shot〔jumped〕 up. // 집세가 8만원으로 올라갔다 The rent has been raised to eighty thousand *won*.
④ [상륙] land ; go〔come〕 ashore ¶ 항구에 올라가다 land at a port
⑤ [재산·밑천이] lose ; be lost ¶ 경마에 5,000원이 올라가다 lose five thousand *won* on a horse race
⑥ [죽다] die ; be dead ; fall off

올라서다 ① [높은 데로 가 서다] get up on a higher place ; mount〔ascend〕 《a platform》; get (up) on ; step up ② [지위가 높아지다] rise to higher level of rank ; mount ; rise ; [출세하다] rise in the world ; raise oneself〔be advanced〕 to 《a higher position》

올라오다 climb ⇨ 오르다, 올라가다

올라타다 ① [탈것에] board 《a train》; go〔come, get〕 on board〔aboard (of)〕 《a ship》; embark on〔in〕 《a ship》; get into〔on〕 《a car》; step into 《a boat》; mount〔ride〕 《a horse》 ¶ 뛰어 올라타다 jump on 《a horse》; jump in 《a bus》; jump into 《a moving car》
② [몸위에] cover ; line ; tread (수탉이)

올랑거리다 ① [가슴이] palpitate ; go pitapat ; pulsate ; flutter ; throb ¶ 무서워서 가슴이 올랑거리다 palpitate with fear ② [물결이] ripple ; ruffle ; roll ¶ 올랑거리는 rolling ; wavy

올랑촐랑 ① [그릇의 물이] slopping from side to side ; [물결이] lapping from side to side ; splashing gently **—하다** slop from side to side ; lap from side to side ¶ 양동이의 물이 올랑촐랑 흔들리다 water slops back and forth in the bucket // 올랑촐랑 물가를 씻고 있는 물결 the waves lapping the shore // 물이 올랑촐랑 흔들린다 Water laps back and forth.
② [경박하게] flightly ; frivolously **—하다** behave frivolously ; act silly ¶ 올랑촐랑 까불다 behave frivolously ; act silly

올려놓다 put 《a thing》 (up) on 《a place, a thing》 ¶ 책을 선반에 올려놓다 put a book (up) on a shelf

올려본각 一角 (angle of) elevation

올록볼록하다 (be) uneven ; embossed ; bossy ; knobbly ; lumpy ; bumpy ; covered with bosses〔protuberances〕

†**올리다** ① [위로] raise ; lift up ; put〔hold〕 up 《one's hand》; elevate ¶ 깃발을 올리다 hoist a flag ; fly〔unfurl〕 a flag // 손을 올리다 hold up〔raise〕 one's hand // 연을 올리다 fly〔send up〕 a kite // 값을 올리다 raise the price // 월급을 올리다 raise one's salary // 관세를 올리다 raise the tariff // 한 급 올리다 promote 《a person》 to a higher class // 지난달 한달 동안만 1만 달러의 순이익을 올렸다 Last month alone we rang up a net profit of one million dollars. // 판매량을 늘리기 위해서는 가격을 더 올려야 한다고 생각합니다 In order to increase sales, I think we must mark up the price.
② [거행] hold ; celebrate ; observe ¶ 결혼식을 올리다 hold a wedding ; celebrate〔have〕 a marriage

③ [드리다] offer ; give ; present ¶ 기도를 올리다 offer a prayer // 선생님에게 책을 올리다 present a book to a teacher
④ [얻다] obtain ; get ; attain ; gain ; win ; secure ¶ 좋은 성과를 올리다 obtain good results ; make a good record // 우리 야구팀은 5점을 올렸다 Our team scored five points〔runs〕.
⑤ [기재] record ; put on record ; enter ; make an entry ¶ 사건을 역사에 올리다 record an event in history // 이름을 올리다 register〔enter〕 one's name // 장부에 올리다 enter〔make an entry〕 in a book // 전화 번호부에 이름을 올리다 put one's name in the telephone directory // 토요일이나 일요일 대기자 명단에 올려 주세요 Put me on your waiting list for Saturday or Sunday, will you?
⑥ [기타] ¶ 칠을 올리다 coat a thing with paint // 질병을 올리다 communicate〔carry〕 a disease ; infect // 머리를 올리다 put〔turn〕 up the hair // 기와〔짚, 슬레이트〕로 지붕을 올리다 roof a house with tiles〔thatch, slate〕 ; tile〔thatch, slate〕 a house〔roof〕 // 환성을 올리다 shout for joy

⁑**올리브** 〖식물〗 an olive
—**유** olive oil

†**올림** ① ⇨ 증정(贈呈) ② [편지에서] Yours very truly, ; Sincerely yours, ; Cordially yours, ¶ 존 올림 Yours very truly, John

올림피아 Olympia

⁑**올림픽** Olympic(s) ¶ 올림픽의 Olympic // 올림픽에 선수를 보내다 send representative athletes to the Olympics // 한국 대표로서 올림픽에 출전하다 represent Korea in the Olympics
— **경기** the Olympics ; the Olympic games —**기** the Olympic flag — **대회** the Olympiad ; the Olympic Games — **성화** the Olympic Torch — **조직 위원회** the Olympic Organizing Committee 《O. O. C》 — **찬가** the Olympic anthem〔hymn〕 —**촌** an Olympic village — **출전 선수** a member of the Olympic team ; an Olympian — **헌장** the Olympic Charter — **회의** the Olympic Congress **국제 기능** — the International Vocational Training Competition **국제 장애자** — the International Paraplegics Olympic Games **동계** — the Olympic Winter Games ; the Winter Olympic Games ; the Winter Olympics **프리** — the Pre-Olympics ; the Pre-Olympic Games **국제 — 위원회** the International Olympic Committee 《I. O. C》 **한국 — 위원회** the Korea Olympic Committee 《K. O. C》

올막졸막 ⇨ 올망졸망

올망 a deep-sea fishing net
—**대** a stick used in casting a net

올망졸망 all sorts〔kinds〕 of little things (in a cluster) ; various sizes of small things (in a cluster) ; in lots of small units ; in clusters —**하다** be of various small sizes ; come in lots of small units ¶ 올망졸망한 어린이들 little children of about the same size // 사과가 올망졸망 여러 개 있다 There are a lot of small apples of about the same size.

올목졸목 ⇨ 올망졸망

올무 a snare ; a trap ; a noose

올바로 uprightly ; honestly ; straightly ; straightforwardly ; frankly ¶ 올바로 살다 live uprightly ; lead an honest life // 올바로 말하다 speak properly〔frankly〕 // 올바로 행동하다 behave properly〔correctly〕 // 올바로 서다 stand upright

올바르다 (be) straight ; upright ; straightforward ; honest ¶ 올바른 사람 an upright person

올밤 an early chestnut

올벼 an early-ripening rice plant

올봄 this spring

⁑**올빼미** an owl ¶ 올빼미 새끼 an owlet // 올빼미 우는 소리 a hoot // 올빼미가 울다 owls hoot〔tu-whit(t), tu-whoo〕

올새 weave ; texture ; a stitch (뜨개질의) ¶ 올새가 거칠다 be rough〔coarse, open〕 in weave // 올새가 가늘다〔굵다〕 have fine〔rough〕 weave

올지다 ⇨ 오달지다

올차다 ① [사람이] (be) substantial ; sturdy ; stout ; peppy ; small but solid ; be of compact build ¶ 올찬 사람 a man of compact〔substantial〕 build
② [곡식이] grow〔become, get〕 ripe and hard early ; ripen early ¶ 올찬 벼 an early-ripening rice plant

***올챙이** a tadpole ; a polliwog 《미》
— **기자** a cub (reporter) 《미·구》 — **작가** a cub〔sucking〕 writer —**배** a protuberant〔protruding〕 belly ; a potbelly

올케 the wife of a girl's brother ; a girl's sister-in-law

올콩 early beans

올통볼통 —**하다** (be) bumpy ; rough ; uneven ; rugged ⇨ 울퉁불퉁하다

올팥 early red beans

올페우스 [신화] Orpheus

***올해** this year ; the current〔present〕 year ¶ 올해는 비가 많이 왔다 We have had a lot of rain this year. // 올해는 풍년이다 This is a plenteous year. // 올해도 며칠 남지 않았다 We have only a few days left before the end of the year.

옭걸다 tie up and hang ; bind

옭다 ① [잡아매다] tie up ; bind ; fasten ¶ 사람을 옭다 bind a person ; tie a person up // 새끼줄로 짐을 옭다 tie a bundle with a rope
② [올가미로] noose 《a rope around the neck of》 ; put the noose on ¶ 염소를 옭다 put the noose on a goat
③ [꾀를 써서 사람을] (en)trap ; (en)snare

옭매다 tie a secure〔fast〕 knot ; fasten

옭매듭 a granny('s) knot

옭아내다 ① [올가미로] put a rope around the neck and drag out ; noose 《an animal, a thing》 out
② [남을 속여서] cheat〔wheedle, swindle, squeeze, do〕《a person》 out of 《a person's money》

옭아매다 tie up ⇨ 옭다 ¶ 짐을 옭아매다 tie up a package // 개를 새끼줄로 옭아매다 tie the rope around a dog's neck

옭히다 ① [올가미에] get roped〔noosed〕; be tangled ¶ 여우가 올가미에 옭히다 a fox is caught in a snare
② [얽히다] be〔get〕 tangled〔entangled, knotted〕 ¶ 실이 옭히어 풀어지지 않는다 Thread is so tangled up that it is impossible to straighten it out.
③ [걸리다] be dragged〔sucked〕 in ; be involved ; be entangled in ; be roped in ; be embroiled in ¶ 그는 살인 사건에 옭히어 큰 욕을 본다 He is mixed up in a murder case and gets a rough going-over.

†**옮기다** ① [이동] move 《to》; remove 《to》; transfer ; shift 《home》 ¶ 의자를 구석으로 옮기다 move a chair to the corner // 발을 옮기다 turn one's steps 《to, toward》; walk on // 주거를 시외로 옮기다 move〔change one's abode〕 to the suburbs // 학교를 옮기다 change schools ; transfer to another school // 그 은행의 본점은 서울로 옮겼다 The head office of the bank was moved to *Seoul*. // 그 사건은 상급 재판소에 옮겨졌다 The case was carried to the higher court.
② [병을] give ; communicate 《a disease to another》; infect 《a person with a disease》 ¶ 감기를 옮기다 give〔pass on〕 one's cold to 《a person》
③ [말을] tell 《to another》; spread (퍼뜨리다) ; pass on ¶ 이 말은 다른 사람에게 옮기지 마라 Don't tell this to anyone. / Keep this secret.

†**옮다** ① move ⇨ 옮기다
② [사람이 병에] be infected 《with a disease》; take ; catch ; contract ; [병이 사람에게] be communicated to ; infect ¶ 병이 옮은 사람 an infected person // 옮기 쉽다 be catching〔infectious, contagious〕 // 남에게서 감기가 옮다 catch a cold from another // 남편의 병을 옮다 catch the disease of one's husband // 아이에게 디프테리아가 옮았다 The child has been infected with diphtheria.
③ [물이] be stained〔smeared〕 《with dye》
④ [말·소문이] spread ; pass on ¶ 말이 옮다 words spread〔pass on〕

옮아가다 ① [이동] move away ; move ; remove ; change quarters ¶ 새집으로 옮아가다 move into a new house // 종로로 옮아가다 move to the *Chongro* district
② [퍼지다] spread ; circulate ¶ 소문이 옮아가다 a rumor spreads // 불이 사방으로 옮아갔다 The fire spread in all directions.

옮아오다 move ⇨ 옮다

옰 compensation ; recompense ; indemnity ; indemnification ; reparations

옳다[1] (be) right ; rightful ; [정당] proper ; reasonable ; [정의] just ; righteous ; [틀림없음] correct ; true ; [정확] exact ; accurate ; [진실] honest ; truthful ¶ 옳게 rightly ; justly ; properly ; correctly ; accurately ; honestly // 옳은 답 a correct answer // 옳은 방법 a proper way ; a correct method // 옳은 사람 a righteous man // 옳은 마음을 가진 사람 a right-hearted〔-minded〕 person // 옳은 자세 a proper posture // 옳은 행위 (a) right conduct // 옳지 않다 be wrong〔improper〕; be unjust ; be incorrect (틀린) ; be inaccurate (부정확) ; be dishonest ; be illegal (위법) // 옳은 일을 하다 do right ; do a right thing ; do what is right // 그의 말이 옳다 He is right〔in the right〕. // 당신의 요구는 옳지 않다 Your demands are not just. // 두 사람 중 누가 옳으냐 Which of the two men is in the right? // 옳소 Hear! /Right on!

옳다[2] [감탄사] Right! /O. K.! /All right! /Right you are! /Right-o! ¶ 옳다 이제 알겠다 Oh, now I get it. // 옳다 됐다 Now I've got it. /That's fine. /I am sure of my game. /I've got it in my power!

옳아 ⇨ 옳다[2]

옳은길 the right road ; the straight path ; the road of righteousness ; righteousness ¶ 옳은길에서 벗어난 짓 an unrighteous act // 옳은길로 인도하다 guide 《a person》 into the right path // 옳은길을 걷다 tread the path of virtue ; pursue an honest career ; be just〔righteous〕

옳은말 true words ; an honest speech ; the truth ; righteous remarks ¶ 옳은말을 하는 사람 a person who speaks truly〔true〕 // 옳은말을 하다 tell the truth ; say right things ; tell what is right

옳지 Good! /Right! /Yes! ¶ 옳지 그만 하면 됐어 Good! That will do.

옴[1] the itch ; scabies ; 〖의학〗 ascariasis ; psora ; scotch fiddle 《속》; mange (가축의)

옴[2] the tiny process around nipple of a new mother

옴[3] 〖물리〗 an ohm ¶ 옴의 법칙 Ohm's law
—계(計) an ohmmeter

옴나위 room to budge ; elbowroom ¶ 옴나위 없다 be jammed〔packed〕 in tight ; have no elbowroom // 전차 안은 너무 사람이 많아서 옴나위 없었다 The streetcar was so closely packed that I could not move.

옴니버스 영화 **—映畫** an omnibus film

옴니암니 miscellaneous〔sundry〕 expenses ; sundries
옴두꺼비 a warty old toad
옴 살 bosom friendship ; intimacy ; one flesh
옴실거리다 swarm 《in, a..bout》; [장소가 주어] crawl 《with》 ¶ 땅에는 개미떼가 옴실거리고 있었다 The ground was crawling with ants.
옴종 —腫 a sore caused by itch ; scabies bumps
옴죽거리다 squirm ; wriggle
옴직거리다 squirm ; wriggle
옴질거리다 ① [오물거리다] mumble ; chew on ② [주저하다] (be) slow〔tardy〕 《in doing》; sluggish ; linger ; dawdle ; dillydally ; shilly-shally ; waver ; hesitate ¶ 옴질거리다가 기회를 놓치다 dally away one's opportunity // 옴질거릴 시간이 없다 We have no time to lose. /Waste no time. /Don't be long about it. /Get wise there. /Make it snappy. // 무얼 그렇게 옴질거리고 있느냐 What are you loitering there for?
옴질옴질 ① [입을] mumbling ; slowly chewing ② [꾸물댐] slowly ; tardily ; lingering ③ [움직임] slowly timidly
옴쭉달싹 with a very slight〔the slightest〕 move ; budging slightly ¶ 옴쭉달싹 않다 do not budge〔stir, move〕 an inch // 옴쭉달싹 못할 지경이다 be in a fix〔pinch〕
옴쭉못하다 [움직이지 못하다] cannot budge 《a thing》; [기를 못펴다] be stuck 《with》
옴츠러들다 shrink up ; cower ; flinch ; quail ; wince ; recoil ⇨ 움츠러들다
옴츠러뜨리다 contract ; shrink up ⇨ 움츠러뜨리다
옴츠러지다 ⇨ 옴츠러들다
옴츠리다 contract ; shrink up ⇨ 움츠리다
옴큼 a handful 《of》
옴키다 ⇨ 움키다
옴파다 bore out (움파다)
옴파리 a small porcelain bowl shaped like an eggplant
옴팍눈 sunken〔deep-set〕 eyes ; [사람] a person with sunken〔deep-set〕 eyes ; a hollow-eyed person
옴패다 get pitted〔dented, sunken〕 ; become hollow ; become depressed ; form a hollow ¶ 옴패인 곳 a sunken place ; a depression // 폭우로 땅이 옴팼다 The ground was pitted by heavy rains. /The rain has caused a depression.
옴포동이같다 [어린애가] (be) plump and dimply ; [옷이] be soft and fluffy ; be plump with cotton padding
***옴 폭** —하 다 (be) hollow ; deep ; sunken ; dented ¶ 눈이 옴폭하다 have deep-set〔sunken〕 eyes
옴폭옴폭 ⇨ 움푹움푹
†**옷** clothes ; garments ; dress (여자의) ; clothing 《총칭》; costume ; a uniform (제복) ; a civilian〔business〕 suit (양복) ¶ 옷을 벗은 naked ; nude ; undressed // 옷 한 벌 a suit of clothes // 어린이 옷 전문 상점 a shop that specializes in children's wear // 옷을 입다〔벗다〕 put on 〔take off〕 one's clothes ; dress〔undress〕 oneself // 옷을 입고 있다 wear clothes〔a dress〕 ; have clothes on // 옷을 입히다 put clothes on 《a person》; clothe 〔dress〕 《a child, servants》 // 옷을 바꿔 입다 change one's clothes // 옷을 입혀주다 〔벗겨주다〕 help 《a person》 into〔off with〕 his robe ; help 《a person》 dress 〔undress〕 himself // 옷이 많다 have a large〔fine〕 wardrobe // 새 옷을 입어보다 try on new clothes // 흰 옷을 입고 있다 be (dressed) in white // 좋은〔초라한〕 옷을 입고 있다 be well〔poorly〕 dressed // 급히 옷을 입다〔벗다〕 throw on〔hurry off〕 one's clothes // 입고 갈 옷이 없다 I have nothing to go in. // 아이가 커서 옷을 입을 수 없게 됐다 The child has outgrown 〔grown out of〕 his garments. // 저 여자는 옷을 멋있게 입는다 She is quite a dresser.
겉— outer garments 속— underwear
옷은 새 옷이 좋고 사람은 옛 사람이 좋다 속담 Old fish, old oil, and old friend are the best.
옷이 날개라 속담 Fine feathers make fine birds. /Apparel makes the men. /The tailor makes the man. /Good clothes open all doors. ☞ ❙ p. 1567 ❙
옷가슴 the breast 《of a coat》; [셔츠의] the shirt front ; the plastron (뗄 수 있는)
옷가지 (several kinds of) garments
옷감 cloth ; [남자의] suit material ; suiting ; [여자의] dress material ; dry goods 《미》; texture (직물) ¶ 얇은 옷감 light stuff ; thin cloth // 옷감을 마르다 cut cloth // 옷감에 물을 들이다 dye cloth
옷거리 the appearance of one's clothes ; one's (outward) appearance
옷걸이 a coat hanger (매다는 것) ; a clothes rack (거는 것)
옷고름 a coat string ; a breast-tie ¶ 옷고름을 매다〔풀다〕 tie〔untie〕 a coat string
옷기장 the length of a garment
옷깃 the collar〔neck〕 of a coat ¶ 옷깃을 세우다 turn up one's collar
옷농 —籠 a clothes chest
옷단 a hem ; a fly ¶ 옷단을 감치다 hem
옷단장하다 —丹粧— dress (oneself) up ; deck oneself out ; doll (oneself) up 《속》
옷보 —褓 ① [보] a cloth for wrapping clothes ; a cloth wrapper ¶ 옷보에 옷을 싸다 wrap up a dress in a kerchief ② [사람] a clothes-conscious person
옷상자 —箱子 a chest〔box〕 of clothes
옷셋집 —貰— a clothes-renting shop ; a rental clothier〔tailor〕

옷

1 의복에 대한 표현

▶clothes — 가장 일반적인 의미의 옷. 평상복 everyday clothes / 작업복 working clothes / 방한복 winter clothes

▶clothing — 의복에 대한 총칭. 의복 한 점 an article of clothing (=a garment; 주로 고급 옷을 뜻함)

▶dress — 주로 장식적인 견지에서의 옷을 뜻한다. 보통 코트나 하의는 제외 되고 부인복의 경우 원피스를 가리킨다. 정장 full dress / 야회복 evening dress / 남자용 주간 예복 morning dress / 결혼예복 wedding dress / 여성용 실내복 house dress / 임신복 maternity dress

▶wear — 특별한 목적을 위해 만들어진 옷. 신사복 men's wear / 아동복 children's wear / 해변에서 입는 옷 beach wear / 하복 summer wear / 운동복 sports wear / 여행복 travel wear / 방문복 visiting wear / 비옷 rain wear / 속옷 underwear

▶suit — wear와 같이 쓰인다. 수영복 bathing suit / (직장의) 근무복 business suit / 우주복 space suit / (남자의) 야회복 dress suit

▶apparel — 주로 겉옷을 말함.

▶attire — 복장·차림새의 뜻.

▶costume — 시대·민족 고유의 의상.

▶garb — 직업·시대·민족의 특수한 복장(양식).

▶castoffs (=hand-me-downs) — 헌 옷.

▶rags — 넝마옷.

▶lining — (특히 garment의) 내피.

▶outfit — 옷 한 벌.

2 옷의 종류

① 양복

▶양복 Western clothes / 신사복 men's clothes / 주문복 a custom-made suit; a suit made to order / 기성복 ready-made clothes; ready-to-wear clothes; off-the-rack suit 《미》 / 고급 부인복 haute couture (프랑스어로 high sewing의 뜻) / 나들이옷 Sunday clothes [best]

② 제복(uniform)

▶학생복 a school uniform / 세일러복 a sailor suit / 군복 a military uniform / 평상복 everyday clothes; casual wear / 사복 plain clothes / 외출복 street clothes; an outdoor dress / (죄수 등에게 징벌용으로 입혔던) 구속복 strait[straight] jacket

③ 예복(ceremonial clothes)

▶(야회용의) 예복 tuxedo[tux 《미》] (★ 주간에 입는 남성용 정장은 morning dress, 준정식 만찬회(black-tie dinner)에서 입는 턱시도에 검은 나비 넥타이 차림은 a black bow-tie, 정식 만찬회(white-tie dinner)에서 입는 연미복에 흰 나비 넥타이 차림옷은 a white bow-tie) / 연미복 a swallow-tailed coat / (대학 졸업식용) 예복 academic costumes[academicals 《영》] (옷만을 지칭할 때는 a gown) / 대학 졸업식용 각모 a mortarboard; a college cap

④ 상의

▶coat — 보통 양복 하의를 말함. 외투를 뜻하기도 한다.

▶jacket — 양복 상의. 가슴 단추가 두줄[한줄]인 양복 상의 a double-[single-] breasted jacket

▶anorak — 모자 달린 상의.

⑤ 바지

▶trousers — 보통 양복 상의를 가리킨다. 양복은 coat, vest, trousers 세 부분으로 이루어짐.

▶pants — 평상복 바지를 가리키나 미국에서는 trousers와 같은 뜻으로도 사용. 헐렁한 바지 slacks (반드시 상의와 한 벌을 이루는 것은 아니다.) / 짧은 바지 shorts / 나팔 바지 bell-bottoms / 헐렁한 바지 baggy pants / 승마용 바지 riding breeches / 바지 멜빵 suspenders 《미》; braces 《영》

⑥ 외투(outerwear)

▶오버, 외투 overcoat / 비옷 raincoat / 방수 외투 mackintosh / 트렌치 코트 trench coat (1차 대전 중 영국군이 참호 전투용으로 만들었던 방수 외투에서 유래) / 소매 없는 외투의 일종 inverness / 먼지막이 겉옷 duster / 팔의 재봉선이 겨드랑에서 목덜미로 나 있는 헐렁한 겉옷 raglan / 재봉선이 어깨에 나 있는 겉옷 set-in sleeve coat / 단춧구멍을 안으로 마감한 긴 자락의 남성용 코트 chesterfield / 폴로코트 polo (본래 경기 관전 때, 선수용으로 입었음) / 더플 코트 toggle coat; duffel (coat) (모자가 달린 긴 코트. 원래 북유럽에서 어로 작업용으로 입었음) / 선원들이 입는 두꺼운 모직의 짧은 코트 pea jacket / 바바리 코트 Burbery (영국 Burbery사의 레인코트)

⑦ 스웨터(sweater)

▶머리로부터 뒤집어 써서 입는 형태의 스웨터 pullover / 앞에 단추가 달린 스웨터 cardigan / 터틀넥 turtleneck / 선원들이 입던 깃이 없는 라운드형 스웨터 crewneck sweater

⑧ 셔츠(shirt)

▶보통 와이셔츠로 불리는 것의 원형은

white shirt / 넥타이 없이 입는 셔츠는 sport shirt / 퍼머넌트 셔츠(주름 가공된 셔츠) permanent shirt / 예복용 와이셔츠 dress shirt / 깃을 단추로 채우게 되어있는 셔츠 button-down shirt (★ 보통 런닝 셔츠라고 불리는 것은 running shirt가 아니라 sleeveless undershirt)

⑨ 속옷·내의(underwear)

▶속옷[내의] underwear; underclothes / (여자·어린이의) 속옷, 란제리 lingerie / 짧은 팬츠 briefs / (권투용) 팬티 trunks; boxer shorts / 드로어즈 팬츠 drawers / 스캔티 scanties (드러나 보이는 속옷) / 속셔츠 undershirt / 속바지 vest 《영》 / 긴 내의 long johns / (여자의) 슬립[《*pl.*》 수영복 《영》] a slip (dress속에 입는) / 브래지어 brassiere; bra / 거들 girdle / 속치마 petticoat / 네글리제 neglige; nightie; nightgown / 파자마 pajamas / 스타킹 hose

③ 입다, 벗다, 신다

▶put on — (옷을) 입다. 1회의 동작을 표현하는 가장 일반적인 말. 「벗다」는 take off. 「벗어 던지다」의 뜻으로는 get off가 쓰인다. wear는 (옷을) 입고 있는 상태를 가리킨다 (=have on).

▶dress — 몸치장, 차림 이란 뜻을 내포하여 옷을 입다, 옷을 입고 있는 상태를 나타낼 때도 쓰인다. 반대어는 undress. 몸에 걸치다[벗다]의 뜻으로는 get into [out of].

▶slip ...on [into] — 옷을 빨리 입을 때의 표현. 반대의 뜻은 slip off[out of]. 바지 등을 입을 때는 step into (반대어는 step out of). 옷을 하나하나 벗다의 뜻으로는 peel off.

④ 영·미의 표현 차이

	(미)	(영)
바지	pants	trousers
신사복	business suit	lounge suit
턱시도	tuxedo	dinner jacket
조끼	vest	waistcoat
잠옷	nightgown	nightdress
파자마	pajamas	pyjamas
화장옷	bathrobe	dressing gown
팬츠	underpants	pants
모닝코트	cutaway	morning dress
멜빵	suspenders	braces
속셔츠	undershirt	vest

옷자락 the lower ends of clothes ; the skirt ; the train ¶ 옷자락을 끌다 trail 〔drag〕 the skirt // 옷자락을 걷어 올리다 tuck up the skirt

옷장 —欌 a clothes chest ; a wardrobe

옷차림 dress ; attire ; getup ; one's (personal) appearance ¶ 옷차림이 훌륭하다〔좋지 않다〕 be well〔ill〕 dressed // 옷차림이 얌전하다 be neat in one's dress ; be neatly turned out ; keep oneself neat and trim ; look neat and tidy // 옷차림이 꾀죄죄하다 be shabbily〔poorly〕 dressed ; be humbly clad // 검소한 옷차림을 하고 있다 be simply dressed // 나는 옷차림에 신경을 안 쓴다 I don't care how I dress〔what I look like〕. // 저 여자는 옷차림이 너저분하다 She is slovenly in her dress.

옷치레 dressing up ; rich attire **—하다** dress up ; wear fine clothes

옹 癰 《의학》 a carbuncle ; an anthrax

옹 翁 an aged〔old〕 man ¶ 도산옹 the old Mr. *Tosan*

옹고집 壅固執 obstinacy ; stubbornness ; bigotry ; a stubborn person (사람)

옹골지다 (be) well-filled ; substantial ; solid

옹골차다 (be) hard ; solid ; sturdy ; firm ¶ 옹골찬 사람 a person of sturdy build

옹구 a pack-saddle

옹구바지 trousers which droop around the ankles

옹그리다 crouch ; squat down ; draw in a limb ¶ 다리를 옹그리다 draw in one's legs // 팔을 옹그리다 pull in one's arms

옹글다 (be) intact ; whole ; unbroken ¶ 옹근 수 an unbroken number ; a whole number

옹긋옹긋, 옹긋쫑긋 sprouting up〔standing out〕 unevenly **—하다** be bristly with points sprouting up unevenly ; bristle

옹기 甕器 pottery with a dark brown glaze ⇨ 오지그릇

옹기옹기, 옹기종기 thickly ; densely

옹기장수 甕器— a pottery dealer ; an earthenware dealer

옹기장이 甕器匠— a potter

옹기전 甕器廛 a pottery shop

옹달 a hollow ; a depression ¶ 옹달에 빗물이 고였다 The rain water has collected in a depression.

—샘 a small spring〔well, fountain〕 **—솥** a small deep iron pot **— 시루** a small deep earthenware steamer **— 우물** a small deep well

옹동고라지다 be shortened〔contracted〕

옹두라지 a small knot (on a tree) ; a gnarl

옹두리 a knot ; a knob ; a gnarl ; a node ; a knar

—뼈 the leg bone 《of cattle》

옹립 擁立 enthroning **—하다** enthrone ; give backing to ; support ; help 《a person》 to a position

옹망추니 ① being all twisted and bent in ; being all crooked and shrunken ② ⇨ 옹춘마니

옹방구리 a small water-jug

옹배기 a tiny earthenware bowl ; a small earthen vessel
옹벽 擁壁 〖토목〗 a breast〔retaining〕 wall ; a revetment
옹색하다 壅塞— ① [궁핍하다] be hard up ; be in straitened circumstances ; be in a fix ¶ 돈에 옹색하다 be hard up for money ; be pinched for money // 옹색하게 살다 be badly off ; live in poverty // 살아가기가 옹색하여지다 be in straightened circumstances // 그들은 옹색한 살림을 하고 있다 They are badly off.
② [좁은] (be) narrow ; cramped ¶ 옹색한 방 a narrow room // 집이 옹색하다 The house is too small.
옹생원 壅生員 a narrow-minded person ; an illiberal person ; a bigoted person
옹송그리다 curl up 《one's body》; crouch ; huddle ; cower ; double up ¶ 추워서 몸을 옹송그리다 huddle oneself up with cold
옹송망송하다 ⇨ 옹송옹송하다
옹송옹송하다 (be) hazy ; confused ; stupefied
옹솥 ⇨ 옹달(—솥)
옹솥 甕— an earthenware pot
옹시루 a small earthenware steamer ⇨ 옹달시루
옹알거리다 mutter ; grumble ; murmur ; babble ; grunt ¶ 혼자서 옹알거리다 grumble〔mutter〕 to oneself
옹위 擁衛 safeguard ; escort —하다 guard ; escort
옹이 a knot ; a node ; a knar ; a gnarl ; a knob ¶ 옹이 있는 gnarled
옹자배기 a tiny pottery〔earthenware〕 bowl
옹잘거리다 mutter ; grumble
옹졸하다 壅拙— (be) narrow-minded ; illiberal ; hidebound ; intolerant ¶ 그는 옹졸한 위인이다 He is a narrow-minded man.
옹종하다 (be) meager and narrow-minded
옹주 翁主 a princess ; a king's daughter by a concubine
옹추 one's bitter enemy ¶ 그들은 서로 옹추다 They are bitter enemies to each other.
옹춘마니 a bigot ; a narrow-minded person
옹크리다 ⇨ 웅그리다
옹하다 ⇨ 옹졸하다
*옹호 擁護 [보호] protection ; safeguard ; [엄호] cover ; [지원] support ; assistance ; backing —하다 support ; back up ; protect ; defend ; safeguard ; cover ; stand by ; take under one's wings〔protection〕 ¶ 옹호 하에 under the protection 《of》 // 정책을 옹호하다 support a policy // 헌정을 옹호하다 defend〔safeguard〕 the constitution // 자기의 권리를 옹호하다 safeguard one's own rights // 자유를 옹호하기 위하여 싸우다 fight in the cause of freedom // 그는 동향인을 극력 옹호한다 He firmly befriends his fellow provincials.
—자 a defender ; a supporter ; a protector ; a backer ¶ 헌정 옹호자 a guardian of constitutionalism
옻 lacquer ¶ 옻칠한 lacquered ; japanned // 옻칠한 제품 a lacquer-ware
옻오르다 관용 be poisoned with lacquer
옻을 칠하다 관용 paint with lacquer ; lacquer ; japan
옻을 타다 관용 be allergic to poison ivy
옻나무 〖식물〗 a lacquer〔varnish〕 tree
옻칠 —漆 varnishing with lacquer —하다 apply lacquer 《to》; lacquer
옻타다 be sensitive〔allergic〕 to lacquer poison
와[1] and ¶ 너와 나 you and I
†와[2] with a great roar ; with a rush ; loudly ¶ 와 웃다 roar with laughter ; burst into laughter // 와 울다 burst out crying // 와 달아나다 run away in a panic // 와 밀려가다 advance on with a rush // 사람들이 우리 집으로 와 몰려왔다 People rushed to my house in crowds.
와[3] [마소를 멈출 때] Whoa ! ; Wo !
와가 瓦家 a tile-roofed house
와각거리다 clatter ; rattle ¶ 돌이 밑에서 와각거렸다 The stones did rattle underneath.
와각와각 rattlingly ; clatteringly ; with a rattling noise
와글거리다 ① swarm ; crowd ; throng ¶ 시장에 사람들이 와글거린다 The market is jammed inside. ② be clamorous〔boisterous, tumultuous, noisy〕 ¶ 와글거리는 사람들 a clamorous crowd of people
와글와글 [북적임] in swarms〔crowds, throngs〕; [시끄럽게] clamorously ; in a boisterous manner ; noisily ¶ 와글와글 떠들다 make a boisterous noise
와닥닥 suddenly ; with a rush ; abruptly ¶ 와닥닥 방에서 뛰어나가다 rush〔bolt〕 out of the room // 와닥닥 일어서다 spring to one's feet
와당탕 thumping ; boisterously ; noisily —하다 make a thumping sound ; make a noise ¶ 아이들이 마루 위에서 와당탕거린다 Children romp around boisterously on the floor.
와당탕퉁탕 boisterously ⇨ 와당탕
와드등와드등 with thud〔thump〕; rumbling and clattering —하다 thump ; clatter
와들와들 shivering ; trembling ¶ 추워서 와들와들 떨다 shiver from cold // 무서워서〔성이나서〕 와들와들 떨다 tremble with fear〔anger〕 // 손이 와들와들 떨려서 쓸 수가 없었다 My hand trembled so much that I could not write.
와락 suddenly ; all at once ; with a rush 〔start, jerk〕 ¶ 문을 와락 열다 jerk a door open // 청중이 와락 몰려 나왔다 The

audience poured out. // 개가 어린애한테 와락 달려들었다 The dog sprang upon the child.
와락와락 jerkily ; with a sudden jerk
와류 渦流 an eddy ; a whirlpool ; a maelstrom ; 『주물』 turbulence **—하다** flow in whirls ; swirl
와르르 ① [사람이] with a rush ¶ 그들은 와르르 역으로 몰려갔다 They rushed to the station. // 군중이 와르르 몰려 들어갔다 The crowd poured〔surged〕 in.
② [물건이] clattering ; crumbling ; all in a heap ¶ 담이 와르르 무너졌다 A wall crumbled all in a heap.
③ [천둥이] rolling ; rumbling ; thundering ¶ 천둥이 와르르 울린다 The thunder rolls〔rumbles〕.
와륵 瓦礫 pieces of broken tile ; broken tiles
와병 臥病 lying in a sickbed **—하다** lie sick in bed ; be ill in bed
와삭거리다 rustle ¶ 와삭와삭 rustlingly // 가랑잎이 바람에 와삭거린다 The dead leaves rustle in the wind.
와삭와삭 with a rustle〔a rustling noise〕 **—하다** rustle
와상 臥牀 a bed ⇨ 침상
와석 臥席 lying in bed ; confinement to one's bed **—하다** lie〔be ill, be sick〕 in bed ; be laid up ; be confined to one's bed
와스스 [떨어짐] with a rustling sound ; [무너짐] crumbling ¶ 마른잎이 와스스 떨어지다 dead leaves fall thick and fast // 모래성이 와스스 무너지다 a sand castle crumbles
와신상담 臥薪嘗膽 struggling against difficulties for the sake of vengeance ; sustained determination and perseverance **—하다** go through unspeakable hardships and privations ¶ 와신상담하기 10년 after ten years of hard struggles against fortune
와싹 ⇨ 우썩
와어 訛語 a false report ; a dialect
와언 訛言 ① a false story ; a groundless rumor ② [사투리] dialect
와우 蝸牛 the snail ⇨ 달팽이
—각(殼) a snail shell ; 『해부』 the cochlea
와음 訛音 a corruption of sound ; a phonetic corruption ; a variant
와이더블유시에이 Y.W.C.A 《Young Women's Christian Association》
와이드 스크린 a wide screen
와이드 프로 『TV·라디오』 an extra-long show 《on TV》
†**와이셔츠** a shirt ¶ 와이셔츠 바람으로 in one's shirt sleeves
와이어 a wire
와이엠시에이 Y.M.C.A.《Young Men's Christian Association》
와이오밍 Wyoming 《Wyo., Wy.》
와이프 a wife 《*pl.* wives》 ; one's wife
와인 wine
와인드업 『야구』 a windup **—하다** wind up
와전 訛傳 a misrepresentation ; a false〔distorted〕 report **—하다** misrepresent ; give a false〔distorted〕 report
와전 瓦全 contenting oneself with safe mediocrity ; completing one's span of life ¶ 와전을 부끄럽게 여기다 be ashamed of having led a safe but mediocre life // 와전하느니보다 옥쇄하라 Better be a broken gem than a whole brick.
와전류 渦電流 『전기』 an eddy current
와중 渦中 a whirlpool ; a vortex ; a maelstrom ¶ …의 와중에 휩쓸려들다 be drawn into the vortex of ; become involved in the vortex of // 전쟁의 와중에 휩쓸려들다 be embroiled in war ; be involved in the maelstrom of war // 정쟁의 와중에 휩쓸리다 be involved in political strife
와지끈 smashing ; crashing ; with a crash **—하다** crash ; go smash ¶ 가구를 와지끈 부수다 smash up furniture
와짝 ① forcefully ; vigorously ¶ 줄을 와짝 잡아당기다 give a rope a vigorous pull ② all at once ; all of a sudden ; abruptly ¶ 날씨가 와짝 추워진다 The weather gets cold suddenly.
와트 ① Watt, James (영 1736~1819) ② 『물리』 a watt (of electric) bulb
—시(時) a watt-hour 《wh., whr.》
와판 瓦版 tile engraving ; 『인쇄판』 a tile block print
와해 瓦解 collapse ; fall ; breakup ; downfall ; falling to pieces ; crumbling ; disintegration **—하다** collapse ; fall to pieces ; disintegrate ; break up〔down〕 ; crumble ¶ 정당의 와해 the collapse of a political party // 로마 제국의 와해 the downfall of the Roman Empire // 내각은 불원간에 와해할 것이다 The Cabinet will soon be dissolved.
왁다그르르 with a rattle **—하다** rattle
왁다글닥다글 rattling **—하다** rattle
왁달박달 rudely ; brusquely **—하다** (be) rude ; brusque ; rough ; wild
왁댓값 heart balm given to a cuckold by an adulterer (구)
왁살스럽다 ⇨ 우악살스럽다
왁스 wax
왁시글 swarming ; thronging ; spreading out in crowds ¶ 왁시글거리다 swarm ; throng ; spread out in crowds
왁시글덕시글 ⇨ 왁시글왁시글
왁시글왁시글 in swarms〔throngs, crowds〕
왁자그르 boisterously ; uproariously ; rowdily ; with much noise **—하다** act boisterous〔rowdy〕 ; make a lot of noise
왁자지껄하다 (be) noisy ; clamorous ; boisterous ; uproarious ; rowdy ¶ 그

문제로 교실 안이 왁자지껄하다 The classroom is in an uproar over the affair.

왁자하다 ① ⇨ 왁자지껄하다 ② ⇨ 왜자하다

왁친 〖의학〗 vaccine

— **주사** a vaccine injection ; (a) vaccination ¶ 왁친 주사를 놓다 vaccinate《a person》 **생—** a live vaccine **유행성 감기 예방—** anti-influenza vaccine

*__완강 頑强__ obstinacy ; stubbornness ; persistence ; doggedness ; tenacity **—하다** (be) obstinate ; stubborn ; dogged ; unbending ; persistent ; tenacious ¶ 완강히 자기설을 주장하다 hold tenaciously to one's own view // 그들은 완강히 저항했다 They offered〔made〕 a stubborn〔stout〕 resistance. /They put up a stiff resistance.

*__완결 完結__ conclusion ; completion ; termination ; finish ; end **—하다** conclude completely ; complete ; terminate ; finish ; end ¶ 완결되다 be completed 〔concluded〕 ; be brought to an end // 사건을 완결 짓다 bring the case to a conclusion // 사전의 편찬은 일단 완결되었다 The compilation of the dictionary has practically been finished.

완경사 緩傾斜 a gentle slope

⁑**완고 頑固** stubbornness ; obstinacy ; bigotry **—하다** (be) stubborn ; stiff-necked ; bigoted ¶ 완고한 노인 a stiff-necked old man

완곡 婉曲 a roundabout way (of speaking) ; circumlocution ; euphemism **—하다** (be) euphemistic ; roundabout ; periphrastic ¶ 완곡히 말하다 insinuate ; say in a roundabout way ; beat about〔around〕 the bush // 그는 완곡하게 말하는 법이 없다 He does not mince matters.

—법 〖수사〗 euphemism : periphrasis

완공 完工 ⇨ 준공(竣工)

완구 緩球 〖야구·크리켓〗 a slow ball

완구 玩具 a toy ; a plaything

—점 a toyshop

완급 緩急 slowness and fastness ; tempo ; high and low speed

— **기호** 〖음악〗 tempo notation **—차** a brake van 《영》

완납 完納 full payment **—하다** pay in full ; pay the whole amount 《of》 ¶ 수업료를 완납하다 pay one's tuition〔fee〕 in full

⁑**완두 豌豆** a pea

완력 腕力 physical〔muscular〕 strength ; brawn ; brute force ¶ 완력으로 이기다 win by force // 완력을 사용하다 use 〔appeal to〕 force ; resort to force〔violence〕 // 우선 완력으로 그들을 이길 도리밖엔 없다 It would be best to subdue them with a strong hand. // 완력으로는 도저히 그를 이길 수 없다 I am no match for him in mere physical strength.

—가 a strong(-armed) man ; a man of muscle ; a muscleman

*__완료 完了__ completion ; conclusion ; termination ; finish ; end **—하다** complete ; finish ; conclude ¶ 완료되다 be concluded ; be completed ; be finished

— **시제** the perfect tense **현재〔과거, 미래〕 — 시제** the present〔past, future〕 perfect tense

완만 緩慢 slowness ; slackness ; dullness **—하다** (be) slow(-moving) ; lax ; slack ; inactive ; dull ; listless ¶ 그는 동작이 완만하다 He is slow-moving. /He is slow in action.

완미 頑迷 asininity ; bigotry ; obstinacy ; stubbornness **—하다** (be) asinine ; bigoted ; stupidly obstinate ; stubborn ¶ 저런 완미한 사람은 드물다 Such a bigoted person is rarely met with. // 그는 완미하여 여론의 동향을 깨닫지 못한다 He is so bigoted in his views that he is blind to the tide of public opinion.

*__완벽 完璧__ perfection ; completeness ; flawlessness **—하다** (be) perfect ; complete ; flawless ; faultless ; ideal ¶ 완벽을 기하다 aim at perfection // 완벽의 경지에 이르다 reach the stage of〔arrive at〕 perfection

완보 完補 supplementation **—하다** complement ; supplement

완보 緩步 a slow walk〔step〕 **—하다** walk slowly

완본 完本 a complete set of books ; complete works

완봉 完封 [항만 따위의] a complete blockade ; [용기 따위의] bottling〔sealing〕 up ; 〖야구〗 a shutout **—하다** blockade completely (항만 따위를) ; bottle〔seal〕 up (그릇 따위를) ; 〖야구〗 shut out ¶ 이런 식으로 계속되면 우리는 완봉패를 당할거다 If it keeps going like this, we're going to be shut out.

완비 完備 perfection ; completion ; complete provision〔arrangement, preparation〕 **—하다** perfect ; complete ; make 《a thing》 perfect ; equip〔furnish〕 completely ¶ 국방의 완비 the completion of national defense // 완비되어 있다 be completely〔thoroughly〕 furnished〔equipped〕 with ; be perfect // 그 호텔은 시설이 완비되어 있다 The hotel is completely furnished. /You will find perfection of accommodation, service and cuisine at the hotel.

완상 玩賞 enjoying ; appreciation ; admiration **—하다** enjoy ; take pleasure in ; appreciate ; admire

†**완성 完成** completion ; perfection ; accomplishment ; consummation **—하다** complete ; perfect ; finish ; accomplish ; bring 《a thing》 to perfection ¶ 발명을 완성하다 perfect an invention // 완성에 가깝다 (be) near completion // 그 빌딩은 가

을에 완성될 예정이다 The building is scheduled for completion in autumn. // 죽기 전에 이 사업을 완성하고 싶다 I hope to see the work accomplished before I die.

— 기일 the date of completion —품 a finished product ; finished goods 자기 — perfection of self

완수 完遂 successful execution ; accomplishment ; completion **—하다** bring to a successful finish〔conclusion〕; accomplish ; complete ; bring off ¶ 직책을 완수하다 perform one's duties // 목적을 완수하다 accomplish one's purpose ; attain one's object

완숙 完熟 full ripeness〔maturity〕**—하다** be fully ripened ; be in full maturity ¶ 완숙해지다 attain〔come to〕full〔complete〕maturity ; ripen into full maturity

— 계란 a hard-boiled egg

완승 完勝 a complete victory ; a sweeping victory **—하다** win a complete victory ; shut out《an opposing team》(야구에서)

완악 頑惡 wickedness ; stubbornness ; obstinacy ; bigotry **—하다** (be) wicked ; stubborn ; obstinate ; bigoted

완역 完譯 a complete translation ; a translation in full **—하다** make a complete translation《of》

완연 宛然 —하다 (be) clear ; obvious ; evident ; patent ; distinct ; vivid ¶ 완연히 clearly ; distinctly ; vividly

완연하다 — (be) wiggly ; snakelike ; serpentine ; winding ; meandering ; sinuous ¶ 완연히 기복하는 산악 rolling mountains

완우 頑愚 stupidity ; dullness ; obtuseness ; obstinacy **—하다** (be) stupid ; dull ; obtuse

완월 玩月 —하다 enjoy〔view〕the moon

완인 完人 [흠 없는] a perfect person ; [병이 나은] a person perfectly recovered

완자[1] a meatball fried in egg batter ; a kind of wonton

—탕 a kind of wonton soup

완자[2] [만자] a swastika ; a gammadion ; a fylfot ; the Buddhist symbol〔cross〕

—창 a window with a swastika-shaped frame

완장 腕章 an armband ; a brassard ; a chevron (계급장)

†**완전 完全** perfection ; completeness ; wholeness ; integrity **—하다** (be) perfect ; complete ; entire ; whole ; finished ; consummate ; integral ¶ 완전히 to perfection ; perfectly ; completely ; wholly ; entirely ; thoroughly // 완전무결한 absolutely perfect ; perfect and faultless // 완전하게 하다 perfect ; complete ; consummate ; make perfect ; bring《a thing》to perfection // 완전하게 되다 be made perfect ; become complete ; be brought〔carried〕to perfection ; be consummated // 완전을 기하다 aim at perfection // 완전한 성공을 거두다 gain a complete success // 완전히 실패하다 fail utterly〔completely〕// 완전히 속다 be completely taken in // 완전의 경지에 달하다 attain to〔reach〕perfection ; make oneself perfect // 나의 영어는 아직 완전치 못하다 My English leaves much to be desired. /My English is far from perfection. // 어떤 일에서나 완전을 바랄 수는 없다 Perfection cannot be expected in anything. // 그 건물은 아직 완전히 끝나지 않았다 The building is not entirely finished yet. // 나는 그 일을 완전히 끝마쳤다 I have finished the work thoroughly.

— 가동(稼動)〔조업〕full operation — 경기 〖야구〗 a perfect game — 고용 full employment — 범죄 a perfect crime — 분석 complete analysis — 연소 perfect combustion — 종지 〖음악〗 the perfect cadence

완전 고용 完全雇用 full employment

완전 무결 完全無缺 absolute perfection **—하다** (be) perfect and faultless ; absolutely perfect ; flawless ¶ 완전 무결한 사람은 없다 No one is perfect and faultless.

완제 完濟 ① [완료] completion ② [완불] full〔complete〕payment ; liquidation **—하다** pay in full ; clear off《one's debts》; liquidate

완주하다 完走— [경기에서] run the whole distance ; stay the course

완초 莞草 〖식물〗 a rush

‡**완충 緩衝** shock-absorbing ; concussion-deadening ; buffing **—하다** buff ; absorb shock ; deaden concussion

—국 a buffer country〔state〕—기 a buffer ; a bumper —물 a fender pile —액 a buffer solution — 장치 a buffer ; a shock absorber ; a fender — 지대 a buffer〔neutral〕zone —판 a deadblock —회로 a buffer circuit

완치 完治 a perfect cure ; a complete recovery **—하다** be completely cured〔recovered〕¶ 3개월 만에 상처는 완치되었다 At the end of three months the last bandages were removed.

완쾌 完快 complete recovery《from illness, of health》**—하다** recover (completely)《from》; be restored to health ; get well ¶ 어쨌든 내 딸은 겨우 완쾌할 수 있었다 Somehow my daughter managed to pull through.

완투 完投 —하다 〖야구〗 pitch〔hurl〕a whole game〔the full nine innings〕; go the full distance〔entire route〕

— 투수 a pitcher who goes the (entire) route

완패 完敗 a complete defeat ; a crushing defeat **—하다** suffer a complete defeat ¶ 완전히 완패당했네 I've been totally wiped out.

완하제 緩下劑 a laxative ; an aperient
완행 緩行 going slow ; running slow **—하다** go slow ; run slow
— 열차 a local train ; a slow train
*완화 緩和** relief ; mitigation ; alleviation ; pacification **—하다** relieve ; mitigate ; alleviate ; ease ; lighten ; mollify ¶ 교통난을 완화하다 relieve traffic congestion // 제한을 완화하다 relax〔lighten〕 restrictions // 학교 증설에 의해서 입학난은 어느 정도 완화될 것이다 The establishment of more schools will somewhat ease the difficulty of entering higher schools.
— 곡선 an easement curve ; a transition curve〔spiral〕 **— 정책** an appeasement policy **—제** a mitigative ; a palliative ; a relaxant **—책** a neutralizing〔an alleviating〕 measure **국제간 긴장 —** an easing of strained relations〔political tensions〕 between nations ; a détente 《프》 **냉전 —** the easing〔relaxation〕 of the cold war **자극 —제** an abirritant
왈 曰 [가로되] said ; quoth ; [소위] so-called ; so called ¶ 공자 왈 Confucius〔The Master〕 said... // 그는 왈 자유주의자다 He is a so-called liberal.
왈(曰) 자가 망하여도 왼다리질 하나는 남는다 속담 It is hard to make an old mare leave flinging.
왈가닥 a (saucy) jade ; a hussy ; a minx ; a tomboy ¶ 그녀는 왈가닥이다 She is a hussy.
왈가닥거리다 clatter ; rattle ¶ 창문이 왈가닥거린다 The window rattles. // 마차가 왈가닥거리며 간다 A cart clatters along.
왈가닥달가닥 rattling and clattering **—하다** rattle and clatter
왈가왈부 曰可曰否 an argument pro and con **—하다** argue pro and con ; argue for and against
왈각거리다 ⇨ 왈가닥거리다
왈딱 suddenly ; abruptly ; unceremoniously ; brusquely ; without warning
왈왈하다 (be) quick-tempered ; hot-tempered ; rough ; violent ¶ 성미가 왈왈하다 be quick-tempered
*왈츠** 《dance》 a waltz
왈칵 all of a sudden ; all at once ; with a jerk ¶ 왈칵 잡아당기다 pull 《a thing》 with a jerk // 왈칵 성을 내다 flare up ; fly into a passion // 왈칵 일어서다 spring to one's feet
왈칵하다 (be) quick-tempered ; hot-brained ; hot-tempered ; irascible
왈패 曰牌 [남자] a roughneck ; a rowdy ; a wild fellow ; [여자] a tomboy ; a hoyden ; a hussy ; a flapper
왔다갔다 coming and going **—하다** come and go ; walk about ; loiter ; stroll ; wander (배회) ¶ 거리를 왔다갔다하다 stroll aimlessly through the streets // 해변을 왔다갔다하다 take a stroll on the beach // 길에 사람들이 많이 왔다갔다한다 There is much traffic in the street. // 그 두 사람 사이에 편지가 여러번 왔다갔다했다 Many letters were exchanged between the two. // 나는 매일 서울과 인천을 왔다갔다한다 Everyday I make several trips between *Seoul* and *Inchon*.
왕 王 a king ; a monarch (군주) ; a ruler (통치자) ; a prince ¶ 왕의 royal // 짐승의 왕 the king of beasts // 자동차왕 an automobile magnate〔king〕 // 꽃 중의 왕 the queen of flowers // 왕을 세우다 set 《a person》 on the throne // 왕을 폐하다 depose〔dethrone〕 a king // 사자는 백수의 왕이다 The lion is (the) king of beasts. // 장미꽃은 백화의 왕이다 The rose is (the) queen of flowers.
†**왕- 王** [큰] large ; big ; king-size ; giant ¶ 왕밤 giant chestnuts
왕가 枉駕 attendance ; presence ; visit ⇨ 왕림
왕가 王家 a royal family
왕개미 王— a Hercules ant ; an army ant ; Camponotus ligniperdus (학명)
왕거미 王— a large spider ; a garden spider ; Araneus ventricosus (학명)
왕게 a king crab ; a horseshoe crab ; a helmet crab ; Alaskan crab ; Paralithodes camtschatius (학명)
*왕겨 王—** chaff ; rice hulls〔bran, husks〕
왕고모 王姑母 a sister of one's father's father
왕고장 王考丈 your〔his, etc.〕 deceased grandfather
왕골 a rush ; a bulrush
— 자리 a rush mat
왕공 王公 kings and dukes ; the nobility 《총칭》
†**왕관 王冠** a crown ; a diadem
†**왕국 王國** a kingdom ; a monarchy
왕궁 王宮 the King's Palace ; the Royal Palace
왕권 王權 royal authority〔prerogatives〕 ; sovereign powers〔rights〕 ; regality ; [왕위] the throne ; royalty ; sovereignty ; the scepter ¶ 왕권을 잡다 hold regal sway
— 신수설 (the theory of) the divine right of kings
왕기 a large ceramic bowl
왕기 王旗 a king's color ; a royal standard
*왕녀 王女** a royal princess ; a princess ; a princely daughter
왕년 往年 the years gone by ; the past ; former years ¶ 왕년의 대 선수 a star player in the days gone by
왕눈이 王— a person with large〔big〕 eyes ; a large-eyed person
왕당 王黨 the Royalists ; the Tories (영국의)
왕대 王— a kind of large bamboo
왕대부인 王大夫人 《your, his》 (esteemed) grandmother

왕대비 王大妃 the Queen Dowager ; the Queen Mother

왕대인 王大人 《your, his》 (esteemed) grandfather

왕도 王道 the royal road ; kingship ; kingcraft ; the rule of right ; righteous government ; the principles of royalty ¶ 왕도와 패도 the rule of right and the rule of might // 왕도로써 다스리다 rule one's people with justice // 학문에는 왕도가 없다 There is no royal road to learning.

왕도 王都 the capital (of a kingdom)

왕둥발가락 王— very coarse and thick cloth

*__왕래 往來__ ① [통행] come-and-go ; comings and goings ; (street) traffic ; passing of people (on the road) **—하다** come and go ¶ 차마의 왕래 the vehicular traffic // 왕래를 금하다 block traffic ; be closed to traffic // 왕래가 빈번한 거리 a busy thoroughfare // 사람의 왕래 the traffic of men ; the pedestrian traffic // 사람의 왕래가 그치다 be deserted // 왕래가 빈번하다 Traffic is heavy. // 왕래가 드물다 Traffic is light. // 이 거리는 왕래가 빈번하다〔적다〕 There is much〔little〕 traffic on this street〔road〕. // 그 곳에서 놀고 있으면 왕래에 방해가 된다 You will obstruct traffic if you play there.
② [친교] intercourse ; correspondence **—하다** associate with ; have intercourse〔keep company〕 with ; exchange letters with (서신 왕래) ¶ 대관들과 왕래하다 be in communication with high officials // 나는 그와 왕래가 있다 I am on visiting terms with him. // 요즘 그 사람하고 편지 왕래가 없다 I have no correspondence with him. // 저런 사람하고 왕래를 해서는 안 된다 Don't keep company with such a man.

왕로 往路 one's way to 《a place》 ; an outward journey〔trip〕 ¶ 왕로에는 배를 탔다 I went there by ship〔boat〕.

왕릉 王陵 a royal mausoleum 《*pl.* -lea》 ; a royal tomb

왕림 枉臨 coming to visit ; deigning to visit ; attendance ; presence ; visit **—하다** come to visit ; deign to visit ; honor 《us》 with a visit ; attend ; visit ¶ 선생의 왕림을 고대하나이다 We look forward to your attendance.

왕립 王立 ¶ 왕립의 royal

왕마디 王— a large knot (나무의) ; a large node (대나무 따위의) ; the biggest knot〔joint〕

왕명 王命 the king's order ; a royal order 〔command〕 ¶ 왕명으로 by royal order // 왕명에 따라 in obedience to a royal command

왕모래 王— coarse sand ; grit

왕밤 王— a large〔giant〕 chestnut

왕방 往訪 paying a visit ; a call **—하다** pay a visit to ; go and see ; call on 《a person》 at 《a place》 ; visit ¶ 왕방한 기자 a pressman who called 《on a person》

왕방울 王— a big〔large〕 bell ¶ 눈이 왕방울 같다 have big eyes ; have eyes like saucers

왕벌 王— a carpenter bee (호박벌) ; a hornet (말벌) ; a queen bee

왕법 王法 the king's law

⁑**왕복 往復** coming and going ; going and returning ; a return〔round〕 《미》 trip **—하다** go and return ; ply between (배가) ; run between ¶ 서울 수원간을 왕복하는 기차 a train running between *Seoul* and *Suwon* // 여기서 부산까지의 왕복 요금은 얼마입니까 How much is the return fare from here to *Pusan*? // 대전까지의 왕복 차표를 주시오 Give me a return ticket for *Taejon*. // 도보로 왕복 시간이 얼마나 걸립니까 How long does it take to walk there and back? // 외길 차표를 드릴까요 왕복으로 드릴까요 Do you want a one-way or a round-trip ticket?
— 비행 a round-trip〔shuttle〕 flight **— 여행** a double journey ; a round trip 《미》 ; a forward and backward journey **— 엽서** a return postcard ; a reply-paid postcard **— 요금** a double fare ; a return fare **— 차비** fare both ways ; round-trip fare **— 차표** a round-trip ticket 《미》 ; a return ticket 《영》 **—편** shuttle service **— 항해** a return voyage

왕복 운동 往復運動 〖기계〗 reciprocation ; an alternating motion
전후 — a stroke

왕봉 王蜂 〖곤충〗 a queenbee ⇨ 장수벌, 여왕벌

왕부 王父 one's grandfather

⁑**왕비 王妃** a queen ; an empress

왕사 王師 [왕의 군사] the Royal army ; [왕의 스승] a King's teacher

왕사 王事 the affairs of the King

왕새우 王— 〖동물〗 a (Yellow Sea) prawn

왕생 往生 death ; 《one's》 end ; extinction of life ; passing to the next world **—하다** die ; depart this life ; pass away (to the next world) ¶ 극락 왕생을 빌다 pray for rebirth in paradise

왕생 극락 往生極樂 going after death to Nirvana〔Buddhist paradise〕 ; euthanasia ; an easy passage into eternity **—하다** go after death to Nirvana ; go to paradise ; die an easy and peaceful death ; pass away peacefully

왕성 王城 the capital of a kingdom

왕성 旺盛 a prosperous〔flourishing, thriving〕 condition ; a fine〔an excellent〕 condition **—하다** (be) excellent ; prosperous ; flourishing ; thriving ; vigorous ; energetic ; full of vigor ¶ 혈기 왕성한 청년 a vigorous〔lusty, hot-blooded〕 youth // 원기 왕성하다 be full of vigor〔energy〕 ; be in high〔excellent〕 spirits // 사기가 왕성하다 be in excellent spirits ; be in high morale // 군의 사기는 매우 왕성하다 The army is highly spirited. // 우리 선수들은 모두가 원기 왕성하다 Our champions are in fine〔prime〕 condition. /Our champions are all full of beans.

왕세손 王世孫 the eldest son of the Crown Prince ; the eldest grandson of the King ⦅in a direct line⦆

왕세자 王世子 the Crown Prince ; the Heir Apparent to the Throne

—비 the consort of the Crown Prince ; the Crown Princess

왕손 王孫 a grandchild of a king ; the royal grandchildren〔descendants〕

왕수 王水 〚화학〛 aqua regia

왕시 往時 old days ; former years

왕신 a cantankerous person ; a cross-grained person

왕실 王室 the royal household ; the royal family〔house〕

왕얽이 王— [새끼의] thick straw weaving ; [짚신] thick-straw sandals

왕업 王業 the rule〔reign〕 of a king ; kingship ; kingcraft ; royal statesmanship ; the royal cause ¶ 왕업을 다하다 identify oneself with the royal cause

왕왕 往往 occasionally ; now and then ; from time to time ; once in a while ; more often than not ; at times ¶ 학생들에게 왕왕 있는 일이지만 as is often the case with students // 이런 일이 왕왕 있다 Such things are apt to happen. // 그런 학생이 왕왕 눈에 띈다 Such a student is not unfrequently met with. // 여자들 가운데는 왕왕 이러한 사상을 가진 사람이 있다 There are not a few women who are imbued with these thoughts. // 그것은 왕왕 있는 일이다 It is a matter of no uncommon occurrence. // 의견의 차이가 왕왕 생긴다 Differences of viewpoint may arise from time to time.

†**왕위 王位** the throne ; the crown ¶ 왕위 계승 succession to the throne // 왕위에 오르다 ascend〔accede to〕 the throne // 왕위를 찬탈하다〔다투다〕 usurp〔contend for〕 the throne // 왕위를 버리다 abdicate the throne ; lay down one's crown // 왕위에서 쫓아내다 dethrone ⦅a king⦆ // 왕위에 있다 be on the throne // 왕위 계승의 다음 차례이다 be next in line of succession to the throne

왕위 王威 Royal prestige〔power〕

†**왕자 王子** a prince ; a royal prince

왕자 王者 a king ; a monarch ; a sovereign ; a ruler ¶ 정구계의 왕자 the champion of the tennis world

왕자 往者 a former time

왕잠자리 王— 〚곤충〛 a large dragonfly ; Anax parthenope (학명)

왕정 王政 the royal regime ; the kingly rule ; monarchy

— 복고 the Restoration of Imperial 〔Royal〕 Rule ; the reestablishment of 〔return to〕 the Imperial regime **— 복고 운동** a monarchy movement **— 복고주의자** a monarchist

***왕조 王朝** a dynasty ¶ 조선 왕조 the *Chosŏn* Dynasty ; the Dynasty of the *Chosŏn* Kings

왕족 王族 the royal family ; the royal line ; royalty ; a member of royalty (개인)

왕존장 王尊長 ⦅your, his⦆ grandfather

†**왕좌 王座** the throne ; [수위] supremacy ; the premier position ; first place ¶ 왕좌를 차지하다 hold the foremost position ⦅among⦆ ; the premier position // 그의 왕좌는 요지부동이다 His premier position is unshaken.

— 결정전 a championship contest〔tournament〕 ; the finals

왕지 〚건축〛 a triangular gable tile

왕지 王旨 the king's〔royal〕 order〔directive〕

왕지네 王— a large centipede

왕지도리 王— 〚건축〛 a beam at the corner of a column

***왕진 往診** a doctor's visit (to a patient) ; a house call by a physician **—하다** go out to see a patient ; make a call on a patient ; visit a patient ; make a professional visit ; go and see a patient at his house ¶ 선생님은 왕진중이십니다 The doctor is away on his round of visits.

—료 a fee for a doctor's visit ; the house-call charge ¶ 의사의 왕진료는 50달러다 The doctor's fee for a visit will be fifty dollars. **— 시간** hours for sick calls〔visiting patients〕 **야간 —** a night call

왕참하다 往參— go and participate ⦅in⦆ ; go to join (in) ⦅a party⦆

왕청되다 be widely disparate ; be poles apart ; be as different as light and darkness

왕콩 王— a big〔large, giant〕 bean

왕토 王土 the royal domain

왕통 王統 the Royal descendants ; the Royal line

왕화 王化 civilizing influence ⦅of a king⦆ ; the benevolent rule of the sovereign

왕후 王后 the queen〔empress〕

왕후 王侯 kings and princes ; princes and lords ; royalty ⦅총칭⦆ ¶ 왕후의 영화 regal splendor // 왕후 같은 생활을 하다 live like a prince // 왕후의 집안에서 태어나다 be born in the purple

†**왜** why ; how ; for what reason〔purpose〕 ; on what ground ¶ 왜냐하면 because ; for ; the reason is // 왜 그런지 without knowing why ; somehow // 왜 그런지 나는 모르겠다 I cannot tell you why. // 왜 늦었느냐 Why were you late ? // 왜 사직을 하느냐 What reasons have you for your resignation ? // 저 여자는 왜 저렇게

울고 있는가 Why is she weeping like that? // 너는 왜 그렇게 웃느냐 What makes you laugh like that?

왜 倭 Japan; Japanese

*왜가리 〖새〗 a common heron

왜간장 倭—醬 Japanese soysauce〔soy〕

왜곡 歪曲 ⇨ 의곡(歪曲)

왜골 a boor; a large fierce person; a rude fellow

왜골참외 a kind of cantaloup(e)

왜구 倭寇 Japanese invaders〔pirates〕; Japanese pirate raiders

왜그르르 crumbly **—하다** (be) crumbly ¶ 밥이 왜그르르하다 rice is too flaky

왜글왜글 ⇨ 왜그르르

왜나막신 倭— 〔게다〕 (a pair of) Japanese clogs〔sandals〕

왜난목 倭—木 ⇨ 내공목(內供木)

왜낫 a fine-bladed sickle; a light sickle with a thin short blade

왜낫 倭— a light sickle with a thin short blade

왜녀 倭女 a Japanese woman〔girl〕

왜놈 倭— a Jap; a Japanese; the Japanese 《총칭》

왜떡 倭— a Japanese cracker; a rice cracker

왜뚜리 a large〔bulky〕 thing

왜뚤삐뚤 zigzag; wiggling; squiggly ¶ 왜뚤삐뚤 걸어가다 go zigzag // 글을 왜뚤삐뚤 쓰다 write crooked letters; write letters in a crooked line

왜림 矮林 a thicket of shrubs

왜말 倭— Japanese; the Japanese language

왜바람 a changeable wind; a fickle wind

왜반물 dark blue dyestuffs

왜색 倭色 Japanese manners (and customs); Japanese ways; things Japanese ¶ 왜색을 일소하다 make a clean sweep of Japanese manners

왜성 矮星 〖천문〗 a dwarf star

왜소 矮小 being short and small; dwarfishness **—하다** (be) short and small; diminutive; dwarfish

왜식 倭式 Japanese style ¶ 순 왜식 주택 a classic Japanese house

왜식 倭食 Japanese-style food; a Japanese (-style) meal; Japanese cooking〔cuisine〕

—집 a Japanese restaurant

왜옥 矮屋 a small flat house

왜이이 倭— a joining of pieces of wood by splicing **—하다** splice 《pieces of wood》

왜인 倭人 a Japanese; the Japanese 《총칭》

왜인 矮人 a midget; a pigmy; a dwarf

왜자기다 behave boisterously; horse around

왜자하다 〔소문이〕 be widespread; be abroad; be rife ¶ 그가 파산했다는 소문이 왜자하다 A rumor is widely abroad that he has gone bankrupt. // 그가 체포되었다는 소문이 왜자하다 A rumor of his arrest is rife.

왜장 倭將 a Japanese general〔commander〕

왜장녀 —女 a virago; a termagant; an Amazon; a female impersonator (가면극에서)

왜적 倭敵 the enemy Japan; the Japanese foe

왜적 倭賊 Japanese invader〔pirates〕

왜정 倭政 Japanese rule: the Japanese reign

—시대 the period of the Japanese administration in Korea (1910~45); the Japanese administration period

왜죽왜죽 with rapid strides ¶ 왜죽왜죽 걷다 walk with rapid strides

왜쭉왜쭉 puckering up the lips ¶ 왜쭉왜쭉 성내다 pucker up one's lips with anger

왜청 倭青 Japanese indigo dye

왜태 —太 〖물고기〗 a kind of large pollack (명태)

왜퉁스럽다 (be) queer and silly

왜틀비틀 zigzag; tottering; reeling ¶ 왜틀비틀 걷다 go zigzag

왜풍 倭風 Japanese style; Japanese manners〔customs〕

왜풍 —風 a changeable wind

왝왝 keck keck!; urp urp!; puke puke! **—하다** keck; retch ¶ 먹은 것을 왝왝 다 게우다 throw〔bring〕 up all one has eaten; vomit〔gag, cat 《영·구》〕 all one has eaten

왱 〔벌 따위〕 with a hum〔buzz〕; 〔돌팔매〕 with a twang; 〔바람〕 with a whistle **—하다** hum; buzz; twang; whistle

왱그랑댕그랑 clink; clank; with a clang; clattering ¶ 종을 왱그랑댕그랑 울리다 clang the bell // 놋그릇들이 왱그랑댕그랑 선반에서 떨어졌다 The brass dishes and bowls fell off the shelf with a loud clatter.

왱왱 whistling; 《boys read》 aloud; noisily **—하다** 〔바람이〕 whistle; 〔책을〕 read aloud; 〔벌레가〕 drone; buzz; boom ¶ 왱왱하는 바람소리 a whistling sound // 바람이 소나무 사이로 왱왱 스친다 The wind whistles through the pine trees. // 아이들이 교실에서 글을 왱왱 읽고 있다 The boys are reading at the top of their voices in the classroom.

외 a cucumber ⇨ 오이

외- 〔홑〕 only; one; single; lone; sole; isolated

—아들 the only son

외 椳 a lath; a lattice-strip

†외 外 ① 〔이외〕 except; but; save; besides; in addition 《to》 ¶ 그 외 the rest // 그 외에 outside of that; except; except for that; in addition; besides // 이들 원인 외에 above and beyond these causes // 이 외에는 아무 것도 가진 것이 없

다 I have nothing but this. //그는 학교 외에는 아무 데도 가지 않았다 He went nowhere except to school. //나 외에 여섯 명의 아이들이 거기에 있었다 Six boys were there besides me. //그 사람 외에는 전원이 갔다 We all went except him. //나는 독서하고 산책하는 일 외에는 아무 할 일이 없다 There is nothing for me to do except to read or take a walk.
② [바깥] outside ; out 《of》 ; outer ; foreign ¶ 시외에 outside the city //권한 외의 행위를 하다 do an act in excess of one's authority

외가 外家 one's mother's maiden home ¶ 외가의 친척 a relative on the mother's side //외가의 할아버지 one's maternal grandfather

외가닥 a single strand

외각 外殼 a shell ; a crust ; an outer covering

외각 外角 〖기하〗 an exterior〔external〕 angle ; 〖야구〗 the outcorner ; the outside

외간 外艱 mourning for a father ¶ 외간을 당하다 go into mourning for one's father
—상(喪) ⇨ 외간

외갈래 a single fork
—길 a road with a single fork

외감 外感 [감기] a cold

외객 外客 a guest ; a visitor

외견 外見 (external) appearance ¶ 외견상(으로는) to all appearance(s) ; externally ; for the sake of appearance ; for show //외견으로 사람을 판단하다 judge 《a person》 by appearance

외겹 one〔a single〕 fold〔layer〕 《of cloth, wood》 ; one ply ¶ 외겹의 single ; one-ply ; onefold

외경 畏敬 awe and respect ; reverence
—하다 revere ; venerate ; reverence ; hold 《a person》 in awe〔reverence〕 ; stand in awe of 《a person》 ¶ 외경할 만한 august ; awful

‡**외계 外界** the external〔outer〕 world ; the outside ; 〖철학〗 external phenomena ; the physical world (정신계에 대한) ¶ 외계와의 교통이 끊어지다 be shut off from the outer world
—론 〖철학〗 externalism

외고리눈 a single eye with white-ringed iris

외고집 —固執 (single-minded) stubbornness ; obduracy ; obstinacy ; mulishness ¶ 외고집의 obstinate ; obdurate ; stubborn ; mulish ; pigheaded ; unyielding
—쟁이 a pigheaded person ; a stubborn 〔an obstinate〕 person ¶ 그는 외고집쟁이다 He is a stiff-necked person.

외골목 a single alley〔back-lane〕

외곬 a single way ; a single track ; a single groove ; an unforked road ; a road without a fork all along ¶ 외곬으로 intently ; simply ; solely ; straightforwardly //외곬으로 생각하는 사람 a person with a one-track mind //외곬으로 생각하다 see things from only one point of view //외곬으로 공부하다 devote oneself to one's studies //그는 그녀만을 외곬으로 생각했다 He conceived a single-minded affection for her.

*****외과 外科** surgery ¶ 외과 수술을 받다 undergo a surgical operation ; be under surgical treatment
— 병동 a surgical ward **— 수술** a surgical operation **— 수술실** an operating room **—용 기구류** surgical instruments **— 의사** a surgeon **— 의원** a surgery **— 조수** a dresser **임상〔정형〕 —** clinical 〔orthopedic〕 surgery

외과피 外果皮 〖식물〗 an exocarp ; an epicarp

외곽 外廓 ① [성] the outer wall (of a walled city) ② [바깥 테두리] an outer ring ; the outer block ; the outline
— 단체 an auxiliary organ ; an outer 〔outside〕 organization ; [관청의] an extra-governmental〔extra-departmental〕 body

†**외관 外觀** (external, outward) appearance ; an outward show〔aspect〕 ; an exterior view ; 〖철학〗 externality ¶ 외관상 externally ; seemingly ; in appearance ; to all appearance(s) //건물의 외관 the exterior of a building //외관을 꾸미다 show off //외관으로 사람을 판단하다 judge (of) 《a person》 by appearance //사물의 외관을 꿰뚫다 pierce beneath the surface of things //외관은 믿을 수 없다 Appearances are deceptive. //그 건물은 외관이 훌륭하다 The building looks fine externally.

외광 外光 〖회화〗 outdoor daylight ; plein air 《프》
—파 화가 a pleinairist

*****외교 外交** diplomacy ; diplomatic relations (관계) ; foreign policy (정책) ; [권유] soliciting ; canvassing ¶ 외교의 diplomatic //외교에 능한 사람 a diplomat ; a diplomatist ; a diplomatic person //외교적 수완 diplomatic talent //외교 관계를 단절하다 break off diplomatic relations 《with》 //외교 관계를 수립하다 establish diplomatic relations 《with》 //외교를 재개하다 revive diplomatic relations 《with》 //분쟁을 외교로 해결하다 settle a dispute by diplomatic negotiations //한국 정부는 외교가 서툴다고 말하는 사람들도 있다 Some say that the Korean Government is wanting in diplomatic skill. //그는 외교관으로서 여러 나라에 주재했었다 He held diplomatic posts in several countries. //회사에서의 나의 일은 외교이다 My work in the company is canvassing. //그는 외교를 아주 잘한다 He is quite a diplomatist.

—가 a diplomatic person ; a diplomatist —계 diplomatic services —관 a diplomat(ist) ; a diplomatic official ; a foreign service officer ¶ 외교관 시험 the Foreign〔Diplomatic〕 Service Examination // 외교관 근무 diplomatic service // 직업 외교관 a career diplomat // 외교관이 되다 enter the diplomatic service — 관계 diplomatic〔foreign〕 relations ¶ 외교 관계를 수립하다 establish diplomatic relations 《with》 // 외교 관계를 끊다 break off〔sever〕 diplomatic relations 《with》 — 교섭〔담판〕 diplomatic negotiations — 기관 the diplomatic machinery〔channels〕 —단 the diplomatic body〔corps〕 ; the corps diplomatique — 단절 diplomatic cessation — 문서 a diplomatic note〔document〕 — 문제 a diplomatic question 〔issue〕 — 백서 a diplomatic white paper — 사령 diplomatic language — 사절단 a diplomatic mission —술 diplomatic skill ; diplomacy —원 a canvasser ; a representative ; a sales agent ; a solicitor 《미》 ; a commercial〔traveling〕 salesman ; a drummer — 정세 a foreign diplomacy situation — 정책 a foreign policy — 특권 a diplomatic privilege 강경〔연약〕 — a strong 〔weak〕 foreign policy 공개〔비밀, 무력〕 — open〔secret, armed〕 diplomacy 달러 — dollar diplomacy 문화〔경제〕 — cultural〔economic〕 diplomacy 초당파 — bipartisan diplomacy

외교 공세 外交攻勢 a diplomatic offensive

외구 畏懼 awe ; reverential fear —하다 be awe-stricken ; be〔stand〕 in awe of ; be struck with awe

외구 外寇 a foreign enemy ; a foreign invader

†외국 外國 a foreign country〔land〕 ; a foreign nation〔power〕 (정치·군사상의) ¶ 외국의 foreign ; alien ; oversea(s) // 외국에서 broad ; overseas // 외국풍의 exotic ; outlandish // 외국 태생의 foreign-born // 외국제의 foreign-made ; of foreign manufacture〔make〕 // 외 국 행 의 foreign-going ; outbound // 외국행 우편물 outgoing mails // 외국에 가다 go abroad // 외국에 있다 be〔stay〕 abroad // 외국에 여행하다 travel abroad // 외국에서 돌아오다 return from abroad // 외국의 침략을 받다 be invaded by a foreign nation // 외국땅을 밟다 set foot on foreign soil // 외국식 생활을 하다 live in foreign style

— 관계 foreign relations — 냄새 outlandish taint — 무역 foreign〔overseas〕 trade — 물품 foreign〔imported〕 goods 〔articles〕 — 배척 antiforeignism — 사절 a foreign envoy — 상사 a foreign firm — 상품 foreign goods —선 a foreign ship ; a foreigner ; foreign bottoms 《총칭》 — 시장 a foreign〔an oversea〕 market — 여행 a foreign travel — 여행비 overseas travel expenses — 영화 전문관 a theater specializing in imported films — 자본 foreign capital — 전보 a foreign telegram ; a cablegram —채(債) a foreign loan —풍 foreign manners ; exotic fashion ; foreignism ; exoticism —항로 a foreign (service) route —환(시세) foreign exchange (rate) —환 관리법 the Foreign Exchange Control Law — 환 시장 foreign exchange market —환 어음 foreign exchange bill

외국 거래 外國去來 foreign trade

*외국어 外國語 a foreign language 〔tongue〕 ¶ 외국어로 in a foreign language // 외국어를 배우기 시작하다 take up a foreign language // 외국어로 자기 생각을 말한다는 것은 매우 어렵다 It is very hard to express oneself in a language that is not one's own. // 그는 외국어를 읽고 쓰고 말할 수 있다 He has a reading, speaking and writing knowledge of a foreign language.

— 대학 a university of foreign languages 제2 — a second foreign language 한국 — 대학 *Hanguk* University of Foreign Studies

⁑외국인 外國人 a foreigner ; a foreign national ; an alien

— 거류지 a foreign settlement — 관광객 a foreign tourist — 등록법 the Aliens Registration Act — 방문객 a foreign visitor — 사회 a foreign community 〔colony〕 — 상사 a foreign firm — 유학생 an overseas student —촌 the foreign quarter of a city — 토지법 〖법〗 the Aliens Landownership Law — 혐오 xenophobia ; zenophobia

외근 外勤 outside duty〔service〕 ; canvassing (외교원의) —하다 be on outside duty ; work outside ¶ 외근의 on outdoor service // 그는 외근입니다 He works outside.

— 기자 a legman ; a reporter — 순경 a patrol(man) —자 a person on outside duty ; a canvasser (외교원) — 직원 an outdoor service employee

외기 外氣 the (open) air ¶ 외기에 쐬다 expose 《a thing》 to the air ; air 《a thing》 // 외기를 쐬다 expose oneself to the air ; take the air ; air oneself

—권(圈) the outer space

외기 노조 外機勞組 the Foreign Organizations Employees Union 《FOEU》

외길 the only road ; a single path

—목 a narrow entrance to a blind alley

외김치 cucumber pickles

외나무다리 a log bridge

외날 a single edge ; a single-edged blade ¶ 외날 면도칼 a single-edged razor

외눈 one eye ; [사람] a one-eyed person

외다¹ [불편하다] be out of the way ; be out of place ; be off to one side ¶ 손이 외다 be out of the way ; be hard to reach ; be unhandy // 손이 왼 곳 a place located out of the way ; a spot hard to reach

외다² [암기] recite ⇨ 외우다

외대다¹ [말을] tell〔relate〕 untruthfully ; give false information

외대다² [푸대접] treat slightingly〔unkindly〕; snub ; give 《a person》 a cold reception ; [배척] reject

외대머리 an unmarried woman who wears her hair as if married

외대박이 ① [배] a single-sail boat ② [애꾸눈이] one-eyed person

외도 外道 [오입] whoring ; [나쁜 길] an evil course ; a wrong course ; deviation from one's proper field **—하다** consort with a whore ; whore ; visit a brothel ; [일탈] go astray ; stray from one's proper field

외돌다 keep aloof ; twist round

외돌토리 a lonely person ; being solitary 〔alone〕 ¶ 외돌토리가 되다 be left alone ; be left to oneself

외동이 an〔the〕 only son

외등 外燈 an outdoor lamp

***외따로** separated ; isolated ; lonely ; all alone ; solitarily ¶ 벌판에 조그만 집이 외따로 서 있다 In the middle of the field (there) stands a solitary cottage. // 그는 도시에서 멀리 떨어져 외따로 산다 He lives a lonely life far away from town. // 그 아이는 다른 애들과 어울리지 않고 늘 외따로 논다 The boy does not mix with other boys but always keeps aloof.

외딴 ① [떨어진] isolated ; separated ; out-of-the-way ¶ 외딴 섬 a solitary island // 외딴집 an isolated house // 외딴 곳에서 살다 live in a secluded place ② [독판침] ¶ 외딴치다 play a one-man show

외딸 an〔the〕 only daughter

외딸다 (be) alone ; solitary ; isolated ; sequestered ; remote ; secluded ; lonely ¶ 외딴 곳 an out-of-the-way place // 그는 외딴 곳에서 산다 He lives in a secluded place.

외떡잎 [식물] a single seed-leaf ; monocotyledon
— 식물 a monocotyledon(ous plant)

외람 猥濫 presumptuousness ; forwardness ; impertinence ; impudence ; audacity **—하다** (be) impudent ; presumptuous ; forward ; impertinent ; audacious ¶ 외람하오나 Allow me to tell you 《that》; I will take the liberty 《of》; I dare say ; It is very presumptuous of me, 《but》 // 외람된 짓을 하다 be presumptuous ; go beyond one's duty 〔power〕; exceed one's authority

외래 外來 ¶ 외래의 foreign ; imported
— 관념 an acquired idea **— 광선** extraneous light **— 사상** foreign〔imported〕 ideas **— 식물〔동물〕** an exotic plant〔animal〕; a denizen ; a colonist **—어** a word of foreign origin ; a borrowed word ; a loan word **—자** a stranger ; an alien ; a visitor **—종** an introduced species **—품** imported goods **— 환자** an outpatient

외력 外力 〖물리〗 external force ¶ 외력이 가해지다 an external force is applied 《to》

외로 leftward ; to the left ; to the left hand ; in the wrong direction ; to the wrong path ; to an evil course ¶ 외로 가다 go to the left ; go astray ; fall into evil ways

외로움 solitude ; loneliness ; isolation

***외로이** all alone ; lonelily ; solitarily ¶ 외로이 살다 lead a solitary life // 외로이 울다 cry all alone // 산 위에 늙은 소나무가 외로이 서 있다 A lonely old pinetree stands on the hill.

⁑**외롭다** (be) lonely ; lonesome ; solitary ; be all alone ¶ 외로운 생활 a lonely〔solitary〕 life // 외로운 나그네 a lonely〔solitary〕 traveler // 외로운 사람 a lonely person ; a person who is left to himself // 남편이 죽어서 그 여자는 외로웠다 She felt forlorn and helpless on the death of her husband. // 낯선 사람들 사이에서 그녀는 외로웠다 She was lonely when among strangers.

외륜 外輪 ① [차의] a tire ② [기선의] a paddle wheel
—선 a paddle〔side-wheel〕 steamer ; a paddle-〔side-〕wheeler

외륜산 外輪山 〖지리〗 somma ; a crater-rim

외마디 [동강] a single piece ; a section ; [소리] a single cry〔sound〕
—설대 a pipe-stem made of a single section of bamboo

외마디소리 a single cry ; an outcry of pain ; a scream ¶ 외마디소리를 지르며 with a cry // 외마디소리를 지르다 scream ; shriek ; utter a piercing cry ; give a shrill cry // 그는 칼에 맞아 외마디 소리를 지르고 쓰러졌다 When the sword hit him, he let out a scream and fell.

†**외면¹ 外面** outward appearance ; the outside ; the exterior
—치레 showing off ; putting on a fair show ¶ 외면치레하다 show off ; make outward show **— 묘사** an external description

***외면² 外面** **—하다** turn away 《one's face》; look away 《from》; avert one's eyes 《from》; cut (dead) ¶ 그는 나를 외면하고 지나갔다 He passed by with his face averted. /He cut me (dead) in the street.

***외모 外貌** (outward) appearance ; external features〔aspect〕; externals ; the exterior ¶ 외모는 우악스럽지만 마음씨는 고운 사람 a good man with a rough exterior 〔appearance〕 // 그는 외모가 단정한 사람이다 He is a man of decent appearance. /

He is always neat in his person. // 사람을 외모로 판단해서는 안된다 You shouldn't judge people by the way they look.
외목 ① ⇨ 외길목 ② [외목 장사] monopoly (business)
외몽고 外蒙古 Outer Mongolia
외무 外務 foreign affairs
—부 the Ministry〔Department〕 of Foreign Affairs ; the Foreign Office —부 장관 the Foreign Minister ; the Minister of Foreign Affairs ; the Secretary of State (국무 장관) 《미》 ; the Foreign Secretary 《영》 —원 a traveling salesman ; a canvasser — 위원회 the Foreign Affairs Committee (국회의) — 차관 the Vice-Minister of Foreign Affairs
외미 外米 foreign〔imported〕 rice ; rice from abroad
외박 外泊 stopping〔staying〕 out —하다 sleep out ; stay out ; stop out ; stop out of the barracks (군인이)
외발제기 playing a shuttlecock with one foot
외방 外方 ① [외국] foreign lands ; foreign parts ② [바깥] outside ③ [서울 밖] districts away from the capital〔*Seoul*〕
—살이 life as a government official out in the provinces
외벌 a single set
— 매듭 a single〔simple〕 knot
외벽 外壁 〖건축〗 an outer wall
‡외부 外部 the outside ; the exterior ¶ 외부의 outside ; external // 외부로부터 from without〔the outside〕 // 외부의 사람 an outsider // 외부로부터의 원조 outside help // 외부에 나타나다 appear on the outside // 외부와 교통이 두절되다 be cut off from the outside world // 비밀이 외부로 샜다 The secret has leaked out. // 외부와의 연락이 두절되었다 Communications with the outside world were cut off. // 외부와의 교섭은 전적으로 지배인이 처리한다 The manager attends to all matters dealing with the general public. // 저 회사는 외부에 나타나지 않을 뿐이지 항상 분규가 있다 The firm has constant troubles, only they are not brought to light.
— 간섭 outside interference — 관계 external relationship — 기생 external parasitism — 부채〔자본〕 an external liability〔capital〕 —성(性) 〖철학〗 outness ; externality — 원조 outside aid — 위험〔손해〕 〖보험〗 external hazard 〔damage〕 — 사람 an outsider — 잡음 external noise — 침략 external aggression
외분 外分 〖기하〗 external division —하다 divide externally
외분비 外分泌 〖의학〗 external secretion
—선(腺) an exocrine gland
외비 外備 defense against foreign invasion
외빈 外賓 [외국 손님] a foreign guest 〔visitor〕 ; [외부 손님] a guest〔visitor〕
외사 外史 ① [외국 역사] history of a foreign country ② [야사] an unofficial 〔unsanctioned〕 history
외사 外事 external〔foreign〕 affairs
—과 the section of foreign affairs ; the foreign affairs section
외사촌 外四寸 a maternal cousin
외삼촌 外三寸 a maternal uncle ; an uncle on one's mother's side
†외상 credit ; trust ; tick 《영·구》 ¶ 외상으로 팔다 sell 《a thing》 on credit〔tick〕 // 외상으로 사다 buy on credit // 외상 장부에 기입하다 enter on the credit note // 외상을 주다 give credit // 외상을 받다 collect a bill // 외상으로 해주시오 Charge it to my account. /Put it on my bill. // 나는 그 선술집에 외상이 30,000원 있다 I owe the public house a 30,000 *won* bill. // 외상으로 살 수 있습니까 Can I buy it on credit ? /Is financing available ?
— 거래 credit transaction —말코지 difficulty in getting things (done) without paying in advance — 매입금 the outstanding balance of credit purchase ; a debt ; accounts payable (지불 계정) — 매출 credit sales ¶ 외상 매출금 a credit account // 외상 매출 계정 charge accounts ; accounts of credit sales — 사절 [게시] No credit given/For cash (down) only. /We do not sell on credit.
— 수금원 a bill-collector —질 buying on credit — 판매 credit sale ; sale〔selling〕 on credit〔tick〕
외상 —床 a table for one ; an individual table ¶ 외상을 받다 get an individual table
외상 外傷 an external wound ; a traumatic injury ; 〖의학〗 trauma ¶ 외상성의 traumatic
외상 外相 the Foreign Minister ⇨ 외무
— 회의 a Foreign Ministers' conference ; a conference at the Foreign Ministers' level
외상 外商 a foreign merchant
외생 外甥 [사위] son-in-law
외서 外書 a foreign book
외선 外線 outside wire ; [구내 전화에 대해] an outside line ¶ 외선 부탁합니다 Give me an outside line, please.
— 공사 outside wiring — 작전 an operation on exterior lines
*외설 猥褻 obscenity ; lewdness ; indecency ; licentiousness ; prurience —하다 (be) obscene ; lewd ; indecent ; licentious ; dirty ; improper ; nasty ¶ 외설한 그림 an obscene picture // 외설한 이야기 indecent talk ; filthy talk ; a risqué story // 외설한 이야기를 하다 have an indecent talk ; talk obscenely ; use indecent language
— 문학 obscene〔immoral〕 literature ;

salacious writings ; pornography — 소설 an obscene〔a hot〕 novel —죄 public indecency ; a morals crime —책〔그림〕 an obscene book〔picture〕 — 행위 an indecent〔a lewd〕 behavior〔act〕

외세 外勢 [형세] external circumstances 〔condition, situation〕; [세력] outside 〔alien, foreign〕 influence〔power〕 ¶ 외세에 의존하다 depend on the power of a foreign country

외소박이 stuffed cucumber pickles

외손 one hand ¶ 외손의 one-handed ; single-handed
—뼉 a single palm —잡이 a one-handed person
외손뼉이 울랴 (속담) It takes two to quarrel.

외손 外孫 a child of one's daughter ; a grandchild by one's daughter ; descendants in the daughter's line
—녀 one's granddaughter ; a daughter of one's daughter —자 one's grandson ; a son of one's daughter

외손지다 get deprived of the use of one hand

외수 外數 deceit ; trick(ery) ; cheat

외숙 外叔 an uncle on one's mother's side ; a maternal uncle

외숙모 外叔母 the wife of one's maternal uncle

외시골 外— outlying〔remote〕 country district ; a remote district

외식 外食 eating〔dining〕 out —하다 dine〔eat〕 out ; board out 《미》
—권(卷) meal ticket ; a meal rationing coupon —자(者) a diner-out

외식 外飾 external ornament ; a show-off —하다 put on outside appearance ; show off

외신 外臣 a foreign subject〔national〕

*외신 外信 foreign news ; a foreign telegram〔message, cablegram〕; an overseas dispatch ¶ 우리는 신문에 의해서 외신을 받다 We depend upon the newspaper for foreign news.
—부장 editor of the foreign news department

외실 外室 an outer room ; man's quarters

외심 外心 〖기하〗 a circumcenter ; an outer center (of a similitude)
—각 an eccentric angle —점 the metacenter

외씨버선 small shapely socks

외아들 an〔the〕 only son

외알제기 a horse〔an ox〕 that drags

†외야 外野 〖야구〗 the outfield
—석 outfield bleachers —수 an outfielder

외양 外洋 the open sea ; the ocean ¶ 외양 항행의 ocean-going
— 조류 an ocean tide — 항행선 an ocean-going steamer

*외양 外樣 (outward) appearance ; aspect

> **참고** **appearance** 눈으로 보았을 때 언뜻 들어오는 전반적인 외양 **aspect** 일정한 때 일정한 조건 속에서 볼 수 있는 외양

¶ 외양은 in appearance ; outwardly // 외양은 부드러우나 though she looks gentle to all appearance ; with all her gentle appearance // 외양치레 putting on a good appearance // 외양을 꾸미다 put up a good front ; keep up appearances ; make show // 외양이 그럴 듯하다 have a good appearance // 사람은 외양으로 판단할 것이 아니다 We should not judge people by their (outward) appearance.

*외양간 a stable (말의) ; a cowhouse 〔shed〕 (소의) ¶ 말을 외양간에 넣다 put a horse in a stable ; stable a horse
소 잃고 외양간 고치다 (속담) Close the barn door after the horse is stolen

외어서다 step aside ; get out of the way ¶ 우리가 외어서니 그가 지나갔다 We stepped aside and he passed on. // 지프차가 온다 외어서라 A jeep is coming, get out of the way.

외연 外延 〖논리〗 extension ; denotation

외연 기관 外燃機關 an external combustion engine

외올 a single strand
—뜨기 single-strand knitwork —베 cloth woven of single strands —실 single-strand thread

외외가 外外家 one's maternal grandmother's home

외욕질 nausea ; vomit〔vomituration〕

외용 外用 external〔topical〕 use〔application〕
—약 a medicine for external〔topical〕 use 〔application〕 only ; an application ; For outward only. (약병에)

외우 外憂 [외간] mourning for the death of a father ; [외환] fears of foreign〔outside〕 invasion

외우 畏友 an esteemed friend

외우다 recite from memory ; learn by heart ; memorize ¶ 시를 외우다 recite a poem // 그걸 잘 외우시오 You must bear it well in your mind. // 그는 말을 외우는 것이 매우 빨랐다 He was very quick in picking up words.

외원 外援 foreign aid〔assistance〕; help from without ; external help

외원 外苑 an outer garden

외유 外遊 foreign travel ; a trip〔tour〕 abroad ; going abroad —하다 travel 〔go〕 abroad ¶ 외유에서 돌아오다 return from one's foreign tour

외유내강 外柔內剛 being gentle in appearance, but sturdy in spirit ; an iron hand in a velvet glove

외음부 外陰部 the vulva ¶ 외음부의 vul-

val ; vulvar
외의 外衣 an outer garment
외이 外耳 external ear ; auricle ; concha
—염 otitis externa ; conchitis
외인 外人 [외국인] a foreigner ; an alien ; [관계 없는 사람] an outsider ; a stranger ; an unrelated person ¶ 이것은 외인이 알아서는 안된다 This is between ourselves.
— 부대 the Foreign Legion — 사회 the foreign community〔colony〕 — 상사 a foreign (business) firm — 여객 명부 an alien manifest —촌 the foreign quarter of a city ; a foreigners' residence area — 출입 금지〔사절〕 [게시] No admittance. /No trespassing. /Keep off ! /Keep out ! 《미》
외인 外因 an external cause ¶ 외인성의 exogenous ; exogenic
외인 강사 外人講師 a foreign instructor 〔lecturer〕 ; a foreign teacher ; a reader 《영》
외자 外字 foreign language
— 신문 a foreign-language newspaper
외자 外資 foreign capital〔currency, money, funds〕
—국 the Foreign Procurement Bureau — 도입 introduction〔importation〕 of foreign capital — 수입 태세 readiness for the induction of foreign capital ; preparation for the receipt of foreign investments — 유입 the inflow〔influx〕 of foreign capital
외장 外裝 [포장] wrapping(s) ; armoring ; 〖전기〗 sheathing (전선의) ; [자동차의] trim ; 〖조선〗 armor ; 〖토목〗 facing
— 검사 packing inspection
외장골 外腸骨 〖해부〗 iliaca external ; the external flank bone
— 동맥〔정맥〕 arteria〔vena〕 iliaca externa
외적 外敵 a foreign enemy〔invader〕 ¶ 외적의 침입을 받다 suffer from foreign invasion〔attack, raid〕
외적 外的 external ; outward
— 증거 a external evidence
외전 外電 a foreign dispatch ; a foreign telegram ; a cable(gram) ¶ 외전이 전하는 바에 의하면 The foreign news says 《that》 ; according to the foreign news
외전 外傳 a supplementary story ; a lateral biography
외접 外接 〖기하〗 circumscription —하다 circumscribe ; be circumscribed
—원 a circumscribed circle ; a circumcircle
외정 外征 a foreign expedition〔campaign〕 —하다 go on a foreign expedition
—군 an expeditionary army
외정 外政 diplomatic〔foreign〕 affairs
외제 外製 ¶ 외제의 of foreign manufacture〔make〕 ; foreign-made
—품 foreign-made articles ; goods of foreign make ; imported articles〔goods〕
외조모 外祖母 a grandmother on one's mother's side ; a maternal grandmother
외조부 外祖父 a grandfather on one's mother's side ; a maternal grandfather
외족 外族 the maternal line of relatives ; a relative on the mother's side
외종 外從 a cousin on one's mother's side ; a maternal cousin
외종 사촌 外從四寸 a cousin on one's mother's side
외주 外周 circumference
외주 外注 an outside order —하다 place an order (with) outside
— 제품 an outside product — 과 a subcontract department
외주물
— 구석 an area where open shacks are clustered ; a shantytown —집 a shabby house that is open to the road ; an open shack
외줄 a single line〔stripe〕
외줄기 a single stalk〔stem〕
외지 外地 a foreign〔an alien〕 land ; an oversea(s) land ; an outlying region ; an external territory ¶ 외지로 건너가다 go abroad ; go overseas
— 근무 overseas service — 수당 an overseas allowance
외지 外紙 a foreign newspaper ; the foreign press 《총칭》
외지다 get isolated〔secluded, sequestered〕 ¶ 외진 산길 a remote mountain trail
외직 外職 a government post away from the capital ; a local〔provincial〕 government post
외진 外診 consultation at a patient's home
*외짝 an odd〔unmatched〕 member of a pair ; a single member〔side, part〕
외쪽 [한 쪽] one side ; a single direction ; [한 조각] a single piece
— 생각 one-sided thinking ; unilateral consideration
외채 single building〔structure, wing〕
—집 a one-wing house
*외채 外債 〖경제〗 a foreign loan (차관) ; foreign bonds (증권) ; an external debt (채무) ¶ 외채를 모집하다 raise〔float〕 a foreign loan // 외채를 많이 빌어 쓰다 borrow heavily abroad // 외채를 상환 못하다 default on foreign loans
— 모집 floatation of a foreign loan — 상환 기금 a redemption fund for foreign 〔external〕 bonds
외척 外戚 a maternal relation ; relatives on one's mother's side
외청도 外聽道 〖해부〗 an external auditory canal
외촌 外村 a village outside a town ; outlying〔outside〕 villages
외축 畏縮 —하다 shrink 《from a difficulty》 ; flinch ; cower 《before a person》 ; be awestruck
*외출 外出 going out ; an outing ; an air-

ing ── 하다 go out (of doors) ¶ 외출을 싫어하는 사람 a stay-at-home // 외출 중에 while one is out // 외출하지 않다 stay at home ; keep indoors ; stop 〔stay〕 in // 외출 준비를 하다 dress oneself for the street ; get ready to go out ; get dressed for going out // 외출을 허가받다 be allowed out // A군 집에 책을 빌리러 갔더니 외출 중이었다 I called at A's to borrow a book and found him out. // 감기가 완전히 나을 때까진 외출해서는 안된다 You must not leave the house till your cold is quite cured. // 어제는 비가 와서 외출할 수 없었다 The rain prevented me from going out yesterday. // 오늘부터 3일간 외출을 금한다 You shall stay at home for three days from today.

─ 금지 confinement (to the barracks) (군인의) ─ 금지령 a curfew (order) ─ 복 a street dress ; street clothes ; outdoor garments ; outdoor clothes ─ 시간 leave-time (군인의) ─ 일 a leave day ; an off-day ─ 허가서 a leave slip ; an exit permit

외측 外側 ⇨ 바깥쪽

외치 外治 [외과적 치료] external medical treatment ; [외교] a foreign policy ── 하다 treat externally ; apply external treatment

†**외치다** shout out ; shout ; utter〔give〕 a cry ; exclaim ; cry〔call〕 out (큰 소리로) ; [비명을 올리다] shriek ; scream ; [소리지르다] yell ¶ 외치는 소리 a scream ; a shriek ; a yell // 살려 달라고 외치다 cry〔yell〕 for help // 찬성이라고 외치다 shout approbation // 반대라고 외치다 clamor against // 찢어지는 소리로 외치다 utter a piercing shriek // 화를 내어 외치다 roar with rage // 목이 쉬도록 외치다 shout oneself hoarse // 기뻐 외치다 shout for joy // 개혁을 외치다 cry for a reform ; advocate reform // 군축을 외치다 cry for disarmament // 남북 통일을 외치다 cry out for the unification of Korea // 그녀는 부인 참정권을 외쳤다 She cried loudly for female suffrage.

외침 a shout ; a cry ; an outcry ; [놀람·감탄의] an exclamation ; [비명] a shriek ; a scream ; [항의의] a clamor ; [노호] a roar ; a howl ¶ 개혁의 외침 a cry〔clamor〕 for reform // 민족의 외침 the voice of the race

외탁 外─ ── 하다 take after one's mother's side in appearance〔character〕 ¶ 그 아이는 성질이 외탁했다 The boy gets his temperament from his mother's side.

외토리 a single person ; a loner ; a solitary〔lonely〕 person ¶ 외토리가 되다 be left alone ; be left to oneself ; be thrown on one's resources〔devices〕

외톨 ① a single ripened chestnut〔garlic bulb〕 ② [외돌토리] a single person on his own resources

─박이 single-bulb garlic (마늘) ; a single-bur chestnut (밤)

외통 ─通 (being) one-way ; [장기] checkmate

‡**외투 外套** an overcoat ; a great-coat ; a topcoat (보통 가벼운) ¶ 외투를 입다〔벗다〕 put on〔take off〕 one's overcoat // 외투를 여기에 맡기십시오 Please check your overcoat here. // 그는 외투를 입은 채 방안에 들어왔다 He entered the room with his overcoat on.

─걸이 an overcoat rack

외판 外販 (a) traveling sale ; canvassing ¶ 트랜지스터의 외판을 하다 go from house to house selling〔peddling〕 transistor radios

─원 a salesman ; a salesperson ; a canvasser ; [여자] a saleswoman ; [지방 순회의] a commercial traveler ; a traveling salesman ; a roadman 서적 ─원 a (door-to-door) salesman in books

외팔 one arm

─이 a one-armed person

‡**외풍 外風** ① [바람] a draught ; a draft ¶ 이 방에는 외풍이 있다 There is a draft in this room.

② [외국풍] foreignism ; exotic fashion ; foreign ways〔manners, style〕

***외피 外皮** an outer cover ; skin ; a rind ; a shuck ; a crust ; a shell (조개 따위의) ; a husk (과일의) ; a hull (곡식의) ; cuticle (피부의)

외할머니 a maternal grandmother ; the mother of one's mother

외할아버지 a maternal grandfather ; the father of one's mother

외항 外港 an outer port〔harbor〕 ; an outport

외항선 外航船 an ocean-going ship ; a ship for overseas service

외해 外海 the open sea ; the high seas ¶ 외해로 나가다 go out into the open sea

***외향성 外向性** 〖심리〗 extroversion ¶ 외향성의 extroversive // 외향성의 사람 an extrovert

외형 外形 an external〔outward〕 form ; shape ¶ 외형이 둥글다 be round in shape

외화 外貨 〖경제〗 [화폐] foreign currency 〔money〕

─ 가득률 a foreign-exchange earning rate ─ 가득액 foreign-exchange earnings ─ 관리 management〔control〕 of foreign currency holdings ─ 대부 foreign currency loan ─ 배척 the boycott of foreign goods ─ 보유고 foreign exchange holdings〔reserve〕 ─ 보유량 an amount of foreign exchange holdings ─ 부족 the scarcity of foreign exchange ; the foreign exchange shortage ─ 시장〔시세〕 foreign exchange market〔rate〕 ─ 어음 a foreign money bill ; a foreign-exchange check ─ 예산 a

foreign exchange budget ― 유출 the diversion〔outflow〕 of foreign currency ― 자금 foreign currency funds ― 절약 foreign currency savings ― 준비 a reserve in foreign currency ― 준비금 foreign currency reserve ― 채권 foreign currency bonds ― 획득 the obtaining of foreign money ; the acquisition of foreign currencies 보유 ― (Korea's) foreign exchange〔currency〕 holdings〔reserve〕
외화 外畫 a foreign film〔movie〕
외환 外換 foreign exchange
― 은행 a foreign exchange bank
외환 外患 fear of foreign〔outside〕 invasion ; foreign〔external〕 troubles ; troubles from without ; the pressure〔invasion〕 of a foreign enemy
내우― internal and external troubles ; trouble from within and without
왹질 ⇨ 외욕질
왼 left ¶ 왼눈 the left eye // 왼쪽 the left (side)
왼구비 a high flight of an arrow
왼낫 a left-handed sickle
왼발 the〔one's〕 left foot
왼소리 news〔rumors〕 of a death ; a report of 《a person's》 death
*왼손 the left hand ¶ 왼손 편 the left side // 왼손으로 글을 쓰다 write with the left hand
왼손잡이 [사람] a left-handed person ; a left hander ; a southpaw ¶ 왼손잡이의 left-handed // 왼손잡이 투수 a left-handed pitcher ; a southpaw 《미·속》
†왼쪽 the left side ¶ 왼쪽에 on the left // 길의 왼쪽에 on the left-hand〔left〕 side of the street // 왼쪽으로부터 쓰다 write from left to right // 왼쪽으로 돌다 turn to the left
왼팔 the left arm
왼편 the left side ¶ 왼편의 left(-hand)
욀총 one's memory〔ability to memorize〕
욋가지 椳― 〖건축〗 lath strips
요[1] ① this little (one) ; these ¶ 요까짓… such a〔little〕 // 요같이 like this // 요놈 you small thing ; you squirt ; you despicable 〔nasty, mean〕 fellow
② [시간적·공간적] right near at hand ¶ 요 근처에 about〔around〕 here ; in this neighborhood // 요 언덕 넘어 정거장이 있다 There is a station right over the hill.
요[2] ① [의문] ¶ 저이는 누구요 Who is he ?
② [단정] ¶ 이것은 호랑이요 This is a tiger.
요 a (quilted) mattress ¶ 요를 깔다〔펴다〕 make a bed ; lay a mattress ; put down〔spread〕 a mattress
요 尿 urine
요 要 the main〔essential, pivotal〕 point ; a summary ; the gist ¶ 요는〔요컨대〕 in the last analysis ; to sum up ; in a word ; in brief ; in short
요가 yoga ¶ 요가의 수련자 a yogi // 요가를 하다 do yoga
요각 凹角 a reentering angle ; a reentrant (angle)
요각 凹刻 an intaglio
― 인쇄 intaglio printing
요강 a chamber pot ; a (night) stool
요강 要綱 the main principle ; a summary ; the general idea ; the outline
지시 ― the essential points for guidance
입학 ― 안내 a list of the entrance requirements (for a college)
요건 要件 [필요 조건] a requisite ; an essential condition〔factor〕 ; [요긴한 일] an important business〔matter〕 ¶ 성공 요건 requisites for success // 요건을 갖추다 fulfil the necessary conditions // 한국 국민된 요건 the conditions necessary for being a Korean // 건강은 성공의 제일 요건이다 Health is the first requisite for success.
요격 邀擊 an ambush ; interception ; a surprise attack ―하다 ambush ; intercept ; attack by surprise
―기 an interceptor (plane) ―용 미사일 an interceptor missile ; an antimissile missile 《AMM》
요결 要訣 [비결] a key ; a secret ; [뜻] an essential meaning ; a vital point 《of》 ¶ 성공의 요결 the secret of success ; the key to success // 건강의 요결은 일찍 일어나는 것이다 Early rising in the morning is a key to good health.
요골 腰骨 the hipbone ; the hucklebone
요관 尿管 [해부] the ureter
요괴 妖怪 a ghost ; an apparition ; a specter ; [괴물] a goblin ; a monster ; a hobgoblin
―담 a ghost〔an uncanny〕 story
요괴스럽다 妖怪― (be) wicked and mysterious ; eerie ; weird ; uncanny
†요구 要求 [요청] a demand ; a claim (권리에 의한) ; [청구] a request ; [필요] a requirement ―하다 demand ; request ; claim ; call for ; call upon 《a person to do》 ; require

> 참고 **demand** 당연한 권리에 의거하여 물건을 강력하게 요구하다 **claim** 물건을 요구할 권리가 있다고 주장하다 **require** 물건을 필요로 하다

¶ 시대의 요구 the needs〔requirements〕 of the times // 정당한 요구 a reasonable claim // 부당한 요구 an unreasonable claim // 임금 인상 요구 a demand for higher wages // 요구에 의해서 on demand ; at 《a person's》 request // 요구에 응하다 accede to 《a person's》 demand ; comply with 《a person's》 request // 사회 개혁을 요구하다 cry for social reform // 손해 배상을 요구하다 present a claim for damages // 나는 그에게 불가능한 것은 요구하지 않는다 I do not expect him to do

impossibilities. // 너의 요구에는 응할 수 없다 I cannot comply with your request. // 회사측은 노동자의 임금 인상 요구에 응하기로 결정했다 The management has decided to meet the demand of the laborers for increased pay. // 국회는 과반수 의원의 요구로 총회를 열었다 The National Assembly called a general meeting at the request of a majority of the members. // 그는 여자들에게 요구하는 게 너무 지나치다 He's just very demanding of women.
—불 payment on demand **—불(拂) 어음** a note〔bill〕 on demand ; a demand bill〔draft〕 **—불 예금** a demand deposit **—서** a written request **—액** amount demanded〔claimed〕 **— 조건** the terms desired **임금 인상 —** a demand for higher wages **은행 —불 어음** a bank demand draft ; a bank D. D.

요구르트 yog(h)urt (우유를 유산균으로 산패(酸敗)·응고시킨 것)

요귀 妖鬼 an evil spirit ; an apparition ; a ghost

†**요금 料金** a charge ; a fee ; a fare ; a rate ¶ 요금을 내다 pay a charge // 요금을 받다 charge // 요금을 안 받다 make no charge ; be free // 요금을 징수하다 collect fees〔a rate, a charge〕 // 잠깐 쓰는 데 100원의 요금을 받았다 He made a charge of one hundred *won* for using it for a few minutes.
— 경쟁 a rate war **— 별납** 〖우편〗 separate payment of postage instead of by affixed postage stamps **— 인상〔인하〕** a raise〔reduction〕 of the charge〔rate〕 ; a charge hike〔cut〕 ; a rate hike〔cut〕 **—(인하) 경쟁** a rate war〔competition〕 ; a ratecutting war **—표** a tariff ; a list of charges ; a price list **— 후납** 〖우편〗 subsequent payment of postage **수도〔전기〕 —** water〔power〕 rate **택시 —** a taxi fare **특별 —** an extra charge

요기 right this place ; right here

요기 僚機 a consort〔comrade, sister〕 plane

요기 療飢 appeasing〔relieving〕 hunger **—하다** appease〔relieve〕 one's hunger ¶ 사과로 요기하다 satisfy one's hunger with apples

요기 妖氣 a weird〔ghostly〕 air

요긴 要緊 essential importance **—하다** be essentially important ; be of vital importance ¶ 일전에 받은 유리 용기는 요긴하게 쓰고 있다 That glass container you gave me is very handy.
—목 a critical position

요까짓 ⇨ 이까짓

요나서 —書 〖성경〗 The Book of Jonah ; Jonah

요녀 妖女 a temptress ; a siren ; an enchantress ; a vampire ; a vamp 《속》

***요다음** next ¶ 요다음의 next // 요다음에 next time

요담 要談 an important (business) talk ; an important conference〔consultation〕 **—하다** have a talk with 《a person》 on important business ¶ 요담 중이다 be in the middle of an important talk // 요담이 있다 have an important matter to discuss

요대 腰帶 ⇨ 허리띠

요도 尿道 〖해부〗 the urethra
— 검사 urethroscopy **—경(鏡)** a urethroscope **—관** the urethral canal **—구(口)** the urethral meatus **—염** urethritis ; inflammation of the urethra **— 절개술** urethrotomy **— 협착** stricture of the urethra

요독증 尿毒症 〖의학〗 uremia ; urine〔uremic〕 poisoning

요동 搖動 shaking ; shake ; rocking **—하다** shake ; quake ; rock ; pitch and roll ¶ 천지를 요동하다 shake heaven and earth

요들 a yodel
— 가수 a yodeler

요때기 — shabby〔dirty〕 bedding

***요란 擾亂** a commotion ; a disturbance ; a fuss ; a bustle **—하다** (be) noisy ; clamorous ; boisterous ; uproarious ; tumultuous ¶ 요란하게 noisily ; boisterously ; clamorously ; uproariously // 요란스럽게 흐르는 강 a roaring and tumultuous river // 요란을 피우다 make 〔raise〕 a fuss 《about, over》 ; raise 〔cause〕 a disturbance // 밖이 요란하다 There is a commotion outside.

요람 要覽 a survey ; a summary ; an outline ; [안내서] a handbook ; a directory bulletin ; catalog ; calendon ¶ 회사 요람 a general survey of a company

⁑**요람 搖籃** a cradle ¶ 요람에서 무덤까지 from the cradle to the grave
—기 the cradle ; babyhood ; infancy ; the inchoate stage **—지** the cradle ; the birthplace ; the home

요략 要略 a resume ; a summary ; an epitome ; an outline **—하다** summarize ; sum up ; epitomize

요량 料量 [짐작] guess ; calculation ; estimate ; [생각] a plan ; an intention ; an idea ; [판단] judgment ; discretion **—하다** guess ; calculate ; plan out ; use one's discretion〔judgment〕 ¶ 내 요량으로는 in my estimation 〔thought〕 // 요량이 맞다 guess right ; be right in one's conjecture // 내 요량으로는 그 계획이 성공할 것 같지 않다 I don't think the plan will prove successful. // 무슨 요량으로 그렇게 말했느냐 What made you say so ?

요러하다 ⇨ 이렇다

요런 such ; this ; like this ¶ 요런 식으로 in this manner〔way〕 ; like this // 요런 식으로 하라 Do like this.

요령 搖鈴 a handbell

***요령 要領** [요점] the point ; the essentials ; the gist ; the pith ; the main point ; [기교] a knack ; the ropes 《속》 ¶ 요령이 있는 사람 a sharp〔shrewd〕 fellow ; a sensible man // 요령이 없는 사람 a tactless man ; a bungling fellow ; a sad sack 《미·속》 // 보고의 요령 the gist〔outline〕 of a report // 요령이 있다 be to the point〔purpose〕 ; be pointed 〔sensible, relevant〕 // 요령이 없다 be pointless〔irrelevant, vague〕 ; be off the point ; say nothing to the point〔purpose〕 // 요령을 터득하다 get the knack 《of》 // 요령 있게 말하다 speak to the point〔purpose〕 // 연습하면 요령을 알게 된다구 Practice will give you the knack of it. // 그 일은 요령을 익히기만 하면 쉬워 It's easy if you just get down a few basic ideas.

요령부득 要領不得 being off the point ; pointlessness ; irrelevancy ; impertinency **— 하다** (be) pointless ; irrelevant ; be beside the point ; be not to the point ¶ 자네 말은 도무지 요령 부득이야 I can't catch〔see〕 your point at all. /I can make neither head nor tail of what you say. /It is hard for me to catch your point.

요로 要路 [고위] an important〔a responsible〕 position〔post〕 ; a high office ; [당국] the authorities ; [길] a principal road ; a main artery 《of traffic》 ¶ 요로에 있는 사람들 those in authority ; the authorities // 요로에 있다 be in authority ; occupy〔hold〕 an important position // 교통의 요로에 있다 be in the main artery of traffic // 요로에 아는 사람이 많다 have many friends in the authorities

요론 要論 an important discourse ; a discussion of importance〔consequence〕 ; a vital argument

요르단 Jordan ¶ 요르단의 Jordanian
— 왕국 the Hashemite Kingdom of Jordan

요리 [요렇게] in this way ; like this ; so ; [요리로] this way ; this direction ; here

†**요리 料理** ① [만들기] cooking ; cookery ; cuisine ; [음식] a dish ; food ; fare **— 하다** cook 《food》 ; dress 《fish》 ; prepare 《a dish》 ¶ 고기와 야채 요리 a plate of beef and vegetables // 불란서식 요리 dishes prepared in French style // 요리를 내다 serve dishes ; set dishes on the table // 요리를 만들다 prepare a dish // 요리를 잘〔못〕하다 be a good 〔poor〕 hand at cookery ; be a good 〔bad〕 cook // 이 요리는 맛이 없다〔좋다〕 This is a poor 〔delicious, palatable〕 dish. // 이 호텔의 요리는 유명하다 The hotel is known for its excellent cuisine. // 요리가 준비되었다 The dishes are ready. // 오늘 요리는 무엇입니까 What is the menu for today ? // 그 여자는 요리 솜씨가 있다 She has the right touch about cooking. // 한국 요리와 비교해 볼 때 미국 요리는 어떻습니까 How do American dishes compare with Korean ones ?

② [처리] management ; handling **— 하다** manage ; handle ; dispose of ¶ 국정을 요리하다 manage〔conduct〕 state affairs ; assume the helm of the state // 일을 요리하다 manage the work
— 교실 a cooking class **— 기구** cooking utensils **—대** a dressing table ; a dresser **— 도구** a cooker ; kitchen 〔cooking〕 utensils **—법** cooking ; cookery ; the culinary art **—사** a cook ; a chef 《프》 ; a cooky (여자) **—장** a kitchen ; a cuisine **—집** a 《Chinese》 restaurant ; an eating house **—책** a cookbook 《미》 ; a cookery book 《영》 **—학** gastrology **— 학원** a cooking school **고급 —** haute cuisine **서양 —** foreign〔Western〕 food〔dishes〕 **야채〔생선〕 —** a vegetable〔fish〕 dish **중화〔한국, 서양〕 —** Chinese〔Korean, Foreign〕 food〔dishes〕

요리조리 here and there ; this way and that way ¶ 요리조리 핑계를 대다 resort to all kinds of excuses ; make one excuse after another // 책임을 요리조리 피하다 be cunning in dodging one's responsibility // 자동차를 요리조리 피하여 가다 thread one's way dodging cars // 여자를 요리조리 꾀다 seduce a girl with all kinds of sweet-talk

요마 妖魔 a goblin ; a demon ; a bogey ; a hobgoblin

요마적 lately ⇨ 이마적

요만 ⇨ 이만

요만것 this small〔little〕 bit ¶ 요만것도 모르느냐 Don't you even know this ?

요만큼 this (little) bit ; to this small extent〔degree〕 ⇨ 이만큼 ¶ 그의 말에는 거짓말이라고는 요만큼도 없다 There is not even the slightest bit of falsehood in what he told me.

요망 妖妄 ¶ 요망스럽다 (be) flighty ; fickle ; frivolous ; capricious ; treacherous

요망 要望 a demand 《for》 ; a desire ; a longing ; a cry 《for》 **— 하다** demand ; desire ; request earnestly ¶ 현대는 이와 같은 인물을 요망하고 있다 The present age demands men of such type. // 혁신을 요망하는 소리가 높다 There is a cry for reform.

요망 떨다 妖妄— act frivolously〔flightily, capriciously〕

요면 凹面 a concave surface ; concave ; concavity
—경 a concave mirror

요모조모 ⇨ 이모저모

요목 要目 principal items ; a syllabus ; a conspectus ; the (main) points
— 색인 an index of principal items 〔topics〕 ; a concordance **교수 —** a syllabus (of lectures) ; a teaching plan (교안)

요무 要務 an important business〔duty, task〕 ¶ 요무를 띠고 on an important business

요물 妖物 [괴물] an uncanny thing ; a goblin ; a hobgoblin ; a monster ; [사람] a wicked person ; a crafty and malicious person

요물 계약 要物契約 a real〔substantial〕 contract

요민 饒民 the people of ample means ; the well-off〔well-to-do〕 subjects〔citizens〕

요밀요밀하다 (be) meticulous ; scrupulous ; circumspect ¶ 요밀요밀한 사람 a meticulous〔scrupulous〕 person

요밀조밀하다 [면밀] (be) meticulous ; scrupulous ; circumspect ¶ 요밀조밀한 필치 a meticulous bit of writing // 요밀조밀한 세공품 elaborate handiwork // 일을 요밀조밀하게 하다 do a thing with meticulous care

요밀하다 要密— [주도] (be) elaborate ; meticulous ; scrupulous ; circumspect ; [세밀] (be) minute ; close ; detailed

요번 —番 this time ⇨ 이번

요법 療法 a remedy ; a method of treatment ; a cure ; a medical treatment ¶ 신경통에 좋은 요법 a good remedy for neuralgia

가정〔정산〕 — home〔psychic〕 treatment 전기 — electropathy 지압 — osteopathy

요변 妖變 [사건] a mysterious happening ; a phantom case ; [행동] suspicious〔questionable, treacherous〕 behavior

—쟁이 a questionable〔untrustworthy, treacherous〕 person

요부 妖婦 an enchantress ; a temptress ; a vamp(ire) ; a siren ; a witch ¶ 요부형의 여자 a woman of the vampire type

요부 饒富 ample means ; easy circumstances ; affluence ; opulence —하다 be well off ; live in comfort ; have ample means

요부 要部 the principal〔main, essential〕 part ¶ 요부를 이루다 form an important part 《of a thing》

요부 腰部 the waist ; the loins ; the hips ; the lumbar〔pelvic〕 region ¶ 요부의 lumbar

요분질 hip-movement (in sexual intercourse)

요사 夭死 an early death ; a premature death —하다 die young〔prematurely, before one's time〕 ; die at an early age ; die an early death ; be nipped in the bud ¶ 그는 요사했다 He died young〔an early death〕.

요사 妖邪 capriciousness ; fickleness ; treacherousness ; wickedness ; craftiness ¶ 요사스럽다 (be) capricious ; fickle ; wicked ; vicious ; wily ; crafty // 요사부리다 behave in a capricious〔crafty〕 way

—꾼 a treacherous person ; a snake-in-the-grass

요사 寮舍 a hostel ; a dormitory ; [불교] a temple dormitory 《for Buddhist monks》

요사떨다, 요사부리다 妖邪— behave in a capricious〔treacherous, wicked〕 way

요사이 ⇨ 요새

요산 尿酸 uric acid

요상 要償 〖법〗 a claim (for damages) ; a claim for compensation —하다 bring a claim for damages ; claim damages

—권 (right of) claim for damages

*요새 recently ; lately ; (in) these days ; nowadays ¶ 요새 사람 men of the present day // 요새 청년 the young people of today〔of these days〕 // 요새 학생 the present-day students // 요새의 경향 the modern〔recent〕 tendency // 요새 일어난 일 a recent event // 그건 요새 일이다 It happened quite recently. // 그녀는 요새 어떻게 지내고 있느냐 How is she these days? // 저런 정직한 사람은 요새 드물다 Such an honest man is rarely to be met with nowadays. // 요새 그를 보지 못했다 I haven't seen him lately. // 그 아가씨는 요새 왔다 The maid is a new comer. // 요새까지 대단히 추웠다 It was very 〔extremely〕 cold until recently.

⁑요새 要塞 a fortress ; a stronghold ; fortification ¶ 하늘의 요새 a flying fortress // 요새를 구축하다 construct a fortress

— 군항 a fortified port — 도시 a fortressed〔fortified〕 city —전 an attack upon a fort ; siege warfare — 지대 a fortified〔strategic〕 zone ; the prohibited area〔limits〕 —포 a fortress gun — 포병 garrison artillery —화(化) fortification

요서 夭逝 a premature death ⇨ 요사(夭死)

요석 尿石 〖의학〗 a urolith ; a urinary calculus

요설 饒舌 garrulity ; loquacity ; volubility ; talkativeness ; the incontinence of speech〔tongue〕 —하다 wag one's tongue ; be garrulous〔loquacious〕

요설 要說 a general statement ⇨ 개설

요성 妖星 ① [불길한 별] an ominous star ② [혜성] a comet ; [유성] a meteor

요셉 〖성경〗 Joseph

†요소 要素 an element ; an important factor ; an essential part ; a constituent ; a requisite (필요 조건) ¶ 생물체의 구성 요소 the elements of living bodies // 생산의 3요소 the three requisites for production // 행복의 요소 a factor of happiness // 훌륭한 정원의 요소 the makings of a good garden // 요소를 이루다 be essential to 《a thing》 ; form an important factor of 《a thing》 ; form an essential part of 《a whole》 // 건강은 행복의 요소다 Health is essential to happiness. // 승리의 제일 요소는 협동이다 Cooperation is the first requisite for victory.

요소 要所 an important position〔post〕 ; a

strategic point〔position〕 ¶ 요소 요소에 at important points // 요소에 경관을 배치하다 post the police at a strategic point

요소 尿素 〖화학〗 urea
—계(計) ureameter **— 수지(樹脂)** urea resins

⁑요술 妖術 magic ; a magical practice ; black art ; witchcraft ; witchery ; tricks ; conjuring ; jugglery ¶ 요술을 걸다 enchant 《a person》 // 요술을 부리다 juggle ; do conjuring tricks ; play a trick (속이다) ; practice black art ; use magic // 요술로 속이다 delude 《a person》 by magical practices
— 방망이 a mallet of luck ; Aladdin's lamp **—쟁이** a juggler ; a conjurer ; a magician (마술사) ; a wizard (남자) ; a witch (여자)

요승 妖僧 a wicked〔vicious〕 Buddhist

요시찰인 명부 要視察人名簿 a black list ; a surveillance list ¶ 요시찰인 명부에 오르다 be put (on) the black list ; be black-listed ; be placed on the black book

요식 要式 formal formalities
— 계약 a formal contract **— 행위** a formal act

요식업 料食業 restaurant business
—자 a restaurant owner〔keeper〕

요신 妖神 Satan ; an evil-spirit ; a devil ; a demon

⁑요약 要約 summary ; condensation ; summing up ; a summary ; a digest ; an epitome **—하다** summarize ; condense ; epitomize ; digest ; sum up ; give an outline of ; abridge ¶ 요약해서 말하자면 in a word ; in brief ; in short ; in sum ; to sum up ; to make a long story short // 그것을 좀더 요약할 수 없니 Can't you boil it down a little ?

요양 療養 medical treatment〔care〕 ; (rest and) recuperation **—하다** recuperate ; receive medical treatment ¶ 병후의 요양 convalescence // 목하 요양 중이다 be now under medical treatment // 전지 요양을 가다 go for a change of air // 그는 동래의 별장에서 요양 중이다 He is recuperating〔staying for the benefit of his health〕 at the villa at *Tongnae*.
—비 medical care expenses **—소** sanitarium 《미》 ; a sanatorium 《영》 ; a convalescent hospital **자택 —** home 〔domiciliary〕 treatment

요언 要言 summarizing the essential points

요얼 妖蘖 [악귀의 재앙] a disaster 〔calamity〕 brought about by an evil spirit

요업 窯業 the ceramic industry ; ceramics〔keramics〕
—가 a ceramist **— 미술** ceramic art ; art from the kilns **—소** a pottery **— 제품** ceramic manufactures ; a ceramic ; ceramics 《복수 취급》 **—학** ceramic engineering

요엘서 —書 〖성경〗 The Book of Joel ; Joel

요연하다 瞭然— (be) clear ; evident ; plain ; obvious ; manifest ¶ 그것은 일목요연하다 It is clear at a glance. /It jumps to the eye. /One can see it with half an eye. /이것을 보면 졸업생의 동태가 일목요연하다 This gives us clear information of the movements of the graduates.

요염 妖艶 voluptuous beauty ; sensual charm ; fascination ; the witchery of a woman's beauty **—하다** (be) bewitching ; voluptuous ; fascinating ; enchanting ¶ 요염한 눈매로 with coquettish eyes // 요염한 모습 a charming 〔bewitching〕 figure // 요염한 미인 a voluptuous beauty

요오드 〖화학〗 iodine ; iodin
— 정량법 iodometry ; iodimetry **—제** an iodine preparation **—팅크** tincture of iodine ; iodine tincture

요요 擾擾 noise and disturbance **—하다** (be) noisy ; uproarious ; tumultuous

요요하다 遙遙— (be) far away〔off〕 ; (far) distant ; remote

요용 要用 useful employment **—하다** make good use of ; put 《a thing》 to a good use
—건 an important matter〔business〕 ; an indispensable article **—품** a necessity ; a must item

요우 僚友 a colleague ; a comrade ; a fellow official ; a fellow worker ; a coworker

***요원 遙遠** (being) very far away ; far distant **—하다** (be) far distant ; fat off 〔away〕 ; remote ¶ 전도 요원하다 [사람이 주어] have a long way to go ; be far from ; have a long way before 《one》 ; [사물이 주어] 《the goal》 be far〔a long way〕 off

요원 燎原 ¶ 요원의 불길 a prairie 〔grass〕 fire ; a wildfire // 요원의 불길처럼 퍼지다 spread〔travel〕 like wildfire

요원 要員 workers required ; needed 〔necessary〕 personnel ; the staff

요율 料率 tariff ; a premium rate (보험료의)

요의 要義 the essentials ; an outline ; a digest ; a constituent

***요인 要人** a key figure ; an important〔a leading〕 person ; a prominent man ; a notable (person)
산업계 — a leading〔key〕 figure of the industrial world ; those essential to various industries **재계 —** a leading person in the financial world **정부 —** key figures in the government ; high government officials

⁑요인 要因 a primary factor〔element〕 ; a chief〔main〕 cause ; a prerequisite

요일 曜日 a day of the week ; a weekday

(일요일을 제외한) ¶ 오늘은 무슨 요일이냐 What day of the week is this? // 정월 초하루가 내년에는 무슨 요일이냐 What day (of the week) does New Year's Day fall on next year?

요임 要任 an important mission〔duty, task〕

*__요전__ [며칠 전] the other day; a few days ago; not long ago; just recently; [전번] last; previous; before; last time ¶ 요전 날 밤 the other evening // 요전 일요일 last Sunday // 요전번 편지 one's last〔previous〕 letter // 바로 요전에 quite recently; only the other day // 바로 요전까지 until quite recently // 요전에 알려드린 바와 같이 as I told you last time; as previously announced // 요전에 만났을 때는 when I saw you last time; the last time I met you // 요전 집보다는 훨씬 좋다 The house is much better than the old one.

요절 夭折 an early〔a premature〕 death **—하다** die young〔early, prematurely〕; die at an early age; die in the prime of life; die before one's time ¶ 그는 요절했다 He died young. /He died an early death.

요절 腰折 —하다 split one's sides with laughter; laugh oneself into convulsions; be convulsed with laughter; die laughing ¶ 요절할 익살 sidesplitting farce // 요절케하다 set〔throw〕《a person》 into convulsions // 참 요절할 일이다 It is really sidesplitting. /How ridiculously amusing!

요절나다 ① [못쓰게 되다] go to ruin; go to pieces; get broken; break down; be wrecked ¶ 요절난 차 a disabled car // 내 시계가 요절났다 My watch has broken // 태풍으로 많은 집들이 요절났다 Many houses were demolished by the typhoon.
② [일이] be spoiled; be demolished; be upset ¶ 우리의 계획이 요절났다 Our plan fell through. /Our plan proved abortive.

요절내다 spoil; ruin; mar; destroy

†**요점 要點** the main〔essential〕 point; the gist; the substance; the pith; the essence; nub 《미》 ¶ 각 학과의 요점 the salient points of each subject // 요점을 따다 summarize // 요점을 잡다 grasp the point of a subject; seize the essence of a matter // 요점을 찌르다 come to the point // 요점을 말하다 give the gist〔essence, pith〕 of // 요점에서 벗어나다 wander from the point; be beside〔off, away from〕 the point // 네 말의 요점을 모르겠다 I do not catch〔get〕 the point of your remarks.

요정 了定 [결정] decision; [결말] conclusion; settlement ¶ 요정짓다 decide 《upon》; conclude; bring 《a matter》 to a close; put an end to

요정나다 관용 be decided; be finished; be concluded; be settled

⁑**요정 妖精** a fairy; a spirit; an elf 《*pl.* -ves》; a nymph ¶ 숲의 요정 a dryad; a wood nymph // 물의 요정 a naiad; a water-spirit

*__요정 料亭__ [요리집] a (Korean) restaurant; [술집] a (Korean) saloon; a *kisaeng* house

요조 窈窕 modesty; chastity; decency **—하다** (be) graceful; refined; modest; chaste; decent ¶ 요조숙녀 a chaste and modest woman; a lady of refined manners

요즈막 recently; lately; theses days; nowadays; last few days

†**요즈음** ① [현금(現今)] nowadays; (in) these days ¶ 요즈음의 젊은이 the young men of today; today's youth
② [최근] lately; recently; of late ¶ 요즈음 일어난 사건 a recent event // 요즈음 그를 못만났다 I haven't seen him lately.

요즘 ⇨ 요즈음

⁑**요지 要地** an important place; a strategic point〔place〕

요지 要旨 [요점] the point; the gist; the substance; [대요] a summary; [취지] the purport ¶ 주의의 요지 the substance〔gist〕 of a doctrine // 요지를 설명하다 explain the gist; set forth the essential points // 연설의 요지를 파악하다 get〔grasp〕 the gist of a speech // 이번 말썽의 요지는 대강 이런 정도다 That's about the gist of what went wrong. // 그러면 바로 요지를 말해 주겠다 Then I'll just go over the main points.

요지경 瑤池鏡 a magic glass; a toy peep-show

요지부동 搖之不動 steadfastness **—하다** be steadfast; be adamantine; be unyielding; be invincible; stand firm

요직 要職 an important post〔position, office〕; a key position ¶ 요직에 취임하다 be appointed to an important post〔office〕 // 정부 요직에 있다 hold an important post in the government

요진 要津 [나루] an important ferry; [요로] a principal〔an important〕 road

요처 凹處 a concave place; concavity

요처 要處 a strategic〔an important〕 point

요철 凹凸 prominence and depression; unevenness; irregularity; ruggedness **—하다** (be) bulgy and hollow; uneven; jagged; rugged
— 렌즈 a concavo-convex lens

*__요청 要請__ request; demand; claim **—하다** demand; ask 《for》; ask 《a person》 to; request; claim ¶ 정당한〔부당한〕 요청 a reasonable〔an unreasonable〕 claim〔demand〕 // 요청에 의하여 on〔by〕 request; at a request of // 시대의 요청에 응하다 meet the needs of the times // 요청을 수락하다 comply with the request //

나에게 무슨 요청이 있느냐 What do you expect me to do? // 그는 연설을 해달라는 요청을 받았다 He was called upon to make a speech. // 나는 그에게 세차례나 보고를 제출하도록 요청하였다 I have asked him three times to send in his report.

요체 要諦 the secret; the cardinal point ¶ 성공의 요체 the secret of success

요추 腰椎 〖해부〗 the lumbar (vertebra) — 마취 lumbar anesthesia

요충 要衝 an important spot ⇨ 요충지

요충 蟯蟲 a threadworm; a pinworm

요충지 要衝地 an important spot〔position, place〕; a point of strategic importance (군사상의) ¶ 지브롤터는 지중해의 요충지이다 Gibraltar is the key point of the Mediterranean Sea.

*__요컨대 要—__ in short; in a word; in sum; in the last analysis; to sum up; to make a long story short; after all; in effect ¶ 요컨대 그는 몽상가다 In short, he is a dreamer. // 요컨대 그 문제는 이렇게 된다 After all, the question boils down to this.

요탓조탓 with all sorts of excuse

요통 腰痛 lumbago; a crick in the back; a lame hip ¶ 요통이 일어나다 have an attack of lumbago // 요통을 앓다 be troubled with〔suffer from〕 lumbago

⁑**요트** a yacht ¶ 요트를 타다 yacht; cruise in a yacht // 요트를 달리다 sail a yacht — 레이스〔경주〕 a yacht(ing) race — 조종자 a yachtsman

요판 凹版 intaglio — 인쇄 intaglio printing

요포대기 — a baby quilt〔coverlet〕

요하 遼河 the Liao-ho (River)

†**요하다 要—** require; need; want; take; demand; call for; have a need of ¶ 휴식을 요하다 need rest // 주의를 요하다 require care // 그곳에 가려면 5천원을 요한다 It costs you five thousand *won* to go there. // 그 일은 대단한 수련을 요한다 The task demands〔calls for〕 great skill. // 커다란 군함을 만들려면 적어도 2년을 요한다 It takes at least two years to build a large man-of-war. // 너의 병은 3주일의 안정을 요한다 Your illness demands three weeks of quiet rest. // 본인의 출두를 요하지 않는다 You need not report〔come〕 in person.

요한 〖성경〗 John — 묵시록〔계시록〕 The Book of the Apocalypse of St. John (카톨릭교); The Book of Revelations of St. John (신교) — 복음 The Gospel according to St. John; John —1서〔2서, 3서〕 The First 〔Second, Third〕 Epistle of St. John

요함 僚艦 a consort (ship); a comrade vessel; a sister ship

요항 要項 essential points; essentials; an important item; the staple; the gist (개요) ¶ 요항을 적어두다 write (down) the points; take〔make〕 notes 《of》 // 노트에 요항을 적어 두어라 Write down the essential points for guidance in your notebook.
상사 — elements in commerce 지도〔지시〕 — the essential points for guidance

요항 要港 an important port; a strategic naval port ¶ 진해는 해군의 요항이다 *Chinhae* is a port of naval importance. 군사 — a port of strategic importance

요해 要害 ① [요새] a stronghold; [요지] a strategic point ¶ 요해 견고한 impregnable; unassailable; secure
② [신체의] the vital parts of the body; a vital part
—지(점) a point of strategic importance; a strategic point

*__요행 僥倖__ luck by chance; chance luck; good luck; good fortune; a lucky chance; a fluke; a godsend; a windfall ¶ 요행으로 by luck; luckily; fortunately; by a fluke // 요행을 바라다 rely on chance // 그것은 요행에 불과하다 It is mere good luck〔a mere fluke〕. // 내가 시험에 합격한 것은 요행이다 It was by chance that I passed the examination. // 그는 요행으로 성공했다 He had the good luck to succeed. /He owes his success to good luck. // 요행으로 그를 만났다 Luckily I met up with him.
—수 a lucky〔happy〕 chance; a piece 〔stroke〕 of good luck; a fortunate move

요혈 尿血 the presence of blood in the urine; hematuria; bleeding in urination —증 〖의학〗 hematuria

요형 凹型 concavity; concave ¶ 요형으로 하다 concave; curve inward

요희 妖姬 a temptress; an enchantress; a vamp; a witch

요힘빈 〖약〗 yohimbine

*__욕 辱__ ① [욕설] abuse; slander; abusive〔foul〕 language; curses; namecalling ——하다 speak ill of 《a person》; call 《a person》 names; speak against 《a person》; abuse; slander; utter curses〔rail〕 《at》; revile 《at, against》 ¶ 뒤에서 욕하다 backbite; speak ill of 《a person》 behind his back // 그는 남의 욕을 잘하는 사람이다 He is a scandalmonger. // 그는 공개 석상에서 나를 욕했다 He railed at me in public. // 누구한테도 욕을 하지 말라 Don't call anyone names. // 상사에게 먼저 말을 해두지 않으면 나중에 그 문제로 욕을 먹을 것이다 You'd better run it by the boss first, or you'll get flak about it later. // 일초만 빨랐어도 그는 우리가 욕하는 소리를 들었을 거야 One second earlier and he would have heard us bad-mouthing him.
② [치욕] shame; disgrace; humiliation; insult ¶ 욕보이다 disgrace; put 《a person》 to shame; humiliate; insult; [능욕하다] rape; violate; abuse // 욕보다

be put to shame ; be insulted ; be humiliated ; be raped ; be violated ; be abused // 욕을 달게 받다 eat humble-pie // 오래 사는 것은 욕이다 To live long is to outlive much.
③ [수고] troubles ; hardships ; pains ¶ 욕을 보다 go through hardships ; have a hard time ; go through the mill ; take pains // 그의 집을 찾는 데 욕봤다 I had a hell of a time looking for his house.

욕 慾 a desire
권세— the will to power 금전— love of money ; desire for wealth〔after riches〕 명예— desire for fame 소유— possessiveness ; possessive instinct 육— sexual desire〔passion〕 지식— a thirst 〔an appetite〕 for knowledge ; hunger after learning ¶ 그는 지식욕에 불타고 있다 He is thirsty for knowledge.

욕가마리 辱— the butt of abuse ; a person deserving of abuse

욕감태기 a person who is called bad names by many people

욕객 浴客 a bathhouse customer ; bathers ; a bathing guest ; a visitor at a spa (온천의)

욕계 欲界 the world of desire ; the greedy 〔avaricious, covetous〕 world

†욕구 欲求 desire ; craving ; urge ; aspiration ; want —하다 desire ; want ; crave 《for》 ; aspire 《after》 ¶ 생의 욕구 the will to live ; craving for life // 성적 욕구 sexual desire // 욕구가 적은 사람 a man of few wants // 욕구를 채우다 fill〔satisfy〕 one's wants // 생리적 욕구를 채우다 satisfy man's natural urge
— 불만 frustration ; unsatisfied desires

욕기 부리다 慾氣— covet ; be greedy ; be avaricious ; be rapacious ; be grasping ¶ 너무 욕기 부리지 마라 You must not be so grasping〔avaricious〕.

욕념 慾念 desire ; want ; appetite ; passions ¶ 욕념을 억제하다 suppress 〔smother, crucify〕 one's desire〔passions〕

욕되다 辱— be a disgrace〔shame〕《to》 ; (be) shameful ; disgraceful ; dishonorable ; discreditable ¶ 욕된 행실 shameful conduct // 학교의 이름을 욕되게 하다 bring disgrace on one's school // 너와 같은 자식은 가문에 욕된다 A son like you is a disgrace〔discredit〕 to our family. // 그런 일을 하면 부모에게 욕된다 If you do so, you will bring shame on your parents.

*욕망 欲望 a desire ; a craving ; an appetite ; (an) ambition (야망) ; wants (욕구) ¶ 욕망을 일으키다 arouse a desire 〔an appetite〕《in a person for a thing》// 욕망을 억제하다 suppress one's desires ; control one's passions // 욕망을 채우다 gratify〔satisfy〕 one's desire 〔want, ambition〕 // 욕망을 품다 harbor an ambition

동물적 — animal appetites

욕먹다 be spoken ill of ; be abused ; be reviled ; be slandered ; be scolded ; be insulted ; be stigmatized ¶ 그는 잘못해서 아버지한테 욕먹었다 He got a scolding from his father for a mistake.

욕보다 ① [곤란] have a hard time ; undergo〔go through〕 hardships ; have a hell of a time ; suffer troubles ¶ 나는 돈 꾸기에 욕봤다 I had a hell of a time getting a loan. // 범인을 잡느라고 욕봤다 I had a hard〔tough, terrible〕 time catching the culprit.
② [치욕] be put to shame ; disgrace oneself ; be humiliated ; be disgraced ; be dishonored ; be insulted ; be abused ¶ 용사는 욕보기보다는 죽음을 택한다 A warrior would choose death before dishonor.
③ [능욕] be raped ; be assaulted ; be violated

욕보이다 ① [치욕] disgrace ; dishonor ; insult ; put 《a person》 to shame ; bring shame on 《a person》 ; humiliate
② [괴롭힘] put 《a person》 to trouble ; give 《a person》 trouble ; abuse
③ [능욕] rape ; assault ; violate ; outrage

⁑욕설 辱說 abuse ; abusive language ; slander ; curses ; swearwords ; vituperation —하다 abuse 《a person》 ; speak ill of ; revile ; call 《a person》 names ; throw insulting words ; vituperate ¶ 마구 욕설을 퍼붓다 curse and swear 《at》 ; call 《a person》 all sorts of names

욕실 浴室 a bathroom ; a bath ; a toilet (room) 《미》

⁑욕심 慾心 [탐욕] greed ; avarice ; covetousness ; rapacity ; cupidity ; acquisitiveness ; (a) desire (욕망) ; [이기심] selfishness ; self-interest ¶ 욕심 많은 greedy ; avaricious ; covetous ; grasping ; rapacious // 욕심 없는 unselfish ; uninterested // 욕심을 부리다 be greedy ; be covetous ; be avaricious ; be grasping // 욕심을 억제하다 control〔mortify〕 one's desire 〔avarice〕 // 욕심에 눈이 멀다 be blind with avarice ; be blinded by greed // 욕심은 한이 없다 Avarice knows no bounds. // 너무 욕심부리지 마라 You must not be so grasping 〔avaricious〕. // 너무 욕심을 부리면 아무것도 얻지 못한다 One who grasps at too much loses all. /Grasp all, lose all.

욕심쟁이 慾心— an avaricious〔a grasping〕 man〔fellow〕 ; a grabber ; [구두쇠] a close-fisted person ; a miser ¶ 욕심쟁이 할머니 a covetous hag ; a skinflint of an old woman

욕의 浴衣 a bathrobe ; a dressing gown ; a bathdress

욕쟁이 a slanderer ; a foul-mouthed〔-tongued〕 person ; a knocker ; [험담꾼] a scandal-monger

욕정 欲情 (a) desire ; craving ; [색욕] passions ; (a) lust ; sexual desire ¶ 욕정에 빠지다 indulge in sexual desire // 욕정을 억제하다 control〔subdue, restrain〕 one's passions ; mortify the flesh ; be continent // 욕정을 채우다 gratify one's lust

욕조 浴槽 a bathtub ; a bath

⁑욕지거리 abusive language ; bad names ; swearwords ; abuse ⇨ 욕설

욕지기 nausea ; qualm ; queasiness ; a sickly feeling ; sickness at the stomach ¶ 욕지기나게 하다 turn one's stomach ; provoke nausea // 그것을 보니 욕지기가 난다 At the sight of it nausea rises in me. /The sight makes〔turns〕 me sick.

욕지기 나다 관용 feel nausea〔sick〕 ; feel queasy 《미》 ; feel sick at the stomach ; one's stomach turns

욕탕 浴湯 a bath house ; a public bath

욕화 浴化 the influence of virtue —하다 be influenced by virtuous examples

욕화 慾火 burning〔ardent〕 desire

욧속 cotton-wool stuffing ; wadding ; batting

욧의 —衣 a mattress cover

욧잇 a bed sheet ; a sheet ; sheeting

†용 用 ① [용돈] pocket money ② [비용] expenses ⇨ 비용 ③ [접미어] for (the use of) ¶ 남자〔여자〕용 for men 〔ladies〕 // 교사용 for the teacher // 자가용 for domestic〔family〕 use ; private ; personal // 어린이용 책 books for children // 교사용 참고서 a teacher's manual // 자가용차 a private〔personal〕 car ; a car for one's personal use

용 茸 [녹용] an antler

⁑용 龍 a dragon

용될 고기는 모이철부터 안다 속담 First impresions are the most lasting. /The first blow is halfly the battle.

용의 꼬리보다 닭의 머리가 낫다 속담 Better be the head of a dog (fox, mouse, lizard) than the tail of a lion. /Better be the head of a pike than the tail of sturgeon. /Better be the head of an ass than the tail of lion. /Better be first in a village than second at Rome.

용가 龍駕 a Royal carriage ; a state carriage

용가마 a large iron pot ; a ca(u)ldron

용가마에 삶은 개가 멍멍 짖거든 속담 Pigs might fly, if they had wings.

†용감 勇敢 bravery ; courageousness ; boldness ; gallantry ; heroism ; valor

> 참고 **brave**는 가장 일반적인 말이며 주로 외견상 「용감한」의 뜻 **courageous**는 「정신적으로 끈질긴 용감함」의 뜻을 포함하고 있고 **bold**는 「대담함」「뻔뻔함」을 강조하는 말

—하다 (be) brave ; courageous ; heroic ; gallant ; valiant ¶ 용감한 사람 a brave〔courageous〕 person // 용감한 행위 a heroic deed ; a deed of heroism // 용감한 기질 chivalrous disposition ; bravery ; gallantry // 용감히 싸우다 fight gallantly〔bravely〕 ; fight a gallant fight // 그는 용감하게 죽었다 He died a brave death. // 그들은 용감하게 적을 공격했다 They made a dashing attack on the enemy.

용강 勇剛 fearless courage ; intrepidity ; stout-heartedness ; stalwartness ; sturdiness —하다 (be) intrepid ; stout-hearted ; stalwart ; sturdy ; brawny lay (down) the keel

용건 用件 business ; matter of business ¶ 급한 용건으로 on urgent〔pressing〕 business // 용건을 묻다 ask 《a person's》 business // 용건이 무엇입니까 What can I do for you ? /What do you want with〔of〕 me ? // 용건을 빨리 말하시오 Come to the point at once. // 무슨 용건이신지 여쭈어 봐도 될까요 May I ask the nature of your business ? /May I ask what this is regarding ?

용고뚜리 a heavy〔chain, hard〕 smoker

*용골 龍骨 [선박의] the keel ; [동물의] mastodon bones ¶ 용골을 설치하다 lay down the keel

—대 the keelblocks — 돌기 〖동물〗 a carina 《*pl.* -nae》 주— the main(-bar) keel

용공 容共 pro-communist

— 사상 pro-communist thought — 정책 a pro-communist policy —파 the pro-communist faction〔elements〕 ; pro-communists

용관 冗官 a supernumerary (of government official)

⁑용광로 鎔鑛爐 a melting〔smelting〕 furnace ; a blast furnace

용구 用具 a tool (공구) ; an instrument (계기) ; implements (기구) ; goods ; an appliance (장치)

가정 — household appliances 골프 — golf things 교육 — teaching aids 운동 — sporting goods

용궁 龍宮 the Dragon Palace ; the palace of the dragon king

용기 用器 [기구] an instrument ; a tool ; [기구의 사용] use of an instrument〔a tool〕

—화 (畫) instrumental〔mechanical〕 drawing

용기 容器 a container ; a vessel ; a receptacle

†용기 勇氣 courage ; bravery ; valor ; pluck ; boldness ; prowess ; nerve ¶ 용기 백배해서 with redoubled〔renewed, fresh〕 courage // 용기가 있다 be courageous ; be brave ; be valiant ; be plucky // 용기가 없다 be pluckless ; be a cow-

ard ; be timid ; be fainthearted ; be lily-livered // 용기를 내다 pluck〔muster, screw, summon〕 up one's courage ; take〔collect〕 heart〔courage〕 ; brace oneself up // 용기를 잃다 lose 《one's》 courage ; be discouraged // 용기를 꺾다 dishearten 《a person》 // 용기를 돋우어 주다 encourage ; give 《a person》 courage ; hearten〔cheer up〕 // 용기를 내어 그를 방문했다 Screwing up my courage, I called on him. // 나는 말할 용기가 없었다 I had not the courage 〔nerve, heart〕 to speak. // 그의 말에 우리는 용기 백배했다 His words inspired us with redoubled courage. // 용기를 내서 그에게 사과해라 Screw up your courage and apologize to him. // 당신 덕분에 용기가 생겼다 You've bolstered my courage.

용기병 龍騎兵 a dragoon

용꿈 a lucky dream ; a dream about a dragon ¶ 용꿈꾸다 dream〔have〕 a lucky dream ; dream about a dragon

용납 容納 toleration ; approval ; allowance ; admission ; permission **—하다** tolerate ; approve ; allow ; admit ; permit ¶ 용납할 수 없는 unpardonable // 지연을 용납치 않다 admit of no delay // 변명을 용납치 않다 allow no excuse

용녀 龍女 the Dragon Princess ; the Princess of the Dragon〔the Sea God〕

용녀 傭女 a maid ; a maidservant ; a hired girl

용뇌 龍腦 refined Borneo〔Sumatra〕 camphor ; borneol ; camphol

용단 勇斷 a decisive measure ; a resolute〔drastic〕 step ; a manly resolution ; a courageous decision ¶ 용단을 내리다 make a resolute decision 《on a matter》 ; give one's resolute decision // 당국의 용단을 요망하다 demand a drastic measure on the part of the authorities

용달 用達 delivery service ; execution of a commission **—하다** deliver 《goods》 ; supply〔provide〕 《goods》 ¶ 용달가다 go on an errand ; run〔go on〕 errands
—사(社) a delivery agent (배달업자) ; a purveyor (조달업자) **—업** the delivery business

용담 用談 [상담] a business talk ; [볼일] business **—하다** talk with 《a person》 on business

용도 用度 expenditure ; expenses
—과 the supplies〔purchasing〕 section 〔department〕

†**용도 用途** use ; service ¶ 용도가 넓다 have many uses ; be used for various purposes〔in various ways〕 // 돈의 용도를 분명히 하다 make known〔account for〕 how the money was spent ; keep account of the money spent

***용돈 用—** pocket money ; spending money 《미》 ; personal expenses ; pin money (아내의) ¶ 나는 용돈이 떨어졌다 I have run out of pocket money. // 아버지는 월 50,000원을 용돈으로 주신다 My father allows me 50,000 *won* a month for pocket money. // 그의 아버지는 그에게 다달이 용돈을 주신다 His father makes him a monthly allowance of pocket money.

용두 龍頭 the stem of a watch

용두레 a large water dipper ; a scoop bucket

용두사미 龍頭蛇尾 anticlimax ; a weak conclusion ; a tame ending ; bathos ; bright beginning and dull finish ; to start off with a bang and to end with a whimper ; He who begins many things, finishes but few. ¶ 용두사미로 끝나다 thin out ; peter out // 그것은 용두사미로 끝났다 It went up like a rocket and came down like a stick.

용두질 masturbation ; onanism ; self-abuse ; self-pollution **—하다** practice masturbation ; masturbate ; commit self-abuse

용략 勇略 courage and strategy ; valor and stratagem ; daring and scheming ; bravery and artifice

†**용량 容量** capacity ; content ; volume ; measure of capacity
—계(計) a capacity meter **— 계수** 〚전기〛 a capacity coefficient ; a coefficient of capacity **— 분석** 〚화학〛 volumetric analysis **— 전류** a capacity current **— 측정법** volumetry **열—** 〚물리〛 the thermal capacity **전기 —** 〚물리〛 electric capacity

용량 用量 [약의] a dose ; dosage

용력 用力 (mental) exertion ; (physical) labor **—하다** exert oneself ; labor ; set one's heart on ; put out〔forth〕 one's strength

용력 勇力 manly strength ; undaunted power ; dauntless〔fearless〕 vigor

용렬 庸劣 mediocrity ; inferiority ; stupidity **—하다** (be) mediocre ; inferior ; stupid ; bungling ; clumsy ; silly ¶ 용렬한 사람 an awkward〔a clumsy〕 fellow // 용렬한 짓 a blunder ; a bungle ; tomfoolery // 용렬한 짓을 해서 미안하오 I am sorry for the blunder I have committed.

용례 用例 an example ; an illustration ; an instance ¶ 용례를 들다 take〔give, show, cite, quote〕 an example ; exemplify ; illustrate

용립 聳立 rising ; soaring ; towering **—하다** rise〔tower, soar〕 high 《over》 ¶ 그것은 서울시 상공 높이 용립하고 있다 It towers (rises) high over *Seoul* city. // 산봉우리가 구름 위에 용립하고 있다 The mountain rears its crest into the clouds.

용마 龍馬 a swift horse ; a fleet steed

용마루 the ridge of a roof
— 높이 〚건축〛 the height of ridge

용마름 the cover(ing) of a roof-ridge or a mud wall

용매 溶媒 〚화학〛 a solvent (agent) ; a

menstruum (pl. -strua)
*용맹 勇猛 intrepidity ; dauntlessness ; valor ; lionheartedness ; courage ; bravery —하다 (be) intrepid ; dauntless ; valiant ; plucky ; lionhearted ; daring ¶ 용맹 과감한 사람 a man of dauntless [fearless] courage
—심 an intrepid [a dashing] spirit
용명 勇名 fame for bravery ¶ 용명을 떨치다 win fame for bravery ; win a great renown
용명 溶明 [영화] a fade-in —하다 fade in
*용모 容貌 a face ; a countenance ; features ; looks ¶ 매력적인 용모 a charming face ; attractive features // 용모가 매우 아름다운 사람 a person of great personal beauty // 용모가 추한 사람 a plain [homely, uncomely] person
용무 冗務 unimportant business [matters] ; a trivial [trifle] business
†용무 用務 business ; a matter of business ; a matter (to be taken care of) ¶ 용무를 띠고 on business // 용무를 마치다 carry out [finish, complete] one's business // 용무 외에는 출입 금지 No admittance except on business. (게시문)
용발 鎔發 [항공] [미사일이 대기권 내에 재돌입할 때의] ablation
*용법 用法 the way to use (a thing) ; the directions for use [using] ; use ; usage ; directions (약품 따위의) ¶ 보통의 용법 the common [ordinary] usage // 전치사의 용법 uses of prepositions // 용법을 모르다 be ignorant of the way to use ; do not know how to use it // 용법을 잘 알고 있다 be familiar with the use of ; be adept in the use of // 용법을 잘 읽고 그 약품을 써라 Apply the medicine after carefully reading the directions.
용벚 a bow wrapped in a cherry bark cover
용변 用便 easing nature ; going to the lavatory [toilet, bathroom] ¶ 용변 후 after stool // 용변을 보다 relieve oneself ; wash one's hands ; go to the closet ; ease nature ; go to stool
용병 用兵 tactics ; manipulation of troops —하다 manipulate [maneuver] the troops ¶ 용병에 능하다 be well versed in tactics
—술 tactics ; strategy ; the science of war
용병 勇兵 a brave soldier ; a soldier of fearless courage
용병 傭兵 a mercenary (soldier) ; hired troops ; subsidiary troops (외국에서 온)
용봉탕 龍鳳湯 soup of carp and chicken boiled together
용부 庸夫 a mediocrity ; an inferior man ; a mediocre [commonplace, stupid] man
용부 勇夫 a brave [courageous] man ; a man of prowess
용불용 用不用 use and disuse
—설 Lamarckism ; the use and disuse theory
용비 用費 expense ; expenditure ; cost ; outlay ¶ 용비를 삭감하다 retrench [slash] the expenditure
용비 冗費 unnecessary [dispensable, avoidable, wasteful, useless] expenditure ¶ 용비를 덜다 curtail [cut down] unnecessary expenses
용사 勇士 a brave man ; the brave ; a man of courage [valor] ; a warrior ¶ 용사중의 용사 the bravest of the brave
용상 龍床 the king's seat ; the (royal) throne
용색 用色 sexual union [intercourse] —하다 have a sexual intercourse
용색 容色 features ; (good) looks ; personal appearance [beauty]
†용서 容恕 pardon ; forgiveness —하다 pardon ; condone ; forgive ; excuse (a person's fault, a person for his fault) ; overlook (a person's fault) ; pass over ; be tolerant of (묵과하다)

> 참고 **condone**은 「죄를 의식적으로 마치 그런 죄를 범하지 않았던 것처럼 너그럽게 용서하다」 **excuse**는 「손위 또는 동등한 입장에서 사소한 죄를 용서하다」 **pardon**은 「관리나 손위의 입장에서 자비나 관용의 행위로서 중대한 죄 특히 법이나 도덕상의 죄를 용서하다」의 뜻 **forgive**는 pardon보다 개인적인 감정의 요소가 강조되어 비난하고자 하는 마음이 없어지고 애정이 다시 돌아온 의미를 포함한 「용서하다」의 뜻

¶ 용서할 수 없는 unpardonable ; inexcusable // 용서 없이 relentlessly ; mercilessly // 용서를 빌다 beg (a person's) pardon ; apologize for // 용서할 수 없는 과실을 용서하다 excuse (a person) for an inexcusable mistake // 죄를 용서하다 forgive (a person's) sins // 용서하십시오 I beg your pardon. /Please pardon me. // 나의 무례를 용서 하십시오 I beg you to forgive my rudeness. // 이번에는 용서할 터이니 다음부터 주의하라 I will overlook your fault this time, so you must be more careful in future. // 너와 나 사이에 용서하고 안하고가 어디있니 There is no need of apology between you and me.
용석 熔石 [지질] lava ; volcanic rock
용선 傭船 ship chartering ; a chartered ship [vessel] —하다 charter [hire] a ship
— 계약서 a charter (party) — 기준 a charter base —료 charterage ; charter money — 시장 a chartering market —업 chartering business —자 a charterer — 중개인 a chartering broker 목재 [곡물] 수송 — lumber [grain] charter 왕복 [편

도〕 — round〔single〕 trip charter 정기 — time charter 정액 — lump sum charter ; charter for a lump sum
용설란 龍舌蘭 〖식물〗 an agave ; a pita
용소 龍沼 a linn ; the basin〔bottom〕 of a waterfall
용속 庸俗 —하다 (be) mediocre ; banal ; ordinary ; common ; commonplace ; vulgar
용솟음 [끓음] boiling up ; [솟음] leaping up ; bubbling up ; gush —치다 [끓다] boil up ; seethe ; bubble up ; [솟다] well (up, forth, out) ; gush〔spring〕 out ¶ 피가 용솟음 치게하다 cause the blood to tingle ; inflame the blood 《of》 ; stir 《a person's》 blood // 샘이 용솟음치듯 한다 A fountain gushes out.
용수 a rice-wine strainer
용수 用水 water ; rainwater (빗물) ; city water (수도) ; well water (우물물) ; irrigation water (관개용) ; using water (사용)
—권 water rights ; [수차 따위의] water power —로 [관개의] an irrigation channel ; [발전소 따위] a flume —지 a reservoir —통 a rain-water tank〔barrel〕
용수뒤 the dregs〔lees〕 of the wine in the bottom of the barrel〔keg, cask〕
용수량 容水量 water capacity
용수철 龍鬚鐵 a spring ¶ 시계의 용수철 the spring of a watch // 그것은 용수철로 움직인다 It works by means of a spring.
— 저울 a spring balance
용신 容身 ① moving (around) —하다 move one's body ¶ 용신 못하다 cannot move about ; cannot stir an inch // 방이 좁아서 용신할 수도 없다 The room is so narrow that I can't even move. ② eking out (one's livelihood) —하다 make a bare living ; eke out a scanty livelihood
용신 龍神 the Dragon God ; the Dragon King
—굿 the Dragon God ritual —제 the Dragon God festival
용심 用心 ① [주의] care ; heed ; caution —하다 attend ; take care 《of》 ; be cautious 《of》
② [심술] malice ; spite
—꾸러기〔쟁이〕 a malicious〔spiteful〕 person
용심 부리다 wreak one's jealousy〔spite〕 《upon》 ; take one's grudge out
용쓰다 ① [기운을 쓰다] put forth efforts ; brace oneself up ; concentrate one's energy ② [참다] endure forcibly
용안 龍眼 〖식물〗 a longan ; Nephelium longana (학명)
용안 龍顔 the royal countenance ¶ 용안을 배알하다 be received in audience by His Majesty〔the King, the Emperor〕
용암 溶暗 〖영화·TV〗 a fadeout ; a dissolve ¶ 용암이 되다 fade out ; dissolve out
*용암 熔岩 〖지질〗 lava ; molten rock ¶ 용암이 분출한다 Torrents of lava pour forth.
—류(流) a stream〔flow〕 of lava ; a lava flow —층(層) a lava bed
용압 溶壓 〖화학〗 solution pressure
용액 溶液 a solution ; a solvent
용약 勇躍 elation ; exultation ; high spirits —하다 exult ; take heart ; become high-spirited ; be animated ¶ 용약하여 in high spirits // 용약 장도에 오르다 go on an expedition in high spirits // 용약 진격을 시작하다 launch a spirited attack
*용어 用語 terminology ; a term ; wording ; phraseology ; vocabulary (어휘) ; diction ; language ¶ 용어에 주의하다 be careful about wording // 용어의 선택 the choice of words〔language〕
관청 — official language ; official jargon 군대 — military parlance 법률 — legal terms〔terminology, jargon〕 ; the language of the law 전문〔학술〕 — technical〔scientific〕 terms〔terminology〕 학생 — schoolboy slang
용언 用言 〖문법〗 a declinable word ; an inflected word
용언 冗言 unnecessary words ; a jest ; a joke ; fun ; kid(ding) 《미·속》
용역단 用役團 service corps
민간 — civilian service corps
용왕 龍王 The Dragon God〔King〕
용왕매진 勇往邁進 advance in a dashing spirit ; dashing forward —하다 advance bravely ; dash forward ¶ 용왕매진의 기상 a dashing spirit // 그는 용왕매진의 기상이 있다 He is full of push and go.
용원 傭員 a temporary employee ; an extra hand
용융 熔融 〖야금〗 fusion ; melting ; smelting —하다 melt ; smelt ; fuse ; dissolve
— 금속 a molten metal — 속도 the melting rate
용융점 熔融點 〖물리〗 a melting point
용의 用意 [조심] care ; precaution ; caution ; prudence ; [준비] preparedness ; readiness ; preparation —하다 take care of ; take precautions ; mind ; plan ; prepare ¶ 용의 주도한 very cautious ; circumspect ; prudent // 용의가 (되어) 있다 be ready 《to, for》 // 한국은 언제라도 신협정의 교섭을 할 용의가 있다 Korea 〔The Government of Korea〕 is ready at any time to negotiate a new agreement.
용의 容儀 manner ; mien ; bearing ; deportment ; demeanor ¶ 용의를 바로하다 draw oneself up ; sit up〔stand up〕 properly〔straight〕
용의 庸醫 a mediocre doctor
*용의자 容疑者 a suspect ; a suspected person ; an alleged culprit〔criminal〕 ¶ 살인 사건의 용의자 a suspect in a murder ; a suspected murderer
†용이 容易 easiness ; ease ; simpleness ;

facility **—하다** (be) easy ; simple ¶ 용이하게 easily ; readily ; with ease 〔facility〕 ; without difficulty // 하기가 용이하다 be easy to do ; be easily done // 용이하게 해치우다 make short work of // 용이한 일이 아니다 It is not easy. /It is no easy matter. // 네 이름을 내세우면 일은 용이하게 될 것이다 Your name will facilitate matters. // 어린애를 기른다는 것은 용이한 일이 아니다 It is hard work to bring up children.

용익권 用益權 〖법〗 a usufructuary right ; a usufruct
—자 a usufructuary

†**용인 容認** toleration ; admission ; approval **—하다** tolerate ; admit ; approve 《of》

용인 庸人 a (man of) mediocrity ; a mediocre person ; an ordinary person

용인 傭人 an employee ⇨ 고용인

용자 勇者 a hero 《*pl.* ~es》 ; a brave 〔courageous〕 man ; a man of valor 〔courage〕 ; the brave 《총칭》

용자 容姿 a figure ; the face and feature ; look ; the features ; appearance ; a carriage ; a form ¶ 품위 있는 용자 an elegant〔a graceful, a fine-looking, a personable〕 figure // 꽃다운 용자 a blooming face ; a face as fair as the May rose // 그 여자의 용자가 시들기 시작했다 Her beauty began to fade.

용자창 用字窓 a lattice window

용잠 龍簪 an ornamental hairpin in the shape of a dragon's head

용잡 冗雜 uselessness ; triviality **—하다** be of no use ; (be) trifling ; trivial ; petty

용장 勇將 a brave general ; a great soldier ¶ 용장 밑에 약졸이 없다 As is the master, so are his men. /Like master, like men.

용장 勇壯 bravery **—하다** (be) brave ; heroic ; gallant ; valiant ¶ 용장한 이야기 a heroic tale ; a story of valor

용재 用材 materials〔persons〕 to make use of ; raw materials ; [재목] timber ; lumber 《미》
—림(林) a timber forest **건축 —** building materials

용재 庸才 mediocre ability ; mediocrity ; a person of common ability ; commonplace capacity

†**용적 容積** capacity (용량) ; volume (체적) ; bulk (부피) ; measurements ; 〖기하〗 content ; cubical〔solid〕 measure 〔content〕 ¶ 용적으로 비교하면 bulk by bulk
—량 the measure of capacity **—법** 〖토목〗 the volumetric method **—톤** a measurement ton **— 톤수** measurement tonnage **— (계산)화물** measurement goods 〔cargo〕 **외부 —** outside measurement **입방 —** cubic capacity

용전 勇戰 brave fighting **—하다** fight heroically〔gallantly, bravely, courageously〕 ; fight a brave fight ¶ 용전 분투하다 fight a battle courageously

용전 여수 用錢如水 spending money like water ; lavish use of money **—하다** spend money like water ; be extravagant ; be too lavish with money

용점 熔點 〖물리〗 the melting point

***용접 鎔接** welding **—하다** weld 《to》 ¶ 금속은 각각 다른 온도에서 용접된다 Different metals weld at different temperatures.
—공 welder **— 공장** a welding shop **—관** a welded pipe **—기** a welding machine ; a welder **—물** a weldment **—법** a welding process **—봉** a welding rod **—제** a welding agent〔flux〕 **가스 —** gas welding **전기 —** electric〔thermit〕 welding

용접 容接 reception ; interview **—하다** receive 《a guest》

용제 溶劑 a solvent

용졸 庸拙 clumsiness ; shabbiness **—하다** (be) clumsy ; shabby ; be below mediocrity ; (be) stupid

용지 a flambeau ; a torch

용지 用紙 paper (to use) ; a (blank) form ; a printed form ; stationery (용전) ¶ 소정의 용지 the printed form
시험 — (a sheet of) examination paper **신문 —** paper (used) for newspapers **신청(원서) —** an application form **전보 —** a telegr-aph form **주문 —** an order blank 〔sheet〕 **투표 —** a ballot (paper) ; a voting paper 《영》

용지 用地 land required 《for works》 ; a lot ; a site (부지) ; a reservation ¶ 용지를 선정하다 choose on a site to use
건축 — a site for a building ; a building lot **군—** a military reservation ; land for military use **농업 —** farmland ; land for agricultural use **목장 —** pasture (land) ; pasturage **주택 —** a housing lot〔site〕 **철도 —** railway land

용지판 —板 〖건축〗 a wainscot ; a wainscotting

용진 勇進 dashing forward ; a brave advance **—하다** dash forward 〔onward〕 bravely ; advance bravely ; push forward vigorously ; make a dash

용질 溶質 solute

용집 sweat stains in socks

용철 鎔鐵 ingot iron〔steel〕
—장 a forge

용출 湧出 gush ; eruption **—하다** gush out〔forth〕 ; erupt ; well 《up》 ¶ 원유의 연간 용출량 the annual yield of crude oil

용출 溶出 〖화학〗 elution **—하다** flow out ¶ 용출시키다 elute (용매(溶媒)로)
—액 〖화학〗 an effluent

용출 聳出 rising〔towering〕 above **—하다** rise ; tower〔rise〕 above ; soar ¶ 산봉우

리가 구름 위에 용출하고 있다 The peak rises above the clouds.
용출 鎔出 〖야금〗 liquation **—하다** liquate out ¶ 용출시키다 liquate (out)
용춤추다 give in to flattery ; be made a cat's paw of 《by》 ¶ 용춤추이다 wheedle 《a person》 into doing ; flatter 〔cajole〕 《a person》 to do
용층줄 a sail rope ; rigging
용퇴 勇退 voluntary retirement〔resignation〕; willing〔graceful〕 retreat〔withdrawal〕 **—하다** retire voluntarily 〔gracefully〕; resign voluntarily ; withdraw gracefully ; bow out 《미》 ¶ 정계에서 용퇴하다 retire from political life // 용퇴해서 후진에게 길을 열어주다 give way to juniors // 그는 이제 용퇴해도 될 나이이다 He is old enough to resign his post. /It is time for him to beat an honorable retreat.
용퉁하다 (be) insensible ; stupid ; stolid
용트림 belching in an affected manner ; a big burp made on purpose **—하다** let out a big burp (on purpose)
용틀임 龍— a dragon picture〔engraving〕 on a building ; dragon embellishments 〔decorations〕
용품 用品 supplies ; an article 《for the use of》
가정 — household goods ; a domestic article 부엌 — kitchen utensils ; kitchenware 사무 — office supplies 일상 — articles for daily use ; daily necessaries 캠프 — an outfit for a camping trip 하이킹 — a hiker's outfit 학교 — school supplies〔requisites〕 화학 실험 — a chemistry set
용필 用筆 ① the use of a brush **—하다** use〔handle〕 a brush ; handwrite
② [운필] the manner of handling the brush ; one's command of the brush ; [필치] a stroke of the brush ; touches ; writing technique (필법) ; brushwork (화가의)
용하다 ① (be) skillful ; be good at ; (be) clever ; dexterous ; deft ; brilliant ¶ 용하게 처리하다 dispose of 《a case》 skillfully // (그림을) 용하게 그리다 draw deftly ; be good at drawing〔painting〕 // 병을 용하게 고치다 be a noted physician // 무엇에나 용하다 be a good hand at all things ; be skillful in everything
② [장하다] (be) admirable ; praiseworthy ; splendid ; brave ; great ; wonderful ¶ 참 용하다 Fine ! /Capital ! /Bravo ! / Splendid ! / Excellent ! /Well done ! // 혼자서 그 일을 다했다니 정말 용한 걸 It is admirable that he did such a great work by himself.
용합 溶合 **—하다** melt together ; melt into ; shade〔fade〕 into
†**용해 溶解** melting ; solution ; liquefaction **—하다** melt ; dissolve ; liquefy ¶ 용해력이 있는 solvent // 용해성의 liquefactive ; liquescent ; soluble // 용해되지 않는 insoluble ; indissoluble // 물에 용해하다 be soluble in water // 지방에 용해하다 be soluble in fat
—도 solubility **—량** meltage **—력** solvency **—성** solubility **— 속도** the velocity of dissolution **—액** a solution **—열** the heat of dissolution **—점** the melting point **—제** a solvent 기계적 — mechanical solution 화학적 — chemical solution
용해 鎔解 [금속의] melting ; fusion **—하다** melt ; fuse ¶ 용해성의 fusible // 비용해성의 infusible // 불에 용해하다 melt in the fire ; be fused by the fire
—로 a smelting furnace **—성** fusibility **—점** the smelting point
용호 龍虎 ① [용과 범] the dragon and the tiger ② [뛰어난 글] a powerful style of writing ③ [두 영웅] the two rival heroes ¶ 용호 상박 a well-matched contest ; diamond cuts diamond ; a Titanic struggle
용화 熔化 melting ; liquefaction ; fusion **—하다** melt ; liquefy ; fuse ; dissolve ¶ 금속의 용화 the fusion of metals
용훼 容喙 making comments 《on》; meddling ; interference **—하다** put in a word 《in》; butt in ; poke one's nose in〔into〕; meddle 《in》; interfere 《in》 ¶ 남의 일에 용훼하다 meddle in another's affairs // 남의 일에 용훼 잘 하는 사람 an officious person ; a meddler ; a busybody
용히 skillfully ; admirably ; splendidly ; remarkably ; eminently
우 all at once ; with a rush ¶ 우하고 몰려오다 rush〔sweep〕 in ; rush to ; throng to ; storm ; besiege // 사람들이 가게로 우하고 몰려왔다 People stormed the shop. // 사람들이 현장에 우 몰려갔다 A crowd of people rushed to the scene. // 바람이 우하고 불었다 There was a sudden gust of wind. // 소낙비가 우 내렸다 A shower came on suddenly.
우 優 [등급] excellent ; an "A" ; superior
우 右 the right ¶ 우로 나란히 [구령] Right dress ! /Eyes right ! // 우향 우 [구령] Right turn !
우 羽 〖음악〗 A scale in the Korean pentatonic ⇨ 우조(羽調)
우각 牛角 cow's horns ; oxhorn
우각 優角 〖기하〗 a major angle〔axis〕; a reflex〔superior〕 angle ¶ 우각의 reflex ; major
우거 寓居 a temporary abode〔residence〕 **—하다** reside〔live〕 temporarily 《at》; take up a temporary abode〔quarters〕
우거 愚擧 a foolish attempt〔act〕; a silly undertaking
우거지 [배추의] the outer leaves of cabbage or other vegetables ; [새우젓의] the dry and tasteless top layer of a crock of

salted shrimps or pickles

*우거지다 grow thick ; overgrow ; be overgrown with ; grow〔be〕 luxuriant ; luxuriate ; be rampant ; flourish ¶ 우거진 잡초 rank weeds // 나무가 우거진 산 a thickly-wooded hill // 잎이 우거진 나무 a nice leafy tree // 풀이 우거진 들 fields densely〔thickly〕 covered with grass // 담에는 담쟁이가 우거져 덮여 있다 The wall is overgrown with vines. // 뜰에는 잡초가 우거져 있었다 The garden was overgrown with weeds. // 산에는 소나무가 우거져 있다 The mountain is overgrown with pine trees.

우거지상 —相 a sour〔wry〕 face ; a scowl ; distorted features ; a frown ; a grimace ; a sullen face ¶ 그는 걱정으로 우거지상을 하고 있다 His brow is knit with worries.

우걱뿔 an inflexed horn ; arched horns —이 an ox with arched〔inflexed〕 horns

우걱우걱 swinging side to side with creaks〔the way a pack animal walks〕

우겨대다 cling stubbornly to ; hang on to ; insist on one's own way ; persist ; hold fast to ¶ 자기 말만 우겨대다 hold fast to one's views // 그는 자기 말이 옳다고 우겨대고 있다 He asserts his statement to be true. // 그는 끝까지 모른다고 우겨댔다 He persisted in denying his knowledge of it.

우격다짐 high-handedness ; forcible compulsion ; coercion ; browbeating —하다 force《a person》 to do ; browbeat ; put pressure《on》 ¶ 우격다짐으로 high-handedly ; forcibly ; by force // 우격다짐으로 모든 일을 하다 resort to high-handed measures in everything // 우격다짐으로 승낙케 하다 force《a person》 into consent // 우격다짐으로 제안을 승낙시키다 browbeat《a person》 into accepting a proposal

우격으로 high-handedly ; against《a person's》 will ; forcibly ; by force〔compulsion〕 ¶ 우격으로 그의 승낙을 받으려는 것은 어리석은 일이다 It is quite silly of you to try to force him to consent.

우견 愚見 ① [자기 의견] my humble opinion〔view〕 ¶ 우견으로는 in my humble opinion ; from my point of view ; to my thinking ② [어리석은 의견] foolish〔stupid〕 opinion

우경 右傾 veering〔turning, tending〕 to the right side —하다 swing to the right ; turn〔lean〕 to the right ¶ 우경화하다 turn rightist

— 운동 a rightist movement —파 the Right Wing〔Wingers〕 ; the Rightist ; the Right — 학생 a rightist student

우계 雨季 the rainy〔wet, moist〕 season ; [열대의] the rains ; 〖지질〗 a pluvial ¶ 우계로 접어 들었다 The wet season has set in. // 열대의 우계가 왔다 The tropical rains came on〔were on us〕.

우곡 紆曲 winding ; twisting ; meandering —하다 (be) winding ; twisting ; tortuous ; zigzag ; take a meandering course

우골 牛骨 cow bones ; oxbone

우구 憂懼 worry ; anxiety ; fear ; dread ; apprehension —하다 worry about ; be anxious over ; fear ; dread ; be apprehensive of〔for〕

우국 憂國 patriotism

— 지사 a patriot — 지정 patriotism ; public spirit ; a patriotic spirit〔sentiment〕 ; [열정] a fire of patriotism — 충정 one's intense patriotism ¶ 우국 충정에서 우러나오다 be motivated by one's ardent patriotic sentiment

우군 右軍 the right wing of an army ; the right-hand troops

우군 友軍 friendly forces ; an allied army

우그러뜨리다 crush〔beat〕 (out of shape) ; make dent in ; push in ; dent ¶ 맥고 모자를 우그러뜨리다 crush a straw hat out of shape // 물통을 우그러뜨리다 dent a bucket

우그러지다 be crushed (out of shape) ; be〔get〕 dented ¶ 우그러진 모자 a battered hat // 자동차 옆이 우그러졌다 The car is dented on the side.

우그렁— ⇨ 오그랑—

우그르르 in swarms ; [물이] with a sizzling sound ; [벌레가] swarming ; in swarms

우그리다 crush ; dent ⇨ 오그리다

*우글거리다 ① swarm ; be crowded ; be alive with ; teem with ¶ 거리에 거지가 우글거린다 The streets swarm with beggars. // 못에 물고기가 우글거린다 The pond teems with fish. /Fish teem in the pond. // 설탕에 개미가 우글거린다 The sugar is alive with ants.

② [끓다] simmer ; boil (up)

우글다 get〔be〕 dented〔crushed out of shape〕

우글부글 bubbling ; simmering —하다 bubble ; simmer

*우글우글[1] in swarms ; alive with —하다 swarm ; be alive with ; teem with ¶ 연못에 붕어가 우글우글하다 The pond is alive with carp.

우글우글[2] ⇨ 우글쭈글

우글쭈글 crumpled ; rumpled ; wrinkled —하다 (be) crumpled ; rumpled ; wrinkled ; withered ¶ 옷에 주름이 우글쭈글 잡혔다 The clothes are all wrinkled led.

우금 a narrow and steep valley with a swift-moving stream

우금 于今 till now ; until now ; up to the present ; by this time

우긋— ⇨ 오긋—

우긋하다 (be) curved〔bent〕 inward slightly

우기 雨氣 signs of rain ; a slight promise

of rain ¶ 우기를 머금은 하늘 a watery sky

우기 雨期 the rainy〔moist, wet〕 season ¶ 우기에 접어들었다 The wet season has set in.

†**우기다** demand one's own way ; force《one's ideas on》; impose《one's views upon》; persist in ; insist on ; assert oneself ¶ 자기 말을 우기다 persist in one's ideas // 자기 의견이 옳다고 우기다 stick to one's own opinion ; hold fast to one's own view ; carry one's point // 그는 자기만 옳다고 우기었다 He insisted he was the only one who was right. // 그는 모른다고 우기었다 He persisted in denying his knowledge of it.

우김성 —性 pigheadedness ; headstrongness ; stubbornness ; egoistic attachment ; obstinacy ¶ 우김성이 많다 be pigheaded ; be headstrong ; be stubborn ; be self-asserting ; be obstinate ; be (self-) opinionated

우꾼하다 [기운이] rise in a sudden burst ; [우기거나 기세올리다]《all the people》 persist〔insist〕 all at once〔in unison〕

우내 宇內 the whole world ; the universe

우는살 an arrow with a turnip-shaped head

우는소리 a complaint ; a whimper —하다 whimper ; whine ; complain

우단 羽緞 velvet ¶ 우단같이 보드랍다 be as smooth as velvet
— 제품 velvet goods — 직기(織機) a velvet loom

우담 牛膽 ox-gall

우당 友黨 a friendly〔an allied〕 party

우당탕 with a reverberating sound ; with a thud〔thump〕; bump ; plump —하다 thud ; go〔come〕 bump ¶ 그는 우당탕 소리 내며 계단을 내려왔다 He clattered down the stairway. // 위에서 발소리가 우당탕 들렸다 I heard heavy footsteps tramping overhead.

우당탕퉁탕 with a thump ; plump ; heavily ; with a thud〔bump〕 —하다 plump ; thud ¶ 우당탕퉁탕 떨어지다 fall plump // 무엇인지 마루에 우당탕퉁탕 떨어졌다 Something fell heavily on the floor.

우대 優待 preferential〔special, handsome〕 treatment ; privileged〔considerate, courteous〕 treatment —하다 treat preferentially ; treat cordially〔considerately〕; show special courtesy toward ¶ 우대받다 be given preferential treatment // 고용인을 우대하다 treat one's employe(e)s considerately // 저 하숙집에서는 학생을 우대한다 That lodging house treats students with kindness.
—권 a complimentary ticket — 승차권 a complimentary pass 교원 —안 a proposal to improve the condition〔a plan for increasing the pay〕 of school teachers

우도 友道 the rules of friendship

우두 牛痘 cowpox ¶ 우두의 vaccinic // 우두를 맞다 take a vaccination ; be vaccinated // 우두를 놓다 vaccinate // 우두가 잘 되었다 The vaccination took well.
— 바이러스 vaccine virus — 백신 (a) vaccine — 자국 a《large》 vaccination scar — 증명서 a vaccination certificate

우두덩거리다 fall down with clatter ; crash《down》

우두덩우두덩 falling down with much clatter

우두둑 [깨물다] crunchingly ; with a crunching sound ; [부러지다] snappingly ; with a snapping sound

우두망찰하다 fluster ; be(come) confused ; be perplexed ; be disconcerted ; be confounded ; be at a loss ¶ 그는 그 소식을 듣고 우두망찰하였다 The news struck him speechless〔dumb〕 for a while.

†**우두머리** [꼭대기] the top ; the head ; [장] a chief ; a leader ; a boss ; the head ¶ 회사의 우두머리 the boss of a company // 우두머리가 되다 assume the leadership《of a party》

***우두커니** absent-mindedly ; vacantly ; blankly ; aimlessly ; with an abstracted air ¶ 우두커니 생각에 잠기다 be lost in thought // 우두커니 바라보다 look vacantly《at》// 그는 창가에 우두커니 서 있다 He is standing idly by the window.

우둔 愚鈍 stupidity ; dullness ; thickheadedness ; silliness —하다 (be) stupid ; dull-witted ; thick-headed ; silly ; heavy

우둔우둔하다 go pit-a-pat ; pound ; throb ; palpitate

우둘우둘 —하다 (be) hard and lumpy ; fibrous ; gristly

우둥퉁하다 (be) stout and fat ; fleshy ; portly ; dumpy

우듬지 a treetop ; the top branches of a tree

우등 優等 the top〔superior〕 grade ; excellency ; superiority ¶ 우등으로 대학을 졸업하다 graduate from a college with honors // 우등으로 합격하다 pass the examination with honors
—상 an honor prize ; a prize for high scholarship ¶ 우등상을 타다 win an honor prize —생 an honor student —장 a diploma of honors ; an honors diploma —재(財) 〖경제〗 superior goods — 졸업생 an honor graduate 품질 — superiority in quality

우뚝 high ; aloft —하다 (be) high ; lofty ; tall ; towering ; [뛰어나다] eminent ; prominent ; conspicuous ; outstanding ¶ 우뚝한 코 a high nose // 서울 상공에 우뚝 솟다 tower〔rise〕 high over the *Seoul*

우뚝우뚝 aloft ; high up —하다 be all

high〔tall, lofty, towering〕 ¶ 그 도시엔 고층 건물이 우뚝우뚝 서 있다 The town bristles with high buildings.

*우라늄, 우란 〖화학〗 uranium 《U, Ur》

우락부락 [난폭] rudely ; roughly ; wildly ; harshly **—하다** (be) rude ; rough ; wild ; harsh ¶ 우락부락 말하다 talk rudely ; utter wild words // 우락부락한 사람 a rough fellow // 우락부락하게 굴다 behave rudely // 그는 우락부락하게 생겼지만 마음은 좋다 He looks wild but he has a tender mind.

우랄 〖지리〗 Ural ; Uralic
—산맥 the Ural Mountains ; the Urals **— 알타이** Ural-Altaic **— 어족** the Uralic language family

우람지다 ⇨ 우렁차다

우람하다 (be) imposing ; grand ; majestic ; magnificent ¶ 우람한 경치 a grand sight // 우람한 저택 a stately〔magnificent, an imposing〕 mansion

*우량 雨量 rainfall ; rain ¶ 우량을 재다 gauge〔measure〕 the rainfall // 어제의 우량은 30밀리였다 We had thirty millimeters of rain yesterday.
—계 a rain gauge ; a pluviometer ; a hyetometer **—도** a hyetograph **— 측정** pluviometry **—학** hyetography

우량 優良 superiority ; excellence **—하다** (be) superior ; excellent ; high grade
—공(工) a skilled operative **— 교사** a competent teacher **— 도서** good〔great, excellent〕 books **—마(馬)** a thoroughbred **— 성적** an excellent result **—아** an ideal〔superior〕 child ; a physically perfect child **— 어음** a fine bill〔paper〕 **—종** a good breed ¶ 우량종의 highbred **—주(株)** blue chips ; blue-chip〔high-grade, high-quality, gilt-edged〕 stocks **—품** superior goods ; articles of superior quality **건강 —아** a prizewinning child in a health contest **최—품** the choicest selection of goods ; the first line

*우러나다 soak out ; come out〔off〕 ¶ 뜨거운 물에 담그면 천 빛깔이 우러날 것이다 In the hot water the dyes of the cloth will come out. // 이 차는 잘 우러난다 This tea draws well. // 잉크 묻은 천을 잉크가 우러나게 물에 담그었다 The ink-stained cloth was put in water for the stain to soak out.

‡우러나오다 spring up ; well up ¶ 진심에서 우러나온 감사 warm〔cordial, heartfelt〕 thanks ; thanks from the bottom of one's heart // 바위 틈에서 물이 우러나온다 Water springs〔gushes〕 from the rock. // 그 여자의 가슴 속에 희망이 우러났다 Hope welled up in her heart.

*우러러보다 [쳐다보다] look up 《at》 ; look upward ; lift the eyes ; [앙모하다] look up to ; admire ; respect ¶ 산을 우러러 보다 look up at the mountain // 우리들은 그를 스승으로 모시고 우러러 보았다 We looked up to him as our teacher. // 사람들은 그의 용감성을 우러러본다 He is admired for his bravery by the people.

우러르다 lift one's head up ; look up

우러리 a wickerwork〔plaited〕 lid

우럭우럭 ① [불이] flaring〔blazing〕 up ; bursting into flames ; furiously ② [술기운이] flushing with drunkenness ¶ 술기운이 얼굴에 우럭우럭 오르다 one's face grows flushed with drunkenness

우렁우렁 thunderingly ; rumblingly **—하다** thunder ; rumble ¶ 천둥이 우렁우렁 울린다 It thunders. /The thunder rolls 〔rumbles〕.

우렁이 a freshwater snail ; a pond〔mud〕 snail

우렁잇속 an inscrutable〔unfathomable〕 inside ¶ 우렁잇속 같다 be inscrutable ; be impenetrable ; be unfathomable

우렁차다 [목소리가] (be) resounding ; resonant ; reverberating ; roaring ; [으리으리하다] magnificent ; imposing ¶ 우렁찬 목소리 a resonant〔resounding〕 voice

‡우레[1] thunder ; thundershower ; thunderstorm ¶ 우레와 같은 갈채 a storm 〔thunder〕 of applause
— 소리 a peal of thunder ; a thunderclap ¶ 우레 소리가 난다 It thunders. /The thunder rolls. // 우레 소리와 번개불이 일어나고 있다 It is thundering and lightening. // 멀리서 우레 소리가 들린다 The thunder is now rumbling in the distance.

우레[2] a birdcall〔whistle〕 used to lure pheasants ¶ 우레(를) 켜다 imitate a pheasant call

*우려 憂慮 worry ; anxiety ; fear ; apprehension ; concern ; care ; solicitude **—하다** worry 《over》 ; be〔feel〕 anxious 《about》 ; be concerned 《about》 ; fear ; dread ; care ¶ 크게 우려할 일 a matter of grave concern // 안부를 우려하다 be anxious for one's safety

우려내다 extort ; wring ; squeeze ; exploit ¶ 돈을 우려내다 squeeze 〔wring, extort〕 money out of 《a person》

우력 偶力 〖물리〗 a couple of forces

우련하다 (be) dim ; obscure ; vague ; faint ; hazy ; misty ¶ 안개로 모든 것이 우련하게 보였다 Everything looked vague in the fog. // 배가 안개 속에 우련하게 나타났다 The ship loomed through the mist.

우로 雨露 rain and dew ¶ 우로를 막다 shelter oneself from the weather // 그는 우로를 피할 곳도 없다 He has no roof over his head.

우론 愚論 [어리석은 의론] a foolish opinion ; an absurd view ; a silly argument ; an absurdity ; nonsense ; [자기 의론의 겸칭] my (humble) opinion 〔view〕 ¶ 우론을 펴다 express〔voice〕 one's foolish opinion

‡우롱 愚弄 mockery ; derision ; scoff ; jeer **—하다** mock 《at》; deride ; ridicule ; make fun〔a fool〕of ; jeer 《at》 ¶ 사람을 우롱하다 hold up 《a person》 to ridicule // 그들이 나를 다시는 우롱하지 못하게 하겠다 I shall not let them make a fool of me again. // 그 어리석은 정치가들은 국민을 우롱하였다 The foolish politicians made a fool of the people. // 사람을 우롱해도 분수가 있지 There is a limit in befooling one.

우료 郵料 postage ; postal charges
— 계기(計器) a postal franker **— 무료** postage free **— 부족** postage due **— 지불필** postage paid **소포 —** the rates of postage on parcels

우루과이 Uruguay ¶ 우루과이의 Uruguayan
— 사람 an Uruguayan

‡우르르 ① [떼지어] all in a group〔crowd〕; all together ; with a rush ; all at once ; stampeding ¶ 그들은 사무실에서 우르르 몰려 나왔다 They poured〔rushed〕out of the office all together〔in a group〕.
② [물 끓는 소리] simmering ; boiling ¶ 물이 우르르 끓고 있다 The water is simmering.
③ [무너지는 소리] all in a heap ; all over ¶ 담이 우르르 무너졌다 The wall came down all in a heap.
④ [천둥소리] rumbling ; thundering ¶ 천둥소리가 먼 데서 우르르 났다 The thunder rumbled in the distance.

우르릉 rolling ; rumbling ; thundering ; booming ¶ 우르릉 울리는 천둥 소리 the roll of thunder ; the rumbling of thunder // 우르릉 울리는 파도 소리 the deep roll of breaking waves

‡우리[1] a cage (맹수의) ; a pen〔corral〕(가축의) ; a fold (양 따위의) ¶ 돼지 우리 a pigsty〔pigpen〕; a hogpen 《미》 // 우리에 든 호랑이 a caged tiger

†우리[2] we ; our (우리의) ; us (우리에게) ¶ 우리 집 my house ; my home // 우리 나라 our country // 우리 한국인 we Koreans

우리[3] [기와 세는 단위] two thousand (tiles)

우리다[1] ① [물에 담가서] soak (out) ¶ 옷에 묻은 잉크를 우리다 soak an ink stain〔spot〕out of clothes ② [우려내다] extort ; squeeze ; wring ¶ 돈을 우리다 wring〔extort〕money out of 《a person》 ③ [때리다] slap hard ; strike ¶ 뺨을 우리다 slap 《a person》 in the face ; give 《a person》 a hard slap

우리다[2] [볕이] stream in

우마 牛馬 oxen and horses ; cattle 《총칭》 ¶ 우마처럼 혹사하다 drive〔work〕《a person》 hard like a horse
—차 carts
우마가 기린 되랴 속담 Once a devil, always a devil. /Once a knave, and ever a knave.

우매 愚昧 stupidity and ignorance **—하다** (be) stupid and ignorant ; silly ; thick-headed ; unenlightened ; uncivilized ¶ 우매한 짓 a folly ; a foolish act〔move〕// 우매한 백성을 선동하다 instigate the mob ; agitate the mob // 우매한 사람들을 계몽하다 enlighten the ignorant

우맹 愚氓 ⇨ 우민(愚民)

우멍거지 〖의학〗 phimosis

우멍하다 be sunken in

우모 羽毛 feathers ; plumes

우목 a wart

우무 vegetable gelatine ; agar-agar

우묵하다 (be) hollow ; dented ; depressed ; sunken ¶ 우묵한 눈 sunken eyes // 우묵한 빰 hollow cheeks // 우묵한 땅 hollow〔sunken, depressed〕ground // 우묵해진다 become hollow ; sink ; fall〔cave〕in

우문 愚問 a stupid〔silly〕question
— 우답 a silly dialogue **— 현답** a wise answer to a silly question

†우물 a well ¶ 우물가 a well-side // 우물물 well water // 우물물을 긷다 draw water from a well // 우물을 파다 dig a well // 우물 안의 개구리는 대해를 모른다 The frog in the well does not know the ocean. /He who is in hell knows not what heaven is. // 한 우물만 파라 결국 둘다 잃게 될 것이다 Don't chase after another. You'll end up losing both of them.
— 굴착기 a well-sinking machine ; a well borer **— 도르래** a pulley of a well **—울** well crib〔tube〕; a curb **— 지붕** a well house **— 치기** well cleaning **— 파기** well sinking〔boring, drilling〕; [사람] a well sinker〔borer, driller〕**— 펌프** a well pump
우물에 가 숭늉 찾는다 속담 To seek hot water under cold ice.

우물 愚物 a fool ; a simpleton ; a blockhead ; a loggerhead ; a dullard ; a dunce

우물거리다[1] [여럿이] swarm 《with》; be crowded 《with》; teem 《with》; wriggle 《about》 ¶ 물통에서 장구벌레가 우물거리고 있다 The water tank teems with mosquito larvae.

우물거리다[2] ① [씹다] mumble ; mouth ¶ 빵 껍질을 우물거리며 씹다 mumble a crust ② [말을] mumble ; murmur ¶ 대답을 우물거리다 mumble the answer // 혼자말로 우물거리다 mumble to oneself

우물귀신 —鬼神 the spirit〔soul〕of a person drowned in a well

우물마루 〖건축〗 a checkered floor

우물반자 〖건축〗 a checkered ceiling

우물우물[1] [여럿이] in a swarm

우물우물[2] [입속에서] mumblingly

우물지다 ① [보조개가] dimple ¶ 그 여자는 웃으면 우물진다 She has a dimple when she smiles. /Her face dimples with a smile. ② [파이다] become hollow ;

form a hollow ; sink ¶ 비가 와서 땅이 우물졌다 The rain formed small hollows in the ground. /The rain formed a pool in the ground.

우물쩍주물쩍 ⇨ 우물쭈물

우물쭈물 hesitantly ; hesitatingly ; indecisively ; with hesitation **―하다** hesitate ; vacillate ; waver ; boggle ¶ 우물쭈물 말하다 speak hesitantly ; speak ambiguously∥우물쭈물 대답하다 make a vague answer∥우물쭈물 일하다 do a slow job ; scamp one's work∥무엇을 할까 우물쭈물하다 hesitate about what to do∥우물쭈물 하지 마라 Waste no time. /Don't delay. / Don't be too slow. ∥계획이 우물쭈물 끝나다 The plan ended up a fade-out.

우뭇가사리 〖식물〗 agar-agar ; Ceylon moss ; Gelidium amansii (학명)

우므러들다 become narrower ; narrow ; pucker

우미 優美 grace ; elegance ; refinement ; prominent beauty **―하다** (be) graceful ; elegant ; refined ; exquisite ; delicate ¶ 고상하고 우미하다 be graceful and high-toned ; be refined and elegant

우미 愚迷 ⇨ 우매(愚昧)

우민 愚民 ignorant people ; the stupid masses

― 정책 an obscurantist policy **― 정치** mobocracy ; mobrale

우민 憂悶 worry ; (mental) agony **―하다** worry oneself 《about》 ; be worried 〔troubled〕 ; be in agony ; be agonized ; agonize

⁑**우박 雨雹** hail ; hailstone ¶ 우박이 오다 It hails.

우발 偶發 accidental〔incidental〕 occurrence **―하다** happen accidentally ; come about by chance ¶ 우발적인 일이 일어나지 않는 한 unless an unforeseen accident occurs

―병 a nadventitious disease **― 사건** an accident ; a contingency ; a chance occurrence **―설** accidentalism **―성** contingency ; eventuality **― 전쟁** an accidental war **― 증상** 〖의학〗 an epiphenomenon 《*pl.* -na》

우방 友邦 a friendly nation〔country〕 ; [맹방] an ally ; an allied nation

우범 소년 虞犯少年 a juvenile liable to committing a crime ; a juvenile with criminal bent

우범 지대 虞犯地帶 a crime-ridden district

우변 右邊 (the edge on) the right side

우보 전술 牛步戰術 stalling tactics

우부 愚夫 a stupid fellow ; a foolish man ; a dolt

우부 愚婦 a stupid〔foolish〕 woman

우부룩하다 (be) dense ; thick ; tufty ; be thick 《with》

우분 牛糞 cow dung ; ox manure

우비 雨備 rain gear ; a rain-coat ; an umbrella ¶ 우비를 입다 put on a raincoat∥우비를 준비하다 prepare for rain

우비 優比 〖수학〗 the ratio of greater inequality

***우비다** poke ; scrape〔scoop〕 out ; bore ; pick ¶ 귀〔코〕를 우비다 pick one's ear〔nose〕∥담뱃대를 우비다 poke a pipe ∥구멍을 우비다 scrape out〔bore〕 a hole

우비어 넣다 twist 《a thing》 into 《a hole》 ¶ 구멍에 막대기를 우비어 넣다 twist a stick into a hole

우비어 파다 scoop out ; hollow out ; scrape out ; gouge ; carve ; [비밀을] ferret out ⇨ 우비다 ¶ 벽에 구멍을 우비어 파다 bore a hole in the wall

우비적거리다 keep poking〔scraping out, boring, picking〕 ¶ 우비적 우비적 poking〔scraping, boring, picking〕∥땅에 구멍을 우비적우비적 파다 go digging a hole in the ground

우비적우비적 poking ; scraping ; scooping ¶ 땅에 구멍을 우비적우비적 파다 go on digging a hole in the ground

우비칼 a scooping〔an engraving〕 knife ; a gouge ; a router

우빙 雨氷 glaze 《미》 ; glazed frost 《영》

우사 牛舍 a cowhouse ; a cowshed ; a cattle shed〔pen〕 ⇨ 외양간

⁑**우산 雨傘** an umbrella ¶ 우산을 쓰다 put up an umbrella ; hold an umbrella∥우산을 접다 close〔fold〕 an umbrella∥우산을 펴다 open an umbrella∥우산을 같이 쓰고 가다 go under one〔the same〕 umbrella ∥그녀는 나에게 우산을 받쳐 주었다 She held her umbrella over my head. ∥바람에 우산이 뒤집혔다 The strong wind turned my umbrella inside out. ∥비 맞지 말고 내 우산 속으로 들어와 Don't get wet. Get under my umbrella. ∥우산을 가져오길 잘 했다 (It's a) Good thing I brought along my umbrella. /I'm glad. I brought along my umbrella. ∥비가 오는데 우산을 갖고 오질 않았어 우산 좀 같이 쓰자 It's raining and I didn't bring an umbrella. Let's share it.

―걸음 walking with a bounce **―꽂이** an umbrella stand **―살** umbrella ribs 〔frames〕 **― 손잡이** the handle〔crook〕 of an umbrella **― 종이** oil paper intended for an umbrella ; umbrella paper **―집** an umbrella sheath〔case〕 **핵(核)―** nuclear umbrella

우상 羽狀 ¶ 우상의 pinnate

⁑**우상 偶像** an image ; an idol ; an icon ¶ 우상을 숭배하다 worship an idol∥우상화하다 idolize ; make an idol of

―교 paganism **― 숭배** idolatry ; idol worship ; iconolatry **― 숭배자** an idolater ; an idol-worshipper **― 파괴** iconoclasm **― 파괴자** an iconoclast **―화〔시(視)〕** idolization

우상 복엽 羽狀複葉 〖식물〗 a pinnate com-

pound leaf
우색 憂色 a worried〔an anxious〕 look ; a melancholy〔gloomy〕 air ; the traces of sorrow《in one's face》 ¶ 우색을 띠다 wear a worried look ; look concerned〔anxious, worried〕 // 얼굴에 우색을 띠고 with a look of anxiety on one's face
우생 優生 ¶ 우생의 eugenic
— 결혼 a eugenic marriage — 보호법 the eugenic protection law — 수술 a eugenic operation
우생학 優生學 eugenics ¶ 우생학적인 eugenic(al)
—자 a eugenist ; a eugenicist
우서 郵書 a letter ; mail ; [단신] a note
우서 愚書 [책] a worthless〔trashy〕 book ; [편지] my letter
†**우선 于先** first ; first of all ; before everything ; in the first place ; to begin with ¶ 우선 건강이다 Health first. // 우선 돈을 마련하여야 한다 First you must raise funds《for the purpose》. // 우선 비용이 문제다 The question of expense takes precedence over all others. // 우선 일을 끝내고 놀기로 합시다 Business first and pleasure afterwards. // 우선 거기에 두어라 For now just put it over there. // 우선은 그들의 반응을 보고 나서 행동 하자 For the moment. Let's wait and see how they respond before we make our next move.
*__우선 優先__ preference ; priority ; precedence —하다 have priority《to, over》; have preference《to》; take preference《of》; take precedence《over, of》; precede ; be prior to ¶ 우선적으로 preferentially ; on the preferential basis // 공익은 사익에 우선한다 Public interest takes precedence of private interest. / Consideration is given to public interest before private interest. // 이 의무는 다른 모든 의무에 우선한다 This duty is prior to all others. // 헌법은 다른 모든 법률에 우선한다 The Constitution is prior to all other laws.
—권 a priority ; a preference ; a prior〔preferential〕 right ¶ 우선권을 얻다 acquire a priority ; take precedence《over, of》; acquire the first claim // 우선권을 주다 give《a person》 a preference《over》; give《a person》 the first refusal — 동의 a privileged motion — 명부《be on》 a priority list — 배당 preference〔preferred〕 dividends — 사항 a priority item〔matter〕 — 순위 the order of priority ; the priority order —제 the priority system —주 preference〔preferred〕 stocks〔shares〕 — 채무 a preferential debt — 취급 preferential treatment — 할당〔원조〕 priority allocation〔assistance〕 공익 — precedence of public interest 최— 사항 a matter of the highest priority 통행 —권 the right of way
우선 郵船 a mail steamer〔boat〕 ; a packet ship〔vessel〕
— 출범일(出帆日) packet day 외국행 — an outgoing mail
우선 외화 優先外貨 preferred foreign currency
— 자금 a preferred foreign currency fund — 제도 the preferred foreign currency system
우선회 右旋回 dextrorotation
우설 愚說 ⇨ 우견(愚見)
우성 優性 〖유전〗 a dominant (character) ; (genetic) dominance ¶ 우성의 dominant
— 법칙 〖생물〗 the law of dominance — 상위 dominant epistasis — 유전 prepotency — 인자 a dominant gene — 전환 〖생물〗 the change of dominance — 형질 a dominant trait〔character〕
우성 偶性 〖철학·논리〗 accident ; accidental quality〔nature〕 ; contingency
우세 shame ; humiliation —하다 be put to shame ; be humiliated ; be subjected to humiliation ¶ 우세스럽다 be humiliating
우세 郵稅 [우표] postage ; postal charges ; rate of postage
‡**우세 優勢** superiority ; superior power ; ascendancy ; predominance ; preponderance —하다 (be) superior (in number or force) ; leading ; predominant ; ascendant ; be far ahead ; come out predominant ; gain in power〔strength〕 ; outnumber ¶ 우세를 보이다 show a preponderance // 우세를 차지하다 prevail over〔against〕 ; get〔gain〕 the better of ; gain the predominating influence ; lead (경기에서) // 그들은 수에 있어서 우리들보다 우세하다 They are superior in number to us. / They outnumber us.
†**우송 郵送** mailing ; posting ; sending by mail —하다 mail ; post ; send by post〔mail〕 ; send through the post
— 금지 a postal ban —료 postage — 무료 post-free ; postage-free —처 명부 a mailing list
우수 ① [덤] an addition ; an extra ; a bonus ; something thrown into the bargain ; a premium ② [우수리] change
우수 雨水 rainwater
우수 右手 the right hand
우수 偶數 an even number ¶ 우수의 even ; even-numbered
†**우수 優秀** superiority ; predominance ; excellence —하다 (be) superior ; predominant ; excellent ; distinguished ¶ 우수한 성적으로 with excellent results ; with honors〔high marks〕 // 우수한 성적을 올리다 get excellent results ; establish〔make〕 fine records // 서울 대학교를 우수한 성적으로 졸업했다 Graduated Phi Beta Kappa from Seoul National University

(이력서 따위에) // 단연 남보다 우수하다 He is definitely superior to the others.

우수 憂愁 melancholy ; gloom ; anxiety ; worry ; distress ; grief ; sorrow ¶ 우수의 melancholy ; gloomy // 우수의 빛 melancholy〔anxious〕air // 우수에 잠기다 be oppressed with sorrow ; be sunk in grief // 그 집은 깊은 우수에 쌓여 있었다 The house was overclouded with a deep melancholy.

****우수리** ① [거스름돈] change ¶ 우수리를 내어주다 give (back) the change // 우수리를 받다 get the change // 우수리가 40원 입니다 That makes forty *won* change. // 우수리는 받아두시오 You may keep the change. /Keep the rest for yourself. // 여기 우수리를 받으세요 Here's your change. // 우수리를 속이다 short-change 《a customer》; give 《a person》 short change

② [단수] an odd sum ; a fraction ¶ 우수리를 떼다 ignore fractions // 우수리 30원만 깎아드리겠습니다 I'll take off the odd thirty *won*. // 우수리 100원을 빼고 5,000원에 드리겠읍니다 I'll knock off the odd hundred *won* and make it a round five thousand.

우수수 《fall》 with a rustle ; rustling down ; 《fall》 in a multitude ; 《scatter》 in great masses **—하다** rustle ¶ 바람에 나뭇잎이 우수수 떨어졌다 A gust of wind shook a multitude of leaves off the trees. // 나뭇잎이 바람에 우수수 떤다 The leaves are rustling in the wind.

우스개 jocularity

우스갯소리 a joke ; a jest ¶ 우스갯소리를 하다 make a joke 《on》 **우스갯짓** clowning ; drollery ; comicality ; waggery

***우스꽝스럽다** (be) ludicrous ; ridiculous ; comic(al) ; facetious ; droll ; laughable ; laughing ¶ 우스꽝스럽게 여기다 think ridiculous // 내 얼굴이 어디가 그리 우스꽝스러우냐 What's funny about my face ? // 우스꽝스러운 짓 하지 마라 Do not make yourself ridiculous. // 그 양복을 입으니까 우스꽝스럽게 보인다 You look funny〔ridiculous〕in that suit.

우스팅 [모직물의] worsted

우습게 보다 despise ; look down on ; treat with contempt ; hold in contempt ; think little of ; disdain ; scorn ; slight ¶ 사람을 우습게 보다 look down upon 《a person》// 돈을 우습게 보다 make light of money // 약한 적이라도 우습게 보지 마라 Don't despise a weak enemy. // 어린애라고 우습게 보지 마라 Don't underestimate him, just because he is a boy. // 부자는 가난한 사람을 우습게 보기 쉽다 The rich are apt to despise the poor. // 오늘날 노동을 우습게 보는 사람은 없다 Nobody now despises honest labor.

****우습다** [재미있다] (be) funny ; amusing ; [가소롭다] laughable ; ridiculous ; ludicrous ; droll ; comic(al) ¶ 우스운 이야기 a funny story // 우스운 몸짓 a comical gesture // 우스운 소리를 하다 say a funny thing // 우습게 들리다 sound funny // 우스운 것을 참다 keep a straight face // 무엇이 그렇게 우스우냐 What is so funny ? /What makes you laugh ? // 우스워 죽겠다 I cannot help laughing. // 그런 양복을 입으니까 우습다 You look funny〔ridiculous〕in that suit. // 모두가 우스워 죽겠다는 듯한 얼굴을 하고 있었다 Every face has a most amused expression on it. // 어찌 우스운지 웃음을 참을 수가 없었다 It was so funny that I could not help laughing.

***우승 優勝** victory ; championship (선수권) **—하다** win a victory〔the championship〕; win (a game) ; come off〔out〕victor〔winner, victorious〕; cop first 《속》 ¶ 우리 팀이 우승했다〔우승기를 탔다〕 Our team won (the championship flag). // 그는 정구에 우승했다 He won〔captured, gained〕the tennis championship. **—기** the championship flag〔banner〕; a pennant **—배** a championship cup ; a trophy (cup) **—배전** a cup tie **— 시합** a championship tournament ; the finals ; a cup event **— 열패(劣敗)** [적자 생존(適者生存)] the survival of the fittest ; The weakest goes to the wall. **—자** a (championship) winner **—자 명부** the honor roll **—팀** a winning 〔championship〕 team **— 후보** a hopeful ; a favorite ; a likely winner (of the championship) // 그는 우승 후보였다 He was a favorite to win. // 우리는 우승을 목표로 한다 We have our sights set on the championship.

우승 열패 優勝劣敗 the survival of the fittest **—하다** The fittest survives. / The superior gains and the inferior loses. / The weakest goes to the wall.

우시장 牛市場 a cattle market

우식 雨蝕 〖지질〗 rainwash

우식 愚息 my son

우심하다 尤甚— (be) extreme ; excessive ; severe ; heavy

우썩 with a steady progress ; with a sudden increase ; with a sudden decrease ¶ 우썩 추워지다 get cold suddenly // 우썩 늘다 [학문·기술이] make steady〔rapid〕progress // 우썩 우썩 자라다 [키가] grow taller and taller // 우썩 우썩 커지다 [사업이] make steady expansion

†우아 優雅 elegance ; refinement ; grace(fulness) ; comeliness ; urbanity **—하다** (be) elegant ; refined ; graceful ; comely ; polite ; urbane ¶ 우아한 문체 a polite〔elegant〕style // 동작이 우아하다 be graceful in manner ; move with grace

우아 [뜻밖에 기쁠 때] Hurrah ! ; Hurray ! ; Wow ! ; [마소를 멈출 때] Soh ! ; Soho !

우악 優渥 graciousness ; benevolence **—하다** (be) gracious ; benevolent

우악스럽다 愚惡— (be) ferocious; cruel; atrocious; violent; wild; rough; rude ¶ 우악스럽게 rudely; roughly; wildly; harshly; gruffly; fiercely // 우악스러운 사람 a rough fellow // 우악스럽게 다루다 handle 《a tool, goods》 roughly // 우악스럽게 생기다 have a ferocious look about one // 일을 우악스럽게 하다 do a crude job // 그는 말버릇이 우악스럽다 He is rough-spoken 〔crude〕.

우안 愚案 my humble opinion〔thought, idea〕 (자기의); a foolish plan

우안 右岸 the right bank (of a river)

우애 友愛 friendship; friendly feeling; fraternity; brotherliness; fellowship; comradeship ¶ 우애롭다 be friendly; be brotherly

—감 a friendly feeling **— 결혼** (a) companionate marriage

우야 雨夜 a rainy evening〔night〕

우양 牛羊 cattle and sheep

우어 [마소를 세울 때] Whoa!; Woback!; Halt there!

우언 寓言 an allegory; a fable

우엉 『식물』 a burdock (weed); Arctium Lappa (학명)

우여 곡절 迂餘曲折 ups and downs; vicissitudes; complications; twistings; meanderings ¶ 인생의 우여 곡절 the vicissitudes of life // 우여 곡절을 겪은 뒤에 after much meandering; after many turns and twists // 우여 곡절을 겪고난 후 교섭이 성립되었다 Agreement was reached after many complications〔much complication〕. // 교섭이 이루어질 때까지는 많은 우여 곡절이 있을 것이다 There will be many complications before they come to terms.

우역 牛疫 a cattle disease〔epidemic〕

†우연 偶然 chance; accident; fortuity **—하다** (be) accidental; casual; fortuitous; incidental ¶ 우연히 by chance 〔accident〕; accidentally; casually; incidentally // 우연의 일치 a coincidence // 우연한 일 an accident // 우연한 발견 a chance discovery // 우연히 만나다 meet by chance; happen to meet; chance upon // 우연히 발견하다 light upon 《a thing》; stumble on 《a fact》 // 나는 우연히 그 자리에 있었다 I was there accidentally〔by chance〕. /I happened to be there. // 그것은 단지 우연에 불과하다 It is nothing but a mere accident. // 나는 그를 서울에서 우연히 만났다 I met him in *Seoul* by chance. /I came across him in *Seoul*. /I met him in *Seoul* accidentally. /I happened〔chanced〕 to meet him in *Seoul*. // 발견은 우연히 된 것들이 많다 Many discoveries were made by accident. // 그와 같은 일치는 우연이 아니다 Such unity is not a mere accident〔does not just happen〕. // 나는 도서관에서 우연히도 진귀한 책을 발견했다 I stumbled upon a rare book in the library. // 우리가 만난 것은 순전히 우연한 일이었다 Our meeting was quite accidental. // 그분의 이번 성공은 결코 우연이 아니다 Chance has nothing to do with his present success. // 우리는 우연히 서로 알게 되었다 Chance brought us into mutual acquaintance. // 우연히 한 말이 그 여자를 노하게 했다 My incidental 〔casual〕 remark made her angry. /The remark I casually let slip angered her. // 나는 그 여자를 어느 파티에서 우연히 알게 되었다 I picked her up at a party. // 요전날 어느 파티에서 그를 우연히 만났다 I ran into him the other day at a party.

—론 accidentalism; casualism; fortuitism **—론자** an accidentalist; a casualist; a fortuitist **— 변화〔변이〕** mutation **—성** contingency; possibility

우연만하다 (be) fairly good; passable ⇨ 웬만하다

***우열 愚劣** stupidity; foolishness; absurdity **—하다** (be) stupid〔silly, foolish, absurd〕

***우열 優劣** superiority and inferiority; merits and demerits; dominance and recessiveness ¶ 우열이 없는 equal; equally〔evenly〕 matched // 우열을 다투다 contend for superiority; struggle〔strive〕 for mastery // 우열을 논하다 discuss merits and demerits 《of things》 // 우열을 따지다 make a discrimination between A and B; put 〔place〕 《one thing》 above 《the other》 // 양자에 우열이 거의 없다 There is little to choose between them. // 양자의 우열은 어떠할까 How does the one compare with the other?

— 법칙 『유전』 the law of dominance **— 전환** 『생물』 the change of dominance

우왕좌왕 右往左往 —하다 go this way and that; move about busily; run 〔move〕 about in (utter) confusion; run pell-mell; rush about to no purpose

우우 ① [바람부는 소리] whistling; howling ¶ 바람이 우우 불고 있다 The wind is whistling〔howling〕. ② [몰려 오는 모양] in crowds; rushingly; with a rush ¶ 우우 도망치다 run away in a panic

우운 雨雲 a rain(-laden) cloud; a precipitation cloud

‡우울 憂鬱 melancholy; dejection; gloom(-iness); dolefulness; low spirits; the blues (속) **—하다** (be) melancholy; doleful; cheerless; dejected; gloomy; be out of〔in low〕 spirits ¶ 우울한 기분으로 with a heavy heart; in a depressed mood // 우울한 날씨 gloomy weather // 우울해지다 be seized with melancholia; feel melancholy // 우울하게 만들다 give 《a person》 a melancholy feeling; make 《a person》 melancholy 〔gloomy〕 // 우울한 얼굴을 하다 draw〔pull〕 a long face; look blue〔long-faced〕 // 비가 오는 날이면 나는 언제나 우울해진다 Rainy weather always depresses me. // 너 우울해 보인다 You look down. // 왜 우울한 얼굴을 하고 있니 Why the long face? / Why so blue? Why so down? /Why the knitted brow? // 왜 그렇게 우울한 표정이냐 Why the long face? /Why so blue? Why so depressed?

—병 melancholy; mental depression —증 melancholia; hypochondria —증 환자 a hypochondriac; a melancholiac —질(質) a melancholic〔atrabilious〕 temperament

우원하다 迂遠— (be) roundabout〔devious, circuitous, circumlocutory〕 ¶ 우원한 방식 a roundabout way of doing《a thing》

†**우월 優越** supremacy; superiority; predominance; preponderance; surpassing **—하다** (be) superior《to》; supreme; preponderant; predominating; surpass; excel《others》in《a thing》 ¶ 우월한 지위를 차지하다 hold a prominent position《in》

—감 a sense of superiority; superiority complex ¶ 우월감을 갖다 have a sense of one's own superiority to《others》// 우월감을 느끼다 feel one's own superiority to《others》; be conscious of one's superiority to // 우월감을 꺾다 wound《a person's》 pride — 콤플렉스 〖심리〗 superiority complex

우위 優位 predominance; a predominant〔higher, superior〕 position; ascendancy; superiority; a position of advantage ¶ 우위를 차지하다 gain〔get〕 an advantage over; gain〔get, obtain〕 the ascendancy; attain superiority over; prevail over // 우위를 유지하다 stay〔be〕 predominant over

***우유 牛乳** (cow's) milk ¶ 우유를 살균하다 pasteurize〔sterilize〕 milk // 우유를 짜다 milk a cow // 우유로 아기를 기르다 feed a baby on cow's milk; bring up a baby on the bottle // 우유를 배달하다 deliver milk

— 배달부 a milkman; a milk roundsman — 배달차〔운반차〕 a milk truck〔cart〕 — 병 a milk bottle —상 〔판매자〕 a milk dealer; a dairyman (착유소의); 〔가게〕 a milk shop — 상자 a milk box — 소독기 a milk-sterilizer 무균 — bacteria-free milk 분말 — milk powder; powder(ed) milk; dry〔dried, desiccated〕 milk 살균 — pasteurized milk 탈지 — skim milk

우유부단 優柔不斷 irresolution; indecisiveness; indetermination; vacillation; shilly-shally **—하다** (be) irresolute; indecisive; wavering; vacillating; hesitant; shilly-shallying ¶ 그는 우유부단한 사람이다 He is an irresolute man. / He does not know his own mind. // 그는 그 문제에 관해 너무 우유부단하다 He's so wishy-washy about the subject.

우유성 偶有性 〖철학〗 accident; accidental quality

우육 牛肉 beef

우음마식 牛飮馬食 heavy eating and drinking; immoderation in food and drink **—하다** drink like a fish and eat like a wolf; be immoderate in drinking and eating; gorge and swill

우의 友誼 friendship; fellowship; friendly relations; fraternity; comradeship ¶ 우의가 두텁다 be a kind〔warm〕 friend to // 우의를 두텁게 하다 promote friendly relations with; cement friendship with《a person》// 우의를 맺다 cultivate〔contract, form〕 a friendship with; become friends with // 우의를 깨뜨리다 violate friendship

우의 羽衣 a robe of feathers ¶ 선녀의 우의 the celestial raiment〔robe〕 of an angel

†**우의 寓意** a moral; a hidden meaning; an implication ¶ 우의적인 allegorical **—하다** satirize; lampoon; squib; innuendo —극 a morality (play) — 소설 an allegory; an allegorical story — 이야기 a parable; a fable

우의 雨衣 a raincoat

우이 牛耳 ① 〔쇠귀〕 the ears of an ox ② 〔우두머리〕 the leader; the head ¶ 그는 한국 금융계에서 우이를 잡고 있다 He has a firm grip on〔is at the helm of〕 the banking business of Korea.

우이를 잡다 관용 take the leadership of; lead; head

우이독경 牛耳讀經 pouring water on a duck's back; to preach to the wind ¶ 나의 충고도 그에게는 우이독경이었다 All my advice fell flat on him.

우익 右翼 ① 〔날개〕 the right wing ② 〔대열〕 the right flank〔column, wing〕 ③ 〔경기〕 the right field (야구의); the right wing (축구의) ④ 〔정당〕 the rightists; the right faction; the right wing ¶ 극단적인 우익 an ultraconservative

— 단체 a right-wing organization —수(手) 〔야구〕 a right fielder — 운동 a Rightist movement; the movement of the Right — 정당 the Right Wing; a Right group; the Rightists 극 — an extreme right-winger; an ultrarightist; an ultraconservative

우익 羽翼 ① 〔깃〕 wings (of birds) ② 〔보좌〕 assistance; aid; help ¶ 우익이 되다 be the right hand《to a person》; assist《a person》

우인 友人 a friend; a companion ⇨ 벗

우인 偶因 an accidental〔an occasional, a contingent〕 cause

—론(論) occasionalism

우인 愚人 a fool; an ass; a dunce; an idiot; a simpleton ⇨ 우자(愚者)

우자 愚者 a fool; a stupid person; a simpleton; an idiot; a dunce ¶ 우자스럽다 be foolish; be stupid; be simple-minded; be idiotic

우작 愚作 ⇨ 졸작(拙作)
우장 雨裝 rain-gear ; rainwear ; a rain outfit ; a raincoat ━하다 put on a raincoat ; prepare for rain ¶ 우장 준비는 되어 있다 be provided with rain-gear
우적 雨滴 a raindrop ; a drop of rain
우적우적 ① ⇨ 우썩 ② [씹다] munching ; crunching ¶ 오이를 우적우적 씹어먹다 munch cucumber ③ [무너지다] creaking ; squeaking ④ [일 따위를] hurriedly
우접 寓接 ⇨ 우거(寓居)
우접다 ① [뛰어나게 되다] become eminent ; become outstanding〔superior〕 ② [이겨 내다] surpass one's superiors ; outstrip one's elders〔teachers〕
*우정 友情 friendship ; friendliness ; fellowship ; friendly feelings ¶ 따뜻한 우정 a warm friendship // 우정이 있는 friendly ; amiable // 우정으로 with friendship ; in a friendly manner // 우정을 두텁게 하다 promote friendship ; cultivate a friendly feeling with 《a person》 // 그는 우정이 깊은 사람이다 He is a friendly sort of fellow. // 그는 친구에 대해서 따뜻한 우정을 가지고 있다 He has a warm heart for his friends.
우정 郵政 postal service〔administration〕
우제 雩祭 a shamanist service to pray for rain
우제 虞祭 a sacrificial rite at the conclusion of a burial
우제 愚弟 My younger brother ; I
우제류 偶蹄類 Artiodactyla
우조 羽調 〖음악〗 *wu* ⇨ the highest note of the Korean pentatonic scale ; C
우족 右族 ① [적자 계통] the legitimate lineage ; the descendants of the legitimate son〔the heir〕 ② [귀족] the nobles〔the noble family〕
우족 右足 the right foot
우졸 愚拙 stupidity ; foolishness ; clumsiness ; folly ━하다 (be) stupid ; clumsy ; foolish ; senseless ; silly
†우주 宇宙 the universe ; the cosmos ; space ; heaven and earth

> 참고 **the universe**는 존재하는 모든 것 **the cosmos**는 정연한 질서로서의 우주를 뜻하며 chaos의 반대 **space**는 모든 사물이 존재하고 운동하는 공간이라는 뜻

¶ 우주의 universal ; cosmic // 우주를 탐험하다 explore space // 우주 여행을 하다 travel outward into space
— 개발 space development — 개발 경쟁 a space race — 공학 space engineering — 과학 space science —관 one's outlook on the universe — 글라이더 a space glider — 로켓 a space 〔cosmic〕 rocket —론 cosmology —모 a space helmet — 발생론 cosmogeny — 보행〔유영(游泳), 산책〕 a spacewalk —복 a space suit — 비행 a space flight ; space flying — 비행사 a spaceman ; a spacewoman ; an astronaut ; a cosmonaut ; a cosmonette (여자) — 산업 the (aero) space industry — 생물학 space biology —선(船) a 《manned》 spaceship ; a spacecraft ; a space vehicle —선(線) 〖물리〗 cosmic rays — 센타 a space center — 소설 space fiction — 속도 space velocity — 시대 the space age〔era〕 —식(食) space foods —어(語) [우주 관계자의 용어] space language ; space talk — 여행 a space trip〔journey, travel, ride〕 ; a travel〔journey〕 in (outer) space — 여행자 a space traveler — 역학 〖물리〗 celestial mechanics ; gravitational astronomy — 연구 space research —운(雲) cosmic clouds — 위성 a space satellite — 의학 space medicine —인 [대기권 밖의 우주에 산다고 하는 사람] a spaceman — 인력 〖물리〗 universal attraction 〔gravitation〕 — 자기(磁氣) 〖물리〗 cosmical magnetism — 정거장 a space 〔satellite〕 station ; a space platform — 중계 ¶ 우주 중계로 via the space relay — 지리학 spatiography —진(塵) 〖천문〗 cosmic dust ; [통속어] star dust — 진화론 cosmogony —총 a space〔propellant〕 gun — 탐험 a space probe ; space exploration — 통신 space communication —학 cosmology —학자 a cosmologist — 항법(航法) space navigation ; astronautics ; astrogation — 협정 a space agreement 대— macrocosm ; macrocosmos 소— microcosm ; microcosmos 은하(銀河) — the Milky Way galaxy〔system〕 국제 — 여행 연맹 the International Astroexpedition Federation ☞ 《p. 1608》
우주 계획 宇宙計劃 a space program〔project〕
우주 병기 宇宙兵器 a space weapon
우죽 a top branch (of a tree) ; the top boughs
우줄거리다 ⇨ 우줄우줄하다
우줄우줄 with a swinging motion ; dancing〔swaying〕 rhythmically ; with a swagger〔rolling gait〕 ━하다 sway〔shake〕 rhythmically ¶ 우줄우줄 걷다 walk with a swagger ; swagger ; roll // 우줄우줄 춤추다 dance up and down
우줅거리다 toddle ; trudge ; waddle ; walk unsteadily
우줅우줅 toddling ; waddling ; trudging ━하다 toddle
우줅이다 persist 《in doing something》 in one's own way ; do willfully〔stubbornly〕 ; take one's own way
우중 雨中 ¶ 우중에 in the rain ; while raining // 우중에도 불구하고 in spite of the rain ; though it is raining // 우중에 나가다 go out in the rain
우중충하다 ① [침침하다] (be) gloomy ;

우주 개발

① 우주 과학과 기술

▶우주 개발 계획 space development project / 우주선 지구호 Spaceship Earth (★ 지구는 자원이 한정된 하나의 우주선과 같다고 보는 새로운 경향) / 우주 공학 기술자 a space engineer / 우주 항공학 space aeronautics / 우주 과학 space science / 우주 의학 space medicine

▶우주 산업 space industry / 우주 개발 위원회 the Space Activities Commission / 미항공 우주국 the National Aeronautics and Space Administration (★ 보통 NASA로 불림) / 유럽 우주국 the European Space Agency(ESA) / 우주 식민지 space colony

▶우주 탐사 space exploration / 우주 탐사기 a space probe / 우주 수송 시스템 space transportation system / 유인 우주 비행 manned space flight / 우주 비행 space flight / 우주 항해 space navigation / 우주 플랫폼[정거장] a space platform [station] / 우주 견인선 a space tug / 우주복 spacesuit; G-suit / 우주식 space foods / 우주선 spaceship; spacecraft / 과학 실험용 우주선 spaceship for scientific experiment; scientific space station

② 궤도(orbit)

▶우주 공간 space; void of space / 궤도 수정 course correction; orbit correction / 정지 궤도 a stationary[geostationary, synchronous] orbit / 대기 궤도 a parking orbit / 지구 궤도 an earth orbit; a circumearth orbit; orbit around the earth / 달 궤도 circumlunar orbit / 인력권 a sphere of gravitation[influence]; a gravitation sphere[field] / (대기권에로의) 재돌입 reentry / 통신 두절 communication blackout / 도킹 docking; line-up / 연착륙 a touchdown; soft landing / 착수(着水) a splashdown / 대기권의 재돌입 reentry / 무중력 상태 weightlessness / 선내(船內) 활동 on-board[in-flight] activities / (우주인의) 선외(船外) 활동 extravehicular activities / 우주 유영 space walk

③ 로켓 · 인공 위성

▶인공 위성 artificial[man-made] satellite / 방송 위성 a broadcasting satellite / 과학 위성 a scientific satellite / 기상 (관측) 위성 weather[meteorological] satellite / 통신 위성 a communication(s)[relay] satellite / 군사 위성 a military satellite / 항행[항해] 위성 navigation satellite / 스페이스 셔틀[우주 왕복선] space shuttle / 측지 위성 geodetic satellite / 해사 위성 marine satellite / 자원 탐사 위성 remote-sensing satellite; earth resources satellite / 스파이 위성 spy satellite

▶다단식 로켓 multistage[multiple stage] rocket / 3단식 로켓 a three-stage rocket / 보조 추진용 로켓 a maneuvering rocket; a service propulsion rocket / 역분사식 로켓 a retrorocket / 달운항 우주선 a lunar spaceship / 부스터[증속(增速) 로켓] a booster rocket

▶로켓 연료 rocket fuel / 탐색기 a probe; an explorer / 달 탐색기 a lunar [moon] probe / 달 착륙선 a lunar module / 선회기 an orbiter / 회수용 헬리콥터 a recovery helicopter

---

somber; dismal; dimly-lit ¶ 우중충한 날씨 gloomy weather // 우중충한 방 a dismal room
② [빛깔이] (be) discolored; faded

우지 a crybaby; milksop

우지 牛脂 beef tallow; suet

우지끈 with a crash〔crack〕 **—하다** crackle; smash; snap ¶ 우지끈하고 큰 나무가 쓰러졌다 A big tree fell down with a crash.

우지끈거리다 make cracking noises ¶ 나무가 우지끈거리며 쓰러졌다 The tree fell〔collapsed〕 with cracking noises.

우지끈뚝딱 with a crack〔crackle, thud, thump〕

우지끈우지끈 with snaps〔cracks, crackles〕 **—하다** make successive cracking noises

우지직 ① [타는 소리] with a crackle; cracking; popping ¶ 우지직 타다 dry straw crackles in the flames ② [부러지는 소리] with a snap〔crack〕

우지직거리다 ① [타다] crackle; crack; pop ② [나무가] creak; crack

우지직우지직 [타는 소리] with crackling〔cracking〕 sounds; [부러지는 소리] with a crack

우직 愚直 simplicity and honesty; stupidity and tactlessness **—하다** (be) stupid and tactless; simple (and honest); stupidly honest; honest to a fault

우질 牛疾 a cattle disease〔epidemic〕;

rinderpest
우집다 look down upon 《a person》 ; despise ; scorn
우짖다 cry loud ; howl ; yell ¶ 우짖는 바람 howling wind
우쩍 ⇨ 와짝
우쩍우쩍 ⇨ 우적우적
우쭉우쭉 [몸을] dancing one's body up and down ; [커지는 모양] rapidly and steadily ; quickly ¶ 우쭉우쭉 자라다 become taller with rapidity
우쭐거리다 ⇨ 우줄우줄하다
우쭐우쭐 ⇨ 우줄우줄
우쭐하다 be proud〔pompous〕; be puffed up 《with》; be elated 《with, by》; hold up one's head ; have a swelled head ¶ 너무 우쭐해할 것 없어 Don't be so proud of yourself. // 성공으로 우쭐해 있다 He is puffed up with his success. // 저 녀석은 조금만 치켜 세워주면 금방 우쭐해 한다 A little flattery and that guy's in high gear.
우차 牛車 an oxcart
우책 愚策 a stupid plan ; a silly step
우처 愚妻 my wife
우천 雨天 rainy〔wet〕 weather ; a rainy〔wet〕 day ¶ 우천으로 인해서 because of〔on account of〕 rain // 우천인 경우 in case of rain ; if it rains // 우천으로 인해서 경기가 연기되었다 Owing to the rain, the game was postponed.
— 순연 postponement〔to be postponed〕 till the first fine day in case of rain **— 접촉** 〖전기〗 weather contact **— 체조장** a gymnasium ; a gym ; a drill hall **— 혼선** 〖전기〗 weathercross
†**우체 郵遞** post ; mail 《미》; postal〔mail〕 service
—국 a post office ; a post 《영》 **—국구(局區)** a postal district ; a postal delivery zone 《미》 **—국(사무)원** a post-office clerk ; a mail〔mailing〕 clerk 《미》; a postal clerk 《영》 **—국 유치** [표기] To be held till called for. **—국장** a postmaster **—부** a mailman 《미》; a mail〔letter〕 carrier 《미》; a postman 《영》 **—통** a post ; a postbox ; pillar〔letter〕 box 《영》; a mailbox 《미》 ¶ 편지를 우체통에 넣다 mail a letter (at a mailbox) **간이 —국** a postal agency **군사 —국** an army〔a fleet〕 post office 《A.〔F.〕P. O.》 **야전(野戰) —국** a field post office **중앙 —국** the Central Post Office **철도 —국** a traveling〔railway〕 post office **특정 —국** a special post office
우측 右側 the right side ; the right hand ¶ 우측에 on the right (side)
— 통행 [게시] Keep to the right. / Walk on right side facing traffic. ¶ 미국에서는 우측 통행이다 Traffic moves on the right in America.
우치 〖의학〗 bleeding piles ; hemorrhoids
우치 a decayed tooth ; caries ⇨ 충치(蟲齒)
우케 grain being dried for grinding
우쿨렐레 〖악기〗 a ukulele
우크라이나 Ukraina
우택 雨澤 a seasonable rainfall ; the benefit〔blessing〕 of rain
우툴두툴하다 (be) rugged ; knotty ; bumpy ; rough ¶ 우툴두툴한 나무 knotty timber // 우툴두툴한 길 a bumpy road // 우툴두툴한 가죽 granulated leather
우파 右派 the right wing〔wingers〕; the right faction ; the Rightists
— 사회당 the right-wing Socialist Party
우편 右便 the right side〔direction〕 ¶ 우편에 on the right side 《of》; on one's right
†**우편 郵便** post ; mail 《미》; postal〔mail〕 service ¶ 다음 우편으로 by the next post〔mail〕 // 우편으로 보내다 send by post〔mail〕; post ; mail // 소포 우편으로 보내다 send 《a thing》 by parcel post
—낭〔가방〕 a mail〔post〕 bag **—료〔요금〕** postage ; postal charges **—물** mailpostal matter ¶ 제1〔2, 3〕종 우편물 the first-〔second-, third-〕class mail // 휴가 중 우편물 배달을 중지해 주십시오 I'd like to put our mail on vasation hold. **— 배달** mail delivery **— 배달 구역** the postal delivery zone〔district 《영》〕; the zone 《미》 **— 배달부** ⇨ 우체부 **— 번호** [전체] the postal〔zip 《미》〕 code ; [개개의] a postal〔zip 《미》〕 code number 《of a postal delivery zone》; a (postal) zone number **— 번호제(도)** the postal zoning system ; the zip code system 《미》 **— 사서함** a post-office box 《POB, P. O. Box》 **— 소인(消印)** a postmark ; a post-office stamp **— 소포** a postal package **— 업무** mail〔postal〕 service **— 엽서** a postal card ; a postal ; [사제(私製)] a post card **— 저금** postal 〔post-office〕 savings ; a postal〔post〕 deposit **— 저금 통장** a postal savings passbook ; a post-office savings bankbook **— 전신환(電信換)** a postal telegraphic transfer **— 제도** the postal system **— 조약** a postal treaty〔convention〕 **— 주문** a mail order **— 집배국** a distributing〔separating〕 post office **—차** [열차의] a post(al)〔mail〕 car ; a mailcoach ; a post van ; [자동차] a mailcoach ; a mail cart 《영》; a mail truck **— 투표** voting by mail **—함** a letterbox 《영》; a mailbox 《미》 **—환** a postal〔post〕 money order 《P. M. O》《미》; a post-office order 《P. O. O》《영》; a money order **가격 표기 —** value-declared post **광고 —** advertisement mail **국유치 —(물)** general delivery mail ; poste restante 《프》; a letter to be called for ¶ 국유치 우편으로 보내다 send 《a person》 a letter poste restante〔to general delivery〕 **군사 —** military〔army〕 post〔mail〕 **내국(외국) —환** an inland〔a foreign〕 money order **등기 —** 《by》 regis-

tered mail〔post〕 만국 — 연합 the International Post Union 배달 불능 — dead letters 선박 — sea post〔mail〕 소포 —료 the rates of postage on parcels 속달 — express mail〔post〕; [편지] a special delivery letter《미》; an express(-delivery) letter《영》 약속 — promissory post 외국〔내국〕 — foreign〔domestic〕 post 〔mail〕 항공 — air mail

우편 요금 郵便料金 postage《on a letter》; the rates of postage〔postal rates〕《on letters》

— 무료 Post-free. /Postage-free. /Free of postal charge. — 후납 Postage will be paid by the licensee〔addressee〕.

우편 집배원 郵便集配員 a mailman《미》; a postman《영》 ¶ 우편 집배원은 하루에 두 번 온다 The mailman comes round twice a day.

†**우표 郵票** a postage-stamp; a stamp ¶ 130원짜리 우표 one hundred (and) thirty *won* stamp // 우표를 붙이다 put a stamp《on》; affix〔stick〕 a stamp; stamp《a letter》// 이 편지에는 얼마짜리 우표를 붙여야 합니까 What is the postage for this letter?

— 수집 stamp collecting; philately ¶ 나의 취미는 우표 수집이다 My hobby is stamp collecting. — 수집가 a stamp collector; a philatelist 반신용 — return postage

우피 牛皮 oxhide; cowhide

우합 偶合 a (casual) coincidence —하다 coincide casually〔incidentally〕; happen to coincide ¶ 단순한 우합 a mere coincidence

우행 愚行 a folly; a foolish act; an act of folly

우향 右向 ¶ 우향 앞으로 가 [구령] Right wheel! // 우향 우 [구령] Right turn 〔face〕!

우현 右舷 〖항해〗 (the) starboard ¶ 우현으로 기울다 list to (the) starboard

*__우호 友好__ friendship; amity; comity ¶ 우호적 friendly; amicable // 우호 관계를 유지하다 maintain friendly relations《with》 —국 a friendly nation — 단체 a friendly organization — 사절 a fraternal delegate — 조약 a treaty of friendship〔amity〕

우화 雨靴 rain shoes; galoshes; overshoes

우화 羽化 ① [벌레의] emergence —하다 grow wings ② ⇨ 우화등선(羽化登仙)

‡**우화 寓話** a fable; an allegory; an apologue

— 작가 a fable writer; a fabler; a fabulist 동물 — an animal fable 이솝 —집 Aesop's Fables

우화등선 羽化登仙 becoming a fairy —하다 ascend to heaven as a Taoist immortal; become a Taoist immortal ¶ 우화등선하는 기분이다 feel as if one were floating〔walking〕 on air

우환 憂患 ① [근심·걱정] trouble; anxiety; worry; apprehension; grief; distress ¶ 우환이 있다 have anxieties; be heavy-hearted; be worried; be grief-stricken ② [병] illness; sickness ¶ 오랜 우환 a long illness; a disease of long duration // 저 집에는 우환이 그칠 날이 없다 Someone is always laid up in that family.

우활 迂闊 ⇨ 오활(迂闊)

우황 牛黃 〖한의학〗 ox bezoar

*__우회 迂回__ a roundabout (way); a circuit; detour —하다 take a roundabout way; make a detour; detour; make a circuit; go round ¶ 5마일을 우회하다 make a detour of five miles // 산을 우회해서 가다 go round a mountain // 우회하시오 Detour. (게시)

— 도로 a bypass; a road bypassing a town — 무역 commodity shunting — 생산 a roundabout method of production; circuitous production —선 a roundabout route

우회로 迂回路 a roundabout〔circuitous〕 way〔route, course〕; a circuit; a detour

우회전 右回轉 (a) right-handed rotation 〔revolution〕; dextrorotation ¶ 우회전의 〔하는〕 right-handed; dextrorotary // 우회전으로 clockwise; in a clockwise direction; with the sun —하다 turn to 〔toward〕 the right; make a right turn

— 금지 No right-turn.

우후 雨後 after the rain; after a rainfall ¶ 우후죽순처럼 나오다 spring〔crop〕 up like (so many) mushrooms after rain; increase with rapidity

욱기 —氣 impetuosity; hot-headedness; hot temper; rashness; wildness ¶ 욱기가 있다 be hot-tempered; be hotheaded; have a wild disposition

욱다 ① [굽다] get bent in; be turned in; be dented ¶ 욱은 그릇 a deep bowl ② [기운이] weaken; fail; get enfeebled 〔enervated〕 ¶ 기운이 욱다 lose one's pep

욱대기다 ① [위협] threaten; scare; intimidate; compel; coerce ¶ 사람을 욱대기어 돈을 받아내다 blackmail《a person》; press《a person》 to pay money // 사람을 욱대기어 일을 하게 하다 bully《a person》 into doing a work ② [딱딱거리다] snap at; snarl at; bark at

욱둥이 a hothead; a rash〔impetuous〕 person; a rough〔wild〕 person

욱박지르다 browbeat; bully; shout down ¶ 욱박질러 말을 못하게 하다 shout《a person》 down

욱시글거리다 swarm together ¶ 많은 개미가 욱시글거리다 innumerable ants swarm round

욱시글득시글 —하다 swarm; throng; teem with

욱시글욱시글 swarming together

욱신거리다 ① [쑤시다] tingle ; throb with pain ; smart ¶ 벌에 쏘인 손가락이 욱신거린다 My finger smarts from a sting. ② [떼가] swarm ; throng ; teem ⟪with⟫
욱신욱신 [북적임] in swarms ; pricking ; [쑤심] throbbing〔smarting〕 with pain
욱실득실 swarming together
욱여들다 gather
욱여싸다 surround ; beset ; wrap ; cover ¶ 도둑 잡으려고 집을 욱여싸다 surround a house to catch a thief ∥ 김치독을 얼지 않도록 짚으로 욱여싸다 wrap a *kimchi* crock up in straw to prevent freezing
욱이다 bend〔turn, batter〕 in ; dent
욱일 旭日 the rising sun ¶ 욱일승천지세이다 be in the ascendent
욱적거리다 jostle all at one place〔all together〕
욱적욱적 in swarms〔throngs〕; hustling and bustling **—하다** ⇨ 욱적거리다
욱죄이다 feel cramped〔squeezed〕
욱지르다 intimidate ; browbeat ¶ 욱질러 말을 못하게 하다 shut ⟪a person⟫ down ; make a person put down
욱질리다 be intimidated ; get browbeaten
욱하다 fall〔get, fly〕 into a passion ; flare up (in anger) ; burn up ; loose one's temper ¶ 욱하기 쉬운 성질 ⟪a man with⟫ an explosive temper ∥ 욱해서 in a fit of passion ; in a (fit of) rage ∥ 그는 욱하는 기질이다 He is hot-〔quick-〕 tempered. / He is quick to anger.
†운 運 [행운] fortune ; luck ; [운명] fate ; one's lot ; destiny ; [기회] chance ; a break ¶ 운이 좋다 be lucky〔fortunate〕∥ 운이 나쁘다 be unlucky〔unfortunate〕∥ 운 좋게 fortunately ; luckily ; by good fortune〔luck〕∥ 운 나쁘게 unluckily ; unfortunately ; by ill luck ∥ 운 나쁘게도 …하다 have the misfortune to ⟪do⟫ ∥ 만약 운이 좋으면 if fortune smiles upon me ∥ 운이 다하다 meet one's doom ∥ 운이 트이다 one's fortune changes for the better ; fortune turns in one's favor ∥ 운이 안 트이다 have constant ill〔bad〕 luck ; luck goes〔runs〕 against ⟪a person⟫ ∥ 운에 맡기다 trust to chance〔luck〕; leave ⟪a matter⟫ to chance ; take the risk ∥ 그는 운이 트이기 시작했다 Fortune has begun to smile upon him. /The wheel of Fortune has begun to roll his way〔to turn in his favor〕. ∥ 누구에게나 운은 한번 돌아오는 것이다 Every dog has his day. ∥ 그런 여자하고 결혼을 하다니 내가 운이 없었지 It was just my luck to many a woman like her. ∥ 운이 좋았어 I was lucky. /I was in luck. /It was a sheer fluke. ∥ 재능이 있으면 언젠가는 운도 따르게 마련이다 Talents are bound to find luck sooner or later.
운 韻 a rhyme〔rime〕 ¶ 운을 맞추다 rhyme ∥ 운이 맞다 rhyme with
운각 雲刻 cloud-shaped carvings on the edges of furniture
운각 韻脚 〚시〛 a (metrical) feet ¶ 운각이 있는 시 rhymed verse
운경 雲鏡 〚기상〛 a nephoscope
운고 雲高 the height of the cloud ceiling **—계〔측정기〕** a ceilometer
운기 運氣 ① [열병] an epidemic fever ② [운수] good luck ; bad luck ; fortune ; misfortune
운김 ① [남은 기운] a trace of warm air 〔vapor〕 ¶ 그 의자에는 먼저 앉았던 사람의 운김이 남아 있었다 The chair was still warm from the person who had been sitting there before me. ② […하는 바람] a sequel ; a consequence (of joint effort) ¶ 운김에 in the wake ⟪of⟫ ; with the circumstance ⟪of⟫ ; affected by
운니 雲泥 [운니지차] a great〔wide〕 difference ⟪between⟫
†운동 運動 ① 〚물리〛 motion ; movement

> **참고** **motion** 움직이고 있는 상태 **movement** 특정한 방향으로 향하여 규칙적으로 움직이는 것

—하다 move ; be in motion ¶ 운동의 법칙 laws of motion ∥ 지구의 이중 운동 the double motion of the earth ∥ 운동중의 물체 a body in motion
② [체육상의] exercise ; recreation ; [경기] sports ; athletics ; games ; a match ; [체조] gymnastics **—하다** take exercise ; exercise ; have〔play〕 a game ¶ 가벼운 운동 light exercise ∥ 운동 부족으로 through lack〔want〕 of exercise ; through insufficient exercise ∥ 운동이 필요하다 need some exercise ∥ 적당히 운동하다 take moderate〔proper〕 exercise ∥ 운동을 좋아하다 be a lover of sports ; be a sports fan ∥ 운동을 하면 식욕이 생긴다 Exercise gives ⟪a person⟫ a good appetite. ∥ 수영은 젊은이에게 좋은 운동이다 Swimming is a fine sport for young people. 운동 좀 하셔야겠습니다 You'd better work out. /You need exercise. ∥ 나는 규칙적으로 운동을 하고 절대로 과식을 하지 않는다 I work out regularly and never pig out.
③ [노력·활동·투쟁] an effort ; [단체적인] a movement ; an agitation ; a campaign ; a drive ; [선거의] electioneering ⟪영⟫ **—하다** make an effort ; conduct 〔carry on, undertake〕 a campaign ⟪for, against⟫ ; campaign ⟪for, against⟫ ; canvass ⟪for⟫ ¶ 독립 운동 an independence movement ∥ 정치〔노동, 학생〕 운동 a political〔labor, student〕 movement ∥ 운동을 일으키다 initiate a campaign ; launch a drive ; start a movement ∥ 취직 운동을 하다 make an effort to obtain a position ; run for a position ∥ 모금 운동을 일으키다 start a campaign for subscription ∥ 시장 배척 운동을 일으키다 start an

agitation against the mayor // 임금 인상 운동을 일으키다 start an agitation for an increase of wages // 그의 유임 운동이 행해지고 있다 Efforts are being made to induce him to remain in office.
—가 an athlete ; a sportsman — 감각 〖심리〗 the motor sensation ; the sensation of movement — 경기 (athletic) sports — 계 the sporting world ; sporting circles — 구점 a sports store〔shop〕 —근 〖해부〗 a motor (muscle) — 기관(器官) 〖해부〗 an organ of locomotion — 기구 sporting〔sport, athletic〕 goods〔equipment, apparatus〕 ; sport outfits — 기사 sports news — 기자 a sports reporter 〔writer, columnist〕 — 능력 capacity for 〔power of〕 locomotion —란 the sports column〔page, section〕 —량 quantity of motion ; 〖물리〗 momentum ; impetus — 마찰 〖물리〗 kinetic friction —모 a sports cap — 방정식 〖물리〗 the equation of motion —복 sports clothes ; sportswear ; a gym suit —부 [신문사의] the sports desk ; [학교의] an athletic club —부장 [대학의] the manager of an athletic club ; [신문사의 체육부장] the director of the department of athletics ; the sports editor —비 campaign funds (자금) ; canvassing expenses (비용) — 선수 an athlete ; a sportsman —성 〖생리〗 motility — 성 실어증 〖의학〗 ataxic〔motor〕 aphasia — 셔츠 a shirt for sports — 시설 sports facilities — 신경 〖해부〗 a motor (nerve) — 실조(失調) 〖의학〗 failure of muscular coordination ; loss of coordination of the muscles ; ataxia — 에너지 〖물리〗 kinetic energy —열 a passion for sports ; love of sports ; an athletic fever — 요법 〖의학〗 an exercise cure ; a movement cure —원 [선거의] a canvasser ; an electioneer 〔electioneering agent〕 ; [정치상의] an agitator ; a campaigner — 자금 campaign funds —장 a playground ; an athletic field — 장애 〖의학〗 motor disturbance — 전위(電位) 〖물리〗 electrokinetic potential — 정신 sportsmanship — 중추 〖해부〗 the motor center — 충동 a motor impulse — 틀 gym equipment —팬 a sports fan 〔enthusiast〕 ; a lover of sports ; a sports-minded person — 팬츠 athletic 〔gym〕 pants〔shorts〕 — 포텐셜 〖물리〗 kinetic potential —학 kinematics — 화 running shoes ; sports〔gymnasium, gym〕 shoes ; sneakers (고무 바닥의) 《미》 —회 a field meet ; an athletic meet 〔meeting〕 금주 — a temperance〔prohibition〕 movement ; a temperance crusade ; a crusade against drunkenness (기금) 모금 — a drive to raise funds ; a fund-raising campaign〔drive〕 반대〔찬성〕 — a campaign against〔for〕 상하 — an up-and-down motion 선거 — an electioneering〔election〕 campaign ; electioneering 실내 — an indoor sport 〔game〕 야외〔옥외〕 — an outdoor sport 〔game〕 ; field sports 종교 — a religious movement 파상(波狀)〔직선〕 — a wavy 〔straight-line〕 motion 회전 — a rotary 〔rotatory〕 motion

운동 부족 運動不足 lack〔want〕 of exercise ; underexercise ¶ 운동 부족으로 through lack〔want〕 of exercise ; through insufficient exercise

운두 the height of shoes〔bowls〕 ¶ 운두가 낮은 신 low-cut shoes // 운두가 높은 신 high-cut shoes

운라 UNRRA 《United Nations Relief and Rehabilitation Administration》 (지금은 폐지되었음)

운명 殞命 death —하다 die ; expire ; breathe one's last

†**운명** 運命 fate ; destiny ; one's lot ; fortune ; doom ; kismet ; luck

> 참고 **destiny, fate, doom**은 전세의 약속과 같은 인력으로 피할 수 없는 초자연적인 숙명을 의미하고 특히 fate와 doom은 죽음 파멸 따위 비참한 결말을 의미한다 **fortune, luck**는 선악 어느편의 운명에도 사용되지만 보통 행운을 의미한다 **lot**은 심지를 뽑아 결정되는 따위의 우연한 운을 의미한다

¶ 운명의 날 the fated〔fatal, fateful〕 day // 운명의 장난 a whim〔an irony〕 of life // 운명의 여신 Fortune ; the (three) Fates // 운명에 맡기다 abandon〔leave〕 《a person, oneself, a thing》 to fate // 운명을 개척하다 improve one's lot ; seek one's fortune // 운명을 같이하다 cast〔throw〕 one's lot 《with》 ; share one's fortune 〔lot〕 《with》 // 운명과 싸우다 strive against fate ; be at odds with fate // 운명이라고 체념하다 resign oneself to one's fate // 운명 지어지다 be destined〔fated〕 to ; be doomed to // 운명을 결정할 때가 왔다 The fatal hour has come. // 어차피 실패할 운명이다 It is doomed to failure.
—론 fatalism —론자 a fatalist —선 [손금] the line of Fate〔Saturn〕

운모 雲母 mica
— 동광 copper mica — 철광 micaceous iron ore —판 a mica plate — 편마암 mica gneiss — 편암 mica schist 〔slate〕 금— phlogopite 백— muscovite 흑— biotite

운무 雲霧 cloud and mist〔fog〕 ¶ 운무에 싸이다 be enveloped in a fog ; be shrouded by cloud and fog

운문 雲紋 a cloudlike〔wavelike〕 pattern ; moiré 《프》

운문 韻文 verse ; poetry ; a poem ¶ 운문을 산문으로 바꿔 쓰다 turn a verse into prose
—극 a verse drama ; a play in verse

†**운반** 運搬 conveyance ; transport ; trans-

portation ; carriage ; portage **—하다** carry ; convey ; transport ; bear

> 참고 **carry** 무거운 것을 들어 나르다의 뜻으로서 가장 일반적으로 쓰이는 말 **bear** 무거운 것에 견디다의 뜻 **convey** 계속 나르다의 뜻으로서 비유적으로 쓰이는 경우가 많다 **transport** 배·비행기·자동차 따위로 장거리를 나르다의 뜻

¶ 철도〔해로〕로 운반하다 convey〔carry〕 by rail〔sea〕// 그 환자는 즉시 병원으로 운반되었다 The patient was immediately taken to a hospital.
—비 transport charges ; carriage ; freight ; portage **—업** transportation〔freight〕 business **—인** a carrier ; a porter (인부) **—차** a cart ; a wagon ; a motor-lorry ; a truck 《미》 **이삿짐 —차** a family-(re)moving van **환자 —차** an ambulance (car)

운봉 雲峰 [구름] a gigantic column of clouds ; a cloud bank ; [산봉우리] a mountain top〔peak〕 wrapped in clouds

운산 雲山 a mountain wrapped〔veiled, shrouded〕 in clouds ; a cloud-wrapped mountain

운산 運算 operation ; calculation **—하다** operate ; work ; calculate ; figure out ; cipher ¶ 운산을 잘하다 be good at calculation〔figures〕// 이 운산은 할 수 없다 I cannot do this sum.

운산무소하다 雲散霧消— scatter and vanish ; vanish like mist ; vanish in smoke ; disappear into thin air

운석 隕石 a meteoric stone ; a meteorite

운성 隕星 a shooting star ; a falling star ; a meteor

운세 運勢 ⇨ 운수(運數)

운속계 雲速計 ⇨ 운경(雲鏡)

****운송 運送** conveyance : transport ; transportation ; shipping ; forwarding ; freight 《미》 **—하다** carry ; transport ; convey ; forward ¶ 운송 중에 on passage // 철도〔배〕로 운송하다 transport 《goods》 by rail〔ship〕
— 계약 a contract of carriage **—기** [석탄 등의] conveyor **—료** carriage ; freight (rates) ; forwarding charges ; haulage **— 보험** transit insurance **—비** cost of transport ; shipping expenses (선편) **—선** a transport (ship) ; a cargo vessel ; a freighter **—업** shipping trade ; transportation business **—업자** a carrier ; a forwarding agent **— 용구** conveyance **—인** a carrier ; a porter **—장** a waybill ; an invoice **—점** a forwarding agency **—차** an express cart〔wagon〕 **— 취급인** a (shipping and) forwarding agent **—품** freight ; goods **— 회사** a transport〔shipping, freight〕 company **소(小)—** express **여객 —** passenger traffic **트럭 —** trucking **해상〔육상〕 —** transportation by sea〔land〕 **화물 —** carriage of goods〔freight〕 ; goods〔freight〕 traffic

†운수 運數 one's star ; luck ; fortune ; chance ¶ 운수가 좋다〔나쁘다〕 be lucky〔unlucky〕 ; fortunate〔unfortunate〕 // 운수가 나빴다 The stars were against it. // 이번에는 운수가 없었다 I have had no luck this time. // 이번에 운수가 좋으면 부자가 될지 모른다 I may be rich at the next turn of the wheel.
— 소관 a matter of chance ; a matter pertaining to luck〔fortune〕

운수 運輸 ⇨ 운송(運送)
— 기관 means of conveyance〔transportation〕 **—국** the traffic department **—량** traffic **— 사업** the transportation business **— 협정** a traffic agreement **— 회사** a transportation〔a shipping, a forwarding, an express〕 company **여객〔철도〕 —** passenger〔railway〕 traffic

운수 노조 運輸勞組 the Traffic Service Workers Union

운신 運身 moving one's body ; movement ; stir **—하다** move about ; stir ¶ 운신조차 못하다 cannot move at all ; cannot stir an inch

운영 雲影 shade of a cloud

운영 運營 operation ; management ; administration **—하다** manage ; run ; operate ; administer ¶ 잡지사를 운영하다 publish〔conduct〕 a magazine // 호텔을 운영하다 run a hotel // 사업을 운영하다 conduct a business
— 규칙 managerial regulations **— 기구** the administrative structure **—비** working expenses **— 위원회** a steering committee (국회 따위의) ; the Committee of Rules (미 하원) **— 자금** working〔operating〕 funds〔capital〕 **국사(國事) —** the conduct of state affairs

운예 雲霓 clouds and rainbow ; a sign of a shower〔rain〕

운용 運用 application ; working ; use ; employment **—하다** apply ; employ ; use ; make use of ; work ; put in practice ¶ 운용할 수 있는 practical ; applicable // 법률의 운용 the application of the law // 자금을 운용하다 employ funds ; invest one's money shrewdly // 제도의 효과는 운용 여하에 있다 The benefit of any legislative measure consists in its wise application. // 실지로 운용해보지 않으면 그 가부는 모른다 Its merits cannot be ascertained unless it is put in practice.
— 자본 working〔functioning〕 capital ; operational funds

운운 云云 so and so ; thus and thus ; and so forth ; and so on ; et cetera 《etc.》 **—하다** say something or other 《of, about》 ; say thus and thus ; say such and such

운유 雲遊 wandering ; roaming **—하다** wander ; roam

*운율 韻律 a rhythm ; a beat ; a cadence ; a metre ¶ 운율의 rhythmical ; metrical // 운율이 없는 rhythmless // 운율에 맞다 be〔sound〕 rhythmical
—학 metrics ; prosody

†운임 運賃 [화물의] goods rates《영》; freight (rates)《미》; portage ; [송료] carriage charges ; shipping expenses ; [짐수레의] cartage ; [사람의] fare ¶ 쌀의 운임 freight rates on rice // 모든 운임은 이쪽에서 부담한다 We send all parcels carriage-paid.
— 가산 가격 cost and freight price《C. & F.》—률 freight〔carriage〕 rates — 무료 [게시] Carriage free. — 보험 freight insurance — 보험료 가산 가격 C. I. F.〔cost, insurance, and freight〕 price — 선불필 carriage〔freight〕prepaid — 수수료 가산 가격 C. F. &C.〔cost, freight, and commission〕 price — 수취인 지불 carriage〔freight〕 forward ; freight to collect ; freight payable at destination ; carriage payable on delivery — 완납 carriage〔freight〕 paid — 청구서 a freight bill《FB》—표 a freight list ; a《railway》 tariff — 할인 환불 freight rebate — 할증(割增) primage — 협정〔경쟁〕 a tariff agreement〔war〕 — 후불 freight to collect 국내〔해양, 항공〕 — inland〔ocean, airway〕 freight 균일 — a uniform fare 반액 — a half fare 배액 — a double fare 보통〔특별〕 — the ordinary〔a special〕 fare 여객 — passenger fares ; passage money 왕복〔편도〕 — a return〔single〕 fare 일〔이, 삼〕등 — the first〔second, third〕 class fare 특정 — an exceptional rate 할인〔할증, 전액〕 — a reduced〔an additional, a full〕 fare 국제 — 동맹 the International Freight Conference 여객 —표 a fare table 화물 — 등급표 a freight rate table

운자 韻字 a rhyming word〔character〕

*운전 運轉 working ; operation ; driving (차량의) ; motion ; revolution (회전) ; running —하다 put〔set〕 in motion ; set《a machine》 going〔working〕 ; run ; work (배를) ; navigate (배·비행기 따위) ; operate (기계를) ; employ (운용하다) ¶ 운전중이다 be in motion ; be driving《a car》// 기계 운전을 계속하다 keep a machine going // 기차를 운전하다 operate〔run〕 a train // 배를 운전하다 work〔navigate〕 a ship // 자동차를 운전하다 drive a car // 운전이 중지되다 be suspended ; be tied up // 이 기계는 전기로 운전된다 This machine is worked by electricity. // 짙은 안개 때문에 모든 열차의 운전이 중지되었다 The railway service has been suspended owing to the deep fog. // 운전중의 버스 운전수에게 말을 걸지 마십시오 Do not talk to the driver while bus is in motion. // 너무 피로해서 꾸벅꾸벅 졸면서 운전을 했다 I was so tired that I was dozing off behind the wheel. // 너는 우험하게 운전해서 같이 타기가 겁난다 You drive so recklessly it's unnerving just to ride with you. // 내 운전 솜씨가 그렇게 나쁘지 않지 I'm not that bad behind the wheel, am I?
— 간격《run on ten-minute》 headway ; intervals — 대 [전차의] a motorman's seat ; [자동차의] a driver's seat〔cab〕 — 면허증 a driver's〔driving〕 license ; a license to drive —사(士) [배의 항해사] a mate ; an officer ; [기계의] an operator〔a runner〕 ; [전차·발동기의] a motorman ; [전차의] a (streetcar) driver〔operator〕 ; [기차의] an engineer ; a locomotive engineer ; a driver ; an engine driver ; [자동차의] a driver〔chauffeur〕 ; [택시의] a cabdriver〔cabman〕 ; a taxi driver ; a cabbie〔cabby〕《구》; [승강기의] an elevator operator〔boy, girl〕 — 시험 [자동차의]《take》 a driving test —자〔인〕 [기계의] an operator — 자본〔자금〕 working capital〔funds〕 ; operational funds — 자산 working assets ; current assets 시— a trial run〔operation〕 ; a road test ; a test run

*운전사 運轉士 [자동차] a driver ; a chauffeur ; [자가용의] a cabman〔cabdriver〕 (택시의) ; [전차] a motorman ; [기차] an engine dirver〔man〕 ; [기계] an operator
— 면허 시험 driver's license test 스페어 — a codriver ; a spare driver《속》

운지법 運指法 『음악』 fingering

운집 雲集 gathering in swarms —하다 swarm ; gather in swarms〔crowd〕 ; crowd ; throng《a place》; flock

운철 隕鐵 meteoric iron

운치 韻致 taste ; refinement ; elegance ; artistic effect ; gracefulness ; harmony of designs ; symmetry of form ¶ 운치 있다 be tasteful ; be elegant ; be graceful // 운치 없다 be tasteless ; be insipid ; be ungraceful ; be unrefined // 운치 없는 사람 a prosaic〔matter-of-fact〕 person // 음산한 겨울 경치에도 운치가 있다 Desolate winter scenery possesses a charm of its own. // 정원이 운치 있게 꾸며져 있다 The garden is tastefully laid out.

운크라 UNKRA《UN Korean Reconstruction Agency》

운크타드 UNCTAD《UN Conference on Trade and Development》

운탄기 運炭機 a coal conveyor

운필 運筆 wielding the writing-brush ; strokes of the brush ; the use of the brush —하다 write ; paint ; draw

*운하 運河 a canal ; a waterway ¶ 운하를 파다 dig〔build〕 a canal // 그 도시에는 운하가 종횡으로 교차하고 있다 The city is crossed by a network of canals.
— 개착(開鑿) canalization ; canalling — 선 a canalboat ; a canal(l)er — 지대 a

canal zone ─ 통과료 canal tolls 선용(船用) ─ a ship canal 수갑식(水閘式)〔해평식(海平式)〕 ─ a lock〔sea-level〕 canal 수에즈 ─ the Suez Canal 파나마 ─ the Panama Canal 파나마 ─ 지대 the Canal Zone

운하 雲霞 clouds and haze ; the spring season

운학 韻學 prosody ; metrics

운항 運航 shipping service ; watertransport operations ─하다 operate ; run ; ply ¶ 인천 목포 간을 운항하는 기선 a steamer that plies between *Inch'ŏn* and *Mokp'o*

운해 雲海 the sea covered by clouds ; a distant place where water and clouds touch ; a sea of clouds

운행 運行 movement ; revolution ; motion ; a march ; race ; operation ; service ─하다 revolve ; go〔move〕 round ; run ¶ 열차의 운행 train service // 천체의 운행 movements of heavenly bodies // 유성은 그 궤도를 운행한다 The planets roll on in their courses.

─ 노선 a 《bus》 route ─ 정지〔중지〕 suspension〔stoppage〕 of the 《bus》 service 열차〔기선, 항공기〕 ─ a train〔a shipping, an airline〕 service 열차 ─ 시간표 a train timetable ; a railroad schedule 《미》 임시 열차 ─ extra train service

운형 雲形 [구름 그림·조각] cloud designs drawn〔engraved〕 ; 〖기상〗 a cloud form ─자 a curved rule ; a French curve

운휴 運休 suspension〔stoppage〕 of the 《bus》 service ¶ 열차가 운휴되었다 The train service stopped. /The train was canceled.

울[1] [떨거지] relations ; relatives ; family ; kinsfolk ; clan ¶ 울을 믿고 행패하다 play the bully, relying on his family to back him up

울[2] ① [울타리] a fence ; an enclosure ; a hedge ¶ 울안에 inside the premises ; in the compound // 울을 치다 fence around 《a house》 ; enclose 《a house》 with a fence ; wall // 울을 뛰어넘다 jump over a fence ; clear a fence // 울 너머로 보다 look over the fence // 울에서 들여다 보다 peep through a fence
② [신발의] the outer rim of shoes

울가망하다 feel〔undergo〕 anxiety ; be concerned about ; apprehend ; feel uncomfortable ; be mindful 《of》 ; trouble oneself 《about》 ; be depressed ; mope

울거미 [얽어맨 것의] an outer rim ; a hoop for a wrapped bundle ; [짚신의] a long rim cord sewing sidewings to sandals

울걱거리다 gargle ; rinse (out) one's mouth ¶ 울걱거리며 양치질하다 gargle 《one's mouth》

울걱울걱 gargling ¶ 울걱울걱 양치하다 gargle

울겅거리다 ⇨ 올강거리다

울겅울겅〔울겅불겅〕 ⇨ 울근울근

울결 鬱結 a pent-up pressure on one's chest ; dejection of mind ; depression ─하다 feel〔be〕 dejected ; be〔feel〕 depressed ; be gloomy ; be distressed ; feel heavy in the chest ; feel oppressed

울골질 intimidation ; frightening by threats ─하다 intimidate ; bully ; show one's teeth ; bulldoze 《미·구》

울근거리다 chew ; mumble

울근불근 ─하다 ① [맞서다] be in discord ; be at war ; be at odds 《with》 ; be on bad terms ; be at sword's point ¶ 그들은 자주 울근불근하나 곧 친해진다 They have frequent quarrels, but they soon make it up again. ② [씹다] chew ; mumble ¶ 질긴 고기를 울근불근 씹다 chew on a tough piece of meat ③ [뼈가] stick out ; (be) bony

울근울근 [씹는 모양] chewing ; mumbling ¶ 질긴 고기를 울근울근 씹다 chew on a tough piece of meat

울금색 鬱金色 saffron (yellow) ; orange color ⇨ 등색(橙色)

울긋불긋 in various〔diverse〕 colors ─하다 (be) colorful ; multicolored ; picturesque ¶ 들에 꽃이 울긋불긋 피었다 The blooming field is ablaze with glaring colors.

울기 鬱氣 gloom ; melancholy ; mental depression ; dolefulness ; low spirit ; pent-up feelings

울꺽 kecking ; coughing (up) ¶ 울꺽 토하다 cough up ; throw up

울남 ─男 a boy crybaby

울녀 ─女 a girl crybaby

†**울다** ① [사람이] cry ; weep ; sob (흐느끼다) ; wail (통곡) ; blubber (엉엉) ; shed tears (눈물 흘리며) ¶ 울면서 with tears in one's eyes ; weeping ; crying // 우는 얼굴 a tearful〔tear-strained, crying〕 face ; weeping eyes // 우는 얼굴을 하다 wear a tearful face // 기뻐서 울다 weep〔cry〕 for〔with〕 joy // 흐느껴 울다 sob ; weep in secret // 엉엉울다 cry bitterly ; blubber // 젖 달라고 울다 cry for one's milk // 어머니 생각이 나서 울다 cry for one's mother // 아파서 울다 cry with pain // 비보를 듣고 울다 weep at sad news // 소설을 읽고 울다 cry over a novel // 울어서 눈이 붓다 have one's eyes swollen with weeping〔crying〕 ; cry one's eyes out // 울며 세월을 보내다 spend one's days in tears ; live in sorrow // 울면서 밤을 새다 weep〔cry〕 all night 《through》 // 울기 시작하다 begin to weep〔cry〕 ; burst〔break〕 into tears ; burst out crying // 그 아이는 과자를 더 달라고 울고 있었다 The child was crying for some more cake. ② [동물이] cry ; bark〔yelp, whine〕 (개) ; mew〔meow〕 (고양이) ; bellow〔low, moo〕 (소) ; neigh〔whinny〕 (말) ; bray (당나귀) ; trumpet (코끼리) ; chatter

〔gibber〕 (원숭이) ; squeak (쥐·토끼) ; growl (곰) ; roar (사자 · 범) ; grunt (돼지) ; bleat (산양·양) ; howl〔snarl〕 (늑대) ; blow (고래) ; crow (수탉) ; cluck〔cackle〕 (암탉) ; gobble (칠면조) ; hoot (부엉이) ; goggle (거위) ; quack (오리) ; coo (비둘기) ; caw〔croak〕 (까마귀) ; whoop (학) ; cuckoo (뻐꾸기) ; warble (종달이) ; croak (개구리) ; sing〔chirp〕 (새·벌레) ; buzz (벌) ; chirrp〔chirr〕 (귀뚜라미)
③ [장판·의복 따위가] get wrinkled ; be shriveled ¶ 내 비단옷이 비를 맞아 울었다 My silk clothes got wrinkled by the raindrops. //종이에 물이 떨어져서 울었다 The drops of water on the paper made small shriveled spots.
④ [종이] ring ; sound ; peal ; toll ; [천둥이] thunder ; rumble ; peal ; roll ¶ 고동이 울다 The sirens blow〔whistle〕. //종이 울다 The bell rings〔tolls〕.
⑤ [기타] ¶ 귀가 울다 one's ears sing〔ring〕//기계가 울다 a machine hums〔buzzes〕//팽이가 울다 a top hums//하찮은 일에 우는 소리를 하다 whine about trifles
울지 않는 아이 젖 주랴 (속담) The squeaking wheel gets the grease.

울대¹ [울타리의] pickets (of a fence)

울대² [새의] the syrinx of a bird

울뚝 impetuously ; rashly **—하다** (be) impetuous ; rash

울뚝불뚝, 울뚝울뚝 with (repeated) impetuosity〔rashness〕

울띠 cross boards of a wooden fence

울렁거리다 ① [두근거리다] palpitate ; throb ; thump ; pound ; beat ; leap ¶ 울렁거리는 가슴 a throbbing heart//기뻐서 가슴이 울렁거리다 one's heart flutters〔throbs〕 with joy//무서워서 가슴이 울렁거리다 one's heart palpitates with fear//그 여자는 그가 온다는 말을 듣고 가슴이 울렁거렸다 Her heart skipped a beat when she heard he was coming.
② [흔들리다] roll ; toss ¶ 물결에 배가 상당히 울렁거렸다 The boat tossed about in the waves quite a bit.
③ [메슥하다] ¶ 속이 울렁거리다 feel nausea ; feel sick〔queasy〕 ; feel sick at the stomach

울렁울렁 ① [가슴이] pitapat ; palpitating ; throbbing ; thumping ¶ 가슴이 울렁울렁 하다 the heart palpitates〔throbs, flutters〕 ② [물결이] tossing ; rolling

울력 combined strength ; cooperation ; collaboration ; joint effort **—하다** join forces ; get together ; make a united effort ; work together ; cooperate ; collaborate ¶ 동네 사람이 울력해서 강에 뚝을 쌓았다 The village people got together and banked up the river.

울룩불룩 rough ; bumpy ; coarse ; uneven **—하다** (be) rough ; bumpy ; coarse ; uneven

울릉대다 threaten ; intimidate ; menace ; frighten ; scare ¶ 죽인다고 울릉대다 threaten 《a person》 with death ; threaten to kill 《a person》//울릉대어 쫓아버리다 scare 《a person》 away//울릉대어 자백시키다 scare 《a person》 into confessing

†울리다 ① [울게 하다] make 《a person》 cry ; move〔touch〕 《a person》 to tears ; grieve 《a person》 ; bring sorrow upon 《a person》 ; break 《a person's》 heart (상심) ¶ 심금을 울리는 이야기 a touching〔pathetic〕 story//그의 웅변이 청중을 울렸다 His eloquence moved the audience to tears. //아이를 울리지 마라 Don't let the child cry !
② [소리나게 하다] ring 《a bell》 ; sound 《a bell, a horn, a trumpet》 ; clang 《a bell, a gong》 ; blow 《a whistle》 ; beat 《a drum》 ; clank 《a heavy chain》 ¶ 종이 울리자 at the ring〔toll〕 of the bell//경적을 울리다 sound the horn〔honker〕 ; toot〔honk〕 a horn//종을 울리다 chime〔sound, clang, toll〕 a bell
③ [명성을] be widely known ; be famous〔popular〕 ; enjoy popularity ; win a reputation ; [세력을] wield 《influence, power》
④ [자동사] ring ; sound ; [반향] resound ; echo : [진동이] reverberate ¶ 종이 울리다 a bell rings//먼 데서 종소리가 울려 왔다 There came the distant toll of a bell. //대포 소리가 산에 울렸다 The report of the gun reverberated through the hills. //이 방은 소리가 울린다 This room echoes.

***울림** a sound ; a noise ; a peal ; a boom ; [반향] an echo ; reverberation ; [진동] a vibration ; a shock ¶ 뇌성의 울림 the boom of distant thunder//말발굽의 울림 the clattering (sound) of horse's hoofs//산울림이 울리다 echoes resound

울먹줄먹, 울멍줄멍 in clusters ; in abundance **—하다** grow in clusters ; be overcrowded with... ; have many children

울밀 鬱密 —하다 (be) luxuriant ; dense ; thick

울바자 straw〔reed〕 fence ; a marshreed screen

울보 a crybaby ; a blubberer

⁑울부짖다 scream ; cry ; shriek ; yell ; utter a cry ; wail ; screech ; [바다·바람이] howl ; roar ; rave ¶ 울부짖는 부녀자들 screaming women and children

울분 鬱憤 pent-up anger ; resentment ; wrath ; grudge ; animosity ; rancor **—하다** (be) pent-up ; resentful ¶ 울분을 터뜨리다 give vent to one's anger//울분을 참다 control one's anger//울분을 풀다 satisfy one's resentment〔grudge〕 ; let off the steam ; vent one's anger〔rancor〕

《on a person》// 울분을 조금이나도 풀려면 좀 쉬기만 해도 될텐데 If only he would enjoy himself a bit to let off a little stream.

울상 一相 a tearful face ; a face about to cry ; weeping eyes ¶ 울상이다 wear a tearful face ; be about to cry ; look sad

울새 〖새〗 a red-tailed robin

울섶 branches〔twigs, brushwood〕 used in making a fence

울세다 have a large family ; have a large number of relatives

울쑥불쑥 sticking here and there ; jagged ; indented ; bumpy **—하다** stick up here and there ; (be) jagged ; bumpy ¶ 산이 울쑥불쑥하다 The mountains are jagged.

울안 a fenced-in place ; an enclosure

울울 鬱鬱 gloom ; melancholy ; cheerlessness **—하다** (be) dejected ; melancholy ; gloomy ; heavy-hearted ; [울창] luxuriant ; exuberant ¶ 울울하게 세월을 보내다 mope one's time away

울울창창 鬱鬱蒼蒼 **—하다** (be) luxuriant ; thick ; dense ¶ 울울창창한 숲 a dense〔thick〕 forest

*__울음__ crying ; weeping ¶ 울음 소리 a tearful voice ; a cry // 울음이 터지다 burst into tears // 울음을 참다 repress one's tears ; gulp down one's tears // 울음을 그치다 stop weeping // 까마귀의 울음 소리는 불길하다는 게 사실이냐 Is it true that the call of a crow is a bad omen?

울적 鬱寂 melancholy ; gloom ; mental depression ; low spirits **—하다** (be) melancholy ; desolate ; depressed ; lonesome ; cheerless ¶ 울적한 날을 보내다 lead a lonely life // 울적한 마음을 풀다 divert〔distract〕 one's mind // 기분이 울적하다 be in low spirits ; be in the blues ; be cast down ; be depressed

울증 鬱症 melancholia ; hypochondria ⇨ 우울(—증)

울짱 a paling ; a palisade ; a stockade ; a wooden barricade ; a fence of stakes ; a picket ; a fence (stakes)

울창 鬱蒼 luxuriant growth ; luxuriance ; exuberance **—하다** (be) luxuriant ; exuberant ; thick ; dense ¶ 울창하게 luxuriantly ; exuberantly ; in luxuriant growth ; thickly ; densely // 울창한 삼림 a thick〔dense〕 forest // 수목이 울창하게 자랐다 The trees have grown thick〔luxuriant〕.

울컥 ① [토하는 모양] 《vomit》 suddenly ; abruptly ② [치미는 모양] 《get angry》 all of a sudden ; with a burst 《of anger》 ¶ 울컥 화가 치밀다 have a fit of anger

*__울타리__ a fence ; a hedge ; an enclosure ; a hurdle ¶ 대울타리 a bamboo fence // 울타리를 친 정원 a fenced-off garden // 울타리를 치다 enclose 《a house》 with a fence ; fence round 《a house》 ; make a fence // 울타리를 뛰어넘다 jump over a fence ; clear a fence

울툭불툭 ⇨ 울퉁불퉁

__울퉁불퉁__ uneven ; rugged ; rough ; bumpy **—하다 (be) uneven ; bumpy 《road》 ; rugged 《features》 ; jagged 《rocks》

울혈 鬱血 〖의학〗 (blood) congestion ; engorgement ¶ 울혈이 생기다 be congested with blood

울화 鬱火 pent-up anger〔resentment〕 ; wrath ¶ 울화가 치밀다 feel a surge of anger〔resentment〕 ; become exasperated〔irritated, impatient〕 ; boil with rage // 울화통을 터뜨리다 let loose one's anger // 울화통이 터지다 burst into a fit of rage ; explode with anger ; lose one's temper

—병 a sickness caused by pent-up anger

욹하다 fly into a rage ; flare up impulsively ; get impetuous ¶ 욹하고 성을 내다 burst into a sudden anger // 그는 걸핏하면 욹한다 He gets like a madman on the slightest provocation.

움¹ [싹] a tiller ; a sprout ; a shoot ; a bud ; an offshoot ; a second growth ¶ 움이 트다 sprout ; shoot ; bud ; tiller

움² [움막] a dugout mud hut ; a dugout mud hole ; a cellar ¶ 움을 파다 dig out a mud hut〔hole〕 // 채소를 움에 묻다 store〔preserve〕 vegetables in a dugout muds cellar // 움에서 살다 live in a dugout mud hut

움돋다 bud ; shoot ; sprout ; put forth shoots ¶ 작약이 움돋기 시작하였다 The peony started to sprout. // 두 사람 사이에 사랑이 움돋았다 Love budded between the two.

움돋이 a tiller ; a bud ; a sprout ; a shoot

움딸 the second wife of one's disowned son-in-law

움막 —幕 a mud hut ; a dugout ¶ 움막살이 life in a mud hut〔dugout〕

움벼 offshoots from the root of a riceplant

움실거리다 swarm ; squirm ; wriggle in great numbers

움쑥 **—하다** (be) dented ; depressed ; hollow

움씰하다 flinch ; draw back 《with fear》 ; shrink ; wince ¶ 주사침을 보고 움씰하다 flinch before a doctor's needle

움죽거리다, 움쭉거리다 ⇨ 움직거리다, 움질거리다

움직거리다 budge ; stir ; move slowly〔slightly〕 ¶ 지렁이가 움직거린다 An earthworm wriggles along. // 움직거리면 너는 죽는다 If you dare budge, you are a dead man. // 잠자던 곰이 움직거리기 시작했다 The bear began to stir from his sleep.

움직씨 a verb ⇨ 동사

†__움직이다__ ① move ; stir ; shift ; change the position 《of》 ; budge ; shake ; act ;

be moved ; be shaken ¶ 움직이지 않는 immovable ; stationary ; fixed // 움직이고 있다 be in motion ; be moving // 움직이지 않고 있다 be at a standstill ; remain stationary ; stay put 《미·구》; 다리를 움직이다 move one's legs // 이가 움직인다 A tooth is loose. // 산들바람이 나뭇잎을 움직였다 A light breeze stirred the leaves. // 상자가 하도 무거워서 아무도 움직일 수 없었다 The box was so heavy that no one could budge it. // 움직이면 죽어 One move and you are a dead man. // 사진을 찍을테니 움직이지 마라 Now I am about to shoot the picture, so please hold still. // 테이블을 움직이지 않게 하시오 Make the table steady. // 움직이지 마라 Stay where you are.
② [기계 따위를] put〔set〕《a machine》in motion ; operate〔run〕《a machine》¶ 이 시계는 움직이지 않는다 This watch does not go〔run〕. // 승강기가 움직이지 않는다 The elevator is not working. // 이 기관은 증기로 움직인다 The engine is driven by steam.
③ [마음을] move ; touch ; affect ; inspire ; influence ; [마음이] be moved 〔touched, affected〕; be influenced 〔swayed〕¶ 감정을 움직이다 affect〔work on〕《a person's feelings》// 쉽게 움직이다 be easily affected〔moved, influenced〕// 돈에 움직이다 be influenced by gold // 돈으로 움직이다 bribe 《a person》// 유혹에 움직이지 않다 be proof against〔do not yield to〕temptation // 마음을 움직여 …하게 하다 move 《a person》to 《do》// 그 광경은 그 여자의 마음을 움직였다 The scene touched〔moved〕her (heart). // 나의 충고는 그의 결심을 움직였다 My advice shook his resolution. // 현재 정치는 사람의 마음을 움직일 힘이 없다 At present politics has not much emotional appeal.
④ [변경하다] change ; alter ¶ 움직일 수 없는 결심 an immovable〔an unshakable, a firm〕resolution // 움직일 수 없는 사실 an undeniable fact // 움직일 수 없는 의지 an immovable purpose

*움직임 [이동] movement ; motion ; [활동] activity ; [동향] trend ; drift ; movement ; development ¶ 세계의 움직임 the trend of the world // 여론의 움직임 the drift of public opinion // 춤추는 사람의 발 움직임 the movement of the dancer's feet

움질거리다 move timidly ; dawdle ; mumble

움집 a dugout hut ; an underground shack ; a cellar used as a residing place ¶ 움집살이하다 live in a dugout hut

움쭉달싹 with a very slight move ; budging ¶ 움쭉달싹 않다 do not budge ; be unshakable ; be unmoved ; remain calm

†움찔 with a flinch —하다 be startled 《at》; be shocked 《at》; come home to 《a person》; shrink back ; wince

*움츠리다 shrink back ; flinch ; crouch ; draw in ¶ 목을 움츠리다 duck one's head // 어깨를 움츠리다 shrug one's shoulders

움칫 with a start〔flinch, jump〕—하다 start ; flinch ; be jumpy ; be startled

†움켜잡다 grab ; grasp ; seize ; clutch ¶ 멱살을 움켜잡다 grasp 《a person》by the throat

*움켜쥐다 seize ; grab ; grip ; clench ; clutch ; grasp ; hold tightly ¶ 손을 움켜쥐다 grasp〔clasp〕《a person's》hand // 정권을 움켜쥐다 grab power ; wield the power

움큼 a handful ¶ 모래〔쌀〕한 움큼 a handful of sand〔rice〕

움키다 clasp ; clench ; grasp ; clutch ; seize ; catch hold of ¶ 밤을 한 움큼 움키다 grasp a handful of chestnuts in one's hand // 독수리가 병아리를 움키었다 An eagle grabbed a chick.

움트다 sprout ; bud ; shoot ; put forth shoots

움파 scallions grown in an underground cellar

움파다 ⇨ 옴파다

움파리 a rudely made underground hut ; a dugout ; a cellar-hovel ; a puddle (물웅덩이)

움패다 get pitted ; become hollow ; form a hollow

움펑눈 deep-set〔sunken, hollow〕eyes ; a person with sunken〔deep-set〕eyes ; a hollow-eyed person
—이 a person with deep-set eyes

*움푹 pitted ; sunken ; dented —하다 (be) sunken ; pitted ; dented ; hollow

움푹움푹 in hollows〔pits, depressions〕—하다 be sunken ; be in hollows ; (be) pitted ¶ 비에 땅이 움푹움푹 패였다 The ground was pitted by the rain.

웁쌀 extra rice put on top of cereals mixed with rice before cooking
웁쌀 얹다 관용 put rice on top of rough grain

웃- the upper ; the above ¶ 웃서랍 the upper drawer // 웃사람 a superior ; a senior

웃간 —間 the upper room ; the room adjoining the main room

웃국 the upper clear part of liquor

*웃기다 make 《a person》laugh ; set 《a person》to laughing ; raise〔provoke〕a smile ; cause a laughter ; excite 《a person's》laughter ; amuse 《a person》¶ 청중을 웃기다 move the audience to laughter // 그만 웃겨라 Stop making me laugh. // 그가 정직하다니 웃기지 마라 He is honest ? What a joke !〔Don't talk nonsense !〕// 네가 음악가가 돼 웃기지 마라 You want to be a musician ? Don't make me laugh.

웃날들다 [날씨가] clear up ; become clear

¶ 웃날들었다 The sky〔It〕 cleared up.
웃녘 the upper part ; the upper side ¶ 웃녘 새악씨 a girl living in the upper village
†**웃다** ① laugh ; smile (미소) ; giggle (낄낄) ; chuckle (껄껄) ¶ 잘 웃는 사람 a good〔easy〕 laugher∥웃는 얼굴 a smiling face∥웃으면서 with a laugh〔smile〕 ; laughing∥소리내어 웃다 laugh loudly∥속으로 웃다 laugh inwardly∥남몰래 웃다 laugh in one's sleeve∥눈물이 나오도록 웃다 laugh till one cries∥웃어넘기다 laugh off〔away〕 《a request》∥웃지 않을 수 없다 cannot help laughing∥웃는 얼굴로 맞이하다 welcome with a smile∥소문만복래 Fortune comes in by a merry gate. ∥그녀는 우는가 하면 곧 또 웃는다 She cries and laughs in quick alternation. ∥그녀는 겉으로는 웃고 속으로는 울고 있다 She cloaks her grief with a smile. ∥그는 그녀를 보고 싱긋 웃었다 He looked at her with a grin. ∥남자 친구에게 차인 것을 웃으면서 이야기할 수 있는 날이 올거야 The time will come when you'll be able to laugh over your boyfriend's leaving you.
② [조소] laugh at ; sneer at ; ridicule ; deride ¶ 무식함을 웃다 smile at 《a person's》 ignorance∥남의 불행을 보고 웃다 make merry over another's mishap∥그의 협박을 웃어버렸다 I laughed at his threats. ∥웃을 테면 웃어봐라 나는 끝까지 해볼 작정이다 You cannot laugh me out of my resolution.
③ [꽃이] bloom beautifully ; be in full bloom ¶ 들에는 꽃들이 활짝 웃고 있다 The field is abloom with flowers.
웃는 낯에 침 뱉으랴 속담 A soft answer turned away wrath. /Good words are good cheap.
웃더껑이 a lid (뚜껑) ; a cover (덮개) ; a flap (호주머니의)
웃도리 ① [상체] the upper part of the body ; [웃옷] a coat ; an upper garment ¶ 웃도리를 벗다 strip to the waist ; remove one's coat
② [십장] a foreman ; a gaffer
웃돈 the difference ; the balance due ¶ 웃돈을 치르다 pay the difference in cash ; make up a difference in cash
웃돌다 exceed ; be more than ; top
웃돛 a topsail ; a topgallant (sail)
웃돛대 a topgallant (mast)
웃목 the upper side of the floor away from the fireplace ; the upper side of a room
웃물 [상류] the upper stream ; the upper waters of a river ; [겉물] water 〔liquid〕 floating on another without mixing with it ¶ 웃물이 돌다 float on the surface without mixing∥웃물이 맑아야 아랫물이 맑다 A servant is only as honest as his master.
웃비 걷다 cease〔stop〕 raining ; hold up 《미》 ; the rain lifts〔ceases, stops〕 ; it clears
웃아귀 the groove at the base of the thumb
웃어른 one's elders
웃옷 ① [거죽옷] an outer garment ; a coat
② [상의] an upper garment
웃을일 a laughing matter ¶ 이것은 웃을일이 아니다 This is a serious matter. / It is no laughing〔joking〕 matter.
†**웃음** a laugh ; laughter ; a smile (미소) ; derision (조소) ¶ 너털 웃음 a horse laugh ; guffaw∥쓴 웃음 a bitter smile∥아첨하는 웃음 a flattering〔an insinuating〕 smile∥억지 웃음 a forced smile∥큰 웃음 a loud〔boisterous〕 laugh ; loud laughter ; guffaw∥헛 웃음 an affected laugh ; a forced laugh ; a feigned smile∥만면에 웃음을 띠고 with a broad smile on one's face ; beaming with a smile∥웃음을 나누다 exchange a smile 《with》 ; enjoy together∥웃음을 짓다 wear a smile∥웃음을 참다 suppress〔repress, resist〕 a smile ; swallow a laugh∥웃음을 터뜨리다 break out into a laugh ; laugh out ; burst out laughing∥웃음을 웃다 smile a smile ; have a laugh∥참다 못해 웃음을 터뜨리다 burst out laughing in spite of oneself∥그 여자는 억지 웃음으로 근심의 빛을 감췄다 She hid her anxiety with a forced smile.
웃음을 사다〔받다〕 관용 incur〔court〕 laughter ; be laughed at ; become a laughing stock ; draw ridicule upon oneself
웃음가마리 ⇨ 웃음거리
*__웃음거리__ a laughingstock ; an object〔a butt〕 of ridicule ; a byword ; a standing jest〔joke〕 ; a subject of derision〔for laughter〕 ¶ 남의 웃음거리가 되다 become〔be made〕 a laughingstock ; make oneself a laughingstock ; be laughed at ; be a standing joke ; make an exhibition of oneself∥웃음거리로 만들다 bring 《a person》 into derision∥그는 친구들 사이에서 웃음거리가 되고 있다 He is the laughingstock〔scorn〕 of his companions. ∥그런 일을 했다가는 남의 웃음거리가 될 것이다 I should be made a laughingstock to do such a thing.
웃음판 a scene of boisterous laughter ¶ 그의 이야기로 좌중에 웃음판이 벌어졌다 At his story the whole party burst into laughter.
웃자리 the upper〔higher〕 seat ; the top seat ; the seat〔place〕 of honor (주빈석) ¶ 웃자리를 차지하다 take the top seat ; sit at the head 《of a table》 ; take the seat of honor ; occupy the place of honor
웃통 the upper half of one's body ; the upper part 《of a thing》 ¶ 웃통을 벗다 strip to the waist ; take off one's coat 〔jacket〕∥그는 웃통을 벗고 나한테 덤벼들었다 He took his coat off and hit into

me.
웅거 雄據 —하다 hold and defend one's own territory
웅건 雄健 majesty and vigor —하다 (be) virile ; stout ; sturdy ; vigorous ¶ 웅건한 문장〔표현〕 a vigorous style〔expression〕// 웅건한 기상 a virile spirit
웅걸 雄傑 a hero ; a great man ; an extraordinary man ¶ 당대의 웅걸 the greatest hero of the age
웅그리다 crouch ; squat ¶ 웅그리고 앉다 squat down ; squat down on one's hams
웅긋쭝긋 sprouting up〔standing out〕 here and there ; bristling —하다 be bristly with points sprouting up here and there ; bristle ¶ 나무 그루가 웅긋쭝긋 서 있다 Stubs of trees stand out here and there. // 굴뚝이 웅긋쭝긋 솟아 있다 The sky bristles with smokestacks.
웅기웅기, 웅기중기 ⇨ 옹기종기
웅담 熊膽 bear's gall
*웅대 雄大 grandeur ; magnificence ; sublimity ; majesty —하다 (be) grand ; magnificent ; sublime ; majestic ¶ 웅대한 경치 a magnificent view ; a grand sight ; a spectacular scene // 웅대한 구상 a grand conception
*웅덩이 a mud puddle ; a pool ; a bog ; a plash ¶ 웅덩이가 많다 be boggy ; be swampy ; be puddly // 웅덩이지다 form a puddle
웅도 雄圖 a grand plan〔scheme〕 ; an ambitious project ¶ 웅도가 수포로 돌아갔다 One has been frustrated in one's great enterprise. /One's dreams have vanished into thin air〔smoke〕.
웅략 雄略 a great plan ; a grand project ; a magnificent scheme ⇨ 웅도
*웅변 雄辯 eloquence ; fluency (of speech) ¶ 웅변의 eloquent ; fluent ; silver-tongued // 웅변을 토하다 speak fluently〔eloquently, with eloquence〕 ; put forth one's eloquence // 웅변은 은이요 침묵은 금이다 Speech is silver, silence is golden. —가 an eloquent speaker ; an eloquent orator — 대회 an oratorical contest —술 oratory ; elocution ; the art of public speaking
웅보 雄— broad-mindedness ; magnanimity ; large-heartedness
웅봉 雄蜂 male bees ; drones
웅비 雄飛 a great leap〔flight〕 ; a flying jump ; a great achievement —하다 take a flying jump ; soar up ; do a great thing ; play an active part 《in》 ¶ 정계에 웅비하다 play an active part in politics ; soar up in politics // 해외에 웅비하다 go abroad with a great ambition ; embark on great ventures abroad
웅성 雄性 maleness ¶ 웅성의 〖식물〗 sterile ; male
— 배우자(配偶者) male gamete — 선숙(先熟) protandry — 식물 a male (plant)
—화(花) a male flower
웅성거리다 make a noise ; buss ; hum ; be noisy ; fuss 《over a matter》 ; gabble ¶ 여럿이서 웅성거리는 소리 the deep hum of a thousand voices ; a babel of voices // 웅성거려서 연설을 한 마디도 들을 수 없었다 I could not catch a word of speech owing to the noise.
웅숭그리다 ⇨ 웅크리다
웅숭깊다 (be) generous ; prudent ; profound ; inscrutable ; subtle ; broad(-minded) ; magnanimous ; deep ; plain ; natural ¶ 웅숭깊은 사람 an unfathomable character ; an inscrutable man ; a deep fellow
웅시 雄視 —하다 look down on predominantly ; glare at superiorly ; hold sway over ; gain an ascendancy over
웅신하다 ① [덥다] (be) warm ; well-heated ② [불기운이] be burning dully
웅어 〖물고기〗 Coilia ectenes (학명)
웅얼거리다 mutter ; murmur ; grumble ; babble ; jabber ¶ 혼자 웅얼거리다 mutter to oneself // 찬이 나쁘다고 웅얼거리다 grumble over the food // 그는 대우가 나쁘다고 웅얼거렸다 He complained about the treatment he had received.
*웅얼웅얼 muttering ; murmuring ; grunting ; grumbling ; complaining ¶ 그 여자는 무엇인가 웅얼웅얼 거렸다 She muttered away to herself.
웅예 〖식물〗 a stamen
웅자 雄姿 a gallant〔majestic〕 figure ; a splendid style ; an imposing form ; a gallant〔brave〕 appearance
†웅장 雄壯 grandeur ; magnificence ; sublimity ; splendor —하다 (be) grand ; magnificent ; sublime ; splendid ¶ 웅장한 경치 a magnificent view ; a grand sight ; a spectacular scene // 웅장한 구상 grand conception // 웅장한 건물 a splendid〔magnificent〕 building
웅절거리다 mutter ; whine ; complain ; whimper ; grunt ; grumble ; bitch ¶ 찬이 나쁘다고 웅절거리다 grumble over the food
웅지 雄志 a great〔noble〕 ambition〔aspiration〕
웅천 an unreliable person
*웅크리다 crouch ; pull in a limb
웅편 雄篇 a masterpiece ; a great literary
웅필 雄筆 an outstanding piece of writing ; a magnificent handwriting
웅혼 雄渾 grandeur ; sublimity —하다 (be) grand ; sublime ; magnificent ¶ 웅혼한 문체 a grand〔sublime〕 style
웅화 雄花 male〔sterile〕 flowers
워걱거리다 clatter
워낙 [본디] by nature〔origin〕 ; constitutionally ; originally ; primarily ¶ 그는 워낙 몸이 약하다 He was born weak. // 그것은 워낙 절이었다 It was originally a temple. // 그는 워낙 온순한 사람이라 난폭

한 짓을 할 리가 없다 He was born good-natured and will never behave rudely.
워낭 a cowbell
워라말 a piebald
워리 [개 부르는 소리] Here doggy! ; Here boy!
워밍업 warming-up ―하다 warm up
워석 rustling
워싱턴 ① Washington, George (미 1732~99) ② [미국의 수도] Washington ③ Washington 《Wash., W.》
워키토키 a walkie-talkie ; a walky-talky
워터 water
― 슈트 a water chute ― 컬러 a water-color ― 탱크 a water tank ― 폴로 water polo
워털루 Waterloo
웍더그르르 with a rattle ―하다 rattle
웍더글덕더글, 웍더글웍더글 rattling ―하다 rattle
원[1] [감탄사] Gosh! ; Gee! ; Goodness! ; Gracious! ; Son of a gun! 《더러운 놈》; Jesus!
원[2] [화폐 단위] a *won* ¶ 백원짜리 동전 a 100-*won* coin
원 元 ① [중국의 왕조] Yuan ② [중국의 화폐 단위] a Yuan
원 員 ① [벼슬] a country magistrate ② a member ; an employee
편집― a member of the editorial staff
원님도 보고 환자(還子)도 탄다 (속담) To catch two pigeons
†원 圓 a circle ¶ 원을 그리다 draw a circle // 원을 그리며 날다 fly in a circle // 3각형 주위에 원을 그리다 draw a circle around a triangle // 서울을 중심으로 원을 그리다 draw a circle with *Seoul* as its center
―운동 circle〔circular〕 movement 〔motion〕
원 願 [소망] a desire ; a wish ; [부탁] a request ; [간청] an entreaty ; [기원] a prayer ―하다 [소망] desire ; wish ; have a desire 《to》; [부탁] ask ; request ; [간청] beg ; entreat ; implore ; [기원] pray ¶ 원을 들어주다 comply with〔grant〕《a person's》 wishes // 원을 이루다 realize〔attain〕 one's wishes ; get one's wish // 미국 가기를 원하다 want to go to America // 의사 되기를 원하다 wish to be a doctor // 큰 사람이 되기를 원하다 aspire to become a great man // 평생의 원을 이루다 realize one's dearest wishes ; have one's cherished hope fulfilled // 모든 일이 원대로 되었다 Everything came out as I hoped it would. // 부모는 그가 의사가 되기를 원했다 His parents wanted him to be a doctor. // 어머니의 원으로 그는 군인이 되었다 At his mother's wish, he became a soldier. // 그는 원에 의해 해임 되었다 He was relieved of his post at his own request.
원- 原 [본디] former ; original ¶ 원경기도 지사 the ex-Governor of *Kyŏnggi* Province // 원주소 original residence
-원 願 an application ; a petition
사직― a (written) resignation 입학― an application for admission
원가 ―價 the *won* value ; price of the *won*
†원가 原價 the cost ; the prime cost ¶ 원가로 팔다 sell at cost (price) // 원가 이하로 팔다 sell below cost
― 계산 cost accounting ― 계정 cost account 공장 ― manufacturing cost 구매 ― purchasing cost 생산 ― cost of production
원거리 遠距離 great〔long〕 distance ; a long range (사정) ¶ 원거리에 at a long distance // 원거리에서 사격하다 shoot at a long range
원격 遠隔 ―하다 be far apart 《from》; be widely separated 《from》; be distant 《from》; (be) far-off ; remote
― 계측기 〖전기〗 a telemeter ―조(調) 〖음악〗 remote keys ― 조작〔조종〕 remote control ― 조종기 a remote control plane ― 측정 telemetering
*원경 遠景 a distant view ; perspective
원고 原告 a plaintiff ; an accuser ; a complainant ¶ 원고측 변호사 an attorney〔a lawyer〕 for the plaintiff
⁑원고 原稿 a manuscript 《MS., *pl.* MSS.》; a copy ; a draft
―료 money for a manuscript ; contribution fee ; copymoney ; payment for copy ― 용지 manuscript paper ; a writing pad (묶은) ; [신문 기자용] a scratch pad 《미》; a scribbling block 《영》 ― 정리계 [신문사의] a copyreader 연설 ― the script for a speech 자필 ― a manuscript written in one's own hand
원광 原鑛 a raw ore ; an ore
원광 圓光 a halo ; a nimbus
원광 遠光 a distant view seen from afar
원교 遠郊 a place remote from a city
원교근공책 遠交近攻策 a policy of befriending distant states and of antagonizing neighbors
원군 援軍 a reinforcement ; relief ¶ 원군을 기다리다 wait for reinforcements // 원군을 보내다 reinforce ; send reinforcements 《to》 // 원군을 요청하다 ask for reinforcements // 부대를 구출하기 위해 원군이 급행했다 Reinforcements were rushed to the relief of the army.
*원근 遠近 far and near ; distance ¶ 원근을 불구하고 regardless of distance // 원근에 따라 다르다 vary according to the distance // 원근에서 모여들다 come flocking from far and near
―도 a scenograph ―법 perspective (representation) ― 조절 〖생리〗 [눈의] accommodation
원금 元金 [밑천] the capital ; [이자의] the principal

원급 原級 the positive degree (문법의) ; the original class〔rank〕 ¶ 원급에 남겨 두다 do not promote ⟪a student⟫ into a higher class // 원급에 머물다 stay down in the same class

***원기 元氣** vigor ; energy ; vitality ; spirits ¶ 원기가 있다 be vigorous〔energetic〕 // 원기가 왕성하다 be in full vigor ; have a flow of spirits // 원기를 회복하다 restore one's energy ; revive one's spirits ; refresh // 원기를 돋우다 invigorate // 원기가 넘쳐 흐르다 brim over with good spirits ; be brimful〔overflowing〕 with vigor // 이 약을 먹으면 원기가 날 것이다 Take this medicine and I am sure it will pep you up.

원기 原器 the primary standard ; the prototype ⟪for weights and measures⟫

원기둥 圓— [기둥] a column ; 〖기하〗 a (circular) cylinder

원내 院內 in〔within〕 the institution〔the Diet, House, Parliament, hospital〕

— 간사 a floor leader ⟪미⟫ ; a ⟪ministerial⟫ whip ⟪영⟫ ; a whipper-in ⟪영⟫ **— 교섭 단체** a floor negotiation group ; a group ⟪of House representatives⟫ large enough to have a legislative bargaining position in the Assembly **— 부총무** the deputy floor leader **— 총무** the leader of the House ; the floor leader ⟪미⟫ ; the (party) whip ⟪영⟫ ¶ 야당〔소수당〕의 원내 총무 the opposition〔minority〕 floor leader // 여당〔다수당〕의 원내 총무 the majority floor leader

원년 元年 the first year ⟪of an era, a king's reign⟫

원념 怨念 a deep-seated grudge ¶ 원념을 품다 bear ⟪a person⟫ a grudge ; have 〔bear, harbor〕 a grudge against ⟪a person⟫

원단 元旦 New Year's Day ¶ 원단의 이른 아침 the early morning of New Year's Day

— 휘호 writing on New Year's Day

원대 遠大 —하다 (be) far-reaching〔-sighted〕 ; great ; grand ¶ 원대한 계획 a far-seeing〔far-sighted〕 scheme ; a great 〔an ambitious〕 plan // 원대한 목적 far-reaching aims ; a long view // 원대한 포부 a great ambition ; a lofty aspiration

원대 原隊 one's (home) unit ¶ 원대에 복귀하다 return to one's unit

원도 原圖 the original drawing

원동 原動 a motive for action ; a prime

—기 a motor ; a prime mover ; a motive power **—기 부착 자전거** a bicycle fitted with a motor ; a motor bicycle ; a motorbike

원동력 原動力 motive power〔force〕 ; the prime〔first〕 mover ; generative power ; driving force ; dynamic ¶ 행동의 원동력 the motive of one's action // 활동의 원동력 the mainspring of activity // 사회의 원동력 the driving force of the world

원두 園頭 melons planted in a field

원두 놓다 관용 plant〔raise〕 melons

원두 부치다 관용 plant a field with melon seeds

원두 圓頭 a spherical head

— 나사 a roundheaded screw **—정(釘)** a bottonhead (rivet) **— 해머** a ball-peen hammer

원두막 園頭幕 a look-out (shed) for a melon field

원둘레 圓— circumference ¶ 원둘레가 1미터이다 be a meter in circumference

***원래 元來** originally ; primarily ; naturally ; by nature ; essentially ; from the first ¶ 그는 원래 정직한 사람이다 He is honest by nature. // 그는 원래 머리가 나쁘다 His head is constitutionally weak. // 인간은 원래 사교적인 동물이다 Man is born a social animal. // 이 책은 원래 아동에게 읽히기 위한 것이다 This book is originally intended for juvenile reading.

원래 遠來 —하다 come from afar ¶ 원래의 손 a visitor from afar

원려 遠慮 long-sightedness ; forethought ; foresight ; prudence ¶ 원려가 없다 be lacking in forethought ; be imprudent // 원려에 근환(近患)없다 Prudence averts danger.

원령 怨靈 a vindictive〔revengeful〕 spirit

원로 遠路 a long way〔distance〕 ; a long journey ¶ 원로를 무릅쓰고 전송해 주셔서 감사합니다 Many thanks for coming all the way to see me off.

원로 元老 an elder〔a senior, a veteran〕 statesman ; [고참] an elder ; a senior (member) ; an old-timer ; a veteran ; [고대 로마의] the conscript fathers ¶ 공업계의 원로 a veteran industrial magnate // 문단의 원로 a literary magnate // 실업계의 원로 an elder〔old-timer〕 in a business circle

—원 the senate (house) **—원 의원** a senator **— 정치** government strongly influenced by elder statesmen **— 회의** conference of the elder statesmen

원론 原論 a theory ; the principles ⟪of⟫ **경제학 —** the principles of economics **의학 —** the principles of medicine

원료 原料 raw material ; materials ¶ 원료가 부족한 나라 a country lacking raw materials // 원료를 확보하다 secure〔procure〕 raw materials // 원료 가격의 앙등으로 물가가 올랐다 The price was raised owing to the appreciation of raw materials.

— 공업 the raw material industry ; the primary product industry **— 분쇄기** a disintegrator **—유** raw〔stock〕 oil

원리 元利 principal and interest ¶ 원리 합계액 an amount with interest added 〔included〕

†**원리 原理** a principle ; a theory ; the fun-

damental truth ; fundamentals ¶ 궁극적 원리 the ultimate principle // 그 근본 원리 the principle upon which it is based // 생활의 지도 원리 the ruling 〔working, guiding〕 principle of life // …을 생활의 원리로 하다 base one's principles of conduct 《on》
근본 ― the underlying〔root〕 principles
원림 園林 a grove ; a garden ; a plantation
원만 圓滿 [완전] perfection ; [만족] satisfaction ; [조화] harmony ; peace ; [원활] smoothness **―하다** (be) perfect ; [조화] harmonious ; amicable ; peaceful ; [성격이] well-rounded ; bland ; suave ; affable ¶ 원만히 harmoniously ; smoothly ; peacefully ; amicably ; satisfactorily // 원만한 가정 a happy〔pleasant〕 home ; a harmonious household // 원만한 신사 a perfect〔an amiable〕 gentleman // 원만한 타협 an amicable agreement // 원만한 태도 smooth〔bland, suave, affable〕 manners // 원만한 해결 an amicable〔a peaceful〕 settlement // 원만하게 살아가다 live in perfect harmony // 쟁의가 원만히 해결되었다 The dispute has been settled amicably. // 그들의 가정 생활은 원만하다 They are in a harmonious condition of home life.
원말 原― an original word
원망 怨望 [원한] grudge ; resentment ; reproach ; spite ; [증오] hatred ; [불평] a grievance ; a complaint **―하다** bear a grudge against 《a person》 ; resent ; reproach ; think ill of 《a person》 ; feel bitter ; make a grievance against 《a person》 ¶ 원망스럽게 reproachfully // 원망스러운 얼굴 a reproachful look // 무정함을 원망하다 feel bitter against 《a person》 for his heartlessness // 자기 자신을 원망하다 reproach oneself // 원망을 사다 incur a grudge // 나를 원망해서는 안된다 You mustn't think ill of me.
원망 遠望 viewing afar ; a hope for the remote future **―하다** view afar ; look afar at
원망 願望 a desire ; a wish ; an aspiration **―하다** desire ; wish (for)
원맨 a dictatorial chief〔leader〕
―쇼 a solo show ; a one-man show ¶ 원맨쇼를 하다 boss it // 사장은 원맨쇼라니까 The president runs a one-man business, you know. **― 정치** one-man rule
원면 原綿 raw cotton
원명 原名 original name ; real name
원모 原毛 raw wool
원모 遠謀 foresight ; forethought ; a far-sighted scheme ; a long-range plan
원목 原木 material wood ; pulpwood (제지용)
원무 圓舞 a waltz ; a circle dance ; a round
―곡 a waltz
원문 原文 the original text (본문) ; the original (원서) ¶ 원문으로 읽다 read 《a novel》 in the original // 원문에 충실하게 번역하다 make a translation faithful to the original ; translate literally ; transliterate
원반 圓盤 a disk ; a discus (투원반 용)
―톱 a circular saw **투―** the discus throw(ing)〔casting〕 ; throwing the discus **투 ― 경기자〔선수〕** a discus thrower
원발 原發 〖의학〗 idiopathy
―병 a primary disease
원방 遠邦 a distant〔remote, far〕 country
원방 遠方 a distant place ; a remote area ; a distance ; a great distance ¶ 원방의 distant ; far-away〔-off〕 ; remote // 원방에 in the distance ; at a distance ; far off ; a long way off // 원방에서 오다 come from a distance // 원방으로 여행가다 make 〔go on〕 a long journey
원배 遠配 exile to a remote place **―하다** exile 《a person》 to a remote place
원범 原犯 [정범] the principal offender ¶ 그 사람이 원범이다 He committed the offense as the principal.
원병 援兵 (troop) reinforcement(s) ; a relieving force ; a relief ¶ 원병을 보내다 send reinforcements 《to》 ; reinforce 〔relieve〕 《an army》
원본 原本 the original (work) ; the original copy〔document〕 ; the text ; 〖법〗 the script (사본에 대해서)
원부 怨府 ¶ 백성의 원부가 되다 become an object〔the focus〕 of common hatred ; expose oneself to popular hatred 〔enmity〕
원부 怨婦 a spiteful woman ; a vindictive woman
원부 原簿 the original register ; 〖부기〗 a ledger
*__원뿔 圓―__ a cone ; a circular cone
― 곡선 a conic (section) **―대** a truncated cone **―면** a conical surface **―형** a cone
원사 寃死 trumped-up〔forged〕 charge **―하다** be put to death on a false charge〔an unfounded accusation〕
원사 遠寫 〖사진·영화〗 a long shot
원사이드 게임 a one-sided game
원산 原産 the origin of a product ¶ 원산지 증명서 a certificate of origin // 커피의 원산지 the home of the coffee plant // 감자는 미국이 원산지이다 The potato is native to America.
―물 primary products **―지** the place 〔country〕 of origin ; the home ; provenance ; the habitat (동식물의)
*__원상 原狀__ the original state ; the former condition ; the status quo ¶ 원상으로 복구하다 restore to the original state 〔the former condition, the status quo〕
원색 原色 a primary color ; original color(s)
― 사진 a heliochrome ; a color picture

3— the three primary colors — 판 a heliotype
원생 原生 〖생물〗 abiogenesis ¶ 원생의 primeval ; primary ; proto
—대(代) the Proterozoic era — 동물 a protozoan — 동물문(門) Protozoa —림 a virgin〔primeval〕 forest ; an old growth — 생물 a protist — 식물 a protophyte — 암석 primary rocks〔minerals〕 —토 residual〔sedimentary, bedrock〕 soil — 품(品) a primary product
원서 原書 the original (work, text) ¶ 셰익스피어를 원서로 읽다 read Shakespeare in the original
원서 願書 an application ; a written request ¶ 원서를 제출하다 send in〔submit〕 an application // 원서를 접수하다 receive〔accept〕 an application
— 용지 an application blank〔form〕 입학 — an application for admission (into a school)
원석 原石 [원광] a raw ore ; an ore ; [가공 전의 보석] rough (stone) ; gemstone ¶ 다이아몬드의 원석 a rough diamond ; a diamond in the rough
원석기 原石器 〖고고〗 an eolith
— 시대 the Eolithic age
원섬유 原纖維 fibrils ; minute〔raw〕 fibers
원성 怨聲 a grievance ; a complaint
†**원소 元素** 〖화학〗 an element ; a chemical element
— 구성 elementary composition — 분석 ultimate〔elementary〕 analysis — 주기율 the periodic law of the elements —파(派) 〖미학〗 elementalism 동위 — an isotope 불안정 — an unstable element 1가(價) — a monad
원손 遠孫 distant descendants
원수 元首 the chief of the state ; a sovereign ; a ruler
⁑**원수 元帥** a (field) marshal (육군의) ; a general of the army 《미》 ; a fleet admiral〔an admiral of the fleet〕 (해군의)
맥아더 — General of the Army Douglas MacArthur
원수 元數 a cardinal number ; the original number ; the first number
원수 員數 the number of persons
원수 怨讐 an enemy ; a foe ; the object of one's grudge〔grievance〕 ¶ 원수지간 mutual enemies // 원수지다 become an enemy 《of》 // 은혜를 원수로 갚다 return evil for good // 원수를 만나다 come across the object of one's vengeance // 친절이 원수가 되었다 My kind intentions turned out harmful after all.
원수를 갚다 [관용] revenge ; take vengeance upon 《a person》
원수폭 原水爆 atomic and hydrogen bombs ; a nuclear bomb
원숙 圓熟 maturity ; mellowness ; ripening ; perfection —하다 (be) mature ; mellow ; ripe ; become perfect ; fully developed ¶ 원숙한 문체 a mellowed style // 원숙한 사람 a man of mellow character // 원숙한 인격 mellowed character // 원숙의 경지에 이르다 attain〔reach〕 maturity // 원숙해지다 come to maturity ; mature ; mellow ; ripen // 나이를 먹으면 인격이 원숙해진다 One's character mellows with age.
†**원숭이** a monkey ; an ape (꼬리 없는) ¶ 원숭이 날 the Day of the Monkey (신일) // 원숭이 해 the Year of the Monkey (신년) // 나무에서 떨어진 원숭이 a fish out of water // 원숭이 상을 한 사람 a monkey-faced man // 원숭이도 나무에서 떨어지는 수가 있다 A monkey may fall from the tree. /Even Homer nods. /A good marksman may sometimes miss.
원시 元是, 原是 ⇨ 본디
원시 原詩 the original poem〔verse〕
†**원시 原始, 元始** the beginning ; origin ; genesis ; the original〔primitive〕 state of nature ¶ 원시적 primitive ; primeval ; original // 원시적 본능 the primitive instinct
— 그리스도교 primitive Christianity — 동물 a protozoan ; a protoplast —림 a virgin〔primeval〕 forest — 사회 primitive society — 산업 the primary industry — 생활 a primitive〔primeval〕 life — 석기 시대 the Eolithic era —성 aboriginality — 세포 〖발생〗 a primordial cell — 시대 the primitive age〔times〕 — 예술 primitive art —용 a protorosaur ; a proteosaur — 인 the primitive man ; the dawn man — 조(鳥) an archaeopteryx — 종교 a primitive religion —주의 〖철학·예술〗 primitivism
원시 遠視 looking far-off at ; [원시안] far-sightedness ; a long-sighted eye ; 〖의학〗 hypermetropia ¶ 원시의 long〔far〕-sighted ; hypermetropic // 원시인 사람 a long-sighted person ; a hypermetrope // 그는 원시인데 그의 아들은 근시이다 He is far-sighted while his son is short〔near〕-sighted.
—경 long-distance glasses ; spectacles for long-sighted eyes ; convex glasses —안(眼) [눈] a hypermetropic〔far-sighted, long-sighted〕 eye ; [사람] a long-sighted person ; a hypermetrope ; a hyperopic —화(畫) a perspective
원심 原審 the original judgment〔decision〕
— 기각〔파기〕 overruling〔overturning, reversing〕 of the original sentence ¶ 원심을 파기하다 reverse〔quash〕 the original sentence〔decision〕
원심 怨心 a bitter feeling ; a heartburning ; a grudge ; a spite ¶ 원심을 품다 have a grudge against 《a person》
원심 圓心 〖기하〗 the center (of a circle)
원심력 遠心力 〖물리〗 the centrifugal force
원심 분리기 遠心分離機 a centrifugal separator ; a centrifuge

원심 탈수기 遠心脫水機 a centrifugal dehydrator
원아 園兒 kindergarten children
원안 原案 the (original) draft (초안) ; the original bill (의안) ; the original plan (계획) ¶ 원안대로 가결하다 pass a bill in its original form // 원안을 수정하다 amend the original bill // 원안을 제출하다 produce a draft proposal // 원안을 지지하다 support〔second〕 the original bill
원안 遠眼 ⇨ 원시(—안)
—경 ⇨ 원시(—경)
원앙 鴛鴦 a mandarin duck ; a pair of love-birds ¶ 원앙의 인연을 맺다 plight one's troth ; vow eternal〔unchanging〕 love
—금 a quilt〔coverlet〕 embroidered with a pair of mandarin ducks ; the marriage bed ; bridal bed ; a quilt with mandarin duck figures on it ¶ 원앙금을 나누다 share the marriage bed —애(愛) the turtledoves' love —침 a pillow embroidered with a pair of mandarin ducks ; a pillow with mandarin duck figures on it ; a couple's pillow
원액 元額·原額 the original sum〔amount〕 ; the principal
원액 原液 an undiluted solution ; a crude liquid
원야 原野 wasteland ; a wilderness ; a moor ; a prairie ; a wild plain
원양 遠洋 an ocean ¶ 원양의 pelagic ; pelagian
— 동물 a pelagian — 부정기선 an ocean tramp — 어업 deep-sea〔pelagic〕 fishery〔fishing〕 — 정기선 an ocean liner — 항로 an ocean line — 항로선 an ocean-going vessel ; an ocean liner — 항해 ocean navigation ; a long cruise ¶ 원양 항해에 나가다 set out on ocean navigation // 원양 항해에 나가 있다 be on a long〔distant〕 cruise 쾌속(快速) —선 an ocean greyhound
원어 原語 the original language〔word〕
원언 怨言 complaint ; reproachful remarks
원엽체 原葉體 a prothallium 《*pl.* -lia》
원영 遠泳 a long-distance swim
*__원예 園藝__ gardening ; horticulture ; floriculture (꽃재배)
—가 a gardener ; a horticulturist — 도구 gardening tools —술 the art〔technique〕 of gardening — 시험소 a horticultural experimental station — 식물 a garden plant — 식물 재배장 a nursery — 용구 gardening tools — 작물 garden products — 잡지 a horticultural〔gardening〕 magazine —장 a nursery — 책력〔달력〕 a gardener's calendar — 학교 a horticultural school —학부 the department of horticulture 가정 — home gardening ; gardening as a pastime
원옥 冤獄 imprisonment on a trumped-up charge
원외 員外 non-membership ; supernumerary (status)
— 교수 a professor extraordinary —자 a non-member ; an extra member
원외 院外 ¶ 원외의 outside the institution〔House, academy, temple, monastery, board, chamber, hospital〕 ; non-parliamentary
—단 the lobby 《미》 ; lobbyism — 단원 a lobbyist ; a ward heeler 《미·구》 — 운동 an outdoor agitation ; lobbying 《미》 ; lobbyism ; lobby ¶ 원외 운동을 벌이다 lobby — 운동자 a lobbyist —자 a lobbyist 《미》 — 자 의견 an outside opinion — 투쟁 an out-of-National Assembly struggle
원용 援用 —하다 claim ; [인용] quote ; [발동] invoke (조문을) ¶ 조항을 원용하다 invoke a clause
원유 原油 crude petroleum〔oil〕
원유회 園遊會 a garden party ; a picnic ¶ 원유회에 초대하다 invite 《a person》 to a garden party // 원유회를 개최하다 give〔hold〕 a garden party
원음 原音 the original pronunciation〔sound〕 ; 〖음악〗 the fundamental tones
원음 遠音 a distant sound
원의 原意, 原義 original intention ; original〔primary〕 meaning
원의 院議 the decision of the House ¶ 원의를 존중하여 in deference to the decision of the House
원의 願意 a desire ; a wish
†__원인 原因__ a cause ; a factor ; [근원] the origin ; the source ¶ 원인과 결과 cause and effect // 원인 불명의 죽음 death of unknown cause // 원인 불명의 화재 a fire of unknown origin // 실패의 원인 the cause of one's failure // 실화의 원인 the origin of a fire // 원인을 밝히다 trace 《a thing》 to its origin // …이 원인이다 be caused by ; originate in〔from, with〕 ; arise〔start〕 from ; come of ; result from ; be due to ; stem from // 주된 원인 a major cause 《for》 // 원인을 분명히 하다 clarify the cause 《of》 // 원인 없이 결과가 생기지 않는다 An effect presupposes a cause. // 이것이 이 사건의 원인이다 This is at the bottom of the trouble. / This stands in a causal relation to the event. // 그 사고의 원인은 운전수의 부주의에 있었다 The accident was due to the carelessness of the driver. // 그 티푸스는 우유가 원인이었다 The typhoid was referable〔assignable〕 to milk. // 그 화재의 원인은 무엇이냐 What started the fire ? // 저 사람은 어떤 원인으로 죽었는지 불명이다 The cause of his death is unknown〔uncertain〕. // 이 소동의 원인은 전적으로 교장의 무능에 있었다 The incompetency of the principal is solely responsible for the disturbances. // 유행성 감기가 원인이 되어 100명이나 죽었다 No less than one-hun-

dred deaths resulted from influenza.
— 결과 cause and effect ; causality ; the cause and effect relationship 《of》 —론 etiology ; the philosophy of causation — 불명병(不明病) an ill-defined disease ; a disease of unknown etiology — 요법 causal treatment 간접 — indirect〔mediate〕 cause 궁극 — the ultimate cause 근본 — the root cause 사망 — the cause of death 주(요) — a major cause 《for》 직접 — direct〔immediate〕 cause 화재 — the origin of a fire

원인 猿人 〚인류〛 an ape-man ; a pithecanthrope ¶ 자바 원인 the Java man

원인 願人 an applicant ; a petitioner

원인 原人 a primitive man

원인 遠因 a remote cause ; an underlying cause ¶ 그것이 전쟁의 원인을 이루고 있다 It is〔forms〕 a remote cause of the war.

원일 元日 New Year's Day

원일점 遠日點 〚천문〛 the aphelion ; the higher apsis

⁑**원자 原子** an atom ; a corpuscle ¶ 원자의 atomic // 물의 분자는 수소 2 산소 1의 원자로 구성되어 있다 A molecule of water consists of two atoms of hydrogen and one atom of oxygen.
—가 atomic value ; valence — 과학 atomic science — 과학자 an atomic scientist — 기기(機器) nuclear power devices —량 atomic weight —로 an atomic pile〔reactor, furnace〕 ; a pile —론 atomic theory ; atomism —론자 an atomist — 물리학 atomic〔nuclear〕 physics — 물리학자 an atomic physicist — 번호 an atomic number —병 an atomic disease —병 환자 a sufferer from an atomic disease — 병기 atomic weapons ; atomic arms — 분열 atomic fission —설 the atomic theory — 세포 a germinal cell — 시계 an atomic clock — 시대 the atomic age —식 an atomic formula — 역학 atomic mechanics —열 atomic heat — 용(容) atomic volume 《at. vol.》 —운 an atomic cloud —전 atomic warfare — 질량 atomic mass — 질량 단위 atomic mass unit — 탄두 an atomic warhead — 파괴 atom smashing — 파괴 장치 an atom smasher —포 an atomic gun〔cannon〕 — 폭발 an atomic explosion — 폭탄 an atom(ic) bomb ; an A-bomb — 폭탄 공격 ¶ 원자 폭탄 공격하다 atom-bomb — 폭탄 발사계 a weaponeer 《미》 — 폭탄 투하 the atomizing 《of Hiroshima》 —학 nucleonics ; atomics —핵 an atomic nucleus ; a nucleus —핵 공학 nucleonics —핵 물리학 nuclear physics —핵 물리학자 a nuclear physicist —핵 반응 nuclear reaction —핵 분열 nuclear fission —핵 실험〔연구자〕 a nuclear test〔researcher〕 —핵 파괴 장치 an atom smasher ; a cyclotron ; a synchrotron —회 radioactive fallout〔ashes〕 다(多)—가(價) multivalence 발전용 —로 a nuclear power reactor

원자

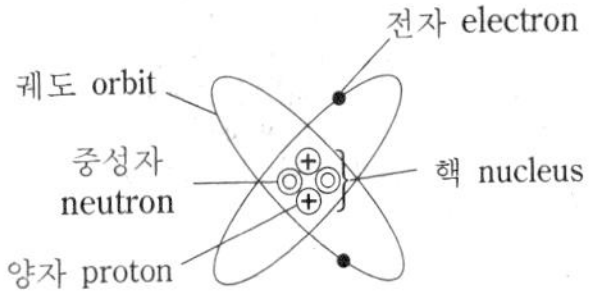

⁑**원자력 原子力** atomic energy ¶ 원자력의 평화적 이용 peaceful uses of atomic〔nuclear〕 energy ; the use of atomic energy for peaceful purposes // 원자력 추진의 nuclear-propelled // 원자력으로 움직이는 atom(ic)-powered ; nuclear-powered
— 관리 atomic control — 국제 관리 the international control of atomic energy — 로켓 a nuclear-powered rocket — 발전 atomic power generation — 발전기 a nuclear generator — 발전소 an atomic power plant —(에 의한) 사고 an atomic accident — 상선 an atomic ship ; a nuclear-powered ship — 시대 the atomic age — 엔진 an atomic engine — 연구소 the Institute of Atomic Energy Research — 연료 atomic〔nuclear〕 fuel — 청 the Office of Atomic Energy 《OAE》 — 위원회 an Atomic Energy Commission 《AEC》 — 잠수함 a nuclear(-powered) submarine — 전쟁 an atomic war — 추진 nuclear propulsion — 평화 이용 계획 the atoms-for-peace program — 항공 모함 an atom-〔a nuclear-〕powered (aircraft) carrier — 협정 an atomic power agreement 국제 — 기구 the International Atomic Energy Agency 한국 — 연구소 Korea Atomic Energy Research Institute

원자재 原資材 raw materials

원작 原作 the original (work)
—자 the (original) author ; the writer ¶ 원작자 미상의 책 a book of doubtful authorship

원장 元帳 a ledger ; a blotter ¶ 원장에 기입〔기장〕하다 enter 《an item》〔make an entry〕 in a ledger
— 잔고 the ledger balance 총계정 — a general ledger

원장 園長 the chief〔head, director〕 《of a zoo, a kindergarten》

원장 院長 the director〔president, superintendent〕 《of a hospital, an institution》

원재판 原裁判 the original judgment
—소 the original court ; the court of the first instance

원저 原著 the original work〔book〕

—자 the author ; the writer
원적 原籍 a permanent abode ; an (original) domicile ; the place of origin
—지 the place of one's domicile ; the domicile of origin
원적 怨敵 a sworn〔bitter〕 enemy ; a deadly〔mortal〕 foe
원적토 原積土 sedentary soil
원전 原典 the original text ; a source book
원점 原點 the starting point ; the origin
원정 遠征 an〔a military〕 expedition ; a campaign ; an invasion (침입) ; a playing tour (운동 선수의) —하다 go on an expedition ; invade ; make a foray ; make a playing tour of (운동 선수가)
—대 ⇨ 원정군(遠征軍) — 시합 an out match —팀 a visiting〔touring〕 team
원정 遠程 a long way ⇨ 원로
원정 園丁 a gardener
원정군 遠征軍 an expedition ; an expeditionary force〔army〕; invaders ¶ 원정군을 조직〔파견〕하다 organize〔dispatch〕 an expeditionary force
원조 元祖 the founder ; the originator ; the father ; the pioneer ; the inventor (발명자) ¶ 양학의 원조 the father of foreign studies // 카스테라의 원조 the original maker of sponge cake
⁂원조 援助 assistance ; support ; help ; aid —하다 assist ; support ; help ; aid ; stand by 《a person》; back up ¶ 원조를 청하다 ask 《a person》 for assistance〔help〕// 원조를 약속하다 pledge one's support // 원조를 얻다 receive〔secure, derive〕 assistance // 나는 그를 원조하고 싶다 I am disposed to help him. // 한국은 외국의 경제 원조를 필요로 한다 Korea is in need of economic assistance from foreign countries.
—국 an aid country —금 an aid fund — 물자 aid goods —자 supporter ; a patron 재정 — financial aid〔help〕 해외 — 계획 a foreign aid plan〔program〕
원조 元朝 (the morning of) New Year's Day ⇨ 원단(元旦)
원족 遠足 ⇨ 소풍(逍風)
원족 遠族 distant relatives
원종 原種 〖생물〗 a pure breed〔stock〕; a germ
원죄 原罪 〖종교〗 original sin ¶ 무원죄의 잉태 Immaculate Conception
원죄 寃罪 a false accusation〔charge〕 ¶ 원죄를 입다 be falsely accused of ; be falsely charged with
원주 圓柱 a column ; a cylinder ¶ 원주상의 columnar ; cylindrical
—면 a cylindrical surface —면 렌즈 a cylindrical lens — 배치법 columniation — 부표(浮標) 〖해양〗 a pillar〔spar〕 buoy — 상체(狀體) [망막내의] a rod — 상피(上皮) cylinder epithelium —체(體) a cylinder — 투영법 cylindric projection
직— a right cylinder 코린트〔이오니아, 도리아〕식 — columns of the Corinthian〔Ionic, Doric〕 style
⁂원주 圓周 circumference
—각 the angle at the circumference —율 the ratio of the circumference of a circle to its diameter ; pi 《π》
원주 原註 original notes
원주 園主 the owner of a garden〔an orchard〕
†원주민 原住民 aborigine ; an indigenous people a native ; [총칭] natives ¶ 원주민과 같은 생활을 하다 go native
— 보호주의 [이주민에 대하여] nativism
원지 原紙 a stencil paper ; a stencil
원지 遠地 remote area
원지 遠志 far-reaching intention ; far-sighted design ; a lofty aspiration ; vast〔great〕 ambition(s)
원지점 遠地點 〖천문〗 the apogee
원진 圓陣 a circle ¶ 원진을 치다 form a circle
원질 原質 an elementary substance ; a protyle
유전 — a gene
원창 圓窓 a round〔circular〕 window
원채[1] by nature ⇨ 워낙
원채[2] 〖건축〗 the main wing of a house ; the main building
원챗집 the main wing of a house ⇨ 몸채
⁂원천 源泉 the fountainhead ; the head spring ; the wellspring ; the source ; the origin ¶ 지식의 원천 the source of knowledge〔information〕
— 과세 taxation at the source (of income) ; withholding 《미》; collection of taxes through withholding ; pay-as-you-earn 《P. A. Y. E》 — 소득세 a withholding tax — 징수 제도 the withholding system
원촌 遠寸 a distant relation ; distant kinship ¶ 원촌이 되는 사람 a distant relative // 그는 나의 원촌이 된다 He is a remote relative of mine. /He is a distant kinsman of mine.
원촌 遠村 a distant〔remote〕 village
원촌 原寸 actual〔natural〕 size
원촌도 原寸圖 a full-scale drawing
원추 圓錐 a cone ; conical shape ; [원추체] a circular cone ¶ 원추형의 conical // 모래 주머니가 원추형으로 쌓여 있다 Sand bags are piled up in conical shape.
— 곡선 a conic (section) — 곡선법 conic sections — 굴절 conical refraction —근(根) a conical root —대(台) a truncated cone ; a frustum of a cone —면 a circular cone —체 a cone —축(軸) the axis of a cone — 투영법 conic projection — 판(瓣)〔진자(振子)〕 a conical valve〔pendulum〕 —형 a cone —형 두부 the nose cone 《of a rocket》 —화(花)〔화서(花序)〕 〖식물〗 a panicle 직(直)〔사(斜), 타(楕), 구상(球狀)〕— a right〔an oblique, an

elliptical, a spherical〕 cone 동초점 ━ 곡선 confocal conics 산개(散開) ━화(花) a lax panicle
원추리 〖식물〗 a day lily ; Hemerocallis aurantiaca (학명)
원추 화서 圓錐花序 〖식물〗 a panicle
원축 原軸 〖기계〗 a driving shaft
원치수 原━數 actual〔natural〕 size
†원칙 原則 a principle ; a fundamental rule〔law〕 ; a (general) rule ¶ 원칙적으로 as a (general) rule ; in principle // 원칙을 세우다 establish a principle // 원칙적으로 동의하다 agree in principle // 원칙에 의거하다 be based on a principle // …하는 것을 원칙으로 하다 make it a rule to 《do》 // 본교 입학자는 원칙적으로 기숙사에 넣기로 되어 있다 Our school expects new students to reside in dormitory.
━ 협정 a formula 근본 ━ a cardinal〔basic〕 principle 기본 ━ ground rules 삼━ 정책 a three-point policy
원컨대 願━ I hope ; I pray ; it is to be hoped〔desired〕 that ; would that ¶ 신이여 원컨대 이 불쌍한 소녀에게 복을 내리소서 Have mercy on this poor girl, O God!
원탁 圓卓 a roundtable
━ 기사단 the Knights of the Round Table (Arthur왕과 그 기사들) ━ 회의 a round-table conference
원태 原態 〖생물〗 a protomorph
원통 寃痛 resentment ; mortification ; chagrin ; vexation ; regret ━하다 (be) resentful ; indignant ; mortifying ; regrettable ; vexing ; chagrined ¶ 원통해하다 regret ; be mortified〔vexed〕 《at》 ; be galled
†원통 圓筒 a cylinder
원판 [원상] the original state of things〔affairs〕 ; [원래] from the first〔beginning, outset〕 ; originally ; by nature
원판 原版 a negative (사진의) ; a film (영화의) ; a (lantern) slide (환등의)
원판결 原判決 the original decision〔judgment〕 ¶ 원판결을 파기하다 reverse the judgment of the lower court ⇨ 원심(原審)
원포 園圃 a vegetable garden ; gardens and fields
원폭 原爆 an atom(ic) bomb ¶ 원폭에 의한 보복 an atomic retaliation〔reprisal〕
━ 기지 an atomic base ━ 실험 atomic testing ; an A-test ━ 실험 정지 an atomic test ban ━전(쟁) an atomic war ━ 희생자 A-bomb victims
원표 元標 the starting point of mileposts ; the zero milestone
원피 原皮 raw hide ; (a) green hide〔skin〕
원피스 a one-piece dress
†원하다 願━ desire ; wish ; want ⇨ 원
*원한 怨恨 grudge ; a bitter〔an ill〕 feeling ; spite ; resentment ; enmity ; malice ; animosity ¶ 원한을 갚다 vent one's spite ; revenge oneself on 《the offender》 ; work off a grudge // 원한을 사다 incur enmity ; earn 《a person's》 grudge ; make an enemy of 《a person》 // 원한을 잊다 forget one's grudge 《against》 // 원한을 품다 bear 《a person》 a grudge ; harbor〔nurse, cherish〕 a gruage ; have a grudge against 《a person》 // 나는 그에게 원한을 품고 있다 I owe him a grudge. // 나는 그에게 아무런 원한도 없다 I bear him no grudge.
원함수 圓函數 〖수학〗 circular function
원항 遠航 ocean navigation ; a long cruise ¶ 원항 중이다 be on a long cruise
원해어 遠海魚 a pelagic fish
원행 遠行 a long〔far〕 journey〔trip〕 ━하다 make〔go on〕 a long journey〔trip〕
†원형 原形 the original form ¶ 원형을 유지하다 retain its original form ; remain intact // 원형을 잃다 lose its original form // 원형을 찾아볼 수 없을 정도로 부서지다 be broken〔destroyed〕 beyond recognition
원형 原型 an archetype ; a prototype ; a model ; a pattern (야금의)
원형 圓形 a round shape〔form〕 ; a circle ; circularity ¶ 원형의 circular ; round ; cycloid ; discoid (식물의) // 원형으로 circularly ; in a circle ; circlewise // 원형으로 만들다 make circular ; circularize // 원형으로 오려내다 cut out (in) a circle
━ 극장 an amphitheater ━엽(葉) 〖식물〗 an orbicular leaf
원형질 原形質 〖생물〗 protoplasm
━체 protoplast ; protoplasmic cell
원호 援護 support ; backing ; relief ; protection ━하다 support ; back (up) ; protect ; give relief〔support〕 to
━ 기금 a relief fund ━ 대상자 a relief recipient ━ 병원 a relief hospital ━ 연금 a relief annuity ━처 the Office of Veterans Administration ━회 a relief society〔association〕 ¶ 상이 군인 원호회가 창립되었다 The Wounded Veterans Relief Association has been established.
원호 圓弧 a circular arc ; an arc of a circle ¶ 원호를 그리다 describe〔trace, draw〕 circular arcs
원혼 寃魂 malignant spirits ; the spirit of 《a person》 put to death on a trumpedup charge ¶ 원혼을 위로하다 solace〔appease〕 the malignant spirits (under the earth)
원화 ━貨 *won* currency
━ 예치율 the *won* deposit rate
원화 原畫 the original painting〔picture, drawing〕 ¶ 반 고흐의 원화 a van Gogh original
원활 圓滑 smoothness ; harmony (융화) ━하다 (be) smooth ; harmonious ; peaceful ; amicable ¶ 원활하게 smooth

ly ; harmoniously ; peacefully ; amicably ; without a hitch (지장없이) // 만사가 원활히 진행된다 Things go on smoothly. /The work progresses smoothly. // 예의는 사회 생활을 원활하게 한다 Good manners serve to oil the wheels of social life.

원훈 元勳 a veteran statesman ; an older statesman (원로) ; a man who has rendered a most distinguished service to his country ; a man of the highest merit

원흉 元兇 a ringleader ; the chief instigator ; the prime mover ; the head〔leader〕《of a gang》

월 [문장] a sentence

월 月 the moon ; a month ; Monday (월요일)

— 평균 a monthly average

월가 —街 Wall Street

****월간 月刊** monthly publication〔issue〕 ¶ 월간의 monthly // 그 잡지는 월간이다 The magazine is issued〔published〕 monthly.

— 잡지 a monthly (magazine)

월간 月間 by the month ; a month-long 《campaign》 ¶ 월간 계약으로 고용하다 hire 《a person》 by the month

월갈 〖언어〗 syntax (문장론)

월경 月經 menstruation ; the menses ; turns ; period ; (monthly) course ; the monthlies ; the flowers ; the monthly flow〔sickness〕; the menstrual cycle ; 〖생리〗 catamenia ¶ 월경의 menstrual // 월경시에 at the period of menstruation ; during one's period // 월경이 있다 have the menses〔monthlies〕; have one's period ; see the flowers // 월경 중이다 be in the flowers ; be unwell ; be off the sports list 《미》 // 월경이 시작되다 one's menses come on ; one's menstruation commences // 월경이 끝나다 one's menstruation ceases // 월경은 보통 28일 만에 시작되고 3일 내지 6일간 계속된다 Menstruation usually occurs every twenty-eight days, and lasts from three to six days.

— 과다 profuse menstruation ; menoruhagia ; hypermenorrhea **—대** a hygienic band ; a sanitary napkin〔towel, belt〕 **—기** the menstrual〔catamenial〕 period **— 불순** menstrual irregularity ; irregular menstruation **— 순조** regular menstruation **— 연령** a menstrual age **— 이상** irregular menstruation **— 장애** disorders of menstruation **— 주기** a menstrual cycle **—통** menstrual colic **— 폐지기** the climacteric ; the menopause ; the turn〔change〕 of life

월경 越境 crossing the border ; border jumping〔transgression〕; violation of the border **—하다** cross the frontier〔border〕; transgress〔violate〕 the border

— 사건 a border incident

월계 月計 a monthly account **—하다** count monthly

—표 a monthly balance sheet

****월계관 月桂冠** laurels ; a laurel crown 〔wreath〕 ¶ 월계관을 차지하다 win laurels ; bear〔carry away〕 the palm // 월계관을 쓰다 be crowned with the laurel of victory ; carry off the honors // 월계관은 그에게 돌아갔다 The laurel of the day fell on his head.

월계수 月桂樹 a laurel tree ; a bay tree ; Laurus nobilis (학명)

월계화 月季花 〖식물〗 the Chinese rose ; Rosa chinensis (학명)

월광 月光 moonlight ; moonshine ; a moonbeam

—곡 the Moonlight Sonata

월궁 月宮 the palace in the moon

월권 越權 arrogation ; abuse of authority 〔confidence〕; going beyond one's powers **—하다** arrogate power ; exceed 〔overstep〕 one's authority ; go beyond one's power ; override one's commission ¶ 그런 짓은 월권이다 You have no warrant for doing that. // 그것은 분명히 너의 월권이다 It is plain that you act beyond your authority in doing so.

— 행위 an (act of) arrogation ; malfeasance

월귤나무 越橘— 〖식물〗 cowberry ; a mountain cranberry ; a bilberry ; Vaccinium Vitis-Idaea (학명)

***월급 月給** a monthly salary〔pay〕; a (monthly) salary〔wage〕; the payroll (지불 급료의 총액) ¶ 많은 월급 a large 〔high〕 salary // 적은 월급 a small salary ; low pay // 월급을 받다 draw〔get〕 a salary // 월급이 오르다 have one's salary raised ; get a rise in one's salary // 30,000원의 일급으로 일하다 work at a salary of 30,000 *won* a day // 월급으로 살다 live on one's salary // 나는 일급이 아니고 월급입니다 I am paid by the month, not by the day. // 너희 아빠 월급만 가지고는 살기가 힘들겠구나 It must be tough to live on your daddy's paycheck alone.

—날 a pay day ; a salary day **— 봉투** a pay envelope **—쟁이** a salaried man 〔worker〕; a white-collar worker **— 지불부(支拂簿)** a payroll ; a pay list **고〔저〕—자** high-〔low-〕salaried man

월남[1] 越南 Vietnam ; Viet-Nam ; Viet Nam ¶ 월남의 Vietnamese

—말 Vietnamese **— 사람** a Vietnamese

월남[2] 越南 [경계를 넘는] coming south over the border ; [북한에서의] coming from North Korea 《over the 38th parallel》 **—하다** come south over the border ; [북한에서] come from North Korea 《over the 38th parallel》; cross the 38th parallel into South Korea

— 동포 north Korean refugees ; the brethren who came from north Korea

월내 月內 ¶ 월내에 within the month ;

in less than a month
월다말 a red horse with a black mane
월단 月旦 ① [초하루] the first day of a month ② [인물평] a character sketch ; comments on personalities
월당 月當 monthly allocation〔distribution, allotment〕; monthly allowance〔share〕
월동 越冬 passing the winter ; wintering **―하다** pass〔tide over〕 the winter ; winter
― 자금 a winter relief fund ; a winter allowance **― 준비** preparations for passing the winter
월드 시리즈 〖야구〗 the World Series
월등 越等 a vast difference in degree **―하다** (be) vastly different ; be poles apart ; be out of the common ; extraordinary ¶ 월등히 out of common〔the ordinary〕; extraordinarily ; exceptionally ; by far // 월등히 낫다 be far better〔superior〕// 월등히 우수하다 be far superior // 월등히 크다 be gigantic ; be huge // 나는 그보다 월등히 못하다 I am not a patch on him. /I cannot hold a candle to him.
월력 月曆 a calendar
월령 月齡 〖천문〗 the age of the (new) moon
월례 月例 ¶ 월례의 monthly
―회 a monthly meeting
월리 月利 monthly interest
월말 月末 the end of the month ¶ 월말에 at the end of the month
―도(渡) monthly-end delivery **― 잔고** monthly balance **― 지불** month-end payment〔settlement〕 ¶ 월말 지불을 하다 pay the monthly bill
월맹증 月盲症 〖수의학〗 periodic ophthalmia
월면 月面 the surface of the moon ; [얼굴] a beautiful face
―도 a selenographic chart ; a selenograph **― 보행** a moon-walk **― 착륙** a 《manned》 lunar landing
월번 月番 [일] monthly duty ; [사람] the person who is on duty for the month
월변 月邊 a monthly interest
월병 月餠 ⇨ 달떡
월보 月報 a monthly report〔bulletin〕; a monthly review ; monthly returns
― 무역 monthly trade returns
월복 越伏 the prolongation of the late dog-day period
월봉 月俸 a monthly salary〔pay〕 ⇨ 월급
월부 月賦 a monthly installment〔payment〕 ¶ 월부로 5천원씩 물다 pay by monthly installment of 5,000 *won* // 3개월의 월부로 사다 buy 《an article》 by three months' installments // 월부로 구두를 한켤레 맞추다 have a pair of shoes made on the monthly installment system // 매월 4만원씩 12개월의 월부 12 monthly payments of 40,000 *won* each // 월부로 살 수 있습니까 Can I buy it on credit ? /Is financing available ?
― 지불 paying by monthly installments
― 판매 an (monthly) installment sale〔plan〕; a hire-purchase system 《영》 ¶ 월부 판매를 하다 sell 《a thing》 on the installment plan **― 판매법** the hire purchase plan 《영》; the installment (paying) system〔plan〕 《미》; installment selling〔sale〕 《미》; the easy payment plan 《미》; the piano system 《미》
월북 越北 ―하다 go to North Korea ; cross the Demilitarized Zone 《DMZ》 into North Korea
월불 月拂 monthly payment **―하다** pay by monthly installments
월비 月費 monthly expenses
월사금 月謝金 [학교 등록금] a monthly school〔tuition〕 fee ; a monthly fee ¶ 비싼 월사금 a heavy charge for tuition // 월사금을 면제하다 remit 《a student》 the fee // 월사금 인상 반대를 외치다 cry against a raise in the regular school fee
월삭 月朔 the first day of a month
월산 月産 a monthly output ; a monthly (amount of) production
월상 月相 〖천문〗 a phase of the moon
월색 月色 moonlight ; moonbeam
월세 月貰 monthly rent ¶ 월세가 얼마입니까 What's the rent ?
월세계 月世界 the moon ; the lunar world
― 여행 a moon trip
월수 月收 [수입] a monthly income ; [빚] a loan at monthly interest ¶ 월수가 800,000원이다 have〔draw〕 a monthly income of 800,000 *won*
월수당 月手當 a monthly allowance
월식 月蝕 〖천문〗 a lunar eclipse ; an eclipse of the moon
개기 ― a total eclipse of the moon **부분 ―** a partial eclipse of the moon
월액 月額 the monthly amount〔sum〕
월야 月夜 a moonlight〔moonlit〕 night
월여 月餘 ¶ 월여간이나 more than a month ; over a month
†월요일 月曜日 Monday
월일 月日 the moon and the sun ; the month and the day ; the date
생년 ― the date of (one's) birth
월전 月前 ¶ 월전에 a month ago
월정 月定 a monthly contract
― 고용 monthly contracted hire〔employment〕 **― 구독료** monthly subscription **― 독자** a monthly subscriber ; a subscriber by the month
월차 月次 every month
월천 越川 crossing〔wading〕 a stream **―하다** cross〔wade〕 a stream
―군 a person who carries others across a stream for a fare
월초 月初 the beginning of a month ¶ 월초에 at the beginning of the month
월출 月出 a moonrise

월컥 ⇨ 왈칵
월파 月波 moonlit waves ; waves in the moonlight
월편 越便 the other〔opposite〕 side ¶ 월편에 on the opposite〔other〕 side
월평 月評 a monthly review〔criticism, comment〕
문단 — a monthly survey of the literary world
월표 月表 a monthly list〔table〕 ; monthly returns
월하 月下 a moonlit spot ; the moonlight
— 빙인 a matchmaker ; a go-between ; Hymen ; Master Cupid
월훈 月暈 a halo〔ring〕 around the moon
웨딩 wedding
— 드레스〔마치〕 a wedding dress 〔march〕
웨이브 [머리의] a wave ¶ 웨이브진 머리 wavy hair
웨이스트 [부인복의] the waist《of a dress》 ¶ 웨이스트가 가는〔가는, 높은〕 large-〔small, high-〕 waisted // 그녀의 웨이스트는 58센티다 Her waist measures 58 centimeters around.
— 라인 one's waistline
웨이스트 볼 〖야구〗 a waste ball
웨이크 섬 Wake Island
‡웨이터 a waiter
웨이트 weight
***웨이트리스** a waitress
웩웩거리다 keck ; retch
웬 what ; what sort of ; what manner of ; what kind of ¶ 웬 사람이냐 Who is the man ? /What is he here for ?
웬걸 O my ! ; Why ! ; Why no ! ; Goodness no ! ; Gee ! ; Gosh ! ¶ (조사해 보니) 웬걸 전과자였어 He turned out to be an ex-convict. // 그래 그녀를 만났나 —웬걸 Well, did you see her ? Gosh, no. // 웬걸 이렇게 많은 사과를 가져 오셨습니까 My goodness gracious ! What a lot of apples you have brought me !
웬곡절 —曲折 what circumstances ; what kind of trouble ; what cause〔reason〕 ¶ 웬곡절로 그리 웃니 What makes you laugh so〔like that〕 ?
웬까닭 ⇨ 웬일
웬만큼 [알맞게] properly ; moderately ; within measure ; [어느 정도] to some extent ; to a certain degree ; [어지간히] passably ; considerably ; fairly ; pretty ¶ 독일어를 웬만큼 하다 speak German fairly well // 웬만큼 마셔라〔먹어라〕 Take it easy on the liquor〔food〕. // 농담도 웬만큼 해라 Do not go too far with your jokes. // 우리의 계획은 웬만큼 성공했다 Our plan was successful to some extent.
웬만하다 (be) passable ; serviceable ; tolerable ; fairly good ; satisfactory ; close to it ¶ 수입이 웬만하다 have a handsome income // 웬만하면 If you like ; if you do not mind ; how about 《doing》 // 웬만하면 술 한잔 합시다 How about having a glass of wine ?
웬셈 ¶ 웬셈인지 나도 모르겠다 I don't know what all this is about.
웬일 what matter ; what cause ; what reason ¶ 웬일인지 for some reason (or other) ; without knowing why ; somehow // 웬일이야 What is all this about ? / What is the matter (with you) ? // 웬일로 왔는가 What has brought you here ? // 나는 웬일인가 하고 뛰어 나가봤다 I ran out to see what the matter was.
웰컴 welcome
웰터급 —級 the welterweight ¶ 웰터급의 선수 a welterweight
웽웽 ⇨ 왱왱
†위 ① [상부] the upper part ; the upside ; the top side ; the above ¶ 위의 upper ; upside ; upward // 위에 above ; over ; upwards // 위에든 이유 때문에 for the reason mentioned above // 바다 위를 날다 fly over the sea // 위로 오르다 rise〔go〕 up // 위를 보다 look upward // 셔츠 위에 스웨터를 껴입다 wear a sweater over one's shirt // 산봉우리가 구름 위에 솟아 있다 The peak rises above the clouds. // 비행기가 하늘 위에 날고 있다 A plane is flying high up in the sky. // 마침내 그들은 그를 배 위로 끌어 올렸다 At last they got him aboard.
② [꼭대기] the top ; the summit ¶ 맨 위의 topmost ; uppermost // 산 위에 on the top of a mountain // 위에서 아래까지 from top to bottom // 위에서 셋째줄 the third line from the top // 저 언덕 위에 집이 있다 A cottage stands atop the hill〔at the top of the hill〕.
③ [표면] the surface ¶ 책상 위에 on the desk // 바다 위에 해파리가 떠 있다 A jellyfish is floating on the surface of the sea.
④ [상위] superiority ; seniority ¶ 위의 higher ; upper ; superior // 남의 위에 서다 lead people ; be the leader of others // 그는 나보다 세살 위이다 He is three years older than I. // 그는 나보다 지위가 훨씬 위이다 He is far above me in rank. // 그는 학교에서 나보다 한 학년 위였다 He was a year ahead of me in school. // 위에는 위가 있다 Greatness is comparative. / Never use the superlative. // 위를 바라보면 한이 없다 Do not compare yourself with those above you. /Do not keep up with Joneses.
위로 진 물이 발등에 진다 속담 Parents are patterns. /One sheep follows another. /If one sheep leap o'er the dyke, all the rest will follow.
위 位 ① [등급] position ; grade ; rank ; situation ¶ 제 1위〔제 2위, 제 3위〕 the first〔second, third〕 position // 2위를 차지하다 hold the second rank
② [신위] souls ¶ 영령 10위 ten heroic

souls

⁑위 胃 the stomach (사람의) ; the paunch (동물의) ; the maw (포유동물의) ; the crop (새의) ¶ 위의 gastric // 위가 튼튼하다〔약하다〕 have a strong〔weak〕 stomach〔digestion〕// 위가 아프다 have a stomachache // 위를 상하다 have a disordered stomach ; put the stomach out of order // 반추동물의 제 1위〔제 2위, 제 3위, 제 4위〕 the paunch〔the honeycomb, the manyplies, the read〕 of a ruminant
—내 촬영술 gastrophotography — 절개(술) gastrotomy — 절제(술) gastrectomy ; gastric resection — 점막 the gastric mucous membrane

위 緯 [위도] latitude ; [씨] woof

위격 違格 disagreement with〔contrariety to〕 established formalities〔rules, forms, styles〕 —하다 be〔run, go〕 contrary to the rule〔form, style〕; contravene the rule

위경 危境 a critical situation ; danger ; a crisis ; jeopardy ¶ 위경에 처하다 face〔be confronted with〕 a crisis // 위경을 헤쳐나가다 tide over〔pass through〕 a crisis

위경 胃鏡 〖의학〗 a gastroscope

위경련 胃痙攣 〖의학〗 stomach cramps ; gastralgia ; convulsion of the stomach

위계 位階 grade of rank(s) ; a (court) rank ¶ 위계가 높은 사람 a person high in rank

위계 危計 a dangerous〔risky〕 plan

위계 僞計 a deceptive plan ; a fraudulent〔feigned〕 stratagem ¶ 위계를 쓰다 use a deceptive scheme

위곡 委曲 details ; full particulars ; the (whole) circumstances ¶ 위곡을 다하다 explain in detail ; enter into details

위공 偉功 a meritorious service ; a great deed〔merit〕; a remarkable〔brilliant〕 achievement ¶ 위공을 세우다 render great services ; achieve a great success

위관 偉觀 a grand〔magnificent〕 sight ; grandeur ; a spectacular sight

위관 尉官 company grade officers 《미》; officers below the rank of major (육군의) ; officers below the rank of lieutenant commander (해군의)

위광 威光 authority ; power ; influence

위구 危懼 fear ; apprehensions ; misgivings —하다 fear ; be afraid of ; be apprehensive over ; have〔entertain〕 misgivings over ; feel uneasy 《about》; be anxious about ¶ 위구심에 사로잡히다 be swayed〔driven〕 by misgivings

위국 危局 a crisis ; a critical situation

위국 爲國 serving〔benefiting〕 one's country —하다 serve〔benefit〕 one's country ; render service to one's country ; be〔do〕 for one's country ¶ 위국지성에서 out of intense patriotic concern for the welfare of the country

위궤양 胃潰瘍 〖의학〗 gastric〔stomach〕 ulcer

위금 僞金 〖화학〗 mosaic gold

위급 危急 an emergency ; a crisis ; an exigency —하다 (be) critical ; crucial ; exigent ¶ 위급시에 in case of emergency ; in an emergency ; in time of crisis // 위급에 대비하다 provide against emergencies // 위급하게 되다 be in peril ; be in imminent danger ; be at stake // 위급을 알리다 spread〔give〕 the alarm ; raise an alarm // 위급할 때는 도와주겠다 I will be by you in the hour of danger.
위급존망지추 (관용) a time of emergency ; a critical moment ; a crisis

⁑위기 危機 a crisis ; an emergency ; a critical moment ; a critical situation ; a crucial hour〔moment〕 ¶ 위기의 critical ; acute // 내각의 위기 a Cabinet crisis // 재정상의 위기 a financial crisis // 위기에 임해서 at the crucial moment ; at a crisis ; in an emergency // 위기에 처하다 come to a crisis〔head〕; be critical ; be in jeopardy ; be at stake // 위기를 벗어나다 get〔pass〕 through a serious crisis ; tide a over crisis
— 돌파 자금 a "crisis-relief" fund —책 an anti-crisis measure

위기 違期 violation〔infringement〕 of the date due〔the appointed time〕 —하다 contravene〔disregard, ignore, fail to keep〕 the date due〔the appointed time〕

위기 圍碁 playing *padook* —하다 play *padook*

위기일발 危機一髮 ¶ 위기일발에(서) at the critical〔psychological〕 moment ; in the nick of time // 위기일발에서 살아나다 have a hairbreadth〔narrow〕 escape ; escape《death》 by a hair's breadth // 위기일발의 순간이었다 That was a close call.

위난 危難 a crisis and peril ; danger ; jeopardy ; distress ¶ 위난을 당하다 encounter〔face, meet〕 a danger // 위난을 면하다 escape danger ; get out of danger

위남자 偉男子 a manly man ; a great man

위니펙 호 —湖 the Lake Winnipeg

위대 偉大 greatness ; mightiness ; grandeur ; magnitude —하다 (be) great ; mighty ; grand ¶ 위대한 국민 a great nation ; a mighty nation // 위대한 업적 a stupendous achievement ; a grand performance // 위대한 인물 a great man ; a master mind

위덕 威德 virtue and influence ¶ 위덕에 굴복하다 submit to 《a person's》 virtuous dignity // 우리는 그의 위덕이 온 천하에 떨쳤음을 알고 있다 We know that his influence is felt all over the country.

⁑위도 緯度 latitude ¶ 위도의 측정 determination of latitude // 위도를 달리하다 be in different latitudes // 그 지방의 위도는 북위 38도이다 The latitude of the region is thirty-eight degrees north.

— 관측소 a latitude observatory — 변화 variation of latitude —선 a parallel — 효과 『물리』 latitude effect 고〔저〕— (지방) high〔low〕 latitudes 지구〔천구〕 — terrestrial〔celestial〕 latitude 지리(학적) — geographic latitude

*위독 危篤 a critical〔serious〕 condition of illness —하다 be dangerously〔critically, seriously〕 ill ; be in a critical condition ¶ 위독해지다 fall into a critical〔dangerous〕 condition ; 《illness》 take a critical〔dangerous〕 turn // 그의 아버지가 위독하다 His father is in a critical condition. // 모친 위독 곧 귀가하라 Mother seriously ill, return immediately. (전문) // 부친이 위독하다는 전보를 받았다 I got a telegram telling me of my father's serious condition.

위락 萎落 withering and falling —하다 wither and fall

위란 危亂 a (national) crisis ; a critical situation —하다 (be) critical ; tumultuous ; be in a critical situation

위략 偉略 an outstanding stratagem ; a splendid tactics ; a grand tactics

*위력 威力 power ; might ; authority ; influence ¶ 위력 있는 powerful ; mighty // 돈의 위력 the power of money // 폭탄의 위력 the power of a bomb // 국가의 위력 the national authority〔influence〕 // 위력을 행사하다 exercise〔wield〕 one's power〔authority〕 《over》 // 위력으로 굴복시키다 bring 《a person》 into submission by a show of one's power // 한국은 동양에서 그 위력을 떨쳐야 한다 Korea ought to make her power felt in the East.

위력 偉力 great power ; mighty force ; great strength

위령 威令 authoritative command〔order〕 ; authority ¶ 위령이 잘 행하여지다 have strong authority 《over the people》 ; be in strong authority 《over》

위령 違令 violation〔infringement, breach〕 of an order〔a decree, a command〕 —하다 violate〔go against, break〕 an order

위령제 慰靈祭 a memorial service ¶ 전몰장병 위령제 a memorial service for the war dead

위령탑 慰靈塔 a cenotaph〔monument〕 ; a memorial tower

†위로 慰勞 ① [치하] appreciation of the services rendered ; recognition〔acknowledgment〕 of 《a person's》 services —하다 appreciate〔recognize, acknowledge〕 《a person's》 services ¶ 위로해 주고자 휴가를 주다 grant holidays in recognition〔acknowledgment〕 of 《a person's》 services // 어제 그를 위한 위로회가 있었다 A dinner was given for him in appreciation of his services.

② [위안] consolation ; solace ; comfort —하다 console ; solace ; comfort ; relieve ; soothe

> 참고 **console** 다소 딱딱한 말이며 상실의 슬픔이나 실망을 덜어주다 **comfort** 사람의 불행이나 비탄을 덜어주다 **relieve** 불행이나 곤궁을 일시적으로 덜어주다 **soothe** 고통을 진정하고 어려움을 덜어주다

¶ 서로 위로하다 comfort each other // 불행을 위로하다 console〔solace〕 《a person》 in his misfortune〔sorrow〕 // 위로의 말을 하다 speak comforting〔soothing〕 words 《to》 ; speak kindly 《to》 // 독서가 나의 유일한 위로다 Reading is my only consolation. /I find my only consolation in reading. // 술은 마음을 위로해준다 Wine makes the heart glad. // 내가 슬플 때 너는 나를 자주 위로해주었다 You often soothed〔consoled〕 me in my sorrow.

—금 a bonus —(의) 말 《speak》 comforting〔smoothing〕 words 《to》 — 연회 a beanfeast 《영 · 속》 — 휴가 a special holiday in appreciation of a person's service

위리 안치 圍籬安置 —하다 enclose 《a banished offender》 in a thorn hedge

위막 胃膜 the coats of the stomach

위망 位望 position and fame〔popularity〕 ; renown

위망 威望 power and fame ; influence and popularity ¶ 위망이 있는 사람 an influential and popular person

위망 僞妄 falsehood (and absurdity)

위명 威名 fame ; renown ; prestige ¶ 위명을 세계에 떨치다 win〔gain〕 (a) worldwide fame // 한국의 위명을 빛내다 show the prestige of Korea

위명 僞名 a false name ; a feigned name ¶ 위명으로 under a false〔feigned〕 name // 그는 Y라는 위명을 사용하고 있다 He goes by the feigned name of Y.

위모레스크 『음악』 a humoresque

위무 威武 authority and armed force

위무 慰撫 pacification ; soothing ; consolation —하다 pacify ; soothe ; console ; appease ; solace ; comfort ; quiet ¶ 노한 사람을 위무하다 pacify 《a person's》 wrath ; calm〔soothe〕 down an angry person

위문 慰問 consolation ; a consolatory visit ; [문병] a call of sympathy〔consolation〕 —하다 console ; pay a visit of inquiry to ; inquire after 《a person's》 health (문병)

—대(袋) a comfort bag〔kit〕 —문 a consolatory letter ; a letter of sympathy —사(使) a messenger of condolence〔consolation〕 —선(船) an amenity ship — 편지〔장〕 a consolatory letter ; a letter of sympathy — 품 a comfort ; an article of comfort ; gifts

‡위반 違反 violation ; infringement ; contravention ; infraction ; a breach 《of a

contract, promise》 —하다 violate 《the law》; infringe; contravene; break 《a promise》; infract; disobey 《orders》 ¶ …에 위반하여 in contravention〔violation〕 of; against // 그는 선거법 위반으로 검거되었다 He was arrested for a breach of the Election Law. // 그는 교통 규칙을 예사로 위반한다 He does not hesitate to violate the traffic regulations. // 그것은 규칙 위반이다 It is against the rule. // 너의 행위는 명령 위반이다 You have acted contrary to orders. // 그것은 계약 조항에 위반된다 It is in contravention of the stipulations.

—자 an offender; a violator; a transgressor — 행위 an offense 교통 — violation of traffic regulations 규칙 — ¶ 그것은 규칙 위반이다 It is against the rule. 명령 — disobedience to an order 법률 — an offense against the law; a violation of the law 선거법 — a violation of the election law 조약 — the infraction of a treaty 주차 — a parking violation 헌법 — an anticonstitutional〔unconstitutional〕 act ¶ 그것은 분명히 헌법 위반이다 It is decidedly against the Constitution.

*위배 違背 violation ⇨ 위반 ¶ 이것은 특허법에 위배된 물품이다 This is an article made in violation of the Patent Law. // 이것은 헌법 정신에 위배되는 일이다 This runs counter to the spirit of the Constitution.

위법 違法 violation of law; illegality; unlawfulness; a foul (play) (경기 따위의) ¶ 위법의 illegal; unlawful // 위법적으로 illegally; unlawfully; against the law // 그런 위법 행위는 처벌을 면할 수 없다 Such an illegal act cannot go unpunished.

—성 illegality —자 a lawbreaker; an offender (against the law) — 처분 illegal disposition〔measures〕 — 행위 an illegal act; an illegality; a delict; an injury (타인의 권리 따위에 대한); [관리 따위의] an irregularity

위벽 胃壁 the wall of the stomach

위병 胃病 a stomach trouble; stomachic disorder ¶ 위병을 앓다 suffer from a stomach trouble

— 전문의(醫) a gastrologer —학 gastrology — 환자 a dyspeptic

위병 衛兵 a guard; a sentinel; a sentry ¶ 위병을 세우다 post a guard

— 교대 changing guard — 근무 guard duty — 사령관 the commander of guards —소 a guardhouse; a guardroom — 장교 an officer of the guard — 텐트 a guard tent

위복 威服 [굴복] submission to power; [정복] subjugation by authority —하다 [굴복] submit to power; [정복] awe 《a person》 into obedience; frighten 《a person》 into submission

위본 僞本 a fabricated book; a spurious copy; a forged book; [해적판] a pirate edition

위부 委付 〖법〗 abandonment —하다 abandon

—자 an abandoner — 조항 an abandonment clause — 통지 a notice of abandonment 피—자 an abandonee

위부 胃部 the gastric region

위사 胃絲 〖동물〗 a gastric filament

위산 違算 miscalculation; an error in calculation; a miscount

위산 胃酸 acid in the stomach

— 결핍증 anachlorhydria — 과다 excess〔excessive〕 acid in the stomach ¶ 위산과다의 hyperacid — 과다증 acid dyspepsia; gastric hyperacidity〔superacidity〕; pyrosis

위산 胃散 medicinal powder for the stomach

위상 位相 〖전기〗 phase

—계(計) a phase meter〔indicator〕 — 공간(空間) 〖수학〗 topological space; 〖물리〗 phase space — 기하학(幾何學) 〖수학〗 topology — 변조 〖전기〗 phase modulation — 속도 〖물리〗 phase velocity — 수학 topology; analysis situs — 정수(定數) 〖물리〗 a phase constant; an initial phase — 조정 phase adjustment — 조정 변압기 a phase compensating transformer —차 phase difference —차 현미경 a phase microscope

위생 衛生 hygiene; sanitation; the preservation of health ¶ 위생의 hygienic; sanitary // 위생상 for reasons of sanitation; for sanitary reason // 비위생적인 음식물 unwholesome food // 위생을 지키다 observe the rules of health // 위생에 주의하다 be careful of one's health; attend to sanitation // 이재민의 위생 상태는 참으로 우려할 바가 있다 The sanitary conditions of the victims are causing great anxiety.

— 경찰 sanitary police — 공학 sanitary engineering —관〔계〕 a health official〔officer〕 — 관념 sanitary thought — 관리자 a health administrator —대 [월경대] a sanitary belt —대 〖군대〗 a medical corps — 도기(陶器) a sanitation〔toilet〕 fixture —반 sanitation detail〔unit〕 —법 hygiene; hygienics —병 a hospital orderly; a medical〔hospital〕 corpsman; a〔an army〕 medic — 보험 sanitary insurance —부(夫) a cesspool man —비 sanitation expenses — 사업(조합) sanitary affairs (association) — 상태 sanitary〔health〕 conditions — 수칙(守則) 《observe》 the rules of health — 시설 sanitary〔health〕 facilities〔arrangement〕 — 시험소 a hygienic laboratory — 식품 wholesome food —실 ⇨ 양호실 — 재료 medical〔hospital〕 supplies; medical impedimenta — 조례 the Sanitary Regulations —컵 [종이로 만든] a sanitary cup —학 hygienics; hygiene; sanitary science —학자 a sanitarian 공중 — public health 노동 — industrial hygiene 정신 — mental hygiene 학교 — school hygiene 비— 식품 unwholesome food

위서 僞書 [편지] a false letter ; [책] an apocryphal book ; a forgery ; a forged writing

위서다 accompany《a bride or groom》; escort ; serve as escort

위석 胃石 〖의학·동물〗 a gastrolith

위선 胃腺 〖해부〗 peptic glands

위선 緯線 a parallel (of latitude)

*위선 僞善 hypocrisy ¶ 위선적 hypocritic(al) // 위선의 탈을 쓰다 play the hypocrite ; do hypocrisy // 나는 위선은 질색이다 Hypocrisy is my abhorrence〔nauseates me〕.

—자 a hypocrite ; a pharisee ; a dissembler ; a wolf in a lamb's skin

위성 衛星 〖천문〗 a satellite ; a secondary planet

—국 a satellite〔dependent〕 state ; a satellite — 궤도 the orbit〔path〕 of a satellite — 도시 a satellite town〔city〕 — 발사 launching of a satellite —선(船) a satellite ship 간첩 — a spy(-in-the-sky) satellite 공중 사찰 — an eye-in-the-sky satellite 과학 — a scientific research satellite 군사 — a military satellite 기구 — a balloon satellite 기상〔통신〕 — a weather〔communications〕 satellite 미사일 탐지 — a missile warning satellite 실용 — a practical satellite 인공 — a man-made〔an artificial〕 satellite 정지 — a stationary satellite 지구 물리 관측 — the Orbiting Geophysical Observatory 통신 —a communication satellite

위세 威勢 power ; might ; influence ; authority ; high spirits ; dash ¶ 위세 있는 powerful ; mighty ; influential // 위세부리다 exercise〔wield〕 one's power《over others》; domineer《over》// 위세를 보이다 make a display of one's influence ; make one's influence felt // 위세를 굴복하다 be awed into obedience // 자네 요즈음 위세가 당당해 보이는군 You've really come up in the world lately, haven't you?

위세척 胃洗滌 gastrolavage ; gastric irrigation —하다 wash out the stomach ; administer a stomach pump《to a person》

위세척기 胃洗滌器 a stomach pump ¶ 위세척기용 고무관 a stomach tube

위수 位數 〖수학〗 the order ; 〖전기〗 a digit

위수 衛戍 a garrison ; border guard (궁경경비)

— 근무 garrison duty —령 the Garrison Decree〔Act〕 —병 border troops ; garrison troops — 병원 a garrison hospital — 사령관 the commandant of a garrison ; the commander of the garrison headquarters —지 a garrison town〔place〕

위스키 whisk(e)y

— 소다 (a) whisky and soda ; (a) high ball《미》

위시 爲始 beginning ; commencing —하다 begin ; commence ; start ¶ 위시하여 including ; and ; as well as ; not to speak of // 김박사를 위시해서 starting with〔including〕 Dr. *Kim* // 서울 시장을 위시해서 많은 인사가 파티에 초대되었다 Many dignitaries, including the Mayor of *Seoul*, were invited to the party.

위식 違式 irregularity ; violation of the forms ; breach of etiquette

*위신 威信 prestige ; dignity ; authority ¶ 중동에서의 미국의 위신 America's prestige in Middle East // 국가의 위신에 관한 문제 a question affecting national prestige // 위신에 관계되다 affect〔compromise, involve〕 one's dignity〔prestige〕// 위신을 잃다 lose one's prestige // 위신을 손상하다 injure the prestige《of》// 위신을 지키다 uphold〔maintain, preserve〕 one's dignity // 나라의 위신을 높이다 enhance national prestige // 정부의 위신이 땅에 떨어졌다 The prestige of the Government is gone.

위신경증 胃神經症 gastric neurosis

위아래 up and down ; the upper and lower ; top and bottom ; [신분] high and low ¶ 위아래로 up and down ; upward and downward // 위아래 구별 없이 both high and low ; irrespective of rank // 위아래가 뒤바뀐 upside down // 위아래로 움직이는 동작 a vertical motion // 위아래로 훑어보다 look《a person》 up and down // 사랑에는 위아래가 없다 Love is a leveler.

위아랫물지다 do not mix up well《with》; liquids seek separate level

위 아토니 胃— 〖의학〗 gastric atony

†위안 慰安 consolation ; solace ; comfort ; amenities —하다 console ; solace ; comfort ; amuse ¶ 생활의 위안 comforts of life // 위안을 구하다 seek comfort〔consolation〕 in《music》// 위안을 제공하다 give comfort to《a person》// 종교에서 위안을 구하다 seek consolation〔solace〕 in religion ; go to religion for solace // 병석에 혼자 있을 때 그의 유일한 위안은 책과 벗하는 것이었다 His sole solace in his loneliness and ill health was the company of books. // 그는 늙은 양친에게 큰 위안이었다 He was a great comfort to his parents in their old age.

—물 a comfort ; a solace —부 a comfort girl〔woman〕; a prostitute (주로 군인을 위한) —소 a service club — 시설 recreation facilities —처 an oasis —회 a recreation meeting ; a beanfeast

위암 胃癌 〖의학〗 cancer of the stomach ; gastroscirrhus ; gastric cancer

*위압 威壓 coercion ; overpowering ; highhandedness ; browbeating —하다 coerce ; overpower ; overawe ; brow-

beat ; bring pressure to bear upon ⟪a person⟫ ; treat with a high hand ¶ 위압적인 high-handed ; overbearing ; coercive ; browbeating // 위압적으로 overbearingly ; coercively ; with a high hand // 위압적으로 복종시키다 force〔browbeat〕 ⟪a person⟫ into submission ; awe ⟪a person⟫ into obedience // 위압당하다 be overawed ⟪by⟫ ; be cowed ⟪before⟫ // 위압되어 복종하다 be coerced into submission

위액 胃液 gastric juice
— (분비)선 a peptic〔gastric〕 gland

위약 胃弱 indigestion ; dyspepsia ; weak digestion **—하다** (be) dyspeptic ; have a weak stomach

위약 違約 a breach of promise〔contract〕 ; a default **—하다** break a promise〔an agreement, an appointment〕 ; infringe a contract ; default ; break one's word ¶ 위약하지 않다 keep one's promise ; act according to what one promises ; be true to one's promise // 오늘 아침 상면할 것을 위약하여 뭐라 사과 말씀을 드려야 할지 모르겠습니다 I beg a thousand pardons for not keeping my appointment with you this morning.
—국 a covenant-breaking state **—금** damages for breach of contract ; a penalty ; a forfeit ; an indemnity **— 보증금** a forfeit **—자** a person breaking a contract ; a defaulter

위양 委讓 transfer ; assignment **—하다** transfer ⟪to⟫

위언 違言 ⇨ 위약(違約)

‡위엄 威嚴 dignity ; stateliness ; majesty ¶ 위엄있는 dignified ; majestic ; august ; stately ; commanding // 위엄이 없는 undignified ; unimpressive ; cheap // 위엄있는 사람 a man of dignified appearance // 위엄을 지키다 maintain〔keep〕 one's dignity // 위엄을 보이다 show one's dignity // 위엄있는 표정을 짓다 make a dignified appearance // 그는 위엄이 없다 He lacks dignity. // 그의 태도에는 어딘지 모르게 위엄이 있다 There is something dignified in his bearing.

위업 偉業 a great undertaking〔enterprise〕 ; a great achievement ; a great work ¶ 공전의 위업 an achievement of unprecedented magnitude // 위업을 성취하다 achieve a great work〔thing〕

위없다 (be) unsurpassed ; unexcelled ; unparalleled ; unrivaled ; unbeatable ; tops

위여 [쫓는 소리] Shoo !

위여일발 危如一髮 ⇨ 위기일발

위연하다 (be) grief-stricken ¶ 위연히 with a sigh ; lamentingly

위열 胃熱 〚의학〛 gastric fever

위염 胃炎 〚의학〛 gastritis ; inflammation of the stomach

위요 圍繞 surrounding ; encircling **—하다** surround ; encircle ¶ 친구들에 위요되어 with one's friends around one // 이 문제를 위요하고 많은 논쟁이 있었다 There were controversies in connection with this subject.

위용 偉容 a grand〔majestic〕 appearance ; a dignified〔stately〕 appearance

‡위원 委員 a member of a committee ; a committeeman ; a commissioner ¶ 위원 조직으로 되어 있다 be organized on the committee system // 다섯명의 위원을 선출하다 elect a committee of five // 위원 근무를 하다 serve on committee // 김씨도 위원의 한사람이다 Mr. *Kim* is〔sits〕 on the committee, too.
— 부탁 commitment ; [국회] devolution **—실** a committee room **—장** a chairman of a committee **— 제도** the committee system **국무 —** a Cabinet Member ; a Minister **부인 —** a committeewoman **상임 —** a standing〔permanent〕 committee **예산 —** the budget committee **운영 —** a steering committee **자격 심사 —** a committee on qualification **접대 —** the reception committee **집행 —** an executive committee **클라스 —** a class secretary

†위원회 委員會 a committee ; a commission ; a board ; a meeting of a committee ¶ 위원회를 소집하다 call a committee meeting // 위원회에 회부하다 submit ⟪a subject⟫ to a committee // 위원회는 5명의 위원으로 구성된다 The committee shall 〔will〕 consist〔be made up〕 of five members. // 이 문제에 관해서 지금 위원회가 열리고 있다 A committee is sitting on this question. // 안건이 위원회를 통과하였다 The bill has passed through the committee.
— 결정 사항 committee findings **— 멤버** a member of the committee **— 소집〔산회〕** ¶ 위원회를 소집〔산회〕하다 call〔discharge〕 a committee meeting **교육 —** the ⟪Seoul⟫ Board of Education **군사 정전 —** the Military Armistice Commission **분과 —** a subcommittee ; [회의] a sectional committee (meeting) **상임 —** a standing committee **소—** a small committee ; a subcommittee **시험 —** an examining body **예산 —** a budget committee **운영 —** a steering committee **자격 심사 —** a committee on qualifications **(적격) 심사 —** a screening committee **조사 —** a commission of inquiry **준비 —** an arrangement committee **직장 —** a shop committee **집행 —** an executive committee **창립〔조사〕 —** an organizing 〔investigation〕 committee **회원 자격 심사 —** a membership committee

위의 威儀 dignity ; stateliness ; a dignified mien ; solemnity ¶ 위의 있는 dignified ; solemn ; stately // 위의를 바로 하고 말하다 speak in a dignified manner ; speak with a solemnity of manner // 고관들이 위의를 갖추고 자리잡고 있었다 Dignitaries were ranged in stately rows.

위의당당 威儀堂堂 a stately manner ⇨ 위풍

위인 偉人 a great man ; a mastermind ; a great mind ; a hero ¶ 학계의 위인 a prodigy of learning // 불세출의 위인 the greatest man that ever lived // 위인이 되다 attain greatness

—전 the life of a great man 학계 — a prodigy of learning

위인 爲人 one's character ; personality ; one's nature ; one's disposition ¶ 소크라테스의 위인 Socrates the man // 위인이 훌륭하다 be a man of good character ; have a fine personality // 그는 위인이 강인하다 He is man of strong character. // 위인이 정직하다 He is honest by nature〔in character〕. // 이 사실은 그의 위인을 말해주고 있다 This fact is characteristic of him. // 그는 거짓말을 할 위인이 아니다 He is not a〔the sort of〕 man to tell a lie.

위인 僞印 a false〔forged〕 seal

†위임 委任 trust ; commission ; charge ; delegation ; authorization ; commitment ; 〖법〗 mandate —하다 entrust 《a person》 with 《a matter》 ; entrust 《a matter》 to 《a person》 ; commission 《a person》 to 《do》 ; authorize〔empower〕 《a person》 to 《do》 ; commit 《a matter》 to 《a person's》 care ¶ 전권을 위임하다 entrust 《a person》 with full powers ; give 《a person》 a carte blanche // 권능을 위임하다 delegate powers to 《a person》 ; invest 《a person》 with powers // 자녀 교육의 임무를 선생에게 위임하다 entrust the duty of educating a child to a teacher // 사무상의 일은 모두 김씨에게 위임하고 있다 I put all business matters under Mr. *Kim*'s charge.

—권 power of attorney — 권한 competency of mandate — 대리 representation of mandate — 명령 a delegated order — 자 the mandator — 제도 a mandate system — 조건 conditions〔terms〕 of entrustment — 투표 proxy voting

위임장 委任狀 a power of attorney ; a procuration ; credentials ¶ 위임장으로 투표하다 vote by proxy

— 쟁탈전 a proxy fight 변호 — a warrant of attorney 주식 양도 — a stock power

***위임 통치 委任統治** mandate ; mandatory rule ¶ 위임 통치를 받다 be under the mandate〔mandatory rule〕 《of》

—국 a mandatory (power〔territory〕) ; a mandatary —권 a mandate —령 territories under mandate ; mandated territories — 영토 territories under mandate ; mandated territories

위자 慰藉 consolation ; solace ; comfort —하다 console ; solace ; comfort ; soothe

—료 consolation money ; a solatium 《*pl.* -tia》 ; alimony ¶ 위자료를 요구하다 demand compensation 《for》

위작 僞作 ⇨ 위조

위작 位爵 peerage ; title and court rank

위장 胃腸 the stomach and intestines 〔bowels〕 ¶ 위장의 gastroenteric ; gastrointestinal // 위장이 튼튼하다 have a strong digestion // 위장을 해치다 injure the stomach and bowels

—병〔장해〕 gastroenteric trouble〔disorder〕 —병학 gastroenterology —약 a medicine for the stomach and bowels —염(炎) gastroenteritis — 하수증(下垂症) gastroenteroptosis

위장 僞裝 camouflage ; disguise —하다 camouflage ; disguise ; disguise oneself 《as》 ; hide by camouflage ¶ 위장된 camouflaged // 거지로 위장하다 disguise oneself as a beggar

— 공장 camouflaged plants — 군함 a dummy warship —망 a camouflage net — 병영 camouflage barracks — 수출 fraud export — 폭탄 a booby trap

위재 偉材 a man of superb talent

위재 偉才 a great talent

위적 偉績 distinguished services ; signal merits ; great exploits ; glorious achievements

위정자 爲政者 an administrator ; a statesman

위조 僞造 forgery ; fabrication ; falsification ; counterfeiting —하다 forge ; counterfeit ; fabricate ; falsify ¶ 위조의 forged ; counterfeit ; spurious // 서류를 위조하다 forge a document // 화폐를 위조하다 counterfeit coins // 수표를 위조하다 forge a check // 그는 위조죄로 기소되었다 He was prosecuted for forgery.

—단 a counterfeit ring — 문서 a spurious document — 수표 a forged check 〔cheque《영》〕 —자 a forger ; a counterfeiter — 증서 a forged bond — 지폐 a spurious bank〔counterfeit, forged〕 note ¶ 위조 지폐를 사용하다 pass a counterfeit note —품 a forgery ; a counterfeit ; a fake ; a spurious article 공문서 — the fabrication of the official documents 문서 —죄 forgery of documents 화폐 —자 a coiner

위족 僞足 〖생물〗 pseudopodium 《*pl.* -dia》

위주 爲主 putting first (in importance) —하다 put first (in importance) ; give the first consideration〔primacy〕 to ; make 《a thing》 the prime object ¶ 영리 위주의 학교 a school run for profit // 자기 위주의 사고 방식 self-centered thinking // 아동 위주의 교육 a child-centered education // 인격의 함양을 위주로 하다 make character-building the prime object ; aim at character-building // 장사에서는 이

득보는 것이 위주다 Profit making is the first consideration in business.

위중 危重 —하다 be in critical condition ; be critically ill ¶ 어머니가 위중하다는 전보가 왔다 I got a wire telling me of my mother's serious condition.

위증 僞證 〖법〗 false testimony ; perjury —하다 perjure oneself ; testify falsely ; bear false testimony 《to》 ; forswear
—자 a perjurer —죄 perjury ¶ 위증죄로 기소되다 be accused of perjury ; be charged with perjury // 위증죄를 범하다 commit (a) perjury

위증 危症 a critical condition of an illness ; a dangerous symptom

위지 危地 a dangerous〔perilous〕 position ; a critical situation ; danger ; peril ; the jaws of death ¶ 위지에서 벗어나다 find one's way out of the danger ; get out of the danger // 위지에 빠지다 get〔run〕 into danger ; fall into the jaws of death // 위지에 빠뜨리다 endanger ; jeopardize // 위지에 뛰어들다 take a risk ; run risks ; put one's head into a lion's mouth

위집 蝟集 gathering in a swarm —하다 swarm ; throng ; crowd〔flock〕 together ; gather in flocks

†**위쪽** the upper direction

위차 位次 rank〔order〕 of seats〔positions〕

위채 the upper wing of a Korean house

위촉 委囑 entrusting ; commission ; request (의뢰) ; charge (담당) —하다 entrust 《a person》 with 《a matter》 ; give a commission to ; commit 《a matter》 to 《a person》 ; request 《a person》 to 《do》 ; put 《an affair》 in charge of 《a person》 ¶ 위촉에 의해 by request ; in compliance with a request ; at the request 《of a person》 // 그것은 전문가에게 위촉해야 한다 It should be entrusted〔committed〕 to an expert.

위축 萎縮 shrinkage ; withering ; shriveling ; contraction ; 〖의학〗 atrophy —하다 wither ; shrivel ; shrink ; cower ; [기관이] become atrophied ¶ 외국 무역을 위축시키다 make foreign trade dwindle 〔decline〕
—병 curl (감자 따위의) —신 〖의학〗 atrophy of the kidney ; the contracted kidney ; nephrosclerosis —위 〖의학〗 the leather-bottle stomach

위층 —層 the upper floor〔story, storey 《영》〕 ; upstairs ¶ 위층방 an upstairs room // 위층에 올라가다 go upstairs // 나의 서재는 위층입니다 My study is upstairs.

*****위치 位置** [장소] a situation ; a location ; [처지·지위] a stand ; a position ; a post ; a place —하다 be situated〔located〕 ; stand ; lie ; rank ¶ 사회 생활에 있어서의 여성의 위치 woman's place in social life // 학교의 위치가 좋다 The school stands in a good situation. /This school is favorably situated〔located〕. /The location of this school is good. // 건축의 위치가 아직 결정되지 않았다 The site for the building is not yet fixed. // 그의 집은 시의 중심부에 위치하고 있다 His house is located in the center〔heart〕 of the city. // 네가 만약 내 위치에 있다면 어떻게 하겠는가 If you were in my place, what would you do ? // 그는 드디어 사장의 위치까지 올라갔다 He was raised to the position of president in the end.
— 감각 〖심리〗 consciousness of bodily position — 결정 〖전기〗 spotting —등 〖항공〗 a position light — 선정 location — 설정 location ; positioning — 에너지 〖물리〗 potential energy — 조절 centering control — 조정 positioning — 천문학 astrometry — 측정기 a position finder

위친하다 爲親— be devoted to one's parents

위칭 僞稱 ⇨ 사칭(詐稱)

위 카메라 胃— gastro-camera

위 카타르 胃— 〖의학〗 catarrh of the stomach ; gastric catarrh

위크 a week
—데이 a weekday —엔드 weekend **위클리** a weekly

†**위탁 委託** trust ; commission ; [상품의] consignment —하다 entrust 《a thing》 to 《a person》 ; entrust 《a person》 with 《a thing》 ; put 《a matter》 in 《a person's》 hand ; commit〔confide〕 to 《a person》 ; consign 《goods》 to 《a firm》

> 참고 **commit** 일반적으로 널리 쓰이는 말이며 보호나 보관을 목적으로 사람이나 물건을 건네다 **consign** 딱딱한 말로 소유권이나 관리권을 정식으로 타인에게 넘겨주다 **entrust** 상대방을 신뢰해서 맡기다 **confide** 개인적인 일을 신뢰를 갖고 타인에게 밝히다

¶ 사무를 위탁받다 be left in charge of the business // 상품의 판매를 위탁하다 consign goods to 《an agent》 // 임무를 대리인에게 위탁하다 depute a task to a proxy // 모든 일을 그에게 위탁했다 I have put everything in his hands.
— 가공 processing of brought-in materials ; processing on commission — 가공품 brought-in materials processed on commission — 권한 the terms of reference —금 money (given) in trust ; trust money —금 소비 embezzlement ; defalcation ; peculation — 모집 [구직자의] commissioning of labor recruitment — 보증금 consignment guarantee money — 사격 firing from a rest〔with the elbow supported〕 — 사무 duties as may be assigned to 《a person》 — 수송품 goods shipped on consignment — 수수료 a consignment fee — 인수인 a trustee ; a principal —자 a truster ; a consignor —

판매 consignment sale ; sale on commission ¶ 상품을 위탁 판매로 보내다 forward goods on consignment ─ 판매인 a commission merchant〔agent〕 ─ 판매〔적송〕품 a consignment ; goods on consignment ─품 consignment goods ; a consignment ; a trust ; an article consigned ─품 매상 계산서 sales account 구매 ─ an indent

위태 危殆 danger ; peril ; jeopardy ; risk ─하다 (be) dangerous ; perilous ; risky ; be at stake ¶ 위태롭게 하다 endanger ; jeopardize ; imperil ; compromise 《one's position》// 그는 생명이 위태롭다 He is in danger of his life. // 아버지께서 갑자기 병이 들었는데 위태롭다는 소식이다 My father suddenly got sick, and they say he may not make it.

위턱 the upper jaw ; a superior maxilla

위통 胃痛 a stomachache ; 〚의학〛 gastralgia

위트 wit ¶ 위트가 있는 witty // 위트가 없는 witless

위패 位牌 a mortuary〔memorial〕 tablet ¶ 조상의 위패 an ancestral tablet

위폐 僞幣 ⇨ 위조(─지폐)

위품 位品 (court) rank ; official rank

‡위풍 威風 a majestic air ; dignified bearing ; a commanding presence ; a stately appearance ¶ 위풍 당당한 majestic ; imposing ; stately // 위풍 당당히 majestically ; in a stately manner // 위풍 당당한 인물 a man of commanding presence ; a majestic figure // 위풍에 압도되다 bow 〔bend〕 to 《a person's》 dignity

위필 僞筆 forged〔feigned, disguised, spurious〕 handwriting ; a forgery ; [그림] a forged picture ─하다 forge ; counterfeit ¶ 위필로 in a forged handwriting

─자 a forger

위하 威嚇 ⇨ 위협

†위하다 爲─ do for the sake of ; do in the interest of ; do in behalf of ; [공경하다] respect ; revere ; look up to ; [소중히 하다] make much of ; take good care of ; value ; esteem ¶ 위하여 for ; for the sake of ; in the interests of ; on behalf of ; in the favor of // 하기 위하여 in order to ; so as to ; so that ; with a view to ; for the purpose of // 너를 위해서 for your own sake // 평화를 위해서 in the interest of peace // 정의를 위해서 in the cause of justice ; for the sake of justice // 몸을 위하다 take care of oneself // 부모를 위하다 take good care of one's parents ; be devoted to one's parents ; honor one's parents // 자기를 위하다 seek one's own interests ; look for one's interests // 어린애를 위하다 be kind to children ; love children // 남편을 위하다 attend to one's husband with devotion ; be devoted to one's husband // 명예를 목숨보다 더 위하다 esteem honor above life // 상을 타기 위해서 열심히 공부하다 study hard in order to get a prize // 돈을 위해 일하다 work for money // 공익을 위해서 일하다 work for the public good // 나라를 위해 죽다 die for one's country // 조국을 위해서 몸을 바치다 lay down one's life for the sake of the fatherland // 남을 위해 일하다 work for the good of others // 그는 집을 짓기 위해 땅을 샀다 He has bought land with a view to building a house. // 이것은 너를 위해서 하는 말이다 I say this for your (own) good. // 그는 통역 시험에 합격하기 위해서 영어 회화를 열심히 공부하고 있다 He is studying English conversation very hard so that he may pass the examination for interpreters. // 당신을 위해서 전력을 다하겠다 I will use all my influence in your favor〔benefit〕.

위하수 胃下垂 〚의학〛 gastroptosis

위학 胃學 gastrology

위해 危害 harm ; injury ; hazard ; danger ; peril ¶ 위해를 가하다 harm ; do 《a person》 harm〔an injury〕 ; inflict an injury 《on》 ; hurt 《a person》 ; endanger ; imperil // 위해를 피하다 keep oneself out of harm's way ; escape unhurt // 이 개는 사람에게 위해를 가하지 않는다 This dog does no harm to man.

─물 a dangerous〔hazardous〕 article ─방지 prevention of danger and peril 〔injury〕 급박 ─ 〚법〛 apparent danger

위헌 違憲 unconstitutionality ; violation of the constitution ─하다 be unconstitutional ; infringe〔breach, violate〕 the constitution ¶ 위헌의 unconstitutional ; against the constitution // 그것은 위헌적인 처사이다 That is an unconstitutional measure.

†위험 危險 danger ; peril ; jeopardy ; hazard ; risk

> 참고 **danger** 일반적으로 쓰이는 말 촉박한 위험 확실한 위험만이라고는 할 수 없다 **peril** 긴박한 또는 일어날 가능성이 있는 위험 **jeopardy** 커다란 위험에 처해 있다는 뜻 **hazard** 우연히 생기는 위험 **risk** 자진하여 부딪치는 위험

─하다 (be) dangerous ; perilous ; hazardous ; risky ; precarious ¶ 위험을 무릅쓰고 in the face of danger ; at the risk 《of one's life》 // 위험한 짓을 하다 fly in the face of danger ; risk one's neck // 위험이 따르다 be attended with danger ; involve some risk // 떨어질 위험이 있다 be in danger of falling // 위험을 무릅쓰다 run a risk ; face a danger ; venture ; take a chance 《미》 // 위험에 직면하다 be in danger ; be at stake ; be in jeopardy // 위험을 느끼다 sense〔suspect, apprehend〕 danger // 위험을 최소한으로 저지하다 minimize the risk 《of fire》 // 위험 천만한 짓

을 하다 perform a hazardous feat ; sleep on a volcano // 그는 위험이 다가오는 것을 몰랐다 He was not aware of the danger threatening him. // 이 사업은 위험을 수반하다 This enterprise involves a lot of risk. // 이제 위험은 한고비 넘었다 The worst danger is now over. // 등산에는 위험이 따르기 마련이다 Mountain climbing is always attended with danger. // 자네가 나를 실망시키지 않을 줄 알기 때문에 위험을 무릅쓰고 결심한 거야 I decided to risk my neck because I know you will not let me down. // 불경기가 계속 되어서 실은 위험한 상황입니다 With this prolonged slump, the situation is actually pretty touch-and-go.
—각(도) a danger angle ; a critical angle — 건축물 a dangerous〔hazardous〕building —률 〖보험〗 the ratio〔percentage〕 of risk —물 a dangerous article ; 〖법〗 a dangerous thing〔object〕; 〖철도〗 explosives and combustibles ; [항해상의] a danger — 박두 danger impending〔pressing〕 — 부담 〖보험〗 risk bearing — 분산 〖경제〗 diversification of risks — 분자 dangerous elements ; risks — 사상 dangerous thoughts〔ideas〕 — 사업 a hazardous enterprise — 상태 a dangerous〔critical〕 condition ; a parlous state —성 riskiness ; jeopardy — 속도 critical speed〔velocity〕; [축(軸)의] whirling speed — 수당 danger allowance —시(視) ¶ 위험시하다 regard《a person, a thing》 as dangerous ; regard《an attempt》 as risky — 신호 a danger signal ; [교통 신호의] a red light ; a stop light《미》; 〖철도〗 a red lamp (야간의) — 신호기 a red flag — 약물 dangerous drugs — 인물 a dangerous man〔character〕; a security risk (국가 안전상의 위험 인물) — 지대〔지역〕 a danger spot〔zone, area〕 — 지점 a danger spot — 직업 hazardous employment — 통보 a danger message — 표지판 a warning (sign) post — 화물〔물품〕 dangerous cargo〔goods〕 — 회전수 the critical (number of) revolutions 고압 전류 — 〖게시〗 Warning ; high voltage
†**위협 威脅** menace ; threat ; intimidation —하다 menace ; threaten ; intimidate ; scare ; frighten

> 참고 **threaten**은 주로 말로 「위협하다」의 뜻이고 **menace**는 몸짓 무기 따위의 수단을 사용하여 「위협하다」의 뜻

¶ 위협적인 menacing ; threatening // 위협적으로 by intimidation ; by threats // 위협적 태도를 취하다 assume a threatening attitude // 위협해서 돈을 빼앗다 blackmail《a person》; extract money from《a person》 by threats // 생활을 위협하다 threaten one's livelihood // 사람을 위협해서 …시키다 bully〔coerce〕《a person》 into《doing》// 그는 나를 죽이겠다고 위협하였다 He threatened to kill me. // 기근이 그 지방을 위협하고 있다 Famine threatens the district.
— 사격 an intimidating fire ; warning shots — 수단 an intimidatory measure —자 an intimidator ; a bulldozer《미》
위화 違和 a physical disorder ; incongruity —감 a feeling of physical disorder ; a sense of incompatibility
위확장 胃擴張 〖의학〗 dilatation of the stomach ; gastric dilatation
위황병 萎黃病 greensickness ; chlorosis
위효 偉效 a great〔signal〕 effect ¶ 위효를 나타내다 produce a marked effect《on》
위훈 偉勳 a great〔brilliant〕 service ; a conspicuous merit ; a great achievement ¶ 위훈을 세우다 accomplish a great achievement ; render distinguished services
윈도우 a window
윈치 a winch ; a crane ; a hoist
윔블든 Wimbledon
— 정구 대회 the Wimbledon
윗- [위의] the upper ; the above ; the outer ¶ 윗학교에 가다 attend a higher institution ; go to the upper school
윗길 superior quality ; better grade ; top grade
윗누이 an elder sister
윗눈썹 upper eyelashes〔lashes〕
윗니 the upper (set of) teeth
윗동(아리) ① ⇨ 웃통 ② [어깨 사이] the span between the shoulders
윗마기 the upper garment ; the top(s) of a garment
윗물 the water of the upper stream《of a river》; the upper waters《of a river》
윗물이 맑아야 아랫물이 맑다 속담 Parents are patterns. /One sheep follows another. /If one sheep leap o'er the dyke, all the rest will follow.
윗배 the upper part of the abdomen ; the stomach
윗변 —邊 〖수학〗 the topside of a polygon
윗사람 one's senior ; one's elder one's superior ; one's better ¶ 한 집의 윗사람 the oldest man in the family // 윗사람에 대한 예의 manners towards a superior // 윗사람에게 순종하라 Obey your betters.
윗수염 a moustache
윗입술 the upper lip
윗잇몸 the upper gum〔toothridge〕
윗자리 the upper〔higher〕 seat ; the top seat ; the seat〔place〕 of honor ; occupy the place of honor
***윙** whizzingly ; with a buzz〔whiz, whir〕 —하다 make a buzz〔whiz, whir〕 ¶ 바람이 윙윙 불어댔다 The wind hissed and raged.
윙윙하다, 윙윙거리다 buzz and buzz ; [바람이] whistle ; [탄알이] ping ; whiz
윙크 a wink —하다 wink《at》 ¶ 윙크하

는 사람 a winker

유 類 ① [무리] a group ; a crowd ② [종류] a sort ; a kind ; a class (부류) ¶ 이런 유의 상품은 현재 품절이다 The goods in this line are now sold out. // 저 사람은 다른 사람과 유를 달리하고 있다 That man is in a class by himself. ③ 〖생물〗 a family ; a genus ¶ 이 동물은 무슨 유에 속하는가 To what genus does this animal belong ?

—유상종 Like attracts like. **거미류** a genus of spider **귤감류** a kind〔variety〕 of orange **장미류** the rose tribe **포유류** Mammalia **하의류** underwear ; underclothes

유 酉 〖민속〗 ① [십이지의] the Sign of the Cock (10th of the 12 Earth's Branches) ② ⇨ 유방(酉方) ③ ⇨ 유시(酉時)

유 有 ① [존재] existence ; being ¶ 무에서 유가 생기지 않는다 Out of nothing, nothing comes.

② [소유] possession ¶ 국유의 state-owned // 민유의 privately-owned

유가 有價 valuableness ; having a fixed price

—물 valuables **— 증권** securities ; stocks and bonds ; a negotiable instrument〔paper〕 **— 증권 상환손(證券償還損)〔익(益)〕** losses〔profits〕 on maturity of securities **— 증권 시장** the stock〔securities〕 market **— 증권 일람표** a portfolio 《*pl.* -s》 《미》 **— 증권 준비** bond〔securities〕 reserve **— 증권 투자** securities investment **정부 발행 — 증권** government securities

유가 儒家 a Confucian (scholar) ; a Confucianist

—서 Confucian literature

유가족 遺家族 a bereaved family

군인 — the families of the war dead ; a war-bereaved family

†유감 遺憾 regret ; a pity ¶ 유감된 일 a matter for regret // 유감스럽게도 to my regret // 유감 없이 most satisfactorily ; to one's heart's content ; fully // 유감스럽다 be regrettable ; be deplorable ; be lamentable ; be pitiable // 유감의 뜻을 표하다 express one's regret // 재능을 유감 없이 발휘하다 give full play to one's abilities // 일이 이렇게 된 것은 유감 천만이다 It is a thousand pities that things should have come to this. // 그가 이미 떠났다는 말을 듣고 유감스러웠다 I heard with regret that he had started already. // 아무런 유감도 없다 I have no regrets. // 이런 사고가 빈발하는 것은 참으로 유감스러운 일이다 It is a matter of sincere regret that such accidents should happen so frequently. // 유감스럽게도 협력할 수가 없습니다 I am sorry I am unable to help you. // 유감스러웠지만 그 제의를 거절하였다 I declined the offer with much regret. // 그는 상인 기질을 유감 없이 발휘하는 장삿군이다 He is a merchant thoroughpaced in his doings. // 유감스러우나 사실이다 It is only too true. // 그거 유감이네 That's a shame.

유감각 지진 有感覺地震 〖지질〗 a felt〔sensible〕 earthquake

***유개 有蓋** having a lid〔top, cover〕 ¶ 유개의 covered ; lidded ; with lid

— 마차〔자동차〕 a closed carriage ; a covered carriage ; a covered wagon 《미》 **—차** a covered cart〔wagon〕 **— 화차** a boxcar 《미》 ; a covered wagon 《영》 ; a roofed〔box〕 wagon ; a goods van

유개념 類概念 〖논리〗 a genus

유객 幽客 a hermit ; a recluse ; an anchorite

유객 遊客 ① [유람객] a tourist ; a man on a pleasure trip

② [건달] a playboy ; a loafer

③ [탕아] a libertine ; a rake ; a debauchee

유거 幽居 [장소] a hermitage ; a solitary〔retired〕 residence ; a sequestered retreat ; [생활] seclusion ; retirement ; a secluded life **—하다** live in seclusion ; lead a retired life

유건 악기 有鍵樂器 a keyed (musical) instrument

유격 遊擊 〖군사〗 a diversion ; a raid ; mobile attack **—하다** divert ; raid

—대 a flying column〔corps, army〕 ; a guerrilla unit ; mobile forces ; a commando group **—병** partisans ; guerrillas ; a ranger ; a commando **—수** 〖야구〗 a shortstop **—전** guerrilla〔a partisan〕 warfare〔war〕 **— 함대** a flying squadron

유견 謬見 a wrong view ; a mistaken notion ; a false idea ; a misunderstanding

유경 幼莖 〖식물〗 a caulicle ; a plumule

유경 幽境 a solitary〔secluded, quiet〕 place〔spot〕

유경 有莖 being caulescent

— 식물 a cormophyte

유계 幽界 the other〔next〕 world ; the world after death ; the world beyond the grave ¶ 유계를 달리하다 go to the better world ; die // 그는 지금 유계를 달리하고 있다 He now lives in the other world.

유고 有故 [사고] an accident ; (a) trouble ; a mishap ; [까닭] cause ; reason **—하다** have (some) trouble ; 《an accident》 happen ; [까닭] have a reason 《for》 ¶ 유고시에 at the time of an accident

— 결석 absence with leave **—시** the time of an accident

유고 遺稿 posthumous works〔manuscripts〕 ; literary remains ; manuscripts left by 《a person》 ¶ 고 A씨의 유고를 출판하다 publish in book form the manuscripts left by the late Mr. A

유고 諭告 ① [타이름] advice ; counsel ;

instructions ; (an) admonition ─하다 admonish ; give instructions ② [포고] a decree ; an ordinance ; a proclamation ─하다 proclaim ; announce
유고 油庫 an oil bunker
유고슬라비아 Yugoslavia ; Yugo-Slavia ; Jugoslavia ; Jugo-Slavia ¶ 유고슬라비아의 Yugoslav ; Yugoslavic ; Yugoslavian
─ 사람 Yugoslav ; a Yugoslavian
유곡 幽谷 deep valley ; a deep〔dark〕 glen
심산 ─ deep mountains and dark valleys
유골 遺骨 [사람의] ashes ; remains ; bones ; [동물의] asheous remains of animals ¶ 유골을 모으다 gather《a person's》remains // 유골을 유골 단지에 담다 put《a person's》ashes in an urn // 유골을 봉안하다 place《a person's》remains in《a temple》
유공 有功 meritoriousness ─하다 (be) meritorious
─ 상패 a medal for merit ─자 a man of merit ─증 a certificate of merit ─ 훈장 the order of merit
유공성 有孔性 porosity ; porousness
─ 석회암 porous limestone
유공충 有孔蟲 〖동물〗 a foraminifer ; Foraminifera (학명)
유과 油菓 oil-and-honey pastry
유곽 遊廓 licensed〔gay, prostitute〕 quarters ; a red-light district (미) ¶ 유곽에 출입하다 frequent houses of ill fame〔gay quarters〕
유관 油管 an oil pipe
유관속 維管束 〖식물〗 a vascular bundle〔strand〕
유관절류 有關節類 〖동물〗 an articulate
유광지 有光紙 glazed paper
*유괴 誘拐 kidnap(p)ing ; abduction ─하다 abduct ; kidnap《a child》; seduce《a girl》; entice《a person》away from《a place》; shanghai ; carry off ¶ 어린애를 유괴하다 kidnap a child
─ 사건 an abduction case ; a snatch case (미) ─자 a abductor ; a kidnap(p)er ─죄 abduction
유교 儒敎 Confucianism ¶ 유교의 감화 Confucian influence // 유교를 믿다 believe in Confucianism
─ 감화 Confucian influence ─도 a Confucian ; a Confucianist ─ 사상 Confucian ideas ─주의 Confucianism ─주의자 a Confucianist
유교 遺敎 ⇨ 유명(遺命)
유구 琉球 Ryukyu (Islands) ; Loochoo(s)
유구 悠久 eternity ; perpetuity ; permanence ─하다 (be) eternal ; everlasting ; perpetual ; permanent ¶ 유구한 옛날부터 from time immemorial
유구 類句 a synonymous phrase
유구무언 有口無言 no excuse to offer ; being unable to say anything ; having no word to say in excuse
유군 幼君 young〔boy〕 king
*유권자 有權者 the holder of a right ; a qualified person ; [선거의] an elector ; a voter ; an eligible voter ; the electorate《총칭》¶ 유권자를 동원하다 recruit voters for the election // 너는 유권자의 자격이 없다 You are not qualified as a voter. // 이 마을의 유권자는 500명이다 Five hundred of the villagers are qualified to vote.
유권 해석 有權解釋 an authoritative interpretation
유근 幼根 〖식물〗 a radicle ; a rootlet
유금류 游禽類 〖새〗 the swimmers ; Natatores (학명)
†유급 有給 ¶ 유급의 paid ; salaried ; stipendiary
─ 고용 gainful employment ─ 외교원 a salaried canvasser〔salesman〕 ─ 위원 salaried〔paid〕 committee man ─자 a salaried person ─직 a salaried office ; a paid position ─ 직업 a paid〔gainful〕 occupation ─ 직원 staff members on the payroll ─ 휴가 a paid vacation〔holiday〕 ; a vacation〔holiday〕 with pay ─ 휴가 수당 a paid-holiday allowance
유급 留級 ─하다 stay two years (or longer) in the same class ; be left back
─생〔자〕 a student remaining in the same class
유기 有期 ¶ 유기의 terminable ; limited ; for a term
─ 공채 a terminable loan〔bond〕 ─ 연금 a terminable〔limited〕 annuity ─형 penal servitude for a definite term ; a sentence for imprisonment for a definite period〔term〕
*유기 有機 ¶ 유기의 〖화학〗 organic // 유기적 organic ; with the parts working in coordination
─ 감각 〖심리·생리〗 organic sensation ─계 the organic world ─ 금속 화합물 an organo-metallic compound ─물 organic matter ; an organism ─ 비료 an organic fertilizer ─ 수은 (화합물) an organic mercury compound ─ 염기 an organic base ─ 영양소 an organic nutritive element ─ 유리 organic glass ─적 세계관 the organic view of the world ─적 통일 the organic unity《of the state》─질 an organic matter〔substance〕 ─질 비료 an organic fertilizer ─체 an organism ; an organic body ; an organized matter ─체설(體說) 〖화학·생물〗 organicism ─토(土) organic soil ─ 화학 organic chemistry ─ 화합물 an organic compound
유기 遺棄 abandonment ; dereliction ; desertion ; exposition ─하다 abandon ; leave《a thing》behind ; desert《a dead body》; expose《a baby》¶ 시체를 유기하고 도망갔다 He ran away leaving the body behind.
─물 an abandoned thing ; a derelict ─선 a derelict ; an abandoned ship (해상의) ─ 시체 an abandoned corpse ¶ 적

의 유기 시체 bodies left by the enemy on the battlefield —자 a deserter 불법 — malicious abandonment 시체 — the abandonment of a corpse 영아 — the exposure of a baby 직무 — neglect of duty

유기 鍮器 brassware

유기음 有氣音 an aspirate ; an aspirated sound

유기적 有機的 organic ; systematic ¶ 유기적 세계관 the organic view of the world // 국가의 유기적 통일 the organic unity of the state

유기하다 誘起— cause ; lead (up) to 《something》; give rise to 《suspicion》

유나 柔懦 effeminacy ; effeminateness ; weakness and timidity —하다 (be) effeminate ; weak and timid

유난 [보통이 아님] unusualness ; uncommonness ; [괴팍] fastidiousness ; fussiness —하다 (be) unusual ; uncommon ; exceptional ; fastidious ; particular ; fussy ¶ 유난히 눈에 띄다 make oneself too conspicuous // 음식〔옷〕에 대해서 유난스럽다 be fastidious〔particular〕 about one's food〔clothes〕 // 올 겨울은 유난스럽게 춥다 It is exceptionally〔unusually〕 cold this winter.

유난 떨다 관용 behave fastidiously

유네스코 UNESCO 《the United Nations Educational Scientific and Cultural Organization》

유녀 幼女 a young〔little〕 girl

유년 酉年 〖민속〗 the Year of the Rooster

*유년 幼年 infancy ; childhood ; boyhood〔girlhood〕; puerility ; juvenility ; a juvenile ; 〖법〗 natural infancy (7세까지) ¶ 유년의 juvenile ; puerile // 유년기의 [지형이] immature // 유년 시대에〔부터〕 in〔from〕 one's early days ; in〔from〕 one's childhood // 나는 유년 시대를 이곳에서 보냈다 I spent my childhood days here.

—공 a child worker — 노동 child labor — 시대〔기〕 infancy ; childhood ; puerility

유념 留念 attention ; consideration ; regard ; mindfulness —하다 bear〔keep〕 《a matter》 in mind ; heed ; regard ; mind ; care about ; attend to ; pay attention to

유뇨증 遺尿症 〖의학〗 enuresis

*유능 有能 ability ; competence ; capability —하다 (be) able ; capable ; competent ; talented ¶ 유능한 사람 a man of ability〔talent〕; a competent man

유니버시아드 〖경기〗 the Universiade

유니버설 universal

유니버시티 a university

유니세프 UNICEF 《the United Nations International Children's Emergency Fund》 (지금은 the United Nations Children's Fund)

유니언 union ; a union

유니언잭 [영국 국기] the Union Jack

유니폼 a uniform

유다 〖성경〗 Judas

†유다르다 (be) uncommon ; unusual ; conspicuous ¶ 유달리 uncommonly ; unusually ; conspicuously ; especially ; particularly // 유달리 눈에 띄다 stand out conspicuously

유단자 有段者 a grade-holder (in judo, fencing, chess)

유당 乳糖 〖화학〗 lactose ; milk sugar

유대 紐帶 a tie ; a band ; relation ¶ 긴밀한 유대를 맺다 come into close relation 《with》 // 상업적 유대를 강화하다 strengthen one's commercial ties 《with》

유대류 有袋類 〖동물〗 the marsupial (animal) ; Marsupialia (학명)

유덕 有德 virtuousness —하다 (be) virtuous ; good ¶ 유덕한 사람 a virtuous person ; a man of virtue ; a good liver

유덕 遺德 posthumous influence ¶ A씨의 유덕 the late Mr. A's virtuous influence

*유도 柔道 judo

— 고단자 a rankholding judo expert〔man〕 —복 a suit for judo practice — 사범 an instructor of judo

유도 誘導 incitement ; inducement ; leading ; 〖전기〗 induction ; 〖화학·수학〗 derivation —하다 induce ; incite ; lead ; 〖화학〗 derive ¶ 사람을 유도하다 induce 《a person》 to 《do》

— 가속기 a betatron — 가열 장치 an induction〔inductive〕 heating apparatus — 결합 inductive coupling —기(機) an induction machine ; an inductor — 기전력 induced electromotive force — 단위 a derived unit —력〔성〕 inductivity —로 〖항공〗 taxiway ; taxi strip — 물질 an inducing substance — 반응 (an) induced reaction — 발전기 an induction generator — 방해 inductive disturbance〔interference〕 — 병기 a guided weapon — 속력 the induced velocity — 신호기 a calling-on signal —자 an inducer ; a conductor — 장치 a guidance system ; guidance control — 전기 induced electricity — 전류 an induced current —체 derivatives — 코일 an induction coil —탄 a (guided) missile — 회로 an inductive circuit 상호 — mutual induction 원격 — teleguidance ; remote control 자기 — self-induction 전기〔자기〕 — electromagnetic〔magnetic〕 induction 정전 — electrostatic induction〔influence〕 지대공 —탄 a surface-to-air missile

유도 儒道 Confucianism

유도 신문 誘導訊問 leading question —하다 lead 《a criminal suspect》 to the point in question ; put a leading question

*유독 有毒 poisonousness ; noxiousness —하다 (be) poisonous ; noxious ; venomous

— 가스 a poisonous〔toxic〕 gas — 균류

(菌類) venomous fungi — 식물 a poisonous〔noxious〕 plant
유독 惟獨 only ; singly ; uniquely ; alone
*유동 流動 a flow ; flowing —하다 flow
—물 liquids ; fluids — 비율 current ratio — 상태 state of flux ; a fluid situation — 성 liquidity ; fluidity ; 〖사회〗 mobility — 식 liquid food ; a liquid ; a liquid diet — 자본 circulating capital — 자산〔자금〕 floating〔liquids, current〕 assets〔funds, money〕 —적 과잉 인구 mobile overpopulation —점 the pour point —체 a fluid ; a liquid — 측정 rheometry
유동 遊動 moving freely
— 원목(圓木) a swinging pole — 활차 a movable pulley ; a freely moving pulley
유동법 類同法 〖논리〗 the method of agreement
유두 流頭 the 15th day of the 6th lunar month ; the *yutwu* festival
유두 油頭 greased〔pomaded〕 hair
— 분면 make-up with cosmetics
유두 乳頭 〖해부〗 a nipple ; a teat ; a mammilla 《*pl.* -lae》 ; a papilla
—륜(輪) areola ; an halo —염 thelitis ; acromastitis —종(腫) a papilloma
유들유들 —하다 (be) brazen ; brassy ; cheeky ; shameless ; pert
유라시아 Eurasia ; Europe and Asia ¶ 유라시아의 Eurasian ; European and Asiatic
— 대륙 the Eurasian Continent — 사람 a Eurasian
유락 流落 —하다 live away from home
유락 遊樂 amusement ; enjoyment ; pleasure —하다 enjoy〔amuse〕 oneself ; make merry ¶ 유락에 빠지다 give oneself up to pleasure ; be given to pleasure
*유람 遊覽 sightseeing ; a sightseeing tour ; an excursion ; a pleasure trip —하다 go sightseeing ; do〔see〕 the sights 《of》 ¶ 유람 여행을 하다 go on a sightseeing tour〔a pleasure trip〕
—객 sightseers ; tourists ; excursionists — 단체 a tourist party ; a sightseeing〔an excursion〕 party — 버스 a sightseeing bus —선 an excursion ship ; a pleasure boat — 안내서 a tourist bureau — 열차 an excursion train —지 a pleasure ground ; a tourist resort — 지도 a tourists' map — 철도 a scenic railway
*유랑 流浪 wandering ; roaming —하다 wander〔roam, rove〕 about ¶ 세계를 유랑하다 roam〔wander, knock〕 about the world // 유랑 생활을 하다 lead a roving 〔wandering〕 life
—민 a nomadic people ; nomads — 민족 nomadic tribes —벽 vagrant habits — 생활 a wandering〔nomadic, Bohemian〕 life ; the life of an exile ; vagabondage ; nomadism —자 wanderer ; a nomad ; a roamer ; a vagabond ; a vagrant
†유래 由來 [기원] origin ; genesis ; [내력] history ; [출처] source ; derivation —하다 originate 《in》 ; result 《from》 ; date back 《to the time of, when》 ; be derived 《from》 ; derive itself〔its origin〕 《from》 ¶ 유래를 더듬다 trace 《a thing》 to its origin ; trace 《a custom》 to its source ; inquire into the origin 《of》 ; study the history 《of》 // 그 이름은 여기서 유래했다 Hence the name.
유랭 油冷 oil cooling
—조(槽) an oil cooling bath — 진공관 an oil-cooled tube
유량 流量 〖물리〗 flux
—계 a flow meter ; a current meter
유량계 油量計 an oil gauge〔meter〕
유러달러 Eurodollars
유럽 Europe ¶ 유럽의 European // 유럽화(化)하다 Europeanize ; Westernize
— (경제) 공동체 the European (Economic) Community 《E. E. C. ; EC》 — 경제 협력 기구 the Organization for European Economic Cooperation 《O. E. E. C》 — 공동 시장 the European Common Market 《E. C. M》 — 대륙 the (European) Continent — 사람 a European — 열강 the European Powers — 정치 공동체 the European Political Community《E. P. C.》
유려하다 流麗— (be) flowing ; elegant ; florid ¶ 유려한 문장 a flowing and elegant style ; a fluent and flowery style
†유력 有力 —하다 (be) powerful ; strong ; influential ¶ 유력한 소식통 some influential quarters ; a reliable source // 유력한 신문〔실업가〕 an influential newspaper〔businessman〕 // 유력한 용의자 a highly probable offender ; a strongly supported suspect // 유력한 증거 valid 〔strong〕 evidence〔proof〕 // 유력한 후보자 a strong candidate // 유력한 정보가 들어왔다 We have obtained reliable information. // 차기 대통령으로는 그가 가장 유력하다 He is the strongest candidate for the next presidential election.
—자 an influential〔a prominent, a leading〕 person ; a man〔person〕 of importance ; a man of influence〔weight〕 ; a potentate
유력 遊歷 a tour ; an itinerancy ; peregrination —하다 tour ; travel about ; make a tour 《of》 ; itinerate ; peregrinate ¶ 세계를 유력하다 make an extensive tour of the world
유렵 遊獵 ⇨ 총렵
—지 a preserve ; shooting〔hunting〕 grounds ; a hunting field
유령 幼齡 the young age
*유령 幽靈 a spirit of the dead ; a ghost ; an apparition ; a specter ; a supernatural visitor ; a phantom ¶ 유령 같은 ghostlike // 유령의 집 a haunted house // 유령이 나오다 be haunted 《by a ghost》 ; a ghost walks on the earth // 그 집에는 유령이 나

온다는 소문이 있다 It is rumored that the house is haunted.
— 도시 a ghost town —선 a phantom ship ; a flying Dutchman — 인구 a bogus〔ghost〕 population ; a fraudulently registered population — 퇴치 ghost hunting — 회사 a bogus company ; a long firm 《영》
유례 類例 a similar example〔instance〕 ; a parallel case ¶ 유례가 없다 be unparalleled ; be unique ; be unexampled ; be unprecedented ; be unconventional // 사상 유례가 없다 be unparalleled〔without parallel〕 in history ; have no parallel in history
유로 달러 Eurodollars
유료 有料 ¶ 유료의 charged ; with fee // 유료이다 be charged for // 입장은 무료입니까 유료입니까 Is the admission free or charged for? // 이 공중 변소는 유료입니다 You must pay for the use of this comfort station.
— 도로 a toll road〔expressway〕 ; a turnpike road — 도서관 a pay library — 변소 pay toilet — 시사회 charged preview — 입장 paid admission — 주차장 a toll parking lot — 직업 소개소 a fee-charging employment exchange — 통화 a chargeable call
유루 遺漏 omission (빠짐) ; a leak (샘) **—하다** be omitted ; leak ¶ 유루 없이 without omission ; thoroughly ; exhaustively
유류 遺留 —하다 leave behind
—물 a thing left (behind) ; lost articles —분(分) 〖법〗 a legal portion of an heir ; a reserve
유류 油類 oil ; all kinds of oil
유리 有理 reasonableness ; rationality **—하다** (be) reasonable ; rational
—수〔식〕 〖수학〗 a rational number〔expression〕 — 지수 a rational index — 함수 〖수학〗 a rational function
†**유리 有利 —하다** (be) profitable ; lucrative ; paying ; [사정 따위가] advantageous ; favorable ¶ 유리한 점 vantage ; a point〔coign〕 of vantage // 유리한 사업 a profitable enterprise ; a paying business // 유리한 조건 advantageous〔remunerative〕 terms // 피고에 유리한 증언을 하다 give testimony favorable to the accused // 보다 유리한 위치에 있다 have advantage over 《a person》 ; have 《a person》 at vantage ; be in a better〔stronger〕 position than // 그는 그 여자에게 유리한 증언을 했다 He testified for her. // 시황은 파는 사람에게 유리하다 The market favors the sellers. // 어두움은 공격에 유리했다 The darkness favored the attack. // 정세는 민주당에 유리하게 전개되었다 Affairs took a turn favorable for the Democratic Party. // 나는 그가 유리한 입장에 있다고 생각한다 I think he has the inside track.
유리 流離 vagrancy ; wandering **—하다** vagabond ; wander〔roam〕 around ; rove — 개걸 roving around begging
유리 遊離 isolation ; separation ; 〖화학〗 extrication **—하다** isolate ; separate ; set free ; be isolated〔separated〕 ¶ 현실에서 유리되다 be isolated〔removed〕 from reality
—가〔전하, 자기〕 free bond〔charge, magnetism〕 — 산소 free oxygen — 상태 a free state — 세포 an isolated〔a free〕 cell — 에너지 〖물리〗 free energy — 염색체 an isolate chromosome — 원자가 free valency —채 〖화학〗 an educt —핵 a free nucleus
†**유리 琉璃** glass ; a pane (창문의) ¶ 시계의 유리 a (watch) crystal 《미》 ; a watch-glass 《영》 // 유리 자르는 칼 a glazier's diamond ; a glass cutter // 깨어진 유리 창 a window with broken panes // 유리를 끼우다 put a pane of glass 《in the window》
— 가게 a glass shop — 공장 a glass factory〔works〕 —관 a glass tube — 그릇 glassware —병 a glass bottle — 섬유 glass wool — 세공 glasswork ; glazing — 잔 a glass — 장수 a glassman ; a glazier — 제품 an article of glass —창〔문〕 a glass window〔door〕 —칼 a diamond pencil ; a cutting〔glazier's〕 diamond — 컵 a drinking glass 색— stained〔colored〕 glass 시계 — a crystal (of a watch) 안전 — safety glass ; nonshatterable glass 창— a windowpane ; broad glass 판— plate glass
유리 瑠璃 〖광물〗 lapis lazuli
—빛 sky〔bright〕 blue ; azure
유리론 唯理論 〖철학〗 rationalism
—자 a rationalist
유린 蹂躪 trampling on ; devastation ; [침해] infringement ; violation ; outrage **—하다** trample on〔down〕 ; tread underfoot ; overrun ; devastate ; [침해] infringe upon 《personal rights》 ; violate ; outrage ¶ 인권을 유린하다 infringe〔trample〕 upon human rights // 적국을 유린하다 overrun〔override, trample down〕 an enemy country // 정조를 유린하다 violate〔dishonor〕 a woman
—자 a devastator ; a harrier 인권 — an infringement upon personal rights
유림 儒林 (the class of) Confucian scholars ; the Confucians
유막 油膜 〖기계〗 an oil film
유만부동하다 類萬不同— be quite different from each other
유망 流網 a drift-net
— 어업 drift-net fishing
*****유망 有望** a bright prospect ; great promise ; rosy prospects ; hopefulness **—하다** (be) promising ; hopeful ; favorable ; have a bright future ; be full of promise ¶ 전도 유망한 청년 a promis-

ing youth ; a young man of (great) promise // 그는 장래가 유망한 사람이다 He is a man of promise.
—주(株) [주식] active stocks ; [사람] an up-and-coming (politician, player)

⁑유머 humor ¶ 유머가 풍부하다 be highly humorous ; be full of〔rich in〕 humor // 유머가 있다 have a (fine) sense of humor — 소설 a humorous novel〔story〕 — 작가 humorous writer〔novelist〕

⁑유머러스 —하다 (be) humorous

유머리스트 a humorist

유면 宥免 pardon ; forgiveness —하다 pardon ; forgive

유면계 油面計 an oil gauge

유명 幽明 [어둠과 밝음] darkness and light ; [이승과 저승] the other world and this world ¶ 유명을 달리하다 pass away ; depart from this life ; die ; join the majority // 그는 이제 유명을 달리하고 있다 He now lives in the other world.

유명 幽冥 [어둠] darkness ; gloom ; [저승] the other world ; the region of the dead ; Hades ¶ 유명객이 되다 depart from this life ; go down to the shades
—계(界) the other world ; Hades ; the region of the dead

유명 遺命 one's will ; one's last〔dying〕 injunctions〔wishes〕 ¶ 아버지의 유명에 의하여 by one's late father's will ; according to one's father's will

⁑유명 有名 —하다 (be) famous ; noted ; famed ; renowned ; celebrated ; well-known ; notorious

> 참고 **famous** 널리 세상의 주목을 끌고 화제에 올라 있다 **renowned** 무엇인가 눈에 띄는 일로써 명성을 얻고 있다 **noted** 특수한 일 (반드시 좋은 일만이 아니라도 좋다)로 널리 알려져 있다 **celebrated** 세상 사람들로부터 많은 존경과 칭찬을 받고 있다 **notorious** 악명으로 널리 알려져 있다

¶ 유명한 사람들 celebrities ; men of distinction // 유명한 소설가 a noted novelist // 유명한 소매치기 a notorious pickpocket // 남북 전쟁에서 유명한 그란트장군 General Grant of Civil War fame // 「바람과 함께 사라지다」로 유명한 마가리트 미첼 Margaret Mitchell of "Gone with the Wind" fame // 유명하게 되다 become famous ; gain distinction ; win fame // 일약 유명하게 되다 leap to fame // 그는 무엇으로 유명한가 What is he famous for ? // 그는 세계적으로 유명한 화학자다 He is a chemist of world-wide fame. /He is a world-famous〔world-renowned, world-famed〕 chemist. // 그는 유명한 작가이다 He is a celebrated author. // 그는 박학으로서 유명하다 He is famous〔noted, celebrated, famed〕 for erudition. /He has a name for his erudition〔great learning〕. // 스위스는 자연미로 매우 유명하다 Switzerland is very famous for its natural beauty. // 에디슨은 발명가로서 유명해졌다 Edison gained〔earned〕 fame as an inventor. // 그 여자는 영화계에서 유명해졌다 She rose to film fame. // 그는 어째서 그렇게 유명해졌는가 What gained him such a reputation ?

유명론 唯名論 〖철학〗 nominalism
—자 a nominalist

유명무명 有名無名 ¶ 유명무명의 사람들 somebodies and nobodies ; people high and low〔humble and famous〕

유명무실 有名無實 —하다 (be) nominal ; titular ; be in name only ¶ 유명무실한 회장 a nominal〔titular〕 chairman ; a chairman in name only // 유명무실한 지도자 a titular leader without any power // 그 회사는 유명무실하다 The company is little more than a name. // 그 조약은 이제는 유명무실하다 The treaty now has become a mere scrap of paper.

유명세 有名稅 a penalty of popularity〔greatness〕 ; a toll of being a celebrity ; *noblesse oblige* 《프》 ¶ 그것은 일종의 유명세이다 That's an instance of noblesse oblige. // 그 정도의 희생은 유명세로서 어쩔 수 없다 Your position involves that kind of sacrifice.

유명인 有名人 a celebrity ; a big-name

유명점 有名店 a famous〔well-known〕 store ; a quality store

유모 乳母 a (wet) nurse ; a nanny 《영》 ¶ 유모를 대다 put 《a baby》 to a nurse ; put〔place〕 《a baby》 under the care of a nurse // 그 아이는 유모가 기르고 있다 The baby is at nurse.
—차 a baby carriage 《미》 ; a pram 《영》

유모 柔毛 〖식물〗 pubes

유목 流木 driftwood ; drifting wood〔logs〕

*유목 遊牧 nomadism —하다 nomadize
—민 a nomadic people ; nomads — 민족 nomadic tribes — 생활 a nomadic life ; nomadism — 시대 the nomadic age

유무 有無 [존재의] existence (and nonexistence) ; presence ; [여부] yes or no ¶ 유령의 유무 the existence of a ghost // 유무상통하다 supply each other's needs ; minister to each other's wants // 출석할 의사의 유무를 묻다 ask 《a person》 whether he will be present or not

유무 遺墨 autographs of a departed person

유문 遺文 posthumous writings ; literary remains

유문 幽門 〖해부〗 the pylorus

*유물 遺物 a relic ; remains ; [유증물] a legacy ; a bequest ¶ 과거의 유물 a relic of the past // 구시대의 유물 antiquities ; a survival of olden days // 석기 시대의 유물 remains〔vestiges〕 of the Stone Age

유물 唯物 ¶ 유물적 materialistic // 유물적으로 해석하다 interpret materialistically
—론 materialism —론자 a materialist —

사관 the materialistic conception of history ; historical materialism 변증법적 —론 dialectical materialism 사적 —론 historical materialism

유미 柳眉 fair〔beautiful〕 eyebrows ; a woman's crescent eyebrows ¶ 유미를 곤두세우다 raise one's eyebrows with anger ; get into a rage

유미 乳糜 〖해부〗 chyle
—관 a lacteal (vessel)

유미 唯美 ¶ 유미의〔적〕 (a) esthetic
—주의(主義) (a) estheticism —주의자 an (a) estheticist ; an (a) esthete —파 the art-for-art school ; (a) esthetes

유민 流民 drifting〔wandering〕 people ; the migrants

유민 遊民 idle people ; idlers ; drones ; nonworkers
고등 — educated idlers

유밀과 油蜜菓 oil-and-honey pastry

유바지 油— oil-cloth trousers ; rain trousers

유박 油粕 ⇨ 깻묵

유발 乳鉢 a mortar

유발 誘發 induction —하다 induce ; cause〔arouse〕 《one's anger》 ; bring about 《an event》 ; give rise to ; set 〔touch〕 off 《a war》 ; land 《one in trouble》
— 방사〔방사능〕 〖물리〗 induced radiation〔radioactivity〕 — 변이(變異) 〖생물〗 an induced mutation

유발 遺髮 the hair of the departed 〔deceased〕

유발승 有髮僧 a monk with an unshaven head

유방 酉方 〖민속〗 the Direction of the Cock ; west

유방 乳房 the (woman's) breast

유배 流配 banishment ; exile ; condemnation of 《a criminal》 to exile —하다 banish〔exile〕 《a person to an island》 ; maroon 《a person by way of punishment》 ¶ 유배에 처하다 condemn 《a person》 to exile ; banish 《a person》 to an island ; transport 《a person》 to a penal colony
—자 an exile ; deportee ; a deported criminal —지 a place of exile

유백 乳白 ¶ 유백색의 milky
—광(光) opalescence

유별 類別 classification ; assortment —하다 classify ; assort ; grade

유별 有別 distinction ; difference —하다 《there》 be a distinction〔difference〕 《between A and B》

*__유별나다 有別—__ (be) distinctive ; different ¶ 유별난 사람 a peculiar person ; a queer man // 유별난 대조 a striking 〔sharp〕 contrast

유보 留保 reservation ⇨ 보류

유복 有福 —하다 (be) blessed ; fortunate ; lucky

*__유복 裕福__ affluence ; opulence ; prosperity —하다 (be) rich ; wealthy ; affluent ; opulent ; well-off ; well-to-do ; prosperous ¶ 유복한 사람 a well-off 〔well-to-do〕 person ; a person in cozy 〔easy〕 circumstances // 유복하게 살다 live well ; be well〔comfortably〕 off ; live in plenty〔clover, abundance〕 // 유복한 가정에 태어나다 be born rich // 유복하게 자라나다 be brought up in luxury

유복자 遺腹子 a posthumous child〔son〕

유복친 有服親 close relatives for whose death one goes into mourning

유부 油腐 《a piece of》 fried bean curd

유부간 有夫姦 adultery (of a wife)

유부 국수 油腐— noodles with fried bean curd

유부남 有夫男 a married man

유부녀 有夫女 a married woman

유불 儒佛 Confucianism and Buddhism

유비 類比 〖철학〗 analogy

유비 油肥 fertilizer made of animal fat

유비무환 有備無患 Prevention is better than cure. /An ounce of prevention is worth a pound of cure.

유빙 流氷 ⇨ 성엣장

유사 [시계의] a hair〔balance〕 spring

유사 有事 emergency ¶ 유사시에 in time〔case〕 of emergency〔need〕 ; in an emergency // 유사시에 대비하다 provide for all emergencies ; prepare for the worst

유사 遺事 reminiscences ; memories (of a dead man) ; [역사의] overlooked historic records〔remains〕

유사 流砂 quicksand ; a drift of sand〔a drifting sand〕

**__유사 類似__ similarity ; resemblance ; likeness ; analogy —하다 be similar 《to》 ; be analogous ; resemble ; be alike ; be akin 《to》

> 참고 **analogous**는 어떤 점에서 대응한다는 뜻으로서 부분적 유사를 의미하며 **similar**는 전면적인 완전한 유사를 말한다

¶ 유사한 similar ; like ; kindred ; analogous // 이 문제는 그것과 유사하다 This question is similar to that. // 그들은 성격이 유사하다 They are alike in character.
— 사건 a similar〔like〕 case — 사항 a like matter — 요법 homeopathy —점 a point of similarity〔resemblance〕 —증 an analogous case of a disease —품 an imitation ¶ 유사품에 주의하시오 Beware of imitations. — 환자 a suspected case

*__유사 有史__ ¶ 유사 이전의 prehistoric ; of prehistoric times // 유사 이래 in history ; since the dawn of history // 유사 이래의 대전쟁 the greatest war in history // 유사 이래 오늘날까지 from prehistoric times to the present

유사 뇌염 類似腦炎 a suspected encephalitis case
유산 有産 (having) property ¶ 유산의 propertied
— 계급 the propertied〔proprietary〕 classes ; property holders ; the bourgeoisie ; the bourgeois class —자 a man of property ; a propertied man ; a bourgeois
유산 乳酸 〖화학〗 lactic acid
—균 lactic ferments —염 a lactate —균 발효유 lactic-acid fermented milk (야쿠르트)
유산 流産 abortion ; miscarriage ; [실패] failure —하다 have a miscarriage〔an abortion〕; miscarry ; abort ; [실패] fail ¶ 그의 계획은 모두 유산되었다 All his plans failed〔miscarried〕. // 그 여자는 유산했다 She had an abortion〔a miscarriage〕.
인공 — artificial abortion〔miscarriage〕
*유산 遺産 an inheritance ; property〔an estate〕 left behind (by a deceased person) ; a legacy ¶ 유산을 남기다〔상속하다〕 leave〔inherit, come into, take over〕 property〔a fortune, an estate〕// 유산을 분배하다 divide 《a person's》 property // 그는 두 아이들에게 많은 유산을 남겼다 He left a large fortune to his two sons. // 나에게는 아버지의 유산이 약간 있다 My father has left me something.
— 관리 administration — 관리인 an administrator ; an administratrix (여자) — 다툼 a quarrel over an inheritance — 분할 partition of the estate — 상속 succession to property — 상속세 succession〔death, legacy〕 duty ; an inheritance tax 《미》 — 상속인 an heir〔heiress (여자)〕 to property ; an inheritor — 수취인 a legatee ; a devisee
유산 硫酸 ⇨ 황산
유산 遊山 a picnic ; an excursion ; an outing —하다 go on〔have〕 a picnic〔an excursion〕; jaunt
—객 a picnicker ; a holiday-maker ; a vacationist
유산탄 榴散彈 a shrapnel (shell)
유삼 油衫 an oilpaper raincoat ; an oilpaper coat
유상 有償 compensation ; 〖법〗 consideration
— 계약 a contract made for a consideration ; an onerous contract — 몰수 confiscation with compensation〔for value〕; onerous confiscation — 원조 credit assistance — 취득 acquisition for value — 행위 a juristic act done for consideration
유상 油狀 ¶ 유상의 oily ; like oil
유상 乳狀 ¶ 유상의 milky ; lacteal ; emulsified
—액 milky juice ; (an) emulsion ; [식물의] latex
유상무상 有象無象 all things in the universe ; [어중이떠중이] the rank and file ; the rabble ; all sorts and conditions of people
유색 有色 ¶ 유색의 colored
—성(星) a colored star — 인종 colored races ; non-white people〔nations〕 —체 〖식물〗 a chromatophore ; a chromoplast
유생 儒生 a Confucian scholar ; a student of Confucianism
유생 有生 ¶ 유생의 living
— 기원설 biogenesis —물 the animate ; life ; living beings
유생 幼生 〖동물〗 larva
— 기관 a larval organ — 생식 paedogenesis
유서 由緖 [내력] a history ; a story ¶ 유서 있는 historic ; storied // 유서 깊은 가문 a historic family ; ancient lineage // 유서 깊은 절 a historic temple // 유서 깊은 땅 a place with its old associations ; a place with a historic background // 이 소나무는 유서가 깊다 This pine tree has a history. // 그는 유서 깊은 가문에서 낳았다 He is of gentle〔good〕 birth.
*유서 遺書 a note left behind by a dead person ; a testament ; a (written) will ¶ 유서를 쓰다 make〔draw up〕 one's will〔testament〕// 유서를 남기고 죽다 die testate // 자살의 이유를 쓴 유서가 있었다 He left a note giving the cause of his suicide.
유서 類書 books of the same kind ; similar books
유석영 乳石英 〖광물〗 milky quartz
유선 有線 cable
— 방송〔중계〕 cable broadcasting〔relaying〕 —식 the wire system — 전신〔전화〕 wire telegraph〔telephone〕 — 통신 communication by wire
유선 乳腺 〖해부〗 the mammary gland
—염 mastitis
*유선형 流線型 streamline ¶ 유선형의 streamlined // 유선형 자동차 a streamlined car〔automobile〕; a streamliner
유설 謬說 [유견] a mistaken〔a wrong, an erroneous〕 remark〔statement〕; a fallacy ; a mistaken opinion ; [오보] a false report ; a wild rumor
유설 流說 ⇨ 유언(流言)
*유성 流星 a shooting star ; a meteor ¶ 야아 유성이다 There goes a shooting star !
—우(雨) a meteoric shower
*유성 遊星 a planet ¶ 유성의 planetary
대— the major planets 소— asteroid ; a planetoid ; a minor planet 외〔내〕— the exterior〔interior〕 planets 1등〔2등〕 — a primary〔secondary〕 planet
유성 有聲 ¶ 유성의 voiced
— 영화 a sound picture〔film〕; a talkie — 음 〖음성〗 a voiced〔vocal〕 sound ; voice — 음화(音化) vocalization ; voicing — 자음 a voiced consonant

유성 油性 an oily〔a greasy〕nature
— 도료 an oil paint — 페니실린 penicillin oil
유성기 留聲器 a phonograph 《미》; a gramophone 《영》 ⇨ 축음기
— 바늘 a phonograph needle ; a stylus 《*pl.* ~es, -li》; a (gramophone) needle
유세 有勢 ⇨ 유력(有力)
†**유세 遊說** stumping〔stump speaking〕《미》; electioneering〔canvassing, a campaign speech〕《영》; [선전] propaganda ; [유세 여행] a stumping tour〔trip〕; a canvassing〔an electioneering〕tour —하다 stump ; take the stump ; go electioneering〔canvassing, campaigning〕; canvass《for a candidate》 ¶ 전국을 유세하다 stump the whole country ; go about the country electioneering // 총리 자신이 유세에 나섰다 The Prime Minister himself set out on a stump tour.
— 계획 a campaign〔stumping〕program —원 a campaign〔stump〕speaker ; an electioneerer ; a stump orator ; a canvasser — 행각 a stump〔speaking〕tour
유세 誘說 coax ; inducement ; solicitation ; persuasion —하다 induce ; solicit ; persuade ¶ 사람을 유세하여 데려가다 coax a person away
유세 有稅 ¶ 유세의 taxable ; dutiable (관세) ; subject〔liable〕to duty〔taxation〕
—지(地) taxable land —품 dutiable〔taxable〕goods〔articles〕; goods subject to duty
유세포 柔細胞 『식물』 a parenchyma(tous) cell
유소 類燒 ⇨ 연소(延燒)
유소 幼少 infancy ; childhood ; a tender age —하다 (be) young ; juvenile ¶ 유소시에 in one's infancy ; in one's childhood ; in one's early days // 유소시부터 from the infant years ; from infancy〔childhood, a child〕; from the cradle
유소성 留巢性 『동물』 [새의] nidicolocity
유속 流速 the speed of a current ¶ 유속이 시속 10킬로미터로 흐르다 the current runs at the speed of 10 kilometers an hour
—계(計) a current meter ; a tachometer — 측정 tachometry
유속 流俗 prevalent customs ; convention ¶ 유속을 따르다 follow the beaten track ; swim with the stream
유속 遺俗 a custom handed down to posterity ; hereditary customs ; tradition ¶ 이것은 고대의 유속이다 This custom is of a very early origin.
유수 有數 —하다 (be) prominent ; leading ; distinguished ; foremost ¶ 그는 우리 나라 유수의 과학자이다 He is one of the foremost scientists in this country.
유수 流水 running water ; a flowing stream ¶ 세월은 정말 유수 같구나 How time flies !
유수 幽囚 confinement ; imprisonment
바빌론 — the Babylonian captivity ¶ 독방에 유수되어 in solitary confinement
유수 幼樹 a young tree〔plant〕; a sapling
유수 幽邃 —하다 (be) secluded ; sequestered ; quiet and retired ¶ 유수한 마을 a quiet and sequestered village
유수류 遊水類 『동물』 the swimmers ; aquatic birds ; Natatores (학명)
유수 정책 誘水政策 『경제』 a pump-priming policy
†**유숙 留宿** lodging ; boarding —하다 lodge《at》; put up《at》; stay《at, in》 ¶ 유숙시키다 put up《a person》at《an inn》; give《a person》accommodation《for the night》
—자 a lodger
유순 柔順 submission ; obedience ; docility —하다 (be) submissive ; obedient ; docile ; meek ; gentle ¶ 유순한 아이들 obedient children // 매우 유순하다 be as gentle〔meek〕as a lamb
유술 柔術 ⇨ 유도(柔道)
유스타키오관 —管 『해부』 the Eustachian tube ; the syrinx 《*pl.* syringes, ~es》
유스 호스텔 a youth hostel
유습 遺習 an old custom ; hereditary customs ; tradition
유시 酉時 『민속』 the Watch of the Cock ① the 10th of the 12 doublehours 《the period between 5 and 7 p. m.》 ② the 19th of the 24 hours 《5 : 30～6 : 30 p. m.》
유시 流矢 a stray arrow
유시 幼時 childhood ; infancy ¶ 유사시에 in one's early days ; in one's infancy〔childhood〕// 유시부터 from infancy〔childhood〕; from a child
유시 諭示 admonition ; instruction ; injunction ; a message —하다 admonish ; instruct ; give an instruction ¶ 대통령의 유시 a presidential instruction〔message〕
유시계 비행 有視界飛行 visual flying ; a visual flight ¶ 유시계 비행을 하다 make a visual flight ; fly VFR
유시류 有翅類 『곤충』 winged insects ; Pterygogenea (학명)
유시무종 有始無終 imperfectness ; incompleteness —하다 (be) incomplete
유시유종 有始有終 —하다 (be) constant ; never-changing ; consistent
유식 有識 scholarly attainment ; scholarship —하다 (be) learned ; educated ; intelligent ; well-informed ¶ 유식하게 말하다 speak in a refined way
— 계급 the learned〔intellectual〕class ; the intellectuals〔intelligentsia〕 —자 an intelligent〔a well-informed〕person ; men of learning ; the wise〔learned〕
유식 遊食 —하다 live in idleness ; live an idle life ; loaf ; eat the bread of idle-

ness
— 생활 an idle life ; a life of ease —자 an idler ; a loafer ; a drone ; a lounger
유신 維新 Revitalizing Reform
— 헌법 Constitution for Revitalizing Reform
유신 遺臣 a surviving retainer ; a minister of the previous dynasty
유신론 唯信論 〖신학〗 solifidianism
—자 a solifidian
†유실 遺失 a lost article —하다 lose (one's articles) ; leave behind
— 신고 a report on lost property —자 a loser ; the owner of a lost property 〔article〕
유실 流失 —하다 be swept〔carried, washed〕 away ; lose to the waves〔to the flood〕 ¶ 다리가〔집이〕 홍수에 유실되었다 A bridge〔house〕 was washed away by the flood.
— 가옥 houses carried away by the floods
유실물 遺失物 a lost article ; lost property ¶ 열차 내의 유실물 an article left〔lost〕 in a train // 수취인이 없는 유실물 an unclaimed lost article
— 광고 a lost advertisement — 보관소 a lost property office ; the lost-and-found (bureau)
유심 有心 attention ; heed ; mindfulness ; carefulness ; caution —하다 pay attention to ; give heed to ; attend to ; heed ; be mindful〔careful, cautious〕 《of》 ¶ 유심히 보다 look mindfully at 《a person》
유심론 唯心論 〖철학〗 spiritualistic ; idealism
—자 a spiritualist ; an idealist
유심적 唯心的 〖철학〗 spiritualistic ; idealistic ; mentalistic
‡유아 幼兒 a baby ; an infant
—기 babyhood — 보험 infantile insurance — 사망률 the infant mortality rate — 살해 infanticide —용 침대 a baby cot
유아 乳兒 a suckling ; a nurs(e)ling ; a baby
— 각기 infantile beriberi —식(食) baby food —원 an infant home
유아 遺兒 [유복자] a posthumous child ; [내버린] an abandoned child ; [고아] an orphan
유아 幼芽 a young sprout ; a germ
유아독존 唯我獨尊 ¶ 천상천하 유아독존 I am my own Lord throughout heaven and earth. /Holy am I alone throughout heaven and earth. /I am not any man's man, but my own.
유아등 誘蛾燈 a light trap ; a luring lamp ; an insect lamp
유아론 唯我論 〖철학〗 solipsism
유아적 唯我的 egoistic
유아차 乳兒車 a baby carriage〔buggy〕 《미》 ; a perambulator 《영》 ; a pram 《영·구》 ¶ 유아차를 밀다 wheel〔trundle〕 a perambulator〔baby carriage〕
유안 留案 a pending question〔problem〕 ; pendency ; pendant ; suspension —하다 leave 《a matter》 in abeyance ; leave 《a question》 undecided
유안 硫安 〖화학〗 ammonium sulphate
유암 乳癌 〖의학〗 cancer of the breast ; mammary cancer
유암 幽暗 gloom ; darkness —하다 (be) dark ; gloomy
유압 油壓 oil pressure
—계 an oil pressure gauge
유액 乳液 ① 〖식물〗 latex ; milky liquid 《in plants》 ② [화장품] milky lotion
유액 誘掖 leading ; guidance ; instruction —하다 lead ; guide ; help ; instruct
유야무야하다 有耶無耶— (be) noncommittal ; vague ; ambiguous ; indecisive ; slapdash ; sloppy ¶ 유야무야하게 되다 be dropped ; be buried in oblivion ; become hazy // 유야무야로 덮어두다 hush up 《a matter》 ; suppress〔smother〕 《a matter》 // 뜻하지 않은 사건으로 교섭이 유야무야하게 되어버렸다 Owing to the unforeseen incident, the negotiations were allowed to drop. // 소문은 유야무야하게 사라졌다 The rumor blew over.
유약 幼弱 —하다 (be) young and fragile
유약 柔弱 weakness ; unmanliness ; fragility ; effeminacy —하다 (be) weak ; effeminate ; fragile ; unmanly ¶ 유약한 체질 a weak constitution // 유약한 인물 a weak character ; a weak-kneed man
유약 釉藥 glaze ; enamel ¶ 유약을 칠하다 enamel ; glaze
유어 幼魚 a young fish
유어 類語 a synonym ; an associate〔a kindred〕 word
유어 游魚 fish disporting themselves ; fish at play
*유언 遺言 a will ; a testament ; one's dying wish ; [구두의] one's last words —하다 make〔leave〕 a will ; will ; express one's dying wish ¶ 유언에 의해서 by 《a person's》 will // 유언을 집행하다 administer 《a person's》 will // 유언을 남기지 않고 죽다 die intestate // 전 재산을 딸에게 물려준다는 유언을 했다 He made a will leaving〔bequeathing〕 all his estate to his daughter.
—자 a testator ; a testatrix (여자) —장 a (written) will ; a testament — 집행자 an executor
유언비어 流言蜚語 a groundless〔wild〕 rumor ; a false report ; a canard 《프》 ¶ 유언비어를 퍼뜨리는 사람 a rumormonger // 유언비어를 퍼뜨리다 spread a (sensational) rumor // 여러 가지 유언비어가 퍼지고 있다 All sorts of rumors are in the air〔noised abroad〕.
유업 乳業 the dairy industry ; dairying

유업 遺業 work left by someone ; an unfinished work ¶ 부친의 유업을 계승하다 carry on the work left unfinished by one's father
유에스 U.S. 《the United States》
유에스에이 U.S.A 《the United States of America》《미국》
*유엔 the U.N.《United Nations》 ¶ 유엔의 승인 U.N. recognition
— 가입 《the Chinese claim to》 membership of the U.N. — 경찰군 the U.N. Emergency Forces 《UNEF》 —군 방송 the Voice of the United Nations Command 《VUNC》 —군 (사령부) the U.N. Forces (Command) — 대사 the 《Korean》 Ambassador to the U.N. — 데이 United Nations〔U.N.〕 Day — 본부 the U.N. Headquarters — 사무 총장 the Secretary-General of the U.N. — 안전 보장 이사회〔국〕 the〔a member of the〕 U.N. Security Council — 총회 the U.N. General Assembly — 한국 대사 the Korean Ambassador to the U.N. — 헌장 the U.N. Charter — 회원국 a U.N. member (nation)
유역 流域 the area drained〔watered〕 by a river ; a drainage basin〔area〕 ; a river valley (큰 강의)
미시시피 — the Mississippi valley 양자강 — the Yangtze valley 한강 하류 — the lower reaches of the *Han* River
유연 柔軟 softness ; pliableness ; suppleness ; flexibleness —하다 (be) soft ; pliable ; supple ; flexible ; tender
—성 softness ; pliability ; suppleness ; pliancy ; pliableness — 체조 light gymnastics ; setting-up exercises ; cal(l)isthenics (미용 체조)
유연 悠然 composure ; self-possession ; repose ; serenity —하다 (be) calm ; composed ; serene ; reposeful ¶ 유연히 with an air〔attitude〕 of perfect composure // 그는 소란 속에서도 유연히 피리를 불고 있었다 He was quietly playing on his flute amidst the confused noises.
유연 油煙 ¶ lamp soot〔smoke〕 ; carbon〔smoke〕 black
유연 類緣 family relation ; 〚생물〛 affinity
유연탄 有煙炭 bituminous〔soft〕 coal
유열 愉悅 joy ; mirth ; gaiety
유영 游泳 swimming —하다 swim ; sail ; [처신] get along ¶ 그는 관계에서 유영하는 법을 알고 있다 He knows how to get along in officialdom.
— 기관 〚동물〛 a natatorial〔swimming〕 organ — 동물 nekton —술 the art of swimming
유예 猶豫 postponement ; deferment ; grace (지불의) ; extension 《of time》 ; delay (지연) ; hesitation (주저) ; [집행유예] a respite ; a reprieve (사형의) —하다 put off ; postpone ; allow〔grant〕 delay〔grace〕 ; defer 《action》 ; give 《a day's》 grace ; hesitate ¶ 유예없이 without (a moment's) delay ; without hesitation
— 기간 [수표의 지불·보험료 불입의] a grace period 《미》 ; days of grace 《영》 ; [채무 이행의 법정] a legal delay — 미결 postponement and suspension 지불 — indulgence ; a grace of payment 집행 — a stay of execution ; a reprieve ; suspension of sentence
†유용 有用 usefulness ; use ; utility ; serviceableness —하다 (be) useful ; valuable ; serviceable ; needed ; be of use ¶ 유용한 사람〔물건〕 a useful man〔thing〕 // 국가에 유용한 인물 a man useful to the state ; a man of service to the country // 돈을 유용하게 쓰다 make the best use of one's money
— 가격 〚경제〛 value in use — 식물 a useful plant
유용 流用 diversion ; appropriation ; misappropriation —하다 divert ; apply ; use 《money》 for other purposes ; appropriate ; misappropriate (부정하게) ¶ 돈을 빚 갚는 데 유용하다 apply money to the payment of a debt // 돈을 다른 데에 유용하다 divert the money to some other purpose // 공금을 유용하다 misappropriate〔make use of〕 government funds
유용종 乳用種 dairy cattle ⇨ 젖소
유우 乳牛 milch cow ; dairy cattle 《집합적》
유원 悠遠 eternity ⇨ 유구
**유원지 遊園地 an amusement park ; a public garden ; a pleasure ground ; a resort
†유월 六月 June
유월 流月 the 6th lunar month
유월 榴月 the 5th lunar month
유월절 踰越節 the Passover
유위 有爲 capability ; ability ; usefulness ; efficiency —하다 (be) capable ; able ; efficient ; promising (유망한) ¶ 유위지사 a man of ability〔great promise〕
유유낙낙하다 唯唯諾諾— do quite willingly〔readily, submissively, meekly〕 ; work at 《a person's》 beck and call
유유도일하다 悠悠度日— live idly〔leisurely〕 ; idle away one's time〔life〕
유유범범 悠悠泛泛 —하다 (be) leisurely ; slow ; tedious
유유상종 類類相從 —하다 Each follows its own kind. /Birds of a feather flock together.
유유아 乳幼兒 infants ; babies
유유자적 悠悠自適 living in easy〔comfortable〕 retirement ; living free from worldly cares
유유하다 悠悠— ① [한가하다] (be) leisurely ; slow ; deliberate ; [침착하다] quiet ; calm ; self-composed ¶ 유유히 quietly ; calmly ; in a leisurely way ; deliberately ; slowly // 유유히 담배를 피우

다 smoke serenely〔at ease〕// 유유히 날을 보내다 pass one's time in idleness ; idle away one's time // 우리는 적을 앞에 두고 유유히 식사를 했다 We sat down composedly to a hearty meal in the face of the enemy.
② [아득하다] (be) boundless ; endless ; vast ; eternal ¶ 유유한 천지 the immense universe

유음 溜飮 〖의학〗 pyrosis ; water brash ; sour stomach

유의 有意 voluntariness ; willingness ; intention **—하다** (be) voluntary ; willing ; intent

유의 油衣 ⇨ 유삼(油衫)

유의 留意 keeping in mind ; heed ; attention ; regard **—하다** bear〔keep〕in mind ; heed ; be mindful of ; regard ; mind ; care about ; pay regard〔attention〕to ; take heed〔account〕of ¶ 유의해서 듣다 hear attentively〔with attention, with care〕// 유의하지 않다 give no heed to ; pay no attention〔regard〕to // 타인의 이익에 유의하지 않다 take no notice of other's interests // 그것은 우리들이 유의할 점이다 It is a point which deserves our attention.
— 사항 matters to be attended to

유의범 有意犯 [범죄] a deliberate〔an intentional〕offense ; [죄인] a deliberate〔an intentional〕offender

유의유식 遊衣遊食 ⇨ 무위(—도식)

***유익 有益 —하다** (be) profitable ; beneficial ; lucrative ; [교훈이 되다] instructive ; edifying ; wholesome ; [유용하다] useful ; serviceable ¶ 유익하게 usefully ; serviceably ; to good advantage // 유익한 교훈 an instructive〔edifying〕discourse〔lesson〕// 유익한 경험 a useful experience // 가장 유익하게 시간을 쓰다 lay out one's time to most advantage ; make the best use of one's time // 개는 인간에게 유익한 동물이다 A dog is a useful animal to a man.

유인 幽人 a hermit ; a recluse
— 생활 a retired life

유인 有人 ¶ 유인의 piloted《aircraft》; manned《spaceship》
— 위성 a manned satellite

***유인 誘引** temptation ; allurement ; inducement ; enticement ; seduction **—하다** tempt ; allure ; lure ; seduce ; decoy ; induce ; entice

> [참고] **lure** 상대방의 욕망을 자극하여 나쁜 일에 이끌어 넣다 **allure** 쾌락을 얻기 위해서 사람을 유인하다 **tempt** 판단력이나 분별심을 잃어버리게 할 만큼 강력한 유인력을 말한다 **decoy** 꾸밈이나 속임수로 덫에 걸리도록 유인하다 **entice** 상대방의 욕망이나 희망을 자극하여 또는 설득에 의하여 유인하다

¶ 유인해 내다 lure《a person》out // 나쁜 짓을 하도록 유인하다 tempt《a person》into evil doing ; lead《a person》astray

유인 誘因 a proximate〔contributing〕cause ; an (immediate) occasion ; a motive ; an inducement ¶ 전쟁의 유인 the cause of war // 유인이 되다 be the cause of ; occasion ; cause ; lead (up) to ; induce

유인 流人 an exile

유인물 油印物 printed〔mimeographed〕matter

유인성 柔靭性 flexibility ; elasticity ¶ 유인성이 있다 be flexible〔elastic〕

유인원 類人猿 an anthropoid (ape)

유일 酉日 〖민속〗 the Day of the Rooster

†**유일 唯一 —하다** (be) unique ; single ¶ 유일무이한 the one and only ; unique ; peerless // 유일한 벗 one's only〔sole〕friend ; the one and only friend one has // 유일의 상속인 the sole heir // 유일의 방책 the only measure left ; one's only resource // 딸의 행복이 내 생애의 유일한 목적이다 The sole object I have in life is to see my girl happy.
—신교 monotheism ; Unitarianism

유임 留任 remaining in office **—하다** remain〔continue〕in office ¶ 유임을 권고하다 advise〔urge〕《a person》to stay in office // 학생들은 교장의 유임 운동을 시작했다 The students started a movement to have their principal remain in office.

유입 流入 (an) inflow ; (an) influx ; incoming **—하다** flow in ; stream in ; come in ¶ 외자의 유입 an inflow〔influx〕of foreign capital

유자 幼者 children ; infants

유자 遺子 ⇨ 유복자

유자 柚子 a citron
—나무 the citron (tree)

유자 遊資 〖경제〗 idle〔unemployed〕capital〔funds〕

유자 儒者 a Confucian (scholar) ; a student of Confucianism

유자격자 有資格者 a (properly) qualified person《for a post》; an eligible ; the qualified《총칭》

유자생녀 有子生女 —하다 bring forth〔give birth to〕many children ; have many children〔sons and daughters〕

유자형 U字形 ¶ 유자형의 U-shaped
— 볼트〔관〕 a U bolt〔tube〕 **— 커브** a hairpin curve〔bent〕

유작 遺作 posthumous works

유장 乳漿 whey ; plasma ; milk serum

유장 悠長 —하다 ① [지리하다] (be) long ; lengthy ; tedious ② [성미·태도가] (be) leisurely ; slow ; deliberate

유저 遺著 a posthumous work〔book〕¶ A씨의 유저 writings of the late Mr. A

유적 遺跡 remains ; relics ; ruins ¶ 로마의 유적 the ruins of Rome // 고대 문명의 유적 the remains〔relics〕of ancient civi-

lization // 역사상의 유적 a place of historic interest ; a historic site〔relic〕// 유적을 방문하다 visit a place of historic interest
유적 幽寂 ―하다 (be) sequestered ; quiet ¶ 유적한 경지 solitude // 유적한 곳 a sequestered place
유적 流賊 a wandering bandit ; a marauder
유적 流謫 exile ; banishment
유전 遺傳 heredity ; inheritance ; hereditary transmission ―하다 be inherited ; be hereditary ; run in the blood 〔family〕; be transmitted 《from parents》 ¶ 유전성의 hereditary ; of hereditary nature ; inherited ; transmissible // 유전에 의한 범죄자 a criminal from heredity // 방사능의 유전적 영향 genetic effects of radioactivity 《on human beings》// 병을 자손에게 유전하다 transmit a disease to one's children // 부모로부터 병이 유전되다 inherit a disease from one's parents // 매독은 유전된다 Syphilis is hereditary. // 저 집안은 정신병이 유전한다 There is hereditary insanity in the family. /Insanity runs in the family.
―론 hereditism ―론자 a hereditarrian ―법칙 the law of heredity ―병 a hereditary disease ; a constitutional disease ―자 a gene ―학 the study of heredity ; genetics ― 형질〔특성, 성향〕 an inherited〔a hereditary〕 character〔quality, tendency〕
유전 油田 an oil field ; a petroleum field ; oil land
― 탐사〔개발〕 oil exploration
유전 流傳 spread ; circulation ; propagation ; dissemination ―하다 be widespread ; spread abroad
유전 流轉 [유랑] vagrancy ; wandering ; [변전] vicissitude ; 〖불교〗 transmigration ; metempsychosis ―하다 wander about ; rove ; roam ; transmigrate (영혼이) ¶ 만물은 유전한다 All things are set in motion and flow. /Impermanency is the nature of things.
유전 誘電 induced electricity
― 물질 a dielectric substance ― 용량 inductive capacity ―자(子) an inductor ―체 a dielectric (substance)
유전기 流電氣 〖전기〗 galvanic〔voltaic〕 electricity
유전스 〖상업〗 usance
유정 有情 warm〔tender〕-heartedness ; sympathetic〔compassionate〕 feelings ; sentience ―하다 be sentient ; warmhearted ; humane ¶ 천지 유정 There is feeling in everything in the universe.
유정 遺精 〖의학〗 involuntary emission of semen ; nocturnal pollution ; wet dreams 《속》
유정 油井 an oil well ; a petroleum well
유제 類題 similar questions
유제 遺制 hereditary system〔institution〕
유제 乳劑 an emulsion
석유 ― petroleum emulsion
유제 油劑 an oily medicine ; an ointment
유제 동물 有蹄動物 an ungulate
유제류 有蹄類 〖동물〗 Ungulata (학명)
유제품 乳製品 a milk product ; dairy products
유조 留鳥 a resident (bird)
유조 遊詔 the king's will ; the king's last wish〔request〕
유조 有助 ―하다 (be) helpful ; useful beneficial
유조 油槽 an oil tank
―선 a〔an oil〕 tanker ; an oiler ―차 a tank car ; an oil car
유족 遺族 a surviving〔bereaved〕 family ; the survivors ¶ 전사자의 유족 the war bereaved // 유족은 처와 두 딸이다 He is survived by his wife and two daughters.
― 보험 survivorship insurance ― 부조 aid to a surviving family ; an allowance to a bereaved family ; survivor's benefits ― 연금 a survivor's pension〔annuity〕 전사 ― the war bereaved
유족하다 裕足― (be) abundant ; well off ; sufficient ; rich ¶ 유족하게 살다 be well off ; live in affluence〔opulence〕 ; live〔be〕 in easy circumstances
유종 有終 having an end ; consummation ―하다 be completed〔finished〕 ; (be) consummate ¶ 유종의 미 crowning glory ; consummation 《of wisdom and virtue》 ; swan song // 유종의 미를 거두다 bring 《a thing》 to a successful conclusion ; crown 《a thing》 with perfection
유종 乳腫 〖의학〗 mastitis
**유죄 有罪 guiltiness ; culpability ; criminality ―하다 be found guilty ; (be) culpable ¶ 유죄를 선고하다 convict 《a person》 of crime ; give 《a person》 the verdict of guilty // 유죄를 인정하다 plead guilty // 유죄라고 인정할 만한 증거가 있다 There is enough evidence to convict him.
―인 a guilty person ― 판결 a judgement of guilty ; a conviction ¶ 유죄 판결을 받다 be convicted ; be found guilty ― 혐의자 a suspected criminal
유죄 流罪 exile ; transportation
―인 an exile
유주 幼主 [임금] a young emperor 〔king〕 ; [주인] a young master〔lord〕
유주무량 有酒無量 unlimitedness in drinking capacity
유주지물 有主之物 an article〔object〕 having an owner〔a possessor〕
유즙 乳汁 milk ; [식물의] latex
유증 類症 similar diseases〔cases〕
유증 遺贈 〖법〗 [동산의] bequest ; bequeathal ; [부동산의] devise ―하다 leave〔give〕 《a thing to a person》 by will ; bequeath (동산) ; devise (부동산) ¶ 그는 조카에게 재산을 유증했다 He left

his nephew a fortune by will.
—물 a bequest ; a legacy —자 a legator ; a devisor 피 —자 a legatee ; a devisee
유지 油紙 oilpaper ; oiled paper
유지 遺志 one's dying〔last〕 wishes〔will〕 ; the desire of a deceased person ¶ 아버지의 유지를 받들어 in pursuance of〔in obedience to〕 one's father's will // 유지를 따르다 follow up the intention of the deceased
유지 遺址 an old site ; remains ; relics ; ruins
†유지 維持 maintenance ; preservation ; upkeep ; sustenance (생계의) ; support —하다 maintain ; keep up ; preserve ; hold (up) ; support ¶ 건강을 유지하다 maintain one's health // 지위를 유지하다 maintain one's position // 사회 질서를 유지하다 preserve the order of society // 체면을 유지하다 maintain one's dignity save face // 평화를 유지하다 maintain〔keep〕 peace // 이 학교는 기부금에 의해 유지되고 있다 The school is entirely supported by subscriptions. // 이 집을 유지하는 데에 연 50만원이 든다 This house costs half a million *won* a year in upkeep〔to keep〕. // 그 학교는 어떻게 유지되고 있는가 How is the school kept up ? // 집안일뿐만 아니라 직업을 유지하기를 바란다면 남편 도움이 필요하다 You need your husband's cooperation if you want to hold down a job as well as keep house.
—비 upkeep〔maintenance〕 expenses〔cost〕 ; (the cost of) maintenance — 위원회 the board of maintenance〔supporters〕 —자 a keeper ; a maintainer ; a supporter — 자금 a maintenance fund — 책 a measure for maintenance
유지 油脂 oil(s) and fat(s)
— 공업 the oil and fat (manufacturing) industry — 식물 an oil plant
유지 乳脂 cream (in milk)
— 비누 curd soap
유지 有志 having intention〔an interest〕 ; having sympathy〔public spirit〕 ; [사람] an interested person〔party〕 ; a volunteer ; a supporter ; a sympathizer —하다 (be) voluntary ; interested ; sympathetic ¶ 유지들에 의해서 기금이 마련되었다 Funds have been collected by people interested. // 유지의 참석을 환영함 All interested persons〔parties〕 are welcome to attend.
— 단체 a voluntary organization — 일동 all the persons concerned 지방 — those who work for the good of the local community ; public-spirited men of the locality
유지질 類脂質 〖화학〗 lipoid
유직 有職 having a job ; being employed
—자 the employed
유진무퇴 有進無退 advance without retreat —하다 be ever-advancing
유질 流質 〖법〗 foreclosure ; mortgage ; forefeit —하다 be foreclosed ; forfeit a pawn
— 공매 처분 a foreclosure sale —물 a forfeited pawn
유착 癒着 〖의학〗 adhesion ; healing (up) ; conglutination ; union —하다 heal up ; adhere ; knit ¶ 상처가 완전히 유착되었다 The wound has completely healed〔closed〕 up.
— 불능 [골절의] nonunion 늑막 — 〖의학〗 pleural adhesion
유착하다 [크다] (be) very big ; huge ; colossal
유찬 流竄 ⇨ 유배(流配)
유찬 類纂 a classified compilation in book form
법규 — a classified compilation of laws
유창 the longer intestine of an ox used for soup
*유창하다 流暢— (be) fluent ; flowing ; smooth ; facile ¶ 유창하게 fluently ; with fluency ; smoothly // 유창한 문장 a flowing〔an easy〕 style // 중국어를 유창하게 말하다 speak fluent Chinese ; speak Chinese fluently〔with fluency〕 // 그는 말이 유창하다 He is a fluent〔ready〕 speaker. // 그의 영어가 유창한 데 놀랐다 I was surprised at the fluency with which he spoke English.
유채 油菜 〖식물〗 a rape
유체 流涕 shedding tears —하다 shed tears ; weep
유체 有體 ¶ 유체의 material ; physical ; tangible ; 〖법률〗 corporeal
— 동산 corporeal movables —물 material things〔objects〕 — 자산 tangible assets〔property〕 ; tangibles ; 〖법〗 corporeal property
유체 流體 a fluid
— 공학 hydraulic engineering — 동력학 hydrodynamics ; fluid dynamics — 압력 fluid pressure — 역학 hydromechanics ; fluid mechanics — 정력학(精力學) hydrostatics
유체스럽다 《one's behavior》 be affected ; (be) priggish ; uncommon ; unusual
유촉 遺囑 entrusting 《a person》 with everything after one's death ; leaving last instructions〔requests〕 —하다 entrust with everything after one's death ; leave a last request
*유추 類推 analogy ; analogical inference ; reasoning by analogy ; analogism —하다 analogize ; reason by analogy ; infer ¶ 유추적 analogic(al) // 일부로써 전체를 유추하다 analogize the whole out of a part
—법 analogy — 진단 〖의학〗 analogism — 추리 reasoning by analogy ; analogism — 해석 analogical interpretation

유축 농업 有畜農業 agriculture with livestock raising as major side line
†유출 流出 outflow ; efflux ; effluence ; drain ; emanation ; extrusion —하다 flow out ; run out ; drain out ¶ 금의 유출 an outflow〔a drain〕 of gold // 금이 유출되다 Gold flows out of the country.
—구 an outlet(물의) ; a debouchment (하천의) —률 the rate of flow —물 effluence ; an emanation ; 〖화학〗 distillate 두뇌 — the brain drain ¶ 과학자들의 미국으로의 두뇌 유출 the brain drain of scientists to America
유충 幼蟲 a larva 《*pl.* -vae》 ¶ 유충의 larval
—기 the larval stage
유취 類聚 grouping in classes〔species〕 ; collecting according to species ; assortment —하다 group in classes ; assort ; classify
유취 乳臭 ⇨ 젖내
유취 만년 遺臭萬年 —하다 leave one's ill fame to posterity
유층 油層 an oil stratum ; a pool of oil
*유치 幼稚 —하다 (be) childish ; puerile ; [미숙하다] crude ; raw ; immature ; primitive ¶ 유치한 생각 a childish〔crude, an infantile〕 idea // 지능이 유치하다 be young in wisdom // 이 나라의 공업은 아직도 유치하다 The industry in this country is still primitive〔in its infancy〕.
유치 誘致 inducement ; luring ; enticement ; allurement —하다 induce ; bring about ; lure ; entice ; attract ¶ 외자를 유치하다 attract foreign capital // 외국인 관광객의 유치책을 강구하다 try to attract foreign tourists
유치 留置 [억류] detention ; custody ; lockup —하다 detain ; keep 《a person》 in custody ; hold ; lock up ; remand ¶ 유치당하다 be detained ; be locked up // 경찰서에 유치하다 take 《a person》 into police custody ; detain 《a person》 at a police station // 그는 조사받기 위해 유치되어 있다 He is held (in custody) for examination.
—권 〖법〗 a lien —료 demurrage — 우편 a poste restante 《프》 —장 a house of detention〔custody〕 ; a detention room ; a police cell ; a lockup — 전보 telegraphe restante 《프》 불법 — 〖법〗 detainer
유치 乳齒 a milk tooth ; the first set of teeth ; one's baby teeth
*유치원 幼稚園 a kindergarten ; an infant school 《영》 ; a preschool 《미》
— 보모 a kindergarten teacher ; a kindergartener — 원아 a kindergarten pupil ; a kindergartener
유침 油侵 oil immersion
—관 an oil-immersed tube〔pipe〕
유칼리나무 a eucalyptus 《*pl.* ~es, -ti》
*유쾌 愉快 pleasure ; delight ; cheerfulness ; enjoyment ; merriment —하다 (be) cheerful ; pleasant ; delightful ; enjoyable ; joyful ; jovial ; happy ; gay ¶ 유쾌하게 pleasantly ; delightfully ; happily ; merrily ; cheerfully // 유쾌한 여행 a pleasant trip // 유쾌한 기질 a pleasant〔cheerful〕 disposition // 유쾌한 사람 a jolly 〔cheerful, pleasant〕 fellow // 유쾌한 이야기 an exhilarating story // 유쾌히 지내다 live happily // 유쾌하게 하루를 보내다 pass the day pleasantly ; have a very enjoyable day // 유쾌하게 이야기를 나누다 have a pleasant talk with 《a person》 // 유쾌하게 웃다 smile happily ; laugh cheerfully // 오늘 밤은 참 유쾌했습니다 We have enjoyed the evening very much. /We have had a very good〔fine〕 time this evening. // 너하고 이야기하고 있으면 참으로 유쾌하다 It is a pleasure to talk with you.
유클리드 Euclid (그 B. C. 300년경)
(비)— 기하학 (non-) Euclidian geometry
유타 遊惰 sloth ; indolence ; laziness
유탄 榴彈 a shell
— 발사기 a grenade launcher —포 〖군사〗 a howitzer
유탄 流彈 a stray bullet〔shot〕 ; a ricochetted bullet ¶ 유탄에 맞다 be struck by a stray bullet
유탈 遺脫 omission (of type) —하다 get〔be〕 omitted
유탕 遊蕩 dissipation ; profligacy ; riotous living ; debauchery —하다 be dissipated ; lead a dissipated〔dissolute〕 life ; be dissolute ; be profligate ¶ 유탕으로 재산을 탕진하다 run through one's fortune in riotous living
— 문학 pornographic literature —아 a rake ; a dissipated person
유태 猶太 Judea ¶ 유태(사람)의 Judaic(al) ; Jewish
—교 Judaism — 민족 the Jews ; Hebrew people ¶ 유태 민족주의 Zionism —인 a Jew ; a Hebrew ¶ 유태인 거리 a ghetto // 유태인 교회 a synagogue
유태 성숙 幼態成熟 〖동물〗 neoteny ; neoteinia
유택 幽宅 a grave ; one's final resting place
유턴 [자동차의] a U-turn —하다 take 〔do, make〕 a U-turn
*유토피아 (a) Utopia ¶ 유토피아의 Utopian
*유통 流通 circulation ; flowing ; currency ; negotiation (어음의) —하다 circulate ; flow ¶ 화폐의 유통 the circulation of money // 공기의 유통 the ventilation of air // 유통하고 있다 (화폐가) be in circulation // 신화폐를 유통시키다 put new coins in〔into〕 circulation // 공기의 유통이 좋다 be well ventilated // 이 방은 공기의 유통이 나쁘다 This room is poorly ventilated.

— 기구 distributive machinery —량 the amount of current money (화폐의) —성 negotiability (어음의) — 속도 [통화의] the rapidity〔velocity〕 of circulation ; circulating velocity — 시장 a circulation market — 어음 a negotiable bill — 자본 circulating〔floating〕 capital — 증권 a negotiable security〔instrument〕 — 질서 distribution order ¶ 유통 질서의 확립 establishment of order in the circulation 《of》 — 혁명 a distribution revolution — 화폐 current money ☞ ❰p. 1657❱

†유파 流派 a school ; a sect

유폐 幽閉 confinement ; incarceration —하다 confine ; shut up ; incarcerate ¶ 유폐되어 있다 be in confinement

유폐 流幣 a current abuse〔evil〕 ; a deep-rooted evil

유포 油布 oiled cotton cloth

*유포 流布 circulation ; spread ; dissemination ; propagation —하다 circulate ; put in circulation ; spread ; disseminate ; get abroad〔afloat〕 ; be widespread ¶ 유포되고 있다 be in circulation ; be current ; be prevalent // 허위의 풍설을 유포하다 circulate〔disseminate〕 false reports // 풍설을 유포하다 set a rumor afloat // 소문이 유포되고 있다 There is a rumor abroad. // 기괴한 풍설이 유포되고 있다 Extraordinary reports are in the air.

유표 遊標 a vernier
—자 a vernier scale

유표 有表 —하다 (be) striking ; conspicuous ; outstanding ; remarkable

유품 遺品 an article left by the departed

유풍 遺風 a custom〔usage〕 handed down from the preceding generations ; an old custom ; hereditary customs ; tradition ¶ 조상의 유풍 a custom handed down by one's forefathers // 봉건 시대의 유풍 a relic of feudalism // 그의 유풍을 따르는 사람이 많다 Quite a few people follow in his footsteps. // 거기에는 봉건 시대의 유풍이 아직도 남아 있다 Some customs of the feudal age still survive there.

유프라테스강 —江 the Euphrates River

유피아이 [미국의 통신사] UPI ; the United Press International

유피화 有被花 〖식물〗 a chlamydeous flower

유하다 柔— (be) soft ; mild ; genial ; amiable ; benign ; carefree ¶ 유한 성질 a placid temper ; a genial disposition

유하다 留— stay ; stop ; put up ; lodge ¶ 여관에 유하다 stop〔put up〕 at a hotel // 부산에서 하룻밤을 유하다 stay in *Pusan* overnight

유학 留學 studying abroad —하다 study abroad ; go abroad for study ¶ 미국 유학중에 during one's stay in the U. S. as a student // 국비로 유학하다 study abroad at government expenses // 다년간 해외에서 유학하다 study abroad for a number of years // 유학을 마치고 귀국하다 return home from 《one's》 studying abroad // 오늘날 미국은 학생 유학의 중심지이다 The United States of America is now the educational Mecca of the world.
—생 a student studying abroad ¶ 외국인 유학생 a foreign student // 재미 한국 유학생 Korean students studying in America

유학 遊學 studying away from 《one's》 home (town) —하다 prosecute one's studies〔study〕 away from home ¶ 해외에 유학하다 go abroad for study

유학 儒學 Confucianism
—자 a Confucianist ; a Confucian scholar

유한 有限 limitedness ; finiteness —하다 (be) limited ; finite
— 급수 a finite series — 법화 limited legal tender — 소수 a finite decimal — 수 a finite number — 직선 a finite straight line — 책임 limited liability — 회사 a limited company

유한 有閑 (having) leisure ; spare time —하다 (be) leisurely ; leisured ¶ 나는 유한 신사 노릇할 만한 여유가 없다 I can not afford to be a gentleman of leisure.
— 계급 the leisure(d) class — 부인 a leisured〔an idle rich〕 woman ; a woman of leisure

유한 流汗 perspiration ; sweat

유한 遺恨 grudge ; rancor ; malice ; enmity ¶ 유한을 품다 owe 《a person》 a grudge ; have a spite〔grudge〕 against 《a person》 // 유한을 갚다 pay off one's old scores ; get even with 《a person》 // 그에게 아무런 유한도 없다 I bear him no grudge.

유합 癒合 ⇨ 유착

유해 遺骸 the remains of the dead ⇨ 유골

⁑유해 有害 harmfulness ; noxiousness ; injuriousness —하다 (be) injurious ; harmful ; noxious ; bad ¶ 건강에 유해하다 be injurious to one's health ; be bad for health // 풍기상 유해하다 be prejudicial〔destructive〕 to public morals // 사회에 유해하다 be detrimental to society // 심신에 유해하다 be harmful both to mind and body // 유해 무익하다 be more injurious than beneficial ; do more harm than good
— 곤충 noxious insects —물 a hazardous article ; a harmful object — 식품 poisonous〔contaminated〕 food (stuff)

†유행 流行 fashion ; vogue ; prevalence (질병의) ; [대유행] craze ; fad (일시적) ; rage —하다 be in fashion ; be in vogue ; be popular ; be widely liked ; prevail ; come into fashion〔vogue〕 ¶ 새 유행 a new fashion // 최신 유행 the latest fashion ; the latest fad〔rage〕 // 일시적인 유행 a (mere) passing vogue // 유행을 따르다 follow the fashion // 유행에 뒤지다 be

유 통·판 매

유통업 distribution industry; merchandising **유통망[경로]** distribution channel [network, system] **시장 조사** market research **시장 점유율** market share **독점 시장** monopoly market **과점 시장(寡占市場)** oligopoly market **카르텔** cartel **카르텔 행위** cartel activity **판매망** sales network[channel, organization] **출하** shipment **창고업** warehousing industry **냉동 트럭** refrigerator truck; refrigerated truck **냉동 창고** cold storage warehouse **체인점** chain store **독점 판매권** franchise[franchisement] system **할인 매점** discount house **백화점의 각 매장** department store counter **매장 감독** [백화점 등의] floorworker; floormanager; shopwalker 《영》 **일용잡화 식료품점** convenience store **상표 맹신** brand loyalty **특매품** loss leader **산지 직판** [농산물] Fresh From The Farm! / Right Off The Farm! **공장 직송** Direct (Shipment) From The Factory! / Right Out Of The Factory! / No Middleman! **고압적 판매** hard sell **충동 구매** impulse buying **특매 상품** [백화점의 손님 끌기용] loss leader

behind the fashion // 유행에 뒤지지 않도록 하다 keep up with the fashion ; keep pace with the current style // 대유행이다 be all〔quite〕 the go〔rage〕 // 유행의 첨단을 걷다 lead〔set〕 the fashion // 최신 유행의 구두를 신다 wear the latest thing in shoes // 이 모자가 유행하고 있다〔유행하기 시작했다〕 This hat is in fashion〔has come into fashion〕. // 짧은 치마가 (대) 유행이다 Short skirts are (all) the vogue. // 요즈음은 작은 시계를 차는 것이 유행이다 It is fashionable to wear small watches now. // 한국에서는 사교춤이 대유행이다 The fad of dancing sweeps Korea. // 유행은 반복한다 Fashion repeats itself. // 독감이 전국에 유행하고 있다 Influenza is prevailing throughout the country. // 콜레라의 유행 때문에 집회가 연기되었다 Owing to the prevalence of cholera, the meeting was postponed. // 쉽게 유행을 따르는 것 같은데요 You're easily swept along by fads, aren't you? // 그것은 지금 젊은이들 사이에서 대유행이다 That's all the rage among young people. // 올해에는 롱스커트가 유행할 것 같다 This year it looks like long skirts are in. // 나로서는 미니스커트가 다시 유행하기를 바란다 Speaking for myself, I'd like miniskirts to make a comeback. // 짧은 머리가 유행이고 긴 머리는 유행이 지났다 Short hair is in, and long hair is out. // 미국에서는 금년 여름에 미니스커트가 유행이다 In the states, miniskirts are the thing this summer. // 1960년대에 미니스커트가 세계적으로 유행했었다 Miniskirts were the craze in the 1960's all over the world.

—어 a word〔phrase〕 in fashion〔vogue〕; a word〔phrase〕 of the minute ; a word〔phrase〕 on every-body's lips ¶ 재건이라는 말이 유행어가 되었다 Reconstruction was the word on everybody's lips. **— 작가** a popular writer

유행 遊行 traveling around **—하다** travel around ; make a tour

유행가 流行歌 a popular song
— 가수 a singer of popular songs ; a popular song singer ; a vocalist ; a crooner

유행병 流行病 an epidemic ; a pestilence ¶ 유행병이 발생하다 an epidemic rages〔breaks out〕

유행성 감기 流行性感氣 influenza ; flu 《속》 ¶ 유행성 감기에 걸리다 be seized with influenza ; have an attack of influenza // 유행성 감기가 퍼지고 있다 There is an epidemic of influenza. // 유행성 감기는 일종의 세균성 질환이다 Influenza is a kind of virus disease.

유행성 뇌염 流行性腦炎 epidemic encephalitis

유행지 流行地 an infected district〔area〕 ¶ 콜레라의 유행지 a cholera-infected district

유향 乳香 frankincense

유현 幽玄 profundity ; abstruseness ; occultness **—하다** (be) profound ; abstruse ; occult ; recondite

유현 儒賢 a Confucian sage

***유혈 流血** bloodshed ; shedding of blood ¶ 유혈의 참사 (an affair of) bloodshed ; a sanguinary accident // 유혈로 끝나다 result in bloodshed

유혈암 油頁岩 oil shale

유형 有形 materiality ; concreteness **—하다** (be) concrete ; material ; corporeal ; tangible
— 무역 visible trade **— 문화재** tangible cultural properties **—물** a material〔concrete〕 object **— 자본** a corporeal capital **— 자산** tangible〔material〕 assets **— 재산** corporeal property **—체** a material body

유형 流刑 banishment ; exile ¶ 유형에 처하다 condemn 《a person》 to exile ; banish ; transport

—수 a transported criminal ; an exile ; a deportee —지 a penal colony〔settlement〕; a place of exile
*유형 類型 a (similar) type ¶ 유형적인 typical
—학 〖심리〗 typology
유형 幼形 〖생물〗 the juvenile form
유형 類形 〖생물〗 analogy ; homoplasy
유형 동물 紐形動物 〖동물〗 Nemertinea ; Nemertea (총칭·학명)
유형무형 有形無形 material(ity) and immaterial(ity) ; visibility and invisibility ¶ 유형 무형으로 그 사람의 도움을 받았다 I received material and moral support from him. /I was supported by him both materially and spiritually.
**유혹 誘惑 temptation ; allurement ; enticement ; seduction —하다 tempt ; lure ; allure ; seduce ; entice ; invite ; attract

> 참고 **allure**는 무엇인가 좋은 것을 미끼로 「유혹하다」라는 뜻이거니와 때로는 유해한 일로 「속여서 유혹하다」의 뜻이 되는 경우도 있다 **lure**는 분명히 나쁜 일로 「속여서 유혹하다」의 뜻 **entice**는 「감쪽같이 속여서 (나쁜 일로) 유혹하다」 **invite**는 사람에 대해서 말할 경우 「의례적으로 초청하다」의 뜻 **attract**나 **tempt**는 「매력을 갖고 유혹하다」의 뜻

¶ 도시의 유혹 the allurements〔temptations〕 of a big city // 바다의 유혹 the lure〔call〕 of the sea // 유혹을 견디다 resist〔withstand〕 temptation // 유혹을 이겨내다 overcome〔get the better of〕 a temptation // 유혹과 싸우다 wrestle with a temptation ; fight〔struggle〕 against a temptation // 유혹에 지다 succumb〔yield〕 to temptation // 유혹에 빠지기 쉽다 be easily led astray ; be easily overcome by temptation
—물 a temptation ((of a drink)) ; a lure ; an invitation ((to death)) ; a decoy —자 a tempter ; an enticer ; a seducer
유혼 幽魂 the spirit of the dead ; a departed soul
유화 油畫 an oil painting〔color〕
—가 an oil painter —구 [채료] oil paints ; oil colors ; oils — 초상 a portrait (painted) in oils ; an oil portrait
유화 柔和 gentleness ; mildness ; meekness —하다 (be) gentle ; mild ; meek ; tender ; bland ¶ 눈매가 유화한 사람 a meek-eyed person // 사람들은 그녀의 유화한 태도가 마음에 들었다 Her suavity of manner pleased all around her.
유화 宥和 appeasement —하다 appease ; pacify
—론자 an appeaser — 정책 an appeasement policy ; a policy of appeasement ¶ 유화 정책은 패배를 뜻한다 Appeasement signifies subjection.
유화 乳化 emulsification
—유 emulsified oil —제 an emulsifying agent ; an emulsifier
유화 類化 assimilation ; 〖생물〗 anabolism
—하다 assimilate ; incorporate
유화 硫化 sulfuration〔sulphuration〕 —하다 sulphurize ⇨ 황화(黃化)
—물 a sulfide — 암모늄〔은, 수소, 철〕 ammonium〔silver, hydrogen, iron〕 sulfide — 작용 sulphurization
유화 식물 有花植物 a flowering plants
유환류 Annulata (학명)
**유황 硫黃 sulfur ; brimstone ¶ 유황의 sulfur(e)ous
— 연고 sulfur ointment —천 a sulfur〔sulfureous〕 spring
유황 악기 有簧樂器 a reed instrument
유회 流會 adjournment of a meeting ¶ 유회되다 be adjourned ; prove abortive // 참석자가 적어서 유회되었다 The meeting was adjourned owing to scanty attendance.
**유효 有效 validity ; availability ; effectiveness ; efficacy ; efficiency —하다 (be) valid ; available ; effective ; efficacious ; good ; sound ¶ 대포의 유효 사정거리 the effective range of a gun // 시간을 유효하게 쓰다 use one's time effectively ; make good use of one's time ; put one's time to good use // 이 계약은 1년 동안 유효하다 This agreement holds good for a year. // 이 기차표는 이틀 동안 유효하다 This train ticket is good〔valid〕 two days. // 세일 가격은 3월 27일까지 유효합니다 Sale prices are good through March 27.
— 기간 the term of validity〔availability〕; the available period — 마력〔압력〕 effective horsepower〔pressure〕 — 사정거리 the effective〔available〕 range — 수요 an effective demand — 숫자 a significant figure — 열량 available heat — 증명 a certificate of validity ; a testimonial — 투표 a valid ballot
유효 적절 有效適切 —하다 (be) effective and well-directed ¶ 유효 적절한 수단을 취하다 take the most effective measures〔steps〕 available
유훈 遺訓 dying injunctions〔instructions〕; the instructions〔teaching〕 of the departed ¶ 조상의 유훈을 받들다 follow the testament left by one's ancestors
유훈자 有勳者 the holder of a decoration
유휴 遊休 idleness ; unemployment ¶ 유휴의 idle ; unused ; unemployed // 유휴물자를 활용하다 desterilize
— 공장 a non-operating plant — 물자 idle commodities — 생산력 idle production capacity — 시설 idle facilities ; unused equipment — 자금 idle〔uninvested〕 money ; floating money〔cash〕; idle〔spare〕 funds ; money to spare — 자본 idle capital〔funds〕 — 자산 idle proper-

ties — 자재 idle materials ; materials lying unused〔idle〕

유흥 遊興 pleasure ; merrymaking ; amusement **—하다** make merry ; have fun ; amuse〔enjoy〕 oneself ¶ 유흥에 빠지다 indulge in pleasures
—가 an amusement center〔quarter〕; gay quarters ; a pleasure haunt **—비** expenses for pleasures ; entertainment costs ; the price of a spree《속》**—세** the entertainment〔amusement〕 tax **—업소** a merry-making place **— 음식세** the tax on amusement, food and drink **—자** a carouser **—장** an amusement quarter **무전 —** merrymaking without money ; eating and drinking without paying

유희 遊戲 ① [놀이] merrymaking ; amusements ; a pastime ② [운동] a game ; sports ; play **—하다** make merry ; amuse oneself ; play ; play (at) a game
— 본능 a sportive instinct ; the play instinct **—실** a recreation hall ; a playroom **—장** a playground

육 六 six ¶ 육분의 1 one-sixth ; a sixth part // 육분의 2 two-sixths

육 肉 flesh ; meat ; beef (쇠고기) ; the flesh ¶ 육과 영 flesh and spirit ; body and soul

육각 六角 six angles ; sexangle ; hexagon ¶ 육각의 hexagonal ; sexangular
—형 hexagon ; sexangle

육감 六感 the sixth sense ¶ 내 육감으로 알 수 있다 My sixth sense tells me that.

육감 肉感 sexual feeling ; sensual pleasure ; voluptuousness ; sensuality ¶ 육감적인 sensual ; sex-appealing ; voluptuous // 육감적인 미인 a voluptuous beauty // 이 그림은 육감적이다 The picture appeals to sensuality.
—주의 sensualism

육갑 六甲 the sexagenary cycle

육개장 肉— soup of chopped beef with various condiments

육경 肉莖 〖동물〗 a stalk ; a footstalk ; a stipe ; a pedicel

육계 肉界 the physical〔sensual〕 world

육계 肉桂 〖식물〗 cinnamon ; cassia bark

육괴 肉塊 a chunk〔lump〕 of meat〔flesh〕; [사람] a fat〔plump〕 person

육교 肉交 carnal relations ; sexual intercourse ⇨ 성교

육교 陸橋 an overpass ; a viaduct ; a girder bridge

†**육군 陸軍** the army ; the military service ; the land forces ¶ 육군의 military ; army // 육군에 입대하다 join〔enter, go into〕 the army ; be drafted into the army (징집) // 육군에서 근무 중이다 be in the military service // 육군에서 제대하다 leave〔be discharged from〕 the army
— 군악대 a military band **— 대장** a general ; an army general **— 대학** a Military Staff College **— 무관** a military attaché (대사관의)《프》**— 병력** land power **— 병원** a military〔an army〕 hospital **— 비행대** the Army Flying〔Aviation〕 Corps **— 사관 학교** the Military Academy **— 사관 후보생** a military cadet **—성** [미국의] the Department of the Army ; [영국의] the War Office **— 장관** [미국의] the Secretary of the Army **— 장교** an army〔a military〕 officer **— 참모 총장** the Army Chief of Staff

육담 肉談 vulgar talk ; immoral language ; a licentious〔lewd〕 story

육대주 六大洲 the Six Continents

육덕 肉德 fatness that would rather make a person virtuous

육도 陸稻 [밭벼] upland rice ; the upland rice plant

육력 戮力 cooperation ; joint effort ; working together **—하다** cooperate with ; work together ; make a united effort

육로 陸路 a land〔an overland〕 route ¶ 육로로 by land ; overland ; by an overland route
— 수송 highway transportation ; transport by land **— 여행** a land〔an overland〕 journey ; travel on〔by〕 land

육류 肉類 flesh ; meat ¶ 육류를 먹지 않다 abstain from flesh and meat

육륜 肉輪 the two〔the upper and lower〕 eyelids

육면체 六面體 a hexahedron《*pl.* ~s, -hedra》¶ 육면체의 hexahedral
정— a regular hexahedron ; a cube

육모 六— a hexagon ; a sexangle ¶ 육모나다 be hexagonal
— 방망이 a six-sided club〔cudgel〕 **—정** a hexagonal pavilion

육묘 育苗 raising seedlings ; seedling culture **—하다** raise seedlings

육미 六味 the six flavors

육미 肉味 flesh food ; meat dishes ¶ 육미를 먹지 않다 abstain from flesh meals〔foods〕
—붙이 meat ; meat dishes

육박 肉薄 closing in upon ; being close at hand **—하다** close in upon《the enemy》; press《the enemy》 hard ; be close〔near〕 at hand ; draw near ; tread close on《a person's》 heels (경기에서) ¶ 적진에 육박하다 carry the fighting to the enemy's camp // 우리 보병이 적군에 육박해갔다 Our infantry closed in upon the enemy.
—전 a hand-to-hand fight ; a close contest〔game〕; a close battle

육발이 六— a person with six toes on a foot

육방망이 a six-pole bier

육방 정계 六方晶系 〖광물〗 the hexagonal system

육배 六倍 six times ; sextuple
육법 六法 the Six Law Codes
— 전서 a Compendium of Laws ; the Statute Books ; a complete book of the six major laws
육보 肉補 nourishing one's body by eating meat ; a meat diet —하다 diet 〔nourish〕 oneself on meat ; eat meat for one's health
육봉 六峰 a hump
육부 六腑 the six viscera〔bowels〕
육분의 六分儀 a sextant
육붕 陸棚 〖지리〗 a continental shelf
육붙이 肉— ⇨ 육미붙이
육산 陸産 land products ; products of the soil
육삼삼제 六三三制 〖교육〗 the six-three-three system of education ; the American type school system
육상 陸上 (on) land ; (on the) ground
— 경기 athletic sports ; field and track events — 경기회 an athletic meet(-ing) ; a field-and-track meet ; a track meet — 근무 [선박 관계] shore duty 〔service〕 ; service ashore ; [항공 관계] ground duty〔service〕 — 동물 a land animal — 부대 a land force — 생활 life on land〔shore〕 — 선수권 대회 the track and field championships — 수송 land carriage〔transportation〕 ; ground〔overland〕 transport — 운송비 overland freight
육색 肉色 flesh color〔tint〕
육서 陸棲 living on land ¶ 육서의 terrestrial ; land-inhabiting
— 동물 terrestrial animals ; a land animal
육성 育成 upbringing ; rearing —하다 rear ; foster ; nurture ; bring up ; raise
— 재배 rearing and cultivating — 회비 school support fees
육성 肉聲 a live voice ; a natural voice ; a (human) voice
육속 陸續 succession ; consecutiveness ; continuance —하다 continue ; be consecutive ; be continuous ¶ 육속하여 successively ; continually ; one after another ; in succession ; consecutively // 육속하여 탈당하다 leave〔resign from〕 the party one after another
육손이 六— a person with six fingers on a hand ; a six-fingered person
육송 陸送 ⇨ 육운
육수 肉水 meet〔beef〕 stock ; gravy
육순 六旬 sexagenarianism ¶ 육순의 sixty-year-old ; sexagenarian
— 노인 a sexagenarian
육시 戮屍 posthumous decapitation —하다 behead 《the dead》 posthumously
육식 肉食 a meat〔flesh〕 diet ; flesh foods ; meat-eating ; flesh-eating (동물의) —하다 eat meat ; eat flesh (동물이) ¶ 육식을 끊다 abstain from meat and flesh // 나는 육식보다 채식을 좋아한다 I prefer a vegetable diet to animal food.
—가 a meat-eater — 동물 a carnivorous〔predatory〕 animal ; predator ¶ 사자는 육식 동물이다 The lion is a beast of prey. —조 a predatory bird ; a bird of prey —충 a predacious insect
육식처대 肉食妻帶 〖불교〗 a Buddhist priest eating meat and taking a wife —하다 [종이] eat meat and take a wife
육신 肉身 the flesh ; the body
**육십 六十 sixty ; threescore ¶ 제 60 the sixtieth // 60분의 1 a sixtieth (part) // 60대의 사람 a sexagenarian
—갑자 the sexagenary cycle
육아 肉芽 〖식물〗 granulation ; proud flesh
—종(腫) granuloma 《*pl.* ~s, -mata》
육아 育兒 infant〔child〕 rearing ; upbringing〔nursing〕 of infants —하다 bring up infants ; rear children
—법 the art of rearing infants —비 childcare expenses — 시간 nursing time —식(食) infant food —실 a nursery (room) —원(院) an orphanage ; an orphan asylum ; a foundling hospital
육안 肉眼 the naked〔unaided〕 eye ¶ 육안으로 쉽게 볼 수 있는 곳에 within easy range of one's eye // 육안으로 보다 see with the naked eye ; examine with the unaided eye // 육안으로는 보이지 않다 be invisible to the naked eye
육양 育養 ⇨ 양육
육양 陸揚 unloading (배에서) ; landing (육지로) ; disembarkation ; discharge —하다 unload ; land ; discharge ; take ashore ¶ 그 배는 육양 중이다 She is discharging her cargo.
육영 育英 education —하다 educate
— 사업 educational work ¶ 그는 육영 사업에 일생을 바쳤다 He devoted his life to education. — 자금 scholarship — 제도 a scholarship system —회 a scholarship society ; an education association
육영 育嬰 upbringing of infants〔children〕 —하다 rear〔bring up〕 children
육욕 戮辱 ignominy ; shame
육욕 肉慾 the carnal desires〔appetites〕 ; the animal passions ¶ 육욕을 채우다 satisfy one's sensual appetites ; gratify one's lusts // 육욕에 빠지다 indulge in〔be given to〕 sensual pleasures // 육욕을 억제하다 restrain one's passions ; be continent
—주의 sensualism ; carnalism
육우 肉牛 beef cattle
육운 陸運 land carriage〔transportation〕 ; overland transportation ; transportation by land
—국 the Land Transportation Bureau — 화물 land-borne goods — 회사 a land transportation company
육자배기 六字— a brisk and lively folk tune (with six words to the line)

육장 六場 [장날] the six market days of the month ; [부사적] all the time
육장 肉醬 beef slices boiled in soy sauce
육적 肉的 fleshly ; physical ; corporal
육적 肉炙 roast meat ; beef slices broiled on a skewer
육전 陸戰 land fighting〔warfare〕 ; a land combat〔battle〕 ; warfare by land
— 법규 the Articles of War
육젓 六— salt-pickled shrimps caught in June
육정 肉情 carnal desire ⇨ 육욕
육정 六情 the six emotions
육종 育種 breeding 《of animals》 ; rearing —하다 breed ; rear
육종 肉腫 〖의학〗 a sarcoma 《*pl.* ~s, -ta》
육중 肉重 —하다 [무겁다] (be) heavy ; weighty ; massive ; bulky ; [말이] (be) exaggerated ; excessive ¶ 육중하게 걷다 walk heavily
육중주 六重奏 〖음악〗 a sextet(te)
육중창 六重唱 〖음악〗 a sextet(te)
육즙 肉汁 beef stock ; gravy
†육지 陸地 land ; the shore ¶ 육지의 동물 a land animal // 육지가 보이다 come in sight of land // 육지에 오르다 go ashore // 육지로 둘러 쌓이다 be landlocked
육지니 育— a fledg(e)ling falcon
육질 肉質 flesh ; [과육] pulpy substance ¶ 다육질의 fleshy
육찬 肉饌 meat dishes
육척 六尺 six feet ¶ 육척 장신의 사나이 a six-footer 《구》 ; a 6-foot man ; a man who is well over six feet tall
*육체 肉體 the flesh ; the body ¶ 육체의 corporal ; bodily ; physical // 육체와 정신 body and spirit ; mind and body // 육체의 고통 physical suffering // 육체적 쾌락 pleasures of the flesh ; sensual〔corporal〕 pleasures // 사람의 육체는 죽어도 정신은 불멸이다 A man's body dies, but his soul is immortal. // 건전한 육체에 건전한 정신 A sound mind in a sound body.
— 관계 sexual relations〔connection, intimacy〕 ; familiarity — 노동 physical 〔manual〕 labor — 노동자 a (physical, muscular) laborer — 문학 sensual〔erotic〕 literature —미 physical beauty ; the beauty of the body — 미인 a woman of great physical beauty ; a curvaceous woman — 소설 a sex novel ; an erotic story —파 a glamour (girl)
육체 肉滯 an indigestion〔a dyspepsia〕 caused by the eating of meat
육초 肉— a tallow candle ; a candle of suet
육촌 六寸 ① [길이] six inches ② [재종] a second cousin
육축 六畜 the six domestic animals
육층 六層 six floors ; floor six
육친 六親 the six family relations
육친 肉親 a blood relative ; one's immediate relative
육탄 肉彈 a human bomb
— 공격 a suicide〔sacrifice〕 attack — 십용사 the ten human bombs —전 storming with human bullets ; a hand-to-hand struggle〔fight〕
육탈 肉脫 losing weight〔flesh〕 ; getting thin〔lean〕 —하다 lose weight ; get thin
육탕 肉湯 meat soup
육태질 陸駄— landed〔shored, unloaded〕 cargo —하다 land 《cargo》 ; unload ; discharge
육통터지다 六通— 《a plan》 fail at the last moment ; collapse on the point of completion
육포 肉脯 jerked (beef) ; jerky ; slices of dried beef
육풍 陸風 a land breeze
육필 肉筆 one's own handwriting ; an autograph ¶ 육필의 편지 a handwritten letter ; a letter in one's own handwriting
육해공 陸海空 land, sea and air
—군 the land, sea and air forces ; the armed forces ; the (fighting) services —군 장병 officers and men of the armed forces — 합동 작전 joint operations of the army, navy and air forces
육해군 陸海軍 the army and navy ; military and naval forces ; the land and sea forces ¶ 육해군의 확장 expansion of armaments on land and sea
육행 陸行 traveling〔going〕 by land —하다 travel〔go〕 by land〔overland〕
육혈포 六穴砲 a pistol ; a six-chambered revolver ; a six-shooter
육회 肉膾 a dish of minced raw beef
육후하다 肉厚— (be) fat ; fleshy ; plump
윤 潤 gloss ; luster ; shine ⇨ 윤기
윤가 允可 the king's sanction〔permission, approval〕 —하다 permit ; approve
윤간 輪姦 a gang〔group〕 rape —하다 rape〔assault, violate〕 a woman by turns ; gang-rape
*윤곽 輪廓 ① [개관] an outline ; a general view ; a sketch ¶ 계획의 윤곽 an outline of a scheme // 영문학의 윤곽 an outline of English literature // 윤곽을 말하다 give an outline〔a rough idea〕 of 《the program》 ; sketch 《something》 ; outline ② [외형] contours 《of human body》 ; outlines 《of a mountain》 ; profile 《of a face》 ; skyline 《of a city》 ¶ 얼굴의 윤곽 the contour of one's face // 윤곽이 뚜렷한 sharply outlined // 인체의 윤곽을 그리다 sketch〔draw〕 the contours of the human body // 그의 얼굴은 윤곽이 뚜렷하다 He has clear-cut features.
윤기 倫紀 moral discipline〔morals and discipline〕 ; moral laws〔regulations〕
윤기 潤氣 gloss ; luster ; polish ; shine ; brightness ; glaze ¶ 윤기있는 머리 glossy〔lustrous〕 hair // 윤기있는 얼굴 a

bright complexion // 윤기가 돌다 have fine luster ; have a good polish // 윤기가 없다 be lusterless〔dull, dry, dim, dingy〕; have no gloss ; [얼굴에] be sallow-complexioned ; look sallow // 그녀의 얼굴은 윤기가 돈다 She has a good color on her face. // 마호가니는 닦으면 윤기가 잘 난다 Mahogany polishes beautifully.

윤나다 潤— be glossy ; be lustrous ; be shiny ; be polished ; be sleek

윤납 輪納 payment in〔by〕 rotation **—하다** pay by turns ; take turns paying

윤내다 潤— gloss ; polish ; shine ; bring out the luster ; give a shine 《to》

윤년 閏年 a leap year ; an intercalary

윤달 閏— a leap month ; an intercalary month

윤독 輪讀 reading by turns **—하다** read by turns ; take turns reading

윤똑똑이 a knowing chap〔fellow〕; a smart guy

*__윤락__ 淪落 ruin ; fall **—하다** be ruined ; go to ruin
—가 a red-light district ; a brothel **—여성** a ruined〔fallen, lost〕 woman ; a delinquent girl

*__윤리__ 倫理 ethics (학문) ; morals ; a code of conduct ¶ 윤리적 ethical ; moral // 윤리적 행위 a moral act // 윤리적 종교 an ethical religion
— 교화 운동 an ethical movement **한국 방송〔신문〕 — 위원회** the Korea Broadcasting〔Press〕 Ethics Committee

*__윤리학__ 倫理學 ethics ; moral philosophy〔science〕
—자 an ethicist ; a moralist **동양 —** Oriental ethics **실천 —** practical ethics

윤몰 淪沒 **—하다** sink ; submerge ; [죄에 빠짐] sink into vice

윤무 輪舞 a circle dance ; a round (dance) ; a waltz
—곡 a rondo

윤번 輪番 turn ; rotation **—하다** take turns ; alternate ¶ 윤번으로 by turns ; in turn ; by rotation ; alternately // 윤번으로 의장이 되다 rotate the chairmanship of the conference
—제 a rotation system

윤삭 閏朔 a leap〔an intercalary〕 month

윤색 潤色 (literary) embellishment ; coloring **—하다** embellish ; color ; adorn ; give color 《to》

윤생 輪生 〖식물〗 verticillation
—엽 verticillate leaves

윤선 輪船 a steamship

윤시하다 輪示— show around ; circulate exhibition

윤월 閏月 ⇨ 윤달(閏—)

윤음 綸音 the king's words ; a royal message

윤일 閏日 a leap〔an intercalary〕 day

윤작 輪作 crop rotation **—하다** rotate crops ¶ 밭을 윤작하다 rotate crops in one's fields

윤전 輪轉 rotation ; revolving **—하다** rotate ; revolve ; turn round
—기 a cylinder press ; a rotary press **초고속도 —** a super-high speed rotary press

윤지 綸旨 the king's words ; a royal message

윤질 輪疾 ⇨ 돌림병

윤차 輪次 ⇨ 윤번

윤창 輪唱 a troll ; a round **—하다** troll ; sing a round

윤척 없다 倫脊— (be) incoherent ; inconsistent ; contradictory ¶ 윤척 없는 말을 하다 talk incoherently ; utter an incoherent remark ; contradict oneself

윤축 輪軸 the wheel and axle

윤택 潤澤 ① [광택] gloss ; luster ; shine ② [풍부] abundance ; plenty ; richness **—하다** be glossy ; shiny ; abundant ; ample ; copious ; plentiful ¶ 윤택한 자금 abundant funds // 윤택한 지식 a great store of knowledge // 윤택해지다 become prosperous // 생활이 윤택하다 live in comfortable circumstances ; be well-off

윤필 潤筆 writing ; painting ; [윤필료] a fee for writing〔painting〕

윤허 允許 royal permission〔sanction〕 **—하다** (be) permitted〔sanctioned〕 《by the king》

윤형 輪形 a wheel-like shape ; a ring ; a circle

윤화 輪禍 a traffic accident ¶ 윤화를 당하다 have a traffic accident ; be injured in a traffic accident

윤활 潤滑 lubrication **—하다** (be) lubricative ; lubricous ; smooth
—유 lubricating oil ; lubricant ; lube (oil) 《미》 ¶ 윤활유의 역할을 하다 help (to) smooth 《the progress of the negotiations》 ; serve to remove the friction 《between》 **— 장치** a lubricating device **—재(材)** a lubricant ; an antifriction **—제** a lubricant

윤회 輪廻 ① [유전] perpetual motion ; constant mutation ② 〖불교〗 the transmigration of souls ; the cycles of life ; metempsychosis 《*pl.* -ses》 **—하다** transmigrate ; make a motion constantly ; rotate
—설 transmigrationism

*__율__ 率 ① [비율] a rate ; a ratio ; a proportion ; a percentage ; 〖물리〗 modulus ; an index ; 〖수학〗 a constant ¶ …의 율로 at the rate of ; on a percentage of // 율을 나타내다 show the percentage〔rate〕 of // 율을 높이다〔낮추다〕 raise〔lower〕 the rate ② [능률] efficiency
고〔저〕— a high〔low〕 percentage〔rate〕 **굴절—** an index of refraction **보험—** insurance rate **사망—** a death rate **요금〔연금, 임금〕—** a scale of charges〔pensions, wages〕 **출산—** a birth rate **팽창—**

a coefficient of expansion 평균— the average rate 할인— the rate of discount

율 律 ① 〖법〗 a law ; a regulation ; commandments (계율) ; discipline (기율) ② [운율] a rhythm ; a meter

도덕— the moral law〔order, code〕 자연— the natural law

율격 律格 ① [규격] a rule ; a statute ② [한시의] rules of versification

**율동 律動 rhythm ; rhythmic movement ¶ 생의 율동 the rhythm of life // 율동적인 미 rhythmical beauty // 빠른 율동으로 연주하다 play in quick rhythm

— 감각 a rhythmical sense —미 rhythmical beauty — 체조 rhythmical gymnastics

율령 律令 a law ; a statute ; an ordinance ; a mandate

율례 律例 an established usage〔precedent〕 of a criminal code ; the penal code ; a statute ; a law

율모기 〖동물〗 a grass snake ; a ring snake

율무 〖식물〗 Job's tears

—쌀 (the involucre of) Job's tears

율문 律文 articles〔provisions〕 of a criminal code

율법 律法 (a) law ; a rule ; [율법] commandments

율시 律詩 a style of Chinese verse

율학 律學 criminal jurisprudence

융 絨 cotton flannel

융기 隆起 a protuberance ; bulging ; rising ; 〖지질〗 upheaval ; elevation —하다 protrude ; upheave ; bulge ; rise

— 산호초 an elevated coral reef — 해안 an uplifted coast

융단 絨緞 a carpet

— 폭격 carpet bombing

융동 隆冬 a severe〔hard〕 winter

융로 隆老 an old person above 70

융모 絨毛 wool ; 〖해부〗 a villus 《*pl.* -li》

융비술 隆鼻術 plastic surgery on the nose ; a rhinoplastic operation

융성 隆盛 prosperity —하다 (be) prosperous ; flourishing ; thriving ¶ 극히 융성하다 be in full flourish ; be at the zenith of prosperity // 그 당시 국운이 크게 융성했다 The nation was in full flourish at that time.

융숭 隆崇 high respect〔regard, esteem, deference〕 ; hospitality —하다 highly respect〔regard〕 ; think highly of ; pay high〔deep〕 esteem to ; entertain warmly 〔cordially〕 ; make 《a person》 welcome ¶ 융숭히 heartily ; cordially ; kindly // 융숭히 대접하다 entertain 《a person》 cordially ; give 《a person》 warm hospitality ; receive 《one's visitors》 kindly

융열 融熱 the heat of fusion

융자 融資 financing ; advance〔accommodation〕 of funds ; a loan —하다 finance 《an enterprise》 ; furnish funds 《to a company》 ; accommodate 《a person》 with funds

—금 a loan — 알선 loan facilitation — 회사 a financing company 구제 — a relief loan 단기 — a short-term loan ; a call loan 《미》 조건부 — conditional financing ; a tied loan

융점 融點 〖물리〗 the melting〔fusing〕 point

융통 融通 ① [유통] circulation 《of capital》 ; accommodation ; financing ; negotiation (어음의) —하다 accommodate 《a persons》 with 《money》 ; circulate ; lend ; provide〔advance〕 money ¶ 돈을 융통해 주다 accommodate 《a person》 with a loan ; advance money 《to a person》 // 500만원을 융통하다 obtain an accommodation of five million *won* // 그는 돈도 없고 또 융통할 수도 없다 He has neither money nor credit.

② [재주·성질] adaptability ; elasticity ; versatility

— 기관 a circulating medium 《*pl.* ~s, -dia》 —력 one's financing ability — 어음 an accommodation bill〔draft, note〕 ; a negotiable paper ; a kite 《속》 —자 an accommodator — 자금 circulating〔floating〕 capital — 증권 a negotiable instrument

융통성 融通性 adaptability ; flexibility ; versatility ; resourcefulness ; negotiability (어음 따위의) ¶ 융통성이 있다 be adaptable ; be flexible ; be versatile ; be resourceful // 융통성 없다 be unadaptable ; lack (in) versatility ; be strait-laced ; be hidebound ; be rigid ; be narrow-minded // 융통성을 발휘하다 adapt oneself to circumstances // 그는 융통성이 많다 He is a man of many resources. / He knows how to adapt himself to circumstances. // 고참 관리들은 융통성이 없다 Superannuated officials cannot prove of use in other walks of life. // 선생님은 그들이 융통성을 좀더 보일 수 있다고 생각하는 거죠 You'd think they could show a little more flexibility, wouldn't you?

융합 融合 fusion ; union ; amalgamation —하다 fuse into one ; unite ; amalgamate

— 유전 blending〔blended〕 inheritance 핵— nuclear fusion ¶ 핵융합 폭탄 a (nuclear) fusion bomb

융해 融解 fusion ; melting ; dissolution —하다 fuse ; melt ; dissolve ; liquefy

—열 the heat of fusion —점 the melting point

융화 融化 deliquescence —하다 deliquesce ; soften ¶ 융화성의 deliquescent

융화 融和 propitiation ; reconciliation ; harmony —하다 propitiate ; be reconciled 《with》 ; harmonize ¶ 융화를 꾀하다 try to be reconciled 《with》 ; take a measure to bring about reconciliation // 저 사람하고는 융화하기 힘들다 Somehow I

cannot hit it off with him.
융흥 隆興 vigorous prosperity ; rise **—하다** rise ; flourish ; thrive ; prosper vigorously
윷 [놀이] the Four-Stick Game ; *yut* **—놀이** playing *yut* ; a game of *yut* **—밭** a quarter of the *yut* board **—짝** the sticks used in playing *yut* ¶ 윷짝 가르듯 흑백을 가르다 discriminate clearly between good and bad〔right and wrong〕 **—판** a *yut* board ; a scene of *yut* playing
윷짝 가르듯 관용 (distinguish) sharply ; clearly
윷놀다 play *yut*
으그러뜨리다 crush 《a thing》 out of shape ⇨ 우그러뜨리다
으그러지다 be crushed out of shape ⇨우그러지다
으깨다 ① [부스러뜨리다] crush (up) ; squash ; smash ② [깨다] mash ; soften up ; beat ; knead (뭉개다)
으끄지르다 crush 《a thing》 up to throw away
-으나 ① [그러나, …하지만] but ; however ; (and) yet ; still ; though ; although ¶ 가고 싶으나 시간이 없다 I should like to go, but I have no time. ② [어쨌든, …간에] ¶ 크나 작으나 regardless of its size // 좋으나 싫으나 해야 한다 You must do it whether or not you like it. ③ [매우 …한] ¶ 넓으나 넓은 바다 a sea that is ever so wide // 높으나 높은 산 such a〔a really〕 high mountain ; ever so high a mountain // 깊으나 깊은 물 water ever so deep
-으나마 but ; however ; though ; still ; yet ; nevertheless ; all the same ¶ 돈은 많이 있으나마 행복하지는 않다 He is rich but not happy.
으늑하다 ① (be) cozy ⇨ 아늑하다 ② (be) secluded ⇨ 으슥하다
-으니(까) ① [원인·이유] as ; so ; since ; because (of) ; for ¶ 시간이 얼마 없으니까 빨리 일을 해치워야 한다 Since there isn't much time, we've got to hurry up to get the thing done. // 이 기둥이 있으니까 집이 안 쓰러진다 This post keeps the house from falling. ② [···했더니] when ; as ; (and) then ¶ 이름을 물으니 김이라 했다 When I asked his name, he said he was *Kim*.
으드득 ① [이가는 소리] **—하다** grate 〔gnash, grind〕 one's teeth
② [깨무는 소리] crunching ; with a crunching sound **—하다** crunch ¶ 그는 으드득 으드득 밤을 깨물어 먹었다 He crunched chestnuts.
으드득거리다 ① [···이] crunch ; be crunchy ② [···을] grit ; grate ; grind 《one's teeth》 ¶ 이를 으드득거리다 grind one's teeth
으드득으드득 ① [깨무는 꼴] crunching ; with a crunch ② [갈리는 꼴] gritting ; grating ; grinding one's teeth (이를)
으드등거리다 bicker ; quarrel ; spat ; fuss ; snarl ; growl ; be at outs〔odds〕 《with one's wife》
으드등으드등 bickering ; fussing ; at odds with each other
으등그러지다 get warped ; warp ; get twisted out of shape
***으뜸** ① [첫째] the top ; the head ; first-rate ; the first (place) ¶ 으뜸으로 합격하다 pass an examination first on the list // 반에서 으뜸가다 be at the head〔top〕 of the class // 영어로는 그가 반에서 으뜸이다 He leads his class in English. // 학자로는 그가 으뜸이다 He is a first-rate scholar. ② [두목] a chief ; a boss ; a leader ; a master
③ [근본] the basis ; the foundation ; the root ; the core ¶ …의 으뜸이 되다 be at the root of... ; form the foundation of... // 건강은 행복의 으뜸이다 Health is the foundation of human happiness.
—음 『음악』 the keynote ; the prime ; the tonic
-으라 [명령·소원] ⇨ -라
-으라고 [명령] ⇨ -라고
-으라는 [···하라는] ⇨ -라는
-으러 [목적] ⇨ -하러
으레 ① [마땅히] customarily ; habitually ; usually ; properly ; naturally ; as a matter of course ; necessarily ; of course ¶ 으레 …해야 한다 it is only fair to 《do》 // 으레 그래야 한다 That is the natural thing to be expected. // 빚진 것은 으레 갚아야 한다 One ought to pay what one owes. // 젊은이는 으레 새 것을 원하기 마련이다 It is quite natural for young men to have a desire for what is new.
② [틀림 없이] always ; invariably ; habitually ; regularly ; usually ; as is one's wont ; all the time ; every time ; without fail ¶ 으레 …하다 make a point of 《doing》 ; be in the habit of 《doing》 ; make it a rule to 《do》 // 비가 왔다 하면 으레 큰 비다 It never rains but it pours. // 그 일에는 으레 위험이 따른다 It is invariably attended by danger. // 그는 월말이면 으레 돈을 꾸러 온다 He never fails to come to me for a loan at the end of every month. // 그들이 아버지를 찾아오면 으레 술자리가 벌어진다 They never call on my father without holding a drinking bout. // 그들은 만나면 으레 싸운다 They never meet without quarreling. /They quarrel whenever they meet.
-으려고 [···하고자] ⇨ -려고
-으려도 ⇨ -려도
-으려면 [···으려 하면] ⇨ -려면
-으련만 ⇨ -련만
-으렴 ⇨ -려무나
으로 by ; with ⇨ 로 ¶ 부산으로 가는 차 a train for *Pusan* // 맨주먹으로 with bare

hands // 배편으로 by ship // 통역으로 as〔in the capacity of〕 an interpreter // 병으로 누워 있다 lie in bed with illness // 연못으로 빠지다 fall into a pond // 왼손으로 쓰다 write with the left hand // 폐병으로 죽다 die of consumption // 헌것을 새것으로 바꾸다 change an old thing to a new one

으로나 ¶ 어느 면으로나 in all respects // 양으로나 질로나 in quantity and〔or〕 in quality

으로는 ¶ 내 생각으로는 in my opinion // 이것으로는 안된다 We can't do it with this. /This won't do. // 내 힘으로는 너를 도와 줄 수가 없다 It is not within my power to help you. // 중학생으로는 키가 아주 크다 He's very tall for a middle school student. // 싸움으로는 그를 당할 사람이 없다 When it comes to a quarrel, none can beat him.

으로도 as〔with〕 ... also〔either, even〕 ¶ 돈으로도 살 수 없는 것 a thing money can't buy // 장군으로도 이름이 나다 be noted as a general also // 그는 시인으로도 화가로도 실패했다 He was a failure both as a poet and as a painter.

으로서 as ; for ⇨ 로서 ¶ 외국인으로서 for a foreigner // 그는 한국 사람으로서는 영어를 잘한다 He speaks fluent English for a Korean.

으로써 ⇨ 로써

으르다 ① [위협하다] threaten ; menace ; intimidate ② [놀라게 하다] scare ; frighten ; terrify ¶ 죽인다고 으르다 threaten 《a person》 with death ; threaten to kill 《a person》 // 을러대어 고백시키다 scare 《a person》 into confession

으르대다 scare ⇨ 으르다

****으르렁** with a snarl〔roar, growl〕

†**으르렁거리다** ① [짐승이] growl ; snarl ; roar ¶ 개가 낯설은 사람에게 으르렁거린다 The dog snarls at a stranger. // 사자가 사납게 으르렁거린다 Lions growl savagely. ② [다투다] wrangle〔dispute, argue〕 with ; quarrel ; feud ¶ 그들은 언제나 으르렁거리고 있다 They are always bickering with each other.

으르르 shivering ; shaking ; quivering ── 하다 shiver ; shake ; tremble ¶ 추워서 몸이 으르르 떨리다 shiver from the cold

으름 〖식물〗 clematis berries ; an akebiseed

── 나무〔덩굴〕 the clematis (shrub, vine)

으름장 intimidation ; browbeating ; threat ── 하다 intimidate ; browbeat ; threaten

-으리까 ⇨ -리까

-으리니 ¶ 그녀는 죽지 않으리니 마음놓게 Take it easy, since she will not die.

-으리라 ¶ 두번 다시 잡히지 않으리라 I will not be caught again.

으리으리 ── 하다 (be) magnificent ; majestic ; imposing ; stately ; awe-inspiring ; solemn ¶ 으리으리하게 in a dignified manner ; solemnly // 으리으리한 저택 a stately mansion // 으리으리한 성당 a magnificent cathedral // 경찰이 집회장을 으리으리하게 경비하고 있었다 An imposing array of police guarded the place of meeting.

-으며 ⇨ -며

-으면 [가설적 조건] if ; when ; whenever

-으면서 ⇨ -면서

-으면서도 ⇨ -면서도

-으므로 ⇨ -므로

으밀아밀 whispering ; (speaking) under one's breath ¶ 으밀아밀 이야기하다 talk in whispers〔secret〕

-으소서 please do, I beg you to do ¶ 저의 간청을 들으소서 Pray listen to my plea.

***으스대다** be proud〔arrogant〕 ; swagger 《about》 ¶ 으스대며 in a lordly manner // 으스대며 걷다 swagger ; strut ; walk with an air // 으스대지 마라 Don't brag !

으스러뜨리다 smash ⇨ 부스러뜨리다

으스러지다 crumble ⇨ 부스러지다

으스름 달밤 a hazy〔misty〕 moonlit night

으스름하다 《moonlight》 (be) hazy ; misty ; faint

으스스 shivering with cold ; with one's blood running cold ── 하다 (be) chilly ; cold ; ghastly ; eerie ¶ 으스스한 날씨 chilly weather // 그 일은 생각만 해도 몸이 으스스하다 It chills my blood to think of it.

***으슥하다** (be) secluded ; retired ; deserted ; lonely ; desolate ; quiet ; hushed ¶ 으슥한 곳 a lonely place // 으슥한 방 a sequestered〔secluded〕 room // 으슥한 숲속에서 in the gloom〔depth〕 of a forest // 밤이 으슥해졌다 The night was getting on〔well advanced〕.

으슬으슬 shivering ── 하다 (be) chilly ; chill ; be rather cold ¶ 오늘은 으슬으슬 춥다 The weather is chilly today.

으슴푸레하다 (be) hazy ; dim ; misty ; vague ¶ 달빛이 으슴푸레하다 The moon shines dimly. // 복도에 등불이 으슴푸레하게 비치고 있었다 A light shone dimly in the passage.

으쓱[1] ── 하다 (be) horrible ; bloodcurdling ; hair-raising ; chilling

***으쓱**[2] ── 하다 perk oneself up ; lift one's head up ; be elated ; be proud ¶ 그는 장관이 되어서 어깨가 으쓱하였다 He was highly elated at becoming a member of the Cabinet.

으쓱거리다 swagger ; strut ; brag ; perk oneself up ; give oneself airs

으악 ① [놀라게] boo ! ② [구토] puke ! (with a puke)

으지적거리다 ⇨ 아지작거리다

으쩍 with a crunch

으츠러지다 get crushed ; get bruised ; be squashed

으크러뜨리다 crush ; crumble ; squash ;

smash
으크러지다 get crushed〔squashed〕
윽물다 clench one's teeth ; set〔grind, gnash〕 one's teeth ; compress one's lips ¶ 그는 이를 윽물고 죽어 있었다 He was found dead with his teeth firmly set 〔shut〕.
윽박다 bully ; browbeat ; oppress ; coerce ; tyrannize《over》
윽박지르다 bully ; browbeat ; shout down ¶ 윽박질러 …시키다 browbeat《a person》into doing《something》// 윽박질러 말을 못하게 하다 shout《a person》down ; intimidate《a person》into silence
은 恩 grace ; favor ⇨ 은공, 은덕, 은혜
†**은 銀** silver ¶ 은(제)의 silver // 은 같은 silvery // 은을 입힌 silver-plated〔-gilt〕// 구리 그릇에 은을 입히다 silver copperware —그릇 silverware —본위 the silver standard —비녀 a silver hairpin 순— pure 〔refined〕 silver ; sterling
-은 ① [형용사 어간에서] ... that〔which, who〕 is ¶ 작은 집 a house that is small ; a small house ② [동사 어간에서] ... that〔which, who〕《one》 did〔has done〕 ¶ 내가 받은 선물 the present that I received // 잘 닦은 구두 well-polished shoes
-은가 [의문] ¶ 어느 것이 나은가 Which is better ?
은가루 銀— silver dust ; powdered silver
-은가보다 seem ; look ¶ 그는 기분이 매우 좋은가보다 He seems (to be) happy. / He looks very happy.
은감 殷鑑 taking warning by another's failure ; a warning ; a lesson ; a caution ; an example
은거 隱居 retirement (from active life) ; sequestration —하다 live〔dwell〕 in retirement ; go into retirement ; sequester 〔seclude〕 oneself from the world ¶ 산중에 은거하다 retire to hermitage in the mountain
은고 恩顧 patronage ; favor —하다 patronize ; favor ¶ 은고를 받다 be patronized《by》; receive favors《from》
은공 恩功 favor ; merits
은광 銀鑛 a silver mine
은괴 銀塊 a silver ingot ; silver bullion
은근 慇懃 ① [정중] politeness ; courtesy ; civility —하다 (be) courteous ; polite ; civil ¶ 은근히 courteously ; politely ; with much courtesy // 은근한 태도 a courteous demeanor // 은근을 다하다 pour one's heart into《something》 ② [다정] intimacy ; friendship —하다 (be) intimate ; be on intimate terms 《with》 ¶ 은근한 우정 a close friendship // 그는 그 여자와 은근한 사이다 He is thick with her.
은근짜 ① a woman of dubious respectability ; an unlicensed prostitute ; a streetwalker ② [의뭉한 사람] a deep one 《속》; a crafty person
은급 恩給 a pension ⇨ 연금
은기 銀器 silverware ; the silver
은니 銀泥 silver dust mixed in a glue ; silver paint
은닉 隱匿 concealment ; secretion —하다 conceal ; hide ; secrete ; shelter ; harbor《a criminal》 ¶ 범인을 은닉하다 harbor a culprit
—물자 concealed goods ; a secret cache of goods 장물 —죄 secretion of stolen goods 중범 —죄 misprison of felony
은닉처 隱匿處 a hiding place ; a cache
은덕 恩德 a benefit ; a favor ; favor and indebtedness ¶ 나는 그가 베풀어주는 은덕에 감사하고 있다 I am grateful for the benefits I receive from him.
은덕 隱德 good done by stealth ; a secret act of virtue〔charity〕 ; a hidden virtue ¶ 은덕을 베풀다 do good by stealth
은도금 銀鍍金 silver-plating —하다 plate with silver ¶ 은도금한 silver-plated〔-gilt〕
*__은둔 隱遁__ retirement《from the world》; seclusion ; sequestration ; withdrawal from ordinary life —하다 retire from the world ; live in retirement〔seclsion〕 ; sequester〔seclude〕 oneself from the world〔society〕
— 생활 a life in seclusion ; a retired 〔sequestered〕 life —자 a recluse ; a hermit —주의 quietism ; monasticism —처 a place of seclusion ; a hermitage
은딱지 a silver case
— 시계 a silver watch
은딴 [땅꾼의 두목] the chief of a group of snake-hunters
은로 銀露 moonlit dew〔dewdrop〕 ; silvery dew
은막 銀幕 the silver screen ; [영화계] the cinema world ; filmdom ¶ 은막의 여왕 a queen of the (silver) screen
은메달 銀— a silver medal
은명 恩命 gracious words〔commands〕 (from the throne)
†**은밀 隱密** privacy ; secrecy —하다 (be) secret ; covert ; confidential ¶ 은밀히 in secret ; in privacy ; confidentially // 은밀히 조사하다 make confidential inquiries // 그와 은밀히 이야기하다 have a private talk with him
-은바 ⇨ -ㄴ바
은박 銀箔 beaten silver ; silver leaf〔foil〕
—지 silver paper
은반 銀盤 ① [소반] a silver plate ② [달] the moon ③ [스케이트장] a skating rink ; an ice rink ¶ 은반의 여왕 a queen of the ice
은발 銀髮 silver (-white) hair ; gray〔grey 《영》〕 hair ¶ 은발의 silver-haired
은방 銀房 a silver shop ; a silversmith's ; a jewelry shop
은방울 a silver bell ¶ 은방울을 굴리는 듯

한 목소리 《in》 a silver(y) voice
은방울꽃 銀— 『식물』 the lily-of-the-valley
은배 銀杯 a silver cup
은백색 銀白色 a silver-white color ¶ 은백색의 silver-white〔-gray〕
은벽 隱僻 —하다 (be) unfrequented ; remote ; secluded
—처 an unfrequented place〔part〕; a retired〔secluded〕 place
은복 隱伏 lying concealed〔hidden〕; lurking **—하다** lie concealed〔hidden〕; lurk
은부 殷富 wealth ; opulence ; abundance **—하다** (be) wealthy ; opulent ; abundant
은분 銀粉 powdered silver ; silver dust
은붙이 銀— silverware 《총칭》
은비 隱庇 concealment by covering ; sheltering ; protection ; shielding **—하다** conceal ; cover 《up》; shelter ; shield ; protect ¶ 증거를 은비하다 suppress〔cover up〕 evidence // 죄상을 은비하다 cover up the traces of a crime
은빛 銀— silver (color) ; silveriness ¶ 은빛의 silver-colored ; silvery
은사 恩師 one's (respected, honored, revered, beloved) teacher ; a teacher to whom one is deeply indebted
은사 隱士 a hermit ; a recluse
은사 隱事 hidden〔private〕 affair ; a secret
은산 銀山 a silver mine
은산덕해 恩山德海 immeasurable favors〔kindness〕; benevolence ; kindliness ; charitableness
은상 恩賞 a gracious reward (by the king) **—하다** reward
은색 銀色 ⇨ 은빛
은서 隱栖, 隱棲 a secluded life ; life in seclusion ; a hermitage **—하다** live in seclusion
은설 銀屑 silver dust
은성 殷盛 prosperity ; flourishingness **—하다** (be) prosperous ; flourishing ; thriving
은세계 銀世界 a silver world ; the whole landscape covered〔blanketed〕 with snow ; a vast snowy scene ¶ 아침에 일어나 보니 온 세상이 은세계였다 I awoke to find the world mantled in a sheet of white snow.
은세공 銀細工 silverwork ; [세공품] silverware
은수저 銀— silver spoons and chopsticks ; silver
은시계 銀時計 a silver watch
은신 隱身 rendering oneself invisible ; hiding oneself **—하다** hide oneself
—처 a hiding-place ; a refuge ; a den (범인의)
은실 銀— silver thread〔strand〕
은애 恩愛 favor and love ; kindness and affection ; tender feeling
은어 銀漁 a sweetfish ; Plecoglossus altivelis (학명)
은어 隱語 secret language ; a jargon ; a cant ; an argot ¶ 은어로 이야기하다 talk in a secret language
은연 隱然 —하다 (be) latent ; hidden ; secret ; behind-the-scenes ¶ 은연한 세력 a latent power ; covert〔hidden〕 influence // 은연중 in secret ; behind the scenes ; secretly ; tacitly // 은연중에 친구를 돕다 help a friend on the quiet // 그는 동료 사이에 은연히 세력을 펴고 있다 He has great influence with his comrades, though he is never obtrusive.
은옥색 銀玉色 light green color
은우 恩遇 beneficial〔favorable〕 treatment ; hospitality **—하다** treat beneficially〔with favor〕; show〔give〕 great hospitality to 《a person》
은원 恩怨 love and hate ; favor and spite〔grudge〕 ¶ 은원을 떠나서 beyond love and hate
은위 恩威 mercy and justice ; leniency and sternness
***은유 隱喩** a metaphor ¶ 은유적으로 metaphorically
은은하다 殷殷— (be) roaring ; booming ; bellowing ; reverberating ¶ 은은히 with roaring〔booming〕 sounds // 은은한 포성 the booming of guns // 멀리서 포성이 은은히 들렸다 A roar of guns was heard in the distance.
은은하다 隱隱— ① [귀에] (be) distant ; faint ; indistinct ¶ 종소리가 은은히 들린다 A sound of a bell is faintly heard. ② [눈에] (be) vague ; dim ¶ 은은히 보이다 be seen dimly〔at a dim distance〕
은의 恩義, 恩誼 a debt of gratitude ; indebtedness and obligation ¶ 은의에 보답하다 repay 《a person》 for his kindness
은익 銀翼 silver wings
은인 恩人 a benefactor ; a patron ; a person who has done one a great favor ¶ 한국 음악계의 대은인 a great benefactor of the musical world of Korea // 그는 나의 생명의 은인이다 I owe him my life. /He saved my life.
은인 隱忍 endurance ; perseverance ; patience **—하다** (be) patient ; endure ; put up with ; suffer in silence ; bear up ¶ 모욕을 당하고도 은인 자중하다 pocket〔swallow〕 an insult // 10년 동안 은인 자중한 보람 있어 마침내 그에게 내각이 돌아왔다 His patient endurance for ten long years was rewarded with an opportunity to form a cabinet.
은일 隱逸 seclusion ⇨ 은둔
은자 銀字 silver letters〔characters〕; letters written in silver paint
****은자 隱者** ⇨ 은사(隱士)
은잔 銀盞 a silver cup
은장 銀匠 a silversmith ; a jewel(l)er
은장도 銀粧刀 an ornamental silver knife

〔sword〕
은장식 銀裝飾 ornamentation〔decoration〕 with silver —하다 ornament〔decorate, adorn, mount〕 with silver
은재 隱才 (a) hidden talent
은저울 銀— a small balance〔steelyard〕 for weighing precious metals
은적 隱迹 abscondence ; concealment of one's traces〔whereabouts〕 —하다 abscond《from》; conceal〔cover〕 one's traces
은전 恩典 a special favor〔grace〕; an act of grace ; a special privilege ¶ 특별한 은전으로 by special grace ; as a special act of grace // 은전을 입다 receive〔be granted〕 special favors
은전 銀錢 a silver coin
은정 恩情 benevolent〔gracious〕 affection ; favor
은제 銀製 [은으로 된] made of silver ; [제품] silverware
은조사 銀造紗 a thin silk made in China
은족반 隱足盤 a flat-bottomed round tray
은종이 銀— silver paper ; tin foil
은줄[1] 銀— [줄] a silver cord
은줄[2] 銀— 〖광산〗 a vein of silver
은진 殷賑 prosperity ; flourishingness ; abundance ; opulence
은짬 secrecy ; privacy
†은총 恩寵 favor ; grace ¶ 신의 은총 the grace of God // 은총을 받다 win《a person's》 favor // 은총을 입다 be in favor with《a person》; stand high in《a person's》 favor // 은총을 잃다 fall from favor ; lose《a person's》 favor ; fall into disfavor
은총이 銀— a horse with white testicles
은침 銀鍼 a silver acupuncture needle
은칭 銀秤 a precious-metal scale〔balance〕
은택 恩澤 grace and benevolent influence ¶ 문명의 은택을 입다 enjoy〔share in〕 the benefits of civilization
은테 銀— a silver rim〔frame〕
— 안경 silver(-rimmed) spectacles
*은퇴 隱退 retirement《from a post》; seclusion《from the world》 —하다 retire《from active life》; withdraw《from public life》; return to private life ¶ 은퇴한 정치가 a retired politician // 정계〔은막〕에서 은퇴하다 retire from politics〔the screen〕 // 은급을 받고 은퇴하다 retire with〔on〕 a pension // 은퇴해서 넉넉하게 살다 retire with a handsome competence
— 경기 a farewell match — 생활 a retired life ¶ 은퇴 생활을 하다 live in retirement ; live a retired〔sequestered〕 life
은파 銀波 the silvery waves ; white waves
*은폐 隱蔽 concealment ; hiding ; suppression —하다 conceal ; hide ; cover up ; suppress ; keep《a matter》 secret〔dark〕 ¶ 사실을 은폐하다 suppress〔cover up〕 a fact // 죄상을 은폐하다 cover up (the traces of) a crime
은피 隱避 concealment ; shelter ; refuge —하다 conceal〔hide〕 oneself ; shelter
*은하 銀河 the Milky Way ; the Galaxy
—계 the galactic system —면 the galactic plane —수 ⇨ 은하 — 좌표 the galactic coordinates
은합 銀盒 a silver bowl with a lid
†은행 銀行 a bank ¶ 은행에 예금하다 deposit money in a bank // 은행과 거래를 트다〔끊다〕 open〔close〕 an account with a bank // 은행에서 돈을 인출하다 draw money from a bank // 은행에 1만 달러의 예금이 있다 have a bank account of $10,000 at a bank
—가 a banker — 감독원 the Bank Inspection Board — 강도 [사람] a bank burglar ; [행위] bank robbery — 거래 bank account ; banking account〔transactions〕 — 계 banking circles —권 a bank note〔bill〕 — 대출 bank advances —법 the Banking Act — 부기 bank bookkeeping — 신용장 a bank credit — 어음 a bank bill〔draft〕 — 업 banking (business) — 영업 시간 banking hours — 예금 bank deposits〔savings〕 — 운용 자금 banking capital〔fund〕 —원 a bank employee〔clerk〕; the staff of a bank《총칭》 — 이자 bank interest (rate) —장 the president of a bank —주 a bank stock — 집회소 a bankers' club — 통장 a bankbook ; a passbook — 할인 bank discount —환 a bank money order ; exchange ; a bank bill ; a banker's draft 국제 결제 — the Bank for International Settlement《B. I. S》 국제 부흥 개발 — the International Bank for Reconstruction and Development《I. B. R. D.》 예금 — a deposit money bank 상업 — a commercial bank 저축 — a savings bank 중앙 — the Central Bank 지방 — a local〔provincial〕 bank 지폐 발행 — a bank of issue 학교 — a school bank 한국 — The Bank of Korea 혈액 — a blood bank
은행 銀杏 a ginkgo nut
— 나무 a gingko tree
은현 隱現 appearing and disappearing —하다 appear and disappear ; come in and out of sight
은혈 銀穴 a silver lode ; a silver mine
은혈 隱穴 an invisible hole〔cave〕; a hidden opening
—못 a double-pointed peg
*은혜 恩惠 favors ; benefits ; a boon ; kindnesses ; a grace ; obligations ¶ 스승의 은혜 the goodness of one's teacher ; obligation one owes to one's teacher // 어버이의 은혜 parental love ; debt to one's parents // 은혜를 잊다 be ungrateful ; lose one's gratitude // 은혜를 갚다 repay〔return〕 another's kindness ; compensate for one's indebtedness // 은혜를 베풀다 do《a person》 a favor ; bestow favors on《a person》 // 은혜를 입다 enjoy the

benefits of ; receive benefits ; be indebted to // 이 은혜는 결코 잊지 않겠습니다 I shall be eternally grateful to you.

은혼식 銀婚式 a silver wedding (anniversary) ¶ 은혼식을 올리다 celebrate 《their》 silver wedding

은홍색 隱紅色 faint pink

†**은화 銀貨** a silver (coin) ¶ 은화 본위로 on a silver basis

— **본위제** the silver standard

은화식물 隱花植物 a cryptogam ; a flowerless plant

은회색 銀灰色 silver gray

은휘 隱諱 concealment ; suppression — **하다** conceal ; suppress ; cover up ; hide

†**을** ① [목적격 조사] ¶ 말을 타다 ride 〔mount〕 a horse // 신문을 읽다 read the newspaper // 가슴을 채이다 get kicked in the chest // 약점을 잡히다 have one's weakness seized〔played〕 upon

② [목표·방향] ¶ 언제 서울을 가느냐 When are you going to *Seoul* ?

③ [어디] ¶ 하늘을 날다 fly (in) the sky // 강을 건너다 cross a river

④ [목적] ¶ 여행을 떠나다 set out on a trip // 영화 구경을 가다 go to see a movie

⑤ [동안] ¶ 두 시간을 잠자다 sleep (for) two hours

⑥ [구어용법] ¶ 앞장을 서다 stand in the van〔lead〕

⑦ [관계] ¶ A군을 상대로 with A for a counterpart〔an opposite number〕 // 그것을 구실로 with (using) that for an excuse // 서울을 중심으로 with *Seoul* as the center // 문법을 중심으로 공부하다 be studying mainly grammar ; be studying with the emphasis on grammar

⑧ [차례] ¶ 수석을 하다 go〔rank〕 first

⑨ [동족 목적어] ¶ 잠을 자다 sleep (a sleep) // 꿈을 꾸다 dream (a dream) // 숨을 쉬다 breathe (a breath)

⑩ [생략·강조] ¶ 하늘에는 영광을, 땅에는 평화를 Glory be in the heaven, and peace on earth ! // 나에게 자유가 아니면 죽음을 달라 Give me liberty, or give me death.

을 乙 the second (둘째) ; B (급수의) ; the latter (후자) ¶ 1학년 을반 the 1st Year, Class B

-을까 ⇨ -ㄹ까

을근거리다 menace ; threaten

을근을근 menacingly ; intimidatingly

을러메다 threaten ; menace ; frighten ; scare ¶ 을러메어 by threats ; by intimidation // 죽인다고〔투옥한다고, 체포한다고〕 을러메다 threaten 《a person》 with death〔imprisonment, arrest〕 // 을러메어 승낙케 하다 threaten 《a person》 into compliance

-을망정 even if〔though〕 ; rather... than ; but ¶ 굶을망정 그에게 청은 안하겠다 Even though I were starving, I would not ask a favor of him. // 죽을망정 그짓은 못하겠다 I would rather die than do it.

을모 a 3-sided corner ; a truncated angle ; a triangular article

을묘 乙卯 〖민속〗 the 52nd binary term of the sexagenary cycle

을미 乙未 〖민속〗 the 32nd binary term of the sexagenary cycle

을밋을밋 tardily ; from day to day ¶ 빚을 을밋을밋 밀어가다 let the debt stand over 〔stay on the books〕 indefinitely

을방 乙方 〖민속〗 east by southeast

을사 乙巳 〖민속〗 the 42nd binary term of the sexagenary cycle

을시 乙時 〖민속〗 the 8th of the 24 hour periods 《6 : 30 - 7 : 30 a. m.》

을씨년스럽다 ① [쓸쓸해 보이다] (be) desolate ; shabby ; wretched ¶ 옷이 너절해서 을씨년스럽다 look wretched with shabby clothes ② [군색] be poorly 〔badly〕 off ; (be) poor ; miserable ¶ 살림이 을씨년스럽다 live in poverty ; live poor ; be poorly〔badly〕 off

을야 乙夜 the second watch at night

을유 乙酉 〖민속〗 the 22nd binary term of the sexagenary cycle

을종 乙種 class B ; second grade

-을지언정 ⇨ -ㄹ지언정

을축 乙丑 〖민속〗 the 2nd binary term of the sexagenary cycle

을해 乙亥 〖민속〗 the 12th binary term of the sexagenary cycle

*‡***읊다** recite〔sing〕 《a poem》 ; write〔compose〕 《a poem》 ¶ 시를 읊다 recite a poem ; compose a poem

읊조리다 recite

†**음 音** ① [소리] a sound ; a note ; a tone ¶ 높은〔낮은〕 음 a high〔low〕 tone // 아름다운 음 a melodious〔musical〕 sound ② [자음] pronunciation (of a Chinese character) ¶ 한자를 음으로 읽다 read Chinese characters phonetically // 이 글자의 음이 무엇이냐 What is the pronunciation of this word ?

음 陰 ① 〖철학〗 Yin ; the negative〔female〕 principle in nature ② 〖수학〗 a negative 〔minus〕 sign ; 〖물리〗 a negative ion ③ [그늘] shade ; [이면] back ; secrecy ¶ 음으로 privately ; indirectly ; secretly ; in secret ; implicitly // 음으로 양으로 publicly and privately ; implicitly and explicitly ; directly and indirectly

음가 音價 phonetic value

음각 陰角 a negative angle

음각 陰刻 intaglio ; (depressed) engraving — **하다** intaglio ; engrave

음감 音感 a sense of sound

— **교육** auditory education ; acoustic training

음건 陰乾 drying 《a thing》 in the shade — **하다** dry 《a thing》 in the shade

음경 陰莖 the penis

— **숭배** phallicism

음계 音界 〖물리〗 the sound field
음계 音階 the (musical) scale ¶ 음계 연습하다 do scales
반— a chromatic scale **장〔단〕—** the major〔minor〕 scale **전—** the gamut ; the diatonic scale **평균 —** a tempered scale
음계 陰界 the world of the dead ; the place of the departed
음곡 音曲 musical performance
— 금지 prohibition of musical entertainments〔performances〕
음공 陰功 hidden merits ; distinguished services behind the scenes〔unknown〕
음극 陰極 the negative pole ; the cathode **—선** the cathode ray **—액** catholyte **—판** a negative plate
음기 陰氣 ① [음울] shadiness ; gloominess ; dismalness
② [찬기운] (a) chill ; cold
음낭 陰囊 the scrotum
음녀 淫女 a lewd woman ; an unchaste woman ; a woman of loose morals
음담 淫談 obscene conversation ; bawdy〔filthy〕 talk ; lewd stories
—패설(悖說) ⇨ 음담
음덕 陰德 hidden〔unostentatious〕 virtue ; kind acts done in secret ¶ 음덕을 베풀다 do good in secret
음덕 蔭德 the ancestor's virtue
음도 音度 pitch
†**음독 音讀** ① reading Chinese characters by their traditional Chinese pronunciation ; the Chinese reading of a character **—하다** read Chinese character phonetically ② reading aloud ; vocal〔loud〕 reading **—하다** read aloud
음독 飮毒 taking poison **—하다** take poison
— 자살 suicide by taking poison
음동 陰冬 a dull and cold〔gloomy, dismal, dreary〕 winter
음락 淫樂 sensual〔carnal〕 pleasure
음란 淫亂 lewdness ; lechery ; lasciviousness ; incontinence **—하다** (be) lewd ; lascivious〔lecherous〕 ; lustful ¶ 음란한 여자 a loose〔lewd〕 woman ; a woman of easy virtue // 어떤 남자가 나한테 음란한 말을 하고 내 엉덩이를 만졌단말야 A man said dirty words and touched my behind.
음란증 淫亂症 ⇨ 색광(一증)
피학대 — masochism **학대 —** sadism
음랭 陰冷 the dark and cold ; gloominess ; dreariness **—하다** (be) dark and cold ; gloomy ; dreary
†**음량 音量** volume (of voice of sound)
음력 陰曆 the lunar calendar ¶ 음력 10월 24일 October 24th of〔according to〕 the lunar calendar // 음력을 쓰다 follow the lunar calendar // 음력으로 날을 세다 reckon the days according to the lunar calendar // 오늘은 음력 설로 우리 한국인에게는 휴일이다 Today is the lunar New Year's day, a holiday for us Koreans.
—설 the Lunar New Year's Day
음료 飮料 a beverage ; a drink ¶ 음료로 적합하다 be fit to drink ; be good to drink // 음료로 쓰다 use for drinking purposes
알코올 — an alcoholic〔a strong〕 drink **청량 —** a cooling drink ; soft drinks **혼합 —** mixed drinks
음료수 飮料水 drinking water ; potable water
음률 音律 tone(s) and rhythm(s) ; music **—학** rhythmics
음매 [소우는 소리] (with a) low ; (with a) moo ¶ 음매 울다 moo ; low
음모 陰毛 pubic hair ; pubes
⁑**음모 陰謀** a plot ; an (underhand) intrigue ; a conspiracy ; machination **—하다** plot ; form a conspiracy ; intrigue ; conspire ; machinate ¶ 음모에 가담하다 be implicated in a plot ; take part in a conspiracy ; get entangled in a plot // 암살 음모를 꾸미다 plot〔conspire〕 against another's life ; plot another's assassination
—가 a schemer ; a machinater ; a mischief maker **—단** a band of conspirators ; a cabal ; a junto **—자** a plotter ; a conspirator ; an intriguer
음문 陰門 the vulva ; the vagina
음물 淫物 a lewd fellow ; a licentious〔lascivious〕 person
음미 吟味 appreciation ; close examination ; critical study ; scrutiny **—하다** appreciate ; examine closely ; investigate minutely ; study critically ; scrutinize ¶ 시를 음미하다 relish poems
음미 淫靡 lasciviousness ; obscenity **—하다** (be) lascivious ; obscene
음반 音盤 a phonograph record ; a disc
음보 音譜 ⇨ 악보(樂譜)
음복 陰伏 **—하다** lie concealed
음복 飮福 **—하다** partake of sacrificial food and drink
음부 音符 a (musical) note ; a (musical) score ; notation ¶ 음부의 길이 time // 음부를 읽다 read (musical) scores〔notes〕 // 음부를 적다 write notes〔musical scores〕 // 음부를 읽을 줄 알다 be able to read notes
음부 陰部 the pubic region ; the pubes ; the private〔secret, privy〕 parts ; the secret 《속》
음부 淫婦 a lewd woman ⇨ 음녀
음부 기호 音部記號 〖음악〗 a clef
음분 淫奔 lewd〔lascivious, unchaste〕 conduct by a woman ; wantonness **—하다** behave lewdly ; act lasciviously
음비 陰秘 sneakiness ; treacherousness **—하다** (be) sneaky ; snaky ; treacherous
음사 淫祠 a shrine dedicated to supersti-

tious worship
음사 淫辭 obscene〔improper, lewd〕 language ; indecent〔nasty, filthy, dirty〕 talk
음사 陰事 ① [비밀] a secret ; confidential〔private〕 affairs ② [성교] sexual intercourse ; coition —하다 have sexual intercourse
음산 陰散 —하다 (be) cloudy and gloomy ; dreary and cold ¶ 음산한 날씨 dismal weather
음색 音色 the quality of a tone ; a tone (color) ; a timbre ¶ 하프와 플루트는 음색이 다르다 The harp and the flute differ in timbre.
— 조절(장치) 〖전기〗 (a) tone control
음서 淫書 an erotic book ; a foul〔lascivious〕 book ; obscene literature ; pornography
*음성 音聲 [목소리] a voice ; 〖언어〗 the phonetics〔sounds〕 of a language ¶ 좋은〔감미로운, 남자다운〕 음성 a good〔sweet, manly〕 voice // 음성을 높이다 raise one's voice // 음성이 좋다 have a sweet〔fine, musical〕 voice // 그는 음성이 부드럽다 He is gentle in voice. /He has a gentle voice.
— 기호 a phonetic sign ; a phonetic notation — 단위 a phone ; a phonetic unit〔segment〕 — 신호 an audio signal — 체계 a phonetic system —학 phonetics —학자 a phonetician
*음성 陰性 negative ; negativity ; dormancy ; passive character ; passivity ¶ 음성의 negative ; dormant // 시험 결과 음성으로 나타났다 The result of the examination was negative.
— 거래 unlawful〔illicit, under-the-table〕 deal〔transaction〕 — 수입 [관리의] spoils ; a perquisite ¶ 음성 수입을 얻다 get perquisites — 원소 an electronegative element — 전대(電帶) negative electrification — 콜레라 dormant cholera
음성학 音聲學 phonetics ¶ 음성학의 phonetic(al)
음소 音素 〖음성〗 a phoneme ¶ 음소의 phonemic
— 기호 a phonemic symbol —론 phonemics — 문자 alphabetic〔phonemic〕 writing — 체계 a phonemic system —화(化) phonemicization ¶ 음소화하다 phonemicize
음속 音速 the velocity〔speed〕 of sound ¶ 음속의 sonic
극초(極超) — hypersonic speed 초— supersonic speed 초—학 supersonics
음송 吟誦 recitation ; a recital —하다 recite
음수 陰數 〖수학〗 a negative number ; a minus quantity ; a minus
음순 陰脣 the labium 《*pl.* -bia》
대〔소〕— the labia majora〔minora〕 ; the major〔minor〕 labia of the vulva
음습 淫習 lascivious habits ; wanton customs ; lecherous ways
음습 陰濕 the dark and damp —하다 (be) dark and damp ; shady and damp
*음식 飮食 food (and drink) ; foodstuffs ; a meal ; refreshments ; eating and drinking ¶ 간단한 음식 light refreshments // 음식의 즐거움 pleasure of the table // 조잡한 음식 humble fare // 음식이 좋다 have a good table // 음식을 절제하다 be moderate in eating and drinking // 음식에 조심하다 be careful about what one eats and drinks // 음식에 조심하라 Be careful about your food〔diet〕. // 그 식당은 음식이 좋다 That restaurant has a good bill of fare. // 나는 음식에 까다롭지 않다 I eat anything offered at table. // 한국 음식 중에서 어떤 것을 가장 좋아합니까 What's your favorite Korean dish?
—용 for table use —용 기구 tableware ; table service —점 an eating house ; a restaurant
음신 音信 news ; tidings ; a letter ; correspondence ; communication ¶ 수주일 동안 그들에게서 음신이 없다 We had not heard from them for weeks. /We were without news for weeks.
음심 淫心 an inclination toward lewdness〔licentiousness〕 ; a zest for lechery
†음악 音樂 music ¶ 음악의 대가 a great musician // 음악적인 musical ; melodious // 음악을 좋아하는 philharmonic ; musical ; music-loving // 음악을 연주하다 play〔perform〕 music // 음악을 배우다 take lessons in music // 음악에 취미가 있다 be musical ; have a taste for music ; be of a musical turn // 음악을 모르다 have no ear for music ; be deaf to music // 저는 음악에는 별로 소질이 없습니다 I don't have a very good ear for music.
—가 a musician — 감독 a music director — 감상실 a music hall —계 musical circles ; the musical world — 교육 musical education —당 a concert hall ; an odeum《*pl.* ~s, odea》 ; a bandstand (야외용) — 사 musical history ; the history of music — 선생 a music teacher ; a music master〔mistress〕 —성 musicality ; musicianship — 애호가 a lover of music ; a philharmonic — 영화 a musical (film) — 콩쿠르 대회 a musical contest — 학교 a music school〔academy〕 —회 a concert ; a musicale (파아티의) 《미》 ; a recital (독창·독주회) ; a musical society (협회) — 효과 musical effects ; the background music 고전 — classical music 교회 — church music 구체 — concrete music ; musique concrète 《프》 극장 — scenic music 실내 — chamber music 절대 — absolute〔abstract〕 music 표제 — program music
음약 淫藥 an aphrodisiac ; a love potion ; a philter ⇨ 미약(媚藥)
음양 陰陽 the cosmic dual forces ; the

male and female principles ; the sun and the moon ; [전기·자기의] the negative and positive (electricity) ¶ 음양의 화합 the harmony of the male and female principles
—각(刻) intaglio and relief —성 polarity ; duality —쟁이〔가〕 a necromancer ; a fortuneteller

음역 音域 compass ; musical range ¶ 음역이 넓은 목소리 voice of great compass

음역 音譯 transliteration —하다 transliterate

음염 淫艶 sensual charm ; voluptuousness

음영 recitation of a (Chinese) poem —하다 recite a (Chinese) poem

음영 陰影 shadow (그림자) ; shade (그늘) ¶ 음영을 던지다 cast a shadow〔gloom〕

음예 淫穢 obscenity and impurity ; indecency —하다 (be) obscene and vulgar

음욕 淫慾 carnal desire ; sensual〔sexual〕 appetite ; lust ¶ 음욕에 탐닉하다 indulge in sensual pleasures // 음욕을 억제하다 restrain〔control〕 one's passion

음용 音容 voice and countenance〔appearance〕

음용 飮用 (for) drinking purpose —하다 drink ; take ; have ¶ 음용에 적합하다 be fit〔good〕 to drink ; be drinkable // 음용에 부적당하다 be unfit for drinking ; be undrinkable
—수(水) drinking water ; water to drink ; [게시] Fit to drink.

음우 陰雨 a dreary rain ; a dismal rain 〔wet〕

음우 a long spell of nasty rainy weather

음운 音韻 [음성] a phoneme ; the phonological structure of a word ; the initial sound and final rhyme of a Chinese syllable
— 조직 sound system —학〔론〕 phonology ; phonemics —학자 a phonologist

‡음울 陰鬱 gloominess ; dullness ; dismalness —하다 (be) gloomy ; dismal ; melancholy ¶ 음울한 날씨 gloomy weather // 음울한 하늘 a heavy〔gloomy〕 sky // 음울한 이야기 a dismal conversation // 음울한 성격 a melancholy temperament 〔disposition〕

음원 音源 a sound source
— 탐지법 sound ranging

음월 陰月 the 4th lunar month

음위 impotence ; impotency

음으로 陰— privately ; implicitly ; indirectly ; secretly ; in secret
음으로 양으로 관용 publicly and privately ; implicitly and explicitly

음읍 飮泣 a sob —하다 sob ; give a sob

음의 音義 the sound and meaning of a Chinese character

음이온 陰— 〖화학〗 a negative ion ; an anion

음일 淫佚 licentious indulgence —하다 give rein to〔indulge in〕 sensual pleasure

음자 音字 a phonetic sign〔character, symbol〕 ; a phonogram

음전 —하다 (be) gentle ; prudent ; well-behaved ; modesty ; decency ¶ 음전한 색시 a nice young lady // 행동이 음전하다 be gentle in manner

음전 音栓 [오르간의] a stop (knob)

음전기 陰電氣 negative electricity

음전자 陰電子 〖물리〗 a negative electron ; a negatron

‡음절 音節 ① 〖언어〗 a syllable ② 〖음악〗 a musical measure ; a bar of music ¶ 단음절의 말 a monosyllabic word // 음절로 나누다 syllabify ; divide into syllables
— 문자 syllabic character ; a syllabary 단〔이·삼·다〕—어 a monosyllabic 〔dis(s)yllabic, trisyllabic, polysyllabic〕 word

음정 音程 a musical interval ; a tone
반— a semi-tone ; a half step 사분— a quarter tone 장〔단〕— a major〔minor〕 (interval) 전— a tone ; a whole step 협화〔불협화〕— a consonant〔dissonant〕 interval

음정증 陰挺症 〖의학〗 a case of fallen uterus ; uterine prolapse

†음조 音調 tune ; rhythm ; melody ¶ 음조의 변화 modulation ; inflection of voice // 아름다운 음조로 in a melodious tune // 음조가 좋다 be euphonical ; be euphonious ; be melodious

음조 陰助 secret assistance —하다 assist secretly ; help by stealth

음종 陰腫 〖의학〗 an ulcer〔a chancre〕 on the surface of the vulva

음주 飮酒 drinking —하다 drink ¶ 음주의 해독 evil effects of drinking // 상습적인 음주자 an inveterate drinker // 음주에 빠지다 be addicted to drinking // 음주로 패가하다 drink one's fortune away // 그는 음주가 과하다 He is too fond of drink.
—가 a drinker —벽 drinking habit ; inebriety — 운전 drunken driving ; driving while intoxicated ¶ 새삼스럽게 말할 필요도 없지만 음주 운전만은 하지 마시오 I don't think I have to tell you that I won't have you drinking and driving. // 그는 음주 운전으로 유죄 판결을 받았다 He was convicted of drunk driving. // 그는 섣달 그믐날 밤에 음주 운전 단속반에 걸려서 혈중 알코올 농도 테스트를 받았는데 통과하지 못했다 On New Year's Eve he was stopped at a sobriety checkpoint and he failed the Breathalyzer test. — 운전자 a drunken driver

음증 陰症 [성격] treacherous character ; [사람] a black-hearted man ; [병] a sickness that becomes worse in the afternoon

음지 陰地 a shady spot ; shaded lot ¶ 양지와 음지 light and shade // 음지에서 온도가 32°였다 The temperature was 32° in the shade.

음지도 양지된다 〔속담〕 Sadness and gladness succeed each other. /Joy and sorrow are next door neighbours. /Bad luck often brings good luck. /The worse luck now, the better another time.
음질 音質 tone quality ; the quality of sound
음차 音叉 a tuning fork
음창 陰瘡 〖의학〗 an ulcer〔a chancre〕 on the vulva
음청 陰晴 cloudy and〔or〕 clear weather —계 a barometer
음축 陰縮 atrophy of the penis
음충맞다, 음충스럽다 ⇨ 음충하다
음충하다 (be) black-hearted ; evil-hearted ; wicked ; crafty ; wily ; insidious ; treacherous ¶ 음충한 사람 a black-hearted person ; a deep one
음치 音痴 tone-deafness ; lack of musical ability ¶ 그는 음치다 He is tone-deaf. ∥ 나는 음치다 I can't carry a tune (in a bucket). /I don't have a very good ear for music.
*음침하다 陰沈— (be) gloomy ; dismal ; dreary ; somber ; melancholy ¶ 음침한 날씨 gloomy weather ∥ 음침한 방 a dismal〔somber〕 room ∥ 그는 항시 음침하다 He is always in the dismals.
음탐 淫貪 a taste for lewdness ; a hunger for lechery —하다 (be) lecherous ; love lustful pleasure
*음탕 淫蕩 debauchery ; licentiousness ; lechery ; profligacy —하다 (be) dissipated ; debauched ; voluptuous ; licentious ; lascivious ¶ 음탕한 풍조 loose morals ; lewd manners
음택 陰宅 a tomb
음통하다 陰通— have one's initial sexual intercourse ; have carnal knowledge ; lose one's innocence〔virginity〕
음파 音波 a sound wave —계 an audiometer — 측정 phonometry — 측정기 a phonometer — 탐지기 a sonar ; a sonobuoy
음판 陰板 〖사진〗 a negative (plate)
음표 音標 〖음악〗 a (musical) note ; notation ¶ 음표의 길이 the length of a musical note ∥ 음표를 적다 write notes〔musical scores〕 ∥ 음표를 읽을 줄 알다 be able to read notes
고— the treble (score) 온— a whole〔full〕 note 《미》 ; a semibreve 《영》 잇단— a group of notes 저— the bass (score) 2분— a half note 《미》 ; a minim 4분 — a quarter note 《미》 ; a crotchet 《영》 8분 — an eighth note 《미》 ; a quaver 《영》 16분 — a sixteenth note 《미》 ; a semiquaver 《영》 32분 — a thirty-second note 《미》 ; a demisemiquaver 《영》 64분 — a sixty-fourth note 《미》 ; a hemidemisemiquaver
음표 문자 音標文字 phonetic alphabet〔notation sign〕 ; a phonogram
만국 — the international phonetic alphabet〔signs〕 《IPA》
음풍 淫風 lascivious customs ; lewd manners ; lecherous ways ; loose morals ⇨ 음습(淫習)
음풍농월 吟風弄月 poetical enthusiasm ; communion with nature —하다 compose poetry
음풍영월 吟風咏月 ⇨ 음풍농월
음하다 淫— (be) lewd ; lustful ; lecherous ; obscene
음하다 陰— [날씨가] (be) cloudy ; [마음씨가] black-hearted ; dark
음해 陰害 —하다 do 《a person》 harm〔an injury〕 secretly
음핵 陰核 the clitoris
음행 淫行 lewd〔immoral, unchaste〕 conduct ; an obscene act
음향 音響 a sound ; a noise ; a report ¶ 음향의 전파 sound propagation ∥ 음향의 효과 a sound〔an acoustic〕 effect ∥ 폭탄이 무서운 음향을 내면서 폭발했다 The bomb went off with a terrific report.
—기 a sounder — 배경 [라디오] acoustic perspective — 설비 sound facilities — 실 [악기의] a sound box — 전파 sound propagation — 조절 [홀의] sound conditioning — 측심 echo sounding — 측심기 an echo sounder ; an echo-sounding device ; a sonic depth finder — 탐지기 a sound detector ; a sound detection gear — 폭탄 a screamer bomb —학 acoustics —학자 an acoustician — 효과 sound〔acoustic〕 effects ; acoustics ; 〖라디오〗 background
음험 陰險 —하다 (be) insidious ; snaky ; crafty ; tricky ; wily ¶ 음험한 사람 an insidious man ; a tricky fellow ∥ 음험한 수단을 부리다 use a treacherous〔an underhand〕 method
음화 陰畫 a negative (print)
음황 淫荒 wild debauchery —하다 (be) wildly debauched
음훈 音訓 the pronunciation and the meaning (of a Chinese character)
음흉 陰凶 wickedness ; treacherousness —하다 (be) cunning ; wily ; crafty ; tricky ; treacherous ¶ 음흉한 사람 a tricky guy ; a crafty fellow
†읍 邑 a town ¶ 읍에 가다 go up to town —사무소 a town office —세 a town tax —장 the mayor of a town —지(誌) a town chronicle ; the history of a town
읍 揖 a low bow〔an obeisance〕 with one's hands in front —하다 bow politely with (joined) hands in front
읍간 泣諫 tearful remonstration〔expostulation〕 —하다 remonstrate〔expostulate〕 with tears
읍내 邑內 《in》 a town ⇨ 읍(邑) ¶ 읍내에 살다 live in the town
읍례 揖禮 ⇨ 읍(揖)
읍민 邑民 the inhabitants of a town ; the

townsmen ; the townspeople ; the townsfolks
읍소 泣訴 ―하다 implore〔supplicate, appeal to〕《a person for mercy》 with tears in one's eyes
읍양 揖讓 [예로써 사양함] declining politely ; courteous concession ; [태도] a courteous and humble attitude ―하다 yield courteously ; assume〔show〕 a courteous and humble attitude
읍청 泣請 a sincere request (with tears) ―하다 implore ; entreat
읍체 泣涕 shedding tears ; sobbing ; weeping ―하다 shed tears ; weep ; sob
읍촌 邑村 towns and villages
응 mmh ; uh-huh ; yes ; yeah ; all right ; O.K. ¶ 응 하고 대답하다 say yes ; give one's consent // 응 꼭 갈게 Oh yes, I will come without fail. // 공원에 가자 응 Let us go to the park, huh?
응결 凝結 congelation ; solidification ; freezing (액체의) ; coagulation (피 따위의) ; condensation (기체의) ; curdling (우유따위의) ; setting (시멘트 따위의) ―하다 congeal ; coagulate ; curdle ; solidify ; freeze ; condense
―기(器) a freezer ―물 a congelation 《of》 ; a coagulation 《of》 ― 시간 setting time ―점 the freezing〔congealing〕 point ―제 a coagulant
응고 凝固 solidification ; congelation (액체가) ; coagulation (혈액 따위가) ; condensation (기체가) ―하다 solidify ; congeal ; coagulate
응그리다 ① [찡그리다] frown 《at, upon》 ; scowl 《at, on》 ② [움켜잡다] clasp ; grab 《at》 ; hold
응급 應急 emergency ―하다 take a temporary expedient ; employ a stopgap measure ¶ 응급의 first-aid ; temporary // 응급 의료진이 곧 도착할 겁니다 Paramedics will be right over.
― 수단〔조치〕 an expediency ; makeshift measures ; stopgap measures ―책 emergency measures
‡응급 치료 應急治療 first aid (treatment) ; emergency treatment ―하다 give first-aid treatment ¶ 응급 치료로 살아난 사람이 많다 Many were saved by first aid.
―소 a first-aid room〔station〕
*응낙 應諾 consent ; assent ; acceptance ; response ―하다 agree 《to》 ; respond 《to》 ; assent 《to》 ; consent 《to》 ¶ 응낙없이 without 《a person's》 consent // 응낙을 청하다 ask 《a person's》 consent // 무리로 응낙시키다 force one's will upon another // 요구를 응낙하다 comply with the request // 그는 계획 변경의 제안에 응낙했다 He assented to the suggested change in plans.
*응달 the shade ; the shady side ¶ 응달에서 쉬다 take a rest in the shade // 응달에 물건을 두다 keep a thing in the shade // (수목 따위) 응달을 만들다 give〔provide, afford〕 shade 《from the warm sun》 // 나무가 있어 집에 응달이 잘 진다 The trees shade the house nicely.
‡응답 應答 an answer ; a reply ; a response ―하다 answer ; reply 《to》 ; respond 《to》 ¶ 노크를 했지만 응답이 없었다 I was unable to get a response to my knocking.
― 악절 〖음악〗 an antistrophe ―자 a respondent 질의 ― questions and answers ; answers to queries
응당 應當 for sure ; without fail ; necessarily ¶ 응당 그렇게 믿어야지 It's natural for you to believe it. // 식사 전에는 응당 손을 씻는 법이다 Be sure to wash your hands before a meal.
응대 應對 ① [응답] a response ; an answer ② [면담] an interview ; personal conversation ―하다 answer ; reply to ; rejoin ; have an interview with ; talk personally with ; meet and talk with ¶ 그가 남을 응대하는 솜씨는 참 능수능란하다 He shows consummate tact in dealing with people.
응대 應對 reception ⇨ 응접
응등그러지다 dry up ; shrink up ; shrivel ; [뒤틀리다] be awry ; be twisted
응등그리다 shrink 《one's body》 ; huddle up ; duck 《one's head》
응력 應力 〖기계〗 stress ; 〖주물〗 internal stress
*응모 應募 subscription (예약) ; application (지원) ; entry (참가) ; enlistment ―하다 apply for ; subscribe to〔for〕 ; enlist ; enter for 《games, a contest》 ¶ 국채 모집에 응모하다 subscribe for government bonds // 응모액이 소요액을 초과했다 The subscription has covered more than the amount required.
― 신청 an application for subscription ― 원고 manuscript entered 《for the prize》 ―자 an applicant 《for a school》 ; a subscriber 《to》 ; an entrant ¶ 현상 논문 응모자 a prize essayist ― 자금 a subscribed capital ― 총액 the total subscription〔sum subscribed〕
응받다 ⇨ 응석받다
응변 應變 ⇨ 임기 응변(臨機應變)
†응보 應報 retribution ; nemesis ¶ 인과응보 As a man sows, so he shall reap.
응분 應分 accordance with one's circumstances〔ability, means〕 ¶ 응분의 appropriate ; proper ; reasonable ; suitable // 응분의 대우를 받다 be given proper treatment
응사 應射 firing back ―하다 return fire ; shoot back
응석 playing on another's affection (어린애가) ―하다 presume upon another's love ; behave like a spoilt child ; play

the baby ⟪to⟫ ¶ 응석부리듯 coaxingly // 응석투로 말하다 speak in a coquettish tone // 우리집 아이는 너무 응석을 부린다 My child has got quite spoilt.

†**응석받다** give in to a child's whims ; indulge ; pamper ; humor ; coddle ; fondle ; spoil

응석받이 a spoilt〔pampered〕 child ¶ 그녀는 그의 부모가 응석받이로 키웠음에 틀림없다 She must have been spoiled by her parents.

응성 應聲 response to a call ; an echo **—하다** response to a call

응소 應訴 acceptance of a legal suit (standing as a defendant) **—하다** accept〔answer〕 a legal suit

응소 應召 answering a call ; being drafted **—하다** answer the call ; get drafted ; obey the calling-up order

—병 a draftee ; a selectee **—율** draft quota

응송 應訟 ⇨ 응소(應訴)

응수 應酬 an answer ; a reply ; a retort ; an exchange (교환) ; a return **—하다** respond ; retort ; return

응수 應手 a countermove ⟪in a game⟫ **—하다** make a countermove

†**응시 應試** applying for an examination ; sitting for an examination ⟪영⟫ **—하다** apply〔sit〕 for an examination ; take〔undergo〕 an examination ¶ 그는 응시하지 않고 입학했다 He entered a school without going through an examination.

—자 a participant in an examination ; an examinee

응시 凝視 a steady gaze ; a stare **—하다** stare at ; gaze at ; watch intently ; look hard at ¶ 그녀는 내 얼굴을 응시하고 있었다 She was looking at me intently in the face.

응신 應信 an answer〔a reply〕 to a signal **—하다** answer〔respond to〕 a signal

응어리 ① [근육의] a stiff muscle ; a knot〔cramp〕 in a muscle ② [속] the pith ; the core ¶ 하루 종일 일해서 팔에 응어리가 생겼다 My arm is stiff from working all day long.

응얼거리다 mutter ; murmur ; grunt

응용 應用 practical application ; adaptation ; practice **—하다** apply ; adapt ; put to practical use ; put into practice ¶ 응용할 수 있는 practicable ; applicable // 응용할 수 없는 inapplicable ; impractical // 널리 응용하다 have wide application // 공식을 응용하다 apply a formula to a particular case // 과학을 일상 생활에 응용하다 apply science to everyday life // 이론을 실제에 응용하다 put a theory into practice // 항해술은 천문학을 응용한 것이다 Navigation is an application of astronomy.

— 경제학 applied〔practical〕 economics **— 문제** a problem (for application) ; an applied question ; material for exercise **— 물리학**〔화학, 과학〕 applied physics〔chemistry, science〕 **— 미술** applied fine arts **— 수학** applied〔mixed〕 mathematics **— 식물학** practical botany

*****응원 應援** aid ; help ; assistance ; support ; reinforcement (원병) ; [경기의] cheering ; rooting ⟪미⟫ **—하다** aid ; help ; assist ; support ; back ; cheer ⟪a team⟫ ; root for ⟪a team⟫ ¶ 후보자를 응원하다 support a candidate // 응원을 청하다 ask ⟪a person⟫ for support ; send for support // 양 대학의 응원단은 자기네 팀을 응원했다 The rooters of both universities cheered their teams. // 이 게임에서 너는 누구를 응원할거니 Who will you root for in this game ?

—가 a rooters' song **—군** reinforcements **—기** a rooters' pennant **—단** a cheering〔supporting〕 party〔squad〕 ; a cheering〔rooting〕 section ; a party of fans〔rooters〕 **—단장** a cheerleader ; a head rooter ⟪미⟫ **—석** a cheering section **— 연설** a campaign speech ; a speech in support **— 연설자** a stump speaker **—자** a supporter ; a backer ; a cheering enthusiast〔fan〕 ; a rooter ⟪미⟫

응전 應戰 taking up a challenge ; a response **—하다** accept ⟪battle, challenge⟫ ; respond to〔return〕 fire ; fight

‡**응접 應接** reception ⟪of a person⟫ ; interview **—하다** receive ⟪a person⟫ ; interview ; see ¶ 손님을 응접하다 receive visitors // 그는 방문객의 응접에 바쁘다 He is busy with visitors.

— 계원 a receptionist **—실** a drawing〔reception〕 room ; a parlor ⟪미⟫

응종 應從 obedience ; compliance **—하다** obey ; comply with

†**응집 凝集** cohesion ; condensation **—하다** cohere ; condense

—력 cohesive power ; cohesion

응징 膺懲 chastisement ; punishment ; penalty **—하다** chastise ; punish ; discipline ¶ 응징군을 파견하다 send out a punitive army

응천 순인 應天順人 obeying the will of heaven and following the voices of the people

응체 凝滯 stoppage ; impediment ; delay **—하다** get stopped ; be impeded

응축 凝縮 condensation ; concentration **—하다** condense ; be compressed

—기 a condenser

응취 凝聚 cohesion ⇨ 응집(凝集)

‡**응하다 應—** ① [답하다] answer ; reply〔respond〕 to ¶ 질문에 응하다 answer a question // 포화에 응하다 return the enemy's fire // 소집에 응하다 answer the call (to the colors) // 의논에 응할 용의가 있다 be willing to discuss the matter ② [승낙하다] accept ; comply with ¶ 쾌히 응하다 comply with a good grace ; give a willing〔ready〕 consent // 초대에 응

하다 accept an invitation // 도전에 응하다 accept〔take up〕 a challenge // 남의 부탁에 쾌히 응하다 comply with 《a person's》 request with pleasure // 제안〔조건〕에 응하다 accept〔agree to〕 the proposal〔terms〕
③ [필요·수요에] meet ; satisfy ¶ 수요에 응하다 meet a demand // 시대의 요구에 응하다 meet the demand of the day〔times〕 // 국가의 위급에 응하다 rise to the national emergency
④ [모집에] apply ; subscribe 《for》 ¶ 회원 모집에 응하다 apply for membership in a society // 학생 모집에 응하다 apply for admission to a school // 현상 논문의 모집에 응하다 enter a prize essay contest
⑤ [따르다] scale ; adjust ; fit ; correspond ; proportion ¶ …에 응해서 in response〔reply, answer〕 to ; in obedience to ; in proportion to ; according to // 처지에 응해서 according to one's means〔position〕 // 필요에 응해서 as the needs of the case demand ; as the occasion arises // 수입에 응해서 소비하다 spend according to one's income ; adjust one's expenditures to one's income // 국력에 응하여 군비를 제한하다 limit the armament to the resources of the country // 죄에 응해서 벌해야 한다 We must fit the punishment to the crime. // 영업세는 가격에 응한다 The sales tax is scaled according to the price.

응혈 凝血 a clot of blood ; coagulated〔clotted, curdled〕 blood ; gore **—하다** clot ; coagulate ; curdle

응화 應和 response **—하다** respond 《to》 ; reply to ; answer ⇨ 화응(和應)

†의 ① [소유·소속·동격] -'s ; -s' ; of ; belonging to ¶ 형의 책 my elder brother's book ; a book of my elder brother // 형님의 소유인 책 the books in my brother's possession ; the books in the possession of my brother ; the books (which) my brother is possessed of ; the books belonging to my brother ; the books owned by my brother ; the books (which) my brother owns // 나〔너, 그, 그녀〕의 친구(의 한사람) one of my〔your, his, her〕 friends ; a friend of mine〔yours, his, hers〕 // 돈의 가치 the value of money ; the monetary value (금전적 가치) // 인간의 가치 a man's worth ; the worth of man // 집의 지붕 the roof of a house ; a housetop // 세계의 뉴스 the news of the world ; the world news // 수상의 비서이다 be secretary to〔the secretary of〕 the Prime Minister // 우리들은 고교의 학생이다 We are students of a high school〔high school students〕.
② [···이 들어 있는, ···으로 되어 있는] ¶ 한 상자의 초콜릿 캔디〔배〕 a box of chocolate candy〔pears〕 // 가득한 한 상자의 사과 a boxful of apples // 한 자루의 귤 a bag of oranges // 세 아름의 나무 단 three armfuls of fagots // 세 다발의 장작 three armfuls of firewood // 유리의 창문 a window of glass ; a glass window pane (유리창) // 은의 장식 an ornament of silver // 나일론의 양말 nylon stockings ; nylons ; stockings made of nylon // 청동의 상 a statue in bronze ; a bronze statue
③ [···에 관한] ¶ 동양 미술의 책 a book on Oriental Fine Arts // 기하의 교과서 a textbook on〔for, in〕 geometry ; a geometry textbook // 태권도의 선생 an instructor of *Taekwondo* // 고대 문학의 권위 an authority on ancient literature // 국제법의 전문가 an expert in〔at〕 international law // 알라스카의 얘기를 하다 give a talk on Alaska // 대수의 시험이 있다 have an examination in algebra
④ [장소·시간] ¶ 세계의 나라들 the countries of〔in〕 the world ; the countries all over the world〔all the world over〕 // 서울의 사람 the people of *Seoul* // 강가의 도시 a town (situated, located) on a river // 나의 이웃사람 a man next (to) me // 오후 9시발의 부산행 급행 the 9 p. m. express for *Pusan*
⑤ [···에 의한, ···으로부터의] ¶ 형님의 편지 a letter from my brother // 고향의 손님 a visitor from home // 극장의 출구 an exit from the theater // 찰스 디킨즈의 소설 a novel (written) by Charles Dickens ; a novel of Charles Dickens ; a Dickens // 이것은 나의 친구(로 부터)의 선물이다 This is a gift (for me) from a friend of mine. // 그는 캘리포니아의 사람이다 He is〔comes〕 from (the State of) California.
⑥ ¶ 내 친구에게 주는 선물 a present for a friend of mine // 문의 열쇠 a key to the door // 문제 해결의 실마리 a clue to the solution of the problem〔for solving the problem, to solve the problem with〕 // 집의 입구 an entrance to a house // 도로의 출구 an exit to the street // 두통의 약 a medicine for headache // 10만원 짜리의 수표 a check〔cheque〕 for 100,000 *won* // 어린이(용)의 책 a book for children // 1년의 계획을 세우다 make plans〔plan〕 for the year // 다과의 시간입니다 It's time for tea.
⑦ [기타] ¶ 검은 옷의 여인 a woman in black〔in a black dress〕 ; [상복의] a woman in mourning〔weeds〕 // 영어의 편지 a letter (written) in English // 15세의 소녀 a fifteen-year-old girl ; a girl of fifteen ; a girl of fifteen years of age // 최대의 겸손 the greatest humility // 미국과 한국의 다른 점 differences between the U.S. and Korea // 반대의 의견을 세우다 form an opinion to the contrary // 남의 머리를 때리다 strike 《a person》 on the head // 남의 팔을 잡다 take〔seize〕 《a person》 by the arm // 남의 뺨을 때리다 slap

〔strike〕《a person》 across the face // 남의 눈을 보다 look 《a person》 in the eye(s)

의 誼 relationship ; friendship ; intimacy ; terms ¶ 의좋은 부부 a devoted〔happy〕 couple // 이웃과의 의 the sentiment of neighborliness // 의좋게 on good terms ; like good friends ; in harmony // 의가 좋다 be on good〔intimate〕 terms 《with》 ; be good friends 《with》 ; be friendly 《with》 // 의가 나쁘다 disagree ; be on bad terms 《with a person》 ; be at loggerheads 《with》 // 의가 상하다 quarrel 《with》 ; fall out 《with》 ; disagree 《with》 // 그들은 의좋게 지내고 있다 They live together in harmony. /They live happily. /They are getting on well with each other. // 그 부부는 의좋게 산다 The couple gets along like a pair of lovebirds. // 그들은 의좋은 친구다 They are very good friends. // 사소한 일로 그 친구들은 의가 상했다 A small matter divided the friends. / They fell out over some trifling matter.

의 義 ① [정의] justice ; righteousness ; loyalty ¶ 의를 위해서 죽다 die for the cause of justice ② [의리] relationship ; ties ; bonds ¶ 군신의 의 the relations of sovereign and subject // 부자의 의를 맺다 contract the relations of father and son

의가 衣架 ⇨ 옷걸이

의가 醫家 a medical man ; a medical practitioner

의거 依據 [증거에 따름] dependence ; dependence on proof〔testimony, evidence〕 ━하다 depend of 《proof》 ; base 《on》 ; according 《to》 ¶ 자료에 의거하여 on the basis〔authority〕 of the data // …의 규정에 의거하여 under the provision

의거 義擧 a worthy〔laudable, noble〕 undertaking ; a heroic〔brave〕 deed (의협적인) ; a movement in the public interest

의걸이 衣— a wardrobe chest (장)

†의견 意見 an opinion ; a view ; an idea ; a suggestion ¶ 의견의 일치 a consensus ; a unanimity of opinion ; an agreement in views ; an accord // 의견의 불일치 a disagreement of opinion ; a lack of consensus // 과격〔온건〕한 의견의 소유자 a man of extreme〔moderate〕 opinions // 의견의 충돌 a conflict of opinions ; a clash (of ideas) // 의견의 대립 a split to opinion // 나의 의견으로는 in my opinion ; I am of the opinion 《that》 ; according to my view // 의견을 말하다 give〔express, state〕 one's opinion ; set forth one's views ; make a few remarks // 의견이 같다 agree with 《a person》 ; be of the same opinion ; see eye to eye 《on a question》 // 의견이 다르다 disagree with // 의견에 찬성하다 favor 《a person's》 ideas // 의견에 따르다 follow〔take〕 《a person's》 advice // 반대 의견을 가지고 있다 have opposite views // 제 의견을 고집하다 stick〔hold〕 to one's opinion // 그의 의견은 보수적이다 His views are conservative. // 그와 나는 언제나 의견이 맞지 않다 He always disagrees with me. // 달리 의견이 있으십니까 Have you anything to say about it? // 그것에 대해선 별로 의견이 없습니다 I have no opinion of my own about that. // 그는 내 의견도 듣지 않고 어리석은 짓을 시작했다 Refusing to take〔Instead of taking〕 my advice, he began the foolish activity. // 자기 의견을 남에게 강요해서는 안된다 You shouldn't force your ideas on other people. // 친구라도 때로는 의견이 맞지 않는다 Even friends sometimes disagree. // 너의 의견 따위는 필요 없어 I don't need your two cents' worth.

의견서 意見書 a written opinion ; a statement of one's views ¶ 의견서를 제출하다 present a written opinion

의결 議決 consultation and decision ; a resolution ; a decision 《of a meeting》 ; [통과] passing 《a vote, a resolution》 ━하다 decide ; decide upon ; resolve ; pass a vote 《of》 ; vote for ¶ 안을 의결하다 vote for a scheme ; vote on a bill ; pass a resolution
━권 a voting right ; the right to vote〔of voting〕 ; franchise ━ 기관 a legislative〔deliberative〕 organ ━문 a letter of resolution ━ 사항 matters for decision〔resolution, deliberation〕

의고 擬古 imitation of ancient style〔form, literature〕 ━하다 write〔compose〕 in (imitation of) ancient style
━문 a (pseudo) classical style ; writings molded on older literature ━주의 classicism (교육상의) ; classicalism (예술상의) ; archaism (조형 미술 따위의) ; pseudoarchaism (사이비 고대주의) ━체 classicism

의곡 歪曲 distortion ; perversion ; falsification ; misconstruction ; misinterpretation ; a strained interpretation ━하다 distort ; warp ; strain ; pervert ; twist ; misconstrue 《a person's words》 ; have a wrong interpretation 《of a matter》 ; look 《a matter》 through colored spectacles ¶ 의곡된 해석 a distorted view ; a biased interpretation ; a strained〔forced〕 interpretation (억지의) // 감정으로 의곡된 판단 a judgment swayed〔influenced〕 by passion // 이것은 사실에 대한 고의적인 의곡이다 It is a wilful distortion of facts.

*의과 醫科 the medical department ; [과정] the medical course ¶ 의과를 졸업하다 graduate from a medical school
━ 대학 a medical college ━ (대)학생 a medical student

의관 衣冠 gown〔clothes〕 and hat ; attire ¶ 의관을 갖추다 be in full dress

의관 衣官 a medical officer

의관 문물 衣冠文物 dress and customs ; the civilization of a nation
의구 依舊 being unchanged —하다 remain unchanged
의구 疑懼 apprehension ; misgivings ; suspicion ; fear ; uneasiness —하다 doubt ; suspect ; apprehend ; fear ¶ 의구하는 마음 misgivings ; apprehensions ; fear // 의구심을 품다 entertain〔have〕 doubts 《about》
의기 意氣 spirits ; feelings ; heart ; vigor ¶ 의기 양양한 triumphant ; exultant ; high-spirited // 의기 왕성하다 be in high spirits ; be high-spirited // 의기 소침하다 be in low spirits ; be depressed in spirits // 의기 충천하다 be in royal〔high, roaring〕 spirits // 아무개의 의기에 감동하다 catch 《a person's》 spirit // 그들은 의기 충천하였다 Their spirits were sky-high. // 아군의 의기는 왕성했다 The morale of our troops ran high. // 나쁜 소식이 우리들의 의기를 꺾었다 The bad news dampened our spirits.
의기 義氣 chivalrous spirit ; chivalry ; heroism ; public spirit ¶ 의기있는 chivalrous ; heroic ; public-spirited // 의기있는 남자 a man of chivalrous spirit ; a public-spirited man
의기 疑忌 suspicion and abhorrence —하다 suspect and abhor ; distrust and avoid
의기 상투 意氣相投 congeniality in spirit〔temperament〕 ; mutual understanding —하다 be of congenial temper ; be of a mind ; fall in with another's temper ¶ 의기 상투한 친구 congenial friends
*의기 양양 意氣揚揚 —하다 (be) triumphant ; exultant ; be in high spirits ¶ 의기 양양하게 exultantly ; proudly ; triumphantly ; with flying colors
의녀 義女 a stepdaughter
의념 疑念 apprehensions ; misgivings ; distrust
⁑의논 議論 [상의] consultation ; conference ; counsel —하다 consult 《with》 ; confer 《with》 ; counsel 《with》 ¶ 의논할 사람 an adviser ; someone to confer with // 오늘은 시간이 없으니까 그 건에 대해서는 후에 따로 의논하자 We don't have any time today, so let's pursue discussion of that question another time.
— 상대 an adviser ¶ 의논할 상대가 없다 have no one to consult with // 의논 상대가 되어 주다 give advice〔counsel〕 《to》
의당 宜當 as a matter of course ; naturally ; properly ; necessarily —하다 (be) natural ; proper ; reasonable ; be of necessity ¶ 의당 받아야 할 것을 받다 have 〔get〕 one's due // 빌린 것은 의당 갚아야 한다 One ought to pay what one owes. // 학생이 선생에게 질문하는 것은 의당한 일이다 It is quite proper that a student should ask questions of his teacher.

의대 衣帶 clothes and belts〔sashes〕
의대 醫大 ⇨ 의과(— 대학)
의도 義徒 a group of righteous〔public-spirited〕 men
†의도 意圖 an intention ; an aim ; a purpose ; a design

> 참고 **intention** 마음 속으로 생각하고 있는 것 반드시 결심한다든가 계획한다든가 하는 의미는 없다 **purpose** 하려고 뚜렷이 생각하고 있는 것 **design** 확실히 계획이나 준비를 하고 있는 마음 속의 계획

—하다 intend 《to do》 ; plan ; aim 《at》 ; design ¶ 살해할 의도를 가지고 with intent to murder 《a person》 // 적의 의도를 꺾다 frustrate the enemy's design
의량 衣糧 clothing and provisions
의량 意量 intention and capacity of mind ; generosity ; motivation and ability
의려 疑慮 apprehensions ; misgivings ; fear —하다 apprehend ; fear
의례 依例 following precedent —하다 follow precedent ; take example 《from》
의례 儀禮 ceremony ; courtesy ; etiquette ¶ 의례적인 ceremonial ; formal // 외교적 의례 diplomatic etiquette // 의례적인 방문을 하다 pay a formal〔courtesy, protocol〕 visit〔call〕
가정 — ritual standards ; folk mores and family rituals
의례건 依例件 a matter of precedent ; customary affairs〔tasks〕
의례히 依例— as usual ⇨ 으레
의론 議論 [논의] argument ; controversy ; discussion ; dispute ; debate

> 참고 **argument** 두 사람 사이의 논쟁으로서 사실이나 이유를 들어 상대방을 설복하려고 든다 **controversy** 단체간의 논쟁으로서 흔히 문장이나 연설의 형식을 빌린다 **dispute** 냉정한 의론이라기보다 감정적인 상호 반박

—하다 argue 《with a person, about a matter》 ; discuss ; dispute ; debate ; contend 《about》 ¶ 빈약한 의론 a flimsy 〔weak〕 argument // 논리 정연한 의론 a consistent argument // 내용이 없는 의론 an argument of little substance // 의론의 여지가 없다 be beyond dispute ; be incontrovertible ; be indisputable // 의론 백출해서 결론을 얻지 못했다 We could not come to a conclusion owing to endless disputes. // 그 일에 관해서 여러 가지 의론이 있었다 Much has been said for and against it.
의롭다 義— (be) righteous ; just ; chivalrous ; public-spirited
의롱 衣籠 a wardrobe
*의뢰 依賴 ① [의지] dependence ; trust ;

reliance ② [부탁] a request ; solicitation **—하다** depend〔rely〕 on ; lean on ; request ; ask ¶ 의뢰하신 대로 at your request∥소송 사건을 변호사에게 의뢰하다 bring a case to a lawyer∥의뢰할 일이 있다 I have a favor to ask of you. ∥이것은 전문가에게 의뢰해야 한다 The matter should be entrusted〔committed〕 to an expert. /We should entrust an expert with the matter.
—료 [변호의] a retaining fee ; a retainer **—서** a written request ; a letter of request ; a letter asking a favor **—심** (a propensity to) dependence ; reliance **—인** a client

의료 醫療 medical treatment〔care〕
— 기관 a medical institution **— 기구** medical〔surgical〕 instruments ; medical appliances **—반** a medical team **— 법인** a medical corporation **— 보험** medical care insurance **— 보험 제도** the medical insurance system **—비** a fee for medical treatment ; medical expenses ; a doctor's bill〔fee〕 **— 사회화 제도** socialized medicine **— 산업** the medical industry **— 시설** medical facilities **—실** a clinic room **—차** a clinic car **—품** medical supplies **국립 —원** the National Medical Center

의료 衣料 clothing ; articles of dress
—비 clothing expense **—품** clothing (items)

의료 수가 醫療酬價 the charge for medical treatment ; a medical fee
— 규정〔기준〕 the rules〔standards〕 for medical fees

⁑의류 衣類 clothes ; dresses ; clothing 《총칭》 ¶ 의류 한 벌 a suit of clothes∥의류 한 점 an article of clothing

의리 義理 ① [도리] (the principles of) righteousness ; a moral sense ; justice ; morality ¶ 의리가 강한 사람 a man of probity∥그는 의리도 인정도 없는 사람이다 He is a brute devoid of all sense of duty and humanity.
② [신의] loyalty ; integrity ; obligation ¶ 의리가 있다 be faithful ; keep faith 《with》∥의리가 없다 have no sense of honor ; be ungrateful ; fail in one's duty ∥의리를 지키다 be loyal to 《a person》 ; do one's duty by 《a person》∥의리상 그렇게 하지 않을 수 없다 I am in duty bound to do so. ∥싫지만 의리상 할 수 없이 일하고 있는 것이다 I am working from a sense of obligation, though I do not like it.
③ [결의] a sworn relation ¶ 형제의 의리를 맺다 swear brotherhood
— 부동(不同) faithlessness ; unreliability

의모 義母 a stepmother ; a foster mother ; a sworn mother

†의무 義務 a duty ; an obligation ; liability ; a responsibility ¶ 의무적인 obligatory ; compulsory∥의무적으로 from a mere sense of duty∥의무가 있다 ought to 《pay》 ; be under an obligation 《to do》 ; be liable for 《service》 ; be obligatory on 《a person》 to 《do》∥의무를 지다 owe a duty to 《one's country》 ; have the obligation to∥의무를 지우다 put 《a person》 under an obligation∥의무를 다하다 do〔discharge, perform〕 one's duty ; undertake〔meet〕 one's obligation∥의무에 어긋나다 swerve from one's duty∥의무를 태만히하다 fail in one's duty ; neglect one's duty∥그는 자기 의무를 충실히 이행했다 He was faithful in the discharge of his duties. ∥아이들을 학교에 보내는 것은 부모의 의무라고 법률에 규정되어 있다 The law obliges parents to send their children to school.
—감 a sense of duty **— 교육** compulsory education **—론** 〖철학〗 deontology **— 면제** excuse from duty **— 연한** an obligatory term of service **— 이행** performance of a duty **—자** 〖법〗 an obligor (채권의) ; a responsible person ; a debtor ; an obligator ☞ ❪p. 1680❫

의무 醫務 medical affairs〔business〕
—실 [학교·공장 따위의] a dispensary ; a medical room

†의문 疑問 a question ; a doubt **—하다** question ; ask ; doubt ¶ 의문이 생기다 a question arises∥의문의 죽음 a mysterious death∥그것은 의문의 여지가 없다 There is no (room for) doubt about it. ∥내가 갈 수 있을지 대단히 의문스럽다 I doubt very much whether I shall be able to come. ∥의문이 있으면 서슴치 말고 질문하십시오 Please feel free to ask me whatever questions you may happen to have.
—문〔대명사〕 an interrogative sentence 〔pronoun〕 **—부〔표〕** a question〔an interrogation〕 mark ; a note〔point〕 of interrogation **—사(詞)** an interrogative **—점** a point in question ; a doubtful〔moot〕 point

의뭉스럽다, 의뭉하다 be more subtle than one might think ; be deeper than one thinks ; (be) subtle

†의미 意味 meaning ; a sense (특수한) ; significance (의의) ; import (취지) ; point (요점) **—하다** mean ; signify ; imply ; import ¶ 의미 없는 insignificant ; meaningless ; pointless ; senseless ; unimportant∥의미 심장한 pregnant ; weighty ; of deep import∥어떤 의미로 in a sense ; in a way∥엄밀한 의미로 in a strict sense∥그의 말의 의미 the import of his remarks∥여러 가지 의미를 가진 말 a word with many meanings∥정치적인 의미를 갖다 have a political significance∥이것은 무슨 의미입니까 What does this mean ? /What is the meaning of this ? ∥실패는 죽음을 의미한다 Failure

의무·필요의 표현

① must do ... 와 have to do ...

조동사 must는 (1) 필요·의무의 「… 하여야 한다; … 하지 않으면 안되다; 꼭 … 해야 한다」 (2) 추정의 「… 이었음[하였음]에 틀림없다」의 두가지 용법으로 대별할 수 있다.

「… 하여야 한다」의 표현에서 must는 말하는 사람의 강한 의지와 주장을 주관적으로 표현하고 have to는 객관적인 필요성을 뜻한다. 구어에서는 have to를 많이 사용한다.

또 must는 활용형이 없는 조동사이다. 그러므로 must의 과거·미래·완료형은 had to, will[shall] have to, had have to를 대신 사용한다. 또한 부정도 do not have to나 need not을 사용한다. must not은 「…해서는 안된다」의 뜻을 지닌 강한 부정이 된다.

¶ 너는 네가 들은 대로 행해야 한다. You must do as you are told. (★ you를 주어로 할 때 must를 쓰면 매우 강한 느낌을 주므로 잘 쓰지 않는다. should를 쓰면 충고조가 된다. 보통 we를 주어로 할 때 쓴다.) // 군인은 군말없이 명령에 따라야 한다. Soldiers must obey orders without question. // 너 그렇게 빨리 가야 하니? — 아니, 아직 안가도 돼. Must you go so soon? — No, I needn't go yet. // 정말 그녀를 만나러 가고 싶지 않지만 가야 할 것 같애. I don't really feel like going to see her but we'll have to, I suppose. // 나는 즉시 편지를 써야 한다. I've got to write a letter right away. (★ have got to가 더 구어적이므로 「즉시」란 의미가 더 강해진다.) // 창문을 닦지 않아도 된다. There's no need to clean the windows. // 서둘러야겠다. We shall have to hurry. // 이제 작별 인사를 해야 할 때입니다. I must say goodby [be going] now. (★ 이렇게 늦게까지 방해가 되어 미안하니 이제 돌아가야겠다의 뜻)

② should do... 와 ought to do...

일반적으로 ought to가 should보다 다소 강한 뜻을 지닌다. should의 경우는 충고나 조건의 의미가 있다. 그러나 대체로 구별없이 쓰이기도 한다. 과거형은 should have done, ought to have done이다. 부정형은 should not, ought not to.

¶ 너는 꼭 진실만을 말해야 한다. You should always tell the truth. // 꼭 그에게 말해야만 되니? — 응, 그래야만 돼. Do you think we should tell him? — Well, we ought to really. // 나는 시험 전에 그 책을 읽었어야 했는데. I should[ought to] have read the book before the examination. // 그에게 돈문제에 관해 얘기 해야 할까? — 응, 하는 것이 좋아. Do you think we ought to tell him about money? — Yes, I think we'd better.

③ have a[be one's] duty to do ... 와 have an obligation ; be obligatory

법률상, 또는 도덕적으로 당연한 공적인 의무에는 duty, 관습, 약속과 같은 개인적인 의무에는 have[be under] an obligation to do ...을 쓴다.

¶ 나는 최선을 다하는 것이 너의 의무라고 생각한다. I feel [think] it's your duty to do your best. // 세금을 내는 것은 모든 시민의 의무이다. It is the duty of every citizen to pay his taxes. / Every citizen has an obligation [is under (an) obligation] to pay his taxes. // 회교도는 하루에 5번 기도해야 한다. For Muslims, it is obligatory to pray five times a day.

④ compulsory 와 mandatory

권한을 가진 자나 법률 등에 의해 강제적으로 그것을 지키지 않아 벌을 받을 때는 compulsory, 강제적이지는 않고 규칙에 의해 제한받는 정도의 부드러운 의미는 mandatory.

¶ 모든 육류와 가금류는 검사를 받아야 한다. Inspection is mandatory for all meat and poultry.

⑤ be bound to do ... 와 be supposed [expected] to do ...

be bound to do...는 「얽매어 있다」, 「…할 의무가 있다」의 뜻이고 be supposed to do...는 「…하기로 되어있다」의 뜻으로 기대가 담겨있다.

¶ 멈춰! 어린아이를 그렇게 흔들어대면 안돼. Stop it! You're not supposed to swing babies around like that. // 너는 매일 여기에 아홉시까지 와야 한다. You are supposed to be here at nine every day. // 무엇 좀 먹어도 될까요? — 물론 드셔야하고 말구요. 당신은 우리의 손님인걸요. Can I help myself to something to eat? — Of course, you're expected to, you're our guest.

spells death. // 이 문장은 무슨 의미인지 모르겠다 I do not understand what this sentence means. /I cannot make sense of this sentence. // 사전을 보면 단어의 의미

를 알 수 있다 A dictionary tells you what words mean. // 당신이 말하는 의미를 모르겠다 I do not see your point. // 다른 말로 하면 의미가 더 분명해질 것이다 A different wording would make the meaning clearer. // 침묵은 동의를 의미할 때가 있다 Silence sometimes implies consent. // 그녀는 의미 심장한 눈초리로 나를 보았다 She glanced at me with some significance in her face. // D. D. 는 무엇을 의미합니까 What does D. D. stand for? // 그런 의미에서 한잔 합시다 Let's drink to that. // 어느 의미로는 그가 말한 것이 아마 옳은지도 모른다 Maybe in a certain sense, what he says is correct.

—론 〚언어〛 semantics

의법 依法 —하다 be pursuant〔conformable〕 to (the) law ; be in accordance with (the) law

— 처단 punishment according to law — 처분 disposition according to law

의병 義兵 an army in the cause of justice ; loyal troops ¶ 의병을 일으키다 raise an army in the cause of justice loyalty

의병 疑兵 camouflaged〔dummy〕 troops

†**의복 衣服** clothes ; garments ; clothing 《총칭》 ¶ 의복 한 벌 a suit (of clothes) // 좋은 의복을 입은 사람들 well-groomed 〔-dressed〕 persons

의부 義父 a stepfather ; a foster father ; a sworn father

의분 義憤 righteous indignation ; public indignation〔rage, resentment〕 ¶ 의분을 느끼다 burn with righteous indignation // 의분을 참다 repress one's righteous indignation

의불합 意不合 disagreement ; incongruity of spirits ; uncongeniality —하다 (be) uncongenial

의붓 step-

—딸 a stepdaughter — 아들 a stepson — 아비 a stepfather — 어미 a stepmother — 자식 a stepchild

의빙 依憑 dependence ⇨ 의거

***의사 意思** an intention ; a purpose ; a mind ; an idea ¶ 의사가 통하다 come to an understanding // 의사를 명백히 하다 speak one's mind // 의사를 수행하다 carry out one's intentions // 그는 귀국할 의사가 없었다 He had no intention of returning to his country. // 둘 사이에는 의사가 소통되지 않고 있었다 The two did not understand each other. /There were misunderstandings between the two. // 나는 그런 의사는 추호도 없다 I have not the slightest intention of doing it. /Nothing is farther from my intention.

의사 義士 a righteous person ; a martyr

의사 義死 dying for the cause of justice ; martyrdom —하다 die for the cause of justice

‡**의사 醫師** a doctor ; a physician (내과의) ; a surgeon (외과의) ; a (medical) practitioner (개업의)

> 참고 doctor는 영국에서는 주로 physician을 가리키지만 미국에서는 surgeon, dentist까지를 포함한 일상어로서 쓰인다 general practitioner는 내과도 외과도 보는 일반 개업의를 말한다

¶ 의사가 되다 become a doctor // 의사를 부르다 send for a doctor ; call in a doctor // 의사의 진찰을 받다 consult〔see〕 a doctor // 의사로서 개업을 하다 practice medicine ; be in medical practice // 의사가 하라는 대로 하는 것이 좋다 You would do well to take your doctor's advice.

— 개업 유자격자 a licentiate in medicine — 국가 시험 the National Examination for Medical Practitioners — 면허증 a medical license ; a physician's diploma 〔license〕 —회 a medical association 〔society〕 단골 — a family doctor ; one's regular physician 돌팔이 — a quack (doctor) ; charlatan

의사 議事 proceedings ; deliberation ; conference ; consultation —하다 deliberate ; confer ; consult

— 규칙 parliamentary rules —당 an assembly hall —록 a minute book ; a report ; minutes ; proceedings ; journals — 목록 an agenda —봉 a gavel — 상정 introduction of business — 일정 the order of the day ; an agenda — 진행 progress of proceedings — 진행 방해 obstruction of proceedings ; filibustering 《미》 ; filibusterism 《미》 국회 —당 the National Assembly Hall ; the Diet Building 《일》 ; the Houses of the National Diet ; the Capitol 《미》 ; the Houses of Parliament 《영》

의사 疑似 ⇨ 유사(類似)

의사 능력 意思能力 mental capacity ¶ 의사 능력이 없다 be devoid of mental capacity

의사 표시 意思表示 declaration of intention —하다 declare one's intention ; declare oneself ¶ 별도로 의사 표시가 없을 때에 in the absence of any different declaration of intention

의상 衣裳 clothes ; clothing ; garb ; dresses ; apparel garments ; costume (특히 연극용) ¶ 연극용 의상 a theatrical 〔stage〕 costume // 의상이 많다 have a large wardrobe // 훌륭한〔소박한, 누추한〕 의상을 입고 있다 be richly〔simply, poorly〕 dressed〔attired〕

—계〔담당〕 〚연극〛 a costumer ; a dresser — 도락 fondness for dress —실 a property room (극장의)

의생 醫生 a physician of the Chinese school ; a herb doctor ; a herbalist

의서 醫書 a medical book ; a book on medicine

†의석 議席 a seat 《in an assembly hall》; a parliamentary seat ; the floor 《총칭》 ¶ 의석에 앉다 take one's seat // 의석을 잃다 lose one's seat // 의석을 보유하다 have 〔hold, keep〕 a seat 《in the House》; sit on the floor of Congress 《미》 // 의석을 획득하다 (선거에서) win seats〔places〕

의성 擬聲 onomatopoeia ; imitating sounds

—법 onomatopoeia —어 an onomatopoeic〔echoic〕 word ; an onomatop(e) ; an onomatopoeia ☞ 《p. 1683》

의세 倚勢 reliance on influence〔power〕 —하다 rely on influence〔power〕; presume on one's influence

의수 義手 an artificial arm〔hand〕

의술 醫術 medicine ; the medical〔healing〕 art ¶ 의술의 medical // 의술은 인술이다 Medicine is a benevolent art. /The physician's is a humanitarian calling.

†의식 衣食 food and clothing〔clothes〕 ¶ 의식을 대주다 provide 《a person》 with food and clothes // 의식을 위하여 일하다 work for one's bread // 의식에 곤란을 받다 find it hard to make a living // 의식이 충분해야 예절을 안다 Well-fed, well-bred. // 그에게는 의식에 부족이 없을 정도의 재산이 있다 He has a fortune sufficient to keep his body and soul together.

‡의식 意識 consciousness ; awareness ; one's senses —하다 be conscious 《of》; feel ; be aware 《of》 ¶ 의식적(으로) conscious(ly) // 의식의 흐름 the stream of consciousness // 의식을 회복하다 recover〔regain〕 one's consciousness ; come to one's senses〔oneself〕 // 의식을 회복시키다 bring 《a person》 to himself // 의식이 뚜렷〔희미〕하다 have a clear〔an indistinct〕 consciousness // 그는 죽을 때까지 의식이 있었다 He remained conscious to the last moment of his life. /He was conscious to the last.

의식을 잃다 관용 lose one's consciousness〔senses〕; become unconscious

의식 儀式 a ceremony ; [예식] formality ; [종교의] a rite ; a ritual ¶ 의식을 거행하다 perform a ceremony // 의식을 생략하다 dispense with ceremony ; drop ceremony

—주의 ritualism

의식주 衣食住 food, clothing〔clothes〕 and shelter〔housing〕 ¶ 의식주에 필요한 물건 the necessaries〔necessities〕 of life // 의식주 이 세가지는 인간 생활에 없어서는 안되는 것이다 Food, clothing and shelter form the requisites of our life. // 그들은 의식주에 부족함이 없다 They are well fed, clad and housed.

†의심 疑心 doubt ; a doubt (의문) ; doubts ; question ; [불신] mistrust ; distrust ; [혐의] suspicion —하다 doubt ; call 《a matter》 in question ; be doubtful 《of, about》; [불신] distrust ; be distrustful 《of》; [혐의] suspect ; regard 《a person》 with suspicion ¶ 의심스러운 점 a doubtful point // 의심스러운 주장 a questionable assertion // 의심을 받고 있는 사람 a suspected person ; a suspect // 의심이 많은 사람 a distrustful person // 의심스럽게 doubtfully ; suspiciously // 의심 없이 without doubt ; doubtlessly ; unquestionably ; beyond doubt ; without question ; no doubt // 의심스럽다 be doubtful ; be questionable ; be uncertain (불확실) ; be open to doubt〔question〕; be suspicious (수상하다) // 의심하지 않다 make〔have〕 no doubt of ; be confident of // 의심이 많다 be distrustful ; be doubting ; be skeptical (회의적이다) ; be suspicious // 의심할 여지가 없다 leave no room〔place〕 for doubt ; admit no doubt ; be beyond〔out of〕 doubt〔question〕; be certain ; there is no doubt about 《it》 // 의심할 여지가 있다 be open to doubt〔question〕; there is room for doubt 《that》 // 의심을 품다 have〔feel, entertain〕 a doubt 《about, on, as to a matter》; be doubtful〔skeptical〕 《about, of a matter》; [혐의를] have suspicion 《against a person》; be suspicious 《about, of》 // 의심을 두다 suspect 《a person》; throw 〔cast〕 suspicion 《on a person》 // 의심을 풀다 dispel〔clear away, remove〕 《a person's》 doubt // 혐의를 풀다 dispel〔clear away〕 suspicion ; clear oneself of suspicion // 의심을 받다〔사다〕 incur suspicion ; fall under suspicion ; be suspected ; be regarded with suspicion of 《crime》 // 의심을 받고 체포되다 be arrested on suspicion // 의심 받고 있다 be under a cloud // 의심이 들게〔생기게〕 하다 make 《a person》 doubt ; arouse a doubt 《in a person's mind》; [혐의를] rouse 《a person's》 suspicion // 의심하는 눈으로 보다 view〔eye〕 《a person》 with suspicion // 의심 받지 않도록 조용히 나가다 go out quietly so as not to excite any suspicion // 당선을 믿어 의심치 않다 be confident of 《a person's》 election // 그가 올지 어떨지 의심스럽다 It is doubtful whether he will come. // 그것에 관해서는 별로 의심할 바 없었다 There appeared little doubt about that. // 우리는 그가 그 여자의 죽음에 관계가 있다고 의심하기 시작했다 We began to suspect him of having a hand in her death. // 그는 자기의 힘을 의심하고 있다 He mistrusts his own powers. // 나는 그의 성공을 의심한다 I doubt his success. /I doubt whether〔if〕 he will succeed. // 나는 그의 수완을 의심한다 I doubt his ability. // 그의 정직을 의심했다 I doubted his honesty〔that he was honest〕. // 그가 범인이 아닌가 하고 의심했다 I suspected that he was the offender. // 나는 내 자신의 귀를 의심했다 I thought I had heard

의성어 · 의태어의 표현

의성어(擬聲語)란 「꼬끼오(cock-a-doodle-do, 똑딱똑딱(ticktack), 윙윙(buzz), 쿵(thud)」 등과 같이 소리를 흉내내어 표현하는 것을 말하고, 의태어(擬態語)는 왁자지껄, 와글와글(hurly burly) 등과 같이 사물의 움직임이나 모양을 흉내내어 만든 말이다. 의성어와 의태어는 영·미의 표현이 다른 것이 많으므로 외어두지 않으면 안된다.

1 종류

① 소리를 반복하는 것

▶(거품이) 부글부글 bubble bubble/(개의) 멍멍 arf arf/칙칙폭폭 choo choo; puff puff 《영》/(자동차의) 빵빵 honk honk/(병아리·새의) 삐악 삐악, 짹짹 peep peep/(돼지의) 꿀꿀 oink oink/(집오리의) 꽥꽥 quack quack

② 앞의 모음을 바꾸어 반복하는 것

▶(종소리의) 땡땡 ding-dong/(빗소리) 후두두; (발소리) 타닥타닥 pitter patter/(당나귀의) 히힝 hee-haw

③ 자음을 바꾸어 반복하는 것

▶(사람의 우는 소리) 흑흑 boo-hoo/왁자지껄, 시끌벅끌 hurly-burly/(먹는 소리) 냠냠 munch crunch

④ 음을 연속하는 것

▶쿨쿨 zzzz/(증기 끓는 소리, 뱀 소리) 슈,쉿 Hissss/(개 으르대는 소리) 그르르 grrrrr

⑤ 소리를 묘사한 것

▶(총소리·문 닫는 소리) 빵, 꽝 bang/(엔진의) 부릉부릉 vroom/(폭발 소리) 펑 boom/(재채기 소리) 에취 a(h)choo; atishoo 《영》/(떨어지는 소리) 쿵, 털썩 fump/(화살 소리) 피융 zing/(총알 소리) 핑 whiz/(무거운 것이 떨어지는 소리) 쿵 thud/(무거운 것이 부딪치는 소리) 쿵, 탁 thump/(활 시위 소리) 핑 twang/(개 등의 소리) 낑낑 whine

⑥ 보통의 명사·동사를 전용하는 것

▶(찢어지는 소리) 짝짝 rip/(뽐내며 걷다) 으쓱으쓱 strut strut/빙글빙글, 뱅뱅 spin spin/(구르다) 딩굴딩굴 roll roll/(문을 쾅 닫다) 쾅 slam/(쪽하고 키스하다) 쪽 smack

⑦ 문장 중에서 동사·명사로 쓰여 지는 것

▶bark (→arf; bowwow)/tick (→ticktack)/hoot (→ hoo hoo)/growl (→ grrrrr) /scream (→eeeek)/plod/giggle

2 표현

¶ 총소리가 빵하고 났다. Bang went the rifle.//그가 지붕에서 쿵하고 떨어졌다. He fell down from a roof with a thud.//교회에서 종소리가 땡그렁땡그렁 울렸다. The church bell rang dingdongs.//문이 바람에 쾅 닫혔다.The door slammed in the wind.//마을의 한 남자가 북을 둥둥 치고 있다. A man from the village is beating the festival drum.//숲속에서 맑은 냇물이 졸졸 흐르고 있었다. In the forest a clear stream was trickling.//시계의 째깍째깍 소리가 어둠 속에서 들렸다. The ticking of the clock was heard in the dark.//한 소년이 첨벙하고 연못으로 뛰어들었다. A boy dived with a splash into the pond.//우리는 강에서 철벅거리며 옷을 빨았다. We splashed away at our clothes in the river.//개가 고기 한 점을 덥썩 물었다.The dog snapped up a piece of meat.//타자기의 달가닥달가닥 소리가 방에서 흘러 나왔다. The clatter of a typewriter came from the room.//처음 교단에 섰을 때 나는 가슴이 두근거렸다. I had butterflies in my stomach the first time I taught a class.//그녀는 하찮은 일에 늘 투덜투덜댄다. She is always whining about trifles.

amiss./I could hardly believe my ears.//나는 그의 정직함을 믿어 의심치 않는다 I am sure of his honesty.//나는 결국 그가 이길 것을 의심치 않는다 I do not doubt that he will win in the end.//나는 그의 성공을 의심하지 않는다 I have no doubt of his success〔that he will succeed〕./I do not doubt (but) that he will succeed.//의심받지 않도록 조심하십시오 Don't let suspicion fall on you.//그 계약에는 뭔가 의심스러운 데가 있다 There's something fishy about that deal.

의아 疑訝 doubt; suspicion; distrust —**하다** suspect; wonder; doubt; mistrust ¶ 의아스러운 듯이 dubiously; suspiciously// 의아스럽다 (be) doubtful; dubious; suspicious//의아스러운 눈으로 보다 eye 《a person》 with suspicion//의아스러운 표정을 짓다 look dubious//그가 왜 그런 짓을 했는지 의아했다 I wondered why he had done〔should have done〕 that.

의안 義眼 an artificial〔a false, a glass〕 eye

의안 議案 a bill ; a measure ¶ 정부가 제출한 의안 a Government bill // 의안을 의회에 제출하다 present〔introduce〕 a bill to the Assembly ; lay a bill before the Congress // 의안을 통과시키다 pass〔approve〕 a bill // 의안을 철회〔수정〕하다 withdraw〔revise〕 a bill // 의안을 채택하다 adopt a bill // 의안을 부결시키다 reject〔kill, vote down〕 a bill // 의안에 찬성〔반대〕하다 endorse〔oppose〕 a measure // 의안은 무사히 통과되었다 The bill has successfully passed.

의약 醫藥 [약] medicine ; physic ; [의술과 시약] medical practice and pharmaceutical dispensing ¶ 그 환자는 의약을 쓰기엔 때가 늦었다 The patient is past medical care.
— 분업 separation of dispensary from medical practice **—품** medical supplies

의업 醫業 the medical profession ¶ 의업에 종사하다 practice medicine // 지씨 집안은 대대로 의업을 직업으로 삼아 왔다 The *Chi's* have been practicing medicine as a family profession.

*‡*의역 意譯** (a) free〔liberal, broad〕 translation **—하다** translate freely ; give a free translation ¶ 그의 번역은 너무 의역에 치우쳤다 His translation is too free.

의연 義捐 contribution ; subscription ; donation 《미》 **—하다** contribute 《money》 to 《a fund》 ; subscribe ; donate
—금 a contribution ; a subscription ; a gift of money ; a donation ; alms ¶ 구제 의연금 모집 collection of subscriptions for relief // 수해 의연금 a relief fund for flood victims // 의연금을 모집하다 invite〔start a campaign for〕 subscriptions ; collect contributions for the relief of 《the flood victims》 **—자** a contributor ; a subscriber ; a donor

의연히 依然— still ; as it was ; as before ; as it used to be ; as ever ; as usual ¶ 의연히 변함없다 remain unchanged // 의연히 게으르다 be lazy as ever // 직물계는 의연히 불경기이다 The weaving〔textile〕 industry is as dull as ever.

의연히 毅然— resolutely ; firmly ; bravely ; boldly ; dauntlessly ¶ 의연한 태도 resolute〔firm, dauntless〕 attitude // 그는 의연히 역경을 견디어 냈다 He heroically〔stoically〕 endured adversity.

의열 義烈 nobility of soul〔spirit〕 ; heroism ; gallantry **—하다** (be) noble ; heroic ; brave ; gallant
— 지사 a man of heroic and noble mind

의예과 醫豫科 the premedical course ; premed(ic) 《미·속》

의옥 疑獄 a (public) scandal ; a criminal case ; a graft case 《미》 ¶ 정치적 의옥 사건 political scandals // 의옥을 일으키다 raise a (public) scandal // 의옥 사건에 관련되다 be involved in a graft scandal

*****의외 意外** surprise ; unexpectation ; an accident ¶ 의외의 [뜻밖의] unexpected ; unforeseen ; unlooked-for ; [우연한] accidental ; [놀라운] surprising // 의외의 일 a surprise ; an unlooked-for event // 의외의 즐거움 an unlooked-for happiness // 의외로 unexpectedly ; contrary to one's expectation ; to one's surprise // 의외로 빨리 sooner than expected ; earlier than was expected // 의외로 생각하다 [놀라다] be surprised 《at》 ; be taken by surprise ; [실망하다] be disappointed // 의외로 어렵다 be more difficult than one may think // 이것은 정말 의외이다 This is quite unexpected. // 그것은 의외의 일이다 That's a surprise to me. // 일은 의외로 빨리 끝났다 The work was done earlier than expected. // 결과가 의외여서 모두 실망했다 The result disappointed us. /We were disappointed at the result. // 그가 낙제했기 때문에 모두 의외로 생각했다 He was flunked, to the surprise of everyone. // 그는 의외에도 전과자였다 He turned out to be an exconvict. // 네가 아직도 여기 있다니 의외이다 I am surprised (that) you still remain here. // 이곳에서 너를 만나다니 참으로 의외이다 It's quite a surprise to see you here. /I little expected that I should see you here. / You are the last person I expected to see here.

의욕 意慾 volition ; will ; desire ¶ 의욕적인 highly motivated ; keenly enthusiastic // 의욕적으로 very enthusiastically ; with a strong will // 공부에 대한 의욕이 대단하다 They are keen on learning. // 이렇게 적은 봉급으로 일에 대한 의욕을 갖기란 어렵다 With such a low salary, it's hard to develop much enthusiasm for your work.
생산 — the will to produce **생활 —** the will to live

의용 義勇 loyalty and courage ; heroism ; bravery for a righteous cause
—군 a volunteer army ; militia **—병** a volunteer soldier ; militiaman

의용 儀容 a mien ; bearing ; presence ; manners ¶ 대단한 의용 a noble mien ; commanding presence // 의용을 갖추다 tidy oneself

의원 醫院 a medical practitioner's office ; a physician's office ; a doctor's office ; a clinic ; a hospital ¶ 김의원 Dr. *Kim's* office
—장 the head physician〔surgeon〕

의원 醫員 the medical staff〔corps〕 ; a member of the medical staff ; a physician

*‡*의원 議員** a member 《of the Assembly》 ; an assemblyman ; a Member of Parliament 《M. P.》 ; a Member of Congress

《M. C.》; a Congressman 《미》 ¶ 의원의 임기 the term of membership // 의원으로 당선되다 be elected a member 《of》 // 의원이 되다 obtain a seat in Parliament
— 생활 one's parliamentary career —석 the floor 《총칭》 — 총회 a general meeting of the Assembly members — 회관 Members' Office Building 국제 — 연맹 the Inter-Parliamentary Union 《IPU》 찬성 — a "yes" man ; a supporter 평— an ordinary〔average〕 member ; a backbencher

의원 議院 the Parliament ; the Assembly Chamber ; the House
— 내각제 the parliamentary government — 제도 the parliamentary system

의원면직 依願免職 dismissal〔retirement〕 at one's own request

의음 擬音 an imitation sound ; [텔레비전·라디오 따위의] sound effects

의의 意義 meaning ; significance ; sense ; import ¶ 의의 있는 significant ; meaningful // 의의 없는 meaningless ; senseless ; insignificant // 의의 깊은 말 a term of profound significance // 그 사업은 그의 생활을 의의 있게 하는 것이다 The work makes his life worth living〔significant〕. // 1776년 7월 4일은 미국인에게는 의의 깊은 날이다 July 4, 1776, is a significant date for Americans.

의의 疑義 a doubt ¶ 의의를 품다 entertain a doubt

의인 義人 a righteous person ; a martyr

의인 擬人 personification ; impersonation ; incarnation —하다 personify ; impersonate

의인법 擬人法 personification ; impersonation ¶ 의인법을 쓰다 personify ; impersonate

†**의자 椅子** [걸상] a chair ; a sofa ; a settee (긴 의자) ; a lounge ; a couch (잠자는) ; an armchair (팔걸이 있는) ; a bench ; a stool (등이 없는) ; an easy chair (안락 의자) ¶ 의자에 걸터 앉다 sit on a chair // 의자에 앉다 take a chair ; have〔take〕 a seat 《미》 // 의자를 한〔두〕줄로 늘어놓다 arrange chairs in a row〔two rows〕 // 이 의자는 앉으면 기분이 좋다〔나쁘다〕 I feel comfortable〔uncomfortable〕 on〔in〕 this chair.
— 커버 a chair cover

의장 衣欌 a wardrobe ; a chest
단층〔이층〕 — a single〔double〕 chest of drawers

의장 衣裝 ⇨ 의상

의장 意匠 a (decorative, an artistic) design ¶ 의장을 고안하다 think〔work〕 out a design
— 등록 registration of design

의장 儀仗 implements〔arms〕 used in the national ceremonies ; a cortege ; a guard ¶ 의장대를 사열하다 inspect an honor guard
—대 a guard〔guards〕 of honor ; an honor guard —병 a guard of honor ; a military escort

‡**의장 議長** the chairman ; the president ; the Speaker (영·미 하원의) ; Mr. Chairman ! (호칭) ¶ 의장이 되다 be in〔take〕 the chair // 의장을 맡아보다 act as chairman at the meeting ; chair the meeting
— 서리 the deputy speaker — 직권 authority of the president 공동 — a cochairman ; a joint chairman 국회 — the Speaker of the National Assembly 부— a vice-speaker ; a vice-chairman 임시 — an acting chairman

의장 議場 an assembly hall ; a chamber ; the House ; the floor (의회) ¶ 의장에서 on the floor of the House // 의장에서 소란을 부리다 make〔create〕 a disturbance in the House

의장 擬裝 ⇨ 위장(僞裝)

의장 儀裝 ceremonial equipage

의장 艤裝 rigging ; fitting out of a ship —하다 rig〔equip, fit out〕 a ship 《for sea》

의적 義賊 a chivalrous robber ; a Robin Hood

의전 儀典 ceremony ; formality ; protocol ; etiquette as practiced on diplomatic occasions
—관 a master of ceremonies ; a ceremonial officer — 비서 a protocol secretary —실 the protocol office

의절 義絶 legal separation ; cutting off relationship ; a breach of friendship —하다 break with 《a friend》

의젓이 stately ; in a dignified〔sober, serious〕 way ; imposingly ; majestically

의젓잖다 (be) undignified ; unimposing ; cheap ; frivolous ; flippant ; imprudent ; indiscreet

의젓하다 (be) dignified ; sober ; well-behaved ; formal ¶ 의젓하게 걷다 walk with slow and stately steps

의정 議定 decision by discussion ; agreement〔arrangement〕 by conference ; arrangement —하다 confer and decide ; confer and agree upon ; arrange
—서 a protocol

의정 議政 [의회 정치] legislature ; parliamentarism ; parliamentary politics〔government〕 ¶ 의정 단상에 서다〔국회 의원이 되다〕 become an Assemblyman〔a member of the National Assembly〕 ; be elected an Assemblyman〔a Representative, a Congressman 《미》〕

의제 義弟 a younger brother-in-law ; a sworn younger brother

의제 議題 a subject〔topic〕 for discussion ; a program 《미》 ; an agenda (전체) ¶ 의제가 되다 come up for discussion ; be placed on the agenda // 의제로 하다 make 《a matter》 a subject for discussion〔an agenda item〕 // 오늘은 아무 의제도 없

다 There is nothing to discuss today.
의제 擬制 〖법〗 a (legal) fiction
— 자본 watered〔fictitious〕 capital
의제 擬製 imitation ; forgery ⇨ 모조(模造), 위조(僞造)
의족 義足 an artificial leg〔limb〕 ; a leg prosthesis
*의존 依存 dependence ; reliance — 하다 depend on ; rely upon ; be dependent upon ¶ 우리는 매일 일어나는 일을 알기 위하여 매스콤에 의존한다 We depend upon the mass media for daily news.
— 관계 〖법〗 reliance 상호 — interdependence ; mutual dependence
의중 意中 one's mind〔heart〕 ; one's inner thoughts〔feelings, heart〕 ¶ 의중의 여인 a girl of one's heart ; a ladylove ; a sweetheart // 의중을 떠보다 sound《a person's》 views ; feel the pulse《of》// 의중을 밝히다 speak one's mind // 저 놈의 의중은 알 수가 없다 That guy's impossible to read.
의증 疑症 doubtfulness ; a suspicious nature
의지 a wrapping for a corpse used in place of a coffin
†의지 依支 a support ; a prop ; a help ; an aid ; assistance ; dependence ; reliance ; a protection ; a shield ; a stay — 하다 lean on ; turn to ; look to ; depend〔rely〕 on〔upon〕 ; trust to ; rest against ; fall back on ¶ 만약의 경우의 의지 the stand-by // 의지할 친구 a friend to turn to // 의지할 곳 없는 helpless ; forlorn // 의지할 곳 없는 신세 one's helpless condition ; the lonely and helpless situation // 의지할 곳 없는 아이 a forlorn〔helpless〕 child // 의지할 수 없다 be unreliable ; be untrustworthy // 의지할 사람이 없다 have no one to turn to 《for help》 ; have no one to depend upon // 지팡이에 의지하여 걷다 walk leaning on〔with the help of〕 one's stick // 그는 양친에게 의지하지 않고 살고 있다 He lives independently of his parents. // 형 밖에 의지할 곳이 없다 I have no one to turn to but my older brother. // 그는 친구를 의지하고 서울에 올라왔다 He came up to *Seoul* seeking help from a friend〔counting on his friend's help〕. // 그 집안은 그에게 의지하여 살았다 He was the main prop and stay of the family. // 그는 벽에 몸을 의지한다 He leans against the wall.
의지 義肢 an artificial limb〔appendage〕
—공(工) an artificial limb maker
†의지 意志 will ; volition ; intention ; purpose ¶ 굳은〔박약한〕 의지 a strong〔weak〕 will // 의지가 강한 사람 a man of strong〔iron〕 will // 의지가 박약한 사람 a man of weak will ; a weak-willed man // 의지가 강하다〔약하다〕 be firm〔weak〕 of purpose // 나는 그것을 내 의지대로 했다 I have done it of〔by〕 my own free will〔quite voluntarily〕.
— 결정 decision making —력 will〔volitional〕 power —주의 〖철학〗 voluntarism 자유 — free will
의지가지없다 have no place〔one〕 to turn to ; be helpless〔homeless〕 ; have no one to rely upon ; have nothing to lean on ¶ 의지가지없는 어린이 a helpless child // 의지가지 없는 처지 one's helpless circumstances // 의지가지없는 사람들 the homeless and helpless people
의처증 疑妻症 a morbid suspicion about one's wife's chastity
의초 affection between brothers and sisters ; fraternity ; fraternal love
의충 意衷 one's mind ; one's heart ; one's intention ; one's idea
의취 意趣 inclination ; mind ; proclivity
의치 義齒 a false〔an artificial〕 tooth ; a denture ¶ 의치를 해서 끼다 have a false tooth put in
—술(術) dental prosthesis
의탁 依託 reliance ; dependence — 하다 rely〔depend〕 on ; turn to ; entrust oneself to ¶ 의탁할 곳 없다 have no place to go to ; be helpless〔homeless〕
의태 擬態 (protective) mimicry ; simulation ; imitation ; mimesis ; camouflage — 하다 simulate ; mimic ¶ 가랑잎 모양으로 의태를 한 나방 moths simulating dead leaves
—색(色) mimic coloration —어(語) mimesis ; a mimetic word 보신(保身)— protective mimicry
의표 儀表 a mien ; demeanor ; bearing ; presence ; deportment ; manners ¶ 당당한 의표 a noble mien ; commanding presence
의표 意表 a surprise ; unexpectedness ¶ 남의 의표를 찌르는 일 things that surprise people // 남의 의표를 찌르다 do something extraordinary ; baffle a person's expectations
†의하다 依— [원인] be due to ; be owing to ; [의존] depend on ; be dependent on ; [근거] be based on ; be founded on ; [수단] appeal to ; use ; have recourse to ¶ …에 의하여 according to ; in accordance with ; pursuant to ; by〔in〕 virtue of ; by ; by dint of ; by means of ; through // 관례에 의하여 according to custom // 당국의 명에 의하여 by order of the authorities // 호의에 의해서 through 《a person's》 kindness // 친구의 주선에 의해서 through a friend's efforts〔good offices〕 // 귀명에 의하여 in accordance〔compliance〕 with your instructions〔order〕 // 직권에 의하여 by virtue of one's office // 요청에 의해서 at 《a person's》 request ; by request // 이 조약에 의하여 in virtue of this treaty // 소문에 의하면 according to rumor ; judging from report // 무력에 의하다 appeal to force // 형법 제

1조에 의하여 처벌할 수 있다 be punishable under Article 1 of the Criminal Code // 그의 성공은 너의 원조에 의한 것이다 His success is due to your support. // 만사가 그의 답변에 의해서 결정된다 Everything turns on his answer. // 그것은 사정에 의해서 달라진다 That depends upon circumstances. // 그의 회복은 전적으로 그녀의 간호에 의한 것이다 His recovery is solely due to her care. // 사상은 언어에 의하여 표현된다 Thoughts are expressed through〔by means of〕 words. // 듣는 바에 의하면 그는 유능한 사람인 것 같다 Judging from reports, he seems to be an able man. // 이들은 시간과 장소에 의해서 달라진다 These things are subject to change with time and place.

⁑**의학 醫學** medical science ; medicine ¶ 의학상의 medical // 의학상으로 medically // 의학을 연구하다 study medicine // 병원에서 의학 실습 근무를 하다 walk the hospital(s) ; intern 《미》 // 한국의 의학은 놀랄 만한 발전을 했다 Korea has made remarkable progress in medical science. **—계** the medical world ; medical circles **— 박사** [사람] a doctor of medicine ; [학위] Doctor of Medicine 《M. D., D. M.》 **—부** the medical department ; medicine faculty ; a medical school 《미》 **—사** [사람] a bachelor of medicine ; [학위] Bachelor of Medicine 《B. M., M. B.》 **—생** a medical student **—서** a medical book **— 실습생** an intern **—자** a medical man ; a doctor

의합 意合 ① [의가 좋음] friendly relationship ; amicability **—하다** be friendly〔amicable〕 ¶ 의합해서 살다 get along amicably ; live in harmony
② [뜻이 맞음] congeniality ; like-mindedness ; a concordance of views **—하다** (be) congenial ; be of the same opinion ¶ 의합하지 않다 disagree with each other ; differ 《from another》 in opinion

⁑**의향 意向** an intention ; an inclination ; a disposition ; [생각] a mind ; an idea ¶ 의향이 있다 be inclined to 《do》 ; intend to 《do》 // 의향이 없다 have no intention of 《doing》 // 의향을 비치다 disclose one's intention // 의향을 묻다 ask 《a person's》 intention // 의향을 타진하다 sound 《a person's》 opinion〔views〕

의혁지 擬革紙 leather paper ; imitation leather

의협 義俠 chivalry ; heroism ; gallantry ; honor ¶ 의협적인 heroic ; chivalrous

의협심 義俠心 chivalry ; a chivalrous spirit ; spirit of righteousness〔justice〕 ; public spirit ; heroism ¶ 의협심이 강한 사람 a chivalrous person ; a man of chivalrous spirit // 의협심이 강하다 be full of chivalry // 의협심을 발휘하다 show chivalrous spirit

의형 義兄 a sworn〔pledged〕 elder brother

의형제 義兄弟 a sworn brother ¶ 의형제를 맺다 form brotherly ties ; swear to be brothers 《with》

***의혹 疑惑** suspicion ; doubt ; distrust ; mistrust ; misgivings

> [참고] **suspicion** 확실한 근거 없이 죄나 잘못이 있다고 믿음 **distrust** 어떤 사람에 대한 신용도가 떨어지고 그 사람의 유죄·허위를 확신하고 있는 것 **doubt** 확신이 없어 결단을 내리지 못하는 것

—하다 suspect ; doubt ; mistrust ¶ 의혹을 품다 entertain〔have〕 a doubt ; harbor suspicion ; have misgivings // 의혹의 눈으로 보다 eye 《a person》 with suspicion // 의혹이 생기게 하다 arouse〔excite〕 suspicions〔misgivings〕 // 의혹을 풀다 dispel〔clear〕 《a person's》 doubt〔suspicions〕

의혼 議婚 discussion〔consultation〕 on marriage〔matrimony〕 ; negotiation of a marriage **—하다** discuss〔negotiate〕 a marriage

의화학 醫化學 medical chemistry

⁑**의회 議會** a national assembly ; the House ; Parliament 《영》 ; Congress 《미》 ; the Diet 《일》 ¶ 제 147차〔금번〕 의회 the 147th〔present〕 session of the National Assembly // 의회를 소집하다 call the National Assembly in session ; convoke a session of the National Assembly // 의회를 해산하다 dissolve the National Assembly // 의안이 의회를 통과했다 The bill has passed the House.
— 공작 lobbying **— 소집** convocation **— 의사록** parliamentary papers **— 정치** parliamentarism ; parliamentary government〔politics〕 **— 제도** parliamentary institutions **—주의** parliamentarism **국민 —** the National Assembly **미국 —** the Congress **영국〔캐나다〕 —** the Parliament of England〔Canada〕 **일본〔덴마크, 스웨덴〕 —** the Japanese〔Danish, Swedish〕 Diet **임시〔특별〕 —** the extraordinary〔special〕 session of the Assembly **한국 —** the National Assembly of Korea

이¹ a person ; a man ; one ¶ 오는 이 가는 이 people coming and passing by // 어떤 이 some person〔man〕 // 김씨라는 이 one *Kim* ; a Mr. *Kim* ; a man named〔called〕 *Kim*

⁑**이²** ① a tooth 《*pl.* teeth》 ; a fang (송곳니) ¶ 이의 자국 a tooth mark ; an impression of teeth // 이의 dental // 이가 없는 toothless // 이가 나다 cut one's teeth ; get a tooth through ; teethe // 이가 좋다〔나쁘다〕 have good〔bad〕 teeth ; have a good〔bad〕 set of teeth // 이가 고르다 have a regular set of teeth // 이가 빠지다 a tooth comes〔falls〕 out // 이를 뽑다 pull〔take

out, extract〕 a tooth // 이를 닦다 brush 〔clean〕 one's teeth // 이가 아프다 have a toothache ; one's tooth aches // 이를 치료하다 have one's teeth treated ; have dental treatment // 이를 쑤시다 pick one's teeth // 이를 부드득부드득 갈다 gnash 〔grind〕 one's teeth // 이가 흔들려 빼야 하겠다 I have a loose tooth ; it will have to come out. // 아이가 이를 갈기〔바꾸기〕 시작했다 The second dentition of the child is just beginning.
② [기계의] the teeth 《of a saw, a gear》; a cog ¶ 이 톱은 이가 많이 빠져 있다 This saw has a lot of teeth missing.
③ [사기 그릇 따위의] broken〔jagged〕 edges 《of a cup, a vase》 ¶ 이가 빠진 접시 a chipped dish
이도 아니 나서 콩밥 먹는다 속담 Learn to say before you sing.
이가 빠지다 관용 chip (off)
이를 악물다 관용 clench〔set, grit〕 one's teeth

이

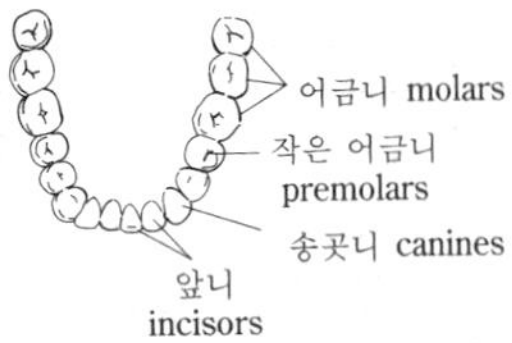

이³ a louse 《*pl.* lice》; vermin (집합적) ¶ 이 투성이의 머리 a lousy head // 이가 끓는 머리 verminous hair // 이가 끓다 be 〔become〕 infested with vermin〔lice〕; become verminous // 이를 잡다 catch 〔hunt〕 lice ; delouse // 이를 없애다 delouse 《the bedding》; rid 《the bedding》 of lice
이 잡듯하다 관용 examine thoroughly 〔one by one〕; comb〔scour〕 《a place for a thing》
†**이⁴** this 《*pl.* these》; present ; current ¶ 이 후 after this ; in future // 이 외에 above this ; besides // 이로써 with this // 이만큼 so much〔many〕 // 이에 불구하고 for all this // 이 2, 3일간 these few〔two or three〕 days // 이 달 this month ; the current〔present〕 month // 이 책 this book // 당신의 이 시계 this watch of yours // 이 바보야 You, stupid ! /You (damn) fool ! / You old donkey !
이 二, 貳 two ; the second (제2의) ¶ 이대 two generations ; two reigns // 2×2=4 two times two makes four
이 利 ① [이득] profit ; gain(s) ¶ 이를 보다 make a profit ; gain // 이가 박하다 give little profit ; do not pay much // 이가 남다 bring profits ; yield a profit // 이 장사는 이가 없다 This business does not pay.
② [유익] benefit ; good ; interests ; an advantage (장점) ¶ 이가 되다 benefit ; profit ; be of use ; do 《a person》 good ; be of advantage 《to》 // 우유는 어린애에게 이롭다 Milk is good for children. // 형세가 이롭지 않다 The chances are against them. // 그런 짓을 해서 무슨 이가 있느냐 What is the profit〔use〕 of doing it ? / What good will it do to do so ?
③ [이자] interest ¶ 고〔저〕리로 at a high 〔low〕 rate of interest // 5푼 이가 붙다 bear interest of 5% ; bear 5 percent interest // 6푼 이로 돈을 꾸다 borrow money at (the rate of) six percent interest
이 里 ① [거리] *ri*, a Korean measurement of distance 《0.244 miles, 약 400 meters》
② [행정 구역] *ri*, the smallest administrative unit ; village ; township
이 釐 ① [돈의 단위] *ri*, one tenth of a *jun* ② [길이의 단위] *ri*, one tenth of a *boon* ③ [무게의 단위] *ri*, one tenth of a *boon*
이 浬 a nautical〔sea〕 mile ; a knot
이 a mile ¶ 이수 mileage
이 理 ① [도리] reason ; [진리] truth ; [공정] justice ¶ 이에 맞지 않는 말을 하다 speak against all reason // 그의 말도 일리가 있다 His view is true in a way ② [원칙] a principle ¶ 음양의 이(치) the principle of duality〔the negative and the positive〕
이가 二價 〖화학·생물〗 bivalance ; divalance ¶ 이가의 bivalent ; double ; 〖화학〗 diatomic
이가 離家 ―하다 leave home〔one's family, one's house〕
이가 원소 二價元素 〖화학〗 dyad ; duad
이간 離間 alienation ; estrangement ―하다 alienate 《a person from another》; estrange 《a person from another》; cause estrangement 《between》; split up ; separate〔sever〕 《husband and wife》; set 《people》 by the ears〔at odds〕; influence〔play〕 《a person》 against 《another》 ¶ 이간당하다 get〔be〕 alienated 《by a person》 // 그는 그 부부를 이간시켰다 He split the couple up.
―쟁이 a mischief-maker ―질 ⇨ 이간 ―책 a discord-producing intrigue ; an alienating measure ; mischief-making ; a splitting maneuver
이갈다 grind〔gnash〕 one's teeth ; grit one's teeth ; [분해서] grind one's teeth with vexation
이같은 such ; the kind〔sort〕 of ; like this ¶ 이같은 일 such a thing (as this) // 이같은 날에 on a day like this ; on such a day (as this) // 이같은 이유로 for such reasons (as mentioned)
이같이 like this ; thus ; so ; in this way 〔manner〕; in such a manner ; so much

¶ 이같이 된 이상 now that things have come to this pass // 이같이 많은 돈 such a big sum of money ; so much money // 그는 이같이 연설했다 He made a speech like this. // 이같이 더운 날은 처음이다 I have never seen such hot weather as this.

이거 [놀람] O ! ; Oh ! ; Good Heavens ! ¶ 이거 야단났네 Here's a pretty kettle of fish ! // 이거 안 되겠군 Good forbid ! // 이거 놀랐는걸 What a surprise ! / Indeed ! /This is a surprise !

이거 移去 removal ; moving away —하다 remove ; move away

이거 移居 removal ; moving ; changing one's residence〔abode〕; migration (이주) —하다 move ; remove ; change one's residence〔abode〕; migrate (외국으로) ¶ 일본으로 이거하다 migrate to Japan

*이것 ① [지시] this ; this thing ; this fact ¶이것으로 with this ; now ; here // 이것뿐 no more // 이것에 반하여 while ; on the contrary // 이것 참 I say ! /Bless my soul ! // 이것 참 야단났군 Gracious heaven ! /Gracious me ! /My gracious ! // 이것은 싫다 I don't like this one. // 네 잘못은 이것뿐이 아니다 This is not the only mistake you have made. // 이것이 인생이다 Such〔This〕 is life. /This is the way life is. // 이것이 바로 축구라는 거다 This is what I call soccer.
② [부를 때] ¶ 이것 좀 봐 I say ! /Say ! 《미·구》/Hey ! /Look〔See〕 here ! // 이것 봐 어디 가는 거야 Here, where are you going ?

이것저것 this and that ; one thing and another ; something or other ¶ 이것저것 생각한 끝에 after a great deal of thinking ; after fully considering the situation // 이것저것 할 것 없이 [떠들 것 없이] with no further ado ; without making a fuss ; [가릴 것 없이] without discrimination // 이것저것 궁리하다 think of this and that ; give consideration to various things ; mull things over // 이것저것 해보다 try one thing or another

이겨내다 overcome 《difficulties》; conquer 《the enemy》; get over 《a disease》; resist 《a temptation》 ¶ 자기를 이겨내다 control〔conquer〕 oneself // 유혹을 이겨내다 overcome a temptation ; put the devil behind one // 병〔곤란〕을 이겨내다 get over one's disease〔difficulties〕

이견 異見 a different view〔opinion〕; a dissenting opinion ; an objection ; a protest ¶ 이견을 품다 hold a different view ; dissent 《from》 // 이견을 제기하다 raise an objection 《to》; make a protest 《to》

이결 已決 a matter already settled ; being already decided ¶ 이결의 decided ; settled
— 사건 matters already decided〔settled〕

이겹실 double-ply thread ; twine (여러겹의)

이경 離京 departure from *Seoul* —하다 leave the capital ; leave *Seoul*

이경 二更 the second watch of the night 《around 10 p.m.》

-이고 ① [두 가지 이상의 사물] and (also) ; and ; or ¶ 이것은 펜이고 그것은 연필이다 This is a pen and that is a pencil. ② [···이나, ···이든] any ; . . . ever ¶ 무엇이고 whichever ; anything // 언제이고 on some〔any〕 occasion // 누구이고 whoever // 그것을 빼놓고는 무엇이고 하겠다 I'll do anything but that.

이골나다 become used〔accustomed〕 to ; get inured to ; grow experienced in ; become skil(l)ful〔good〕 at

*이곳 this place ; here ¶ 이곳에 here ; in this place // 이곳으로 here ; to this place ; hither // 이곳으로 오신지 얼마나 되십니까 How long have you been here ? // 이곳을 지나실 때는 한번 들러 주시오 Drop in please when you come this way.

이공 理工 science and engineering
—과 the department of science and engineering — 대학 a college of science and engineering — 학부 the faculty of science and engineering

이과 耳科 〖의학〗 otology
— 전문의(醫) an ear specialist ; an otologist ; an aurist

이과 理科 [학문] science ; [과목] the science course ; [학부] the science department
— 대학 a college of science

이관 移管 transfer of control〔jurisdiction〕 —하다 transfer the superintendence 〔control〕《to》 ¶ 국고에 이관하다 transfer to the national treasury
군원(軍援) — transfer of the Military Assistance Program

*이교 異教 [기독교에서 본] heathenism ; [이단] heresy ; heterodoxy ¶ 이교의 pagan ; heathen ; heretical ; heterodoxical
—국 a heathen country ; heathendom ; pagandom —도 a pagan ; a heathen ; a heretic ; an infidel ; a gentile (이방인) — 주의 paganism

이구동성 異口同聲 a unanimous voice ; common consent ¶ 이구 동성으로 with one voice〔mouth〕; with one consent 〔accord〕; by common consent ; unanimously ; 《cry》 in chorus // 이구동성으로 인정하다 recognize without a dissenting voice // 사람들은 이구 동성으로 그를 칭찬했다 They praised him with one accord.

이국 異國 a strange land ; a foreign country〔land〕; an alien land ¶ 이국적인 exotic // 이국에 묻히다 die in a foreign land
—인 a foreigner ; a stranger — 정취〔정

서〕 an exotic mood ; exoticism ; foreign sentiment —풍 exoticism ; foreign〔alien〕 customs

이군 二軍 〖야구〗 a farm〔scrub〕 team ; a farm
— 선수 a farm hand ; rookie

이궁 離宮 ① [태자궁] the palace of the Crown Prince
② [별궁] a detached palace ; a royal villa ; a secondary palace

이권 利權 rights and interests ; privileges ; concessions (광산·철도의) ; vested rights ¶ 이권에 급급한 사람 a concession hunter ; a grafter 《미》 // 아랍 지방에서의 미국의 유전 이권 the United States oil interests in the Arab League States // 이권을 획득하다 acquire rights〔concessions〕 // 이권을 포기하다 renounce one's interests // 광산 개발의 이권을 양보하다 grant 《foreigners》 mining concessions
— 양도〔회복〕 transfer〔recovery〕 of rights〔concession〕 — 추구 grafting ; grabbing ; hunting for concessions — 획득 acquisition of concessions ; graft 《미》

이글루 [에스키모인의 얼음집] an igloo

이글이글 《burn》 lively ; deeply flushed
—하다 (be) burning ; blazing ; glowing ; [얼굴이] flushing ¶ 이글이글 타는 태양 a blazing sun // 이글이글 타는 눈 eyes burning with passion // 숯불이 이글이글 탄다 The charcoal burns brightly. // 전신이 이글이글했다 My body was all of a glow. // 그녀의 얼굴이 부끄러워서 이글이글 달아올랐다 Her face was deeply flushed with shame.

이금 泥金 gold dust mixed with glue ; gilt paint

이급 二級 the second class
—주(酒) second-grade wine —품 second-class goods ; seconds

이기 利己 self-interest ; selfishness ; egoism ¶ 이기적인 selfish ; egoistic ; self-seeking ; self-interested // 이기적이 아닌 disinterested ; selfless ; unselfish // 이기적인 동기에서 from a selfish motive // 그는 이기적인 사람이다 He has an eye to the main chance. /He is guided by self-interest.
—심 egoistic〔selfish, egocentric, self-centered〕 mind —주의 egoism ; selfishness ; self-interest —주의자 an egoist ; an egotist

이기 利器 ① a convenience ; a device ¶ 문명의 이기 a modern convenience ; a factor of civilization // 문명한 오늘날 전화는 필요 불가결의 이기다 In these civilized days the telephone is a most necessary apparatus. ② [재능] (practical) ability ; (useful) talent
③ [연모] a sharp-edged tool

이기 理氣 〖철학〗 the basic principles and the atmospheric force of nature ; the predisposition of nature (toward good or bad luck)

†이기다[1] ① [승리하다] win 《a battle》 ; gain a victory 《over》 ; hold the field ; have the best of it ; [쳐부수다] defeat ; beat ; triumph 《over》 ; prevail 《against, over》 ; [정복하다] conquer ¶ 싸움에 이기다 win a battle ; win〔gain〕 the day // 적을 이기다 defeat〔beat〕 the enemy ; win over the enemy // 카드놀이에서 이기다 win at cards // 시합에 이기다 win the game // 재판에 이기다 win a lawsuit // 겨우 이기다 win by a narrow margin // 논쟁에 이기다 get the better of 《a person》 in an argument // 쉽게 이기다 win an easy victory 《over》 ; walk over // 5대 3으로 이겼다 We won, 5 to 3. // 그는 선거에서 겨우 이겼다 He won the election by a narrow margin.
② [극복하다] overcome ; surmount ; get over ¶ 병〔곤란〕을 이겨내다 get over〔overcome〕 one's disease〔difficulties〕 // 유혹을 이겨내다 overcome a temptation

이기다[2] ① [반죽하다] knead 《flour》 ; mash 《potatoes》 ; work 《mortar》 ¶ 진흙을 이기다 knead clay ② [짓찧다] mince ; chop ; pound into pieces ¶ 고기를 이기다 mince meat ③ [기타] beat ; paddle 《the wash》

-이기에 ⇨ -기에 ②

이기죽거리다 talk nonsense ; make invidious〔sly, insinuating〕 remarks ; talk at ; carp

이기죽이기죽 《talk》 invidiously ; with sly hints ; insinuatingly ; carping

이김수 a winning move

이까짓 this kind of ; such a 《trifle》 ; so trifling〔slight, little, small〕 ¶ 이까짓 것 such a trifle // 이까짓 돈 such a trifling sum of money // 이까짓 일을 갖고 크게 떠벌리지 마라 Don't make a fuss over such a trifle. // 이까짓 것 하고 깔본 것이 잘못이었다 I did wrong in making light of the matter.

이깔나무 a kind of larch (tree)

†이끌다 [지도] guide ; lead ; [인도·안내] guide ; conduct ; show〔usher〕 in ; introduce 《a person》 into 《a room》 ; shepherd 《a crowd》 ; [인솔] lead ; head 《a party》 ; be at the head of ; [지휘] command〔lead〕 《an army》 ¶ 후진을 이끌다 lead the younger generation // 사람을 바른 길로 이끌다 guide〔lead〕 a person's steps in the path of righteousness ; put〔set〕 the man on the right road // 서재로 이끌다 usher into〔conduct to〕 the study // 폭도를 이끌고 at the head of a rebellion // 군대를 이끌다 command〔lead〕 an army // 노구를 이끌고 in spite of one's old age

이끌리다 be guided ; be led ; be headed ; [정에] be tied〔drawn, moved〕 《by》 ¶ 선생님에게 이끌리어 led〔headed〕 by a teacher // 이끌리어 가다 be led away ; be taken along // 육친의 정에 이끌리어 by the ties of parent and child

이끗 利— a clue〔chance〕 of gaining 〔making〕 profit ; the first step for profit ; the beginning of making gains

*이끼[1] moss ; a lichen ; 〖식물〗 a liverwort ¶ 이끼낀 나무 mossy trees // 이끼가 끼다 moss grows 《over a rock》 ; be mossy ; be moss-grown // 굴러다니는 돌에는 이끼도 안낀다 A rolling stone gathers no moss.

이끼[2] Oh ! ; Oh my ! ; Dear me ! ; What a fright ! ¶ 이끼 이건 또 뭐야 There ! What's that ? // 이끼 순경이 온다 Look ! There comes a cop.

이끼나 Oh ! /Oh my ! // Oh my goodness ! /My ! /My eye ! /Oh dear ! / Gracious me !

이나 ① [그러나] but ; (and) yet ; while ; though ; although ¶ 그의 말은 사실이나 행동이 나빴다 He spoke the truth, but what he did was bad.
② [정도] as many〔much, long, far〕 as ; no less than ; about ; around ¶ 두 시간쯤이나 about two hours // 그는 나에게 50,000원이나 주었다 He gave me no less than 50,000 *won.* // 나는 50리나 걸었다 I walked as far〔long〕 as 50 *ri.* // 그는 죽은 것이나 다름없다 He is as good as dead. // 나는 겨우 의사나 전할 수 있다 I can barely express my ideas.
③ [선택] or ; and ; either... or ¶ 공책이나 연필 notebooks and〔or〕 pencils // 이 집이나 저집이나 다 같다 This house and that one are both alike. // 이군이나 내가 가야 한다 Either Mr. *Lee* or I must go. // 어느 것이나 좋다 I don't care which. // 어느 것이나 좋은 것을 가져라 Take whichever〔whatever〕 you like. // 커피나 마실까 Let's have something, say a cup of coffee. /What do you say to having a cup of coffee ?

이나마[1] [아쉬운 대로] although 《it is》 ¶ 한 달에 만원이나마 저축하고 싶다 I wish to save money, say a minimum of ten thousand *won* a month. // 초라한 집이나마 내 집을 하나 가졌으면 좋겠다 I wish I had a house of my own however humble it might be.

이나마[2] [이것이나마] although〔even though〕 it is this

이날 ① [오늘] today ; this day ¶ 이날에 이르기까지 until〔to〕 the present ; so far ; up to this time ; (up) to date // 내년 이날 this day next year // 이날에 이르기까지 그의 행방이 불명이다 His whereabouts is unknown to this day. ② [특정한 날] that day ; the very〔same〕 day ; on the day in question ¶ 이날의 연사 the speaker of the day // 이날 날씨는 맑았다 The occasion was favored by fine weather.

이날저날 this day and that day ; from day to day ; day after day ¶ 이날저날 미루어 나가다 put off from day to day ; keep putting 《it》 off day after day // 이날저날 살아가다 live from day to day

이남 以南 south of 《*Seoul*》 ; South Korea ¶ 서울 이남 south of *Seoul* ; *Seoul* and southward ; from *Seoul* south // 38선 이남 south of the 38th Parallel

이남박 a rice-washing bowl ; a wooden bowl with grooves running around the inside (used for washing rice)

†이내 ① [곧] soon ; presently ; at once ; right away ; immediately ; instantly ; straight away ; right away ; as soon as... ¶ 이내 가야한다 I must go right away〔at once〕. // 이내 돌아오겠다 I'll be back in a moment. // 그는 이내 죽었다 He died soon after〔a short time later〕. // 그는 이내 왔다 He was not long in coming. // 그는 나를 보자 이내 달아났다 The moment he saw me he ran off.
② [그후 내처] ever since ; ever afterward ¶ 집을 떠난 후 이내 소식이 없다 I have had no news from him ever since he left home.

이내 以內 within ; inside 《 of》 ; not exceeding ; less than ; not more than ; inside the limit ¶ 1주일 이내 within a week ; inside of a week // 3마일 이내 less than three miles // 5,000원 이내의 금액 a sum not exceeding 5000 *won* // 3일 이내에 돈을 돌려주겠다 I will pay back the money within three days.

이냥 as it is ; as it stands ; in this way ; with no change ; as one is ¶ 이냥 둬두다 leave 《it》 as it is ; leave 《a thing》 off (as it is) ; leave 《a thing》 intact // 이냥 가겠다 I will go as I am. // 이냥이라도 좋다 I am all right as I am.

이네(들) these people ; they

이년 this bad girl〔woman〕 ; this chit ¶ 이년(아) You bitch ! /You slut !

이년 二年 two years ¶ 이년마다 biennially ; every two years // 그는 지금 대학 이년생이다 He is now a sophomore.

이념 理念 an idea ; an ideology ; a doctrine (교리) ¶ 이념적 ideological // 이념분쟁 a ideological quarrel〔dispute〕

이노베이션 (an) innovation

이놈 this (damn) guy ; this man〔fellow〕 ¶ 이놈아 You rascal ! /You rat ! /You villain ! /You scoundrel !

이농 離農 rural exodus —하다 give up farming ; departure village

이뇨 利尿 urination ; excretion of urine —하다 urinate ; promote urination — 곤란 difficulty in urination ; difficult urination〔diuresis〕 —제 a diuretic ; a hydragogue

-이니 and ; or ; with ; and so on〔forth〕 ¶ 공책이니 연필이니 잘 간수를 안 하다 do not take good care of notebooks and pencils and things like that // 과로니 영양 부족이니 하다 그는 병에 걸렸다 His overwork and undernourishment caused him to be ill.

-이니(까) as〔since〕 it is ; you see ; so ¶ 의사가 외출중이니 한 30분 기다려 주시겠습니까 Since the doctor is out, could you wait about 30 minutes? // 저녁이 다 준비된 모양이니 식당으로 가십시다 As the dinner seems to be ready, let's go to the dining room. // 오늘은 일요일이니까 학교에 갈 필요가 없다 Today is Sunday, so we don't have to go to school.

이니셜 one's initials ¶ 이니셜로 서명하다 initial 《a document》

이니셔티브 initiative ¶ 이니셔티브를 잡다 take the initiative 《in》 // …에게서 이니셔티브를 빼앗다 take the initiative away from...

이닝 〖야구〗 inning(s)

†**이다**[1] ① [지정하는 말] be ¶ 개는 충실한 동물이다 A dog is an honest animal.
② [되다] come ; be ¶ 이번 생일에는 만 열살이다 I shall be〔am coming〕 ten years old next birthday.
③ [수량] number ; weigh ; measure ; cover ¶ 키가 6피트이다 be six feet tall ; measure 6 feet in height // 그것은 1미터이다 It measures one meter. // 그 대지는 100평이다 The lot covers 100 *pyung*. // 학생은 1,000명 이상이다 The students number over〔exceed〕 1,000.

이다[2] [머리 위에] carry〔put〕 on the head ¶ 물동이를 머리에 이다 carry a water jar on one's head

이다[3] [지붕을] tile 《a roof》 (기와로) ; thatch (이엉으로) ; shingle (판자로) ; slate (슬레이트로) ¶ 짚으로 인 집 a straw-thatched cottage

이다음 next ¶ 이다음에 next ; next time ; another time // 이다음의 next // 이다음은 네 차례다 It's your turn next.

이다지 to this extent〔degree〕 ; so large ; so much ; thus ¶ 이다지 많이 so many ; so much // 이다지 오래 so long // 이다지 아침 일찌기 at this hour of morning // 이다지 눈이 많이 올 줄은 몰랐다 I did not expect so much snow here. // 기차가 왜 이다지 늦담 Why is the train so damn late? // 이다지 어려울 줄은 몰랐다 I did not expect it to be so difficult. // 이다지 잘 되리라고는 생각치 않았다 I did not expect to succeed so well. /I did not bargain for such success.

이단 異端 heresy ; paganism ; heterodoxy ; heathenism ¶ 이단의 heretical ; pagan ; heathen // 이단시하다 regard as a heretic // 이단을 주창하다 express a heretical view〔doctrine〕
—설(說) a heretical view〔doctrine〕 **—자** a heretic ; a heathen

이단 二段 ¶ 이단의 double ; two-stage
— 여과(濾過) two-stage filtration **— 표제(標題)** two-line heading

*__이달__ this month ; the current〔present〕 month ; instant 《inst.》 ¶ 이달 봉급 this month's pay ; one's pay for this month // 이달(분) 신문대 a newspaper subscription for the month // 이달 호 the current number〔issue〕 // 이달 15일 《on》 the 15th inst. ; the 15th of this month // 이달 그믐께 about the end of this month // 이달 중에 in the course of this month ; before the end of this month

*__이대로__ as it is ; as it stands ; as one is ; intact ; untouched ¶ 이대로 내버려 둘 수는 없다 I can't leave the matter as it is. /I can't leave the matter as it is. /I can't pass the matter over unnoticed〔unattended〕. // 나는 이대로 좋다 I like it this way. /I am all right as I am. // 이대로 두시오 Leave it as it is. // 이대로 가겠다 I will go as I am. // 이대로 두시오 Leave it as it is. // 이집은 이대로 5000만원에 팔린다 This house will sell for fifty million *won* as it stands. // 이대로 간대면 그는 대단한 사람이 될 것이다 If he goes on at this rate, he will do well. // 이대로 열흘만 비가 더 계속되면 전서울 시내는 홍수가 날 것이다 If it keeps on raining at the present rate for ten more days, the whole city of *Seoul* will be flooded.

이데아 〖철학〗 an idea ¶ 이데아적인 ideal

*__이데올로기__ ideology ¶ 이데올로기의 ideological // 이데올로기의 분열〔상충〕 an ideological split〔conflict〕 《between》 // 그것은 이데올로기의 차이다 That means a difference in ideology between us.

이도 吏道 the duty of officials
— 쇄신 renovation of officialdom

이동 異同 difference and sameness ; distinction ; difference ¶ 당신은 A와 B와의 이동을 말할 수 있습니까 Can you distinguish〔tell〕 A from B?
— 식별 identification

†**이동 移動** movement ; transfer ; locomotion ; migration ; drift **—하다** move ; transfer ; migrate ; travel ¶ 이동식의 movable ; portable ; traveling
— 경찰 mobile police ; highway police **— 극단** an itinerant theatrical troupe **— 노동자** a migratory laborer **— 도서관** an itinerant〔a traveling〕 library ; mobile library ; a bookmobile 《미》 **—력** locomotive faculty〔power〕 **—률** turnover rate ; drift (조류·기류 따위의) **— 무대** a movable〔sliding〕 stage **— 병원** a hospital on wheels ; a mobile hospital **— 신고** a report of removal **— 장치** a shifter **— 전람회** a mobile show〔exhibition〕 **— 진료소** a traveling clinic **— 촬영** a moving shot **— 통신** mobile communication **인구 —** the movement〔drift〕 of population 《to a place》

이동 異動 a change ; (an) alteration ; shifting ¶ 사원의 이동 changes in the

staff ; personnel changes // 내각〔개각〕의 이동 a reshuffle of the Cabinet // 이동을 실행하다 make changes 《in, at》 // 관리의 이동이 빈번히 발표되다 Changes of officials are〔Reshuffling of government personnel is〕 frequently announced. // 지방 관리의 이동이 있을 예정이다 Changes among local officials are expected.
대— a wholesale change ; a shake-up 《미》 ; a sweeping shift 인사 — changes of personnel ; reshuffling of personnel

이동 以東 east of 《*Seoul*》 ¶ 이동에〔은, 의〕 east of 《*Seoul*》 ; 《*Seoul*》 and eastward // 서울 이동 east of *Seoul* ; *Seoul* and eastward ; from *Seoul* east

이동성 移動性 ¶ 이동성의 rambling ; roving
— 고기압(高氣壓) 〖기상〗 migratory anticyclone — 류머티즘 rambling rheumatism

이드거니 plentifully ; in rather large quantity〔amount〕 (after a long interval)

이드르르 glossily ; lustrously ; brightly —하다 (be) glossy ; lustrous ; bright ; polished ; [피부 따위가] soft and delicate ; soft and shiny

† **이득 利得** gain ; profit ; benefit ; returns ; 〖법〗 issue (부동산 따위의) ¶ 부당하게 이득을 취하다 profiteer
부당 — profiteering ; excess profit ; 〖법〗 unjust enrichment 부당 —세 the excess profits tax 부당 —자 a profiteer

이든지 whether... or ; either... or ; or ; no matter 《who, what, when, where, how》 ⇨ 든지 ¶ 무엇이든지 whatever ; anything (무엇이든지 하나) ; anything and everything (무엇이든지 다) // 정말이든지 거짓말이든지 whether it is〔be〕 true or not // 한국 사람이었든지 미국 사람이었든지 whether he was a Korean or an American // 그가 누구이든지 whoever〔no matter who〕 he may be // 이것이든지 그것이든지 마음 대로 가져라 You may take either this one or that. // 택시든지 버스든지 타고 가자 Let's go by cab or bus.

이들이들하다 (be) glossy ⇨ 이드르르하다

이듬[1] [다음] next ; the following ¶ 이듬날 the next day ; the day after

이듬[2] [농사의] the second hoeing ; the second weeding ; the second plowing —하다 give 《a field》 a second hoeing 〔weeding, plowing〕

이듬해 the next〔following〕 year ; the year after

이듭 a two-year-old 《ox, horse》

이등 二等 the second class〔grade, prize, place〕 ; the second ¶ 이등의 second ; second class〔rate〕 // 이등이 되다 finish second ; [경기에서] be a runner-up ; win the second prize // 이등으로 졸업하다 graduate second in one's class // 이등을 타고 여행하다 travel second-class ; travel second-cabin (배의)
—병 [육군·해병] a (second class) private ; [해군] a seaman apprentice ; an ordinary seaman ; [공군] an airman —상 the〔a〕 second prize〔award〕 — 승객 a second-class passenger —차〔차표, 선실〕 a second-class car〔ticket, cabin〕 —품 seconds ; second-grade articles 〔goods〕

이등변 삼각형 二等邊三角形 〖수학〗 an isosceles triangle

이등분 二等分 bisection —하다 divide equally〔in half〕 ; divide into two equal parts ; bisect 《a line》 ¶ 이등분한 halved ; bisected // 나는 사과를 이등분하였다 I cut an apple into two equal parts.
—선 a bisector

이디엄 an idiom

이디오피아 Ethiopia ¶ 이디오피아의 Ethiopian
— 사람 an Ethiopian

이따 [이따가] after a while ; after a short time ; a little later ¶ 이따 내게로 오게 Come see me a little later. // 이따 다시 오겠습니다 I will come again after a while.

‡**이따금** from time to time ; sometimes ; (every) now and then ; occasionally ; once in a while ; at intervals ; as often as not ; on and off ¶ 이따금 오다 come occasionally〔now and then〕 // 이따금 만나다 see 《a person》 now and then // 이따금 소식을 듣다 hear from 《a person》 once in a while

이따위 such 《a thing》 as this ; a thing 〔person〕 of this sort ; such ; like this ; of this kind〔sort〕 ; this kind〔sort〕 of ¶ 이따위 일 such a job as this ; a job like this ; a job of this kind ; this kind of job // 이따위로 in this manner ; like this // 이따위 짓은 두 번 다시 안하겠다 I will never do such a thing again.

* **이때** at this time〔moment, juncture, point〕 ; now ; then ; on this occasion ¶ 이때에 at this time〔moment〕 // 바로 이때(에) at this very moment // 이때까지 until now ; to this time ; up to this day // 바로 이때 한 여자가 다방으로 들어왔다 At this point a woman came into the tearoom. // 달아날 준비를 할 때는 이때다 Now is the time for us to make ready to flee.

이똥 tartar ; the yellow on one's teeth

-이라 it is and (so) ¶ 지배인이 외출중이라 비서에게 말을 전하고 왔다 The manager was out, so I left a message with his secretary.

이라고 ⇨ 라고 ¶ 네가 가는 곳이 어디라고 말했느냐 Where did you say it was that you are going ? // 이것은 무엇이라고 하느냐 What do you call this ? // 저것이 장미라고 하는 꽃이다 That is a flower called the rose.

이라고는 [···라고 하는 것은] that (one) says it is ; called ; [이렇다할] as for (the one that is called) ¶ 그를 위인이라고는

할 수 없다 We cannot say he is〔He is anything but〕 a great man. // 호주머니에 돈이라고는 한 푼도 없었다 There was not a single penny in my pocket.

이라는 that is (called) ¶ 심이라는 사람 a man named〔called〕 *Sim* // "청년"이라는 잡지 a magazine called〔titled〕 the "Rising Generation"

-이라니 ¶ 김군이라니 어느 김군 말이냐 Which *Kim* are you talking about? // 저 사람이 새로 온 선생이라니 Just think of his being our new teacher! // 친척이라니 누구 말인가 Whom do you mean by a relative? // 아 벌써 정오라니 Can it be (true) that it is noon already?

이라크 Iraq ; Irak ¶ 이라크의 Iraqi **—말** Iraqi **— 사람** an Iraqi

이락 利落 ¶ 이락의 ex dividend〔interest〕 **— 채권** 〖증권〗 an ex div. bond

이란 Iran ¶ 이란의 Iranian **—말** Iranian **— 사람** an Iranian

-이란 [이라고 하는] that is (called) ; [이라고 하는 것은] "as for (the one that is called)" ¶ 신이란 무엇인가 What is God? // 도둑이란 남의 물건을 훔치는 놈이다 A thief is a wretch who steals the property of others.

이란성 二卵性 ¶ 이란성의 biovular **— 쌍둥이** 《one of》 fraternal twins

-이람 Do you mean to say that it is? ; really? ¶ 그런 놈도 사람이람 Would you call the likes of him a human being? // 그가 무슨 상관이람 That's none of his business?

이랑[1] the ridge and furrow 《of a field》

이랑[2] and ; or ; what with ¶ 이 일이랑 저 일이랑 with one thing and another

이래 they say ; I hear ¶ 그는 도둑놈이래 It is said that he is a thief. /They call him a thief. // 그의 이름은 존이래 I hear his name is John. /They say his name is John.

†**이래 以來** [그후] since ; since then ; after that ; [금후] in future ; after this ; hereafter ¶ 그때 이래 줄곧 ever since // 저는 전쟁 이래 줄곧 여기 있었다 I have been here ever since the war. // 작년의 폭풍은 1935년 이래의 최대 폭풍이었다 Last year's storm was the severest one that has ever visited our country since 1935. // 금년 여름은 10년 이래의 최고 더위였다 We have had the hottest summer (ever experienced) in the past ten years.

이래도 ¶ 겉보기엔 이래도 나는 아직 40이 다 Old as I may appear, I haven't turned forty yet. // 이래도 김양 저래도 김양이었다 It was Miss *Kim* this and Miss *Kim* that.

이래라저래라 ordering 《a person》 to do this and to do that ; ordering 《people》 about ¶ 이래라저래라 참견이 심하다 He is always poking into other people's business and telling them what to do. // 어디 감히 이래라 저래라 하는 거야 How dare you try to boss me around?

이래 봬도 such as I am ; humble as I am ; whatever you may take me for ; I don't know what you take me for, but... ; in spite of my appearance ¶ 이래 봬도 나는 행복해요 Such as I am, I am happy. // 이래 봬도 나는 예술가야 I am an artist, humble as I am.

이래저래 with this and that ; one thing or another ; one way or another ; in various ways ; somehow or other ¶ 이래저래 바쁘다 I am busy with one thing or another. // 이래저래 2만원이 필요하다 I need 20,000 *won* for this and that. // 이래저래 신세만 진다 I am much obliged to you.

이랬다저랬다 this way and that way ; (be) changeable ; fickle ; unreliable ¶ 이랬다저랬다 마음이 늘 변하다 be fickle as a cat's eye ; be unstable〔unreliable, unpredictable〕 // 너무 이랬다저랬다 말아라 Don't be so fickle. // 그는 말을 이랬다저랬다 한다 He says first one thing and then the opposite.

이러 [우마를 모는 소리] Get up! /Giddap! /Haw! (왼쪽으로 돌릴 때)/Gee-ho! /Gee-up! /Gee-wo!

이러구러 ① [우연히] unexpectedly ; accidentally ; by chance ¶ 이러구러 그녀를 만나게 되었다 I happened〔chanced〕 upon her. /It so happened that I met her.
② [세월이] meantime ; meanwhile ; before one knows ; before one is aware ; unawares ; unnoticed ¶ 이러구러 10년이 지났다 Ten years have passed all too soon. // 이러구러 가을이 왔다 Fall has stolen up on us.

이러나저러나 at any rate ; in any case ; at all events ; anyhow ; anyway ¶ 이러나저러나 살아야겠다 At all events, I must live. // 이러나저러나 해보겠다 At any rate, I will try. // 그것이 내게는 이러나저러나 마찬가지다 It is all one to me. // 이러나저러나 기차로 서울까지 가자 Anyhow, let's take the train as far as *Seoul*. // 이러나저러나 그에게 미안하다 Be that as it may, I am sorry for him.

이러니저러니 this or that ; something or other ¶ 이러니저러니 말할 것 없이 without saying this or that ; without ado ; without raising useless questions ; with a good grace // 이러니저러니 말하다 say things ; criticize ; raise objection ; make complaints // 지금 와서 이러니저러니 해야 소용 없다 It is too late now to raise any objections. // 이러니저러니 하는 것이 세상이다 People will talk. /They will say something or other.

이러다 do〔say, think〕 this way ¶ 이러다가는 이달에 못 끝나겠다 At this rate it will not be finished this month. // 서둘러라 이러다 기차 놓칠라 Hurry up, or we will miss train.

이러루하다 《it》 seem to be this way ; be like〔as〕 this (one) ; be similar to this

이러므로 for this reason ; so ; therefore ; accordingly ; hence

이러이러하다 be so and so ; such and such ¶ 이러이러한 사람 such and such a person // 이러이러한 이유로 for such and such reasons ; for certain reasons // 이러이러한 경우에는 이러이러하게 말하라고 일러 두시오 Tell him to say so and so on such and such an occasion.

이러저러하다 ⇨ 이러이러하다

이러쿵저러쿵 this or that ⇨ 이러니저러니

이러하다 be this way ; be like this ; be as follows ¶ 사실인즉 이러하다 The fact is this. // 대통령이 발표한 담화는 이러하다 The statement issued by the President is as follows.

†**이럭저럭** ① somehow or other ; in one way or another ; somehow ¶ 그들은 이럭저럭 살아가고 있다 They are making a living by some means or other. // 이럭저럭 뒤떨어졌다 He somehow dropped behind. // 지붕을 고치는 데 이럭저럭 5백만 원이 들었다 With one thing or another, it cost me 5,000,000 *won* to repair the roof.

② [어느덧] unawares ; unnoticed ; before one knows ; in no time ¶ 이럭저럭 겨울 방학이 지나가버렸다 The winter vacation has passed all too soon. // 이럭저럭 봄이 왔다 Spring has stolen up on us. // 집을 떠난지 이럭저럭 10년이 지났다 Somehow ten years have passed away since I left home.

†**이런** ① [이러한] such ; such... as ; like this ; of this kind〔sort〕; this kind〔sort〕 of ¶ 이런 고로 for this reason // 이런 때에 at a time like this ; at such a time // 이런 사정인즉 such being the case // 이런 재미 있는 책은 읽은 적이 없다 I have never read such an interesting book. // 이런 일이 이렇게 되리라고는 생각도 못했다 I didn't think things would come to this. /Just think that I should ever come to this.

② [감탄] Oh dear ! /Goodness ! /Oh my ! /Why ! /What a surprise ! /Well, well ! ¶ 이런 라이터를 안 가지고 왔군 Oh dear, I forgot to bring my lighter with me. // 이런 비가 오네 Ah ! It rains. // 이런 그건 아주 쉬워 Why, it's quite easy !

이런저런 this and that ; one thing or another ; something or other ¶ 이런저런 일로 바쁘다 I am busy with one thing and another. // 이런저런 일로 돈이 필요하다 I need money for this and that.

이렁성저렁성 like this and like that ; somehow or other

이렁저렁 ⇨ 이럭저럭

***이렇게** thus ; so 《many, much》; like this ; in this way〔manner〕 ¶ 이렇게 나쁜 so bad // 이렇게 된 바에는 since it has come to this // 이렇게 비가 와도 for all this rain // 이렇게 해라 Do it this way. // 나는 일이 이렇게 될 줄 알았다 I knew things would come to this. // 태어나서 이렇게 유쾌한 적은 없었다 I have never had such a pleasant time in life.

†**이렇다** be like this ⇨ 이러하다

이렇다저렇다 this or that ⇨ 이러니저러니

이렇든저렇든 whether it is this or that ; at any rate ; in any case ; in any event ; anyhow ; anyway

이렇듯 thus ; like this ; so 《large》 ¶ 이렇듯 많은 so many〔much〕// 이렇듯 잘 될 줄 몰랐다 I did not expect to succeed so well.

이렇지 않다 (be) not like this ¶ 예전엔 이렇지 않았다 Things were different in the old days. // 내가 떠났을 때는 이렇지 않았다 It was not like this when I left.

이레 [날짜] the seventh day (of the month) ; [일곱날] seven days ; [이레째] the seventh day

이렛날 ⇨ 이레

***이력 履歷** one's personal history ; one's career ; one's antecedents ; one's past ; one's record ; one's background ¶ 이력이 훌륭한 사람 a man of good antecedents // 이력이 좋다〔나쁘다〕 have a good〔poor〕 record of service // 나는 그의 이력을 알고 있다 I know his antecedents 〔personal history〕. // 이력에 오점이 찍히다 leave a spot on one 's record // 그의 이력은 전연 모른다 His past life is a sealed book to me. // 이런 직업도 너의 이력의 하나가 된다 Such a job will make an important item in your history.

—서 a résumé ; a personal history〔statement〕; a curriculum vitae 《라》; a record of one's life ¶ 이력서를 첨부해서 지원서를 제출하다 present an application along with one's curriculum vitae **— 현상** 〖물리〗 hysteresis

이령수 prayer said loudly to 《a god》 while rubbing one's hands in supplication

이례 異例 an exception ; a singular〔an exceptional〕 case ; an unprecedented case ; an anomaly ; unconventionality ¶ 이례의 exceptional ; singular ; unprecedented (전례가 없는) ; unconventional // 그의 승진은 이례다 His promotion is exceptional. // 이것은 이례적인 일이다 This is rare case. /This kind seldom happens, if any. // 이 추위는 3월로서는 이례적이다 This cold weather is exceptional for March.

-이로다 ⇨ 로다

이로되 it is but ; though it is ¶ 사장은 사장이로되 실권이 없는 사장이다 Though he is the president, he has no power. // 밥은 밥이로되 선밥이다 It sure is boiled rice, but it is undercooked.

이로부터 ① [시간] from now on ; from this time on ; in (the) future ; hereafter ; henceforth ¶ 이로부터 죽 from now〔here〕 on // 이로부터 몇 달 동안 for a few months ahead〔from now〕
② [이유·결과] from this cause ; hence ; as a result of this ¶ 이로부터 여러 문제가 일어났다 Out of this many questions arose.

이로써 with this ; hereby ; herewith ¶ 이로써 보건대 seeing that〔this〕; in view of these 《facts》

이론 異論 an objection ; a dissent ; a different〔an opposite〕 opinion〔view〕 ¶ 이론 없이 without any objection ; unanimously // 이론이 있다 have an objection 《to》; object to 《the plan》 // 이론이 없다 have no objection 《to》 // 이론을 제기하다 raise an objection 《to, against》; object 《to》; take exception〔objection〕 《to》 // 이론이 있습니까 Have you any objection to it ? // 이 일에 대해서 하등 이론이 있을 리가 없다 There can be no two opinions as to this matter.

†이론 理論 a theory ¶ 이론적 theoretical // 이론상 theoretically ; in theory ; on paper // 이론을 세우다 theorize ; advance a theory // 이론을 실천하다 put one's theory into practice ; reduce a theory to practice // 이론과 실제와를 일치시키다 reconcile theory and practice // 너의 계획은 이론상 좋으나 그대로 될까 Your plan is very well in theory, but will it work〔is it workable〕? // 이론과 실제와는 반드시 일치하지는 않는다 Theory and practice do not always go hand in hand. // 실천이 따르지 않는 이론은 아무 소용이 없다 Theory without practice will serve for nothing.
—가 a theorist ; a theoretician — 경제학 theoretical economics — 과학〔물리학, 천문학, 화학〕 theoretical science〔physics, astronomy, chemistry〕 — 생계비 theoretical cost of living ; wages based on calorific needs — 수학 abstract mathematics — 투쟁 a theoretical〔an ideological〕 dispute〔quarrel〕

이롭 a seven-year-old 《ox, horse》

*이롭다 利— (be) good 《for》; do 《a person》 good ; [유익한] (be) beneficial 《to》; [유리한] (be) advantageous 《to》; favorable 《to, for》; [도움이 되는] (be) helpful 《to, for》; instructive ¶ 이롭지 않다 be bad 《for》; do 《a person》 harm ; be harmful〔injurious〕 《to》; be against 《a person's》 interest ; be disadvantageous〔unfavorable〕 《to》 // 그렇게 하면 너에게 이로울 것이다 It will do you good to do so. // 그렇게 하면 너에게 이롭지 못하다 It would be against your interest to do so. // 침묵을 지키는 것이 너에게 이롭다 It would be to your interest〔advantageous to you〕 to keep silence.

이롱 耳聾 deafness
—증 a symptom of deafness

이루 by any means ; by no means ; 《cannot》 possibly ; 《cannot》 by any possibility ; 《none》 at all ; not nearly 《so... as》; utterly ¶ 이루 말할 수 없는 indescribable ; unspeakable ; beyond description // 이루 헤아릴 수 없는 numberless ; countless ; unaccountable ; innumerable // 그 참상은 이루 말로 표현할 수 없었다 The disaster was beyond all description. /The misery of the scene beggars description.

이루 耳漏 『의학』 otorrhoea ; discharge from the ear

이루 二壘 『야구』 the second base ; the middle sack 《미·속》
—수 a second baseman ; a second baser 〔sacker〕 —타 a two-base hit ; a two-bagger〔-baser〕; a double (hit) ¶ 이루타를 치다 hit a two-bagger ; bang out a double ; double

†이루다 ① [성취] accomplish ; achieve ; attain ; effect ; [실현] realize ; [완성] complete ; finish ; [실행] fulfil(l) ; carry out ¶ 이룰 수 없는 소망 an unattainable desire // 이룰 수 있는 attainable ; realizable // 목적을 이루다 achieve one's purpose〔end〕; make good one's purpose ; effect one's intention // 소망을 이루다 realize one's desire // 대사를 이루다 achieve a great work〔deed〕 // 너는 소망을 이루었다 You have had your wish.
② [형성] make ; form ; constitute ¶ 부를 이루다 make a fortune // 사회를 이루다 form society // 좋은 자연항을 이루다 form a good natural harbor // 이런 원소가 모여서 물질계를 이루는 것이다 These elements combine to constitute the material universe.

이루어지다 ① [성취·실현] get〔be〕 accomplished〔done, achieved, attained, effected, realized〕 ¶ 뜻이 이루어지다 one's purpose is realized // 대사업이 이루어졌다 Great things were accomplished. /A great deed was achieved. // 나의 오랜 소원이 마침내 이루어졌다 My long-cherished desire is at last accomplished.
② [형성] be formed〔made up, constituted, composed of〕

이룩하다 [건립·수립] erect ; build ; set up ; establish ; found ; [성취] accomplish ; achieve ; complete ¶ 나라를 이룩하다 erect〔set up, establish〕 a new state 〔nation〕 // 새 살림을 이룩하다 set up a household ; establish〔create〕 a house // 큰 일을 이룩하다 achieve a great work // 어떠한 일이 있어도 이 일은 이룩할 결심이다 Nothing shall prevent me from accomplishing this. /I am determined to go through with the undertaking.

이류 二流 ¶ 이류의 second-class ; second-rate ; minor ; inferior

— 소설가 a second-rate novelist — 시인 a minor poet — 작가 a second writer

이류 異類 different kinds〔species〕; varieties

— 개념 〖논리〗 a disparate concept —항 〖수학〗 a dissimilar term

이류 감각 異類感覺 disparate sensation

*이륙 離陸 a take-off ; a hop-off ; taking 〔flying〕 off ; leaving the ground —하다 [비행기가] take〔hop〕 off ; take the air ; leave the ground ¶ 이륙과 착륙 연습을 하다 practice taking-off and landing

— 시간〔거리〕 take-off time〔distance〕 —지 a take-off point — 활주 a take-off 〔taking-off〕 run

이륜 彝倫 [인륜] humane duties ; morality ; moral duties〔principles〕; ethics and morality (인륜, 도덕)

이륜 二輪 [수레의] two wheels ; [꽃의] two flowers ¶ 이륜의 two-wheeled (수레의) ; double-flowered (꽃의)

—차 a two-wheeled vehicle ; a two-wheeler ; a cart

이르다[1] [시간이] (be) early ; premature ¶ 이른 아침〔봄〕 early morning〔spring〕// 아침 이르게 early in the morning// 아직 이르다 It is quite early yet. // 잘 시간이 아직 이르다 It is too early for bed. // 한 시간이 이르다 We are an hour too soon. // 금년은 벼가 이르다 The rice crop is early this year. // 그것에 대한 평가를 내리기는 아직 이르다 The Jury is still out on that. // 계획했던 것보다 더 이른 것 아냐 Isn't that sooner than you'd planned ?

†이르다[2] ① [도착] reach ; arrive 《at, in》; get 《to》 ¶ 이르는 곳마다 everywhere one goes ; throughout// 목적지에 이르다 reach〔arrive at, get to〕 one's destination // 이 길로 가면 부산에 이른다 This road leads to *Pusan*. // 여기서 1킬로 가면 폭포에 이른다 One kilometer along this road, and you will come to a waterfall. /One kilometer to a waterfall. // 덕행은 행복에 이르는 길이요 악덕은 불행에 이르는 길이다 Virtue leads to happiness, and vice to misery.

② [정도·범위] reach ; extend to ; come to ; lead to ; end〔result〕 《in》 ¶ 오늘에 이르기까지 (up) to this day ; until now ; up to the present time// 4월에서 5월에 이르기까지 from April to May// 믿기에 이르다 come to believe 《it》// 실패하기에 이르다 end〔result〕 in one 's failure// 자살하기에 이르렀다 go so far as to commit suicide// 그는 실패해서 결국 파산하기에 이르렀다 The failure has resulted in his bankruptcy.

이르다[3] ① [알리다] let 《a person》 know ; inform ; report ; tell ; [고자질] tell on 《a person》 ; inform〔peach〕 《a person against another》 ¶ 미리 이르다 give notice beforehand// 이르지 않고 두다 leave 《a person》 uninformed ; keep 《a person》 ignorant 《of a matter》// 선생님에게 이르다 tell one's teacher on 《a person》

② [가라사대] say ¶ 옛날에 이르기를 an old saying has it that// 성경에 이르기를 심령이 가난한 자는 복이 있다고 했다 The Bible says "Blessed are the poor in spirit."

이르집다 ① [뜯어벗기다] pull off ; peel ; pick ¶ 장판귀를 이르집다 pick at the end of the floor paper

② [날조] make up ; fabricate ; cook up ; fake up ; frame up ¶ 사건을 이르집다 frame up an affair ; make up an incident

③ (지난일을) rake up 《a person's》 past deeds ; dig up 《all》 the facts of 《a person's》 past life

이른모 〖농업〗 young rice plants transplanted early

이른바 what is called ; what you〔we, they〕 call ; as it is called ; so-called ; quote-unquote ¶ 이른바 멘델의 법칙 what is called the Mendelian law// 속담에 이른바 as a proverb runs ; as is proverbially said// 저런 여자가 이른바 전후파 여성이다 Such a woman is what we call a postwar girl. // 그들은 이른바 보호색이라고 하는 것으로 자신을 방어한다 They protect themselves by what is called protective coloring.

이를테면 so to speak ; as it were ; in other words ; [요컨대] in a word ; in short ¶ 그는 이를테면 살아 있는 사전이다 He is, so to speak〔as it were〕, a walking dictionary. // 인생이란 이를테면 아침 이슬과 같은 것이다 Our life is, so to speak, a morning dew. /Our life may be likened to a morning dew.

†이름 ① [성명] a name ; a full name ; [실명·통칭] a given〔personal, Christian〕 name ; a first name 《미》; [애칭] a pet name ; [성] a surname ; a family name ¶ 인국이란 이름의 사나이 a man named *Inkook* ; a person by the name of *Inkook* // 이름을 알 수 없는 unidentified ; nameless// 이름을 짓다 name 《a person》; give a name 《to》; christen// 이름을 대다 tell〔give〕 one's name ; [타인의] mention 《a person's》 name// 이름을 따다 take 《a person's》 name// 이름을 묻다 ask 《a person's》 name// 이름을 부르다 call 《a person》 by name// 이름을 바꾸다 change one's name// 이름을 빼다 take one's name off 《the list》// 이름을 속이다 assume another's〔a false〕 name ; give a wrong name// 아버지의 이름을 따서 짓다 name 《one's child》 after 《his father》// 예수의 이름으로 기도하다 pray in Jesus' name// 아버지의 이름으로 장사하다 do business under the name of one's father. // 그 사람의 이름만 알고 있다 I only know him by name. // 우리는 서로 경칭은

빼고 이름만 부르는 사이다 We are on a first-name basis. // 그런 이름 가진 사람 여기 없는데요 There is no one here by that name.
② [명칭] a name ; a title ; a designation ¶ 이름만의 nominal ; only in name // 이름에 합당하지 않다〔부합하다〕 be untrue〔true〕 to one's name // 그는 이름만의 의사다 He is a doctor only in name. // 그는 「살아 있는 사전」이란 이름으로 통한다 He goes by the name of "a walking dictionary". // 보고서에는 세 사람의 이름이 언급되어 있었다 Three persons were named in the report.
③ [명성] a (good) name ; reputation ; fame ; [악명] notoriety ¶ 이름있는〔없는〕 사람 a man of (no) name ; a famous〔nameless〕 person // 다소 이름이 알려진 사람 a man of some reputation // 이름도 없는 마을 a small and insignificant town ; a one-horse town 《미》 // 이름이 알려지다 be well-known〔noted, famous, notorious (악명으로)〕 // 이름도 없다 be nameless〔obscure, unknown, worthless (보잘 것 없다)〕 // 이름이 나다 become famous〔renowned〕 // 이름을 남용하다 take 《a person's》 name in vain // 이름 높다 be famous〔noted, celebrated, well-known, notorious (악명으로)〕; [탁월한] be distinguished〔eminent〕 // 이름을 후세에 남기다 leave a name behind ; hand down〔bequeath〕 one's name to posterity ; make one's name immortal // 이름을 더럽히다 sully〔disgrace, spoil〕 《a person's》 name〔reputation〕 // 사람은 죽어도 이름은 남는다 Man lives but for one generation, his name for many. /A man dies but his name remains.
④ [구실] a pretext ; a plea ; a excuse ; [명목] a cause ¶ 정계 혁신이라는 이름으로 on the pretext〔plea〕 of political reform // 자선이란 이름 아래 under the pretext〔mask〕 of charity
이름을 날리다〔떨치다〕 관용 get〔win〕 a name ; have one's name up ; make〔get, win〕 oneself a name ; gain fame ; win〔obtain〕 distinction
이름을 팔다 관용 trade on one's fame ; take advantage of one's popularity ; prostitute one's reputation
이름씨 a noun ; a substantive
이름표 一標 a nameplate ; a name card ; a name tag ¶ 이름표를 달다 attach〔affix〕 a name tag 《to》; attach an identification tag 《to a child》 // 그 아이는 이름표를 달고 있지 않았다 The child wore no tag to identify him.
이리[1] [물고기의] soft roe ; milt
†**이리**[2] 〖동물〗 a wolf ; Canis lupus (학명) ¶ 이리 떼 a pack of wolves
***이리**[3] ① [방향] this way ; this direction ; this side ; here ¶ 이리 오십시오 This way, please. /Please, come this way. // 이리 앉아라 Sit here. // 이리 오신지 얼마나 됩니까 How long have you been here? ② [이렇게] in this way ; like this ; so ¶ 이리 많이 so many〔much〕
이리듐 〖화학〗 iridium 《Ir》
이리오너라 Hello, there. ¶ (문간에서) 이리오너라 하고 부르다 knock at the door ; call for admission
이리이리 so and so ; such and such ¶ 이리이리 하라고 말하다 tell 《a person》 to do such and such
***이리저리** [이쪽저쪽으로] this way and that ; here and there ; [이렇게 저렇게] like this way and that ; [곳곳에] in places ; [사방으로] all about ¶ 이리저리 돌아다니다 wander〔roam, ramble〕 about ; loaf around // 이리저리 흐트려 놓다 litter 《things》 about 《a room》 // 이리저리 살펴보다 look this way and that ; look around 《미》; look about 《영》 // 책을 이리저리 찾다 look high and low for a book
이리하다 say〔read〕 like this ⇨ 이러하다
이리 호 一湖 Lake Erie
‡**이마** the forehead ; the brow ¶ 넓은〔좁은〕이마 a broad〔narrow〕 forehead ; a high〔low〕 brow // 이마가 좁은 사람〔교양이 낮은 사람〕 a low-browed person // 이마의 땀을 닦다 mop one's brow // 이마를 찌푸리다 knit〔bend, wrinkle〕 one's brow // 그들은 이마를 맞대고 의논했다 They laid〔put〕 their heads together. // 사람은 이마에 땀흘려 일해서 살아야 한다 Man must live by〔in〕 the sweat of his brow. **―받이** striking with the head ; butting ; running into 《a thing》 **―빼기** ⇨ 이마
이마마하다 be as much as this ¶ 이마마한 손해는 대수롭지 않다 Such a small loss is nothing to me.
이마적 recently ; lately ; of late ; these days ; nowadays ¶ 언제나 이마적은 날씨가 변하기 쉽다 The weather is changeable at this time of (the) year.
이만 this〔so〕 much〔many, large, long, wide〕; [정도] to this extent〔degree〕; this far〔high〕 ¶ 오늘은 이만하자 Let us stop here today. /So much for today. /Let's call it a day. // 이만한 크기〔높이〕였다 It was about this big〔tall〕.
이만저만 [정도] 《not》 to just this extent or that ; 《hardly》 to any limited degree ; in no small degree ; not a little ; [수] in no small number ; [양] in no small quantity ¶ 이만저만한 사람 such and such a person/she is no everyday beauty/She is a girl of unsurpassed beauty. // 이만저만 놀라지 않았다 be not a little surprised // 이만저만 귀찮지 않다 be no small trouble // 이만저만 미인이 아니다 She is quite a beauty. // 이만저만 춥지 않다 It is quite cold. // 영어를 이만저만 잘하지 않는다 He speaks English quite well. /His English is quite good. // 저분에

게 이만저만 신세를 지지 않았다 I owe him a great deal. // 그는 음악을 이만저만 좋아하지 않는 것 같다 He seems to have no small delight in music.

*이만큼 this much〔big, long〕; so much〔many〕; to this extent〔degree〕¶ 이만큼 이면 된다 This much will do. /This much is enough, I think. // 2층에 이만큼 책이 또 있다 I have just as many books upstairs as here. // 이만큼 꾸짖으면 조금은 정신 차릴 것이다 I believe so much scolding will open his eyes to his faults. // 이만큼 공부하면 합격할 것이다 If I work so hard, I shall pass the examination. // 그 못의 깊이는 이만큼이다 The pond is about this deep〔so deep〕. // 이만큼 영문을 잘 쓰는 사람은 별로 없다 Few people can write English so well.

이만하다 be this much ; be as much〔big, long〕as this ; be to this extent〔degree〕¶ 이만한 추위가 뭐냐 What does this cold matter? // 내 책상은 이만하다 My desk is this large. // 이만한 손해는 아무것도 아니다 Such a small loss is nothing to me. // 둑이 이만하면 철옹성이다 The dike is strong as can be. // 누가 내 수첩 못봤어 이만한 크긴데 Has anybody seen my schedule book? It's about this big?

이맘때 about〔around〕this time ; at this time〔moment, point〕of day〔night, year〕¶ 이맘때에는 by this time ; about this time // 작년〔내년〕이맘때 at this time last〔next〕year // 어제〔내일〕이맘때 at this time yesterday〔tomorrow〕// 나는 어제 이맘때 도착했다 I came here about this time yesterday. // 내일 저녁 이맘때 또 찾아 뵙겠습니다 Tomorrow evening at this time, I'll come and see you again. // 이맘때는 도서관은 벌써 닫았을 것이다 By now〔this time〕the library must have already closed. // 내일 이맘때까지 고칠 수 있겠습니까 Can you fix it by this time tomorrow?

이맛살 wrinkles on〔in, across〕the brow〔forehead〕¶ 이맛살을 찌푸리다 knit〔bend, wrinkle〕one's brow ; frown

이맛전 ¶ 이맛전이 넓다 have a broad forehead

이맞다 be in gear《with》; gear《into, with》; mesh《with》; engage《with》;《teeth》occlude ; fit《in》¶ 이맞추다 engage ; clutch

이매 移買 buying new land after selling out the land one owns elsewhere

이매지네이션 imagination

이며 〔조사〕and ; or ; and/or ¶ 책이며 돈이며 몽땅 잃었다 I have lost money, books, and everything. // 그는 작가이며 학자다 He is both a writer and a scholar. /He is a writer and scholar.

이면 〔조사〕if〔when〕it is ; as for ; in case ¶ 이런 경우 당신이면 어떻게 하겠소 What would you do in such a case? // 여기서 한 3분이면 간다 It's about three minutes (walk) from here.

*이면 裏面 〔뒤쪽〕the back ; the reverse ; the other side : 〔내면〕the inside ; the background ; the inside story ¶ 어음의 이면 the back of a bill // 인생의 이면 the dark〔seamy〕side of life // 이면의 사실〔사정〕inside facts〔affairs〕// 사회의 이면 the dark side of society // 이면에서 활약하다 play an active part in the background // 이면에서 조종하다 act as a wirepuller behind ; pull the wires

— 공작 behind-the-scene〔backstage〕maneuvering〔maneuvers〕; underground activities ; wirepulling — 부지(不知) a person displaying lack of judgment〔behaving indiscreetly〕—사 an inside history ; an account from within — 사정〔사실〕the inside affairs〔facts〕¶ 이면 사정에 밝은 사람 those on the inside — 생활 one's intimate〔private〕life — 술책 wirepulling

이면 二面 ① 〔두개의 면〕two faces ; two sides ② 〔신문의〕the second page ¶ 이면의 two-sided // 이면은 경제란이다 The second page is devoted to financial affairs.

—각 〖수학〗dihedral angle — 기사 items on the second page —성 two-facedness ; two-sidedness

이면 경계 裏面境界 the details and merits of a case ¶ 이면 경계를 알다 know the details and merits of a case ; know the fact of a matter and can judge whether it is right or wrong // 그는 이면 경계에 밝은 사람이다 He is a man of a fair judgement.

이명 異名 another name ; a second name ; an alias ; 〔별명〕a nickname ; sobriquet

이명 耳鳴 ringing〔singing, buzzing, drumming〕in the ears

—증 〖의학〗tinnitus

이명법 二名法 〖생물〗binomial〔binominal〕nomenclature

이모 姨母 one's mother's sister ; a maternal aunt

이모부 姨母夫 an uncle (who is the husband of one's mother's sister) ; the husband of one's maternal aunt ; a maternal uncle-by-marriage

이모작 二毛作 two crops a year ; two-crop farming ; semiannual crops ; double-crop —하다 raise two crops《of rice》a year

— 지대 a two-crop area

이모저모 various sides ; this angle and that ; every facet〔side, view〕of《a matter》¶ 문제를 이모저모로 생각하다 study〔consider〕all the aspects〔angles〕of a problem ; study a matter from all sides〔angles〕

이목 耳目 [귀와 눈] eye and ear ; [주의] public attention〔notice〕 ¶ 이목을 피하다 avoid public notice ; shun publicity
이목을 끌다 관용 attract〔arrest〕 public attention ; command public attention ; catch the public eye

이목구비 耳目口鼻 ear, eye, mouth, and nose ; [용모] features ; looks ; a face ; a countenance ¶ 이목구비가 반듯하다 have regular features ; be regular-featured // 이목구비가 반반하다 have good〔pretty〕 features

이몽가몽 a trance ; dreaminess —하다 feel as if in a dream ; be in a trance ; (be) dreamlike ; dreamy ; dim ; vague ; faint ; indistinct

이무기 a monster serpent ; a python

*이문 利文 profit ; gain ; returns ¶ 적은 이문 small〔little〕 profit // 이문이 있는 장사 a lucrative〔profitable〕 business // 이문이 있다 be profitable ; be lucrative ; be paying ; pay // 이문이 적다 give〔yield〕 little profit ; do not pay much // 이문이 없다 be unprofitable ; do not pay // 이문을 보다 profit 《by, at, from》 ; make〔fetch〕 a profit 《on》 // 큰〔상당한〕 이문을 보다 make large〔good〕 profits

이문 異聞 a strange news ; a strange report〔rumor〕 ; curious information ; queer〔strange〕 stories〔tales〕

*이물 the bow ; the prow ; the head ; the stem ¶ 이물에서 고물까지 from stem to stern

이물 異物 a different thing ; an alien〔a foreign〕 substance

-이므로 ⇨ -므로

†이미 ① [벌써] already ; now ; yet ; any longer ¶ 이미 때가 늦다 It is now too late. // 이미 답을 알고 있다 We already know the answer. // 이미 서울에 다녀 왔다 I have been in *Seoul* already. // 내가 정거장에 도착했을 때 기차는 이미 떠나버렸다 When I arrived at the station, the train had already started〔left〕.
② [앞서] previously ; before(hand) ¶ 이미 말한 바와 같이 as previously stated〔mentioned〕 ; as aforementioned

†이미지 an image ¶ 이미지를 향상시키다 improve the image 《of a company, a new starlet》 // 이미지를 바꾸다 change one's image

이미지즘 〖문예〗 imagism ⇨ 사상(—주의)

이민 移民 [이주] emigration (출국), immigration (입국) ; [이주자] an emigrant (외국에 간) ; an immigrant (외국에서 온) ; a settler (개척지의) —하다 emigrate 《into, to》 (외국으로) ; immigrate 《into, to》 (국내로) ; plant settlers 《on》 ¶ 많은 사람이 미국으로 이민간다 A large number of people emigrate to America from this country. // 매년 많은 이민이 합중국으로 왔다 Many immigrants came to the United States each year.
— 관리 사무소 (출입국 관리 사무소) an immigration office 《미》 — 교섭 negotiations for immigration —단 a group of emigrants (to Brazil) — 문제 an emigration〔immigration〕 problem —법 immigration〔emigration〕 law — 보호법 the Emigrants Protection Act —선 an emigrant〔immigrant〕 ship — 제한 restriction of immigration — 제한법 the Immigration Restriction Law

이바지 —하다 ① [공급하다] supply 《with》 ; provide 《with》 ; serve 《with》 ; furnish 《with》 ¶ 재료를 이바지하다 furnish 《a person》 with materials ; supply 《a factory》 with materials // 양식을 이바지하다 provide 《a person》 with food
② [공헌하다] contribute 《to, toward》 《peace》 ; render service 《to》 ; make a contribution 《to》 ; do much 《for》 ; make 《for》 ¶ 크게 이바지하다 make a great contribution 《towards peace》 ; do much 《for peace》 ; do a major service 《to peace》 ; do great service 《to》 // 한국의 경제 발전에 이바지하다 contribute to the economic growth of Korea // 그것은 인구 문제의 해결에 크게 이바지할 것이다 That will do much for solving the population problem. // 그분이 교육계에 이바지한 바가 실로 컸다 His contributions to the cause of education were really great. // 그는 한국 과학계에 이바지한 바가 크다 He has rendered great services to the science of Korea.

이박자 二拍子 〖음악〗 binary time

이반 離反 estrangement ; desertion ; alienation ; defection 《from a person》 ; disaffection —하다 be estranged〔alienated〕 《from》 ; be disaffected 《toward》 ¶ 민심이 현 정부로부터 이반하고 있다 The public are alienated from the present Government. /The Government has lost the support of the public.

*이발 理髮 [깎음] haircutting ; a haircut ; [다듬기] hairtrimming ; hairdressing —하다 get〔have〕 a haircut ; have one's hair cut〔trimmed〕 ; [이발사가] cut〔trim〕 《a person's》 hair ¶ 이발을 해야 겠다 I must have a haircut. /I must have my hair cut. /I must go to a barber (shop).
— 기계 a hair-clipper —사 a barber ; a hairdresser 《영》 ; a tonsorial artist 《미》 —소 a barber's (shop) ; a barbershop 《미》 —업 barbering ; hairdressing — 요금 the charge for〔price of〕 a haircut ; a barber fee — 용구 hairdressing implements〔tools, appliances〕

이밥 plain boiled rice

이방 異邦 an alien country ; a foreign country〔land〕
—인 an alien ; a foreigner ; a stranger ; 〖성경〗 a Gentile

이방성 異方性 〖물리〗 aeolotropy ; anisotropy ¶ 이방성의 anisotropic ;

aeolotropic
— 용액 an anisotropic liquid
이배 二倍 double ; twice ; twofold —하다 double
*이번 [금번] this time ; [최근] recently ; lately ; [현재의] present ; new ; now ; [다음번] next time ; [머지 않아] shortly ; soon ; [다음의] next ; [지난번의] last ; recent ¶ 이번 사건 the current〔present〕incident // 이번 선생님 this new teacher // 이번 시험 the coming〔next〕examination ; the last〔recent〕examination (지난번) // 이번만 just this time ; for this once ; once for all // 이번 갈 때 데려다 주시오 Take me there (the) next time you go. // 이번부터는 주의하겠습니다 I will be more careful after this. // 이번은 네가 갈 차례다 Now it is your turn to go. // 이번에 미국에 갈 예정입니다 I am going to America shortly. // 이번에는 그는 꼭 성공한다 He is sure to succeed this time. // 이번만 더 설명해주겠다 I shall explain it once for all.
이번 二番 number two ; No. 2 ; the second
— 타자 the second batter〔hitter〕
이법 理法 (a) law ; (the) order ; principles and rules ; propriety and decorum ¶ 자연의 이법 the order of nature ; natural laws
이베리아 반도 —半島 the Iberian Peninsula
*이변 異變 [사고] an accident ; mishap ; [재앙] a disaster ; a calamity ; [변고] an extraordinary phenomenon ¶ 기후의 이변 an unusual change in the weather // 금융계의 이변 a disturbance in financial circles // 태양의 이변 an extraordinary phenomenon in the sun // 그에게 어떤 이변이 일어난게 아닐까 I fear that something has happened to him.
이변 색성 二變色性 [동물] dichroism ; dichromatism ¶ 이변 색성의 dichroic ; dichromatic
이변 유전자 易變遺傳子 『생물』 a mutable gene
*이별 離別 parting ; separation ; divorce (이혼) —하다 part《with a person》; separate《from a person》; [이혼] divorce《one's wife》¶ 이별의 슬픔 the wrench〔sorrow〕of parting // 이별을 고하다 say〔bid〕《a person》good-bye ; bid farewell to《a person》// 이별을 애석해 하다 be loath〔sorry〕to part《with a person》// 그는 처와 이별했다 He has left〔divorced, put away〕his wife.
—가 a farewell song ; a song of farewell
—주 a farewell drink
이병 罹病 contraction《of a disease》; suffering《from illness》—하다 contract〔take, catch, get〕a disease ; suffer from illness
—률 the attack rate ; the (rate of) incidence《of influenza》; a disease incidence rate ; an occurrence ratio —자 a patient ; sufferers《from cholera》; cases《of typhoid fever》; victims《of a disease》
이보다《more, less, better, worse》than this ¶ 이보다 앞서 prior to this ; before this // 이보다 낫다 be better than this // 이보다 더한 불행은 없다 There can be no greater misfortune than this.
이복 異腹 a different mother
— 동생 a younger sibling by a different mother ; a half brother〔sister〕— 형제 brothers by a different mother ; half brothers〔sisters〕
이본 異本 [진본(珍本)] a rare book ; [다른 책] a different version ; a copy of a different edition
이 봐 Hi ! /Hey ! /Say ! /I say ! /Look here ! /Haloo !
이부 異父 a different father
— 형제〔자매〕uterine brothers〔sisters〕; brothers〔sisters〕by different fathers ; half brothers〔sisters〕
이부 二部 ① two parts ; [제2의〔부〕] the second part〔section〕; part two ¶ 이부로 나누어지다 be divided into two parts
② [두권] two copies ¶ 이 사전 이부 two copies of this dictionary
③ [야간부] a night school〔class〕
이부 利附, 利付 ¶ 이부의 interest bearing ; with〔cum〕interest
— 공채 an active〔interest-bearing〕bond 확정〔불확정〕— fixed〔variable〕interest bearing 5분 — 공채 5% interest-bearing bond
이부 수업 二部授業 instruction in two shifts ; the double-shift school system ¶ 이부 수업을 받는 아동 a half-timer // 이부 수업을 하다 adopt the double-shift school system ; instruct《school children》in two shifts ; operate double shifts
이부자리 bed clothes (and mattress) ; bedding ¶ 이부자리를 펴다 lay〔make〕a bed // 이부자리를 개다 fold up〔put away〕the bedding〔bedclothes〕
이부제 二部制 a two-shift《school》system ¶ 이부제로 일하다 work on the two-shift system
— 수업 ⇨ 이부 수업 — 학교 a school operated on the two-shift system
이부 합주 二部合奏 a duet ¶ 이부 합주를 하다 perform a duet
이부 합창 二部合唱 a chorus in two parts ¶ 이부 합창을 하다 sing〔chorus〕《a song》in two parts
이북 以北 north of《*Seoul*》; North Korea ¶ 38선 이북 north of the 38th parallel // 이북에서 온 사람 a man from North Korea
이분 二分 —하다 divide《a thing》into〔in〕two (parts) ; halve ; bisect《a line》

¶ 이분의 일 one half // 이분의 이박자 alla breve 《이》// 천하를 이분하다 share the control of the land with 《another》

—법 『논리』 dichotomy —음표 a half-note ; a minim 《영》

이분자 異分子 a heterogeneous element ; an alien〔a foreign〕 element ; an outsider

***이불** [이부자리] bedding ; bedclothes ; [누비 이불] a quilt ; [침대 덮개] counterpane ; coverlet ; [홑이불] a sheet ¶ 이불을 덮다 put on a quilt // 이불을 펴다〔걷다〕 make〔put away〕 the bed // 이불을 뒤집어 쓰다 pull one's bedclothes over one's head

이불 깃 보아가며 발 뻗친다 〈속담〉 Stretch your arm no further than your sleeve will reach. /Everyone stretches his legs according to the length of his coverlet.

이불리간 利不利間 regardless of profit or loss

이불줄 『광산』 a horizontal vein of ore

이브¹ [저녁] the eve ; the previous evening ; [전야제] the festivities on the previous evening 《of》

이브² [아담의 아내] Eve

이브닝 드레스 an evening dress

이브닝 코트 an evening coat

이비 理非 the rights and wrongs ; the relative merits

이비 耳鼻 ear and nose

—과 otorhinology —인후 ear, nose and throat —인후과 otorhinolaryngology

이빨 ⇨ 이²

이쁘다 (be) pretty ⇨ 예쁘다

이사 移徙 house-moving ; removal ; a move —하다 change one's residence 〔abode〕 ; move〔remove〕 《to, into》 ¶ 새집으로 이사하다 move into a new house // 서울로 이사하다 move to *Seoul* // 내일 정오까지는 이사하겠습니다 We shall move in by tomorrow noon. // 어디로 이사하시는지 알려주십시오 Let me know where you are moving to // 채용이 되면 이사할 수 있습니까 Can you relocate in case you're hired by us ? // 너 상당히 먼 곳으로 이사했지 You moved a distant away, didn't you ?

— 비용 removal expenses

이사 二死 『야구』 two outs ¶ 이사 만루 two down, bases filled

이사 理事 a director ; [공공 단체〔대학·법인〕의] trustee ¶ 이사가 되다 obtain a seat on the board of directors

—관 a grade-Ⅱ-A official ; a bureau-chief-grade official ; a commissioner —장 the chief director ; the chairman of the board of directors ; the director general —회 a board of directors ; the governing body ; a council 대표 — a representative director 상무 — an executive director 전무 — a managing director ; an executive director 국제 연합 —국 a member of the Council of the United Nations 상임〔비상임〕 —국 a permanent〔nonpermanent〕 member (nation) 《of the Security Council》

이사 —하다 lead 《a person》 by the nose ; have 《a person》 at one's beck and call ; turn 《a person》 round one's little finger ; order about

이사야서 —書 『성경』 The Book of Isaiah ; Isaiah 《Isa.》

이사이 these days ; nowadays ; lately ; recently ; of late

이삭 an ear 《of grain》 ; a spike ; a head ¶ 이삭을 줍다 glean 《a field》 // 이삭이 나오다 be in the ear ; come into ears

벼〔보리〕— an ear of rice〔barley〕 ¶ 보리이삭이 다 나왔다 The ears of barley are all out.

이산 離散 dispersion ; scattering ; breakup ; separation —하다 be dispersed ; be scattered ; be broken up ; separate ¶ 일가가 이산의 비운에 처했다 The family had the misfortune to be broken up.

— 가족 dispersed families ¶ 이산 가족 찾기 운동 the search campaigns for families separated ; a campaign for reunion of dispersed family members // 이산 가족의 재결합 reunion of one's dispersed family members

이산화 二酸化 『화학』 dioxide

— 탄소〔질소〕 carbon〔nitrogen〕 dioxide

이삼일 二三日 two or three days ; a few days ; a couple of days

이삼차 二三次 two or three times

***이상 以上** ① [수량·정도] more than ; over ; above ; beyond ; and upward ; upward of ¶ 10년 이상 more than ten years ; over ten years ; ten years or more〔and upward〕 // 50 이상 100까지 50 through 100 ; 50 up to 100 // 500원 이상 1,000원까지 from 500 *won* to 1,000 *won* // 6세 이상의 아동 children over six years old // 수입 이상의 생활을 하다 live beyond one's income〔means〕 ; do not cut one's coat according to one's cloth // 예상이상이다 exceed one's expectation // 이 이상 참을 수 없다 That's the limit. // 그 이상은 모른다 I know nothing beyond that. // 그 이상 말할 것이 없다 I have nothing further〔more〕 to say. // 이 이상 바라는 것은 무리다 You cannot reasonably wish for more. // 나는 이 이상 잘 할 수 없다 This is the best I can do. // 더 이상 말하고 싶지 않다 Period !

② [위에 말한] above-mentioned ; stated above ¶ 이상 말한 사실 the fact mentioned above // 이상 말한 바와 같이 as (is) mentioned〔stated〕 above // 이상은 그의 연설의 대요이다 The above is the gist of his speech.

③ [···한 바에는] since ; now that ; seeing that ¶ 약속을 한 이상 since you have promised // 살아 있는 이상 일을 해야 한다

So long as we live, we must work. // 졸업을 한 이상 부모님에게 폐를 끼쳐서는 안 되겠다 Now (that) I have finished school, I must live independently of my parents. /Now I am out of college, I must be on my own. // 일단 결정한 이상 절대 변경해서는 안된다 Once it is decided, it should never be changed.

†**이상 異常** strangeness ; queerness ; oddity ; abnormality ; extraordinariness **—하다** [기이] (be) strange ; queer ; odd ; [보통과 다름] unusual ; uncommon ; abnormal ; extraordinary ; [수상] suspicious ¶ 이상한 이야기이지만 strange to say // 이상하게 들리다 sound strange // 머리가 이상하다 be out of one's mind ; be off one's head // 그거 이상하다 That's strange. // 이상한 일도 다 있지 How can a thing like that happen, I wonder ? // 그 옷을 입으니까 이상하다 You look funny〔ridiculous〕 in that suit. // 그 모자는 이상하다 That hat doesn't match〔go very well with〕 the dress. // 그의 행동이 이상하다 His behavior is suspicious.

— 건조 abnormal〔unusual〕 aridity ; abnormal dryness **— 난동(暖冬)** an abnormally warm winter **— 반응** allergy **— 비대** 〖의학〗 hypertrophy **— 식욕** 〖의학〗 a perverted appetite **— 심리** abnormal mentality **—아** an abnormal child

†**이상 異狀** [몸의] indisposition ; an abnormal condition〔symptom〕 ; [불건전] unsoundness ; [정신의] derangement ; abnormality ; [고장] an accident ; disorder ; something wrong ; [변화] change ¶ 이상이 있다 be abnormal〔unsound, affected〕 ; be out of order (기계가) ; be indisposed (사람이) // 이상이 없다 be sound〔normal, usual〕 ; be all right ; be in good order〔condition〕 // 정신에 이상이 있다 be mentally deranged // 아무런 이상이 없다 Nothing is the matter. // 맥박과 체온에 이상이 없다 Your pulse and temperature are normal. // 뼈에는 이상이 없다 The bone is not affected at all. /The bone is all right. // 서부 전선에 이상 없다 All (is) quiet on the Western Front. // 당신의 검사 결과에서는 어떤 이상도 보이지 않았습니다 Your test results showed nothing that would be considered out of the ordinary.

정신 — mental derangement

⁑**이상 理想** an ideal ; the goal (of ambition) ; the ultimate object ¶ 이상적 ideal // 이상적인 남편〔가정〕 an ideal husband〔home〕 // 이상화하다 idealize // 이상을 추구하다 pursue〔follow〕 an ideal // 이상을 세우다 set up〔entertain〕 an ideal // 이상에 달하다 attain〔reach〕 one's ideal // 이상을 실현하다 realize one's ideal // 이상에 맞다〔적합하다〕 meet〔conform to〕 one's ideal // 이상이 높다 aim high // 이상에서 멀다 be far from one's ideal // 그 여자는 이상이 높다 She has a lofty ideal. // 그는 나의 이상적인 남편이다 He is a man after my own heart. // 그는 교사로서 이상적이다 He is as good a teacher as can be. // 그는 이상적인 교육가이다 He is a model of what an educator ought to be. // 이상적인 남자를 찾기란 쉬운 일이 아니다 It's not easy to find a Prince Charming.

—가 an idealist ; a utopian **—주의** idealism **—주의자** an idealist **—파** the idealistic school **—향** a Utopia ; an ideal land **—형** 〖사회〗 an ideal type

이상야릇하다 異常— (be) strange ; queer ; odd ; funny

이상화 理想化 idealization **—하다** idealize ; sublimate

이색 二色 two colors

— 인쇄 two-color printing **—판** a two-color plate

이색 異色 ① a different color ② [색다른 것] novelty ¶ 이색적 (be) novel ; conspicuous ; unique ; figure〔stand out〕 prominently // 이색적인 화가 a unique artist

— 인종 a race of a different color **— 작가** a unique novelist **— 작품** a unique 〔novel〕 work

이생 —生 this life(-time) ; this world

이서 以西 west of 《*Seoul*》 ; westward ¶ 서울 이서 west of *Seoul* ; *Seoul* and westward ; from *Seoul* west

이서 裏書 endorsement **—하다** endorse **—인** an endorser **공동 —** a joint endorsement **기명식 —** a special endorsement **피—인** an endorsee

이선 離船 leaving the ship **—하다** leave the ship ; go ashore

이설 異說 a different view〔theory〕 ; a divergent view〔opinion〕 ; a heterodoxy ; a heresy ¶ 이설을 펴다 give a different opinion ; raise an objection 《to》 // 이 문제에 관하여 이설이 분분했다 Many conflicting opinions have been expressed on this subject.

†**이성 理性** reason ; reasoning power ; rationality ; 〖철학〗 Logos ¶ 이성적 rational ; reasonable // 이성이 없는 irrational ; reasonless // 이성과 경험에 비추어 in the light of reason and experience // 이성에 호소하다 appeal to one's reason // 이성을 잃다 lose one's reason // 이성이 결핍되다 be devoid of reason ; be unreasonable // 그의 이성에 물으면 알 일이다 His reason will tell him.

— 동물 rational creatures **—론** rationalism **순수 —** pure reason

이성 異姓 a different surname ; a different family name

***이성 異性** ① the other〔opposite〕 sex ¶ 이성을 알다 know a woman〔man〕 ; have connection with the other sex // 그는 이성간에 교제가 넓다 He has a large

acquaintance of the opposite sex.
② [다른 성질] different nature ; 〖화학〗 isomerism
—애 heterosexual love
이성지합 二姓之合 the union of two families (in marriage)
이성화 異性花〖식물〗 a heterogamous flower
이세 二世 ①〖불교〗 the present and the future world
② [인명 뒤에] the Second ; Junior
③ [다음 세대] a second〔next〕 generation ¶ 미국 태생 한국인 이세 an America-born Korean // 이세 국민 the children of the next〔coming〕 generation ; a second-generation // 필립 이세 Philip Ⅱ ;Philip the Second
이솝 우화 Aesop's Fables
이송 移送 transfer ; removal ; transportation —하다 transfer ; remove ; transport ¶ 사건의 이송 removal〔transfer, transmission〕 of a case
이수 離水 —하다 leave the water ; take 〔hop〕 off from the water
이수 里數 ① [거리] the mileage ; the distance ② [마을 수] the number of villages
이수 履修 completion 《of a course of study》 —하다 complete ; finish ; go through ¶ 본과를 이수하다 complete 〔study〕 the regular course
이수 移囚 transfer of a prisoner
이수 利水 irrigation ; water utilization
— 공사 irrigation work
이수 異數 [예우] an exceptionally cordial reception
—성 〖동물〗 aneuploidy ; heteroploidy
이수 離愁 sorrows of parting ; the pain of parting
이순 耳順 sixty years old ; the sixtieth year (of age) ; [사람] a sexagenarian ¶ 이순에 달하다 attain one's sixtieth year of age
이스라엘 Israel ¶ 이스라엘의 Israeli
— 사람 an Israelite ; an Israeli ; the Israelites 《총칭》
이스탄불 Istanbul
이스터 Easter ⇨ 부활재〔제〕
이스트 yeast
—균 a yeast plant
이스파니아 ⇨ 스페인
이슥하다 《the night》 be far advanced ¶ 이슥한 밤에 late at night ; deep in the night // 밤이 이슥하도록 일하다 work far into the night〔till late at night〕 // 밤이 이슥해진다 The night gets late〔advances〕. /The evening deepens. // 밤이 이슥하도록 잠이 오지 않았다 Sleep did not come to me till late at night〔the night was far advanced〕.
*이슬 ① dew ; dewdrops (방울진) ¶ 이슬 맺힌 꽃 dewy flowers ; dew-laden flowers // 이슬 같은 목숨 man's ephemeral life // 이슬에 젖다 be wet with dew // 이슬을 털다 brush the dew // 교수대의 이슬로 사라지다 end one's days on the gallows〔gibbet〕 // 이슬이 내린다 Dew falls.
② [눈물] tear-drops ; tears ¶ 이슬지다 《one's eyes》 become tearful
—점 〖물리〗 the dew point
이슬라마바드 Islamabad
이슬람 Islam ¶ 이슬람의 Islamic
—교 Islam ; Mohammedanism ¶ 이슬람교도 an Muslim ; a Mohammedan
이슬받이 ① [때] the time when dew begins to form ; dewfall ② [도롱이] a grass kilt worn as protection from dew ; a dew-kilt ③ [사람] a person who clears the way of dewdrops for another ; a dew-clearer ④ [길] a dew-laden path
*이슬비 a drizzle ; a mizzle ; a misty rain ; a fog rain ¶ 종일토록 이슬비가 내렸다 It drizzled from morning till night.
이승 this world ; this life ; this existence ¶ 이승의 괴로움 the trial of this life // 이승에서 in this world // 이승을 떠나다 die ; pass away ; depart this life
이승 二乘 square ⇨ 자승
이식 利息 interest ⇨ 이자
— 계산 calculation of interest — 계정 the interest account —법 the rule of interest — 제한법 the Interest Restriction Act ; the Usury Act — 조견표(早見表) a ready reckoner (of interest)
이식 利殖 money-making ; increase of wealth ¶ 그는 이식에 눈이 밝지 못하다 He knows little of the art of making money.
—법 a money-making scheme ; the secret of moneymaking
*이식 移植 transplantation ; [식물의] naturalization ; [피부의] grafting —하다 transplant 《a flower》 ; [식물을] naturalize ; [피부를] graft ¶ 외국의 식물을 마당에 이식하다 colonize foreign plants in a garden
—기(機) a transplanter — 수술 transplantation surgery 근육 —법〔수술〕 flesh (and muscle) transplantation (operation) 심장 — (수술) a heart transplant〔graft〕 (operation)
이신동체 異身同體 one flesh ¶ 부부는 이신동체이다 Man and wife are one flesh.
이신론 理神論 deism
이실직고 以實直告 reporting〔speaking out according to〕 the truth ; telling the truth —하다 report〔tell, speak out according to〕 the truth
이심 二心 [두 마음] duplicity ; [배신] treachery ; [변덕] fickleness ¶ 이심을 품다 play a double game ; wean two faces // 그가 이심을 품고 있지 않은지 의심스럽다 I suspect him of duplicity.
이심 異心 [다른 마음] a different intention 〔mind, heart〕 ; [배신] a treasonous intention〔thought, idea, design〕 ; treachery ; duplicity (두 마음)

이심 已甚 excessiveness ; immoderateness ; excessive harshness〔severity, perverseness〕 **—하다, —스럽다** (be) excessive, excessively harsh〔severe〕

이심 離心 〖수학〗 eccentricity ¶ 이심적 eccentric

—각 an eccentric angle —권〔궤도〕 an eccentric orbit —율 eccentricity

이심전심 以心傳心 immediate communication 《of truth》 from one mind to another ; telepathy ; tacit understanding ; communion of mind with mind ¶ 이심전심으로 telepathically ; tacitly ; by tacit understanding

†이십 二十 twenty ; a score ; the twentieth (제20의) ¶ 20대 여자 a woman in her twenties // 20년에 한번의 vigesimal ; vicennial // 나의 20대는 지났다 My twenties have passed.

이십사 二十四 twenty-four ¶ 이십사 시간 이내 within twenty-four hours // 이십사 시간 내내 《work》 (a) round the clock ; all day and night // 이십사 시간 내내의 (a) round-the-clock

— 시간제 the twenty-four-hours system ; the around-the-clock system — 시간 조정 a round-the-clock operation

이십사 절기 the twenty-four seasons on the lunar calendar

이십오시 二十五時 the twenty-fifth hour

이아치다 [손해를 끼치다] cause damage ; lead to loss ; harm ; injure ; spoil ; ruin ; [방해되다] be a hindrance ; stand in one's way ; [방해하다] hinder ; obstruct ; nterfere 《with》

이악하다 be mercenary ; be keen〔greedy〕 for gain ; be wide-awake to one's own interest ; (be) shrewd ; sharp ; smart ; clever ¶ 이악한 아이 a smart boy

이안 렌즈 二眼— twin lenses

이안 리플렉스 二眼— 〖사진〗 a twin-lens reflex (camera)

이알 a grain of plain boiled rice

이알이 곤두선다 (속담) Don't be so cocky.

이앓이 toothache ; odontalgia ¶ 이앓이를 하다 have〔suffer from〕 a toothache

이앙 移秧 transplantation of rice seedlings ; rice planting ; rice transplantation **—하다** plant out the rice ; transplant the rice (-plants)

이야 only if it be ; if (it be) ; when it comes to ; even ; indeed ¶ 뒷일이야 누가 알 수 있으랴 When it comes to the future, who can tell ? /No one knows what will happen in the future. // 그 사람이야 훌륭하지 He is indeed a fine man. // 풍경〔경치〕이야 한국 따라갈 나라가 없지 For〔As for〕 scenery, there is no country like Korea.

†이야기 ① [담화] a conversation ; a talk ; a discourse ; [잡담] a chat ; a gossip **—하다** speak 《to a person》 ; converse 《with a person》 ; talk 《to a person》 ; chatter 《with a person》 ; gossip 《about a person, matter》 ; have a talk〔chat〕 《with a person》 ¶ 쓸데 없는 이야기 an idle talk (객담) // 이야기를 잘하는 사람 a good talker〔speaker〕 ; a talkative person (수다쟁이) // 우리들끼리 이야기인데 between you and me // 이야기를 걸다 speak to ; address oneself to // 이야기를 들려주다 give a talk 《to a person》 // 낚시질 이야기를 하다 talk about fishing // 그 사람과 이야기를 시작하다 enter into conversation with him // 너와 잠깐 이야기하고 싶다 I want a little talk with you. /Just a word with you. // 수업중에 이야기하지 마라 Don't gossip in the class. // 그렇다면 이야기가 통한다 Now you're talking. // 그것은 이야기가 다르다 It is another story now. // 그이만 이야기하게 하지 마라 Don't let him monopolize the conversation. // 그 이야기는 없었던 걸로 해 주시오 Let's just forget we ever had that talk, okay ?

② [화제] a topic (of conversation) ; the subject **—하다** talk 《about, on》 ; tell ; speak 《of, about》 ¶ 이야기를 바꾸다 change〔turn〕 the subject ; talk about something else // 할 이야기가 많다 I have many things to tell you. // 이제 그 이야기는 그만 둡시다 Let us say no more about it. // 본 이야기로 되돌아갑시다 Let's come〔hark〕 back to the subject. // 여행에 관한 이야기라면 그리스에 가 본 적이 있습니까 Talking of travel, have you been to Greece yet ?

③ [사실·허구] a story ; a tale ; an account (사실담) ; a legend (전설) ; a statement **—하다** tell 《a story》 ; give an account 《of a matter》 ; relate ; narrate 《a story》 ¶ 전쟁에 관한 이야기를 하다 give an account of a battle // 그 이야기만큼 재미있는 이야기를 알고 있습니까 Can you match that story ? // 그것은 이야기가 안된다 It is out of the question.

④ [소문] talk ; a rumor ; a report ; hearsay **—하다** say ¶ 어떤 사람들의 이야기에 의하면 some say 《that》 // …라는 이야기이다 The story goes〔runs〕 《that》 ; It is said〔rumored〕 《that》 ; They say〔I hear〕 《that》 // 나는 이야기를 들어서 알고 있다 I know it by hearsay. // 좋은 이야기가 있다 I will tell you what. /Tell you what.

⑤ [진술] a statement **—하다** state ; relate ; tell ¶ 의견〔입장〕을 이야기하다 state one's view〔case〕 // 그녀의 이야기는 매우 듣기 힘들었다 Her statement was very hard to hear.

⑥ [기타] a negotiation (교섭) ; a consultation (상담) ; an agreement (합의) ; understanding (의사소통) **—하다** [상담] talk with 《a person》 about 《a matter》 ; consult with 《a person》 ; discuss 《a matter》 with 《a person》 ¶ 이야기가

되다 arrive at〔come to〕 an arrangement with 《a person》; reach〔come to〕 an understanding with 《a person》// 이야기가 상통하다 have〔keep〕 a good understanding with 《a person》// 그 일에 관해서 당신과 할 이야기가 있다 I want to have a word with you about the matter. // 이야기가 다르지 않습니까 It is against our agreement. /That's not our understanding. // 그와의 이야기가 막다른 골목에 이르렀다 The negotiations with him have come to a deadlock. // 그와 만나 이야기하려면 언제쯤이 가장 좋습니까 When is the best time to approach him? // 숙박비는 무료라는 이야기였는데요 We were given to understand that free accommodation(s) would be supplied.

— 상대 a companion; someone to talk to ¶ 좋은 이야기 상대 a good〔boon〕 companion // 이야기 상대가 되다 keep 《a person》 company // 이야기 상대가 없다 I have no one to talk to. —쟁이 a story-teller; a teller of tales —책 a storybook —투 one's way〔manner〕 of talking 이야깃 주머니 a person with lots of interesting things to tell

이야깃거리 a topic〔theme, subject〕 of conversation; something to talk about ¶ 이야깃거리가 되다 become a subject of conversation; be talked〔gossiped〕 about

이야말로¹ this very one〔thing, person〕; this indeed ¶ 이야말로 바로 내가 찾던 책이다 This is the very book (that) I have been looking for. // 이야말로 정당한 비평이라고 할 수 있다 This indeed can be called just criticism.

이야말로² [조사] the very; precisely; just; indeed; exactly; no other than ¶ 그것이야말로 내가 찾고 있던 것이다 That is the very thing〔just the thing〕 that I wanted. // 이번이야말로 어떻게든 잘해야 하겠다 I must succeed this time or never.

이양 移讓 transfer; handing over; relinquishment —하다 transfer; hand over; relinquish ¶ 정권을 이양하다 turn over the reins of government

이어 俚語 [비어] vulgarity; [속어] colloquialism; slang

이어 移御 change of the king's residence —하다 change the king's residence

*이어링 an earing

이어받다 [재산·성질을] inherit; be heir to; [지위를] succeed to; accede to; take over ¶ 아버지의 사업을 이어받다 succeed to one's father's business // 그녀는 아버지의 지능과 어머니의 우아함을 이어받았다 She was an heir to her father's intelligence and her mother's grace. // 그 과부가 농장을 이어받았다 The widow inherited the farm.

이어(서) subsequently; continuing; (going) on; following; next; (soon) after ¶ 연이어 one after another; in succession // 화가 연이어 닥쳐온다 Disasters come treading on each other's heels.

이어지다 get joined on; be continued; be connected; be linked ¶ 남북 아메리카는 파나마 지협으로 이어져 있다 North and South America are connected by the Isthmus of Panama. // 전화가 이어졌다 The call was put〔came〕 through. /The connection was made.

이어차 Yo-ho! /You-heave-ho! ¶ 이어차 이어차 짐을 나르다 carry a load with the cry of yo-heave-ho

*이어폰 an earphone ¶ 라디오를 이어폰으로 듣다 listen to a radio by earphone

이언 俚諺 a proverb; a maxim; a saying

이언 二言 duplicity; double-dealing —하다 break〔go back on〕 one's word 〔promise〕; be double-tongued

이언정 though; although; even if

이엄이엄 continuously; uninterruptedly; without a break

*이엉 straw thatch ¶ 이엉집 a (straw-) thatched house // 지붕에 이엉을 잇다 thatch a roof with straw; thatch

이에 hereupon; thereupon; whereupon; on this; hence; meanwhile; accordingly; immediately after that; consequently

이에서 than this; compared with this ¶ 이에서 더한 불행은 없다 There can be no greater misfortune than this.

이에짬 a joint; a point of attachment; juncture; junction; connection

이여 ¶ 서울이여 잘 있거라 Adieu〔Goodbye〕 to *Seoul*.

이여 爾餘 the rest; the other(s)

이여차 Yo-ho!; Yo-heave-ho! ¶ 이여차 이여차 짐을 나르다 carry a load with the cry of yo-heave-ho

이역 異域 ① [이국] a foreign〔an alien〕 country〔land, part〕 ② [먼곳] a remote place; a different village ¶ 이역에서 죽다 die in an alien land

이역 二役 two roles〔parts〕; a double role ¶ 일인 이역을 하다 play a double role; take two parts

이역본 異譯本 another〔a different〕 version; a variation

이역시 —亦是 this too〔also, again〕; as well; likewise ¶ 이 역시 가짜다 This, too, is an imitation.

이연 離緣 divorce; legal separation; the dissolution of marriage〔adoption〕 —하다 [처와] divorce 《one's wife》; renounce one's marriage vows; [양자와] cancel adoption; disown 《one's adopted son》 ¶ 그는 처와 이연했다 He has divorced〔put away, left〕 his wife. —장 a letter of divorce

이연 移延 postponement —하다 postpone; put off; defer

이연발 二連發 [총] a double-barreled gun ; a double-chambered rifle

이연하다 怡然— (be) joyful ; glad ¶ 이연히 joyfully ; gladly ; rejoicingly

이열 二列 two rows ; a double line ; a double file〔column〕 ¶ 이열로 in two rows〔ranks〕; in double file ; two abreast // 이열로 행진하다 march two abreast // 이열로 늘어서다 form two rows

이열 怡悅 joy ; joyfulness ; rejoicing ; delight **—하다** (be) joyful ; glad ; delighted

이열치열 以熱治熱 Like cures like. /One poison drives out another. /The smell of garlic takes away the smell of onions. /Fight fire with fire.

이염 耳炎 〖의학〗 otitis ; inflammation of the ear

중〔내, 외〕— otitis media〔interna, externa〕

이염화물 二鹽化物 〖화학〗 a bichloride

이영차 ⇨ 이여차

이오늄 〖화학〗 ionium 《Io》

이오니아 Ionia ¶ 이오니아의 Ionian ; Ionic

— 사람 an Ionian

이온 〖화학〗 an ion ¶ 이온화하다 ionize

— 교환 수지(樹脂) an ion exchange resin **—층** an ionosphere **양—** a cation ; a positive ion **양성(兩性) —** a dipolar ion ; a zwitterion **음—** an anion ; a negative ion〔a negatively charged ion〕

이온화 —化 ionization **—하다** ionize ¶ 이온화된 ionized ; polar

이와전와 以訛傳訛 transmitting errors ; perpetuating mistakes **—하다** transmit errors ; perpetuate mistakes

*__이완 弛緩__ relaxation ; laxity ; slackness ; 〖의학〗 atony **—하다** slacken ; relax ; be slackened ; lax

이왕 已往 the past ; bygones (이왕지사) ¶ 이왕의 past ; bygone // 이왕에 already ; now that ; as long as ; since ; once // 이왕지사는 묻지 말자 Let bygones be bygones. // 이왕에 가기로 했으면 가야지 Once you have decided to go, you had better go. // 이왕에 늦었으니 천천히 가자 It is already late, so let's take our time. // 이왕에 일을 시작했으니 다 마치도록 해라 Now that you have started the job, try to finish it. // 이왕에 할 바엔 큰 일을 해라 If you do anything at all, do something great. // 이왕이면 유효하게 돈을 써라 If you must spend money, spend it usefully. // 이왕이면 나하고 같이 가자 As long as you are going anyway, come along with me. // 이왕이면 영어를 배우겠다 As long as I am about it〔While I'm at it〕 I might as well take English.

이왕지사 已往之事 ⇨ 이왕(已往)

†**이외 以外** [제외] except ; save 《for》; but ; outside 《of》; aside〔apart〕《from》; other than ; beyond ; [그외에] besides ; in addition 《to》; aside〔apart〕《from》《미》 ¶ 일요일 이외에 except on Sunday // 월급 이외에 besides〔in addition to, aside from〕 one's salary // 도둑질 이외에는 무엇이나 다 했다 I did everything except stealing. // 가족 이외는 아무도 비밀을 몰랐다 No one knew the secret outside my family. // 그 이외에 다른 방법이 없다 There is no other way than that. /This is the only way. // 그 이외의 일은 아무것도 모른다 I know nothing beyond〔except〕 that. /I know only this. /This is all I know. // 회원 이외는 입장 금지 No admittance except for members. /Members only. // 영어 이외에 독일어를 한다 He speaks German in addition to English. // 나 이외에 모두 갔다 All went there except me. // 나 이외에 여섯 사람이 갔다 Six people went there besides me. (나도 갔다)

이욕 利慾 greed ; avarice ; covetousness ; cupidity ; love of gain〔money〕 ¶ 이욕 때문에 for the sake of gain // 이욕을 떠나서 without any desire of gain // 이욕을 좇다 be greedy of gain ; be avaricious ; be covetous ; be mercenary // 이욕에 눈이 멀다 be blinded by avarice ; be tempted〔allured〕 by gain // 그들은 모두 이욕과 명성에 골몰하고 있다 They are all absorbed in pursuing worldly fame and gain.

†**이용 利用** use ; utilization **—하다** make use 《of》; use 《a thing》 to good advantage ; make the most〔best〕《of》; utilize ; take advantage 《of》; avail 《oneself of》; turn 《a thing》 to〔good〕 account ¶ 폐물 이용 the utilization of waste material // 여가를 이용하다 make (good) use of one's leisure // 기회를 이용하다 avail oneself of〔make the best of〕 an opportunity // 천연 자원을 이용하다 exploit natural resources // 자기의 재능을 최대한으로 이용하다 use one's talents to the best advantage ; make the most of one's talents // 이용할 가치가 있다〔없다〕 be of utility〔no utility〕 value // 나의 책을 마음대로 이용하십시오 My library is at your disposal. // 우리는 댐을 건설해서 수력을 이용한다 By building dams we harness water. // 여름 휴가를 이용해서 유럽을 여행했다 I made a tour of Europe, availing myself of the summer vacation. // 영어로 말할 수 있는 기회를 최대한 이용하도록 노력하시오 Try and make use of every opportunity of speaking English. // 그는 언제나 나를 이용하려고 한다 He is always trying to make a cat's paw of me. // 그는 중역의 지위를 잘 이용해서 여러 가지 부정을 범했다 He committed various irregularities, taking full advantage of his position of director. // 롯데 백화점을 이용해 주셔서 감사합니다 Thank you for shopping (at) Lotte.

—률 coefficient of utilization **—법** utilization ; a use ; a way to use ; how to use 《a book》 —자 a user ; [도서관의] a visitor ; a reader 폐품 — the utilization of waste material

이용 理容 ⇨ 이발 (理髮)

이용 가치 利用價値 usefulness ; utility value ; value in use ¶ 이용 가치가 있다 be of utility value

이우다 give 《someone》 a hand〔a help〕 to get〔carry〕 something on the head

이울다 ① [시들다] wither ; droop ; fade ; wilt ; deflate ¶ 꽃들이 이울었다 The flowers have withered // 풍선이 이울었다 The balloon deflated.
② [달이] wane ; be on the wane ¶ 달이 이울어 가고 있다 The moon is waning.
③ [쇠퇴] decline ; fall off ; wane ; fail ; decay ; be going down ; be sinking ¶ 저 나라의 국위〔국운〕도 이울고 있다 The prestige of that country is on the decline. // 해가 이울고 있다 The sun is going down.

†이웃 the neighborhood ; [집] next door 〔house〕 ; [사람] a neighbor ; a neighborhood ¶ 이웃의 neighboring ; next ; adjoining // 한 집 건너 이웃 next door but one // 두 집 건너 이웃 two doors from 《one》 // 이웃 사람 a neighbor // 이웃간이다 be neighbors // 서로 이웃간이다 be next door to each other ; adjoin each other // 그녀는 내 이웃에서 산다 She lives in the house next to me. /She lives next door to me. // 식탁에서 너의 이웃에 있었던 분은 누구인가 Who was your neighbor at table ? // 내 바로 이웃은 존스 부인입니다 My immediate neighbor is Mrs. Jones.

이웃집 a next-door〔a neighboring〕 house ; a neighbor's house ; the house next door ¶ 우리 이웃집 my neighboring house ; the house adjacent to ours

이원 利源 source of gain〔profit〕

이원 二元 duality
—론 dualism — 방송 simultaneous broadcast by two stations

이원권 以遠權 the beyond (traffic) right (항공 협정상의)

이원제 二院制 a bicameral system ; a two-chamber (house) system

†이월 二月 February 《Feb.》

이월 移越 carrying forward —하다 carry forward 《a sum, an account balance》 ¶ 전기 이월금 a balance carried forward from the last account // 다음 연도로 이월하다 carry 《a sum》 forward to next year
— 손익 『상업』 losses and profits brought forward — 잔액 『상업』 [전기로부터의] balance brought forward (from the last account) ; [차기로의] balance carried forward (to next year)

이위 二位 [석차] the second place ; [사람] a runner-up ¶ 2위다 rank second ; stand second on the list ; hold the second place ; be (a) runner-up // 근소한 차로 2위가 되다 make a close friend 《in a race》

†이유 理由 [까닭] a reason ; a cause ; a ground (근거) ; [동기] why ; motive ; [구실] a pretext ; an excuse ¶ 충분〔빈약〕한 이유 a good〔slender〕 reason // 이유 없는 공포심 groundless fears // 이유가 있어서 with good reason // 이유 없이 without reason〔good cause〕 ; without provocation〔occasion〕 // …의 이유로 by reason of ; on the ground(s) of〔that〕 ; on account of ; because of ; for // 어떤 이유로 for some reason or other // 여러 가지 이유로 for several reasons // 어떤 이유를 붙여 on some pretext or other ; on one pretext or another // 건강상의 이유로 for reason of health // 이유가 될 만한 justifiable ; reasonable ; excusable // 어떤 이유가 있더라도 on any account ; irrespective of reason // …할 만한 충분한 이유가 있다 have (every) reason for〔to do〕 ; there is (every) reason for // 내가 사과해야 할 이유가 없다 There is no reason why I should apologize. // 그가 그렇게 한 이유를 모르겠다 The reason why he did it is obscure to me. // 이유가 뭔지 궁금하네요 I wonder why. // 사람들이 이유 없이 너를 구두쇠라고 부르는게 아니다 They don't call you a skinflint for nothing.
—서 a statement of reasons ; an explanatory statement

이유 離乳 weaning ; ablactation —하다 wean 《a child》 from the breast〔from its mother〕 ; ablactate 《a baby》 ¶ 조기 이유가 더 흔해지고 있다 Early weaning is becoming more common.
—기 the weaning period —식(食) a weaning diet ; baby food

이윤 利潤 profit ; gain ; returns ; a profit margin ¶ 상당한 이윤을 올리다 make a good profit
— 분배 제도 a profit-sharing system ; industrial〔labor〕 copartnership —율 a profit rate ; a rate of profit — 증권 a profit-sharing security — 통제〔추구〕 control〔pursuit〕 of profits 한계〔초과, 정상〕 — marginal〔excess, normal〕 profits

이율 利率 the rate of interest ; interest ¶ 이율 인상〔인하〕 rise〔reduction〕 in interest rates ; an increase〔a decrease〕 in interest rates // 이율을 인상〔인하〕하다 raise〔lower〕 the rate of interest
법정 — the legal rate of interest 은행〔시장〕 — the bank〔market〕 rate 협정 — the conventional rate of interest

이율 배반 二律背反 antinomy

†이윽고 after a while ; before long ; soon after ; in a short time ; presently ; shortly ¶ 그는 이윽고 왔다 It was not long before he came.

이음 connection
— 철물 a clampjoint metal —판 a joint bar ; a splice plate

이음 異音 〖음성〗 an allophone
*이음매 a joint ; a juncture ; a join ; a commissure ; a seam ¶ 이음매가 없는 jointless ; one-piece ; seamless // 이음매가 헐거워졌다 The joint has got loosened.
†이의 異義 [뜻] a different meaning ; [주의] a different principle
이의 異意 a different opinion〔view〕
*이의 異議 [반대] an objection ; an exception ; [항의] a protest ; [불찬성] a dissent ; 〖법〗 a demurrer ¶ 이의 없이 with one consent〔accord〕; without objection〔dissent〕; unanimously // 이의가 있다〔없다〕 have an〔no〕 objection 《to》 // 이의를 말하다 object 《to》 ; raise an objection 《to》 ; protest 《against》 ; take exception 《to》 ; dissent 《from》 // 이의를 제기〔신청〕하다 make〔file, lodge〕 a protest 《against》 // 종업원들은 밤일에 이의를 제기했다 The workers objected to working nights. // 그 동의는 이의 없이 채택되었다 The motion was adopted unanimously. // 이의 없습니까 Have you any objection? // 이의 없는 것으로 인정합니다 I see no objection.
— 제기〔신청〕 a formal objection ; an exception ; a demurrer — 제기인〔신청인〕a demurrant
†이익 利益 ① [이윤] profit(s) ; gain(s) ; returns (수익) ; [매상고] turnover ; proceeds ¶ 이익이 있는 profitable ; lucrative ; paying // 이익이 없는 unprofitable ; profitless // 이익이 적다 give〔yield〕 little profit ; do not pay much // …으로 이익을 얻다 profit 《by, at, from》 ; make〔fetch〕 a profit 《on》 // 이익을 분배하다 give 《a person》 a profit participation // 이익 분배를 받다 participate〔have a share〕 in the profit // 나는 그 거래로 1,000달러의 이익을 얻었다 I made a profit of a thousand dollars on the transaction.
② [도움] benefit ; good ; [편리] advantage ; [유리] interests ¶ 공동의 이익 common interest // 공공의 이익 the public interests // 이익이 있는 beneficial ; advantageous // …의 이익을 위하여 for the benefit of ; in the interests of ; for one's good // 상호간의 이익을 위하여 for mutual advantage〔interest〕 // 이익에 반하다 be against one's interests // 이익을 주다 benefit ; do 《a person》 good // 사회의 이익을 도모하다 labor〔work〕 for the public good // 자기의 이익을 도모하다 look after〔to〕 one's own interests // 그는 분규를 틈타 이익을 보려 했다 He tried to fish in troubled waters. // 그렇게 하는 것이 당신의 이익이다 It is to your advantage to do so. // 그런 말을 해서 무슨 이익이 있는가 What is the use〔good〕 of saying such a thing? // 지난달에 우리는 큰 이익을 올렸다 We rang up a huge profit last month.
— 교환 reciprocity ; give and take —금 a profit ; gains ¶ 당기 이익금 profits for the term // 순이익금 a net〔clear〕 profit // 총이익금 a gross profit — 배당〔분배〕 distribution of profits ; profit sharing — 배당금 a dividend 미배당 — undivided profit 부정 — illicit gains
이인 二人 two persons〔men〕 ; two-man —분 a double order〔portion〕 — 삼각(三脚) 경주 a three-legged race —승 a two-seater —조 《a comedy》 duo —칭 〖문법〗 the second person
이인 異人 ① [기재] a genius ; a wizard 《미·구》 ; a man of no common ability
② [다른 사람] different people
동명 — a different person with the same name ; one's namesake
이인종 異人種 an alien〔a different〕 race ¶ 이인종간의 결혼 interracial〔mixed〕 marriage
이임 離任 —하다 leave〔quit〕 one's post
이입 移入 importation ; introduction —하다 bring in 《from》 ; import ; introduce — 노동자 an immigrant worker —자 an incomer ; an immigrant — 조직 〖식물〗 transfusion tissue 감정 — 〖심리〗 empathy
이자 the spleen ; the pancreas (췌장)
이자 —者 this man〔fellow, guy〕
*이자 利子 interest ¶ 높은〔싼, 5부〕이자로 at a high〔low, 5 percent〕 interest // 무이자로 without〔free of〕 interest // 이자가 붙다 yield〔bear, draw〕 interest // 이자를 붙여 돈을 빌려주다 put one's money out at interest // 이자를 붙여 빚을 갚다 pay a debt with interest // 우편 예금의 이자는 얼마입니까 What is the rate of interest for postal savings? // 은행 이자는 얼마입니까 How much interest do they give at the bank?
— 계산서〔산출표〕 an interest note〔table〕 — 소득 the income from interest — 수입 interest receipts — 증권 an interest-bearing security — 지불 interest payment — 평형세 the interest equalization tax — 학설 a theory on interest 미불 — interest unpaid 연체〔사채, 은행, 확정〕 — overdue〔debenture, bank, fixed〕 interest
이자락 利子落 ex interest 《ex int.》 ; interest off ; less〔minus〕 interest
이자부 利子附 ¶ 이자부의 interest-bearing ; with〔cum〕 interest
— 공채 an active〔interest-bearing〕 bond — 증권 an interest-bearing security 정액 — 증권 a fixed interest-bearing security
이자 택일 二者擇一 alternative ; selecting one alternative —하다 choose between the two
이작 裏作 a secondary crop ; a winter crop
이작 移作 change〔replacement〕 of one's farm tenant with another —하다 change one's farm tenant with another ;

replace one's farm tenant by another
이장 移葬 exhuming and burying elsewhere —하다 exhume and bury in another place ; change the burial site
이장 里長 the head of a village
이재 罹災 suffering 《from a calamity》 ; affliction —하다 suffer 《from a calamity》 ; fall victim 《to a calamity》
— 구호금 a (disaster) relief fund —민 the sufferers (from) ; the afflicted people ; the victims (of) —율 〖보험〗 the frequency of loss — 지구 the afflicted 〔stricken, affected〕 districts〔area〕
이재 理財 management of financial affairs ; economy ; finance ¶ 이재에 능숙하다 be adept at〔in〕 moneymaking ; be a shrewd man of business ; be efficient at financial affairs
—가 an economist ; a financier —국(局) the Financial (Management) Bureau
이재 異才 a remarkable〔brilliant〕talent
이재발신 以財發身 advancement in life 〔career〕 through wealth
이적 異蹟 a miracle ; a wonder ; a mystery ¶ 이적을 행하다 work〔perform〕 miracles ; do wonders // 이적을 나타내다 achieve a miracle // 이적이 나타난다 A miracle is wrought. /A miracle occurs 〔happens〕.
이적 移籍 transfer of one's name and records to another's family register ; transference of census registration ; a change〔an entry〕 of permanent domicile —하다 transfer one's name and records to another's family register ; transfer〔change〕 one's permanent domicile〔family register〕 《to》
이적 離籍 removal of one's name and records from the family register —하다 remove one's name and records from the family register
이적 利敵 benefiting the enemy —하다 benefit〔profit〕 the enemy
— 행위 acts benefiting〔advantageous to〕the enemy ; an act to serve the interest of the enemy
†이전 以前 former times〔days〕 ¶ 이전에 before ; formerly ; once // 훨씬 이전에 long ago ; a long time ago // 이전의 previous ; former ; old ; prior // 이전과 같이 as before // 그는 이전의 그가 아니다 He is not what he used to be. /He is not what he once was. // 그는 이전에는 고등학교의 선생님이었다 He was formerly a high school teacher. /He used to teach at a high school. // 우리는 훨씬 이전부터 서로 알고 있다 We have known each other for a long time. // 그는 이전에 어디에 살고 있었습니까 Where did he live before?
이전 移轉 removal ; moving 《미》 ; transfer ; transference (권리의) —하다 remove ; move ; transfer ¶ 다른 집으로 이전하다 move into another house // 위의〔다음〕 주소로 이전했다 We have moved to the above〔following〕 address.
— 등기부 a transfer book — 통지〔공고〕 a removal notice ; a notice of change of address
이전 利錢 gain ; profit ; interest
이절 二折 ¶ 이절의 twofold ; twicefolded
—(판)본 a folio
†이점 利點 an advantage ; a point of advantage ; a vantage point ¶ 이 기계의 이점 advantages claimed for this machine // 이 기계에는 많은 이점이 있다 This machine has many advantages. // 이 기계는 값이 싸다는 이점이 있다 This machine has the advantage of cheapness.
이접 移接 moving 《of residence》 ; change 《of one's abode》 ; removal —하다 (re) move ; change one's residence
이정 里程 mileage ; distance ¶ 부산까지의 이정 the distance to *Pusan*
—표(表) a table〔list〕 of distances —표(標) a milestone ; a milepost
이정 釐正 arrangement ; correction —하다 arrange 《in proper shape》 ; put in order ; correct ; right ; put right
†이제 now ⇨ 지금 ¶ 이제부터는 결코 같은 잘못을 저지르지 않겠다 From now on I will never make the same mistake. // 이제야 말로 절호의 기회다 It's now or never. // 이제야 그가 왔다 He has just come at long last. // 이것은 내가 이제까지 읽은 소설 중에서 가장 재미있다 This is the most interesting novel (that) I have ever read.
이제와서 now ; after so long a time ; when it is too late ¶ 이제와서 취소도 할 수 없다 It is too late to cancel it. // 이제와서 어쩔 수 없다 Nothing can be done now. /It can't be helped now.
이조 移調 〖음악〗 (a) transposition
— 악기 a transposing instrument
이조 李朝 the *Yi* Dynasty
이족 異族 [이인종] a different race 〔tribe〕 ; an alien race ; [이성] a different clan ; a different surname ; [이혈] a different blood
이종 移種 transplantation ; transplanting —하다 transplant ; plant out
이종 姨從 cousins by a maternal aunt
이종 異種 a different kind〔species〕 ; a variety ; heterogeneity
— 교배〔번식〕 hybridization ; cross〔out-and-out〕 breeding — 구조 〖생물〗 heterology — 피질 〖의학〗 allocortex
이종 二種 the second class
— 우편물 the second-class mail (matter)
*이주 移住 moving ; removal (전거) ; [사람·동물의] migration ; [외국으로] emigration ; [외국에서] immigration —하다 move 《미》 ; remove 《영》 ; migrate ; emigrate 《to》 ; immigrate 《into》 ¶ 브라질로 이주하다 emigrate to Brazil

—민 a settler ; [외국으로 가는] an emigrant ; [외국에서 온] an immigrant
이주 移駐 transference —하다 move ; transfer
이주간 二週間 two weeks ; a fortnight
이주걱거리다 make invidious remarks ; carp ; prattle
이죽거리다 prattle ; make invidious remarks ⇨ 이기죽거리다
*이중 二重 duplication ; doubleness ¶ 이중의 double 《meaning》 ; twofold ; duplicate ; dual // 이중의 뜻 double meaning // 이중으로 doubly ; twice over ; over again // 이중 바닥의 double-bottomed ; double-soled // 이중으로 하다〔되다〕 double ; duplicate // 이중 역할을 하다 perform a double service // 이중으로 포장하다 wrap 《a thing》 double // 이중 기입하다 make an entry twice over // 요금을 이중으로 치르다 pay a charge twice over // 이중의 목적을 달성하다 fill a dual〔twofold〕 purpose // 이중일이 되었다 The work is to be done all over again.
— 가격 a double price — 가격제 the double-〔two-〕price system ; the two-tier market system — 결합 a double bond — 결혼 bigamy — 과세 double taxation — 구조 〖경제〗 dual (industrial) structure — 국적 dual nationality —극 〖화학·물리〗 a dipole — 노출 double exposure — 모음 a diphthong — 방송 dual broadcasting — 부정 〖문법〗 a double negative — 생활 a double life —성 dualism ; duplicity — 외교 dual diplomacy — 의식 〖심리〗 double consciousness — 인격 a dual personality ; 〖심리〗 double personality — 인격자 a double-faced person ; a Jekyll and Hyde —주 a duet ; a duetto —창(唱) a duet —창(窓) a storm window — 촬영 an overlap —턱 a double chin ¶ 이중턱의 double-chinned
이즈막 ⇨ 요즈막
이즈음 these days ; lately ; recently ; of late ¶ 이즈음의 청년 the young people of today // 이즈음의 학생 the present-day students // 이즈음의 경향 the modern 〔recent〕 tendency // 이즈음의 사건 a recent event // 이즈음까지 till recent times ; until lately〔recently〕 // 이즈음 그녀는 어떻게 지내고 있습니까 How is she these days ?
이즘 [주의·설] an ism
이지 異志 ⇨ 이심(異心)
이지 理智 intellect ; reasoning power ; intelligence ¶ 이지적 intellectual // 이지의 번득임 flashes of intellect // 이지적인 얼굴 an intelligent〔intellectual〕 face // 이지로 판단하다 judge by intellect // 저 사람은 감정보다 이지적인 사람이다 He is a man of mind rather than of heart.
—주의 intellectualism
이지다 grow big ; develop ; mature ; get fat
*이지러지다 break off ; chip ; [달이] wane ¶ 달이 이지러져 간다 The moon is waning. // 저 유리컵들은 모두 이지러졌다 Those glasses are all chipped.
이지렁스럽다 be unabashedly deceitful ; be not so sweet as one looks ; be a devil with an angel's face
-이지마는 but ; however ; though
이직 移職 change of occupation —하다 change one's job〔occupation〕 ; take up another employment
이직 離職 separation from one's position 〔service〕 ; loss of employment —하다 leave〔quit〕 one's job
—률 a separation rate
이직자 離職者 the jobless ; the unemployed ; a person out of work
이진법 二進法 the binary scale
이질 姨姪 the children of one's wife's sister
이질 痢疾 〖의학〗 dysentery
아메바성 — amoebic dysentery
이질 異質 ① [성질이] heterogeneity ② [재주] a distinctive〔outstanding〕 quality〔talent〕 ; an unusual man ¶ 이질의 heterogeneous
이질풀 痢疾— 〖식물〗 the crane's-bill ; Geranium nepalense (학명)
이집트 Egypt
— 공화국 the Republic of Egypt
이징가미 a broken piece〔chip, fragment〕of porcelain〔earthenware〕
*이쪽 this side〔way〕 ; our side ¶ 이쪽으로 오십시오 This way, please. // 이쪽으로 나오시는 일이 있으면 들려주십시오 If you come this way, don't fail to drop in. // 은행은 이쪽에 있다 The bank is on this side of the street.
이차 二次 ① [두번째] the second ; secondary (부차) ② 〖수학〗 quadratic ¶ 그런 일은 이차적인 문제다 A question like that is of secondary importance.
— 대전 the second World War ; World War Ⅱ — 방정식 a quadratic equation — 전지 a secondary battery —회 an after-feast (연회) ; a second meeting ¶ 이차회를 갖다 have another feast〔spree〕
이차피 ⇨ 어차피
이착 二着 the second place ; a runner-up —하다 finish second ; come in second
이착륙 離着陸 take-off and landing ⇨ 이륙, 착륙
이채 異彩 a conspicuous color ¶ 이채를 띠다 be conspicuous ; show brilliance ; cut a conspicuous〔brilliant〕 figure ; stand out 《from others》 // 그는 반에서 이채를 띠고 있다 He cuts〔makes〕 a brilliant 〔conspicuous〕 figure in his class. // 그는 독특한 수염으로 이채를 띠고 있었다 He caught our eyes with his characteristic beard.
이처럼 thus ; like this ; in this way〔manner〕 ; this much ; so much ¶ 이처럼 많

이 so many〔much〕// 이처럼 아침 일찍이 at this hour of (the) morning // 이처럼 왕림해주셔서 감사합니다 Thank you for coming like this. // 이처럼 재미있는 일은 없다 Nothing is more interesting than this.

이첩 移牒 transfer of notification ; notification to the authorities concerned ; communication ―하다 transmit《an order, information》to the office〔official〕concerned ; notify《of, that》; refer《to》; communicate《to》

이체 동심 異體同心 two in body but one in mind ¶ 이체 동심이다 be of one mind ; acting perfect harmony〔accord〕; cooperate heartily〔closely〕《with》

이초 二秒 two seconds

이초 離礁 ―하다 get off the rock〔reef〕; refloat ¶ 이초시키다 refloat ; get《a ship》off the rocks

이초점 二焦點 ¶ 이초점의 bifocal《lens》

이촉 the root of a tooth ; a fang

이축 移築 〖건축〗 removing and reconstruction

이출 移出 shipment ; export ; clearance ―하다 ship《out of》; export
― 신고서 [세관의] a declaration of clearance

이출혈 耳出血 〖의학〗 aural hemorrhage

이취 泥醉 dead drunkenness ―하다 get dead〔beastly, blind〕 drunk ; be boozy《구》

*이층 二層 the second floor〔story〕《미》; the upper storey《영》; the first floor〔storey〕《영》

> 참고 영국에서는 1층을 **ground floor** 3층을 **the second floor** 라고 함

¶ 2층에〔으로〕 upstairs // 2층 방 an upstairs room // 2층에 올라가다 go upstairs // 2층에서 내려오다〔떨어지다〕 come〔fall〕 downstairs // 그 집은 2층이다 The house has two stories. // 그의 침실은 2층에 있다 His bedroom is upstairs. // 그들의 아파트는 그 빌딩 2층에 있다 Their apartment is on the second floor of the building.
―집 a two-storied〔two-story〕 house

이치 理致 reason ; principle ¶ 이치로 판단하여 on reason // 이치에 맞다 stand to reason ; be reasonable ; accord with reason // 이치를 말하다 reason with《a person》// 이치에 맞는 말을 하다 speak〔talk〕 reason // 이치를 설명하여 고집을 꺾다 reason《a person》out of his obstinacy // 아이에게 이치를 말해도 허사다 It is no use reasoning with a child. // 네 말도 충분히 이치가 있다 There is a lot of truth in what you say.

이치다 ⇨ 이아치다

이칭 異稱 another name ; another title ; a by-name ; an alias

이커서니 oof ; heave ; yo-heave-ho ; yo-ho

이퀄 equal ¶ 5×4=20 Five times four is twenty. // 8÷2=4 Two goes into eight fourtime. // 2+3=5 Two and three make〔makes, is, are〕 five. // 7－4=3 Four from seven leaves three.

이키나 Wow ! /Oh ! /Oh, my goodness !

이타 利他 altruism ¶ 이타적 altruistic
―주의 altruism ―주의자 an altruist

이탄 泥炭 peat ; turf ¶ 이탄같은 peaty
―층 peat deposits

*이탈 離脫 secession ; separation ―하다 secede《from》; break away《from》; leave〔bolt from〕《a party》¶ 당에서 이탈하다 secede from the party // 직장을 이탈하다 desert one's job ; walk out on one's job《미》
―자 a seceder ; a bolter 국적 ― the renunciation of one's nationality 금본위 ― abolition of the gold standard

이탈리아 Italy ¶ 이탈리아의 Italian
―말 Italian ― 사람 an Italian

이탓저탓 with this excuse〔complaint〕 and that ; on one pretext〔excuse〕 or another

이태 two years ¶ 이태 동안 for a couple of years

이태리 伊太利 ⇨ 이탈리아

*이탤릭 〖인쇄〗 italics ; italic type ¶ 이탤릭으로 하다 italicize

이토 泥土 mud ; mire
―암 clay rock ; pelite ―층 a dirt bed

이토록 so〔this〕 much ; like this ¶ 이토록 부탁을 하는데도 for all my asking // 영어 가르치기가 이토록 힘들 줄은 몰랐다 I little dreamed that it was so〔pretty, awfully〕 hard to teach English.

이통 耳痛 earache ; otalgia ¶ 이통이 나다 have a pain in the ear
―제 an otalgic

이튿날 [다음날] the next〔following〕 day ; the day after ; the second day (of the month) ¶ 이튿날 아침 the next morning 불이 난 이튿날에 on the day following〔succeeding〕 the fire

이틀[1] ① two days ¶ 이틀마다 every two days ; every other day ② [초 이틀] the second day (of the month) ¶ 정월 초 이틀 the second of January〔Jan. 2nd〕

이틀[2] ① [치조] an alveolus ; the sockets of teeth ② [의치] a dental plate ; a full denture ¶ 이틀을 해넣다 insert a plate ; fix a denture

이틀거리 〖한의〗 a tertian fever ; malaria ¶ 이틀거리에 걸리다 be taken with tertian fever

이판암 泥板岩 shale

이팔 二八 sixteen
―청춘 a sixteen-year-old ; sweet sixteen ; a boy〔girl〕 in the flower of youth

이페리트 〖화학〗 yperite ; mustard gas

이편 ① [이쪽] this side ; this way ¶ 우체국은 길 이편에 있다 The post office is on

this side of the street.
② [자기] his side ; our side ; we ; I ¶ 이편의 잘못 my〔our〕 fault ; a fault on my〔our〕 part // 축구에서 이편이 이겼다 We won the football game.

이풀 rice-paste

이풍 異風 [모양] strangeness ; novelty ; strange appearance ; [이속] a strange〔quaint〕 custom

이핑계저핑계 with this excuse and that excuse ; on one pretext〔excuse〕 or another

*****이하 以下** ① [수량] less than ; under ; below ; not exceeding ; [정도] under ; below ; beneath ¶ 50 이하 [50을 포함] 50 and less ; 50 and below ; [50을 제외] less than〔below〕 50 // 표준 이하 below the mark // 영도 이하 below zero // 6세 이하의 아이들 children under six years of age // 5,000원 이하의 벌금 a fine not exceeding 5,000 *won* // 평균 이하의 강우 the rainfall below the average // 중류 이하 below the middle class(es) // 평균 이하이다 be below the average〔par〕 // 성적이 예상 이하이다 The result falls below what was expected.
② [하기] the following ; the rest ¶ 이하 …라 칭함 hereinafter referred to《as》// 이하 생략 The rest is omitted. // 이하에 준함 The same rules apply correspondingly to the following.

이하부정관 李下不整冠 Avoid anything suspicious. /Don't get suspicious. /Keep〔stay〕 away from suspicion.

이하선 耳下腺 the parotid gland
—염 parotitis ; mumps

이학 理學 ① physical science ② [철학] philosophy ; metaphysics (형이상학)
— 박사 a doctor of science《D. Sc.》 **—부** Department of Science ; the Science Faculty **—사** a bachelor of science《B. Sc.》 **—자** a scientist

이한 離韓 one's departure from Korea **—하다** leave〔depart, go away from〕Korea

이할 二割 twenty percent

이함 離艦 〖공군〗 take-off《of an aircraft》 from a ship《such as an aircraft (carrier)》

이합 離合 meeting and parting ¶ 정당의 이합집산 alignment of political parties
—집산 meeting and parting

이합사 二合絲 double-ply thread

이항 二項 ¶ 이항의 binomial
— 방정식 a binomial equation **—식** a binomial (expression) **— 정리** the binomial theorem

이항 移項 〖수학〗 transposition **—하다** transpose

이해 this year ; the current〔present〕 year ⇨ 올해, 금년 ¶ 이해는 풍년이 들 것 같다 We shall probably have a good harvest this year. // 이해도 며칠 남지 않았다 We have only a few days left before the end of the year. /The year is drawing to a close. /New Year's Day is coming on us.

*****이해 利害** interests ; gain and loss ; advantages and disadvantages ; concern ¶ 이해 관계자 the persons concerned ; the interested parties // 이해를 초월한 disinterested // 이해의 일치 identity〔community〕 of interests // 이해의 충돌 a clash〔conflict〕 of interests // 이해에 관계되다 affect one's interests // 이해를 같이하다 have common interests with others // 이해관계가 있다 have an interest in the matter
—득실 advantages and disadvantages ; gains and losses ¶ 무엇이든지 이해득실이 없는 것은 없다 Everything has its merits and demerits〔faults〕. **— 상반** both gain and loss ; both advantages and disadvantages ; both benefit and harm ¶ 이해 상반하다 be both profitable and unprofitable〔favorable and unfavorable, advantageous and disadvantageous〕

†**이해 理解** understanding ; comprehension ; apprehension ; appreciation **—하다** understand ; comprehend ; catch ; grasp ; see get ; make out ; apprehend ; appreciate ¶ 이해하기 어려운 difficult to understand ; beyond one's comprehension // 이해하는 사람 a man of understanding〔sense〕 // 이해하는 친구〔남편〕 a sympathetic friend〔husband〕 // 이해하는 아내 an understanding wife // 이해할 수 있다 be understandable〔comprehensible〕 ; make sense ; can be appreciated // 이해하기 쉽다 be easy to understand ; be easily understandable // 이해하기 어렵다 be incomprehensible ; be hard〔difficult〕 to understand ; be abstruse // 이해하지 않다 have no understanding ; lack sense〔understanding〕 // 이해가 느리다〔빠르다〕 be slow〔quick〕 of apprehension〔understanding〕 // 이해가 부족하다 do not fully understand ; want〔lack〕 sympathy // 이해를 깊이하다 deepen one's understanding // 상호 이해를 증진하다 promote〔increase〕 mutual understanding // 올바르게 이해하다 have a right〔proper〕 understanding《of》// 잘 이해하다 have a good grasp《of》// 음악을 이해하다 appreciate music ; have a good ear for music // 나로선 네가 말한 바를 이해할 수 없다 I can't catch your meaning. /I don't understand〔get〕 you. // 그는 교육에 대한 이해가 없다 He has no idea of education. /He does not know what education is. // 나는 그렇게 이해가 느린 집단을 보지 못했다 I've never seen a group so slow on the uptake. // 최근에 당신은 이해가 매우 빠른것 같다 You're sharp as a tack lately, aren't you ? // 우리 딸은 사물에 대한 이해가 빠르다 Our little girl picks things up fast.

이해력 理解力 the faculty of comprehension ; the understanding ; the power to understand ; sense ¶ 이해력이 둔하다〔빠르다〕 be slow〔quick〕 of understanding // 이해력을 기르다 cultivate the power of understanding

이해심 理解心 understanding ; consideration ; sympathy ¶ 이해심이 있다〔없다〕 be considerate〔inconsiderate〕 《of》 ; be sympathetic〔unsympathetic〕 《about》

이해 타산 利害打算 [계산] calculation 〔reckoning〕 of the loss and gain〔the profits and losses〕 ; [욕심] self-interest ; selfishness ; interestedness ¶ 이해 타산에서 《act》 from selfish motives ; guided by self-interest

이핵 二核 ¶ 이핵의 binuclear ; binucleate(d)

†**이행 履行** performance 《of a duty》 ; fulfilment 《of a promise》 ; discharge 《of an obligation》 ; execution 《of a contract》 ; observance 《of a treaty》 **—하다** fulfil ; perform ; carry out ; make good ; discharge ; execute ; put into practice ¶ 의무의 이행 performance of a duty // 약속을 이행하다 fulfil〔make good, stand to〕 one's promise ; keep one's engagement ; carry out a pledge // 계약을 이행하다 live up to〔execute, fulfil, abide by〕 a contract // 채무를 이행하다 discharge one's liabilities // 그는 약속을 이행하지 않는다 He does not abide by his promise. /He has broken his word. // 그는 훌륭히 약속을 이행했다 He was as good as his word.

—자 a performer ; an executer

이행 移行 switching over ; veering **—하다** switch over to ; veer to (풍향이) ; shift to (위치가)

이향 異鄕 a foreign country ⇨ 타향

이향 離鄕 departure from one's native place ; leaving one's home **—하다** leave one's native place ; leave home

이형 異形 〖생물〗 heteromorphy ; heteromorphism

— 배우자 anisogamete ; a heterogamete **— 세포** an idioblast **— 염색체** a heterochromosome

이호 二號 number two ; No. 2 ; [첩] a concubine ; a (kept) mistress ; one's secondary wife

‡**이혼 離婚** divorce ; the dissolution of marriage **—하다** divorce ; be〔get〕 divorced from ; have one's marriage annulled (법률적으로) ¶ 합의〔협의〕 이혼 a divorce by agreement〔consent〕 // 이혼을 청하다 seek〔claim〕 a divorce // 남편과 이혼하다 divorce one's husband // S부부를 이혼시키다 divorce Mr. S and Mrs. S // 요새 그 나라에서는 결혼한 부부 세 쌍 중 한 쌍은 결국 이혼한다 Every third marriage ends up in divorce in that country nowadays.

—계 a report〔notice〕 of divorce ¶ 이혼계를 내다 notify one's divorce ; send in a divorce notice **— 소송** a divorce suit ; a suit〔an action〕 for divorce ¶ 이혼 소송을 제기하다 file a suit〔petition〕 for divorce ; start divorce proceedings ; sue for divorce **— 수속** a divorce procedure 〔formalities〕 **— 신고** a divorce notice ¶ 이혼 신고를 하다 notify of one's divorce ; send in a divorce notice **—자** a divorcee ; a divorced person

이화 李花 plum blossoms

이화 梨花 pear blossoms

이화 異化 〖사회·음성〗 dissimilation ; 〖생물〗 catabolism **—하다** dissimilate

이화 수분 異花受粉 〖식물〗 cross-pollination **—하다** cross-pollinate

이화 수정 異化受精 〖식물〗 cross-fertilization ; allogamy **—하다** cross-fertilize

이화 작용 異化作用 〖생물·생리〗 dissimilation

이화학 理化學 physics and chemistry ; physico-chemistry ¶ 이화학의 physicochemical

— 교실 a science room ; a science theater **— 기계** physical and chemical appliances〔apparatus〕 **— 연구소** a physicchemical research institute

이환 罹患 ⇨ 이병

이환 耳環 an earring ⇨ 귀엣고리

이회 二回 twice ; two times ¶ 제2회의 the second // 1일 2회 twice a day // 주 2회 twice a week ; semiweekly // 월 2회 twice a month ; semimonthly // 연 2회 semiannually

***이후 以後** after this ; henceforth ; in the future ; hereafter ; from now〔this time, today〕 on ¶ 그 이후 since then ; after that time ; afterward(s) ; thereafter // 그 이후에 생긴 일 subsequent events // 종전 이후 벌써 50년이 되었다 It is already fifty years〔Fifty years have already passed〕 since the end of the war.

익곡 溺谷 〖지리〗 a drowned valley

익년 翌年 the following〔succeeding〕 year ; the next year

‡**익다** ① [과일·기회 따위가] ripe ; be〔get, grow, become〕 ripe ; mellow ; mature ¶ 익은 ripe ; mature ; mellow // 익지 않은 unripe ; green // 너무 익은 overripe // 공격의 기회가 익다 be ripe for the assault // 사과가 딸 만큼 익었다 The apples were ripe enough to be picked.

② [익숙하다] be〔get, become〕 used 〔accustomed, inured, habituated〕《to》 ; be familiar 《with》 ; be experienced 《in》 ; get〔be〕 skilled 《in》 ; become skillful ¶ 익은 accustomed ; practiced ; familiar ; experienced // 익지 않은 unaccustomed ; new ; unfamiliar ; unexperienced // 눈에 익은 얼굴 a familiar face // 귀에 익은 벗의 목소리 the familiar voice of one's companions // 익은 솜씨로 with

experienced hands ; with clever hands ; skillfully // 눈〔귀〕에 익다 be accustomed to see〔hear〕; get used to seeing〔hearing〕// 거친 일에 익다 be inured to drudgery // 그는 도시 생활에 익지 않았다 He is unused〔unaccustomed〕 to city life.
③ [음식이] be〔get〕 cooked ; be done ¶ 잘 익은 well-done ; well-cooked // 너무 익다 be overdone ; be cooked too much // 알맞게 익다 be done to a turn // 이것은 잘 익지 않았다 This is only half boiled〔done〕./This is underdone.
④ [장·술이] become seasoned ; be matured ; ferment ; mature ; age
익은 밥먹고 선소리한다 〔속담〕 Eat well-done rice and say half-baked things. /Talk immaturely〔foolishly〕.
벼는 익을 수록 머리를 숙인다 〔속담〕 The boughs that bear most hang lowest.

익더귀 〖새〗 the female Asiatic sparrow hawk

*__익명 匿名__ anonymity ; pseudonymous names ¶ 익명의 anonymous // 익명으로 anonymously // 익명의 편지 an anonymous letter // 익명으로 기고하다 contribute to 《a magazine》 anonymously
—광고 a blind advertisement **—기부** anonymous contributions **—기증** an anonymous gift **—비평** unsigned criticism **—사원** a silent partner **—자** an incognito ; an anonym **—작가** an anonym ; an anonymous author〔writer〕 **—조합** an anonymous association **—투고** an unsigned〔anonymous〕 contribution **—투서** an anonymous letter **—투표** a secret ballot

익모초 益母草 〖식물〗 a motherwort ; Leonurus sibiricus (학명)

익반죽하다 knead flour with hot water

:익사 溺死 (death from) drowning **—하다** be drowned (to death) ¶ 그는 수영 중에 익사했다 He was drowned while bathing. // 그는 익사할 뻔했다 He was near being drowned.
—자 a drowned person ; a case of drowning **—체** the body of a drowned person

*__익살__ drollery ; waggishness ; jocularity ; pleasantry ; comicality ; clownery ; a joke ; a jest ; humor ¶ 익살 떨다〔부리다, 피우다〕 crack jokes ; jest ; talk humorously ; be comical ; play the fool // 익살스럽다 be funny〔waggish, facetious, comical, clownish〕; droll // 익살스럽게 이야기하다 speak humorously // 원숭이가 자전거 탄 것이 참 익살스러웠다 The monkey looked so funny on the bicycle. // 그는 언제나 익살을 부린다 He is always clowning〔having his joke〕.
—꾼 a jokester ; a wag ; a funnyman ; a humorist ; a buffoon ; a clown ; a harlequin ; a comic ; a comedian

익수 **—手** an old hand ; a skilled person

†**익숙하다** [능숙] (be) skilled〔experienced, practiced〕; skillful ; be good 《at》; be a good hand at ; [잘 알다] (be) familiar ; be well acquainted 《with》; be well versed 《in》; be at home in ¶ 익숙한 일 a familiar job // 익숙하지 않은 장사 an unfamiliar business // 미국 사정에 익숙한 사람 a man familiar with things American // 익숙한 손으로 with a practiced hand // 이 길에 익숙하오 Do you know this road well? // 곧 익숙해질 것이다. You'll soon get used to it. // 지금은 이 고을에 익숙해졌다 I'm used to this town by now. // 그는 그런 일에는 익숙하다 He is a practiced hand〔quite experienced〕 in such things. // 영어에 점점 익숙해지는 것 같다 I think I'm getting better and better in English.

익숙히 well ; with skill ; skil(l)fully ; proficiently ; adroitly ; expertly ; with sure〔practiced〕 hand ; like an old-timer〔a veteran〕

익스프레셔니즘 expressionism ⇨ 표현

익애 溺愛 dotage **—하다** dote upon ; love 《a person》 to idolatry ; lavish one's love upon

익야 翌夜 the next〔following〕 evening〔night〕

익우 益友 a good companion ; a useful friend ¶ 익우를 고르다 choose one's companions from among worthy people

익월 翌月 the next month ; the following〔ensuing〕 month

익은이 a well boiled piece of meat

익일 翌日 the next〔following, succeeding〕 day ¶ 편지를 낸 익일 그는 도착하였다 He arrived the day after the letter was posted.

익장 翼長 〖항공〗 the wingspan ; the wingspread

익조 益鳥 a beneficial〔useful〕 bird

익충 益蟲 a useful〔beneficial〕 insect

익히 ⇨ 익숙히 ¶ 익히 알다 know well〔fully, thoroughly〕; be well aware〔informed〕 of 《a fact》; be familiar〔well acquainted〕 with 《a matter》; be at home in〔on〕 // 이 점은 여러분도 익히 알고 있을 줄 압니다 I think you are all well aware of it.

†**익히다** ① [과일을] make ripe ; ripen ; mature ; mellow ; [술·간장을] brew ; ferment ; mature ; age 《soysauce, wine》; [음식을] cook ; boil ¶ 선 과일을 익히다 ripen green fruit // 술을 익히다 brew rice wine // 감자를 익히다 boil potatoes // 고기를 잘 익히다 get the meat well done
② [익숙] make oneself familiar with ; acquaint oneself with ; accustom oneself to ; habituate oneself to ; learn (by heart) ; practice ¶ 귀를 익히다 train the ear // 자동차 운전을 익히다 learn how to drive a car // 영어 회화를 익히다 practice

English conversation // 몸을 추위에 익히다 inure oneself to cold // 영화는 영어 회화를 익히는 데 좋다 Movies give you good practice in learning English.

인 仁 perfect virtue ; selflessness ; humanity ; humaneness ; goodness ; goodwill ; benevolence ; charity ¶ 인의예지신(仁義禮知信) benevolence, righteousness, propriety, wisdom and sincerity // 자기를 희생하며 인을 이루다 sacrifice oneself for the good of others

인 印 a seal ; a stamp

인 燐 〖화학〗 phosphorus ¶ 인의 phosphorus ; phosphoric

인 寅 [인방] the Direction of the Tiger 《northeast-by-east》 ; [인시] the Watch of the Tiger ; the 3rd of the 12 double-hours

-인 人 a man ; a person
문화— a cultured man 한국— a Korean

인가 人家 a house ; a dwelling house ; a human habitation ¶ 인가가 드물다 be sparsely-populated // 인가가 많다 be crowded with houses ; be thickly inhabited

인가 隣家 a neighboring〔an adjoining〕 house ; a neighbor's ; the next door

인가 認可 confirmation ; affirmation ; authorization ; approval ; permission ; sanction —하다 sanction ; authorize ; give a permit ¶ 인가된 학교 an authorized〔accredited〕 school // 인가를 받다 obtain〔secure〕 sanction〔authorization〕 ; get〔take out〕 a license // 경찰에 인가를 신청하다 apply for the approval of the police authorities
— 영업 a licensed business — 증서 a certificate ; a permit ; a license ; written authority

인가 印加 〖전기〗 impression —하다 impress
— 전압 impressed〔applied〕 voltage ; impressed electromotive force

인가난 人— a dearth〔shortage〕 of qualified people

인각 印刻 carving ; engraving —하다 carve ; engrave
—사 a seal engraver

†인간 人間 a human being ; a man ; a mortal ; [인류] man ; mankind ; humanity ¶ 인간의 human ; mortal // 인간 도처에 유청산이라 Opportunity awaits a man everywhere. // 인간 만사 새옹지마(塞翁之馬)라 Inscrutable are the ways of Heaven. // 그는 인간이 되지 않았다 He is a depraved character. // 인간은 만물의 영장이다 Man is lord of creation. // 그들도 인간이다 They are human beings even as we are.
— 개조 reform in humanity —계 the world of mortals ; the terrestrial world —고 (common) sufferings of man ; human sufferings ; the bitterness of life — 고락 the delights and sorrows of life — 관계 human relations — 국보 a living national treasure — 기계 a human machine — 도크 a clinical survey 《of the aged and middle-aged》 ; a complete physical examination ; a medical check-up 《미》 ¶ 인간 도크에 들어가다 be in hospital〔get oneself hospitalized〕 to undergo a complete physical examination — 문화재 human cultural assets — 미(味) (touches of) humanity ; a human touch ; humanity ; humaneness — 사회 human society ; the community of men —성 human nature ; humanity — 송충 a human caterpillar ; an illegal tree-feller —애 human love — 존중 respecting man's life and dignity — 중심주의 anthropocentricism — 탐구 the study of man — 폭탄〔어뢰〕 a human bomb〔torpedo〕 — 혐오 misanthropy ; misanthropism

인간화 人間化 humanization —하다 humanize ; make human
비— dehumanization ¶ 비인간화하다 dehumanize

인감 印鑑 a seal-impression ; a specimen impression of one's seal
— 도장 one's legal〔registered〕 seal — 신고〔계〕 the registration of a seal impression ¶ 인감계를 하다 have one's seal impression registered — 증명 a certificate of one's seal impression

인갑 鱗甲 ① [비늘과 껍데기] a scale and a shell ② [비늘 모양의 껍데기] a scale armor ; a scutum (동물) ¶ 인갑이 있는 (동물) scutate ; scutellate

인건비 人件費 personnel expenses 〔expenditure〕 ; labor cost ; wages

인걸 人傑 a distinguished person ; an eminent man〔character〕

†인격 人格 personality ; character ¶ 인격적 감화 moral influence // 인격을 함양하다 build up one's character // 인격을 존중하다〔무시하다〕 respect〔disregard〕 《a person's》 personality // 그것은 인격 문제이다 It's a question touching my honor.
— 교육〔양성〕 character building ; formation of character —권 personal rights — 문제 a matter of personality — 분열 dissociation〔division, disintegration〕 of a personality — 상실 depersonalization —자 a man of character —주의 personalism —화 impersonation ; personification
다중— multiple personality 무— impersonality 이중— a double personality 전— one's whole personality 비—화 depersonalization

인견 引見 —하다 receive (in audience) ; grant 《a person》 an interview ; give audience 《to a person》 ¶ 내객을 인견하다 receive callers

인견 人絹 artificial silk ; rayon
—사 rayon yarn

인경 a large brass gong used as a curfew bell ¶ 인경을 치다 toll the curfew

인경 隣境 [이웃과의 경계] a boundary ; a border ; [이웃지방] a vicinity ; a vicinage ; environs ; a neighborhood ¶ 서울의 남쪽 인경 the Southern environs of *Seoul* // 서울과 그 인경의 사람들 people in *Seoul* and its vicinity

인계 引繼 handing over 《one's duties》; taking over 《another's duties》; transfer of business ; transfer of control〔administration〕; succession 《to》 **—하다** hand over 《one's duties to》; take over 《another's duties》; transfer 《one's business to》 ¶ 사무를 인계받다 take over the official duties

인고 忍苦 endurance ; stoicism ¶ 인고의 생애 a stoic life

인골 人骨 a human bone

*__인공 人工__ art ; human skill ; human work ¶ 자연과 인공 nature and art // 인공의 artificial ; unnatural // 인공적으로 artificially // 인공을 가하다 work 《on》; improve by human skill // 인공 호흡이 시행되었다 Artificial respiration was tried upon him. // 자연계에는 인공으로 모방할 수 없는 것이 많다 There are many things in nature which defy human ingenuity to imitate them.

— 감미료 artificial sweetening **— 강우** rainmaking ; artificial rain **— 건조** 〖토목〗 artificial seasoning ¶ 인공 건조재 artificially seasoned〔kiln-dried〕 wood **— 두뇌** a mechanical brain **— 두뇌학** cybernetics **—물** an artifact **—미** man-created beauty **— 배양** artificial culture **— 부화** artificial incubation **— 수정** a test-tube insemination **— 수정아** a test-tube baby **— 수태** artificial conception **— 영양** artificial feeding ; bottle-feeding ¶ 인공 영양의 유아 a bottle-fed baby **— 위성** an artificial satellite ; an earth satellite **— 유산** (induced) abortion **— 일광** artificial daylight〔sunlight〕 **— 접종** artificial infection **— 진주** an artificial〔imitation〕 pearl **— 태양등** an artificial sunlight〔daylight〕 lamp ; a mercury〔vapor〕 lamp **— 통풍** artificial draft **— 피임법** artificial contraception **—항** an artificial harbor **— 향료** synthetic perfumes **— 혜성** an artificial comet **— 호흡** artificial breathing〔respiration〕 **— 호흡기** an artificial respiratory machine〔apparatus〕; a pulmotor **— 혹성** a man-made planet

인과 因果 [원인·결과] cause and effect ; [응보] retribution ¶ 피할 길 없는 인과 inevitable retribution // 인과는 돌고 돈다 The wheel is come to full circle. 《속》

— 관계 a causal sequence〔nexus〕; dependence of effect on cause ; causal relation〔dependence, chain〕; the interactions〔relation〕 of cause and effect ; causation ; causality **—성** causality **—율** the law of cause and effect ; causality ; the law〔principle〕 of causality〔causation〕 **—응보** a reward in accordance with a deed ; retributive justice in the universe ; retribution ; karma (윤회) ¶ 이것은 그의 청년 시대의 부절제와 방종의 인과응보다 He is only reaping what he has sown in his youth of uncontrolled vice and licentiousness.

인광 燐光 phosphorescence ¶ 인광을 발하다 emit phosphorescence

인광 燐鑛 〖광석〗 phosphate ore〔rock〕 **—체** a phosphorescent body

인교 隣交 friendly〔intimate〕 relations with one's neighbors ; friendship〔intimacy〕 with a neighboring country ; good neighborly relations 《with》

— 정책 a good neighbor policy

†**인구 人口** population ¶ 인구가 조밀〔희박〕한 지역 a densely〔sparsely〕populated district // 인구 100만의 도시 a city with a population of one million // 인구의 증가〔감소〕 an increase〔a decrease〕 in population // 인구 조사를 하다 take a census of the population // 미국 인구가 얼마나 되는지 아십니까 Do you know what the USA population is ?

— 과소 underpopulation **— 과잉** overcrowding ; congestion of population ¶ 인구 과잉 지역 an overpopulated〔overpeopled, overcrowded〕 district ; a congested area **— 동태** the movement of population **— 동태〔정태〕 통계** dynamic〔static〕 statistics of population **— 문제** the population problem ¶ 인구 문제 연구소 a population research institute **— 밀도** density of population ; population density **— 부양력** 《the land's》 capacity to support the population **— 정책** population policy **— 조사** a census **— 증가율** the rate of increase in population **— 통계** vital statistics **— 통계학** demography **— 폭발** (a) population explosion **과잉 —** surplus〔excess, overflowing〕 population **노동 —** the labor population 《of *Seoul*》 **부동 —** a floating population **적정 —** an optimum population

인구어 印歐語 Indo-European language

인국 隣國 a neighboring country〔province (국내의)〕 ¶ 인국간의 우의 relations of good neighborhood

인군 仁君 a benevolent〔gracious, munificent〕 sovereign〔ruler〕; a gracious lord ¶ 세종 대왕은 인군이었다 King *Sejong* was noted for his munificence.

*__인권 人權__ the rights of man ; human〔personal〕 rights ¶ 인권을 유린하다 trample upon human rights // 인권을 침해당했다고 진술하다 allege encroachment upon personal rights

— 문제 a question affecting human rights **— 선언** the Declaration of Human Rights **— 옹호** safeguarding〔defending〕

human rights〔civil liberty〕 ¶ 인권 옹호 위원 a commissioner for the Protection of Fundamental Human Rights // 인권 옹호 협회 the Civil Liberty Association // 인권 옹호 활동 civil liberty activities — **유린** an outrage upon personal rights **기본적** — the fundamental human rights

:**인근 隣近** the neighborhood ; the vicinity ¶ 인근의 neighboring ; nearby

인금 人— one's personality ; one's personal worth ¶ 인금이 잘나다 have a good personality ; have capability // 인금이 못나다 be worthless〔useless〕

†**인기 人氣** popularity ; popular favor ; public interest ¶ 인기 있는 popular ; favorite // 인기가 없는 unpopular // 인기를 얻다 gain in public favor ; win popularity // 인기가 있다 be popular ; enjoy popularity ; be in favor // 인기가 떨어지다 lose〔fall in〕 popularity // 인기를 회복하다 recover one's popularity // 그는 갑작스레 인기를 얻었다 He grew rapidly into favor. // 그는 동료 사이에 대단히 인기가 있었다 He enjoyed popularity with 〔among〕 his fellow workers.

— **경쟁** a popularity contest — **배우** a star ; a popular actor ; a box-office star ; a stage favorite — **선수** a star player — **소설** a sensational〔catching〕 novel — **연기자** a show stopper — **작가** a popular〔star〕 writer —**주(株)** active 〔popular〕 stocks ; blue chips — **투표** a popularity〔straw〕 vote

인기척 an indication of a person being around ¶ 인기척이 있다 show indications of people being around〔approaching〕 // 누가 따라 오는 인기척이 있다 I hear someone following me. // 그 집에는 인기척이 없었다 The house showed no signs of life.

인꼭지 印— the handle of a seal

인끈 印— the cord attached to the handle of a seal ; a seal-chain

인날 人— the seventh of January (in the lunar calendar)

인내 人— the smell〔body odor〕 of a human being

:**인내 忍耐** patience ; perseverance ; endurance ; fortitude

> 참고 **patience**는 일반적인 말 **perseverance**는 곤란 장애를 넘어서 적극적으로 행동하는 의미를 포함한다 **endurance**는 고통을 이겨내는 능력을 뜻한다

—**하다** endure ; put up with 《an insult》 ; bear patiently ; persevere 《in》 ; be patient with 《a person》 ¶ 인내성 있는 patient ; persevering ; stoical // 인내력 없는 lacking in patience // 인내할 수 없다 have no patience with 《a person》 // 그것을 하는 데는 많은 인내력이 필요하다 It requires much perseverance to do it.

인년 寅年 〖민속〗 the Year of the Tiger

인대 靭帶 〖해부〗 a ligament ¶ 인대의 ligamentous

— **관절** a syndesmosis 《*pl.* -ses》 — **장치** ligamentous apparatus

인더스 강 —**江** the Indus River

인덕 人德 natural〔innate〕 virtue ; being blessed with friendly people ¶ 그는 인덕이 있다 He has been blessed with people who are willing to help him.

인덕 仁德 benevolence ; goodness ; humanity

-**인데** it is and〔but〕 ¶ 이것은 내 책인데 보고 주게 This is my book, return it to me when you are through with it. // 좋은 곳인데 Why, it's a very nice place !

인덱스 [색인] an index ; a finding list ; [목차] a table of contents ; [지수] an index ; an indicator ; a measure

인덴트 indent ¶ 인덴트로 하다 〖인쇄〗 indent 《the first line》

인도 人道 ① [인륜] humanity ¶ 인도에 반한 죄 a crime against humanity // 인도적 humanitarian ; humane // 인도를 위해 for humanity's sake ; in the interest 〔cause〕 of humanity // 인도적 견지에서 from a humanitarian point of view // 인도를 짓밟다 commit an outrage on humanity // 인도에 어긋나다 be contrary to humanity ; be inhumane

② [보도] a pavement 《영》 ; a sidewalk 《미》 ; a footpath

—**교(橋)** a footbridge —**교(敎)** the religion of humanity — **문제** a question touching〔affecting〕 humanity — **주의** humanitarianism ; humanism — **주의자** a humanist

:**인도 引渡** delivery (of goods) ; transfer (of property) ; surrender (죄인의) ; extradition (외국으로부터 죄인을) —**하다** deliver ; transfer ; turn〔hand〕 over ¶ 상품의 인도 the delivery of goods // 인도받다 take delivery of 《a thing》 from 《a person》 // 재산을 인도하다 transfer one's property 《to》 // 시체를 유족에게 인도하다 deliver 《a person's》 body to his family // 도둑을 경찰에 인도하다 hand〔turn〕 over a thief to the police

— **부족** short delivery —**식** a hand-over ceremony —**일** a settlement〔delivery〕 day — **장소** a place of delivery —**증** a bill of parcels —**필** delivered ; transferred **도착항** — free port of destination **본선** — free on board 《F. O. B.》 **현장** — spot delivery **범인** — **조약** an extradition treaty

†**인도 引導** guidance (지도) ; introduction (선도) —**하다** guide ; introduce ; lead ¶ 그는 하녀의 인도를 받아 응접실에 들어갔다 He was guided by a maidservant into the drawing room.

—**자** a guide (안내자) ; an introducer (선도자) ; a backer (후원자)

인도 印度 India ¶ 인도의 Indian
— 공화국 the Republic of India —교 ⇨ 힌두교 —말 [공용의] Hindustani ; [북인도의] Hindi — 사람 an Indian ; [힌두교 신자] a Hindu —양 the Indian Ocean — 철학 Hindu〔Hindoo〕 philosophy 동〔서〕—제도 the East〔West〕 Indies

인도게르만 어족 —語族 Indo-Germanic languages

인도어 indoor
— 골프장 an indoor practice teeing ground ; a driving range — 스포츠 indoor sports

인도유럽 어족 —語族 the Indo-European family of languages

인도차이나 Indo-China

인동 忍冬 dried honeysuckle stems and leaves (used in herbalist remedies)
—초 a (Japanese) honeysuckle ; Lonicera japonica

인동광 燐銅鑛 〖광물〗 libethenite

인두 ① [바느질] a small heart-shaped iron with a long handle ② [납땜] a soldering iron
—질 ironing ; [납땜] soldering ¶ 인두질하다 iron ; solder —판 an ironing board

인두 咽頭 〖해부〗 the pharynx 《*pl.* ~es, pharynges》
—염 pharyngitis

인두겁 人— human mask ; human shape ; the covering of a human ¶ 그는 인두겁만 썼지 사람이 아니다 He is a brute in human form.

인두세 人頭稅 a poll tax ; capitation taxes ¶ 인두세를 받다 levy a poll tax

인둘리다 人— get dizzy from overcrowding ; feel sick〔faint〕 from the jostling of a crowd

인들 granted that it be〔is〕 ; even though it be〔is〕 ¶ 세살 먹은 아이인들 even a little child // 내일인들 늦으리 Tomorrow is never too late. // 그런 욕을 듣고는 아무리 착한 사람인들 가만 있겠느냐 Anyone, however gentle, would get angry at such abusive language.

†**인디언** an Indian ; a Red Indian
아메리카 — an American Indian

인디오 an American India ; an Amerind

인력 人力 human power〔strength〕 ; manpower ; human agency (자연에 대하여) ¶ 인력으로 할 수 없다 be beyond the power of man ; be humanly impossible
— 감사 manpower inspection

인력 引力 gravitation (지구의) ; magnetism (자기의) ; attraction (물질간의) ¶ 인력의 법칙 the law of gravitation // 인력 있는 attractive ; magnetic // 조수의 간만은 달의 인력에 기인한다 The ebb and flow of the tide are due to the gravitation of the moon.
만유 — universal gravitation 모세관 — capillary attraction 반대 — counterattraction 지구 — terrestrial gravitation ; gravity

인력거 人力車 a rickshaw ¶ 인력거로 by rickshaw // 인력거로 가다 go by rickshaw // 인력거를 타다 take〔ride in〕 a rickshaw
—군 a rickshaw-man ; a rickshaw puller

인례 引例 a quotation ; a cited〔quoted〕 example —하다 give〔adduce〕 quotations

*****인류 人類** the human race ; human beings ; mankind ; man ¶ 인류의 human ; racial // 인류의 행복 the happiness of mankind ; human happiness ; man's happiness // 전 인류의 복지를 증진하다 promote the welfare of all mankind
— 발달사 the history of human progress —사 the history of man — 사회 human society —애 love for humanity〔mankind〕 — 역사 human history —학 anthropology ¶ 인류학상의 문제 an anthropological question // 인류 학자 an anthropologist // 문화 인류학 cultural anthropology // 자연〔형질〕 인류학 physical anthropology

인륜 人倫 [도덕] morality ; morals ; [인도] humanity ¶인륜을 어기다 transgress moral laws
— 도덕 ethics and morality

인마 人馬 men and horses ¶인마의 왕래 the traffic of men and horses // 인마가 함께 골짜기로 떨어졌다 They fell into the valley, men and horses.

인마궁 人馬宮 〖천문〗 the Archer ; Sagittarius

인마좌 人馬座 〖천문〗 the Centaur ; Centaurus

인망 人望 popularity ¶ 인망 있는 popular // 인망이 없는 unpopular // 인망이 높다 enjoy a high reputation // 인망을 얻다 win〔gain, attain, acquire〕 popularity ; become popular // 인망을 잃다 lose one's popularity ; forfeit people's esteem ; fall in popular favor〔public estimation〕
—가 a popular person〔character〕 ; a person of wide〔good〕 reputation ; an idol of the people

인면 人面 a human face ¶ 인면수심 a beast with a human face ; man in face but brute in mind

인멸 湮滅 extinction (자연적) ; destruction (고의적) —하다 be extinct (자연히) ; destroy〔do away with〕 (고의로) ¶ 증거를 인멸하다 destroy the proof ; stifle evidence

*****인명 人命** human life ; a life ¶인명의 손해 a loss of lives // 많은 인명을 희생하여 at a great sacrifice of life // 인명을 구조하여 표창받다 be given public recognition for saving lives // 인명을 구조하다 save a life // 인명에 관계되다 affect people's lives ; endanger life // 인명을 존중하지 않다 have no regard for human life // 위험에 빠진 인명을 구하다 rescue 《a person》 whose life is in danger // 그 광산 사고로 다수의 인명이 희생되었다 The mine accident cost

many lives〔took a terrible toll of lives〕.
인명 人名 a person's name
—록 a directory ; a Who's Who (서명)
—부 a roll ; a list of names ; a name list ; a directory — 사전 a biographical dictionary — 색인 the name index ; the index of persons
인모 鱗毛 〖식물〗 a ramentum 《pl. -ta》 ; 〖곤충〗 a scale hair
†인문 人文 human knowledge〔inquiry〕; civilization (of mankind) ; culture ; liberal arts ; the humanities ¶ 인문의 발달 the advance of civilization
— 과학 cultural sciences ; humane studies〔learning〕; Kulturwissenschaft 《도》
—주의 humanism —주의자 a humanist
— 지리 human geography ; anthropogeography —학부 a humanity faculty ; the school〔department〕 of humanities — 학파 the humanists
†인물 人物 [사람] a man ; a person ; an individual ; [인품] personality ; what one is ; [민완가] a man of ability ; [인격자] a man of character ; [작품중의] a character ¶ 위대한 인물 a great man〔mind, soul〕; a man of〔high〕 great caliber∥작은 인물 a low man ; a man of low caliber ∥위험 인물 a dangerous character∥(외교관으로서) 좋지 않은 인물 persona non grata 《라》∥인물을 양성하다 build character∥유명한 인물을 배출하다 turn out men of note∥인물을 보증하다 vouch for a person's character∥인물 본위로 결혼하다 marry for character∥어떤 인물입니까 What sort of a man is he ? ∥훌륭한 인물이다 He has a fine personality.
— 가난 a shortage〔dearth〕 of talented men — 묘사 character painting〔portrayal, portraiture〕; character sketch — 시험 a character〔personality〕 test — 양성 character building ; training of men of ability —평 personal criticism ¶ 인물평을 하다 make a character sketch 《of a person》 —화 a figure painting ; [초상화] a portrait — 화가 a portrait painter 등장 — dramatis personae ; (stage) characters ; the cast
인물 고사 人物考査 a character test 〔examination〕
인민 人民 the people ; [공중] the public ; citizens ¶ 인민의 권리 the people's rights ; the civil rights∥인민의 인민에 의한 인민을 위한 정치 a government of the people, by the people and for the people∥인민을 보호하다 protect the people
— 공사(公社) [중국의] a people's commune — 공화국 a people's republic — 광장 the People's Plaza —당 the People's Party — 민주주의 a people's democracy ¶ 인민 위원회 the Council of People's Commissars∥외교 인민 위원 the People's Commissary for Foreign Affairs — 재판 a people's court ; a kangaroo court — 전선 the people's〔popular〕 front — 정부 the people's government — 정치 government by〔for, of〕 the people — 주권 popular sovereignty — 투표 a plebiscite ; a referendum 《pl. ~s, -da》
— 해방군 the People's Liberation Army
인박이다 fall〔get〕 into the habit of 《doing》; be addicted to ¶ 인박인 사람 a habitual user 《of》
인발 印— the imprint〔impression〕 of a seal
인방 隣邦 a neighboring〔an adjacent〕 country ¶ 인방의 친선 《relations of》 good neighborhood∥우리의 인방인 일본 Japan, our neighbor ; our neighbor Japan
인방 引枋 the lintel (of a door, window) ; a molding ; a cornice ; a baseboard
상— the upper lintel ; the crosspiece 중— a molding ; a cornice (halfway up a wall) 하— the lower lintel (of a door or window) ; the baseboard (of a room) ; skirting
인방 寅方 〖민속〗 the Direction of the Tiger〔northeast-by-east〕
인보 印譜 a collection of seal impressions
인보 隣保 a neighbo(u)r ; neighborhood ; a neighborhood association
—관(館) a settlement house — 사업 settlement〔social〕 work
인보이스 〖상업〗 an invoice
인복 人福 the good fortune to have kind friends
인본 印本 a printed book
*인본주의 人本主義 〖철학〗 humanism
—자 a humanist
인봉 印封 ① stamping with an official seal ② locking up an official seal after hours
—하다 stamp and seal ; lock up the seal
인부 人夫 a sundry laborer ; a coolie ; [운반부] a porter ; a carrier
— 십장 a foreman ; a coolie-master 선로 — a trainman ; a railway worker
인부 認否 approval or disapproval
인분 人糞 feces ; human excrements ; ordure ; night soil
— 비료 human manure ; night soil for manure
인비 人秘 secrecy of personal affairs
인비 燐肥 ⇨ 인산 (비료)
인비늘 人— scaly skin (on a human) ; skin peelings ; dandruff ; scurf
인사 人士 people ; men of society ; persons
†인사 人事 ① greetings ; salutation ; [절] a bow ; a kowtow ; a salutation ; [감사] thanks ; gratitude ; acknowledgment ; [예절] manners ; etiquette ; courtesy
—하다 greet ; salute ; make a bow ; thank ; acknowledge ; make a present (in acknowledgment) ¶ 인사하다 bow ;

make a bow《to a person》; make 〔drop〕 a curtsy (여자가) // 작별 인사를 하다 say good-bye // 인사를 받다 receive a bow《of one's student》// 정중히 인사하다 bow politely ; bow low // 모자를 벗고 인사하다 take one's hat off to《a person》// 고맙다고 인사하다 bow one's thanks ; express one's thanks〔gratitude〕《to》// 인사를 알다〔모르다〕 have good〔no〕 manners // 그렇게 하는 것은 인사가 아니다 It is bad manners to do so. // 그녀에게 인사말씀 전해주시오 Thank her for me. // 두분이 인사를 하셨습니까 Have you met each other? // 인사드리지 못했는데 제 이름은 김기수입니다 I don't think we've met yet. My name is *Kim kisu.* // 오늘은 격식을 차린 인사 따위는 집어치웁시다 Let's dispense with such formal exchanges today.

② [사람이 하는 일] human affairs ; what men can do ¶ 인사를 다하고 천명을 기다리다 do one's best and leave the rest to Providence

③ [직원 관계] personal affairs ; personnel

— **계장** a personnel manager —**과**〔**국, 부**〕 the section〔bureau, division〕 of personnel ; the personnel (affairs) section〔bureau, division〕 — **관리**〔**행정**〕 personnel management〔administration〕 —**권** the right of personnel management — **기록** a personnel record —**란** a personal column ; 'Personals' — **비밀** secrecy of personal affair — **상담란** a personal affairs column ; a human relations column ; an advice column — **상담소** a private affairs consultation office — **성** courteousness ; sociability — **소송** a personal suit — **위원회** the National Personnel Commission ; [일반적으로] a personnel committee — **이동** personnel changes ¶ 부장은 올해 대대적인 인사 이동이 있을 거라고 말했다 The manager was saying there are going to be some major personnel shifts this spring. —**장** a greeting card ; [전임·이전 따위의] a notice **작별** — a farewell address ; a valediction ; parting words ☞ ❰p. 1722❱

인사 교류 人事交流 an interchange of personnel《between》¶ 부처간의 인사 교류 interministerial personnel reshuffle

†**인사말 人事—** greetings ; compliments ; [식사(式辭)] an address

인사불성 人事不省 ① unconsciousness ; a coma ② having no sense of propriety ¶ 인사불성의 unconscious ; comatose ; senseless // 인사불성이 되다 become unconscious ; lose consciousness〔one's senses〕; pass out《미·속》

***인산 燐酸** 〖화학〗 phosphoric acid

— **비료** phosphatic fertilizer〔manure〕; superphosphate —**석회** phosphate of lime —**염** phosphate —**칼리** potassium phosphate — **칼슘** calcium phosphate

인산 因山 a state〔national〕 funeral

인산인해 人山人海 hordes of people ¶ 집 앞에 인산인해를 이루고 있다 A big crowd was gathered in front of the house.

인삼 人蔘 ginseng (used as a geriatric tonic)

***인상 人相** a look ; features ; personal appearance ; a cast of countenance ; physiognomy ¶ 천한 인상 a low cast of countenance // 인상이 좋지 않은 사내 a man of evil physiognomy ; an evil-looking man ; a hard-featured〔ill-favored〕 man // 인상을 보다 read〔judge〕 one's character by the face ; read one's countenance ; tell fortunes by physiognomy // 그는 부하 직원을 몹시 부려먹은 사람 같은 인상을 주었다 He struck me as a slave driver.

—**서** the description of one's looks ; a personal description ¶ 인상서와 부합하다 answer〔fit, meet〕 the description of a person —**학** physiognomy ; metoposcopy —**학자** a physiognomist

***인상 引上** ① [끌어 올림] pulling〔drawing〕 up —**하다** pull〔draw〕 up

② [가격 따위의] raising ; a raise ; (an) increase ; an upward revision —**하다** increase ; raise ; hike ; up《구》¶ 가격이 1,000원으로 올랐다 The price was raised to 1,000 *won.*

임금〔**물가**〕 — a raise〔rise, hike〕 in wages〔prices〕 **임금** — **요구** a demand 〔request〕 for higher wages〔a wage hike〕 **세금** — tax hike

‡**인상 印象** impression ; imprint ¶ 좋은 인상 a good〔favorable〕 impression // 깊은 인상 a deep〔profound〕 impression // 잊을 수 없는 인상 an unforgettable impression // 후기 인상파의 사람 the post impressionists // 인상적 impressive // 인상을 주다 give an impression ; make an impression《on a person》; impress《a person》// 인상을 받다 receive〔get〕 an impression // 인상을 남기다 leave an impression behind // 좋은〔깊은〕 인상을 주다 impress《a person》 favorably〔deeply〕; make a good〔deep〕 impression on《a person》// 그의 연설은 청중에게 깊은 인상을 주었다 His speech produced a deep impression on the audience. // 그의 인상이 깊이 남아 있다 His image is deeply impressed on my mind. // 그 시절의 인상은 조금도 안 남아 있다 I have no recollection of those days. / Nothing of those days remains in my memory.

—**주의** impressionism —**주의자** an impressionist —**파** the impressionist school《미》; the impressionists **첫**— the first impression ¶ 그의 첫인상이 나빴다 He made a bad first impression. // 한국의 첫인상은 어떻습니까 What is your first impression of Korea?

인사의 표현

① 만났을 때

¶ 오전 0시부터 정오까지의 인사 Good morning! / Morning! // 정오부터 저녁 시간(12시부터 업무 종료)까지의 인사 Good afternoon! / Afternoon! // 저녁 무렵(6시 이후 혹은 업무가 끝난 후)부터 자정까지의 인사 Good evening! / Evening!

② 아는 사이일 때

¶ 안녕 Hello [Hi]! / Hi there! (★오전·오후 관계없이 아주 친한 사이일 때) // 어떻게 지내니? How are you? // 가족들도 안녕하시지요? How's your family? // 어떻게 지내십니까? How's everything with you? // 요즈음 어떠십니까? How have you been lately?

③ 구면일 때

¶ 다시 만나서 반갑습니다. Good to see you (again)! / It's good [great] to see you! / How [Very] nice to see you (again). // 그래, 요즈음 어때? How's things? / How goes it with you? (★허물없는 사이에) // 좋아 보이네요. In good shape, are you. // 정말 오랜만입니다. Long time no see! / It's been a long time (since I saw you last). / I haven't seen you for a long time.

④ 헤어질 때

¶ 안녕. Good-by(e). / So long. (★허물없는 사이에 쓰고 보통 윗사람에게는 쓰지 않음.) / Good night. (★밤에 헤어질 때) // 또 뵙겠습니다. (I'll) See you again[later]. // 잘 가. (I'll) See you. // 조심해. Take care. // 이제 가봐야겠습니다. I'm afraid I'd better say good-bye [be going now].

⑤ 응답

¶ 잘 있어, 고마워. I'm fine, thank you. / Very well, and you. / Quite well, thank you. // 그럭저럭, 그저그래. So-so, thanks. / Mustn't grumble. / Can't complain. / Not so[too] bad. / Pretty fair. // 나는 아주 좋아. I'm extremely well, thank you. / I'm in excellent health, thank you. / I'm very well indeed, (thank you).

⑥ 안부를 전할 때

¶ 아버님 [어머님]께 안부 좀 전해 주십시오. Please say hello to your father [mother] for me. (★허물없는 사이에) / Please give my best regards[wishes] to your father[mother]. / Please remember me to your father[mother]. (★ 격식을 차릴 때)

⑦ 편지

¶ 여러분 안녕! Dear all. / Hi, everybody! // 사랑하는 …에게. Dear[My dear] Jane. / Dearest[My dearest] Judy. / Darling[My darling] Tom. (★ 사랑하는 연인 사이) / Dear Sir. / Dear Madam. (★받는 이를 확실히 모르는 곳에 보낼 때)

인상 鱗狀 ¶ 인상의 scale-like ; scaly ; squamous

인새 印璽 a royal seal

인색 吝嗇 stinginess ; parsimoniousness ; niggardliness **—하다** (be) stingy ; miserly ; tight-fisted ; close-fisted ; parsimonious ¶ 인색한 사람 a miser ; an old screw ; a tightwad 《속》 ; a stingy fellow ; a close-fisted fellow // 인색하게 굴지 마라 Don't be so stingy. // 우리 사장은 어찌나 인색한지 보너스 주는 일이 없다 My boss is so cheap that he never gives bonuses. // 그는 어찌나 인색한지 자선 단체에 땡전 한 푼 기부하지 않는다 He is so cheap that he never gives a penny to charities. // 그는 돈 쓰는 데에 인색하다 He keeps track of every penny he spends.

†**인생 人生** man's〔human〕 life ; life ; human existence ¶ 인생의 목적〔의의〕 the aim〔meaning〕 of life // 인생에 지치다 find life a bore // 인생을 낙관하다 take an optimistic〔a cheerful〕 view of life ; look on the bright side of life // 인생을 비관하다 take a pessimistic〔gloomy〕 view of life ; look on the dark side of life // 인생은 꿈이다 Life is but an empty dream. // 인생 무상 Red at morn, dead at eve. **—관** one's view of life ; one's theory 〔conception〕 of life ; an outlook on〔attitude toward〕 life **— 기록** a human document **— 문제** the problems of life **— 여로〔항로〕** life's journey ; the voyage 〔path〕 of life **— 철학** the philosophy of life **— 행로** the tenor〔path〕 of one's life ; one's course of life ; stages in a man's career

인생 겨우 오십 년 〖속담〗 Life is but a span.

인생은 뿌리없는 평초 〔속담〕 Life is a pilgrimage.
인생 칠십 고래희 〔관용〕 A man seldom lives to be seventy.
인서트 〖영화〗 an insert
인석 人石 the two stone statues before a (king's) grave
인석 茵席 mats ; woven-reed seats
—장이 a reed weaver ; a mat maker
인선 人選 the selection of a suitable person —하다 select a suitable person 《of》 ¶ 각료의 인선 the selection of Cabinet members // 후임은 목하 인선중이다 His successor is now under consideration. /They are now looking for his successor. // 인선난이다 The difficulty lies in the choice of men〔the personnel〕.
:인성 人性 human nature ; humanism ; human instinct (본능)
—론 Treatise of Human Nature —주의자 a humanist —학 ethology
인성 人聲 a human voice
인성 靭性 tenacity ¶ 인성의 tenacious ; tough
인성 燐性 ¶ 인성의 〖화학〗 phosphoric
인성만성 ① 〔군집〕 bustling ; crowded with people ; in a hubbub〔an uproar, a tumult〕 ② 〔혼미〕 losing consciousness ; dizzily ; passing out ; fainting —하다 (be) dizzying〔giddy, confused〕
인세 印稅 a royalty ; the stamp duty ¶ 저자에게 인세를 지불하다 pay the author a royalty 《on his work》 // 1할의 인세로 출판을 계약하다 contract for publication with 10 percent royalties
인솔 引率 —하다 lead ; command ; have in charge ¶ …에 인솔되어 under the command〔leadership〕 of 《a person》 ; led〔headed〕 by 《a person》
—자 a leader ; a person in charge ; a guide ; a captain
†인쇄 印刷 printing ; typography ; presswork —하다 print ; put into print ¶ 인쇄의 잘못 a typographical error ; a misprint // 인쇄에 붙이다 send 《a book》 to print // 인쇄가 선명하다〔나쁘다〕 It is clearly〔poorly〕 printed. // 인쇄중이다 It is in (the) press. // 그건 인쇄가 잘못된 것입니다 That's a typo.
—공 a pressman ; a printer —공장 a printing house ; a print shop —국 Printing Bureau —기 a printing machine ; a press —물 printed matter ; prints (미) —소 a printing house〔office, shop〕 —술 (the art of) printing ; typography —업 printing (business) —용지 printing paper —인 a printer ; a typographer —잉크 printing〔printer's〕 ink —체 문자 a print letter ; a disjoined〔printing〕 hand —판 a printing plate ; a press plate 삼색—법 the three-color process 수색(數色)동시 —법 stenochromy 착색 — colored printing
인수 人數 the number of persons ; numerical strength ¶ 대〔소〕 인수 a large〔small〕 number of people // 그들의 인수는 10명이었다 They were ten in number.
인수 印綬 the ribbon(s) on an official seal ; the seal-chain〔-cord〕
인수 引水 conducting water —하다 conduct water
인수 因數 〖수학〗 a factor
—분해 factorization ; resolution into factors ; factor analysis ¶ 인수 분해하다 solve〔resolve, break up〕 《a number》 into factors 소(素)— a prime〔common〕 factor
*인수 引受 〔부담·담당〕 undertaking ; charge ; 〔수락〕 acceptance ; 〔환어음의 보증〕 guaranty ; security —하다 undertake ; take charge of ; answer for ; hold oneself responsible for ; take over ; accept guarantee
—거절 non-acceptance ; dishonor —단 an underwriting syndicate —어음 an accepted〔acceptable〕 bill —은행 an accepting〔undertaking〕 bank —인 a guarantor ; a surety (보증자) ; a claimer ; a claimant (시체, 분실물의) 조건부〔단순〕 — qualified〔clean, absolute〕 acceptance
인순 因循 ① 〔머뭇거림〕 vacillation ; irresolution ; shilly-shally —하다 vacillate ; be irresolute ; shilly-shally ② 〔보수적임〕 conservatism —하다 be conservative
인술 仁術 a benevolent art ; the healing art ; the science of medicine ¶ 의술은 인술이다 Medicine is a benevolent art.
인슈트 〖야구〗 an inshoot
인슐린 〖약〗 insulin
—쇼크 insulin shock
인스턴트 instant 《coffee》 ¶
—식품 precooked food ; convenience food
인스피레이션 inspiration ¶ 인스피레이션을 얻다 get〔receive〕 inspiration 《from》 ; be inspired 《by》
인습 因習 convention ; conventionalism ; 〔전통〕 tradition ; 〔낡은 풍습〕 a long-established custom ; ¶ 인습적인 conventional ; traditional // 인습적 도덕 conventional morality // 인습을 지키다 follow a long usage // 인습을 타파하다 break a long-established usage ; do away with conventionalities // 그는 인습에 사로잡혀 있다 He is a slave to convention.
인시 寅時 the Watch of the Tiger ; the 3rd of the 12 double-hours (=the period between 3 : 00 and 5 : 00 a. m.) ; the 5th of the 24 hours (=3 : 30-4 : 30 a. m.)
인시류 鱗翅類 〖곤충〗 Lepidoptera (학명) ¶ 인시류의 곤충 the lepidopteron
:인식 認識 recognition ; cognizance ; 〔이

해] understanding **—하다** recognize ; cognize ; understand ; appreciate ¶ 옳게 인식하다 have a correct understanding 《of》; look at 《a matter》 in the right light ; show a true perception 《of》// 현상에 대한 인식이 결여되어 있다 They have little understanding of the present situation. // 그것은 현 정세에 대한 그의 인식 부족의 증거이다 It proves that he has little understanding of the present situation.
—력 cognitive faculty〔power〕 **—론** 『철학』 epistemology ; the theory of knowledge **—부족** lack of understanding 〔knowledge〕 **—비판** 『철학』 critique of cognition **—작용** 『철학·심리』 cognition **—표** 『군사』 an identification tag〔disk〕; a dog tag 《속》

인신 人身 the human body ; one's person **—공격** a personal attack〔criticism〕 **—매매** human〔flesh〕 traffic ; the slave trade ; traffic in human cargo **—보험법** the Protection of Personal Liberty Act ; the Habeas Corpus Act 《영》 **—보호 영장** a (writ of) habeas corpus

인신 人臣 a subject ⇨ 신하(臣下)

인심 人心 a man's mind〔heart〕; people's mind ; the hearts of the people ; the public mind ; popular sentiments ; public feeling ¶ 인심이 좋다 be good-hearted ; be genial ; be generous // 인심을 얻다 win the heart of the people // 인심을 살피다 perceive the drift of public sentiment // 항구의 인심은 대개 사납다 The people of a seaport town are usually rough-tempered.
—소관 dependence on one's mind ; a matter of consideration

인심 仁心 a benevolent heart ; kindheartedness ; benevolence ; humaneness

인아 人我 oneself and others
—일체 the unification〔integration〕 of oneself and others

인애 仁愛 a kind love ; humane affection

인양 引揚 pulling up ; salvage (난파선의) ; recovery (시체의) **—하다** pull up ; salvage ; recover ¶ 침몰선을 인양하다 salvage〔salve〕 a sunken ship
—작업 salvage work〔operations〕

***인어 人魚** a mermaid (암컷) ; a merman (수컷)

†**인연 因緣** [인과] cause and occasion ; karma ; fate ; fatality ; destiny ; [연분] tie ; affinity ; bond ; a relation ; [유래] origin ; history ¶ 이것도 인연이다 There is an act of providence. // 돈과는 인연이 없다 Money and I are strangers.
인연을 끊다 관용 break off relations ; cut a connection

인영 人影 [사람의 그림자] a human shadow ; the shadow of a person ; [사람의 모습] a figure ; a form

인영 人影 the imprint〔mark〕 of a seal

인욕 忍辱 fortitude ; forbearance ; endurance

:**인용 引用** quotation ; citation **—하다** quote 《from》; cite 《an instance》; refer to (참조)

> 참고 **quote** 그 사람의 이름을 밝히고 다른 사람의 말을 인용하다 **cite** 증거로서 저자 저서 절 제목 페이지 따위를 듦 내용은 인용하지 않는다

¶ 인용구의 출처를 밝히다 identify a quotation ; trace a quotation to its original source **—구〔문〕** a quotation **—부** a quotation mark **—서** reference books ; books referred to **—점** inverted commas

인용 認容 admission ; acknowledgment **—하다** acknowledge ; admit

***인원 人員** [사람의 수효] the number of persons ; [직원] the personnel ; the staff ¶ 인원 과잉이다 be overstaffed // 인원 부족이다 be understaffed〔undermanned〕; be short of hands // 인원을 줄이다〔늘리다〕 reduce〔increase〕 the personnel
—구성 personnel setup **—배치표** a personnel allotment table **—점호** a roll call ; the muster ¶ 인원 점호를 하다 call the roll ; hold a muster **—정리** a personnel cut〔reduction〕; a trimming of the personnel **가동 —** available hands

인원 人猿 [사람과 원숭이] men and apes
—동조설(同祖說) the theory of human descent from common ancestors with the apes

인위 人爲 human work ; human power 〔agency〕; artificiality ¶ 인위적 도태 『생물』 artificial selection // 인위적 artificial // 인위적으로 artificially ; by artificial means

인유 人乳 human milk

인유 引喩 an allusion **—하다** allude

인육 人肉 human flesh
—시장 a slave market ; a house of prostitution

***인의 仁義** benevolence and righteousness ; humanity and justice ¶ 인의 충효 humanity, justice, loyalty and filial piety

인일 寅日 『민속』 the Day of the Tiger

인자 因子 a factor
—분석 『심리』 factor analysis **가속도 —** 『경제』 an accelerator **유전 —** 『유전』 a factor ; a gene

***인자 仁慈** charity ; benevolence **—하다** (be) charitable ; benevolent ; gracious

인자 仁者 a benevolent person ; a man of goodwill

인자 人子 [아들] a son ; [예수] the Son of Man

인자 印字 printing ; typing ; [그 글자] a printed letter ; a typewritten letter
—기 ⇨ 타자기 **—전신기** a printing telegraph ; a teletype (writer)

:**인장 印章** a seal ; the imprint of a seal (인발) ¶ 인장을 위조하다 counterfeit a seal
—위조 forgery of a seal **—위조인** the

counterfeiter of a seal **위조** — a forged seal

인재 人材 a man of ability ; a competent person ; talent 《집합적》 ¶ 인재를 등용하다 open the offices to the talented // 천하의 인재를 모으다 attract all the talent of the world // 당신은 숨은 인재이다 You are a diamond in the rough.

— 등용 selection of fit persons for higher positions **—주의** the merit system

인재 印材 materials to make seals

인적 人的 (being) human ¶ 인적 자원 manpower ; human resources // 한국은 인적 자원이 풍부하다 Korea is rich in human resources.

— 손해 the loss of manpower

인적 人跡 human traces〔tracks, footsteps〕 ¶ 인적이 끊어진 uninhabited ; out-of-the-way ; desolate

인절미 cake made from glutinous rice

:인접 隣接 contiguity ; adjacency **—하다** be contiguous 《to》 ; lie adjacent 《to》 ; be〔lie, stand〕 close by ¶ 인접한 마을 neighboring towns and villages

—지 adjacent〔adjoining〕 land ; an adjacent area ; the immediate vicinity

†인정 人情 ① human desire〔passions〕 ; human nature
② humaneness ; sympathy ; humanity ¶ 따뜻한 인정 the milk of human kindness // 인정 있는 사람 a warm〔tender-hearted〕 person // 인정이 넘치는 친절 heart-warming hospitality // 인정이 있다 be humane ; be kind ; be sympathetic ; have a feeling heart // 인정스럽다 be warm-hearted ; be kindhearted ; be tender-hearted ; be sympathetic ; be considerate ; be thoughtful // 인정에 끌리다 be moved to pity ; be prompted by pity ; be moved with compassion ; be touched with pity // 인정을 알다 know the secrets of the human heart ; have a knowledge of human nature // 그의 행동은 인정에 어긋난다 His conduct goes against everything human. // 그러한 일은 인정상 할 수 없다 I can't find it in my heart to do so. // 그렇게 생각하는 것이 인정이다 It is human nature to think so. /It is quite natural that one should think so. // 쾌락을 추구하는 것이 인정이다 The desire to pursue pleasure is but natural to the human mind. // 그것이 인정이다 That's (what is called) human nature. // 어디에 가나 인정에는 변함이 없다 Human nature is the same everywhere〔all over〕. // 세상 인정은 얼음장같이 차다 The public are cold as ice to me. // 어디 가나 인정은 있다 People aren't as bad as they're made out to be. // 인정머리라곤 How cold can you get ?

—극 a human-nature play **—미** a human touch ; human appeal ; humanity **— 풍속** the customs and manners 《of a people》

인정이 없다 관용 be unfeeling ; be cold-hearted ; be heartless ; be inhumane

인정 仁政 benevolent government〔administration, rule〕 ¶ 인정을 베풀다 govern with benevolence

†인정 認定 recognition (승인) ; acknowledgment ; confirmation (확인) ; approval ; sanction ; authorization (공인·인증) **—하다** recognize ; acknowledge ; admit ; confirm ; approve ; authorize

> 참고 **acknowledge** 내심으로 인정하고 있는 사실을 못마땅하나마 인정하다 (보기) They have acknowledged defeat. (그들은 드디어 패배를 인정하였다)
> **admit** 외부의 힘에 의하여 또는 자기의 양심이나 판단에 따라 사실을 인정하다

¶ 시인으로 인정을 받다 be acknowledged as a poet // 무죄로 인정하다 presume 《a person's》 innocence ; presume 《a person》 to be innocent // 그 배우는 곧 일반의 인정을 받게 되었다 The actor soon won recognition from the public.

— 사채 an authorized bond **—서** a certificate ; a written recognition 《of championship》 **문교부 — 교과서** textbooks authorized by the Ministry of Education

인정법 人定法 〖법〗 a man-made law ; an enactment

인정 신문 人定訊問 identity questioning ; an identity interrogation **—하다** question〔interrogate〕 the identity 《of the accused》

인제 now ; after such a long time ; from now〔this time〕 on ¶ 인제라도 even now ; still // 인제라도 늦지 않다 It is not too late to do so. // 인제 그렇게 안 하겠습니다 I will never do so in the future. // 인제 와서 그런 말 해야 소용없다 There's no use saying such a thing now〔when it's too late〕. // 인제야 그이가 왔다 He has just come at long last.

:인조 人造 human work ; artificiality ¶ 인조의 artificial ; imitation (모조) ; synthetic (합성)

—견(사) artificial〔art, synthetic〕 silk〔thread〕 ; rayon (yarn) 《미》 **— 고무** synthetic rubber **—금** imitation gold ; Dutch metal ; oroide **—미(米)** artificial〔man-made, imitation〕 rice **— 버터** margarin(e) ; artificial butter **— 비료** an artificial fertilizer〔manure〕 **—빙** artificial ice **— 상아(석)** imitation ivory〔stone〕 **— 석유** synthetic oil〔petroleum〕 **— 섬유** a synthetic〔chemical〕 textile ; staple fiber **—육** synthetic meat **— 인간** a man-made〔mechanical〕 man ; a robot **— 진주** an artificial〔an imitation, a false〕 pearl **— 피혁** synthetic〔American〕 leather **—호** an artificial lake

†인종 人種 a human race ; human species

¶ 인종적 racial ; ethnological (인종학상의) ; ethnical // 인종적 감정 racial〔color〕 feeling // 인종 차별 racial discrimination ; segregation // 인종적 편견 a racial〔color〕 prejudice
— 개량 improvement of the race ; the production of fine (human) offspring ; racial eugenics — 문제 the race problem ; the color question〔problem, issue〕
— 차별주의 racism — 차별주의자 a racist ; an advocate of racial discrimination — 평등 racial equality — 폭동 a race〔color〕 riot —학 ethnology ; the science of races 백색 — the white race〔people〕 황색 — the oriental race〔people〕 흑색 — the Negro race〔people〕

인종 忍從 submission ; self-surrender ; resignation —하다 submit to ; resign oneself to

인주 印朱 red stamping ink
—함 an inkpad case

인주머니 印— a seal-bag ; a container for a seal

인줄 人— ropes hung across the door to guard against evil spirits

인중 人中 philtrum ; dimple in the upper lip

인중독 燐中毒 phosphorous poisoning ; phosphorism

인즉 to speak of ; speaking of ; as for ¶ 사실인즉 in fact ; to tell the truth // 글씨인즉 명필이다 When it comes to the handwriting, that is excellent. // 말인즉 옳소 What he says is true.

-인즉 since〔as〕 it is ⇨ -인지라(서)

인증 引證 quotation ; citation —하다 quote《a fact》; cite ; adduce《an instance》

인증 認證 certification ; authentication ; validation ; confirmation —하다 certify ; authenticate ; attest ; confirm
—관 an attestation official —식 an (Imperial) attestation ceremony ; an investiture ceremony

인증 人證 the testimony of a witness

인지 人智 human knowledge〔intelligence〕 ¶ 인지의 발달 the advancement of human knowledge // 인지가 미치지 않는 beyond human knowledge

†인지 印紙 a (paper) stamp ¶ 인지를 첨부하다 affix a stamp《to》; put a stamp《on》; stamp《a paper》// 인지로 납부하다 pay in stamps // 500원짜리 인지를 붙이시오 Put a five hundred *won* stamp on it.
— 세법 the Stamp Act — 수입 stamp revenue — 판매소 a stampseller's office ; [게시] Stamps on sale ; Stamps sold here. 수입 — a revenue stamp ; fiscal stamp

*인지 認知 (legal) recognition ; acknowledgment —하다 recognize (legally) ; acknowledge ¶ 사생아를 인지하다 recognize an illegitimate child (as one's own)

-인지 [막연한 의문] I wonder《if, whether, how, what, when, who, where》¶ 도대체 그런 일이 있을 수 있는지 How can that be, I wonder ? // 그가 누구인지 잘 모르겠다 I wonder who he is.

-인지라(서) as it is ; since it is ¶ 그는 어린애인지라 보살펴 주어야 한다 As he is a young boy, he needs looking after. // 자네가 묻는 것인지라 이야기하지 Since you ask, I will tell you.

인지상정 人之常情 human nature ; humaneness ; humanity

*인질 人質 a hostage ; a (personal) security ¶ 인질로 잡다 take〔hold〕《a person》 as a hostage

인찰지 印札紙 ruled〔lined〕 paper

인책 引責 —하다 take the responsibility on oneself ; hold oneself responsible ; assume〔shoulder〕 the responsibility ¶ 인책 사임하다 assume the responsibility and resign one's post

*인척 姻戚 a relative〔relation〕 by marriage ; a relative on one's mother's side ; one's in-law(s)《미》¶ 인척 관계이다 be related by marriage // 당신은 대통령의 인척이 됩니까 Are you related to the president ? // 나는 대통령과 아무 인척 관계도 아니다 I'm no relation to the president.

*인체 人體 the human body ; (human) flesh ¶ 인체에 위해를 가하다 inflict a bodily injury on《a person》// 인체에 영향을 끼치다 affect the human body
— 구조 the structure of the human body — 기생충 a human parasite — 모형 an anatomical model of the human body ; [인형] a lay figure ; a manikin — 실험 an experiment on a human body ; a living body test — 측정 anthropometry — 학 somatology — 해부학 human anatomy — 화석 an anthropolite ; an anthropolith

인촌 隣村 the neighboring village

인축 人畜 man and beast ; humans and animals ¶ 인축 무해 No harm to man and beast

인출 引出 [예금 따위의] withdrawal ; drawing out —하다 draw out《from》; withdraw ¶ 은행에서 저금을 인출하다 withdraw one's savings from the bank // 은행에서 수표로 10만원을 인출하다 draw a check on the bank for 100,000 *won*
— 초과 overdraft 특별 —권 special drawing rights《SDR》

†인치 an inch《in.》¶ 6인치 반 six and a half inches ; six inches and a half

인치 引致 taking《a person》 into custody —하다 take《a person》 into custody ¶ 운전수는 본서로 인치되어 취조를 받았다 The driver was taken to the police station and questioned.

인칭 人稱 〖문법〗 grammatical person ¶ 제 1〔2, 3〕 인칭 the first〔second, third〕 person

— 대명사 a personal pronoun
인커브 〖야구〗 an incurve
인터내셔널 international
—리즘 internationalism
인터뷰 an interview — 하다 interview 《a person》; have an interview 《with》 ¶ 인터뷰하는 사람 an interviewer // 인터뷰받는 사람 an interviewee
인터체인지 an interchange
인터폰 an interphone ; an intercom
인터폴 the Interpol (국제 형사 경찰 기구)
인턴 [수련의] an intern ¶ 인턴으로 근무하다 intern 《at》; serve one's internship 《at》
— 제도 the internship system
인테르 〖인쇄〗 lead ⇨ 공목
인텔리(겐치아) an intellectual ; an educated man ; a highbrow 《미·구》; [경멸적] an egghead 《미》; [총칭] the intelligentsia ; the intellectuals ¶ 창백한 인텔리 a palefaced intellectual // 그는 인텔리다 He is an intellectual.
인토네이션 〖음성〗 intonation
인파 人波 a surging crowd (of people) ¶ 인파가 밀려왔다 The crowd surged in.
인파이터 〖권투〗 an infighter
인편 人便 (through) the agency of a person ¶ 인편으로 by〔through〕 a person // 인편으로 보내다 send 《a thing》 by someone
인품 人品 personality ; character ¶ 인품이 좋다 have a fine personality〔looking〕 // 인품이 좋은 사람 a man of respectable appearance // 인품이 야비하다 have a coarse personality
:인플레(이션) 〖경제〗 inflation ¶ 인플레를 초래하다 cause inflation // 인플레를 막다 check〔curb, counter, curtail〕 inflation // 인플레를 피하다 avoid inflation // 인플레 경향의 완만화 slowdown of the inflationary trend
— 경기 an inflation boom — 경향 an inflationary trend〔tendency〕 — 대책 anti-inflation(ary) measures — 상태 an inflationary situation — 정책 an inflation policy 악성 — vicious〔unsound〕 inflation 잠행성 — creeping inflation
인플루엔자 〖의학〗 influenza ; grippe ; flu 《속》 ¶ 인플루엔자에 걸리다 suffer from influenza
인피 人皮 human skin
인피 靭皮 〖식물〗 bast
— 섬유 liber ; phloem〔bast〕 fiber
인하 引下 reduction ; lowering ; a cut — 하다 lower ; bring down ; reduce ; cut (down) ¶ 가격을 인하하다 cut a price down ; reduce〔lower〕 the price 《to》
물가 — a reduction of price 임금 — a reduction in wages ; a wage cut 물가 — 운동 a cut-the-price movement ; a price cut campaign
인하다 因— be due 《to》; be caused 《by》; be attributable 《to》; come 《from》; be a consequence 《of》 ¶ 인하여 therefore ; hence ; consequently ; accordingly // 병으로 인해서 결석하다 be absent because of illness // 사고로 인하여 죽다 die from〔on account of〕 an accident
인해 人海 a human sea ; a sea of people
— 전술 human sea〔wave〕 tactics 〔sweep〕; infiltration tactics
인행 印行 publication — 하다 print
인허 認許 recognition ; approval ; authorization — 하다 recognize ; approve ; authorize
†인형 人形 a doll ; a puppet ; a figure ¶ 인형 같은 doll-like
—극 a doll play ; a puppet show ; a marionette performance — 극장 a puppet〔marionette〕 theater
인형 仁兄 [편지에서] Dear Friend
인혜 仁惠 [자비] graciousness ; benevolence ; mercy ; [자선] charity
인화 燐火 a phosphorescent light ; an elf fire ; a jack-o'-lantern ; a will-o'-the-wisp ; the glow〔glimmer〕 of a firefly
인화 人和 harmony among men ; peace and amity within 《the nation》; 《national》 concord
인화 印畫 a print (of a photograph) — 하다 print (a photograph) ; make a print 《of》
—지 photographic (printing) paper ; sensitized paper
인화 引火 ignition ; catching fire — 하다 ignite ; catch〔take〕 fire ¶ 인화하기 쉽다 be inflammable ; be ignitable
— 물질 the inflammables —성 (in-)flammability ; ignitability —점 the flashing〔flash, inflammation, ignition〕 point —점 시험 a flash test —점 시험기 a flash 〔flashing point〕 tester
인환 引換 exchange ; change — 하다 exchange ; change
—권 an exchange ticket ; a coupon
인회석 燐灰石 〖광물〗 apatite
인회토 燐灰土 〖광물〗 phosphorite
인후 仁厚 humanity and generosity
인후 咽喉 the throat ¶ 인후의 faucal ; guttural
—병 a swelling〔swollen〕 sore throat —염 a sore throat — 카타르 catarrh of the throat
†일 ① work ; employment ; a task ; [직업] a job ; an occupation ; [사무] business ; [근무] duties ; [사명] mission — 하다 work ; labor ¶ 하루일 a day's work // 나날의 일 one's daily〔routine〕 work // 어려운 일 a difficult task ; a hard job // 급한 일 urgent business // 일하러 가다 go to work // 일을 하고 있다 be at work // 일에 착수하다 set to work // 일이 없다 have nothing to do ; [실업] be out of work ; have no employment〔job〕 // 일을 찾다 look 〔hunt〕 for work〔employment〕 // 일을 얻다 get a job ; find work // 일을 쉬다 stay

away from work // 일을 치우다 close〔knock off〕one's work // 일을 급히 하다 rush one's work // 일을 시키다 put 《a person》 to work // 일을 맡다 accept〔take〕a job // 유흥을 일삼다 be given (up) to pleasure // 일이 손에 잡히지 않다 be unable to bring oneself to work // 오늘은 할 일이 많다 I have many things to do today. // 우리는 관청 일을 하고 있다 We are working for government offices. // 이것은 쉬운 일이 아니다 This is no easy task. // 그는 요새 술 마시는 것이 일이다 He does nothing but drink these days. // 댁은 무슨 일을 하십니까—식당을 하고 있습니다 What line of business are you in? I run a restaurant. // 나는 두 가지 일을 하고 있다 I work two jobs. // 그는 일을 잘하고 있나 How is he doing at work?
② [건(件)] a matter ; a thing ; an affair ; a fact ; a proposition ; a job 《속》; something ; what ; that ¶ 불쾌한 일 an unpleasant matter ; an ugly job ; something unpleasant // 귀찮은 일 an awkward proposition // 돈에 관한 일 a money matter ; a matter of money // 그 일이라면 for that matter // 학교 일에 관해서 이야기하다 speak about the school affairs // 내 일은 걱정 말라 Don't trouble yourself about me. // 네가 참견할 일이 아니다 That's none of your business. // 참 이상한 일이다 It is a curious thing, indeed. // 무슨 일이냐—어디 아프냐 What's the matter with you? Are you sick or something?
③ [사정] circumstance ; [사태] things ; matters ¶ 어떤 일이 있더라도 under any circumstances ; come what may // 극히 사소한 일로 화내다 get angry on the slightest provocation〔for nothing〕// 일이 이쯤 되었다 Things have come to such a pass. // 무슨 일이라도 있니 Anything the matter?
④ [사건] an incident ; an occurrence ; an event ; [사고] an accident ; [분규] trouble ¶ 일 없이 without incident〔accident〕; peacefully ; smoothly ; quietly ; without let or hindrance // 일이 생기면 in (case of) emergency // 일을 저지르다 cause〔make〕trouble // 일은 그 시합에서 발단했다 The trouble originated in a game.
⑤ [경험] experience ¶ 그곳에는 한번 가본 일이 있다 I once visited there. // 아직 가르쳐본 일이 없다 I am not experienced in teaching.
⑥ [계획·사업] a plan ; a business ; an errand ; a scheme ; a project ; a program ; an undertaking ¶ 일을 꾸미다 make a plan ; form a scheme // 일을 진행시키다 carry on a program // 일이 척척 잘 되어간다 The plan is on a fair way to success.

일 日 a day ¶ 3일 three days // 5월 2일 the 2nd of May ; May 2 // 단 2,3일에 in a brief period of two or threedays

일 一 one ¶ 일등 first ; number one ; first class // 일인 일표 one man one vote // 제일 the first // 헨리 1세 Henry I〔the first〕

일가 一家 ① [가정] a household ; a home ; [가족] a family ; [일가친척] one's kinsfolk ¶ 일가의 family ; household // 일가를 가지다〔이루다〕have〔make〕a home of one's own // 일가를 유지하다 support one's family // 댁내 일가 여러분 안녕하십니까 Are all of your family well?
② [학파] a school ; [대가] an authority ¶ 일가를 이루다 establish a school of one's own // 이 방면에 있어서 일가를 이루다 be an authority in this field
— 단란 a happy family〔home〕circle ; the pleasures of a happy〔sweet〕home
— 몰살 annihilation of an entire family
— 문중 one's close and distant relatives ; one's kinsfolk **—붙이** family relations ; relatives ; one's kinsfolk **— 친척** one's kinsfolk **— 화합** harmony in a family

일가 一價 〖화학〗 univalence ; monovalence ¶ 일가의 univalent ; monovalent ; monatomic
— 원소 a monad

일가견 一家見 a personal〔private〕view ; one's own opinion

일가족 一家族 one family ; the whole family

일각 一刻 a moment ; a second ; a minute ¶ 일각을 다투다 not a moment (is) to be lost ; (there is) no time to lose // 일각을 아끼다 grudge even a minute // 일각이 천금 Every moment is precious. /Time is money. // 일각 여삼추(如三秋) A minute is like three years〔seems like a lifetime〕.

일각 一角 a corner ; a section
— 대문 a front gate with two posts and a roof **—수(獸)** a unicorn **— 중문** an inner〔an included〕gate with two posts and a roof

*__일간 日刊__ daily publication〔issue〕¶ 일간의 daily
— 신문 a daily newspaper ; a daily 《미》

일간 日間 (in) a few days ; (within) a couple of days ; (in) the near future ¶ 일간 가겠소 I'll come one of these days. // 일간 결혼하겠지 He will get married by and by〔before long〕.

일간두옥 一間斗屋 a small one-room house ; a hut ; a humble house

일갈 一喝 a thundering cry **— 하다** thunder 《at》; cry in a thunderous voice ; thunder 《out》; cry in a voice of thunder ¶ 그의 일갈을 듣고 그들은 계획을 포기했다 They shrank from the attempt at his thundering cry〔thunderous condemnation〕.

일개 一箇 one ; a piece ¶ 일개의 one ; single // 일개 천원 1,000 *won* a piece 〔each〕 // 나는 일개 가난한 학생이다 I am but a poor student.

일개 一介 ¶ 일개의 mere ; only // 나는 일개의 가난한 학생에 지나지 않는다 I am nothing but〔no more than〕 a struggling student.

일개인 一個人 an individual ; a private person ¶ 나 일개인의 생각 my personal 〔private〕 view // 일개인의 individual ; personal ; private // 일개인으로서 as an individual ; individually ; personally // 일개인의 자격으로 in one's private〔individual〕 capacity ; in the character〔capacity〕 of an individual〔a private citizen〕

일거 一擧 one effort ; one action ¶ 일거에 at a〔one〕 stroke ; by one effort ; at one coup // 일거에 일을 결정하다 decide 《a matter》 by one effort // 적을 일거에 쳐부수다 beat〔crush〕 the enemy at a blow

일거 逸居 an idle life ; a leisurely life **―하다** lead an idle life ; live in leisure ; live a leisurely life

일거리 a piece of work ; a job ; things to do ¶ 나날의 일거리 one's routine work // 하루의 일거리 a day's work // 편한〔고된〕 일거리 light〔hard〕 work // 일거리가 있다 have work to do ; have business to attend to // 일거리가 없다 be out of work ; have nothing to do // 일거리를 주다 assign a task to 《a person》 // 일거리를 맡기다 entrust 《a person》 with a task // 요즘 일거리가 별로 많지 않다 We are kind of slow these days.

일거무소식 一去無消息 no tidings since departure ¶ 일거무소식이다 I have never heard from him since he left.

일거수일투족 一擧手一投足 ① a slight motion ; a slight effort ② ⇨ 일거일동

일거양득 一擧兩得 attaining two advantages at one move ; killing two birds with one stone〔bolt, sling〕 ; to catch two pigeons with one bean. ¶ 그렇게 하면 일거양득이다 It serves two ends.

일거일동 一擧一動 one's every action ; every movement 《of a person》 ; everything one does ¶ 남의 일거일동을 주시하다 watch every movement of 《a person》 // 그는 일거일동을 소홀히 하지 않는다 He is prudence itself〔is all prudence〕.

일건 一件 an affair ; a matter ; an item
― 기록〔서류〕 the papers relating to the affair

일격 一擊 a blow ; a stroke ; a hit ¶ 일격에 at a〔one〕 blow ; with one stroke 〔blow〕 ; by a (single) blow // 일격을 가하다 give〔deal〕 《a person》 a blow ; strike 《a person》 a blow // 그는 얼굴에 일격을 가했다 I landed〔dealt〕 him a blow on the face.

†일견 一見 a look ; a sight ; a glance ; a glimpse **―하다** take〔have, cast, get〕 a glance 《at》 ; catch a glimpse 《of》 ; have a squint 《at》 ¶ 일견하여 at first sight ; at the first glance ; at one view ; apparently ; outwardly ; to all appearance // 신사 같았다 He had the outward appearance of a gentleman. // 일견하여 쉬울 듯했다 At first sight it seemed quite easy. // 백문이 불여일견이다 A hundred hearings are not worth one seeing. /One picture is worth a thousand words.

일결 一決 ① decision ; agreement ② bursting (of a dam, dike) **―하다** reach an agreement ; come to a decision ; 《a dam, dike》 burst

일계 一計 a plan ¶ 일계를 생각해내다 think〔work〕 out a plan

일계 日系 ¶ 일계의 of Japanese ancestry
― 미국인 a Japanese American

일계 日計 daily account ; daily expenses
―표 〖상업〗 daily trial balance

일고 一考 consideration ; thought **―하다** consider ; think of〔about〕 ; think over ; take into consideration ; give a thought 《to》 ¶ 일고의 여지가 있다 leave room for consideration // 이것은 일고를 요하는 문제다 This is a matter for consideration.

일고 一顧 notice ; attention ; consideration ¶ 일고의 가치도 없다 It is beneath notice. /It does not deserve even a passing notice. // 일고의 가치가 있다 It is worth our attention.

일고동 a vital point (of a thing, an affair) ; the pivot ; the crux

일고삼장 日高三丈 late morning ; broad daylight ; late in the day

일곱 seven ¶ 일곱 이레 the 49th day after a baby's birth // 일곱번째 the seventh

일공 日工 day labor ; a day laborer ; a day's wage

일과 一過 ―하다 [지나가다] pass away ; [눈을 거침] run one's eyes through 《a book》 ; glance〔run〕 (one's eyes) over 《the papers》 ¶ 일과성의 temporary ; transitory ; fugitive // 태풍 일과후 after the typhoon passed through

일과 日課 a daily lesson ; a daily work 〔task〕 ; the daily routine〔round〕 ¶ 그는 매일 아침 산보하는 것을 일과로 삼고 있다 He makes a point of taking a walk every morning.
―표 a daily schedule ; a schedule (of lessons)

일곽 一郭 a block

***일관 一貫** consistency ; coherence **―하다** run through ; be consistent ¶ 일관된 consistent ; coherent // 일관하여 consistently ; all the way through // 시종 일관된 정책 a consistent〔coherent〕 policy // 초지를 일관하다 go through with〔carry out〕 one's original idea // 그는 시종일관 학문에

전념했다 He was constant in his devotion to learning.
—성 consistency ; coherence — 작업 integrated〔vertical〕 work ; a through process
일괄 一括 a bundle ; a lump —하다 make〔tie up〕 into a bundle ; bundle up ; [총괄하다] sum up ¶ 일괄하여 in a lump ; collectively ; en bloc 《프》 ; summarily // 세개의 의안을 일괄하여 의제로 했다 The three bills were brought up en bloc〔together〕 for discussion.
— 계약 a contract in bulk ; a blanket contract ; a package deal — 구입 a blanket purchase — 배급 collective rationing — 사표 en masse resignations — 소송 a wholesale suit ; a package suit — 제안 a package proposal — 지불 a lump-sum payment ; a payment in lump sum — 타결 a package〔an overall〕 settlement — 판매 (a) sale by bulk
:**일광 日光** sunlight ; sunshine ; sunbeams ; the rays of the sun ¶ 일광에 소독하다 expose 《a thing》 to the sun // 일광에 말리다 dry in the sun
— 반사기 a heliotrope — 발동기 a solar 〔sun〕 motor — 소독 sterilization by sunning ; disinfection by sunlight — 요법 heliotherapy —욕 a sunbath ; sunbathing ¶ 일광욕을 하다 bathe in the sun —욕실 a solarium 《*pl.* -ria》 ; a sun-room ; a sun parlor — 절약 daylight saving 자연〔인공〕 — natural〔artificial〕 sunlight 직사 — direct sunlight
일구 一區 a section ; a district ; a division ; a block ; a ward
일구 逸球 〖야구〗 a passed ball —하다 miss a catch
일구난설 一口難說 being difficult to explain in a word ; being unexplainable 〔indescribable〕 in a word
일구다 ① raise (topsoil) ; clear (land) ; bring under cultivation ② 《a mole》 raise a mound ; burrow in
일구월심 日久月深 lapse of time [부사적] earnestly ; intently ; with all one's heart —하다 days and months go by
일구이언 一口二言 a double-tongue —하다 contradict oneself ; be double-tongued ; talk out of both sides of the mouth
일국 一國 a nation〔country〕
일군 一軍 ① [전군] the whole army 〔force〕 ; [일개 군] an army ② [제1군] the First Army ¶ 일군의 지휘관 a commander-in-chief // 일군 사령관 the Commander of the First Army
일군 一郡 one county
*__일그러지다__ (be) distorted ; contorted ; twisted ¶ 일그러진 distorted ; contorted ; awry
일근 日勤 daily service〔work, duty〕 —하다 do〔be on〕 duty every day ; work every day
일금 一金 《the sum of》 money
— 5천원 (the sum of) five thousand *won*
*__일급 一級__ the first class
—품 first-class goods ; an article of the first〔highest〕 quality
일급 日給 daily wages ; a day's wage ; per diem 《미》 ¶ 일급 30,000원 a day's wage of 30,000 *won* // 일급으로 일하다 work by the day // 일급으로 지불하다〔고용하다〕 pay〔hire〕 《a person》 by the day
— 노동자 a day laborer ; a day wage man —제 the day-rate plan
일긋거리다 shake ; be tottering ; be quivery ; be shaky ; be rickety ¶ 책상 다리가 좀 일긋거린다 The legs of the table are a bit shaky.
일긋일긋 totteringly ; shakily ; unsteadily
일기 一期 [기간] one term ; [일생] one's span of life ; one's whole life ; one's lifetime ¶ 60세를 일기로 죽다 die at (the age of) sixty ; die aged 60
— 배당금 a regular〔quarterly〕 dividend
일기 一騎 a single horseman
†__일기 日記__ a diary ; a journal ¶ 일기를 적다 keep〔write〕 a diary ; [기입하다] write 〔record〕 《the matter》 in one's diary ; make an entry in one's diary
— 문학 diaries (as a branch of literature) —장 a diary ; a daybook ; a summary book 여행 — one's diary of a trip ; a travel diary ; an itinerary 영문 — an English diary 학생 — a student diary
*__일기 日氣__ the weather ¶ 좋은〔궂은〕 일기 fine〔bad〕 weather // 일기가 좋으면 weather permitting ; if the weather is favorable // 일기가 좋든 나쁘든 in fair weather or foul // 일기를 예보하는 것은 쉽지 않다 It is not easy to forecast the weather.
— 개황 a general weather condition — 불순 (being) unseasonable ; unsettled ; changeable — 예보 a weather forecast 〔report〕 ¶ 내일의 일기 예보 the weather forecast for tomorrow // 라디오에서 일기 예보를 듣다 listen to the weather forecast over the radio
일기 一技 an art ; a skill
일인 — one man, one skill
일기당천 一騎當千 a match for a thousand ; a matchless warrior
일기죽거리다 ⇨ 얄기죽거리다
일긴하다 一緊— (be) most important ; be of vital importance ; (be) momentous ; essential 《to》
일깨우다 convince 《a person》 of ; waken 《a person》 to ; open 《a person's》 eyes to ; make 《a person》 aware of : tell 《a person》 about ¶ 그의 잘못을 그에게 일깨워 주었다 I brought to his attention what he had done wrong.
일껏 with (much) effort〔trouble〕 ; at great pains ¶ 일껏 번 돈을 쓰지 않으면 안 되었다 I had to spend my hardearned

일기

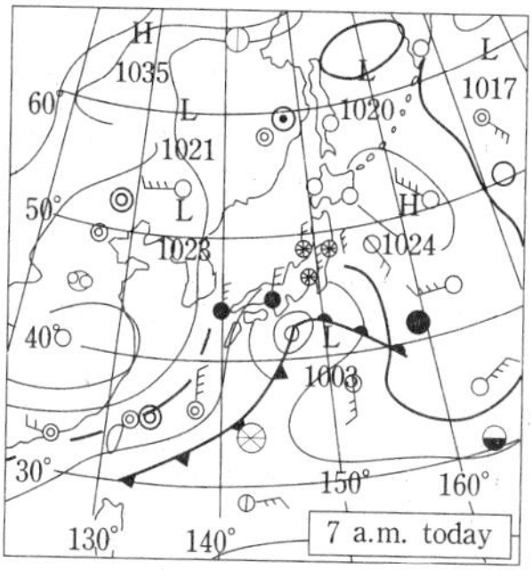

H 고기압 high (atmospheric) pressure
L 저기압 low (atmospheric) pressure
○ 매우 맑음 clear
◒ 뇌우 thunderstorm
● 비 rain
⦶ 맑음 fair
◎ 구름 cloudy
⊙ 안개 fog
∞ 연무 haze
⊗ 눈 snow
⟋ 바람 방향과 속도 wind direction and speed
─●─●─●─ 온난 전선 warm front
─▲─▲─▲─ 한랭 전선 cold front

money. // 일껏 찾아오신 것을 제가 없어 죄송했습니다 I was very sorry to miss your call. // 일껏 오라고 했는데 그는 안 왔다 He did not come, though I told him to.

일꾼 ① [품팔이] a workman ; a worker ; a laborer ; a coolie ; a navvy (막일의) ② [역량 있는 사람] an able man〔hand〕; a man of ability ¶ 그는 사회의 큰 일꾼이 될 것이다 He will become a pillar of society.

게으른 일꾼 밭고랑 세듯 (속담) Idle folks lack no excuses.

일끝 one end〔the start, the finish〕 of a job〔an event〕; (a bit〔a piece〕 of) trouble ¶ 일끝을 맺다 finish the matter up ; tie up the loose ends

일난 풍화 日暖風和 warm weather and gentle breeze ; [좋은 날씨] fair〔fine〕 weather **── 하다** (be) warm and breezy ; fine ; fair

일년 一年 a〔one〕 year ¶ 일년의 yearly ; annual // 일년내 all the year round ; throughout the year // 일년마다 every year ; annually // 일년에 한 번씩 once a year ; annually // 일년에 두 번씩 twice a year ; semiannually // 일년지계는 정초에 있다 New Year's Day is the key of the year.

─감 a tomato **─생** a first-year〔-grade〕 boy〔girl〕; [대학 등의] a freshman 《미》 **─초** an annual (plant)

일념 一念 a will ; a prayer ; an earnest desire ; an ardent wish ¶ 일념으로 with a concentrated mind ; with a whole heart ; whole-heartedly // 일념으로 기도하다 pray from one's whole heart // 일념은 하늘에 통한다 Faith will move a mountain.

일다[1] happen ; spring up ; ascend ¶ 물결이 일다 waves rise // 바람이 일다 the wind rises ; a wind comes up

일다[2] [일구다] bring 《land》 under cultivation ; clear 《the land》; break up 《the soil》

일다[3] clear out useless elements ; scour ; clean out ; wash ¶ 금을 일다 wash for gold ; pan gold // 쌀을 일다 wash rice

일단 一旦 once ; [잠깐] for the moment ¶ 일단 유사시에 in case of emergency // 일단 결심한 이상 once you have made up your mind // 일단 한 약속을 충실히 이행해야만 한다 A promise once made should be faithfully kept. // 그 사건은 일단 끝났다 The case was closed for the moment.

일단 一端 one end (한쪽 끝) ; a part (일부) ¶ 소감의 일단을 피력하다 express a fragment of one's impression // 그의 성격의 일단을 알게 되다 get a glimpse of his character

†일단 一團 a body ; a group ; a party ; a

band ; a gang (패거리) ; a troupe (극단) ¶ 일단의 관광객 a party of tourists // 악당의 일단 a pack〔gang〕 of villains // 일단이 되어 in a body ; en masse 《프》 // 일단을 조직하다 form〔make, organize〕 a party

일단 一段 ① [단계] one stage ; the first stage ② [계단의] a step ③ [급수] a grade ; the first grade ④ [글의] a passage ; a paragraph

일단락 一段落 a pause (쉼) ; a conclusion (결말) ; a chapter ¶ 이것으로 일단락지었다 With this we have completed the first stage of the work. /We have come to the end of a chapter.

*****일당 一黨** a ring ; partisans ; participators ; adherents (to a cause) ; the same ; a gang ¶ 일당이 체포되었다 All the fellow-conspirators were nabbed.

— 국회 a one-party legislature **— 독재** one-party rule〔dictatorship〕

일당 一堂 ¶ 일당에 회합하다 meet together (in a hall)

일당 日當 daily allowance ; daily pay 〔wages〕 ; per diem 《미》 ¶ 여비 일당 daily travel(ing) allowance // 일당 삼만원을 지불하다 pay〔grant〕 30,000 *won* a day // 일당으로 일하다 work by the day

일당백 一黨百 a match for a hundred ; one (person) that is worth a hundred (persons)

일당 일파 一黨一派 a party or a faction ¶ 일당 일파를 초월한 정책 a supraparty policy // 일당 일파에 치우치지 않다 be nonpartisan ; have the crossbench mind

일대 一代 a〔one〕 generation ; one's lifetime ; one's whole life ¶ 일대의 영웅 the greatest hero of the day〔age〕 // 일대에 재산을 이루다 make a fortune in one's lifetime // 이것은 일대의 실책이다 This is the greatest mistake I have ever had.

—기 a life story ; a life ; a biography

일대 一隊 a party ; a company 《of soldiers》 ; a bevy 《of school girls》 ; a troop 《of children》 ; a gang 《of robbers》

일대 一帶 the whole area〔district〕 ; the neighborhood 《of》 ; a region ; a zone 《of forest》 ¶ 일대의 whole ; throughout // 그 근처 일대 the whole neighborhood // 그 지방 일대에 all over the district // 서울 일대에 all over *Seoul*

일대 一大 one great〔large〕 ¶ 일대 성황 a great prosperity

일대사 一大事 a matter of great importance〔grave concern〕 ; a serious〔grave〕 affair ; an emergency ¶ 국가의 일대사 an affair of vital importance to the State // 일대사가 일어났다 A serious thing has happened.

일대일 一對一 one to one ¶ 일대일의 승부 a single combat〔fight〕 ; a single field ; a man-to-man fight // 그 선거는 A씨와 B씨의 일대일의 대결이다 The election is an exclusive contest between A and B. /A and B are running neck and neck 《for the governorship》. // 어제 사장하고 일대일로 면담을 했다 I had a one-on-one talk with the boss yesterday.

일더위 early heat ; early hot weather

일도양단 一刀兩斷 cutting in two with one stroke of the sword ; decisiveness

—하다 cut 《a thing》 in two with a slash of the sword ; cut the Gordian knot ¶ 일도양단의 조치를 취하다 take a drastic〔decisive〕 measure ; solve a problem once for all

일독 一讀 reading through once ; a perusal **—하다** read 《a book》 through ; peruse ¶ 일독의 가치가 있다 The book is worth reading. /That is a rewarding book.

일동 一同 all the persons present〔concerned〕 ; all (of us, them) ¶ 우리들 일동 all of us ; we all // 일동 모두 함께 in a body // 일동을 대표하여 on behalf of all // 일동 모두 승낙했다 They all gave consent.

가내 — all one's family **사원 —** the whole company **회원 —** all the members

일동일정 一動一靜 every bit of conduct〔movement, motion〕

일되다 mature〔grow, ripen〕 early ¶ 일된 아이 a precocious child // 금년은 벼가 일된다 The rice crop are early this year.

일득일실 一得一失 one merit and one demerit ; an advantage set off by a disadvantage ¶ 일득일실은 당연한 것이다 Where there is good, there is evil.

*****일등 一等** the first class ; the first rank 〔grade〕 ; the first place ¶ 일등의 first-class ; first-rate ; top grade 《미》 // 일등석을 타다 travel first-class ; [선박의] travel in the first cabin // (비행기) 일등석에 타본 일이 있니 Have you ever flown first class ? // 나는 일등을 했다 I was first. /I finished first. /I placed first. /I won first place.

—국 a first-class power **— 기관사** the first engineer **—병** a private first class 《pfc.》 **—성** a star of the first magnitude **— 수병** a leading seaman **— 승객** a first-class passenger **—차〔차표〕** a first-class carriage〔ticket〕 **— 침대** a first-class berth **— 통신사** a chief〔first〕 (wireless) operator **—품** a first-class article ; the finest stuff (품질)

일등상 一等賞 the first prize ; a blue ribbon ¶ 일등상을 타다 win (the) first prize ; win first place

일떠나다[1] leave〔set out〕 (on one's way) early in the morning

일떠나다[2] [일어나다] spring〔start, jump, leap, bound〕 to one's feet ; spring〔leap, jump〕 up ; stir〔rouse〕 up

일락 逸樂 pleasure ; ease ; comfort ¶ 일락에 잠기다 indulge in pleasure

— 생활 a life given up to pleasure
일락서산 日落西山 the sun setting on the western hills —하다 the sun sets on the western hills〔in the west〕
일란성 一卵性 [형용사적] monozygous ; monovular
— 쌍생아 monovular twins ; an identical twin
†일람 一覽 a look ; a view(ing) ; a perusal ; a summary ; an outline ; a prospectus ; a catalog —하다 take a look at ; take a view of ; peruse 《a book》 ; run (one's eyes) through ¶ 일람 후 10일불의 payable 10 days after sight∥일람불 어음 a bill payable at sight〔on demand〕 ; a sight bill∥보고서를 일람하십시오 Please look through the report.
—표 a table ; a chart ; a list 대학 — a university catalog〔prospectus〕
일람불 一覽拂 ¶ 일람불의 payable at sight ∥일람불 어음을 발행하다 draw a bill 〔draft〕 at sight〔on demand〕
— 어음 a bill〔draft〕 (payable) at sight 〔on demand〕 ; a sight bill 《S/B》 ; a demand draft ; a sight draft
일러두기 explanatory notes ; introductory remarks
일러두다 request ; bit ; order ; tell ¶ …하라고 일러두다 tell〔order, request〕 《a person》 to 《do》
일러바치다 tell〔carry〕 tales 《about, against》 ; inform 《an elder, a superior》 ; tell on ; tattle (학생이) ¶ 내가 한 일을 선생님께 일러바치다 tell our teacher on me
일러주다 let 《a person》 know ; tell 《a person》 ; inform ; report ; notify ; tip off 《about》 ; advise ; admonish ; teach ; inculcate ; instruct ¶ 다음부터 더 조심하라고 일러 주어라 Tell him to be more careful from now on. ∥출발 시간을 일러주시오 Please let me know the time of your departure.
일렁거리다 bob up and down ; toss ; rock (on the waves)
일렁일렁 bobbing up and down ; tossing ; rocking 《on the waves》
일렉트론 〖물리〗 electron
일력 日曆 a daily pad calendar
†일련 一連 a series 《of》 ; a chain 《of》 ; a succession 《of》 ; a ream 《of paper》 ¶ 일련의 successive ; connected ; joined∥일련의 사건 a chain of events
— 번호 consecutive〔serial〕 numbers
일련탁생 一蓮托生 a pledge to rise or sink together ; sharing the fate of another
*일렬 一列 a line ; a row ; a rank ; a file (세로의) ¶ 일렬로 in a row〔line〕 ; in a single file∥(매표소 따위에서) 일렬로 줄서다 stand in single file ; form a queue
일례 一例 an example ; an instance ; one instance from many ¶ 일례를 들면 for example〔instance〕 ; to cite〔give〕 an example〔instance〕∥이것은 일례를 든 데 불과하다 This is only an instance out of〔among〕 many.
일로 一路 [길] a straight road ; [곧장] one road ; straight ¶ 일로 평안하시기를 빌다 wish 《a person》 bon voyage∥일로 호놀룰루를 향하여 고향을 떠났다 He left home direct for Honolulu.
일루 一壘 〖야구〗 the first base
—수 the first baseman —측 스탠드 the right stand —타 a〔one〕 timer ; a base hit ; an ordinary
일루 一縷 a thin wreath 《of smoke》 ; a ray〔gleam〕 《of hope》 ¶ 일루의 희망 a ray〔gleam〕 of hope∥일루의 희망을 갖다 cling to one's last hope∥일루의 희망도 없다 There is not the faintest hope. ∥그가 죽었기 때문에 일루의 희망마저 없어졌다 His death deprived me of the last hope.
‡일류 一流 first class〔rank, rate〕 ; top-notch ; [독특] peculiarity ; unique ; [유파] a school ¶ 그는 재계에서 일류 인물이다 He is the foremost man in the financial circle. /He is a leading financier.
— 가수 a top class singer —교 a prestige school — 극장 a first-class theater — 기술자 a topnotch〔an A-1〕 engineer —병 a first class kick ; a fad〔passion〕 for top class ¶ 학부모들은 일류병에 걸려 있다 The pupils' parents are on the first class school kick. — 선수 a ranking player — 신문 leading newspapers — 신사 a gentleman of the best standing — 음악가 an A-1 musician — 작가 a first-rate writer ; a name writer ; one of the best〔leading〕 writers — 정치가 a politician of the first rank — 학자 a scholar of highest standing — 회사 leading companies
일류미네이션 illumination ¶ 일류미네이션 장치를 한 illuminated
일륜 一輪 ① [꽃의] a (single) flower ② [바퀴의] a wheel
— 롤러 〖토목〗 a single-wheel roller —차 a monocycle ; a wheelbarrow — 활차 a gin block
일륜 日輪 the sun
일륜차 一輪車 a monocycle ; [손수레] a wheelbarrow
일률 一律 [균등] uniformity ; evenness ; equality ; indiscrimination (무차별) ¶ 일률적으로 uniformly ; [무차별로] indiscriminately ; [전체적으로] as a whole ; sweepingly∥그런 문제는 일률적으로 생각할 수는 없다 We cannot think of them in the same light.
일리 一理 some reason ; some truth ¶ 그것도 일리가 있다 There is some truth 〔reason〕 in it. ∥그가 그렇게 한 것도 일리는 있다 He has a reason for doing so. ∥일리가 있는 말이군 You got a point there.

일리노이 Illinois 《Ill.》
일리일해 一利一害 an advantage offset by a disadvantage ; one merit and one demerit ¶ 그것에는 일리일해가 있다 It has its advantages and disadvantages. // 일리일해는 세상사다 Where there is good, there is evil. /Where there light is, there shadow is.
일막 一幕 one act
—극 a one-act play
일말 一抹 a spray ; a wreath ; [소량] a touch 《of》 ; a shadow 《of》 ; a suspicion 《of》 ; a tinge 《of》 ¶ 일말의 연기 a wreath of smoke // 일말의 불안 a touch 〔tinge, shadow〕 of uneasiness // 일말의 애수 a slight feeling of sadness // 그의 눈에는 일말의 불안이 감돌고 있었다 There was a look of uneasiness in his eyes.
일망 一望 a sweep of the eye **—하다** command a sweeping〔whole, an unbroken〕 view of ; take the whole in one view ¶ 그 언덕에서는 시 전체가 일망지하에 보인다 From the hilltop one can take 〔obtain〕 a bird's-eye view of the whole town. /The hill commands a panoramic〔full〕 view of the town.
일망무제 一望無際 endlessness ; boundlessness **—하다** (be) endless ; boundless ¶ 일망무제한 바다 a boundless (expanse of the) ocean
일망타진 一網打盡 a wholesale arrest ; a roundup **—하다** make a wholesale arrest 《of》 ; round 《them》 up
일매지다 (be) even ; uniform ; be all alike ¶ 풀밭을 일매지게 깎다 trim the lawn evenly
일맥 一脈 a vein ¶ 일맥 상통하다 have a thread of connection 《with》 ; have something to do with // 양자간에는 일맥상통한 점이 있다 There is a thread of connections between the two.
일면 一面 [반면] one side〔hand〕 ; [전면] the whole surface ; [양상] an aspect ; a phase ; [신문의] the first page ¶ 시대상의 일면 a sign of the times // 일면적 one-sided // 일면에 all over // 얼굴 일면에 all over the face // 일면적인 판단은 공평치가 않다 A one-sided judgment is not fair. // 상자의 일면은 유리다 One side of the box is glass. // 네가 말하는 것은 일면의 이유가 있다 What you say contains some truth. // 하늘 일면에 먹구름이 덮여있다 The sky is covered all over with dark clouds. // 그의 행동은 비난을 받을 것이나 일면 동정할 점도 있다 His action is to be blamed, but, on the other hand we must sympathize with him, too.
일면식 一面識 a sight acquaintance ; a bowing〔nodding〕 acquaintance ¶ 일면식도 없는 사람 an utter stranger ; a man whom one has never met // 일면식이 있다 be slightly acquainted 《with》 // have a bowing acquaintance 《with》 // 그와는 일면식도 없다 He is a complete stranger to me. /I have never met him.
일면여구 一面如舊 being very friendly (like old pals) at the first meeting
일면지분 一面之分 ¶ …와 일면지분이 있다 know 《a person》 slightly
일명 一名 [한사람] a person ; [별명] another〔a second〕 name ; an alias ¶ 스미드 일명 심프슨 Smith, alias Simpson // 일명에 대하여 만원의 회비 subscription of 10,000 *won* each // 타이피스트 일명 채용 Wanted : a typist. // 이군은 일명 세돌이다 *Sedol* is another name of Mr. *Lee.* / Mr. *Lee* goes by the name of *Sedol.*
일명 一命 a life ¶ 일명을 바치다 offer 〔lay down〕 one's life 《for one's country》
일모 日暮 [일몰] sunset ; nightfall ; sundown ; [황혼] dusk ; twilight ; [저녁때] evening ; before nightfall ¶ 일모전〔후〕 before〔after〕 sunset〔sundown〕 // 일모까지 돌아오다 come back by sunset〔sundown〕 ; come back before the sun sets
—도궁(途窮) loneliness and woe ; senile decay
일모작 一毛作 a single crop ¶ 그 지방은 일모작이다 That is a single-crop district.
— 전답 a single-crop field
일목 一目 a glance ; a look ; one eye ¶ 일목요연하다 be clear at a glance ; be as clear as day ; be obvious
일몰 日沒 sunset ; sundown 《미》 ¶ 일몰후〔전〕에 after〔before〕 sunset
일무 一無 nothing ; not even one
—가관(可觀) nothing worth seeing **—소득** no profit〔gain〕 at all **—소식** no tidings〔news〕 at all ; not a single word
일문 一門 a family ; a house ; a clan ; one's folks
일문 日文 Japanese script〔writings〕
일문 逸聞 an anecdote
일문일답 一問一答 answering questions one after another ; question and answer ; an interview **—하다** give an answer to each question ; give an interview ; answer questions
일물 逸物 an excellent thing ; a superb article ; a thing of the first rate ; a masterpiece
일미 一味 a superb flavor
일박 一泊 a night's lodging **—하다** put up for a night ; stay overnight ; pass a night 《at》 ; stop for the night ¶ 일박의 손님 an over-night〔a one-night〕 guest // 일박료 일등 40,000원 40,000 *won* for the first class charge per night
— 여행 an overnight trip ¶ 일박 여행을 하다 make an overnight trip
†**일반 一般** ¶ 일반의 [전반의] general ; [보편의] universal ; [통례의] common ; usual ; [대중의] popular // 일반적 교양 general〔liberal〕 culture // 일반화된 용어 a household word // 일반적인 지식 general knowledge // 일반 사람들 the general

public ; the public at large ; the man in the street // 일반적 경향 a general tendency // 일반적으로 generally ; in general ; as a rule ; at large ; on the whole // 일반적으로 말하면 generally speaking // 일반화하다 generalize ; popularize // 일반에 알려져 있다 be generally〔universally, popularly〕 known // 일반에 알리다 make 《it》 generally known // 일반에 공개하다 open 《a garden》 to the public // 아이들은 일반적으로 과자를 좋아한다 Children in general are fond of candy. // 이것이 일반의 의견이다 That is the common opinion of all. // 여성은 일반적으로 아이들을 좋아한다 Women generally love children. // 성적은 일반적으로 우수하다 The results are on the whole excellent. // 나는 고속도로를 안 타고 일반 도로로만 왔다 I didn't take the freeways. I came by surface streets only.

— **감각** 〖심리〗 general sensation — **개념** a general concept〔idea, notion〕 ; a universal — **교서** the State of Union Message (to Congress) — **교양 과목** the subjects for general education — **국민** the general public — **규정** a general〔universal〕 rule ; general provisions — **대중** the general public ; the public at large — **독자** common readers —**론** general consideration — **명사(名辭)** a general term —**법** a general law 〔statute〕 — **사면** a general pardon —**석** [극장 따위의] a general admission seat —**성** generality — **원칙** broad 〔general〕 principles — **입찰** open public tender〔bid〕 — **투표** a popular vote ; a referendum 《*pl.* ~s, -da》 —**화** generalization ; [보급] popularization — **회계** the general account

일발 一發 [총 따위의] a (single) shot 〔pop〕 ; [탄알의] a round ¶ 일발의 총성 the report of a gun〔shot〕 // 일발로 at a shot

일방 一方 [한쪽] one side ; [딴쪽] the other side ; [상대방의] one party ; the other party ¶ 일방에 치우치다 lean to one side

— **무역** a one-way trade — **통행** one-way (traffic) ¶ 그 길은 일방 통행이기 때문에 들어갈 수가 없다 That's a one-way street, so we can't turn in. — **통행로** a one-way street〔road〕

일방적 一方的 one-sided ; lopsided ; unilateral ¶ 일방적인 독립 선언 unilateral declaration of independence // 조약을 일방적으로 파기하다 abrogate a treaty one-sidedly // 우리는 7회에 대거 6점을 올려 그때까지의 접전을 일방적인 시합으로 만들었다 We poured in 6 points in the seventh inning and turned what had started as a close game into a rout.

일배 一杯 a cup 《of tea》 ; a glass 《of beer》 ; a cupful ; a glassful

일번 一番 the first ; the best ; No. 1 ¶ 일번의 first ; foremost ; top // 학급에서 일번이다 be at the head〔top〕 of the class // 일번으로 합격하다 pass an examination first on the list

— **열차** the first train — **타자** 〖야구〗 a lead-off man

일벌 〖곤충〗 a worker (bee) ; a working bee

일변 一變 a complete change **—하다** change completely〔altogether〕 ; undergo a complete change ¶ 태도를 일변하다 change front〔one's attitude〕 // 성격이 일변했다 He has changed completely in character. // 국면이 일변했다 The situation has taken a new aspect. // 원자 무기의 발명은 전술을 일변시켰다 The invention of atomic weapons has revolutionized strategy〔warfare〕.

일변 日邊 daily interest ; interest per diem

일변도 一邊倒 the wholehearted〔complete〕 devotion to one side ; doing the utmost for one side alone ¶ 대미(對美) 일변도이다 be absolutely for America ; be in exclusive support of America ; be out-and-out pro-America

— **정책** a lean-to-one-side policy

일별 一瞥 a glance ; a look ; a glimpse **—하다** glance 《at, toward》 ; cast a look 《at》 ; catch〔get〕 a glimpse 《of》 ¶ 일별하여 at a glance // 일별할 가치도 없다 be beneath notice // 그는 일별했을 뿐이다 He only gave it a glance.

일별 一別 parting **—하다** part 《from》 ; separate 《from》 ¶ 일별 이래 since we met last ; since I saw you last

일보 一步 a〔one〕 step ; a pace ¶ 일보 일보 step by step // 개선의 제일보 the first step toward improvement // 일보 앞서다 take a step forward ; go a step ahead // 붕괴 일보 전에 있다 be on the brink of ruin // 일보 물러나다 take a step back(ward) ; yield a step ; concede a point

— **전진** a step forward

일보 日報 a daily report ; [신문] a daily (newspaper) ¶ 동아일보 the *Dong-A Daily News*

일보다 take care of a business ; handle a job ; work

일본 日本 Japan ¶ 일본의 Japanese // 일본식으로 in Japanese style // 일본화하다 Japanize

— **뇌염** Japanese encephalitis —**말** Japanese ; the Japanese language — **사람** a Japanese 《*pl.* Japanese》 ; the Japanese (people) 《총칭》 — **요리** Japanese dishes〔cooking, cuisine〕 —**학** Japanology

일본할미꽃 〖식물〗 a Pulsatilla ; an anemone ; Pulsatilla cernua (학명)

일봉 一封 an enclosure ; an envelope enclosing money as a gift ¶ 금일봉을 보

내다 make 《a person》 a gift of money ; grant 《a person》 an envelope containing money

일봉 日捧 daily collection 《of money》 ━하다 collect 《money》 daily

†일부 一部 a part ; a portion ; a section ; a division ; a (single) copy 《of a book》 ; a complete set ¶ 일부의 partial ; divisional ; sectional // 일부의 사람들 some people // 일부를 이루다 form (a) part 《of》 // 일부를 수정하다 amend partially〔in part〕; make partial amendment 《of》 // 일부는 금속으로 되어 있다 It is made partly of metal.

— 결정 partial decision — 수정 partial amendment — 용선 a partcargo charter — 인사 some people ; certain circles — 주권국 a state having partial sovereignty ; a semi-independent country

일부 日附 ⇨ 날짜

—인(印) a date stamp

일부 日賦 a daily payment〔installment〕 ¶ 일부로 갚다 pay by daily installment〔payment〕

—금 daily installment〔payment〕 — 판매 sale on daily installment terms

일부 一夫 one man ; one husband ¶ 일부의 monogamous

—다처 polygamy ; polygyny ; plural marriage ¶ 일부다처의 풍습 polygamic customs // 일부다처주의자 a polygamist —이처 bigamy ; having two wives —일처주의자 a monogamist —종사 serving but a single husband —종신 having but a single husband during life

*일부러 [고의로] on purpose ; intentionally ; [짐짓] knowingly ; wittingly ; [특히] specially ; expressly ¶ 일부러 …하다 《do》 on purpose ; take pains to 《do》 ; go to the trouble to 《do》 ; go out of one's way to 《do》 // 그는 일부러 모른 체했다 He would not understand me. // 그 일 때문에 일부러 왔다 I am here for that express purpose. // 너를 보려고 일부러 서울에 왔다 I've come all the way to *Seoul* to see you. // 일부러 거기 갈 것은 없다 You don't have to go there on purpose. // 일부러 그런 수고 할 필요 없어요 Don't bother ! /Don't go to that trouble. // 그래 넌 일부러 날 위해 복사를 했구나 So you went to all the trouble of making a copy for me ?

일부 변경선 日附變更線 the (international) dateline

:일부분 一部分 one part〔portion, section, division〕 ¶ 일부분의 partial ; sectional

일부토 [한줌의 흙] a handful of soil ; [무덤] a grave ; a tomb

일분 一分 [시간] one minute (of an hour) ¶ 일분 일초 every minute and second

일비 日費 daily expenses〔expenditure〕

일비지력 一臂之力 a muscle〔bit〕 of strength ; a helping hand ; an assistance

일사 一事 one thing ; a single item

—부재리 prohibition against double jeopardy —부재의 the principle of not deliberating the same measure twice during the same session of the Assembly

일사 一死 〖야구〗 one out ¶ 일사 만루가 됐다 The bases were loaded with one out.

일사 逸史 history unknown to the world ; an unofficial history

일사 逸事 a fact unknown to the world ; a hidden fact ; an anecdote

일사반기 一四半期 the first quarter

일사병 日射病 sunstroke ; heatstroke ; heat prostration ¶ 일사병에 걸리다 have sunstroke ; be sunstruck

일사분기 一四分期 ⇨ 일사반기

일사불란 一絲不亂 being in perfect order ; being shipshape ━하다 be in perfect〔strict〕 order ; (be) shipshape ¶ 일사불란한 논지 a thoroughly consistent argument // 일사불란하게 in perfect〔strict〕 order

일사천리 一瀉千里 dashing flow of torrents ; rapid advance ¶ 일사천리로 with lightning speed〔rapidity〕; with a rush ; in great haste // 일사천리로 일을 처리하다 dispatch business at full gallop ; make short work of it // 의안을 일사천리로 통과시키다 rush through a bill

일삭 一朔 one〔a〕 month

일삯 wages ⇨ 임금

일산 日産 [생산고] daily output〔production〕; [일본산] Japanese products ; Japan-made ; (of) Japanese make

일산화 一酸化 ¶ 일산화의 monoacidic

—물 monoxide —질소 nitrogen monoxide —탄소 carbon monoxide

일삼다 make it one's business to 《do something》; [전념] devote oneself to ; engage in ; [탐닉] give oneself up to ; indulge in ¶ 술 마시는 것을 일삼다 do nothing but drink ; be given to drink

:일상 日常 everyday ; daily ; usually ; usual ; ordinary // 그것은 일상 다반사이다 It is a daily event.

—복 everyday dress —사 an everyday experience〔occurrence, affair〕 — 생활 everyday〔daily〕 life —어 everyday language — 업무 daily business ; routine work

일색 一色 [한빛] one color ; [미인] a distinguished beauty ¶ 천하 일색 a peerless beauty (in the world) // 그 위원회는 공화당 일색이었다 The committee seats were exclusively occupied by Republicans.

—화 a monochrome ; a monotint

†일생 一生 one's lifetime ; one's (whole) life ; throughout one's life ; as long as one lives ; to the end of one's life ¶ 일생의 lifelong ; for life // 일생의 한 a lifelong regret // 일생의 일 one's life work //

일생에 한번 once in a lifetime // 일생을 통하여 from the cradle to the grave ; from birth to death ; during one's lifetime // 일생 독신으로 지내다 remain single all one's life // 일생을 안락히 보내다 spend one's life in easy circumstances // 일생을 바치다 devote〔dedicate, consecrate, give〕 one's life 《to a cause》 // 일생을 그르치다 make a failure of one's life ; wreck one's chances in life ; ruin one's career // 나는 일생 그날을 잊지 못할 것이다 I shall not forget that day as long as I live〔to the end of my life〕.

— 사업 one's life work **— 소원** one's lifelong desire ; a desire cherished for life **— 일사** living and dying ; life and death

일서 逸書 a scattered and lost book

일석이조 一石二鳥 killing two birds with one stone〔bolt, sling〕 ; serving a double purpose ; to catch two pigeons with one bean

일선 一線 a line ; [전선] the fighting line ; the front ¶ 제 일선에 서다 take the lead

일설 一說 one report〔opinion, view, version〕 ; another opinion ¶ 일설에 의하면 according to another opinion 〔report, view, version〕

일성 一聲 a voice ; a cry ; a shout

일세 一世 a generation ; a lifetime ; the time ; the age ; the day ; the first (of a dynasty) ; senior ¶ 헨리 1세 Henry I〔the first〕 // 일세의 호걸 the greatest hero of the day

일세기 一世紀 one〔a〕 century ; 100 years

일세대 一世代 a〔one〕 generation

일세 일대 一世一代 ¶ 일세 일대의 of one's〔once in a〕 lifetime // 일세 일대의 대작 one's life's masterpiece

일소 一笑 a laugh ; a smile ¶ 일소하여 with a laugh〔smile〕

일소에 붙이다 관용 laugh 《a matter》 off 〔away, down〕 ; dismiss〔carry off〕 《a matter》 with a laugh

*__일소 一掃__ a (clean) sweep ; a cleanup **—하다** sweep〔wash〕 away ; clear 《a place of》 ; make a clean sweep 《of》 ; drive off ; deterge (나쁜 것을) ¶ 다년간의 폐습을 일소하다 clear away abuses of many years' standing // 적을 일소하다 clear 《the place》 of the enemy // 의심을 일소하다 clear away doubts // 부패 분자를 일소하다 make a clean sweep of the corrupt elements

†**일손** work in hand ; [일 솜씨] skill ; performance ; a skillful hand ; skill at a job ; [사람] a hand at work ; a help ; a worker ¶ 일손을 쉬다 take a work break // 일손이 오르다 improve in one's skill // 일손이 떨어지다 fall off in one's skill // 일손이 모자라다 be short-handed ; be undermanned

일수 日收 a loan collected by daily installment ; moneylending at daily interest ; daily earnings

—장이 a moneylender who collects by daily installment

일수 日數 the number of days ; time ; a day's luck ¶ 치료 연일수 days of treatment // 일수가 사납다 have a bad day // 일수가 좋다 The day is lucky.

일수판매 一手販賣 sole agency ; monopoly

일숙박 一宿泊 a night's lodging ¶ 일숙박 1등 3만원 thirty thousand *won* for the first class charge per night // 전주에 일숙박 여행을 하다 make an overnight trip to *Chŏnju*

일순 一旬 ten days

일순 一巡 a round ; a patrol (경관의) **—하다** make a round〔tour〕 《of》 ; take a round ; walk over〔round〕 《a museum》 ; patrol

일순간 一瞬間 an instant ; a moment ; a flash ; a twinkling ¶ 일순간의 momentary // 일순간에 in an instant〔a moment〕

일습 一襲 [의복의] one suit (of clothes) ; a complete outfit ; [도구의] a set ¶ 화장품 일습 a toilet set // 겨울옷 일습 a suit of winter clothes ; a winter suit // 일습의 a set of 《teacups》 ; a suit of 《clothes》

일승일패 一勝一敗 victory and defeat ¶ 일승일패의 승부 a seesaw match

일승일패는 병가상사라 속담 A stumble may prevent fall.

일시 日時 day〔date〕 and time

†**일시 一時** [한때] at one〔a〕 time ; once ; [잠시] for a time〔while〕 ; [임시로] temporarily ; [동시에] all together ; at the same time ¶ 일시적 방편 a temporary expedient〔measure〕 ; a stopgap // 일시적 분노 the anger of the moment // 일시적 인기 a mere mushroom〔transient〕 popularity // 일시적 경기 one-time prosperity // 일시적 충동 the impulse of the moment // 일시적 현상 a passing phenomenon // 짐을 일시 맡기다 leave one's luggage at a cloakroom 《미》 ; have one's baggage checked // 학생들이 일시 떠들기 시작했다 The students got noisy all at once. // 그는 일시 여기에 살았었다 He lived here for a time. // 그는 일시에 갑부가 되었다 He became a millionaire overnight. // 일시불로 내야 합니까 Do I have to pay in a lump sum?

—금 a lump sum allowance **—불** payment in a lump sum ; a lump sum payment **— 차입금** a temporary〔short-term〕 loan ; a floating debt

일시동인 一視同仁 [박애] universal benevolence ; [공평] impartiality ¶ 일시동인의 impartial ; cosmopolitan

일시에 一時— all of a sudden ; [동시에] at a time ; at the same time ; [갑자기] suddenly ; all at once ; abruptly

일시키다 set〔put〕《a person》 to work ; make 《a person》 work ; work

일식 日蝕 a solar eclipse ; an eclipse of the sun

일식경 一息耕 a good(ly) while ; quite some time

:**일신 一新** renovation ; renewal ; a reform ; a revolution **—하다** change completely ; renovate ; reform ; revolutionize ¶ 면목을 일신하다 assume a new aspect ; undergo a complete change // 생활을 일신하다 begin a new life

일신 日新 daily renovation〔improvement〕 **—하다** be renovated daily ; undergo a daily improvement ; undergo a change day after day

일신 一身 oneself ; one's self〔body〕 ; one's life ¶ 일신을 걸고 at the risk of one's life // 일신의 이익을 꾀하다 consult one's own〔personal〕 interests // 일신을 바치다 offer〔devote〕 oneself 《to》

— 이역 (taking charge of) two duties at the same time **— 일가** oneself and one's family

일신교 一神教 monotheism ¶ 일신교의 monotheistic

—도 a monotheist

일신상 一身上 ¶ 일신상의 personal ; private // 일신상의 일로 상담하다 consult 《a person》 about one's personal affairs // 그것은 나의 일신상의 일입니다 This is personal to myself. /The matter is my business. // 일신상의 문제에 언급하는 것을 용서해 주십시오 You will pardon the personal reference.

일심 一審 the first instance〔trial, court〕 ¶ 일심에서 무죄가 되다 be acquitted〔free of charges〕 at the first trial

— 재판소 the court of the first instance

일심 日甚 daily intensification **—하다** get worse day by day ; get more serious from day to day

일심 一心 one mind ; a whole mind ; wholeheartedness ; concentration〔absorption〕 of mind 《on one thing》 ¶ 일심으로 빌다 pray with one's whole heart // 전국민이 일심이 되다 The whole nation unites as one.

—동체 being one in body and spirit ; two hearts beating as one ; one flesh

일심불란 一心不亂 one's whole heart ; heart and soul ; undivided attention ; single-hearted devotion **—하다** give one's whole mind〔heart〕 《to》 ; put one's heart and soul 《into》 ; devote oneself 《to》 ; concentrate upon ¶ 일심불란으로 absorbedly ; with one's whole heart ; whole-heartedly ; intently

일심 전력 一心專力 one's whole mind〔heart〕 and all one's best〔utmost〕 ; all possible efforts **—하다** do one's very best〔utmost〕 ; do all one can ; make every possible efforts ¶ 일심 전력으로 with one's whole heart and all one's might〔energies〕

일쑤 habitual practice ¶ …하기가 일쑤이다 be always doing 《something unpleasant》 // 거짓말하기가 일쑤다 He tells a lie every time he turns around. // 저 애는 울기가 일쑤다 She's a constant crybaby.

일안 리플렉스 一眼— a single-lens reflex (camera)

일야 日夜 day and night ; night and day

일약 一躍 [명사적] one bound〔leap, jump〕 ; [부사적] at a (single) bound ; at a jump ; (all) of a sudden ; at〔with〕 a leap ¶ 일약 유명하게 되다 spring〔leap〕 into fame〔eminence〕 // 그 소설을 써서 일약 문단에 이름을 떨쳤다 He leaped into literary eminence by writing that novel. // 평사원에서 일약 사장이 되었다 From a mere clerk he became president at a bound.

일양 一樣 uniformity ; evenness ; similarity ; equality

일양일 一兩日 a day or two ¶ 일양일간 for a couple of days // 일양일 중에 in a day or two

일어 日語 Japanese ; the Japanese language

†**일어나다** ① [기상] rise (from one's bed) ; get up ; get out of bed ; leave one's bed (병상에서) ¶ 일찍 일어나는 사람 an early-riser // 아침 일찍 일어나다 get up early in the morning // 병석에서 일어나다 get up from a sickbed ; leave one's sickbed // 내가 일어날 시간이다 It's time for me to get up.

② [일어나다] get up ; stand up ; pick oneself up ; regain one's feet ; arise ; recover one's legs ¶ 벌떡 일어나다 spring〔leap, start〕 to one's feet

③ [자지 않고 있다] lie awake ; sit up ; stay up ¶ 어젯밤은 일이 있어서 늦도록 일어나 있었다 Work kept me up till late last night.

④ [발생] happen ; occur ; break out ; arise ; take place ¶ …이 일어날 것만 같다 It's in the cards 《that》 // 그것은 지난달에 일어났던 일이다 It took place〔occurred〕 last month. // 그것은 자주 일어난 일이다 It is a common occurrence. /It occurs very often. // 전쟁이〔화재가〕 일어났다 A war〔fire〕 broke out.

⑤ [원인] arise〔spring, result〕 from ; come of ; originate 《in, from, with》 ; be caused 《by》 ¶ 이 병은 부절제로 일어난다 This disease originates from〔has it's origin in〕 intemperance. // 사고는 부주의에서 자주 일어난다 Accidents are often caused by carelessness.

⑥ [발흥] spring up ; come into being ; arise ; [융성] prosper ; flourish ; be prosperous ; revive ¶ 나라가 크게 일어나다 a nation rides the wave of a great prosperity // 제2차 대전 후 많은 신생국이

일어났다 A great many nations have sprung up since World War Ⅱ. // 최근 각종 공업이 일어났다 Various industries have sprung up lately.
⑦ [불이] be kindled ; be made ; 《a fire》 burn ; get lively ; 《a flame》 rise ¶ 불이 잘 일어난다 The fire is burning lively.
⑧ [바람이] rise ; blow ; come up ¶ 바람이 일어나기 시작한다 The wind is getting up〔rising〕.

†**일어서다** stand up ; rise to one's feet ; [분기] be stir oneself ; brace oneself (up) ; rise (up) ¶ 자리에서 일어서다 rise from one's seat // 벌떡 일어서다 spring〔leap, jump〕 to one's feet // 비틀비틀 일어서다 stagger to one's feet // 간신히 일어서다 struggle to one's feet // 무기를 들고 일어서다 rise in arms // 압제에 반항하여 일어서다 rise against oppression // 그는 농촌을 구제하고자 일어섰다 He set himself to save the agricultural village. // 일어섯 Rise ! /Everybody up ! // 일어서기 전에 딱 한잔만 더 주세요 Give me just one more for the road.

일어탁수 一魚濁水 One man's mistake 〔error, misconduct〕 does damage 〔injury, mischief〕 to many.

일억 一億 a hundred million

일언 一言 a (single) word ; one word **— 하다** speak〔say〕 a word 《about》 ; pass a remark ; put in a word ¶ 남자의 일언 a man's word (of honor) // 일언지하에 거절하다 refuse that by a single word // 남아 일언은 중천금이다 A word of honor is as good as a bond.
—반구 a single word ¶ 그는 일언반구의 인사도 없이 떠나버렸다 He left us without a single word of farewell. **—일행** every word and deed〔act〕

일언이폐지 一言以蔽之 One sentence can cover the whole.

일없다 (be) unwanted ; needless ; there is no need for ; no use for ¶ 옷은 일없으니 돈으로 주십시오 I don't want clothes, give me money. // 그런 것은 일없다 I don't want such a thing.

일여덟 seven or eight

일염기산 一鹽基酸 monobasic acid

일염색체 一染色體 〖유전〗 a monosome

일엽 一葉 one leaf ; one leaf〔sheet〕 of paper
—지추(知秋) knowing autumn from (the fall of) a single leaf ; A straw shows which way the wind blows. **—편주** a light skiff ; a small boat

일요 日曜 ⇨ 일요일
—판 a Sunday edition **— 학교** a Sunday school **— 화가** a Sunday painter

†**일요일 日曜日** Sunday ¶ 일요일 이외의 날 the weekdays // 다음 일요일에 next Sunday ; on Sunday next // 일요일도 없이 일하고 있다 We are working without a day's rest
—판 a Sunday edition

일용 日用 everyday〔daily〕 use ¶ 일용의 daily ; of daily necessity
— 기구 ordinary utensils ; utensils for daily use **— 사전** an everyday〔all-purpose〕 dictionary **—품** daily necessities ; articles for daily use

일우 一隅 a corner ; a nook ¶ 일우에 in a〔one〕 corner ; in a nook

일울다 《cocks》 crow early (in the morning)

일원 一圓 [일대] the whole place 〔area〕 ; the neighborhood ; a tract 《of land》 ; a zone 《of forest》 ¶ 그 근처 일원 the whole neighborhood

일원 一元 (being) unitary ¶ 일원적 unitary ; single ; 〖철학〗 monistic // 일원화 하다 unify
—론 monism **—설** monogenesis

†**일원 一員** a member ¶ 사회〔클럽〕의 일원 a member of society〔club〕

일원제 一院制 the unicameral system ; the single-chamber system ¶ 일원제의 의회 a unicameral legislature

일원화 一元化 unification ; centralization **— 하다** unify ; centralize

†**일월 一月** January 《Jan.》

†**일월 日月** the sun and the moon ; [때] time ; days ; years
—성신 the sun, the moon, and the stars **—식** solar and lunar eclipse(s)

일위 一位 [첫째] the first〔foremost〕 place ; the premier position ; No. 1 ; the first rank ¶ 일위를 차지하다 take 〔hold〕 the foremost place ; rank 〔stand〕 first ; be at the top ; head the list ; lead // 그는 항상 학급에서 1위이다 He is always at the top of his class. // 미국은 수출국 중 제1위를 차지하고 있다 America ranks first〔holds the foremost position〕 among the exporting countries.

†**일으키다** ① [세우다] raise ; get up (-right) ; set up ; help〔pick〕 《a person》 up ¶ 몸을 일으키다 rise ; get up // 일으켜 세우다 make 《a person》 stand // 아이를 일으켜 주다 help a child to his feet // 도와 일으키다 help〔lift〕 《a person》 to his feet ; help 《a person》 up
② [깨우다] wake up ; call ; rout out ; awaken ¶ 깊은 잠에서 일으켜지다 be aroused out of a sound sleep // 6시에 일으켜 주시오 Please wake〔call〕 me at 6.
③ [창시] start 《a school》 ; initiate ; commence ; open ; begin ; bring about ; give rise to ; undertake ; set afoot ; establish ; found ; reestablish ¶ 사업을 일으키다 promote an enterprise // 학교를 일으키다 establish〔found〕 a school // 운동을 일으키다 start a movement ; set a movement on foot ; launch a drive〔campaign〕 // 회사를 일으키다 form a company
④ [야기] cause ; breed ; raise ; bring about〔on〕 ; lead to ; give rise to ; pro-

voke ; invite ; arouse ¶ 의심을 일으키다 raise a doubt // 전쟁〔대소동〕을 일으키다 bring about war〔great commotion〕 // 폭동을 일으키다 raise a riot // 흥미를 일으키다 excite〔arouse〕《a person's》 interest // 발작을 일으키다 have a fit 《of apoplexy》 // 소송을 일으키다 bring a suit〔an action〕《against a person》

⑤ [불을] kindle ; make up 《a fire》 ; build 《a fire》 ¶ 불어서 불을 일으키다 blow up the fire

⑥ [번영] ¶ 나라를 크게 일으키다 bring a nation to great prosperity

⑦ [발생] generate 《electricity》 ; produce 《heat》 ; raise ; excite ¶ 전기를 일으키다 generate electricity

일의대수 一衣帶水 a tiny ribbon of water ; a narrow stream〔strait〕 ; a narrow streak of water

일익 日益 daily ; everyday ; day by〔after〕 day ; from day to day ¶ 사태가 일익 악화하다 the situation is getting worse by the day // 일익 더워집니다 It is growing hotter everyday. /It is getting hotter and hotter.

일익 一翼 a part ; a role ¶ 일익을 담당하다 bear a part

†**일인 一人** one person
—당 for each (person) ; per head ¶ 일인당 100원 a hundred won for one person **— 독재** one-man〔personal〕 dictatorship **—분** a portion for one person ; one helping (식사의) **—승 비행기〔자동차〕** a single seater **— 이역** a double role **— 일기(—技)** one man, one skill **— 지도 체제** a unitary leadership

일인 日人 a Japanese ; the Japanese 《총칭》

일인자 一人者 the first(-ranking) person ; the greatest〔leading〕 person ; the first among one's peers ; the pick ¶ 그는 현대 작가의 일인자이다 He stands foremost among the writers of today. // 그는 연극계의 일인자이다 He takes a premier stand in the theatrical world.

일인칭 一人稱 〖문법〗 the first person

일일 一日 a〔one〕 day ; the first day (of a month) ¶ 제 일일 the first day // 일일이 천추 같다 feel as if one day were years **— 일선** a good deed a day **—학(瘧)** quotidian ague ; diurnal malaria

일일 日日 every day ; daily ⇨ 매일 ¶ 일일의 everyday ; daily

*****일일이** [하나씩] one by one ; individually ; separately ; [상세히] in detail ; in full ; [모두] everything ; in everything〔every case〕 ¶ 일일이 조사하다 examine 《a thing》 one by one // 일일이 설명하다 explain in detail〔point by point〕 // 일일이 보고하다 report in full // 일일이 트집잡다 find fault with everything 《a person》 does // 그는 내가 하는 일에 일일이 간섭하다 He meddles with me in every blessed thing I do.

일일지장 一日之長 superiority ; be a little ahead of (a person) ¶ 나는 이점에서 너보다 일일지장이 있다 I am a bit your senior in this line.

일임 一任 — 하다 leave 《a matter》 in the hands 《of》 ; leave 《a matter》 to 《a person》 ; trust 《a person》 with a matter ; commit 《a matter》 to 《a person's》 care ¶ 자네에게 일임하네 I leave it to you. /I leave the matter in your hands.

일자 日字 [날짜] a date ; [날수] the number of days ¶ 일자는 얼마 걸립니까 How long〔many days〕 will it take ?
— 변경선 a date line

일자리 a job ; a position ¶ 일자리를 찾다 seek a job ; look for a position // 일자리를 얻다 get a job ; find a position ; obtain employment

일자무식 一字無識 utter ignorance
—꾼 an illiterate person

일자이후 一自以後 since then till now ; from that time on ; ever since (줄곧)

일잠 going to bed early ¶ 일잠 자다 go to bed〔retire〕 early

일장 一場 a spell of action ; a scene ¶ 일장의 연설을 하다 make〔deliver〕 a speech ; address
— 연설 a speech ; an address ¶ 일장 연설을 하다 make〔deliver〕 a speech ; address 《an audience》 **—춘몽** a spring〔an empty〕 dream **— 통곡** a spell of weeping ; a (good) cry **—풍파** a spell of wind and waves

일장일단 一長一短 merits and demerits ; strength and weakeness ¶ 일장일단이 있다 have both merits and demerits

일재 逸材, 逸才 superior talent

일전 日前 the other day ; some time ago ; a few days ago ; recently

일전 一戰 a battle ; an engagement ¶ 적과 일전하다 fight a battle with an enemy ; have a game (경기)

일전 一轉 a complete change ; a turn **— 하다** [회전] turn round ; [일변] make a complete change

†**일절 一切** all ; wholly ; entirely ; altogether ; absolutely ¶ 일절 …하지 않다 never 《do》 ; not at all // 사례는 일절 받지 않습니다 I decline any form of reward. // 외상은 일절 사절합니다 We never sell on credit. /Positively no credit.

일절 一節 a section ; a paragraph ; a passage ; a verse ; a stanza (시의) ; a syllable (음절) ¶ 제3장 제1절 Chapter Ⅲ, section 1

일점 一點 a point ; a dot ; an article (한 개) ; one

일점홍 一點紅 a member of the fair sex at a men's party ⇨ 홍일점

일정 日程 the day's program〔schedule〕 ; [의사] the order of the day ; the calendar ; [의안] the agenda ¶ 일정에 올리다

〔넣다〕 place 《a bill》 on the order of the day ; place on the calendar // 일정을 변경하다 alter a day's program

†**일정 一定 ━하다** be fixed〔set, settled〕; be regular〔established, uniform〕 ¶ 일정한 목적 a definite object // 일정한 서식 a prescribed〔set〕 form // 일정한 수입 a regular income // 일정한 식사 시간 the regular hour for eating // 일정한 일 a steady job ; a regular work // 일정한 표준 a fixed standard // 일정하게 하다 standardize ; unify ; secure a unity of // 복장을 일정하게 하다 standardize the clothing

일정 불변 一定不變 ¶ 일정 불변의 invariable ; constant ; permanent // 일정 불변의 방침 a definite and unchanging policy

*__일제 一齊__ ¶ 일제히 altogether (다같이) ; all at once (동시에) ; in chorus ; simultaneously (이구동성으로) // 일제히 외치다〔말하다〕 shout〔say〕 in chorus〔unison〕 // 일제 사격을 하다 fire a volley ; volley 《at》

━ 검거 a roundup ; a wholesale〔blanket〕 arrest **━ 사격** volley firing ; a simultaneous discharge

일제 日帝 Japanese imperialism ; imperialist Japan ¶ 일제하에 under the rule of Japanese imperialism ; under the Japanese (imperialistic) rule

일제 日製 Japanese make ; Japanese manufacture ¶ 일제의 of Japanese make ; made in Japan ; Japanese // 일제 화장품 Japanese-made cosmetics

일조 一朝 ¶ 일조에 in a day // 일조 유사시에 in case of emergency ; in time of need

━일석 one morning or one evening ; a brief space〔span〕 of time ¶ 로마는 일조일석에 이루어지지 않았다 Rome was not built in a day.

*__일조 日照__ sunshine ¶ 일조 시간은 일년에 2천 5백 시간이다 be blessed with 2,500 hours of sunlight annually

━계 a heliograph **━권** a right to enjoy sunshine **━ 시간** the duration of sunshine ; sunshine duration **━율** the percentage of sunshine

일조 一助 ¶ 일조가 되다 be a help 《to》; be helpful ; be of a help 《toward》

*†__일족 一族__ [친족] all one's family and relatives ; kinsmen ; the whole clan ; [가족] the whole family

*__일종 一種__ a kind ; a sort ; a species ; a variety ¶ 동물의 일종 a species of animal // 제 일종 우편물 first-class mail // 일종의 a kind〔sort〕 of ; of a kind〔sort〕 // 벼는 풀의 일종이다 The rice plant is a kind〔variety〕 of grass. // 그는 일종의 천재이다 He is a genius of a kind〔sort〕.

일좌 一座 [온좌석] the party ; the (whole) company ; all those〔the persons〕 present

*__일주 一周__ a round ; a tour ; a circumnavigation ; a lap **━하다** go〔walk, travel〕 round ; make a round ; make a tour 《of》 ; circle ; circuit ; sail round ; circumnavigate 《the globe》 ¶ 세계를 일주하다 go〔travel〕 round the world ; make a tour of the world ; make a round-the-world trip // 세계 일주 비행을 하다 make a round-the-world flight // 지구는 1년에 태양을 일주한다 The earth goes〔revolves〕 round the sun once a year.

━기(期) 〖천문〗 a period **━기(忌)** the first anniversary of one's death **━년** the first anniversary **━ 여행** the round trip ¶ 세계 일주 여행 a round-the-world trip

일주 一週 a week ¶ 일주 노동 시간수 work(ing) week // 일주 1〔2〕회(의) once〔twice〕 a week // 일주일의 휴가 a week's leave〔holiday, vacation〕

━ 5일제 the five-day work week

일주년 一週年 a full year

━ 기념 the first anniversary 《of》 ¶ 창립 일주년 기념 행사를 하다 observe the first anniversary of the opening〔foundation〕 《of the school》

일주야 一晝夜 a whole day and night

일주 운동 日周運動 diurnal motion

일중 日中 noon ; noontime ; midday

†**일지 日誌** a diary ; a journal ⇨ 일기

일직 日直 day duty ; day watch **━하다** be on day duty

━ 장교 an officer of the day ; an orderly officer 《영》

일직선 一直線 a straight line ¶ 일직선으로 straight ; in a straight line ; in a beeline // 일직선으로 나아가다 advance in a straight line // 서울에서 일직선으로 가서 50마일이다 It is 50 miles in a straight line from *Seoul*. // 비행기는 도시의 상공을 일직선으로 가로질렀다 The plane flew in a beeline across the city.

일진 日辰 the binary designation of the day according to the sexagenary cycle ; the day's luck (운수) ¶ 일진이 사납다 This is not a lucky day for me.

*__일진 一陣__ [진지] a military camp ; the van (of an army) ; the vanguard ; [한바탕의] gust〔puff〕 of wind

━ 광풍 a strong gust〔blast〕 of wind ¶ 창으로 일진 광풍이 불어 들어와 촛불이 모두 꺼졌다 A gust of wind blowing in at the window put out all the candles. **━ 청풍** a puff of breeze

일진월보 日進月步 steady progress ; rapid advance ¶ 일진월보하는 progressive ; ever-〔rapidly-〕advancing

일진일퇴 一進一退 advance and retreat ; ebb and flow **━하다** advance and retreat ; ebb and flow ; be everchangeful〔everchanging〕 ; fluctuate ¶ 일진일퇴의 now advancing and now retreating ; everchanging ; fluctuating ; seesaw // 일진일퇴의 승부 a seesaw game // 그의 병세는 일진일퇴하고 있다 Sometimes he gets

a little better but then he has a relapse 〔gets worse〕
일쩝다 (be) annoying ; irksome ; (I) am annoyed
일쭉얄쭉 smooth and slippery ; slipping easily this way and that (like fine textured cloth) **—하다** slip〔slide〕 easily this way and that ; give way easily
일찌감치 earlier ⇨ 일찌거니
일찌거니 a little early ; rather early ¶ 좀 일찌거니 a little〔bit〕 earlier 《than》// 일찌거니 떠나다 make〔get off to〕 a little earlier start // 물론 일찌거니 와주면 더욱 좋다 Of course, if you're a bit earlier, all the better.
일찍 early ⇨ 일찍이 ¶ 좀 일찍 a little〔bit〕 earlier // 일찍 피는 early flowering // 일찍 일어나다 rise〔get up〕 early // 일찍 떠나다 make an early start // 기차가 10분 일찍 도착했다 The train arrived ten minutes ahead of time.
†**일찍이** ① early ¶ 일찍이 일어나다 get up early // 일찍이 죽다 die young // 그는 일찍이 부모를 여의었다 He lost his parents at an early age.
② [전에] earlier ; once ; at one time ; formerly // 일찍이 들어본 일이 없다 I have never heard of such a thing. // 그 여자는 일찍이 여배우인 적이 있었다 She was at one time〔formerly〕 an actress.
일차 一次 one time ; once ; the first ; 〚수학〛 linear ¶ 일차의 first ; primary
— 반응 〚화학〛 a first-order reaction **— 방정식** an equation of the first degree ; a linear〔simple〕 equation **— 시험** a primary examination ; [예비 시험] a preliminary examination **— 전류** the primary current **— 전지〔코일〕** the primary battery〔coil〕
일착 一着 ① [경주의] the first arrival ; the first in ; the first to arrive〔come in〕 **—하다** come in first ; finish first ; be the first to come in ; win the first place ② [옷의] a suit 《of clothes》 ¶ 하복 일착 a summer suit ; a suit for summer wear // 일착분의 복지 a pattern of woolen cloth
일책 一策 a plan ; an idea ; a move ¶ 일책을 생각해 내다 devise〔think out〕 a plan // 일책을 내놓다 suggest a plan ; make a suggestion // 그것도 일책이다 That's a good idea, too. // 나에게 일책이 있다 I have got a plan. // 일책이 떠올랐다 I hit upon a plan.
일처다부 一妻多夫 polyandry ¶ 일처다부의 polyandrous
일척 一擲 —하다 throw〔cast〕 away ; abandon
일천 日淺 being a few days old **—하다** be a few days old ; (be) short ; be not long ¶ 취직한지 아직 일천하다 It is not long since he got his job. // 회사는 창립한지 아직 일천하다 It is only a short time since the company was founded.
†**일체 一體** one body ; a single body ¶ 일체가 되어 in a body ; as a man ; as one body ; en bloc // 부부는 일체다 Husband and wife are one flesh.
—식 구조 〚건축〛 monolithic construction **— 양면론** the double aspect theory **—화** unification ; integration
*__일체 一切__ all ; everything ; the whole ; [부사적] entirely ; wholly ; altogether ¶ 일체의 비용 the whole cost 《of》// 일체의 관계를 끊다 cut off all relations 《with》// 사건의 진상은 일체 비밀로 되어 있다 Absolute secrecy is preserved as to the actual state of the matter. // 본건에는 일체 관계가 없다 I have nothing whatever to do with this affair. // 그 노인은 전쟁으로 일체의 재산을 잃었다 The old man lost all〔the whole of〕 his property because of the war. // 외상 일체 사절 Positively no credit.
일체 중생 一切衆生 all living beings 〔things〕 ; all creatures ; all life〔flesh〕 ; the whole of (all) mankind
일촉즉발 一觸卽發 a touch-and-go situation ; a situation full of dynamite〔ripe for explosion〕 ; a delicate situation ; a condition of simmering rebellion〔anger〕 ¶ 양국간의 관계가 일촉즉발의 위기에 있다 Things are strained to the breaking point between the two countries.
일촌광음 불가경 一寸光陰不可輕 Improve every minute. /Even a moment of time must not be slighted.
일축 一蹴 —하다 [걷어차다] kick ; [거절하다] turn down ; refuse〔reject〕 flatly ; [이기다] beat〔win〕 easily ¶ 상대를 가볍게 일축하다 [경기에서] beat easily ; brush off lightly // 그의 제안을 일축했다 I spurned〔turned down〕 his proposal.
일출 逸出 ① [빠져 나옴] escape ; yaw ② [뛰어남] ⇨ 걸출(傑出) **—하다** escape 《from a place》 ; run away 《from》 ; force one's way out 《of a place》
일출 溢出 effusion ; overflow ; 〚의학·지질〛 extravasation **—하다** overflow ; flow 〔run〕 over 《the banks》 ; effuse
일출 日出 sunrise
일취월장 日就月將 daily progress and monthly advance (as in study) **—하다** make progress day after day and month after month ; make steady progress ¶ 일취월장의 progressive ; ever-advancing
일층 一層 ① [건물의] one story ; the ground-floor 《영》 ; the first floor 《미》 ② [더욱] more ; still more ; all the more ; only the more ¶ 일층 힘이 드는 일 a (much) harder work // 일층 노력하다 make greater efforts ; work harder (than ever)
†**일치 一致** agreement ; accord ; [조화] harmony ; [통일] unity ; [부합] correspondence ; [협력] cooperation ; 〚문법〛

[수·성·인칭 따위의] concord ; agreement ; [시제의] sequence (of tenses) **—하다** agree 《with》; accord 《with》; be at one 《with》; harmonize 《with》; correspond 《to, with》; unite ; cooperate ¶ 의견의 일치 consensus of opinions // 일치된 united ; unanimous ; harmonious // 일치하여 unitedly ; unanimously ; in union ; as one man // 동의를 만장 일치로 가결하다 carry a motion without dissent // 이상과 실제는 결코 일치하지 않는다 The ideal and the real never coincide. // 그의 행동은 약속과 일치하지 않다 His actions are not in keeping with his promises. // 그 법안은 만장 일치로 가결되었다 The bill was passed unanimously by common consent.
— 단결 union ; solidarity ; harmonious cooperation **—점** a meeting point ; a point of convergence〔concurrence, getting together〕; the common ground **—협력** united〔combined〕 efforts ; cooperation

일컫다 ① call ; name ; style ; designate ¶ B라고 일컫는 사람 a man named B // 스스로 대학자라고 일컫다 style oneself as a great scholar // 미인이라고 일컬어 진다 She is reputed to be a beauty.
② [칭찬하다] praise ; commend ; admire ; laud ; pay tribute to ¶ 모든 사람이 그의 덕을 일컬었다 Everybody extolled his supreme virtue.

*__일탈 逸脫__ omission (by mistake) ; deviation ; departure **—하다** deviate 《from》; omit ; depart 《from》 ¶ 오랜 습관에서의 일탈 a radical departure〔deviation〕 from long-standing customs

일터 a job site ; a workshop ; one's office ; a construction site (공사장)

일통 一通 a copy 《of》
서류 — one document

일통 一統 unification **—하다, 치다** unify ; unite ; bring 《a country》 under sway

일파 一派 [유파] a school ; [파당] a party ; [종파] a sect ; a faction ¶ 일파를 이루다 create a school ; found a new sect (종교의)

일패 一敗 a single defeat
—도지(塗地) a complete〔crushing〕 defeat ; an overwhelming reverse 《at the hands of》 ¶ 일패도지하다 meet with complete defeat ; suffer a crushing defeat

†**일편 一片** a〔one〕 piece ; a bit ¶ 일편의 양심 a bit〔modicum〕 of conscience
—단심 a sincere heart ; sincerity ¶ 일편단심의 sincere ; single〔true, whole〕-hearted

일편 一篇 a piece ¶ 일편의 시 a piece of poetry

일평생 一平生 all one's life ; all days of one's life ; [부사적] all one's life〔days〕; throughout〔all through〕 one's life ; to the end of one's days〔life〕; from the cradle to the grave ¶ 일생의 일 a life-work // 일평생에 한번 once in a lifetime // 일평생을 통하여 from birth to death // 연구에 일평생을 바치다 give a lifetime to the study 《of》; devote one's life 《to》 // 일평생 독신으로 지내다 remain single all one's life〔to the end of one's life〕 // 그는 일평생 행복하게 지냈다 He was happy all his life. // 그것은 그의 일평생의 큰 실수였다 That was the gravest blunder in his life.

일폭 一幅 a scroll ¶ 일폭의 명화 a notable painting // 동양화 일폭 a scroll of Oriental painting // 그 광경은 마치 일폭의 그림과 같다 The scene looks like a picture scroll spread out.

일표 一票 a vote ; a ballot
일인 —주의 one man one vote principle

일품 一品 an article ; [한개] a piece ; [요리] a dish ; a course
— 요리 a one-course dinner〔service〕; a one-dish meal〔dinner〕; [선택 요리] dishes à la carte (프) **천하 —** an article of peerless quality ; a unique article ; a nonesuch

일품 逸品 an article par excellence ; an excellent thing ; an unusual〔rare〕 article

일필 一筆 one stroke of a brush〔pen〕
—휘지 dashing off with one stroke of a brush ¶ 일필휘지하다 write with one stroke of a brush

†**일하다** work ; labor ; toil ; [근무하다] be employed ; serve 《a person》; be in the service〔employ〕 《of》 ¶ 먹고 살기 위해 일하다 work for a living // 지나치게 일하다 work too hard ; overwork 《oneself》 // 너무 일해서 병나다 work oneself ill // 열심히 일하다 work hard // 일해가며 대학을 나오다 work one's way through college // 일하고 있다 He is working〔at work〕. // 20년간 그 회사에서 일했다 He was employed in〔in the service of〕 the company for twenty years. // 일하지 않는 자는 먹지 말라 No work, no pay. /If any does not work, neither should he eat.

일한 日限 a date ; a fixed time ; an appointed day〔time〕 ¶ 일한 내에 within the time set // 일한을 정하다 fix〔set〕 the date〔term〕; give time-limits // 일한을 연기하다 extend the time〔term〕 // 계약의 일한이 마감된다 The contract expires. // 지불 일한이 된다 The payment〔bill〕 is 〔falls〕 due.

일할 一割 ten percent ; 10% ¶ 일할 할인 ten percent discount

†**일행 一行** ① [동아리] a party ; a company ; one's suite (수행원) ; a troupe (흥행단) ¶ 관광단 일행 a tourist party // 수상 일행 the Premier and his suite〔party〕 // 일행의 사람들 the members of a party // 일행에 참가하다 join the party ; be a

member of the party // 일행은 3명이었다 The party consisted of three (members). ② [한줄] a line ; a row ; a line of verse (시의) ¶ 일행 띄어서 쓰다 write on every other line

일현금 一弦琴 a one-stringed instrument ; a monochord

일혈 溢血 〖의학〗 extravasation ; effusion of blood ⇨ 뇌일혈

뇌— cerebral h(a)emorrhage ; (a stroke of) apoplexy

일호 一號 No. 1 ; number one

일호 一毫 a hair's breadth ; the smallest fraction ; a bid ; a trifle ¶ 일호도 (not) in the least ; (not) a jot〔whit, bit〕

—반점(半點) ⇨ 일호(一毫)

∗∗일화 逸話 an anecdote ¶ 그에게는 재미있는 일화가 있다 An amusing anecdote is told of him.

—집 an an ecdotage

일화 日貨 Japanese goods (상품) ; Japanese money (화폐) ¶ 일화 배척 a boycott of〔against〕 Japanese goods

일확천금 一攫千金 making a big fortune on a single occasion〔with one swoop〕

—하다 make a big fortune at one stroke ; get rich quick ¶ 일확천금적인 사업 a get-rich-quick business // 일확천금을 꿈꾸다 dream of making a fortune at one stroke

일환 一環 a link ¶ 일환을 이루다 form a part 《of》; be a link in a chain 《of》// 계획의 일환을 이루다 form a part of the program

∗일회 一回 one time ; once ; a game ; a round ; an inning ¶ 제일회 회합 the first meeting // 일주에 일회 once a week // 일회 내지 수회 one or more times // 단 일회로 시험에 합격하다 succeed in an examination at one's first attempt

—분 a dose (of medicine) **— 승부** a contest of single round **—전** [첫번째 시합] the first game ; [토너먼트의] the first round

일후 日後 in the future ; in days to come

일훈 日暈 ⇨ 햇무리

일흔 seventy ; three score and ten ¶ 일흔 일곱 seventy-seven

일희일비 一喜一悲 alternation of joy and grief〔laughter and tears〕; being now glad, now sad ; a mingled〔mixed〕 blessing **—하다** have joy and sorrow in quick alternation ; have a mixed sensation of joy and depression ; be now glad, now sad ¶ 선거가 시작되어 후보자들은 일희일비의 상태다 Now that the poll〔voting〕 is going on, candidates are agitated, now being optimistic, now pessimistic. // 아버지의 병세는 지금 일희일비의 상태이다 Father's condition is now encouraging, now alarming. /Father's condition varies between good and bad.

†읽다 read ; peruse (정독하다) ; [암송] recite ; [경문 따위를] chant 《a sutra》 ¶ 읽기 reading ; reading lessons // 읽고 쓰기 reading and writing // 읽을 거리가 없는 잡지 a magazine with little content // 고교생이 꼭 읽어야 할 책 a must book for high-school students // 읽기 쉬운 easy to read ; readable ; legible (필적, 인쇄 따위) // 소설을 읽으면서 울다 cry〔weep〕 over a novel ; be moved to tears by a novel // 정신들여 읽다 peruse ; read carefully〔with care〕// 널리 읽다 read widely // 소리 내어 읽다 read aloud ; read out〔off〕// 읽어주다 read to 《a person》// 다 읽다 read through 《a book》// 신문에서 읽다 read about 《a matter》 in a newspaper // 한자 한자 음미하며 읽다 dwell on each word ; read word by word // 이 책을 다 읽었다 I have done with this book. // 이 책은 주의 깊게 읽을 가치가 있다 The book is well worth careful perusal. // 그 여자는 악보를 유창하게 읽을 줄 안다 She can read music fluently. // 당신이 모든 것을 정확히 받아 썼는지 확인하기 위해서 그런데 다시 좀 읽어 주시겠어요 Will you read it back to me to make sure you got everything correct ?

읽히다 get 《a person》 to read ; have 《a person》 learn ; set 《a person》 to reading ¶ 널리 읽히는 책 a widely-read book // 어린아이들한테 논어를 읽히다 get children to read the Confucian Analects

†잃다 lose ; miss ; be deprived〔bereft〕 of (빼기다) ¶ 잃어 버린 물건 a lost article ; things lost ; a thing dropped by mistake 《on the road》// 기회를 잃다 miss〔lose〕 an opportunity // 희망〔직업, 생명〕을 잃다 lose one's hope〔position, life〕// 면목을 잃다 lose one's face ; bring disgrace upon oneself // 길을 잃다 get lost ; lose oneself // 아버지를 잃다 lose one's father ; be bereft of one's father // 집을 잃다 be left homeless ; be dispossessed of one's home (빼기다) // 잃을 뿐 얻음이 없다 We have everything to lose and nothing to gain. // 그 여자는 전쟁중에 아들 셋을 잃어버렸다 She lost three sons in the war. // 그는 경마에서 돈을 상당히 잃었다 He lost a large amount of money in horse racing. /He suffered a heavy loss in horse races. // 그는 자유를 잃어버렸다 He was deprived of his freedom. // 한번 잃은 시간은 두번 다시 오지 않는다 Time, once lost, is never to be recovered. // 그들은 국민적 특색을 잃어버린 것같이 여겨진다 They seem to have divested themselves entirely of their national traits.

잃어버리다 ⇨ 잃다

임 one's beloved〔sweetheart〕; one's love〔lover〕 ¶ 옛임 one's old flame // 임 그리운 마음 a heart pining for an absent love // 임 향한 일편단심이야 가실 줄이 있으랴 How can my devotion to my lord possibly vanish !

임도 보고 뽕도 딴다 [속담] To catch two pigeons with one bean. /To kill two birds with one stone〔bolt, sling〕.

임 壬 ① the 9th of the 10 Heaven's Stems ② [임방] north-by-northwest ③ [임시] the last of the 24 hour periods《10 : 30~11 : 30 p. m.》

임간 林間 the interior of a forest〔wood〕 ¶ 임간에서 in a wood〔forest〕
— 학교 an open-air〔outdoor〕 school ; a camping〔forest〕 school ; a school in the wood

임갈 굴정 臨渴掘井 lack of foresight ; short-sightedness

임검 臨檢 an official inspection ; a search ; a visit of inspection ; a domiciliary visit〔search〕; [급습] a (police) raid ; a surprise visit ; boarding (배의)
—하다 visit and inspect ; make a search of《a room for something》; raid ; make a raid《on》; pay a surprise visit《to》; board (배를) ¶ 임검을 행하다 conduct a spot inspection // 현장을 임검하다 make an official inspection of the site〔scene〕// 선박의 임검을 행하다 search a ship ; institute a search on vessels
—반 a raiding party ; [배의] a boarding party —증 a certificate of inspection

임계 臨界 critical
—각 critical angle —량 critical mass — 상태〔점〕 the critical state〔point〕 — 실험 장치 a critical assembly — 온도〔고도, 압력〕 critical temperature〔altitude, pressure〕

임관 任官 appointment《to an office》; an entrance into office ; an installation ; commission (장교의) —하다 be appointed《to an office》; be installed in《an office》; be gazetted《as》; be commissioned ; receive one's commission (군인이) ¶ 임관의 인사 an inaugural address // 임관되다 get appointed《to an office》; be commissioned (무관) // 소위로 임관하다 be commissioned a second lieutenant
—식 a ceremony of one's installation ¶ 임관식을 행하다 hold an inaugural ceremony ; inaugurate — 장교 a commissioned officer

임균 淋菌 a gonococcus《*pl.* -cocci》
—성 안염 gonorrheal ophthalmia —성 요도염 gonorrheal urethritis

임금 a king ; a ruler ; a sovereign ; a monarch

†**임금** 賃金 wages ; pay ¶ 임금을 얻다 get〔earn〕 wages // 임금을 지불하다 pay (wages) // 임금을 올리다〔내리다〕 raise〔lower, cut down〕 wages〔the fares〕// 임금이 싸다〔비싸다〕 Labor is cheap〔dear〕.
— 격차 wage disparity — 노동 work for wages — 노동자 a wage earner — 대장 a wage ledger — 동결 freezing of wages —률 a wage〔pay〕 rate〔scale〕 — 마감일 the closing day for the payroll — 물가 체계 the wage-price structure — 베이스 a wage base — 생활자 a wage earner〔slave〕 — 수준 a wage level — 안정 wage stabilization — 연동제 the sliding scale wage system — 인상 a wage increase ; a pay raise ; a wage boost〔hike〕《미》 ¶ 임금 인상을 요구하다 demand higher wages〔pay〕 — 인하 a wage decrease〔cut, reduction〕 — 정책 a wage policy — 제도 the wage system — 지불일 a payday — 지수 a wage index — 철칙 the Iron Law of Wages — 통제 wage control — 통제령 the Wage Control Ordinance — 투쟁 a struggle for higher wages — 형태 a wage payment plan ; a method〔form〕 of wage payment
기본 — basic wages 기준 — the standard〔basic〕 wage 능률 — efficiency wages ; wages based on efficiency 명목 — nominal wages 시간 — time wages 실질 — real wages ; take-home (pay)《미》 전시 특별 — war wages 지역별 — regional wage differentials 최고〔최저, 생활〕 — maximum〔minimum, living〕 wages 최저 —제 the legal minimum wage system

임기 任期 one's term of office〔service〕; one's tenure (of office) ; a term of membership (의원의) ¶ 임기중 during one's term〔tenure〕 of office // 임기를 연장하다 extend one's term // 임기를 마치다 wind up one's service ; finish up one's tenure of office // 그의 임기는 끝났다 His term of office has expired. // 대통령의 임기는 5년이다 The President holds office for five years. /The President's tenure of office is five years. /The (length of the) Presidential tenure is five years.
— 만료 completion〔expiration〕 of one's term of office

임기응변 臨機應變 adaptation to circumstances —하다 act according to the circumstances ; adapt oneself to circumstances〔the moment〕 ¶ 임기응변의 extemporaneous ; expedient ; emergency // 임기응변으로 extemporaneously ; as the occasion demands ; according to circumstances // 임기응변의 재주가 있다 have the ability to accommodate oneself to circumstances ; be resourceful ; be full of resources // 임기응변의 조치를 취하다 take such a step as the occasion demands ; take emergency measures ; rise to the occasion ; resort to a temporary expedient ; take measures suited to the occasion // 경우에 따라서는 임기응변만 부리시오 Just take care of each situation as the occasion demands, will you?

‡**임대** 賃貸 (receiving money by) lease (부동산의) ; letting out on hire (기구 따위의) ; hiring out (물품의) ; charter (배

의) ; location (부동산의) —하다 lease ; hire 《out》 ; rent ; locate (토지·가옥따위를) ; hire out 《a boat》 ; let 《a thing》 out on hire ; charter 《a ship》

— 가격 rental value ; value of lease — 계약 a lease contract —료 rent ; charterage (배의) ; the charge for hire —물 a hired article —인 a lessor ; a leaseholder —지 leased land —차(借) lease ; letting and hiring ; charter (배의)

임대 책중 任大責重 weighty〔heavy〕 responsibility —하다 be weighty〔serious, heavy〕 in responsibility

임독 淋毒 〖의학〗 gonorrhoeal infection ; a clap 《속》

—균 a gonococcus 《*pl.* -cocci》 —성 관절염〔안염〕 gonorrheal rheumatism 〔opthalmia〕

임률 賃率 rate ; [화물의] freight rates ; [노임의] a wage scale

임립 林立 —하다 stand close together ; bristle ¶ 항구에 돛대가 임립해 있다 The harbor bristles with masts.

임면 任免 appointment and dismissal —하다 appoint and dismiss〔remove〕

—권 the power to appoint and to dismiss

‡임명 任命 appointment ; nomination ; designation ; commission (무관의) —하다 appoint 《a person to〔as〕 ; nominate 〔name〕 《a person for a position》 ¶ 그는 외무부 장관으로 임명되었다 He was appointed Minister of Foreign Affairs. // 정부는 그를 비서관으로 임명했다 The government appointed him to the post of secretary.

—권 the appointing power —식 a ceremony of appointment ; an investiture

임목 林木 a forest tree

†임무 任務 a duty ; an office ; a task ; official duties ; mission (사명) ¶ 중요 임무 an important duty ; a grave task〔mission〕 // 신문의 임무 the function of a newspaper // 특별 임무를 띠고 on special service ; on a special mission // 임무를 수행하다 discharge〔carry out〕 one's duties ; accomplish one's allotted task // 임무를 짊어지다 take up the task ; take over the duties // 임무를 게을리 하다 neglect one's task // 그는 임무 수행중 부상했다 He was injured in the discharge of his duty. // 그는 가끔 임무를 소홀히 한다 He is now and then neglectful〔negligent〕 of his duties.

임무관 林務官 a (government) forester ; an inspector of state〔government〕 forests ; a forestry officer

*임박 臨迫 approaching ; impending —하다 draw near ; approach ; impend ; be at hand ; be on the point〔brink〕 of ¶ 눈앞에 임박한 위험 a pressing danger // …에 임박하여 at the last moment ; on the point〔verge〕 《of》 // 기한이 임박했다 The time draws near. // 그는 사기(死期)가 임박했다 He is dying〔on the verge of death〕. // 시험이 임박했다 The examination is near at hand. // 여행 출발의 날이 임박했다 The day when I start for my journey is drawing near〔near at hand, approaching〕.

임방 壬方 north-by-northwest

임부 妊婦 a pregnant woman ; a woman with child ; an expectant mother (초산의)

—복 a maternity dress〔robe, gown〕

임사 臨事 —하다 meet with an affair ; have an affair at hand

임삭 臨朔 the last month of pregnancy ; the month of parturition ; the month in which childbirth is due〔expected〕 —하다 come to one's time 《of parturition》 ¶ 임삭의 여자 a parturient woman // 그녀는 이 달이 임삭이다 Her time comes this month. /She is going to have a baby this month.

임산물 林産物 forest products

임산부 妊産婦 pregnant women and nursing mothers

*임상 臨床 〖의학〗 clinic ¶ 임상의 clinical // 임상적으로 clinically // 임상 진찰하다 clinically examine ; pursue a clinical examination

— 강의 clinical lecture〔instruction〕 ; bedside instruction ; a clinic — 교수 clinical instruction — 병리학 clinical pathology — 실험〔실습〕 (bedside and) clinical demonstration〔training〕 — 심문 a clinical examination —의(醫) a clinician ; a therapist — 의학 clinical medicine ; clinics — 일기 a physician's diary — 진단 (a) clinical diagnosis —진찰 a clinical examination

임석 臨席 attendance ; presence —하다 attend ; be present 《at》 ¶ 임석 하에 with 《a person》 in attendance ; in the presence of 《a person》

— 경관 a policeman present —자 a person present ; [총칭] those present ; the attendance

임술 壬戌 〖민속〗 the 59th binary term of the sexagenary cycle

임습 霖濕 humidity〔dampness〕 during the rainy season

임시 壬時 〖민속〗 the last of the 24 hour periods 《10 : 30—11 : 30 p. m.》

†임시 臨時 ¶ 임시의 temporary ; special ; extra ; extraordinary ; pro tempore 〔pro tem〕 《라》 // 임시의 일 an odd job ; casual labor // 임시로 temporarily ; specially ; extraordinarily // 임시로 고용하다 engage 《a person》 temporarily // 임시 고용원을 채용하지 그러세요 Why don't you hire temps?

— 결정 a tentative decision — 고용인 a temporary employee ; an extra hand ; a casual worker —공(工) a casual laborer — 구호 본부 a temporary rescue headquarters — 국회 an extra session of the National Assembly ; an extraordinary session of the Diet — 급여 extra pay — 낭패 failure 《of a plan》 at the critical moment ¶ 임시 낭패하다 fail at the critical moment — 뉴스 a news special ; a special newscast ¶ 지금 TV에서 임시 뉴스 방송을 하고 있어 They've got a special newscast on TV right now. —법 『법』 a temporary law —비 extraordinary 〔emergency〕 expenses — 소집 an emergency call-up — 수당 a special〔an extra〕 allowance — 수입〔지출〕 extraordinary income〔disbursement〕 — 시험 a special examination — 열차 a special train — 영업소 a temporary office ; temporary (office) quarters — 예산 a provisional budget — 외상 the interim Foreign Minister — 의장 an acting chairman — 정부 a provisional government — 증간 an extra edition〔number〕 《of a magazine》 — 지출(비) extraordinary expenditure ; a contingent outlay ; incidental expenses — 처변(處變) ⇨ 임기응변(臨機應變) — 총회 an extraordinary general meeting — 휴업 a special〔an extra〕 holiday ; [게시] No Business Today.

임시 변통 臨時變通 management of an unforeseen matter through a makeshift —하다 make shift with 《a thing》 ; make 《a thing》 do for the present ; resort to a temporary expedient ; temporize ¶ 임시 변통의 makeshift ; impromptu ; temporary // 임시 변통으로 만든 책상 an impromptu desk // 임시 변통의 방책 a stopgap measure. // 이것으로 임시 변통할까 한다 I am thinking of using this as a makeshift. // 그것으로도 임시 변통이 될 것이다 That will serve as a stopgap〔temporary substitute〕. // 그 돈으로 위기를 임시 변통할까 한다 I shall tide over the crisis with that sum.

임시 채용 臨時採用 [임시로] temporary employment ; [시험적으로] probation ; adoption on〔under〕 probation —하다 employ 《a person》 temporarily ; take 〔admit〕 《a person》 on probation ; employ 《a person》 on trial

임신 壬申 『민속』 the 9th binary term of the sexagenary cycle

*__임신 妊娠__ pregnancy ; conception ; gravidity ; foetation —하다 become〔be〕 pregnant 《with a child》 ; be in the family way ; conceive ¶ 임신한 여자 a pregnant woman // 임신중에 during the period of maternity // 그녀는 임신했었다 She was in the family way. // 임신 5개월이다 She is in the fifth month of pregnancy〔five months pregnant〕.
— 조절 birth control — 중독증 toxemia of pregnancy — 중절 artificial abortion 자궁외 — extrauterine〔ectopic〕 pregnancy

임야 林野 forests and fields ; a forest land ; a woodland

임어 臨御 the royal presence ; a royal visit —하다 《the king》 make a visit 《to》 ¶ 임금의 임어 아래 with the king in attendance ; in the presence of His Majesty

임업 林業 forestry
— 경제 forestry economy —과 a forestry course (학교의) — 기술원 a forestry technician — 시험장 a forestry experiment station

임오 壬午 『민속』 the 19th binary term of the sexagenary cycle
—군란 the *Im-o* Military Revolt of (June) 1882

임용 任用 appointment ; employment —하다 appoint 《a person》 to a post
— 후보자 명부 a list of eligible candidates for appointment 공무원 —령 the Official Appointment Regulations 특별 —령 the Special Appointment Ordinance

임우 霖雨 ⇨ 장마

임원 任員 an officer ; an official ; an executive (미) ; a person in charge ; the board 《총칭》
—석 an officer's seat — 선거 the election of officers — 회의 a meeting of officers ; the staff meeting

*__임의 任意__ option ; discretion ; voluntariness ¶ 임의의 free ; optional ; voluntary // 임의의 3각형 any triangle // 임의로 of one's own accord ; at will ; at one's pleasure ; as one pleases // 임의로 행동하다 do as one pleases ; act at one's discretion // 임의로 하게 하다 leave 《a matter》 to 《a person's》 discretion // 임의로 처분해도 좋다 You can do with it as you please. // 가고 안 가고는 임의다 You can suit yourself about going or remaining.
—법 voluntary law — 선택 option ; free choice —성(性) voluntariness ¶ 자백의 임의성 the voluntariness of one's confession — 양도 『법』 voluntary conveyance — 자백 voluntary confession — 추출법(抽出法) the random sampling method — 출두 voluntary appearance — 퇴직 voluntary retirement〔resignation〕

임인 壬寅 『민속』 the 39th binary term of the sexagenary cycle

†__임자__¹ [소유자] the owner ; the possessor ; [경영자] the proprietor ¶ 임자 없는 ownerless ; belonging to nobody // 임자 없는 집 a vacant house // 임자 있는 여자 a married woman ; another's wife // 가게의 임자 the proprietor of a shop // 임자가 바뀌다 change hands〔ownership〕 (집·물품 따위) // 이 집의 임자는 누구요 Who owns this house? // 이 가게들은 모두 임자가 같다 These stores are under the same proprietorship. // 저 여자 임자 있니 Is she spoken for?
—말 『문법』 the subject (of a sentence)

—씨 〖문법〗 substantive elements ; nouns
임자² ① [자네] you ; old man〔fellow〕 ② [부부간] (my) dear ; darling ; honey
임자 壬子 〖민속〗 the 49th binary term of the sexagenary cycle
임장 臨場 attendance ; presence ; appearance《on the scene》; a visit **—하다** attend ; visit ; be present《at》; appear
임전 臨戰 going into battle ; presence at a battle **—하다** go into action ¶ 임전 준비를 하다 clear for action ; clear the decks for action
—무퇴 knowing no retreat at a battlefield — 태세 preparation for action ; military preparedness
임정 臨政 a provisional government ⇨ 임시 정부 ¶ 임정 요인 key figures of the provisional government
임정 林政 forestry administration〔management〕
임종 臨終 ① the hour of death ; the dying hour ; one's last moments of life ; [죽음에 다달음] facing death ; standing in the presence of death ¶ 임종의 last ; dying ; deathbed // 임종의 말 one's last〔dying〕 word // 임종의 고백 a deathbed confession // 임종이 다가왔다 The end is near.
② [부모의] attendance〔presence〕 at one's parent's deathbed **—하다** wait upon one's parent's deathbed ; be present at the moment of one's parent's death ¶ 아버지가 돌아가실 때 임종 못한 것이 원통하다 I regret I could not be present at my father's deathbed.
임지 任地 one's post ; the place of one's appointment ¶ 신임지 one's new post // 임지로 향하다 proceed to〔leave for〕 one's new post // 임지에 있다 be at one's post // 임지에서 죽다 die at one's post
임직 任職 appointment to an office
임진 壬辰 〖민속〗 the 29th binary term of the sexagenary cycle
—(왜)란 Japanese Invasion of Korea in 1592
임질 —하다 carry《loads》on the head
임질 淋疾 〖의학〗 gonorrh(o)ea ; clap《속》 ¶ 임질에 걸리다 suffer from gonorrhoea
—균 a gonococcus《*pl.* -cocci》 — 환자 a gonorrheal patient ; a case of gonorrhea
임차 賃借 hire ; hiring ; (paying money as) lease (부동산의) **—하다** lease (land) ; hold a lease《on land》; hire《a car, a boat》; take a lease《of a building》
— 가격 the value of lease —권 the right of lease ; a lease —료 rent ; hire (that one pays) — 부동산 leasehold estate —인 a hirer ; a lessee ; a leaseholder (차가·차지인) ; a tenant —지 leased land
임치 任置 a deposit **—하다** deposit《in a bank, with a person》; leave《a thing》with《a person》
—자 a depositor ; a truster — 증서 a deposit certificate
임파 淋巴 〖해부〗 lymph ¶ 임파의 lymphatic
—관 a lymphatic vessel —관염 inflammation of the lymphatics ; lymphangitis —선 a lymph(atic) gland ; a lymph node —선염(腺炎) lymphadenitis —선종(腺腫) lymphadenoma — 세포 a lymph cell ; a lymphocite —액 lymph —절 lymph node〔gland〕
임하다 任— [임명하다] appoint《a person Mayor》; nominate《a person to a post》; institute〔install, put, place〕《a person in an office》; [장교에] commission《a person as colonel》⇨ 임명
임하다 臨— ① [면하다] face《on》; front《on》; look out《upon》; border《on》 ¶ 시냇가에 임한 집 a house on the stream // 바다에 임해 있다 face the sea // 파리는 센 강에 임한 도시이다 Paris is a city (standing) on (the banks of) the river Seine.
② [당면하다] stand〔be〕 in the presence of ; face ; be confronted by ; meet ¶ 이 때에 임하여 at this moment〔juncture〕 // 죽음에 임하여 on one's deathbed // 출발에 임하여 한마디 인사말씀을 올립니다 At the moment of my departure I should like to say a few parting words. // 아무리 침착한 사람일지라도 그러한 위기에 임하면 침착을 잃는 법이다 Were a man ever so calm, he would lose his presence of mind if confronted by such a crisis.
③ [임석] attend ; be present《at》; present oneself《at》 ¶ 개회식에 임하다 attend〔be present at〕 the opening ceremony // 지사는 졸업식에 임하여 일장의 연설을 했다 The Governor made an address at the graduation ceremony.
임학 林學 forestry ; dendrology
—자 a dendrologist ; a forestry expert
임항선 臨港線 a boat-train line ; a harbor railway
임항 열차 臨港列車 a boat train
임항 철도 臨港鐵道 ⇨ 임항선
임해 臨海 the seashore ; the seaside
— 공업 지대 a coastal industrial zone〔region〕 — 실습 marine practice — 실험소 a marine (biological) laboratory — 지역 littoral districts — 학교 a seaside school
†**입** ① the mouth ; lips (입술) ; 〖해부〗 os《*pl.* ora》 ¶ 예쁜 입 a pretty mouth // 한입에 at a gulp〔mouthful〕 // 입을 벌리고 with one's mouth open〔agape〕 ; openmouthed ; agape // 입을 벌리다 open one's mouth // 입을 다물다 shut one's mouth ; hold one's tongue // 입을 오므리다 purse one's lips // 손등으로 입을 씻다 wipe one's mouth with the back of one's hand // 입에서 구린내가 나다 have foul

〔bad〕 breath // 입을 딱 벌리고 바로보고 있었다 He stared at it with his mouth wide open. // 그의 입가에 미소가 떠 올랐다 A smile came to his lips. // 그 소문은 그의 입에서 나왔다 He is the man who spread the rumor. // 좋은 약은 입에 쓰다 Good medicine is bitter in the mouth〔to the taste〕. // 입을 대고 하는 인공 호흡을 할 줄 아십니까? Do you know how to do mouth-to-mouth resuscitation? // 입 좀 닥쳐 Shut up! /Shut you big mouth! / Button your lip! /Zip your lip!
② [말씨·말투] tongue ; speech ; words ¶ 입에 담을 수 없는 not to be spoken 〔mentioned〕; unmentionable // 입을 모아 in chorus ; in unison // 입 밖에 내다 disclose ; betray ; reveal ; mention ; express // 입이 사납다 be foul-mouthed ; be slanderous ; have a sharp tongue (독설가) // 그는 그것에 대해서 아무말도 입 밖에 내지 않았다 He said nothing about it. /He kept it to himself. // 너는 입만 살았다 You are bold in word only. // 그 소문이 모든 사람 입에 올랐다 The rumor is on everybody's lips. // 입은 재앙의 근원이다 Let not your tongue cut your throat. /Out of the mouth comes (the) evil. /Least said soonest mended. // 그는 떠벌이기는 잘 하지만 입뿐이다 He talks mighty fine, but it is all talk (and no deed).
③ [식구] a mouth (to feed) ; a dependent ¶ 입을 줄이다 reduce the number of mouths to feed // 우리 집은 입이 셋이다 We are a family of three.
④ [미각] taste ; palate ¶ 입에 대지도 않다 leave《wine》untasted // 음식이 입에 맞지 않는다 This food is not to my liking〔taste〕. /This food does not suit my taste〔palate〕.
⑤ [부리] a bill (넓적한) ; a beak (갈구리 모양의)
산 입에 거미줄 치랴 속담 Everyday brings its bread with it.
입에 쓴 약이 병에도 좋다 속담 No pains, no gains. /Bitter pills may have blessed effects.
입에 맞다 관용 suit one's taste〔palate〕; be to one's taste
입에 오르내리다 관용 be spoken of ; be talked〔gossiped〕 about ; be on the tongues〔lips〕 of《people》
입이 가볍다 관용 be talkative ; be glib-tongued ; be voluble
입이 무겁다 관용 be slow of speech ; be taciturn ; be reticent

입가 the sides of the mouth ; parts near the mouth ¶ 입가에 미소를 띠우고 with a smile about one's mouth〔lips〕

입가심 **—하다** take off the aftertaste ; take away a bitter〔an unpleasant〕 taste of《medicine》¶ 약을 먹고 사과로 입가심하다 eat an apple to chase the medicine taste

입각 入閣 joining〔entry into〕 a Cabinet **—하다** accede to the Ministry ; become a Cabinet member ; take office 〔a seat〕 in the Cabinet ¶ 교육부 장관으로 입각이 확실하다 It is certain that he will join the Cabinet as Minister of Education.

†**입각 立脚** **—하다** be based〔founded, grounded, built〕《on》; take one's ground《on》; rest on the basis《of》¶ 사실에 입각하다 be based on facts // 법률은 개개인의 존엄성에 입각하여 제정되어야 한다 Laws should be enacted from the standpoint of individual dignity.
—점 a standpoint ; a viewpoint ; [입장] a footing ; a scaffold

입감 入監 confinement ; imprisonment **—하다** be sent to prison〔jail〕; be imprisoned ¶ 입감 중이다 be in jail 〔prison〕; be serving a term (in prison)

입거 入渠 entering a dock ; docking **—하다** go into (a) dock ; enter a dock ¶ 입거중이다 be in dock
—료 dockage **—시설** docking accommodations ; docking facilities

입건하다 立件— book《a person》on a charge《of》; prosecute a person《for》¶ 경찰은 과실 치사 혐의로 그를 입건했다 Police booked him on a charge of accidental homicide.

입견하다 立見— see standing ; see《a play》in〔from〕 the gallery

입경 入京 arrival in the capital city ; coming up to *Seoul* **—하다** arrive in *Seoul* ; enter the capital city

입고 入庫 warehousing (상품의) ; entering the car-shed《for the night》(차량의) **—하다** put into a warehouse ; store ¶ 상품의 입고 warehousing of goods

입공 入貢 paying tribute **—하다** pay tribute

입관 入棺 placing〔putting〕 a body in a coffin **—하다** place〔put〕 a body in a coffin ¶ 입관 준비를 하다 lay out《a corpse》
—식 the rites of placing the body in a coffin ; the coffin rites

입교 入敎 entering a faith〔the church〕 **—하다** enter the church

입교 入校 ⇨입학

†**입구 入口** an entrance ; a way in ; a gateway ; an entry《to a river》; Way In (게시) ¶ 방의 입구 the door of a room // 항구 입구 the mouth of harbor // 동굴입구 the inlet〔mouth〕 of a cavern // 터널의 입구 the approach〔entrance〕 to a tunnel // 입구에서 at the entrance ; at the door // 입구에 서 있지 말라 Don't stand in the doorway.

입구 入寇 invasion ; a raid **—하다**《a foreign enemy》invade ; raid ; encroach 《on》; make an inroad《into》

입국 入國 entrance〔entry〕 into a country

—하다 enter a country ; gain entrance into a country ; be admitted into the country ¶ 입국을 거절하다 deny〔refuse〕 《a person》 admission into a country // 입국이 허가되다 be admitted into〔to〕 the country // 그들은 입국을 금지 당하였다 They were prohibited entry into the country.
— 금지 prohibition of entry — 비자 an entry visa — 수속 formalities for entry — 허가 an entry permit 불법 — unlawful 〔illegal〕 entry 재— reentry ; reentrance

입국 立國 the founding〔establishment〕 of a state —하다 found〔establish〕 a state ¶ 산업 입국 the establishment of a state on the basis of industries // 입국의 대본 the principles upon which a state is founded

입궁 入宮 —하다 enter the palace ; [궁녀가 됨] become a court lady ; [장기에서] checkmate the king

입궐 入闕 attendance at the Royal Court —하다 proceed〔go〕 to the Royal Court ; visit the Royal Palace

입금 入金 [수령금] receipts ; receipt of money ; money received ; [내금] part payment ; payment on account —하다 receive 《some money》 ; [내금으로서 지불] pay in part〔on account〕 ¶ 다달의 입금 [수취] monthly receipts ; [지불] monthly payment // 만원만 입금했다 He paid 10,000 *won* on account.
— 전표 [은행의] a receive〔deposit, credit, paying-in〕 slip 일부〔전액〕 — part〔full〕 payment

입길 the mouth of one who speaks ill of another's fault
입길에 오르내리다 [관용] be disputed by others

입김 the steam of breath ¶ 입김을 불다 blow on 《frozen hands》 // 유리창이 사람의 입김에 흐려졌다 The windowpanes were steamed up with people's breath. // 그는 언 손에 후후 입김을 불었다 He blew on his frozen hands.

입납 入納 [편지의] please deliver to ¶ 김씨댁 입납 To Mr. *Kim*

입내[1] mimicry ¶ 남의 입내를 내다 mimic another ; imitate another's way of speaking
—쟁이 a mimic(ker)

입내[2] [구취] mouth odo(u)r ; (the smell of) one's breath ¶ 입내가 나다 have a foul breath ; [입을 주어로] smell

입노릇 eating ; munching ; having a bite ¶ 입노릇을 하다 have a bite ; eat ; munch

-입니다 ⇨ -이다

†입다 ① [옷을] put on ; don ; get into ; slip on ; [입고 있다] wear ; have on ; be dressed in ¶ 내가 입고 있는 외투 the overcoat I have on // 제복을 입고 있는 사람 a man in uniform // 급히 옷을 입다 put on one's clothes〔dress oneself〕 hurriedly // 옷을 입은 채 자다 sleep in one's clothes // 웃옷을 입다 put on one's jacket // 새로 맞춘 옷을 입어보다 try on one's new clothes // 양복을 입다 wear〔dress in〕 European clothes // 옷을 잘 입다 be well dressed ; dress well // 그 옷은 당분간 더 입을 수 있다 It has plenty of wear in it. // 매일 입기에 좋다 It is good for everyday wear. // 9시에 시작하는 모임에 그 양복을 입고 가야 한다 I have to wear the suit to a meeting that starts at 9. // 너는 저 여자가 이런 장소에 어울리지 않게 옷을 입고 있다고 생각지 않니 Don't you think she is inappropriately clothed at a place like this ? // 네가 입고 있는 그 옷 참 멋있다 That's a stylish outfit you have on. // 파티에는 무엇을 입고 가니 What are you wearing to the party ?
② [은혜를] owe ; be indebted to ; be due to ; enjoy 《a person's》 patronage ; be favored 《with》 ; [손해를] suffer 《a loss》 ; sustain 《damage》 ¶ 상처를 입다 receive a wound ; get injured // 은혜를 입다 receive favor ; be placed under an obligation ; share in the benefit // 재난을 입다 meet a misfortune〔calamity〕 // 피해를 입다 suffer the loss 《of crops》 // 적은 큰 손해를 입고 퇴각했다 The enemy retreated with great loss. // 나의 성공은 그의 조력에 힘 입은 바가 크다 I owe my success to his help.
③ [상을 입다] be in〔go into〕 mourning 《for》

입단 入團 joining an organization —하다 join〔enter〕 an organization

입담 skill at talking ; volubility ; the impact of one's words ¶ 입담이 좋다 be glib ; be voluble // 입담이 사납다 be foul- tongued

입당 入黨 joining a political party ; accession to a party —하다 join a (political) party ¶ 민주당에 입당하다 join〔affiliate oneself with〕 the Democratic Party
—자 an incoming member ; admissions

입대 入隊 enlistment ; enrollment ; joining the army —하다 join〔enter〕 the armed service ; enlist in the army〔navy〕 ; be recruited
—식 the ceremonial parade of〔a ceremony of welcoming〕 new recruits —자 a recruit

입덧나다 lose one's taste for food (as from pregnancy) ; lose one's appetite

입도 入道 becoming a Taoist —하다 become a Taoist

입도 선매 立稻先賣 pre-harvest sale of rice crop —하다 sell rice before the harvest

입동 立冬 the onset of winter ; one of the 24 seasonal divisions 《 around 7th November》

입되다 be a gourmet ; be fastidious

(about food) ; have a dainty palate
입뜨다 (be) reticent ¶ 그는 입이 뜨다 He is a man of few words.
*입력 入力 [전기의] power input ; [전자 계산기의] input
입례 立禮 [선 채로 하는] a salute in a standing posture ; [일어서서 하는] standing up and making a bow
입론 立論 argument ; argumentation ―하다 argue ; make〔put forward〕 an argument ¶ 훌륭한 입론 a good argument // 그의 입론은 충분한 근거가 있다 His argument is well grounded〔sound〕. // 정당한〔확고한〕 입론 irrefutable and just argument
입막음하다 forbid 《a person》 to speak ; stop 《a person's mouth》 ; impose silence on 《a person》 ; bind 《a person》 to secrecy ; gag 《a person》 ¶ 입막음하는 돈 hush money ; a bribe
*입맛 appetite ; taste ; palate ¶ 입맛이 있다〔없다〕 have a good〔no〕 appetite // 입맛을 잃다 lose one's appetite // 입맛을 돋우다 stimulate〔excite, provoke, arouse〕 one's appetite // 식사 전에 단 것을 먹어 입맛을 떨어뜨리다 spoil one's appetite by eating sweets just before dinner // 조금 운동하면 입맛이 난다 A little exercise will give you an appetite. // 내 입맛에 꼭 맞는다 It tastes just right to me. // 그 여자는 입맛도 매우 까다롭고 옷을 고르는 데도 매우 까다롭다 She is very fussy about food and very picky about cloths.
입맛이 떨어지다 관용 one's appetite fails
입맛 다시다 [음식을 보고] smack one's lips ; lick one's chops ; lick one's lips ; [못마땅하여] click one's tongue ¶ 입맛 다시며 먹다 eat smacking one's lips ; eat with much gusto // 사과를 보고 입맛 다시다 lick one's chops at the sight of an apple ; one's mouth waters at seeing an apple // 남의 행동이 못마땅해서 입맛 다시다 click one's tongue 《at a person's behavior》
입맛 쓰다 taste bitter ; feel wretched ¶ 낙제해서 입맛이 쓰다 feel miserable for failing the examination // 실패해서 입맛이 쓰다 He is chagrined at his failure.
입맞추다 kiss ; give 《a person》 a kiss ; press one's lips against ; osculate ; smack ¶ 사람의 손에 입맞추다 kiss 《a person's》 hand // 뺨에 입맞추다 kiss 《a person》 on the cheek // 입술에 입맞추다 press a kiss upon 《a person's》 lips // 쪽 소리나게 입맞추다 give a smacking kiss // 사랑의 입맞춤을 하다 kiss 《her》 with love // 입맞추고 헤어지다 kiss 《a person》 good-by ; kiss off
입매 [음식] a dab of food ; [일] a slapdash job ―하다 take〔eat〕 just a little dab ; do a slapdash job ; pretend to do a job
입맷상(床) a small table of food served to appease one's hunger before a formal banquet
입멸 入滅 entering nirvana ; death (of a Buddhist saint)
입모습 shape of the mouth ¶ 입모습이 예쁜 소녀 a sweet-mouthed girl // 그 여자는 입모습이 예쁘다 She has a lovely mouth.
입목 立木 a standing〔growing〕 tree
입묘 入廟 transferring the mortuary tablet to the family shrine after the second anniversary of 《a person's》 death ―하다 transfer《the mortuary tablet》 to the family shrine
입묵 入墨 tattooing ―하다 tattoo ¶ 등에 입묵하다 have one's back tattooed // 바른 팔에 용의 입묵이 있다 have a dragon tattooed on one's right arm
⁑입문 入門 entrance into a private school ―하다 enter a private school ; become 《a person's》 pupil
―료 an initiation〔admission〕 fee ―서 a guide ; a manual ; a primer ; an elementary textbook ¶ 이 책은 영어 회화의 입문서이다 This book serves as a first step in〔portal of entry to〕 English conversation. ―식 an initiation 경제학 ― an introduction to economics ; the fundamentals of economics 문학 ― an introduction to the study of literature 산술 ― a primer of arithmetic 영작문 ― a first manual of English composition 희랍어 ― a Greek primer
입바르다 (be) plain-spoken ; outspoken ; straightforward ¶ 입바른 소리 plain speaking ; a straight talk // 입바른 사람 a plain-spoken person ; an outspoken person // 입바른 소리를 하다 speak plainly ; call a spade a spade ; speak without reserve ; speak directly
입밖 ¶ 입밖에 내다 disclose ; tell ; mention ; betray ; reveal ; divulge // 비밀을 입밖에 내다 let out〔divulge, reveal〕 a secret // 한 마디도 입밖에 내지 마라 Say nothing to any one. /Breathe not a syllable of it to any one. // 이 일은 절대로 입밖에 내서는 안된다 Be sure and keep your mouth shut about this. /Mind you don't blab about this.
⁑입방 立方 〖수학〗 cube ; cubic
―골 〖해부〗 a cuboid (bone) ―근 the cube root ― 미터 a cubic meter ― 배적(倍積) duplication of a cube ― 용적 volume ; cubic content(s) ―체 a cube ; a solid ; a regular hexahedron 정―체 a regular solid
입방아찧다 nag 《at》 ; find fault ; pick 《on》 ¶ 입방아찧는 사람 a shrew ; a nagging〔sharp-tongued〕 woman
입버릇 a way〔habit〕 of saying ; one's manner of speech ; one's favorite phrase ; one's favorite〔pet〕 saying ¶ 입버릇이 나쁜 foul-tongued ; evil-mouthed // 입버릇처럼 말하다 always say ; never fail to say ; be in the habit of saying // …이라고

말하는 것이 입버릇이 되어 있다 He always says ((that))/He is in the habit of saying ((that))//그 말이 그의 입버릇이 되어 있다 That's his favorite phrase. /That's his pet expression. //아버지는 「정직은 최선의 정책」이라고 입버릇처럼 말씀하셨다 Father used to say "Honesty is the best policy."

***입법 立法** legislation ; lawmaking ¶ 입법의 legislative ; lawmaking//입법의 취지 the purpose of legislation//입법과 행정의 구별 distinction between the legislative and executive//입법 정신에 위배되다 be contrary to the spirit of legislation
— 고문 a legislative councilor **—권** legislative power ; lawmaking power ¶ 입법권을 행사하다 exercise the legislative power **— 기관** a legislative organ ; a legislative body **—부** the legislature ; the legislative body **— 자** a legislator ; a lawmaker **— 회의** a legislative council **경제〔사회, 노동〕—** economic〔social, labor〕 legislation

입병 —病 a sore mouth ; a mouth infection

입불 入佛 enshrining of a Buddhist image **—하다** enshrine a Buddhist image
— 공양 services performed for enshrined Buddhist image

입비 立碑 —하다 raise〔erect〕 a monument((to the memory of a person))

입비뚤이 a person with a twisted mouth

입사 入社 entering〔joining〕 a company **—하다** enter〔join〕 a company〔firm〕 ; enter the service ((of)) ¶ 다수의 입사 시험 희망자 a big waiting list of applicants for the employment examinations//모 대회사에 입사하다 join a certain big company//입사를 허가하다 take a new member into a company ; admit〔initiate〕 ((a person)) into a society//동아일보사에 입사하다 join the *Dong-A* Daily News//입사를 환영합니다 Welcome aboard
— 시험 an examination〔a test〕 for service in a business company ; an entrance 〔employment〕 examination ; [인물 시험] a character test〔a personal interview〕 for entering a company ¶ 입사 시험이 너무 쉬웠던 것 같다 The company recruitment exam must have gotten too easy.

입사 入射 〖물리〗 incidence ⇨ 투사 ¶ 입사의 incident
—각 an incidence angle ; an angle of incidence **— 광선** a ray of light incident ((upon a mirror))

입사 入絲 inlaying silver-thread decorations on metal dishes ; damascening **—하다** inlay silver-thread decorations ; damascene

입사 立嗣 designating heir **—하다** designate ((a person)) as heir

입산 入山 retiring to a mountain to enter the priesthood **—하다** become a bonze ; enter〔join〕 the Buddhist priesthood ; renounce the world

입산 수도 入山修道 mountaineering asceticism
—사 a monk who leads an ascetic life in the mountains ; a mountaineering ascetic

입상 入賞 winning a prize **—하다** win 〔get, receive, carry off〕 a prize ¶ 일등으로 입상하다 win〔take〕 the first prize
—시(詩) a winning poem **—자** a prize-winner ; a winning contestant **—화** a prize picture

입상 立像 a standing statue〔statuette〕

입상 粒狀 ¶ 입상의 granular ; granulous ; graniform
—과(果) 〖식물〗 an acinus ((*pl.* -ni)) **—반(斑)** 〖천문〗 [태양 광구면의] a granule **—설탕** granular sugar **— 전분〔석회암, 백운석〕** granular starch〔limestone, dolomite〕 **— 조직** granular texture

입석 立席 [극장의] the gallery ; [극장·버스 따위의] standing room ; room for standing ¶ 입석도 만원이다 There's no room even for standing.
— 손님 a standee

입선 入選 —하다 be accepted ; be selected ; be a successful competitor ¶ 그의 그림이 국전에 입선했다 His painting was accepted for this year's National Art Exhibition.
— 논문 a winning essay **— 소설** a winning novel **—자** a winner ; a winning 〔successful〕 competitor〔candidate, contestant〕 **—작** a winning piece of work

입성 [옷] clothes ; garments ; clothing ((총칭))

입성 入城 an entry into a castle ; a triumphal entry into a fortress **—하다** enter a castle ; make a triumphal entry into a fortress
—식 formal〔triumphal〕 entry

입성수 —星數 telling one's fortune by the shape of the mouth

입센 Ibsen, Henrik (노르웨이 1828～1906)

입소 入所 entrance ((into)) ; admission ((to)) ; [교도소에] imprisonment ; internment ; confinement ; incarceration **—하다** enter ((an institute)) ; be admitted ((to an institute)) ; be put in〔into〕 prison ; be sent to〔cast into〕 prison〔jail〕 ; be imprisoned ¶ 입소 중이다 be in prison 〔jail〕//입소시키다 put〔cast〕 ((a person)) into prison ; commit ((a person)) to a prison//수회죄로 2년 입소하다 serve two years (in jail) for bribery

입속말 a murmur ; a mutter ; muttering **—하다** mutter (to oneself) ; grumble ((at, over, about)) ; murmur ((at, against)) ¶ 투덜투덜 입속말하다 grumble (oneself) //혼자 입속말하다 mutter to oneself //입속말로 대답하다 mumble the answer

†입수 入手 receipt ; being brought into possession ; obtainment **—하다** receive ;

get ; obtain ¶ 입수되다 come to hand ; be procured〔obtained〕
— 경로 means of acquisition —난 difficulty of obtaining ¶ 입수난이다 be hard to obtain〔get〕
입숟가락 a crude unpolished spoon
†입술 the lips ¶ 윗〔아랫〕 입술 the upper〔under, lower〕 lip // 터진 입술 chapped lips // 두꺼운〔얇은〕 입술 thick〔thin〕 lips // 입술을 깨물다 bite one's lips // 입술을 빨다 lick one's lips // 입술을 비죽거리다 make a lip ; pout one's lips // 입술을 오므리다 purse one's lips
— 소리 『언어학』 labial sounds
입시 入侍 an audience with the king — 하다 have an audience with the king ; be presented to the king
*입시 入試 an entrance examination ; the examinations for entrance 《to a higher school》 ; a matric (대학에의) ¶ 입시 준비를 하다 prepare for an entrance examination // 입시를 치르다 take〔sit for, undergo, face〕 an entrance examination // 입시에 합격하다 (successfully) pass an〔one's〕 entrance examination (for a university)
— 문제 ⇨ 입학 시험 문제 — 지옥 exam hell ; the narrow gate to an upper school
입시울 the edge of the mouth
입식 立食 ① [서서 먹는 식사] a stand-up meal〔collation, lunch, dinner〕 ; a perpendicular 《영·속》 —하다 have a stand-up meal ; eat 《while》 standing
— 식당 a buffet ; a stand-up luncheon stall —회 a stand-up dinner party
입신 立身 a rise in the world ; establishment of oneself in life ; success in life —하다 rise in the world ; succeed〔advance, rise〕 in life ; get on〔forward〕 in life ; rise to distinction ¶ 입신을 꾀하다 seek one's fortune // 입신의 길을 열다 get a chance to better oneself ; open a prospect // 자신의 운명을 개척하여 입신하다 carve one's way to fortune // 입신의 기회를 얻다 get a chance in life // 그는 급사로부터 사장의 자리에까지 입신했다 He worked his way up from an errand boy to the head of the firm.
— 양명 rising in the world and gaining fame — 출세 success in life ; a successful career ¶ 입신 출세주의 the cult of success ; careerism // 입신 출세주의자 a (social) climber ; a status seeker // 입신 출세담 an up-from-the-bottom story
입신 入神 divineness ¶ 입신의 inspired ; divine // 입신의 기예(技藝) exquisite art ; divine skill
입심 boldness〔brazenness〕 in words ; volubleness ; eloquence ¶ 입심이 좋다 be bold〔brazen〕 in words ; talk big ; be glib〔voluble, loquacious, eloquent〕
입싸다 be rash of speech ; (be) glib (-tongued) ¶ 그는 입이 싸서 탈이다 He is too ready to speak.
입쌀 unglutinous rice
입씨름 bickering ; (exchange of) high words ; a brawl ; a dispute ; an argument —하다 bicker ; have high words 《with》 ; argue 《with》 ; dispute 《with》 ; quarrel
입씻기다 give money to have 《a person》 keep his mouth shut ¶ 그한테 1만원을 주고 입씻겼다 I gave him 10,000 *won* to keep his mouth shut.
입씻이 ① [입씻기는] hush money ; a gold muzzle ② ⇨ 입가심
입아귀 the corner(s) of the mouth
*입안 立案 drafting ; setting up 《a plan, a scheme》 —하다 plan ; frame ; devise ; form〔make, map out〕 《a plan》 ; draw up ; originate ; work out ¶ 규약을 입안하다 draw up regulations // 운동 방침을 면밀히 입안하다 map out the lines of one's campaign carefully // 이것은 내가 입안한 것이다 This was planned by me. /The idea originated with me.
—자 a planner ; an originator ; a framer ; a designer ; a drafter ; a deviser ¶ 도시 계획의 입안자 a city planner
입양 入養 adoption ; adopting 《a person》 as one's child〔son〕 ; being adopted into 《a person's》 family
입어권 入漁權 an entrance right to a fishing lot ; a right of entry into a fishing ground ; the common of piscary〔fishery〕
입어료 入漁料 charges for fishing in another's piscary
입언 立言 expression of one's opinion〔view〕 ; a proposition ; a proposal —하다 express one's opinion〔view〕 ; propose ; make a proposition〔proposal〕
입영 入營 enrollment ; enlistment ; entering barracks —하다 join〔enlist in〕 the army ; enter barracks ¶ 입영중이다 be in the army ; be serving with the colors
입옥 入獄 imprisonment —하다 be sent to prison〔jail〕 ; be imprisoned
입욕 入浴 bathing ; a hot bath —하다 take〔have〕 a (hot) bath ; bathe 《oneself》 ¶ 입욕시키다 give 《a baby》 a bath
*입원 入院 hospitalization ; being in hospital ; admission into a hospital —하다 enter a hospital ; be taken to hospital ; be hospitalized (미) ¶ 입원 중이다 be in (the) hospital // 입원을 권하다 advise 《a person's》 transfer to a hospital // 입원을 신청하다 apply for admission to a hospital // 입원 가료를 요하다 require treatment in (a) hospital // 그는 입원 치료를 요한다 He requires hospital treatment. // 나는 입원한 사람한테 갖다 줄 것을 찾고 있습니다 I'm looking for something to give to a hospitalized person.
—료 charges for hospital accommodation
— 일수 days of hospital treatment — 절

차 arrangements for entering a hospital ; formalities connected with admission to a hospital — 치료 hospital treatment〔care〕 — 환자 an inpatient ; an inmate of a hospital ¶ 지난 달 입원 환자는 30명이었다 There were 30 admissions last month.

‡입자 粒子 〖물리〗 a particle
—량 particle weight 중(重)— 〖물리〗 a heavy (atomic) particle ; a baryon

‡입장 入場 admission ; entrance ; admittance —하다 enter ; get in ; be admitted 《into》 ; get admission ¶ 입장을 허락하다 admit 《a person》 // 입장을 거절하다 refuse admission ; turn away // 공중의 입장을 허락하다 be open to the public // 입장료를 받다〔안받다〕 charge an〔no〕 admission // 입장 못한 자가 500명 이상이다 More than 500 people could not get in. // 입장자가 많았다 There was a very good attendance. // 여기는 외국인의 입장을 금하고 있다 This place is off limits〔out of bounds〕 to foreigners. // 무용자 입장 금지 No admittance except on business.
—권(權) ingress ; entrée 《프》 ; right of admission —권(券) an admission 〔entrance〕 ticket ; [역의] a platform ticket ¶ 입장권을 발행하다 issue admission tickets —권 소유자 a ticket holder —권 판매소 a booking office〔window〕 《영》 ; a ticket office〔counter〕 《미》 —료 an admission fee〔charge〕 ; a door fee (도박장의) ¶ 입장료를 지불하다 pay admission — 무료 Admission (is) free. / There is no charge for admission. —세 an admission〔amusement〕 tax —식 an entrance〔opening〕 ceremony —자 a visitor ; a spectator ; [총칭] an attendance 무료〔특별〕 —권 a complimentary ticket ; an order ; a free card〔pass〕 유료 —자 a paid attendance

†입장 立場 a position ; a situation ; [견지] a standpoint ; a point of view ; a ground ; an angle ¶ 괴로운 입장에 있다 be in a difficult situation // 입장을 밝히다 make one's position clear // 다른 입장에서 논하다 discuss from a different angle 〔point of view〕 // 미묘한 입장에 있다 be placed in a delicate position // 자기의 입장을 지키다 hold one's ground ; maintain one's position // 타인의 입장에 서서 생각하다 place〔put〕 oneself in another's place〔shoes〕 // 우리는 그들과 대등한 입장에 있다 We are on an equal footing with them. // 그것에 관해서는 나는 아무런 말도 할 수 없는 입장에 있다 I am not in a position to say anything about it.

입장단 —長短 humming along to dance rhythm ¶ 입장단을 치다 hum along to dance rhythm

입적 入寂 entering nirvana ; the death of a Buddhist priest ⇨ 입멸

입적 入籍 entry in a family register —하다 have 《a person's》 name entered in the family register

입전 入電 a telegram received ; a cable message received ¶ 워싱턴으로부터의 입전에 의하면 according to a cablegram from Washington

입절 立節 proving〔maintaining〕 one's faithfulness unto death ; fidelity to one's principle —하다 prove〔maintain〕 one's faithfulness throughout one's life ; stick to one's colors

입정 入定 〖불교〗 ① [선정(禪定)에 들어감] calm contemplation 《of a Zen priest》 ② [중이 죽음] ⇨ 입적(入寂)

입정 入廷 entrance into the courtroom —하다 enter the courtroom

입정 놀리다 keep one's mouth busy ; eat incessantly between meals

입정사납다 (be) foul-tongued〔foul-mouthed〕 ; abusive ; [탐내다] greedy ; voracious

입조 入朝 attendance at〔a visit to〕 the Royal Court —하다 attend the Royal Court ; be present at the Royal Court

입주 入住 —하다 move in ; take possession of 《a house》
— 가정 교사〔식모〕 a resident tutor 〔maid〕 —자 an occupant of a house ; a tenant —제 a living-in system

†입증 立證 (giving) proof ; demonstration ; establishment 《of a fact》 ; substantiation 《of one's statement》 —하다 prove ; give proof ; bear out ; establish 《a fact》 ¶ 입증하는 사실 facts corroborative of 《a crime》 // 유죄를 입증하다 prove 《a person》 guilty // 무죄를 입증하다 establish one's innocence // 사실을 입증하다 establish the〔a〕 fact // 우수성을 입증하다 demonstrate the superiority 《of》 // 역사가 이것을 입증한다 History bears this out.
— 자료 supporting evidence

입지 立地 location (of industry)

입지 立志 determination to make a success in life ; making a strong resolution ; fixing one's aim in life ; decision of purpose in life —하다 determine to make a success in life ; make a strong resolution ; fix one's aim in life
— 소설 an edifying〔inspiring〕 novel —전(傳) the biography of a self-made man ; a success story ¶ 입지전 속의 인물 a self-made man

입지 조건 立地條件 conditions of location ¶ 입지 조건이 좋다〔나쁘다〕 be conveniently〔inconveniently〕 located ; be in a favorable〔an unfavorable〕 situation ; be located favorably〔unfavorably〕

입직 入直 one's turn for night duty ; one's turn in office —하다 take one's turn for night duty〔in office〕

입질 [낚시에서] a bite

입짓 moving one's lips ; mouthing ; eating

¶ 입짓을 하다 make a mouth
입짧다 have a small〔feeble, weak〕 appetite ; eat sparingly ¶ 입짧은 사람 a spare〔light, small〕 eater ; a small feeder
입찬말, 입찬소리 bragging ; hot air 《속》 ¶ 그는 자기의 기술을 입찬말로 지껄였다 He bragged about his skill.
†**입찰 入札** a tender 《영》 ; a bid ; bidding 《미》 **—하다** tender〔bid〕 for ; offer〔submit, deliver〕 a tender ; put in tenders ; hand in a bid ; make a bid 《for》 ¶ 입찰에 붙이다 sell 《a thing》 by (public) tender // 입찰을 모집하다 invite tenders ; call for bids // 최고 입찰자에 불하되다 be sold to the highest bidder // 남보다 싸게 입찰하다 underbid others // 상기 입찰 희망자는 1주일 내에 신청할 것 Any person who desires to bid for the above shall apply within a week. // 신교사 건축 입찰을 받음 Tenders〔Bids〕 are invited for the new schoolbuilding.
— 가격 the price tendered ; bidding price **— 공고** a notice of tender 《for engineering work》 **— 기일** time appointed for handing in tenders **—법** tender system **— 보증금** a security for a tender〔bid〕 **—서** a tender ; a bid ; a sealed proposal **—일** the day of tender **—자** a bidder 《미》 ; a tenderer **경쟁〔일반〕 —** a public〔an open〕 tender ; sealed tenders〔bids〕 ; competitive bids **지명 —** a private tender ; tender of specified contractors **최고〔최저〕 —** the highest〔lowest〕 tender〔bid〕 **공사 — 광고** an advertisement of tender for engineering work
입천장 —天障 the palate ; the roof of the mouth ¶ 입천장의 palatine
입체 立替 payment in advance ; payment for 《a person》 **—하다** pay in advance ; pay for 《a person》 ¶ 적은 돈을 입체하다 make 《a person》 a little advance // 입장료를 입체하다 pay the admission for 《a person》 // 그에게 여비를 충분히 입체해 주었다 I made a large advance to meet his traveling expenses.
—금 an advance ; a disbursement
***입체 立體** a solid (body) ¶ 입체의 cubic ; vertical ; solid // 입체적 cubic ; vertical ; solid // 입체적 three-dimensional // 입체적으로 in three dimensions // 경작지의 입체적 이용 intensive cultivation // 대도시의 입체적 팽창 the vertical expansion of great cities
—각(角) a solid angle **—감** cubic effect **— 교차** a two〔multi〕-level crossing (도로의) **— 교차(도)로** a freeway ; a flyover roadway **— 기하학** solid geometry **— 묘사** cubic〔solid〕 delineation **—미** solid beauty **— 방송** a stereophonic〔binaural〕 broadcast **— 사진** a stereo(scopic) picture ; stereoscopic photography ; stereo photograph **— 영화** a three-dimension〔3-D〕 film〔movie, picture〕 ; a Cinerama 《미》 **— 음향** stereophonic sound **—전** three-dimensional warfare **—파** 〖미술〗 [작풍] cubism ; [단체] the cubists ¶ 입체파 예술가 [화가·조각가] a cubist // 입체파 회화 a cubist picture **— 현미경** a stereomicroscope
입초 立哨 sentry duty ; standing watch ¶ 입초서다 stand〔keep〕 watch〔guard〕 ; stand〔be〕 on sentry // 입초를 세우다 post a sentry // 입초를 교대시키다 relieve a sentry
—병 a sentry
입초 入超 an excess of imports (over exports) ; an unfavorable〔adverse〕 balance of trade
입추 立秋 onset of autumn 《one of the 24 seasonal divisions》
입추 立錐 ¶ 강당은 만원으로 입추의 여지도 없었다 The hall was crowded〔packed〕 to capacity〔overflowing〕. // 강연회는 입추의 여지도 없는 성황이었다 The lectures were greeted with a packed house. // 그들의 콘서트는 항상 입추의 여지가 없는 것 같아 I hear their concerts are always packed to capacity.
입추의 여지도 없다 [관용] be filled to capacity〔overflowing〕 ; be closely packed ; be densely crowded
입춘 立春 onset of spring ; one of the 24 seasonal divisions 《around 3~4 February》
입태자 立太子 the official investiture of a Prince as Heir Apparent to the Throne **—하다** officially invest the Crown Prince
입평 立坪 a cubic *pyung* (=6.008 cubic meters)
입하 立夏 onset of summer ; one of the 24 seasonal divisions 《around 5~6 May》
입하 入荷 arrival〔receipt〕 of goods ; a fresh supply of goods **—하다** arrive ; be received ¶ 약 20톤의 야채가 입하하였다 About 20 tons of vegetables were received.
— 통지 an arrival notice
†**입학 入學** admission to school ; entrance into school ; [대학] matriculation **—하다** enter a school ; be admitted into〔to〕 a school ¶ 입학을 지원하다 apply to a school for admission // 입학을 허가하다 admit 《a person》 into a school〔college〕 // 본 대학에 입학하려면 시험을 치러야 한다 Entrance to this college is by examination only. // 우리 딸을 이 학교에 입학시키고 싶은데요 I want to have my daughter enrolled at this school.
— 규칙 the admission rules ; the regulations governing the admission of candidates to the school **—금** an entrance〔a matriculation〕 fee **—기** the admission period **—난** difficulty in obtaining school admission **—생** a new student ; an

entering student — 수속 registration for admission — 시험 an entrance examination ; the examinations for entrance ¶ 입학 시험을 치다 take〔sit for〕 an entrance examination — 시험 문제 entrance examination questions —식 an entrance ceremony — 원서 an application for admission — 자격 entrance requirements ; requirements for admission — 절차 entrance formalities — 지원자 a candidate〔an applicant〕 for admission 《to》 — 허가 admission 《to a school》 재— reentrance ; readmission

*입항 入港 entry into port ; arrival in port ; docking —하다 come into port ; make port ; arrive in a port ; dock 《at》 ; enter port ¶ 입항 중이다 be in port // 부산에 입항하다 put in at *Pusan* ; dock at *Pusan* // 그 배는 오늘 입항할 예정이었다 The boat was scheduled to make port today. // 우리 배는 내일 오전 9시 인천에 입항한다 Our ship will make〔put into〕 *Inch'ŏn* at nine tomorrow morning.

—선 incoming〔inbound〕 vessels —세 port〔harbor〕 dues〔fees〕 ; keelage 《영》 — 수속 clearance inwards — 수수료 an entrance fee — 신고 an entrance notice

입향순속 入鄕循俗 When you enter a foreign place, follow its customs. /When in Rome do as the Romans do.

입헌 立憲 constitutionalism ¶ 입헌적인 constitutional // 입헌적으로 constitutionally ; on constitutional lines // 입헌적 수단으로 through constitutional means // 입헌 사상을 고취하다 inculcate constitutional ideas 《in the people》

—국 a constitutional country — 군주 정체 constitutional monarchy — 민주 정체 constitutional democracy — 정치 constitutional government ¶ 입헌 정치를 운용하다 conduct〔work〕 constitutional government —주의 constitutionalism

입회 入會 admission 《to membership》 ; joining ; entrance —하다 join〔enter〕 《a club, a society》 ; associate 《oneself》 with a society ; become a member 《of》 ¶ 입회를 허락하다 admit 《a person》 to membership // 입회를 신청하다 apply for membership // 입회 신청을 받다 receive applications for admission // 그는 학우회에 입회했다 He was initiated into the fraternity. /They initiated him into the fraternity. // 누구나 입회할 수 있음 The membership is open to all.

—권(權) 〚법〛 (right of) common —금 an entrance fee —식 initiation — 신청자 an applicant for membership —자 an entrant ; a person admitted to membership 신—자 a new member

입회 立會 presence ; attendance ; [거래소의] a session ; a call —하다 be present ; attend ; witness ¶ 증인 입회하에 in the presence of a witness // 입회를 요청하다 request〔ask for〕 《a person's》 presence 《at》 // 입회 진찰을 하다 have a joint consultation 《with another surgeon》 // 식에는 삼촌이 입회했다 The ceremony was witnessed by my uncle.

— 경관 a policeman present〔in attendance〕 — 시간 market hours —인 a witness (증인) ; a teller (개표의) —장 the floor ; the boardroom 《미》 — 재판 a mixed court — 중지〔정지〕 suspension of a session〔of exchange〕 — 증인 an attester〔attestor〕 전장〔후장〕 — the morning〔afternoon〕 session

*입후보 立候補 candidacy 《미》 ; candidature —하다 stand as a candidate for 《an election》 ; run for 《an election》 ; come forward as a candidate 《for》 ; run for 《President》 《미》 ; stand for 《Parliament》 ¶ 입후보를 선언하다 announce one's candidacy 《for the National Assembly》 // 국회 의원으로 입후보하다 run for election to the National Assembly // 입후보를 사퇴하다 decline the nomination for candidature // 입후보를 단념하다 give up one's candidature // 서울에서 입후보하다 run as a candidate in *Seoul*

— 등록 registration of one's candidacy — 사퇴 withdrawal of one's candidacy —자 a candidate 《for》 이중 — double candidacy

†입히다 ① [옷을] clothe ; dress ; put on ¶ 옷을 입히다 put clothes on 《a person》 // 저고리를 입혀보다 try a coat on 《a person》 // 오버를 입혀주다 help 《a person》 on with his overcoat

② [도금] plate ; coat ; gild ¶ 주석을 입히다 coat 《copper》 with tin // 반지에 금을 얇게 입히다 plate〔wash〕 a ring with gold // 이것은 순금입니까 그렇지 않으면 입힌 것입니까 Is this pure〔solid〕 gold or only plated ?

③ [씌우다·올리다] cover ; veneer (베니어판을) ; coat (당의를) ¶ 사탕을 입힌 sugar-coated 《tablet》 // 정제에 당의를 입히다 coat tablets with sugar // 가마니를 입히다 cover 《a thing》 with a straw mat

④ [죄·손해 따위] charge〔fix〕 《guilt on a person》 ; fasten 《a crime on a person》 ; inflict 《injury upon》 ; cause 《damage to》 ; subject 《a person》 to ¶ 손해를 입히다 inflict losses upon 《a person》 // 죄를 입히다 fasten〔fix〕 the guilt upon 《a person》

잇¹ a mattress ; a cover

베갯— a pillow-slip〔-cover, -case〕

잇² 〚식물〛 the safflower

잇다¹ [지붕을] roof ; thatch (이엉으로) ; shingle (널빤지로) ; tile (기와로) ; slate (슬레이트로) ¶ 기와를 다시 이어야 하겠다 We must have our roof retiled. // 그 집은 짚으로 이어져 있다 The cottage roof is thatched with straw.

†잇다² ① [접속] join 《one thing to anoth-

er》; put together ; connect ; link ¶ 두 개를 잇다 join two things together // 실을 잇다 piece threads together // 파편을 이어 붙이다 put the broken pieces together // 두 가닥의 새끼를 잇다 tie together two pieces of rope // 뼈를 이어 맞추다 set a broken bone // 객차를 잇다 join〔couple〕 a passenger car with 《a train of cars》// 책상 다리를 잇다 fix the leg of a table (by adding to it) // 책상을 이어 붙이다 place the table end to end
② [계속] continue ; ensue ; follow ; keep up ; keep on 《with》 ; go on 《with》 ; [계승] succeed to ; carry on ; inherit ; take over ; [유지] preserve ¶ 이어서 in succession ; one after another ; continually ; successively // 10시간 이어서 for ten hours at a stretch〔on end, running〕 // 아버지의 뜻을 잇다 carry on one's father's cherished plan // 가업을 잇다 succeed to the family business // 노래를 잇다 sing on // 이야기를 잇다 continue to talk ; go on talking ; keep up a conversation // 왕위를 잇다 succeed to the throne // 목숨을 겨우 잇다 live barely ; keep body and soul together // 홍수에 이어서 전염병이 발생했다 Pestilence followed on the heels of the flood. // 그는 자기 뒤를 이을 자손이 없다 He has no heir. /There is no one to carry on his family〔to inherit his property〕.

잇달다 follow one after another ; go 〔come, appear〕 in succession ; continue ; ensue ; keep on ; be continuous ¶ 잇달아서 continually ; successively ; in succession ; one after another〔the other〕 // 10시간 잇달아 for ten hours running〔at a stretch, on end, together〕 // 잇달아 3회 이기다 win three consecutive〔straight〕 victories〔games〕 // 불행이 잇달다 have a run of ill luck // 살인 사건이 잇달아 신문에 보도됐다 A succession of homicidal cases filled the paper every day. // 밤은 낮에 잇단다 Night follows〔succeeds〕 day. // 잇달아 총회가 있었다 Then a plenary meeting followed.

잇닿다 continue ; go on ; be continuous 《to》; be connected to ¶ 거실은 침실에 잇닿아 있다 The sitting room opens into a bedroom.

잇대다 ① [계속] continue ; keep up ; go on 《with》; carry on ; go ahead ¶ 잇대서 continuously ; without a break ; at a stretch // 며칠이고 잇대서 for days on end // 몇개월이고 잇대서 for months at a time // 세번 잇대서 three times running〔in succession〕 // 말을 잇대다 go on talking ; keep up a conversation // 종을 잇대어 치다 strike a bell continuously // 그는 3시간 잇대어 연설했다 He spoke for three hours at a stretch. // 10일간 잇대어 눈이 왔다 It kept on snowing for ten days. / The snow lasted〔continued, kept up〕 for ten days.
② [이어대다] put together ; join ; add to ¶ 잇댄 부분 an added part // 기관차를 객차에 잇대다 couple a locomotive with passenger cars

잇따르다 ⇨ 잇달다

잇몸 a gum ; a teethridge ¶ 잇몸의 종기 a gumboil ; a small abscess on the gum // 잇몸을 드러내고 웃다 (show one's teeth and) grin

잇새 the crevice〔an opening〕 between teeth ¶ 잇새에 끼다 get 《a shred of meat》 stuck between the teeth // 잇새에 고기가 끼었다 I got a shred of meat stuck between my teeth.

잇소리 〖음성〗 ⇨ 치음

잇속 [이의] the shape of one's teeth ¶ 잇속이 좋다〔나쁘다〕 have a regular〔an irregular〕 set of teeth

잇속 利— source of profit〔gains〕 ¶ 잇속 있는 장사 a profitable business // 잇속이 있다 be profitable ; be lucrative // 잇속이 없다 be unprofitable

잇자국 a tooth mark ; an impression of teeth ; a bite ¶ 잇자국이 나다 have 〔show〕 a tooth mark

잇줄 利— a profitable line ; a lucrative connection ; a road to gains

잇집 the socket of a tooth

있는 그대로 [사실대로] as it is ; [솔직히] frankly ; honestly ; plainly ; [과장없이] without exaggeration ¶ 사실을 있는 그대로 말하다 state a fact just as it is ; give an honest statement〔account〕 of fact ; tell〔speak〕 the truth

†**있다** ① [존재하다] be ; there is〔are〕 ; exist ; be in existence ¶ 산 위에 집이 있다 There is a house on the hill. // 책은 책상 위에 있다 The book is on the table. // 신은 있다 God is〔exists〕. // 그런 일이 어디 있담 That is impossible. /How can such things be? // 옛날에 어진 임금이 있었다 Once there lived a wise king. // 나는 그에게 있는 그대로 말했다 I told him everything just the way it is. // 네가 할 일은 네 자신의 있는 그대로를 그들에게 보여 주어야 하는 것뿐이다 All you have to do is to show them your real self.
② [머무르다] stay ; stop ; remain ¶ 있다가 after a while // 좀 더 있으면 a little bit later on // 너 여기 있거라 You stay here. // 좀 더 있거라 Stay a little longer. // 너 어디 있었니 Where have you been? // 그는 아저씨 댁에 있다 He is staying at his uncle's.
③ [위치하다] [산·건물이] stand ; [도시·나라가] lie ; [길·강이] be ; be situated ; be located 《미》; run ¶ 강가에 있는 절 a temple standing by the river // 포토막 강변에 있는 벚꽃 나무 the cherry trees along the Potomac // 그 섬은 목포의 서남 100 마일 지점에 있다 The island is〔lies〕 100 miles southwest of *Mokpo*. // 중국은

한국 서쪽에 있다 China lies to the west of Korea. // 학교는 어디에 있느냐 Where is the school situated〔located〕? // 산 뒤에 시내가 있다 Behind the hill there runs a brook.
④ [···에] consist 《in》; lie 《in》; reside 《in》 ¶ 행복은 자기 본분을 다하는 데 있다 Happiness consists in trying to do one's duty. // 성공은 노력에 있다 Success depends on labor. // 주권은 의회에 있다 Sovereignty resides in the Assembly. // 허물은 그에게 있다 The blame rests with him. /He is to blame. /It is his fault.
⑤ [소유하다] have ; possess ; own ; [부여되다] be blessed with (좋은 것을) ; be cursed with (나쁜 것을) ¶ 아들이 둘 있다 have two sons // 좋은 기억력이 있다 He is blessed with a good memory. // 그의 딸은 음악 재주가 있다 His daughter is endowed with musical talents. // 천식이 있다 He is cursed with asthma.
⑥ [팔다] sell ; keep ; carry 《미》; have ¶ (이 가게에) 비누 있습니까 Do you sell soap ? // (당신의 가게에) 미국 담배가 있습니까 Do you carry American cigarettes ?
⑦ [거행되다] be held〔given〕; take place ; come off ; open ; sit ; meet (회의가) ¶ 학교에서 음악회가 있었다 There was a concert at the school. // 다음 회는 언제 있느냐 When is the next meeting to be held ? // 곧 시험이 있다 An examination will take place〔be held〕 shortly. // 어제 기하 시험이 있었다 We had an examination in geometry yesterday.
⑧ [발견되다] be found ; be got ¶ 어디 있더냐 Where did you find it ? // 전화책이 어디 있었느냐 Where did you find the telephone book ? // 이 잡지라면 어디에나 있다 You can get this magazine at any shop.
⑨ [발생하다] there is〔are〕; happen ; occur ; break out ; arise ; take place ; come about ¶ 무슨 일이 있던지 no matter what happens ; come what may // 화재가 있었다 A fire broke out (yesterday night). // 호우가 있었다 There was a heavy rain. /We had a heavy rain. // 그 부부 사이에 무슨 일이 있었는지 나는 모르겠다 I don't know what has passed between that couple.
⑩ [경험하다] have experience ¶ 그를 한번 만난 적이 있다 I have met him once before. // 거기에 한번 간 일이 있다 I have once been there. // 학교에서 가르친 일이 있습니까 Have you ever taught at the school ?
⑪ [포함되다] contain ; bear ; include ¶ 과목 중에 프랑스어가 있다 French is included in the curriculum. // 그 책에 저서 목록이 있다 The book contains a bibliography. // 이 책에는 재미있는 이야기가 많이 있다 This book contains many interesting stories.
⑫ [부속] have 《a thing》 attached to 《it》; [설비가] be equipped〔fitted, provided〕 《with》 ¶ 우리 학교에는 기숙사가 있다 Our school has a dormitory attached to it. // 그 집에는 목욕탕이 있다 The house is provided with a bathroom.
⑬ [재산] be rich〔wealthy〕 ¶ 있는 사람 a well-off person // 있는 집에 태어나다 be born rich ; be born in a rich family〔of rich parents〕
⑭ [동작의 계속] be 《doing》; [상태의 존속] be ; remain ¶ 그는 독서하고 있다 He is reading. // 그녀는 일을 하고〔놀고〕 있다 She is at work〔play〕. // 아버지는 장사를 하고 있다 My father is engaged in business. // 담이 무너져 있다 The wall is broken.
⑮ [상태] go ; keep ; remain ¶ 서 있다 keep standing // 맨발로 있다 go barefoot // 먹지 않고 있다 go without food // 독신으로 있다 remain single

있음직하다 (be) possible ; probable ; likely ¶ 있음직한 일 a possibility ; a probability // 있음직하지도 않은 impossible ; improbable ; unlikely // 그런 일은 있음직하다 It may possibly happen.

잉걸불 a lively burning charcoal fire

잉글랜드 England ⇨ 영국(英國)

잉꼬 〖새〗 a macaw

잉부 孕婦 a pregnant woman ; a woman with child〔in pregnancy〕

잉손 仍孫 posterity of the seventh generation

잉아 threads used to hold up the warp while weaving ; warp ties

잉앗대 a warp-tie stick 《on a loom》

잉어 a carp 《*pl.* carps》; carp 《총칭》

잉여 剩餘 a surplus ; an overplus ; the remainder ; a margin
— **가치** surplus value —**금** a surplus (fund) ; balance in hand — **농산물** farm surpluses — **산물〔식량〕** surplus products〔food〕

잉잉 with whimpers ¶ 잉잉 울다 whimper ; mewl

잉존 仍存 —**하다** retain〔keep〕 as before

잉카 Inca
— **문명** the Incan Civilization — **사람** an Inca(n) — **제국** the Inca Empire —**족(族)** the Incas

†**잉크** ink ¶ 잉크 얼룩 an ink blot〔stain, spot〕 // 펜과 잉크로 쓰다 write in〔with〕 ink ; write with pen and ink // 펜촉에 잉크를 찍다 dip a pen in ink // 잉크가 번지다 ink runs〔spreads〕 // 잉크로 지우다 ink out // 잉크를 흡수하다 dry ink 《with blotting-paper》; blot out (ink)
—**병** an ink bottle —**스탠드** an inkstand — **지우개** an ink eraser **등사** — copying ink **만년필(용)** — ink for the fountain pen **불변색** — indelible ink ; safety ink **인쇄〔제도〕** — printing〔drafting〕 ink

잉태 孕胎 conception ; pregnancy —**하**

다 conceive ; get〔become, be〕 pregnant 《with child》

†잊다 ① [망각] forget ; be forgetful 《of》 ; [사물이 주어] escape 《a person's》 memory ; pass from 《a person's mind》 ¶ 잊을 수 없는 날 a never-to-be-forgotten day // 잘 잊어버리는 사람 a forgetful person ; a person with a short memory // 잊지 말고 without forgetting ; without fail // 잊지 않도록 for remembrance sake ; lest you should forget // 잊기 잘 하다 be forgetful〔oblivious〕 // 사람의 이름〔얼굴〕을 잘 잊다 have a bad memory for names〔faces〕 // 본분을 잊다 be unmindful of one's duty // 근심 걱정을 잊고 일하다 work unmindful of cares and worries // 그의 이름을 잊었다 I forgot his name. /His name has slipped from my memory. // 그 일을 완전히 잊어버렸다 I have forgotten all about it. /The event has quite gone out of my mind. // 잊지 말고 회답을 해주시오 Be sure to answer my letter. // 당신의 은혜는 결코 잊지 않겠습니다 I shall never forget your kindness. // 이 교훈을 항상 잊지 마라 Always keep〔bear〕 this lesson in mind. // 깜박 잊었다 I forgot. /It slipped my mind.
② [단념] take〔keep〕 one's mind off ; put out of one's mind ; dismiss 《a thing》 from one's mind ; think no more 《of, about》 ¶ 그 일은 다 잊어버려라 Don't think about it any more. /Forget all about it. // 나는 그녀를 잊을 수 없었다 I couldn't put her out of my mind // 한잔 마시고 걱정을 잊어라 Wash down your troubles with wine. /Drink away your cares.
③ [놓고 오다] leave 《a thing》 behind ; forget 《a thing》 ¶ 가지고 오는 것을 잊다 forget to bring〔take〕 《a thing》 // 나의 책을 집에서〔기차에서〕 잊고 안 가져 왔다 I left my book at home〔in the train〕.

잊어버리다 completely forget ¶ 비디오 게임을 할 때는 완전히 시간을 잊어버리는구나 You completely lose track of time when you play video games.

잊히다 escape one's memory ; pass out of 〔slip〕 one's mind ¶ 잊히지 않는 일 an unforgettable event // 그녀가 잊히지 않았다 She was always on my mind. /I couldn't put her out of my mind. // 이 애가 있어 죽은 아내의 일이 잊히지 않는다 This child is an eternal reminder of my departed wife.

*잎 a leaf 《*pl.* leaves》 ; a blade (풀의) ; a needle (침엽) : foliage 《집합적》 ; leafage 《집합적》 ¶ 잎의 무성한 좁은 길 a leafy lane // 잎이 진 나무 a naked tree ; a tree denuded of leaves // 잎이 없는 leafless ; bare ; naked 《tree》 // 잎이 나오기 전에 꽃이 피는 precocious // 잎이 나오다 be in leaf ; the leaves are out // 잎이 지다 become leafless ; be bare〔stripped〕 of leaves // 나뭇잎이 모두 졌다 The leaves are all gone off the trees.

잎

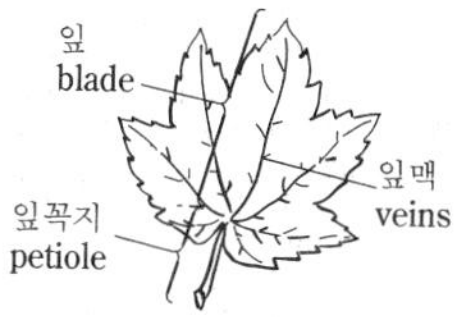

잎나무 brushwood

잎담배 leaf tobacco

잎맥 『식물』 a vein (of a leaf) ; a nerve ; a nervure

잎사귀 a leaf ; a leaflet

잎사귀머리 beef tripe

잎새 ⇨ 잎

잎샘 a cold spell in the early spring ; lingering cold in the leafing season ━하다 get cold in leafing time

잎자루 『식물』 a petiole

잎줄기 『식물』 a cladophyll ; a phylloclade ; phyllocladium

잎파랑이 『식물』 chlorophyl(l) ⇨ 엽록소

ㅈ

자[1] ① [단위] a Korean foot ; a *ja* 《a unit of length, 0.33m》 ② [도구] a ruler ; a rule ; a measure ; a square ; a yardstick ¶ 자로 재다 measure with a rule // 자로 잰 것처럼 as precisely as a square ; like clockwork // 자로 재서 팔다 sell 《cloth》 by the measure
만곡〔원형〕— a curved rule **미터—** a meter rule **티—** a T-square

자[2] [감탄사] Come on ! /Come now ! / Here ! /Here you are ! ¶ 자 한잔 들게 Come on, have a drink. // 자 덤벼라 Come on ! // 자 가자 Come, let us go ! // 자 들어오시오 Please come in ! // 자 너의 선물이다 Here's a present for you. // 자 자 울지마 There, there ! Don't cry. // 자 같이 하자 Come, let us all do it. // 자 쏠테면 쏘아라 Go ahead and shoot, if you are going to.

†**-자** ① [하자 마자] as soon as ; no sooner than ; when ; on ; at ¶ 그녀는 나를 보자 울음을 터뜨렸다 On seeing me, she burst into cry. /No sooner had she seen me than she burst into cry. /As soon as〔(The) first thing〕 she saw me, she burst into cry. /Hardly〔scarcely〕 had she seen me when〔before〕 she burst into cry. /She burst into cry at my sight.
② let (us) ¶ 가자 Let's go. // 먹자 Let's eat. // 앉자 Let's sit down.

자 子 [아들] a son ; a child ; [선생] the master ; [십이지의] the sign of the Rat ; [공자] Confucius
—년 the Year of the Rat **—방** the north **—시** midnight

자 字 ① [글자] a character ; a letter ; an ideograph (한자 따위) ② [이름의] a pseudonym ; another name ; an alias ; a nickname ¶ 글자를 빼다〔보태다〕 erase 〔add〕 a character // 영어라고는 한자도 모르다 do not know a word of English
영— English characters **한—** Chinese characters

자 者 ① [사람] a person ; one ; a fellow ; a guy ; a chap ¶ 그자 he ; that fellow // 박이란 자 one〔a〕 *Park* ; a man named *Park* // 그 자리에서 죽은 자도 있다 Some were killed on the spot. // 가난한 자는 복이 있나니 Those who are poor shall be blessed.
② [것] a thing ; that ; this ¶ 전자와 후자 the former and the latter

자 自 from ¶ 자 오전 10시 지 오후 3시 from 10 a.m. to 3 p.m.

자 紫 purple ; violet ; [자수정의] amethyst

자가 自家 [집] one's own house〔family〕 ; [자기] one's self ; self
— 당착 self-contradiction **— 발전 장치** an independent (electric) power plant **— 시설** one's own facilities ¶ 자가 시설을 갖춘 출판사 a publishing firm with its own printing plant **— 전염** autoinfection **— 중독** autointoxication ; self-poisoning

자가 광고 自家廣告 self-advertisement

자가사리 〖물고기〗 a kind of catfish ; Liobagrus mediodiposalis (학명)
자가사리가 용을 건드린다 [속담] Fools rush in where angels fear to tread.

자가 생식 自家生殖 〖식물〗 autogamy ¶ 자가 생식의 autogamous

*__자가용 自家用__ ① [개인용] (for) private use ; personal use ; family use (가정용) ② [자가용차] a private car〔automobile〕 ; an automobile for one's personal〔private〕 use ¶ 자가용으로 부산까지 데려다 주겠다 I'll drive you down to *Pusan* in my car.
— 운전사 a chauffeur in one's employ **— 족** those who have a car of their own ; [자신이 운전하는] owner drivers

자가 치료 自家治療 doctoring oneself ; self-treatment ; home treatment ; domestic medication **—하다** doctor〔treat〕 oneself ; be one's own doctor ; try home treatment

‡**자각 自覺** consciousness ; self-consciousness ; awakening (각성) ; [정신 병자의] insight **—하다** become〔be〕 conscious 〔aware〕 《of》 ; awake to ; realize ¶ 자기 힘을 자각하다 realize〔feel〕 one's own strength // 죄를 자각시키다 awaken 《a person》 to a sense of sin // 국민의 자각을 기다리다 wait for the self-awakening of the nation // 내 자신의 부족함을 자각하고 있다 I am conscious〔well aware〕 of my want of ability.
— 증상 subjective symptom ; the patient's complaints ; symptoms of which the patient is conscious

자간 子癎 〖의학〗 eclampsia

‡**자갈** gravel ; pebbles ; shingle ; ballast ; macadam ¶ 길에 자갈을 깔다 gravel the road
—길 a gravel road **—밭** gravelly field ; shingle **— 보도** a gravel walk **—차** a gravel truck **— 채굴장〔터〕** a gravel pit **— 하치장** a gravel yard

자갈색 紫褐色 purplish brown

자강 自彊 strenuous efforts **—하다** make strenuous efforts

—불식 ceaseless endeavors —술 the art of health building〔physical fitness〕 —책 how〔plan〕 to make strenuous efforts
자개 mother-of-pearl ; nacre ¶ 자개 박은 장 a cabinet inlaid with mother-of-pearl // 자개를 박다 inlay with mother-of-pearl
— 그릇 a wooden bowl inlaid with mother-of-pearl — 단추 pearl buttons — 일꾼 a shellworker — 세공 《an article of》 mother-of-pearl work
자개미 [겨드랑이의] a depression in either side of the armpit ; [오금의] a depression in either side of the hollow of the knee〔of the crook of the arm〕
자객 刺客 an assassin ; an assassinator ¶ 그는 자객 손에 죽었다 He fell a victim to an assassin. /He met the death at the hands of an assassin. /He was assassinated.
***자격 資格** qualification ; requirement ; [능력] capacity ; competence ; [회원의] eligibility ¶ 개인 자격으로 in a private capacity // …의 자격으로 in the capacity of // 자격이 있다 be qualified 《to do, for》 ; have qualification 《for》 ; be entitled 《to do, to a seat》 ; have a right 《for》 (권리) ; be eligible 《for》 // 자격이 없다 be disqualified〔unqualified〕 《for》 ; have no right 《for》 ; be ineligible 《for》 // 자격을 주다 qualify 《a person》 for // 자격을 박탈하다 disqualify 《a person》 《from》 // 자격을 잃다 be disqualified 《for, as》 // // 교원의 자격을 얻었다 He obtained a teacher's license. // 당신은 회원 자격이 있다 You are eligible to membership. // 나는 당신의 친절을 받을 자격이 없다 I am unworthy of your kindness. // 그는 그 일을 할 자격이 없다 He has no qualification for the work. // 그는 그것을 비평할 자격이 있다 He is competent to criticize it. // 그는 팀의 주장으로서 충분한 자격이 있다 He has excellent qualifications for a team captain. // 다음 모임부터는 개인 자격으로 참가할 것이다 I'll take part in the next meeting in a prirate capacity.
—상실 disqualification ; incapacitation — 시험 a qualifying examination — 심사 an examination of qualifications ; screening ; an examination of the applicants' 〔candidates'〕 qualification —증(명서) a certificate of qualification 교원 — a teacher's license ; a license for teaching 《in the high school》 선거 — qualifications as a voter 선거인 — qualifications for an elector ; the elective franchise 입학 — entrance requirements 입회 — requirements for membership 피선거 — eligibility 무 —자 a disqualified〔an incompetent〕 person ; an unlicensed person 유—자 a qualified〔competent〕 person ; a licensed〔an eligible〕 person
자격지심 自激之心 a guilty conscience ; a feeling of self-accusation ¶ 그건 그의 자격지심에서 나온 말이다 He said that out of self-accusation〔dissatisfaction〕.
자결 自決 ① self-determination ② [자살] suicide — 하다 determine for〔by〕 oneself ; decide by〔for〕 oneself ; commit suicide ; kill oneself
민족 — self-determination of races
자경 自警 self-warning ; vigilance ; caution
자경단 自警團 civil militia ; a vigilance committee ; vigilante corps 《미》
—원 a vigilante 《미》 ; a vigilance committee member
자경마 들다 hold the reins for oneself while riding
자계 自戒 self-discipline — 하다 admonish oneself
자계 磁界 ⇨ 자장(磁場)
자고 慈姑 〖식물〗 the arrowhead plant ; Sagittaria sagittifolia (학명)
자고 〖새〗 a partridge
자고깨면 whenever one awakes from one's sleep ; all the time ; every (waking) minute ; from morning till night ; ever ; always
자고로 自古— from ancient times ; from time immemorial ; from old times ; traditionally ¶ 자고로 내려온 풍습 time-honored〔long-established〕 customs // 자고로 한국인은 백의를 즐겨 입었다 We Koreans traditionally have preferred to wear white clothes.
자고새면 when the days breaks〔dawns〕 ; if only another day breaks
자공 自供 a (voluntary) confession — 하다 confess ; 〖법〗 depose ; make a deposition ¶ 자공시키다 elicit a confession 《from a person》
자괴지심 自愧之心 a sense of shame ¶ 자괴지심이 있다 have〔feel〕 a sense of shame ; be sensible to shame
자구 행위 自救行爲 〖법〗 self-help
†**자국** a mark ; a print ; a scar ; a trace ; a track ; a trail ¶ 긁힌 자국 a scratch // 수레가 지나간 자국 the trace〔track〕 of a wagon // 연필로 지운 자국 traces of erased pencil marks // 시체에서 폭행의 자국을 발견할 수가 없었다 The body bore no traces of violation. /There were no marks of violation on the body.
눈물 — traces of tears 발— a footprint 이빨 — teeth-marks 총상 — the mark of a bullet-wound 핏— blood stains
자국 自國 one's (own) country ; one's native land ; one's fatherland〔motherland〕 ; home ¶ 자국의 native ; home ; domestic // 자국제의 home made
—민 one's fellow countrymen ; one's compatriots —어 one's mother〔native〕 tongue ; one's own language ; the vernacular (language)
자국나다 get marked ; make a print〔an impression〕 《in, on》 ; form a scar ;

ㅈ

leave a trace〔track〕
자국눈 a snowfall barely enough to leave footprints ; a light fall of snow
자국물 water gathered in footprints ; a small puddle
자국 밟다 follow the tracks of ; trace 《a person》; follow a spoor (짐승의)
***자궁 子宮** 〖해부〗 the womb ; the uterus
— **발육 부전증** uterine hypoplasia **—벽** the uterine wall **—병** a uterine disease **—비대** uterine hypertrophy **—암** uterine cancer ; cancer of the womb **—염** uteritis ; metritis **—외 임신** extrauterine 〔ectopic〕 pregnancy〔conception〕 **— 전굴(前屈)〔전경(前傾)〕** anteversion〔anteflexion〕 of the uterus **— 절개(술)** hysterotomy **— 출혈** uterine hemorrhage ; metrorrhagia **—통(痛)** metralgia ; hysteralgia **— 후굴(後屈)〔후경(後傾)〕** retroflexion〔retroversion〕 of the uterus
자궁 내막 子宮內膜 the endometrium
— **소파(술)** hysterotrachelectasia **—염** endometritis
자귀[1] [연장] an adz
—질 wielding an adze ¶ 자귀질하다 wield an adze **자귓밥** chips from an adze
자귀[2] [개병] a dog ailment caused by overeating
자귀[3] [짐승의 발자국] a spoor ; a trail ; tracks (of wild animals) ¶ 자귀 짚다 track 《an animal》
자구 字句 words and phrases ; terms ; [표현] expressions ; wording ; phrasing ; phraseology ¶ 자구의 verbal // 자구의 해석 interpretation of words and phrases // 자귀대로 해석하다 interpret literally // 자귀에 얽매이다 be letterbound ; adhere to the letter 《of the law》// 자귀에 충실한〔구애되지 않는〕 번역 (a) literal〔free〕 translation // 자귀를 수정하다 amend phraseology ; make verbal modification // 자귀를 바꾸다 change the wording ; make some change in the wording
자귀나무 〖식물〗 a silk-tree ; Albizzia julibrissin (학명)
자귀짚다 trace〔track, spoor〕 《an animal》
자그락거리다, 짜그락거리다 ⇨ 지그럭거리다
자그르르, 짜그르르 simmering
자그마치 [자그마하게] somewhat small 〔little〕; in a smallish way ; [적지 않게] not a little ; no less〔fewer〕 than ; as much〔many〕 as ¶ 술을 자그마치 마셔라 Don't drink too much. // 그 열차 사고에 자그마치 20명의 사상자가 났다 As many as twenty passengers were killed and wounded in that train wreck.
자그마하다 (be) smallish ; be of a somewhat small size ; be rather on the small side ¶ 키가 자그마한 사람 a person of smallish stature
자그맣다 ⇨ 자그마하다
†**자극 刺戟** a stimulus ; an impetus ; a spur ; an incentive ; stimulation ; excitement **—하다** stimulate ; give an impetus 《to》; excite ; incite 《a person》; spur 《a person on》; irritate ¶ 자극적 exciting ; sensational // 자극이 없는 생활 a dull〔monotonous〕 life // 도시 생활의 자극 the excitements of town life // 자극이 강하다 be exciting ; be thrilling ; be sensational // 자극을 받다 be under impetus from ; be receiving impetus from // 신경을 자극하다 get on 《a person's》 nerves // 자극을 찾다 look for some excitement ; seek a thrill // 칭찬하는 것은 정신적인 자극이 된다 Praise can be a mental tonic. // 활발히 걸으면 혈액 순환이 자극된다 Brisk walking stimulates the circulation. // 흥미는 연구의 자극이 된다 Interest is an incitement to study. // 나에게 도시 생활은 자극이 강하다 City life irritates my nerves. // 그를 너무 자극하지 않는 편이 좋다 You'd better not get him too stirred up. // 내 아내도 자극을 받았다 My wife's caught the bug too.
— **감응성** 〖생물〗 irritability **—물** a stimulus ; a stimulant ; an incentive ; an excitant ; an exciter ; an incitant **— 반응대(反應帶)** 〖심리〗 stimulus-response bonds **—역** 〖심리〗 the stimulus〔absolute〕 threshold **— 완화제** an abirritant **— 요법** stimulation therapy **— 운동** 〖동·식물〗 (a) paratonic movement ; a taxis 《*pl.* taxes》; tropism **—제** a stimulant ; an excitant ; an irritant **—취(臭)** 〖화학〗 irritating smell〔odor〕; irritant odor
자극 磁極 a magnetic pole
—단(端) a pole tip **—성** magnetic polarity **— 전단(前端)〔후단(後端)〕** a leading〔trailing〕 pole tip **전—** electromagnetic pole
자금 自今 from now on ; henceforth ; hereafter ; in future
‡**자금 資金** funds ; capital ; money ¶ 풍부한 자금 ample funds // 자금의 해외 도피 the flight of capital // 자금이 부족하다 be short of funds // 자금을 내다 finance 《an enterprise》// 자금을 융통하다 accommodate 《a person》 with money // 자금을 조달하다 raise the capital〔funds〕// 그는 아주 적은 자금으로 장사를 시작했다 He started business with a small capital. // 그는 그 재단에서 나오는 적은 자금으로 연구 중이다 He is carrying on his study on funds granted by the foundation. // 누가 그 여행의 자금을 댑니까 Who is going to finance the trip? // 자금 부족으로 공사가 중지되었다 Lack of funds halted the work.
— **고갈** fund starvation **— 공급** funding ; financing ; bankrolling **—난** financial difficulty ; stringency of capital **— 동결** freezing of funds **— 부족** insufficiency〔shortage〕 of funds **— 수급 계획** a

ㅈ

funds supply and demand program — 조달 운동 a campaign for raising funds ; a fund-raising campaign〔drive〕 — 통제 control of funds — 회전 turnover of capital 건축〔계절, 운동, 장학, 구제〕 — a building〔seasonal, campaign, scholarship, relief〕 fund 유동 — floating money 적립〔준비〕 — reserve funds 회전〔운영〕 — revolving〔working〕 funds

자금거리다 be gritty to the teeth

자금화 資金化 capitalization —하다 capitalize ; convert 《goods》 into money

자급 自給 self-supply〔-support, -sustenance〕 ; self-sufficiency —하다 support oneself ; supply oneself ; provide for oneself ; be self-sufficient ¶ 자급하는 self-supporting

— 경제 self-sufficient economy ; autarky — 경제주의 autarky — 국가 a self-sustaining〔-supporting〕 country — 비료 self-sufficing manure — 정책 a self-supporting policy

자급자족 自給自足 self-sufficiency〔-containment〕 ¶ 자급자족의 self-sufficing〔-sufficient〕 // 식량의 자급자족 foodstuff self-sufficiency

— 경제 self-sufficient〔-sustaining〕 economy —주의〔정책〕 a self-supporting and self-sufficient policy

자긍 自矜 [자찬] self-praise ; self-admiration ; [자부] self-conceit ; pride —하다 pride oneself 《on》 ; sing one's praise

†**자기 自己** oneself ; self ; ego ¶ 자기의 one's own ; personal ; private // 자기 스스로 personally ; in person ; for oneself (독력으로) ; by oneself (혼자) // 자기 자신을 반성하다 reflect on oneself // 자기 자신을 알다 know oneself // 자기 이익을 도모하다 seek〔pursue〕 one's own interest // 자기 자신을 소개하다 introduce oneself // 자기 선전을 하다 seek〔court〕 publicity // 자기 신분을 밝히다 identify oneself

— 감응 〖전기〗 self-induction — 감정 self-feeling — 결정 self-determination ; 〖철학〗 freedom — 경멸 self-contempt — 계시 self-revelation — 관찰 self-observation — 극복 self-conquest — 기만 self-deception — 도취 self-absorption〔-intoxication〕 ; 〖정신 분석〗 narcissism ; narcism (자기 도취증) — 독소 〖의학〗 autotoxin — 동형(同型) 〖물리〗 automorphism —류 one's own style〔way, fashion〕 — 만족 self-contentment〔-satisfaction〕 ; self-complacency〔-sufficiency〕 — 모순 self-contradiction — 반성 self-reflection〔-scrutiny〕 ; self-survey — 발견 self-discovery — 방위 self-defense〔-protection〕 ; self-preservation — 방전(放電) self-discharge — 변호 self-vindication〔-justification〕 ; an excuse — 보존 self-preservation — 본위 egotism ; egoism ; egocentricity — 본위자 an egoist ; an egotist — 부정 self-denial ; self-negation — 분석 self-analysis — 비판〔비평〕 self-criticism — 상실 loss of self — 선전 self-advertisement — 성찰 self-examination — 소개 self-introduction — 소외 self-alienation〔-estrangement〕 — 수양 self-culture — 숭배 autolatry ; self-worship — 신뢰 self-reliance〔-trust〕 — 실현 self-expression ; self-fulfilment ; 〖윤리〗 self-realization — 암시 autosuggestion — 억제 self-restriction ; self-control — 연민 self-pity — 원인 〖철학〗 causa sui — 유도(誘導) 〖전기〗 self-induction — 자본 equity capital — 접종 〖의학〗 autoinoculation — 주장 self-assertion — 중독 〖의학〗 autotoxemia ; autotoxis ; autointoxication ; autotoxicosis — 중심 self-centeredness ; selfishness — 중심벽(中心癖) egocentrism ; egotism — 최면 autohypnotism ; autohypnosis — 통제 self-command — 활동 self-activity — 혐오 self-hatred〔-hate, -abhorrence〕 — 희생 self-sacrifice

자기 自棄 self-abandonment ⇨ 자포자기

***자기 磁氣** magnetism ¶ 자기를 띤 magnetic // 자기를 띠게 하다 magnetize ; make a magnet of // 자기를 없애다 demagnetize — 감응 magnetic induction — 검출기 a magnetoscope —계(計) a magnetometer — 나침의 a magnetic compass — 녹음〔녹음기〕 magnetic recording〔a magnetic recorder〕 —량 magnetic charge — 렌즈 magnetic lens —력 magnetic force — 방위〔편차〕 magnetic amplitude〔declination〕 — 북극 the magnetic north — 유도 magnetic induction — 인력〔작용〕 magnetic attraction〔action〕 — 자오선〔적도〕 the magnetic meridian〔equator〕 — 저항 reluctance ; magnetic resistance — 체(體) magnetic ; paramagnet ; paramagnetic — 측정 magnetometry — 폭풍 [지자기의 급변] a magnetic storm —학 magnetics ; magnetism —학자 a magnetist — 화학 magnetochemistry — 회로 magnetic circuits 잔류 — residual magnetism 지(地)— terrestrial magnetism

자기 自記 ① [자기가 씀] writing by oneself ② [자동 작용] self-register —하다 write by oneself ; register (automatically) ¶ 자기의 self-registering〔-recording〕

— 검력기(檢力器) a dynamograph — 기압계 a barograph — 미압계(微壓計) a microbarograph — 수위계(水位計) a hydrograph — 심도계(深度計) a depth recorder — 온도계〔우량계〕 a self-registering thermometer〔rain gauge〕 — 온도기압계 a thermobarograph — 풍속계 an anemograph — 풍향계 a recording wind vane — 한란계〔검조기(檢潮器)〕 a self-registering thermometer〔tidegauge〕 — 형기(衡器) a registering scale

‡**자기 瓷器** porcelain ; china (ware) ; crockery

ㅈ

자기앞 수표 自己─手票 a cashier's check ; a bank〔banker's〕 check

자깝스럽다 assume a grown-up person's air ; act like a man ; (be) precocious

*자꾸 repeatedly ; frequently ; always ; again and again ¶ 그는 수업중에 자꾸 잠만 잔다 He frequently sleeps in class. // 그 아이는 자꾸 돈만 달란다 The child keeps asking for money. // 그는 자꾸 나에게 구혼했다 He eagerly proposed me to marry him.

-자꾸나 let us ; let's ; how about〔shall we〕…? ¶ 두고 보자꾸나 Let's wait and see. // 한잔 하자꾸나 Let's have a drink, shall we?/How about a drink?

자끈 with a crack ⇨ 지끈

*자나깨나 day and night ; awake or asleep ¶ 자나깨나 그 일을 잊을 수가 없다 I cannot forget that waking or sleeping. // 그는 자나깨나 그 일만 생각하고 있다 The thought is ever present in his mind. /It engrosses his attention all the time.

자낭 子囊 a seed bag ; an ascus ; a sporangium

—과(果) an ascocarp —군(群) a sorus 《*pl.* -ri》 —균(菌) an ascomycete ; a sac fungus —반(盤) an apothecium 《*pl.* -cia》 ; a discocarp — 포자 an ascospore

자네 you

자녀 子女 children ; sons and daughters ; offspring ¶ 자녀의 교육비 the educational expenditure of one's children

자년 子年 〖민속〗 the Year of the Rat

자늑자늑 —하다 (be) soft-moving ; gentle ; swaying

자닝하다, 자닝스럽다 be beyond misery ; be too piteous to see 《one's misery》

*자다 ① [잠을] sleep ; fall asleep ; doze off (잠깐) ; go to sleep ; [잠자리에 들다] go to bed ; retire ¶ 낮잠을 자다 take a nap〔siesta〕 // 늦잠을 자다 sleep late ; oversleep // 푹 자고 있다 lie〔be〕 fast asleep // 정신 없이 자다 sleep like a dog〔log〕 // 자지 않고 간호하다 keep vigil over 《a sick child》 ; watch〔sit up〕 with 《an invalid》 // 어젯밤은 한잠도 못 잤다 I could not sleep a wink last night. // 간밤에 잘 잤어 Did you have a good night's sleep?

② [정지하다] go〔die〕 down ; subside ; calm down ; become quiet〔still〕 ; stop ; run down ¶ 바람이 잤다 The wind has died down. // 폭풍우가 잤다 The storm has abated. // 시계가 잔다 The watch has run down〔stopped〕.

③ [성교하다] have sexual intercourse

자는 호랑이 불침 놓기 〔속담〕 Let sleeping dogs lie. /Wake not a sleeping lion.

자단 紫檀 〖식물〗 a red sandalwood

자담 自擔 personal charge ; self-responsibility —하다 take charge 《of something》 personally〔in person〕 ; bear 《one's own expense》 ; pay 《one's own way》 ; take care of 《one's own share》 ¶ 비용은 자담한다 Each man has to bear his expense.

자당 自黨 one's (own) party〔faction, clique〕 ¶ 자당에 포섭하다 bring 《a person》 over to one's party

자당 蔗糖 cane sugar ; saccharose

자당 慈堂 your〔his, her〕 mother

자독 自瀆 self-pollution ; masturbation ; self-abuse ; onanism

*자동 自動 automatic action〔movement, operation〕 ; automatism ; intransitivity —하다 move automatically ; act〔work〕 by itself ¶ 자동식의 automatic ; self-acting ; self-operating // 반 자동식의 semi-automatic // 자동적으로 automatically ; mechanically // 이 기계는 자동적으로 작업을 한다 The machine works by itself.

—계 a meter (물·가스 등의 계량계) ; [속도의] an autometer ; a speedometer —계단 an escalator — 금전 출납기 an automatic paying machine — 급유 장치 a self-oiling arrangement — 급탄기 an automatic〔a mechanical〕 stoker — 기계 an automatic machine ; an automaton —기중기 a jenny — 면역 〖의학〗 active immunity —(식)문 an automatic door —변속 장치 an automatic transmitter —설 〖철학〗 automatism —성 〖생물〗 automaticity ; 〖생리〗 automatism — 소방 장치 sprinkler system — 소화기(消火器) an automatic fire-extinguisher ; a self-sprinkler — 송신기 an automatic transmitter — 수신기 an automatic receiver —스타터 a self-starter —식 전화 a dial telephone ; an automatic telephone ; a pay-phone —식 차단기〔소총〕 an automatic cutout〔rifle〕 — 안마기 a vibrator — 안정 장치 〖항공〗 stabilizer ; a stabilizing apparatus — 엘리베이터 an automatic elevator ; a self-help elevator —연결기 an automatic coupler — 운동 〖식물〗 automatic movement — 유도 장치 a homing device — 작용 an automatic action — 장치 an automaton 《*pl.* ~s, -ta》 — 전철기(轉轍機) an automatic switch — 점멸 장치(點滅裝置) an automatic switch ; a flasher — 제동기 an automatic brake — 제어 〖기계〗 automatic control — 제어 장치 servomechanism — 조작(操作) automatic operation ; 〖기계〗 automation — 조정(調整) self-adjustment — 조정기 an automatic regulator — 조종 장치(操縱裝置) 〖항공〗 an automatic pilot ; a gyropilot — 직기(織機) an automatic loom〔weaving machine〕 — 판매기 a slot machine ; an automatic vending machine ; an automat (식당의) — 폐색 신호 〖철도〗 an automatic block signal — 행동설 [동물의] automatism — 허가제 an automatic approval system — 현상 〖심리〗 automa-

tism — 화기(火器) automatic firearms — 화재 경보기 an automatic fire alarm 담배 — 판매기 an automatic tobacco vending machine
*자동사 自動詞 an intransitive verb
자동 승인 自動承認 automatic approval —제 the automatic approval system — 품목 immediate import liberal items
†자동차 自動車 a (motor) car ; an automobile《미》; an auto《미·속》¶ 자갈을 가득 실은 자동차 a fully loaded gravel truck // 자동차를 운전하다 drive a car〔an automobile〕// 자동차에 타다 ride in a car // 자동차로 가다 go out motoring // 자동차로 서울에 가다 go to *Seoul* by car // 자동차에서 내리다 get off a car // 나는 그를 내 자동차에 태워주었다 I gave him a ride〔lift〕 in my car. // 아버지는 자동차로 일터에 가신다 Father drives to work. // 그는 나를 집까지 자동차로 데려다 주었다 He drove me home in his car. // 그는 자동차로 어린이를 치었다 He hit a child with his car. // 저는 자동차 부속품 장사를 하고 있습니다 I'm in the auto parts business.
— 경주 a motor〔an auto〕 race — 경주 선수 a racing driver ; a car racer — 경주장 a motor racecourse ; a motordrome — 공업〔산업〕 the auto〔automotive〕 industry — 도둑 [사람] an auto lifter ; a car thief ; [사건] autotheft — (전용) 도로 a driveway ; a motorway ; an auto〔a motor〕 road ; a road for motoring ; a turnpike (road) — 매매업자 a motor〔an automobile〕 dealer — 메이커(제조 업자) an auto maker ; an automobile〔a car〕 manufacturer — 번호판 a number plate ; a license〔licence〕 plate — 사고 a motoring accident —세 a private auto〔an auto〕 tax — 속도계 a speedometer ; an autometer — 손해 배상 책임 보험 automobile third-party liability insurance — 쇼 an auto(mobile) show — 수리 공장 an auto-repair shop ; a garage — 여행 a motor trip — 여행자 an autoist ; a motorist —왕 a motorcar magnate ; an automobile king —용 라디오 a car radio — 운전 면허증 a driver's license〔licence〕 — 운전수 an automobile〔a motor〕 driver ; a chauffeur (남자) ; a chauffeuse (여자) — 이용 인구 the motoring population — 주차장 a parking place〔lot〕 — 차고 a garage — 학원(교습소) a driving school ; a driver training school ; a motor school — 행렬 a motorcade — 회사 an automobile〔automotive〕 company 고물 — a jalopy ; a flivver 살수(撒水) — an automobile sprinkler 영업용 — a taxicab ; motorcars for business use ; trade cars 자가용 — a private car 전기 — an electromobile ; an electric motorcar 전세 — an automobile for hire 화물 — a truck《미》; a (motor) truck ; an autotruck ; an automobile truck ; a (motor) lorry 화물 — 운송업 trucking business ☞《p. 1766》
*자두 〖식물〗 a plum
— 나무 a (damson) plum
자드락 the decline of a hill
—길 a hill path
자드락거리다, 짜드락거리다 ⇨ 지드럭거리다
자득 自得 ① [만족] self-complacency ; self-satisfaction ② [터득] apprehension ; understanding —하다 (be) self-complacent ; feel〔be〕 self-satisfied ; apprehend ; understand
자등 紫藤 〖식물〗 the purple wisteria
자디잘다 (be) very small ; tiny ; fine ; be of a very small size ¶ 자디잔 사람 a petty-minded person ; a meticulous〔overscrupulous〕 person // 글씨를 자디잘게 쓰다 write microscopically
자라 〖동물〗 a snapping〔mud, soft-shelled〕 turtle ; a〔an alligator〕 terrapin —목 깃 [스웨터 따위의] a turtle neck — 자지 [작은] a shrivelled-up〔an impotent〕 penis ; [팽대하는] a deceptively small penis —풀 〖식물〗 a kind of frogbit
자라 보고 놀란 가슴 소댕 보고 놀란다 [속담] Once bitten, twice shy. /A burnt child dreads the fire. /A scalded cat〔dog〕 fears cold water.
*자라다[1] ① [성장하다] grow up ; be bred ; be brought up ¶ 모유로 자란 아이 a child raised on mother's milk // 우유로 자란 아이 a bottle-fed child // 좋은 집안에서 자란 사람 a well-bred person ; a well brought-up person // 도시〔시골〕에서 자란 city〔country〕-bred // 자라서 어른이 되다 grow into manhood〔a man〕 ; grow to maturity // 너무 자라서 옷이 작아지다 outgrow one's clothes // 이 나무는 아주 크게 자랄 거요 This tree will grow to a great size. // 그는 자랄 대로 자랐다 He has reached his full growth. // 태양 광선이 없으면 식물은 자라지 않는다 Plants will not thrive without sunshine.
② [증가하다] increase ; gain ¶ 이자가 자라다 yield〔bear〕 interest // 그 도시의 인구가 급속히 자라고 있다 The city is rapidly increasing in its population. /The population of the city is rapidly growing.
자라다[2] ① [충분하다] (be) enough ; sufficient ¶ 천원 있으면 자라겠다 One thousand *won* will be sufficient〔will do〕. // 의자가 다섯 개만 더 있으면 자라겠다 Five more chairs will be enough to go round.
② [도달하다] reach ; come up ; get to ¶ 손이 자라는 곳에 within one's reach // 힘이 자라다 be within one's ability〔power〕 // 내 힘이 자라는 대로 하겠다 I will do it to the best of my ability.
자락 the lower edges〔the ends〕 of garments ; the hem of a cloth〔garment〕 ¶ 바지 자락을 걷어 올리다 tuck up one's

자동차 운전

① 표현

▶핸들 steering wheel (★자전거 핸들은 handle bar) ¶운전석에 앉다 get [sit down] behind the wheel // 핸들을 잡다 take the wheel // 차를 운전하고 있는 사람 the man at the wheel // 핸들을 꺾다 wheel right [left]; turn the steering wheel

▶가속기 accelerator ¶가속기를 밟다 step [press down] on the accelerator // 속도를 내다 step on the gas 《미》 // 가속기에서 발을 떼다 release the accelerator; take one's foot off the gas pedal

▶클러치 clutch (pedal) ¶클러치를 밟다 engage the clutch // 클러치를 풀다 disengage the clutch // 클러치가 들어가 있다 The clutch is in.

▶기어 gear ¶기어 레버 gear shift; gear lever 《영》 // 고속 기어 high gear // 후진 기어 reverse (gear) // 최고속 기어 top gear // 저속기어 bottom gear // 4단 기어차 a car with four gears // 기어를 고속으로 놓다 shift into high gear; gear up // 기어를 후진으로 놓다 shift the transmission into reverse // 그는 차에 기어를 넣고 차를 발진시켰다. He put the car in gear and drove away.

▶브레이크 brake ¶에어 브레이크 air brake // 풋브레이크 foot brake // 핸드[보조] 브레이크 hand brake // 브레이크를 밟다 put on [apply] the brakes; press the brake pedal // 브레이크를 풀다 take off the brakes; take one's foot off the brakes // 브레이크를 과도하게[자주] 밟다 ride the brakes // 급브레이크를 밟다 slam[jam] on the brakes; jam the brakes on; brake suddenly

▶방향지시기 blinker; turn signal; winker 《영》

▶미등 tail light

▶펜더 fender; wing 《영》

② 잘못된 표현

▶사이드 브레이크 hand brake 《영》; parking brake 《미》 / 핸들 steering wheel / 백미러 review mirror / 프론트 글래스, 앞유리 windshield 《미》, windscreen 《영》 / 노클러치 automatic transmission / 와이퍼 windshield wiper / 클랙슨 horn (★클랙슨(klaxon)이라 불리는 경적기는 상표명.)

---

trousers

자락자락 impertinently; impudently; saucily ¶ 보자 하니 자락자락 더 한다 I have been overlooking it, but now his rudeness is getting worse.

자란자란 to the brim; brimfully ⇨ 지런지런

†**자랑** self-praise; vanity; boast; brag; pride **—하다** be proud〔boastful, vain〕 of; brag〔boast〕 of; make a boast of; pride oneself on; take pride in ¶ 자랑하는 사람 a braggart; a boaster // 자랑스러운 얼굴 a boastful look // 자랑스럽게 boastfully; proudly // 자기 나라를 자랑하다 boast about one's own country // 그녀가 아들을 자랑하는 것도 당연하다 She may well be proud of her son. // 그 배우는 얼굴 잘 생긴 것이 자랑이었다 The actor piqued himself on his good looks. // 양친은 그가 자랑이었다 He was the pride 〔boast〕 of his parents. // 그것은 우리 나라로서는 자랑할 만한 기록이 아니다 It is not a proud record for our country. // 그는 자기 정원을 자랑스럽게 보고 있었다 He looked with pride at his garden. // 그는 늘 자기 자랑을 늘어놓는다 He always blows his own horn.

자랑거리 a source of pride; something one is proud of; a feather in one's cap ¶ 새로 산 모자가 그 여자의 자랑거리다 The new hat is her pride and joy. // 이 사진은 나의 자랑거리이다 This photograph is my pride and joy.

자래 [알 주머니] a double egg case

†**자력 資力** means; (financial) resources; capital; funds ¶ 자력이 있는〔없는〕 사람 a man of〔without〕 means // 자력에 따라 according to one's means // 자력의 부족으로 from lack of funds // 그는 새차를 살만한 자력이 없었다 He could not afford to buy a new car.

자력 自力 one's own strength; self-effort; one's own exertion ¶ 자력으로 by one's own efforts; by oneself; single-handed // 자력으로 하다 do for oneself; do with one's might // 자력 갱생하다 work out one's salvation by one's own effort // 자력으로 세상을 살아가다 carve out a career for oneself

자력 磁力 〖물리〗 magnetism; magnetic force ¶ 자력의 magnetic // 자력으로 magnetically

— 검출기(檢出機) a magnetoscope **—계** a magnetometer **— 기록** a magnetogram **— 기록기** a magnetograph **— 녹음기** a magnetic recorder **—선** a line of magnetic force **— 전화기** a magnetotelephone

ㅈ

자로 磁路 〖물리〗 a magnetic circuit〔path〕
***자료 資料** material ; data 《*sg.* datum》 ¶ 자료를 수집하다 collect material〔data〕 // 자료를 제공하다 furnish data
—실 [신문사 등의] a morgue 《미》 **—통계국** the Data and Statistics Bureau **근본—** basic raw materials ; source materials **연구—** research materials〔data〕 **통계—** statistical data ; materials for statistics
†자루¹ [주머니] a (gunny) sack ; a bag ¶ 자루에 넣다 put 《a thing》 into a bag
쌀— a rice bag
***자루²** [손잡이] a handle ; a haft ; a hilt (칼 따위의) ; a shaft (창 따위의) ; a helve ¶ 낫에 자루를 달다 put a handle on a sickle
권총 — a revolver handle **도끼 —** the helve of an ax **빗—** a broomstick **칼 —** the handle of a knife ; the haft of a dagger ; the hilt of a sword
자루³ [세는 단위] a piece〔cake, stick〕 《of India ink》 ; a pair 《of scissors》 ¶ 연필 두 자루 two pencils // 분필 다섯 자루 five pieces of chalk
자류 磁流 〖물리〗 magnetic flux
— 철광(鐵鑛) 〖광물〗 pyrrhotite ; magnetic pyrites
‡자르다¹ ① [칼 따위로] cut (off) ; chop ; sever (절단하다) ; hash (잘게) ; saw (off) (톱으로) ; clip ; snip ; shear (가위로) ; carve (식탁에서 닭고기 따위를) ; slice ; slash ; strip ; shave (얇게) ¶ 둘로 자르다 cut in〔into〕 two // 싹을 자르다 nip the bud // (사람의) 목을 자르다 cut〔strike〕 off 《a person's》 head // 약간 자르는 것이 훨씬 보기가 낫겠어요 A little trim would make it look much better. // 적당한 길이로 잘라 주세요 Medium cut, please. // 이 정도 길이로 잘라 주세요 Leave〔Make〕 them this long. // 짧게 잘라 주세요 Short cut, please.
② [거절하다] refuse flatly ; give a flat〔point-blank〕 refusal ; spurn 《a demand》 point-blank〔bluntly〕
③ [적당히 끝맺다] end〔finish, drop〕 at a proper time ; break〔call, leave, knock〕 off at the right moment
자르다² tie up ; tighten ⇨ 조르다
자르랑거리다 ⇨ 쩌르렁거리다
자르르, 짜르르 dribbling ; dripping ⇨ 지르르, 찌르르
†자리¹ ① [좌석] a seat ; one's place ¶ 창가의 자리 a seat next to the window // 자리에 앉다 take one's seat ; seat oneself 《at a table》 ; be seated ; sit down // 자리에서 일어나다 rise〔get〕 up from one's seat // 자리를 가리키다 motion to a seat // 자리에 앉히다 place 《a person》 in a seat ; seat 《a person》 // 자리를 잡아두다 keep〔secure〕 a seat 《for a person》 ; reserve a seat (예약) // 자리를 비우다 clear〔vacate〕 the seat // 양보하다 offer〔give〕 one's seat to 《a lady》 ; make room 《for a person》 // 이 자리 비었습니까 Is this seat occupied? /Has anybody taken this seat? /Is this seat vacant〔free〕? // 잠깐만 제자리 좀 봐주시겠습니까 Would you save my place for a minute, please?
② [여지] room ; space ¶ 자리를 내다 make room 《for》 // 자리를 많이 차지하다 occupy much space ; take up room // 자리를 만들다 make room ; leave space // 자리를 채우다 fill〔bridge〕 a gap // 한 사람 더 들어갈 자리가 있다 There is room left for one more.
③ [현장] the spot ; the occasion ¶ 살인 사건이 있었던 자리 the scene of murder // 그 자리에서 on the spot ; then and there // 그 자리에서 체포되다 be arrested on the spot // 그 자리에서 그렇게 말했어야 했다 You should have said so then and there.
④ [위치] a situation ; a position ; a location ; a site (대지) ¶ 자리가 좋다〔나쁘다〕 be well〔ill〕-situated // 집이 좋은 자리에 있다 Your house is nicely situated. // 자리가 좋으면 장사가 잘 된다 The locality brings a great deal of business.
⑤ [지위] a position ; a post ; an office (관직) ¶ 책임 있는 자리 a position of responsibility // 중요한 자리 an important position // 장관 자리 a cabinet position ; a portfolio ; ministership // 자리에서 물러나다 resign one's post ; give up one's office // 그 학교에 선생 자리가 하나 났다 There is an opening for a teacher at that school.
⑥ [계산상의] a figure ; a reed (주판의) ; [숫자의] unit ; place ¶ 자리를 틀리게 잡다 misplace a figure ; calculate on a wrong unit // 한 자리 내리다 take a figure down one place
⑦ [안정된 상태] settling down in life ; establishment ; stability ¶ 자리가 잡히다 get into a groove ; get on the (right) track ; settle down ; establish oneself ; get in the saddle // 정부가 이제는 자리가 잡히었다 The government is in the saddle now. // 그는 늘 떠돌더니 이제는 자리가 잡힌 모양이다 He was a regular "rolling stone", but now he seems to have settled down and found his place in life. // 모든것이 자리 잡히었다 Everything is in its place. /Everything is under control. // 그는 이제 선생으로 자리 잡히었다 He is now an old hand at teaching.
⑧ [자국] a mark ; an impression ¶ 총에 맞은 자리 《the mark of》 a bullet wound // 개한테 물린 자리 a scar from a dog bite // 이것은 종두맞은 자리다 This is a vaccination scar.
⑨ [깔개] a mat ; a mattress ; a cushion ; bed(ding) ¶ 자리를 보다 make〔lay〕 a bed // 자리를 걷다 put away a bed
자리² 〖천문〗 constellation ¶ 오리온자리

ㅈ

the (constellation of) Orion // 큰곰자리 the Great Bear ; the Big Dipper ; Ursa Major

자리 自利 self-interest ; personal gain 〔profit〕 ; one's own interest ¶ 자리적 self-seeking ; selfish

자리개 a thick straw-rope ; a sheaf-rope **—질** binding sheaves ; threshing

자리끼 bedtime drinking-water ; drinking water placed on the bedside for night use

자리보전 —保全 lying in one's sickbed **—하다** lie in〔keep to〕 one's sickbed ; be sick in bed

자리수 a cipher ¶ 다섯 자리수 a number of five ciphers

자리옷 night clothes ; a nightgown ; a nightdress ; pajamas ; a sleeping garment ¶ 자리옷 차림으로 in one's night clothes

자리자리 —하다 smart ; tingle ; (be) sore ; numb ¶ 다리가 자리자리하다 I have pins and needles in my feet. // 손가락이 자리자리하다 My fingers smart.

†**자리잡다** take one's place ; place oneself ; occupy a position ¶ 시청은 시의 중앙에 자리잡고 있다 The City Hall stands in the center of the city.

자립 自立 [독립] independence ; self-reliance ; [자활] self-support ; self-sustenance **—하다** establish oneself ; become independent ; stand on one's own feet ¶ 자립할 수 없는 국민 people not able to stand by themselves // 자립한 independent ; self-supporting // 자립하여 independently ; on one's own account // 자립해서 장사를 하다 do business on his own account
— 경제 economical independence ; self-supporting economy **—어(語)** an independent word

자릿자릿 —하다 [저리다] (be) benumbed ; [쑤시다] tingling ; [마음조이다] thrilling ; suspenseful ; thrilled

자마구 pollen 《of cereals》

-자마자 as soon as ; no sooner. . . than . . . ; hardly〔scarcely〕. . . when〔before〕 . . . ; directly ; immediately 《on, upon》 ; the moment〔minute, instant〕 ¶ 아침에 일어나자 마자 as soon as one gets up ; on getting up // 집에 돌아오자 마자 the moment one comes home ; as soon as one comes home // 그는 나를 보자마자 나가 버렸다 He had no sooner caught sight of me than he went out. /The moment he saw me he went out.

자막 字幕 [영화의] a title ; a caption **— 설명** a cut-in ; a subtitle ; an insert title **의장(意匠) —** an art title

자막대기 a measuring stick ; a yardstick ; a foot rule

자만 自滿 self-satisfaction ; self-complacence **—하다** be self-satisfied〔-complacent〕

†**자만 自慢** self-conceit ; self-admiration ; self-praise ; self-applause ; vanity ; pride ; boast

> **참고** **pride**는 자기의 가치·소유물·행위 따위에 대한 만족 그것이 적당하면 자존심이 되지만 지나치면 만심·존대가 된다 **conceit**는 자기의 업적이나 능력에 대한 과대한 평가 **vanity**는 자기의 풍채·업적 따위로 다른 사람으로부터 칭찬 받고자 하는 마음

—하다 be proud of ; brag〔boast〕 of ; make a boast of ; pride oneself 《on》 ¶ 그녀는 자기의 용모를 은근히 자만하고 있다 She inwardly prides herself on her good looks.

자만심 自慢心 (self-) conceit ; self-sufficiency ; self-opinion ; vanity ; ego 《구》 ¶ 자만심이 강하다 be full of conceit ; think no small beer of oneself

자망 刺網 a gill net **— 어선** a gill netter

†**자매 姉妹** sisters **— 결연** establishment〔setting up〕 of sisterhood relationship〔ties〕 ¶ 자매 결연을 맺다 set up sisterhood relationship 《with》 **— 기관** sister agencies **— 도시** a sister city 《to》 **— 도시 결연** a sister-city affiliation **—편** a sister〔companion〕 volume 《to》 **— 학교** a sister school **—함** a sister (war) ship **— 형제** an affiliated company **친(親) —** sisters german

자맥질 ⇨ 무자맥질

자메이카 Jamaica ¶ 자메이카의 Jamaican **— 사람** a Jamaican

자멸 自滅 self-destruction ; self-ruin ; suicide ; natural decay **—하다** destroy 〔ruin, kill〕 oneself ; bring destruction upon oneself ; perish ¶ 자멸적 self-destructive ; suicidal // 자멸을 초래하다 lead to self-destruction // 정치적 자멸을 하다 commit political suicide // 그 회사는 현 상태로 내버려 두면 불원 자멸할 것이다 That company will soon be ruined, if it is left as it is.

***자명 自明** self-evidence **—하다** (be) self-evident ; obvious ; self-explaining ; axiomatic (al) ¶ 자명한 이치 a self-evident truth ; a truism ; an axiom // 권리에는 의무가 수반한다는 것은 자명의 이치다 It is axiomatic that there can be no right without a corresponding obligation.

‡**자명종 自鳴鐘** an alarm clock

자모 字母 ① [음표 문자] an alphabet ; a letter ; a syllabic ② [활자] a matrix 《*pl.* -trices》 ; a printing type

자모 慈母 an affectionate〔loving〕 mother ¶ 학생들을 사랑함이 자모와 같다 She has a mother's〔motherly〕 affection for her pupils.

자모음 子母音 vowels and consonants

자못 very ; greatly ; exceedingly ; remarkably ¶ 그 일은 자못 어렵다 It is an exceedingly hard job.
자문 諮問 a question ; an inquiry ; consultation **—하다** inquire ; put〔submit〕 a question to ; consult ¶ 자문에 응하다 provide advice and suggestion as requested // 회의에 자문하다 refer 《a matter》 to a conference
— 기관 a consultative body ; an advisory organ **—안** a draft put for deliberation **— 위원회** an advisory committee
자문 自問 —하다 question〔ask〕 oneself
자문자답 自問自答 a soliloquy ; a monologue **—하다** answer one's own question ; talk to oneself ; soliloquize ; think aloud
†**자물쇠** a lock ; a padlock ; a snap lock (자동) ; a snap bolt ¶ 문에 자물쇠를 잠그다 lock〔padlock〕 the door // 자물쇠를 열다 unlock // 자물쇠가 잠겨 있다 be locked ; be on the lock // 자물쇠를 잠가 놓다 keep 《a thing》 locked // 자물쇠가 잠겨 있지 않다 be off the lock ; be unlocked // 자물쇠를 비틀어 열다 force a lock ; wrench away〔open〕 a lock // 자물쇠가 잘 안 잠긴다 The lock won't catch. // 이 문은 자동적으로 잠긴다 This door locks automatically.
자미 滋味 ① [맛좋고 자양분 있는 음식] a dainty ; a delicacy ; rich food ; nourishment ② [좋은 맛] daintiness ; savoriness ③ ⇨ 재미
자바 Java
—어〔인〕 Javanese **— 커피** Java coffee
자바라 〖악기〗 small cymbals
③ [이탈] fall away 《from》 ; drop away 〔off〕
자박 〖광업〗 a nugget of gold
자박거리다 walk softly ¶ 자박자박 with soft steps
자반 salted dry fish
— 뒤집기 writhing in agony ¶ 자반 뒤집기 하다 toss about 《in sickness》 ; suffer from pain ; writhe in agony
†**자발 自發** ¶ 자발적 spontaneous ; voluntary // 자발적으로 spontaneously ; voluntarily ; on one's own initiative ; of one's 〔its〕 own accord ¶ 자발적으로 사직하다 resign voluntarily
—성 spontaneity ; spontaneousness
자발없다 (be) restless ; impatient ; rash ; hasty ; impetuous
자방 子方 〖민속〗 the Direction of the Rat 《north》
자방 子房 〖식물〗 an ovary (of a plant)
자배기 a round and large pottery bowl
⁑**자백 自白** confession (고백) ; avowal ; admission ; acknowledgment (자인) ; penance **—하다** confess 《to》 ; make a confession ; own up ; admit ¶ 죄를 자백하다 confess one's guilt ; confess to a crime // 깨끗이 자백하다 make a clean breast 《of》 ; make a full confession 《of》 // 자백시키다 force〔compel〕 a confession from 《a person》 ; force 《a person》 into confession
자벌레 〖곤충〗 a looper ; a measuring worm
자법 子法 a filial law ; an adopted law
자변 自辨 —하다 pay one's own expenses ; pay out of one's own pocket ; pay oneself
자복 子福 ¶ 자복이 많은 사람 a person blessed with many children
자복 自服 ⇨ 자백(自白)
⁑**자본 資本** capital ; a fund ¶ 자본가와 노동자 capital and labor // 자본의 부족 lack of funds // 자본의 축적 an accumulation of capital // 자본의 집중 centralization of capital // 자본금 2억원의 회사 company capitalized at two hundred million *won* // 자본을 투자하다 invest〔lay out, put〕 capital 《in an enterprise》 // 자본화하다 capitalize // 자본을 공급하다 provide capital 《for》 ; finance 《an undertaking》 ; supply〔furnish〕 《a person》 with capital 〔funds〕 // 자본을 축적하다 accumulate capital // 자본을 놀려두다 let capital lie idle // 자본을 회전시키다 employ〔rotate〕 capital // 자본을 대다 finance 《an undertaking》 // 천만원의 자본으로 장사를 시작하다 start business with a capital of ten million *won* // 그 회사의 자본금은 2백만 달러였다 The company was capitalized at $2,000,000.
—가 a capitalist ; a financier **— 계수(係數)** a capital coefficient **— 구성** capital composition ; capital structure **—금** (a) capital ; a share capital (주식 자본) ; capital stock 《미》 **— 도피** a flight of capital ; a capital flight **—론** [서명(書名)] the Capital **— 설비** capital equipment **— (과)세** capital levy **— 소득** capital income **— 수출** capital export **— 시장** capital market **— 유입** influx〔inflow〕 of capital **— 유출** capital outflow **— 이동** movement of capital **— 잉여금** capital surplus **—재** capital goods **— 조성** capital construction **— 초과** overcapitalization **— 투자** capital investment **— 합동** a consortium 《*pl.* ~s, -tia》 **—화(化)** capitalization **— 환원** capitalization **가징(加徵)〔가변(可變)〕 —** callable〔variable〕 capital **공칭(公稱) —** authorized〔nominal〕 capital **과잉 —** surplus capital **금융〔공모(公募), 고정, 독점〕 —** financial 〔subscribed, fixed, monopolistic〕 capital **매판 —** a comprador capital **미발행(未發行) —** unissued capital **미징(未徵)〔미납〕 —** uncalled〔unpaid〕 capital **보류〔자기, 수권(授權)〕 —** reserve〔owned, authorized〕 capital **불변(不變)〔외국, 의제(擬製)〕 —** constant〔foreign, fictitious〕 capital **사회〔타인, 도피, 등록〕 —** social overhead〔borrowed, flight, regis-

ㅈ

tered〕 capital 산업 — industrial capital 운전 — working capital〔funds〕 유동 — circulating〔liquid, floating〕 capital 유휴 — unemployed capital 주식 — a share capital 준비 — unemployed〔reserve〕 capital ; reserve fund 차입 — a loan capital 투하 — invested capital 회전 — working〔revolving〕 capital

자본주의 資本主義 capitalism
— 경제 capitalistic economy — 국가 a capitalist country〔nation〕; a capitalistic state —자 a capitalist — 제도 the capitalistic system — 진영 the capitalist camp 국가 — state capitalism 독점 — monopolistic capitalism 산업 — industrial capitalism 수정— modified〔revised〕 capitalism 신— neocapitalism

자볼기 being whipped〔lashed〕 by one's wife ; verbal lashing from one's wife ¶ 자볼기 맞다 take a beating〔verbal lashing〕 from one's wife ; be henpecked

자봉침 自縫針 a sewing machine ⇨ 재봉틀

자봉틀 自縫— a sewing machine ⇨ 재봉틀

자부 子婦 a daughter-in-law

***자부 自負** (self-) conceit ; self-esteem ; self-importance ; pride **—하다** be (self-) conceited ; be self-confident ; be self-important ; be proud ; flatter oneself 《that》

자부 慈父 a loving〔an affectionate〕 father

자부락거리다 ⇨ 지부럭거리다

⁑**자부심 自負心** self-conceit〔-confidence, -esteem, -importance〕; pride ¶ 자부심이 강한 self-conceited〔-confident, -important〕// 자부심을 상하다 hurt〔wound〕 《a person's》 pride

자부지 the handle of a plow

자북 磁北 magnetic north
—극 the North Magnetic Pole

자분자분 ⇨ 저분저분

자비 ［탈것］ any man-carried vehicle (such as a sedan chair)

자비 自費 one's own expense〔charge〕 ¶ 자비로 at one's own expense // 자비 출판하다 publish 《one's book》 at one's own expense // 자비로 세계 일주 여행하다 make a round-the-world trip at one's own expense
—생 a private〔self-paying〕 student

⁑**자비 慈悲** ［인정］ mercy ; ［자선］ charity ; benevolence ; ［동정］ compassion ; pity **—하다** (be) merciful ; benevolent ; kind〔tender〕-hearted ; compassionate ; humane ¶ 자비를 베풀다 have〔take〕 mercy 《on a person》; have〔take〕 compassion 《on a person》; show mercy 《to a person》; do 《a person》 an act of charity
—심 a merciful heart ; mercy ¶ 저 친구는 자비심도 인정도 없다 He is a stranger to pity or mercy. /He has a heart of stone.

***자빠뜨리다** make 《a person》 fall on his back ; knock〔pull, push, throw〕 《a person》 down on his back ¶ 나무를 자빠뜨리다 fell a tree // 전기 스탠드를 자빠뜨리다 knock a desk lamp down // 집을 자빠뜨리다 pull down a house

***자빠지다** ① ［넘어지다］ fall on one's back ; tumble over backward ; tumble down ¶ 빙판 위에 자빠지다 fall down on the ice // 바람에 나무들이 자빠졌다 The wind knocked down many trees.
② ［하는 일 없이］ lie down ; lay oneself down ; stretch oneself out ; lounge ¶ 늘 자빠져 놀다 loaf away one's time〔days〕; lead an idle life // 늘 자빠져 있지 말고 일 좀 해라 Stop lollygagging around and do some work.

자빡 refusal ; rejection ¶ 자빡대다 flatly〔plainly, absolutely〕 refuse ; turn down // 자빡맞다 be refused point-blank ; be given a brush-off ; be positively turned down ; be flatly opposed

자빡뿔 a crooked〔twisted〕 oxhorn

***자산 資産** property ; a fortune ; estate ; means ; assets (부채의 반대말) ¶ 자산과 부채 assets and liabilities // 자산의 동결 freezing of assets // 자산을 만들다 make〔amass〕 a fortune // 자산을 남기다 leave an estate
—가 a wealthy〔rich〕 person ; a man of property〔wealth〕 — 계정 assets account — 목록 assets — 상태 one's financial standing — 소득 assets income — 재평가 revaluation of property 고정 — fixed assets 동결 — frozen assets 무형〔유형〕 — intangible〔tangible〕 assets 비공언 — undeclared assets 소모〔수익〕 — wasting〔live〕 assets 실(實)〔명목(名目)〕 — actual〔nominal〕 assets 유동 — circulating〔floating〕 assets ; current assets ; liquid assets 은닉 — hidden assets 총— nominal assets 활동 — active assets 현금〔자본〕 — cash〔capital〕 assets

⁑**자살 自殺** suicide ; self-destruction **—하다** kill oneself ; commit suicide ; take one's own life ¶ 자살적 suicidal // 자살할 목적으로 with suicidal intent // 자살을 기도하다 attempt suicide // 권총 자살하다 shoot and kill oneself ; shoot oneself to death // 음독 자살하다 commit suicide〔kill oneself〕 by taking poison // 타살이 아니라 자살로 판명되었다 It was found to be a case of suicide, not of murder. // 그것은 그에게 있어서 정치적 자살 행위이다 It is a political suicide for him.
—광(狂) suicidal mania ; thanatomania — 미수 attempted suicide — 미수자 a would-be suicide — 방조 aiding and abetting suicide — 방조죄 the crime of aiding self-destruction —자 a suicide — 행위 a suicide act 집단 — mass suicide 철도 — killing oneself on the railroad

ㅈ

tracks
자살 刺殺 stabbing to death —하다 stab 《a person》 to death ¶ 자살당하다 be stabbed to death
자상 仔詳 details ; particulars ; minuteness —하다 (be) detailed ; minute ; meticulous ; be in detail ¶ 자상히 in detail ; minutely ; in full
자상 刺傷 a stab ; a pierced wound
자상 행위 自傷行爲 self-inflicted injury ; injuring〔crippling〕 oneself 《to avoid military service》
자새 a small reel
—질 reeling
자색 姿色 beauty 《in a woman》 ; comeliness ¶ 자색이 아름답다 be beautiful // 그 여자는 자기 자색을 자랑한다 She prides herself on her good looks.
자색 紫色 purple ; violet
자생 自生 [우연 발생] autogenesis ; spontaneous generation ; [야생] wild〔natural〕 growth —하다 grow wild〔naturally, spontaneously〕 ; be autogenous ¶ 자생의 autogenous ; spontaneous ; [야생의] wild ; native 《plants》 // 이 지방에서는 포도가 자생한다 Vines grow naturally in this district.
— 식물 native〔wild, voluntary〕 plants — 작물(作物) native〔wild, voluntary〕 crops
자서 自序 the author's preface —하다 write one's own preface 《to one's work》
자서 自署 an autograph ; a signature ; a sign manual —하다 affix one's signature ; sign one's name ; autograph ¶ 자서를 한 사진 an autographed〔signed〕 photograph // 책에 자서하다 autograph a book
자서 字書 자전(字典)
자서 自敍 writing one's own story —하다 write one's own story
자서 自書 one's own writing ; an autograph —하다 write in one's own hand ; autograph
*자서전 自敍傳 an autobiography ; one's life story ¶ 자서전체의〔로〕 autobiographical(ly) // 자서전을 쓰다 write the story of one's own life ; write one's own life ; write one's life story
— 소설 autobiographical novel ; a fictionized autobiography — 작자 an autobiographer
⁑자석 磁石 a magnet ; a compass (지남철) ; a loadstone (천연 자석) ¶ 자석성의 magnetic // 자석 상호간의 작용 reciprocal action of magnets // 자석의 인력 magnetic attraction // 자석은 철을 잡아당긴다 Magnet attracts iron.
— 발전기 a magnetogenerator ; a magnetodynamo —벨 a magnetobell —식 〖전화〗 the magneto system —식 교환기 a magneto switchboard —식 전화기 a magneto telephone set 막대〔말굽〕 — a bar〔horseshoe〕 magnet 일시(—時)〔영구〕 — a temporary〔permanent〕 magnet 장(場)— a field magnet 천연 — a natural magnet ; a loadstone
자석영 紫石英 an amethyst ⇨ 자수정
⁑자선 慈善 charity ; benevolence ; philanthropy ; almsgiving (자선 행위) ¶ 자선의 charitable ; benevolent ; philanthropic // 자선을 위해서 for charity's sake ; for charitable purposes // 가난한 사람에게 자선을 베풀다 give alms to the poor // 사람에게 자선을 행하다 dispense charity to people // 그의 전재산을 자선 사업에 바쳤다 He gave all he had to charity.
—가 a charitable person ; a philanthropist — 기관 a philanthropic institution — 기금 a charity fund — 냄비 a charity pot — 단체 a philanthropic〔charitable〕 organization ; a social service organization — 목적 ¶ 자선 목적으로 for charitable purposes ; for the sake of charity — 무도회 a charity ball — 병원 a charity hospital — 사업 charitable〔philanthropic〕 work — 상자 a charity〔poor〕 box —시 a (charity) bazaar — 시설 a charitable institution —심 a charitable spirit ; benevolence — 음악회 a charity〔benefit〕 concert — 판매장 a charity〔benefit〕 bazaar — 학교 a charity school — 행위 an act of charity〔humanity〕 ; charities ; benefactions — 흥행 a benefit〔charity〕 play〔performance〕 — 흥행 입장권 a charity ticket
자선 自選 self-selection —하다 [자기 선정] elect oneself ; vote for oneself ; [작품을] make a selection from one's own work
— 시집 a collection of poems selected by the author —집 the author's (own) selection〔anthology〕 — 투표 self-vote
자설 自說 one's own view〔opinion〕 ¶ 자설을 주장하다 maintain one's opinion ; persist in one's view〔opinion〕 // 자설을 굽히다 give up one's view ; change〔switch〕 one's opinion ; turn one's coat (변절하다) ; revise one's thinking // 자설을 고집하다 stick〔hold fast〕 to one's opinion
자성 自省 self-examination ; reflection (반성) ; introspection (내성) —하다 examine oneself ; reflect ; introspect ¶ 자성의 reflective ; introspective
자성 資性 (a) nature ; (a) disposition
*자성 磁性 magnetism ¶ 자성의 magnetic // 자성을 띠게 하다 magnetize
— 산화철 magnetic oxide of iron — 인력 polarity —체 a magnetic substance〔body, material〕 반—체 a diamagnetic (body)
자성 雌性 〖생물〗 femininity ; femaleness
— 식물 a pistillate plant ; a female
*자세 仔細 minuteness ; details ; ins and outs —하다 (be) minute ; detailed ; distinct ¶ 자세히 minutely ; in detail ; in full // 자세한 이야기〔지도〕 a detailed

ㅈ

account〔map〕// 자세한 일〔것〕(full) details ; particulars ; further information // 자세히 묻다 question 《a person》 minutely // 자세히 설명하다 give a full explanation ; explain in full〔in detail〕// 자세히 말하다 give a detailed〔full〕 account of 《a matter》// 자세한 것은 편지로 말씀드리겠습니다 I will give you full information by letter. /I'll write you a letter all about it. // 이 사전이 저 사전보다 설명이 자세하다 This dictionary gives fuller explanation than that. // 더 자세한 것은 지배인에게 문의하십시오 For further details〔particulars〕 I must refer you to my manager. // 참 자세히도 알고 있네 그려 You certainly are well informed (about the matter). /You talk like a book. // 그로부터 일의 자세한 전말을 들었다 I got a full account from him.

†**자세 姿勢** a posture ; a pose ; an attitude (태도) ; a carriage (몸가짐) ¶ 올바른 자세 a correct carriage〔pose of body〕// 앉은 자세로 in a sitting posture // 자세가 좋다〔나쁘다〕 have a fine〔poor〕 carriage // 자세를 취하다 posture ; pose // 자세를 바꾸다 change one's posture〔position〕// 자세를 바로잡다 straighten oneself // 방어 자세를 취하다 take the posture of defense // 차려 자세를 취하다 stand at attention // 편한 자세로 앉다 sit in a comfortable position // 자세에 주의하라 Be careful of your posture.

— 검사 a posture examination **— 반응** posture reflex **고—** a haughty〔high-handed〕 attitude ¶ 고자세를 취하다 act high-handedly ; take a high-handed policy **기본 —** 〖체조〗 a basic position **방어 —** a posture of defense **사격 —** 《take up》 the stance for firing the gun **저—** a humble〔meek〕 attitude ¶ 저자세를 취하다 behave oneself humbly **직립 —** an erect〔upright〕 position〔posture〕

자세 藉勢 relying on "pull" **—하다** rely on "pull" 《with》 ¶ 자세하고서 on the strength of some connections

자속 磁束 〖물리〗 magnetic flux

⁑**자손 子孫** sons and grandsons ; progeny ; descendants ; posterity ; offspring ¶ 자손에게 전하다 hand down 《a thing》 to posterity // …의 자손이다 be descended from〔a descendant of〕 《a person》

자수 自手 (with) one's own hands ; in person ; for oneself ; (being) unaided ; without help

— 삭발 cutting one's hair with one's own hands ; [비유적] tackling difficulties unaided **— 성가** making a home by one's own hand ; making one's own fortune ¶ 자수 성가한 사람 a self-made man

***자수 自首** self-surrender ; self-denunciation ; voluntary surrender〔denunciation〕 **—하다** give oneself up 《to the authorities》; surrender (oneself) 《to》 ¶ 그는 경찰에 자수했다 He delivered himself 〔gave himself up〕 to the police.

자수 自修 self-study ; self-teaching ; self-culture **—하다** teach oneself ; study for oneself ; study without a teacher ; practice oneself

자수 刺繡 embroidery **—하다** embroider ; do embroidery 《on》 ¶ 손으로〔기계로〕 자수한 스웨터 a hand-〔machine-〕 embroidered sweater // 금실로 화조(花鳥)를 자수하다 embroider patterns of birds and flowers in gold thread

—본〔무늬〕 embroidery designs **—실** embroidery thread **—자(者)** an embroiderer **—틀** an embroidery frame ; a taboret **금은 —** gold and silver embroidery **손〔기계〕—** ¶ 손〔기계〕 자수한 hand〔machine〕-embroidered

자수정 紫水晶 an amethyst

자숙 自肅 self-discipline ; self-control **—하다** exercise self-discipline〔-control〕; check oneself from 《going too far》

자습 自習 self-study ; self-teaching **—하다** teach oneself ; study for oneself

— 문제 [방과후의] homework ; home task〔exercises〕 **— 시간** study hours **—실** a study (hall)

자습서 自習書 a self-teaching〔"teach yourself"〕 manual ; a key ; a crib 《영·속》; a pony 《미·속》 ¶ 수험생의 자습서 the examinee's book // 자습서의 사용은 금지 되어 있다 The use of cribs is prohibited.

영문법 — English Grammar Self-Taught

자승 自乘 square **—하다** square 《a number》; multiply 《a number》 by itself ¶ 9의 자승은 81이다 The square of 9 is 81. /Nine squared makes eighty-one.

—근 a square root **—멱** the square 《of 16》; the second power **—법** involution **—비** duplicate proportion **—수** a square number

자승자박 自繩自縛 falling into a trap set by oneself ; to sow the wind and reap the whirlwind ; as you make your bed, so you must lie on it **—하다** be caught in one's own trap ; be hoist with one's own petard ; fall into a trap set by oneself ¶ 그 따위 짓은 자승자박하는 거나 마찬가지다 That would prove suicidal for him. /Such an act would make him the prisoner of his own deed. // 그 사람 자승자박하고 있는거야 He is just pulling the noose around his own neck.

자시 子時 the Watch of the Rat 《the period between 11 p. m. and 1 a. m.》

자시다 eat ⇨ 먹다

자시하 慈侍下 having one's widowed mother to support

⁑**자식 子息** ① [자녀] one's children ; one's sons and daughters ¶ 자식이 없다 be childless ; have no children // 자식이 셋 있다 have three children

② [욕] a creature ; a guy ; a chap ; a fellow ; a bloke ¶ 개 자식 son of a bitch 〔gun〕// 이 후레 자식 You wretch ! // 저 자식은 사기꾼이다 That guy is a damn swindler.

†**자신 自身** one's self ; oneself ¶ 자신의 (one's) own // 나자신 myself // 나자신의 my own ; of my own // 자신이 (by) oneself ; in person (몸소) // 자신이 하다 do it oneself // 자신의 생명을 내걸다 risk one's life // 자신의 나갈 길을 개척하다 make one's way in the world

†**자신 自信** self-confidence ; confidence **—하다** be confident of 《success》 ; have confidence in oneself ; be assured 《of, that》 ¶ 자신 있는 태도 a confident〔self-confident〕 manner // 자신 없는 사람 a man without self-confidence // 자신이 있다 be confident of 《success》 ; have confidence in oneself ; be assured 《of, that》 // 자신이 없다 lack assurance ; be diffident // 자신만만하다 be full of confidence ; have a lot of confidence in oneself // 자신을 얻다〔잃다〕 gain〔lose〕 confidence in 《one's own ability》 // 자신을 가지고 말하다 speak with confidence // 그는 자기의 실력에 자신을 가지고 응시했다 He sat for the exam with confidence in his capacity. // 나는 성공할 자신이 있다 I feel confident of success. /I feel confident that I shall succeed. // 그는 성공할 자신이 없다 He is not sure of success. // 나는 자신만만하다 I'm brimming with confidence.

자실 自失 losing one's wits ; being dazed ; abstraction ; absent-mindedness **—하다** lose one's wit ; lose consciousness ; be stupefied ; be dazed ; be self-abstracted ¶ 망연 자실하다 be distrait ; be stupefied ; be entranced ; be dazed // 망연 자실하여 어찌 할 바를 모르다 be quite at a loss what to do

자실체 子實體 『식물』 a fruit body

자심 滋甚 getting worse ; aggravation

자아 now ; come ; here ; well ⇨ 자

자아 自我 self ; ego ¶ 자아의 해방 emancipation of ego // 자아의 완성 the perfection of self // 자아의 몰각 self-effacement // 자아가 강한 egotistic ; egoistic ; selfish ; self-centered

— 관념 the sense of self **— 망각** self-effacement **— 보존** self-preservation **— 비판** self-criticism〔-accusation〕 **— 억제** self-repression **— 완성** the perfection of self **— 의식** self-consciousness **—주의** egoism ; egotism **—주의자** an egoist **— 해방** the emancipation of self〔ego〕 **이중 —** the double self

자아내다 ① [실을] reel off ; spin ¶ 고치에서 실을 자아내다 reel silk off cocoons // 솜에서 실을 자아내다 spin thread out of cotton ② [액체·가스 따위를] extract 《liquid, gas》 by machine ; suck out ; pump out ③ [느낌 따위를] evoke ; arouse ¶ 동정심을 자아내다 evoke 《a person's》 sympathy // 물의를 자아내다 evoke criticism // 슬픔을 자아내다 make 《a person》 feel sad // 의심을 자아내다 arouse suspicion // 불의는 언제나 의분을 자아낸다 Injustice always arouses indignation.

자아올리다 suck up 《water》 ; pump up ; draw up

자안 慈眼 merciful eyes

‡**자애 慈愛** affection ; love ; benevolence ; kindness ¶ 어머니의 자애 the love of mother 《for her children》 ; a mother's love // 자애 깊은 affectionate ; loving ; benevolent ; kind // 그는 어릴 때부터 부모의 자애를 모르고 자랐다 From his childhood he has been a stranger to parental affection.

자애 自愛 self-love ; self-regard ; selfishness ; egoism **—하다** take care of〔look after〕 oneself〔one's health〕 ¶ 아무쪼록 자중 자애 하시기를 앙망합니다 Please take good care of yourself. /I pray that you may get on well and strong〔be good for yourself〕.

— 도덕설 the selfish theory of morals **—주의** egotism ; egoism

자약 自若 —하다 (be) self-possessed ; composed ; calm ; compose oneself ¶ 자약하게 calmly ; composedly ; coolly ; with composure ; with self-possession // 자약한 태도로 일에 처하다 take things coolly // 자약하게 죽음을 맞다 meet〔face〕 one's death calmly ; accept death with perfect equanimity

자양 滋養 nutrition ; nourishment ; alimentation ¶ 자양분이 많다 be full of nutrient ; be nutritious ; be nourishing // 밀은 자양분이 많다 Wheat contains a great deal of nutriment〔nutritious matter〕.

— 가치 nutritive value **— 과다** supernutrition ; hypertrophy **—물** nutritious food ; nourishment ; a nutrient **—분** a nutritious element ; nutritious matter ; nutrient

자양화 紫陽花 『식물』 a hydrangea

자업자득 自業自得 natural consequence of one's (mis)deeds ; the natural outcome of one's acts **—하다** reap the fruits of one's actions ; reap the harvest of one's sowing ; [고생하다] stew in one's own juice ¶ 자업자득으로 알고 체념하게 You must take the consequences of your own deeds. /You must lie on the bed you have made. // 그 사람 자업자득이다 It serves him right. /He had it coming to him. /He deserves it. /He got his just deserts.

자업자득이다 속담 As one sows, so one reaps. /As a man sows, so he shall reap. /To sow the wind and reap the whirlwind. /As you make your bed, so you must lie on it.

†**자연 自然** nature ¶ 자연과 인생 nature and man // 자연의 natural ; [자발적] spontaneous ; [꾸밈 없는] unartificial ; unaffected ; [야생의] wild // 자연히 naturally ; [저절로] of itself ; in the course of nature ; [자발적으로] spontaneously ; of one's own accord ; [본능적으로] instinctively // 자연의 섭리에 의하여 by provision of nature // 자연적 결과로서 as a natural result // 자연스럽다 be natural // 자연히 생기다 come of itself // 자연으로 돌아가다 return to nature // 자연을 사랑하다〔즐기다〕 love〔enjoy〕 nature // 자연을 벗삼다 commune with nature ; take to nature // 자연히 되어가는 대로 맡기다 leave《a matter》 to take its natural〔own〕 course // 상처가 자연히 아물었다 The wound healed all by itself. // 아프리카의 대자연과 접한 감상이 어떠한가 How did it feel to commune with nature in Africa?

— **건조** natural seasoning —**계** the natural〔physical〕 world ; (the realm of) nature — **공원** a natural park — **과학** natural science — **과학자** a natural scientist —**관** a view of〔an outlook on〕 nature — **대수(對數)** 〖수학〗 natural〔Napierian〕 logarithm — **도태** natural selection —**력(力)** [자연계의 작용] (a) natural agency ; [풍력·수력 등] the forces〔power〕 of nature ; elemental forces — **묘사** description of nature —**물** a natural object —**미** natural beauty ; the beauty of nature — **발생** spontaneous generation ; 〖생물〗 abiogenesis ; autogenesis — **발화** spontaneous combustion 〔ignition〕 — **방사능** natural radioactivity —**법** the natural law — **법칙** the law of nature ; the natural laws — **보호** conservation〔preservation〕 of nature ; protection of natural environment — **보호론〔주의〕자** a conservationist — **분리** avulsion —**사(死)** 《die》 a natural death — **사회** natural society —**색** a natural color —**석(石)** a living〔native〕 rock — **소멸** natural extinction —**수** 〖수학〗 natural number — **숭배** nature worship〔cult〕 — **숭배자** a nature worshipper —**시** a nature poem — **시인** a nature poet —**식** eating natural foods — **식품** natural foods — **신교(神敎)** deism — **신학** natural theology — **신학자** a natural theologian — **연소** spontaneous combustion — **요법** naturopathy ; physiotherapy ; physical therapy — **유량** a rate of flow — **은〔유황〕** native silver〔sulfur〕 —**인** a natural man〔person〕 — **자원** natural resources — **정복** man's mastery over nature — **종교** natural religion ; naturism (자연을 숭배하는) —**주의** naturalism —**주의자** a naturalist — **증가(增價)** 〖경제〗 a natural increase in the value 《of one's land》 ; an unearned increment — **지리(학)** physical geography ; physiography — **철학** [고대 그리스 등의] natural philosophy — **현상** natural phenomena — **환경 보전법** the Natural Environment Conservation Act — **휴회** a spontaneous recess **원생림** — **보호** the conservation of a virgin forest **한국** — **보호 협회** the Nature Conservation Society of Korea

자연 紫煙 tobacco-smoke

자엽 子葉 a seed leaf ; a cotyledon ; a seminal leaf ; a seed lobe

자영 自營 self-management ; self-sustenance —**하다** do 《business》 independently〔on one's own account〕 ¶ 자영의 self supporting ; independent // 자영으로 장사하다 run a business on one's own account // 아버지로부터 독립해서 자영하고 있습니다 I am now carrying on business myself independently of my father.

— **발전소** an isolated powerhouse — **사업** an independent enterprise

***자오선 子午線** the meridian

자오의 子午儀 a meridian transit instrument

자오환 子午環 〖천문〗 meridian circle

***자욱하다** (be) thick ; dense ; heavy ¶ 자욱하게 in thick clouds ; thickly ; densely ; obscurely // 자욱한 안개 a thick 〔dense〕 fog // 방안에 연기가 자욱하다 The room is clouded with smoke.

자외선 紫外線 ultraviolet rays〔light〕

— **요법** the ultraviolet light therapy — **치료** (an) ultraviolet treatment — **현미경** an ultraviolet microscope

자용 自用 —**하다** put〔turn〕 to private use ; appropriate 《a thing》 to oneself 〔private purposes〕 ¶ 자용의 for one's own use ; private ; for personal〔private〕 use

자우 慈雨 a seasonable rain ; a welcome 〔good, beneficial〕 rain ¶ 한천(旱天)의 자우 a looked-for rainfall during the dry season

자욱하다 (be) dense ⇨ 자옥하다

자운 紫雲 auspicious purple clouds

자웅 雌雄 male and female ; the sexes ; [승패] victory or defeat ; supremacy ; mastery ¶ 자웅 양성의 bisexual // 자웅을 결하다 fight a decisive battle 《with》 ; try conclusions 《with》 ; fight to a finish ; fight it out // 자웅을 다투다 contend〔vie〕 for supremacy ; strive for mastery // 자웅을 감별하다 determine the sex 《of a chicken》

—**눈** a pair of eyes that are not the same size —**눈이** a person whose eyes do not match — **도태〔선택〕** sexual selection — **동주(同株)** monoecism — **동체(同體)** hermaphrodite — **이주(異株)** dioecism

자원 自願 volunteering —**하다** volunteer 《for》 ¶ 자원해서 voluntarily // 종군을 자원하다 volunteer for military service

—자 a volunteer

*자원 資源 resources ¶ 자원이 풍부하다 be full of resources ; be rich〔abundant〕 in resources // 자원을 개발하다 develop〔exploit〕 the resources // 국가의 자원을 고갈시키다 drain a country of its resources

— 개발 resource development — 보호〔애호〕 conservation of resources — 혁명 resource revolution 광물 — mineral resources 국가 — national resources 물적 — material〔visible〕 resources 미개발 — undeveloped〔dormant〕 resources 석유 — oil resources 수— water resources 인력 — manpower resources 인적 — human resources 지하 — underground resources 천연 — natural resources

자원소 字原素 〖물리〗 a daughter element

자위[1] a large reel

자위[2] the fixed position in which an object is lodged ; a fixed〔quiet, undeveloped〕 position〔state〕 ¶ 태아의 자위가 돌았다 The fetus has started to move〔quicken〕. // 바위가 마침내 자위돌기 시작했다 The rock gave a little at last. // 밥이 자위나 돌아야 움직이겠다 I think I'll sit here a little bit until the food settles. /I'm too full to move.

자위 뜨다 관용 budge ; stir ; leave〔make, show〕 a slight opening

자위[3] the white〔yolk〕 of an egg ; the white〔colored part〕 of the eye ¶ 눈의 흰〔검은〕 자위 the white〔pupil〕 of the eye

자위 自慰 ① self-consolation —하다 comfort oneself ; flatter oneself (자부하여) ¶ …이라고 생각하고 자위하다 comfort oneself with the thought 《that》 ② 〔수음〕 solitary vice ; masturbation ; self-abuse ; onanism ¶ 자위 과도의 희생자 a victim of solitary excesses // 자위 행위를 하다 practice masturbation ; masturbate

자위 自衛 self-defense〔-protection, -preservation〕 —하다 protect〔defend〕 oneself ¶ 자위의 self-protecting〔-preserving, -preservative〕 // 자위상 in〔by way of〕 self-defense // 자위권을 주장하다 claim the defense right 《of the nation》 // 자위책을 강구하다 take a step to protect〔defend〕 oneself ; think out the means of self-preservation // 자위를 위하여 사람을 죽이다 kill a man in self-defense

—권 the right of self-defense〔-protection〕 ; the defense right 《of the nation》 ; the right to defend oneself —권 발동 invocation of self-defense power —대 the Self-Defense Forces (일본의) —력 capacity for self-defense — 본능 the instinct of self-protection ; the protective instinct — 수단 a measure of self-defense — 전력 war potential for self-defense ; self-defense war potential —책 a self-protecting policy — 행동 actions for self-defense〔for one's own protection〕 항공〔육상, 해상〕 —대 〔일본의〕 the Air〔Ground, Maritime〕 Self-Defense Force

자위 磁位 〖전기〗 a magnetic potential

†자유 自由 freedom ; liberty

> 참고 **freedom**은 속박 억압 따위가 없는 것 **liberty**는 과거의 속박 제한 따위로부터 해방된 상태를 암시하는 말이며 따라서 freedom보다 소극적 상대적이다

¶ 자유의 천지 a land of freedom // 천부의 자유권 natural liberty // 신앙의 자유 freedom of worship〔religion〕 // 언론의 자유 freedom of speech // 출판의 자유 freedom of the press // 의지의 자유 freedom of the will // 자유화 liberalization 《of trade》 // 자유의 나라 영국 England, the nurse of liberty // 자유로이 freely ; at will 〔liberty〕 ; at one's pleasure ; as one likes〔wishes, pleases〕 // 자유롭다 be free 〔liberal, unrestricted〕 // 자유로운 몸이 되다 be set at liberty ; be set free // 자유로 사용하다 make free use 《of one's car》 // 자유 행동을 허가하다 give 《a person》 a free hand ; let 《a person》 have his own way // 자유 행동을 취하다 act for oneself // 자유를 구속하다 restrain 《a person's》 liberty // 자유를 부르짖다 cry for liberty // 자유를 옹호하다〔획득하다〕 defend 〔obtain〕 one's liberty // 언론의 자유를 억제하다 curb free speech // 자유를 주다 give 《a person》 liberty // 자유 재량에 맡기다 give 《a person》 a free hand ; leave to the discretion of 《a person》 // 생명보다 자유를 존중하다 prize freedom more than life ; prize liberty above life // 영어를 자유로이 말하다 have a good command of English // 오후는 대개 자유입니다 I am free generally in the afternoon. // 가든지 안 가든지 네 자유다 You are free to go or stay as you please. // 누구나 자유롭게 의견을 말할 수 있다 Each member will be at liberty to state his own views. // 자유는 자칫하면 방종으로 흐른다 Liberty often degenerates into lawlessness. // 자유 아니면 죽음을 달라 Give me liberty or give me death. // 이 세상 만사가 뭐든지 네 자유대로 되는 게 아니야 We cannot have our will〔way〕 in everything in this world.

— 결사 a voluntary association — 결혼 free marriage〔union〕 ; common-law marriage — 경쟁 free〔open〕 competition ; competition open to all ; 〔규칙이 없는〕 a go-as-you-please race — 교육 liberal education — 국가 a free state〔country, nation〕 —권 civil liberties — 기업 a free enterprise — 기업가 a free enterpriser — 기업 경제 free-enterprise economy — 노동 free〔casual〕 labor — 노동자 a free〔casual, day〕 laborer — 노동 조합

ㅈ

a free trade union —당 the Liberal Party ; the Liberals — 당원 a Liberal ; a member of the Liberal Party — 도(度) 〚물리·화학〛 the degree of freedom — 도시 a free city — 독서 free〔voluntary〕 reading — 독서 시간 a free-reading 〔browsing〕 period — 독서실 a browsing room — 무역 free trade — 무역주의 free trade — 무역주의자 a free trader — 무역항 a free port —민 free people ; a yeoman (영국 역사상의) — 민권론 democratic rights — 민주당 the Liberal Democratic Party ; the Liberal Democrats — 민주당원 a Liberal Democrat ; a member of the Liberal Democratic Party — 방임 non-interference ; 〚경제〛 laissez-〔laisser-〕faire — 방임주의 the principle of laissez-faire ; a let-alone policy — 범위 [견해·행동 등의] latitude — 보유권(保有權) freehold — 사상 liberal ideas 《in politics》 ; free〔liberal〕 thought — 사상가 a free thinker ; a liberal thinker —석(席) an unreserved seat — 선택 free choice — 선택 과목 an elective〔optional 《영》〕 subject — 세계 [공산권에 대하여] the free world —시 free verse — 에너지 〚물리〛 free energy — 연구 free inquiry ; independent investigation ; individual research — 예금 (a) free (account) deposit ; free savings — 의지 free will〔volition〕 ; spontaneity — 의지론〔설〕 the doctrine〔theory〕 of free will ; indeterminism — 의지론자 an indeterminist ; a libertarian — 이민 a free emigrant〔immigrant〕 —인 a freeman — 임용(任用)〔연애〕 free appointment〔love〕 —재 free goods — 재량 latitude ; discretion ; a free hand — 전자(電子) 〚물리〛 a free electron — 전화(電化) 〚물리〛 free charge — 종목 [체조의] free exercises —주의 liberalism ; [종교상의] latitudinarianism —주의 경제〔경제학〕 liberalistic economy〔economics〕 — 주의자 a liberalist ; a liberal ; a latitudinarian ; a libertarian — 지역 free soil (미국 역사상의) — 직업 a liberal profession — 직업인 a professional man — 진동 〚전기·건축〛 free vibration〔oscillation〕 — 진영 free World ; the Western Camp — 천지 a land of freedom — 토의 (a) free discussion —투(投) 〚농구〛 a free throw — 판매 free sale —항〔시장〕 a free port〔market〕 — 항해권 〚국제법〛 freedom of the seas — 해방 setting free ; emancipation ; liberation — 행동 free 〔independent〕 action ¶ 자유 행동을 취하다 act at one's own discretion ; act for oneself // 자유 행동을 허락하다 give 〔allow〕 《a person》 a free hand // 자유 행동을 할 수 있다 have〔get〕 a free hand — 행동권 free〔independent〕 action ; a free hand ; freedom of action〔movement〕 — 행위자 a free〔voluntary〕 agent —형 freestyle (수영의) —형 수영 선수 a freestyler —화(化) liberalization ; freeing 《of trade》 —화(畫) a free drawing — 활주〔경제〕 free skating〔economy〕 개인 — personal liberty 신—주의 neoliberalism

자유 의사 自由意思 free will ; one's voluntariness ¶ 자유 의사로 at will ; of one's own accord〔free will〕 ; voluntarily // 네 자유 의사에 맡긴다 You may do as you please.

자유자재 自由自在 —하다 (be) free ; unrestricted ¶ 자유자재로 quite freely ; at one's pleasure ; at will ; with perfect freedom ; as one pleases // 자유자재한 필치 free and bold hand // 그는 영어를 자유자재로 구사한다 He has a good command of English.

자율 自律 self-control ; self-regulation ; 〚철학〛 autonomy ¶ 자율적 autonomous ; autonomic (생리의)
—성 autonomy — 신경 〚생리〛 an autonomic nerve — 신경계 the autonomic nervous system — 신경 불안정증〔실조증〕 autonomic ataxia〔imbalance〕

자음 字音 the sound〔pronunciation〕 of a word〔character〕 ¶ 한자의 자음 pronunciation of a Chinese character

*__자음__ 子音 〚음성〛 a consonant ⇨ 닿소리 ¶ 자음의 consonantal

자의 自意 one's own will〔volition〕 ¶ 자의로 voluntarily ; of one's own accord

자의 字義 the meaning〔signification, sense〕 of a word ¶ 자의대로 literally // 자의대로의 해석 a literal interpretation ; a word-for-word translation // 자의대로 해석하다 interpret a word literally

자의 恣意 wilfulness ; self-will ; waywardness ; arbitrariness ¶ 자의로 wilfully ; waywardly ; arbitrarily // 자의로 행하다 act wilfully ; have one's own way

자의식 自意識 self-consciousness ; self-awareness ¶ 자의식이 강하다 be highly self-conscious // 자의식을 발달시키다〔버리다〕 develop〔cast aside〕 self-consciousness

자이레 the Republic of Zaire

자이로스코프 a gyroscope

자이로컴퍼스 a gyrocompass

자이언트 a giant

자인 自認 self-acknowledgment ; admittance —하다 acknowledge 《oneself beaten》 ; admit 《one's fault》 ; own oneself 《to be inferior》 ¶ 잘못했음을 자인하다 own 〔acknowledge〕 oneself to be in the wrong ; admit one's fault // 피고는 유죄를 자인했다 The accused made acknowledgment〔confession〕 of his guilt.

자인 自刃 suicide (by the sword) ; self-murder〔-destruction〕 —하다 commit suicide (with a sword) ; stab oneself with a sword ; stab oneself to death ; die by one's own hand ; die upon one's own sword

자인력 磁引力 〖물리〗 magnetic attraction

자일 *Seil* 《도》 ; [등산용] a rope

자일 子日 〖민속〗 the Day of the Rat

자임 自任 pretension ; self-regard **—하다** regard〔look upon〕 oneself 《as》 ; consider oneself 《to be》 ; fancy oneself 《to be》 ¶ 학자로 자임하다 fancy oneself a scholar // 사회 사업가로 자임하다 pose as〔flatter oneself that he is〕 a social worker

자자 藉藉 —하다 [소문 따위가] be widespread ; be spread abroad ; create public sensation ¶ 칭찬이 자자하다 win wide admiration

자자손손 子子孫孫 one's children and grandchildren ; posterity ; descendants ; offspring ; generation after generation (대대로) ¶ 자자손손 전하다 hand 《a thing》 down to posterity // 자자손손 전해지다 go down to posterity

자작 自作 ① one's own work〔production, composition〕 **—하다** make〔write〕 by oneself ¶ 자작의 of one's own making 〔writing, composition〕 // 자작한 시 one's own poem ; a poem of one's own composition // 자작 자연(自演)하다 act in 〔direct〕 a play of one's own writing ; [음악을] play a piece of one's own composition // 논문은 자작이어야 한다 Essays must be original.
② [농업] cultivation of one's own farm **—하다** cultivate one's own farm ¶ 자작한 감자 potatoes of one's own growing **—농** an independent〔a landed〕 farmer ; a yeoman 《영》 ; an owner farmer〔cultivator〕 ; a land-owning tiller **— 소설** a novel of one's own writing〔from one's own pen〕 **—시** one's own poem **— 자급** making by oneself and supplying oneself ; self-sustenance

자작 自酌 pouring wine for oneself ; self-service **—하다** pour wine for oneself ; serve oneself

***자작 子爵** a viscount
— 부인 a viscountess

자작거리다 toddle along〔about〕 ; totter along ; stagger along ¶ 자작거리며 with tottering steps ; totteringly // 서너 걸음 자작거리다 make a few tottering steps

자작나무 〖식물〗 the white birch ; Betula platyphylla (학명)

자작자작 《sounding》 almost dry **—하다** sound almost dry

자작지얼 自作之孼 a calamity brought upon oneself ; the natural consequence of one's (mis) deeds ; the natural outcome of one's acts ; a sorrow of one's own making

자잘하다 be all tiny〔minute〕 ; be small all alike

자장 磁場 〖물리〗 a magnetic field

***자장가 —歌** a lullaby ; a cradle song ; a nursery song ¶ 자장가를 불러서 아기를 재우다 lullaby〔sing〕 a baby to sleep // 자장가를 들으며 자다 fall asleep to a lullaby

자장자장 hushaby(e) ; rockaby(e) ¶ 자장자장 잘 자라 Hushaby〔Rockaby〕 baby, go to sleep now.

자재 資材 materials ; resources
—과 supply section **—국(局)** [운수] the Materials Bureau ; [통신] the Supplies Bureau **건축 —** construction〔building〕 materials **전쟁 —** war material **펄프 —** pulp wood

자재 資財 ⇨ 자산(資産)

자재 自在 [존재] self-existence ; [자유] unrestrictedness ; freedom **—하다** (be) free ; unrestricted ¶ 자재로 quite freely ; at will〔pleasure〕 ; as one pleases ⇨ 자유자재

자저 自著 one's own work

자저 自邸 one's (own) residence ; one's home

자적 自適 self-satisfaction ; complacency ; self-contentment **—하다** be self-satisfied ; be complacent ¶ 유유자적하다 live in free and easy retirement ; lead a free and quiet life

자전 字典 a dictionary ; a lexicon
한한(漢韓) — a dictionary of classical Chinese, explained in Korean

자전 磁電 〖물리〗 magnetoelectricity

자전 自傳 an autobiography

자전 自轉 rotation **—하다** rotate〔revolve, turn〕 on its own axis ¶ 지구의 자전이 밤과 낮을 생기게 한다 The revolution of the earth causes day and night.

⁑자전거 自轉車 a bicycle ; a cycle ; a bike 《속》 ; a unicycle (1륜) ; a tricycle (3륜) ¶ 자전거 타는 사람 a bicycle rider ; a cyclist // 자전거를 타다 ride (on) a bicycle // 자전거로 가다 go by bicycle ; go on a bicycle // 자전거를 탈 줄 아시오 Can you cycle ? /Can you ride a wheel ? 《미》
— 경기〔경주〕 a bicycle race **— 도둑** bicycle theft **— 선수** a cyclist ; a cycler ; a bicycle rider ; a wheelman **— 여행** a bicycle trip ; a cycling tour **—점** a bicycle shop ; a bicycle-house〔-shed〕 **경주용 —** a racing bicycle **이인승(二人乘) —** a tandem bicycle **일륜(一輪) —** a unicycle

자전관 磁電管 〖물리〗 magnetron

자전지계 自全之計 a measure of self-protection

자절 自切 〖동물〗 [도마뱀 따위의] autotomy ; self-amputation

자정 子正 midnight

자정 작용 自淨作用 [물의] self-purification ; [토지의] autopurification ¶ 자연의 자정 작용 natural purification ; the self-cleansing action of nature

자정향 紫丁香 〖식물〗 a lilac

ㅈ

자제 子弟 sons ; children ; young people ¶ 김씨의 자제 Mr. *Kim's* son // 명문의 자제 sons of an illustrious family

†**자제 自制** self-control〔-mastery, -repression, -restraint, -command〕 **—하다** control〔restrain〕 oneself ; be master of oneself ; exercise self-restraint ¶ 자제력 없는 사람 a man lacking self-control // 자제력이 있다 have self-control // 자제력을 잃다 lose one's self-control ; fly off the handle ; let oneself go // 현명한 사람은 자기의 행위와 쾌락을 자제한다 The wise man exercises restraint in his behavior and enjoyment.

—력 the power of self-control〔-restraint〕 ; command over one's temper ¶ 네가 발끈해서 자제력을 잃으면 일의 결말이 나지 않는다 When you fly off the handle, you lose sight of the consequences.

자제 自製 one's own making ; one's own manufacture ¶ 자제의 made by oneself ; of one's own making ; homemade (자가제의)

—품 an article of one's own making

자조 自嘲 self-scorn

*__자조 自助__ self-help〔-reliance〕 ; self-dependence ¶ 자조의 정신 the spirit of self-help // 자조는 최선의 도움 Self-help is the best help.

—론 "A Treatise on Self-Help" **— 정신** self-help spirit ; the spirit of self-help

자조 문학 自照文學 literature which reflects the writer himself (like diaries and familiar essays)

자족 自足 self-sufficiency **—하다** (be) self-sufficient ¶ 자족의 self-sufficing〔-sufficient〕 // 한국의 공업은 자족의 경지에 이르렀다 Korea's industry has attained the state of self-sufficiency.

— 경제 self-sufficient〔-sufficing〕

자존 自存 self-existence

자존 自尊 self-respect ; self-esteem ; self-importance (자긍) ; pride **—하다** respect〔esteem〕 oneself ; have self-respect ; be self-conceited ; be proud

—가 a self-respecting person

†**자존심 自尊心** self-respect ; pride ¶ 자존심이 강한 사람 a man of great self-respect // 자존심이 있다 be self-respecting ; be proud // 자존심이 없다 be prideless // 자존심이 모자라다 lack (the spirit of) self-respect // 자존심을 손상하다 hurt〔wound〕 《a person's》 pride // 자존심을 잃다 lose one's self-respect // 그는 자존심이 강하다 He has much self-respect. // 국민적 자존심의 유지가 긴요하다 We must maintain our national self-respect.

⁑**자주** often ; frequently ; repeatedly ¶ 자주 있는 일 a common〔an every day〕 affair // 청년들에게 자주 있는 과오 a blunder (that) young men are apt to make // 자주 자주 ever so often ; repeatedly // 학생들에게 자주 있는 일로서 as is usual with students // 자주 다니다 frequent 《a theater, a bar》 // 자네들은 자주 만나나 Do you see much of each other? // 최근 철도 사고가 자주 일어난다 Railway accidents are frequent of late〔lately〕.

자주 自主 independence ; autonomy ¶ 자주 독립의 정신 the spirit of independence // 자주적 independent ; autonomous ; free ; [자발적] voluntary // 자주적으로 of one's own free will ; voluntarily // 자주성이 없다 lack independence 《in one's way of thinking》

— 교육 self-active education **—국** a sovereign ; an independent state **—권** autonomy ; sovereign rights ¶ 자주권의 상실 frustration of autonomy **— 규제** self-imposed control **— 독립** independence ; autonomy **— 무역** active commerce〔trade〕 **—성** independence ; sovereignty **— 외교** an independent foreign policy **— 행로** an independent way of life **관세 —권** customs〔tariff〕 autonomy

자주 紫朱 maroon (color) ; purple ; violet (color)

— 꼴뚜기 a person with a purplish face **—물** purple〔maroon〕 dye

자주 국방 自主國防 self-reliance of national defense ; self-defense of one's country

—력 self-reliant defense〔security〕 potential **— 태세** go-it-alone defense posture

자주장 自主張 [자기 주장] self-assertion ; self-assertiveness (태도) ; [자기 나름대로 하기] keeping one's own way 《of doing》 **—하다** have〔go〕 one's own way ; assert oneself ; do as one pleases〔likes〕

자주포 自走砲 a self-propelled gun ; self-propelled artillery 《총칭》

—가(架) a self-propelled mount **—병** self-propelled artillery

⁑**자줏빛 紫朱—** purple〔violet〕 color ¶ 자줏빛으로 물들이다 dye 《a thing》 purple // 추워서 그의 입술이 자줏빛이 되었다 His lips turned purple with cold.

자중 自重 self-love〔-respect〕 ; taking care of oneself ; [신중] prudence ; circumspection **—하다** take care of oneself ; respect oneself ; be prudent ; be cautious ; be circumspect

자중지난 自中之亂 a fight among themselves ; an internal strife〔dissension〕

자지 the penis ; the cock 《미·속》

자지러뜨리다 shrink ; double 《up》 ¶ 우스워서 몸을 자지러뜨리다 double up with laughter

자지러지다¹ shrink ; cower ⇨ 지지러지다 ¶ 놀라서 자지러지다 shrink with fright ; be frightened

자지러지다² [그림·조각·음악 등이] (be) exquisite ; superb ; charming ; fascinat-

ing
자지레하다 ⇨ 자질구레하다
자지리 ⇨ 지지리
*__자진 自進__ **—하다** volunteer ¶ 일을 자진해서 하다 do a job of one's own accord // 자진 입대하다 volunteer for military service // 그는 자진해서 책임을 맡았다 He was willing to take the responsibility.
— 신고 기간 the voluntary reporting period
자질 measuring **—하다** take measurement ; measure
자질 資質 (natural) disposition ; temperament ; quality
자질구레하다 (be) evenly small ; petty ; trifling ¶ 자질구레한 일 a trifling matter ; a trifle
자질자질 almost dried-up
자차분하다 (be) fine and tangled
자찬 自讚 self-praise ; self-admiration ; self-applause **—하다** praise〔admire〕 oneself ¶ 신문에 자찬의 광고를 내다 insert one's puffs in the papers
자채(벼) a variety of early-ripening rice plant
—볏논 early rice fields
자책 自責 self-accusation〔-reproach, -condemnation, -blame〕 **—하다** accuse oneself of ; blame oneself for ; feel guilty about ¶ 자책하는 마음 a guilty conscience ; pangs〔prick〕 of conscience ; remorse (양심의 가책) // 자책의 마음으로 괴로워하다 have〔suffer from〕 a guilty conscience ; be conscience-stricken
—감〔심〕 a guilty conscience ; [가책] pangs〔prick〕 of conscience ; [후회] remorse ¶ 자책심〔감〕에 사로 잡히다 have〔suffer from〕 a guilty conscience ; be conscience-stricken ; be seized with remorse **—점(點)** 〚야구〛 earned run
자처 自處 [자살] suicide ; [자임] pretension ; assumption ; [처리] self-determination **—하다** [자살하다] kill oneself ; commit suicide ; [체하다] look upon oneself as ; pose as ; fancy oneself ; [처리하다] decide〔determine〕 oneself
자처울다 cackle convulsively ; crow faster and faster
자천 自薦 self-recommendation **—하다** recommend oneself
자철 磁鐵 〚광물〛 magnetic iron
자철광 磁鐵鑛 magnetite
자청 自請 volunteering **—하다** volunteer 《for》; offer oneself 《as》 ¶ 자청해서 of one's own accord〔free will, free choice〕 ; willingly ; voluntarily // 자청해서 힘든 일을 맡다 volunteer a difficult job
†**자체 字體** the shape〔form〕 of a character〔letter〕 ; type ; print ¶ 정자체로 명료하게 쓰다 write clearly in the square style
자체 自體 oneself ; itself ; one's own body (제 몸) ¶ 그 자체의 무게로 쓰러지다 fall of its own weight // 그 생각 자체가 어리석다 The idea itself is absurd.
자초 自招 **—하다** bring〔draw〕 upon oneself ; incur 《blame》 ; court 《danger》 ¶ 재앙을 자초하다 bring calamity upon oneself ; court disaster // 화를 자초하다 bring misfortune on oneself
자초지종 自初至終 the whole story ; all the details ; full particulars ¶ 자초지종을 듣다 hear the whole story // 자초지종을 알다 know everything about it ; know the ins and outs of a matter // 자초지종을 이야기하다 give full particulars 《of》 ; give a complete account 《of》
자촉 반응 自觸反應 〚화학〛 autocatalysis
자총이 〚식물〛 a kind of purple onion
자축 自祝 celebration by oneself **—하다** celebrate 《an event》 by oneself
자축거리다 limp ⇨ 저축거리다
자춤거리다 limp slightly ⇨ 저춤거리다
자춤발이 a lame person ; a cripple
†**자취** a trace ; a track ; a vestige ; a trail ; marks ; signs ; one's whereabouts ¶ 영화의 옛 자취 traces of former glory // 자취를 감추다 disappear ; cover up one's tracks ; conceal one's whereabouts ; vanish into the air // 자취를 남기다 leave one's traces behind // 그의 자취를 찾을 수 없다 I can find no trace of him. // 지난날의 영화는 그 자취도 없다 Of it former glory not a vestige remains.
자취 自炊 cooking food for oneself **—하다** cook for oneself ; do one's own cooking ; cook one's own food ; board oneself
자취 自取 **—하다** bring upon oneself ¶ 자취 기화하다 bring the calamity on oneself // 위험을 자취하다 court danger
자치 〚물고기〛 a kind of salmon
*__자치 自治__ self-government ; self-administration ; autonomy ; home rule **—하다** govern oneself ¶ 자치의 self-governing ; autonomous // 학생에게 자치를 허용하다 allow students to govern themselves // 그들은 자치를 모른다 They do not know how to govern themselves.
—구 an autonomous district〔region〕 **—권** autonomous rights ; autonomy **— 기관** an organ of self-government **— 단체** a self-governing body **— 도시** a corporate town **—령** a self-governing dominion **— 식민지** a crown colony ; a dominion ; a self-governing colony **— 정신** the spirit of self-government **—제** the self-governing system ¶ 시의 자치제 municipalization **— 제도** the system of self-government **—체** a self-governing community〔body〕 **— 행정** self-governing administration **—회** a student council (학생의) **대학 —** university autonomy **지방 —** local〔provincial〕 self-government **시 —체** a municipal corporation ; a municipality **완전 —국** a fully self-governing state **지방 —체** a local self-gov-

ㅈ

erning body
자치기 (any one of several kinds of) stick-tossing〔-hitting〕 games
자치동갑 —同甲 one's senior〔junior〕 by one year ; one's contemporary ; people (of) about the same age
자친 慈親 one's (loving) mother
자침 自沈 scuttling〔sinking〕 one's own ship〔boat〕 —하다 scuttle (one's own boat)
자침 磁針 a magnetic needle
— 검류계(檢流計) a needle galvanometer — 검파기(檢波器) a magnetic detector —로(路) a magnetic course — 방위 magnetic bearing — 편차도 a magnetic variation chart 무정위(無定位)〔북지(北指)〕 — an astatic〔a north-pointing〕 needle
자칫 at the slightest slip ; with the slightest provocation ¶ 자칫 목숨을 잃을 뻔 하다 come near losing one's life // 자칫하면 성내다 get mad on the slightest provocation // 자칫하면 비가 오겠다 It looks like rain at any moment.
자칭 自稱 —하다 profess oneself 《to be》 ; call〔style〕 oneself 《a poet》 ; represent oneself 《as》 ; claim to be 《a lawyer》 ¶ …라고 자칭하다 assume the title 《of》 // 변호사라고 자칭하다 profess oneself to be a lawyer // 그는 백만 장자를 자칭한다 He calls〔styles〕 himself a millionaire.
— 문학사 a self-styled〔-appointed〕 Master of Arts — 시인 a would-be〔self-styled〕 poet — 신사 a self-styled gentleman — 어학자 a professed〔pretended〕 linguistic student — 의인(義人) a self-styled righteous person
자카르타 Djakarta ; Jakarta
자켓 a jacket ; a sweater ; [스웨터] a jersey ; a pullover
자크 a zipper ; a zip (fastener) ; a slide fastener 《미》 ⇨ 지퍼
자타 自他 oneself and others ; 〖문법〗 transitive and intransitive verbs ¶ 자타의 관계 one's relation with others ; relations between oneself and others // 자타가 모두 both oneself and others // 자타의 구별을 명백히 하다 draw a line of demarcation between oneself and others // 그는 자타가 다 인정하는 위대한 학자이다 He is generally admitted to be a great scholar. /It is commonly acknowledged that he is a great scholar.
자탁 藉託, 藉托 ⇨ 칭탁
자탄 自嘆 —하다 complain〔grieve〕 to oneself ; feel grief for oneself
자태 姿態 a figure ; personal appearance ¶ 아름다운 자태 a beautiful figure
자택 自宅 one's own house〔home〕 ; a private residence ¶ 자택에서 at one's home
— 구금 house arrest — 요법 a home treatment〔remedy〕 — 요양 convalescing at home ; home treatment — 진료 (medical) consultation at a doctor's office — 집무제 the system of home transaction of office business
자토 瓷土 kaolin ; crockery〔china〕 clay
자통 自通 —하다 master 《a thing》 by oneself ; achieve〔accomplish〕 《a thing》 by oneself
자퇴 自退 leaving 《one's post》 voluntarily〔willingly〕 ; voluntary resignation ; [입후보 따위의] voluntary withdrawal —하다 leave 《one's post》 of one's own accord ; relieve oneself of one's post ; resign willingly〔voluntarily〕
자투리 odds and ends of yardage ; remnants of dress goods ; a piece of cloth
자파 自派 one's own party〔faction〕
자판 自判 —하다 become self-evident ; become clear of itself ; reverse the original decision (상급 재판소에서)
자판 自辦 —하다 [일을] handle 《a matter》 personally ; dispose of oneself ; [비용을] pay one's own expense ; pay oneself
자폐선 自閉線 〖수학〗 a folium 《*pl.* -lia》 ; a looped curve
자폐증 自閉症 〖심리〗 autism
*자포자기 自暴自棄 desperation ; despair ; self-abandonment —하다 become〔grow〕 desperate ; abandon oneself to despair ; give oneself up to despair ¶ 그는 사랑에 실패하여 자포자기가 되었다 Disappointed in love, he lost all incentive to self-esteem. // 여기까지 왔는데 자포자기라니 Now that I have come this far, I don't give a damn.
자폭 自爆 self-destruction ; blowing oneself up ; suicidal〔self-blasting〕 explosion —하다 [배가] scuttle oneself ; be scuttled ; [비행기가] dash one's plane into an enemy position ; destroy oneself
자풀이 [계산] estimating the yard-price of cloth ; [판매] selling cloth by the yard —하다 estimate the yard-price of ; sell by the yard
자품 資稟 (natural) disposition ; inherent character ; nature
*자필 自筆 one's own handwriting ; an autograph ; a holograph ¶ 자필로 in one's own handwriting ; autographically
— 유언 a holograph will — 이력서 a curriculum vitae〔personal history〕 in one's own handwriting — 증서 a holograph — 편지 an autograph letter ; a holograph letter — 헌사(獻詞) an autographed dedication
자학 自虐 self-torture〔-torment〕 —하다 torture oneself
— 행위 a cruelty to oneself
자학자습 自學自習 teaching oneself ⇨ 자습, 독학(獨學)
자해 字解 a glossary
자해 自害 suicide ; self-injury —하다 kill

oneself ; commit suicide ; injure〔hurt〕 oneself

자행 恣行 waywardness ; willfulness ; self-indulgence —하다 do as one pleases ; have one's own way ; indulge 《in》

자형 字形 the shape of a character ; type ; print

*자형 姊兄 an elder sister's husband ; a brother-in-law

자형 慈兄 a kind-hearted elder brother

자혜 慈惠 charity ; benevolence ; philanthropy

— 병원 a charity〔public〕 hospital ; a free clinic —원 a charity institution ; an almshouse

자화 磁化 〖물리〗 magnetization —하다 magnetize

자화상 自畫像 a self-portrait ¶ 자화상을 그리다 paint one's own portrait

자화 수분 自花受粉 〖식물〗 self-pollination

자화 수정 自花受精 〖식물〗 self-fertilization

자화자찬 自畫自讚 self-laudation〔-admiration, -praise〕 —하다 praise〔admire〕 oneself ; blow one's own trumpet ; ring one's own bell ¶ 그는 늘 자화자찬을 한다 He always blows his own horn.

자활 自活 self-support —하다 support oneself ; earn one's (own) living ; provide for oneself ¶ 자활하는 여자 a woman who fights her own way in the world // 자활의 길을 열어 주다 put 《a person》 in the way of getting his living

자회사 子會社 an affiliated company ; a subsidiary company ; a daughter firm ¶ 그는 자회사에 근무하게 되었다 He was farmed out to a subsidiary.

자획 字劃 the number of strokes in a Chinese character

작 勺 a unit of measure (⇨ 1/10 *hob*)

작 作 [작품] a work ; a production ; [농작] a harvest ; a crop ; a yield

걸— a wonderful piece of workmanship 로댕 — a work by Rodin ; a Rodin 이모— two crops a year ¶ 이모작의 첫번째〔두 번째〕 경작 the first〔second〕 crop 평— an average crop 풍— a good crop 《of rice》 ; a rich harvest 《of wheat》 흉— a bad crop 《of rice》 윤동주 —시 a poem written by *Yun Dong-joo*

작 昨 yesterday

작 爵 peerage ; a degree of nobility ; rank

—위 peerage ; a titular rank ; title and court rank 오등— the five degrees of peerage

†작가 作家 a writer ; an author ; an artist

— 협회 a writers' association 신진 — a rising〔young〕 novelist 여류 — a lady〔fair, woman〕 writer〔novelist〕 ; an authoress 인기 — a popular〔favorite〕 writer ; [전문가들에게] an in-writer ; [대중에게] an out-writer

작가 作歌 song writing ; versification —하다 write a song ; compose a song

작고 作故 decease ; death —하다 die ; decease ; pass away ¶ 작고한 the late // 작고한 사람들 the deceased

*작곡 作曲 (musical) composition —하다 compose〔write〕 the music ; [가사를] set 《a song》 to the music

—가 a composer — 기술 compositional technique (S씨 작시) Y씨 — (words by S), music by Y

작금 昨今 these days ; recently ; lately ¶ 작금의 recent ; new // 작금의 추위 the recent〔present〕 cold // 작금에 시작된 것이 아니다 It is of no recent date.

— 양년(兩年) both last and this year — 양일(兩日) both yesterday and today

작년 昨年 last year ; the past year ¶ 작년의 오늘 today last year

— 여름 last summer

†작다 [크기가] (be) small ; little ; tiny ; be of small size ; [사소한] petty ; trifling ; trivial ; insignificant ; [연소한] young ; little ; [낮은] low ; [마음이] narrow-minded ; small-minded ; [얼마 되지 않는] slight ; minor ; small ¶ 작은 사람 a man of small caliber ; a small-minded person // 작은 일 a trifle ; a trivial matter ; a small affair // 작은 아이들 little ones ; little kids // 작은 목소리 a low voice // 키가 작은 사람 a short person // 담이 작다 be timid ; be cowardly // 작아지다 become smaller ; dwindle ; diminish // 이 모자는 나에게는 작다 This hat is too small〔tight〕 for me. // 옷이 어린애에게 작아졌다 The child has outgrown its clothes. // 이 회사도 처음에는 아주 작았었다 The company started from a small beginning. // 그가 작았을 때부터 알고 있다 I have known him from a child. // 우리 집에는 작은 아이들이 둘 있습니다 We have two little ones. // 라디오를 좀 작게 하라 Please turn the radio down a little.

작은 것부터 큰 것 이룬다 〈속담〉 From small beginnings came great things. / Everything has its seed.

작다리 a man of small〔low, short〕 stature 〔height〕 ; a (very) short person ; a little fellow ; a shorty 《미·구》

작달막하다 (be) stumpy ; be rather short 《of stature》

작달비 a torrential〔pouring〕 rain ; a downpour

작당 作黨 forming a gang —하다 band together ; form a gang〔group, league〕

작대 作隊 —하다 form ranks〔a column〕 ; line up ¶ 작대하여 in line〔procession〕 ; in formation

작대기 a rod ; a pole ; a crossing (지움표)

작대기바늘 a big needle

작도 作圖 drawing figures ; 〖기하〗 construction —하다 draw figures ; construct

ㅈ

— 문제 a problem for construction ; a construction
작동 昨冬 last winter
작동 作動 functioning ; working —하다 function ; operate ; work ; run ; go ¶ 작동하기 시작하다 begin to work ; go into action
작두 斫— a fodder-chop ; a straw-cutter
—질 chopping〔cutting〕 fodder
작두콩 〖식물〗 a horse bean
작란 作亂 ① [난리를 일으킴] —하다 start a war ; raise a rebellion ; rise in revolt ② ⇨ 장난
작량 酌量 consideration ; allowance ; extenuation —하다 consider ; take into consideration ; extenuate ; make allowance 《for》
작렬 炸裂 explosion —하다 explode
작례 作例 an example 《of》 ; a model 《of》 ¶ 작례를 보이다 give an example
작말 作末 pulverization —하다 pulverize ; reduce to〔grind into〕 powder ; powder ¶ 곡물을 작말하다 grind 《corn》 into flour
작명 作名 naming ; dubbing ; christening —하다 name ; dub ; christen
*작문 作文 composition ; writing —하다 make a composition ; write 《a theme》 ¶ 작문 연습을 하다 practice the art of composition ; practice in writing // 봄이라는 제목으로 작문을 짓다 write a composition on the spring
— 시간 a composition lesson — 제목 a subject for composition ; a theme 영— English composition 자유 — free〔voluntary〕 composition
작물 作物 crops ; farm products ¶ 작물의 씨를 뿌리다 sow crops 《in a field》 // 작물을 재배하다 raise〔grow〕 crops
작박구리 an upturned horn
작반 作伴 traveling〔going〕 together ; keeping company —하다 keep company 《with》 ; go〔travel〕 together ; accompany ; make friends with
작배 作配 pairing off ; making a match ; getting married —하다 pair off ; make a match 《of》 ; marry
작법 作法 composition ; method ; making a law〔rule, regulation〕 —하다 make a law〔rule〕
작벼리 the pebbly sands
⁑작별 作別 leave-taking ; farewell (visit) ; a parting call —하다 take leave ; bid farewell ; say good bye ; pay 《a person》 farewell visit ; go for a parting call ¶ 작별 인사 a farewell〔parting〕 speech〔call, greeting〕 // 친구와 작별하다 take leave of one's friends // 이제 작별해야겠습니다 I must say good-bye. /I think I must be going now.
작보 昨報 the previous〔yesterday's〕 report ¶ 작보한 바와 같이 as reported〔stated〕 in yesterday's issue〔report〕
작부 作付 planting —하다 crop〔plant, sow〕 《a field with barley》 ; put seeds in the ground
— 면적 the acreage under cultivation ; the area under crop
작부 酌婦 a barmaid ; a waitress
작사 作詞 [짓기] lyric making ; writing songs〔words〕 ; [가사] words ; lyric lines —하다 [유행가 따위를] write lyrics
—자 a lyric writer ; a songwriter
작사리 a prop
*작살 a harpoon ; a fish spear
작성 作成 framing ; drawing up ; preparation —하다 draw up ; frame ; write out ; make out ¶ 계약서를 두 통 작성하다 make out a contract in duplicate // 증서를 작성하다 draw up a deed // 이 신청서를 작성하신 후 다시 오십시오 Fill this application form out and come back, please.
—법 the art of verse making ; versification 유언서 — making a written will〔one's will〕
작시 作詩 versification ; verse making —하다 verse ; versify ; compose a poem ; write a verse
—법 the art of verse making ; how to write〔compose〕 poems
작신거리다 importune ; tease for 《a thing》 ; cling 《to a person》 begging for
작신작신 teasing for 《a thing》 ; clinging and begging ; importuning
작심 作心 resolution ; determination —하다 make up one's mind ; determine ; resolve
—삼일 a short-lived resolve ; an unsteady plan
작야 昨夜 last night
작약 芍藥 〖식물〗 a peony
작약 炸藥 an explosive ; gunpowder
작약 雀躍 dancing〔leaping〕 for joy —하다 jump〔dance, leap〕 for joy ; exult 《over》
작업 作業 work ; operations ; fatigue duty (군대의) —하다 work ; conduct operations ¶ 작업을 시작하다 begin〔start, commence〕 operations ; get down to work // 작업을 중지하다 suspend operations // 작업 중 while at work ; while working ; on the job
— 강도 intensity of work — 검사 〖심리〗 a performance test — 공정(工程) a working process — 관행(慣行) work habits — 교대 a work shift — 능률 operation〔work〕 efficiency — 명령 a job order —모 a fatigue cap —반 a work〔working〕 detail —복 a fatigue uniform (군대의) —비 working expenses — 수입 working receipts ; operation revenue — 시간 working hours —실 a workroom ; an operation room —원 a worker ; an operator —장 a workshop ; a works ; [광산 등의] workings — 조건

work conditions ; requirements — 중지 기간 a down〔work stoppage〕 period — 허가 work permit —화 work shoes — 환경 working environment — 회계 operation account — 훈련 on-the-job training

‡작업복 作業服 a working clothes〔dress, garments〕; a working uniform ; a jumper (선원의) ; fatigue dress〔clothes〕(군인의)

작열 灼熱 white heat ; incandescence ; scorching heat —하다 become red〔white〕 hot ; be burning ¶ 작열하는 사랑 a passionate〔burning〕 love // 작열하는 모래 사장 burning sands // 작열하는 태양 a scorching〔broiling〕 sun

†작용 作用 action ; operation ; effect ; working ; [기능] function ; process —하다 act〔operate, work〕《on》; exert action《on》; function ¶ 자연의 작용 natural operation // 산의 작용 the actions of an acid // 태양열이 인체에 미치는 작용 the action of the sun's heat upon the human body // 물의 작용으로 by the action of water // 서로 작용하다 interact

—량 〖물리〗 action —량 변수 an action variable — 범위 the working realm —선(線)〔구(球), 점〕〖물리〗 a line〔sphere, point〕 of action — 양자(量子) 〖물리〗 quantum of action — 중심 〖물리〗 the center of action 기계 — the working of a machine 동화 — the process of assimilation 반(反)— reaction 상호 — an interaction 심리 — a mental process 인력(引力) — the influence of gravity 정신 — operation of the mind 화학 — chemical action〔process〕

작월 昨月 last month

작위 爵位 peerage ; title and rank of nobility

작위 作爲 artificiality ; 〖법〗 commission ; feasance ¶ 작위의 intentional ; deliberate // 작위의 죄 a sin of commission

— 동사 〖문법〗 a factitive〔causative〕 verb 《cause him to fall의 cause 같은 것》 —범 a commissive crime 부— nonfeasance ; omission

작은곰자리 〖천문〗 the Little Bear ; the Ursa Minor ; the Little Dipper

작은꾸리 the smaller〔inner〕 beef foreshank

작은마마 〖의학〗 chicken-pox ; varicella

작은말 〖언어〗 a "light isotope" of a word

작은아버지 an uncle ; a younger brother of one's father

작은어머니 an aunt ; the wife of one's father's younger brother

작은집 ① [아들·동생의 집] one's son's〔younger brother's〕 house ; a branch〔collateral〕 family ② [첩의 집] the house of one's concubine

작의 作意 [창작 의욕] a creative impulse ; [창작 취향] a central theme ; a motif 《프》

작인 作人 a sharecropper ; a tenant farmer

작일 昨日 yesterday

*작자 作者 [소작인] a sharecropper ; [저자] an author ; a writer ; [위인] personality ; a person ; a guy ; [살 사람] a buyer ; a purchaser ¶ 작자가 없다 have no demand ; find no buyers

작작[1] properly ; moderately ; not too much ¶ 술을 작작 마셔라 Do not drink too much. // 농담도 작작 해라 Do not go too far with your joke.

작작[2] [소리] ⇨ 짝짝 ④

작작 綽綽 —하다 (be) free and easy ; leisurely ; unconstrained ¶ 여유 작작하다 be free and easy ; have a great reserve of energy ; have plenty in reserve ; have more than enough

작잠 a tussah (worm)

*작전 作戰 (military) operations ; maneuvers ; tactics ; strategy

> 참고 **tactics**는 개개의 전투에 있어서의 계획·전술을 말하고 **strategy**는 전체적 작전 계획을 말한다

¶ 작전상 tactically ; strategically // 작전상 중요한 of strategic importance // 작전을 짜다 elaborate〔consider〕 a plan of operations // 작전을 잘못하다 commit a tactical error // 작전을 변경하다 change one's tactics

— 개시일 the D-day — 계획 a plan of campaign〔operations〕 ¶ 작전 계획을 세우다 map out a plan of campaign — 구역 an operating area — 기지〔근거지〕 a base〔center〕 of operations — 명령 an operation order — 목표 the objective of operations — 비행 an operational flight — 준비 완료《report》(a state of) operational readiness — 지도 an operational map — 책임 전술 지역 〖군사〗 the tactical area of operational responsibility 《TAOR》 — 회의 a council of war 공격 — offensive〔active〕 operations 공동 — concerted operations ; combined action 공〔수〕세 — active〔passive〕 operations ; offensive〔defensive〕 operations 공중 — airborne operations 도양 — overseas operations 방어 — a defensive operations 양동 — the feint operation 해양 — overseas operations 현상 유지 — holding operations

†작정 作定 a decision ; a determination ; an intention ; a thought ; an idea ; a plan ; a purpose —하다 decide ; determine ; intend 《to do》; make up one's mind 《to do》; plan ; propose ¶ 차를 팔기로 작정하다 decide to sell one's automobile // 그는 아들에게 목사를 시킬 작정이다 He intends his son for the church. // 그는 여행갈 작정이다 He is planning to make a tour.

ㅈ

작조 昨朝 yesterday morning
작주 昨週 last week
작차다 be full 《of》; be filled 《with》; [기한이] fall due; expire; mature
작첩 作妾 —하다 take〔keep〕 a concubine〔mistress〕
작추 昨秋 last autumn
작춘 昨春 last spring
작태 作態 —하다 assume an attitude 〔air〕 《of》; take up〔adopt〕 an attitude 《of》; put on an 《unconcerned》 air; put on a show of 《doing》; affect; [옷차림 따위를] tidy (up) oneself; get (oneself) up
작파 作破 —하다 give up 《trying》; leave off 《work》; abandon; call off; withdrawing》; leave off 《work》: abandon; call off; withdraw
작폐 作弊 —하다 make trouble; make a nuisance
†작품 作品 a (piece of) work; a product; a (literary) production ¶ 예술 작품 a work of art // 문학 작품 a literary work // 아동들의 작품 pupils' products // 디킨스의 작품을 읽은 일이 없다 I have read none of Dickens. // 셰익스피어의 작품을 읽어 보았습니까 Did you ever read Shakespeare? —집 the works 《of Thomas Hardy》 문예 — a literary work 우수 영화 — 《his》 outstanding screen achievements
작풍 作風 a (literary) style; a style of writing ¶ 작풍을 모방하다 model one's style on 《another's》
작하 昨夏 last summer
작황 作況 a harvest; a crop; a yield — 보고 a crop report〔return〕 — 예상 crop〔harvest〕 prospects
작희 作戲 an interruption; a hindrance; a disturbance —하다 hinder; disturb; interrupt; interfere; ruin 《other's fun》
작히나 ⇨ 오죽
잔 盞 a cup; a wine cup〔glass〕; a goblet (받침이 달린) ¶ 찻잔 a teacup // 잔을 주다 offer a cup // 잔을 비우다 drain〔drink off〕 a cup // 잔을 엎다 turn over a cup // 물을 한 잔 마시다 drink a glass of water // 잔을 주고 받다 exchange cups // 잔에 술을 따르다 fill a cup with wine // 손님은 벌써 세 잔이나 마시셨습니다 You've had two refills already, sir.
잔을 받다 [관용] accept a cup
잔을 돌리다 [관용] pass the cup round
*잔 殘 the remainder; the remnant; leavings; the residue; the balance (잔금 따위); the surplus (잉여); the rest (나머지)
잔가시 fine bones of fish
잔가지 a twig; [꽃가지] a sprig; a spray
잔걸음 walking within a short distance ¶ 잔걸음치다 walk back and forth within a short distance; [잰 걸음으로] walk with mincing steps
잔고 殘高 the balance; the remainder —장(帳) a balance book —표 a balance sheet (대차 대조표) — 회계 balance 은행 예금 — the〔one's〕 balance at the bank 이월 — the balance carried over 〔carried forward, brought forward〕; the balance forward 주문 — the balance of an order 차감 — the balance 현금 — the cash balance
잔고기 small fish; small fry
잔고기 가시 세다 [속담] No viper so small, but has its venom.
잔교 棧橋 ① [산간의] bridges laid across ravines ② [부두의] a pier; a jetty; a landing stage
잔글씨 a small character; a fine letter ¶ 잔글씨로 쓰다 write in small letters 〔characters〕
잔금 fine〔thin〕 wrinkles; fine〔small〕 lines
잔금 殘金 the balance; the remainder; the rest ¶ 잔금을 치르다 pay the balance // 잔금은 모두 이것뿐입니다 This is all the money left.
잔기 殘期 the remainder of a period 〔term〕
잔기침 a slight cough; a hack; a hacking cough ¶ 잔기침하다 hack; emit a hacking cough
잔꾀 little selfish wiles; petty guile
잔누비(질) close〔fine〕 quilting
잔다리밟다 rise to a high position step by step
잔당 殘黨 remnants (of a defeated party)
잔대 盞臺 a saucer for a wine cup
잔도 棧道 a plank road
†잔돈 small change; loose money; loose cash ¶ 잔돈으로 치르다 pay in small change // 천원짜리를 잔돈으로 바꾸다 change a thousand-*won* bill // 5,000원짜리를 잔돈으로 바꾸고 싶습니다만 Would you break this five-thousand *won* bill for me? // 잔돈 좀 줄까 Shall I give you some small change?
잔돈푼 [용돈] pocket money; pin money (여자의); [푼돈] odd money; petty cash; a small sum of money ¶ 잔돈푼이나 벌기 위해서 as an aid to one's pocketbook
잔돌 a pebble
잔드근하다 ⇨ 진드근하다
잔등(이) the back ⇨ 등
†잔디 (a patch of) lawn —깎이 기계 a lawn mower; [수동식] a hand mower; [동력식] a power〔motor〕 mower —밭 a lawn; a grassplot ¶ 잔디밭을 깎다 mow the lawn // 잔디밭에 물을 주다 sprinkle the lawn // 잔디밭에 들어가지 마시오 Keep off the grass. —밭 살수기(撒水器) a lawn sprinkler grass; turf; sod ¶ 잔디를 심다 turf; put 《a yard》 in turf
잔디밭에서 바늘 찾기 [속담] Like a needle in a bottle of hay.
잔뜩 to capacity; till full; to the fullest; extremely; to the utmost ¶ 잔뜩 마시다

〔먹다〕 drink〔eat〕 one's fill // 잔에 술을 잔뜩 붓다 fill the glass to the brim with wine // 잔뜩 흥분하다 be extremely excited ; be excited in the extreme ; be highly wrought up // 잔뜩 노려보다 look hard at《a person》; stare《a person》in the face ; look straight at《a person》; fix one's eyes on《a person》// 잔뜩 기대하다 eagerly look forward to《seeing him》// 얼굴을 잔뜩 찌푸리다 scowl ; make a very sour face ; draw up one's face (고통으로) // 잔뜩 노기를 띠다 be black with anger // 눈에 눈물이 잔뜩 고였다 Her eyes are filled〔brimming〕 with tears. // 잔뜩 먹었더니 배가 터질 것 같다 I have had more than enough. // 그는 눈물을 잔뜩 참았다 He struggled to hold his tears back.

잔루 殘壘 〖야구〗 runners left on base **—하다** be left on base

잔류 殘留 **—하다** remain behind

— 감각 〖심리〗 aftersensation **— 그룹** a group ordered to remain **—물** residue ; residuum《*pl.* -dua》; leavings ; remnants ; sediment ; dregs (찌꺼기) **— 부대** the remaining forces **—선**(線)〔**자화**(磁化)〕 residual rays 〔magnetization〕 **— 자기**(磁氣) residual magnetism

***잔말** small talk ; useless talk ; small complaints ; bitching (속) ; mutter ; nag ; a scolding **—하다** complain ; grumble ; nag ; scold ; chatter ¶ 잔말 말고 파시오 Cut the patter and sell it. // 잔말 말고 일해라 Cut the chatter and get down to work. // 그 여자는 잔말이 많다 That woman is constantly nagging.

잔망 殘亡 ⇨ 잔멸

잔망 孱妄 being infirm and rash〔feeble and stupid〕 **—스럽다, —하다** be feeble and stupid (for one's age)

잔멸 殘滅 ruin ; decline ; decay **—하다** go to ruin ; perish ; decline ; decay

잔명 殘命 the remainder of one's doomed life

잔무 殘務 remaining affairs〔business〕; unsettled affairs ¶ 잔무를 정리하다 wind up the affairs《of a company》; clear up the remaining business

잔물결 little waves ; ripples

잔밉다 (be) provoking ; hateful ; detestable

잔반 殘飯 leftover rice〔food〕; the leavings〔remains〕 (of a meal)

잔병 —病 sickliness ; constant slight sickness ¶ 잔병꾸러기 a sickly person // 잔병치레 getting sick frequently // 잔병이 많다 be sickly ; be constantly sick // 그는 어렸을 때부터 잔병을 늘 앓는다 He has been sickly from childhood.

잔병 殘兵 the remnants of a defeated army ; remnant troops

잔부 殘部 the remainder ; the remnant ; the rest ; what is〔are〕 left

잔부끄럼 bashfulness ; diffidence ¶ 잔부끄럼을 타다 be bashful

잔상 殘像 〖심리〗 an afterimage

잔서 殘暑 the lingering summer heat

잔설 殘雪 the remaining〔unmelted〕 snow ; snow of yester year

잔셈 a small account ¶ 잔셈은 나중에 하자 Let's settle small accounts later on.

잔소리 small talk ; small complaints ; a scolding ⇨ 잔말 **—하다** scold ; rebuke ; lecture ; chide ; give《a person》a scolding ; give an earful (미·속) ¶ 그는 내게 호된 잔소리를 했다 He really gave me a chewing out.

—꾼 a chatterbox ; a nagger ; a prattler ; a glib speaker ; a talkative〔wordy, verbose, voluble, loquacious〕 person

잔속 the intimate details ; the insides ; the inside information ¶ 잔속을 알다 know the insides《of, on》; have an intimate knowledge《of》

잔손 elaborate〔detailed〕 handwork ; a little touch ; minute attention〔care, trouble〕 ¶ 잔손이 가는 일 a troublesome job // 잔손이 많이 들다 require care ; take a lot of trouble ; demand a lot of little fine touches // 방을 꾸미는 데 잔손이 많이 들었다 It took a lot of little touches for me to get this room decorated.

—질 a small touch ; a final touch

잔솔 a young pine

—밭 a young〔little〕 pine grove〔wood〕; a grove of young pines

잔술 盞— liquor by the cup ; draft liquor

—집 a drinking-house〔pub〕 that sells draft liquor

잔심부름 sundry errands〔jobs〕

잔악 殘惡 atrocity ; cruelty **—하다** (be) atrocious ; cruel

잔액 殘額 the balance ; the remainder

이월 — the balance carried over **차감 —** the balance

잔약 孱弱 frailness ; delicateness ; feebleness ; weakness **—하다** (be) frail ; delicate ; fragile ; weak ¶ 잔약한 남자 a man of frail constitution

잔업 殘業 overtime work **—하다** work overtime ; work extra hours

— 수당 pay for overtime ; overtime pay ; an allowance for overtime work

잔여 殘餘 the remainder ; the rest

—액 the balance ; the remainder ; the residue **— 재산** remaining〔surplus〕 assets ; 〖법〗 the residue〔residuum〕 (of one's estate) ; a residuary estate ; residual property **— 재산 상속자** a residuary legatee

잔열 殘熱 ① a lingering fever ; remaining warmth〔heat〕 ② ⇨ 잔서(殘暑)

잔영 殘影 traces ; relics

잔용 —用 〔용돈〕 pocket money ; pin money (부녀자의) ; spending money

잔월 殘月 a waning moon ; a morning

ㅈ

moon
*잔인 殘忍 cruelty; brutality; atrocity; inhumanity —하다 (be) cruel; brutal; heartless; atrocious; merciless ¶ 잔인한 짓 a cruel act; a cold-blooded act // 잔인한 사람 a cruel〔brutal〕person // 잔인한 짓을 하다 do a cruel thing; commit cruelties // 잔인하게 대하다 treat 《a person》 cruelly; be cruel to 《a person》; be hard on 《a person》 // 그런 짓을 하는 것은 잔인하다 It is cruel to do such a thing.
— 무도 abominable cruelty; inhumanity
—성 one's brutal nature
잔일 small matters; fine details
잔입 the limited appetite one has on getting out of bed ¶ 잔입이라 입맛이 없다 I don't feel like eating because I just got out of bed.
잔자누룩하다 (be) calm; quiet ¶ 소동이 가라앉아 잔자누룩하다 The riot is over and everything is quiet now.
잔작하다 be backward for one's age; be underdeveloped for one's age
잔잔하다 (be) quiet; calm; still ¶ 잔잔한 바다 a quiet sea
잔잔하다 潺潺— (be) murmuring ¶ 잔잔한 시냇물 a murmuring stream // 잔잔히 흐르다 flow murmuringly; murmur along
잔재 殘滓 [찌끼] waste matter; dregs (액체의) ¶ 일제의 잔재 vestiges of Japanese imperialism
잔재미 a subtle pleasure; a pleasure in a small way ¶ 잔재미를 보다 get a subtle pleasure 《from》; have a nice little time of it
잔재비 ① [처리] ability to do a bit of intricate work ② [일] applying oneself to the small details of a large job
잔재주 a petty artifice; a trick; a device ¶ 잔재주가 있는 smart; smartish; shrewd; tricky // 잔재주를 부리다 resort to petty tricks
잔적 殘敵 the remnants of a defeated enemy; stragglers ¶ 잔적을 소탕하다 mop up stragglers
잔적 殘賊 the remaining bandits; the rest of the insurgents ¶ 잔적을 소탕하다 round up the bandits still at large
잔전 —錢 small change ⇨ 잔돈
잔존 殘存 survival —하다 be still alive; be extant; survive; [잔류하다] be left; remain ¶ 잔존자 a survivor // 잔존하는 surviving; extant
— 기관 a vestigial〔residual, rudimentary〕organ — 동물 relic fauna — 동물〔식물〕군 relic fauna〔flora〕 —물 a hangover; a survival — 생물 a relic —자 a survivor —종(種) 〖동물·식물〗 a relict; a relic
잔주 drunken grumbling —하다 grumble while drunk
잔주 —註 detailed notes〔annotations〕; copious notes
잔주름 fine wrinkles
—살 skin with fine wrinkles in it 눈꼬리 — crow's-feet
잔줄 a fine line
잔질다 (be) weakhearted〔fainthearted〕
잔챙이 a small variety; a small one; small fry; small potatoes; peanuts; children ¶ 고기 잔챙이 small fish; small fry // 잔챙이들은 밖에서 놀아라 You kids go play outside.
*잔치 a feast; a banquet; a party ¶ 생일 잔치 a birthday party // 혼인 잔치 a wedding feast // 환갑 잔치 the banquet given on one's sixtieth birthday // 잔치를 열다 give a banquet
잔칼질 mincing; chopping —하다 mince; chop ¶ 고기를 잔칼질하다 mince meat
잔털 fine hairs
잔판머리 the last stage; the wind-up; the close; the denouement ¶ 연극의 잔판머리 the denouement of a play // 회의 잔판머리에 가서 주먹 싸움이 벌어졌다 Just as the meeting was winding up, a fist-fight broke out.
잔풀나기 a person boastful of his first little success; [이른 봄] early spring
잔풀호사 —豪奢 luxury beyond one's means
잔품 殘品 the remaining stock(s); unsold stock〔goods〕 ¶ 잔품이 얼마 없다 The stock is running short〔low〕.
— 정리 a clearance sale
잔학 殘虐 cruelty; brutality; atrocity; inhumanity; outrage —하다 cruel; atrocious; brutal; inhuman; outrageous; ruthless ¶ 잔학한 짓 a brutal act; brutalities; atrocities // 잔학하게 대하다 treat 《a person》 cruelly〔brutally〕; subject 《a person》 to inhuman treatment
잔해 殘骸 remains (유해); a carcass (동물의); [파괴물] a wreck; wreckage ¶ 비행기의 잔해 the wreck of an airplane
잔향 殘響 〖물리〗 reverberation〔echo〕
잔허리 the small of the back
*잔혹 殘酷 cruelty; brutality; atrocity; heartlessness; ruthlessness —하다 (be) cruel; brutal; heartless; atrocious; merciless; ruthless ¶ 잔혹한 짓 a cruel act; a cold-blooded act // 잔혹한 사람 a brutal〔cruel〕person // 잔혹한 짓을 하다 do a cruel thing; commit cruelties
잔화 殘火 remaining fire; embers
잔흔 殘痕 a (remaining) trace〔mark〕; scar
잗갈다 grind up finely; grind into powder
잗널다 gnaw into fine bits
잗다듬다 trim smooth〔fine〕; nip off neatly
잗다랗다, 잗닿다 (be) extremely fine〔small〕
잗달다 (be) narrow-minded; petty; infe-

rior ; stingy
잔젊다 look younger than one's years ; look young for one's age
잔주름 fine creases〔folds〕 in clothes ¶ 잔주름을 잡다 make fine creases
잔타다 grind 《beans, etc.》 fine ; grind into powder
†잘[1] ① [익숙·능란] well ; skilfully ; nicely ; excellently ; expertly ; splendidly ¶ 영어를 잘하다 speak English well∥노래를 잘 부르다 sing well∥요리를 잘하다 be a good cook∥피아노를 잘 치다 play the piano well∥그 말 잘했다 That is well said.∥참 잘했다 Well done ! /Good man ! /Good for you ! 《미》∥나는 잘 못한다 I can't do it well.∥말 좀 잘해 주시겠습니까 Would you put in a word for me, please ?
② [충분히] well ; thoroughly ; in full ; fully ; carefully ; closely ; soundly ¶ 잘 생각하다 think hard ; give much thought to∥잘 눈여겨 보다 look at 《a thing》 carefully ; observe closely ; have a good look at∥잘 듣다 listen to 《a person》 carefully∥잘 자다 sleep soundly〔well〕 ; have a good night∥잘 익지 않았다 It is not properly cooked.∥그를 잘 안다 I know him well.∥내가 더 잘 안다 I know him better (than you).∥잘 모르겠다 I don't know for certain.∥잘 흔들어서 사용하시오 Shake well before using.∥자신을 잘 반성하라 Look well at yourself.
③ [편히] well ; satisfactorily ; favorably ¶ 잘 살다 be well off ; live well∥잘 지냈니 How have you been ?∥잘 있거라 Good-bye !∥간밤에 잘 잤어 Did you have a good night's sleep ?
④ [곧잘] readily ; easily ; [자주] often ; frequently ; a lot ¶ 잘 웃다 laugh readily ; be fond of laughing∥잘 싸우다 be apt to pick quarrels with others∥그는 화를 잘 낸다 He is apt to get angry. /He gets angry readily.∥그는 극장에 잘 간다 He goes to the movies a lot.∥요즘 비가 잘 온다 It rains often these days.∥눈이 잘 내린다 Snow falls quite often.
⑤ [기타] ¶ 잘 생기다 be good-looking∥옷이 잘 어울리다 a dress fits nicely∥너 잘 왔다 You did well to come !∥마침 잘 왔다 You've come at just the right time !
잘 자랄 나무는 떡잎부터 알아본다 속담 First impressions are the most lasting. / The first blow is halfly the battle.
잘[2] [억] a hundred million
잘[3] [모피] the fur of the sable ; sable (fur)
잘강잘강 chewing ; gnawing ⇨ 질겅질겅
잘게 finely ; fine ; closely ; to〔in〕 pieces ; [좀스럽게] narrow-mindedly ; pettily ¶ 잘게 썬 양파만 넣으면 요리가 끝이다 Just add some finely chopped onion and it's ready to serve.
잘그랑 with a cling ; jingling ; rattling —하다 cling ; jingle ; rattle
잘금거리다 trickle ; dribble ⇨ 질금거리다
잘깃하다 ⇨ 질깃하다
잘끈 tight ; fast ; firm ¶ 꾸러미를 잘끈 동이다 tie a package up tight∥허리끈을 잘끈 매다 tie one's sash tight
잘나다 ① [잘 생기다] (be) handsome ; good-looking ¶ 잘난 사내아이 a handsome boy∥잘난 풍채의 청년 a fine-looking young man
② [뛰어나다] be of excellent caliber ; (be) distinguished ; great ¶ 잘난 사람 a distinguished〔great〕 person ; a person of excellent caliber∥잘난 체하다 put on〔give oneself〕 airs ; assume an air of importance∥잘난 체하고 말하다 speak with an air of importance〔in a lordly manner〕 ; speak conceitedly 〔cockily〕
③ [반의적] (be) worthless ; useless ; good-for-nothing ¶ 이런 잘난 책을 무엇하러 읽느냐 I don't see why you are reading such a "great work"〔stupid book〕 as this.
*잘다 (be) fine ; small ; tiny ; minute ¶ 잔모래〔자갈〕 fine sand〔gravel〕∥글씨를 잘게 쓰다 write closely∥잔 글씨를 쓰다 write small characters〔letters〕∥잘게 자르다 cut 《a thing》 fine∥고기를 잘게 썰다 chop meat into small pieces ; mince meat∥그는 사람이 잘다 He is a small-minded〔fussy〕 man.
*잘되다 go well ; come out well〔successfully〕 ; [번영] prosper ; thrive ; [진척] make good progress ¶ 모든 일이 잘되어 간다 Everything is going on well.∥도로 보수 공사는 잘되어 가고 있다 The road repair is making progress steadily 〔rapidly〕.∥금년은 벼가 잘된다 The rice plants are doing nicely this year.∥그의 집안이 잘되어 간다 His family is thriving.∥그는 외국에 나가 잘되었다 He went abroad and prospered.∥조금만 있으면 일이 잘되어 갈 것이다 A little more and things will go on smoothly.∥전쟁 후 장사가 전처럼 잘되어 가지 못한다 After a war, business never goes quite so smoothly as before.
잘똑거리다 limp ⇨ 절뚝거리다
잘똑하다 be pinched in
잘뚜마기 the slender part〔narrow part〕 (of a thing such as a gourd) ; the neck ; the small
잘라 내다 cut off ; cut out〔away〕 ; cleave ; whittle down ; tear off
잘라 말하다 say〔state〕 positively ; say definitely ; declare ; affirm ; give one's word ; assert
잘라매다 bind fast ; tie fast ; fasten tightly ¶ 허리끈을 잘라매다 tie one's sash tight∥사람의 양다리를 잘라매다 tie 《a person's》 feet together∥범인을 잘라매다 tie a criminal with cords∥그의 손발을 잘라매어라 Bind him hand and foot.
잘라먹다 ① eat by cutting〔breaking〕 into

ㅈ

pieces ; cut and eat ¶ 떡을 잘라먹다 break a cake and eat it

② [떼먹다] bilk ; make 《a borrowed thing》 one's own ; leave 《a bill》 unpaid ¶ 빚을 잘라먹다 welsh on 《a person's》 debt // 외상을 잘라먹다 bilk〔ignore〕《a person's》 bill // 그는 늘 남의 것을 잘라먹는다 He is always keeping borrowed things. // 빚을 잘라먹을 셈이냐 Do you mean to disown your debt?

잘라버리다 [나무 따위를] clear〔cut, chop〕 away

잘랑거리다 jingle ; clink ; tinkle

잘랑잘랑 clink ; jingle

잘래잘래, 짤래짤래 shaking one's head

잘록잘록, 짤록짤록 pinched〔sloped〕 in (in many places) ─하다 (be) pinched〔sloped〕 in (in many places)

잘록하다 (be) slender ; narrow ; (be) constricted (in the middle) ¶ 잘록한 허리 a slender waist // 박은 허리가 잘록하다 A gourd has a neck〔narrows in the middle〕. // 이 옷은 허리가 너무 잘록하다 The dress is too much pinched in at the waist.

잘름거리다 ⇨ 짤끔거리다, 절뚝거리다

잘리다 ① be snapped ; be cut (off) ; be broken ¶ 목이 잘리다 be decapitated〔beheaded〕; get fired ; get the axe // 연실이 잘렸다 The string of the kite has broken〔snapped〕. // 이 통나무는 잘 잘리지 않는다 This log won't chop. // 그는 자동차에 치여서 팔이 잘리었다 He was run over by a car and lost one arm.

② [떼이다] lose (a thing by lending or entrusting to a person) ; be cheated out of ; have a loan uncollected ¶ 나는 그한테 책을 잘리었다 I lost a book by lending it to him. // 저녀석한테 10,000원 잘렸다 He has bilked〔swindled〕 me out of ten thousand *won*.

†잘못 [과실] a fault ; a mistake ; [악의 없는] an error ; blame (과실의 책임) ; a slip (작은 잘못) ; a blunder (큰 잘못) ; a failure ; a wrong ; [부사적] by mistake ; wrongly ; erroneously ; mistakenly ─하다 mistake ; make a mistake ; commit〔make〕 an error ; be mistaken 《in》 ; do wrong ; do amiss〔wrongly〕 ; blunder ; misdo ¶ 조그만 잘못 a slight slip // 큰 잘못 a gross fault ; a blunder // 잘못된 정책 the wrong policy ; a mistaken (political) course // 잘못된 생각 the wrong idea ; a misjudgment // 잘못해서 by mistake // 잘못되다 go wrong〔amiss, awry〕 // 잘못을 고치다 mend one's ways // 잘못을 사과하다 apologize 《to a person》 for one's fault // 잘못에 빠지다 fall into error // 잘못을 저지르다 commit〔make〕 an error〔a mistake〕 // 잘못을 지적하다 point out an error // 잘못을 발견하다 detect errors〔mistakes〕 // 잘못을 피하다 avoid a mistake // 잘못을 되풀이하다 repeat an error // 잘못이 많다〔적다〕 be full of〔free from〕 mistakes // 사람의 잘못을 캐다 find out 《a person's》 fault // 잘못 쓰다 make a mistake in writing ; miswrite // 그것은 나의 잘못이다 It is my fault. /I am to blame for it. // 잘못이 있으면 고쳐라 Correct errors, if any. // 잘못을 타인의 탓으로 돌리지 마라 Don't put〔lay〕 the blame on another. // 잘못해서 전주행 기차를 탔다 By mistake I took a train bound for *Chŏnju*. // 저런 남자를 믿은 것이 나의 잘못이었다 It was my mistake that I trusted such a fellow. /I did wrong in trusting such a fellow. // 잘못된 일을 해 놓았다 I have done something wrong. // 그렇게 생각해도 크게 잘못은 없을 게다 We shall not greatly err if we assume so. // 그 여자를 남자로 잘못 보았다 I mistook her for a man. // 모든 일이 잘못되었다 Everything went wrong. // 그 사람의 판단에 잘못이 없다 He is infallible〔unerring〕 in his judgment. // 정부가 이런 정책을 쓰는 것은 잘못이다 It is a big mistake for the Government to adopt such a policy. // 이 작문에는 잘못이 아주 많다 This composition bristles with〔is full of〕 mistakes.

잘바당 ⇨ 철버덩

잘박 with a splash ─하다 splash ; make a splash

잘박거리다 splash ¶ 물 속을 잘박거리며 걷다 splash one's way through the water // 잘박거리며 시내를 건너다 splash across the stream

잘박잘박 with splash after splash ; splashing ¶ 잘박잘박 걷다 splash along

†잘생기다 (be) good-looking ; beautiful ; handsome ; fair ¶ 잘생긴 남자 a good-looking〔handsome〕 man // 잘생긴 여자 a beautiful〔a charming, an attractive〕 woman

잘싸닥 with a slap〔spank〕

*잘싹 with a slap ; with a spank ; with a bang ─하다 spank ; make a spanking sound ; slap ; bang ; crash ; slam ; thwack ¶ 볼기를 잘싹 치다 spank 《a person》 on the bottom // 따귀를 잘싹 갈기다 slap 《a person》 in the face

잘싹거리다 keep spanking〔slapping〕 ; bang and bang ; slam and slam

잘싹잘싹 spanking〔slapping〕 away ; banging and banging ; slamming and slamming

잘쑥거리다, 짤쑥거리다 ⇨ 절뚝거리다

잘쑥하다, 짤쑥하다 ⇨ 잘록하다

잘잘, 짤짤 [끓다] bubbling ; simmering ; seething ; boiling ; [치맛자락 따위가] dragging (on the ground) ; [쏘다니다] darting about ; going around hurriedly ; [흔들다] shaking ; jingling 《in one's hand》 ; [윤기가] (being) oily ; greasy ; glossy ; glistening ; sleek ; be well-fed ¶ 치맛자락을 잘잘 끌다 drag the

ㅈ

ends of one's skirt // 물이 잘잘 끓는다 The water is simmering. // 방바닥이 잘잘 끓는다 The floor is hot. // 그는 열이 있어 몸이 잘잘 끓는다 His body is burning with fever. // 어디를 그렇게 잘잘 돌아다니니 What are you doing, darting about so much?

잘잘거리다 ⇨ 짤짤거리다

잘잘못 right and wrong ; merits and demerits ¶ 잘잘못간에 (regardless of whether) right or wrong ; for good or (for) bad // 잘잘못을 헤아리다 discriminate the right〔good〕 from the wrong〔bad〕 // 잘잘못간에 싸울 것 없다 No matter who is right or wrong, you shouldn't quarrel.

잘카닥 ⇨ 짤까닥

잘코사니 goody-goody ¶ 잘코사니 그래싸지 Goody, goody! Serve him right.

잘크라지다 get crushed in ; wilt

잘팍 with a squish〔squash, slosh〕 **—하다** [진흙이] give a squish

잘팍거리다 [진흙이] squish and squash ; slosh away

잘팍잘팍 squishing and squashing ; sloshing away

*__잘하다__ do well〔skillfully, expertly, right, nicely〕; be skil(l)ful〔good, clever, expert〕; [자주] do a lot ; do often ¶ 잘해야 at best ; at most // 영어를 잘하다 speak English well ; be proficient in English // 계산을 잘하다 be good at figures // 말을 잘하다 be a good speaker // 요리를 잘하다 be a good cook // 피아노를 잘하다 play the piano well // 재담을 잘하다 be good at punning // 웃기를 잘하다 laugh a lot // 그가 그르고 네가 잘했다 He is wrong and you are right. // 참 잘했다 Fine! /Well done! /Bravo! /Good for you! // 잘한다 Way to go! /Good job! // 우산을 가져오길 잘했다 (It's a) good thing I brought along my umbrella. /I'm glad I brought along my umbrella.

‡__잠__ sleep ; a nap (낮잠) ; a doze (졸음) ; slumbers (선잠) ¶ 잠자는 약 a sleeping drug〔potion, pill〕 // 깊은〔얕은〕 잠 a deep〔light〕 sleep // 잠에서 깨다 awake〔start〕 from one's sleep // 잠자다 sleep ; go to sleep // 잠들다 fall asleep // 잠을 못 이루다 fail to get to sleep ; be sleepless ; be wakeful // 이 약은 잠을 오게 한다 This medicine will induce sleep. // 잠을 못 자서 머리가 아프다 I spent a restless night and now I have a headache.

낮— a nap (아침) **늦—** late rising **늦—꾸러기** a late-rising person ; a late riser ; a lie-abed ; a sleepyhead

잠결 while asleep ¶ 잠결에 in one's sleep ; while asleep // 잠결에 듣다 hear half asleep // 잠결에 「불이야」 하는 소리를 들었다 Half asleep and half awake, I heard the cry "Fire!" // 잠결에 총소리를 들었다 In my sleep I heard the sound of a rifle shot.

잠구 蠶具 sericultural equipment

잠귀 one's hearing while asleep ; one's auditory sensation in sleep ; one's wakeability ¶ 잠귀가 밝다 awake from one's sleep at the slightest noise ; sleep lightly ; be a light sleeper // 잠귀가 어둡다 sleep heavily ; be a heavy sleeper // 잠귀로 듣다 hear while one is asleep // 그는 잠귀가 밝다 He sleeps with one eye open.

*__잠그다__[1] [자물쇠를] lock ; lock up ; fasten (the lock of) ¶ 문〔서랍, 집, 방〕을 잠그다 lock a door〔drawer, house, room〕 // 쇠를 잠그다 turn a key on // 수도를 잠그다 turn off the water〔the faucet〕 // 너는 분명히 문에 자물쇠를 잠그었느냐 Are you sure you locked the door? // 차 안에 열쇠를 놔두고 문을 잠그었습니다 I'm locked out of my car.

*__잠그다__[2] [물에] immerse ; soak ; steep ; dip ; submerge ; sink ; [밑천을] invest 《money》 in a permanent holding ; sink (funds) ¶ 머리를 물 속에 잠그다 immerse〔plunge〕 one's head in the water // 스폰지를 더운 물에 잠그다 soak a sponge in hot water // 광산업에 돈을 잠그다 sink money in the mining industry

잠기다[1] lock ; be locked ; be fastened ¶ 이 문은 저절로 잠긴다 This door locks automatically. /This is a self-locking door. // 문이 잠기어 있다 This gate is locked. // 문이 잠기지 않는다 The door won't lock.

잠기다[2] ① [물 속에] sink ; be submerged 《under water》 ; go down to 《the bottom》 ¶ 물에 잠기다 sink〔dip, be submerged〕 under water // 바다 밑에 잠기다 sink to the bottom 《of the sea》 // 잠기지 않게 해두다 keep 《a thing》 afloat // 집들이 물에 잠겼다 the houses were sunk under water.

② [목이] get〔become, grow〕 hoarse〔husky, harsh〕 ¶ 잠긴 목소리 a hoarse voice // 목이 잠기도록 떠들다 talk oneself hoarse

③ [생각 따위에] be absorbed〔engrossed, immersed〕 in ; be intent〔bent〕 on ; be given to ¶ 명상에 잠기다 be lost in meditation // 공상에 잠기다 indulge in reverie ; give 《full》 indulgence to the vagaries of imagination // 아름다운 생각에 잠기면서 집으로 돌아갔다 With these sweet thoughts I went home.

④ [돈이] 《capital》 be tied down ; be sunk

*__잠깐__ (for) a little while ; (for) a moment〔minute〕; (for) some time ¶ 잠깐 있으면 in a short time // 잠깐 있다가 after a while ; in a little time // 잠깐 여유를 주십시오 Kindly wait a little longer. // 잠깐 기다리십시오 Wait a few moments, please. // 잠깐 뵐 수 있습니까 May I see you for

ㅈ

a minute? //잠깐 다녀 오겠다 I won't be gone long. //잠깐 잊어 버렸다 I forgot for the moment.

잠깨다 awake (from one's sleep) ; wake up

잠꼬대 talking in one's sleep ; sleeptalking ; [실없는 말] silly talk ; nonsense ; bosh **—하다** talk in one's sleep ; say silly things ; twaddle ; talk nonsense ; talk rubbish ; talk bosh

***잠꾸러기** a sleepyhead ; a great〔heavy〕 sleeper ; a late riser ; a lie-a-bed ; a slug-a-bed

잠동무 a bedfellow〔buddy〕

잠두 蠶豆 〖식물〗 a broad〔horse〕 bean

†**잠들다** ① [잠자다] fall〔drop〕 asleep ; drop〔go〕 off to sleep ; sink〔fall〕 into a slumber〔sleep〕 ¶ 깊이 잠들다 fall fast asleep //아기가 울다가 잠들었다 The baby cried itself to sleep.
② [사망하다] die ; pass away ; be dead ; rest ¶ 영원히 잠들다 go to one's long sleep ; take one's last sleep

잠란 蠶卵 a silkworm egg〔seed〕
—지(紙) a silkworm-egg card ; an egg card

잠망경 潛望鏡 a periscope

잠매 潛賣 an illicit sale ; black-marketing ; smuggling **—하다** sell secretly ; smuggle ; black-market(eer)

***잠바** a jacket ; a jumper
—스커트 a jumper (dress)

잠박 蠶箔 a silkworm raising〔rearing〕 basket ; a sericultural basket〔shelf〕

잠방이 farmer's knee-breeches

잠복 潛伏 concealment ; hiding ; ambush ; [병의] incubation ; latency **—하다** conceal oneself ; lie hidden ; hide 〔lurk〕 《in, under》 ; [병이] lie dormant ; be latent ¶ 시내에 잠복해 있다 be in hiding in the city ; remain in concealment in the city
— 근무(하다) (be on the) ambush (sentry) duty **—기** the period of incubation ; the latent period **—성** latency **—성 보균자** a healthy〔contact〕 carrier **—성 비타민 결핍증** a subclinical vitamin deficiency **—성 질환** a latent disease **—성 촉매** 〖화학〗 a latent catalyst **—아(芽)** 〖식물〗 a latent bud **— 장소** [범인의] a shelter ; a hideout ; an Alsatia ; [동물의] a shelter ; cover ; a blind [사냥꾼의] **— 초소** an ambush sentry box

잠비아 Zambia

잠뿍 heavily loaded ¶ 짐을 잠뿍 싣다 bear a heavy load

잠사 蠶絲 silk yarn〔thread〕
— 수출업자 조합 a silk yarn exporters' association **— 시험장** the Sericulture Experiment Station **—업** silkreeling〔sericultural〕 industry **—업법(業法)** the Sericultural Industry Act **— 전문학교** a college of sericulture

잠상 潛商 a smuggler ; a black marketeer

잠세력 潛勢力 potential energy ; latent force

****잠수 潛水** diving ; submerging ; submergence **—하다** dive ; go under water ; make a dive ; submerge
— 공작원 〖군대〗 a frogman **— 기구** an aqualung 《호흡기》 ; a diving apparatus **— 모** a diving helmet **— 모함** a submarine tender **—병** submarine sickness **—복** a diving suit〔dress〕 **—부** a diver **—시험** a diving test **—업** diving **—업자** a diving contractor **—영법** subaqueous〔underwater〕 swimming **—종(鍾)** a diving bell **—함** a submarine ¶ 잠수함으로 공격하다 submarine 《a convoy》 **—함 승무원** a submariner **—함 탐지기** an asdic ; a sonar **공격형 —함** a hunterkiller submarine **대(對) —함용 로켓 폭탄** an anti-submarine rocket (bomb) **대잠(對潛) —함** a submarine-killer submarine

†**잠시 暫時** a short while ; a (little) while ; for a (little) while ; for some time ¶ 잠시간 (for) a short while〔time〕 ; (for) a (little) while //잠시 후에 after a while ; a little later ; sometime after ; in a little time //잠시 기다려 주십시오 Please wait just for a little while.

잠식 蠶食 encroachment ; an inroad ; invasion **—하다** encroach 《upon》 ; make an inroad 《upon, into》 ; gain 《on》 ¶ 영토를 잠식하다 encroach on the territory 《of another country》 //외국의 시장을 잠식하다 make inroads into foreign markets //산은 금속을 잠식한다 The acid eats away the metal.

잠실 蠶室 a silkworm-raising〔rearing〕 room

잠아 蠶蛾 〖곤충〗 a silkworm moth (누에나방)

잠약 —藥 a sleeping drug〔medicine〕 ; [정제] a sleeping pill〔tablet〕

잠언 箴言 an aphorism ; a maxim ; an apo(ph)thegm ; 〖성경〗 the proverbs ¶ 솔로몬의 잠언 the Proverbs of Solomon

잠업 蠶業 sericulture ; the sericultural industry
— 시험장 a sericultural laboratory

잠열 潛熱 [지하의] latent heat ; [인체의] dormant temperature

***잠옷** night clothes ; pajamas ; [남자용] a night shirt ; [부인·어린이용] a night gown ; a night dress

잠입 潛入 infiltration **—하다** smuggle oneself 《into》 ; sneak〔filter, steal〕 《into》 ¶ 무장 간첩이 서울에 잠입해 있다 The armed agents have infiltrated into *Seoul*.

†**잠자다** ① [수면] sleep ; go to sleep ; fall asleep ; take a nap〔siesta〕 (낮잠) ; go to bed (취침) ¶ 잠자는 아기 a sleeping child //잠자는 약 a sleeping drug〔draught, pill〕 //잠잘 시간 time to sleep ; bedtime

(취침 시간) // 늦도록 잠자다 sleep late // 잠자지 못하고 밤을 새우다 pass a wakeful〔sleepless〕 night // 잠자지 않고 병을 간호하다 keep vigil over 《a sick child》; watch〔sit up〕 with 《an invalid》// 노천에서 잠자다 sleep in the open air // 잠 좀 자라구 Get some sleep.
② [이불·머리 따위가] be pressed down; be smoothed down; be compressed ¶ 이불 솜이 잠자다 The cotton of the quilt is well set. // 머리가 잠자다 My hair got nicely set〔took a nice set〕.

*잠자리¹ a dragonfly
—과(科) Libelluidae —목(目) Odonata 고추 — a red dragonfly

잠자리² a sleeping place; a bed; bedding; [동침] sleeping together; sharing the same bed 《with》 ¶ 잠자리를 펴다 make a bed // 잠자리를 걷다 put away bedding // 잠자리에 들다 go to bed; turn in 《구》// 잠자리에서 일어나다 get out of bed // 잠자리에서 책을 읽다 read in bed // 잠자리를 같이하다 sleep together; share the same bed 《with》// 그는 집에 도착하자마자 일찍 잠자리에 들었다 As soon as he got home, he went out like a light.

*잠자코 without a word; in silence; [이의 없이] without objection; obediently; [무단] without leave; without notice ¶ 잠자코 있다 keep silence〔mum〕; keep one's mouth shut; say nothing at all // 잠자코 서 있다 be standing in silence // 잠자코 가버리다 go away without a word〔saying anything〕// 잠자코 바라보다 stand by (방관) // 잠자코 시키는 대로 하다 be ordered about without a show of resistance (무저항) // 잠자코 하라는 대로 하라 Do as I tell you without question. // 이 일에 대해서는 잠자코 있어라 Keep quiet〔mum〕 about this. // 왜 그 일을 잠자코 있었니 Why have you kept it from me? // 잠자코 있어라 Silence! /Shut up! /Cut it out! 《미·구》/Keep your mouth shut! // 그의 무례한 짓을 이 이상 잠자코 있을 수 없다 I cannot stand〔put up with〕 his insolence any longer.

*잠잠하다 (be) quiet; still; deserted ¶ 잠잠하게 quietly // 거리는 잠잠하다 All is quiet in the street. / The street looks deserted.

*잠재 潛在 latency; dormancy; potentiality —하다 be〔lie〕 latent〔dormant〕; lie hidden ¶ 잠재적 latent; dormant; subconscious; potential
— 구매력 latent purchasing power — 능력 latent faculties —력 potential energy ¶ 잠재력을 발달시키다 develop the powers latent within one — 세력 potentia〔latent〕 power — 수요 potential demand — 실업 latent〔potential, invisible〕 unemployment — 실업자 the potential〔latent, invisible〕 unemployed — 의식 subconsciousness; coconsciousness (부의식) — 의식적 subconscious — 자아(自我) the subliminal self — 자원 potential resources — 전력 war potentials — 주권 residual sovereignty 성욕 —기 a latency period

잠재우다 ⇨ 재우다[1,2]

잠적 潛跡 concealing oneself —하다 disappear; hide〔efface〕 oneself; get out of sight; vanish; cover one's traces

잠정 暫定 ¶ 잠정의 provisional; tentative; temporary // 잠정적 합의 a provisional agreement // 잠정적으로 provisionally; tentatively; temporarily; for the time being // 잠정 조치를 취하다 take tentative measures〔steps〕
— 내각 a caretaker cabinet; a stopgap government —안 a tentative plan — 예산 a provisional budget — 임금 변경 an interim wage change — 조약 a provisional treaty — 조치 a temporary step; an interim〔a stopgap, a tentative〕 measure — 협정 〖외교〗 a protocol; a temporary〔a tentative, a working, an interim〕 agreement

잠종 簪種 silkworm eggs
— 개량 silkworm species improvement

잠지 a baby's penis

잠지 蠶紙 a silkworm-egg card

잠투세 a baby's peevishness before〔after〕 sleep —하다 get peevish〔fret〕 before〔after〕 sleep ¶ 이 아이는 잘 때마다 잠투세를 한다 This baby is always fighting sleep.

잠투정 ⇨ 잠투세

잠포록하다 it is cloudy and still〔windless, calm〕

잠함 a caisson; a pontoon
— 공법 the caisson method —병 caisson〔diver's〕 disease; the bends 《미·구》 목조 — a wood pneumatic caisson

잠항 潛航 submarine voyage; navigation under water —하다 dive〔move, navigate〕 under water ¶ 잠항 신기록을 세우다 make〔create〕 a new immersion record of 《60 hours》
— 어뢰 a submarine torpedo — 시간 underwater time —정 a submarine —정 방어망 an anti-submarine net

잠행 潛行 traveling in disguise —하다 travel incognito〔in disguise〕 ¶ 잠행적 활동 underground activities // 지하에 잠행하다 go underground

잡가 雜歌 vulgar songs; a folk song (민요)

잡감 雜感 miscellaneous thoughts〔impressions〕 《of》

잡거 雜居 mixed residence〔living〕 —하다 live〔reside, dwell〕 together
— 구금(拘禁) imprisonment without solitary confinement —지 a mixed-residence quarter —화 a polygamous flower

잡건 雜件 miscellaneous matters〔affairs, items〕; the miscellanies; sundries

ㅈ

잡것 雜— [사물] miscellaneous things ; odds and ends ; miscellaneous junk ; [사람] a low〔vulgar〕 fellow ; a churl ; a menial ; a cad ; a ribald ; a yahoo ; rag-tag (and bobtail)

잡계정 雜計定 〖부기〗 sundry〔miscellaneous〕 accounts ; miscellaneous credits (대변) ; miscellaneous debts (차변)

잡곡 雜穀 (miscellaneous) cereals ; minor grains〔cereals〕 ; corn

— 도매상 a corn factor ; grain broker 《미》 **—밥** boiled rice and cereals **—상** a dealer in cereals ; a corn merchant 〔dealer, chandler〕

잡교 雜交 〖생물〗 (inter) crossing

잡귀 雜鬼 fiends ; demons ; evil spirits ; sundry evil spirits

잡균 雜菌 various〔sundry〕 germs〔bacteria, bacilli〕

잡급 雜給 sundry payments ; miscellaneous allowances

잡기 雜技 miscellaneous games ; [노름] gambling

—꾼 a gambler **—판** a gambling place ; a gaming house

잡기 雜記 miscellaneous notes ; miscellanies

—장 a notebook ; an exercise book

잡낭 雜囊 a haversack ; a provision bag ; 〖군사〗 a duffel〔duffle〕 bag

잡년 雜— a loose woman ; a slattern ; a slut ¶ 이 잡년아 You slut !

잡념 雜念 worldly〔earthly〕 thoughts ¶ 잡념을 버리다 dismiss〔banish〕 worldly thoughts from one's mind

잡놈 雜— a low〔vulgar〕 fellow ; a churl ; a cad ; a ribald ; a yahoo

ㅈ

***잡다**[1] ① [손으로] catch ; get ; take ; [쥐다] seize ; hold ; take hold of ; grasp ; grip ; clutch ¶ 공을 잡다 catch a ball // 멱살을 잡다 seize 《a person》 by the neck 〔breast of his coat〕 // 손을 잡다 take 《a person》 by the hand ; grasp 《a person's》 hand // 팔을 잡다 seize〔hold〕 《a person》 by the arm // 잡으려고 손을 내밀다 reach for 《a thing》 // 날아가는 공을 잡다 make a snatch at a flying ball // 꼭 잡고 놓지 마라 Don't release〔let go〕 your hold〔grip〕 on it. // 다치지 않도록 손잡이를 잡는게 좋다 Better hold on to the strap so you don't get hurt. // 이 여행 가방을 바꾸어 잡을게요 Let me change my grip on this suitcase.

② [체포] catch ; arrest ; seize ; capture ; [포획] catch ; get ; take ; seize ¶ 도둑을 잡다 catch〔seize, arrest〕 a thief // 새를 잡다 catch a bird // 고기를 잡으러 가다 go fishing // 적병을 잡다 capture an enemy (soldier)

③ [권력·기회 따위를] take ; seize ; assume ; wield ¶ 기회를 잡다 seize upon an opportunity // 돈을 잡다 come into money // 정권을 잡다 come into〔be in〕 power // 권력을 잡고 있다 have power

④ [담보로] hold 《a thing》 in pawn〔on mortgage〕 ; take 《a thing》 on security 〔mortgage〕 ¶ 저당 잡고 on mortgage // 저당을 잡고 돈을 꾸어주다 lend money on security〔mortgage〕 // 자동차를 잡고 돈을 꾸어 주다 lend money on a car // 집을 저당으로 잡고 있다 hold a mortgage on a house

⑤ [결정] fix ; decide ; settle ; determine ; [선정] choose ; [예약] reserve ; book ¶ 골라 잡다 choose〔pick up, select〕 《a thing》 // 날짜를 잡다 fix the date 《for》 // 일자리를 잡다 get a job ; find a position ; obtain employment // 여관에 방을 잡다 get a room at a hotel // 극장에 자리를 잡아 두다 reserve a seat at a theater

⑥ [결점을] find 《fault》 ; pick〔point〕 out 《a person's defects》 ; look for 《a fault》 ¶ 물건의 흠을 잡다 pick a hole in an article // 사람의 흠을 잡다 find fault with 《a person》 // 말트집을 잡다 find fault with 《a person's》 remark // 약점을 잡다 hold a sword over 《a person's》 head ; take advantage of 《a person's》 shortcomings

⑦ [기타] ¶ (논에) 물을 잡다 conduct water ; irrigate // 실증을 잡다 get〔have〕 a positive proof // 장소를 잡다 occupy 〔take up〕 much room〔space〕 // 좋은 자리를 잡다 secure a good place // 초를 잡다 draft ; draw the outlines ; sketch // 택시 잡느라고 혼났다 I had a heck of a time flagging down a cab.

잡다[2] [요량] estimate〔put〕 《the expenses》 at 《500 thousand *won*》 ; make an estimate 《of》 ; compute 《one's losses》 at 《20 million *won*》 ¶ 줄 잡아서 at a rough estimate // 최대한으로 잡아서 at the highest estimate ; at most // 최소한으로 잡아서 at the lowest estimate ; at least // 지나치게 많이 잡다 overestimate // 지나치게 적게 잡다 underestimate

잡다[3] ① [죽이다] butcher ; kill 《animals》 ; slaughter ¶ 돼지를 잡다 butcher a hog

② [모함] plot against 《a person》 ; slander ; ensnare ; entrap ¶ 사람 잡을 소리 그만해 Stop slandering me.

③ [불을] put out〔extinguish〕 《a fire》 ; get〔put, bring〕 《a fire》 under control ¶ 물〔모래〕로 불을 잡다 quench a fire with water〔sand〕

④ [마음을] get a grip on oneself ; steady 《one's mind》 ; settle down ; hold 〔get, put〕 《one's passion》 under control ; collect〔calm〕 oneself ¶ 들뜬 마음을 잡다 hold the rein over one's mind ; keep a firm hand on oneself // 마음을 잡고 공부하다 study in a settled frame of mind〔with concentration〕

잡다[4] ① [굽은 것을] make straight ; straighten out〔up〕 ; unbend ¶ 굽은 바늘

을 (바로) 잡다 make a bent needle straight // 굽은 화살을 (바로) 잡다 straighten out a bent arrow
② [주름을] make ((a crease)) ; fold 〔arrange〕 ((in pleats)) ¶ 바지에 주름을 잡다 crease trousers // 치마에 주름을 잡다 pleat〔shirr〕 a skirt

*잡다 雜多 —하다 (be) miscellaneous ; various ; sundry

*잡담 雜談 gossip ; small talk ; chit-chat ; idle〔empty〕 talk —하다 gossip((with a person about a thing)) ; chat ((with)) ; have an idle talk ; have a chat ((with)) ; chatter ; have a chin ((미·구)) ¶ 잡담으로 시간을 보내다 pass time gossiping〔in small talk〕 // 나는 그와 얼마 동안 잡담을 했다 I had a chat with him for some time. // 일 이야기는 곧 끝났지만 잡담이 길어졌다 Our talk about work was over in no time, but then we got caught up in small talk.
우물가 — kitchen gossip ; backfence talk ((속))

잡답 雜沓 bustle ; congestion ; throng ; crowdedness —하다 be crowded 〔thronged, congested〕 ((with people)) ; be bustling〔full of bustle〕 ¶ 잡답한 거리 a crowded〔thronged, bustling〕 street // 잡답한 시간 the rush hour(s) // 왕래가 잡답하다 The street is busy with traffic. / The street is congested. / There is much traffic in the street.

잡도리 supervision ; management ; control —하다 supervise ; superintend ; oversee ; take care of

*잡동사니 various things ; all sorts of things ; miscellaneous articles ; sundries ; odds and ends ¶ 그런 잡동사니들을 너저분하게 모아 어찌 할건가 Just what do you plan to do with that assortment of junk you've collected?

잡되다 雜— [천하다] (be) vulgar ; low ; mean ; coarse ; crude ; indecent ; [부정하다] wanton ; lewd ; licentious ¶ 잡된 사람 a low〔vulgar〕 fellow // 잡된 생각 wanton〔slovenly, indecent〕 thoughts

잡록 雜錄 a miscellany ; miscellaneous records

잡말 雜— dirty talk ⇨ 잡소리

잡맛 雜— an impure taste ; a taste other than the original

잡매다 ⇨ 잡아매다

잡목 雜木 miscellaneous〔inferior〕 wood ; scrubs
—림 a thicket of assorted trees ; a copse ; a coppice

잡무 雜務 miscellaneous〔odd〕 business 〔duties〕 ; routine work ; sundry duties ; odds and ends to do ¶ 신변의 잡무 miscellaneous personal affairs // 잡무에 몰리다 be pressed with routine work // 잡무에 바쁘다 be busy with this and that

잡문 雜文 a literary medley〔miscellany〕 ; miscellanies ; miscellanea ; [수필] an essay
—가 a miscellanist

잡물 雜物 [불순물] impurities ; foreign matters〔ingredients〕 ; [잡다한 물건] miscellaneous things〔articles〕 ; sundries ; miscellany

잡박 雜駁 confusion ; medley ; disunity ; looseness ; incoherence —하다 be in confusion ; lack unity〔organization〕 ; (be) loose ; desultory ; slipshod ¶ 잡박한 생각 loose ideas // 잡박한 의론 a loose argument // 잡박한 지식 unsystematic 〔scrappy〕 knowledge

잡배 雜輩 a low fellow ; vulgar people ; small fry ; the ruck ; the ragtag and bobtail

잡병 雜病 various diseases

잡보 雜報 general〔miscellaneous〕 news ; sundry reports ; miscellaneous paragraphs
—난 the general-news column(s)

잡부 雜夫 an odd(-job) 〔a handy〕 man ⇨ 잡역부(雜役夫)

잡부금 雜賦金 miscellaneous fees ¶ 잡부금을 일소하다 prohibit the collection of miscellaneous fees

잡비 雜費 miscellaneous〔sundry, incidental〕 expenses ; incidentals ; sundries ¶ 잡비를 덜다 exclude the incidental expenses // 잡비가 꽤 많이 든다 Sundries come up to a considerable amount.
— 계정 a petty expenses account

잡사 雜事 miscellaneous affairs

잡살뱅이 odds and ends ; odd-come-shorts ; lumber ; junk ((미·구)) ; a jumble ; a medley

잡살전 —廛 a seed(s) store

잡상스럽다 雜常— [음탕] (be) lewd ; lecherous ; licentious ; wanton ; obscene ; [상스럽다] vulgar ; low ; mean ; base ; indecent ; sordid ; gross ¶ 그녀의 거동은 숙녀로서 너무 잡상스럽다 Her manners are too gross for a lady.

잡상인 雜商人 merchants〔tradesmen〕 of all kinds ; miscellaneous〔various〕 merchants〔traders〕 ¶ 잡상인 금지 No soliciting.

잡색 雜色 [빛깔] various colors ; variegation ; [사람] all kinds of people ; a motley crew ¶ 잡색의 parti-colored ; variegated ; varicolored ; motley

잡생 雜生 promiscuous growth —하다 grow promiscuously

잡서 雜書 miscellaneous books ; a book on miscellaneous subjects

잡석 雜石 [소용이 적은 돌] stones of little use ; [허드렛돌] riprap ; rubble ; broken stones

잡설 雜說 idle talk ⇨ 잡소리

잡세 雜稅 miscellaneous〔sundry, various〕 taxes

잡소리 雜— [외설한] obscene〔dirty〕

ㅈ

talk ; foul〔indecent, broad〕 talk ; smut ; [잡담] useless〔idle〕 talk ; prattle ; nonsense

잡손질 雜— idle fingering ; useless touching ; playing〔idling〕 with one's fingers ; unnecessary work〔handling〕 **—하 다** play with one's fingers

잡수당 雜手當 miscellaneous allowances

잡수입 雜收入 miscellaneous income 〔revenue〕 ; sundry receipts

잡술 雜術 witchcraft ; trickery

잡숫다 ① [먹다의 공대어] eat ; drink ; have ; partake 《of》 ¶ 많이 잡수시오 Help yourself, please. ② [제사를] perform an ancestor-memorial service

잡스럽다 雜— (be) indecent ; loose ; wanton

잡식 雜食 a mixed diet ; polyphagia **—하다** live on a mixed diet ; be omnivorous ¶ 잡식의 omnivorous ; polyphagous **—성** polyphagia **—성 동물** a polyphagous animal ; an omnivore

잡신 雜神 evil spirits ⇨ 잡귀

잡심 雜心 worldly thoughts ⇨ 잡념

잡아가다 take〔walk〕 《a suspect to a police station》 ; haul〔bring〕 《a person》 before 《a police authority》

잡아내다 [결점 따위] point out 《mistakes》 ; pick at 《flaws》 ; criticize 《shortcomings》 ; [밖으로] throw 《a person》 out 《of the door》 ; pull out

†**잡아당기다** [끌다] pull ; draw ; tug ; stretch (팽팽하게) ; pull back (뒤로) ; jerk (갑자기) ¶ 귀를 잡아당기다 pull 《a person》 by the ear // 홱 잡아당기다 pull with a jerk // 밧줄을 홱 잡아당기다 give the rope a jerk // 그 장난꾸러기가 고양이 꼬리를 잡아당겼다 The naughty boy pulled the cat by the tail. // 나무꾼들이 무거운 통나무를 쇠사슬로 잡아당겼다 The woodsmen dragged the heavy log by a chain. // 잭은 제인의 땋은 머리를 쭉 잡아당겼다 Jack yanked Jane's pigtail.

잡아들이다 drag〔draw〕 in〔into〕 ; bring 〔talk〕 in ; arrest ; imprison ¶ 도둑을 잡아들이다 arrest〔catch, capture〕 a thief

†**잡아떼다** ① [손으로] pull〔set〕 《a thing》 apart ; take off ¶ 의자의 다리를 잡아떼다 take a leg off a chair
② [모른다고] feign〔pretend〕 ignorance〔to be ignorant〕 ; play the innocent ; brazen〔face〕 《it》 out ; dissemble ; put a bold face 《on a matter》 ¶ 아무리 물어봐도 모른다고 잡아뗐다 However much I asked, he persisted in feigning ignorance.

*****잡아매다** tie up ; bind ; fasten ¶ 책을 한데 잡아매다 tie books up in a bundle ; bundle up books

잡아먹다 ① [먹다] slaughter and eat ; butcher and eat ; devour (짐승이) ¶ 잡아 먹느냐 잡아먹히느냐의 싸움 a life and death struggle ; a war of survival // 뱀은 개구리나 쥐를 잡아먹고 산다 The snake lives on frogs, mice, and rats. // 뱀은 개구리를 잡아먹는다 Snakes prey on frogs. ② [괴롭히다] torment ; torture ¶ 그는 나를 잡아먹을 듯이 야단이다 He is needling me all the time. // 그는 나를 잡아먹지 못해 야단이다 He has it in for me.

잡아뽑다 pluck〔pick, pull, tear〕 (off) ¶ 머리를 잡아뽑다 tear〔rend〕 one's hair // 새의 털을 잡아뽑다 pick〔pluck〕 a fowl ; pick feathers from a fowl // 풀을 잡아뽑다 pluck up weeds ; weed 《a garden》

잡아찢다 tear off ; rend ; rip ; pull up

잡아채다 snatch〔switch〕 (away) 《something》 from〔out of〕 《a person's hand》 ; twitch ; wrest 《from》 ; take by force ; strip 《a person》 of 《a thing》

잡어 雜魚 small fish ; small〔lesser, young〕 fry

잡역 雜役 miscellaneous〔sundry〕 services ; odd jobs ; chores 《미》 ; 〖군사〗 fatigue duty
—부(夫) an odd (job) man ; a handy man **—부(婦)** a maid-of-all-work ; a charwoman (날품팔이)

잡용 雜用 sundry expenses ; sundry uses

잡은것 〖광산〗 mining tools

잡을손 뜨다 be lazy〔slow, sluggish〕 in one's work ; (be) slow-handed

‡**잡음 雜音** noises ; [라디오의] static ; jarring and grating ; jamming ; [이의] dissenting voices ; objections ¶ 도시의 잡음 city noises // 라디오에서 잡음이 난다 The radio program is interrupted by static. /The radio is affected by static. // 우리 전화기는 잡음이 많이 난다 My phone has lots of static.

잡음씨 〖문법〗 a copula

잡이 a note ; a guide (지침) ; remarks (for reference)

잡인 雜人 an outsider

잡일 雜— miscellaneous affairs ; chores (일상의) 《미》

잡제 雜題 [문제] miscellaneous problems ; [제재(題材)] miscellaneous subjects〔themes〕

잡종 雜種 a cross ; a hybrid ; a half breed ; a mixed breed ; a mongrel ¶ 잡종의 cross〔half〕-bred ; hybrid ; miscellaneous // 잡종의 말 a crossbred horse // 잡종의 개 a mongrel (dog) // 잡종을 만들다 cross 《one breed》 with 《another》 ; cross 《two breeds》 ; interbreed ; hybridize // 너의 개는 순종이니 잡종이니 Is your dog a purebred or a mutt?
— 강세 〖생물〗 heterosis ; hybrid vigor **—개** a mongrel (dog) **—말** a crossbred horse **—성** hybridity **—세(稅)** miscellaneous local taxes **— 제 1 대** the first filial generation

잡좆 a furrow-depth adjuster (of a plough)

잡죄다 ① [잡도리하다] supervise ; super-

intend ; oversee ; take care of
② [독촉하다] hurry ; rush ; hasten
잡증 雜症 complications (in an illness)
†**잡지 雜誌** a magazine ; [전문적] a journal ; [정기 간행물] a periodical ¶ 잡지를 구독하다 take (in) a magazine ; subscribe for〔to〕 a magazine // 잡지를 편집하다 edit a magazine // 잡지에 기고하다 write for a magazine // 이것은 과학 잡지이다 The magazine is devoted to science.
— **기사** a magazine article — **기자** a magazine writer — **진열 선반** a periodical〔magazine〕 rack — **편집자** a magazine editor **경제** — an economics magazine **계간** — a quarterly (magazine) **고급** — a quality magazine **대중〔여성〕** — a popular〔woman's〕 magazine **동창회** — an alumni bulletin **문예〔종합〕** — a literary〔general〕 magazine **문학** — a literary journal **상업** — a commercial journal **소년·소녀** — a teen-age magazine **월간〔주간〕** — a monthly〔weekly〕 magazine **월 2회 발행** — a fortnightly ; a bimonthly magazine **의학** — a medical journal **지방** — a local magazine **평론** — a review **학술** — a learned journal
잡지출 雜支出 miscellaneous〔sundry〕 expenditures〔disbursements〕
잡차래 boiled oddments of beef
잡채 雜菜 a mixed dish of vegetables and beef
‡**잡초 雜草** weeds ; coarse〔weedy〕 grass ¶ 잡초가 우거진 weedy 《yard》 ; weed-grown〔-infected〕 ; 《a garden》 rank with weeds // 잡초를 뽑다 weed 《a garden》 // 마당에 잡초가 우거졌다 Weeds have overrun the garden.
— **제거기** a weeder —**밭** a place overgrown with weeds
***잡치다** spoil ; mar ; ruin ; hurt ; make a mess〔muddle〕 of ; upset 《the applecart》 ¶ 기분을 잡치다 hurt 《a person's》 feeling ; offend 《a person》 // 계획을 잡치다 upset 《a person's》 plan // 입맛을 잡치다 spoil 《a person's》 appetite // 졸렬한 식자로 원문을 잡치다 mangle a text by poor typesetting // 흥을 잡치다 spoil 《a person's》 pleasure // 그 사고로 우리 예정을 잡쳤다 The accident messed up our schedule. // 비가 와서 휴일을 잡쳤다 The rain spoiled my holiday. // 단 한번 실수로 그의 일생을 잡쳤다 Just a single failure ruined his life.
잡칙 雜則 miscellaneous rules〔regulations〕
잡탕 雜湯 ① [음식] a hotchpotch〔hodgepodge〕 ; a porridge of rice and vegetables ② [뒤범벅] a medley ; a hotchpotch ; a jumble ; a melange ; a muddle ¶ 잡탕의 medley ; mixed ; promiscuous // 잡탕의 책 an odd collection of books // 잡탕이 되다 be jumbled together ; be mixed up

—**밥** rice mixed with fish and vegetables
잡풀 雜— weeds ⇨ 잡초
잡품 雜品 miscellaneous articles ; sundries
잡혼 雜婚 a mixed marriage ; a promiscuous marriage ; an intermarriage —**하다** intermarry ¶ 흑백 인종의 잡혼 white and black intermarriage
— **번식** 〖생물〗 panmixia —**제** promiscuity
잡화 雜貨 miscellaneous〔sundry〕 goods ; sundries ; general merchandise ; [식료잡화] grocery ; [선하의] general cargo ¶ 잡화를 적재하고 with a cargo of general merchandise ; with a general cargo
—**상** a grocery business ; [사람] a general dealer ; a grocer ¶ 잡화상을 경영하다 be in the grocery line —**점** a general shop〔store〕 ; a grocery (store) ; a grocer's ; a variety shop〔store〕 ; a notions counter
***잡히다¹** ① [손에] be caught〔arrested, seized, taken up〕 ; fall into the hands of ¶ 경관에게 잡히다 be caught〔nabbed〕 by the police // 포로로 잡히다 be taken captive // 새가 한 마리 잡혔다 A bird was caught. // 속도 위반으로 잡혔다 I got caught speeding.
② [담보로] put〔give〕 《a thing》 in〔at〕 pawn ; have 《a thing》 taken as security ; pawn〔mortgage〕 《a thing》 ¶ 그 집은 800만원에 저당잡혀 있다 The house is mortgaged for 8,000,000 *won*.
③ [결점·흉을] have 《a weakness》 discovered ; be taken advantage of ; have to listen to complaints about 《one's shortcomings》 ¶ 사람에게 흉을 잡히다 be spoken ill of ; be cavilled at ; have 《something》 harped on // 사람에게 흠을 잡히다 have one's weakness found out by 《a person》 ; have 《a person》 take advantage of one's shortcomings
④ [기타] ¶ 물이 잡히다 water is held // 모양이 잡히다 take a form // 균형이 잡히다 be well-balanced // 시내는 다시 질서가 잡혔다 Order was restored to the city.
잡히다² [도조가] get estimated at ; be rated ¶ 도조가 30섬 잡혔다 The farm rent is rated at thirty bushels in kind.
잡히다³ ① [모해에] fall into 《a person's scheme, plot》 ; get trapped ; be maneuvered into ; get taken in ¶ 남의 꾀에 잡히다 be caught〔taken in〕 by 《a person's》 scheme ; play into the hands of a person
② [불이] 《a fire》 be held〔put, brought〕 under control ; be quenched ; be extinguished
③ [마음이] 《one's mind》 turn steady ; settle down ; 《one's passion》 be held〔put〕 under control
잡히다⁴ ① [굽은 것이] get〔be〕 straightened out〔up〕 ; be made straight
② [주름이] get〔be〕 creased〔pleated〕 ;

ㅈ

get〔be〕 wrinkled ¶ 주름이 잘 잡힌 바지 well creased trousers // 주름이 잘 잡힌 치마 a well pleated skirt // 이마에 주름이 잡히다 have wrinkles on one's forehead

잡힐손 handiness ; serviceableness ¶ 잡힐손 있는 사람 a serviceable person ; a handy man ; a Jack of all trades

잣 pine-nuts ; Pinus koraiensis (학명)
—가루 ground〔chopped〕 pine-nuts **—기름** pine-nut oil **—나무** a big cone pine ; a Korean white pine ; Pinus pentaphylla (학명) **—송진** pine sap〔resin〕

잣눈[1] scale ; graduation

잣눈[2] [눈] a foot-deep snow

‡**잣다** ① [물을] pump up ; suck up ; draw up ② [실을] spin ¶ 목화를 자아 실을 만들다 spin cotton into yarn // 목화에서 실을 자아 내다 spin thread out of cotton

잣박산 a honey cake of rice flavored with pine nuts

잣새 〖새〗 a crossbill ; Loxia curvirostra (학명)

잣송이 a pine cone (containing nuts)

잣엿 pine-nut taffy

잣죽 —粥 a gruel made of rice and pine-nuts

잣징 a tiny〔small〕 hobnail

장 [게딱지 속의] crab-spawn ; tomalley ; lobster liver

장 帳 a curtain ; a tent

†**장 長** ① [우두머리] the head ; the chief ; the chieftain ; the boss 《미》 ; the director ; the chairman ; the commander (사령관) ¶ 한 집안의 장 the head of a family // 만물의 장 the lord of all creation // 그는 남의 장이 될 그릇이 못된다 He is not competent to lead 〔stand above〕 others.
② [장점] a merit ; a strong〔good〕 point ; an advantage ¶ 장을 취하고 단을 보충하다 adopt another's strength and overcome one's weakness // 일장 일단이 있다 Each merit has its demerit. /Each advantage has its own disadvantage.

장 將 a general ; a commander ; [지도자] a leader ¶ 일군의 장 a commander of an army // 장이 되다 take command 《of an army》 ; take the leadership

†**장 張** a leaf 《of a book》 ; a sheet 《of paper》 ; a piece 《of paper》 ; a page ¶ 오십 원짜리 우표 두장 two fifty-*won* stamps // 책을 한장 한장 넘기다 turn over the leaves of a book

†**장 章** [책의] a chapter ; [기장] a sign ; a mark ; a badge ; an emblem ; [인장] a seal ¶ 제 1 장 the first chapter ; Chapter I // 한국에 관한 장 the chapter on Korea // 이 책의 문학 비평의 장은 특히 재미 있다 The chapter of literary criticism in this book is particularly interesting. // 100달러짜리 두 장, 50달러짜리 다섯 장, 그리고 20달러짜리 열 장 주십시오 Give me two hundreds, five fifties and ten twenties, please.

†**장**[1] **場** a market ; a fair (정기적인) ¶ 장날 a market〔fair〕 day // 장 보러 가다 go to market // 장에 물건을 내다 take commodities to market // 다음 장은 10일에 선다〔열리다〕 The next market is on the 10th. // 어디에서 주로 장을 보십니까 Where do you usually go grocery shopping ?
장이 서다〔열리다〕 관용 A fair is held.

장[2] **場** [장소] a place ; a ground ; a track ; a field ; [공간] room ; space ; [연극의] a scene ; [물리에서] a field ¶ 골프장 a golf links // 제 3 장 the third scene ; scene Ⅲ // 자장(磁場) the magnetic field

장 腸 the intestines ; the bowels ; the entrails ¶ 장의 intestinal ; enteric // 장이 나쁘다 have a bowel trouble ; have weak intestines
—병(病) a bowel disease ; an intestinal trouble **—통(痛)** a pain in the intestines **대(소)—** the large〔small〕 intestine

장 醬 [간장] soy ; soy sauce ; soya ; [간장과 된장] soy and bean paste ¶ 내 손에 장을 지지겠다 I'll eat my hat.

장 欌 a wardrobe ; a chest of drawers ; a cabinet ; a closet ; a cage
새— a bird cage **옷—** a wardrobe ; a chest of drawers

장 臟 the five vital organs of the body 《heart, liver, lungs, kidney, spleen》 ; the vitals ; the viscera ; the internal organs

-장 丈 [척도] a measure of length 《10 *ja*》 ; [존칭] an esteemed elder ¶ 노인장 an elderly person // 춘부장 your venerable father

-장 狀 a letter
소개— a letter of introduction **초대—** a letter of invitation ; an invitation **추천—** a letter of recommendation

장가 [결혼] a marriage ; a wedding ; taking a wife ; getting a bride ; [집] the bride's house ¶ 장가들다 marry ; get married ; take a wife // 장가들이다 marry 《a son》 to a woman ; get 《a son》 married // 장가들었느냐 Are you married ? / Do you have a wife ?

장가 長歌 a long poem〔song〕

장가처 —妻 one's legal wife ; one's first wife

†**장갑 掌匣** 《a pair of》 gloves ; 《a pair of》 mittens (벙어리 장갑) ; a muffle (권투용) ; a gauntlet (승마·크리켓용) ¶ 장갑을 끼다〔벗다〕 put on〔take off〕 one's gloves ; pull on〔off〕 one's gloves // 장갑을 낀 채 악수하다 shake hands 《with a person》 with one's gloves on

장갑 裝甲 armor ; an armor plate **—하다** armor ; arm ¶ 장갑한 armored ; ironclad
— 부대 an armored corps ; a panzer (division) **— 사단** a panzer division —

순양함 an armored cruiser — 자동차〔열차〕 an armored (motor) car〔train〕 —판 an armor plate — 포대 an armed 〔armored〕 battery —함 a cuirassed〔an armored〕 ship
장강 長江 a long river
장거 壯擧 a great〔fine〕 undertaking ; a daring enterprise ; a heroic attempt ; a brilliant scheme ¶ 세계 일주 비행의 장거 the grand project of a round-the-world flight
장거리 場— a market street
*장거리 長距離 a long distance ; a long range
— 경주 a long-distance race ; a cross-country race — 버스 a long-distance (touring) coach — 비행 a long-distance flight — 선수 a (long-) distance runner — 전화 a long-distance call〔telephone〕 — 전화료 the rates for long-distance calls — 탄도탄 a long-range ballistic missile —포 a long-range gun — 폭격기 a long range bomber
장검 長劍 a long sword
장결석 腸結石 『의학』 enterolite
장결핵 腸結核 『의학』 intestinal tuberculosis
장경 長徑 [타원의] the major axis
장경성 長庚星 『천문』 the evening star ; the Hesperus
장골 壯骨 a muscular man ; stout-built physique
장공 長空 the vast sky
⁑장과 漿果 『식물』 a berry
†장관 壯觀 a grand sight ; a magnificent 〔marvelous〕 spectacle ; a spectacular sight ; grandeur ; splendor ; imposing spectacle ¶ 나이아가라 폭포의 장관 the grand panorama of Niagara Falls // 장관을 이루다 present a grand sight〔a magnificent spectacle〕 // 천하의 장관이다 be one of the grandest sights imaginable
†장관 長官 a minister ; a Cabinet minister ; a Cabinet member ; a Secretary (미국의) ; [우두머리] a chief ; a head ; a governor ¶ 장관이 되다 become a minister
국무 — the Secretary of State 《미》 국방〔외무〕 — the Minister of Defense 〔Foreign Affairs〕 교육부 — the Minister of Education 지방 — a provincial governor
장관 將官 [육군] a general (officer) ; [해군] a flag officer ; an admiral
장관 腸管 『해부』 the intestinal tract
장광 長廣 length and width
—설 a long-winded talk ; a mighty tongue ¶ 장광설을 늘어놓다 make 〔deliver〕 a long(-winded) speech ; harangue —창 a large, elongated window for light in a warehouse
†장교 將校 an officer ; a commissioned officer ¶ 장교와 사병 officers and men
—단 an officer corps — 식당 an officers' mess hall 고급 — a high-ranking officer 사병 출신 — a commissioned officer promoted〔risen〕 from the ranks ; a ranker 육〔해〕군 — a military〔naval〕 officer
장구 *a Changku* ; a double-headed drum pinched in at the middle ; a drum shaped like an hourglass
— 대가리 a long protruding head ; a person with a long protruding head — 매듭 a kind of slipknot
장구 長久 a long period of time ; a long time ; eternity —하다 (be) long (-ranged) ; lasting ; be of long standing ¶ 장구지계 a long-run〔far-reaching〕 plan ; a perpetual policy // 장구한 시일이 지난후 after the lapse of many a year // 장구한 시일을 요하다 require a long period of time // 무운 장구를 빌다 wish 《a person》 good luck in war
장구 葬具 articles used at funerals ; funeral necessaries〔items〕 ; a funeral outfit
장구 長驅 riding far on horseback ; pursuing the enemy a great distance ; a long march ; a long drive —하다 ride a great distance ; make a long drive ; pursue the enemy a great distance
장구 長軀 tall stature ; towering height
장구 裝具 [사람의] an outfit ; equipment ; accouterments ; [말의] harness ; trappings ; [화장 도구] a toilet set
장구 章句 the chapter and verse ; a passage
장구벌레 a mosquito larva 《*pl.* -vae》
장구채 ① a *changku* drumstick ② 『식물』 Melandrium firmum (학명)
장국 醬— [맑은 국] clear soup ; [간장을 탄] soup flavored with soy (sauce)
—밥 rice served in beef soup
장군 an earthenware jar
장군 將軍 a general ; [장기의] "check" in chess
장군목 將軍木 a crossbar of a palace gate
장군풀 『식물』 a kind of medicinal rhubarb plant ; Rheum coreanum (학명)
장궁 長弓 a bow covered with horn
장궤양 腸潰瘍 『의학』 an intestinal ulcer
장귀틀 長— 『건축』 a main prop under floor boards
장금 場— the market price ¶ 장금이 오르다〔내리다〕 The market rises〔falls〕.
장기 長技 special skill ; one's strong point ; one's favorite performance ; one's forte ¶ 그의 장기는 뭣이냐 What is his speciality ?
장기 miasma ; pestilential vapors ; malaria
장기 臟器 the internal organs ; the viscera ; the bowels
장기 將棋 (the game of) chess ¶ 장기를 두다 play chess ; have a game of chess
— 놀이 a game of chess —짝 a chessman ; a man ; a piece —판 a chessboard

*장기 長期 a long time〔period, term, date〕 ¶ 장기의 long(-dated) ; protracted ; prolonged
— 거래 long-term transaction ; dealings in futures — 계획 a long-range plan — 공채(公債) a long-term (public) bond — 대부 a long-term loan — 사채(社債) a long-term bond — 신용 long-term credit — 어음 a long-dated bill — 예보 a long-range weather forecast —전 a long〔protracted〕 war — 정책 a long-range〔-term〕 policy — 증서 a long-term bond — 채무 a long-term debt — 체류 a long〔prolonged〕 stay — 흥행 a long run
장기 결근 長期缺勤 a long-term absence
—자 a long-term absentee
장기 근속 長期勤續 long service ; years of labor
—자 a long-term employed person
장기튀김 將棋— repercussion ; falling like a house of cards〔a row of dominoes〕 ¶ 장기튀김이 되다 fall down one after another
장김치 醬— vegetables〔*kimchi*〕 pickled in soy sauce
장군 將軍 a general ; [장기의] "check" in chess
장꾼 場— marketeers ; marketers ; market crowds
장끼 〖새〗 a cock pheasant
장나무 a long stick ; a pole
장나무에 낫걸이 (속담) As oak is not felled at one stroke.
†장난 [놀이] a game ; play ; [희롱] mischief ; prank ; a joke ; [실없는 일] trifle ; fun ; hobby —하다 play ; toy (손으로) ; trifle ; play a trick ; play a practical joke ¶ 어린 아이들의 장난 children's games // 어린 아이 같은 장난 childish mischief // 장난으로 for fun〔a joke〕 ; as a pastime〔hobby〕 // 장난으로 말하다 speak in fun ; joke // 공을 가지고 혼자 장난하다 amuse oneself with a ball // 탄환을 잰 총을 가지고 장난하다 fool〔toy〕 with a loaded gun // 불장난을 하다 play with fire // 사람한테 장난하다 play a trick on 《a person》 // 장난으로 꽃을 기르다 raise flowers as a hobby // 시계줄을 가지고 장난하다 toy with one's watch chain // 그 아이는 언제나 장난만 한다 That boy is always up to some mischief. // 그는 한창 짓궂은 장난을 칠 나이다 He's just at the height of his mischief-making. // 장난으로 했다 치더라도 그건 좀 심했다 Even if it was only meant in fun, that's awful.
†장난감 a plaything ; a toy ; a sport (놀림감) ¶ 장난감 같은 집 a toy〔matchbox〕 of a house // 장난감이 되다 be made a plaything 《by》 // 장난감을 가지고 놀 나이가 아니다 You have outgrown your playthings.
— 가게 a toy shop — 기차〔피스톨〕 a toy train〔pistol〕 — 돈 play money — 말 a toy horse — 상자 a toy box — 성(城) a castle in miniature 어른 — an adult toy
장난기 playfulness ; mischievousness ; (a) pleasantry ; mischief ¶ 장난기 어린 눈 eyes beaming with mischief // 장난기 어린 웃음 an impish smile
‡장난꾸러기 [일반적으로] a mischief (-maker) ; a rogue ; a jokester ; a joker ; a prankster 《미·구》 ; a cutup ; [짓궂은] a practical joker ; [아이] a mischievous 〔naughty〕 boy ; a naughty rouge
장난꾼 ⇨ 장난꾸러기
장난치다 romp (about) ; frisk (about) ; have a lark 《with》 ; run one's rigs ; play 〔sport〕 with ; joke ; make fun〔sport〕 of ; get funny with 《a person》
장날 場— a market day
장남 長男 the eldest son
장남하다 [자녀가] be all grown up ; (be) matured ; be well mannered
장내 場內 the inside of the hall〔grounds, premises〕 ¶ 장내에서 in the hall ; in the grounds ; on the premises // 장내는 입추의 여지도 없다 There is no standing room in the hall.
장내기 場— goods for market
장녀 長女 the eldest daughter
장년 長年 the prime of manhood〔life〕 ¶ 장년의 사람 a man in the prime of life // 장년 시대에 in〔at〕 the prime of life // 장년에 달하다 reach manhood ; attain the prime of manhood
—기(期) 《in one's》 manhood ; 《in》 the prime of the life
*장뇌 樟腦 camphor ¶ 장뇌를 넣다 camphorate
—산(酸) 〖화학〗 camphoric acid —유 camphor oil —정(精) spirit of camphor 정제(精製) — refined camphor 조제(粗製) — crude camphor
장닉 藏匿 concealment ; sheltering ; harboring —하다 conceal ; shelter ; harbor
—자 a concealer
장님 a blind man ; the blind ¶ 눈뜬 장님 an unlettered〔illiterate〕 person // 장님이 되다 become〔go〕 blind ; lose one's sight // 타고난 장님이다 be born blind
장님이 장님을 인도한다 (속담) When the blind lead the blind, both shall fall into the ditch.
장다리 a flowering stalk (of radishes, cabbages) ¶ 장다리가 나다 go〔run〕 to seed
— 무 a seed radish
장단 長短 [길이] the long and the short ; length ; [장단점] merits and demerits ; advantages and disadvantages ; [박자] rhythm ; beat ; time ¶ …의 장단을 생각하다 consider the relative merits of // 사물에는 모두 장단이 있다 Things have good and bad points of their own. // 사람

은 누구나 장단을 가지고 있다 Everyman has his merits and demerits. // 장단이 상쇄된다 His merits and demerits offset each other. // 그는 발로 장단을 맞추고 있다 He is beating time with his feet.

장단점 長短點 merits and demerits〔faults〕; strength and weakness ⇨ 장단(長短)

장담 壯談 assurance ; a positive statement ; assertion ; guarantee ; vouching **—하다** assure ; vouch《for》; give one's word《for》¶ 그것이 사실임을 나는 장담한다 I affirm it to be a fact. // 나는 어떻다고도 장담 못하겠다 I cannot commit myself either way.

장대 壯大 —하다 (be) big and strong ; stout ; sturdy ; grand ; magnificent ¶ 장대한 사람 a mighty man // 장대한 건물 an imposing building

†**장대 長—** a pole ; a rod ; a swipe〔sweep〕 **— 높이 뛰기** jumping with a pole ; a pole jump ; a pole vault《미》 **— 높이 뛰기 선수** a pole jumper〔vaulter〕 **대나무 —** a bamboo pole

장대 長大 —하다 (be) huge ; immense

장도 壯途 an ambitious undertaking〔course〕; an important mission ¶ 장도에 오르다 start on the ambitious course // 북극 탐험의 장도에 오르다 embark on the enterprise of an Arctic expedition

장도 壯圖 a grand scheme〔attempt〕; a great undertaking ; a brilliant project ; a daring enterprise ¶ 세계 일주 비행의 장도 the grand project of a round-the-world flight

장도 粧刀 an encased ornamental knife

장도감치다 張都監— raise a storm

*__장도리__ a hammer ¶ 장도리의 대가리 a hammer-head // 장도리의 자루 the handle of a hammer // 장도리로 치다 hammer // 장도리로 못을 박다 drive in a nail with a hammer ; hammer a nail in
노루발 — a claw-hammer

장독 a crock〔jar〕 of soy ; a soy jar
—간 a place to keep jars of soy sauce **— 소래기** the lid of a soy sauce crock

장독대 醬—臺 a jar stand ; a terrace where soy sauce crocks are placed

장돌림 場— a traveling marketeer ; a roving market dealer

장돌뱅이 場— ⇨ 장돌림

장두 —하다 compare《two routes》to see which is the shorter

장두 長頭 a longhead ; dolichocephaly

장두 檣頭 a masthead ¶ 국기를 장두에 올리다 hoist the national flag at the masthead // 장두 높이 펄렁거리다 fly from the masthead
—등(燈) a top light ; a top lantern

장등 長燈 —하다 keep a light on all through the night ; burn light till late at night

장딴지〖해부〗the calf (of the leg)

장떡 醬— rice-cake made with soy sauce

‡**장래 將來** the future ; the time to come ; the prospect ; [부사적] in future ; some day〔time〕 ¶ 장래가 촉망되는 청년 a promising young man ; a young man with bright prospects // 장래의 future ; prospective // 가까운 장래에 in the near future ; at no distant date // 장래를 생각하다 think of the future // 그는 장래를 촉망받고 있다 Future greatness is expected of him. // 그는 장래가 유망하다 He has a great future before him. /He is a promising youth. // 장래에 대한 너의 계획은 무엇이냐 What's your plan for the future? // 출판 사업은 장래가 대단히 유망하다 The publishing business has great prospects.
— 계획 a plan for one's future **—성** a prospect ; possibilities ¶ 장래성 있는 promising ; likely ; with a bright future // 한국 산업의 장래성 Korean industrial possibilities // 장래성이 있다 [장사가] It has great (commercial) possibilities. / [사람이] He has bright prospects. // 이 작가는 장래성이 있다 The author shows promise of better things.

‡**장려 壯麗** splendor ; grandeur ; magnificence **—하다** (be) splendid ; magnificent ; grand ; imposing

‡**장려 奬勵** encouragement ; promotion ; stimulation ; incitement **—하다** encourage ; stimulate ; promote ; incite ¶ 공부를 장려하다 encourage《a person》to work hard // 저축을 장려하다 encourage saving ; encourage《a person》in saving // 그것은 영어 연구를 장려하게 될 것이다 It will serve as an impetus to the study of English. // 이 학교에서는 여러 가지 운동을 장려하고 있다 This school encourages all sorts of athletic sports.
—급(給) incentive wages **—금** a subsidy ; a bounty **—자** a promoter ; a supporter **수출 —금** a bounty on exports ; an export bounty **연구 — 보조금** grants for the encouragement of research **증산 —금** a bounty for increased production

장력 張力〖물리〗tension
표면 — surface tension

장렬 壯烈 —하다 (be) heroic ; brave ; gallant ; sublime ¶ 장렬한 행동 brave〔heroic〕 deeds // 장렬한 죽음을 하다 die gloriously ; die a heroic death

장렬 葬列 a funeral procession ; a funeral cortege

‡**장례 葬禮** a funeral (ceremony) ; a funeral service ; funeral rites ¶ 장례를 거행하다 hold a funeral ; perform a funeral service ; pay the last honors《to》
—비 funeral expenses **—식** funeral services〔rites〕 **— 위원** a person in charge of funeral arrangements ; a funeral commissioner **— 위원장** the chief funeral commissioner **—차** a funeral car ; a

hearse
*장로 長老 an elder ; a senior ; a superior ; [교회의] an elder ; a presbyter
— 교회 the Presbyterian Church — 회의 [미개인 부락 등에서의] a council of elders 외교계 — an elder of the diplomatic service
*장롱 欌籠 a wardrobe ; a bureau 《미》 ; a dresser
장루 檣樓 a crow's nest
장르 a genre 《프》
장리 掌理 management ; direction ; control ; supervision —하다 manage ; direct ; control ; administer
장리 長利 an annual interest of fifty percent
장림 長霖 a long rainy season ; a long spell〔stretch〕 of rainy weather
*장마 the rainy spell in (early) summer ; a spell of rainy weather ¶ 장마가 지다 the rainy season sets in // 장마가 걷히다 the rainy season is over
— 전선 a seasonal rain front —철 the rainy〔wet〕 season
장마루 長— 〖건축〗 a floor made of long planks (instead of inlaid blocks)
장막 帳幕 a tent ; a curtain ; a hanging ¶ 밤의 장막 the mantle of night〔darkness〕 // 철〔죽〕의 장막 the iron〔bamboo〕 curtain // 장막을 치다 pitch a tent ; hang a curtain // 장막을 늘어뜨리다 hang 《a window》 with a curtain // 신비의 장막에 싸이다 be wrapped〔shrouded〕 in mystery
*장만 [음식 따위의] preparation ; [마련] arrangement ; procurement ; acquirement —하다 prepare ; provide oneself 《with》 ; buy ; make ; get ; ready ¶ 돈을 장만하다 make〔raise, get〕 money // 옷을 새로 장만하다 have a new suit made ; buy a new suit // 점심을 장만하다 prepare luncheon // 집을 장만하다 get〔buy〕 a house // 돈을 장만하지 못했다 have no money prepared // 옷을 많이 장만했다 have a lot of clothes prepared // 그 여자는 시집가려고 옷을 많이 장만해 두었다 She has prepared many dresses for her marriage.
장맞이 —하다 lie in ambush 《for》 ; ambush ; waylay
†장면 場面 a scene ; a situation (연극의) ; a place (장소) ; spectacle (광경) ¶ 연애 장면 a love scene // 장면이 바뀌다 the scene shifts ; the scene changes
장명 長命 a long life ; longevity ; macrobiosis —하다 (be) long-lived ; macrobian
장명등 長明燈 a hanging lantern at the end of the eaves〔on the gate〕
*장모 丈母 the wife's mother ; a man's mother-in-law
장목 pheasant plumes on the top of a flagpole
—비 a brush made of pheasant plumes ; pheasant-tail duster
장목 長木 lumber ; timber
장문 長文 a lengthy piece of writing ; a long article ; a long letter (편지) ¶ 장문의 전보 a long telegram
장문 掌紋 the lines of the palm ¶ 장문을 보다 read one's palm ; practice palmistry
장문 —門 a wide-open gate〔door〕
장물 贓物 stolen goods〔articles, property〕 ¶ 장물을 은닉하다 secrete stolen goods
— 고매(故買) buying〔purchasing〕 goods with full knowledge that they are stolen goods — 고매자 a receiver ; a fence — 아비 a fence 《속》 ; a hot goods broker — 취득 receiving stolen goods ; fencing ¶ 장물 취득하다 receive〔purchase〕 stolen goods
†장미 薔薇 a rose ¶ 장밋빛의 rosy ; rose-colored // 가시 없는 장미는 없다 Every rose has its thorns.
—나무 a rose tree〔bush〕 —꽃 장식 a rosette —색 rose color ; rose pink ¶ 장미색의 rosy ; rose-colored〔-tinted〕 —원 a rosery ; a rose garden —유〔향유〕 rose oil ; attar of roses — 재배 전문가 an expert grower of roses — 전쟁 〖서양사〗 the Wars of the Roses 들— a wild rose ; a brier 장밋빛 입술 rose-red lips ; rose lips ¶ 장밋빛 입술의 rose-lipped
장미 壯美 sublime beauty ; grandeur ; sublimity ; magnificence —하다 (be) sublime ; grand ; magnificent
장미계 長尾鷄 〖새〗 a long-tailed rooster
장바구니 場— a shopping basket ; a kit
장바닥 場— the market area ; a market place
장반자 長— 〖건축〗 a plank ceiling
장발 長髮 long hair ; a long-haired person ¶ 장발의 long-haired
—적(賊) 〖역사〗 the Taiping —적(의) 난 the Taiping rebellion —족(族) a "hippie" style long-haired youth
장방형 長方形 a rectangle ; an oblong ¶ 장방형의 rectangular ; oblong
‡장벽 障壁 a fence ; a wall ; a barrier ¶ 장벽을 쌓다 raise a barrier // 장벽을 없애다 let down the bars
관세 — a tariff wall 언어 — a language barrier
장벽 腸壁 the intestinal wall
장변 場邊 interest on a loan for a period of five days 《from one market to the next》 ; a loan at high interest ¶ 장변 놀이하다 lend money at high interest ; practice usury ; be a loan shark
장병 長病 a long-standing disease ; a chronic disease ¶ 장병을 앓다 suffer from a chronic disease // 그는 장병 끝에 죽었다 He died after a lingering illness.
장병 將兵 officers and men ; soldiers
장보 長— a stretcher beam ; an unsupported room-length beam

장보기 場— marketing ¶ 장보기를 끝내다 complete all purchases
장보다 場— go to market ; go shopping ; [팔기 위해] open a booth at a market
장복 長服 constant use of a medicine ; habitual use (of a medicine) **—하다** use 《a medicine》 constantly ; take habitually
장본 張本 the origin ; the root ; the (fatal) cause ¶ 그 정당에 든 것이 그가 망한 장본이었다 His joining that party was what led to his downfall.
장본 藏本 one's collection of books ; one's library
장본인 張本人 the ringleader ; the prime mover ; an originator ; the author ¶ 그가 그 소동의 장본인이다 He is the very author of the riot.
장부[1] a tenon ; a dovetail
—촉 이음 mortise and tenon joint **장붓구멍** a mortise
장부[2] 〖농업〗 [가래의] the handle of a spade with pull-ropes ; [장부군] the handle holder of a spade
장부 丈夫 a full-grown man ; a mighty man ; a manly man
대— a manly man ; a hero
장부 帳簿 an account book ; a register (등기부) ¶ 장부에 기입하다 book ; enter accounts // 장부를 끝막다 close the books // 장부를 검사하다 inspect the books ; audit the accounts ; check the records
— 가격 book value **— 감사** auditing **— 검사** auditing **—계** a bookkeeper ; an accountant ¶ 장부계 일을 보다 be in charge of bookkeeping **—외 자산** nonledger〔concealed〕 assets **— 정리** adjustment of accounts **— 조직** a system of books **상업 —** trade books **이중 —** double bookkeeping
장부끝 帳簿— the balance of accounts ; a balance (account) ¶ 장부끝을 맞추다 make the accounts balance ; make (both) ends meet
장부 대조 帳簿對照 [대조] balancing accounts ; [기장] keeping accounts ¶ 장부 대조를 하다 balance accounts
장비 葬費 funeral expenses
*__장비 裝備__ equipment ; outfit ; fitting **—하다** equip 《a ship》 with ; fit out 《a ship》 ¶ 우수한 장비를 갖춘 부대 well-equipped troops // 그 군함은 10인치 포 9문을 장비하고 있다 The warship carries nine 10-inch guns.
야영 — camp equipage **전(全)—** ¶ 전장비의 full-rigged 《ship》 **중—** heavy equipment ¶ 중장비의 heavily equipped 《division》
†**장사** trade ; business ; commerce ; a transaction (거래) **—하다** engage in business ; be in business ; do business ; deal in 《some goods》 ¶ 수지맞는 장사 a paying business // 수지 안 맞는 장사 a nonpaying business // 쌀장사를 하다 deal in 《rice》 // 장사를 시작하다 go into〔start〕 a business ; set up〔start〕 in business // 장사를 배우다 learn a trade // 장사를 그만두다 give up business // 장사를 바꾸다 change one's business〔trade〕 // 장사를 잘하다〔못하다〕 be a good〔bad〕 businessman // 월 10만원 벌이의 장사를 하고 있다 make〔do〕 a business of a hundred thousand *won* per month // 장사가 번창하다 drive a roaring trade ; one's business prospers // 장사가 전혀 안되다 be put out of business // 그건 장사가 안된다 It does not pay. /It is not a paying business. // 그는 장사를 하고 있다 He is (engaged) in business. // 무슨 장사를 하고 있느냐 What (kind of) business 〔trade, line〕 are you in ? // 이 장사는 제법 수지가 맞는다 This business pays well 〔gains a good profit〕. // 저는 자동차 부속품 장사를 하고 있습니다 I'm in the auto parts business.
— 도구 one's stock in trade ; one's kit **— 부진** 《suffer from》 business depression **— 요령(비결)** a trick of the trade **—치** a peddler ; a trader **—판** trade ; commercial〔business〕 pursuits **장사꾼** a trader ; a merchant ; a dealer **장사꾼 근성** a mercenary spirit **장사꾼 기질(의식)** professionalism
장사 葬事 a funeral (service) ; a burial ¶ 장사 지내다 hold a funeral ; bury
장사 壯士 a muscular man ; a strong man ¶ 힘이 장사다 be as strong as Hercules
장사진 長蛇陣 a long line〔file, row〕 ; a long queue ¶ 장사진을 치다 form a long line〔queue〕
장살 長— the perpendicular strips of a lattice
장살 杖殺 —하다 flog〔club, bastinado〕 《a person》 to death
장삼 長衫 a Buddhist monk's robe
장삼 이사 張三李四 every "Tom, Dick and Harry" ; everybody ; the common crowd
장삿날 葬事— a funeral day
장삿속 a commercial spirit ; a mercantile mind ¶ 장삿속을 떠나서 from a noncommercial〔disinterested〕 motive ; apart from gain
장상 藏相 [재무장관] the Finance Minister ; the Minister of Finance ; the Chancellor of the Exchequer 《영》 ; the Secretary of the Treasury 《미》
장상 掌狀 ¶ 장상의 palmate(d) ; digitate(d)
—엽 a palmate leaf
장색 匠色 a handicraftsman ; a craftsman ; an artisan
장생 長生 long life ; longevity **—하다** live long ; enjoy longevity〔a long life〕 ¶ 불로 장생의 비결 the secret of perpetual youth

장생불사 長生不死 eternal life ; eternal longevity ; immortality **—하다** enjoy eternal life ; share immortality ¶ 장생불사의 영약 the elixir of life

⁑**장서 藏書** a collection of books ; one's library **—하다** collect books ; build a library ¶ 10,000권의 장서를 모으다 accumulate a library of ten thousand volumes **—가** a book collector ; a bibliophile ; the owner of a well-stocked〔large, fine〕 library **—광** bibliomania ; a bibliomaniac **— 목록** a library catalogue **—벽** bibliomania **—인(印)〔기호〕** an ownership stamp〔mark〕 **— 점검** general stocktaking **— 정리** setting〔putting〕 one's library to rights **— 충실 도서관** a well-stocked library **—표** a bookplate ; a book label

장서 長逝 —하다 die ; pass away

장석 長石 〚광물〛 feldspar ; felspar

장선 長線 〚건축〛 an underfloor support beam ; underflooring

장선 腸線 a catgut ; a gut

장성 將星 generals

장성 長成 growth ; maturity **—하다** grow up ; grow to maturity ¶ 장성해서 어른이 되다 grow into an adult

장성 長城 a long wall
만리 — the Great Wall of China

장세 場稅 a market tax

†**장소 場所** a place ; a spot ; [위치] a location ; a position ; [부지] a site ; a lot ; [좌석] a seat ; [공간] room ; space ¶ 회합하는 장소 a place of〔for〕 meeting // 장소가 나쁘다 be badly〔inconveniently〕 located // 장소가 좋다 be well〔conveniently〕 situated〔located〕 // 장소를 선정하다 select a site // 좋은 장소를 잡다 get a good seat〔place〕 // 넓은 장소를 차지하다 occupy〔take up〕 much room〔space〕 // 장소가 좋아서 장사가 잘 된다 The locality brings a great deal of business. // 새 공장을 세우는 데 적합한 장소를 마련하고 싶다 We want a suitable location for a new factory.

장속 裝束 costume ; dress ; attire **—하다** be dressed ; dress oneself

장손 長孫 the eldest grandson by the eldest son

장송 長松 a tall pine tree (나무) ; a long pine board (목재)

장송 葬送 escorting a funeral ; attending a funeral **—하다** escort a funeral ; attend a funeral
—곡 a funeral〔dead〕 march

***장수** a tradesman ; a merchant ; a dealer ; a seller ; [행상인] a peddler
생선 — a fishmonger **술—** a wine dealer **책—** a bookseller

장수 張數 the number of leaves〔sheets〕

***장수 長壽** long life ; longevity ; macrobiosis **—하다** live long ; enjoy longevity ¶ 장수의 비결 the secret of longevity
— 소망자 an age-seeker **—약** the elixir of life **—자** a macrobian **— 혈통〔집안〕** a long-lived family

장수 將帥 a general ; a commander-in-chief

장수로 長水路 〚수영〛 a long〔50-meter〕 course〔lane〕

장수벌 將帥— 〚곤충〛 a queen bee

장시간 長時間 many long hours ; long time ¶ 장시간에 걸쳐 for (many) hours // 장시간 회담하다 have a long talk 《with》

장시세 場市勢 the market price〔rate〕 ; quotations ; the market

장시일 長時日 a long (period〔space〕 of) time ; years ¶ 장시일에 걸쳐서 for a long time // 장시일을 지나서 after many years ; after the lapse of many a year

⁑**장식 裝飾** decoration ; adornment ; ornament(ation) ; dressing (가게의) **—하다** decorate ; adorn ; ornament ; dress ; trim ¶ 장식에 사용하다 use for decoration // 방을 꽃으로 장식하다 decorate a room with flowers // 시내는 국기로 장식되어 있다 The city is decorated with flags. // 이 접시는 단순한 장식으로서 실용적이 못 된다 This (China) dish is only for show and not for practical use.
—계 a person in charge of decoration **— 물〔품〕** an ornament ; a decoration **— 미술** decorative art〔painting〕 **—법** ornamentation ; decoration **—비** decoration expenses **—술** decorative art **— 예술** (a) decorative art **—용 전구** a decoration light bulb **— 유리** ornamental glass **—음** 〚음악〛 a grace (note) **—자** an interior decorator (실내의) ; a window dresser (가게의) **— 조명** decorative illumination **—주의** ornamentalism **—품** decorations ; ornaments ; trinkets (장신구) **—화** a decorative painting **무대 —** stage decoration **실내 —** interior decoration **실내 —가** an interior decorator

장식 粧飾 sprucing oneself up ; decking oneself out **—하다** ornament ; adorn ; deck out ¶ 보석으로 몸을 장식하다 deck oneself out with jewels ; bejewel oneself
—품 personal ornaments ; fancy goods

장식 葬式 a funeral service〔ceremony, rite〕 ⇨ 장례

장식 문자 裝飾文字 [무늬 글씨 따위] a flourish ; a scroll ; a quirk ; a tag ¶ 장식 문자를 쓰다 flourish

장신 長身 a tall stature〔figure〕

장신구 裝身具 personal ornaments ; accessories ; trinketry

장아찌 slices of radish or cucumber dried and seasoned with soy

장악 掌握 —하다 hold ; grasp ; command ; seize ; secure ; hold sway 《over》 ¶ 정권을 장악하다 come into power ; assume the reins of the government // 실권을 장악하다 hold real power ; be in the saddle // 제공권을 장악하다 secure the command of the air ; win the air

장안 長安 a capital city ¶ 서울 장안 *Seoul,* the capital city

*‡*장애 障碍** an obstacle ; a hindrance ; a difficulty ; an impediment ; a hitch ; hurdles (운동 기구) ; troubles (병) ¶ 장애가 되다 be〔stand〕 in the way〔a person's way〕 ; impede ; hinder // 장애를 극복하다 surmount an obstacle ; overcome 〔get over〕 a difficulty // 장애가 생기다 A hitch arises.

—물 an obstacle ; an obstruction ; a hurdle (경기의) ; a (jumping) bar (경마의) ; a bunker (골프의) ¶ 장애물을 뛰어넘다 hurdle ; clear the hurdles // 장애물을 제거하다 remove obstacles〔impediments〕 **—물 경주** an obstacle race ; hurdles ; a steeplechase (경마의) **교육 —** a barrier to education **기능 —** a functional disease **뇌—** a brain injury ; brain trouble ¶ 뇌장애자 a brain-injured person **무역 —** a trade barrier **방사선 —** radiation sickness **언어 —** a speech defect ; an impediment in one's speech **위장 —** gastroenteric trouble〔disorder〕 **정서 —** an emotional disorder **중대 —** a serious obstacle **신체 —자** a disabled person ; the physically handicapped (person) **정신 —자** a mentally handicapped person

장액 腸液 intestinal juices〔secretions〕

장액 漿液 serum

장야 長夜 a long night ; the long nights of winter

장약 裝藥 charging gunpowder ; charge **—하다** charge 《a gun》 with powder

장어 長魚 an eel ; a common eel

— 구이 eels〔loaches〕 split and broiled 〔grilled〕 in soy ; broiled eels **— 덮밥** a bowl of eel and rice **—밥** eel and rice **—집** an eel restaurant

장어 章魚 [낙지] a small octopus

*‡*장엄 莊嚴** grandeur ; solemnity ; sublimity ; stateliness **—하다** (be) magnificent ; solemn ; grand ; sublime ; impressive ; awe-inspiring ¶ 장엄한 장면 an impressive scene〔sight〕 // 아주 장엄하다 be most sublime〔impressive〕

— 미사 a High Mass

장여 長— 〚건축〛 a strip of wood supporting a beam

장염 腸炎 〚의학〛 enteritis

장염전 腸捻轉 〚의학〛 a twist in the intestines ; volvulus (축념)

장영창 長映窓 〚건축〛 a long sliding window

장옷 a kind of long hood formerly worn by Korean women

장외 場外 ¶ 장외의〔에〕 outside the hall 〔ground〕 ; 〚주식〛 off-board ; off-floor ; outside the (exchange) market ; 〚경마〛 off-course〔-track〕 《betting》 // 장외에(서) outside the hall〔arena, grounds〕 ; on the curb

— 거래 〚주식〛 [상장 증권의 장외 거래] off-board transactions ; transaction on the third market **—주** an unlisted stock ; an over-the-counter stock **— 홈런** an out-of-the-park homer

장용제 腸溶劑 〚약〛 enteric coating

장용지 長— 〚건축〛 a piece of wood to brace the wall

장원 壯元 a person who won the first place in the higher civil service examination (사람) ; the highest passing mark in the state examination (등급) **—하다** win the first place in the state examination

***장원 莊園** a manor

장유 長幼 old and young ¶ 장유 유서하다 The younger should give precedence to the elder. / Elders first.

장유 醬油 soy ; soy and sesame oil

장으리 〚식물〛 a variety of millet

장음 長音 a prolonged sound ; 〚음성〛 a long vowel〔syllable〕

—계 〚음악〛 the major (scale) ; the gamut **—부** 〚언어학〛 a macron ; a length mark ; a "long" mark ¶ 장음부를 붙이다 put a macron 《over a vowel》 **변—부** a circumflex

장읍 長揖 **—하다** make a deep bow

장의 葬儀 a funeral (service) ; funeral rites ; obsequies ¶ 성대한 장의 an extravagant funeral // 장의를 치르다 hold a funeral service // 장의에 참석하다 attend the funeral

—식 비용 funeral expenses **—사(社)** an undertaker's shop ; a funeral parlor 《미》 **— 위원** a person in charge of funeral arrangements ; a funeral commissioner **— 위원장** the chief funeral commissioner **—장(場)** a funeral hall

장의자 長椅子 a sofa ; a couch ; a lounge ; a bench

-장이 -er ; -monger ; a dealer ; a man who does

장인 丈人 the wife's father ; a man's father-in-law

***장인 匠人** an artisan ; a workman ; a craftsman

장일 葬日 the day of the funeral

장자 長子 the eldest son

— 상속권 the right of primogeniture **— 상속법** primogeniture

장자 長者 [어른] an elder ; one's superior〔senior〕 ; [부자] a rich〔wealthy〕 man ; a millionaire ; [덕망가] a man of moral influence ; an elder of virtue ¶ 장자를 존경하다 respect one's superiors // 장자를 받들어 모셔야 한다 The young should willingly give their services to the old.

백만 — millionaire **억만 —** a billionaire

***장작 長斫** firewood ¶ 장작을 패다 chop 〔split〕 firewood // 장작을 지피다 feed a fire with firewood

—개비 a piece of (fire) wood ; a billet

장장 長長 very long ; at great length ; tediously (지루하게)
—추야(秋夜) the long nights of autumn **—하일(夏日)** the long days of summer
장재 將材 a man of《real》general timber
장전 charge《of a gun》; loading **—하다** load〔charge, feed〕a gun
장전 欌廛 a furniture store
장절 章節 chapters and verses ¶ 장절로 나누다 divide into chapters and verses
†**장점 長點** a merit ; a good〔strong〕point ; a forte ; a virtue (미덕) ; graces ; an advantage (이점) ¶ 장점과 단점 merits and demerits ; strength and weakness∥그것이 그의 장점의 하나다 It is one of his good〔strong〕points.∥용기와 인내가 그의 장점이다 Courage and endurance are his good points.∥그는 신제품의 많은 장점을 선전했다 He claimed〔advertised〕many advantages for the new product.
장정 壯丁 an able-bodied man ; a sturdy youth ; an adult ; [징병 적령자] a young man of conscription age
— 검사 a physical examination of conscripts **— 명부** a list of conscripts
*‡**장정 裝幀** binding《of books》; book cover design **—하다** bind ; design (표지를) ¶ 견고한 장정 durable binding∥A씨가 장정한 책 a book designed by Mr. A∥그 책은 가죽 장정이다 The book is bound in leather.∥책의 장정이 아담하다 The book is neatly〔smartly〕bound.∥장정이 한국식이다 It is bound in the Korean way.
—소 bindery **—자** a designer ; binder **금박 가죽 —** binding in full leather with gilt letters **모로코 가죽 — 책자** a book bound in morocco leather
장정 長程 a long way ; a great distance ¶ 장정 5천 마일 a distance of 5,000 miles
장정 長征 a long march
장제 葬制 the funeral institution
장조 長調 〖음악〗 a major key
장조림 醬— beef boiled in soy
장조모 丈祖母 the wife's grandmother
장조부 丈祖父 the wife's grandfather
장조카 長— the eldest son of one's eldest brother
장족 長足 a great stride〔pace〕; a long foot ¶ 장족의 진보 rapid progress∥장족의 진보를 하다 make remarkable〔rapid〕progress ; make rapid strides
장족편 醬足— ox-hoof jelly seasoned with soy
장졸 將卒 officers and men
장주릅 場— a market broker ; a middleman
장죽 長竹 a long (smoking) pipe
장중 掌中 ¶ 장중에 in one's hands〔possession, power〕; within one's grip〔power〕; at《a person's》mercy (지배 하에)∥장중이 있다 be in《a person's》hands ; hold《a person, a thing》in the hollow of one's hands ; be at《a person's》nod∥…의 장중에 들어가다 fall into《a person's》hands〔possession〕; play into the hands of《a person》
— 보옥 a jewel (in one's hands) ¶ 딸을 장중 보옥처럼 기르다 love one's daughter as the apple of one's eye
장중 莊重 solemnity ; gravity ; impressiveness **—하다** (be) solemn ; grave ; impressive ; sublime ; serious ¶ 장중하게 solemnly ; gravely ; with solemnity∥장중한 광경 an impressive scene∥장중한 음악 solemn music∥장중한 어조로 in a solemn tone∥의식은 장중하게 거행되었다 The ceremony was conducted with solemnity.
장중적증 腸重積症 〖의학〗 invagination
장지 a paper sliding door ; a sliding door ¶ 장지를 열다〔닫다〕open〔shut〕a paper sliding door
—문 a paper sliding door **— 종이** sliding-screen paper **—틀** the sliding-door frame **유리 —** a glass-fitted screen **종이 —** a paper screen ; a paper-sliding door
장지 長指 the middle finger
장지 將指 the middle finger (손가락) ; the big〔great〕toe (발가락)
장지 壯志 a grand ambition ; a lofty aspiration ¶ 장지를 품다 entertain a great ambition
장지 葬地 a burial place〔ground〕
장질 長姪 the eldest son of one's eldest brother
장질부사 腸窒扶斯 enteric fever《영》; typhoid fever《미》 ¶ 장질부사의 typhoid ; typhoidal
—균 a typhoid bacillus《*pl.* -lli》 **— 예방 주사** antityphoid inoculation **— 환자** a (case of) typhoid
장차 將次 in (the) future ; someday
장차다 長— [길다] (be) straight and long ; [멀다] far ; distant
장창 長槍 a long spear〔lance〕
장채 長— long poles (of a sedan chair)
장책 長冊 an accounting book ; a ledger ¶ 장책을 달다 keep books∥장책에 달다 enter in the books〔accounts, ledger〕
장처 長處 a strong point ; one's forte
장척 丈尺 a ten-foot rule
장천 長天 the boundless〔vast〕sky
장총 長銃 a (long-barreled) rifle
장축 長軸 〖수학〗 the major axis
장출혈 腸出血 〖의학〗 enterohemorrhage
장취 長醉 being drunk all the time ; incessant drunkenness **—하다** be always drunk
장취 將就 progressiveness ; development ; growth **—하다** progressdevelop ; drive ahead
—성 an enterprising〔a progressive〕spirit ; possibility of future growth
장치 場— a loan on which interest is to be paid every market day

*장치 裝置 equipment ; installation ; contrivance ; provision ; mounting (대포의) ; an apparatus —하다 equip 《a ship》 with ; install ; mount 《a gun》 ; fit 《a house》 with ; arrange ; place
급수 — a feeding apparatus 난방 — a heating apparatus 냉방 — air-conditioning apparatus〔equipment〕 무대 — the stage setting 무전 — a wireless installation〔apparatus〕 ¶ 무전 장치가 되어 있다 be equipped with a wireless ; carry a wireless equipment 방화 — anti-fire provision ; fire prevention equipment 발화 — an ignition device ¶ 자동 발화 장치가 되어 있다 It is so contrived as to ignite automatically. 스테레오 — stereo equipment 안전 — a safety device〔apparatus〕 전기 — electrical equipment
장침 長針 a long needle ; [시계의] the long hand ; the minute hand
장침 長枕 a long pillow that serves as an armrest ; an armrest
장카타르 腸— 〖의학〗 intestinal catarrh
장쾌 壯快 being exciting ; splendidness ; thrillingness —하다 (be) stirring ; thrilling ; exciting ¶ 장쾌한 거사 a stirring〔an exciting〕 attempt
장타 長打 〖야구〗 《hit》 a long hit
—자 a long-ball hitter
장타령꾼 場打令— a singing beggar strolling about market places
장탄 裝彈 charging —하다 load 《a revolver》 ; charge 《a gun》
장탄식 長嘆息 a long〔heavy, deep〕 sigh —하다 draw a long〔deep〕 sigh ; heave〔give〕 a heavy sigh
장터 場— a market site〔place〕
*장티푸스 腸— typhoid〔enteric〕 fever ; typhoid ; enteric (영)
—균 a typhoid bacillus〔germ〕 — 예방 주사 antityphoid inoculation — 환자 a typhoid ; a case of typhoid fever
장파 長波 a long wave
— 라디오 a long-wave radio set — 라디오 수신기 a long-wave radio set — 방송 a long-wave broadcast
장판 場— a market place〔square〕 ; a crowded〔thronged〕 place ; a place swarming with people
장판 壯版 a floor covered with laminated paper
—방 a room with paper-covered floor —지 laminated paper lacquered with bean oil
장편 長篇 a long work 《of art》 ; a long piece
— 만화 영화 a feature-length cartoon film — 소설 a novel ; a full-length novel — 영화 a long film ; a full-length film ; a feature (film)
장편 掌篇 a conte 《프》 ; a very short piece of writing〔story〕
— 소설 a conte 《프》 ; a short story

장폐색증 腸閉塞症 〖의학〗 enterostenosis ; intestinal obstruction
장포 場圃 a kitchen〔vegetable〕 garden
장품 贓品 stolen goods ⇨ 장물
장피 獐皮 the skin of a roe deer
장피살 〖건축〗 a lattice piece with a back shaped like an iris stalk
장하 裝荷 〖전기〗 loading —하다 load
— 케이블 a loaded cable — 코일 a loading coil
장하다 長— (be) excellent 《at, in》 ; proficient 《in》 ; skillful ; good 《at》 ; adept ¶ 장한 생각 a splendid〔shrewd, bright〕 idea
*장하다 壯— [훌륭하다] (be) great ; splendid ; glorious ; brave (용감하다) ; admirable ; praiseworthy ; [굉장하다] grand ; magnificent ; [놀랍다] wonderful ; surprising ¶ 장하게 싸우다 fight bravely // 장한 죽음을 하다 die an honorable death // 일등상을 탔다니 참 장하다 It is splendid that you have taken first prize.
장학 奬學 encouragement〔promotion〕 of learning〔study〕 —하다 encourage learning
—금 a scholarship ¶ 장학금 제도를 마련하다 create〔found, establish〕 a scholarship // 장학금으로 해외에 파견되다 be sent abroad on a scholarship // 장학금을 얻다 win〔gain〕 a scholarship — 기금 a scholarship fund —사〔관〕 a school inspector ; a school commissioner —생 a scholarship student — 자금 a scholarship fund
장한 壯漢 a strong man
장해 障害 an obstacle ; a hindrance ⇨ 장애
장행회 壯行會 a farewell party ; a send-off party〔dinner〕 ¶ 장행회를 열다 hold〔give〕 a send-off〔farewell〕 party 《for a person》
장혈 獐血 blood of a roe deer
장형 杖刑 flogging —하다 flog
장형 長兄 the eldest brother
장화 長話 a long talk
†장화 長靴 high boots ; boots (미)
장황 張皇 —하다 (be) lengthy ; tedious ; long and boring ; dull ¶ 장황한 문장 a diffuse〔verbose〕 style // 장황한 연설 a tedious discourse ; a tirade // 그 자동차 판매 사원은 새 모델에 관해 장황한 선전을 늘어놓기 시작했다 The car salesman started a song and danced about the new model.
잦다¹ [기울다] lean backward(s) ; get sway-back(ed)
잦다² [졸아들다] ⇨ 찾아들다
*잦다³ [빈번하다] (be) frequent ; incessant ¶ 왕래가 잦은 길 a busy〔bustling〕 street // 요즈음은 화재가 잦을 때다 Fires are frequent at this time of the year. // 요즈음 시내 각처에서 살인 사건이 잦다고 한다

Murder cases are frequently reported from various parts of the city.

잦뜨리다 bend back〔backwards〕; throw back

잦바듬하다 lean back

잦아들다 run dry ; keep sinking ; boil down (끓어서) ¶ 비가 안 와서 호수의 물이 잦아들고 있다 The lake is sinking with the drought.

잦아지다 dry up ; be boiled dry ; sink ; go down

잦은걸음 a quick pace ; quick〔short〕 steps ¶ 잦은걸음으로 with quick〔rapid〕 steps ; at a brisk pace

잦추다 press 《a person for》; urge 《a person to do》 ¶ 대답을 하라고 잦추다 press 《a person》 for an answer // 빚을 갚으라고 잦추다 press 《a person》 for the payment of a debt

잦추리다 ⇨ 잦추다

잦혀놓다 [뒤집다] turn over〔up〕; turn upside down ; lay 《a thing》 face down ; [뒤로 미루다] put〔lay〕 aside ; leave out ; reserve ¶ 돈 문제는 잦혀놓고 apart from the problem of expense // 접시를 잦혀놓다 turn over a plate // 책을 잦혀놓다 lay a book open // 하던 일을 잦혀놓고 친구를 맞다 meet a friend laying aside what one was doing // 급하지 않은 일은 잦혀놓고 급한 일을 먼저 하라 Put aside what can be done later and do the urgent thing first.

잦혀지다 [뒤집히다] be turned over ; lie face down〔upside down〕 ¶ 책이 잦혀져 있다 A book lies open.

잦히다[1] [뒤집다] turn over〔down〕; turn upside down ; lay 《a thing》 face down ; [몸을 뒤로] pull back ; lean backwards ; bend back ¶ 책을 잦히다 open a book ; turn over leaves of a book // 접시를 잦히다 turn a plate over〔upside down〕 // 어깨를 잦히다 pull back one's shoulder

잦히다[2] [밥을] stew ; simmer ; hang the rice over a slow fire

⁑재[1] [타고 남은] ashes ¶ 재 같은 ashy ; ashen // 타서 재가 되다 be reduced to ashes ; lie in ashes〔rubble〕 // 죽어서 재가 되다 be cremated

—떨이 an ash tray —통 an ash can 《미》; an ash bin 《영》 담뱃— cigarette ashes ¶ 담뱃재를 털다 shake off the ashes from one's cigarette

재[2] [고개] a ridge ; a (mountain) pass ¶ 재를 넘다 cross a ridge ; cross over a pass ; go over a hill

재 災 a calamity ; a disaster ; a misfortune

재 齋 [불공] the Buddhist service for the deceased ¶ 재를 올리다 have a service performed〔offered〕 for the repose of a soul〔the dead〕

재 財 [부] wealth ; riches ; [금전] money ; [재산] a fortune ; assets (자산) ; [재물] property ; commodities ; 〖경제〗 goods

생산— producer's goods 소비— consumer's〔consumption〕 goods

⁑재- 再 again ; re-

재- 在 situated in 《a place》; resident in 《a city》

—미 교포 [한인] Korean residents in America

재가 在家 —하다 stay at home ; retire from public life ; live in retirement

—승(僧) a married Buddhist priest

재가 再嫁 a second marriage ; remarriage —하다 marry again ; remarry

*재가 裁可 sanction ; approval —하다 sanction ; approve ; give sanction 《to》 ¶ 재가를 바라다 submit 《a matter》 to 《a person's》 sanction // 재가를 얻다 obtain 《a person's》 sanction

재간 才幹 ability ; talent ; capability ; caliber ¶ 재간 있는 able ; talented ; gifted ; resourceful // 학식 재간이 남보다 뛰어나다 excel both in talent and attainments

말— the gift of gab 손— manual skill ; dexterity

재간 再刊 republication ; reprint ; reissue ; second edition —하다 republish ; reprint ; reissue

*재갈 a bit

재갈먹이다〔물리다〕 관용 bit a horse

재갈매기 〖새〗 a herring gull

재감 在監 imprisonment ; staying in prison —하다 be in prison〔jail, gaol 《영》〕; be imprisoned

—자 a convict ; a prison inmate ; a prisoner —중 《be》 in prison〔jail〕

재감염 再感染 reinfection

재강 the sediment〔lees〕 of fermented liquor

—장 soy steeped in liquor lees —죽 a gruel made with liquor lees and sticky rice

재강아지 [재투성이의] a dusty〔ash-covered〕 puppy ; [잿빛 털의] an ashy〔ash-colored〕 puppy ; a gray puppy ¶ 재강아지 눈감은 듯하다 be (done) without any trace〔change〕 whatsoever

*재개 再開 reopening ; resumption —하다 open again ; reopen ; reconvene ; resume ¶ 교섭을 재개하다 reopen〔resume〕 negotiations // 무역을 재개하다 reopen foreign trade

재개의 再改議 a second amendment —하다 make a second amendment

재거 再擧 a second attempt ; beginning again —하다 make another attempt ; try again ; renew one's attempt

⁑재건 再建 rebuilding ; reconstruction ; rehabilitation —하다 rebuild ; reconstruct ; rehabilitate ¶ 한국을 재건하다 reconstruct Korea

—비 rebuilding expenses — 정비 reconstruction and reorganization 경제 — economic reconstruction 산업 — industrial

reconstruction
재건축 再建築 reconstruction ; rebuilding —하다 reconstruct ; rebuild
재검사 再檢査 re-examination ; reinspection —하다 reinspect ; re-examine ; examine over again ; recheck
재검토 再檢討 reappraisal ; re-examination ; review —하다 re-examine ; reappraise ; review ; take a new look at
재결 裁決 decision ; judgment ; arbitration ; verdict (배심원의) —하다 give a decision〔judgment〕; arbitrate ; decide ¶ 재결을 바라다 ask《a person》for a decision // 재결에 따르다 abide by a decision
—권 a casting vote —서 a written verdict〔judgment〕
재결합 再結合 reunion ; recombination —하다 reunite《with》; recombine ; rejoin together ¶ 이산 가족의 재결합 reunion of one's dispersed family members
재경 在京 —하다 be〔reside〕in *Seoul* ; stay in *Seoul* ¶ 재경의 벗 a friend in *Seoul* // 재경 중에 while in the capital〔in *Seoul*〕; during one's stay in *Seoul*
— 동창생 alumni in *Seoul* — 외국인 foreign residents in *Seoul*
재경 再耕 —하다 till《a field》a second time ; plow again ; replow ; retill
재경 財經 finance〔financial administration〕and economy
재경기 再競技 a rematch
재계 財界 [금융계] the financial world ; financial circles ; [경제계] the economic world ; [실업계] the business world ¶ 재계의 위기 a financial crisis // 재계의 재건 economic rehabilitation // 재계는 공황 상태에 있다 The financial world is panic-stricken. // 재계는 활기를 띠고 있다 The financial world shows signs of activity.
— 거물〔주요 인물〕 a financial magnate ; a leading magnate in financial〔business〕circles ; a leading financier〔businessman〕; a man of financial influence ; a tycoon (미) — 경기(景氣) the financial situation — 불황 business depression — 사정 financial affairs — 안정〔불안〕 financial stability〔unrest〕 —인 [금융가] a financier ; [실업가] a businessman ; [자본가] a capitalist
재계 齋戒 purification ; ablution —하다 purify oneself ; perform purification ¶ 목욕 재계하고 기도 드리다 offer prayers after performing purification
*재고 再考 reconsideration —하다 reconsider ; think twice ; think better《of》; give《a matter》second thoughts ¶ 재고한 후에 on reflection ; on second thoughts // 재고를 요함 ad referendum (라) // 재고를 재촉하다 urge《a person》to reconsider // 사직의 건은 재고해 보시오 I would advise you to reconsider your intended resignation. // 재고의 여지가 없다 There is no room for reconsideration.
재고 在庫 stock ; the stockpile ¶ 재고의 in store ; in stock // 재고품 목록 a stock list ; an inventory ; a catalogue // 재고가 부족하다 do not have sufficient quantities in stock ; the stock has run short // 재고가 있다 have〔keep〕《articles》in stock ; 《the articles》be in store〔stock〕; be kept in the storehouse ; be on hand // 솔직히 말씀드리면 그 물건은 재고가 너무 쌓여서 밑지고 파는 겁니다 Honestly, we are overstocked on that item, so we are selling it below cost. // 재고 정리를 하느라고 TV를 본전에 판다고 하더군요 They said they were selling those TV sets at lost to get rid of an overstock. // 그때는 재고가 많이 있을 것입니다 I think we'll have plenty of them in stock by then.
—량 the total stock — 장부 a stock book — 조사 inventory ; stocktaking — 증가율 a rate of inventory building — 투자 inventory investment —품 goods in stock〔a storehouse〕; stored goods ; stock〔goods〕in store ; stock〔goods〕on〔in〕hand —품계(品係) a stock clerk
재고 정리 在庫整理 clearance ; inventory adjustment
— 대매출 a clearance〔stocktaking〕sale —품 clearance goods
재곤두치다 fall headlong〔head over heels〕; tumble down
재공연 再公演 a repeat performance ; replaying ; reopening ; a rerun —하다 repeat《the same play》; present〔stage〕《a play》again ; show《a play》again ; replay ; rerun
재관 在官 ⇨ 재직(在職)
재교 再校 the second proof —하다 read the second proofs ; proofread a second time ¶ 재교를 요하다 require a second proof // 재교를 요함 Second proof required.
재교부 再交付 reissue ; renewal《of a certificate》; regrant —하다 reissue《a passport》; renew
재교육 再教育 re-education ; retraining —하다 re-educate ; retrain ¶ 재교육을 받다 be re-educated ; be retrained
재구성 再構成 reconstruction ; reorganization ; reconstitution ; —하다 reconstruct ; reorganize ; reconstitute
재구속 再拘束 〖법〗 (a) remand —하다 remand《a person》(in custody)
재군비 再軍備 rearmament ; remilitarization —하다 rearm ; remilitarize《a country》
— 계획 remilitarization〔rearmament〕program
재귀 再歸 return ; reflection ; recurrence ; relapsing —하다 return ; come〔go〕back
— 대명사 a reflexive pronoun — 동사 a

reflexive verb — 반응 〖의학〗 a recurrent reaction —열 〖의학〗 recurrent〔relapsing〕 fever — 용법 the reflexive use

재규어 〖동물〗 a jaguar

재근 在勤 holding office ; staying in office —하다 hold office〔a post〕; serve ; work ¶ 지방 재근의 관리 officials resident in the provinces∥서대문 경찰서에 재근하다 hold a post in *Sudaemun* Police Station

**재기 才氣 a flash of wit ; talent ¶ 재기가 발랄하다 be very witty〔clever〕; be of brilliant talent

재기 才器 [재간] talent ; gift ; ability ; capability ; [사람] an able〔a talented, a gifted〕 man ; a man of talent

재기 再起 a comeback ; rising again ; [회복] recovery ; restoration ; rally —하다 come back ; rise again ; recover ; restore ; rally ¶ 재기 불능이다 be beyond recovery∥그는 재기 불능이라고들 한다 His recovery is pronounced hopeless〔impossible〕./His chance of recovery is said to be hopeless.

재깍 with a click ; with a snap

재깍거리다 keep clicking

재깍재깍 [소리] with repeated clicks〔snaps〕 with repeated bumps〔thuds〕; [일 처리를] with dispatch ; speedily ; quickly ¶ 재깍재깍하기를 좋아하는 사람 a chatterer

재깔거리다 be talkative ; be loquacious ; talk garrulously ; jabber ; gibber ; gabble ; chatter

재깔이다 talk garrulously ; jabber

재깔재깔 garrulously ; chattering ; talkatively ; loquaciously

**재난 災難 [불행] a misfortune ; [재액] a calamity ; a disaster ; a fatality ; [불의의 사고] an accident ; a catastrophe ; a mishap ¶ 불의의 재난 an unforeseen〔unforeseeable〕 accident∥접종하는 재난 a chapter of accidents ; a series of misfortunes∥재난을 당하다 meet with a misfortune〔an accident〕∥재난을 면하다 escape a disaster〔calamity〕

재넘어 a violent wind blowing from a mountain

재녀 才女 [재주가 뛰어난] an intelligent〔a talented〕 woman ; a woman of ability

재년 災年 a year of calamity ; a year of famine

**재능 才能 talent ; ability ; capability ; aptitude ; capacity ; faculty ; gift

> 참고 **ability**는 어떤 일을 능란하게 할 수 있는 능력을 가리키는 말 **capability**는 어떤 일을 하는 데 있어서의 실제적 수완 **capacity**는 사물을 이해하는 능력 **faculty**는 어떤 특수한 능력 **gift**는 천부의 재능 **talent**는 특수한 분야에 있어서의 타고난 재능

¶ 숨은 재능 a hidden talent∥어학적 재능 a linguistic talent∥재능 있는 able ; talented ; capable∥재능 있는 사람 an able〔a talented〕 man ; a man of parts∥재능을 발휘하다 display one's ability〔talents〕; give full play to one's ability∥그는 그것을 할 재능이 있다 He has the ability to do it. ∥그는 천성적으로 재능이 풍부하다 He is richly gifted by nature.

*재다[1] ① [자로] measure ; gauge ; survey (측량하다) ; sound (수심을) ¶ 자로 재다 take measurements with a ruler∥키를 재다 measure one's height∥바다의 깊이를 재다 take soundings in a sea ; sound a sea∥산의 높이를 재다 measure the height of a mountain∥체온을 재다 take one's temperature∥그 가치는 돈으로 잴 수 없다 Its value cannot be measured by money.

② [헤아리다] calculate ; give careful consideration ; view ¶ 일을 재서 하다 carry out one's plan with discretion∥여러 가지 각도로 재보다 view 《a matter》 from various angles

③ [염탐하다] spy upon 《a person》; sound〔investigate〕 《a person》 on a subject ; feel out 《a person's》 view ¶ 형세를 재다 feel out the situation∥회사의 내정을 재다 investigate the inside affairs of a company∥사람의 마음을 재다 sound (out) a person ; tap a person's opinion

④ [탄환을] load 《a gun》; charge ; feed 《a gun》 ¶ 나는 총에다 탄환을 쟀다 I charged the gun with a shot.

⑤ [으시대다] be proud of ; be boasted of ; be high-browed ¶ 그것은 잴 만한 일이 못된다 That is nothing to be proud of. ∥너무 재지말고 그 사진을 보여 줘 Stop making such a big deal of it and show it to us.

⑥ [재우다] press ; smooth 《down》; lodge (사람을) ¶ 머리를 재다 set one's hair ; smooth one's hair down∥솜을 재다 have the cotton pressed

⑦ [쟁이다] pile on〔up〕; put in layers ; lay one thing on another ¶ 높이 재다 pile up high∥쌀가마를 재다 pile up bags of rice

**재다[2] [동작이] (be) quick ; nimble ; agile ; alert ; [입이] talkative ; loose-tongued ¶ 손이 잰 사람 a person with nimble fingers∥걸음이 재다 have quick steps∥입이 재다 be talkative〔loose-tongued〕; have a ready tongue

재단 財團 a foundation

— 법인 a foundation ; a foundational juridical〔juristic〕 person — 법인 학교 an endowed school 국제 — an international consortium 금융 — a syndicate 록펠러 — the Rockefeller Foundation 카네기 국제 평화 — the Carnegie Endowment for International Peace

재단 裁斷 [재결] decision ; judgment ; [마

름질] cutting —하다 judge ; decide ; rule ; cut (마르다) ¶ 재단을 내리다 pass judgment 《on》// 재단에 맡기다 leave 《a matter》 to 《a person's》 judgment
—기 a cutter ; a cutting machine —법 cutting —사 a cutter —판 a cutting board

재담 才談 a witticism —하다 talk wittily

재당숙 再堂叔 one's father's second cousin

재당질 再堂姪 a second cousin's son

재덕 才德 talent and virtue ¶ 재덕을 겸비한 부인 a virtuous and talented lady // 재덕을 겸비하다 be both talented and virtuous

재독 再讀 reading again ; a second reading —하다 read again ; reread ; reperuse

재돌입 再突入 [대기권으로의] re-entry 《into the atmosphere》 ¶ (로켓이) 대기권으로 재돌입하다 re-enter the atmosphere
— 조종 장치 re-entry controls

재동 才童 a clever child ; a child of talent ; an infant prodigy

재두루미 〖새〗 a white-naped crane

재떨이 an ash tray

재래 在來 ¶ 재래의 usual ; common ; ordinary ; traditional ; conventional // 재래의 것과는 전혀 다르다 It is very different in nature from the existing kind.
— 무기 conventional weapons — 방침 《along》 the line(s) one has pursued 〔followed〕 so〔thus〕 far — 습관 traditional usage —식 conventional type —종 a native kind ; the natural species —종 딸기 native strawberries

재래 再來 a second coming〔advent〕; reincarnation —하다 come again ¶ 예수의 재래 the Second Advent of Christ // 예수 재래설 Adventism

재래 齎來 bringing about〔on, forth〕 —하다 bring ; bring about〔on, forth〕 ¶ 불행을 재래하다 bring about a misfortune

재략 才略 resources ; tact ; parts ¶ 재략이 있다 be resourceful ; be tactful ; be adroit

재량 裁量 discretion ; decision ¶ …의 재량으로 at 《a person's》 discretion // …의 재량에 맡기다 leave 《a matter》 to 《a person's》 discretion ; give 《a person》 a free hand〔rein〕 《in a matter》
— 처분 discretional〔discretionary〕 disposition 자기 — 《at》 one's own discretion 자유 —권 discretionary power 〔authority〕

재력 財力 financial power〔ability, status, means〕; wealth ; competence ¶ 재력 있는 사람 a man of means 〔wealth〕

재련 再鍊 [쇠의] resmelting ; reforging ; [목재·석재의] refinishing 《wood》; retouching —하다 reforge ; resmelt ; refinish ; retouch

재록 載錄 —하다 record ; put on record ¶ 재록되어 있다 be given 〔found〕 《in a glossary》

재록 再錄 —하다 re-record ; record again ; record anew

재롱 才弄 (baby's) cute tricks ¶ 재롱을 부리다 act cute ; do cute things
—둥이 a cute baby ; a sweet baby doing cute things

†**재료 材料** stuff ; material ; raw material (원료) ; data (자료) ; ingredients (성분) ¶ 풍부한〔빈약한〕 재료 abundant〔scanty〕 materials // 재료를 공급하다 supply〔furnish〕 《a person》 with materials ; afford data 《for》// 재료를 조달하다 procure〔get〕 materials // 재료를 수집하다 collect 〔amass〕 materials 《for》// 이 집은 좋은 재료를 썼다 This house is built of good materials.
—비 the cost of materials ; the material cost — 시험 material testing — 시험기 a material testing machine — 역학 the strength of materials — 창고 a material store —표 a material list ; a bill of materials 건축 — building〔construction〕 materials 기제(旣製) — manufactured materials 비(낙)관 — a disheartening〔an encouraging〕 element〔factor〕 실험 — materials for experiments

재료 강도 시험 材料强度試驗 a test on the strength of materials

재류 在留 residence ¶ 재류의 resident ; living 《in, at》 —하다 reside ; dwell ; stay
—민 the residents — 외국인 foreign residents 《in, at》; resident aliens 《in》 ¶ 서울의 재류 외국인 foreign residents in *Seoul*.

재리[1] [나막신의] a spike〔calk, cleat〕 (on clogs)

재리[2] [땅꾼] a young snake-catcher ; [구두쇠] a miser ; a niggard ; a skinflint ; a screw

재리 財利 property and profit

재림 再臨 a second coming 〔advent〕; reincarnation —하다 come again ; be reincarnated ¶ 그리스도의 재림 the Second Advent of Christ // 그리스도 재림설 Adventism // 그는 모짜르트의 재림이라 하겠다 He is "a second Mozart."

재명 才名 talent and fame ; fame for one's talent ¶ 재명을 떨치다 win fame for one's talent ; be well known as a man of talent

***재목 材木** wood ; timber 《영》; lumber 《미》; a log (통나무) ¶ 재목을 벌채하다 lumber
—상 a timber〔lumber〕 dealer〔merchant〕; a timber〔lumber〕 trader〔wholesaler〕; a wholesale dealer in lumber〔timber〕; the lumber business — 운반선 a lumber carrier — 적재장 a lumberyard 《미》; a timberyard 《영》 —차 a lumber〔timber〕 wagon〔truck〕

재못 〖건축〗 a peg wedge
재무 財務 financial affairs
— **감독관** a comptroller (of the treasury) — **고문** a financial advisor —**관** a financier ; a finance secretary ; a financial commissioner〔agent〕 — **관리** financial management —**부** the Ministry of Finance ; the Exchequer《영》; the Department of the Treasury《미》 —**부 장관** the Minister of Finance ; the Chancellor of the Exchequer《영》; the Secretary of the Treasury《미》 —**성(省)** [미국의] the Department of the Treasury ; the Treasury Department — **위원회** the Finance Committee — **제표(諸表)** financial statements — **행정** financial administration
재무장 再武裝 rearmament —**하다** rearm
도덕 — 운동 Moral Rearmament Movement《MRA》
재무진동 〖광물〗 ashen iron-ore ; iron ash
*****재물 財物** property ; means ; effects ; goods ; treasures ; a fortune ¶ 재물에 눈이 어두워지다 be dazzled by riches // 남의 재물을 빼앗다 rob《a person》of his property
***재미** amusement ; enjoyment ; fun ; interest ; [만족] satisfaction ; [취미] hobby ; comfort ¶ 재미있는 사람 a man of humor // 재미있는 이야기〔책〕 an interesting〔amusing〕 story〔book〕// 재미없는 소문 unpleasant〔unsavory〕 rumors // 재미있다 be interesting ; be amusing ; be enjoyable ; be pleasant // 재미없다 be uninteresting ; be dull ; be insipid ; be unpleasant // 그는 그 연극이 별로 재미없었다 He was little amused by the play. // 그는 낚시질의 재미를 모른다 He cannot see the fun of fishing. // 결과는 재미없었다 The result was unsatisfactory. // 이 책을 재미있게 읽었다 I have read this book with great interest. // 이거 재미가 적은데 The prospects are not encouraging. /Things are getting worse. // 수술 결과가 아무래도 재미없다 The result of the operation is far from reassuring. // 요즈음 장사 재미가 어떻습니까 How is your business getting along ? // 그의 건강이 재미없다 His health is in poor shape. // 낚시질이 그의 유일한 재미다 Fishing is his sole comfort. // 그는 재미로 꽃을 기른다 He grows flowers for a hobby.
재미를 보다 관용 have fun〔a good time〕
재미를 붙이다 관용 take interest〔pleasure〕 in ; be interested in
재미 在美 residing in America ¶ 재미의 in America // 재미 중에 while in America // 재미 중이다 be in America
— **교포** Korean residents in America ; Korean people (residing) in America — **유학생** Korean students studying in America

재민 災民 the afflicted people ; the sufferers ; the victims of calamity〔disaster〕 ¶ 재민을 구호하다 carry out the relief of victims of a disaster
— **구호금** disaster relief fund **한해** — sufferers from the drought
재받이 an ashpan ; an ash receiver (난로의)
***재발 再發** [병의] relapse ; recurrence ; return ; recrudescence ; [재발송] a second dispatch〔sending〕《of a letter》 —**하다** [병이] recur ; relapse ; return ; [다시 보내다] send out〔dispatch〕 again ¶ 그 열병은 재발할 염려가 없다 There is no fear of a return〔relapse〕 of the fever. // 그는 늑막염이 재발했다 He has relapsed into pleurisy.
재발견 再發見 rediscovery ; recovery —**하다** rediscover ; recover
재발급 再發給 reissuance ; (a) reissue —**하다** reissue《a licence》
재발족 再發足 starting anew —**하다** start out again ; begin anew〔afresh〕
재발행 再發行 reissue —**하다** reissue
재방송 再放送 rebroadcast(ing) —**하다** rebroadcast
재배 再拜 bowing twice ; a second bowing〔obeisance〕 ; [편지 끝에] "Sincerely yours" ; "As ever" —**하다** bow twice
†**재배 栽培** cultivation ; culture ; growing ; raising —**하다**cultivate ; grow ; raise ; rear ¶ 토마토를 재배하고 있는 토지 the tomato growing land ; the area under tomato cultivation // 그는 과일을 재배하고 있다 He is growing〔raising〕 fruit. // 이 지방에서는 담배가 널리 재배되고 있다 Tobacco is widely cultivated in this part of the country.
— **고무** plantation rubber —**법** a method of cultivation —**자** a grower ; a cultivator —**종** agricultural species **고무** — rubber culture **과수** — fruit growing ; pomiculture **담배** — tobacco farming〔raising〕 **촉성(促成)** — forcing (culture) **국화** —**법** a method of chrysanthemum culture ; how to rear〔cultivate, grow〕 chrysanthemums
재배분 再配分 ⇨ 재분배(再分配)
재배치 再配置 reassignment ; relocation ; realignment ; rearrangement —**하다** reassign ; relocate ; realign
재벌 財閥 a financial clique ; plutocracy ; the plutocrats ¶ 재벌의 횡포 plutocratic despotism
카네기 — the Carnegie financial interests〔plutocracy〕
재범 再犯 a second offense (죄) ; a second conviction ; a second offender (범인) —**하다** commit a second offense
재벽 再壁 〖건축〗 second coating〔plastering〕 ; overplastering —**하다** coat〔plaster〕 again ; reface
재변 才辯 a witty remark ; wit ; [구변]

oratorical talent ; eloquence ; the gift of gab 《구》 ¶ 재변이 좋다 have a fluent〔ready〕 tongue

재변 災變 a calamity ; a disaster

재보 財寶 riches ; valuables ; treasures ; wealth ; precious things

재보험 再保險 reinsurance ; reassurance (생명 보험의) **—하다** reinsure ; reassure

—자 a reinsurer **— 조항** a reinsurance clause **— 중개인** a reinsurance broker **비례 —** quota share reinsurance **의무 —** obligatory reinsurance **임의 —** facultative reinsurance **자동 —** automatic reinsurance **초과액 —** excess(-of-loss) reinsurance **총괄 —** general reinsurance **특정 —** specific reinsurance **할당 —** reinsurance by quota **피—자** the reinsured

재복무 再服務 re-enlistment ; extension of one's military service **—하다** reenlist ; extend one's military service

⁑**재봉 裁縫** sewing ; needlework ; tailoring **—하다** sew ; do needlework ¶ 재봉을 잘〔못〕하다 be clever〔awkward〕 in sewing // 여자는 재봉을 잘한다 She is handy with the needle.

— 가위 a pair of sewing scissors **—과** a sewing course **— 교수** instruction in needlework **— 도구** sewing things〔requisites〕 **— 도구통** a housewife **— 레슨** a lesson in sewing **—사** a tailor ; a tailoress (여자) ; a dress-maker (부인복의) **—새** 〖새〗 a tailorbird **— 선생** a sewing master〔mistress〕 **—실〔대〕** a sewing room〔table〕 **— 학교** a sewing school

재봉쇄 再封鎖 reblocking ; refreezing **—하다** reblock ; refreeze

재봉틀 裁縫— a sewing machine ¶ 재봉틀로 박다 sew 《a thing》 by machine // 이건 손으로 꿰맨 겁니까 재봉틀로 한 것입니까 Was the sewing done by hand or by machine ? /Is this handsewed or machine-sewed ?

— 기름 sewing-machine oil **— 바늘〔실〕** a sewing-machine needle〔thread〕 **발—** a pedal-operated〔treadle〕 sewing machine **손—** a hand sewing machine **전기〔고주파(高周波)〕 —** an electric〔a high-frequency〕 sewing machine

재분배 再分配 redistribution ; reallotment **—하다** redistribute ; reallot ¶ 부의 재분배 redistribution of wealth

*__재빠르다__ [동작이] (be) quick ; nimble ; agile ; alert ; [성질이] quick-witted ; smart ; sharp ; shrewd ¶ 재빠른 사람 a shrewd person // 재빠르게 quickly ; nimbly ; agilely ; alertly ; (as) quick as thought ; like winking 《속》 // 재빠른 동작 an agile〔alert〕 movement // 재빠르게 움직이다 move smartly // 손이 재빠르다 have nimble fingers

재빨리 quickly ; rapidly ; promptly ; fast ; without delay ; at once

재사 才士 a man of talent〔ability〕 ; a man of parts ; a clever person ; a wit

— 가인 wit and beauty **— 다병** Men of genius are often of delicate health.

†**재산 財産** property ; a fortune ; an estate ; assets (자산) ¶ 전 재산 one's whole fortune // 먹고 살 만한 재산 a competence // 재산을 만들다 make〔amass〕 a fortune // 재산을 이어받다 inherit〔succeed to, come into〕 a fortune // 재산을 몰수하다 confiscate property // 재산을 탕진하다 run through one's fortune // 재산을 청산하다 wind up an estate ; liquidate // 재산을 노리고 결혼하다 marry 《a man, a girl》 for 《his, her》 fortune ; marry for money // 국민의 생명과 재산을 보호하다 protect the life and property of nationals // 100만원의 재산을 남기다 leave an estate of a million *won* // 당신의 재산은 얼마나 됩니까 How much are you worth ? // 만일 너에게 갑자기 큰 재산이 생기면 어떻게 하겠니 What would you do if you suddenly came into a fortune ?

—가 a man〔person〕 of wealth〔fortune, means, property〕 ; a wealthy〔rich〕 person ; a man of (large) substance **— 계정** 〖부기〗 assets and liabilities account **— 관리** property management ; administration〔custody〕 of property **— 관리인** an administrator〔a custodian〕 of property **—구(區)** a financial ward **—권** property right ; the right to own〔to hold〕 property **—권 설정〔이전〕** settlement〔transfer〕 of the title to a property **— 매각손(賣却損)** 〖부기〗 loss on sale of property **— 매각익(賣却益)** 〖부기〗 profits on assets sold **— 목록** an inventory (of property) ; a list of property **— 반환 청구** a claim for recapture of property **— 배당〔소득〕** a property dividend〔income〕 **—법** the law of property **— 보전** preservation of property **— 보존 회사** a property holding corporation **— 분리〔인도, 보증, 처분, 검사〕** separation〔delivery, undertaking, disposition, inspection〕 of property **— 분여(分與)** distribution of property ; settlement **— 상속** succession to 《a person's》 property **— 상태** one's financial conditions〔position〕 ; the financial status〔standing〕 《of a firm》 **— 선취권** a (prior) lien on property **—세** property tax 《미》 ; capital levy 《영》 **—세법** 〖법〗 the Capital Levy Act **— 손해 보험** property damage insurance **— 양도** conveyance of an estate **— 이전세** a tax on transfer of properties **— 이전자** 〖법〗 a transferor **— 전환** conversion of property **— 증가세** (a) property increase〔increment〕 tax **— 차압** attachment〔seizure〕 of property **— 청구권 기금** the Property Claims Fund **— 청산** liquidation of property ; property liquidation **— 평가** property valuation〔appraisal〕 **— 평가손**

(評價損) 〖부기〗 losses from appraised assets — 평가익(評價益) 〖부기〗 an income from appreciation of assets — 피양도인(被讓渡人) an assignee ; a transferee —형(刑) a pecuniary punishment — 회계 〖부기〗 a property〔an assets and liabilities〕 account 개별 — a several estate 개인〔공공〕 — individual〔public〕 property 공유 — common〔joint〕 property ; an estate in common ; a joint estate 국유 — state-owned〔national〕 property 사유 — private property ; peculium 《*pl.* -lia》 세습〔상속〕 — hereditary〔heritable〕 property ; hereditament ; a heritage ; a patrimony 알— net assets 유형〔무형〕 — tangible〔intangible〕 property 증여(贈與) — a settlement

재살 災煞 disaster due to taking an inauspicious direction

재삼 再三 two or three times ; [부사적] more than once ; repeatedly ; again and again ; often ; frequently ¶ 재삼재사 over and over again // 재삼 시험하다 try again and again ; make several attempts ; try and try again // 재삼 말해도 듣지 않는다 He turns a deaf ear to my repeated warnings.

재상 在喪 being in mourning 《for one's parent》

재상 宰相 the prime minister ; the premier (under the king)

재상영 再上映 a rerun ; a repeat 〔revival〕 ; a reshowing 《of a movie》 —하다 rerun ; repeat

재색 才色 wit and beauty ¶ 재색을 겸비하다 be beautiful and talented ; have both wit and beauty

****재생 再生** restoration to life ; revival ; resuscitation ; rebirth ; a return to life ; [폐물의] rejuvenation ; remaking ; reproduction ; regeneration ; reclamation —하다 revive ; resuscitate ; return to life ; [폐물을] remake ; rejuvenate ; regenerate ; reproduce ; reclaim ¶ 머리 털의 재생 regrowth of hair // 재생의 은혜를 입다 owe 《a person》 one's life // 재생의 감이 있다 feel greatly relieved // 이 알루미늄 깡통은 재생해서 쓸 수 있다 This aluminum can is recyclable.

— 고무 reclaimed rubber —기(器) 〖전기〗 a regenerator —로(爐) a regenerative furnace —법 a reproduction process — 불량〔능〕성 빈혈 〖의학〗 aplastic〔aregenerative〕 anemia — 산업 the reproductive industry — 섬유 regenerated fiber — 섬유소 regenerated cellulose —식 검파(式檢波) 〖무선〗 regenerative detection — 양모 reworked wool — 장치 [보일러의] a regenerative apparatus ; [녹음·녹화의] playback equipment — 터빈 a regenerative turbine

재생산 再生産 reproduction —하다 reproduce

—론(論) the theory of reproduction 축소〔확대〕 — reproduction on a regressive〔progressive〕 scale

***재선 再選** reelection ; a second selection —하다 reelect ; select a second time ¶ 재선되다 be reelected 《Mayor, to the Assembly》

재선거 再選擧 (a) reelection ; a recall election ¶ 재선거를 실시하다 hold a reelection〔recall election〕

재선적 再船積 re-exportation ; reshipment —하다 re-export ; reship ; return ; ship back

— 신청서 an application for reshipment — 인가서 a reshipment permit —표 a reshipping slip —품 reshipments ; returned goods — 화물 a return cargo

재설 再說 recapitulation ; a repeated explanation —하다 explain again ; recapitulate

재세 在世 being alive ; living ¶ 재세의 living ; in life // 재세 시에 during one's lifetime ; while one was alive // 재세 중에 그를 알고 있는 사람들 people who knew him in life

재소자 在所者 a prisoner ; a prison inmate ; the criminal population 《총칭》

재송 再送 resending ; reforwarding —하다 send again ; resend ; reforward

— 전보 a retransmitted telegram (재송된) ; a telegram to be retransmitted (재송할)

***재수 財數** luck ; fortune ¶ 재수 좋은 사람 a lucky〔fortunate〕 person // 재수가 좋다 be fortunate ; be lucky // 재수가 없다 be unlucky ; be unfortunate ; be out of luck // 재수없게 unluckily ; unfortunately ; by ill luck // 재수가 트였다 Fortune has begun to smile upon him. / The wheel of fortune has begun to roll his way. // 재수도 되게 없군 What a stroke of luck ! // 너는 재수가 좋다 You're in luck.

재수없는 포수는 곰을 잡아도 웅담이 없다 [속담] The bread never falls but on its buttered side.

재수 再修 —하다 cram to repeat a college entrance exam ¶ 또 한해를 재수해야 하는구나 Ah, me. another extra year of cramming for entrance exams.

—생 a student who failed a college-entrance exam and has been cramming to try again ; [유급생] a repeater 《미》

재수입 再輸入 reimport ; reimportation —하다 reimport

— 면허장 a reimport permit (세관의) ; a bill of store — 신고서 a reimport declaration —품 reimported articles ; reimports

재수출 再輸出 re-export ; re-exportation —하다 re-export

—품 re-exports ; goods re-exported〔for reexport〕 ; re-exported articles

재승 박덕 才勝薄德 superior talents and

inferior virtue ―하다 be more talented than virtuous

재시합 再試合 a return game 〔match〕 ; rematch (of a game)

재시험 再試驗 a re-examination ; a retest ―하다 re-examine ; examine〔test〕 again ; give〔have〕 a make-up test

재식 才識 talents and knowledge ; ability and discernment〔intelligence〕

재식 栽植 planting (trees) ―하다 plant ; set

재실 再室 [후실] a second wife ; 『건축』 a house built with used timbers

재심 再審 re-examination ; [재판의] retrial ; a new trial ―하다 re-examine ; try over again ; hear again ; have a new trial ¶ 재심을 청구하다 apply for a new trial

― 법원 a court of review ―사 (a) reexamination ; (a) review ― 소송 an action for renewal of procedure

재심문 再審問 [증인의] re-examination

*재앙 災殃 [재난] a disaster ; a calamity ; [불행] a misfortune ; evils ¶ 재앙을 당하다 meet with a misfortune 〔calamity〕 // 재앙을 자초하다 bring a calamity upon oneself // 재앙을 피하다 keep off a misfortune

재액 災厄 a calamity ; mishap ; a misfortune

재야 在野 ―하다 be out of power 〔office〕 ¶ 재야의 명사 distinguished men out of office // 재야 10년에 이르다 spend ten years in〔with the〕 opposition

―당 a non-Government party ; the Opposition ; the outs ; a party out of office〔power〕 ― 시대 ¶ 재야 시대에 when〔while〕 (one is) out of power

재약하다 ―藥― load 《a gun》 ; charge

재양 載陽 ―하다 dry 《starched silk》 on a board

―틀 a drying device ―판 a drying-board

재연 再燃 recrudescence ; recurrence ; revival ; resuscitation ―하다 revive ; break up again ; come to the fore again ; burn up again (불이) ¶ 문제의 재연 resuscitation of a problem // 사랑의 재연 rekindling of love // 인플레의 재연 recurrence of inflation // 문제가 재연되었다 The problem has come to the fore again.

재연 再演 a second presentation ; an encore (프) ; rerunning (of a movie) ―하다 present〔produce〕 again ; give an encore ¶ 재연을 청하다 encore 《a song, a singer》 ; call〔cry〕 for an encore

재영 在營 ¶ 재영중의 during one's military service

― 기간 the period of active service

재예 才藝 talent and accomplishments ¶ 재예가 출중하다 be highly accomplished

재외 在外 (being) abroad ; overseas

― 공관 embassies and legations abroad ― 대리점 an agency abroad ― 동포〔교포〕 Korean residents〔nationals〕 abroad ; overseas Koreans ; Koreans remaining abroad ― 부채 overseas liabilities ― 사무소 an overseas agency ― 연구원 a research student abroad ― 예금 foreign deposits ― 자산〔재산〕 overseas〔external〕 assets ― 크레디트 a foreign credit ; a credit in a foreign country ― 투자 foreign investments

재욕 財慾 greediness〔desire〕 for wealth ¶ 재욕이 많다 be greedy for wealth

재우 fast ; quickly ; nimbly ; agilely

*재우다[1] [자게 하다] put 《a person》 to sleep ; induce sleep ; make 《a person》 sleep ; afford 《a person》 lodging ; give 《a person》 bed ; put 《a baby》 to bed ; lull 《a child》 to sleep ¶ 노래를 불러 재우다 sing 《a baby》 to sleep // 자장가를 불러 아이를 재우다 lullaby a child to sleep // 하룻밤 재우다 give 《a person》 a night's lodging ; give 《a person》 a bed overnight ; take 《a traveler》 in for the night

재우다[2] [재다] load with ; press down ⇨ 재다

재우치다 finish up quickly ; dispatch 《work》 ; make short work 《of》

재원 財源 financial〔economic〕 resources ; a revenue source ; funds ¶ 재원이 없다 be at a loss for a source of revenue // 재원이 풍부하다 be abundant in resources // 재원을 구하다 look for a source of revenue // 전쟁으로 나라의 재원이 거의 고갈했다 The war has nearly drained the country of its resources. // 대우를 개선하고 싶어도 재원이 없다 We have no means to finance the desired raise in the wages.

재원 才媛 a talented girl ; an accomplished woman ; [학문이 있는] a girl with scholastic ability ; a woman of literary accomplishments

재위 在位 being upon the throne ; the period of one's reign ―하다 be on the throne ; reign ¶ 재위 시에 in one's reign // 재위 30년에 after a reign of 30 years // 엘리자베스 1세 재위 중에 during the reign of Queen Elizabeth I // 재위 5년에 서거하시다 die in the fifth year of 《one's》 reign

재음미 再吟味 (a) re-examination ; a review ―하다 re-examine ; review

재의 再議 reconsideration ; rediscussion ―하다 reconsider ; discuss again ¶ 일사 부재의의 원칙 a principle not to deliberate the same measure twice during the same session // 재의에 붙이다 submit 《a matter》 for reconsideration // 재의가 불필요하다 The matter needs no reconsideration.

재인 才人 ① [재사] a man of talent ⇨ 재사 ② [광대] an acrobatic tumbler

재인식 再認識 a new understanding 《of》 ; reperception ; reappraisal ―하다

renew understanding ; see 《a matter》 in a new light ; take another look 《at》 ; look into further ; have a new understanding 《of》 ; reperceive ¶ 정세를 재인식하다 have a new understanding of the situation

재일 在日 residing in Japan
— **교포** Korean residents in Japan — **조선인 총연맹** ⇨ 조총련 — **한국 거류 민단** the Korean Residents Association in Japan

재임 在任 being in office —**하다** be in office ; hold office〔a post〕 ¶ 재임 시에 while in office ; during one's term 〔tenure〕 of office

재임 再任 reappointment —**하다** be reappointed

재입국 再入國 re-entry 《into a country》 —**하다** re-enter
— **허가서** a reentry permit

재입학 再入學 readmission 《to a school》 ; reentrance ¶ 재입학을 허가하다 readmit 《a boy to a school》

재자 才子 a man of talent〔ability〕 ; a man of parts ; a wit ; a clever man
— **가인** wit and beauty — **다병** Men of genius are often of delicate health

재작 裁酌 ⇨ 재량

재작년 再昨年 the year before last

재작일 再昨日 the day before yesterday ⇨ 그저께

재잘거리다 chatter ; prattle ; babble ; gabble ; gibber ; cackle ; blather ; jabber ; prate ¶ 재잘거리는 사람 a tattling 〔prattling〕 person ; a tattler // 재잘거리는 여자〔아이〕 a chatterbox

⁑**재잘재잘** chatteringly ; tattlingly ; garrulously ; glibly ; volubly

재재거리다 ⇨ 재잘거리다

재재작년 再再昨年 three years back 〔ago〕 ; two years before last ; the year but one before last

재재하다 (be) garrulous ; talkative ; chattering

재적 在籍 enrollment —**하다** be on the register〔roll〕 ¶ 이 반은 재적 학생 수가 52명이다 This class has 52 pupils on the register. // 이 학교의 재적 학생 총수는 2,000명이다 The school has a total enrollment of two thousand. // 그 대학에는 중국 학생이 다수 재적하고 있다 The university has a large registration of Chinese students.
—**자** [학생] students on the register

재적 材積 overall measurement of a piece of lumber

재전환 再轉換 reconversion 《of industries》

⁑**재정 財政** finances ; financial affairs 《of a company》 ; economy ¶ 재정적 부채 financial obligations // 재정적 원조 financial support〔help〕 // 재정적 지불 불능 economic insolvency // 재정상의 financial ; fiscal // 재정상 이유로 on financial grounds. // 재정이 곤란하다 be in a state of pecuniary embarrassment ; be in financial difficulty // 재정이 풍부하다 be well off ; be in abundant circumstances // 재정을 정리하다 adjust the finances ; put one's finances in order // 재정을 확립하다 put the finances 《of a company》 on a firm basis // 재정 상태를 개선하다 improve one's financial status〔position〕 // 국가 재정을 재건하다 rebuild〔reconstruct〕 the national economy // 그는 재정적으로 곤란하다 He is in a bad way financially. /He is in financial difficulties〔trouble〕. // 그런 사치는 재정상 할 수 없다 I cannot afford such luxury. /My means cannot afford such luxury.
—**가** a financier ; a financial man — **감독** financial control — **계획** a financial 〔fiscal〕 program〔plan〕 — **고문** a financial advisor — **긴축** retrenchment in finance ¶ 재정 긴축을 하다 tighten one's belt〔purse strings〕 —**력** financial 〔purse-string〕 power —**면** financial aspects — **문제** a financial question 〔problem〕 —**법** the Finance Act — **법안** a finance bill — **보고** a fiscal report —**상태** the financial standing〔conditions〕 — **연도** a fiscal 〔financial〕 year — **연설** a financial address — **인플레** inflation caused by budgetary deficit — **자금** financial funds ; funds for public finance — **전문가** a financial expert — **정리** financial reform ; readjustment of financial affairs — **정책** a financial〔fiscal〕 policy —**통(通)** a financial expert — **통계** finance statistics — **투융자** treasury loans and investments — **투자** (a) financial investment — **핍박** financial straits〔pressure, stringency〕 —**학** the science of finance ; (public) finance —**학 연구가** a student of finance — **학자** a financier — **혼란** financial derangement **가정** — family finances ¶ 가정 재정을 쥐다 hold the strings to the family purse **건전** — sound〔balanced〕 finance **국가** — national finance ¶ 국가 재정을 쥐다 hold the strings to the government purse **시(市)**— the city finance〔purse〕 **적자** — red-ink 〔unbalanced〕 finance **지방** — local (government) finance **흑자** — balanced finance

재정 再訂 revision —**하다** revise
—**판** a second revised edition

재정 裁定 decision ; arbitration ; adjudication —**하다** decide ; arbitrate ; adjudicate
—**비(費)** 〖노동〗 arbitration expenses — **서(書)** an award —**안(案)** 〖노동〗 an arbitration draft〔proposal〕 —**자** an adjudicator — **조항[노사간의]** an arbitration clause —**환** arbitrated exchange

재제 再製 remanufacture ; reproduction

—하다 remake ; remanufacture ; rework ; reproduce
— 고무 reclaimed rubber —염(鹽) refined salt — 원모(原毛) shoddy —품 reclaimed〔made-over〕 goods ; rebuilt〔reprocessed, remodeled〕 articles

재조 在朝 ¶ 재조의 now in power〔office〕; governmental // 재조 재야의 명사 noted people in and out of official life

재조사 再調査 re-examination ; reinvestigation —하다 re-examine ; reinvestigate

재조직 再組織 reorganization —하다 reorganize

재종 再從 a second cousin
—간 second-cousinship —손 the grandson of a cousin —수 the wife of a second cousin —숙 a second cousin of one's father —제(弟) a (younger male) second cousin —조 a cousin of one's grandfather — 조모 the wife of one's grandfather's cousin —질(姪) a son of one's second cousin —형(兄) a(an) (older male) second cousin

†재주 [재능] ability ; talent ; gifts ; parts ; [솜씨] skill ; dexterity ¶ 재주 있는 talented ; capable ; gifted // 재주 없는 talentless ; dull-witted ; stupid // 재주 있는 사람 a man of talent〔ability〕; a talented man // 재주를 발휘하다 display one's ability〔talent〕// 재주를 부리다 exercise one's talent ; give full play to one's ability // 재주를 피우다 prostitute one's talent // 그는 어학에 재주가 있다 He has a talent for language. // 현재의 지위에서는 충분히 재주를 발휘할 수 없다 His present position gives little scope to his ability.
재주는 곰이 넘고 돈은 되놈이 번다 (속담) One beats the bush and another catches the birds. /Two dogs strive for a bone, and a third run away with it.

재주 在住 residence —하다 live ; reside ; be resident ¶ 서울 재주의 외국인 foreign residents in *Seoul* ; foreigners living in *Seoul*
—자 a resident

재주 齋主 〖불교〗 the person who requests a Buddhist priest to perform a service for the soul of the dead

재주껏 to the best of one's ability ; to the top of one's bent ; as far〔best, much〕 as one can

재주꾼 a person of high talents ¶ 그는 대단한 재주꾼이다 He is clever to fingernails〔highly intelligent〕.

재주 넘기 a somersault ; a somerset

재주 넘다 turn〔make, do, cut, cast, perform〕 a somersault ; somerset ; turn〔do〕 a handspring ; turn (head over) heels

재주문 再注文 renewal of an order ; a repeat commission ; 〖상업〗 a repeat order ; a reorder —하다 renew an order ; reorder

재중 在中 ¶ 재중의 containing // 재중의 물건 the contents《of》// 견본 재중 "Samples" // 사진 재중 "Photographs (only)"

⁑재즈 〖음악〗 jazz ; ragtime music ; razzmatazz《속》
— 밴드 a jazz band — 음악 jazz music —팬 a jazz fan ; a cat《속》; a hip

재지 才智 talent ; tact ; intelligence ¶ 재지 있는 clever ; talented ; intelligent // 재지에 찬 full of wisdom〔wit〕; tactful ; resourceful

재지니 再— a two-year old falcon

재직 在職 —하다 hold office ; be in office〔service〕 ¶ 재직 중의 판사 a judge in active service // 재직 중에 (while) in office // 본교에 재직한 지 20년이 되다 He has served this school for twenty years.
— 연한〔기간〕 one's tenure of office ; one's period of service in a position —자 the holder of a position ; an incumbent

재질 才質 natural endowment ; natural gifts ; talent

재질 材質 the quality of the lumber〔wood〕

재차 再次 [부사적] twice ; again ; a second time ; [두번째로] for the second time ; [한번 더] once more ; once again ¶ 재차의 방문 one's second visit // 재차 시도하다 try again ; make another〔a second〕 attempt // 재차 갈채가 일어났다 The cheering was renewed.

*재채기 sneezing ; a sneeze —하다 sneeze

재천 在天 existing in Heaven ¶ 재천의 in Heaven ; heavenly // 인명은 재천이다 Life and death are providential

재청 再請 a second request ; an encore《프》; [동의에 대한] seconding —하다 request a second time ; encore ; second《a motion》

⁑재촉 pressing ; urging ; demand —하다 press《a person for》; urge《a person to do》; request ; demand ¶ 대답을 재촉하다 press《a person》 for an answer // 빚을 재촉하다 urge《a person》 to pay a debt // 식사를 재촉하다 call for a meal // 재촉하지 않으면 그는 일을 안 한다 He will not do anything unless he is pressed. // 그는 빚을 조금도 재촉하지 않았다 He was very easy with me over the debt.

재촬영 再撮影 〖사진〗 a retake —하다 rephotograph ; retake ; take《a picture》 over again

재출발 再出發 a restart ; a fresh〔new〕 start —하다 make a restart ; make a fresh〔new〕 start〔departure〕; start a fresh

재취 再娶 remarriage (after the death of one's first wife) —하다 remarry ; marry again ; take《another woman》 to wife (after the death of one's first wife)

*재치 才致 wit ; cleverness ; resources ;

tact ¶ 재치 있는 사람 a man of tact ; a tactful〔witty〕 person // 재치가 있다 be quick-witted〔witty, resourceful, tactful, smart, clever〕// 그는 어떤 역할이라도 재치있게 소화해낼 수 있다 He can tackle any role with ease.

재침략 再侵略 reinvasion **—하다** reinvade

재탄 滓炭 dust coal ; (char) coal dust

재탕 再湯 [다시 달임] redecoction ; a second brew 《of the same decoc-tion》 ; [개작] a (literary) rehash ; an adaptation **—하다** decoct again ; make a second brew 《of》 ; make a rehash 《of》 ¶ 재탕한 커피 a second brew of the same grounds of coffee // A 박사 논문의 재탕 a rehash of Dr. A's treatise

재통고 再通告 renotification **—하다** renotify 《a person of a matter》 ; notify 《a person》 again

재통용 再通用 [통화의] remonetization ¶ 재통용시키다 remonetize

재통일 再統一 reunification **—하다** reunify

재투자 再投資 reinvestment **—하다** reinvest ; plow back 《the profits of a business》 ¶ 토지에 재투자하다 reinvest one's money in land

재투표 再投票 revoting **—하다** take a vote again ; renew voting

재티 cinders ; ashes ¶ 재티가 튀다 cinders fly // 재티가 눈에 들어가다 get cinders in one's eye

재판 再版 [중판] reprint ; a second edition〔impression〕 ; [반복] a repetition 《of a past event》 **—하다** reprint ¶ 재판 2천 부 a second impression of 2,000 copies // 재판을 하게 되다 run into a second edition // 재판을 연출하다 repeat 《a person's》 folly ; follow in 《a person's》 wake

†**재판 裁判** justice ; [공판] a trial ; hearing ; [판결] judgment ; decision **—하다** administer justice ; judge 《a person, a case》 ; try 《a person, a case》 ; decide on 《a case》 ; pass judgment on 《a person》 ; adjudicate〔give a decision〕 upon 《a case》 ¶ 공평한 재판 fair justice ; impartial judgment // 재판을 받다 be tried ; stand trial 《for murder》 ; go on trial // 재판을 걸다 lay〔submit〕 《a case》 before the court ; bring a suit against 《a person》 // 재판을 열다 hold a court // 재판에 붙이다 put 《a case》 on trial // 재판에 이기다〔지다〕 win〔lose〕 a suit // 그 사건은 재판 중이다 The case is on trial. / The matter is pending in court. // 재판은 피고의 승소로 끝났다 The case was decided in favor of the defendant.

—관 a judge ; the bench 《총칭》 **—관 소추 위원회** [국회의] the Impeachment Committee **—관 직무 정지** suspension of a judge's functions **—관 탄핵법** the Impeachment of Judges Act **—관 탄핵 재판소** a Court of Impeachment of Judges **—관 회의** a judicial assembly **—구** a judicial district **—권** jurisdiction ; imperium **— 비용** judicial costs **— 수속** legal procedure〔proceedings〕 **—일** a court day **—장** the presiding〔chief〕 judge ; the chief justice 《미》 **—지(地)** the venue **— 확정 채권〔채무〕** a judgment credit〔debt〕 **— 확정 채무자〔채권자〕** a judgment debtor〔creditor〕 **궐석 —** judgment by default **모의 —** a mock trial **약식 —** a summary trial **인민 —** a people's court ; a kangaroo court 《미·구》 **정식 —** a formal trial **확정 —** final judgment

재판매 再販賣 resale

— 가격 resale price **— 가격 유지** resale price maintenance 《rpm》 **— 가격 유지 정책〔계약〕** a resale price maintenance policy〔contract〕

재판서 裁判書 court records ; a written judgment ; the document of a judgment

***재판소 裁判所** a court of justice〔law〕 ; a law-court ; a court-house ¶ 재판소에 출두하다 come into court ; appear in court

재편 再編 ⇨ 재편성

재편성 再編成 reorganization ; reforming ; reshuffle ; revamps **—하다** reorganize ; reform ; reshuffle ; revamp

재평가 再評價 revaluation ; reassessment ; reappraisal **—하다** revaluate ; reassess

—액 the revaluation amount **— 적립금** revaluation reserves **자산 —** revaluation〔reassessment〕 of property **자산 —법** the Assets Revaluation Law

재포장 再包裝 repacking **—하다** repack

재포장 再鋪裝 〖토목〗 resurfacing **—하다** pave again ; resurface

재필 才筆 a brilliant pen ; a clever〔facile〕 style

재하 在荷 stock ; goods (in stock) ; goods on hand ; stored goods ; the inventory ¶ 시장은 재하 과잉 상태다 The market is overstocked.

재하자 在下者 a subordinate ; a person who is under one's authority

재학 才學 ability and learning ; talent and scholarship ¶ 재학을 겸비하다 excel in both ability and learning

***재학 在學** being in school **—하다** be in school〔college〕 ; attend school〔college〕 ¶ 재학 중에 while in〔at〕 school〔college〕 ; during one's school〔college〕 days

— 기간 the period of attendance at school **—생** the students ; an undergraduate (대학의) **— 증명서** a certificate of studentship

재할인 再割引 a rediscount **—하다** rediscount 《a bill》

— 어음 a rediscount bill **—율** a rediscount rate

재합성 再合成 resynthesis **—하다** resynthesize ; synthesize again
재해 災害 [재난] a disaster ; a calamity ; an accident (사고) ¶ 재해의 연속 a series of accidents ; a spell of ill luck // 재해를 입다 suffer from a disaster ; meet with an accident // 금년은 재해가 많은 해였다 This year has been indeed remarkable for frequent disasters.
— **구호법** the Disaster Relief Act — **대책** countermeasures against natural calamities — **방지** prevention of disasters — **보험〔보상〕** accident insurance〔compensation〕 — **복구비** natural disaster relief expenditure〔fund〕 — **수당** a casualty〔an accident〕 allowance —**지** the stricken〔afflicted, affected, suffering, devastated〕 district **중앙 — 대책 본부** the Central Disaster Relief Center
재행 再行 a bridegroom's first visit to his bride's home after the wedding ceremony **—하다** pay a first visit 《to one's bride's home》
***재향** 在鄕 the countryside ; the country ; rural districts
— **군인** a veteran (soldier) 《미》 ; an ex-soldier ; [총칭] soldiers on the reserve list ; reservists — **군인회** (Korean) veterans Association
재허가 再許可 renewal of permission ¶ 재허가를 받다 have permission renewed
***재현** 再現 reappearance ; a second appearance ; reemergence ; revival ; rea dvent **—하다** reappear ; appear again ; reemerge ; come back ; revive ; [재생] reproduce ; repeat (반복)
—**부** 〖음악〗 recapitulation —**성** 〖화학〗 reproducibility
재혼 再婚 a second marriage ; a remarriage ; a deuterogamy ; a digamy **—하다** marry again ; remarry ¶ 재혼을 권하다 advise 《a woman》 to remarry
—**자** a remarried person ; a deuterogamist ; a digamist
재화 才華 (a) brilliant talent
재화 災禍 [재난] a calamity ; a disaster ; [불행] a misfortune ; an evil ¶ 재화를 당하다 meet with a misfortune // 재화를 자초하다 invite〔court〕 disaster ; bring evil 〔disaster, misfortune〕 upon oneself // 재화를 피하다 keep off a misfortune
재화 財貨 [상품] goods ; commodities ; [재산] property ; wealth
재화 載貨 《a ship's》 cargo ; shipment
— **용적** measurement capacity
재확인 再確認 reaffirmation ; reconfirmation **—하다** reaffirm ; confirm again ; reconfirm
재회 再會 meeting again ; reunion **—하다** meet〔see〕 《a person》 again ¶ 재회를 기약하다 promise to meet again // 재회를 기약하고 갈리다 say au revoir ; part in the hopes of meeting again // 재회는 기약하기 어렵다 We may not meet again. / God knows when we may be brought together again.
재흥 再興 revival ; restoration ; reestablishment ; rehabilitation (부흥) **—하다** revive ; restore ; reestablish ; rehabilitate ¶ 민족 문화의 재흥 rehabilitation of national culture // 폐가를 재흥하다 revive an extinct family
—**자** a reviver ; a restorer
잭 [기중기] a jack ; [트럼프] the knave ; the jack
잭나이프 a jackknife
잰지 〖조개〗 a scallop
***잼** 《apple, strawberry》 jam ¶ 잼 바른 빵 bread and jam
잼버리 a jamboree
잽 〖권투〗 a jab ¶ 잽을 먹이다 jab 《one's opponent》
잽싸다 (be) nimble ; agile ; quick
잿길 [언덕빼기의] a steep road
잿더미 a lump of ash ¶ 잿더미로 화하다 be burnt〔reduced〕 to ashes
잿물¹ lye ; [가성소다] caustic soda
잿물² [도자기용] glaze ; enamel ¶ 도자기에 잿물을 올리다 put glaze on pottery
잿박 a container for fertilizer ash
잿밥 齋— rice offered to Buddha ¶ 부처에게 잿밥을 올리다 offer rice to Buddha
잿불 a fire turning to ashes
잿빛 ash color ; gray 《미》 ; grey 《영》 ¶ 잿빛이 도는 grayish ; ashy // 얼굴이 잿빛이 되다 one's face turns ashen
쟁 箏 [악기] a kind of 13-stringed musical instrument
쟁 錚 [꽹과리] a gong
쟁강 [금속 소리] (with) a clank ; (with) a clink **—하다** give a clank〔clink〕
쟁강거리다, 쨍강거리다 clank ; clink
쟁강쟁강 clinking ; clanging ; clashing ; clanking
쟁개비 a small 《iron》 pan〔pot〕
쟁그랍다 (be) crawly ; creepy ⇨ 징그럽다
***쟁기** a (Korean) plow ; a plough 《영》
—**질** plowing〔ploughing〕 **쟁깃술** the blade-guard of a plow
쟁단 爭端 a cause〔source〕 of strife〔dispute, discord〕
쟁론 爭論 a dispute ; a quarrel ; a controversy ; an altercation ; an argument **—하다** dispute 《with》 ; have a quarrel〔an argument〕 《with》 ; quarrel 《with》 ; have (high) words 《with》 ¶ 쟁론을 시작하다 get into an argument with 《a person》 over 《a matter》
***쟁반** 錚盤 a tray ; a salver ; a server
쟁의 爭議 a dispute ; conflicts ; a controversy ; a trouble ¶ 쟁의를 일으키다 start a dispute ; strike // 쟁의를 조정하다 mediate a dispute // 양자의 쟁의를 해결하다 settle a dispute between the two // 경영주와 종업원 간에 쟁의가 일어났다 A dispute 〔conflict〕 arose between the manage-

ment and the employees.
—권 the right to〔of〕 strike —단 the strikers — 위원 a dispute committee —점 the point at issue — 참가자〔불참가자〕 a participant〔nonparticipant〕 in a dispute — 행위 actions taken in a labor〔trade 《영》〕 dispute — 행위 방법 규제법 the Act to Regulate Strikes 《in Electricity Enterprises and Coal Mines》 노동— a labor dispute 소작 — disputes between landowners and tenant farmers ; tenant disputes

쟁이다 heap〔pile〕 up ; make a neat pile of 《things》 ; accumulate ¶ 고기를 쟁이다 leave sliced meat in piles〔stacks〕 // 돌을 쟁이다 lay one stone upon another // 쌀가마가 쟁여져 있다 Bags of rice are piled up.

쟁쟁하다 錚錚— [뛰어나다] (be) prominent ; eminent ; outstanding ; leading ; conspicuous ; foremost ; first class ; crack 《구》 ¶ 쟁쟁한 인물 an outstanding man ; a prominent figure ; a leader // 쟁쟁한 영문학자 a prominent English scholar // 당내의 쟁쟁한 인물 one of the shining lights of the party // 쟁쟁한 명선수 a crack player

쟁쟁하다 ① [귀에 남다] linger 〔ring〕 《in one's ears》 ¶ 그의 말소리가 아직도 귀에 쟁쟁하다 His words still linger〔are still ringing〕 in my ears.
② [소리가] (be) clear ; have a nice ring to it ; (be) sonorous ; resonant ¶ 쟁쟁한 목소리 a clear (ringing) voice

쟁점 爭點 a point at issue〔in dispute〕 ; a point of contention ; an issue ¶ 법률〔사실〕상의 쟁점 an issue of law〔fact〕

쟁첩 a small (brass) plate

쟁취 爭取 —하다 win ; gain ; obtain ; secure ; score ¶ 독립〔승리〕을 쟁취하다 win one's independence〔a victory〕

쟁탈 爭奪 a struggle ; a contest ; a competition ; a scramble —하다 struggle 〔scramble, fight, contest〕 for ¶ 정권의 쟁탈 a struggle〔scramble〕 for political power
—전 a scramble 《for》 ; a contest 《for》 ; a struggle 《for》 ¶ 지금 그 도시의 쟁탈전이 벌어지고 있다 A battle for the possession of the city is now in progress. 데이비스컵 —전 a competition for the Davis Cup 선수권 —전 a championship tournament ; a pennant race 우승패 —전 a contest for the championship trophy 진지 —전 a struggle for a position

쟁투 爭鬪 a strife ; a struggle ; a fight ; a combat —하다 fight ; struggle ; strive

쟁퉁이 [거만한] a haughty person ; [가난한] a grumpy person ; a person who has let poverty make him mean and cross

쟁패전 爭霸戰 a struggle〔fight, contest〕 for supremacy ; a championship game (경기의)

저[1] ① [나] I ; me ② [자기] self ; oneself ¶ 저희들 We // 저의 의견으로는 in 〔according to〕 my opinion

저[2] [악기] a flute

†**저**[3] [지칭] that 《*pl.* those》 ; the ¶ 저 사람 that man〔woman〕 // 저것 that (one) // 저 집들 those houses

***저**[4] [감탄사] well ; I say ; say 《미》 ¶ 저 최선생님 I say, Mr. *Choi* // 저 잠깐 실례합니다만 Excuse me, but // 누가 이 짓을 했나—저 제가 아닙니다—그럼 누구야—저 모르겠습니다 Who did this ? Please, I didn't. Who did it, then ? Well, I don't know.

저 著 one's writings (저술) ; (written) by ¶ 송박사 저 (written) by Dr. *Song*

저 箸 [젓가락] 《a pair of》 chopsticks

저가 低價 a low〔moderate〕 price ⇨ 염가(廉價)

저각 底角 〖기하〗 a base angle

저간 這間 that time ; then ; that occasion ¶ 저간의 사정 the circumstances of the occasion〔the days〕

저감 低減 (a) reduction ; (a) diminution ; (a) decrease —하다 reduce ; diminish ; decrease

저같이 like that ; (in) that way ; so ¶ 저같이 해라 Do like that. // 그 아이를 저같이 호되게 꾸짖지 않아도 좋을 텐데 He shouldn't have scolded the boy so severely.

저개발 低開發 underdevelopment
—국 an underdeveloped country ; less-developed countries ⇨ 개발 (도상국가) — 지역 an underdeveloped area

저것 that ; that thing 《over there》 ; that one ¶ 이것 저것 this and that ; one thing and〔or〕 another // 그 외의 이것 저것 that or what not // 이것 저것 생각한 끝에 after a great deal of thinking // 이것 저것 생각해 보면 taking everything into consideration ; putting this and that together // 저것 봐 Look there !

저격 狙擊 shooting ; sniping ; sharpshooting —하다 shoot〔fire〕 《at》 ; snipe 《at》 ¶ 저격을 당하다 be shot 《by》
—대 a sharpshooting squad —병 a sniper ; a sharpshooter —용 소총 a sniper rifle —자 a shooter

저고리 a coat ; a Korean jacket ¶ 저고리를 입다〔벗다〕 put on〔take off〕 one's coat

저곡 貯穀 storing crops —하다 store crops ; have crops in store
—미 stored rice ; rice held in stock

저공 低空 a low sky〔altitude〕 ¶ 저공으로 비행하다 fly low ; fly at a low altitude
— 비행 low flying ; a low-altitude flight ; low-level flying — 폭격 low-altitude bombing 초— 비행 hedgehopping 《속》

저광수리 〖새〗 a goshawk

†**저금** 貯金 saving (행위) ; savings (돈) ; a

deposit **—하다** save ; lay〔put〕 by 《money》 ; deposit 《in the bank》 ; have money 《in the bank》 ¶ 저금을 찾다 draw one's savings // 저금을 다 써 버리다 exhaust one's savings // 은행에 20만원 저금이 있다 have 200,000 *won* (deposited) in the bank ; have a bank account of 200,000 *won* // 월급 중에서 저금하다 save 《a sum》 out of one's salary

—통 a savings box ; a (piggy) bank **—통장** a (savings) bankbook ; a deposit passbook **우편 —** postal savings **은행 —** a bank deposit **자유 —** free (account) savings **적립 —** installment savings

저금리 低金利 low interest ; cheap money **— 정책** a cheap〔an easy〕 money policy

저급 低級 low grade〔class〕 ; inferiority **—하다** (be) low ; low-grade ; low-toned ; inferior ; vulgar (야비한) ¶ 저급한 노래 a vulgar song ; a cheap tune // 저급한 소설 a vulgar novel ; a penny-a-line novel // 저급한 영화 a film for lowbrows // 저급한 취미 low taste

— 신문 a gutter press **— 음식점** a low-class eating house **— 인간** vulgar people **—품** low-grade articles

⁑**저기** that place ; there (저곳) ¶ 저기에 there ; over〔up, down〕 there ; yonder // 저기까지 there ; as far as there // 여기 저기 here and there ; from place to place // 저기 있는 저 건물이 정거장입니다 The building over there is the station. // 그를 본 적이 있니—저기에 그가 있잖아 Flave you seen him? Yes, there he is.

저기압 低氣壓 low (atmospheric) pressure ; a (barometric) depression ; [기분] bad temper〔humor〕 ¶ 저기압의 중심 the center of a depression // 저기압의 내습 the approach of a depression // 정계의 저기압 a political storm center // 저기압이 발생했다 A low pressure system developed. // 저기압이 남동으로 진행하고 있다 A low pressure area is traveling southeast. // 사장님이 오늘 아침 저기압인 것 같다 The boss seems to be down〔in a bad mood〕 this morning.

— 지방 a low-pressure area **열대〔온대〕 —** a tropical〔an extratropical〕 cyclone

저까짓 that kind of... ; such a... ; so trifling〔trivial, slight, small, worthless, poor〕...

저나마 although it is (nothing more than) that ¶ 저나마 그대로 (poor, worthless, trivial) as that is〔may be〕 // 구두가 낡았지만 저나마 신을 수 밖에 없다 I have to put on that pair of shoes, worn out as they are.

저냐 panfried food ; a sauté ; a sautéed dish

쇠고기 — beef sauté ; sautéed beef

저냥 (in) that way ; (in) the same way as that ; as that is〔was〕 ; still ; with no change ; with no letup ¶ 저냥 (내버려) 두다 leave 《a thing, a person》 as it〔he〕 is // 어린아이를 저냥 비 맞힐 수가 있느냐 How can you leave the child out in the rain like that?

⁑**저널리스트** a journalist

⁑**저널리즘** journalism

저네 those people (over there) ; they 〔them〕

†**저녁** ① evening ¶ 오늘〔어제, 내일〕 저녁 this〔yesterday, tomorrow〕 evening // 저녁에 in the evening // 다음날 저녁(에) the next 〔following〕 evening // 저녁이면 흔히 of an evening // 저녁이 될 무렵에 toward evening

② [식사] the evening meal ; supper ; dinner ¶ 저녁에 초대하다 invite to dinner // 저녁을 짓다 prepare supper // 저녁에 갈비를 먹다 eat〔have〕 short-ribs for dinner // 저녁 먹고 가지 그래 Stay for the dinner, please.

—놀 the evening glow ; sunset colors **—종** the evening bell

저녁때 evening (time) ; dusk ; sunset ; eventide ¶ 저녁때에 in the evening ; toward(s) evening ; at dusk // 저녁때까지는 by evening // 저녁때에 귀가하다 return home towards evening

⁑**저녁밥** supper ; the evening meal ¶ 저녁밥을 먹다 take supper ; sup // 저녁밥을 짓다 prepare supper ; get dinner ready

저놈 that damn guy (over there) ; he 〔him〕 ; that damn thing

저능 低能 low intelligence ; feeble〔weak〕-mindedness ; mental deficiency ; imbecility ; idiocy ; moronism **—하다** (be) feeble〔weak〕-minded ; mentally weak ; backward ; retarded ; moronic ; imbecile

—아 a feeble〔weak〕-minded child ; an imbecile child **—아 교육** the education of the feeble-minded

저다지 so ; so much ; like that ; to that extent〔degree〕 ¶ 저다지도 완고한 사람은 일찍이 본 일이 없다 He is the most obstinate fellow I have ever seen. // 저다지 서둘 것이 무엇 있담 What's the hurry! // 저다지 울 필요가 없다 She needn't cry like that.

***저당 抵當** mortgage ; security ; collateral **—하다** mortgage ; hypothecate ; give 《a thing》 as security ¶ 저당잡다 take 《a thing》 as security // 집을 저당잡히다 mortgage one's house // 저당을 잡고 돈을 빌려 주다 lend money on security〔mortgage〕 // 이 집은 3,000만원에 저당잡혀 있다 There is a mortgage of thirty million *won* on the house. // 그 토지를 저당잡고 3,000만원 빌려 주었다 I advanced thirty million *won* on the lot.

—권 mortgage ; hypothec **—권 설정** settlement of mortgage **—권 설정자** a mortgagor ; a mortgager **—권자** a mortgagee **—권자 조항〔화재 보험 증권상의〕** a mortgagee clause — 대부금 a loan on security ; a mortgage loan —물 a security ; a pledge ; a pawn — 보험 mortgage insurance — 정리 consolidation of mortgage — 증권법 the Mortgage Certificate Act — 증서 a mortgage bond 근(根)— fixed collateral 동산 — chattel mortgage 부가(付加)〔부(副)〕 — collateral〔secondary〕 security 이중 — double mortgage 1번〔2번〕 — first〔second〕 mortgage 총괄 — blanket security 무— 대금(貸金) an unsecured loan 토지 — 대금(貸金) a loan secured on landed property

저대로 at it is〔stands〕; like that ¶ 저대로 두다 leave it just as it is ; leave it alone

저도 低度 a low degree

저도 모르게 in spite of oneself ; unconsciously ; unwittingly ; involuntarily ; instinctively ; unknowingly ; unintentionally ¶ 저도 모르게 실수하다 make a mistake unconsciously

저돌 recklessness ; foolhardiness ; rashness —하다 rush recklessly ; make a reckless〔wild〕 rush ; make a headlong rush ¶ 저돌적인 rash ; foolhardy ; reckless // 저돌적으로 recklessly ; foolhardily ; precipitately

저들 those people (over there) ; they 〔them〕

저따위 of that sort〔kind〕; that kind 《of》; that sort 《of》 ¶ 저따위 사람 a man like him ; the likes of him ; his like // 저따위는 처음 본다 I have never seen such a person in all my life. // 저따위 집은 사서 무엇하냐 What are you buying that sort of shabby house for ?

저라 [소 모는 소리] Haw !

저락 低落 fall ; decline (시세의) ; depreciation —하다 fall ; go down ; depreciate ; decline ¶ 달러의 저락 the decline of the dollar // 저락의 기미가 보이다 have downward tendency ; be on the fall 〔decline〕

대— a slump

저러하다 be like that ; be that way

저런[1] such ; so ; that (sort of) ; like that ¶ 저런 사람 such a man ; a man like him ; the like of him // 저런 책 a book of that kind // 저런 여자 a woman like her // 저런 모자 that sort of cap // 저런 좋은 집 so fine a house // 저런 어리석은 사람 such a foolish man as he // 저런 정직한 사람 such an honest man as he // 저런 짓을 하다 do such a thing

저런[2] [감탄사] Oh dear ! /O my ! /Good heavens ! /Goodness ! /Good gracious ! / Good grief ! /Indeed ! /Golly ! /By Jove ! ¶ 저런 벌써 11시야 Why ! It is eleven. // 저런 그 집의 번지를 잊었군 By Jove ! I have forgotten the number of the house.

저렇게 like that ⇨ 저런[1]

저렇다 be like that ⇨ 저러하다

저력 底力 latent〔potential〕 energy ; reserve of force ¶ 경제적 저력 economic staying power // 저력 있는 of preserving strength ; energetic // 저력 있는 목소리 a deep (tone of) voice // 저력이 있다 have sufficient bottom

저렴 低廉 cheapness ; moderateness ; a low price —하다 (be) cheap ; low-priced ; moderate ; inexpensive ¶ 저렴한 값 moderate prices // 저렴한 물품 low-priced articles〔goods〕

저류 底流 an undercurrent ¶ 의식의 저류 subconscious current

저르렁거리다, 쩌르렁거리다 clang and clang ; tinkle and tinkle ; jingle and jingle

저리 [저렇게] so ; like that ; in that way ; to that extent ; [방향] that way ; that direction ; over there ; there ; thither ¶ 이리 저리 here and there // 저리 가거라 Over there ! /Go away ! // 어린애를 저리 데리고 가거라 Take the baby away. // 저리 가면 어디냐 Where does that road over there lead to ? // 저리 좀 비키시오 Step aside, please.

저리 低利 low interest ; a low rate of interest ¶ 저리로 대부하다 put out 〔lend〕 money at a low rate of interest — 금융 cheap credit — 대금〔대부〕 a low-interest loan ; a loan at cheap interest — 자금 low-interest funds 〔loans, credit〕; easy money 《미》 — 자금 정책 an easy-money program

저리다 [손발이] be〔fall〕 asleep ; be benumbed ; become numbed ; [쑤시다] be〔feel〕 sore ; have a dull pain ¶ 저린 발 benumbed feet // 온 뼈마디가 저리다 feel pain in all one's joints // 추워서 손이 저린다 My hands are benumbed 〔asleep〕 with cold. // 다리가 저리고 쑤신다 I have pins and needles in my legs.

저마 紵麻 ramie ; China Grass ; Boehmeria nivea (학명)

***저마다** each one ; everyone ¶ 저마다 제가 옳다고 한다 Every man claims that he himself is right. // 저마다 먼저 나가느라고 서로 떼민다 Everybody is pushing everybody else trying to get out first.

저만저만 to that extent〔point〕; that much ; tolerably —하다 (be) that much ; tolerable ; fair ; ordinary ; commonplace

저만큼 so ; like that ; so much ; that much ; to that extent ¶ 저만큼 고집 센 친구는 본 적이 없다 He is the most obstinate fellow I have ever seen. // 저만큼 영어를 하면 좋겠는데 I wish I could speak English that well.

저만하다 be that much〔so much〕; be to that extent ; be as much as that ¶ 저만한 인물 a man of that caliber // 저만한 미인 such a beautiful girl ; a woman of such great beauty // 저만한 돈이 있는데도 with all that money ; for all one's riches // 저만하면 충분하다 That much is good enough for me. // 저만한 학자이면서도 교만하지 않았다 For all his scholarship he was not proud of himself.

저맘때 about〔around〕 that time ; at that time of day〔night, year〕 ¶ 나도 저맘때는 무척 장난꾼이었다 I was quite a naughty boy when I was his age.

⁑**저명 著名** prominence ; eminence ; distinction **—하다** (be) well-known ; eminent ; noted ; prominent ; celebrated ; famous ; notable ; distinguished ¶ 저명한 실업가 an eminent man of business

— 인사 a person of fame ; a man of distinction ; a notable

저목장 貯木場 a timberyard ; a lumberyard 《미》

저목지 貯木池 a timber pond

저물가 低物價 low prices

— 정책 a low-price policy

*__저물다__ [해가] grow〔get〕 dark〔dim〕 ; 《the sun》 set ; 《night》 fall ; 《the day》 close ; [끝나다] draw to a close ; end ; come to an end ¶ 저물도록 till a late hour ; far into the night // 해가 저물기 전에 before (it is) dark〔dusk〕 // 해가 저문다 Night〔Evening〕 falls. /Night sets in. /The day draws to a close. // 6시에 해가 저물었다 Night fell at six. // 우리들은 저물기 전에 귀가했다 We arrived home before dark. // 도중에서 해가 깜빡 저물었다 Night and darkness overtook us on the way. // 이 해도 다 저물었다 This year has come to a close. // 이제 열흘이면 올해도 다 저문다 Only ten days are left before the year is out.

저미 低迷 hanging low **—하다** hang low ¶ 암운이 저미한다 Dark clouds hang low.

저미다 slice ; cut thin ¶ 저며내다 slice off〔away〕 // 고기를 얇게 저미다 cut meat into thin slices

†**저버리다** go back on ; turn one's back on ; back down ; forsake ; desert ; break 《one's promise》 ¶ 은혜를 저버리다 go back on one's obligation // 약속을 저버리다 back down on a promise // 처자를 저버리다 forsake one's wife and children // 남편을 저버리다 desert〔leave〕 one's husband // 기대를 저버리다 be contrary〔do not come up〕 to 《a person's》 expectations ; disappoint 《a person》

저벅 (with) a heavy footstep

저벅거리다 tramp ; trample ¶ 병정들이 저벅거리고 지나가는 소리가 들리었다 Soldiers were heard tramping by.

저벅저벅 with heavy footsteps ; tramping ¶ 저벅저벅 걷다 walk heavily〔with heavy steps〕

저번 這番 last ; last time ; the other day ; some time ago ; lately ; previously ¶ 저번의 last ; recent ; previous ; of the other day // 저번 일요일 last Sunday ; on Sunday last // 저번 주인 one's former master // 저번 내각 the preceding Cabinet // 저번에 만났을 적에 when I saw him last ; the last time I saw him // 저번에 알려 드린 바와 같이 as I let you know last time ; as previously announced

저변 底邊 the base

저분저분하다 [씹히는 모양] (be) soft and chewy ; [성질이] pliable ; gentle ; sociable ; amiable ; [먹음직한 모양] 《look》 appetizing ; tempting ; delicious-looking

저상 沮喪 dejection ; depression of spirits ; discouragement ; demoralization ; damp **—하다** be dejected ; be depressed ; be disheartened ; be discouraged ; be dispirited ; be in low spirits ; be despondent ¶ 의기 저상된 모습으로 with a dejected air ; pulling a long face ; looking blue〔gloomy〕 // 의기를 저상시키다 damp〔depress〕 《a person's》 spirits ; dishearten 《a person》 // 적군은 의기가 저상되어 있다 The enemy troops are demoralized.

저서 著書 one's writings ; a book ; a (literary) work ¶ 영국인의 저서 a book of English authorship // 그는 저서가 많다 He has written many books. // 그것은 누구의 저서인지 모른다 The book is anonymous〔of unknown authorship〕.

저선 底線 〖기하〗 the base ; the base line

저성 低聲 a low voice〔tone〕 ; a subdued voice ¶ 저성으로 in a low voice ; in an undertone ; sotto voce 《이》

저성능 低性能 low efficiency

저소득 低所得 a small income

—자 a person who draws a small income ; people in the lower brackets of income **—층** the low-income bracket〔group〕 ; the lower brackets of income

⁑**저속 低俗** vulgarity ; baseness **—하다** (be) vulgar ; base ; low ¶ 그는 말씨가 저속하다 He is vulgar in his speech.

저속도 低速度 a low speed ; 〖사진〗 time lapse ¶ 저속도의 low-speed ; slow moving // 저속도로 《film》 at a low speed ; in low gear // 저속도로 촬영한 영화 a time-lapse〔slow-speed〕 film

— 기어 [자동차의] low gear

*__저수 貯水__ reservoir water ; storage of water **—하다** keep (water) in store ; build up a reservoir

—량 pondage ; the volume of water kept in store **—조(槽)** a (water) tank **— 조직** [식물의] a (water-) storage tissue **—지** a (storing) reservoir **—탑(塔)** a water tower

저수 底數 〖수학〗 a base ; a radix (기수)

저수위 低水位 the low-water level

— 경보기 a low-water alarm

†**저술 著述** writing (of books) ; authorship ; literary work〔pursuits〕; [저작물] a work ; a book ; one's writing **—하다** write 《a book》 ¶ 중국에 관한 저술 a book〔work〕 on China // 역사에 관해서 저술하다 write on history // 저술로 생활하다 live by the pen
—가 a writer ; [남자] an author ; [여자] an authoress ; a lady-writer **—업** the literary profession ; the profession of letters ¶ 저술업에 종사하고 있다 He is engaged in literary work.

저습 低濕 —하다 (be) low and moist **—지** a low, swampy place

저승 the world beyond ; the other〔next〕 world ; the world〔life〕 to come ; a better land ¶ 저승으로 가다 depart this life ; pass away (into the other world) ; go to Heaven ; die ; join the majority // 저승에서 부모님이 틀림없이 기뻐할 것이다 Your parents must be looking down (from heaven) with delight.

저쑵다 bow 《to a god》; kneel down〔fall on one's knees〕 in worship

저압 低壓 low pressure ; low tension 〔voltage〕
—부(部) a locality of low pressure ; a low area **— 전류** a low-tension current **— 증기 기관** a low-pressure steam engine **—측(側)** the low-tension side **— 회로〔케이블, 코일〕** a low-tension circuit〔cable, coil〕

저액 低額 small amount
— 소득자 a person of small income ; a small-income earner **— 소득층** the low(er) income classes〔bracket〕

저어새 〖새〗 a blackfaced spoonbill

저어하다 be afraid ; fear ¶ 늦을까봐 저어합니다 I am afraid〔I fear〕 that I will be late.

저열 低熱 a low (bodily) temperature ; a slight fever

저열 低劣 vulgarity ; baseness **—하다** (be) base ; vulgar ; mean ; low

저온 低溫 a low temperature
— 건류 low-temperature carbonization **— 경화(硬化)** 〖화학〗 cold cure **—계(計)** 〖물리〗 a cryometer **— 공업** the low-temperature manufacturing industry **— 냉동** low temperature refrigeration **— 유지 장치** 〖물리〗 a cryostat **— 소독〔살균〕** pasteurization at a low-temperature **— 연료** cryogenic fuels **— 요법** cry(m)otherapy **— 처리법** [통조림] cold pack **— 코크스** coalite **—타르** low-temperature tar **—학** cryogenics **극(極)—** a very low temperature **극— 물리학** very low temperature physics

†**저울** [천칭] a balance ; 《a pair of》 scales ; [대저울] a weighing beam ; a beam scale ; a steelyard ¶ 저울에 달다 weigh 《a thing》 in the balance〔on a scale〕 // 저울을 후하게〔모자라게〕 주다 give good〔short〕 weight // 두 개의 사실을 저울질해 보다 compare 《A》 with 《B》
—눈 the notches of a beam **—대** a balance beam ; a weighing beam **— 접시** a scale ; a pair of scales **—추** a weight ; the weight of a balance **—판** a scale **부정(不正) —** an unlawful balance

저울질 weighing ; scaling **—하다** weigh ; scale ; put on the scales ; [비교 고찰하다] weigh 《an argument》 with 《another》; compare 《A》 with 《B》

저위 低位 a low position〔rank〕; a low degree

저유 貯油 storage of oil
—소 a storing place for oil ; an oil reservoir **— 시설** facilities for storing oil **— 탱크** a storage tank

저육 猪肉 pork
—구이 roast pork

저율 低率 a low rate ¶ 저율의 이자 low interest ; a low rate of interest

저음 低音 ① 〖음악〗 bass ; a low-pitched sound ② [낮은 목소리] a low voice ¶ 저음으로 sotto voce 《이》; in an undertone // 전화에서는 네 목소리가 저음으로 들린다 On the phone your voice sounds low.
— 가수 a low-voiced singer ; a bass ; a contralto (여성의) **— 나팔** a bassoon **— 부** bass ; besso 《이》

저의 底意 one's original purpose ; one's real intention ; one's will〔motive〕 ¶ 저의를 알 수 없다 I can't understand what you really mean to do.

저이 that person ; he〔him〕; she〔her〕 ¶ 저이들 those people ; they〔them〕

저인망 底引網 a dragnet ; a trawlnet
— 어업 dragnet fisheries

저임금 低賃金 low wages
— 정책 a low-wage policy

저자 [시장] a market ; a fair ⇨ 장[1]

†**저자 著者** a writer ; [남자] an author ; [여자] an authoress ¶ 소설의 저자 the author of a novel // 저자 불명의 책 a book of unknown〔uncertain〕 authorship // 그 소설의 저자라고 주장하다 claim the authorship of the novel

저자세 低姿勢 ¶ 저자세를 취하다 assume a low posture ; take〔adopt〕 a low〔humble, modest〕 attitude

***저작 著作** [저서] a book ; a work ; [저술] writing ; authorship ; literary work 〔production〕 **—하다** write 《a book》; compose
—가〔자〕 a writer ; an author **—가 협회** the Authors' Association **—권** copyright **—권 등록** copyright registration ; Copyright registered. (등록필) **—권법** the Copyright Act **—권 사용료** a royalty **—권 소유** All rights reserved. /Copyrighted. **—권 소유자** a copyright holder **—권 심사회** the Copyright Compensation Council **—권 침해** an infringement of copyright ; (literary) piracy **—권 침해자** a

(literary) pirate —물 a (literary) work ; writings 국제 —권 international copyright 문예 —권 literary and artistic copyright 문예 —권 대리인 a literary agent

저작 咀嚼 chewing ; mastication —하다 chew ; masticate ¶ 음식을 저작하다 masticate〔chew〕 one's food well
—구(口) 〖곤충〗 the manducatory apparatus ; a mandible —근(筋) 〖해부〗 a muscle of mastication —력 digestive power — 운동 〖의학〗 masticatory movement

저잣거리 the streets 《of a city, town》 ; a shopping center ; the downtown

*저장 貯藏 store ; keeping ; storing ; preservation —하다 store ; keep ; lay up ; keep 《things》 in store ; set aside ; preserve ¶ 저장해 둔 in store // 겨울 준비로 식량을 대량 저장하다 lay up large stocks of food for the winter // 오래 저장하기 어렵다 be of limited storage life
—고(庫) a storehouse ; storage house —고(高) the amount of stock ; [곡물의] visible supply —물〔품〕 stored goods ; stores ; stock —미(米) stored rice ; set-aside rice —소 a storing place ; a repository ; a preservatory ; storage facilities —실 a storeroom — 야채 preserved vegetables 냉동 — cold storage ; refrigeration 식료품 —실 [상선(商船)의] a lazaretto 《*pl.* ~s》 ; a lazaret(te)

저적거리다 drag 《oneself》 along ; [아기가] toddle ; totter

저적에 last time ; the other day ; previously

저적저적 dragging one's weary feet ; totteringly ; with tottering〔unsteady〕 steps —하다 drag one's weary feet ; totter 〔toddle〕 along

*저절로 of itself ; by itself ; of its own accord ; spontaneously ; automatically ¶ 촛불이 저절로 꺼졌다 The candle went out of itself. // 충치가 하나 저절로 빠졌다 A decayed tooth has come out of itself. // 그 사람 앞에서는 저절로 고개가 수그러진다 I can't help bowing in respect for him.

저조 低調 ① [소리] a low tone ; an undertone ② [침체] dullness ; inactiveness ¶ 저조의 low-toned ; low-pitched ; low-keyed ; [침체한] dull ; lagging ; inactive // 저조를 나타내다 show lack of enthusiasm // 공장 가동이 아직은 저조하다 The factories now operate at a whisper. // 시황이 저조하다 The market is sluggish. /The trade is dull.

저조 低潮 (a) low tide ; low water ¶ 저조에 at low tide
— 수준표(水準標) a low-water mark 최— the neap (tide)

*저주 詛呪 a curse ; imprecation ; execration ; a malediction ; an anathema ; a backward blessing —하다 curse ; imprecate evil 《upon》 ; pronounce an anathema 《against a person》 ; execrate ; wish ill of 《a person》 ¶ 저주 받은 doomed ; cursed // 저주 받고 있다 be under a curse ; carry a curse // 세상을 저주하다 curse the world // 그는 나를 저주하고 있다 He wishes me evil. // 그놈을 저주한다 My curse shall be on his head.

저주파 低周波 low〔audio〕 frequency

†저지 沮止 obstruction ; hindrance ; impediment ; retardation ; interception —하다 obstruct ; hinder ; check ; hamper ; hold back ; retard ; impede ; block ; intercept ¶ 발달을 저지하다 check the growth ; arrest the development // 진보를 저지하다 impede〔retard, block〕 the progress ; halt the advance // 적의 진격을 저지하다 check the enemy's advance ; hold the enemy in check

저지 低地 low(-lying) land ; lowlands

저지난 before last time ; the one before last ¶ 저지난번 the time before last

저지레 spoiling ; ruining ; marring —하다 spoil ; ruin ; mar

저지르다 do ; commit 《an error》 ; spoil ; ruin ; mar ¶ 또 무슨 일을 저지를지 알 수 없다 There is no knowing what he will be up to next.

*저쪽 that side〔direction〕 ; over there ; the other side〔direction〕 ¶ 저쪽에 there ; over there ; yonder ; that way // 저쪽으로 가라 Go there. /Go away. // 불평이 이쪽에서도 저쪽에서도 나왔다 Complaints came from all quarters. // 저쪽을 봐줄 수도 없고 이쪽을 봐줄 수도 없고 입장이 난처하다 I am in a dilemma〔fix〕, unable to satisfy both sides.

저차 低次 ¶ 저차의 〖수학〗 of a lower order

저처럼 like that ⇨ 저같이

저촉 抵觸 conflict ; collision ; contradiction ; infringement —하다 conflict 〔collide〕 《with》 ; be in conflict 《with》 ; be contradictory〔contrary〕 《to》 ; be incompatible 《with》 ¶ 규칙에 저촉하다 be contradictory to the regulations // 법령에 저촉하다 be in conflict with the laws and regulations // 협약에 저촉하다 be in contravention of a treaty // 법에 저촉하는 짓은 하지 않았다 I have done nothing contrary to the law.

*저축 貯蓄 saving ; laying-by ; hoarding ; savings (저금) —하다 save ; lay by 〔aside〕 ; put by ; store up ; hoard ¶ 저축심 있는〔없는〕 사람 a provident〔an improvident〕 man ; a thrifty〔thriftless〕 person // 저축심이 있는 saving ; thrifty // 저축을 장려하다 encourage savings // 수입중에서 얼마를 저축하다 save 《a sum》 from〔out of〕 one's income
— 성향 a propensity to save — 예금 a savings deposit — 운동 a savings campaign

저축거리다 limp ; hobble ¶ 저축거리며 limping ; hobbling
저축심 貯蓄心 the spirit of saving ; thriftiness
저축 은행 貯蓄銀行 a savings bank
—법 〖법〗 the Savings Bank Act **상호 —** a mutual savings bank
저춤거리다 limp ; hobble ¶ 저춤거리며 limping ; hobbling
저퀴 an evil spirit causing illness
저퀴 들다 관용 be afflicted by a disease-bearing spirit
저큼 never repeating a mistake ; learning from one's slip〔error〕
저탄 貯炭 a stock (pile) of coal
—소〔장〕 coal yard〔depot〕; a coaling station ; a bunker (배의)
‡**저택 邸宅** a mansion ; a residence ¶ 훌륭한 저택 a lordly〔stately〕 mansion ; a fine home 《미》; a fine house // 시골에 훌륭한 저택이 있다 Have a beautiful place in the country
—가(街) residential quarters
저통 箸筒 a chopstick stand〔holder〕
†**저편** that side〔direction〕 ⇨ 저쪽 ¶ 중대한 일이 아니면 우리는 바다 저편에서 일어나는 일에 대해 신경을 쓰지 않는다 Unless it's something major, we don't care what happens on the other side of the ocean.
저포 紵布 ramie cloth ⇨ 모시
저하 低下 a fall ; a drop ; lowering ; decline ; depreciation (가치의) ; deterioration (품질의) **—하다** fall ; drop ; depreciate ; deteriorate ¶ 도덕의 저하 moral degeneracy // 수준의 저하 a lowering of standards // 품질의 저하 a falling-off in quality 《of goods》; quality deterioration // 능률을 저하시키지 않고 without loss of efficiency // 생산을 저하시키다 curtail production
저학년 低學年 the lower classes〔grades, forms〕
†**저항 抵抗** ① [반항] resistance ; opposition (반대) ; defiance ; struggle **—하다** resist ; oppose ; stand against ; offer resistance 《to》; struggle with〔against〕; defy ; antagonize ; fight〔contend〕 against ; withstand ¶ 최후의 저항 a last-ditch stand // 저항하기 어려운 irresistible // 공격에 저항하다 resist an attack ; withstand an attack // 유혹에 저항하다 resist temptation // 완강히 저항하다 offer stubborn resistance // 저항을 받다 meet with resistance // 권위에 저항하다 revolt〔mutiny〕 against authority // 피해자는 상당히 저항한 것 같다 There are signs of strong resistance having been made by the victim. // 제 아무리 저항해도 소용 없다 There is no struggling against it. // 사원들의 저항이 심해서 일이 순조롭게 진척되지 않고 있다 Things aren't going too smoothly, since the employees are strongly opposed. ② 〖물리〗 resistance ¶ 공기의 저항을 감소 시키다 dwindle〔lessen〕 the air resistance
—기(器) a resistor **—력** (power of) resistance ; resisting power〔force〕; resistivity ; resistibility **—률** moment of 〔specific〕 resistance **— 상자** a resistance box **—손(損)** 〖전기〗 ohmic loss **— 용접** resistance welding **— 운동** the resistance **— 운동자** a resister ; a member of the resistance **—자** a resistant ; a resister **— 코일** a resistance coil **고유 —** resistivity **공기 —** the air resistance **내〔외〕—** internal〔external〕 resistance **마찰 —** frictional resistance **소극적 —** 〖정치〗 passive resistance **전기 —** electric resistance **상관 — 자** 〖군사〗 a mutineer **상관 —죄** mutiny **전기 —계** an ohmmeter **전기 — 압력계** an electric resistance pressure gauge **전기 — 온도계** an electrical resistance thermometer **최소 —선** a line of least resistance
저항라 紵亢羅 (sheer) ramie cambric
저해 沮害 obstruction ; impediment ; check **—하다** obstruct ; check ; impede ; retard ; hamper ; stunt ; block ¶ 발달을 저해하다 hamper〔impede, check〕 development // 활동을 저해하다 hinder 《a person's》 activity // 그것은 세계 평화를 저해한다 It is an obstruction to world peace.
저혈압 低血壓 low blood pressure ; hypotension ¶ 그녀는 저혈압이다 She has low blood pressure.
저희들 we ¶ 저희들의 our // 저희들을 us
적[1] [때] the time 《when》; 《on》 the occasion ¶ 옛적에 once upon a time ; in the old days // 필요할 적에 in case of need // 그가 왔을 적에 내가 없었다 When he came to see me, I was out.
적[2] [떨어진 조각] a partial splinter 《of stone, wood》; a chip
적 賊 [도둑] a thief ; a robber ; [역적] a rebel ; an insurgent ; a traitor
†**적 敵** an enemy ; a foe ; [적수] an opponent ; an antagonist ; a rival ; a match ¶ 적의 enemy('s) ; hostile // 상업상의 적 a business rival // 인도의 적 an enemy to humanity // 적을 공격하다 attack the enemy // 적을 만들다 make an enemy // 적을 사랑하다 love one's enemy // 적에게 붙다 go over to the enemy // 그를 적으로 삼다 have him for an enemy // 너는 그의 적이 될 수 없다 You are no match for him. /You've got no chance against him. // 그가 가는 곳에 적이 없다 He has no enemies wherever he goes.
적 積 〖수학〗 [승적] the product ; [면적] the area ¶ 35와 20의 적을 구하다 multiply 35 by 20 // 42는 6과 7의 적이다 42 is the product of 6 by 7.
누— continued product
적 籍 [호적] the census register ; a domicile ; [단체의] membership ¶ 적을 두다

register ⟪in *Seoul*⟫ ; be enrolled ⟪at a university⟫ ; become a member ⟪of a party⟫ // 적을 넣다〔빼다〕 have one's name entered in〔removed from〕 the register // 이 학교에는 2,000명의 학생이 적을 두고 있다 The school has 2,000 students on the register. /The school has a registration〔an enrollment〕 of 2,000 students.

적 的 ① [목표·대상] a target ; a mark ; an object ; a focus ¶ 비판의 적 the target of criticism // 선망의 적이 되다 become an object of envy // 조소의 적이 되다 become a laughingstock ; be the butt of derision ; become an object of ridicule

② [접미어] -ic ; -ical ; -like ; a sort of ¶ 경제적 economic(al) // 동양적 Oriental // 세계적 worldwide ; all over the world // 직업적 professional // 가급적 so far as possible // 구체적으로 concretely // 문화와 군사와의 교량적 역할 the role of a sort of cultural and military bridge

적가 嫡家 the main family

적갈색 赤褐色 a reddish brown color

적개심 敵愾心 a hostile feeling ; hostility ; enmity ; animosity ¶ 적개심을 품다 have a hostile feeling ⟪against⟫ ; have animosity ⟪against⟫ // 적개심에 불타서 influenced by a hostile feeling // 적개심을 일으키게 하다 arouse〔rouse〕 the animosity ⟪of⟫

적객 謫客 a person in exile ; an exile ; a person banished

적거 謫居 exile ; banishment **—하다** be in exile ; live in exile

적격 適格 conformity to the standard 〔qualification〕 ; a proper qualification ⟪for⟫ ; competence ; eligibility ; fitness

—성 eligibility **— 심사 위원회** a screening committee ⟪미⟫ **—자** a qualified person ; a competent〔an eligible〕 person **—품** proper〔standard, acceptable〕 goods

적곡 積穀 storing of grains **—하다** store grain

적공 積功 building up merit **—하다** build up merit

적과 摘果 **—하다** thin out the superfluous fruits

적괴 賊魁 the ringleader ; the chief of a gang of robbers〔rebels〕

적교 吊橋 a suspension bridge

적구 赤狗 the Reds ; a communist ; a commie

적국 敵國 the enemy〔hostile〕 country ; the enemy ; a hostile power

—어 the language of the enemy

적군 赤軍 the Red Army

적군 賊軍 rebels ; a rebel army ; insurgents

적군 敵軍 the enemy (troops, force)

적굴 賊窟 a den of robbers

적권운 積卷雲 an alto-cumulus

⁑**적극 積極** the positive ¶ 적극적(으로) positive(ly) ; active(ly) ; constructive(ly) // 적극적 공격 an active offense // 적극적 원조 positive aid // 적극적인 태도로 나오다 take up a positive attitude // 적극적으로 원조하다 give positive aid to ⟪a person⟫ // 적극적으로 활동하다 work on positive lines ; be very active // 정부는 재정에 관해서 적극적 방침을 취하기로 했다 The government has decided upon a positive financial policy.

—성 positiveness ¶ 적극성이 없다 lack something positive **— 정책** a positive policy **—주의** positivism ; activism **—주의자** a positivist ; an activist

적금 赤金 [금과 구리의 합금] a reddish copper-gold alloy ; [구리] copper

적금 積金 installment savings

적기 敵機 an enemy〔a hostile〕 plane

적기 赤旗 a red flag ; the Red Flag

적기 摘記 a summary ; an epitome **—하다** summarize ; sum up ; epitomize

적기 適期 ¶ 적기의 timely ; opportune // 지금이 적기이다 the present is most opportune for ⟪doing something⟫

적꼬치 炙— a skewer

⁑**적나라 赤裸裸** nakedness ; nudity ; [솔직] frankness ; plainness ; straightforwardness **—하다** (be) nude ; bare ; [솔직] frank ; plain ; open ¶ 적나라한 사실 a naked〔bald〕 fact // 적나라하게 plainly ; frankly ; without reserve // 적나라하게 고백하다 frankly confess ; make a clean confession ; make a clean breast of it ; own up

적남 嫡男 a legitimate son

적녀 嫡女 a legitimate daughter

적년 積年 many years ; an accumulation of years ¶ 적년의 of many years ; of long standing // 적년의 공 efforts〔labor〕 of many years // 적년의 노고 years of labor // 적년의 폐해 an evil of long standing

†**적다¹** [기록하다] write (down) ; record ; put〔take〕 down ; note ; make a memorandum of ¶ 연필로 적다 write with a pencil ; write in pencil // 영어로 적다 write in English // 잉크로 적다 write in ink // 수첩에 적다 make a note in one's note book // 대장에 금액을 적다 enter an account in a ledger // 그는 매일 일기를 적고 있다 He keeps a diary every day.

⁑**적다²** [수가] (be) few ; be of small number ; [양이] little ; be of small quantity ; [한정되다] (be) limited ; [드물다] rare ; be few and far between ; [많지 않다] (be) scarce ; scant(y) ; [부족하다] wanting ; short ⟪of⟫ ; be not sufficient 〔enough〕 ¶ 적지 않은 not a few〔little〕 ; no small ; much ; considerable // 적지 않은 손해 a considerable loss // 적지 않게 greatly ; considerably ; deeply // 적게 잡아도 at the lowest estimate // 적어지다 decrease ; diminish ; fall off ; dwindle //

점점 적어지다 diminish by degrees ; taper off // 수입이 적다 have a small income // 그것보다 적다 less than that // 칼로리가 적다 be low〔poor〕 in calories // 비용을 적게 하다 reduce〔cut down〕 expenses // 이런 예는 적다 Such instances are few and far between. // 100세까지 사는 사람은 적다 Few live to be one hundred years old. // 이렇게 정직한 사람은 적다 Such an honest man is rarely to be met with. // 그의 조력을 적지 않게 입었다 I owed much〔not a little〕 to his assistance.

적다마 赤多馬 a chestnut horse ; a sorrel horse ; a bay (horse)

적당 賊黨 a gang of thieves〔rebels〕 ; a band of robbers ; bandits

†**적당 適當** fitness ; suitableness ; suitability ; propriety ; appropriateness **—하다** (be) fit ; suitable ; proper ; right ; appropriate

> 참고 **fit** 가장 널리 쓰이는 말 목적 용도에 필요한 성질과 자격을 구비하고 있다 **suitable** 어떤 특수한 상황 목적 사태에 필요한 성질을 구비하고 있다 **proper** 본래 그 자체에 속한다고 생각되는 성질을 구비하고 있다 **appropriate** 어떤 특수한 사람 목적 상황 따위에 특히 적합하다

¶ 적당하게 suitable ; properly ; [임의로] as you think fit〔proper, right〕 // 적당한 직업 a suitable calling // 아이들에게 적당한 책 a proper book for children // 적당한 때에 at a proper time // 적당히 대답을 해 주십시오 Answer him as you think fit. // 적당한 길이로 깎아 주세요 Medium cut, please. // 의사가 술을 적당히 마시라고 하지 않던가 Didn't the doctor tell you to go easy on the alcohol ? // 아직 적당한 남자를 만나지 못했어요 I haven't met Mr. Right yet. // 나도 적당한 여자를 아직 찾지 못했다 I haven't met Miss. Right, either.

‡**적대 敵對** hostility ; antagonism **—하다** show hostility 《toward》 ; be antagonistic 《to》 ; oppose ; be hostile 《to》
—국 a hostile country **— 행위** hostile action ; hostilities ¶ 공공연한 적대 행위 open hostilities

적대시 敵對視 regarding with hostility **—하다** be hostile 《to》 ; regard with hostility ; look upon 《a person》 as an enemy ¶ 적대시하는 태도 hostile attitude

적대하 赤帶下 〚한의〛 bloody leucorrh(o)ea

‡**적도 赤道** the equator ¶ 적도 직하의 equatorial // 적도 직하에서 directly on the equator // 적도에서의 지구의 주위 the circumference of the earth at the equator
— 무풍대 the zone of the equatorial calm ; the doldrums **—선(線)** the equator **— 아프리카** Equatorial Africa **—의(儀)** an equatorial telescope **— 전선** an equatorial front **—제(祭)** the ceremony of crossing the equator〔line〕 **— 해류** the Equatorial current **열(熱)—** the thermal equator **자기(磁氣) —** the magnetic equator **지구〔천구〕 —** the terrestrial 〔celestial〕 equator

적도 賊徒 a group of thieves

적도 適度 proper degree〔amount〕 ; moderation ; temperance ; measure

적도 기니 赤道— Equatorial Guinea
— 공화국 the Republic of Equatorial Guinea

적동 赤銅 〚광물〛 red copper
—광 cuprite ; red copper ore

적란운 積亂雲 a cumulo-nimbus

적량 適量 a proper quantity ; a proper dose (약의)

적량 積量 carrying capacity ; tonnage ¶ 배의 적량 the carrying capacity of a vessel ; a ship's tonnage

적령 適齡 the right〔suitable〕 age 《for》 ¶ 적령기에 이르다 reach〔attain〕 the suitable age ; be old enough 《to marry》
결혼 — the marriageable age **징병 —** the military age ; draft age **징병 —자** a person liable to〔eligible for〕 military service ; a person of enlistment〔military〕 age

적례 適例 a good〔an apposite〕 example ; an apt〔a typical〕 instance ; a case in point ¶ 적례를 들다 cite an apt instance ; quote a case in point // 적례를 보이다 aptly illustrate // 다음 것이 적례이다 The following is an example in point.

적록 摘錄 a summary ; a compendium **—하다** summarize ; sum up ; epitomize

적리 赤痢 dysentery ; bloody flux ¶ 적리는 보통 여름에 발생한다 Dysentery usually comes in summer.
—균 a dysentery bacillus 《*pl.* -li》 **— 증상** a dysenteric symptom **— 환자** a dysentery patient **아메바 —** amoebic dysentery

적린 赤燐 red〔amorphous〕 phosphorus

적립 積立 accumulation ; reserving ; laying〔putting〕 by **—하다** save up 《money》 ; lay〔put〕 by〔aside〕 ; accumulate ; amass ; reserve ¶ 나는 한달에 8,000원씩 적립하고 있다 I lay aside 8,000 *won* every month. // 그는 봉급의 일부를 매달 적립하고 있다 He saves up part of his salary every month.
—금 a reserve (fund) **— 배당금** accumulated dividend **— 저금** installment savings **법정 —금** a legal reserve **별도 —금** a special reserve

적마 赤魔 a Red demon ; the Red menace

적막 寂寞 loneliness ; desolation ; solitude **—하다** (be) lonely ; dreary ; desolate ; deserted ¶ 적막감 a lonely feeling // 적막한 광경 a dreary〔desolate〕 sight

적면 赤面 blushing ; a blush **—하다**

blush 《with〔for〕 shame》; turn red; flush red; color up

적멸 寂滅 annihilation; death; Nirvana —하다 be annihilated; pass away; die; attain Nirvana

적모 嫡母 one's father's legal wife

적목질 赤木質 heartwood

적몰 籍沒 confiscation; forfeiture —하다 confiscate; forfeit; seize

적바르다 [서술적] be〔come〕 almost to the standard〔limit〕; be nearly enough

적바림 —하다 make〔take〕 a note of; jot down; note; record

적반하장 賊反荷杖 The thief turns on the master with a club./Save a stranger from the sea, and he'll turn your enemy./Save a thief from the gallows and he'll cut your throat.

—자 a denunciator

적발 摘發 disclosure; exposure; prosecution (고발) —하다 disclose; expose; lay bare; prosecute; unmask ¶ 부정 사건을 적발하다 expose〔lay bare〕 a scandal // 위반자를 적발하다 prosecute an offender; bring an offender to book // 은닉 물자를 적발하다 uncover〔sound up〕 hoarded goods

적발 something jotted down; a note; a jotting

적법 適法 legality; lawfulness —하다 (be) legal; lawful ¶ 적법이다 be lawful // 적법이 아니다 be unlawful

— 목적 lawful purposes — 상속인 the rightful heir 《to》 — 처치 a lawful measure — 행위 a legal〔lawful〕 act

적병 敵兵 the enemy soldier〔troops〕; the enemy

적부 適否 propriety; suitability; fitness ¶ 인물의 적부 the fitness of a person // 장소의 적부 the suitability of a place // 직업의 적부 employment aptitude // 처치의 적부 the propriety of a step // 적부를 판단하다 judge whether a thing is proper or not

적부적 適不適 ⇨ 적부(適否) ¶ 사람에 따라 적부적이 있다 Some are fitted for the work, but others are not.

적분 積分 〖수학〗 integral calculus ¶ 적분의 integral

— 곡선 an integral curve — 방정식 an integral equation —법 integration — 부호 the sign of integration; the integral sign — 인수 an integrating factor —학 integral calculus — 함수 integral function 면— surface integral 선(線)— curvilinear integral

적분 積忿 pent-up indignation〔rancor〕 ¶ 적분을 풀다 vent〔give vent to〕 one's pent-up rancor 《on》

적비 賊匪 bandits; brigands; rebels

적빈 赤貧 abject〔dire〕 poverty; indigence; destitution; penury —하다 be in dire poverty; suffer from utter destitution ¶ 적빈하기 짝이 없다 He is〔lives〕 in dire poverty./He is as poor as a church mouse.

적산 敵産 enemy property ¶ 적산을 몰수하다 confiscate enemy property

— 관리인 an enemy property administrator

적산 積算 addition; integration —하다 add up; integrate

—법 integration —표 a reckoning table

적삼 an unlined summer jacket ¶ 적삼 벗고 은가락지 낀다 behave improperly; act beyond one's means

적색 赤色 [빛깔] red color; red; [공산주의] communism; Red ¶ 적색의 red (-colored)

— 러시아 Red Russia — 리트머스 시험지 red litmus paper — 분자 a Red — 시험지 red test paper — 안료 red pigment — 테러 Red terrorism — 혁명 a Red revolution

적서 嫡庶 legitimate children and illegitimate children

적선 積善 accumulation of virtuous deeds; building up merits; practice of charities —하다 accumulate virtuous deeds; build up merits; practice charities

적선 敵船 an enemy ship

적선지대 赤線地帶 a red-light district; prostitute quarters

적설 積雪 drifted snow; deep snow; snowdrifts ¶ 적설이 2피트에 달했다 The snow lay〔was〕 2 feet deep./We had a snowfall of 2 feet.

—량 a snowfall — 조사 a snow survey — 한랭지 a snowy and cold area

적설초 積雪草 〖식물〗 a ground ivy

적성 赤誠 sincerity; singleness of heart

적성 適性 aptitude

— 검사 an aptitude test ¶ 적성 검사를 받다 undergo a quality test 직업 — vocational aptitude 진학 — 검사 an academic aptitude test

*적성 敵性 hostility; enmity ¶ 적성을 나타내다 manifest hostility〔enmity〕

— 감염 〖국제법〗 infection — 국가 a hostile country

적세 敵勢 the strength of the enemy; the morale of the foe ¶ 적세를 무찌르다 shatter the enemy morale

적소 謫所 a place of exile; the place that one is banished to

적소 適所 the right〔proper〕 place; a proper〔suitable〕 position ¶ 적재적소 the right man in the right place

적손 嫡孫 a legal posterity; a legitimate grandson〔grandchild〕

적송 積送 shipment; [위탁 판매를 위한] consignment —하다 ship; forward; consign

—인 a shipper; a forwarder —품 consigned〔consignment〕 goods; a consignment —품 대장 a consignment ledger 〔invoice〕

적송 赤松 ⇨ 소나무

적쇠 a grill ; a grid ⇨ 석쇠

‡적수 赤手 a bare hand ; an empty hand ; naked fists ¶ 적수로 without the use of any weapon ; unarmed ; barehanded ; [독력으로] single-handed // 적수 공권으로 거부가 되다 make an enormous fortune starting with nothing

— 공권 empty hands and naked fists ; being without any financial support

적수 敵手 a match ; an opponent ; a rival ; a competitor ; an antagonist

호— a good rival〔match〕; a worthy opponent

적수 笛手 a flutist ; a fifer

적습 敵襲 an enemy attack ¶ 적습을 받다 be attacked〔raided〕 by the enemy

‡적시 適時 ¶ 적시의 timely ; opportune

— 안타 〖야구〗 a timely hit

적시 敵視 enmity ; hostility —하다 be hostile 《to》; have hostility 《toward》; look upon 《a person》 as an enemy ; regard 《a person》 with hostility

‡적시다 wet ; drench ; moisten ; dampen ; soak ; [정조를] defile ; deflorate ; rob of chastity

> 참고 **wet** 일반어 **drench** 액체를 부어서 완전히 적시다 **soak** 액체 속에 담가서 충분히 적시다

¶ 옷을 적시다 get one's clothes wet // 수건을 적시다 wet a towel // 눈물로 소매를 적시다 wet one's sleeves with tears

적신 賊臣 a rebel ; a traitor ; a conspirator

*적신호 赤信號 a red〔danger〕 signal ; a red light ; a stoplight

적실 的實 exactness ; preciseness ; accuracy —하다 (be) accurate ; exact ; precise

적실 嫡室 the legal〔legitimate〕 wife

적심 floating of timber down a river

적심 積心 〖건축〗 small (bits of wood) sticks put on top of the mud plaster to give a slope to a Korean roof

적심 赤心 one's true heart ; sincerity

적심 賊心 [도둑질의] a thieving〔larcenous〕 propensity ; propensity of larceny ; [해치려는] malicious intent ; an evil intention ; malice ; ill will ; [반역심] a treasonous intention ; rebellious spirit 〔heart〕

‡적십자 赤十字 the Red Cross

— 구호반 the Relief Corps of the Red Cross Society —기 the Red Cross flag — 병원 the Red Cross Hospital —사 the Red Cross Society —사 간호사 a Red Cross nurse —사 사원 a member of the Red Cross (society) — 사업 Red Cross work —일 Red Cross Day —장(章) a Red Cross medal — 조약 the Red Cross Convention 청소년 — the Junior Red Cross 《J. R. C.》 남북 — 회담 Talks between the South and North Korean Red Cross Societies 대한 —사 the Korean National Red Cross Society 《KNRC》 만국 —사 the International Red Cross

적악 積惡 accumulated wickedness ; a long course of evil life ; a series of evil deeds —하다 accumulate wickedness ; practice evils ; heap up wickedness

적약 適藥 a specific (remedy, medicine) ; a good remedy

적어도 at (the) least ; at a minimum ¶ 적어도 1만원은 들 것이다 It will cost you at least 10,000 *won*.

적업 適業 the right vocation ; a good line of work 《to be in》

적역 適役 a fit post ; a suitable office ¶ 그 일에는 그가 가장 적역이다 He is the right man for the work.

적역 適譯 an exact rendering ; an adequate〔a proper〕 translation ¶ 한국 말에는 이 단어의 적역이 없다 There is no exact Korean equivalent to this word.

적연 寂然 —하다 (be) lonely ; lonesome ; desolate ; deserted

적열 赤熱 red heat —하다 heat 《iron》 to red heat ; make red-hot

적외선 赤外線 infrared rays

— 램프 an infrared lamp — 분광기 an infrared spectrometer — 사진 infrared photography — 요법 infrared therapy — 필름〔건판〕 an infrared film〔sensitive plate〕

적외선 방사 赤外線放射 〖물리〗 infrared radiation

적요 摘要 a summary ; an outline ; an epitome ; a synopsis ; a compendium

—란 the remarks column —서 a statement ; a docket (소송의)

적요하다 寂寥— (be) desolate ; lonely ; lonesome

†적용 適用 application —하다 apply 《to》 ¶ 법의 적용 the application of a law // 적용의 범위 the limit of application // 적용할 수 있는 applicable // 법의 적용을 그르치다 make a wrong application of the law // 일반적으로 적용되다 be universally applicable ; be of general application // 이 규정은 기숙생에게 적용된다 The regulations are applied to the boarders. // 이 설명은 모든 경우에 적용되는 것이 아니다 This explanation will not apply to〔in〕 all cases.

적운 積雲 a cumulus

적울 積鬱 deep melancholy ; deep-seated 〔deep-rooted, accumulated, built-up〕 gloom ; the blues —하다 be congested with melancholy ; smoulder

적원 積怨 a built-up grudge ; bitter resentment ; deep-seated rancor

적위 赤緯 〖천문〗 declination

적위군 赤衛軍 the Red Guards ; the Red

Army
적은집 a concubine's house ; a mistress ; a kept woman ; a concubine ¶ 적은집을 두다 keep a mistress
‡적응 適應 fitness ; suitability ; adaptation —하다 fit ; be fit for ; be suited to ; be adapted too ¶ 적응시키다 fit 《a person a thing》 for ; adapt 《a thing》 to // 새 환경에 적응하다 adapt oneself to new circumstances // 그녀는 환경에 잘 적응한다 She adapts herself to her environment.
—설 〖생물〗 an adaptation theory —성 adaptability ; flexibility —증 diseases for which medicine is efficacious — 형질 an adaptative character
‡적의 敵意 animosity ; enmity ; hostility ; hostile feeling ¶ 적의 있는 hostile ; antagonistic ; unfriendly // 적의를 품다 entertain〔harbor〕 a hostile feeling 《against》 // 적의를 보이다 show hostility 《against》 ; manifest animosity 《toward》
적의 適宜 appropriateness ; suitableness ; suitability —하다 (be) fit ; fitting ; proper ; right ; suitable ¶ 적의한 조치를 취하다 take proper steps
적이 somewhat ; to some extent ; in some measure ; slightly ¶ 그 소식에 적이 안심되오 I was slightly relieved at the news.
적이나 at the very least ; ever so little ; a little at least ; if at all possible ¶ 적이나 후회하니 다행이다 I am glad he was sorry a little at least.
적임 適任 fitness 《to the post》 ; suitability ; competence ¶ 적임의 fit〔suitable〕 《for the office》 ; competent 《for》 ; efficient
—자 a well-qualified person ; the right man 《for the position》 ¶ 그는 이 일에 적임자이다 He is well fitted for this work.
—자 선택 selection of the right sort of officials —증 a certificate of competency 부—자 an unqualified〔incompetent〕 person ; an incompetent 최—자 the very man〔just the man〕 for 《the post》 ; the best man for 《the job》
*적자 赤字 red letters ; [결손] red figures ; a deficit ; a loss ¶ 적자가 되다 show a loss ; run into red figures ; be in the red // 적자를 메우다 cover〔make up〕 the deficit
— 경영 deficit operation — 공채 a deficit-covering bond — 노선 a railroad line operated at a deficit — 보전(補塡) a deficit covering — 생활 red-ink living — 수당 a deficit-covering allowance — 예산 an unbalanced budget — 요인 deficit causing factors — 운영 deficit operation — 융자 deficit-covering financing — 인생 a financially hard-pressed life — 잔액 a red balance — 재정 deficit finance ; a financial deficit ; "red-ink" finance — 지출 deficit spending 대— a heavy〔yawning〕 deficit 수지 — an adverse balance of payments
적자 赤子 a baby ; an infant
적자 嫡子 a legitimate child〔son〕
적자 適者 a fit person ; the fit
— 생존 the survival of the fittest ¶ 적자생존의 법칙 the law of the survival of the fittest
적장 敵將 the enemy's general ; the enemy commander ; the commander of the enemy force
적재 適材 a person fit for the post ; the right man
— 교육 talent〔personality〕 instruction〔education〕 — 적소 the right man in the right place ¶ 적재적소에 배치하다 put the right man in the right place〔a round peg in a round hole〕
적재 摘載 —하다 give a summary of ; give an excerpt〔extract〕 from ; reprint an extract from
†적재 積載 lading ; carrying ; loading —하다 load ; lade ; carry ; take on〔in〕 ¶ 배에 화물을 적재하다 load〔lade〕 a ship with goods // 우편물 및 승객을 적재하다 take on mail and passengers
— 능력 carrying〔loading〕 capacity —량 carrying capacity — 배수량 load displacement — 톤수 capacity〔freight〕 tonnage — 화물 cargo on board
적적하다 寂寂— (be) lonely ; lonesome ; solitary ; desolate ; deserted ¶ 적적한 감 a lonely feeling ; loneliness ; lonesomeness // 적적한 곳 a lonely place // 적적하게 지내다 lead〔live〕 a lonely life // 이 방은 가구가 없어서 보기에 적적하다 This room looks bare〔empty〕 without furniture. // 말동무가 없어서 적적하다 I feel lonely having no one to talk to. // 당신이 없어서 무척 적적했었다 We missed you badly.
적전 敵前 ¶ 적전의 in front〔the face〕 of the enemy // 적전에 가까워지다 face〔appro-ach〕 the enemy // 적전에서 도망가다 turn one's back to the enemy ; fly before the enemy
— 도하 a forced crossing of a river (against an enemy) ¶ 적전 도하를 하다 force the passage of a river against an enemy ; cross a river under the enemy's fire — 상륙 a landing in the face of the enemy — 상륙용 주정(上陸用舟艇) an assault boat〔barge〕
†적절 適切 pertinence ; appropriateness ; propriety ; felicity (표현의) —하다 (be) pertinent ; fit ; fitting ; apt ; adequate ; pr oper ; appropriate ; well-timed ; opportune ¶ 적절한 말 a felicitous〔an apt〕 remark〔expression〕 // 적절한 비유 a fitting comparison // 적절한 비평 a pertinent criticism // 적절한 예 an apt instance ; a good example // 이 경우에 적절한 말 words appropriate for the occasion // 적절하지 않다 be impertinent ; be unfit ; be

inadequate ; be irrelevant // 그의 제의는 이 사건에 가장 적절하다 What he proposes is most pertinent to the matter in hand.
적정 敵情 the movements of the enemy ¶ 적정을 살피다 reconnoiter the enemy's movements〔positions〕
적정 適正 propriety ; appropriateness ; reasonableness —하다 (be) proper ; appropriate ; right ; reasonable ; normal ; fair
— 가격 reasonable〔fair〕 prices —량정(量定) the just appreciation《of responsibility》 — 통화량 optimum money supply —화(化) rationalization
적조 赤潮 a red〔reddish brown〕 tide ; red water
적조 積阻 silence ; neglect to write ; being remiss in writing —하다 be silent ; be remiss in writing ; be a poor correspondent ¶ 오랫동안 적조했습니다 Pardon me for my long silence.
적중 的中 a hit ; a good hit —하다 [맞다] hit《the mark》; make a good hit ; [예언 따위가] come true ; turn out true ; [상상이] guess right ; make a good guess ; [계략이] take ; work ¶ 적중하지 않다 miss the mark ; go wild // 네 활〔총알〕이 표적에 적중했다 You hit the mark. // 너의 예언이 적중했다 Your prophecy〔prediction〕 came true. // 내 상상이 적중했다 I was right in my conjecture. / I guessed right. / My hunch was right on target.
적중 敵中 the middle of the enemy ¶ 적중에 돌입하다 rush into the enemy camp
적지 敵地 an enemy〔the hostile〕 land〔territory, country〕 ¶ 적지에 침입하다 advance into the enemy's country
적지않은 not a few〔little〕; extraordinary ; unusual ; uncommon ; [많은] many ; much ; immense ¶ 적지않은 돈 no small money ; a sizable amount〔sum〕 of money // 적지않은 기부 a substantial contribution // 나는 그에게 적지않은 신세를 졌다 I owe him a great deal.
적지않이 [수] in no small numbers ; not a few ; [양] in no small quantities ; not a little ; [정도] not a little ¶ 적지않이 놀라다 be not a little surprised // 적지않이 수고하다 take no little pains
적진 敵陣 the enemy camp ; the enemy's position ; the enemy line ¶ 적진을 돌파하다 break through the enemy line // 적진을 무찌르다 attack the enemy's position
적처 嫡妻 a legitimate wife
적철광 赤鐵鑛 〖광물〗 hematite
적체 積滯 the piling-up (of goods to be handled) ; accumulation ; backlog —하다 accumulate ; pile up ; form a backlog
적출 積出 shipment ; forwarding —하다 ship off ; send off ; forward
—인 a shipper — 통지서 an advice of shipment —항 the port of shipment 석탄—항 a coal-shipping port
적출 摘出 extracting ; an extract ; picking〔taking〕 out —하다 extract ; pick〔take〕 out ¶ 상처에서 총알을 적출하다 remove〔extract〕 the bullet from a wound
적출 嫡出 a child born of the legal wife
적취 積聚 ① ⇨ 적체(積滯) ② 〖한의〗 chronic indigestion
적치 積置 —하다 pile up ; heap ; amass
적침 赤沈 [의학] the precipitation of blood
— 검사 a blood precipitation〔sedimentation〕 test
적탄 敵彈 the enemy's shells〔bullets〕 ¶ 적탄을 무릅쓰고 in the face of enemy fire // 적탄에 쓰러지다 fall under the enemy fire ; be killed by an enemy bullet
적토 赤土 red earth〔soil〕; clay
적통 嫡統 the line of descent〔the descendants〕 from the legal wife ; the main line of descent
적틀 炙— a ritual vessel for shish kebab
적파 嫡派 descendants from the legal wife ; the main line of a family
적평 適評 a just criticism ; an appropriate comment ; an apt remark ¶ 적평을 내리다 make a pertinent remark《on》
적폐 積弊 a deep-rooted evil ; an evil of long standing ; accumulated evils ¶ 적폐를 일소하다 clean up old〔deep-rooted〕 evils
적포도주 赤葡萄酒 red wine
*적하 積荷 a load ; a freight ; a cargo ; [적재] loading ; shipping ; lading
— 명세서 a freight list — 목록 a shipping invoice ; a manifest (배의) — 보험 insurance on cargo — 비용 loading costs ; cargo costs — 수령증 a shipping receipt — 안내 an advice of shipment —항 a port of loading〔shipment〕
적하 滴下 dropping ; dripping —하다 drop ; drip ; distill ; dribble ; fall in drops
— 주유기 a drop oiler
적함 敵艦 an enemy warship〔vessel〕; hostile craft
†적합 適合 suitability ; fitness ; appropriateness ; conformity ; agreement —하다 (be) suitable ; fit ; compatible ¶ 목적에 적합하다 suit one's purpose ; be suited to one's purpose // 그는 악역에 적합하다 He's perfect in the role of the villain.
적혈 赤血 red blood
—구 〖의학〗 a red blood cell ; a red blood corpuscle — 소다 〖화학〗 ferricyanide of soda —염 〖화학〗 potassium ferricyanide
적형 嫡兄 an elder brother (born of the legal wife)
적화 赤化 communization ; Bolshevization ; sovietization —하다 communize ; Bolshevize ; infect《a person》 with

Bolshevik ideas ¶ 적화를 방지하다 check the spread of communism
— 선전 Red〔Bolshevik〕 propaganda — 운동 a Red〔Bolshevik〕 movement — 위협 the red menace
적화 赤禍 the red peril
적확 的確 exactness ; precision ; accuracy ; infallibility **—하다** (be) precise ; accurate ; exact ; infallible ¶ 말의 적확한 뜻 the exact meaning of a word // 적확한 방법 a correct method // 적확한 숫자 exact figures // 적확한 증거 a positive proof
적환 積換 trans(s)hipment ; reshipment **—하다** trans(s)hip ; reship
—비〔화물〕 a transshipment charge 〔cargo〕 — 하물(荷物) transshipment goods — 허가증 a transshipment permit
적회 積懷 a pent-up longing to see someone
적흑색 赤黑色 a reddish black (color)
적히다 be recorded ; be put on record ; be written down ¶ 역사에 적혀 있다 be recorded in history
전[1] [가장자리] an extended rim 《of a jar》
전[2] [나무·풀] a rakeful ; a bunch
전 田 a field ; a farm ⇨ 밭
전 典 a code ; a ceremony
†**전 前** [앞] the front ; the presence (사람의) ; [편지 따위에서] Dear ; Sir ; [부사적] before ; to ; till ; under ; ago ; [과거] the past ; the last time ¶ 전 주 the last week // 전 주소 one's former address // 전 페이지 the preceding page // 전날 밤 the night before // 어머님 전 Dear Mother // 수일 전에 a few days ago // 출발 전에 before one's departure // 이틀 전에 미리 two days in advance // 5시 15분 전에 at a quarter to〔before〕 five // 해가 뜨기 전에 before the sunrise // 전에 말한 바와 같이 as previously stated // 전에 그것을 들은 일이 있다 I have heard it before. // 그는 전과 다름이 없었다 He has not changed since. // 그것은 오래 전 일이다 It happened a long time ago.
전 煎 grilled food ¶ 전을 부치다 grill ; prepare a grilled dish // 생선전을 부치다 grill fish
전 廛 a shop ; a store ; a stall
전 錢 [돈] money ; a coin ; [단위] a hundredth part of one *won*
동— a copper (coin, piece) 백동— a nickel (coin)
전- 全 all ; whole ; entire ; total ; complete
—교 the whole school ; all the school — 국민 the whole nation —그리스주의 Pan-Hellenism —미 all America —미주의 Pan-Americanism —미 회의 the Pan-American Congress —3권 《be》 complete in three volumes —세계 the whole world —아시아 회의 the Pan-Asiatic Conference —재산 one's entire fortune —페이지 삽화 a full-page illustration —한국 all-Korea
-전 傳 [전기] a life ; a biography ; a chronicle ¶ 위인전 the lives of great men // 그리스도전 A Life of Christ
-전 殿 a hall ; a palace ; a sanctum
궁— a palace 복마— an abode of demons ; pandemonium 불— a Buddhist sanctum〔temple〕 신— a shrine
-전 戰 a war ; a battle ; [경기의] a game ; a match
공중— an air battle〔war〕 ; an air combat ; air fighting 근대— modern warfare 시가— street fighting 육박— a hand-to-hand fight ; a close combat
전가 轉嫁 [재혼] a second marriage ; remarriage ; [죄·책임의] imputation **—하다** [재혼하다] marry again ; remarry ; [책임 따위를] impute 《a crime to a person》 ; shift 《on》 ; lay〔throw〕 《the blame on a person》 ¶ 책임을 전가하다 shift responsibility on 《a person》 // 전책임을 부인에게 전가하다 throw the entire blame on one's wife // 나에게 책임을 전가하지 말아라 Don't pass the buck to me.
전가 傳家 —하다 pass on one's house to one's son ; transfer the headship of a house to one's son ¶ 전가의 hereditary
—지보 an heirloom —지보도(之寶刀) an heirloom sword ; a sword treasured in the family ; a trump card ; one's last resort
전가 田家 a farmhouse ; a rural cottage
전가 全家 the whole family ; all the family
— 양천(良賤) the whole household without exception
전각 全角 〖인쇄〗 an em
전각 殿閣 a royal palace
전각 前脚 forelegs ⇨ 앞다리
전각 篆刻 seal engraving **—하다** engrave a seal
—가 a seal engraver
전간 癲癇 〖의학〗 epilepsy ¶ 전간의 epileptic // 전간을 일으키다 have an epileptic fit
***전갈 全蠍** 〖동물〗 a scorpion
—좌 〖천문〗 the Scorpion
†**전갈 傳喝** a (verbal) message **—하다** give a (verbal) message ; send〔deliver〕 a (verbal) message
⁑**전개 展開** unfolding ; development ; expansion ; deployment (군대의) **—하다** unfold ; develop ; evolve ; spread out ; unroll ¶ 국면의 전개 the development of the situation // 국면의 전개를 기다리다 await developments // 정국이 신속히 전개되었다 The political situation developed rapidly. // 넓은 전망이 눈 앞에 전개된다 A wide panorama spreads out before me. // 이 사건은 앞으로 어떻게 전개될까 What will be the future developments of the affair ?
—도(圖) 〖기하〗 a development figure —

면 〖기하〗 development〔developable〕 surface —부(部) 〖음악〗 the development (section) —식 an expansion 국면 — the development of the situation ¶ 국면 전개를 기다리다 await developments 신국면(新局面) — ¶ 신국면 전개를 하다 take a new turn ; make a fresh development 이동 — ¶ 부대를 이동 전개하다 redeploy troops《from Europe to the Pacific》 종렬(縱列) — ¶ 종렬 전개하고 있다 be deployed in depth 횡대 — deploy (ahead) into line

전갱이 〖물고기〗 a horse mackerel ; a saurel

전거 典據 authority ; source ; reference ¶ 신뢰할 전거 reliable authority // 전거를 들다 name〔cite〕 authority // 명백한 전거를 보이다 give chapter and verse // 전거를 명백히 하다 verify one's reference

전거 奠居 decision on one's place of residence

전거 轉居 removal ; a change of abode 〔address〕 —하다 remove ; move ; change one's abode〔address〕 ; transfer one's residence《to》 ¶ 전거를 통지하다 notify change of address ; give notice of removal // 금번 표기 장소로 전거하였습니다 I have lately removed to the address given on the front.

전거리 bunches of firewood twigs ; fagot

전건 電鍵 a《telegraph》 key ; a tapper —반 a keyboard 계(繼)— a relay key

전게 前揭 ¶ 전게의 show above 〔before〕 ; aforenamed ; aforecited ⇨ 전기(前記)
—서 op. cit.《opus citatum《라》》 ¶ 전게서 중에 op. cit.《opere citato《라》》

전격 電擊 [충격] an electric shock ; [급습] a lightning attack —하다 attack rapidly ; blitz(krieg) ¶ 전격적 lightning // 전격적으로 공격을 받다 be blitzed ; be attacked with a blitz // 런던을 전격하다 make a lightning attack on London
— 공습 an air blitz — 요법 electric shock therapy — 작전 blitzkrieg〔lightning〕 tactics —전 a lightning war ; blitzkrieg 《도》 공중 —전 an air lightning war ; an air blitzkrieg

*전경 全景 a complete view ; a bird's-eye view ; the whole view ; a general〔an extensive, a panoramic〕 view ; a panorama ¶ 경기장의 전경 a general view of the grounds // 서울의 전경을 보다 see the whole view of *Seoul* // 언덕 위에서 그 도시의 전경을 볼 수 있다 The hill commands a panoramic view of the town.
— 사진 a panoramic photograph — 사진기 a pantoscope ; a pantoscopic camera 시가지 — a panoramic view of the town

전경 前景 the front view ; the foreground ¶ 그 사진의 전경에 옛 다리가 있다 We see an old bridge in the foreground of the picture.

전고 典故 an authentic precedent

전고 傳告 —하다 tell ; inform《of》 ; report

전고 銓考 consideration〔deliberation〕 in selecting ; (deliberate) selection〔choice, screening〕 —하다 select〔make choice, screen〕 deliberately

전곡 田穀 dry field grain〔crop〕

전곡 錢穀 money and grain

전곡 녹음 全曲錄音 (a) full-length recording

전곡 연주 全曲演奏 (a) full-length play 《of》

전골 beef with vegetables cooked in casserole
—틀 a casserole (pan)

†전공 專攻 a specialty ; a major ; a special subject of study —하다 study specially ; major《in》 ; specialize《in》 ; make a specialty《of》 ¶ 대학에서 경제학을 전공하다 specialize in〔take up〕 economics at the university
—과 a postgraduate course — 과목 a subject of special study ; a major《미》 ¶ 무슨 과목을 전공하고 있습니까 What are you majoring in? — 논문 a monograph — 분야 a major field of study

전공 戰功 distinguished war services ; military merit ; meritorious services in war ¶ 전공을 세우다 distinguish oneself in war ; render distinguished military services

전공 前功 a former merit ; past services

전공 電工 an electrician ; an electrical engineer

전과 全科 the whole curriculum ; the full〔complete〕 course ¶ 전과를 마치다 complete the whole required course
— 의사 a general practitioner

전과 前科 a previous conviction ; a criminal record ¶ 전과 3범의 사람 a person with three previous convictions // 그는 전과가 있다 He has been previously convicted. /He has a criminal record.
— 수범자(數犯者) a man with〔who has〕 several (previous) convictions ; a person who has been convicted several times —자 an ex-convict ; a former convict ; an old offender ; a marked man《미》 ; a relapsed criminal — 전무자(全無者) a man with〔who has〕 no (previous) court 〔police〕 record (whatever) 절도 — ¶ 절도 전과가 있다 have been previously 〔once〕 convicted of theft

전과 戰果 war results ; military achievements ¶ 혁혁한 전과를 거두다 achieve brilliant results in war ; make great gains in war ; make marked military achievements // 전과를 확대하다 improve the fruits of (a) battle

전과 轉科 change of one's major study ; change of one's service branch in the army —하다 change one's course ((to)) ; transfer to another branch

전관 專管 exclusive jurisdiction〔management〕 —하다 have exclusive jurisdiction ((over)) ; have power ((over))

— 수역 an exclusive〔restrictive〕 fishing zone〔waters〕

전관 前官 ① [전임자] the predecessor ((in a post)) ¶ 전관은 누구였는가 Who preceded you in the post? /Who held the post before you?

② [자신의] one's former post ¶ 전관 예우(禮遇)를 받다 be granted the privileges of one's former post

⁑**전광 電光** electric light ; (a flash of) lightning ; a bolt ¶ 전광 석화와 같이 like a flash of lightning ; as quick as lightning ; with lightning speed // 전광을 내다 emit electric sparks

— 간판 an electric sign ((of a store)) — 뉴스 a sky sign (광고의)

전광 癲狂 lunacy ; insanity ; madness

전교 轉交 delivery〔transfer〕 through a person (물건을) ; sending ((a letter)) in care of a person (편지를) —하다 send ((a thing)) by〔through〕 ((a person)) ; send ((mail)) in care of ((a person)) ¶ A씨 전교 B씨 귀하 Mr. B, care of〔c/o〕 Mr. A (겉봉에) // 전교로 편지를 내다 address a letter in care of ((a person))

†**전교 全校** the whole school ¶ 전교 제일의 근면한 학생 the most diligent student in the whole school

—생 all the students of a school ; the whole student body — 일등생 the most diligent〔hardworking〕 student in the whole school

전교¹ 傳敎 [포교] propagation (of religion) ; missionary work ; mission (work) ; propagandism —하다 propagate ((a religion)) ; mission ; propagandize

—자 a propagator ; a propagandist ; a missionary (worker)

전교² 傳敎 [왕명] a royal ordinance〔order〕 —하다 issue a royal ordinance

⁑**전구 電球** an electric bulb ; a light bulb ¶ 40와트의 전구 a 40-watt bulb // 끊어진 전구 a burnt-out light bulb // 전구 하나가 나갔다 One of the bulbs is burned out.

—선 a filament ¶ 전구선이 끊겼다 The filament has burnt out〔broken〕. /The electric bulb snapped. 가스 — a gas-filled bulb 금속선 — a metal(l)ic-filament bulb 백열 — an incandescent bulb 불투명 유리 — a frosted bulb 색— a colored bulb 섬광 — a flash bulb 소형 — a miniature bulb ; a decoration〔fancy〕 bulb 알— a naked light bulb 탄소선 — a carbon-filament bulb

전구 前驅 a forerunner ; a precursor ; an outrider ; the van ; the vanguard

— 증상 premonitory symptoms ((of)) ; 〖의학〗 a prodrome — 증상적 단계 a prodromal stage

전국 全— undiluted liquor〔soysauce〕 ¶ 전국의 pure ; undiluted

— 간장 pure soysauce —술 raw spirit

전국 全局 the whole aspect〔field〕 ((of affairs)) ; the general situation ; the general state ((of affairs)) ¶ 전국을 살피다 take in the general situation ; take a broad view of things

전국 全國 the whole country〔nation〕 ¶ 전국의 nationwide ; national // 전국에 all over the country ; throughout the nation // 전국적으로 on a national scale // 전국적으로 유명한 사람 a man with a national reputation // 전국적으로 운동을 일으키다 launch a nationwide movement // 전국적으로 퍼지다 spread all over the nation // 전국에서 모이다 come together from all over the country // 전국 대회를 열다 hold a national conference

—구 the national〔nationwide〕 constituency —구제(區制) the national constituency system — 대회 [정당의] a national convention ; [스포츠의] a national athletic meet — 동맹 a national federation —민 the whole〔entire〕 nation — 방송 a nationwide broadcast ; a national network broadcast —적 national ; nationwide ; countrywide ¶ 전국적 공황〔강우〕 a general panic〔rainfall〕 // 전국적 단체 an organization nationwide in its scope // 전국적 운동 a campaign on a nationwide〔national〕 scale ; ((start)) a nationwide movement〔campaign〕 — 조합 a national union — 중계(방송) a nationwide hookup ¶ 전국 중계 방송되었다 The broadcast was carried on a national network. —지(紙) a national newspaper — 체육 대회 a national athletic meet — 출판물 목록 a national bibliography〔catalogue of publications〕 — 학교 도서관 협의회 Korea School Library Association ((KSLA))

전국 戰國 a country at war ; a country in civil war

— 시대 the age of civil wars

전국 戰局 the war situation ; the state〔aspect〕 of the war ; the tide of war ¶ 전국이 변하다 the war situation changes // 전국이 호전하다 the tide of war turns in one's favor

전군 全軍 the whole〔entire〕 army 〔force〕

전권 全權 plenary〔absolute〕 power〔authority〕 ; plenipotentiary powers ¶ 전권을 위임하다 invest〔entrust〕 ((a person)) with full powers // 전권을 장악하다 have full powers ((over)) // 회사의 전권을 잡다 hold absolute power over the company

— 대사〔공사〕 an ambassador〔a minister〕 plenipotentiary — 위원 a plenipotentiary — 위임장 a commission of full

powers 특명 — 대사 an ambassador extraordinary and plenipotentiary
전권 專權 an exclusive right ; arbitrary power ; supreme power —하다 exercise〔wield〕 an exclusive right
전권 全卷 the whole book ; the entire volume ; the whole reel (영화의) ¶ 전권을 통하여 from cover to cover ; throughout the book
전권 前卷 the preceding volume
전극 電極 an electrode ; a pole ; [양극] positive ; [음극] negative
전근 轉勤 transference 《to another office》 —하다 be〔get〕 transferred to 《another office》 ¶ 부산 지점으로 전근 명령을 받다 be transferred to the *Pusan* branch // 그는 회사의 뉴욕 지점으로 전근했다 He has been transferred to the New York branch office of his company.
전근 轉筋 a cramp
전근대적 前近代的 premodern
전기 前記 ¶ 전기의 above-mentioned ; foregoing ; aforementioned ; said // 전기의 금액 the said sum // 전기와 같이 as said〔mentioned〕 above ; above-mentioned // 전기의 장소에 이전하다 move to the above address
전기 前期 the former term ; the first term ; the preceding〔first〕 half year (반년) ; the first semester (2학기제의 1학기)
— 결산 settlement for the first half year — 시험 the first term examination — 이월금 the balance brought 〔carried〕 over from the last account — 이월 이익〔결손〕금 the surplus〔deficit〕 at the beginning of a period
†전기 電氣 electricity ¶ 전기의 electric ; electrical // 전기를 일으키다 generate electricity // 전기를 켜다 turn〔switch〕 on the electric light // 전기를 끄다 turn 〔switch〕 off the electric light // 방에는 전기가 켜져 있었다 A light was burning in his room. // 이 전선에는 전기가 통해 있다 This wire is live〔charged with electricity〕.
— 감응 electric induction — 검사원 an electricity checker〔inspector〕 — 경보기 an electric alarm — 계기(計器) an electric meter — 계산기 an electric calculator —공 an electrician — 공사 electric work — 공업 electric industry — 공예학 electrotechnology ; electrotechnics — 공학 electrical engineering — 광학 electrooptics — 기계 an electric machine — 기계공 an electrician — 기관차 an electric locomotive — 기구 an electric device〔appliance〕 ; electric apparatus〔outfit〕 — 기구 수리 ¶ 전기 기구 수리를 하다 do electrical repairs — 기구점 an electric(al) goods〔appliance〕 store — 기사 an electrical engineer ; an electrician — 난로 an electric heater — 난방(법) electric heating — 난방기 an electric (air) heater — 냉장고 an electric refrigerator〔freezer〕 — 다리미〔담요〕 an electric iron〔blanket〕 —대(帶) [의료] a galvanic belt — 도금 electroplating ; [금] electrogilding ¶ 전기 도금을 하다 electroplate ; galvanize — 도금기 an electroplater — 도금물(鍍金物) an electroplated article — 도체 an electric conductor — 동력계 an electric dynamometer —량 quantity of electricity — 레인지 an electric range —력 electric force〔intensity〕 —력계(力計) an electrodynamometer —로 an electric furnace 〔oven〕 —료 electric(-al) charges 〔rates〕 ; electricity〔power〕 rates ; [전등료] electric light rates — 마사지 electromassage — 마취 electronarcosis — 메스 a radio knife — 면도 an electric shaver — 미싱 an electrical sewing machine — 발동기 an electric motor ; an electromotor — 방사 electric radiation — 방사기 an electric radiator — 방석 a heating pad —법 galvanoplasty ; galvanoplastics — 변위(變位) electric displacement — 복사기(輻射機) an electric radiator — 복사 난로 an electric glow heater — 복사로(輻射爐) an electric radiant heater — 분석 electroanalysis — 분해 electrolysis — 분해 기록 a polarogram — 분해물 an electrolyte — 분해 자기기(分解自記器) a polarograph —불 an electric light — 불꽃 a sparkler — 사업 the electric (supply) enterprise ; the electrical enterprise 〔industry〕 — 사업법 the Electricity Enterprises Act — 사업 회사 an electric enterprise company — 사자기(寫字機) a telewriter — 사형 electrocution —석(石) 〖광물〗 tourmaline ; turmaline —석 집게 tourmaline tongs — 설비 electric installation 〔equipment〕 — 세탁기 an electric washing machine —소(素) 〖물리〗 an effluvium 《*pl.* -via, ~s》 — 소작(燒灼) 〖의학〗 galvanocautery — 소제기 an electric vacuum cleaner —솥 an electric rice-cooker — 스탠드 a desk lamp — 스토브 an electric stove〔heater〕 ; an electric fire 《영》 — 스파크 an electric spark — 시계 an electric clock〔watch〕 — 식각(술) glyphography — 식각사(蝕刻師) a glyphographer — 식각판(蝕刻版) a glyphograph — 야금(법) electrometallurgy — 역학 electrodynamics — 온도계 a telethermometer — 완구 an electric toy — 요금 electric charges〔rates〕 ; power rates — 요법 electric treatment ; electropathy — 요법의(療法醫) an electrotherapist —욕(탕) an electric bath — 용광(법) electric smelting — 용량 electric capacity — 용접 electric welding — 용접기 an electric welder — 의자 an electric chair ¶ 전기 의자에 앉다 be electrocuted ; get the chair 《미·속》 // 전기 의자에 앉히다 electrocute ; send 《a

prisoner》 to the electric chair — 이발기 an electric hair clipper — 자격(刺激) electrostimulation — 자동차 a battery car ; an electric automobile〔car〕 — 자석 an electromagnet — 장치 electric apparatus — 저항 electric resistance — 저항계 an ohmmeter — 저항 압력계 an electric resistance pressure gauge — 저항 온도계 an electrical resistance thermometer — 전도 electrical conduction — 전도율 electric conductivity — 절연체 an electric insulator — 제어 electric control — 제어기(制御器) an electric controller — 제판(製版) electrotypy ; galvanoplasty — 제판공 an electrotyper — 제품 an electric(al) appliance ; an electric apparatus — 제품 회사 an electrical products firm — 조명 electric illumination — 주전자 [물끓이는] an electric kettle — 진공 수진기(眞空收塵機) an electric vacuum cleaner — 진동 electric oscillation — 진동기 an electric oscillator — 집진(集塵) 장치 an electric precipitator — 철도 an electric railway ; an electric tramway — 철도 회사 an electric railway〔traction〕 company — 축음기 an electric gramophone ; a radiophonograph — 치료 ¶ 전기 치료하다 〖의학〗 fulgurate —침[외과용] an electric needle — 침투 electroosmosis ; electroosmose ; electroendosmosis ; electroendosmose — 탐광 electric prospecting — 토스터 an electric toaster —톱 a power saw — 통신 telecommunication ; electric(al) communication — 통신 학부 the department of telecommunication —판(版) 〖인쇄〗 an electrotype ; an electroplate ; an electro 《*pl.* -s》《구》; a galvanograph ¶ 전기판으로 하다 electrotype ; electro 《구》 —판공 an electrotyper —판술(版術) electrotyping ; electrotypy ; galvanography ; galvanoplasty —판 조각기 an electrograph —포(砲) an electric gun — 표백(법) electric〔electrolytic〕 bleaching — 풍로 an electric hot plate〔cooker〕 —학 the science of electricity ; electric science ; electricity ; electrology —학자 an electrician — 합성 〖화학〗 electrosynthesis — 해리(解離) 〖물리〗 electrolytic dissociationionization — 화로 an electric foot warmer — 화학 electrochemistry — 화학 공업 electrochemical industry — 화학 당량(化學當量) electrochemical equivalent — 회로 an electric circuit — 회사 an electric(al) company 공중 — atmospheric electricity 동 — dynamic〔voltaic, kinetic, current〕 electricity 마찰 — frictional electricity 수력〔화력〕 — hydraulic〔steam power〕 electricity 양〔음〕— positive〔negative〕 electricity 열— thermal electricity 유— galvanic electricity 자— magnetic electricity 정— static electricity 가정(용) — 제품〔기구〕 household electric(al) appliances

전기 電機 electrical machinery and appliances ; electrical equipment〔supplies〕
— 공업 electrical machinery industry — 학교 an electrotechnological school — 회사 an electrical manufacturing〔engineering〕 company

†전기 傳記 a life ; a biography ; a life history
—담 a biographical story — 문학 biographical literature —물 biographical writings — 소설 a fictional biography — 소설가 a fictional biographer — 영화 a film biography — 작가 a biographer

전기 轉機 a turning point ¶ 생애의 전기 the turning point in one's life // 정국에 일대 전기를 가져 오다 mark〔make〕 a turning point in the political situation // 그것은 새 생활에의 전기가 됐다 That was the turning point of my career.

전기 轉記 posting —하다 post 《an item》 ¶ 대장에 전기하다 post 《an item》 in the ledger

전기 戰記 a record〔an account〕 of war ; a war〔military〕 history

전기 戰機 the time for fighting〔battle〕 ; military secret ¶ 전기가 무르익었다 The time is ripe for a battle. /The time has matured for opening hostilities.

전기 소설 傳奇小說 a novel ; a romance

전기줄 電氣— an electrical wire〔cord〕 ⇨ 전선(電線)

전나귀 〖동물〗 a lame〔limping〕 ass〔donkey〕

*전나무 〖식물〗 a fir (tree)

전날 前— the other day ; some〔a few〕 days ago ; recently ; previously ; formerly ; before ¶ 전날부터 for some days past // 전날 말씀 드린 바와 같이 as I informed you the other day

전남편 前男便 one's former husband ; one's late husband (죽은) ; one's divorced husband

전납 前納 payment in advance ; advance payment ; prepayment —하다 pay in advance ; prepay

전납 全納 payment in full ; full payment —하다 pay in full

전낭 錢囊 a purse ; a moneybag

전내 殿內 ① [내부] the inside of the palace ② [신위] a spirit tablet for praying and fortune-telling

전내기 全— pure〔undiluted〕 liquor

전내기 廛— [날림물건] cheap〔crude, coarse, poor, plain〕 articles〔goods〕

전년 前年 the previous year ; the years before ; last year (작년) ¶ 전년 여름에 in the previous summer // 전쟁이 일어나기 전년 the last prewar year
—도 the previous (fiscal) year

전념 專念 concentration of mind ; close attention ⇨ 전렴

전뇌 前腦 〖해부〗 the forebrain ; the prosencephalon

⁑전능 全能 omnipotence **—하다** (be) omnipotent ; almighty ¶ 전능의 신 the Almighty (God) ; the Omnipotent

전능력 全能力 all one's ability ; [공장 따위의] full capacity ¶ 전능력을 기울이고 as much as one can do ; as best one can ; to the best of one's ability ; [공장 따위가] at full capacity ; to capacity // 전능력을 기울이다 put one's heart and soul into one's work ; [공장에서] operate〔run〕 at full capacity

전다 煎茶 an infusion of tea **—하다** boil tea

전단 全段 [신문의] a whole〔an entire〕 page ; the whole space ¶ 전단을 전쟁 기사로 메우다 devote a whole page to war news

— 표제 a banner (headline) 《미》 ; a bannerline

전단 前段 the preceding paragraph ; previous portion ; a foregoing part

전단 剪斷 a shear ; shearing **—하다** nip ; cut ; cut with scissors ; shear

—기 a shearing machine ; a shearer

전단 傳單 a leaflet

전단 戰端 the cause of war ; the opening of hostilities ; hostile operations ¶ 전단을 열다 open hostilities ; take up arms against

전단 專斷 arbitrary decision ; arbitrariness **—하다** act arbitrarily〔on one's own authority〕 ; act high-handedly〔at one's own discretion〕 ¶ 전단의 조치 an arbitrary measure // 그는 재임중 전단의 행패가 많았다 He abused his authority while in office.

전달 前— last month ; the preceding month ; the previous month

⁑전달 傳達 delivery ; conveyance ; transmission **—하다** deliver ; forward ; convey ; notify ; announce ¶ 음향의 전달 traveling of sound // 명령을 전달하다 serve 《a person》 with an order // 취지를 정부에 전달하다 communicate the purport to the government // 음향의 전달은 광천보다 늦다 Sound travels slower than light. // 내 의사를 전달하려 했을 뿐이다 I was just trying to get my point across.

전담 全擔 the whole responsibility ; complete charge **—하다** take full〔complete〕 charge 《of》 ; assume full responsibility ; be wholly responsible 《for》 ¶ 비용을 전담하다 be charged with the whole cost

전담 專擔 the exclusive responsibility 〔charge〕 **—하다** take whole〔exclusive〕 charge 《of》 ; be fully responsible 《for》 ¶ 비용을 전담하다 be charged with the whole cost

전답 田畓 paddies and dry〔upland〕 fields ; paddy fields〔rice fields〕 and ordinary fields

***전당 典當** pawn(ing) ; a pledge ¶ 전당에 잡혀 있다 be in〔at〕 pawn ; be in pop 《영·속》 ; be in hock 《영·속》 // 그는 시계를 6,000원에 전당 잡혔다 He pledged his watch for six thousand *won*.

—물 a pawned article ; an article in pawn ¶ 전당물을 찾다 redeem a thing in pledge **—포** a pawnshop ; a pawnbroker's shop ; a spout 《미·속》 ; a popshop 《미·속》 ¶ 전당포에 드나들다 frequent a pawnshop **—표** a pawn ticket **공설 —포** a public〔municipal〕 pawnshop

전당 잡다 [관용] take 《a thing》 in pawn 〔pledge〕 ; hold 《a thing》 in pledge

전당 잡히다 [관용] pawn ; pledge ; put 《a thing》 in pawn

전당 殿堂 a temple ; a sanctuary ; a hall ; a mansion ; a palace ¶ 학문의 전당 a hall〔sanctuary〕 of learning

전당 대회 全黨大會 the national convention 《of a party》 ; a party convention

— 의장 the chairman of the party (national) convention **연례〔격년〕 —** an annual〔a biennial〕 (party) convention

전대 戰隊 a (naval) squadron ; a battle corps ¶ 수뢰 전대 a torpedo boat flotilla

전대 纏帶 a money belt (허리에 차는) ; a wallet

전대 轉貸 underlease ; sublease ; underletting **—하다** [토지를] sublease ; underlease ; [가옥을] underlet ; sublet ; subrent ¶ 집을 전대하다 sublet a house

—인 a sublessor **—차(借)** subletting ; sublease

전대 前代 former generations ; former ages ¶ 전대 미문의 unheard-of ; unprecedented ; record-breaking // 전대 미문의 대홍수 an unheard-of flood ; a record flood // 이것은 전대 미문의 일이다 We have never heard of this before. / This is something new under the sun.

전대야 a brass basin with an extended rim

전도 全道 the whole province ¶ 전도에 all over〔throughout〕 the province

전도 全島 the entire island ¶ 전도에 all over〔throughout〕 the island

전도 前途 one's future ; prospects ; an outlook ; [여정] the journey before one ; the distance to cover ¶ 전도 유망한 청년 a promising young man ; a young man with a bright future // 전도가 요원하다 have a long way to go (사람이) ; be far off (사물이) // 전도를 걱정하다 be anxious about one's future // 전도를 그르치다 spoil one's future〔career〕 // 전도를 내다보다 see one's course clearly ; look ahead into the future // 전도를 축복하다 wish 《a person》 success // 그는 전도가 유망하다 He has a bright future before him. // 전도가 어둡다 We have a dark future before us. // 우리의 전도는 다난하

다 Our future is full of difficulties. /We have many difficulties ahead of us. ∥너의 전도는 양양하다 The world lies all before you. ∥그 일은 전도가 신통치 않다 The enterprise has rather dark prospects. ∥우리의 전도는 아직도 요원하다 We are yet far from our object〔goal〕. ∥도중 하차는 전도 무효임 No stopover on this ticket.

전도 前渡 [돈의] payment in advance ; advance payment ; [물품의] delivery in advance
—금 advanced money ; an advance ; an advancement

전도 前導 leading the way ; guidance —하다 guide ; lead
—자 a guide ; a leader ¶ 그는 문명의 전도자였다 He was in the van of civilization. —함 a guide ship

***전도 傳道** mission〔missionary〕 work ; evangelical work ; propagation —하다 preach ; propagate ; engage in mission work ; evangelize ¶ 기독교를 전도하다 engage in Christian mission work
— 부인 a Bible woman ; a lady evangelist —사 a preacher ; a missionary ; an evangelist — 사업 missionary work —서 〖성경〗 The Book of Ecclesiastes ; Ecclesiastes 《Eccl., Eccles.》 — 여행 an evangelical tour — 학교 a mission〔missionary〕 school — 회사 a missionary society ; a mission board 국내〔해외(海外)〕— home〔foreign〕 missions

전도 奠都 establishment of the capital —하다 establish〔set up〕 the capital

전도 顚倒 inversion ; turning upside down ; an upset ; reversal ; upsetting —하다 overturn ; invert ; reverse ; upset ; turn over〔upside down〕 ; lose one's head (정신이) ¶ 본말을 전도하다 put the cart before the horse ; invert the order ∥정신이 전도되다 be upset ; lose one's balance〔head〕 ∥놀라서 정신이 전도되다 be frightened out of one's wit ∥그는 그 소식을 듣고 정신이 전도됐다 He was very much upset by the news.

전도 全圖 a complete〔whole〕 map〔drawing, diagram〕
서울 — a complete map of *Seoul* 세계 — the world map

전도 傳導 conduction (열 따위의) ; transmission (음향 따위의) —하다 conduct ; transmit ¶ 열을 전도하다 conduct heat
—기 an intermedium —도(度) conductivity —력 conductive power ; conductivity — 방전(放電) conductive discharge —성 conductivity —율 conductivity —전류 conduction〔galvanic〕 current —체 a conductor ; a transmitter 부(不)— ¶ 부전도의 nonconducting 열— heat conduction 초(超)(전기)— superconduction

전동 電動 electromotion ¶ 전동(식)의 electromotive ; electric-powered
— 개폐기 a motor-operated switch —력 electromotive force — 발전기 a motor generator (set)

전동 轉動 revolution ; rotation ; rolling —하다 revolve ; rotate ; turn ; roll

전동 a quiver for arrows

전동기 電動機 an electromotor ; an electric motor
— 부하(負荷)〔회로〕 a motorload〔circuit〕 가감 속도(加減速度)〔교직 양용(交直兩用)〕— an adjustable speed〔a universal〕 motor 교류— an alternating current motor 반발(反撥) — a repulsion motor 유도 — an induction motor 직류 — a direct current motor

전동자 電動子 an armature (of a motor)

전두 前頭 the forehead ; 〖해부〗 the sinciput ¶ 전두부의 sincipital ; proce-phalic
—골 the frontal (bone) —낭 〖생물〗 a frontal sac ; a ptilinum 《*pl.* -na》 —부 the front ; the forehead —엽 the frontal lobe

전두리 the circumference of a rim ; the edge of a rim 《of jar, lid》

전등 電燈 an electric light〔lamp〕 ¶ 전등을 설치하다 have electric lights installed ∥전등을 켜다 turn〔switch〕 on an electric light ∥전등을 끄다 turn out〔switch off〕 the electric light ∥집에는 전등이 들어와 있다 The house is electrically lighted. ∥그는 전등을 켜 놓은 채 잠 들었다 He fell asleep with the light on.
—갓〔코드〕 a lamp shade〔cord〕 —선 an indoor wire for the lamplight ; [실내] a lamp cord〔wire〕 — 스위치 체인 a light chain —알 a light bulb — 장식 an electric illumination 고촉광 — a high-powered lamp 꽃— an electrolier (장식용) 소형 — a fairy lamp〔light〕 알— a bare electric light 장식 — a decoration (electric) lamp ; decoration lighting 회중 — a flashlight

전등 前燈 a headlight ; a headlamp ⇨ 헤드라이트

전라 全裸 total nudity ; stark nakedness ¶ 전라의 stark-naked ; nude 《picture》 ; 《a girl》 in the nude ; with nothing on ∥전라가 되다 be stripped stark-naked ∥전라로 헤엄치다 swim with nothing on〔in the altogether〕

전락 轉落 fall ; downfall ; [주식] slump ; drop ; [타락] degradation —하다 fall ; degrade ; have a setback ¶ 창부로 전락하다 sink〔be reduced〕 to prostitution ∥100원으로 전락하다 fall〔slump〕 to 100 *won*

전란 戰亂 wars ; hostilities ; disturbances ; strife ¶ 전란의 위협 the threat of war ∥전란의 유럽 war-torn Europe ∥전란이 일어나다 a war breaks out
대— a great war ; a cataclysm

‡전람 展覽 exhibition ; show(ing) ; display —하다 exhibit ; show ¶ 전람에 내놓다 exhibit ; put 《a thing》 on exhibition 〔view〕 // 훌륭한 그림이 전람되어 있다 Fine pictures are on show.
—실 a showroom ; a salon —자 an exhibitor —품 exhibits ; a showpiece —회 an exhibition ; a show ¶ 전람회를 열다 hold an exhibition // 전람회에 출품하다 exhibit 《articles》 in a display —회장 an exhibition gallery〔hall〕 국화 —회 a chrysanthemum show 미술 —회 an art exhibition 순회 —회 a circulating exhibition

전래 傳來 transmission ; introduction (외래) —하다 be transmitted ; be handed down 《from》 ; be introduced 《from》 ¶ 전래의 traditional ; hereditary ; inherited // 불교의 전래 the introduction of Buddhism // 선조 전래의 가보 an heirloom ; patrimonial goods // 선조 전래의 검 a sword handed down from generation to generation in the family // 전래지풍 traditional manners〔customs〕 // 불교는 인도에서 전래했다 Buddhism was introduced from India.

*전략 戰略 strategy ; stratagem ; tactics (전술) ¶ 전략적 strategic // 전략적으로 strategically ; from a strategic point of view // 전략을 세우다 work out a strategy // 전략적 후퇴 a strategic retreat // 전략상의 목적으로 for strategic purposes // 전략으로 이기다 outmaneuver 《a person》 // 이 상품을 팔 전략을 세우자 Let's try to map out a strategy for selling this product.
—가 a strategist — 공군 a strategic air force ; the Strategic Air Command (미국의) — 공군 총사령부 the Strategic Air Command 《SAC》 — 단위 a strategical unit — 목표 a strategic target — 물자 strategic materials — 미스 a strategic error — 육군[미군의] the Strategic Army Corps 《STRAC》 — 작성자 a strategy-maker —적 지점 a strategic point —적 퇴각 a strategic retreat〔withdrawal〕 — 폭격 strategic bombing — 회의 a strategy meeting

전략 前略 the preceding passages omitted ; the preface omitted —하다 omit the preface

전량 全量 the whole quantity

전량 錢糧 money and provisions

전량계 電量計 a coulometer ; coulombmeter ; voltameter

*전력 全力 all one's power〔strength, might, energies〕 ; all-out effort ; one's best ¶ 전력을 다하여 with all one's might ; with might and main ; to the best of one's ability // 전력을 다하다 do one's best ; do everything in one's power ; exert oneself to the utmost // 전력을 기울이다 devote〔give〕 one's heart and soul 《to》 // 전력을 다하여 싸우다 fight desperately // 학생은 전력을 다하여 공부하지 않으면 안된다 Students should devote their best efforts to their studies.

전력 專力 concentration of one's energies 〔powers〕 —하다 concentrate one's energies〔powers〕 on 《the object》 ; devote oneself to ; put one's whole energy into 《one's work》

*전력 電力 electric power〔energy〕 ; electricity ; power ¶ 10만 마력의 전력 100,000 electrical horsepower // 전력을 공급하다 supply electric power
—계 a wattmeter — 공급 supply of electric power ; (electric) power supply — 공사 power supply works — 관리〔통제〕 control of electric power ; power control — 기근 power famine — 낭비〔절약〕 waste〔economy〕 of electric power — 부족 an electric power shortage — 사업 the (electric) power industry — 사정 the (electric) power condition — 생산 electric-power production —선 a power line — 소비 power consumption — 수송〔분포〕 (electric) power transmission〔distribution〕 — 요금 power rates ; an electric fee — 융통 interchange〔intersupply〕 of electricity — 제한 power restriction —채(債) electric power company bonds — 통제 power control — 평균 분배(법) load shedding —학 electrodynamics — 할당제 the electric power allocation system — 회사 an electric power company 공업용 — industrial electric power 10만 마력 — 100,000 electrical horse-power 수력 발전 — 생산량 hydroelectric power output

전력 戰力 fighting power〔strength〕 ; war 〔military〕 potential〔capacity〕
—원(源) [재정적·물리적인] the sinews of war — 유지〔상실〕 the maintenance 〔loss〕 of war potential — 증강 the strengthening of war potential 미사일 — missile capability

전력 戰歷 war experience ; a war career 〔record〕 ; a battle record

전력 前歷 one's past〔previous〕 record ; one's previous history ; one's antecedents ¶ 전력을 조사하다 inquire into a person's past record // 그의 전력은 은행원이다 He once served in a bank.

전렴 專念 concentration of mind ; undivided attention ; close attention —하다 give〔devote〕 oneself 《to》 ; be absorbed 〔engrossed〕 《in》 ; concentrate on〔upon〕 ¶ 공부에 전렴하다 devote oneself to one's study ; concentrate one's whole mind upon study // 생업에 전렴하다 work hard to get living

전령 電鈴 an electric bell ¶ 전령을 누르다 ring an electric bell

전령 傳令 [사람] a messenger ; an orderly ; [명령] an official message ; a written official order —하다 carry orders

《to》; deliver〔convey〕 an official message ¶ 전령을 보내다 send a message ; send an orderly
— 근무 an orderly duty — 기병 a cavalry orderly 기마(騎馬) — a dispatch rider
전례 典禮 ceremony ; ritual
*전례 前例 a precedent ; a former〔previous〕 example ¶ 전례 없는 일 an unprecedented matter ; an unheard-of affair // 전례에 의해서 according to a precedent // 전례가 없다 There is no precedent for this. /It is without a precedent. // 전례를 만들다 set〔make, create〕 a precedent // 전례에 따르다 follow a precedent ; follow suit // 전례를 깨뜨리다 violate〔depart from〕 the precedent ; break the precedent // 전례로 삼다 take《a thing》 as a precedent
전류 電流 an electric current ; a voltaic current ; a flow of electricity ¶ 전류가 통한 철사 a live wire ; a wire charged with electricity // 전류를 통하다 turn on electricity ; send〔apply〕 an electric current ; make contact // 전류를 끊다 turn off the electricity ; shut off the current ; break the contact
— 강도 current intensity〔strength〕 —계 a galvanometer ; an ammeter — 단속기 an interrupter — 단위 a current unit — 밀도 current density — 발생 yield of current — 역류(逆流)〔분류(奔流)〕 reversal〔rush〕 of current — 전환기 a commutator — 제한기 a current limiter — 차단기 a contact breaker〔limiter〕 — 측정 galvanometry ; measuring —칭(秤) a current balance —학 galvanism — 회로 a current circuit 고〔저〕압 — a high〔low〕 voltage current 과(過)〔강(强), 누(漏)〕— an excess〔a heavy, a leakage〕 current 교〔직〕류 — an alternating〔a continuous〕 current 무효(無效)〔맥동(脈動), 열(熱)〕— a wattless〔pulsating, thermo-electric〕 current 실효(實效)〔순(順), 순환(循環)〕 — an effective〔a forward, a circulating〕 current 양(陽)— a positive current 합성〔역(逆), 자화(磁化)〕— a resultant〔an inverse, a magnetizing〕 current 가정 —계 a house meter 무정위(無定位) —계 an astatic galvanometer
전륜 前輪 a front wheel
— 구동(驅動) front (wheel) drive
전리 電離 〖물리〗 ionization ; electrolytic dissociation — 하다 ionize
— 상자 an ionization〔ion〕 chamber — 압력계 an ionization gauge — 용압(溶壓) electrolytic solution pressure — 장치 an ionizer —층 the ionosphere ; an ionization layer
전리품 戰利品 a (war) trophy ; 〔약탈품〕 booty ; spoils (of war) ; loot
전립 氈笠 a soldier's felt hat
전립선 前立腺 〖해부〗 the prostate (gland)
— 비대 enlargement of the prostate gland — 비대증 prostatomegaly — 수술 ¶ 전립선 수술을 받다 undergo a prostate operation —염 prostatitis — 절제 prostatectomy
전마선 傳馬船 a lighter ; a barge ; a baggage boat ; a tender
전말 顚末 〔상세〕 particulars ; details ; a full account ; 〔경위〕 the course of events ; 〔사정〕 the circumstances ¶ 사고의 전말을 이야기하다 give a full account of an accident // 전말을 상세히 보고하다 report all the circumstances in detail // 사직하게 된 전말을 설명하다 explain the circumstances which led to one's resignation
—서 an account ; a report
†전망 展望 a view ; a prospect ; an outlook ; observation — 하다 view ; have a view《of》; look out on〔over〕; observe ¶ 앞으로의 전망 the future prospect // 산정에서의 전망 a view from the mountain top // 전망을 방해하다 obscure the view // 전망이 좋다 have a good prospect ; have〔command〕 a fine view《of the sea》
—경(鏡) ⇨ 잠망경 —대 an observation platform —탑 an observation tower —차 an observation car ; a parlor car 《미》 — 초(哨) an observation post ; a lookout 미술계〔정계〕 — a view of the art〔the political〕 world
전맞춤 廛— goods for sale ordered from the factory ; special-order goods ; a special order
전매 轉賣 resale — 하다 resell
*전매 專賣 monopoly ; monopolization — 하다 monopolize ; make a monopoly of ¶ 술을 정부의 전매로 하다 make the sale of liquor a government monopoly
—권 monopoly ; exclusive rights —익금(益金) profits of the monopoly enterprise —인 a monopolist — 제도 the monopoly system —주의 monopolism — 청 the Monopoly Bureau —품 〔정부의〕 (government) monopoly goods ; monopolies ; 〔특허품〕 a patented article 알코올〔소금, 담배〕 —법 the Government Monopoly in Alcohol〔Salt, Tobacco〕 Act 정부 —품 Government monopoly goods
전매 특허 專賣特許 a patent ¶ 전매 특허를 얻다 take out〔get〕 a patent《on》; patent《an article》// 전매 특허를 인가하다 grant a patent // 전매 특허를 출원하다 apply for a patent
—권 patent rights —권 소유자 a patentee —권 출원중(出願中) 〔표지〕 Patent applied for. /Patent pending. — 등록부 a patent roll〔register〕 — 수여자(授與者) a patentor —인 a patentee —증 letters patent —품 a patented article
전면 前面 the front ; the foreground (전경) ; the facade (건물의) ¶ 전면에 in

front 《of》; in the foreground // 전면의 적 the enemy in front // 전면을 돌로 장식하다 be fronted with stone
— 공격 a frontal attack — 면적 〖기하〗 the frontal area — 조망 a front view — 저항 〖항공〗 head resistance 의식 — the foreground of consciousness

†전면 全面 the whole〔entire〕 surface ¶ 전면에 걸쳐 all over the surface
— 강화 an all-out〔overall〕 peace (treaty) — 광고 a full-page advertisement — 전쟁 an all-out〔a full-scale, a full-sized〕 war — 파업 an overall strike — 핵전쟁 an all-out nuclear war

전면적 全面的 ¶ 전면적인 all-out ; overall ; general ; wholesale ; full-scale ; extensive ; complete // 전면적으로 extensively ; completely ; in a wholesale way ; in full measure // 전면적인 변경 sweeping changes // 전면적인 통제 full control // 전면적인 협력 wholehearted〔all-out〕 cooperation // 전면적인 개정을 하다 make a sweeping〔an overall〕 revision 《of the regulations》// 전면적인 동의를 하다 give a blanket consent 《to》// 전면적으로 지지하다 give solid〔wholehearted〕 support to 《a person》

*전멸 全滅 complete〔total, wholesale〕 destruction ; annihilation ; extermination —하다 be completely〔totally〕 destroyed ; be annihilated ; be wiped out ¶ 전멸시키다 destroy completely〔totally〕 ; annihilate ; wipe out // 그 도시는 전멸했다 The whole town was wiped out. / The town was totally destroyed. // 연대는 전멸했다 The whole regiment was annihilated.

전명 電命 telegraphic instructions

전모 全貌 the whole aspect ; the whole affair ; the whole picture 《of》 ¶ 전모를 밝히다 give the entire picture 《of》; get the full story of 《a matter》// 그것으로 사건의 전모가 밝혀졌다 It throws light upon the whole affair.

전모 剪毛 wool shearing —하다 shear wool

전몰 戰沒 death in battle〔on the battle field〕 —하다 be killed in action ; die〔fall〕 in war〔battle〕
— 용사 the war dead ; the fallen heroes —자 the war dead —자 묘 a fallen soldier's tomb —자 위령 ¶ 전몰자 위령을 하다 honor the memories of the war dead — 장병 [개인] a fallen soldier ; the war dead 《총칭》

전무 全無 total nonexistence ; total lack ; total absence —하다 be wholly lacking〔wanting〕 ¶ 나는 법률 지식이라고는 전무합니다 I have not the least knowledge of law.

전무 專務 special〔exclusive〕 duty ; [회사의] a managing director ; an executive director

전무식 全無識 utter ignorance ; complete illiteracy —하다 (be) utterly ignorant 〔illiterate, unlearned, uneducated〕 ¶ 전무식자 an utter ignoramus ; an ignorant person

전무후무 前無後無 the unprecedented 〔unparalleled〕 in history ; the unique ; the epoch-making ; the record-breaking —하다 (be) unprecedented ; unheard-of ; record-breaking ; unique ¶ 전무후무의 대발견 an epoch-making discovery // 전무후무한 명가수 the greatest singer of all times // 이번과 같은 전쟁은 전무후무일 것이다 There has never been and never will be such a war as this.

전문 全文 the whole sentence ; the whole statement (성명서 따위) ; the full text (조약 따위) ¶ 조약의 전문 the full text of a treaty // 전문을 인용하다 quote a whole sentence // 편지의 전문을 게재하다 give the letter in full

전문 前文 the above〔foregoing〕 sentence 〔statement〕 ; the preamble (조약문 따위의)

전문 前門 a front gate

전문 電文 a telegraphic message ; a telegram ; [문구] the wording of a telegram —체(體) telegraphese

†전문 專門 a specialty ; a special work ; a special branch of science ; a special object of pursuit ; a major (subject of study) ¶ 전문의 special ; expert // 전문으로 specially ; professionally ; technically // 심장 전문의 a heart specialist // 전문적 지식 technical〔professional〕 knowledge // 전문화하다 specialize // 전문으로 연구하다 specialize in 《law》; make a special study of // 전문가의 의견을 듣다 take professional advice // 그것은 나의 전문이 아니다 It is out of my field. /It is not in my line. // 그는 영어를 전문으로 공부하고 있다 He devotes himself to the study of English. // 그의 전문은 화학이다 His specialty is chemistry. /He majors in chemistry. // 러시아어는 내 전문이 아니다 Russian is outside my field.
—가 a specialist 《in》; an expert 《on》; [아마추어에 대한] a 《golf》 professional — 과목 a special (ized) subject〔study〕 — 과정 a specialized course — 교육 technical〔professional〕 education — 기술 expert skill ; expertise — 기술자 a technical expert ; a professional worker ; an expert — 단체 a professional organization — 도서관 a special〔subject〕 library — 메이커 manufacturers specialized in the production 《of...》 — 병원 a special hospital — 서적 a technical book ; special works ; a subject series (전문 총서) —어 a technical term ; technology ; jargon (동업자끼리만 아는) — 위원 [국회 등의] an expert committee (전체) ; a technical expert ; an expert member

〔adviser〕 **—의** a medical specialist ¶ 전문의의 진찰을 원하다 seek the advice of a medical specialist **— 잡지** a technical 〔recondite〕 magazine ; a learned journal **—적 직업** a profession **—점** a specialty store **— 조사원** a technical researcher **—지(誌)** a technical journal〔magazine〕; a magazine dealing with a special field **—지식** expert〔technical〕 knowledge ; expertise **— 직원** an expert official **— 학교** a college ; a special〔professional〕 school **—화(化)** specialization

전문 傳聞 hearsay ; a report ; a rumor **—하다** learn by hearsay ; learn from others ; know at secondhand ¶ 전문한 바에 의하면 according to what I hear ; according to rumor
— 증거 hearsay evidence **— 증인** a hearsay witness

전문 錢文 money

전문 轉聞 hearsay ; a report ; a rumor **—하다** hear〔learn〕 from others ; learn 〔know〕 by hearsay〔report〕

전물 奠物 offerings (to God, to Buddha)

전미 全美 all America ; the entire United States ; the whole of America

전미련하다 全— (be) utterly stupid

전박 前膊 a forearm

전반 前半 the first half ¶ 5회의 전반전 the top〔first half〕 of the fifth inning (야구의)
—기 the first half year

전반 全般 the whole ; the all ; general ¶ 전반적 whole ; general ; over-all // 전반적으로 generally // 국민 전반 the people at large // 사회 전반 the world at large // 과학 전반에 걸쳐 있다 It covers the whole field of science.

전반사 全反射 〖물리〗 total reflection

*‡***전방 前方** the front ; forward area ; the front line ¶ 전방의 front ; forward // 전방에 ahead ; in front ; forward // 100미터 전방에 one hundred meters ahead
— 기지 〖군사〗 an advance base **— 지휘소** command post 《CP》

전방 廛房 a shop ; a store

전방석 氈方席 a felt cushion

전방향 全方向 ¶ 전방향(성)의 〖물리·전기〗 omnidirectional
—성 안테나 an omnidirectional antenna

전배 前杯 earlier〔beforehand〕 drinking ⇨ 전작

전번 前番 the other day ; last time ¶ 전번의 last ; previous ; former // 전번에 last ; last time ; before this ; previously ; sometimes ago ; lately ; recently // 전번에 만났을 때 when I saw him last // 전번에 상경했을 때에는 1주일 밖에 체재하지 않았다 The last time I came to *Seoul*, I stayed only a week.

전범 戰犯 [죄] war crimes ; [사람] a war criminal ¶ A급 전범 an A-class war criminal
— 법정 a war crimes court **— 용의자** a suspected war criminal ; a war crime suspect **—자** a war criminal

전범 典範 ① [모범] a model ; a standard ② [법] a law ; a code

전법 戰法 tactics ; strategy ; a plan of campaign

전벽 全壁 a blind〔blank〕 wall

전변 轉變 changeableness ; variableness ; mutation **—하다** change ; vary ; mutate ¶ 유위 전변 the vicissitudes of life

전별 餞別 giving a farewell party ; sending off ; farewell **—하다** send 《a person》 off ; bid farewell 《to》
—사 a farewell address〔speech〕 **— 징표** ¶ 전별 징표로서 이걸 드립니다 Kindly accept this as a token of my best wishes for your journey. **—회** a farewell party〔dinner, feast〕

전병 煎餠 pancakes

전병사 戰病死 death caused by a disease〔an illness〕 while at war **—하다** die of an illness while at war
—자 non-battle casualties ; the dead from diseases contracted at the front

전보 塡補 supplement ; complement ; filling up ; making up **—하다** supplement ; complement ; fill ; make up 《a deficiency》 ¶ 결손을 전보하다 make up a deficit

전보 轉補 transfer(ence) ; shuffling **—하다** transfer ¶ 전보되다 be transferred to another position

전보 戰報 war news ; a war report ; war intelligence

†**전보 電報** a telegram ; a wire ; [무전의] a radiogram ; dispatch ; [해외] a cable (-gram) **—하다** telegraph ; wire ; cable ; send a telegram〔wire〕 ¶ 전보로 by wire〔telegraph, cable〕 // …라는 보고의 전보 a telegram reporting 《that》 // 전보를 배달하다 deliver a telegram // 전보가 분실됐다 Your telegram has miscarried. // 전보로 간호사를 부르겠습니다 I will telegraph for a nurse. // 서울에 가라는 전보가 왔다 They cabled me to go to *Seoul*.
—국 a telegraphic office **—란** telegraphic news columns **—료** a telegram fee 〔charge〕 **— 배달 [사람]** a telegram deliverer **— 배달계** a (postal) telegraph messenger **— 사무** telegraph service 〔business〕 **— 송달지(送達紙)** a delivery form **— 암호장(暗號帳)** a cable〔telegraphic〕 code **— 약호** a telegraphic address ; a cable code address **— 어음** a telegraphic remittance〔transfer〕 **— 용지** a telegram form **— 취급국** a telegraph office **국내 —** an inland〔a domestic〕 telegram **무전 —** a radio(tele)gram ; a wireless (telegram) **보통문 — [**암호 아닌**]** a telegram in plain language **서신 —**

a letter telegram 《LT》; a day letter **시간외(時間外) —** a late telegram〔message〕 **신문 —** a newspaper dispatch **암호 —** a code telegram **외국 —** a foreign telegram **재송(再送)〔지급, 친전〕 —** a redirected〔an urgent, a confidential〕 telegram

†**전복 顚覆** overturn(ing); subversion; [정부 따위] overthrow(ing); [선박] capsizal **—하다** overthrow; overturn; capsize; swamp; keel over (배가) ¶ 내각을 전복시키다 overthrow the Cabinet // 배를 전복시키다 capsize a boat // 열차를 전복시키다 overturn a train // 배가 전복했다 The boat capsized.

전복 全鰒 〖조개〗 an ear shell; an abalone; an ormer; a sea-ear
건(乾)— a dried abalone

전봇대 電報— a telegraph pole; telephone pole

†**전부 全部** all; the whole; [부사적] all; in full; in its entirety; altogether; in all; all told ¶ 전부의 all; whole; entire; complete; total; every // 학생 전부 all the students; the entire student body // 원고를 전부 읽다 read a manuscript through // 이야기를 전부 듣다 hear 《a person》 out; hear 《a person》 to the end // 빚을 전부 갚다 pay one's debts in full // 전부 다섯권이다 There are five volumes in all. /It is complete in five volumes. // 전부해서 얼마입니까 How much is it altogether? // 전부해서 50,000원 되겠습니다 The total comes to 50000 won.

전부 前部 the front part; the fore; the front ¶ 배의 전부 the fore part of a ship // 최전부에 in the forefront

전부 前夫 one's former husband ¶ 전부의 자식 a child by her former husband

전부 轉付 transference; 〖법〗 assignment **—하다** transfer 《to》; assign; [채무를] delegate
—명령 an assignment order **일부〔총〕—** partial〔general〕 assignment

전분 澱粉 starch; farina; dextrin(e) ¶ 전분질의 starchy; farinaceous

전비 戰費 war expenditure〔funds〕; the cost of war

전비 戰備 war〔warlike〕 preparations; preparations for war; war preparedness ¶ 전비를 갖추다 prepare for war; make warlike preparations

전비 前非 one's past error〔sin, misdeeds〕 ¶ 전비를 뉘우치다 see the error of one's way; repent of one's previous misdeeds 〔error, sin〕

전사 前史 [옛 사서(史書)] a history (book) of antiquity〔old times〕; the history of the preceding age

전사 全史 a complete history

‡**전사 戰士** a soldier; a fighter; a warrior; a combatant ¶ 자유의 전사 a champion of liberty // 무명 전사의 묘 the tomb of an unknown soldier
산업 — an industrial worker

전사 戰死 death in battle〔action〕 **—하다** be killed in action〔battle〕; die〔fall〕 in battle〔on the battlefield〕 ¶ 명예롭게 전사하다 die a glorious death on the battlefield
—상자 the war dead and wounded; war casualties **—자** a fallen soldier; the war dead; the fallen in war〔battle〕; those killed〔fallen〕 in battle **명예 —** a glorious〔heroic〕 death on the field of battle; a glorious death in action

전사 轉寫 transcription; copying **—하다** transcribe; copy 《from》
—기 a transcriber **— 잉크〔용지〕** transfer ink〔paper〕 **—지** transfer paper; a flimsy **—화(畫)** a transfer

전사 戰史 a military history ¶ 전사에 남다 be mentioned in war history // 제2차 세계 대전 전사 a history of World War Ⅱ

전삭 前朔 last month; ultimo 《ult.》

전산기 電算機 ⇨ 전자(계산기)
소형 — a microcomputer

전상 戰傷 a war wound **—하다** be wounded in war〔action, battle〕
—병 a wounded soldier **—병자(病者)** war invalids **—자** the war wounded (총칭); a wounded veteran; a war wounded

전색맹 全色盲 total color blindness; 〖의학〗 achromatopsia

전생 前生 〖불교〗 a former〔previous〕 existence; a former life; preexistence ¶ 전생의 약속 predestination; destiny; fate; karma // 전생의 인연 karma relations (from a previous life); fate; predestination // 전생의 죄 sins committed in one's previous existence〔birth〕

전생애 全生涯 one's whole〔entire〕 life ¶ 전생애를 통하여 throughout〔in all〕 one's life; from cradle to grave

전서 篆書 a seal character; writing in seal characters

전서 全書 a complete book
백과 — an encyclopedia **육법 —** a compendium of laws; a statute book

전서 前書 one's previous〔foregoing〕 letter; the first letter
고린도 — The First Epistle of St. Paul to the Corinthians; I Corinthians 《I Cor.》

전서 傳書 transmittance〔conveyance〕 of a communication〔letter〕
— 비둘기 ⇨ 전서구(傳書鳩)

전서구 傳書鳩 〖새〗 a carrier〔homing〕 pigeon
— 통신 communication〔sending messages〕 by carrier pigeons; pigeon post
— 통신서 a pigeongram

전선 全線 the whole line (of a railroad)

†**전선 電線** an electric wire; an electric cord; a cable; a telephone〔telegraph〕 wire〔line〕
— 가설 ¶ 전선 가설을 하다 lay (on)

electric wires —망 a power grid — 부설 laying of cables 견(絹)〔지(紙)〕 — a silk-〔paper-〕covered wire 해저 — a submarine cable

전선 戰船 a warship

전선 戰線 the front〔battle〕 line ; the fighting〔firing〕 line ; the front ¶ 전선에 나가다 go to the front ; be in the firing line // 적의 전선 후방에 behind the enemy lines // 적의 전선을 돌파하다 break through the enemy line // 공동 전선을 펴다 present a united〔common〕 front ; make common cause with 《a person》

— 개편〔재정리〕 readjustment of the battle line — 통일 〖노동〗 unification of the labor front 공동 — a united front ¶ …에 대한 공동 전선을 펴다 form a united front against 노동 — the labor front 외교 — 《on》 the diplomatic front 인민 — a popular〔people's〕 front

전선 前線 [일선] the front line ; [기상] a front ¶ 전선의 장병 officers and men at the front // 병력을 전선으로 보내다 send troops up to the front line

강우 — a rain front 극— a polar front 온난 — a warm front 한랭 — 통과 the passage of a cold front

전선병 傳線病 [스타킹 따위의] a run ; a runner 《미》 ; a ladder 《영》 ¶ 전선병이 나다 develop a run ; run ; [사람이 주어] get a run in one's stockings // 전선병이 나지 않는 양말 runproof〔ladderproof〕 stockings // 전선병이 난 양말 stockings with runs in them ; laddered stockings

＊＊전설 傳說 a tradition ; a legend ; a myth ; legendary ¶ 전설적 traditional ; legendary ; mythical // 전설에 의하면 according to tradition〔legend〕 ; legend says〔runs〕 《that》 // 그는 전설적 인물에 불과하다 He is nothing but a legendary person.

— 시대 a legendary age〔period〕

전설 前說 one's previous view〔opinion, statement, doctrine〕 ; theories〔views, doctrines〕 of predecessors ¶ 전설을 고수하다 hold〔stick〕 to one's former views // 전설을 번복하다 change one's former views

전성 展性 〖물리〗 malleability ¶ 전성이 풍부하다 be malleable

＊＊전성 全盛 the height〔zenith〕 of prosperity〔power〕 —하다 be at the height〔zenith〕 of one's prosperity ; be at its full glory ; be flourishing ¶ 그의 전성시에 in his best days // 그 도시의 전성기는 지났다 The heyday of the city is over. // 그녀의 전성기는 이미 지나갔다 She's already passed her peak.

— 시대 the palmy days ; the heyday ; the golden age ¶ 그 작가는 자연주의 전성 시대에는 크게 날렸다 The novelist enjoyed great popularity in the days when naturalism reigned supreme in this country.

전성 轉成 transformation ; transmutation —하다 be transformed 《into》 ; change 《into》

—어 [파생어] a derivative ; [외래어] a loanword

전성관 傳聲管 《speak into》 a voice tube〔pipe〕 ; a speaking tube

전세 前世 ① [전대] former time ; former generations ; past ages ; prehistoric ages ② a former life ⇨ 전생

전세 傳貰 the lease of a house〔room〕 on a deposit basis ¶ 전세 놓다 lease a house〔room〕 on a deposit basis // 전세 내다 take〔hold〕 a house〔room〕 by lease on a deposit basis

전세 專貰 reservations 《미》 ; booking ; engagement ¶ 전세 내다 engage 《a whole boat》 ; book ; reserve 《미》 ; make reservations // 버스를 전세 내다 hire〔charter 《구》〕 a bus // 전세 [게시] Reserved. /Engaged.

— 버스〔비행기, 열차〕 a chartered bus〔plane, train〕

전세 戰勢 the progress of a battle〔campaign〕 ; the war situation ¶ 전세가 불리하다 The war is not going in our favor.

전세계 全世界 the whole world ¶ 전세계에 all over〔throughout〕 the world ; the world over // 전세계의 여성 women throughout the world ; women the world over // 전세계에 이름이 알려진 사람 a world-famous man // 전세계에서 모이다 come from all parts of the world // 전세계에서 선발되다 be selected from all the nations of the world // 전세계를 놀라게 하다 astonish the whole world

전세계 前世界 a prehistoric age ; the world before now〔this〕 ¶ 전세계의 유물 antediluvian

전세기 前世紀 past centuries

전소 全燒 total destruction by fire —하다 be completely〔entirely, totally〕 destroyed ; be burned down 《to the ground》 ¶ 그 집은 전소하였다 The house was completely destroyed by fire.

전속 專屬 —하다 belong exclusively 《to》 ; be under the exclusive control 《of》 ¶ KBS 전속 악단 an orchestra attached to KBS ; the KBS orchestra

— 가수 a singer attached to〔under exclusive contract with〕 《KBS》 — 관할 exclusive jurisdiction — 관할구 an exclusive jurisdiction — 극작가 a playwright belonging to〔who writes specially for〕 《a company》 — 부관 the aide-de-camp — 선(船) a tender 극장 — 오케스트라 a house orchestra

전속 轉屬 transference ; transfer of a census register —하다 be transferred 《to》 ; transfer a census register

전속력 全速力 full〔top〕 speed ¶ 전속력으로 at full speed ; [사람이] at the top of one's speed ; as fast as one can ; [말이] at full gallop ; [배가] under full steam ; at full sail // 전속력을 내다 develop〔gather, put forth〕 full speed // 전속력으로 뛰다 run at full speed ; sprint (단거리 경기에서)

전손 全損 total loss
— 담보 security for total loss only《T. L. O.》; free of all average《F. A. A.》 추정 — constructive total loss 현실 — actual total loss

†전송 餞送 seeing《a person》off ; a send-off **—하다** see《a person》off ; give a send-off ¶ 그는 성대한 전송을 받았다 He was given a good send-off. // 그를 전송하기 위하여 많은 사람들이 정거장에 모였다 A large crowd gathered at the station to see him off.
—사 a farewell address〔speech〕 —인 persons present for a send-off —회 a farewell party

전송 轉送 forwarding ; transmission **—하다** forward ; transmit ¶ 편지를 A씨에게 전송하다 forward a letter to Mr. A // 본인 앞으로 오는 편지는 전부 전송해 주십시오 Kindly forward all the letters addressed to me.
— 방식 a transmission device —처 a forwarding address

전송 電送 electrical transmission **—하다** telegraph ; wire《a message》; transmit
— 사진 a telephotograph ; wireless transmission of pictures ; a wirephoto (유선의) 사진 — telephoto service ; radiophoto transmission ; wireless transmission of pictures ; phototelegraphy ; telephotography ¶ 사진 전송을 하다 transmit a picture by radio〔wireless〕; radio a photo 사진 —용 전파 a radiophoto carrier wave 사진 — 장치 a telephoto apparatus

전수 傳受 [전하여 받음] being handed down〔over〕; receiving ; inheriting (물려받음) ; [기술 따위의] being instructed〔initiated〕 **—하다** [전하여 받다] be handed down〔over〕; receive ; inherit ; [기술 따위를] receive instruction ; be instructed〔taught〕; be initiated into
—자(者) an initiate ; the initiated《총칭》

전수 傳授 [전하여 줌] handing down〔over〕; transmission ; conveyance ; [기술 따위] instruction ; initiation **—하다** [전해 주다] hand down〔over〕; transmit ; convey ; [기술 따위를] instruct ; give instruction《in》; initiate ; tell ; show ¶ 비법을 전수하다 initiate《a person》into the secrets〔mysteries〕
—자(者) an initiator (기술 따위의)

전수 全數 the total number〔figure〕; the whole ; unanimity ; [부사적] all ; totally ; unanimously

전수 專修 exclusive study ; specialization **—하다** make a special study《of》; major《in》《미》; specialize《in》
—과 a special course 영어 —과 the special English course

전수금 前受金 an advance《received on contract work》

전술 全— ⇨ 전내기

전술 前述 ¶ 전술의 above(-mentioned) ; foregoing ; preceding // 전술한 바와 같이 as stated〔mentioned〕 above

†전술 戰術 tactics ; the art of war ; a plan of campaign ¶ 전술상의 tactical // 전술적으로 tactically // 교묘한 전술 a brilliant〔clever〕 tactic // 전술상의 오산 a tactical miscalculation // 전술로 이기다 outgeneral
—가 a tactician — 공군 tactical air forces — 단위 a tactical unit —용 항공기 tactical aircraft —적 핵병기 a tactical nuclear weapon — 전환 a shift in tactics — 지정학 geostrategy — 지정학자 a geostrategist 고등 — grand tactics 국지(局地) — minor tactics

전습 傳襲 inheritance ; descent **—하다** inherit ; descend

전승 全勝 a complete victory **—하다** win〔gain〕 a complete victory ; whip〔sweep〕 the field ; make straight wins
—군 an ever-victorious army

전승 傳承 transmission ; tradition **—하다** transmit from generation to generation ; hand down《on》
— 문학 oral literature — 문학 연구자 a folklore expert 민간 — folklore

전승 戰勝 a victory ; a triumph **—하다** win〔gain〕 a victory ; be victorious ; carry〔win〕 the day ¶ 전승을 빌다〔축하하다〕 pray for〔celebrate〕 the victory
—국 a victorious country — 기념일 an anniversary of a victory — 기념품 a war trophy —자 a victor ; the victorious — 축하회 a victory celebaration

전시 全市 the whole city ¶ 전시에 파급되고 있다 It spreads all over the city. // 전시민 all the citizens ; entire citizenry

†전시 展示 exhibition ; display **—하다** exhibit《a thing》; put《a thing》on display〔view〕 ¶ 여러 가지 상품이 전시되어 있다 A variety of things are displayed for sale.
—관 [박람회 등의] a pavilion —물 an exhibit ; exhibition《총칭》 —회 an exhibition〔a show, a display〕 ¶ 전시회를 열다 hold an exhibition〔a show, a display〕 —회장 an exhibit hall〔room〕 — 효과 a demonstration effect 교과서 —회 a textbook exhibition 한복 —회 Korean dress show

전시 戰時 wartime ; time of war ¶ 전시에 during the war ; in wartime // 전시나 평시를 막론하고 whether in peace or in war
— 경기 a war boom — 경제 wartime economy — 공채 a war-loan〔-bond〕 — 국제법 international law in time of war ; law of war (전쟁법) — 국채 a

wartime bond — 근무 해제 deactivation ¶ 전시 근무 해제를 하다 deactivate — 금제품 contraband of war — 내각 a war cabinet — 배상 위원회 [UN의] the War Reparations Committee — 보상 war indemnity〔compensation〕 — 보상 특별 조치 special measures for war indemnity — 보험 war risk insurance — 산업 the wartime industry — 상태 a state of war〔belligerency〕 — 수당 war bonus — 이득세 the War Profit Tax — 재정 wartime finance — 정원(定員) war establishment〔strength, footing〕 — 체제 war structure ; war basis — 특례 a wartime exception — 특별 수당 a special wartime allowance — 편성〔편제〕 war organization〔footing〕

전시대 前時代 former ages〔times〕; past generations

전식 電飾 (decorative) illumination —하다 illuminate (decoratively)

전신 全身 the whole body ; one's whole〔entire〕 being ¶ 전신에 all over the body ; from head to foot ; from top to toe // 전신이 떨리다 shake all over // 전신에 화상을 입다 burn oneself all over // 전신에 식은 땀이 났다 The cold sweat broke out all over me. // 마지막 장면에서는 전신에 전율을 느꼈다 During the last scene I had goose bumps all over. // 어쩌다가 운동을 했더니 전신이 쑤신다 I exercised for a change, and now I ache all over.

— 동맥 systemic arteries —력 all one's strength — 마취 general anesthesia — 매독 syphilis of the system —병 a general disorder ; a constitutional disease — 부종 anasarca — 불수 total paralysis — 사진 a full length (picture) —상(像)〔화상(畫像)〕 a full-length〔full-size〕 figure〔portrait〕 ¶ 전신상을 그리다 paint《a person》full length — 쇠약 general prostration — 순환 systemic circulation —욕(浴) a full bath — 운동 exercise of the whole body —적(的) 〖의학〗 systemic — 침례 [그리스도교] total immersion

전신 前身 one's former〔past〕 self ; one's antecedents ¶ 고려 대학교의 전신인 보성 전문 학교 the *Bosung* (College), the predecessor of (the present) Korea University // 전신을 조사하다 investigate〔inquire into〕《a person's》 antecedents〔past life〕; check up (on)《a person's》 record

†**전신 電信** telegraph ; [해저 전신] cable ; a cablegram ¶ 전신으로 by telegraph〔cable〕 // 전신을 치다 telegraph ; wire ; cable // 부산과의 전신이 회복되었다 Telegraphic service with *Pusan* was resumed. // 전신이 두절되었다 Telegraphic communication was interrupted.

— 가설 ¶ 전신 가설을 하다 lay a telegraph wire ; establish a telegraph service —계 a telegraph clerk —국 a telegraph office —기 a telegraphic instrument ; a telegraph apparatus〔set〕 — 기사 a telegraphic engineer〔operator〕 —대 a telegraph corps ; communications outfit —료 telegram charges —법 telegraphy — 사무 telegraphic service —선 a telegraphic wire〔line〕 —술 telegraphy — 암호 a telegraphic code — 암호장(暗號帳) a telegraphic code book — 약호 a telegraphic〔cable〕 address — 약호 문자 a code word — 요금표 a tariff for telegraphic messages (해외) — 용어 cablese — 인자기(印字機) a teletypewriter ; a teletype — 전화 공통 장치 a phonophore〔phonopore〕 —주 a telegraph pole —환 a telegraphic transfer《T. T.》; a telegraphic remittance〔money order〕 — 회사 a telegraph company — 회선 a telegraphic circuit 무선 — wireless telegraphy 해저 — a cable 해외 —환 a cable order〔transfer〕

전신 前信 one's last letter ¶ 전신에서 말씀드린 바와 같이 as I informed you in my last (letter)

전신 轉身 turnover —하다 change over《from. . . to. . .》; give up one's old principle〔doctrine〕 for another ; find one's way to a new course

전신 감각 全身感覺 coen(a)esthesis ; coen(a)esthesia

전실 前室 one's former〔divorced〕 wife — 자식 the children of one's former wife

전심 全心 one's whole heart〔soul〕 ¶ 전심을 다하여 with one's whole heart〔soul〕 // 전심 전력을 경주하다 put one's heart and soul into《one's work》

***전심 專心** concentration of mind ; undivided attention ; the whole heart —하다 devote〔bend〕 oneself《to》; put heart and soul《into》; force〔concentrate〕《one's mind》upon〔on〕 ¶ 전심으로 wholeheartedly ; with all one's heart and soul ; devotedly

전아 典雅 elegance ; refinement —하다 (be) graceful ; refined ; elegant

전압 電壓 voltage ; electric pressure ¶ 높은〔낮은〕 전압 a high〔low〕 voltage // 전압을 올리다〔낮추다〕 increase〔drop〕 voltage — 강하 a drop of electric pressure —계 a voltmeter —량 voltage —선 a pressure wire — 전류계 a voltameter — 조절기 a (an automatic) pressure regulator 낙하 — [계전기(繼電器)의] drop-away voltage 사용〔단자(端子), 정(定)〕 — working〔terminal, constant〕 voltage 이상(異常)〔시험〕 — abnormal〔test〕 voltage

전압력 全壓力 〖물리〗 the full〔total〕 pressure

전액 全額 the total〔full〕 amount ; the sum total

— 국고 부담 ¶ 전액 국고 부담으로 하다 The total amount is defrayed out of〔borne by〕 the national treasury. —

납입 full payment ; payment in full — 납입필 주(納入畢 株) a fully paid〔a paid-up〕 stock — 담보 full coverage — 보험 full〔whole〕 insurance — 영수서(領收書) a receipt in full — 준비 제도 the total〔simple〕 reserve system — 지급 장학금 [여비·체재비 등 일체 포함] an all-expenses-paid〔all-expense〕 scholarship 급료 — full pay

전야 前夜 the previous night〔evening〕; the night〔evening〕 before ; an eve ; last night ¶ 결혼 전야 the night before the wedding // 크리스마스 전야 Christmas Eve // 혁명 전야에 on the eve of a revolution // 전야제를 지내다 celebrate the eve《of a school festival》

—제 an eve 전쟁 발발〔혁명〕— the eve of the battle〔revolution〕

전야 田野 fields ; cultivated fields

전약 前約 a previous engagement〔appointment〕; a prior agreement ¶ 전약이 있다 have a previous engagement

전약 煎藥 a (medical) decoction ; a decoction of medicinal herbs

전어 錢魚 〖물고기〗 a gizzard〔hickory〕 shad ; Konosirus punctatus (학명)

전언 傳言 a (verbal) message ; word —하다 send〔bring〕《a person》 word ¶ 전언을 남기다 leave word〔a message〕// 전언을 부탁받다 be asked to give a message // 저 사람에게 전언이 있다 I have a message for him.

전언 前言 one's previous remarks〔words, statement〕 ¶ 전언을 취소하다 withdraw〔take back〕 one's words ; retract〔cancel, revoke, recant〕 one's words // 전언을 번복하다 go back on one's words ; swallow〔eat〕 one's words

전업 轉業 change of business〔trade, occupation, employment〕 —하다 change one's business ; change from one employment to another

—자 a person who (has) changed his occupation〔trade〕 — 자금 funds for occupational change

전업 專業 speciality ; special〔principal〕 occupation ; monopoly ¶ 외국 무역을 전업으로 하다 specialize in foreign trade ; make a speciality of foreign trade

—자 a specialist ; a monopolist

전업 電業 the electrical industry

전역 戰役 a war ; a battle ; a campaign

전역 全譯 a complete〔whole〕 translation ; an unabridged translation —하다 translate《a book》 in full〔completely〕

— 성서 a complete translation of the Bible

전역 戰域 a war zone ; a battle area ; a war area ; a range of (military) operations ; a theater of war ¶ 전역을 확대〔축소〕하다 extend〔reduce〕 the range of operations

전역 全域 [지역]《through》 all the area〔the whole (district)〕;《in》 all parts《of》; [영역] the whole field〔all the sphere〕; [범위] the gamut《of experience, business》

전역 轉役 〖군사〗 transfer《from active service to the first reserve》; [제대] discharge from military service —하다 be transferred《from the active list to the reserve list》; [제대하다] be discharged〔dismissed〕 from military service ¶ 전역시키다 transfer《a person》 to the first reserve ; place〔register〕《a person》 on the reserve list

전연 全然 entirely ; completely ; wholly ; altogether ; utterly ¶ 전연 모른다 I do not know it at all. /I know nothing about it. // 그것은 전연 실패였다 It was a complete failure. // 전연 모르는 사람이다 He is a perfect〔an utter〕 stranger to me. // 나는 그 일에 대해서는 전연 모른다 I have not the remotest〔slightest〕 idea of it. // 그것은 전연 거짓말이다 That is all a lie. // 그것은 전연 너의 잘못이다 That is entirely your fault. // 나는 그의 의도를 전연 모른다 I am in complete ignorance of his intentions.

전열 電熱 electric heat

—기 an electric heater (난방용) ; an electric range〔stove〕 (요리용) ; heating equipment (장치) ; a hotplate 유효(有效) —면(面) the effective electric heating surface

전열 前列 the front rank〔row〕 ¶ 전열 왼편에서 다섯번째 the fifth from the left in the front row〔rank〕

전열 戰列 a battle line ; a line of battle ¶ 전열에 참가하다 join the line of battle // 전열을 이탈하다 leave the line of battle

⁑**전염 傳染** infection ; contagion ; communication —하다 be infectious ; be contagious ; be catching ; be communicated ¶ 전염성의 infectious ; contagious ; communicable ; epidemic // 하품은 전염한다 Yawning is infectious〔catching〕. // 디프테리아는 전염됩니까 Is diphtheria contagious〔catching〕? // 그는 전염 예방을 위해서 격리되었다 He was isolated to prevent infection.

— 계통 the trace of an epidemic — 독소 a virus ; a contagium《*pl.* -gia》 —성〔력〕 contagiousness ; virulence —원(源) a source of infection —질 contagium 공기 — aerial〔airborne〕 infection 직접〔간접〕 — direct〔indirect〕 infection 접촉 — contact infection

전염병 傳染病 an infectious〔a contagious〕 disease ; an epidemic

—기(旗) [배의] a quarantine〔yellow, sick〕 flag —동(棟)〔실〕 an isolated ward — 병원 a hospital for contagious diseases ; a quarantine ; an isolation hospital —소(巢) a pesthole — 연구소 the Infectious Diseases Research Laborato-

ry〔Institute〕 — 예방법 the Infectious Diseases Prevention Act — 유행지 a plague spot ; a tainted district — 환자 a case of infectious disease ; an infectious case ; people with contagious diseases
전옥 典獄 the governor of a prison 〔gaol〕 ; the warden of a prison 《미》 ; the chief jailer
전와 轉訛 corruption 《of a word》 —하다 be corrupted 《into》
—어 a corrupt word ; a corruption
전완 前腕 the forearm
전용 專用 exclusive use ; private use —하다 use exclusively ; be for private use ¶ 전용의 exclusive ; private (개인의) // 고객 전용 주차장 Customer Parking Only. // 이 전화는 내선(內線) 전용이다 The telephone is only for in-house calls.
—권 the sole right of use —기 a plane for one's personal use ¶ 대통령의 전용 비행기 a presidential plane〔jet〕 — 도로 a driveway —선 an industry〔a business〕 track ; a line for the owner's exclusive use —선 an exclusive line (전화의) ; an official line (관청의) —실 a private cabin (배의) ; a stateroom —전(栓) a private tap〔stopcock, hydrant〕 (수도의) ; home waterpipes —차 a private car ; a car for one's personal use
전용 轉用 diversion ; appropriation ; misappropriation —하다 divert ; use 《money》 for other purposes ; misappropriate ; peculate ¶ 자금을 전용하다 divert funds to other purposes
전우 戰友 a comrade(-in-arms) ; fellow soldiers ; a buddy 《미》
전운 戰雲 war clouds ¶ 전운이 감돈다 War clouds hang heavy 《over Europe》.
전원 田園 farms ; fields ; fields and gardens ; [시골] the country ; rural district ; [교외] suburbs ¶ 전원의 rural ; pastoral
—곡(曲) 〖음악〗 a pastorale 《*pl.* -li》 — 도시 a garden city — 문학 idyllic〔pastoral〕 literature — 생활 country〔rural〕 life ¶ 전원 생활을 하다 lead a rural life ; live in the country — 생활주의자 a ruralist —시 an idyl ; a pastoral — 시인 a pastoral poet — 지방 rural country 〔districts〕 — 취미 ¶ 전원 취미를 즐기다 taste the pleasures of rural life — 클럽 a country club
전원 電源 sources of (hydraulic) electricity
— 개발 the development of power resources —차(車) a power generating car —함(函) 〖통신〗 a power pack
전원 全員 all members ; the entire staff ; the whole crew ; all hands ¶ 전원의 승낙 unanimous consent // 전원 일치로 unanimously // 전원 출동하다 be present in full force
전원 全院 [국회] the whole House ; both Houses (양원(兩院)) ¶ 전원 위원회를 개최하다 hold a committee of the whole House ; the whole House sits in committee
전월 前月 last month
전위 前衛 〖군사〗 an advance guard ; a vanguard ; [정구의] a forward〔net〕 player ; [축구·농구의] a forward ¶ 전위를 보다 play forward ; play at the net
— 미술〔문학〕 avant-garde art〔literature〕 — 영화 an avant-garde picture —전(戰) advance-guard fighting —파 an avant-gardist
전위 傳位 abdication of the throne ; demise of the crown —하다 abdicate 〔demise〕 the throne
전위 電位 〖물리〗 electric potential ¶ 양〔음〕 전위 positive〔negative〕 potential
— 강하 a potential drop —계 an electrometer —차 a potential difference —차계(差計) a potentiometer 대지(大地) —ground〔earth〕 potential 양〔음〕— positive〔negative〕 potential 유동(流動) — a potential of flow 상한(象限)〔비틀림〕 —계 a quadrant〔torsion〕 electrometer 접촉 —차 contact potential
전위 轉位 transposition ; dislocation ; displacement ; 〖수학〗 inversion
*전유 專有 exclusive possession —하다 have 《a room》 to oneself ; possess exclusively ; monopolize
—권 an exclusive right ; monopoly —자 a sole〔private〕 owner
전유 煎油 (pan-)frying —하다 fry
—어(魚) fried fish
*전율 戰慄 shudder ; shivering ; [공포] terror ; horror —하다 shudder 《at》 ; shudder〔shiver〕 with fright ; tremble with fear ¶ 전율할 horrible ; terrible ; shocking ; frightful ; bloodcurdling ; hair-raising // 전율할 광경 a horrible〔bloodcurdling〕 sight // 전율시키다 make 《a person》 shudder ; make 《a person's》 flesh creep ; give 《a person》 the creeps
전음 全音 〖음악〗 a whole tone
—계 the whole-note scale ; the whole gamut —부 a whole note ; a semibreve —정 a whole step〔tone〕 대〔소〕— the major〔minor〕 tone
전음 顫音 〖음악〗 trill
전의 專意 concentration of mind ; undivided attention —하다 devote oneself 《to》 ; put one's heart and soul 《into》
전의 轉義 a derivative meaning 《of a word》 ; a figurative meaning
전의 戰意 an intention to fight ; the will to fight ; hostile〔aggressive〕 intention ; a fighting spirit ¶ 전의가 없다 have no intention to fight ; have no fighting spirit // 전의를 잃다 lose one's fighting spirit
전의 銓議 [조사] inquiry ; examination ; investigation ; [심의] consideration ;

deliberation —하다 inquire into ; examine ; investigate ; consider ; deliberate over ¶ 엄중히 전의하다 make a strict examination ; subject 《a person》 to a cross examination
전이 轉移 change ; transition ; [병원체의] transfer 《of a disease-producing agency》 from an original site of disease to another part of the body —하다 change ; spread (by metastasis) ; 〚의학〛 metastasize
전인 前人 a predecessor ; former people ¶ 전인 미답의 unprecedented ; unexplored ; original ; unique // 전인 미답의 삼림 a trackless〔virgin〕 forest
전인 全人 the whole man ; a well-rounded person
— 교육 education for the whole man
전인격 全人格 one's whole personality ¶ 전인격을 경주하다 put one's whole personality 《into》 ; devote oneself 《to》 ; go heart and soul into 《work》
전일 前日 the other day ; a few days ago ; previously ; formerly ; before ; some time ago ¶ 출발 전일 the day before one's departure // 전일부터 since the day before
전일 專一 the whole mind ; concentration —하다 concentrate one's whole mind 《upon》 ; devote oneself 《to》
전일제 全日制 a full-time system
*전임 專任 full-time service〔employment〕 ; exclusive duty ; sole charge —하다 be in sole charge ; be regular
— 강사 a full-time lecturer : [대학의] an instructor 《미》 — 교사 a full-time teacher
전임 前任 [사람] one's predecessor ; a former official ; [자리] the post previously occupied ; a previous appointment —자 a predecessor 《in a post》 —지 one's former〔last〕 post
전임 轉任 transference ; change of post —하다 be transferred 《from, to》 ¶ …에 전임을 명하다 transfer 《a person》 to ; order 《a person's》 transference 《to》 // 파리에서 런던으로 전임되다 be transferred from Paris to London
—자 a person transferred —지 one's new post
전입 轉入 transference ; [타지방으로부터의] moving in〔into〕 —하다 be〔get〕 transferred 《from》 ; move into
—생 a student〔pupil〕 transferred from another school — 신고 a moving-in notification
전입학 轉入學 transfer of school —하다 enter a school from another ; be transferred to a school from another
†전자 前者 ① [the latter에 대하여] the former ; [this에 대하여] that ; [the other에 대하여] the one ; 〚법〛 the prior〔antecedent〕 party ¶ 전자와 후자 the former and the latter ② [지난 번] the other day ; some time〔a few days〕 ago ; last time ; previously ¶ 전자에 만났을 때 when I saw 《him》 last
전자 篆字 a seal character
전자 專恣 arbitrariness ; high-handedness ; despotism —하다 treat high-handedly ; tyrannize 《over》 ; take high-handed measures
*전자 電子 an electron ; electronic
—가(價) electrovalence ; electrovalency ; ionic valence — 계산기 a computer〔computer〕 ; an electronic computer〔calculator〕 ; a computing machine ; an electronic data processing machine 《EDPM》 — 계산기 사용 electronic data processing 《EDP》 — 계산기화(計算機化) computerization — 공학 electronics ; electronic engineering — 공학 제품 회사 an electronics company〔firm〕 —관(管) an electron tube — 광학 electron optics — 교환기 [전화의] an electronic exchanger — 기기(機器) an electronic machine ; [집합적] electronic equipment — 기상 관측 spherics — 기체 electron gas — 냉동 electronic refrigeration ; thermo-electric cooling — 냉방 electro-cooling — 두뇌 an electronic brain — 레인지 an electronic〔a microwave〕 oven — 렌즈 an electron lens — 망원경 an electron telescope — 방사 corpuscular radiation — 방출 〚물리〛 electron emission — 번역기 an electronic translator〔translating machine〕 — 볼트 〚원자 물리〛 an electron volt 《EV, eV, ev, e. v.》 — 사진 electrophotography — 산업 electronics industry — 산업 노동자 an electronic worker —설 the electron theory — 악기 an electronic (musical) instrument — 오르간 an electronic organ —음 an electronic sound — 음악 electronic〔electrophonic〕 music — 장치 an electronic device — 조명 electroluminescence — 조종 장치 electronic controls 《of an airplane》 —총 [텔레비전] an electron gun — 친화력 electron effinity — 핵공학(核工學) nucleonics — 현미경 an electron microscope— 현미경 사용법 electron microscopy 양— a positron ; a positive electron 주사(走射) — 현미경 a scanning electron microscope 천〔백만, 십억〕 — 볼트 a kilo〔million, billion〕 electron volt ; KEV〔MEV, BEV〕 항공 — 공학 avionics
전자 電磁 ¶ 전자의 electromagnetic
— 감응〔유도〕 electromagnetic induction —기 electromagnetism — 기력 electromagnetic force — 기학(氣學) electromagnetism ; electromagnetics — 단위 an electromagnetic unit —력 electromagnetic force —석 an electromagnet — 유체 역학(流體力學) magnetohydrodynamics —장(場) an electromagnetic field —

적 자연관 an electromagnetic view of nature —파 electromagnetic waves —파 반사법 echolocation

전작 田作 dry field farming ; [농작물] farm crops ; dry field crops

전작 前酌 liquor previously taken ; previous intoxication ¶ 나는 전작이 있다 I have already taken some (cups of liquor).

전장 全長 the total length ; an over-all length ¶ 전장 52미터이다 It is 52 meters in length. /It has a total length of 52 meters.

전장 田庄 one's farmstead ; fields in one's possession

전장 戰場 a battlefield ; a field of battle ; the front ; a battleground ¶ 전장으로 가다 go to the front ; take the field // 전장의 이슬로 사라지다 be killed in battle ; fall on the field of battle

전장 電場 [물리] an electric field

전장 前章 the preceding〔foregoing〕 chapter ; the last〔prior〕 chapter ; the chapter before

전장 前場 [증권] the morning stock market session ; the first call

전재 轉載 reprinting ; reproduction —하다 reprint《from》; reproduce《from》; take《from》¶ 미국 잡지에서 전재하다 reprint《the article》from an American magazine

— 금지 Copyright reserved. /Reproduction (in part or whole) forbidden〔prohibited〕.

전재 戰災 war damage ¶ 전재를 입다 suffer war damages // 전재를 면하다 escape war damages

— 가족 a bombed-out family — 건물 a war-battered building — 고아 war orphans — 도시 a war-ravaged city —민 war victims〔refugees〕 — 부흥 rehabilitation of war — 유민(流民) displaced persons ; DP's《미군·속》 —자 war (-damage) sufferers ; bombed-out people ; war victims — 지구 a war-damaged area ; a war-torn area

†전쟁 戰爭 a war ; warfare ; hostilities ; a battle ; a fight ; a combat —하다 make〔wage〕 war《against》; take up arms《against》; [개전하다] go to war《with》; [전투하다] fight《with, against》; fight a battle ¶ 전쟁의 원인 the cause of war // 전쟁의 참화 the calamity of war // 전쟁 전의 pre-war // 전쟁 후의 post-war // 전쟁중 during the war ; in wartime ; [교전] while fighting ; during the battle // 전쟁중의 at war《with》; belligerent ; warring // 전쟁에 나가다 go to war〔the front〕 // 전쟁에 이기다 win a war ; be victorious // 전쟁에 지다 lose a war // 전쟁에 대비하다 prepare for defense // 전쟁을 일으키다 bring on war ; appeal to arms ; resort to war // 전쟁을 포기하다 renounce war // 전쟁을 수행하다 conduct war // 전쟁 이야기를 하다 talk war // 전쟁 놀이를 하다 play soldiers〔war〕 // 전쟁이 일어나다 a war begins〔breaks out〕 // 전쟁 중이다 We are at war《with》. // 전쟁이 끝나가다 A war comes to an end.

— 경기 a war〔wartime〕 boom — 고아 a war orphan — 공포증 warphobia — 기분 an atmosphere of war ; a war atmosphere ; the war spirit — 놀이 ¶ 전쟁 놀이를 하다 play at make-believe war ; play at soldiers — 능력 war potential — 도발 warmongering — 도발자 a warmonger — 모리 war profiteering — 모리배 a war profiteer — 문학 war literature —물 [서적류] a war book ; [소설] a war novel ; [영화] a war film — 미망인 a war widow — 범죄 war crimes — 범죄자 a war criminal — 법규 the laws of war — 사생아 a war baby — 상태 a state of war ; belligerency — 상태 종결 선언 a declaration of the termination of the state of war — 상해 보험 war casualties insurance — 소설 a war novel — 신부 a war bride ; a GI bride —열 a war fever — 영화 a war film — 재판 a war-criminals trial — 재판소 a war-criminals court — 전〔후〕 ¶ 전쟁 전〔후〕의 prewar〔postwar〕 — 종식전 a war to end war — 지도자 a war leader — 참화 the calamity of war ; war calamities — 추방 the outlawry of war — 포기 the renunciation of war — 포기 조항〔헌법〕 a war-renouncing article〔constitution〕 ; a "no-war" article〔constitution〕 — 피로증 battle fatigue — 행위 an act of war ; warfare — 협력자 war collaborators —화(畫) a battle picture〔piece〕 — 확대 expansion〔escalation, enlargement, widening〕 of a war — 희생자 a war victim — 희생자 구제 자금 the war victims' relief fund 구주(歐洲) — the great European War ; World War I ; the First World War 국내 — a civil war 냉〔열〕— a cold〔hot, shooting〕 war 대— a major〔massive〕 war 세계 — a global〔world〕 war 소규모 — a brush-fire war 장기 — a protracted〔long-drawn(-out)〕 war 전면 — a total〔an all-out〕 war 침략 — an aggressive war

전쟁터 戰爭— ⇨ 전장(戰場)

전적 戰跡 an old battlefield ; the scene of a former battle ; vestiges of war

전적 轉籍 transfer of one's place of domicile ; transfer of one's family register —하다 transfer one's domicile

†전적 全的 [형용사적] total ; whole ; entire ¶ 전적으로 totally ; wholly ; entirely ; utterly // 전적인 지지 full support

전적 典籍 classical books ; books ; records

전적 戰績 a military〔war〕 record ; [경기의] results ; a record ; a score ¶ 혁혁한

전적 a brilliant (war) record

전전 前前 former times ; the one before last ¶ 전전줄에 two rows ahead ((of ours))
—날 two days before〔earlier〕; [그저께] the day before yesterday —달 the month before last —번 the time before last

전전 輾轉 tossing about in bed —하다 toss about in bed ; roll

전전 轉轉 —하다 [임자를 바꾸다] pass through many hands ; change hands many times ; [헤매다] wander from place to place ; roam about ; [구르다] roll ; go rolling ¶ 이 직장 저 직장을 전전하다 change one's employment from place to place // 이 학교 저 학교를 전전하다 change from school to school

전전 轉戰 —하다 go to another theater of war ; fight in one place after another ; take part in various battles

전전 戰前 prewar days ¶ 전전의 prewar ; antebellum ((라)) // 전전에 before the war ; prior to the war // 전전의 상태 prewar〔antebellum〕conditions // 전전에 비하여 compared with the prewar days // 전전파이다 belong to the prewar generation

전전긍긍 戰戰兢兢 trembling from fear ; trepidation ; timidness ; nervousness —하다 be trembling with fear ; be filled with trepidation ; be timid ; be nervous ; be gingerly ¶ 스캔들이 폭로되지 않을까 하고 그는 전전긍긍하고 있다 He is in constant fear lest the scandal (should) come to light.

전절 前節 the foregoing〔preceding〕paragraph

전정 前程 the distance to be covered in one's travel ; the way ahead

전정 前庭 [앞뜰] a front garden ; a front court〔yard〕; [귀] the vestibule

전정 剪定 pruning ; trimming —하다 prune ((a tree)) ; trim
— 가위 pruning〔topiary〕shears ; ((a pair of)) secateurs —기(器) a pruner ; a trimmer —낫 a pruning hook —술 topiary art

*전제 前提 〖논리〗 a premise ; a proposition —하다 set forth beforehand ; premise ; assume ¶ …을 전제로 하고 on the assumption ((that)) ; on the premise ((that)) ; assuming ; supposing
— 조건 a precondition ; a prior condition 가정(假定) — an assumed premise 대— a major premise〔proposition〕 소— a minor premise〔proposition〕

†전제 專制 absolutism ; despotism ; autocracy —하다 be absolute ; be despotic ; be autocratic ; be arbitrary ; tyrannize ; act the tyrant to〔over〕
—국 an absolute monarchy — 군주 a despot ; an autocrat ; a tyrant ; an absolute〔a despotic〕monarch — 군주 정체 an absolute〔a despotic〕monarchy —자 an absolutist ; a dictator — 정치 despotic government ; autocracy — 정치국 a country under despotic government ; a despotism —주의 absolutism ; despotism —주의자 an absolutist

전제동 全制動 〖스키〗 double stemming ; snowplowing ¶ 전제동을 걸다 snowplow

*전조 前兆 a sign ; an omen ; a precursor ; a portent ; a presage ; a foreboding ; a premonition ¶ 비가 올 전조 a sign of rain // 좋은 전조 a good omen // 전쟁의 전조 portents of war // 전조이다 be a sign ((of)) ; foretell ; betoken ; augur ; be ominous of

전조 前條 the preceding〔foregoing〕article〔paragraph〕

전조 前朝 a former〔previous〕dynasty

전조 轉調 〖음악〗 transition ; modulation

전조등 前照燈 a headlight ; a headlamp

전족 纏足 foot-binding

전죄 前罪 a previous crime〔conviction, sin〕

전주 電柱 an electric pole ; telegraph〔telephone〕poles

전주 電鑄 electrotyping —하다 electrotype

전주 錢主 a creditor ; a money owner

전주 轉住 a change of abode〔address〕 —하다 change abode〔address〕; transfer one's residence ; move

전주 前週 last week ; the preceding〔previous〕week ; the week before ¶ 전주의 오늘 this day last week

*전주 前奏 a prelude ; an overture ; an introduction ¶ 세계 대전의 전주 a prelude to the World War
—곡 an overture ; a prelude

전주르다 take〔have〕a breather〔rest〕 ¶ 전주르고 나서 after a pause

전중 典重 courteousness ; civility —하다 (be) courteous ; civil ; well-mannered

전중이 a prisoner ; a convict ; a jailbird ((미·구))

전지 田地 cultivated land ; fields ; rice-field ; farms

전지 全紙 the whole uncut paper ; the whole of the paper ¶ 이 기사로 전지를 메웠다 The paper is full of accounts of this affair.

전지 全知 omniscience ¶ 전지의 all-knowing ; omniscient

전지 電池 an electric cell ; a battery ¶ 전지에 충전하다 charge a battery // 전지가 닳았다 The battery is run down.
— 개폐기〔회로, 열(列)〕 a battery switch〔circuit, group〕— 세력 battery energy —실(室) a battery room〔compartment, space, tank〕 — 용량 battery capacity — 인입선(引入線) a battery lead-in wire — 작용〔강도〕 battery action〔strength〕 — 전압〔전류〕 battery voltage

〔current〕 — 점화 장치 a battery ignition system — 충전 battery charging — 케이스 a cell case 건— a dry battery〔cell〕 아연 공기 — a zinc-air battery 액— a galvanic battery (로켓) 연료 — a fuel cell 2차 — a secondary cell〔battery〕 중추〔국부, 선〕 — a central〔local, line〕 battery 축— a storage battery 화학 — a chemical cell

전지 戰地 the battlefield ; the front
— 군대 the troops at the front — 근무 field〔active〕 service — 수당 a field allowance ; [장교의] batmoney 《영》

전지 轉地 a change of air ; a change of climate —하다 go 《to a place》 for a change of air ; try a change of air ¶ 여름철에 도시에서 시골로 전지하는 것은 아이들에게 좋다 A change from the city to the country in the summer is good for children.
— 요양 treatment by a change of air ¶ 전지 요양하다 go away 《to a place》 for one's health — 요양소 a sanatorium ; a sanitarium ; a convalescent camp〔hospital〕

전지 剪枝 lopping ; trimming ; pruning —하다 lop ; trim ; prune

전지전능 全知全能 omniscience and omnipotence —하다 (be) omniscient and omnipotent ¶ 전지전능하신 신 Almighty God ; the Almighty

전직 轉職 change of employment〔occupation〕 ; change of post —하다 change one's occupation〔employment〕 ; change from one official post to another ; be transferred to another post ; take up another kind of job ¶ 실업계에서 문학계로 전직하다 leave business for literary work
—자(者) a person who has given up his job for a new one ; a newcomer (to a company from another workshop) ; a "job-converter"

전직 前職 one's former occupation〔job〕 ; the office〔post〕 held previously ; one's former office
— 장관 an ex-minister

†전진 前進 an advance ; a forward movement ; moving forward —하다 advance ; proceed ; move forward ; make headway ; go〔push〕 ahead

> 참고 **advance** 일정한 목표를 향하여 전진하다 **proceed** 일정한 지점으로부터 전진하다

¶ 전진 운동을 일으키다 begin a forward movement // 전진 명령을 내리다 order 《troops》 to advance ; give orders for advance
—각(角) 〖항공〗 a sweepforward (주익(主翼) 앞 가장자리의) ; an angle of advance ; an angular advance — 기지 an advance base ; an outpost ; [공군의] an advance air base ; an air-head —력 driving power ; propulsive force — 명령 《give》 orders for advance ; advance〔march〕 orders ¶ 전진 명령이 내렸다 March orders were given. / The order came to march. // 전진 명령을 기다리고 있었다 They were waiting for the go-ahead. — 부대 the foremost troops (of an army) ; an advance unit 《of the infantry》 — 사령부 an advance headquarters — 운동 a forward movement ; forward motion — 저지 [미식 축구] charge ¶ 전진 저지를 하다 check the advance 《of the enemy》 — 해상 기지 a forward floating base 일보 — ¶ 일보 전진하다 take a step forward

전진 戰陣 battle array ; battle formation ; a military camp ; [전법] tactics ; strategy

전진 戰塵 the dust of combat〔battlefield〕 ¶ 전진을 씻다 wash off the dust of combat

전진 轉進 change of one's course ; the shifting of position ; transfer —하다 change one's course ; shift the position ; be transferred

전질 全帙 a complete set (of books)

전집 全集 one's complete works ; a complete collection ¶ 디킨즈 전집 Dickens' complete works
—물 a complete works series 개인 — complete works of an individual (writer) 라틴 시— the (entire) corpus of Latin poetry 셰익스피어 — the complete works of Shakespeare ; a complete edition〔set〕 of Shakespeare's works

전짬 全— a pure and thick thing

‡전차 電車 an electric car ; a tramcar 《영》 ; a streetcar 《미》 ; a trolley car ; an electric train ¶ 전차를 타다 take a streetcar〔tramcar〕 // 전차에서 내리다 get off a streetcar // 지금은 전차가 다니고 있습니다 Streetcars 〔Tramcars〕 run there now. // 여기는 전차의 운행이 편리하다 This place is convenient for electric cars.
—길 a street with a tramway〔car line〕 —삯 carfare ; tram-fare 《영》 —선〔궤도〕 a streetcar line〔track〕 ; a car line 《미》 ; a tramline 《영》 ; a tramway 《영》 —역 an electric railway station — 운전수 a motorman — 정류장 a streetcar stop 《미》 ; a tram stop 《영》 — 종업원 a trolleyman 《미》 ; a carman 《미》 ; a tramwayman 《영》 — 차고 a car house 《미》 ; a tram shed 《영》 — 차장 a streetcar conductor

전차 前借 borrowing in advance ; an advance ; a loan —하다 borrow in advance ; receive 《money》 in advance ; obtain an advance

—금 a loan ; money borrowed in advance
전차 轉借 subletting ; sublease ; subtenancy —하다 sublet ; sublease ; borrow at second hand
—인 a sublessee ; a subtenant ; an undertenant
*전차 戰車 a tank
— 공격용 비행기 antitank aircraft ; a tank buster 《속》 — 공격차 a tank destroyer —대 a tank corps 《TC》 ; a tank unit — 대장 the commander of a tank corps —병 a tankman — 부대 tank forces ; a fleet of tanks — 승무원 a tank crew —장 a tank commander — 장교 a tank officer — 장애물 a tank barrier —전 a tank battle ; tank warfare —포 a tank gun —호 a tank trap ; an antitank trench 경(輕)— a light〔female〕 tank 고속경(高速輕) — [제1차 대전 때 연합군이 사용한 전차] a whippet (tank) 대(大)— a supertank 대지뢰(對地雷) — a flail tank 무선 조종 — a radio controlled tank 소형(小型) — a midget tank 수륙 양용(水陸兩用) — an amphibian tank 중(重)— a heavy〔male〕 tank 초중(超重) — a monster〔mammoth〕 tank 대(對)— 박격포 a piat 《projector infantry antitank》 대(對)—포 an antitank gun ; [집합적] antitank artillery
전착 顚錯 upsetting ; confusion —하다 upset ; turn upside down ; put the cart before the horse ; get things mixed up〔messed up〕
전채 戰債 war debt(s) ; war bonds
전책임 全責任 full〔entire, complete〕 responsibility ¶ 전책임을 지다 assume 〔bear, shoulder〕 full responsibility 《for》 ; accept complete responsibility 《for》
전처 前妻 one's former wife ; one's divorced wife (이혼한) ; one's late wife (죽은) ¶ 전처의 소생이 넷 있다 have four children by one's previous marriage
전천후 全天候 all-weather
—기(機)〔요격기, 카메라〕 an all-weather plane〔fighter, camera〕 — 농업 all-weather agriculture — 도로 all-weather highway — 비행 all-weather flying
전철 前轍 a precedent
전철을 밟다 관용 tread in another's step ; follow another' s example ; follow in the footsteps〔wake〕 of another
전철 轉轍 —하다 switch ; shunt
—기 points 《영》 ; a switch 《미》 —기 손잡이 a pointer —봉(棒) a switchbar —수 a pointsman〔switchman〕 — 표지〔신호〕 a point〔switch 《미》〕 indicator〔signal〕 자동 —기 an automatic〔safety〕 switch
전철 電鐵 an electric railway
— 회사 an electric railway company ; a traction company
전첨후고 前瞻後顧 looking before and behind〔after〕 ; circumspection ; hesitation —하다 look before and behind 〔after〕 ; reflect on〔think of〕 the consequences ; take〔assume〕 a cautious〔prudent〕 attitude ; think twice ; be irresolute〔hesitant〕
전첩 戰捷 a victory ; a triumph —하다 win a victory
—국 a victorious power〔country〕 — 기념일 a victory day ; an anniversary of a victory — 기념품 a memorial of a victory ; a victory〔war〕 trophy — 축하회 war rejoicings
†전체 全體 the whole ¶ 전체의 whole ; entire ; general // 전체적으로 generally ; in general ; on the whole ; as a whole // 전체에 걸쳐 all over ; throughout // 전체 15명이다 There are fifteen people in all. // 이 작품들은 개별적이 아닌 전체로 고찰하지 않으면 안 된다 The works should be considered not separately, but as a whole. // 전체적인 느낌은 좋았지만 인상에 남는 것이 없었다 Taken as a whole, it wasn't bad, but neither was there anything that leaves a lasting impression.
—도(圖) a general view〔drawing〕 —론(論) 〖철학·심리〗 holism —적 문제 an overall problem — 전쟁 a total〔an all-out〕 war —주의 totalitarianism —주의 국가 a totalitarian state〔country〕 — 회의 a plenary session ; a general meeting
전초 前哨 an outpost ; an advance post
— 기지 an advance base — 부대〔근무〕 outpost troops〔duty〕 —선 the outpost line —전 a (patrol) skirmish ; an outpost action ¶ 총선거의 전초전 a skirmish of the general election // 이것은 전초전에 불과하다 This is just a prelude to what we expect to be.
전축 電蓄 a record player ; a phonograph ; a (an electric) gramophone
라디오 겸용 — a radiophonograph ; a radiogram 《영》 ; a radio gramophone 스테레오 — a stereophonic gramophone
전출 轉出 moving out ; transfer (of post) —하다 move out (of) ; be transferred to ¶ 방계 회사에 전출하다 to be transferred to a subsidiary company
—계〔신고〕 a moving-out notification — 증명 certification of moving out —지 a place of moving out —처 a new address
전충 塡充 filling ; tamping ; plugging —하다 fill up ; tamp ; plug
전취 戰取 win (a war) ; achieve ; gain
전취 前娶 one's former wife ⇨ 전처(前妻)
전치 全治 complete cure〔recovery〕 ; full recovery —하다 be completely cured 〔recovered〕 ; recover completely ¶ 전치 2주일의 부상 an injury which will take two weeks to heal completely // 상처가 전치되었다 The wound healed completely. // 그렇게 하면 전치될 것입니다 It will

effect a complete cure.

전치 前齒 a front tooth ; a fore-tooth ⇨ 앞니

전치 轉置 transposition **—하다** transpose ; dislocate ; displace ¶ 전치할 수 있는 displaceable ; transposable

—법 〖문법〗 hyperbaton

⁑**전치사 前置詞** a preposition ¶ 전치사적 용법 a prepositional〔prepositive〕 use // 이 동사에는 어떤 전치사가 필요한가 What preposition is required after this verb ?

—구 a preposition〔prepositional〕 phrase **— 대용구** a phrase preposition **—적 용법** a prepositional〔prepositive〕 use

전칙 典則 a law ; a rule ⇨ 법칙

전칭 全稱 the generic ; the universal

— 긍정 a universal affirmative **— 명사(名辭)** a general term **— 명제** a universal proposition **— 부정** a universal negative **— 판단** a universal judgment

전쾌 全快 complete recovery ; [전치] complete cure **—하다** get well ; recover from 《one's illness》 ; be (completely) restored to health ; be perfectly〔completely〕 cured ¶ 전쾌되었습니까 Have you quite recovered ? // 하루 빨리 전쾌하시기를 빕니다 Let me wish you a speedy return to health.

전토 田土 cultivated lands ; fields ⇨ 전답

전토 全土 the whole land〔territory, country〕 ¶ 전토에 all over〔throughout〕 the land

⁑**전통 傳統** tradition ; convention ; succession (계승) ¶ 전통적인 traditional ; conventional // 전통적으로 traditionally ; conventionally // 30년의 전통이 있는 학교 a school of 30 years' tradition // 전통에 구애되지 않다 be bound by no tradition // 전통에 묶인 tradition-bound〔-ridden〕 // 전통을 깨뜨리다 break〔defy, violate〕 tradition // 전통을 따르다 follow tradition // 전통을 무시하다 ignore tradition // 전통을 존중하다 set store by tradition

—주의 traditionalism ; conventionalism **—주의자** a traditionalist **— 중시자(重視者)** a tradition-minded person

전통 箭筒 ⇨ 전동(箭筒)

전퇴직율 轉退職率 the separation rate

†**전투 戰鬪** combat ; war ; battle ; campaign ; engagement ; encounter ; skirmish

> 참고 **combat** 가장 일반적인 말 **war** 장기에 걸친 전쟁 상태 **battle** 상당 기간 그리고 꽤 넓은 범위에 걸쳐 대대적으로 행해지는 전투 **campaign** 어떤 목적을 갖고 행해지는 일련의 작전이며 그동안 여러번의 battle이 있을 수 있다 **engagement** 전군의 전투에도 소부대의 충돌에도 사용되지만 다소 딱딱한 말 **encounter** 우연의 충돌 **skirmish** 부대간의 우연한 충돌

—하다 fight 《a battle》 ; battle ; have a fight〔battle〕 ¶ 전투를 시작하다 commence〔open〕 hostilities ; get into action // 전투를 중지하다 suspend hostilities ; break off a battle // 전투에 참가하다 take part in an engagement // 전투 준비를 하다 prepare for action ; clear for action (군함이)

— 개시 [구령] Action ! ¶ 전투 개시하다 start warlike action 《against》 **— 교련** combat drill ; battle practice ; field training **—기** a fighter ; a fighting plane **—기 파일럿** a fighter〔combat〕 pilot ; a fighter jockey 《구어》 **— 대형** battle formation〔array〕 **—력** fighting power 〔strength, efficiency〕 ¶ 전투력을 상실시키다 put 《a ship》 out of action ; disable 《a ship》 **—모** a field〔fatigue〕 cap **—복** a combat uniform ; a battle jacket 〔dress〕 ; battle fatigues 《미》 ; battle dress 《영》 **— 부대** a combat unit **— 부서** one's battle〔action〕 station ; [해군] general quarters **— 부서표(部署表)** [해군] a quarter bill **— 비행** combat flying **— 비행복** an anti-G suit ; a G suit (가속도의 영향을 방지하기 위해 사용하는) **— 사령소(司令所)** [미 육군] a command post 《C. P.》 (전장의) **— 서열(序列)** the order of battle **— 신경증** shell shock **—용 항공기** combat aircraft **—용 휴대 식량** combat ration **—원** a combatant ; a combat 〔combatant〕 soldier ; a fighting man ; a fighter ; a combat crew (항공기의) ; [집합적] combat personnel **— 장루(檣樓)** [군함의] a fighting〔military〕 top **— 준비** fighting trim ; preparation for action **— 지구** a battle zone **— 지휘관** a combat commander〔leader〕 **— 태세** combat readiness **— 폭격기** a fighter-bomber **—함** a battleship ; a battlewagon 《미》 **— 행위** action ; combat〔military〕 action ; a hostile act ; an act of hostility ; hostilities **— 행위 이외 근무** noncombat service **—화** combat shoes **— 훈련** battle practice ; field〔combat〕 training **— 휴지선** a cease-fire line **공격〔방어〕 —** offensive〔defensive〕 operations **야간 —** night fighting **보병 — 부대** a combat infantry troop **육상 — 부대** a ground combat unit **제공(制空) —기** an air-superiority〔a strategic〕 fighter

전파 全破 complete destruction **—하다** destroy completely ; raze ; demolish

— 가옥 a razed〔completely destroyed〕 house

전파 電波 an electric wave ; a radio wave ¶ 전파를 통하여 over the radio ; on the air

— 감시 monitoring of radio waves ; radio regulatory monitoring **— 강도** radio field intensity〔strength〕 **—계** a wave meter **— 관리** radio regulation ; radio wave control **— 망원경** a radio telescope — 방해 jamming — 병기 radio equipment —성(星) a radio star — 수상경(受像鏡) [레이더의] a radarscope —원(源) a radio source — 조종 radio control — 천문학 radioastronomy — 천문학자 a radioastronomer — 탐위(探位) radio fix —탐지경(探知鏡) a plan position indicator ; PPI — 탐지기 a radar ; a radiolocator — 탐지기계(探知機係) a radar man〔operator〕 — 탐지기 방해기 a resnatron — 탐지기 항공술 teleran — 탐지법 radiolocation — 파장 wave length — 항법(航法) radio navigation 라디오 — a check beam (조종사가 착륙 전에 위치를 확인하기 위한) 신호 — 〖통신〗 a (radio) beam 수중 — 탐지기 a sonar

전파 傳播 spread ; propagation ; circulation ; diffusion ; dissemination —하다 propagate ; transmit ; spread ; disseminate ; circulate ¶ 열의 전파 transmission of heat // 음의 전파 propagation of sound // 병독의 전파 dissemination of disease germs // 음파는 공기 속을 전파한다 Sound waves are propagated through the air. // 그것은 병을 전파시키는 매개체이다 It is a vehicle for the spread of disease.

전파 수신기 全波受信機 an all-wave receiver〔radio set〕

전판 全— all ; the whole ; the entire lot ¶ 가진 것을 전판 잃었다 He lost his all. // 전판 거짓말이다 It is a downright lie from start to finish.

전패 戰敗 a defeat (in war) —하다 be defeated in a war ; lose a war
—국 a vanquished country ; the vanquished ; the defeated

전패 全敗 a complete defeat ; a crushing〔total〕 defeat ; a rout —하다 be completely defeated 《in》 ; sustain a crushing defeat ; lose all games

전편 全篇 the whole book〔volume〕 ; the whole reel (영화의) ¶ 전편을 통해서 from cover to cover ; throughout the books

전편 前篇 the first part〔volume〕

전폐 全廢 total abolition —하다 abolish ; do away with ¶ 노예 제도의 전폐 the abolition of slavery
—론 abolitionism —론자 an abolitionist

전포 廛鋪 a store ; a shop

전포 傳布 ⇨ 전파(傳播)

전폭 全幅 the full width (of cloth) ; the whole piece (of cloth) ¶ 전폭적 full ; utmost ; wholehearted // 전폭적으로 fully ; to the utmost // 전폭적인 동정 wholehearted sympathy // 전폭적인 지지를 하다 give 《a person》 full〔whole-hearted〕 support // 전폭적인 신뢰를 하다 trust 《a person》 whole-heartedly

전폭기 戰爆機 a fighter-bomber

전표 傳票 a chit ; a slip ; ticket ; a bill ¶ 지불〔수납〕 전표 a paying-out〔a receiving〕 slip // 전표와 교환으로 지불하다 pay money in exchange for a slip // 전표를 떼다 sign〔give〕 a chit ; issue a voucher
—식 회계법 the slip system of accounting — 지불 제도 the chit system (현금 지불에 대하여) 매도(賣渡) — a sales check〔slip〕 수납(收納) — a receiving slip 예입(預入) — [은행의] a deposit 〔paying-in 《영》〕 slip 지불 — a payment voucher〔slip〕

전표 錢票 a note〔bill〕 (payable) to (the) bearer ; a bearer cheque

전하 電荷 〖물리〗 an electric charge

전하 殿下 His〔Her〕 Royal Highness ; Your Highness ¶ 영국 황태자 전하 His Royal Highness the Prince of Wales

†전하다 傳— ① [전달하다] convey ; report ; deliver ; communicate ; transmit ; impart ; tell ; [열·빛 따위를] conduct ; transmit ¶ 신문이 전하는 바에 의하면 according to the newspaper reports // 허위 보도를 전하다 give〔spread, circulate〕 a false report // 말을 전하다 convey a message // 출석할 뜻을 전하다 notify 《a person》 of one's intention to be present // 배운 것을 전하다 pass what one has learned to others // 이 말을 그에게 전하시오 Please convey this message to him. // 나한테 전화하라고 그에게 전해 주십시오 Will you tell him to give me a ring? // 신문이 그 사건을 자세히 전하고 있다 The paper reports the affair in full. // 부인께 인사 말씀 전해 주십시오 Please remember me to your wife. /Give your wife my kind regards.
② [전수하다] give ; initiate (비결을) ; impart (지식 따위를) ; teach ; introduce ¶ 비결을 전하다 initiate 《a person》 into the secrets // 제자에게 지식을 전하다 impart knowledge to one's disciples // 틀림없이 전하겠습니다 I will make sure he gets the message.
③ [남겨주다] hand down ; bequeath ; leave ¶ 가보로 전해진 칼 a sword handed down as an heirloom // 자손에게 전하다 hand down 《a thing》 to posterity // 그것은 예부터 우리에게 전해온 풍속이다 It is a custom handed down to us from ancient times.

전학 轉學 change〔transfer〕 of school —하다 change from one school to another ; change schools〔one's school〕 ¶ 우리 아들을 덴버의 한 학교로 전학을 시키려고 합니다 I'd like to have my son transferred to a school in Denver.
—생 a student〔pupil〕 transferred from another school

전학급 全學級 the whole class

전함 戰艦 a battleship ; a warship

전항 前項 the preceding clause ; the foregoing paragraph ; 〖수학〗 the antecedent

전해 前— the preceding〔previous〕 year ; last year (작년)

전해 電解 〖화학〗 electrolysis —하다

electrolyze ¶ 전해의 electrolytic
— 검파기 an electrolytic (wave) detector —물〔액, 질〕 an electrolyte — 분리〔분석, 부식(腐蝕), 정련(精練)〕 electrolytic dissociation〔analysis, etching, refining〕 — 소다 electrolytic soda — 아연〔염〕 electrolytic zinc〔soda〕 —조(槽)〔통〕 an electrolytic bath〔cell〕; an electrolyzer — 콘덴서〔정류기(整流器)〕 an electrolytic condenser〔rectifier〕 —형계기(形計器) an electrolytic meter

전해듣다 傳— hear from others ; know〔learn〕 by〔from, on〕 hearsay ¶ 전해들은 말 hearsay // 그것은 전해들어서 알았네 I have got it by hearsay.

전해지다 傳— ① [전승되다] be handed down ; be transmitted ; come down 《from one's ancestors》; go down 《to posterity》; descend 《from father to son》 ② [전달되다] be conveyed ; be transmitted ; be carried ; come across to ; [퍼지다] spread ; pass ; travel ; [소문이] get abroad〔about〕; be circulated ; get〔take〕 wind ; be reported ; be told
③ [전래하다] be introduced 《into Korea》; be brought 《to Korea from India》

전행 專行 —하다 do 《a thing》 at one's own discretion〔judgment〕; act on one's own authority

전향 轉向 conversion ; turning ; changing direction ; switching course —하다 be converted 《to》; turn 《to》; swing〔switch〕《to》; [개심하다] mend one's way ; reform ¶ 전향을 맹세하다 swear to renounce one's views // 우익으로 전향하다 swing to the right // 실업가로 전향하다 turn into a businessman // 그는 급진파로부터 보수파로 전향했다 He turned from Radical to Conservative.
—륜(輪) 〖기계〗 a fifth wheel —자 a convert ; a turncoat — 장치 [기류·가스 조절용] a deflector —점 a turning point

†**전혀** 全— entirely ; completely ; utterly ; wholly ; totally ; altogether ¶ 전혀 모르는 사람 an utter〔a total〕 stranger // 전혀 들은 바 없다 hear nothing of // 전혀 거짓말이다 be a downright lie // 그 사람을 전혀 모른다 I do not know him at all. // 나는 전혀 상관이 없다 I have nothing to do with it. // 그 계획은 전혀 실패였다 The plan was a complete failure. // 동정심이라고는 전혀 없다 He has not a particle of sympathy. // 기계에 관해서는 전혀 모른다 I know nothing whatever about mechanics. // 전혀 모르겠다 I have not the slightest idea. /Not the slightest. /Not the vaguest. /Not the foggiest. // 나는 운동을 전혀 하지 못한다 I'm a total klutz at sports.

†**전형** 典型 a model ; a pattern ; a specimen ¶ 전형적 typical (대표적) ; model (모범적) // 전형적 한국인 a typical Korean

전형 銓衡 screening ; selection ; choice —하다 select ; make choice of ; screen ¶ 전형 중이다 be under consideration // 전형에 누락되다 be left out of selection // 제1차 전형에 통과하다 get through the first selection
— 기준 a criterion for selection — 위원(회) a selection committee ; a screening committee — 테스트 a screening test

전호 前號 the preceding〔last〕 number〔issue〕 ¶ 전호에서 계속되다 be continued from the last issue

†**전화** 電話 a telephone ; a phone —하다 telephone ; phone ¶ 전화로 by telephone ; over the telephone // 전화로 불러내다 call 《a person》 on the phone ; give 《a person》 a ring ; ring up 《a person》 // 전화로 이야기하다 talk over〔by〕 the telephone // 전화를 끊다 ring off ; hang up the receiver // 전화를 가설하다 install a telephone // 전화가 걸리다 be called up〔wanted〕 on the phone // 전화를 받다 answer the telephone ; come to the telephone for 《a person's》 call // 전화를 받는 분은 누구입니까 Who's speaking? // 전화가 잘 들리지 않는다 The voice is not distinct. // 전화가 잘 들리지 않습니다 조금 더 큰 소리로 말해주시오 I can't hear you. Will you speak louder, please? // 전화가 잘 들린다 The connection is clear. // 전화 받으셔요 A phone for you. / You're wanted on the phone. // 전화가 통화중 The number is engaged. 《영》/The line is busy. 《미》 // 전화를 끊지 말아 주시오 Hold the line, please. // 전화를 사용해도 좋습니까 May I use your phone? // 그 전화는 수화기가 제대로 놓여있지 않아서, 제가 수화기를 제대로 놓으라고 신호를 보냈습니다 That phone was off the hook, so I signaled them to put it back on the hook. // 내가 나가 있는 동안 나를 찾는 전화가 걸려 오면 900-2424로 전화하라고 전해 주십시오 If someone calls for me while I'm out, please have him call 900-2424. // 당신이 나가 있는 동안에 톰 베이커라는 사람한테서 전화가 왔었다 While you were out, a Tom Baker called for you. // 그는 지금 다른 전화를 받고 있다 He is on another line. // 톰 119에 빨리 전화 좀 해줘 Tom, dial 119 quickly. // 그녀가 있는 곳은 전화가 되지 않는다 I can't get through to her on the phone. // 이 전화는 불통이다 This telephone line is interrupted. /The telephone is out of order. / The wire〔line〕 is dead.
— 가설료 charge for telephone installation — 가입 ¶ 전화 가입을 신청하다 subscribe for telephone service — 가입자 a (tele)phone subscriber — 교환국 a telephone exchange office ; a telephone central office 《미》 — 교환원 a telephone

operator —국 a telephone office — 국번 an exchange number —기 a telephone ; a phone 《속》 — 도수계(度數計) a telephone service register — 도수제(度數制) the message rate system of the telephone service —료〔요금〕 telephone charges — 목소리 a voice heard over the telephone — 번호 a (tele) phone number — 번호부 a telephone directory ; a (tele) phone book — 상대 the person on the other end of the line —선 a telephone wire〔line〕 — 수화기 a (telephone) receiver —술(術) telephony — 신청 an application by telephone —실 a telephone room ; a (tele) phone booth — 전보 a telephone telegram — 전언(傳言) a telephone message — 중계기 a telephone repeater 공무용 — an official telephone 공중 — a public 〔coinbox〕 (tele) phone ; a pay phone 구내 — an interphone 국제 — international telephone service 급설(急設) — an urgent telephone installation 벽(壁)— a wall telephone 시내〔외〕 — a local〔trunk〕 call 실내 — an interphone ; a room-to-room telephone 외래(外來) — an incoming call 자동 — a dial phone 장거리 — a long-distance call 《미》 직통 — a trunk call ; [미·소간의] the direct communications link ; the hot line〔telephone〕 탁상 — a desk〔cradle〕 telephone 호출 — ¶ 호출 전화를 걸다 make a beeper call 공중 —실 a public telephone station 〔booth〕 ; a call box 《영》 직업별 — 번호부 a classified telephone directory 탁상 —대 the cradle 해저 —선 an undersea telephone cable

☞ ◀p. 1857▶

전화

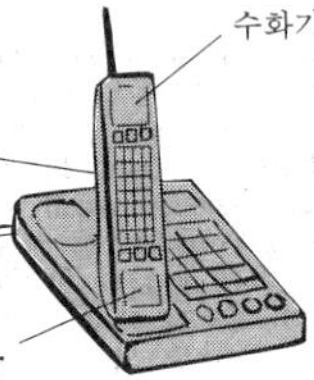

전화 戰禍 the horrors〔ravages, disaster〕 of war ¶ 전화 속의 월남 war-torn Vietnam // 전화에 휩쓸리다 be ravaged by war // 유럽을 전화로부터 구하다 save Europe from war

전화 戰火 war fire ; fire and sword ¶ 전화의 확대 the spread of the war

전화 轉化 change ; transformation —하다 change ; be transformed

전화 電化 [철도·가정 따위를] electrification —하다 electrify 《a railway》 ; install electrical appliances 《in one's house》 ¶ 철도의 전화 electrification of railways

— 계획 an electrification scheme〔project, program〕 — 구간 an electrified section — 사업 an electrification work 〔undertaking〕 — 주택 an electricified home

전화위복 轉禍爲福 Bad luck often brings good luck. /A misfortune turns into a blessing.

*전환 轉換 conversion ; turnover ; switch-over ; diversion ; (기분의) ; change —하다 convert ; divert ; change ; turn ¶ 180도의 전환 a complete about-face // 노래를 불러서 기분을 전환하다 divert oneself in singing // 전시 산업을 평화 산업으로 전환하다 switchover war industries to peace ones // 주의를 다른 데로 전환하다 turn one's attention to〔from〕 // 상심하고 있는 그 여자의 기분을 어떻게 하면 전환시킬 수 있을까 How can we divert her thoughts from her sad loss?

— 가치 〖경제〗 a conversion factor 〔value〕 —기 (器) a commutator ; a switch —기(期) a turning point ; a transition period〔stage〕 ¶ 전환기의 한국 Korea in transition // 일생의 전환기 a turning point in one's life —기 문학 literature at the turning point — 레버 〖철도〗 a switch lever〔bar〕 —로(爐) a converter〔convertor〕 (reactor) —비 (比) conversion ratio — 사채(私債) convertible bond — 스위치 a change-over switch —주(株) a convertible stock 방향 — a switch 배치 — a reshuffle ; a shake-up ; transposition ; redistribution 180도 — ¶ 180도 전환을 하다 execute a 180-degree turn ; take a right about-face ; make a complete about-face 산업 — industrial reconversion 성— sex transformation 주의〔기분〕 — diversion

전황 戰況 [전투 상황] the progress of a battle ; [전국] the military〔war〕 situation ¶ 전황을 보고하다 report on the military situation

— 뉴스 war news〔reports〕 ; news from the front

전회 前回 the last time〔occasion, session〕 ; the last installment (연속물의) ¶ 전회의 last ; previous ; preceding // 전회의 강의 the last〔previous〕 lecture // 전회까지의 개요 an outline up to the last installment // 전회에 이어 그 책의 이야기를 하겠습니다 I will resume the story of the book where I left off.

전회 轉回 revolution ; rotation ; evolution —하다 revolve ; rotate

전횡 專橫 arbitrariness ; despotism ; tyranny —하다 act arbitrarily ; take

전 화

① 전화기

▶전화(기) telephone; phone (★전화를 설치하다 install a telephone; 가입자측에서는 have a telephone installed) / 수화기 earpiece; receiver / 송화기 mouthpiece; transmitter / 다이얼식 전화 dial telephone / 누름단추식 전화 push-button telephone

▶공중전화 public[pay] telephone / 공중전화 박스 public[pay] telephone booth / 전화가입자 telephone subscriber / 공동가입전화 party line[telephone] / 즉시 직통전화 pickup phone; hot line / 회의전화 conference call / 국제전화 international call

▶전용선(專用線) leased wire / 도청방지전화 scrambler telephone / 무선전화 radiophone; radiotelephone; radio-telephone / 이동전화 mobile radio telephone; mobile radiophone / 호출기 (pocket) beeper; (radio) pager / 자동응답전화 answering service (machine); (automatic) telephone message recorder / 콜웨이팅 전화 call-waiting telephone (★통화중에도 다른 전화가 걸려 온 것을 알리는 전화) / 가정 전화번호 home (telephone) number / 회사전화번호 office (telephone) number

▶전화국 telephone exchange (station) / 전화교환원 operator / 교환대 switchboard / 사설 교환대 private branch exchange / 시외국번(局番) long-distance number[code]; area code / 대표번호 pilot number / 내선 extension / 직업별 전화부(電話簿) the yellow pages; the Yellow Pages / 시내전화 local call / 장거리 [시외] 전화 long-distance [out-of-city] call; trunk call 《영》

② 전화번호 읽기

전화번호는 원래 숫자를 그대로 읽는다. 03-203-4141은 o[óu]-three, two-o-three, four-one-four-one으로 읽는다. 0는 영국에서는 nought로 읽기도 한다. 또한 끝에서 두자리씩 끊어서 읽기도 한다. 6345는 sixty-three, forty-five, 526은 five-twenty-six로 읽는다. 내선 235번은 Extension two-three-five.

③ 전화 표현

¶ 여보세요 hello (★ 발음은 [həlóu], 악센트 위치에 주의.) // 브라운입니다 This is Brown (speaking). / Brown speaking[calling].

¶ 브라운씨 댁입니까? Is this the Brown residence? / Is this Mr. Brown's home [residence]? (★ 전자는 정중한 표현.) // 브라운씨 집에 있습니까? Is Brown at home [in]? / Is Brown there? / May I speak to [with] Brown, please? // 예, 접니다. Speaking. (★ 전화로 찾는 사람이 지명되었을 경우에 쓴다. 여성일 경우에는 This is she.를 쓰기도 한다.) // 전화번호가 잘못되었습니다. 몇 번에 거셨습니까? I'm afraid you have the wrong number. What number are you calling? // 실례지만 누구십니까? Who's calling, please? (★ Who are you?는 실례되는 표현이므로 사용하지 않는다. 그러나 Who's this?는 가벼운 회화에서 쓰인다.) // 통화 중입니다. The line is busy. // 브라운씨는 지금 없습니다. He[Brown] is out [not here] (right now).

¶ 뭐라고 전해드릴까요? Would you like [care] to leave a message? // 아닙니다. 나중에 다시 걸겠습니다. No, thank you. I'll call back later. // 그분에게 전화를 드리라고 이를까요? Shall I have her call you back? // 잠깐만 기다려 주십시오. Can you wait a minute, please? / One moment, please. (★ 전자가 많이 사용된다. 후자도 많이 사용되나 전화 교환원 등이 많이 쓰는 편.) // 전화를 끊지 말고 기다려 주십시오. Hold the line, please. // 성함이 뭐라고 하셨지요? What did you say your name was? // 내선 512번 부탁합니다. Extension 512, please. (★ 512는 five-one-two 또는 five-twelve로 읽는다.) // 외선으로 걸어주십시오. Give me an outside line, please. // 브라운 박사 부탁합니다. Please connect me with Dr. Brown. // 그녀를 전화로 호출하여 주십시오. Please get her on the phone. // 나 지금 공중 전화로 하고 있어 I'm calling from a pay telephone. / I'm using a pay telephone.

---

high-handed measures; tyrannize over 《a person》; be despotic

*__전후 前後__ [순서] order; sequence; [앞과 뒤] front and rear; [부사적] before and behind; in front and in the rear; before and〔or〕 after; about; around; for so; approximately ¶ 전후 10년간 for 10 years off and on // 대전 전후 before and after the World War // 전후하여 closely one upon the other // 전후의 생각도 없이 regardless of the consequence; recklessly; thoughtlessly // 전후로 움직이

다 move back and forth // 전후를 모르게 되다 become unconscious ; lose consciousness // 전후도 모르게 술을 마시다 drink oneself unconscious ; be dead drunk // 전후 좌우를 살피다 look about 〔around〕《one》// 전후를 망각하다 forget oneself ; be beside oneself《with rage》// 전후를 돌보다 reflect on the consequences // 순서의 전후가 바뀌다 The order is inverted. // 그는 20세 전후이다 He is about 20 years old. // 전후의 관계로 말의 뜻을 알 때가 많다 You can often tell the meaning of a word from its context.

전후 戰後 postwar days ¶ 전후의 post-war ; after the war ; post-bellum《라》; après guerre《프》// 전후의 한국 postwar Korea // 전후의 문제 post-bellum questions〔problems〕// 전후 수년간 for several years after the war // 전후 20년이 경과하였다 Twenty years have passed since the end of the war.

— 상태 postbellum conditions — 최고〔최저〕 the postwar high〔low〕 —파 the après guerre〔postwar〕 generation — 프랑스 France after the war ; postwar France

전훈 電訓 telegraphic instructions〔order〕

전희 前戱 (sexual) foreplay

***절**[1] [사찰] a Buddhist temple ¶ 절에 불공 드리러 가다 go to a temple to worship 《Buddha》; visit a temple for worship

***절**[2] [인사] a bow ; salutation (경례) ; an obeisance ; a kowtow —하다 bow ; make an obeisance ; salute ¶ 큰 절 a bow on ceremonial occasions // 공손히 절하다 bow politely ; make a low bow

†**절 節** 〖문법〗 a clause ; a paragraph ; 〖물리〗 node ; [절개] loyalty ; chastity ; 〖경제〗 an item ¶ 제1절 Paragraph One

-절 節 [접미어] a season ; a festival day 개천— the Foundation Day of Korea 성탄— Christmas Day

-절 折 folding ¶ 12절 duodecimo ; 12mo // 32절판 thirty-twomo ; 32mo // 2절로 하다 fold in two〔half〕; double《a sheet》 down

절가 折價 [값을 정함] fixing〔settling〕 a price ; [값을 깎음] bargaining ; haggling —하다 fix〔settle〕 a price ; bargain 〔haggle〕 over the price ; beat down the price

절간 a Buddhist temple ; a temple building ⇨ 절

절감 切感 —하다 feel keenly〔acutely, painfully, heartily, sincerely〕 ¶ 외국어의 필요성을 절감하다 feel keenly the necessity of linguistic knowledge

절감 節減 reduction ; retrenchment ; curtailment ; economy —하다 reduce ; retrench ; curtail ; cut down ¶ 경비를 절감하다 cut down〔curtail〕 expenses ; retrench in expenditures

경비 — curtailment of expenditure

***절개 切開** incision ; operation ; removal —하다 incise ; operate《on》 ¶ 종기를 절개하다 incise a tumor // 암을 절개하다 remove a cancer // 환부를 절개하다 cut out the affected part

— 수술 an〔a surgical〕 operation —침 a needle 십자 — crucial incision 위—술 gastrotomy 제왕 — 수술 Caesarean operation

절개 節槪 fidelity《to one's principles》; honor ; integrity ¶ 절개 있는 chaste ; loyal ; integral // 절개를 지키다 preserve chastity〔integrity〕; remain faithful

절검 節儉 economy ; thrift ; frugality —하다 economize ; save

절경 絶景 a superb view ; a wonderful〔a charming, an enchanting〕 view ; picturesque〔fine〕 scenery ; a scenic masterpiece ¶ 천하의 절경 scenery beyond description ; a superb view ; scenery unparalleled〔unrivalled〕 in the world

절계 節季 [연말] the end of the year ; the year end ; [계절의 끝] the end of a season

절골 折骨 a broken bone ; a bone fracture —하다 break a bone ; suffer a fractured bone

절교 絶交 break of friendship ; a rupture ; breaking relation —하다 cut 〔drop〕 one's acquaintance ; break off with《a person》; renounce friendship ; break relations ¶ 이제 너와는 절교다 I will no longer have anything to do with you. /I am through with you.

—장(狀) a letter of breaking off ; a Dear John (letter) (여자가 남자에게 보낸)《미·속》

절구 a mortar ¶ 절구에 찧다 pound《rice》 in a mortar // 그 여자는 절구통이다 She is built like a wash-tub〔silo〕.

—돌 a millstone ; a burstone —질 pounding grain in a mortar —통 the body of a mortar 절굿공이 a (wood) pestle ; a pounder ; a stone-headed hammer

절구 絶句 a Chinese quatrain (한시의)

절국대 〖식물〗 a kind of globethistle

‡**절규 絶叫** a scream ; an exclamation ; an ejaculation —하다 ejaculate ; scream ; exclaim ; cry out ; shout ¶ 정계의 정화를 절규하다 cry loudly〔raise a cry〕 for the purification of the political world

절그렁 with a clink ; jingling ; rattling —하다 clank ; clink ; jingle ; rattle ¶ 열쇠를 절그렁거리다 rattle one's keys

절기 絶忌 abhorrence ; abomination —하다 abhor ; abominate

절기 絶奇 exquisiteness ; excellence —하다 (be) exquisite ; excellent

절기 節氣 the subdivisions of the seasons ; the 24 solar terms

절기 絶技 [연기] an admirable performance〔acting〕; a miraculous feat ; [기

술] wonderful skill ; excellent technics
절꺼덕 with a snap〔click〕 **—하다** make a snap ; click ; slap ; slurp ¶ 절꺼덕거리다 snap〔click〕 away ; slap and slap // 자물쇠를 절꺼덕 잠그다 click the door shut ; fasten a lock with a snap
절꺼덩 ⇨ 절꺼덕
절꺽 ⇨ 절꺼덕
절다¹ [소금에] be salted ; be seasoned with salt
절다² [발을] hobble ; walk lame ; limp ¶ 발을 저는 lame ; crippled ; limping // 바른편 다리를 절다 limp in the right leg // 다리를 절며 가다 limp〔hobble〕 away // 다리를 절며 걷다 limp along ; walk with a limp // 부상자는 다리를 절며 가버렸다 The wounded man hobbled away. // 그는 발을 절기 때문에 활동적인 일을 하지 못했다 His lame foot disqualified him for active work.
†**절단 切斷, 截斷** cutting ; severance ; abscission ; amputation (수족의) **—하다** cut (off) ; sever (from) ; amputate ; chop ¶ 둘로 절단하다 cut 《a thing》 in two // 전선을 절단하다 cut off a telegraph line // 발을 절단하다 amputate 《a person's》 leg (의사가) ; have one's leg amputated (환자가) // 무릎을 절단하다 have one's leg amputated at the knee
—기 a cutting machine ; a cutter **—도** a drawing in section **—면** a section ; 〖제도〗 a cutting plane **— 방법** a cutting process **—선** 〖제도〗 a cutting-plane line **— 수술** amputation **— 신호** a disconnecting signal **—자** an amputator **—칼** a catling **— 환자** an amputee **2등분 —** ¶ 2등분 절단하다 cut 《a thing》 in two **양수 양각(兩手兩脚) — 환자** a basket case ; a quadruple amputee **팔 — 환자** an arm amputee
절대 絶大 hugeness ; immensity **—하다** (be) greatest ; highest ; tremendous ; immense
†**절대 絶對** absoluteness ¶ 절대로 absolutely ; unconditionally ; positively ; imperatively // 절대적인 absolute ; unconditional ; positive ; imperative ; categorical // 절대 금연 Positively No Smoking. // 주차 절대 금지 Positively No Parking. // 우리 팀이 절대적으로 유리하니까 반드시 이길 거다 With an overwhelming advantage like this, there's no way we can lose.
— 개념 absolute concept **— 고도〔밀도, 습도〕** absolute altitude〔density, humidity〕 **— 공간** absolute space **— 과반수〔다수〕** an absolute majority ¶ 절대 다수로 by an absolute majority // 절대 다수를 점하다 get〔win, enjoy〕 an absolute majority **— 군주제** an absolute monarchy **—권(력)** absolute authority〔right, power〕 《over》 **— 권력자** a despot ; an autocrat ; an absolutist **— 금주** total abstinence **— 금주가** a total abstainer ; a teetotaler **— 단위** 〖물리〗 an absolute unit **— 대표권** exclusive representation **— 등급** 〖천문〗 absolute magnitude **—량** absolute quantity ¶ 식량 절대량을 확보하다 secure the absolutely needed quantity〔supply〕 of food **—론자** an absolutist **— 명령** 〖철학〗 a categorical imperative ; a peremptory command **— 반대** positive opposition ¶ 절대 반대다 be positively against 《a person's plan》 // 절대 반대 입장을 취하다 stand positively against 《it》 ; take an attitude of positive opposition 《to》 **— 복종** absolute〔unconditional〕 obedience **— 불변** ¶ 절대 불변의 immutable ; permanent **—선(善)** the absolute good **— 소유권** absolute ownership **— 속도** absolute velocity **—아(我)** 〖철학〗 absolute ego **— 안정** a complete〔an absolute〕 rest ¶ 환자는 절대 안정을 요한다 The patient must be kept absolutely at rest. **—압(력)** 〖물리〗 absolute pressure **— 영도** 〖물리〗 absolute zero **— 온도** 〖물리〗 absolute temperature **— 운동** 〖물리〗 absolute motion **— 원리** an absolute principle **— 음감(音感)** (the sense of) perfect〔absolute〕 pitch **— 음감 교육** training in the perfect〔absolute〕 pitch **— 음고(音高)** 〖음악〗 perfect〔absolute〕 pitch **— 음악** absolute〔abstract〕 music **—자** 〖철학〗 the Absolute ; the absolute being **—적 실업** absolute unemployment **—적 영장** a peremptory writ **—적 요소〔사항〕** an absolute **—적 존재** the absolute being ¶ 신은 절대적 존재이다 God is the absolute being. **—주의** 〖철학·경제〗 absolutism **— 진리** an absolute truth **— 측정** absolute measurement **—치(値)** 〖수학〗 the absolute value ; the modulus 《*pl.* -li》
절대 絶代 ① [옛날] ancient times ; remote ages〔antiquity〕 ; prehistoric days ② ⇨ 절세
*⁑***절도 節度** moderation ¶ 절도를 지키다 be moderate 《in drinking》 ; use〔exercise〕 moderation
절도 絶島 a desert〔lonely, an isolated〕 island ; a solitary island
절도 竊盜 a thief ; a larcenist ¶ 시계 절도의 혐의로 on a charge of the larceny of a watch ; on suspicion of the larceny of a watch // 절도질하다 steal ; commit a theft ; be guilty of larceny // 그는 절도 혐의로 잡혔다 He was arrested on the suspicion of theft.
—광〔성벽(性癖)〕 kleptomania ; [사람] a kleptomaniac **—범** larceny ; theft ; a larcenist **—죄** larceny ; theft **— 행위** a larcenous act
절따(말) a red〔sorrel, bay〕 horse
절뚝거리다 limp ; hobble ; walk lame ; walk with a limp ¶ 약간 절뚝거리며 걷다 walk with a slight limp
절뚝발이 a cripple ; a lame person
⁑**절뚝절뚝** limping ; hobbling ; with lame

steps
절량 농가 絶糧農家 a food-short farm household ; food-short farmers ¶ 절량 농가의 구호 대책을 세우다 map〔work〕 out relief measures for food-short farmers
절렁거리다, 쩔렁거리다 clink ; jingle ; make tinkling〔clinking〕 sound
절레절레 shaking one's head
절로 ① automatically ⇨ 저절로 ② there ⇨ 저리로
절룩거리다 ⇨ 절다²
절륜 絶倫 ─하다 (be) peerless ; matchless ; unequalled ; unsurpassed ¶ 정력이 절륜한 사람 a man of untiring〔indefatigable, unbounded〕 energy ; a man of hustle
⁑**절름발이** a lame person ; a cripple ; a halt 《고어》 ¶ 절름발이의 lame ; limping ; crippled ; game 《leg》 // 절름발이가 되다 become lame ; become crippled ; go〔fall〕 lame
*__절름거리다__ ⇨ 절다²
절망 切望 a earnest desire ; longing ; an eager wish ; an entreaty ─하다 desire〔hope〕 earnestly ; be anxious 《for, to》 ¶ 그녀는 가기를 절망하고 있다 She is anxious to go.
⁑**절망 絶望** despair ; hopelessness ─하다 despair 《of》 ; lose〔give up〕 hope 《of》 ; be driven to despair ¶ 절망적 hopeless ; desperate // 절망시키다 make 《a person》 despair ; drive 《a person》 to despair ; throw 《a person》 into despair // 정세는 절망적이다 The situation is hopeless. // 그는 절망하고 있는 것 같았다 He appeared (to be) in despair. // 반드시 절망이라고 할 수는 없다 There is still some hope. // 그는 절망한 끝에 자살했다 Despair drove him to suicide. /He took his own life out of despair. // 환자는 절망적이다 The patient's life is despaired of. // 전도는 아주 절망적이다 There is not a slim chance〔a gleam of hope〕 before us.
절맥 絶脈 〖의학〗 a pulse that has ceased to beat ─하다 a pulse stops 〔ceases〕 to beat
절멸 絶滅 extinction ; extermination ; eradication ; annihilation ─하다 stamp〔root〕 out ; wipe out ; annihilate ; exterminate ; eradicate ; become extinct ; die out ; cease to exist ¶ 소아마비의 절멸 the stamping out of polio
절명 絶命 death ; the end of life ─하다 die ; expire ; breathe one's last ; pass away ¶ 두 시간 후에 절명했다 He passed away two hours later.
절목 節目 a subdivision ; a section ; a paragraph
절묘 絶妙 exquisiteness ; superbness ; excellence ─하다 (be) superb ; exquisite ¶ 절묘한 재주 a miraculous feat // 절묘한 필치 an exquisite touch
절무 絶無 nought ; none at all ; nil ; nothing ; total absence ─하다 be none at all ; (be) nil ; totally absent ¶ 그런 일은 절무라고 하여도 좋다 It is next to impossible that such a thing should happen.
절물 節物 seasonable goods ; things in season
절미 絶美 surpassing〔matchless, peerless〕 beauty ; exquisiteness
절미 節米 rice saving ; economy of rice consumption ─하다 economize on rice ; save rice
─ **계획** a rice-saving program ─ **운동** a movement for rice saving
*__절박 切迫__ urgency ; pressure ; imminence ; impendence ; acuteness ; tension ─하다 draw near ; be near at hand ; approach ; impend ; press ; (be) imminent ; be acute ; grow tense ¶ 절박한 urgent ; pressing ; imminent ; acute ; tense ; strained ; serious // 시간이 절박하다 Time presses. // 기일이 절박하다 The time is drawing near. // 사태가 절박하다 The situation is acute〔serious〕.
절반 折半 a half ─하다 halve ; divide into halves ; cut in halves ¶ 이익을 절반하다 share the profit equally ; go halves〔fifty-fifty〕 on the profit
절버덕, 절벅 with a splash〔plash〕 ¶ 절버덕거리다 splash ; plash // 진창 속을 절버덕거리며 지나가다 splash through mud
절벅절벅 splashing ; plashing ; with splashing sounds ¶ 물구덩이를 절벅절벅 걸어가다 slosh〔splash〕 through the puddles
*__절벽 絶壁__ [낭떠러지] an inaccessible precipice ; a (sheer) cliff ; a bluff ; [사람] a deaf person ; a dull〔stupid〕 person ¶ 절벽 위의 등대 a lighthouse on a bluff // 절벽을 기어오르다 scale〔climb up〕 a cliff // 절벽에서 추락하다 fall over a precipice
절부 節婦 a chaste woman ; a virtuous woman
절사 節士 a man of integrity〔fidelity, loyalty〕
절사 節死 ─하다 die for the sake of one's integrity ; die a martyr to one's cause
절삭 切削 cutting
─ **공구** a cutting tool
절색 絶色 an unsurpassed beauty ; a woman of peerless〔matchless〕 beauty ; the fairest of the fair ; the loveliest of all ; a paragon of beauty
절세 絶世 [비길 데 없음] the unequalled in the world ; the peerless ; the matchless ; [세상과 등짐] retirement from the world ─하다 retire from the world ¶ 절세의 미인 a paragon of beauty ; a rare beauty ; the fairest of the fair
절손 絶孫 ─하다 let one's family line

die out ; have〔leave〕 no posterity
절수 節水 water saving ; economization of water ―하다 economize (in) water
절승 絶勝 fine scenery ; superb scenic beauty ; unsurpassed〔breathtaking〕 scenery
절식 絶食 [단식] fasting ; self-starvation ; abstinence from food ; [절곡] lacking food ―하다 fast ; abstain from food ; go without food ¶ 절식하여 죽다 starve oneself to death ; die of self-starvation
― 요법 a fast cure ; a fasting treatment
절식 節食 temperance〔moderation〕 in eating ; a spare diet ―하다 eat moderately〔sparingly〕 ; be temperate in eating
절식 絶息 expiring ―하다 expire ; breathe one's last (breath) ; gasp out one's life ; die
절신 絶信 [서신을 끊음] cessation of corresponding ; [소식이 끊어짐] hearing no news from 《a person》 ―하다 cease to correspond ¶ 절신되다 hear nothing from 《a person》// 그녀와는 10년 전에 헤어진 뒤로 절신되었다 I have not heard〔I have heard nothing〕 from her since I parted from her ten years ago.
절실 切實 ―하다 (be) urgent ; immediate ; real ; sincere ; earnest ¶ 절실하게 acutely ; keenly ; urgently ; appositely ; heartily ; sincerely // 절실한 소원 an earnest desire // 필요성을 절실히 느끼다 feel keenly the necessity of 《it》
†절약 節約 economy ; husbandry ; frugality ; saving ; thrift

> 참고 **saving**은 장래를 위하여 저축해 두는 것 **economy**는 노력 돈 시간 따위를 함부로 하지 않는 것 **frugality**는 특히 먹을 것 비용 따위를 저축하기 위하여 따로 모아 두는 것 **thrift**는 돈이나 물건 따위를 조심해서 사용하는 뜻으로서 economy 보다 뜻이 강하며 economy는 frugality 보다 뜻이 강하다

―하다 economize 《in》 ; dispense with ; spare ; save 《on》 ; be economical 〔frugal〕 of ; curtail ; retrench 《in》 ; practice economy ¶ 충분히 절약하여 with strict economy // 모든 절약을 하다 practice every retrenchment // 경비를 절약하다 cut (down) expenses ; save down expenditure // 음식을 절약하다 save on food // 1년에 500만원을 절약할 수 있다 A saving of 5,000,000 *won* a year can be effected.
― 장치 an economizer ; a save-all ; a saver 경비〔비용〕 ― economy in expenditures 시간 ― economy of time 일광 ― daylight saving 자원 ― ¶ 자원 절약을 하다 nurse resources 전기 ― ¶ 전기 절약을 하다 economize in (electric) power 연료 ―기 a fuel economizer
절연 絶緣 severing relations ; breaking off one's connection ; insulation ; isolation ―하다 sever one's connection with 《a person》 ; break with ; wash one's hands off ; insulate ; isolate ¶ 과거와 절연하다 break with the past // 그와 절연했다 I have done with him. /I am through with him.
―기(器) an insulator ; a (cut-off) switch ―기(機) an insulating machine ― 내력(耐力) dielectric strength ―선 an insulated wire ― 시험〔시험기(試驗器)〕 an insulation test〔tester〕 ―유(油) insulating oil ―재(료) an insulating material ― 저항 insulation resistance ―지(紙)〔바니시, 왁스〕 insulating paper〔varnish, wax〕 ―체 〖전기〗 an insulator ; an isolator ; a non-conductor ― 테이프 a friction〔an electric〕 tape 유(油)〔공기〕― oil〔air〕 insulation 면(綿) ―선(線) a weatherproof wire
절연 節煙 temperance〔moderation〕 in smoking ―하다 smoke less ; be moderate〔temperate〕 in smoking
절요 絶要, 切要 importance ; urgency ―하다 (be) important ; urgent
절용 節用 frugality ; economy ; thrift ; frugal use ―하다 use frugally ; economize 《on》 ; be frugal of ; save ; be sparing of
절원 絶遠 a far distance ; remoteness ―하다 be far away〔off, distant〕 ; (be) remote
절음 絶飮 abstinence from drinking ; total abstinence ; temperance ; teetotalism ―하다 give up drinking ; abstain from drinking ¶ 절음을 장려하다 promote temperance
절음 節飮 temperance (in drinking) ; moderation in drinking ―하다 be temperate in drinking ; drink in moderation
절의 節義 fidelity to one's principle ; integrity ; honor ¶ 절의를 지키다 adhere 〔be loyal〕 to one's principle
*절이다 [소금에] preserve 《pickle》 with salt ; salt down ; souse 《a thing》 ; corn 《meat》 ¶ 절인 배추 salted cabbage // 생선을 소금에 절이다 preserve fish with salt ; salt fish
절일 節日 a festival ; a holiday
절장보단 絶長補短 ―하다 use another's strength to shove oneself up ; utilize one's good points to make up for one's weakness
절재 絶才 extraordinary〔matchless〕 talents ; rare gifts
절전 節電 economy in power consumption ; power saving ―하다 economize (in) power〔electricity〕
― 운동 power-saving movement
절절, 쩔쩔 [끓는 모양] simmering ; boiling
절절이 節節― word by word ; each word ; phrase by phrase ; paragraph by

paragraph ; verse by verse
절절하다 切切— (be) earnest ; eager ; ardent ¶ 절절한 사랑의 편지 an ardent love letter // 절절히 호소하다 appeal earnestly〔ardently〕
†**절정 絶頂** [산 꼭대기] the summit ; the top ; [정점] the height ; the zenith ; the peak ; the crest ; a climax ¶ 경기의 절정 the peak of prosperity // 불경기의 절정 the depth of depression // 절정에 달하다 gain〔attain〕 the (very) summit // 인기 절정에 서다 be〔stand〕 at the peak of one's prosperity // 물가고가 절정에 달했다 We have reached the peak of high prices.
⁑**절제 節制** temperance ; temperate living ; self-restraint ; moderation《in drinking》 **—하다** be temperate《in》; be moderate《in》; abstain from (술 따위를) ; (be) continent (성욕을) ¶ 절제하여 moderately ; temperately // 음식을 절제하다 be moderate in eating and drinking
절제 切除 〖의학〗 resection ; excision ; [의과의] erasion ; a surgical removal **—하다** excise ; cut off ; resect ; guillotine (편도선을)
신경 **—술** neurotomy 폐 **—술** pneumonectomy
절제술 切除術 ⇨ 절제
위**—** gastrotomy
절조 節操 integrity ; honor ; faith ; fidelity ; chastity ¶ 절조가 없는 사람 an unprincipled man // 절조를 지키다 preserve one's integrity ; keep one's principles ; keep one's chastity (여자가)
절족 동물 節足動物 〖동물〗 an arthropod ; Arthropoda (학명)
절종 絶種 extinction of species ; an extinct species **—하다** a species dies out ; a kind becomes extinct
절주 節酒 moderation in drink ; temperance **—하다** be moderate in drink ; practice temperance
절지 絶地 a most remote region
절지동물 節肢動物 〖동물〗 an arthropod
⁑**절차 節次** process ; formalities ; procedure ; proceedings (소송의) ¶ 법률상의 절차 legal formalities // 입학 절차 entrance formalities // 절차를 밟다 go through formalities ; take steps〔proceedings〕// 절차를 밟지 않다 neglect the procedure ; fail to take steps // 정식 절차를 밟다 go through due formalities // 수출입 절차에 정통하다 be familiar with export-import procedure // 그것은 단지 절차상의 문제이다 It is just a matter of procedure.
—법 an adjective law 소송 **—** legal procedure
절차탁마 切磋琢磨 cutting and polishing things such as precious stones ; learning by close application ; indefatigable assiduity in one's learning and virtuous conduct **—하다** apply oneself closely《to one's study》

절찬 絶讚 extolment ; great admiration **—하다** speak in the highest terms of 《a person》; be loud in praise of ; extol ¶ 절찬을 받다 win great admiration ; enjoy the highest praise ; be loudly applauded // 절찬을 받을 만하다 deserve the highest terms of praise ; cannot be overpraised // 그의 발명에 절찬을 아끼지 않는다 My highest praise goes to his invention.
절창 絶唱 excellent singing (노래) ; an excellent reading of poetry (시)
절처봉생 絶處逢生 finding one's way out of a desperate situation ; having a narrow escape from the jaws of death
절충 折衷 a compromise ; eclecticism **—하다** compromise with ; make a compromise ¶ 노사 쌍방의 절충으로 쟁의가 해결되었다 The strike came to a settlement through a compromise between labor and management. // 이 집은 한·양식 절충식 집이다 The house is a compromise between Korean and foreign (styles).
—법 an eclectic method **—설** eclecticism ; a compromise on conflicting views **—안** a compromise plan〔suggestion, proposal〕 **—자** an eclectic ; an eclectist **—주의(主義)** eclecticism **—파〔자〕** an eclectic **— 학파** 〖철학〗 the Eclectic School
절충 折衝 [외교·담판] negotiation ; conference ; parley ; [침입을 막음] checking the enemy's advance〔invasion〕 **—하다** negotiate〔bargain〕 with 《a person》 about ; negotiate〔confer〕 with ; check 〔defend〕 the enemy ¶ 절충을 거듭한 후에 after prolonged negotiations // …에 관하여 절충 중이다 negotiations are going on〔are in progress〕 about ; be under negotiations
절취 竊取 theft ; larceny ; stealing ; abstraction **—하다** steal ; abstract ; purloin
절취선 切取線 the line along which to cut 《a section》 off ; [절선] a dotted line ; [바늘 구멍] perforated line ¶ 절취선이 있는 종이〔우표〕 perforated paper〔stamps〕
절치 切齒 the gnashing of teeth ; rage **—하다** grind〔gnash〕 one's teeth with vexation ¶ 절치부심(腐心)하다 grind one's teeth with vexation ; feel〔be〕 deeply chagrined《at》
절친 切親 a close friendship ; intimacy **—하다** (be) intimate《with》; close ; be on the best〔warmest〕 terms《with》
절커덕, 절컥 ⇨ 절꺼덕, 절꺽
절터 a temple site ; a site of temple
절토 切土 〖토목〗 cutting ; cutting the ground
절통 切痛 **—하다** (be) most regrettable ; bitterly mortifying
절판 絶版 **—하다** be out of print ; print no more copies of《the book》 ¶ 절판되

다 go out of print // 이 책은 절판되었다 The book is out of print.
절편 a rice cake with a flower pattern imprinted
절품 絶品 an exquisite piece of work ; a unique article ; a rarity ; a paragon ; a nonpareil
절품 切品 absence of stock **—하다** be out of stock ; be sold out ¶ 절품이 되다 run out of stock ; the stock runs out // 현재 절품이 되어 주문을 받지 못하겠습니다 We cannot meet your orders owing to absence of stock.
절피 thread reinforcing a bowstring to fit the nock of an arrow
절필 絶筆 [마지막 글] one's last writing ; [끊음] giving up writing ; putting down one's pen **—하다** give up writing ; put down one's pen
절핍 切逼 pressure 《for money》; stringency ; tightness 《of money》 **—하다** (be) pressing ; tight ; stringent
절핍 絶乏 exhaustion ; drain **—하다** get〔be〕 exhausted ; be drained ; give out
절하 切下 reduction ; devaluation (평가의) **—하다** cut down ; reduce 《to》 ¶ 평가 절하하다 devaluate ; devalue // 원화를 2할 절하하다 devalue the *won* by 20 percent
평가 — 〖경제〗 devaluation
절한 絶汗 one's last〔dying〕 sweat (on the forehead)
절해 絶海 the farthest seas ¶ 절해의 고도 a lonely island in the distant sea
절호 絶好 ¶ 절호의 splendid ; grand ; capital ; first-rate ; the best ; golden // 절호의 기회 a golden〔rare〕 opportunity ; an excellent chance // 절호의 시기 the time of all times // 절호의 일기 perfect weather 《for》 // 절호의 기회를 놓치다 let slip a capital opportunity
절후 節候 the subdivision of the seasons
†**젊다** (be) young ; youthful ; [손아래] younger ; junior ¶ 젊음 youth ; youthfulness // 젊은이 a young man ; the youth // 젊었을 때부터 from one's youth〔one's earliest year〕 // 젊었을 때에는 when young ; in one's youth // 젊었을 동안에 while young // 젊어 보이다 look young ; be youthful-looking // 나이에 비해서 젊다 look〔be〕 young for one's age // 젊어서 죽다 die young〔at an early age〕 // 젊어지다 become〔grow〕 younger // 열살이나 젊어진 것 같다 feel ten years younger // 젊은 기분이다 be young in spirit // 그는 아직 젊지마는 생각은 벌써 늙었다 He has an old head on young shoulders.
†**젊은이** a young person〔man〕 ; a youth ; a youngster ; a lad (남자) ; the young 《총칭》; young people ¶ 요즈음 젊은이들은 버르장머리 없다 Young people have no manners these days. // 젊은이들을 위해서 길을 열어 줘야 한다는 생각이 든다 I just feel that I should make way new blood.
젊음 youth ; youthfulness ¶ 젊음을 유지하다 remain〔stay〕 young ; retain one's youthfulness
점 占 divination ; fortune-telling **—하다** tell(one's) fortune ; divine ; forecast ¶ 점치다 consult a fortuneteller ; have one's fortune told
—쟁이 a fortuneteller ; a diviner **꿈—** divination by means of dreams **성명—** onomancy **성서—** bibliomancy **수상(手相)—** palmistry **숫자—** arithmancy **인상(人相)—** divination by the features **제비—** sortilege ; divination by lot
†**점 點** ① [반점] a spot ; a speck ; a speckle ; a dot ¶ 태양의 흑점 sunspots // 흰점 박힌 검정개 a black dog with white spots // 한점의 구름도 없는 하늘 sky without a speck of cloud // 검은 점이 하늘에 나타났다 A black speck was seen in the sky.
② [표기] a point ; a dot ; a mark ¶ 점을 찍다 dot ; mark with a dot ; point
③ [점수] a mark ; a point ; a grade ; a run (야구) ; a goal (축구) ¶ 60점 60 marks // 좋은 점을 받다 get a good mark // 점을 매기다 mark ; give marks // 점이 후하다 be generous in marking // 점이 박하다 be severe in marking // 영어에서 70점을 받다 get a grade of 70 in English // 100점 만점에서 80점 맞다 get 80 points out of 100 // 5회에 3점을 얻다 score three runs in the fifth inning // 그는 95점이었다 His mark was 95.
④ [논점] a point ; a respect ; a reason ; a score ¶ 좋은 점 a strong〔good〕 point ; a merit ; a forte // 나쁜 점 a weak point ; a defect ; a fault // 품질의 점에 있어서 in respect of quality // 좋은 점도 있고 나쁜 점도 있다 have both merits and demerits // 이 점에 있어서는 아무것도 할 말이 없다 I have nothing to say on this score〔in this respect〕. // 나는 모든 점에서 네가 틀렸다고 생각한다 I think you are wrong in every respect.
⑤ [입장] a point of view ; a standpoint ¶ 상업상의 점에서 보면 from a commercial point of view〔standpoint〕 // 모든 점에서 보다 view〔look at〕 《a matter》 from every point of view〔angle〕
⑥ [지점] a point ; an extent (범위) ¶ 출발점 the starting point // 교차점 a crossing // 어느 점까지 to what extent ; how far
⑦ [수효] items ; a piece ¶ 의류 수점 several pieces of clothing // 의류 10점을 도둑맞다 have ten pieces of dress stolen
⑧ [소수점] a decimal point
⑨ 〖화학〗 a point ¶ 비등점 the boiling point // 융해점 the melting point
⑩ [바둑의] a piece (돌) ; a cross (판의 눈목)
⑪ [피부의] a birthmark ; a macula ; a mole (검은)

—선 a dotted line
-점 店 a store ; a shop 《영》
양복— a tailor's (shop) ; a tailor shop 《미》
점가 漸加 a gradual increase —하다 increase gradually ; accelerate
— 속도 acceleration of velocity —약(藥) a cumulative medicine
점감 漸減 a gradual decrease —하다 diminish〔decrease〕 gradually ; dwindle
점강 漸降 a gradual decline〔fall〕 ; (a) decrescendo 《*pl.* ～s》 《이》
†점거 占據 occupation ⇨ 점령
불법 — unlawful〔illegal〕 occupation
점검 點檢 inspection ; examination ; a roll call (인원의) —하다 inspect ; examine ; take a roll call of 《men》 ¶ 엔진을 철저히 점검해 보시는 게 좋을 겁니다 You'd better check out the engine thoroughly.
— 매매 sale on approval —자 an inspector 불시 — a spot check〔test〕 순회 — ¶ 순회 점검을 하다 make the walk-around inspection 《of the aircraft》 엔진 — an engine checkup 인원 — ¶ 인원 점검을 하다 call the roll ; take a roll-call 《of a class》 피복 — inspection of clothing
점고 漸高 a gradual rise〔elevation〕 —하다 rise〔ascend, increase〕 gradually
점괘 占卦 a divination sign ¶ 점괘가 좋다〔나쁘다〕 have a good〔an ill〕 divination sign
점근 漸近 a gradual approach —하다 approach gradually ; draw near
— 곡선 an asymptotic curve — 급수 〖기하〗 asymptotic series —산(법) successive approximation —선 〖기하〗 asymptotic curve —원 〖기하〗 asymptotic circle — 원뿔 〖수학〗 an asymptotic cone — 전개 asymptotic expansion
점대 占— divining-rods ; the lots〔sticks〕 cast for divination
점도 粘度 [점성(粘性)] viscosity ; [점성률] a coefficient of viscosity
점도표 占圖表 〖수학〗 a point chart
점두 店頭 a shop〔store〕 front ; a shop〔show〕 window (진열장) ¶ 점두를 파괴하다 damage a shop front
— 거래 〖주식〗 an over-the-counter transaction — 광고 a window advertisement — 매매 〖주식〗 over-the-counter dealings — 장식(술) window dressing〔trimming〕 — 장식사 a window dresser〔trimmer〕 — 장식 진열 window display — 판매 over-the-counter dealings
점둥이 點— [개] a brindled dog ; [사람] a person with a birthmark〔mole〕
점등 點燈 lighting —하다 light ; light a lamp ; turn〔switch〕 on a lamp ¶ 점등후 after dark
— 시간 the lighting hour — 장치 lighting system 가로〔옥외〕 — street 〔exterior〕 lighting
점등 漸騰 a gradual rise 《of price》 —하다 rise gradually
점락 漸落 a gradual fall 《of price》 ; moderate decline 《of price》 —하다 sag ; decline ; fall gradually
점력 粘力 viscosity ; stickiness
†점령 占領 occupation ; possession ; capture —하다 take ; occupy ; hold ; seize ; capture ; take possession of ; be in occupation of
—국 the occupying nation —군 the army of occupation ; occupation forces —비 occupation costs — 시대 the occupation years〔days〕 — 정책 an occupation policy —지 an occupied territory ; a territory under occupation — 지대 a zone of military occupation 군사 — military occupation 도시 — the capture of a city
점막 店幕 an inn ; a tavern
점막 粘膜 a mucous membrane ; a mucosa
— 분비물 rheum ; a mucous discharge
—선 a mucous gland
점멸 點滅 flickering —하다 flicker ; be on and off ; make flicker ; switch on and off
—기 a switch —등 an on-and-off light ; a flasher
점묘 點描 a sketch ; depiction〔description〕 of parts ; a partial depiction ; a spot(-ty) description ; 〖미술〗 painting with dots ; pointillism —하다 depict ; portray ; delineate
—주의 〖미술〗 pointillism — 화가 a pointillist — 화법 pointillism 인물 — personal sketches ; the (personal) profile 《of》
점박이 點— [동물] a dapple〔brindled〕 animal ; [사람] a person with a birthmark〔mole〕 ; [웃음거리] a laughingstock
점보 ① [거대한 것] a jumbo 《*pl.* ～s》 ② 〖사진〗 [프린트] a jumbo-sized 《photographic》 print ; [장치] the apparatus for making jumbo-sized prints
— 제트기〔로켓〕 a jumbo jet〔rocket〕
점서 占書 a book on divination ; a fortune(-telling) book
점석 苫席 a mourners' straw mat
점선 點線 a dotted line ; a perforated line ¶ 점선으로 표시된 부분 the part shown in dotted line // 점선을 긋다 draw a dotted line
점성 粘性 viscosity ; cohesion
점성 占星 divination by the stars ; horoscope
—가 an astrologer ; a stargazer —학〔술〕 astrology
†점수 點數 marks ; the number of marks ⇨ 점 ¶ 점수를 많이 따다 get good marks ; make a good score // 점수를 매기다 give marks ; mark
영어 — marks for English
점술 占術 the art of divination ; prognos-

tication ; fortune-telling

점신세 漸新世 〖지질〗 the Oligocene Age

†점심 點心 lunch(eon) ¶ 점심을 먹다 take〔have, eat〕 lunch ; lunch // 점심을 싸 가지고 다니다 bring one's own lunch

— 그릇 a lunch-box — 나절 the forenoon —때 lunch time ; noontime ; noon — 시간 the noon recess // 나는 매일 점심을 싸 가지고 다니기로 했다 I decided to brown-bag it every day.

점심바치다 點心— 〖민속〗 (a shaman) offer lunch (to the goddess of childbirth *samsin*) to pray for the long life of a baby

점안 點眼 —하다 apply eyewash 《to》 ; drop lotion in the eyes

—기 an eye dropper —수(水) an eye lotion ; eyewash

점액 粘液 mucus ; viscous fluid〔liquid〕 ¶ 점액성의 mucus ; viscous ; sticky

— 대변 liquid stool —변(便) mucous stool〔evacuation〕 — 분비 secretion of mucus — 분비선 a slime-gland —산(酸) 〖화학〗 mucic acid —선 a mucous gland — 세포 a mucilage cell —소(素) mucin — 수종(水腫) a myx(o)edema 《*pl.* -mata》 — 아메바 myxamoeba —질 a phlegmatic temperament ¶ 점액질의 사람 a person of phlegmatic temperament

점원 店員 a shop-assistant 《영》 ; a (shop) clerk 《미》 ; [판매원] a salesman 《*pl.* -men》 ; a saleslady 《영》 ; a salesgirl 《미》

*점유 占有 possession ; occupation ; occupancy —하다 occupy ; possess (oneself of) ; take possession of ; seize upon

—권 a possessory right —물 a thing possessed ; a possession ; property — 보전 preservation〔protection〕 of possession — 신고 an avowry —자 an occupant ; a possessor ; a seizer ; an occupier — 재산 personal property — 침탈(侵奪) 〖법〗 disseizin ; disseisin — 회복 recovery of possession 불법 — detention ; deforcement

점입가경 漸入佳境 approaching the climax —하다 grow more exciting ; approach the climax ; become more and more interesting

점자 點字 braille (points) ; raised letters ¶ 점자를 읽다 read braille type // 점자로 발행하다 publish 《a book》 in raised type〔braille〕

— 독법 finger-reading —법 the braille — 서사기(書寫器) a braille writer — 악보 braille music —책 books in braille〔raised letters〕 — 투표 a braille ballot

*점잔 a dignified air ¶ 점잔만 빼는 상사를 만나면 괴롭다 It's a pain when you've got a boss who always stands on his dignity.

점잔 부리다 관용 assume a dignified air ; behave in a genteel way ; put on airs

*점잖다 (be) dignified ; well-bred〔-behaved〕 ; respectable ; genteel ; decent ; grave ¶ 점잖은 사람 a fine gentleman // 점잖게 굴다 behave like a gentleman ; behave oneself // 점잖지 못하다 be disrespectable〔ill-bred, ill-mannered, misbehaved〕 // 점잖은 말을 쓰다 use refined〔graceful〕 language

점재 點在 —하다 be scattered〔studded, interspersed, dotted〕 《with》 ¶ 호반에는 별장들이 점재하고 있다 The lake side is dotted with villas.

점쟁이 占— a fortune-teller ; a diviner ; a prognosticator

점적 點滴 drops ; drippings ; [물방울] a drop of water ; [빗방울] raindrops

—기 a dropper —약 medicinal drops

*점점 漸漸 more and more (많이) ; less and less (적게) ; by degrees (차차) ; little by little ; bit by bit ; step by step ; by inches ; gradually ; increasingly ¶ 점점 더워지다 be getting hotter ; grow hotter by degrees // 점점 나빠지다 go from bad to worse // 점점 적어지다 grow less and less // 길은 점점 험해졌다 The road became steeper and steeper. // 이야기는 점점 재미있게 된다 The story is getting more and more interesting. // 높이 올라갈수록 공기는 점점 더 희박해진다 The higher we climb, the thinner the air is.

점점이 點點— [여기저기] here and there ; scattering ; sporadically ; [하나씩] item by item ; one by one ; article by article ¶ 물건을 점점이 세다 count 《articles》 one by one // 마을에 집이 점점이 흩어져 있었다 The village was dotted with houses.

점주 店主 a store-owner ; a shopkeeper ; the proprietor (of a store)

점증 漸增 a steady〔gradual〕 increase —하다 increase gradually〔steadily〕 ; rise steadily〔by degrees〕

점지 blessing 《a person》 with a son —하다 [신불(神佛)이] bless 《a person》 with a son

점직하다 (be) ashamed ; feel shame ; feel sorry

점진 漸進 gradual progress ; gradations ; slow but steady advance —하다 progress〔advance〕 gradually ; make gradual progress ; move step by step ¶ 점진적 gradual ; moderate

—주의 moderatism ; moderate principles ; gradual progressivism —주의자 a moderatist

점찍다 點— fasten〔set〕 one's eyes on 《a person》 ; mark out〔down〕 《a thing》 for 《some purpose》 ; [골라서] single 〔pick〕 out 《a house for hire》 ; fix one's choice on 《a person》 ¶ 범인으로 점찍다 suspect 《a person》 of a crime ; throw〔cast〕 suspicion 《on》

*점차 漸次 gradually ; by steps〔degrees〕 ;

little by little ; step by step ¶ 점차 나아지다 be getting better gradually ; show gradual improvement // 점차 퇴각하다 make a gradual retreat // 점차 진보하다 make gradual progress

*점착 粘着 viscosity ; adhesion ; cohesion —하다 stick〔adhere〕《to》; glue (together)
— 계수(係數) an adhesion coefficient —력 adhesive power ; adhesiveness ; viscosity —선(腺) an adhesive gland —성 adhesion ; viscosity ; stickiness ¶ 점착성의 cohesive ; sticky ; gluey // 점착성이 없는 inadhesive — 세포 an adhesive〔a glue〕 cell —제 an adhesive ; a gluing agent — 테이프 an adhesive tape 불(不)— 시험(試驗) a tack-free test

점철 點綴 —하다 dot ; be scattered〔studded〕《with》; intersperse ¶ 그곳엔 인가가 점철해 있다 The place is dotted with houses. // 바다에는 뱃불이 반딧불처럼 점철해 있다 The sea is studded with the glow-worm lights of the shipping.

점층법 漸層法 〖문법〗 climax ; gradation

*점치다 占— ⇨ 점(占)

*점토 粘土 clay ¶ 점토질의 clayey
—상(像) a figure in clay ; a clay figure — 세공(물) clay work —암 clay stone —질 모르타르 fireclay mortar — 채굴장 a clay pit —층 a clay layer —판(板) a clay tablet 백(白)— potter's clay 유(油)〔가소성(可塑性)〕— fat clay

점퇴하다 漸退— recede〔withdraw, retreat〕 gradually

점파 點播 sowing seeds with spaces between ; sowing in clusters

점판암 粘板岩 clay-slate stone ; argillite

점퍼 ⇨ 잠바

점포 店鋪 a shop 《영》; a store 《미》 ¶ 점포를 내다 open〔start〕 a shop ; keep a store // 점포를 닫다 close〔shut〕 up a store ; give up one's business // 큰 길에 점포를 내다 keep a store in the avenue
— 정리 판매 a going-out-of-business sale

점프 a jump —하다 jump

점하다 占— occupy ; hold ; take ; form ; account for ¶ 중요한 지위를 점하다 hold〔occupy〕 an important position // 3할을 점하다 form〔account for〕 30 percent // 제1위를 점하다 rank first // 의회에서 과반수를 점하다 have〔command〕 a majority in the Assembly // 그 회의에는 부인들이 다수를 점하고 있었다 Ladies predominated at the meeting.

점호 點呼 (a) roll call —하다 call〔take〕 the roll ; muster out ¶ 인원을 점호하다 take a roll call of men
일조〔일석〕— 〖군사〗 the morning〔evening〕 roll call 임시〔불시(不時)〕— a check〔surprise〕 roll call 지명(指名)— ¶ 지명 점호를 하다 call off the names 《of》

점화 點火 ignition ; lighting —하다 ignite ; light ; fire ¶ 다이너마이트에 점화하다 fire〔set off〕 a charge of dynamite
—관 an ignition tube —기 a lighter ; a firer —약 priming powders — 장치 a spark(ing)-plug ; an igniter —전(栓) a spark plug —지 fidibus ; a paper spill — 코일 an ignition coil 발파 — 장치 [광산의] portfire

접 [100개] a hundred 《fruit, bulbs, tubers》 ¶ 감 한 접 a hundred persimmons

접 a graft ; grafting ¶ 접붙이다 graft ; ingraft ; engraft ; put a graft into 《a stock》 // 자두 나무에 배를 접붙이다 graft the pear upon the plum

접각 接角 〖기하〗 a contiguous〔an adjacent〕 angle

접객 接客 reception of a guest ; entertaining a guest —하다 receive 《a guest》; welcome ; entertain 《a guest》
—부(婦) a cateress ; a serving girl ; a (restaurant) hostess

접객업 接客業 the service trade ; a personal service occupation〔trade〕; entertaining business
—자 an owner〔a proprietor〕 who runs entertainment business ; hotel and restaurant keepers

접견 接見 an interview ; a reception —하다 receive 《a person》; have an interview with 《a person》; give an interview
—실 an audience chamber〔room〕 —일 a reception day ; one's at-home day (사교상의)

접경 接境 a border (line) ; a border land (area) ; a boundary ; a frontier

접골 接骨 bonesetting —하다 set (a fractured or broken) bone
—술 the art of bonesetting —의 a bonesetter

†접근 接近 approach ; access ; closeness ; proximity ; approximation —하다 approach ; draw〔get〕 near ; (be) adjacent 《to》; come〔get〕 close ; (be) contiguous 《to》; adjoin ¶ 접근하기 쉬운 사람 an easily approachable〔accessible〕 person // 접근하기 어렵다 be difficult of access ; be inaccessible ; be unapproachable // 한일 양국의 접근을 도모하다 bring about better relations between Korea and Japan // 시일이 접근하다 The time draws near.
— 비행 ¶ 접근 비행하다 buzz 《another plane》 — 유속(流速) approach(ing) velocity —전 infighting (권투의) ; a close combat

접낫 a small sickle

†접다 [종이·옷 따위를] fold (up) ; strike 《a tent》; furl〔hand〕 《sail, a flag》; wrap up ; double ¶ 우산을 접다 fold up〔shut, close〕 an umbrella // 종이를 네겹으로 접다 fold paper into four leaves // 부채를 접

다 fold〔close〕 a fan∥그는 페이지의 구석을 접었다 He turned down the corner of the page. /He dog-eared the page

*접대 接待 reception ; welcome ; entertainment ── 하다 receive《guests》; entertain ; welcome ; treat ; serve ; wait on ¶ 손님을 접대하다 receive〔entertain〕 guests ∥접대를 잘하다 be hospitable ; be of good service

─ 담배 cigarettes〔cigars〕 offered to guests ─부 a cateress ; a serving girl ; a waitress ─비 reception expenses ─실 a reception room ─원 a receptionist ─ 위원 a reception committee ─일 a reception day

*접두사 接頭辭 〖문법〗 a prefix《to》 ¶ 접두사 붙이기 prefixation

접두어 接頭語 ⇨ 접두사(接頭辭)

접등 ─燈 a folding〔collapsible〕 lantern〔lamp〕

접때 not long ago〔before〕 ; the other day ; a few days ago〔earlier〕 ¶ 접때부터 for some days past∥접때 편지에 in one's late letter∥접때 만났을 때 the last time one saw《a person》

*접목 接木 grafting ; a grafted tree (나무) ── 하다 graft《trees》 together ; graft《a tree》 on《another》

*접미사 接尾辭 〖문법〗 a suffix

접미어 接尾語 ⇨ 접미사(接尾辭)

접변 接變 〖언어〗 progressive assimilation (of sounds) ── 하다 undergo〔show〕 progressive assimilation

접본 a stock〔stem〕 ; a grafted tree

접붙이다 接─ graft ⇨ 접목(-하다)

접빈 接賓 reception (of a guest) ; service for customers ── 하다 receive a guest ; entertain a guest

접사 接辭 〖언어〗 an affix

접선 接線 〖기하〗 a tangent (line) ; [접촉] a contact ── 하다 make contact《with》; contact ¶ 접선의 tangential

접속 接續 connection ; joining ; junction ── 하다 connect《with》; join《on》; link ; adjoin ¶ 본선에 접속된다 It connects with the main line.

─곡 〖음악〗 a medley ; a fantasia ; a potpourri (프) ─기 a circuit closer ─사 〖문법〗 a conjunction ; a connective (word) ─ 상자 a joint〔connection〕 box ─선 a connecting line ─역 a junction (station) ; a union station ─ 연관(鉛管) 〖전기〗 a lead sleeve ─ 플러그 〖전기〗 a connecting plug ─항 a port of connection 납땜 ─ a soldered joint 케이블 ─ a cable joint

접수 接受 receipt ; acceptance ── 하다 receive ; accept ; be in receipt of ; pick up (무전을) ¶ 무전을 접수하다 pick up a wireless message

─계 an information man ; a receptionist ─구 an usher's window〔desk〕 ; an inquiry office ─ 번호 a receipt number ─처 an information office 원서 ─ 기간 the time for application

접수 接收 seizure ; requisition ; taking over ── 하다 take over ; take control of ¶ 접수되어 있다 be under requisition ; be taken over∥철도를 접수하다 take over a railway∥건물이 점령군에게 접수되었다 The building was taken over by the occupation army.

─ 가옥 a requisitioned house ─ 해제 release ; derequisition

†접시 a plate (평평한) ; a dish (움푹한) ; a platter (큰) ; a saucer (받침 접시) ; a scale (저울의) ¶ 고기 한 접시 a dish of meat∥굴 한 접시 a plate of oysters∥음식을 접시에 담다 dish up〔out〕 food∥음식을 접시에 담아서 내놓다 serve food on a plate〔in a dish〕∥접시를 씻다 wash dishes

나무접시 놋접시 될까 (속담) Once a devil, always a devil. /Once a knave, and ever a knave.

접시꽃 〖식물〗 a hollyhock ; Althaea rosea (학명)

접신 接神 ── 하다 be possessed by〔with〕 a spirit

─론 theosophy

접안 接岸 ── 하다 [배가] come alongside the pier〔quay, berth〕

접안경 接眼鏡 an ocular (piece) ; an eyepiece

접안 렌즈 接眼─ ⇨ 접안경

접어 接語 〖문법〗 an affix

접어넣다 fold in ; turn〔tuck〕 in ; make a tuck in ; [3각 따위를] telescope ; [접어 끼우다] insert

접어들다 enter ; set in ; [세월이] approach ¶ 가을로 접어들다 the autumn (season) draws near〔approaches〕∥이달에 접어들더니 몹시 춥다 The weather has been extremely cold since the beginning of this month. ∥경제가 불경기로 접어든건 아닌지 모르겠군 I'm wondering if we are all heading toward a recession.

접어 주다 [너그럽게 보아 주다] overlook《a person's fault》 ; tolerate ; pass over ; shut〔close〕 one's eyes to ; [유리한 조건을 붙여주다 (바둑 따위에서)] give an advantage of ; give a head start of ¶ 자네 행위를 이번만은 접어 주겠네 I will overlook your behavior for this once. ∥나는 자네에게 다섯점 접어 주겠네 I will give you a five point advantage《in playing *Badook*》.

접의자 摺椅子 a folding〔collapsible〕 chair ; a camp chair

접자 摺─ a carpenter's rule ; a jointed measuring stick ; a folding ruler

접전 接戰 a hand-to-hand fight ; close (-range) fighting ; [선거] a close contest ; [경기] a close〔hard〕 game ── 하다 fight hand-to-hand〔at close quarters〕 ; [경기에서] have a close contest〔game〕 ¶ 접

전 끝에 after playing a seesaw game // 그 시합은 의외로 접전이 되었다 It came out a closer match than any one had thought possible.

접점 接點 『기하』 a point of contact

‡접종 接種 inoculation ; vaccination **—하다** inoculate ; vaccinate
— 요법 a vaccine cure — 재료 inoculum —침(針) a vaccinating lancet 병균 — ¶ 병균 접종을 하다 inoculate 《a person》 with viruses 비시지 접종 — inoculation of BCG 《Bacillus Calmette-Guérin》 예방 — preventive inoculation

접종 接踵 **—하다** follow on the heels of ; come〔follow〕 in the wake of ; occur one after another ; arise in succession ¶ 크고 작은 사건들이 접종하여 일어났다 Events, great and small, occurred in (rapid) succession.

접지 『전기』 ground〔earth〕 connection ; grounding ; a ground ; an earth **—하다** earth
—선 a grounding〔an earthing〕 conductor — 장치 an earthing device ; a ground system

접지 摺紙 folding paper ; paper〔sheet〕 folding **—하다** fold paper (to bind a book)
— 기계 a folding machine ; a folder

접지 a branch graft(ing) ; a slip

접질리다 get sprained ; be wricked ¶ 발목을 접질리다 have one's ankle sprained

접착 接着 『화학』 adhesion ; glueing ; 『식물』 syndesis **—하다** stick to ; adhere to —력 adhesive strength —성 adhesive property —제 adhesives ; a bonding〔an adhesive〕 agent

접책 摺册 a folding book ; a folder

접척 摺尺 ⇨ 접자

접첨접첨 with fold after fold ; into many folds **—하다** fold over and over

†접촉 接觸 contact ; touch ; 『기하』 tangency ; contingence ; osculation **—하다** touch ; make contact ; come in〔into〕 contact〔touch〕 《with》 ; be close 《to》 ¶ 접촉을 계속하다 keep in touch〔contact〕 with 《a person》 // 접촉을 잃다 get out of touch with 《a person》 // 청년들과 접촉을 계속함으로써 through contact with young people // 세상과 접촉을 끊다 be out of touch with the world // 사람들과 자주 접촉하여 경험을 쌓다 acquire experience of the world from frequent contact with people // A를 B에 접촉시키다 bring A into contact with B // 그는 사업상 여러 층의 사람들과 접촉한다 The nature of his business throws him into contact with all sorts of men.
—각 a contact angle — 감염 contagion — 곡선 an osculating curve —기(器) 『전기』 a contactor —대(帶) a contact zone —면(面) a contact surface — 반응 a catalysis — 반응력 catalytic power —법 the contact process — 변성암 a contact metamorphic rock — 변성 작용 『화학』 contact catalysis — 변환(變換) 『수학』 contact transformation —부(部) [기계 따위의] a contacting part — 분석 『화학』 catalytic analysis — 분해 『화학』 catalytic cracking — 분해 장치 a catalytic cracker — 비행 contact flying ; a contact flight —성(性) 알레르기 『의학』 contact allergy —성 질환 a contagious disease —원(圓) 『수학』 an osculating circle —자(者) 『의학』 a contact —자(子) 『전기』 a contact maker — 작용 『화학』 contact catalysis — 전기 contact electricity — 전위차(電位差) contact potential difference — 전이(轉移) 『의학』 a contact metastasis 《*pl.* -ses》 —점 a point of contact〔tangency〕 —제 『화학』 a contact agent — 조사 [성병 따위의] contact tracing —편(片) 『기계』 a contact segment ; a contactor — 평면 『수학』 an osculating plane — 한계표 『철도』 a clearance post —호(弧) an arc of contact 개인적 — personal contact〔touch〕 단시간(單時間) — [적과의] a brush

접치다 fold ; furl (우산을) ; collapse (책상을)

접치이다 get folded

접침 摺枕 a folding〔collapsible〕 pillow〔headrest〕

접칼 摺— a folding knife ; a pocketknife

접칼 a grafting knife

접피술 接皮術 skin graft(ing) ; transplantation of skin

†접하다 接— ① [접촉하다] be close 《to》 ; come in contact〔touch〕 《with》 ; [인접하다] touch ; border on ; adjoin ; be adjacent 《to》 ¶ 러시아에 접한 소국 small nations bordering the Russia. // 환자와 접하다 come in contact with sick people // 동쪽은 태평양과 접해 있다 It is bounded by the Pacific on the east. // 집들이 서로 접해 있다 The houses adjoin each other.
② [응접하다] receive ; see ; have an interview 《with》 ¶ 방문객을 접하다 receive〔see〕 callers // 많은 사람을 접하다 come in contact with many people // 문학에 접하다 have〔get〕 access to literature
③ [받다] receive ; have ; get ¶ 부고에 접하다 hear of 《a person's》 death ; receive the news of 《a person's》 death

*접합 接合 union ; joining ; junction **—하다** unite ; connect ; join ; put together
—구(具) 『건축』 a connector — 렌즈 a cemented lens —면(面) commissure —부(部) a copula — 세포 zygosis — 식물 a zygophyte —자 〔체〕 zygote 〔zygospore〕 —재(材) a binder —제(劑) glue — 혈관 inosculation

접히다 ① [접다] get folded ; be furled ② [바둑에서] take a handicap ; receive odds ¶ 세 겹으로 접히다 be folded in

three // 두 점이 접히다 take odds of two points
젓 pickled〔salted〕 fish〔shrimps, etc.〕
—국 pickling brine ; pickle juice —국지 brine-soaked radishes 새우— pickled shrimps ¶ 새우젓을 담다 pickle shrimps 조개— pickled clams
젓가락 (a pair of) chopsticks
— 통 a chopstick holder〔case〕
젓갈¹ ⇨ 젓
젓갈² ⇨ 젓가락
젓갖 a leash (attached to a hawk's jess)
†젓다 ① [배를] row ; work at oars ; scull ; paddle ② [액체를] stir ; churn ; beat ; whip ③ [손을] sign ; gesticulate ; [머리를] shake ¶ 배를 젓다 row〔oar〕 a boat // 한번 크게 젓다 row a (long) stroke // 달걀을 젓다 beat up an egg // 고개를 젓다 shake one's head ; say "no" // 한 사람 한 사람이 다 열심히 노를 저었다 Each man pulled hard at the oars.
젓대 〖악기〗 a flute ; the body of a flute
젓조기 yellow corbinas for pickling
정¹ [쇠연장] a chisel ; a burin
정² [참으로] really ; indeed ; quite ; very
정³ 丁 ① [십간(十干)의] the fourth of the ten celestial stems〔calendar signs〕 ② [차례의] the fourth ; No. 4 ; D ; [등급의] the fourth grade ; grade D
정⁴ 正 [옳음] justice ; righteousness ; 〖수학〗 [정수] positive (number) ; plus
정⁵ 情 [감정] feeling ; [정서] emotion ; [애정] love ; affection ; [정조] sentiment ; [열정] passion ; [인정] human nature ; [동정] sympathy ; compassion ; [심정] heart ¶ 부부의 정 conjugal affection // 그리운 정 longing ; yearning // 어머니에 대한 정 affection for one's mother // 아이들에 대한 어머니의 정 a motherly affection toward children // 정을 주다 set one's affections on 《a person》 // 여자와 정이 들다 become attached to〔grow fond of〕 a girl // 정이 많다 be warmhearted〔kind-hearted〕
오는 정이 있어야 가는 정이 있다 (속담) To give one as one gets.
정 亭 [정자] an arbor ; cottage ; a bower ; [요정] a restaurant
정 町 [거리] a unit of distance 《c. 109 m》 ; [면적] a unit of area 《c. 99 ares》
정 鉦 〖악기〗 a gong
정 整 [금액] net〔neat〕 amount ¶ 3만원정 a clear 30,000 *won*
정 錠 a tablet ; a tabloid
정 艇 a boat ¶ 제7호정 No. 7 boat
정 精 ① [정수] ⇨ 정수(精髓) ; [정액] ⇨ 정액(精液) ; [정기] ⇨ 정기(精氣) ② [정령] a spirit ; a sprite
정 靜 quiet ; peace ; inactivity ¶ 동중정(動中靜)이다 Rest amidst motion./Perpetually unmoved in the mind while constantly moving with the world.
정가¹ —하다 harp on bygones
정가² 〖식물〗 a kind of pigweed〔goosefoot〕
정가 正價 a normal〔true, fair〕 price ; (net) price
†정가 定價 a fixed〔set, definite, marked〕 price ; the price ¶ 정가에 팔다 sell at the fixed price ; make no reduction // 정가의 1할을 빼다 make〔allow〕 a discount of 10 per cent on regular prices // 정가를 붙이다 set a price 《on a thing》 // 정가를 올리다〔내리다〕 raise〔lower〕 the price // 이것은 정가 5백원입니다 This is priced at five hundred *won*. // 값이 비싼 물건을 정가대로 다 주고 사면 바가지를 쓴 기분이 든다 If I pay a full price for a big-ticket item, I feel like being ripped off.
—표(票) a price tag —표(表) a price-list ; a priced catalog(ue) —표 가격 list price
정가극 正歌劇 a grand opera ; opera seria 《이》
정각 正刻 the exact time ; [부사적] just ; sharp ¶ 정각 5시에 just at five ; at five sharp〔exactly〕 // 정각 1시에 오너라 Come at one o'clock sharp〔at exactly one o'clock〕. // 매시 정각 Every hour on the hour. // 그는 늘 정각에 나타난다 He always shows up right on the dot.
정각 定刻 the appointed〔fixed〕 time ; scheduled time (기차 따위의) ¶ 기차가 정각에 도착하였다 The train came on time. // 일을 정각에 시작하여야 한다 We should always be on time at work. // 그는 오늘 정각보다 30분 늦었다 He is half an hour behind time today. // 그는 정각에 돌아오지 못했기 때문에 벌받았다 He was punished as he failed to return by the appointed time. // 서울에서 오전 7시 30분에 출발하여 오후 8시 30분까지 매시 한 편씩 있습니다 동경에서는 오전 8시부터 오후 9시까지 매시 정각에 출발합니다 The first flight from Seoul is at 7 : 30 in the morning and thereafter every hour at 30 minutes past the hour until 8 : 30 in the evening. From Tokyo, the plane departs every hour on the hour from 8 a. m. until 9 p. m.
정각 頂角 〖기하〗 a vertical angle
정간 停刊 suspension of publication ; discontinuance of publication —하다 suspend publication ; stop issue ¶ 신문의 정간을 해제한다 release the suspension of a newspaper
정간 井間 a checker square ; a check ; a square
—지 a squared-paper underlay (used as a writing guide)
정갈스럽다 ⇨ 정갈하다
정갈하다 (be) neat and proper ; clean ; smart ; trim ; dapper ; tidy ; snug ¶ 방을 정갈하게 치우다 keep a room neat and clean
정감 情感 feeling ; emotion ; sentiment ¶ 정감을 나타내다〔감추다〕 show〔conceal〕

one's feelings // 정감에 호소하다 appeal to 《a person's》 feelings
정강 政綱 a political principle〔creed〕; [정당의] a policy ; a party platform ; a plank (조목) ¶ 신당의 정강 the platform of a new party
정강마루 the ridge of the shin
정강말 riding shanks' mare〔pony〕; a hike 《미》 ¶ 정강말하다 go on a walking tour ; foot it ; ride〔go on〕 shanks' mare ; walk ; hike 《미》
*정강이 the shin ; shank ¶ 정강이뼈 the tibia ; a shinbone // 정강이를 차다 kick 《a person》 in the shin
— 받이 leg-guard (경기용의) ; greave (갑옷의)
정객 政客 a politician
정객 正客 the guest of honor
*정거 停車 ⇨ 정차
†정거장 停車場 a railroad〔railway〕 station ; a depot 《미》; a stand (자동차 따위의) ¶ 갈아 타는 정거장 a junction〔transfer〕 station // 다음 정거장은 어디요 What is the next stop ?
— 구내 the station yard〔premises〕 — 대합실 a station waiting room 중간 — an intermediate station 중앙 — [런던의] the Central Station
정격 正格 a proper form〔formality〕; regularity ¶ 정격의 regular ; correct ; orthodox
— 활용 a regular conjugation
정격 定格 〖전기〗 rating
— 전류 a rated current
정견 定見 [견해] a definite view〔opinion〕; [학설] a fixed opinion ; [정책] a fixed policy ; [주의] a fixed principle ; [확신] a conviction ¶ 정견이 있는〔없는〕 사람 a man of〔without〕 settled convictions // 그에게는 정견이 없다 He has no definite view.
정견 政見 one's political views ; the platform (정당의) ¶ 정견의 차이 political differences // 정견을 발표하다 state〔set forth〕 one's political views // 정견을 달리하다 have different political views ; differ 《from a person》 in political views
— 발표회 a meeting for the announcement of one's political views ; a campaign meeting — 방송 broadcast of political opinions
정결 貞潔 chastity ; faithfulness —하다 (be) chaste and pure ; faithful ¶ 정결한 부인 a chaste〔faithful〕 wife
정결 淨潔 cleanliness ; neatness —하다 (be) clean and neat ; undefiled ; sanitary ¶ 정결히 하다 clean up ; cleanse ; make〔keep〕 clean // 부엌을 정결히 하다 keep the kitchen clean
정경 情景 [민망한 광경] a pathetic〔touching〕 scene〔sight〕
정경 政經 politico-economic (s) ; political economy ; politics and economics
— 분리 원칙 the principle of separation of political matters from economic matters —학부 the Department of Politics and Economics
정경 正經 ① [정도] the path of righteousness〔virtue〕; the straight path ; the right track ② 〖기독교〗 the canon ; the canonical books (of the Bible) ; the canonized books
정경 분리 政經分離 the separation of economy and politics —하다 separate〔sever〕 economy from politics
—론 divisibility of politics and economy
— 정책 a policy separating economy from politics
정계 淨界 an undefiled place ; holy confines
정계 正系 a legitimate line ; direct lineage〔descent〕
정계 政界 the political world ; political circles ¶ 정계의 거물 a great figure in politics // 정계의 원로 an eldest statesman // 정계의 불안 political unrest // 정계의 움직임 a political trend // 정계에 들어가다 enter〔go into〕 politics // 정계에서 은퇴하다 retire from political life // 정계의 사정에 통하다 be familiar with political affairs // 그는 정계에 있다 He is in politics.
정계 定界 a (fixed) boundary ; delimitation ; demarcation —하다 fix the boundaries ; delimitate ; demarcate the frontier line
정곡 正鵠 the main point ; the mark ; the bull's-eye ¶ 정곡을 찌르다 hit the mark ; hit the nail on the head ; be to the point // 정곡을 잃다 miss the mark ; be not to the point
정골 整骨 ⇨ 접골(接骨)
정공 正攻 a frontal attack —하다 make a frontal attack ; fight openly and squarely ; play fair ¶ 양면 정공법 a double frontal attack
정과 正果 fruits preserved in honey
정과 正課 (a subject of) the regular curriculum ; a required course ¶ 정과 외의 과목 an extra-curricular subject
정관 定款 articles of association〔incorporation〕; a statute ¶ 정관으로 규정되다 be fixed by the articles of association
정관 靜觀 serene contemplation ; watchful waiting —하다 watch ; await calmly〔watchfully〕; wait and see ; contemplate ¶ 되어가는 형편을 정관하다 await developments watchfully〔calmly〕 // 정관적 태도를 취하다 take〔assume〕 a wait-and-see attitude
—적 태도 a wait-and-see attitude 《toward》 — 정책 a policy of watchful waiting ; a wait-and-see policy —주의 a wait-and-see policy
정관 精管 〖해부〗 a spermaduct ; a seminal duct
— 수술 vasectomy

정관사 定冠詞 the definite article
부— the indefinite article
정광 精鑛 〖야금〗 a concentrate
정교 政敎 [정치와 종교] church and state ; religion and politics ; [정치와 교육] politics and education ; state and school
— 분리 the separation of church and state〔religion and politics〕 — 일치 the union of church and state
정교 情交 [친교] intimate friendship ; intimacy ; [육체 관계] illicit intercourse〔relations〕 ; sexual intimacy ; a liaison —하다 form a friendship ; have intimate relations ; become intimate 《with》 ; have illicit intercourse 《with》 ; establish a liaison
⁑정교 精巧 elaborateness ; exquisiteness ; ingenuity ; delicacy —하다 (be) elaborate ; exquisite ; delicate ; ingenious ; fine ¶ 정교한 기계 an elaborate〔a delicate〕 machine // 당신 스웨터는 무늬가 정교하군요 Your sweater has an intricate pattern.
정교 正敎 orthodoxy
—회 the Orthodox Church
정교사 正敎師 a regular teacher ; a licensed teacher
†정구 庭球 (lawn-) tennis —하다 play tennis
—계 the tennis world ¶ 정구계 제1인자 a net ace —공 a tennis-ball —부 the Lawn Tennis club — 선수 a tennis player — 선수권 a tennis championship ; a net title — 시합 a (lawn-) tennis match —장 a (lawn-) tennis court 경〔연〕식 — hard〔soft〕 ball tennis 단식 — tennis singles 복식 — tennis doubles
정국 政局 the political situation ¶ 정국의 위기 a political crisis // 정국의 추이 a political development // 정국을 수습하다 save a political situation // 정국을 담당하다 assume the helm of government // 정국을 타개하다 break a political deadlock
— 안정〔불안정〕 the stability〔instability〕 of a political situation 국제 — international political situation
정권 政權 political power ; power ; the reins of government ¶ 중국의 공산당 정권 the Communist regime in China // 클린턴 정권 the Clinton administration // 정권에 대한 욕심 the lust for political power // 정권을 잃다 go out of power // 정권을 유지하다 stay in power // 정권을 장악하다 come to〔into〕 power ; take〔seize〕 power ; rise to power ; take the reins of government // 공화당이 정권을 장악하고 있다 The Republican Party is in power〔the saddle〕.
— 교체(交替) a change of regime ¶ 평화적인 정권 교체 a peaceful turnover of political power —욕(欲) ambition〔desire〕 for political power — 장악 ¶ 정권 장악을 하고 있다 be in power — 쟁탈 a scramble for political power — 획득 accession to power 괴뢰 — a dummy government
정규 定規 [규칙] the fixed〔established〕 regulation〔rule〕 ; [자] a rule ; a ruler ; a square ; a standard
†정규 正規 regularity ; formality ; legality ¶ 정규의 regular ; legal ; proper // 정규의 수속을 밟다 go through the prescribed〔legal〕 formalities〔due procedure〕 // 정규의 교육을 받지 못했다 He has not received formal school education.
— 곡선 〖통계〗 a normal〔probability〕 curve — 교육 regular〔formal〕 school education —군 a regular army — 루트 a regal channel —병 a regular (soldier) — 수속 the regular procedure —전 regular warfare
정극 正劇 a traditional〔legitimate, conventional, an orthodox〕 drama
정근 精勤 diligence ; industry ; regular attendance —하다 (be) diligent ; industrious ; be attentive to one's duties
—상 a prize for good attendance ¶ 그는 정근상을 탔다 He won a prize for regularity. —자 a person regular in attendance — 증서 a certificate of regular attendance
정글 a jungle
—짐 [운동 시설] a jungle gym
정금 正金 [정화] specie ; bullion〔specie〕 money ; [순금] pure gold ; solid gold ; bullion ; [현금] cash ; hard money ¶ 정금으로 지불하다 pay in cash // 정금으로 바꾸다 cash 《a bill》 ; turn 《a bond》 in cash ; encash
— 결핍 shortage of specie — 수송점 a specie point — 은행 a specie bank
정기 正氣 [바른 기풍] a fair and equitable spirit ; uprighteousness ; [천지의 원기] the spirit which animates and controls the universe
*정기 定期 a fixed time〔term, period〕 ; a regular interval ; a stated period ; 〖상업〗 the option market ¶ 정기의 fixed ; regular ; periodical // 정기로 periodically ; at regular intervals ; at stated periods
— 간행 a periodical publication — 간행물 periodicals ; periodical publications — 검사 a periodical inspection — 공연 [오케스트라의] a subscription concert — 공연 시즌 a subscription season — 국회 a regular session of the National Assembly —권 a commutation ticket ; a season ticket —권 사용자〔통근자〕 a commuter 《미》 ; a commutation passenger 《미》 ; a season-ticket holder 《영》 —금 money payable periodically ; the installments of the amount payable periodically ; a regular allowance — 대부 a time loan ; time money — 매매 time transactions — 보험 term insurance —불(拂) payment on

term ; a periodic payments —불 어음 a term〔time〕 bill —선(船) a (regular) liner ; a packet (boat) —성(性) periodicity — 승차권 a commutation〔season〕 ticket — 시험〔휴업, 검사〕 a regular examination〔holiday, inspection〕 — 연금 a terminable annuity — 열차 a regular train — 예금 a time〔fixed〕 deposit — 예금자 a time depositor — 운행 [버스의] a regular run — 조사 a routine checkup — 진단 a medical checkup at regular intervals — 집회 a regular meeting — 차입(借入) time money — 총회 a regular general meeting —풍(風) periodical winds — 항공 a scheduled flight ; regular airplane service — 항공기 an air liner — 항공로 an air route〔line〕 ; an airway — 항로〔운행〕 a regular line〔run〕 — 항해 regular steamer service — 휴가 regular〔periodic〕 holidays — 휴업일 a scheduled holiday

정기 精氣 essence ; spirit and energy

정나미 情— attachment ; affection ; fondness ; liking

정나미가 떨어지다 관용 be disgusted 《with》

정남 正南 due south

정남 貞男 a male virgin ; a sexually inexperienced man

정낭 精囊 a seminal vesicle ; a spermatic sac

정녀 貞女 a chaste woman ; [처녀] a virgin ; a maiden

정년 丁年 full age ; legal age ; majority ¶ 정년에 달하다 come〔be〕 of age ; be of legal age ; attain one's majority // 정년에 미달하다 be under age ; be in minority

정년 停年 the age limit ; retirement age ¶ 정년에 달하다 reach the age limit // 정년제를 두다 set an age limit // 정년으로 퇴직하다 retire due to age

—법 the age-limit law ; the retiring age law —제 the age-limit system — 퇴직 retirement due to the age limit

정념 情念 sentiments ; passions

정다각형 正多角形 an equilateral〔a regular〕 polygon

정다면체 正多面體 a regular polyhedron

정다시다 情— have bitter experiences ; be very careful not to repeat a blunder that one has been heavily scolded for ¶ 나는 그 일에는 정다셨네 Don't you ever think I will do it again !

정담 政談 a political talk〔chat〕 ; a discussion of politics

정담 情談 a friendly talk ; [남녀 간의] lovers' talk ; a tête-à-tête 《프》

정담 鼎談 a three-man talk ; a tripartite talk

***정답다 情—** (be) friendly ; affectionate ; tender ; loving ¶ 정다운 관계 intimate relations // 정다운 미소 an endearing smile // 정다운 누이〔편지〕 an affectionate sister〔letter〕 // 정다운 인사 warm greetings // 손님을 정답게 맞다 receive a visitor warmly // 아이들을 정답게 바라보다 look fondly〔wistfully, longingly〕 at one's children // 그 부부는 정답게 지낸다 They are an affectionate couple.

정당 正堂 the main hall〔building〕

†정당 正當 justness ; propriety ; lawfulness

—하다 (be) just ; right ; proper ; reasonable ; lawful ¶ 정당한 이유 없이 without good〔just〕 reason // 정당한 수단으로 by fair means // 정당한 법적 수속을 밟지 않고 without due process of law // 정당화하다 justify 《one's action》 // 정당하게 평가하다 do justice to // 사람을 정당하게 취급하다 give 《a person》 his due // 그는 정당하다 He is right〔justified, justifiable〕. // 그의 처벌은 정당하다 He deserves the punishment. // 목적은 수단을 정당화한다 The end justifies the means.

— 방위 legitimate self-defense ; legal defense — 행위 a lawful act —화(化) justification

†정당 政黨 a political party ¶ 정당 출신의 각료〔수상〕 a party minister〔premier〕 // 정당에 관계가 없는 non-partisan // 정당에 적을 두다 belong to〔be a member of〕 a political party // 정당에 관계하고 있지 않다 be not connected with any political party // 정당을 만들다 form a new political party

— 강령 a party platform 《미》 ; a party program 《영》 — 관계 party〔political〕 affiliations — 내각 a party cabinet ¶ 정당 내각을 조직하다 form a cabinet on party lines — 대회 a party convention — 법 the Political Party Law —색(色) a political coloring —원(員) a member of a political party ; a party man — 정치 party politics〔government〕 — 조직 party organization 계급 — a political party representing a particular social class 국민 — a popular party ; a political party representing the interests of all classes of citizens 급진 — a radical party 기성 — the existing political parties 보수 — a conservative party 양대 — both major political parties 진보 — a progressive party 혁신 — a reformist party 양대 — 주의 a two-party system 초—적 supra-party 《foreign policy》 ☞ ❙p. 1873❙

정대 正大 uprightness ; fairness ; justice

—하다 (be) fair ; just ; fair and square ; upright

정도 正道 justice ; the right〔true, orthodox〕 path ¶ 정도를 밟다 tread the path of virtue // 정도에서 벗어나다 stray from the right path // 사람을 정도로 이끌다 lead a person into the right path

정도 精度 precision ; accuracy ¶ 정도가 높다 be very accurate ; be highly precise

정도 征途 [정벌] a military expedition ;

정 당

정당(政黨) political party
정당 강령(政黨綱領) party platform [program]
보수 정당(保守政黨) conservative party
중도 정당(中道政黨) middle-of-the-road party; centrist party (★ 드물게 center party라고도 한다.)
혁신 정당(革新政黨) reformist party
당수(黨首) party leader [chairman]
당 조직(黨組織) party bureaucracy
당 대회(黨大會) party congress ⦅미⦆
당 노선(黨路線) party line
당 간부(黨幹部) party leaders; senior party members
간부회(幹部會) caucus ⦅미⦆
당 기관지(黨機關誌) party organ
당리당략(黨利黨略) party politics
당원(黨員) party member [man]
정규 당원(正規黨員) regular [registered] member
일반 당원(一般黨員) rank-and-file members (of the party); the rank-and-file; the general membership
당의 분열(分裂) split [split-up, break up] of a party
탈당하다(脫黨) withdraw [secede] from a party; leave [bolt, desert] a party
탈당자(脫黨者) secessionist [bolter, deserter] from a party
당내 파벌(黨內派閥) intraparty faction
파벌 투쟁(派閥鬪爭) factional struggle [squabble, dispute, war]
주류파(主流派) mainstream (faction); main streamer; main current

[여행] a journey; travel ¶ 정도에 오르다 go on an expedition〔a journey〕

†**정도 程度** [도] grade; degree; [분량] measure; [비율] rate; [범위] extent; [한도] limit; [표준] standard; level; [적도] moderation ¶ 정도 문제 a matter〔question〕 of degree // 생활 정도 the standard of living // 중학 정도의 학교 a school of the middle-school standard // 입학 시험의 정도 the standard of an entrance examination // 손해의 정도 the extent of the loss〔damage〕 // 어느 정도까지 to some degree; up to a certain point; to what extent // 정도의 차는 있어도 more or less // 정도를 높이다〔낮추다〕 raise〔lower〕 the standard // 정도를 지키다 keep within bounds; use moderation // 정도를 넘다 get out of bounds〔hand〕; be excessive; go beyond bounds〔limits〕 // 더운 정도가 아니다 "Hot" is not the word. // 네 말엔 어느 정도 진리가 있다 There is a certain degree of truth in what you say. // 불가능이라 해도 좋을 정도다 It is next to impossible. // 술을 마시는 것도 좋지만 정도 문제다 You may drink, but you must use moderation. // 이 책은 정도가 높다 This book is of higher standard // 그 정도다 That's probably about right. // 그 정도는 아니라고 생각한다 I don't think it was all that great. // 편안한 친구니까 그 정도까지 하지 않아도 괜찮다 He's just an old friend. There's no need to go out of your way for him.
생활 — the standard of living **지능** — an intellectual standard.

정독 精讀 careful reading; perusal; intensive reading **—하다** read carefully 〔with care〕; peruse

†**정돈 整頓** order; arrangement; adjustment **—하다** arrange; put in order; set〔put〕 to rights; order; adjust ¶ 정돈되어 있다 be in good shape〔order〕 // 정돈되어 있지 않다 be in disorder // 방을 정돈하다 arrange a room; put a room to rights〔in order〕 // 그의 방은 언제나 깨끗이 정돈되어 있다 His room is always in apple-pie order.

정돈 停頓 a standstill; a deadlock; a stalemate **—하다** come to a standstill; reach a deadlock; reach the end of the road ¶ 정돈 상태에 있다 be at a standstill // 정돈 상태를 타개하다 break the deadlock〔stalemate〕; bring a deadlock to an end // 전국이 정돈되었다 The military situation came to a standstill. // 내각이 이제 정돈 상태에 있다 The government is at a deadlock. // 그의 사업은 자금 부족으로 일시 정돈되었다 His business was embarrassed for a time by lack of funds.

정동 正東 due east

정동 精銅 refined copper

정동사 定動詞 〖문법〗 a finite verb

정들다 情— become attached ⦅to⦆; become familiar ⦅with⦆; become intimate ⦅with⦆; come to like〔love〕; acquire affection ⦅for⦆ ¶ 정든 님 one's beloved; one's love; one's lover // 정든 학생들 one's beloved students // 여자와 정들다 become fond of〔fall in love with〕 a girl // 그는 정든 부모 슬하를 떠나 외국 유학을 떠났다 He left his beloved parents and went abroad to study.

정들이다 like; love; take to; become attached to

정떨어지다 情— be disgusted 《with》; fall out of love 《with》; be disaffected 《with》; get sick of ¶ 정떨어지는 이야기 a disgusting story // 여자한테 정떨어지다 fall out of love with a girl; one's affection is turned from a girl // 그 녀석 미련한 데 정이 뚝 떨어진다 I am quite disgusted at〔with〕 his stupidity.

정란 靖亂 suppression; repression —하다 suppress a rebellion; quell〔put down〕 a revolt

정랑 情郞 a lover; a sweetheart

정략 政略 politics; political tactics; a political game〔move〕; a political maneuver ¶ 정략적 political // 정략적 책동 a political move // 그것은 일시의 정략에서 나온 조치이다 It is a measure dictated by political expediency.
—가 a political tactician — 결혼 a marriage of convenience

정량 定量 a fixed quantity; a standard capacity; a dose (내복약의)
— 분석 quantitative analysis

정려 精勵 diligence; industry; assiduity; close application —하다 apply oneself closely 《to》; be industrious; be diligent; be assiduous ¶ 직무에 정려하다 apply oneself closely to one's duties; attend diligently to one's duties

*정력 精力 energy; vigor; vitality; stamina ¶ 정력 왕성한 energetic; vigorous // 정력 절륜의 사람 a man of enormous energy〔vigor〕; an energetic person // 정력을 집중하다 put all one's energies into 《one's work》 // 정력이 다하다〔을 낭비하다〕 exhaust〔waste, dissipate〕 one's energy // 정력을 돋우다 invigorate; energize // 그는 활동가이며 정력가이다 He is active and energetic. // 그는 공부에 있어서는 무서운 정력가이다 He is frightfully energetic at his studies.
—가 a man of energy〔pith〕

정력 감퇴 精力減退 a decline in energy

정력학 靜力學 ⇨ 정역학

정련 精練 good training〔drill〕 —하다 drill〔train〕 well
— 가마 a boiling kier〔keir〕 —병 trained troops —용 비누 scouring soap —제 a scouring agent

정련 精鍊 refining; smelting (구리의); tempering (철의) —하다 refine; smelt; purify
—로(爐) a smelting〔reducing〕 furnace —소 a refinery; a smelting works; a smeltery —업 the refining industry —업자 a refiner 진공 — vacuum refining

†정렬 貞烈 chastity; virtue —하다 (be) virtuous; chaste
— 부인 a lady of virtue; highly virtuous 〔very chaste〕 lady

*정렬 整列 standing in line; a parade; an array; a lineup —하다 stand〔form〕 in line; be drawn up; line up; get into line ¶ 정렬하여 기다리다 wait in line // 도로에 정렬하다 line the route // 5열로 정렬하다 be drawn up five lines deep

정령 政令 a government〔a cabinet〕 ordinance〔order, decree〕

정령 精靈 a soul〔of the deceased〕; the spirit; the ghost
—설 『철학』 animism; spiritualism — 숭배 spiritism

†정례 定例 fixed rule〔regulation〕; a usage; a custom; a precedent ¶ 정례의 usual; customary; ordinary; regular // 정례에 따라 according to usage
— 국무 회의 a regular Cabinet meeting — 기자 회견 a regular press conference〔interview〕

정로 正路 ① [대로] the main road ② [올바른] the true〔right, orthodox〕 path; righteousness; the right principle

정론 正論 a sound〔just〕 argument; a fair view ¶ 자네 주장이 정론이야 I admit the justice of your argument. /You are right.

정론 定論 an established theory; an established〔settled〕 view〔opinion〕

정론 政論 political arguments〔discussions〕; politics ¶ 정론을 하다 discuss current political affairs〔matters〕; talk politics

정류 停留 a stop; stoppage —하다 stop; halt; make〔come to〕 a stop
— 기호 『음악』 a hold; a pause —장 a stop; a stopping place; a station; a stand; a depot 《미》 버스 —장 a bus stop 전차 —장 a car stop; a tram stop

정류 精溜 『화학』 rectification; refinement; purification —하다 rectify; purify; refine
—관(管) a rectifying column — 주정 refined spirits; rectified alcohol

정류 整流 rectification (of electricity) —하다 rectify; adjust
— 검파기 a rectifying detector —기 rectifier —자 a commutator —자 전동기 a commutator motor — 작용 rectifying action — 전류 a rectified current — 진공관 a rectification tube 전파(全波)〔반파(半波)〕 — full-〔half-〕wave rectification 수은〔알루미늄〕 —기 a mercury〔an aluminum〕 rectifier 전환(轉換) —기 a commutator rectifier 접해(接解)〔전해(電解)〕 —기 a contact〔an electrolytic〕 rectifier

정률 定率 a fixed rate
— 감가 상각법(減價償却法) the declining balance method of depreciation —세 proportional taxation

정률 定律 『물리』 a fixed law

정리 正理 truth; reason; logic ¶ 정리에 맞는 행동 a righteous act

정리 廷吏 a court clerk

정리 定理 a theorem ¶ 다항〔2항〕식 정리 polynomial〔binomial〕 theorem

*정리 整理 arrangement; regulation;

adjustment ; readjustment ; disposal —하다 regulate ; arrange ; put in order ; adjust ; readjust ; straighten out ; dispose of ¶ 가사를 정리하다 adjust one's household affairs // 교통을 정리하다 regulate〔control〕 traffic // 부채를 정리하다 clear off one's debts // (회계) 장부를 정리하다 adjust accounts // 유고를 정리하다 arrange《a person's》 posthumous manuscripts // 재정을 정리하다 readjust〔straighten〕 one's finances〔financial affairs〕// 인원을 정리하다 reduce〔cut down〕 the staff // 이 서류 좀 정리하여 보관해 주세요 File these papers, please. // 재고 정리 세일 Clearance sale. // 이사한 뒤에 정리는 다했니 Have you gotten things organized since your move? // 나는 생각을 정리할 수가 없었다 I wasn't able to pull my thoughts together.
— 공채 a consolidated public loan ; funded loans — 기금 consolidated funds — 번호 a reference number —부(部) 〖신문〗 the copydesk —부원 a copyreader ; a deskman —부장 the copy editor —안(案) a readjust —자 an adjuster — 자금 consolidated capital —장(欌) a commode ; a filing cabinet ; a chest of drawers —표(票) an order ticket —품 [파산 따위로 인한] distress goods〔merchandise〕 경지 — the readjustment of (rice-) fields 구획 — city〔town〕 planning 인원 — curtailment of personnel ; reduction of the staff 행정 — administrative readjustment 문서 —계 a filer

정리 情理 reason and sentiment〔feeling〕; heart and mind ; humanity ¶ 정리를 다하여 타이르다 reason with《a person》; expostulate《with a person》《on》 // 정리를 다하여 타일렀지만 그는 듣지 않았다 He would not listen to reason, however hard I might try (to persuade him). // 그것이야말로 정리를 겸하였다 하겠습니다 Indeed it may be called an example of justice combined with mercy.

정립 鼎立 a triangular position —하다 take〔be in〕 a triangular position ; be in a three-cornered contest ; stand in a trio ¶ 당시 3국은 서로 정립하고 있었다 At that time the three countries were opposed to one another.
—전 a three-cornered contest

정립 定立 〖논리〗 a thesis《*pl.* theses》

†정말 正— truth ; reality ; a fact ; [부사적] really ; truly ; in truth ; in earnest ; seriously ; quite ; indeed ; very ¶ 정말 같은 likely ; plausible ; specious // 정말 같은 이야기 a likely story // 정말 같은 거짓말 a plausible lie // 정말은 really ; in fact ; as a matter of fact // 정말로 알아듣다 believe ; take seriously // 정말로 말하자면 to tell the truth ; truth to tell // 정말을 말하다 speak the truth // 정말로 아름답다 It is really beautiful. // 정말인지 모르겠다 I wonder if it is true. // 그녀는 그의 말을 정말로 들었다 She believed him〔what he said〕. // 정말 감사합니다 I thank you very much. // 정말일까 Can it be true? // 그 소문이 정말일까 Is there any truth in the rumor? // 정말 잘한다 That really takes the cake!

정말 丁抹 ⇨ 덴마크

정맥 精麥 barley cleaning ; [보리] cleaned barley —하다 clean barley
—기 a barley processor ; a barley-〔wheat-〕cleaning machine

*‡정맥 靜脈 〖해부〗 a vein ¶ 정맥의 venous ; veiny // 정맥 내의 intravenous
— 경화증 phlebosclerosis — 계통 the venous system —류(瘤) a varix《*pl.* varices》; a varicosity ; varicocele —압(壓) venous pressure —염(炎) phlebitis — 울혈 venous congestion〔stasis〕; venosity — 주사 a venous injection —혈 venous flood 소— a veinlet 안면 — a facial vein 요(腰)— the lumbar veins

†정면 正面 the front side ; the frontage ; the front ; the facade ¶ 정면의 front ; frontal // 정면에 in front of // 정면에서 본 얼굴 a full face // 정면의 입구 the front entrance // 정면에 앉다 sit in front // 정면 공격하다 make a frontal attack // 정면 충돌하다 collide head-on《with》; have a head-on collision《with》// 정면으로 반대하다 be (dead) against《a matter》; publicly oppose // 바람을 정면으로 받다 face the wind // 보통 사람이 강타를 정면으로 받는다면 병원에 실려갈 것이다 If an ordinary person took a blow full force, he'd be off to the hospital.
— 공격 a frontal attack —도 a front view —석 the front bench (의회 따위의) ; the dress circle (극장의) ; the stalls (극장의)
건물 — the front〔facade〕 of a building

정명 定命 ① [숙명] fate ② [수명] the predetermined length of life ; one's span of life ; the destined duration of life
—론 fatalism ; determinism —론자 a fatalist ; a determinist

정모 正帽 a full dress hat ; a formal hat

정묘 丁卯 〖민속〗 the 4th year of the sexagenary cycle ; the Year of the Hare

정묘 精妙 exquisiteness ; fineness ; ingenuity —하다 (be) exquisite ; fine ; subtle ; delicate

정무 政務 [국무] affairs of state ; state affairs ; [공무] official business ; administrative work ¶ 정무를 보다 administer the affairs of state ; attend to official business
—관 an administrative official — 위원 a political committeeman ; a political committee《총칭》 — 차관 a parliamentary vice-minister

*정문 正門 the front gate ; the main entrance ¶ 정문으로 들어가다 go〔come〕

in at the main gate
정문 正文 the (official) text ¶ 조약의 정문 the text of a treaty
정문 頂門 the crown of the head ; the pate ¶ 정문에 일침을 놓다 give an admonition to the point
— **일침** an incisive remonstrance ; a vital warning ; a home thrust ; a finger on the sore spot ; a piercing reproach
정물 靜物 inanimate objects ; still life
— **사진** a still photo ; a still-life picture —**화** a picture of still life —**화가** a still-life painter
정미 丁未 〖민속〗 the 44th binary term of the sexagenary cycle
정미 精米 rice polishing ; rice cleaning ; polished rice —**하다** polish 〔clean〕 rice
—**기** a rice-polishing〔cleaning〕 machine
—**소** a rice mill
정미 精美 refined beauty ; supreme beauty ; elegance ; exquisiteness —**하다** (be) exquisitely〔exceedingly〕 beautiful
정미 精微 fineness ; delicacy ; minuteness ; subtlety —**하다** (be) minute ; fine ; delicate ; subtle
정미 正味 net content ; net weight ¶ 정미 1파운드 one pound net
†**정밀 精密** minuteness ; precision ; accuracy —**하다** [세밀하다] (be) minute ; close ; detailed ; precise ; [정확하다] precise ; exact ; accurate ¶ 정밀히 minutely ; closely ; thoroughly ; in detail ; elaborately ; precisely ; exactly ; accurately // 정밀한 보고 a minute report // 정밀한 조사 a close investigation // 정밀한 지도 a detailed map // 이 기계는 정밀히 검사되었다 A thoroughgoing inspection has been made with this machine.
— **검사** close examination 《of》 — **계기(計器)** a precision gauge — **계획** a detailed plan — **공업** precision manufacture — **공작 기계** a precision machine tool — **과학** an exact science — **기계** a precision instrument — **선반(旋盤)** a precision lathe — **지도** a detailed map — **폭격** precision〔pinpoint〕 bombing —**화** a miniature
정밀 靜謐 tranquility ; peace —**하다** (be) tranquil ; peaceful
***정박 碇泊, 渟泊** anchorage ; anchoring ; mooring —**하다** cast〔come to〕 anchor ; moor ; berth ¶ 항구에 정박하고 있는 배 a ship (lying) at anchor in the harbor // 정박 중이다 be〔lie〕 at anchor
— **기간** lay days —**등** a riding lamp —**료** anchorage dues ; demurrage —**선** a ship at anchor —**세(稅)** anchorage ; berthage ; ground ; groundage 《영》 —**소** an anchorage ; a moorage ; a berth — **위치** a berth — **일수 초과 할증금(日數超過割增金)** demurrage —**지** an anchorage —**항** an anchorage harbor **초과** — demurrage
†**정반대 正反對** direct opposition ; the exact reverse ; just the opposite ¶ 정반대의 diametrical ; opposite〔opposed〕 ; quite contrary to ; reverse // 정반대로 diagonally〔directly〕 opposite 《to》 ; diametrically // 정반대의 방향으로 in the opposite direction // 그것과 이것과는 정반대이다 It is the other way round. /It is just the opposite. // 너의 의견과 그녀의 의견이 정반대니 내가 난처하다 I'm in a bind because your opinion and hers are diametrically opposed.
정반합 正反合 〖철학〗 thesis-antithesis-synthesis
정방 丁方 south by west ; south-southwest
정방 精紡 (fine) spinning
—**기** a (fine) spinning machine〔frame〕
정방형 正方形 a (regular) square ; a perfect〔an exact〕 square ¶ 정방형의 square ; quadrate // 정방형으로 자르다 cut square
정배 定配 exile ; banishment —**하다** banish ; exile ¶ 정배 가다 go into exile // 정배 보내다 condemn 《a person》 to exile ; exile 《a person》
정백 精白 pure white (순백)
—**당(糖)** refined sugar —**미** polished 〔cleaned〕 rice —**소(所)** a (rice) refinery ; a rice mill
정벌 征伐 [원정] an expedition ; [전쟁] a campaign ; [정복] conquest ; subjugation ; [징벌] chastisement —**하다** subjugate ; conquer ; march against (the enemy) ; send an expedition (army) against
정범 正犯 the principal offense〔offender〕 ; the chief criminal ; the main culprit ; a principal (in a crime)
—**자** the principal offender
정법 定法 an order ; an established〔a fixed〕 rule ; a convention ; the usual way
정변 政變 a coup d'état 《프》 ; a political change〔crisis〕 ; [내각 경질] a change of Government ; a ministerial change
정병 精兵 picked〔élite〕 troops ; the flower of the army
†**정보 情報** information ; intelligence ; a report ; news ; [밀고] a tip-off ; dope ¶ 정보를 얻다 obtain information 《about》 // 정보를 누설하다 divulge〔reveal〕 information ; spill the dope 《구》 // 정보에 통해 있다 be in the know 《구》 // 외무부 정보에 의하면 according to information received at the Foreign Office // 무슨 정보 없나 Have you got any news ? / (Is there) Any news ?
—**가** [경마 따위의] a tip-off man ; a dopester ; a tipster — **경로〔루트〕** a channel of information ; [기밀의] a pipeline — **장교** an intelligence officer —

공학 information engineering — 과학 the science of information —국 the (Cabinet) Information Board — 기관 the secret (intelligence) service ; a counter-intelligence corps — 누설 a leakage of information —망 an intelligence network —부 the information〔intelligence〕 bureau ; [외무성 따위의] the Public Information Division —부〔과, 계〕원 the information personnel — 산업 the information〔communications〕 industry — 수집 information gathering — 수집함(收集艦) an intelligence vessel〔ship〕 — 이론 information theory —화 사회(化社會) an information-oriented society 중앙 —국 [미국의] the Central Intelligence Agency《CIA》 중앙 —부장 the Director of the Central Intelligence Agency ; the CIA Director

정보 町步 ⇨ 정(町)

정복 正服 a formal dress ; formal attire ; a uniform

— 경찰관 a policeman in full uniform

*정복 征服 conquest ; subjugation ; mastery —하다 conquer ; subjugate ; overcome ; subdue ; reduce ; make a conquest of ; gain the mastery of ¶ 정복할 수 없는 unconquerable ; invincible // 세계를 정복하다 conquer〔make a conquest of〕 the world // 에베레스트산을 정복하다 conquer Mt. Everest

—욕 lust for conquest —자 a conqueror ; a subjugator ; a vanquisher

정복 淨福 pure (and restful) happiness ; beatitude

정복 整復 〖의학〗 reposition ; reduction —하다 reduce ; reset ; redress

정본 正本 the original〔legal, formal〕 copy ; the text ¶ 정본과 사본 the original and the copy

정부 正否 right and wrong ¶ 정부를 확인하다 ascertain whether it is right〔correct〕 or wrong〔not〕

정부 正副 principal and assistant ; [서류의] original and copy ; senior and junior ¶ 정부 2통 duplicate copies ; original and copy // 정부 2통을 제출하다 submit《an application》 in duplicate

—의장 the speaker and vice-speaker ; the president and vice-president —통령 the president and vice-president

†정부 政府 the government ; the administration ; [내각] the ministry ¶ 정부의 governmental ; ministerial // 정부의 소재지 the seat of government // 신정부를 수립하다 set up〔establish〕 a new government // 현정부를 타도하다 overthrow the present government // 정부를 지지〔공격〕하다 support〔attack〕 the government

— 당국 the government authorities — 보조금 government subsidies —안 a government measure〔bill〕 — 종합 청사 the Integrated Government Building 연립 — a coalition government 연방 — a federal government 임시 — an interim〔a provisional〕 government 중앙 — the central government 지방 — the local government

정부 情夫 a sweetheart ; a lover ; a paramour ; an adulterer

정부 情婦 a mistress ; a paramour

정부 貞婦 a chaste〔virtuous〕 woman ; a woman of virtue ; a faithful wife

정부 正負 〖수학〗 positive and negative ; plus and minus

정북 正北 due north

정분 情分 a cordial friendship ; affection ; intimacy ¶ 정분이 있다 be on terms of intimacy // 이 학교의 선생과 학생 사이에는 정분이 결여되어 있는 것 같다 It seems that familiarity is wanting between teachers and students of this school.

정비 正比 〖수학〗 direct ratio ⇨ 정비례

정비 正妃 the legitimate queen〔empress〕 ; the first wife《of an emperor, a king, a prince》

정비 整備 complete equipment ; consolidation ; improvement —하다 put in good order ; keep in order ; fully equip ; equip completely ; maintain ; consolidate ¶ 전선을 정비하다 consolidate the front // 사업을 정비하다 consolidate various undertakings // 인원을 정비하다 reshuffle the personnel《of》 // 이 차는 완전히 재정비한 차입니다 This is a completely overhauled car.

—군 a fully equipped army — 불량 poor maintenance —원 〖항공〗 a groundman〔ground crew〕 기업 — business reorganization ; readjustment of enterprises 그라운드 —원 [경기장의] a groundkeeper ; a ground(s)man 자동차 —공 a car mechanic 제트기 —원 a member of a ground crew for jets 지상(地上) —원 a member of a ground crew〔staff《영》〕 항공기 조립 —공 a rigger 항만 — 계획 a harbor improvement project

정비례 正比例 direct proportion〔ratio〕 —하다 be in direct proportion《to》; be directly proportional《to》 ¶ 정비례해서 in direct proportion《to》

정비례 定比例 constant〔definite〕 proportion

정빈 正賓 a guest of honor

정사 丁巳 〖민속〗 the 54th year of the sexagenary cycle ; the Year of the Serpent

정사 正史 authentic history

정사 正使 a senior envoy ; the chief delegate

정사 正邪 right and wrong ; good and evil 정사를 막론하고 whether right or wrong // 정사를 구별하다 distinguish〔know〕 right from wrong ; discriminate between right and wrong

정사 政事 governmental〔political〕 affairs ;

[정무] administrative business ¶ 정사를 다스리다 manage the affairs of state

정사 情死 a love suicide ; a double suicide (for love) **—하다** die together for love ; commit a double suicide ¶ 그들은 정사했다 The lovers killed themselves together.

— 미수 an attempted double suicide 억지 — a forced double suicide

정사 情事 a love affair ; a romance ¶ 정사를 알다 understand love // 정사에 눈뜨다 become sexually awakened ; become adolescent

혼외 — extramarital intercourse

정사 靜思 meditation ; contemplation **—하다** meditate ; contemplate ; ponder

정사 精査 minute investigation ; careful examination **—하다** look closely into ; examine carefully ; investigate minutely ; scrutinize

정사 精舍 a cloister ; [남자의] monastery ; [여자의] nunnery ; convent

정사 情史 a love story ; a romance

정사 淨寫 neat copying ⇨ 정서(淨書)

정사각형 正四角形 〖수학〗 a (regular) square ; a perfect〔an exact〕 square

정사면체 正四面體 a regular tetrahedron

정사영 正射影 〖기하〗 an orthogonal projection

—법 orthography

정사원 正社員 a regular member ; a full member of the staff

정산 精算 exact calculation ; an accurate account ; [결산] settlement of accounts **—하다** settle accounts ; keep an accurate account

—서 a statement of accounts —액 an adjusted amount —인 an average adjuster 운임 —소 a fare adjustment office

정삼각형 正三角形 a regular〔an equilateral〕 triangle

†정상 正常 normalcy ; normality **—하다** (be) normal ¶ 정상적 normal // 정상이 아닌 abnormal ; irregular // 정상의 심리 상태 normal mentality // 정상으로 돌아가다 return to normalcy〔normal condition〕 // 컨디션이 아직 정상으로 돌아오지는 않았지만 무리하지 않으면 괜찮다 My condition isn't quite back to normal yet, but I'm all right as long as I don't overdo it.

— 가격 a normal price — 능률 normal efficiency — 상태 normal state — 속도 a normal speed — 심리 상태 normal mentality — 운전 normal operation —위(位) a normal position〔posture〕 — 호흡 eupnea —화 normalization 국교 —화 normalization of diplomatic relations 《with》

정상 政商 a businessman with political 〔party〕 affiliations ; a businessman having special connections with a political party or clique〔faction〕

—배 a political hack ; a racketeer ; businessman with party ties

정상 情狀 condition ; circumstances ¶ 정상을 참작해서 in consideration of the (extenuating) circumstances // 정상을 참작하다 take the circumstances into consideration

정상 頂上 the top ; the summit ; the peak ; [작은 산의] the crest ; [극점] the climax ; the zenith ; the acme ; the apex

> 참고 **top**은 산 이외에도 수목·기둥·머리의 정상 따위 널리 쓰이지만 **summit**는 일반적으로 산 이외에는 쓰이지 않는다

¶ 정상을 정복하다 gain〔get to〕 the summit // 물가는 1월이 정상이었고 그 뒤부터 상당히 하락하였다 Prices declined considerably from the high peak of January. // 불경기도 이것이 정상일 게다 Perhaps we have got to the bottom〔bedrock〕 of the depression.

—급 회담 a summit-level conference — 회담 a summit talk〔conference〕 산 — the top of a mountain

정상파 定常波 〖물리〗 a stationary wave

정상화 正常化 normalization **—하다** normalize ; be normalized

국교 — normalization of diplomatic relations

정색 正色 [얼굴·태도] a serious countenance〔mien〕 ; seriousness ; earnestness ; a solemn air ; a serious〔grave〕 look **—하다** maintain a serious countenance ; show one's seriousness〔earnestness, sincerity〕 ; assume a solemn air ; wear a sober look ; put on a grave look

정색 반응 呈色反應 〖화학〗 color reaction

정서 淨書 a fair〔clean〕 copy ; neat writing **—하다** copy〔write out〕 fair ; make a fair〔clean〕 copy 《of》

정서 正書 square-hand〔printed style〕 characters **—하다** write in the square style ; write square-hand

—법 orthography

정서 情緖 emotion ; feeling ; heartstring ; sentiment ¶ 면면한 정서 tender sentiments // 정서가 면면하다 be overcome with emotions ; have a tender feeling 《for》

정서 正西 due west

정석 定石 [바둑 따위에서] formulas 〔rules〕 in the game of *Baduk* ; established tactics ; [원칙] the cardinal principle ; [비유적] a formula ¶ 정석대로 두다 play by the book // 정석으로 하다 make it a rule 《to》 // 그것은 범인 수사의 정석에 불과하다 That's only the ABC of tracing〔running down〕 a criminal.

정선 精選 careful selection **—하다** select carefully〔with care〕 ; single〔pick〕 out ; discriminate (in choosing) ¶ 이번 신입

사원은 모두 정선되었다 This year's new team members are the cream of the crop.
—품 choice goods ; select〔picked〕 goods

정선 停船 stopping of vessel ; quarantine (검역을 위해서) —하다 stop ; heave to ; haul to ; hold 《a vessel》 in quarantine ¶ 정선을 명하다 stop a vessel ; order a ship to heave〔haul〕 to ; detain a ship // 안개 때문에 정선하였다 The ship was brought to a stop in the fog.

정선 汀線 the beachline ; the shoreline

*정설 定說 an established theory ; [개인의] a definite opinion ; settled conviction ¶ 정설을 뒤집어 엎다 overthrow an established theory

정성 精誠 [성의] true heart ; sincerity ; earnestness ; devotion ¶ 정성어린 선물 a gift with one's best wishes // 정성껏 with one's utmost sincerity ; with one's whole heart ; elaborately // 정성들이다 exert oneself to the utmost ; put the whole mind to ; elaborate // 그는 우리를 정성껏 대접했다 He did his utmost to entertain us. // 그 여자는 온 정성을 다하여 그 일을 했다 She did it with all her heart. // 자식의 취직으로 신세를 진 데 대한 제 정성입니다 It's just a token of my appreciation for all your help in finding my son a job.

정성 분석 定性分析 〖화학〗 qualitative analysis

정세 情勢 [정황] the state of things 〔affairs〕 ; situation ; conditions ; circumstances ; [징조] circumstances ; appearances ; indications ; signs ¶ 유럽의 정세 the European situation // 정세의 변화 the change of situation ; a change in the situation // 세계 정세 the world situation // 정세의 악화 deterioration〔worsening〕 of a situation // 지금 정세로는 according to the present situation ; as matters stand now ; judging by the situation // 정세를 판단하다 judge〔size up〕 the situation // 정세에 대처하다 meet conditions // 정세를 관망하다 watch the development of situation // 그것이 정세를 일변시켰다 That altered the situation. // 정세가 어떤지 확실히 말해 주시오 Tell me exactly how matters stand. // 정세는 이미 변했다 This is no longer the case. // 내란이 가라앉을 것 같은 정세가 아니다 There is no appearance〔prospect〕 of the rebellion subsiding.

정세 精細 minuteness ; detail —하다 (be) minute ; detailed ; thorough ¶ 정세하게 minutely ; closely ; in detail // 정세한 검사 close examination // 정세한 계획 a detailed plan ; a blueprint // 정세한 계획을 세우다 make a blueprint 《of》 ; blueprint

정세포 精細胞 〖생물〗 a sperm〔male generative〕 cell ; a spermatoblast

정소 精巢 a spermary ; seminal glands ; a testicle

‡정수 定數 [수] a fixed number ; a quorum ; a quota ; [운명] destiny ; fate ; 〖수학〗 a constant ; an invariable ¶ 정수 미달시에는 unless a quorum is present // 정수를 넘다 exceed the fixed number // 정수에 달하다 make up the fixed number
— 비례 constant proportion

‡정수 精粹 pureness ; purity —하다 (be) pure ; genuine

*정수 精髓 marrow ; essence ; quintessence ; pith ; gist ; core ¶ 동양 문화의 정수 the essence of the Eastern Culture // 종교의 정수 the essence of religion // 교육의 정수 the spirit of education

정수 渟水 stagnant〔standing〕 water ⇨ 정수(靜水)

정수 精水 semen ; spermatic fluid ⇨ 정액
— (세척)법 〖사진〗 stand washing —압(壓) hydrostatic pressure — 역학 hydrostatics

정수 淨水 clean water

정수 井水 well water

정수 正數 a positive number

정수 正手 [바둑·장기의] the proper move

정수 整數 an integral〔a whole〕 number ; an integer

정수리 頂— the crown of the head ; the vertex

정수 식물 挺水植物 an emerged〔aquatic〕 plant

*정숙 貞淑 chastity ; female virtue ; feminine modesty —하다 (be) chaste ; virtuous ; modest ¶ 정숙하기로 이름이 높다 have a reputation for womanly virtue

정숙 靜肅 silence ; stillness ; quiet(ness) ; hush —하다 (be) silent ; still ; quiet ; hushed ¶ 정숙히 하여라 Keep quiet. /Don't make a noise. /Be silent. // 집회는 정숙하였다 The meeting was orderly.

정승 政丞 a minister of State ; a prime minister (in the Kingdom of Korea)

정시 丁時 〖민속〗 the 14th of the 24 hour periods 《=12 : 30~1 : 30 p. m》

정시 正視 looking straight ; 〖의학〗 stigmatism —하다 look 《a person》 in the face ; look straight〔squarely〕 at ¶ 사실을 정시하다 look at a fact squarely
— 렌즈 an orthoptic lens —안 emmetropia — 연습 orthoptic exercises

정시 定時 fixed〔regular〕 time ; a stated 〔scheduled〕 period ¶ 정시의 regular ; scheduled // 정시에 regularly ; periodically ; on scheduled time // 정시 운행하다 move on schedule ; operate regularly // 정시에 도착하다 arrive on schedule // 정시에 발차하다 leave at the scheduled time〔on schedule〕

정시 외 定時外 ¶ 정시 외의 overtime // 정시 외에 일하다 work overtime
— 근무 overtime work

정시제 定時制 〖교육〗 the part-time

(schooling) system ¶ 정시제의 part-time
— 고교 a part-time high school — 과정 the part-time course

†정식 正式 formality ; due〔proper, regular〕 form ¶ 정식의 formal ; regular ; due ; official ; proper // 정식으로 formally ; properly ; regularly ; duly ; in due〔proper〕 form // 정식의 수속 a formal process〔step〕 // 정식의 교육〔교섭〕 formal education〔negotiations〕 // 정식의 경우에 on formal occasions // 정식으로 소개받다 be formally introduced // 정식으로 결혼을 제의하다 make a formal proposal of marriage to 《a girl》 // 정식으로 방문하다 make a formal call 《at, on》 ; pay a formal visit 《to》
— 결혼 legal marriage — 계약 a formal agreement — 교섭 formal negotiations — (학교) 교육 regular schooling ; regular school education — 당원 a full〔regular, card-carrying〕 party member — 만찬회 a dress-up dinner — 수락 formal acceptance — 식사 a regular dinner — 재판 《apply for》 a formal trial — 통지 a formal notice

정식 定式 [규정] an established〔a prescribed〕 form ; a formula ¶ 정식의 formular ; regular ; formal

정식 定食 table d'hôte 《프》 ; a dinner à prix fixe 《프》 ; [집에서의] a regular meal 《breakfast, lunch, supper》

정식 整式 〖수학〗 an integral expression

정식 程式 〖수학〗 a formula ; forms

†정신 精神 mind ; spirit ; soul ; will ; intention ; mentality ; motive ; genius

> 참고 **mind**는 「지력」 **spirit**는 soul보다 더욱 육체와의 독립을 강조한 말로써 「영혼」이라는 뜻 **soul**은 육체가 멸한 뒤에도 멸하지 않는다는 「혼」의 뜻이며 때로는 spirit를 대신할 수 있다 **will**은 「의지」, **intention**은 「의도」, **motive**는 「동기」, **mentality**는 「심성」, **genius**는 「시대의 경향 풍조」의 뜻

¶ 정신적인 mental ; moral ; spiritual // 정신적으로 mentally ; morally ; spiritually // 정신이 썩은 corrupt ; depraved // 고결한 정신의 high-minded ; noble // 정신적 사랑 Platonic〔spiritual〕 love // 정신적 지원 moral support // 정신적 타격 a mental blow〔shock〕 // 정신적 유산 mental heritage // 정신적 피로 brain weariness ; mental fatigue // 정신의 이상 mental disorder ; alienation // 사랑의 정신 the spirit of love // 고상한 정신 a noble mind ; high spirit // 비열한 정신 a base mind ; a mean spirit // 정신에 이상이 없다 be of sound mind ; be mentally sound // 정신을 발달시키다 develop the mind // 정신을 향상시키다 elevate one's mind〔soul〕 // 정신을 단련하다 train the mind // 정신을 쏟다 devote one's heart and soul to 《a work》 // 정신을 집중하다 concentrate one's attention on 《a thing》 // 그는 장사에서 손해를 보아 정신이 이상해졌다 His loss in business affected his mind. // 건전한 정신은 건전한 육체에 깃든다 A sound mind in a sound body. // 정신 일도 하사 불성 Where there is a will, there is a way. // 누구를 비방하려는 정신은 추호도 없다 Nothing is farther from me than to detract from other's merits. // 법률의 자구에 구애받지 말고 그 정신을 따르라 Do not stick to the letter of the law, but obey its spirit. // 남의 집 차고 진입로에다가 차를 주차시키다니 당신 정신 나갔소 What's the big idea of parking your car in my driveway ? // 나는 오늘 내 정신이 아니야 I'm not myself today. // 곧 정신이 들 테니까 걱정마세요 He will come to soon. Don't worry. // 첫 해외 여행이라 짐을 꾸리는 등 여러 가지로 정신을 못 차렸다 This being my first trip overseas, I'm all in a flurry, what with packing and everything.
— 감응 psychomancy ; (mental) telepathy — 감정 a psychiatric test —계 the mental〔moral, spiritual〕 world — 과로 mental overstrain — 과학 the science of mind ; mental science — 교육 moral education — 구조 one's mental make-up〔structure〕 — 기능 a psychic〔mental〕 function — 기능 쇠퇴 failure of a psychic function — 노동 brain〔mental〕 work — 노동자 a brain〔mental〕 worker —력 mental power ; spiritual strength —론 idealism ; spiritualism — 묘사도 〖심리학〗 a psychograph — 무장 mental〔spiritual〕 armament — 문명 moral〔spiritual〕 civilization — 문화 moral〔spiritual〕 culture — 물리학 psychophysics — 물리학자 a psychophysicist — 박약 mental weakness ; weak-mindedness ; feeblemindedness ; low intelligence — 박약아 a feebleminded child — 박약아 시설 a home for feebleminded children — 박약자 a feebleminded〔weak-minded〕 person ; a mentally deficient person — 발생학 psychogenesis — 변조(變調) mental aberration —병 a mental disease〔trouble〕 ; a disease of the mind ; a psychosis 《*pl.* -ses》 ; psychopathy — 병동(病棟) a psychiatric〔psychopathic, psychotic〕 ward — 병리학 psychopathology — 병리학자 a psychopathologist — 병원 a mental hospital —병 의사 a psychiatrist ; a psychiater ; a psychopathist ; a mental specialist ; an alienist —병 유전 a taint of insanity —병자 a mentally deranged person ; an insane〔a demented〕 person ; a lunatic ; a psychopath ; a psycho —병질자 a psychopath —병학 psychiatry ; psychopathy —병 학자 a psychiatrist ; a psychiater —병 환자 a mental〔psychopathic〕 patient — 분석

psychoanalysis — 분석학자 a psychoanalyst — 분열증 schizophrenia ; split personality — 분열증 환자 a schizoid — 상태 a mental condition ; a state of mind — 생활 spiritual life — 수양 mental culture〔training〕 — 생물학 psychobiology — 생물학자 a psychobiologist — 생리학 psychophysiology — 생리학자 a psychophysiologist — 신경증 psychoneurosis — 신경증 환자 a psychoneurotic — 신체 의학 psychosomatic medicine ; psychosomatics — 신체증 a psychosomatic disorder — 신체증 환자 a psychosomatic (patient) — 안정제 a tranquil(l)izer — 약물학 psychopharmacology — 역학 psychodynamics — 연령 mental age — 외과 psychosurgery — 외과의 a psychosurgeon — 요법 psychotherapy ; mental healing — 요법가 a psychotherapist — 위생(학) mental hygiene — 의학 psychiatry ; mental〔psychologic〕 medicine — 이상 mental disorder ; psychosis — 이상자 an insane person ; a lunatic ; a psycho — 일도 하사불성(一到何事不成) Nothing is impossible to a determined mind. — 작용 mental operation〔process〕 — 장애 mental disorder〔derangement〕 —적 공백 a spiritual vacuum —적 사랑 Platonic love —적 유산 spiritual〔mental〕 heritage —적 지지〔압박〕 moral support〔pressure〕 —적 타격 a mental blow ; a (mental) shock —적 힘 moral〔spiritual〕 force — 전류계(電流計) [거짓말 탐지기] a psychogalvanometer —주의 idealism ; spiritualism —주의자 an idealist ; a spiritualist — 진단(학) psychognosis — 착란 a mental storm — 측정 psychometry — 통일 concentration of mind ; mental concentration — 피로 mental fatigue ; brain fag — 현상 a mental phenomenon 과학적 — a scientific mind 독립 — the spirit of independence 애국 — a patriotic spirit 입법 — the spirit of legislation 프로테스탄트 — Protestant ethos 헌법 — the spirit of the constitution 의사(擬似) — 분열증 schizothymia

정신 艇身 a boat's length ¶ 일 정신의 차로 지다 lose the race by a boat's length

정신 挺身 volunteering —하다 offer oneself ; volunteer ; go ahead of others ¶ 난국에 정신하다 offer oneself〔volunteer〕 to undertake the difficult task

정신차리다 ① [의식을] recover〔regain〕 consciousness ; recover one's senses ; come〔return〕 to (oneself) ② [긴장하다] collect one's mind ; strain〔string〕 one's nerve ; pay attention ; be all attention ¶ 그를 한번 정신차리게 해줄 필요가 있다 He wants screwing up.

정실 貞實 fidelity ; faithfulness —하다 (be) faithful ; true ; devoted

정실 正室 the lawful〔legal〕 wife

정실 情實 private circumstances ; a special connection ; personal〔private〕 considerations ; favoritism ¶ 정실에 흐르다 be influenced by personal considerations // 정실을 배제하다 set〔put〕 aside all personal considerations // 그는 조금도 정실을 허용치 않는다 He is deaf to all private considerations. // 그는 정실에 의해서 승진됐다 He got promoted through favoritism. — 인사(人事) favoritism

정악 正樂 〖음악〗 classical music ; court music

정안 定案 a definite plan ¶ 아직 정안은 없다 We have not yet any definite plan.

정압 定壓 constant〔fixed〕 pressure

정애 情愛 affection ; love

정액 定額 a fixed amount ; a specified amount ¶ 정액에 달하다 come up to the specified amount
—등 a fixed-rate lamp —량 a ration — 반제(返濟) amortization —세 a fixed amount tax — 소득 a fixed income — 예금 a fixed deposit ; a deposit by installments — 임금 a fixed wage — 저금 fixed amount savings —제 a flat sum system —제 요금 a flat rate

정액 精液 semen ; sperm ; spermatic fluid —관 a spermaduct — 사출 a seminal emission —소(素) spermatin —학 spermatology —학자 a spermatologist

정야 靜夜 a silent〔quiet〕 night

정약 定約 an agreement ; an understanding ; a contract ; a promise —하다 make〔give〕 an agreement〔a contract〕 ; agree ; promise

정양 靜養 rest ; recuperation ; convalescence (병후의) —하다 rest quietly ; recuperate ; take a rest ¶ 정양차 for a rest ; for (the benefit of) one's health

***정어리** 〖물고기〗 a sardine
— 통조림 canned sardines

정언적 定言的 〖논리〗 categorical ¶ 정언적 명제 a categorical proposition // 정언적 판단〔명령〕 categorical judgment〔imperative〕

정업 正業 honest employment ; a legitimate〔respectable〕 business

정업 定業 a regular〔fixed〕 occupation 〔employment〕 ¶ 그는 정업이 없다 He has no fixed occupation.

정역학 靜力學 〖물리〗 statics

정연 整然 orderliness —하다 (be) orderly ; regular ; systematic ; coherent ¶ 정연히 in good order ; in an orderly way ; shipshape ; systematically // 이론 정연히 설교하다 be perfectly logical in one's argument // 모든 것이 정연히 놓여 있다 All are arranged in nice order.

정열 情熱 passion ; ardor ; fervor ; enthusiasm ¶ 정열적 passionate ; ardent // 정열적인 사람 a passionate person // 정열에 불타다 burn with passion

정염 正鹽 normal salt
정염 情炎 burning passion ; flaming love 〔desire〕 ¶ 정염에 불타다 burn with passion
정예 精銳 the pick ; the flower ; [군인] picked〔crack〕 soldiers〔troops〕 ¶ 정예 부대 a crack contingent
정오 正午 (high) noon ; midday
†정오 正誤 correction ; rectification —하다 correct an error ; rectify ¶ 신문에 정오를 요청하다 write to a newspaper requesting correction of an error
—표 errata ; corrigenda ; a list of printer's errors
정온 定溫 fixed temperature
—기(器) a thermostat — 동물 a homoiothermic animal —층 invariable stratum
정온 靜穩 calmness ; tranquility ; serenity —하다 (be) calm ; tranquil ; quiet
정욕 情慾 sexual desire ; lust ; passion ; carnal desire ¶ 정욕의 노예 a slave of passion // 정욕의 억제 restraint〔control〕 of passion // 정욕을 만족시키다 gratify one's lust // 정욕을 실컷 채우다 indulge in one's sexual desires ; give rein to one's passion // 정욕을 억제하다 control one's sexual desires // 정욕에 지배되다 be swayed by passion // 정욕을 일으키게 하다 inflame 《a person》 with desire // 정욕은 억제하기 어렵다 Passions are hard to control.
정용 定容 〖물리〗 constant volume
— 비열 specific heat at constant volume
— 사이클 a constant-volume cycle
정용 整容 —하다 tidy one's appearance ; tidy oneself up
정우 丁憂 losing one's parents ; mourning for one's parents
정우 政友 a political friend
정원 正圓 a perfect circle〔ring, round〕 ; being perfectly round
정원 定員 a regular staff ; the personnel ; the full strength ; capacity (수용 능력) ; a quorum (정족수) ¶ 버스의 정원 the seating capacity of a bus // 정원 외의 supernumerary // 정원에 달하다 reach the regular number // 정원에 미달하다 lack the quorum // 정원 이상의 승객을 태우다 carry more passengers than the seating capacity allows // 이 사무실의 정원은 30명이다 The regular personnel of this office is 30. // 출석자 수가 정원 미달이어서 집회가 연기되었다 The meeting was adjourned for want of a quorum.
— 배치 allocation of the authorized strength — 초과 exceeding capacity ; overcrowdedness 연대(聯隊)〔선박〕 — the full complement of a regiment〔ship〕 입학 — an entrance quota 전시〔평시〕 — war〔peace〕 strength〔establishment〕
정원 庭園 a garden ; [넓은] a park ¶ 정원을 만들다 lay out a garden
— 공사 landscaping — 부지 a garden plot —사 a gardener — 살수기(撒水器) a garden sprinkler —수 a garden tree —술 (landscape) gardening 옥상 — a roof garden
정월 正月 January ; the first month of the year ¶ 정월 초하루 New Year's Day
정위치 定位置 one's regular position ; a fixed position
정유 丁酉 〖민속〗 the 34th binary term of the sexagenary cycle
정유 精油 refined oil
— 공장 an oil refinery —관 an oil pipeline
정육 精肉 fresh meat ; dressed meat
—상 a butcher ; a meatman —업 the meat industry
정육면체 正六面體 a regular hexahedron
정윤 正閏 [평년과 윤년] normal and leap years ; [왕위] legitimacy
정은 正銀 pure〔solid〕 silver
정음 正音 correct pronunciation of a letter
†정의 正義 right ; justice ; righteousness ¶ 정의의 righteous ; just // 정의의 싸움 a righteous war ; fighting for a rightful cause // 정의감이 강한 사람 a man with a strong sense of justice // 정의를 위하여 폭력과 싸우다 fight for〔in the cause of〕 justice against force // 정의는 마침내 승리한다 Right will prevail in the end. // 힘이 정의다 Might is right.
—감 a sense of justice ¶ 정의감이 강하다 have a strong sense of justice
:정의 定義 a definition ¶ 자유란 말의 정의 a definition of the word "liberty" // 정의를 내리다 define 《a word》 ; give a definition // 명확한 정의를 내리다 form a clear definition 《of》 // 신사의 정의는 예의를 아는 사람인 것이다 A gentleman is defined as one who knows manners. /Good manners define the gentleman.
정의 情誼 (ties of) friendship ; fellowship ; friendly feelings ; affections ¶ 깊은 정의 deep friendship // 정의가 두텁다 be very friendly ; be kind and warmhearted ; be heartwarming // 정의를 다하다 do 《a person》 a kindness〔good turn〕 // 그는 정의를 모르는 사람이다 He is lacking in friendly feelings.
정의 精義 [뜻] the exact meaning ; [해석] an (a detailed) exposition ; a (full) commentary ¶ 민법 정의 a Commentary on the Civil Law
정의 情意 emotion and will ; sentiment
정의 상통 情意相通 mutual understanding〔feeling, affection〕 ; amorous connection (남녀간의) —하다 enjoy〔come to〕 mutual understanding〔affection〕 ; become intimate (남녀가)
정인 情人 a sweetheart ; a sweetie ; [유부녀·유부남] a paramour ⇨ 정부(情夫, 情婦)
정일 定日 the fixed date〔day〕 ; the ap-

pointed day ¶ 정일에 on the fixed date

정자 晶子 〖광물〗 a crystallite

정자 正字 a correct letter ; an unsimplified character

정자 精子 spermatozoon ; antherozoid
—낭 a spermogonium —론 spermism —론자 a spermist — 발생 spermatogenesis ; spermatogeny —선 (腺) a sperm gland ; a spermary — 세포 a spermatid — 은행 a sperm bank —핵 a sperm nucleus — 형성 spermatogenesis

*정자 亭子 a pavilion ; an arbor ; a summerhouse
—나무 trees planted around a pavilion 〔summerhouse〕 ; a big tree serving as a shady resting place in a village

정자각 丁字閣 a "T"-shaped house for sacrifice before a royal tomb

정자법 正字法 〖문법〗 the orthography ¶ 정자법의 orthographic (al)

정자형 丁字形 T-form〔-shape〕 ; the figure T ¶ 정자형의 T-shaped // 정자형의 자 a T square

정작 a real fact ; truth ; actuality ; reality ; [부사적] truly ; really ; actually ; practically ¶ 정작 있던 일 an actual occurrence // 정작 말하면 to tell the truth // 정작으로 믿다 believe 《a thing》 to be true // 정작 화가 난다 I am very angry with him. // 정작 알아보니 거짓말이었다 Upon actual investigation, it turned out to be a false report. // 그의 대답은 정작 사죄나 다름 없다 His reply is, in fact, an apology. // 정작 사려고 하면 살 수 없다 When you actually try to buy things, they are not to be found.

†정장 正裝 full dress ; formal dress ; a suit ; a dress suit ; full uniform —하다 be in full dress ; be formally attired ; dress formally ; be in full uniform ¶ 정장을 요하는 모임 a dress affair ; a white-tie function // 정장하실 필요는 없습니다 No dress.

정장 艇長 [보트의] a coxswain ; a cox 《구》 ; a skipper ; [수뢰정 따위의] a captain

정장석 正長石 〖광물〗 orthoclase

정장제 整腸劑 medicine for intestinal disorders

정재 淨財 estate〔property, money〕 for votive offerings ; an offertory ¶ 정재를 희사하다 make a votive offering of money〔property〕 《to a temple》 // 정재를 모으다 collect alms ; take up a collection

정쟁 政爭 a political strife〔controversy, dispute〕 ¶ 정쟁의 도구로 삼다 make a political issue of 《a thing》

*정적 靜的 (being) passive ; quiet ; calm ; static (al)

정적 靜寂 stillness ; silence ; solitude ; quiet —하다 (be) still ; silent ; quiet ¶ 죽음과 같은 정적 dead〔death-like〕 silence ; silence like the grave // 밤의 정적 perfect stillness of the night // 정적을 깨뜨리다 break the silence // 정적을 깨뜨리는 것은 시계 소리뿐이었다 Silence was only broken by the ticking of the clock.

정적 政敵 a political opponent〔enemy, foe, adversary〕

정적 正嫡 ① [본처] a legitimate wife ② [적자] a legitimate child ; a child born in legal marriage〔in lawful wedlock〕

정전 正殿 a palace for the king's morning audience ; the royal audience chamber

정전 政戰 political warfare〔war〕 ; a political maneuver ; a political campaign

정전 停電 interruption of electric power ; an electricity〔a power〕 failure ; the giving out of the electric power ; a tie up (전차의) —하다 the power gives out ; the (electric) current is off ; 《the cars》 be tied up ¶ 전차가 정전되었다 The streetcar was tied up. // 요즈음은 정전이 잦다 We often have no electric light at night these days. // 천둥으로 정전됐다 The thunderstorm caused power failure. // 정전으로 깜깜해졌다 The electricity failed, and everything was blacked out.

정전 停戰 a cease-fire ; the suspension 〔cessation〕 of hostilities〔arms〕 ; a truce ; an armistice —하다 suspend hostilities ; have a truce ¶ 정전을 명하다 order to suspend hostilities
— 교섭 a cease-fire negotiation — 명령 a cease-fire order — 선상 충돌(線上衝突) clashes along the truce〔cease-fire〕 line — 연락원 a cease-fire liaison officer — 위원회 a cease-fire committee — 제의 a cease-fire proposal — 협정 an armistice〔a ceasefire〕 agreement ¶ 정전 협정을 체결하다 conclude a truce — 회담 a cease-fire conference〔parley〕 ; a truce talk

정전 正典 〖기독교〗 the canon ; the canonical books (of the Bible) ; the canonized books

정전기 正電氣 ⇨ 양전기(陽電氣)

정전기 靜電氣 〖물리〗 static electricity

정전류 定電流 constant current

정전압 定電壓 constant voltage

정절 貞節 faithfulness ; fidelity ; constancy ; chastity ; devotion ¶ 정절한 faithful ; constant ; devoted // 정절한 아내 a faithful〔devoted〕 wife // 남편에게 정절하다 be devoted〔faithful〕 to one's husband // 정절을 지키다 lead a chaste life

정절 正切 a tangent ⇨ 정접

*정점 頂點 a vertex ; the summit ; the peak ; the top ; the height ; [극치] the climax ; the zenith ; the apex ¶ 3각형의 정점 the apex of a triangle // 영화의 정점에 있다 be at the height〔zenith〕 of one's prosperity

정점 定點 〖기하〗 a definite〔fixed〕 point

정접 正接 〖수학〗 a tangent ¶ 정접의 tangential ; tangental
— 검류계 a tangent galvanometer — 눈금판 a tangent scale

†**정정 訂正** correction ; rectification ; [개정] revision —하다 correct ; rectify ; revise ¶ 오류를 정정하다 correct errors // 그는 의견을 정정해야만 했다 He had to amend his opinion.
— 부호 a note of correction —자 a corrector ; a reviser — 재판 the revised second edition —판 a revised edition

정정 政情 political conditions〔affairs〕; the political situation ¶ 정정의 안정 the stability of the political situation // 정정이 불안하기 때문에 on account of the unsettled political situation // 정정에 정통하다 be familiar〔conversant〕 with political conditions

정정 당당 正正堂堂 —하다 (be) fair and square ; open and aboveboard ¶ 정정 당당히 fairly (and squarely) ; openly // 정정 당당한 논쟁 a full-dress debate // 정정 당당한 승부 a fairly contested match // 정정 당당하게 싸우다 play fair〔on the square〕; fight openly and squarely // 그 여자의 태도는 정정 당당하였다 Her attitude was open and aboveboard.

정정법 政淨法 the Political Purification Law

정정하다 亭亭— [노익장이다] (be) hale and hearty ; vigorous ; active ; [우뚝 솟다] be standing lofty and alone ¶ 정정한 노인 a man in his robust old age ; a hale old man // 그는 90을 넘었으나 아직도 정정하다 He has turned 90 and is still an active man.

:**정제 錠劑** a tablet ; a tabloid ; a pill ¶ 비타민 정제 a vitamin tablet

*__정제 精製__ refining —하다 refine ; purify ¶ 정제한 refined 《sugar, oil》 // 정제한 상품 choice goods
— 공장 a refinery —당〔식염〕 refined sugar〔salt〕 —법 a refining process —소 a refinery —업자 a refiner —유 refined oil —품 a refined article〔product〕

정제 整除 〖수학〗 divisibility ¶ 정제되는 (exactly) divisible // 정제되지 않는 indivisible
—수 an aliquot part ; an exact divisor

정제 整齊 regularity ; symmetry —하다 arrange in regular order ; make symmetrical〔regular, even, uniform〕

정조 正條 express provisions〔clauses, stipulations〕
—식 〖농업〗 checkrowing

정조 貞操 chastity ; constancy ; faithfulness ; honor ¶ 정조를 지키다 remain faithful 《to one's husband》 // 정조를 팔다 sell one's chastity ; prostitute oneself // 정조를 중히 여기다 prize chastity // 정조를 바치다 surrender one's chastity to ; give oneself to 《a man》 // 정조를 유린하다 defile〔trifle with〕 a girl's chastity ; seduce〔dishonor, ruin〕 a girl // 정조 관념이 희박하다 have a weak sense of virtue
—대(帶) a chastity belt — 유린 (a) violation of chastity

정조 情操 feeling ; sentiment ¶ 고상한 정조 a noble sentiment
— 교육 culture of aesthetic sentiment

정조 情調 a mood ; a tone ; an atmosphere
시골 — the rural atmosphere 이국 — an exotic atmosphere ; exoticism

정조 正租 unhulled rice

정족 鼎足 the legs of tripod ¶ 정족지세 a triangular position

정족수 定足數 a fixed number

정종 正宗 refined rice *sool*〔wine〕

정좌 靜坐 quiet sitting ; meditation —하다 sit quietly ; sit in meditation
—법 a meditation cure ¶ 정좌법을 행하다 practice abdominal respiration in a sitting posture

정좌 正坐 sitting up straight —하다 sit upright 《on one's seat》; sit up straight

정좌 鼎坐 sitting in a triangle —하다 sit in a triangle

정주 定住 settlement ; domiciliation ; one's fixed residence —하다 domiciliate ; settle down ; establish a domicile ¶ 서울에 정주하다 settle down〔make one's home〕 in *Seoul* // 그들은 영국에 정주했다 They have settled in England.
—지(자) a permanent home〔resident〕

*__정중 鄭重__ courtesy ; politeness ; civility ; consideration ; care (주의) —하다 (be) courteous ; polite ; civil ; careful ¶ 정중히 courteously ; politely ; with civility // 정중한 대접 hospitable treatment ; a courteous reception // 정중한 말로 in courteous words〔terms〕 // 정중히 대하다 treat 《a person》 courteously ; treat 《a person》 with consideration

정중 正中 the very middle
—선 〖해부〗 a median line — 신경 a median nerve

†**정지 停止** a stop ; stoppage ; suspension (중지) ; interruption (중절) —하다 stop ; interrupt ; suspend ¶ 지불을 정지하다 suspend payment // 발행〔영업〕을 정지하다 suspend publication〔business〕 // 전투 행위를 정지하다 suspend hostilities // 연극 기타 일체의 흥행을 정지하다 suspend theaters and all other forms of entertainment // 상업은 정지 상태에 있다 Business is at a standstill.
— 가격 a pegged〔stopped〕 price — 경례 a salute at attention — 기간 the period of suspension — 반응 cessation reaction ; termination —선 a stop line ; a clearance post — 신호 a stop signal — 위치 the place where 《a car》 stops ; a stop position —점 a stationary point ; the end point — 조건 〖법〗 a condition

precedent —파(波) a standing wave 자발적 — [핵실험의] a voluntary moratorium 《on nuclear tests》 지급〔발행, 영업〕 — suspension of payment〔publication, business〕

정지 靜止 quiescence ; stillness ; stationariness ; standstill —하다 rest ; stand still ; be at〔come to〕 a standstill ; be stationary ¶ 정지 자세 the posture of repose // 자연계의 어느 것도 한시도 정지하는 일이 없다 Nothing in nature stands still for a moment.

정지 整地 [건축을 위한] leveling the ground ; land readjustment ; [경작을 위한] soil preparation —하다 readjust the land 《for construction》 ; prepare the soil 《for planting》

†정직 正直 honesty ; uprightness ; frankness ; straightforwardness ; honor ; integrity

> 참고 **honesty** 타인에 대해서 공정한 것 즉 다른 사람의 물건을 훔친다든가 속인다든가 거짓말을 하지 않는 것 **honor** 자기의 지위나 계급에 속하는 것으로서 당연히 요구되는 도덕을 충실히 지키는 것 **integrity** 행동보다도 인격에 대해서 쓰이는 말 정사 선악에 관한 높은 규준을 견지하여 그 규준에서 벗어나는 일은 결코 하지 않는 것

—하다 (be) honest ; upright ; square ; straightforward ¶ 정직하게 honestly ; squarely ; frankly // 정직해 보이는 honest-looking // 정직하게 말하자면 to be frank〔honest〕 with you // 너에게는 정직하게 말하겠다 I shall be quite honest with you. // 정직한 사람은 제대로 인정을 못 받는 세상이다 Honesty does not pay in this world. // 정직은 최선의 정책이다 Honesty is the best policy. /Plain dealing is a jewel. // 아이들은 정직하다 Children speak the truth.

정직 停職 suspension from office〔duty〕 ¶ 정직을 명하다 suspend 《a person》 from office ; order 《an official》 suspended // 그는 정직당했다 He was suspended from office.

정직 定職 a regular occupation ; a fixed employment ; a steady job ¶ 정직이 없는 불규칙한 생활 a desultory life without regular occupation // 정직을 얻다 find a regular employment // 정직이 없다 have no regular occupation〔employment, calling〕 // 정직을 가지고 있다 have a regular occupation

정진 精進 concentration of mind ; assiduity ; close application ; [금욕] abstinence from flesh ; [종교적] religious purification —하다 devote oneself 《to》 ; apply oneself 《to》 ; abstain from flesh ; strive to ¶ 문학 연구에 정진하다 devote oneself to the study of literature

정진 挺進 —하다 go ahead of the others ; dash forward

—대 an advance corps

정질 晶質 〖화학〗 crystalloid ¶ 정질의 crystalloidal

정차 停車 a stop ; stoppage ⇨ 정거

†정착 定着 fixation ; [사진의] fixing —하다 fix ¶ 그는 간신히 2루에 정착했다 He finally found himself at second base.

—금 resettlement funds —도(度) fixity —망 a fixed shore net〔trap〕 —물 a fixture —액 〖사진〗 a fixing solution —제 〖사진〗 a fixing agent

†정찬 正餐 a formal dinner

정찰 正札 a price label ; a price mark〔tag〕 ¶ 5,000원 정찰이 붙은 상품 an article marked five thousand *won* // 정찰이 붙은 상품 a price-tagged article // 정찰을 붙이다 mark a price ; mark 《goods》 in plain figures // 1,000원이라는 정찰이 붙어 있다 be marked "a thousand *won*" // 정찰제 에누리 없음 Marked price and no overcharge. /One price and no reduction.

— 가격 a marked price ; a net price —제 a price tag system ; a fixed price system ¶ 정찰제 판매 sale at a fixed〔set, labeled〕 price

:정찰 偵察 reconnaissance ; scouting ; patrol —하다 reconnoiter ; scout ; patrol ¶ 적정을 정찰하다 feel〔reconnoiter〕 the enemy // 정찰하러 가다 go scouting // 정찰 임무를 띠고 출발하다 start charged with reconnoitering duties〔on scouting service〕

—기 a scout plane —대 a reconnoitering party ; a patrol team —병 a scout — 비행 a reconnaissance flight ¶ 정찰 비행을 하다 make〔go on〕 a scouting〔reconnoitering〕 flight — 순양함 a scout cruiser —자 a reconnoiterer ; a scout ; a scouter 《미》 ; an observer — 장치 reconnaissance equipment —전 a reconnoitering〔scouting〕 skirmish 강행(强行) — reconnaissance in force 공중 — aerial reconnaissance 사진 —기 a photo-reconnaissance plane

정찰 精察 close inspection〔examination〕 —하다 examine〔inspect〕 closely

정채 精彩 luster ; color ; [생기] liveliness ; vitality ; spirit ¶ 정채가 있는 colorful ; vivid ; lively // 정채가 없는 lifeless

:정책 政策 a policy ; political measures ¶ 정책상의 문제 a matter of policy // 정책의 변경 a change of policy // 한국의 대미 정책 Korea's policy towards the U. S. A. // 정책을 수립하다 frame〔formulate, shape〕 a policy // 정책을 쓰다〔채택하다〕 employ〔adopt〕 a policy // 정책을 바꾸다 change a policy // 정책을 실행하다 carry out a policy // 신정책을 발표하다 announce〔publish〕 a new policy // 현내각의 정책은 적절치 않다 The policy of the present

Cabinet is not appropriate.
— 강령 a platform — 결정 a policy decision — 결정 회의 a policy conference — 노선 party line 《미》 — 논쟁 a policy argument — 위원회 a policy planning committee ; the Policy Board — 입안자 a policy maker〔planner〕 — 전환 policy switch — 협정 a policy agreement ; an agreement on policies — 획정 policy-making 경제 — an economic policy 대미(對美)— 《Korea's》 policy toward America ; the American policy 《of Korea》 사회〔상업, 산업〕 — a social〔a commercial, an industrial〕 policy 외교〔대외〕 — a diplomatic〔foreign〕 policy

정처 正妻 a lawful〔legal〕 wife ; one's (legally) wedded wife ¶ 정처로 삼다 make an honest woman of her

정처 定處 a fixed place〔abode〕 ; a definite destination ¶ 정처 없이 with no definite objective in view ; aimlessly // 정처 없는 나그네 길에 오르다 set out on a journey with no definite objective in view

정철 精鐵 refined iron

정철 正鐵 wrought iron ; pure iron ore

정청 政廳 a government office〔house〕

정체 正體 [본성] the true character ; identity ; true colors ; [원래 꼴] a natural shape ; one's original form ¶ 정체 불명의 strange ; mysterious ; funny // 정체 불명의 사람 a total stranger ; a nondescript ; a suspicious person ; an unidentified person // 정체를 감추다 wear〔put on〕 a mask // 정체를 파악하다 find 《a person》 out // 정체를 폭로하다 debunk // 정체를 나타내다 show oneself in true colors ; show one's colors ; show the cloven hoof

정체 政體 the form〔system〕 of government ; the political system ¶ 정체를 변경하다 change the form of government
공화 — a republican system〔form〕 of government 군주 — monarchy 민주 — democracy 입헌〔전제〕 — a constitutional〔dictatorial〕 form of government 절대 군주 — an absolute〔a despotic〕 monarchy

*__정체 停滯__ [쌓임] accumulation ; [혼잡] congestion ; [침체] stagnation ; [자금·화물의] a tie-up ; [지불의 지연] falling into arrears —하다 stagnate ; pile up ; accumulate ; be tied up ; fall into arrears ¶ 정체된 stagnant ; sluggish // 자금의 정체 a tie-up of funds // 화물의 정체 a congestion〔an accumulation〕 of goods // 사무가 정체되다 business is (seriously) delayed // 전쟁 때문에 무역이 정체되어 버렸다 The war caused a paralysis of trade. // 금융이 정체되어 있다 The money market is sluggish.

정초 正初 the first ten days of January ¶ 정초에 early in January

정초 定礎 the laying of the cornerstone〔foundation stone〕 —하다 lay the cornerstone of a building

정축 丁丑 〖민속〗 the 14th binary term of the sexagenary cycle

정축 正軸 a principal axis ; an orthoaxis ; an orthodiagonal

정충 精蟲 a spermatozoon 《*pl.* -zoa》

정충 貞忠 loyalty ; fealty ; devotion

정취 情趣 [기분] mood ; [느낌] sentiment ; [아취] artistic effect 《of a painting》 ; charms ; charming effect ; a romantic touch ; flavor ¶ 정취 있는 charming ; appealing ; tasteful // 그 정취가 이 책에 잘 나타나 있다 That sentiment is well displayed in this book. // 그의 그림에는 사람을 매혹할 만한 정취가 있다 There is something in his paintings which appeals to our imagination.
서울 — the *Seoul* atmosphere 이국 — an exotic mood ; exoticism 일말의 동양적 — an Oriental touch

†**정치 政治** politics ; government ; administration ; political affairs ¶ 정치적인 political // 정치적으로 politically // 정치적 수완 statesmanship ; political ability // 정치적 자유 political freedom〔liberty〕 // 정치의 빈곤 lack of proper government // 밝은 정치 clean politics // 정치에 대한 불신 distrust in politics // 정치에 관계하다 enter〔go into, be in〕 politics // 정치를 하다 assume the helm of state ; take the reins of the government ; administer〔conduct〕 the affairs of state // 정치를 논하다 talk politics // 정치상의 문제로 삼다 make a political issue 《of》 // 정치 운동에 참가하다 take part in a political campaign〔movement〕
—가 a politician ; a professional politician — 결사 a political organization〔association〕 —계 the political world ; political circles — 공작 political maneuvering —과 a course in political science —광(狂) [사람] a politicomaniac — 권력 political authority — 기관 an organ of government ; the political machinery — 기구 a political structure a body politic — 기자 a political writer — 깡패 political hoodlums ; a political henchman — 단체 a political organization〔body〕 — 도덕 political morality —란 a political column — 문제 a political issue〔question〕 —범 political offense ; a political offender — 사상 political ideas — 사찰 political surveillance — 생명 a political life — 생활 a political career〔life〕 — 연감 a politician's yearbook —열 political fever — 운동 a political campaign〔movement, agitation〕 — 자금 political funds — 정화(淨化) a political clean-up ; the purification of politics — 조직 a political system ; a body politic — 테러 political terrorism — 투쟁 a political struggle ; political strife — 평론가 a publicist —학 political science ; politics —학자 a polit-

ical scientist — 헌금 a political donation — 협상 political negotiations — 활동 political activities 과두 — oligarchy 관료 — bureaucratic 금권 — plutocracy 독재 — despotic government 무단 — the rule of the saber 우민〔폭민〕 — ochlocracy ; mobocracy 정당 — party politics 혁신 — reformist politics 유엔 총회 특별 — 위원회 the Special Political Committee of the UN General Assembly ☞《p. 1888》

정치 定置 fixation ; settling ; stationary ──하다 station

—망 a fixed shore net ; a stationary net —망 어업 fixed shore net fishing ; stationary net fishery

정치 精緻 [정교] exquisiteness ; fineness ; [섬세] delicacy ; [미세] minuteness ──하다 (be) exquisite ; fine ; delicate ; minute

정치 情致 a charming effect ; a romantic touch ; appealing

정치 鼎峙 triangular position ──하다 stand in a trio ; be in a triangular position ¶ 3파 정치전 a three-cornered fight〔contest〕

정칙 正則 a regular system ; regularity ; normality ¶ 정칙의 regular ; proper ; formal ; systematic // 정칙의 영어 연구 a systematic study of English

— 영어 correct〔normal, proper, natural, good〕 English — 용액 a regular solution — 함수 a regular function

정칙 定則 a law ; an established rule

정크 a (Chinese) junk

정탐 偵探 scouting ; spying ; espionage (군사상의) ──하다 spy (on) ; investigate ; inquire into《a thing》

—군 a spy〔scout〕 ; a secret detective

정태 靜態 stationariness ¶ 정태의 static(-al) ; stationary

— 경제학 static economics — 사회학 static sociology — 통계학 static statistics

정태 情態 sycophancy ; adulation ; servile flattery

정토 征討 subjugation ⇨ 정벌

정토 淨土 paradise ; the promised〔holy〕 land ; the Buddhist Elysium

:정통 正統 [혈통] legitimacy ; orthodoxy ; [왕위] lineal descent of royalty ¶ 정통적인 legitimate ; orthodox

—극 a legitimate drama —주의 legitimism —주의자 a legitimist —파 the orthodox school〔party〕 ¶ 정통파의 신앙 the orthodox faith ; orthodoxy — 학파 the orthodox school

정통 精通 complete knowledge ──하다 know thoroughly ; be familiar with ; be well acquainted with ; be well versed in ; be well posted on 《미》 ; be at home in 《미》 ; be well informed 《of, on》 ; have a thorough knowledge 《of》 ¶ 그는 한국의 사정에 정통하다 He is well acquainted with Korean affairs. // 그는 정치〔문학〕에 정통하다 He is well versed in politics〔literature〕. // 그는 3개 국어에 정통하다 He is an expert in three languages.

정퇴 停退 deferment ; postponement ──하다 postpone ; defer ; put off

정파 政派 a group〔clique〕 (within a political party)

정판 整版 〖인쇄〗 recomposition ──하다 recompose

정평 定評 a reputation ; a settled opinion ; public acknowledgment ¶ 정평 있는 acknowledged ; recognized // 정평 있는 인물 a man of established reputation // 그는 대학자라는 정평이 있다 He has the reputation of being a great scholar. /He is recognized as a great scholar. // 그는 작가로 이미 정평이 있다 He is a writer of established reputation. // 그의 시간 엄수는 정평이 있다 He is famous for his punctuality. // 그것은 일반의 정평이다 That is what everybody says.

정평 正評 a right〔fair, pertinent〕 criticism ──하다 criticize properly〔pertinently〕

정표 情表 a love token ; a token 《of》 ; a keepsake ; a memento ¶ 애정의 정표 a token of one's love and affection // 감사의 정표로서 in token〔as a token〕 of one's gratitude ; as a mark of one's appreciation of 《a person's》 service

정품 精品 choice goods ; articles of the best quality

정풍 整風 rectification

— 운동 the rectification movement (중공의)

정하다 淨— (be) clear ; clean ; pure

정하다 呈— [제출하다] present 《a petition to authorities》 ; prefer 《a request》 ; send in ; turn in 《a report》

†정하다 定— [결정] decide 《on》 ; fix ; settle ; determine ; [협정] arrange ; agree upon ; [날짜를] set ; appoint ; [선정] choose ; [결심] resolve ; determine ; be resolved〔determined〕 ; [규칙] lay down ¶ 법령이 정하는 바에 따라 as provided by the law // …하기로 정하다 make it a rule to 《do》 ; make a point of 《doing》 // 값을 정하다 fix〔set〕 the price // 날을 정하다 fix a date // 직업을 정하다 choose〔decide on〕 one's occupation // 태도를 정하다 define one's attitude // 법을 정하다 lay down a law

정학 停學 suspension from school ; rustication (영국 대학의) ¶ 3일간의 정학 three days' suspension from school // 정학 처분을 받았다 He was suspended from school.

— 처분 suspension from school 무기 — suspension of attendance for an indefinite period

정한 定限 [기한] a definite period of time ; a limited time ; [한도] a fixed limit ; a fixed degree ; limit

정 치

정치는 politics와 government를 쓰며 「정치를 하다」, 「정치가 나쁘다」 등으로 쓸 경우의 정치는 politics보다도 government를 쓰는 것이 적절한 경우가 많다. 「정치에 종사하다」는 be [engage] in politics / play politics / do politicking으로 쓰고 「국민의, 국민에 의한, 국민을 위한 정치」는 government of the people, by the people, for the people로 쓴다. play politics는 「술책을 쓰다」의 뜻이 있으므로 「정치에 종사하다」의 뜻으로 쓸 때는 주의할 필요가 있다.

▶**현실(적) 정치** practical politics **금권 정치** money [moneyed] politics; bankroll [bankrolled] politics (★때로는 plutocracy [plu:tákrəsi]가 쓰이지만 이것은 「부유 계급에 의한 정치」의 뜻으로 이 말 자체에 부정, 독직 따위의 개념이 없으므로 money politics와 구별된다.) **정치 이념** political belief [ideal, concept]

▶**정치가** politician; statesman; politico; pol (★권력을 추구하는 정치가나 윤리의식이 결여된 「정치꾼」은 politico를 쓴다. pol은 politician의 단축형으로 「늙은 너구리 같은 정치인」의 뜻이 포함되어 있다.) **관료 정치가** bureaucrat-turned politician

▶**정당 정치** party politics [government] **원내 총무** party whip **열성 당원** party man **(정당의) 정책 노선** party line **정치 자금** political fund[money] **정치 자금 규제법** the Political Fund Control Law **정치 헌금** political donation [contribution] **정치 단체** political organization [group] **공인(公認)정치 단체** (officially) registered political organization **미공인 정치 단체** yet-to-be registered political organization **비공인 정치 단체** officially unrecognized political organization; private political organization **정치적으로 이용하다** politicize ¶야당은 소비자 운동을 정치적으로 이용하는 데 성공했다. The Opposition party has successfully politicized consumerism.

▶**정권** (political) power; government; regime; administration **정권을 잡다** come into (the seat of) power; take [gain] power **정권 쟁탈** power struggle [scramble, schism, squabble]; struggle [scramble, maneuvering] for power **정권 교체** change of power [government] **보수 정권** conservative government **혁신 정권** reformist [renovationist, progressive] government **중도 정권** centrist[middle-of-the-road] government **연립(연합) 정권** coalition government ¶양당은 연립 정권을 수립했다. The two parties went into coalition to form a government.

▶**여당** party in power; ruling party **야당** opposition; the Opposition (party)

▶**체제** the establishment; (political) system **반체제** anti-establishment; anti-system **쿠데타** coup d'état[kú:deitá:]; coup [ku:] ¶그들은 무혈 쿠데타를 일으켰다. They pulled [staged] a bloodless coup.

▶**혁명** revolution **혁명가** revolutionist; revolutionary **혁명 위원회** junta [húntə, dʒʌ́ntə] 《쿠데타 직후의 임시 정부》 **반혁명** counter-revolution **숙청** purge ¶그는 당내의 정적들을 숙청했다. He purged the party of his political enemies. **소리 없는 대중** silent majority

---

정한 精悍 intrepidity ; fierceness **— 하다** (be) dauntless ; intrepid ; fierce ; fearless

정해 丁亥 〖민속〗 the 24th binary term of the sexagenary cycle

정해 正解 a correct answer〔solution, interpretation〕; correct understanding **— 하다** give〔send〕 a correct answer 〔solution〕; understand〔interpret, apprehend〕 correctly
—자 one who gives a correct answer

정해 精解 precise〔accurate〕 solution 〔interpretation〕 **— 하다** solve〔interpret〕 precisely

정해지다 定— [결정되다] be decided ; be settled ; be determined ; be fixed ; [규정되다] be laid down ; be provided ; be established ¶ 그것은 다 미리 정해져 있었다 It was all arranged beforehand. // 공급은 수요에 따라 정해진다 Demand determines supply.

정향 丁香 clove buds ; Syringa palibiniana (학명)
—나무 a kind of clove tree ; a kind of lilac bush

정향 진화 定向進化 〖생물〗 orthogenesis

정현 正弦 〖기하〗 a sine (of an angle)
— 곡선 a sine curve **— 법칙** 〖수학〗 law of sine **—파** 〖물리〗 sine wave

정혈 精血 lifeblood

정형 正刑 (a) capital punishment ; (a) death penalty ; the punishment of death

정형 整形 〖의학〗 a plastic operation ; [모양] remodelling ; transfiguration
— 병원 an orthopedic hospital **— 수술** orthopedic treatment ; plastic operation ¶ 정형 수술을 받다 undergo a plastic surgery〔operation〕 **— 외과** orthope-

dics ; orthopedic surgery ¶ 미용 정형 외과 cosmetic surgery — 외과의 an orthopedist ; an orthopedic surgeon

정형 定型 a set pattern ; a (fixed, regular) type ; a definite form ; standard ¶ 정형적 typical
—시 a fixed form of verse —열 〖의학〗 typic fever —화 standardization

정형 定形 a fixed〔regular〕 form〔shape〕

정혼 定婚 arranging a marriage ; affiance ; betrothal ; engagement —하다 arrange a marriage ; betroth

정혼 精魂 soul ; spirit ⇨ 정령(精靈)

정화 正貨 specie ¶ 정화로 in specie
— 보유고 specie holdings — 수송점 a gold〔specie〕 point — 유출〔유입〕 an outflow〔inflow〕 of specie — 준비 specie 〔gold〕 reserve ; gold coverage — 지불 specie payment — 현송 specie shipment

정화 情火 the passion of love ; the fire of passion〔love〕 ; the flame of love ¶ 정화가 불타다 burn with passion〔love〕

정화 情話 [대화] lover's talk ; [이야기] a love story ; a romance

정화 淨火 a sacred fire

정화 淨化 purification ; a cleanup —하다 purify ; purge ; cleanup
— 설비 sewage disposal facilities ; sanitation facilities — 운동 a purge ; a cleanup movement — 작용 〖정신 분석〗 abreaction ; catharsis — 장치 a purifier ; an apparatus for purifying — 탱크 a water-purifier tank ; a tank for purifying water ; a septic tank

†정화 精華 the essence ; the flower ; the glory ¶ 기사도의 정화 the flower of chivalry

정화수 井華水 water drawn from the well early at dawn

†정확 正確 correctness ; accuracy ; exactness ; precision ; exactitude —하다 (be) correct ; exact ; accurate ; right ; precise

> 참고 **correct**는 일반적인 말로서 오류를 포함하지 않은 **accurate**는 의미가 강하여 진실 표준에 완전히 일치한 **precise**는 세부에 이르기까지 정확한 **exact**는 엄밀히 정확한 **right**는 정당한으로서 원래는 도덕적인 의미가 강하였다

¶ 정확한 기계 a precise instrument // 정확한 발음 correct pronunciation // 정확한 시간 correct〔exact〕 time // 정확한 영어 good English // 정확한 지도 an accurate map // 보도의 정확 the veracity of information // 정확하게 말하자면 to be exact ; correctly〔precisely〕 speaking // 과학적인 정확성으로 with scientific exactitude〔precision〕 // 정확한 것은 모른다 I don't know for certain. // 그 시계는 정확하다 The clock keeps correct〔good〕 time.

†정확 精確 precision ; accuracy ; exactitude ; exactness —하다 (be) accurate ; precise ; exact ¶ 정확한 지도 an accurate map // 시계처럼 정확히 with clockwork precision // 정확한 관찰을 하다 make accurate observations // 네 추측은 정확하게 맞아 떨어졌다 Your guess was right on the money. /Your guess was right on the nose.

정황 政況 the political situation〔outlook〕

정황 情況 conditions ; circumstances ; a situation ; the state of things ¶ 지금 정황으로는 under these circumstances ; as matters stand ; as things go

정황 증거 情況證據 〖법〗 circumstantial 〔direct〕 evidence ¶ 그 증거를 단순한 정황 증거로 경시하다 belittle the evidence as purely circumstantial // 그는 정황 증거로 유죄를 선고받았다 He was convicted on circumstantial evidence.

정회 停會 suspension of a meeting ; [의회의] prorogation ; [휴회] adjournment —하다 suspend ; prorogue ; adjourn

정회 情懷 affectionate remembrances ; fond recollection ; dear memories

정회원 正會員 a regular member ¶ 정회원의 자격 full membership

정훈 政訓 [군(軍)에서] troop information and education
— 요원 T. I. E. personnel

정휴일 定休日 a regular〔set〕 holiday

정히 正— exactly ; precisely ; surely ; certainly ; no doubt ; truly ; really

†젖 [유방] the breast(s) ; [유즙] milk ¶ 소젖 cow's milk // 어머니 젖 mother's milk // 소 젖을 짜다 milk a cow // 소 젖이 잘 나오다 be in (the) milk ; milk well // 젖을 빨다 suck milk // 젖을 주다 nurse 《a baby》 ; give the breast to // 젖이 마르다 one's breasts run dry // 젖이 잘 나오다 make the milk flow easily // 젖이 붓다 the breast is swollen // 젖을 떼다 wean 《a baby from its mother》
—가슴 the breast(s) ; the bosom —꼭지 the teat(s) ; the nipple(s) —형제 a foster〔milk〕 brother

젖내 [냄새] the smell of milk ¶ 젖내 나다 be (still) suckling ; be (still) in swaddling clothes ; be babyish〔childish, puerile, immature, green〕

젖니 a milk〔deciduous, baby, calf's〕 tooth ; the first set of teeth

†젖다 get wet〔soaked, drenched〕 ; be damp ; be moistened ; be dank ; be moist ; be humid

> 참고 **damp** 습기가 많아 흔히 불쾌한 감정이 따른다 **dank** 습기가 있어 차고 불쾌한 느낌을 준다 **moist** 기분이 좋을 정도의 습기로서 damp보다 물기가 적다 **humid** 공중의 고도에 있는 습기의 상태를 말하며 문어 또는 전문어로 쓰인다 **wet** 물에 젖은 상태

¶ 젖은 옷〔땅〕 wet clothes〔ground〕// 비에 젖다 get wet in the rain // 땀에 젖다 be wet with perspiration // 물에 젖다 get wet ; be soaked // 함빡 젖다 be wet〔soaked〕 to the skin ; be soaking wet // 귀에 젖다 ring in one's ears ; be familiar to one's ear ; be impressed on one's mind ; soak〔be soaked〕 in thoroughly // 귀에 젖도록 타이르다 admonish again and again ; drum a lesson into《a person's》 head // 아버지의 말씀이 귀에 젖었다 Father's words are still ringing in my ears. // 네 말은 귀에 젖도록 들었다 That's enough out of you.

젖동생 —同生 a foster brother〔sister〕

젖떨어지다 be〔get〕 weaned ¶ 젖 떨어진 아이 a weaned child ; a weanling

젖떼기 a weaned child〔animal〕

젖떼다 wean ; cease to suckle

젖뜨리다 ⇨ 잦뜨리다

젖먹이 a suckling child ; a suckling ; a baby

젖멍울 [젖샘] the mammary gland ; [멍울] mastitis ¶ 젖멍울이 서다《a girl, a woman》 suffer〔fill out〕 from mastitis

젖몸살 mastitis ¶ 젖몸살을 앓다 suffer from mastitis ; have inflamed mammary glands

젖버듬하다 ⇨ 잦바듬하다

젖병 —瓶 a nursing bottle ; a nurser

젖부들기 meat from the breast〔udder, bag〕; teat of an animal

젖빛 milk white ¶ 젖빛의 milk-white
— **유리** frosted〔ground〕 glass

젖빨이 동물 —動物 ⇨ 포유(哺乳) 동물

젖소 a milch〔milking〕 cow

젖어머니, 젖어미 a wet nurse

젖통 ⇨ 젖통이 ¶ 젖통이 큰 여자 a girl with big breasts ; a blowsy〔bosomy〕 girl ; a bust-bomb

젖통이 the breast(s)

젖히다 ① turn over《leaves of a book》; turn down ② pull back《one's shoulders》; lean backwards ¶ 가슴을 뒤로 젖히고 턱을 끌어 당겨라 Push out your chest and pull in your chin. ③ fling《a door》 open ; open wide ④ put aside《one's work》; lay aside ; set apart

제[1] [저기] that place ; there ; over there ¶ 제 있는 건물이 우리 학교입니다 The building over there is our school.

제[2] [저·자기] I ; self ; oneself ; [자기의] one's own ; my ; my own ¶ 제가 결정한 self-determined // 제가 좋아하는 일 self-imposed work // 제 일로 on one's private business // 제 이익만 생각하다 look to one's own interest // 제 일은 제가 해야 한다 One should look after one's own business. // 제 모자입니다 It is my hat. // 제가 했습니다 I myself did it. // 제 딴은 잘한 셈이다 He believes〔fancies〕 himself to have done well. // 제 딴은 시인이라고 생각한다 He thinks he is a poet. / He is a would-be poet.

제 눈에 안경 속담 Beauty is in the eye of the beholder.

제 도끼에 제 발등 찍힌다 속담 In trust is treason. /Trust makes way for treachery. /Trust is the mother of deceit.

제 발등 불을 먼저 끄랬다 속담 Skeer your own fire. /Meddle not with another man's matter.

제 버릇 개 줄까 속담 It is hard to break a hog of an ill custion.

제 祭 [제사] a religious service ; [축제] a festival ; a fete
기념 — a commemoration **50년 —** a jubilee **100년 —** a centennial anniversary ; a centenary **200년—** a bicentenary

제 題 a subject ⇨ 제목

제 弟 [자칭] I ; [아우] a younger brother

제 除 subtraction ⇨ 제법 ; exclusion ⇨ 제거

제 帝 an emperor

제 諸 many ; several ; various ; diverse ; manifold ¶ 제비용〔경비〕 expenses ; costs ; charges ; overhead // 제형 dear friends ; gentlemen

제 第 -th ; number ; No. ¶ 제일〔이, 삼〕 the first〔second, third〕// 제삼국 the third power〔country〕// 제 5조 제 3항 Clause Ⅲ, Article Ⅴ // 제삼자 a third party〔person〕; an outsider

-제 劑 a medicine ; a drug ; a remedy for
소화— an aid to digestion ; a stomach remedy

-제 制 a system ; an organization ; an institution ¶ 8시간제 the eight-hour system // 4년제 대학 a four-year college

-제 製 make ; manufacture ¶ 영국제의 of English make ; made in England // 목제의 wooden ; made of wood // 강철제의 made of steel // 외국제의 물건 articles of foreign manufacture〔make〕

제가 齊家 governing a family ; managing a household **—하다** govern a family ; manage a household

제가 諸家 [여러 학자] various〔many〕 masters ; all the schools (of art) ; [친척들] the whole family ; all the relatives

제각 除却 ⇨ 제거(除去)

제각각 —各各 ⇨ 제각기

제각기 —各其 each ; respectively ; separately ; individually ¶ 사람은 제각기 장단점이 있다 Each man has his merits and faults. // 그 회의에 참석한 학생들은 제각기 의견을 제시했다 Each student present at the meeting expressed his opinion.

제감 除減 deduction ; subtraction **—하다** deduct ; take away ; subtract

제강 製鋼 steel manufacture ; steel making
—법 a steel making process **—소** steel works **—업** the steel industry **—업자** a steelman ; a steelmaker

†**제거 除去** exclusion ; removal ; elimina-

tion ; omission ; eradication —하다 exclude ; remove ; get rid of ; eliminate ¶ 수술에 의한 난소의 제거 an operative removal of the ovary // 생활의 낭비를 제거하다 eliminate the wastefulness of life // 폐풍을 제거하다 do away with evil practices // 장애물을 제거하다 remove obstacles // 원인을 제거하다 get rid of the cause

제것 one's own property ; one's (private) possession ; what one possesses ¶ 제것이 되다 fall into one's hands〔possession〕; [사람이 주어] come by《a thing》 // 제것으로 만들다 make《a thing》one's own ; take《a thing》to oneself ; have《a thing》for one's own ; possess oneself of《a thing》; appropriate (for oneself)

제겨디디다 stand〔step〕on tiptoes

제겨차다 kick hard

제격 —格 becoming〔being suitable, proper, etc.〕to one's status ; befitting one's station ¶ 그 일은 그에게 제격이다 He is just the man for the job. /He is the right person for the work.

제고 提高 —하다 raise ; uplift

제고장 one's native place ; the (original) home

제골 蹄骨 〖해부〗 a coffin bone (말의)

제곱 〖수학〗 square ; squaring —하다 square《a number》; multiply《a number》by itself

—근 a square root ¶ 제곱근을 구하다 extract the square root《of》; find the square《of》 // 3은 9의 제곱근이다 Three is the square root of 9. —근 풀이 evolution ; extraction of a square root ¶ 제곱근 풀이하다 extract the square root《of》

†**제공 提供** offer ; proffer —하다 offer ; make an offer ; proffer ; furnish ¶ 그 물건을 만원에 제공하다 offer the article at ten thousand *won* // 그에게 100만원을 제공하다 offer him a million *won* // 정보를 제공하다 furnish information

— 가격 the price offered —자 a《blood》donor 실비 — offered at cost

제공권 制空權 the mastery〔command〕of the air ; air supremacy ¶ 제공권을 잡다〔잃다〕win〔lose〕the air ; secure〔lose〕the command of the air

제과 製菓 confectionery

—업 the confectionery industry —업자 a confectioner — 회사 a confectionery company

제관 祭官 a priest ; an officiating priest ; [참례자] those who participate in sacrifices

제관 帝冠 a crown ; a diadem

제관 製罐 can manufacturing ; canning《미》; tinning《영》

제구 祭具 utensils used in religious services

제구 諸具 various articles〔utensils, tools, fixtures〕

제구력 制球力 〖야구〗 control ¶ 제구력이 없다〔있다〕lack〔have good〕control of the ball

제구실 one's function ; one's duty (의무) ; one's duties (직무) ; one's obligation ; one's share〔bit〕; [병] the usual epidemic diseases that every child has to go through ¶ 제구실을 하다 do one's bit ; prove adequate ; be worth one's salt ; have one's measles〔smallpox, scarlet fever〕/// 제구실을 하게 되다 become an adult ; become independent ; become a self-supporting man // 제구실 못하다 be not worth one's salt // 선생은 가르치는 것이 제구실이다 The business〔duty, function〕of the teacher is to teach.

†**제국 帝國** an empire ¶ 제국의 imperial

—주의 imperialism ; expansionism《미》¶ 제국주의적 imperialistic // 반 제국주의 감정 anti-imperialist sentiment —주의자 an imperialist ; an expansionist 로마— the Roman Empire

제국 諸國 all〔various, many〕countries〔states〕

제군 諸君 gentlemen ; my friends ; my lads (부하에게) ; [연설의 경우] Ladies and Gentlemen !

제권 판결 除權判決 judgement of exclusion

제규 制規 rules ; regulations

제금 〖국악기〗 small cymbals

제금 提琴 a violin ; a fiddle

—가 a violinist ; a fiddler

제기[1] [유희] a kind of shuttlecock game played with the feet ¶ 제기를 차다 play shuttlecock

제기[2] shucks ; damn it ; confound it ; fie ¶ 제기랄 Damn it ! /Go and hang it ! // 제기 빌어먹을 자식 Go to hell ! // 제기 비싸기도 하다 It's damn expensive !

제기 祭器 dishes〔utensils〕used in religious services

제기 提起 [제의] proposal ; [소송] institution ; [항의] lodging ; [발언] suggestion —하다 present ; propose ; institute ; lodge ; bring《forward》; [문제 따위를] start ¶ 소송을 제기하다 institute〔lodge, file〕a lawsuit // 이론을 제기하다 raise a question in argument

제기다[1] ① [지르다] kick with (the) toe ; nudge with (the) elbow ; toe ; elbow ② [연장으로] cut with light repeated strokes ③ [물을] pour《water》a little at a time

제기다[2] ① [눈에] have〔get〕a white spot in the pupil of an eye ② [살짝] slip out ; sneak away

제기랄 ⇨ 제기[2]

제깐에 ⇨ 제딴은

제꺽 ⇨ 재깍

제너레이션 a generation

제네바 Geneva ; Geneve

제다 製茶 tea manufacture〔making〕
— 공장 a tea factory —업 the tea manufacturing industry
:제단 祭壇 an altar ; the seat of religious service
제당 製糖 sugar-manufacture〔-refining〕
— 공장 a sugar mill〔refinery〕 —소 a sugar-manufactory —업 the sugar-manufacturing industry — 회사 a sugar-manufacturing company
제대 除隊 discharge from military service ; demobilization —하다 be discharged from military service ; be demobilized ; be mustered out 《미》
— 명령 a ticket —병 a discharged soldier — 휴가 (제대 직전의) a terminal leave 만기 — an honorable discharge 명예〔불명예〕 — honorable〔dishonorable〕 discharge 의가사〔의병〕 — discharge from service due to family hardships〔illness〕 ; a hardship〔compassionate〕 discharge
제대 梯隊 〖군사〗 an echelon
제대 臍帶 〖해부〗 the umbilical cord (탯줄)
제대로 as it is ; as it should ; as one please ; in one's own way ; intactuntouched ; smoothly ; without a hitch ; in orderly fashion ¶ 제대로 두다 leave it as it is ; let it alone // 제대로 하게 하다 let 《a person》 do as he pleases // 일이 제대로 되다 One's work goes well. // 일이 제대로 되면 내달에는 끝나겠다 If all goes well, this job will be finished next month. // 그건 네가 집을 나서기 전에 제대로 아침 식사를 하지 않기 때문이야 That's because you don't eat a proper breakfast before you leave the house.
*제도 制度 a system ; [시설] an institution ; [조직] an organization ; [질서] an order ¶ 영국의 문물 제도 English culture and institutions // 우리 교육 제도의 결함 defects in our educational system // 신제도하의 교육 education under the new system // 제도를 바꾸다 change the system // 제도를 시행하다 enforce a system ; put a system〔an institution〕 in operation〔practice〕 // 제도를 폐지하다 abolish the system // 제도를 개선하다 improve〔reform〕 the system
—사(史) an institutional history —주의 institutionalism 결혼 — the marriage institution 교육 — the educational system 구(舊)— the ancient regime ; the fossil 군대 — military organization 문물 — culture and institutions 사회 — the social system 의회 — the parliamentary system〔regime〕 현행 — the existing system ; the existing order of things
제도 製陶 pottery manufacture ; porcelain making
—술 the ceramic〔fictile〕 art ; ceramics ; pottery
제도 製圖 draughtsmanship ; drafting ; cartography ; 〖기하〗 drawing —하다 draw ; draft
—가 a draughtsman ; a draftsman 《미》 — 기구 drawing instruments ; a (mechanical) drawing set —실 a drawing〔drafting〕 room — 용구 draftsman's outfit — 용지 drafting〔drawing〕 paper —판 a drawing board ; a trestle board
제도 諸島 a group of islands ; an archipelago
남양 — The South Sea Islands
제도 濟度 salvation ; redemption —하다 save ; redeem ¶ 제도하기 힘들다 be past salvation ; be beyond〔past〕 redemption
제도화 制度化 institutionalization —하다 institutionalize ¶ 제도화되다 be institutionalized
제독 制毒 protection against poison —하다 counteract (poisonous effects) ; rid of noxious influence ; neutralize a poison ; serve as an antidote
제독 提督 an admiral ; a commodore 《미》
제독 除毒 ⇨ 해독(解毒)
제독주다 制毒— humble〔humiliate〕 《a person》 ; take 《a person》 down a notch〔peg〕 or two ; cut 《a person's》 comb ; unnerve
제동 制動 braking ; [전기] damping —하다 brake 《a car》 ; damp
—근(筋) 〖조개〗 a catch muscle — 레버 a safety lever —력 braking〔damping, arresting〕 power —수 a brakeman —자 a damper — 장치 a damping device ; an arresting gear —차 〖철도〗 a brake van —활강 glissade (스키의)
제동기 制動機 a brake ¶ 제동기를 걸다 apply〔put on〕 the brakes // 제동기를 푼 채로 달리다 run with the brakes off
공기 — an air brake 동력 — a power brake 비상 — an emergency brake 수동 — a hand brake 자동 — an automatic brake 자력 — a magnetic brake 전기 — an electric brake 진공 — a vacuum brake
제등 提燈 a paper lantern ¶ 제등 행렬 a lantern procession〔parade〕
제등수 諸等數 〖수학〗 a compound number
제딴은 as for one ; for one's part ; for oneself ; in one's own opinion ¶ 제딴은 큰 학자로 믿고 있다 He is a savant in his own estimation. /He is a self-styled scholar. // 제딴은 아주 열심히 공부하는 것으로 알고 있다 He fancies himself to be working very hard.
제때 an appointed〔a scheduled, a proper〕 time ¶ 제때에 식사하다 have regular meals ; be regular in one's diet // 제때를 노리다 watch for the proper time // 기차는 제때에 도착했다 The train arrived on schedule.
제라늄 〖식물〗 a geranium
*제련 製鍊 refining ; tempering ; smelting —하다 refine ; smelt ; purify ¶ 제련용

노 a smelting furnace
—소 a refinery ; a smelting works —업 the refining industry —업자 a refiner
제령 制令 regulations ; laws
제례 祭禮 religious ceremonies ; sacrificial rituals —하다 observe religious ceremonies
:제로 zero ¶ 내 화학 지식은 제로나 마찬가지다 I know practically nothing about chemistry. // 그는 교사로서는 제로다 As a teacher, he is a complete failure. /He must be given zero as a teacher.
— 게임 〖정구〗 a love game ; 〖야구〗 a shut-out
제록스 [상표명] Xerox ¶ 제록스로 복사하다 xerox (a copy) ; make a Xerox copy
제마 製麻 manufacture of hemp —하다 manufacture hemp (goods)
— 회사 a hemp-dressing company
제막 除幕 unveiling —하다 unveil ⟪a bust, a statue⟫
—식 the ceremony of unveiling ; the unveiling ceremony ⟪of a statue, bust⟫
제매 弟妹 younger brothers and sisters
제멋 one's own taste〔way, fancy, style〕
제멋대로 ⇨ 멋대로
제면 製綿 ginning cotton —하다 gin cotton
제면 製麵 manufacturing noodles —하다 manufacture〔make〕 noodles ; make vermicelli
—기 a noodle-making machine
*제명 除名 expulsion ; dismissal from membership —하다 expel ⟪from⟫ ; strike〔take〕 a name off the list〔roll〕 ; dismiss ⟪a person⟫ from membership ¶ 제명되다 be struck off the list ; be expelled from membership // 회원을 제명하다 dismiss ⟪a person⟫ from membership // 자유당은 S씨의 제명을 결의했다 The Liberals have decided to strike Mr. S's name off the roll. // 그는 그 회에서 제명당했다 He was expelled from the society.
제명 題名 a title ¶ "서울의 밤"이라는 제명의 영화 a picture entitled 'A Night in *Seoul*' // …의 제명으로 출판되다 be published under the title ⟪of⟫
제모 制帽 a regulation〔uniform, school〕 cap ¶ 제복 제모의 학생 a student in uniform
제목 題目 a subject ; a theme ; a title (책의) ; a heading〔headline〕 ; caption (사진의) ¶ 작문의 제목 the subject of composition // 「자유」라는 제목의 논문 an essay entitled 'Liberty' // 제목을 붙이다 give a title to ; entitle ⟪a book⟫ // 제목은 자유이다 Subjects can be chosen freely.
제문 祭文 a funeral oration〔ode〕
제물 [국물] the water in which food was cooked ; soup left after food is cooked ; [순수한 것] something genuine
제물 祭物 an offering ; a sacrificial offering ; things offered in sacrifice
제물낚시 an artificial fishing-fly ; a fly
제물로 ⇨ 제물에
제물에 of its〔one's〕 own accord ; of itself ; by itself ¶ 상처가 제물에 나았다 The wound healed of itself.
제바람 its own influence ; one's own fault ¶ 제바람에 of itself ; by oneself
제반 諸般 all sorts ¶ 제반의 various ; several ; all ; every // 제반의 정세 all circumstances ; general state of things // 제반의 준비를 갖추다 make every preparation
제반미 祭飯米 rice (to be cooked and) offered in memorial service
제발 kindly ; please ; if you please ; pray ; I beg ; [반드시] by all means ¶ 제발 문을 닫아 주십시오 May I trouble you to shut the door ? // 제발 용서하세요 Excuse me, please. /I humbly beg your pardon. // 제발 좀 조용히 해 주게 For goodness' sake, don't start making a noise about it. // 제발 농담 좀 그만두어라 Don't go too far with your jokes, please. // 제발 살려 주십시오 Spare me〔my life〕, please.
제발 덕분에 —德分— for mercy's 〔God's, goodness'〕 sake ; please for my sake ¶ 제발 덕분에 살려 주십시오 Spare me〔my life〕 for mercy's〔Peter's〕 sake. // 제발 덕분에 그를 관대히 처분해 주십시오 Please, show him your leniency.
제방 堤防 a bank ; an embankment ; a dike〔dyke〕 ; a levee ⟪미⟫ ¶ 제방을 구축하다 build a dike // 제방이 무너지다 a dike breaks
— 공사 bank revetment ; banking ; riparian works ; shore-protection works
제방 諸邦 ⇨ 제국
제백사 除百事 laying aside everything ; neglecting everything else —하다 lay everything aside ; throw〔put〕 aside everything ¶ 제백사하고 before everything else ; above all things // 제백사하고 찾아 뵙겠습니다 I'll let everything else go and visit you.
제번 除煩 saving trouble ; [편지 서두] without ceremony —하다 save trouble ; be without ceremony
제벌 除伐 〖임업〗 improvement〔salvage〕 cutting
제법 quite ; fairly ; considerably ; pretty ; rather ¶ 제법 중대한 일 a matter of no small consequence // 제법 좋은 수입 a handsome income // 제법이다 be better than expected ; be good beyond expectation // 제법 덥다 be quite〔rather〕 warm // 제법 늦다 be fairly late // 제법 시간이 걸리다 take a great deal of time // 영어를 제법 하다 have a fair knowledge of English ; speak English fairly well // 그 여자는 정구도 제법한다 She is not half bad at tennis. // 그는 제법 문장가이다 He is

very much of a writer. // 그 친구 제법이야 He is not a man to be despised. /He is a man of no mean ability.
제법 除法 〖수학〗 division
제법 製法 a method〔process〕 of manufacture ; a manufacturing process〔method〕; [과자·요리의] a recipe 《for》 making a cake. 》
†제복 制服 a uniform ; a regulation dress ; [고용인의] livery ; [법관 따위의] a gown ¶ 학교의 제복 a school uniform // 제복의 경관 a uniformed policeman // 제복을 입은 uniformed ; in uniform // 학교에는 제복을 입고 가지 않으면 안된다 We have to go to school in uniform.
제복 除服 going out of mourning ; end 〔expiration〕 of mourning period ━하다 leave off mourning ; go out of mourning
제복 祭服 priest's ritual robes ; sacrificial robes ; [카톨릭교] a pallium ; a pall
제복 제모 制服制帽 a regulation cap and uniform ¶ (학교의) 제복 제모 차림으로 in school cap and uniform
제본 製本 bookbinding ━하다 bind 《a book》 ¶ 제본 중이다 be at the binder's // 제본이 잘 되어 있다 be well bound // 이것을 제본해 주십시오 I want to have the book bound.
━소 a bookbindery ; a bookbinder ━업 the bookbinding industry 고급 양장 ━ high quality hard-cover bookbinding
†제분 製粉 milling ; pulverizing ; grinding ━하다 mill ; pulverize ; grind
━기 a mill machine ━소 a flour mill ━업 the milling industry ━업자 a miller ━ 회사 a flour mill company
제본사 製本絲 darning-thread ; binding thread ; lashing
제붙이 one's own people ; one's relatives 〔kinsfolk, family circle〕
†제비[1] a lot ; a lottery ; a raffle ; a lottery ticket (표) ¶ 제비 뽑다 draw lots // 제비에 맞다 draw a winning number ; draw a prize // 제비에 떨어지다 draw a blank // 제비 뽑아 결정하다 decide〔choose〕 by lot // 누가 갖게 되나 제비뽑자 Let's draw lots to see who can have it. // 제비가 맞았다 The lot fell upon me.
‡제비[2] 〖새〗 a swallow ¶ 제비가 왔다고 여름이 되는 것은 아니다 One swallow does not make a summer.
‡제비꽃 〖식물〗 a violet ; a pansy
제비꿀 〖식물〗 a sandalwood plant
제비추리 beef from the inside ribs
제비턱 (a person with) a chubby chin ; a double chin
제빙 除氷 deicing ━하다 deice
제빙 製氷 ice manufacture
━기 an ice(-making) machine ; a refrigerator ━소〔공장〕 an ice-plant〔-manufactory〕 ━업자 an ice manufacturer ; an ice-man 《영》 ━ 회사 an ice (-manufacturing) company 인공 ━ manufacture of (artificial) ice
제사 祭祀 a religious service ; sacrificial rites ; a sacrifice ¶ 제사를 지내다 perform a religious service〔sacrificial rite〕
━날 a sacrificial day
제사 製絲 spinning ; silk-reeling〔-manufacture〕; filature ━하다 draw silk ; make thread
━공 a silk-reel worker ━ 공장 a filature ; a silk mill ━ 기계 a reeling machine ━업 the silk-reeling industry ━업자 a silk manufacturer
제사 第四 the fourth
━ 계급 [무산자] the proletariat ; [언론인] the fourth estate ; journalists
제산 除算 division ━하다 divide
제산제 制酸劑 an antacid〔antiacid〕 (agent)
제살붙이 ⇨ 제붙이
제살이 self-support ━하다 support oneself ; earn〔make〕 one's own living
제삼 계급 第三階級 the bourgeoisie ; the third estate
제삼국 第三國 the third power〔country〕
제삼자 第三者 a third person ; the disinterested party ; an outsider
제삿날로 of one's own accord ; according to one's own desires
제상 祭床 a table used in a religious 〔memorial〕 service ; a sacrificial table
제상 除霜 defrosting ; deicing ━하다 defrost ; deice
━ 장치 a defroster ; a deicer
제석 除夕 New Year's Eve ; the watch night ⇨ 제야
제석 祭席 a mat used in religious〔memorial〕 services ; a sacrificial mat
제석 帝釋 ① 〖민속〗 the Harvest God (a shamanistic deity) ② ⇨ 제석천(帝釋天)
━풀이 〖민속〗 the shamanistic rite celebrating the Harvest God
제석천 帝釋天 〖불교〗 Sakra devánám Indra 《범》
제설 諸說 diverse views〔opinions〕; various theories ¶ 이 사건에 대하여는 제설이 분분하다 Various views are expressed on this affair.
제설 除雪 snow removal ━하다 remove snow
━기 a snowplow ━ 작업 snow removing work ━차 a snowplow car〔locomotive〕 러셀식 ━ 기관차 a Russel plow〔plough〕
제성 帝城 an imperial palace
제세 濟世 salvation〔relief〕 of the world ━하다 save〔relieve〕 the world
━ 안민 saving the world and relieving the people
제소 提訴 instituting〔filing〕 a lawsuit ━하다 bring a lawsuit against ; sue ; file a suit
━자 a suitor ; a complainant
제수 弟嫂 one's younger brother's wife ; a sister-in-law

제수 除數 〖수학〗 the divisor ; the number to be divided by
제수 祭需 things needed in the sacrificial service ; expenses of the sacrificial service
제수당 諸手當 sundry〔various〕 allowances
제술 製述 literary composition ―하다 compose 《literary works》 ; write
제스처 a gesture ¶ 정치〔외교〕적 제스처 a political〔diplomatic〕 gesture // 단순한 제스처에 불과하다 It's simply a gesture.
제습 除濕 ―하다 dehumidify
―기(器) a dehumidifier
제승 制勝 (a) victory ; a win ―하다 win〔gain〕 a victory 《over》 ; earn〔chalk up〕 a win 《over》
†제시 提示 presentation ―하다 〖법〗 exhibit ; present ¶ 제시하는 대로 at〔on〕 presentation
―금 show money ― 기간 time of presentation ―부 〖음악·연극〗 exposition ―불 payment at sight ―불 어음 a sight〔demand〕 bill ― 어음 〖상업〗 enfaced paper ―자 [제출 물건의] 〖법〗 an exhibitor
제시간 ―時間 the appropriate〔proper, scheduled〕 time ¶ 제시간에 발차(發車)하다 leave at a scheduled time〔on schedule〕 // 제시간에 대지 못하다 be late 《for》 ; miss // 회장(會長)까지 간신히 제시간에 대어 갔다 I got to the place of meeting just in time.
제실 帝室 the royal house〔family〕
제씨 弟氏 your〔his〕 esteemed younger brother
제씨 諸氏 gentlemen ; Messrs.
†제안 提案 a proposal ; a proposition ; a suggestion ; an overture

> 참고 **proposal** 상대방으로부터 찬부의 결정을 받기 위하여 내놓는 계획이나 제안 **proposition** 논의 증명 따위를 위하여 내놓는 진술이나 명제 그러나 상업 용어로서는 전자와 구별하지 않는다

―하다 propose ; make an overture ; bring forward ; suggest ¶ 제안을 가결〔부결〕하다 adopt〔reject〕 a proposal // 제안을 설명하다 enunciate the proposition // 그는 그 모임에서 새 계획을 제안할 것이다 He will propose a new plan at the meeting. // 그 피크닉은 그 여자의 제안이었다 The picnic was her suggestion.
― 설명 enunciation of a proposal ―자 a proposer ; a sponsor 반대 ― a counterproposal ; a counteroffer 공동 ―자〔국〕 cosponsors〔joint sponsors〕 of a proposal ☞ ❪p. 1896❫
제암성 制癌性 ¶ 제암성의 anticarcinogenic ; carcinolytic (암세포 파괴의)
제압 制壓 oppression ; mastery ; domination ―하다 control ; gain control over ; dominate ; domineer over
제액 題額 writing an inscription on a tablet
제야 除夜 New Year's Eve ; the watch night ¶ 제야의 종소리 a watch-night bell // 제야의 종을 울리다 ring out the old year
제약 製藥 [제조] manufacture of medicines ; pharmacy ; [약] a manufactured medicine〔drug〕 ―하다 manufacture drugs〔medicines〕
― 공장〔회사〕 a pharmaceutical factory〔company〕 ―업자 a drug manufacturer ; a pharmacist ― 화학 pharmaceutical chemistry ― 회사 a pharmaceutical〔drug〕 company
제약 制約 [조건] condition ; [속박] a restriction ; a limitation ―하다 control ; limit ; restrict ¶ 제약적 판단 〖철학〗 conditional judgment // 시간의 제약을 받다 be restricted by time // 유형 무형의 제약을 받다 be curbed physically and spiritually 《from》 // 인생에는 여러 가지 제약이 있다 Life is hampered by a variety of restrictions.
― 명제 〖논리학〗 a conditional proposition ―적 판단 〖철학〗 conditional judgment
제어 制御, 制馭 control ; governing ; domination ; mastery ; management ―하다 control ; master ; govern ; manage ; bring under control ; hold in check ¶ 제어하기 쉽다 be easy to control ; be controllable ; be manageable // 제어하기 어렵다 be hard of control ; be uncontrollable ; be unmanageable // 제어력을 잃다 lose control 《of》
―기 〖전기〗 a controller ―력 (power to) control ―봉 a control rod (원자로의) ― 부분 장치 [전자 계산기의] the control unit
제언 提言 ⇨ 제의
제언 堤堰 a dam ; a barrage ; a weir ¶ 제언을 쌓다 construct〔build〕 a dam 《across a river》 ; dam 《up》
제언 題言 a prefatory motto ; an epigraph
제역 除役 exemption from military service ―하다 exempt 《a person》 from military service
제염 臍炎 〖의학〗 inflammation of the navel
제염 製鹽 salt manufacture ―하다 manufacture salt
―소 a saltern ; a salt manufactory〔works〕 ―업 the salt industry 자가 ― nonprofessional salt manufacturing ; salt manufacture for private consumption
제오 第五 the fifth ; number five 《No. 5》
― 성병 the fifth venereal disease ―열 the fifth column〔columnist〕
제오공화국 第五共和國 the Fifth Republic
*제왕 帝王 an emperor ; a monarch ; a sovereign

제안 · 권고

영어의 제안·권고 표현에는 you를 주어로 하여 직접 상대방에게 행하는 것과 we를 주어로 하여 발언자도 포함하여 간접적으로 상대방에게 나타내는 방법이 있다. 「… 하지 않겠습니까?」의 일반적인 표현은 Will [Would] you..., (please)? ; Shall we ...? ; Let's....가 가장 일반적 표현이고, I'd like you to..., (please.) / Would you mind..., (please)? / Why don't we...? / What about...? / I suggest[propose] .... / May[Might] I suggest ..., (then)? / Would you care to...? 등과 같은 표현도 쓸 수 있다.

1 Will you..., Won't you...?

「…하지 않겠습니까?」라고 상대방을 이끄는 부드러운 표현. Will you...?는 주로 상대방에 대한 의뢰를 나타낸다. Won't you...?는 긍정적인 답변을 기대하지만, Will you...?는 그렇지 않다.

¶ 커피 한잔 더 드시겠습니까? Will [Won't] you have another cup of coffee? (=Have another cup of coffee, won't you?)

2 Let's...(, shall we?)

「…합시다」의 뜻으로 허물없는 사이에 쓰는 가장 일반적인 표현.

¶ 수영하러 갑시다. — 그럽시다. Let's go for a swim. — Yes, let's (do that).

(1) 긍정의 경우

Let's ....에 대한 답변은 긍정일 경우에는 Yes, let's.가 가장 전형적이긴 하나 보통은 Yes, let's do that. / OK. / All right. / That's good idea. / Yes, I'd like that. / That sounds good. 등으로 대답하는 것이 보통이다.

(2) 부정의 경우

No, let's not. 이 형식에는 맞지만 너무 딱딱한 표현이므로 보통은 Sorry, but I don't have (the) time. / No, I don't think so. / (No.) I'd (really) rather not. / (Sorry, but) not today [right now, this time]. / I'm not too sure (about that). 등이 사용된다.

Let's ....에 속하는 부가 의문문은 shall we로 한다.

¶ 한잔 할까요? — 좋지. Let's have a drink, shall we? — OK.

Shall we ...? 만으로 권고·제안의 뜻을 나타낼 수 있다.

¶ 안으로 들어 갈까요? — 좋은 생각이야. Shall we go in? — That's a good idea.

3 How[What] about...ing?

상대방에게 제안·권고할 때는 How, 상대방의 감상과 의견을 구할 때는 What으로 구별하기도 하나 대부분 같은 뜻으로 쓰인다. 다만 《미》에서는 How를 많이 쓰는 편이다. 답변은 Yes, let's. / No, let's not.을 제외하고는 Let's ....와 같다.

¶ 드라이브하는 것 어때? — 거 좋지. How [What] about going for a drive? — That would be [sounds] great. (★ 사정이 있어서 거절할 때는 I'm afraid I can't.... / I'm sorry, I can't.... / Unfortunately,.... / Actually,.... 등으로 한다.) // 산보하러 갈까요? — 미안하지만 안되겠는데요. 지금 치과에 가봐야 합니다. How [What] about (going for) a walk? — I'm sorry I can't. I must see the dentist right now. (★ about 다음에 going for가 생략될 수도 있음.)

보다 정중한 표현으로는 How would you like...?가 있다.

4 Why don't you [not]...?

허물없는 사이에서 쓰이고 웃사람에게는 쓰지 않는 것이 보통이다.

¶ 샤워하지 않을래? — 응, 나도 할거야. Why don't you [not] have a shower? — All right. I will. // 자 앉지 그래. — 응. Why don't you sit down? — OK. // 그의 조언을 구하는 게 어때? — 글쎄, 마음이 내키질 않아. Why don't you [not] ask his advice? — Well, I never thought of it.

5 We will[might]....

화자가 대표하여 간접적으로 제안하는 방식

¶ 그 계획은 포기하는 것이 어떨까. We might give up the plan. // 다시 한 번 해보는 게 어때요? — 예, 해보지요. We'll try (it) once more [again], won't we? — Yes, we will.

6 had better[best] do....

「…하는 것이 좋다」의 뜻. 주어가 you일 때는 강한 충고·명령이 된다. 강요의 뜻이 내포되어 있어서 윗사람에게는 쓰지 않는다. 이에 비해 You should...는 부드러운 제안의 뜻을 가지고 있다. had better의 부정은 had better not이다. 회화에서는 보통 ...'d better의 단축형이 사용된다. better 뒤에는 동사의 원형이 쓰이는 것에 주의.

¶ 그를 바로 만나보는 것이 좋겠습니다. You'd better see him now. // 지금은 그녀를 만나지 않는 것이 좋겠습니다. You'd better not see her now.

같은 better를 사용하여 좀 더 부드럽게 표현할 수도 있다.

¶ 2, 3일 휴가를 내면 어떨까요. It might be better for you to take a few days off.

자신도 포함하여 간접적으로 제안할 때는 we를 사용한다.

¶ 집에 있는 것이 좋겠죠. I think we'd better stay (at) home.

⑦ may[might] as well....

「…하여도 좋겠지」, 「…하는 것이 좋겠다」의 뜻. might를 쓰면 「차라리 …하는 것이 좋겠다」의 뜻으로 완곡한 표현이 된다.

¶ 마음을 정하는 것이 좋다. You may [might] as well make up your mind. // 그에게 사실을 말하는 것이 좋겠다. We might as well tell him the truth. // 그에게 그녀를 도와달라고 하는 것이 어떨까. We might ask him to help her.

should [ought to]를 쓰면 충고의 뜻이 강해진다.

¶ 담배는 피우지 않는 것이 좋습니다. You should [ought to] quit smoking.

⑧ What do[would] you say to ...ing?

「…하는 것이 어때?」의 뜻으로 격의없는 사이에서 쓰고 say 뒤에는 절이 올 수도 있다.

¶ 오늘 저녁은 밖에서 먹는 게 어때? — 나쁘지 않은데. What do [would] you say to eating [we eat] out this evening? — Not so bad. (★ Suppose we eat out this evening.이라고 하면 한층 허물없는 표현이 된다.)

⑨ propose, suggest, advise

적극적으로 제안할 때는 propose, 약간 조심스럽게 제안할 때는 suppose, 상대방에게 권할 때는 advise를 쓴다.

¶ 그는 휴식을 제안했다. He proposed that we rest. / He proposed taking a rest. / He proposed that we (should) take a rest. // 그는 내게 담배를 끊을 것을 권했다. He advised me that I (should) quit smoking. (★ that 이하의 should는 생략되는 경우가 많다. 이 경우 주어와 관계없이 동사는 원형을 쓰는 것에 주의.)

— 신권설 the theory of the divine right of kings — 절개 수술 『의학』 a caesarean operation

†**제외 除外** exclusion ; exception ; [면제] exemption

—하다 except 《from》 ; make an exception of ; exclude 《from》 ; exempt 《a person》 ¶ …을 제외하고 with the exception of // 명단에서 제외하다 except 《a person's》 name from a list // 회원에서 제외하다 exclude 《a person》 from membership // 제외되다 be ruled out // 배심 의무에서 제외하다 exempt 《a person》 from jury duty

—례 an exception ; an exemption ¶ 원칙에 대하여 제외례를 만들다 make an exception to the rule — **조항** an escape clause

제요 提要 a compendium ; an epitome ; a summary ; a résumé 《프》 **—하다** summarize ; epitomize ¶ 물리학 제요 elements of physics

—서 a manual

제욕 制慾 control of passion〔appetites〕; self-control **—하다** mortify〔control〕 one's passions ; regulate one's desires ; be ascetic ; control oneself

—주의 asceticism

제우스 [그리스 신화] Zeus

제웅 a straw effigy for exorcism

제위 帝位 the throne ; the crown ¶ 제위에 오르다 ascend〔accede to〕 the throne // 제위를 계승하다 succeed to the throne // 제위를 양보하다 abdicate the throne 《in favor of another》 // 제위를 빼앗다 usurp the throne // 제위를 노리다 aspire to the throne ; aim at the crown

제위 諸位 gentlemen

제위 祭位 the enshrined deity ; a deity worshipped ; a deity for worship

제유 製油 oil manufacture **—하다** manufacture oil

—소 an oil factory

제유법 提喩法 『수사』 synecdoche

제육 pork ; hog-meat

—구이 roasted thin pork chops **—전** a pork butcher〔shop〕

제육감 第六感 the sixth sense ¶ 제육감으로 안다 I know that by instinct. / My sixth sense tells me that.

제융 製絨 wool weaving

— 공장 a woolen factory ; a wool mill

†**제의 提議** a proposal ; a proposition ; an offer ; an overture ; [제언] a suggestion

—하다 propose ; offer ; make an overture ; move ; suggest ; make a proposal ¶ 강화의 제의 a peace overture // …의 제의로 at the motion〔instance〕 of // 계획을 제의하다 propose a plan // 강화를 제의하다 make overtures for peace // 제의에 동의하다 agree to 《a person's》 proposal ; accept a suggestion put forward by // …이라는 제의가 있다 It is proposed 《that》 // 이 회의에 제의할 것이 있다 I have a proposal to make to this meeting.

—자 a proposer ; a mover

‡**제이 第二** the second ; the secondary ; the second best ¶ 제이의 the second ; [또 하나의] a second ; another ; [중요성이] secondary ; of second〔minor〕 importance // 제이의 천성 a second nature

// 제이의 고향 one's second〔adopted〕 home // 제이의 문제 a matter of secondary importance ; a secondary consideration
—군 〖야구〗 the second string —당 the second largest party — 인칭 〖문법〗 the second person —종 우편(물) second-class mail (matter) — 주제 〖음악〗 the subsidiary (theme) —차 산업 혁명 the Second Industrial Revolution —차 세계 대전 World War Ⅱ ; the Second World War —차 제품 secondary products

제인 諸人 all people ; the public

제일 [자기 일] one's own〔personal〕 affair ; one's personal concern ; one's business ¶ 그는 친구가 받은 모욕을 제일처럼 분개했다 He got enraged at the indignity his friend had been subjected to, as if he himself had suffered it. // 그는 친구가 성공했다는 소식을 듣고 제일처럼 자랑스러워 했다 He heard of the success of his friend and felt a sort of personal pride.

제일 除日 the last day of the year

제일 祭日 a sacrificial day ; the day for holding a〔an ancestor worship〕 sacrifice

⁑제일 第一 number one 《No. 1》 ; the first ; the best ; leading ; [부사적] most ; best ¶ 제일의 first ; initial ; primary ; [중요한] prime ; principal ; chief ; leading ; [으뜸인] the greatest ; the best // 제일 앞〔뒤〕의 foremost〔hindmost〕 // 제일 나쁜〔좋은〕 the worst〔best〕 // 제일 아름다운 the most beautiful // 제일 먼저 first ; firstly ; in the first place ; first of all ; before everything else // 제일류의 first-class〔-rank, -rate〕 ; top-notch 《미》 // 안전 제일 safety first // 귀국 제일성 the first public speech after one's return from abroad // 세계 제일의 부자 the richest man in the world // 제일위를 차지하다 stand〔rank〕 first ; hold the foremost place ; lead all the rest // 그것이 제일 중요하다 It is of primary importance. // 이곳이 한국 제일의 명승지이다 It is the most picturesque place in Korea. // 나는 그가 제일 만나기 싫다 He is the last man I want to see. // 그 여자는 영어가 학급에서 제일이다 She leads the class in English. // 성공에는 인내가 제일이다 Perseverance is the first essential to success. // 미국은 공업과 상업에 있어 세계 제일의 나라이다 America holds the first rank in the world for industry and commerce.
—과 the first lesson ; lesson one —기 the first term〔period〕 ; the first stage (병의) —기 불입 payment of the first installment —당 the leading〔dominant〕 party —보(步) the first〔initial〕 step ; a start ; [시작] the beginning ¶ 제일보를 내딛다 (make a) start — 서기 the First Secretary (of the Communist Party) —선 the first〔foremost〕 line ; the fighting line —심 the first trial ¶ 그는 제일심에서 이겼으나 제이심에서 패소했다 He won the case at the first hearing, but was defeated at the second. — 야당 the major opposition party —위 the first (rank) —의 the first principle〔definition〕 ; the first meaning —인자 the first(-ranking) man ; the leading person ¶ 그는 현대 작가 가운데 제일인자이다 He stands foremost among the writers of the day. —인칭 〖문법〗 the first person —종 우편 first class mail (matter) —차 세계 대전 the First World War ; World War Ⅰ —착(着) the first to arrive〔to reach the goal〕 ; the first in the race

제자 弟子 a disciple ; a pupil ; an apprentice ; a student ¶ 제자로 들어가다 become 《a person's》 pupil ; be apprenticed to 《a person》 // 제자를 두다 take pupils〔apprentices〕

제자 諸子 [호격] you ; gentlemen ; [아들] one's sons ; [현자·철인] masters ; sages
— 백가 all philosophers and literary scholars

제자 題字 a motto〔an inscription〕 at the head of a book

⁑제자리 the proper place ; the original place ¶ 통화가 끝난 후에는 수화기를 제자리에 도로 놓으세요 Replace phone when finished.
— 걸음 marking time ; a standstill ; a stalemate ¶ 제자리 걸음하다 [군대나 물가가] mark time ; be at a standstill ; be in a stalemate — 넓이〔높이〕뛰기 a standing broad〔high〕 jump

제작 制作 a work ; a production —하다 make ; turn out ; produce 《a work of art, etc.》 ¶ 제작중이다 be at work 《on a picture》
—실 a workshop ; an atelier ; a studio

***제작 製作** manufacture ; production —하다 manufacture ; make ; produce ; turn out ¶ 비행기를 제작하다 make 〔turn out〕 airplanes // 우리들의 새 공장은 상품을 대량으로 제작하고 있다 Our new factory is turning out a large quantity of goods.
— 번호 the factory number —비 production cost(s) —소 a factory ; a works ; a workshop ; a plant ; a mill —자 a maker ; a manufacturer ; a producer (영화의) —품 a manufactured article ; manufactured goods ; products ; output 영화 — the production of films 공동 —자 a co-producer 국립 영화 —소 the National Film Production Center 영화 —자 a film〔cinema〕 producer 한국 영화 —가 협회 the Association of Korean Movie Producers

제잡담 除雜談 —하다 leave off idle talk ; stop〔cease〕 one's idle talk ; cut (out) the chit-chat ¶ 제잡담하고 without palaver ; without useless words ; with no worthless words

같은 better를 사용하여 좀 더 부드럽게 표현할 수도 있다.

¶ 2, 3일 휴가를 내면 어떨까요. It might be better for you to take a few days off.

자신도 포함하여 간접적으로 제안할 때는 we를 사용한다.

¶ 집에 있는 것이 좋겠죠. I think we'd better stay (at) home.

⑦ may[might] as well....

「…하여도 좋겠지」, 「…하는 것이 좋겠다」의 뜻. might를 쓰면 「차라리 …하는 것이 좋겠다」의 뜻으로 완곡한 표현이 된다.

¶ 마음을 정하는 것이 좋다. You may [might] as well make up your mind. // 그에게 사실을 말하는 것이 좋겠다. We might as well tell him the truth. // 그에게 그녀를 도와달라고 하는 것이 어떨까. We might ask him to help her.

should [ought to]를 쓰면 충고의 뜻이 강해진다.

¶ 담배는 피우지 않는 것이 좋습니다. You should [ought to] quit smoking.

⑧ What do[would] you say to ...ing?

「…하는 것이 어때?」의 뜻으로 격의없는 사이에서 쓰고 say 뒤에는 절이 올 수도 있다.

¶ 오늘 저녁은 밖에서 먹는 게 어때? — 나쁘지 않은데. What do [would] you say to eating [we eat] out this evening? — Not so bad. (★ Suppose we eat out this evening.이라고 하면 한층 허물없는 표현이 된다.)

⑨ propose, suggest, advise

적극적으로 제안할 때는 propose, 약간 조심스럽게 제안할 때는 suppose, 상대방에게 권할 때는 advise를 쓴다.

¶ 그는 휴식을 제안했다. He proposed that we rest. / He proposed taking a rest. / He proposed that we (should) take a rest. // 그는 내게 담배를 끊을 것을 권했다. He advised me that I (should) quit smoking. (★ that 이하의 should는 생략되는 경우가 많다. 이 경우 주어와 관계없이 동사는 원형을 쓰는 것에 주의.)

— **신권설** the theory of the divine right of kings — **절개 수술** 〖의학〗 a caesarean operation

†**제외 除外** exclusion ; exception ; [면제] exemption

—하다 except 《from》 ; make an exception of ; exclude 《from》 ; exempt 《a person》 ¶ …을 제외하고 with the exception of // 명단에서 제외하다 except 《a person's》 name from a list // 회원에서 제외하다 exclude 《a person》 from membership // 제외되다 be ruled out // 배심 의무에서 제외하다 exempt 《a person》 from jury duty

—례 an exception ; an exemption ¶ 원칙에 대하여 제외례를 만들다 make an exception to the rule — **조항** an escape clause

제요 提要 a compendium ; an epitome ; a summary ; a résumé 《프》 **—하다** summarize ; epitomize ¶ 물리학 제요 elements of physics

—서 a manual

제욕 制慾 control of passion〔appetites〕 ; self-control **—하다** mortify〔control〕 one's passions ; regulate one's desires ; be ascetic ; control oneself

—주의 asceticism

제우스 [그리스 신화] Zeus

제웅 a straw effigy for exorcism

제위 帝位 the throne ; the crown ¶ 제위에 오르다 ascend〔accede to〕 the throne // 제위를 계승하다 succeed to the throne // 제위를 양보하다 abdicate the throne 《in favor of another》 // 제위를 빼앗다 usurp the throne // 제위를 노리다 aspire to the throne ; aim at the crown

제위 諸位 gentlemen

제위 祭位 the enshrined deity ; a deity worshipped ; a deity for worship

제유 製油 oil manufacture **—하다** manufacture oil

—소 an oil factory

제유법 提喩法 〖수사〗 synecdoche

제육 pork ; hog-meat

—구이 roasted thin pork chops **—전** a pork butcher〔shop〕

제육감 第六感 the sixth sense ¶ 제육감으로 안다 I know that by instinct. / My sixth sense tells me that.

제융 製絨 wool weaving

— **공장** a woolen factory ; a wool mill

†**제의 提議** a proposal ; a proposition ; an offer ; an overture ; [제언] a suggestion

—하다 propose ; offer ; make an overture ; move ; suggest ; make a proposal ¶ 강화의 제의 a peace overture // …의 제의로 at the motion〔instance〕 of // 계획을 제의하다 propose a plan // 강화를 제의하다 make overtures for peace // 제의에 동의하다 agree to 《a person's》 proposal ; accept a suggestion put forward by // …이라는 제의가 있다 It is proposed 《that》 // 이 회의에 제의할 것이 있다 I have a proposal to make to this meeting.

—자 a proposer ; a mover

*⁑**제이 第二** the second ; the secondary ; the second best ¶ 제이의 the second ; [또 하나의] a second ; another ; [중요성이] secondary ; of second〔minor〕 importance // 제이의 천성 a second nature

// 제이의 고향 one's second〔adopted〕 home // 제이의 문제 a matter of secondary importance ; a secondary consideration
—군 〖야구〗 the second string —당 the second largest party — 인칭 〖문법〗 the second person —종 우편(물) second-class mail (matter) — 주제 〖음악〗 the subsidiary (theme) —차 산업 혁명 the Second Industrial Revolution —차 세계 대전 World War Ⅱ ; the Second World War —차 제품 secondary products

제인 諸人 all people ; the public

제일 [자기 일] one's own〔personal〕 affair ; one's personal concern ; one's business ¶ 그는 친구가 받은 모욕을 제일처럼 분개했다 He got enraged at the indignity his friend had been subjected to, as if he himself had suffered it. // 그는 친구가 성공했다는 소식을 듣고 제일처럼 자랑스러워 했다 He heard of the success of his friend and felt a sort of personal pride.

제일 除日 the last day of the year

제일 祭日 a sacrificial day ; the day for holding a〔an ancestor worship〕 sacrifice

*****제일 第一** number one 《No. 1》 ; the first ; the best ; leading ; [부사적] most ; best ¶ 제일의 first ; initial ; primary ; [중요한] prime ; principal ; chief ; leading ; [으뜸인] the greatest ; the best // 제일 앞〔뒤〕의 foremost〔hindmost〕 // 제일 나쁜〔좋은〕 the worst〔best〕 // 제일 아름다운 the most beautiful // 제일 먼저 first ; firstly ; in the first place ; first of all ; before everything else // 제일류의 first-class〔-rank, -rate〕 ; top-notch 《미》 // 안전 제일 safety first // 귀국 제일성 the first public speech after one's return from abroad // 세계 제일의 부자 the richest man in the world // 제일위를 차지하다 stand〔rank〕 first ; hold the foremost place ; lead all the rest // 그것이 제일 중요하다 It is of primary importance. // 이곳이 한국 제일의 명승지이다 It is the most picturesque place in Korea. // 나는 그가 제일 만나기 싫다 He is the last man I want to see. // 그 여자는 영어가 학급에서 제일이다 She leads the class in English. // 성공에는 인내가 제일이다 Perseverance is the first essential to success. // 미국은 공업과 상업에 있어 세계 제일의 나라이다 America holds the first rank in the world for industry and commerce.
—과 the first lesson ; lesson one —기 the first term〔period〕 ; the first stage (병의) —기 불입 payment of the first installment —당 the leading〔dominant〕 party —보(步) the first〔initial〕 step ; a start ; [시작] the beginning ¶ 제일보를 내딛다 (make a) start — 서기 the First Secretary (of the Communist Party) —선 the first〔foremost〕 line ; the fighting line —심 the first trial ¶ 그는 제일심에서 이겼으나 제이심에서 패소했다 He won the case at the first hearing, but was defeated at the second. — 야당 the major opposition party —위 the first (rank) —의 the first principle〔definition〕 ; the first meaning —인자 the first(-ranking) man ; the leading person ¶ 그는 현대 작가 가운데 제일인자이다 He stands foremost among the writers of the day. —인칭 〖문법〗 the first person —종 우편 first class mail (matter) —차 세계 대전 the First World War ; World War Ⅰ —착(着) the first to arrive〔to reach the goal〕 ; the first in the race

제자 弟子 a disciple ; a pupil ; an apprentice ; a student ¶ 제자로 들어가다 become 《a person's》 pupil ; be apprenticed to 《a person》 // 제자를 두다 take pupils〔apprentices〕

제자 諸子 [호격] you ; gentlemen ; [아들] one's sons ; [현자·철인] masters ; sages
— 백가 all philosophers and literary scholars

제자 題字 a motto〔an inscription〕 at the head of a book

*****제자리** the proper place ; the original place ¶ 통화가 끝난 후에는 수화기를 제자리에 도로 놓으세요 Replace phone when finished.
— 걸음 marking time ; a standstill ; a stalemate ¶ 제자리 걸음하다 [군대나 물가가] mark time ; be at a standstill ; be in a stalemate — 넓이〔높이〕뛰기 a standing broad〔high〕 jump

제작 制作 a work ; a production —하다 make ; turn out ; produce 《a work of art, etc.》 ¶ 제작중이다 be at work 《on a picture》
—실 a workshop ; an atelier ; a studio

*__제작 製作__ manufacture ; production —하다 manufacture ; make ; produce ; turn out ¶ 비행기를 제작하다 make 〔turn out〕 airplanes // 우리들의 새 공장은 상품을 대량으로 제작하고 있다 Our new factory is turning out a large quantity of goods.
— 번호 the factory number —비 production cost(s) —소 a factory ; a works ; a workshop ; a plant ; a mill —자 a maker ; a manufacturer ; a producer (영화의) —품 a manufactured article ; manufactured goods ; products ; output 영화 — the production of films 공동 —자 a co-producer 국립 영화 —소 the National Film Production Center 영화 —자 a film〔cinema〕 producer 한국 영화 —가 협회 the Association of Korean Movie Producers

제잡담 除雜談 —하다 leave off idle talk ; stop〔cease〕 one's idle talk ; cut (out) the chit-chat ¶ 제잡담하고 without palaver ; without useless words ; with no worthless words

shop —자 a platemaker ; a photoengraver 사진 — photoengraving 전기〔철(凸)판〕 — an electrotype〔a stereotype〕 process

제팔 第八 the eighth

제패 制覇 conquest ; mastery ; supremacy ; domination ; championship (경기의) —하다 conquer ; rule ; gain supremacy 《over》 ¶ 제패를 목표로 하는 싸움 a struggle for supremacy // 제패를 겨루다 contend for supremacy〔championship〕 // 우주의 제패를 다투다 fight for the supremacy of space

—전(戰) a struggle for supremacy, a championship game〔tournament, series〕 (경기의) 공중 — the mastery of the air 세계 — domination of the world ; world hegemony〔conquest〕

제폐 除弊 —하다 get rid of abuses ; do away with abuses

제폭제 制爆劑 〖기계〗 an antiknock ; an antidetonator

제표 除標 〖수학〗 a division mark〔sign〕 《÷》

제표 製表 tabulation —하다 tabulate

제풀로, 제풀에 ⇨ 제물에

†제품 製品 manufactured goods〔articles〕 ; manufactures ; finished goods ¶ 영국 제품 English〔British〕-made goods ; goods of English make // 외국 제품 an article of foreign make ; foreign products ; imported goods // 국내 제품 home products // 어느 회사 제품을 염두에 두고 계십니까 What make do you have in mind ? // 우리 제품의 우수성을 선전하는 것이 중요하다 It's important to make a pitch for our products. // 어느 회사 제품을 염두에 두고 계십니까 What make do you have in mind ? // 우리 제품의 우수성을 선전하는 것이 중요하다 It's important to make a pitch for our products.

— 규격 표준화 standardization of manufactures — 목록 a catalog(ue) of products〔finished goods〕 — 원가 the cost (of products)

제하 臍下 ¶ 제하의 under the navel

— 단전 the abdomen ; the center of the abdominal region

제하다 除— 〔제외하다〕 exclude ; except ; leave out ; 〔빼다〕 deduct ; subtract ; subduce ; 〔나누다〕 divide ; 〔제거하다〕 eliminate ; get rid of ¶ 제하고 except ; but ; save ; exclusive of // 세금을 제하고 8만원의 수입 an income of 80,000 *won* after taxes // 여기 계신 분은 제하고 excepting those present ; the present company excepted // 전항의 규정에 의한 경우를 제하고 apart from cases stipulated in the provisions of the preceding paragraph // 봉급에서 제하다 deduct 《a sum》 from one's salary // 10에서 5를 제하면 5가 남는다 Five from ten leaves five. /Ten minus five equals five.

제한 際限 〔끝〕 limits ; bounds ; an end

†제한 制限 limit ; restriction ; limitation —하다 restrict ; limit ; set limits 《to》 ; put a limitation 《on》 ; put restriction 《upon》 ¶ 제한 없이 without limit〔restriction〕 ; unrestrictedly // 연령의 제한 age limit // 제한 내〔외〕 within〔beyond〕 the limits // 제한 내〔외〕에서 행동하다 act within〔beyond〕 the limits // 제한부로 under certain restriction // 제한의 범위를 넘다 go out of bounds // 경비를 제한하다 restrict expenses // 산아를 제한하다 practice birth control // 제한을 완화〔해제〕하다 relax〔lift, remove〕 restriction // 회원은 200명으로 제한되어 있다 Its membership is limited to 200. // 그의 식사는 빵과 물만으로 제한되었다 His food was restricted to bread and water.

— 방식 a method of limitation — 속도 a speed limit ; regulation speed — 송전(送電) power limit ¶ 제한 송전하다 limit the supply of electricity — 시간 the time limit ; the restricted〔limited〕 hours ; the deadline 《for》 — 인수 qualified acceptance — 전쟁 a limited war ; limited warfare — 한자 the restricted set of Chinese characters ; the limited number of Chinese characters designated for daily use — 회사 a restricted concern 군비 — armament limitation 산아 — birth control 생산 — a curtailment of output 수입 — import restrictions 《on》 연령〔시간〕 — an age〔a time〕 limit 전력 — restriction on〔of〕 (electric) power consumption

제해권 制海權 the control〔rule〕 of the sea ; the command〔mastery〕 of the sea ¶ 제해권을 잡다 rule〔command〕 the sea ; have〔secure〕 the command of the sea // 제해권을 잃다 lose the command of the sea

제행 諸行 〖불교〗 all things in the universe ; all worldly things ; 〔고행〕 (various) ascetic practices ¶ 제행 무상 All is vanity. /Nothing is certain in this world.

제향 祭享 a sacrificial〔religious〕 rite ; a religious service

제헌 制憲 establishment of a constitution —하다 establish a constitution

— 국회 the Constitutional Assembly —절 Constitution Day ; Constitution(-al) Promulgation Day

제혁 製革 tanning ; leather manufacturing —하다 manufacture leather

—소(所) a tannery —업 the tanning industry ¶ 제혁업자 a tanner

제현 諸賢 (Ladies and) Gentlemen

제형 梯形 a trapezoid ; an echelon formation

제형 諸兄 (my dear) friends

제형 蹄形 a hoof shape ; U-shape ¶ 제형의 hoof-shaped ; U-shaped

— 자석 a horse shoe magnet —체 an ungula ; a truncated cone

제호 題號 a title ⟪of a book⟫ ¶ 제호를 붙이다 give a title ⟪to a book⟫ ; entitle ⟪a book⟫
제화 製靴 shoemaking
—공 a shoemaker **— 공장** a shoemaking factory **—업** the shoe industry
제회 際會 an encounter ; meeting **—하다** meet ; face ; confront ; encounter ; fall in with ¶ 위기에 제회하다 face a crisis ; be confronted by an emergency // 그는 국가 위기에 제회하여 공을 세웠다 He distinguished himself in the national crisis.
제후 諸侯 feudal lords〔princes〕
제휴 提携 helping each other ; cooperation ; concert ; coalition **—하다** join hands ⟪with⟫ ; act in concert ⟪with⟫ ; cooperate ⟪with⟫ ; move in harmony ; tie up ⟪with⟫ ¶ 제휴하여 in concert ; in cooperation // 제휴하여 운동을 일으키다 join hands to start a movement // 그는 노동당과 제휴했다 He identified himself with the Labor Party.
— 회사 an affiliated concern **기술 —** a technical tie-up
젠장 Damn ! /Hang〔Damn〕 it ! /Pshaw ! / Hell !
젠체하다 put on〔give oneself〕 airs ; assume an air of importance ; stand on one's dignity ; think highly of oneself ; be puffed up with pride ¶ 젠체하는 affected ; conceited // 젠체하는 사람 a dude // 젠체하고 걷다 walk in an affected manner // 그는 언제나 젠체한다 He always puts on airs. // 너무 젠체 말아라 Don't give yourself such airs. // 그의 젠체하는 꼴이 아니꼽다 His affected manners are quite provoking. // 그는 젠체하는 버릇이 있다 He has a habit of holding his head too high.
젠틀맨 a gentleman ⇨ 신사
****젤라틴** ⟦화학⟧ gelatin(e)
‡**젤리** jelly
젯날 祭— ⇨ 제일(祭日)
젯메 祭— sacrificial rice
젯밥 祭— cooked rice that has been offered in sacrifice
젱그렁거리다, 쩽그렁거리다 jangle ; clang ; clank ; be jangling ; clangour ¶ 젱그렁젱그렁 clang-clang ; with a clang
조¹ ⟦식물⟧ millet ; a millet seed (알)
조² that little ⟪things over there⟫ ¶ 조놈 that little man〔guy, so-and-so〕
조 組 [작은 집단] a company ; a band ; a group ; a party ; a team
****조 兆** a million million ; a billion ⟪영⟫ ; a thousand billion ⟪미⟫ ; a trillion ⟪미⟫
조 調 [곡조] an air ; a tune ; meter ; [접미어] an air〔manner, attitude〕 of ¶ 장난조로 jokingly // 시비조로 defiantly // 비난조로 critically ; with an air of censure
조 朝 [왕조] a dynasty ; a reign ¶ 이조때에 in the (reign of the) *Yi* Dynasty
조 條 an article ; an item ; a clause ¶ 제7조 Article 7 // 제5조 제3항 Clause 3, Art. 5 // 소년법 제24조 1항 1호 Item 1 of Para. 1 of Art. 24 of the Juvenile Law
-조 造 made ; built ¶ 석조 가옥 a stone〔stone-built〕 house ; a stone-building // 연와조의 가옥 a house built of brick ; a brick house
조가 弔歌 a dirge ; an elegy ; a lament ; a funeral song
†**조가비** a clam shell ; a shell ¶ 조가비를 줍다 gather〔pick up〕 shells
— 세공 shellwork
†**조각** a piece ; a bit ; a strip ; a slip ; a slice ; a scrap ; a cut ; [고기 따위의] a chop ; [파편] a fragment ; a shrapnel ¶ 조각 구름이 하늘을 달리고 있었다 Snatches of clouds were scudding across the sky.
빵— a scrap〔crumb〕 of bread **유리 —** a broken piece of glass ; a splinter **종잇—** a piece〔scrap, slip, strip〕 of paper **포탄 —** (bomb) shell fragments
****조각 彫刻** sculpture ; carving ; engraving

> **참고** **sculpture**는 돌·나무·금속·진흙 따위 **carving**은 나무·상아 따위 **engraving**은 금속·돌·나무 따위의 표면에 새긴 조각

—하다 sculpture ; carve ; engrave ¶ 나무로 상을 조각하다 carve an image in wood
—가 an engraver ; a carver ; a sculptor ; a sculptress (여자) **—도** a chisel ; [동판의] a graver ; a burin ; a carving knife **—물** a (piece of) sculpture ; an engraving ; a carving ; [집합적] statuary **—술** sculptural art ; sculpture ; [조소(彫塑)의] the plastic-engraving art ; [목제의] xylography ; [밀랍의] cerography ; [동판의] chalcography ; [전기판의] glyphography ; [보석의] glyptography ; [보석·조개·상아 따위의] glyptics **—판** engravings
조각 組閣 formation〔organization〕 of a cabinet〔ministry〕 **—하다** form〔organize〕 a cabinet〔ministry〕
— 본부 the Cabinet organization〔formation〕 headquarters
조각나다 be broken to pieces ; split in pieces ; break into splinters ; splinter ; break ; [갈라지다] split ; cleave ; [의견 따위가] have a difference in opinion ¶ 두 조각나다 break〔be broken〕 in two
조각달 a crescent〔new〕 moon ; a waxing moon (상현) ; a waning moon (하현)
조각보 odd ends〔pieces〕 of cloth ⟪for wrapping⟫ ; patchwork wrapping-cloth ; scraps of cloth ; odd-come-shorts ; remnants
— 이불 a crazy〔patchwork〕 quilt **— 세공** patchwork ; crazy work

조각조각 in〔to〕 pieces〔bits, fragments, shreds〕 ¶ 조각조각 찢다 tear (a letter) to pieces // 조각조각 부서지다 break to pieces // 헝겊을 조각조각 이어서 이불을 만들다 make〔piece together〕 a patchwork quilt

조간 朝刊 a morning edition〔paper〕 ¶ 조선 일보의 조간 the morning edition of the *Chosun-Ilbo*

— **신문** a morning paper

조간 遭艱 losing one's parents ; becoming a mourner **—하다** lose one's parents ; go into mourning for one's parents

조갈 燥渴 thirst ¶ 조갈이 나다 feel〔get〕 thirsty

—증 a disease attended by great thirst

조감도 鳥瞰圖 a bird's-eye-view ; an airplane view

조감독 助監督 an assistant director (영화의)

조갑 爪甲 finger〔toe〕 nails

조강 糟糠 distiller's grains and rice-bran ; chaff and bran ¶ 조강지처 a wife who has shared one's difficulty and poverty ; one's good old wife // 조강지처 불하당 One should not divorce the old wife married in penury. /One should respect his wife who has shared his adversity.

조강 粗鋼 crude steel

*__조개__ a shellfish ; a clam ¶ 조개를 잡다 dig out shellfish

—구름 a cirrocumulus cloud **—껍데기** a shell ¶ 조개껍데기를 줍다 gather shells **—무지** a shell-heap ; a shell-mound **—탄** oval briquettes

조개잡이 [썰물 때에 하는] shell gathering (at low tide) **—하다** gather shellfish 〔sea shells〕 ¶ 조개잡이를 가다 go gathering sea shells

조객 弔客 a caller〔visitor〕 for condolence

—록 the list of callers for condolence ; a guest book for condolers

조갯살 clam meat

†**조건 條件** a condition ; a term ; a stipulation ¶ 회원의 조건 conditions of membership // 계약의 조건 the terms of contract // 매매의 조건 terms of sale // 노동 조건 a labor condition // 부대 조건 a collateral condition // 필수 조건 a precondition ; a prerequisite // 첫째 조건 the first prerequisite // 조건부의 conditional ; qualified // 조건부로 conditionally ; on condition 《that》 // 무조건으로 unconditionally // 조건부 매매 conditional sales // 조건부 계약 a conditional contract // 조건부 인수 conditional acceptance // 가혹한 조건으로 on ironbound conditions // 공평한 조건으로 on fair terms // 조건을 붙이다 attach〔annex〕 a condition 《to》 ; make conditions // 어둡기 전에 귀가한다는 조건으로 그는 딸의 외출을 허가했다 He allowed his daughter to go out on condition that she would come back before dark. // 채용은 전부 조건부로 하기로 한다 Any initial appointment shall be considered conditional. // 나는 약간의 조건부로 동의할 수 있다 I can agree with some reservation. // 그는 유리한 조건으로 채용됐다 He was employed on favorable terms. // 네가 도와 준다는 조건으로 인수하겠다 I will undertake it on condition that you help me.

—문 〖문법〗 a conditional sentence **— 반사** a conditioned reflex〔response〕 **—법** 〖문법〗 the conditional mood **강화〔화해〕 —** the terms of peace〔settlement〕 **악—** unfavorable conditions **지급 —** terms of payment **해제 —** a condition subsequent

조것 ⇨ 저것

조격 阻隔 isolation ; separation ; estrangement **—하다** be〔become〕 estranged 《from each other》 ; be cut off ; be isolated

조경 造景 landscape architecture〔gardening〕

—술 landscape architecture **—가** a landscape architect〔gardener〕

조경 潮境 [한류와 난류의] the junction line between two ocean currents

조계 早計 rashness ; a premature scheme 〔plan〕 ¶ 조계의 premature ; rash ; too hasty // 그렇게 생각하는 것은 조계이다 This is too hasty a conclusion. /Don't jump to that conclusion. /It would be premature to think so.

조계 租界 a concession ; a settlement

공동 — the International Settlement (상해의) **영국 —** a British concession **외국 —** a foreign settlement〔concession〕

조고 祖考 one's deceased grandfather

조곡 弔哭 **—하다** wail in mourning

조곡 組曲 〖음악〗 a (musical) suite

조공 朝貢 tribute ; bringing a tribute 《to a country》 **—하다** bring a tribute to a country ; pay tribute

—국 a tributary state

조공 租貢 payment of taxes **—하다** pay taxes

조공 彫工 ⇨ 조각가

조관 朝官 a court official ; a courtier

조관 條款 a stipulation ; a provision ; an article ; a clause ; an item ¶ 최혜국 조관 a most-favored-nation clause

조광 粗鑛 (an) ore ; (an) unwrought metal

조광 躁狂 frenzy ; raving madness ; a mad〔wild, violent〕 excitement ; 〖의학〗 mania

조광권 租鑛權 a mining right〔concession〕 ; the royalty

조교 調敎 《horse》 breaking〔training〕 **—하다** train〔break in〕 《a horse》

—사 a 《horse》 trainer ; a horsebreaker

조교 助敎 an assistant (teacher, instructor)

조교 弔橋 ⇨ 적교(吊橋)
조교 照校 collation **—하다** collate **—전보** a collated telegram **—표** [거래소의] a comparison slip ; an exchange ticket
조교수 助敎授 an assistant professor
조구 釣具 fishing tackle〔gear, rig, equipment, things〕; a rod and line
*__조국 祖國__ the fatherland ; one's mother country ; one's native land ; one's homeland ¶ 조국을 위하여 싸우다 fight〔rise in arms〕 for one's fatherland // 조국을 방위하다 defend one's fatherland // 해외에서 조국을 그리다 be nostalgic for one's mother country while on foreign soil **—근대화** modernization of the fatherland **—애** [애국심] patriotism ; love for one's motherland〔(own) country〕
조국 肇國 founding a state〔nation〕 **—하다** found a nation〔state〕
조규 條規 a stipulation ; articles ; provisions ; regulations《of a law》 ¶ 헌법 조규에 따라 under the terms of the Constitution
*__조그마하다__ (be) small ; tiny ; smallish ; be of a rather small size ¶ 조그마하게 on a small scale ; in a small size ; in a small way // 조그마한 가게 a petty shop // 조그마한 일 a small matter ; a trifle // 조그마한 일에 성을 내다 get angry over trifles // 조그맣게 짜르다 cut small // 조그맣게 시작하다 make a small beginning // 조그맣게 장사를 시작하다 start a small business // 그 회사는 처음엔 조그마한 회사였다 The company started from a small beginning.
조그만큼 [양] just a little ; in small quantities ; [정도] slightly ; a little
†**조금** ① [양] a small quantity ; a little ; a dash ¶ 아주 조금 just a little ; in small quantities // 조금 더 just a little more // 조금씩 little by little ; bit by bit ; in small doses ; a little at a time // 술을 조금 마시다 have〔take〕 a drink or two // 후추를 조금 넣어서 맛을 내다 season with a dash of pepper // 돈이 조금 필요하다 I want some money. // 조금밖에 남아 있지 않다 There is but little left. // 전 직장에서 일년에 1200만원을 받았으니까 그것보다는 조금 더 기대하고 있습니다 I made 12 million *won* per year at my last employment so I am expecting a little more than that // 이 화물을 한번에 조금씩 운반합시다 Let's carry this cargo in a little at a time.
② [수] a small number ; a few ¶ 아주 조금 just a few ; in small numbers // 조금 더 a few more《pieces》// 이 작문에는 틀린 곳이 조금 있다 There are some mistakes in this composition. // 이 책에는 오식이 조금밖에 없다 There are only a few misprints in this book.
③ [정도] somewhat ; rather ; a bit ; a little ; slightly ; to a slight degree ; to a small extent ; [명사적] something ¶ 조금도 (not) in the least ; (not) at all // 조금 놀라서 in some surprise ; a little surprised // 조금의 차로 by a narrow margin // 조금의 차로 이기다 win《a game》by a whisker // 조금이라도 돈이 있으면 if he has any money // 조금이라도 친절심이 있으면 if you have a spark of kindness in you // 뭣이든지 조금은 알고 있다 He knows a bit of everything. /He knows something〔a little〕 of everything. // 조금 아팠다 I felt a touch of pain. // 그의 영어는 조금 서투른 데가 있다 His English leaves something to be desired. // 그는 반성의 기미라고는 조금도 보이지 않았다 He hasn't shown the slightest bit of remorse. // 저 그림은 조금 오른쪽으로 기울어져 있는 것 같다 That picture looks like it's tilted slightly to the right.
④ [시간] a moment ; a minute ; a (little) while ; a second ¶ 조금 전에 a little while ago // 조금 있으면 in a little while ; in a short time ; a little later ; shortly ; soon // 조금 기다려라 Wait a minute. // 조금 있다 오십시오 Call again a little later. // 조금이라도 빠른 편이 좋다 The sooner, the better. // 그는 할 일이 있어서 조금 일찍 집에 갔다 He had something to do, so he went home a little early. // 조금 전에 얘기하고 있었던 사람은 누구지 Who were you talking to just now?
⑤ [거리] a little way ; a short distance ¶ 조금 떨어져서 a little way off ; at a short distance // 조금씩 전진하다 advance inch by inch // 강을 따라 조금 가다 go a little way along the river
조금 潮減 the neap tide ; the neap
조금 彫金 [술(術)] chasing ; metal-carving **—사** a chaser
조금도 《not》 in the least ; 《not》 at all ; 《not》 in any degree ; 《not》 a bit ; 《not》 the slightest ¶ 조금도 쓸모가 없다 be of no use at all ; be good for nothing ; be absolutely useless // 그것에 대해서는 조금도 모른다 I know nothing about it. // 그것은 조금도 예기치 못한 일이다 That is the last thing I expected. // 그에게는 영어 지식이 조금도 없다 He has not the least〔slightest〕 knowledge of English. // 그것에 대해서는 조금도 걱정하고 있지 않다 I'm not in the slightest〔not at all〕 anxious about it. // 조금도 염려 마세요 Don't worry about a thing. // 조금도 안 변했구나 You haven't changed a bit.
†**조급 躁急** a hasty〔quick〕 temper ; impatience ; impetuosity **—하다** (be) impatient ; impetuous ; hasty ; quick-tempered ; short-tempered ¶ 조급히 impetuously ; hastily ; impatiently // 조급한 사람 a person of impetuous disposition ; a hasty person ; a hothead // 중요한

일이니까 너무 조급하게 진행시키지 않는 편이 좋겠다 It's an important job, so you'd better not push things too fast.

조기¹ 〖물고기〗 a yellow corvina ; Pseudosciaena manchurica (학명)
—젓 pickled〔salted〕 yellow corvina

조기² ⇨ 저기

조기 弔旗 a mourning flag ; a flag at half-mast ; a flag draped with black ¶ 조기를 달다 hang a flag draped in black ; hang〔hoist〕 a flag at half-mast

조기 早起 early rising —하다 get up early ; rise early in the morning ¶ 조기하는 습관이 붙다 get the early-rising habit

조기 早期 an early stage〔period〕
— 강화 early peace settlement — 발화 [내연 기관의] preignition — 사용 an early use ; advance use — 치료〔진단〕 early treatment〔diagnosis〕 ¶ 조기 진단을 받다 be diagnosed in good time ; consult with a doctor at an early stage — 타결 early rapprochement ; an early settlement of issues (pending between...)

조기 경보망 早期警報網 an early warning system

조기 교육 早期敎育 《receive》 early education

‡**조끼¹** a waistcoat 《영》 ; a vest 《미》
— 적삼 a sleeved vest

조끼² [맥주 따위의] a pitcher ; a jug ¶ 맥주 한 조끼 a jugful of beer

조난 遭難 a disaster ; an accident ; [파선] a shipwreck —하다 meet with a disaster〔an accident〕 ; be in distress ; [파선] be wrecked ¶ 폭풍우로 조난하다 be wrecked in a storm
— 구조선 a rescue boat ; [항공기의] a crash boat —선 a ship in distress ; a wrecked ship ¶ 조난선을 구조하다 go to the rescue of a ship in distress — 신호 a signal of distress ; a distress signal ; an SOS call ; a distress call (무전의) ¶ 조난 신호를 하다 send out an SOS —자 a victim ; a sufferer ; [생존자] a survivor ¶ 철도 사고의 조난자 victims of a railroad accident // 조난자의 이야기를 듣다 hear the account of a survivor —지 the place of a disaster ; a disaster area — 현장 the scene of a disaster 〔an accident〕

조다지 ⇨ 저다지

조달 早達 [빠른 출세] success〔advancement〕 in one's early age ; a rapid rise ; [조숙] precocity ; maturity ; early〔premature〕 development —하다 rise rapidly in the world ; succeed〔attain distinction〕 in one's early age ; mature young ; grow early ; be precocious

조달 調達 [공급] supply [관청에서] procurement ; [식량·일용품 따위의] provision ; [자금] raising ; [주문의] execution ; fulfil(l)ment —하다 supply 《a thing》 ; provide 《food》 ; raise 《money》 ; execute 《an order》
—과 the purchasing〔supplies〕 section —기관 a procurement agency — 요구 [주둔군의] a procurement demand 《P. D.》 —청 the Office of Supply 해외 — offshore procurement

조당 粗糖 raw〔crude〕 sugar

조대 a clay〔bamboo〕 pipe

조대 粗大 —하다 [거칠다] (be) coarse ; rough ; gross ; unpolished

조도 調度 proper management of matters〔affairs, business〕 ; [살림] making a proper living ; [경비] expenses ; expenditure —하다 manage matters properly ; make a proper living ; spend money

조도 照度 intensity of illumination
—계 an illuminometer ; a photometer (광도계)

조독 爪毒 an inflammation caused by scratching ; infection from scratching

조동사 助動詞 〖문법〗 an auxiliary verb

조라기 strips of hemp ; tow ; hards

조라떨다 bungle by a rash〔hasty〕 act ; make a mess〔muddle, hash, mush〕 of it ; upset the apple cart

조락 凋落 withering ; [영락] downfall ; reduced circumstances ; [몰락] decline ; decay ; fall —하다 [시들다] fade ; wither ; [영락] be in reduced circumstance ; [쇠퇴] decay ; decline ; wane ; be ruined ¶ 자연주의 문학의 조락 the decay of the naturalist school in literature

조락노 a tow rope ; a hemp string

조란 鳥卵 a bird's egg

조람 照覽 ¶ 신이여 조람하옵소서 Heaven be my witness ! /I call Heaven to witness 《that...》

조랑조랑 in cluster ⇨ 주렁주렁

조략 粗略 coarseness ; crudeness ; plainness —하다 (be) coarse ; crude ; rough ; plain ; poor

조량 照亮, 照諒 discernment ; discrimination ; insight ; knowing thoroughly —하다 discern ; discriminate ; know thoroughly

조러하다 be like that ⇨ 저러하다

조력 助力 aid ; assistance ; help ; support (후원) ; cooperation (협력) —하다 help ; aid ; assist ; give〔render〕 《a person》 assistance 《in, at》 ¶ 당신의 조력에 의하여 with〔by〕 your kind assistance // 친구의 조력을 바라다 ask for a friend's help ; turn to a friend for aid〔help〕 // 외부의 조력은 필요치 않다 I do not need assistance from outside.
—자 a helper ; an assistant ; a supporter ; a friend

조력 발전소 潮力發電所 a tidal (power) plant

조련 操練 training exercises ; military drill ; maneuvers —하다 drill ; train

조령모개 朝令暮改 an unsettled course of action ; lack of principle ; changeableness ; unpredictability ; unreliability **—하다** change an order frequently ¶ 조령모개의 정책 a fickle〔an erratic〕 policy ; inconsistency of policy

조례 弔禮 condolatory etiquette〔manners〕; the forms observed for condolence

조례 條例 an ordinance ; regulations ; rules ; law ; an act ¶ 조례를 반포〔취소〕하다 issue〔revoke〕 regulations〔an ordinance〕
— 위반 a violation of regulations **시(市)—** a municipal ordinance **철도 —** the railway law〔regulations〕

조례 照例 reference to the precedents 〔former examples〕 **—하다** refer to a precedent

조로 朝露 the morning dew ; [무상] transiency ¶ 조로와 같은 세상사 transient affairs of this life // 인생은 조로와 같다 Man's life vanishes like the dew. /Life is but a span.

조로 早老 premature old age ¶ 조로한 prematurely old

조로 a watering pot ; a sprinkling can ; a sprinkler ¶ 조로로 초목에 물을 주다 water plants with a watering pot

조로아스터 〖종교〗 Zoroaster
—교 Zoroastrianism **— 교도** a Zoroastrian

조롱 鳥籠 a (bird) cage ; a cage for birds

⁑조롱 嘲弄 ridicule ; mockery ; sneer ; derision **—하다** jeer ; ridicule ; deride ; laugh〔sneer, jeer〕 at ; make fun of ; mock ; make a fool of ; make sport〔fun〕 of

조롱박 〖식물〗 a bottle gourd ; a calabash ; a cucurbit ; a water dipper made of a gourd

조롱복 —福 little〔small〕 luck ¶ 조롱복을 타고나다 be born with little luck ; be born under an unlucky star

조롱이 〖새〗 a sparrow hawk
황— a kestrel

조루 早漏 premature ejaculation **—하다** ejaculate prematurely

조류 鳥類 birds ; fowls ; the feathered tribe ¶ 수류와 조류 fur and feather
—상(相) [생태] the avifauna〔bird fauna〕 《of a region》 **—학** ornithology ; birdlore **— 학자** an ornithologist

조류 潮流 [해류] a tide ; an ocean〔a tidal〕 current ; [풍조] the tide ; a current ; a trend ; tendency ¶ 세상 조류에 역행하다 go against the current of the times // 세상 조류에 따르다 go with the stream of the times // 시대 조류에 역행할 수는 없다 There is no swimming against the current of the times.

***조류 藻類** 〖식물〗 seaweeds ; Algae (학명) ¶ 조류의 algoid
—학 phycology ; algology **—학자** an algologist ; a phycologist

조륙 造陸 〖지질〗
— 운동 epeirogenic movements **— 작용** epeirogeny

조르기 〖유도〗 choking techniques ; strangle hold

조르다 [죄다] tie up ; tighten ; wring ; strangle ; [요구] importune ; tease 《for》; ask〔press〕 《a person to do》; [재촉] press 《a person》 for ; urge 《a person to do》; request ; demand ¶ 허리띠를 조르다 tie〔fasten〕 a belt // 사달라고 조르다 ask 《a person》 to buy 《a thing》 // 빚을 빨리 갚으라고 조르다 urge 《a person》 to pay a debt ; press 《a person》 for payment of a debt

조르르, 쪼르르 trickling ; dribbling ; running

조르륵, 쪼르륵 ⇨조르르, 쪼르르

조름 [아가미의] the gill slits〔gill pouches〕 of a fish

조리 in that way there ; that way ; right over there ⇨ 저리 ¶ 조리 돌아가면 책방이 하나 있다 There is a bookstore just around the corner.

조리 條理 logic ; reason ¶ 조리 있는 reasonable ; logical ; consistent // 조리에 닿지 않는 unreasonable ; absurd ; incoherent ; illogical ; unjustifiable // 조리에 닿다 stand to reason ; be reasonable ; be logical // 그가 방금 말한 것은 조리가 서지 않는다 What he says just isn't logical.

***조리 調理** [조섭] care of the health ; recuperation ; [처리] proper disposition ; appropriate disposal〔handling〕 of a matter ; [요리] cooking ; cookery **—하다** take care of one's health ; recuperate ; [요리하다] cook ; prepare food ; [처리] deal with a matter properly 〔appropriately〕
—대 a dresser ; a kitchen table **—법** the art of cooking ; cookery ; cuisine **—사** a cook **—실** a cuisine ; a kitchen

조리개 [끈] a thin cord ; a tightening string ; [사진기의] the iris (of a camera lens)

조리다 boil down ¶ 생선을 간장에 조리다 boil fish down in soy // 과일을 조리어 잼을 만들다 boil fruit down into jam

조리돌리다 drag 《a malefactor》 along the streets to expose 《him》 to public shame

조리복소니 [망침] a thing all hacked-up〔ruined〕; a piece of hackwork

조리차하다 spend〔use〕 sparingly ; stint ; be sparing of

조리치다 take〔have〕 a short nap ; catch cat naps

조림 hard-boiled food
고기 — hard-boiled beef **통—** canned food

조림 造林 afforestation ; forestation **—하다** (af)forest ; reforest ; plant trees ¶ 조

림을 장려하다 encourage afforestation
— 면적 an afforestation area — 장려 encouragement of afforestation —지 afforested land ; [삼림] a plantation —학 forestry

†조립 組立 construction ; [조직] organization ; set-up ; [기계의] assembling —하다 put together ; construct ; set up ; assemble ¶ 배를 조립하다 assemble a ship
— 건축 prefabrication ¶ 조립 건축물 〚건축〛 a set〔prefab〕 building —공(工) an assembler ; an assemblyman ; an assembly technician ; 〚기계〛 an erector ; a fitter — 공장 an assembly plant — 도면 an assembly〔erection〕 drawing〔diagram〕 —식 침대 a fold-up bed — 주택 a prefabricated house ; a house on the knockdown plan ; a prefab 《구》 — 책장 a sectional〔knockdown〕 bookcase —포(砲) a built-up gun 근대 — 산업 modern assembly industries

조릿조릿 —하다 be in thrilling suspense

조마 調馬 horse-training〔-taming〕 ; horsebreaking —하다 break〔train, tame〕 a horse
—사 a horse trainer — 연습 horse training exercise —장 a riding ground ; a paddock

조마조마 nervously ; uneasily ; anxiously ; in thrilling〔breathless〕 suspense ; with a beating heart —하다 feel nervous ; be uneasy ; be kept in suspense ; be in a flutter ; be fidgety〔agitated, edgy〕 ¶ 사람을 조마조마하게 하다 put 《a person》 into a flutter ; keep 《a person》 in suspense // 밤에 홍수나 나지 않을까 조마조마하면서 지냈다 We passed the night in the great fear of a flood. // 딸이 낙제할까봐 조마조마하다 He is nervous at the thought that his daughter might fail in the exam. // 그가 첫무대에서 노래 부르는 것을 보면서 조마조마했다 I felt uneasy watching him sing in his first performance.

조막 a fist size ¶ 조막만하다 be the size of a fist

조막손이 a person with a withered hand

조만간 早晩間 sooner or later ; in time ; by and by ; in the long run ¶ 조만간에 나는 면직될 것이다 I am going to be fired sooner or later. /My dismissal is a question of time now.

조만하다 ⇨ 저만하다

†조망 眺望 a view ; a prospect ; a lookout 《전망》 —하다 take〔command〕 a view of ; look out over〔on〕 ¶ 그 언덕은 조망이 좋다 There is a good view from the hill. /The hill commands a fine prospect. // 나무가 조망을 가로막다 The tree obstructs the view.

조망 鳥網 a fowler's〔fowling〕 net ; a bird net

조매 嘲罵 a jeer ; abuse ; revilement ; insulting remarks —하다 jeer at ; revile against ; ridicule ; flout

‡조명 照明 lighting ; illumination —하다 illuminate ; light up ¶ 조명이 좋지 않다 It is poorly lighted〔illuminated〕.
— 공학 illumination engineering — 기구 an illuminator ; [집합적] lighting apparatus ; luminaire 《프》 —등 《street, tunnel》 lighting —탄 a flare(bomb) ; a light bomb ; a star shell — 효과 lighting effects 무대 — stage lighting〔illumination〕 직접〔간접〕 — direct〔indirect〕 illumination

조명 助命 sparing 《a person's》 life ; [포로의] quarter ; [죄수의] clemency —하다 spare 《a person's》 life ; give quarter to 《a prisoner》 ¶ 조명을 애원하다 ask for 《a person's》 life ; appeal for mercy ; [전쟁 포로가] ask〔cry〕 for quarter

조명 朝命 [조정의 명령] a Royal〔an Imperial〕 command ; government order

조명 詔命 a Royal order〔command〕 ¶ 조명을 받들어 in obedience to a Royal order

조명나다 have a bad reputation ; have an ill name ; be notorious

조모 祖母 a grandmother

조모 朝暮 morning and evening

조목 條目 an article ; a clause ; an item ¶ 일람표에 기입된 열 가지 조목 ten items on the list // 조목별로 기입하다 itemize

조몰락거리다 finger 《a toy》 ; fumble with〔at〕

조무 朝霧 morning mist〔fog〕

조무래기 ① [물건] small articles ; sundries ; odds and ends ② [아이] small children ; little kids ; kiddies ; small fry

조문 弔問 a call of condolence —하다 make a call of condolence ; call 《at a place》 to express condolence
—객 a caller for condolence ; a condolence caller ; a condoler ; a person calling to express his sympathy —사(使) a messenger of condolence

조문 弔文 a funeral address ; a memorial address ; a tribute to one's memory

조문 條文 [본문] the text 《of regulation》 ; [조항] provision ¶ 헌법의 조문 the text of the Constitution // 조문에 있는 바와 같이 as stipulated in the text // 조문에 명기되어 있다 be expressly stated in the text 《of the law》

조물주 造物主 the Creator ; the Maker (of the universe) ; the Supreme Being ; God

조미 調味 seasoning ; flavor —하다 season ; flavor ; give flavor to
—료 a seasoning ; a condiment ; a flavoring ; dressing materials ; spices

조미 造米 hulling rice —하다 hull rice ; make〔turn out〕 processed rice

*조밀 稠密 density —하다 (be) dense ;

populous ; close ; crowded ¶ 인구 조밀한 지방 a densely populated〔a crowded〕 district // 이 도시는 인구가 조밀하다 This city is densely populated. // 그 근처는 인가가 조밀하다 Houses are closely crowded in that neighborhood.

‡**조바심**¹ threshing millet **—하다** thresh ears of millet

조바심² worry ; anxiety ; uneasiness ¶ 그는 조바심을 치면서 보고 있었다 He watched it with his heart in his mouth.

조바위 a women's winter hat (with earflaps)

조박 糟粕 [술찌꺼기] brewer's grains ; lees ; draff ; [옛 학문의] dregs ; lees ; leavings ¶ 고인의 조박을 핥다 imitate old masters ; merely follow the footsteps of one's predecessors

조반 朝飯 breakfast

조반기 早飯器 a brass bowl with a lid

조발 調髮 [머리를 땋음] plaiting hair ; [이발] a haircut ; hair-dressing **—하다** [땋다] plait〔braid〕 one's hair ; make one's hair into a plait ; [이발하다] get a haircut

조발성 早發性 〖의학〗 precociousness
— 치매(痴呆) schizophrenia ; dementia praecox

조밥 cooked millet
조밥도 많이 먹으면 배 부르다 〔속담〕 Grain by grain, and the hen fills her belly.

조방 助幇 pandering ; pimping ; procuration ¶ 조방을 보다 act as a pander ; pander ; pimp
—꾼〔구니〕 [오입판의] a pander ; a pimp ; a procurer ; [놀이동무] a children's attendant〔nurse, companion〕

조방가새 ⇨ 조뱅이

조방 농업 粗放農業 extensive agriculture〔farming〕

조백 早白 growing gray early in one's life ; premature growth of gray hair **—하다** 《one's hair》 turn gray early in one's life ; have gray hairs while young

조뱅이 〖식물〗 a kind of thistle

조법 助法 〖법〗 subsidiary laws

조변석개 朝變夕改 changeableness ; variableness ; fickleness **—하다** change constantly ; take an unsettled course of action ; keep changing〔revising, revamping〕

조병창 造兵廠 an arms factory ; an arsenal ; an armory (미)

조복 朝服 a court dress ; an official dress〔costume〕 ; court attire

조부 弔賻 [조문과 부의] condolence and presents for funeral expenses

*__조부 祖父__ a grandfather
—모 grandparents **증—** a great grandfather

조분 鳥糞 bird droppings ; guano (해조의)
—석(石) guano (deposit)

조붓하다 be a bit narrow ; be on the narrow side

조비 祖妣 one's deceased grandmother

조사 弔詞 a funeral address ; words of condolence ; a memorial address (영결식에서의)

조사 助詞 an auxiliary word ; a particle

조사 措辭 wording ; phraseology ; diction
—법 syntax

조사 早死 a premature〔an early, an untimely〕 death **—하다** die young ; die an early death ; die at an early age ; die before one's time ¶ 술 때문에 조사했다 Wine brought him to an early death.

조사 祖師 the founder of a religious sect〔a school〕

조사 釣師, 釣士 [낚시꾼] an angler ; a rodster

조사 照査 (an) examination by reference 《to》 ; a check (up) ; verification ; collation **—하다** check ; check up (on) 《미》 ; examine by reference 《to》 ; verify ; collate

조사 照射 irradiation **—하다** irradiate ¶ 뢴트겐을 조사하다 apply X-rays 《to》 ; X-ray 《a person's chest》

†**조사 調査** inquiry ; examination ; investigation ; [연구] research ; a census (인구 따위의)

> 〔참고〕 **investigation** 진상을 규명하기 위하여 상세히 조사하는 것 **examination** 사실을 알기 위하여 세밀히 관찰하기도 하고 실험하기도 하는 것 **inquiry** 질문하여 조사하는 것

—하다 inquire〔look〕 《into》 ; investigate 《into》 ; examine 《into》 ; take a census ¶ 조사한 바 upon investigation // 조사 중이다 be under investigation // 원인을 조사하다 inquire into the cause ; investigate the cause // 인물을 조사하다 examine into one's character // 실업 상태를 조사하다 take a census of unemployment // 조사 결과 그것은 단순한 소문으로 판명됐다 Upon investigation it was found to be a mere rumor. // 우리는 당신의 신용 상태를 조사해 봐야겠습니다 We have to check out your credit.
— 결과 findings on〔upon〕 inquiry〔investigation, survey〕 **—관** an examiner ; an investigator **—국** the Research Bureau **— 보고** a report of investigation ; an investigative report ; a surveyor's report **—부〔실〕** an inquiry section ; [신문사의] the finding department ; a morgue (미) **— 사항** matters for investigation **—서** a written investigation **— 용지〔표〕** a questionnaire (정부·신문사 따위의) **—원** an investigator ; an examiner **— 위원** an examiner ; an investigator ; a fact finder ; [국회의] a research secre-

tary — 위원회 a committee of inquiry〔investigation〕 — 자료 data for research〔investigation〕

조산 早産 premature birth — 하다 give premature birth to ; bear prematurely
—아 a prematurely born infant ; a premature infant

조산 造山 an artificial mound (in a garden) ; a miniature hill — 하다 build an artifical mound (in a garden) ; build a rock garden

조산원 助産員 a midwife ; a maternity nurse

조산원 助産院 a maternity hospital

조삼모사 朝三暮四 swindling by a clever trick ; a confidence game ; imposture ; deception

*조상 祖上 an ancestor ; a forefather ¶ 조상의 ancestral // 조상 전래의 ancestral ; hereditary // 조상을 숭배하다 worship ancestors // 조상의 이름을 더럽히다 bring disgrace upon the good name of one's fathers

조상 彫像 a (carved) statue ¶ 대리석 조상 a statue of marble
—사 a sculptor ; a statuary ; a carver —술 sculpture ; the statuary art

조상 弔喪 condolence — 하다 condole with 《a mourner》

조상 早霜 an early frost — 하다 have an early frost

조상굿 祖上— 〖민속〗 a shamanistic rite for one's ancestors

조상 부모 早喪父母 ⇨ 조실부모

조상육 俎上肉 meat〔a fish〕 ready to be chopped on a block ; a person brought〔driven〕 to bay

조새 a metal oyster-shucker

조색 調色 mixing colors
—실〔장치〕 [염색] an ager —판 a (painter's) palette 이중 — double toning

조색 기구 阻塞氣球 a barrage balloon

조생종 早生種 〖농업〗 a precocious species

조서 弔書 a letter of condolence

조서 詔書 a royal rescript〔edict〕

조서 調書 a protocol ; a record ; written evidence ¶ 조서의 작성 drawing up of a protocol // 조서를 작성하다 put a deposition on record

조석 朝夕 morning and evening ; [식사] morning meal and evening meal
—반 breakfast and supper

조석 潮汐 [간만] ebb and flow ; [조수] a tide

조선 朝鮮 ⇨ 한국

*조선 造船 shipbuilding ; ship construction — 하다 build〔construct〕 a ship ¶ 여객선의 조선비 the cost of building a passenger boat // 조선용 강철 steel for ship construction
—계(界) the shipbuilding world〔circles〕 — 계획 a shipbuilding program —공 a shipbuilding worker ; [선장(船匠)] a shipwright ; a ship〔shipbuilding〕 carpenter — 기사 a marine engineer〔architect〕 ; a shipbuilder ; a naval architect — 능력 shipbuilding capacity —대(臺) shipway ; [경사진] a slip —소 a dockyard ; a shipyard ; a shipbuilding yard —술(術) shipbuilding —업 the shipbuilding industry ; shipbuilding —학 naval architecture ; ship building — 회사 a shipbuilding company 대한 — 공사 Korea Shipbuilding Corporation

조섭 調攝 care of the health ⇨ 조리(調理)

조성 造成 make ; manufacture ; production ; construction — 하다 make ; manufacture ; produce ; build up

조성 組成 formation ; composition ; constitution — 하다 compose ; constitute ; form ; make up
—물 a composite ; a composition —분 a component (part) ; a constituent (element) —체 an organism

조성 助成 [조장] furtherance ; fostering ; promoting ; [기여] aid ; assistance — 하다 help ; further ; aid ; assist ; promote ; contribute to ; make for ; subsidize
—금 a (promotional) subsidy ; a bounty ; a grant ; a (government) grant-in-aid 《*pl.* grants-in-aid》 ; a conducement fund ¶ 조성금을 지급하다 subsidize — 산업 a spoonfed〔an artificially encouraged〕 industry 개간 —비 a reclamation subsidy〔subvention〕

조성 早成 early attainment〔achievement〕 ; [조숙] precocity ; early maturity — 하다 attain〔achieve〕 early ; develop〔grow, mature〕 early

조세 租稅 taxes ; taxation ¶ 조세의 경감 a reduction in〔of〕 taxation // 조세를 부과하다 impose〔levy, lay〕 a tax upon // 조세를 바치다 pay taxes // 조세를 징수하다 collect taxes // 조세를 면제하다 exempt 《a person》 from taxes // 과중한 조세에 시달리다 groan under the heavy burden of taxation
— 수입 internal〔inland〕 revenue — 징수 tax collection — 체납 tax delinquency

조소 嘲笑 a scornful〔derisive〕 laugh ; a sardonic smile ; ridicule ; derision ; sneer — 하다 laugh scornfully ; ridicule ; laugh at ; sneer at ; jeer at ; mock ¶ 조소를 사다 incur〔excite〕 ridicule ; bring ridicule upon oneself // 조소를 당하다 be mocked and derided ; be jeered〔laughed〕 at ; excite ridicule // 그는 동네 사람들의 조소거리였다 He was a laughingstock of the whole town.

조소 彫塑 carving and modeling ; a clay model
—가 a plastic artist

조속기 調速機 a governor ; a speed regulator

자동(自動) — an automatic speed regulator
조속히 早速— an soon as possible ; at the earliest possible moment ; at your earliest convenience
조손 祖孫 grandfather and grandson
‡조수 助手 an assistant ; a helper ¶ 대학의 조수 a tutor // 외과의 조수 a surgeon's mate ; a surgical assistant // 운전 조수 an assistant driver // 조수로 일하다 serve as an assistant
조수 鳥獸 birds and beasts ; fur and feather
*조수 潮水 the tides ; tidal〔tide〕 water
—표 tide table
*조숙 早熟 early maturity ; premature growth ; premature development ; prematurity ; precocity —하다 mature〔ripen〕 early ; grow early ¶ 요즘 아이들은 나이에 비해서 조숙하다 Kids these days are advanced for their age.
—아 a precocious〔forward〕 child
조술 祖述 exposition ; commentation ; propagation —하다 expound ; comment 《upon a text》 ; propagate ¶ 맹자가 공자의 설을 조술했다 Mencius propagated Confucian doctrines.
—자 an expounder〔a propagator〕 (of one's master's doctrines) ; an exponent
조습 燥濕 dryness and dampness ; aridity and humidity
조시 弔詩 an elegy
조식 朝食 breakfast
조식 粗食 a plain diet ; coarse〔simple〕 food ; poor〔meager〕 fare ; a frugal meal —하다 live on plain fare〔diet〕 ; take simple meals ¶ 조식에 익숙해지다 become accustomed to plain fare
—가 a man on a frugal diet
조신 朝臣 court officials ; a courtier
*조신 操身 carefulness of conduct〔behavior〕 ; circumspection —하다 be careful of oneself ; exercise circumspection
조실부모 早失父母 losing one's parents early in life —하다 lose parents early in life ¶ 그는 조실부모 했다 His parents passed away early in life. /He lost his parents at an early age.
†조심 操心 [주의] heed ; care ; carefulness ; [경계] caution ; precaution ; guard ; [신중] prudence ; discretion ; circumspection —하다 take care 《of》 ; be careful 《about》 ; take precaution 《against》 ; guard 《against》 ; look out ; be watchful against 《temptation》 ; be prudent ; be circumspect ¶ 조심하여 carefully ; cautiously ; with care // 조심하고 있다 be on one's guard ; be on the alert ; be wide awake ; keep one's eyes open // 조심해서 걷다 walk with care // 도둑을 조심하다 be on guard against thieves // 조심하라고 이르다 warn 《a person》 against // 불조심하다 mind the fire ; take precaution against fire // 몸조심하다 take care of oneself ; be careful of one's health // 조심하십시오 Talk care. /Be careful. // 길 조심 Watch your step. // 그 사람의 행동에 조심하라 Keep a sharp lookout on his behavior. // 소매치기 조심 Beware of pickpockets. /Beware of purse-snatchers. /Be alert for purse-snatchers. // 차 조심하십시오 Watch out for cars. /Look out for cars. // 발을 조심해라 Watch your step. // 사기꾼을 조심하시오 Be alert to con artists. /Beware of con artists. // 오늘 우리 회사 사장님이 회사 사무실을 시찰차 방문하시니 여러분은 각별히 행동에 조심하기 바랍니다 Today our company president is coming to this office on all inspection tour. So you guys mind your p's and q's.
—성 cautiousness ; circumspectness
불— precaution against fire ; [게시] Watch out for fires ! ; Fire danger ! ; Inflammable ! ; Flammable !
조쌀하다 [노인 얼굴이] (be) nice and clean ; have a nice clean old face
조아 爪牙 claws and teeth ; clutches and fangs ; [신하] a right-hand man ; trusted retainers ; [긴요한 물건] an indispensable thing
조아리다 knock one's forehead on the floor〔ground〕 ; kowtow ; give a deep bow
조아팔다 sell in small lots〔quantity〕 ; break up into small lots to sell
조악 粗惡 coarseness ; crudeness
—하다 (be) coarse ; crude ; be of poor〔inferior〕 quality ¶ 품질이 조악하다 It is of inferior〔poor〕 quality
조암 광물 造岩鑛物 rock-forming minerals
조앙 早秧 early seedlings of rice
조야 粗野 rusticity ; coarseness ; rudeness ; vulgarity ; grossness —하다 (be) coarse ; rough ; rudevulgar ; unpolished ; rustic ¶ 조야한 말씨 coarse speech〔language〕 // 조야한 사람 a man of rough manners
조야 朝野 the government and the people ; the whole nation ¶ 조야의 명사 men of distinction both in and out of government // 조야가 일심 합력하여 the whole nation moving with one accord 〔as one man〕 ; the whole nation making a united effort
‡조약 條約 a treaty ; a convention ; an agreement ; a pact ¶ 조약의 조인 the signing of a treaty // 조약상의 권리〔의무〕 treaty rights〔obligations〕 // 조약을 체결하다 conclude〔enter into〕 a treaty 《with》 // 조약을 지키다〔위반하다, 개정하다〕 observe〔break, revise〕 a treaty // 조약을 폐기하다 denounce a treaty // 미국과 조약을 체결하다 conclude a treaty with America

— 가맹국 a signatory country —국 a treaty power ; a (treaty) signatory ; a pact member — 규정 the treaty provisions〔terms, stipulations〕 — 비준 the ratification of a treaty —안 a treaty draft — 원안 a protocol — 체결권 treaty-making powers 기본 — a basic relations treaty 보호 — a protectorate treaty 불가침 — a Nonaggression Treaty〔Pact〕 수호 — a Treaty of Peace and Amity 잠정 — a temporary〔working〕 agreement ; a modus vivend 《라》 평화〔통상〕 — a peace〔commercial〕 treaty 포츠머스 — the Treaty of Portsmouth 헤이그 — the Hague Convention 현행 국제 — international conventions existing

*조약돌 a gravel ; pebbles

조어 造語 [말] a coined word ; a coinage ; a nonce word (임시 변통의) ¶ 이것은 B씨의 조어이다 This word was coined by Mr. B. /This is a word of Mr. B's coinage.

—법 word formation — 성분 the constituent elements〔components〕 of a compound

조어 助語 〖문법〗 a grammatical particle ; an expletive

조어 釣魚 fishing ; angling —하다 fish ; angle

— 대전(大全) [책 이름] the Complete Angler

조언 造言 ⇨ 거짓말

†조언 助言 advice ; counsel ; a suggestion ; a hint —하다 advise ; counsel ; give 《a person》 advice〔counsel, hint〕 ; suggest ¶ 조언을 구하다 ask advice of 《a person》 ; seek advice from 《a person》 // 조언을 받아들이다 take〔listen to〕 《a person's》 advice

—자 an adviser ; a counsellor

조업 操業 work ; operation —하다 operate ; work ¶ 조업을 정지하다 cease operations // 조업을 단축하다 cut down 〔reduce, curtail〕 operations // 그 공장 조업률은 6할이다 The factory is operating at 60 percent of capacity.

— 개시 a〔the〕 start-up〔beginning〕 of operations — 단축 shorter-time〔curtailed〕 operation ; reduction〔curtailment〕 of operation〔working hours〕 —비 operation expenses — 일수 days operated — 제한 output restriction — 중지 a〔the〕 shutdown of operations ; a〔the〕 cessation of work 완전 — (be in) full operation ¶ 그 공장은 완전 조업을 하고 있다 The mill is running full time. 8시간 — an eight-hour run 《of a factory》

조역 助役 [일] an assistant action ; [보좌하는 사람] a supporting role ; an assistant stationmaster (역의) ; a helper —하다 help〔assist〕 《a person》

—꾼 an assistant for rough work

조연 助演 supporting〔assisting〕 performance —하다 play a supporting role

—자 a supporting player ; a member of the supporting cast ; a supporting actor 〔actress〕 ; [오페라·발레에서] a figurant 《프》 (남자) ; a figurante 《프》 (여자)

조영 造營 building ; (a) construction ; (an) erection —하다 build ; erect ; construct

—물 buildings ; structures

조예 造詣 attainments ; scholarship ¶ 학문에 조예가 깊은 사람 a man of great erudition // …에 조예가 깊다 have a profound〔a deep〕 knowledge of 《literature》 ; be (well) versed in 《history》 ; be at home in ; possess high attainments 《in》

†조용하다 [잠잠하다] (be) quiet ; silent ; still ; calm ; tranquil ; serene ; peaceful ; [태도가] soft ; gentle ; graceful ; [한적하다] deserted ; [평안하다] restful ¶ 조용히 quietly ; calmly ; peacefully ; softly ; gently // 조용한 관중 a silent audience // 조용한 목소리 a gentle voice // 조용히 이야기하다 speak in a calm tone // 조용히 하다 keep quiet〔still〕 ; be silent // 조용해지다 become〔grow〕 still ; quiet down ; [바람 따위가] abate ; subside // 조용히 살다 lead a quiet life // 2·3분 동안 조용히 해 주십시오 Keep quiet for a few minutes. // 장내는 쥐죽은 듯이 조용해졌다 Hushed silence reigned over the room. /The hall became as silent as death. // 조용해라 Quiet! /Be quiet!

조우 遭遇 [만남] encounter ; meeting ; [임금의 신임] winning royal confidence —하다 meet 《with》 ; encounter ; run into ; come across〔upon〕 ; win royal confidence ¶ 적과 조우하다 encounter the enemy // 폭풍우와 조우하다 run into a storm ; be overtaken by a storm // 불행에 조우하다 meet with misfortune // 곤란에 조우하다 meet〔be confronted〕 with a difficulty

—전 an encounter ; an engagement

조운 漕運 marine transportation ; shipping ; carriage by sea ; freighting —하다 transport〔carry〕 by sea

—선 a cargo vessel ; a transport (ship) ; a freighter —업 marine transportation business ; shipping business 〔trade〕 —업자 a shipping agent

조울병 躁鬱病 〖의학〗 a manic-depressive sickness

— 환자 a manic-depressive

조원 造園 landscape gardening —하다 make〔lay out〕 a garden ; landscape

—가 a landscape gardener〔architect〕 ; a garden designer —술 landscape gardening〔architecture〕 ; (the art of) landscaping

조위 弔慰 (the expression of) condolence —하다 condole with 《a person》 ; offer one's condolence to 《a person》 ¶ 조위

전보를 치다 telegraph one's condolence ((to))
—금 condolence money ; a solatium for bereavement

조육 鳥肉 chicken ; poultry meat

조율 調律 tuning ; harmony ; intonation —하다 put ((a piano)) in tune ; tune ¶ 이 피아노는 조율해야겠다 This piano needs tuning.
—기 a key ; a regulator —료 a charge for tuning ((a piano)) —사 a (piano) tuner

조은 朝恩 the King's benevolence ; the Royal graces〔favor〕

조음 調音 [목소리의] articulation ; modulation ; [악기의] tuning —하다 articulate ; tune ¶ 나는 매달 피아노 조음을 한다 I have the piano tuned every month.

조응 照應 correspondence ; agreement accordance —하다 agree〔accord〕((with)) ; correspond ((to)) ; be in accordance ((with))

조의 朝議 a Court〔Cabinet〕Council ¶ 조의에서 의결했다 The Cabinet came to a decision.

조의 弔意 [유족에 대한] condolence ; [고인에 대한] a mark of respect to the dead ¶ 조의를 표하다 express one's condolence // 조의를 표하여 휴업하다 be closed as a mark of respect to the dead

조인 鳥人 an airman ; a birdman ; an aviator

⁑**조인 調印** signature ; signing ; sealing —하다 affix〔set〕one's seal ((to)) ; put one's seal ((on)) ; affix〔put〕one's signature ((to)) ; sign ((a note, a treaty))
—국 a signatory (power) —식 a signing ceremony ; a ceremony of signing —자 a signer ; a signatory — 장소 the place of signature 가— the initial signature

조자리¹ ⇨ 주저리

조자리² [대문의] the hinge pivot-piece of a door

조작 造作 [제조] manufacturing ; construction ; [날조] fabrication ; concoction ; invention —하다 [날조] fabricate ; forge ; fake ; invent ; make up ; concoct ; trump up ; cook up 〔devise〕(안출하다) ; [만들다] construct ; manufacture ¶ 조작된 소문 a cooked-up rumor // 조작된 민의 fabricated public opinion // 그 정보는 선동적인 신문의 조작이다 The report is an invention of sensational newspapers. // 그것은 순전히 그가 조작한 이야기이다 The story is a pure invention on his part.
—설 a fabrication ; a made-up story —자 a fabricator

*__조작 操作__ (an) operation ; handling ; management ; (a) manipulation —하다 operate〔work〕((a machine)) ; manipulate ((the market)) ; manage ((a boat)) ; handle ; rig ((the market)) (부정으로)
시장 — market manipulation〔operation〕

조작거리다 ⇨ 주적거리다

⁑**조잡 粗雜** coarseness ; rudeness ; crudeness —하다 (be) rough ; coarse ; rude ; crude ; gross ¶ 조잡한 생각 a crude idea // 조잡한 건물 a crude building // 조잡한 사람 a coarse man

조장 助長 promotion ; furtherance —하다 promote ; foster ; further ; make for ; be conducive ((to)) ¶ 운동은 건강을 조장한다 Exercise promotes health. / Exercise is conducive to health. // 그 조약은 평화를 조장했다 The treaty made for peace. // 정부는 국내 산업 조장의 대책을 세웠다 The government took measures to promote domestic industry.

조장 組長 a head ; a foreman

조재 造材 cutting and processing of logs ; logging
—자 a logger ; a woodcutter ; a lumberjack

조전 弔電 a telegram of condolence ; telegraphic condolence ¶ 조전을 치다 send a telegram of condolence ((to))

조전 操典 a drill book ; a drill manual

⁑**조절 調節** regulation ; adjustment ; control ; governing ; modulation ; tuning (악기의) ; tuning in (라디오의) —하다 regulate ((a machine)) ; adjust ((prices)) ; control ((birth)) ; govern ; modulate ((one's voice)) ; tune ((a piano)) ; tune in ((the radio)) ¶ 목소리의 조절 the modulation of one's voice // 물가의 조절 the regulation〔control〕of prices
—기 a regulator ; an adjuster ; a governor ; a modulator (라디오의) —망 a guide〔trail〕rope —미(米) ((release)) (government-held) rice to cushion a rice price hike —익 [항공] an adjusting plane —전(栓) a regulator cock —판 [기계] a regulator〔control〕valve 미가(米價) — the regulation〔control〕of the price of rice 남북 회담 — 위원회 the South-North Coordinating Committee

조정 朝廷 the (royal) court

조정 調停 mediation ; arbitration —하다 mediate ((a dispute)) ; arbitrate ((between parties)) ¶ 분쟁을 조정하다 mediate a dispute // 조정에 붙이다 submit ((a matter)) to arbitration // 조정 역할을 하다 take the trouble of mediation // 아버지와의 의견차를 조정했니 Did you settle your differences with your father? // 그들은 한동안 싸우고 있었지만 결국은 의견 차이를 조정할 수 있었다고 생각해 They were fighting for a while, but I guess they managed to patch things up.
—서 a consent decree (법원에서 작성하는) — 신청서 a written application for mediation —안 a mediation〔compromise〕plan ; an arbitration proposal — 역할 a mediation role — 위원 a mediator ; an arbitrator ; a member of a mediation committee —자〔인〕a mediator ;

an arbitrator ; an intervener ; a peacemaker — 재판 court arbitration 강제〔임의〕 — compulsory〔voluntary〕 arbitration (가정)분쟁 — grievance mediation

조정 調定 settlement —하다 settle
— 세액 the tax amount settled —필 settled

†조정 調整 regulation ; adjustment ; control ; coordination —하다 regulate ; adjust ; coordinate ¶ 세금의 연말 조정 the year-end adjustment of taxes // 가격을 조정하다 adjust the price 《of》 // 외교 문제를 조정하다 adjust diplomatic affairs
—기 a regulator ; [가스의] a governor —실 [라디오·TV] a control room 미(微)— [라디오·텔레비전] fine tuning

조정 漕艇 rowing ; boating —하다 row a boat
— 경기 a boat race

조제 粗製 crude〔coarse〕 manufacture —하다 manufacture coarse articles
— 남조 mass production of inferior articles ; quick and careless manufacture ; sacrifice of quality to quantity ; slipshod manufacture in large quantities — 설탕 raw〔unrefined〕 sugar —품 a crude〔an inferior〕 article ; coarse manufactures ; an article of inferior〔poor〕 quality

*조제 調劑 preparation〔compounding〕 of medicine —하다 prepare medicine ; make up a prescription ; fill a prescription (처방에 의해) ¶ 조제시키다 have the prescription filled
—법 pharmacy —사 a pharmacist 〔pharmaceutist〕 ; an apothecary ; a chemist ; a druggist 《미》 —실 a pharmacy ; a dispensary —학 pharmaceutics

조제 調製 making 《to order》 ; preparation (조합) ; manufacture ; execution (주문품의) —하다 make ; prepare ; compound ; execute
—법 a recipe — 식품〔식품점〕 delicatessen〔a delicatessen store〕 《미》 —품 a preparation

조조 早朝 early morning ¶ 조조에 early in the morning // 내일 조조에 early tomorrow morning

조조하다 躁躁— (be) impetuous ; impatient ; hasty ¶ 조조하게 굴다 be in a hurry ; do without deliberation

조졸 早卒 ⇨ 조사(早死)

조종 弔鐘 a funeral bell ; a knell

조종 祖宗 the royal ancestors

†조종 操縱 control ; management ; operation ; manipulation —하다 manage ; control ; handle ; operate ; manipulate ; steer ; pilot (비행기를) ; drive (차를) ; pull the wires (배후에서) ¶ 조종하기 어렵다〔쉽다〕 be hard〔easy〕 to manage〔control〕 // A씨 조종의 자동차로 in a motorcar driven by Mr. A // 기계를 조종하다 operate a machine // 비행기를 조종하다 pilot〔fly〕 an airplane // 남편을 마음대로 조종하다 twist〔turn〕 one's husband around one's finger // 여자에게 조종당하다 be tied to a woman's apron strings // 교묘하게 조종하여 …시키다 maneuver 《a person》 into 《doing》 // 조종 불능이 되다 [사람이] lose control of 《a car》 ; [물건이] get out of control ; become uncontrollable〔unmanageable〕
—간 a control stick〔lever〕 ; a joy stick 《속》 —법 operation ; control —사 a pilot ; an aviator ; an aviatrix (여자) —석 a pilot seat ; a cockpit ; a flight deck —자 a manager ; a manipulator ; an operator ; [자동차의] a driver ; a steersman — 장치 a steering〔controlling〕 gear ; controls 공동 — 장치 dual controls (연습 비행기의) 부—사 a copilot 자동 — 비행기 a pilotless plane

조주 助奏 『음악』 an o(b)bligato

조주 助走 an approach run 《for the broad jump》
—로 a runway ; an approach — 스타트 a flying start

조준 照準 aim ; aiming ; laying ; sight —하다 aim ; lay ; take aim〔a sight〕 ; sight ¶ 대포의 조준각 the elevation of guns // 조준 연습 사격 a sighting shot // 조준이 틀리다 be faulty at aim // 200 미터에 조준을 맞추다 sight the gun for 200 meters
—각 an elevation 《of a gun》 —기(器) a sight —기(機) training gear ; a laying apparatus — 망원경 a sighting telescope — 상수 collimation constant —선 a line of sight —수 [군함의] a gun-layer 《영》 ; a pointer —의(儀) an alidad(e) — 폭격 precision〔pinpoint〕 bombing 《미》 상하 — laying for elevation 전시(全視) — panoramic sight 직접 — direct laying

조지다 ① [단단히 맞추다] fix tightly ; tighten up ; screw up ¶ 사개를 조지다 screw〔make, fix〕 a joint tight ② [단속하다] exercise strict control 《over》 ; make double-sure ; hold 《a person》 to ; bear down on

조지아 Georgia 《Ga.》

조지타운 Georgetown

†조직 組織 [결성] organization ; formation ; [구성] construction ; structure ; make-up ; [체계·제도] system ; [생물] tissue —하다 form ; organize ; constitute ¶ 조직적 systematic ; methodical // 조직적 살인 systematic murder // 조직적으로 systematically ; methodically ; on system // 조직화하다 systematize // …로 조직되다 be made up〔composed of〕 ; consist of // 내각〔회사〕을 조직하다 form a Cabinet〔company〕 // 조직을 개편하다 reorganize // 조직적으로 연구하다 make a systematic study of 《English》 // 조직적으로 일을 하다 work systematically ; be systematic in one's work // 이 회는 어떻게 조직되어 있습니까 What is the constitu-

tion of the society? // 인체의 조직은 7년마다 완전히 일신된다 The tissues of the human body are completely renewed every seven years.
— 노동자 organized labor〔worker〕 —력 organizing ability; systematizing talent; capacity for organization —망 the network of a system — 변경 transformation — 위원회 an organizing〔organization〕 committee —자 an organizer —책 a chief organizer —체 an organism; an organic body —표 [선거의] block votes 《of》 —학 〖생물〗 histology —화 systematization ¶ 조직화하다 systematize 경제 — economic structure 사회 — social structure; the structure〔fabric, setup〕 of society 세포〔근육, 신경〕 — cellular〔muscular, nervous〕 tissue

조짐 [장작 평수] firewood piles (of four cubic feet)

조짐 兆朕 symptoms; signs; indications; an omen; a foreboding ¶ …의 조짐이 있다 show signs 《of》; betoken; forebode

조짚 millet straw(s)

†조차 even; too; in addition; into the bargain ¶ 너조차 그럴 줄은 몰랐다 I didn't know that even you would do that. // 분묘가 어디인지조차 알지 못한다 I cannot even tell where the grave is. // 점심도 못 먹고 저녁조차 굶었다 I did not eat any lunch and then skipped dinner as well.

조차 操車 (railway) operation —하다 operate 《a locomotive》
—계 a train dispatcher; a yardman —계장 a yardmaster —장 a switchyard; a shunting yard; a marshaling yard; a classification yard 《미》

조차 潮差 tidal range; the range of tide

조차 租借 lease 《of territory, of a house》 —하다 lease; obtain a lease on 《an island》 from; lease 《a territory》 from ¶ 영국 조차지 a British-leased territory
—권 lease; leasehold —지 leased territory〔ground〕; a leasehold

조착 早着 —하다 arrive at〔in〕 《ten minutes》 ahead of schedule〔time〕

조찬 粗餐 a plain〔coarse〕 dinner

조찬 朝餐 breakfast ⇨ 조반

조처 措處 management; conduct; arrangement; settlement; disposition —하다 manage; conduct; arrange; settle; dispose 《of》 ¶ 적절한 조처 a measure suited to the occasion; a proper step〔measure〕 // 재빨리 조처하다 take prompt action 《on》 // 필요한 조처를 하다 take necessary measures〔action, step〕

조척 照尺 ⇨ 가늠(—자)

조청 造淸 grain syrup; molasses

조촉 弔燭 a funeral candle

조촐하다 [아담하다] (be) snug; cozy; neat; [단정하다] dapper; refined; elegant; neat; tidy; decent; [해사하다] graceful; fair; handsome ¶ 조촐한 용모 neat and elegant appearance // 조촐한 집 a trim house

조촘거리다 hesitate ⇨ 주춤거리다

조총 鳥銃 a fowling piece; a matchlock; a firelock

조총 弔銃 a volley of rifles at a funeral service ¶ 조총을 놓다 fire a volley for the dead

조총련 朝總聯 Chochongnyŏn, the pro-*Pyŏngyang* federation of Korean residents in Japan ⇨ 조련(朝聯)

조추 早秋 early autumn〔fall〕

조춘 早春 early spring

조충 條蟲 a tapeworm; a taenia
—류 tapeworms; Cestoda —(구제(驅除))약 a taeniafuge; a taeniacide

조치 thick broth; heavy soup

조치 措置 management ⇨ 조처

조치개 a necessary accessory〔adjunct〕; an essential accessory

조칙 詔勅 a royal edict〔proclamation, rescript, message〕 ¶ 조칙을 내리다 issue a royal message

조칫보 a stew dish; a thick-stew bowl

‡조카 a nephew ¶ 조카의 아들 a grand-nephew // 그는 내 조카뻘이다 He stands to me in the relation of nephew.
—딸 a niece — 며느리 a nephew's wife —뻘 the relation of nephew — 사위 a niece's husband

조커 [카드놀이] a joker

조타 操舵 steering; steerage —하다 steer
—기 the steering gear — 명령 a helm order —수 a steersman; a quartermaster; a helmsman —술 steersmanship; steering —실 a pilot house; a steering house; a wheelhouse — 장치 a steering gear

조탁 彫琢 [보석의] carving; chiselling; polishing (gems) —하다 carve; chisel; polish

조탄 粗炭 coarse〔low-grade〕 coal

조탕 潮湯 a hot sea-water bath

조퇴 早退 leaving early; leaving 《office, school》 earlier than usual —하다 leave 《office, school》 earlier than usual ¶ 세 시간 일찍 조퇴하다 get〔take〕 three hours off; leave 《work》 three hours early

조판 組版 typesetting; composition —하다 set up type; do typesetting ¶ 조판되어 있다 be in type

조팝나무 〖식물〗 a bridal wreath

조팝나물 〖식물〗 hawkweed

조편성 組編成 organizing〔forming〕 into groups —하다 organize〔form〕 into groups

*조폐 造幣 coinage; mintage —하다 mint; stamp coin
— 각인 mintage mark —국 the mint; the Mint Bureau —국장 the

Director〔Treasurer《미》〕 of the Mint Bureau — 비가(比價) the mint par of exchange 한국 — 공사 the Korea Mint Corporation
조포 弔砲 an artillery salute (for the dead)
조품 粗品 coarse products ⇨ 조제품
조피 Japanese peppercorns
— 나무 the Japanese pepper ; the prickly ash
조하 早夏 early summer
조하 朝霞 morning mist
조하다 躁— (be) hasty ; quick-tempered ; impatient
조함 造艦 naval shipbuilding ; naval construction
— 계획 a naval construction program — 능력〔경쟁〕 naval shipbuilding capacity 〔rivalry〕
조합 調合 [약 따위의] mixture ; compounding ; mixing ; preparation ; [조미] seasoning ; flavoring —하다 mix ; compound ; prepare ; make up ; [조미하다] season ; dress
—물〔제〕 a mixture ; a preparation ; a concoction
*조합 組合 an association ; a league ; a union ; a partnership (합자의) ; a guild ; 〖수학〗 a combination ¶ 조합을 만들다 organize an association ; form a partnership // 조합에 가입하다 join the association // 조합에 가입시키다 admit 《a person》 into the association ; take 《a person》 into partnership
— 간부 a union leader〔official〕 — 관리 union administration — 규약 the articles of an association ; a union charter〔constitution〕 — 기구 union structure —비〔활동〕 union dues〔activities〕 — 운동 union activities〔movements〕 —원 a member of the association〔union〕 ; a union member ; a partner ; a syndicate member ; a copartner ; a unionist —장 a union president — 조직 union organization —주의 unionism — 지도자 a union leader 구매 — a consumers' purchase cooperative association 노동 — a trade union 《영》 ; a labor union 《미》 산업별 — an industrial〔a vertical〕 union 생산〔소비〕 — a producers'〔consumers'〕 cooperative 어용 — a company(-kept) union 직업별 — a craft〔horizontal〕 union 판매 — marketing〔selling〕 cooperative association 협동 — a cooperative association〔union〕 ; a co-op 《구》
조합 照合 verification ; collation ; comparison ; check up —하다 verify ; collate 《with》 ; check up ; tally 《with》 ; compare 《with》
조합 교회 組合敎會 the Congregational Church
†조항 條項 [법률 따위] articles ; clauses ; [항목] provisions ; items

계약 — a contract clause 무효 — 〖법〗 an irritant clause ; an irritancy 인수 — the provisions for acceptance
조해 潮解 〖화학〗 deliquescence —하다 deliquesce
조행 操行 manners ; behavior ; deportment ¶ 조행이 바른 학생 a student of good conduct // 조행이 좋다 be well conducted // 조행이 나쁘다 be dissolute in conduct
조현 朝見 an audience with the King ; a levee —하다 be received in audience 《by His Majesty》 ; be granted〔have〕 an audience with 《the King》
조혈 造血 hematosis ; hematopoiesis ; sanguification —하다 increase〔make〕 the blood
*조형 造形 mo(u)lding ; modeling —하다 mould ; shape ; model
— 미〔예〕술 the formative〔plastic〕 arts
조혼 早婚 an early marriage —하다 marry early〔young〕 ; marry at an early age ¶ 조혼을 장려하다 encourage early marriage // 요즘 젊은이에겐 조혼이 유행하고 있다 Nowadays, early marriage prevails among the young.
조혼전 助婚錢 the wedding expenses paid by the groom for a poor bride
조홍 潮紅 flush (in the face) ; blushing
조화 弔花 floral tributes ; an offering of flowers
조화 造化 creation ; nature ¶ 조화의 신 the Creator ; the Maker of the Universe // 조화의 묘 the wonders of nature // 조화의 장난 a freak of nature
조화 造花 an artificial flower ; an imitation flower
†조화 調和 [일치] harmony ; accord ; agreement ; [음색의] symphony ; [균형] symmetry —하다 harmonize with ; agree with ; be consistent 《with》 ; be in keeping 《with》 ¶ 조화된 harmonious ; [균형이 잡힌] symmetrical // 조화되지 않은 inharmonious ; asymmetrical ; out of keeping 《with》 ; discordant // 조화되어 harmoniously ; in agreement // 조화시키다 harmonize ; conciliate // 조화를 결하다 lack harmony ; disagree // 커튼의 빛깔이 방과 조화되어 있다 The color of the curtain harmonizes with the room.
— 운동 〖물리〗 harmonic motion — 중항〔비례, 함수, 수열〕 〖수학〗 harmonic mean〔proportion, function, progression〕
조환 弔環 [체조의] (the) flying rings ; the rings
‡조회 照會 inquiry ; reference ; communication —하다 inquire 《of a person》 ; make reference 《to》 ¶ 직접 조회하다 write direct to 《a person》 // 나에 관해서는 A 씨에게 조회하시오 I refer you to Mr. A as to my character. // 그 쪽에 조회 중이다 We are in communication with

them.
—장 《send out》 a letter of inquiry —처 [신원·신용 따위의] a reference
조회 朝會 a morning meeting ; the morning session in school 《for moral instruction and physical exercise》 —하다 have a morning meeting
조후 潮候 a tide period
— 관측 tidal prediction —차 a tidal difference
조흔 爪痕 a nail-mark ; a scratch ; a crescent spot (made by pinching)
조흔 條痕 a streak ; a stria
조흥 助興 —하다 add to the fun 《of》; heighten the interest 《of》
족 ⇨ 죽²
족 足 a foot ; [동물의] a cloven foot ; a hoof ; the leg (소의) ; the shank (돼지의) ; the trotter (양의) ¶ 돼지족 pettitoes
-족 族 [가족] a family ; [족속] kinsmen ; relatives ; [생물의] a family ; [종족] a tribe ; a race
몽고— The Mongol tribe
족내혼 族內婚 endogamy ¶ 족내혼의 endogamous ; endogamic
족대 足臺 a step ; a stool ; a footstool
족대기다 [볶아치다] hurry〔urge, compel, force, constrain, press〕《a person》 to do 《a thing》; [우겨대다] persist in 《one's opinion》; insist ; force 《one's idea》; [깨뜨리다] break ; mangle ¶ 하인들을 족대기어 일을 시키다 force servants to work // 대문을 족대기어 열다 break the gate open
족두리 a black crown-like headpiece worn by women on formal occasions
족두리풀 〖식물〗 wild-ginger plant ; Asiasraum heterotropoides (학명)
족발 足— a pork hock
족벌 族閥 a clan ; a clique
— 정치 clan government
족벌주의 族閥主義 nepotism
—자 nepotist
족보 族譜 a genealogical table ; a clan register ; genealogy ; a pedigree ; a family-tree
족생 簇生 gregarious growth —하다 grow gregariously〔in cluster〕
— 식물 a social〔gregarious〕 plant
족속 族屬 [가족] a family ; [일가] kinsmen ; relatives ; a clan
*족쇄 足鎖 fetters ; shackle (for the feet) ¶ 족쇄를 채우다 fetter ; shackle ; put 《a person》 in stocks
족인 族人 clansmen〔kinsmen〕; relatives
족자 簇子 a hanging picture〔scroll〕
—걸이 a pole with hooks for hanging a scroll
족자리 handles on both sides of a pot
족장 族丈 an elder of a clan
족장 族長 a patriarch ; the head of family〔tribe〕
— 시대 the patriarchal age ; patriarchy ; patriarchalism
족적 足跡 a footprint ; footmarks ; traces ¶ 족적을 남기다 leave one's footprints
족제 族弟 younger brothers in relation
족제 族制 clanship ; the system of relationship
족제비 〖동물〗 a weasel
족족 ⇨ 죽죽
-족족 [마다] every〔each〕 time ; whenever ; time 《that》 ¶ 오는 족족 whenever 〔as often as〕 one comes ; each〔every〕 time one calls // 그들은 만나는 족족 악수한다 They never meet without shaking hands. /They shake hands every time they meet. // 친구들을 만나는 족족 이 말을 전해주시오 Give this information whatever time you meet your friends.
족지 足指 the toes ⇨ 발가락
족집게 (hair-)tweezers ¶ 족집게로 털을 뽑다 pluck a hair out with tweezers
족척 族戚 kindred ; relatives
족출 簇出 —하다 spring up in clusters ; mushroom (up) ¶ 그 시대에는 위인이 족출했다 The age was highly productive of great men.
족치다 ① [작게 만들다] chop ; hack ¶ 갈비를 족치다 chop short ribs
② [차차 줄이다] waste ; fritter ¶ 가산을 족치다 waste〔fritter〕 away one's patrimony
③ [깨뜨리다] destroy ; mangle ¶ 의자를 족치다 break a chair
④ [족대기다] compel ; press ¶ 사람을 족쳐서 시키다 force 《a person》 to work
족친 族親 kinsmen ; relatives
족탕 足湯 soup made with foot and knuckle (of beef) ; beef-foot soup
족편 足— calf's-hoof jelly〔gelatin, agar-agar〕
족하 足下 [편지의 존칭] Sir ; Esquire
‡족하다 足— [충분하다] (be) sufficient ; enough ; adequate ; suffice ; serve ; answer ; do ¶ 5,000원이면 족하다 Five thousand *won* will do. // 마음이 족하다 He is satisfied with it. // 그것으로 족하다 That will do. // 자격이 족하다 He is fully qualified. // 한번 보면 족하다 A glance at it is quite enough. // 그와는 족히 문학을 논할 만하다 He is well worth talking literature with.
족히 足— enough ; sufficiently ; in plenty ; fully ; well (worth) ¶ 족히 만 명은 수용할 수 있다 be large enough to accommodate ten thousand people // 족히 볼 만하다 be well worth seeing // 족히 다섯 시간은 걸린다 It takes you a full five hours. // 적어도 2만 달러는 족히 들 겁니다 It will cost me a cool 20 grand at least.
존 a zone
†존경 尊敬 respect ; esteem ; honor ; veneration ; reverence ; deference ; a high

> 참고 **respect**는 사람에게 경의를 표하거나 의지·생각·약속 따위를 존중한다는 의미에서 가장 널리 쓰이는 말 **esteem**은 마음으로부터 존경한다는 뜻으로 사람에게도 물건에게도 사용된다 **honor**는 사람의 명예를 인정하고 공경하는 것 **reverence**는 황송해하며 존경하는것

regard —하다 respect ; honor ; venerate ; revere ; have a (high) regard for ; hold 《a person》 in (high) esteem〔respect〕; look up to 《a person》; pay deference 《to》 ¶ 존경할 honorable ; estimable ; respectable ; worthy of respect // 존경심에서 out of respect 《for》; in deference 《to》; out of courtesy 《to》// 존경을 받다 win respect ; command esteem // 저 사람을 선배로서 존경하고 있다 I respect him as my senior. // 그는 시인으로서 존경받고 있다 He is highly regarded as a poet. // 그는 여자를 그다지 존경하지 않는다 He does not esteem women highly.

존공 尊公 your esteemed father

존귀 尊貴 nobility —하다 (be) high and noble

존당 尊堂 your esteemed mother

존대 尊待 treatment with respect —하다 treat with politeness〔respect〕; respect ; (be) polite 《to》; hold 《a person》 in (high) esteem ¶ 존대받다 be esteemed〔held in esteem〕

—어 a term of respect ; an honorific

존대인 尊大人 your (esteemed) father

존득거리다, 쫀득거리다 (be) sticky ; glutinous ; adhesive ; elastic ; rubbery ; tough

존득존득, 쫀득쫀득 moist and sticky ; tough and clammy

존립 存立 existence ; life ; remaining〔being〕 independent —하다 exist ; be in existence ¶ 국가의 존립을 위협하다 threaten the national existence

— 기간 〖법〗 duration

존망 存亡 life and death ; existence ; destiny ; fate ¶ 위급 존망의 때 a crisis ; a critical moment // 국가 존망지추에 in this time of national crisis // 국가의 존망에 관한 문제다 It is a question of life or death for the nation. /The national existence is at stake.

존부 存否 existence and inexistence ¶ 존부를 확인하다 ascertain the existence 《of》; find out whether 《a person》 is alive or not

존비 尊卑 the high and the low ; aristocrat and plebeian ¶ 존비 귀천 할 것 없이 without distinction of rank ; irrespective of rank

— 귀천 high and low ; noble and mean

존속 存續 continuance ; continued existence ; continuation ; duration —하다 continue to exist ; last ; continue ; keep up

존속 尊屬 〖법〗 an ancestor

— 살인 the killing of a lineal ascendant

— 살해 a parricide ; [부친] patricide ; [모친] matricide 직〔방〕계 — a lineal〔collateral〕 ascendant

존속친 尊屬親 〖법〗 lineal consanguinity

존숭 尊崇 reverence ; veneration ; respect ; worship —하다 reverence ; respect ; revere

존심 存心 —하다 bear〔keep〕 in mind ; take 《a thing》 to heart

존안 尊顔 your (esteemed) face

***존엄 尊嚴** dignity ; majesty ; augustness ; sanctity —하다 (be) dignified ; majestic ; august ; sacred ; solemn ¶ 법의 존엄 the dignity of law // 법의 존엄을 지키다 uphold the majesty of the law // 존엄을 손상하다 impair the dignity 《of》// 신의 존엄을 더럽히다 be guilty of profanation ; blaspheme against God

존영 尊影 your esteemed〔noble〕 portrait〔picture〕

존의 尊意 your esteemed opinion〔view idea〕

존자 尊者 a (Buddhist) priest of eminent virtue ; a saint

존장 尊長 the (venerable) elder

†존재 存在 existence ; subsistence ; being —하다 exist ; subsist ; be ; be in existence ; be present ; remain (잔존하다) ¶ 신의 존재 the existence of God // 존재 이유 reason for being ; raison d'être 《프》 // 존재하고 있는 existent ; extant ; existing // 존재하지 않다 be nonexistent ; be out of existence // 존재를 인정받다 win recognition ; be recognized // 존재를 인정하지 않다 ignore 《a person》; take no notice of 《a person》// 그것은 지금도 존재하고 있다 It is still in existence. // 그런 인물은 역사상 존재하지 않는다 Those characters have no place〔existence〕 in history. // 그는 야구계에서는 잊을 수 없는 존재이다 He is a notable figure in baseball circles. // 그것들은 더 이상 존재하지 않는다 They are history.

—론 〖철학〗 ontology —물 an existence ; a being —부 〖음악〗 an episode —사 〖문법〗 an infix — 의의 the significance〔meaning〕 of existence 《of》 — 이유 reason for being ; justification for existence —자 〖철학〗 *an ens* 《*pl. entia*》; a being

존저 尊邸 your house

존절 frugality ; saving ; thrift —하다 economize 《on》; be economical〔sparing〕 《of》; be frugal ; be thrifty

존존하다, 쫀쫀하다 (be) finely woven ; be of fine weave

†존중 尊重 respect ; esteem ; regard ; deference —하다 respect ; esteem ; value ; appreciate ; hold dear ; think highly 《of》; hold in high respect〔esteem〕; set store 《by》; have a high regard 《for》

> 참고 **value** 가치가 있다는 것을 인정하여 높이 평가하다 **appreciate** 그 가치를 이해하고 그것을 감상할 수 있기 때문에 높이 평가하다 **esteem** 존중하고 동시에 경애하다

¶ 존중할 만한 estimable ; respectable ; worthy of esteem // 존중하지 않다 pay no regard to ; have no regard for ; set no value on // 의사〔권리〕를 존중하다 respect 《a person's》 wishes 〔rights〕// 명예를 생명 이상으로 존중하다 hold honor dearer than one's life // 여론을 존중하다 pay regard to public opinion

존체 尊體 your esteemed self〔health〕

존치 存置 retention ; maintenance **—하다** retain ; maintain

존칭 尊稱 a title of honor〔respect, esteem〕; an honorific title **—하다** address honorifically

존택 尊宅 your esteemed house

존폐 存廢 maintenance or abolition ; existence ; continuation〔retention〕 **— 문제** the question of maintenance or abolition 《of the institution》; the problem of keeping or discarding

존필 尊筆 your esteemed writing

존한 尊翰 your esteemed letter

존함 鏡啣, 尊銜 your (honorable) name

존형 尊兄 you

존호 尊號 eulogistic posthumous title of a king〔queen〕

존후 尊候 (the state of) your health

졸 〖화학〗 sol ; colloidal solution

졸(卒) [장기의] a Korean-chess pawn ¶ 졸을 잡다 take a pawn

졸가 拙家 my house〔home〕; my abode

졸가리 dry bits of twig ; a stripped stalk 〔stem〕 ⇨ 줄거리

졸경 卒更 [순라] a night patrol ; [밤새의 고민] tossing about in bed

졸경치(르)다 卒更— have bitter experiences ; have a hard〔bad〕 time of it 《with a person》; pay dearly 《for》

졸계 拙計 a foolish plan ; a poor scheme

졸고 拙稿 an unworthy manuscript of mine ; my manuscript

졸곡 卒哭 ① [삼우제 뒤의] a sacrificial ceremony performed following the third sacrifice after burial ② [석달 뒤의] a sacrificial ceremony performed in the third month after burial

졸공 拙工 a clumsy〔poor〕 workman

졸깃졸깃, 쫄깃쫄깃 —하다 (be) sticky ; chewy

졸년 卒年 the year of 《a person's》 death **— 월일** the date of death

***졸다¹** doze ; take a nap ; fall into a doze ; [깜박] drop (off) into a doze ; [앉아서] fall asleep〔nap〕 in one's seat ; drop asleep ; drowse ; snooze ¶ 책을 읽다가 졸다 doze over a book // 청중의 대부분은 졸고 있었다 Most of audience were asleep. // 너무 피로해서 꾸벅꾸벅 졸면서 운전을 했다 I was so tired that I was dozing off behind the wheel.

졸다² [물 따위가] get boiled down ; be boiled dry

†**졸도 卒倒** a swoon ; a fainting fit ; a faint ; fainting ; 〖의학〗 syncope **—하다** fall down in a swoon ; faint ; swoon ; fall unconscious ; go into fits ¶ 공포 때문에 졸도했다 The fright made her sink down in a swoon. // 졸도할 뻔했다 He was on the point of swooning.

졸도 卒徒 one's soldiers ; men under one's charge ; privates ; the rank and file ; [변변치 못한 사람] small fry 《총칭》 ¶ 졸도들은 거들떠 보지도 않고 ignoring the presence of the rank and file

졸들다 be〔get〕 hampered in development ; be stunted ; be shriveled ; be withered ¶ 비가 안 와서 배추가 졸들었다 All the cabbages were shriveled from lack of rain.

졸때기 [일] a small-scale affair ; a petty job ; [사람] a petty〔an unimportant〕 person ; a stupid little fellow

졸라대다 badger 《a person to do》; tease〔importune〕 《a person for》; clamor 《for》 ¶ 사달라고 졸라대다 ask 《a person》 to buy 《a thing》// 과자를 달라고 졸라대다 clamor for candy // 결혼하자고 졸라대다 tease 《a person》 to marry 《one》

***졸라매다** tie up ; fasten ; tighten ; constrict ; strangle ¶ 허리띠를 졸라매다 tie 〔fasten〕 a belt // 목을 졸라매어 죽이다 strangle 《a person》 to death

졸래졸래 flippantly ; forwardly ; pertly ; frivolously ¶ 졸래졸래 돌아다니다 gad about // 꼬마는 졸래졸래 엄마 뒤를 따라 갔다 The child trotted along after his mother.

졸렬 拙劣 clumsiness ; inexpertness ; awkwardness ; unskillfulness **—하다** (be) poor ; clumsy ; awkward ; inexpert ¶ 졸렬한 수단 a bungling step ; a clumsy means // 졸렬한 외교 poor diplomacy

졸론 拙論 [자기의] my unworthy view 〔treatise, comment, opinion〕; [보잘 것 없는] an absurd view ; a silly argument

졸리다¹ [남에게] be〔get〕 teased 〔pestered, pressed, coaxed, annoyed, importuned〕 by 《a person for something》; be badgered by 《a person to do》; [매이다] be tightened〔fastened, strangled〕

***졸리다²** feel sleepy ; grow drowsy ; be heavy with sleep ¶ 졸려 보이는 sleepily ; drowsily ; sleepy-looking // 졸린 듯이 sleepily ; drowsily // 졸려서 죽겠다 I feel dead tired.

졸막졸막 in various small sizes〔quantities〕 **—하다** (be) motley ; be diverse in size ¶ 졸막졸막한 나무들 a group of various sized trees

졸망졸망 —하다 (be) small-sized ; be all bumpy ¶ 졸망졸망한 아이들 a bunch of small children // 감나무에 감이 졸망졸망 열려 있다 The persimmon tree is laden with persimmons.

졸문 拙文 [자기 글] my unworthy writing〔composition〕 ; [졸렬한 글] a poor〔clumsy〕 writing

졸밥 a bit of pheasant meat fed to a falcon to arouse his hunting desires

졸병 卒兵 a common soldier ⇨ 병졸

졸보 拙甫 a good-for-nothing

졸부 猝富 sudden riches ; an overnight millionaire ; a nouveau riche 《프》

졸사 猝死 sudden death **—하다** die suddenly ; drop〔fall〕 dead

졸사간 猝乍間 (in) a moment

졸서 卒逝 passing (away) ; dying ; decease **—하다** pass away ; depart this life ; decease

졸속 拙速 ¶ 졸속의 rough-and-ready ; knocked-up ; hasty // 졸속을 존중하다 prefer speed to elaboration

—주의 a rough-and-ready method〔rule〕

졸시 拙詩 a doggerel (verse) ; a poor poem ¶ 졸시를 짓다 write〔compose〕 a doggerel

졸아들다 shrink ; boil away ⇨ 줄어들다

졸아붙다 [물 따위가] get boiled dry ; be boiled down

졸아지다 be boiled away ; be contracted ; be reduced ; shrink ¶ 빨아서 졸아지다 shrink in the wash

***졸업 卒業** graduation **—하다** complete a course ; finish school ; graduate at 《a school》 《영》 ; be graduated 《from》 《미》 ¶ 졸업하면 after〔upon〕 graduation // 대학을 졸업하다 graduate from〔at〕 a university // 중학교를 졸업하다 finish 〔complete〕 the junior high school 〔lower secondary school〕 // 수석으로 졸업하다 graduate first on the list // 그는 의과를 졸업했다 He was graduated in medicine 《at a university》. // 그런 것은 벌써 졸업했다 He has gone beyond that sort of thing. // 그 여자는 우등으로 대학을 졸업했다 She graduated from a college with honors.

—논문 a graduation thesis **—반** 《students of》 the graduating class **—생** a graduate ; [남자] an alumnus 《*pl.* -ni》 ; an old boy ; [여자] an alumna 《*pl.* -nae》 ; an old girl ¶ 대학 졸업생 a university graduate〔man〕 // 졸업생 명부 a list of the graduates // 300명의 졸업생을 내다 turn out 300 boys〔girls〕 // 1977년도의 졸업생이다 He graduated with the class of 1977. **—시험** a graduation examination **—식** a graduation ceremony ; the graduation exercises ; the commencement (ceremony) 《미》 **—장** a diploma ; a certificate of the completion of a school course ; a parchment ; a sheepskin 《미·구》

졸연하다 猝然, 卒然— (be) sudden ; abrupt ; unexpected ¶ 졸연히 suddenly ; abruptly ; all of a sudden ; unexpectedly ; all at once

졸음 sleepiness ; drowsiness ¶ 졸음이 오다 feel sleepy〔drowsy〕 // 졸음을 깨다 shake off sleepiness // 졸음을 깨기 위해 산보하다 take a walk to keep oneself awake ; walk off one's sleepiness

졸이다 [고기 따위를] boil down ; [마음을] feel anxious〔nervous〕 ¶ 고기를 간장에 졸이다 boil beef down in soy sauce // 마음을 졸이다 be fidgety〔agitated, edgy, on edge〕 ; be held in suspense ; be excited ; be nervous〔uneasy, anxious〕 《of》 ; worry

졸자 拙者 ① [「나」의 겸사말] I ② [용렬한 사람] a stupid〔foolish〕 fellow

졸작 拙作 [졸렬한] a poor work ; trash ; rubbish ; [자기의] an unworthy work of mine

졸장부 拙丈夫 a small-minded man, a petty little fellow ; the chicken-hearted ; a man of small caliber

졸저 拙著 [자기 작품] my humble 〔unworthy〕 work ; [보잘것없는 작품] a poor composition ; a poor book〔work〕

졸졸 [물이] trickling(ly) ; murmuring (ly) ; [사람을] 《follow a person》 persistently ; hanging on ; sticking close ; tagging along ¶ 시냇물이 졸졸 흐르다 a brook murmurs along // 수돗물이 졸졸 나오다 water trickles down from the faucet // 어린아이가 어머니를 졸졸 따라 다닌다 The child is always tagging at his mother's heels.

졸중 卒中 〖한의〗 apoplexy

졸중풍 卒中風 〖의학〗 apoplexy ¶ 졸중풍에 걸리다 be seized with apoplexy

졸지 猝地 ¶ 졸지에 suddenly ; abruptly ; all of a sudden ; unexpectedly // 졸지에 파산을 당하다 become bankrupt all of a sudden

졸직 卒直 —하다 (be) narrow-minded and rigid ; illiberal and unadaptable

졸참나무 〖식물〗 a queritron ; Quercus serrate (학명)

졸책 拙策 ① [졸계] a poor policy〔plan〕 ② [자기 계책] my humble plan

졸필 拙筆 [악필] a poor〔bad〕 hand ; poor (hand)writing ; [악필가] a person with poor handwriting ; a poor writer ; a scribbler ; [자기 필적] my unworthy handwriting

졸하다 卒— die ; pass away ; decease

졸하다 拙— [재주 없고 용렬하다] (be) clumsy ; awkward ; bungling ; poor ; [졸

직하다] narrow-minded ; illiberal ; hidebound ¶ 졸한 사람 a narrow-minded person
졸한 猝寒 sudden cold ; a sudden chill
좀[1] 〖곤충〗 a moth ; a bristle tail ; a bookworm ¶ 좀 먹은 moth-eaten // 책이 다 좀 먹었다 The books are all worm-eaten.
좀[2] [그 얼마나] how ; how much ; surely ; indeed ; no doubt ; certainly ; presumably ; I dare say ; I am sure ¶ 좀 걱정하셨겠어요 You must have felt very anxious. // 좀 장관이었겠습니까 What a grand sight it must have been ! // 자네 얼굴을 보시면 어머님께서 좀 기뻐하시겠나 How glad your mother will be to see you ! // 좀 시장했겠나 You have been hungry, I dare say.
좀[3] [남에게 청할 때의 「부디」「제발」의 뜻으로] (if you) please ; kindly ; pray ; I beg ¶ …을 좀 해주십시오 Be good enough to 《do》.../Be so good〔kind〕 as to 《do》.../Do me the goodness to 《do》... // 문 좀 닫아주십시오 May I trouble you to shut the door ? /I will thank you to shut the door. // 누군지 좀 가 봐 Go (and) see who it is. // 불 좀 빌려주십시오 Please give me a light. // 확답을 좀 부탁합니다 Please give us a definite answer. // 책 좀 빌려주시겠습니까 —네 그러세요. May I borrow your book ? Go right ahead. // 그렇게 좀 해주십시오. I hope you will do so. // 길 좀 묻겠습니다 Would you tell me the way 《to》... // 부탁이 좀 있습니다 I want to ask a favor of you. /I have a favor to ask of you. /Will you do me a favor ? // 내 말 좀 들어봐 Just listen to me.
좀- petty ; small
좀것 [사람] a small-minded man ; a man of small caliber ; [물건] small things ; trifles
좀꾀 petty wiles ; little〔cheap〕 tricks ¶ 좀꾀를 부리다 play cheap tricks ; resort to petty wiles // 좀꾀가 많다 be full of little tricks
좀노릇 a petty job ; trifling work
좀놈 a petty person ; a man of small caliber
좀더 [양] a little more ; [수] a few more ; [시간] a little longer ¶ 좀더 있으면 다섯 시다 It is close on 5. // 좀더 가자 Let's go farther〔further〕.
좀도둑 a sneak (thief) ; a filcher ; a snatcher ; a snapper ; a porch climber 《미·속》 ; a cat burglar 《영·속》 ¶ 우리가 집을 비운 동안에 좀도둑이 들었다 The house was broken into while we were away.
—질 petty theft ; pilfering ¶ 좀도둑질하다 filch ; pilfer ; commit petty theft ; sneak ; snatch
좀말 small talk ; a narrow-minded remark
좀먹다 get moth-eaten ; be worm-eaten ; get destro yed little by little from within
좀바 Zomba
좀생원 —生員 a narrow-minded〔an illiberal〕 person ; a petty poltroon
좀생이 〖천문〗 the pleiades ; [잔 물건] small things
좀스럽다 [성질이] (be) small-minded ; petty ; [규모가] small ; be on a small scale ; (be) insignificant ¶ 좀스러운 사람 a petty person // 좀스러운 일 petty jobs ; trifles // 좀스럽게 별것 다 알려고 한다 Why are you so curious to know about such petty matters ?
좀약 mothballs ¶ 좀약을 넣어 두다 mothball 《clothes》
†**좀처럼** [여간해서] rarely ; seldom ; least likely ; [쉽사리] easily ; lightly ; readily ¶ 이 지방은 좀처럼 눈이 안 온다 It seldom snows in this region. // 저런 천재는 좀처럼 없을 것이다 Such a genius is rarely to be met with. // 그는 좀처럼 거기에 가지 않는다 He hardly ever goes there. // 문이 좀처럼 열리지 않는다 The door will not open easily. // 그의 승낙은 좀처럼 얻기 힘들 것이다 I am afraid, he will not give a ready consent. // 좀처럼 말이 나오지 않아 I just can't seem to bring myself to tell him.
좀첸것 a so-so thing ; an ordinary thing ; one that is (barely, merely) adequate ; an unimpressive〔unremarkable〕 thing ; "Just any old thing" ¶ 그 문제는 좀첸것으로는 풀 수가 없다 The problem can't be solved by an ordinary method.
좀팽이 a petty little person ; a small-minded person ; a thing too small to be worth looking at
†**좁다** [폭이] (be) narrow ; [면적이] small ; limited ; [갑갑하다] close ; tight ; confined ; [마음이] narrow-minded ; illiberal ¶ 좁은 마당 a narrow yard // 좁은 활동 무대 a limited sphere of activity // 좁은 문 a strait gate // 좁은 안계 a narrow horizon // 좁은 소견 a small mind // 마음이 좁은 사람 a narrow-minded person ; a man of narrow views // 좁아지다 become narrower // 그는 마음이 좁다 He is narrow-minded. // 우리 집은 좁다 We are cramped for room. // 세상은 따지고 보면 좁은 것이다 This is a small world after all. // 이 옷은 품이 좁다 This coat is tight under the arm. // 우리 나라는 땅은 좁고 인구는 많다 Our country is limited in area and densely populated. // 나는 일 때문에 교제 범위가 좁다 I'm so tied to my work that I don't have much of a social life.
좁다랗다 (be) narrow and close ; rather narrow
좁쌀 hulled millet
—뱅이 a petty person — **여우** a petty and cunning person ; a foxy little man — **영감** a petty old man

좁쌀풀 〖식물〗 a loosestrife ; Lysimachia davurica (학명)
좁쌀만큼 아끼다가 담돌만큼 해 본다 속담 To spoil〔lose〕 the ship〔sheep, ewe, hog〕 for a half penny worth of tar.
†좁아지다 become〔get〕 narrow ; narrow ; contract
좁혀지내다 live〔groan〕 under oppression
†좁히다 make narrow ; restrict ; [족대기다] force ; constrain ; compel ; press ; urge ¶ 문제의 범위를 좁히다 limit the field of a problem
종¹ a servant ; a slave ; a thrall ¶ 종의 근성 a servile spirit // 종의 신분 slavery ; bondage ; thraldom ; serfdom // 종으로 삼다 make a slave 《to, of》 // 종과 같이 부리다 put 《a person》 to practically slave labor ; use 《a person》 at one's beck and call // 종과 같이 일하다 work like a slave ; drudge // 종으로 팔리다 be sold for a slave
종² [파 따위의] (the end of) a stalk (of scallion, garlic)
종 縱 length ¶ 종의 vertical ; longitudinal // 종으로 lengthwise ; lengthways ; vertically // 종으로 자르다 cut 《a thing》 lengthways
⁑종 種 [종류] a sort ; a kind ; a class ; a category ; a variety ; [분류 단위] a species ; [종자] a seed ; a grain ; [동물] a breed ; a stock ¶ 종의 기원 the Origin of Species // 각종의 every variety of // 각종의 나비 every species of butterfly // 일종의 귀금속 a kind of precious metals // 일종의 독특한 향기 a unique aroma // 외국종의 말 a horse of foreign breed // 이것은 장미의 일종이다 This is one variety of rose. // 당신의 개는 무슨 종입니까 What breed is your dog?
—마 a stallion ; a breeding horse —우 a bull ; breeding cow 잡— hybrid ; cross-bred
종 終 the end ; the finish
†종 鐘 a bell ; a buzzer ; a doorbell (현관의) ; a handbell (손종) ; a gong (징) ; [한조로 된 교회의] chime ; carillon ¶ 종의 추 a clapper // 종치는 방망이 a wood bell-hammer // 종을 울리다 ring a bell // 종을 치다 strike a bell // 종이 울린다 A bell tolls〔rings〕.
—소리 a sound of a bell
종- 從 [사촌] a second-degree relative ¶ 종형 one's cousin
-종 宗 a religious sect ; a denomination ¶ 조계종 the *Choge* sect
종가 宗家 the head〔main〕 family ; the head〔original〕 house
종가래 a small spade〔plow, shovel〕
종가세 從價稅 an ad valorem duty ¶ 종가세율 an ad valorem tariff // 종가 5부의 관세 an import duty of 5 percent ad valorem
종각 鐘閣 a belfry ; a bell tower
종간 終刊 ⇨ 폐간(廢刊)
—호 the final number
종개 〖물고기〗 a (Yalu) loach
종개념 種概念 〖논리〗 species ; specific concept〔notion〕
종견 種犬 a breeding dog
⁑종결 終結 an end ; a close ; conclusion ; termination ; consummation (완결) —하다 end ; come〔be brought〕 to an end〔a close〕 ; be concluded ; be settled ; terminate ¶ 전쟁의 종결 the end of the war // 토론의 종결 the conclusion of a discussion // 종결시키다 bring 《a matter》 to an end // 전쟁을 종결시키다 bring the war to a conclusion〔an end〕
종경 終境 the borderland ; a remote region ; a frontier
종계 種鷄 ⇨ 씨닭
종고 種鼓 a bell and drum
종고모 從姑母 a female cousin of one's father
종곡 終曲 〖음악〗 a finale
종곡 種穀 seed grain〔corn 《영》〕
종관 縱貫 running〔penetrating〕 lengthwise —하다 penetrate〔run through〕 lengthwise ¶ 종관 철도 the railway running through 《the land》 // 그 산맥이 반도를 종관하고 있다 A long range of mountains runs through the peninsula.
†종교 宗教 (a) religion ; a faith ; a creed ; a cult ¶ 종교적 religious ; ecclesiastical ; spiritual // 종교적 감정 religious feeling // 종교를 믿다 believe in a religion ; profess〔embrace〕 a religion // 종교를 박해하다 persecute a religion // 종교를 금하다 ban〔proscribe〕 a religion // 종교를 전도하다 propagate a religion ; spread a faith // 종교에 위안을 구하다 seek solace〔consolation〕 in religion // 저 사람들은 각각 종교가 다르다 They are followers of different faiths.
—가 a religionist ; a clergyman ; a man of religion ; a religious man — 개혁 religious reformation ; 〖역사〗 the Reformation —계 the religious world ; religious circles —광〔사람〕 a religious crank〔maniac, fanatic, enthusiast〕 ; [병] religious mania〔madness〕 — 교육 religious education —극 a religious drama ; [유럽 중세의 기적극] a mystery ; a miracle play — 단체 a religious body〔organization〕 ; a spiritual corporation — 문제 a religious question〔problem〕 — 문학 religious literature —사 the history of religions —심 a religious spirit —열 religious enthusiasm〔fever〕 — 재판 the Inquisition — 전쟁〔운동〕 a religious war〔movement〕 — 정치 theocracy — 철학 philosophy of religion —학 the science〔study〕 of religion ; theology (신학) —화(畫) a holy〔sacred, religious〕 picture — 회의 a religious conference〔congress〕 ; an ecclesiastical meeting 기성 — estab-

lished〔existing〕 religions 민족 — the religion of a people 자연〔계시〕 — natural〔revealed〕 religion
종교 음악 宗教音樂 sacred music ¶ 종교 음악을 연주하다 play〔perform〕 sacred music
종구라기 a small gourd
종국 終局 an end ; a close ; a conclusion ; a termination ; [바둑의] the end of a game ; a finale ¶ 종국의 final ; ultimate ; eventual // 종국의 승리 ultimate victory // 종국에 가서는 after all ; ultimately ; in the long run // 종국에 가까와지다 draw to a close // 종국을 고하다 end ; come〔be brought〕 to an end ; be concluded〔settled〕 // 전쟁도 드디어 종국을 고했다 The war came to an end at last. // 그 회담은 만족할 만한 종국을 보리라 The negotiations will arrive at a satisfactory termination〔conclusion〕.
— 판결 final judgment〔decision〕
종군 從軍 following the army ; going to the front — 하다 serve in a war ; take part in a campaign ; go to the front ; see active service ; accompany the army (비 전투원이) ¶ 종군을 지원하다 apply〔petition〕 for permission to go to war // 그는 2차 대전에 종군했다 He served〔saw active service〕 in World War Ⅱ.
— 간호원 a war〔military〕 nurse — 기자〔기장〕 a war correspondent〔medal〕 — 상인 a sutler —자 a campaigner ; a camp follower (비전투원)
종굴박 a small gourd
종극 終極 finality ; extremity ; the ultimate ¶ 종극의 final ; ultimate ; extreme
종기 腫氣 a swell(ing) ; a boil ; a tumor ; an abscess ¶ 목에 종기가 났다 A swelling came out on the neck.
악성 — a malignant tumor
종기 終期 the end (of a term) ; the close ; the termination
종날 〖민속〗 the starting day of the year's farming ; the 1st of February in the lunar calendar
종내 終乃 [마침내] at last ; at length ; finally ; after all (결국) ¶ 그는 종내 가버렸다 He went away at length. // 그는 종내 오지 않았다 He did not come after all. // 그는 병상에 눕더니 종내 일어나지 못했다 He lay on a bed of illness, never to rise again.
종내기 種— a breed ; a stock ; a strain ; a variety ; a species ¶ 종내기가 같다〔다르다〕 be of the same〔a different〕 breed
종년 a servant〔slave〕 girl
종놈 a servant ; a slave
종다래끼 a small bamboo basket
***종다리** ⇨ 종달새
종다수 從多數 following〔agreeing to〕 the views of the majority — 하다 follow the views of the majority ¶ 종다수 취결하다 pass a resolution〔decide a matter〕 by majority vote
종단 終端 a terminus 《*pl.* -nuses, -ni》 ; a terminal ; an end
종단 宗團 the religious order〔fraternity〕
종단 縱斷 vertical section ; [분할] a division ; a split — 하다 cut vertically〔longitudinally〕 ; run through (산맥 따위가) ; traverse ¶ 종단적 vertical ; longitudinal // 종단을 획책하다 attempt at dividing〔splitting up〕 《the existing party arrangement》
—면 〖수학〗 a longitudinal〔vertical, lengthwise〕 section ; 〖건축〗 a profile
종달거리다 grumble ; complain
***종달새** a skylark ; a lark
종답 宗畓 paddy fields that produce the crop used in the ancestral sacrifices of the clan
종당 從當 as a matter of course ; from the very nature of things ; after all ; in the end
종대 the stalk 《of garlic》
종대 縱隊 a column ; a file ¶ 2열 종대로 in double columns // 1렬 종대로 in Indian file ; in single file // 종대를 짓다 form a column
— 행진 a march in a column 사열 — a quarter column ; a column of fours 이열 — double file〔column〕 ; a double file column 일렬 — a (single) file ; an Indian file 중대 — a company column 측면 — a column of a flank
종댕기 a pigtail ribbon
종독 腫毒 a malignant〔virulent, noxious〕 tumor〔growth〕
종돈 種豚 a breeding pig
***종두 種痘** vaccination for smallpox ; inoculation — 하다 vaccinate ; inoculate with vaccine ¶ 종두를 받다 be vaccinated 《for smallpox》 // 종두가 잘 되었다 The vaccination has taken.
—기(器) a vaccinator —료 a vaccination fee —의(醫) a vaccinator ; inoculator — 증명서 a vaccination certificate
종두지미 從頭至尾 [부사적] from head to tail ; from beginning to end
종란 種卵 a hatchery egg ; a fertilized egg used for breeding
종람 縱覽 inspection ; reading (열람) — 하다 inspect 《a factory》 ; visit ; read ¶ 종람시키다 exhibit ; throw 《a thing》 open to public inspection // 종람을 환영〔거절〕하다 invite〔decline〕 inspection
—권 an admission ticket ; a pass — 사절 No visitors (are) allowed〔admitted〕. ; Inspection declined. ; No admission. —실 an exhibition room ; a reading room (신문 따위의) —자 a visitor ; [도서의] a reader ; a spectator
종래 從來 [부사적] hitherto ; up to now ¶ 종래의 usual ; customary ; traditional // 종래에 hitherto ; until now ; up to now〔present〕 // 종래와 같이 as in the past ;

as usual ; as before ; as ever // 종래에 없었다 There has never been (up to now).
종량세 從量稅 a specific commercial duty〔tariff〕
종량 요금제 從量料金制 the meter-rate system
*종려 棕櫚 〖식물〗 a hemp palm ; a palm —수 the palm tree —유 palm oil —잎 a palm leaf
종렬 縱列 a column ; a file ; a train ¶ 소〔중, 분〕대 종렬로 platoons〔companies, sections〕 in column // 종렬로 행진하다 defile // 종렬을 이루다 form a file
종론 宗論 a polemic ¶ 종론을 벌이다 polemize 《against》 ; engage in polemics 《against》
*종료 終了 an end ; a close ; a conclusion ; [완료] completion ; [기간의] expiration ; [임대차·연금 따위] cesser —하다 [마치다] close ; end ; complete ; conclude ; [끝나다] come to an end ; be completed〔concluded〕 ¶ 세계 대전이 종료했다 The World War is over〔came to an end〕.
종루 鐘樓 a bell tower ; a belfry
†종류 種類 a kind ; a sort ; a class ; [동·식물의] a species ; a variety ; [형] type ¶ 같은 종류 the same kind〔sort, description, variety〕 // 다른 종류 different kinds ; a different kind of things // 이 종류의 꽃 flowers of this kind // 이런 종류의 범죄 crimes of this nature // 이런 종류의 사기 this type of swindling // 모든 종류의 all kinds〔sorts〕 of ; of every description // 세 종류로 나누다 divide 《things》 into three classes // 종류 별로 나누다 classify // 개에도 여러 종류가 있다 There are dogs and dogs. // 해초는 5,000의 종류가 있다 There are 5,000 different species of seaweed. // 50원 100원 500원의 세 종류가 있다 The three denominations are 50 *won*, 100 *won* and 500 *won*.
종마 種馬 a stallion ; a breeding horse
종막 終幕 the last act 《of a play》 ; an end ; a close ¶ 종막이 가까와지다 draw to a close // 종막이 되다 the curtain falls〔drops〕 ; come to an end
종말 終末 an end ; a close ; a conclusion ¶ 종말을 고하다 come to an end
—관(觀)〔론(論)〕 〖종교〗 eschatology
종매 從妹 a female younger cousin
종목 種目 an item ; a line ; an event (경기의)
영업 — lines〔items〕 of business 주요 — 〖경기〗 main events
종묘 種苗 [싹을 기름] planting a seedling ; [묘목] a seedling〔sapling〕 ; a young plant —하다 plant (a seedling)
—장 a field for seedlings ; a nursery (garden) — 회사 a nursery company
종묘 宗廟 the ancestral shrine of the royal family
종무 宗務 religious affairs
종무 終務 the closing of offices for the year ; the end of the year's business
종물 從物 〖법〗 an accessory (thing)
종반 宗班 the royal clan
종반전 終盤戰 [바둑·장기의] the end game ; [선거 등의] 《get into》 the last 〔final〕 phase〔stage〕 《of an election campaign》
종발 鍾鉢 a small bowl
종배 終杯 the last wine cup〔glass〕 in drinking
종배 終— the last brood〔litter〕
종범 從犯 participation in a crime ; aiding and abetting ; accessory ¶ 종범의 accessory 《to》 // 살인죄의 종범 accessory to murder
—자 an accessory〔accessary〕 《to a crime》 ; an accomplice 사전(事前)〔후〕(後)— an accessory before〔after〕 a fact
종법 宗法 clan rules ; a code of clan regulations ; a clan code〔constitution〕
종별 種別 classification ; assortment —하다 classify ; divide into classes ; assort
종복 從僕 a servant ; an attendant
종부 從夫 obedience to one's husband —하다 be obedient to one's husband ; obey one's husband faithfully
종사 宗嗣 the descendant〔heir〕 of the main family of a clan
종사 從死 killing oneself to follow 《a person》 in death ; suttee (아내의) —하다 die in attendance on 《a person》 ; follow to the grave
†종사 從事 —하다 [전념함] devote oneself to ; [집무에] engage in 《business》 ; pursue 《a calling》 ; follow 《a profession》 ; practice 《medicine》 ; attend to 《a business》 ; carry on 《trade》 ; employ oneself 《in writing books》 ¶ …에 종사하고 있다 be engaged in〔occupied with〕 // 그는 무슨 직업에 종사하고 있습니까 What business is he engaged in? /What is he by occupation〔profession〕? // 그는 신문 사업에 종사하고 있습니다 He is engaged in newspaper work.
종사 縱射 a raking fire ; an enfilade —하다 rake 《with fire》 ; enfilade
—포 a raker — 포대 an enfiladed battery
종산 宗山 a mountain〔hill〕 where a clan's graveyard is located ; a family graveyard
종상하다 終喪— ⇨ 탈상하다
종서 縱書 vertical writing —하다 write vertically ; write in vertical lines
종선 從船 a small boat attached to a ship ; a dinghy
종선 縱線 a vertical line ; [악보의] a bar
종성 終聲 [언어] a final consonant
종성 鐘聲 the sound〔peal〕 of a bell
종성 宗姓 the royal family ; the relatives of the king
종소원 從所願 compliance with 《a per-

son's》 request ── 하다 comply with 《a person's》 request ; grant a request 〔favor〕 ; answer〔hear〕 a prayer

†종속 從屬 subordination ; dependency ── 하다 be subordinate〔subject〕 《to》 ; be dependent on〔upon〕 ¶ 종속적인 subordinate ; dependent ; secondary ; subsidiary ; auxiliary // 종속시키다 subordinate 《a thing》 to 《a person》

─ 관계 subordinate relationship ─구〔절〕 『문법』 a subordinate phrase 〔clause〕 ─국 a vassal state ; a dependency ; an appanage ─ 변수 『수학』 a dependent variable ─ 접속사 『문법』 a subordinate conjunction

종손 宗孫 the eldest grandson of the main family

종손 從孫 the grandson of one's brother ; a grandnephew

종손녀 從孫女 the granddaughter of one's brother ; a grandniece

종숙 從叔 a male cousin of one's father

종숙모 從叔母 the wife of a cousin of one's father

종시 終始 ① [처음과 끝] the beginning and the end

② [내내] throughout ; all through ; from beginning to end ; from start to end ¶ 종시 일관한 정책 a consistent policy // 종시 일관하여 consistently ; from first to last // 종시 일관하다 be consistent ; be constant // 종시 잠자코 그들의 토론을 듣고 있었다 He remained silent from first to last listening to their discussion. // 그는 종시 일관하여 세계 평화를 제창했다 He made it his consistent aim to work hard for the peace of the world.

종시 終是 ⇨ 끝끝내

종시속 從時俗 conforming to the times ; following the manners and ways of the age ── 하다 conform to the times ; follow the manners and ways of the day ¶ 그의 행위는 종시속적이 아니다 His doings are unconventional.

종식 終熄 cessation ; eradication ; extirpation (근절) ── 하다 cease ; come to an end ; quiet down ; be brought to close ; be eradicated〔extirpated〕

¶ 종식시키다 put an end〔a stop〕 to 《war》 // 그 병은 완전히 종식되었다 The disease was stamped out altogether.

종신 宗臣 ① [원훈] a distinguished minister of state ② [왕족] a minister from the royal family

종신 終身 ① [한평생] a whole life ; a life ② [임종] being at one's parent's death bed ③ [죽음] the end of life ; one's death ── 하다 be at one's parent's death bed ; be with one's parent at his death ¶ 종신 징역을 살다 serve a life sentence // 종신 징역을 언도받다 be sentenced to life imprisonment ; be given a life sentence // 늦게 와서 부상에 종신 못했다 I arrived too late to see my father alive.

─ 고용 제도 the life(long) employment system ─ 생명 보험 straight 〔whole, ordinary〕 life insurance ─ 연금〔은급〕 a life annuity〔pension〕 ─ 재산 a life estate ─직(職) a life tenure (of office) ; an office for life ─ 징역 life imprisonment ─ 징역자 a lifer 《속》 ─형 a life sentence〔term〕 ; penal servitude for life ─ 회원 a life member

종실 宗室 the Royal family ; descendants in the male line from the founder of the dynasty

종심 終審 『법』 the final trial〔judicial examination〕

─ 법원 the court of last resort

종씨 宗氏 a clansman (of the same surname)

종씨 從氏 [자기의] a paternal cousin older than oneself ; [남의] a paternal cousin of an esteemed person

종아리 the calf of the leg ¶ 종아리를 때리다 lash 《a person》 on the calf

─뼈 『해부』 a fibula ; a splint bone ─채 a switch ; a cane 《미》

종아리를 맞다 관용 get whipped on the calf (as punishment)

종알거리다 mutter ; grumble〔complain〕 《about》 ¶ 혼자 종알거리다 mutter to oneself

종애 鍾愛 ── 하다 love dearly 〔like the apple of one's eye〕 ; have a deep affection 《for》 ; pour one's affection 《on》

종야 終夜 all night ; the whole night ; all the night through

종양 腫瘍 a tumor

─학 oncology 악성〔양성〕 ─ a malignant 〔benign〕 tumor

종어 宗魚 『물고기』 Leiocassis dumerili (학명)

종언 終焉 [임종] the end (of life) ; [종말] an end ; a close ; expiration ; completion ── 하다 die ; end ; come to an end ; be brought to a death ; finish ¶ 종언을 고하다 come to an end ; be brought to a close

종업 從業 work in service ; attending to one's work ── 하다 be employed〔in the service, in employment〕 ; work ; [쉬고 있던 사람이] return to work ; resume work

─ 금지 prohibition〔prevention〕 of work ─ 시간 working hours ─원 [한 사람] an employee ; an operative ; a (service) worker ; men 《총칭》 ; (all) hands ; regular force ; a working staff ¶ 종업원 조합 a workers〔an employe〕 union // 종업원 주식 소유제 employee stock ownership // 종업원용 엘리베이터 a service elevator〔lift 《영》〕

종업 終業 the end〔conclusion〕 of work ; completion〔close〕 of work ; [학교의] the close of a school term ── 하다 complete

〔finish, end〕 a work
— 시간 the closing hour〔time〕 —식 the closing ceremony〔exercises〕 —일 [학교의] the last day of school
종연 終演 the end of a show ¶ 오후 10시 종연 The curtain falls〔drops〕 at 10 p. m. // 그 쇼는 국가와 함께 종연하였다 The show ended with the national anthem.
종요로이 importantly ; necessarily ; indispensably
종요롭다 (be) important ; indispensable ; pivotal
종용 慫慂 inducement ; coaxing ; persuasion ; suggestion ; advice —하다 coax ; prevail on ; persuade ; suggest ; advise ; urge ¶ 자수를 종용했다 I advised him to surrender himself to the police. // 친구의 종용으로 생명 보험에 들었다 I took out〔bought〕 a life insurance policy at my friend's suggestion.
종용하다 從容— (be) calm ; serene ; composed ; undisturbed ⇨ 조용하다
종우 種牛 a seed bull ; a breeding cow
종위 從位 ⇨ 종속(從屬)
— 접속사 〖문법〗 a subordinate conjunction
종유 種油 [평지의] rape (seed) oil ; colza oil ; [씨의] seed oil
종유동 鍾乳洞 a stalactite grotto〔cave, cavern〕
종유석 鍾乳石 stalactite
종의 腫醫 〖한의〗 a herb doctor specialized in tumors〔abscesses〕
†종이 paper ¶ 종이 한 장〔다섯 장〕 a sheet〔five sheets〕 of paper // 종이 조각 a piece〔scrap, strip, slip〕 of paper // 종이에 싸다 wrap〔do up〕 《things》 in paper // 벽에 종이를 바르다 paper the wall // 종이를 뜨다 make paper // 이 종이에 주소를 쓰시오 Write your address on this paper.
—관 a paper tube —꾸러미 a paper parcel〔package〕 — 운반대 〖인쇄〗 a delivery board —접기 paper work — 제품 paper products —쪽 a piece〔scrap, strip, slip〕 of paper —컵 a paper cup — 케이블 a paper(-cored) cable — 타월〔벨트〕 a paper towel〔belt〕 — 테이프 a paper tape ; [환영·환송용의] paper streamers — 표지 a paper cover 색— colored paper
종이 한 장의 차이 관용 a very slight difference
종인 宗人 a clansman ; a clan member
종인 從因 a secondary〔an incidental〕 cause ; a by-cause
*종일 終日 all day ; all day long ; all the day long ; all through the day ; all the day through ; throughout the whole day ; from morning to〔till〕 night ¶ 종일토록 공부하다 study all day long // 종일 부재이다 He is away from home all day. // 종일 독서하고 지냈다 I spent the whole day in reading. // 비가 와서 종일토록 집에 있었다 I have been at home all day long because of rain. // 하루 종일 질질 끌 셈이냐 We haven't got all day.
종자 宗子 the eldest son of the main〔head〕 family
종자 從者 a follower ; a vassal ; an attendant ; a servant ; a retinue〔suite〕 (수행자) ¶ 많은〔적은〕 종자를 데리고 with a large〔small〕 following〔suite〕
종자 種子 [식물의] a seed ; [동물의] a breed ; a stock ; a strain ¶ 종자가 좋다 be of a good stock // 종자가 나다 run〔go〕 to seed ; seed // 가축의 종자를 받다 breed from 《a stock》 // 종자를 받고자 기르다 keep for breeding (purposes)
종자매 從姉妹 female cousins
종작 the gist〔point〕 ; the rough idea
종작없다 (be) pointless ; desultory ; senseless ; nonsensical ; absurd ; inconsistent ¶ 종작없는 말 senseless remarks ; nonsense // 그의 지금 말은 종작없는 말이다 There is no logic〔neither rhyme nor reason〕 in his last remark.
종잘거리다 prattle ; mutter ⇨ 종알거리다
종잡다 get the gist〔point〕 ; get a rough idea ; roughly understand ¶ 그의 말을 종잡을 수 없었다 I couldn't make out what he was saying. // 당신의 말은 종잡을 수가 없다 I have not the remotest idea of what you mean. // 그의 설명을 들었으나 전혀 종잡을 수 없었다 I was none the wiser for his explanation.
종장 終章 the last of the 3 verses of a (*sijo*) poem ; the last part of a song
종장 宗匠 a master ; a teacher ; an instructor ; a scholar
종적 蹤迹 one's traces〔whereabouts〕 ¶ 종적을 감추다 disappear ; cover one's trail ; leave no trace behind ; abscond 《from》 ; drop from sight ¶ 사내 아이가 종적을 감춘 지 수일이 됩니다 The boy has been missing from his home for some days.
종전 宗田 dry fields that produce the crop used in the ancestral sacrifices of the clan that owns them
종전 從前 ¶ 종전의 previous ; former ; old ; usual // 종전에 hitherto ; heretofore ; formerly ; before // 종전과 같이 as usual ; as before ; as in the past ; as heretofore ; as hitherto ; as ever ; as of old ; as of yore // 종전의 관계 one's past connections // 종전 예와 같음 be same as before // 그는 모든 것이 종전 그대로라고 믿고 싶었다 He wanted to believe that everything was exactly as it had been before. // 그는 모든 것이 종전 그대로이기를 원했다 He wanted everything to be the way it had been.
종전 終戰 the end of the war ; the termination〔cessation〕 of hostilities —하다 the war ends〔comes to an end〕 ¶ 종전 후의 postwar // 종전 당시에 at the time of

the war's end // 종전 후의 젊은이들 post-war youngsters
종절 從節 〖문법〗 a subordinate〔dependent〕 clause
*종점 終點 the terminal (point) ; the terminus ; the terminal (station) 《미》
— 설비 terminal facilities 버스 — the last stop of a bus ; the end of the bus line 열차 — a rail(road) terminal
종제 從弟 a younger cousin of paternal side
종조 宗祖 the founder 《of a sect》 ; the originator ; the father
종조모 從祖母 a grandaunt ; the wife of one's granduncle
종조부 從祖父 a granduncle ; a great uncle
종족 宗族 a clan ; a family ; kindred
종족 種族 a race ; a tribe ; [동·식물의] a family ; a species ; a genus
— 보존 preservation of the species — 본능 racial instinct ¶ 종족 보존의 본능 the instinct of preservation of the species —(적) 집단〔사회〕 an ethnic group〔society〕 —학 speciology
종졸 從卒 a soldier servant ; an officer's servant ; an orderly 《미》
종종 with short, quick paces ; with hurried steps ¶ 종종거리다 walk with hurried steps
†종종 種種 a variety of things ; different kinds ; [부사적] now and then ; occasionally ; often ¶ 종종 친구를 찾다 visit a friend every now and then // 종종 놀러 오십시오 Come and see us often. // 그에게서는 종종 소식이 있습니다 I hear from him once in a while.
종종걸음 a quick pace ; short and quick steps ; hurried steps ; mincing steps
종종 걸음치다 (관용) walk with short, quick paces〔mincing steps〕
종종머리 a hairdo with three triple braids on either side joined at the end with a ribbon
종종모 〖농업〗 a thickly seeded rice-seed plot
종종이 〖인쇄〗 ellipsis ; leaders
종주 宗主 a suzerain ¶ 종주권을 요구하다 claim the suzerainty on 《a country》
—국 a suzerain (state) —권 suzerainty ¶ 종주권을 요구하다 claim suzerainty 《on》
종주 縱走 mountain-range〔-ridge〕 traversing —하다 traverse ¶ 알프스를 종주하다 climb the length of the Alps
종중 宗中 the families of the same clan ¶ 종중답 the paddy fields owned by a clan
종지 a small dish〔bowl, cup〕
종지 宗旨 the main purport ; the fundamental meaning ; a tenet ; principles
†종지 終止 stop ; termination ; end ; cessation —하다 terminate ; end ; stop ; come to an end ; cease
—부 a period ; a full stop ¶ …에 종지부를 찍다 put an end to… —사(辭) the sentence-final form 불완전 — 〖음악〗 an imperfect〔a half〕 cadence 완전 — 〖음악〗 a perfect〔full〕 cadence
종지뼈 the kneecap ; the patella
종진 縱陣 a column ; a line ahead ¶ 종진으로 in a line ahead ; in a single file // 종진을 치다 form a column
종질 slavery ; bondage —하다 serve as a servant〔slave〕 ; be a slave
종질 從姪 a (male) cousin's son
종질녀 從姪女 a (male) cousin's daughter
종짓굽 ① [종지뼈 언저리] the rim of the kneecap ② [쟁기의] the part that protrudes from the end of the under ridge of a plow
종짓굽 떨어지다 (관용) start toddling ; find its feet
종짓굽아 날 살려라 (관용) Let's get out of here.
종차 種差 a specific difference
*종착역 終着驛 a terminal station ; a terminus
종창 腫脹 a swelling ; a boil ; an intumescence
종처 腫處 a boil ; an abscess
종척 宗戚 the paternal and maternal relatives of the king
종축 種畜 breeding stock
*종축 縱軸 ① 〖수학〗 the axis of ordinates ② 〖기계〗 a spindle ; a vertical shaft
종친 宗親 the royal family ; kindred of the king
종콩 〖식물〗 a kind of small white bean
종탑 鐘塔 a bell tower ; a belfry
종파 宗派 the main branch of a family ; 〖종교〗 a sect ; a denomination
—심(주의) sectarianism — 싸움 sectarian strife
종파 種— sowing ; seeding
종피 種皮 the testa
*종합 綜合 synthesis ; generalization ; 〖철학〗 colligation —하다 synthesize ; integrate ; put together ¶ 종합적 synthetic ; composite // 종합적으로 synthetically // 종합해서 생각하다 think collectively // 각종 보고를 종합하다 put various reports together
— 개발 overall〔comprehensive〕 development — 경기 all-round games〔events〕 — 계획 a comprehensive plan ; an all-out plan — 기하학 synthetic geometry — 대학 a university — 메이커 a comprehensive〔an all-around 《미》〕 《automobile》 maker — 명사 a collective noun — 병원 a general hospital — 선수권 the all-round championships — 소득세 a composite income tax — 예술 synthetic 〔composite〕 art — 잡지 an all-round magazine —주의 synthesism — 철학 synthetic philosophy — 판단 (a) syn-

thetic judgment 개인 — 〖체조〗 individual combined (exercises)
종헌 終獻 the last〔third〕 libation in a sacrifice (in a memorial service)
종형 從兄 an elder (male) cousin
종형제 從兄弟 (male) cousins
종회 宗會 a family〔clan〕 meeting ¶ 종회를 가지다 hold a family meeting
종횡 縱橫 length and breadth ¶ 종횡으로 lengthwise and breadthwise ; in all directions // 종횡 무진으로 freely ; at will ; right and left
좆 the penis ; the dick 《미·속》
좆심 virility ; sexual prowess
†좇다 follow ; run after ; conform to ; obey ; abide by ¶ 순서를 좇아 in order // 지시〔명령〕을 좇아 in accordance with 〔according to〕 《a person's》 instructions 〔orders〕 // 법을 좇아서 in accordance with the law // 관습을 좇아서 in conformity with custom ; according to custom // 뒤를 좇다 follow 《a person》 ; run after 《a person》 // 유행을 좇다 follow the fashion // 명령을 좇다 obey 《a person's》 order // 사람의 의사를 좇다 bow to another's will // 선례를 좇다 follow a precedent // 충고를 좇다 take〔follow, act upon〕 《a person's》 advice // 법을 좇다 conform to the law ; observe the law // 관습을 좇다 follow〔conform to〕 the custom ; toe the line // 결정을 좇다 abide by the decision // 대량 생산에 있어서는 미국을 좇아 갈 수 없다 In mass production, it is impossible to keep up with America.
†좋다¹ ① (be) good ; fine ; nice ¶ 좋은 사람과 나쁜 사람 good men and bad // 좋은 집〔그림, 길, 책〕 a good house〔picture, road, book〕 // 좋은 소식 good news // 좋은 집안 a good family // 좋든 나쁘든 for better or for worse // 사람이 좋다 be good-natured〔-humored〕 // 그것이 그의 좋은 점이다 That's one good thing about him. // 날씨가 좋다 It's a lovely day. // 그는 머리가 좋다 He is bright〔smart, clever〕. // 좋은 생각이다 That's a good〔capital〕 idea. // 친구 좋다는 게 뭔가 What are friends for?
② [유익] (be) beneficial ; favorable ; good ¶ 천식에 좋은 약 a medicine efficacious for asthma // 건강에 좋다 be good for (the) health // 류머티즘에 좋다 be good for rheumatism // 치통에 좋다 be good for toothache // 먹기에 좋다 be good to eat // 우유는 어린아이한테 좋다 Milk is good for children.
③ [적당] (be) right ; proper ; suitable ; good ¶ 그 지위에 좋은 사람 a good man for the post // 좋을 대로 하다 do as one pleases ; suit oneself // 어찌하면 좋을지 모르겠다 I don't know what to do. // 이곳은 휴식하기에 좋지 않다 This is not a good place to rest in.
④ [기교] (be) good ; skilled ; able ¶ 손재주가 좋다 be dexterous ; be good 〔clever〕 with one's hands // 필적이 좋다 write a good hand // 화술이 좋다 be a good talker // 영어 실력이 좋다 have a good command of English // 그는 입담이 좋다 He has great conversational power.
⑤ [기호] like ; [비교] (be) better ; preferable ; [선택] (had) better ; like better ; prefer ¶ 나는 과일이 좋다 I like fruits. // 이것이 훨씬 좋다 This is far 〔much〕 better (than that). // 나는 배보다 사과가 좋다 I like apples better than pears. // 나는 차보다 커피가 좋다 I prefer coffee to tea. // 봄과 가을과 어느 쪽이 좋으냐 Which do you like better, spring or autumn? // 빨리 하면 할수록 더욱더 좋다 The sooner done the better. // 너는 비행기로 가는 게 좋다 You (had) better go by plane. // 곧 병원에 가보는 게 좋다 You had better go to a doctor at once. // 어디로 가는 게 좋을까 Where'd I better go? // 해보지 않는 편이 좋다 You (had) better not try. // 더 이상 이곳에 있지 않는 게 좋다 We had better not remain here any longer.
⑥ [소원] wish ; hope ; desire ¶ 그 소식이 정말이 아니라면 좋겠다 I wish the news may not prove true. // 그래 내가 죽으면 좋겠니 So, do you wish me dead? // 살아 생전에 그것을 보았으면 좋겠다 I wish I may live to see it. // 100만원이 있다면 좋겠다 I wish I had a million *won*.
⑦ [(…해도) 상관 없다] may ; do not mind 《doing》 ; do not care 《if》 ¶ 정원에 들어가도 좋습니까—네 좋습니다 May I go into the garden? Yes, you may. // 내 사전을 써도 좋다 You may use my dictionary if you like. // 어느 것이나 좋으니 하나 다오 Give me one please, any one will do. // 그가 없어도 좋다 I can do very well without him. // 얼마라도 좋으니 돈 좀 꾸어다오 Lend me whatever sum you can spare. // 어떻게 되어도 좋다 I don't care what happens. // 남들이 무어라 말해도 좋다 I don't mind〔care〕 what others say about me. // 100원이든 1,000원이든 좋으니 제발 사주십시오 Please do buy it, whether it costs one hundred *won* or a thousand *won*.
⑧ [(…하지 않아도) 좋다] need not 《do》 ; do not have to ¶ 점심을 가지고 오지 않아도 좋다 You do not have to bring your lunch. // 내일 오지 않아도 좋다 You don't need to come tomorrow. / You need not come tomorrow. // 그러지 않아도 좋았었다 You need not have done it. // 일부러 설명 안 해도 좋다 You need not trouble yourself to explain.
좋다² [느낌] Good! /Well! /All right! / O.K.! ; [환성] Whee! /Whoopee! ¶ 돈 걸자구—좋다 (You are gone to) Bet? All right! // 좋다 하자 Very well〔All right, O.K.〕, I'll do it.

좋아지내다 ① [친하게] be intimate〔familiar〕 with 《a person》; be on intimate〔familiar, good〕 terms with 《a person》 ¶ 좋아지내게 되다 become intimate with 《a person》
② [사랑하다] be in love〔have tender relations〕 with; be thick with ¶ 두 사람은 서로 좋아지낸다 They love each other. /They are lovers.

좋아지다 ① [상태가] become〔grow〕 better; [아름다와지다] become finer〔more beautiful〕 ¶ 날씨가 좋아진다 The weather clears up. //경기가 좋아진다 Business is improving〔looking up〕. //건강이 작년보다 좋아졌다 She became healthier than she was last year. //그는 병이 좋아지고 있다 He is in the convalescent stage. /He is picking up. //자네는 나이가 들수록 얼굴이 더 좋아지는 것 같아 It seems like the older you grow, the better you look.
② [좋아하게 되다] get〔come, learn〕 to like 《a thing》; become〔grow〕 fond of; take a fancy〔liking〕 to ¶ 점점 좋아지다 develop a liking 《for》//난 이 집이 좋아졌어요 I've become fond of this house. /I have taken a fancy to this house.

†**좋아하다** ① like; be (very) fond of; love (사랑하다); have a great fancy〔liking, taste〕 for; [특별히] be partial to; [주로 음식을] have a weakness for 《apples》; [주로 의문문·부정문에] care for; [딴 것보다] prefer one thing to another ¶ 좋아하는 책 one's favorite book//음악을 좋아하다 like〔be fond of, delight in〕 music //차보다 커피를 좋아하다 prefer coffee to tea; like coffee better than tea//그리 좋아하지 않다 do not care much for〔to do〕 it//네가 좋아하건 말건 시키겠다 I will have you do it whether you like it or not. //그들은 서로 좋아하는 사이다 They are in love with each other. //춤 좋아하세요 Do you care for social dancing? //전혀 안 좋아합니다 No, I don't care for it. //그녀는 커피를 아주 좋아한다 She is partial to coffee. //그는 술을 아주 좋아한다 He has a weakness for liquor. //무엇이 좋아서 그런 짓을 했느냐 Why did you choose to do that? //저 남자의 얼굴이 요즈음 사람들이 좋아하는 형인 것 같다 He's got the kind of face they seem to go for these days.
② [유쾌해하다] be pleased 《with》; be delighted〔take delight〕 《in doing》; rejoice〔be rejoiced〕 《about, to do, that》; be glad 《about, to do, that》 ¶ 장난치며 좋아하는 아이들 boys taking delight in doing mischief//껑충껑충 뛰며 좋아하다 jump for joy//그는 그 말을 듣고 무척 좋아했다 He was much pleased to hear that. //그 소식에 모두들 좋아했다 All were delighted at the news. //그 개는 꼬리를 치고 좋아했다 The dog wagged his tail for joy. //그는 그 여자가 거기 가는 것을 좋아하지 않는다 He doesn't like her to go there. /He doesn't like the idea of her going there.

좋이 well; nicely; fully; properly; suitably; rightly; rather; considerably ¶ 돈 천만원은 좋이 모았을 걸 I guess he has fully made ten million *won*. //그는 60세는 좋이 넘었을 것이다 He must be well over〔past〕 sixty. //역까지 좋이 2마일이 된다 It is a good two miles to the station.

좋지 않다 ① [도덕상] (be) bad; evil; wrong; immoral; sinful ¶ 좋지 않은 일 a wrong; an evil deed//좋지 않은 짓을 하다 do wrong; commit a sin〔crime〕
②[악하다] (be) bad; evil; wicked; ill-natured; malicious; villainous; roguish ¶ 좋지 않은 사람 a wicked man; a rascal
③ [해롭다] (be) bad; harmful; injurious; detrimental ¶ 눈에 좋지 않다 be bad for〔be injurious to〕 the eyes
④ [품질이] (be) bad; inferior; be of low grade; be of inferior quality
⑤ [머리가] (be) poor; weak
⑤ [날씨가] (be) bad; foul; inclement
⑥ [불길] (be) ill; unlucky; ominous ¶ 좋지 않은 징조 a bad〔an ill〕 omen
⑦ [건강이] (be) ill〔sick〕; be〔feel〕 unwell
⑧ [평판이] (be) bad; ill; unsavo(u)ry
⑨ [기분이] feel unwell〔poorly, ill, indisposed〕; be〔feel〕 out of sorts

좌 左 (the) left; the left side ¶ 좌와 같다 be as follows; be given below; the following is〔are〕//좌향 좌 Left turn!

좌 座 a seat; throne; base; [성좌] a constellation; [극단] a theatrical company; a troupe ¶ 스칼라좌 La Scala//대웅좌 the Great Bear; the Big Dipper; Uras Major

좌각 左脚 the left leg

좌객 座客 the guests (who are) present

좌경 左傾 an inclination to the left; communistic leanings; Bolshevization **—하다** incline to the left; become leftish ¶ 좌경적 leftist(-leaning); radical; Red; Bolshevized//좌경 색채를 띤 잡지 a journal of leftist coloring
— 문학 leftist literature **— 분자** radical〔leftist〕 elements; the left; the radicals **— 사상** leftist thinking; radical thoughts **— 운동** a left movement **—파** left〔radical〕 elements; the left **—파 지도자** a left-wing leader **— 학생** a radical〔Red〕 student; a student inclining〔leaning〕 toward〔to〕 the left

좌고 坐高 one's height when seated; one's sitting height

좌고우면 左顧右眄 looking to left and right; looking around; irresolution; vacillation ¶ 좌고우면 갈피를 잡지 못하다 waver (in one's attitude); vacillate; be irresolute ; sit on the fence 《미》

좌골 坐骨 the hipbone〔hucklebone〕; the ischium
— 신경 the sciatic nerve — 신경통 sciatic neuralgia ; sciatica ; hip gout

좌골 挫骨 a broken bone — 하다 have a bone broken

좌기 左記 ¶ 좌기의 undermentioned ; the following // 좌기와 같이 as undermentioned〔underwritten, follows〕
— 사람 the following persons

좌단 左袒 taking sides with ; siding with ; backing ; supporting — 하다 support ; identify oneself with
— 자 a supporter ; a friend

좌담 座談 [식탁에서의] table-talk ; conversation ¶ 정치문제의 좌담회 a symposium on politics // 좌담식으로 말하다 speak informally // 좌담에 능하다 be a good talker〔conversationalist〕
— 회 a round-table talk ; a discussion meeting ; a symposium 《*pl.* ~s, -sia》 ¶ 좌담회를 갖다 hold a symposium 《on》; have a discussion meeting 라디오 — a radio forum〔round table〕《on traffic accidents》 정치 — a symposium on politics

좌뜨다 excel by far ; surpass others ¶ 생각이 좌뜨다 have a far better idea than anyone else

좌르륵 with a great rush ; with a splash ¶ 좌르르 흐르다 pour〔run〕 down ; rush〔gush〕 out // 물이 좌르르 나오다 water comes rushing out

좌방 左方 the left

좌변 左邊 the left side

좌불안석 坐不安席 being unable to sit comfortably〔still〕《from anxiety》 ¶ 좌불안석이다 be ill at ease ; feel out of place ; be unable to rest ; fidget // 그와 함께 있으면 좌불안석이다 I feel ill at ease in his company.

좌상 挫傷 a sprain ; a wrench ; a contusion ; a fractural injury ; a fracture

좌상 坐像 a seated〔sitting, sedentary〕 figure〔image, statue〕

좌상 坐商 keeping a shop ; [사람] a shopkeeper (as contrasted with a hawker)

좌상 座上 ① ⇨ 좌중 ② [연장] the elder in a company〔party〕

좌서 左書 [쓰는 양식] writing from left to right ; [왼손으로] left-handed writing

†좌석 座席 [자리] a seat ; [비행기의] a cockpit ; [교회의] a pew : [앉을 장소] (sitting) room ¶ 천명의 좌석이 있는 강당 an auditorium with seating accommodation for one thousand // 좌석순으로 in the order of sitting // 좌석에 앉다 seat oneself 《at a table, in a chair》; take〔have〕 one's seat // 좌석을 잡다 get〔take, secure〕 a seat 《in a bus》 // 좌석을 잡아두다 reserve a seat // 내일 오후의 좌석을 예약합니다 Keep me a seat for tomorrow afternoon. // (열차) 좌석은 전부 예약됐음 All seats are taken.
— 권 a ticket — 만원 [극장의 게시] Standing Room Only 《S. R. O.》 — 버스 a (reserved) seat bus — 번호 the seat number — 수 seating capacity〔accommodation〕 — 일람도 the sitting plan — 정원(수) seating capacity〔accommodation〕 — 지정권 a reserved-seat ticket

좌선 坐禪 sitting in Buddhist meditation — 하다 sit in meditation〔contemplation〕

좌선회 左旋回 rotation to the left ; levorotation ; levorotatory — 하다 rotate〔turn〕 to the left

좌수우봉 左授右捧 giving and taking〔exchanging〕 on the spot — 하다 exchange on the spot

좌시 坐市 a marketplace
— 터 a marketplace

좌시 坐視 — 하다 stand idly 《by》; look (on) with indifference ¶ 차마 좌시할 수 없다 I cannot sit idle watching it.

좌식 坐食 eating the bread of idleness — 하다 live in idleness

좌안 左岸 the left bank (of a river)

좌약 坐藥 a suppository

좌업 坐業 a sedentary occupation〔work〕; a sitting-down job

좌완 투수 左腕投手 a southpaw (pitcher) ; a lefty 《미·속》

좌욕 坐浴 a sitz〔hip〕 bath

*좌우 左右 ① (the) right and left ; [옆] one's side
② [시중 드는 사람] one's attendants ; people in attendance — 하다 [지배하다] command ; control ; dominate ; sway ; have 《a person》 under one's thumb ; have a free hand ; [영향을 주다] affect ; influence ; have an influence upon ¶ 좌우의 right and left ; on both sides ; [사상의] rightist and leftist // 좌우로 from side to side ; right and left ; [양쪽에] on both sides // 길의 좌우에 on either side〔on both sides〕 of the road // 좌우로 흔들리다 roll from side to side // 좌우를 둘러보다 look around // 좌우되다 be under the control 《of》; be swayed 《by》; be influenced 《by》 // 시장을 좌우하다 control〔gain control of〕 the market // 일국의 운명을 좌우하다 hold sway over the destinies of a nation // 감정에 좌우되다 be carried away by one's own feeling

좌우 座右 ¶ 좌우에 by one's side ; at one's elbow ; at hand // 좌우에 갖추다 keep 《a thing》 at hand〔one's elbow〕; keep 《a thing》 handy
— 명 a favorite〔one's〕 motto 《*pl.* -(e)s》

*좌우간 左右間 anyhow ; anyway ; in any circumstance ; in any case ; in any event ; at any rate ¶ 좌우간 그렇게 합시다 I will do so, anyway. // 좌우간 그의 일은 끝났다 He has finished the work

somehow (or other). // 좌우간 준비 만은 해두자 In any case〔At all events〕, I will make preparations for it. // 좌우간 무슨 일인지 가보자 Anyway, let's go there and find out what has really happened.

좌우고면 左右顧眄 ⇨ 좌고우면

좌우 균제 左右均齊 symmetry

좌우익 左右翼 [군대의] the left and right wings of an army ; the left and right column ; [사상의] the left and right wing(er) ; the leftists and the rightists

좌익 左翼 [대형] the left wing〔flank〕 ; [주의] the left wing ; [사람] a leftist ; a left winger ; [야구] the left field ¶ 좌익의 leftwing ; leftist // 좌익 사상에 물들다 be tinctured with radicalism

—**군** 〖군사〗 the left column —**단체** a leftist organization ; a group of radicals —**분자** a left-wing element ; a leftist faction —**사상** leftism ; radicalism —**소아병** a puerile leftish sentiment —**수** 〖야구〗 a left fielder —**운동** a leftist〔radical〕 movement **극**— the extreme left(wing)

좌장 座長 the chairman ; the president ; [흥행의] the proprietor ; the boss ; [한자리에서의 어른] the senior person present (in a seated group)

좌장 坐杖 a T-shaped armrest

좌전 座前 ⇨ 좌하

*__좌절 挫折__ a setback ; a breakdown ; a collapse ; frustration ; a reverse 《of one's fortune》 ; an eclipse ; ruin ; [용기의] discouragement —**하다** [계획이] get ruined ; be upset ; breakdown ; collapse ; fall through ; suffer a setback ; get frustrated ; be thwarted ; [용기나 기력이] get discouraged〔disheartened, daunted〕 ¶ 계획이 좌절되다 a plan is ruined〔upset〕 // 계획을 좌절시키다 frustrate 《a person's》 plan // 공격이 좌절되다 an attack is frustrated ; an attack suffers a setback // 그 운동은 좌절됐다 The movement received a setback〔was frustrated〕.

—**감** frustration

좌정 坐定 —**하다** sit ; be seated ; take a seat

좌종 坐鐘 a table clock

좌중 座中 the whole assembly ; the company present

좌지우지 左之右之 —**하다** command ; control ⇨ 좌우하다

좌처 坐處 one's seat ; the place where one sits

좌천 左遷 downgrading ; relegation ; demotion —**하다** be downgraded 〔demoted〕 ; relegate ; consign 《a person》 to an inferior position ; be relegated (좌천되다) ¶ 그의 이번 발령은 좌천이다 His new appointment is a demotion〔a change for the worse〕.

좌초 坐礁 running aground ; stranding —**하다** run aground〔ashore, on a rock〕 ; strand ; strike a rock ; go on a reef ; take the ground ¶ 좌초한 배 a stranded ship // 부산 앞바다에서 좌초했다 The ship ran aground on the coast of *Pusan*.

좌측 左側 the left (side) ¶ 길의 좌측에 on〔to〕 the left (side) of the street

—**통행** [게시] Keep to the left.

좌파 左派 the left wing ; the left faction (of a party) ; [사람] the left wingers ; the leftists

—**사회당** the leftist Socialists ; the left faction〔left-wingers〕 of the Socialist Party

좌판 坐板 a low bench ; a board to sit on

좌편 左便 the left side ; the left

좌편광 左偏光 [편광하기] left-handed polarization ; [빛] left-handed polarized light

좌표 座標 〖수학〗 coordinates ¶ 각〔직각, 사각, 곡선, 구면〕 좌표 angular〔rectangular, oblique, curvilinear, spherical〕 coordinates

—**계**(系) 〖수학〗 the coordinate system ; a system of coordinates ; 〖물리〗 a frame of reference —**기하학** coordinate geometry —**축** the axis of coordinates ; a coordinate axis **가로**— the abscissa 《*pl.* ～s, -sae》 **각〔구, 점〕**— angular〔spherical, punctual〕 coordinates **곡선〔구면〕**— curvilinear〔spherical〕 coordinates **극**— polar coordinates **데카르트〔평행〕**— Cartesian coordinates **세로**— the ordinate **직각〔사각(斜角)〕**— rectangular 〔oblique〕 coordinates

좌하 座下 [편지의] Mister 《Mr.》 ; Esquire 《Esq.》

좌향 左向 ¶ 좌향좌 Left turn〔face〕! (구령) // 좌향 앞으로 가 Left wheel !

좌향 坐向 [집·묘의] an exposure ; an aspect

좌현 左舷 port ; port side ¶ 좌현으로 기울다 list to port // 좌현에〔으로〕 on the portside // 방향을 좌현으로 잡다 give 《the vessel》 port helm

좌회전 左廻轉 turning left ; a left turn —**하다** turn to the left ; make a left turn ¶ 좌회전 금지 No left turn. (게시)

좌흥 座興 amusement〔entertainment〕 of the company ; fun ¶ 좌흥으로 in〔for〕 fun ; by way of joke ; to amuse〔entertain〕 the company // 좌흥으로 이야기를 한자리 하다 tell a short story for the entertainment of the company

좍 ① broadly ; extensively ¶ 소문이 좍 퍼졌다 The rumor has got abroad. /The rumor spread in a flash.

② widely ¶ 문을 좍 열다 fling a door wide open

③ pouring down ¶ 비가 좍 퍼붓는다 It rains heavily〔hard, in showers〕. /The rain is pouring down in buckets〔bucketfuls〕.

좍좍 ① [비가] 《it rains》 in torrents〔sheets, buckets〕 ¶ 비가 좍좍 온다 It's raining cats and dogs.
② [물이] with a gush〔rush〕; gushing; flowing freely ¶ 물을 좍좍 끼얹다 shower〔water over〕《the grass》
③ [시원히] with ease; fluently; sonorously ¶ 좍좍 읽다 read fluently

좔좔 with a gush〔rush〕; gushing; flowing freely ¶ 좔좔거리다 gush; pour down // 물이 좔좔 흐르다 《water》 run freely; 《water》 gush along

좨기 a cake of cooked vegetables〔flour〕

좨치다 ⇨ 죄어치다

좽이 [투망] a casting-net

†**죄 罪** [법률상의] a crime; [종교·도덕상의] a sin; [악덕] a vice; [과실·허물] blame; fault; [벌] (a) punishment; (a) penalty; [유죄] guilt; [반칙] an offense; transgression ¶ 죄 있는 guilty; blamable; culpable; sinful // 죄 없는 not guilty; blameless; innocent // 간음의 죄 the sin of adultery // 죄 받을 짓 a sinful act // 죄를 범하다 commit a crime; be guilty of a crime〔an offense〕; commit a sin (정신적인) // 죄를 캐다 inquire into one's crime // 복죄(服罪)하다 submit to a sentence; plead guilty; admit an offense // 죄를 씌우다 fasten the crime on〔upon〕《a person》; put〔lay〕 the blame on 《a person》 // 죄를 (남에게) 돌리다 blame 《a person》 for the failure; lay the failure at 《a person's》 door // 스스로 죄를 뒤집어 쓰다 take the guilt upon oneself; hold oneself blamable // 죄를 자백하다 confess oneself to be guilty // 죄받을 짓을 하다 do a sinful thing // 죄를 받다 meet with〔suffer〕 punishment // 문죄하다 accuse 《a person》 of a crime; bring a charge against 《a person》 // 죄인을 미워하지 않고 죄를 미워하라 Condemn the offense and not its perpetrator. // 이 실패는 누구의 죄냐 Who is to blame for the failure?/Who is responsible of the failure? // 내가 무슨 죄를 범했단 말이오 In what have I offended?/I haven't done anything wrong./I am not to blame.
죄는 지은 대로 가고 물은 트는 대로 간다 [속담] Every sin brings its punishment with it.

죄과 罪過 an offense; sin (죄악); a fault〔an error〕 (과오) ¶ 죄과가 없는 사람 an innocent〔a guiltless〕 person // 죄과 없는 사람을 벌하다 punish 《a person》 for nothing

죄과 罪科 an offense; a crime; guilt; [처형] punishment ¶ 죄과를 묻다 make inquiry into a crime

‡**죄다**[1] ① tighten (up); stiffen; strain; stretch; string ¶ 나사를 죄다 tighten (up) a screw // 바이올린 줄을 죄다 tighten up the strings of a violin // 느슨한 줄을 죄다 tighten (up) a loose rope; stretch a rope tight // 다 좋은데 허리 부분이 너무 죄는 거 아니야 The dress is not bad, but isn't it a little tight around the waist?
② [마음을] feel anxious〔nervous, uneasy, tense〕; tense up ¶ 마음을 죄다 be fidgety〔edgy〕; be held in suspense; be nervous〔uneasy, anxious〕 // 마음을 죄면서 경과를 지켜 봤다 I kept watching with breathless anxiety how it would turn out.

죄다[2] all; wholly; entirely; altogether ¶ 죄다 자백하다 confess everything // 이것이 죄다인가 Is this all?/Are these all? // 죄다해서 만원이 된다 It amounts to ten thousand *won*. // 당신께 죄다 맡깁니다 I'll leave the whole matter〔the matter entirely〕 in your hands./I'll leave it all to you.

죄명 罪名 the name of a crime〔an offense〕; a charge ¶ 사기의 죄명으로 on the charge of fraud; charged with fraud // 애매한 죄명으로 on no definite charge

죄목 罪目 the name of a crime〔an offense〕; a charge ¶ 사기의 죄목으로 on a charge of fraud; charged with fraud

죄밑 a guilty conscience; a sense of guilt; remorse for one's crime ¶ 죄밑을 느끼다 have qualms of conscience; have a guilty〔an uneasy, a bad〕 conscience; be conscience-stricken; be stung by conscience

죄받다 罪— be punished〔condemned〕 《for》 ¶ 죄받을 짓 a sinful act // 죄받아야 하다 be liable to〔responsible for〕 punishment

죄벌 罪罰 punishment〔a penalty〕 for a crime

죄상 罪狀 the circumstances of a crime; the nature of a crime; criminality; guilt; charge ¶ 죄상을 묻다 inquire into 《a person's》 guilt // 죄상이 명백해지다 be proved guilty // 죄상을 자백하다 confess one's crime〔guilt〕 // 죄상을 부인하다 plead not guilty
— 항목서 a bill of particulars〔indictment〕 (배심원에 의한 판결 전의); an indictment

죄송 罪悚 regret; feeling sorry **—하다** (be) sorry 《for》; regret ¶ 죄송하지만 I am sorry to trouble you, 《but》/Excuse me, 《but》 // 기다리게 해서 죄송합니다 I am very sorry to have kept you waiting. // 죄송하지만 이것을 김씨에게 전해주십시오 I am sorry for troubling you, but please hand this to Mr. *Kim*.

†**죄수 罪囚** a prisoner; a convict; a jailbird; an inmate

죄악 罪惡 [종교상] a sin; [법률상] a crime; [도덕상] a vice ¶ 죄악의 소굴 a den of iniquity // 죄악을 범하다 commit a sin〔crime〕 // 시간의 낭비는 일종의 죄악이다 Waste of time is a sort of sin.

—감 a sense of guilt〔sin〕; a guilt feelings
죄암죄암 Grab it, grab it!
죄암질 playing "grab it"
죄어들다 become〔get〕 tight〔tightened〕; contract; shrink ¶ 세탁해도 죄어들지 않는다 This is unshrinkable (in the wash)./This won't shrink in the wash.
†죄어치다 [죄다] tighten; shrink; draw; contract; [몰다·족대기다] press; urge; rush; dun
죄업 罪業 〖불교〗 act that will lead to sin; a sin; an iniquity ¶ 죄업 많은 여자 a sinful woman // 죄업을 쌓다 commit many sins; live a sinful life
죄이다 [물건이] get tightened; be drawn up; [마음이] feel anxious 〔uneasy, nervous〕; be tense
죄인 罪人 a criminal; a convict; an offender; a culprit; [종교·도덕상의] a sinner; a transgressor; an evildoer
죄임성 —性 suspense; fidget(s); eager expectation
죄장 罪障 〖불교〗 sins; sin and retribution ¶ 죄장의 소멸을 위하여 in expiation of one's sins
죄적 罪迹 proofs〔traces〕 of guilt; evidence of a crime ¶ 죄적을 인멸하다 destroy evidences of one's crime // 죄적을 들추다 trace out a crime // 죄적을 감추다 cover (up) the traces of guilt; leave no traces of a crime
죄주다 罪— punish; penalize; subject 《a person》 to punishment〔penalty〕
죄증 罪證 proofs〔evidence〕 of guilt; witness ¶ 죄증을 인멸하다 destroy all the proofs of one's guilt
죄질 罪質 the nature of a crime〔an offence〕
죄짓다 罪— commit a crime〔an offense〕; [종교상의] do sinful things; commit sins
죄책 罪責 [죄의 책임] liability〔responsibility〕 for a crime ¶ 죄책을 묻다 charge with a crime
죄형 법정주의 罪刑法定主義 the principle of "nulla poena〔nullum, crimen〕 sine lege"; the principle of legality
*죔쇠 a kind of vise〔clamp〕; a clamper
죔틀 a vise
†주 主 [주인] one's master; one's employer; [수령] a chief; [신] the Lord; the Savior; [주요 부분] the main〔chief〕 part; the principal part ¶ 주가 되는 main; chief; principal // 주로 mainly; chiefly; in the main; principally; [대개] mostly; for the most part; generally // 그들의 성공은 주로 근면의 덕택이다 Their success is mainly due to their assiduity. // 여기 학생들은 주로 지방 출신이다 The students are, for the most part, from the provinces.
†주 州 a province; a state (미국의) ¶ 뉴욕 주 the State of New York // 주립 대학 a state university
†주 註 an annotation; foot notes; comments; explanatory notes; commentary ¶ 주를 달다 annotate; make note on; comment on; annex notes to 《a book》
†주 株 ① [주식] a share; a stock 《미》; an interest 《in a business》

> 참고 **stock**은 개인 출자의 총액을 말하고 **share**는 일정한 단위로 분할한 한 단위주를 말한다 미국에서는 양쪽의 뜻으로 stock을 사용하지만 「100주」와 일정한 주수를 말할 경우에는 share를 사용한다

¶ 인기 있는 주 active〔popular〕 stocks // 주가의 상승〔하락〕 a rise〔fall〕 in shares // 주를 모집하다 offer stocks for subscription // 주를 사다 buy〔invest in〕 stocks; buy an interest 《in a business》 // 주 시세의 변동 the fluctuation of shares in price // 그 회사는 7,000주로 조직되었다 The company was established with 7,000 shares.
② [그루] ¶ 나무 한 주 a tree // 장미 한주 one rose plant
—가 the price of a stock; a stock price
—권 a share〔stock〕 certificate; a share; a stock 《미》 —주 a share-holder 《영》; a stockholder 《미》 구— old shares 신— new shares 실— real stocks 우량— blue-chip〔gilt-edged〕 stocks 우선〔보통〕— preference〔common〕 shares 은행— bank stocks 인기— active〔popular〕 stocks 전액 불입— a full-paid〔paid-up〕 stock
†주 週 a week ¶ 금주 this week // 내〔전〕주 next〔last〕 week // 몇 주동안 for (many) weeks // 주초에 at the beginning of the week
주 朱 vermilion; Chinese red; 〖광물〗 cinnabar
주 洲 a sandbank; [대륙] a continent 삼각— a (river) delta 아시아— the Continent of Asia 5대— the Five Continents
주- 駐 resident〔stationed, staying〕 《in》 ¶ 주한의 resident〔stationed〕 in Korea // 주한 미국 대사 the U. S. Ambassador to Korea
주가 株價 the price〔value〕 of a stock
주간 主幹 the (chief) manager; the superintendent; [편집의] the managing〔chief〕 editor —하다 manage 《affairs》; [편집을] edit 《a magazine》
†주간 週刊 a weekly; weekly publication — 잡지 a weekly magazine ⇨ 주간지 (週刊誌)
*주간 晝間 daytime; day ¶ 주간에 in the daytime; during the day
— 근무 day-duty; daywork; work on a day shift — 노동 daytime labor —선 〖전기〗 a daytime line — 인구 the daytime population 《of》

주간 週間 a week
— 논평 a weekly review 교통 안전 — Traffic Safety Week 방범 — Crime Prevention Week 인권 강조 — Human Rights Week
주간지 週刊誌 a weekly (magazine)
시사 — a weekly newsmagazine ; a newsweekly 여성 — a women's weekly
주강 鑄鋼 cast steel
—업 steel casting
주객 主客 [사람] host and guest ; [사물] principal and auxiliary ¶ 주객이 전도한 preposterous // 주객이 전도됐다 The relations are reversed. // 주객 전도이다 The tables are turned. /That is putting the cart before the horse. /That is contrary to the usual order.
—간 between host and guest — 전도 putting the last before the first ; putting the cart before the horse
주객 酒客 a drinker ; a tippler ; a thirsty soul
⁑주거 住居 residing ; a dwelling ; a habitation ; a residence ; an abode —하다 dwell ; reside ; live 《in》 ; inhabit
—비 housing expenses — 수당 a living allowance —인 an occupant of a house ; a resident ; an inhabitant ; a dweller — 지역 a residential area〔district〕 — 침입 home-breaking ; violation of domicile
주거니받거니 exchanging 《wine cups》 ¶ 주거니받거니하며 마시다 hobnob〔have a hobnob〕 《with》
주걱 a large flat wooden spoon (used for scooping rice) ; a rice scoop
—뼈 the shoulder blade ; the spadebone ; the scapula —상(相) a pushed-in face —턱 a jutting chin
주검 [시체] remains ; a corpse ; a dead body ¶ 주검을 묻다 bury a body
*주격 主格 〚문법〛 the nominative〔subjective〕 case
주견 主見 one's own opinion〔view〕 ; an independent idea ; a firm conviction ; a fixed view
주경야독 晝耕夜讀 farm by day and study by night
주고도 走高跳 the running high jump
주고받다 give and take ; exchange ; reciprocate ¶ 선물을 주고 받다 give presents to each other // 인사를 주고 받다 exchange greetings〔civilities〕
주공 奏功 success ; efficacy —하다 succeed ; be successful ; [주효하다] be effective ; take effect
주공 鑄工 a caster ; a cast-iron worker
주관 主管 management ; supervision —하다 supervise ; manage ; superintend ; have charge of
— 사항 matters in one's charge —자 a superintendent ; a supervisor
*주관 主觀 subjectivity ; subjectiveness ; [자아] the subjectivity ; ego ¶ 주관적 subjective // 주관적으로 subjectively // 주관적 비평 subjective criticism // 주관적으로 말하자면 subjectively speaking // 주관적으로 보다 take a subjective view of 《a thing》 ; look at 《a thing》 subjectively // 주관에 치우치다 be too subjective
—론 subjectivism —성 subjectivity
주관화 主觀化 subjectification ; subjectivization —하다 subjectify ; subjectivize
주광 酒狂 [상태] drunken disorderliness ; [사람] a disorderly drunk ; a boozer
주광색 전구 晝光色電球 a daylight〔daytime〕 lamp
주광성 走光性 〚생물〛 phototaxis
⁑주교 主敎 [교직] a prelate ; a primate ; a bishop ; an archbishop (대주교) : [주요 종교] the principal religion
— 관구 a diocese — 제도 episcopacy — 제 주의 Episcopalianism —직(職) episcopate ; bishopric 대— an archbishop 총(總)— 〚그리스 정교〛 the Ecumenical Patriarch
주교 舟橋 a pontoon bridge ; a floating bridge
주구 走狗 [앞잡이] a tool ; a cat's paw ; a puppet ; [사냥개] a hound ; a hunting dog ¶ 공산당의 주구 a mere tool of the communists // 남의 주구가 되다 be made a cat's paw of
주구 誅求 exaction ; extortion —하다 exact ; extort ; squeeze ; lay under tribute ⇨ 가렴주구
주군 主君 one's (liege) lord ; one's master
주군 駐軍 stationing troops
주권 株券 a share certificate ; a stock certificate ; a share ¶ 주권을 현금으로 바꾸다 cash shares
가— a script 가명 — a registered share 무기명 — a share certificate to bearer 예비 — an unissued stock certificate 전액 불입— a full-paid share
⁑주권 主權 sovereignty ; sovereign 〔supreme〕 power〔rights〕 ; supremacy ¶ 주권을 잡다 rule〔reign〕 supreme // 주권 재민 Sovereignty rests with the people. // 주권을 침해하다 violate sovereignty
—국 a sovereignty ; a sovereign state — 자 the sovereign ; the ruler ; the chief of a state — 재민론(在民論) the doctrine that sovereignty rests with〔resides in〕 the people ; the doctrine of democratic 〔popular〕 sovereignty — 침해 infringement of sovereignty 공동 — joint sovereignty ; condominium
*주근깨 freckles ; flecks ; 〚의학〛 lentigo 《*pl.* -gines》 ¶ 주근깨가 있는 얼굴 a freckled face // 주근깨가 끼다 freckle ; get freckled
주금 株金 a share ; a stock (투자금 총액) ¶ 주금 불입의 청구 a call on shareholders // 주금을 불입하다 pay up one's shares

// 주금을 모집하다 call in shares ; call for payment of shares
— 계정 capital account ⟪a/c⟫
주금 鑄金 casting
주금류 走禽類 〖새〗 runners ; cursorial birds ; Cursores (학명)
주급 週給 weekly wages〔pay, salary〕
— 제도 the weekly payment system ¶ 저 회사에선 주급제(도)를 실시한다 They are paid by the week in that company.
주기 酒氣 the influence of alcohol ; intoxication ¶ 주기를 띠고 있다 be under the influence of alcohol〔liquor〕 ; smell of liquor
**주기 週期 a periodic time ; a period ; a cycle ; periodicity (주기성) ¶ 주기적 periodic(al) // 주기적으로 periodically // 유성의 주기 the period of a planet // 주기적으로 순환하다 move in a cycle ; circulate periodically // 이 현상은 주기적인 것이다 This phenomenon occurs periodically.
—성(性) periodicity —성(星) a periodic star —율 the periodic law ¶ 주기율표 〖화학〗 a periodic table — 전류 a periodic current — 함수〔반응, 운동〕 a periodic function〔reaction, motion〕 — 혜성 〖천문〗 a periodic comet 원소 —표 〖화학〗 a periodic table of elements
주낙 a (fishing) reel and line with multiple hooks ¶ 주낙으로 고기를 잡다 fish with a reel and line with multiple hooks
주년 周年 an anniversary ; a whole year ¶ 8주년 the eighth anniversary
주뇌 主腦 the brains ; the leaders ⇨ 수뇌
주눅들다 feel timid ; lose one's nerve ; feel out of place ¶ 나는 그 사람 앞에 나가기만 하면 주눅이 든다 I feel small in his presence. /I lose my nerve in front of him.
주눅좋다 (be) brazen-faced ; impudent ; shameless ; unabashed
주니 tediousness ; weariness ; boredom ¶ 주니가 나다〔주니를 대다〕 be tired of ; get sick of ; be bored with
주니어 a junior
— 스타일 〖양재〗 junior〔teenage〕 style
†주다[1] give ; give away ; present ; bestow ; confer ; grant ; donate ; provide

> 참고 **give** 「주다」의 일반어 **bestow** (너그러운 체 하면서) 무상으로 주다 **present** 정식으로 (때로는 의식을 갖추어) 주다 증정하다 **confer** 윗 사람이 영예나 특권을 주다 **grant** 요망에 따라서 주다 **donate** 자선 또는 신앙 때문에 주다

¶ 주는 사람 a giver ; a donator // 먹을 것을 주다 give ⟪a person⟫ something to eat // 거지에게 동냥을 주다 give to beggars // 닭에게 모이를 주다 feed the chickens // 가진 돈을 다 털어 주다 give away all the money one has // 일거리를 주다 provide work ⟪for a person⟫ // 상을 주다 award a prize // 박사 학위를 주다 confer the doctorate ; give the doctor's degree // 학생한테 숙제를 주다 assign homework to students // 타격을 주다 give a blow to ⟪a person⟫ // 암시를 주다 drop a hint // 자금을 주다 furnish ⟪a person⟫ with funds // 고통을 주다 cause pain to ⟪a person⟫ // 손해를 주다 inflict a loss on ⟪a person⟫ // 영향을 주다 exert influence ⟪on⟫ // 힘 주어 말하다 accentuate ; speak with emphasis ; emphasize one's words // 고기 한 근에 2,000원 주다 pay 2,000 *won* for a ***keun*** of meat // 다달이 5,000원씩 주다 allow ⟪a person⟫ 5,000 *won* a month // 이것을 네게 주겠다 This is for you. // 그는 내게 기회를 주지 않았다 He offered me no chance. // 이 실패는 그의 사업에 큰 타격을 주었다 This failure dealt a heavy blow to his business.
주다[2] 〔조동사〕 do for ⟪a person⟫ ¶ 모자를 사주다 buy a hat for ⟪one's daughter⟫ // 문을 열어주다 open the door for ⟪a person⟫ // 아내에게 외투를 입혀주다 help one's wife on with her coat // 영어 편지 한 장 써주십시오 Please write a letter in English for me.
주단 紬緞 silks and satins ; silk goods
주달 奏達 —하다 report ⟪a matter⟫ to the throne
주담 酒痰 〖한의〗 a kind of stomach upset following heavy drinking
주당 周堂 〖민속〗 a malignant spirit which is shunned during wedding festivals
주당 酒黨 a drinker
주대 a fishing line and pole ; a rod and line
주도 周到 —하다 (be) cautious ; prudent ; exhaustive ; thoroughgoing ; scrupulous ; circumspect ¶ 용의주도한 계획 an alert and cautious plan ; the plan prepared to the minutest details
주도 主導 leading ; taking the initiative
—하다 lead ; assume leadership of
—권 leadership ; initiative ¶ 주도권을 잡다 take the leadership〔initiative〕 // 러시아는 동구 지역에서 주도권을 잡고 있다 Russia wears the pants in the East. —자 a leader ; a prime mover ; a moving spirit
주독 酒毒 alcoholic poisoning ; alcoholism ¶ 주독이 오르다 get a red spot on one's face
—코 a red nose (from drinking)
주독 駐獨 ¶ 주독의 resident〔stationed〕 in Germany
— 한국 대사 the Korean Ambassador to〔in〕 Germany〔at〔in, to〕 Bonn〕
주동 主動 motive power ; leadership —하다 take the lead〔initiative〕
—자 a prime mover ; the originator ; the leader ¶ 주동자가 되다 take the leading part
주되다 主— be the head of ; take the lead of ; lead others ⟪in some work⟫ ¶ 아무

도 주되어서 일하는 사람이 없다 None takes the initiative in working. // 그가 주되어서 일을 했다 He played the most active part in it.

주두 柱頭 〖식물〗 a stigma ; [대접받침] a capital ; a headpiece on a column

주두라지 ① ⇨ 주둥이 ② ⇨ 말씨

*__주둔 駐屯__ stationing ; staying ; posting **—하다** be stationed ; station ; post ; stay

—군 stationary troops ; occupation army ; a garrison (수비대) **—지** a post ; an army post

주둥아리 ⇨ 주둥이

*__주둥이__ [입] the mouth ; lips ; tongue (말) ; [부리] a bill (편편한) ; a beak (매부리 따위) ; [물건의] a mouth(piece) ¶ 주둥이가 큰 병 a large-mouthed jar // 주둥이를 놀리다 wag one's tongue ; prattle ; chatter ; babble // 저 친구는 주둥이가 사납다 He has a foul tongue.

주둥이가 싸다 관용 be glib-tongued 〔talkative〕

주라 朱螺 〖악기〗 a conch shell painted red and used as a horn to blow on

주라통 朱螺筒 the gullet (of an ox) ; the esophagus

주란 酒亂 drunken frenzy

주란사 —紗 cloth woven from gassed cotton thread

주람 周覽 a widespread tour of inspection〔observation〕 **—하다** go on a round of inspection〔sightseeing〕

주랑 柱廊 a parvis(e) ; a colonnade

— 현관 a portico 《*pl.* ~(e)s》

주량 酒量 one's drinking capacity ¶ 주량을 줄이다 drink less (wine) ; cut down on one's drinking // 주량이 늘다 gain drinking capacity // 주량이 크다 be a heavy drinker

주럽 [피로] fatigue ; weariness ; exhaustion ; [주접] stunting ; blight ¶ 주럽떨다 rest from one's fatigue ; rest oneself

주렁주렁 in abundance ; in clusters ¶ 가지에는 주렁주렁 열매가 달려 있다 The branches are heavily loaded with fruit.

주력 主力 the main force〔strength, body〕 ¶ 군의 주력 the main army // 적의 주력이 아군의 좌측에 육박했다 The enemy's main force pressed on our left flank.

— 부대 main-force unit ; hard-core unit **—전** a major engagement ; the clash of the main forces **—주** 〖주식〗 leaders ; leading issues〔shares〕 **—함** a capital ship **— 함대** the main fleet

주력 呪力 magical power ; mana ; medicinal power (병을 고치는)

주력 注力 putting forth strength ; concentrating one's effort **—하다** concentrate 《one's effort on something》 ; exert oneself for ; make efforts ; give one's mind to 《something》 ¶ 그는 영어 공부에 주력했다 He devoted〔applied〕 (his) energies to the study of English. /He concentrated his energies on the study of English.

주련 柱聯 a verse couplet carved or written on a plank which is put on a pillar

주렴 珠簾 a window blind woven with strings of beads ; beaded hanging screen

주례 主禮 ① officiating at〔presiding over〕 a ceremony ¶ 베이커 목사님이 주례를 보실 거야 Rev. Baker will officiate at the wedding. ② [사회자] an officiator ; a master of ceremonies ; the one in charge of a ceremony

— 목사 an officiating pastor〔minister〕

⁑__주로 主—__ mainly ; chiefly ; principally ; primarily ; in the main ; [대개] generally ; mostly ; for the most part ¶ 그것은 주로 나의 과실이다 It is largely my fault. // 그것은 주로 너의 책임이다 You are mainly responsible for it. // 길 양쪽의 집들은 주로 석조 건물이었다 The houses on either side of the street were for the most part built of stone.

주로 走路 a track ; a course

주루 走壘 〖야구〗 base running ¶ 주루를 잘하다 be good at base running

주루 酒樓 a drinking shop

주룩주룩, 쭈룩쭈룩 ① [주름이] with wrinkles〔rumples, folds〕 ② [비가] pouring hard ; in sudden downpours ¶ 주름이 주룩주룩진 노파 an old withered woman // 주름이 주룩주룩지다 be all wrinkled ; have wrinkles on it ; be withered 〔crumpled, rumpled〕 // 비가 주룩주룩 온다 The rain keeps pouring down.

주류 主流 the main current〔stream〕 ¶ 미국사의 주류 the main current in American history

—파 the mainstream faction ¶ 공화당의 주류파 the mainstream〔faction〕 of the Democratic Republican Party **반 —파** anti-mainstream group

주류 酒類 alcoholic liquors ¶ 주류의 판매 liquor selling

주류 駐留 ⇨ 주둔(駐屯)

주륙 誅戮 capital punishment ; execution **—하다** punish 《a person》 with death ; execute

주르르, 쭈르르 trickling ; dribbling ¶ 주르르 흐르다 trickle down ; flow out // 가지에서 물이 주르르 흘렀다 Water trickled down in drops from the branches. // 그 여자의 뺨에서 눈물이 주르르 흘렀다 Tears streamed〔rolled〕 down her cheeks.

†__주름__ [얼굴의] wrinkles ; furrows ; [눈 가장자리의] crow's feet ; [물건의] creases ; rumples ; folds ; [옷의] a plait ; a fold ¶ 주름 잡힌 얼굴 a wrinkled〔lined〕 face ; a withered face // 주름을 잡다 plait ; pleat ; crease ; fold // 주름이 잡히다 become wrinkled〔crumpled, rumpled〕 // 주름을 펴다 smooth out ; unrumple // 주름을 없애다 remove wrinkles // 다리미로 옷의 주름을 펴다 iron out the wrinkles in

one's dress // 노인의 이마에는 깊은 주름이 져 있었다 Deep furrows lined the old man's forehead. // 그 여자의 눈가에 주름이 지기 시작했다 She is beginning to get wrinkled round her eyes. // 이 웃옷은 어깨에 주름이 져 있다 This coat puckers at the shoulders. // 주름이 지지 않게 옷을 싸시오 Pack the dresses so that they may not crease.
— 상자 bellows (on a camera) — 치마 a pleated skirt

*주름살 [구김살] wrinkles ; [접은 줄] pleats ; folds ; creases ¶ 이마에 주름살을 짓다 knit〔pucker up〕 one's brows // 옷에 주름이 잡히다 one's clothes are wrinkled.

**주름잡다 ① plait ; crease ⇨ 주름 ② [지배] manage ; control ; take the lead 《in》 ¶ 금융계를 주름잡다 have a firm grip on the banking business // 바다를 주름잡는 자가 세계를 지배한다 Those who have command of the seas have control of the world.

주릅 [거간] a broker ; a commission-merchant〔-agent〕 ; a go-between ; an intermediary ; a middleman
집— a real estate agent ; a rental agent
주릅 들다 관용 act as a broker

주리 the leg-screw ; torture ⇨ 주리틀다

주리다 be〔go〕 hungry ; starve ; be famished ; [갈망] be hungry for〔after〕 ; hanker after ; hunger〔thirst〕 for〔after〕 ¶ 주린 hungry ; famished ; starved // 지식에 주리다 be thirsty for〔after〕 knowledge // 사랑에 주리다 hanker after love // 처자를 주리게 하다 let one's family go hungry ; leave one's family to starve // 주린 자는 음식을 가리지 않는다 Nothing comes amiss to a hungry man. / Nothing is unpalatable to a hungry stomach. /Hunger is the best sauce.

주리 틀다 impose leg-screw torture ; torture a suspect by twisting his legs with two sticks inserted between them

주립 州立 state(-established) ; province (-established) ; provincial
— 대학 a state〔provincial〕 university

주릿대 [형구] the wooden sticks used for leg-screw torture ; [사람] a bad man ; a wicked〔an evil〕 person
주릿대 안기다 관용 inflict a cruel punishment on

주마 走馬 a running horse ; [달림] driving a horse —하다 drive a horse ; gallop a horse
—가편(加鞭) whipping an already galloping horse ; unrelenting industry 〔drive〕 —간산(看山) giving a hurried 〔cursory〕 glance —등 a revolving lantern ¶ 여러가지 생각이 주마등처럼 스쳐갔다 In her eyes many pictures came and went. —창(瘡) 〖한의학〗 boils that spread all over the body

주막 酒幕 an inn ; a tavern ¶ 주막에 들다 put up at an inn
— 거리 a road with taverns on it — 주인 an innkeeper

**주말 週末 the weekend ¶ 주말에 on weekends (언제나) ; over the weekend (이번 주말에) // 주말을 온양에서 지내다 weekend at *Onyeang* ; stay at *Onyeang* over the weekend // 이번 주말은 나 좀 쉴까 해 I think I'll take this weekend off.
— 여행 a weekend trip — 여행자 a weekender

주맥 主脈 [산맥] the main mountain range ; 〖식물〗 a costa 《*pl.* -tae》 ; a midrib

주맹 晝盲 〖의학〗 day blindness ; hemeralopia

*주머니 a moneybag ; a pocketbook ; a bag ; a sack ; a pouch (작은) ; a pocket (호주머니)

> 참고 **bag**은 직물·가죽·종이 따위로 만들어진 주머니를 말한다 **sack**는 거친 헝겊 또는 강한 재료로써 만들어진 포대이며 곡물·밀가루·감자·석탄·야채 따위를 넣는 데 사용된다

¶ 주머니에서 끄집어내다 take 《money》 out of one's purse // 주머니가 든든하다 have a long〔heavy, plump, well-filled, well-lined, fat〕 purse〔pocket〕 // 손을 주머니에 넣고 서 있다 stand keeping one's hands in one's pocket // 주머니 속이 텅 비다 be penniless // 나는 주머니 사정이 좋지 않다 I have a tight pocketbook. /I have a tight budget. // 나는 요즘 주머니 사정이 별로 좋지 않다 I am a little short lately.
—끈 purse strings —돈〔밑천〕 pocket money (reserved for an emergency) —칼 a pocketknife 돈— a moneybag ; a purse 뒷— a hip pocket 속— an inside pocket 저고리〔바지〕 — a coat〔trouser〕 pocket
주머니를 털다 관용 empty one's purse to the last penny ; clear one's purse out

**주먹 a fist ; the bunch of fives ¶ 주먹만 한 돌 a fist-sized rock〔stone〕 // 주먹을 쥐다 clench〔double up〕 one's fist // 주먹을 쥐고 사람을 치다 strike 《a person》 with a clenched〔closed〕 fist // 주먹으로 탁자를 치다 bang the table with one's fist // 빈 주먹으로 장사를 시작하다 start in business empty-handed〔without any capital〕
—밥 a rice ball — 싸움 a fist fight —심 the power of one's fist 《to hit, grasp, figure》 ; [완력] physical strength ; force —장 〖건축〗 a pole plate with a fist-shaped head —코 a snob nose

주먹구구 —九九 [손가락 셈] finger counting ; [어림] rule of thumb ; rough estimate ; approximate figures ¶ 주먹구구로 어림하다 estimate by rule of thumb ; make a rule-of-thumb estimate

주먹다짐 ① [때림] striking 《a person》

with one's fist ; fisticuff ; a fist fight ② [완력] threats of violence ; intimidation ; shaking one's fist **—하다** strike ⟪a person⟫ with one's fist ; take one's fists to ⟪a person⟫ ; give ⟪a person⟫ a taste of one's fists ; threaten ; intimidate ¶ 그는 그 노인에게 주먹다짐했다 He rained blows on the old guy.

*__주먹질__ (a bout of) fisticuffs ; fist-fighting ; an exchange of blows ; [권투에서] rally **—하다** strike〔beat〕⟪a person⟫ with one's fist ; give ⟪a person⟫ a good punch ; exchange blows ; come to blows with ; come to fisticuffs ; have a fight ¶ 주먹질을 시작하다 begin to fight ; get into a fight ⟪with⟫ ; fall〔come〕to blows ; take to one's fists // 두 사람은 하마터면 주먹질을 시작할 판이었다 They narrowly missed a fist fight.

주멸 誅滅 extermination (of a family as a penalty) **—하다** exterminate (as a penalty)

주명 主命 [군주의 명] one's lord's command ; [주인의 명] one's master's order

주명곡 奏鳴曲 〚음악〛 a sonata

주모 酒母 [술밑] distiller's grains ; yeast ; ferment ; [술집의] a barmaid

주모 主謀 heading a conspiracy〔scheme, plot〕; taking the lead in a conspiracy **—하다** lead a conspiracy〔scheme, plot〕; stir up ; organize
—자 a ringleader ; the author ⟪of a plot⟫ ; a prime mover ; a leader ; the instigator ¶ 이 반란의 주모자는 누구냐 Who led the mutiny ? // 저 사람이 틀림없이 주모자일 것이다 He must be at the bottom of the affair.

주목 〚식물〛 a yew (tree) ; Taxus cuspidata (학명)

*__주목 注目__ attention ; notice ; note ; observation **—하다** pay attention to ; watch ; observe ; keep an eye on ; take notice of ; direct〔turn〕one's attention ¶ 주목할 만한 noteworthy ; remarkable ; significant ; striking // 주목할 만하다 be worthy of notice ; be worth noticing ; merit attention // 주목을 받지 않다 be unnoticed // 세인의 주목을 받다 attract〔arrest, draw, engage〕public attention // 가련한 고아의 모습이 일동의 주목을 끌었다 The poor orphan occupied the attention of the whole company. /All the eyes of the company were turned to the poor orphan. // 그는 경찰에서 주목받고 있다 He is under the eye of the police. // 그 일의 귀추가 대단히 주목되고 있다 The development is being watched with keen interest.

주무 主務 management ; chief control of an affair ; the official〔person〕in charge ; a manager **—하다** have chief control ; be in charge of ⟪an affair⟫
—부 competent ministry **—자** a person in charge ; the chief official ⟪in charge of affairs⟫ ; a supervisor **— 장관〔관청〕** the competent Minister〔authorities, office〕

주무르다 [손으로] finger ; fumble with ; [안마하다] massage ; [농락하다] inveigle ; entice ; cajole ; coax ; have ⟪a person⟫ in hand ; make a puppet of ⟪a person⟫ ¶ 어깨를 주무르다 massage ⟪a person's⟫ shoulder // 마음을 마음대로 주무르다 have ⟪a person⟫ completely under one's control ; have ⟪a person⟫ under one's thumb // 남자를 마음대로 주무르다 make sport of a man

†**주무시다** go to bed ; retire ⇨ 자다 ¶ 어젯밤 잘 주무셨습니까 Did you have a good sleep last night ?

주묵 朱墨 vermilion Chinese〔India〕ink ; red ink

주문 主文 [판결] the text ; 〚문법〛 the principal clause

*__주문 呪文__ a magic formula〔chanting〕; an incantation ; a conjuration ; a spell ; a charm ; a curse ¶ 주문을 외우다 make an incantation ; chant a spell ; say the magic words ; mutter charms // 주문에 사로잡히다 be bound by a spell

†**주문 注文** [마춤] an order ; ordering ; an indent (주문서) ; [요구] a request ; a wish **—하다** order ⟪a thing⟫ from ; give ⟪a person⟫ an order for ⟪a thing⟫ ; place an order with ⟪a person⟫ ; indent for ⟪goods⟫ ¶ 주문한 손님 a client // 어려운 주문 an unreasonable request // 주문하시는 대로 곧 upon receipt of your order // 주문에 따라 in compliance with〔in obedience to〕an order // 주문을 받다 take〔book〕orders // 주문에 응하다 fill〔accept〕an order ; comply with ⟪a person's⟫ request // 주문에 따라 만들다 make ⟪a thing⟫ to order // …의 주문이 많다 have a large order ⟪for⟫ // 주문이 쇄도하다 have a rush of orders (from many directions) // 주문을 권유하다 canvass for orders // 주문을 취소하다 cancel〔revoke, withdraw〕an order // 주문을 받고 있다 have ⟪something⟫ under order // 이 구두는 주문해서 만든 것이다 This pair of shoes is made to order. // 귀사의 주문에 성심껏 응해 드리겠습니다 Your order will receive our best attention. // 그것은 어려운 주문이다 It is a difficult bill to fill. /That is a tall order. // 그런 주문은 무리이다 That is too much to ask. // 만사 우리의 주문대로 되어간다 Everything is turning out just as we wish. // 주문하셨습니까 Are you being waited on ? /Are you being helped ? /Are you being served ? /Did you order ? // 주문하시겠습니까 May I take your order ? // 주문받으세요 Can you take our order, please ? // 무엇을 주문하시겠습니까 What would you like ? /What will it be ?
—복 a suit made to order ; a custom〔bespoke〕suit ⟪미⟫ **—서** an order

sheet ; an indent (외국에서의) — 잔고 unexecuted orders ; a backlog (of orders) ⦅구⦆ —장(帳) an order book —장이 a canvasser —처 [주문자] the orderer ; [인수자] the receiver of an order —표 an order pad (한 장씩 떼어 쓰는) —품 goods ordered ; [미제품] an article on order ; [기제품] an article made to order 견본 — a sample order 무조건 — an open order 분할 — a give-out〔split〕 order 재— a repeat order 확정 — a firm order 우편 — 거래 orders by post ; mail order business

주문 奏聞 —하다 report ⦅a matter⦆ to the throne

주물 鑄物 cast-iron ware ; a cast-iron product
— 공장 a foundry

주물 呪物 a fetish ¶ 주물의〔숭배적인〕 fetishistic
— 숭배 fetishism — 숭배자 a fetishist

주물럭거리다 finger ; fumble with

주물럭주물럭 fingering ; fumbling ; kneadingly

주미 駐美 ¶ 주미의 stationed〔resident〕 in America
— 한국 대사 the Korean Ambassador to〔in〕 the United States of America

†주민 住民 inhabitants ; residents ; dwellers
— 등록 resident registration — 등록법 〖법〗 the Residents Registration Act — 등록증 a certificate of residence —세 the inhabitants' tax 원— the natives ; the aborigines

주밀 周密 completeness ; cau-tiousness ; prudence ; thoroughgoing preparation —하다 (be) scrupulous ; cautious ; prudent ; exhaustive ; careful ¶ 주밀하게 circumspectly ; scrupulously ; carefully ; cautiously ; meticulously // 주밀한 설계 thoroughgoing design

주반 酒飯 liquor and cooked rice

주발 周鉢 a brass rice-bowl
— 뚜껑 the lid of a brass rice-bowl 통— a cheap brass rice-bowl

주방 廚房 a kitchen ; a cookroom ; a cuisine
—장 a head cook ; a *chef* ⦅프⦆ ☞ ⦗p. 1939⦘

주배 酒杯 a wine cup ; a wine glass

주버기 a lump ; a mass ; being full ⦅of⦆ ; being covered ⦅with⦆ ¶ 얼굴에 분이 주버기로 붙었다 Her face was caked with powder.

주번 週番 weekly duty
— 사관 the officer of the week

주벌 誅罰 punishment ; chastisement —하다 punish ; chastise

주벌 誅伐 a punitive expedition —하다 send a punitive expedition ⦅against rebels⦆

주범 主犯 the principal offense ; the principal offender (사람)

주법 主法 the principal〔major〕 laws

주법 走法 (a form of) running

주법 奏法 〖음악〗 (the style of) rendition ; execution ; how to play ⦅a clarinet⦆ ¶ 주법이 좋다〔나쁘다〕 be well〔badly〕 executed

주법 呪法 incantation ; enchantment

주벽 酒癖 one's behavior under the influence of alcohol ; a drinking habit ¶ 주벽이 나쁘다 be quarrelsome in one's cups ; be a quarrelsome〔vicious〕 drinker ; be a bad drinker

주변 adaptability ; resourcefulness ; tactfulness ; flexibility ; versatility ; shiftiness ; ability to shift about ¶ 주변이 있다 be resourceful ; be on the ball ; be quick on one's feet // 그는 말 주변이 좋다 He has the gift of gab. / He has a silver tongue. // 그는 돈도 없고 주변도 없다 He is neither rich nor versatile.

⁑주변 周邊 a circumference ; 〖기하〗 a perimeter (평면도의) ; [토지의] environs ; outskirts ¶ 서울 및 그 주변에 in and around *Seoul* ; in *Seoul* and its outskirts〔suburbs〕

주병 酒餠 wine〔liquor〕 and rice cake

주병 駐兵 stationing troops —하다 station〔keep〕 troops

주병 州兵 [미국의] a National Guardsman ; the National Guard ⦅총칭⦆

주보 週報 [신문] a weekly (periodical) ; [보고] a weekly bulletin

주보 酒甫 a drunkard ; a heavy drinker ; an alcoholic

주보 酒保 a canteen ; a post exchange ⦅P. X.⦆

주복 主僕 master and servant ; valet and master

주봉 主峯 the highest〔main〕 peak (of the mountain)

주부 主部 the main〔a principal〕 part ; 〖문법〗 a subject

⁑주부 主婦 the mistress〔lady〕 of a house ; a housewife ; [하숙집의] the landlady ; [안주인] the hostess

주부코 a red bulbous nose ; a whisky nose

주불 駐佛 ¶ 주불의 resident〔stationed〕 in France
— 한국 대사 the Korean Ambassador to〔in〕 France〔at〔in, to〕 Paris〕

주붕 酒朋 a boon companion ; a drinking pal

주비 〖식물〗 a variety of millet

주비 籌備 arrangement ; preparation —하다 arrange ; prepare ⦅for⦆
— 위원회 a preparatory committee ; an arrangements committee

주빈 主賓 the guest of honor ; the chief〔principal〕 guest ; the honor guest ¶ …을 주빈으로 만찬회를 베풀다 give a dinner party in honor of ⦅a person⦆

주 방

① 주방 설비

▶개수대 kitchen (sink)/바닥에 까는 고무 매트 sink mat/설거지 통 sink stopper/수도꼭지 faucet; tap 《영》/수도꼭지를 틀다 open[turn] the faucet/수도꼭지를 잠그다 close the faucet; turn the water off/수도꼭지를 열다 turn the water on/배수관 drain/배수 찌꺼기 처리기 disposer; garbage disposer[disposal]/이조식 [삼조식] 개수대 double [triple] sink/접시 선반 plate rack

▶조리대 kitchen table (★ 주방 한 가운데 있는 것을 말하며 개수대와 붙어 있는 것은 counter)

▶가스대 gas range (★ range보다는 stove를 많이 쓴다; cookstove)/화구 burner/화구 전체 cooktop (★ 전기를 사용하는 것은 electric stove)/생선 굽는 석쇠 grill (★ 밀폐형은 broiler)/전자레인지 microwave range (★ 오븐으로 …을 굽다는 bake ... in the oven.)/환기 장치 ventilator

▶냉장고 refrigerator (★ 생략하여 fridge라고도 한다. 윗칸에 냉동실이 있는 것은 top-freezer refrigerator, 캐비넷형 냉장고는 side-by-side refrigerator)

▶찬장 cupboard (부착형) (★이동이 가능한 것은 cabinet, 식당에 있는 찬장은 sideboard)

② 주방용품

▶식기(류) tableware/식기 세척기 dishwasher/밥솥 rice cooker/찻숟갈 teaspoon/숟갈 tablespoon/접시 dish (★ 식탁에서 각자가 덜어먹는 접시는 plate, 고기나 생선 요리를 낼 때 쓰는 커다란 접시는 platter)/식칼 kitchen knife/도마 cutting board; chopping board 《영》/교반기 whisk; (egg) beater/국자 soup ladle/강판 grater/깡통따개 can opener/(코르크 마개 따는) 타래 송곳 corkscrew/체 strainer; sifter/쇠격자, 석쇠 grid/(조리용) 소쿠리 colander (주로 금속제)/주걱 ladle

▶유리잔 glass/유리잔류 stemware/맥주잔 stein 《미》; jug/컵 cup/(구멍뚫린) 조미료통 caster/계량컵 measuring cup/계량스푼 measuring spoon/받침달린 잔 goblet

▶쥬서 juicer/(전기) 믹서 mixer; blender/레몬즙기 lemon squeezer/얼음통 ice pail; ice bucket/얼음집게 ice tongs (★ 각설탕은 ice cube sugar, 냉장고의 각얼음은 ice cube)

▶(손잡이와 주둥이가 있는) 물주전자 pitcher/찻주전자 teakettle

▶받침접시 saucer (★ 받침접시로 받힌 찻종 a cup and saucer)/(여과기 달린) 커피끓이개 percolator/수프 접시 soup plate/밥그릇 rice bowl/토스터 toaster/냄비 pan/프라이팬 frying pan; skillet 《미》 (★ 뚜껑이 달리고 안이 깊은 것은 saucepan)/(도기 또는 유리로 만든) 식탁용 냄비 casserole/젓가락 chopsticks/포크 fork (★ 끝이 두가닥인 것은 two-pronged fork)

▶행주 kitchen towel (★ 접시닦는 행주는 dish towel; dishcloth 《영》)/종이 행주 paper towel/(철제) 수세미 steel wool

▶(프라이팬용) 뒤집개 turner; spatula/찜통 steamer/(반죽을 미는) 밀대 rollingpin/랩 clear-plastic wrap/알루미늄 포일 aluminium foil

③ 조리 용어

▶자르다 cut/저미다 cut up/강판에 갈다 grate/난도질하다 shred/고기 등을 썰다 chop/잘게 썰다 mince/얇게 썰다 slice/(고기를 주사위꼴로) 토막내다 dice; cube

▶(감자 등을) 짓찧다 mash/눌러 부수다 crush/껍질을 벗기다 pare; peel/갈다 grind

▶섞다 mix/재료를 가볍게 뒤섞다 toss/젓갈로 뒤섞다 stir/(전체가 균일한 질·농도가 되도록) 휘젓다 blend/거품기로 뒤섞다 beat/크림 등을 거품이 나도록 휘젓다 whip/(소금 등을) 흩뿌리다 sprinkle/(밀가루 등을) 입히다 coat

▶석쇠를 사용하여 굽다 grill; broil 《미》/바베큐로 굽다 barbecue/야채, 빵, 케이크 등을 굽다 bake/데우다 heat; scald/고기를 굽다 roast/얇게 저민 빵을 굽다 toast/약한 불로 굽다 panbroil

▶끓이다 boil/저온·약한 불로 볶다 braise/여러 가지 재료를 넣고 끓이다 stew/약한 불에 지글지글 끓이다 simmer

▶냉동하다 freeze/냉장하다 refrigerate/(냉장고에) 얼리다 chill/(실온에서) 식히다 cool

▶(기름에) 튀기다 fry; deep-fat fry; deep-fry (★ 튀긴 고기는 fritter)/(가루를 묻히지 않고 날로) 튀기다 French-fry/살짝 튀기다 shallow-fry; pan-fry; sauté 《프》/휘저어 볶다 stir-fry/노릇노릇하게 튀기다 brown/양념하다 season

—석 the seat of honor
주사 主事 a junior official ; the clerical staff 《총칭》
주사 主辭 〖논리〗 the subject (of a sentence)
*주사 注射 injection ; inoculation (접종) —하다 inject ; inoculate 《a person》 with ; syringe ; give an injection 《of》 ¶ 모르핀 주사를 놓다 inject morphia // 피하 주사를 놓다 inject 《medicine》 hypodermically〔under the skin〕 // 장티푸스의 예방 주사를 맞다 be inoculated with an anti-typhoid vaccine ; be inoculated〔injected〕 against typhoid ; get a shot against typhoid // 그 환자는 주사 힘으로 연명하고 있다 The patient barely lives due to the influence of the injection. // 우리 아들은 주사맞는 것을 싫어해서 내가 그 애의 손을 잡아 끌고 의사에게 갔다 Our son hates shots, So I had to drag him by the hand to the doctor.
—기 an injector ; a syringe —약 an injection ; a vaccine —침 an injection syringe ; a needle 근육〔정맥, 피하〕 — intramuscular〔intravenous, hypodermic〕 injection 예방 — preventive injection
주사 朱砂 〖광물〗 cinnabar
주사 走査 [텔레비전의] scanning —하다 scan
—면(面) a scanning area —밀도 scanning density —선〔점〕 a scanning line〔spot〕 —장치 a scanning apparatus —진폭 scanning frequency
주사 酒邪 disorderly conduct under the influence of alcohol ; delirium tremens ¶ 주사가 있는 사람 a vicious drinker ; a quarrelsome drinker
주사 紬絲 silk thread
주사 酒肆 a drinking shop ; a tavern
주사니 silks
—것 silk garments
*주사위 a die 《*pl.* dice》 ¶ 주사위의 눈 the spot on a die ; a pip // 주사위를 던지다 throw〔cast, shoot〕 a die
— 놀이 diceplay ¶ 주사위 놀이를 하다 play at〔cast〕 dice ; shoot craps
주사위는 던져졌다 관용 The die is cast.
주산 主山 a guardian mountain (located to the north of a town or a grave)
주산 珠算 abacus calculation ; calculation on the abacus —하다 count〔figure〕 on an abacus
— 경기 an abacus contest
주산물 主産物 principal〔major, prime〕 products ; main products
주산지 主産地 a chief〔main〕 producing district〔place〕
주살 an arrow with a string attached to its nock
—질 shooting an arrow with string-attached
주살 誅殺 the death penalty —하다 put 《a traitor》 to death ; kill ; slay
주상 主上 the Sovereign ; the King ; His Majesty
주상 主喪 the chief mourner ; the chief officiator in an ancestor-memorial service
주상 奏上 a report to the King〔Throne〕 ⇨ 주달(奏達)
주상 酒傷 illness from drinking alcohol
주상 柱狀 ¶ 주상의 pillar-shaped ; columnar
주색 朱色 vermilion
주색 酒色 wine and women ; dissipation and debauchery ; sensual pleasures ¶ 주색에 빠지다 give oneself up to wine and women〔liquor and sex〕 ; be addicted to sensual pleasures ; indulge in〔lead〕 a voluptuous life
— 잡기 wine, women and gambling
주서 朱書 rubrication ; writing in red —하다 write in red ink ; rubricate ; mark〔color〕 with red
주석 主席 [사람] the head ; the chief ; [자리] the top〔head〕 seat ; [중국의] the President
주석 柱石 a pillar ; a foundation-stone (주추) ; a mainstay ; a main prop ¶ 일가의 주석 the pillar of a family // 국가의 주석 the pillar of a state
주석 朱錫 tin ¶ 주석을 입히다 tin
—박(箔) tin foil — 제품 tinware
주석 註釋 an annotation ; notes ; comments ; a commentary —하다 annotate ; comment 《on》 ; expound ¶ 주석을 달다 annotate ; append notes 《to a book》
—자 an annotator
주석 酒席 a banquet ; a feast ; a drinking party ¶ 주석에 배석하다 wait〔serve〕 at a banquet // 주석을 베풀다 give a banquet
주석 酒石 〖화학〗 (crude) tartar
—산(酸) tartaric acid —영(英) cream of tartar
주선 周旋 [알선] good offices ; kind offices ; [추천] recommendation ; [중개] agency ; (inter) mediation —하다 recommend ; use one's influence〔one's good offices〕 ; act as an intermediary〔agent〕 ; find〔get〕 《a thing for a person》 ¶ …의 주선으로 through 《a person's》 good offices // 직업을 주선해주다 get〔find〕 《a person》 a position // 친구의 주선으로 이 직장을 얻었다 I've got this job through the good offices of a friend.
—료 brokerage ; commission —업 brokerage ; employment agency (고용인의)
—인 an agent ; an intermediary ; a go-between (중매인) ; a broker ; a real-estate agent (토지·가옥의)
주선 酒仙 a hard drinker ; a son of Bacchus
주섬주섬 one by one ¶ 옷을 주섬주섬 싸다 pack one's clothes one by one
주성분 主成分 the chief〔main〕 ingredient ; the principal element ¶ 이 약은 옥도가 주성분이다 The chief ingredient of

this medicine is iodine.

주세 酒稅 a tax on liquor ; liquor-tax
—법 the Liquor Tax Law

****주소 住所** a dwelling (place) ; a residence ; an abode ; an address ; 〖법〗 a domicile ¶ 주소가 부정하다 have no fixed abode ; be a vagrant ; be a floater 《미》 // 주소 성명을 말하다 give one's name and address // 주소를 변경하다 change one's domicile〔address〕 // 주소를 정하다 take up one's residence〔abode, quarters〕 // 주소는 어디입니까 What is your address ? /Where do you live ? // 주소 변경 신고서 하나 얻을 수 있을까요 Could I have a change of address form ?
—록 an address book ; a directory **— 불명** address unknown **— 성명** one's name and address ¶ 주소 성명을 말하시오 Give me your name and address. **— 이전 신고** a report of one's removal

주술 呪術 incantation ; sorcery

주스 juice ; fruit juice ; fruit-flavor soft drink
오렌지 — orange juice

주시 注視 a staring gaze ; close observation ; scrutiny **—하다** gaze steadily ; fix one's eyes on ; observe 《a person》 closely ; watch〔look at〕《a thing》 carefully ; scrutinize ¶ 온 세계의 주시의 대상이 되다 become the cynosure of the world // 정전 회담은 온 세계가 주시하는 가운데 지금 파리에서 속개되고 있다 The peace talks〔negotiations〕 are being kept open in Paris with all the world observing.

****주식 株式** shares 《영》 ; stocks 《미》 ¶ 주식의 발행 issue of shares // 주식을 매매하다 deal in stocks〔shares〕 // 주식을 모집하다 offer stocks for subscription // 주식의 명의 변경을 정지하다 suspend transfers of stocks ; close the transfer books
— 거래 stock trading **— 발행** a stock issue ¶ 주식 발행액 the issue prices of shares **— 배당** a stock dividend **— 분할** a stock split **— 시세** stock quotations **— 시장〔거래소〕** a stock market〔exchange〕 ; a bourse (유럽에서) **— 액면** the face-value of a stock **— 양도** transfer of shares **— 응모** a stock subscription **— 자본** capital stock **— 중매업** stock-broking **— 중매인** a stockbroker ; a stock speculator (투기자) **— 청산** clearing of stocks **— 청약서** an application for stocks **— 투자** investment in stocks **— 할당** allotment of shares **— 합자 회사** a joint-stock limited partnership **— 회사** a joint-stock company ; corporation 《미》

주식 酒食 food and drink
—점 a tavern ; a restaurant

주식 晝食 lunch ; luncheon

주식 主食 the principal〔staple〕 food ; a staple article of food ¶ 쌀을 주식으로 하다 They live largely on rice. /Rice is the staple food for them.

주신 酒神 the god of wine ; [로마 신화] Bacchus ; [그리스 신화] Dionysus

주심 主心 fixed principles ; firm character ; backbone ; one's iron will ⇨ 줏대

주심 主審 the chief umpire〔referee〕

주아 主我 egocentrism ; self ; ego
—주의 egoism

주아 珠芽 〖식물〗 a bulbil ; a bulblet

주악 奏樂 playing music ; a musical performance **—하다** play〔perform〕 music ¶ 악대의 주악 band music // 국가주악리에 amid the playing of the national anthem
—자 a performer ; a player

주안 主眼 the principal〔first, primary〕 object〔aim〕 ; the chief end〔aim〕 ; the object in view ; the principal point ¶ …에 주안을 두다 aim at // 인격 함양을 주안으로 하다 make character-building the first object 《of education》 // 주안으로 하는 것은 …이다 It aims at 《the conquest of》 /The primary object in view is 《to cultivate their moral character》.
—점 the essential point ; the keynote

주안 酒案 [술상] a liquor table ; a table with wine and some eatables

주야 晝夜 day and night ¶ 주야 교대로 in day and night shifts // 주야 겸행하다 work day and night ; work without rest // 주야 골몰하다 be busy day and night
— 은행 a day-and-night bank **—장천** day and night ever passing ; unceasingly **— 평분선** the equinoctial (line) **일(—)—** (for) twenty-four hours ; twice around the clock

주약 主藥 the principal〔main〕 ingredient ; the base

주어 主語 〖문법〗 the subject (of a sentence)

주역 主役 the leading part〔role〕 ; the lead ; [배우] the leading actor〔actress〕 ; the star ; hero〔heroine〕 ¶ 주역을 맡다 take the leading part〔role〕 in ; play the lead ; star 《in a play》 // 그는 정계의 주역이다 He is playing a leading part on the political stage.

주역 周易 [역경] the Book of Changes

주연 主演 starring ; playing the leading part **—하다** play the leading part〔role〕 in ; star 《in a play》 ¶ 제임스딘 주연 starring James Dean ; James Dean starring
—자 a leading actor〔actress〕 ; a star ; the star player ; a leading man〔lady〕

***주연 酒宴** a feast ; a drinking bout〔party〕 ; a carousal ; a revel ¶ 주연을 열다 give〔hold〕 a banquet〔feast〕 // 주연은 지금 한창이다 The banquet is at its height〔peak〕.

주연 周延 〖논리〗 distribution **—하다** distribute ¶ 주연적인 distributive
—칙(則) the rule of distribution

주연 酒筵 a drinking party ⇨ 술자리
주연 周緣 the fringe ; the rim
주영 駐英 ¶ 주영의 resident〔stationed〕 in England
— 한국 대사 the Korean Ambassador to the Court of St. James's〔at〔in, to〕 London〕
주옥 珠玉 [보석] a jewel ; a gem ; jewelry (집합적) ¶ 주옥 같은 글 a beautiful composition ; a writing of rare beauty // 주옥 같은 시 a gem of a poem // 주옥편 a masterpiece ; a jewel of a literary work // 주옥이 아로새겨져 있다 be inlaid〔embellished, adorned〕 with gems
***주요 主要 —하다** (be) chief ; principal ; leading ; essential ; important ; staple ; capital ; foremost

> 참고 **chief** 지위·중요성 따위에 있어 첫째이며 다른것들은 종속적인 입장에 있는 것을 의미한다 **principal** 타인을 지도하는 사람 또 중요성 크기에 있어 다른것보다 우월한 것에 대해서 쓰인다 **leading** 다른 사람의 선두에 선다는 뜻이 우세하다 **foremost** 다른 것〔사람〕을 제쳐놓고 첫째로 나선다는 뜻 **capital** 같은 종류의 것들 가운데 수위에 선다는 뜻

¶ 주요한 작가 leading〔prominent〕 writers // 금주의 주요한 행사 main events of the week // 주요한 역할을 하다 play a prominent part // 주요하지 않다 be unimportant ; be nonessential // 한국의 주요 관광 명소는 어디입니까 What is the major tourist attractions in Korea ?
— 경기 종목 the main events《of today》 **— 도시** major〔principal〕 cities **— 목적** the main object **—부** the principal part ; the head and front **— 산물** staple products ; the leading products《of Korea》 **— 산업** key industries **— 성분** the main〔principal〕 ingredients **— 수입품** the staple for import **— 수출품** chief〔principal〕 exports **—역** main〔principal〕 stations **— 원인** main cause〔reason〕 **— 인물** a central figure **—점** the main point
주워내다 take out ; pick put ; single〔sort〕 out ; select ¶ 주워넣다 pick up and put in // 나쁜 것들을 주워냈다 He took out the bad ones. // 돈을 호주머니 속에 주워넣었다 He picked up the money on the floor and put it in his pocket.
주워담다 pick up〔gather up〕 and put〔stuff〕 in ¶ 그녀는 흩어진 성냥 개비를 상자에 다시 주워담았다 She picked up the scattered matches and put them back into the box.
주워대다 enumerate glibly ; mention all sorts of things ¶ 거짓말을 주워대다 make up lies
주워듣다 overhear ; pick up《a bit of information》 ; learn of ; get wind of ¶ 남한테 주워들은 지식 knowledge picked up from others // 남한테서 이야기를 주워듣다 pick a story up from others
주워먹다 pick up and eat ; grab a bite to eat ¶ 돌아다니며 주워먹다 go around pecking
주워모으다 gather up ; collect ; rake up ; scrape up ¶ 여기저기서 주워모아 만원을 만들었다 I have scraped together a sum of ten thousand *won*.
주워섬기다 chatter〔rattle on, spiel, shoot off one's mouth, carry tales〕 about all sorts of things ; give an endless spiel on everything one knows
***주위 周圍** [언저리] the circumference ; the girth ; [환경] the surroundings ; environment ; [부근] the environs ; the vicinity ; the neighborhood ; 〚기하〛 a periphery ¶ 주위의 surrounding ; attendant // 읍의 주위 the environs of a town // 주위의 사람들 those around one ; one's close associates ; those close to one ; one's surroundings // 주위의 사정 circumstances ; surroundings ; environment (환경) // 주위를 재다 girt // 주위에 울을 치다 fence around《a house》// 이 호수는 주위가 얼마나 되나 What is the circumference of this lake ? // 주위가 약 14마일 된다 The lake is about fourteen miles in circumference. // 저 친구는 주위 사람들이 싫어한다 He is hated by his surroundings.
주위 主位 the head〔top〕 place ; the main〔leading〕 position
주유 周遊 a tour ; a round trip **—하다** tour ; make a round trip ; go on a tour ; take a pleasure trip ¶ 세계를 주유하다 make a trip around the world
주유 舟遊 boating ; a cruise ⇨ 뱃놀이
주유 注油 oiling ; lubrication ; [급유] oil supply **—하다** oil ; lubricate ; [급유] fill ; feed ¶ 한번은 그 영화 배우가 주유소에서 직접 자기 차에 주유하는 것을 보았다 I once saw the movie star gassing up his car personally at a filling station.
—기(器) a lubricator **—소** an oil〔a gasoline〕 station ; a filling station ; a service station
주육 酒肉 wine and meat ; wine and some eatables
주은 主恩 [임금의] royal benevolence ; the favors of one's lord ; [주인의] one's master's favor ; [신의] the grace of God
***주음 主音** [음악] the keynote ; the dominant note ; the tonic
주의 主意 [요지] the point ; a gist ; a tenor ; [목적] an object ; a purpose ; [의미] the main meaning〔purport〕 ¶ 주의적 volitional
—론 〚철학〛 voluntarism
주의 主義 a principle ; a doctrine ; a theory ; an ism ; a cause ; [방침] a policy ;

a rule ; a line ; a system ; a basis ¶ 주의가 있는〔없는〕 사람 a man of principle〔no principle〕// 근본의 주의 a guiding〔an underlying〕 principle // 주의로서 on principle ; as a matter of principle // 주의를 위해서 죽다 die for one's cause ; sacrifice one's life to one's principle // 주의를 굽히다 deviate from one's principles // 주의를 지키다 be true〔live up〕 to one's principles // 주의에 의해서 행동하다 act on principle // …을 주의로 하고 있다 make it principle to《do》// 주의가 없다 He is unprincipled. // 주의에 반한다 It is against one's principle. // 그 학교는 돈벌이 주의이다 That school is a money making enterprise. // 나는 돈을 빌리거나 빌려주지 않는 주의이다 I have always made it a principle never to borrow nor to lend money.

감각— sensationalism 개관— objectivism 공화— republicanism 비관— pessimism

*주의 注意 ① [주목] attention ; notice ; heed —하다 pay attention〔heed〕 to ; notice ; heed ; attend to ; take note of ; [귀를 기울이다] listen to ¶ 주의하여 attentively ; with attention // 주의할 만한 noteworthy ; significant ; remarkable // 주의를 끌다 attract〔draw, engage〕《a person's》 attention // 주의를 환기하다 call《a person's》 attention《to》; bring《a matter》 to《a person's》 notice // 주의를 딴 곳으로 쏠게 하다 divert《a person's》 attention from《a matter》

② [조심] (a) care ; watchfulness ; caution ; [경고] (a) warning —하다 take care ; have a care ; be careful《of, about》; be watchful《of, against》; look out for ; guard《against》; [경고하다] warn《a person》 against ; caution《a person》 against ¶ 주의 깊은 careful ; cautious ; watchful ; wary ; gingerly // 주의하여 carefully ; with care ; warily ; gingerly ; cautiously // 주의가 부족한 careless ; negligent // 건강에 주의하시오 Take care〔Be careful〕 of your health. // 길을 횡단할 때는 차에 주의하시오 When you cross a street, look out for cars. // 계집애는 주의하여 키우지 않으면 안된다 Girls should be reared with great care. // 한마디 주의하고 싶다 I should like to give you a word of caution. // 나쁜 친구들에 조심하라고 그에게 주의시켰다 I warned〔cautioned〕 him against evil companions. // 기차에 주의 [게시] Beware of the train. // 외투나 우산에 주의 Not responsible for overcoats and umbrellas. // 모조품 있음 등록 상표에 주의 [광고] Look out for our trademark, avoid〔beware of〕 imitations. // 개천에 주의하시오 Mind the ditch. // 먹는 것에 주의하고 있니 Do you watch what you eat?

③ [충고] advice ; suggestion —하다 advise ; counsel ; suggest ¶ 잠깐 주의 말씀드립니다 Let me give you a piece of advice.

④ [흥미] interest —하다 be interested in ¶ 주의를 끌다 arouse interest // 그것은 지대한 주의를 끌고 있다 The event is arousing much interest.

— 기호 caution mark —력 attentiveness —보 『기상』 a《storm》 warning — 사항 suggestions ; hints —산만 distraction —서 notes ; instruction — 인물 a suspicious〔dangerous〕 character ; a person under observation〔the eyes of the police〕

주의 周衣 a Korean-styled overcoat ⇨ 두루마기

주의자 主義者 an ideologist

주익 主翼 the main plane (of an airplane)

주인 主人 [가장] the head〔master〕 of a family ; [남편] one's man ; one's husband ; [손님에 대하여] the host ; the hostess (여자) : [여관·음식점 따위의] the landlord ; the landlady (여자) ; the proprietor ; [고용주] an employer ; the master ; [물건의 주인] the owner《of goods》 ¶ 주인과 손님 host and guest // 주인과 하인 master and servant // 주인을 섬기다 serve one's master // 주인 노릇하다 act as host〔hostess〕; play host〔hostess〕// 주인인 체하다 assume a proprietary air

상점 — a shop keeper 여관 — an innkeeper ; a hotel keeper

주인 主因 a principal〔primary, leading〕 cause ; the prime factor ; the main reason ¶ 너의 실패의 주인은 태만에 있다 Your failure is mainly due to your negligence.

주인공 主人公 [가장] the head《of a family》; the master《of a house》; [소설·영화 따위의] a hero ; a heroine (여자)

주인집 主人— one's employer's〔master's〕 house ¶ 주인집에서 쫓겨나다 be out of one's master's favor ; be dismissed

주일 週日 a week ¶ 1주일 전의 오늘 today week // 다음 주일 next week ; the following week // 1주일 후의 내일 만납시다 I'll meet you tomorrow week.

주일 主日 the Lord's day ; a holiday ; the Sabbath (유태교의)

— 학교 a Sunday school

주일 駐日 ¶ 주일의 stationed〔resident〕 in Japan

— 미국 대사 the United States Ambassador to Japan — 한국 대사관 the Embassy of the Republic of Korea to Japan

주임 主任 the person in charge ; the head ; the chief ; the manager ¶ 주임을 명하다 put《a person》 in full charge《of a department》// 주임이다 He is in charge of a section. /He is the head of a section.

— 교사 the teacher in charge (of a

class) — **교수** a head professor ¶ 영어과 주임 교수 the chief instructor of English ; the head of the English department — **기사** the chief engineer

*__주입 注入__ pouring 《into》; [약 따위의] injection ; instilment ; [사상의] infusion ; instillation ; infiltration ; [공부 따위의] cramming **— 하다** pour〔put〕 into ; [약을] inject ; impregnate ; [고취하다] infuse 《a spirit into a person's mind》; instill a sentiment in 《a person》; implant 《a principle in a person's mind》; imbue 《a person with an idea》; [공부 따위를] cram

—식 cramming method of teaching **—식 교육** cramming education

주자 鑄字 type casting〔founding〕; [활자] a metal movable〔printing〕 type **— 하다** cast〔found〕 《metal types》

—소 a type foundry

주자 走者 [야구 따위에서] a runner ¶ 주자를 내보내다 send a runner 《to》

주자 奏者 a player 《of a musical instrument》

주장 主張 assertion ; contention ; maintenance ; [고집] insistence ; persistence ; [주창] advocacy ; [권리로서] a claim [견해] one's opinion ; one's doctrine **— 하다** assert ; maintain ; contend ; claim ; persist 《in》; insist 《on》; [창도하다] advocate ¶ 권리를 주장하다 assert one's rights ; insist on one's rights // 자기의 설을 주장하다 assert oneself ; stand on one's opinion ; stick to one's guns ; stick out for one's right // 산아 제한을 주장하다 advocate birth control // 자기 주장을 관철하다 carry〔gain〕 one's point ; have one's own way // 무죄를 주장하다 insist on one's innocence ; plead 《a person's》 innocence (변호사가) // 주장을 굽히다 compromise // 전쟁은 불가피하다고 주장하다 He maintains that war is inevitable.

—자 [권리의] a claimant ; [주의의] an advocate **자기 —** self-assertion ; assertiveness

주장 主將 the captain (경기단의) ; a chief general ; the commander-in-chief (군의)

*__주장 主掌__ [관장] charge ; management ; [담당자] 《the person, officer》 in charge **— 하다** take charge of ; have 《a matter》 in charge ¶ 사무를 주장하다 take charge of〔supervise〕 business affairs // 국정을 주장하다 administer the affairs of state // 이것은 그의 주장 사무이다 This is the work〔duty〕 in his charge.

주재 駐在 residence ; stay **— 하다** reside 《at, in》; be stationed 《at》; stay ¶ 주재의 resident 《at, in》

—국 the country of residence **—관** a resident officer〔official〕; an official〔officer〕 resident in a country **—원** [신문사의] a resident reporter **마닐라 — 한국 영사** the Korean Consul at Manila

주재 主宰 superintendence ; supervision **— 하다** superintend ; supervise ; preside over ; have control over ¶ …주재의 위원회 a committee under the presidency 《of》// …의 주재 하에 under the superintendence〔supervision, presidency〕 《of》// 회의를 주재하다 preside over a meeting // 김 박사가 주재하는 잡지 a magazine edited〔run, controlled〕 by Dr. *Kim*

—자 the chairman (회의의) ; the presiding officer (관청의)

주저 主著 one's main〔chief〕 (literary) work

*__주저 躊躇__ hesitation ; indecision ; vacillation **— 하다** hesitate ; waver ; falter ; vacillate ; be irresolute ; think twice 《about doing》; be hesitant ; hang back

> 참고 **hesitate** 아직 결심이 서지 않아 급속히 행동으로 옮길 수 없다 **falter** 용기가 결여되어 회의적으로 되다 **waver** 결심을 지속시킬 수 없어 어떻게 해야 할지 망설이다

¶ 주저하면서 hesitatingly ; falteringly ; reluctantly ; with hesitation // 주저하지 않고 without hesitation // 아무 주저 없이 without slightest hesitation // …함을 주저하지 않다 have no scruples 《about》; do not stick 《at》// 나는 주저하지 않고 …이라고 말한다 I have no hesitation in saying 《that》// 그것을 인정하는데 주저하지 않는다 I make no bones about admitting that. // 그는 목적을 관철하기 위해서는 어떤 일도 주저하지 않는다 He will stick〔stop〕 at nothing to gain his end. // 초대에 응할까 말까 다소 주저했다 I felt〔had〕 some hesitation in accepting the invitation.

주저롭다 be hard up ; be destitute 〔pressed, pinched, strained〕 《for》 ¶ 돈에 주저롭다 be hard up for money

주저리 a messy bundle ; a thing suspended〔hanging〕 in disorder

주저앉다 [털썩 앉다] sit down plump ; [정착하다] plant oneself down ; settle down ; [함몰하다] collapse ; crumble ¶ 의자에 털썩 주저앉다 sink〔drop〕 into a chair // 땅 바닥에 털썩 주저앉다 plump 〔flop〕 down on the ground // 지붕이 주저앉다 a roof caves〔falls〕 in // 그는 사직하려는 생각을 버리고 그 자리에 주저앉았다 He stayed on in his office and gave up the idea of resigning.

주저앉히다 [의자 따위에] force 《a person》 to sit down ; [못 떠나게] make 《a person》 stay on

주적거리다 [아는 체하다] show off piddling knowledge ; parade〔make a display of〕 one's ignorance ; be pedantic ; brag of insufficient learning ; [어린 아이가] toddle

주전 主戰 advocating war ; pro-war **— 하**

다 advocate war
—론 a pro-war argument ; advocacy of war ; jingoism ; war-mongering ¶ 주전론자 a war advocate ; a jingoist ; a war-monger — 투수 〖야구〗 the chief pitcher ; an ace hurler〔pitcher〕
주전 鑄錢 coinage ; mintage —하다 mint ; coin ; strike coin
주전거리다 snack between meals
주전부리 snacking between meals —하다 take a snack between meals
주전자 酒煎子 a (copper, brass) kettle ; a teakettle
— 주둥이〔뚜껑〕 the spout〔lid〕 of a kettle
주절 主節 〖문법〗 the main〔principal〕 clause
주절거리다 ⇨ 중얼거리다
주점 酒店 a wine shop ; a liquor store ; a grog shop ; a tavern ; a pub 《영·속》
주점 主點 the principal〔main〕 point ; an important point
주접 stunting ; abortion
—꾼〔뱅이〕 a troublesome drunkard ; a bad drunk ; a drunken brute
주접들다 get stunted〔blighted〕 ; be in bad shape ¶ 주접든 나락 stunted rice plants // 영양 부족으로 주접들다 be in bad shape through lack of nourishment
주접스럽다 《be》 greedy ; voracious ; ravenous ; starving ; gluttonous
주정 酒酊 disorderly conduct under the influence of liquor ; drunken rowdiness —하다 act in a drunken and disorderly way ; be a bad drunk
주정 酒精 alcohol ; spirits ; a hard liquor 《미》 ¶ 주정의 alcoholic ; spirituous
—계(計) an alcoholometer — 수준기 a spirit level — 음료 alcoholic beverages 〔drinks〕
주정 舟艇 a boat ; a craft
상륙용 — a landing craft
주정설 主情設 〖철학〗 emotionalism
주제 [몰골] mean attire ; seedy appearance ⇨ 주제꼴 ¶ 이런 주제로 남 앞에 나갈 수가 없다 I simply cannot appear before company looking like this. // 남자인 주제에 울다니 Be a man and stop crying!
*주제 主題 [주제목] the main〔principal〕 subject ; the subject matter ; [작품의] the theme ; the motif ¶ 주제의 subjective (주제목의) ; thematic (작품의) // 주제의 전개 thematic development // 한국의 시골 생활을 주제로 희곡을 쓰다 write a play based on the rural life of Korea
—가 a theme song
주제꼴 shabby〔humble, wretched〕 appearance〔looks〕 ¶ 주제꼴 사납다 have a shabby appearance ; be impertinent 〔cheeky〕 // 할줄 모르는 주제꼴에 무턱대고 좋아하다 be crazy about 《a thing》 at which he is poor hand ; be enthusiastic 《for a thing》 though a poor hand at it // 주제꼴 사납게 이래라 저래라한다 He has the effrontery to keep telling me what to do.
*주제넘다 《be》 forward ; cheeky ; smart-alecky ; saucy ; conceited ; impudent ; impertinent ; have the effrontery to ; put 《oneself》 forward ¶ 주제넘게 impertinently ; impudently ; presumptuously ; obtrusively // 주제넘은 놈 an impudent〔a saucy〕 fellow ; a conceited pup ; a snob ; a smartaleck // 주제넘은 계집애 a saucy girl ; a flapper // 주제넘게도 …하다 have the cheek〔impudence〕 to 《do》 // 주제넘은 말을 하다 talk fresh〔saucy〕 ; have a saucy tongue ; give cheek // 주제넘은 소리 마라 Don't say such saucy things. /None of your cheek〔impudence, lip〕. /Mind your own business. // 너는 10세의 소년으로서는 너무 주제넘다 You've got too much cheek for a boy of ten.
주조 主調 the keynote ; the dominant note
주조 酒造 brewing rice-wine —하다 brew
—업 the brewing industry —장 a brewery
*주조 鑄造 casting ; founding ; [화폐] minting ; mintage —하다 cast 《metal types》 ; found 《a bell》 ; mint〔coin〕 《money》 ; strike 《a coin》
—비 coinage charges —소 a foundry —업 foundry —인 a founder ; a caster —화폐 a metallic coin
주조 主潮 the main current ; the main tide ¶ 아시아 문명의 주조 the main current of Asian civilization
주조정실 主調整室 〖라디오·텔레비전〗 a master control room
주종 主從 employer and employee ; master and servant ; lord and retainer 〔vassal〕 ; the principal and subordinate
— 공생 〖생물〗 helotism — 관계 the relation between master and servant
주주 株主 a shareholder 《영》 ; a stockholder 《미》 ¶ 회사의 주주 stockholders in〔of〕 a company
—권 the voting right of stockholders — 명부 a stockholders' list — 배당금 dividends to the stockholders — 의결권 the voting right of stockholders — 총회 a general meeting of stockholders 개인〔법인〕 — an individual〔institutional〕 stockholder 대— a heavy stockholder 안정 — a strong stockholder
주중 駐中 ¶ 주중의 stationed〔resident〕 in China
— 한국 대사 the Korean Ambassador to China
주지 主旨 the general purport ; the main meaning ; the gist ; the point
주지 住持 the resident〔head〕 priest (of a Buddhist temple)

주지 周知 ¶ 주지의 well〔widely〕-known ; established ; known to all 〔everybody〕; patent to the world // 주지의 사실 a matter of common knowledge ; a well-known fact ; a fact patent to the public // 주지하는 바와 같이 as everybody knows ; as is generally known

주지육림 酒池肉林 a sumptuous repast 〔feast, banquet〕; "mountains of meat and lakes of wine"

주지주의 主知主義 intellectualism
—**자** an intellectualist

주차 駐箚 residence ; stay —**하다** reside 《in, at》; be stationed 《at》 ¶ 주차의 resident ; residing ; stationed ; accredited to // 미국 주차 프랑스 대사 the French Ambassador (accredited) to the United States // 동경 주차 한국 공사 the Korean Minister at Tokyo
—**관** a resident 《at》 —**지** diplomatic stations (외교관의)

*__주차 駐車__ parking —**하다** park 《a car》 ¶ 어디에 주차할 수 있습니까 Where can we park?
—**금지** "No Parking (Here)." [게시] —**미터** a parking meter —**위반** parking violation —**장** a parking place〔lot〕《미》; a car park 《영》

주착 主着 a definite view ; a fixed opinion
—**망나니**〔**바가지**〕 a wishy-washy〔indecisive, injudicious, indiscreet〕 person

주착없다 主着— (be) indecent ; immodest ; ungentlemanly ; have no definite opinion of one's own ; (be) wishy-washy ¶ 주착없이 말하다 talk senselessly 〔pointlessly〕; talk without rhyme〔reason〕 // 주착없는 짓을 하다 behave disgracefully

주찬 酒饌 food and drink ⇨ 주효(酒肴)

주찬 晝餐 lunch ; luncheon

주창 主唱 advocacy ; promotion —**하다** advocate ; promote ; pioneer ; advance ; set forth ¶ 김씨의 주창으로 at the instance of Mr. *Kim* // 평화를 주창하다 advocate peace
—**자** an advocate ; a promoter ; a prime mover ; an exponent ; a pioneer ; a standard-bearer

주철 鑄鐵 cast iron
—**소** an iron foundry〔works〕

주청 奏請 petitioning the king —**하다** petition the king 《for》

주체 a burden ; a bother ; a handful —**하다** cope with〔take care of〕 one's burden

주체 主體 the subject ; the main body ; [중심] the core ; the nucleus ; 〖법〗 the main constituent ¶ 주체의 〖철학〗 subjective // 주체적인〔으로〕 independent(ly) // 권리의 주체 the subject of rights // 운영의 주체 the central operating body
—**성** [주관] subjectivity ; subjecthood ; [독립성] autonomy ; independence ¶ 주체성을 확립하다 establish one's subjecthood —**세력** the main group〔stream〕 《of》

주체 酒滯 indigestion from〔caused by〕 drinking

주체궂다 ⇨ 주체스럽다

주체못하다 be unable to take care of 《one's trouble》; be hard to deal with ; have too many〔much〕; have more than enough ; (be) superabundant ¶ 그는 주체못할 만큼 돈이 많다 He has more than enough money〔more money than he knows what to do with〕. // 그는 너무 먹어서 주체를 못했다 He had such a full stomach that he could hardly take care of himself. // 은퇴한 이후로는 시간이 주체못할 정도로 많다 Ever since I retired, I have lots of time on my hands.

주체스럽다 be beyond one's capacity 〔control〕; be too much for one ; be hard to handle ; (be) unmanageable 〔unwieldy〕 ¶ 이 아이는 거칠어서 데리고 다니기가 주체스럽다 It is beyind me to take this wild child with me. // 그 워드프로세서는 너무나 많은 기능이 있기 때문에 나로서는 약간 주체스럽다 The word processer has got so many complicated functions it is a little bit more than I can handle.

주쳇덩어리 a thing〔person〕 that is hard to handle〔manage〕; "a real problem (on one's hands)" ¶ 집안의 주쳇덩어리 the black sheep of〔in〕 the family

주최 主催 auspices ; sponsorship —**하다** sponsor ¶ …의 공동 주최로 under the joint auspices 《of》 // 그 자선 바자는 A신문사 주최였다 The charity bazaar was held under the sponsorship of〔sponsored by〕 the A press. // 그 시합은 대한 테니스 협회 주최로 거행되었다 The contest was held under the auspices of the Korean Lawn Tennis Association.
—**국**〔**단체**〕 the host nation〔organization〕
—**자** the sponsor ; the promoter

주추 柱— a foundation〔base〕 stone ; a cornerstone ; [비유적] a (main) prop ; a support ¶ 국가의 주추 the main prop 〔cornerstone〕 of a state ; the pillar of a state

주축 主軸 the principal〔main〕 axis

*__주춤거리다__ shrink〔fall, hold〕 back ; flinch ; wince ; hesitate ; hang a leg ; shy 《at》; [당황] be at a loss ; be indecisive ¶ 주춤거리면서 hesitantly ; shrinkingly ; staggeringly ; waveringly // 살까 말까 주춤거리다 hesitate to buy // 무서워서 주춤거리다 shrink with fear // 뱀을 보자 잠시 주춤거렸다 On seeing the snake, he held back for a while.

주춤병 —病 dilatoriness ; balkiness ; inability to get things done

주춤주춤 hesitantly ; falteringly ; waveringly

주춧돌 柱— a foundation stone ; a footstone ; a cornerstone
주치 主治 having a patient in charge ; being in charge of the treatment of a patient
—의(醫) the physician in charge ; the attending physician ; the physician in attendance on 《a person》 ; [가정의] a family doctor ; one's private doctor — 효능 the chief virtue (of a medicine)
*주택 住宅 a (dwelling) house ; a residence ; housing 《총칭》 ¶ 주택용 건물 a residential building // 브라운 씨 주택 the Brown home 《미》 ; Mr. Brown's house 《영》 // 그 건물은 주택으로는 부적당하다 The building is not fit to live in. // 급속히 증가하는 인구에 주택을 공급한다는 것은 어려운 문제다 It is a difficult problem to provide housing for a rapidly increasing population.
—가 a residential street ¶ 문화주택가 modern living quarter — 공사 the Housing Corporation — 구역〔지구〕 a residential district〔quarter, section〕 ; uptown — 금융 금고 the Housing Loan Bank —난 a housing shortage ¶ 주택난으로 고생하다 suffer from scarcity of houses〔the housing shortage〕 — 문제 the housing problem —비〔수당〕 the housing expenses〔allowance, facilities〕 — 시설 residential problem —지 a residential section〔quarter〕 (of a town, city) — 행정〔정책〕 the housing administration〔policy〕 간이〔조립〕 — a prefabricated house ; a prefab 《미》 공영 — a city-built〔-owned〕 house 근로자용 — houses for the working class 모델 — a model dwelling 문화 — a modern dwelling 호화 — a luxurious〔deluxe〕 house〔mansion〕 ; a palatial mansion 한국 — 은행 the Korea Housing Bank
☞ ◖p. 1948◗
주토 朱土 red clay〔earth〕
주특기 主特技 one's principal accomplishment
주파 走破 —하다 run ; cover ¶ 3마일을 30분에 주파하다 cover〔run〕 three miles in half an hour
주파 周波 a cycle ; a wave ; periodicity ¶ 350 내지 550 사이클의 주파수로 방송하다 broadcast in the band〔frequency〕 of 350～550 cycles
—계 a frequency meter —대 a frequency band — 변조 〖방송〗 frequency modulation 《FM》 —수 frequency — 조정 amplitude modulation —(수) 증폭기〔변환기〕 a frequency amplifier〔changer, converter〕 장〔단, 전〕— a long 〔short, all〕 wave 가청 —수 〖전기〗 audible frequency ; audio frequency 《A. F., a. f.》 고〔저〕—수 high〔low〕 frequency
주판 籌板, 珠板 an abacus ¶ 주판을 잘 놓다 be clever with one's abacus // 주판으로 계산하다 reckon〔count〕 on an abacus
—알 counters ; beads (on the abacus)
주판을 놓다 관용 use〔work〕 the abacus
주포 主砲 the principal battery ; the main armament
주폭도 走幅跳 the running broad jump
주피터 [로마 신화의] Jupiter
주필 主筆 the chief editor ; the editor in chief
부— a subeditor 《영》 ; an associate editor 《미》
주필 朱筆 a vermilion-brush ; a brush used for writing in red ink ¶ 주필을 가하다 correct ; revise
주한 駐韓 ¶ 주한의 stationed〔resident〕 in Korea
— 미군 the U. S. Armed Forces in Korea — 외교 사절단 the diplomatic corps in Korea — 일본대사 Japanese Ambassador to Korea
주항 周航 circumnavigation ; sailing round —하다 sail round ; circumnavigate ¶ 세계를 주항하다 circumnavigate〔sail around〕 the globe
세계 — a voyage round the world ; a round-the-world trip
주항라 紬亢羅 sheer silk
주해 註解 a note ; an explanatory note ; an annotation ; a commentary ; a comment ; an exposition —하다 comment upon ; make notes upon ; annotate ¶ 주해를 단 책 an annotated edition // 주해가 붙은 annotated ; with notes
—서 a pony 《학생 속어》 ; a crib 《영》 —자 an annotator ; a commentator
주행 舟行 going by boat ; traveling by ship ; navigation —하다 go by boat ; sail along ; navigate
주행 走行 traveling ; covering —하다 travel 《from A to B》 ¶ 차의 주행 마일수를 조사하다 check the mileage of a car
— 거리 the distance covered 《in a given time》 ; [마일로 나타낸] mileage ; milage
주행 周行 ⇨ 주유(周遊)
주행 동물 晝行動物 a diurnal animal
주향 酒香 the aroma〔bouquet〕 of wine
주형 主刑 the principal penalty
주형 鑄型 a mold ; a cast ; [활자의] a matrix〔die〕 ¶ 주형을 뜨다 cast (a mold) // 주형에 붓다 pour into a mold
주호 酒豪 a hard〔heavy〕 drinker ; a tippler ; a bibber
주혼 主婚 officiating at a marriage —하다 officiate at a marriage
—자 the officiator at a wedding
주홍 朱紅 scarlet ; bright orange color
주화 鑄貨 coinage ; minting ; mintage ; coins —하다 coin ; mint ; strike coins
— 능력 minting capacity
주화론 主和論 advocacy of peace ; pacifism
—자 an advocate of peace ; a pacifist
주황 朱黃 orange color

주 택

단순한 「가옥, 주택」의 뜻으로는 보통 a house를 쓰고 가족 생활의 개념이 포함되면 home을 쓰는 것이 보통이다. 단, 미국에서는 home을 house와 같은 「가옥, 주택」의 뜻으로 쓰는 경우도 있다.

이밖에 거주하는 집(주소를 둔)의 뜻으로는 a residence(★ 실제로는 고급주택의 개념이 있음), a dwelling house로 쓰기도 한다.

① 주택의 종류

▶단독 주택 a detached house; an independent house (★ 두 채가 나란히 붙은 집 a duplex (house) ((미)), a semidetached house ((영)) / 단층집 house of [with] one story; one-storied [one-story] house / 이층집 house of [with] two stories; two-storied[two-story] house (★ ((영))에서는 storey를 쓴다. 특히 floor를 쓸 때 ((미))에서는 the first floor, the second floor로 쓰지만 ((영))에서는 the ground floor, the first floor로 쓴다.) / 목조 주택 a wooden house / 목골조 주택 a half-timbered house / 벽돌집 a brick house / 서구풍 주택 a Western-style house / 이동 주택 a mobile home[a camper, a trailer house, a motor home] / 공영(公營) 주택 public housing

▶집단 주택 town house / 주택 단지 a housing development; estate ((영)) / 아파트 단지 apartment complex / 공단 주택 public housing / 밀집가옥 cluster house / 주민회관 community house [room]

▶아파트 (전체) an apartment house; a block of flats ((영)) (★아파트 한 가구는 an apartment; flat ((영))) / 저급한 아파트 tenement (house) / (엘리베이터가 없는) 저층 아파트 walk-up ((미)) / (목욕탕과 침대가 딸린) 한 칸짜리 아파트 efficiency apartment; studio apartment / (침실·거실 겸용의) 한 칸짜리 아파트 bed-sitter ((영)) / 가구 딸린 아파트 furnished apartment / 고층 아파트 high-rise apartment / (정원이 딸린) 2, 3층의 아파트 garden apartment / 분양 아파트 co-op; coop; cooperative / 임대식 아파트 mansionette (★임대 아파트의 임대료는 rent, 부금은 deposit, 매매할 때의 웃돈 gift money, key money, premium, 계약금은 down payment)

▶아파트 관리인 superintendent; super ((미)); custodian; janitor / 관리비 maintenance cost [charge] / 공유 면적 common area / 베란다 balcony

▶부동산 중개소[인] real estate agency[agent]; realtor

▶맨션 mansion (★본래 개인의 대저택을 가리킨다.) / (분양용) 고급 맨션 condominium; condo ((영))

▶전셋집 a house for rent; rental house; to let ((영)) / 분양 주택 a house built for sale / 규격화된 주택 tract house / 세입자 boarder; lodger / 불법입주자 squatter / 차용자 tenant

② 가옥 구조

▶현관 entrance / (입구의) 돌출부 porch / 현관문 the front door / 현관안의 홀 (entrance) hall

▶응접실 parlor; drawing room (★ 대저택 외에는 응접실이 따로 없고 일반 가정에서는 거실에서 손님을 맞이함)

▶거실 living room; family room; sitting room ((영)) / 침실 bedroom / 어린이 방 children's room; nursery / 서재 study; library / 식당 dining room / 벽장 closet

▶주방 kitchen (★개수대·조리대 등을 갖춘 간이 부엌은 kitchenette)

▶욕실 bathroom / 욕조 bathtub / 샤워실 shower room / 수세식 변기 toilet / 세면대 washbowl(washbasin ((영))) (★ 수세식 변기는 flush toilet, 재래식은 cesspool)

▶ 도난 경보기 burglar alarm / 주거 면적 living space / 주택 사정 housing situation / 주택 부족 housing shortage

---

주효 酒肴 food and wine; viands and beverages; liquor and some eatables 〔side dishes〕; [술안주] appetizers served with drinks; an accompaniment for wine ¶ 주효로 대접하다 offer ((a person)) food and drink; entertain ((a person)) at a repast // 약주 주효로선 최고다 It is a capital accompaniment of rice wine.

주효 奏效 [성공] fruition; success; [유효] efficacy **—하다** succeed; take effect; bear fruit; prove effective; be effectual〔fruitful, successful〕; tell; work well ¶ 그의 시도는 주효하지 않았다 His attempt proved ineffectual. // 이 위협은 군중에게 크게 주효했다 This threat had a noticeable effect on the crowd.

주휴 週休 a weekly holiday

주흥 酒興 conviviality; merrymaking 〔joviality, merriment, hilarity〕 over one's cups ¶ 주흥에 겨워 under the influence of wine; heated by wine // 주흥을 돋다 heighten〔increase〕 conviviality //

주홍을 깨뜨리다 wetblanket〔dampen〕 conviviality // 그 일 때문에 모처럼의 주홍이 깨지고 말았다 That brought a chill over the merriment.

죽¹ ten pieces ¶ 접시 한 죽 (a set of) ten plates

죽² ① [차례로] in a row〔line〕 ¶ 차례로 죽 서다 stand in a line // 그들은 그 책들을 죽 늘어 놓았다 They ranged the volumes line upon line. // 죽 나가시오 Keep straight on. // 그들은 죽 늘어섰다 They made an array. // 그는 죽 불행을 만났다 He met with a succession of disasters.
② [계속해서] all during ; throughout ; all the time ¶ 아침부터 죽 all through the morning // 여기 와서 부터 죽 여기서 살고 있다 I have lived here ever since I came. // 그는 3일 동안 죽 지각했다 He has been late for three days in a row. // 그는 역까지 죽 달렸다 He ran all the way to the station. // 지금까지 죽 기다렸습니다 I have been waiting for you all this while. // 그 논문을 죽 읽어봤다 I have read the article all the way through. // 그 전세 계약은 10년을 죽 유효하다 The lease runs for ten years.
③ [멀리] far ; away ¶ 죽 저멀리 far away from here ; far in the distance ; way down there 《미·속》 // 죽 뒤처지다 lag far behind // 죽 찾아보다 search far and wide
④ [찢다] with a rip ¶ 손수건을 죽 찢다 rip a handkerchief // 봉투를 죽 찢다 tear open an envelope // 책에서 한 페이지를 죽 찢어내다 rip a page out of a book
⑤ [처지다] droopingly ¶ 그의 머리가 쿠션 쪽으로 죽 처졌다 His head slowly sagged down onto the cushion.
⑥ [완전히] recede〔retreat〕 completely 〔all down the line, readily, easily〕 ¶ 큰물이 죽 빠졌다 The flood receded completely. // 조수가 죽 빠져서 해변가의 험한 물구덩이를 조사할 수 있었다 As the tide receded, we were able to explore the rocky pools on the beach. // 기운이 죽 빠져버렸다 I am utterly exhausted.
⑦ [대강] quickly ; roughly ; briefly ¶ 죽 훑어보다 look〔glance, run〕 through ; look over 《a letter》 // 그 책을 대강 죽 보다 run〔skim〕 through the book

죽 粥 (rice-) gruel ; porridge ; hot cereal ; pap ¶ 죽을 끓이다 cook hot cereal // 죽을 먹다 eat gruel // 죽 끓일 것도 없다 cannot afford even to make porridge ; live in sad poverty // 죽도 못먹을 지경이 되다 be reduced to a crust // 그것은 식은 죽먹기다 That's nothing. /This sort of thing is a cinch.

죽사발이 웃음이요 밥사발이 눈물이라 속담 Better a dinner of herbes where love is than a stalled ox where hate is.

죽 竹 bamboo

죽간 竹竿 a bamboo pole

죽기 竹器 bamboo-ware ; bamboo-dish 〔-vessel〕

죽는소리 ① [불평·비탄] a doleful complaint ; a grievance ; a plaintive〔feeble〕 protestation ; grumble **一하다** make complaints ; complain 《about》 ; whine ; express discontent ; bemoan〔lament〕 one's hard lot〔fate〕 ; dwell on grievances ¶ 그들은 하고 싶은 것을 할 틈이 없다고 죽는소리한다 They constantly complain that they cannot find time to do what they want to do. // 죽는소리 하지 마라 Never say die ! /Stop talking defeat.
② [비명] a shriek ; a scream ; a screech ¶ 죽는소리를 지르다 utter a shriek ; screech // 아파서 죽는소리를 지르다 give a cry of pain ; shriek with pain

†죽다 ① [사망] die ; pass away ; be gone ; leave the world ; [아어] join the majority ; go to one's eternal home ; sink into the grave ; return to Mother Earth ; [숨지다] expire ; breathe one's last ; [목숨을 잃다] be killed ; [전쟁·사고 따위로] lose one's life ; suffer death ; meet one's death ; [목숨을 버리다] lay down one's life ; give up one's life ; throw away one's life ; yield one's life ; [자살하다] kill oneself ; commit suicide ; take one's own life ; do away with oneself
¶ 죽은 친구〔개〕 a dead friend〔dog〕 // 죽은 아버지 the deceased father // 죽은 사람 the deceased ; a dead person ; dead persons // 죽어 있다 be dead ; be lifeless ; have no life ; be inanimate (생기가 없다) // 죽느냐 사느냐의 문제 a matter of life and death // 죽도록 to the end〔last〕 ; to the last hour of one's life // 죽을 각오로 at the risk of one's life // …으로 죽다 die of ; die from ; die with // 수치〔기쁨, 슬픔〕의 나머지 죽다 die with shame〔joy, grief〕 // 목매어 죽다 die by hanging // 물에 빠져 죽다 be drowned // 얼어〔타〕 죽다 be frozen〔burned〕 to death // 굶어 죽다 be starved to death // 원인 모르게 죽다 die from some unknown cause // 철도 사고로 죽다 be killed in a railway accident // 전쟁에서 죽다 be killed in the war // 음독하여 죽다 kill oneself by taking poison // 재직 중에 죽다 die in office // 바다〔집〕에서 죽다 die at sea〔in one's bed, a natural death〕 // 빚을 많이 지고 죽다 die greatly in debt // 30세에 죽다 die at (the age of) thirty〔thirty years of age, when he was thirty〕 // 젊어서〔늙어서〕 죽다 die young 〔old〕 // 곧 죽다 die instantly // 갑자기 죽다 die suddenly // 거지가 되어 죽다 die a beggar // 미쳐 죽다 die a lunatic // 무참히 죽다 die〔meet with〕 a violent death // 편안히 죽다 die an easy death // 웃으면서 죽다 greet〔face, meet〕 one's death with a smile // 술을 너무 마시고 죽다 drink oneself to death // 죽을 지경이다 be in a tight position ; be in a corner // 그들은 그 여자

를 죽은 것으로 쳤다 They had given her up for lost〔dead〕. // 그는 죽은 것이나 같다 He is almost〔as good as〕 dead. // 그는 죽은 것처럼 거기 누워 있었다 He lay there like one dead. // 그는 죽어가고 있다 He is almost to die〔dying, at the point of death〕. // 그 노인의 친구는 이미 많이 죽어 버렸다 The old man outlasted many of his friends. // 그는 아들이 출세하는 것을 보고 죽었다 He lived to see his son rise in the world. // 더워서 죽겠다 The heat is killing me. // 그가 보고 싶어 죽겠다 I am dying to see him. // 심심해서 죽겠다 I am bored to death. // 아이고 죽겠다 My, it's murder ! // 그녀가 보고 싶어 죽겠다 I'm dying to see her. // 불경기 때문에 죽을 지경이다 This recession is killing me. /This recession is murder.
② [초목이] wither ; die ; perish ; be blasted (서리 따위로) ¶ 죽은 잎 withered〔dead, dried〕 leaves // 이 나무는 죽었다 This tree is dead.
③ [기(氣)가] be dejected〔dispirited, crestfallen〕 ; be out of spirits ; have no life ; be lifeless ; [풀기가] be thin of starch ¶ 죽은 빛 a dull〔drab〕 color // 그 당시 그는 풀이 죽어 있었다 He was in low spirits then.
④ [멎다] run down ; stop ¶ 시계가 죽었다 The clock has run down〔stopped〕.
⑤ [꺼지다] go out ; die out ¶ 죽어가는 불 a dying fire // 불이 거의 죽었다 The fire is nearly out.
⑥ [야구에서] be (put) out ; [장기·바둑에서] be captured〔lost〕
죽고 보면 여섯 자 [속담] Six feet of earth make all men equal.
죽기가 설운 것이 아니라 늙는 것이 섧다 [속담] Fear of death is worse than death itself.
죽어 보아야 저승을 알지 [속담] Nothing venture, nothing win.
죽어 영 이별은 문 앞마다 한다 [속담] Death is the black camel that kneels before every door. /Every door may be shut but death's door.
죽어야 명(名)이 난다 [속담] A fair death honours the whole life.
죽은 자는 말이 없다 [속담] Death men tell no tales.

죽담 a stone wall
죽대 〖식물〗 a Solomon's-seal ; Polygonatum lasianthum (학명)
죽데기 side-splits from whole logs
죽도 竹刀 a bamboo knife〔sword〕
죽도화나무 〖식물〗 a Japan globeflower ; Kerria japonica (학명) ; a yellow rose (속명)
죽떼다 ⇨ 죽지떼다
죽력 竹瀝 〖한의〗 tabasheer (juice from heated green bamboo, used as medicine)
—고 a tabasheer poultice
죽렴 竹簾 [대발] bamboo blinds ; a bamboo hanging-screen
—지우 a childhood friend ; a friend from childhood ; an old chum ; an old playmate
죽림 竹林 a bamboo grove
죽마 竹馬 a child's hobbyhorse ; stilts
죽머리 the shoulder one puts an archer's bow to
죽물 粥— thin porridge〔gruel〕
죽바디 shank beef
죽방울 ① [장난감] a diabolo ② [도구] a tool for making purse strings
죽비 竹扉 [사립문] a bamboo gate
죽살이 (a matter of) life and death ¶ 죽살이치다 make desperate〔frantic〕 efforts
죽세공 竹細工 a bamboo work ; bambooworking ; bamboo ware
—사(師) a bamboo-ware maker
죽순 竹筍 a bamboo shoot〔sprout〕 ¶ 우후죽순같이 나오다 spring〔crop〕 up like mushrooms after rain
죽술 粥— a few spoonfuls of porridge ¶ 죽술이나 먹고 살다 live a meager life
죽어라하고 [필사적으로] desperately ; frantically ; [목숨을 걸고] for life ; [전력을 다해] as hard as one can ; with all one's might
죽어지내다 live under oppression ; live a life of subjugation ; live in constant fear ¶ 그는 아내 앞에 죽어지낸다 He lives under his wife's thumb. // 우리는 그 선생 앞에서 죽어지냈다 The teacher was very oppressive to us.
죽여버리다 do away with 《a person》 ; do 《a person》 in ; put 《a person》 to death ¶ 죽여버린다고 위협하다 threaten 《a person》 with death
죽엽 竹葉 a bamboo leaf
죽은목숨 ① [살 길 없는] a living corpse ; a life as good as dead ; a person beyond the realm of hope〔help〕 ; a hopeless case ; a person as good as dead
② [자유를 잃은] a person living at another's mercy ; an enslaved life
죽을둥살둥 desperately ; frantically ; tooth and nail ¶ 죽을둥살둥 싸우다 fight against 《enemy》 tooth and nail // 죽을둥살둥 일을 하고 있다 He is now working away like one possessed.
죽을병 —病 a fatal〔mortal〕 disease ¶ 죽을병에 걸리다 suffer from a mortal disease
죽을뻔살뻔 with bare life ; for one's (dear) life ; by the skin of one's teeth ; at the peril of one's life ; within an inch of one's life ; having a close shave (with death) ¶ 죽을뻔살뻔 내빼다 escape with bare life ; escape life and limb ; escape by the skin of one's teeth ; have a narrow escape
죽을상 —相 an agonized look ; a frantic

〔desperate〕 look

죽을힘 ¶ 죽을힘을 다하여 desperately ; frantically // 죽을힘을 다하여 싸우다 fight a desperate fight ; fight to the death

*죽음 death ; decease ; demise (높은 사람의) ¶ 죽음의 공포 the fear of death // 죽음으로 속죄하다 atone for 《a crime》 with death // 죽음에 직면하다 face death ; be face to face〔be faced〕 with death // 죽음을 각오하다 prepare for death ; be ready to die // 죽음을 면하다 escape death // 죽음을 재촉하다 hasten one's death // 개죽음을 하다 die a dog's death ; die to no purpose〔avail〕 // 비열한 죽음을 하다 die an ignoble death // 죽음은 때를 가리지 않는다 Death keeps no calendar. // 죽음은 쉽고 삶은 어렵다 It is harder to live than to die. // 죽음은 평등하다 All are equal in the grave.

죽음의 재 관용 radioactive dust〔ashes〕 ; atomic dust ; fallout

죽의 장막 竹—帳幕 the Bamboo Curtain

†죽이다 ① [살해] kill ; slay ; murder (모살) ; slaughter ; butcher (도살) ; put 《a person》 to death ; take 《a person's》 life ; put an end to another's life ; make 〔do〕 away with 《a person》 ¶ 목졸라 죽이다 strangle 《a person》 to death // 때려죽이다 beat 《a person》 to death // 독으로 죽이다 poison 《a person》 to death // 사람을 죽이다 kill〔slay, murder〕 a man // 소를 죽이다 butcher 〔slaughter〕 a cow // 죽인다고 협박하다 threaten 《a person's》 life // 죽이려고 하다 attempt 《a person's》 life ; make an attempt on 《a person's》 life // 움직이면 죽인다 Stir a step and you're a dead man.

② [억제] hold〔keep〕 back ; restrain ; suppress ; repress ¶ 숨을 죽이고 with bated breath // 감정을 죽이다 suppress 〔repress〕 one's feelings // 숨을 죽이다 hold one's breath // 발소리를 죽이다 muffle one's steps // 적의 기세를 죽이다 put a damper on enemy's spirit

③ [잃다] suffer the death〔loss〕 of ¶ 전쟁에 아이를 죽이다 lose a son in the war // 나무를 죽이다 blight〔blast, destroy, let wither〕 a plant // 병으로 소를 죽였다 He lost a cow from disease.

④ [멈추다] stop ; let go out ¶ 엔진을 죽이다 stop a motor // 불을 죽이다 put out a fire〔light〕

죽일 놈 Rascal ! ; Wretch ! ; S. O. B. ! ¶ 이 죽일 놈아 Damn you ! /Be damned to you. // 그 놈 죽일 놈이군 He is a rascal, indeed.

죽자꾸나하고 neck or nothing〔naught〕 ; desperately ; frantically ; as if one's life depends on it ¶ 죽자꾸나하고 헤엄치다 swim for one's life // 죽자꾸나하고 해봐 Go at it hammer and tongs〔heart and soul, tooth and nail〕.

죽장 竹杖 a bamboo cane〔stick〕

—망혜(芒鞋) a bamboo cane and straw shoes

죽장구 竹— a bamboo-bodied drum

죽장기 —將棋 a poor chess player ; a poor hand at chess ¶ 죽장기를 두다 play a poor hand at it

죽재 竹材 bamboo

죽젓개 粥— a porridge-stirrer ; a ladle

죽젓개질 interfering ; getting in the way ; stirring up trouble —하다 interfere ; get in the way ; interrupt

죽죽, 쭉쭉 ① [줄줄이] in rows〔lines〕 ; row after row ; in streaks ¶ 줄을 죽죽 긋다 draw line after line // 흰줄이 죽죽 그어져 있다 be banded with white strips ; be streaked with white

② [거침없이] briskly ; directly ; rapidly ; in sheets ; in showers ¶ 죽죽 내리 읽다 read straight on // 죽죽 나아가다 push on ; advance rapidly ; go ahead at a rapid space // 비가 죽죽 내린다 The rain comes down in sheets.

③ [갈기갈기] into shreds ; in〔to〕 pieces ¶ 죽죽 찢다 tear to pieces

죽지 a shoulder blade ; a scapula ; the shoulder joint

날갯— the joint of a wing 어깻— the shoulder joint 팔— the upper arm

죽지 떼다 ① [활을 쏘고] lower one's shoulder after shooting an arrow ② [배후를 믿고] act overbearing ; be imperious ; be stuck-up ; put on airs

죽창 竹窓 a window of bamboo latticework

죽창 竹槍 a bamboo spear

죽책 竹柵 a bamboo palisade〔stockade, fence〕

죽총 竹叢 a bamboo bush〔thicket〕

죽치 goods sold by the tens〔dozens〕 ; wholesale coarse products ; massproduced goods

죽치기 wholesale (trade) ¶ 죽치기로 사다〔팔다〕 buy〔sell〕 wholesale

죽치다 live in seclusion ; shut oneself up in ; confine oneself in 《one's house》 ; remain indoors ¶ 집안에 죽치고 있다 remain〔stay, be〕 indoors ; keep〔be shut up in〕 the house // 시골에서 죽치고 지내다 lead a secluded life in the country

죽침 竹針 a bamboo〔knitting〕 needle

죽통 竹筒 a bamboo tube

죽통 粥筩[구유] a feeding trough

죽피 竹皮 bamboo sheath

— 방석 a cushion made of bamboo sheaths

준 準 『인쇄』 ⇨ 교정(校正)

준- 準 quasi- ; semi- ; associate

—결승 a semifinal —독립국 a quasi-sovereign state —동사 『문법』 verbals —사법적 권력 quasi-judicial power —현행범 a quasi-flagrant offense —회원 an associate member

준거 準據 [따름] conformity ; [전거]

authority cited ; standard referred to —하다 be based upon ; follow (the lines of) ; conform to ; be made uniform with ¶ 준거하여 in conformity《to》; in accordance《with》; on the authority《of》// …의 준거하는 바를 밝히다 give the authority《of》// 그 주장이 무엇에 준거하느냐는 밝히지 않고 있었다 Authority for that statement was not named. // 준거할 규정이 없다 We have no rule to go by.

준걸 俊傑 a man of eminent ability ; a great man ; a hero

준결승(전) 準決勝(戰) a semifinal game ¶ 준결승전 출전 선수 a semifinalist // 준결승전에 진출하다 go on to〔play in〕the semifinals

준골 俊骨 an eminent physique ; a man of eminent physique〔ability〕

준공 竣工 completion (of a construction work) —하다 be completed〔finished〕 ¶ 준공에 가깝다 be nearing completion ; be near completion
—기 the time of completion —식 the ceremony for the completion《of a building》

준교사 準敎師 an assistant teacher

준금치산 準禁治產 quasi-incompetence
—자 a quasi-incompetent (person)

준급 準急 ⇨ 준급행 (열차)

준급행(열차) 準急行(列車) a semi-express (train) ; a local express《미》

준돈 [돈치기의] the given coin to hit

준동 蠢動 wriggling ; squirming ; despicable acts ; activities —하다 wriggle ; squirm ; [책동] be active ¶ 간첩〔불평 분자〕의 준동 activities of the espionage agents〔discontented elements〕

준득준득 —하다 (be) sticky ; resilient and glutinous ; tough and tenacious

준령 峻嶺 a high and steep peak ; a dangerous high range

준례 準例 a precedent ; a model case〔example〕

준론 峻論 a serious〔rigorous〕discussion ; a sharp〔stringent〕criticism

준마 駿馬 a swift〔fleet〕horse〔steed〕; an excellent horse

준말 a shortened word ; an abbreviation

준물 俊物 a man of eminent ability〔personality〕; a great character

준법 峻法 stringent law

준법 遵法 lawabiding ; obeying the law
— 정신 the lawabiding spirit ¶ 준법 정신을 앙양하다 promote lawabiding spirit
— 투쟁 a lawabiding struggle

준별 峻別 a sharp〔nice〕distinction ; a discrimination —하다 make a sharp distinction《between A and B》

준봉 峻峰 a steep peak ; a lofty mountain

준봉 遵奉 observance —하다 observe ; obey ; follow ; adhere to ; conform to ; abide by ; live up to ¶ 국법을 준봉하다 obey〔abide by〕the laws of the country ⇨ 준수(遵守)

*준비 準備 preparation (s) ; (preliminary) arrangements ; readiness ; [예비] provision ; reserve —하다 prepare ; arrange《for》; provide for ; make preparation〔arrangement〕《for》; get ready《for》; [기계를] gear ¶ 군대의 전투 준비 preparation of troops for battle // 미리 준비한 연설 a set speech // 준비하지 않았던 연설 (즉석의) an extempore〔off-the-cuff〕speech ; ad-libbing // 준비의 preparatory ; preparative ; preliminary ; reserve〔spare〕(예비의) // 준비 없는 unprepared ; offhand // 준비된 be ready ; be prepared《for》; be all set《미·구》// 만반의 준비를 하다 get everything in readiness《for》// 식사 준비를 하다 provide (for) a dinner ; get a dinner ready // 시험 준비를 하다 prepare (oneself) for an examination ; make preparations for an examination // 여행 준비로 바쁘다 be busy getting ready for one's journey // 준비됐느냐 Are you ready? // 준비 다 됐다 Everything is ready. // 이것으로 준비가 됐다 Thus the stage is set for it. // 식사 준비가 다 됐습니다 The meal is ready. // 준비하는 데 시간이 얼마나 걸리느냐 What time will be required for preparation? // 여기는 대학 입학을 준비하는 학교입니다 This school is fitting students for college. // 만일을 위해서 준비해 두어야 한다 We must provide against a rainy day. // 곧 준비된다 It won't take me long to get ready.
— 공사 preparatory work — 교육 preparatory education ; [시험의] cramming —금 a reserve fund — 기간 a preparatory〔breaking-in〕period — 단계 a preparatory stage — 서면 〖법〗 preparatory documents —실 an outfit room ; a retiring〔dressing〕-room — 완료 (We are) All set (to go). — 운동 warming up — 위원 a committee of arrangements ; an arrangement committee 시험 — preparations for examinations 여행 — preparations for a trip

준비 은행 準備銀行 a reserve bank
연방 — the Federal Reserve Bank

준사 俊士 a man of eminent ability ; a great man ; a talented man ; a boy wonder《미》¶ 그 학교는 수많은 준사를 배출했다 The school has turned out many men of talent.

준사관 準士官 a warrant officer

준사원 準社員 a junior employee ; an associate member

준설 浚渫 dredging —하다 dredge《a river》
—기 a dredger ; a dredging machine ; a dredge —선 a dredge(r) ; a dredging boat — 인부 a dredger — 작업 dredging work〔operations〕

준세대 準世帶 a quasi-household

준속사 準速射 semi-rapid firing〔fire〕

준수 遵守 observance ; compliance ; conformity —하다 observe ; adhere to ; abide by ; conform to ; follow ; obey ¶ 준수하는 사람 an observer // 법률의 준수 law-observance // 법률을 잘 준수하는 국민 a law-abiding people // 법률〔규칙〕을 준수하다 observe the law〔rules〕// 저희는 정찰제를 엄격히 준수합니다 We go strictly by the price tag.

준수 俊秀 superior talent and elegance —하다 excel in talent and elegance ; (be) superior and refined ¶ 준수한 prominent ; outstanding ; distinguished

준순 逡巡 shrinking back ; recoiling ; hesitation —하다 shrink back ; recoil ; hesitate ; be irresolute

준승 準繩 a carpenter's ink line ; a marking line ; a plumb line ; [기준 법칙] a fixed rule ; a fixed form ; a norm ; a rule (of conduct)

준어 俊魚 [준치] a kind of shad

준엄 峻嚴 strictness ; sternness ; rigidity —하다 (be) severe ; rigorous ; strict ; stern ; stringent ; relentless ¶ 준엄한 태도 a stern attitude // 준엄한 검열 the strict censorship 《of movie films》// 준엄한 얼굴을 하다 look stern

준열 峻烈 severity ; rigor ; sternness —하다 (be) rigorous ; stern ; severe ; relentless ; ruthless ; scathing ¶ 준열한 논고 a scathing address〔argument〕// 준열한 비판 sharp criticism

준용 準用 —하다 apply 《provisions, rules》 correspondingly 《to》 ; apply with necessary modifications ¶ 이 경우에는 …에 관한 본조의 규정을 준용한다 The provision of this article with respect to 《the penal code》 shall apply in this case.

준우승 準優勝 a victory in the semifinals —자 a winner of the semifinals

준위 准尉 a sub-officer ; a warrant officer 《W. O.》

*준장 准將 a brigadier general (육군) ; a commodore (해군) ; an air-commodore (공군)

준재 俊才 [사람] a brilliant〔talented〕 man ; a man of talent ; [재주] eminent ability〔talent〕

준절 峻截, 峻切 [높고 험함] precipitousness ; steepness ; [위엄] sternness ; strictness ; rigidity ; dignity —하다 [높고 험함] (be) steep ; precipitous ; [위엄] stern ; strict ; rigid ; dignified

준족 駿足 [말] a swift horse ; [사람] a swift runner ; a talented man ⇨ 준재(俊才)

준준결승 準準決勝 a quarter-final (game)

준지 準紙 [교정쇄] corrected pageproof

준치 〖물고기〗 a kind of shad fish ; Ilisha elongata (학명)

준칙 準則 a standing rule ; working rules ; regulations ; a criterion ; a standard ¶ 법률은 행위의 준칙이다 Law is the rule of conduct.

준평원 準平原 a peneplain

준하다 準— [비례] be proportionate〔proportional〕《to》 ; be in proportion to ; [준용] apply correspondingly 《to》 ; [기준] follow ; be based upon ; conform to ; [상응] correspond to ¶ …에 준하여 in accordance with ; in proportion to // 이하 이에 준함 It applies correspondingly to the following cases. // 이익은 출비에 준한다 The profit is proportionate to the amount spent.

준행 遵行 following in accordance with an order〔the rule〕; observance —하다 follow in accordance with an order〔the rule〕 ¶ 법을 준행하다 observe laws

준험 峻險 steepness ; precipitousness —하다 (be) steep ; precipitous ; rugged

준현행범 準現行犯 〖법〗 a quasi-flagrant offense

준회원 準會員 an associate member

*줄¹ [끈] a rope ; a cord ; a string (연·악기 따위의) ; a line (전화·낚시 따위의) ; [선] a line ; a stripe ; [수준] level ; [열] a row ; a line ¶ 생명의 줄 a lifeline // 가는〔굵은〕 줄 a thin〔thick〕 line // 이 줄의 맨 끝 집 the last house on this side // 한 줄로 늘어선 나무 a line of trees // 밑에서부터 다섯째 줄 the fifth line from the bottom // 줄을 지어 in a line〔row, file〕// 한 줄 걸러 on every other line // 줄을 치다 stretch a rope // 줄을 긋다 draw a line // 한 줄로 서다 stand in a queue // 줄을 바꾸다 begin a new line // 줄에 걸리다 be caught in a line // 믿는 줄이 끊어졌다 My last hope has gone. // 거기가 줄의 맨 끝인가요 Is this the end of the line? // 줄을 서 계신 것입니까 Are you in line? // 줄이 얼마나 긴가 좀 보시오 See how long the line is.
전기— electric cord ; power line 전화— a telephone wire

줄² [쇠를 깎는] a file ; a rasp (굵은) ¶ 줄로 쓸어 미끈하게 하다 file 《a thing》 smooth

줄³ 〖식물〗 the wild rice ; the Indian rice ; the water-oat ; Zizania latifolia (학명)

줄⁴ [방법] the how ; the way how to ; [예상] the assumed fact ; likelihood ¶ 글 쓸 줄 모르다 do not know how to write // 헤엄칠 줄 알다 know how to swim // 나는 그가 결석한 줄 알았다 I thought〔supposed〕 that he was absent from school. // 너를 여기서 만날 줄이야 꿈에도 생각 못했다 I never dreamed I would run into you here.

줄거리 [가지] a stalk ; a stem ; a leaf-stalk ; [골자] outline ; a plot ¶ 도중에 이야기의 줄거리를 놓쳤다 Halfway through I lost the thread of the story.

줄걷다¹ ⇨ 줄밑걷다

줄걷다² [줄타다] walk 《on》 a tightrope

줄걸리다 have ⟪a person⟫ walk a tightrope
줄곧 all the time ; all through ; constantly ; consecutively ; continually ; from start to finish ¶ 아침부터 줄곧 all through the morning // 지금까지 줄곧 기다리고 있었다 I have been waiting all the while. // 그후 줄곧 여기서 살고 있었다 I have lived here ever since.
줄글 prose
줄긋다 draw a line ; line〔rule〕 paper ; line through ; run a line through ; underline
*__줄기__ [나무 따위의] a trunk ; a stem ; a stalk ; a cane ; [물줄기] a stream ; a current ; a vein (혈관의) ; [산의] a range ; [소나기의] a shower ; a downpour ¶ 한 줄기의 광선 a streak〔ray〕 of light // 한 줄기의 연기 a column of smoke **강—** the course of a river **물—** a water course ; a stream of water **산—** a range of mountains
줄기줄기 ① [시냇물이] in streams 〔streamlets〕 ¶ 물이 줄기줄기 흐르다 water flows in streamlets ② [산이] in ranges〔chains〕 ¶ 산이 줄기줄기 뻗어 나가다 a mountain spreads out into ranges
줄기직 a rush mat which is put under a coffin
줄기차다 (be) strong ; vigorous ; be bursting with vitality ; [계속하다] incessant ; constant ; continuous ¶ 줄기차게 비가 내리다 rain incessantly〔hard〕 ; pour down // 줄기차게 항거하다 offer a stout resistance // 시냇물이 줄기차게 흘러간다 The stream rushes along exuberantly.
줄깃줄깃, 쫄깃쫄깃 —하다 (be) chewy ; sticky
줄나다 [감산하다] be produced in less than estimated quantity ; fall short of the production goal
줄남생이 a row of tortoises (basking in the sun on a riverbank) ¶ 사람들이 줄남생이처럼 앉아 있다 People are sitting there like bumps on a log.
줄넘기 rope-skipping ; rope-jumping **—하다** skip〔jump〕 rope ; turn a skipping rope
*__줄다__ [감소하다] decrease ; diminish ; lessen ; fall ⟪off⟫ ; dwindle ; run low ; subside ; [축소하다] shrink ; contract ; draw ¶ 빨아도 줄지 않다 be unshrinkable // 요새 체중이 줄었다 I have lost much weight of late. // 샘물이 줄었다 The water in the well got low. // 구두가 줄어 들었다 My shoes have tightened. // 그의 재산이 줄어서 거의 없어졌다 His property dwindled down to practically nothing. // 회원이 200명으로 줄었다 The membership has fallen〔dwindled〕 to 200.
줄다리기 a tug of war **—하다** play at a tug of war
줄달다 follow one after another ; continue in unbroken succession ¶ 줄달아서 successively ; one after another ; in succession ; one upon the heels of another // 줄달아 생기다 spring up like so many mushrooms // 불행이 줄단다 One misfortune followed on the heels of another. /I have a crop of troubles.
줄달음질 running ; dashing ; darting **—하다** run hard ; rush ; dart ¶ 집 밖으로 줄달음질쳐 나가다 dash out into the street
줄담배 ¶ 줄담배를 피우다 chainsmoke // 줄담배를 피우는 사람 a chainsmoker
줄대다 keep ⟪a thing⟫ running〔flowing〕 without interruption ; go on ; keep on ¶ 줄대서 continuously ; uninterruptedly ; in succession ; in a row // 줄대어 서다 stand in a row〔line, file〕 ; line〔queue〕 up
줄드리다 [줄을 걸다] hang a rope ; [줄을 꼬다] make〔twist, strand〕 a rope
줄띄우다 stretch out a rope ⟪to measure a distance, take an angle, etc.⟫
줄띠 [목줄띠] the throat muscles
줄먹줄먹 in various small sizes〔quantities〕 ⇨ 졸막졸막
줄멍줄멍 small things in a group ; all bumpy ⇨ 졸망졸망
줄모 rice seedlings bedded out in lines 〔rows〕 ; row-planted rice seedlings ¶ 줄모를 심다 bed out young rice plants in lines
줄목 key-point (of a matter) ; a chief 〔main, turning〕 point ; the highlights
줄무늬 a stripe ¶ 줄무늬의 striped
줄무더기 a medley ; a motley (of colors) ; a patchwork
— 형제 brothers of different mothers
줄무지 a (lower-class) funeral procession in which close friends or family members serve as pallbearers
줄밑걷다 trace〔find out〕 ⟪the source of a rumor⟫
줄바둑 a poor game of *paduk* ; [사람] a poor paduk-player
¶ 줄바둑을 두다 play〔have〕 a poor game of *paduk*
—꾼 a poor player of *paduk*
줄밥[1] [매의 먹이] the feed attached to an end of the string given a falcon during its training period ¶ 줄밥에 매로구나 serve another's interest through one's own greed
줄밥[2] [줄질할 때의] (metal) filings
줄방귀 a succession of breaking wind ; breaking wind time after time
줄방석 —方席 a rush seat-mat
줄버들 a row of willows
줄불 a string of fire-crackers
줄사닥다리 a rope ladder
줄어들다 dwindle away ; grow smaller ; shrink ; diminish ; decrease ¶ 점점 줄어들어 없어지다 dwindle away into nothing // 인구가 10만으로 줄어들다 the popula-

tion falls to 100,000 // 이것은 빨면 줄어들까요 Do you think this will shrink if washed?

줄어지다 ⇨ 줄어들다

***줄이다** [감소시키다] reduce ; decrease ; diminish ; lessen ; [삭감하다] shorten ; curtail ; cut ; [축소하다] abbreviate ; abridge ; [단축하다] contract ; boil down ¶ 줄인 말 an abbreviation ; a shortened word // 문장을 줄이다 condense a sentence // 비용을 줄이다 retrench〔cut down〕 expenditure // 저고리를 줄이다 take in a coat // 3분의 2로 줄이다 reduce by two thirds // 두 줄로 줄이다 boil down 《an article》 into two lines // 고기를 줄이고 야채를 더 먹다 eat less meat and more vegetables // 선택 범위를 사립 대학으로 줄여야 할 것 같다 Maybe I should narrow my choices down to private colleges. // 어떻게 하면 체중을 좀 줄일 수 있을까 I wonder how I can take off some weight. // 끓기 시작했으니까 불을 줄여라 It's started boiling, so turn down the heat.

줄자 a measuring tape〔a tape measure, a tapeline〕 ¶ 줄자로 재다 tape-measure

줄잡다 make a conservative〔moderate, low〕 estimate 《of》 ; estimate conservatively ; underestimate ¶ 줄잡아서 at a moderate estimate // 최하로 줄잡아서 at the lowest estimate // 비용을 줄잡다 make a rock-bottom estimate of the expenses // 이것은 줄잡아서 들어야 한다 It must be taken with a grain of salt. // 기부금의 액수가 줄잡아서 100만원쯤 된다 The total sum of the contributions is conservatively estimated at a million *won*.

줄줄[1] ceaselessly in a stream ; profusely ¶ 땀을 줄줄 흘리다 swelter ; perspire profusely // 상처에서 피가 줄줄 흐르고 있었다 The wound was bleeding profusely.

줄줄[2] [막힘없이] smoothly ; without stopping ; fluently ¶ 시를 줄줄 외우다 recite a poem fluently

줄줄이 in row after row ; all in rows ; all rows

줄짓다 [정렬하다] be in a row ; stand in (a) line ; [줄을 짓다] line up ; rank ¶ 일렬로 줄짓다 stand in a line // 줄지어 서게 하다 have 《them》 get into〔stand in〕 line // 그 거리에는 멋진 집들이 줄지어 있다 A row of fine buildings lines the street.

줄참외 the striped cantaloup

줄치다 draw a line ; rule〔line on〕 paper ; [빨랫줄 따위를] stretch a rope

줄타기 (tight) rope dancing〔walking〕 ; a tightrope feat〔act〕 ; funambulism **—하다** walk a tightrope ; walk〔dance〕 on a tightrope ; tightrope ¶ 위태위태한 줄타기를 하다 run a risk ; walk a high wire ; make a risky attempt ; engage in a touch-and-go business ; go out on a limb 《구》

— 광대 a tightrope walker〔dancer〕 ; a ropedancer ; a funambulist

줄타다 walk on a (tight) rope

줄통 〖광산〗 one of the ore veins leading from an ore rock ¶ 줄통뽑다 (be so elated that one) pulls up the lapel of one's undergarment and lets it be seen at the neck ; be elated

줄팔매(질) (stone-) slinging ; a sling (of a stone)

줄팽팽이 staying taut〔stiff〕

줄행랑 —行廊 [행랑채] the front wing of a house ; the outhouses (하인의 숙소) ; [도망] running away ; flight ; absconding ¶ 줄행랑 치다 run away ; take flight ; dart off

줌 [분량] a handful ; a fistful ; a grip ; a grasp ; [활의 줌통] the handle of a bow ¶ 한줌의 모래 a handful of sand

줌뒤 the back of the hand with which one holds the handle of a bow

줌밖 ¶ 줌밖의 out of hands〔clutches, grasp, control〕 ; uncontrollable〔unmanageable, ungovernable〕

줌밖에 나다 get〔be〕 out of person's hands〔clutches, grasp, control〕 ; be uncontrollable〔unmanageable, ungovernable〕 ¶ 아무의 줌밖에 나다 be freed from〔slip out of〕 a person's grasp

줌벌다 be too big to hold in a hand ; be beyond one's grasp ¶ 라켓의 손잡이가 줌벌다 The grip of the racket is too thick to get my fingers around.

줌손 the hand with which one holds a bow

줌안에 들다 fall〔slip〕 into a person's hands〔clutches, grasp, control〕 ; slip under a person's control ; be controllable〔manageable, governable〕 ¶ 아무가 줌안에 들다 have a person under one's control〔in one's clutches〕

줌통 [활의] the handle of a bow

***줍다** pick up ; gather 《shells》 ; collect (거두다) ; find 《a purse》 ¶ 모자를 줍다 pick up one's hat // 이삭을 줍다 glean ; gather ears of corn // 그것을 주워다오 Please, pick it up for me.

줏대 the metal rim of a wheel

줏대 主— fixed principles ; strength of character ; moral fiber ; backbone ; a definite opinion ; a settled conviction ¶ 줏대 있는 사람 a man of principle ; a man of steady〔firm, strong〕 character // 줏대가 없다 lack backbone〔moral fiber〕

중 a monk ; a bonze ; a Buddhist priest ¶ 중이 되다 enter the priesthood ; become a priest

중 中 ① [중앙] the center ; the middle ; [중위] medium ; average ¶ 중의 medium ; average ; mediocre ; middling // 중키의 사람 a man of medium height // 중이상〔이하〕이다 be above〔below〕 the average // 학력은 중이다 His scholarship

is average.
② [동안] during ; through ; within ; in the course of ; while ¶ 내월 중에 within〔in the course of〕 next month // 병중에 during one's illness ; while one is ill // 여행 중에 on one's journey // 부재중에 during〔in〕 one's absence
③ [진행중] under ; at ; in course〔process〕 of ¶ 건축 중의 집 a house under〔in course of〕 construction // 식사 중이다 be at table // 공사 중이다 be under construction ; be in process〔course〕 of construction // 일이 진행 중이다 The work is in progress〔going on〕. // 통화 중이다 Line (is) engaged. /Line is busy. 《미》 // 그는 근무 중이다 He is on duty. // 나는 지금 목욕 중이다. I'm in the middle of taking a bath.
④ [중에서] among ; in ; out of ; of ¶ 10중 8, 9는 in nine cases out of ten ; ten to one
⑤ [내내] all over ; throughout ¶ 오전중 all through the morning

중 重 [겹] fold ; [무게] weight ; [중요] heavy ; important ¶ 이중의 twofold ; double ; two-ply // 삼중의 threefold ; treble ; triple ; three-ply // 5중탑 a five-storied pagoda // 중기관총 a heavy machine gun // 중폭격기 a heavy bomber // 이중으로 쌓다 put one above the other // 이 반지는 세 돈 중이다 This ring weighs 3 *don*.

중가 重價 a great〔high, dear〕 price ⇨ 중값

중가산금 重加算金 heavy additional money

중간 重刊 republication ; reprint ; reissue **—하다** republish ; reprint ; reissue

*__중간 中間__ the middle ; midway ; halfway ; midterm (중간의) ¶ 중간의 middle ; intermediate ; stop-gap ; [잠정적] temporary ; interim (기한 전의) // …의 중간에 서다 mediate between ; act as a go-between for 《two parties》 // 대전은 서울과 부산의 중간에 있다 *Taejŏn* lies halfway between *Seoul* and *Pusan*. // 이런 경우에는 중간에 사람을 세워서 이야기하는 것이 최선이다 In cases like this it's best to have somebody act as a go-between.
— 결과 interim findings **— 경기(景氣)** a temporary〔passing〕 boom **— 계급** the middle class **— 고사** a midterm examination **—권〔층〕** the mesosphere (대기의) **— 노선** neutrality ¶ 중간 노선을 취하다 take a middle-of-the-road〔neutral〕 attitude〔course〕 **— 무역** intermediate trade **—물** a medium ; an intermediate **— 보고** an interim report **— 상인** a middle man ; a broker **—색(色)** a neutral tint **— 선거** off-year election 《미》 **— 소설** a middlebrow novel **— 시험** intermediate examinations ; midterm examinations **—역** an intermediate station **—음** 〖음악〗 an intertone ; an intermediate tone **— 이득** intermediary profiteering **—자** 〖물리〗 ⇨ 중간자(中間子) **— 정책** the middle-of-the-road policy **— 지층** 〖지질〗 intercalary strata ; an interstratification **— 착취** intermediary exploitation ; kickback 《미》 **—층** the middle class(es) ; middlebrows 《취미 등의》 **—파** the neutrals ; a middle-of-the-roader

중간자 中間子 〖물리〗 a mes(otr)on **뮤—** a mu-mesotron ; a muon **중—** a heavy meson

중간치 中間— [물건] an average article ; an article of medium size〔price, quality〕

중간파 中間派 the neutrals ; the independents ; the middle-of-the-roaders

중갈이 中— 〖농업〗 fall vegetables sown in summer

중갑판 中甲板 the middle deck

중값 重— a great〔high, dear〕 price

*__중개 仲介__ intermediation ; mediation (조정) **—하다** mediate ; intermediate 《between two parties》 ; act as go-between ; intercede ¶ …의 중개로 through the intermediation 《of》 // 중개 역을 하다 act as a go-between〔an intermediary〕
—국 a mediating power **— 기관** a medium ; an agency **—물** a medium ; a channel **— 수수료** brokerage (commission) **—인〔자〕** an intermediary ; a middleman **— 판매** sale on commission

중개업 仲介業 a brokerage ; the brokerage business ; [주선업] agency
—자 a broker ; a middleman ; a jobber ; a commission merchant

중거리 中距離 a medium distance〔range〕 **— 경주** a middle-distance race **— 선수** a middle-distance runner **— 탄도탄** an intermediate range ballistic missile 《IRBM》 ; a medium-range ballistic missile 《MRBM》

중견 中堅 [사람] the backbone ; the mainstay ; the nucleus ; [군사] the main body ; a centerfield (야구의) ¶ 회사의 중견이 되다 form〔prove oneself〕 the backbone of a company // 중산 계급은 국가의 중견이다 The middle class forms the backbone of the nation.
— 샐러리맨 salary earners of middle standing **— 소득층** those in the middleincome bracket **—수** 〖야구〗 a centerfielder **— 인물** a leader ; leading figures ; an animating spirit **— 작가** a writer of medium standing

중경상 重輕傷 serious and slight injuries〔wounds〕 ; major and minor casualties
—자 seriously and slightly injured persons

중계 中繼 relay ; hook up 《미》 **—하다** relay

—국 a relay station — 무역 intermediate〔transit, entrepôt《프》〕 trade — 방송 relay ; hook-up《미》 ¶ 전국 중계 방송을 하다 broadcast over a nation-wide hookup〔network〕 —선 [철도의] a junction line —항 a transit port — 회로 〖전기〗 a junction circuit 무대 — a drama relayed from the stage 실황 — relay of actual conditions 현장 — relay from the spot〔scene〕

*중고 中古 ① [물건] a second hand article ¶ 중고의 slightly old ; second-hand ; little used // 중고 책상 a second-hand desk // 중고의 것을 사다 buy《a thing》(at) second-hand
② 〖역사〗 the middle age ; medieval times ¶ 중고의 medieval
—품 a slightly used article ; secondhand goods ¶ 신품과 다름 없는 중고품 slightly used but almost brand-new〔as good as new〕

중고기 〖물고기〗 a kind of freshwater carp

중고 연령자 中高年齡者 persons of middle or advanced age

중공업 重工業 heavy industry

중과 衆寡 odds ; disparity in numbers ¶ 중과부적이다 We are outnumbered〔overcome by numbers〕. /There is no fighting against such odds.

중과세 重課稅 ⇨ 중세(重稅)

중과피 中果皮 〖식물〗 the mesocarp

중괴탄 中塊炭 coal in medium-size lumps

중구 中歐 Central Europe

중구 衆口 public rumor ; popular criticism ¶ 중구난방이다 It is difficult to stop the voice of the people.

중구미 the elbow of the arm with which one holds an archery bow

중국 中國 China ¶ 중국의 Chinese
— 공산당 the Chinese Communists —말 Chinese ; the Chinese language — 사람 a Chinese《*pl.* Chinese》; the Chinese《총칭》 —학 sinology ; study of things Chinese〔Chinese culture〕 —학자 a sinologist ; a sinologue ; a China scholar 자유 — Nationalist China
☞ ◀p. 1958▶

중궁 中宮 the queen

중궁(전) 中宮(殿) ⇨ 왕후(王后)

중권 中卷 the middle〔second〕 volume (of a set of three)

중근동 中近東 the middle and Near East

중금고 重禁錮 imprisonment with〔at〕 hard labor

중금속 重金屬 a heavy metal

중급 中級 an intermediate grade
— 영어 intermediate English —품 fair average quality

중기 中期 the middle (years)《of an era》; [세포 분열의] the metaphase

중기 重機 ⇨ 중기계(重機械), 중기관총

중기계 中機械 heavy machinery

중기관총 重機關銃 a heavy machine gun

중길 [물건] an article of medium quality ; medium goods ; average-grade goods ; middlings

중깃 中— 〖건축〗 a small reinforcing post inside a wall

중난하다 重難— (be) exceedingly difficult ; serious

중남미 中南美 Central and South Amer-ica
— 사람들 Latin Americans — 자유 무역 연합 Latin American Free Trade Association《LAFTA》

*중년 中年 middle age ; mid-life ¶ 중년의 middle-aged // 중년을 지난 여자 an elderly woman // 중년에 죽다 die middle-aged
—기 the middle years of one's life — 신사 a middle-aged gentleman — 여자 a woman past her prime —층 middle-aged (people)

중노동 重勞動 heavy labor ¶ 중노동을 하다 engage〔be engaged〕 in heavy labor
—자 a heavy worker

중노인 中老人 ⇨ 중늙은이

중농 中農 a middle-class farmer

중농 정책 重農政策 an agriculture-first policy

중농주의 重農主義 physiocracy
—자 a physiocrat

중뇌 中腦 the midbrain ; mesencephalon

중늙은이 an elderly person ; a middle-aged person

중다 衆多 —하다 be of great number ; (be) numerous

중다리 〖식물〗 a variety of early-ripening rice plant

중다버지 long tufty hair ; a child with such hair

†중단 中斷 discontinuance ; suspension ; interruption —하다 discontinue ; interrupt ; suspend ; break continuity
시효 — 〖법〗 suspension of prescription

중단 中段 the landing (계단의) ; the middle (중앙부) ; the middle tier (상·하단에 대해) ¶ 중단의 침대 a middle berth

†중대 重大 importance ; gravity ; seriousness —하다 (be) important ; serious ; weighty ; momentous ; be of great importance ¶ 중대한 문제 an important〔a serious, a vital〕 question // 중대한 책임 grave responsibility // 중대한 사건 a serious〔grave〕 affair // 중대시하다 take a serious view of // 중대하여지다 become serious ; aggravate
— 관심사 a matter of the utmost concern — 성명 an important statement〔announcement〕 ¶ 중대 성명을 발표하다 announce〔make public〕 a serious statement

중대 中隊 a company (보병·공병) ; a battery (포병) ; a squadron (비행)
— 교련 company drill —장 a company commander ; a captain 기병 — a troop 보병 — an infantry company 비행 — a squadron 포병 — a battery

중 국

중화인민공화국 the People's Republic of China 전국인민대표대회[全人大] the National People's Congress 중국 공산당 the Communist Party of China 당주석 chairman 《정식 명칭은 chair man of the central committee of the Chinese Communist Party 당 중앙위원회 주석》 총서기 General Secretary 문화대혁명 the Great Proletarian Cultural Revolution (★ the (Great) Cultural Revolution으로 약칭하기도 함) 홍위병(紅衛兵) Red Guard 문혁파(文革派) cultural revolutionist 주자파(走資派) capitalist-roader 실권파 people in authority; the bureaucrats; the pragmatists; the pragmatic bureaucrats 혁명파 revolutionists; revolutionaries 모택동(毛澤東) Mao Zedong 모택동사상 Mao Zedong Thought 인민복 Mao jacket[tunic] 오성홍기(五星紅旗) 《국기》 the Five-Starred Red Flag 천안문(天安門) the Tien An Men 인민해방군 the People's Liberation Army 죽(竹)의 장막 the Bamboo Curtain 대자보(大字報) wall poster; big-character poster 경극(京劇) Beijing Opera 북경대학(北京大學) Beijing University 인민일보(人民日報) the People's Daily (★중국 공산당 기관지) 중국일보 China Daily (★영자신문) 사인방(四人幇) the Gang of Four; the Four Brigands; the Shanghai Mafia (★ 江靑, 王洪文, 長春橋, 姚文元) 청천백일기(靑天白日旗) the Sun-in-the-Blue-Sky Flag

중대가리 [머리] a shaven head; a tonsure; a close-cropped head; [사람] a person with a close-cropped head

중대님 中— pantleg-ties just below the knee

중대문 中大門 the inner gate

중대시 重大視 taking 《a matter》 seriously **—하다** attach great importance to 《an affair》; take 《a matter》 seriously; take a serious view of 《a matter》; regard 《a situation》 as serious

중대화 重大化 aggravation **—하다** become serious; have serious developments; aggravate; assume serious proportions

중덜거리다 grumble 《on, about》; complain 《of》

⁑중도 中途 halfway; midway; mid-course ¶ 중도에서 halfway; midway; in the middle // 중도에서 그만두다 stop in the middle of 《work》; do things by halves; stop working halfway // 중도에서 돌아서다 turn back halfway 일의 중도에서 쓰러지다 break down in the middle of one's work

중도 中道 [중용] the middle path; the middle-of-the-road; mean; moderation ¶ 모든 것에는 중도라는 것이 있다 There is a happy medium in everything.

— 정책 the middle-of-the-road policy

—파 a middle-of-the-roader

중도위 a broker; a middleman

중도 퇴학 中途退學 leaving school in mid-course **—하다** leave school in mid-course ¶ 대학을 중도 퇴학한 청년 a young man who got only halfway through college

중독 中毒 poisoning; toxication; toxic effect ¶ 중독성의 poisonous; toxic // 중독되다 be poisoned 《by》 // 생선에 중독됐다 The fish disagreed with me. // 그는 연탄 중독으로 죽었다 He was poisoned to death by the gas of a briquet. // 아들한테 컴퓨터를 한 대 사다주었는데 그 애는 이제 컴퓨터 중독이 되었어요 I bought my son a computer, and now he's hooked on it.

—사 death from poisoning ¶ 가스 중독사하다 be poisoned to death by gas **—성** toxicity; toxic; poisonous ¶ 중독성 빈혈 toxic anaemia **—증(症)** toxicosis **— 증상** toxic symptoms **식—** poisoning from eating; food poisoning **아편 —** opiumism; opium-poisoning **알코올 —** alcoholism

중동 中— the middle part 《of a thing》; the waist 《of the body》 ¶ 생선의 중동 the center cut of the fish // 중동이 길다〔짧다〕 be long-waisted〔short-waisted〕

—끈 the belt to a skirt; a sash

중동 中東 the Middle East

— 조약 기구 the Middle East Treaty Organization 《M. E. T. O.》

중동 仲冬 the eleventh month in the lunar calendar; midwinter

중동무이 中— leaving something half-done〔unfinished〕; stopping halfway **—하다** leave 《things》 half-done〔unfinished〕; give up halfway; go halfway

중동바지 中— women's pants with unlined waist and lined legs

중동치레 中— [장식] ornamental trappings worn on the waist

중두리 中— a small earthenware jar

중등 中等 [급] the middle〔second〕 class 〔grade〕; [질] medium quality; [중위] the average; mediocrity ¶ 중등의 middle; medium; average // 성적이 중등 이

상〔이하〕이다 one's school record is above〔below〕 average

— 교육 secondary education — 교원 a secondary school teacher — 학교 a secondary school

중략 中略 an ellipsis ; an omission (of interior parts) ; syncopation ; "omitted" — 하다 omit the interior parts ; skip

중량 重量 weight ¶ 중량 한도를 초과한 하물 overweight luggage // 중량감이 있는 massive ; weighty // 항공 우편의 중량 air mail poundage // 중량이 10파운드이다 weigh ten pounds

— 감각 weight sensation — 급 권투 선수 a heavy-weight boxer — 부족〔초과〕 a short〔over〕 weight — 분석 gravimetric analysis — 제한 weight〔《미》 load〕 limits — 측정 gravimetry — 톤 weight ton ; deadweight tonnage — 화물 a weight cargo ; a deadweight 가감 — changeable weight 총— gross weight

중량급 中量級 the middle weight class

⁑**중력 重力** gravity ; gravitation ¶ 중력의 법칙 the law of gravity

— 가속도 acceleration of gravity — 단위 a gravitational unit — 댐 a gravity dam — 법칙 the law of gravity — 전지 a gravity cell — 제어 gravity control — 중심 the center of gravity — 탱크 a gravity tank — 파 〖물리〗 a gravity〔gravitation〕 wave — 학〔론〕 barology 무— 상태 gravity-free state

중령 中領 a lieutenant colonel (육군·해병) ; a commander (해군) ; a lieutenant colonel ; a wing commander 《영》 (공군)

중로 中老 middle age ; [사람] a middle aged〔an elderly〕 person ; a man past his prime ¶ 중로의 elderly ; middle-aged

중론 衆論 public opinion ; the voice of the people ¶ 중론에 의하여 결정하다 refer 《a matter》 to public opinion

***중류 中流** [흐름의 복판] the middle of the river ; mid-stream ; [사회] the middle class ¶ 강 중류에 작은 섬이 있다 There is an isle halfway up the river.

— 가정 a middle-class family — 계급 the middle class

중리 重利 [복리] compound interest ; [큰 이익] a large〔heavy〕 profit

⁑**중립 中立** neutrality ; neutralization — 하다 stand neutral ; sit on the fence ¶ 호의적 중립 friendly neutrality // 중립을 선언하다 declare neutrality // 중립을 지키다 adhere to neutrality ; observe〔keep, maintain〕 neutrality // 중립을 취소하다 revoke neutrality

— 국 a neutral power〔state〕 ; a neutral ¶ 중립국기〔선〕 a neutral flag〔ship〕 // 중립국 영해 neutral waters — 보장 security of neutrality — 선언 declaration of neutrality — 성 neutrality ; impartiality — 위반 a violation of neutrality — 정책 a neutrality〔neutralist〕 policy — 조약 a neutrality pact — 주의 neutralism — 지대 a neutral zone — 파 a neutral faction〔party〕 ; the neutralists — 화 neutralization ¶ 중립화 해소 deneutralization // 중립화하다 neutralize 무장 — armed neutrality 엄정 — strict neutrality

중망 衆望 popular expectation (기대) ; public confidence (신망) ; popularity ¶ 중망을 얻다 be the center of popular hopes ; enjoy public confidence // 중망을 한몸에 모으다 win a great popularity // 중망에 어긋나지 않다 meet public expectation // 중망을 얻어 대통령에 입후보하다 candidate for the presidential election with popular support

중매 仲媒 matchmaking (결혼) ; a matchmaker ; a go-between — 하다 serve as a matchmaker ; act as (a) go-between

— 결혼 a marriage arranged by a go-between — 인 a matchmaker ; a go-between

중매 仲買 brokerage — 하다 act as (a) broker ¶ 매매 및 중매업 a general merchant and commission agent

— 구전 a broker's commission — 상 the business of a broker ; brokerage — 인 a broker ; a middleman ; a jobber ; a commission agent〔merchant〕 — 점 a brokerage house〔firm〕

중목 衆目 public attention ; all the eyes ¶ 중목을 모으다 become the focus of public attention

— 소시(所視) what every eye saw ; the cynosure of all eyes ¶ 중목소시가 되다 be the cynosure of all eyes

중문 重文 〖문법〗 a compound sentence

중문 重門 the inner gate

중미 中米 rice of medium quality ; moderately polished rice

중미 中美 Central America ; Middle America ¶ 중미의 나라 a Central American country

중바닥 the central〔downtown〕 area

중바랑 a monk's knapsack

중반전 中盤戰 [선거 따위] the middle phase 《of an election campaign》 ; [바둑·장기 따위] the middle game ¶ 선거가 중반전에 접어들었다 The election campaigning is now at its height.

중발 中鉢 a small rice-bowl made of brass

중방 中枋 〖건축〗 a middle molding〔cornice〕 of a wall

***중배 中—** [중복] a bulged-out middle ; [동물의] an animal born after the first litter

중배 부르다 (관용) be bulged out in the middle ; be potbellied

중배끼 a kind of fried honeycake

중벌 重罰 severe punishment ; heavy penalty ¶ 중벌에 처하다 sentence 《a person》 to a severe punishment

중범 重犯 [중범죄] felony ; [거듭 저지름] repetition of crimes ; [사람] a perpetra-

repeated offense
중병 重病 a serious〔severe〕 illness ¶ 퍽 중병이다 be very〔seriously〕 ill // 중병에 걸리다 get〔fall, be taken〕 seriously ill ; be attacked by a serious illness
— 환자 a serious case
중보 重寶 a treasure of great value ; a priceless treasure ¶ 가전(家傳)의 중보 a treasured heirloom
중복 中伏 the middle period of the dog-days
중복 中腹 [산의 중턱] the mountain's breast ; the mid-slope of a mountain ; [중배] a bulged-out middle ¶ 중복에 halfway up〔down〕 a hill // 그 산의 중복 위는 눈에 쌓여 있다 The upper half of the mountain is enveloped〔blanketed〕 in snow.
*중복 重複 overlapping ; repetition (반복) ; duplication —하다 overlap ; duplicate ; be repeated ; be double ¶ 중복된 overlapping ; duplicate ; [어구 따위가] pleonastic ; tautological // 중복을 피하다 avoid overlapping〔duplication〕 // 일이 중복되었다 Work is duplicated.
— 계정 overlapping account —물 a duplicate — 보험 double insurance
중부 中部 the central〔middle〕 part〔portion〕 ; the center〔middle〕 ; the heart
— 갑판 the middle deck — 지방 the central districts ; the Middle West 《미》
— 태평양 mid-Pacific
중부 仲父 an uncle ; one's father's elder brother
중분 中分 [등분] bisection ; division into halves ; [중년의 운수] one's luck at middle age —하다 bisect ; divide into halves
중불 中佛 Sino-French 《rapprochement》
중뿔나다 中— intrude ; intermeddle ; be officious〔meddlesome, impertinent, presumptuous〕 ¶ 중뿔난 사람 a meddler ; an officious person ; a busybody // 중뿔나게 말하다 make uncalled-for〔impertinent〕 remarks
중사 中士 a sergeant ; a sergeant first class (육군·해병) ; a petty officer first class (해군) ; a technical sergeant (공군)
*중산 계급 中産階級 the middle class ; the petit bourgeoisie 《프》 ; [사람들] the middle classes ; middle class people ¶ 중산 계급의 시민 a middle-class citizen ; a bourgeois
중산모 中山帽 a bowler 《영》 ; a derby 《미》
*중상 中傷 slander ; calumny ; aspersion ; defamation —하다 slander ; defame ; calumniate ; throw〔fling〕 mud at 《a person》 ; asperse ; stab 《a person》 in the back ¶ 중상적 slanderous ; calumnious // 중상적 보도 a slanderous report // 그는 남을 중상하기 좋아한다 He is a scandalmonger.
—자 a slanderer ; a scandalmonger
중상 重賞 high prize ; a liberal reward
중상 重傷 a serious〔severe, major〕 wound〔injury〕 ¶ 중상을 입다 receive〔sustain〕 a serious wound ; be seriously〔badly〕 wounded // 중상을 입히다 inflict a severe injury〔wound〕 on 《a person》 // 그는 중상을 입고 쓰러졌다 He succumbed to a severe wound. // His wounds proved fatal.
—자 a seriously wounded〔injured〕 person
중상 重喪 double mourning 《losing both parents within three years》
중상 中商 a broker ; a middleman
중상주의 重商主義 mercantilism ; the mercantile system
중생 衆生 mankind ; human beings ; the world ; living things ¶ 중생의 제도를 위하여 in order to save mankind
중생 重生 〖기독교〗 second birth ; rebirth —하다 be born again ; be reborn
중생대 中生代 the Mesozoic (Age, Era)
중서부 中西部 [미국] the Middle West ; the Midwest ¶ 중서부의 the Middle Western
중석 重石 tungsten ; scheelite
중석기 시대 中石器時代 〖고고〗 the Mesolithic period〔era〕 ; the Middle Stone Age
중선거구 中選擧區 a medium electoral district
—제 the medium constituency (electorate) system
중설 衆說 public opinion
중성 中性 〖문법〗 the neuter gender ; 〖화학〗 neutrality ; 〖생물〗 sexlessness ¶ 중성의 남자 a sexless man
— 반응 a neutral reaction —염 neutral salt —자 a neutron —화(花) a neutral flower
중성 中聲 〖언어〗 the medial of a Korean orthographic syllable ; the vowels (and semivowels) of a Korean syllable
중성자 中性子 〖물리〗 a neutron
광— a photoneutron 열— a thermal neutron
중성화 中性化 neutralization —하다 neutralize
*중세 中世 the middle ages ; medieval times ¶ 중세의 medieval
—기 the Middle Ages —사 〖역사〗 medieval history — 암흑 시대 the Dark Ages
중세 重稅 a heavy tax ; heavy〔excessive〕 taxation ¶ 중세를 부과하다 impose a heavy tax 《on》 // 중세에 시달리다 groan〔labor〕 under the heavy burden〔load〕 of taxation // 중세를 부담하다 bear a heavy duty
중소 中蘇 Sino-Soviet
— 분쟁〔이념 논쟁〕 the Sino-Soviet con-

flict〔ideological dispute〕

중소 기업 中小企業 small and medium enterprises

— 경영자 minor enterprisers **— 은행** the Medium Industry Bank **— 자금** bank loans for medium and small enterprises

중소 상공업자 中小商工業者 medium and small traders and manufacturers

중속환이 —俗還— an ex-monk

중송아지 中— a full-grown calf

중쇠 中— ① [걸립패의] the second〔middle〕 gong player in a folkband ② ⇨ 맷돌중쇠

중수 重修 repairing 《a building》; remodeling; restoration **—하다** repair; remodel; restore

중수 重囚 a felon

중수 重水 〖화학〗 heavy water

중수소 重水素 heavy hydrogen

중순 中旬 the second〔middle〕 ten days of a month ¶ 5월 중순에 about the middle of May; in mid-May // 내월 중순에 about the middle of next month

중시 重視 serious consideration; taking a serious view 《of》 **—하다** attach importance to; take a serious view 《of》; lay stress on 《a point》; value〔think, make〕 much 《of》 ¶ 중시할 것이 못되다 be of little account // 당국은 이 사건을 중시하고 있다 The authority is taking a serious view of this incident.

중시하 重侍下 looking after both parents and grandparents

중신 重臣 a senior statesman; a chief 〔key〕 retainer

— 회의 a conference of senior statesmen

***중심 中心** [복판] the center〔heart, middle〕; [초점] the focus; [중핵] the nucleus; the core; [중추] the pivot; [중점] stress; emphasis; importance; [평형] balance

> 참고 **center**는 「점」 **middle**은 「부분」 **heart**는 가장 「중요한 부분」에 대해서 말하는 것이 보통이다

¶ 도시의 중심 the center〔hub〕 of a city // 공업의 중심 an industrial center // 중력의 중심 the center of gravity // 문제의 중심 the crux of a problem // 태풍의 중심 the center〔eye〕 of a typhoon // 금융의 중심 the pivot of financial operations // 중심을 벗어난 out of center〔focus〕; eccentric // …을 중심으로 하여 with 《a person》 as the central figure; centering around 《a thing》; with priority given to 《a thing》; laying stress on 《a thing》 // 중심을 잃다 lose one's balance // 중심이 되어 일하다 lead others in some work; take the lead in some work // 한 발로 몸의 중심을 잡다 balance oneself on one leg // 그 도시는 학문의 중심지이다 The city is a center of learning. // 한국에서는 가족이 사회의 중심이다 The family is the nucleus of the community in Korea. // 당신의 의론은 중심을 벗어나 있다 Your argument is beside the mark〔point〕. // 중심이 되어 일할 사람이 없다 None takes the initiative in working. // 그 협회는 그가 중심이 되어 조직되었다 The association was organized with him as a leader.

— 과제 the key subject **—력** a centripetal force **— 사상** the central idea **—선** a center-line **— 세력** central force **— 시도(示度)** 〖기상〗 the central pressure ¶ 중심 시도 1,000밀리바 1,000 mb. at the central pressure **—지** a center; a central place ¶ 미술의 중심지 an art center // 교통의 중심지 a transport〔rail (road)〕 center // 공업의 중심지 a center of industry // 상업의 중심지 a commercial center // 학문의 중심지 a seat of learning **—축** the central axis

중심 重心 the center of gravity; the centroid

—법 the method of elastic center **—축** the (principal) central axis

중심 송곳 中心— a three-pronged gimlet

중심 인물 中心人物 the central〔focal〕 figure; a key man; the leader; the brain; the ringleader ¶ 혁명의 중심 인물 the central figure of a revolution

중씨 仲氏 a middle brother; the second eldest brother

중압 重壓 (heavy) pressure; [부담] heavy burden **—하다** press hard ¶ 중압을 가하다 bring pressure to bear 《upon a person》; subject 《a person》 to pressure

—감 an oppressive feeling ¶ 사소한 실수라도 하면 신경에 중압감이 온다 Even the slightest mistakes can be quite a strain on the nerves.

†**중앙 中央** the center; the middle; the heart ¶ 중앙의 central; middle; mid // 중앙에서 in the middle〔center〕 // 도시의 중앙 the center of the city // 중앙에 모이다 concentrate; centralize

— 공무원 훈련원 the Central Official Training Institute **— 관상대** the Central Meteorological Observatory **— 노동 위원회** the Central Labor Relations Committee **— 돌파** a frontal breakthrough **— 문단** literary circles in the metropolis **— 방송국** a central〔key〕 radio station **—부** the central part **—선** [철도의] the Central Line **— 시장** the central market **— 아시아** central Asia **— 우체국** the Central Post Office 《CPO》 **— 전화국** the central telephone office **— 정보부** the Central Intelligence Agency 《CIA》 ¶ 중앙 정보부장 the Director of the Central Intelligence Agency; the CIA Director **— 정부** the central government **—지(紙)** a metropolitan newspaper **— 집행 위원회** a central executive committee **—청** the

Capitol building (in *Seoul*) ¶ 중앙청 광장 the Capitol plaza — **행정** state administration

중앙 집권 中央集權 centralized authoritarian rule ¶ 중앙 집권화 centralization of power // 중앙 집권화되다 be centralized **—제** centralism ¶ 중앙 집권제로 하다 centralize

중야 中夜 midnight

중언(부언) 重言(復言) (a) repetition ; a repeat ; reiteration **—하다** say over again ; repeat (the same thing) ; reiterate

중얼거리다 mutter to oneself ; grumble 《at, over, about》; murmur 《at, against》 ¶ 대우가 나쁘다고 중얼거리다 grumble at the poor treatment // 무어라고 혼자 중얼거리다 mutter something to oneself

*__중얼중얼__ muttering ; murmuring ; grumbling ¶ 중얼중얼 혼자 말하다 mutter to oneself

중역 重譯 a translation from a translation ; a retranslation **—하다** retranslate

중역 重役 a director (of a company) ; an executive (간부) ; a swivel-chair man (중역급의 사람) ¶ 중역이 되다 obtain a seat on a board of directors **—회** the board of directors ; the directorate — **회의** a meeting of directors ; a directors' meeting — **회장** the chairman of a board of directors **회사** — a high executive (of a company)

중엽 中葉 the middle part (of a period) ¶ 16세기 중엽 the mid-sixteenth century // 고려 중엽에 about the middle of the time of *Koryŏ* Dynasty

중외 中外 the inside and the outside ; home and abroad ¶ 중외의 domestic 〔home〕 and foreign ; internal and external ; home and abroad // 중외에 at home and abroad ; in all parts of the world // 중외에 선언하다 declare〔announce〕 to the world // 명성을 중외에 떨치다 win a worldwide reputation

†**중요 重要** importance ; consequence **—하다** (be) important ; momentous ; weighty ; essential ; cardinal ; be of importance 〔consequence, moment〕 ¶ 중요한 사람 a person of importance〔consequence〕// 중요한 지위 an important position // 중요한 상품 staple commodities〔products〕// 중요한 사항 an important matter 〔affair〕; a matter of consequence 〔moment〕// 중요한 서류 valuable〔important〕 documents // 중요한 문제 a serious 〔an important〕 question // 중요한 물자 critical materials // 중요한 회의 a major session // 오늘 신문의 중요 기사 the highlights〔highlighted news〕 in today's paper // 정부의 중요 발표 an important release of the government // 중요하지 않다 be of little〔no〕 importance // 정부에서 중요한 위치를 차지하다 hold a key post in the government // 그 일은 그다지 중요하지 않다 The matter is of little importance. // 그 따위 일은 여기서는 별로 중요하지 않다 That does not count. /It is neither here nor there. // 오늘 우리가 상담할 사람은 중요한 고객이니까 지난번 같은 허물없는 태도는 삼가해 주시오 The person we're talking to today is a valued client, so don't adopt the familiar attitude you did last time.
— 기사 news of value ; front page news ; the highlights 《in today's paper》 **— 도시** principal cities **— 사항** an important matter ; a matter of consequence 〔moment〕 **— 산물** stable products **— 산업** the key〔major〕 industry **— 서류** important documents〔papers〕 **—성** importance ; gravity ¶ 그것은 문제로서는 중요성이 없다 It cuts a small figure in the matter. **— 인물** a very important person 《VIP》; [핵심 인물] a key person **— 참고인〔증인〕** a key witness ; [용의자] a key suspect

*__중요시 重要視__ **—하다** attach great importance to ; make〔think〕 much of ; take a serious view of ¶ (사람이) 대단히 중요시되다 be held in high repute ; carry great prestige // 나는 우정을 무엇보다도 중요시한다 I value friendship above everything else.

중용 中庸 moderation ; the happy golden mean ; the middle-of-the-road ¶ 중용의 moderate ; reasonable ; mean ; middle // 중용을 벗어난 immoderate // 중용을 취하다 take the golden mean ; hit〔strike〕 the happy mean ; strike an average // 중용을 지키다 practice the virtue of the golden mean ; keep to the middle path ; exercise〔use〕 moderation // 그 일에는 중용을 지키는 것이 필요하다 It is a question of the happy medium. // 언동에 중용을 취함은 미덕이다 It's virtuous to practice temperance in one's conduct and speech.
—지도(之道) the middle path ; the golden mean

중용 重用 promotion to a responsible post **—하다** promote 《a person》 to a responsible post ; appoint 《a person》 to a position of trust ¶ 중용되다 be taken into confidence 《by one's superior》// 중용되고 있다 hold an important position 《in a company》

중우 衆愚 the vulgar〔ignorant〕 crowd ; the mob ; the blind populace
— 정치 mobocracy ; ochlocracy ; mob rule

중원 中元 the 15th day of the seventh lunar month

중원 中原 [들판의] the center of a field ; [나라의] the midlands ; [경쟁장] the field of contest ¶ 중원에서 패권을 다투다 compete for the supremacy in a country

†**중위 中位** ¶ 중위의 medium ; middle ;

average
—수 〖수학〗 the median
중위 中尉 a first lieutenant (육군의) ; a sublieutenant (영해군의) ; a lieutenant junior grade (미해군의)
중위 中衛 〖배구〗 the middle guard ; 〖미식 축구〗 the halfback ; the snapback
중유 重油 heavy oil ; crude petroleum 〔oil〕 ; diesel oil
중은 重恩 great kindness ; great benefits 〔favor, grace〕 ¶ 중은을 입다 receive great favor〔kindness〕
중음 重音 〖음성〗 a double sound
중음 中音 〖음악〗 mezzo-soprano ; [여성] contralto ; [남성] baritone
— 기호 the mean〔alto〕 clef —부 the mean
중의 衆意 public〔popular, general〕 opinion ¶ 그가 적임자라는 점에 중의가 일치했다 It is universally admitted that he is suitable for the post.
중의 衆議 a general consultation〔deliberation〕 ; public discussion ¶ 중의에 의하여 결정하다 decide according to the majority of votes〔public opinion〕 // 곧 출발하자는 데에 중의가 일치했다 It was unanimously agreed that we should start at once.
중이 中耳 the mid-ear ; the tympanum 《*pl.* -na》
—염 tympanitis ; otitis media
중이층 中二層 the mezzanine (floor)
중인 重因 a principal cause ; a prime factor
중인 衆人 many people ; the people ; the public ; the multitude ¶ 중인 앞에서 in the presence of the whole〔company〕 ; in public〔company〕 // 중인환시 중에 모욕하다 insult 《a person》 in public
중인방 中引枋 ⇨ 중방
중일 中日 China and Japan ¶ 중일의 Chinese-Japanese ; Sino-Japanese
— 관계 the relations between China and Japan — 전쟁 the Chinese-Japanese War
중임 重任 ① [중한 책임] a heavy responsibility ; an important duty〔mission〕 ; a responsible post (중요 위치) ; a position of trust ¶ 중임을 맡다 take a heavy trust 〔responsibility〕 ; take upon oneself an important task // 중임을 띠고 있다 be entrusted with an important mission ; have a heavy responsibility on one's shoulders // 나는 이런 중임을 감당 못한다 I am not equal to such an important duty. ② [재임] reappointment ; reelection (재선) —하다 be reappointed ; be reelected ¶ 그의 중임을 반대하지 않는다 I have no objection to his reappointment.
중장 中章 the middle of the 3 verses of a *shijo* poem ; the middle part of a song
중장 中將 a lieutenant general (육군) ; a vice admiral (해군) ; a lieutenant general (공군) 《미》 ; an air martial 《영》
중장비 重裝備 heavy equipment ¶ 중장비한 heavily equipped 《division》
***중재 仲裁** arbitration ; mediation ; intercession ; peacemaking —하다 arbitrate 《between》 ; mediate〔intervene, intercede〕 《between》 ; act as a peacemaker ; intercede with 《a person》 for 《one's friend》 ¶ 싸움의 중재를 하다 mend〔arbitrate, mediate〕 a quarrel ; make peace between two quarreling parties // 중재에 회부하다 submit〔refer〕 《a matter》 to arbitration // 중재를 제의하다 offer mediation // 중재를 의뢰하다 solicit 《a person's》 mediation ; ask for arbitration // 중재로 쟁의를 해결하다 settle a dispute by arbitration
— 결정 an award — 위임 계약서 an arbitration bond ; a submission bond —인 a mediator ; an arbitrator — 재정 an arbitration draft〔proposal〕 — 재판 arbitration — 재판소 an arbitration tribunal 〔court〕 — 조약 an arbitration treaty 강제〔임의〕 — compulsory〔voluntary〕 arbitration
중전 中殿 the queen
—마마 Her Majesty the Queen
중전기 重電機 heavy electric machine 〔equipment〕
중전차 重戰車 a heavy tank
중절 中絶 interruption ; stoppage ; discontinuance ; intermission ; suspension ; abeyance —하다 be interrupted ; be stopped ; be suspended ; be held up ; be dropped ; fall into abeyance ¶ 중절된 집안을 재흥하다 restore a family line
임신 — (artificial) termination of pregnancy ; lawful〔artificial〕 abortion
중절모 中折帽 a soft hat ; a felt hat ; a wide-awake (hat)
— 배급 priority rationing ; rationing
중점 中點 the middle point ; the median (point) ; the central point ; the center
중점 重點 [강조] emphasis ; stress ; [중요] importance ; [우위] priority ; [중심점] the pivotal point ¶ 중점적으로 in priority ; preponderantly // 중점을 두다 lay emphasis〔stress〕 on ; emphasize ; give 〔place〕 priority to // 중점적으로 조사〔연구〕하다 concentrate upon the subject
— 배급 priority rationing ; rationing on priority basis — 생산 priority production —주의 a preferential policy ; a priority system
중정 重訂 the second revision ; a re-revision —하다 revise twice
중정 中正 impartiality ; fairness ¶ 중정한 impartial ; fair ; unbiased // 중정한 의견 an unbiased opinion
중정석 重晶石 〖광물〗 barite
중조 重曹 bicarbonate of soda ; sodium bicarbonate ; baking soda 《속》
중죄 重罪 felony ; a grave〔capital, seri-

ous〕 offense〔crime〕 ¶ 중죄의 felonious //중죄를 범하다 commit a grave〔serious〕 offense
—(범)인 a felon — 재판 a trial for felony
*중주 重奏 a duet(t)
육— a sextet(te)
중중거리다 mutter ⇨ 중얼거리다
중증 重症 a serious case ¶ 그는 중증이다 He is a serious case.
— 심신 장애아 a severely-handicapped child — 환자 a serious case ; a patient with an advanced disease ¶ 중증 환자실 an intensive-care room
†중지 中止 stoppage ; suspension ; interruption ; suppression (금지) —하다 stop ; suspend ; suppress ; call off 《a game, a strike》; put the lid on 《속》 ¶ 중지되다 be suspended ; be stopped ; come〔be brought〕 to a standstill //연설을 중지시키다 stop the speaker //그 협상은 중지 상태다 The negotiations are at a standstill. /The negotiations are kept in abeyance. //회의가 중지되었다 The meeting was canceled. /The meeting was adjourned. //그는 일을 중지하지 않을 수 없었다 He had to leave off his work. //경기가 우천으로 중지되었다 The match was called off〔halted〕 owing to rain. //나는 해외 여행할 생각을 중지했다 I have given up the idea of going abroad. //그의 행동을 중지시키겠다 I will stop his action. //얼마동안 신문 배달을 중지시킬까요 How long would you like your paper put on hold? //휴가 중 신문 배달을 중지시켜 주십시오 I'd like to put our newspaper on vacation hold.
중지 中指 the middle finger
중지 衆智 wisdom of the many ¶ 중지를 모으다 seek counsel〔ask advice〕 of many people
중지상 中之上 the higher class of the medium grade ; B plus ; the higher class of the fair grade
중지중 中之中 the middle class of the medium grade ; B
중지하 中之下 the lower class of the medium grade ; B minus ; the lower class of the fair grade
중직 重職 an important〔a weighty〕 office ; a responsible post〔position〕; a position of trust ¶ 중직을 맡다 hold〔occupy〕 a responsible〔an important〕 post
중진 重鎭 [문진] a heavy paperweight ; [사람] a man of influence ; a prominent figure ; a leader ; a leading man ; an authority (학계의) ¶ 저작계의 중진 an outstanding figure in the book-writing world //영어학계의 중진 a leading scholar of English ; an authority of English //그는 정계의 중진이다 He is one of the leading figures in our political circles.
중진국 中進國 a semideveloped country〔nation〕
중질 中帙 [상품 따위의] medium quality ¶ 중질의 medium ⇨ 중길
중창 中— the middle layer of a shoe sole
*중창 重唱 『음악』 a part song
사— a vocal four ; a (vocal) quartet(te)
중채 中— 『건축』 a building between the main building and the outer building
중책 重責 [책임] a heavy responsibility ; [책망] a severe rebuke ; a severe reprimand ¶ 중책을 맡다 assume a heavy responsibility
중천 中天 midair ; the midheaven ; the zenith ¶ 달이 중천에 걸려 있다 The moon hangs high in the sky.
중첩 重疊 [중복] reiteration ; [겹쳐 쌓임] being piled up one on another —하다 be piled up one on another ; be heaped up ; be amassed ; be repeated〔reiterated, duplicated〕 ¶ 산악이 중첩하여 하늘을 찌를 듯이 솟아 있다 Mountain upon mountain soars into the sky.
중추 中秋 the fifteenth day of the eighth month by lunar calendar ; a harvest festival ; mid-autumn day
중추 仲秋 mid-autumn ; the eighth lunar month
— 명월 the harvest moon
중추 中樞 the center ; the pivot ; the focus ; the nucleus ; the backbone ; the main prop ¶ 중추의 central ; leading ; pivotal //상업의 중추 an artery of trade //산업의 중추 a hub of industry //사회의 중추 the mainstay of society //중추적 인물 a central〔pivotal〕 figure
— 산업 a pivotal〔key〕 industry — 신경 the central nerve — 인물 a leading figure ; a key man ; a mainstay
중축 中軸 the axis ; the pivot
중춘 仲春 the second lunar month ; the middle of spring
중측연 重測鉛 『측량』 [심해용] deep-sea lead
중층 中層 the middle storey〔stratum, layer, class, floor〕
중치 中— [품질] an article of medium〔average〕 quality ; middlings ; medium (quality) goods ; [값] a medium-priced one ; [크기] a medium-sized one
중치막 a man's outer coat with large sleeves
중침 中針 a medium-sized needle
중크롬산 重—酸 『화학』 dichromic acid
—염 dichromate ; bichromate
중키 middle height ; medium stature〔size〕 ¶ 그는 중키의 미남자였다 He was a handsome man of medium height.
중탄산 重炭酸 『화학』 bicarbonate
—소다 bicarbonate of soda ; sodium bicarbonate —염 bicarbonate —칼리 bicarbonate of potassium
중탕 重湯 cooking〔warming up〕 in a double boiler —하다 cook〔warm up〕 in a

double boiler

중태 重態 a serious〔grave, critical〕 condition ; a critical state〔stage〕 ¶ 중태이다 be seriously ill ; be in a serious condition // 중태에 빠지다 fall into a critical condition ; [병이 주어] take a serious turn // 그는 폐병으로 중태이다 He is seriously ill with consumption. // 그는 부상해서 중태에 빠졌다 He was wounded and in a critical condition.

중턱 中— [산의] the mountain's breast ; the mid-slope of a mountain ¶ 중턱에 halfway up〔down〕《a hill, a mountain》 // 그 산의 중턱 위는 구름에 덮여 있었다 The upper half of the mountain was enveloped in clouds.

중토 重土 〖화학〗 baryta

중톱 a medium-sized saw

중퇴 中退 leaving school in mid-course ; dropping out of school **—하다** leave school in mid-course ; leave school without finishing a complete course ; leave a university without graduating (대학을) ; drop out of school ¶ 대학을 중퇴한 청년 a young man who got only halfway through college ; a young man who gave up a university course halfway

—율 a school dropout rate **—자** a school dropout

중파 中波 〖전파〗 a medium electric wave

중파 中破 half-damage **—하다** half-damage

중판 中判 〖사진〗 medium size ¶ 중판 사진 a photo of cabinet size

중판 重版 a second edition ; a reprint **—하다** reprint ; print the second edition ¶ 그 책은 중판에 중판을 거듭했다 The book went into many editions.

중편 中篇 [제2권] the second part《of three parts》; the second〔middle〕 volume ; [중편의 글] a medium-length story

— 소설 a medium-length story

중평 衆評 public〔popular, general〕 opinion〔criticism〕 ; common talk (평판) ¶ 중평이 각색이다 Public opinion is divided. // 그 연주는 실패였다는 것이 중평이다 The performance was voted a failure.

중포 重砲 a heavy gun

—병 heavy artillery 《총칭》 ; a heavy artillery man **— 연대** a heavy artillery regiment

중포격 重砲擊 heavy bombardment **—하다** bombard heavily

중폭 中幅 medium width

중폭격 重爆擊 heavy bombing **—하다** bomb heavily

—기(機) a heavy bomber

중품 中品 medium quality (goods)

중풍 中風 〖의학〗 palsy ; paralysis ¶ 중풍의 palsied ; paralytic // 중풍에 걸리다 be stricken with paralysis ; have a stroke of paralysis

중하 仲夏 the fifth lunar month ; midsummer

중하 重荷 [짐] heavy burden ; [부담] heavy responsibility

중하다 重— [무겁다] (be) heavy ; [병이] serious ; critical ; [일이] grave ; important ¶ 중한 죄 a grave charge // 중한 벌 a heavy punishment // 중한 책임 a heavy responsibility // 중한 지위 an important position ; a key post // 병이 중하다 be seriously ill

중학교 中學校 a junior high school 《미》 ; the lower secondary school 《총칭》 ; a middle school ¶ 중학교에 다니다 attend a middle school // 중학교를 졸업하다 finish〔leave〕 a junior high school ; complete the junior high school course

— 과정 a junior high (school) course

— 학생 ⇨ 중학생

중학생 中學生 a junior high school student〔boy, girl〕 ; a middleschool student〔boy, girl〕

중합 重合 polymerization ; polymerism

중항 中項 〖수학〗 the mean

비례 — the mean proportional

중핵 中核 the kernel ; the core ; the nucleus ¶ 가정은 사회의 중핵을 이룬다 The family is the nucleus of the community.

중허리 中— 〖음악〗 a kind of popular ballad that starts off as a *pyeong shijo* and then abruptly changes form in the middle

중형 重刑 a heavy penalty ; a severe punishment ¶ 중형에 처하다 sentence 《a person》 to a severe punishment // 중형을 과하다 inflict heavy penalty upon 《a person》 ; punish 《a person》 severely

중형 仲兄 one's second eldest brother

중형 中型 a medium〔middle〕 size ¶ 중형의 middle-sized

중혼 重婚 bigamy ; double marriage **—하다** commit bigamy ; marry 《a person》 bigamously ¶ 중혼의 bigamous // 중혼죄를 범하다 commit bigamy ; be guilty of bigamy

—자 a bigamist **—죄** bigamy

***중화 中和** neutralization (화학적) ; counteraction ; [평형] equability **—하다** neutralize ; counteract ¶ 중화성의 counteractive // 산을 염기로 중화시키다 neutralize acid with a base // 둘은 서로 중화한다 One neutralizes the other.

—점 the neutral point **—제(약)** a counteractive ; a counteragent

중화 中華 China

—민국 the Republic of China ; Nationalist China **— 요리** a Chinese dish **— 요리법** Chinese cookery **— 요리책** a Chinese cookbook **— 인민 공화국** the People's Republic of China (중공)

중화기 重火器 heavy weapons

중화학 공업 重化學工業 the heavy chemical industry

중환 重患 a serious illness
―자 a serious case ; one who is seriously ill

중후 重厚 courtesy and generosity **―하다** (be) courteous and generous ; grave and lenient〔gentle〕 ¶ 중후한 신사 a courteous and generous gentleman // 그는 중후한 사람이다 His personality is gentle and sincere.

중흥 中興 restoration ; revival ; rehabilitation **―하다** revive ; restore ; rehabilitate ¶ 쇠퇴한 가운을 중흥하다 revive the collapsed fortunes of the family
―지주(之主) a restorer 《of a kingdom, a dynasty》 ; a revivalist

중히 重― with care ; with caution ; with respect ¶ 중히 여기다 [소중히] value ; hold dear ; make〔think〕 much of ; set a high value on ; [주의] take good care of ; [존중] respect ; honor // 중히 여기지 않다 make light〔little〕 of ; have no regard for // 사람을 중히 쓰다 appoint 《a person》 to a post of trust ; give 《a person》 an important position // 물건을 중히 간수하다 take good care of a thing // 건강을 무엇보다 중히 여기다 set health before everything else // 생명보다 명예를 중히 여기다 put honor before life // 부모를 중히 여기다 be filial〔devoted〕 to one's parents

중힘 中― [활에서] the second sturdiest bow

‡쥐[1] a rat ; a mouse 《*pl.* mice》 ¶ 쥐잡기 운동 an anti-rat drive // 이 고양이는 쥐를 잘 잡는다 This cat is a good mouser. / This cat is very good at catching mice.
―약 ratsbane ; raticide **집〔들〕―** the house〔field〕 mouse
독 안에 든 쥐와 같다 ⟨속담⟩ be like a rat in a trap

쥐[2] [경련] a cramp ; a jerk ; convulsions ¶ 쥐나다 have a cramp ; be seized with a cramp

쥐구멍 a rathole ; a mousehole ¶ 쥐구멍을 찾다 seek a loophole〔hiding place〕 // 어디 쥐구멍이라도 있으면 들어가고 싶은 심정이다 I feel like crawling into a hole somewhere. // 부끄러워서 쥐구멍이라도 있으면 들어가 숨고 싶었다 I felt inclined to sink into the ground with shame. /I was so overwhelmed with shame that I wished the floor would open and engulf me.
쥐구멍에도 볕들 날이 있다 ⟨속담⟩ It is a long lane that has no turning. /Fortune knocks at our door by turns. /Every cloud has a silver lining. /Fortune knocks once at least at every man's gate. /Every dog has his day.

쥐꼬리 a rattail ¶ 쥐꼬리만한 a mere particle of ; a modicum of ; an atom of // 쥐꼬리만한 월급 a low〔small〕 salary ; poor〔little〕 pay // 쥐꼬리만하다 be very small // 쥐꼬리만한 월급을 보고 일하자니 우스꽝스럽다 It is ridiculous for me to work for such a small salary
―톱 a kind of long thin saw

쥐나다 [부끄러워서] blush (with shame) ; [경련] have a cramp〔jerk〕 ¶ 부끄러워서 얼굴에 쥐날 지경이었다 She felt as if her face were colored to the roots of her hair.

쥐눈이콩 〖식물〗 a kind of small bean ; Rhynchosia volubilis (학명)

†쥐다 hold ; take〔get〕 hold of ; grasp ; clasp ; seize ¶ 사람의 손을 꽉 쥐다 hold 《a person's》 hand tightly // 주먹을 쥐다 clench〔double, close〕 one's fist // 비밀을 쥐다 hold 《a person's》 secret ; have the goods on 《a person》 (속) // 권력을 쥐다 have power // 정권을 쥐다 come into〔be in〕 power // 돈을 쥐다 come into money

쥐대기 a clumsy craftsman

쥐덫 a mousetrap ; a rattrap ¶ 쥐덫을 놓다 set a trap for rats // 쥐덫으로 쥐를 잡다 catch a mouse with a mousetrap

쥐똥나무 〖식물〗 a privet

쥐라기 ―紀 〖지질〗 the Jurassic period

쥐락펴락 controlling 《a person》 perfectly ; make a puppet of a person ; twist〔turn〕 a person round one's (little) finger ; have a person perfectly under one's control ; have〔keep〕 a person on a string ; have a string on a person ¶ 청중을 쥐락펴락하다 play on the audience // 남편을 쥐락펴락하다 dominate one's husband

쥐머리 a kind of short ribs

쥐며느리 〖곤충〗 a sow bug

쥐방울 〖식물〗 a Dutchman's pipe

쥐뿔같다 (be) worthless

쥐살 foreshank of beef

쥐새끼 a young rat ¶ 쥐새끼 같은 놈 a paltry fellow

쥐색 ―色 dark gray

쥐숨듯이 without leaving any trace

쥐알봉수 a smart fellow ; a shrewd guy ; a crafty fellow ; a sly dog

쥐약 ―藥 rat poison ; raticide

쥐어뜯다 pluck (off) ; pick ; tear (off) ¶ 머리털을 쥐어뜯다 tear〔rend〕 one's hair // 닭털을 쥐어뜯다 pluck〔pick〕 chicken

쥐어주다 [돈을] slip (money) into 《a person's》 hand〔pocket〕 ; [팁을] tip 《a porter》 ; [뇌물을] grease〔tickle〕 《a person's》 palm ; oil 《a person's》 hand ; bribe ; tickle 《a person》 in the palm (구) ¶ 1만원을 쥐어 주다 give 《a person》 a 10,000 *won* bribe

쥐어짜다 ① [액체] press〔squeeze〕 out ; extract ② [머리·목소리] press out ¶ 목소리를 쥐어짜다 strain one's voice ③ [착취하다] extort ; squeeze ¶ 돈을 쥐어짜다 extort money from 《a person》 ④ [조르다] importune

쥐어흔들다 grab and shake ; brandish ; wave ; sway ; swing ¶ 정계를 쥐어흔들다 hold sway over the political world // 어깨를 쥐어흔들다 shake 《a person》 by the shoulder
쥐엄나무 〖식물〗 the honey locust (tree)
쥐엄발이 a shrivel(l)ed foot ; a person with a shriveled foot
쥐엄쥐엄 ⇨ 죄암죄암
쥐엄질 [젖먹이의 재롱] the way a baby opens and closes its hands
쥐여지내다 be placed under 《a person's》 control ; live in the grips of 《a person》 ; live under 《a person's》 thumb ¶ 그는 아내에게 쥐여지낸다 He is dominated by his wife. /He is a henpecked husband. /He is kept under his wife's thumb.
쥐오줌풀 〖식물〗 the common valerian (plant)
쥐이다 get grabbed ; be caught〔held〕
쥐잡듯이 one by one ; individually ; thoroughly **—하다** comb〔scour〕 《a place for a thing》 ¶ 한집한집 쥐잡듯이 수색했다 They went the rounds of inquiry from door to door.
쥐정신 —精神 amnesia ; a short〔weak〕 memory ; forgetfulness
쥐젖 a (small) wart
쥐죽은 듯하다 be still as a stone ; be silent as the grave ; (be) hushed and still ; be in a deathly silence ¶ 쥐죽은 듯이 고요한 한밤중 the dead hours (of the night) // 교실 안은 쥐죽은 듯이 조용했다 The class was as silent as the grave.
쥐참외 〖식물〗 a snake gourd ; Trichosanthes cucumeoides (학명)
쥐치 〖물고기〗 a filefish ; a foolfish ; leatherfish
쥐코밥상 —床 a frugal meal ; a poor 〔humble〕 table
쥐코조리 a narrow〔little〕-minded person ; a small-minded man ; a petty person
쥐통 〖의학〗 cholera ¶ 쥐통이 돌다 have 〔be in the grip of〕 a cholera epidemic
쥐포육장수 —脯肉— a petty miserly person ; a mean fellow
쥐해 the Year of the Rat
쥔 the master ⇨ 주인(主人)
쥘대 a small round stick used in quilting
쥘부채 a folding fan ¶ 쥘부채꼴의 fan-shaped
쥘손 a handle ; a grip ; something to hold on to
쥘쌈지 a tobacco pouch
즈런즈런 in affluence ; in abundance ; plentifully **—하다** (be) affluent ; opulent ; abundant ; plentiful ¶ 살림이 즈런즈런하다 be well off ; lead an abundant life ; live in clover
즈음 the time ; an occasion ¶ 이즈음 now ; nowadays ; lately ; these days // 그즈음 at that time ; on that occasion // 그녀가 여학교에 다닐 즈음에 나는 대학생이었다 At the time (when) she was a high school girl, I was a college boy.
즈음하여 when ; at the time 《of》 ; in case 《of》 ¶ 이때에 즈음하여 at this time // 위험에 즈음하여 in case of danger // 어려운 때 즈음하여 in time of need // 이별에 즈음하여 at parting from you
즈크 doek 《네》 ; duck ; canvas
—신 〔화(靴)〕 canvas shoes ; tennis shoes
†즉 卽 [곧] namely ; that is (to say) ; to wit ; so to speak ; [바로] just ; precisely ; exactly ; nothing but ; neither more nor less ¶ 작문의 법칙 즉 문법 the rules of composition or grammar // 당신의 출세가 즉 나의 출세이다 Your success means my success. // 이것이 즉 내가 원했던 것이다 This is just a thing I wanted. // 여기가 구세주 즉 예수가 난 곳이다 This is the place where the Savior, that is, Christ was born.
-즉 if ; when ; then ; on ¶ 알아본즉 거짓이었다 On inquiry, the report proved false. // 네 말을 들은즉 참 안됐다 I am sorry to hear that.
†즉각 卽刻 on the spot ; at once ; right away ; instantly ; immediately ; in a moment ¶ 즉각 승낙하다 give a ready consent ; accept immediately // 즉각 대답하다 give a ready answer ; make an immediate reply // 즉각 거절했다 I declined then and there.
즉결 卽決 an immediate〔a prompt, a quick〕 decision ; 〖법〗 summary judgment〔dealing, action〕 ; snap judgment 《미》 **—하다** decide on the spot〔immediately〕 ; 〖법〗 try〔deal with〕 summarily ¶ 즉결 즉행 prompt decision and execution
— 재판 a summary decision〔judgment〕 ¶ 즉결 재판소 a summary court **— 처분** summary conviction
즉낙 卽諾 a ready consent **—하다** readily consent to ; give a ready consent 〔nod〕
즉납 卽納 immediate〔prompt〕 payment **—하다** pay immediately
즉단 卽斷 immediate〔prompt〕 decision **—하다** decide immediately〔on the spot〕
즉답 卽答 a ready〔a prompt, an immediate〕 answer **—하다** reply on the spot ; give a ready answer ¶ 즉답을 앙망합니다 We ask for your prompt reply. /Your prompt answer is requested. // 그 질문에 즉답할 수는 없다 I cannot answer that question offhand.
즉매 卽賣 spot sale **—하다** sell on the spot
—장 a sale(s)room **— 전시회** an exhibition and spot sale 《of pictures》

즉사 卽死 instantaneous death **—하다** die on the spot ; be killed instantly ¶ 토끼가 일격에 즉사했다 A blow at the hare proved instantly fatal. // 어린애가 자동차에 치어 즉사했다 A child was run over by a car and killed on the spot.
—자 a person killed instantly
즉살 卽殺 killing promptly ; killing outright **—하다** kill on the spot ; kill outright
즉석 卽席 ¶ 즉석의 immediate ; ready ; instant ; prompt ; impromptu ; improvised ; offhand(ed) // 즉석에서 offhandedly ; instantly ; impromptu ; on the spot ; immediately // 즉석 연설을 하다 speak extempore ; make an impromptu speech ; make a speech offhand // 즉석에서 시를 짓다 extemporize a poem // 즉석에서 대답하다 answer immediately〔offhand〕// 즉석에서 의견을 말하다 give an offhand opinion 《on》
— 연설 an impromptu〔offhand〕 speech ¶ 즉석 연설을 하다 speak extempore ; make an impromptu speech **— 연주자** an improviser **— 요리** a quick〔an instant, an improvised〕 dish **— 커피** instant coffee
†**즉시 卽時** at once ; immediately ; instantly ; without delay ; right away〔off〕; directly ¶ 그는 즉시 허락했다 He gave me a ready consent. // 이 문제는 즉시 해결해야 한다 The question calls for an immediate solution. /This is an urgent question.
— 거래 direct〔spot〕 transaction **—불** spot〔immediate, down〕 payment **—불 어음** a sight bill **— 인도** spot delivery **— 통고** an immediate notice **— 통화** direct distance dialing 《D. D. D.》 **— 항고** an immediate complaint
즉영 卽詠 improvisation ; [즉영시] an impromptu poem **—하다** improvise a poem
즉위 卽位 accession to the throne ; enthronement **—하다** come〔accede〕 to the throne ; ascend the throne
—식 a coronation (ceremony) ¶ 즉위식을 행하다 hold a coronation ceremony
즉응 卽應 prompt conformity〔agreement〕; immediate adaptation **—하다** conform immediately 《to》; (immediately) adapt oneself 《to》; meet (immediately) ¶ 즉응하여 in immediate conformity with ; in immediate response to // 시대에 즉응한 교육 education adapted promptly to the times // 시대의 요구에 즉응하다 promptly meet the needs of the times
즉일 卽日 the same〔very〕 day ¶ 즉일로 on the same〔very〕 day // 즉일로 돌아오다 return on the same day // 결혼 즉일로 부부싸움을 하다 make a (domestic) scene on the very wedding day
즉전 卽錢 cash down ; spot〔ready〕 cash
즉전 즉결 卽戰卽決 a lightning war plan ; blitzkrieg operations
즉조 卽祚 enthronement ⇨ 즉위
즉좌 卽座 ⇨ 즉석(卽席)
즉행 卽行 ① [곧 감] prompt departure ② [곧 행함] prompt execution ; immediate operation **—하다** depart at once ; go promptly ; [실행] carry into immediate execution〔operation〕; carry out promptly〔immediately〕; act at once ¶ 옳다고 생각하는 일을 즉행하라 Do at once what you think is right.
즉효 卽效 immediate effect 《of medicine》 ¶ 즉효가 있다 produce〔have, take〕 immediate effect ; [고통이 없어지다] give immediate relief ; afford instantaneous relief
—약 a quick〔an instant(aneous)〕 remedy ; a quick cure
즉흥 卽興 extempore amusement ¶ 즉흥적 impromptu ; extempore ; extemporary ; improvisatory // 즉흥적으로 짓다 compose 《a poem》 extempore ; improvise
—곡 an impromptu **—시** an impromptu poem ; an extempore verse **— 시인** an improviser ; an improvisator
즐거움 pleasure ; enjoyment ; delight ; happiness ; joy ¶ 독서의 즐거움 the pleasure of reading // 인생의 즐거움 the pleasure〔joy, enjoyment〕 of life // 가정 생활의 즐거움 the amenities of home life // …을 즐거움으로 삼다 delight in ; take pleasure〔delight〕 in // 인생의 즐거움이 없어졌다 The charm of life is gone.
즐거이 pleasantly ; delightfully ; merrily ; cheerfully ; joyfully ¶ 하루를 즐거이 보내다 have a nice day // 즐거이 지내다 live〔lead〕 a happy life // 즐거이 놀다 enjoy oneself // 즐거이 맞이하다 welcome with joy ; receive 《a person》 with open arms
†**즐겁다** (be) pleasant ; delightful ; cheerful ; merry ; joyful ; glad ; happy ¶ 즐거운 설 a happy new year // 즐거운 옛날 the good old days // 즐거운 추억 a pleasant memory // 즐거운 때나 괴로운 때나 in pain or pleasure ; rain or shine // 즐겁게 하다 please ; delight ; amuse // 이런 것을 보면 즐거웠던 옛 생활이 생각난다 This reminds me of my past happy days〔of the good old times〕. // 매우 즐거웠습니다 I enjoyed every minute of it. // 오늘 밤은 아주 즐겁게 보내자 Tonight let's pull out all the stops and have ourselves a good time.
즐겨 ① [소망하여] by〔from〕 choice ; willingly ; [자진하여] willing to 《do》; of one's (own) free will ¶ 즐겨 독서하다 take pleasure in reading
② [종종] often ¶ 즐겨 그림을 그리다 care to paint a picture frequently
†**즐기다** enjoy oneself 《over》; take pleasure〔delight〕 in ; amuse oneself 《with》;

make merry ; take a fancy to〔for〕; be fond of ¶ 독서를 즐기다 enjoy reading ; enjoy oneself by reading // 음악을 즐기다 be fond of music // 인생을 즐기다 enjoy life // 보고 즐기다 take pleasure in looking 《at》 // 같이 즐기다 share one's joy with company

즐비 櫛比 ―하다 stand closely together ; form a line ; stand in a continuous row ¶ 그 거리의 한쪽엔 서점이 즐비하게 서 있다 On one side of the street is an unbroken succession of book shops.

즐풍목우 櫛風沐雨 the storms of life

*즙 汁 juice (과실의) ; sap (초목의) ; latex (고무 나무의) ¶ 즙내다 express〔press out〕 juice 《from grapes》 ; squeeze〔extract〕 juice 《from a lemon》 // 즙이 많은 juicy ; succulent // 즙이 많은 배 a pear full of juice ; a juicy pear

포도〔사과〕― grape〔apple〕 juice

즙나다 汁― [익숙해지다] get skilled ; become expert 《in》 ; attain proficiency ; improve oneself 《in》

즙내다 汁― extract〔squeeze, press〕 juice ; juice ¶ 사과를 즙내다 juice〔press the juice out of〕 an apple

즙액 汁液 juice ¶ 즙액이 많은〔없는〕 juicy〔juiceless〕

증 症 ① [증세] symptoms ② [화증] anger ③ [싫증] disgust ; dislike ¶ 무서움증이 나다 show signs of fear // 싫증이 나다 feel a repugnance 《to》

증 證 [증거] proof ; evidence ; testimony ; [증서] a certificate ; a warrant

차량 등록― vehicle registration card 학생― a student identification〔card〕

증 贈 presentation ; proffering

저자― "With the Compliments of the Author." (책에 서명하여)

†증가 增加 an increase ; addition ; augmentation ; expansion ; a gain ; a rise ; growth (인구 따위) ―하다 increase 《in》 ; rise ; grow ; swell ; multiply ¶ 작년의 3할 증가 an increase〔a gain〕 of 30% over that of last year // 증가되고 있다 be on the increase // 수가 증가하다 increase in number // 인구가 400만으로 증가하다 go on increasing in population to four millions // 요즘 사고와 범죄가 놀랄 만큼 증가하고 있다 Nowadays accidents and crimes augment in an alarming way. // 우리 나라의 무역은 해마다 증가한다 The trade of our country grows larger every year. // 지난 달 우리 매상이 상당히 증가했습니다 Our sales picked up considerably last month.

― 소득세 increased income tax ―액 the amount increased ―율 the rate of increase ― 이익 increased profits ― 자본 additional capital 인구 ― (an) increase in population 자연 ― a natural increase〔increment〕 ; an increase by natural growth

증간 增刊 [발행 증가] increasing printing〔publication〕 ; [간행물] a special〔an extra〕 number 《of a magazine》 ; an extra edition〔issue〕

―호 a special issue

증감 增減 increase and decrease ; rise and fall ; addition and reduction ; variation ; fluctuation (변동) ―하다 increase and decrease ; add and reduce ; rise and fall ; vary ; fluctuate ¶ 수입은 달마다 증감이 있다 The receipts vary with the month. // 하천의 물은 조수의 간만에 따라 증감한다 The river rises and falls with the tide.

*증강 增强 reinforcement ; augmentation ; increase ―하다 reinforce ; increase ; augment ¶ 공군을 증강하다 reinforce the air force // 수송력을 증강하다 augment the carrying capacity 《of the railway》

†증거 證據 evidence ; proof ; witness ; testimony ¶ 물적 증거 material evidence // 결정적인 증거 conclusive evidence〔proof〕 ; a clinching〔decisive, final〕 proof // 충분한 증거 abundant〔sufficient〕 evidence ; ample proof // 불충분한 증거 insufficient evidence // 제1차적 증거 an original evidence // 확실한 증거 certain〔convincing, trustworthy, corroborative〕 evidence ; a strong〔positive〕 proof〔testimony〕 // 반대의 증거 a contrary proof ; evidence against a case // 증거가 없어서 for lack of evidence ; in the absence of evidence // 확실한 증거에 따라서 on trustworthy evidence // 증거를 제출하다 produce evidence〔proof〕 ; present〔bring forward〕 evidence〔testimony〕 // 증거를 내세우다 adduce〔give〕 evidence // 증거를 제공하다 afford〔furnish〕 proof // 증거를 모으다 collect〔gather〕 evidence ; accumulate proofs // 증거로서 예를 들다 give examples in evidence // 증거가 박약하다 The evidence is slender. // 그가 유죄라는 증거는 조금도 없다 There is no evidence of his guilt. // 그에게 불리한 증거는 전혀 없다 There is not the slightest evidence against him. // 증거가 명백하므로 판사는 그의 유죄를 선고했다 The evidence against him, being clear the judge declared him guilty. // 그는 아무런 증거도 없는데 감금되었다 He was imprisoned on no evidence. // 무슨 증거로 그 따위 소리를 하느냐 On what authority do you say so? // 하품은 졸린 증거이다 Yawning is a sign of sleepiness.

―금 a deposit ; deposit money ― 능력 admissibility of evidence ―물 (a piece of) evidence ; an exhibit ― 보전 preservation of evidence ― 서류 documentary evidence ― 인 a witness ; a testifier ; an attestor ― 인멸 destruction of evidence ¶ 증거 인멸하다 destroy evidence // 증거 인멸을 꾀하다 try to hide traces of the crime ― 자료 corroborative facts ― 조

사 taking of evidence 간접〔내적〕 — indirect〔internal〕 evidence 정황 — circumstantial evidence

증결하다 增結— make an additional connection (of a passenger or freight car) to a train ¶ 객차를 2량 증결하다 add two passenger cars to a train

*증권 證券 [유가] securities ; [상업상의] an instrument ; [주식의] a certificate ; [해운 관계] a bill ; [증서] a document ; a deed ¶ 증권화하다 convert 《funds, deposits》 into securities ; fund 《debts》 (부채 따위를)

— 거래법 the Securities Exchange Law — 거래소 a stock exchange ; the Securities Exchange ¶ 한국 증권 거래소 the Korea Stock Exchange — 거래원 a bill broker ; a (licensed) stock broker ¶ 증권 거래원 수수료 brokerage ; commission — 매매 dealing in bonds and securities — 소유자 a security holder — 시장 the securities market —업 security business ¶ 증권업자 a security dealer — 인수 회사 an underwriting company ; an underwriter — 인지 a revenue stamp — 회사 the security corporation 국고 — a treasury bond 《미》 ; an exchequer bond 《영》 대용 — collateral securities 선적 — shipping documents 선하 — a bill of lading 《B/L》 유가 — securities 유통 — a negotiable instrument 정부 발행 — government securities 창고 — a warehouse receipt

증권 거래 證券去來 a dealings in stocks

증급 增給 an increase〔advance〕 of〔in〕 wages〔pay, salary〕 ; increased pay 〔wages〕 ; a raise of wages ; a pay raise —하다 increase〔raise〕 《a person's》 pay ; give 《a person》 a pay raise ¶ 증급을 요구하다 demand〔ask for〕 higher wages〔pay〕

†증기 蒸氣 steam ; vapor ¶ 증기를 일으키다 get up〔put on, generate〕 steam // 증기를 막다 shut〔turn〕 off steam // 증기가 통하고 있다 The steam is on.

—관(管) a steam pipe — 기관 a steam engine — 기관차 a steam locomotive — 난로 a steam heater — 난방 steam heating —력 steam power — 목욕 a steam bath — 브레이크 a steam brake —선 a steamer — 소독 steam disinfection —실 a steam chest〔chamber〕 — 실린더 a steam cylinder —압 steam〔vapor〕 pressure〔tension〕 — 압력 steam pressure — 운전 기계 a steam-worked〔-operated〕 machine ; steam machinery 《집합적》 — 터빈 a steam turbine

증답 贈答 present-giving ; an exchange of presents〔gifts〕 —하다 exchange gifts 〔presents〕 ; give presents to each other —품 a gift ; a present 신년〔성탄〕 — a New Year's〔Christmas〕 gift

†증대 增大 enlargement ; increase ; augmentation —하다 enlarge ; increase ; augment ; swell ; enhance

— 모세포 〖생물〗 an auxocyte —판 an enlarged edition〔number〕 — 포자(胞子) 〖생물〗 an auxospore —호 an enlarged number

증량 增量 (an) increase in quantity —하다 increase the quantity 《of》

*증류 蒸溜 distillation —하다 distill ¶ 해수를 증류하여 진수(眞水)로 만들다 distill fresh water from sea water

—관 a distiller tube —기 a distiller ; a retort —수 distilled water —액 distillate ; distillation — 장치 distillatory apparatus —주 a spirituous liquor ¶ 증류주 양조장 a distillery

†증명 證明 proof ; evidence ; [증언] testimony ; attestation ; [확증] authentication [논증] demonstration

> 참고 **proof**는 뚜렷한 결론을 끄집어 낼 수 있을 정도로 완전하고 납득이 가는 증명 **evidence**는 밝히는 것 사물을 증명하거나 반증하는 모든 종류의 것들을 가리키는 넓은 의미의 말

—하다 [실증하다] prove ; show ; bear out ; [증언하다] testify to ; bear witness to ; [입증하다] verify ; demonstrate ; [진짜임을] authenticate ; [신원을] identify ¶ 학설을 증명하다 demonstrate a theory // 범죄를 증명하다 bear witness to a crime // 무죄를 증명하다 establish 《a person's》 innocence // 문서를 증명하다 attest a document // 품행 방정함을 증명하다 testify to 《a person's》 good conduct // …의 시체임을 증명하다 identify the body as that of 《a person》 // …을 증명함 This is to certify 《that》 // 그것을 증명할 수 있느냐 Can you prove it ?

—서 a certificate ; a testimonial (인물, 자격 따위의) ¶ 건강 증명서 a health certificate // 신분 증명서 an identification card // 원산지 증명서 a certificate of origin

증모 增募 an increased recruiting 〔enrolling〕 —하다 [군인 따위를] recruit a larger enlistment ; raise extra troops ; [학생 따위를] receive larger enrollment ; increase the number 《of students》 to be admitted ; raise extra

*증발 蒸發 evaporation ; volatilization ; vaporization —하다 evaporate ; vaporize ; escape〔fly off〕 in vapor ; steam (물이) ¶ 증발하기 쉬운 volatile ; vaporable // 증발시키다 evaporate 《milk》 ; vaporize

—계 vaporimeter — 계수 a factor of evaporation (보일러의) —(건조)기 an evaporator ; a vaporizer — 농축(화) graduation —열 evaporation heat — 용량 the evaporative capacity — 응축기 an evaporative condenser — 접시 an evaporating dish

증발 增發 [열차의] operation of an extra train ; [통화의] an increased issue **—하다** [열차를] operate an extra train ; increase the railway service ; [통화를] issue additional paper money ¶ 임시 열차를 증발하다 operate〔run〕 a special train 《for skiers》// 지폐를 증발하다 issue additional paper money

증배 增配 [배당의] an increased dividend ; a bonus ; [배급의] an increase of rations ; a ration increase ; an extra ration **—하다** [배당을] declare an increased dividend ; pay an increased dividend ; [배급품을] increase the rations ; distribute extra rations
—미(米) extra rations of rice

증병 增兵 reinforcement ; additional dispatch 《of troops》 **—하다** reinforce ; dispatch reinforcements

증보 增補 an enlargement ; a supplement **—하다** enlarge ; supplement ¶ 증보 개정하여 재판하다 produce a reprint with additions and emendations
개정 —판 a new edition revised and enlarged

증봉 增俸 a salary increase ; an increase of salary ; a raise〔rise〕 in salary **—하다** increase〔raise〕 the salary

증빙 證憑 evidence ; proof ; witness ; authority (근거)
— 서류 documentary evidence

증산 增産 increased production〔output〕 ; production increase ; an increased yield (농산물의) **—하다** increase〔boost〕 production ; produce a greater amount 《of》 ¶ 쌀의 증산 an increased yield of rice // 석탄의 증산 계획 a plan for increasing coal output // 식료품 증산이 급했다 It was of burning necessity to turn out foodstuffs in increasing amounts.
— 계획 a program for the increased production 《of》 **— 운동** a drive for production increase

증상 症狀 [징후] symptoms ; [병세] the condition of a patient ¶ 유행성 감기의 증상을 나타내다 develop〔show〕 symptoms of influenza
객관〔자각〕 — objective〔subjective〕 symptoms **중독 —** toxic symptoms

증서 證書 a deed ; a paper ; a bond (채무의) ; a voucher (영수증 따위) ; a certificate (증명서) ; a diploma (졸업 증서) ; a bill (상업상의) ¶ 증서와 교환으로 in exchange for a bond // 증서를 쓰다 draw up〔prepare〕 a deed // 증서를 담보로 잡다 hold the deeds as security // 계약은 증서로 해주시오 I want to have the contract in writing.
국채 — government bonds **예금 —** a certificate of deposit **졸업 —** a diploma **차용 —** an IOU ; a bond of debt

증설 增設 an increase 《of buildings》 ; extension of installations ; enlargement 《of parks》 **—하다** increase ; establish more 《schools, parks》 ; install more ¶ 전화를 증설하다 install more telephones

증세 症勢 symptoms ; the condition of a patient (용태) ¶ 독감의 증세를 나타내다 develop symptoms of influenza // 폐렴의 증세가 있다 have symptoms of pneumonia // 증세가 좋아졌다 His condition improved〔took a turn for the better〕.

증세 增稅 an increase of〔in〕 taxation ; increased taxes **—하다** increase〔raise〕 taxes〔taxation〕 ¶ 1할 증세 a ten percent increase in taxation // 10억원이 증세되었다 Taxes were increased by a thousand million〔billion〕 *won*.
— 계획 an increased taxation plan **—안** an increased taxation bill

증손 曾孫 a great-grandson ; a great-grandchild
—녀 a great-granddaughter **—부** the wife of one's great-grandson **—서** the husband of one's great-granddaughter **—자** ⇨ 증손

증쇄 增刷 an additional printing **—하다** print in addition ¶ 1만 부를 증쇄하다 print an additional 10,000 copies

증수 增水 the rising〔swelling〕 of the river ; flooding **—하다** rise ; swell ; be swollen ¶ 강이 현저하게 증수되었다 The river has remarkably swollen. // 큰 비로 강이 정상 수위에서 3미터나 더 증수됐다 The river water stands three meters above normal level after the heavy rain.
—기 the annual flooding period **—표** a floodmark

증수 增收 an additional increase ; [수입의] increased income〔revenue, receipts〕 ; [농산물의] an increased yield **—하다** increase in receipts〔income, products〕 ¶ 작년의 같은 달에 비하여 약 4퍼센트의 증수이다 It shows an increase of about 4 percent over the same month of last year.

증수회 贈收賄 (official) corruption ; bribery
— 사건 a bribery case

*__증식 增殖__ multiplication ; increase ; propagation **—하다** increase ; multiply ; propagate ¶ 증식성의 proliferous
—로(爐) a breeder ; a reactor **— 속도** a multiplication〔proliferation〕 rate **병적 —** [피부 조직의] vegetation

증압 增壓 **—하다** raise〔get up〕 the pressure 《of》
— 반사 〚생리〛 a pressor reflex

증액 增額 the increased amount ; (an) increase 《of》 ; augmentation ; the increment **—하다** increase ; raise ; augment 《an amount》 ¶ 봉급을 팔십만원으로 증액하다 increase 《a person's》 salary to 800,000 *won* // 교육비의 증액을 요구하다 ask an additional sum for educational expenses // 임금의 증액을 요구한다 We demand an increase in our wages. /We ask for a wage hike.

*증언 證言 verbal evidence ; testimony ; witness ; [증언 조서] deposition —하다 testify〔depose〕《to》; attest《to》; bear witness to ; give evidence ; swear to ¶ …임을 증언하다 testify〔bear testimony〕 to the fact《that》// 유리한 증언을 하다 give evidence in favor of《a person》// 무죄를 증언하다 testify to《a person's》 innocence // 증인은 자기가 아는 범위내에서 증언하지 않으면 안 된다 A witness must depose to such facts as are within his own knowledge.
—대 the witness stand ¶ 증언대에 서다 take the witness stand —서 a written testimony —자 a witness

*증여 贈與 donation ; gift ; presentation —하다 give ; present《a thing》to《a person》; donate
—물 a gift ; a present —세 a donation〔gift〕tax —자 a giver ; a presenter ; a donator ; a donor — 재산 a donated property 피—자 〖법〗 a donee ; a donatory

*증오 憎惡 hatred ; abhorrence ; detestation —하다 hate ; abhor ; detest ; loathe ¶ 증오할 hateful ; detestable ; abhorrent ; loathsome ; odious ; execrable // 증오를 사다 incur《a person's》 hatred // 증오심을 갖다 bear hatred towards《a person》// 증오의 눈으로 그를 보았다 They looked at him with hatred in their eyes. // 혐오는 곧 증오로 변한다 Dislike easily rises into hatred.

증원 增員 an increase of the staff〔personnel〕 —하다 increase the staff〔personnel〕 ¶ 50명을 65명으로 증원하다 increase the staff〔personnel〕 from 50 to 65

증원 增援 reinforcement —하다 reinforce ¶ 수비대를 증원하다 reinforce a garrison
—대(隊) reinforcements

증유 贈遺 donation ⇨ 증여

증음기 增音器 a sound amplifier ; [오르간의] a knee swell

증익 增益 [증가] (an) increase ; [기업] increased profits ; (an) increase in profit
—률 a rate of profit increase

증인 證人 a witness ; a testifier ; a deponent ; an eyewitness ; an attestor ; a surety (보증인) ¶ 살아 있는 증인 a living witness // 위증하는〔신뢰할 수 있는〕 증인 a lying〔trustworthy〕 witness // 증인이 되다 testify〔depose〕《to a fact》; bear witness to〔of〕; give evidence (법정에서) ; stand surety for《a person》(신원의) // 증인으로 하다 call〔take〕《a person》 to witness // 증인을 소환하다 call a witness // 한 남자가 증인으로서 출두했다 A man presented himself as a witness.
— 대심권(對審權) the right of confrontation —석 the witness stand〔box〕
— 조사 (an) examination of witnesses

증인 證印 a seal affixed to a document ; an evidential seal

증자 增資 an increase of capital ; a capital increase —하다 increase the capital ¶ 10억원을 20억원으로 증자하다 increase the capital from a billion to two billions
—주(株) additional shares 무상 — free issue of new shares 유상 — issue of new shares to be purchased

증적 證跡 evidence ; traces ; vestiges ¶ 범죄의 증적 evidence of a crime // 증적을 남기다 leave traces〔marks〕// 증적을 인멸하다 destroy the evidence《of a crime》

†증정 贈呈 presentation ; with the compliments of the author (증정자의 서명) —하다 present《a person with a thing, a thing to a person》; make a present of《a thing》 ¶ 꽃의 증정 a floral gift ; a floral tribute (조화의) // 그는 회원으로부터 금시계를 증정받았다 A golden watch was presented to him by the members.
—본(本) a presentation ; a complimentary〔free〕 copy —사(辭) a presentation speech —식 the presentation ceremony —자 a giver ; a presenter —주(株) a bonus share —품 a present ; a gift

증정 增訂 supplementing〔enlarging〕 and correcting〔revising〕 —하다 revise and enlarge ; supplement and correct
—판 a new edition ; a revised and enlarged edition

증조 曾祖 ⇨ 증조부

증조고 曾祖考 [돌아간] the deceased great-grandfather

증조모 曾祖母 a (paternal) great-grandmother

증조부 曾祖父 a (paternal) great-grandfather

증조비 曾祖妣 [돌아간] the deceased great-grandmother

증좌 證左 corroborative evidence ⇨ 증거

증주 增註 additional notes ; an increase of annotations —하다 make additional notes〔annotations〕; append additional notes ; enlarge annotations

증지 證紙 a certificate stamp

증진 增進 increase ; promotion ; advancement ; improvement ; furtherance —하다 increase ; promote ; further ; contribute《to》 ¶ 사회 복지의 증진 promotion of social welfare // 건강을 증진하다 promote〔build up〕 health ; conduce〔be conducive〕 to health // 실력을 증진하다 improve one's ability // 능률을 증진하다 increase the efficiency // 식욕을 증진하다 promote〔sharpen〕 one's appetite // 국제친선의 증진에 따라서 with the advancement of closer international relations

증징 增徵 collection〔imposition〕 of additional taxes〔dues〕 ¶ 세금을 증징하다 levy additional taxes《on》; collect additional dues《from》

증축 增築 enlargement of a building ; a new extension on an old building ; an annex(e) ―하다 extend〔enlarge, add to〕 a building ; build an annex(e) 《to the main building》 ; make extensions
― 공사 extension work ―비 the cost of extending a building

증파 增派 reinforcement ―하다 send 〔dispatch〕 additional troops〔ships〕 ; send reinforcements ; reinforce 《an army》

증편 蒸― steamed rice-cake with yeast in it
―틀 a cake steamer

증폭 增幅 amplification ―하다 amplify
― 장치〔기〕 an amplifier ― 정수(定數)(율) an amplification constant (factor) 검청(檢聽) ―기 a checking amplifier 음성〔고주파, 가청주파, 고조파(高調波)〕 ―기 a speech〔a high-frequency, an audio frequency, a harmonic〕 amplifier 직선〔이중〕 ― linear〔dual〕 amplification

증표 證票 a voucher

증험 證驗 a trial ; a test ; an attempt ―하다 try ; attempt ; have a try

증회 贈賄 bribery ; graft ; corruption (증수회) ―하다 bribe ; corrupt ; offer a bribe to 《a person》 ; grease〔gild, oil〕 《a person's》 palm
― 사건 a bribery〔graft〕 case ―자 a briber ; a bribe-giver ―죄 bribery ¶ 증회죄를 범하다 commit bribery // 증회죄로 고소되다 be charged with bribery

증후 症候 symptoms ; conditions ⇨ 증세

증후군 症候群 〖의학〗 a syndrome

지 〔동안〕 since ; from ; after ¶ 그들이 이혼한 지 5년이 된다 It is five years since they were divorced. // 그들이 떠난 지 10분 후에 우리는 출발했다 We started ten minutes after they had left.

지 至 to... ; till ¶ 자 오전 10시 지 오후 3시 from 10 a. m. to 3 p. m.

지 肢 the limbs

지 知 intelligence ; intellect

지 智 wisdom

†-지 ① 〔부정〕 do not ; be not ¶ 나는 가고 싶지 않다 I do not want to go. // 아직 도착하지 않았다 They have not yet arrived. // 그는 영리하지 않다 He is not an intelligent man. // 꽃이 아름답지 않다 The flower is not beautiful. // 염려하지 마시오 Don't worry. // 잊지 말고 편지하시오 Don't forget to write the letter.
② 〔의문〕 ¶ 그들은 형제지 They are brothers, aren't they? // 너 지금 열살이지 You are ten now, aren't you? // 저 불쌍한 애를 누가 돌보지 Who cares for the poor little child?
③ 〔종결형의 반말〕 ¶ 인제 자지 Suppose we go to bed! // 나도 대강 들었지 I've heard the outline of it, you know. // 이만하면 되겠지 This will do, I believe.

지가 地價 land prices ; the price of land ; 〔대장의〕 the value of land ; land value ¶ 지가가 오른다 Land rises in price.
법정 ― the assessed value of land

지가 紙價 the price of paper ¶ 그 책은 낙양의 지가를 올렸다 The book sold immensely well.

*지각 知覺 〔인식〕 perception ; 〔의식〕 consciousness ; 〔감각〕 sensation ―하다 perceive ; feel ; be conscious of ¶ 지각있는 sensible ; discreet ; prudent // 지각없는 insensible ; sleepy ; imprudent ; thoughtless // 지각이 생기다 reach the age of reason ; arrive at the age of reason 〔discretion〕 // 지각이 생기기도 전에 아버지를 잃다 lose one's father before one can remember // 나이가 그만하면 지각이 날 때도 되었다 You are old enough to have more sense than that.
― 과정 a perceptual process ― 기관 the organs of perception ― 대상 a percept ― 동사 〖문법〗 verbs of perception ―력 perceptibility ; sensibility ― 마비 paralysis of sensation ― 상실 stupefaction ― 신경 sensory nerves ― 착란 mental derangement

⁑지각 遲刻 lateness ; being late ; coming late ; tardiness ―하다 be〔come〕 late ; be behind time ; come late ¶ 학교에 지각하다 be late for〔at〕 school // 직장에 지각하다 reach one's office late // 지각한 변명을 하다 make an excuse for being late // 학교에 지각 않고 가다 go to school in time ; be in time for school // 오늘 아침 학교에 10분 지각했다 I was ten minutes behind time for school this morning. /I was late for school by ten minutes this morning. // 지각하지 마라 Don't be late. /Don't be tardy.
―계 a report for being late ; a late report ―생 a tardy student ―일수 the number of days late ―자 a latecomer

지각 地殼 the (earth's) crust ; the lithosphere
― 구조학 tectonic geology ― 운동 crustal activity ― 이동설 diastrophism ― 평형 isostasy ― 화성론(火成論) the Plutonic theory ; Plutonism ― 화학 geochemistry 해양〔대륙〕 ― the oceanic 〔continental〕 crust

⁑지갑 紙匣 〔종이갑〕 a box made of paper ; 〔돈지갑〕 a purse ; a moneybag ; a pocketbook ¶ 가죽 지갑 a leather pocketbook // 두둑한 지갑 a well-lined purse ; a plump purse // 지갑이 가볍다 have a light purse // 지갑에 넣다 put 《money》 into one's purse

지검 地檢 a district public prosecutor's office

지게 an A-frame ; an A-frame carrier ; a coolie rack 《for carrying things》 ; a *chigeh*
― 꼬리 strings on an A-frame 지겟가지

the two prongs of an A-frame 지겟다리 the legs of the A-frame carrier 지겟작대기 an A-frame carrier pole
지게를 지다 관용 carry the A-frame on one's back
지게꾼 an A-frame man ; a burden carrier ; one who carries things with an A-frame
지게미 [술의] lees ; residue left after rice liquor is drained ; [눈곱] gum in the corner of the eye ; [비듬] dandruff
지게질 carrying things on an A-frame ─하다 carry things on an A-frame
지견 知見 knowledge ; insight ⇨ 식견
지견 智見 wisdom and knowledge
지겹다 (be) tedious ; wearisome ; tiresome ; disgusting ; detestable ; loathsome ; odious ¶ 일이 지겹다 I am sick of this work. /I became disgusted with the work. /I am fed up with the work. // 그런 말은 듣기에도 지겹다 It is disgusting even to hear. // 그녀는 이제 지겹다 I am sick and tired of her.
지경 枝莖 the branches〔sprigs〕 and stalks
지경 地境 ① [경계] a boundary ; a border ② [형편] a state ; a situation ; circumstances ; a condition ¶ 이웃 땅과의 지경 the boundary with the neighboring land // 지경을 정하다 fix the boundary 《of》 ; draw the line of demarcation // 지경에 있다 be on the point〔brink〕 《of》 ; be about to ; face (직면하다) // 파면할 지경이다 stand on the brink of ruin // 너무 슬퍼서 울음이 터질 지경이었다 She felt so sad that she stood on the verge of bursting into tears.
지계 地階 the basement (지하실) ; the ground floor (1층)
지계 持戒 〖불교〗 observing the Buddhist commandments
지계 地界 [지경] a boundary ; a border ; [불교] the world on earth ; the terrestrial world
지고 至高 supremacy ; sublimity ─하다 (be) highest ; supreme ; most sublime ; loftiest
지골 肢骨 bones of the extremities
지골 指骨 a phalanx ; a phalange
지공 至恭 the utmost reverence〔esteem, deference〕 ─하다 (be) most reverent 〔deferential〕
지공무사 至公無私 supreme〔perfect〕 fairness and impartiality ─하다 (be) absolutely fair〔just〕 ; strictly impartial
지공지평 至公至平 supreme〔strict, perfect〕 fairness ; absolute justice ─하다 (be) absolutely fair
지공품 紙工品 paper wares
지관 地官 a geomancer ¶ 지관을 찾아가서 묏자리를 물어 봤다 I went and found a geomancer and asked him for a lucky site for burials.
지괴 地塊 [지질] a block ; a landmass
─운동 the block movement
지교 至交 eternal friendship ; deep 〔close〕 friendship ; friendship in need
지교 智巧 wisdom and ability ─하다 (be) intelligent and able ; wise ; sagacious
†지구 地球 the earth ; the globe ¶ 지구의 인력〔자기〕 terrestrial gravitation 〔magnetism〕 // 지구의 공전 the revolution of the earth around the sun // 지구의 자전 the rotation of the earth on its axis // 지구는 서에서 동으로 회전한다 The earth rotates from west to east.
─ 구조학 geognosy ─ 물리학 geophysics ─ 발생학 geogony ─ 역학 geodynamics ─ 위도 geographical latitude ─의(儀) a (terrestrial) globe ─인 an earthian ; an earthman ; an earthling ─ 중심설 the geocentric theory ─ 화학 geochemistry 국제 ─ 관측년 The International Geographical Year 《IGY, I. G. Y.》
지구 地溝 a rift (in the earth) ; a trough ; a graben
─대(帶) a rift valley ; a graben
†지구 地區 [지역] a district ; a region ; an area ; a zone ; a section 《미》 ; [대지] a lot
─ 경계 a zonal frontier (베를린 따위의) ─당 a (electoral) district party chapter ; a (party's) constituency chapter ¶ 지구당 위원장 the chairman of a district party chapter ; a district leader 《미》 경인 ─ the *Seoul-Inchŏn* district 〔area〕 상업〔오락, 주택〕 ─ a business 〔an amusement, a residence〕 zone
지구 知舊 an old acquaintance ; an old friend ; an old crony ; a bosom friend
‡지구 持久 persistence ; endurance ; sustenance ─하다 sustain ; stay ; endure ; persist
─력 endurance ; staying power ; tenacity ; stamina ─전 a long drawn out struggle〔war〕 ; a war of attrition ; a protracted war ¶ 지구전으로 들어가다 get into the stage of position warfare ─책 dilatory tactics ; a Fabian policy ¶ 지구책을 강구하다 form a plan for holding out
지구 과학 地球科學 earth science
─자 an earth scientist
지국 支局 a branch〔district〕 office
─장 a branch manager ; the head 〔manager〕 of a branch 신문사 ─ a branch office of a newspaper
지궐련 a cigarette
지그럭거리다 grumble to one's annoyance
지그럭지그럭 grumbling ; complaining
지그르르 simmering
지그리다 shut〔close〕 a door softly〔lightly〕
지그시 ① [참는 모양] patiently ; with patience ; perseveringly ; persistently ¶ 아픔을 지그시 참다 endure〔stand〕 pain

stoically // 웃음을 지그시 참다 (patiently) stifle〔suppress〕 one's laughter ; swallow a laugh ; keep〔hold〕 back one's smile // 그는 울고 싶은 것을 지그시 참았다 He resisted an impulse to cry out. ② [(슬그머니) 누르거나 당기는 모양] gently ; softly ; calmly ; quietly ; stealthily ¶ 옷소매를 지그시 당기다 quietly〔gently〕 pull〔tug〕 《a person》 by the sleeve // 여자의 손을 지그시 당기다 pull a girl's hand stealthily // 눈을 지그시 감다 close one's eyes gently

지극 至極 **—하다** (be) extreme ; utmost ; exceeding ; be at the utmost ¶ 지극히 very ; extremely ; exceedingly ; highly // 지극히 중요한 문제 a problem of the greatest importance ; a very important matter // 지극한 가난 dire poverty // 지극히 아름다운 경치 a scene of exceeding beauty // 지극히 건강하다 be very healthy〔well〕 // 지극히 힘들다 be extremely difficult // 그는 어머니에게 효성이 지극하다 He shows the greatest devotion to his mother. /He is very filial to his mother.

지근 支根 rootlets ; radicles

지근 至近 ¶ 지근 거리에서 at close range〔quarters〕 ; within〔at〕 point-blank range

—탄(彈) a near hit〔miss〕 《on》 ; [폭탄] a close-falling bomb

지근(덕)거리다 ① [집적거림] annoy ; harass ; tease ; bother ; pester ; make a nuisance 《of》 ; needle ¶ 아무에게 지근거리다 needle a person // 지근거리며 돈을 달라고 하다 pester 《a person》 for money ② [씹다] chew softly ③ [머리가] have a shooting pain 《in one's head》

지글거리다 sizzle ; simmer ; seethe ; bubble up

지글지글 sizzling ; simmering ; bubbling ; seething

†**지금 只今** the present time ; now ; [부사적] at present ; for the present ; now ¶ 지금의 present // 지금까지 up to date〔the present〕 ; by this time ; till now // 지금부터 from now on ; after this ; hence // 지금의 대통령 the current President // 지금의 상태 the existing state of things // 지금까지 없던 사건 an unprecedented event // 지금으로부터 10년 전 ten years ago // 지금으로부터 50년 후 fifty years hence // 지금이나 옛날이나 in these days as in those ; for all ages // 지금 생각해 보면 when I think of〔look back to〕 it now // 지금 같아서는 as the matter stands ; as things are // 지금도 still ; even now ; to this day // 지금은 봄이다 It is spring now. /Spring is come now. // 지금 와서 그런 소리를 해야 쓸 데 없다 It is of no use to say such a thing now when it is too late. // 지금부터라도 늦지 않다 It is not too late even yet. // 아버지가 지금 돌아오셨다 Father came back just now. // 10년 전보다 지금의 생활이 훨씬 편안하다 We are much better off now than ten years ago. // 지금부터 세 시까지 자유이다 I will〔shall〕 be free until three o'clock. // 지금부터 2주일 후에 여름 방학이 시작된다 The summer vacation begins two weeks hence.

지금 地金 ingot gold ; free gold ; ground metal ; bullion (화폐의)

— 본위제 a bullion standard

지금거리다 chew gritty ; be gritty〔feel sandy〕 to the teeth ¶ 밥이 지금거리다 the rice is gritty

⁑**지금껏** so far ; till now ; all this while ¶ 지금껏 알려지지 않은 비밀 a secret hitherto unknown to the world // 이것은 지금껏 읽은 책들 중에서 가장 재미있다 This is the most interesting book I have ever read. /I have never read such an interesting book (as this). // 만사가 지금껏 잘 돼 왔다 Everything has been in order so far.

지금지금 ¶ 지금지금 씹히다 chew gritty

지금쯤 只今— (about) this time ; at the time of day〔night, (the) year〕 ¶ 내일〔어젯밤〕 지금쯤 at〔about〕 this time tomorrow〔last night〕 // 지금쯤 그는 과연 무엇을 하고 있을까 What can he be doing now ?

지급 支給 [공급] provision ; grant ; purveyance (식료품의) ; supply ; [지불] payment ; allowance **—하다** give ; grant ; allow ; furnish〔supply, provide〕 《a person》 with 《a thing》 ¶ 의식을 지급하다 supply 《a person》 with food and clothing // 여비를 지급하다 provide 《a person》 with travel(ling) expenses // 월급 58만원을 지급하다 give 《a person》 a monthly salary of 580,000 *won*

— 기준 인상 raising of the pay standard

—액 an allowance ; the amount supplied

—품 articles supplied ; supplies

지급 至急 utmost urgency ; exigency **—하다** (be) urgent ; pressing ¶ 지급히 urgently ; promptly ; immediately ; at once ; without delay ; with dispatch ; with all haste〔speed〕 ; as soon as possible // 지급 친전이라고 써 있는 편지 a letter marked "private and urgent" // 지급한 용무 urgent〔pressing〕 business // 지급편으로 보내다 send 《a letter》 by express〔special delivery〕 // 그 일은 지급하다 The matter is pressing. // 지급으로 해주시오 I want to have it finished with all possible dispatch. // 이것은 지급히 해결해야 할 문제다 The matter must be settled without delay.

— 우편 express mail **— 전보〔전화〕** an urgent telegram〔call〕

***지긋지긋하다** ① [싫증] (be) tedious ; wearisome ; tiresome ¶ 지긋지긋한 강연 a tedious〔boring, wearisome〕 lecture // 지긋지긋한 날씨 abominable weather // 비

가 지긋지긋하게 온다 We have had enough of rain. // 정치 싸움은 이제 지긋지긋하다 I am fed up with political bickering.
② [잔인하다] (be) loathsome ; detestable ; odious ; repulsive ; horrible ¶ 지긋지긋한 광경 a horrible sight // 생각만 해도 지긋지긋하다 It makes me sick even to think of it.

*지긋하다 be advanced in years ; be well up in years ¶ 나이가 지긋한 사람 a man well advanced in years // 나이가 지긋한 분이 그게 무슨 짓이오 You are old enough to be more prudent.

지기 地氣 vapor of the earth ; vapor

지기 地祇 the gods of earth
천신— the gods of heaven and earth

지기 志氣 spirit and will ; sentiment ¶ 애국의 지기 spirit of patriotism ; patriotic sentiment // 지기 상합하다 come to mutual understanding ; be of congenial temper

지기 紙器 a paper container

지기 知己 a bosom friend ; an intimate 〔appreciative〕 friend

-지기[1] an area of land ; a measure of land
닷마— a plot of and that takes five *mal* of seed 두 섬— a stretch of land requiring two *sŏm* of seed

-지기[2] [사람] a keeper ; a guard ¶ 산지기 a forest ranger // 능지기 a grave caretaker〔keeper〕 // 문지기 a gatekeeper

지기지우 知己之友 an appreciative friend ; an intimate〔a bosom, a close〕 friend ; friend

지꺼분하다 ① [눈이] (be) dirty ; gummy ② [어수선하다] (be) disorderly ; untidy ; scattered ¶ 지꺼분한 눈 gummy eyes // 지꺼분한 것들 shabby things // 지꺼분하게 늘어놓다 litter 《things》 up

지껄거리다 ⇨ 지껄이다

지껄이다 chatter ; gabble ; jabber ; gibber ¶ 잘 지껄이는 garrulous ; glibtongued ; talkative ; loquacious // 그는 연방 지껄여댔다 He went on talking with a flow of eloquence. // 그만좀 지껄여라 Hold your tongue.

지끈 with a snap〔crack, crash〕

지끈지끈 ① [부러지는 소리] with a snap ; snappingly ② [아픈 모양] ¶ 골치가 지끈지끈 아프다 I have a splitting 〔racking〕 headache.

지나 支那 [중국] China ⇨ 중국

†지나가다 ① ⇨ 지나다 ① ② ⇨ 지나다 ②

†지나다 ① [통과하다] pass by ; go past ; pass through ¶ 문앞을 지나다 pass by the door // 숲 속을 지나다 go through a woods // 기차는 이미 대구를 지났다 The train has already passed *Taegu*. // 지나가는 길에 한번 들르시오 Please drop in sometime when you are passing by. / When you happen to pass by, drop in and see us.
② [경과하다] pass ; elapse ; go on ; go by ¶ 지난 날 past days ; days gone by ; olden times ; the other day // 지난 달 last month // 지난 밤 last night // 지난 일 the past ; bygones ; a past event ; a thing of the past // 시간이 지남에 따라 as time goes on // 오랜 시일이 지났다 A long time has passed. // 지난 일은 어쩔 수 없느니라 Let bygones be bygones. / What has been done, has been done. // 봄이 지나고 여름이 왔다 Spring passed into summer.
③ [초과하다] expire ; terminate ; be out ; exceed ; go beyond ; go far ¶ 계약기한이 지났다 The contract has expired. // 지원 마감이 어제로 지났다 The time for application expired yesterday. // 그는 일개 학생에 지나지 않는다 He is nothing but a student. // 졸다가 두 정거장이나 지나가 버렸다 I was carried two stops beyond my destination while napping.

지나새나 all the time ; day in day out ; night and day ; always ; at all times ¶ 그녀는 지나새나 남편한테 바가지를 긁었다 She yapped at her husband morning and night.

지나오다 [통과하다] pass by〔through〕 ; come along〔through〕 ; get through ; [겪다] go through ; undergo ¶ 많은 시련을 지나오다 go through hardships // 지나온 일을 생각하다 remember things gone by // 지금 지나온 정거장 이름은 무엇입니까 What is the name of the station we have just passed ?

지나지 않다 be nothing but. . . ; be no more than. . ; [다만 …일 뿐] only ; merely ¶ 그것은 구실〔핑계〕에 지나지 않는다 It is a mere excuse. /That is an excuse. // 그저 해야 할 일을 한 데 지나지 않는다 I only have done what I ought to (do).

†지나치다 ① [과도] go too far ; go to extremes ; carry 《a joke》 too far ; do too much ; overdo 《a thing》 ; go to excessive lengths ¶ 지나친 excessive ; immoderate ; undue ; inordinate // 지나치게 excessively ; immoderately ; to excess ; to an undue extent ; unduly ; too // 지나친 요구 inordinate demands // 지나치게 공부하다 study too hard ; overwork oneself // 지나치게 술을 마시다 drink too much ; drink to excess // 지나치게 먹다 eat too much ; overeat (oneself) // 운동을 지나치게 하다 take too much exercise // 지나치게 영리하다 be clever to a fault〔weakness〕 // 지나치게 공부를 해서 병이 났다 He worked himself ill. /He made himself ill by overworking. // 어떤 운동이든 지나치게 하면 심장에 장애가 온다 Excess in any exercise strains the heart. // 자넨 지나치게 겸손해 You are too modest. /You carry modesty too far. // 그것은 지나치다 That is too much. /It is unfair. /It is mean of

you to do such a thing. // 다이어트도 도가 지나치면 위험하다고 한다 They say a diet can be dangerous if you overdo it.

② [지나가다] pass by ; go past ; pass through

지난 last ¶ 지난 일들 (things of) the past ; bygones // 지난 겨울 last winter // 지난 해 last year // 지난 밤 last night

지난 至難 extreme difficulty **—하다** (be) most difficult ; very hard ; be next to impossible ; (be) extremely difficult ¶ 지난한 과제이다 It is a task of extreme difficulty.

지난날 old days〔times〕; bygone days ; days gone by ¶ 지난날의 추억 the memory of old days ; old memories // 지난날을 그리워하다 think dearly of the good old days // 나는 지난날의 내가 아니다 I am not what I used to be. // 지난날은 좋았다 Things were better in the old days. // 저 것을 보니 지난날이 생각난다 That reminds me of the past. // 지난날을 회고하다 look back on the past

지난달 last month ; ultimo《ult.》¶ 지난달 5일에 on the 5th (of) last month ; on the 5th ult.

지난번 last ; last time ; some time ago ; the other day ; before this ¶ 지난번의 of the other day ; last ; previous ; recent ; former // 지난번에 받은 편지 the last letter received // 지난번에 알려 드린 바와 같이 as I let you know last time // 지난번 만났을 때 when I saw him last // 지난번에 자네한테 말 안 했던가 Haven't I told you before? // 지난번 상경했을 땐 1주일밖에 체재하지 않았다 The last time I came to *Seoul*, I stayed only a week.

지난주 —週 last week ¶ 지난주의 오늘 this day (last) week ; today week ; a week ago today // 지난주의 월요일 last Monday (week) ; a week ago last Monday

지날결 on one's way《to》; while passing ; in passing ; when going by ¶ 지날결에 사람을 데리러 들르다 call for《a person》as one goes along // 지날결에 잠깐 들렀습니다 I just dropped in to see you while passing by.

지남 指南 guidance ; instructions ; a guide book

—석 a magnet **—극(極)** [자석의] the south (-seeking) pole

지남철 指南鐵 a magnet

지남침 指南針 a magnetic needle

— 방위 a compass bearing

지낭 智囊 a man of great wisdom and talents ; the brain ¶ 지낭을 쥐어짜다 cudgel〔rack〕one's brains

*__지내다__ ① [세월을] spend〔pass〕one's time ; lead a life ; get along ; [생활하다] live ; make a living ; earn one's living ; support oneself ¶ 독서로 지내다 spend one's time in reading // 즐거이 지내다 have a good time // 과부로 지내다 live in widowhood // 호화스럽게 지내다 live in luxury // 요즈음 어떻게 지내십니까 How are you getting along these days? // 월급으로 지낼 수 있나 Can you get along on your pay? // 적은 월급으로 겨우 지낸다 He ekes out a living on a tiny salary. // 품을 팔아서 그날그날 지낸다 He lives from hand to mouth〔from day to day〕. // 외투 없이는 이번 겨울은 지낼 수 없을 것이다 You cannot go through the winter without an overcoat. // 나머지 반년을 어떻게 지낼 것인가 How shall I tide over the next six months? // 어떻게 지내셨습니까 How have you been getting along?

② [치르다] hold ; observe ¶ 장사를 지내다 hold a funeral // 제사를 지내다 perform ancestral rites

③ [겪다] pursue〔follow〕a career ; serve ; go through ; experience ¶ 교사를 지내다가 지금은 출판사의 편집 위원을 하고 있다 He has been a teacher but he is now on the editorial staff of a publishing company. // 그는 한때 국회 의원을 지냈다 He was once〔at one time〕a member of the National Assembly.

④ [교제하다] associate《with》; consort《with》¶ 친하게 지내다 be on intimate terms《with》

지내듣다 listen to《a person》inattentively ; take no notice《of》; pay no〔little〕attention to ; pass over《a thing》unnoticed ¶ 지내들어서는 안될 말 a remark that cannot be passed over in silence // 남의 충고를 지내듣다 give a deaf ear to《a person's》advice // 그것은 지내들을 수 없는 말이다 I cannot pass it over〔let it pass〕. /I cannot pass it unnoticed.

지내력 地耐力 〖건축〗 the bearing power〔capacity〕of the soil

지내보다 ① [겪어보다] go through ; experience ; get acquainted with ; get on with ¶ 사람은 지내보아야 안다 It takes time to really get to know a person. // 지내보니 좋은 친구더라 On further acquaintance, I found him a jolly fellow. // 같이 지내보았으나 별로 재미 있는 친구가 못 된다 I have gone through him but he interested me little.

② [건성으로 보다] fail to notice ; disregard〔ignore〕 indulgently ; lose sight of ; miss seeing ¶ 너무 졸려서 가장 재미 있는 장면을 지내보고 말았다 I was so sleepy that I lost sight of the most interesting scene. /I was so sleepy that I missed seeing the most interesting scene.

지네 〖동물〗 a centipede

지네고사리 〖식물〗 a Japanese woodfern

지네철 —鐵 〖건축〗 a metal cramp

지노 紙— a paper string ¶ 지노를 꼬다 twist paper into a string

*__지느러미__ a fin ; pinna《*pl.* ～s, -nae》

—발 a flipper ; a pinna 《*pl.* ~s, -nae》 등〔가슴, 꼬리〕— a dorsal〔pectoral, caudal〕 fin 배— a ventral fin

‡지능 知能 intelligence ; intellect ; mental faculties〔powers〕 ¶ 지능적 intellectual ; mental // 지능을 계발하다 develop one's intellectual powers ; improve one's mind // 저 아이는 지능이 모자란다 That child is feeble-minded.
— 검사 an intelligence〔a mental〕 test ; an I. Q. test —률〔계수〕 〖심리〗 an intelligence quotient 《IQ, I. Q.》 — 발달 기준 the norm —범 an intellectual offense〔crime〕 — 연령 the I. Q. age ; the mental age — 정도 an intellectual standard — 지수 intelligence quotient

†지니다 [휴대하다] carry 《with》 ; have 《with》 ; [소유하다] keep ; preserve ; maintain ; possess ; own ; [간직하다] hold ; entertain ; cherish ; harbor (악 의 따위를) ¶ 비밀을 지니다 cherish a secret // 집을 여러 채 지니다 own many houses // 생각〔의문〕을 지니다 entertain an idea〔a doubt〕 // 대망을 지니다 cherish〔have〕 a great ambition // 돈을 지니고 있지 않다 I have no money with 〔about, on〕 me. // 그는 신념을 지니고 나가리라 믿습니다 // I believe he will hold to his convictions. // 인간은 이성을 지니고 있다 Man is endowed with reason. // 그는 단도를 항상 지니고 있다 He always carries a dagger with him. // 그녀는 가요계의 인기를 한 몸에 지니고 있다 She enjoys a reputation in the world of popular song.
지닐성 —性 the quality of carrying〔preserving, remembering〕
지닐 재주 a good memory

†지다¹ [패배하다] be〔get〕 defeated ; be beaten ; lose ; [굴복하다] be overcome with ; yield 《to》 ; submit 《to》 ; give in 《to》 ; succumb to ; [열등하다] be inferior 《to》 ; be second 《to》 ¶ 유혹에 지다 yield to temptation // 경기에 지다 lose in a contest // 토론에 지다 be put down in an argument ; be argued down // 당당히 지다 take it on the chin ; be a good loser // 더위에 지다 succumb to the heat // 진 것을 인정하다 admit defeat ; throw in the towel ; throw up the sponge // 재주로는 누구한테도 지지 않는다 As far as talent is concerned, he is second to none. // 그런 사람에게는 지기 싫다 I don't want to give in to someone like him. // 영어는 누구에게도 지지 않는다 In English he is second to none (in the class). // 힘으로는 그에게 안 진다 I equal him in physical strength.

지다² [등에] bear ; carry on the back ; [의무를] owe ; be indebted 《to》 ; be under an obligation 《to》 ; incur ; [책임을] take upon〔on〕 oneself ; bear ; shoulder ; assume 《a responsibility》 ¶ 무거운 짐을 지다 bear a heavy burden // 쌀 가마니를 등에 지다 carry a bag of rice on one's back // 빚을 지다 owe money ; run into debt // 신세를 지다 be indebted to 《a person》 ; owe 《a person》 a debt of gratitude // 책임을 지지 않다 hold no liability 《for》 // 그가 전책임을 지곤 했다 He did it on his responsibility. // 내가 전책임을 지겠습니다 I assume all responsibility. // 우리 청년들은 무거운 책임을 지고 있다 A great responsibility rests upon us young men.

†지다³ ① [잎·꽃이] fall ; fade and fall ; be shed ; be gone ¶ 지기 시작하다 begin to fall // 곧 꽃이 지겠지 The flowers will soon be gone. // 벚꽃은 이제 지고 없을 것이다 The cherry blossoms must have fallen. // 잎이 바람에 졌다 The leaves were scattered by the breeze. // 나뭇잎이 지고 있다 The leaves are fluttering down.
② [해·달이] set ; sink ; go down ¶ 해가 서쪽에 질 무렵 when the sun sets in the west // 달이 졌다 The moon has set. // 해는 동쪽에서 떠서 서쪽으로 진다 The sun rises in the east and sets in the west.
③ [얼룩 따위가] be stained ; get spotted ¶ 얼룩이 지다 become stained // 칼라에 얼룩이 져 있다 Your collar has a stain on it.
④ [없어지다] come off ; be removed ; be taken out ; fade away ¶ 아무리 빨아도 때가 지지 않는다 The dirt will not come out, however hard I may try to wash it off.
⑤ [장마 따위] set in ; begin ¶ 장마가 지다 The rainy season has begun〔set in〕.
⑥ [그늘 따위가] cast a shadow ; shade ; get shaded〔shady〕 ¶ 그늘진 길 a shady path // 그늘이 지다 shade ; cast a shadow ; get shady // 나무 때문에 집에 그늘이 너무 진다 The trees overshadow the house.

지다⁴ [되어가다] become ; grow ; get ¶ 추워지다 get cold // 좋아지다 [호감] begin〔get〕 to like 《a thing》 // 어두워지다 become dark ; darken // 밤이 길어진다 The nights are growing longer. // 그는 그녀가 싫어졌다 He has fallen out of love with her.

-지다¹ [되다] be ; become ; get to be ; grow ; make ; change ; turn into〔out〕 ; develop ; be reduced 《to》 ¶ 추워〔더워〕지다 get colder〔warmer〕 // 좋아〔나빠〕지다 get better〔worse〕 // 창백해지다 turn pale // 풀어지다 get loose // 엉클어지다 get tangled // 부러지다 break // 일기가 좋아졌다 The weather has turned out fine. // 우유가 시어졌다 The milk has turned (sour). /The milk has gone sour. // 그는 화가 나서 낯이 붉어졌다 He went red with anger. // 폭풍우는 점점 심해졌다 The storm grew more and more severe.

-지다² [접미사] ¶ 기름지다 be fatty // 언덕지다 be hilly // 뼈지다 be bony

지다위 [의지] dependence ; reliance ; [전가] imputation —하다 [의지하다]

depend〔rely〕 on ; [전가하다] impute 《a crime to a person》 ; shuffle off a responsibility on 《a person's》 shoulders ; lay a responsibility on another

지당 至當 propriety ; justice ; reasonableness **—하다** (be) proper ; right ; fair ; natural ; reasonable ¶ 지당한 요구 a reasonable demand // 지당한 조처 a proper measure // 그렇게 하는 것이 지당하다 It is right of you to do so. /You ought to do so. /It is proper that you should do so.

지대 〚불교〛 the travel bag of a Buddhist monk

†지대 地帶 a zone ; a region ; a belt **공장 —** an industrial area **구릉 —** hilly districts **녹화 —** a green belt **미작 —** a rice-producing district **비무장 —** a demilitarized zone 《D. M. Z.》 **사막〔산악, 삼림〕 —** a desert〔mountainous, forest〕 area **안전〔위험〕 —** a safety 〔danger〕 zone **요새 —** a fortified zone **주택 —** a residential area〔zone〕 **중립 —** a neutral zone

지대 至大 —하다 (be) great ; immense ; vast ; enormous ¶ 지대한 관심사 a matter of great interest〔concern〕 // 그 문제에 대해서 지대한 관심을 갖다 be greatly interested in the matter

지대 址臺 a foundation ; groundwork **—석** foundation stones

‡지대 地代 land〔ground〕 rent ¶ 지대를 받다 collect ground rents // 지대로 생활하다 live on the revenue from lands

지대 支隊 a detached force ; a detachment (of troops)

지대 紙袋 ⇨ 봉지(封紙)

지대공 地對空 ¶ 지대공의 ground-〔surface-〕to-air **— 미사일** a ground-to-air missile

지대기 〚불교〛 the garments of an itinerant monk

지대지 地對地 ground〔surface〕 to ground 〔surface〕 **— 미사일** a ground to ground missile

지더리다 (be) mean ; vile ; low ; gross ; vulgar ; dirty ¶ 품성이 지더리다 be low-minded ; be a man of vile character

지덕 地德 the auspicious effect of a site

지덕 知德 knowledge and virtue ¶ 지덕을 갖춘 사람 a man of knowledge and virtue

†지도 地圖 a map ; an atlas (지도책) ; a chart (해도) ; a plan (시가 따위의) ¶ 5만분지 1지도 a map on a scale of one to fifty thousand // 벽에 거는 지도 a wall map // 지도를 그리다 draw a map // 지도를 보다 read〔consult〕 a map // 지도를 찾다 look up 《a place》 on a map // 지도에 나와 있지 않다 It is not on the map. // 벽에는 비 자국이 지도처럼 얼룩져 있었다 Rain water traced maps on the wall. // 그 나라는 지도에서 말살되었다 The country was wiped off the map. **— 제작(법)** cartography **— 제작자** a cartographer ; a map-maker **—책** an atlas **—학** cartology **구면(球面)—** a globular map **괘—** a wall map **등고선 —** a contour map **백〔암사〕—** a blank map **역사 —** a(n) historical map **윤곽 —** an outline〔a key〕 map **접—** a folding map **축척 —** a map on a reduced scale **항공 —** an aerial map

†지도 指導 guidance ; directions ; leadership **—하다** guide ; direct ; coach ; lead ¶ A씨의 지도 아래 under Mr. A's guidance〔leadership, direction〕 // 지도의 임무를 맡다 assume leadership ; undertake to guide 《a person》 // 지도를 청하다 look to 《a person》 for guidance // 잘못 지도하다 misdirect ; misguide // 연구를 지도하다 guide 《a person's》 research work ; guide 《a person》 in his research // 지도적 역할을 하다 play a leading〔prominent〕 part 《in》 // 연극을 지도하다 coach a play **— 교사** a guidance teacher **— 교수** a tutor ; an (academic) adviser **—권** leadership ; hegemony ; ascendency 《over》 **—반** a guiding group **— 방침〔원리〕** a guiding principle **—법** a method of guidance **—부** a guidance division **—서** a manual ; a guide (book) **—안** a guidance plan ; a teaching plan (학과의) **— 요강** a (teacher's) manual for student guidance **—원** an instructor ; an advisor **— 위원** a direction committee **—자** a leader ; a director ; a coach **— 정신** a guiding spirit **집단 —** collective guidance 〔leadership〕

지도력 指導力 the capacity as a leader ¶ 위대한 지도력을 지니다 have a great leadership

지도리 a hinge ; hook-and-eye hinges

†지독 至毒 —하다 (be) vicious ; venomous ; spiteful ; [심하다] severe ; intense ; extreme ; terrible ; awful ; cruel ¶ 지독한 구두쇠 an awful miser // 지독한 말 vicious remarks // 지독한 사람 a very determined person // 지독한 여자 a spiteful woman // 지독한 더위 intense heat // 지독한 추위 severe〔bitter〕 cold // 지독한 짓 an atrocious act // 지독하게 공부하다 study awfully hard // 지독한 감기에 걸리다 catch a nasty cold // 그는 지독한 근시이다 He is dreadfully nearsighted. // 오늘은 지독하게 춥다 It's unbelievably cold today.

지돌이 a tight corner (on a cliff path)

지동 地動 [지진] an earthquake ; an earth tremor ; [공전·자전] the revolution and rotation of the earth **—하다** have an earthquake **—설** the Copernican theory ; the heliocentric theory

지두 指頭 the finger tips ; the tip of a finger

지둔 遲鈍 stupidity ; dullness ; slowness **—하다** (be) dull-witted ; sluggish ;

slow ; stupid ; thick-headed
지둔 至鈍 extreme stupidity **—하다** (be) extremely stupid〔dull〕
지둥 an earthquake ⇨ 지동
지드럭거리다, 찌드럭거리다 annoy ; pester ; tease ; needle ; pick on
지득 知得 acquisition of knowledge **—하다** know ; learn
지등 紙燈 a paper-covered lamp
지등롱 紙燈籠 a paper lantern
지딱 hurriedly and at random ; recklessly ¶ 지딱지딱하다, 지딱거리다 do 《it》 hurriedly〔in haste〕
지라 [비장] the spleen ; the milt
지란지교 芝蘭之交 sweet and noble friendship
지랄 an epileptic fit ; (an attack of) epilepsy ; a fit 《of hysteria》 **—하다** behave rampageously ; get out of line ; go crazy ; have fit ; get hysterical
—병 〖의학〗 epilepsy ; an epileptic fit **—병 환자** an epileptic **—쟁이** [간질쟁이] an epileptic ; [변덕쟁이] a capricious〔an unreliable, an irresponsible〕 person
지략 智略 cleverness ; strategy ; resourcefulness ¶ 지략이 풍부한 사람 a resourceful mind ; a man of resources // 지략이 풍부하다 be resourceful
지러지다 be stunted ; wither ; wilt ; shrivel
지런지런 ① [넘칠 듯] brimful ② [닿을락 말락] scraping close ; almost touching
지렁이 〖동물〗 an earthworm
지렁이도 밟으면 꿈틀한다 속담 Even a worm will turn. /Even a fly has its anger. /Tread on a worm and it will turn.
*__지레¹__ a lever ; a handspike ¶ 지레로 물건을 움직이다 raise a thing with a lever
— 작용 leverage ; purchase
지레² [미리] in advance ; beforehand ¶ 지레 알리다 let 《a person》 know beforehand〔in advance〕; give prior 〔advance〕 notice // 돈을 지레 찾아 쓰다 get an advance of money
지레질 levering **—하다** lever ; raise with a lever
지레짐작 guesswork ; conjecture ; prejudgment ; hasty conclusion **—하다** guess ; conjecture ; speculate ; foreguess ; judge ; make a hasty conclusion ¶ 쌀값이 오를 것을 지레짐작하고 쌀을 사두다 buy up rice in anticipation of a rise in price // 승패란 지레짐작할 수 없다 The fate of a battle cannot be foreseen. // 지레짐작이 맞았다 My guess was right.
지레채다 know beforehand ; foresee ; perceive in advance ¶ 남의 이야기를 지레채다 guess the point of another's story in advance
지렛대 a lever ⇨ 지레¹
지려 智慮 prudence ; wisdom
지력 地力 fertility of soil
— 체감 decreasing fertility
⁑**지력 智力** mental capacity〔faculty〕; intellectual power ; intellect ; mentality ¶ 지력이 발달한 intelligent ; intellectual // 12세의 지력밖에 없다 He has the mentality of a 12 year-old. /His I. Q. 〔mental〕 age is not above 12.
지력 地歷 geography and history
지력선 指力線 a magnetic curve ; lines of force
지령 指令 an order ; a notice ; a directive ; an instruction **—하다** order ; notify ; direct ; give instructions ¶ 파업 지령을 내리다 call〔declare〕 a strike ; instruct the workers to go on strike // 지령을 기다리다 wait for instructions
—서 written instructions〔orders〕 **— 코드〔카운터, 정수(定數)〕** [전자 계산기의] an instruction code〔counter, constant〕 **비밀 —** a secret order
지령 紙齡 the issue number of a periodical
지로 支路 a branch〔side〕 road ; a bypath ; a byway ; a byroad ; an offshoot
지론 至論 a most reasonable opinion
지론 持論 one's pet theory ; a stock argument ; a cherished opinion〔view〕 ¶ 지론대로 행하다 act out one's opinion // 지론을 굽히지 않다 stick〔hold fast〕 to one's opinion ; persist in one's view // …이 나의 지론이다 My theory is 《that》; I hold 《that》
지뢰 地雷 a land〔ground〕 mine ¶ 지뢰를 묻다 lay〔charge〕 a mine // 지뢰를 밟다 strike a mine
— 공병 a miner **— 지대** a mine field **— 탐지기** a mine detector **—함** a caisson **— 화약** blasting powder **촉발 —** a mechanical contact mine
⁑**지루하다** (be) tedious ⇨ 지리하다
지류 支流 a tributary ; a branch stream ¶ 한강의 지류 a tributary to the *Han* river
지르다¹ [소리를] holler ; yell ; scream ; cry aloud ¶ 고함을 지르다 yell ; shout ; holler // 비명을 지르다 shriek ; scream ; let out a shriek // 오라고 소리 지르다 shout 《to a person》 to come // 사람 살리라고 소리 지르다 yell〔cry〕 for help // 「도둑이야」하고 소리 지르다 shout 〔scream〕 "Thief!" // 연설을 시작하려 했으나 청중이 소리를 지르는 바람에 할 수 없었다 He wished to begin his speech, but he was shouted down.
지르다² ① [손·발로] kick ; give 《a person》 a kick ; knock ; strike ; give 《a person》 a blow ¶ 공을 지르다 kick a ball // 얼굴을 지르다 strick 《a person》 across the face // 발로 옆구리를 지르다 give a kick on side
② [꽂다] insert ; thrust ¶ 빗장을 지르다 bolt〔bar〕 a door // 머리에 비녀를 지르다 stick a hairpin in one's hair // 만년필을 주머니에 지르다 clip a fountain pen onto

one's pocket
③ [불을] set fire to ¶ 집에 불을 지르다 set a house on fire
④ [길을] take a shorter way ; cut across ¶ 길을 질러가다 take a shortcut
⑤ [나무의 순을] cut off ; snip ; nip ¶ 순을 지르다 cut off the buds
⑥ [돈을] bet ; stake ¶ 판에 돈을 지르다 lay a bet 《on the gambling table》; put money down
⑦ [앞지르다] get the jump on 《a person》; grab the initiative ¶ (앞)질러 대답하다 cut in before 《a person》; has a chance to reply // (앞)질러가다 go ahead of 《a person》
⑧ [냄새가 코를] stink ; smell nasty

지르되다 grow slowly ; be of slow growth

지르디디다 stand on tiptoe (서다) ; walk on tiptoe (걷다)

지르르, 찌르르 [기름기 따위가] dribbling ; dripping ; glossy with grease ; [뼈마디가] with a dull pain 《in the joints》 ¶ 개기름이 지르르 도는 얼굴 one's face glossy with grease

지르박 [춤의 하나] jitterbug

지르신다 slip 《shoes》 halfway on ; wear shoes half-on ; wear socks slipped down over the heels

지르잡다 hold the soiled part of a garment (and wash it off) ¶ 지르잡아 빨다 wash off a spot

지르코늄 〖화학〗 zirconium 《Zr》

지르콘 〖광물〗 zircon
—산 a zirconic acid

지르퉁하다 (be) sulky ; sullen ; pouting ; morose ; ill-humored ¶ 지르퉁해지다 turn sulky // 그는 지르퉁하니 말이 없었다 He was in a sulky mood and did not say a word.

⁑**지름** a diameter
반— a radius 《*pl.* -dii, ~es》; a semidiameter ⇨ 반경

†**지름길** a shortcut ; a shorter way ¶ 제일의 지름길 the shortest way // 지름길로 가다 take a shortcut ; cut across 《a field》 // 정거장으로 가는 지름길을 가르쳐 주시오 Show me a shortcut to the station.

지름 시조 —時調 a *shijo* poem recited with the first verse especially high

지릅뜨기 a glaring eye ; a person with glaring eyes

지릅뜨다 glare ; make 《one's eyes》 glare ; give a strong stare 《at》 ¶ 성이 나서 눈을 지릅뜨다 glare at 《a person》 with anger

지리 地利 [유리한 지세] geographical advantage ; advantage of locality〔situation〕; [토지에서의 이익] profit from land ¶ 지리를 점하다 be on favorable ground ; occupy a vantage ground

⁑**지리** 地理 a geographical feature ; topography ; geography (지리학) ¶ 지리학상의 geographical // 그곳의 지리에 밝다 be familiar with that place ; know the geography of the place
—적 위치〔분포, 조건〕 geographical position〔distribution, conditions〕 **—책** a geography (book) **—학** geography **—학자** a geographer **군사 —학** military geography **동물 —학** zoogeography **상업 —학** commercial geography **수리(數理) —학** mathematical geography **식물 —학** phytogeography **역사 —학** historical geography **인문 —학** descriptive geography **자연〔정치〕 —학** physical〔political〕 geography

지리다[1] [냄새가] smell of urine ¶ 지린내 smell of urine

지리다[2] [조금 싸다] wet〔soil〕 one's pants

지리멸렬 支離滅裂 incoherence ; inconsistency ; breaking up in pieces ; separation ; split **—하다** (be) contradictory ; incoherent ; inconsistent ; disjointed ; chaotic ¶ 지리멸렬한 연설 a disjointed speech // 지리멸렬되다 fall into a chaotic condition ; go to pieces // 그의 연설은 지리멸렬했다 He got balled up in his speech.

지리하다 支離— (be) tedious ; dull ; boring ; tiresome ; monotonous ; wearisome ; [사람이 주어] be bored ; be tired 《of》; become weary 《of》; find 《a matter》 dull ¶ 지리한 여행 a monotonous journey // 지리한 이야기 a tedious〔dull〕 talk // 지리한 일상 생활 an insipid daily life // 지리한 나머지 to kill the time ; by way of beguiling the time // 지리하게 하다 bore 《a person》 // 지리해 하는 것 같다 look bored // 나는 지리하다 I have a dull time. /Time hangs heavy on my hands. / Time passes heavily. // 지리해 죽겠다 I am bored to death. // 이 책은 지리하다 This book bores me. // 일이 지리하다 I am tired of this work. /This work bores me. // 교장 선생의 연설은 참 지리했다 We were bored to death by the principal's speech.

지린내 the smell of urine ; a stale smell 《of laundry》

-지마는 though ; although ; yet ; nevertheless ; notwithstanding ¶ 나이가 어리지마는 분별이 있다 Though he is young, he is discreet. /He is young, but he is discreet. // 그렇지마는 당신에게 찬성할 수는 없다 I cannot agree with you, however. // 여자지마는 남자에 못지 않다 Woman as she is, she is equal to a man.

-지만 ⇨ -지마는

지망 志望 wish ; desire ; choice (선택) ; aspiration ; ambition **—하다** wish ; desire ; aspire 《to》; choose ; prefer ¶ 교사 지망자 a prospective〔would-be〕 teacher // 제1〔2〕 지망교 the school of one's first〔second〕 choice // 지망대로 as one wishes // 지망하는 직업을 기입하라

State the profession preferred. // 외교관을 지망하고 있다 He wishes to be a diplomat. /He has a desire to become a diplomat. // 나는 1차 지망한 대학에 합격했다 I passed the exam for my first-choice university.
—자 an applicant ; a candidate ; an aspirant — 학과 the desired course 〔subject of study〕 — 학교 the school of one's choice ; the school preferred 제1〔제2〕— one's first〔second〕 preference〔choice〕
지망지망 carelessly ; heedlessly ; neglectfully ; indifferently ; rashly —하다 (be) careless ; thoughtless ; indifferent
지맥 支脈 [지선] a spur ; an offset ; a feeder (광산의) ; [산맥의] a branch〔an offshoot〕 of a mountain range ¶ 철도의 지맥 a spur line 《미》 ; a feeder line
지맥 地脈 a vein 《of rock, ore》 ; a (mineral) vein
지면 知面 acquaintance ⇨ 면식(面識) ¶ 지면있는 well-acquainted ; familiar
†**지면 地面** the surface 《of land, the earth》 (지표) ; the ground (지상) ; land (토지) ; a lot (건축용의) ¶ 넓은 지면 a large tract of land // 지면에 주저앉다 squat on the ground // 지면에 눈이 2미터나 쌓여 있다 The snow lies two meters deep on the ground.
지면 紙面 paper ; space (여백) ¶ 지면이 허락하면 if space permits〔allows〕 // 지면 관계로 for want of space ; on account of space considerations // 지면을 확장하다 increase the printed columns of a paper
지면 誌面 the space〔pages〕 of a magazine〔journal, periodical〕 ¶ 지면에 in a magazine // 지면을 통해 through a magazine
지멸있다 (be) steady ; faithful ¶ 지멸있게 steadily ; constantly ; faithfully ; persistently
지명 地名 the name of a place ; a geographical designation〔name〕
— 사전 a geographical dictionary ; a gazetteer
지명 知名 a wide reputation ¶ 지명의 noted ; notable ; distinguished ; eminent ; well-known ; celebrated // 지명 인사 a man of fame ; a celebrity ; a well-known person // 지명 작가 an eminent author〔writer〕
지명 知命 knowing the decrees of Heaven 《as Confucius did at the age of fifty》 ; [50세] the age of fifty years —하다 know the decrees of Heaven ; know one's own destiny
†**지명 指名** naming ; nomination ; designation —하다 name ; nominate ; designate ¶ 지명된 사람 a nominee ; a designate // 지명순으로 in order of the persons called〔mentioned〕 // 전범자로 지명되다 be designated as a war criminal // 의장으로 지명하다 nominate 《a person》 for chairman // 대통령 후보자로 지명되다 be nominated for President // 만일 내가 지명을 받으면 옆에서 가르쳐 줘 If I get called on, I'll expect a little help on the side.
—권 the right of nomination — 수배 arrangements for the search for an identified criminal — 수배인 a most wanted criminal — 입찰 a tender by specified bidders ; a private tender —자 a nominator — 통화〔전화〕 a person-to-person call — 투표 a roll call vote ; a vote by yeas and nays〔roll call〕 피—자 a nominee
지모 智謀 practical ingenuity ; resourcefulness ¶ 지모가 풍부한 사람 a man of resources // 지모가 풍부하다 be resourceful ; be full of resources
지목 地目 the classification of land ; land category
— 변경 re-classification of land ; a change in the category of land
지목 指目 pointing out ; indication —하다 point out ; indicate ; designate ; put the finger on ; spot ¶ 범인으로 지목하다 spot 《a person》 as the culprit // 그는 그 사건의 용의자로 지목받고 있다 He is spotted as a suspicious character of the offense.
지묘 至妙 (supreme) exquisiteness ; superbness —하다 (be) exquisite ; superb ¶ 지묘한 작전 the superb execution of stratagem
지묵 紙墨 paper and ink (-stick)
지문 指紋 a fingerprint ; a finger mark ¶ 지문을 남기다 leave one's fingerprints 《on》 // 지문을 채취하다 take 《a person's》 fingerprints ; fingerprint 《a person》 // 지문을 남기지 않도록 장갑을 끼다 wear gloves to avoid leaving fingerprints
— 기록 a fingerprint record —법 the fingerprint (system) ; dactyloscopy ; [지문학] dactylography — 원지 finger print forms — 전문가 a fingerprint expert — 현출기(顯出器) an insufflator 와상(渦狀)〔궁상(弓狀), 제상(蹄狀)〕 — a whirl〔an arch, a loop〕 fingerprint
지문 地文 the physical features and changes of the earth ; [지문학] physical geography ; physiography
—학자 a physiographer
지물 地物 ¶ 지물을 이용하여 숨다 shelter oneself behind a natural feature on the earth ; 〖군사〗 take cover
지물 紙物 paper goods ; various kinds of paper
—포 a paper goods store
지미 至微 utmost minuteness ; extreme fineness —하다 (be) extremely minute〔fine, detailed〕
지미 至美 supreme〔superb〕 beauty —하다 (be) supremely beautiful
지미 地味 the quality〔nature〕 of soil ¶ 비옥한 지미 fertile〔rich〕 soil
지반 地盤 ① [땅바닥] the ground ¶ 단단

한 지반 firm〔solid〕 ground // 물렁한 지반 soft〔flimsy〕 ground // 지반을 굳히다 solidify〔harden〕 the foundation // 이 근처는 지반이 물러서 지진이 있을 때는 위험하다 The ground about here is not firm, so it is dangerous in an earthquake.
② [근거] the foundation ; the base ; [세력 범위] a sphere of influence ; a constituency 《영》 ; a position (지위) ; a territory (영역) ¶ 민자당의 지반 a Democratic Liberal Party's territory〔constituency〕 // 이것이 그의 성공의 지반이 되었다 It laid the foundation for his success. // 지반을 구축하다 lay the foundation ; nurse one's constituency (정당이) // 농촌을 지반으로 하여 입후보하다 run for the Assembly with agricultural districts as one's constituency // 확고한 지반을 닦다 establish one's firm foothold 《in society》

지반 池畔 a pondside
—석 a foundation stone — 침몰 ground 〔land〕 subsidence

지반자 紙— 〖건축〗 a papered ceiling

지발 폭탄 遲發爆彈 a delayed-action bomb ; a time bomb

†**지방 脂肪** fat ; grease ; lard (돼지의) ; speck (고래 따위의) ; suet (소·양 따위의) ¶ 지방질의 sebaceous ; fatty // 지방이 많은 음식물 fatty food // 그는 지나치게 지방분이 많다 There is surplus fat in his body. /He is obese.
— 결핍증 a fat-deficiency disease — 과다 excess of fat ; obesity —분 fatty matter ; a fatty〔sebaceous〕 substance — 분비선 an oil gland — 분해 〖화학〗 lipolysis —선 the sebaceous glands — 세포 a fat cell — 조직 adipose tissue — 침착 deposit of fat — 침착증 〖의학〗 lipomatosis

†**지방 地方** a locality ; a district ; a region ; a section 《미》 ; [시골] the country ; the provinces 《영》 ; [부근] the neighborhood ; the vicinity ¶ 지방적 local ; sectional ; provincial // 이 지방 this part〔section〕 of the country ; these parts // 서울 지방 *Seoul* and the nearby // 부산 지방 the *Pusan* district // 지방적 편견 localism ; provincialism
— 검사 a district attorney — 검찰청 a district public prosecutor's office — 경찰 the local〔provincial〕 police — 공무원 a local public service employee 〔worker〕 — 관청 the provincial government office —기관 a local administrative organ — 기사 local news — 단체 a local body — 법원 a district court ¶ 지방법원 판사 a district judge —병 〖의학〗 an endemic (disease) ; [가축의] an enzootic (disease) — 분권 decentralization of power — 사투리 a local accent〔dialect 《방언》〕 ; a brogue ¶ 지방 사투리가 심하다 speak with a brogue〔broad provincial accent〕 —색 local color ; localism —세 local rates 《영》 ; a local tax 《미》 — 순회 a provincial tour ; barnstorming 《미·구》 —시 local time — 신문 a local newspaper — 은행 a local〔provincial〕 bank — 의회 a local assembly ¶ 지방의회 의원 a local assembly man — 자치 local self-government〔autonomy〕 ; home rule ¶ 지방 자치 단체 a local autonomous entity // 지방자치법 〖법〗 the Local Government Act — 장관 a provincial governor — 재정 local〔provincial〕 finance — 정책 a local policy —주의 provincialism ; regionalism —판〔신문〕 a provincial edition 〔paper〕 — 행정 local administration —화 localization ¶ 지방화하다 localize

지방 紙榜 an ancestral tablet made of paper

지방질 脂肪質 ¶ 지방질의 fatty ; sebaceous ; adipose // 지방질이 많다 be fatty

†**지배 支配** [관리] control ; superintendence ; [처리] management ; [지휘] direction ; [통치] rule ; government — 하다 control ; rule ; govern ; direct ; dominate ; have control of ; manage ; sway ¶ 지배를 받다 be (put) under the control〔rule〕 of ; be subject to 《laws》 // 운명을 지배하다 sway the destiny 《of》 ; be master of one's fortune // 세론을 지배하다 sway〔lead〕 public opinion // 감정에 지배되다 be influenced by a passion // 세계를 지배하다 dominate the world // 환경에 지배되다 be at the mercy of circumstances〔environment〕 // 해상을 지배하는 자가 세계를 지배한다 Those who have command of the seas have control of the world. // 일국의 운명을 지배할 중대 문제이다 This is the serious problem which will decide the fate of the country.
— 계급 the ruling〔governing〕 class —권 one's control〔sway, hold〕 《over》 ; management ; supremacy — 능력 〖체육〗 physical intelligence —력 one's control 〔sway〕 《over》 ; one's hold 《over, on》 ; one's grip 《on》 — 민족 a master race — 자 a ruler ; a dominator ; a master ; a governor ; an administrator —질 〖생물〗 archoplasm

지배 遲配 [우편물] delay in mail delivery

지배인 支配人 a manager ; an executive ; a superintendent ¶ 호텔의 지배인 the manager of a hotel ; a hotel manager
— 대리 an acting manager 부— an assistant manager ; a submanager 여— a manageress 총— a general manager

지벅거리다, 찌뻑거리다 stumble along ; walk with difficulty

지벅지벅 stumbling ; with difficulty ¶ 지벅지벅 걷다 stumble along

지번 地番 a lot number

지벌 地閥 social standing and (noble) lineage

지벌 —罰 divine punishment ; a curse ; an evil spell
지범거리다 pick up one by one
지범지범 picking 《them》 up one by one
지변 地變 an extraordinary geographical phenomenon ; a natural calamity ; cataclysm ; a terrestrial upheaval ; the convulsion of nature
지병 持病 a chronic disease ; an old complaint ¶ 나의 지병은 두통이다 Headache is a chronic disease with me.
지보 至寶 most valuable treasure ; a most valuable assert ¶ 국가의 지보 a great national asset // 산업계의 지보 the pride of industrial circles
⁑**지보 地步** one's stand ; (a) standing ; (a) foothold ; (a) footing ; a position ; ground
지복 至福 the highest good ; the supreme bliss ; beatitude
지부 支部 a branch 《of a society, an association》 ; a chapter ¶ 적십자사 서울 지부 the *Seoul* chapter of the Red Cross Society
—장 the manager of a branch office ; the president〔director〕 of a local chapter 도〔지방〕— a provincial 〔district〕 subdivision
지부럭거리다 annoy ; pester ; tease ; needle ; make fun of ¶ 지부럭지부럭 annoying ; pestering ; teasing
지부지기 〖식물〗 a roof-tile moss
지분 脂粉 rouge and powder ; cosmetics ¶ 지분의 향기 an odor of cosmetics // 지분질하다 paint and powder one's face ; make up one's face
—내 an odor of cosmetics
지분거리다 [썹히다] be disagreeable 〔unpleasant〕 to chew ; [귀찮게 굴다] tease ; annoy ; pester
지분지분 ⇨ 지분거리다
†**지불 支拂** payment ; defrayment ; settlement ; discharge —하다 pay ; defray ; discharge ; disburse ; clear (빚을) ; honor (어음을) ; repay〔settle〕 (부채를) ; redeem (채권을) ¶ 지불을 청구하다 ask 《a person》 to pay ; ask for payment // 지불받는 사람 a payee // 지불을 거절하다 refuse payment // 지불을 정지하다 stop 〔suspend〕 payment // 지불 기한이 되다 fall〔become〕 due ; mature // 지불 기한이 지나다 be overdue // 지불을 연기하다 postpone〔put off〕 one's payment 《for the bill》 // 지불 의무가 있다 be liable for // 그 은행에서 어음을 지불하다 honor the check at the bank // 수선비는 건물의 소유자가 지불해야 한다 Cost of repairs is chargeable to the owner of the building.
— 거절 refusal of payment —고 the amount paid〔payable, due〕 —계 a paying cashier〔teller〕 — 기일 the date of payment ; the pay day (봉급일) ; the maturity (어음의) — 능력 ability 〔capacity〕 to pay ; solvency ; payment capability — 명령 an order for payment — 방법 the terms of payment — 보증 a certificate of payment — 보증 수표 a certified check 《미》 — 불능(자) insolvency〔an insolvent〕 — 승낙 a guarantee for payment —액 the amount payable〔paid〕 — 어음 a bill〔an account〕 payable — 연기 postponement of payment — 유예 a moratorium 《*pl.* ~s, -ria》 ; postponement of payment ¶ 지불 유예 기일〔기간〕 period of grace ; a moratorium —인 a payer ; a drawee (수표의) — 전표 a payment slip — 정지 suspension of payment ; bank suspension (은행의) ; a moratorium (비상시의) — 조건 terms of payment — 준비금 a reserve fund (for payment) — 준비 제도 [은행의] a reserve requirement system —지 the place of payment ; a domicile — 지시서 a cashier's check — 청구서 a written application for payment — 협정 a payment agreement
†**지붕** a roof ; the house-top (옥상) ¶ 기와로 지붕을 이다 roof a house with tiles ; tile the roof // 지붕이 새다 the roof leaks
기와 — a tiled roof 둥근 — a dome 초가 — a thatched roof
지브롤터 Gibraltar (스페인의 항구)
— 해협 the Strait of Gibraltar
지뿌드드하다 (be) uncomfortable ; be out of sorts ; (be) indisposed ¶ 몸이 지뿌드드하다 feel uncomfortable ; be unwell // 입이 지뿌드드하다 have a poor appetite // 지뿌드드한 날씨이다 It is a heavy day.
지사 支社 a branch (office)
지사 志士 a patriot
우국— a patriot
*__지사 知事__ a (provincial) governor ¶ 지사직 governorship
— 관사 gubernatorial mansion〔residence〕 — 선거 a gubernatorial election
⁑**지상 地上** the ground ¶ 지상의 earthly (천국에 대한) ; on (the) earth // 지상에서 on〔above, over〕 the ground〔earth〕 // 지상의 생활〔낙원〕 an earthly existence 〔paradise〕 // 나무의 높이는 지상 5미터이다 The tree rises 5 meters above ground.
—경(莖) 〖식물〗 an aerial stem — 공격 a ground attack —군 a ground〔land〕 army —권 superficies ; surface rights ¶ 지상권 소유자 a superficiary — 근무 ground service — 낙원 an earthly paradise ; a heaven〔paradise〕 on earth — 병력 land power ; ground strength 〔force〕 — 부대 a ground troops〔unit, forces〕 —수 〖광산〗 surface water — 유도 착륙 방식 〖항공〗 a ground control approach method — 작전 a ground operation —전 ground warfare ; land war — 정비원 [비행기 따위의] a ground man ; a mechanic ; [총칭] a ground crew — 통신국 [항공 연락용 무

선국] an aeronautic(al) station — 포화 ground fire
지상 地象 terrestrial phenomena
지상 紙上 (on) paper ; (in the) newspaper ¶ 지상의 논쟁 paper warfare ; a paper battle // 지상에 by letter (편지에) ; in print (인쇄로) ; through the press (신문에) // 본지상에서 in our columns
— 공론 mere paper talk — 논전 paper warfare — 상담난 a personal advice column — 투표 a straw vote〔ballot〕
지상 誌上 (in) a magazine ¶ 지상에 in a magazine〔journal〕 // 차호 지상에서 발표함 To be made public in the next number〔issue〕.
지상 至上 supremacy ¶ 지상의 highest ; supreme ; utmost // 예술 지상주의 the art-for-art principle // 인생의 지상 목적 the supreme end of life
—권 supremacy ; supreme power ; sovereignty — 명령 a supreme order ; 〖철학〗 a categorical imperative 백인 —주의자 a white supremacist 예술 —주의 the art-for-art principle ; art for art's sake
지상 地相 [토지의 형세] configuration of the ground ; the lay of the land ; [토지의 감정] geomancy
—학 physiography
지상선 地上仙 Taoist immortals living on earth (신선) ; a minion of fortune (운명의 총아)
지새다 the day breaks ; it dawns
지새우다 awake〔stay up〕 all night ; see the night out
지서 支署 a branch office ; a substation
경찰 — a police substation〔box〕
지석 誌石 a memorial stone
지석묘 支石墓 〖고고〗 a dolmen ; a cromlech
지선 支線 a branch line 《of railroad》 ; a local line (지방 철도의) ; a feeder line (항공로의)
지선 至善 the supreme good —하다 (be) extremely good
지성 至誠 perfect〔absolute〕 sincerity ; devotion ; wholeheartedness ; one's true heart ¶ 지성껏 faithfully ; sincerely ; with one's whole heart and soul // 지성을 보이다 manifest〔show〕 one's sincerity // 지성이면 감천이라 Sincerity moves heaven. // 그녀는 시부모를 지성껏 모셨다 She served her husband's parents with devotion.
†지성 知性 intellect ; intelligence ¶ 한국의 지성(인들) the intellectuals of Korea // 인간의 지성 human intelligence // 지성에 호소하다 appeal to one's intelligence
지성소 至聖所 〖성경〗 the sanctuary ; the holy of holies ; sanctum sanctorum
지세 地貰 ground〔land〕 rent ; rent
지세 地勢 terrain (군사상의) ; topography ; geographical feature ; physical aspect ; geographical position (위치) ¶ 지세상 topographically
지세 地稅 a land tax
지소 至小 (being) infinitesimal —하다 (be) minute ; microscopic ; infinitesimal ; very small ; extremely small
지소 支所 a branch (office) ; a substation
지소사 指小辭 〖문법〗 a diminutive
†지속 持續 continuance ; continuation —하다 continue ; last ; keep up ; sustain (버티다) ; maintain ¶ 지속적 lasting ; continuous // 연구를 지속하다 keep up one's study // 생명을 지속하기 위해서는 공기가 필요하다 Air is necessary to support life. // 결심은 잘 하지만 지속하는 일이 없다 He makes good resolutions indeed, only he never keeps on with them.
— 기간 duration ; period of life — 기호 〖음악〗 a tenuto 《*pl.* -tos, -ti》 —력 tenacity ; sustaining power ; persistency —성 durability —전 a retaining action —파 a continuous wave
지속 遲速 slowness and celerity ; speed ; swiftness ¶ 일의 지속 the speed of one's work
지수 止水 stagnant water ; standing〔still〕 water
지수 指數 a numerical index ; 〖수학〗 an exponent
— 급수〔함수, 방정식〕 an exponential series〔function, equation〕 물가 — a price index 불쾌 — a discomfort index 생활비 — the index figure of the cost of living
지순 至純 absolute purity —하다 (be) absolutely pure
지순 至順 supreme gentleness〔docility〕 —하다 be as meek as a lamb ; (be) meek ; gentle
지술 地術 〖민속〗 geomancy
지스러기 waste ; trash ; refuse ; remnants ; odds and ends
실— waste threads 인간 — dregs of humanity
†지시 指示 directions ; instructions ; orders ; indication —하다 direct ; instruct ; [가리키다] show ; indicate ; point out ¶ 지시 하에 under 《a person's》 directions〔instructions〕 // 지시에 따라서 in accordance with 《a person's》 directions ; under instructions 《from》 // 지시에 따르다 follow 《a person's》 instructions
— 계기〔전력계, 표지〕 an indicating instrument〔wattmeter, sign〕 — 기속 〖항공〗 indicated airspeed 《IAS》 — 대명사〔형용사〕 〖문법〗 a demonstrative pronoun〔adjective〕 —등 a pilot lamp ; an indicator light —서 directions ; an order —약 〖화학〗 an indicator —판 a notice board ; finger post
†지식 知識 knowledge ; information (견문) ; attainments (소양) ; learning (학문) ; understanding (이해) ¶ 일반적 지식 general knowledge〔information〕 // 심

오한 지식 a profound〔deep〕 knowledge // 최신 지식 up-to-date knowledge〔information〕 // 해박한 지식 a broad〔comprehensive〕 knowledge ; an extensive knowledge // 피상적인 지식 a superficial〔shallow〕 knowledge // 빈약한 지식 a poor〔meager, limited〕 knowledge // 불완전한 지식 an imperfect knowledge ; incomplete information // 변변찮은 지식 a little knowledge ; a smattering knowledge 《of English》 // 어학의 지식 linguistic attainments〔knowledge〕 // 지식이 많은 사람 a well-informed person // 법률의 지식이 있다 have legal knowledge ; be legally enlightened // 지식을 얻다 get〔gain〕 knowledge ; acquire〔obtain〕 information ; derive one's knowledge 《from》 ; extract information 《from》 // 지식을 연마하다 improve one's mind〔knowledge〕 // 단편적인 지식 a fragmentary〔scrappy〕 knowledge // 초보적인 지식 an elementary〔a rudimentary〕 knowledge // 전문적 지식 expert〔professional〕 knowledge〔information〕 // 산 지식 a work〔serviceable, practical〕 knowledge // 읽을〔쓸〕 수 있는 정도의 영어 지식 a reading〔writing〕 knowledge of English // 영어의 지식이 충분하다 He has a good knowledge of English. // 세상 일에 대한 지식은 조금도 없다 He knows nothing of the world.
— 계급 the intellectual class ; the intellectuals ; the intelligentsia ; the highbrows 《구》 **— 산업** the knowledge industry **—인** an intellectual ; a highbrow 《구》 : an egghead 《속》 **기초 —** a basic〔foundation〕 knowledge **신 —** 《acquire》 new〔up-to-date〕 knowledge〔information〕 ; advanced ideas **예비 —** preliminary〔previous〕 knowledge

지식욕 知識慾 a thirst for knowledge ; an appetite for knowledge ; intellectual appetite ; a desire to learn〔for learning〕 ; love for learning ¶ 지식욕에 불타다 have a voracious appetite for knowledge ; have a thirst for knowledge ; be thirsty〔hungry〕 for knowledge ; thirst〔hunger〕 for knowledge

지신 地神 the god of the earth

지실 知悉 complete knowledge〔information〕 **—하다** have a complete knowledge of ; be perfectly acquainted with ; be fully informed of〔on〕 ¶ 그 소문은 세상이 지실하는 바다 People are fully informed of the gossip.

지실 [재난] (a) disaster ; a calamity ; [불행] (a) misfortune

지심 地心 the core〔center〕 of the earth

지싯거리다 badger 《a person》 to do ; insist upon ; ask for persistently ; keep begging ; importune

지싯지싯 《ask for》 persistently ; insistently ; importunately

지아비 a husband

지아이 a GI 《*pl.* GI's》 《Government Issue》

지악 至惡 —하다 (be) most wicked ; atrocious ; devilish ; diabolical ; [악착하다] stubborn ; tough ; hard ¶ 지악한 놈 a devil ; a fiend // 지악한 수단 villainous measures ; atrocious tricks // 지악스럽게 일하다 make frantic〔desperate〕 effort ; work hard ; toil and moil

지압 地壓 a ground pressure ; an earth pressure

지압 요법 指壓療法 finger-pressure therapy〔cure〕 ; manual therapeutics ¶ 지압요법을 행하다 practice〔perform〕 the finger-pressure treatment

지애 至愛 a deep love

지약 持藥 a medicine for one's habitual use ¶ 지약으로 쓰다 take 《some medicine》 regularly

지양 止揚 〚철학〛 sublation ; aufheben 《도》 **—하다** sublate

지어내다 [꾸며내다] cook up ; coin ; frame up ; make up 《a story》 ; fabricate ; invent ; forge ¶ 지어낸 말 a made-up〔cooked-up, fabricated〕 story // 하루에 옷을 열 죽씩 지어내다 produce ten suits of clothes a day // 새 말을 지어내다 create〔make up〕 a new word // 없는 이야기를 지어내다 make up a story out of whole cloth

지어땡이 a game in which each player gets 5 cards〔dominoes〕 at a time, with three of them used to make a *mudae* 《10, 20 score》 and the remaining two used for matching other players

지어먹다 gather 《one's wits》 ; apply〔gather〕 《one's mind》 ¶ 마음을 지어먹다 gather one's wits ; give〔apply〕 one's mind 《to》 ; keep one's mind 《on》

지어미 a wife

지어붓다 pour 《into》 ¶ 녹인 납을 거푸집에 지어붓다 pour molten lead into a mold

지언 至言 a wise〔good〕 saying ; most reasonable remarks

지엄 至嚴 extreme strictness〔sternness〕 **—하다** (be) extremely strict〔stern, rigid〕 (be) extremely strict〔stern, rigid〕

지업상 紙業商 [상점] a paper store〔shop〕 ; [상인] a dealer in paper

지에밥 steamed rice used for brewing rice wine

지엔피 the G. N. P. 《gross national product》

†지역 地域 an area ; a region ; a territory ; a zone ¶ 지역적 local ; regional // 광대한 지역 a vast area // 지역별로 by regional groups // 지역에 따라 다르다 vary in different localities
—구 [선거의] local constituencies〔electorates〕 **— 단체** a territorial〔local, regional〕 society〔group〕 **— 대표** the delegation〔delegates〕 of a district〔region〕 ; [조합의] local union delegates

regional director —사회 a (local) community —수당 a district allowance —연구 an area study (학문의 한 분야) —제 [도시 계획] zoning —차 regional differences 공업 — a manufacturing area 방화 — a fire zone

지역권 地役權 〖법〗 easement ; (real) servitude
—자 a servitude holder

지연 紙鳶 a kite

†지연 遲延 delay ; tardiness ; retardation ; postponement —하다 delay ; be overdue ; be late ; be put off ; be behind time with 《one's payment》 ; be retarded ; retard ¶ 오래 지연된 long-deferred // 예정보다 2주일이나 지연하여 two weeks behind the schedule // 출발이 지연되다 be delayed in one's departure // 오래 지연한 후에 우리는 그 일을 완성했다 After much delay, we finished the work.
— 작전 stalling〔delaying〕 tactics〔operations〕 —책 a delaying move ; a dilatory measure

지연 단체 地緣團體 a territorial〔territorially organized〕 society

지연 사회 地緣社會 a territorial society

지열 地熱 the heat of the earth ; the subterranean heat ¶ 지열의 geothermal

지열 止熱 the abatement〔removal, alleviation〕 of fever ; dropping of temperature —하다 the temperature falls〔goes down〕 ; break a fever

지엽 枝葉 [가지와 잎] branches and leaves ; [중요치 않은 일] minor details ; nonessentials ¶ 지엽적인 minor ; unessential ; of minor importance // 지엽으로 흐르다 enter into unimportant details ; deviate from the main course ; digress〔diverge〕 from the subject
— 문제 a side〔an off〕 issue ; a subordinate problem ; an irrelevant matter ; a mere detail〔trifle〕

*지옥 地獄 hell ; Hades ; the inferno ; the infernal regions ¶ 지옥과 극락 heaven and hell ; Hades and Paradise // 지옥 같은 infernal ; hellish // 지옥에 떨어지다 go to hell // 지옥에 떨어뜨리다 condemn 《a person》 to hell ; let 《a person》 fall into hell // 지옥도 극락도 이승에 있다 Heaven and hell exist in this world. /Heaven and hell are but the two phases of life.
교통 — a (terrific) traffic jam 생— a hell on earth ; a living hell ; an earthy〔a mundane〕 hell ; an inferno 《*pl.* ~s》 시험 — the torture of examination ; the examination evil

지온 地溫 [토양의] soil temperature ; [지면의] ground temperature

지요 地— a mattress on which a body is laid in a coffin

지용 智勇 wisdom and courage ; sagacity and valor ¶ 그는 지용을 겸비한 명장이다 He is a great general who combines wisdom with valor. /He is a general remarkable for both wisdom and valor.

지용성 脂溶性 〖화학〗 fat-solubility ; liposolubility

지우 知友 a close friend ; a bosom friend ; an intimate acquaintance

지우 知遇 warm friendship ; favor ; warm hospitality —하다 treat 《a person》 with warm hospitality〔consideration, treatment〕 ¶ 지우를 입다 enjoy the favor of 《a person's》 acquaintance ; be favored with 《a person's》 recognition // 지우를 감사히 여기다 be impressed by another's warm friendship ; be thankful for another's appreciation // 지우에 보답하다 requite 《a person's》 patronage〔favor〕

지우개 an eraser ; a cleaner ; a wiper
칠판 — a blackboard eraser

†지우다[1] ① [등에] put 《a thing》 on 《a person's》 back ; make 《a person》 bear〔carry〕 ; saddle 《a person》 with ¶ 무거운 짐을 지우다 burden 《a person》 ; lay〔put〕 a burden upon 《a person》 // 사람을 얻어서 짐을 지웠다 We engaged a worker to carry our luggage.
② [부담시키다] charge 《a person with a duty》 ; lay a duty upon 《a person》 ; lay a burden upon 《a person》 ; entrust 《a person with a task》 ¶ 책임을 지우다 [책임 전가] shift〔place〕 the responsibility on to 《a person》 ; lay the blame on 《a person》 // 큰 임무를 지우다 entrust 《a person》 with a grave task // 빚을 남에게 지우다 let 《a person》 bear one's debt

*지우다[2] [지워 없애다] erase ; rub〔wipe〕 out ; cross〔strike〕 out ¶ 글씨를 지우다 erase a word ; cross out a word // 칠판을 지우다 erase a blackboard // 옷에 묻은 자국을 지우다 wipe a stain off clothes // 명부에서 이름을 지우다 strike a name off the list // 장부에서 지우다 cross out〔liquidate〕 an account

지우다[3] [숨을] die ; expire ; breathe one's last ; [꽃을] scatter〔strew〕 flowers ; [아이를] have a miscarriage

지우다[4] [이기다] defeat ; beat ; overcome ; overpower ; get the better of ; outdo ; outplay ; outtake ; outpoint (점수를) ¶ 논쟁에서 적수를 지우다 argue one's rival down // 축구에서 상대방을 지우다 beat〔outplay〕 one's opponent in football // 씨름에서 상대방을 지우다 overmatch 《a person》 in wrestling

지우다[5] [형성하다] form ; make ¶ 원을 지우다 form a circle // 세무를 지우다 form a triangle // 그늘을 지우다 shade ; cast shade upon // 눈물을 지우다 shed tears

지우산 紙雨傘 an (oil) paper umbrella

*지원 支援 support ; back up ; bolster up —하다 support ; back up ; bolster up ; give〔lend〕 support ¶ 정신적 지원 moral support // 지원하에 with the support 《of》 ; under the auspices〔sponsorship〕

《of》// 지원을 청하다 ask 《a person's》 support ; ask 《a person》 to support
— 부대 backup〔support〕 forces ; a support troop — 연설 [선거의] a campaign speech 《for a candidate》 —자 a supporter ; a sponsor ; a patron

지원 志願 [지망] desire ; aspiration ; application (신청) ; volunteering (자원)
— 하다 wish ; desire ; apply 《for》 ; volunteer 《for》 ¶ 입학 지원자 an applicant for entrance to a school // 입학을 지원하다 apply for admission〔enrollment〕 to a school // 간호부를 지원하다 volunteer one's service as a nurse // 종군을 지원하다 volunteer for military service // 지원을 받아 주다 grant 《a person's》 application
—서 a written application —병 a volunteer — 제도 a volunteer system ; voluntary enlistment 《미》 —자 an applicant ; [후보자] a candidate ; a volunteer ; an aspirant

†지위 地位 [신분] position ; status ; standing ; rank ; [직업] a position ; a situation ; a post ; a place ; an office ¶ 지위 있는 사람 a man of position〔rank〕 // 사회적 지위가 높은 사람 a man of high social standing // 유리한 지위 an advantageous position // 책임 있는 지위 a responsible position // 교사의 지위 a position as a teacher // 좋은 지위를 얻다 get〔obtain〕 a good position // 지위를 잃다 lose one's station〔position〕 // 높은 지위를 차지하다 occupy〔hold〕 a high social position // 지위를 향상하다 improve one's position // 좋은 지위를 버리다 throw〔give〕 up a good place // 여자의 사회적 지위를 향상시키다 raise〔elevate〕 woman's status in society // 그는 지위도 있고 돈도 있다 He has both position and money.

지위지다 ① [병으로] get〔become, grow〕 thin〔emaciated, weak, haggard〕 《from illness》 ; lose vigor ; be enfeebled ; be exhausted ; be worn-out ; lose flesh 〔weight〕 ¶ 지위진 얼굴 a haggard 〔worn〕 face ; a rawboned〔gaunt, lean〕 figure ; an emaciated face // 병으로 몹시 지위지다 become worn-out from illness // 그는 자꾸만 지위져 간다 He is growing weaker day after day.
② [살림이 줄다] decline ; fall ; sink ; wane ; be reduced ¶ 지위져 가고 있다 be on the wane〔decline〕 // 가운이 지위지기 시작한다 One's fortune begins to ebb 〔fall〕. /One begins to sink in fortune. // 가세가 지위지기 시작했다 The family is going downhill. // 주인이 죽은 후로 가게는 지위졌다 Since the proprietor's death, the store has declined.

지육 智育 intellectual〔mental〕 training ; mental education〔culture〕 ¶ 지육에 치우치다 overemphasize mental education

지은 知恩 being conscious of a kindness sense of gratitude ; being grateful 《to》
— 하다 be grateful〔thankful〕 to 《a person's》 kindness〔favor〕 ; feel indebted to ¶ 지은 보은하다 repay〔requite〕 《a person's》 favor〔kindness〕

지은이 the writer ; the maker ; the one who wrote〔made〕 《it》

*지의 地衣 〖식물〗 a lichen

지이 地異 a convulsion of nature ; a natural disaster ⇨ 지변(地變)

지인 知人 an acquaintance ¶ 지인지감(之人之鑑) good judgment of human nature 〔character〕 // 나의 지인인 미국인 an American of my acquaintance // 지인이 많다 have a wide acquaintance ; have a large circle of acquaintances // 이 도시에는 지인이 하나도 없다 I am an utter stranger in this city.

지인용 智仁勇 wisdom, benevolence and valor

지일 至日 the solstices ; [동지] the winter solstice ; [하지] summer solstice

지자 智者 a wise man ; a man of wisdom ; a sage ; the wise 《총칭》 ¶ 지자불혹이다 A wise man knows his own mind. // 지자도 천려의 일실이 있다 No one is wise of all times. /Even Homer sometimes nods.

지자 知者 a man of intelligence ; a man of knowledge and experience

지자기 地磁氣 terrestrial magnetism

지장 支障 difficulty (곤란) ; [장애] impediment ; hindrance ; obstacle ; obstruction ; harm (해) ¶ 지장이 없으면 if it is convenient to you // 지장이 있다 be hindered ; be impeded ; be prevented ; be interrupted // 지장이 없다면 내일 너를 만나겠다 I will see you tomorrow, should nothing intervene. // 걷는 데는 지장이 없다 I feel〔have〕 no difficulty in walking. // 무슨 지장이 있어서 못 왔나 Did anything prevent you from coming? // 지장이 있어서 오늘 못 떠났다 Something prevented me from leaving today.

지장 指章 a thumb impression ; a thumbmark ; a thumbprint ¶ 지장을 찍다 seal 《a document》 with the thumb

지장 紙帳 a paper mosquito net

지장 智將 a resourceful general

지저거리다 [새가] sing ; chirp ; chirrup ; twitter ; warble ; [사람이] prattle ; chatter

*지저귀다 twitter ; chirp ; chatter ; chirrup ; warble (꾀꼬리 따위) ¶ 새가 지저귀는 소리 a bird's chirpings // 참새처럼 지저귀다 chatter like sparrows

지저깨비 [잔 조각] a chip of wood

‡지저분하다 (be) messy ; disordered ; messed up ; untidy ; dirty ; soiled ; unclean ; filthy ¶ 지저분한 방 a room in a mess ; a messed-up room // 지저분한 거리 a dirty street // 지저분하게 먹다 eat in a messy way

지적 地籍 acreage ; area 《of land,

ground》; the acreage of a lot
— 측량 a cadastral survey
지적 地籍 a land register ; the record of land registration
—도 a land registration map
†지적 指摘 pointing out ; indication —하다 point out ; indicate ; lay〔put out〕 a finger on ¶ 잘못을 지적하다 point out mistakes // 남의 약점을 지적하는 것은 쉬운 일이다 It is easy to put one's finger on 《a person's》 weakness. // 고객에게 잘못된 점을 지적당하는 것은 곤혹스러운 일이다 It is embarrassing to have a client point out our mistake.
‡지적 知的 ¶ 지적인 intellectual ; mental ; brainy // 지적 생활 intellectual life // 지적 작용 intellection // 지적 활동 mental activity // 지적인 일 brain work
지전 紙廛 a paper goods shop
지전 紙錢 paper money (지폐) ; currency notes ; a (bank) note ; a bill 《미》 ; soft money 《미·속》 ¶ 지전 뭉치 a stack〔roll〕 of notes ; a wad of paper money // 100원 짜리 지전 a hundred *won* note〔bill〕 // 지전으로 100만원 one million *won* in notes
지전류 地電流 〖전기〗 an earth current
지절 志節 principle and constancy 〔faith〕 ; integrity
지절 肢節 a joint ; an articulation
지절거리다 chatter ; gabble ; wag one's tongue ; talk volubly〔glibly〕 ; rattle on ⇨ 지껄이다
지점 地點 a spot ; a point ; a place ; a position ¶ 유리한 지점 a vantage point
예정 — the intended spot 중추 — pivotal〔key〕 point
지점 支店 a branch office〔shop, house〕 ¶ 한국 은행 광주 지점 the *Kwangju* Branch of the Bank of Korea // 지점을 개설하다 open〔establish〕 a branch office 《in, at》 // 지점에 전근되다 be transferred 〔assigned〕 to a branch office
—장 the manager of a branch office ; a branch manager
지점 支點 [지레의] a fulcrum ; 〖건축〗 a bearing
지정 知情 understanding〔knowing〕 of 《a person's》 situation〔position, plight〕 —하다 understand〔know〕 《a person's》 situation〔plight〕
†지정 指定 appointment ; designation ; assignment ; specification ; authorization —하다 appoint ; designate ; assign ; name ; specify ; authorize ¶ 지정한 appointed ; designated ; specified ; named ; authorized // 지정한 물건 an article specified // 지정한 시간에 at the appointed hour // 지정한 대로 as specified ; according to the specifications // 방을 지정하다 assign a room to 《a person》 // 날짜와 장소를 지정하다 appoint a day and a place
— 공장 a designated plant〔factory〕 — 대리인 an authorized agent —사(詞) a copula (word) — 상인 an authorized merchant ; a purveyor —석〔권〕 a reserved seat〔ticket〕 — 시간〔장소〕 the designated hour〔place〕 ; the appointed time〔place〕 — 여관 a designated hotel —인 〖법〗 an appointer —일 a designated day ; specified date — 통화 a designated〔specified〕 currency — 항구 a designated port ; a port named — 후견인 a designated guardian
지정 至情 [정분] close intimacy〔friendship〕 ; [충정] one's sincere heart ; sincerity ; deep feelings ¶ 지정에 감동되다 be moved〔touched〕 by 《a person's》 sincerity
지정가 指定價 〖상업〗 the limits ¶ 지정가 이하로 below the limits // 지정가에 달하다 reach the limits
구입 — buying limits 매각 — selling limits
지정거리다 linger ; take one's time 《about something》 ; delay ¶ 준비하느라고 지정거리다 take time in one's preparation
지정지미 至精至微 utmost minuteness —하다 (be) extremely minute〔fine, detailed〕
지정지밀 至精至密 utmost precision (minuteness) —하다 (be) extremely minute〔precise, exact, detailed〕
지정지정 lingering ; taking one's time ; delaying
지정학 地政學 geopolitics
—자 a geopolitician
지조 志操 principle ; purpose ; constancy ; integrity ¶ 지조가 고결한 사람 a man of (high) principles // 지조가 굳다 have a firm purpose ; be firm of purpose // 지조가 약하다 be weak of purpose // 지조를 지키다 be faithful〔devoted〕 to one's principles
지조 地租 a land tax ; the tax on land
지족 知足 contentment ; knowing satisfaction —하다 be content with ; be satisfied with ¶ 행복은 지족에 있다 Happiness lies in contentment.
지존 至尊 His Majesty (the King) ; the Throne
‡지주 支柱 a pillar ; a support ; a prop ; a stay ¶ 일가의 지주 the prop and stay of a family // 지주를 세우다 prop up ; stay ; support
‡지주 地主 a landowner ; a landlord ; a landholder
— 계급 the landed〔propertied, proprietary〕 class ; landocracy ; the landowning classes〔gentry〕 ; [희언(戱言)] the lords of the soil — 기질 landlordism 대— a large〔great, big〕 landowner ; a squire ; an extensive property ; a lord of broad acres 부재 — an absentee landowner 〔landlord〕 소— a small〔petty〕 landowner ; a squirelet 여— a landlady ; a pro-

prietress
지주 持株 one's (stock) holdings ; one's shares
— **회사** a holding company
지주 蜘蛛 〖동물〗 a spider
—**류** the arachnid ; Arachnida (학명)
지중 地中 ¶ 지중의 underground ; subterranean // 지중의 in〔under〕 the ground〔earth〕 // 지중의 보물 a buried〔an underground, a hidden〕 treasure // 지중에 묻히다 be buried in the earth // 지중에서 파내다 dig 《a thing》 out of the ground ; unearth 《treasures》
—**선** a subterranean line — **송전선** an underground transmission line — **온도계** an underground thermometer
지중해 地中海 the Mediterranean (Sea) ¶ 지중해(연안)의 Mediterranean
‡**지지 支持** support ; backing ; maintenance ; upholding —**하다** support ; stand by ; uphold ; hold ; prop up ¶ 민중의 지지 popular support // 세론의 지지 the backing〔support〕 of public opinion // 공화당을 지지하다 uphold the banner of the Republican Party // 입후보자를 지지하다 boost〔support〕 a candidate // 지지를 받다 have 《a person》 at the back // …의 주장을 지지하다 support〔second〕 《a person's》 claim〔contention〕 // 국민의 지지를 얻다 have the support of the people // 지도자를 전적으로 지지하다 back the leader to the hilt
— **가격** a support price (농산물의) —**력** 〖공학〗 bearing power —**물** a support ; a supporting structure —**자** a supporter ; an upholder ; a backer
지지 地誌 a topography ; a geographical description ¶ 지지의 topographic(al)
—**학자** a topographer
지지 遲遲 slowness ; lagging ; tardiness —**하다** (be) slow ; tardy ; lagging ¶ 지지하게 slowly ; tardily ; languidly // 지지부진하다 make slow progress ; go at a snail's pace
지지난달 the month before last
지지난밤 the night before last
지지난번 —番 the time before last
지지난해 the year before last
지지다 〔끓이다〕 stew ; 〔기름으로〕 sauter 《프》 ; panfry ; 〔머리를〕 frizzle ; curl one's hair with heated tongs ; singe one's hair ; 〔인두 따위로〕 burn ; sear ; scorch ¶ 생선을 지지다 stew fish // 저냐를 지지다 make fish sauté // 고기를 지지다 panfry meat // 인두로 상처를 지지다 sear a wound with a hot iron // 머리를 지지다 frizzle〔curl〕 hair ; put a wave into hair
지지랑물 rusty drippings from the thatch roof
지지러지다 〔놀라서〕 shrink ; flinch ; quail 《at, before》 ; cower ; 〔병으로〕 weaken ; grow feeble〔weak〕 ; be debilitated ⇨ 자지러지다
지지르다 ① 〔내리누르다〕 press ; weigh 《on》 ¶ 돌로 지지르다 weigh 《a thing》 with a stone // 잘 지지러지지 않는다 The weight doesn't work well.
② 〔억누르다〕 keep〔hold, pin〕 down ; overbear ; check ; curb ; overpower ¶ 사람의 기를 지지르다 cow 《a person》 // 그는 내가 제기하는 이의를 모조리 지질렀다 He overbore whatever objections were raised by me. /He overbore all my objections.
지지리 awfully ; frightfully ; shockingly ; terribly ; unbearably ; horribly ; exceedingly ¶ 지지리 못생기다 be awfully ugly (-looking) ; be downright stupid // 지지리 고생하다 go through terrible〔unbearable〕 hardships
지지콜콜이 inquisitively ⇨ 미주알고주알
†**지지하다** (be) trifling ; trivial ; poor ; worthless ; rubbish ; scummy 《미》 ¶ 지지한 책 a worthless book ; a dull book // 지지한 일에 시간을 보내다 waste time over trivial〔small〕 matters // 지지한 일로 걱정하다 worry about trifles ; bother one's mind over a trivial matter // 인생을 지지하게 느끼다 grow weary〔get sick〕 of life ; lose faith〔interest〕 in life ; find life a bore
지직하다 〔반죽 따위가〕 be on the wet side
지진 地震 an earthquake ; a shock (of earthquake) ; a terrestrial tremor〔disturbance〕 ¶ 대지진 a big〔severe〕 earthquake ; a terrible shock // 지진의 earthquake ; seismic ; seismal // 지진의 중심 the epicenter ; the seismic center // 그것은 지난 몇 해 동안 없었던 무서운 지진이었다 It was the sharpest earthquake we have experienced for some years past.
—**계** a seismograph ; a seismometer ; an earthquake recorder — **관측** seismometry ; seismography ; seismological observation —**대** an earthquake〔a seismic〕 zone〔belt〕 —**도** a seismogram — **보험**〔**화재**〕 an earthquake insurance 〔fire〕 —**학** seismology —**학자** a seismologist ; a seismographer — **현상** seismism ; earthquake phenomena **단층**〔**심해, 심발(深發)**〕 — a dislocation〔deep-sea, deep-focus〕 earthquake **함몰** — a downfall earthquake **해저** — a submarine 〔an underwater〕 earthquake **화산** — a volcanic earthquake
지진아 遲進兒 a (mentally) retarded child ; a backward child
지질 地質 the nature〔quality〕 of soil ; geological features ¶ 지질학상의 geological
— **공학** geotechnology —**도** a geological map — **분석** a soil analysis — **시대** the geographical age ; geologic eras — **연구소** the Geological Survey office — **조사** a geological survey

지질리다 [눌리다] get pressed ; be weighted《with》[억압당하다] be overpowered ; be quailed ; cower
지질지질 **—하다** (be) watery ; soft
지질컹이 a stunted fellow ; a weak-spirited person ; a scrubby thing
지질펀펀하다 (be) even ; level ; flat ; smooth ; [질듯하고 넓다] wet and open ¶ 지질펀펀한 길 a smooth road // 지질펀펀한 들 a broad expanse of swampy field
지질하다 [지리하다] (be) tedious ; boresome ; wearisome ; tiresome ; [신통치 않다] good-for-nothing ; worthless ; wretched ¶ 지질한 놈 a good-for-nothing fellow ; a worthless fellow // 지질한 연설 a poor〔dull〕speech // 지질한 소리하다 talk nonsense ; say silly things // 지질한 일생 a dull life // 그의 연설은 지질했다 His speech was long and boring. // 지질한 일로 시간을 낭비했다 I have spent time doing a trivial task.
*__지질학 地質學__ geology ¶ 지질학적인 geologic(al) // 지질학상(으로) geologically
—자 a geologist **고대 —** paleogeology **구조 —** structural〔tectonic〕geology **해저 —** submarine〔ocean bottom〕geology
지짐거리다 be rainy ; be wet ; rain off and on ¶ 이번 달은 지짐거리는 날이 많았다 We have had many rainy days this month.
지짐이 a stew ¶ 고기 지짐이 meat stew
지짐지짐 raining off and on
지짐질 making griddlecakes ; pan-frying **—하다** pan-fry
지참 遲參 last attendance ; late arrival《at a meeting》**—하다** arrive〔come〕late ; be behind time
—자 a late-comer
지참 持參 bringing ; bearing **—하다** bring《a thing》with ; take《a thing》with ; carry ; bear ; fetch ¶ 도시락을 지참했느냐 Have you brought lunch with you? // 수렵에 참가할 사람은 엽총을 지참할 것 One who wants to join in the hunting should carry a shotgun.
—금 a dowry ; a marriage portion ; a dot ¶ 지참금을 붙여서 딸을 시집보냈다 They married off their daughter with a dowry.
—인 the bearer ¶ 지참인불《a cheque》payable to (the) bearer // 지참인불 수표 a bearer cheque ; a cheque to the bearer // 지참인불 어음 a bill〔note〕(payable) to (the) bearer
지척 咫尺 a very short distance ¶ 지척을 분간할 수 없을 만큼 어두운 밤 a pitch-dark night // 지척지간이다 be very close ; be within a foot // 지척을 분간할 수 없을 만큼 안개가 짙었다 The fog was so dense that nothing was to be seen an inch ahead.
지척거리다 drag along ; plod ; trudge ; plod one's weary way
지척지척 dragging ; plodding ; trudging ¶ 지척지척 걷다 plod along ; walk with dragging feet
지천 至賤 **—하다** [천하다] (be) most humble ; very vulgar〔low, mean〕; [많다] abundant ; in excess ¶ 그는 지천한 집안에서 태어난 사람이다 He is a man of very humble birth. // 그런 사람은 지천으로 있다 You can find such a man at every turn.
지청 支廳 a branch office
지청구 **—하다** reproach〔blame〕《a person》without any reason ; have a grudge against〔think ill of〕《a person》without foundation
지체 lineage ; birth ; family stock ; pedigree ¶ 지체가 높은 of good lineage ; of noble birth // 지체가 낮은 of humble birth
지체 肢體 the limbs and the body ¶ 지체가 부자유한 lame ; crippled
— 부자유아 a crippled child
지체 遲滯 delay ; deferment ; retardation ; arrear **—하다** delay ; be retarded ; defer ; hold off ; be overdue ¶ 지체 없이 without delay ; without loss of time ; immediately ; promptly // 세금을 지체 없이 납부하다 pay tax without delay // 우리는 모두 월급 지불이 지체되고 있다 We are all behind in our payment.
— 일수 days in arrears
지초 芝草 a kind of iris ; Formes japonicus (학명)
지촉 紙燭 paper and candles
지축 地軸 the axis of the earth
†**지출 支出** [비용] expenses ; expenditure ; appropriation ; [수입에 대한] disbursement ; outgo ; outlay **—하다** expend ; pay ; disburse ; appropriate ; defray ¶ 수입과 지출 revenue and expenditure ; incomings and outgoings // 예산외 지출 defrayment unprovided for in a budget ; extra-budgetary expenditures // 예비비에서 지출하다 pay《a sum》out of the reserve fund // 건축비로 100만원을 지출하다 appropriate〔make an appropriation of〕one million *won* for the construction of // 국고에서 지출하다 disburse from the treasury // 지출을 삭감하다 curtail〔cut down〕expenditure // 정부 지출 삭감 spending cut
지출 持出 carrying out ; taking out **—하다** take out ; carry out ¶ 도서의 지출을 금하다 forbid《a person》to take out books
*__지층 地層__ a geological stratum《*pl.* strata》; a layer
—학 stratigraphy
지치 〖식물〗 a gromwell
지치 智齒 a wisdom tooth
†**지치다**[1] [힘이 빠지다] be exhausted ; be fatigued ; be worn out ; be〔get〕tired ¶ 몹시 지치다 be tired〔worn〕out ; be dead tired ; be used up // 지쳐서 자리에 들다 go

to bed fatigued // 나는 아주 지쳤다 I am tired to death. /I am all run down. /I'm dead beat. // 나는 지쳐서 털썩 주저앉았다 I sank exhausted. // 어두운 등불 밑에서 독서하면 눈이 지친다 Reading in a poor light taxes the eyes.

지치다² [소나 말이] have a watery stool (지쳐서)

지치다³ [얼음을] slide on〔over〕; skate on ¶ 얼음 지치기 skating ; sliding // 얼음을 지치는 사람 a〔an ice〕skater // 얼음을 지치다 skate〔slide〕on the ice // 눈 위를 지치다 slide〔skate〕on the snow // 얼음 지치러 가다 go skating

지치다⁴ [문을] close《a door》without locking ; shut a door softly〔lightly, gently〕

지친 至親 [아주 친함] close friendship ; [친족] close relatives ; members of one's immediate family **—하다** (be) very close〔intimate〕

지친것 an old-time retiree ; a rejected person

선생 — an old fogy retired from a teaching position

†지침 指針 [자석의] a compass needle ; [기계의] an indicator ; a pointer ; an index ; [시계의] a hand ; [지표] a guide ¶ 생활의 지침 a guiding principle in one's life

—면 a dial (나침판 따위의) **—서** a guide(book) **압력 —** an indicator diagram **수험 —서** a guide to examinations ; a guide book for examinees

지칭 指稱 designation **—하다** designate ¶ 반역자로 지칭되다 be designated〔labeled〕as a traitor

†지켜보다 [주시하다] watch (intently) ; stare〔gaze〕《at》; [보호하다] watch《over》; [확인하다] make sure《of, that...》; ascertain ; [목격하다] witness ; see with one's own eyes ¶ 끝까지 지켜보다 watch《a happening》to the end《of it》; see《it》through // 사건의 추이를 지켜보다 watch the development of events ; follow the evolution of events

†지키다 ① [방어하다] defend《from, against》; protect ; guard ; hold ¶ 나라를 지키다 defend the country // 자기를 지키다 defend oneself // 자기의 이익을 지키다 protect〔look after〕one's own interest ② [감시하다] watch ; keep watch《for》; guard ¶ 가게를 지키다 tend a shop // 문을 지키다 guard the door // 집을 지키다 look after〔take care of〕a house // 엄중히 지키다 watch《a person》closely ; keep a close eye《on a person》// 사람의 거동을 지키다 watch〔keep an eye on〕another's movements // 양떼를 지키다 watch a flock of sheep ③ [고수하다] cling to《a cause》; keep ; maintain ; hold fast to《one's principle》; stick to ; remain faithful (절개를) ¶ 평화와 질서를 지키다 maintain〔keep, preserve〕peace and order // 중립을 지키다 observe neutrality // 절개를 지키다 remain faithful to one's loyalty〔allegiance〕; keep one's integrity ; maintain chastity // 구습을 지키다 hold fast to old custom ④ [약속 따위를] keep《to》; abide《by》; observe ; live up《to》¶ 법을 지키다 observe〔keep, abide by〕the law // 신용을 지키다 keep up one's credit // 약속을 지키다 keep one's word // 주의를 지키다 adhere〔act according〕to one's principles // 배움을 지키다 live up to《a person's》teachings // 본분을 지키다 stick〔keep〕to one's lot in life ; fulfill one's duty // 예의를 지키다 observe good manners // 침묵〔시간〕을 지키다 keep silence〔the time〕// 규칙을 지키다 stick〔keep〕to the regulations // 지금부터는 시간을 잘 지키겠습니다 I'll be prompt from now on. // 그는 약속을 잘 지키는 사람이다 He is a man of his word. /He is as good as his word. // 저희는 정찰제를 엄격히 지킵니다 We go strictly by the price tag.

지탄 指彈 —하다 [손가락을 튀기다] fillip ; make a fillip ; flip ; flick ; [배척하다] shun ; ostracize ; send《a person》Coventry ¶ 그는 모든 사람에게 지탄받고 있다 He is shunned by all.

†지탱 支撐 maintenance ; preservation ; support **—하다** keep (up) ; maintain ; sustain ; preserve ; prop up ; support ; bear up ; hold out ¶ 건강을 지탱하다 preserve one's health // 이 이상 지탱할 수 없다 can hold out no longer // 환자는 내년까지 지탱 못할 것이다 The patient will not survive another year. // 점포를 지탱할 수 없어서 폐업했다 Being unable to maintain the shop any longer, he shut it up. // 그들은 적의 공격을 3개월 간 지탱했다 They held out for three months against the attack of enemy troops. // 사실상 그 한 사람 때문에 회사가 지탱하고 있었는데 He's practically the only reason the company is holding out.

지통 止痛 allaying〔relieving, killing〕pain **—하다** allay〔relieve, kill〕pain

—약〔제〕 an anodyne ; a pain-killer

지파 支派 a lateral branch ; a sect ; an offshoot ; a branch〔descendant, scion〕of a family〔race〕

지판 地板 [관의] the bottom piece of a coffin

지팡막대 ⇨ 지팡이

†지팡이 a stick ; a cane《영》; a walking stick ¶ 지팡이를 짚고 다니다 carry a cane // 지팡이에 의지하다 hang on〔lean upon〕one's stick // 지팡이를 짚고 걷다 walk with a stick

대— a bamboo cane **등산용 —** an alpenstock

지퍼 a zipper ¶ 지퍼를 채우다 zip《up》;

run up the zipper∥지퍼를 끄르다 unzip 《a coat》∥상의의 지퍼를 채우다 zip up one's coat ; zip one's coat on∥바지 지퍼가 열렸다 Your fly is open.

지편 紙片 a piece of paper ; a slip of paper ; a strip of paper

*__지평 地平__ the horizon ; the skyline ; ground level

—각 a horizontal angle —경〔축〕 a horizon glass〔axis〕 —면 the horizontal plane — 부각 the dip of the horizon —선 the horizon ; a horizontal line ; the skyline ¶ 지평선상에 above the horizon ; on the horizon (접하여) — 시차 the horizontal parallax 시(視)〔진(眞), 인조〕— the apparent〔rational, artificial〕 horizon 지리〔천문〕 — the sensible〔astronomical〕 horizon

지평 地坪 area ; acreage of land

†**지폐 紙幣** paper money〔currency〕; a (bank) note ; a bill 《미》; soft money 《미·속》 ¶ 지폐 뭉치 a roll of bills∥1,000원 짜리 지폐 a thousand-*won* note∥지폐로 5만원 fifty thousand *won* in notes∥지폐를 발행하다 issue paper money∥지폐를 회수하다 recall bank notes∥지폐를 남발하다 issue paper money excessively

— 남발 an excessive issue of paper currency — 발행 issue of paper money ; note issue — 발행고 a note issue — 발행권 the right of issue ; the note-issuing right — 발행 은행 a note-issuing bank ; a bank of issue — 본위 paper standard — 유통고 a note circulation 불환 — an inconvertible note 소액 — a bank note of small denomination 위조 — a counterfeit〔forged〕 note 태환 — a convertible note

지폭 紙幅 the width of paper

지표 指標 an index ; a directing post ; a guide post ; 〖수학〗 characteristic

지표 地表 the earth's surface

지푸라기 a piece of straw ; a straw

물에 빠진 사람은 지푸라기라도 잡는다 〔속담〕 A drowning man will catch at a straw.

지프 [자동차] a jeep

지피다[1] burn ; kindle ; make〔build, light〕 a fire ; feed a fire ¶ 석탄〔장작〕을 지피다 burn coal〔wood〕∥난로에 불을 지피다 make a fire in the stove∥아궁이에 불을 지피다 get a fire going in the fireplace∥지필 것이 없다 have nothing to make fire with ; run out of fuel

지피다[2] [신통하다] get inspiration from a divine power ; be inspired

지필 紙筆 paper and pens〔writing brushes〕

—묵 paper, writing brushes and inkstick ; paper, pens and ink

‡**지하 地下** ¶ 지하의 underground ; subterranean∥지하에 below ground ; underground ; in the grave (묘 속에)∥지하에 잠들다 sleep in the grave ; rest in peace∥지하에서 일하다 work underground∥지하에 잠입하다 go underground ; go into hiding∥지하에 묻다 bury〔lay〕 underground∥지하 200미터까지 파다 dig in the ground to the depth of two hundred meters

—경(莖) 〖식물〗 a subterranean stem ; a rootstock ; a rhizoma — 공작 underground operations〔maneuvering, activities〕 —근 a subterranean root —도 an underground passage ; a subway 《영》; an underpass 《미》; 〖축성〗 a postern ; a gallery (광산의) — 목표 an underground 〔a buried〕 target (미사일 공격 따위의) — 상가 an underground shopping center —선 an underground wire〔cable〕; a subterranean line — 세포 an underground cell —수 subterranean〔underground〕 water — 수로 a culvert — 수위 an underground water level ; [지하 수면] the water table — 식물 a geophyte —실 a basement ; a cellar ; an underground room〔cellar〕; [고대 건축의] a hypogeum 《*pl.* -gea》 — 운동 an underground movement〔activity〕 — 자원 underground resources — 정부 an underground〔an invisible, a hidden〕 government〔cabinet〕 — 조직 an underground organization 《of France in World War Ⅱ》 — 철도 an underground (railway) 《영》; a subway 《미》; the Tube (런던의) ; the Metro (파리의) — 핵실험 an underground nuclear test — 활동 underground activities

‡**지하철 地下鐵** the subway 《미》; the underground (railway) 《영》; [런던의] the tube 《영·구》 ¶ 지하철로 가다 go by subway〔underground〕; go by tube ; go by sub 《미》∥지하철을 타다 take a subway train ; take the underground∥지하철을 내리다 get off a subway train

—역 a subway station〔stop〕 《미》; an underground〔a tube〕 station

지학 地學 physical geography

지한 知韓 pro-Koreanism

—파 the pro-Korean 《group》

지함 紙函 a cardboard box ; a carton

지해제 止咳劑 a cough medicine ; [정제의] a cough lozenge

지핵 地核 the centrosphere ; the nucleus 〔core〕 of the earth

지행 知行 knowledge and conduct 〔behavior〕

지향 指向 a fixed direction ; pointing —하다 point to 《a place》; head for 〔toward〕 ¶ 지향 없이 aimlessly

—도(圖) a pattern —성 안테나〔이득〕 a directional antenna〔gain〕 — 송〔수〕신 direction transmission〔reception〕 — 전파 a radio beam

지향 志向 intention ; aim ; inclination —하다 intend to ; point to

지현 至賢 supreme sagacity —하다 (be)

most sagacious〔wise〕

지혈 止血 stopping of bleeding ; stanching **—하다** stop bleeding〔hemorrhage〕; stanch
—대 a tourniquet —면 styptic cotton —법 styptic treatment ; stanching ; a hemostatic method —제 a hemostatic (agent) ; a styptic (agent)

지협 地峽 an isthmus 《*pl.* ～es, -mi》; a land bridge ; a neck of land ¶ 지협의 isthmian // 파나마 지협 the Isthmus of Panama

지형 地形 topography ; the lay〔lie〕of the land ; natural〔geographical〕features ; configuration of the ground ¶ 지형(학)상의 topographical
— 답사 〖지질〗 reconnaissance ; survey —도 topographical map〔chart〕; a relief map — 측량 a topographical survey — 판단 estimation of land〔ground〕—학 geomorphology ; topography ; morphology

지형 紙型 a paper mold ; papier-mâché mold ¶ 지형을 뜨다 make a paper mold ; take a papier-mâché mold

†지혜 智慧, 知慧 intelligence ; wisdom ; wits ; sagacity ; resourcefulness ¶ 지혜 있는 wise ; intelligent ; sagacious ; resourceful // 지혜 없는 unintelligent ; unwise ; stupid ; dumb 《미·속》// 지혜를 짜내다 rack one's brains // 지혜를 빌리다 pick 《a person's》 brain ; steal 《a person's》 thunder // 지혜가 생기다 grow wise ; grow in wisdom // 그런 짓을 하는 것을 보니 너도 지혜가 없다 It is unwise of you to do so.

지호 指呼 beckoning **—하다** beckon 《to a person》 ¶ 지호지간(之間)이다 be within hail〔call, hailing distance〕; be near at hand

지화 指話 《use》 finger〔hand〕 language
—법〔술〕 dactylology

지화자 a shout to mark time in accompanying singing or dancing ; corresponding to hand clapping

지환 指環 a ring ⇨ 가락지, 반지

지황 地黃 〖식물〗 the foxglove

지효 至孝 the utmost filial piety

†지휘 指揮 command ; orders ; [지시] direction ; instructions ; leading **—하다** command ; assume〔take〕command of ; order ; lead ; give orders〔instructions〕; head ; conduct (악단을) ; direct ; manage ; control ; marshal (행진을)

> 참고 **conduct** 자기의 수완 지식 경험 따위를 동원하여 직접 감독 지휘하다 **direct** 지휘 감독하는 대상 보다는 지휘하는 쪽을 강조하는 말 **manage** 본인이 직접 세부의 일에 관여하여 솜씨있게 전체를 운영하다 **control** 제어하고 통솔하다

¶ 지휘 하에 under the command〔direction〕of // 지휘를 받다 take orders from ; be under 《a person's》 command ; be presided over by // 지휘를 바라다 ask orders 《from》; ask for instructions // 음악회를 지휘하다 conduct a concert // 만사에 그분의 지휘를 받아야 한다 You must follow his directions in everything. // 20인의 부하가 그 장군의 지휘하에 있다 He has twenty men under the general's command.
— 계통 a chain of command —관 a commander ; a commanding officer —권 (the right of) command — 기술〔법〕〖음악〗 conduction technique — 능력 command ability (군인 따위의) —대 〖음악〗 a podium 《*pl.* -dia》; a raised platform —도 an officer's sword ; a parade sword —봉 a baton —자 a commander ; a director ; a leader ; a conductor (음악의) ; a cheer leader (응원단의)

⁑직 職 [일자리] employment ; work ; a job ; a position (지위) ; [직업] a calling ; an occupation ; a trade ; [직무] duties ; [관공직] an office ¶ 직을 주다 give 《a person》 work〔employment〕; give 《a person》 a position // 직을 해임시키다 relieve 《a person》 of his post〔office〕; dismiss ; fire (미) // 직을 얻다 get a job〔position〕《with a firm》; find work〔a job〕; obtain employment // 직을 잃다 lose one's position〔job〕; be thrown out of work〔employment〕// 직을 구하다 seek work ; look for a job

직 直 ① [당번] duty ; watch ; guard ② [곧은] straight ; upright ; perpendicular ; direct
일— day duty ; day watch

†직각 直角 a right angle ¶ 직각의 rectangular ; right-angled // 직각으로 at a right angle 《to》; perpendicular 《to》// 직각을 이루다 be at right angle 《to》
—기 〖측량〗 a cross-staff 《*pl.* -staves》 — 삼각형 a right-angled triangle —선 a perpendicular line ; a normal (line) — 원기둥 〖수학〗 a right cylinder — 원뿔 〖수학〗 a right circular cone —자 a square —추 a right pyramid

직각 直覺 intuition ; the sixth sense (제육감) ; direct perception ¶ 직각적 intuitive ; intuitional // 직각력이 있는 시인 an intuitive poet // 직각적으로 알다 know by intuition
—력 intuitive power —설 〖철학·윤리〗 intuition(al)ism ; 〖윤리〗 intuitivism — 판단 intuitive judgment

직간 直諫 direct admonition〔remonstrance, reproof〕 **—하다** reprove 《a person》 face to face ; admonish directly〔openly, without fear〕

직감 直感 intuition ; immediate perception **—하다** perceive immediately ¶ 직감적으로 intuitively ; by intuition // 직감에 의

존하다 rely upon one's intuition // 직감으로 알다 learn〔perceive〕 intuitively

직거래 直去來 direct〔spot〕 transaction〔deal〕 ¶ 외국인과 직거래하다 deal directly with foreigners

직격 直擊 a direct hit

—탄 a direct hit (bomb) ¶ 직격탄에 맞다 be directly hit by a bomb ; suffer a direct hit from a bomb

직결 直結 direct connection ; direct coupling (전기) —하다 connect〔link, couple〕 directly 《with》 ¶ 직결되다 be connected directly 《with》 ; be linked directly 《with》 // 국민과 직결되어 있다 be linked directly with the citizens

***직경 直徑** a diameter ; the distance across ¶ 직경 5미터 five meters in diameter // 직경이 3미터이다 be〔measure〕 three meters in diameter ; have a diameter of three meters // 이 호수는 직경 5리이다 The lake is five *ri* across.

직계 直系 the direct line〔descent〕 (of a family) ; a direct descendant (사람) ¶ 직계의 lineal // 직계 비속〔존속〕이 없는 without issue ; sine prole 《라》 // 직계이다 trace direct descent 《from》 ; be descended in a direct line 《from》

— 가족 family members in a direct line — 선조 a direct〔lineal〕 ancestor — 자손 direct〔lineal〕 descendants ; descendants in the direct line — 존속〔비속〕 a lineal ascendant〔descendant〕 — 혈족 a lineal relation — 회사 a directly affiliated concern ; a direct affiliate ; a controlled company

직계 職階 position-class

—급(給) job-classified〔-oriented〕 wages —제(制) the job classification system ; a job-ranking system ; a classified civil service system (관청의)

직고 直告 informing〔reporting〕 truthfully —하다 inform〔report〕 truthfully

직공 職工 a workman ; a worker ; a factory hand ; a mechanic

— 기질 artisan spirit —복 working clothes ; overalls —장 a foreman ; an overman

직공 織工 a weaver

***직관 直觀** intuition ; the sixth sense

— 교수 〖교육〗 an object lesson —력 intuition ; intuitive power —상(像) 〖심리〗 an eidetic image ; [집합적] eidetic imagery —성 〖철학〗 immediacy 순수 — 〖철학〗 pure intuition

직관주의 直觀主義 〖철학·수학〗 intuition(al)ism

—자 an intuition(al)ist

직구 直球 〖야구〗 a straight ball ¶ 직구를 던지다 drive

직권 職權 official authority ; official power ; duties of office ; functions ; competence ¶ 직권 외의 outside one's authority ; extraofficial // 직권에 의하여 in virtue of one's office // 직권을 남용하다 abuse one's authority // 직권을 침해하다 encroach on another's functions // 직권을 행사하다 exercise one's authority // 직권 외의 짓을 하다 overstep one's authority // 직권을 위임하다 authorize 《a person to do》 ; invest 《a person》 with the authority // 의장의 직권으로 퇴장을 명령한다 On my authority as chairman, I order you to leave the room.

— 남용 misfeasance ; wrongful exercise of authority ; abuse of one's authority — 알선〔조정〕 compulsory conciliation〔arbitration〕 conducted by virtue of one's authority as 《Chairman of the Mediation Committee》

직급 職級 the class of one's position ⇨ 직계(職階)

직기 織機 a (weaver's) loom ; a weaving machine

수동〔자동〕 — a hand〔an automatic〕 loom

직나무 〖식물〗 the Chinese juniper

직날 〖한의〗 the day when one has an attack of malaria ; a malarial day

직녀 織女 ① [사람] a woman weaver ② [직녀성] the star Vega in the constellation Lyra

***직능 職能** function ¶ 의회의 직능 the function of the parliament

— 검사 performance test —급 pay according to function ; wages based on job evaluation — 대표(제) vocational 〔professional〕 representation (system)

직달 直達 direct delivery —하다 deliver 《a thing》 direct 《to a person》 ; hand 《him a letter》 personally

직답 直答 a prompt〔ready〕 answer 〔reply〕 ; a direct〔personal〕 answer ; an immediate answer〔reply〕 —하다 give a ready answer offhand ¶ 귀사의 직답을 앙망합니다 Your prompt reply will be obliged〔appreciated〕 by us. // 나는 너의 직답을 들어야겠다 I would have your ready answer.

직력 職歷 one's business〔professional〕 career〔experience〕

직렬 直列 〖전기〗 (an electrical) series

— 변압기 a series transformer — 회로 a series circuit

직로 直路 a straight road ; a direct route

직류 直流 〖전기〗 direct current 《D. C.》 ; continuous current ; series flow

— 고〔저〕압 배전 the direct current high 〔low〕 tension system — 발전기〔발동기, 전압기〕 a direct current dynamo〔generator, converter〕 — 회로 a direct current circuit

직류 直溜 straight distillation

— 가솔린 straight(-run) gasoline

***직립 直立** standing erect〔upright, straight〕 —하다 stand erect〔straight, upright〕 ¶ 직립한 straight ; upright ;

erect // 직립하여 upright ; erect ; in an erect posture ; in an upright position // 직립 부동의 자세를 취하다 stand at attention ; stand erect and stiff // 그 바위는 수면에서 50척이나 직립하고 있다 The rock rises perpendicularly fifty feet high sheer out of the water.

—경 〖식물〗 an erect stem —면〔선〕 〖수학〗 a perpendicular plane〔line〕 — 원인 (猿人) an ape man ; [자바 원인] *Pithecanthropus erectus* (학명) ; Java man —체 a vertical style —체 서법 vertical penmanship

직매 直賣 direct sales ; spot〔hand-to-hand〕 sales **—하다** carry out direct sales ; sell direct 《to》 ; sell directly

—소〔점〕 a direct sales depot〔store〕

†**직면 直面 —하다** face ; confront ; see 《a person》 face to face ; be confronted by〔with〕 ¶ 위험에 직면하여 in the face of danger // 직면하고 있는 문제 problems that are now being faced 《by》 // 죽음에 직면하다 face〔be confronted by〕 death // 그는 파멸에 직면하고 있다 Ruin stares him in the face. // 그는 파멸에 직면하고 있다 Ruin stares him in the face. // 그는 어려운 문제에 직면하였다 He was faced〔confronted〕 with a difficult question.

직명 職名 (the name of) an occupation (직업명) ; an official title (직함)

†**직무 職務** (a) duty ; duties ; a function ¶ 직무상의 official // 직무상 officially ; as a matter of duty // 직무를 수행하다 perform〔carry out, discharge〕 one's duties ; fulfill one's duties ; do one's work // 직무를 분담하다 divide duties // 직무를 게을리하다 neglect one's duties // 직무 수행중 쓰러지다 die in the pursuit of one's duties ; die in harness // 그것은 네 직무에서 벗어나는 것이다 You overstep your authority to do so.

— 규정 office regulations — 내용 job specifications — 분석(표) a job analysis (sheet) — 수당 a service allowance ; an allowance〔wages〕 attached to a post — 유기 dereliction〔delinquency〕 of one's duty ¶ 직무 유기로 고소당하다 be charged with dereliction of one's duty — 정지 a suspension of performing one's duties — 집행 performance of one's duties ¶ 직무 집행을 방해하다 interfere with 《an official》 in the performance of his duty — 태만 《on a charge of》 neglect〔dereliction〕 of duty

⁑**직물 織物** woven stuff〔goods〕 ; textile (fabrics) ; cloth

— 공업 textile industry — 공장 a textile factory〔mill〕 —류 woven goods ; drapery —상 a draper — 시장 the cloth market —업 [판매] a drapery ; drygoods business ; rag business (속) ; the textile trade ; [제조] textile manufacturing〔manufacture〕 —업 조합 a textile manufacturers' association — 원료 textile materials — 직공 a clothworker 면〔견, 모〕— cotton〔silk, woolen〕 fabrics

직방체 直方體 a rectangular parallelepiped〔parallelopipedon〕

직배 直配 [배달] direct delivery〔service〕 ; [배급] direct distribution **—하다** deliver〔distribute〕 directly

직부 織婦 a woman weaver ⇨ 직녀(織女)

직분 職分 (a) duty ; duties ; a sphere (본분) ¶ 교사의 직분 duties of a teacher // 직분을 다하다 do one's duty ; discharge one's duties // 직분을 지키다 be true〔faithful〕 to one's duty

직사 直射 [포화의] direct fire ; frontal fire ; direct rays (of the sun) (일광의) **—하다** [포화를] fire directly 《upon》 ; [태양 따위가] shine〔fall〕 directly upon ¶ 일광의 직사를 받다 be exposed direct to the sun

— 광선 a direct ray of light —포 a direct-firing gun ; a gun firing point-blank

직사각 直四角 a regular square

***직사각형 直四角形** 〖수학〗 rectangular form ; a rectangle ; an oblong

직사주의 直寫主義 〖미술·문예〗 literalism ¶ 직사주의적인 literalistic

—자 a literalist

직삼 直蔘 ginseng dried in its original shape

직삼각형 直三角形 〖수학〗 a right (-angled) triangle

직상 直上 ① [바로 위] right above ; directly overhead ② [올라감] ascending〔climbing〕 straight up **—하다** rise perpendicularly ; ascend straight up

직석 直席 extemporaneous(ness) ; impromptu ⇨ 즉석

***직선 直線** a straight line ; a beeline ¶ 직선의 straight ; rectilineal // 직선으로 in a straight line ; in a beeline // 직선을 긋다 draw a straight line

— 구간 〖측량〗 a tangent — 기선(基線) straight base-line —미 lineal beauty — 운동 rectilineal movement ; a straight-line〔rectilineal〕 motion — 코스 a straight course ; a beeline 《미》 ; 《in》 a straightaway —형 a rectilineal〔rectangular〕 figure

직선거리 a distance in straight line

직설 直說 straight talk ; plain speaking ; frankness **—하다** talk frankly〔straight from the shoulder〕 ; speak out ; speak up ; speak without reserve

***직설법 直說法** 〖문법〗 the indicative mood

직성 풀리다 直星— be satisfied〔gratified〕 ; feel relieved ¶ 직성이 풀리지 않다 be not satisfied ; feel regret 《for》

직세 直稅 a direct tax

—과 the direct tax section

직소 直訴 a direct appeal〔petition〕 **—하**

다 appeal directly ¶ 직소를 기도하다 attempt a direct appeal

직소 直所 a guard box ; the guard('s) room

직소 職所 the place of one's work ; one's office ; one's post

직속 直屬 directly belonging 《to》; being directly attached **—하다** be under direct control 《of》; belong directly 《to》 ¶ 직속의 under immediate〔direct〕 control 《of》// 송씨는 나의 직속 상관이다 Mr. *Song* is the senior officer I directly belong to.

직손 直孫 direct〔lineal〕 descendants ; descendants in the direct line

직송 直送 direct delivery **—하다** send direct(ly) 《to》 ¶ 하와이에서 직송된 파인애플들 pineapples sent directly from Hawaii

직수굿하다 (be) docile ; obedient ; quiet ; reserved ; submissive ; tame ¶ 직수굿한 어린이 a docile〔meek〕 child // 직수굿하게 명령에 따르다 submit to an order ; obey meekly

직수입 直輸入 direct import〔importation〕 **—하다** import 《a thing》 direct 《from》 **—무역** direct import trade **—상** a direct importer **—품** direct imports ; articles imported direct from abroad

직수출 直輸出 direct export〔exportation〕 **—하다** export 《goods》 direct 《to》 **—상** a direct exporter **—품** direct exports

직시 直視 looking 《a person》 in the face ; direct vision **—하다** look squarely〔straight, full and square〕 《on》; look 《a person》 face to face ; look 《a person, a thing, a fact》 in the face ¶ 사태를 직시하다 face〔envisage〕 a matter squarely ; confront a problem boldly // 현실을 직시하다 face up to reality // 그는 사실을 직시하지 않고 있다 He buries his head in the sand.

직시류 直翅類 〖곤충〗 Orthoptera (학명)

직신 稷神 the god of agriculture ; Ceres

직신거리다 tease persistently for ⇨ 작신거리다

직심 直心 straightforwardness (솔직) ; [정직] honesty ; uprightness ; an honest heart ¶ 직심스럽다 be honest ; be straight ; be straightforward

직언 直言 plain speaking ; direct〔frank, open〕 speech ; a straight talk **—하다** speak plainly〔bluntly, frankly, directly〕 to ; speak without reserve ; speak out ¶ 직언하자면 to be frank // 삼가 직언드립니다 Forgive my plain speaking.

—가 an outspoken person ; a plain dealer ; a plainspoken〔free-spoken〕 person

†직업 職業 an occupation ; a calling ; a vocation ; a work of life ; a job ; a profession ; a trade ; (a line of) business ; a career (이력)

> 참고 **occupation**은 가장 일반적인 말 **calling**은 천직으로서 「신의 명령에 의한 일」이라고 하는 것이 원래의 의미 **vocation**은 calling보다 고상한 말 **profession**은 변호사 교사 따위 주로 학문적 지식을 필요로 하는 것 **trade**는 손의 훈련을 필요로 하는 직업을 가리킨다

¶ 직업적 professional ; vocational // 직업을 선택하다 choose one's profession〔trade〕 // 직업에 종사하다 follow an occupation〔a calling〕 ; take up a career (특히 여자가) // 직업으로 하다 make a business〔profession〕 《of》 // 직업을 주다 give employment to 《a person》 // 그는 일정한 직업이 없다 He has no regular occupation. // 나는 직업상 자주 여행을 해야 한다 The nature of my calling requires a good deal of traveling. // 그의 직업은 목수다 He is a carpenter by profession. // 지난주까지만 해도 두 개의 직업을 가지고 있었는데 지금은 실업자입니다 Only last week I worked two jobs, but now I'm unemployed. // 직업이 무엇입니까 What do you do (for a living) ? /What's your occupation ? /What business are you in ? / What line of work are you in ? /What's your line ? /What's your job ? // 그녀는 직업을 바꾸길 잘한 것 같다 It seems that changing jobs was the right move for her.

—경력 a work record ; one's business〔professional〕 career〔experience〕 **—군인** a professional〔career 《미》〕 soldier〔military officer〕 **—별 전화번호부** a classified telephone directory **—병** an occupational〔industrial〕 disease ; a vocational disease **—보도** vocational guidance〔training〕 ¶ 직업 보도소 the Public Vocational Training Agency **—분야** fields of work **—상담** employment counseling ; a vocational counsel **—선수** a professional (player) ; a pro 《*pl.* ~s》 《구》 **—소개소** an employment agency〔exchange〕 ; a labour exchange 《영》 ; a placement bureau 《미》 **—안내란** wanted columns ; a "help-wanted" column (신문의) **—안정** employment security **—안정소** an employment security office **—야구** professional baseball ¶ 직업 야구단 a professional baseball team // 직업 야구 선수 a professional baseball player ; a pro ballplayer 《미·구》 **—여성** [전문 기술을 가진] a professional〔career〕 woman ; a working woman ; a woman〔female〕 worker ; an office girl (사무원) **—의식** professional consciousness〔sense〕 **—적성** vocational aptitude ¶ 직업 적성 검사 a vocational aptitude test **—전선** the struggle for jobs **—정치가** a professional politician **—조합** a trade union 《영》 ; a labor union 《미》 **—학교** a vocational〔trade〕 school **—화** professionalization ¶ 직업화하다 professionalize

직역 職域 one's occupation ; one's post ¶ 직역 별로 by occupation group

직역 直譯 a literal translation ; a word for word translation ; direct translation **—하다** translate literally〔word for word〕; translate mechanically ; metaphrase ¶ 직역적 metaphrastic

—주의 literalism **—체〔문체〕** metaphrastic style

직영 直營 direct management〔control, operation〕 **—하다** manage〔control, operate〕 directly ¶ 회사 직영 식당 the restaurant under direct management of the company // 정부의 직영 사업 an enterprise under government management

직왕 매진 直往邁進 —하다 push boldly forward ; push on to the front

⁑**직원 職員** the staff 《총칭》; the personnel ; the faculty (대학 따위의) ; [개인] a staff-member ; an employee ¶ 내무부 직원 an official of the Ministry of Home Affairs // 직원의 이동 a personnel change ; a change in the staff ; a reshuffle of personnel // 50 인의 직원 a staff of 50 men // 그는 그 중학교의 직원이다 He is on the staff of the middle school. // 너희 사무실에는 직원이 3명이니 Your office has a staff of three ?

— 공제 조합 a mutual aid association of personnel **— 명부** a staff register〔list〕; a list of officials ; a personnel directory ; a roster 《of a firm》 **—실** a faculty room ; an instructors' room **— 일동** all the members of the staff ; all the staff **— 회의** a staff meeting ; a faculty meeting (대학의) **— 훈련** staff training

직원주 直圓柱 〖기하〗 a right cylinder

직원추 直圓錐 〖기하〗 a right circular cone

직유 直喩 a simile

직인 職印 an official seal ; [정부의] a government seal

직임 職任 duties of a post

직장 直腸 〖해부〗 the rectum 《*pl.* -ta》 ¶ 직장의 rectal

—경(鏡) 〖의학〗 a rectoscope **—선** the rectal gland **—암〔궤양〕** cancer〔ulcer〕 of the rectum **—염** procititis **—탈** prolapse of the rectum ; prolapsus recti

직장 職場 one's place of work ; one's work place ; one's work site ; one's job ; one's post ; [공장] a workshop ¶ 직장을 지키다 stick to one's post // 직장을 이탈하다 desert〔walk off〕 one's job // 직장 결혼을 하다 marry a man〔woman〕 working in the same place // 어느 직장에 나가십니까 Where do you go to work ? // 전 직장에서 일년에 1200만원을 받았으니까 그것보다는 조금 더 기대하고 있습니다 I made 12 million *won* per year at my last employment. So I am expecting a little more than that.

— 대표 [노동 쟁의의] a shop deputy〔steward, chairman〕 **— 대회** a (work-) shop rally〔meeting〕 **— 보도(輔導)** training within industry 《T. W. I》; an on-the-job training **— 복귀(운동)** back-to-work (movement) ¶ 직장 복귀령 a "return-to-work" order ; a "haltstrike" order **— 투쟁** a workshop struggle〔strife〕 **— 포기** job desertion ; a walkout 《미》; a strike ; desertion of one's post〔job〕

직장 織匠 a skilled weaver

직장 職長 a foreman

직장 職掌 the division of official duties ; duties ; functions ¶ 직장상의 official ; functional // 그는 직장 관계로 그 방면에 익숙하다 His duties have made him familiar with those circles.

직재 直裁 [직접] a direct〔personal〕 decision ; [즉시] a prompt〔an immediate〕 decision **—하다** make direct decision ; decide personally ; decide immediately〔on the spot〕 ¶ 직재를 바라다 submit 《a matter》 to direct decision

직전 直前 just〔immediately〕 before ; just prior to ¶ 시험 직전에 just before the examination ; on the eve of the examination // 제1차 세계 대전 발발 직전에 on the eve of World War Ⅰ // 일이 너무 많아 몸이 고장나기 일보 직전이다 I've taken on so many jobs that I'm on the verge of a breakdown.

직절 直節 fidelity ; loyalty ; integrity ; faithfulness

†**직접 直接** immediateness ; direct contact ; [부사적] directly ; immediately ; firsthand ; at firsthand ; personally ; in person ¶ 직접적 direct ; immediate ; personal ; firsthand (본인으로부터 직접 얻은) // 직접의 원인 an immediate cause // 직접의 영향 a direct effect // 직접 얻은 정보 a firsthand information // 직접 편지를 내다 write direct to 《a person》 // 직접 면회하다 see 《a person》 personally // 직접 관계가 있다 have immediate〔intimate〕 connection with ; be directly concerned in // 그 일을 내가 직접 보았다 I saw it with my own eyes. // 나는 그 사람과 직접 관계는 없다 I have no direct connection with him. // 직접 본인으로부터 들었다 I have got the news at firsthand.

— 거래 direct dealings **— 교섭** direct〔face-to-face〕 negotiation ¶ 직접 교섭을 하다 have direct negotiations with **— 매매** spot sales **— 목적어** 〖문법〗 direct object **— 선거** direct election **—성** 〖철학〗 immediacy **—세** a direct tax **— 심문** 〖법〗 the examination in chief **— 원인** an immediate occasion〔cause〕 **— 입법** direct legislation **— 조명** direct illumination **— 행동** 《a》 direct action **— 화법** 〖문법〗 direct narration〔speech〕

직접 담판 直接談判 a direct negotiation ; a personal consultation ―하다 negotiate directly 《with a person》 ; consult personally 《with a person》 ; have a personal interview 《with a person》

직제 職制 office organization ; staff organization ; rules for allotting duties ; service regulations ¶ 직제를 개정하다 reorganize an office ; revise the office regulations // 직제를 근대화하다 streamline the organization

직제자 直弟子 an immediate pupil ; a direct disciple

직조 織造 weaving ―하다 weave
―기 a loom ―소 a weaving shop ; a textile

직종 職種 a type〔kind〕 of occupation ; an occupational category ; job series ¶ 직종별로 by job classification ; by occupation // 그는 자신이 지원한 직종에서 5년간 일한 경험이 있다 He has 5-year experience in the type of work he's applying for.
―별 임금 prevailing wages by occupation ― 부호〔기호〕 an occupational code ―분류 occupational〔job〕 classification

직주로 直走路 a straight track

직직[1] ⇨ 작작[2]

직직[2] ① [긋는·찢는 소리] with repeated written strokes or tearing of paper ② [대소변의] with repeated sounds of bird-droppings

직직거리다, 찍찍거리다 keep dragging 〔scuffing〕 one's shoes

직진 直進 ―하다 go right on ; make straight for ; make a straight drive 〔advance〕 on ; go straight ahead

직차 職次 the order of official ranks

직책 職責 responsibilities of office ; duty ; duties ; functions ¶ 직책을 다하다 discharge〔perform〕 one's duties // 직책을 중히 여기다 have a strong〔keen〕 sense of duty〔responsibility〕 // 그것은 과장으로서의 자네 직책일세 As the chief of your section you are responsible for it. // 그는 직책을 위해서는 어떠한 위험도 두려워하지 않았다 He was ready to face any danger when duty called.

직토 直吐 ―하다 confess ; make a frank statement 《of a affair》 ; tell the (whole) truth

직통 直通 direct communication ; a direct service ; [신호의] a direct code ―하다 communicate directly〔direct〕 《with》 ; be in direct communication 《with》 ; [길이] lead directly to ; [교통 수단이] have a through〔direct〕 service ¶ 직통으로 가다 go to 《*Pusan*》 without changing cars 〔transfer〕 // 이 열차는 전주 직통이다 This train goes direct to *Chŏnju*. /This is a through train to *Chŏnju*. // 직통 열차〔전차〕가 개통되었다 A direct railway 〔tramway〕 service has been opened. // 양 도시간에는 직통 열차가 개통할 것이다 A direct train service will be opened between the two cities.
― 전화 a trunk call ; a direct telephone service ; a telephone for direct communications 《with, between》 ¶ 직통 전화선 a direct telephone line ; [정부 수뇌간의] a hot line

직품 職品 the grades of official ranks

직필 直筆 [사실 대로] writing plainly 《on a matter》 ; writing in frank language ; [붓을 세워서] holding the brush upright while writing ; [직접] writing direct for oneself ―하다 [사실대로] write plainly 《on a matter》 ; write in frank language ; [붓을 세워서] write holding a brush upright ; [직접] write direct for oneself

직하 直下 [바로 아래] directly〔just, right〕 under ; [내려감] a perpendicular fall ; falling plumb down ―하다 fall perpendicularly ; fall plumb down ¶ 적도 직하 directly〔right〕 under the equator // 급전직하하다 make a rapid〔swift〕 movement ; take a rapid turn // 수백척 아래로 직하하다 fall plumb down several hundred feet

직하다 直― [바르다] (be) right ; upright ; [고지식하다] simple and honest ; simpleminded ; straightforward

†**-직하다** be likely 《to》 ; be probable 《to》 ; be worth ; seem ¶ 있음직한 이야기 a likely story // 나는 그가 있음직한 곳은 모두 찾아보았다 I looked for him in every likely place. // 그가 함직한 일이다 That's like him. /I should not be surprised if he did that.

직할 直轄 direct control〔jurisdiction〕 ; immediate supervision ―하다 control directly〔immediately〕 ; hold under direct jurisdiction ¶ 문교부 직할 학교 a school under the direct control〔supervision〕 of the Ministry of Education // 직할로 만들다 transfer 《a thing》 to the direct control 《of》 // 시의 직할이 되다 come under the direct control of the municipality

직할시 直轄市 a city under the direct control〔supervision〕 of the government

†**직함 職銜** the title of a position ; one's official title ¶ 직함이 있는 사람 a man of title // 그는 아무 직함도 없다 He has no handle to his name.

직항 直航 [배의] a direct voyage〔service〕 ; [비행기의] a non-stop flight ―하다 sail direct〔straight〕 《for》 ; be bound 《for Hong Kong》 direct ; make a non-stop flight 《to》 ¶ 그 배는 부산을 출항하여 마닐라로 직항했다 The steamer left *Pusan* for Manila.
―로 a direct line〔service〕 ―선 a direct steamer〔boat〕

직행 直行 going straight〔direct〕 ; [바꾸어 타지 않고] running straight through ; [무정차] going non-stop ―하다 go straight〔direct〕 《to》 ; [기차가] run through 《to》 ¶ 직행차로 가다 go by a

through train ⟪to⟫ ; go through ⟪to⟫ // 사고 현장에 직행하다 rush right〔straight〕 to the scene of the accident // 바꾸어 타지 않고 직행하다 go through without changing // 이 열차는 전주까지 직행한다 This train goes through to *Chŏnju.* // 나는 부산까지 직행하려 한다 I plan to head straight for *Pusan.*
— 열차〔버스〕 a through〔direct〕 train〔bus〕

직후 直後 ¶ 직후에 immediately〔directly, right〕 after // 종전 직후 directly after (the termination of) the war ; in the immediate postwar days

진 [술] gin ¶ 진피스 gin fizz // 진토닉 gin and tonic

진 辰 the Sign of Dragon ⟪the 5th of the 12 Earth's Branches⟫ ; [방향] the Direction of the Dragon ⟪southeast-by-last⟫ ; [시간] the Watch of the Dragon ⟪the 5th of the 12 double-hours ; the hours from 7 o'clock to 9 (o'clock) in the morning⟫ ; [해] the Year of the Dragon

진 —津 [나무의] resin ; gum ; [생리 작용의] secretion ; [담배의] nicotine ; tar ¶ 담뱃대가 진으로 막혔다 The pipe is clogged up with tar.
담배 — (tobacco) tar ; nicotine 송 — pine resin

진 陣 [진형] a battle array ; battle formation ; [진영] a (military) camp ; [진지] a position ; [대열] lines ; ranks ¶ 진을 치다 pitch a camp ; encamp ; be stationed〔quartered〕 ; camp ; occupy a position // 진을 철거하다 strike camp ; withdraw from a position // 진을 정비하다 organize〔equip〕 the battle array
장사— a long line〔queue〕 ¶ 오페라 입장권을 사려고 장사진을 치고 있다 They queue up to buy tickets for the opera.

진 眞 true ; real ; genuine
—상 the truth ; the real facts ¶ 진상을 폭로하다 disclose the real facts

＊**진가 眞價** true〔real〕 worth ; true〔intrinsic〕 value ; true merit ¶ 교육의 진가 the true value of education // 진가가 있다 have intrinsic value // 진가를 인정하다 appreciate ⟪a person⟫ as his true worth ; recognize ⟪a person's⟫ real worth // 진가를 발휘하다 prove one's worth // 진가를 의심하다 doubt the true worth

진가 眞假 the true and〔or〕 the false ; the real and the fake ; genuineness ¶ 진가를 구별하다 judge the true or the false ⇨ 진위(眞僞)

진간장 —醬 nicely aged soy sauce ; thick soy

진갈이 plowing wet fields after rain ; tillage of fields right after a rainfall —하다 plow wet fields after rain ; till fields right after a rainfall

진감 a shock ; a shake —하다 [흔들다] shake ; shock ; [흔들리다] be shocked ; be shaken ¶ 세계를 진감시킨 대사건 a world-shaking event

진갑 進甲 the 62st birthday ; the sixty-second anniversary of one's birth
— 잔치 the celebration of one's 62st birthday

진강 進講 a lecture before His Majesty ; a lecture in the Royal presence —하다 give a lecture in the Royal presence

진개 塵芥 dust and dirt ; rubbish ; refuse

진객 珍客 a rare guest ; a welcome visitor

진걸레 a wet scrub cloth ; a wet mop ; a wet floorcloth〔house cloth〕

진격 進擊 an attack ; a drive ; an advance ; a charge ; a push —하다 make a drive against ; attack ; advance on ; charge ⟪at, on⟫ ; move against ; storm
—군 an attacking force ; a storming party — 명령 the order to advance ; a go-ahead ⟪미·구⟫

진경 眞境 the actual state of things ; the actual facts of a case ; the real condition〔state〕 ; [경계] the real borderline

진계 塵界 the dusty world ; this world ; this temporal world ; everyday life

진곡 陳穀 grain that is kept over ; old and stale grain

진공 進攻 an attack ; a drive ⇨ 진격
— 작전 advance〔advancing〕 operations

진공 進供 —하다 present ⟪local products⟫ to the King

진공 進貢 tribute —하다 pay〔send〕 tribute

＊**진공 眞空** a vacuum ¶ 진공의 vacuous ; hollow // 진공으로 하다 make ⟪a thing⟫ vacuous // 진공이 되다 form a vacuum
— 건조 vacuum〔suction〕 drying ; [목재의] seasoning — 건조기 a vacuum drier —계 a vacuum gauge〔indicator〕 —관 a (vacuum) tube ; an electron(ic) tube ; a thermionic ; a vacuum valve ⟪영⟫ ¶ 라디오의 진공관 a radio valve〔tube〕 // 텔레비전의 진공관 a kinescope —대(臺) an air pocket — 방전 『전기』 vacuum discharge — 브레이크 a vacuum brake — 전구 a vacuum lamp — 제동기 a vacuum brake — 청소기 a vacuum cleaner〔sweeper〕 ; a vacuum ⟪구⟫ — 펌프 a vacuum pump

진과 珍果 rare〔uncommon〕 fruit

진과 珍菓 rare dainties ; rare sweets〔delicacies〕

진과 眞果 『식물』 the true fruit

진구렁 a mud hole ; a slough ; a quagmire ; a dog ¶ 진구렁을 터벅터벅 걷다 trudge in the mire // 진구렁에 빠지다 fall in a mud hole ; be bogged down // 진구렁에서 나오다 pull oneself out of the mire

진구리 the side ; the flank

진국 眞— ① [국물] undiluted liquor ;

soysauce ; genuine liquid
② [사람] a simple-hearted person ; an honest person ; a genuine person
진군 進軍 march ; advance ―하다 march〔advance〕《against the enemy, on Paris》; make a drive《against》¶ 진군을 명령하다 order the advance ; give the order to advance // 진군 중이다 be on the march // 진군 나팔을 불다 sound the advance // 보무 당당하게 진군하다 march in a stately manner
―가 a march ; a marching song
진권 進勸 recommendation ―하다 recommend
진귀 珍貴 preciousness ; valuableness ; pricelessness ―하다 (be) rare and precious ; valuable ; priceless
†진급 進級 promotion ―하다 be〔get〕promoted《to》; win〔obtain〕promotion ¶ 진급시키다 promote《a person》to ; advance《a person》to // 그는 진급이 빠르다〔늦다〕He is rapid〔slow〕in promotion. // 그는 상사로 진급되었다 He was promoted sergeant. /He was promoted to the rank of sergeant. // 그 학생들은 내년 봄에 대학 2년생으로 진급한다 The students will be promoted to the sophomores next spring.
― 상신(上申) a recommendation for promotion ― 시험 an examination for promotion 명예 ― a brevet (군인의)
*진기 珍奇 rarity ; novelty ; curiosity ; singularity ―하다 (be) rare ; novel ; curious ; singular ; queer ; strange ¶ 진기한 책 a rare book // 진기한 현상 a rare occurrence ; a strange phenomenon // 보고 듣는 것들 모두가 진기했다 Everything I saw and heard was new to me.
진기 珍器 a rare article ; a curious〔precious〕vessel ; an uncommon receptacle ; a rarity ; a curio
진기 振起 stimulation ; animation ; rousing ―하다 stir up ; stimulate to action ; rouse ; shake up ; animate
진기 津氣 stickiness ; viscousness ; viscosity ; persistency ¶ 진기가 있는 쌀 glutinous rice // 진기가 있다 be sticky〔viscous, viscid, glutinous〕// 그 쌀은 진기가 있다 The rice is rich in gluten. // 이 고약은 진기가 없어졌다 This plaster has lost its adhesiveness.
진나다 津― ① [진이 나다] sap exudes ; secrete gum〔resin〕② [시달려] get pestered《by a person》
진날 a rainy〔wet〕day ¶ 진날 나막신 wooden shoes for a rainy day ; visiting a long-neglected friend in time of need // 진날에 대비하다 provide for〔against〕a rainy day
진념 軫念 the king's care〔concern, anxiety, solicitude〕―하다《the king》kindly show concern〔solicitude, anxiety〕
진노 震怒 ire ; wrath ; rage ; violent anger ―하다 burst with anger ; be enraged ¶ 신의 진노 the wrath of God
진눈¹ bleary eyes
진눈² sleet ; wet snow
*진눈깨비 sleet ; snow mixed〔mingling〕with rain ¶ 진눈깨비 오는 날 a sleet day // 진눈깨비가 오고 있다 Sleet is falling.
*진단 診斷 diagnosis《*pl.* -ses》―하다 diagnose《as》; make a diagnosis of ; examine ¶ 의사의 진단을 받다 consult a doctor ; undergo a medical examination // 암이라고 진단하다 diagnose《a person's illness》as cancer // 심장병으로 인한 사망으로 진단하다 pronounce《a person》dead of heart attack // 잘못 진단하다 make a faulty diagnosis
― 기술 diagnostic technique ―서 a medical certificate ; (a written) diagnosis ―학 diagnostics ¶ 진단학자 a diagnostician 건강 ― a medical examination〔checkup〕조기 ― an early diagnosis〔checkup〕
진달 進達 forwarding ; transmission ―하다 forward ; transmit
진달래 『식물』 the azalea
진담 珍談 an interesting story ; an amusing tale ; a funny story ; a strange tale ; [일화] an anecdote ; news ¶ 이솝우화에는 진담이 많다 There is a lot of amusing stories in Aesop's Fables.
진담 眞談 serious talk ; solemn〔earnest〕talk ¶ 농담을 진담으로 듣다 take a joke seriously // 내 말은 진담이다 My talk is not a joke. // 이번에는 진담이다 I mean business this time. // 너 그말 진담이냐 Do you really mean it?
진답 陣畓 fallow paddy〔rice〕fields
진대 bothering《a person》by parasitism ; sponging ; pestering ¶ 진대 붙이다 parasitize ; sponge // 그 여자는 나에게 진대 붙는다 She sticks to me as a bur〔leech〕.
진도 進度 the rate of progress ¶ 학과의 진도 progress of classwork // 이 학급은 수학 진도가 뒤떨어져 있다 This class is backward in mathematics. // 한국은 경제 성장 진도가 빠르다 Korean economy shows a rapid advancement toward its higher status.
―표 a teaching schedule《for the year〔term〕》(학과의) ; a progress chart 학과 ― the progress of classwork
진도 震度 seismic intensity ¶ 진도 6의 강진 a very strong earthquake of six degrees intensity
진동 the armhole (of a sleeve)
*진동 振動 vibration ; oscillation ; swing (시계추의) ―하다 vibrate ; oscillate ; swing ¶ 진동을 일으키다 set up a vibration〔swinging motion〕
―계 a vibration gauge ; a vibrometer ; a vibroscope ―기(機) 『공학』 a vibrator ―기(器) 『전기』 a vibrator ; an oscillator ―막(膜) 『동물』 a timbal (매미 따위의)

—수 the number of vibrations ; an oscillation frequency ; a pitch — 시간 the oscillation time —자 〖물리〗 a vibrator (오실로그래프의) ; a trembler ; an oscillator〔oscillations〕 — 전류 oscillation〔oscillating〕 current — 주기〔위상〕 the period〔phase〕 of vibration —판 a diaphragm ; tympanum 《*pl.* ~s, -na》 (전화기의)

†진동 震動 [지진 따위의] a shock ; a quake ; a tremor ; [폭발 따위의] concussion ── 하다 shake ; quake ; vibrate ; quiver ¶ 가옥〔열차〕의 진동 the shaking of house〔train〕 // 진동시키다 shake ; vibrate // 진동을 느끼다 feel a shock // 가옥이 진동하다 The house shakes. /The house is rocked. (심히) // 이 자동차는 진동이 적다 This motorcar drives smoothly.
—계 a vibroscope —수 the number of vibrations — 시간 the duration of a shock 〔vibration〕 (지진의) —파 an earthquake wave

진동항아리 〖민속〗 ① [무당의] a tablet in a shaman's home before which gods and the spirits of ancestors are worshiped ② [항아리] a vase where some money and rice are kept as a token to insure peace and prosperity

진두 陣頭 (at) the head of an army ; the front ¶ 진두에 서다 be in the forefront 《of》 ; lead the van 《of》 ; be at the head 《of》

진두 지휘 陣頭指揮 command exercised by the head of an army ── 하다 act as the leader of an army ; lead an army

진둥한둥 busily ; in a hurry〔flurry〕 ; confusedly ; helter-skelter ; like a busy bee ── 하다 hurry (up) ; hasten ; busy oneself with ; fluster oneself ; be flurried ¶ 진둥한둥 하루를 보내다 pass a busy day // 진둥한둥 밥을 먹다 take a hasty〔hurried〕 meal

진드근하다 (be) very staid ; sedate ; sober ; earnest ; quite quiet ¶ 진드근히 very sedately ; soberly ; earnestly

진드기 〖동물〗 a tick ; a mite ; a louse ¶ 진드기 같은 사람 a barnacle ; a hanger-on // 진드기에 물리다 be bitten by a tick // 진드기같이 달라붙다 fasten on 《a person》 like a tick ; cling to 《a person》 like a leech
개〔소〕— a dog〔cattle〕 tick

진득거리다 ① [들러붙다] be sticky ; keep sticking〔holding on, adhering〕 ② [검질기다] resist cutting ; (be) stubborn ; tough ; steadfast ; unyielding

진득이 gravely ; sedately ; with dignity ; in earnest ; patiently ; calmly ; soberly ; quietly

진득진득 stubborn(ly) ; unyielding(ly) ── 하다 (be) sticky ; adhesive ; clammy ; gluey ; viscous ; tacky

진득하다 (be) quiet and serious ; staid ; sedate ; dignified ; grave ; earnest ; patient ; quiet ; calm ; composed ¶ 진득하게 gravely ; dignifiedly // 진득한 사람 a man of dignified presence // 그는 언제 봐도 진득하다 He always appears dignified. /He is a deep-seated person. 《속》 // 그는 나이가 어려서 진득한 데가 없다 He lacks dignity, being still young. /He is too young to have (any) weight of character.

진디 〖곤충〗 a plant louse ; an aphid
—등에 a gnat ; a sandfly 진딧물 a plant-louse-infested spot ; a nest of aphides ¶ 진딧물 내리다 get infested with aphides ; swarm with plant lice

진땀 津— sweat of anxiety ; greasy sweat ; sticky sweat ¶ 진땀이 나다 sweat hard ; undergo terrible hardships // 아파서 진땀을 흘리다 sweat hard in agony // 그 시험에는 진땀을 뺐다 That examination had me sweating.

진력 盡力 effort ; exertion ; endeavor ; [알선] good offices ; services ; assistance ── 하다 make an effort ; exert oneself ; use one's influence ; [타인을 위하여] render 《a person》 services ; endeavor ¶ S씨가 진력해준 덕분에 through the efforts〔good offices〕 of Mr. S // 그는 나를 위해서 진력해 주었다 He made every effort to help me. // 그는 일생을 아프리카에서 전도사업에 진력하였다 He devoted his life to mission work in Africa.

진력나다 盡力— be sickened 《of》 ; be sick 〔quite tired〕 《of》 ¶ 진력나는 강의 a boring 〔tedious, tiresome〕 lecture // 단것도 너무 자주 먹으면 진력난다 Sweets served too often cloy the palate.

†진로 進路 a course ; a direction ; a way ; a path ¶ 진로를 잃다 lose one's course // 진로를 잘못 들다 take a wrong course // 진로를 개척하다 carve one's way 《through, to》 // 후진에게 진로를 열어주다 make way for one's juniors // 진로를 방해하다 bar〔block〕 《a person's》 way // 진로를 벗어나다 yaw ; turn up the right course // 진로를 바꾸다 change〔alter〕 one's course ; change the course of 《the vessel》 ; veer // 진로를 오른쪽으로 바꾸다 veer to the right // 진로를 북으로 잡다 take a northerly course // 태풍의 진로 안에 들다 be in the path of a typhoon // 진로를 따르다 keep track 《of》 // 빙산이 배의 진로를 가로 막고 있다 Icebergs lie in the course 〔track〕 of a steamer. // 우리는 진흙길을 헤치고 진로를 찾아야 했다 We had to pick our way along the muddy path.

*진료 診療 medical examination and treatment ── 하다 diagnose and treat ; give medical treatment ¶ 진료를 받다 receive (medical) treatment ; be treated ; consult one's doctor
—소 a clinic ; a medical office ; [공장 따위에 부속한] a dispensary ; an infirmary — 시간 consultation hours —실 consultation room ; a medical office

진루 陣壘 〖군사〗 (the site of) a military camp ; a position

진루하다 進壘— 〖야구〗 advance ¶ 1루에 진루하다 advance〔move up〕 to first base

†**진리 眞理** (a) truth ; a fact ¶ 보편적 진리 a universal truth // 과학의 진리 the truths of science // 영구 불변의 진리 eternal truth // 진리의 탐구자 a seeker after (the) truth // 진리를 탐구하다 seek after (the) truth // 그것은 진리이다 It is a truth. // 그의 말에는 어느 정도의 진리가 있다 There is some〔an element of, a grain of〕 truth in what he says.

진맥 診脈 feeling the pulse for diagnosis ; examination of pulse **—하다** feel the pulse 《of》 ; take〔examine〕 the pulse 《of》

진면목 眞面目 one's true character ¶ 진면목을 발휘하다 reveal〔show〕 one's true character ; appear〔come out〕 in one's true colors ; [진가를 발휘하다] give full play〔justice〕 to one's ability〔gifts〕

진멸 殄滅 annihilation ; extermination **—하다** annihilate ; exterminate ; wipe out ; bring to nothing

진목 珍木 a rare tree

진묘 珍妙 queerness ; oddity **—하다** (be) queer ; odd ¶ 진묘한 생각 a fantastic idea // 진묘한 표정을 짓다 put on a queer face

진무 鎭撫 pacification ; appeasement ; placation ; conciliation **—하다** pacify ; placate ; appease ; calm ; quell ; quiet ¶ 흑인 폭동을 진무하다 pacify the Black riot // 신의 노여움을 진무하다 propitiate a deity // 알렉산더 대왕은 정복민들을 진무하기에 성공했다 Alexander the Great achieved a success in pacifying the conquered.

진묵 眞墨 superior Chinese ink-stick ⇨ 참먹

진문 珍聞 news (새로운) ; a strange〔curious〕 story (기담) ; a revelation (새로운 사실) ¶ 무엇인가 진문이 있는가 What is the news of the day? // 진문이 있다 I have something new to tell you. // 그것은 진문이다 That's quite news to me.

진문 珍問 a strange〔an extraordinary, incomprehensible〕 question
— 진답 an incomprehensible question and a garbled reply

진문 陣門 the gate to a military camp ; a camp gate

진물 ooze from a sore ; secretions from a sore ¶ 진물이 나다 a sore oozes〔waters〕

진물 眞物 a genuine article ⇨ 진짜

진물진물 all inflamed ; gangrenous ; blistered ; bleary **—하다** (be) sore ; be all inflamed ; ulcerated ; septic ; bleared

진미 珍味 a (food) of delicate flavor ; a delicacy ; a dainty ; a rich diet ¶ 계절의 진미 all the delicacies of the season // 산해의 진미 a sumptuous feast ; all sorts of dainties // 피크닉 바구니에는 온갖 진미가 들어 있었다 There were dainties of every kind in the picnic basket. // 상은 산해의 진미로 꽉 차 있다 The table groans with dainties of many kinds.

진미 眞味 [참 맛] true taste ; [참 뜻] a true meaning〔sense〕 ; genuine appreciation ¶ 동양화의 진미를 알다 appreciate what Oriental painting is all about

진미 陳米 old stale rice

진발 muddy〔dirty〕 feet〔shoes〕 ¶ 진발로 마루에 올라서다 soil the floor with muddy feet〔shoes〕

진발 進發 a start **—하다** march off ; start ; leave

진방 辰方 〚민속〛 the Direction of the Dragon 《southeast-by-east》

진배없다 (be) equal 《to》 ; equivalent 《to》 ; similar 《to》 ; be as good as ; be no worse than ¶ 새것이나 진배없다 be as good as new // 오락도 일에 진배없이 필요하다 Recreation is no less necessary than work. // 이것은 외제품에 비해서 조금도 진배 없다 This compares quite well with foreign-made articles. // 어제도 추웠었다—오늘에 진배없이 추웠다 It was very cold yesterday—as much〔as cold〕 as it is today.

진버짐 eczema ; a watery ringworm ¶ 진버짐이 난 얼굴 an eczematous face

진범 眞犯 the true culprit ⇨ 진범인

진범인 眞犯人 the true culprit ; the real criminal〔offender〕 ¶ 진범인은 아직 잡히지 않고 있다 The real criminal is still at large.

진법 陣法 disposition of troops ; battle formation ; plan of campaign ; tactics
방어〔공격〕— defensive〔offensive〕 disposition

진보 珍寶 a treasure ; a precious article ; valuables ; precious things

†**진보 進步** progress ; advance ; advancement ; improvement ; progression

> 참고 **progress** 비교적 현저한 발달을 말하지만 **advance**는 전진을 의미하여 진보의 정도 여하에 구애받지 않는다

—하다 progress ; advance ; make progress 〔headway〕 ; improve ¶ 과학의 진보 the advancement of science ; scientific advance // 진보적 progressive ; up-to-date // 진보적 의견 an advanced view // 굉장한 진보를 하다 make great progress〔advance〕 ; make rapid strides // 학문이 진보하다 make progress in one's studies // 그의 연구는 조금도 진보가 없다 He has made no progress in his studies. // 이것은 정치에 있어 하나의 진보다 This marks a step forward in politics.
—당 the Progressive Party **—주의** progressivism **—주의자** a progressive ; progressionist **—파** the progressives ; [진영] the progressive camp ; [보수당 내의] the progressive group 《within the Conservative Party》

진본 珍本 a rare book

진본 眞本 [책의] the original copy ; an authentic piece of writing ; [서화의] a genuine writing〔painting〕 ; an unforged piece of painting

진부 眞否 truth or falsehood ; authenticity ; genuineness ; the real facts ; truth ¶ 진부간에 whether truth or falsehood // 진

부를 확인하다 ascertain the reality ; ascertain whether it is true or not
진부 陳腐 platitude ; commonplaceness ; banality ; triteness **—하다** (be) commonplace ; old-fashioned ; trite ; stale ; hackneyed ; worn-out ; out-of-date ¶ 진부한 말 a trite〔threadbare〕 remark // 진부한 격언 a hackneyed saying // 진부한 생각 an old-fashioned idea // 진부한 표현 a trite expression // 진부한 말을 하다 make a commonplace〔trite〕 remark // 그의 이론은 모두 진부하고 평범하다 His arguments are all cut-and-dried.
진사 a one-eyed person ⇨ 애꾸눈이
진사 眞絲 ⇨ 명주실
진사 眞事 a rare incident ⇨ 진사건
진사 陳謝 an apology **—하다** apologize to 《a person for》 ; express one's regret ; tender one's apology ; beg pardon of ¶ 진사를 요구하다 demand an apology 《from》 // 그는 내 차에 손해를 입힌 데 대하여 진사했다 He offered his apology for damaging my car.
진사 進士 a person who has only passed the first examination for office
진사건 珍事件 a rare case ; a strange affair ; a mysterious event〔occurrence〕 ; a curious event ; a rare incident
진산 鎭山 a guardian mountain
진상 眞相 the truth 《of a matter》 ; the real〔true〕 facts ; the real state of affairs ¶ 진상을 파악하다 get at the truth〔real state of affairs〕 // 진상을 규명하다 inquire into the actual state of things ; get down to the bed-rock // 진상을 말하다 lay bare the truth 《of a matter》 // 사건의 진상을 밝히다 reveal 〔disclose〕 the real facts of the case // 언젠가는 진상이 밝혀진다 The truth will be out someday.
— 조사 fact finding ¶ 진상 조사단〔조사위원회〕 a fact-finding mission〔committee〕
진상 進上 presenting to the king local produces〔products〕 as tribute from the country **—하다** present to the king ; offer up **—물** a present to the king ; an offering to the king
진서 珍書 a rare book ; a treasured volume ¶ 진서를 찾아 다니다 hunt for〔up〕 rare books
진선 津船 a ferryboat ; a ferry
진선미 眞善美 truth, goodness and beauty ; the true, the good and the beautiful
진선진미 盡善盡美 most virtuous and most beautiful ; perfect ; excellent **—하다** (be) most virtuous and most beautiful ; perfect ; excellent
진설 珍說 a strange〔ridiculous〕 opinion
진설 陳設 arranging the dishes of food ; preparing a table of eatables (for memorial service) **—하다** set out ; arrange ; prepare a table of eatables (for memorial service)
진성 眞性 [천부] one's inborn nature ; one's true character ; [진짜] genuineness ¶ 진성의 genuine // 진성 호열자 a genuine case of cholera ; true cholera
— 뇌염 a genuine encephalitis ¶ 진성 뇌염 환자 a genuine encephalitis case ; a genuine case of encephalitis **— 콜레라** a genuine case of cholera ; true cholera
진세 塵世 the world ; this world ; this mortal life ; this carnal world ; this dirty world ¶ 진세의 worldly ; earthly ; mundane // 진세를 멀리하고 살다 live far from the bustle and hustle of life // 진세를 벗어나다 seclude oneself from the world ; keep aloof from the world // 진세가 싫어지다 be weary〔sick〕 of life // 진세를 버리다 forsake〔retire from〕 the world
진세 陣勢 [진용] battle array〔formation〕 ; [군세] forces ; troops ¶ 진세를 벌리다 array one's men
진소위 眞所謂 really ; truly ; verily ; in fact ; in truth ; indeed
진속 塵俗 the world ; this world ; this earthly life
진솔 [새옷] brand-new clothes ; [모시옷] ramie-cloth garments made in spring or fall
진수 珍羞 rare dainties ; delicacies ; food of delicate flavor
—성찬 rich viands and sumptuous fare ; all sorts of delicacies ¶ 오늘은 진수성찬이군요 You've fixed quite a meal today.
진수 眞髓 the essence ; the quintessence ; the gist ; the core ; the pith ; the kernel ; the essential ; the soul ; the spirit ¶ 시의 진수 the essence of poetry // 불교의 진수 the essentials of Buddhism // 입센의 진수 quintessence of Ibsen // 교육의 진수 the spirit of education // 간결은 기지의 진수다 Brevity is the soul of wit.
⁑**진수 進水** launching **—하다** be launched ; launch 《a ship》 ; set 《a ship》 afloat ¶ 진수시키다 launch
—대 the launching platform〔ways〕 ¶ 배가 진수대를 떠나다 leave the ways **—식** a launching ceremony ¶ 진수식을 올리다 launch 《a ship》 ; hold a launching ceremony // 진수식은 S조선소에서 거행되었다 She was launched from the S dockyard.
진수 眞數 antilogarithm 《antilog》
†**진술 陳述** a statement ; a declaration ; [증언] a testimony **—하다** state ; declare ; explain ; set forth ; make a statement ¶ 선장의 진술에 의하면 according to the statement made by the captain // 의견을 진술하다 state〔set forth〕 one's views // 허위 진술하다 make a false statement // 증인은 피고에게 불리한 진술을 했다 The witness gave testimony against the defendant.
—서 a (written) statement〔declaration〕
진시 辰時 〚민속〛 the Watch of the Dragon ① the 5th of the 12 double hours 《7–9 a. m.》 ② the 9th of the 24 hours 《7 : 30–8 : 30 a. m.》
진시 眞是 truly ; really ; surely ; verily ; in

reality
진신 (leather) rain shoes
진신 搢紳 government officials ; high officials ; court nobles ; gentry
진신발 [신] muddy shoes〔boots〕 ⇨ 진발
†**진실 眞實** truth ; truthfulness ; sincerity ; reality ; fact **—하다** (be) true ; truthful ; real ; sincere ; honest ; genuine ; faithful ¶ 진실로 truly ; really ; in fact ; in reality ; sincerely ; heartily ; honestly // 진실하지 않은 insincere ; faithless ; unfaithful ; false ; feigned // 진실을 말하다 tell 〔speak〕 the truth // 진실로 동정하다 feel real sympathy // 진실하게 대하다 act sincerely 《towards a person》 ; show fidelity 《to a person》 // 그의 말에 진실이라고는 조금도 없다 There is no truth in what he says.
진실성 眞實性 fidelity ; allegiance ; loyalty ; devotion ; [성명 따위의] the truth ; [보고서 따위의] the authority ; credibility ; veracity ¶ 진실성을 의심하다 doubt the truth 《of》 // 그의 진실성은 의심할 여지가 없다 His veracity is unquestioned.
*__진심 眞心__ the whole〔true〕 heart ; sincerity ¶ 진심으로 from (the bottom of) one's heart ; heartily ; sincerely ; with one's whole heart and soul // 진심에서 우러나오는 경의 a tribute from the bottom of one's heart // 진심으로 일을 하다 do a work with devotion ; devote oneself to a work ; do a work with one's whole heart // 진심을 토로하다 speak out of one's heart ; lay one's heart open to // 진심으로 감사하다 thank 《a person》 whole-heartedly〔cordially, heartily〕 ; thank 《a person》 from (the bottom of) one's heart // 진심으로 환영합니다 We welcome you with whole heart. // 진심으로 하는 말이에요 You mean it? // 진심으로 하는 말이야 I mean it. /I mean business.
진안 ⇨ 진위(眞僞)
진알 進謁 an audience ; presenting oneself to a superior **—하다** have an audience of ; present oneself (to a superior) ; be received in audience by His 〔Her〕 Majesty ; visit ¶ 그는 로마 교황을 진알했다 He was received in audience by the Supreme Pontiff.
†**진압 鎭壓** suppression ; repression ; subjugation **—하다** suppress ; repress ; quell ; subdue ; subjugate ; put down ¶ 폭동을 진압하다 quell a riot ; put down 〔suppress〕 a rebellion
—책(策) a repressive measure **폭동 —경찰** the helmeted〔riot〕 police
진앙 震央 the seismic center〔focus〕 ; the epicenter ; the earthquake center
진애 塵埃 dust ; dirt ¶ 진애 속에 묻히다 be buried in dust
—계 a dust counter
진액 津液 resin ; sap ; juice ¶ 진액이 나는 resinous ; juicy ; sappy // 단풍 나무에서 진액이 나오기 시작한다 The sap is beginning to rise in the maple-trees. // 고무 나무는 자르면 진액이 나온다 A gum tree bleeds when cut.
진언 進言 counsel ; advice ; offering one's view ; a suggestion ; a proposal ; a proposition **—하다** counsel 《a person》 ; advise 《a person》 ; suggest ; propose
진언 眞言 the words〔sayings〕 of Buddha ; holy words
진역 震域 an old name for Korea
진연 塵煙 a cloud of dust
⁑**진열 陳列** exhibition ; show ; display ; arrangement **—하다** exhibit ; display ; put on show ; [배열하다] arrange ; place 《things》 on exhibition〔view〕 ¶ 진열되어 있다 be on display〔view, show〕 ; be placed on show // 박물관에는 정교한 중국 도자기가 진열되어 있다 There is a fine exhibit of Chinese porcelain in the museum.
—관 [통산(通產)] the Exhibition House ; a museum ; [회화의] a (picture) gallery **—대** a display stand〔counter〕 **—실** a show〔display〕 room **—장**〔**상자, 선반**〕 a showcase〔a display rack〕 **—창** a show window〔case〕 **—품** an exhibit ; articles on display〔show〕 **상품 —관** a commercial museum
진영 陣營 a camp ; an encampment ; quarters ; a bloc ¶ 양진영간에서 중립을 지키다 stand in the right middle of both blocs // 공산 진영에 가담하다 join the Communist camp // 당신과 나는 정치적 진영이 다르다 You and I belong to different political camps.
동서 양— the camps of the East and the West ; the East and West camps ; the two power blocs of the world ; the major Powers of the East and the West ¶ 동서 양진영간의 긴장 the tension between the two camps of the East and West **민주 —** the democratic camp **반공 —** the anti-communist camp **보수**〔**혁신**〕 **—** the conservative〔progressive〕 camp
진영 眞影 a portrait ; a true image ; a picture ; a likeness ¶ 고종 황제의 진영 a portrait of Emperor *Kojong*
진옥 眞玉 genuine jade
진옴 watery itch ; watery scabies
진외가 陳外家 the parents' home of one's paternal grandmother
진용 陣容 (a) battle array ; (battle) formation ; disposition ; [야구 따위의] a line-up ¶ 교수 진용 the teaching staff ; the faculty (of a university) // 새 내각의 진용 the line-up〔make-up〕 of the newly formed cabinet // 진용을 갖추다 line up for battle ; put 《troops》 in battle formation
진원지 震源地 the seismic〔earthquake〕 center ; the epicenter ; the focus of an earthquake ; [비유적] the center of the

disturbance ¶ 진원지는 제주도 부근이었다 The center of the disturbance lay near *Cheju-do.* // 그 사건의 진원지는 서울이었다 The event originated in *Seoul.* /*Seoul* was the fountainhead of the event.

진위 眞僞 truth or falsehood ; truth ; authenticity ; genuineness or spuriousness ¶ 진위를 조사하다 examine〔ascertain〕 the genuineness《of》// 진위를 분별하다 discriminate truth from error // 소문의 진위를 확인하다 confirm (the truth of) a report // 나로서는 진위를 보증할 수 없다 I can't say positively whether it is true or false. // 이 보고의 진위는 확실치가 않다 This report is of dubious authenticity.

진의 眞意 [본심] one's real intention ; one's true motive ; [참뜻] the true meaning ¶ 그의 진의가 무엇인지 알 수 없다 I can't see what he really means. // 나의 진의는 바로 거기에 있다 That is what I really mean.

진의 眞義 the true meaning〔sense, significance〕

진인 眞因 the real cause〔motive, ground, reason〕 ¶ 그들의 이혼의 진인은 분명치 않다 The true motive for their divorce remains unknown.

진인 眞人 a true man

진일 wet housework ; chores in which one's hands get wet

진일 盡日 ⇨ 종일(終日)

진입 進入 penetration ; entry 《into a place》 ; a drive 《on a place》 ; 〖기하〗 admission **—하다** march〔penetrate〕 into ; enter ; go into ; make one's way into ; advance into ¶ 진입 금지 No entering.

—구 an admission part **—등(燈)** an approach light **—로** 〖기계〗 an admission passage **— 지시기** 〖철도〗 an approach indicator **—판** an admission valve **지상 관제 — 방식** 〖항공〗 the ground-controlled approach system 《G. C. A.》

진잎 leaves of vegetable

—밥〔죽〕 rice〔porridge〕 cooked with vegetable leaves

***진자 振子** a pendulum

진자리 ① [바로 그 자리] the place ; the spot ¶ 진자리에서 then and there ; on the spot ; [즉석에서] extempore ② the spot where a child was just born or a spot soiled by a person just died ③ a spot soiled by a child's urine or feces

진작 ① [곧] on the spot ; offhand ; immediately ; directly ; promptly ; on that occasion ¶ 왜 진작 말하지 않았느냐 You might have said so then and there. // 진작 왔으면 만났을 것을 Had you come earlier, you might have met her.

② [더 일찍] earlier ¶ 진작 갔어야 했다 You should have gone there at once. // 진작 알려 주었으면 좋았을 것을 You should have informed me of this earlier.

진작 振作 stimulation ; rousing **—하다** promote ; arouse 《a person to activity》 ; awaken ¶ 사기를 진작시키다 stir up the morale 《of troops》

진작 眞斫 oak firewood

진장 珍藏 keeping as treasure ; treasuring **—하다** treasure (up)

—서 one's prized〔treasured〕 book **—품** treasured possessions

진장 陳醬 aged soy-sauce ; long-stored blackish soy

진재 陳材 〖한의〗 aged medicinal herbs

진재 震災 an earthquake disaster ; an earthquake (지진) ¶ 진재민 구호 the relief of earthquake victims // 진재의 예방 prevention of earthquake disaster // 진재를 당하다 be in an earthquake // 진재로 전멸하다 be wiped out by an earthquake

—지 an earthquake zone ; a quake-stricken district

진저리 ① [떨림] a shiver after urinating ; a quiver ; a shudder ; a thrilling ¶ 진저리 나다 shiver after urinating ; tremble 《for fear》 ; be sickened of // 진저리 치다 shudder ; be horrified ; quiver 《with emotion》 ② disgust ⇨ 진절머리

진저리고사리 a kind of fern

진저 에일 [음료] ginger ale

진적 珍籍 a rare book ⇨ 진서

진적 眞蹟 ① real traces〔relics, vestiges〕 ② ⇨ 진필(眞筆)

진전 進展 development ; progress ; evolution ; march ; advance **—하다** develop ; (make) progress ; march ; shape up (미) ¶ 전국의 진전과 더불어 with the progress of the war // 일의 진전 여하에 따라 according to the development of the affairs // 연구에 진전을 보다 advance in one's studies // 진전이 빠르다 make a rapid progress ; proceed rapidly // 원활하게 진전되다 go on smoothly ; make good progress // 사건의 진전 the march of events // 만사 잘 진전되고 있다 Everything is shaping out well. // 앞으로 이 문제는 어떻게 진전되어 갈 것인지 What will be the future development of this question? // 영어로 말을 할 정도로 진전되었습니까 Has your English come along far enough so that you can speak it?

진절머리 disgust ; repugnance ; dislike ; aversion ¶ 진절머리 나다 be sick of ; be disgusted with ; feel a repugnance to // 진절머리 나게 하다 make 《a person》 sick of 《a thing》 ; bore 《a person》 to death // 저 남자에게는 진절머리가 난다 He wearies〔bores〕 me to death. // 이제 비에는 진절머리가 났다 We have had enough of rain. /We are fed up with rain. // 그는 힘드는 공부에 진절머리가 났다 He began to feel aversion to hard study. // 나는 그 일에 거의 진절머리가 난다 I am about sick of that business.

***진정 眞正** genuineness ; authenticity —

하다 (be) genuine ; authentic ; real ; true ; pure ¶ 진정한 종교 a true religion // 진정한 의미에서 in the true sense of the word // 그 사람이야말로 진정한 애국자다 If there is a true patriot, he is the one.

진정 眞情 true feeling ; true heart ; genuine sentiment ¶ 진정의 true ; sincere ; earnest // 진정으로 truly ; seriously ; in earnest ; from one's heart // 진정을 털어놓고 이야기하다 have a heart-to-heart talk 《with a person》 // 진정을 토로하다 express one's genuine feeling ; unbosom oneself to 《another》 ; speak from one's heart // 편지에는 그의 진정이 깃들어 있다 His whole heart and soul is in the letter.

진정 陳情 a representation ; a petition ; an appeal —하다 petition ; make a representation〔petition〕《to the Government》 ; lay 《a matter》 before 《the authorities》 ; lobby for 《미》 ¶ 진정을 받아들이다 accept a representation〔petition〕 // 진정을 각하하다 reject〔turn down〕 a petition〔representation〕

—단 [국회의] a group of lobbyists 《미》 ; a lobby —서 a written petition ; a petition ; a memorial ¶ 진정서를 제출하다 present〔submit, lodge〕 a petition 《to the Government》 — 위원회 a petition committee —자 a petitioner 의회 — 운동자 a lobbyist

진정 鎭定 suppression ; repression ; subdual —하다 suppress ; repress ; put down ; subdue ; tranquil(l)ize ¶ 반란을 진정하다 stamp out a rebellion // 그 정도로는 국민의 분노를 진정시키기에 충분치 않다 That won't be enough to mollify the public's ire.

†진정 鎭靜 quiet ; calm ; tranquility ; pacification —하다 become calm〔quiet〕 ; calm〔quiet〕 down ; [고통 따위가] be relieved〔appeased〕 ; be allayed ; be soothed ¶ 마음을 진정시키다 calm oneself down ; preserve a tranquil mind // 진정하시오 Don't get excited ! /Calm yourself. /Cool it. /Calm down. /Simmer down. // 그 지방의 소동은 진정되었다 Tranquility has been restored in that district.

— 작용 〖의학〗 sedation (특히 진정제 따위에 의한) —제 a sedative ; a tranquilizer ; a calmative ; a depressant

진정 進呈 presentation —하다 give ; present 《a person with a thing, a thing to a person》 ; make 《a person》 a present of 《a thing》 ¶ 물건을 진정하다 give〔present〕 《a person with a thing》 // 김씨에게 진정함 To〔Presented to〕 Mr. *Kim* // 견본 무료 진정함 Samples are presented free. (광고) // 필요하시면 일부 진정하겠습니다 If you want it, I will make you a present of a copy.

—자 a presenter 견본 무료 — [광고] Write for free samples. /Samples sent free on application. 경품 — [광고] premiums offered 무료 — a free gift

진종일 盡終日 the whole day ; all day (long) ; all through the day ; throughout the day ; from morning to〔till〕 night ¶ 진종일 기다리다 wait for 《a person》 the livelong day

†진주 眞珠 a pearl ¶ 진주 캐는 사람 a pearl diver〔fisher〕 // 진주 같은 광택 a pearly luster

—병 〖수의〗 pearl disease —색 pearl gray — 세공 pearl work — 양식 pearl culture ; the culture of pearls — 양식장 a pearl farm〔bed〕 — 조개 a pearl oyster〔shell〕 — 채취 pearl fishing 모조 — an imitation pearl 양식 — a cultured pearl 인조 — an artificial〔false〕 pearl 흑〔분홍색〕 — a black〔pink〕 pearl

진주 進駐 advancing and staying ; occupying 《a place》 and staying —하다 advance〔march〕 into 《Tokyo》 and stay ; make an entry into 《Tokyo》 ; be stationed

—군 the Occupation Forces ; the army of occupation ¶ 진주군에서 일하다 work for〔be in the employ of〕 the Occupation Army ; work 《as a clerk》 in an Occupation office

진주만 眞珠灣 Pearl Harbor

진중 珍重 —하다 (be) valuable ; precious ; treasured ¶ 진중히 여기다 highly esteem〔value〕 ; prize ; treasure ; set great store by ; make〔think〕 much of // 기념품으로 진중히 여기겠습니다 I shall prize it as a keepsake.

진중 陣中 ¶ 진중에서 at the front ; in the ranks ; in camp ; in the field // 적의 진중에 난입하다 rush into the ranks of the enemy

— 근무 field duty ; duties in the field — 생활 a camp life — 위문 an inquiry after 《a person's》 health at the front ; a comfort bag (위문품) — 일기 a staff diary ; a field〔war〕 diary

진중 鎭重 —하다 (be) sedate ; gentle ; reserved ; grave ; dignified ; imposing ¶ 진중한 발걸음으로 with a dignified step ; with a solemn pace // 그는 언행이 진중하다 He is prudent in his behavior.

진지 meal ; rice ¶ 진지 잡수셨습니까 Have you had your meal ?

진지 陣地 a position ; an encampment ; quarters ¶ 진지를 펴다 take up a position // 진지를 철수하다 evacuate〔withdraw from〕 a position ; decamp ; break camp // 진지를 사수하다 defend a position to the last // 적의 진지를 점령하다 capture an enemy position // 아군은 분전하여 적의 진지를 탈취했다 After desperate fighting we dislodged the enemy from his position. // 완강한 저항을 시도한 끝에 적은 진지를

철퇴했다 After stubborn resistance the enemy evacuated its〔his〕 lines.
—전 position operations ; position warfare ; position-war — 철퇴 decampment ; evacuation of a position 가설 — a temporary position 기관총 — a machine-gun nest 본— the main position 포병 — an artillery position

†**진지 眞摯** seriousness ; sincerity ; soberness ; earnestness —하다 (be) serious ; sincere ; sober ; earnest ; grave ; single-minded ¶ 진지하게 earnestly ; in earnest ; single-mindedly // 진지한 사람 a serious〔serious-minded〕 person ; a man of sober habits // 진지한 노력 an earnest effort // 진지한 태도 a serious attitude // 진지하게 생각하다 take 《everything》 seriously〔soberly, gravely, earnestly〕 // 진지한 얼굴을 하다 look grave〔sober〕 // 진지하게 말하다 speak in earnest ; speak with gravity // 진지하게 일하다 work earnestly (열심히) ; work conscientiously (양심적으로) ; work seriously // 진지하게 살다 live honestly ; live straight // 그 일은 진지하게 생각할 필요가 있다 It requires grave〔sober〕 reflection. // 나는 농담으로 한 말을 그는 진지하게 받아 들였다 He took seriously what I meant for a joke. // 아무리 여러 번 경고해도 그는 진지하게 받아들일 기미를 보이지 않는다 No matter how often I warn that guy, he shows no sign of having taken it to heart.

진지러지다 [움츠리다] flinch ; shrink 《from》 ; quail 《at, before》 ; cower 《before》 ; [생물이] weaken ; grow weak ; be enfeebled ; fail in health ; [병자가] sink

진진 津津 —하다 (be) brimful ; brim with ; be full of ; (be) overflowing ¶ 맛이 진진하다 be tasteful // 흥미 진진하다 be highly interesting ; be an unfailing fountain of interest

진집 a gap ; a crevice ; an opening ; an aperture ; a crack ¶ 진집이 나다 develop〔have〕 a crack〔an opening〕 // 그로 말미암아 두 사람의 우정에 진집이 났다 That has caused a crack in their (bond of) friendship.

†**진짜** a genuine〔real, sterling〕 article ; a real thing ¶ 진짜의 genuine ; true ; real ; natural (인공에 대하여) ; authentic // 진짜 고려 자기 a genuine piece of *Koryo* pottery // 진짜 진주 a natural pearl // 진짜 커피 honest coffee // 진짜와 가짜를 분별하다 tell the real from the false ; distinguish〔tell〕 the imitations from the originals // 이 장미의 조화는 꼭 진짜 같다 These artificial roses are quite lifelike. // 그는 학생 때부터 두각을 나타내더니만 역시 진짜 실력이 있었군 He shone as a student, and I guess he was for real after all.

진찰 診察 (a) medical examination 〔advice〕 ; diagnosis (진단) —하다 examine ; see 《a patient》 ; diagnose ¶ 진찰을 받다 see〔consult〕 a doctor // 나는 어제 눈을 진찰받았다 I had my eyes examined yesterday. // 그들이 나를 진찰해 본 결과 내게 이상은 없다고 했다 They checked me over and told me there's nothing wrong.
—권 a consultation ticket —료 a medical 〔doctor's, consultation〕 fee〔charge〕 ; a fee for medical advice ¶ 진찰료 10,000원 Ten thousand *won* for the consultation fee. — 시간 consultation hours —실 a consultation〔consulting〕 room ; an examining room —일 a consultation day 무료 — [게시] Consultation free.

‡**진창** mud ; a muddy place ¶ 진창 속에 내던지다 throw 《a thing》 into the mud // 진창에 넘어지다 fall in the mud // 진창속에 빠지다 [비유적] be bogged down ; get stuck in a bog ; be in a bad fix
—길 a muddy road

진채 眞彩 a deep-color pigment

진척 進陟 ① [일의] advance ; progress —하다 [일이] progress ; make (good) progress ; advance ¶ 진척중이다 be under way ; be in progress ; be on foot // 진척시키다 hasten ; carry forward // 진척하지 않다 make no progress ; be slow in progress // 이 건축 공사는 진척이 없다 This building work makes little progress. // 도로 공사는 착착 진척되고 있다 The road work is making progress steadily〔rapidly〕. // 사장의 수행원으로 이쪽저쪽 끌려다니다 보니 일을 전혀 진척시키지 못했다 I've had to accompany the president all around, so I haven't made any headway with my work.
② [계급이] promotion ; advancement ; rise (in rank) —하다 be promoted 〔advanced〕 《to》 ; rise (in rank) ¶ 그는 진척이 빠르다 He is rapid in promotion.

진천동지 震天動地 —하다 shake the sphere〔earth and sky, heaven and earth, whole universe〕 ; make the whole world wonder ; rend the air (특히 음향이) ¶ 진천동지의 world-shaking ; astounding ; marvelous // 진천동지의 대사건 a most sensational〔extraordinary〕 event ; a rare event ; an event of a rare kind // 진천동지의 위업을 이루다 accomplish a startling〔sensational〕 achievement ; set the river〔Thames〕 on fire

진체 振替 transfer ; change 《of funds》 ¶ 진체 구좌 번호 a postal transfer account number ; a postal remittance number // 진체 저금 구좌 서울 1번 Postal Transfer Account No. 1 *Seoul* // 진체로 송금하다 send a money by transfer

진출 進出 advance ; 〖군사〗 debouchment ; [진입] entry ; penetration —하다 advance ; debouch 《into》 ; [발전하다] enter〔penetrate〕 《into》 ¶ 국산품의 해외

진출 export of home goods // 한국의 베트남에의 진출 the Korean advance into Vietnam // 여성의 정치 방면에의 진출 the entry of women into the political sphere of the community // 문단에 진출하다 make one's debut in letters // 해외 시장에 진출하다 make inroads into foreign market // 정계에 진출하다 enter into politics // 미국 시장에 진출하다 push into the American market

진충 盡忠 loyalty ; fidelity ; allegiance

진충보국 盡忠報國 loyalty and patriotism —하다 be loyal and patriotic ; practice loyalty and render service to one's country

진췌 盡悴 ⇨ 진력(盡力) —하다 devote oneself 《to a task》

진취 進取 progressiveness ; enterprise —하다 (be) progressive ; pushing ; enterprising ¶ 진취의 기상 a progressive〔enterprising〕spirit ; a spirit of enterprise // 진취의 기상이 왕성하다 be endowed with a progressive〔enterprising〕spirit // 네가 진취적인 자세를 취하면 네 앞길을 방해하는 것은 아무것도 없다 As long as you adopt an aggressive approach, nothing can stand in your way.

진취 進就 making gradual progress〔development〕—하다 progress gradually 《in》
—성 a progressive〔an enterprising〕spirit

진치다 陣— encamp ; pitch〔form〕a camp ; take up a position

진탕 —宕 to one's heart's content ; as one likes ; freely ¶ 진탕 먹다〔마시다〕eat〔drink〕one's full

진탕 concussion ; shock ; percussion —하다 get a shock〔concussion〕; give a shock ; shake
— 배양 〖생물·화학〗 shake〔shaking〕culture 뇌— cerebral concussion ; the concussion of the brain

진토 塵土 dust and soil

진통 陣痛 labor pains ; travail ; throes ; pangs of childbirth (분만시의) ¶ 진통의 발작 an onset of labor pains // 진통중이다 be in labor // 진통을 느끼다 suffer throes 《of childbed》; feel pains // 진통이 시작되다 begin to labor ; have〔feel〕labor pains ; suffer the pains〔throes〕of childbirth // 그 나라는 지금 혁명의 진통기에 있다 The country is now in the throes of revolution.

진통 鎭痛 alleviation〔soothing〕of pain —하다 relieve the pain
—액 a liquid anodyne —제 an anodyne ; an analgesic ; a pain-killer ; a pain-killing drug ; a balm

진퇴 進退 [운동] advance and retreat ; movement ; [거동] one's attitude ; one's course of action ; [거취] resigning and remaining in office ¶ 진퇴를 결정하다 decide on one's course of action // 진퇴의 자유를 잃다 be stalled ; be stranded ; lose one's freedom of movement // 진퇴를 같이 하다 cast in one's lot with 《a person》; act in line with // 진퇴를 그르치다 take the wrong course // 이것은 장관의 진퇴에 관한 문제이다 The matter affects the Minister's position.

*진퇴양난 進退兩難 a dilemma ; a (tight) fix ; a predicament ¶ 진퇴양난이다〔이 되다〕be (placed〔put〕) in a dilemma 《between》; be in a fix ; be〔find oneself〕between two fires ; face pressure from two sides // 두 사람 사이에 끼여 진퇴양난이다 Placed between them, I find my position very awkward.

진퇴유곡 進退維谷 ⇨ 진퇴양난

진티 the cause 《of a trouble》; the beginning ; the start ¶ 그 일이 틀린 진티가 여기 있다 This is what made the plan fail.

진파선 震波線 〖물리〗 a seismic ray

진펄 a bog ; a swamp ; a marsh

진폐증 塵肺症 〖의학〗 pneumoconiosis

진폭 振幅 〖물리〗 the amplitude (of vibration)
— 변조 〖전기〗 amplitude modulation 《AM》 — 평형 제어 〖전기〗 amplitude balance control

진폭 震幅 the amplitude of an earthquake

진풀 wet starch

진품 珍品 a rare〔priceless〕article ; a curio ; a rarity

진피 stubbornness ; wil(l)fulness ; obstinacy ¶ 진피부리다 act stubbornly〔willfully〕

진피 陳皮 〖한의〗 dried orange peel

진피아들 an extremely ugly-looking person

진필 眞筆 one's own handwriting ; an autograph ; a genuine writing ¶ 이것은 진필이냐 위필이냐 Is this writing forged or genuine?

†진하다 津— [빛깔이] (be) dark ; deep ; [국물 따위가] thick ; heavy ; strong ; rich ¶ 진한 빛 dark color // 진한 푸른 빛 deep blue ; navy blue 《미》 // 진한 갈색 dark〔deep〕brown color ; a dark shade of brown // 진한 차〔커피〕strong tea〔coffee〕 // 진한 국 thick soup // 진하게 화장한 얼굴 a thickly powdered face // 차를 진하게 하다 make tea strong // 화장을 진하게 하다 make up heavily

진하다 盡— [다하다] be exhausted ; be spent ; be used up ; come to an end ; run out ¶ 기운이 진하다 feel exhausted // 수단이 진하다 exhaust one's resources ; have played one's last card // 식량이 진하다 We have run out of provisions. /The provisions have run out.

진학 進學 —하다 enter upon studies ; enter a school of higher grade ; contin-

ue one's studies at a higher level ¶ 대학에 진학하다 go on to university // 진학을 지망하다 apply for admission to a school of higher grade // 우리 딸은 의과대학으로 진학할 겁니다 My daughter is going on to medical school. // 아버지는 내가 대학원에 진학하는 데 동의하셨다 My father agreed to let me go on to graduate school.
— 적성 검사 a scholastic〔an academic〕 aptitude test — 지망자 applicants for admission〔a student wishing to go on〕 to a school of higher grade
진합 眞蛤 〖조개〗 a kind of razor clam
진합 태산 塵合泰山 Many a mickle makes a muckle. /Many drops make a shower.
진항 進航 sailing out —하다 sail out ; steam ahead ; proceed
진해 震駭 terror ; horror ; alarm —하다 be alarmed ; be terrified ; be frightened
진해제 鎭咳劑 a cough remedy〔mixture〕
†진행 進行 progress ; advance ; motion ; march ; movement —하다 progress ; make progress〔headway〕; advance ; proceed ; go on ; run (기차 따위가) ; move ; be in motion ¶ 진행중의 기차 a moving train ; a train in motion // 착착 진행하다 make steady progress ; progress steadily // 진행이 빠르다〔느리다〕 make rapid〔slow〕 progress // 순조롭게 진행하다 progress favorably // 의사를 진행시키다 filibuster 《미》 // 교섭이 진행중이다 Negotiations are going on〔in progress〕. // 일의 진행이 신속하다 The progress of the work is rapid. // 운동은 현재 진행중이다 The movement is now under way. // 일이 잘 진행되고 있다 The work is in full swing〔well advanced〕.
—계(係) a program director — 상황 the progress of 《the research》 — 신호 〖철도〗 a clear〔a proceed〕 signal —파 〖전기·공학〗 a traveling〔progress〕 wave —형 〖문법〗 the progressive form 의사 —계 a person charged with expediting the proceedings 《of a conference》; a steering committee ; [사회자] the master of ceremonies
진행주 a wet dishcloth
진허리 the hollow back of the waist ; the small of the back
진헌 進獻 presentation to the King —하다 present 《a thing》 to the King
—물 a tribute of respect to the King
진현 進見, 進現 —하다 enter the presence of the King ; present oneself at court
진형 陣形 battle formation ; battle array 공격 — offense disposition 방어 — defense disposition 전투 — battle formation
진혼 鎭魂 repose of the soul
—곡 requiem —제 a service for the repose of the deceased〔departed soul〕; [카톨릭] a requiem (mass)
진홍 眞紅 crimson ; scarlet ¶ 진홍의 crimson ; cardinal // 진홍색 옷을 입다 be robed in crimson
‡진화 進化 evolution (생물의) ; development (발달) —하다 evolve ; develop ¶ 진화하여 사람이 되다 evolve into man // 사람은 원숭이로부터 진화했다 Man has evolved from the ape.
—론 the theory〔doctrine〕 of evolution 〔descent〕; the evolution(ary) theory ; Darwinism —론자 an evolutionist ; a Darwinian 수렴 — convergent evolution 점변(漸變) — anamorphosis 정향 — orthogenesis
진화 鎭火 putting out a fire —하다 extinguish ; put out ; get〔bring〕 under control ¶ 불은 얼마 안 가서 진화되었다 The fire was soon extinguished〔brought under control〕.
진휼 賑恤 relief ; almsgiving —하다 relieve 《famine》
—금 alms
‡진흙 mud ; mire ; dirt ; [차진 흙] clay ¶ 진흙 덩어리 lumps of clay // 진흙 투성이의 muddy ; miry ; covered with mud // 진흙 구렁 a mudhole // 진흙에 빠지다 stick in the mud
진흙땅 a bog ; a morass ; morasses of mud ; a marsh ; marshy ground
진흙탕 (morasses of) mud ¶ 진흙탕이다 be muddy〔miry〕
진흥 振興 promotion ; development ; encouragement ; advancement —하다 develop ; grow ; [조성하다] promote ; advance ; forward ; encourage ¶ 애국심을 진흥하다 rouse patriotism // 무역을 진흥하다 promote〔stimulate〕 foreign trade // 산업의 진흥을 꾀하다 promote the development of industry
—책 measures for the promotion 〔advancement, furtherance〕《of》 경제 — 계획 a program of economic buildup 대한 무역 — 공사 the Korea Trade Promotion Corporation 《KOTRA》
질 potter's clay ; unglazed clay
-질 (the act of) doing ¶ 양치질 rinsing the mouth // 톱질 sawing
질 帙 [책갑] a folding case for books ; a book-wrapper
질 膣 the vagina ; the vaginal canal
—경(鏡) a vaginal speculum ; a colposcope —관〔막〕 〖동물〗 a vaginal canal 〔tunic〕 —구〔벽, 부〕 the vaginal opening〔wall, region〕 —염 vaginitis ; colpitis
†질 質 [품질] quality ; stuff ; [소질] nature ; [성격] character ; [기질] temperament ; fiber ¶ 질적인 qualitative // 질적으로 qualitatively // 질이 좋은 석탄 coal of excellent quality // 양보다 질 quality before quantity // 질이 좋다〔나쁘다〕 be of good〔poor〕 quality // 질을 향상시키다 raise the quality of // 질을 떨어뜨리다

debase the quality of // 양보다 질이 중요하다 Quality matters more than quantity. // 담배 질이 떨어져 간다 The quality of tobacco is declining.

질겁하다 be appalled ; be astounded ; be frightened ; be scared ; start ; take fright ; be surprised ; be startled ; be taken aback ¶ 질겁할 일 a surprising〔an amazing〕event // 그것을 듣고〔보고〕질겁을 하다 be surprised at the news〔sight〕// 질겁해서 소리를 지르다 cry out in consternation // 도둑이 개 짖는 소리에 질겁해서 달아났다 The burglar was frightened away by the barking of the dog.

질겅질겅 ¶ 질겅질겅 씹다 chew ; gnaw ; masticate

질경이 〖식물〗 a plantain

질곡 桎梏 fetters ; bonds ; a yoke ; shackles ¶ 질곡에서 벗어나다 shake off fetters ; break the fetters 《of》; cast〔fling, throw〕off the yoke // 구습의 질곡에서 벗어나다 set oneself free from the fetters of old conventions

질구 疾驅 —하다 ride fast ; drive 《a horse》 fast

질권 質權 the right of pledge ¶ 질권을 설정하다 establish the right of pledge
— 설정자 a pledger〔pledgor〕; a mortgager **—자** a mortgage creditor ; a pledgee ; a pawnee ; a mortgagee

질그릇 unglazed earthenware ; clayware

질근질근 [꼬는 모양] (weave a string or rope) slowly ; leisurely ; idly ; [씹는 모양] chewing ; gnawing

질금거리다, 찔금거리다 trickle ; dribble ; fall off and on ¶ 걸핏하면 눈물을 질금거리다 be maudlin

질금질금, 찔끔찔끔 dribbling, oozily ¶ 질금질금 나오다 [고름따위] ooze out ; be oozy

질급 窒急 —하다 be appalled ⇨ 질겁하다

질긋이 ① [참는 모양] patiently ; forbearingly ; with patience〔forbearance〕; perseveringly ; without letup ¶ 치통을 질긋이 참다 bear the toothache patiently〔with stoical resignation〕
② [슬그머니] (pulling) gently ; softly ¶ 소매를 질긋이 잡아 당기다 tug gently at 《a person's》 sleeve

질기다 [물건이] (be) tough ; durable ; lasting ; rigid ; [성질이] tenacious ; persisting ; tough ¶ 질긴 고기 tough meat // 질긴 옷감 durable cloth // 성질이 질기다 be tenacious by nature // 이런 옷감은 질기지 않다 This kind of cloth does not wear long. // 스테이크가 질기다 The steak is tough.

질기둥이 [물건] tough material ; [사람] man of tenacity ; a tough fellow

질기와 an unglazed roof tile

질깃질깃, 찔깃찔깃 —하다 (be) pertinacious ; tough ; tenacious

질깃하다 (be) rather〔somewhat〕tough

질끈 tying tight ; firmly ¶ 질끈 동여매다 bind〔tie〕《a thing》 tightly // 수건을 머리에 질끈 동여매다 wear〔tie〕a towel around one's head tightly

질나발 —喇叭 an earthen trumpet

질냄비 an earthen pot ; a casserole ¶ 질냄비로 콩을 볶다 parch〔roast〕beans in an earthen pot

질녀 姪女 a niece

질다 [반죽이] (be) soft ; watery ; [땅이] muddy ; slushy ; wet ¶ 진길 a muddy road // 밥이 너무 질다 The rice has come out too soft.

질동이 a clay〔an earthen〕jar

질둔 質鈍 [투미함] clumsiness ; stolidity
—하다 (be) clumsy ; stolid ; dull

질뚝배기 a large earthen〔clay〕bowl

질량 質量 mass ; quantity of matter ¶ 질량불변의 법칙 the law of the constancy of mass // 질량을 측정하다 gauge mass
— 단위 a mass unit (원자의) **— 분석기** a mass spectrometer〔spectrograph〕**— 불변의 원칙** the law of constancy〔conservation〕of mass **—수(數)** mass number **—차(差)** mass defect

질러가다 take a shortcut ; take a shorter way ; cut across 《a field》 ¶ 질러가는 길 a shorter road ; a shortcut // 질러가다 go by a shortcut

질러먹다 eat food before it is well cooked

질러오다 come by a shortcut

질레 〖양재〗 gilet (프) ; a vest ; a dickey

질료 質料 〖철학〗 substance ; matter ; material

질름거리다, 찔름거리다 [넘치다] brim over ; flow over the brim ; [조금씩 주다] give bit by bit〔little by little〕¶ 질름 질름〔찔름찔름〕little by little ; bit by bit ; (by) piecemeal ; in small doses〔quantities〕

질리다¹ [채이다] be〔get〕kicked ; get hit ; be struck ¶ 정강이를 질리다 be kicked in the shin // 옆구리를 질리다 get a kick on the side

질리다² ① [진력나다] become disgusted with ; get sick of ; become fed up with ¶ 이 일에는 질렸다 I am fed up with this work. // 날마다 국수만 먹는 데 질렸다 I am sick and tired of eating noodles everyday. // 길고 피곤한 출퇴근에 질렸다 The long and tiring commute is getting to me. // 겨울산에 질렸다 I've had enough of the mountains in winter.
② [파랗게] turn pale ; lose〔change〕color ¶ 무서워서 파랗게 질리다 be white with fear // 노여워서 파랗게 질리다 be white with rage // 얼굴빛이 새파랗게 질리다 one's face goes ashy pale // 무서워서 새파랗게 질렸다 She turned white〔pale〕with fear.
③ [기가] cower ; be cowed ; be over-

awed ¶ 그는 아버지 앞에서는 기가 질려서 말 한 마디 못한다 When his father is present, he loses his nerve and cannot say a word.
④ [물감이] dye unevenly ¶ 옷감에 물이 질리다 A cloth gets dyed unevenly.
⑤ [값이 먹히다] take ; cost ¶ 이 책은 100원이 질렸다 This book cost me 100 *won.*

†**질문 質問** a question ; a query ; an inquiry ; an interrogation ; an interpellation (의회에서 장관에게) **—하다** ask ⟪a person⟫ a question ; put a question to ⟪a person⟫ ; question ; interrogate ¶ 질문의 연발 a barrage of questions // 넘겨짚는 질문 a catch question ; a tricky question // 급소를 찌른 질문 a searching〔pertinent〕 question // 질문을 퍼붓다 rain questions ⟪on a person⟫ // 질문에 답하다 answer a question // 질문을 종결하다 bring interpellation to a close // 질문 공세를 받다 be piled〔flooded〕 with questions // 그는 나에게 질문을 했다 He asked me a question. /He asked a question of me. **—서** a written inquiry ; an interrogation ; a questionnaire ⟪프⟫ (조사용의) **—자** a questioner ; an interrogator ; interpellator (국회에서의) **—전** interpellations **— 조사** [정보 입수를 위한] (a) debriefing ; [통계 조사를 위한] questionnairing **축조 —** article by article interpellation

질물 質物 a pawn ; a pledge

질박 質樸, 質朴 simplicity ; plainness **—하다** (be) simple (and unadorned) ; plain ; simple and honest ; homely ; unsophisticated ¶ 질박한 미풍 a laudable habit of simplicity // 질박한 풍습 simple manners // 질박한 촌사람 a simple〔simpleminded〕 villager ⇨ 소박하다

질벅거리다 (be) wet and soft ; muddy ¶ 길이 매우 질벅거렸다 It was a very muddy walk. ⇨ 질척하다 (질벅거리다)

질번질번하다 (be) abundant ; plentiful ; rich ; wealthy ; affluent ¶ 질번질번하게 richly ; abundantly ; plentifully ; amply ; in affluence // 질번질번하게 살다 be well off ; live in clover

질병 —瓶 an unglazed earthenware bottle

질병 疾病 a disease ; a sickness ; a malady ; a disorder ¶ 소화기 계통의 질병 a disorder of the digestive system

질부 姪婦 the wife of a nephew

질빵 a shoulder-pack strap ; a backstrap ; a sling (총의) ¶ 질빵을 지다 have a backpack strapped across one's chest

질사 窒死 death from suffocation ⇨ 질식 **—하다** be suffocated to death

질산 窒酸 nitric acid

질색 窒塞 [몹시 싫음] disgust ; detestation ; abomination ; abhorrence ; dismay ; shock **—하다** disgust ; detest ; loathe ; abhor ; be appalled ; be shocked ¶ 아주 질색하는 것 one's pet aversion // 아부하는 사람은 질색이다 I loathe flattery. /I hate to be flattered. // 그의 무식에 질색했다 He showed an appalling ignorance. // 그런 짓은 질색이다 Such an act is abhorrent to my feelings. // 엉뚱한 값에 질색했다 I was shocked〔dismayed〕 at the exorbitant price. // 나는 단 것은 딱 질색이다 I don't care for sweets. // 전쟁은 질색이다 I want nothing more to do with war. // 더위는 질색이야 I can't stand hot weather.

질서 秩序 order ; system ; method ; regularity ¶ 질서 있는 orderly ; systematic ; methodical // 질서 없는 disorderly ; unsystematic ; unmethodical // 질서 정연하게 in good order ; in an orderly manner ; systematically // 질서를 유지하다 maintain〔observe, keep〕 order // 질서를 확립하다 establish order // 사회 질서를 문란하게 하다 disturb public order // 질서를 회복하다 restore order // 질서가 정연하다 be in perfect〔systematic〕 order ; be shipshape ; be in an apple pie order // 질서가 문란하다 be in disorder ; be out of order // 시내의 질서가 회복되었다 Order was restored to the city.

⁑**질소 窒素** nitrogen
— 가스 nitrogen gas **— 공업** nitrogen industry **— 비료** nitrogenous fertilizer 〔manure〕 **— 순환** the nitrogen cycle **— 전구** a nitro-filled lamp **— 포화(飽和)** nitrification **— 폭탄** a nitrogen bomb **— 화합물** a nitrogenous compound **공중 —** atmospheric〔air〕 nitrogen **과산화 —** nitrogen proxide **산화 —** nitric oxide **석회 —** nitrolime〔calcium cyanamide〕 **아산화 —** nitrous oxide

질솥 an earthenware kettle

질시 嫉視 jealousy ; regarding with jealousy〔dislike〕 ; jealous looks **—하다** look on ⟪a person⟫ with dislike ; regard ⟪a person⟫ with jealousy ; keep a jealous eye ⟪on⟫ ¶ 질시를 받다 be regarded with jealousy

⁑**질식 窒息** suffocation ; asphyxiation **—하다** be suffocated ; be choked ; be smothered ¶ 질식시키다 suffocate ; asphyxiate ; choke ; stifle ; smother // 질식하여 죽다 be suffocated to death ; die from suffocation
— 가스 asphyxiating gas ; [탄갱내의] blackdamp ; chokedamp **—사(死)** death from〔by〕 suffocation ¶ 질식사하다 die from suffocation ; choke to death

질실 質實 simplicity and sincerity **—하다** (be) simple and sincere〔honest〕

질역 疾疫 an epidemic ; a plague

질염 膣炎 〚의학〛 vaginitis

질의 質疑 a question ; an interrogation ; an inquiry **—하다** question ; inquire of ; interrogate ¶ 질의 응답 후에 의안이 표결에 붙여졌다 After questions and answers the bill was put to the vote.

— 응답 question and answer — 응답란 the "Answers to Questions" column — 응답 시간 a question period 대정부 — an interpellation

질의 質議 debate ; discussion ; argument — 하다 discuss ; debate ; argue

질의 연설 質疑演說 [국회에서] an interpellation ¶ 질의 연설을 하다 address an interpellation

질적 質的 qualitative ¶ 질적으로 qualitatively // 질적으로 양적으로 quantitatively as well as qualitatively ; both in quality and in quantity

†질주 疾走 speeding ; running rapidly ; a scamper ; a scud — 하다 run fast〔at full speed〕; speed (away) ; scamper ; scud ¶ 질주하는 자동차 a speeding motorcar // 맹렬한 속도로 질주하다 run at a breakneck speed ; ride held for leather

*질질 ① [끄는 모양] trailingly ; draggingly ② [흐르는 모양] dribbling ; oozing ¶ 질질 끄는 병 a long illness ; a protracted disease // 질질 끌다 drag ; draggle ; [미루다] prolong ; protract ; drag on // 기름이 질질 흐르다 ooze oil // 치마를 질질 끌며 걷다 walk with a trailing skirt // 오줌을 질질 싸다 dribble urine // 재판이 질질 끌었다 The trial dragged on〔along〕. // 손질을 잘 해서 가구에 윤기가 질질 돈다 All the furniture glistens from constant care. // 전쟁이 질질 오래 끌었다 The war dragged on. // 그의 병이 오래도록 질질 끌었다 He was long in recovering from his illness.

질질거리다 roam around ; tramp ; gad about

질책 叱責 rebuke ; reproof ; reproach ; reprimand — 하다 reprove ; rebuke ; reprimand ; call 《a person》 to task 《for doing》; chide ; reproach ; scold ¶ 질책을 받다 be reproved ; be reprimanded ; be called to task ; receive a reprimand // 부주의를 질책하다 reproach〔reprimand, reprove〕 《a person》 for his carelessness

질책 帙册 books enclosed in a case ; a set of books

질척거리다 be muddy ; be miry ; [죽 모양으로] be mushy ; be soppy ; [눈이 녹아] be slushy ¶ 길이 몹시 질척거렸다 It was a very muddy walk.

질척질척 all soft and wet ; muddily ; sloppily ¶ 질척질척한 밥 rice boiled too soft // 질척질척해지다 become sloppy

질척하다 (be) wet and soft ; muddy ¶ 반죽이 질척하다 the dough is too wet and soft ; dough is too gooey // 길이 질척하여 우리는 간신히 목적지에 도착하였다 The roads were so muddy that we could reach our destination with great difficulty.

질커덕거리다 ⇨ 질컥거리다, 질척거리다

질컥하다 (be) muddy ; sloppy

질크러지다 get〔be〕 crushed in

질타 叱咤 scolding — 하다 scold ; give 《a person》 a scolding

질탕관 —湯罐 an earthenware pot

*질투 嫉妬 jealousy ; envy ; a green eye — 하다 be jealous ; regard 《a person》 with jealousy ¶ 질투가 많은 jealous ; envious ; green-eyed // 질투한 나머지 from jealousy ; out of envy // 질투에 눈이 어두워서 blinded by jealousy ; in a fit of jealous rage // 질투를 일으키다 feel jealous of ; become envious of // 질투를 품다 nurse jealousy against 《a person》 // 그 여자는 질투한 나머지 살인을 했다 Jealousy drove her to commit murder.

—심 jealousy ; envy ¶ 그것을 보고 울컥 질투심이 일어났다 Green envy filled her heart at the sight.

질퍼덕거리다, 질퍽거리다 squish and squash ; slosh away

질퍽 (be) muddy ; sloppy ¶ 길이 질퍽하다 The road is muddy.

질퍽질퍽 ⇨ 질퍼덕거리다

질펀하다 ① [넓다] (be) broad and level ; wide and flat ② [게으르다] (be) sluggish ; slovenly ; idle ③ [그득하다] (be) numerous ; immense ; enormous ¶ 질펀한 들 a broad expanse of fields // 방에 질펀하게 누워 있다 sprawl around the room // 질펀하게 게으름 피우다 be a sluggish idler ; be slothful // 질펀하게 누워서 세월을 보내다 live an idle life ; dawdle one's time away

*질풍 疾風 a rushing wind ; a gust ; a gale ; a hurricane ; a violent wind ; a squall ¶ 질풍같이 like the wind ; with lightning speed // 질풍같이 달아나다 flee on the wings of the wind

— 경초(勁草) a man who never yields his integrity even in adversity — 노도 the storm and stress ; Strum und Drang 《도》

질항아리 a clay (water-)jar

질호 疾呼 shout ; calling out — 하다 shout ; call out ; yell ; vociferate ¶ 대성질호하다 call out in a loud voice // 대성질호하며 격려하다 shout encouragement

질화물 窒化物 〖화학〗 a nitride

질환 疾患 a disease ; an ailment ; a trouble ; a disorder ; a malady ; a complaint ¶ 눈〔흉부〕의 질환 an eye〔a chest〕 trouble

질흙 [진흙] mud ; [차진 흙] clay ; potter's clay ; unglazed clay

†짊어지다 ① [짐을] bear ; carry 《a thing》 on the back ; shoulder ② [의무 따위] be charged with 《duty》; take 《a trust》 upon oneself ; owe 《a debt》; bear ; assume 《a responsibility》; incur 《debts》 ¶ 무거운 짐을 짊어지다 bear a heavy burden // 빚을 많이 짊어지다 be heavily in debt // 책임을 짊어지다 assume〔shoulder〕 a responsibility // 우리 청년들은 무거운 책임을 짊어지고 있다 A great responsibility rests upon us young men. // 나는 그 이상 책임을 짊어질

수 없다 I can not be saddled with any more responsibilities. // 그는 책임을 짊어지고 사직했다 He took the responsibility 〔blame〕 upon himself and resigned. // 그는 중요한 책임을 짊어졌다 He was charged with an important duty.

†**짐** a load ; a burden ; [뱃짐] a cargo ; [기차의] goods ; freight 《미》 ; [수화물] luggage ; baggage 《미》 ; [부담] a burden ; a charge ¶ 석탄 짐 a load of coal // 등에 진 짐 a pack on one's back // 짐을 싣다 load 《a cart》 // 짐을 부리다 unload 《a ship》 // 짐을 풀다 unpack 《a package》 // 짐이 과중하다 be overloaded // 짐을 가볍게 하다 lighten the load // 짐이 되다 be a burden to 《a person》 // 그 일은 나에게 너무 무거운 짐이다 The task is too heavy a burden to carry out. // 그 희소식이 마음의 짐을 벗겨주었다 The good news took a load off my mind. // 그것은 너의 짐을 무겁게 할 따름이다 It will only increase your burden. // 나는 자전거로 무거운 짐을 운반하다가 균형을 잃고 넘어졌다 I was carrying a heavy load on my bicycle, when I lost my balance and fell.

짐 朕 I ; Me ; We ; Us ; Our Royal Person

짐꾸리기 packing ; package ; pack ¶ 짐꾸리기가 쉽다〔어렵다〕 pack well〔badly〕 // 그는 짐꾸리기에 바쁘다 He is busy packing.

짐꾼 a porter ; a luggage porter ; a red cap (역의)

짐마차 —馬車 a cart ; a wag(g)on

짐바리 a load on the packsaddle ; a pack on a pack animal

짐받이 [트럭] a bed ; [자전거·오토바이의] a carrier

짐배 [화물선] a cargo boat ; a freighter ; [거룻배] a lighter ; a barge

짐수레 [손수레] a cart ; [짐마차] a wagon ; a dray ¶ 짐수레에 싣다 load a cart 《with goods》 // 짐수레를 끌다 draw a cart

짐스럽다 (be) burdensome ; cumbersome ; troublesome ¶ 짐스럽게 여기다 find 《it》 burdensome

†**짐승** a beast ; a brute (야수) ; an animal (동물)

짐자동차 —自動車 a (transport, delivery) truck ; a van ; a lorry

⁑**짐작** guess ; conjecture ; inference ; estimation ; [판단] judgment ; discretion **—하다** guess ; conjecture ; infer ; gather 《from》 ; judge ¶ 눈짐작 eye measure ; measure by eye // 손짐작 measuring roughly with one's hands // 내 짐작으로는 in my estimation〔imagination〕 // 내 짐작이 틀리지 않으면 if I guess right // 짐작이 가다 come to form an idea of // 짐작이 맞다 guess right ; be right in one's conjecture // 짐작에 맡기다 leave 《a matter》 to 《a person's》 conjecture // 짐작이 안가다 be unable to form any notion of // 짐작해서 해라 Do it at your own discretion. // 겉으로 보아 나이가 40이라고 짐작했다 Judging from his appearance, I guessed his age to be forty. // 말투로 짐작컨대 생계가 어려운 것 같다 I gather from his words that he is badly off. // 이제 대강은 짐작이 간다 Now I think I get the picture.

짐짐하다 [맛이] (be) salty and untasty ; tasteless ; [마음에] weigh on one's mind ; lie at one's heart ; get on one's nerves ; (be) nervous ; uncomfortable ¶ 시험이 언제나 짐짐하다 Examinations weigh on my mind at all time. // 그 사건에 관한 일이라면 좀더 짐짐하다 I don't feel very good about the whole affair.

짐짓 purposely ; on purpose ; deliberately ; intentionally ; by design ¶ 짐짓 냉정한 태도를 취하다 deliberately assume an indifferent attitude // 그는 짐짓 못 알아듣는 체했다 He would not understand me. // 그는 짐짓 모르는 체했다 He affected ignorance.

짐짝 a package ; a pack ; a parcel ; an item of freight〔baggage〕

짐차 —車 [기차] a goods wagon〔van〕 ; a freight car ; a truck (자동차)

†**집¹** ① [사람의] a house ; residence ; a dwelling(-house) ; a home

> 참고 **house**는 「가옥」 **home**은 「가정」 **residence**는 법률 용어, 훌륭한 「저택」의 뜻으로 사용된다 **dwelling-house**는 「살림집」이라는 뜻임

¶ 넓은〔좁은〕 집 a large〔small〕 house // 붉은 지붕의 집 a red-roofed house ; a house with a red roof // 석조 집 a stone house ; a house built〔made〕 of stone // 쓰러져가는 집 a house ready to tumble down // 집 없는 사람들 houseless〔homeless〕 people // 집안에서 in the house ; within doors // 집에 있다 stay〔be〕 at home // 집을 세내다 rent a house // 집을 짓다 have a house built (남으로 하여금) ; build a house (자기 손으로) // 집까지 바래다주다 walk 《a person》 home // 밤 10시까지는 집에 들어와야 한다 I want you home by 10 p.m. // 나 혼자 집에 있어요 I'm home alone. // 우리가 휴가 가 있는 동안 집 좀 봐주시겠습니까 Could you house-sit for us while we are gone on vacation? // 그는 내가 2년 전에 우리집을 팔아 달라고 부탁했던 부동산 중개인이다 He is my real estate broker whom I listed my house with a couple of years ago.

② [가족·가정] a home ; a family ; a household ¶ 큰집 the main branch of a family // 집을 비우다 be〔stay〕 out ; be away from home // 집 생각이 나다 get homesick ; think of home // 부잣집에 태어나다 be born rich ; be born with a silver

spoon in the mouth // 집안 일을 처리하다 manage one's family affairs
③ [동물의] a nest ; a home ; a lie ¶ 개집 a kennel // 거미집 a cobweb // 벌집 a beehive // 새집 a nest ; a bird's-nest
④ [물건의] a case ; a box ; a protector ¶ 두꺼비집 a fuse box // 벼룻집 an ink-stone box // 아기집 a womb // 칼집 a sheath ; a scabbard
⑤ [바둑의] a cross
집과 계집은 가꾸기 탓 [속담] A good husband makes a good wife. /A good Jack makes a good Jill.

집² one's spouse 《wife or husband》 ; [첩] a concubine ; a kept mistress ¶ 전줏집 one's concubine from〔in〕 *Chonju* // 우리 집 사람은 유치원의 보모다 My wife is a kindergarten〔nursery-school〕 teacher.

집³ juice ⇨ 즙

-집 集 collections 《of writings》
단편— collected short stories **서간—** a collection of letters ; collected letters **수필—** a collection of essays

집 輯 a series ¶ 제1 집 the first series

가시다 [민속] purify a house of evil spirits (after a funeral)

***집게** tongs ; tweezers ; forceps ; nippers ; pliers ¶ 집게로 집다 pick up with nippers // 집게로 못을 뽑다 pull a nail out with pliers
부— fire tongs

***집게발** claws (of crustaceans) ; pincers ¶ 집게발로 집다 nip with its claws (게가)

집게벌레 an earwig

집게뼘 the length between extended thumb and index finger

***집게손가락** the index finger ; the forefinger ; the first finger

집결 集結 concentration ; collection ; assembly **—하다** concentrate ; gather ; collect ; mass ¶ 병력의 집결 a troop concentration // 병력을 집결하다 build up troops ; rally forces // 국경에 많은 비행기를 집결하다 concentrate many planes along the border
—소 a concentration center **—점** a concentration point **부대 —지** 〖군사〗 an assembly area〔place〕 ; [출동을 위한] a staging area ; a rendezvous

집계 集計 a total **—하다** add〔sum〕 up ; total ¶ 집계를 내다 find the total of ; total
— 개념 〖경제·통계〗 an aggregate concept **—표** a tabulation ; a summary sheet

집광기 集光器 〖광학〗 a condenser

집괭이 a domestic〔pet, house〕 cat

집괴 集塊 a mass ; a cluster

집구석 within〔around〕 the house ; indoors ¶ 집구석에 박혀 있다 stay〔keep〕 indoors ; keep to the house ; be stuck indoors

집권 執權 grasping political power ; seizure of political power ; coming into power **—하다** come into power ; hold

집

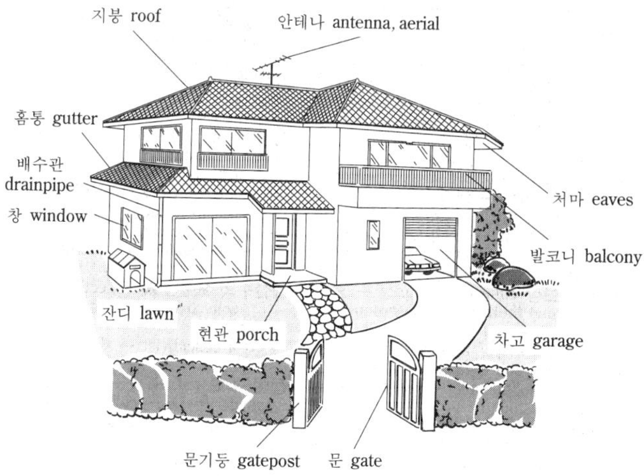

the reins of power ; take the helm of state affairs
—당(黨) the party in power
집권 集權 centralization of power〔authority〕 —하다 centralize the power
중앙 — centralization of power ; centralized authoritarian rule ¶ 중앙 집권 제도 centralized administration
집금 集金 collection of money ; bill collecting —하다 collect money〔bills〕 ⇨ 수금(收金)
집기 什器 ⇨집물 ¶ 사무용 집기 office fixtures
집나다 ① a house is put on sale ② [바둑] a nest is formed ; a square is made
집내다 ① empty〔vacate, clear〕 a house ; put a house on sale ② [바둑] form a nest ; make a square
집념 執念 concentration of one's attention ; tenacity of purpose —하다 concentrate one's mind ; keep one's mind on ; be intent upon ; devote one's attention to ¶ 연구에 집념하라 Control your attention and concentrate it upon your research.
*집다 pick up ; take up ; [가리키다] point 《at》; [집어먹다] eat ¶ 집게로 집다 pick up with tongs // 길에 떨어진 돈을 집다 pick up a coin on the street // 안주를 집다 eat side dishes
†집단 集團 a group ; a mass ; a collective body ¶ 집단적으로 collectively ; as a group // 집단화하다 collectivize // 집단을 이루다 form a group
— 강도 organized burglary ; a gang of burglars〔robbers〕 — 검거 mass arrest ; wholesale arrest ; a rounding up 《구》 — 결근 mass〔collective〕 absenteeism — 결혼 a group marriage — 경기 〖체조〗 a mass game — 경영 community management — 노동〔사업〕 group work — 농장 a collective farm ; [구소련의] a kolkhoz 《*pl.* -zy, -zes》; [이스라엘의] a kibbutz 《*pl.* -zim》 — 대표제 group representation — 발생 a mass outbreak 《of dysentery》 — 보험 group insurance — 살인 multiple murder — 생활 collective life ; group life ; living〔life〕 in a group ; [생태] aggregation — 소개(疏開) group 〔mass, collective〕 evacuation — 심리 mass〔group〕 psychology ; herd instinct — 안전 보장 collective security — 요법 〖심리〗 group therapy — 의식 group consciousness — 이민 mass〔collective〕 emigration — 자살 a suicide pact — 자위 collective self-defense — 주택 group houses ; row houses — 중독 mass 《food》 poisoning — 지도 collective 〔group〕 guidance〔leadership〕 ¶ 집단 지도 체제 a collective leadership system — 토론 group discussion — 폭행 mob violence —화 collectivization
집달관 執達官 a bailiff ; a process-server
집대성 集大成 achieving a synthesis ; integration into a greater whole ; summation —하다 make a synthesis of ; be comprehensive of ; embrace ; sum up ; integrate
집도 執刀 performance of a surgical operation —하다 perform a surgical operation ¶ 수술은 김 박사 집도로 행하여졌다 The operation was performed by Dr. *Kim.*
집돼지 a (barnyard) pig
집들이 a housewarming (party) ¶ 집들이를 하다 give a housewarming (party)
집록 集錄 compilation of various data ; a collection 《of one's writings》 —하다 compile various data ; collect
집류 執留 confiscation of an embezzler's properties —하다 confiscate (an embezzler's properties)
집무 執務 the performance of one's official duties ; execution of one's business —하다 work ; attend to one's business ; conduct business ; beat one's business ; conduct business ; beat one's desk ¶ 집무 시간 후 out of〔after〕 office hours // 집무의 경험 experience in office routine // 집무 중이다 be at one's desk ; be on duty // 집무에 다망하다 be pressed by business
— 시간 office〔business, working〕 hours
— 요령 a guide to office routine
집문서 —文書 a house deed ; deed papers ; a title deed ¶ 집문서를 잡히고 돈을 빌리다 loan money with the deed for security
집물 什物 household furniture and utensils ; miscellaneous household goods
집배 集配 collection and delivery —하다 collect and deliver ¶ 편지 집배인 a postman ; a mailman
집비둘기 a dove ; a house〔domestic〕 pigeon
집뼘 ⇨ 집게뼘
*집사 執事 a steward ; a manager ; [교회의] a deacon ; a deaconess (여자)
집산 集散 reception〔gathering〕 and distribution —하다 receive〔collect, gather〕 and distribute
—지 a collecting〔receiving〕 and distributing center ; a trading center ; an entrepôt 《프》
집산주의 集産主義 collectivism ¶ 집산주의의 collectivistic // 집산주의화하다 collectivize
—자 a collectivist — 제도 the collectivist system
집성 集成 gathering together into a systematic whole ; collection ; compilation —하다 gather and form into ; compile ; collect
‡집세 —貰 a rent ; a house-rent ¶ 비싼〔싼〕 집세 a high〔low〕 rent // 밀린 집세 back rent ; arrears of rent // 집세를 내다

pay 《a sum》 in rent ; pay for the house // 집세를 올리다〔내리다〕 raise〔lower〕 the rent // 집세를 안받고 집을 빌려주다 let a house rent-free

*집시 a gypsy 《미》 ; a gipsy 《영》
—족 the Gypsies

집심 執心 devotion ; attachment —하다 be devoted 《to》 ; be attached 《to》

집안 ① [가족·친척] a family ; a household ; a home ; one's relatives〔kin〕 ¶ 온 집안 the whole family ; all the family // 집안만이 아는 비밀 a secret known only within the family circle // 집안의 큰일 a matter of concern to the family // 그의 집안은 좋은 집안이다 He is from a well-known family. // 그는 집안도 좋고 교양도 있다 He is well-born and well-bred. // 집안의 수치를 밖에 드러내지 마라 Wash your dirty linen at home. // 그는 어느 집안 사람이냐 Of what family is he sprung? // 지금은 집안의 귀천을 따지는 시대가 아니다 We live in an age when birth and extraction are of little〔no〕 account. ② [집 속] the inside〔interior〕 of a house ¶ 집안의 공기 the indoor air // 집안에서 기른 house-broken // 집안을 치우다 clean the house up // 집안에 틀어박히다 remain indoors
— 싸움 a domestic quarrel ; a family squabble〔trouble〕 — 식구 a household ; a family —일 housework

집안 사람 my wife

집안 심부름 domestic chores ; errands around the house —하다 do domestic chores ; see to domestic affairs ; do errands around the house

집알이 a courtesy visit to a newly-moved family —하다 make the first visit on 《a person's》 new house ; visit 《a person's》 new house for the first time.

집약 集約 —하다 integrate ; be intensive ¶ 집약적 intensive // 집약적 방법 an intensive method
— 농업〔어업〕 intensive agriculture 〔fishery〕

집어넣다 ① ⇨ 넣다 ② [투옥] throw 《a person》 into prison ; imprison ¶ 가방에 서류를 집어넣다 stuff the documents into a briefcase // 도둑놈을 감옥에 집어넣다 throw a thief into prison ; put a thief in jail

집어등 集魚燈 a fish-luring light

집어먹다 [음식을] eat with one's fingers ; pick up and eat ; [착복하다] pocket ; make off with ; swipe ; embezzle ; misappropriate ¶ 대금을 집어먹다 pocket 〔peculate〕 a large sum // 공금을 집어먹다 embezzle public money ; divert public money into one's own pocket // 그는 그 돈의 일부를 집어먹었다 Some of the money stuck to his fingers.

집어삼키다 [먹다] pick up and swallow ; drink in ; [가로채다] usurp ; make off with ; swipe ; embezzle ; appropriate unlawfully ; seize ¶ 한 입에 꿀꺽 집어삼키다 gulp down ; swallow at one gulp // 공금을 집어삼키다 embezzle public funds // 남의 재산을 집어삼키다 seize 《a person's》 property ; dispossess 《a person》 of his property

집어세다 [함부로 먹다] eat greedily 〔ravenously〕 ; eat up ; [닦달하다] urge ; reproach ; carp at ; [남의 것을] embezzle ; usurp ; make off with ; swipe ¶ 순식간에 국수 세 그릇을 집어세다 devour three bowls of noodles in a moment // 대수롭지 않은 실수를 집어세다 carp at minor errors // 친구의 돈을 집어세다 make off with a friend's money

집어주다 ① [물건을] pass ; reach ¶ 설탕 좀 집어주세요 Pass the sugar please. // 연필 좀 집어주시오 Please, reach me the pencil. ② [뇌물을] offer a bribe ; bribe 〔corrupt〕 《a person for》 ¶ 집어주고 입을 막다 bribe 《a person》 into secrecy // 집어주고 매수하다 buy off 《a person》 // 집어주고 응낙받다 bribe 《a person's》 compliance // 그는 관리에게 집어주고 그것을 시켰다 He bribed the officials into doing it.

집어치우다 [중지하다] stop 《doing》 ; cease 《to do, doing》 ; discontinue ; leave off ; bring a matter to an end ; [단념하다] give up ; abandon ; [사직하다] resign ; quit ¶ 일을 집어치우다 lay aside one's work ; leave off one's work // 완전히 집어치우다 bring to a full stop // 이야기를 집어치우다 leave off talking ; drop the subject // 싸움을 집어치우다 break up a fight // 공부를 집어치우다 give up one's studies // 노예 제도를 집어치우다 abolish slavery // 회사를 집어치우다 leave 《the service of》 the company ; resign from office // 집어치워 Cut it out! // 제발 그 이야기 좀 그만 집어치워라 Will you please drop that subject? // 농담은 집어치우고 진짜 이유를 말해 봐라 Joking aside, what's the real story?

집어타다 take ; get on ⇨ 타다 ¶ 택시를 집어타다 take〔get〕 a taxi

집오리 a tame duck ; a barnyard duck ; a (domestic) duck ; a drake (수컷) ¶ 집오리가 운다 A duck quacks.

집요 執拗 obstinacy ; persistence ; pertinacity ; tenacity —하다 (be) obstinate ; stubborn ; persistent ; tenacious ¶ 집요하게 stubbornly ; obstinately ; tenaciously ; persistently // 집요한 반항 stubborn resistance // 집요한 질문 inveterate〔tenacious〕 questions // 집요하게 돈을 재촉하다 make an importunate demand for payment

집음기 集音機 a parabolic reflector

집장사 ¶ 집장사의 집 a ready-built house // 집장사를 하다 sell ready-built houses

집적 集積 accumulation ; pile —하다 accumulate ; pile up ; conglomerate

*집적거리다 [참견하다] meddle 《with》; dabble; have a finger 《in》; poke one's nose 《into》; [건드리다] tease; make a nuisance of oneself; needle; provoke ¶ 남의 일에 집적거리다 meddle with 《a person's》 business; poke one's nose into 《a person's》 affairs // 개를 집적거리다 tease a dog // 사람을 집적거리다 needle〔provoke〕 a person

집적집적 ⇨ 집적거리다

집정 執政 governing; administration; [사람] an administrator; a ruler ─하다 hold the power of state; govern; administrate

집주 集註 a variorum edition

집주름 a house broker; a real estate agent; a rental agent

*집주인 ─主人 [임자] the owner of a house; a landlord〔landlady〕; [가장] the head of a family; the master of a house ¶ 이 집의 집주인은 누구요 Who owns this house? // 집주인이 세든 사람의 신세를 진다 The landlord is overshadowed by his tenant.

*집중 集中 concentration; convergence; centralization ─하다 concentrate 《one's attention》 upon〔on〕; centralize 《power》 upon; mass 《troops》; converge 《upon》; focus 《on》 ¶ 정력의 집중 concentration of energy // 주의를 집중하다 concentrate one's attention 《on》 // 그는 자기 일에 정신을 집중 못하는 사람이다 He can never concentrate upon his work.

─ 공격 a concentrated attack ─ 배제 decentralization; deconcentration ─ 안타 〖야구〗 a clouting spree; an avalanche〔a rally〕 of hits ─ 포화〔사격〕 a concentrated〔converging〕 fire ─ 폭격 saturation bombing 《on Hanoi》 《미》 ─ 하중(荷重) 〖전기·기계〗 concentrated load ─ 호우 a localized torrential downpour

집쥐 〖동물〗 the common house rat

집진기 集塵器 a dust collector

집집 every door; each and every house; house after house ¶ 집집이 from door to door; in every house; at every door // 국기가 집집이 걸려 있다 The national flag is flying at every house.

집착 執着, 執著 [애착] attachment; excessive fondness; [고집] tenacity; persistence ─하다 cling〔stick, hold fast〕 to; be attached to; be fond of ¶ 삶에의 집착 tenacity for life // 삶에 집착하다 cling to life // 구습에 집착하다 stick to old customs

─력 tenacity; pertinacity; adhesion ─심 [끈질김] tenacity of purpose; [애착심] attachment 《to, for》

집찰 集札 〖철도〗 collection of tickets

─ 계원 a ticket collector〔taker〕

집채 (the bulk of) a house ¶ 집채 같다 be as large as a house; be of great size 〔bulk〕 // 집채 같은 파도 a billow; a big 〔giant〕 wave // 집채 같은 황소 a bull about the size of a house; an enormous bull

집치레 ⇨ 집치장(治粧)

집치장 ─治粧 the interior decoration of a house ─하다 decorate (the interior of) a house; do the interior decorating ¶ 집치장이 좋다 be nicely decorated

집터 a house site; a lot ¶ 집터를 닦다 level a site for a house // 집터를 사다 buy a lot for a building

─서리 the spare space around a house 〔building〕

집토끼 a tame rabbit

집파리 a housefly

집필 執筆 writing ─하다 write; pen ¶ 잡지에 집필하다 write for a magazine

─료 payment for writing; remuneration for one's copy; copy money ─자 [저자] the author; the writer; [투고자] a contributor

집하 集荷 gathering of goods; goods gathered ─하다 gather goods; collect cargos

*집합 集合 gathering; collection; a gathering; a meeting; an assembly ─하다 gather; collect; assemble; meet; congregate ¶ 군대를 집합시키다 gather an army // 그들은 대광장에 집합했다 They assembled themselves in the plaza. // 우리는 그를 전송하기 위해 여기에 집합했다 We are assembled here to see him off. // 우리는 정거장에 집합하기로 되어 있다 We are to meet at the station.

─ 나팔 a muster call ─론 〖수학〗 the theory of sets; the set theory ─ 명령 a gathering cry ─ 명사 〖문법〗 a collective noun ─ 시간 the hour of meeting ¶ 집합 시간은 한시로 정해졌다 The time for our rendezvous was fixed for one o'clock. ─ 장소 a meeting〔assembly〕 place; a rendezvous ─점 〖기하〗 a concurrence ─체 an aggregate ─ 표상(表象) 〖사회〗 a collective representation 무한〔유한〕 ─ 〖수학〗 an infinite〔a finite〕 set

집합과 集合果 〖식물〗 a mutiple fruit; a syncarp

집해 集解 a collection of commentaries; a variorum edition

*집행 執行 execution; enforcement; performance ─하다 execute; carry out; enforce; perform; carry into effect; hold (거행하다) ¶ 직무를 집행하다 perform〔discharge〕 one's duties // 형을 집행하다 execute a sentence // 장례를 집행하다 hold a funeral // 공무원이 공무 집행과 관련하여 선물을 받는 것은 불법이다 It's illegal for a government official to accept a present in connection with conducting his official duty.

—관(官) an executor ; a bailiff — 기간 the term of execution — 기관 an executive organ〔body〕 — 기일 the date of〔fixed for〕 execution — 연기 영장 a reprieve — 영장〔명령〕 a writ〔an order〕 of execution — 위원회 an executive committee —자 an executor ; [회사 업무의] an executive 《미》 — 절차 execution procedure — 정지 suspension of executant — 처분 an execution measure — 판결 judgement of execution 강제 — compulsory execution 영장 — commitment 사형 —인 an executioner

집행 유예 執行猶豫 probation ; [일시적 연기] a stay of (an) execution ; respite ; [판결] a suspended sentence —하다 place 《a person》 on probation ; allow 《a person》 to go on probation ; [일시적으로] grant 《a person》 a stay of execution ¶ 집행 유예부 금고 1년형 a suspended jail sentence of one year // 징역 6개월 집행 유예 2년에 처하다 be sentenced to six months in jail with a two year stay of execution // 1년의 집행 유예중이다 He is on probation for a year.

집형 執刑 execution of a sentence —하다 execute a sentence

†집회 集會 a meeting ; an assembly ; a gathering ; a congregation —하다 meet together ; gather ; assemble ; congregate ¶ 집회의 자유 freedom of assembly —소 [집회 장소] a meeting〔gathering〕 place ; a (place of) rendezvous ; [회관] an assembly hall〔room〕 ; a clubhouse — 신고 a notice of an assembly — 참가자 a participant in a meeting ; a rallier (대집회의) 불법 — an unlawful assembly 옥〔야〕외 — an open-air meeting ; an out-of-door gathering

집히다 get picked up ; be held between one's fingers ; can be held in one's hand ¶ 바늘이 잘 집히지 않는다 The needle is hard to pick up.

짓 [행위] an act 《of behavior》 ; behavior ; conduct ; a motion ; a gesture ; a movement ¶ 손짓 a motion of the hand ; a wave ; a hand signal // 몸짓 a gesture ; gesticulation // 눈짓 a sign with the eyes ; a look ; an eye-sign ; a look ; an eye-signal ; eyeing // 나쁜 짓 bad conduct // 이게 무슨 짓이냐 Where are your manners? // 너 하는 짓은 밤낮 그 모양이다 Nothing you do ever amounts to anything. // 누구 짓인지 대강 안다 I have a rough idea who it could be.

짓거리 [흥에 겨운] an act〔a gesture〕 out of merriment ; [짓] an act ; a deed ; a doing

짓고땡이 ① ⇨ 지어땡이 ② [뜻대로 됨] a smooth going of a job

짓궂게 annoying(ly) ; insistent(ly) ; nagging

짓궂다 (be) ill-tempered ; ill-natured ; [공교롭다] unlucky ; unfortunate ; cursed ¶ 짓궂은 사람 an ill-natured person // 짓궂은 비 the cursed rain // 짓궂은 짓을 하다 be unkind to 《a person》 // 짓궂은 장난을 치다 carry a practical joke // 또 그 짓궂은 장난 전화다 It is one of those prank calls again.

짓나다 frolic ; cut a caper ; disport oneself

*짓누르다 weigh down ; press down ; [억누르다] put down ; [마음을] weigh heavily on 《one's mind》 ¶ 짓눌러 뭉개다 crush ; smash ; squash // 슬픔에 짓눌린 grief-stricken 《man》 // 전쟁의 쓰라림에 짓눌린 사람들 people weighed down by the war

짓다¹ ① [만들다] make ; manufacture ¶ 옷을 짓다 have a suit made // 구두를 짓다 make shoes (자기가) ; have one's shoes made (시켜서) // 그 옷은 어디에서 지었습니까 Where did you get your clothes made?

② [건조하다] build ; construct ; make ¶ 벽돌로 지은 집 a brick house ; a house built of brick // 집을 짓다 build 《oneself》 a house // 새가 집을 지었다 The bird built a nest. // 그 집은 태풍을 견디어 낼 수 있도록 지어져 있다 The house is constructed to resist typhoons. // 새로 지은 고층 건물이 관광 명소가 되었다고 들었습니다 I heard a newly-built high-rise building has become a tourist attraction.

③ [작성하다] write ; compose ; make ¶ 책을 짓다 write a book // 작문을 짓다 write a composition // 시를 짓다 compose a poem // 그는 자기가 지은 것이 아니라고 말했다 He denied the authorship. // 「우주비행사」라는 말은 누가 지었습니까? Who coined the word "astronaut"?

④ [밥을] boil ; cook ; prepare ; [약을] prepare ; compound 《medicines》 ; fill a prescription (처방에 의해서) ¶ 밥을 짓다 boil rice ; cook rice // 저녁을 짓다 prepare〔cook〕 supper // 약을 짓다 prepare medicine ; make up〔fill〕 a prescription (처방에 따라)

⑤ [열을] form ; make ; constitute ¶ 원을 지어 in a circle // 열을 지어 in a line〔row, queue〕 // 원을 짓다 form a circle // 열을 짓다 form a line〔queue〕 ; line up ; draw up

⑥ [재배·경작] cultivate ; grow ; raise ; farm ; rear ¶ 밭을 짓다 farm a field // 채소를 짓다 raise〔grow, cultivate〕 vegetables // 벼농사를 짓다 grow〔raise〕 rice ; till a rice-field // 보리 농사를 짓다 raise〔grow〕 barley

⑦ [죄를] commit ; be guilty 《of》 ¶ 죄를 짓다 commit a crime ; commit a sin (도덕상의 죄) // 그는 죄를 지었다 He is guilty of the crime. // 벌이 무서워서 죄를 짓지 않는 자가 많다 The fear of punishment deters many people from crime.

⑧ [표정 따위] show ; express ; look 《glad, sad》 ¶ 지은 웃음 a forced smile ; a smirk // 미소를 짓다 smile ; wear〔put forth〕 a smile // 눈물 짓다 be moved to tears ; one's eyes swim with tears // 슬픈 표정을 짓다 take on a sad look
⑨ [결말 따위] settle ; solve ; [사물이 주어] come to a settlement〔decision〕 ¶ 일의 결말을 짓다 settle〔wind up〕 a matter ; bring an affair to a conclusion // 양국간의 국경 문제는 원만히 해결 지어졌다 The problem about the boundary between the two countries has come to a peaceful settlement.
⑩ [허구] make up ; invent ; fabricate ¶ 지어낸 이야기 a made-up〔an invented〕 story ; an invention

짓다² [유산] miscarry ; abort ¶ 아기를 짓다 have a miscarriage

짓둥이 gesticulation ; behavior ; deportment ; conduct

짓마다 smash ; break to pieces ; beat hard ; crush ¶ 세간을 짓마다 smash up furniture // 그릇을 짓마다 smash plates to pieces // 사람을 주먹으로 짓마다 smash a person with one's fist

짓먹다 eat one's fill 《of》 ; eat a stomachfull

짓무찌르다 smash ; crush ; beat ; rout ¶ 적을 짓무찌르다 crush〔smash〕 the enemy

†**짓밟다** trample on〔down〕 ; tread down 《under foot》 ; overrun ; override ; devastate ; ravage ; lay a place waste (황폐) ; infringe on (침해) ¶ 꽃을 짓밟다 trample flowers down // 인권을 짓밟다 infringe〔trample〕 upon human rights // 적을 짓밟다 trample on an enemy // 국토를 짓밟다 override〔overrun〕 the country // 민의를 짓밟다 override the wishes of the people

짓밟히다 (be) downtrodden ; trampled 〔trod〕 underfoot ; trampled〔trod〕 down ; tramped under one's foot 〔feet〕 ; ridden over ; run over ¶ 짓밟혀 죽다 be trampled to death // 우리들의 권리는 짓밟힐 것이다 We shall have our rights trampled under foot.

짓부수다 batter ; crush (down) ⇨ 짓마다 ¶ 돌을 짓부수어 시멘트로 만들다 crush down stone into cement

짓씹다 chew thoroughly ; masticate ; crunch

***짓이기다** mash ; beat to a pulp ; knead to a mash ¶ 감자를 짓이기다 mash potatoes // 사람을 짓이기다 beat 《a person》 to a jelly // 진흙을 짓이기다 knead clay

짓적다 be ashamed 《of oneself》

짓짓이 every doings ; all conducts〔acts〕

짓찧다 [곡식 따위를] pound 《rice》 ; pulverize ; crush down ; [이마 따위를] strike ; hit ; knock ; bump 《one's head》 against 《the wall》 ¶ 고추를 절구에 짓찧다 pulverize red pepper in a mortar // 돌을 짓찧어서 시멘트를 만들다 crush down stone into cement

***징¹** [악기] a gong ¶ 징을 치다 strike a gong

†**징²** [구두의] a hobnail ; a clout nail ¶ 구두에 징을 박다 put〔get〕 heel and toe plates on one's shoes

징거두다 [바늘로] baste ; stitch slightly ; sew loosely〔with long stitches〕 ; [미리 준비하다] make advance preparation ; make arrangements ¶ 찢어진 바지 무릎을 징거두다 sew the ripped knees of trousers temporarily // 내일 할 일을 징거두다 make preparation for tomorrow's work

징건하다 (be) stodgy ; feel heavy on the stomach ¶ 음식이 너무 기름져서 속이 좀 징건하다 The dinner was so rich that I feel stuffy.

징걸이 a shoemaker's jack

징검다리 stepping stones 《across a stream》 ¶ 징검다리를 건너다 walk across over the stepping stones

징검징검 [꿰매는 모양] sewing loosely ; [걷는 모양] striding ; with long stride ¶ 징검징검 꿰매다 sew loosely // 징검징검 걷다 stride ; stalk ; walk with long steps

징경이 〖새〗 the osprey ; the fish hawk

징계 懲戒 disciplinary punishment ; discipline ; reprimand **—하다** punish ; reprimand ; discipline ; submit 《a person》 to disciplinary action ¶ 징계 처분을 받다 be submitted to a disciplinary measure // 그는 징계 처분을 받을 것이다 Disciplinary action will be taken against him.
— 동의 a motion for disciplinary measures 《against a person》 **— 면직** a disciplinary dismissal **— 위원(회)** a disciplinary committee **— 재판〔처벌〕** a disciplinary trial〔punishment〕 **— 조치** 《take》 a disciplinary measure **— 파면** a disciplinary dismissal〔disposition〕

징그다 tack ; baste ; sew loosely〔with long stitches〕

징그럽다 (be) crawly ; creepy ; repulsive ; odious ; hideous ¶ 징그러운 벌레 creepy insects // 징그러운 느낌 a creepy sensation // 징그러운 광경 a repulsive sight // 보기만 해도 징그럽다 The sight made me crawly. // 이런 징그러운 것을 어떻게 먹나 I would not eat odious stuff like this.

징글징글하다 ⇨ 징그럽다

징기스칸 요리 (a) Mongolian mutton barbecue

징두리 the foundation〔lower part〕 of a house

징모 徵募 recruiting ; enlistment ; levy **—하다** recruit ; enlist ; levy ; raise ¶ 강제 징모하다 press 《a person》 into service

징발 徵發 levy ; commandeering ; requisition **—하다** commandeer ; press into service ; requisition ; forage ; put〔bring〕《a thing》 under requisition ¶ 징발되다 be placed under requisition // 징발을 면하다 be exempted from requisition // 거마를 징발하다 press carriages and horses into service // 정부에서 자동차를 징발했다 The government commandeered motorcars 〔pressed motorcars into service〕.

—권 the right of requisition —대 a foraging party —령 a requisition order —법 the Requisition Law —병 a forager — 보상 compensation for commandeered properties —선 a requisitioned ship 식량 — requisition for provisions

징벌 懲罰 discipline ; punishment ; chastisement ; penalty —하다 punish ; discipline ; chastise ; penalize ; subject 《a person》 to discipline ¶ 징벌을 동의하다 make a motion for disciplinary measures 《against a person》

— 규정 a disciplinary provision — 동의 a motion for disciplinary measures 《against a person》 — 위원회 a disciplinary committee

*징병 徵兵 conscription ; enlistment ; recruitment ; levying ; draft(ing) ; (compulsory) military service —하다 draft ; conscript ¶ 징병을 면제받다 be exempted from military service // 징병을 기피하다 evade conscription ; evade the draft 《미》 ; escape military service // 징병 제도를 실시하다 establish a conscription system // 스위스에는 징병 제도가 없다 Conscription is not practiced in Switzerland.

— 검사 a physical examination for conscription —관 a conscription〔recruiting〕 officer ; a recruiter —구 a recruiting district — 기피 evasion of conscrip-tion ; evasion of the draft ; draft dodging〔evasion〕 — 기피자 a slacker 《미》 ; a draft dodger〔evader〕 《미》 — 면제 exemption from conscription〔military service〕 ; exemption from the draft 《미》 ; draft exemption — 연령 《be of》 draft age — 유예 draft deferment temporary exemption from conscription〔military service〕 — 적령 conscription〔military〕 age ; the draft age 《미》 — 제도 the conscription〔draft〕 system 선발 —제 [미국의] the selective service system 《S. S. S》

징세 徵稅 tax collection ; the levy of taxes —하다 collect taxes ; raise taxes ; levy 〔impose〕 taxes 《upon》

—관 a tax official〔collector〕 — 기구 a tax collection system — 목표 a tax collection goal 원천 — collection at source 〔of withholding tax〕

*징수 徵收 collection ; levy —하다 collect ; levy ; charge ; assess ; impose 《on》 (과하다) ¶ 세금을 징수하다 collect taxes // 부가 징수하다 levy additional 《taxes》 ; collect additional dues〔fees〕

— 가능 예상액 an estimated collectable amount —계 a collection unit —료 a collection fee —율 a tax collection rate —액 the collected amount 원천 — collection at the source ¶ 이렇게 많은 세금을 원천 징수당하다니 괴롭다 It hurts to have this much tax withheld.

징악 懲惡 reproval of vice ; chastisement〔punishment〕 for evil doers —하다 chastise vice ; punish the wicked

권선— reproval of vice and promotion of virtue ; encouraging good and punishing evil ; politic〔poetic〕 justice ¶ 권선 징악극 a morality play ; a moralizing〔didactic〕 drama // 권선 징악 소설 a didactic novel

징역 懲役 penal servitude ; imprisonment with hard labor —하다 serve in prison ; be in jail ¶ 징역가다 be sent to jail ; go to in jail // 2개월의 징역 선고를 받다 be sentenced to two month's imprisonment // 3년의 징역을 마치다 finish three years' prison term // 판사가 한 죄수에게 5년 징역형을 선고했다 The judge sentenced a convict to five years in prison.

무기 — penal servitude for life ; life imprisonment with hard labor ¶ 무기 징역수 a lifer ; a life timer 유기 — penal servitude for a definite term ¶ 유기 징역형 a sentence for imprisonment for a definite period〔term〕

징역살이 懲役— a prison life ; a life behind bars ; imprisonment —하다 serve time ; be doing penal servitude ; serve a sentence (of penal servitude)

징용 徵用 draft (for work) ; drafting ; commandeering ; requisition —하다 draft ; commandeer ; requisition ¶ 징용가다 be drafted

—권 the requisitioning power of the government —선 a requisitioned ship —자 draftees — 해제 derequisition

징잡이 a gong player

징장구 a gong and a drum

*징조 徵兆 symptoms ; an indication ; a foreboding ; an omen ¶ …의 징조가 있다 show signs of ; give indications of ; be ominous of ; forebode // …의 징조가 농후하다 There is every indication 《that》 // 전염병의 징조가 있다 There are signs of the prevalence of epidemics.

징집 徵集 [징모] levy ; enlistment ; recruitment ; [수집] collection ; gathering —하다 levy ; enlist ; recruit ; call up〔out〕 ; raise ; muster ; [수집하다] collect ; gather

— 기피 evasion of conscription ; draft dodging — 기피자 a slacker ; a draft dodger —령 orders for calling up〔out〕 — 면제 exemption from enlistment — 연기 postponement of enlistment — 유예 temporary draft exemption

징치 懲治 correction ; castigation ; discipline —하다 correct ; castigate ; discipline

징크스 jinx ¶ 징크스를 깨뜨리다 break〔smash〕the jinx
징크철판 —凸版〖인쇄〗a zinc relief
징크판 —版〖인쇄〗zinc plate
†**징후** 徵候 [병의] a symptom ; [일반적] a sign ; an indication ; a foretoken ; an omen ; a token

> 참고 **sign** 어떤 일이 일어날 것을 객관적으로 알 수 있는 징후 **omen** 특히 종교적·미신적인 면에서 보아 특이한 일 무엇인가 이상한 일이 일어날 것을 예시한다고 생각되는 것 **token** 어떤 성질이나 감정이 외부에 나타난 징후 **symptom** 병이나 혼란 따위가 외부에 나타난 징후

¶ 폭풍의 징후 an indication of a storm // 징후가 나타나다 show〔exhibit〕signs ; [병의] develop symptoms // 검은 구름은 비가 올 징후이다 A dark cloud is a sign of rain. // 그것은 감기의 징후이다 It is a symptom of cold.
—학 symptomology
†**짖다** [개가] bark ; bay (사냥개가) ; howl (늑대가) ; [까마귀] caw ; croak ¶ 짖는 소리 a bark ; a howl // 달을 보고 짖다 bark at〔against〕the moon (공연히 떠들다) // 낯선 사람 보고 짖다 bark at a stranger // 짖는 개는 물지 않는다 Barking dogs seldom bite. // 우리 집 개는 짖기는 잘하나 좀처럼 물지 않는다 Our dog's bark is worse than his bite. // 까마귀가 짖는다 A crow caws〔croaks〕.
†**짙다** [색채가] (be) dark ; deep ; rich ; [안개 따위가] dense ; thick ; [숲·머리털 따위가] thick ; [액체가] heavy ; rich ¶ 짙은 푸른 빛 a deep blue // 짙은 숲 a thick forest // 짙은 안개 thick fog // 짙은 머리털 thick hair // 짙게 하다 thicken ; deepen ; make strong // 차를 짙게 하다 make tea strong // 짙게 화장하다 powder one's face thick ; make up heavily // 무대에 서는 사람들은 왜 저렇게 짙은 화장을 하고 있는 거지 Why do people on the stage always put on such thick make-up ?
짙푸르다 (be) deep blue ¶ 짙푸른 호수 a sapphire lake // 짙푸른 옷을 입고 있다 be dressed in deep blue // 하늘은 짙푸르게 개어 있었다 The sky was clear and deep blue.
‡**짚** straw ¶ 짚을 묶다 tie up straw in sheaves // 짚을 깔다 spread straw ; litter down (외양간에) // 짚으로 만든 종이 straw paper // 짚으로 싸다 wrap up in straw // 짚을 넣은 요 a straw mattress ; a pallet ; a palliasse // 짚을 썬 여물 chaff // 짚으로 만든 인형 a straw man ; a man of straw
밀— wheat straw **벼—** rice straw **밀—모자** a straw hat
짚가리 a rick ; a stack of straw ¶ 짚가리를 쌓다 rick ; stack ; pile straw (sheaves) in a stack
짚나라미 shredded bits of straw
짚다 ① [맥 따위를] feel ; take ; examine ¶ 맥을 짚다 feel〔take, examine〕the pulse ; put fingers on the pulse // 열이 있나 이마를 짚어보다 feel one's forehead to see if one has fever
② [지팡이를] use ; carry ¶ 지팡이를 짚다 use a stick // 지팡이를 짚고 걷다 walk with a cane〔stick〕
③ [짐작하다] figure《out》; guess ; count on the fingers ¶ 달수를 짚다 count the months on one's fingers // 육갑을 짚다 count the sexagenary cycle on one's fingers
④ [손을 받치다] put ; rest ¶ 돗자리에 손을 짚다 put one's hands on the mat // 책상 위에 팔꿈치를 짚다 rest one's elbows on the desk
짚단 a sheaf of straw
짚둥우리 a straw basket
짚뭇 a bundle〔sheaf〕of straw
짚북더기 a scattered heap of straw
짚불 a straw fire ¶ 짚불을 피우다 make fire with straw
짚세공 straw work
짚수세미 a scrub brush made of straw ; a straw scrubber
짚신 straw sandals〔shoes〕¶ 짚신을 삼다 make straw sandals // 짚신을 신다 wear〔put on〕straw shoes // 짚신을 신고 in straw shoes ; with straw shoes on
짚신도 제날이 좋다 속담 Merry your like.
짚신장이 헌신 신는다 속담 None more bare〔worse shod〕than to shoemaker's wife and the smith's mare. /The shoemaker's son always goes barefoot.
헌 짚신도 짝이 있다 속담 Every Jack has his Jill.
짚신감발 wearing〔putting on〕one's foot-cloths and straw shoes ; equipping oneself for a walking trip **—하다** wear〔put on〕one's foot-cloths and straw shoes ; equip oneself for a walking trip
짚신나물〖식물〗an agrimony
짚신벌레〖동물〗a paramecium《*pl.* -cia》
짚여물 chopped straw ; chaff
짚이다 [마음에] (happen to) know of ; have in mind ¶ 짚이는 곳 a likely place // 짚이는 데가 없다 have no idea《of》
짚자리 a straw mat ¶ 짚자리를 짜다 weave a straw mat
짚재 ashes from burnt straw
짚절단기 chaffcutter
짚펄프 straw pulp
짜개 a piece of bean split in two
— 김치 a pickle dish made of cucumber cut into small pieces and salted without stuffing **— 황밤** split chestnuts **콩—** split beans〔peas〕
짜개다 split ⇨ 쪼개다
짜금짜금 chewing loudly with relish
짜깁기 invisible mending **—하다** mend《the trousers》invisibly

짜깁다 [짜깁기하다] mend invisibly ; [짜듯이 깁다] darn ¶ 양말을 짜깁다 darn socks ; stop socks from running

짜끔거리다 chew loudly (showing enjoyment of food) ; munch with relish ; smack one's lips (while eating)

***짜다**[1] ① [맛이] (be) salty ; briny ② [마음이] (be) unpleasant ; displeased ¶ 짠 맛 a salty taste // 짠 반찬 salted〔salty〕 foods // 마음이 짜다 feel unpleasant

***짜다**[2] ① [만들다] piece together ; put 《things》 together ; assemble ; construct ; make ¶ 책상을 짜다 make a table // 부분품을 완성품으로 짜 맞추다 assemble the parts into a complete unit ② [편성하다] form ; organize ; prepare ¶ 편을 짜다 make up a party ; form a faction // 영어반을 짜다 form an English class // 편을 짜서 놀다 play sides // 계획을 짜다 form a plan // 해가 바뀌자마자 즉시 계획을 짜 볼까 Shall we start planning something right after New Year's ?
③ [한통이 되다] unite 《with》 ; cooperate 《with》 ; enter into partnership ; collude 《with》 ¶ 남과 짜서 together with 《a person》 ; in league with 《a person》 ; in cahoot(s) // 남과 짜고 장사하다 associate with 《a person》 in business // 그들은 서로 짜고 공금을 횡령했다 They got together and embezzled public funds in cahoots.
④ [실·끈으로] weave ; spin ; knit ¶ 비단을 짜다 weave silk cloth // 털실로 양말을 짜다 knit stockings out of wool
⑤ [물기를] wring ; compress ; squeeze ; press ; rack ¶ 젖은 옷을 짜다 wring (out) wet clothes // 옷을 짜서 물을 빼다 squeeze water from the clothes // 우유를 짜다 milk a cow // 귤에서 즙을 짜다 press the juice out of an orange // 올리브에서 기름을 짜내다 press oil from olives // 여드름은 짜지 않는 것이 좋다 그것은 상처 자국을 남길거야 You had better not pop the pimple. It'll leave a scar.
⑥ [억지로] press out ; squeeze ; cudgel〔rack〕 one's brains ¶ 이 문제를 풀기 위해 머리를 짜내고 있는 중이다 I am now racking my brains to solve this problem.
⑦ [착취] exploit ; squeeze ; extort ; exact ¶ 돈을 짜내다 squeeze〔wring, extort〕 money out of 《a person》 // 한푼도 남김 없이 짜내다 bleed 《a person》 white // 빈민에게서 중세를 짜내다 squeeze the poor with heavy taxes
⑧ [눈물을] weep ; cry ; sob ¶ 그녀는 하루 종일 눈물을 짜고 지냈다 She did nothing but cry all day long. // 그 이야기는 모든 사람의 눈에서 눈물을 짜내게 했다 The story drew tears from all those present.

짜드락나다 be discovered〔detected〕 ; be found out ; be disclosed〔revealed, exposed〕

짜들다 be hardened 《by bitter experience》 ⇨ 찌들다

짜디짜다 (be) very〔pretty〕 salty

짜뜰름짜뜰름 piece by piece ; little by little

-짜리 ① [가치] worth ; value ¶ 만 원짜리 지폐 a 10,000 *won* bill ② [양] amount ¶ 삼십 파운드짜리 설탕 a thirty-pound bag of sugar ③ [입은 사람] a person wearing. . . ¶ 양복짜리 the fellow in the suit

짜릿하다 [맛이] (be) pungent ; piquant ; spicy [마음 따위가] tingling ; prickling ; aching ; smarting

짜부라지다 ⇨ 찌부러지다

짜이다 ① [규모·규격 등이] be in harmony〔keeping〕 with ; bear〔be in〕 proportion to ; match well ② [조직·이론 등이] get formed〔organized, framed, structured〕 ¶ 조직이 잘 짜이다 be well organized // 이론이 잘 짜이다 a theory is well framed〔nicely structured〕

짜임 [맞추어] being put〔pieced〕 together ; formation ; composition ; structure ; constitution ; assembly ; [부서의] system ; organization
—새 the make ; structure ; the way something is put together

짜증 ill humor ; (a hot, a quick, a short) temper ; irritability ; irascibility ; petulance ; grumbles ¶ 사소한 일에도 짜증을 잘 내는 성질 a hair-trigger temper // 짜증을 내다〔짜증이 나다〕 fret ; show temper ; be cross ; be peevish ; be vexed // 짜증이 나게 하다 offend ; ruffle ; ruffle 《a person's》 feathers ; irritate

짜하다 (be) widespread abroad ; well aired〔circulated〕 ¶ 그 소문이 짜하게 퍼졌다 The rumor spread like a wildfire.

짝[1] one of a pair〔couple〕 ; one of a set ; a partner ; a counterpart ¶ 양말 한 짝 an odd sock // 장갑 한 짝 an odd glove // 짝이 맞지 않는 신 an odd pair of shoes // 짝을 맞추다 pair ; make a pair of ; match // 내 구두 한 짝이 보이지 않는다 I cannot find the other shoe of mine. // 누구에게나 짝이 있는 법이다 Every Jack must have his Jill.

짝[2] [갈비의] a side of beef〔pork〕 ribs ; [곳·꼴] place ; shape ; look ¶ 아무짝에도 못 쓴다 It is no good anywhere. // 그게 무슨 짝이냐 What a shame it is !

짝[3] [소리] ripping ; tearing ; [여는 모양] wide open ¶ 편지를 짝 찢다 tear a letter // 문을 짝 열다 fling the door wide open

짝귀 ears which are not the same size ; [사람] a person who has one ear bigger than the other

짝눈 one's mismatched〔mismated〕 eyes ; one's eyes irregular〔different〕 in size
—이 a person whose eyes are different in size

짝맞다 match

짝맞추다 match ; make a pair of 《two things》

짝사랑 one-sided love ; unrequited love

—하다 love in vain ¶ 그의 사랑은 짝사랑이었다 His love was never returned〔was unreciprocated〕.

짝수 —數 an even number

짝신 an unmatched〔a mismated〕 pair of shoes ; wrongly paired shoes

짝없다 [비길 데 없다] (be) matchless ; incomparable ; [주책 없다] preposterous ; incongruous ¶ 짝없는 말 preposterous remarks // 기쁘기 짝없다 be happy beyond measure

짝자게 〖식물〗 a kind of lilac

짝자꿍 a baby's hand-clapping —하다 clap hands

짝자꿍이 ① [다툼] a clash ; a fight ; a commotion ; a scene —하다 clash〔fight〕 with each other ¶ 짝자꿍이 일다 raise a commotion ; make a scene ② [밀계] a secret scheme —하다 secretly scheme

짝자래나무 〖식물〗 a kind of buckthorn

*짝짓다 pair ; make a pair 《of》 ; match ; make a match ; mate ¶ 남녀를 짝지어 주다 mate a woman with a man // 새를 짝지어 주다 mate a bird // 춤추기 위해 이분들을 짝지어 주시오 Just pair those people for the dance. // 댄서들은 두 사람씩 짝지어졌다 The dancers were paired off.

짝짝 ① [입맛을] ¶ 그는 수프에 입맛을 짝짝 다셨다 He smacked his lips over the soup. ② [끈끈한 것이] ¶ 젖은 옷이 몸에 짝짝 달라붙는다 My wet clothing clings to my body. ③ [찢는 소리] ¶ 옷자락을 짝짝 찢다 rip up 《one's clothes》 // 종이를 짝짝 찢다 tear up paper into scraps〔pieces〕 ④ [신발을] ¶ 신발을 짝짝 끌다 drag one's shoes

짝짝거리다 smack one's lips ; lick one's chops ¶ 짝짝거리며 먹다 smack one's lips while eating ; eat with much gusto

짝짝이 an unmatched〔odd〕 pair ; a wrongly matched pair ¶ 짝짝이 양말을 신다 wear mismatched〔mismated〕 socks // 이 구두는 짝짝이다 These shoes are odd〔mismated, mismatched, wrongly paired〕. / These shoes do not make a pair.

짝채우다 make a set ; match ; mate ¶ 찻잔 하나를 사서 짝채우다 buy a teacup to match the set

짝패 (one's) mate〔partner〕 ; a pal

짝하다 become a partner ; partake ¶ 짝해서 in partnership 《with》 // 친구와 짝해서 장사하다 run a business in partnership with a friend

짠맛 a salty taste

짠물 salt water ; brine ; seawater

짠지 radish preserved with salt

짠하다 (be) bitterly regretful ; touching ; pitiful ; feel depressed〔sad〕

짤까닥 ① with a click〔snap〕 ② with a slap ¶ 짤까닥거리다 click〔snap〕 away ; give a snap〔click〕 ; slap and slap // 사진을 짤까닥 찍다 snap a picture // 자물쇠를 짤까닥 걸다 click the door shut // 뺨을 짤까닥 때리다 slap 《a person》 on the face

짤까당 with a click〔clang, chink, snap〕 —하다 click ; give a snap

짤깍 ⇨ 짤까닥

짤끔거리다 ⇨ 잘금거리다

짤끔짤끔 ① ¶ 물이 물 꼭지에서 짤끔짤끔 나왔다 The water trickled from the faucet. ② ⇨ 찔름찔름²

짤따랗다 (be) shortish ; rather short ; be on the short side

짤라뱅이 an undersized thing ; a shrunk article ; a dwarf ; a runt ; a midget ; a miniature

짤막짤막 ¶ 그는 짤막짤막하게 글을 썼다 He wrote choppy sentences. ⇨ 짤막하다

짤막하다 (be) shortish ; choppy ; be on the short side ¶ 짤막한 인사말 a brief address

짤짜리 blackless slippers ; scuffs

짤짤거리다 go around hurriedly ; dart about

짤짤이 a person who dashes about〔runs around〕 unceremoniously

짧게 short ; close ; briefly (간단히)

짧다 ① (be) short ; brief ; be of brief duration (기간이) ¶ 짧은 기간 a short (period of) time // 짧은 일생 a short span of life ; a brief life // 짧게 말하면 in short ; to be brief ; to make a long story short // 머리를 짧게 깎았다 I had my hair cut short. /I had a close crop. // 다섯자 짧다 be short by five feet // 손톱을 짧게 깎다 cut one's nails close // 짧게 하다 shorten ; make〔cut〕 short // 짧아지다 It shortens〔gets short〕. // 인생은 짧고 예술은 길다 Life is short, art is long. // 날이 점점 짧아져 간다 The days are getting shorter. // 이번 회의는 기간이 짧다 The present conference is of short duration. // 짧게 깎아 주세요 Short cut, please. ② [부족] (be) inadequate ; wanting ; short ; be not enough ; be short of ; be in want of ¶ 밑천이 짧다 be short of funds

짬 ① [겨를] leisure ; leisure time〔hours〕 ; free〔spare〕 time ; time to spare ¶ 짬짬히 at odd moments ; in one's spare moments // 짬이 있다 be free ; be not busy ; be at leisure // 짬이 없다 have no leisure ; have no time to spare // 짬만 있으면 낚시질을 했다 Every spare moment was spent in angling. ② [틈] crack ; interstice ; a crevice ; an opening

짬뽕 [뒤범벅] a mixture ; a medley ; [중국 음식] a Chinese-style hotchpotch cooked chiefly with noodles

짬짜미 a secret promise —하다 make a secret promise ; promise secretly

짭짤찮다 ① [점잖지 못하다] (be) unrefined ; coarse ; vulgar ; low ; indecent ;

gross ② [시원찮다] (be) worthless ; inferior ; poor
짭짤하다 (be) nice and salty ; have a good salty taste to it ¶ 짭짤한 고기 반찬 a nicely salted meat dish // 짭짤한 글 a pointed article // 짭짤한 사람 a man of salty humor
짭짭 licking one's chops ; smacking one's lips ¶ 짭짭 입맛을 다시다 lick one's chops ; smack one's lips // 짭짭거리며 먹다 smack one's lips while eating
짯짯하다 ① [성질이] (be) tough ; hard ; resistant ② [나뭇결 따위가] (be) crisp ③ [빛깔이] (be) crisp ; bright ; clean
짱알거리다 ⇨ 찡얼거리다
짱짱하다 (be) sturdy〔stout〕
-째[1] [차례·등급] ¶ 둘째 형 the second eldest brother // 첫째로 졸업하다 graduate at the head of one's class // 여기 온 것은 이번이 세번째다 This is the third time I have been here.
-째[2] [그대로] together〔along〕 with ; as it is ; inclusive of ¶ 사과를 껍질째 먹다 eat an apple, peel and all // 생선을 가시째 삼켜버리다 devour a fish, bones and all // 나무를 뿌리째 뽑다 pull up a tree by the roots // 그는 술을 병째로 마신다 He drinks out of a bottle.
***째다** ① [찢다·절개하다] tear 《up》 ; rip ; cut open ; cleave ; incise ¶ 종기를 째다 lance a boil // 칼로 주머니를 째다 cut one's pocket open with a knife
② [부족하다] (be) insufficient ; be short of ¶ 식량이 째다 run short of provisions // 손이 째다 be short of help〔hands〕 // 연료가 째기 시작하다 be running〔getting〕 out of fuel ; the fuel is running short
③ [작다] (be) tight ; firm ; too small ¶ 짼 모자 a tight hat // 신이 째다 one's shoes pinch // 이 옷은 너무 짼다 The suit is too tight for me. // 구두가 째서 아프다 I feel the pressure of the shoes on my feet.
째마리 [물건] rubbish ; scum ; trash ; junk ; dregs ; [사람] human waste〔debris〕 ; dregs of population ; dross of mankind ; a bum 《미》 ; the scum of society 《미》 ; a hobo
째보 [언청이] a harelipped person ; [경망한 자] a frivolous person ; a flattering fellow
째어지다 split ; tear ; rend ; burst ; rip ; cleave ; crack (금이 가다) ¶ 길게 째어진 눈 long slanted eyes // 둘로 째어지다 be split in two // 쉽게 째어지다 tear easily // 네 옷이 째어졌다 Your clothes are torn. // 깃발이 바람에 조각조각 째어졌다 The flag was torn to ribbons by the wind.
째푸리다 ⇨ 찌푸리다
짹소리 a chirp ; a tweet ⇨ 찍소리 **— 하다** give a chirp〔tweet〕
짹짹거리다 tweet ; twitter ; chirp
쨍 with a clink〔clank〕 ¶ 칼과 칼이 쨍 부딪쳤다 The swords clanked.
쨍그랑 with a clink〔clank, clang〕 **— 하다** clink ; clank ; clang ; give a clink〔clank〕
쨍그랑거리다 clink ; clank ; clash ; jingle
쨍그리다 ⇨ 찡그리다
쨍쨍 blazing(ly) ; bright(ly) ; glaring(ly) **— 하다** (be) bright ; blazing
쨍쨍거리다 mutter ; grumble ⇨ 찡찡거리다
쩌렁쩌렁하다 (be) resonant ; sonorous ; full and ringing ¶ 그의 목소리는 전화로 들어도 쩌렁쩌렁하다 He has a resonant voice even on the phone.
쩌르렁 with a clang〔ring, tinkle〕
쩌르렁쩌르렁 with clang after clang
쩌쩌 ① [혀 차는 소리] Tsk tsk tsk ! ② [소 몰 때] Haw !
-쩍다 feel ; have〔give〕 a feeling 《of》 ¶ 겸연쩍다 be abashed ; be bashful // 미심쩍다 be doubtful ; be suspicious // 미안쩍다 be embarrassed
쩍말없다 leave nothing to be said ; have nothing to complain 《of》 ; (be) perfect ; have nothing better
쩍쩍 ⇨ 짝짝 ① ②
쩍쩍거리다 smack one's lips ; lick one's chops ¶ (입을) 쩍쩍거리며 먹다 smack one's lips while eating
쩍하면 on the slightest movement ; easily ; with the slightest provocation
쩔거덩 ⇨ 짤까당
쩔그렁 ⇨ 절그렁
쩔뚝거리다 ⇨ 절뚝거리다
쩔쩔매다 be at one's wit's end ; be at a loss 《what to do》 ; be bewildered ; be confused ; be in a tight box ; do not know what to do ¶ 돈이 없어 쩔쩔매다 be hard up for money // 바빠서 쩔쩔매다 be pressed with business ; be snowed under with work // 상관에게 쩔쩔매다 be shaken up by one's superior // 그는 어떻게 해야 좋을지 몰라서 쩔쩔맸다 He was frightened out of his wits.
쩝쩝 ¶ 입맛을 쩝쩝 다시다 lick one's chops ; smack one's lips ; [못마땅할 때] click〔clack〕 one's tongue ⇨ 쩝쩝하다
쩝쩝거리다, 쩝쩝하다 lick one's chops ; smack one's lips ¶ 쩝쩝거리며 먹다 smack appreciative lips 《over〔on〕 a dish》
쩡쩡 ① [권세가] ¶ 그는 정계에서 쩡쩡 울리고 있다 He is gaining influence in the political world. ⇨ 쩡쩡거리다 ② [소리가] with a snap (튀기며) ; with a crack ¶ 얼음이 쩡쩡 갈라진다 The ice breaks with a crack.
쩡쩡거리다, 쩡쩡대다 be influential ; be powerful ; have great〔exercise one's〕 influence 《over, with, on》
쩡쩡하다 [소리가] flip ; snap ; crack (깨지며)

쩨쩨하다 [인색] (be) stingy ; niggardly ; miserly ; close-fisted ; tight-fisted ; parsimonious ; illiberal ; [다랍다] (be) low ; mean ; humble ; shabby ; poor ; [시시하다] (be) worthless ; valueless ; unworthy ¶ 쩨쩨한 사람 a miser ; a stingy person ; a niggard // 쩨쩨한 생각 a narrowminded idea ; a contracted idea // 쩨쩨한 소리 하지 말라 Don't be stingy. /Be liberal.

***쪼개다** split ; divide ; part 《a thing into》 ; cleave ; smash ¶ 나무를 쪼개다 split wood // 도끼로 장작을 쪼개다 chop wood with an ax // 둘로 쪼개다 cut〔divide〕 in two // 8을 4로 쪼개다 divide 8 by 4 // 그는 도끼로 통나무를 쪼갰다 He clove the log with an ax. // 이 과자를 셋으로 쪼개어 하나씩 나누자 Let's divide this cake into three and each take one piece.

쪼개지다 split ; break ; divide ; get split

쪼그랑박 a stunted gourd

쪼그랑할멈 a withered old woman

쪼그리다 crush ⇨ 쭈그리다

쪼글쪼글 ⇨ 쭈글쭈글

쪼다 [모이를] peck 《at》 ; pick up ; [돌 따위를] chisel ¶ 새가 콩을 쪼다 a bird pecks at beans // 징으로 돌을 쪼다 cut a stone with a chisel

쪼들리다 be troubled〔annoyed〕 ; be oppressed ; be straitened ; be in distressed condition ¶ 돈에 쪼들리다 be straitened〔pressed〕 for money // 일에 쪼들리다 be pressed with business // 빚에 쪼들리다 be harassed with debts

쪼아먹다 peck at and eat ; pick

쪽[1] [낭자] a chignon ¶ 쪽지다 do one's hair up in a chignon

쪽[2] [조각] a piece ; a slice ; a cut ¶ 빵 한 쪽 a slice of bread

쪽[3] [방향] a direction ; a side ; a way ¶ 동쪽 the east // 오른쪽 the right side // 이쪽 this way // 양쪽 both sides // 위쪽 the upper side // 우리쪽 our side // 길을 걸을 때는 왼쪽으로 가시오 Keep left when walking along the street. // 길을 건널 때는 양쪽을 잘 살펴라 Look both ways carefully before crossing the street.

쪽[4] [늘어선 모양] in a row ; in a line ¶ 쪽 고르다 be all of equal size ; be uniform〔equal〕 // 쪽 늘어서다 stand in a row

쪽[5] 〖식물〗 the indigo plant

쪽마루 a veranda of one or two floorboards〔planks〕

쪽매 parquetry-work ; parquet ¶ 쪽매 붙임하다 inlay parquet strips on (a base board) // 쪽매질하다 make〔decorate〕 (a wooden vessel) with parquet strips ; make (a parquet vessel)

쪽문 一門 a wicket

쪽박 a small gourd ; a gourd dipper

쪽반달 一半一 a kite with a colored crescent ornament on its top

쪽발이 a thing which has only one leg left ; a one-legged thing ; a cloven foot

쪽빛 indigo (blue) ; indigotin ; deep-violet blue

쪽소매 a desk with drawers on one side

— 책상 ⇨ 쪽소매

쪽자 一字 〖인쇄〗 a single piece of printing type made by combining parts taken from other pieces

쪽잘거리다 nibble〔chew〕 by bits ; eat half-heartedly

쪽지 一紙 a slip of paper ; a tag ; a label ¶ 쪽지에 몇 자 적다 jot a few words down on a slip // 배달 불능의 쪽지가 붙어서 편지가 돌아왔다 The letter came back with a tag explaining its nondelivery.

쪽찌다 do up (one's hair) in a chignon ¶ 쪽찐 머리 a (round) chignon

쫄딱 completely ; wholly ; altogether ; utterly ¶ 쫄딱 망하다 be completely ruined ; be totally spoiled

쫄딱쫄딱 [옹졸] small-scale ; petty ; [조금씩] doing a little at a time ; bit by bit

—하다 (be) small-scale ; petty ; be done in little bits

쫄래둥이 a flippant〔frivolous〕 child ; a flippant and mischievous boy

쫑그리다 [귀를] cock〔prick up〕 《its》 ears ⇨ 쫑긋거리다

쫑긋거리다 [입을] move〔purse〕 the lips ; move the lips ; [귀를] prick up 〔strain, cock〕 one's ears ¶ 입을 쫑긋거리다 move the lips ; curl one's lip ; make a lip // 귀를 쫑긋거리다 strain〔prick up, cock, move〕 one's ears

쫑긋쫑긋 ⇨ 쫑긋거리다

쫑알거리다 ⇨ 종알거리다

쫓기다 be chased〔run after, pursued〕 ; be driven〔ousted, expelled, removed〕 [일에] be pressed 《with business》 ; feel the pressure of business ¶ 돈에 쫓기다 be pressed for money // 일에 쫓기다 be pressed with work〔business〕 // 직장에서 쫓겨나다 be dismissed〔fired〕 from one's post // 동네에서 쫓겨나다 be ousted from the village ; be driven out of a village

***쫓다** ① [쫓아버리다] drive away ; drive 《a person》 out of ¶ 파리떼를 쫓다 drive away flies // 고양이를 쫓다 shoo a cat away // 군중을 쫓다 disperse a crowd // 방에서 쫓아내다 drive〔turn〕 《a person》 out of the room // 거지를 쫓아내다 turn away a beggar from one's door // 세든 사람을 쫓아내다 eject〔evict〕 a tenant out of one's home // 자리에서 쫓아내다 oust 《a person》 from office // 하인을 쫓아내다 give a maid the sack // 학교에서 학생을 쫓아내다 expel a student from school
② [뒤쫓다] run after 《a person》 ; chase ; pursue ; give chase to ¶ 도둑을 쫓다 run after a thief // 적의 함대를 쫓다 give chase to the enemy's fleet // 후퇴하는 적을 쫓다 follow a retreating enemy // 뒤를 바싹 쫓아가다 follow close upon the

heels《of》// 적의 뒤를 바싹 쫓아가다 closely pursue the enemy
③ [따르다] follow ; follow suit ¶ 유행을 쫓다 follow〔run after〕 the fashion // 충고〔명령〕를 쫓다 follow《a person's》 advice〔orders〕// 외국의 관례를 쫓다 follow in the footsteps of foreign practice
④ [따라가다] catch up with ; keep up with ; compete with ¶ 앞서 가는 사람을 쫓아가다 catch up with《a person》 ahead // 먼저 가시오 곧 쫓아갈 테니 You go on, I will catch you up. // 내가 너무 빨리 걸어서 그가 쫓아오지 못했다 I walked too fast for him to catch up with me. // 요리 솜씨로는 그녀를 쫓아갈 사람이 없다 No one can match her cooking.

쫓아보내다 [돌려보내다] drive back〔out〕; send away ; turn《a person》 from the door ; turn away ¶ 그녀가 시집에서 친정으로 뛰쳐나오자 어머니는 그녀를 다시 시집으로 쫓아보냈다 When she ran home to mother, she was sent packing back to her husband.

쫙 ⇨ 좍

쬐다 ① [볕이 비치다]《the sun》 shine ② [볕·불에] expose to the sun ; put over the fire ¶ 햇볕에 쬐다 be bathed in the sun ; bask in the sun ; take the sun // 손을 화로에 쬐다 warm one's hands over a brazier // 손수건을 불에 쬐어 말리다 dry a handkerchief over〔at〕 a fire // 이불을 햇볕에 쬐다 expose bedding to the sun ; air bedclothes

쭈그러뜨리다 press〔squeeze〕 out of shape ; crush ; crumple ¶ 모자를 납작하게 쭈그러뜨리다 crumple a hat flat

쭈그러지다 be crushed ; be crumpled ; be〔get〕 pressed〔squeezed〕 out of shape ; [살기가] be withered ; grow gaunt ; shrivel ¶ 쭈그러진 얼굴 a worn face // 쭈그러진 손 a shriveled hand

쭈그렁이 [물건] a thing crushed out of shape ; [사람] a withered old person

쭈그리다 [쭈그러뜨리다] crush ; [몸을] crouch ; squat ; bend low ; stoop ¶ 쭈그리고 걷다 walk with a stoop // 불을 쬐려고 쭈그리다 stoop〔lean〕 over the fire

쭈글쭈글 —하다 (be) crumpled ; rumpled ; wrinkled ; withered ¶ 쭈글쭈글한 바지 crumpled trousers // 노인의 쭈글쭈글한 수족 the shrunken limbs of old age // 쭈글쭈글하게 하다 crumple ; wrinkle ; rumple ; crease ; crush《clothes》

쭈뼛 —하다 ① [솟다] stand on end ; stand up ; stand erect ; bristle up
② [주저하다] (be) shy and hesitant ; timid ¶ 머리끝이 쭈뼛하다 have one's hair stand (up) on end《at a sight》

쭈뼛쭈뼛 hesitantly ; diffidently ; timorously ; nervously —하다 (be) shy and hesitant

쭉정이 empty heads of grain ; blasted〔blighted〕 ears

쫑그리다 prick up ears ; cock〔raise, move〕 the ears

쭝얼거리다 ⇨ 중얼거리다

쭝쭝거리다 express discontent ; grumble《at》; complain《of》; mutter《at, about》

-쯤 about ; almost ; some ; more or less ; or so ¶ 지금쯤 by now ; by this time // 네 시쯤 about〔around〕 four o'clock // 내일쯤 by tomorrow // 연 1할 2부쯤 about〔something like〕 12 percent a year // 나이가 50쯤 되다 be about fifty (years old) ; be〔look〕 fiftyish《미》// 두 시쯤 만나자 I will see you around two.

쯧쯧 [못마땅함] tut, tut ! sucks ! ¶ 쯧쯧하고 그는 혀를 찼다 "Tut, tut !" He clicked his tongue.

찌 ① [부전] a tag ; a slip ; a label ¶ 찌를 붙이다 tag ; label
② [낚시] a float ; a cork ; a quill ¶ 찌를 달다 tie〔fasten〕 a float《to》

찌개 dish served in the pot ; a pot stew
생선 — fish pot-stew

찌그러뜨리다 crush ; squash ; batter

찌그러지다 be crushed ; be battered ; be withered ¶ 찌그러진 코 a bashed-in nose // 찌그러진 얼굴 distorted features

찌그럭거리다 ⇨지그럭거리다

찌그렁이 stubborn insistence ¶ 찌그렁이 부리다 stubbornly insist on one's own way

찌근덕거리다 ⇨ 지근덕거리다

찌글거리다 ⇨ 지글거리다

찌글찌글 with a sizzling sound ⇨ 지글거리다

찌긋거리다 [눈을] wink《at a person》; [옷을 당기다] pull《a person》 by the sleeve

찌긋이 with a frown〔grimace〕

찌긋찌긋 ⇨ 찌긋거리다

찌긋하다 ① ⇨ 찡긋거리다 ② [눈이] (be) distorted ; contorted ; skew ; awry

찌꺼기 dregs ; remnants ; [커피의] grounds ; [가라앉은] sediments ; settlings ¶ 타고 남은 찌꺼기 cinders // 팔다 남은 찌꺼기 remainders ; remnants

찌끼 dregs ; lees ⇨ 찌꺼기

찌다¹ [살이] grow fat ; gain〔put on〕 weight ¶ 살찐 fat ; stout ; plump // 돼지를 살찌게 하다 fatten a pig // 그는 너무 살이 쪘다 He is overweight. // 살이 쪄서 외투가 작아졌다 The overcoat is too small for me now since I have grown stouter. // 너 살이 찌는 것 같다 I'm afraid you're getting overweight.

찌다² [날씨가] be sultry ; be humid ; get steaming〔boiling〕 hot ¶ 찌는 듯한 더위 the sweltering heat // 찌는 듯이 덥다 It is boiling〔steaming〕 hot. // 오늘도 푹푹 찔 모양이군 Looks like another scorcher〔sizzler〕 today. // 푹푹 찌는군 What a scorcher〔sizzler〕!

찌다³ [김으로] steam ; cook by steam ; heat with steam ¶ 감자를 찌다 steam

potatoes
찌다⁴ [베다] cut ; mow ¶ 낫으로 나뭇가지를 찌다 cut off branches with a sickle
찌다⁵ [흙탕물이] overflow a field
찌득찌득하다 (be) tough ; sticky ; hard (to crack)
찌들다 ① [때가 끼다] get dirty ; be smudged ② [고생으로] get thin 《from》; be careworn ; be worn out ¶ 그녀는 어려운 살림에 찌들었다 Hardship of life has left its trace on her face. /Her face was worn out by hardship of life.
찌르기 a thrust ; a push ; a jab ; [검 따위의] a lunge ; a stab ; 〖펜싱〗 a punto 《*pl.* ～s》
찌르다 ① [칼 따위로] pierce ; prick ; thrust ; stab ¶ 칼로 찌르다 stab 《a person》 with a sword // 목을 찌르다 stab 《a person》 in the throat // 단도로 심장을 찌르다 stab the heart with a dagger // 바늘로 찌르다 prick 《one's finger》 with a needle
② [비밀을] inform 《against》; report ; tip off ¶ 공범자를 찌르다 betray one's accomplice // 경찰에 찌르다 tip the police off
③ [냄새가] stink ; smell nasty ¶ 불쾌한 냄새가 코를 찔렀다 An offensive smell assailed my nostrils.
④ [감정을] hurt 《a person's feelings》; offend 《a person》; stir 《a person's emotion》 ¶ 아픈 곳을 찌르는구나 You hit me on a sore spot. // 그의 말이 가슴을 찔렀다 His remark hit home
⑤ [돈을] invest ; lay out ; put 《money》 in ¶ 장사에 밑천을 찌르다 invest one's money in a business
찌르레기 〖새〗 a starling
찌르륵 with a slurp (as through a straw)
찌르륵거리다 keep slurping
찌르릉 ¶ 찌르릉하고 초인종을 울리다 ring the doorbell // 찌르릉 찌르릉 소리나다〔울리다〕 tinkle ; jingle
찌무룩하다 (be) sullen ; sulky ; be in a bad temper ¶ 찌무룩한 얼굴을 하다 look displeased〔sullen, cross, morose, moody〕
찌부러뜨리다 deflate ; crush ; crumple ¶ 모자를 찌부러뜨리다 crush a hat
찌부러지다 get〔be〕 deflated〔crushed, crumpled〕; be squashed ; collapse ; be ruined ¶ 찌부러진 공 a crushed ball
찌지 —紙 a marker ; a tag
찌푸리다 [날씨가] cloud over ; get〔be〕 cloudy ; [얼굴을] frown ; scowl ; make a face ; wrinkle up ; make a grimace ¶ 찌푸린 날씨 cloudy weather // 얼굴을 찌푸리고 with a grimace〔frown, wry face〕// 이마를 찌푸리다 wrinkle up one's brow // 얼굴을 찌푸리다 make a wry face ; pull faces ; grimace // 그는 아파서 얼굴을 찌푸렸다 His face was distorted with pain.
찍 ① [미끄러지는 모양] slidingly ¶ 찍 미끄러지다 slide〔slip〕 down ② [선 따위를 긋는 모양] ¶ 선을 찍 긋다 draw a line with a (vigorous) stroke
찍다 ① [도장을] stamp ; seal ; impress 《a signature》; imprint (인각) ¶ 도장을 찍다 set a seal 《to》; fix a seal ; stamp a seal // 편지에 소인을 찍다 imprint a postmark on a letter // 서류에 도장을 찍다 affix one's seal to a document // 세일 가격은 40,000원인데 정규 가격을 찍으셨네요 The sale price is 40,000 *won* but you rang up the regular price.
② [묻히다] dip 《into》 ¶ 잉크를 찍다 dip the pen into ink // 설탕을 찍어 먹다 eat 《a thing》 with sugar
③ [점찍다] place 《a dot》; mark 《with a point》; dot ¶ 소수점을 찍다 place a decimal point
④ [눈여겨 두다] mark out ; keep an eye on 《a person》; have an eye to ; single〔pick〕 out ¶ 그 세명이 수상하다고 점찍어 두었다 I have an eye to those three, whom I suppose to be the offenders. // 난 그를 범인으로 점 찍고 있다 I have spotted him the culprit. // 도둑이 전부터 그 집을 털려고 점 찍고 있었다 The robber had marked out the house for burglary. // 이 나무들은 내년에 벨 것으로 점찍어 놓았다 These trees have been earmarked for cutting next year.
⑤ [도끼 따위로] chop 《with an ax》; hew ; hack (조각조각) ; cut ; [차표를] punch ¶ 도끼로 나무를 찍어 넘어뜨리다 chop a tree down with an ax // 차표를 찍다 punch a ticket ; have one's ticket punched
⑥ [찔러 꿰다] catch with a hook ; pierce ; thrust ¶ 작살로 고기를 찍다 spear a fish // 갈고리로 나무를 찍다 hook a log
⑦ [사진을] photograph ; take a photograph 《of》; shoot ; snap ; [다른 사람이] have〔get〕 one's photograph taken ¶ 사진을 찍다 take a picture〔snapshot〕; have one's a picture taken // 영화를 찍다 take a motion picture ; shoot picture ; film // 나는 개의 사진을 찍었다 I took a picture of my dog. // 비디오 좀 찍어 주시겠어요 Could you videotape me, please ?
찍소리 a chirp ; a tweet ; [한마디] a word ; a syllable ; a single word ¶ 찍소리 없이 without a word ; without complaining ; in silence // 찍소리 없이 복종하다 obey without a whimper // 찍소리도 못하게 하다 silence ; floor ; put 《a person》 to silence ; beat 《a person》 all hollow // 그 말에 찍소리도 못했다 He couldn't utter a syllable in reply. /He was nonplused〔completely silenced〕. /It was a staggerer to him. // 분명히 그 친구는 그 사업건으로 김씨와 입씨름을 벌일 때 찍소리도 못할 만큼 당했을거야 Apparently he was talked down by Mr. *Kim* in an argument over

the new project.

찍어당기다 hook and pull ; hook in

찍어매다 stitch up ; sew〔patch〕 together ¶ 터진 곳을 찍어 매다 stitch up a tear

찍히다 ① [인쇄되다] be printed

② [도장 따위] be〔get〕 sealed〔stamped, impressed〕; [차표가] get punched ¶ 런던의 소인이 찍힌 편지 a letter postmarked from London〔bearing the London postmark〕

③ [지목받다] be marked out〔down〕 for ; be spotted ¶ 범인으로 점찍히다 be suspected as the offender // 그에게 찍히면 마지막이니까 주의를 해야 한다 If he turns against you, it's the end of the line, so be very careful.

④ [사진이] be taken ; come out ¶ 이 사진은 잘 찍혔다 This photo has come out well〔is taken well〕.

찐덥다 have nothing to be ashamed of ; have an easy conscience

찐득거리다 ⇨ 진득거리다

찐빵 steamed bread

찐쌀 rice processed by steaming unripe grains

찐하다 feel depressed〔sad, blue, regretful〕

찔끔하다 be startled ; be alarmed ; be intimidated ; get struck with fear ¶ 나는 그의 말에 찔끔했다 His words came home to me. // 아버지 묻는 말씀에 찔끔했다 My heart stood still at father's question.

찔레 〖식물〗 the wild〔brier〕 rose

—나무 a wild rosebush

찔름찔름[1] brimfully

찔름찔름[2] piecemeal ; in dribs and drabs ¶ 돈을 찔름찔름 주다 give money out piecemeal // 돈을 찔름찔름 쓰다 use one's money in dribs and drabs

찔리다 be stuck ; be pricked ; be pierced ¶ 손을 가시에 찔리다 get a hand pricked by a thorn // 칼에 등을 찔려 죽다 be stabbed in the back to death // 스스로 돌이켜서 양심에 찔리는 바 없다 As I look into my heart, I have nothing to be ashamed of.

찔찔 ⇨ 질질

찜 a steamed〔boiled〕 dish ; hard-boiled food ; fomentation (찜질)

닭— steamed chicken 삼치— hard-boiled bonitos

찜부럭 petulance ; ill humor ; peevishness ; fretfulness ¶ 찜부럭 내다 be fretful ; be touchy ; be irritable ; get cross

찜질 fomentation ; applying a poultice —하다 foment ; poultice ; apply a hot〔cold〕 pack to ¶ 얼음 찜질 apply an ice pack // 얼음 찜질 apply an ice pack // 더운 물수건으로 무릎을 찜질하다 apply a hot towel to the knee

찜쪄먹다 be more so ; be worse ¶ 그도 바보지만 그의 동생은 형 찜쪄먹는 바보다 He's a fool, but his younger brother is a bigger one.

찜찜하다 feel constrained〔embarrassed, awkward〕; feel ill at ease ; be uncomfortable ¶ 말하기가 찜찜하다 find it awkward〔hard〕 to say 《that...》

찜통 —桶 a steamer

찝찔하다 (be) saltish ; [못마땅하다] unsatisfactory ; disagreeable

* **찡그리다** frown ; scowl ; make a wry face ; make a grimace ; distort one's face ¶ 그는 아픔에 못이겨 얼굴을 찡그렸다 His face was distorted with pain. // 그는 말을 하지 않고 얼굴만 찡그렸다 He made no reply, but simply scowled. // 그녀는 밤낮 찡그리고만 있다 She is always frowning. // 왜 찡그리고 있느냐 Why the knitted brow? // 그는 몹시 찡그린 얼굴을 하고 있다 His face is so drawn.

찡긋거리다 wink at ; warn by knitting one's brows ; twist〔wrinkle〕 one's face at 《a person》

찡기다 be crumpled ; be rumpled ; be wrinkled ; be creased

찡등그리다 twist (one's face) up into a scowl ; scowl hard

찡얼거리다 [불평] grumble ; murmur ; complain ; [어린애가] whimper ; whine ; be fretful

찡얼찡얼 ⇨ 찡얼거리다

찡찡거리다 [불평] grumble 《at》; complain 《of》; murmur 《at, against》; whimper ¶ 대우가 나쁘다고 찡찡거리다 complain of ill treatment

찡찡이 a person who sounds odd because of a nasal polyp

찡찡하다 [겸연쩍다] (be) awkward ; uncomfortable ; [코가 막혀] stuffy ; blocked ; clogged

찢기다 get〔be〕 torn〔rent, ripped〕 ¶ 갈기갈기 찢기다 be torn to ribbons // 둘로 찢기다 be split in two // 옷이 철조망에 걸려서 찢겼다 His clothes were ripped on barbed wire. // 그 여자의 마음은 슬픔으로 갈기갈기 찢겼다 Her heart was rent with grief.

* **찢다** tear ; rend ; rip ; split ; cleave ; sever ¶ 갈기갈기 찢다 tear into threads〔to pieces〕 // 신문지를 찢다 tear a newspaper // 둘로 찢다 split 《a thing》 in two // 편지를 갈기갈기 찢다 tear a letter to pieces // 자루를 찢어 열다 rip a bag open

찢뜨리다 let 《a piece of paper》 tear ; cause 《a piece of paper》 to tear (in two) by accident

찢어 발기다 tear to threads〔pieces〕

찢어지다 be torn ; be rent ¶ 가슴이 찢어지는 듯한 heart-rending〔-aching〕 // 잘 찢어지다 tear easily // 갈기갈기 찢어지다 be torn into shreds〔pieces〕 // 찢어지게 가난하다 have not a shirt to one's back ; be as poor as a church-mouse

찧다 [곡식을] pound 《rice》; hull ; husk ; ram ¶ 절구에 쌀을 찧다 pound rice in a mortar // 엉덩방아를 찧다 come down flop on one's buttocks // 코방아를 찧다 fall flat on the ground // 벽에 이마를 찧다 ram one's head against a wall // 찧고 까불다 make fun〔game, sport〕 of 《a person》 // 함께〔섞어〕 찧다 pound 《fish》 to a jelly // 문에 머리를 찧다 knock one's head against〔on〕 the door // 그는 넘어질 때 머리를 되게 찧었다 He got a nasty knock on the head when he fell.

ㅊ

차 此 [이것] this ; these ; present ; current ¶ 차제에 now ; on this occasion ; at this juncture〔time〕// 차로써 now ; with this ; here // 차로써 보면 in view of these facts

†**차 茶** [음료] tea ; green tea (녹차) ; black tea (홍차) ; [나무] a tea plant ; [잎] tea leaves ¶ 첫물 달인 차 the first infusion of tea // 차를 끓이다 make〔prepare, fix〕 tea // 차를 따르다 pour tea into a cup // 차를 한 잔 마시다 take〔drink〕 a cup of tea // 손님에게 차를 내다 offer〔serve〕 《a person》 tea // 차를 마시며 이야기하다 talk over a cup of tea // 차가 나왔다 Tea was served. // 진한〔엷은〕 차를 좋아한다 He likes his tea strong〔weak〕. // 차가 잘 우러난다〔우러나지 않는다〕 The tea draws 〔doesn't draw〕 well.
—거르개 a tea strainer **—관** a teakettle ; a teapot **—그릇** a tea set **—나무 밭** a tea plantation〔garden〕 **—숟가락** a teaspoon **— 주전자(받이)** a teapot (stand) **— 찌끼** tea〔coffee〕 grounds **가루—** powdered tea

†**차 車** [일반적으로] a vehicle ; [자동차] a (motor-) car ; a taxi (cab) ; an automobile ; a truck ; [기차] a (railway) carriage ; [화차] a freight car ; [장기] a chariot ¶ 석탄〔사과〕 한 차 a carload of coal〔apple-boxes〕// 자가용차 a car of one's own // 차로 가다 go by car〔train〕// 차〔택시〕를 타다〔잡다, 부르다〕 take〔get, hail〕 a car // 차로 나르다 carry 《goods》 in a car〔truck〕// 그를 사무소로 가는 도중에 태우고 갔다 I picked him up on the way to my office. // 차가 지나가며 먼지를 냈다 The car raised a cloud of dust when it passed by. // 어디를 가나 서로 부딪칠 정도로 차가 많고 조금 가다가 서고 조금 가다간 서고 한다 It's bumper-to-bumper and stop-and-go everywhere. // 내 차의 오른쪽 여기저기가 쭈그러지고 긁히고 했어 The passenger side of my car got dents and scratches all over. // 차를 혼자 타고 다니는 사람들이 너무 많다 There are too many solo drivers. // 이 차는 휘발유를 참 많이 소비합니다 This car is a gas guzzler. // 이거 몇 년도 차지요 What model year is this car ? // 중고차 매매인에게서 고물차를 산 것 같아 I think I got a lemon from the used car dealer.
— 번호판 a number plate ; a license plate **— 사고** vehicular accidents **—삯** fare ; hire ; [운송료] carriage ; cartage **전세 —** a rental car

차 差 [차이] difference ; [불일치] disparity ; inequality ; [변화] variation ; [차별] discrimination ; 〖수학〗 the remainder ; [차감의] balance ; [간격의] a gap ; [매매 가격의] margin ¶ 품질의 차 difference in quality // 연령의 차 disparity in〔of〕 age // 역량의 차 discrepancy in ability // 임금의 차 wage differentials // A · B간의 차 difference between A and B // 차가 있다 differ from ; there is a difference from. . . // 차가 없다 differ little from // 2점 차로 이기다〔지다〕 win〔lose〕 by two points // 빈부의 차가 심하다 There is a big gulf between the rich and the poor. // 한란의 차가 심하다 There are great changes of (fluctuations in) temperature. // 그들간에는 천양지차가 있다 They are as like as chalk and cheese. // 1점 차로 졌다 We lost by one run.

차 次 ① [계제] on the point〔verge〕 of 《doing》 ; by the way ; as ; when ¶ 가려던 차에 그가 왔다 He came when I was just about to leave. // 시장에 갔던 차에 아주머니집에 들렀다 I called at my aunt's on my way to the market.
② [목적] for the purpose of ; with the intention of ; in order to ; so that ; (so as) to ¶ 인사차 내방하다 pay a courtesy call〔visit〕 ; come to pay one's respects // 요양차 …에 가다 go 《to some place》 for a change of air // 사업차 홍콩에 갔다 He went to Hong Kong on business.
③ [다음의] next ; the following ; below ; sub
④ [순서] order ; sequence ; degree (수학의) ¶ 1〔2〕차 코일 a primary〔secondary〕 coil // 1차 방정식 a simple equation ; an equation of the first degree // 제2차 대전 World War Ⅱ // 제3차 내각 the third Cabinet // 수삼차 읽다 read several times // 1차 시험에 합격했다 He passed the primary examination.
—기 next term **—석** the next seat ; [관리 따위] an official next in rank ; an assistant ; [수상자] the runner-up **편집 —장** a sub-editor

차가 借家 a rented house ; a house on lease ; [빌리는 일] taking a house for rent **—하다** rent a house ; live in a rented house ; take a house on lease
—료 a house rent **—인** a tenant

차가다 carry off ; snatch away ; run away with ; [유괴] kidnap ¶ 매가 병아리를 차갔다 An eagle swooped down upon a chicken and snatched it away. // 날치기가

부인의 핸드백을 차갔다 The pick pocket snatched the handbag from〔out of〕 a lady's hand.
차간 車間 a train compartment
— 거리 the distance between (two) cars going in the same direction ¶ 차간 거리를 지키다 observe the proper distance between cars
*차감 差減 —하다 strike a balance ; balance ¶ 차감을 계산하다 balance 《an account》; offset ; strike a balance // 손익을 차감하다 balance the profit and loss
— 계정 balance ; striking a balance — 잔액 a balance
차갑다 be as cold as ice ; be ice-cold // 차가워지다 become〔get〕 cold // 차가운 눈으로 쳐다보다 look at 《a person》 coldly
차견 借見 —하다 borrow and see〔read〕
‡차고 車庫 [자동차의] a garage ; [전차의] a car shed〔barn〕; [기차의] a train depot ¶ 전차를 차고에 넣다 house tramcars // 자동차를 차고에 넣다 put a car into a garage ; garage 《a car》
차고음 次高音 〖음악〗 mezzo-soprano
차곡차곡 in orderly fashion ; neatly ; squarely one after another ¶ 차곡차곡 쌓다 pile up one by one neatly // 차곡차곡 문제를 풀다 solve a problem step by step〔systematically〕
*차관 次官 a vice-minister ; an undersecretary 《영》; an assistant secretary 《미》
—보 an assistant secretary 《미》 문교부 — the Vice-Minister〔Deputy Minister〕 of Education 사무 — a permanent vice-minister 정무 — a parliamentary vice-minister 국방부 —보 the Assistant Deputy Minister of Defense
차관 借款 a loan ¶ 차관을 신청하다 apply〔ask〕 for a loan // 차관을 체결하다 contract a loan // 차관을 제공하다 grant〔extend, supply〕 a credit 《to》
— 계약 a loan contract (국제적) —단 a consortium 《*pl.* -tia, ～s》 — 융자 credit financing — 업체 a firm using foreign loans ; a firm〔company〕 constructing factories with foreign loans — 협정 a loan agreement 개발 — a development loan ; a DLF loan 공공〔재정〕 — a public〔financial〕 loan 민간〔상업〕 — a commercial loan 연불 — a delayed payment loan 장기〔단기〕 — a long-term〔short-term〕 loan 현금 — cash loan ; loans in cash
차관 茶罐 a tea caddy〔canister〕
차광 遮光 —하다 shade〔shield〕 the light ; hinder〔intercept〕 the light ; cover the light over
—기 a flash suppresser (on a gun) —막 [등화 관제용] a blackout curtain (창문의) ; a shade (등불 주위의) ; [텔레비전·카메라용의] a flag — 스크린 an occulter — 장치 a shutter ; shading ; an iris shutter (사진기의) —판 a glare shield (on aircraft)
*차근차근 in orderly fashion ; neatly ; minutely ; compactly ; in detail ; attentively ; carefully ; scrupulously —하다 (be) minute ; compact ; attentive ¶ 몹시 차근차근하다 be overscrupulous // 성질이 차근차근한 사람 a scrupulously careful person // 책을 차근차근 쌓아놓다 stack the books up carefully〔in good order〕 // 일을 차근차근 처리하다 dispose of a matter methodically〔systematically〕 // 차근차근 설명하다 explain in detail〔one after another〕 // 차근차근 역설하다 inculcate ; dwell on at length // 그는 차근차근 그 여자의 잘못된 생각을 뉘우치도록 노력했다 He tried to talk her out of her silly ideas. /He tried patiently to convince her of her error. // 처음부터 차근차근히 검토해 봅시다 Let's go over it step by step from the beginning.
차금 差金 〖증권〗 difference ; margin ; balance
— 거래 dealing in difference — 결재 making up differences — 투기 speculating
차금 借金 a debt ; borrowings ⇨ 빚
차기 次期 the next term〔period〕
— 대통령 the President for the next term ; the next President — 이월 [부기에서] Carried forward. 《c/f》 — 정권 the next Administration
차깔하다 ¶ 문을 차깔하다 close〔shut〕 a door securely
차꼬 shackles ; fetters ¶ 차꼬를 채우다 put 《a person》 in fetters // 그는 차꼬를 차고 있다 He has fetters on.
차꼬막이 [용마루의] crescent-shaped tiles placed at both sides of the ridge of a tiled house ; [박공머리의] a square rafter and tile fitted to the edges of a gable
차끈차끈하다 feel chills ; feel freezing cold
차끈하다 (be) very cold ; feel chilled〔very cold〕
차남 次男 one's second (eldest) son
차내 車內 the inside〔interior〕 of a car〔train〕 ¶ 차내에서 in the car ; on the train
— 금연 No smoking in the car ! — 통화 장치 an intercommunication system ; an intercom 《구》 — 회견 an interview in the train
차녀 次女 one's second (eldest) daughter
†차다¹ [한랭] (be) cold ; chilly ; icy ¶ 찬물 cold water // 찬바람 a chilly〔cold〕 wind // 차디찬 사람 a cold-hearted〔an icy〕 person // 차지다 become〔get〕 cold〔chill〕 // 얼음장같이 차다 be ice-cold ; be as cold as ice // 해진 후에는 기온이 차다 The temperature is chilly〔goes down〕 after sundown.
†차다² [충만] fill (it) up ; be full of ; be filled with ; [달이] (be) full ; be at the

full ; wax ; [조수가] rise ; flow ; [기한이] expire ; be out ; fall〔become〕 due ; run out ¶ 꽉〔빽빽히〕 들어차다 be jammed ; be tightly packed ; be overcrowded // 마음에 차다 be satisfied 《with》 ; meet with satisfaction ; prove〔be〕 satisfactory // 마음에 안 차다 prove〔be〕 unsatisfactory ; leave something〔much〕 to be desired // 활기차다 be brimful of vigor // 배가 차다 one's stomach is full // 전도가 희망에 차다 one's future is full of hope // 앞길은 위험에 차 있다 Our way (ahead) is full of danger. // 그 아이의 눈은 눈물로 가득 차 있다 The child's eyes are filled〔brimming〕 with tears. // 조수가 차 있다 The tide is on the flow. /The tide is in. // 그의 임기는 내달에 찬다 His term of office will expire next month. // 내달로 지불 기한이 찬다 The payment will come due next month. // 달이 차서 사내아이를 낳았다 When her time came she gave birth to a boy. // 달도 차면 기운다 A flow will have an ebb. /Every flood〔tide〕 hath its ebb.

†**차다³** [발로] kick ; give a kick 《at》 ¶ 공을 차다 kick a ball // 개를 차다 give a kick at a dog // 혀를 차다 click one's tongue 《over》 // 차이다 be〔get〕 kicked // 차서 넘어뜨리다 kick 《a person》 down ; kick 《a thing》 over // 문을 차서 열다 kick the door open // 자리를 차고 일어서다 shake the dust off one's feet ; leave one's seat bruskly ; stamp out of the room // 그는 내 정강이를 찼다 He kicked me on the shin. // 내가 가난한 월급쟁이라고 여자 친구가 나를 차 버렸어 My girl friend has dumped me because I'm a poor salaried worker. // 왜 그렇게 좋은 여자를 찼니 Why did you dump a nice girl like her? // 그 여자는 결국 그 사람을 찼다 She ended up dumping him.

차다⁴ [패용] put on ; fasten on ; carry ; wear ¶ 칼을 차다 wear a sword at one's side ; gird on a sword // 훈장을 차다 pin on〔wear〕 a decoration // 패물을 차다 wear trinkets // 시계를 차다 strap on〔wear〕 a watch

차닥거리다 paddle ; keep paddling〔slapping, beating〕 ; [바르다] paste haphazardly ; slap together ⇨ 처덕거리다

차단 遮斷 interception ; isolation ; quarantine (검역) **—하다** cut〔shut〕 《a person》 off from ; intercept ; isolate ¶ 적의 퇴로를 차단하다 intercept the enemy's retreat // 그 섬을 외계와의 교통에서 차단하다 cut off the island from communication with the outside world
—기 a circuit breaker ; [건널목의] a crossing〔lifting〕 gate **— 용량** 『전기』 an interrupting〔breaking, rapturing〕 capacity **— 장치** a cut-off **교통 —** suspension of traffic ; [검역의] quarantine

차대 次代 the coming〔oncoming〕 generation

차대 車臺 a car-body ; a chassis

차도 差度 improvement (of sickness) ; convalescence ; recovery ¶ 차도가 있다 be getting better ; convalesce ; progress favorably ; take a turn for the better ; improve // 그의 병은 차도가 있다 He is recovering from his illness. /He is getting better. // 앓고 있던 아이가 어머니의 간호로 많은 차도가 있었다 Under his mother's care the sick child mended quickly.

∗**차도 車道** a road〔carriage〕 way ; a car lane ; a traffic lane ; a driveway

차돌 quartz ; silicates ¶ 차돌 같은 사람 a man of firm〔steady〕 character
— 모래 silica sand ; glass silica

차동 差動 『물리』 ¶ 차동의 differential
— 장치 differential gear(ing) **— 전동기** a differential motor **— 전류계** a differential galvanometer **— 전위계** a differential electrometer **— 코일** a differential coil **— 톱니바퀴** a differential gear

차드 Chad (아프리카 공화국)

차등 此等 these (things)

차등 差等 grade ; gradation ; graduation ; difference ; discrimination ¶ 차등이 있다 be different in grade(s) // 차등을 매기다 grade ; graduate ; discriminate
— 세율 a graded tariff ; a graduated tax scale

차디차다 be ever so cold ; icy ; be as cold as ice ; be cold as can be

∗**차라리** rather ; preferably ¶ 차라리 …하는 것이 좋다 You had better... ; I would rather... ; I should prefer... to // 이쪽이 차라리 낫다 This would be better. /I'd rather take this one. /I prefer this one. // 이런 고통 속에서 사느니 차라리 죽는 것이 낫다 I would rather die than live in this agony. // 그렇게 하려면 차라리 안하는 것이 낫다 It would be better not to do it at all than to do it that way.

차란차란 [차다] completely filling (it) up ; [드리우다] drooping〔hanging〕 low ¶ 차란차란한 머리채 long braid of hair ; a long pigtail〔queue〕 // 물이 독에 차란차란 차다 A jar is brimful of water.

차랑거리다 move〔swing〕 gently ; tinkle ; ting ¶ 열쇠 뭉치를 차랑거리며 걷다 walk along clinking a bunch of keys // 긴 머리채가 차랑거린다 Her long pigtail sways on her back.

차랑차랑 ① ⇨ 치렁치렁 ② [소리] clinking ; rattling ; ting-a-ling ; ting-ting

차량 車輛 vehicles ; cars ; a (railway) carriage ; trucks ; rolling stock (화차, 객차) 《총칭》 ¶ 한 차량분의 화물 a carload
— 갑판 the wagon deck (열차 도선의) **— 검사** vehicle (maintenance) inspection ; safety inspection **— 계중기** a track scale **— 고장** a car trouble ; a breakdown **— 등록(증)** vehicle registration

ㅊ

(card) — 번호판 [자동차의] a (license) plate — 연결기 a car coupler — 정비 vehicle maintenance — 제작 the manufacturing of vehicles — 회사 a rolling stock (manufacturing) company 철도 — railroad cars

차려 [구령] Attention! ¶ 차려 자세를 취하다 come to attention ; stand at〔to〕 attention ; place oneself in an attitude of attention

차려입다 dress (oneself) up ; be gaily dressed ; be dressed up ¶ 화려하게 차려 입다 be gaudily dressed ; overdress (oneself)

차력 借力 —하다 enhance one's physical strength by taking a tonic

차렵 thin wadding〔padding〕
—것 thinly wadded〔padded〕 clothes

⁑차례 次例 ① [번] order ; sequence ; arrangement ; precedence ¶ 차례로 in (good) order ; one by one ; one after another〔the other〕 ; in turn ; by turns ; in regular sequence // 차례를 따라 according to the order〔program〕 ; in regular order // 차례를 기다리다 wait for one's turn // 차례가 뒤바뀌다 be out of order ; be in wrong order // 차례를 바꾸다 change the order ; follow the wrong order // 차례로 서다 stand in order // 연령〔키〕 차례로 서다 stand in order of age〔height〕 // 내 차례가 왔다 My turn has come round.
② [횟수] time ; round ¶ 한〔두〕 차례 once〔twice〕 // 세 차례 thrice ; three times // 여러 차례 several times // 책을 세 차례 읽다 read a book three times // 한 차례 이기다 win one round of a game
③ [목차] a table of contents ¶ 차례를 달다 attach a table of contents to 《a book》 // 차례를 만들다 compile〔draw up〕 a table of contents
—표 a program

차례 茶禮 ancestor-memorial services ; a brief family-memorial service

차례차례 次例次例 one by one ; one after another ; [순서로] in turn ; [이어서] in succession ¶ 카드를 번호대로 차례차례 놓다 arrange the cards in numerical order // 차례차례 돌려가며 한턱씩 내다 take turns treating one another // 선착순으로 차례차례 받다 be accepted in order of application

차롓걸음 次例— proceeding in due order〔course, succession〕 ; proceeding step by step ¶ 차롓걸음으로 해치우다 get a thing done without a skip

차로 遮路 cutting off communications ; obstruction〔blocking〕 of the road —하다 bar〔obstruct〕 the passage ; block the road ; stop the traffic

차로 叉路 a crossroads ; a forked road

차륜 車輪 a wheel ; a rundle
— 거리 wheel track〔tread〕 — 제동기 a wheel brake 착륙 — a landing wheel

차르랑 [쇳소리] with a clink ; with a rattle —하다 give a clink〔rattle〕

차르랑거리다 clink ; rattle

⁑차리다 ① [준비] make ready ; prepare for ¶ 살림을 차리다 establish a home // 점포를 차리다 set up a shop // 잔치를 차리다 give a feast〔banquet〕 // 아침밥을 차리다 prepare breakfast ; get breakfast ready // 차려놓다 set ; set〔put〕 up ; put〔place〕 in position // 부장님이 회사 그만두고 새 회사 차린다며 The manager's quitting and starting up a new company?
② [외관을] equip oneself 《with》 ; dress up ¶ 옷을 차려입다 dress up // 외모를 차리다 show up ; make a show
③ [간직] maintain ; preserve ¶ 인사를 차리다 observe decorum // 체면을 차리다 keep up appearances // 제 욕심을 차리다 seek a personal profit〔personal advantage, selfish end〕
④ [정신을] pull oneself together ; collect oneself ; concentrate one's attention ; be wide awake ¶ 정신을 차려 일하다 devote one's attention to the task at hand ; do the job carefully〔attentively〕

차림새 [준비] outfit ; furnishing ; preparation ; arrangement ; the setup ; [옷차림] one's manner of dressing ; one's clothes ; make-up (분장) ; [풍채] air ; appearance ; look ¶ 훌륭한 차림새의 부인 a well-dressed woman // 차림새가 얌전하다〔난하다〕 be neatly〔loudly〕 dressed // 그는 차림새에 개의치 않는 사람이다 He is quite indifferent to〔careless about〕 his personal appearance. // 그 여인은 차림새에 신경을 많이 쓴다 She takes much care in dressing. // 차림새만 봐도 그 여자의 성격을 알 수 있었다 Her appearance betrayed her character. /You could judge her character through her outfit.

차림표 [식단] a menu ⇨ 메뉴

차마 too... to ; for (all) the world ¶ 차마 견딜 수 없는 모욕 an intolerable〔unpardonable〕 insult // 차마 볼 수 없는 비참한 광경 a most pitiful sight // 차마 …할 수 없다 have not the heart to ; cannot bear〔stand〕 to ; be reluctant〔loath〕 to 《do》 // 나는 차마 그것을 들을 수 없다 I cannot stand hearing〔to hear〕 it. // 나는 차마 그것을 볼 수 없다 I cannot bear the sight of it. // 그의 농담은 차마 들을 수 없다 I can't stand his jokes. // 그에게 차마 화를 낼 수 없었다 We do not have the heart to be angry at him.

차마 車馬 horses and vehicles ¶ 차마의 통행 vehicular traffic
— 통행 금지 "No Horses and Vehicles (Allowed)."

차멀미 car sickness —하다 get〔be〕 carsick ; have car sickness

차면 遮面 hiding one's face ; putting a wall〔screen〕 between people

—담 a screening wall
차명 借名 using〔assuming, taking〕a person's name **—하다** use〔assume, borrow, take〕a person's name
차바퀴 車— a wheel ; a rundle ¶ 차바퀴 밑에 깔리다 be run over〔knocked down〕 by 《a car》// 차바퀴가 빠졌다 The wheel has come off.
차반 a sumptuous repast ; a fine〔nice〕 dish
차반 茶盤 a tea tray ; a tea board ; a tea serving tray
차버리다 kick away〔off〕; give 《a person》 a kick ; [거절하다] reject 《a request》; refuse ; turn down 《a proposal》 ¶ 애인을 차버리다 jilt one's lover // 그 녀석을 차 버려 Reach him a kick.
차변 借邊 the debtor 《Dr.》; the debit side (부기의) ¶ 차변에 기입하다 debit 《a sum》 against〔to〕《a person》; enter 《a sum》 to the debit of 《a person》
— 계정〔잔고〕 debtor account〔balance〕 **— 기입** a debit entry **—란** a debit side **—표** a debit〔debtor〕 note
*__차별 差別__ distinction ; discrimination ; partiality ; difference (차이) **—하다** draw〔make〕 a distinction《between》; discriminate《between, against》; distinguish ; differentiate ; be partial ¶ 차별 없이 without distinction ; indiscriminately ; fairly ; impartially // 차별하는 discriminative ; discriminatory ; discriminating // 차별 없는 indiscriminate // 선악의 차별쯤은 나도 안다 I know right from wrong.
— 고용 discrimination in employment **— 고용 조건** discriminatory hiring requirements **— 관세(關稅)** differential duties ; a discriminative tariff (세율) **— 대우** discriminative treatment ¶ 차별 대우를 하다 treat 《a person》 with discrimination ; discriminate against 《a person》// 차별 대우를 받다 be treated discriminatingly **— 임금** differential wages **— 임금 제도** a differential wage rate system **계급적 —** class distinction **인종 —** racial discrimination ; [흑인에 대한] (racial) segregation ; [남아 연방의] apartheid ¶ 인종 차별하지 마시오 Cut that racial discrimination out ! **인종 — 철폐** abolition of racial discrimination
차부 車夫 a cart-drawer
차분하다 (be) calm ; composed ; quiet ; subdued ; self-possessed ¶ 차분한 태도 a quiet attitude ; a calm manner // 마음을 차분히 가라앉히다 calm〔compose〕 oneself ; keep cool ; gather one's wits
차비 車費 [운임] carfare ; train〔railway, bus〕 fare ; charges ; [운반료] carriage ; cartage ¶ 서울까지의 왕복 차비는 얼마입니까 ? What is the fare to *Seoul* and back ? // 차비로 쓸 잔돈이 있습니까 Any small change for the fare ?
차비 差備 [준비] preparations ; (preliminary) arrangements ; outfit ; equipment ; provision ; [의도] intention **—하다** prepare ; make preparations〔arrangements〕; get〔make〕 ready ¶ 아무 차비도 없이 without any preparation // 여행갈 차비다 I am going (to go) on a trip.
차사 差使 [옛 제도] an official sent to arrest a criminal ; a messenger (sent by a governor)
함흥— a messenger who either never returns or is greatly delayed in coming back
차서 次序 order ; system ; arrangement ¶ 차서대로 앉다 be seated in 《their》 proper order of precedence
차석 次席 the next〔second〕 seat〔position〕; the second in command ; [관리] an official next in rank ; an assistant 《manager, director》; an associate ; [경기] the second winner ; the runner-up ¶ 차석에 앉다 sit next to ; rank next to (계급) // 과장 부재 시에 차석이 대리한다 The chief being absent, the official next in rank acts in his behalf
— 검사 [차장 검사] an associate public prosecutor **— 서기** a sub-head clerk **— 판사** an associate〔a side〕 judge
차선 次善 the second〔next〕 best
—책(策) the second〔next〕 best policy
차선 車線 a (traffic) lane ¶ 차선을 지키다 keep to one's lane ; stay in one lane // 4차선의 도로 a four-lane road
— 분리 channelization ; the segregation of traffic **— 분리대(帶)** a divisional strip **— 분리선** a lane-dividing line ; a stripe **—폭** lane width **— 하중(荷重)** lane load(ing)
차송 差送 dispatch **—하다** dispatch ; despatch ; send
차수 差數 disparity ; balance ; difference (in number)
차수 次數 『수학』 degree
차승 差勝 ⇨ 치승(差勝)
차아 次兒 a second child
차아- 次亞 hypo- ¶ 차아황산 hyposulfurous acid
차지 『축구』 charge
차트 [도표] a chart ¶ 차트로 만든다 make a chart 《of》; chart
차압 差押 ⇨ 압류(押留)
차액 差額 difference (in amount) ; balance ; margin ¶ 큰〔적은〕 차액 a wide〔narrow〕 margin // 원가와 매가와의 차액 margin ; difference ; spread (미) // 가격의 차액 the difference between two prices // 차액이 얼마인가 What is the balance ? // 차액의 증감은 사업의 성과를 말한다 The loss or gain of the balance shows the outcome of business.
†**차양 遮陽** an awning around the eaves, a pent roof ; [창의] a blind ; [모자의] the visor of a cap ¶ 차양이 넓은 모자 a broad-brimmed cap // 차양을 내리다 pull

ㅊ

the blind(s) down
차용 借用 borrowing ; loan **—하다** borrow ; have〔get〕 a loan《of》 ¶ 돈의 차용을 부탁하다 ask《a person》for a loan of money ; apply to《a person》 for an advance of money // 일금 100만원을 차용함 I. O. U. one million *won.* // 10,000원 가량 차용할 수 있을까요 Can you accommodate me with a loan of ten thousand *won* or so?
—금 borrowed money ; a loan **— 증서** an I. O. U. ; a bond of debt〔loan〕 ¶ 만원에 대한 차용 증서를 쓰다 write an IOU for 10,000 *won*
차원 次元 〖수학〗 a dimension ¶ 제4차원 the fourth dimension // 제3차원의 three-dimensional // 차원이 다르다 be entirely different
차월 借越 an outstanding debt ; a debt balance ; [수표의] an overdraft ; overdrawing **—하다** overdraw ; let a debt stand over ; leave a debt outstanding ¶ 차월금이 어느 정도인가 How much of the debt is still outstanding? // 그의 차월금은 약 만원으로 남아 있다 About ten thousand *won* remains to the debt of his account.
차위 次位 the second rank〔place〕 ; [경기의] a runner-up ¶ 차위를 차지하다 hold the second place // 차위상을 받다 win the second prize ; become a second prize winner
차이 差異 difference ; [구별] distinction ; [불균형] disparity ; [부동] dissimilarity ¶ 숫자의 차이 a numerical difference // 신분의 차이 disparity in social standing〔status〕 // 능력의 차이 discrepancy in ability // 현저한 차이 a striking〔remarkable, sharp〕 contrast // 차이로 구별하다 distinguish by a difference // 양자간에는 천양지차가 있다 They are poles asunder. /They are as opposite as two poles. // 양자간에는 아무 차이도 없다 There is no difference between the two. // 소문과 실제로 보는 것과는 큰 차이가 있다 There is all the difference between seeing and hearing. // 그렇게 걱정할 정도로 차이는 없다 Not enough of a difference to worry about.
—법 the method of difference **—점** a point of difference
차익 差益 marginal profit(s)
차인군 差人— an employee (of a merchant)
차일 遮日 a sunshade ; a (sun-)blind ; an awning ; a marquee ; a tent ¶ 차일을 치다 shade〔protect〕 a thing from the sun ; fix a marquee ; pitch a tent // 창문의 차일을 내리다 pull the blinds down
차일피일 此日彼日 —하다 put off from day to day ; delay day by day ; procrastinate ¶ 차일피일 미루고 지불하지 않다 delay payment time and again on one pretext or another
차임 a chime
—벨 a chime bell
차임 差任 [부동산·건물의] (a) rent ; [물건의] hire
차입 差入 —하다 send in《a thing》to a prisoner
—물 things sent in to a prisoner **— 식사** a lunch sent into a prisoner
차입 借入 borrowing ; loaning **—하다** borrow ; obtain《money》on loan
—금 a loan (of money) ; borrowed money ; a debt **일시 —금** a temporary loan ; 〖회계〗 a floating〔an unfunded〕 debt **장기 —금** a long-term debt
차자 次子 one's second son
차작 借作 [대작] ghostwriting ; a composition written for another《글》 **—하다** ghostwrite ; write for another
—자 a ghost-writer
차장 茶欌 a tea cabinet ; a cupboard for tea-things
차장 次長 a vice-chief〔-director〕 ; a deputy〔assistant〕-chief
— 검사 the assistant prosecutor general **편집 —** a senior editor ; an associate editor
차장 車掌 a conductor《미》 ; a guard《영》
—대(臺) the conductor's platform **—실** the conductor's compartment
차점 次點 the second highest mark〔number of points〕 ; the next〔second〕 score ; [경기] the second place winner ; the runner-up ; [선거] the second largest number (of votes) ¶ 차점으로 당선하다 stand second on the list of successful candidates // 5백표로 차점이 되었다 He polled 500 votes, heading the list of unsuccessful candidates. // 그는 차점자보다 5만표를 더 얻었다 He obtained more than 50,000 votes over his nearest competitor.
—자 [경쟁의] the runner-up《*pl.* runners-》 ; the second place winner ; the person who gets the second highest mark〔score〕 ; [선거의] the candidate with the next highest number ; the second successful candidate
차제 此際 now ; on this occasion ; at this junction〔time〕 ; under these circumstances ¶ 차제에 여러분에게 감사의 인사를 드립니다 I will take this opportunity of thanking you for helping me. // 차제의 최선책은 이것이다 This is the best policy to cope with the situation. /This is the best way to handle the situation.
차조 〖식물〗 glutinous millet
차조기 〖식물〗 a purple perilla plant ; *Perilla nankinensis* (학명)
차조밥 boiled glutinous millet
차좁쌀 hulled glutinous millet
차종 茶鍾 a teacup ; a tea bowl ¶ 차종에 차를 따르다 serve〔pour〕 tea into a cup
차주 車主 the owner of a car〔vehicle〕

차주 借主 a borrower ; a debtor ; a hirer ; [부동산] a renter ; a tenant ; a lessee
차주전자 茶酒煎子 a teapot
차중 車中 ① [찻속] in(side) a car〔train〕 ② [차 탄 동안] while aboard《a train》; while in the car
─담 an informal interview on the train
차중음 次中音 〖음악〗 tenor
†**차지 ─하다** hold ; occupy ; take ; have ; [가지다] capture ; seize ; take possession 《of》; make 《a thing》 one's own ; keep 《a thing》 as one's own ¶ 최후의 승리를 차지하다 win the final victory // 수석을 차지하다 sit at the top 《of one's class》// 3할을 차지하다 form 30 percent 《of》// 높은 지위를 차지하다 hold〔secure〕 a high position // 중요한 자리를 차지하다 occupy an important position // 과반수를 차지하다 have a majority // 땅을 차지하다 take possession of the land ; occupy the land // 독차지하다 monopolize ; have solely to oneself // 그는 제1위를 차지했다 He took the first place. /He ranked first. // 미국은 자동차 생산으로 1위를 차지한다 America ranks top in the production of automobiles. // 그 가구는 많은 공간을 차지할 것이다 The furniture would take up much space.
차지 借地 leased land ; rented ground ; a leasehold ; lease of land
─권 (right of) lease ; leasehold **─료** a ground rent **─법** the Leased Land Law **─인** a tenant ; a leaseholder ; a lessee **─ 증서** a land lease
⁑**차지다** [쌀, 밀 따위가] glutinous sticky ; [끈기가 있는] tenacious ; persistent ; stick-to-itive ¶ 차진 쌀〔밀〕 glutinous rice〔wheat〕// 차진 사람 a man of tenacity // 이 쌀은 차지다 The rice is rich in gluten. // 그는 차지지가 못하다 He sticks to nothing. /He lacks tenacity of purpose.
차질 蹉跌 stumbling ; a failure ; a miscarriage ; a deadlock ; a snag ; a setback ¶ 계획의 차질 a fiasco in the plan 《of》// 차질을 일으키다 fail ; stumble ; miscarry ; fall through ; be deadlocked ; reach a deadlock // 사업에 차질이 생겼다 The business struck a snag. // 차질이 생겨 아직 입금을 하지 못했다 There was a slipup and we still haven't paid.
차질다 ⇨ 차지다
†**차차 次次** [점점] gradually ; by and by ; by degrees ; little by little ; increasingly ; more and more ; less and less ; [나중에] later on ; afterwards ; in (due) time ; with the lapse of time ¶ 차차 높은 지위로 올라가다 be promoted to a higher position step by step // 차차 약아지다 《people》 become clever more and more // 차차 가까이 접근하다 get into close touch with 《a person》 in due time // 차차 추워진다 It is getting colder by and by 〔colder and colder〕. // 낮시간이 차차 길어진다 The daytime grows longer and longer. // 저금이 차차 불〔줄어 들〕었다 My savings have become more and more 〔less and less〕. // 차차 익숙해질 거야 You will get used to it by degrees. // 차차 말씀드리지요 I will let you know later on〔by and by〕. // 자세한 것은 차차 알게 될 것이오 All the details will be known in time.
차차차 〖음악〗 cha-cha(-cha) ¶ 차차차를 추다 cha-cha ; dance the cha-cha
차창 車窓 a car〔train〕 window ¶ 차창 밖을 내다보다 look out of the carriage window // 차창으로 내다보이는 풍경 the scenery seen from a car window
차체 車體 a frame ; a (car-)body ; a chassis
─ 검사 checking an automobile **─ 제조** coachwork **─ 중량** the tare
*__차축 車軸__ an axle
차출 差出 [일시적 전근] (a) temporary transfer **─하다** send on loan 《an employee of one department to another department》
차츰차츰 gradually ; by degrees ; step by step ; little by little ; inch by inch ; by and by ; more and more
차치 且置 setting〔putting〕 aside ; leaving unmentioned〔untouched〕; besides **─하다** let alone ; set〔put〕 aside〔apart〕 ¶ 차치하고 exclusive of ; apart from ; to say nothing 《of》
차치 물론 且置勿論 ⇨ 차치하다
차탁 茶托 a teacup holder ; a saucer 《for a teacup》
차탄 嗟歎 [탄식] sigh ; lament(ation) ; grief ; [감탄] admiration **─하다** lament ; sigh ; admire
차편 車便 a (public) conveyance ; 《by way of》 a vehicle ¶ 차편을 이용하다 avail oneself of a vehicle // 차편으로 여행하다 travel by (a) vehicle // 거기 가려면 어떤 차편이 있습니까 What kind of conveyance is available to go there?
차폐 遮蔽 cover ; shelter ; shielding ; 〖군사〗 defilade **─하다** cover ; shelter ; defilade ; shield 《from radioactivity》
─막 a blackout curtain **─물** cover ; shelter ¶ 차폐물 뒤에 숨다 draw into cover **─ 진지** a covered position **─ 케이블** 〖전기〗 a screened(-conductor) cable **─ 포대(砲臺)** a masked battery
차폭 車幅 the breadth of a car
─ 제한 a breadth limit
*__차표 車票__ a (railroad, bus, streetcar) ticket〔pass〕 ¶ 3일간 유효 차표 a ticket with a three-day time limit // 차표 파는 곳 a box office ; a booking office // 차표를 끊다 buy〔get〕 a ticket // 차표를 찍다〔개찰하다〕 punch tickets // 차표를 조사하다 examine tickets // 차표를 팔고 있다 The

ticket window is open. // 부산까지의 2등 차표 한 장을 주시오 Please give me a second-class (ticket) to *Pusan*.
— 브로커 a ticket broker ; a scalper 《미》 — 판매계 a ticket agent 《미》 ; a booking clerk 《영》 — 판매소 a booking office 《영》 ; a ticket office 《미》 ; [창구] a ticket〔booking〕 window 당일 — a day ticket 왕복 — a return-ticket ; a round-trip ticket 《미》 편도 — a one-way ticket 《미》 ; a single ticket 자동 — 판매기 a passometer ; a passimeter 《영》

차필 借筆 having 《a person》 write for one —하다 have 《a person》 write for one

차하다 (be) insufficient ; be not enough ; be short (of)

차하지다 差下— be inferior to ; be worse than ; be below ; fall behind

차한 此限 ¶ 단, 그 경우에는 차한에 부재함 This rule, however, does not apply to the case.

차항 次項 the following clause ¶ 차항 참조 confer 《cf.》 the next item〔clause〕

차형 次兄 one's second elder brother

차호 次號 the next issue〔number〕 ; the forthcoming issue
— 계속 (to be) continued (in the next issue) — 완결 (to be) concluded (in the forthcoming issue)

차환 借換 conversion ; refunding —하다 renew 《a debt》
— 공채 a converted loan — 발행 a conversion issue

차회 次回 next time ; the following occasion ; the following sequence ; [경기] the next game〔match〕 ¶ 차회의 next
— 완결 to be concluded in our next (issue) — 흥행 the next performance

차회 此回 this time

⁑차후 此後 after this ; henceforth ; hereafter ; from now on ; [장래] in (the) future ; for the future ¶ 차후에는 더 조심해라 Be more careful in future.

착 closely ; tightly ; sticking fast ; low ; deep ¶ 착 들러붙다 stick fast to // 착 가라앉은 목소리 a subdued〔deep, low〕 voice

착 着 ① arrival ; reaching ; getting to ⇨ 도착 ¶ 5일 인천착의 배 the ship due at *Inch'ŏn* on the 5th ② [경주] order of arrival ¶ 1착이다 be the first to finish〔arrive〕 ; come in first // 2착이다 be a runner-up // 그는 3착이었다 He finished third.

착각 錯角 [기하] alternate angles

착각 錯覺 an (optical) illusion ; a hallucination ; misunderstanding —하다 have〔be under〕 an illusion 《that》 ; become the victim of an illusion ; misunderstand ; misjudge ¶ 착각을 일으키다 be hallucinated ; be under a hallucination ; become a victim of an illusion ; have an illusion ; be confused into thinking 《that》 // 착각하고 있다 cherish〔be possessed with〕 the illusion 《that》 // 사람을 도둑으로 착각하다 mistake 《a person》 for a robber // 너는 나를 딴 사람으로 착각하고 있다 You've got me mixed up with somebody else.

착검 着劍 [호령] Fix bayonets ! —하다 fix a bayonet ; carry a sword ; wear a sword

착공 着工 starting (construction) work —하다 start〔begin〕 work ¶ 본 철도 공사는 내주에 착공한다 Construction work on this railway line begins next week.
—식 [건물의] a ground-breaking ceremony ; [배의] a keel-laying ceremony — 일자 the date of the start〔commencement, embarkment〕 of construction work

착근 着根 —하다 take〔strike〕 root ; find roots 《in》 ; root

착념 着念 keeping in mind ; paying attention to —하다 keep in mind ; pay attention to

착란 錯亂 distraction ; derangement ; aberration ; [무질서] disorder ; disarrangement ; confusion —하다 be distracted ; get confused ; be deranged ; aberrate ¶ 정신이 착란하다 go distracted ; go〔run〕 mad ; lose one's mind ; be mentally deranged // 정신을 착란시키다 drive 《a person》 distracted ; derange 《a person's》 mind
— 상태 a state of dementia ¶ 일시적으로 착란 상태가 되다 become temporarily insane 정신 — dementia ; mental derangement〔aberration〕

착렬 錯列 〖수학〗 alternation

착륙 着陸 landing ; alighting —하다 land ; alight ; make a landing ; reach the ground ¶ 불시 착륙하다 make a forced〔an emergency〕 landing // 도중 착륙하다 make a stop en route〔on the way〕 ; stop off〔over〕 《at》
—료(料) landing charges — 보조 시설 a landing aid —장 a landing field〔ground〕 ; a landing strip ; an airstrip — 장치 a landing gear ; undercarriage — 지시기 a landing indicator — 지점 a touchdown point 불시 — an emergency landing 야간 — 《make》 a night landing 연(軟)— soft landing 지상 유도 — the ground-controlled approach 무 — 비행 a non-stop flight 중도 —지 a way〔intervening〕 station ; a staging post

착모 着帽 putting on〔wearing〕 a hat —하다 put on〔wear〕 a hat

착발 着發 arrival(s) and departure(s) —하다 arrive and depart ; [총] percuss
— 시간표 a (railway) timetable ; a (railroad) schedule 《미》 — 신관(信管) a percussion fuse —탄 a percussion shell

착복 着服 ① clothing ② [횡령] embezzlement ; peculation ; misappropriation —하다 embezzle ; misappropriate ;

divert to one's private use ; pocket ¶ 출납계원이 은행돈 5만불을 착복했다 The cashier embezzled $50,000 from the bank. // 그는 거액의 공금을 착복했다 He embezzled a large sum of public money. // 그는 이익을 전부 착복했다 He pocketed all the profits. // 그는 회사 기금을 착복하였다 He helped himself to company funds. // 여러 국회의원들이 공금을 착복한 적이 있다 Several congressmen have had their hands in the till at one time or another.

착빙 着氷 icing《on an airplane》 **—하다** ice forms on ; [물체가 주어] ice (up)

착살맞다 (be) stingy ; mean ; nasty ; petty ; meticulous ¶ 착살맞은 짓 a niggardly thing to do // 조그마한 일에 착살맞다 be fussy about trifling things

†**착상 着想** (hitting on) an idea ; a conception ; a turn of thought **—하다** conceive an idea ; hit on an idea ¶ 좋은〔독창적〕 착상 a clever〔an original〕 idea // 착상이 좋다 be cleverly conceived ; be a clever conception〔idea〕 // 그의 문장의 착상은 기발하다 His writings are marked by originality of ideas. // 참 좋은 착상이다 That's a good idea.

착상 着床 〖생물〗 [수정란(受精卵)의] implantation **—하다** become implanted《on the uterine wall》

†**착색 着色** coloring ; coloration ; painting **—하다** color ; paint ; tint
—기(機) a tinter **—도기** painted china **—목판** a color woodcut **—법** coloring **—사진** a colored photograph **—석판쇄** a chromo ; a chromolithograph **—유리** stained glass **—제** a coloring agent **—화** a colored picture ; a colored print (색쇄)

착생 着生 〖생물〗 insertion

†**착석 着席** taking a seat **—하다** take a〔one's〕 seat ; take a chair ; sit down ; be seated ¶ 착석 순으로 in the order of seats // 착석하고 있다 be seated ; be in one's seat // 착석시키다 seat《a person》; induce《a person》 to take a seat // 여러분 착석해 주시오 Please be seated, gentlemen〔ladies〕. /Take your places, gentlemen !

착선 着船 arrival of a ship〔vessel〕 **—하다** arrive《at》

†**착수 着手** start(ing) ; commencement ; setting about ; outset **—하다** start ; commence ; begin ; set about《business》; set to《work》; put one's hand to ; put《work》 in hand ¶ 착수하고 있다 have《work》 in hand // 새 사업에 착수하다 embark〔start〕 on a new enterprise // 그 일〔조사〕에 착수하다 set about the work〔making inquiries〕 // 곧 일에 착수하겠다 I'll launch out on my work at once. /I'll set to work at once. // 공사는 아직 착수되지 않고 있다 No start has yet been made with the work. // 새로운 사업에 착수했다 A new undertaking has been set on foot. // 착수금이 10만원 필요하다 We want 100,000 *won* to start the work with.

착수 着水 splashdown (우주선의) ; alighting on the water **—하다** alight〔land〕 on the water ; splash down (우주선이)

착수금 着手金 a retaining fee ; a deposit ; bargain money (약조금) ; [시작하는] money paid to initiate work

착신 着信 arrival of the post〔mail〕 ; [전신] a message received
—국(局) a receiving〔the destination〕 post office

†**착실 着實** **—하다** (be) steady (and honest) ; sound ; steady-going ; trustworthy ; faithful ; [부유] be well-off ; moneyed ¶ 착실한 부자 quite a rich person ; a well-heeled person // 착실한 사람 a reliable〔trustworthy〕 person // 착실한 생각 a solid〔sober〕 view // 착실한 영업 방법 a sound business management // 착실한 자본 a substantial amount of capital // 일을 착실히 하다 do one's work faithfully // 장사를 착실하게 하다 do〔conduct〕 business on a sound basis // 어쩌면 그렇게 착실한 사람이 신세를 그르치는 그런 행동을 할 수 있을까 How could such a serious-minded man throw his life away like that ?

착안 着眼 aim ; notice ; attention ; observation ; conception **—하다** have an eye on ; pay attention to ; take notice of ; fix one's eyes upon ; aim at ¶ 착안이 좋다 be right in one's way of looking at the matter ; have an accurate observation ; pinpoint the right thing ; be a clever conception // 그가 그것을 착안한 것은 참 잘한 것이다 It is to his credit that he perceived it. // 그 사업의 유망성에 착안해서 투자했다 As the business looked promising, he invested money in it.
—점 the point aimed at ; the point of one's observation ; a point of view ; one's viewpoint ¶ 이것이 문제의 착안점이다 This is the aspect〔point〕 of the question which we must consider.

착암기 鑿岩機 a rock drill

착염 錯鹽 a complex salt

‡**착오 錯誤** a mistake ; an error ; a misapprehension **—하다** err〔make a mistake〕《in》; slip ¶ 착오에 빠지다 fall〔drift〕 into an error
시각 — an optical illusion ; hallucination **시대 —** anachronism **시행(試行) —** 〖심리〗 trial and error **언어 —증** paraphasia

†**착용 着用** putting on ; wearing **—하다** wear ; put on ; have on ¶ 제복을 착용하고 있다 be in uniform // 등교시는 제복을 착용하여야 한다 The students must attend school in uniform. // 참석자는 예복 착용을 바람 Full dress to be worn〔is in

ㅊ

order〕.
—품 (wearing) apparel ; habiliment
착유 搾乳 milking —하다 milk 《a cow, a goat》 ¶ 착유하는 여자 a milkmaid ; a dairymaid
—기 a milking machine — 동물 a dairy animal —용 가축 dairy stock —장 a dairy
착유 搾油 oil expression —하다 press 〔express〕 oil 《from》 ; extract oil by pressing
— 공장 an oil mill —기 an oil press 〔mill〕
착의 着衣 getting dressed ; dressing —하다 put on clothes ; dress
착임 着任 arrival at one's post —하다 arrive at one's post
착잡 錯雜 confusion ; intricacy ; involution ; tangle ; disorder —하다 (be) confused ; tangled ; mixed together ; involved ; intricate ; complicated ; perplexing ¶ 착잡한 사건 a complicated affair // 그 여자의 표정은 착잡한 심정을 나타내고 있었다 Her face betrayed a mixture of emotions within.
착전 着電 the arrival of a telegram (전신의 도착) ; telegram received (도착한 전신)
착정 鑿井 digging a well ; well-drilling〔-sinking〕 —하다 dig〔bore〕 a well
착종 錯綜 entangling ; intricacy ⇨ 착잡
착좌식 着座式 〖카톨릭〗 an enthronement
착지 着地 [체조 따위에서의] landing —하다 land 《on the mat》 ¶ 착지에 성공〔실패〕하다 make a good〔poor〕 landing
착착 steadily ; in orderly fashion ; step by step ; slow but sure ¶ 착착 진척하다 make steady progress ; progress steadily // 사업은 착착 진행되고 있다 The business is steadily progressing〔is well under way〕.
*착취 搾取 ① extortion ; exploitation —하다 exploit ; extort ; squeeze ; sweat 《one's workers》 ¶ 자본가의 착취 capitalist exploitation // 식민지를 착취하다 exploit a colony // 돈을 착취하다 screw 《a person》 out of his money
② [과즙] squeezing out ; extraction —하다 squeeze out ; extract ¶ 오렌지에서 즙을 착취하다 squeeze〔press〕 juice from 〔out of〕 oranges
— 계급 the exploiting class — 노동 sweated labor ; sweat shop labor — 산업 sweated industry — 제도 the sweating system 중간 — intermediary exploitation 피 — 계급 the exploited class
착탄 거리 着彈距離 the range of a gun ; gunshot ; shooting〔firing〕 distance ¶ 착탄 거리내〔밖〕에 있다 be in〔out of〕 range // 착탄 거리내에 오다〔밖으로 나가다〕 come within〔go out of〕 range // 착탄 거리를 재다 find the range // 이 포의 착탄 거리는 6마일이다 This gun has the range of 6 miles.
착탄 지점 着彈地點 an impact area
착하 着荷 arrivals ; arrival〔receipt〕 of goods ¶ 춘기 착하물 대매출 the opening sales of the spring assortment just in
— 인도〔지불〕 delivery〔payment〕 on arrival
*착하다 (be) nice ; good ; virtuous ; gentle ; kind ; [온순] meek ; obedient ; docile ¶ 착한 사람 a man of sincerity ; a good man // 착한 아이 a meek〔docile, good〕 child // 착한 일 a good deed ; a virtuous act ; virtue // 착하게 nicely ; gently ; virtuously ; benevolently // 마음이 착하다 be kindhearted ; be of good〔nice〕 disposition ; have a sweet temper // 착한 관리자로서 남을 다루다 treat others with the care of a good manager // 그는 마음은 착하지만 센스가 모자란다 He has a good heart but poor sense.
착하지 着荷地 the destination ¶ 착하지를 정하다 destine 《goods》 ; fix the destination
착함 着艦 [비행기의] deck-landing ; [귀함] rejoining one's ship —하다 [비행기가] land 《on a carrier, on the deck of a ship》
착항 着港 arrival (in port) —하다 make port〔harbor〕 ; arrive in port〔harbor〕 ; put〔get〕 into port
— 가격 landed terms
찬 贊, 讚 praise ; eulogy ; panegyric ; a legend ¶ 그림에 찬을 쓰다 write a panegyric over〔under〕 a painting ; write a sentence〔poem〕 on a painting in praise of it
찬 饌 a side dish ; relishes ; dishes served to go with rice ¶ 찬이 많다 have many side dishes
—거리 side-dish makings ; groceries
찬가 讚歌 a hymn ; a doxology
찬가게 饌— a pickle shop ; a grocer's (store)
찬간 饌間 a kitchen ; a pantry where side dishes are prepared
찬간자 a white-faced bluish horse
찬광 饌— a grocery storage ; a pantry ; a kitchen cupboard
찬국 soup (made from water, soy sauce, and vinegar)
찬기 cold air ; chilly atmosphere ¶ 찬기가 가시다 warm slightly // 찬기를 쏘이다 expose 《a thing》 to cold air
찬동 贊同 approval ; approbation ; support ; endorsement —하다 approve 《of》 ; support ; give one's approval ; endorse ¶ 찬동을 얻어서 with 《a person's》 approval〔support〕 // 찬동을 구하다 ask 《a person's》 approval 《of a plan》 // 찬동을 얻다 obtain 《a person's》 approval ; meet 《a person's》 approval // 찬동의 뜻을 표하다 express one's approval
*찬란 燦爛 brilliancy ; brightness ; resplendence ; radiancy ; glitter —하다 (be)

brilliant ; shining ; bright ; glittering ; gorgeous ; dazzling ; resplendent ; radiant ; glorious ; splendid ; lustrous ¶ 찬란한 문화 the glorious civilization // 찬란한 별 glittering stars // 찬란한 보석 a brilliant〔radiant〕 jewel // 찬란한 업적 a splendid accomplishment // 찬란한 장식 a glittering decoration // 찬란하게 빛나다 shine bright〔brightly, brilliantly〕 // 찬란한 승리가 그에게 안겨졌다 A brilliant victory fell to him. // 미스 코리아가 입은 의상은 매우 호화 찬란하다 The dress worn by Miss Korea looks so gorgeous and radiant.

찬립 簒立 usurpation of the throne **—하다** usurp〔seize〕 the throne

찬모 饌母 a woman cook (in charge of making side dishes)

찬무대 a cold current〔flowing, flow〕; the Arctic〔Antarctic〕 Current

찬물 cold water ¶ 나는 매일 아침 운동을 하고 나서 찬물로 샤워를 합니다 I take a cold shower after exercising every morning.

찬물을 끼얹다 관용 pour cold water ; take a cold shower ; [비유적] discourage

***찬미 讚美** praise ; glorification ; extolment ; admiration ; adoration **—하다** praise ; glorify ; extol ; eulogize ; chant hymns of praise to ; admire ; adore ¶ 신을 찬미하다 praise God〔the Lord〕; give praise〔glory〕 to God // 인생을 찬미하다 sing praise of life // 사람의 덕을 찬미하다 extol〔eulogize〕《a person's》 virtue

—자 an admirer ; an adorer

찬미가 讚美歌 a hymn ; a psalm ¶ 찬미가를 부르다 chant a psalm

찬바람머리 the (time of) setting in of the chill winds of autumn ; the early autumn ¶ 찬바람머리가 되었다 An autumn breeze begins to blow.

찬반 양론 贊反兩論 pros and cons

찬밥 cold boiled-rice

찬방 饌房 a store room for food supplies ; a service room ; a pantry

찬부 贊否 approval or disapproval ; yes or no ; ayes or noes ; for and against ; pros and cons ¶ 찬부의 논쟁 arguments for and against〔pros and cons〕 // 찬부를 결정하다 approve or disapprove ; [투표로] vote on 《a matter》 // 찬부를 묻다 put 《a matter》 to a vote // 찬부는 동수였다 The ayes and noes were equally divided among the members.

— 양론 pros and cons ; arguments for and against ¶ 찬부 양론을 듣다 listen to the pros and cons of 《the matter》 // 그 의안에 대해서는 찬부 양론이 있다 They are arguing for and against the bill.

찬사 讚辭 a praise ; words of praise ; a eulogy ; a panegyric ; a compliment ; kind remarks ¶ 찬사를 드리다 praise ; pay 《a person》 compliments ; compliment 《a person》 on ; eulogize ; pay tribute to 《a person》; speak of 《a thing》 in terms of high praise // 찬사를 아끼지 않다 be unsparing of〔in〕 one's praise

찬상 讚賞 admiration ; praise ; applause **—하다** admire ; praise ; applaud ; laud

⁑찬성 贊成 approval ; approbation ; agreement ; assent ; support ; endorsement ; favor ; patronage **—하다** [계획에] approve of 《a plan》; give one's approval to 《a plan》; [의견에] agree to 《a person's opinion》; agree with 《a person》; be agreeable to ; subscribe to 《a person's view》; assent to 《a person's opinion》; [의안·동의에] support 《a bill》; second 《a motion》; vote for 《a measure》; vote aye to 《a proposal》; favor ; be in favor of 《a reform》; endorse 《a plan》; [지지하여] take interest in 《a project》 ¶ 찬성을 얻어서 with the approval of 《a person》 // 만장 일치로 찬성하다 consent unanimously ; reach unanimous agreement // 동의에 찬성하다 second a motion // 찬성을 구하다 ask 《a person's》 support〔approval〕; beg 《a person's》 suffrage // 찬성을 얻다 win〔get, meet with〕 《a person's》 approval ; be consented // 자기 의견에 찬성시키다 win 《a person》 round to one's view // 영화 보러 가는 데 찬성하다 agree to go to the movies // 찬성이다 I am for it. /I am in favor of it. // 너의 의견에 찬성한다 I agree to your opinion. /I am for〔with〕 you. // 너는 이 일에〔나에게〕 찬성이냐 불찬성이냐 Are you for it〔with me〕 or against it〔me〕? // 찬성 100에 불찬성은 50이었다 There were 100 ayes and 50 noes. /A hundred were for and fifty were against. // 그는 찬성한다고 고개를 끄덕였다 He nodded in approval. // 찬성하는 분은 손을 들어 주시오 All those in favor, signify by raising your hands. /The ayes are requested to hold up their hands. // 그런 난폭한 방식에는 찬성할 수 없다 I can't go along with strong-arm tactics like that. // 나는 그 생각에 찬성이야 I go along with that idea.

—론 a supporting argument ¶ 찬성론과 반대론이 대립되었다 They argued for and against the plan. **— 연설** a speech in support of 《a measure》 ¶ 그는 그 동의에 찬성 연설했다 He spoke for〔in support of〕 the motion. **—자** a supporter ; an advocate ; a seconder **— 투표** a vote in favor of 《a motion》 ¶ 찬성 투표를 하다 vote for〔in favor of〕 《a bill》; cast a favorable〔an aye〕 vote for 《a measure》

—파 the consenting party

찬송 讚頌 praise ; glorification ; extolment ; admiration ; a eulogy ; an encomium **—하다** praise ; glorify ; chant hymns of praise to ¶ 하느님을 찬송하다 give

glory to God ; praise God ; sing God's praises // 사람의 덕을 찬송하다 extol 《a person's》 virtue
—가 a hymn ; a psalm ¶ 찬송가를 부르다 chant a psalm ; sing a hymn —가집 a hymnbook ; a hymnal
찬술 撰述 writing ; composing —하다 write ; compose ; compile
찬술 纂述 editing ; compilation —하다 edit ; compile
찬스 a chance ; an opportunity ⇨ 기회 ¶ 절호의 찬스 a capital chance ; a golden opportunity // 찬스를 잡다〔만들다, 얻다〕 seize〔make, get〕 a chance // 찬스를 놓치다 lose〔pass up〕 a chance // 자 지금이 찬스야 Now's your chance. // 우리가 달아날 찬스가 있을까 Is there any chance of our escape ?
— 메이커 a heads-up player —볼 a set-up ; a ball so played〔pitched〕 as to give one's opponent a good chance
***찬양 讚揚** praise ; commendation ; admiration ; laudation —하다 praise ; admire ; commend ; laud ¶ 찬양할 만하다 be worthy of praise ; be praiseworthy ; be commendable // 높이 찬양하다 admire highly ; speak in high terms ; praise to the skies // 말로 다 찬양할 수 없다 be beyond all praise // 그들은 소리높이 그를 찬양했다 They were loud in his praise (s).
찬역 簒逆 usurpation ; seizure —하다 usurp ; seize
찬연 燦然 brilliancy ; radiancy ; resplendence —하다 (be) brilliant ; resplendent ; radiant ¶ 찬연한 빛 brilliant light // 찬연히 빛나다 shine〔glitter〕 brilliantly
찬위 簒位 ⇨ 찬탈(簒奪)
찬의 贊意 approval ; approbation ¶ 찬의를 표하다 express one's approval
찬이슬 cold dew ¶ 찬이슬 맞은 놈 a rascal with the cold dew (of night) on him ; a thief
***찬장 饌欌** a pantry chest ; a cupboard ; a sideboard
찬조 贊助 support ; backing ; advocacy ; patronage ; approval ; [후원] sponsorship ; auspices ; endorsement ; approval ; [장려] encouragement —하다 support ; patronize ; render assistance ; advocate ; sponsor ; endorse ¶ A씨의 찬조하에 supported by Mr. A // 찬조 출연하다 appear as a guest star // 찬조를 얻다 obtain〔have〕 《a person's》 patronage〔endorsement〕 // 찬조를 구하다 solicit 《a person's》 support
—금 a contribution ; a donation — 연설 a supporting speech ¶ 지방 유세에서 찬조 연설을 했다 He appeared as a guest speaker at a barnstorming rally. —자 a supporter ; an assistant — 출연 appearance as a guest (artist) — 회원 a supporting member ; a patron member
찬찬 ⇨ 친친
찬찬하다 [꼼꼼하다] (be) meticulous ; very attentive ; considerate ; punctilious ; scrupulous ; thorough ; cautious ; [침착] calm ; composed ; quiet ; self-possessed ; placid ¶ 그는 성격이 아주 찬찬하다 He is very calm and attentive.
찬찬히 ① [침착하게] staidly ; deliberately ; calmly ; [꼼꼼히] carefully ; cautiously ¶ 찬찬히 준비하다 make thoroughgoing preparations ② [천천히] slowly ; leisurely ¶ 찬찬히 하다 take one's time 《in doing》
찬칼 饌— a small kitchen knife ; a carving knife ; [식탁용] a table-knife
찬탄 讚嘆 admiration ; praise ; applause ; laudation —하다 admire ; praise (highly) ; extol ; speak highly of ; be filled with admiration ¶ 찬탄할 만하다 [가치가 있다] be worthy of the highest admiration ; merit the highest praise
찬탈 簒奪 usurpation (by a subject) ; seizure —하다 usurp ; seize ¶ 왕위를 찬탈하다 usurp a throne
—자 a usurper
찬평 讚評 praising and criticizing ; a favorable criticism〔comment〕 —하다 comment〔criticize〕 favorably
찬합 饌盒 a dish〔box〕 for keeping side dishes ; a tier of side-dish boxes fitting one upon the other
찰 [곡식] sticky ; glutinous ; [형편] persistent ; extreme
찰가난 [적빈] extreme〔dire〕 poverty
—뱅이 a very poor person
찰거머리 〖동물〗 a leech ¶ 찰거머리 같은 사람 a barnacle ; a hanger-on ; a leech
찰 것 foodstuff made from glutinous grain ; glutinous〔sticky〕 eatables
찰과상 擦過傷 an abrasion ; a scratch ¶ 찰과상을 입다 have〔sustain〕 a scratch
찰교인 —敎人 a firm〔fanatic〕 believer 《in》
찰그랑 ⇨ 절그렁
찰기 —氣 stickiness ; glutinousness ; glutinosity ¶ 이 국수는 찰기가 좋다 These noodles have a good consistency.
찰기장 glutinous (Chinese) millet
찰깍 [붙는] sticking tight〔close, fast〕 ; [소리] with a slap〔snap〕 ¶ 젖은 옷이 몸에 찰깍 달라붙다 wet clothes cling tight to one's body // 사람을 찰깍 때리다 slap 《a person》 // 찰깍 잠그다 fasten 《a lock》 with a snap
찰깍거리다 keep slapping〔snapping〕
찰깍쟁이 a real〔nasty, mean〕 miser
찰깍찰깍 ① [붙는 모양] all sticking tight〔close, fast〕 ② [소리] with slap after slap ; snapping and snapping
찰나 刹那 a moment ; an instant ; a juncture ; the very moment ¶ 찰나적 쾌락 momentary pleasure // 유리창을 연 찰나 the minute〔instant〕 I opened the win-

dow // 그 찰나에 at that very moment ; at that juncture // …하려는 찰나에 on the point of 《doing》 ; on the spur of the moment ; impulsively // 찰나에 살다 live in the present ; live on (momentary) impulses ; enjoy the present moment
—주의 impulsiveness ; momentalism ; (the philosophy of) gathering rosebuds while you may

찰담쟁이 an incurable〔irremediable〕 syphilitic (person)

찰딱거리다 cling 《to》 ; stick 《to》

찰떡 rice cake made of glutinous rice ; glutinous rice cake

찰락거리다 trickle

찰락찰락 trickling

찰랑 lapping ; splashing ; with a splash
—하다 ⇨ 찰랑거리다

찰랑거리다 [쇠붙이] jingle ; clink ; tinkle ; [물] lap ; slop ; slosh ¶ 주머니 돈을 찰랑거리다 jingle the coins〔one's money〕 in one's pocket // 독 안의 물이 찰랑거린다 The water in a jar is slopping from side to side.

찰랑찰랑 ⇨ 찰랑거리다

찰바닥거리다 splash ; slop ; dabble 《one's legs in the water》 ¶ 찰바닥거리며 호수로 들어가다 splash one's way into the lake // 아이들은 웅덩이 속에서 찰바닥거리기를 좋아한다 Some children love slopping about in puddles.

찰밥 cooked glutinous rice

찰방 splash(ingly) ; splatter(ingly) ; dabbling(ly)

찰벼 a rice plant which yields glutinous rice

찰부꾸미 a fried ricecake made of ground glutinous rice

찰상 擦傷 an abrasion ; a scratch ; a graze

찰쇠 a metal ring fitting around a gate pivot

*⁑***찰싹** with a slap〔spank〕 ; splashingly ¶ 찰싹 때리다 spank ; slap 《a person on the face》 // 찰싹 매질하다 crack a whip on〔over〕 // 바둑을 찰싹 놓다 place one's *paduk*-piece with a click

찰쌈지 a tobacco pouch carried on one's side

찰짜 an overscrupulous person

찰찰 brimming over ; overflowing ¶ 주전자의 물이 찰찰 끓어 넘친다 The water in the kettle is boiling over.

찰찰 察察 —하다 (be) exact ; punctilious ; meticulous

찰흙 clay

참[1] [참으로] really ; truly ; in truth ; indeed ; in fact ; actually ; surely ; [감탄] oh ; well ; ugh ; now ¶ 참 춥다 It is awfully〔terribly〕 cold today. // 그 여자는 참 미인이다 She's ever such a beautiful woman. // 도와 주셔서 참 고맙습니다 It was very kind indeed of you to help me. /A thousand thanks for your kind help. // 참 재미 있었다 I had such a good time, indeed. // 참 별꼴이야 Fiddlesticks ! /What nonsense ! / How odd it is ! // 참 오늘이 일요일이지 Oh — it's Sunday, isn't it ? // 참 그렇구나 How true that is !

참[2] truth ; reality ; actuality ; genuineness ; [성실] sincerity ; fidelity ; [사실] a fact

참- [접두어] true ; real ; genuine
—말 a true remark ; the truth ; a (real) fact **—사람** a true man ; an honest man **—사랑** a true love

참 站 [장소] a post town ; a post station ; a stage ; a stop ; a resting place ; [시간] a rest period ; a break ; a recess ; [계단] the landing 《of the stairs》 ¶ 하는 참에 at the point of 《doing》 ; just when // 내가 나가려는 참이었다 I was just about to leave home.

†**참가 參加** participation ; joining ; adherence ; entry **—하다** participate 《in a project》 ; take part 《in a discussion》 ; join 《in a movement》 ; enter 《a war》 ; enter (for) 《a contest》 ; be a party to ¶ 참가를 신청하다 send an entry // 운동〔동맹파업〕에 참가하다 join a movement〔strike〕 // 경기에 참가하다 take part〔participate〕 in a game // 사람을 경기에 참가시키다 enter 《a person》 for a race // 60개국이 그 조약에 참가하고 있다 Sixty countries are parties to the treaty.
—교(校) an entrant school **—국〔팀〕** a participating nation〔team〕 **—료** an entry fee **—자** a participant ; a participator ; an entrant ; an entry **—자 명단** an entry
불— nonparticipation

참게 〖동물〗 a king crab ; a horse-shoe crab

⁑**참견 參見** interference ; meddling ; participation ; taking part ; association **—하다** interfere 《in a matter, with a person》 ; meddle 《in》 ; step 《in》 ¶ 참견 잘하는 사람 an officious person ; a meddlesome person ; a meddler // 남의 일에 참견하다 meddle〔interfere〕 in other people's affairs ; poke one's nose into another's business // 쓸데 없는 참견 마라 Mind〔Attend to〕 your own business. // 네가 참견할 일이 아니다 This is none of your business. // 그 여자는 무엇에든 참견한다 She meddles with everything. // 참견하지 마시오 Stay out of this. /Keep your nose out of this. / Butt out. 《속》

참경 慘景 a terrible〔horrible〕 sight ; a frightful scene ; a disastrous spectacle

⁑**참고 參考** reference ; information ; [참조] consultation ; comparison **—하다** refer to 《a book》 ; consult ¶ 참고가 되다 be of (great) value ; be a good guide ; be suggestive ; serve as a good reference ; furnish 《one》 with much information // 주석을 참고하다 consult〔refer to〕 the notes

ㅊ

// 문헌을 참고하다 refer to the literature ; consult a document // 참고로 for reference ; for one's information // 후일의 참고로 간직하다 keep it for future reference // …을 참고로 하여 with reference 《to》; in the light 《of》// 참고로 말한다 I say this only by way of suggestion〔for your information〕. // 사전은 어학 공부에 많은 참고가 된다 A dictionary is very useful〔helpful〕 in studying language. // 당신이 한 일에 대해서 참고의 말을 해줄 수 있는 사람들의 이름을 좀 적어 주십시오 Give me some references on your work, please. // 저 자료는 참고가 되었습니까 Did those reference materials do you any good? // 대충 한번 훑어보았는데 참고는 되지 않았다 I gave them a once-over, but they weren't much help.

— 문헌 a bibliography ; literature cited —물(物) a specimen —서 a reference book ; a book of reference (책끝 따위의) — 서류 reference documents —인 a reference ; [증인] a witness — 자료 reference materials —품 a specimen for reference

참고둥 〚조개〛 a rock shell ; Rapana thomasiana (학명)

참관 參觀 a visit ; (a visit of) inspection **—하다** visit ; see ; inspect ; make an inspection 《of》 ¶ 참관이 허락되다〔허락되지 않다〕 be open〔closed〕 to visitors // 학교〔수업〕를 참관하다 visit a school 〔class〕 at work // 공장을 참관하다 pay a visit of inspection to the workshops // 개표를 참관하다 witness the ballot-counting

—인 a visitor ; [선거 따위의] a witness —일 a visiting day —자 명부 a visitors' book

참괴 慙愧 shame ; humiliation ; [회한] compunction **—하다** feel shame 《at》; be ashamed 《of, to》 ¶ 참괴시키다 put 《a person》 to shame〔the blush〕

참극 慘劇 a tragedy ; a catastrophe ; a tragic event ¶ 참극의 현장 the scene of a tragedy // 참극을 빚어내다 enact a tragedy

참기름 sesame oil ¶ 참기름을 치다 season 《food》 with sesame oil

참깨 sesame ¶ 참깨를 찧다 grind sesame seeds

—씨 a sesame seed ; sesame

†**참나리** 〚식물〛 a tiger lily ; a crumble lily ; Lilium lancifolium (학명)

참나무 a kind of oak ; Quercus serrata (학명)

참녜 參— participation ⇨ 참여

*__참다__ bear ; endure ; put up with ; have patience with ; be patient ; persevere ; stand ; tolerate ; forbear 《to do, doing》; [자제하다] suppress ; repress ; control oneself ¶ 참을 수 있는〔없는〕 (un) bearable ; (in) tolerable // 참을성 있는 patient ; persevering ; long-suffering // 억지로 참다 endure beyond 《one's》 strength // 꾹 참다 possess one's soul in patience ; bear 《an ache》 with stoical resignation // 치통을 참다 endure toothache // 웃음을 참다 suppress one's laughter ; keep〔hold〕 back one's laughter // 노여움을 참다 suppress one's anger ; restrain one's wrath ; pocket an insult〔affront〕 // 뒤 마려운 것을 참다 resist the call of nature ; put〔hold〕 off a bowel movement // 오줌 마려운 것을 참다 contain one's urine ; put off relieving oneself // 배고픔을 참다 bear〔stand〕 hunger // 물 마시고 배고픔을 참다 satisfy one's hunger with water // 참고 또 참다 bear and forbear ; bear to the best of one's capacity // 참다 못하여 unable to hold back〔control〕 《a thing》 any longer ; impatient of // 참지 못하게 되다 exhaust one's patience ; one's patience become exhausted // 이 이상 참을 수 없다 I can't bear〔stand〕 this any longer. /This is the last straw. /I won't stand for such treatment. /This is too much for me. // 술 마시고 싶은 것을 꾹 참았다 I forbore my thirst for drink. // 참으시오 Keep your temper. / Have〔Practice〕 patience. // 싫어도 참아야 한다〔참으시오〕 If you don't like it, you may lump it. // 그는 나를 참을 수 없을 정도로 학대했다 He ill-treated me beyond all bearing. // 그에게는 더 이상 참을 수 없다 I have lost patience with him. /I can't endure〔stand〕 him any more. // 당분간 이 조건으로 참아 주시오 Put up with these terms for the time being. // 하루만 더 참아 주세요 Please bear with me another day. // 참지 말고 내 자리로 와요 Quit trying to put on a good face and come on over to my place.

참을 인(忍)자 셋이면 살인도 면한다 속담 Patience is the best buckler against affronts. /Patience is a virtue.

참담 慘憺 misery ; tragedy ; disaster ; wretchedness ; distress **—하다** [비참] (be) miserable ; terrible ; frightful ; tragic ; wretched ; [가련] pitiful ; pitiable ; miserable ¶ 참담한 광경을 이루다 present a gruesome spectacle〔scene〕 // 참담한 패배를 당하다 suffer a crushing defeat // 참담한 꼴을 보니 끔찍하다 be frightened to see a wretched plight // 참담한 죽음을 하다 die a miserable death // 그 때문에 농사는 참담했다 It has wreaked havoc with the crops.

참답다 ⇨ 참되다

참당 參堂 a visit to a temple〔shrine〕 **—하다** visit a temple〔shrine〕

참대 〚식물〛 a long-jointed bamboo ; Phyllostachys bambusoides (학명)

참돔 〚물고기〛 a red sea-bream ; Chrysophrys major (학명)

†**참되다** (be) true ; honest ; faithful ; sin-

cere ; truthful ; upright ; right-minded ; genuine ¶ 참된 사람 a genuine〔a sincere, an honest〕 person // 참된 우정〔친절〕 true friendship〔kindness〕 // 참된 용기 genuine courage // 참된 친구 a faithful friend

참뜻 true meaning ; sincere intention

참따랗게, 참딸게 truly ; faithfully ; truthfully ; sincerely ; really ; genuinely

참람 僭濫 presumptuousness ; presumption ; forwardness **—하다** (be) presumptuous ; arrogant

참렬 參列 attendance ; presence ; participation **—하다** attend《a ceremony》; take part《in》; go to ¶ 장례식에 참렬하다 attend〔go to〕 a funeral

—자 an attendant ; those present《총칭》 ¶ 다수의 참렬자 a large attendance

참례 參禮 attending a ceremony ; attendance ; presence ; participation **—하다** attend《a ceremony》; take part《in》; share《in》

참말 a true remake ; a fact ; a real fact ; an authentic story〔account〕; the truth ¶ 참말로 truly ; really ; certainly ; indeed ; very // 참말은 to tell the truth ; in fact ; in reality // 참말로 믿다 believe (to be true) ; accept (as true) ; take seriously // 참말로 놀라다 be really surprised // 그게 참말인가 Is that true? /Do you mean what you say? // 그게 참말일까 Can that be true? /I wonder if it is true. // 정직이 제일이란 참말이다 It is true〔It is truly said〕 that honesty is the best policy. // 너 참말로 말 잘했다 You have spoken well, indeed. // 그는 참말로 신사다 He is, in a true sense of the word, a gentleman.

참망 僭妄 presumption ; recklessness ; audacity ; assumption ; unreasonableness **—하다** (be) presumptuous ; audacious ; assumptive ; reckless ; unreasonable

참먹 an ink-stick of good quality ; Chinese ink of superior quality

참모 參謀 the staff《총칭》; a staff officer (개인) ; [상담역] an adviser ; a brain truster

—부 the General Staff (Office) **—역** a brain truster ; an adviser **—장** the chief of staff **— 장교** a staff officer **— 총장〔차장〕** the Chief〔the Vice-Chief〕 of the General Staff **— 회의** a staff conference ; a briefing **선거 —** an adviser in an election campaign **연합 — 본부** the Joint Chiefs of Staff

참모습 —貌襲 one's true face ; one's true character〔colors〕 ¶ 참모습을 드러내다 throw off one's disguise ; throw off the mask

참밀 『식물』 common wheat

참바 a heavy rope

참밥 站— a snack ; a workbreak snack

참배 參拜 worship ; visiting a place of worship **—하다** (go and) worship at〔pray before, pay homage to〕 a temple〔shrine, national cemetery〕

—자 a visitor《to a shrine》

참벌 a honeybee

참변 慘變 a disastrous accident ; a tragic incident ; a disaster ¶ 참변을 당하다 suffer a disastrous accident

참빗 a fine-tooth(ed) bamboo comb

***참사 慘死** a tragic death **—하다** meet with a tragic death ; be killed《in an accident》 ¶ 교통 사고로 참사하다 be killed in a traffic accident

참사 慙死 **—하다** die of〔from〕 shame ¶ 남을 참사시키다 shame a person to death

참사 參事 a secretary ; an advisor ; a councilor

—관 a councilor ; an adviser ¶ 대사관의 참사관 the councilor of an embassy **—회** a council

참사 慘事 a disaster ; a tragedy ; a disastrous〔terrible〕 accident

참사람 a true〔an honest〕 man ¶ 참사람이 되다 reform oneself ; turn over a new leaf ; become a sincere man ; live an honest life

참살 斬殺 beheading ; decapitation **—하다** behead ; decapitate ¶ 참살당하다 have one's head cut off ; be beheaded ; be decapitated

참살 慘殺 murder ; slaughter ; massacre **—하다** murder cruelly ; slaughter ; butcher ; massacre ¶ 일가족을 참살하다 murder〔wipe out〕 the whole family

— 사건 an atrocious murder case **— 시체** a mangled body〔corpse〕 **—자** a murderer ; a slayer

참상 慘狀 a terrible〔dreadful〕 sight〔scene〕; a wretched spectacle ; a pitiable〔miserable〕 state of affairs ; a sad situation ¶ 기근의 참상 the misery of a famine // 참상을 빚어내다 present a terrible sight〔spectacle〕; be in a miserable〔wretched〕 condition // 이재민의 참상은 가슴 아프다 The condition of the sufferers is most pitiable. // 전쟁 직후의 광경은 참상 그대로를 나타냈다 The scene after the battle presented a horrible spectacle.

****참새** a sparrow ¶ 참새처럼 재잘거리다 chatter like a sparrow // 참새가 울다 a sparrow chirps〔twitters〕

—떼 a flock of sparrows

참서 讖書 a book of prediction ; a prophetic book

참석 參席 attendance ; presence ; participation **—하다** be present《at》; present oneself《at》; attend ; take part《in》 ¶ 회의에 참석하다 attend〔be present at〕 the meeting〔conference〕 // 참석자가 많다〔적다〕 have〔there is〕 a large〔small, poor〕 attendance

—자 persons present ; attendance ; an

attendant (개인)

참선 參禪 the Zen-Buddhist meditation ; study of the Zen cult〔sect〕 ━하다 study and practice the Zen cult〔meditation〕 ; meditate

—자 a Zen practicer

참섭 參涉 meddling ; interference ; tampering ━하다 meddle〔interfere〕《in, with》; intervene《in》

참소 讒訴 a false charge ; (a) slander ; calumny ━하다 make a false charge《against》; make a false representation《of》

—자 a slanderer ; a calumniator

참수 斬首 beheading ; decapitation ━하다 behead ; decapitate ¶ 참수당하다 have one's head cut off ; be beheaded

—대 a scaffold ; a guillotine

참숯 hardwood charcoal ; charcoal made of oak wood

참 스쿨 a charm school

참신 嶄新 newness ; freshness ; originality ; novelty ━하다 (be) novel ; original ; up-to-date ; brand-new ; new and striking ¶ 참신한 교수법 an up-to-date method of teaching // 의장(意匠)이 참신하다 It is new and striking〔original〕 in design.

참언 讒言 a false charge〔representation〕; a slander ; a calumny ; a defamation ━하다 slander ; calumniate ; defame ; make a false representation

—자 a slanderer ; a calumniator

참언 讖言 a prediction ; a prophecy

*참여 參與 participation《in public affairs》 ━하다 participate in ; take part in ; join in ; have a share〔hand〕 in ; have anything to do ; concern oneself in〔with〕 ¶ 국정에 참여하다 take part in the conduct of state affairs ; take part in the national government // 이익 배당에 참여하다 share in the profits // 분배에 참여하다 come in for a share // 경영에 참여할 권리를 가지다 have the right to participate in management ; have a voice in management // 네가 참여할 바 아니니다 You have nothing to do with this. /It is none of your business.

—권 the right to participate ; a voice —자 a participant

참연 嶄然 ━하다 (be) prominent ; conspicuous ; preeminent ; unrivaled

참예 參詣 worship ; a visit to a temple〔shrine〕; a pilgrimage ━하다 visit〔worship at〕 a temple〔shrine〕; make〔go on〕 a pilgrimage《to》

—자 a visitor ; a worshiper ; a pilgrim (순례자) ¶ 경내는 참예자로 번잡하였다 The precincts were crowded with worshipers.

참외 a melon

— 넝쿨 a melon vine —밭 a melon field〔patch〕

참월 僭越 presumptuousness ; presumption ; forwardness ━하다 (be) presumptuous ; arrogant ; insolent

참위 僭位 ━하다 usurp the throne

†참으로 really ; truly ; indeed ; how ¶ 참으로 아름다운 그림 a truly beautiful picture // 그 소식을 들으니 참으로 기쁘다 I am really very pleased to hear the news. // 요즈음 내 수면 시간은 참으로 적다 My hours of sleep are now very few indeed. // 그는 참으로 위대한 정치가였다 He was a truly great politician.

참으아리 〖식물〗 sweet autumn clematis

†참을성 patience ; perseverance ; fortitude ; endurance ; forbearance ¶ 참을성 있는〔있게〕 patient(ly) ; persevering(ly) // 참을성이 없다 be impatient ; lack patience // 참을성 있게 기다리다 wait with patience〔forbearance〕 // 그는 참을성이 없다 He sticks to nothing. /He is a rolling stone.

참의원 參議院 the Senate ; the Upper House ; the House of Councilors

— 의원〔의장〕 a member〔the President〕 of the House of Councilors〔the Upper House〕 — 의원 사무국 the Secretariat of the House of Councilors

참작 參酌 consideration ; deliberation ; allowance ; qualification ; reference ━하다 take into consideration〔account〕; make allowances for ; consult ; refer to ; deliberate ¶ 정상을 참작하다 make allowances for the circumstances ; take account of the circumstances // 실정을 참작하여 in view of the actual circumstances《of》 // 연령을 참작하지 않고 without reference to age // 나이가 어리다는 점을 참작해야 한다 You must make allowances for his youth. /You must take his youth into consideration. // 이 사실을 참작해 주시오 Please take consideration of this fact.

참작약 —芍藥 〖식물〗 a Chinese peony

참전 參戰 participation in〔entry into〕 a war ━하다 participate in〔enter, join〕 a war ¶ 미국의 참전 America's entry into the war // 연합국 측으로 참전하다 enter the war on the Allied side

참정 參政 participation in government ━하다 participate in government

참정권 參政權 the right to vote ; political rights ; suffrage (rights) ; franchise ¶ 참정권을 부여하다 give〔grant〕 the suffrage《to》; enfranchise

—론자 a suffragist — 반대자 an antisuffragist — 부여 enfranchisement — 획득 the acquisition of the franchise 여성 — woman suffrage 여성 — 운동자 a suffragette

*참조 參照 reference ; comparison ━하다 refer《to》; compare《with》 ¶ 참조하라 see ; confer《cf.》; vide《v.》 // 해당 항목 참조 quod vide《q. v.》 // 35페이지 참조

See〔Confer〕 page 35. // 각주 참조 Refer to footnotes. /See footnotes.
전후 — cross reference
참조기 〖물고기〗 a yellow corvenia ; Pseudosciaena manchuria (학명)
참주 僭主 a usurper (of the throne) ; a tyrant ; a despot
참죽나무 〖식물〗 a kind of red oak ; Cedrela sinensis (학명)
참참 站站 a rest ; a recess ; repeated stops〔breaks〕 ; every relay station ¶ 참참이 at intervals ; leisurely
참척 慘慽 the sad bereavement〔loss〕 of a child〔grandchild〕
참척 보다 관용 be bereaved of one's child〔grandchild〕
참척하다 be absorbed〔lost〕 in ; be devoted to ; devote oneself to
참칭 僭稱 arrogation to oneself of a title〔rank〕 ; claiming the title 《to》 ; an unjustified title —하다 assume the title 《of》 ; claim the title 《to》 ; usurp the name 《of》
참패 慘敗 a miserable defeat ; a crushing〔a serious, an overwhelming〕 defeat ; [경기의] a skunk ; [야구의] a shut-out —하다 suffer〔sustain〕 a crushing defeat ; be routed ; [경기에서] be beaten utterly〔all hollow〕 ; [야구에서] be shut out (영패) ¶ …와의 싸움에서 참패하다 meet with a disastrous defeat in a battle 《with》
참하다 [얌전하다] (be) nice and pretty ; mild ; quiet ; meek ; modest ; reserved ; good(-tempered) ; [말쑥하다] trim ; tidy ; neat ; smart ¶ 참한 색시 a nice〔gentle〕 young lady ; a neat young lady // 참한 집 a neat〔snug〕 house // 참하게 굴다 behave nicely
참하다 斬— cut off 《a person's》 head ; behead
참학 慘虐 cruelty ; brutality ; atrocity ; inhumanity ; savagery —하다 (be) cruel ; savage ; brutal ; atrocious ¶ 참학한 행위 a brutal act ; brutalities ; atrocities
참한하다 —限— wait till the due date
참해 慘害 heavy damage ; havoc ; ravage ; a disaster ; a holocaust ¶ 원자폭탄의 참해 the horrors of an atomic bomb // 참해를 입히다 work havoc 《with》 ; do heavy damage 《to》 // 참해를 입다 suffer severely from 《a storm》
참형 慘刑 a cruel〔terrible〕 punishment
참형 斬刑 execution〔death〕 by beheading ; decapitation ; beheading ¶ 참형에 처하다 punish by beheading ; decapitate ; behead
**참호 塹壕 a trench ; a dugout ; a foxhole ; an entrenchment ¶ 참호를 파다 dig〔make〕 a trench〔foxhole〕 ; throw up〔open〕 trenches
— 공사 trench fortification works — 굴착용 삽 an entrenching shovel — 생활 life in the trenches —선 a line of trenches ; a trench line ; entrenchment —열 trench fever — 작업 trenchdigging operations —전 trench warfare 가(假)— a dummy trench
참혹 慘酷 cruelty ; terribleness ; misery ; wretchedness ; pitiableness ; distress —하다 (be) cruel ; brutal ; atrocious ; miserable ; wretched ; tragic ; sad ; pitiable ; pathetic ; touching ¶ 참혹한 사람 a cruel〔brutal〕 person // 참혹한 생활 a wretched life // 참혹한 행위 a cruel act ; a cold-blooded act // 참혹한 죽음을 당하다 die in great misery // 참혹한 짓을 하다 do a cruel thing ; commit cruelties // 참혹하게 다루다 treat 《a person》 cruelly ; be cruel to 《a person》 ; be hard on 《a person》
참화 慘禍 a terrible disaster〔misfortune〕 ; calamity ; horrors ¶ 전쟁의 참화 the horrors〔ravages〕 of war // 전쟁의 참화를 입다 suffer the ravages of war
참회 參會 attendance 《at a meeting》
—하다 attend 《a meeting》 ; be present at 《a meeting》 ¶ 다수의 참회자가 있었다 There was a large attendance. / There were a large number of attendants. // 각국에서 대표가 참회했다 All the countries were represented at the meeting.
*참회 懺悔 [고백] confession ; [회오] repentance ; penitence ; contrition —하다 [고백하다] confess ; make a confession ; [회오하다] (be) penitent ; repent 《of one's sins》 ¶ 참회의 눈물 penitential tears // 참회의 생활 a penitential〔a penitent's〕 life // 죄를 참회하다 confess one's sins // 신부에게 참회하다 confess one's sin to a priest〔father〕 // 참회하여 죄의 용서를 받다 be confessed of a crime // 고백은 참회의 표시이다 Confession is one mark of repentance.
—록 a confession ; [책 이름] The Confessions —자 a confessant ; a penitent — 청문실(聽問室) a confessional
참획 參劃 participation in planning —하다 participate〔have a hand〕 《in the planning of a program》
찹쌀 glutinous rice
찹찹하다 ① [물건이] be neatly piled〔heaped〕 up ; be stacked in good order ② [마음이] (be) composed ; calm〔cool〕 and serene ; self-possessed
찻감 茶— tea material
찻길 車— ① [궤도] a train track ; a car track ; a railway line ② [차도] a roadway ; a carriageway ; a driveway 《미》 ; a pavement 《미》
찻물 茶— tea (to drink) ; [녹차] green tea ; [홍차] black tea ; [커피] coffee ¶ 진한〔묽은〕 찻물 strong〔thin, pale〕 tea // 찻물이 잘 우러나다 The tea brews〔draws〕 well.

찻삯 the fare (on train, streetcar)
*찻숟가락, 찻숟갈 茶— a teaspoon ¶ 찻숟갈로 하나 a teaspoonful 《of sugar》
찻잎 茶— tea leaves
*찻잔 茶盞 a teacup
†찻종 茶鍾 a teacup ; a teabowl ¶ 차를 찻종에 따르다 pour tea into a cup
찻집 茶— a tea-house〔-stall〕; a tea-shop ; a tearoom ⇨ 다방
창¹ [구멍] a hole (made in paper or cloth) ; a tear ; a rent ¶ 저고리에 난 창 a hole in the coat
창² [구두의] a shoe sole ; sole leather ¶ 창을 갈다 resole 《shoes》; repair a sole ; put a new sole
구두— a shoe sole 밑— an outer sole 속— an inner sole 안— a liner
⁑창 槍 a spear ; a javelin (던지는) ; [기병의] a lance ¶ 창으로 찌르다 spear 《a person》; thrust a spear // 창을 놀리다 wield〔take〕 a spear
—고달 the butt end of lance —끝 a spearhead —던지기 javelin throw〔throwing〕 (경기) —자루 a spear handle〔shaft〕
창 瘡 syphilis ⇨ 창병
창 窓 a window ; [올리고 내리는] a sash window ; [선반의] a port ¶ 창을 열다 open a window ; raise a window (위로) // 창을 닫다 close a window ; lower a window (아래로) // 창밖을 보다 look out of a window // 창으로 넘겨다보다 peep in at the window // 창가에 서다 stand by the window // 창에서 얼굴을 내밀다 stick one's head out of the window // 창을 열어 주시겠습니까 Will you please open the window? /Would you mind opening the window? // 창을 열어도 좋습니까 Would you mind my opening the window? / Would you mind if I open the window? // 그는 창밖의 젖은 지붕을 봤다 She looked through the window at the wet roofs. // 내 방의 창은 정원〔거리〕을 향하고 있다 My windows look out into the garden〔on the street〕.
—틀 a window frame 유리— a glass window 이중— a double window
창가 娼家 the house of a prostitute ; a bawdy house ; a brothel ; a house of ill fame ; a cathouse 《미·속》
창가 唱歌 singing ; a song ; vocal music ¶ 창가를 잘하다〔못하다〕 be good〔bad〕 at singing ; be a good〔bad〕 singer
—대 a choir —집 a collection of songs
창간 創刊 the first edition〔publication〕; foundation 《of a journal, periodical》 —하다 found ; start ¶ 1945년 창간 Founded in 1945. ; First published in 1945.
— 기념호 a special number in commemoration of the foundation 《of the journal》 —호 the initial〔first〕 number〔issue〕 of 《a magazine》 ¶ 창간호를 발행하다 issue its first number ; publish the first edition

창갈이 resoling ; sole-repairing —하다 resole (shoes) ; tap
창건 創建 establishment ; founding ; foundation ; embarkment ; inauguration —하다 establish ; found ; organize ; start ; embark ; inaugurate ; bring into existence ¶ 그 단체는 한국동란 직후에 창건되었다 The organization was established right after the Korean War.
창견 創見 an original view ; originality ¶ 창견이 풍부하다 be original ; be fertile ; have a creative mind // 그것은 A씨의 창견이다 It was originated by Mr. A.
*창고 倉庫 a warehouse ; a storehouse ; [동양의] a go-down ; [군수품의] a magazine ¶ 창고에 보관하다 warehouse 〔store〕 《goods》
— 계원 a warehouse keeper ; a storekeeper —료 warehouse charges —업 warehousing (business) — 인도 ex warehouse ; ex store — 증권 a warehouse bond —품 【부기】 stores — 회사 a warehouse〔storage〕 company 보세— a bonded warehouse 일반〔특수, 사설〕— a general〔special, private〕 warehouse
*창공 蒼空 the blue sky ; the blue expanse of heaven ; the vault of heaven ; the firmament ¶ 창공을 날다 fly in the sky
창구 創口 the lips of a wound ; a cut ; a wound ; a gash
창구 艙口 a hatch ; a hatchway
창구 窓口 a window ; a wicket ¶ 매표 창구에서 at a ticket window // 창구의 서비스(를 개선하다) (give better) service at the window
— 계원 a clerk at the window 출납 — a cashier's〔teller's (은행의)〕 window〔cage〕
창궁 蒼穹 the blue sky ; the vault of heaven ; the blue heavens ; the welkin ⇨ 창공 蒼空
창궐 猖獗 rage ; fury ; rampancy —하다 rage ; be virulent ; be rampant ; be rife ; go on the rampage ¶ 콜레라가 전국적으로 창궐하다 Cholera is prevalent throughout the country. // 유행성 감기가 그곳에 창궐하고 있다 The flu〔influenza epidemic〕 is raging very fiercely there.
창극 唱劇 a Korean classical opera
창기 娼妓 a prostitute ; a harlot ; a street-girl ; a whore ; a white slave 《미》 ¶ 가난 때문에 창기로 팔리다 be driven by poverty to white slavery
창기병 槍騎兵 a lancer
창끝 a spearhead ; the point of a spear
창나무 the rudderstick of a boat
창난젓 salt-pickled pollack tripe
창녀 娼女 a prostitute ; a whore ; a harlot ; a street-girl ¶ 창녀 노릇하다 sell oneself as a prostitute // 창녀집에 드나들다 frequent a prostitute quarter
창달 暢達 a fluency ; activity ; liveliness ;

briskness ¶ 언론의 창달 the promotion of the freedom of speech

창당 創黨 formation of a political party **—하다** form〔organize〕 a political party **— 당원** a charter member of a party **— 이념** founding ideology (of a party) **— 정신** the spirit〔principles〕 underlying the formation of the party

창대 槍— a spear-handle〔-shaft〕

창던지기 槍— 〖경기〗 javelin (throw) ; a javelin-throwing contest ¶ 창던지기를 하다 throw a javelin // 그녀는 창던지기에서 57미터로 우승했다 She won the javelin with a toss of 57 meters.

— 선수 a javelin thrower

창도 唱導 advocacy **—하다** advocate ; advance ; preach ; uphold ¶ 자유를 창도하다 espouse the cause of liberty // 신학설을 창도하다 advance a new theory // 금주를 창도하다 advocate temperance

—자 an advocate ; an exponent ; a proponent ; an apostle

창독 瘡毒 the infectious boil ; virus of the boil

†창립 創立 founding ; foundation ; establishment ; creation ; formation **—하다** found ; establish ; form ; organize ; set up ¶ 1900년 창립 Established in 1900. // 창립한 지 얼마 안된다 It is not very long since the company was formed.

— 10주년 기념일 the tenth anniversary of the founding 《of the school》

— 위원〔사무실〕 the organizing committee〔office〕 **—자** the founder **— 총회** the inaugural〔first general〕 meeting **— 취지서** the prospectus

창만 脹滿 〖의학〗 abdominal dropsy

창망 蒼茫 vastness of an expanse of water ; the boundless expanse of water ; the blue sea **—하다** (be) vast ; boundless

†창문 窓門 a window ; a porthole (배의)

창밖 窓— ¶ 창밖에 outside the window // 창밖을 내다보다 look out (of) the window // 창밖의 경치를 바라보다 enjoy the shifting scenes outside the carriage window

창받다 [구두의] put a sole on a shoe ; [양말의] put a patch on a sock

창백 蒼白 pallor ; paleness ; pallidness ; whiteness **—하다** (be) pale ; pallid ; white ; livid ¶ 창백해지다 turn pale〔white〕 // 그는 안색이 몹시 창백하다 He is looking awfully washed out.

창병 瘡病 syphilis ; pox 《속》 ; venereal diseases 《총칭》 ⇨ 매독 梅毒

창부 倡夫 an actor

창부 娼婦 a prostitute ; a whore ; a harlot ; a street-girl ¶ 창부 생활을 하다 prostitute oneself ; walk the street

창살 窓— [문의] a lattice (work) ; a lattice strip ; a grating ; a grille ; [감옥의] iron bars ¶ 창살 없는 감옥 a prison without bars

—문 a latticed door **가로 —** a bar **세로 —** a cross-rib of a window

창상 創傷 a cut ; a wound by an edged weapon ; a gash ; an injury

창생 蒼生 the people ; the populace ; the masses ; the subjects

창설 創設 establishment ; foundation ; creation **—하다** establish ; found ; create ¶ 학교를 창설하다 found a school // 그 회사는 창설된 지 얼마 되지 않았다 It is not very long since the company was established.

—자 the founder ; the organizer

창성 昌盛 prosperity ; flourishing ; thriving **—하다** prosper ; thrive ; flourish

창세 創世 the creation of the world

—기 《성경》 the Genesis

창술 槍術 spear (s) manship

창시 創始 origination ; commencement ; initiation ; foundation **—하다** initiate ; originate ; found ; create ¶ 그것은 A씨가 창시했던 것이다 It originated with〔It was invented by〕 Mr. A.

—자 an originator ; a founder ; an initiator

창안 創案 [생각] an original idea〔plan〕 ; an originality ; [입안] origination ¶ 그것은 그〔우리 회사〕의 창안이다 The idea originated with him〔our firm〕.

—자 the originator ; the inventor

창알거리다 ⇨ 칭얼거리다

창애 a trap ¶ 창애에 걸리다 get caught in a trap

쥐— a rattrap ; a mousetrap

창업 創業 the commencement of an enterprise ; establishment ; foundation ; inauguration ; [건국] founding a nation ; 〔dynasty〕 **—하다** start 《a new enterprise》 ; start business ; begin operations ; establish ; found ¶ 창업의 어려움 initial difficulties // 창업 50주년을 기념하다 celebrate its fiftieth anniversary // 창업은 쉬우나 끝까지 유지하기가 어렵다 The difficulty is not to start an enterprise but to carry it to final success. // 어떤 사업에 있어서나 창업 당시의 난관은 각오하지 않으면 안된다 We must be prepared for a certain difficulty in starting any enterprise.

—비 initial〔starting〕 expenses **—자** the founder

창연 蒼然 **—하다** [푸르다] (be) blue ; bluish ; [어두컴컴하다] dim ; gloomy ; gray ; shady ; somber ; [고색] antiquated ¶ 고색이 창연하다 be black with age ; antique ; hoary with antiquity ; venerable

창연 悵然 dejection ; gloom (iness) ; depression **—하다** (be) dejected ; gloomy ; depressed ; dispirited ; downcast ¶ 창연히 sadly ; sorrowfully ; mournfully

창연 蒼鉛 〖화학〗 bismuth 《Bi》

창유리 窓琉璃 a windowpane

— 닦개 (자동차의) a windshield washer

창의 創意 an original idea ; originality (of thought) ¶ 그것은 전적으로 그의 창의에 의한 것이다 It is entirely original with him. /That comes entirely from his originality.
—력 an initiative spirit ; initiativeness ¶ 창의력이 풍부한 사람 a man of great originality // 창의력이 없다 lack originality // 그는 창의력이 풍부하다 He is rich in originality. / He has a great creative talent.

창이 創痍 a cut ; a wound ; a bruise ¶ 만신창이가 되다 be thoroughly hurt 〔injured〕; be covered all over with wounds ; have cuts all over one's body ; [비판] be the object of criticism

창일 漲溢 overflow ; inundation **—하다** overflow ; flood ; inundate

***창자** 〖해부〗 intestines ; bowels ; the entrails ; guts ¶ (동물의) 창자의 intestinal ; enteric // 창자가 끊어지는 듯이 아프다 have a splitting pain in the intestines ; have stitches in the side (옆배가)

†**창작 創作** creation ; origination ; original 〔creative〕 work (작품) ; [저작] creative writing **—하다** create ; write an original work ¶ 창작에 종사하다 engage in creative writing〔original work〕// 창작 분야에서 활약하다 [문학] play an active part in the field of creative literature // (접수는) 창작에 한함 [모집 조건] Only original work is accepted〔available〕.
—가 a creative writer ; an author (저자) ; a novelist (소설가) **—력** creative power ; originality **—욕** an appetite for writing ; the will to write **—품** a creation ; an original work ; an original production (제작) ; a literary work ; a novel ; a fiction

창제 創製 invention ; origination **—하다** invent ; originate

†**창조 創造** creation **—하다** create ; call into being ¶ 창조적 creative ; originative // 천지 창조 이래 since the creation of Heaven and Earth // 창조의 재능 creative genius // 창조적 진화론 creative evolutionism // 하느님이 최초에 천지를 창조하셨다 In the beginning God created the heaven and the earth.
—력 creative power **—물** a creature ; creation 《총칭》 **—설** creationism **—성** creativity **—자** a creator ; [신] the Creator **천지 —** Creation ¶ 천지 창조 이래 since the Creation of the world〔of Heaven and Earth〕

창졸 倉卒 suddenness ; unexpectedness ; precipitation ; hurry

창졸간 倉卒間 ¶ 창졸간에 in the midst of great hurry ; at a moment of precipitation〔rush, haste〕// 창졸간에 찾아뵙지도 못하였습니다 I was in such a hurry that I could not pay you a visit.

창증 脹症 abdominal dropsy ; ascites

창창하다 蒼蒼— [빛깔] (be) deep blue ; azure ; deep green ; [장래가] long ; wide ; broad ; bright ; prosperous ; rosy ¶ 창창한 대해 the blue〔vast, boundless〕 sea ; the deep // 그는 장래가 창창한 청년이다 He is just a young man who has the world before him〔who is in the prime of youth〕. // 우리 갈 길이 창창하다 We still have a long, long way to go.

창천 蒼天 the blue sky ; the (vault of) heaven ; the firmament

창칼 ① ⇨ 찬칼 ② [작은 칼] a small knife

창턱 窓— a windowsill

†**창틀 窓—** a window frame ; a sash (아래위로 여닫는 창의) ; a reveal (자동차의)

창파 滄波 big waves ; billows
만경 — the vast expanse of waters ; the endless waves ; the billowy sea

창포 菖蒲 〖식물〗 a sweet flag ; a calamus
—꽃 an iris flower **—원** a garden of irises

***창피 猖披** shame ; disgrace ; ignominy ; dishonor ; infamy ; humiliation **—하다** (be) ashamed ; shameful ; ignoble ; ignominious ; discreditable ¶ 창피한 일 a shame ; a disgrace // 매우 창피한 일 a burning〔crying〕 shame ; a deep disgrace // 창피를 아는 사람 a man of honor // 창피를 알다 be sensible to shame ; have a sense of shame // 창피를 무릅쓰다 disgrace oneself ; humiliate oneself ; be put to shame ; bring disgrace upon oneself // 창피를 주다 put 《a person》 to shame ; humiliate 《a person》 ; bring 《a person》 into contempt ; insult // 창피를 당하다 be put to shame ; be humiliated // 창피를 참다 suppress the feeling of shame ; tolerate an insult // 오래 살다 보면 창피한 일도 많다 To live long is to outlive much. // 아이구 창피해 What a shame ! // 무슨 창피니 Shame on you ! / Shame ! // 창피스러워 말 못하겠다 I would be ashamed to say that. // 그것은 남자로서는 창피(한 일이)다 A man must be ashamed of it. // 네가 그런 짓을 하면 온 집안이 창피를 당한다 If you do such a thing, you will bring shame on our whole family.

창하 倉荷 warehouse goods
— 증권 a warehouse certificate

창해 滄海 the vast blue sea ; the ocean ; the deep ; the vast expanse of waters
— 일속(一粟) a mere drop in the bucket〔ocean〕

창호 窓戶 windows and doors

창호지 窓戶紙 window-paper ; sliding screen paper ; paper for sliding doors ¶ 창호지를 바르다 paper a sliding door

창화 唱和 a chorus **—하다** sing〔cry, give〕 in chorus ; join (in the chorus)

창황 倉皇 ¶ 창황하게 hastily ; in a great hurry ; in a rush // 창황하게 떠나다 leave hastily〔in great haste〕

— 망조(罔措) a flurry ¶ 창황 망조하다 be panic-stricken ; be upset

†찾다 ① [발견] seek for〔after〕; search 《for》; hunt (up) ; trace ; look for〔up〕; follow up ; look out for ; locate ¶ 찾고 있다 be searching〔looking〕 for ; be on the look out for ; be in quest of // 찾아 다니다 search〔look〕 about for 《a thing》// 사람을 찾다 look for a person // 집을 찾다 locate a house // 집안에서 찾다 search a house 《for something》// 서랍 속을 찾다 rummage (in) the drawer for 《a name-card》// 호주머니를 찾다 fumble〔feel〕 one's pocket 《for a coin》// 일자리를 찾다 hunt for a job ; look for work // 잃은 아이〔개, 지갑〕를 찾다 search for〔trace〕 a lost boy〔dog, purse〕// 단서를 찾다 search for clues // 연고를 찾다 hunt up connections ; look out for a link // 그는 전셋집을 찾고 있다 He is looking〔hunting〕 for a house to let〔a house for rent 《미》〕. // 누구를 찾고 계십니까 Who〔Whom〕 are you looking for? // 나는 열쇠를 찾으려고 그의 호주머니를 뒤졌다 I searched his pockets for the key. // 나는 포켓 안의 지갑을 (더듬어서) 찾았다 I felt in my pocket for my purse. // 지도로 그 도시를 찾았다 I looked up the town on the map. // 경찰은 그 남자를 찾기 위하여 온 도시를 수색했다 The police combed the city〔streets〕 for the man. // 그들은 먹을 것을 찾아다녔다 They looked〔searched〕 about for food. // 그들은 길 잃은 아이를 찾으러 나섰다 They went in search of a lost child. // 실례하지만 베이커라는 사람이 제임스 테일러를 찾으면 나한테 보내주세요 Excuse me. If a Mr. Baker asks for James Taylor, please direct him to me. // 그 커리숍에서 어떤 사람이 나를 기다리고 있는데 좀 찾아주시겠습니까 I have a person waiting for me in the coffee shop. Could you please page him for me? // 마이크로〔안내 방송으로〕 사람 좀 찾아주시겠습니까 Could you please hare a person paged for me? // 콘택트 렌즈를 같이 찾아주지 않을래 Will you help me hunt for my contact?

② [저금을] draw ; [임대물을] redeem ; take out ¶ 은행에서 만원을 찾다 draw ten thousand *won* from the bank // 은행예금을 찾다 draw on one's bank account ; draw one's savings from the bank // 전당포에서 반지를 찾다 redeem one's ring from the pawn shop // 우체국에서 소포를 찾다 go to the post office to pick up a parcel // 잘 생각해 보면 그에 대한 대답을 찾을 수 있을 거야 I think you can come up with the answer to that if you'll really think about it.

③ [방문] call at 《a place》; call on 《a person》; visit ; drop in ; look in ¶ 그는 나를 찾아왔다 He came to see me. // 이쪽으로 오시는 길에 종종 찾아 주십시오 Please drop in (on us) when you come this way. // 어제 시골서 친척이 찾아왔다 I had a visit yesterday from a relative from the country.

④ [사전을] consult 《a dictionary》; look up ¶ 사전에서 단어를 찾다 look up a word in a dictionary

†찾아내다 find out ; discover ; detect ; locate ; look〔hunt〕 for ; seek ¶ 사망 원인을 찾아내다 trace the cause of 《a person's》 death // 군중 속에서 찾아내다 spot 《a person》 in the crowd // 소문의 출처가 그라는 것을 찾아냈다 The rumor was traced back to him. // 내 책을 찾아내시오 Please find me my book. / Please find my book for me. // 오래된 서류 가운데서 이 종이를 찾아냈다 I discovered this paper among some old documents of my own. // 잘 생각해 보면 그에 대한 대답을 찾아낼 수 있을 거야 I think you can come up with the answer to that if you'll really think about it.

찾을모 a merit ; value ; a feature that makes it worthwhile to visit ¶ 그 산의 절경은 찾을모가 있다 The beautiful scenery of that mountain is worth visiting. // 그 여자에게는 하등 찾을모가 없다 There is nothing in her.

채¹ [북·장구의] a drumstick ; [채찍] a whip
말— a whip ; a switch 종아리— a switch (to use on the legs) 총— a horsehair duster 파리— a fly swatter

채² bearing poles ; [수레의] shafts
가마— a palanquin pole 상여— the pallbearers' poles on a funeral bier

채³ a building of a group of connected buildings ¶ 집 두 채 two houses // 집채 같은 바위 a rock as big as a house
딴— a separate building〔wing〕 사랑— a detached building〔the detached wing of a house〕 used for a reception room 큰— the main building〔house〕

채⁴ [물이 고루 안 먹음] uneven dye ; spotty〔streaky〕 coloring

채⁵ the length of a long and slender object ; [머리채] a tress of hair

채⁶ shredding〔mincing〕 vegetables ; shredded vegetables ; vegetable shreds〔chops〕 ¶ 오이를 채치다 shred a cucumber 《for salad》

채⁷ [아직] incomplete ; (not) yet ; as yet ; so far ; [겨우] only ¶ 사과가 채 익지 않았다 Apples are not quite ripe. // 그의 소설 작품은 채 완성되지 못했다 He has not yet finished his novel. // 이 건물은 지은 지 한달이 채 못된다 It is less than a month that〔since〕 the building was built. // 그것은 채 자리가 잡히지 않았다 It is not yet on the right track.

채⁸ just as it is ; intact ; as it stands ; with no change ¶ 사람을 산 채로 묻다 bury 《a person》 alive // 뼈 채로 다 먹다

ㅊ

eat〔devour〕 bones and all // 통 채로 삼키다 swallow 《a thing》 without chewing it // 뿌리 채 뽑다 pull up by the roots // 선 채로 있다 keep standing // 나는 옷을 입은 채 잠들어버렸다 I fell asleep with my clothes on. // 그들은 웃옷을 벗은 채 테이블 둘레에 앉아 있었다 They were sitting around the table with their coats off. // 그는 포켓에 손을 넣은 채 바라보고 있었다 He was looking on with his hands in his pockets. // 나는 대구까지 선 채였다 I was kept standing as far *Taegu*. // 그는 방 안에서 가운을 입은 채였다 He kept his gown on in the room. // 신발을 신은 채로 들어오십시오 Please come in with your shoes on. // 파이프를 입에 문 채 말하지 마라 Don't speak (with a) pipe in (your) mouth. // 앉으신 채로 계십시오 Please keep your seats. // 문을 연 채로 잠들었다 He slept with the door (left) open.

채 菜 vegetable salad

채결 採決 ballot-taking ; a vote ; a roll-call 《미》 ; a division 《영》 **—하다** take a ballot〔vote〕 《on a question》 ; call the roll on ; put 《a matter》 to a vote ; decide by a roll-call vote ; divide ; take a roll-call ¶ 채결을 요구하다 call for a division〔a roll call〕 // K씨의 수정안은 채결의 결과 120대 21표로 부결됐다 An amendment by Mr. K went to a division and was defeated by 120 to 21. // 목요일 밤 채결 예정 The vote is to be taken Thursday night.

채고추 long slices of pepper

*__채광__ 採鑛 mining **—하다** mine ; dig for minerals

— 공학 mine engineering —권 mining rights — 야금학 (the science of) mining and metallurgy —학 mine engineering —학자 a mining expert

채광 採光 lighting **—하다** take in light ; light ¶ 채광이 좋은 방 a well-lighted room // 채광을 좋게 하다 improve〔better〕 lighting

—창 a skylight window 천연 —법 natural lighting system

채굴 採掘 mining ; digging ; exploitation **—하다** mine 《gold, silver, coal》 ; dig ; exploit ; work 《a mine》 ; [경영] operate ¶ 금광의 채굴 the operation〔exploitation, working〕 of a gold mine // 석탄〔금〕을 채굴하다 mine〔dig〕 coal〔gold〕

—권 mining〔mineral〕 rights ; a mineral concession —량 the output 《of a gold mine》 —료 mining rent —장 a stope —지 diggings — 출원인 a digging applicant — 출원지 an area of land intended for digging in an application

채권 債券 a (loan) bond ; a debenture ; a note ¶ 채권을 발행하다 issue bonds

— 소유자 a bondholder — 시장 a bond market —액(額) the face value of a bond 개발 — a development bond 국고 — a treasury〔an exchequer〕 bond 기명 — a registered bond 무담보 — a plain bond 유기한〔무기한〕 — a redeemable〔perpetual〕 bond 유통 — a negotiable bond 장기〔단기〕 — a long〔short〕-term bond 저축 — a (savings) debenture 투자 — an investment bond 할증금부 — a premium-bearing debenture

*__채권__ 債權 credit ; claim ; an obligatory right ¶ 그에 대하여 나는 채권이 있다 I am his creditor. /He owes me some money. // 고 L씨에 대하여 채권이 있는 자는 본인에게 명세서를 제출하시기 바랍니다 All persons having claims against the estate of Mr. L. deceased, are hereby required to send particulars thereof in writing to me.

— 계출 기간 the period for reporting obligations —국 a creditor power〔nation〕 — 담보 security for an obligation —법 the law of obligations — 순위 the order of credit — 신고 기간 the period for reporting obligation — 압류 garnishment ¶ 채권 압류인 a garnisher — 양도 cession〔assignment, transfer〕 of an obligation —자 a creditor ; an obligee —표 a list of claims 무기명 — an obligation (performable) to bearer 지명 — an obligation with a named obligee

채귀 債鬼 a dun ; a dunning creditor ; a creditor ¶ 채귀에 시달리다 be dunned ; be tormented〔harassed〕 by creditors〔dunners〕

채그릇 goods made of wicker ; wicker-ware

채근 採根 [식물] digging〔pulling〕 roots out ; [원인] finding out〔tracing back〕 the origin ; [채무] pressing ; urging ; hounding 《for the repayment》 ; dunning **—하다** [식물] dig 《roots》 out ; pull out ; [원인] find out ; trace back ; [채무] press〔urge〕 (the payment of a debt) ; dun

채금 採金 gold mining **—하다** mine gold

—자 a gold digger —지 a gold field

채꾼 a boy drover〔driver〕 ; a young cow-boy

채끝 [고기] beef flank

‡**채널** [텔레비전] a channel ¶ 채널 9에서 on channel 9 // 4채널 스테레오〔레코드〕 a 4-channel stereo〔record〕 // 채널 다툼 a dispute over which television program 《they》 should watch // 채널 11로 돌리다 turn on channel 11 // 채널을 고르다 pick up〔select〕 a channel // 채널을 바꾸다 change the channel // 그 채널은 잘 나오지 않았다 The channel was weakly received.

채다¹ ① get〔be〕 kicked ¶ 말에 채다 get kicked by a horse ② [도난] get snatched〔seized, robbed〕

채다² [눈치를] sense ; suspect ; spot ;

ㅊ

smell ; scent ; get scent〔wind〕 of ; get wise to ; take hint of ¶ 아무에게도 눈치채지 않고 without attracting any attention ; with no one the wiser ; unnoticed // 사람이 싫어하는 것을 눈치채다 sense《a person's》 dislike

채다³ [훔치다] snatch ; seize ; filch ; pilfer ; [잡아 당기다] pull with a jerk ; [정도] accelerate ¶ 낚싯대를 잡아 채다 jerk one's fishing rod out // 남의 손에서 …을 채다 filch〔snatch〕《a thing》 from a person's hand // 값이 채다 prices rise // 날치기가 돈지갑을 챈다 A pickpocket walks〔makes〕 off with the purse.

채다⁴ fasten ; complete ; satisfy ⇨ 채우다

채단 綵緞 silks

채독 a large paper-lined wicker basket in the shape of a deep jar

채독 菜毒 food poisoning from vegetables ; a vegetable-born〔hookworm〕 disease ¶ 채독에 걸리다 suffer from a vegetable-born disease

채둥우리 a large wicket basket

채뜨리다 ① [당기다] give a sudden pull《on a thing》 ② [빼앗다] snatch〔jerk〕《a thing》 away

채련 donkey leather

채록 recording in a book ― 하다 select〔extract〕《a passage》 and put《it》 on record ; record ¶ 채록되어 있다 [사전이 주어] contain《a word》; [어구가 주어] be given〔found〕《in a dictionary》

채롱 ―籠 a kind of box-shaped wicker basket ; a hamper

채료 彩料 the colored pigment ; water paint ¶ 채료를 칠하다 paint

― 그릇 a palette ―붓 a paint brush ―상자 a paint box ― 접시 a paint palette (한 벌의) 수채화 ― water colors 유화 ― oil colors

채마 菜麻 garden vegetables

채마밭 菜麻― a green farm ; a kitchen garden ; a truck farm ; a garden for vegetables ¶ 채마밭을 가꾸다 take care of〔keep〕 the green garden // 채마밭에 거름을 주다 fertilize〔manure〕 the green farm

채면기 採綿器 a cotton picker

채무 債務 a debt ; a financial obligation ; liabilities ; indebtedness ¶ 채무가 있다 be liable to《a person》 for debts ; owe《a person》 some money ; stand in debt // 채무를 이행하다 pay〔settle〕 one's debt ; meet one's obligation〔liabilities〕; discharge one's obligations

―국 a debtor nation〔country〕 ― 면제 waiver of obligation ― 명의 a title of debt ― 상환 redemption of a debt ― 소멸 expiration of an obligation ― 이행 fulfillment of an obligation ―자 a debtor ― 초과 liabilities exceeding the assets 고정 ― fixed liabilities〔indebtedness〕 보증 ― a suretyship obligation 연대 ― a joint obligation

채문 彩紋 a design ; figures (of colors)

채반 ―盤 ① a wicker tray ② [진미] delicacies (which a bride takes to her parents or parents-in-law)

채반상 ―盤相 (a person with) a flat and round face

채받이 beef shoulder

채발 a long and narrow foot ; a slender foot

채벌 採伐 cutting down (trees) ; felling ; deforestation ; lumbering ― 하다 cut down ; fell ; chop down ; lumber ; clear ground

― 시기 the felling season ; the cutting period ―자 a feller ; a lumberjack ; a wood cutter

채변 polite hesitancy (to accept something) ¶ 너무 채변 말고 많이 잡수시오 Help yourself. / Dig in a lot. 《미·속》 // 채변말고 받아 Come on, just take it.

*채비 ―備 preparations ⇨ 차비

채산 採算 doing accounts ; (commercial) profit ¶ 채산이 맞다 pay ; be profitable〔paying〕; be remunerative // 채산점 이하 below prime cost // 채산이 맞지 않다 do not pay ; be unprofitable ; be unremunerative // 채산에 맞추어 사다 buy on a yield basis

― 가격 a remunerative price ―성 payability ―점 break-even point 독립 ― self-support ; self-sustenance 독립 ―제 the self-supporting accounting system

채색 菜色 [빛깔] a green〔vegetable〕 color ; [굶주린 얼굴빛] a starved look

†채색 彩色 coloring ; painting ; coloration ; variegated colors ; a color scheme (배합) ; shading ― 하다 color ; paint in colors ; decorate ¶ 채색한 colored ; painted // 프리즘은 오색이 영롱한 채색을 벽에 반사한다 A prism reflects all the colors of a rainbow on the wall. // 들은 가지가지 꽃으로 채색되어 있다 The field is variegated with all kinds of flowering plants.

―감 (artist's) colors ; paints ― 도판 a colored plate ― 인쇄 color printing ―판 chromatic printing ; a colored print ―화 a colored picture ; a painting

*채석 採石 stone-cutting ; quarrying ― 하다 quarry〔cut〕 stones

―공(工) a quarry man ; a quarrier ―권(자) (an owner of) the stone quarrying rights ―기 a quarrying machine ―장 a quarry ; a stone pit ―장이 a quarry man ― 해머〔망치〕 a knapping hammer

채소 菜蔬 vegetables ; greens ; truckfarm products ¶ 채소를 가꾸다 grow greens ; raise vegetables

― 가게 a greengrocer's (shop) ; a vegetable shop ―밭 a vegetable〔kitchen〕 garden ; a truck farm ― 요리 greens ; a dish of cooked green vegetables

ㅊ

채송화 菜松花 〖식물〗 a garden portulaca ; a rose moss ; Portulaca grandiflora (학명)
채식 菜食 living on vegetables ; a vegetarian diet ; vegetable diet〔food〕 ―하다 live on vegetables
―광 a vegetarian craze ― 동물 a herbivorous〔grass-eating〕 animal ―주의 vegetarianism ―주의자 a vegetarian
채약 採藥 gathering〔collecting〕 medical plants〔herbs〕 ―하다 gather medical herbs
†채용 採用 [채택] adoption ; acceptance ; introduction ; use ; [임용] engagement ; appointment ; employment ―하다 adopt 《a plan》 ; accept 《a proposal》 ; introduce 《a system》 ; use ; [임용] employ ; engage ; appoint ; take 《a person》 into service ¶ 신교수법을 채용하다 adopt a new method of teaching // 서기로 채용하다 employ 《a person》 as a clerk // 임시로 채용하다 appoint 《a person》 on probation // 우리는 그때그때의 필요에 따라 임시 직원을 채용한다 From time to time as the need arises, we take on part-time help.
― 시험 an examination for service ― 신청 an application for a position ― 조건 hiring specifications〔qualification, requirements〕 ― 통지 a notification of employment 〔appointment〕 ― 후보자 prospective employee 가〔임시〕― appointment on trial 가〔임시〕 ―자 a candidate on probation
†채우다¹ lock ; fasten ; hook (훅을) ¶ 자물쇠를 채우다 fasten a lock // 문을 채우다 lock the door // 단추를 채우다 button (up) one's coat ; fasten a button // 칼을 채우다 (차게 하다) make〔let, have〕 《a person》 wear〔carry〕 a sword // 지퍼를 채우다 run up a zipper
채우다² put〔keep〕 in cold water〔on ice〕 ; ice ; chill ; refrigerate (냉동) ¶ 냉장고에 채우다 keep 《a thing》 in an icebox // 맥주를 물에 채우다 soak the bottles of beer in icy water // 생선을 얼음에 채우다 keep fish on ice // 수박을 찬물에 채우다 keep a watermelon in cold water
채우다³ [기한을] complete 《a term》 ; fulfill ; [욕심을] satisfy ; gratify ; look after only ; [충만] fill ; fill up ; [수효를] make up for ¶ 계약 기한을 채워 일하다 see one's contract through ; fulfill one's contract ; work until a contract period expires // 제 배만을 채우다 satisfy only one's own appetite ; look after only one's own interest // 욕심을 채우다 satisfy〔gratify〕 one's desire // 사복을 채우다 enrich one's pocket ; enrich oneself ; feather one's nest // 요구(조건)를 채우다 meet the conditions 《of》 ; satisfy〔fulfill〕 the demand // 술잔을 채우다 fill a wine glass ; fill a glass with wine // 쌀부대〔가마니〕를 채우다 fill up a rice bag // 공복을 채우다 satisfy one's hunger 《with》
채우다⁴ make〔let〕 《a person》 wear 《a thing》
채운 彩雲 glowing〔iridescent〕 clouds ¶ 채운으로 덮이다 be covered with golden clouds
채원 菜園 ⇨ 채전
채유 採油 extracting oil ; drilling for oil ―하다 drill for oil ; extract oil 《from olives》
―권 oil concessions〔rights〕 ; drilling right ― 원료 oil(-bearing) seeds
채유 菜油 rapeseed oil ; colza oil
채이다¹ [빼앗기다] get 《a thing》 snatched 〔seized〕 ; have 《a thing》 filched〔pilfered〕
채이다² [눈치를] get 《a thing》 sensed 〔suspected, spotted, found out, detected〕 ¶ 둘의 사랑이 남한테 눈치채였다 The love between the two was sensed by others.
채자 採字 type-picking ―하다 pick type ; set type
채잡다 take charge of ; take over ; preside over ¶ 일을 채잡다 take charge of matters ; take things in hand
채전 菜田 a vegetable garden ; a kitchen garden ; a market garden ; a truck farm
채전에 a long time ago ; long before
†채점 採點 marking ; grading ; rating ; scoring ―하다 mark ; give marks ; grade ; score ¶ 시험지를 채점하다 grade examination papers // 100점 만점으로 채점하다 mark〔score〕 examination papers on the basis of 100 points // 채점이 후〔박〕하다 generous〔strict〕 in marking ; be a good 〔bad〕 marker
―부 a grade-〔mark-, score-〕book ―자 a marker ; a scorer ― 카드 [경기에서의] a scorecard ; a tally card 《미》 ―표 a list of marks ; a grade list
채종 採種 gathering the seeds ―하다 gather (the seeds)
―기 seeder ―밭 field for seed-raising ― 식물 plants grown for seeds
채주 債主 a creditor ; an obligee
채지다 get〔be〕 dyed unevenly〔spottedly〕 ; be streaky in coloring
채질 whipping ; lashing ; flogging ; scourging ; urging on ; spurring on ―하다 whip ; lash ; flog ; urge〔spur〕 on ; press ; encourage ¶ 사람을 채질하다 flog 《a person》 // 말을 채질하다 whip a horse
채집 採集 collection ; collecting ; gathering ―하다 collect ; gather ; make a collection 《of》 ¶ 식물을 채집하다 collect plants ; gather herbs // 나비를 채집하다 collect〔catch〕 butterflies for specimens // 식물〔곤충〕 채집하러 가다 go botanizing〔bugging〕
―가 a collector (of specimens) ― 지점 [동식물이 발견된] a station 곤충 ― insect

ㅊ

collecting ; bugging ; bug hunting 식물〔광물〕 — collection of plants〔rocks〕 약초 — a collection of herbs 곤충 —망 a butterfly catcher 식물 —통 a vasculum 《*pl.* ~s, -la》

‡**채찍** a whip ; a lash ; a rod ; a cane ¶ 채찍으로 말을 때리다 whip a horse // 채찍을 휘두르다〔울리다〕 wield〔crack, swish〕 a whip

‡**채찍질** whipping ; lashing ; urging on —하다 whip ; lash ; spur〔urge〕 on ; encourage ¶ 달리는 말에 채찍질하다 [매질] whip a willing horse ; [격려] urge on a willing person ; make 《a person》 redouble his efforts ; lash 《a person》 into fresh exertion

채취 採取 picking ; gathering ; extraction ; gleaning —하다 collect ; gather ; fish 《pearl》 ; extract 《alcohol, radium》 ; mine 《coal》 ¶ 해초를 채취하다 gather seaweed // 고구마로부터 주정을 채취하다 extract alcohol from sweet potatoes

—기 the picking season —자 picker ; a gatherer ; a collector 진주 —장 pearl fisheries

채치다[1] [속도·가격이] speed ; accelerate ; advance 《in price》 ; quicken ; rise ; go up ¶ 값이 갑자기 채치다 prices jump

채치다[2] [채찍질] whip ; lash ; flog ; [독촉] urge ; spur on ; lash ¶ 말을 채치다 whip a horse // 사람을 채치다 urge〔press〕 《a person》

채치다[3] [당기다] jerk ; pull violently ; snatch ¶ 사람의 팔을 채치다 jerk at 《a person's》 arm // 손에 쥔 것을 채치다 snatch 《a thing》 from 《a person's》 hand

채치다[4] mince ; slice ; chop up ¶ 무우를 채치다 shred a radish // 잘게 채치다 cut〔chop〕 fine

채칼 菜— a chef's knife ; a knife for chopping〔mincing〕

채탄 採炭 coal mining —하다 mine coal —량 the output of coal — 목표 a goal 〔target〕 in coal mining —부 a coal miner ; a pitman —소 a colliery ; coalmine

***채택 採擇** adoption ; choice ; selection —하다 adopt ; select ; pick up ¶ 청원의 채택 adoption of a petition // 결의원을 채택하다 adopt a resolution // 채택 여부를 결정하다 vote upon 《a bill》 ; decide upon 《a matter》 // 그 교과서는 몇몇 학교에서 채택되고 있다 The textbook is used 〔adopted〕 in several schools.

채편 —便 the side of a drum to be struck ; the beating side

채플 a chapel ¶ 채플에 나가다〔빠지다〕 keep〔miss〕 a chapel

채필 彩筆 a paintbrush

채혈 採血 blood-gathering〔-collecting〕 ; drawing blood —하다 gather 〔collect〕 blood 《from a donor》 — 기관 a blood-gathering agency — 용구 blood collecting equipment

채화 彩畫 a painting ; a colored picture 수— a watercolor (painting) ; a painting in watercolors 유— painting in oil colors

채화 菜花 rape blossoms ; flowers on vegetables

†**책 冊** a book ; a volume ; [작품] a work ¶ 경제학의 책 a book on economics // 책을 쓰다 write a book // 책을 읽다 read a book // 책을 내다 publish〔put out〕 a book // 책장을 넘기다 turn over the pages of a book // 한 책으로 묶다 bind up in one volume // 논문을 책으로 내다 publish essays in book form // 한 책으로 편집하다 compile 《data》 into a book // 책장 사이에 꽂아두다 keep 《a thing》 between the leaves of a book // 이 책은 참 잘 썼다 This book is well〔wonderfully〕 written. // 그 분은 많은 책을 썼다 He is the author of many books. // 형에게는 책이 많다 My brother has a large library. // 그는 책을 많이 읽었다 He is well-read.

—갑(匣) a slipcase —궤(櫃) a bookshelf — 뚜껑 a book cover

책

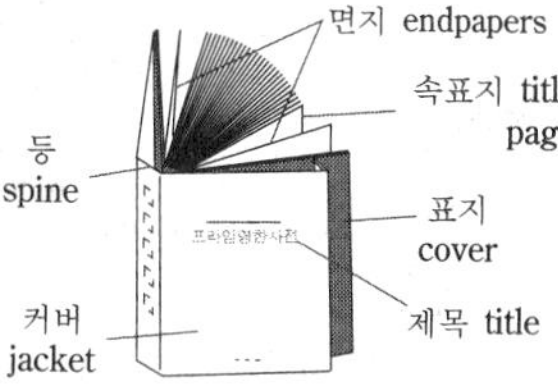

책 柵 ① [울] a fence ; a railing ; a palisade ; a stockade ; a paling ¶ 책을 두르다 set〔put〕 up a fence 《round》 ; fence 《round, around》 ; palisade 《a place》 ; enclose 《a place》 with a palisade ② [둑의] a long dike

책 責 [책임] responsibility ; liability ; [책망] reproach ; blame ; charge —하다 reproach ; call to account

책 策 a scheme ; a plan ; means ; measures

궁여지— a shift ; the last expedient 대응— countermeasures 해결— a means of settling a problem

책가위 冊— a dust jacket ; a book cover

책갑 冊匣 a bookcase ; a case for books〔a book〕

책값 冊— the price of a book ; a book price

책권 冊卷 a volume ; a book ¶ 그는 책권이나 가졌다 He has quite a lot of books. / He has a large library.

책궤 冊櫃 a bookshelf

책글씨 冊— penmanship used for hand-

ㅊ

written books ; a handwriting style used for books
책꽂이 冊— a bookshelf ; a bookcase
책동 策動 maneuvers ; machination ; scheming —하다 maneuver ; machinate ¶ 배후에서 책동하다 maneuver behind the scenes ; pull the wires
—가 a schemer ; a plotter ; a wire-puller ; a machinator ; a Machiavellian
책등 冊— the back〔backbone, backstrip, shelfback〕 of a book
책뚜껑 a (book) cover
‡책략 策略 a stratagem ; an artifice ; a trick ; a plan ; a plot ; a scheme ; a policy ; a frame up 《미》 ; maneuvers ¶ 당을 분열시키는 책략 a trick to split a party // 여러 가지 책략을 쓰다 use every artifice ; use every trick ; resort to every possible stratagem
—가 a tactician ; a schemer ; an artful man ; a strategist — 매매 〖주식〗 strategic operations
책력 冊曆 an almanac ; a book-calendar
*책망 責望 reproof ; reproach ; rebuke ; reprimand ; censure ; blame ; charge —하다 scold 《a person for》 ; give 《a person》 a scolding ; call〔take, bring〕 《a person》 to task 《for》 ; find faults with 《a person》 ; give 《a person》 a good talking-to ¶ 책망을 받다 be scolded ; get a scolding ; receive a reproof〔reprimand〕 ; draw a reproof from ; be called to task // 부주의를 책망하다 blame〔reprimand, reprove〕 《a person》 for his carelessness // 아주 엄하게 책망하다 rebuke 《a person's》 ingratitude // 행실을 책망하다 reproach 《a person》 with his bad manner〔behavior〕 // 자신을 책망하다 blame 〔reproach〕 oneself
책모 策謀 a stratagem ; a scheme ; [음모] an intrigue ⇨ 책략
책무 責務 [의무] duty ; obligation ; [책임] responsibility ¶ 가족에 대한 책무 one's duty to one's family // 책무를 다하다 discharge one's obligation ; do one's duty
책받침 a pad inserted under a notebook sheet ; an underlay
‡책방 冊房 a bookstore ; a bookshop ; a bookseller's
— 주인 a bookseller ; the proprietor of a bookshop
책벌 責罰 punishment ; penalty (법률상의) ; retribution —하다 punish ; inflict punishment 《on》 ¶ 책벌받다 be punished ; receive〔bear, suffer〕 punishment
책벌레 冊— [벌레] a bookworm ; [사람] a bookworm
책보 冊褓 a book wrapper ; [보자기] a (cloth) wrapper ; a wrapping cloth ; a kerchief ¶ 책보에 싸다 wrap in a kerchief
— 꾸러미 a bundle ; a parcel in a wrapper

책사 策士 a schemer ; a man of resources ; a tactician ; a machinator
†책상 冊床 a writing table ; a desk ¶ 책상을 두드리다 bang the table ; rap on the table // 책상에 앉다 sit at one's desk
—보 a table cloth ; a desk cover 사무용 — an office desk 양소매 — a kneehole desk
책상다리 冊床— legs of a table〔desk〕 ; [앉음새] sitting cross-legged ; sitting with one's legs crossed ¶ 그는 책상다리를 하고 앉아 있었다 He was sitting cross-legged.
책상물림 冊床— a naive academic ; a novice from the ivory tower ; an inexperienced person ¶ 그는 정말 책상물림이다 He is green in his job. /He knows nothing of the world.
책송곳 冊— a book maker's awl
책실 冊— bookbinding thread
책싸개 冊— a book wrapper ; a dust jacket
책씻이 冊— [책례] treating one's teacher and friends in celebration of the completion of a course —하다 treat one's teacher and friends upon finishing a course
책원지 策源地 a base〔center〕 of operations ; a strategic base ¶ 폭동의 책원지 a hotbed of commotion〔riot〕
‡책임 責任 responsibility ; [의무] duty ; [부담] obligation ; liability ; [죄의] blame ¶ 중대한 책임 heavy〔high〕 responsibility // 의무이행의 책임 responsibility for the fulfilment of obligations // 일가족 부양의 책임 a family responsibility // 법률에 대한 책임 responsibility under the law // 전쟁의 책임 war guilt ; responsibility〔accountability〕 for war // 사고에 대한 책임 liability for an accident // 책임 있는 회답 a responsible answer // 책임 있는 지위 a responsible post ; a position of trust // 책임이 없는 아이 an irresponsible child // 책임이 있다 be responsible for ; be answerable〔accountable〕 for 《a person》 // 책임을 지다 bear 〔assume, shoulder〕 the responsibility 《for, of》 ; hold oneself responsible for // 책임을 지우다 hold 《a person》 responsible 《for》 ; pass the buck to 《미·구》 ; place the blame upon 《a person》 // 책임을 떠맡다 undertake〔accept〕 the responsibility 《for》 ; take the responsibility for 《the matter》 ; charge oneself with // 책임을 느끼다 feel responsible ; be sensible of the responsibility // 책임을 완수하다 fulfill〔serve〕 one's responsibility ; do〔discharge〕 one's duty // 책임을 묻다 call 《a person》 to account // 책임을 추궁하다 be called to account ; get blamed 〔reproached〕 for ; be taken to task // 책임을 회피하다 avoid〔evade, shirk〕 one's responsibility // 책임을 해제하다 absolve 《a person》 from responsibility // 책임을 갚

이하다 share the responsibility《with》// 자기 책임으로 하다 act on one's own responsibility // 책임은 네게 있다 You are responsible〔answerable〕 for it. // 버스 운전사는 여객의 안전에 대한 책임이 있다 The driver of a bus is responsible for the safety of the passengers. // 남편은 처의 부채에 대하여 책임이 있느냐 Is a husband liable for his wife's debts? // 유아는 자기 행동에 대한 책임이 없다 An infant is unaccountable〔not accountable〕 for his actions. // 이 책임은 누구에게 있느냐 Who shall be responsible for it? /Where shall we place the responsibility for it? // 전책임은 나에게 있다 The sole responsibility is mine. // 가족을 부양한다는 것은 큰 책임이다 Supporting a family is a great responsibility. // 이 방의 청소는 네 책임이다 You are responsible for the sweeping of this room. /It is your duty to sweep this room. // 그 사고에 대하여 그는 책임지기를 거절한다 He refuses to take any responsibility for the accident. // 자제분의 안전에 대해서는 내가 책임을 지겠소 I will answer for the safety of your son. // 그의 빚은 내가 책임집니다 I am liable for his debts. // 나한테 책임을 미루지 마라 Don't pass the buck to me. // 모든 책임은 내가 지겠다 The buck stops with me. /The buck stops here. // 우리는 우리가 한 일에 대해 책임을 진다 We stand behind our job. // 너에게도 책임이 있었다 You were at fault too, you know. // 이제는 너도 책임을 져야 할 위치에 도달했다 You're reached a position of responsibility now.
— 관념〔감〕 a sense of responsibility〔duty〕 — 교료(校了)〖인쇄〗 [표시] O. K. with corrections —내각 a responsible Cabinet — 보험 liability insurance —자 a responsible person ¶ 여기 책임자는 누구냐 Who is in charge here? —전가 imputation ; buck-passing《미·구》— 준비금 legal (liability) reserve — 해제 absolution ; release from responsibility ; freedom from responsibility — 회피 evasion of responsibility 공동(보증) — collective (reserve) responsibility 무— irresponsibility 연대 — collective responsibility 유한〔무한〕 — limited〔unlimited〕 liability 전— the whole responsibility

책자 冊子 a book ; a pamphlet ; a leaflet ; publications

책잡다 責— find fault with ; take to task for ; blame《a person》¶ 파약을 책잡다 reproach《a person》 for his breach of promise

책잡히다 責— get blamed〔reproached〕 for ; be found fault with ; be called to account ; be taken to task ¶ 약속 불이행으로 책잡히다 be blamed for breaking one's promise // 직무 태만으로 책잡히다 be taken to task for neglecting one's duty // 일을 못하면 책잡힐 걸세 He will come to you anyway if you don't do a good job.

****책장 冊欌** a bookcase ; a bookshelf ; a bookchest

책장 冊張 a leaf of a book ; the pages ¶ 책장을 넘기다 turn over the pages〔leaves〕 of a book

책점 冊店 a bookstore ; a bookshop ; a bookseller's

책정 策定 [예산 따위] appropriation ; [가격 따위] fixing《prices》 **—하다** appropriate ; allot ; earmark《for》 ¶ 가격을 책정하다 fix a price // 연구비로서 얼마의 금액을 책정하다 earmark a sum of money for research work
—량〔액〕 a quota 봉급 — arrangement of a salary scale

책치레 冊— book decoration

책하다 責— ⇨ 책망하다

****챔피언** a champion ; a champ《속》 ¶ 스케이트의 세계 챔피언 the skating champion of the world // 챔피언이 되다 win〔gain〕 a championship
—십 a championship

챗국 a cold soup with shredded radish in it

챗열 a whiplash ; a whipcord

챙 a visor ; an eave awning ⇨ 차양

챙기다 [모으다] gather (all together) ; collect ; [짐꾸리다] pack ; [정리] put《things》 in order ; take care of ¶ 물건을 챙기다 tidy things up after one has used them // 서류를 챙기다 arrange〔put〕 papers in order // 소지품을 챙기다 pack〔collect〕 one's belongings // 원고를 챙겨서 보내드리지요 I will get the manuscript in order and send it to you.

처 處 a place ; [기구] an office
과학 기술— the Ministry of Science and Technology 근무— one's place of employment ; one's office 총무— the Ministry of General Affairs

처 妻 a wife ; one's better-half (해학적) ; a spouse (배우자) ¶ 그 여자를 처로 삼다 make her one's wife // 처를 얻다 take〔get〕《to oneself》 a wife ; take《a woman》 to wife ; marry a woman
악— a bad wife 조강지— a good wife ; a wife who has shared one's difficulties
소더러 한 말은 안 나도 처더러 한 말은 난다 〔속담〕 Confide in an aunt and the world will know.

처가 妻家 the house of one's wife's parents ; one's wife's old home
—살이 living at one's wife's house

처결 處決 settlement ; decision ; disposal ; disposition ; arrangement **—하다** settle ; decide ; dispose of ; arrange

처깔하다 keep the door tightly shut ; shut the door fast

처남 妻男 a brother of one's wife ; a brother-in-law

ㅊ

처넣다 [밀어넣다] push〔shove〕 into ; stuff ; cram ; eat ; [투자] put into ; invest〔sink〕 in ¶ 책을 상자에 처넣다 pack one's books into a box // 떡을 입에 처넣다 shovel down rice cake // 형무소에 처넣다 cast〔clap, fling, throw〕 《a culprit》 into prison // 전 재산을 증권에 처넣다 put all one's fortune into stocks

처네 a quilt ; a coverlet ; a comforter ; a coverlet for carrying a baby on one's back

‡처녀 處女 a virgin ; a maiden ; a maid ; [처녀성] virginity ¶ 처녀의 virgin ; maiden // 처녀다운 maidenly ; maidenlike ; virginal // 처녀답게 like a maiden ; in a maidenlike manner // 처녀로 늙은 여자 women who have retained their virginity // 처녀성을 잃다 lose one's virginity ; lose one's silken snood // 처녀성을 빼앗기다 be deflowered ; be deprived of her virginity〔virgin purity〕
—궁 〖천문〗 the Virgin〔Virgo〕 —림 a maiden forest —막 〖해부〗 the hymen ; the maidenhead ; the virginal membrane —봉 an unclimbed peak — 비행(항해) a shakedown flight〔cruise〕 ; a maiden flight 〔voyage〕 — 생식 〖동물〗 parthenogenesis —설 (virgin) untracked snow ; untrodden snow —성 virginity ; virginhood ; maidenhood —작(품) one's maiden〔first〕 work —지 virgin soil ; virgin earth — 출판 a maiden publication

처넙 ⇨ 처분

처단 處斷 decision ; settlement ; disposition —하다 decide ; settle ; deal with ; punish ¶ 엄중 처단하다 deal with 《an offender》 severely

처대다 ① [대주다] keep supplying ② [땔감을] put on the flames ; burn on a fire

처덕 妻德 the virtue of a wife ; one's wife's help

처덕거리다 slap ; flap ; keep slapping 〔flapping〕 ¶ 빨래를 처덕거리다 paddle the laundry

처덕처덕 [빨래를] pitapat ; paddling ; slapping ; beating ; [바름] pasting up haphazardly ; thick(ly) ¶ 분을 처덕처덕 바르다 paint one's face thick

처든지르다 eat ; shove〔shovel〕 down 《food》 ; dig in

처때다 burn (a fire) high

처뜨리다 hang down ; droop ; let droop ¶ 귀를 처뜨린 개 a dog with drooping ears // 어깨를 처뜨리다 droop one's shoulders // 선배를 처뜨리고 승진하다 be promoted over the heads of one's seniors

처란 a bird shot ; a thing shaped like a bird shot

처량 凄涼 —하다 [황량하다] (be) desolate ; bleak ; dreary ; deserted ; [구슬프다] plaintive ; lonely ; lonesome ; melancholy ; solitary ; mournful ; sad ¶ 처량한 광경 a desolate scene ; a pathetic sight ; a ghastly view // 처량한 벌판 a wind-swept〔desolate〕 plain ; a wilderness // 처량한 노래 a plaintive song // 처량한 모습 a lonesome〔wretched〕 look // 처량한 심사 melancholy〔pensive〕 mood

*처럼 like ; as ; as if ; as ... as ; so ... as ¶ 평상시처럼 as usual // 거지처럼 보이다 look like a beggar // 눈처럼 희다 be as white as snow // 물은 수정처럼 맑다 The water is as clear as crystal. // 그는 억만장자나 된 것처럼 말한다 He talks as if he were a billionaire. // 물이 쇠를 녹슬게 하는 것처럼 게으름은 마음을 좀먹는다 As water rusts iron, idleness rusts the mind. // 그것은 네가 생각하는 것처럼 간단하지는 않다 It is not so simple as you think. // 네가 미치지 않은 것처럼 그도 미친 사람은 아니다 He is no more mad than you are. /He is not mad any more than you are. // 학생 때처럼 긴 여름 휴가를 얻었으면 좋겠다 I wish we could take long summer vacations like when we were students.

처렁거리다 clang ; jingle ; tinkle ; keep clinking〔rattling〕 ¶ 처렁처렁 clanging (-ly) ; jingling(ly) ; tinkling(ly)

처르렁거리다 ⇨ 차르랑거리다

†처리 處理 handling ; treatment ; disposal ; transaction ; dealing ; administration ; management ; arrangement ; settlement ; manipulation ; discretion —하다 handle ; treat ; manage ; take care of ; dispose of 《a thing》 ; transact ; deal with ; settle 《a matter》 ; get rid of ; bring 《a matter》 to a conclusion ¶ 처리되다 be settled ; be disposed of // 사무를 처리하다 conduct 〔transact〕 business // 자기 일을 스스로 처리하다 take care of one's own business // 사건을 처리하다 deal with a matter // 가사를 처리하다 run a household ; manage household affairs // 복잡한 사건을 잘 처리하다 handle a complicated problem well // 사건의 처리 방법을 알다 know how to deal with the affairs // 조속한 시일내에 처리해 주십시오 I want you to settle the matter as soon as possible. // 이것은 네가 적당히 처리하기 바란다 I leave the matter to your discretion. // 지난 달에 끝내지 못한 일을 처리하고 있다 I'm making up for all the work I didn't get done last month. // 그 일을 어떻게 처리하지 What should we do about that matter? // 이 정도 분량이라면 3일에 처리할 수 있다 If this is all there is, I can handle it in three days.

*처마 the eaves ¶ 처마에서 떨어지는 빗물 raindrops falling from the eaves // 처마 밑에 under the eaves // 처마 밑에서 비를 잠시 피하다 take brief shelter from rain under the eaves
—끝, 처맛기슭 the edge of the eaves

처매다 bandage up thoroughly

처먹다 devour ; shovel into one's mouth ;

ㅊ

dig in ; tuck in ; eat greedily ; shove 〔shovel〕 down ¶ 처먹어라 Dig in! / Tuck in!

처먹이다 feed immoderately ; stuff

***처방 處方** a prescription ; a recipe ; a formula **—하다** prescribe ¶ 처방을 쓰다 write〔make out〕 a prescription ; prescribe《medicine for a person》// 처방에 의해서 조제하다 make up〔dispense, prepare〕 a prescription ; fill a prescription // 이 약은 의사 처방 없이는 조제하지 않음 This medicine is obtainable only on a physician's prescription. // 화장품 처방 cosmetic formulas

—전 a (medical) prescription (slip) ¶ 처방전에 의하여 조제해 받다 receive medicine according to a prescription // 그런 항생제는 처방전 없이는 바로 팔 수 없습니다 We can't sell those antibiotics over the counter. **— 조제** [표시] Prescription filled **— 조제소** a dispensary

처벌 處罰 punishment ; penalty **—하다** punish ; discipline ; inflict punishment《on》 ¶ 처벌받다 be〔get〕 punished ; receive〔bear, suffer〕 punishment ; be visited with punishment ; be brought to book // 교통위반으로 처벌받다 be punished for violation of the traffic regulations // 처벌받지 않다 go unpunished ; go〔get off〕 scot-free // 엄중히 처벌하다 punish severely ; deal severely with《a person》 ; inflict severe〔heavy〕 punishment《on》// 처벌을 면하다 escape punishment

처부모 妻父母 one's wife's parents ; one's parents-in-law

****처분 處分** disposal ; disposition ; dealing ; management ; proceeding ; action ; a measure ; [처벌] punishment **—하다** dispose of ; deal〔do〕 with ; take action ; manage ; punish (처벌) ¶ 토지〔재산〕를 처분하다 dispose of one's land〔property〕 // 쓰레기를 처분하다 get rid of junk ; make a clean sweep of old stuff // 위반자를 엄중히〔관대히〕 처분하다 deal with an offender severely〔leniently〕 // 적당한 처분을 바랍니다 Deal with him as you think fit. // 그 소년을 어떻게 처분해야 할지 모른다 They don't know what to do with the boy.

—품 clearance goods ; distress goods 〔articles〕 ; articles to be disposed of **공매 —** disposition by public sale **매각 —** disposal〔disposition〕 by sale **부당 —** an unwarrantable proceeding〔measure〕 ; wrongful dealing **체납 —** disposition for failure in (tax) payment ; a process for the recovery of taxes in arrears

처사 處士 a retired gentleman ; a scholar in retirement

처사 處事 management《of an affair》 ; transaction ; disposal ; conduct ; handling a matter ; an action ¶ 처사를 잘하다 take a proper step ; deal with《a matter》 properly // 처사를 그르치다 take a wrong measure ; make an error in dealing with an affair

처삼촌 妻三寸 one's wife's uncle

처상 妻喪 one's wife's death ; mourning for one's wife

처서 處暑 one of the 24 seasonal divisions occurring about the end of August

처세 處世 conduct of life **—하다** conduct oneself ; carry oneself ; get on in the world ¶ 그는 처세가 능하다 He is worldly wise. /He is a man of the world. // 그는 처세할 줄 모른다 He is lacking in worldly wisdom. // 정직과 근면은 그의 처세 방법이다 Honesty and diligence are the guiding principles of his life.

—술〔법〕 the art of living ; the secret of success in life ; worldly wisdom ; one's way of living ; how to get on in the world **—훈(訓)** the rules of conduct in life ; the lessons of life ; maxim ; the (guiding) motto for one's life

처소 處所 [장소] location ; a place ; [거처] a living place ; a residence ; [행방] whereabouts ¶ 처소를 찾아내다 locate ; follow up《a person's》 residence // 그의 처소는 아직 모른다 His whereabouts is〔are〕 still unknown.

— 불명 an unidentified location **임시 —** a temporary residence〔abode〕

처시하 妻侍下 a henpecked husband ; petticoat government ; being henpecked ¶ 그는 처시하에 산다 He is tied to his wife's apron-strings. /The wife is the ruler in his home.

처신 處身 one's conduct ; behavior ; deportment ; demeanor **—하다** behave 〔manage〕 oneself ; carry oneself ¶ 처신이 단정하다 be well-behaved〔-conducted〕 ; be of good behavior ; behave oneself well // 불한당처럼 처신하다 behave oneself like a scoundrel // 점잖게 처신하다 play a noble part ; bear oneself gracefully

처신사납다 處身— (be) disreputable ; discreditable ; loose in morals ; ill-conducted ¶ 처신사나운 남자 a sloven ; a libertine ; a loose liver // 처신사나운 여자 a slut ; a loose woman〔girl〕 ; a woman of loose morals // 그는 상처 이후로 처신사나운 생활을 한다 Ever since he lost his wife, he has been living a disreputable life.

처신 없다 處身— (be) undignified ; ungentlemanly ; unbecoming ¶ 처신 없는 사람 a person〔man〕 with no dignity // 처신 없는 일 an undignified act〔behavior〕 // 처신 없는 짓 cheap conduct // 그런 것은 처신 없는 짓이다 It would be ill-becoming for you to do such a thing.

처연 悽然 —하다 (be) pathetic ; sad ; sorrowful

ㅊ

처외편 妻外便 one's wife's maternal family ; the maternal relatives of one's wife

처우 處遇 treatment **—하다** treat ; deal 〔do〕 with

— 개선 improvement〔betterment〕 of labor conditions ; increase of pay ; raising salary ¶ 처우 개선을 하다 raise 〔increase〕《a person's》 pay ; give better treatment《to workers》

†처음 the first ; the beginning ; the start ; the opening ; the outset ; the origin (기원) ; [초기] the early stage ¶ 처음의 first ; initial ; original // 처음으로 first ; for the first time // 처음에 at first ; firstly ; to begin with ; at the start〔outset〕// 생전 처음으로 for the first time in one's life // 처음부터 끝까지 from (the) beginning to (the) end ; from start to finish // 맨 처음 the very beginning // 처음 계획 the original plan // 처음부터 다시하다 do it all over again ; begin afresh // 처음이 중요하다 A good beginning is half the battle. /Well begun is half done. // 나는 이곳이 처음입니다 I have never been here before. // 처음에는 실패했다 I failed in it at first. // 이것이 처음이자 마지막이다 This is the first and the last. // 처음에 무엇을 할까요 What shall I do to begin with ? // 처음엔 다 그런 법이지 We all started that way. // 그 회사는 처음에는 아주 작은 규모였다 The company began in a small way. // 이 도시에는 처음 오세요 Are you new in town ? // 서울에는 처음이십니까 Is this your first time in *Seoul* ? // 처음부터 다시 시작해야 합니다 I have to start from scratch.

처자 處子 a virgin ; a maiden ⇨ 처녀

처자 妻子 one's wife and children ; one's family ¶ 처자를 부양하다 support〔provide for〕 one's family // 처자를 버리다 discard〔desert〕 one's wife and children

처장 妻葬 [장사] the funeral of one's wife ; [처산] the grave of one's wife

처재 妻財 one's wife's property ; one's wife's dowry (지참금 따위)

처쟁이다 heap up ; pile up ; stack ¶ 입구에는 쌀 가마니가 처쟁여 있었다 Bags of rice were piled up at the entrance.

처절 悽絶 extreme sadness ; ghastliness ; gruesomeness **—하다** (be) ghastly ; gruesome ; lurid ; extremely weird ; ominous ¶ 처절한 광경 a gruesome scene 〔picture〕

처제 妻弟 a sister-in-law ; a younger sister of one's wife

처조모 妻祖母 the grandmother of one's wife

처조부 妻祖父 the grandfather of one's wife

처조카 a nephew of one's wife

처족 妻族 the relatives〔family〕 of one's wife

†처지 處地 ① [형편] a situation ; a condition ; circumstances ; one's standing〔status〕 ; one's means〔lot〕 ¶ 비참한 처지 a miserable〔pathetic, wretched〕 situation ; a hard plight ; a fix // 어색한 처지에 놓여 있다 be (placed) in an awkward situation ; be in a fix // 네 처지가 제일 부럽다 I wish I were in your shoes. // 내 처지에 그런 사치는 바랄 수 없다 I can't afford such luxury. /My circumstances will not allow me such luxury. // 내가 네 처지라면 그렇게 하지 않을 것이다 If I were in your place, I would not do that. // 그의 처지가 되어봐라 Try to put yourself in his place.

② [사이] relations ; terms ; a footing ¶ 우리는 서로 말을 놓고 지내는 처지다 We are on friendly terms with each other.

처지다 [가라앉다] sink ; sag ; go down ; dip (지층이) ; precipitate (용해물이) ; [늘어지다] hang ; droop ; lower ; [뒤떨어지다] left〔fall〕 behind ; draggle (낙오) ; [남다] stay behind ; remain ; linger ¶ 귀가 처진 개 a flap-eared dog // 축 처진 어깨 drooping〔sloping〕 shoulders // 버드나무의 처진 가지 the pendent branches of a willow // 혼자 뒤처지다 remain behind all alone // 기운이 처지다 sink into feebleness ; one's spirits droop // 열매가 많이 열려서 가지가 축 처져 있다 The branches are drooping under the weight of the fruits. // 경주에서 처지다 drop〔fall〕 behind in the race // 눈꼬리가 살짝 처진 것이 아주 귀엽다 The slight droop in the outer corners of her eyes is very cute.

처지르다 ¶ 밥을 처지르다 devour〔munch〕 voraciously ; shovel in rice ; stuff one's stomach // 불을 처지르다 make a big 〔huge〕 fire // 난로에 석탄을 처지르다 shovel coal into a stove

처질 妻姪 one's wife's niece ⇨ 처조카

처참 處斬 decapitation ; beheading ; cutting the head off ¶ 처참을 당하다 be beheaded ; be decapitated

처참 悽慘 ghastliness ; wretchedness ; gruesomeness **—하다** (be) ghastly ; gruesome ; lurid ; grim ; appalling ; wretched ¶ 처참한 광경 a grim〔an appalling〕 scene ; a heart-rending sight // 처참한 생활 a wretched life // 처참한 얘기 a tragic〔sad, touching〕 tale〔story〕 // 처참한 최후를 마치다 meet with a tragic end〔death〕 ; die a miserable death // 전쟁터는 처참했다 The battle ground presented a ghastly sight. // 처참한 싸움이었다 It was a bloody battle.

처창 悽愴 —하다 (be) extremely miserable〔tragic, sad, sorrowful〕

처처 處處 several〔various〕 places ; this and that part ; several parts ; from place to place ¶ 처처에 in several places ; in places ; here and there ⇨ 곳곳

처첩 妻妾 wife and concubine

처치 處置 [처리] disposition ; dealing ; management ; disposal ; [방책] action ; proceeding ; a measure ; a step **—하다** deal with ; dispose of ; take measures 〔steps, action〕 ; get rid of ; do away with ¶ 적절한 처치 an appropriate〔adequate〕 measure ; a proper step ; a measure suited to the occasion // 처치 곤란이다 do not know what to do with // 단호한 처치를 하다 take strong measures〔a decisive step〕 // 적절한 처치를 하다 take necessary measures〔steps〕 ; take necessary action ; take a proper step ; deal with 《a matter》 properly // 적당히 처치하다 deal with 《a matter》 as one thinks fit ; act at one's discretion // 일을 신속히 처치하다 deal summarily with ; take prompt action on // 책상을 어딘가에 처치해야겠다 We have to move the table away somewhere.

처편 妻便 ⇨ 처족(妻族)

처하다 處— ① [이르다] be placed ; get faced with ; [다루다] cope with ; deal with ; manage ; conduct oneself ; act ¶ 역경에 처하여 in〔under〕 adversity // (어떤 경우에) 처하여 when ; at the time of ; in case of ; on occasion of ; in time of // 어려운 사정에 처해 있다 be in a fix ; be in adversity ; be under unfavorable circumstances // 위기에 처하다 face a crisis ; rise to a crisis // 난관에 잘 처하다 deal with〔tide over〕 a difficult situation nicely
② [처벌] sentence ; condemn ; punish ¶ 사형에 처하다 sentence 《a person》 to death ; punish 《a person》 with death // 절도범을 6개월 형에 처하다 sentence a larcenist to six months' imprisonment // 구류에 처하다 order detention for 《a person》
③ [대처하다] ⇨ 대처(對處)

처형 妻兄 a sister-in-law ; an elder sister of one's wife

처형 處刑 punishment ; [형의 집행] execution **—하다** punish ; execute ¶ 처형을 받다 be punished〔executed〕 // 가스 처형을 받다 be executed in a gas〔lethal〕 chamber // 그는 전기 처형을 당했다 He was electrocuted.
—대 a scaffold ; the gallows **—장** an execution-ground

척[1] pretense ⇨ 체[2]

척[2] [달라붙음] tight ; fast ; clingingly ; closely ; [축늘어짐] droopingly ; sluggishly ; languidly ; [선뜻] without hesitation〔delay〕 ; right off ; quickly ; speedily ; readily ; easily ¶ 척 달라 붙다 cling tight 《to one's body》 // (풀이 손에) 척 달라 붙다 《paste》 stick fast 《to one's hand》 // 안경을 척 쓰다 put on one's glasses imposingly // 돈을 척 내걸다 bet one's money without hesitation // 문이 척 열린다 The door flies open. // 나뭇가지가 척 늘어져 있다 The branches of the tree droop low.

척[3] ① 〖기계〗 a vise ② [지퍼] a zipper

척 隻 ¶ 수척의 선박 a few ships〔vessels〕 // 배 한척 a vessel ; a ship // 한 척분의 뱃짐 a shipload // 군함 한 척을 출동시키다 dispatch a warship

척 尺 a Korean foot ¶ 척수가 길다〔짧다〕 be long〔short〕 in length // 척수가 모자라다 be wanting in length ; be short of measure // 척으로 재서 팔다 sell 《cloth》 by the yard〔measure〕

척각 隻脚 one leg ¶ 척각인 사람 a one-legged person

척결 剔抉 gouging out ; hollowing out ; scraping out ; laying bare ; exposing **—하다** gouge〔hollow〕 out ; scrape out ¶ 부정 사건을 척결하다 expose a scandal

척골 蹠骨 〖해부〗 metatarsus 《*pl.* -si》

척골 脊骨 the backbone ⇨ 척추골

척도 尺度 a (linear) measure ; a rule ; a scale ; a gauge ; a yardstick ; an index ; a barometer ; a standard ; a criterion ¶ 문명의 척도 an index〔barometer〕 of civilization // 척도가 되다 be〔constitute〕 a measure 《of》 ; be a yardstick 《for》

척량 脊梁 the spinal column ; the ridge of the spine ; the line of the backbone ¶ 한반도의 척량인 태백산맥 the chain of the *Taeback* mountains that forms the backbone of the Korean peninsula

척박 瘠薄 barrenness ; sterility ; infertility 《of soil》 ; meagerness **—하다** (be) barren ; sterile ; infertile ; meager ; poor ¶ 척박한 땅 barren soil〔land〕

척분 戚分 kinship ; close feeling among relatives

척사 擲柶 the *yut* ⇨ 윷

척살 刺殺 stabbing 《a person》 to death ; 〖야구〗 touching out **—하다** stab 《a person》 to death ; 〖야구〗 put〔touch〕 《a runner》 out ; catch 《a runner》 ¶ 주자〔러너〕가 방심하고 있는 사이에 척살하다 catch a runner asleep at the base ; catch a runner napping

척선 隻船 a ship ; a vessel

척수 隻手 one hand ; a single hand ¶ 척수로 single-handed(ly) ; all alone

척수 脊髓 〖해부〗 the spinal cord〔marrow〕 ; pith ; the medulla spinalis (학명) **— 마비** spinal paralysis **—막염** cerebrospinal meningitis **—병** a spinal complaint〔trouble〕 **— 신경** spinal nerves **—액** the spinal fluid **—염** myelitis **— 주사** a spinal injection **— 카리에스** vertebra caries ; tuberculosis of the spine ; Pott's disease **뇌—** cerebrospinal medulla **뇌—막염** cerebro-spinal meningitis〔fever〕

척식 拓殖 colonization ; exploitaion **—하다** colonize ; settle ; establish a colony **— 은행** a colonial bank **—자** a colonist **— 회사** a colonization company

척신 隻身 ¶ 척신으로 alone ; by one-

ㅊ

self ; unaided ; without a companion ; singlehanded
척안 隻眼 one eye ¶ 척안의 사람 a one-eyed person
척주 脊柱 〖해부〗 the spinal column ⇨ 척추
척지 尺地 [작은 땅] a foot of land ; [가까움] a foot away ; a stone's throw
척지다 隻— come to hate each other ¶ 그 사람과 척진 일은 없다 I have no grudge against him.
척짓다 隻— create a situation leading to mutual hatred ; sow the seeds of discord
척척 ① [잘되는] quickly ; rapidly ; steadily ; promptly ; with dispatch ; readily ; easily ¶ 어려운 문제를 척척 풀다 solve a hard question easily // 질문에 척척 대답하다 answer questions readily // 일은 척척 진행 중이다 The work is making steady progress. /The work is well under way. // 척척 말해버려라 Speak out. /Tell me quick ! / Out with it.
② [달라붙는] stick to〔on〕 ; adhere to ¶ 불로 척척 붙이다 stick 《a thing》 on with paste // (책장이) 척척 달라붙다 《the leaves》 stick together
③ [쌓는] heap by heap ; high ¶ 쌀가마니를 척척 쌓다 stack up rice bags ; pile〔heap〕 up rice bags // 서류가 책상 위에 척척 쌓여 있다 Papers are piled high on the desk.
④ [감기는] coil by coil ; twining ; clinging ¶ 척척 감기다 twine〔coil〕 itself round ; twist about ; cling to
⑤ [개키는] fold by fold ; in orderly fashion ¶ 옷을 척척 개키다 fold up one's clothes
척척하다 (be) wet ; damp ¶ 척척한 옷 wet clothes // 비에 척척하게 젖다 get wet in the rain ; be wet from the rain
척추 脊椎 〖해부〗 the vertebra 《*pl.* -brae, -bras》 ; the backbone ; the spinal column
—골 the backbone ; the spine ; the chine ; the vertebra **— 동물** Vertebrata (학명) **— 마취** spinal〔medullary〕 an(a)esthesia **— 만곡** spinal curvature **—염** spinitis **— 전만(前灣)** lordosis **— 카리에스** vertebra caries **— 후만** kyphosis **무— 동물** invertebrate animals
척축 斥逐 expulsion ; ouster ; ejectment **—하다** drive〔turn〕 out ; expel ; oust ; eject
척출 斥黜 —하다 dismiss〔remove〕 from office ; oust
척출 剔出 extraction ; removal ; excision **—하다** extract ; excise ; remove
—기 an extractor **난소 —** removal of an ovary
척탄 擲彈 〖군사〗 a (hand) grenade
—병 a grenadier ; a grenade〔bomb〕 thrower **—통(筒)** a grenade〔bomb〕 thrower ; a grenade discharger〔launcher〕
척토 尺土 a foot of land ; an inch of land ; a small bit of land
척하다 ⇨ 체하다
척후 斥候 〖군사〗 [임무] reconnaissance ; patrol duty ; [사람] a scout ; a patrol ; a reconnoitering soldier ¶ 척후를 내보내다 send out scouts
—대 a reconnoitering party **—전** skirmishes of scouts ; a patrol encounter ; an affair of outposts **전투 —** a combat patrol **정찰 —** a reconnoitering patrol **추적 —** a contact patrol
†**천** [피륙] cloth ; woven stuff ; a fabric ¶ 고급 천 fine quality of cloth // 천을 끊다〔사다〕 buy a piece of cloth // 천을 짜다 weave cloth
천 天 ⇨ 하늘
†**천 千** a thousand ¶ 2천의 학생 two thousand students // 천분의 1 a〔one〕 thousandth // 수천의 thousands of 《people》 // 천배의 a thousand times ; thousandfold // 천배로 하다 increase thousandfold // 천에 하나 one in a thousand
천 薦 recommendation ⇨ 천거 ¶ …의 천으로 on〔at〕 one's recommendation ; through〔by〕 recommendation 《of》
***천개 天蓋** the lid of a coffin ; a coffin lid
천객만래 千客萬來 —하다 have an interminable succession of visitors ¶ 저 가게에는 천객만래하고 있다 That store draws a lot of customers.
****천거 薦擧** recommendation **—하다** recommend ; put in a good word for 《a person》 ¶ 그를 이 자리에 천거할 수 있습니까 Can you recommend him for this post ?
천격 賤格 mean style ; mean character ; [사람] a person of low birth ¶ 천격스럽다 be mean〔low, base〕
천견 淺見 a shallow view ; little knowledge ; my (humble) view〔opinion〕
— 박식 little experience and small learning
천계 天界 the heaven ; the sky
천계 天啓 a divine revelation ; revelation from Heaven
천고 千古 remote antiquity ; eternity ¶ 천고 불멸의 eternal ; everlasting ; immortal // 천고의 명언 an eternal truth // 천고의 명장 greatest general that ever lived
천고마비 天高馬肥 ¶ 천고마비의 계절 the season of "high sky and plump〔stout〕 horses"
천골 賤骨 a person of low birth ; a mean look ; a mean countenance
천공 天空 the sky ; the firmament ; the heaven ¶ 천공을 날다 fly high in the air
천공 天功 Nature's work ; wonders of Nature
***천공 穿孔** boring ; perforation ; punching ; drilling **—하다** bore ; drill ; punch
—기 a boring machine ; a drill ; a perfo-

rator ; a key punch (계산기 카드의) ; [외과용] a trepan — 카드 a punch(ed) card (계산기용)

천구 天球 the celestial sphere
—도 a celestial map —의(儀) a celestial globe — 적도 the celestial equator

†천국 天國 Heaven ; Paradise ; the kingdom of Heaven ¶ 천국의 heavenly // 지상의 천국 an earthly heaven ; a heaven on earth // 천국에 가 있다 be in Heaven // 천국에 가다 go to Heaven

천군만마 千軍萬馬 (many) thousands of troops and horses ¶ 천군만마의 사이를 누비다 fight〔be in〕 many battles ; be an old campaigner ; be a seasoned veteran

천극 天極 the celestial poles

천근 淺近 shallowness ; superficiality — 하다 (be) shallow ; superficial ; short-sighted ¶ 좋은 과학자일수록 천근한 관측을 하지 않는다 Every good scientist will have a deep observation.

천금 千金 a thousand pieces of gold ; a lot of money ; fortune ¶ 일확천금 making a big fortune with one swoop〔at one stroke〕 // 천금을 주고도 사지 못할 물건 an invaluable article // 남아일언은 중천금이다 A word of honor is as good as a bond.

천기 天氣 weather
—도 a weather map〔chart〕 ; a synoptic (weather) chart

천기 天機 the secrets of nature ; the hidden plans of Providence ; a state secret ; [기밀] a deep secret ; a precious secret ; [타고난 기지] native〔innate, inherent〕 wit ¶ 천기를 누설 마라 The secret should not be divulged. /It must be kept (a) secret.

천기 喘氣 a light case of asthma

천길 千— a thousand fathoms ; [헤아릴 수 없는 깊이] bottomlessness

천녀 天女 a heavenly maid ; a celestial nymph

천녀 賤女 a woman of humble〔low〕 birth ; a lowly woman thousand years ; a millennium

천년 千年 a thousand years ; a millennium
— 만년 thousands of years ; eternity ; [부사적] forever ; for countless ages

천단 淺短 shallowness ; superficiality — 하다 (be) shallow〔superficial〕

천단 擅斷 arbitrary decision ; arbitrariness — 하다 decide arbitrarily〔decide at one's own discretion〕 ¶ 너무 천단적이다 act arbitrarily ; act on one's own authority ; lay down the law

천당 天堂 Heaven ; Paradise ; the heavenly kingdom ¶ 천당가다 go to Heaven ; die ; pass away

천대 賤待 contemptuous〔scornful〕 treatment ; inhospitable〔cold〕 reception — 하다 treat 《a person》 with contempt ; slight ; give〔show, turn〕 the cold shoulder ¶ 천대받다 be treated contemptuously ; be despised // 천대받을 짓을 하다 incur the contempt of others // 가난하다고 그 소년은 천대받았다 The boy was looked down upon because he was poor.

천더기 賤— a despised person ; a child of scorn ¶ 천더기 노릇하다 be treated as a child of scorn

천덩거리다 [끈기있는 액체 따위가] keep dripping in drops

천덩천덩 dripping in sticky drops

천도 天桃 a mythical peach that is said to grow in Heaven

천도 天道 the way of Heaven ; Providence ; the way of Providence ; the laws of God ; divine justice ¶ 천도가 무심하구나 Alas ! God is indifferent.

천도 遷都 transfer of the capital ; moving the seat of government — 하다 transfer the capital ; move the seat of government

천도교 天道教 the religion of *Chŏndokyo* ; the *Chŏndokyo* religion

천동 天動 thunder ; a thunderbolt

천동설 天動說 the geocentric theory ; the Ptolemaic theory

⁑천둥 thunder ¶ 천둥이 울린다 It thunders. /The thunder rolls and rumbles.
— 소리 a peal of thunder ; rolls of thunder

천둥벌거숭이 a rough and tumble amateur ; a man of reckless valor ¶ 그는 천둥벌거숭이다 He is an impetuous daredevil.

천둥지기 天— rice paddies that depend solely on rainfall for water

천랑성 天狼星 〖천문〗 Sirius

천래 天來 ¶ 천래의 heavenly ; divine ; inspired // 천래의 음악 heavenly〔divine〕 music // 천래의 목소리 a voice from above // 천래의 재능 a heavenly gift

천량 money and food ; possessions ¶ 천량이 다 떨어지다 have run out of money and food

천려 淺慮 lack of prudence ; indiscretion ; thoughtlessness

천려일실 千慮一失 a slip〔an oversight〕 of a wise man ; a mere oversight

천렵 川獵 fishing (in a river) ; river fishing — 하다 fish in a river

천로역정 天路歷程 The Pilgrim's Progress

천루 賤陋 lowness ; meanness ; vulgarity — 하다 (be) despicable ; nasty ; mean

천륜 天倫 morals ; moral laws ¶ 천륜에 어그러지다 violate〔transgress〕 moral laws

천리 千里 a thousand *ri* ; a long distance
천릿길도 한 걸음부터 속담 A journey of a thousand miles must begin with the first step. /High buildings have low foundations.

천리 天理 natural law〔principle〕; a law of nature ¶ 천리에 어긋나다 go against nature

천리마 千里馬 a horse so swift that it can make a thousand *ri* a day ; an excellent horse

천리안 千里眼 clairvoyance ; second sight ; foresight ; insight ; penetration ¶ 천리안을 가진 사람 a clairvoyant (남자) ; a clairvoyante (여자) ; a person gifted with second sight // 그 여자는 천리안이다 She has clairvoyant powers.

천마 天馬 a flying horse ; Pegasus

*천막 天幕 a tent ; marquee (큰) ; a pup tent (작은) ; a belltent (원추형의) ; an awning (배의) ¶ 천막을 치다〔걷다〕 pitch〔strike〕 a tent ; pitch〔break〕 camp — 기둥 an awning stanchion — 생활 camp life ; a nomadic life (유목 생활) ¶ 천막 생활을 하다 live under canvas ; camp out —촌 a tent〔camp〕 village

천만 千萬 ten million (수효) ; a myriad (무수) ; [부사적] very much ; exceedingly ; extremely ¶ 천만 뜻밖의 일 quite an unexpected thing // 유감 천만이다 It is really regrettable 《that》; It is quite deplorable 《that》; It is much to be regretted 《that》 // 천만의 말씀입니다 Not at all. /Don't mention it. /You are welcome. // 천만에요 My pleasure. /The pleasure was all mine.
— 장자 a billionaire ; a multimillionaire

천만고 千萬古 remote antiquity ; eternity (영원) ; most ancient days

천만금 千萬金 millions of money ¶ 천만금을 다준대도 싫다 I wouldn't do that for all the world.

천만년 千萬年 ten million years ; myriad years ; a long long time

천만다행 千萬多幸 being extremely fortunate ; being very lucky ; a piece of colossal good fortune ; capital luck —하다 (be) extremely fortunate ; very lucky ¶ 천만다행으로 luckily〔fortunately〕 enough ; by good luck // 천만다행으로 다치지 않았다 By a lucky chance, I escaped unhurt. // 시험에 합격해서 천만다행이었다 He was fortunate enough to pass the examination. // 천만다행이다 Thank God !

천만 뜻밖 千萬— ¶ 천만 뜻밖의 quite unexpected ; unlooked-for ; unforeseen ; unanticipated ; unsuspected ; quite surprising ; [우연한] accidental // 천만 뜻밖의 일 a great surprise ; a bolt from the blue // 천만 뜻밖의 사건 an unforeseen occurrence ; an accident 천만 뜻밖의 장소에서 만나다 meet a person where least expected // 천만 뜻밖에 unexpectedly ; beyond〔contrary to〕 one's expectation ; surprisingly enough ; (all) of a sudden // 이건 천만 뜻밖이다 What a surprise ! // 이런 일은 천만 뜻밖이다 Who would have thought this ! /I am unprepared for this.

천만번 千萬番 tens of thousands of times ; ever so many times ; over and over again ; repeatedly ¶ 천만번 죽어 마땅하다 The likes of you cannot die too often.

천만부당 千萬不當 being utterly unjust ; absolute injustice —하다 (be) utterly unjust ; absolutely unfair ; exceedingly unreasonable ¶ 천만부당한 발언 an absolutely unreasonable〔inappropriate〕 remark

천만사 千萬事 all things ; all kinds of affairs ; everything ; all matters ; all ¶ 천만사가 다 뜻대로 되지 않는다 All things go wrong.

천만세 千萬世 all ages ; countless generations ¶ 천만세에 걸쳐 for all ages to come ; throughout ages ; forever

천만세 千萬歲 eternity ⇨ 천만년

천만에 千萬— ① [겸사] Not at all. ; Don't mention it. ; You are welcome. ② [부당] Never happen. 《미·구》; Certainly not. ; Far from that. ; Oh, no !

천만 의외 千萬意外 ⇨ 천만 뜻밖

천만인 千萬人 tens of millions of people ; countless numbers of people ; so many people

천만층 千萬層 all levels ; innumerable 〔various〕 ranks〔classes, grades〕 ¶ 물건도 천만층이다 There is an endless variety of articles in the world.

천만층 千萬層 all levels ; innumerable 〔various〕 ranks〔classes, grades〕 ¶ 물건도 천만층이다 There is an endless variety of articles in the world.

천명 天命 ① one's allotted span of life ¶ 천명이 다하다 complete the natural span of life ; come to one's journey's end ; die a natural death
② fate ; destiny ; Providence ¶ 천명에 따르다 resign oneself to fate // (나이 50에) 천명을 알다 know Heaven's will (at 50) ; submit to Heaven's will ; take life philosophically // 인사를 다하고 천명을 기다리다 do one's best and leave the rest to Providence // 모든 것은 천명이다 All our fortunes are ordained by Providence.

천명 闡明 clarification ; elucidation —하다 make clear ; elucidate ; declare ; throw light 《on》 ¶ 그는 정치에 관심이 없다고 천명했다 He proclaimed that he was indifferent to politics.

천묘 遷墓 moving〔relocating〕 a grave ; transfer of a grave —하다 move〔relocate〕 a grave

*천문 天文 astronomy ; [현상] astronomical phenomena ¶ 천문학상의 astronomical // 천문학적 숫자에 달하다 reach astronomical figures
—년〔조수〕 astronomical year〔tide〕 — 단

ㅊ

위 astronomical chronology ―대 an astronomical observatory ―도 an astronomical chart ― 망원경 an astronomical telescope ―시〔일〕 astronomical time〔day〕 ―학 astronomy ― 학자 an astronomer ― 항법 celestial navigation ; astronavigation

천문동 天門冬 〖식물〗 a kind of asparagus ; Asparagus cochincinensis (학명)

천물 天物 natural products

천민 賤民 a man of humble〔lowly〕 birth ; the poor ; the underprivileged ; the low-class people ; an outcast

*천박 淺薄 shallowness ; superficiality ―하다 (be) shallow ; superficial ; crude ¶ 천박한 사람 a shallow-witted〔-hearted〕 person // 천박한 지식 superficial knowledge // 천박한 학문 a little learning ; a smattering 《of philosophy》 // 천박한 생각 a half-baked idea ; a superficial view

천방지축 天方地軸 recklessness ; foolhardiness ; rashness ; precipitation ; [부사적] headlong ; recklessly ; rashly ; in a stupid hurry ; helter-skelter ; hurry-scurry ¶ 천방지축 날뛰다 rush recklessly ; make a headlong rush // 천방지축 뛰쳐나가다 bundle out ; rush out of door in consternation

천배 千倍 a thousand times ; a thousandfold ¶ 천배로 하다 increase a thousandfold

천백번 千百番 ever so many times

*천벌 天罰 the wrath of God ; Heaven's judgment〔justice〕 ; divine punishment〔vengeance〕 ; Nemesis ¶ 천벌을 받다 be punished by Heaven ; be visited with Heaven's judgment // 그것은 천벌이다 It's Heaven's justice. // 전에는 역병을 인간의 죄에 대한 천벌로 여겼다 Plague was formerly regarded as a visitation of God for the people's sins.

천변 川邊 a riverside ; a bank of a river ; the edge of a stream ¶ 천변의〔에〕 along a river // 천변의 풍경 river (side) scenery // 천변에 살다 live along a river

천변 天變 extraordinary phenomena in the heavens ; a natural disaster〔calamity〕
― 지이 the disturbances of the elements ; a convulsion of nature

천변 千變 ⇨ 천변만화(千變萬化)

천변만화 千變萬化 innumerable〔incalculable〕 changes ; kaleidoscopic changes ; immense〔infinite〕 variety ―하다 change endlessly ; make kaleidoscopic changes ¶ 천변만화하는 경치 shifting scenes

천병만마 千兵萬馬 vast numbers〔hordes〕 of infantry and cavalry ; a big army

천보 賤― (a) mean〔humble〕 nature ; (a) vulgar〔base〕 disposition ; bad manners

천복 天福 a heavenly blessing ; benediction ¶ 천복을 받다 be blessed by Heaven

천부 天賦 innateness ; a natural gift ; native ability ; endowment ¶ 천부의 natural ; inherent ; gifted ; inborn ; endowed // 천부의 권리 a God-given right ; the natural〔absolute〕 rights of man // 천부의 재능 an inherent〔a native〕 talent ; a gift of nature ; natural talent ; genius // 천부의 재능을 발휘하다 display one's talent
―론 nativism ― 인권 natural〔inherent, absolute〕 rights of man

천부 賤夫 a man of low〔humble〕 birth

천부당만부당 千不當萬不當 being utterly unreasonable ⇨ 천만부당

천분 天分 [천성] nature ; [특질] sphere ; province ; [천부의 재능] a natural gift ; talents ; endowments ¶ 천분이 있다 be talented〔gifted〕 ; be endowed with talents // 천분을 발휘하다 display one's talents ; give full play to one's natural endowments // 그는 기지의 천분이 갖추어져 있었다 He was endowed with wit.

*천사 天使 an angel ¶ 천사 같은 angelic ; seraphic ; cherubic ; cherublike // 천사 같은 목소리 an angelic voice // 천사의 계급 the angelic order
―장(長) an archangel 대― a seraph 《*pl.* ～s, -phim》 소― a cherub 《*pl.* ～s, -bim》 수호〔호위〕― one's good genius

천사 만고 千思萬考 deep meditation ; mature consideration ; careful deliberation ―하다 deliberate carefully ; ponder carefully 《on》

천사슬 天― doing things nature's way ; letting nature take its course

천산 天産 natural production〔products〕
―물 natural products〔produce〕 ¶ 갖가지 천산물이 풍부하다 be rich in natural products of all kinds

천산갑 穿山甲 〖동물〗 a pangolin ; a scaly anteater

천산지산 with all sorts of excuses ; profuse excuses ¶ 핑계를 천산지산 늘어놓다 come out with〔make, produce〕 all sorts of excuses

천상 天上 the heavens ; paradise ¶ 천상의 heavenly ; celestial // 천상의 음악 heavenly music
― 천하 heaven and earth ; the whole world ; under the sun
천상 천하 유아 독존 〔관용〕 I am my own Lord〔Holy am I alone〕 throughout heaven and earth.

천상 天象 an astronomical phenomenon

천상바라기 天上― a person who has always his eyes on the ceiling ; a squint-eyed person

천상의 天象儀 a planetarium

천생 天生 what is destined〔preordained〕 by Heaven ; what is natural ; [부사적] by nature ; as ever ¶ 천생의 natural ; born ; designed by nature // 천생의 시인 a

born poet // 천생의 음악가이다 He is a musician by nature. // 천생 그럴 수 밖에 딴 도리가 없었다 There was no other alternative. /We had no choice left.
— 배필 a predestined marriage ; a well-matched couple — 연분 marriage ties preordained by Providence ; match made in heaven
천석꾼 千石君 a person who has a crop of 1,000 bags of rice ; a wealthy landlord ; a large〔great〕 land owner
천성 天性 nature ; natural disposition ; [기질] a temperament ; [본능] an instinct ¶ 천성의 natural ; instinctive // 사람의 천성 human nature // 천성이 정직하다 be honest by nature // 천성이 온순하다 have a gentle disposition // 습관은 제2의 천성이다 Habit is a second nature. // 사태를 낙관하는 것은 내 천성에 맞지 않는다 It's not in my nature to take things easy.
천세 千歲 eternity ; a thousand years ; distant future ¶ 천세 불멸의 immortal // 이름을 천세에 남기다 win (an) immortal fame
천세나다 [상품 따위가] be in great demand ; be at a premium ; be very popular
천세력 千歲曆 a one hundred year almanac ; a century almanac ; a perpetual calendar
천수 天壽 ⇨ 천명(天命) ①
천수 天數 the natural span of life ¶ 천수를 다하다 live one's allotted span of life ; die a natural death ; [기운] fate ; destiny
천수 天水 rain water
—답(畓) ⇨ 천둥지기
천수 泉水 spring water ¶ 천수로 된 연못 a spring-fed pond
천시 天時 ① [기회] a good〔golden, favorable〕 opportunity ; a good time ¶ 천시를 포착하다 seize an opportunity ; take the tide as it offers ② [자연 현상] the times and seasons
천시 賤視 contempt ; disregard ; disdain ⇨ 멸시
천식 喘息 〖의학〗 asthma
— 환자 an asthmatic (patient)
천신 天神 the gods of heaven
—지기(地祇) the gods of heaven and earth
천신 薦新 offering〔presenting〕 a new product to the gods —하다 offer〔present〕 new fruits to the gods
천신만고 千辛萬苦 all sorts of hardships and privations ; hard work ; severe trials —하다 undergo〔go through〕 all sorts of hardships and privations ; have a hard time ; work hard ¶ 천신만고하여 아이를 기르다 manage to bring up one's child under difficulties
천심 天心 the will of Heaven ; the divine will ; providence ; [하늘의 조심] the zenith ¶ 천심은 헤아릴 수 없다 Inscrutable are the ways of Heaven. // 인심은 천심이다 The voice of people (is) the voice of God.
천안 天顔 the Royal countenance ; the King's face〔visage〕 ¶ 천안을 뵙다〔배알하다〕 be received in audience by〔be presented to〕 the King〔Emperor〕
천앙 天殃 Heaven's punishment ; divine retribution ; the wrath of God ¶ 천앙을 받다 be punished by Heaven
천애 天涯 [하늘의 끝] the horizon ; the skyline ; [아득한 땅] a strange land ; a far-off country ¶ 천애의 고아 a lonely orphan // 천애 고독의 몸 a stranger in a strange land ; a person without a single relative
천양 天壤 Heaven and Earth ¶ 천양지간(之間) the whole universe ; the space between heaven and earth // 천양지판(之判) extreme opposition ; miles of difference ; all the difference in the world // 조금 인내하느냐 마느냐로 성공과 실패라는 천양지판이 생긴다 A little perseverance makes all the difference between success and failure. // 그들의 사고나 관념에는 천양지판이 있다 In thought and ideas they're poles asunder.
천양지차 天壤之差 extreme opposition ; all the difference in the world ; poles apart ; as different as night and day ¶ 두 사람 사이에는 천양지차가 있다 There is all the difference (in the world) between them. /They are poles asunder〔worlds apart〕 in opinion〔in social standing〕.
천언만어 千言萬語 innumerable〔countless〕 words ; endless arguments
천업 賤業 a mean occupation ; low-pay business ; humble work ; drudgery (고된 일) ; a dirty job
—부(婦) a prostitute ; a street girl
천여 天與 a godsend ; Heaven's gift ¶ 천여의 heaven-sent ; providential
천역 賤役 a mean task〔job〕 ; a humble role
†천연 天然 nature ; natural state ; being natural ; [자발] spontaneity ¶ 천연의 natural ; spontaneous ; [야생의] wild // 천연의 미 natural beauty ; the beauty of nature
— 가스 natural gas — 기념물 a natural monument —물 a natural substance 〔object〕 ; the natural form (of a thing) —미 natural beauty ; the beauty〔charm〕 of nature —색 natural color(s) ; technicolor —색 사진 color photograph ; [영화] a technicolor film —석 native rock — 수(水) natural water — 자원 natural resources
천연 遷延 delay ; procrastination ; postponement —하다 delay ; put off ; postpone ; procrastinate ¶ 천연할 수 없다 (it) admit of no delay ; be extremely urgent

ㅊ

—책 a dilatory policy〔motion〕; a delaying move ; a time-gaining measure

천연덕스럽다 be natural〔unaffected〕; be unmoved ⇨ 천연스럽다

천연두 天然痘 smallpox ¶ 천연두에 걸리다 be infected with smallpox ; contract smallpox ; come down with smallpox

—균 a smallpox germ〔virus〕 **— 자국** a pockmark **— 환자** a case of smallpox ¶ 천연두 환자 3명 three cases of smallpox 자반성 — black smallpox

천연스럽다 天然— (be) natural ; unartificial ; unaffected ; [태연] be unmoved ; calm ; quiet ; cool ; composed ¶ 천연스런〔스럽게〕 calm(ly) ; cool(ly) ; fearless(ly) ; undaunted(ly) ; nonchalant(ly) ; with utter indifference ; as if nothing had happened // 천연스러운 자세 a natural pose ; a calm attitude ; a nonchalant air // 천연스러운 안색 a natural expression of face // 욕설을 듣고도 천연스러웠다 He did not turn a hair at the abuse. // 마치 아무 일도 없었던 것처럼 천연스레 나타났다 He turned up as if nothing had happened.

천엽 千葉 the reticulum of a ruminant ; the tripe of an ox's stomach ¶ 천엽의 double-petalled ; double-flowered

— 수선(水仙) a double daffodil

천왕성 天王星 Uranus

천왕지팡이 天王— a tall person ; a lamppost 《속》; a daddy-longlegs

천외 天外 ① [하늘의 바깥] ¶ 천외에 beyond the heavens ② [퍽 먼곳] farthest regions

천우신조 天佑神助 the divine care ; the grace of Heaven ; Providence ¶ 천우신조로 by the grace of God // 천우신조로 어려움을 피하다 escape providentially // 이것은 천우신조라 할 수 있다 This is like providence.

천운 天運 destiny ; fate ; fortune ; one's lot ; one's star ¶ 천운에 맡기다 trust to chance〔luck, Providence〕

천원 泉源 a springhead ; a fountainhead

천은 天恩 the blessing of Heaven ; the grace of god ; Royal favor ; the king's grace

천의 天意 the divine will ; the will of heaven ; God's will ; Providence ¶ 천의에 따르다 obey〔follow, bow to〕 the will of Heaven // 천의에 어긋나다 be against〔be contrary to〕 the will of Heaven〔the divine will〕

천의무봉 天衣無縫 perfect beauty with no trace of artifice ¶ 천의무봉의 flawless ; perfect

천인 天人 heaven〔God〕 and man ; heavenly phenomena and human affairs ; a man of talent(s) ; a beautiful woman ; a heavenly being ; a fairy ; an angel ¶ 천인이 공노할 죄다 It is an offense against God and man.

천인 賤人 a man of humble origin〔birth〕; a lowly man

천일 天日 the sky and the sun ; [햇빛] sunlight ; sunshine

—염 bay salt ; sun-dried salt **— 제염** salt manufacturing by spontaneous evaporation

천일 千日 a thousand days

— 기도 devotions for a thousand days

천일야화 千一夜話 the Arabian Nights ; The Thousand and One Nights

천일초 千日草 〖식물〗 a globe amaranth ⇨ 천일홍

천일홍 千日紅 a globe amaranth

천입 擅入 breaking and entering ; trespassing ; an intrusion **—하다** break into ; trespass ; enter by force ; force one's way in

천자 天子 an emperor ; a sovereign ; [하늘의 아들] the Son of the God〔Heaven〕

천자 天資 natural endowments〔talent, ability〕; (a) nature ¶ 천자 총명한 endowed with high intelligence

천자 千字 the Thousand (Chinese) Characters

—문 the Thousand Characters Text ; a primer of Chinese characters

천자만태 千姿萬態 an endless variety of forms ; multifariousness ¶ 천자만태의 multifarious

천자만홍 千紫萬紅 a colorful display (of flowers) ; a resplendent variety of beautiful flowers ; all sorts of colorful flowers ¶ 정원에 꽃이 천자만홍으로 피었다 The garden is a riot of color with the flowers in full bloom. /The garden is gorgeous with variegated flowers in full glory.

천잠 天蠶 a wild silkworm

—사 silk from the wild silkworm ; gut ; catgut (낚싯줄 실)

†**천장 天障** the ceiling ¶ 둥근 천장 a dome ; a cupola // 천장에 매달려 있다 hang from the ceiling // 천장이 높다 have a high ceiling ; this room is high // 천장에 파리가 붙어 있다 There is a fly on the ceiling.

—등(燈) a ceiling light **— 선풍기** a ceiling fan

‡**천재 天才** [재능] genius ; talent ; a natural gift〔endowment〕; [사람] a genius ; a prodigy ¶ 천재적 talented ; gifted // 어학의 천재 a linguistic genius ; a talented linguist // 천재 기질을 발휘하다 display one's genius〔natural talent〕; give fullplay to one's genius // 돈 버는 천재다 He has a genius for making money. // 천재 기질의 사람이다 He is something of a genius.

— 교육 genius education **—아** a gifted child ; an infant prodigy ; a boy〔girl〕 wonder 《미》

‡**천재 天災** a (natural) calamity ; a natural disaster ; an act of God ¶ 천재를 만나다

ㅊ

be visited by a natural calamity ; meet with disaster

천재 千載 a thousand years ¶ 천재 일우의 기회 a rare opportunity ; the chance of one's lifetime ; a chance in a thousand ; the best day of one's lifetime ; a once-in-a-lifetime chance // 천재 일우의 호기를 놓치다 miss a golden〔rare〕 opportunity

천재지변 天災地變 a natural calamity〔disaster〕 ¶ 천재지변이 자주 일어나다 be often visited by natural calamities

천적 天敵 a natural enemy

*__천정 天頂__ the zenith ; the height
— 거리 〖천문〗 the zenith distance **—의(儀)** a zenith telescope **—점(點)** the zenith

천정 天定 what has been preordained by Heaven ; Providence ⇨ 천생(天生)

천정부지 天井不知 skyrocketing ¶ 천정부지로 올라가는 물가 skyrocketing living costs

천제 天帝 God ; Heaven ; the Creator ; Providence

천조 天助 Heavenly help ; Providential help ; help from above

천조 踐祚 accession (to the throne) **—하다** ascend〔accede to〕 the throne

천주 天主 the Lord of Heaven ; God ; the Creator
—경(經) ⇨ 주기도문

천주교 天主教 Roman Catholicism
—국 a Catholic nation **— 신부** a Roman Catholic father **— 신자** a Roman Catholic **—학** Roman Catholicism **—(교)회** the Roman Catholic Church

†**천지 天地** ① [하늘과 땅] heaven and earth ; the heavens and the earth ; [우주] the universe ; [세계] the world ② [사회] a world ; a sphere ¶ 천지의 창조주 the Creator // 천지가 뒤집혀도 though the heavens fall // 천지를 진동시키다 shake earth and sky // 천지에 맹세하다 swear by heaven and earth // 자유의 천지 a free land // 새 천지를 개척하다 find a new world for oneself ; seek one's fortune in a new world // 양자의 사이에는 천지의 차이가 있다 There is all the difference in the world between the two. / They are poles〔worlds〕 apart. // 천지간 만물 중에 사람이 가장 귀하다 Man is the noblest of all creatures in the world.
— 만물 all creatures ; the creation ; the universe ; universal〔all〕 nature **대—** a macrocosm **별—** a world by itself ; a world of its own **새—** a new world ; a new sphere of activity **소—** a narrow〔limited〕 sphere ; a microcosm

천지 天池 the crater lake on Mt. *Paektu*

천지 개벽 天地開闢 the beginning of the world ¶ 천지 개벽 이래 ever since the world began

천지신명 天地神明 gods of heaven and earth ¶ 천지신명의 가호 the protection of god ; the grace of Heaven // 천지신명에 맹세하다 swear by the gods of heaven and earth ; call Heaven to witness

천지인 天地人 heaven, earth and man ; the three orders of heaven, earth and man

천지판 天地板 the cover and bottom boards of coffin

**__천직 天職__ a calling ; a (real) vocation ; a mission ; a duty ¶ 천직을 발견하다 find〔discover〕 one's real vocation // 여자의 천직은 가정이다 Women's place is in the home. // 나는 이 일을 천직으로 알고 있다 I feel a call to this work.

천진난만 天眞爛漫 (heaven-given) simplicity and innocence ; innocence ; naiveté ; naiveness ; artlessness ; open-heartedness ; spontaneity **—하다** (be) simple and innocent ; naive ; artless ; unaffected ; unsophisticated ; open-hearted ¶ 천진난만한 어린이 a simple and innocent child // 천진난만한 사람 a naive person // 천진난만한 태도 an unsophisticated〔unaffected〕 attitude // 그의 행동에는 천진난만한 데가 있다 He had a sort of naiveté〔naivety〕 and openness of demeanor.

천질 天質 one's innate nature ; natural disposition ; a temperament (기질)

천차만별 千差萬別 infinite variety〔gradation〕 ¶ 천차만별의 an infinite variety of ; of various kinds // 천차만별의 사람 all sorts of people ; various kinds of people // 사람의 마음은 천차만별이다 So many men, so many minds.

천착 穿鑿 boring ; excavation ; search ; inquiry ; exploration ; investigation **—하다** bore ; excavate ; search ; seek for ; inquire〔look〕 into ; explore ; investigate ¶ 남의 사사일을 천착하다 dig〔pry〕 into a person's private affairs // 천착하기 좋아하다 be fond of prying ; be inquisitive

천착 舛錯 —하다 (be) ill-natured ; mean-spirited ; [얼굴] mean-looking ; vulgar ; ugly ¶ 천착스러운 사람 a vixenish person // 천착한 얼굴 an ugly face ; vulgar features

천창 天窓 a skylight ; a scuttle

**__천천하다__ (be) slow ; tardy ; unhurried

†**천천히** slowly ; without haste ; leisurely ; gradually ¶ 천천히 말하다〔걷다〕 speak〔walk〕 slowly // 천천히 서류를 조사하다 examine papers at leisure // 좀 더 천천히 말씀해 주십시오 Please speak more slowly. // 천천히 하시오 Take your time about it. /Take plenty of time. /Take it easy. /Take your time. There's no rush.

천첩 賤妾 ① concubine of low birth ② [부인의 자칭] I

천체 天體 a heavenly body ; a celestial sphere ; an orb ¶ 천체의 운동 movements of heavenly bodies

ㅊ

— 관측 astronomical observation — 기상학 astrometeorology —도 a celestial map — 망원경 an astronomical telescope — 물리학 astrophysics — 사진 the photograph of a star〔heavenly body〕 — 사진술 astrophotography — 역학 gravitational astronomy — 운동 the movement of heavenly bodies — 좌표 celestial coordinates — 측량 uranometry —학 uranography

천추 千秋 a thousand years ; many years ¶ 천추의 한 a matter of great regret // 하루를 천추같이 …을 기다리다 wait impatiently for 《a person》; look forward to 《a thing》 with longing // 이름을 천추에 남기다 immortalize one's name ; leave one's name to posterity
— 만세(萬歲) ⇨ 천만년

천축 天竺 (an old Chinese name for) India

천출 賤出 an illegitimate child ; a bastard

천층만층 千層萬層 countless classes ; all levels

*천치 天癡 an idiot ; an imbecile ; a moron ; a fool ; a simpleton

†천칭 天秤 ⇨ 천평칭

천칭 賤稱 deprecation ; a deprecatory term〔word, name〕; derogation

천태만상 千態萬象 all kinds of forms and figures ; a great diversity

천트다 薦— ① get〔be〕 recommended for〔to〕
② try for the first time ; embark on (an unexperienced work) ¶ 장사를 천트다 try business for the first time ; attempt a business career

천편일률 千篇一律 monotony ; grooviness ; lack in variety ¶ 천편일률의 monotonous ; stereotyped // 그의 말은 천편일률적이다 He always harps on the same string.

천평칭 天平秤 a balance ¶ 천평칭에 달다 weigh 《a thing》 in a balance

천품 天稟 natural disposition ; temperament ; innateness ; [천질] natural gifts 〔endowments〕 ¶ 천품의 재능이 있는 작가 a gifted〔talented〕 author // 천품이 뛰어나다 be endowed with high intelligence〔great talents〕 // 천품을 발휘하다 display one's natural talents

천하 天下 the universe ; the earth ; the world ; the whole country ; the whole land ; the public ¶ 천하의 대세 the general world situation〔trend〕 // 천하의 영웅 the greatest hero of the world // 천하의 공론 a universal opinion // 천하없어도 whatever happens ; under any circumstances // 천하에 under the sun ; in the world // 천하에 (둘도) 없는 unique ; unequaled ; unparalleled ; matchless ; peerless // 천하에 호령하다 dictate to the world // 천하에 무적이다 have no rival〔be unrivaled, be peerless〕 in the world // 천하에 이름을 날리다 spread one's name around the world ; become world-famous // 천하를 잡다 rule over the land ; come to power ; become the ruler of the country ; take over the state // 천하를 통일하다 unify a country ; bring the whole country under one's rule // 천하를 정복하다 conquer the world // 지금은 금융 자본가의 천하다 The monetary capitalists are now having their own way.

†천하다 賤— [비열] (be) base ; mean ; despicable ; contemptible ; [창피] shameful ; ignoble ; [신분] low ; humble ; vulgar ; [흔함] plenty ; cheap ¶ 천하지 않다 be respectable ; be decent // 천한 직업 a humble calling // 천한 신분 a humble station in life ; one's lowly status // 천한 말투 a vulgar expression // 그는 천한 집안에서 태어난 사람이었다 He was a man of humble birth〔origin〕.

천하 명창 天下名唱 an excellent singer 〔vocalist〕; a world famous singer

천하일색 天下一色 a woman of matchless beauty

천하 일품 天下一品 a unique article ; the best specimen in existence ¶ 천하 일품이다 be peerless ; be unique ; be unequaled in the world // 그것은 천하 일품이다 There is nothing like it in the world. // 그의 영어 실력은 천하 일품이다 He stands unchallenged in his knowledge of English.

천하장사 天下壯士 a matchless warrior ; the strongest man on earth ; a Hercules ; an Atlas ¶ 기운이 천하장사다 He is a pillar of strength.

천학 淺學 superficial knowledge〔learning〕 ¶ 천학 비재를 불구하고 in spite of my lack of knowledge and ability

천행 天幸 god's blessing〔favor〕; a piece of good luck〔fortune〕; a godsend ; a boon ¶ 천행으로 luckily ; fortunately ; by good luck ; as luck would have it // 네가 살아난 것은 천행이다 You must bless your stars that you have escaped !

천험 天險 a natural stronghold ; a natural barrier for defense ¶ 천험을 의지하다 take to a natural stronghold

천형병 天刑病 leprosy
—자 a lepra ; leprosy ⇨ 나병

천혜 天惠 Heaven's blessing ; God's blessing〔favor〕; a gift of nature ; a natural advantage ; a boon

천화 天禍 the wrath of Heaven ; a visitation of God

천후 天候 the weather ⇨ 기후(氣候) ¶ 전천후의 all-weather
전— 비행기 an all-weather airplane

†철¹ [계절] a season ; the time ¶ 여름철 summer ; the summer season // 벚꽃 피는 철 the cherry season // 제철의 옷 the clothes of the season // 철 이른〔늦은〕 사과 early〔late〕 apples // 제철이 아닌 out of

season ; unseasonable // 철에 뒤진〔철이 지난〕 behind the season // 제철을 만나다 be in one's heyday〔one's prime〕; have one's best days // 철을 따라 옷을 바꿔 입다 change one's clothes according to the season // 지금은 버섯이 한창 나오는 철이다 Mushrooms are now in season.

사— the four seasons ⇨ 사철

철² [분별] discretion ; prudence ; sense ; good sense ; wisdom ¶ 철이 없다 have no sense〔discretion〕; be indiscreet〔thoughtless, foolish〕// 철이 들다 become sensible〔wise〕// 그는 아직 철이 덜 들었다 He is still immature in his way of thinking.

철나자 망령난다 ㈜속담 Life is half spent before we know what it is.

†**철 鐵** iron ; steel (강철) ¶ 철의 iron ; steel // 철의 폐(肺) an iron lung // 철의 장막 the Iron Curtain // 철을 포함하다 contain iron

철 綴 binding ; filing —하다 bind ; file ¶ 책을 철하다 bind a book // 서류〔신문〕를 철해 놓다 keep papers〔newspapers〕 on file

서류— a file (of documents, papers) 신문— a newspaper file

철각 鐵脚 iron legs ¶ 철각을 자랑하는 선수 a runner of iron legs

철갑 鐵甲 an iron covering ; [더께] a coating ; a crust —하다 form a coating ; coat

—선 an ironclad ship 먹— a coating of ink 흙— a coating of mud〔clay〕

철강 鐵鋼 steel

—업 the steel industry — 제품 steel manufactures

철갱 鐵坑 an iron mine

철거 撤去 [퇴거] withdrawal ; [제거] removal ; [명도] evacuation ; clearing away —하다 withdraw ; evacuate ; remove ; clear away ¶ 구주로부터 군대를 철거하다 withdraw troops from Europe // 장애물을 철거하다 remove the obstacles

—령 an order to evacuate

철겹다 be behind the season ; be out of season ; unseasonable ¶ 철겨운 꽃 a flower late for the season ; late flowers // 철겨운 날씨 unsettled〔crazy〕 weather

철골 a skinny〔bony, thin, meager〕 appearance ¶ 철골이 되다 become emaciated〔skinny〕; be reduced to a mere skeleton

철골 鐵骨 an iron〔a steel〕 frame ; a steel skeleton

— 건물 a steel-frame〔-skeleton〕 building — 공사 steel-frame work — 구조 a cage ; steel-frame structure ; skeleton construction — 목선 a composite ship

철공 鐵工 an ironworker ; an ironsmith ; a blacksmith

—소〔장〕 an ironworks ; an iron foundry ¶ 철공소〔장〕 주인 an ironmaster

철관 鐵管 a iron pipe〔tube〕 ¶ 철관을 묻다 lay iron pipes (underground)

수도 — an iron water pipe ; a water main

철광 鐵鑛 an iron mine ; [광석] iron ore

—천(泉) a ferruginous spring ; chalybeate spring〔waters〕 니(泥)— clay ironstone

철교 鐵橋 an iron bridge ; a railway bridge (철도의) ¶ 철교를 놓다 build〔construct〕 an iron bridge

철군 撤軍 ⇨ 철병(撤兵) ¶ 철군의 규모와 일정 the size and timetable of the pull out (of the troops)

철권 鐵拳 a strong fist ¶ 철권을 먹이다 use one's fist on 《a person》; strike 《a person》 with one's fist // 철권 세례를 퍼붓다 rain blows upon 《a person》 // 철권으로 제재를 가하다 administer fist law

— 제재 a fist-law〔toco 《영·속》〕 to 《a person》; taking the law into one's fists ; a fist punishment

철궤 鐵櫃 a steel safe ; an iron (money-) box

철그렁 clinking ; with a clink ¶ 철그렁 소리나다 clink ; clank

철근 鐵筋 steel reinforcing

— 절단기 a bar cutter — 콘크리트 steel〔ferro〕 concrete ; reinforced concrete ; beton armée 《프》 ¶ 철근 콘크리트 건물 a steel-concrete building

철금 鐵琴 a glockenspiel ; a carillon

철기 鐵器 ironware ; hardware 《미》

— 시대 〖고고학〗 the Iron Age

철기 鐵騎 an armored horseman ; brave cavalry

철꺽 sticking tight ; with a slap〔snap〕 ¶ 철꺽 때리다 slap 《a person》 // 철꺽 잠그다 fasten a lock with a clap // 철꺽 달라붙다 stick fast〔tight〕; cling tight

철끈 綴— a binding string〔strip〕

철나다 become sensible〔wise〕; attain the age of discretion ; cut one's wisdom teeth ¶ 철날 나이 an age of discretion // 이젠 철날 때가 아니냐 You ought to know better at your age.

†**철도 鐵道** a railroad 《미》; a railway ; rail ¶ 5천 마일의 철도 5,000 miles of railroad // 철도 편에 부치다 send by rail // 철도를 부설하다 build〔construct〕 a railroad // 철도가 통하다 have a railroad ; a railroad runs

— 공사 railroad (construction) work — 공안관 a railway public peace officer ; [집합적으로] the railway police — 공학 railway engineering — 기관사 a locomotive engineer 《미》; an engine driver on the railway 《영》 — 노선 a railroad track〔line〕 —망(網) a network of railroads — 부설 the construction〔building〕 of railways ; railroading 《미》 — 부설권 a railway charter — 사고 a railroad accident — 선로〔궤도〕 a railroad〔railway〕 track ; a (railroad) line ; [집합적] trackage — 수송 transportation by rail — 시설〔서비스〕 railway service ; a railroad

《미》 ━ 안내소 a railroad information bureau 《*pl.* ~s, ~x》 《미》; a railway inquiry office 《영》 ━ 여객 a railroad passenger ━ 여행 railroad traveling; a railroad journey; railroading 《미》 ━ 연락 railway connections ━ 우편 the railroad post service ━ 운임 a railroad 〔train〕 fare (여객의); railroad freight rates (화물의) ━ 인부 a trackman; a linesman ━ 자살 committing suicide by throwing oneself before a train ━ 조례(條例) the railway law ━ 종업원 a railway worker〔operative, official〕; a railroader 《미》; a railroad man 《미》; a railroad employee 《미》; a railway servant 《영》 ━청 the Office of (Korean National) Railroads ━ 침목 crossties; ties; sleepers ━편 transportation by rail ━ 화물 railway goods; freight 《미》 고가 ━ an elevated〔overhead〕 railroad 고속 ━ a high-speed railroad 관광 ━ a scenic railway 광궤〔협궤〕 ━ a broad-〔narrow-〕 gauge railroad 국유 ━ a government 〔state〕 railway 군용 ━ a military railroad 단선〔복선〕 ━ a single-〔double-〕track railroad; a single〔double〕 line of rails 사설 ━ a private railroad 시외〔교외〕 ━ a suburban railway 전기 ━ an electric railroad

철도 경비대 鐵道警備隊 railway guards

철두철미 徹頭徹尾 being thorough〔exhaustive〕; thoroughness; [부사적] from beginning to end; from start to finish; to the core; in every way; every inch; through and through; out and out; completely; all ━하다 (be) thorough〔thoroughgoing, exhaustive〕; complete; out and out ¶ 철두철미한 악한 an out-and-out rascal 〔scoundrel〕// 철두철미 반대하다 oppose in every particular; be dead set against it

철들다 become sensible〔wise〕 ⇨ 철나다

철떡거리다 slop from side to side; splash; keep lapping〔slopping〕; drag; trail ¶ 젖은 옷이 철떡거리다 one's wet clothing slings to one's body

철럭거리다 trickle

철렁거리다 keep jingling; clink; tinkle; keep lapping〔slopping〕 ⇨ 찰랑거리다

철로 鐵路 a railroad ⇨ 철도 ¶ 철로 바탕 a rail(road) bed

철록어미 a heavy〔chain〕 smoker

철리 哲理 the philosophical principles (of anything); the philosophy ¶ 철리를 탐구하다 study the philosophy of the matter// 철리를 실천하다 put one's philosophy into practice

철마 鐵馬 a (railway) train

철망 鐵網 a wire-gauge〔cage〕; a fireguard (난롯가의); a wire-screen; wire netting 《총칭》 ¶ 철망을 치다 cover 《a thing》 with wire netting
━ 가시 barbed wire ━문 a wire-door 〔-screen〕

철매 soot ⇨ 검댕, 그을음

철면 凸面 a convex surface
━경〔렌즈〕 a convex mirror〔lens〕

철면피 鐵面皮 a brazen face; brazenfacedness; impudence; audacity; cheek 《속》 ¶ 철면피의 impudent; audacious; cheeky; brazen-faced// 철면피하게도 …하다 have the impudence〔face, nerve〕 to 《do》// 그는 철면피한 놈이다 He is a cheeky〔brazen-faced, audacious〕 fellow.

*철모 鐵帽 a helmet; a steel〔iron〕 cap

철모르다 have no sense〔discretion〕; lack judgment; be thoughtless; be simple-minded〔innocent〕 ¶ 철모르는 애 an innocent child; a thoughtless child// 철모르는 애의 일이니 용서하시오 Please forgive his behavior, he is only a child.

철문 鐵門 an iron gate

*철물 鐵物 hardware 《미》; ironware; ironwork; ironmongery; metal fittings
━ 세공 metal work ━ 장수 an ironmonger; a hardwareman 《미》; hardware dealer ━전 a hardware shop 《미》; an ironmonger 《영》

철바람 a seasonal wind; a monsoon

철버덕 with a splash ━하다 ⇨ 철벅거리다

철버덕거리다 ⇨ 철벅거리다

철버덩 with a plop ¶ 물에 철버덩 빠지다 fall plop into the water

철벅거리다 splash 《about》 ¶ 철벅거리며 내를 건너다 splash across the stream

철벅철벅 splashing(ly); dabbing; splish-splash; with splashing ¶ 철벅철벅 물속에 들어가다 splash into the water

철벽 鐵壁 an iron wall; an impregnable fortress ¶ 철벽의 impregnable; invulnerable// 철벽 같은 진 an impregnable position
금성 ━ an impregnable fortress〔castle〕

철병 撤兵 withdrawal〔evacuation〕 of troops ━하다 withdraw troops; evacuate ¶ 철병을 요구하다 demand troop withdrawal(s); demand evacuation// 월남에서 철병하다 withdraw troops from Vietnam

철봉 鐵棒 an iron rod〔bar〕; a crowbar; [체조용] an exercise bar; a horizontal bar ¶ 철봉을 하다 exercise on the horizontal bar

철부지 ━不知 a mere child; just a child; a person who has no sense〔who lacks good sense〕; a person of immature judgment; a stupid〔foolish〕 person ¶ 아무 것도 모르는 철부지 just a child who does not know his own mind// 철부지 노릇을 하다 behave like a mere child; play a fool; act thoughtlessly// 그는 모든 면에서 아직 미숙한 철부지이다 He's still just an immature youth with a superficial view of everything.

철분 鐵分 iron content ¶ 철분이 있다 contain iron ; (be) ferric ; ferrous ; chalybeate ; ferruginous // 철분을 함유한 물 chalybeate water // 철분이 많다〔적다〕 be rich〔poor〕 in iron ; be high〔low〕 in iron

철빈 鐵貧 extreme〔dire, abject〕 poverty ; destitution ―하다 (be) very poor ; destitute ; indigent

†철사 鐵絲 a wire ; wiring ¶ 철사를 뽑다〔만들다〕 draw a wire ; draw metal into wire

― 그물 a wire net ― 세공 wirework 가시 ― barbed wire

철삭 鐵索 a cable ; a wire rope ; a cable-way

철상 撤床 clearing the offertory table ―하다 clear (the offertory table)

철새 a seasonal〔migratory〕 bird

철색 鐵色 iron blue ; steel blue

철색 鐵索 an iron cable ; a wire rope

철석 鐵石 iron and stone ; 〔굳음〕 adamant ; firmness ; solidity ¶ 철석 같은 adamantine ; resolute ; indomitable ; steadfast // 철석 같은 마음 an iron〔an adamantine〕 will

철석간장 鐵石肝腸 a hard heart ; a firm mind ; an adamant resolution ¶ 철석간장을 녹이다 disarm one's hardheartedness ; make one's firm purpose waver ; captivate (a man)

철석영 鐵石英 〖광물〗 ferruginous quartz

철선 鐵線 (iron) wire

철설 鐵屑 scrapiron ; ferrous scrap ; iron filings (쇠의 줄밥)

철쇄 鐵鎖 〔자물쇠〕 an iron lock ; 〔쇠사슬〕 an iron chain

*철수 撤收 evacuation ; withdrawal ―하다 withdraw ; evacuate ¶ 군대를 철수시키다 withdraw the troops

―자 an evacuee 전면 ― a total withdrawal

철시 撤市 closing up shop ; suspension of business ―하다 close up shop ; close market place ; suspend business ¶ 철시하여 파업하다 go on strike closing all the stores // 처사에 항의하여 도시가 철시하다 A community closes up shop in protest against the measure.

철심 鐵心 a firm mind ; an iron will ; 〔기계의〕 an iron core ; a metal supporting frame ¶ 철심들이 안경테 a spectacle frame with a metal support inside

철썩 with a splash ; with a thud〔slam, slap〕 ; plump ; heavily ¶ 철썩 떨어지다 fall down with a thud〔bump〕 // 철썩 주저앉다 sit down heavily 《on a chair》 // 머리를 철썩 때리다 slap 《a person》 on the head ; flap

철썩거리다 lap ; splash ; spank ¶ 철썩거리며 해안에 부딪치는 파도 the water lapping the shore

철썩철썩 〔파도 소리〕 splashing ; plashing ; 〔때리는 소리〕 spanking ; slapping ; banging ; slamming ¶ 바닷물이 해안에서 철썩철썩 파도 치고 있다 The waves are lapping〔beating〕 the beach.

철아령 鐵啞鈴 iron dumbbells

철안 鐵案 an immutable conclusion ¶ 철안을 내리다 give a final decision 《on a case》

*철야 徹夜 an all-night vigil ; sitting up all night ; an all-night sitting ―하다 sit〔be〕 up all night ; keep vigil ¶ 철야하여 병자를 간호하다 sit up all night with a patient // 철야하여 시험 공부하다 cram for the examination throughout the night ; sit up all night preparing oneself for the examination // 철야하여 회의하다 have an all-night conference

― 운행 〔버스 따위〕 all-night service ¶ 철야 운행하다 be run all night long ― 작업 all-night work

철없다 have no sense〔discretion〕 ; (be) indiscreet ; lack judgment ; (be) thoughtless〔foolish〕 ¶ 철없는 애 a mere child // 철없는 말 a thoughtless remark // 철없는 짓을 하다 act thoughtlessly〔foolishly〕 ; behave like a mere child

철옷 clothes of〔for〕 the season ; seasonal attire ¶ 철옷으로 갈아 입다 change the clothes of the season

철옹산성 鐵甕山城 ⇨ 철옹성(鐵甕城)

철옹성 鐵甕城 a strong〔an impregnable〕 fortification ; an ironclad bastion ¶ 철옹성 같다, 철옹성이다 be very〔ever so〕 strong

철완 투수 鐵腕投手 a pitcher with an iron arm

철요 凸凹 convexity and concavity ; convex and concave ; unevenness ; irregularity

철음 綴音 the sound of a syllable

철의 장막 鐵—帳幕 the Iron Curtain ¶ 과학의 철의 장막 the Iron Curtain on science // 철의 장막을 허물다 tear down the Iron Curtain

철인 哲人 a man of wisdom ; a sage ; a philosopher

철인 鐵人 an iron man

*철자 綴字 spelling ; orthography ―하다 spell ¶ 단어를 철자하다 spell a word // 철자가 틀리다 be misspelled ; misspell a word

―법 a spelling system ; the rules of orthography 한글 ―법 the rule of Korean orthography

철재 鐵材 iron (material) ; an iron frame ¶ 철재로 집을 짓다 build a house with iron frames

*철저 徹底 thoroughness ; exhaustiveness ―하다 (be) thorough ; thoroughgoing ; exhaustive ¶ 철저한 thorough ; thoroughgoing ; thoroughpaced ; exhaustive ; out-and-out ; through-and-through ; downright ; dyed-in-the-wool // 철저한 각오 firm determination // 철저한

공산주의자 a hardcore communist ; a dyed-in-the-wool communist // 철저한 대책 a radical〔drastic〕 measure // 철저한 애국자 a patriot to the core // 철저한 연구 a thorough〔an exhaustive〕 study // 철저한 자유주의자 a liberal to the core ; an out-and-out liberal // 그의 검약은 철저하다 His thrift is thoroughgoing. // 일을 철저하게 하다 make a thorough job (of it) ; do a job thoroughly ; go all the way // 철저하게 전시(全市)를 수색하다 comb the whole city

철저히 徹底— thoroughly ; thoroughgoingly ; completely ; exhaustively ¶ 철저히 연구하다 exhaust《a subject》; probe《a matter》 to the bottom // 철저히 조사하다 make a thorough investigation of《a matter》// 철저히 싸우다 fight to the bitter end // 철저히 패배하다 be soundly defeated

철정 鐵釘 a〔an iron〕 nail

철제 鐵製 (made of) iron ; steel ; iron make ; [철제품] an iron ; iron-work ; iron ware ; hardware ¶ 철제의 iron ; steel // 건물용 철제품 ironwork for buildings

— **기구** an iron tool ; ironwork

철제 鐵劑 〖약〗 iron ; an iron preparation

철제 鐵蹄 [편자] a horseshoe ; [말] a strong〔swift〕 horse ; a sturdy and gallant steed ¶ 철제에 유린되다 be overrun by the cavalry

철조망 鐵條網 wire-entanglements ; barbed-wire entanglements (가시 철조망) ¶ 철조망을 치다 set〔put up〕 barbed-wire entanglements // 철조망을 뚫고 가다 break through wire-entanglements

철주자 鐵鑄字 (a) metal type (for printing)

철쭉 a royal azalea ; rhododendron (Schlippenbachii) (학명)

—**꽃** royal azalea blossom

철창 鐵窓 [창] a steel-barred window ; [감옥] prison bars ; a prison ; a jail ¶ 철창에서 신음하다 pine behind (the) iron bars // 철창에 갇히다 be placed behind the prison bars ; be imprisoned

— **생활** life behind the bars ¶ 철창 생활 10년 ten years in prison

철찾다 suit the season ; be seasonable

철책 鐵柵 an iron〔an iron-wire〕 fence ; an iron railing〔impalement〕 ¶ 철책을 두르다 put an iron fence around《a thing》 // 철책으로 사람을 못 들어오게 하다 keep people away with a wire fence

철천지원 徹天之寃 a lasting regret ; an inveterate grudge ; deep-rooted enmity ¶ 철천지원을 풀다 vent one's inveterate grudge // 철천지원을 품다 have〔nurse〕 a deep-rooted rancor《against》; have a blood feud《against》; cherish an implacable hostility《toward》

철천지한 徹天之恨 ⇨ 철천지원

철철 brimming over ; overflowing ¶ 철철 넘치다 brim over ; run over ; overflow // 철철 넘치도록 to the brim ; to the full // 철철 넘도록 붓다 fill to overflow〔brim over〕 the pot

철철이 each and every season ; at each season ; around the calendar ¶ 철철이 피는 꽃들 flowers of each season

철총이 a horse with bluish-gray hair spotted with white

철추 鐵椎 an iron hammer ⇨ 철퇴

철칙 鐵則 an iron(clad) rule ; a strict regulation

철커덕 with a snap ; with a click〔clink〕 ; rattling ¶ 문을 철커덕 잠그다 lock the door with a rattling sound〔click〕

철탑 鐵塔 a steel tower ; [고압선용의] a pylon

철통 鐵桶 a steel tub ; an iron pail ¶ 철통 같은 방위진 an impenetrable defense〔protection〕 cordon // 철통 같은 경계 strict watch // 철통 같다 be perfectly provided against ; be well protected ; be on strict watch〔guard〕 (경비) ; be strong〔impregnable〕 // 수도 방위 태세는 철통 같다 The defense system of the capital is just perfect.

철퇴 撤退 evacuation ; withdrawal —**하다** evacuate ; withdraw《from》; clear《out of》 ¶ 병력을 진지에서 철퇴시키다 withdraw troops《from a position》// 군대는 그 도시에서 철퇴했다 The soldiers evacuated the town.

— **명령** an evacuation order ¶ 그 도시로부터의 철퇴 명령을 받다 be ordered out of the city —**자** an evacuee **부분** — a partial pullout ; a thinout **전면** — a general pullout

철퇴 鐵槌 an iron hammer ¶ 철퇴를 가하다 deal a hard〔heavy〕 blow《to》; deal a sledge-hammer at《a person》; crack down on // 당국은 저속 영화에 철퇴를 내렸다 Indecent films were banned by the authorities.

철판 凸板 a relief ; [인쇄] relief printing — **인쇄** letterpress ; relief〔anastatic, surface〕 printing — **잉크** letterpress〔typographic〕 ink **백악** — a graphotype **아연** — a zinc relief

철판 鐵板 an iron〔a steel〕 plate ; a sheet of iron

—**공(工)** a plater — **사진** a ferrotype ; a tintype

철편 鐵鞭 an iron rod〔cane〕

철편 鐵片 a piece〔scrap〕 of iron

***철폐 撤廢** abolition ; removal —**하다** abolish ; remove ; do away with ¶ 차별대우를 철폐하다 do away with〔abolish〕 the discrimination // 이민 제한을 철폐하다 let down《their》 immigration barriers

철필 鐵筆 a pen ; a stencil pen ; a stylus《*pl.* ～es, styli》; a metallic pencil ¶ 철필로 쓰다 write with a (stencil) pen

—대 a penholder —촉 a pen point
철하다 綴— file ; bind ¶ 서류를 철하다 file papers // 서류를 철해놓다 keep papers on file
*철학 哲學 philosophy ¶ 철학을 공부하다 study philosophy // 철학(적으로 생각)하다 philosophize ; think philosophically
— 개론 an introduction to philosophy ; an outline of philosophy — 박사 a Doctor of philosophy 《Ph. D》 —자 a philosopher — 체계 a system of philosophy 귀납〔연역, 경험〕 — inductive 〔deductive, empirical〕 philosophy 도덕 — moral philosophy 동양〔서양〕 — Oriental〔Occidental〕 philosophy 분석 — analytical philosophy 비판 — critical philosophy 사변 — speculative philosophy 사회 — social philosophy 실존 — existential philosophy ; existentialism 실증 — positive philosophy ; positivism 실험 — experimental philosophy 역사 — philosophy of history 연상 — association philosophy 예술〔언어〕 — philosophy of art〔language〕 인생 — philosophy of life 자연 — natural philosophy 직관 — intuitive philosophy 처세 — a philosophy of living
철혈 鐵血 blood and iron
— 재상 the Iron Chancellor ; Bismark (별명) — 정책 a blood-and-iron policy
철형 凸形 convex(ity)
철환 鐵環 an iron ring
*철회 撤回 withdrawal ; recall ; repeal ; retraction —하다 withdraw ; recall ; repeal ; retract ¶ 사표를 철회하다 withdraw one's resignation // 자주 발언을 철회하다 withdraw〔take back〕 one's words // 법령을 철회하다 repeal the law // 요구를 철회하다 retract〔recede from〕 one's demand
첨가 添加 adding ; annexing ; (an) addition —하다 add ; annex ; append ; affix ¶ 단서를 첨가하다 add 《something》 as a postscriptum ; add a postscript to // 원금에 이자를 첨가하다 add the interest to the principal // 책에 색인을 첨가하다 add〔append〕 an index to a book
—물 an addition ; an annex —어 an agglutinative language
첨계 檐階 terrace stones ; stone steps
—돌 individual terrace stones ; a (stepping) stone
*첨단 尖端 a (pointed) tip〔end, head〕 ; a fine point ; the spearhead ¶ 첨단적 ultramodern ; up-to-date ; up-to-the-minute ; the newest ; the latest // 신사조의 첨단 the newest trend〔current〕 of thought ; the latest ideas // 유행의 첨단 an up-to-date fashion ; the latest thing // 유행의 첨단을 걷다 set the fashion // 시대의 첨단을 걷다 be in the van of the new era
첨대 籤— a piece of bamboo used as a marker ; the (bamboo) slip〔stick〕 cast for divination ¶ 첨대를 꽂다 put the bamboo slip between 《the leaves of a book》
첨망 瞻望 looking up ; lifting one's face upwards —하다 look up at ; lift one's face upwards to
첨벙 with a splash ¶ 첨벙 뛰어들다 jump into 《water》 with a splash
첨병 尖兵 a (military) spearhead ; an advance guard point
첨부 添附 appending ; annexing —하다 append ; annex ; accompany 《a thing》 with ¶ 첨부의 accompanying // 원서에 이력서를 첨부하여 제출하다 submit an application with one's personal history
—물 a supplement — 사진〔서류〕 the accompanying photograph〔document〕
첨삭 添削 correction ; revision —하다 correct ; look over ; revise ¶ 작문을 첨삭하다 correct a composition
—료 a correction fee
첨서 添書 an addition 《of a note》 ; an added note ; a supplementary note ; a postscript —하다 add (as a note) ; insert ; append
첨예 尖銳 sharpness ; acuteness ; being radical —하다 [급격] (be) acute 〔sharp〕 ; [급진적] radical ¶ 첨예한 미소 관계 acute〔tense〕 relations between America and Soviet Russia
— 분자 radicals ; extremists ; extreme 〔radical〕 element ; the radical part
첨예화 尖銳化 —하다 [분쟁 따위가] become〔get〕 acute〔tense〕 ; be aggravated // 첨예화하는 분쟁 a sharpening conflict
첨자 籤子 ① [장도집의] metal pins (that keep a belt-knife from slipping out of its sheath) ② ⇨ 점대
첨작 添酌 pouring additional wine into an offertory cup ; putting more 《wine》 in ¶ 술을 두번 첨작하다 add more wine to the cup twice
첨지 籤紙 a piece of paper used as a marker ; a tag ; a card
첨차 檐遮 〖건축〗 a crenel(le) ; crenels ; crenel(l)ation
첨첨 layer on layer ; pile after pile ; heap upon heap ; on and on ¶ 책을 첨첨 쌓다 pile up books
첨탑 尖塔 a spire ; a pinnacle ; a steeple ; (회교 사원의) a minaret
첨하 檐下 under the eaves ¶ 첨하에서 비를 피하다 take shelter from the rain under the eaves
첩 妾 a concubine ; a (secret) mistress ¶ 첩을 두다 keep a secret mistress // 첩 노릇을 하다 be 《a person's》 concubine
—살림 living with a concubine
첩 貼 a pack (of herb-medicine) ; a package (of prepared herbs) ¶ 약 두 첩 two packages of prepared herbs

첩 帖 an album ; a (note) book
견본— a sample book 발췌— a scrapbook 사진— a photo album
첩경 捷徑 ① [지름길] a nearer way ; a shortcut ; [쉬운 길] a short〔quick, easy〕 way ; a royal road ; a simplified method ¶ 영어를 배우는 첩경 a quick way to learn English // 성공에의 첩경 a shortcut to success // 학문에는 첩경이 없다 There is no royal road to learning.
② [부사적] be apt to〔tending to〕; be liable to ; be prone to ; easily ¶ 돈은 꾸어 주면 첩경 잃기 쉽다 If you lend money, you are liable to lose it.
첩데기 妾— ⇨ 첩(妾)
첩로 捷路 a shortcut ; a shorter way
첩며느리 妾— the concubine of one's son
첩모 睫毛 ⇨ 속눈썹
— 난생(亂生) introverted eyelashes — 난생증 〚의학〛 trichiasis — 탈락 〚의학〛 deplumation
첩박다 lock the door〔gate〕; board up ¶ 문을 첩박다 board a door up
첩보 捷報 news of a victory ¶ 첩보를 올리다 report the victory《of…》 to the throne
첩보 諜報 intelligence ; secret information
— 기관 an intelligence organization 〔agency, office〕; a secret service —망 an intelligence〔espionage〕 network ; a spy ring〔net〕 —부 the intelligence bureau〔department〕; a counter-intelligence office《C. I. O.》(미군) —원 an intelligence officer〔man〕; a secret agent
— 활동 espionage activities ¶ 철의 장막 뒤에서 첩보 활동을 하다 play cloak-and-dagger behind the Iron Curtain
첩부 貼付 pasting ; sticking ; affixing ; applying (고약) —하다 put《a stamp》 on ; paste ; stick ; apply《a plaster》 ¶ 편지에 우표를 첩부하다 stick〔put〕 a stamp on a letter ; stamp a letter
—약 a medicine for external application
첩서 捷書 a report of victory
첩실 妾室 a concubine
첩약 貼藥 a pack of prepared herb medicine ; medical herbs in package
첩자 諜者 a spy ; a secret agent ; an (espionage) agent ; [경찰·고용주의] a stool pigeon《미·속》 ¶ 공산주의 첩자들의 …으로의 침투 communist (espionage) agents' infiltration into. . . // 첩자 노릇하다 engage in espionage
첩장가 妾—
첩장가 들다 [관용] take a concubine (with due ceremony)
첩지 an ornamental hairpin (worn on ceremonial occasion)
첩지머리 ① [첩지를 쓴] one's head with an ornamental hairpin on ② [머리 모양] a girl's hairdo with the side hairs plaited so that the ends cover her ears
첩첩 喋喋 volubly ; glibly ; loquaciously
—하다 (be) prattling ; talkative ; chattering
첩첩 疊疊 fold upon fold ; layer upon layer ; pile upon pile ; in piles ¶ 구름이 첩첩이 쌓이다 clouds hang in great bunches〔heaps〕// 산이 첩첩이 쌓이다 have mountains lie range after range
— 산중 the heart of mountains rising one above another ; the depths of mountains ¶ 첩첩 산중에 살다 live in the heart of mountains — 수심 anxiety on anxiety ; worry on top of worry ¶ 첩첩 수심에 싸이다 have a lot of anxiety ; have worries upon worries
첩출 疊出 —하다 arise〔happen〕 one after another ; arise〔happen〕 in succession
첩치가 妾置家 concubinage —하다 keep a mistress〔concubine〕 in a house
첫 - the first ; new ; maiden ; starting ; beginning
—글자 an initial (letter) —아이 one's first(-born) child —차 the first car〔bus, train〕 —항해 a maiden voyage
첫가을 early autumn ; the beginning of autumn
첫걸음 [걸음] the first step ; a start ; [초보·기본] elements ; rudiments ; the ABC《of》; the first steps ¶ 영어 첫걸음 elementary〔beginner's〕 English ; "First steps in English" ; a "primer of English" (책이름) // 성공에의 첫걸음 the first step to success // 첫걸음을 떼어 놓다 set one's foot《on》; mark the first step《in》; take an initial step ; make a start
첫겨울 early winter ; the beginning of winter
첫고등 the first chance〔opportunity〕; the very start ¶ 첫고등에 at the start // 첫고등에 실패하다 make an unsuccessful start
첫공개 —公開 the first public exhibition《of the shrine's treasures》
첫공연 —公演 the première〔first public〕 performance ⇨ 초연(初演)
첫국밥 the first meal after childbirth ¶ 첫국밥을 먹다 take seaweed soup and rice for the first time after childbirth
첫기제 —忌祭 the first anniversary of one's parent's death after the three years' mourning period
첫길 an unaccustomed course〔route〕; one's first trip (to a place) ; a road one is on for the first time ¶ 첫길이 되어 생소하다 I am not familiar with the road.
첫나들이 [아이의] going out for the first time after its birth ; [신부의] the first visit of a bride to her native home after marriage
첫날 the first day〔night〕; the opening day〔night〕 ¶ 연극의 첫날 the opening day〔première〕 of a play // 회의의 첫날 the opening session
첫날밤 the bridal night ; the night of one's

wedding ; the first night of a married couple
첫낯 an unfamiliar face ; a stranger ; a first meeting ¶ 첫낯에 그런 청을 할 수 없다 I can't make such a request of him on our first meeting.
첫눈[1] [일견] the first sight〔look, glance, glimpse〕 ¶ 첫눈에 at first look〔glance〕; on sight // 나는 첫눈에 그 여자한테 반했다 I fell in love with her at first sight.
첫눈에 들다 관용 be attracted at first sight
첫눈[2] the first snow of the season
첫더위 the first heat of the year ; the first spell of hot weather ¶ 첫더위가 시작되다 the first hot weather sets in
첫돌 [사건의] the first anniversary ; [사람의] the first anniversary of a baby's birthday
첫딸 a female firstborn ; one's first(-born) daughter
첫마디 an opening remark〔word〕; the first word ; an initial remark ¶ 첫마디를 끌어내다 open one's word ; open the conversation // 첫마디를 잘못하다 make a false start // 첫마디부터 맹렬히 정부의 무능을 공격했다 He opened his speech with a severe attack against the incompetency of the government. // 그의 첫마디는 "왜 왔느냐"였다 His first word to me was, "Why did you come here?"
첫말 the first word〔remark〕⇨ 첫마디
첫머리 [시작] the beginning ; the start ; the first (part) ; the outset ¶ 책을 첫머리부터 읽다 read a book from the beginning // 첫머리부터 완벽할 수 없다 You can expect to be perfect from the outset.
첫무대 —舞臺 one's first appearance《on the stage》; one's début ¶ 첫무대를 밟다 make one's début
첫물 [옷] new clothes worn for the first time ; a first wear ; a first wearing
첫밗 the outset ; the start ¶ 첫밗에 at the start〔outset〕
첫발 the first step《to, toward》; an initial step ¶ 첫발을 내디디다 take〔make〕 the first step
첫밥 the first feeding (of silkworms) ¶ 첫밥을 주다 feed (silkworms) for the first time
첫배 the first litter ; the first hatch
— **돼지** the first litter of pigs — **병아리** the first hatch of chickens
첫번 —番 a first time ; the first time ¶ 첫번부터 from the first〔start〕// 첫번에는 at first ; at the outset〔start〕// 첫번 보고 서로 사랑하게 됐다 They fell in love at first sight. // 내가 연단에 선 것은 이것이 첫번입니다 This is the first time that I have ever stood on the platform.
— **경험** the first experience — **시험** the first examination ; a first trial
첫봄 early spring ; the beginning of spring
첫사랑 a〔one's〕 first love ; one's first lover〔sweetheart〕 ¶ 첫사랑에 실패하다 lose one's first love ; be disappointed in the first love // 첫사랑에 빠지다 fall in love for the first time
첫새벽 early dawn〔morning〕 ¶ 첫새벽에 before dawn ; in the early dawn ; in the gray〔dawn〕 of the morning // 첫새벽같이 일어나다 get up very early in the morning
첫서리 the first frost (of the season)
첫선 the first appearance ¶ 첫선을 뵈다 appear〔be put out〕 for the first time
첫소리 [초성] an initial sound ; an initial consonant (in a Korean orthographic syllable) ; [첫마디] the first word〔remark〕
첫손자 —孫子 one's first grandchild
첫솜씨 a first try of one's skill ; the first attempt〔performance〕; a green hand ¶ 첫솜씨치고는 잘 되었다 You have done pretty well for a greenhorn.
첫술 the first spoonful of food (at meals) ¶ 첫술을 뜨다 take one's first spoonful of food at meals // 첫술에 배부를 수 없다 You must not expect too much at your first attempt.
첫아들 one's first(-born) son ¶ 첫아들을 얻다 get a boy as one's first child
첫얼음 the first freeze (of the season)
첫여름 early summer ; the beginning of summer
첫이레 the seventh day after the birth of a baby
첫인상 —印象 one's first impression ¶ 첫인상이 좋다 give a good〔favorable〕 first impression // 첫인상을 말하다 give one's first impression《of Korea》// 그 사람의 첫인상이 어땠니 How did he strike you? / What kind of first impression did he make on you?
첫잠 a sleep one has just fallen into ; the first stage of sleep ¶ 첫잠을 달게 자다 fall into a good sleep // 첫잠에서 깨다 wake up soon after one has gone to sleep for the night
첫정 —情 a first affection〔love, attachment〕 ¶ 서로 첫정이 들다 fall in love with each other for the first time // 첫정을 끝내 잊지 못하다 can't get over one's first attachment at all
†**첫째** the first ; the foremost ; number one《No. 1》 ¶ 첫째의 the first ; primary ; foremost ; leading // 첫째(로) first (of all) ; firstly ; above all ; in the first place ; to begin with // 첫째로 시간을 지켜라 Above all, you should be punctual. // 첫째가 되다 stand〔rank〕 first《among》// 경쟁에서 첫째가 되다 have the lead〔come in first〕 in a race // 건강이 첫째다 Health is above everything else. // 첫째 난관은 돌파했다 We have managed to overcome the first

obstacle. // 그는 학급에서 첫째이다 He tops his class. /He is at the head〔top〕 of his class. // 그녀가 첫째로 도착했다 She was the very first to arrive. /She arrived sooner than anyone else. // 첫째 그 사람의 외모가 마음에 들지 않는다 To begin with, I don't like his looks.

첫추위 the first cold of the winter ; the first spell of cold weather ¶ 첫추위가 닥치다 the first cold weather sets in

첫출근 一出勤 one's first attendance〔presence〕 (to the office) ¶ 첫출근을 하다 attend one's office for the first time

첫출발 一出發 the first start ; the very beginning ¶ 인생의 첫출발 one's first start in life // 첫출발이 좋아야 된다 You've got to have a good start to begin with.

첫출사 一出仕 entering government service for the first time ; the beginning of one's official career

첫출전 一出戰 one's first campaign ; a maiden battle ¶ 첫출전하다 make〔set out upon〕 one's first campaign

첫판 [경기·시합의] the first round ; the beginning ¶ 첫판 씨름에 지다 get beaten in the first round of wrestling

첫판 一版 the first edition〔printing〕 ¶ 책의 첫판을 발간하다 publish the first edition of a book

첫항해 一航海 [배의] a maiden voyage ; [사람의] one's first voyage

첫해 the first year ¶ 미국 생활의 첫해 the first year of my life in America

— 권농 typical amateur approach to a problem ; awkwardness due to the lack of skill

첫해산 一解産 a woman's first delivery (of a child) ¶ 2개월이면 첫해산을 할 것이다 She is going to be a mother in a couple of months.

첫행보 一行步 one's first errand〔visit〕 ; [장사] one's first venture at peddling〔hawking〕 ¶ 첫행보에 상당한 이를 보았다 He made a considerable profit on his first peddling trip.

첫혼인 一婚姻 a first marriage **—하다** get married for the first time

첫흥행 一興行 the first public presentation of a play〔performance〕

청 a membrane

갈대(대)— the white membrane inside a reed **귀—** the drum membrane ; the eardrum **목—** the vocal cords〔bands〕 **코—** the septum of the nose

청 靑 blue (color)

청 請 a request ; a favor ; one's wishes **—하다** ask ; beg ; request ; appeal ; solicit ; plead ; make a request ¶ 간절한 청 an earnest request ; an entreaty // 원조를 청하다 ask《a person's》 assistance ; call for help // 참석을 청하다 ask〔request〕《a person》 to attend // 청을 듣다 grant a request ; comply with〔accede to〕 a request ; do《a person》 a favor // 청을 들어 주지 않다 turn down〔refuse〕 a request ; turn a deaf ear to a request // 청이 하나 있어요 I have a favor to ask of you. // 청이 무엇이오 What is your request ?

청을 넣다 관용 ask a favor indirectly ; make a request through another

청 廳 a hall ; a building ; [대청] the main floored room

—사 an office〔a government〕 building **구—** a ward office **시—** the City Hall **조달—** Office of Supply **중앙—** the Capitol building〔Hall〕

청가 請暇 [요청] application for leave ; [휴가] leave of absence ; furlough ¶ 청가를 얻다 get〔be〕 granted of absence ; get a vacation // 2주일의 청가원을 내다 apply for two weeks' leave of absence

청가뢰 靑— 〖곤충〗 a green Spanish fly ; a cantharides ; a blister beetle

‡**청각** 聽覺 auditory〔acoustic〕 sense ; the sense of hearing ¶ 훌륭한 청각 a fine sense of hearing // 청각을 날카롭게 하다 keep one's ears wide open

— 기관 the auditory〔hearing〕 organ **— 신경** auditory〔acoustic〕 nerves **— 심상** an auditory〔acoustic〕 image **—형** [기억형의 하나] the auditory type

청각채 靑角菜 〖식물〗 a kind of seaweed used to flavor *Kimch'i* ; Gloiopeltis furcata (학명)

청강 聽講 attending a lecture ; attendance at a lecture **—하다** listen to〔attend〕 a lecture ; audit a course ; sit in on a class ¶ 많은 사람의 청강이 예상된다 A large attendance is expected.

—료(권) an admission〔attendance〕 fee〔ticket〕 **— 무료(자유)** Attendance〔Admission〕 (is) free. (게시) **—생** an irregular〔special〕 student ; [방청자] an auditor (대학의) 《미》 **—자** an auditor ; a listener ; audience《총칭》; attendance ¶ 청강자가 많다〔적다〕 have a large〔small〕 attendance〔audience〕 **—증** an attendance〔admission〕 ticket

청개구리 靑— 〖동물〗 a tree frog ; a green frog ; a tree toad

청객 請客 inviting guests **—하다** invite a guest

†**청결** 清潔 cleanness ; cleanliness ; neatness ; purity ; personal cleanliness (개인의) **—하다** (be) clean ; neat ; sanitary ¶ 몸과 마음이 청결하다 be pure in body and mind // 청결하게 하다 clean (up) ; cleanse ; make〔keep〕 clean ; sweep away〔out〕 // 부엌〔몸〕을 청결히 하라 Keep the kitchen〔your body〕 clean.

청경 우독 晴耕雨讀 **—하다** work in the field in fine weather and read at home in wet weather ; take every opportunity to improve oneself

청계 〖민속〗 a plague demon
청계 淸溪 a clear〔limpid, pellucid〕 stream
청고 淸高 integrity and loftiness ; uprightness and purity **—하다** (be) upright and lofty ; pure and cleanhanded
청공 靑空 the blue〔azure〕 sky ⇨ 청천(靑天)
청과 靑果 vegetables and fruits ; fruits ; greens ; green stuff
— 시장 a vegetable and fruit market ; a produce market **—점** a green grocery ; a vegetable and fruit dealer
청관 聽官 the auditory organ(s) ; the organ of hearing
*__청교도 淸敎徒__ a Puritan ¶ 청교도의 Puritanical
—주의 Puritanism **— 혁명** the Puritan Revolution
†**청구 請求** [요구] demand ; [청원] request ; [변상 따위] claim ; [신청] application **—하다** ask〔apply〕 《 for》 ; request ; demand ; claim ¶ (변상 따위를) 청구할 수 있는 claimable // 청구에 응하여 at 《a person's》 request ; in compliance with 《 a person's》 request ; on demand 〔application, request〕 ; in response to a claim // 돈〔견본〕을 청구하다 demand payment // 청구에 응하다 meet 《a person's》 demand ; comply with 《 a person's》 request // …에 손해 보상 지불을 청구하다 demand〔claim〕 payment from 《a person》 for damages
—권 a claim ; a right of claim ¶ 한국의 대일 재산 청구권 Korea's property claims against Japan **— 번호** a call number (도서관에서 책의) **—불 어음** a demand draft〔bill〕 **—서** a bill ; a written claim ; [신청서] an application (form) ¶ 나중에 청구서를 보내시오 Bill me later. **—액** the amount asked〔claimed〕 **—인** an applicant ; a claimant ; a demandant **손해〔배상〕 —** a claim for damages〔reimbursement〕 **지불 —** a demand for payment
청구 靑丘 green hills ; another name for Korea
청구멍 請— [연줄] an "in" ; a pull ; connections ¶ 좋은 청구멍 a good〔the right〕 connections
청국장 淸麴醬 fermented soybeans
—국 soup with fermented soybeans
청기 靑旗 a blue flag
청기와 靑— green tiles〔slates〕
— 장수 a man who keeps the tricks of his trade secret ; a specialist
청꾼 請— an influence peddler
청널 廳— the floorboards of a main hall
청녀 靑女 ① [서리의 신(神)] a goddess of frost ; Jack Frost ② [서리] frost
†**청년 靑年** young man ; a youth ; [총칭] young people ; the youth ; the younger 〔rising〕 generation ¶ 그는 전도 유망한 청년이다 He is a promising young man. // 청년기란 모험과 대담의 시대다 One's youth is the time of adventure and daring.
—기 adolescence **— 남녀** young men and women ; youths and maiden ; young people **— 시대** one's young days 〔years〕 ; one's youth ; one's salad days ¶ 그는 청년 시대에는 두드러지지 않았다 He was not conspicuous in his youth 〔when he was young〕. **— 신사** a young gentleman **— 운동** a youth movement **—회〔단〕** a young mens' association ; a young people's group **— 회의소** the Junior Chamber **기독교 —회** Young Men's Christian Association 《YMCA》 **기독교 여자 —회** Young Women's Christian Association 《YWCA》
청녹두 靑綠豆 〖식물〗 a tiny green pea 〔chickpea〕 with black shell
청녹색 靑綠色 bluish green
청담 淸淡 purity and honesty ; integrity ; uprightness ; disinterestedness ; simplicity **—하다** (be) honest ; disinterested ; upright ; clean-handed ; plain ; simple ¶ 청담한 사람 a man of integrity
청담 晴曇 relative clearness〔cloudiness〕 of the sky
청대 靑— 〖식물〗 green〔unripe〕 bamboo
청대콩 靑— green〔unripe〕 bean ; roasted unripe beans with their shells on
청도 靑島 Tsingtao
청도 聽度 audibility
—계 an audibility meter
‡**청동 靑銅** bronze
—기(器) bronze ware **— 세공** work ; a bronze **— 시대** the Bronze Age **— 주물** bronze casting **— 화로** a bronze brazier **알루미늄〔망간, 텅스텐〕 —** aluminum 〔manganese, tungsten〕 bronze
청둥 호박 a fully-ripened pumpkin
청등롱 靑燈籠 a lantern made of blue silk ⇨ 청사 등롱
청등홍가 靑燈紅街 a red-light〔brothel〕 district ; gay quarters
청딱다구리 靑— a Korean black-naped green woodpecker
청람 晴嵐 heat haze ; heat waves (in the air)
청랑 晴朗 (weather) clearness ; serenity ; pleasantness **—하다** (be) clear ; fair ; serene ¶ 날씨가 청랑하다 The weather is fine. /It is a fine day.
청량 淸涼 coolness ; being cool and refreshing **—하다** (be) clear and cool ; refreshing ; crisp ¶ 청량한 날씨 nice cool weather
— 음료(수) a refreshing〔cooling〕 drink 〔beverage〕 ; a refrigerant ; a carbonated 〔an aerated〕 drink ; a soft drink 《미》 ; (soda) pop ; mineral water ; the dishwater 《속》 **— 음료점** a soft-drink stand ; a soda fountain **—제** a refresher ; a cooler ; a refrigerant

청력 聽力 the hearing ability ; the sense 〔power〕 of hearing ; audition ¶ 청력이 좋다 have a keen sense of hearing // 청력을 잃다 lose one's hearing
—계 an audiometer ; a sonometer — 시험 a hearing test — 측정 audiometry
청렬 淸冽 —하다 (be) clear ; limpid
청렴 淸廉 integrity ; uprightness —하다 (be) honest ; upright ; cleanhanded ; incorruptible ¶ 청렴한 사람 a man of integrity ; a pure-hearted man
청렴 결백 淸廉潔白 ⇨ 청렴
청령 淸令 —하다 receive〔listen to〕《a person's》 orders
청료 靑蓼 a kind of smartweed
청룡도 靑龍刀 a broad Chinese sword ; a scimitar with a blue-dragon figure on it
청루 靑樓 a brothel ; a house of an ill fame ; a whorehouse ¶ 청루에 드나들다 frequent brothels
청루 주사 靑樓酒肆 brothels and bars ; gay quarters
청류 淸流 a clear〔limpid〕 stream
청매 靑梅 a green plum
청맹과니 靑盲— an amaurotic eye〔person〕; an eye that is blind though it looks perfect
청명 淸明 serenity ; brightness ; fineness ; fairness —하다 (be) fine ; fair ; bright ; clear ¶ 청명한 하늘 a clear 〔crystalline〕 sky // 청명한 일기 bright weather // 청명한 달 a bright moon
청문 聽聞 audience ; audition —하다 listen to ; hear
—회 a hearing
청밀 淸蜜 honey
청바지 靑— blue jeans ¶ 청바지 복장을 한 십대들 the teenagers in blue jeans
청백 淸白 uprightness ; integrity ; innocence ; purity —하다 (be) upright ; honest ; clean-handed ; incorruptible ¶ 청백한 관리 a clean-handed〔an uncorrupted〕 government officer // 청백한 사람 a man of spotless integrity ; a man of pure heart and clean hands // 돈에 청백하다 be honest in financial matters // 청백하기 때문에 항상 동료들로부터 따돌림을 받는다 He is left out alone from his friends because he has too much integrity to get involved in shady deals.
—리(吏) a cleanhanded government officer
청백 靑白 blue and white ¶ 청백으로 나뉘어 게임을 하다 play one side against the other in a game
—전 a match〔game〕 between blue and white camps
청병 請兵 asking for a dispatch of troops —하다 request (a dispatch of) troops
청병 淸兵 a Chinese soldier
청부 請負 a contract《for work》; contracted work ¶ 청부 맡다 have a contract《for》// 청부 맡기다 give《a person》a contract for《building, a house》; put out to contract ; have a work done by contract
— 가격 a contract price — 계약 a contract — 공사 contract job〔work〕 — 살인자 a hired assassin〔killer, murderer〕 — 업자 a contractor ; 〖법〗 an independent contractor — 입찰 a contract tender — 전쟁 a proxy war 건축 —업자 a building contractor ; a housebuilder 토목 건축 —업자 an engineering and construction contractor
청빈 淸貧 honest〔honorable, noble〕 poverty ¶ 청빈한 생활 poor but honest living // 청빈에 만족하다 be satisfied to be poor but honest // 청빈을 감수하다 be contented with honest poverty
청사 靑史 history ; the annals ¶ 청사에 이름을 남기다 leave one's name in history ; go down in history // 이름이 청사에 빛나다 be famous in history ; one's name is immortalized in history
청사 靑絲 blue yarn〔thread〕
청사 廳舍 government〔office〕 buildings
청사 등롱 靑紗燈籠 a lantern covered with blue silk in the middle and with red silk at both ends
청사진 靑寫眞 a blueprint ; [구상] conception ¶ 청사진을 뜨다 make a blueprint of
— 도면 a blueprinted plan —법 blueprinting (process) ; cyanotype — 지도 a blueprint map
청산 靑山 green〔blue〕 mountains ¶ 인간도처 유 청산 A green hill fit for one's burial place is to be found anywhere. /A man's fortune can be sought anywhere in the world. /Opportunity awaits a man everywhere.
청산 靑酸 (hydro) cyanic acid
— 가스 hydrocyanic acid gas —염(鹽) cyanide ; prussiate — 중독 hydrocyanic poisoning —칼리 potassium cyanide ; cyanide of potassium
†청산 淸算 [정리] liquidation ; [셈의] settling〔squaring, clearing up〕 accounts ; paying off ; clearing —하다 pay off ; clear ; liquidate ; go into liquidation ¶ 채권 채무의 청산 square〔pay off〕 one's debt // 회사를 청산하다 liquidate a company // (회사가) 청산중이다 be in receivership ; be in the hands of a receiver // 인생을 청산하다 kill oneself ; put an end to one's life // 과거를 청산하다 liquidate〔have done〕 the past // 자살하여 죄를 청산하다 pay for one's sin with one's life ; commit suicide for atoning one's crime
— 거래 [증권에서] future transaction — 계정 an open account —서 a statement of liquidation ; a balance sheet (결산서) —인 a liquidator ; a balancer (청산서를

만드는) — 협정 a clearing agreement — 회사 a company in liquidation 강제〔임의〕 — forced〔voluntary〕 liquidation
청산유수 靑山流水 fluency ; eloquency ; a fluent tongue ¶ 청산유수같이 fluently ; smoothly ; with fluency // 청산유수로 이야기하다 speak very fluently ; be a fluent speaker
청상 淸爽 —하다 (be) fresh and cheerful ; refreshing
청상 과부 靑孀寡婦 a young widow
†청색 靑色 blue〔green〕 color ; blue ; green — 사진 ⇨ 청사진
청색 신고 靑色申告 [소득세의] blue return ; a blue paper report《on business income》 ¶ 청색 신고하다 file a blue return
청서 淸書 a fair〔clean〕 copy ; making a fair copy —하다 make a fair copy《of》; copy out neatly
청서 靑書 [영국 의회 따위의 보고서] a Blue Book
‡청소 淸掃 cleaning ; sweeping ; dusting —하다 clean ; sweep ¶ 청소가 잘 된 clean-kept ; tidy // 집안을 청소하다 clean up a house ; have〔do〕 a housecleaning // 오물을 청소하다 collect〔clear away〕 the night soil
— 도구 scrubbing things —부 a cleaner ; a sweeper ; [가로의] a scavenger ; a janitor ; a street sweeper〔cleaner《미》〕; [먼지의] a dustman ; [부엌 찌꺼기의] a garbage man〔collector〕; [변소의] a night soil man ; a charwoman (여자) ; a scrub woman《미》 —차 a scavenger's〔refuse〕 cart ; a garbage wagon〔truck〕 전기〔진공〕 —기 a vacuum cleaner〔sweeper〕
청소년 靑少年 young boys and girls ; teenagers ; juveniles ; youth ; the younger generation
—기 an adolescent period —단 a teenager group ; teenagers' association — 범죄 juvenile delinquency ; offenses committed by juvenile
청송 靑松 a green pine (tree)
청수 淸秀 handsomeness —하다 (be) handsome ; fair
청수 淸水 clear〔pure〕 water
청순 淸純 purity —하다 be pure and innocent ¶ 청순한 처녀 a pure and innocent girl
청술레 靑— 〖식물〗 a kind of pear with green skin
청승 signs of a wretched fate ¶ 청승궂다〔청승스럽다〕 ⇨ 청승맞다
—살 excess flesh afflicting a miserable old man
청승 떨다 관용 act like fortune's orphan
청승꾸러기 a jinx ; a person with bad luck written on his face ; a sad-looking person ; a loser
청승맞다《one's face or manner》 be suggestive of ill luck ; (be) ominously sorrowful ; wretched ; miserable ¶ 청승맞은 노인 a pitiful old man // 청승맞게 울다 wail in an ominously sorrowful manner
청시 聽視 (TV) viewing ⇨ 청취, 시청
청신 淸新 freshness ; novelty —하다 (be) fresh ; new ¶ 청신한 기풍 a new and fresh tide〔style〕 // 청신미가 있는 문체 a style marked by freshness // 청신한 데가 없다 lack freshness // 청신한 기운을 불어넣다 infuse〔inspire〕 new life into《a person》 // 그 인상은 이미 청신한 맛을 많이 잃었다 The impression has already lost much of its freshness. // 그의 이야기는 청신한 데가 있다 His conversation is fresh and stimulating.
청신경 聽神經 the auditory〔acoustic〕 nerves
청신남 淸信男 a male Buddhist believer〔follower〕
청신녀 淸信女 a female Buddhist believer〔follower〕
청신호 靑信號 a green traffic signal ; a green light ¶ 청신호가 켜져 있다 The

청소

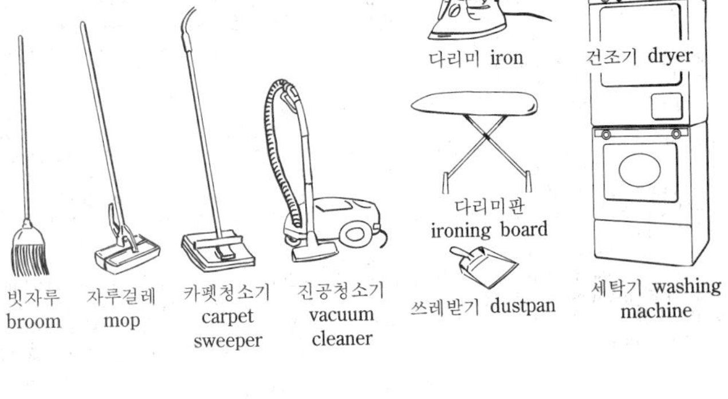

light is on for "go".

청실 靑— cordials ; sweetener ; invigorating liquor

청아 淸雅 elegance ; grace ; refinement **—하다** (be) elegant ; graceful ; refined ¶ 청아한 음악 elegant music // 청아한 목소리 a clear ringing voice

청야 淸夜 a clear〔bright〕 night

청야 聽野 a field of hearing

청약 請約 (an) application **—하다** subscribe《for bonds》; send a subscription

— 기한 a time limit for application —서 a written application ; [용지] an application form〔blank〕 —자 an applicant ; a proposer —처 a place for application

*청어 靑魚 〖물고기〗 a herring

—알 herring roe —회 raw herring 훈제— a red herring ; [배를 갈라 처리한] a kippered herring ; a kipper ; [통째 말린] a bloater

청어 淸語 Manchu ; the Manchu language

청연광 靑鉛鑛 〖광물〗 linarite

청옥 靑玉 sapphire

청올치 dried inner bark of arrowroot ; a string made of the inner bark of arrowroot

—끈 a string made of arrowroot bark

청와 靑瓦 [참개구리] a leopard frog ; [청개구리] a tree frog

청와대 靑瓦臺 *Chŏng Wa Dae* the (Korean Executive) Presidential Mansion ; the Presidential Residence of the Republic of Korea

청요리 淸料理 a Chinese dish ; Chinese cookery ; Chinese food

—집 a Chinese restaurant ; a chop suey house《미》

청우 晴雨 fair or rainy weather ; rain or shine ¶ 청우에 불구하고 rain〔wet〕 or shine ; whether it may rain or not ; regardless of the weather ; in any weather ; in all weathers

청우계 晴雨計 a barometer ; a weatherglass ; a rainglass ¶ 청우계가 올라〔내려〕 가다 The barometer rises〔falls〕.

청운 靑雲 [구름] blue clouds ; [고위] high ranks〔offices〕 ¶ 청운의 뜻을 품은 청년들 the aspiring youth // 청운의 뜻을 품다 aspire after greatness〔distinction〕

—객 an ambitious man ; a man of great ambitions

청원 請援 asking for assistance〔help〕; calling for aid〔rescue〕 **—하다** ask《a person》 for assistance〔help〕; appeal〔turn〕 to《a person》 for help

*청원 請願 a petition ; an application ; a request **—하다** petition ; make petition ; present〔lodge, submit〕 a petition ; file a petition《with》; ask ; request ; apply for ¶ 청원을 정부에 제출하다 present a petition to the government // 정부에 보호를 청원하다 petition the government for protection // 청원을 들어주다 grant〔accede to, comply with〕 a petition // 청원을 각하하다 turn down〔reject〕 a petition // 학교 신설을 청원하다 petition for the establishment of a new school

— 경찰관 a policeman specially detailed to protect《a person's》 body —법 the Petition Law — 사항 petition matter —서 a (written) petition〔application〕 — 심의 위원회 a petition committee —자 a petitioner ; an applicant

청유 淸遊 a pleasant outing ; a picnic ; a pleasure excursion〔trip〕 **—하다** go on a pleasure excursion ¶ 하루의 청유 a one-day pleasure trip ; a day's outing

청음 淸音 〖문법〗 [닿소리] a voiceless sound〔consonant〕; a surd sound ; [목소리] a clear〔silvery〕 voice

청음기 聽音機 a sound detector ; an audiphone

청의 靑衣 [푸른 옷] blue clothes ; [천한 사람] a man of low birth

청이불문 聽而不聞 hearing and yet paying no attention《to》; turning deaf ears《to》 **—하다** turn a deaf ear《to》

청일 淸日 Sino-Japanese ; China-Japan

— 전쟁 the Sino-Japanese War

청일 淸逸 purity and loftiness **—하다** (be) pure ; lofty

청자 靑瓷 celadon porcelain

—색 celadon green — 향로 an incense burner of celadon porcelain 고려 — *Koryŏ* celadon (porcelain)

청장 請狀 a letter of invitation ; a formal invitation ; an invitation (card) ¶ 청장을 내다 send an invitation // 청장을 받다 get an invitation ; be invited

청장 廳長 the Administrator〔Director-General〕《of the Office of Forest》

청재 淸齋 purification

청전 靑田 green rice-fields ; paddy-fields under crop ; unripe rice-fields ; [입도] the standing rice

— 매매 dealing in unharvested rice crop — 선매 [팔기] selling rice before the harvest ; [사기] buying rice before the harvest

청절 淸節 [정조] chastity ; [절조] fidelity ; faithfulness

청정 淸淨 purity ; cleanness ; cleanliness **—하다** (be) pure ; clean ; stainless ; undefiled ; immaculate ¶ 청정 결백한 마음 a pure and undefiled heart // 청정 순박한 처녀 a pure and innocent girl // 청정하게 하다 purify ; cleanse

—액 a cleaning solution〔fluid〕 — 야채 clean vegetables — 재배 parasite-free cultivation ; sanitary〔germ-free〕 culture ; [수경법] hydroponics —제 a purifier ; a detergent 혈액 —제 blood-purifier

청조 靑鳥 [새] a grosbeak ; a blue bird ;

[사자] a messenger ; [편지] a letter

청조 淸朝 〖역사〗 the Ch'ing〔Manchu〕 dynasty ; the Manchu court

청종 聽從 obeying ; listening 《to》 ; following **—하다** obey ; listen 《to》 ; follow ¶ 부모의 명령을 청종하다 obey one's parents

청주 淸酒 clear strained rice wine

청죽 靑竹 a green bamboo ; [마르지 않은] a newly-cut bamboo ; unseasoned bamboo

⁑**청중 聽衆** an audience ; hearers ; auditors ; the attendance ; the crowd (in attendance) ¶ 많은 청중 a large audience〔attendance〕 // 많은 청중에게 연설하다 speak to a large audience // 5천의 청중을 끌다 attract〔draw〕 an audience of 5,000 // 청중을 열광시키다 arouse〔move〕 one's audience to enthusiasm

—석 an auditorium ; an audience seat ; a seat in the audience

청지기 廳— a manager of the household of high official ; a steward

청직 淸直 serenity ; integrity ; honesty ; uprightness **—하다** (be) honest ; upright ; just ; clean-handed ¶ 청직한 사람 a man of integrity ; an upright man

청진 聽診 auscultation ; stethoscopy **—하다** auscultate ; stethoscope ; examine with a stethoscope

—기 a stethoscope ¶ 청진기를 대다 apply a stethoscope 《to》 // 청진기로 진찰하다 examine with a stethoscope ; stethoscope

청질 請— asking a favor ; currying favor **—하다** ask a favor ; court a person's influence 《on one's behalf》

청참외 靑— a green melon

청처짐하다 (be) slow ; sluggish ¶ 청처짐한 걸음 a slow pace ; a snail's pace

청천 靑天 the blue sky〔heaven〕 ; a clear〔cloudless〕 sky ; the vault of heaven

청천 淸泉 a clear〔clean, crystal〕 spring

청천 晴天 fine〔fair〕 weather ; an unclouded〔a cloudless〕 sky ¶ 청천이 계속되다 have a spell of fine weather

청천 백일 靑天白日 clear〔fair, fine〕 weather ; a clear day ; a blue sky ; innocence ¶ 청천 백일의 벼락 a bolt from the blue ; a sudden and unexpected disaster // 청천 백일의 몸이 되다 be proven innocent ; be cleared of an unjust〔a false〕 charge

청천 벽력 靑天霹靂 a bolt from the blue ; a thunderbolt from a clear sky ¶ 청천 벽력으로 out of the blue ; like a bolt from the blue // 그것은 청천 벽력과도 같았다 I came like a bolt from the blue sky. /It was a bolt out of the blue. // 그 소식은 상업계에는 청천 벽력이었다 The news came like a thunderclap on the commercial world.

청첩 請牒 an invitation (card) ; a letter of invitation ; an invite 《구》

—장(狀) ⇨ 청첩(請牒) ¶ 청첩장을 내다 send an invitation (card) // 청첩장을 받다 get an invitation ; be invited **결혼 —장** a wedding invitation

청청하다 靑靑— (be) bright green ; verdant ; blue ¶ 청청한 대 bright green bamboos // 산에 나무가 청청하다 A hill is nicely wooded.

청초 靑— a blue kite with a white top

청초 靑草 green grass ; [담배] green tobacco ¶ 썬 청초 cut〔shredded〕 green tobacco

청초 淸楚 neatness ; tidiness ; smartness **—하다** (be) neat and tidy ; smart ; nice ¶ 청초한 여자 a nice-looking girl // 청초한 옷 neat〔smart〕 clothes // 청초하게 차리고 있다 be neatly dressed

청촉 請囑 asking ; begging ; a request ⇨ 청탁(請託)

청추 淸秋 fine autumn weather ; a bright autumn ; [음력 8월] the 8th month by the lunar calendar

청춘 靑春 youth ; the springtime of life ; bloom of youth ; the heyday of youth ¶ 청춘의 youthful ; young ; adolescent // 청춘의 정열 ardor〔enthusiasm〕 of youth // 허송한 청춘 a misspent youth // 청춘의 꿈과 야망 the dreams and ambitions of youth // 청춘의 피를 끓게 하다 stir up youthful blood // 청춘의 정열에 불타다 burn with youthful ardor

—기 adolescence ; one's adolescent period **— 남녀** adolescent〔teenage〕 boys and girls **— 시대** one's youth ; one's youthful days〔teens〕 ; the morning〔prime〕 of youth

청춘 소년 靑春少年 a young man〔boy〕 ; a lad ; a young in the bloom of youth

청출어람 靑出於藍 Blue comes from indigo... (but is bluer). /A pupil excels his master.

청취 聽取 hearing ; listening ; receiving ; picking up〔catching〕 a sound signal **—하다** listen to ; give a hearing 《to》 ; hear ; catch ; listen in〔to〕 ¶ 라디오를 청취하다 listen to the radio // 증언을 청취하다 hear evidence // 무선 전신을 청취하다 pick up a wireless message

—료 a (radio) listener's fee **— 시험** a hearing test ; an audition **—자 참가 프로** audience participating program ; a participation show **— 장치** a receiving set〔apparatus〕 ; a radio (receiver) **라디오 —자** a radio listener ; a radio audience

청취 테스트 聽取— an audition ¶ 청취 테스트를 하다 audition 《a person》 ; give an audition // 청취 테스트를 받다 audition

청치 靑— ① [푸른 쌀] bluetinged〔less ripe〕 grains of rice ② [얼룩소] a spotted bluish-gray cow

청칠 靑漆 green〔blue〕 paint〔lacquer〕

청컨대 請— (if you) please ; pray ; I

hope ; I wish (I could) ; It is to be hoped 《that》 ⇨ 청하다
청탁 淸濁 purity and impurity ; good and bad ; likes and dislikes ¶ 물의 청탁 the (relative) purity〔clarity〕 of water // 청탁을 가리지 않다 be broad-minded and tolerant of〔tolerate〕 all kinds〔sorts〕 of (men)
청탁 請託 asking ; begging ; solicitation ; entreaty ; supplication **—하다** ask ; beg ; request ; entreat〔beseech〕 《a person to do》 ; solicit 《for》 ; supplicate 《a person for》 ¶ 긴한 청탁 an urgent 〔important〕 request // 기고를 청탁하다 solicit contribution // 취직자리를 청탁하다 ask 《a person》 to get a job for one // 청탁을 들어주다 comply with〔grant, accede to〕 a request // 청탁이 하나 있습니다 I have a favor to ask of you.
청태 靑苔 [이끼] green moss〔lichen〕 ; [김] seaweed ; laver
청파 靑— a green scallion (planted in autumn)
청편지 請便紙 a letter of solicitation ; a letter asking favors ; a letter of favor
청포 靑布 blue hemp cloth
청포 淸泡 green-lentil jelly
청풍 淸風 a cool〔refreshing〕 breeze ; a fresh wind
—명월 a fresh wind and a bright moon
†**청하다 請—** [부탁] ask ; request ; demand ; [간청] beg ; entreat ; apply ; [초빙] invite ; ask ¶ 청을 받고 at 《a person's》 request ; in compliance〔accordance〕 with 《a person's》 request // 청하지 않은 손님 an uninvited guest // 청을 받아들이다 comply with〔grant〕 a request // 손님을 집에 청하다 invite〔ask〕 a guest to one's home // 조력을 청하다 ask 《a person》 for help ; call for help // 면회를 청하다 ask for〔request〕 an interview ; ask to see 《a person》 ; ring the bell ; knock at the door // 의사를 청하다 send for a doctor ; call in a doctor // 그는 음식을 청했다 He begged for a meal. // 청할 것이 한 가지 있다 I have a favor to ask of you. // 오늘밤 미국인 부부를 저녁 식사에 청했다 We are asking an American couple to have dinner with us this evening.
청한 淸閑 quiet ; tranquility **—하다** (be) quiet ; tranquil
청향 淸香 noble fragrance〔odor〕
청허 聽許 approval ; sanction ; grant **—하다** give assent 《to》 ; grant 《a person's request》 ; sanction ; approve
청혼 請婚 a proposal〔an offer〕 of marriage **—하다** propose 《a marriage》 to ; ask for〔seek〕 a marriage ; ask one's hand in marriage ¶ 이씨집에 청혼하다 propose to the *Lee* family // 청혼을 승낙하다 accept 《a person's》 proposal of marriage
—자 a suitor ¶ 청혼자가 없다 No man has asked for her hand. **—장** a letter proposing a marriage
청혼 請魂 〖불교〗 invocation of the spirit (of a dead person) **—하다** invoke the spirit
청홍 靑紅 blue and red
— 치마 blue and red skirts
청훈 請訓 a request for instructions **—하다** ask 《the government》 for instructions
—서 a (written) request for instructions
청흥 淸興 an innocent enjoyment ; a good clean fun
*__체__[1] a sieve ; a sifter ; a strainer ¶ 석탄치는 체 a (coal) bolter ; a screen // 체로 치다 sieve ; sift ; screen ; weed out // 밀가루를 체질하다 pass flour through a sieve
체[2] pretense ; pretending ; false show **—하다** pretend 《illness, to be ill》 ; affect 《ignorance》 ; feign ; make believe ¶ 죽은 체하다 feign〔sham〕 death // 안 들리는 〔자는〕 체하다 pretend not to hear〔to be asleep〕 // 보고도 못본 체하다 pretend not to see ; [눈감아 주다] blink〔wink〕 at 《a fault》 ; [딴 곳을 보다] look the other way ; [길에서] ignore〔cut〕 《a person》 in 〔on〕 the street ; give 《a person, thing》 the go-by // 그는 책을 읽고 있는 체했다 He made a feint at〔of〕 reading. /He feigned that he was reading.
체[3] Pshaw ! /For shame ! /Tsk !
체 體 [몸·형체] physique ; constitution ; frame ; body ; object ; [방식] style ¶ 체가 크〔작〕다 be of big〔small〕 build 〔frame〕 // 체가 잡히다 take〔get into〕 shape
건강— a healthy body **기업—** an enterprise
체 滯 indigestion ; stomach disorders ⇨ 체증
체가 遞加 acceleration ; successive increase ; increase in order **—하다** increase in order〔successively〕 ; accelerate
체감 遞減 successive diminution ; decrease in order ; deceleration **—하다** decrease in order ; diminish successively ¶ 수확 체감의 법칙 the law of diminishing returns
— 속도 (a) slowdown speed **수익〔효용〕—** diminishing returns〔utility〕
*__체격 體格__ physique ; structure of body ; build ; frame ; make ; setup ; construction ¶ 좋은 체격 a fine physique ; a good constitution // 가냘픈 체격 a slight build ; a delicate physique // 체격이 훌륭하다 be a fine-built man ; have a splendid〔fine〕 physique // 그는 운동가의 체격이다 He has the build of an athlete.
— 검사 a physical〔medical〕 examination ; health inspection ; a (physical) checkup 《미》 ; a physical examination ¶ 체격 검사를 하다〔받다〕 hold〔undergo〕 a physical examination // 체격 검사에 합격하

다〔떨어지다〕 pass〔fail in〕 a physical examination

†**체결 締結** conclusion ; contracting **—하다** conclude contract ; enter into《a contract》 ¶ 평화 조약을 체결하다 conclude a peace treaty《with》// 차관 계약을 체결하다 contract a loan contract

체경 滯京 staying in the capital city **—하다** stay in *Seoul*〔in the capital〕

체경 體鏡 a large looking-glass ; a full-length glass

†**체계 體系** a system ; an organization ¶ 체계적(으로) systematic(ally) // 체계를 세우다 systematize ; organize ; formulate a system // 그의 강의는 체계적이다 His lectures are well organized〔systematic〕.
사상〔철학〕 — a system of thought〔philosophy〕

체계 遞計 moneylending ; usury
—돈 money used for lending at interest
— 집 a money lender's ; a loan office ; a financial association

체공 滯空 remaining〔staying〕 in the air **—하다** stay in the air
— 기록 a duration〔flight〕 record — 비행 an endurance flight — 시간 duration of flight

체관 諦觀 seeing clearly ; a philosophic view ; [체념] resignation **—하다** see clearly ; be resigned

체구 體軀 the body ; the frame ; physical constitution ¶ 체구가 건장한 사나이 a man of magnificent〔strong〕 physique // 체구가 장대〔왜소〕하다 have a gigantic〔small〕 frame ; be large-limbed〔of small build〕

체구 滯歐 staying in Europe ; a stay〔sojourn〕 in Europe ¶ 체구중에 while (staying) in Europe

체급 體級 〖스포츠〗 weight ¶ 권투의 체급 boxing weight

체기 滯氣 the symptoms〔an indication〕 of indigestion ; dyspepsia ¶ 체기가 있다 have an indication of indigestion ; suffer from indigestion

체납 滯納 delinquency in payment (of taxes or duties) ; non-payment ; deferred payment **—하다** fail to pay ; default ; be delinquent in paying ¶ 세금을 체납하다 fail to pay one's taxes ; get behind on one's taxes // 집세가 3개월 체납되어 있다 His rent is three months in arrears. /He is three months behindhand with the rent.
—금 arrears ; arrearages — 상습자 a habitual delinquent — 세금 taxes in arrear(s)〔default〕; tax arrear(s) ; back〔delinquent〕 taxes —액 an amount in arrear(s) —자 a defaulter ; a delinquent ; [세금의] a tax delinquent ; a delinquent taxpayer ¶ 체납자 명부 a delinquent list — 처분 delinquency disposition ; handling of back taxes〔dues〕; disposition for failure to pay《taxes》; coercive collection ¶ 체납 처분비 the disposition fee for arrears // 체납 처분하다 make an attachment《on a person's property》 for unpaid taxes ; institute a process for the recovery of back taxes — 회비 back dues (of membership)

체내 體內 the interior of the body ¶ 체내의 in the body ; in the system
— 골격 〖동물〗 an endoskeleton — 기생충 an endoparasite ; an entozoon《*pl.* -zoa》; an entoparasite — 당분 body〔tissue〕 sugar — 수정 entosomatic〔internal〕 fertilization

***체념 諦念** ① [체관] clear vision ; apprehension of the truth ; spiritual enlightenment **—하다** apprehend the truth
② [단념] resignation ; renunciation **—하다** renounce ; resign《from》; give up ¶ 운명이라고 체념하다 resign oneself to《one's fate, misfortune》; meet one's fate with resignation // 해외로 가는 것을 체념하다 give up the idea of going abroad

체능 體能 physical fitness〔aptitude〕
— 검사 a physical placement test

체대 體大 being big in body〔frame, build〕 **—하다** be of big build〔frame〕; be large-limbed ; have a huge body

체대 替代 [교체] replacing〔changing〕 in turn **—하다** change〔replace〕 in turn

체득 體得 [체험] getting〔learning〕 by experience ; realization ; [이해] comprehension ; [숙련] mastery **—하다** get〔learn, realize〕 by experience ; realize ; master ; comprehend ¶ 불교의 교리를 체득하다 master Buddhist doctrines // 요령을 체득하다 learn the knack of《a trade》 // 학설의 깊은 이치를 체득하다 realize the true meaning of a theory ; learn the underlying meaning of a theory by experience // 기계 다루는 요령을 체득하다 master an instrument

체량 體量 (body) weight ⇨ 체중

체력 體力 physical strength〔stamina〕; body strength ¶ 체력이 강〔약〕하다 have a strong〔weak〕 body // 체력을 기르다 develop〔build up, train〕 one's (physical) strength // 저 선수도 체력이 떨어졌다 That athlete's lost some of his stamina.
— 검정〔검사〕 an examination of physical strength — 시험 a test of strength — 양성 the development of physical strength ; physical training —장(章) physical charter ; medal for brawn ; a physical strength medal ¶ 체력장제 physical strength measurement system ; physical charter system — 평정 physical capacities appraisal

체루 涕淚 falling tears

†**체류 滯留** (a) stay ; a visit ; (a) sojourn **—하다** stay ; stop《at a hotel, with a person's》; make a stay ; sojourn ¶ 서울 체류 중에 during one's stay in *Seoul* ;

while one is〔was〕 in *Seoul* // 10일간의 체류 a ten days' stay〔visit〕 // 오래 체류하다 stay for a long time // 호텔에 체류하다 stay〔put up〕 at a hotel ; be a guest at a hotel
— 일수 the length of one's visit —자 a sojourner ; a《hotel》guest ; a visitor ; a stayer —지 the temporary place of residence ; the place of sojourn
체리 [버찌] a cherry
체맹 締盟 conclusion of a treaty〔an alliance〕 —하다 conclude (a treaty of alliance) ; ally oneself《with》
—국 a treaty power ; [조인국] a signatory (power)
체머리 shaking one's head to and fro ; a shaky head
체머리 흔들다 관용 have a shaky head
체메 a shameless〔cheeky, audacious〕 man
체메다 fix a sieve net on its frame ; make a sieve
체면 體面 one's face ; prestige ; dignity ; honor ; reputation ; a good name ¶ 체면상 for honor's sake ; to save one's face // 체면을 유지하다 keep up〔maintain〕 one's dignity〔prestige〕; save one's face // 체면을 손상하다 lose face ; disgrace oneself ; hurt〔impair〕 one's honor // 체면을 소중히 여기다 respect one's honor // 국가의 체면을 손상시킨 자 a disgrace to one's country // 체면이 있다 be honorable〔respectable, dignified〕 // 체면이 없다 disregard one's honor〔reputation, good name〕 // 그것은 체면 문제다 It is a matter of face. /It is a point of honor. // 사람이 체면이 있어야지 You should have some sense of honor.
체모 體貌 honor ; prestige ⇨ 체면
체모 體毛 hair
체미 滯美 staying〔residing〕 in America —하다 stay in America ¶ 체미 중에 while (staying) in America
체발 剃髮 shaving one's head ; tonsure —하다 shave one's head ; enter the Buddhist priesthood ; become a Buddhist monk
체벌 體罰 corporal punishment ¶ 체벌을 가하다 inflict corporal punishment on《a person》
체법 體法 a calligraphic style〔art〕; a calligraphic brushmanship
체불 滯拂 a delay in payment ; delayed payment《of wages》
체불 임금 滯拂賃金 overdue wage ; wage unpaid ¶ 체불 임금의 청산을 요구하다 call for clearance of overdue wages
체비지 替費地 ① a city-owned land for auction ② a newly-developed land for residential area
체색 體色 [동물의] the color of the body
체선료 滯船料 demurrage
체성 감각 體性感覺 somatic sensation
체세포 體細胞 a somatic cell
체소 體小 —하다 be small in body〔frame, build〕; be of slight build ¶ 체소한 사람 a man of small build
체송 遞送 conveyance ; forwarding —하다 convey ; send by post ; mail ; forward
‡**체스** [서양 장기] chess
—판 a chessboard
체신 遞信 communications
—부 the Ministry of Communications —사무 post and telegraphic service(s)
체액 體液 body fluids ; humors
—류(流) 정지 〖의학〗 stasis — 병리학 humoral pathology 사(四)— the four cardinal humors
체약 締約 [협약] a convention ; a treaty ; an agreement ; [체맹] the conclusion of a convention —하다 conclude《a treaty》
—국 treaty powers
체언 體言 an uninflected word ; a noun ; a substantive
체열 體熱 body heat ; [동물의] animal heat ¶ 체열을 발산하다 give off body heat
***체온 體溫** (body) temperature ; body heat ¶ 체온을 재다 take one's temperature // 체온이 오르다〔내리다〕 one's temperature rises〔falls〕 // 체온이 높다〔낮다〕 one's temperature is high〔low〕 // 그의 체온은 정상이다 His temperature is normal. // 그 여자의 체온은 36도 6부이다 Her temperature is 36.6°〔thirty-six point six degrees〕.
—계 a (clinical) thermometer ¶ 항내(肛內) 체온계 a rectal thermometer — 곡선 a temperature curve — 소산(消散) 〖생리〗 thermolysis — 조절 작용 regulation of body temperature —표 a fever〔temperature〕 chart
체용 體用 ① [본체와 작용] the thing and its functions ② [원리와 응용] a principle and its application ③ 〖문법〗 [체언과 용언] substantives and inflectionals
체위 體位 [체격] a physical standard ; physical condition ; physique ; [자세] a posture ; a position of the body ¶ 체위의 physical // 체위의 향상 improvement of physical condition // 국민 체위의 저하 deterioration in the national physique // 체위를 향상시키다 improve the physique ; elevate〔raise, better〕 the physical standards《of a nation》
— 저하 physical deterioration — 적성 physical fitness — 향상 운동 a "keep fit" movement 평균 — the physical average《in the country》
체육 體育 physical education〔training〕; [과목] physical exercise ; gymnastics ; athletics ¶ 체육을 장려하다 encourage physical training
—가 a physical culturist〔educator〕; [운동가] an athlete —관 a gymnasium《*pl.*

～s, -sia》 a gym 《구》 ―단체 an athletic organization ―대회 an athletic meet(ing) ―부(장) (the director of) the department of athletics ―일 Sports Day ―지도자 a physical director ―회 an athletic association〔club〕 ¶ 대한 체육회 the Korea Amateur Sports Association 《K. A. S. A》

체읍 涕泣 crying ; weeping and wailing ―하다 wail ; weep ; shed tears

체인 a chain ; [자동차의] a tire chain
―스토어 a chain store 《미》 ; a multiple shop 《영》

체인지 a change
―오브 페이스 〖야구〗 a change-up ; a change of pace

체장 體長 the length ¶ 그들은 체장이 대체로 같다 They are all about the same in stature.

체재 體裁 [생김새] style ; [외형] form ; appearance ; show ; [꾸밈새] makeup ; getup ; setup ; format ¶ 책의 체재 the format〔getup〕 of a book // 체재가 훌륭하다 have nice appearance ; be of good style ; have a fine format // 체재가 나쁘다 be indecent〔unseemly, awkward〕 // 체재를 갖추고 있다 have proper form〔style〕 // 이 책은 체재가 아담하다 This book is of elegant format.

체재 滯在 staying ; (a) stay ⇨ 체류

체적 體積 volume ; cubic volume〔measure〕 ; capacity ¶ 2입방 미터의 체적 a volume of 2 cubic meters // 체적을 구하다 cube
―계 a volumenometer ; a stereometer ―측정 volumenometry ; stereometry ―팽창 cubical expansion ―학 stereometry

체전 遞傳 sending forward ; passing on ; sending by mail ―하다 send forward ; pass on

체전부 遞傳夫 a letter-carrier ; a mailman 《미》 ; postman 《영》 ⇨ 우체부

체절 體節 〖동물〗 an arthromere ; a metamere ; a somite ; a segment ¶ 체절의 arthromeric ; metameric ; somital ; segmental
―구성 segmentation ―기관 a segmental organ ―제 metamerism

체제 體制 setup ; formation ; constitution ; organization ; a system ; a structure ; an order ¶ 신〔구〕체제 a new〔an old〕 system // 사회의 체제 the structure〔fabric〕 of a society // 신경제 체제 a new economic structure // 군대의 편성 체제 the organization of an army // 산업의 전시 체제 wartime industrial mobilization
―경제 an economic structure 전시― a war footing ¶ 전시 체제로 바뀌다 be reorganized on a war footing 정치― a political system〔dispensation〕

*체조 體操 gymnastics ; gym ; physical〔gymnastic, athletic〕 exercises ; physical training ―하다 practice gymnastics ; have〔do〕 physical〔gymnastic, athletic〕 exercises
―교사 a gym(nastic) teacher ; a gymnast ; a drill master ―기구 gymnastic apparatus〔devices〕 ―선수 a gymnast ―팀 a gymnastic team 기계― heavy〔apparatus〕 gymnastics 도수― free gymnastics 라디오― radio gymnastic exercises 미용〔유연〕― calisthenics ; setting-up exercises 율동― eurhythmics ; rhythmic gymnastics〔calisthenics〕 ; light〔simple〕 gymnastics

*체중 體重 (body) weight ¶ 체중을 달다 weigh〔measure〕 oneself // 체중이 60킬로이다 weigh 60 kilograms // 체중이 늘다〔줄다〕 gain〔lose〕 in weight // 당신은 체중이 얼마입니까 How much do you weigh ? / What's your weight ? // 체중계에 올라서 주세요 Step on the scale, please. // 나는 키에 비해서 체중이 모자란다 I'm underweight for my height.

체증 滯症 indigestion ; dyspepsia ; digestive disorders ¶ 체증에 걸리다 suffer from indigestion
―환자 a dyspeptic patient〔case〕

체증 遞增 gradual increase ―하다 increase gradually

체지 體肢 one's trunk and limbs ; one's body〔frame〕 ¶ 체지가 온전하다 be able-bodied // 체지가 크다 be huge-limbed ; have a large body

체진 滯陣 encampment ―하다 continue to camp ; be encamped ; be in camp

체질 sieving ; screening ; sifting ―하다 sieve ; pass 《a thing》 through a sieve ; sift ; screen

*체질 體質 (physical) constitution ; habitude ¶ 체질의 constitutional // 체질상의 결함 physical〔constitutional〕 defects // 폐병 체질의 사람 a man predisposed to consumption ; a constitutional predisposition to consumption
―개선 improving one's physical constitution ; [단체·기업 따위의] radical reform ; revamping ; overhauling ¶ 대기업의 체질을 개선하다 improve the constitution of big enterprises ―변환약 an alterative

체취 體臭 body odor(s) 《B. O.》 ; one's personal smell ¶ 체취가 심하다 have strong body odor // 그의 작품에는 그의 체취가 풍긴다 His work reveals his idiosyncrasy.

체크 ① [대조 검사] collation ; check(up) ―하다 check〔tick〕 (off) ; mark ; [짐 따위를 맡기다] place a check 《beside》 ② [수표] a check 《미》 ; a cheque 《영》 ③ [체크 무늬] checks ; checkers ; cross stripes

체통 體― (the bulk of) the body

체통 體統 an official's decency ; dignity ; prestige ; honor ⇨ 체면

체팽창 體膨脹 cubical expansion

†**체포** 逮捕 arrest(ment) ; apprehension ; capture —**하다** arrest ; place《a person》under arrest ; capture ; seize ; take《a person》into custody ; nab《구》; cop《속》¶ 아직 체포되지 않고 있다 be still at large // 그는 혐의를 받고 체포되었다 He was placed under arrest upon suspicion // 그에게 체포령이 내리었다 He is under a warrant of arrest. /There is warrant out for him. // 지난주 경찰은 3명의 은행 강도를 체포했다 The police picked up three bank robbers last week.

—**령** a mandate for an arrest ; a warrant for an arrest ¶ 그에게 체포령이 내리었다 There is a warrant (of arrest) out for 〔against〕 him. — **(영)장** a warrant of arrest〔apprehension〕; a bench warrant

‡**체하다** pretend《to do, to have done》; make believe ; feign ¶ 안 들리는 체하다 pretend not to hear // 모르는 체하다 affect ignorance ⇨ 체[2]

체하다 滯— have a digestive upset ; suffer from indigestion ; sit〔lie〕 heavy on the stomach ¶ 아침 먹은 것이 체했다 What took for breakfast lies heavy on my stomach.

체한 滯韓 staying in Korea —**하다** stay in Korea

체험 體驗 (one's personal) experience(s) —**하다** experience (personally) ; undergo ; go through ¶ 어려운 고난을 체험하다 go through many hardships // 노동 생활을 체험하다 experience a life of labor // 직접 체험해서 알다 learn by direct and actual experience

—**담** a story of one's personal experiences —**주의** empiricism

체현 體現 embodiment ; personification ; impersonation —**하다** embody ; personify ; impersonate

체형 體形 a form ; a figure

체형 體刑 a jail sentence ; penal servitude ; [처벌] corporal punishment ¶ 체형을 과하다 impose a jail sentence ; sentence《a person》to penal servitude ; inflict corporal punishment on《a person》

체화 滯貨 [화물의] the accumulation of freight ; freight congestion ; [상품의] the accumulation of stocks〔goods〕; stockpiles of goods —**하다** accumulate ; be held up ; pile up ¶ 체화를 일소하다 clear out the accumulated goods // 각 역마다 체화가 심하다 There is a great accumulation of freights at every station.

첼로 〖악기〗 a (violon) cello

— **연주자** a cellist

쳇다리 a support on which a sieve is laid while in use ; sieve-frame legs

쳇바퀴 the rim of a sieve〔bolter〕; the frame of a sieve ¶ 쳇바퀴에 체를 매달다 fix a sieve net on its frame

쳇발 [베틀의] a stick placed across the already woven part of cloth on the loom to keep it in shape

쳇불 the meshes of a sieve ; a sieve net

쳐가다 collect and take away ; sweep away ; dip up and cart away ¶ 쓰레기를 쳐가다 clear away garbage〔rubbish〕// 소외양간의 두엄을 쳐가다 clean a cow-shed of manure

쳐내다 take away ; remove ; clean up ; clear ; [체로 쳐서] sift〔sieve〕 out ¶ 뜰의 눈을 쳐내다 clear the yard of snow ; shovel away the snow from the yard // 변소를 쳐내다 clean up a toilet ; take away the night soil

쳐넣다 throw〔cast, fling〕 in ; dump into ¶ 감옥에 쳐넣다 cast〔throw〕《a person》into prison // 잠옷을 뭉뚱거려 반침에 쳐넣다 bundle one's night clothes into the closet

쳐다보다 look up ; turn up the eyes ; cast an upward glance ¶ 하늘을 쳐다보다 look up at the sky ; raise one's eye's to heaven // 사람의 얼굴을 쳐다보다 look up at《a person's》face

쳐들다 lift up ; raise ; hold up ; heave ; hoist ; [지적] hold out ; point out〔to〕; refer to ¶ 무거운 돌을 쳐들다 heave a heavy stone // 손을 번쩍 쳐들다 raise〔put up〕 one's hand high // 부끄러워 고개를 쳐들지 못하다 cannot hold up one's head for shame ; cannot look《a person》in the face because of shame // 남의 결점을 쳐들다 point to〔refer to〕《a person's》defects ; find fault with《a person》

쳐들어가다 raid ; make a raid on ; invade ; penetrate into

쳐바르다 [페인트 따위를] daub all over ; bedaub ; besmear ; [얼굴에] paint〔powder〕《one's face》thick(ly)〔heavily〕; use (too) much makeup ¶ 분을 쳐바르다 plaster《one's face》with powder ; be thickly powdered ; be heavily painted

쳐박다 ① [때려박다] drive〔strike〕 in 〔into〕; ram down《a stake》; wedge in (쐐기 따위를) ¶ 말뚝을 쳐박다 drive in a stake〔pile, picket〕 ② [물속에] douse ; dowse ; dip ; plunge ; duck

쳐버리다 sweep〔take〕 away ; clear ; remove ; clean up ¶ 쓰레기를 쳐버리다 clean up garbage ; cart rubbish off

쳐주다 ① [셈하다] estimate ; value ; rate ; reckon ; calculate ¶ 집 값을 100만원으로 쳐주다 appraise〔value〕 a house at one million *won* // 돈을 쳐주다 pay the bill ② [인정하다] acknowledge ; treat《as》; look upon《as》¶ 이겼다고 쳐주다 regard《a person》as the winner // 나는 그의 지력과 수완을 높이 쳐준다 I have a high opinion of his intelligence and ability.

쳐죽이다 beat〔strike, knock〕《a person》to death ; strike dead

‡**초** a candle ; a taper

—심지 the wick (of a candle) ; a candlewick —장수 a candler 밀— honey wax ; a wax candle 양— a candle

*초 秒 a second ¶ 초속 20미터 a velocity〔speed〕 of 20 meters a〔per〕 second
—침 a second-hand

초 草 ① a draft ; drafting —하다 draft ; make a draft ; draw〔write〕 up ¶ 편지의 초를 잡다 draft a letter ; write a draft of one's letter // 법안의 초 a draft of a bill ② [초서] cursive writing ; a cursive hand ¶ 초를 잘 쓰다 be good at cursive brushmanship

초 醋 vinegar ¶ 초에 절이다 pickle in vinegar // 초친 요리 a vinegared dish
—간장 soy sauce mixed with vinegar —김치 spring vegetables pickled in vinegar

초 初 the beginning ; the commencement ; the first ¶ 내월 초에 early next month // 초하루 the first of the month // 학기 초 the beginning of the school term

초 抄 an extract〔excerpt〕 ; a selection ¶ 괴테 시초 selected poems of Goethe

초- 超 super- ; ultra- ; sur- ; hyper- ; transcendental ¶ 초경험적 transcendental ; metempirical // 초현대적 ultramodern // 초자연적 supernatural // 초인간적 superhuman // 초고속도 ultrahigh speed // 초고속도 촬영기 an ultrahigh speed camera // 초현실주의 surrealism

초가 草家 a straw-〔grass-〕roofed house ; a house with straw-thatched roof
— 삼간 a small cottage ; a three-room thatched house

초가 樵歌 a woodcutter's song

초가을 初— early autumn〔fall〕 ; the beginning of autumn

초감각적 超感覺的 extrasensory ; supersensible ; pretersensual
— 개념 a transcendental concept

초강초강하다 [얼굴이] (be) lean ; thin ¶ 초강초강한 얼굴 a thin face

초개 草芥 bits of straw〔grass〕 ; a worthless thing ¶ 초개 같다 be worthless (as bits of straw) // 초개 같은 인생 a worthless life ; a humble life

초겨울 初— early winter ; the beginning of winter

초견 初見 seeing〔reading〕 for the first time ; a first view〔sight〕 —하다 see 《a thing》 for the first time

초경 初經 [첫 월경] menarche

초경 初更 the first watch (of the night) ; early evening

초경 初耕 『농업』 the first tilling〔plowing〕 ; a preliminary tilling —하다 till〔plow〕 once ; give a preliminary tilling

초경험론 超經驗論 『철학』 metempiricism ; metempiric(s)
—자 a metempiricist ; a metempiric

초계 哨戒 patrolling —하다 patrol ¶ 초계 중에 on patrol
— 부대〔기, 선〕 a patrol force〔plane, line〕 —정 a patrol〔picket, vedette〕 boat ; a PT boat

초고 草稿 a rough copy ; a draft ; notes ; a manuscript ¶ 강의의 초고 notes for a lecture // 연설의 초고 a rough copy of a speech // 초고를 만들다 draft ; prepare〔make〕 a draft // 초고를 보고〔보지 않고〕 연설하다 speak from〔without〕 notes
강의 — notes for a lecture 연설 — a rough copy of a speech

초고속도 超高速度 《at》 superhigh〔ultrahigh〕 speed ¶ 초고속의 superspeed 《flight》
— 촬영기 a superhigh-〔a hyperhigh-, an ultrahigh-〕speed camera

초고속 도로 超高速道路 a superhighway 《미》 ; a motorway 《영》 (expressway, freeway, throughway, turnpike를 총칭함)

초고주파 超高周波 superhigh frequency 《S. H. F., SHF》 ; ultrahigh frequency 《U. H. F., UHF, u. h. f., uhf》

초고추장 醋—醬 vinegared red pepper paste

*초과 超過 excess ; surplus —하다 exceed ; be in excess 《of》 ; be more than ¶ 인구의 초과 overpopulation // 화폐의 초과 발행 overissue〔excessive issue〕 of currency // 연령을 초과하다 exceed the age limit ; be over the regular〔required〕 age // 정원을 초과하다 exceed the fixed number of people // 수요가 공급을 초과한다 The demand exceeds the supply.
— 근무 overtime work ; extra duties — 소득 excess income —액 a surplus ; an excess 《of》 — 이득세 an extra profits duty《E. P. D.》 ; an excess profit tax 수출〔수입〕 — an excess of exports〔imports〕 ; favorable〔unfavorable, adverse〕 balance of trade 인원 — an excessive number of people

초교 初校 the first proof-reading ; the first proof(-sheet) (교정쇄) ¶ 초교를 보다 read the first proof

초국가 超國家 a superstate ¶ 초국가적인 supernational ; supranational
—주의 ultranationalism —주의자 an ultranationalist

초군 樵軍 a woodcutter ; a woodman

초극 超克 conquest —하다 conquer ; overcome〔surmount, get over〕 《a difficulty》 ; tide over 《a crisis》

초근목피 草根木皮 roots of herbs and barks of trees ; coarse and miserable food ¶ 초근목피로 연명하다 barely manage to stay alive with the aid of〔eating〕 herb-roots and tree-barks

초급 初級 a primary grade〔class〕 ; the lowest〔beginner's〕 class
— 대학 a junior college — 영문법 English Grammar for Beginners — 학교 a primary〔an elementary〕 school

초급 初給 a starting〔initial, beginning〕 salary ¶ 초급은 6만원이었다 I began 〔started〕 with a salary of sixty thousand *won*. /My salary was sixty thousand *won* at the start. /My beginning salary was sixty thousand *won*.

***초기 初期** the early days〔period〕; the first〔initial, incipient〕 stage ; an early stage ¶ 초기의 early ; initial ; incipient // 이조 초기 the early years of the *Yi* dynasty // 초기의 암 incipient cancer ; cancer in its early stages // 셰익스피어의 초기 작품 Shakespeare's early works // 문명의 초기 the early stage of civilization // 병의 초기 the early stage of a disease ; the beginning of a disease // 병은 초기에 치료하여야 한다 Disease should be treated at the very beginning.
— 결핵 early〔incipient〕 T. B. **— 작품** one's early works **— 침윤** 〖의학〗 primary infiltration

초김치 醋— early spring vegetables pickled in vinegar

초꽂이 a sconce (for candlesticks)

초나흗날, 초나흘 初— the fourth day of the month

초년 初年 [첫해] the first year ; [초기] early years ; [생애의] one's young days ; the early part of one's life ; one's early years ¶ 운수가 초년에는 길하고 만년에는 흉하다 be destined to be lucky in early years but unlucky in later years
—급 the beginners' class ; the first-year class ; the early grades **—병** a raw recruit ; a new conscript **—생(生)** a mere beginner ¶ 이 일에 나는 초년생이다 I'm a mere beginner in this business.
초년 고생은 은 주고 산다 〔속담〕 Experience is the best teacher. /Experience keeps a dear school.

초념 初念 one's original intention〔purpose〕 ⇨ 초지

초노급함 超弩級艦 a superdreadnought

초다짐 初— —하다 eat just a bite to ease〔assuage〕 one's hunger before mealtime ; snack before mealtime

초단 初段 the first grade ¶ 유도 초단자 a first grader in *Yudo* // 바둑 초단자 a first-grade player of *Paduk*

초단파 超短波 microwaves ; ultrashort waves
— 가열론〔학〕 radiothemics **— 방송** frequency modulation〔FM〕 broadcasting **— 수〔송〕신기** an ultrashort wave receiver〔transmitter〕

초닷새, 초닷샛날 初— the fifth day of the month

초당 草堂 a thatched cottage separated from the main building of a house (and usually used for a study)

초당 안보 기구 超黨安保機構 a suprapartisan〔nonpartisan〕 organization for national security

초당파 超黨派 super〔supra〕partisan ; bipartisan
— 내각 a suprapartisan〔coalition〕 cabinet **— 외교** a supraparty〔bipartisan〕 diplomacy **— 정부** an all-party government

초대 初— a greenhorn ; a green hand ; a novice ; a beginner ¶ 골프에 있어서는 그는 아직 초대다 He is still a beginner〔greenhorn〕 in golf.

***초대 招待** invitation **—하다** invite〔ask〕《a person》 to ; be host to ¶ 만찬회에 초대하다 invite《a person》 to a dinner party // 초대에 응하다〔거절하다〕 accept 〔decline〕 an invitation // 초대를 받다 be invited《to a dinner》; receive an invitation《to》
—객 an invited guest **— 경기** invitation game **—권** an invitation card ; a complimentary ticket ; a courtesy card **—석** a reserved seat for an invited guest **— 시합** an invitation(al) match **—연** a dinner party ; a feast ; a banquet **— 외교** diplomacy conducted by inviting people in high offices **—일** [전시회 따위의] a preview day **— 작가** the invited artist **—장** a letter of invitation ; an invitation (card) ¶ 초대장을 내다 send〔issue〕 an invitation **—전(展)** [그림 따위의] a preview 《미》; a private view

초대 初代 the first generation ; the founder ; the originator ¶ 초대의 the first // 초대 대통령 the first President // 초대 회장 the first president of the association // 본대학의 초대 총장은 A박사였다 Dr. A was the first president of this university.

초대국 超大國 [미국·소련 같은] a superpower ; a superstate

초대면 初對面 the first meeting〔interview〕《with》 ¶ 초대면인 사람 a stranger // 그 사람하고는 그때 초대면이었다 Then I met him for the first time. /He had been a stranger to me until then.

초대작 超大作 a superproduction ; [영화의] a superfilm ; a suprafeature film ¶ 백만 달러의 초대작 a one-million-dollar "Super Special"

초대형 超大型 ¶ 초대형의 extra-large ; out-size(d) 《구》
— 여객기 a superliner

초동 樵童 a boy woodcutter ; a wood-boy

초동 初冬 the beginning of winter ; early winter

초두 初頭 the beginning ; the outset ; the first ; the start ¶ 20세기 초두 the outset of the 20th century // 사업 초두에 실패하다 fail at the very beginning of an undertaking

초들다 mention ; refer to ; enumerate ; cite ¶ 남의 결점을 초들다 mention〔bring up〕 a person's shortcomings

***초등 初等** ¶ 초등의 elementary ; primary

—과 an elementary course — 교육 elementary〔primary〕 education — 기하학 elementary geometry —반 a beginners' class
*초등 학교 初等學校 a primary〔an elementary〕 school ; a public school 《미》
— 과정(過程) an elementary course of study — 교사 an elementary school teacher ; a public school teacher 《미》 — 아동 a pupil ; a schoolboy〔schoolgirl〕
초라니 〖민속〗 an exorcist who appears in woman's dress at a court rite
초라떼다 get snubbed〔squelched〕 ; be put in one's place ; be humbled ; be defeated
†초라하다 (be) shabby ; miserable ; wretched〔poor〕-looking ; seedy ; shoddy ; run-down (looking) ; beat-up (looking) ; mean ; dirty ¶ 초라한 집 a shabby〔run-down, sorry-looking〕 house ; a shoddy building // 초라한 옷 shabby clothes // 초라하게 살다 be poorly〔badly〕 off // 그는 행색이 초라했다 He looked seedy. /He was poorly dressed.
†초래 招來 —하다 bring about〔on〕 ; cause ; incur ; lead ; give rise to ¶ 전쟁을 초래하다 lead to war // 물가 등귀를 초래하다 cause an advance in the prices of commodities // 결과를 초래하다 bring about〔lead to〕 a result // 위험을 초래하다 invite〔bring on〕 danger // 그는 무모한 짓으로 화를 스스로 초래한 꼴이 되었다 He has, in a sense, courted disaster by his own reckless conduct. // 원칙을 고수하는 데에는 잘못된 게 없으나 완고함도 도를 넘어서면 주위의 비난을 초래한다 There's nothing wrong with holding to principles, but when you get too stubborn it only invites criticism all around.
초략 抄略 plunder ; ravage ; pillage ; spoliation —하다 plunder ; ravage ; spoliate
초려 焦慮 [초조] impatience ; [걱정] worry ; trouble —하다 be impatient 《to do》 ; be anxious 《for》 ; be too eager 《for》 ; be in a fidget
초련 an early crop to be used until the regular harvest time
초련 初鍊 a rough-planed〔hewn〕 board ; preliminary arrangements
초련 初戀 ⇨ 첫사랑
초례 醮禮 a marriage ceremony ; a wedding ; nuptials ¶ 초례를 지내다 celebrate a wedding ; hold nuptials
—청 a wedding hall
초로 草路 a path across a meadow〔grassfield〕
초로 草露 dew on the grass ¶ 초로와 같은 인생 a life as fleeting as the dew on the grass ; transient life
초로 初老 the age of forty years ; the beginning of middle age ¶ 초로의 신사 an elderly gentleman
초록 抄錄 an abstract ; an extract ; a summary ; an excerpt —하다 excerpt ; extract ; make a summary〔an abstract〕 of ¶ 시사 초록 a summary of current affairs
†초록 草綠 grass-green ; green
—빛 green color — 치마 a green skirt
초롱 a tin plate container ; a tin 《영》 ; a can 《미》 ; [용량] a canful〔bucketful〕 (of liquid) ¶ 물 두 초롱 two pails of water
석유 — a kerosene can〔tin〕 ; an oil can
초롱 —籠 a silk-covered lantern ; a lantern of gauze ; a hand-lantern
초롱꽃 〖식물〗 a (dotted) bellflower
초름하다 (a share) be small ; be less than due amount〔quantity〕 ; be not enough ; be hardly ample ; be wanting ; be short of ¶ 초름한 몫 a share smaller than others // 밥이 그릇에 초름하다 There isn't enough rice to fill a bowl.
초립 草笠 a straw hat (worn by a young married man of below twenty)
초립동 草笠童 a very young married man (wearing a straw hat) ; a young adult
초막 草幕 a straw-thatched hut
초만원 超滿員 being overly filled-up ¶ 초만원이다 be filled to overflowing〔capacity〕 ; be packed with people ; be jampacked
초매 草昧 primitiveness ; a primitive〔an uncivilized〕 state ; [혼란] chaos ; confusion ; disorder ; disorganization
초면 初面 the first meeting〔interview〕 ; seeing〔meeting〕 for the first time ¶ 초면의 사람 a stranger ; a casual acquaintance // 초면의 강산 a strange country〔place〕 // 초면의 인상 one's first impression // 초면의 인사 greetings on a first meeting // 초면이다 meet 《a person》 for the first time ; have never met before
초면 炒麵 chow mein ; Chinese fried noodles
초멸 剿滅 mopping up 《a gang of thieves etc.》 —하다 mop up 《a gang》 ; extirpate ; destroy
초모 招募 recruitment ; enlistment —하다 recruit ; enlist 《soldiers》 ; raise 《armies》 ; assemble 《an army》 ¶ 방을 내걸어 의병을 초모하다 put out notices calling for volunteers to serve against 《rebels, the enemy》
초모 醋母 [초산균] mother-of-vinegar
*초목 草木 trees and grass ; plants ; vegetation ¶ 초목이 없다 be bare of vegetation // 산천 초목 mountains and streams, plants and grass ; nature // 초목이 우거지다 have lush vegetation
초문 初聞 the latest〔last〕 news ; hot news ¶ 금시 초문이다 That's quite news to me. /I have never heard of it before.
초미 焦眉 emergency ; urgency ; imminence ¶ 초미의 urgent ; pressing ; imminent ; burning // 초미의 문제 an

urgent question ; a pressing〔burning〕 question
조미지급 (관용) an urgent need ; a pressing necessity ; an urgency
초민 焦悶 distress ; impatience ; worry ; miserableness ―하다 be worried 《about》 ; be concerned 《about》 ; (be) impatient ; be sad at heart
초반 初盤 the opening part 《of a game, of *Paduk*》
초밥 醋― Japanese vinegared rice delicacies
초방 初枋 『건축』 the first cornice-moulding added after setting up a pillar
초배 初褙 the underpapering of a wall ; the first coat of wallpaper ―하다 underpaper ; paste the first coat of wallpaper on ¶ 벽을 초배하다 underpaper a wall
*초벌 初― the first ; the primary ⇨ 애벌
―김 the first weeding ―도배 ⇨ 초배(初褙)
초범 初犯 the first offense
―자 a first offender
초범 初凡 extraordinariness ; being out of the common ―하다 be extraordinary ; be uncommon ; be out of the common 〔ordinary〕 ; be of an unusual order
초벽 初壁 an inner first coat of plaster 《on a wall》 ; the first plastering ―하다 plaster the first coat on 《a wall》
초병 哨兵 a sentinel ; a sentry ; a military guard
―근무 sentry-duty ―선 a sentry line
초병 醋甁 a vinegar bottle
―마개 [비유적] a very sour person
*초보 初步 first steps ; the first stage ; elements ; rudiments ; the ABC('s) ; a primer ; a beginners' course ; the beginning ; the start ¶ 초보의 elementary ; rudimentary // 초보용의 《a book》 for beginners // 영어 초보 a primer of English ; First Steps in English // 산술의 초보 the elements〔rudiments〕 of arithmetic ; the ABC's of arithmetic // 초보 영어 elementary English // 초보 지식 the rudimentary〔elementary〕 knowledge 《of》 // 물리학을 초보부터 배우다 start with the ABC of physics ; know the ABC of physics // 기계학의 초보를 알다 have the rudiments of mechanics // 그는 영문법의 초보도 모른다 He lacks even a rudimentary knowledge of English grammar. /He is ill-grounded in English grammar.
―영어 elementary English ―자 a beginner ; a novice ; a green hand ; a greenhorn ¶ 초보자를 위한 for beginners // 이 산은 등산 초보자에게는 이상적이다 This mountain is ideal for inexperienced climbers. 경제학 ― the ABC of economics 산술 ― the rudiments〔elements, ABC〕 of arithmetic 식물학 ― 지식 an elementary〔rudimentary〕 knowledge of botany
초복 初伏 the first day of dog days ; the beginning of the hottest period ; the first period of summer doldrums
초본 抄本 an abstract ; an extract
호적 ― an abstract of the census register
초본 草本 herbs ; aceous plants ¶ 초본의 herbal
―경(莖) a herbaceous system ―대(帶) a floral zone ―식물 a herbaceous plant
초봄 初― early spring ; the beginning of spring ¶ 초봄부터 from early spring
초봉 初俸 a starting〔an initial, a commencing〕 pay〔salary〕 ; a starter 《미·속》 ¶ 초봉은 80만원이었다 I started with a salary of 800,000 *won*. // 초봉은 대개 어느 정도로 생각하고 계십니까 What kind of starting pay do you have in mind?
초부 樵夫 a woodcutter
초분 初分 [초년 운수] one's star〔fortune, lot〕 in the early days〔years〕 ¶ 초분이 무척 좋다 have a swell run of luck in one's early years
초빙 招聘 invitation〔employment〕 《with due respect》 ; engagement ―하다 engage ; employ ; extend a call to 《a person》 ¶ …의 초빙을 받고 at the invitation 《of》 // 초빙을 받다 receive an offer of employment 《a position》 // 초빙에 응하다 accept the offer of a position ; receive a call // 전문가를 초빙하다 engage the service of an expert ; call in a specialist // 정부 고문으로 초빙하다 employ 《a person》 as an adviser to the government
초사 焦思 worry ; anxiety ; restlessness ―하다 worry over ; be anxious about ; be troubled by
초사흗날, 초사흘 初― the third day of the month
초산 初産 a woman's first childbirth 〔delivery〕 ¶ 초산은 난산이었다 Her first delivery was a difficult one.
―부 a primipara ; a woman who has had her first childbirth
초산 硝酸 nitric acid ⇨ 질산
초산 醋酸 acetic acid
―균 an acetobacter ―염 an acetate 빙― glacial acetic acid
*초상 肖像 a portrait ; a likeness ¶ 황제의 초상 an effigy of the Emperor // 초상을 그리게 하다 sit for one's portrait ; have one's portrait painted
초상 初霜 the first frost of the season
초상 初喪 (a period of) mourning ¶ 초상을 당하다 go into〔put on, take to〕 mourning
―집 a house〔family〕 in mourning
*초상화 肖像畫 a portrait ; a picture ; a portrait painting (화법) ¶ 유화의 초상화 a portrait in oil
―가 a portrait painter
초색 草色 [색깔] green color

초생 初生 the beginning of a month ; being newborn
—달 a new〔young〕 moon ; a crescent (moon) ¶ 초생달 모양의 crescent (-shaped) —아 a new-born child
초서 草書 the cursive〔running〕 style of brushmanship〔penmanship〕; [글씨] cursive characters ¶ 초서체 활자 script type
—체 the cursive style ; grass characters
초석 硝石 (potassium) nitrate
칠레 — nitrate of soda
초석 礎石 a foundation stone ; a cornerstone ; a foundation ¶ 민주정치의 초석을 놓다 lay a cornerstone (in the foundation) of democracy
초석 草席 a straw mat
초석 礁石 a reef ; a submerged〔sunken〕 rock
초설 初雪 the first snow (of the season)
초성 初聲 an initial sound
초소 哨所 a guard〔sentry〕 post ; [검문하는] a checkpoint
감시 — an observation point
초속 初速 initial velocity
초속 秒速 a velocity per second ¶ 초속 20미터 a speed of 20 meter a second
초속 超俗 unworldliness ¶ 초속적인 unworldly ; supermundane // 초속적인 생활을하다 live a supermundane life // 그는 초속적이다 He keeps aloof from the world.
초속도 超速度 super〔ultra〕high speed
— 윤전기 a superhigh speed rotary press
초순 初旬 the first third〔ten days〕 of a month ¶ 초순에 early in 《May》; at the beginning of a month
시월 — the beginning of October
*초승 first days (of the month)
—달 a new〔young〕 moon ; a crescent (moon) ¶ 초승달이 하늘에 떠 있다 The young moon hangs in the sky.
초시계 秒時計 a microchronometer ; a stopwatch
초시류 鞘翅類 Coleoptera ¶ 초시류의 coleopterous // 초시류의 곤충 a coleopteron 《*pl.* -ra》
초식 草食 grass-eating ; living on grass ; eating vegetables —하다 eat grass ; live on grass〔vegetables〕 ¶ 초식의 grass-eating ; graminivorous ; herbivorous
—가 a vegetarian — 동물 a grass-eating〔herbivorous〕 animal ; a herbivore — 류 a herbivorous animal ; a herbivore
초실 初室 ① [집] a newly built house ② ⇨ 초취(初娶)
‡초심 初心 one's original intention〔purpose, aim〕; greenness (미숙) ; [초심자] a beginner ; a greenhorn ; a novice ; the uninitiated 《총칭》 ¶ 초심의 inexperienced ; uninitiated ; inexpert ; green // 스키의 초심자 a novice skier // 그 일에 있어서의 전적인 초심자 the rankest novices 〔mere beginners〕 in the business
—자 ⇨ 초심(初心) ¶ 초심자를 위한 for beginners
초심 焦心 worry ; anxiety
초심 初審 the first trial〔hearing〕
— 재판소 a court of first instance
초싹거리다 ⇨ 추썩거리다
초아흐레, 초아흐렛날 初— the ninth day of the month
초안 草案 a (rough) draft ¶ 헌법 초안 the draft of constitution // 초안을 기초하다 draft〔frame〕 a bill ; prepare a draft
민법 — a draft civil code 법률 — a draft of a law 법안 — a draft bill
초안 硝安 ammonium nitrate
— 폭약 an ammonium nitrate explosive
초야 草野 an out-of-the-way place ; the boondocks ; the backwoods ; a remote corner of the country ¶ 초야에 묻혀 살다 live in seclusion ; live in absolute privacy ; remain in private life
초야 初夜 the first half part of a night ; [첫날밤] the first night ; a bridal night ; a wedding night
초여드레, 초여드렛날 初— the eighth day of the month
초여름 early summer ; the beginning of summer ¶ 초여름에 early in summer
초역 抄譯 an abridged translation ; translation of selected passages ; a selected translation —하다 translate selected passages 《from》 ¶ 파우스트 초역 a translation of selections from the Faust
*초연 超然 aloofness ; detachment ; transcendence —하다 stand〔keep〕 aloof from 《a matter》; be unconcerned ; be above ; rise above 《the world》 ¶ 초연하게 aloof ; in solitary supremacy ; with a detached manner // 초연히 대중과 섞이지 않다 keep aloof from the crowd // 정치〔돈 문제〕에서 초연하다 be〔rise〕 above party politics〔money matters〕
—주의 the policy of isolation ; a standoff policy〔attitude〕
초연 初演 a première 《프》; the first performance ; one's debut on the stage (배우의) ¶ 이 나라에서의 초연 the first performance of a play in this country
초연 招宴 an invitation to a party —하다 invite〔ask〕 《a person》 to a party
초연 硝煙 gunsmoke ; the smoke of battle ¶ 초연 탄우 속에 in the thick of the fight(ing) ; in the midst of the gunsmoke and bullets
초열흘날 初— the tenth day of the month
초엽 初葉 the early years〔days〕; the beginning ; the initial phase ¶ 20세기 초엽에 in the early part of the 20th century
초엽 草葉, 蕉葉 【건축】 a bracket ; a corbel ; a console
초엿새, 초엿샛날 the sixth day of the

month
초오 草烏 〖식물〗 monkshood ; wolfsbane
초옥 草屋 a grass-roofed house ; a straw-thatched hut
초원 草原 a plain ; a grassland ; a prairie (북미의) ; a pampas (남미의) ; a steppe (러시아·중앙 아시아의)
†초월 超越 [탁월] superiority ; (super-) excellence ; transcendence —하다 transcend ; excel ; surpass ; stand〔be〕above ; be superior to ¶ 초월적 transcendental // 세속을 초월하다 rise above the world // 인력을 초월하다 transcend human power
—론 transcendentalism — 철학 transcendental philosophy ; transcendentalism — 함수 a transcendental function
초유 初有 ¶ 초유의 first ; initial ; original // 초유의 일 an unheard-of event // 이것은 우리 나라 초유의 일이다 This is really unexampled〔unprecedented〕 in the history of this country.
초음속 超音速 〖물리〗 supersonic speed ; hypersonic speed (음속의 약 5배이상의 속도) ¶ 초음속의 supersonic
—도계(度計) a Mach meter ; a machometer — 비행 supersonic flight — 수송기 a supersonic transport 《SST》 — 제트기 a supersonic jet plane
초음파 超音波 〖물리〗 supersonic〔ultrasonic〕 waves ¶ 초음파의 supersonic ; ultrasonic
— 발생기 an ultrasonic generator — 위저상(僞底像) 〖해양〗 the deep scattering layer 《DSL》 —학 supersonics ; ultrasonics
초이레, 초이렛날 初— the seventh of a month
초이튿날, 초이틀 初— the second of a month
초인 超人 a superman ¶ 초인적 superhuman // 초인적인 노력 superhuman〔Herculean〕 efforts
—격 superhumanity —적 superhuman ; preterhuman —적 노력 superhuman efforts —주의 supermanism
초인종 招人鐘 a call-bell ; a (door-) bell ; a buzzer
초일 初日 the first〔opening〕 day ; an opening ; [연극의] the première 《프》 ; the opening night of a show
초읽기 秒— countdown —하다 count down
초임 初任 the first appointment ¶ 초임 인사를 하다 make an inaugural address
— 교원 a newly appointed teacher —급 an initial salary ; an entrance wage ; a starting salary ¶ 초임급 10만원이었다 I started off〔began〕 with a salary of hundred thousand *won*.
초입 初入 [어귀] an entrance ; an entry ; an approach ; a way in ; the mouth ; [처음 들어감] the first entrance ¶ 초입에서 at the entrance
—길 the first entrance to a road 길— an entry to a road 동리 — an entrance〔approach〕 to a village ; the outskirts of a village
초자 硝子 ⇨ 유리(琉璃)
*초자연 超自然 supernaturalness ; supernatural agencies ¶ 초자연적인 supernatural ; preternatural
—력 supernatural forces —주의 supernaturalism
초잡다 草— make a draft 《of》 ; draft ¶ 연설을 초잡다 draft a speech
초장 初場 〖음악〗 the first movement ; [글] the first chapter ; the first of the verses of a Korean *sijo* poem
초장 初場 ① [시장의] the opening〔morning〕 market〔session, sale〕 ; the first session〔call〕 ¶ 시세가 높은 초장 〖증권〗 opening with higher quotations ② [첫머리판] the outset ; the start ; the beginning ¶ 초장에는 실패했다 I failed at first.
초장 醋醬 soysauce mixed with vinegar and pine-nut meal
초장파 超長波 〖통신〗 very low frequency 《V. L. F.》
초재 草材 native medicinal herbs
초저녁 初— early (in the) evening ; the early hours of evening ¶ 초저녁 잠이 들다 fall asleep early in the night // 그는 초저녁잠이 많다 He is a man who sleeps〔goes to bed〕 early in the evening. // 아직 초저녁이었다 The night was still young.
초적 草笛 a grass harp ; a grass blade vibrated between the lips
초전기 焦電氣 pyroelectricity
초전도 超電導 〖전기〗 superconduction
—성 superconductivity —체 a superconductor
초절 超絶 transcendence ; supremacy ; [탁월] excellence —하다 transcend ; excel ; surpass
—주의(론) transcendentalism —주의자 a transcendentalist
‡초점 焦點 a focus 《*pl.* ~es, -ci》 ; a focal point ¶ 초점을 맞추다 focus ; bring to a focus ; adjust the focus 《of》 // 초점이 맞다 be in complete focus // 공격의 초점이 되다 bear the brunt of an attack // 그의 말은 초점이 흐리다 His remark is beside the point. // 카메라 초점이 맞지 않았거나 셔터를 누를 때 카메라가 흔들렸다 Either your camera was out of focus or you shook it when pressing the shutter.
— 거리 the focal distance — 거리 측정 focometry ; focimetry — 거리 측정기 a focometer ; a focimeter —면 a focal plane —면 개폐 장치 a focal plane shutter — 심도(深度) the depth of a focus 고정 — 〖사진〗 a fixed focus 자동 — self-focus(s)ing 허(虛)〔주(主), 실(實)〕— a virtual〔principal, real〕 focus

⁑초조 焦燥 anxiousness ; impatience ; irritation ―하다 (be) impatient ; irritated ; anxious ¶ 초조하게 impatiently // 초조한 기분으로 in an impatient mood // 초조한 마음 an anxious state of mind // 초조해 하다 be impatient 《over》 ; fret ; be irritated ; grow anxious // 귀환을 초조하게 기다리다 wait impatiently for 《a person's》 return // 시험 결과를 몰라서 초조해하다 be anxious to know the result of an examination // 그 여자는 지각할까봐 초조했다 She was anxious lest she should be late for school. // 그렇게 초조해할 것 없다 You have nothing to fret about like that. // 내가 초조하지 않도록 네가 생각하고 있는 것을 말해 줘 Don't keep me dangling. Tell me what you think.

초조 初潮 the first menstruation ; the first menses

초종 初終 the whole period of mourning (from beginning to end) ¶ 초종이 끝나다 have gone through due formalities of mourning // 초종을 치르다 go through due formalities of mourning

초주검되다 初― be all but dead ; be more dead than alive ; be half-dead ; [남의 손에] be half-killed ; be nearly〔all but〕 killed ¶ 초주검되게 얻어맞다 be thrashed〔flogged〕 within an inch of one's life

초지 初志 one's original intention〔purpose〕 ¶ 초지를 관철하다 carry out one's intention ; accomplish one's original purposes // 초지를 버리다 desist from one's intention ; give up one's original aim // 초지를 굽히지 않다 stick to〔abide by〕 one's original intention // 초지일관하다 accomplish one's original intention

초지 草紙 paper used in preparing a rough copy〔draft〕

초지 草地 grassland ; a grassy place 〔plain〕 ; a green (field) ; [목초지] a pasture ; a meadow

초지니 初― a 2-year-old falcon

초진 初診 the first medical examination ―료 fee for the first medical examination ; the fee charged for a patient's first visit (besides that charged for his medical examination) ― 환자 a new patient 〔client〕

초집 抄輯 (a collection of) excerpts 〔abstracts〕 ―하다 excerpt 《from》 ; extract 《from》 ; make an abstract 《of》 ― 법안 extracts of bills ; a copy of extracted bills

초집 抄集 a call ; a summons 《*pl.* -es》 ; convocation ―하다 call ; summon ; convene ; convoke ; issue a call 《to》

초집 草集 literary drafts ; a collection of manuscripts
시문(詩文) ― (a collection of) manuscripts of one's literary works

초창 草創 origination ; beginning ; the start ; an early stage ¶ 사업의 초창 the beginning of a business〔an enterprise〕 ―기 infancy ; the pioneer days ; an early 〔initial〕 stage ¶ 인류의 초창기 the early days of mankind ; the most ancient days of human history

†초청 招請 invitation ―하다 invite 《a person》 to ; ask 《a person》 to ¶ 초청을 받다 be invited ; be asked 《to a dinner》 // 초청에 응하다 accept an invitation // 초청 받지 않고 가다 go uninvited // 초청 받고 오다 come by invitation // 강사를 초청하다 invite〔call in〕 a lecturer // 각국 대표를 평화 회의에 초청하다 call the representatives〔delegates〕 of each country to the Peace Conference
― 경기 an invitation game ―국 an inviting nation〔power〕 ―장 an invitation (card) ; a letter of invitation ¶ 초청장을 보내다 extend an invitation to 《a person》 피―국 an invited nation〔power〕

초체 草體 the cursive〔running〕 style of brushmanship ; [글자] a cursive character ¶ 초체로 쓰다 write in a cursive hand〔style〕
― 활자 script type

초추 初秋 early autumn〔fall〕 ; the beginning of autumn

초춘 初春 early spring ; the beginning of spring

초출 抄出 extraction ; excerption ; selection ―하다 make an extract 《from》 ; extract 《from》 ; excerpt 《from》 ; select 《from》 ; single out

초출 初出 appearing for the first time ; the first (of the season)
― 참외 the first melon of the season

초출 超出 excellence ; remarkableness ; outstandingness ; eminence

초췌 憔悴 haggardness ; emaciation ―하다 (be) haggard ; emaciated ; thin ; gaunt ; worn-out ¶ 얼굴이 초췌한 thin-faced ; haggard // 그는 모습이 초췌하다 He looks haggard. // 초췌하여 피골이 상접하다 He is very thin〔nothing but skin and bone, a bag of bones〕.

초취 初娶 one's first wife

초치 招致 (an) invitation ; a summons ―하다 summon ; invite ¶ 외국 대사를 회담에 초치하다 summon an ambassador for a conference

초친놈 a worthless playboy ; a rake of no promise

*초침 秒針 a second-hand (of a watch)

초콜릿 chocolate ; [한 개의] a chocolate ; a stick〔bar〕 of chocolate ¶ 초콜릿빛 chocolate ; chocolate-colored ; dark brown

초크 [백묵] chalk

초탈 超脫 transcendence ; detachment ; aloofness ―하다 transcend ; rise above the ways of the world ¶ 초탈한 태도 a disinterested attitude // 속세를 초탈하다

keep aloof from the world ; rise above the ways of the world

초토 焦土 scorched〔parched〕 earth ; burnt ground ¶ 초토화되다 be burnt to the ground ; be reduced to ashes // 아름다운 거리는 전쟁 때문에 초토화되었다 War turned the beautiful streets into ruins.
— 정책〔전술〕 the scorched-earth policy〔tactics〕

초특급 超特急 a superexpress (train) ¶ 초특급으로 by a superexpress (train)

초특작 超特作 a superproduction ; [영화의] a superfilm ; a suprafeature film ¶ 100만 달러 짜리 초특작 a one-million-dollar "Super Special"

초특작품 超特作品 a superfilm ; a superproduction ; a special feature

초판 初— the first edition ¶ 초판으로 5천 부 인쇄하다 print a first edition of 5,000 copies
—본(本) a copy of the first edition ; a "first-edition"

초피 貂皮 marten ; sable

초필 抄筆 [가는 붓] a fine (writing) brush

초하 初夏 early (in the) summer ; the beginning of summer

초하다 抄— [베끼다] copy ; transcribe ; [엮다] abstract ; make an abstract 〔extract〕 of

초하다 草— make a draft《of, on, from》; draft〔draw up〕《a bill》; write in rough form ¶ 법안을 초하다 draft a bill // 연설문을 초하다 draft out an address

초하룻날 初— the first (day) of the month

초학 初學 [처음 배움] first learning ; start of studies ; [초학의 학문] the rudiments ; elements ; a beginner's course ¶ 초학의 elementary ; rudimentary // 아직 초학이라 별로 배운 것이 없습니다 I am just a beginner and haven't learned much yet.
—자 a beginner ; a novice ; a tyro

초학 初瘧 the first attack of malaria

초한 初寒 the first cold of the season ; the first spell of cold weather

초함 哨艦 a patrol ship〔boat〕; a picket warship ⇨ 초계

초행 初行 a first trip〔journey〕 ¶ 유럽은 초행입니다 This is my first visit to Europe.
—길 a road new to one ; one's first trip

초현대적 超現代的 ultramodern

초현미법 超顯微法 ultramicroscopy

초현실주의 超現實主義 surrealism
—자 a surrealist

초혜 草鞋 straw sandals ⇨ 짚신

초호 礁湖 a lagoon

초혼 初昏 the evening dusk ; twilight ¶ 초혼이 되다 dusk falls

초혼 初婚 one's first marriage ¶ 그 여자는 45세의 초혼이었다 She married for the first time at (the age of) forty-five.

초혼 招魂 invocation of the spirit of a deceased —하다 invoke the spirit of the deceased (calling his name three times)
—제 a memorial service for the war dead ; Decoration Day

초화 草花 a flowering plant

초환 招還 recall ; summons —하다 recall ; summon〔order〕 home

초회 初回 the first time〔round〕
—(불입)금 [월부의] the first installment ; down payment ¶ 초회불입금 없는 월부 No money down.

촉 鏃 a pointed part ; a point ; [살촉] an arrow-head ; a steel point ; [펜촉] the pen ; the nib of a pen
만년필— the tip of a fountain pen 펜— a penpoint ; a nib

촉 燭 candlepower ; candlelight

촉각 觸角 〖곤충〗 a feeler ; an antenna《*pl.* -nae》; a tentacle ¶ 달팽이의 촉각 a horn of a snail

촉각 觸覺 a sense of touch ; tactile〔tactual〕 sense

†**촉감 觸感** tactile sensation〔impression〕; (the sense of) touch ; feel ¶ 촉감이 부드럽다〔딱딱하다〕 [사물이 주어] feel soft 〔hard〕 to the touch // 촉감이 좋다 [사물이 주어] be pleasant to the touch // 그것은 나무 같은 촉감이 있다 It feels like wood.

촉관 觸官 the touch〔tactile〕 organ ; the sense of touch

촉광 燭光 candlelight ; [강도] candlepower ¶ 30 촉광의 전구 a thirty candlepower bulb

촉구 促求 stimulating ; giving impetus 《to》; [요구] insisting ; pressing ; urging ; [격려] spurring

촉구하다 促求— [조르다] urge ; press ; [요구하다] demand ; call upon《a person to do》 ¶ 대답을 촉구하다 press《a person》 for an answer

촉규 蜀葵 [접시꽃] a rose mallow ; a hollyhock
—화(花) ⇨ 촉규

촉급 促急 pressure ; urgency ; imminence —하다 (be) pressing ; impending ; urgent ¶ 촉급한 문제 a matter of great urgency // 촉급한 용무로 on urgent business

촉노 觸怒 —하다 incur the displeasure of《one's superior》; touch off the anger of an elder ; provoke《a person》 to anger

촉대 燭臺 a candle-stick ⇨ 촛대

촉더데 鏃— [화살촉의 마디] the knot of an arrowhead ; the arrowhead point

촉돌이 鏃— an arrowhead vise ; a device used to insert or remove an arrowhead

촉력 燭力 candle power

촉뢰 觸雷 —하다 touch〔strike〕 a torpedo〔mine〕

촉루 燭淚 guttered candlewax

촉망 嘱望 expectation ; hope **—하다** expect〔hope〕 much from 《a person》 ; entertain expectations 《of》 ; hold expectations 《for》 ¶ 촉망할 만한 청년 a promising〔likely〕 young man ; a young man of much promise // 가장 촉망되는 학생 the most likely student to succeed // 모두가 그에게 촉망하고 있다 He is the hope of every man. // 그 사람은 크게 촉망받고 있다 Much is expected from him. /It is thought there is a great future for him. // 그는 장래가 촉망되는 사람이다 He is a man of promise.

촉매 觸媒 a catalyst ; a catalyzer
—독 catalytic poison **— 반응** catalysis **— 방지제** anti-catalyst **—법** the contact 〔catalytic〕 process **— 작용** catalysis **부(負)—** 〖물리·화학〗 a negative catalyst 〔catalyzer〕 ; an anticatalyst **항(抗)—** an anticatalyst

촉모 觸毛 a feeler ; tentacle ; an antenna (*pl.* -nae)

촉박 促迫 urgency ; imminence ; tensity **—하다** (be) imminent ; urgent ; pressing ¶ 시일이 촉박하다 A set-date is near at hand.

촉발 觸發 contact detonation ; [감동] an excitement ; an emotion 《stirred by》 ¶ 감정이 촉발되다 be stirred〔moved, excited〕
— 수뢰 a contact mine **— 장치** a contact-detonating device

촉새 〖새〗 a black-faced bunting ; Emberiza spodocephala
— 부리 a thing with the shape of a beak ; a person with a beak-shaped mouth

촉성 促成 promotion of growth **—하다** promote〔hasten〕 the growth 《of》 ; stimulate〔foster〕 the realization 《of》
— 재배 forcing culture ¶ 야채의 촉성 재배 intensive cultivation of vegetables **— 재배 야채** forced vegetables **— 재배용 온실〔온상〕** a forcing house〔bed〕

촉수 觸手 〖동물〗 a feeler ; a tentacle ; [접촉] touching ¶ 촉수 엄금 Hands off.
촉수를 뻗치다 관용 extend its tentacles

촉수 觸鬚 a feeler ; a tentacle ; a palp ; a barbel ; a palpus

촉언 囑言 verbally entrusting another with one's future affairs **—하다** ask 《a person》 to look after one's (future) affairs

촉지 觸知 tactile perception **—하다** feel ; perceive by touch ¶ 촉지할 수 있는 palpable ; tangible // 촉지할 수 없는 impalpable ; intangible

***촉진 促進** promotion ; speeding up ; furtherance ; acceleration ; facilitation ; hastening ; hurrying up **—하다** promote ; press for ; accelerate ; hasten ; speed up ; expedite ¶ 평화를 촉진하다 promote peace // 신운동을 촉진하다 give impetus to the new movement // 회복을 촉진하다 hasten its recovery // 실현을 촉진하다 hasten〔quicken〕 the realization // 식욕을 촉진하다 quicken〔stimulate〕 the appetite // 문명의 진보를 촉진하다 expedite the progress of civilization

촉진 觸診 〖의학〗 palpation **—하다** palpate ; examine by the hand

촉처 봉패 觸處逢敗 failure in every attempt〔turn〕 **—하다** fail in every attempt〔turn〕

촉촉하다 (be) moist ; damp ⇨ 축축하다

촉탁 囑託 entrusting〔charging〕 《a person》 with an affair ; commissioning ; commission ; part-time engagement ; [사람] a part-time employee ; a non-regular staff **—하다** entrust〔commission〕 《a person》 with 《a matter》 ; give 《a person》 charge of ¶ 대학 교수에게 외교 문제 연구를 촉탁하다 commission a university professor to study diplomatic problems
— 관리 a part-time employee of a government office **— 교원** a part-time teacher **은행 —** a part-time employee of a bank **학교 —의** a part-time school doctor

촌 寸 ① [단위] a Korean inch (치) ; a unit of linear measurement
② [촌수] a degree of kinship (especially on the father's side)
사— a cousin **삼—** an uncle

촌 村 a village ; a rural community ; the country side ; a rural district ¶ 촌에서 살다 live in the country
—사람 a villager ; village folk〔people〕 ; the inhabitants of a village **—살림** country〔rural, provincial〕 living

촌가 寸暇 a little〔moment's〕 leisure ; a little spare moment ¶ 촌가에 at odd moments // 촌가를 아끼어 독서하다 read at odd moments from one's work // 촌가라도 이용하다 make use〔take advantage〕 of odd moments // 촌가라도 헛되이 해서는 안 된다 You must make use every available time.

촌가 村家 a country house ; a village house

촌각 寸刻 a moment ⇨ 촌음

촌거 村居 country life ; rural living **—하다** live〔dwell〕 in the country

촌공 寸功 a bit of merit ; a small service ¶ 촌공도 없다 be devoid of the least merit

촌극 寸劇 a short dramatic performance ; a dramatic sketch ; a little piece of a side-show ; a skit

촌극 寸隙 a spare moment ; just a little while

촌길 村— a country lane〔road〕

촌내 寸內 near relatives

촌놈 村— a country fellow ; a country cousin ; a rustic ; a rube ; a boor ; a backwoodsman ; a country bumpkin ¶

촌놈의 티가 나다 have the earmarks of a peasant ; wear a rustic air ; have a bit of the country about one ; have hayseed in one's hair

촌뜨기 村— a countryman ; a peasant ; a hillbilly ; a hayseed ; a rustic ¶ 촌뜨기 같은 여자 a boorish〔countrified-looking〕girl∥촌뜨기 짓을 하다 commit untraveled men's blunders

촌락 村落 a village ; a hamlet

촌로 村老 a village senior〔elder〕

촌목 寸— a carpenter's notched marking tool

촌민 村民 villagers ; village folk〔people〕; inhabitants of a village

촌백성 村百性 country people〔folk〕

촌백충 寸白蟲 a tapeworm ; a taenia ⇨ 촌충

촌보 寸步 a few steps ¶ 피로해서 촌보도 옮길 수 없다 I am so tired that I can't move an inch.

촌부 村婦 a country woman

촌부자 村夫子 ⇨ 촌학구(村學究)

***촌사람 村—** a country person ; an inhabitant of the country ; a rural dweller

촌샌님 村— an aged countryman ; a village senior ; a country gentleman

촌수 寸數 the degree of kinship〔consanguinity〕; the distance of blood relationship ¶ 촌수를 캐다 trace the degree of kinship∥촌수가 멀다〔가깝다〕 be distant〔near〕 in kinship

촌스럽다 村— (be) farmerly ; countrified ; rustic ; boorish ; farmlike ¶ 촌스럽게 in country fashion

촌시 寸時 a moment ; an instant ; a second

촌외 寸外 a distant relative

촌음 寸陰 a moment ; an instant ; the slightest space of time ¶ 촌음을 아끼다 improve every minute〔moment〕; value each instant ; do not waste a single moment

촌장 村庄 a country house ; a rustic dwelling ; a cottage ; a country-seat ; a villa

촌장 村長 a village headman〔chief〕

촌전 척토 寸田尺土 a small farm〔field, lot〕

촌지 寸地 a smallest piece of land

촌지 寸志 a token of good will ; a slight token of gratitude ; a trifle present ¶ 촌지이니 받아주십시오 This is just a token of my gratitude, please accept it.

촌진 寸進 —하다 inch (oneself) ; advance inch by inch

촌철 寸鐵 a small weapon ; [경귀] a pithy saying〔remark〕; an epigram ; a bit of wit ¶ 촌철 살인의 경귀 a witty remark piercing home ; a very pithy remark∥몸에 촌철도 지니지 않았다 haven't the smallest weapon on one ; be quite unarmed ; be with naked fists〔hands〕

— 살인(殺人) [경구] a pithy epigram〔saying〕 touching《a person》 to the quick **—집(集)** a collection of epigrams

촌촌 村村 ¶ 촌촌 걸식 begging around from village to village∥촌촌이 돌아다니다 go around all the villages

촌충 寸蟲 a tapeworm ; a taenia

— 구제약 a taeniacide ; a taeniafuge **—류** tapeworms

촌탁 忖度 —하다 guess what is in《a person's》 mind ; sense《a person's》 feelings ; conjecture ¶ 자기 마음으로 남을 촌탁하다 judge others in terms of oneself ; measure other's corn by one's own bushel

촌토 寸土 an inch of ground〔territory〕; the smallest piece of land ¶ 촌토도 양보하지 않다 cede not an inch of ground〔territory〕; won't yield

촌퇴 寸退 —하다 inch (oneself) back

촌티 村— a smack〔taste, air〕 of the country《about a person》 ¶ 촌티나다 have a touch〔air〕 of the country about one ; have hayseed in one's hair

촌평 寸評 a brief comment《on》; a brief review《of》 **—하다** make a brief comment

촌학구 村學究 [촌부자] a village schoolmaster ; a rural pedagogue ; a rustic moralist ; [옹졸한 사람] a narrow-minded〔an obstinate〕 villager

촐랑거리다 ① [행동] act frivolous ; be irresponsible ; be flippant ; be slopping ¶ 촐랑거리며 돌아다니다 gad about ; flit〔flitter〕 about ② [물이] toss about ; splash ; lap ; slop ¶ 독의 물이 촐랑 거린다 The water in a jar is slopping from side to side.

촐랑이 a rash person ; a frivolous character

촐랑촐랑 ⇨ 촐랑거리다

촐싹거리다 act〔be〕 frivolous ; frolic ; [부추기다] agitate ; stir up ; make《a person》 restless

촐싹촐싹 ⇨촐싹거리다

촐촐 with an empty stomach ; without eating anything at all **—하다** be somewhat hungry ; feel a bit empty ¶ 촐촐 굶다 starve ; be absolutely famished∥촐촐하니 요기나 하세 Let's drop in somewhere to fill up our empty stomach, will you?

촘촘하다 (be) close ; dense ; thick ¶ 모를 촘촘하게 심다 plant rice seedlings close together∥촘촘한 박음새 close stitching ; close stitches∥일을 촘촘하게 하다 do an elaborate〔a painstaking〕 job of it

촛국 醋— an over-vinegared dish

촛농 —膿 guttered candle〔wax〕; drops of wax ; streams of melted wax running down a candlestick ¶ 촛농이 흐르다 (a candle) gutters down

*촛대 —臺 a candlestick ; a candlestand ; a candle holder ¶ 촛대에 초를 꽂다 fix a candle in a candlestick
*촛불 candle-light ¶ 촛불을 켜다〔끄다〕 light up〔put out〕 a candle // 촛불로 책을 읽다 read by candle-light
총 [말의] the hairs of a horse's mane
*총 總 all ; whole ; entire ; total ; general ; gross ; overall
—계산 a final〔full〕 settlement —소득 the gross income —수입 gross receipts ; the gross revenue ; the gross income —액 the total amount ; the whole sum —예산 the total budget ; the general estimates —인구 the total population 《of *Seoul*》 —자본 the total amount〔sum〕 of capital ; the fund total —지배인 a general manager —지출 total expenditures —지휘 the supreme command —지휘관 a commander-in-chief ; a supreme commander —톤수 the aggregate〔gross, total〕 tonnage —퇴각 a general〔full〕 retreat —파업 a general strike ; a genest
†총 銃 a gun ; a rifle ; firearms ¶ 총을 겨누고 with a rifle at the ready ; leveling one's rifle 《at》 // 총을 쏘다 fire〔shoot〕 a gun // 총을 메다 shoulder a gun // 총을 들다 take (up) a gun ; present a gun ; present arms
—신(身) the barrel of a gun 기관— a machine gun ; a maxim (gun) 단발— a single-loader 새— a fowling piece ; a bird gun 소— a rifle ; a musket ; small firearms 쌍대— a double-barreled gun 연발— a magazine-rifle ; a repeater 자동소— an automatic rifle 전장(前裝)— muzzle-loader ; a muzzle-loading rifle 후장(後裝)— a breechloader
총 寵 ⇨ 총애
총가 銃架 a rifle stand ; a gun rest 〔mount〕
총각 總角 a bachelor ; an unmarried man
처녀 — young people (of both sexes) ; young men and women
총감 總監 an inspector general ; a superintendent general ; a commissioner
총감독 總監督 〖야구〗 a general manager
총감투 a cap made of horsehair
*총검 銃劍 rifles and swords ; [무기] arms ; [총에 꽂는 칼] a bayonet ; sidearms ¶ 총검을 꽂다〔빼다〕 fix〔unfix〕 bayonets // 총검으로 찌르다 bayonet
—도(道)〔술〕 bayonet fencing〔drill, exercise, practice〕 —돌격 a bayonet charge
총격 銃擊 (rifle) shooting
—전(戰) (을 벌이다) gunfight
총결산 總決算 total〔final〕 settlement of accounts ; total liquidation ; final balancing of books —하다 settle〔balance〕 an account totally ; liquidate all ¶ 연말에 수입 지출을 총결산하다 balance the receipts and disbursements at the end of the year // 과거를 총결산하다 liquidate the past
총경 總警 a police superintendent
†총계 總計 a total ; the total ; the aggregate ; the gross ; [부사적] in all 〔total〕 ; all told ; all together ; by the gross〔lump〕 —하다 total ; totalize ; sum〔count, add〕 up ¶ 총계하면 약 7만원이 된다 The total amounts〔comes〕 to about 70,000 *won*. /It makes a total of 70,000 *won*.
총공격 總攻擊 a general〔all-out〕 attack 〔offensive〕 —하다 make a general attack 《on》 ; attack 《the enemy》 in full force ; open〔launch〕 a general offensive 《on》 ¶ 전전선에 걸쳐 총공격을 하다 launch an all-out offensive along the entire front
총괄 總括 generalization ; summarization ; summing up ; bracketing〔lumping〕 together ; a summary —하다 generalize ; summarize ; sum up ¶ 총괄적 general ; summary ; all-inclusive ; blanket // 총괄하면 in the lump ; as a whole ; en masse // 총괄해서 말하자면 generally speaking ; as a whole ; to sum up ; the long and short of it is... // 대체적인 총괄 a sweeping generalization
— 가격 a blanket price — 개념 a colligated concept(ion) ; an overall concept — 보험 comprehensive〔blanket〕 insurance — 운임 lump-sum freight — 의안 an omnibus bill ; a blanket clause — 저당(抵當) 〖법〗 a general〔blanket〕 mortgage — 조항 a blanket clause — 질의 [국회 따위에서의] a general interpellation
총구 銃口 the muzzle of a gun〔rifle〕
— 뚜껑 a muzzle cap — 마개 a plug
총군 總軍 the whole army
총급 悤急 a big hurry ; being very busy —하다 be in a hurry ; (be) very busy
총기 聰氣 brightness ; intelligence ; sagacity ; spark (of intelligence) ; sense ; wit ; a good memory ; retentiveness ¶ 총기가 있다 be bright〔intelligent〕 // 총기가 없다 be dull〔unintelligent〕 // 총기가 좋다 have a good〔retentive〕 memory // 그는 총기라고는 전혀 없다 He hasn't a lick of sense about him.
*총기 銃器 small arms ¶ 총기를 잘 다루다 be a good gun-handler
— 수리 field-stripping —실 a gun room ; an armory
총꾼 銃— a gunner ; a hunter ; a gunman ; a rifleman
총냥이 a thin person with large bulging eyes and a protruding mouth ; a foxy person
총대 銃— a gun stock ; the barrel〔barrel-mounting〕 of a gun
총대 總代 a representative ; a deputy ; [대변자] a spokesman ¶ 총대가 되다 represent // …의 총대로서 in〔on〕 behalf of ; representing // 회사의 총대가 되다

represent the company
총대리인 總代理人 a general agent 《at a place for a company》
총대리점 總代理店 a general agency ⇨ 총대리인(總代理人)
총대우 a hat(-top) made of horsehair 〔oxhair〕
총대장 總大將 [총사령관] a commander-in-chief 《*pl.* commanders-》; [두목] a leader; a captain; a boss
총댕이 銃— ⇨ 총군
†**총독 總督** a governor-general; a viceroy
— 지위〔직, 임기〕 governor-generalship; viceroyalty; viceroyship 인도 — 〖영국사〗 the Viceroy of India
총동원 總動員 a general mobilization —하다 make〔effect〕 a general mobilization 《of》 ¶ 총동원되어 in a body; in full force; all together // 총동원을 실시하다 mobilize the entire army // 산업계를 총동원하다 mobilize all of industry // 전학교가 총동원되어 식목했다 All the teachers and students took part in planting trees.
—령 orders for the mobilization of the entire army 국가 — national mobilization
총득점 總得點 the total score; total points〔runs, goals〕 made ¶ 총득점 10점을 얻다 score 10 in all
총람 總覽 a comprehensive〔an exhaustive〕 bibliography 《of, on》
총람 總攬 superintendence; general control —하다 superintend; oversee; preside over; control; supervise
총량 總量 [액] the total amount; [양] the total weight
총력 總力 total strength; the aggregate power; all one's energy; one's might and main ¶ 총력을 다하여 with all one's might
— 외교 a total diplomacy —전 a total〔totalitarian〕 war
총렵 銃獵 shooting 《미》; hunting 《영》; sporting —하다 hunt (with a gun); shoot ¶ 총렵(하러) 가다 go shooting 〔hunting〕 // 총렵을 금하다 prohibit hunting
— 금지기 the closed season —기 the hunting season; the open season — 면허장 a hunting〔shooting〕 license —법 a game law —복(服) a shooting coat —세 a hunting tax
총론 總論 an introduction; general remarks; a general summary; an outline ¶ 총론에서 각론으로 들어가다 proceed from the general principles〔a summary〕 to the details〔particular〕
민법 — an introduction to the study of civil law 화학 — the elements of chemistry
총론 叢論 a collection of treatises〔essays〕
문학 — a collection of essays on literature

총류탄 銃榴彈 a rifle grenade
총리 總理 ① [총관리] general overseeing 〔control〕; superintendence; presiding over —하다 preside over; oversee; control; superintend ¶ 국무를 총리하다 preside over〔run〕 affairs of state
② [수상] the premier; the prime minister
— 관저 the Prime Minister's official residence — 비서과 the Prime Minister's Secretariat —실 the Office of Premier —직 premiership 국무 — the Prime Minister 부(副)— the Deputy Prime Minister
총림 叢林 a dense wood; a bush; a grove; a thicket; a jungle
총망 悤忙 hurry; precipitation; being very busy —하다 be in a hurry; be in haste; (be) hurried; flurried ¶ 총망히 in a great hurry; hurriedly; in precipitation; hurry-scurry // 총망중에 그것을 잊어버렸다 I forgot it in my hurry.
총명 聰明 brightness; intelligence; sagacity; wisdom; a good memory —하다 be bright〔intelligent, sagacious, wise〕; have a good〔sharp, retentive〕 memory ¶ 총명이 불여둔필(不如鈍筆) No memory is the equal of even a dull pencil.
총목록 總目錄 the table of contents; a (general) catalog; a full list
총무 總務 [일] general affairs〔business〕; [사람] a manager; a director; an executive ¶ 국회 여〔야〕당 원내 총무 the majority〔minority〕 leader of the National Assembly; a floor leader; a legislative leader // 학우회 총무 a manager of the students' association
—과〔국〕 the general affairs section 〔bureau〕 —부 the general affairs department〔division〕 —부장 the chief of the general affairs department〔division〕 —처 the Ministry of Government Administration —처 장관 the Minister of Government Administration —회 [정당의] the Executive Council 원내 — a floor leader; a whip 학생회 — a manager of the students' association
총민 聰敏 cleverness; keenness; smartness and quickness —하다 (be) clever (and keen); smart and quick; sharp
총반격 總反擊 an all-out〔a full-scale〕 counterattack —하다 mount a general counteroffensive
총받이 銃— the firing line; the front line
총보 總譜 a score ¶ 연주를 들으며 총보를 보다 follow the score while listening to the music
총복습 總復習 [학과의] a general review of one's lessons; [연극의] a dress rehearsal —하다 [학과를] make a general review of one's lessons; go over all one's lessons; [연극을] make a dress

rehearsal
총본산 總本山 the head temple (of a Buddhist sect)
총부리 銃— the muzzle (of a rifle) ¶ 총부리를 겨누다 point〔aim at〕 a gun
총사 叢祠 〖민속〗 a shrine to various goods
총사 銃士 a musketeer ¶ 삼총사 The Three Musketeers (책이름)
총사냥 銃— shooting ⇨ 총렵(銃獵)
총사령관 總司令官 the commander-in-chief ; the supreme commander
총사령부 總司令部 the general headquarters 《G. H. Q.》
총사직 總辭職 general resignation ; resignation in a body〔en masse, en bloc〕 **—하다** resign in a body〔en masse〕 ¶ 내각 총사직 the resignation of the Cabinet // 내각이 총사직한다는 소문이 떠돌고 있다 There is a rumor that the Cabinet is going to resign en bloc〔en masse〕.
총살 銃殺 shooting 《a person》 to death ; execution by shooting **—하다** shoot 《a person》 to death ; execute 《a criminal》 by shooting ¶ 총살 당하다 be shot dead〔to death〕 ; be executed by a firing squad ; die before a firing squad
총살형 銃殺刑 execution by a firing squad〔shooting〕 ¶ 총살형을 선고받다 be sentenced to face〔die before〕 a firing squad
총상 銃傷 a bullet〔gunshot〕 wound ¶ 팔에 총상을 입다 receive〔have〕 a bullet wound in the arm // 총상으로 죽다 die from a bullet wound
총상 화서 銃狀花序 〖식물〗 a racemous inflorescence ; a raceme
복(複)— a compound raceme **소(小)—** a racemule ; a small raceme
총색인 總索引 a general index 《to a book》
총생 叢生 fasciculation ; dense〔thick〕 growth ; fascicle **—하다** grow dense〔thick〕 ; cluster ¶ 총생한 fasciculate ; fasciated ; fascicled
총서 叢書 a series (of books) ; a collection of books ; a library ¶ 총서로 출판되다 be published in a series
가정 — a home library **영문학 —** a series of English Literature
총선거 總選擧 a general election **—하다** hold a general election ; appeal〔go〕 to the country
총설 總說 introduction ; general remarks ⇨ 총세 백명 one hundred men in all〔all told〕 ; 《a party》 100 strong
총소리 銃— the report of a gun ; a gunreport ; a gunshot ¶ 총소리를 듣다 hear the report of a gun ; hear a shot
총손질 銃— cleaning of a gun ¶ 총손질 사고 a gun-cleaning accident
총수 總帥 the supreme leader ; the commander-in-chief
총수 總數 the total (number) ; the aggregate ¶ 총수 2,000이다 The total number is 2,000. /They number〔are〕 2,000 in all.
총수입 總收入 a gross〔total〕 income ; gross earnings
총수 화서 總穗花序 〖식물〗 a botryose inflorescence ¶ 총수 화서의 botryose
총신 銃身 (the bore of) the barrel of a gun ⇨ 총열
총신 寵臣 one's favorite retainer〔subject〕 ; a court favorite ; a minion
총아 寵兒 a favorite〔pet〕 child ; a favorite ; a darling ¶ 문단의 총아 a popular writer ; the star of the literary world // 시대의 총아 the lion of the day ; the man-of-the-day // 운명의 총아 a Fortune's favorite ; a pampered child of Fortune
***총안 銃眼** a loophole (to shoot through) ; a crenel ; an embrasure ; an eyelet ¶ 총안이 있는 crenellated // 총안을 내다 crenellate
총알 銃— a bullet ; a shot ¶ 총알을 잰 총 a loaded gun // 총알을 재우다 load〔charge〕 a gun ; load with a bullet // 총알을 빼다 extract the ball 《from》 ; unload a gun // 총알에 맞아 죽다 be killed by a bullet ; be shot dead // 총알이 다리에 박히다 get a bullet in the leg // 적에게 총알을 퍼붓다 rain bullets on the enemy ; subject the enemy to fire // 총알이 벽을 꿰뚫었다 A bullet went through a wall.
— 구멍 a shot hole ; a bullet hole **— 자국** a bullet mark ; a shot hole ¶ 그 선체에는 총알 자국이 나 있다 The hull is riddled with shot holes〔bullet marks〕.
총애 寵愛 favor ; good graces ; love ; patronage ; affection **—하다** love tenderly ; show 《a person》 favor ; lavish care on 《a person》 ; make a favorite 《of》 ; treat with great favour ; pet ¶ 총애하는 favorite // 총애를 받다 win 《a person's》 favor ; be in 《a person's》 favor〔good graces〕 // 총애를 잃다 lose 《a person's》 favor ; fall into disfavor 《with》
총액 總額 the total〔sum〕 amount ; the sum〔grand〕 total ; [부사적] in all ; in total ; in the aggregate ¶ 예산 총액 the total budget // 총액이 100만원이 된다 It amounts to a million *won* in the aggregate. /It totals〔aggregates〕 a million *won*.
— 2백만원 2,000,000 *won* in total **수출 무역 —** the total volume of export trade ; the total exports **예산 —** the total budget
총열 銃— the barrel of a gun
— 소제기 a jag
총영사 總領事 a consul general 《*pl.* consuls general》 ¶ 총영사의 직(職) consulate general
—관 a consulate general ¶ 뉴욕주재 한국 총영사관 Korean Consulate General in

New York
총우 寵遇 special favor ; patronage ; good graces **—하다** show special favor ¶ 총우를 받다 enjoy 《a person's》 special favor ; be in 《a person's》 good graces ; be a favorite with 《a person》
총원 總員 the whole〔total〕 number (of persons) ; the (entire) personnel ; all members ; [배의] all hands ; [부사적] in all ; all told ¶ 총원 100명 100 persons in all // 총원 경기에 참가하다 all (hands) join in a game // 총원 갑판으로 All hands on deck ! // 총원 기상 All hands turn out !
총의 總意 a common will ; general opinion〔sentiment〕 ; consensus (of opinion) ¶ 국민의 총의 the (collective) will of the people // 총의는 개정에 반대다 The consensus is against revision.
총의치 總義齒 a full set of false teeth ; a full denture
총자본금 總資本金 the nominal〔authorized〕 capital ; [등기필의] the registered capital
총장 總長 ① [학교] the president ; the chancellor (영국 대학의) ¶ 서울 대학교 총장 the President of the Seoul University
② [사무 총장] the secretary-〔director-〕general ¶ 국제 연합 사무 총장 the Secretary-General of the United Nations
③ [군대의] the chief of staff ¶ 육군 참모 총장 the Chief of Staff 《of the R. O. K. Army》 // 참모 총장 the Chief of the General Staff
총재 總裁 a president ; a governor ¶ 총재의 직 presidency ; governorship // 한국은행 (부)총재 the (vice-)governor of the Bank of Korea // 대한 적십자사 총재 the president of the Korean Red Cross Society // 총재가 되다 assume the presidency of
총점 總點 [시험 따위의] the (sum) total of one's marks ; [경기의] the total score ¶ 총점이 …에 이르다 one's marks total〔amount to〕...
총좌 銃座 a gun emplacement〔position〕
총죽 叢竹 a bamboo grove
총중 叢中 ¶ 총중에 amidst a crowd〔multitude ; throng〕 // 만록 총중 홍일점 a woman in a men's party // 만록 총중의 홍일점 격이었다 She was the only woman (that was) present among male members.
총중량 總重量 gross weight
총지배인 總支配人 the general manager
총지출 總支出 gross〔total〕 expenditure
총지휘 總指揮 the high〔supreme〕 command **—하다** take the supreme command of 《an army》
—관 ⇨ 총사령관
총질 銃— shooting ; firing **—하다** shoot 〔fire〕 (a gun)
총집 叢集 **—하다** crowd ; throng ; [새가] flock together ; [벌레가] swarm
총창 銃創 a gunshot wound ; a bullet wound
***총채** a horsehair duster ¶ 총채질하다 dust 《a thing》
총첩 寵妾 one's favorite mistress
****총체 總體** all ; the whole ¶ 총체적으로 generally ; in general ; generally speaking ; on the whole
총총 悤悤 hurriedly ; hastily ; in haste ; in a hurry ; quickly **—하다** (be) hasty ; hurried ; rushed ¶ 총총한 여행 a hurried journey // 총총히 briskly ; quickly ; hurriedly // 총총히 가버리다 hurry away 〔off〕 ; beat a hurry retreat
총총 蔥蔥 thickly ; dense(ly) ¶ 나무가 총총 들어서 있다 be planted close together ; be densely wooded // 모를 총총 심다 plant young rice seedlings close together
총총 叢叢 densely ; numerously **—하다** (be) dense ; crowded ; numerous ¶ 하늘에 별이 총총 박혀 있다 The sky is studded〔strewn〕 with stars.
총총걸음 a quick pace ; quick steps ; hurried walking ¶ 총총걸음으로 at a quick〔brisk〕 pace ; with quick short steps // 그 여자는 총총 걸음으로 사라졌다 She hurried away with mincing steps.
총총들이 蔥蔥— close ; tight(ly) ¶ 나무를 총총들이 심다 plant trees close to each other
총출동 總出動 general mobilization **—하다** be all mobilized ; be all called out ¶ 군대의 총출동 the general mobilization of troops // 어젯밤의 대화재에 소방차가 총출동했다 All the fire engines turned out in〔at〕 the big fire last night.
총칙 總則 general rules〔provisions〕
민법 — the general provisions of the civil code
총칭 總稱 a general name ; a generic term ; an overall designation **—하다** give a general name to ; call〔name〕 collectively ¶ 이들을 초식 동물이라고 총칭한다 Herbivora is the general term for these animals. /These are known generically as Herbivora.
총칼 銃— a gun and a sword ; fire arms
****총탄 銃彈** a bullet ; a shot
총톤수 總—數 a gross tonnage
총통 總統 a president ; a chancellor ; a generalissimo ; the Führer 《도》 ¶ 장개석 총통 *Chiang Kai-shek,* the Generalissimo ; president *Chiang Kai-shek*
총퇴각 總退却 a general〔full〕 retreat **—하다** make a general retreat ¶ 총퇴각 중이다 be in full retreat
총파 銃把 the grip 《of a gun》 ; [소총의] the small of the butt ; [권총의] the hand
총파업 總罷業 a general strike ¶ 총파업에 들어가다〔을 하다〕 go on a general strike ; call a general strike // 총파업을 선

언하다 declare〔proclaim〕 a general strike
총판 總販 sole agency〔trade〕 **—하다** make an exclusive sale of ¶ 총판을 특약하다 make〔enter into〕 a special contract for the sole agency
총평 總評 a general survey〔review, critique〕 ¶ 스포츠계의 총평 a general review of the sporting circles
총포 銃砲 guns ; fire-arms
—공(工) a gunman ; a gunmaker ; a gunsmith **—(상)점** a dealer in firearms ; a gun shop **—점주(店主)** a dealer in firearms ; a gun dealer **—화약류 단속법** the Firearms & Explosive Control Law
총피 제본 總皮製本 full〔whole〕 binding ¶ 총피 제본의 full-bound ; whole-bound ; bound in full leather
총할 總轄 general control〔supervision〕 ; superintendence **—하다** superintend ; preside over ; have general control 《over》
총합 總合 synthesis ; generalization ; gathering together **—하다** synthesize ; gather together ; piece〔put〕 together ; generalize ; integrate ; coordinate ¶ 총합적으로 synthetically // 총합하여 생각하다 think collectively // 이것 저것 총합해서 보면 piecing〔putting〕 this and that together ; taking one consideration with another ; all in all ; by and large
총화 銃火 rifle-fire ; gun-fire ¶ 총화를 무릅쓰고 under fire ; defying〔braving〕 the enemy's gun-fire // 총화를 교환하다 exchange fire with 《the enemy》
총화 總和 a total amount ; a sum〔grand〕 total **—하다** total ; sum up ; count up
총화 정치 總和政治 politics of integration
총회 總會 a general meeting ; a plenary session〔sitting〕 ; [종교의] a synod ¶ 총회의 의제로 올리다 submit 《a matter》 to the discussion of a general meeting // 결의를 총회에 붙이다 leave the decision up to a general meeting
유엔 — the U. N. General Assembly **임시〔정례〕 —** an extraordinary〔ordinary〕 general meeting **주주 —** a general meeting of stockholders〔shareholders〕 **창립 —** an inaugural assembly〔general meeting〕
총희 寵姬 one's favorite mistress
†**촬영 撮影** photographing ; picture-taking ; [영화] filming **—하다** take a photograph〔picture〕 of ; photograph ; photo ; snapshot ; film 《a scene》 ; shoot ; make a film of ¶ 사진을 촬영하다 take a photograph // 야외 촬영가다 go on a location // 내 사진을 촬영했다 I had〔got〕 my photograph taken. /I sat for a photograph. // 촬영이 금지되어 있다 Photographing is prohibited〔forbidden〕. /The use of a camera is not allowed.
— 감독 a movie director **—기** a moving-camera ; a movie camera **— 기사** a movie photographer ; a cinematographer ; a cameraman **— 기술** camera technique ; camera work ; cinematography **— 대본** a continuity **—(용) 대본 작자** a continuity writer **—소** a cinema〔film〕 studio ; a lot 《미》 **— 속도** crankspeed **— 시간** shooting time **—실** a studio **—자** a cameraman ; a photographer **부감(俯瞰) —** a crane〔boom〕 shot **실내 —** indoor photographing **야간 —** night photographing **야외 —** a location **옥외 —** outdoor photographing **재(再)—** a retake ; rephotographing ; reshooting **적외선 — 장치** an infrared imaging system
최- 最 the most ; the extreme ; ultra- ¶ 최하등의 the worst // 최적의 the most fitted〔suitable〕
—남 the southernmost **—남단** the southernmost **—첨단(尖端)** the spearhead **—하등** the worst
최강 最強 the strongest ¶ 최강의 the strongest 《team》 ; the most powerful 《nation》
*****최고 最高** maximum ¶ 최고의 the highest ; supreme ; maximum ; superlative // 최고의 인파 a record turnout // 올 여름 최고의 더위 the hottest weather (that) we have had this summer // 물가 지수가 최고에 달했다 The price index hit〔reached〕 a new high. // 게 요리는 이 식당이 최고야 Nothing beats this place for crabs.
— 가격 the highest〔top〕 price ; top dollar ¶ 당신의 집을 최고 가격으로 팔아드리겠습니다 I'll sell your house for top dollar. **— 가치** tops in value ; the highest value **— 간부** the executive **— 고문** a supreme advisor **—권** imperium ; absolute〔supreme〕 power **— 권위** the highest〔supreme〕 authority **— 기관** the highest organization〔institution, agency〕 **— 기록** the highest record ; a new〔an all-time〕 high ¶ 최고 기록을 깨뜨리다 break〔smash〕 the record **— 기온** the maximum temperature ¶ 오늘의 최고 기온은 34°였다 The maximum temperature today was 34 degrees. **—도** the highest degree ¶ 최고도로 이용하다 use 《one's talent》 to the highest degree ; make the best 《of one's talent》 **— 법규** the supreme law **— 법원** 〖카톨릭〗 the Rota **—봉** ⇨ 최고봉(峰) **— 사령관** the supreme commander ; the commander-in-chief **— 사령부** the highest〔supreme〕 command **—상** the highest〔first〕 prize ; a top-drawer award **— 속도** (a) maximum〔top〕 speed **— 수뇌 회의** a summit conference **— 수준** the highest watermark ¶ 최고 수준을 보이다 be the highest watermark **— 수훈 선수** 〖야구〗 the most valuable player 《MVP》 **— 열도** the maximum heat **—음** 〖음악〗 the treble ; soprano **— 임금** the highest wages ; the

wage ceiling — 임금제 the maximum wage system — 재판소 the Supreme Court 《미》 —점 the highest〔top〕 point ; [경기의] the highest score ; [시험의] the highest mark ¶ 그는 시험에서 최고점을 땄다 He gained the highest marks in the examination. // 그는 최고점으로 국회 의원에 당선됐다 He was elected a member of the National Assembly by the greatest number of votes. —조 [조수의] the high watermark ; [정점] the climax ; the zenith ; the acme ¶ 최고조에 달하다 reach〔hit〕 the climax // 최고조 상태다 be in full swing ; [사람이 주어] be in top form ; be at the tiptop of 《one's profession》 — 지휘관 the Supreme Commander — 책임자〔수뇌자〕 [정부 따위의] the highest〔chief〕 executive —층 the uppermost stratum —품 the best stuff ; tops — 품질 top〔the best〕 quality — 학부 the highest seat〔institution〕 of learning ¶ 최고 학부에서 배우다 study at a university — 한도 the maximum limit ; the highest limit ; the maximum ¶ 가격을 최고 한도로 인상하다 raise the ceiling for the price — 한란〔온도〕계 a maximum thermometer — 회의 the supreme council

최고 催告 notification ; demanding ; [지불의] call —하다 notify ; press 《a person》 for 《payment》

최고급 最高級 the highest〔top〕 grade 〔class〕 ¶ 최고급의 of the highest grade 〔order〕 ; top-level〔-ranking〕 ; first-rate ; best ; finest
—품 an article of the highest quality

최고 득점 最高得點 the highest point ; the highest〔top〕 mark(s) (시험의) ; a possible (경기) ; the highest poll (투표의) ¶ 최고 득점을 하다 get〔gain, win〕 the highest mark(s) ; score a possible (운동 경기에서) // (사격의) 800 야드에서 최고 득점을 올리다 score a possible at the 800 yards // 최고 득점으로 당선되다 be elected 《to the National Assembly》 with the highest poll〔with the largest number of vote, at the head of poll〕

최고봉 最高峰 ① [봉우리] the highest peak ② [비유적] the highest authority ; the acme ¶ 피아노의 최고봉 the greatest pianist // 영시의 최고봉 the highwater mark of English poetry // 현대 문학의 최고봉 the highest level of contemporary literature

최고위 最高位 the highest rank ; the top place ¶ 최고위를 차지하다 hold (the) top place ; rank first

최고 위원 最高委員 a member of the supreme council ; a supreme (council) member
대표 — the chairman of the supreme council ; the supreme representative ; the party president —회 the supreme council of a party

최귀 最貴 —하다 (be) most valuable ¶ 최귀 최선의 것들 things of the most valuable and the best

†최근 最近 [때의] the latest ; the nearest ; the most recent ; the latest date ; [거리의] the nearest〔shortest〕 ; [부사] lately ; in recent years ¶ 최근의 [시간] latest ; last ; recent ; up-to-date ; [거리] the nearest ; the shortest // 타임지의 최근호 the latest number〔current issue〕 of Time // 최근 5년간 in these〔the last〕 five years // 최근 출판된 책 a book recently published ; a recently published book // 최근에 그를 만나지 않았다 I haven't seen him lately. // 그 여자는 최근에야 여기 왔다 She has only come here just recently. // 최근까지 아주 더웠다 It was very hot until recently. // 최근에 언제 그를 보았습니까 When did you see him last ?
— 거리 the shortest distance — 소식 the latest news — 유행 the latest〔up-to-date〕 fashion —작 one's last〔latest〕 work — 작품 the latest works — 정보 the latest information

최근세 最近世 recent times ; the modern period ¶ 한국 최근세사 a History of Modern Korea

최급 最急 —하다 (be) most urgent 〔pressing〕 ; exigent ; burning
—무(務) the most urgent〔pressing〕 matter〔business〕 ; a matter of paramount urgency ; a matter demanding the most immediate attention ; an exigency

최긴 最緊 —하다 (be) most important ; essential ; indispensable ; vital ¶ 최긴한 문제 the most important question〔problem〕

최다 最多 being most numerous ; the maximum ; the greatest in number 〔quantity〕 ¶ 최다의 수〔액〕 the greatest〔largest〕 number〔quantity〕 // 최다의 군중 the largest crowd〔mob〕

최다수 最多數 the maximum ; the greatest number ; the largest majority ¶ 최다수의 결의 the decision of the largest majority // 최다수의 최대 행복 the greatest happiness of the greatest number

최단 最短 the shortest ; the nearest (distance) ¶ 최단의 the shortest // 이 길은 샌프란시스코로 가는 최단의 코스입니다 This is the shortest course〔cut, route〕 to San Francisco.
— 거리 the shortest〔nearest〕 distance ¶ 최단 거리를 가다 go the nearest way ; take the shortest course — 시일 the shortest time

최단 조업 最短操業 the daily operations 《of a mill》 for the shortest possible time —하다 cut down〔curtail〕 the operations 《of a mill》 to the minimum

†최대 最大 the greatest ; the biggest ; the largest ; the maximum ¶ 최대의 the greatest ; maximum (최대한) // 최대 다수

의 최대 행복 the greatest happiness of the greatest number // 최소의 노력으로 최대의 능률을 올리다 find the maximum efficiency with the minimum of labor // 최대 속력이 시속 120마일에 이르다 attain a maximum speed of 120 miles an hour // 최대의 노력을 기울이다 exert every effort 《in》; make every possible effort ; do one's very best

— 강우량 the maximum rainfall — 공약수 the greatest common measure 《G. C. M.》 —량 the largest〔maximum〕 amount — 속도 the highest〔maximum〕 speed — 압력 the maximum pressure — 장력(張力) the maximum tension —한(도) the maximum — 한(도) 능률 the maximum of efficiency — 확률 측정법 〖통계〗 maximum likelihood estimation

†**최대 한도 最大限度** the maximum ¶ 최대 한도의 비용 the maximum expense 〔allowance〕 // 최대 한도의 능률을 내다 put out〔have, show〕 the maximum efficiency ; make every effort to 《do》 // 최대 한도의 속력을 내다 run with the maximum speed // 최대 한도로 활용하다 make the maximum use 《of》 // 건축비의 최대 한도는 600만원이다 The building cost must not exceed 6,000,000 *won.* /The maximum appropriation for building is six million *won.*

최량 最良 the best ; the most excellent ; the supreme ; the ideal ¶ 품질 최량이다 be〔stand〕 supreme in quality ; be the best〔highest〕 quality ; be top in quality

최루 催淚 causing〔producing〕 tears
— 가스 tear gas —탄 a tear bomb ; a lachrymatory bomb ¶ 경찰은 데모하는 군중을 최루탄으로 저지했다 The city police stopped the crowd in demonstration by using teargas bomb. — 피스톨 a tear-gas pistol

최면 催眠 hypnosis ; hypnotic〔induced〕 sleep ; hypnogenesis ; somnolency ¶ 자기 최면 self-hypnotism
— 상태 a hypnotic spell〔state〕; hypnosis ; hypnotism ¶ 최면 상태에 빠지다 be hypnotized // 최면 상태에서 깨우다 dehypnotize ; break the hypnotic spell — 상태자 a hypnotic ; a person under hypnosis — 요법 a hypnotic cure ; hypnoanalysis —제 a sleeping drug〔tablet〕 —학 hypnology

최면술 催眠術 hypnotism ; mesmerism ¶ 최면술의 mesmeric ; hypnotic // 피최면술자 a hypnotic subject ; a person under hypnosis // 최면술을 걸다 mesmerize ; hypnotize ; exercise a mesmeric power over // 최면술에 걸리다 be hypnotized 〔mesmerized〕; go into〔fall under〕 hypnosis // 연사의 웅변에 청중은 마치 최면술에 걸린 듯했다 The speaker's eloquence hypnotized the audience.
—사 a hypnotist ; a mesmerist — 수면 somnipathy — 요법 a hypnotic treatment ; hypnotherapy — 피술자(被術者) a hypnotic subject 자기 — self-hypnotism

최면제 催眠劑 a sleeping pill〔drug〕; a soporific ¶ 자살하기 위하여 최면제를 과도히 먹다 take over-doses of sleeping pills to take one's own life

최북 最北 the northernmost ¶ 최북의 northernmost
—단 the northernmost tip〔extremity〕

***최상 最上** the best ; the finest ; the highest ¶ 최상의 the best ; the finest ; the highest ; supreme ; top-notch ; A-one // 최상의 행복 the supreme happiness ; bliss // 최상의 품질 the best〔choicest, top〕 quality
—권 supreme power ; supremacy —급 〖문법〗 the superlative degree ; [학교] the top class —급생 a senior (student) —등 the top grade ; the first order ; the highest class ; A-1 —선(善) the supreme good ; *Summun bonua* 《라》 —층 the uppermost story (of a building) ; the top floor ; [계급] the upper-crust ; high society ; the social elite —품 an article of the highest〔best〕 quality ; the best stuff — 행복 the supreme happiness

최서 最西 the westernmost

최선 最善 the highest good ; [노력] the best ; one's (level) best ¶ 최선의 노력을 다하다 do one's best〔utmost〕; put〔exert〕 one's best efforts ; do everything in one's power ; to do one's level best 《구》 // 그로서는 최선을 다했다 He did the best that was in him. // 최선을 다해보겠습니다 We'll see what we can do. // 최선을 다해보고 안되면 다시 생각하겠다 I'll give it my best shot, and if I can't hack it, I'll decide what to do then. // 최선을 다했기 때문에 어떤 결과가 나도더라도 후회는 없다 I gave it my best shot, so I have no regrets no matter how it turns out.

최선 最先 the first ; the foremost ; the head ; out in front ¶ 최선으로 도착하다 arrive first ; arrive ahead of others // 최선으로 달리다 run at the head ; run ahead

최성기 最盛期 the golden age〔days〕; the height of prosperity ; the zenith ; the prime ; the season ¶ 남자 40이면 최성기에 있다 A man of forty is in the prime of life. // 사과는 지금이 최성기다 Apples are in seasons now.

‡**최소 最小, 最少** the smallest ; the fewest ; the minimum ; the least ; [부사적] at the least ; at the minimum ¶ 회사의 인원을 최소한으로 줄이다 minimize the numbers of the company workers // 비용을 최소한으로 줄이다 reduce expenses to the minimum // 최소의 노력으로 최대의 효과를 올리다 achieve a maximum of efficiency with a minimum of effort // 최

소한 5년은 걸리겠다 It will take five years at least〔at the minimum〕.

— 곡률(曲率)〔작용, 속박〕 원리 〖물리〗 the principle of least curvature〔action, constraint〕 — 공배수 the least common-multiple《L. C. M.》 — 공분모 the least common denominator — 노력 a minimum of effort —량 the minimum quantity — 비용 the least expense —액 the smallest sum〔amount〕 — 자승법 〖통계〗 the method of least squares — 저항 the least resistance — 전류 a minimum current — 치사량 the minimum lethal dose — 한도 the minimum ; the bottom limit — 혈압 minimum blood pressure

최신 最新 ¶ 최신의 the newest ; the latest ; up-to-date ; up-to-the-minute // 사실 이것은 가장 최근에 시장에 나온 최신 제품입니다 As a matter of fact, this is a state-of-the-art product just out on the market.

— 뉴스 red-hot news —식 the newest〔latest〕 type〔style〕 —식 군함 a warship of the newest type —식 유행 the latest fashion ; the newest fashion —식 호텔 a hotel with the latest improvements ; an ultramodern hotel — 유행 모자〔수트〕 a new-look hat〔suit〕 —형 the latest〔newest〕 model

최신세 最新世 〖지질〗 the Pleistocene epoch ¶ 최신세의 Pleistocene

최심 最甚 the most extreme〔excessive〕 ; the severest〔heaviest〕 ; the worst —하다 (be) most extreme〔excessive〕 ; severest ; heaviest ; worst ¶ 피해가 최심하다 suffer the worst damage

최악 最惡 the worst ¶ 최악의 경우에는 at the worst ; if things come to the worst // 최악의 경우에 대비하다 prepare oneself for the worst // 최악의 경우가 도래하였다 The worst has come to the worst. // 최악이었다 The pits. // 최악의 사태가 나면 회사는 언제라도 부동산을 팔 수 있다 If worst comes to worst, the company can always sell off its real-estate assets. // 최악의 경우에는 철야를 해서 다시 만들어 내는 수 밖에 없다 If worst comes to worst, we'll just have to stay up all night and make them again.

—형 the worst〔severest〕 punishment

최우등 最優等 being most excellent ; superiority ; the top(-notch) grade ; the highest class ¶ 최우등의 the most excellent ; the best ; superior head // 최우등으로 졸업하다 graduate with top honors〔the greatest distinction〕

—생 a top student ; a top-honors man ¶ 우리 아들은 대학을 최우등생으로 졸업했다 My son graduated summa cum laude from his university. —품 the most excellent stuff ; an article of superb quality ; A-1 goods ; a choice article

최우수 最優秀 the very best ; the unsurpassed ; an A1 ; an ace —하다 (be) (very) best ; most excellent ; ace ¶ 최우수한 비행사 an ace of aces // 최우수한 학자 the best scholar

최유제 催乳劑 a galactagogue ; a lactagogue

최음제 催淫劑 an aphrodisiac (medicine)

최장 最長 the longest ; the oldest ¶ 최장의 (the) longest // 최장 다섯자를 넘지 못하다 do not exceed five feet at the longest

— 거리 the longest distance — 교량 the longest bridge —년자 the oldest person

최저 最低 the lowest ; the lowermost ; the minimum ¶ 최저액으로 견적하다 make a minimum estimation ; estimate at a minimum // 월급이 최저 십만원은 된다 The salary is 100,000 *won* at the lowest. // 오늘의 최저 기온은 10도에서 14도 사이로 떨어지겠지만 바람 때문에 실제 체감 온도는 영하로 훨씬 떨어질 거라는 예보야 Today's low will drop to the lower 10's, they forecast, but the wind chill will be way below zero. // 최저 기온은 영하 15도다 It reaches a low of fifteen degrees below zero.

— 가격 the minimum〔lowest〕 price ; the floor〔bottom〕 price ¶ 최저 가격으로 드리겠습니다 I'll give you a rock-bottom price. — 경매 가격 a reserved price — 기록 the lowest record ; a new〔an all-time〕 low 《미·구》 — 보증 소득 guaranteed minimum earning — 생활 a minimum standard of living — 생활비 a minimum cost of living — 수익점 〖경제〗 the margin — 연령 the minimum〔lowest〕 age — 온도계 a minimum thermometer — 음부 〖음악〗 bass — 임금 the minimum wage — 임금법 the Minimum Wages Act — 임금제 the legal minimum wage system — 필요 조건 minimum requirements — 한란계 a minimum thermometer

최적 最適 (being) the best suited ; best fitted ; most suitable ; most agreeable

—격자 a best-fitted person — 규모 [기업 등의] the optimum size — 기준 the optimum standard ¶ 최적 기준 임금 the optimum standard wages — 속도 the optimum speed — 온도〔밀도〕 the optimum temperature〔density (인구의)〕 — 조건 the optimum (condition) —화(化) 〖경제〗 optimization

최전방 最前方 ⇨ 최전선

최전선 最前線 the frontmost line(s) ; the foremost front ; the advance〔first〕 line ; the line of battle

최종 最終 ¶ 최종의 last ; final ; terminal // 최종까지 to the last〔end〕 // 최종에 가서 in the end

— 결정 the final decision — 목적 ultimate object — 무기〔병기〕 the ultimate weapon — 수용자(需用者) an end user — 시험 the final〔last〕 examination —안

the final program〔plan〕 — **열차〔차〕** the last train〔car〕 — **용도** 〖경제〗 end use — **일** the last day ; the closing day ¶ 최종일의 회의 the last-day session // 흥행의 최종일 the leave-taking day of a theatrical performance — **침전지(沈澱池)** [상수도] a final settling tank —**회** the last round ; the last inning(s)

최초 最初 the very first ; the very beginning ; the start ; the outset ¶ 최초의 first ; original ; initial // 최초에 first (of all) ; in the first place ; to begin〔start〕 with // 최초의 경험 one's first〔new〕 experience // 최초의 계획 the original plan // 최초의 목적 one's primary object // 최초의 3년간 the first three years // 최초의 사건 the first happening // 최초에는 그럴 계획이 아니었다 It wasn't the original plan to do so. // 급료는 최초에 60만 원이며 차차 승급할 수 있다 You will start at 600,000 *won*, but will get a gradual raise.

최하 最下 the lowest ; the most inferior ; the worst ¶ 최하의 the lowest ; the worst // 그는 인간으로서는 최하다 He is a low-down good-for-nothing.
— **가격** the minimum〔lowest〕 price —**급** the lowest grade〔class〕 ; the worst —**급생** a student of the lowest class —**등** the lowest class〔grade〕 —**등품** an article of the worst quality〔lowest grade〕 ; the worst stuff —**류** the lowest stream —**부** the lowest part ; the foot ; the bottom — **연령** the minimum〔lowest〕 age —**위** the lowest rank〔position〕 ; [야구] the tail end —**위팀** the tailender —**층** the lowest class〔grade, stratum〕 ; [건물의] the lowest story (of a building) ; the ground floor —**층 계급** the lowermost class —**품** the worst stuff ; an article of the lowest grade〔quality〕

최혜국 最惠國 the most favored nation
— **대우** most-favored-nation treatment — **조관(條款)〔약관(約款)〕** the most-favored-nation clause — **조약** a most-favored-nation treaty

최호하다 最好— like〔love〕 best〔most〕 ; be the best ; be the finest

최확치 最確値 〖측량〗 the most probable value

최활 a flexible stick used as a cloth stretcher on a loom

최후 最後 ① the last ; the end ; the conclusion ¶ 최후의 the last ; final ; closing ; ultimate // 최후로 lastly ; finally ; in conclusion ; in the end // 최후까지 to the last end // 최후의 심판 the Last Judgment ; the great〔last〕 account ; doom // 최후의 희망 one's last hope // 이 책의 최후의 2페이지 the last two pages of this book // 최후의 한 방울까지 마시다 drink to the last drop // 최후의 승리를 얻다 win in the long run ; win an ultimate victory // 강의를 최후까지 듣다 sit out the lecture // 영화를 최후까지 보다 sit through the movie // 최후의 5분간이 중요하다 The last five minutes determines the issue. // 그는 최후로 한 마디 했다 He said a few words in conclusion. // 최후로 그 사람을 한번만 더 보고 싶다 I would like to see him again one last time. // 그들은 최후까지 싸웠다 They fought to the last〔end〕. / They fought it out.
② [죽음] one's death〔end〕 ; one's fate ¶ 비참한 최후를 마치다 meet〔face〕 a tragic end ; die a tragic death // 최후를 지켜보다 watch 《a person》 die ; be present at 《a person's》 deathbed ; see 《a person's》 last
— **결과** a final issue — **노력** a last spurt effort — **만찬** 〖기독교〗 the Last Supper — **수단** the last resort〔resource〕 ; the ultimate〔final〕 step ; an extreme measure — **순간** the last〔critical〕 moment ¶ 최후 순간에 우리를 저버리다니 그 사람답다 It was like him to fail us at the last minute. — **승리** the final〔ultimate〕 victory — **심판** the Last Judgment ; the Great Assize — **운명** one's (final) destiny ; one's (ultimate) fate — **저항** a last-ditch resistance — **점검** a last-minute check-up — **통첩** an ultimation ; a final note ¶ 최후 통첩을 보내다 send〔deliver〕 an ultimatum

추 錘 [저울의] a weight ; a poise ; [낚싯줄의] a bob ; a sinker ; [먹줄의] a plumb ; a plummet ; [시계의] a pendulum weight ; the bob of a clock ¶ 추를 달다 weight 《a thing》 // 낚시추를 달다 weight a line

추가 追加 an addition ; [추가물] an addendum 《*pl.* -da》 ; an appendix 《*pl.* ~es, dices》 (부록) ; supplement —**하다** add〔append〕 《a thing》 to another ; supplement ¶ 추가의 additional ; supplementary // 예산에 추가하다 supplement a budget // 주문을 추가하다 add to one's order // 차표를 2인분 추가하다 obtain tickets for two more persons
— **가협정(假協定)** a provisional supplementary arrangement — **공사** additional works — **관세** an additional duty — **기입** 〖부기〗 a postentry — **녹음** 〖영화〗 rerecording — **배당** a supplementary dividend — **비용** additional expenses — **시험** a supplementary〔make-up〕 examination ¶ 추가 시험을 보다 take a make-up test — **예산** a supplementary budget — **예산안** a supplementary budget bill — **조항** an added article ; a rider ; a codicil — **주문** an additional order — **지출** a supplementary appropriation

추가 경정 예산 追加更正豫算 a revised supplementary budget ¶ 추가 경정 예산을 편성하다 draft〔formulate〕 a revised supplementary budget

추간 追刊 additional publication **—하다** publish in addition
추거 推擧 recommendation ⇨ 추천
추격 追擊 pursuit ; chase ; a follow-up attack **—하다** pursue ; give chase 《to》; press (hard) 《on》 ¶ 적을 맹렬히 추격하고 있다 be in hot pursuit of the enemy ; be pressing hard on the enemy **—기** a pursuit plane ; a pursuer ; a chaser **—전** a running fight ; a battle of pursuit **—포** 〖해군〗 a chase gun ; a (bow) chaser **정미(正尾) —** 〖해군〗 stern chase
추격 붙이다 追擊— ① [습진(習陣)시키다] hold〔carry out〕 maneuvers ; do military exercise ; hold a sham battle 〔fight〕
② [이간시키다] make 《persons》 quarrel ; make 《a person》 quarrel with 《another》; alienate〔estrange〕《a person》 from 《another》; put 《a person》 into dispute with 《another》
추경 秋耕 autumn plowing
추경 치다 관용 plow in autumn ; till a field in autumn ; do the autumn〔fall〕 plowing
추경 秋景 autumn scene ; autumnal scenery
추계 秋季 autumn ⇨ 추기(秋期)
— 운동회 an autumn sports〔athletic〕 meet〔meeting〕
추계 推計 estimation
—지(紙) stochastic paper **—학** stochastics ; the theory of statistical inference **— 학자** a stochastician ; an inductive statistician **— 한도〔한계〕** 〖총계〗 a stochastic limit
추고 推敲 polish〔improvement〕 (of writing) ; elaboration (of writing) ; choice of diction **—하다** polish ; improve ¶ 추고에 추고를 거듭하다 work hard to polish out 《the composition》// 추고의 여지가 있다 admit of further polish
추고 推考 inference ; deduction ; deliberation **—하다** infer ; deduce ; deliberate ; investigate ¶ 당신 말로 추고하건데 당신은 이 계획에 반대인 것 같다 I should infer from your remark that you are against this plan.
추곡 秋穀 the harvested〔an autumn〕 grain〔rice〕
— 수매 a purchase of autumnal harvest grain by the government
추골 椎骨 〖해부〗 a vertebra 《*pl.* -brae, ~s》
추괴 醜怪 ugliness ; grotesqueness **—하다** (be) ugly ; grotesque
추교 醜交 an illicit connection ; an evil relation ; an improper relation ; a liaison ¶ 추교의 소문 a rumor of a scandalous relation // …와 추교를 맺다 have an illicit〔a scandalous〕 relation 《with》; have a very ugly affair 《with》
추구 追求 pursuit ; chase ; running after ; going into thoroughly **—하다** pursue ; seek〔search〕《after, for》; run after ; go into thoroughly ; press hard ¶ 행복의 추구 the pursuit of happiness ; the search for happiness // 추구하여 in quest of ; in pursuit of // 죄상을 추구하다 press 《a person》 to confess his crime ; go after〔dig into〕 the facts of a crime // 그는 지위와 권력 추구의 일생을 보냈다 He spent his whole life in pursuit of rank and power.
추구 追究 thoroughgoing study ; close inquiry ; thorough investigation **—하다** inquire into 《a matter》 closely ; cross-examine ¶ 문제를 추구하다 study a problem thoroughly // 진리를 추구하다 seek truth
추구 推究 thinking through 《a matter》; inference **—하다** infer ; inquire into 《a matter》 thoroughly
추궁 追窮 close inquiry ; pressing hard ; thorough investigation **—하다** go after ; probe to the bottom ; press 《a person》 hard ¶ 책임을 추궁하다 call 《a person》 to account
추근추근 tenaciously ; persistently ; doggedly ; demandingly **—하다** (be) dogged ; tenacious ; persistent ; importunate ; demanding ¶ 추근추근한 사람 a dogged person ; a nuisance // 추근추근 …하다 be persistent〔tenacious, demanding〕 in doing // 여자를 추근추근 쫓아다니다 keep after〔pester〕 a girl ; pursue a girl doggedly // 추근추근 묻다 pester 《a person》 with questions // 아이는 할머니에게 캔디를 달라고 추근추근 졸랐다 The child teased his grandmother for some candy.
추급 追及 overtaking ; catching up 《with》 **—하다** overtake ; catch up 《with》
추급 追給 supplementary pay ; additional grant〔allowance〕 **—하다** provide as supplementary pay ; supply additional grant〔allowance〕
추기 秋氣 an indication of autumn (in the air) ; a sign of autumn ; the early chill of autumn
추기 秋期 an autumn ; fall 《미》
추기 追記 an additional note ; an addendum ; an epilog(ue)
추기 樞機 the most important affairs (of state) ; the helm of the state ; the vital part (of a thing) ¶ 추기에 참여하다 take part in the deliberation of the most important state affairs
—경 a Cardinal (of the Roman Church)
— 경 회의 the Consistory
추기다 [꾀다] instigate ; stimulate ; entice ; seduce ; tempt ; [선동하다] incite 《a person》 to do ; egg 《a person》 on ; stir up ; [개 따위를] set 《a dog》 on〔at〕《a person》 ¶ 추겨서 싸우게 하다 egg 《a person》 on

to fight // 그들은 노동자들을 추겨서 파업하도록 꾀했다 They tried to instigate the workers to go on strike.

추깃물 water from a rotting corpse ; cadaveric fluid

추남 醜男 an ugly (looking) man ; an ill-favored man

추납 追納 supplementary pay(ment) ; a follow-up payment

추녀 the eaves ; the protruding corners of Korean eaves ¶ 추녀 끝에 매달린 고드름 icicles hanging from the eaves

추녀 醜女 an ugly woman ; an unlovely woman

추념 追念 commemoration ; remembrance **—식** a commemoration ceremony

추다[1] [찾아내다] find out ; recover ; get back ; rummage out ; worm out (비밀 따위를) ; [추리다] arrange〔put〕 in order ; set rights ; square (up) ; [올리다] pull up ; lift ¶ 비밀을 추어내다 worm out ⟪a person's⟫ secrets // 짚을 추(어내)다 pick straws ⟪weeding out the short unwanted ones⟫ // 몸을 추다 lift oneself up

추다[2] praise ; speak highly of ¶ 공부 잘한다고 추(어주)다 praise ⟪a student⟫ for his good marks

추다[3] dance ¶ 춤을 추다 dance (a dance) ; perform a dance // 장단에 맞추어 춤을 추다 dance to the music〔a melody〕 // 폴카를 추다 dance a polka // 남의 장단에 춤을 추다 dance to someone else's tune ; dance to ⟪a person's⟫ piping ; be made a puppet by another ; be manipulated // 다음에는 저와 추시지 않겠습니까 May I have the next dance with you ?

추단 推斷 [판단] inference ; deduction ; [처단] judgment ; decision ; punishment **—하다** infer〔deduce, gather〕 (from evidence) ; [처단] render judgment on ; mete out punishment for ¶ 기지의 사실로부터의 정당한 추단 legitimate inference from known facts // 그의 말투로 보아서 그가 이 조건에는 불복인 것으로 추단된다 I gather from his words that he is not satisfied with the terms. // 이들 사실로부터의 추단은 극히 명확하다 The inference from these facts is quite〔perfectly〕 obvious.

추담 醜談 filthy〔indecent, nasty, foul〕 talk ; a dirty story ; a smutty story ¶ 추담을 하다 tell an obscene story ; talk filth〔smut〕

추대 推戴 —하다 have ⟪a person⟫ as head〔president, director〕 ; be under (the presidency of) ¶ N 박사를 교장으로 추대하다 have Dr. N as〔for〕 the director of the school // 그 구락부는 이 박사를 회장으로 추대하고 있다 That club is under the presidency of Dr. *Lee*.

추도 追悼 mourning ; lamentation **—하다** mourn for〔over〕 ⟪a person⟫ ; lament ⟪a person's death⟫

—가 an elegy ; a requiem **—문** a memorial writing **—사** a memorial address〔tribute〕 ; a funeral oration ¶ 추도사를 하다 pay a tribute to the memory of ⟪a person⟫ **—시** an *in memoriam* poem ; a monody **—식** a memorial service ; a memorial ceremony ¶ 고 케네디 대통령 추도식 the memorial service for the late President Kennedy // 10월 10일에 Y씨의 추도식을 개최하오니 참석을 바랍니다 We are going to hold a meeting in memory of Mr. Y on the tenth of October, so we ask you to be present at it. **—회** memorial services

추돌 追突 a rear-end collision ; a bump ; a rear-ending **—하다** dash〔bump, clash〕 ⟪against a thing⟫ from behind ; collide ⟪with a thing⟫ from behind ; run into ⟪a car⟫ from behind ; telescope into ⟪another car⟫

추락 墜落 a fall ; a crash ; a plunge **—하다** fall ; drop ; crash ; plunge ¶ 지상에 추락하다 crash ; fall to the ground // 거꾸로 추락하다 fall headlong to the ground // 추락사하다 be killed in a fall // 비행기 추락으로 죽다 be killed in an airplane crash // 기차에서 추락하다 fall from a train // 위신이 추락되다 lose one's prestige〔authority〕 ; be humiliated

— 비행기 a crashed plane **—사** death from a fall **— 지점** [비행기의] the crash site

추량 秋涼 autumnal cold ¶ 추량지절(-之節) cold autumn weather

추량 推量 guess ; conjecture ⇨ 추측

추레하다 (be) shabby ; poor-looking ¶ 차림새가 추레하다 be in seedy clothes

추려내다 pick out ; single out ; weed out ⇨ 추리다

추력 推力 thrust ; impellent〔driving〕 force ¶ 발사시의 추력 a lift-off thrust // …의 추력을 내다 generate〔yield, develop〕 a thrust of...

추렴 collection of money ; raising of money ; [각자 부담] sharing the expenses ; going Dutch ; a Dutch treat **—하다** collect〔raise〕 money ; make up a purse ; pass a hat around ; have a Dutch treat ; go Dutch ¶ 돈을 추렴해서 결혼 선물을 사다 raise money〔pass a hat around〕 to buy a wedding present〔gift〕 // 돈을 추렴해서 술을 마시다 drink on a Dutch treat // 점심을 각자 추렴으로 결정하다 decide to go Dutch on the luncheon // 소풍 가는 비용을 추렴하다 pool the expenses for a picnic

—술 a drinking party that goes Dutch ; a Dutch treat drinking party

추렴새 collecting together ; contributing jointly ; a share ; a contribution ¶ 추렴새가 많다 A share is large.

추록 追錄 a postscript ; a supplement ; an addition **—하다** supplement ; add

추론 推論 reasoning ; inference ; deduc-

tion —하다 reason ; infer ; deduce ; draw deduction from
—식 〖논리〗 syllogism

추루 醜陋 filthiness ; being dirty and unsightly ; foulness —하다 (be) filthy and ugly ; foul

추리 beef flank

추리 推理 reasoning ; inference ; deduction —하다 reason ; infer ; deduce ; figure out ¶ 순서적으로 추리해 나가다 follow out a train of reasoning // 결론을 추리하다 infer a conclusion
—력 reasoning power ; the power〔faculty〕 of reasoning — 소설 a mystery〔detective〕 story ; a whodunit 《미》 간접 — indirect inference 귀납〔연역〕 — inductive〔deductive〕 inference 연결 — combined〔compound〕 syllogism 직접 — direct〔immediate〕 inference

추리다 pick out ; choose ; select ¶ 추리고 추린 picked ; choice // 추려내다 select ; pick out ; single out // 짚을 추리다 pick straw (weeding out the short) // 좋은 것만을 추리다 pick out the best ones // 선수를 한 사람만 추릴 수는 없다 It is impossible to single out one player.

추림 秋霖 a long spell of rain in autumn

추맥 秋麥 autumn-sown barley ; the late barley

추명 醜名 a bad reputation ; notoriety ; a scandal ¶ 추명을 사다 make oneself notorious ; make a bad name for oneself

추모 追慕 —하다 cherish the memory of a deceased person ¶ 선친을 추모하다 look back upon the memory of one's late father with reverence and affection // …을 추모하여 비를 세우다 set up a monument to the memory 《of》

추문 醜聞 a scandal ; a scandalous report ; ill fame ; ignominy ¶ 추문을 일으키다 make〔cause〕 a scandal ; give rise to a scandal // 그에게는 추문이 붙어다닌다 He is the object of continual〔frequent〕 scandal.
— 거리 a scandalous affair ; a source of scandal ; an object of public scandal

추물 醜物 [물건] an ugly〔dirty, filthy, foul〕 object ; [사람] an ugly person ; a dirty〔filthy〕 fellow

추미 追尾 pursuit ; chase ; shadowing —하다 follow ; pursue ; shadow ; dog 《another's》 steps
— 공격 an attack from the rear ; a tail attack — 미사일 a homing missile 자동 — 장치 a homing device

추밀 樞密 important secret ; affairs of state
— 고문관 a Privy Councillor ; (영국의) a member of the Privy Council —원 the Privy Council —원 의장 the President of the Privy Council

추방 追放 expulsion ; banishment ; deportation ; driving out ; exile ; purge (공직에서) —하다 expel ; banish ; deport ; exile ; purge ¶ 피추방자 a person in exile ; a purgee // 공직으로부터 추방하다 remove 《a person》 from public offices〔life〕 // 국외로 추방당하다 be exiled〔deported〕 from the country // 불량 당원을 추방하다 purge a party of undesirable members ; purge an undesirable member from the party
—령 a deportation order (국외) ; a purge directive (공직) —자 a purgee —해제 depurge ; clearing of purge 악서(惡書) — 운동 a campaign aimed at doing away with harmful publications 외국 —자 an exile ; an expatriate ; an expellee

추백 追白 ⇨ 추서

추병 追兵 a pursuing party〔force〕 ; soldiers in chase〔pursuit〕 ¶ 추병이 오래지 않아 이를 것이다 The pursuers will be upon us quickly.

추부 醜婦 an ugly〔ill-favored〕 woman

추분 秋分 the autumnal equinox
—날 the Autumnal Equinox Day —점(點) the autumnal equinox

추비 追肥 (applying of) additional fertilizer

추사 秋思 autumnal sentiment〔thoughts〕

추산 推算 calculation ; computation ; estimate —하다 put ; estimate (at) ; calculate ¶ 그 이득은 2백만불로 추산된다 The gain is estimated at 2 million dollars.

추삼삭 秋三朔 the three autumn months

추상 推想 guess ; conjecture ; imagination ; inference ; surmise —하다 guess ; conjecture ; infer (from) ; imagine ¶ 도저히 추상할 수 없다 It is past all conjecture. // 그것은 추상에 불과하다 It is mere guesswork.

추상 抽象 abstract ; abstraction ¶ 추상적 abstract ; nonobjective ; metaphysical // 추상적으로 abstractly ; in the abstract // 추상적 관념 an abstract concept〔idea〕 // 추상적으로 말하면 speaking in the abstract〔in the general terms〕 // 시간의 개념을 추상하다 abstract the notion of time
—론 an abstract argument ; generalities ¶ 추상론을 하다 deal with things in the abstract — 명사 an abstract noun —미 abstract beauty — 예술 abstract〔nonrepresentational〕 art —파 abstractionism ¶ 추상파의 그림 an abstract picture —파 화가 an abstractionist ; an abstract painter〔artist〕 —화 abstract painting

추상 秋霜 [서리] autumn frost(s) ; [준엄] severity ; sternness ; mercilessness ¶ 추상 같은 sever ; rigorous ; relentless // 추상 같은 명령 a stern order // 추상 같은 형벌 a severe punishment // (검사의) 추상 같은 논고 a most relentless argument

추상 追想 retrospection ; recollection ; reminiscence ⇨ 추억 ¶ 험난했던 과거를

추상하다 look back on one's wretched past
—록 reminiscences

추색 秋色 autumnal scenery ; autumn colors〔tints〕; a sign of autumn ¶ 추색을 탐방하다 visit a place for its splendidness in autumn ; inspect〔enjoy〕 the autumnal scenery // 추색이 짙다 There is a definite sign of autumn.

추서 追書 a postscript《P. S.》

추서 追敍 posthumous honors **—하다** confer posthumous honors on《a person》; be promoted to《general》 posthumously

추서다 recover (from illness) ; get well again ; be restored to health ; recruit〔rally, regain〕《one's health》; get around ¶ 그는 이제 완전히 추섰다 He is now completely restored in health. /His health is now quite restored. // 병자는 곧 추설 것이다 The patient will soon come round.

추석 秋夕 the harvest〔moon〕 festival (on the 15th of August by the lunar calendar)

추선 追善 a mass for the dead ; a requiem mass ; a memorial service **—하다** hold a (requiem) mass for the dead ; have masses said for the repose of《a person's》 soul ; perform〔hold〕 memorial services

추세 趨勢 tendency ; trend ; drift ; current ; tide ¶ 일반적 추세 a general tendency ; the trend of events ; the current of the world // 자연의 추세 the course of nature // 세론의 추세 the trend of public opinion // 세상의 추세에 따르다 swim with the current // 추세에 맡기다 let things〔matters〕 take their own course // 물가는 하락〔상승〕의 추세가 있다 Prices are tending downwards〔upwards〕. /The tendency is toward lower〔higher〕 prices. // 세계 정세의 추세로 보아 전쟁이 일어날 듯 하다 The tendency of the world affairs〔situation〕 is toward war.
— 효과 [경제의] a trend effect **물가 —** a price trend **시대 —** the current of the times **여론 —** the trend〔set, tendency〕 of public opinion

추소 秋宵 an autumn evening〔night〕

추소 追訴 a supplementary legal suit **—하다** bring a supplementary suit《against》

추속 醜俗 unseemly customs ; ugly〔foul〕 manners

추수 追隨 association ; company ; intercourse ; fellowship ; friendship **—하다** associate with ; hold intercourse with ; keep company with ; mix with ; get on〔along〕 with

추수 秋收 (autumn) harvesting ; a harvest ; gathering a harvest **—하다** harvest ¶ 추수 때 a harvest time // 곡식을 추수하다 harvest crops ; reap ; gather (in) a harvest // 밭에서 옥수수를 30석 추수하다 harvest〔reap〕 30 bags from a corn field
— 감사절 Thanksgiving Day

추스르다 pick and trim ; set in order ; put into shape ; take good care of ; [구스르다] cajole ; coax ; fawn upon ¶ 짚을 추스르다 pick straw and trim them (weeding out the short ones) // 일을 추스르다 straighten matters out ; deal with an affair nicely // 백성을 잘 추스러 다스리다 get the people under complete control

추습 醜習 a vice ; indecent practices

추시 追諡 a posthumous title〔name〕 **—하다** confer a posthumous title

추시 趨時 keeping pace with the times ; keeping abreast of the times

추신 抽身 —하다 get free from〔of〕《business》; free oneself from〔of〕《work》

추신 追伸 an added note ; a postscript《P. S.》

추심 推尋 —하다 take〔get, receive〕 back what is one's own ¶ 은행에서 돈을 추심하다 draw one's money from one's bank ; receive payment
—금 money collected ; exactions **—료** collection charge **— 어음** a collection bill **— 위임 배서(背書)** endorsement for collection **— 은행** a collection bank

추썩거리다 [어깨를] keep shrugging ; [옷] rock up ; pull up ¶ 어깨를 추썩거리다 shrug one's shoulders from time to time // 옷을 추썩거리다 keep pulling up one's coat

추썩추썩 ⇨ 추썩거리다.

추악 醜惡 [행위] abominableness ; foulness ; scandalousness ; vileness ; [모습] ugliness ; unsightliness **—하다** (be) vile ; foul ; abominable ; ugly ; unsightly ; obscene ; filthy ; dirty ¶ 추악한 간판 an unsightly sign // 추악한 놈 an abominable person ; a viper ; a loathsome creature // 추악한 짓 a dirty trick // 추악한 소문 a scandalous rumor

추앙 推仰 reverence ; adoration ; respect ; worship **—하다** adore ; worship ; respect ; revere ; look up to ¶ 그는 이순신 장군을 추앙하고 있다 He is a great admirer of General *Lee Sun-Shin*.

추야 秋夜 an autumn night ¶ 추야장 긴긴 밤 the live-long autumn night

추양 秋陽 the autumn sunshine ; the autumn sun

추어 鰍魚 a mudfish ; a loach ⇨ 미꾸라지
—탕 loach soup

추어내다 expose ; disclose ; uncover ; reveal ; dig up ; dig out ; find out ; seek out ⇨ 들추어내다

추어올리다 ① pull up ; lift up ; hoist ¶ 치마를 추어올리다 pull up one's skirt ② [사람을] praise ; speak highly〔in high terms〕 of ; cry up to the skies ¶ 자기

친구를 추어올리다 rave about〔of〕 one's friend
추어주다 praise ; laud ; extol ; compliment ; flatter ; cajole ; wheedle ¶ 일을 잘했다고 추어주다 praise《a person》for doing a good job // 몹시 추어주다 praise 〔extol〕 to the skies // 추어주어 싫다는 사람은 없다 Nobody takes offense at a compliment.
***추억 追憶** remembrance ; recollection ; retrospection ; memory ; reminiscence **—하다** recall ; recollect ; go over in one's mind ; take a retrospective glance backward ¶ 슬픈 추억 a painful reminiscence ; a sad memory // 추억케 하다 make 《a person》 reminiscent of the past ; remind 《a person》 of old days ; carry one's thoughts back to the past ; be reminiscent of past // 어린 시절의 추억에 잠겨 있다 be absorbed in memories of one's childhood // 영원히 추억할 만한 가치가 있다 deserve permanent remembrance
—거리 a remembrancer ; a reminder ; a memento **—담** reminiscences ; memoirs
추업 醜業 shameful occupation ; prostitution ; a life of shame ; a shameful life 〔trade〕 ¶ 추업에 종사하다 live a life of shame〔vice〕 ; earn money on the street **—부** a woman on the streets ; a street walker ; a street girl ; a prostitute
추완 追完 〖법〗 subsequent accomplishment **—하다** complement ; subsequently complete
추요 樞要 importance ; vitality **—하다** (be) important ; vital ; critical ¶ 추요한 인물 a pivotal figure // 추요한 지위를 점하다 have〔occupy〕 an important position
추우 秋雨 an autumn rain
추운 秋雲 an autumn cloud
추워지다 grow〔get〕 cold(er) ; get〔become〕 chilly ; cool down ¶ 으스스 추워지다 take〔catch〕 a chill
추워하다 be susceptible to the cold ; complain of the cold ¶ 그는 곧잘 추워한다 He is terribly susceptible to the cold.
추원 追願 an additional petition 《to a god》 **—하다** pray that one more wish be fulfilled ; make an additional petition 《to a god》
추월 秋月 the autumn moon
추월 追越 —하다 [앞지르다] outrun ; pass 《another in the race》 ; outstrip ; outpace ; pass 《another motorcar》 ahead (자동차 따위가) ; outsail〔outsteam〕 (배가) ; have〔get〕 the heels of ; shoot ahead ; get〔be〕 ahead of 《another》 ; leave 《another》 behind ¶ 그 배가 보트에 추월당했다 The ship dropped〔fell〕 astern of the boat. // 스포츠카가 우리 차를 추월했다 A sports car overtook ours.
— 금지 [게시] No Passing. 《미》 ; Overtaking Prohibited. 《영》 ; No Overtaking.
— 금지 구역 a no-passing zone
***추위** the cold ; coldness ; cold weather ; a chill ; chilliness ¶ 살을 에이는 듯한 추위 biting〔piercing〕 cold // 이런 추위에 in this cold (weather) // 추위에 견디다 bear the cold // 추위타는 사람 a person who is sensitive to the cold // 추위에 떨다 shiver with cold // 추위를 느끼다 feel a chill ; have a cold fit ; get chilly // 추위를 막다 keep out〔off〕 the cold // 추위가 심하다 It is very cold. /It is bitterly cold. /The cold is intense. // 그날은 굉장한 추위였다 It was bitterly cold on that day.
추위 타다 관용 be sensitive〔susceptible〕 to the cold ; get cold easily
추이 推移 (a) transition ; (a) change ; progress ; development ; the turn〔course, trend〕 of affairs **—하다** change ; undergo a change〔transition〕 ; shift ; progress ; make progress ; advance ¶ 시대의 추이에 따라 with the change of times // 사태의 추이를 관망하다 watch the development of events ; see how the wind blows // 그는 그 정치 운동의 추이에 관심이 있었다 He interested himself in the progress of the political campaign.
추인 追認 confirmation ; ratification **—하다** confirm ; ratify
추자 楸子 pondweed ; a walnut
추잠 秋蠶 autumn silkworms ¶ 추잠을 놓다 raise silkworms in autumn
추잡 醜雜 filthiness ; obscenity **—하다** (be) dirty ; indecent ; obscene ; nasty ; foul ; filthy ; scurrilous ; disgusting ; loathsome ¶ 추잡한 사람 an indecent〔a filthy〕 person // 추잡한 짓 a dirty trick // 추잡한 그림 an obscene picture // 추잡한 이야기 filthy〔indecent〕 talk
추잡 麤雜 crudity ; coarseness ; crudeness **—하다** (be) crude ; coarse ; rough
추장 推奬 recommendation ; commendation **—하다** recommend ; commend ¶ 추장할 만하다 be worthy of commendation
추장 酋長 a chief ; a chieftain
추저분하다 醜— (be) dirty and messy ; filthy ; slovenly ¶ 추저분한 방 a messy room // 추저분한 누옥 a drab little hut
†추적 追跡 chase ; pursuit ; tracing ; following 《after》 **—하다** pursue ; give chase 《to》 ; follow 《after》 ¶ 살인범의 추적 the chase after a murderer // 도둑을 맹렬히 추적하다 follow the thief in hot pursuit // …을 추적 중이다 be in pursuit 《of》 ; be on the track 《of》 // 우리는 지방민의 추적을 받고 도망쳤다 We ran off with the natives following at our heels.
— 검사 a follow-up **—권(權)** [외국선 따위에 대한] the right of hot pursuit **—기** a pursuit plane **— 기지** [인공위성 따위의] a tracking station **— 비행** ¶ 추적 비행을 하다 fly chase 《on》 **— 원소** a tracer element **—자** a pursuer ; a pursuing

party〔force〕; a chaser —자(子) 〖화학〗 a tracer — 조사 a follow-up

추전성 趨電性 〖생물〗 electrotaxis ; galvanotropism ¶ 추전성의 electrotactic ; galvanotropistic

추절 秋節 autumn ; fall 《미》; the autumnal season ; autumnal days

추접 醜— —하다 (be) nasty ; filthy ; foul ; indecent ; obscene ; low-down ; sordid ¶ 추접스러운 놈 a dirty fellow ; a low-down good-for-nothing ; a mean-spirited fellow // 추접스러운 이야기 filthy talk // 추접스럽게 굴다 behave in a mean fashion // 그는 돈에 대해서는 추접하다 He is mean about money〔over money matters〕. // 그의 이름은 말하기조차 추접스럽다 I would not foul my tongue with his nasty name.

추접지근하다 (be) rather dirty ; unclean ; filthy

추젓 秋— tiny shrimps salted in autumn

*추정 推定 deduction ; presumption ; assumption ; inference —하다 presume ; assume ; infer ¶ 추정적 presumptive ; assumed // 사실의 추정 presumption of fact // 추정을 내리다 draw a deduction // 추정이 들어맞다 be right in one's assumption // 유죄로 추정하다 presume 《a person》 to be guilty // 그 여자의 추정 연령은 20세이다 She is supposed to be twenty years old. // 네가 말하는 것은 단지 추정에 불과하다 What you say amounts to a mere presumption.

— 가격 the presumed value 《of an article》 —량 an estimated volume — 범죄 a constructive crime — 상속인 an heir presumptive〔apparent〕 — 점유 constructive possession — 증거 presumptive evidence

추종 追從 obeying ; servile following ; imitation (모방) —하다 follow ; follow in 《a person's》 wake ; be servile to ; lick 《a person's》 heel〔boots〕; wait on hand and foot ¶ …에 있어서 추종을 불허하다 be without a peer ; be unrivaled ; be second to none // 공정한 재판관은 세론에 추종하지 않는다 An honest judge cannot be servile to public opinion. // 그는 누구의 말이든지 추종한다 He is at everyone's beck and call.

추증 追贈 posthumous conferment of honors

추지 推知 inference ; conjecture ; deduction —하다 conjecture ; guess ; surmise ; infer

추지다 (be) wet ; damp ; moist ; humid

*추진 推進 propulsion ; drive —하다 propel ; drive forward ; promote (사업을) ¶ 이 운동의 추진 세력 the driving force of this movement

—기 a propeller ; a screw propeller —력 propulsive force ; driving force ; impulse ¶ 추진력이 강하다 have a positive drive (사람) ; have a powerful driving force (동력) // 기획력과 추진력을 갖춘 사람 a man with initiative and drive — 모체(母體) a nucleus 《*pl.* -clei》 —용 연료 a propellant (로켓의) —제(劑) [로켓 따위의] a propellant — 축(軸) a thrust〔screw〕 shaft 분사 — 비행기 a jet-propelled plane

추징 追徵 additional charge ; supplementary collection —하다 make an additional charge ; collect in addition ; collect as a supplement〔surcharge, penalty〕

—금 money collected in addition —세 a penalty tax — 처분 punishment by imposing a penalty tax

추찰 推察 guess ; conjecture ; inference ; surmise ; [동정] sympathy ; consideration —하다 guess ; gather ; conjecture ; surmise ; sympathize 《with》 (동정) ¶ 추찰이 맞다〔안맞다〕 guess right〔wrong〕 // 추찰이 틀리지 않다면 if one's guess is not mistaken // 그의 말로 추찰컨대 I gather from his words 《that》 // 남의 마음을 추찰하다 read 《a person's》 mind ; enter into 《a person's》 feelings

*추천 推薦 recommendation ; nomination (지명) —하다 recommend 《for, to》; say a good word 《for》; put in a good opinion 《of》; propose (회원으로) ; nominate (지명) ¶ 김씨의 추천으로 on〔at〕 the recommendation of Mr. *Kim* // 문교부 추천 영화 a film recommended by the Education Ministry // 교장으로 추천하다 recommend 《a person》 as principal // 회원으로 추천하다 recommend〔propose, sponsor〕 《a person》 for membership // 후보자를 추천하다 put up〔nominate, adopt〕 a candidate // 친구를 박씨에게 추천하다 recommend a friend to Mr. *Park* // 좋도록 추천해 주시오 Please say a good word of me. // 당신이라면 쾌히 추천하겠소 I will gladly recommend you.

—생 a recommended student — 연설 《make》 a speech to recommend 《a person》 《for》 — 입학제 a system of admitting students into colleges upon the recommendations of high school presidents —자 a recommender ; a proposer ; an introducer ; a nominator —장 a letter of recommendation — 후보 a recommended candidate 피—자 a recommendee ; a nominee

추첨 抽籤 drawing lots ; a drawing ; a lottery —하다 draw〔cast〕 lots ; hold a lottery ¶ 추첨으로 순번을 결정하다 choose〔determine〕 turns by lot // 추첨에 당선되다 draw a lot ; have got a lucky number

—권 a lottery ticket (회전식) —기 a lottery wheel — 번호 a lottery number — 부(付) cum〔ex〕 drawing —제 the lottery system ¶ 추첨제의 중학 입시 the middle school lottery system — 판매 a raffle ¶ 추첨 판매의 복권 a ticket on raffle

추체 錐體 a conical form

추초 秋草 autumn grass〔plants, weeds〕

***추축 樞軸** a pivot ; an axle ; an axis ; a pivotal point ; a cardinal point ; the center (of point)

—국 an Axis power 반—국 the anti-Axis powers

추출 抽出 abstraction ; 〖화학〗 extraction —하다 draw ; abstract ; extract

— 견본 a sampling —률 〖제분〗 an extraction rate —물 an extract —법 a sampling process — 산업 extract industry —용 용제〔용매〕 〖화학〗 an extractant — 조사 a sample survey 임의 —법 a random sampling method 층화(層化) —법 stratified sampling ; a stratified sampling method

†**추측 推測** guess ; conjecture ; supposition ; presumption —하다 guess ; suppose ; conjecture ; surmise ¶ 추측대로 as supposed ; as conjectured // 내 추측으로 in my guess〔estimation〕 // 추측이 맞다〔어긋나다〕 guess right〔wrong〕 ; be right〔wrong〕 in one's conjecture // 추측에 지나지 않다 be mere guesswork // 한 사실에서 한 결과를 추측하다 infer a result from a certain fact

— 기사 a speculative news story〔article〕 — 항법(航法) dead reckoning

추켜들다 raise ; hold up ¶ 돌을 추켜들다 hold〔lift〕 up a rock // 사람을 추켜들다 hold 《a person》 up // 어린이를 추켜들다 raise〔lift〕 a boy aloft

추켜잡다 lift up ; hold up ¶ 치맛자락을 추켜잡다 hold up one's skirt to keep it from dragging

추키다 lift〔hold〕 up

추탕 鰍湯 loach soup ⇨ 추어탕

추태 醜態 [행동] a shameful conduct ; disgraceful behavior ; [상태] an unseemly sight ; an offensive appearance ; a scandalous condition ¶ 추태를 부리다 behave in a shameful〔disgraceful〕 manner ; conduct oneself disgracefully // 추태를 폭로하다 reveal its scandalous condition // 집안의 추태를 드러내다 wash one's dirty linen in public

추토 追討 —하다 hunt down and kill ; track down and dispose of

—군 a punitive force ¶ 추토군을 파견하다 dispatch a punitive force 《against the rebels》 —사(使) a general appointed to liquidate rebels

추파 秋波 an amorous glance ; an ogle ; an ogling look ¶ 추파를 던지다 cast an amorous glance 《at》 ; make (sheep's) eyes at ; make a pass 《at》 《속》 ; leer〔ogle〕 《at》

추풍 秋風 the autumn wind

— 낙엽 falling leaves in autumn winds ¶ 많은 군사들이 포화 속에 추풍 낙엽처럼 쓰러졌다 Soldiers were felled by the gunfire like so many leaves falling in the autumn wind.

추풍 醜風 unseemly customs

추하다 醜— ① [불결] (be) dirty ; filthy ; foul ; unclean ; squalid ; shabby ② [비루] (be) mean ; base ; disgusting ; abominable ; loathsome ¶ 추한 관계 an illicit connection ; an improper relation // 추한 사람 a filthy person ; a meanspirited person ; a low-down good-for-nothing // 추한 옷 soiled〔shabby〕 clothes // 추한 집 a squalid〔shoddy〕 house ; a dirty shack // 추한 이야기 filthy〔indecent〕 talk // 추한 관계를 맺다 have an illicit connection〔evil relation〕 with

추하다 — (be) coarse ; crude ; rough ; untidy ¶ 추한 물건 crude〔coarse〕 stuff

추한 醜漢 an ugly fellow〔guy〕 ; a low-down type

추해당 秋海棠 〖식물〗 a begonia ; an elephant's-ear

추행 醜行 an indecent act ; disgraceful 〔scandalous〕 conduct ; misconduct ¶ 추행을 적발하다 bring a scandal to light ; expose a scandal // 여자에게 추행하다 assault a girl ; rape a girl or a woman

추행 追行 following suit —하다 follow suit ; follow

추향 趨向 a trend ; a tendency ⇨ 경향

추호 秋毫 a bit ; a hair ¶ 추호도 (not) in the least ; (not) at all ; (not) a bit ; (not) the slightest // 추호도 의심 않는다 I have not the slightest doubt. // 그것을 훔칠 생각은 추호도 없었다 I hadn't the slightest intention to steal it. // 내 말에는 추호도 거짓이 없다 I mean everything I say. /Cross my heart, I'm not telling a lie. // 그에게는 양심 따위는 추호도 없다 He has not a spark〔an ounce, an atom〕 of conscience.

추화 秋花 autumn flowers

추확 秋穫 the harvest

추회 追懷 recollection ; reminiscence ; retrospection ¶ 옛날을 추회하다 look back upon the old days ; recollect the past

—담 reminiscences

추후 追後 ¶ 추후에 later on ; afterwards ; by and by // 추후 통고가 있을 때까지 until further notice // 추후에 전화하겠습니다 I'll (tele)phone you later on. // 추후에 자세한 이야기를 하겠습니다 I will write you about the details later on.

추흥 秋興 pleasures〔delights〕 of autumn ; autumn fun

축¹ the group〔bunch〕 of people〔things〕 ¶ 축에 끼이지 못하다 cannot associate with others on an equal footing ; be unequal 《to》 // 그는 똑똑한 축에 든다 He is one of the clever ones.

축² droopingly ; sluggishly ; loosely ; languidly ¶ 축 늘어진 귀 drooped〔drooping, droopy〕 ears // 어깨가 축 늘어지다 one's shoulders droop ; have drooping shoulders // 개가 혀를 축 늘어 뜨리고 있었다 The dog lolled out his tongue. // 줄이 한가운데가 축 늘어져 있다 The rope is slack in the middle. // 그 여자는 피부가 축 처져 있다 Her skin is loose.

축 丑 the Sign of the Ox ; the Direction of the Ox (축방) ; the Watch of the Ox (축시)
—일 the Day of the Ox

축 祝 ① a written prayer ⇨ 축문 ② celebration ; congratulation ⇨ 경축

축 逐 [바둑] being cornered always by one move

축 軸 [굴대] an axis ; an axle (차의) ; a shaft (기계의) ; a pivot ; a spindle (두루마리의) ; a roller ; rolls of paper ; a roll ¶ 편지 종이의 축 a roller for letter paper // 종이 두축 two rolls of paper // 지구는 그 축을 중심으로 24시간에 일회전한다 The earth makes one revolution on its axis every twenty-four hours.
—거(距) 〖기계〗 wheelbase **— 마력** 〖기계〗 shaft horsepower **—물(物)** [두루마리] a scroll (picture) **—받이** a bearing ; a pillow (block) **—받이 공** a bearing ball **—받이 대** a bearing stand **—받이 메탈** a bearing metal **—받이 압력** bearing pressure **—받이 용수철** a bearing spring **—색(索)** 〖해부학〗 an axon ; an axis cylinder **—선(線)** 〖기계〗 an axis ; 〖조선〗 a shaft line **세로—** a vertical〔longitudinal〕 axis **주—** the principal axis **지—** the axis of the earth **횡〔수평〕—** a horizontal〔traverse〕 axis

축 縮 shortage ; deficiency ; deficit ; lack ; shrinkage ; reduction ⇨ 축나다 ¶ 5백원의 축 a deficit of 500 *won*

‡**축가 祝歌** a festive song ; a carol (크리스마스) ; an epithalamium (결혼식)

축가다 縮— ⇨ 축나다

축감 縮減 reduction ; decrease **—하다** be decreased〔reduced〕

축객 逐客 **—하다** turn〔get, drive〕 a guest〔visitor〕 out ¶ 문전 축객하다 deny oneself to a visitor ; turn away a visitor (at the door) ; be not at home to a caller

축견 畜犬 a house dog
—세(稅) a dog tax

†**축구 蹴球** football ¶ 축구를 하다 play football〔soccer〕
— 경기 a soccer〔football〕 game **—계** the world of soccer〔football〕 **—공** a soccer ball ; a football **— 선수** a football player ; a footballer **— 시합** a football game **—장** a football field〔ground〕 ; a gridiron **— 팀** a football team ; the 《Harvard》 eleven **럭비식 —** Rugby football ; Rugger 《구》 **미식 —** American football ; gridiron 《미·구》 **아식 —** Association football ; soccer 《구》

축구장

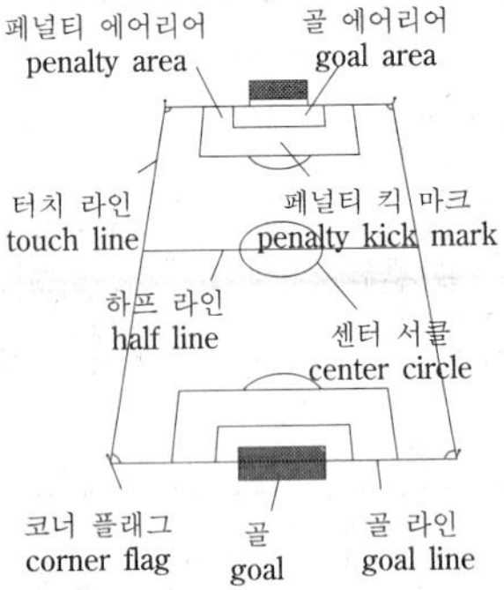

축국 蹴鞠 [놀이] football ; [그 공] a football ¶ 축국을 하다 play football

축나다 縮— decrease ; run low ; lack ; be deficient ; fall〔become〕 short of ¶ 돈이 5백원 축난다 The sum comes short by 500 *won*. /There is a deficit〔shortage〕 of 500 *won*. // 공부를 너무하여 그는 몸이 축났다 He lost some weight due to his hard study.

축내다 縮— spend 《a certain amount, part of a sum》 ¶ 1,000원에서 100원을 축내다 spend 100 *won* of the 1,000 *won*.

축년 丑年 〖민속〗 the Year of the Ox

축년 逐年 year after year ; from year to year

축농증 蓄膿症 〖의학〗 ozena ; empyema

축다 become wet ; get damp

축대 築臺 a terrace ; an elevation ; stone embankment ¶ 축대를 쌓다 build a ground high up with stone enforcement **위험 —** an embankment in dangerous conditions

축대 軸臺 〖기계〗 a pillow (block)

축도 縮圖 a reduced drawing〔copy〕 ; a miniature copy ; a tabloid edition ¶ 인생의 축도 an epitome of life // 표준 세계 지도의 축도 a reduced-size edition of the standard map of the world // 축도를 그리다 make a miniature copy 《of》
—기 a pantograph ; an eidograph

축도 祝禱 benediction ¶ 축도를 하다 pronounce a benediction

축록 逐鹿 running for a high position ; competition for a high office ; [정권 다툼] a scramble for political power
—전 competition for a position ; an election campaign

축류 畜類 livestock ; domestic animals

축문 祝文 a written prayer《for the deceased》; a memorial address (offered at memorial services of one's ancestors) ¶ 축문을 읽다 recite a written prayer
축받이 ⇨ 베어링
축발 蓄髮 letting one's hair grow long **—하다** let one's hair grow long
축방 丑方 〖민속〗 the Direction of the Ox (northeast-by-north)
축배 祝杯 a toast ; a drink in celebration ¶ 축배를 들다 [건배] drink a toast ; drink《to a person's》 success or health ; [축하] drink in celebration of《the victory, success》; [앞날을 위하여] drink success to《a person》// 서로 축배를 들다 toast each other // 축배를 들자고 말하다 propose a toast《for, to》// 김씨의 도미를 축하하기 위하여 축배를 들다 drink a toast for Mr. *Kim* to celebrate his going to America
†**축복 祝福** blessing ; blessedness ; benediction **—하다** bless ; call a blessing upon ; give〔pronounce〕 benediction ¶ 축복 받은 blessed // 축복 받은 나라 a blessed〔god-favored〕 country // 전도를 축복하다 wish《a person》 luck〔success〕// 목사가 교인을 위하여 축복하였다 The pastor blessed the congregation.
— 기도 〖기독교〗 a benediction ; a blessing ¶ 축복 기도를 올리다 pronounce the benediction《upon the congregation》
축사 縮寫 drawing on a smaller scale ; scaling down ; an abridged〔a reduced, a miniature〕 copy **—하다** draw〔copy〕 on a smaller scale ; make a reduced copy
—도 a reduced drawing **— 사진** a small-size〔reduced-size〕 photograph **— 지도** a scale map ¶ 1,000 분의 1 축사 지도 a map on the scale of one to a thousand
축사 祝辭 a congratulatory address〔speech, message〕; greetings ; congratulations ¶ 축사를 하다 deliver a congratulatory address ; offer one's congratulations ; congratulate〔felicitate〕《a person》 on《a matter》// 축사를 받다 receive〔be given〕 a congratulatory message
결혼 — wedding congratulations
축사 畜舍 a stall ; a stable ; a cattle shed
축산 畜産 stock raising〔breeding, farming〕; livestock farming ; [가축] domestic animals ; livestock
—국(局) the Livestock Bureau **— 박람회** a livestock exhibition〔fair, show〕 **— 시험장** a livestock experiment station〔center〕 **— 식품** livestock products〔foodstuffs〕 **—업** (the business of) stock breeding ; livestock industry **—업자** a livestock raiser ; a rancher **— 자금** (government) loans for livestock industry **—장** a (live) stock farm ; a stud farm ; a ranch **— 장려** encouragement〔promotion〕 of stock raising **— 조합** a stock-raisers association **—학** zootechny ; animal husbandry **—학부** the department of animal husbandry
축생 畜生 [금수] animals ; beasts ; a brute ¶ 축생만도 못한 놈 a man no better than a brute ; a brute (of a man)
—계(界) World of Beast **—도(道)** devildom ; incest ; the World〔Hell〕 of the Beasts ; the tormenting purgatory
축석 築石 piles of stones ; a cornerstone (주춧돌)
— 공사 rockwork ; terracing with stones
*__축성 築城__ fortification ; construction of a castle **—하다** build〔construct〕 a castle ; fortify
—가 a fortifier **—술** (the art of) fortification **—학** (the science of) fortification
축성 祝聖 benediction ; consecration ; sanctification **—하다** consecrate ; sanctify ; bless
—식(式) consecration ; Benediction **성당 —** the consecration of a church
*__축소 縮小__ abridgment ; reduction ; curtailment ; retrenchment **—하다** reduce ; cut down ; retrench ; curtail ¶ 군비를 축소하다 reduce armaments // 사업을 축소하다 reduce business // 경비를 축소하다 cut down〔reduce, retrench〕 expenses // 인원을 축소하다 cut〔reduce〕 the personnel
— 사진 필름 a microfilm **—판** a tabloid edition **군비 —** (partial) disarmament ; arms reduction
축쇄 縮刷 printing in smaller type **—하다** print a reduced-size edition
—판 a reduced-size edition
축수 祝手 invocation by prayer ; imploration ; supplication **—하다** invoke by prayer ¶ 병을 낫게 해 달라고 축수하다 implore God〔Gods〕 to heal one of a disease ; pray to God for the recovery of one's health
축수 祝壽 wishing《a person》 a long life **—하다** wish《a person》 a long life ; congratulate《a person》 on his long life
축승 祝勝 celebration of a victory ; rejoicing over a victory
축시 丑時 the Watch of the Ox ; the period between 1 and 3 a. m.
축어 逐語 verbalism ¶ 축어적(으로) word for word ; verbatim ; literal(ly)
—(번)역 a word-for-word〔literal〕 translation
*__축연 祝宴__ a feast ; a banquet ¶ 축연을 열다 hold a banquet〔feast〕 in celebration of《the event》; give a feast to celebrate《the event》
축열 蓄熱 ¶ 축열식의 regenerative
—기(器) 〖기계〗 a regenerator **—로** a regenerative furnace
축우 畜牛 a domestic cow〔ox〕; cattle
축원 祝願 praying ; a prayer ; supplication ; invocation **—하다** pray ; say〔utter〕 a prayer ; offer (up) a prayer ; supplicate ¶ 세계 평화를 축원하다 pray

for the peace of the world
—문 a written prayer

:축음기 蓄音器 a phonograph 《미》; a record player; a gramophone 《영》 ¶ 축음기에 취입하다 sing〔speak〕 into a phonograph; record a song // 축음기를 틀다 play a record; turn the phonograph on // 판이 자동적으로 바뀌는 축음기 a phonograph with an automatic record changer — 바늘 a phonograph needle; a stylus — 음악 canned music; phonograph music; recorded music; music on records〔disks〕; transcribed music —판 a record; a disk 고성능 — a high fidelity phonograph; a hifi 라디오 겸용 전기 — a radiophonograph; a radiogram(ophone) 전기 — an electric phonograph

축의 祝意 celebration (사물에 대한); congratulation (사람에 대한) ¶ 축의를 표하여 in honor of; in celebration of // 축의를 표하다 offer〔extend〕 one's congratulations〔felicitations〕 on 《a person's birthday, success》; congratulate〔felicitate〕 《a person》 on 《his success》; celebrate // 모든 기관은 그날 축의를 표하고 휴업한다 All firms will be closed in honor of the occasion〔event〕.

축의 祝儀 a festival; a celebration ⇨ 축전

축이다 wet; moisten; dampen; dip ¶ 목을 축이다 wet one's whistle; quench one's thirst // 수건을 축이다 wet a towel // 충분히 축이다 give it a thorough soak

축일 祝日 a festival (day); a fête day; a gala day; a flag〔red-letter〕 day

축일 逐一 [상세히] in full (detail); minutely; [하나하나] one after another; one by one; from point to point; item by item; word for word; in order ¶ 법안을 축일 토의하다 discuss the bills one by one // 축일 실례를 들다 mention〔cite〕 examples one by one; enumerate examples // 축일 보고하다 make a detailed report

축일 逐日 day after day; day by day; daily; every day ¶ 축일 증가하다 increase by the day

축장 蓄藏 hoarding; storage; accumulation 《of》 **—하다** hoard; store; keep; lay up

축재 蓄財 the accumulation of wealth〔riches〕; money-grubbing; accumulated wealth; amassed wealth **—하다** amass; make money; accumulate riches; amass a fortune ¶ 그는 축재에 급급하고 있다 He is striving hard after wealth. —자 a moneymaker; a thrifty person 부정 —자 an illicit fortune maker

:축적 蓄積 accumulation; storing up; stockpiling; amassment **—하다** accumulate; amass; store (up); stockpile; pile up; hoard (up); put to reserve ¶ 자본의 축적 the accumulation of capital // 원시적 축적 primitive accumulation // 지식을 축적하다 accumulate a store of knowledge // 재산의 축적에 전념하다 devote oneself to the accumulation of riches —물 accumulation — 배당 an accumulated dividend — 잉여금 accumulation surplus 자본 — accumulation of capital 자본 —론 the theory of capital accumulation

축전 蓄電 storage of electricity **—하다** store ¶ 축전식 검전기 a condensing electroscope

축전 祝典 a festival; festivities; a celebration; a commemoration; festive celebration ¶ 축전 기분 a festive mood // 축전 행사 festive activities // 크리스마스의 축전 Christmas festivities; the festival of Christmas // 창립 20주년 축전을 베풀다 hold〔keep, make〕 a celebration of the 20th anniversary of the founding 《of a school》
기념 — a commemoration festival ¶ 50주년 기념 축전을 올리다 hold a celebration of the 50th anniversary 《of》 25〔50, 60〕년 — the silver〔golden, diamond〕 jubilee

축전 祝電 a congratulatory telegram〔message〕; a wire of congratulation〔felicitation〕; a telegram of good wishes ¶ 축전을 치다〔보내다〕 send a congratulatory telegram〔message〕 to 《a person》; telegraph〔cable〕 one's congratulations to 《a person》

축전 縮戰 de-escalation

축전기 蓄電器 〖전기〗 an electric condenser
가변 — a variable condenser 결합 — a coupling condenser 고정〔공기〕 — a fixed〔an air〕 condenser 글라스 — a glass condenser 용량 — a capacity condenser

축전지 蓄電池 〖전기〗 a storage battery

축정 築庭 (landscape) gardening **—하다** make〔layout〕 a garden; engage in landscape gardening

축정 畜政 [축산 행정] livestock administration

축제 築堤 banking〔embanking〕 a river **—하다** embank (a river); dike; construct a riverbank
— 공사 embanking; embankment works

:축제일 祝祭日 a public〔national〕 holiday; a fête day; a gala day

축조 逐條 article by article; clause by clause; item by item; point by point; seriatim
— 심의〔토의〕 an article-by-article〔a clause-by-clause〕 discussion ¶ 축조 심의하다 discuss article by article; consider the articles seriatim; take the items up one by one

축조 築造 building; construction **—하다** build; construct; erect ¶ 축조 중이다 be under〔in course of〕 construction

축지다 縮— [사람의 가치가] discredit oneself ; fall into discredit ; sink (in one's estimation) ; [몸이] grow weak ; be run down ; lose weight ; fail in health ¶ 앓아서 몸이 축지다 lose some weight due to illness // 축질 노릇을 왜 하려느냐 Why would you do such a discreditable thing ?
축지법 縮地法 a magic method of contracting space ; "Seven-League Boots"
축짓다 軸— make a pivot ; fix an axle ¶ 종이로 축짓다 roll paper into a roll
축차적 逐次的 ⇨ 순차
축처지다 [어깨 따위가] droop low ; [천장이] sag low ; [나뭇가지가] hang down low ; [머리카락이] trail ; [모자테 따위가] slouch
축척 縮尺 a reduced scale
—도(圖) a map on a reduced scale — 5만분의 1 [지도 따위의 기재] Scale : 1/50,000 — 5만분의 1 지도 a map drawn on a scale of 1 to 50,000 — 7분의 1 모형 a one-seventh model 《of》 대(大)—도 a large-scale map 《of a small area》 소(小)—도 a small-scale map 《of a large area》
축첩 蓄妾 keeping a concubine〔mistress〕; concubinage —하다 keep a concubine ¶ 축첩 공무원을 파면하다 fire a government official who keeps a concubine
— 제도 concubinage
축축 all drooping〔sagging, hanging down〕 low ; drooping all the time ¶ 나뭇가지가 축축 늘어진다 The branches all droop low.
*__축축하다__ (be) slightly〔moderately〕 wet ; moist ; damp ; humid ; clammy ; sticky ; dampish ¶ 축축한 공기 moist air // 축축한 옷 wet clothes // 축축하게 축이다 moisten ; dampen ; make 《a thing》 damp〔moist〕// 등골에 땀이 축축하다 His back is damp with sweat. // 빨래가 이슬에 축축하다 The laundry is moist with dew. // 땅이 축축해서 씨뿌리기에 알맞다 The field is moderately wet and just right for sowing.
축출 逐出 driving out ; expulsion ; deportation —하다 drive〔turn, send, put〕 out ; kick out ; rout out 《of home》; oust 《from a position》; eject ; expel ¶ 축출을 당하다 get driven〔run, kicked〕 out ; be expelled // …을 집 밖으로 축출하다 turn 《a person》 out of the house ; show 《a person》 the door ; give 《a person》 the gate // 당에서 축출하다 expel〔oust〕《a person》 from the party // 선동자를 회장에서 축출하다 eject an agitator from a meeting
축판 縮版 ⇨ 축쇄(—판)
축포 祝砲 a salute (of guns) ; a cannon salute ; a feu de joie ¶ 21발의 축포를 놓다 fire〔give〕 a salute of twenty-one guns ; salute with twenty-one guns
*__축하__ 祝賀 congratulation ; celebration ; felicitation ; rejoicing ; (congratulatory) greetings —하다 congratulate〔felicitate〕《a person》 on ; greet [일을] celebrate ; keep (a festival) ¶ 축하의 congratulatory // 축하하여 in celebration of ; in honor of // 축하할 일 a matter for congratulation // 축하의 말 congratulations ; congratulatory remarks〔greetings〕// 전승을 축하하다 celebrate a war victory // 친구의 결혼을 축하하다 felicitate a friend on his marriage // 축하의 말을 하다 offer one's congratulations ; make a congratulatory speech // 축하합니다 Congratulations ! // 크리스마스를 축하합니다 Merry Christmas to you ! // 삼가 성공을 축하드립니다 Please accept my sincere congratulations on your success.
—객 a congratulator — 선물 a congratulatory gift — 인사 one's congratulations 《on an event》; a congratulatory address —장 a letter of congratulation ; a congratulatory note ; a greeting card ; a greeting —회 a celebration ; a congratulatory entertainment ; a reunion in celebration of an event ¶ 결혼 축하회 a wedding celebration〔reception〕// 축하회를 열다 hold a celebration ; give a party (in celebration) 전승(戰勝) — rejoicings over a victory ; (a) celebration of a victory
축하다 縮— (be) wilted ; languid
축합 縮合 〖화학〗 condensation —하다 condense
—물 a condensate ; a condensation product — 반응 a condensation reaction — 산소 a condensing enzyme — 수지 condensation resin —제 a condensing agent
축항 築港 harbor construction —하다 construct a harbor
— 공사 harbor work(s) ¶ 축항 공사를 시작하다 start harbor construction〔improvements〕; begin to improve the harbor
춘경 春耕 spring plowing
춘경 春景 spring scenes〔scenery〕
춘계 春季 spring ⇨ 춘기
춘곤 春困 fatigue in the spring tide ; languor〔lassitude〕 which affects people in spring ; "spring fever"
춘광 春光 spring scenes ⇨ 춘색
춘궁 春宮 the Crown Prince ; the Prince Imperial
춘궁기 春窮期 the farm hardship period ; the season of spring poverty〔shortage〕; spring cessation to the peasants ; the spring austerity
춘기 春機 spring ; the spring season ; springtime
— 방학 the spring vacation — 운동회 a spring athletic meet

춘기 春期 sexual desire
춘기 발동기 春機發動期 the age of puberty ; adolescence ; the period of sexual awakening ¶ 춘기 발동기에 달하다 arrive at puberty ; become adolescent
춘난 春暖 spring warmth ; the warmth of spring ; genial〔balmy〕 weather of spring ¶ 춘난지절 (春暖之節) warm spring weather
춘뢰 春雷 a spring thunder
춘맥 春麥 early〔spring-sown〕 barley
춘면 春眠 drowsiness〔fatigue〕 in the spring ; sleep on a spring morning
춘몽 春夢 spring dreams ; visionary fancies ; a spring fantasy ; an empty dream ¶ 그의 계획은 일장의 춘몽으로 돌아갔다 His plan ended up as nothing but a springtime fantasy. /All his ideas came to naught.
춘복 春服 clothes for spring wear ; spring wear
춘부장 春府丈, 椿府丈 your (honored) father
춘분 春分 the vernal〔spring〕 equinox ¶ 춘분의 날 the Spring〔Vernal〕 Equinox Day
춘사 春思 spring sentiments〔musings〕 ; feelings of spring ; spring fever ; a surge of lust ; lewd thoughts ; thoughts of sex
춘사 椿事 an accident ; a mishap ; [대춘사] a disaster ; [비극] a tragedy ¶ 춘사의 희생자 the victims of the accident // 춘사를 만나다〔당하다〕 have〔meet〕 a great accident // 공장에 춘사가 발생했다 An unexpected accident happened〔occurred〕 at the factory.
춘산 春山 mountains in springtime
춘삼월 春三月 March of〔in〕 the lunar month ¶ 춘삼월 호시절 the pleasant days of spring ; the mild weather of spring
춘색 春色 spring scenery ; the vernal beauty of nature ; a sign〔hint, indication〕 of spring ¶ 춘색을 탐방하다 inspect the spring scenery // 춘색이 한창이다 Spring is now at its height.
춘설 春雪 spring snow
춘소 春宵 a spring evening〔night〕 ¶ 춘소의 일각은 천금과도 같다 One hour of a spring is worth a thousand pieces of gold.
춘수 春水 spring water
춘수 春愁 spring sadness ; melancholy aroused in springtime
춘신 春信 tidings of spring ; signs〔tokens〕 of spring ; news of flowers (화신)
춘심 春心 spring sentiment(s) ; lustful desires
춘야 春夜 spring night
춘약 春藥 an aphrodisiac (dose) ; a sexual stimulant
춘양 春陽 spring sunshine ; the spring sun ; [철] the spring season ; the spring tide
춘우 春雨 a spring rain〔drizzle〕
춘일 春日 a spring day
춘잠 春蠶 spring silkworms ; a spring breed of silkworms ¶ 춘잠을 치다 raise silkworms in spring
춘절 春節 the spring season ; the springtime
춘정 春情 sexual〔carnal〕 desire ; sexual urge ; lust ; passion ¶ 춘정을 돋우다 excite sexual desire ; be suggestive ; be provocative
춘초 春初 early spring ; the beginning of spring
춘추 春秋 spring and autumn ; [세월] years ; [연령] age ; years ¶ 춘추가 기울다 decline in age〔one's years〕 // 춘추가 몇이십니까 What is your age, sir ? /How old are you, sir ?
—복 a suit for spring〔autumn〕 wear ; spring and autumn wear ; between-season wear
춘추 필법 春秋筆法 the guiding principle of Confucius in writing the Annals ¶ 춘추의 필법을 빌면 according to the Confucian way of criticism
춘파 春播 **—하다** sow in spring
춘풍 春風 the spring breeze〔wind〕 ¶ 춘풍에 돛단 듯하다 Everything goes all right〔smoothly〕.
— 추우 the spring wind and the autumn rain ; a year ; years come and gone **— 화기(和氣)** balmy spring weather
춘하추동 春夏秋冬 the four seasons ; all the year round ; always
춘한 春寒 the lingering cold in spring
춘화 春花 spring flowers
춘화 春畫 an obscene〔licentious, dirty, filthy〕 picture ; a pornography
춘화도 春畫圖 ⇨ 춘화(春畫)
춘화 현상 春化現象 〖식물〗 vernalization
춘흥 春興 the charms〔pleasures〕 of spring ; the spring fever ; the lure of spring ¶ 춘흥에 겨워하다 be overjoyed with the charms of spring
출가 出家 leaving home ; entering the Buddhist priesthood **—하다** leave home ; become a bonze〔a Buddhist priest〕 ; join the priesthood ; renounce the world ; take the veil (수녀원으로)
출가 出嫁 a woman's being married ; marriage ; wedding **—하다** (a woman) be married to ¶ 출가시키다 marry one's daughter off ; get a daughter married // 김씨 가문으로 출가했다 get married to one of the *Kims* // 출가 외인 A married daughter is no better than a stranger.
출간 出刊 publication ; issue ⇨ 출판(出版)
출감 出監 release from prison **—하다** be released〔discharged〕 from prison ⇨ 출옥
출강 出講 **—하다** lecture ; give lectures 《at a school》

*출격 出擊 a sally ; a sortie ; going out to attack〔raid〕 ━하다 sally forth ; make a sortie ; set out to make an assault

출결 出缺 ¶ 출결을 알려 주십시오 Kindly let me know whether you will be present or not.

출경 出京 leaving the capital ; [상경] going to the *Seoul* ━하다 leave〔go to〕 the capital ; leave the capital and go to the country side ; go to the capital from the country

출계하다 出系— get adopted ; become an heir of another family (leaving one's own) ¶ 삼촌집에 출계하다 be adopted by one's uncle

출고 出庫 taking goods out of the warehouse ; delivery

— 가격 a factory〔store〕 price —세 the delivery tax — 지시서 a delivery order

출관 出棺 ━하다 take a coffin out of the house 《of a dead person》

*출구 出口 an exit ; a way out ; a gateway ; an outlet ¶ 극장의 출구 the exit of a theater // 출구는 이쪽입니다 This way out. // 그는 둘러보며 출구를 찾았다 He looked around for a way out.

— 콕 〖기계〗 a delivery cock —판(瓣) 〖기계〗 an outlet valve 바깥 — a street door 비상 — fire escape〔exit〕

출구 出柩 taking a coffin out of the house ━하다 carry a coffin out of the house

출국 出國 ━하다 depart from the country ; leave the country

— 허가 an exit〔a departure〕 permit

출근 出勤 attendance 《at office》 ━하다 go(come) to the office ; show up at 〔for〕 work ; attend the office ; report ¶ 8시에 출근하다 come〔go〕 to the office at 8 ; report (for duty) at 8 // 회사에 출근하다 show up at one's desk in the (company) office // 출근하고 있다 be at the office〔at his desk〕 // 오늘은 출근했다 be on duty today // 출근이 불규칙하다 be irregular in attendance // 출근이 늦어지다 be late for the office // 그는 오늘 출근하지 않았다 He is off today. // 그래서 시차 출근을 하고 있다 That's why I work staggered hours.

—부 an attendance book〔record〕 ; a time book ¶ 출근부에 도장을 찍다 sign 〔register〕 one's name in the attendance book ; punch the time clock — 상태 the relative absenteeism ; attendance (state, figures) ; condition of attendance — 수당 an attendance allowance — 시간 the hour for reporting ; the time to attend the office ; the office-going hour —율 (non-)absentee rate〔ratio〕 —일 one's working day ; the office day —일수 the number of attendance —자 an attendant ; a nonabsentee ; attendance 《총칭》 ; those on the job〔at their desks〕 오후 — 《be on》 the afternoon shift

출금 出金 defrayment ; payment ; drawing (예금의) ; contribution (기부의) ; [출자] investment ━하다 pay ; draw out ; contribute 《to》 ; invest money 《in》 ¶ 결혼 선물하는 1불 출금에 응하다 chip in a dollar to buy 《a person》 a wedding present

—액 the amount of contribution〔investment〕 —자 [출자자] an investor ; a financier — 전표 a payingout slip

*출납 出納 [금전] receipts and payments〔disbursements, expenses〕 ; revenue and expenditure ; incomings and outgoings ; depositing and drawing ¶ 출납을 맡아보다 take〔be in〕 charge of accounts ; hold the purse strings // 현금 출납을 하다 handle the cash ; be a cashier〔teller〕 // 국고의 출납을 관할하다 take charge of Government revenues and disbursements〔payments〕 ; hold the purse strings of the Government

—계 a cashier ; [은행] a teller — 공무원 an accounting official ; a paymaster — 관리 an official in charge of accounts —부 a cashbook ; an account book — 정리기 the settlement period

출동 出動 going〔moving〕 out ; [군대·경관의] mobilization ; [함선] sailing ━하다 be mobilized ; be called out ; set out ; sail ; go into action (활동) ¶ 군대〔경찰〕의 출동 the mobilization of troops 〔police〕 // 군대〔경찰〕의 출동을 명하다 order〔call〕 out troops〔police〕 // 출동 준비를 하다 hold itself〔themselves〕 in readiness for action ; get ready to move // 출동 준비를 명하다 order to be ready to move ; order to stand by ; order standby mobilization // 전차가 출동했다 Tanks went into action.

출동 명령 出動命令 an order for moving〔going〕 《out, in》 ¶ 육군의 출동 명령 marching orders // 해군의 출동 명령 sailing orders // (요격기의) 긴급 출동 명령 a scramble order // 출동 명령을 내리다 give an order for moving 《on, out, in》

출두 出頭 appearance ; presence ; attendance ━하다 appear ; attend ; report oneself 《at》 ; present oneself 《at》 ¶ 본인이 출두하다 appear〔report〕 in person // 본사에 출두하다 report〔present oneself〕 at the head office // 법정 출두의 통지를 받다 be ordered to appear in court // 피고의 출두 없이 재판하다 hold a trial with the accused absent

— 명령 a summons 자진〔임의〕 — (형식으로) (in the form of) voluntary appearance 재판소 — 명령 《issue》 a summons to appear in court

출람 出藍 excelling〔surpassing〕 one's master〔teacher〕 ¶ 출람지재 a person who excels his teacher ; a pupil greater than his master

출렁거리다 lap ; slop ; slash ; roll ; swell ¶ 기슭에 출렁거리는 물결 little waves lapping (against) the shore // 물이 독안에서 출렁거린다 The water in a jar is slopping from side to side.

‡**출력 出力** generating power〔capacity〕; output of power ¶ 출력 300킬로와트 발전기 a 300 kilowatt dynamo // 출력이 작다〔크다〕 have a small〔large〕 output

출렵 出獵 —**하다** go hunting〔shooting〕

출루하다 出壘— 〖야구〗 get to 《first》 base ¶ 출루해 있다 be on 《the second》 base (러너가 주어) ; have 《two》 on (base) (팀이 주어) // 선두 타자가 4구로 출루했다 The first batter got to first base on four balls.

출마 出馬 ① [말타고 감] —**하다** go out 〔forth〕 on horseback
② [입후보] running for office ; coming forward as a candidate —**하다** run for office ; stand〔come forward〕 as a candidate ¶ 선거에 출마하다 run〔stand〕 for election // 국회 의원 선거에 출마하다 run 〔stand〕 for the National Assembly

‡**출몰 出沒** appearing and disappearing —**하다** make frequent appearances ; come and go ; frequent ; pop in and out ; haunt ¶ 호랑이가 출몰한다 Tigers lurk there. // 해상에 적선이 출몰한다 Enemy ships show up from time to time 〔frequently〕 on the sea.

출무성하다 ① [굵기가] have about the same thickness at the top and at the bottom ② [대가리가] (be) even ¶ 출무성한 묘목들 young trees of even height

†**출발 出發** departure ; leaving ; starting —**하다** leave ; start ; set out 《from a place, for one's home, on one's travel》; take one's departure ; make a start 《in the morning for a place》; [배가] embark ; [비행기가] take〔hop〕 off ¶ 출발에 즈음하여 on the departure ; at the outset // 빨리 출발하다 make an early start ; start early // 부산으로 출발하다 leave〔start〕 for *Pusan* // 부산을 출발하다 leave *Pusan* ; start from *Pusan* // 여행에 출발하다 start on a journey // 배로 출발하다 embark 《for America》 in a〔on a, by〕 steamer // 출발을 잘못하다 make a bad start ; make a wrong start in life (인생의) ; make a false start (경기에서) // 출발을 연기하다 postpone〔put off, defer〕 one's departure // 버스는 이미 출발했다 The bus has already gone〔started, left〕. // 비행기는 오후 3시에 뉴욕으로 출발합니다 The plane takes off for New York at 3 p. m. // 곧 출발하는 것이 좋다 You had better set out right now.
—**계** [경기의] a starter — **시간** the starting time ; the time of departure ¶ 출발 시간이다 It is time to depart. — **신호** a starting〔leaving〕 signal — **신호원** [경기의] a starter —**역** a starting station —**일** the date of one's departure —**점** the starting point ; the point of departure ¶ 그들은 출발점에 섰다 They lined up for the start.

†**출범 出帆** sailing (away) ; departure —**하다** [배·사람이 주어] sail 《from *Inch'ŏn* for Manila》; put off 《on a long voyage》; put to sea ; [배가 주어] set sail 《from *Inch'ŏn* for San Francisco》; leave〔clear〕 (a) port ; leave 《*Inch'ŏn* for Singapore》 ¶ 배는 수일 후에 출범합니다 The ship sails off in several days. // 기선의 뱃고동 소리는 출범을 알린다 The steam-whistle signals the time of departure.
—**기** a Blue Peter ; a sailing signal flag — **명령** sailing orders — **시간** sailing time ¶ 출범 시간은 오후 4시다 The sailing time of the boat is 4 p. m. —**일** the sailing day ; the date of sailing —**표** a sailing schedule

출병 出兵 the dispatch of troops —**하다** send〔dispatch〕 troops ; send a military expedition ¶ 호주군의 월남 출병 the dispatch of Australian troops to Vietnam
—**론** the argument for an expedition

출분 出奔 abscondence ; decampment ; elopement (사랑의 도피) —**하다** run away ; fly 《a place》; abscond ; decamp ; bolt
—**자** an absconder ; a runaway

출비 出費 expenses ; outlay ; outgo ; expenditure ¶ 출비를 절약하다 cut down on expenses ; curtail expenses ; squeeze pennies // 이 계획은 많은 출비가 필요하다 The projects require very heavy expenditure. // 물가 앙등으로 출비가 증가한다 The expenses increase as the commodity prices rise high.

출사 出仕 going into government service〔office〕 ¶ 40에 처음 출사하다 enter government service for the first time at forty

출사 出社 —**하다** go〔come〕 to office

출사 出師 the dispatch of troops ; an expedition —**하다** dispatch the troops ; send an expedition

출사 出寫 a photographing visit

출산 出産 child birth ; delivery ; parturition —**하다** give birth to ; be delivered of ¶ 출산 예정일이 언제입니까 When is your baby due?
— **경력〔경험〕** one's parity —**율** (a) birth rate — **촉진제** a parturifacient — **축하** a celebration of a birth ; congratulations on a birth — **휴가** a maternity leave ¶ 그 분은 지금 출산 휴가 중이신데요 She is on maternity leave. **첫** — one's first childbirth

출상 出喪 carrying the coffin out of the house —**하다** carry the coffin out of the house ¶ 오후 3시 자택 출상 The funeral procession will leave the house at 3 p. m.

†**출생 出生** birth ; childbirth **—하다** [낳아지다] be born ; [낳다] give birth to ; be delivered of ¶ 미천〔고귀〕한 출생 a person of low〔noble〕 birth // 남아의 출생 the birth〔arrival〕 of a baby boy // 둘째 아들로 출생하다 be born the second son // 출생을 축하하다 congratulate 《a person》 on the birth of a child (타인이) ; celebrate the birth of a child (자기가) // D씨 부부에게 여아가 출생했다 A daughter was born to Mr. and Mrs. D.
—계 the registration〔report〕 of a birth **—률** (a) birth rate **— 신고** the report〔registration〕 of a birth ¶ 출생 신고하다 register one's birth **— 연월일** the date of one's birth **— 증명서** a birth certificate **—지** the place of one's birth ; one's birthplace

출생후 出生後 since one's birth ; (in) all one's born days ¶ 출생후 죽 서울에서 살고 있다 I have lived in *Seoul* since I was born.

†**출석 出席** attendance ; presence **—하다** be present 《at》 ; attend 《at》 ; present oneself at ¶ 출석을 부르다 call the roll〔names〕 ; make a roll call // 출석하지 않다 absent oneself from ; stay 《away》 // 출석이 불규칙하다 be irregular in attendance // 회의에 출석하다 attend〔be present at〕 a meeting // 회원이 다수 출석했다 A large number of members were present. /It was attended by a large number of members. // 출석하시기 바라나이다 Your presence〔attendance〕 is requested. // 회원의 출석이 아주 나빴다 The attendance of the members were very slim〔thin〕.
—률 the percentage〔number〕 of attendance **—부** an attendance book ; a roll (book) **— 요구서** 〖법〗 a summons **— 일수** the number of one's attendances **—자** a person present ; attendants ; those present ; an attendance 《총칭》 ¶ 출석자가 많다〔적다〕 have a large〔small〕 attendance **— 정지** suspension of attendance **—표** a table of attendance **전원 —** complete attendance ; non-absence ¶ 저 클래스는 오늘 전원 출석하고 있다 That class has perfect attendance today. **다수〔소수〕 —자** a large〔small〕 attendance

출선 出船 [출범] sailing out ; setting sail ; weighing anchor ; [떠나는 배] an outgoing ship〔vessel〕

출세 出世 success in life ; rising in the world ; (career) advancement **—하다** have great success in life ; rise in the world ; make one's way in life ; attain distinction ; rise to a high position〔prominence〕 ¶ 출세한 사람 a successful person ; a success // 입신 출세의 노력가 a social climber // 출세할 기회를 놓치다 miss a chance to get ahead in life // 출세가 빠르다 make a rapid rise ; rise rapidly in the world // 출세를 방해하다 stand in the way of 《a person's》 advancement // 사장으로 출세하다 rise to the head of the company // 그는 꼭 출세할 것이다 He is bound to success in life. // 재능만 있으면 출세한다 All careers are open to talent. /Talent is all it takes to make you a success in this world. // 가난한 집에 나서 크게 출세했다 Born of a poor family, he made his way in the world.
— 계단 the ladder of success **— 비결** secrets of social success〔a successful life〕 **—욕(慾)** ambitions for success

출세작 出世作 [작품] the work which (has) brought 《a person》 into prominence ; one's maiden success-piece ¶ 그것이 그의 출세작이었다 The work was the beginning of his fame. / The work made him famous〔brought him fame〕.

출소 出所 release 《from prison》 ⇨ 출옥 **—하다** be released〔discharged〕 from prison ; leave〔come out of〕 prison
—자 a released convict

출소 出訴 —하다 institute a lawsuit 《against a person》 ; bring〔file〕 an action 《against a person》 ; sue 《a person for something》 ; go to law 《with a person》
— 기한 a time limit for bringing an action **—자** a suitor

출수 出穗 ¶ 출수하다 come into ears ; ear (up)
—기 the earing season

출신 出身 [태생] a native ; [졸업] a graduate ; [가문] origin ; birth ; affiliation ¶ 대학 출신이다 be a college graduate // 군부 출신이다 be 《a person》 of the military clique // 정당 출신의 장관 a minister affiliated with a political party ; a party Minister // 그는 제주도 출신이다 He is a native of *Cheju-do.* /He comes from *Cheju-do.* // 어디 출신입니까 제주도입니다 Where are you from? —I come〔am〕 from *Cheju-do.*
—자 [학교의] a graduate ; [남자] an alumnus 《*pl.* -ni》 ; [여자] an alumna 《*pl.* -nae》 **—지** one's native place ; one's home (town) **—(학)교** one's alma mater **관료 —** ex-government officials **군부 —** a person of the military clique **군인 —** a former military man **농민 —** ¶ 우리 사장은 농민 출신이다 The president of our concern comes from peasant stock. **대학 —** a college〔university〕 graduate ¶ 서울대학 출신 a graduate of *Seoul* National University // 그들의 5할은 대학 출신이다 Fifty percent of them are of university origin. **명문 —** (a person of) noble birth **서울 —** (a person of) *Seoul* birth ¶ 서울 출신이다 come from *Seoul*

출아 出芽 germination ; sprouting ; budding **—하다** germinate ; sprout ; bud ; put forth buds

출애굽기 出—記 〖성경〗 The Book of Exo-

dus ; Exodus 《Exod.》
출어 出漁 going out fishing **—하다** go out fishing ; sail out for fish
— 구역 a fishing area〔ground〕 **—권** the fishing right **—기** the fishing season
출연 出捐 contribution ; donation ; subscription **—하다** donate ; contribute
—금 a contribution ; a donation ; an endowment
†**출연 出演** one's appearance on stage ; one's performance ; [첫출연] debut **—하다** appear 《on the stage》 ; act ; play ; [노래하다] sing ; [연설하다] speak ; make a speech ¶ 스타 총출연 an all-star cast// 처음으로 출연하다 make one's first appearance 《on the stage, in the film》 ; make one's debut ; make one's first entry upon the stage// 그 극〔극장〕에 출연하다 appear in the play〔at the theater〕// 춘향으로 출연하다 appear as〔play the role of〕 *Chun-hyang*
— 계약 a booking〔contract〕 **—료** performance fee **—자** the players ; the performers ; the singers ; the speakers ¶ 주요한 출연자 the leading actor〔actress〕 ; the main player **고별 — [공연]** one's farewell appearance〔performance〕
출영 出迎 meeting ; reception (영접) **—하다** receive ; greet ; meet 《a person》 ; go〔come〕 (out) to meet 《a person》 on arrival ¶ 많은 친지의 출영을 받다 be met〔received〕 by many friends 〔people〕 at 《a place》// 출영 군중이 그 광장에 꽉 찼다 The plaza was bursting with the welcoming〔cheering〕 crowd.
출옥 出獄 discharge〔release〕 from prison **—하다** get released〔discharged〕 from prison ; be set free ; come out of prison ¶ 만기 출옥하다 be discharged upon expiration of one's term// 그는 10년 형기를 마치고 출옥했다 He was released after serving a sentence of 10 years' confinement.
—자 a released convict ; an exconvict **가—** release on parole ; provisional release
출원 出願 application ; submitting application **—하다** apply for ; make an application for ¶ 특허 발부를 출원하다 apply (to the patent office) for a patent// 여권 발부를 출원하다 submit an application for (the issuance of) a passport// 증명서의 발부를 출원하다 apply (to the authorities) for a certificate〔license〕
— 기한〔마감〕 the deadline〔time limit〕 for application **— 번호** the application number **— 수속** the procedure of application **—자** an applicant **광업 —자** a mining applicant **특허 —중** Patent applied for. /Patent pending.
출유 出遊 an outing ; an excursion **—하다** make an outing〔excursion〕
출입 出入 coming and going ; going in and out ; entrance and exit **—하다** go 〔come〕 in and out ; enter and leave ; frequent ¶ 출입하는 배 incoming and outgoing vessels// 출입하는 상인 one's regular〔usual〕 tradesman// 출입을 허가하다 admit into ; permit to come in and go out ; [장소가] be on limits// 방의 출입을 금하다 forbid 《a person》 the room// 사람의 출입이 많다 (lots of people) come and go ; have a lot of visitors// 극장 출입을 자주하다 go to the theater frequently// 자유로 출입할 수 있다 have〔be allowed〕 free access to (a house)// 손님의 출입이 많다 Visitors are constantly coming and going (from the house)./There is a continuous stream of visitors.// 주인님은 출입하시고 안계십니다 The master has gone out and not come home yet.// 학생의 도서관 출입을 허용함 Free access is allowed to the library to any student.
—구 the entrance ; a gateway ; a doorway **—국(國)** entry into, and departure from, the country **—국 관리** immigration control〔management〕 ¶ 출입국 관리법 the Immigration Control Law// 출입국 관리국 the Exit and Entry Control Bureau ; the Immigration Bureau **—권** an admission ticket **— 금지** Off limits. /No trespassing. ¶ 출입 금지 장소 an off-limits place// 미성년자 출입 금지 No minors.// 학생 출입 금지 No students. /The place is off-limits to students. **— 상인** one's regular tradesman **— 선박** incoming and outgoing vessels **—증** an admission ticket
출자 出資 financing ; investment ; contribution **—하다** invest〔put〕 money into ; finance (an enterprise) ¶ 주식에 출자하다 invest one's money into stocks// 박씨가 출자한 사업이다 This business is financed by Mr. *Park*.
—금 an investment ; money invested **—액** the amount of investment **—자** an investor ; a financial backer **— 증권** an investment certificate **공동 —** a joint investment ; a joint venture (합작 투자) **개인 — 사업** a privately financed enterprise
출장 出張 an official tour〔trip〕 ; a business trip ; going on business **—하다** go on a business〔an official〕 trip ; travel on business ¶ …에 출장중이다 be in 《a place》 on a business trip// 출장 명령을 받다 receive an order to go to 《a place》 ; be ordered〔dispatched〕 to 《a place》 on official business// 응급 치료를 위하여 간호사가 출장해 있었다 Nurses were on duty to give first-aid.// 출장이 어땠니 How was your business trip?
— 교수 a visiting〔an extension〕 professor **— 명령** an order to go on an official〔a business〕 trip **—소** an agency ; a branch office **— 여비** traveling expens-

es ; a traveling allowance —원 an agent ; a commercial traveler ¶ 세관 출장원 a man sent from the custom house
—지 the place which one visits on business ; the destination of one's business trip — 지도 (giving) lessons at one's pupil's home — 촬영 ⇨ 출사(出寫)

†**출장 出場** appearance in a place ; participation ; taking part in —하다 take part 《in》 ; participate 《in》 ; appear ; be present 《at》 ¶ 경기에 출장하다 enter a race ; take part in an athletic contest // (말을) 경마에 출장시키다 run her〔him〕 in a horse race
— 선수 a participating athlete ; an entrant ; the entry 《총칭》 — 유자격자 a qualifier 《for an event》 —자 a participant ; an entrant 《총칭》 ¶ 다수의 경기 출장자 many participants in the contest 〔game〕 — 자격 qualification 《for the finals》

출전 出典 a source ; a source book ; the origin ; the provenance ¶ 출전을 밝히다 give〔indicate〕 the source ; give authorities 《for a statement》

출전 出戰 going to the war〔the battle field〕 ; departure for the front ; [경기의] participating in a game —하다 go to the front ; serve on active duty ; participate〔take part〕 in athletic games ¶ 경기에 출전하다 play〔take part〕 in an athletic contest // 선수권을 쟁취하기 위하여 출전하다 enter for an event to win the championship
— 선수 an entrant ; a participating athlete —자 participants ; entrants

출정 出廷 appearance in court ; a court appearance —하다 appear in court ; attend court ; be in court ¶ 출정을 명하다 summon 《a person》 to appear in court〔at the court〕 // 재판을 받기 위해 출정하다 be brought to court for trial // 피고가 출정치 않으면 in case of nonappearance of the defendant
— 명령 garnishment —일 the court day

출정 出征 departure for the front ; expedition —하다 depart for〔go to〕 the front ; go to war ; serve in the war ; take the field (군대가) ¶ 출정해 있다 be at the front〔in the field〕 // 의용군으로 출정하다 go to war as a volunteer
— 가족 the family of a soldier at the front〔in the battle〕 —군 an army in the field ; troops at the front — 군인 a soldier at the front — 병사 가족 the family of a soldier at the front ; a service-man's family

출제 出題 setting〔giving〕 questions 《for examination》 ; presenting problems ; [문제] the questions〔problems〕 in the examination —하다 set〔give〕 questions 《for examination》 ; present problems ; make up a question ¶ 출제 문제들은 비교적 다루기 쉬웠다〔어려웠다〕 The questions in the examination were considerably easy〔difficult〕.
—자 an examiner

출중 出衆 distinction ; superiority ; eminence ; prominence —하다 be outstanding ; be by far the best ; excel ; surpass ¶ …에 출중하다 excel 《a person》 in 《studies, sports》 // 딴 사람보다 출중하다 tower high above one's fellows ; stand out above the others ; have an advantage over others // 그는 출중한 인물이다 He is an outstanding figure〔a prominent person〕. // 그는 출중한 재간을 가졌었다 He was endowed with extraordinary talents. // 그는 출중하게 공부를 잘한다 He is by far the best student.

출진 出陣 going to war —하다 go to battle ; take the field

출차 出差 〖천문〗 evection

출찰 出札 issue of a ticket
—계 a ticket clerk 《미》 ; a booking clerk 《영》 —소〔구〕 a ticket office ; a ticket window〔booth〕 ; a booking office

출창 出窓 a bow window ; a bay (window)

⁑**출처 出處** source ; origin ; provenance ¶ 뉴스의 출처 the source of (the) news 〔information〕 // 출처가 확실한 authentic ; reliable // 출처를 밝히다 disclose 〔authenticate〕 the source ; cite authority // 소문의 출처를 밝히다 trace (the source of) a report // 그 보도의 출처는 공표되지 않았다 The source of that information is withheld. // 이 글의 출처는 셰익스피어이다 This is quoted from Shakespeare.

출초 出超 an excess of exports (over imports) ; a favorable balance of (trade) ¶ 10월에는 1억불의 출초였다 We had a favorable trade balance of one hundred million dollars in October. / The excess of exports over imports in October was one hundred million dollars.

출출하다 be with empty stomach ; be 〔feel〕 somewhat hungry ¶ 출출한 김에 in one's hunger // 출출한 배에 술 한잔 하다 drink on an empty stomach

출타 出他 an outing ; being away from home —하다 go〔be〕 out 《on a visit》 ¶ 출타 중에 in〔during〕 one's absence ; while one is away〔absent〕 // 출타하고 안 계신다 He has gone out and is not back yet. // 출타 중이라 실례했습니다 I am very sorry I was not in 《home, office》 when you called on me.

출탄 出炭 coal production ; production of coal —하다 produce coal
—량 coal output

출토 出土 —하다 [사물이 주어] be excavated〔unearthed, exhumed, dug out〕 《at a site, from the ruins of...》 ; be found 《at》 ; [장소가 주어] produce ; yield
—품 an unearthed〔excavated〕 article ;

a〔an archaeological〕 find

†**출판 出版** publication ; publishing ; issue **—하다** publish ; put〔bring〕 out ; issue ; print ¶ 출판의 자유 freedom of the press // 출판을 시작하다 embark on〔undertake〕 the publication 《of》 // 출판되다 be published ; come〔be〕 out // 그의 신작이 출판되었다 His new book is out. // 그는 출판업계의 거물이다 He is the leading figure in the field of publication.

—계(界) the publishing world ; publishing circles **—권** the right of publication ; publication right ; a copyright **—기념회** a party in celebration〔honor〕 of the publication of a book **— 목록** a catalog(ue) of publications **—물** a publication **—법** the publication law ; the press law **—부(部)** a publishing department **—부수** the number of issues **—비** publishing costs **—사** a publishing company 〔house, firm〕 **— 신고** a report of publication **—업** the publishing business **—업자** a publisher **—자** a publisher ; a publishing house〔firm〕 **— 조건** terms of publication **— 허가** a license to publish 《a book》 ; 〖카톨릭〗 imprimatur **— 협회** the publishers' association **예약 —** publication by subscription **자비 —** publication on one's own account **한정 —** limited publication

출판권 出版權 the right of publication ; publication rights ; copyright ⇨ 판권 ¶ 출판권의 소유〔침해〕 ownership〔an infringement〕 of copyright // 출판권을 양도하다〔받다〕 hand〔take〕 over the copyright

†**출품 出品** exhibition ; display ; [물건] an exhibit **—하다** exhibit ; display ; put on exhibition〔view, show〕 ; show on exhibition ¶ 박람회에 출품하다 submit for exhibition ; send an exhibit to the fair ; participate in the exposition // 그림을 전람회에 출품하다 exhibit one's pictures at a public show

—국 an exhibiting country **— 목록** a catalog(ue) of exhibits **—물** an exhibit ; an article of exhibit ; display items **—자** an exhibitor **— 점수** the number of exhibits **— 품목** a list of exhibits〔items for display〕

출하 出荷 shipment ; shipping ; forwarding **—하다** forward 《goods》 ; ship ; make a shipment 《to》 ¶ 화물을 출하하다 ship goods from (*Seoul* station)

— 기관 a shipping agency **— 단체〔공동조합〕** a marketing organization〔cooperative〕 **— 안내〔통지〕** an advice〔a note〕 of shipment ; a shipping advice ; a consignment note **—자** a shipper ; a forwarder **—지** the place of shipment **—처** [목적지] the destination ; [하수인(荷受人)] the consignee

출학 黜學 expulsion from school **—하다** expel 《a student》 from school ¶ 출학당하다 be expelled from school ; be sacked

출항 出港 leaving port ; departure (of a ship from a port) **—하다** leave port ; sail from 《a port》 ; set sail ; clear ¶ 부산을 출항하다 leave *Pusan* // 출항을 허가하다 give 《a ship》 clearance ; give clearance papers // 출항을 정지하다 lay an embargo on a ship // 배는 리스본을 출항한 지 4일되었다 The ship was four days out from Lisbon.

— 명령 an order for sailing **—서** a bill of clearance ; a clearance paper **—선** an outgoing vessel ; clearances 《총칭》 **—세** a clearance fee ; clearance dues **— 수속** clearance formalities ; clearance outward ¶ 출항 수속을 하다 clear a ship 《at the custom house》 **— 정지** a port embargo **—지** the outport ; the clearance station **— 통지〔증〕** a clearance notice〔permit, certificate〕 **— 허가** a clearance permit

출항 出航 a take-off ; departure **—하다** leave ; sail from ; take off

출향 出鄕 departure from one's hometown **—하다** leave〔depart from, bid adieu to〕 one's home〔native place〕

†**출현 出現** appearance ; advent ; apparition ; arrival **—하다** appear ; make one's appearance ; turn up ; come into being ¶ 구세주의 출현 the advent〔coming〕 of a savior // 제트기의 출현 이후 여행이 가속화되었다 Since the advent of jet aircraft, travel has been sped-up.

*‡**출혈 出血** bleeding ; loss of blood ; hemorrhage (내출혈) ; sacrifice **—하다** bleed ; lose blood ¶ 출혈을 막다 stop the bleeding ; stanch blood ; stanch a cut ; control the hemorrhage // 다량의 출혈을 보다 bleed badly〔freely〕 ; blood flows profusely // 출혈적인 판매 a sacrifice〔below-cost〕 sale ; dumping // 출혈 다량으로 중태이다 He is seriously ill from heavy loss of blood〔profuse bleeding〕.

— 경쟁 [업계의] a cutthroat competition ; dumping **— 매출 중** [가게 앞의 게시] Sacrifice Sale **—성 침윤** 〖의학〗 bleeding infiltration **— 수주(受注)** accepting orders at a sacrifice **— 수출** below-cost export **— 작전** a "bleed-them-white"〔"bleed-the-enemy"〕 strategy **—증** bleeders' disease **— 판매** a sacrifice〔below-cost〕 sale **내—** internal hemorrhage **뇌—** cerebral hemorrhage **혈관 —** a discharge of blood from a blood vessel

출화 出火 an outbreak of fire **—하다** a fire breaks out〔starts, occurs〕 ¶ 출화의 원인 the origin〔cause〕 of a fire // 어젯밤 저 호텔에서 출화했다 There was a fire at the hotel last night. /A fire broke out at the hotel last night.

출회 出廻 circulation of goods ; supply 《of commodity》 **—하다** goods flow out 《to

the market》; circulate
—고 visible supply —기 a season for active movement in a commodity

춤¹ [분량] a grip ; a grasp ; a handful ¶ 모〔짚〕 한 춤 a handful of rice seedlings〔a bunch of straw〕

춤² height of a rim ¶ 병의 춤이 높다 The vase is tall.

춤³ trouser〔waist〕 tops ¶ 허리춤에 손을 넣다 put one's hands in one's trouser tops

†춤⁴ [무용] dancing ; a dance ¶ 춤추다 dance 《a dance》; [나비가] flutter about ; [새가] circle ; wheel // 춤을 잘 추다 be a good dancer // …의 곡에 맞추어 춤추다 dance to the tune〔melody〕《of》// 기뻐 춤추다 dance for joy // 남의 장단에 춤을 추다 dance to 《a person's》 tune ; be manipulated ; be made a puppet 《of》; be at 《a person's》 beck and call
— 선생 a dancing master〔mistress〕 어깨— shoulder dancing 엉덩이— a hula〔hip〕 dance

†춥다 (be) cold ; chilly ; feel cold ¶ 추운 날씨 cold weather ; a freezing day // 추운 지방 a cold area〔country〕// 몹시 추운 겨울 a severe〔cold〕 winter // 추워지다 get〔grow〕 cold // 추워서 떨다 quiver from cold ; shiver with cold // 추워하다 be sensitive to the cold ; complain of the cold // 날씨가 춥다 It is (very) cold. // 추워서 죽겠다 I am freezing to death. /I am dying of the cold. // 지난 겨울은 몹시 추웠다 We have had a severe winter. // 살을 에는 듯이 춥다 It is piercing〔biting〕 cold. // 오늘도 굉장히 춥겠군요 Looks like it's going to be another freeze today.

충 蟲 an insect ; a bug ; a worm ; a moth

충 衝 〖천문〗 opposition

충간 忠諫 a loyal remonstrance ; pleading with one's master from a loyal motive
— 하다 plead with 《one's master》 from a loyal motive

†충격 衝擊 (an) impact 《on》; (a) shock 《to》; percussion ; a trauma — 하다 shock ; strike against ; bombard ¶ 충격을 주다 shock 《a person》; give 《a person》 a shock ; make 《a person》 jump // 충격을 받다 get〔feel〕 a shock // 그의 죽음은 그녀에게 큰 충격을 주었다 His death was a great shock to her.
—력 shock power — 시험 an impact〔a percussion〕 test — 실속(失速) 〖항공〗 shock stall — 요법 shock treatment〔therapy〕 —음 a crashing sound — 전류 an impulse〔impulsive〕 current (of electricity) —파 a shock wave —파음 [초음속 항공기 따위의] a sonic boom

충견 忠犬 a faithful dog

†충고 忠告 [조언] advice ; counsel ; suggestion ; [간언] admonition ; remonstrance ; exhortation ; [경고] (a) warning ; (a) caution — 하다 advise ; give 《a person》 advice ; warn ; give warning ; admonish ; counsel ¶ 충고를 구하다 ask advice 《of a person》; seek the advice 《of a person》// 충고를 듣다 follow〔take〕 《a person's》 advice ; act upon 《a person's》 advice // 충고를 어기다 act against 《a person's》 advice // 충고를 무시하다 disregard〔ignore, take no heed of〕 《a person's》 advice ; do against 《a person's》 counsel // 술을 마시지 말라고 충고하다 advise 《a person》 not to drink ; warn against drinking // 자네에게 충고하겠네 Let me give you a few pieces of advice. // 왜 나의 충고를 듣지 않는거지 Why do you turn a deaf ear to my admonition?
—자 an adviser ; a counselor

충군 忠君 loyalty〔devotion〕 to one's sovereign〔king〕
— 애국(愛國) loyalty and patriotism — 애국 지사 a loyalist and patriot ; a man who is loyal and patriotic — 애민(愛民) loyalty and love of the people

충근 忠勤 loyal〔devoted〕 service ; faithfulness — 하다 render loyal service ; discharge〔do〕 one's duty faithfully

충나다 蟲— get infested with 《worms》

충노 忠奴 ⇨ 충복(忠僕)

‡충당 充當 appropriation ; making up ; filling up ; meeting 《the demand》; supplying 《a deficiency》 — 하다 replenish ; fill up ; make up ; appropriate ; supply ; allocate ¶ 생활비에 충당할 돈 money to meet one's living expenses ; money earmarked for living expenses // 돈을 어떤 목적〔사업〕에 충당하다 appropriate a sum to a purpose〔an enterprise〕// 공원의 일부를 운동장으로 충당하다 devote part of the park to a playground // 돈을 빚 갚는 데 충당하다 apply money to the payment of a debt

†충돌 衝突 a collision ; a clash ; [불일치] a conflict ; a discord ; [전투] an encounter — 하다 collide with〔against〕; come into collision with ; run〔strike〕 against〔into〕; clash with ; conflict with ¶ 의견〔이해〕의 충돌 a clash〔collision〕 of views〔interests〕// 부자간의 충돌 a friction between father and son // 공중 충돌 a collision in mid air // 정면 충돌 a head-on collision // 휴전선에서의 양군의 충돌 encounters between two armies at the truce line // 그의 차가 나무와 충돌했다 He ran his car into a tree. // 버스와 택시가 저 모퉁이에서 충돌했다 A bus collided with a taxi at the corner. // 두 대의 차가 저 커브에서 충돌했다 Two cars crashed on that curve. // 어제 여기서 큰 열차 충돌 사고가 있었다 There was a horrible smash on the railway here yesterday. // 그의 자동차는 충돌해서 많이 망가졌다 His car was badly dented in a collision. // 가두에서 경찰과 학생의 충돌이 있었다 There was a fight on the street between the

police and students. // 야당은 정부와 그 문제로 정면 충돌했다 The opposition party clashed head-on with the government over the question. // 그는 아무와도 잘 충돌한다 He is apt to fall out with anybody.
감정 — an emotional〔a temperamental〕 clash 《between, with》 군사적 — a military collision 《between》 무력 — an armed conflict 《with, between》 삼중〔이중〕 — a three-way〔double〕 collision 유혈 — a sanguinary collision 측면 — a broadside collision

‡**충동 衝動** ① an urge ; an impulse ; an impetus ¶ 성적 충동 a sexual urge〔drive〕; the sex drive // 충동적으로 on impulse ; impulsively ; on the spur of the moment // 충동적으로 사람을 죽이다 kill 《a person》 on the spur of the moment // 일시적 충동에 못 이기다 give in to the impulse of the moment // 충동을 느끼다 feel the urge to 《do》 // 젊은이는 노인들보다 더 충동적이다 The young are liable to be more impulsive〔impetuous〕 than the aged. // 집을 순간적인 충동으로 살 수는 없다 You can't buy a house on the spur of the moment.
② [교사·선동] instigation ; incitement —하다 instigate ; stir up ; urge ; set 〔egg〕 《a person》 on ¶ 충동하는 사람 an instigator // 충동하여 도둑질을 하게 하다 instigate〔get〕 《a person》 to steal
— 터빈 an impulse turbine 추상 — [예술상의] an abstract impulse

충동적 衝動的 impulsive ¶ 충동적인 사람 an impulsive person ; a man of impulse // 충동적으로 impulsively ; on impulse

충량 忠良 loyalty and honesty

충렬 忠烈 unswerving loyalty ; faithfulness —하다 (be) loyal and true ; devoted and faithful

충령탑 忠靈塔 a memorial to fallen heroes ; a monument for the war dead

충류 蟲類 the insect family ; worms ; insects

***충만 充滿** abundance ; fullness ; repletion —하다 be full 《of》 ; be filled〔crowded〕 《with》 ; (be) abundant ¶ 충만시키다 fill〔replete〕 《with》 // 정력이 충만하다 be full of energy ; be all energy // 그 안내서는 유익한 기사로 충만하다 The guidebook is replete with useful information.

충매 蟲媒 〖식물〗 entomophily
—화 an entomophilous flower

충복 忠僕 a faithful〔devoted, dutiful〕 servant ; a henchman

†**충분 充分** —하다 (be) sufficient ; enough ; ample ; good ; thorough ; satisfactory ¶ 충분한 수입 an ample income // 충분한 이유 a good〔an adequate〕 reason // 충분한 식량 sufficient provisions // 충분한 조사〔고려〕 a full〔thorough〕 investigation〔consideration〕 // 우리는 시간이 충분했다 We were in plenty of time. /We had ample time at our disposal. // 그 배는 2개월 간의 항해에 충분한 식량을 실었다 The ship had a sufficiency of provisions for a voyage of two months. // 이 방의 크기는 우리의 큰 모임을 수용하기에는 충분하지 않다 The room is inadequate for our large group. // 그만하면 충분합니다 That's enough. // 하루에 2달러면 충분하다 Two dollars a day will do.

충분히 充分— [정도] enough ; sufficiently ; fairly ; thoroughly ; in its fullness ; to the fullest measure ; without restraint ; [풍부하게] amply ; copiously ; plentifully ; in plenty ; [만족하게] satisfactorily ; to one's satisfaction ; to one's heart's content ¶ 충분히 생각한 후에 after 〔upon〕 due consideration // 충분히 표준에 달하다 be well up to the standard // 충분히 그 직위를 담당하다 be adequate to one's post // 성공할 가망이 충분히 있다 be in a fair way to succeed // 여기서 5마일은 충분히 된다 It is a good five miles from here.

충비 充備 complete preparation —하다 prepare completely〔adequately〕

충사 忠死 a loyal death —하다 die for one's loyalty

충색 充塞 filling up ; congestion —하다 fill up ; congest

***충성 忠誠** loyalty ; devotion ; faithfulness ; fidelity ; sincerity ; patriotism ¶ 충성스럽다 be loyal〔faithful, patriotic, devoted, true〕 // 충성을 다하다 be loyal 〔faithful, devoted〕 《to》 ; render devoted service // 충성을 맹세하다 pledge loyalty ; make a pledge of allegiance
— 선서(宣誓) [공무원 따위의] a loyalty oath

충수염 蟲垂炎 appendicitis
— 수술 appendectomy

충순 忠純 faithfulness and simplicity ; honesty —하다 (be) faithful ; honest ; true

충순 忠順 loyalty ; fidelity ; devotion —하다 (be) dutiful ; obedient

충신 忠臣 a loyal subject ; a faithful retainer ; a loyalist ¶ 충신은 두 임금을 섬기지 않는다 A faithful retainer will not serve two masters. // 충신은 효자 가문에서 나온다 A filial son makes a loyal subject.

충신 忠信 fidelity ; loyalty ; faithfulness ; devotion

†**충실 忠實** faithfulness ; devotion ; honesty ; fidelity ; faith —하다 (be) faithful ; honest ; devoted ; loyal ; trusty ; true ¶ 충실하게 faithfully ; truly ; honestly // 충실한 벗 a faithful friend // 올바른 목적에 충실한 사람 a man of sterling honesty of purpose // 충실하게 일하다 serve〔work〕 faithfully ; work like a horse〔nigger〕 // 직책에 충실하다 be faithful〔devoted〕 to

one's duties // 그 영화는 원작에 충실하다 The film is true〔faithful〕 to the original (work). // 그는 자기 자신에 충실했다 He was faithful to his principles.
—도 [통신] fidelity ; [텔레비전 영상의] linearity 고(高)—도 수신기 a high-fidelity〔hi-fi〕 receiver

충실 充實 [실질] substantiality ; fullness ; [충족] repletion ; replenishment ; [완비] completeness ; perfection **—하다** (be) full ; replete ; complete ; rich ; substantial ¶ 국방의 충실 completion〔perfection〕 of national defense // 내용이 충실한 저술 a substantial work // 건강의 충실을 도모하다 try to build up perfect health // 생활 내용을 충실하게 하다 enrich one's experiences // 충실한 생활을 하다 live a full life // 책의 내용이 충실하다 a book is substantial〔very rich〕 in content

*****충심 衷心** one's true heart ; one's inmost feelings〔heart〕 ¶ 충심으로 from the bottom of one's heart ; cordially ; with one's whole heart ; heartily ; wholeheartedly ; sincerely // 충심으로부터의 환영 a hearty〔cordial〕 welcome〔reception〕 // 충심에서 우러나오는 동정 heartfelt〔hearty〕 sympathy // 충심으로 사랑하다 love with one's whole heart // 충심으로 감사합니다 I thank you from the bottom of my heart.

충심 忠心 loyalty ; fidelity ; allegiance ; integrity ¶ 충심이 지극하다 (be) loyal ; true ; faithful ; devoted

충심 衝心 〖의학〗 heart failure

충애 忠愛 [충성과 사랑] loyalty and love ; devoted affection ; [충군 애국] loyalty and patriotism

충양돌기 蟲樣突起 〖해부〗 the vermiform appendix
—염(炎) appendicitis — 절제 수술 appendectomy

충언 忠言 honest〔good〕 advice ; counsel **—하다** give good counsel ; advise ¶ 충언은 역이(逆耳)라 Unpleasant advice is a good medicine. /Good advice is harsh to the ear. /Honest advice jars on the ear.

충영 a gall ; an insect gall
— 곤충 a gall insect 유두상(乳頭狀) — a nipple gall

충요 衝要 an important〔strategic〕 place ⇨ 요충(要衝)

충욕 充慾 gratifying one's desire〔lust〕 **—하다** gratify〔please, satisfy〕 one's desire

충용 忠勇 loyalty and courage〔valor〕 **—하다** (be) loyal and courageous〔brave〕

충용 充用 appropriation ; application ⇨ 충당 **—하다** appropriate 《to, for》 ; apply 《to》 ; earmark 《for》

충원 充員 supplement of the personnel ; [군사] reserves ; recruits ; drafts (보충인원) **—하다** supplement the personnel ; levy ; recruit
— 계획 a levy plan — 소집 calling out the reserves ; a levy in mass ; a general levy

충의 忠義 loyalty ; devotion ; faithfulness ; fidelity ; allegiance ¶ 충의 있는 loyal ; faithful ; devoted // 충의를 다하다 be faithful〔devoted〕 to 《one's master》 ; show loyalty〔fidelity〕 to 《one's lord》
— 지사 a man of loyalty and uprightness

충이다 shake up and down〔from side to side〕 ; joggle 《something》 in ¶ 쌀자루를 충이다 shake a rice bag from side to side ; joggle rice in the bag

충일 充溢 overflow ; exuberance ; affluence ; abundance ; adequacy ; sufficiency **—하다** overflow ; be full 《of》 ; be overflowing 《with》 ; be affluent〔abundant〕 《in》 ; be exuberant

충재 蟲災 damage from insects ⇨ 충해

충적 沖積 〖지질〗 ¶ 충적의 alluvial
—곡(谷) an alluvial valley —기 the alluvial epoch〔period〕 —물 alluvium ; alluvial matter — 물질 alluvial material — 선상지(扇狀地) an alluvial fan —제(堤) a levee —지 an alluvion —층 the alluvial layer —토 alluvial soil — 퇴적물 alluvial deposits — 평야 an alluvial plain ; a foodplain

충전 充塡 filling (up) ; replenishment ; plugging (충치·구멍 따위를) **—하다** fill up ; stop (up) ; replenish ; plug ¶ 화약을 충전하다 tamp powder // 충치에 고무를 충전하다 plug〔fill〕 a decayed tooth with gum
—기 a plugger ; a filling machine — 세포 〖식물〗 complementary cells — 재료 tamping ; gob —제(劑) a filler

충전 充電 an electric charging ; electrification **—하다** electrify ; charge 《an accumulator, a storage battery》 with electricity
—기 a charger —소 a charging station — 장치 charging equipment — 전지〔전류〕 a charging battery〔current〕 과(過)— overcharge 재— recharging 전지— battery charging 세류(細流) —기 a trickle charger

충절 忠節 faithfulness ; loyalty ; fidelity ; allegiance ; devotion ¶ 충절을 다하다 serve with loyalty ; be loyal〔devoted〕 to 《one's lord》

충정 衷情 one's true feeling〔heart〕 ; one's inmost〔deepest〕 feeling ¶ 충정에서 우러나오는 동정 heartfelt sympathy // 충정을 털어놓다 open one's heart to 《a person》 ; unbosom oneself

충정 衝程 〖기계〗 a stroke

충족 充足 sufficiency ; adequacy ; satisfaction ; fullness ; being enough **—하다** (be) sufficient ; adequate ; satisfactory ; full ; enough ¶ 충족적 조건 sufficient condition // 충족 이유의 원리 〖철학〗 principle of sufficient reason // 살아가기에

충족한 수입 enough income to get along on // 충족시키다 fill ; fulfill ; meet ; satisfy // 조건을 충족시키다 meet the requirements ; satisfy the conditions // 식욕을 충족시키다 satisfy one's appetite fully

충직 忠直 uprightness ; faithfulness ; honesty **—하다** (be) faithful ; honest ; upright ; true ¶ 충직한 마음 a true heart ; an honest mind // 그는 주인에게 충직한 머슴이다 He is a servant true to his master.

충천 衝天 —하다 rise〔soar〕 high up ; go sky high ¶ 의기가 충천하다 one's spirit soars to the skies ; be in high spirits ; be feeling sky-high // 흑연이 충천한다 A cloud of dense smoke shoots up into the sky. /Black smoke goes sky high.

충충 ① [걸음을] (walking) fast ; hastily ; briskly ; with a brisk step ¶ 걸음을 충충 걷다 walk at a fast clip ; breeze along ② [물이] full and deep ¶ 물이 충충 고이다 water gathers full and deep

충충하다 ① [빛깔이] (be) dark ; gloomy ; shady ; dim ¶ 충충한 빛 dark color // 충충한 방 a gloomy〔dimly-lit〕 room

② [물이] (be) full and deep ¶ 우물에 물이 충충하다 A well has plenty of water in it.

충치 蟲齒 a decayed tooth ; [상태] decay of teeth ; 〖의학〗 caries ¶ 충치가 먹다〔생기다〕 get a decayed tooth ; have a tooth decay // 충치가 두 개 있다 have two decayed teeth // 충치를 치료하다 treat a decayed tooth // 충치를 예방하다 prevent tooth-decay ; prevent teeth from decaying

충해 蟲害 a plague of vermin ; insect pests ; fly ; damage from insects ; vermin damage ; a blight ¶ 충해를 입다 be damaged by insects ; be blighted ; be infested by vermin // 콩에 충해가 많았다 There has been a great deal of fly on the beans.

충혈 充血 congestion ; hyperemia ; engorgement ; afflux (of blood) 《to the head》 **—하다** be congested (with blood) ; be blood-shot ; be engorged ¶ 충혈한 눈 blood-shot eyes // 충혈한 뇌 a congested brain // 충혈성의 congestive // 충혈시키다 congest ; engorge ; cause congestion

— 소퇴(消退)〔제거〕제 a decongestant **— 증상** congestive symptoms **뇌—** the congestion of the brain **동맥성 —** arterial congestion

충혼 忠魂 [전사자의 넋] the loyal dead ; the war dead ; [충의심] a loyal soul〔spirit〕 ; loyalty ¶ 충혼을 위로하다 propitiate the loyal dead

—비 a monument to the loyal dead〔war dead〕

충혼탑 忠魂塔 a memorial to fallen heroes ; a monument for the war dead

충효 忠孝 loyalty and filial piety ¶ 충효 쌍전(雙全)하다 be at once a loyal subject and a filial son

췌관 膵管 〖해부〗 a pancreatic duct

췌론 贅論 an idle〔a futile〕 argument ; a verbose〔redundant〕 argument

췌액 膵液 pancreation ; pancreatic juice **—소** pancreatin

췌언 贅言 superfluous〔redundant〕 words ; needless remarks ; tautology ; pleonasm ; redundancy ¶ 췌언이 많다 be redundant ; be verbose ; be pleonastic // 교육의 중요성은 췌언할 필요가 없다 There is no need of a pleonasm on the importance of education. /There is no need to dwell upon〔to reiterate〕 the importance of education.

췌장 膵臟 the pancreas ⇨ 지라

— 결석(結石) a pancreatic calculus 《*pl.* -li》 ; a pancreatolith **—액** pancreatin **—염** 〖의학〗 pancreatitis **— 절개술** pancreatotomy ; pancreatectomy

취 〖식물〗 a fragrant edible wild aster

취 嘴 a (woodwind) reed

취객 醉客 a drunkard ; a sot ; a drinksodden fellow ; a drunken man ; a toper ; a tippler ; a boozer

취결 就結 [어음의] drawing (of bills) **—하다** draw ¶ …앞으로 어음을 취결하다 draw a bill upon 《a person for a sum》

환어음 — a money-order exchange

취관 吹管 a blowpipe

— 돌기 〖동물〗 a siphonal process **— 분석** blowpipe analysis

취광 醉狂 drunken frenzy ; delirium tremens ; [사람] a drunken man ; a drunk ; a drunkard ; a boozer ; a lush 〔souse〕 《속》

†취급 取扱 [사람의] treatment ; [물건·사무의] dealing ; handling ; manipulation (교묘한) ; management (관리) **—하다** [사람을] treat ; [물건을] deal with ; handle ; [매매하다] deal in ; [사무 따위를] conduct ; manage ; carry out ; deal with ¶ 난폭한 취급 rough handling // 공평한 취급 impartial treatment // 사회 문제를 취급한 소설 a novel that treats of social problems // 취급하기 쉽다 be handy ; be easy to handle ; be manageable〔wieldy〕 ; be easy to manage // 취급하기 편리하다 be easy to work〔manipulate〕 ; be convenient to handle // 신사로 취급하다 treat 《a person》 as a gentleman // 사무를 취급하다 transact business ; manage affairs // 외환을 취급하다 deal in foreign exchange // 전보를 취급하다 accept〔take in〕 telegram // 조심해서 취급하다 handle 《it》 with care // 어린애로 취급하다 treat 《a person》 as a little child // 손님으로 취급받다 be treated as a guest // 우리는 그 물건을 취급하지 않습니다 We don't carry that item. // 취

급하는 상품이 늘어났기 때문에 가게를 조금 넓히고 싶다 We've increased the volume of merchandise we handle, so I'd like to expand the store a little.
—량 the volume of business ; the total of dealings —법 treatment ; how to treat 〔deal with〕《a person》 — 설명서 [기계류의] an instruction manual —소 an office ; an agency — 시간 service hours ; hours of attendance —인 an agent ; a person in charge —점 a store dealing in 《a particular item》; a distributor — 주의 [포장 표기] Handle with care. /Fragile. 공평 — a fair〔square〕 deal 소화물 — parcels consignment 수하물 —소 a luggage〔baggage 《미》〕 office 전보 —역[게시] Telegrams Accepted 화물 —소 a freight agency 《미》; a forwarding agency 《영》 화물 —인 a freight agent 《미》; a forwarding agent 《영》

취기 醉氣 effects of drink ; tipsiness ; intoxication ; inebriation ¶ 취기가 돌다 become tipsy ; feel the effect of drink ; get drunk ; the liquor begins to show its effect // 취기가 만면하다 one's face glows with the wine // 취기가 가시다 become sober ; sober down〔up〕 // 취기를 이기지 못하다 be overcome by the effects of the liquor ; fall dead drunk ; pass out (drunk) // 파티에서 마신 맥주 때문에 약간 취기가 있다 I'm feeling a little high from the beer I drank at the party.

취기 臭氣 an offensive〔odious〕 smell ; a bad〔foul, nasty, fetid, filthy〕 odor ; a stench ; a stink ¶ 취기를 없애다 destroy the bad odor 《of》 // 취기가 코를 찌른다 It stinks (to heaven). /It is offensive to the nose. /It has an offensive smell.

취담 醉談 a talk〔speech〕 under the influence of liquor〔alcohol〕; drunken words ¶ 취담이 진담이다 In wine there is truth. // 취담이니 나쁘게 생각치 마오 Don't take me seriously. I am drunk.

취대 取貸 borrowing and lending ; debt(s) and credit(s) ; a loan —하다 borrow and lend

취도계 醉度計 a drunkometer

*취득 取得 acquisition ; purchase (상속 이외의) —하다 acquire ; obtain ; come into possession of ; purchase ; take (재산을) ¶ 소유권을 취득하다 acquire the ownership 《of》
— 가격 acquisition cost —권 ownership —물 an acquisition — 본능 the acquisitive instinct —세 an acquisition tax — 시효 an acquisitive prescription —자 an acquisitor 권리 — acquisition of rights 부동산 —세 the real property acquisition tax

취락 聚落 a settlement ; a community ; a colony

취렴 聚斂 exploitation ; sweating ; squeezing ; exaction ; overtaxation —하다 exploit ; sweat 《people》 ; squeeze 《money out of people》; overtax

취로 就勞 —하다 set to work ; work ; find work〔employment〕 ¶ 취로 중이다 be at work
— 일수〔시간〕 working days〔hours〕 —표 a work card〔slip〕

취리 取利 moneylending ⇨ 돈놀이
—업자 a moneylender ; an usurer

취면 就眠 —하다 go to sleep ; fall asleep ; go to bed ; turn in ; retire

취목 取木 a layer ; [취목하기] layering ; layerage —하다 lay〔layer〕 《a tree》

†취미 趣味 taste ; interest ; relish ; zest ; hobby ¶ 세련된 취미 refined taste // 취미가 광범한 사람 a man of versatile 〔catholic〕 tastes // 문학 취미 literary taste // 취미 생활 a dilettante life // 골동품〔음악, 문학, 우표〕 취미 interest in antiques 〔music, literature, stamp collection〕 // 취미가 있다 have good taste in ; be interested in // 취미가 없다 have no interest for ; have no relish〔taste〕 for // 취미에 맞다 suit〔meet, appeal to〕 one's taste // 취미를 붙이다 develop a taste ; acquire in interest // 취미를 잃다 lose one's interest〔taste〕 // 취미가 서로 다르다 have quite different tastes // 취미를 향상시키다 elevate〔nourish〕 one's taste〔interest〕 // 취미가 공통한 데가 많다 have many interests in common ; have a similar taste in many aspects // 사람마다 취미가 서로 다르다 Everybody to his own taste. // 우리는 같은 취미를 가지고 있다 We have congenial tastes. /My tastes are congenial with yours. // 그것은 내 취미에 맞지 않는다 It is alien to my tastes. // 그것은 취미로는 좋지만 직업으로는 흥미가 없다 It may be nice as a hobby, but will lose its interest as a job. // 너도 뭔가 취미를 하나 갖지 그러니 Why don't you take up something as a hobby?
— 강좌 lectures on artistic topics — 문제 a matter of taste — 원예 horticulture 〔gardening〕 for pleasure〔as a hobby〕 고급〔속악〕 — refined〔vulgar, loud〕 taste 독서 — interest in reading ; the pleasure of reading 악— bad〔barbarous〕 taste 전원 — the pleasure of rural life

취병 翠屛 a quickset door〔screen〕
취병 틀다 관용 make a quickset door 〔screen〕

취사 炊事 kitchen work ; cooking ; cookery —하다 cook ; do (the) cooking
—계 a cook — 당번 the cook's duty ; a kitchen police (군대의) — 도구 cooking〔kitchen〕 utensils —장 a community kitchen (공동의) ; a kitchenette (아파트의)

*취사 선택 取捨選擇 adoption (or rejection) ; choice ; option ; selection —하다 adopt or reject〔take or leave〕;

choose ; select ; make one's option 〔choice〕 ¶ 취사 선택의 자유 freedom of choice // 취사 선택을 그르치다 make the wrong choice ; make a mistake in the choice 《of》 // 적절히 취사 선택되다 [사물이 주어] be properly selected ; [사람이 주어] be judicious in one's selection // 취사 선택에 망설이다 be at a loss which to take〔choose〕 《from among》 // 취사 선택을 마음대로 하세요 You may take it or leave it at your pleasure.

—권 a right of selection ; an option

취산 화서 聚繖花序 〖식물〗 centrifugal inflorescence ; cyme

취색 翠色 verdure ; jade color

취생몽사 醉生夢死 "living like a drunkard and dying like a dreamer" ; dreaming one's life away **—하다** dream 〔slumber〕 one's life away ; pass through life in dreamy state ; drone one's life away ; live to no purpose ¶ 취생몽사하는 사람 a happy-go-lucky fellow ; a lotus-eater

취석 臭石 stinkstone

취소 臭素 〖화학〗 bromide 《Br》

—산 bromic acid —산염(酸鹽) a bromate —산 칼륨 potassium bromate —수 bromine water — 적정(滴定) bromometry — 중독 bromism ; bromine poisoning —지 bromide paper — 처리 ¶ 취소 처리하다 brominate ; bromize — 칼리 bromide of potash ; potassium bromide

:취소 取消 [계약·주문] cancellation ; retraction ; rescission ; annulment (무효) ; withdrawal (철회) **—하다** cancel ; retract ; rescind ; withdraw ; revoke ; recall ; take back ; reverse (법률) ¶ 기사의 취소 withdrawal of a statement 《in a newspaper》 ; cut out // 주문의 취소 cancellation of an order // 판결의 취소 annulment〔revocation〕 of a sentence // 취소할 수 있는 retractable ; revocable ; recallable // 취소할 수 없는 irrevocable ; beyond recall〔revoke〕 // 약속을 취소하다 retract 〔withdraw〕 from an engagement // 초대를 취소하다 cancel invitation // 말을 취소하다 withdraw〔take back〕 one's words // 명령을 취소하다 revoke an order // …에 반대했던 말을 정식으로 취소하다 make a formal retraction of what one said against... // 취소합니다 I take it back. // 그들은 그로 하여금 그 말을 취소하게 했다 They made him eat his words. // 그러나 성함과 전화 번호를 주시면 예약이 취소되는 방이 생기는 대로 연락드리겠습니다 We'll give you the first cancellation if you leave your name and phone number, though. // 그 여자에 대해서 한 말을 취소할겁니까 Are you going to take back what you said about her?

— 가능 신용장 a revocable (letter of) credit —권 right of rescission ; the right of rescind —권부 신용장 a revocable letter of credit — 명령 a countermand order — 불능 신용장 an irrevocable letter of credit — 신청 ¶ 취소 신청을 하다 request a retraction 계약 — rescission of a contract 면허(증) — revocation of a license 예약 — ¶ 예약 취소를 하다 cancel a reservation

취쌈 rice wrapped in aster leaves

취안 醉眼 drunken eyes ; eyes dim with drink ¶ 취안이 몽롱하여 with one's eyes heavy〔blurred〕 with drinking ; dazed by liquor

취안 醉顔 the face of an intoxicated person ; a drunken face〔look〕 ; a face flushed with liquor

취약 脆弱 fragility ; frailty ; brittleness ; flimsiness **—하다** (be) weak ; fragile ; frail ; delicate ; tender ; brittle (바삭바삭하다) ¶ 취약한 몸 a delicate〔frail〕 body

— 지역〔지점〕 〖군사〗 a vulnerable area 〔point〕

취언 醉言 ⇨ 취담(醉談)

취업 就業 employment ; entering a profession ; working ; [일의 시작] going to work ; commencement of work **—하다** enter a profession ; be employed ; go 〔begin〕 to work ; set about〔start〕 work ¶ 취업중이다 be at work // 내년 봄부터 취업할 예정이다 plan to operate (the business) from next spring

— 규칙 the rules of employment ; office〔shop〕 regulations —률 the percentage of employment ¶ 금년도 대학 졸업자들의 취업률이 좋다 The percentage of employment among the college graduates shows a favorable trend this year. — 상태 the state of employment — 시간〔일 수〕 working hours〔days〕 ; hours 〔days〕 worked — 연령 working age — 정지 suspension — 제한 restriction on employment —지 location〔place〕 of employment 불완전 — underemployment 야간 — night work ; the night shift 완전 — full employment 해외 — overseas employment

취역 就役 commission (군함) ; servitude (징역) **—하다** go into commission ; be placed in commission ; get a commission ; enter servitude ¶ 취역 중의 《a warship》 in commission // 미국 항로에 취역하다 be placed on the American line

취연 炊煙 《a wisp of》 kitchen smoke

취옥 翠玉 an emerald

취와 醉臥 —하다 lie dead-drunken

취용 取用 borrowing **—하다** borrow

취우 驟雨 a shower ; a passing rain ¶ 취우를 만나다 be caught in a shower // 취우가 일과하다 [소나기가] a shower passes ; [사건이] a stormy event comes to end

취음 取音 —하다 borrow the sounds 《from Chinese characters》 in transcribing

취의 趣意 [의미] sense ; import ; effect ; purport ; meaning ; [목적] an object ; a purpose ; [요지] the point ; the drift ; the gist ; the substance ¶ 연설의 취의 the substance of 《a person's》 speech // 방문의 취의 the object of one's visit // 그런 취의의 편지 a letter to that effect

‡취임 就任 inauguration ; induction into office ; installation ; assumption of office **—하다** take office 《as》 ; take up one's post〔one's duties〕 as ; be installed ; be inaugurated ¶ 취임을 발표하다 announce the assumption of one's post // 취임을 수락하다 accept an appointment // 취임을 선서하다 take the oath of office // 교수로 취임하다 take up a professorship // 대통령으로 취임하다 take office as president

—식 an installation ; an inauguration ; an induction ; an inaugural ceremony **—인사** an inaugural address **대통령 —일** the Inauguration Day

취입 吹入 —하다 have 《one's speech, etc.》 recorded ; make a record 《of》 ; put on a record〔disk, tape〕 ; speak〔sing〕 into a gramophone ¶ 그의 연설〔노래〕을 취입했다 His speech〔song〕 was recorded on the phonograph〔gramophone〕.

취재 取才 selection〔picking out〕 of talented persons ; finding talent **—하다** pick out〔select〕 talented persons ; find talent

취재 取材 subject selection ; choice of subject ; selection of material **—하다** collect〔gather〕 data 《on the case》 ; cover 《a fire》 (신문 기자가) ¶ 신문의 취재 data for the newspaper ; news material

—(담당) 구역 one's newsbeat **— 기자** a newshound ; a news reporter ; a legman **— 범위** coverage **—원** a news source **— 활동** legwork (미·구) ¶ 정치 관계의 취재 활동 political legwork // 취재 활동 범위 the scope of news coverage activities

취조 取調 investigation ; inquiry ; examination ; research **—하다** investigate ; inquire 《into》 ; examine ¶ 취조 중 under examination (사람을) ; pending inquiries (사건) // 일단 취조한 뒤에 after due investigation // 엄중히 취조하다 conduct strict examination // 경찰의 취조를 받다 be examined〔inquired〕 under the police // 혐의자를 취조하다 examine a suspect

—관 an examining official **—실** [경찰서의] an interrogation room

취종 取種 selection of good seed〔breed〕 **—하다** select good seed〔breed〕

취주 吹奏 blowing ; playing **—하다** play (on)〔blow〕 《the flute》 ¶ 트럼펫을 취주하다 blow〔play〕 a trumpet

—악 wind-instrument music **— 악기** a wind instrument **— 악대** a brass band ; a band of wind-instrument players **—자** a player

취중 醉中 ¶ 취중에 in drink ; when (one was) drunk ; under the influence of liquor // 취중에 실수하다 make a drunken slip ; make a mistake while in one's cups // 취중에 진담한다 One often tells the truth when drunk. /There is truth in wine. /In vino veritas. /What soberness conceals drunkenness reveals.

— 사고 a drunken accident **— 운전** drunken driving ; driving 《a car》 while intoxicated〔under the influence of liquor〕 ; drink-and-driving 《offense》 **— 운전자** a drunken driver

취중 就中 [무엇보다도] above all ; among other things ; before everything〔anything else〕 ; most of all ; [특별히] particularly ; in particular ; especially ¶ 취중 언행에 조심해야 한다 First of all, behave yourself. // 취중 경제 부흥이 가장 긴요한 문제이다 Above all, the economical rehabilitation is the most essential matter.

†취지 趣旨 [생각] an opinion ; an idea ; [목적] an object ; a purpose ; an aim ; a gist ; [의의·요지] a sense ; a tenor ; a meaning ; a purport ; an import ; effect ¶ 질문의 취지 the purport of a question // 연설의 취지 the tenor of a speech // 법률의 취지 the intent of the law // …한 취지의 연설을 하다 make a speech to the effect 《that》 // 회 설립의 취지 the object of setting up a society // 독립 선언의 취지를 설복시키려고 하다 try to persuade the gist of the Declaration of Independence // 본회의 설립 취지는 빈민 구제에 있다 The society has been organized with the relief of the poor for its main object. // 그 취지를 그에게 전하겠다 I will tell him to that effect.

—서 a prospectus **내방 —** the object of one's call **담화 —** the drift〔gist〕 of a discourse

‡취직 就職 employment ; entrance into office ; getting a job ; going to work **—하다** get〔find, obtain〕 a job ; find a work ; be appointed to 《a position》 ; get〔secure〕 a position 《in》 ; enter the service 《of》 ; assume〔take up〕 an office (관직에) ¶ 취직을 시키다 get 《a person》 employed ; place 《a person》 in a position ; place 《a person》 in the service of 《a company》 // 취직처를 찾다 look for a place to work ; seek for a job ; try to find an employment // 취직을 알선하다 help 《a person》 get a job // 무역 회사에 취직하다 be employed in the trading company // 금년 졸업생들이 거의 다 취직하였다 The graduates of this year have almost been placed. // 고등 학교 때의 선생님이 내가 취직하는 데에 물심 양면으로 도와 주셨다 My old high school teacher spared no effort to help me land a job.

—계 [학교의] an employment officer ; a vocational advisor —난 the difficulty of finding employment〔work〕; job shortage ¶ 이러한 취직난에 직업을 갖게 된 것만도 고맙게 생각하시오 Just be glad you were able to get a job at all in this tight job market. —률 the rate of placement — 상담소 the employment office — 시험 an employment examination — 신청〔지망〕 an application for a position — 운동 a job hunting —원 a job application〔bid〕 — 자리 a job ; an opening ; a position ; a place ; a situation ; employment — 지원자 the applicant for a position —처 the place of employment

취진 驟進 rapid promotion —하다 be promoted rapidly ; move ahead rapidly

취처 娶妻 marriage ; taking a woman to〔as〕 wife —하다 get married to a woman ; take a woman〔girl〕 in marriage ; marry《a woman》

취체 取締 [통제] control ; [단속] regulation ; supervision ; [관리] management —하다 control ; supervise ; oversee ; keep control over ; manage ¶ 취체의 대상 a subject of control // 취체의 강화 rigid enforcement of regulations // 취체 불철저의 건으로 견책받다 be reprimanded for lack of supervision
— 관청〔기관〕 a regulatory agency — 규칙 regulations for the control of ; disciplinary rules —역 a director —역 사장 the president《of a business company》 —역 회장 the chairman of the board of directors —인(人) a controller ; a regulator ; a supervisor ; an overseer 전무 —역 a managing director

***취침 就寢** going to bed ; going to sleep —하다 go to bed ; retire ; turn in ¶ 취침 중 while (one is) asleep ; in bed ; at bedtime // 취침 전에 before retiring
— 시간 bedtime ; time to go to bed

취태 醉態 drunken behavior ; drunkenness ¶ 취태를 부리다 put on a drunken display ; hit the booze and become wild《미·속》

취택 取擇 choice ; selection ; picking out —하다 pick out ; choose ; select ¶ 취택하기를 망설이다 be at a loss which to choose

취하 取下 withdrawal —하다 withdraw ; drop ; abandon ¶ 신청을 취하하다 withdraw one's application // 소송을 취하하다 drop〔withdraw〕 a legal case〔suit〕

†취하다 取— ① [채용] adopt ; take ; assume ¶ 강경한 태도를 취하다 assume〔take〕 a firm attitude // 방침을 취하다 take〔adopt〕 a course // 조치를 취하다 take action〔measures〕 // 최후의〔극단적인〕 수단을 취하다 resort to the last〔an extreme〕 measure // 공세를 취하다 assume the offensive
② [선택하다] prefer ; choose ; pick ; take ¶ 달리 취할 길 the alternative // 그 책보다는 이것을 취하다 prefer this book to that // 작은 것을 취하다 choose〔take〕 the smaller one // 많은 가운데서 하나를 취하다 choose〔pick〕 one out of many // 굴욕보다 죽음을 취하다 choose death rather than humiliation
③ [섭취] take ; have ¶ 자양물을 많이 취하다 take plenty of nourishment
④ [꾸다] borrow ; lend ¶ 돈을 취하다 borrow money // 돈을 취해주다 lend money

†취하다 醉— ① [술에] get drunk ; become intoxicated ; get tipsy ; be in one's cups ; have a jag on ¶ 취하여 drunk ; under the influence of drink // 취한 체하고 feigning〔pretending〕 to be drunk // 거나하게 취하다 be a bit tipsy // 곤드레만드레 취하다 be drunk like a fish〔fiddler〕 ; be dead drunk ; be good and loaded《미·속》 // 술취해 넉두리하다 get maudlin in drunk ; grumble in one's cups // 술에 취한 손님은 구내에 더 있을 수 없습니다 Customers who had one too many are not allowed to stay on the premises. // 당신은 취했다 You had one too many (drinks). // 나는 벌써 상당히 취했어 I'm already pretty high. // 몇 잔 마셨더니 벌써 좀 취하는데 I'm already beginning to feel these drinks. // 나는 포도주 한 잔을 마셔도 취한다 I get high on a mere glass of wine.
② [배·차 따위에] get〔feel〕 sick ; be nauseated ¶ 차〔비행기, 배〕에 취하다 get〔be〕 car〔air, sea〕sick // 그는 배에 취하지 않는다 He is a good sailor.
③ [중독] get poisoned ¶ 담배에 취하다 get sick from smoking ; smoke oneself sick
④ [열중] be elated ; be exalted ; be intoxicated ; get fascinated ¶ 여자에 취하다 be charmed by a woman // 성공〔승리〕에 취하다 be elated〔beside oneself〕 with success〔victory〕 // 음악에 취하다 be lost in (the ecstasy of) the music // 환희에 취하다 be in the raptures of happiness ; be beside oneself with happiness

취학 就學 school attendance ; entering school —하다 enter a school ¶ 취학시키다 send to〔put in〕 school
—률 the percentage of school attendance — 아동 schoolchildren — 연령 the school age 미— 아동 a preschool child

취한 醉漢 a drunken fellow ; a drunkard ; a tippler ; a winebibber

취한 取汗 inducing perspiration ; sweating out (a cold) —하다 sweat out

취항 就航 putting out to sea ; sailing ; commission ; service —하다 put out to sea ; set sail ; start on a voyage ; enter service ; go into commission (새 배가) ; be put on《the line, route》 ¶ 취항시키다 place《a ship》 in commission〔ser-

vice〕; commission a ship // 샌프란시스코 항로에 취항하다 be put on the San Francisco line〔route〕
—선 a vessel in commission

취향 趣向 [기호] taste ; liking ; fondness ; [경향] 《follow one's artistic》 bent ; inclination ¶ 취향에 맞는 favorite 《color》; to one's taste〔liking, mind〕 // 취향에 맞다 suit〔be to〕 one's taste ; please〔suit, hit〕 one's fancy // 누군가 이것을 내게 주었지만 내 취향에 맞지 않는다 Somebody gave this to me, but it doesn't suit my taste.

취화 臭化 bromination —하다 brominate —물 a bromide — 수소 hydrogen bromide 《HBr》 — 암모늄 ammonium bromide ; bromide of ammonium —은 silver bromide 《AgBr》

취흥 醉興 conviviality ; joviality〔merriment, hilarity〕 over one's cups ; the fun of being drunk ¶ 취흥에 겨워 excited 〔elated〕 under the influence of drink ; in drunken delight ; heated by wine // 취흥을 돋우다 heighten〔increase〕 the conviviality // 그 소식은 모처럼 올랐던 취흥을 깨쳐버렸다 The bad news threw a chill upon the merrymaking party.

측 側 the side ¶ 양측 both sides ; the two sides ; either〔each〕 side // 유엔측 the UN side // 공산측 the communist side // 주주측에서는 아무 이의도 없었다 There was no objection on the part of the shareholders.

측각 測角 measurement of an angle
—계 an angle meter ; a goniometer —술 goniometry 접촉 —기 a contact goniometer

측간 廁間 a toilet shed ; an outhouse 《미》 ⇨ 뒷간

측거의 測距儀 a range finder

측근 側根 〖식물〗 a lateral root

측근 側近 the surroundings ; around 《a person》 ¶ 측근에 모시다 stand by 《a person's》 side ; attend 《on》 // 측근에 아무도 없다 have nobody around ; be unaccompanied〔unattended〕; be alone

측근자 側近者 close associates ; an entourage ; persons close to 《a person》; one's staff members ; brain trusters ¶ 대통령의 측근자 persons close to the President ; the President's associates // 대통령의 측근자에 의하면 according to those close to the President

측도 測度 measurement (of degree) ; gauging —하다 measure ; gauge

***측량 測量** measurement ; [토지의] surveying ; a survey ; [수심의] sounding ; [헤아림] estimation ; guess —하다 measure ; take measurements of survey ; make a survey of ; sound ; [마음] estimate ; guess ; sound ; conjecture ¶ 토지를 측량하다 survey land // 수심을 측량하다 sound the sea ; take the water depth // 산의 높이를 측정하다 measure (the height of) a mountain // 철도를 가설하기 위해 측량을 하다 make a survey for a new railway line // 사람의 마음을 측량하다 fathom 《a person's》 mind // 측량할 수 없다 be immeasurable〔unfathomable, inscrutable〕 // 신의 섭리는 측량할 수 없다 The ways of Heaven are inscrutable. // 감사한 마음 이루 측량할 수 없습니다 You can't guess how grateful I am to you. // 주택 부지를 측량하다 survey house lots
—기 surveying instrument — 기사 a (land) surveyor ; a surveying engineer — 기술 surveying technique ; mensuration —대 a leveling pole —도 a survey map —반 a surveying corps〔squad〕 —부 the survey department —사(士) a surveyor registered —선(船) a survey(ing) ship 고저(高低)〔수준(水準)〕 — leveling 기선(基線) — a base line measurement 사진〔항공〕 — a photo〔an aerial〕 survey 삼각 — triangulation 지지(地誌)〔지형〕 — a topographical survey 토지 —(술) land surveying 사진 —법 photogrammetry 수심 —기 a depth-sounding apparatus 육군 — 지도 an ordnance map〔sheet〕 육지 —부 the (land) survey department ; the Ordnance Survey 《영》

†측면 側面 the side ; the flank ; [기하] the lateral face ¶ 측면의 side ; flank ; lateral // 건물의 측면 the side of a building // …의 측면사(史) a sidelight on the history 《of》 // 측면에서 보다 take a side view of 《a thing》; look at from the side // 측면에서 원조하다 give indirect aid 《to》; aid 《a person》 indirectly // 측면에서 적을 공격하다 attack the enemy in the flank // 측면을 들이받다 hit broadside // 하마터면 트럭에 측면으로 받힐 뻔했지 I was almost hit broadside by a truck.
— 공격〔방어, 행진〕 a flank attack 〔defense, march〕 —관 a side〔lateral〕 view ; an objective view —도 a side〔lateral〕 view〔elevation〕; a profile —사(史) byways〔bypaths〕 of the history 《of》 — 운동 a lateral movement — 충돌 a broadcollision

측면 測面 measuring the surface area 《of》
—계(기) a planimeter —법 planimetry

측문 仄聞 —하다 hear casually ; learn by hearsay ¶ 측문한 바에 의하면 according to what we have heard by chance ; I hear〔understand〕 《that》

측미계 測微計 a micrometer

측백나무 側柏— 〖식물〗 an Oriental arbor vitae ; a thuja ; Biota Orientalis (학명)

측보기 測步器 a pedometer

측사 側射 a flanking fire

측사기 測斜器 a clinometer

측산 測算 calculation ; estimation —하다 calculate ; estimate

측선 側線 [철도의] a sidetrack ; a siding ;

[물고기의] the lateral lines ¶ 측선에 넣다 sidetrack 《a train》
측수 測水 sounding (depths) ; plumbing —하다 sound the depth
측심 測深 sounding the depth —하다 sound 《the sea》; plumb ; take sounding —기 a sounder ; a depth finder ; [상표명] a fathometer —봉(棒)〔관(管)〕 a sounding rod〔pipe〕 — 연추(鉛錘) a plummet
측아 側芽 『식물』 a lateral bud ; an axillary bud
측연 惻然 —하다 be compassionate 〔sympathetic〕 ¶ 측연히 생각하다 pity ; commiserate〔sympathize〕 with
측연 測鉛 a sounding lead ; a plumb ; a plummet ; a lead ¶ 측연을 던져 넣다 cast the lead
—선(線) a sounding line ; a lead line ; a fathom line —수(手) a lead(s) man
측열기 測熱器 a calorimeter
측우기 測雨器 a rain(fall) gauge ; a pluviometer ; a udometer
측원기 測遠器 a range〔position〕 finder ; a telemeter
*측은 惻隱 —하다 (be) compassionate ; pitiable ; pitiful ; pathetic ; touching ¶ 측은지심 compassion ; pity ; mercy ; natural sympathy // 측은히 여기다 sympathize ; compassionate ; commiserate ; have compassion[pity] on ; feel pity 《for》// 측은한 마음이 들다 be overwhelmed 〔touched〕 with pity 《for》; feel compassion〔pity〕 for 《a person》; take pity on 《a person》; be touched with pity 《for》; feel compassion compassion ; touch one's heart
측음 側音 sidetone
측음기 測音器 a sonometer ; a phonometer
측전기 測電器 an electrometer
측점 測點 [측량의] a surveying station ; a measuring point
측정 測定 measurement ; survey (토지의) ; sounding ; fathoming ; plumbing (수심의) ; calibration (구경 따위의) —하다 measure ; gauge ; survey ; sound ; calibrate ¶ 거리를 측정하다 measure the distance ; take a measurement of the range // 수심을 측정하다 sound the sea ; fathom the depth of water // 정확히 측정하다 take an accurate measurement 《of》 —기(器) a measuring instrument —기구 a measuring apparatus —법 a method of measurement ; mensuration 거리 — ¶ 거리 측정하다 find〔measure〕 the distance 《to》 구경 — calibration 속력 — ¶ 속력 측정을 하다 determine the velocity 《of》 수심 — sounding ; fathoming ; plumbing 시간 — chronometry 열량 — calorimetry 토지 — a land survey ; land surveying 시간 —법 chronometry
측정 測程 a log
—선 a log line —의〔기〕 a log —판 『해양』 a log chip
측지 測地 land surveying ; geodetic survey —하다 measure land ; survey land —선(線) a geodetic〔geodesic〕 line —위성(衛星) a geodetic〔an earth-mapping〕 satellite —학 geodesy —학자 a geodesist
측추 測錘 a plumb ; a sounding lead
측판 測板 a surveying table
측표 測標 a (depth) mark
측화산 側火山 『지질』 a parasitic volcano ; a parasitic cone ; a new volcanic hump
측후 測候 a meteorological observation —하다 make a meteorological observation ; observe the weather
—관 a weather forecaster ; a weatherman ; a meteorologist —소 a meteorological station〔observatory〕 ; a weather bureau
츱츱하다 (be) impudent ; brazen-faced ; dirty ¶ 그는 츱츱하게 남의 물건을 자꾸 달란다 He keeps asking me for things shamelessly.
†층 層 [계급] a grade ; a class ; [건물의] a storey 《영》 ; a story ; a (numbered) floor ; a flight (of stairs) ; [계단의] a stair 〔staircase〕 ; [지층] a layer ; a stratum 《*pl.* -ta》; a bed (석탄 따위의) ; [광맥] a vein ; a seam (of ore) ¶ 1〔2, 3〕층 the first〔second, third〕 floor 《미》 ; the ground〔first, second〕 floor 《영》// 2층집 a two story〔two storied〕 house ; a house of two stories // 그 건물은 지상 9층 지하 4층이다 The building has nine floors above ground and four underground. // 사무실은 6층에 있다 The office is on the sixth floor. // 승강기는 각 층마다 멈춘다 The elevator〔lift〕 serves〔stops at〕 every floor. 대기 상(大氣上)— the upper layers of the atmosphere 사회— the social classes〔strata〕 사회 중간— the middle classes of society 사회 최하— the lowest social stratum 석탄— a coal bed〔seam〕 연령— an age group〔bracket〕 중생(中生)— the Mesozoic stratum 지식— the intellectual class ; the intellectuals ; the intelligentsia 상— 사회 the upper classes ; upper-class society
층각 層閣 a many-storied building
층계 層階 [층층다리] steps ; stairs ; a staircase ; a stairway ; a step〔stair〕 (층계의 하나) ; a flight of stairs〔steps〕 ; doorsteps (입구의) ¶ 높은 층계 tall 〔long〕 stairs // 가파른 층계 a steep staircase // 15단의 층계 a flight of 15 steps // 층계 꼭대기〔아래〕 the top〔bottom〕 of stairs // 층계를 오르내리다 go up and down the stairs // 긴 층계를 오르다 go up a long flight of steps〔stairs〕
—참 the landing (place) 회전 — a winding stair

층나다 層— show〔have〕 (a structure of) layers ; be terraced ; become differentiated〔uneven〕 ; (be) differential ; graded ; uneven ¶ 연령이〔결과가〕 층나다 there is disparity in age〔results〕∥머리를 층나게 깎다 cut one's hair uneven

층널 層— a layer board

층대 層臺 steps ; a stairway ; a flight of stairs ; a terrace ⇨ 층층대

층돌 層— a touchstone ; a Lydian stone ; a stone for assaying gold

층등 層等 gradation ; grade ; difference

층루 層樓 a many-storied building〔turret〕 ; a building several stories high

층류 層流 『물리』 laminar〔streamline〕 flow

층면 層面 the surface of the stratum ; the stratification plane

층상 層狀 ¶ 층상의 stratiform ; stratified **— 격자(格子)** 『물리』 a layer lattice **—암** a stratified rock **—운** a stratiform cloud

층새 層— the quality of gold ¶ 층새를 가리다 assay gold ; grade gold

층생첩출 層生疊出 **—하다** appear in succession ; crop up ; mushroom

층수 層數 the number of layers〔floors, stories, storeys 《영》〕

층암 절벽 層岩絶壁 a rocky cliff〔slope, precipice〕 ; an overhanging cliff

층애 層崖 a stratal precipice〔cliff〕

층운 層雲 『기상』 a stratus 《*pl.* -ti》 **고—** an altostratus

층위 層位 『지질』 a (soil) layer〔stratum〕 ; a horizon **—학** stratigraphy

층적운 層積雲 『기상』 a roll cumulus ; a stratocumulus 《*pl.* -li》

층지다 層— have layers ; be terraced ; become differentiated ; be graded ; uneven ⇨ 층나다

층집 層— a building〔house〕 of more than one story〔floor〕 ¶ 2〔3〕층집 a two-〔three-〕storied building

층층 層層 layer upon layer ; pile after pile ; all stories ¶ 돌을 층층이 쌓다 pile up stones

층층다리 層層— a flight of steps ; a staircase ; stairs

층층대 層層臺 a flight of steps ; a stairway ; a staircase ; stairs ¶ 높은 층층대 a long stairway∥가파른 층층대 a steep staircase∥층층대를 오르내리다 go up and down the stairs **나사 —** a spiral staircase ; screw stairs

층층 시하 層層侍下 having both parents and grandparents alive ¶ 층층 시하의 며느리 a daughter-in-law who has to serve the parents and grandparents of her husband

층하 層下 disrespect ; discrimination ; partiality ¶ 층하를 두고 사람을 대하다 discriminate against 《a person》 ; treat 《a person》 with less respect than others ; disrespect

층화 層化 stratification ⇨ 층상 **— 추출법** stratified sampling

치[1] [길이의 단위] a Korean inch ; a *ch'i* 《3.03030cm》

치[2] [분량] a portion ; a ration ; a fixed quantity ; a share ; [것] stuff ; things ; goods ; [사람] a fellow ; a guy ¶ 이달치 the amount〔charge, rent, income〕 for this month∥하루치의 식량 food for one day∥상〔중, 하〕치 top〔medium, low〕 grade stuff∥중간치 in-between things 《in size, in price》∥파치 defective goods ; damaged〔broken〕 articles∥이 치〔저 치〕 this〔that〕 fellow ; this〔that〕 guy∥저 치가 그렇게 말했다 That guy told me so.

치 値 [수(數)] numerical value ¶ 치를 구하다 seek〔find〕 the value

치 齒 a tooth ⇨ 이

치가 治家 home management **—하다** manage a home ; take care of one's home affairs

치가 置家 ⇨ 첩치가

치가 떨리다 齒— gnash〔grind〕 one's teeth with indignation〔vexation〕 ; be tense with indignation ¶ 그 여자는 그에 대한 생각만 하면 치가 떨렸다 She set her teeth when she thought of him.

치감 齒疳 『의학』 Riggs' disease ; pyorrhea alveolaris

치감다 lift up〔raise〕 and wind ; wind upward

치강 齒腔 a dental cavity

치경 齒莖 the teethridge ; the gum(s)

치경음 齒莖音 『음성』 an alveolar consonant

치고 when it comes to ; as for ; be that as it may ¶ 그것은 그렇다치고 be that as it may ; well, let me see∥그는 나이치고는 크다〔작다〕 He is big〔small〕 for his age.∥그는 나이치고는 늙어 보인다 He looks oldish considering (that) he is so young.∥여자치고 자기 밥을 짓지 않는 사람은 없다 Every woman does her own cooking.∥비밀치고 탄로 안 나는 것이 없다 There is nothing so secret but it comes to light.∥사람치고 결점 없는 사람 없다 No one is without his faults. / There is no one but has some faults.∥제 정신 가진 사람치고 아무도 의심할 수 없을 것이다 No one in his senses could doubt it.

†**치고는** [···을 감안하면] considering ; seeing ; [···의 자격으로는] as ; for ¶ 미국인치고는 한국어를 잘하다 speak fluent Korean for an American∥그는 아마추어치고는 노래를 잘 부른다 He sings very well as amateur singers go.∥새로 들어온 사람치고는 일을 썩 잘했다 Considering〔Seeing〕 that he is new to the job, he has done very well.∥한국 사람치고는 꽤 키가 크군요 Pretty tall for a Korean.

치골 恥骨 the pubis ; the pubic bones

치골 癡骨 a fool ; a simpleton ; an idiot ;

a dunce
치골 齒骨 〖의학〗 the dentine (of a tooth)
*치과 齒科 dental surgery ; dentistry ; dental service
— 교정학(矯正學) orthodontics ; orthodontia — 기공(技工) a dental technician — 기공학 prosthodontia — 기구 dentists' tools ; dental instruments — 대학 a dental college — 방사선학 radiodontia — 병원 a dental clinic ; a dental hospital — 보존학 operative dentistry — 위생 dental hygiene — 위생사(士) a dental hygienist —의(사) a dentist ; a dental surgeon〔practitioner〕 — 의원 a dentist's (office) ; a dental office 〔clinic〕 — 치료 dental treatment —(의)학 dentistry ; odontology — 학생〔조수〕 a dental student〔assistant〕
치관 齒冠 the crown (of a tooth)
치구 馳驅 —하다 [말을 달리다] ride fast ; [뛰어다니다] run about ; [활동하다] play an active part 《in》 ; exert oneself 《for another》
치국 治國 ruling a nation ; governing a country
—책 statecraft ; statesmanship
치근 齒根 the root of a tooth ; a dental root ; a fang
—관 a pulp canal (of a tooth) —막 the alveolar〔dental〕 periosteum
치근거리다 annoy ; pester ; bother ; tease ¶ 치근거리는 사람 a dogged person ; a nuisance
치근치근하다 ⇨ 치근거리다
치긋다 stroke upward ; make an upward stroke (in writing) ¶ 획을 치긋다 make an upward stroke
-치기 (playing) a game ¶ 딱지치기 a game of slap-match // 돈치기 a kind of money-throwing game
치기 稚氣 senselessness ; foolishness ; childishness ¶ 치기에 가득 찬 childish ; puerile ; with a childish show of (one's) ability
†치다1 [때리다] strike ; hit (겨냥해서) ; beat (계속해서) ; slap (손으로) ; smite (세게) ; thrash ; punch (주먹으로) ; give a blow ; hammer (망치로) ¶ 치고 받고 하다 give 《a person》 cuffs and butts // 치고 차고 하다 give 《a person》 cuffs and kicks // 되게 치다 strike 《a person》 heavily ; give 《a person》 a heavy blow // 머리를 치다 strike〔hit〕 《a person》 on the head 《with a stick》 // 북을 치다 beat a drum // 종을 치다 ring the bell // 손뼉을 치다 clap one's hands // 못을 치다 hammer a nail ; drive in a nail // 공을 치다 hit a ball // 몽둥이로 치다 hit with a club // 시계가 3시를 치다 a clock strikes three // 물장구를 치다 paddle one's feet in water // 종치는 소리가 들린다 I hear the bell ringing. // 연주라고 이야기했을때 내 말은 기타를 서투르게나마 조금 칠 수 있다는 뜻이다 By playing, I mean I can strum the guitar a little.
치다2 [공격] attack ; assault ; defeat ; conquer ; charge ; condemn ¶ 적을 불시에 치다 attack the enemy by surprise ; make a surprise attack ; surprise the enemy // 신문에 사람을 치다 denounce 《a person》 in the newspaper ; attack〔hound〕 《a person》 in the newspaper ; write against 《a person》 // 눈보라치다 snow drifts hard ; have a snowstorm ; a blizzard rages over // 물결치다 waves rise ; undulate ; wave ; roll // 벼락이 친다 Lightning strikes〔flashes〕. // 벼락이 나무를 친다 Lightning〔A thunderbolt〕 strikes a tree.
치다3 ① [나무] prune ; trim ; cut off ; slice ; cut into pieces ; peel ; rind ¶ 나무가지를 치다 prune the branches off // 잔디를 치다 trim lawn grass // 채를 치다 shred 《radishes》 // 묵을 치다 cut jelly into pieces // 밤을 치다 skin chestnuts // 약간만 쳐 주세요 Just a trim, please. (이발)
② [체질하다] sift ; sieve ; pass through a sieve ; screen ¶ 가루를 체에 치다 sift flour (through a sifter) // 쭉정이를 쳐 내다 sift grain from chaff
치다4 [깨끗이 하다] clean (out) ; remove ; carry〔take〕 away ; get rid of ; dredge ¶ 똥을 치다 remove the human waste〔dung〕 // 우물을 치다 clean a well // 개천을 치다 dredge a ditch // 논을 치다 turn a field into a rice paddy ; create a paddy
치다5 ① [사육] raise ; keep ; rear ¶ 누에를 치다 rear silkworms ; engage in sericulture // 닭을 치다 raise〔rear〕 chickens // 돼지를 치다 raise hogs
② [새끼를] breed ; reproduce ¶ 개가 새끼를 친다 A dog whelps〔pups〕. // 새는 봄에 새끼를 친다 Birds breed in the spring.
③ shoot out ; spread ¶ 나무가 가지를 친다 A tree spreads branches.
④ keep ¶ 하숙을 치다 keep a lodger 〔roomer〕
†치다6 [양념] put〔pour〕 into ; mix with ; season with ¶ 음식에 양념을 치다 season food with spice // 음식에 소금을 치다 put salt into food ; salt food // 나물에 참기름을 치다 season vegetables with sesame oil // 떡에 콩가루를 치다 sprinkle bean powder on rice cake
치다7 [휘장·천막] put up ; hang ; draw ; attach ; fasten ¶ 모기장을 치다 put up a mosquito net // 커튼을 치다 stretch〔draw〕 a curtain // 창에 커튼을 치다 hang a window with a curtain // 천막을 치다 pitch 〔put up, set up〕 a tent // 병풍을 치다 put up a screen // 각반을 치다 wear gaiters // 문에 거적을 치다 cover a door with a straw mat // 철조망을 치다 construct〔put up〕 wire entanglements
치다8 weave ¶ 돗자리를 치다 weave a mat

//허리끈을 치다 braid a belt//휘갑을 치다 buttonhole ; bind the hole

치다⁹ do ; perform ¶ 어린애들이 장난을 치다 the children are at play//피아노를 치다 play (on) the piano//화투를 치다 shuffle cards (섞다) ; play cards (놀다) //헤엄을 치다 swim ; have a swim//물장구 치다 paddle one's feet in water//용두질을 치다 masturbate

***치다¹⁰** ① [셈] count ; reckon ; figure ; value ; appraise ; estimate ; calculate ¶ 셈을 치다 figure〔cast〕 accounts//총경비를 100만원으로 치다 estimate the total expenditures at one million *won*//집 값을 5백만원으로 치다 value the house at five million *won*

② [여김] consider ; regard ; admit ; grant ; suppose ¶ 그 돈은 없어졌다고 치자 Let us regard the money as gone. //네가 대통령이 됐다고 치자 무엇을 처음 하겠느냐 Let's suppose you were the President, what would you do first ?

치다¹¹ [차가] run over〔down〕; knock 〔turn〕 down ¶ 치고 도망친 자동차 a hit-and-run car//(사람을) 치고 도망하다 hit and run//치어 넘어 뜨리다 knock《a person》 down//치어 죽이다 kill《a person》 by running over ; knock down《a person》 to death//자동차에 치이다 be run over〔down〕 by a car

치다¹² ① [전보를] send《a person》 a telegram ; telegraph to《a person》

② [시험을] take〔sit for, undergo〕 (an examination) ¶ 시험칠 준비를 하다 prepare〔read, study〕 for an examination

③ [소리치다] shout ; raise one's voice

-치다 do hard ¶ 밀치다 push〔thrust〕 hard//넘치다 overflow ; flow (over) ; brim over//해치다 spoil ; mar ; damage //몰아치다 urge forward〔on, onward〕 (마소 따위를)

치다꺼리 [처리] looking after ; tidying up ; dealing with ; taking care of ; management ; conduct ; [조력] help ; aid ; providing **—하다** manage ; dispose of ; take care of ; look after ; help ; aid ; assist《a person》 in doing ¶ 손님을 치다꺼리하다 entertain guests//살림을 치다꺼리하다 manage a house ; take care of the housekeeping//친구의 장례식을 치다꺼리하다 provide〔arrange〕 a funeral for a friend//치다꺼리가 남아 있다 The matter awaits winding up.

치닫다 run up ; go up ; rush up ; run uphill ; ascend (언덕을) ; run upstairs (계단을) ¶ 새가 하늘 높이 치닫다 a bird soars sky high//계단을 한꺼번에 3단씩 치달아 올랐다 He ran up the stairs three at a time.

치대다 [위에 대다] put on the upper side ; [문지르다] rub ; knead ¶ 판자를 치대다 fix a piece of board on the upper side (of a wall) //배를 좀더 치대다 moor the boat a bit farther up//반죽을 치대다 knead dough//빨래를 치대다 rub laundry

치도곤 治盜棍 a club for flogging a criminal

치독 治毒 anti-toxic remedy ; counterpoison ; treatment for poison **—하다** counteract〔neutralize〕 poison ; treat for poison ; mithridatize (면독제를 써서) ¶ 식중독을 치독하다 neutralize the effects of food poisoning

치독 置毒 administration of poison ; poisoning **—하다** administer poison ; put poison《in food》

치둔 癡鈍 stupidity ; dumbness ; dullness **—하다** (be) stupid ; dumb ; knucklehead ; dull-witted

치뜨다 raise〔lift〕 (one's eyes) ¶ 눈을 치뜨다 lift up one's eyes ; look up

치뜨리다 [볏단을] toss up ; throw up ; pitch up ¶ 볏단을 둑으로 치뜨리다 toss sheaves of rice up on the bank〔dike〕

치뜰다 (be) mean ; dirty ; ugly ¶ 치뜬 놈 a mean fellow

치란 治亂 suppression of a rebellion 〔revolt〕; [평화와 전란] peace and〔or〕 war **—하다** suppress a rebellion ; put down a revolt

치런치런 overflowing ; dragging ; trailing

치렁거리다 drag ; trail ; hang down ; droop ; drag on ; [날짜] be prolonged 〔protracted〕; drag it out ¶ 치렁거리는 머리채 a long pigtail//바람에 치렁거리는 가지 branches swaying in the breeze//치맛자락이 치렁거리다 one's skirt drags// 버드나무 가지가 치렁거리다 willow branches droop low〔hang down droopingly〕//체재 일자를 치렁거리다 protract one's stay indefinitely

치렁치렁 ⇨ 치렁거리다

치렁하다 (be) drooping ; dragging ; hanging (down) ¶ (땅에) 치렁한 버들가지 drooping willow branches that almost sweep the ground

치레 make-up ; beautifying ; embellishment ; adornment ; ornament **—하다** embellish ; adorn ; decorate ; deck〔dress〕 up ; smarten up ; doll〔pretty〕 up ¶ 옷을 치레하다 dress up ; be in full feather//얼굴을 치레하다 touch〔make〕 up on one's face ; work on〔makeup to〕 one's face// 집을 치레하다 beautify〔prettify〕 a house //겉치레하다 make show ; keep up appearances ; save appearances//겉치레로만 하다 do for mere form's〔appearance's〕 sake

치련 治鍊 temper ; forging ; smelting **—하다** temper ; forge ; anneal ; smelt

†치료 治療 medical treatment〔attention〕; medical cure ; remedy **—하다** cure ; heal ; treat《a disease, a person for》; cure《a patient of, a disease》; give medical treatment ; attend to ¶ 치료를 받다 be treated ; undergo (medical) treatment ; be placed under medical care ; receive medical attention // 상처를 치료하다 treat an injury ; dress a wound // 병을 치료하다 cure a disease ; have one's disease treated // 눈을 치료받다 have one's eyes treated // 응급 치료를 하다〔받다〕 give〔receive〕 first aid // 병원에서 치료를 받다 be treated at the hospital // 치료 중이다 be under the care〔attention〕 of a doctor ; be under (medical) treatment // 의사의 치료로 완쾌하다 gain a complete recovery under the treatment of a doctor // 치료를 게을리하다 neglect to have proper medical care // 치료할 수 없는 병 an incurable disease // 치료할 수 없다 be beyond medical treatment ; be hopeless **—대(臺)** a treatment table **—법** a curative means ; (a method of) medical treatment ; a remedy ; a cure ; therapeutics **—비** doctor's bills ; a medical 〔doctor's〕 fee ; the hospital expenses ; [배상의] smart money **—소** the clinic ; an infirmary **—자** a curer **— 재료** materials for medical treatment **—학** therapeutics **— 효과** remedial〔curative〕 value **물리 —** physical therapy **민간 —** a popular remedy **심리 —** a psychical cure **자가 —** doctoring oneself ; home treatment ; self-treatment **전 기 —** electrotherapy **폐병 —** treatment for consumption

치루 痔漏 〚의학〛 piles ; hemorrhoids

치루 痔瘻 〚의학〛 anal fistula

치루 〚동물〛 [티베트 영양(羚羊)] a chiru

치룽 a deep wicker basket ; a crate **—장수** a peddler with wares in a round wicker basket

치룽구니 a good-for-nothing ; a nut ; a fool ; a simpleton ; an ass ; a dunce

†**치르다** [돈을] pay 《off》 ; make payment ; pay one's bill ; square〔settle〕 one's accounts ; [경험] experience ; undergo ; carry out ; go through ¶ 돈을 치르다 pay away money // 현금으로 치르다 pay in cash〔ready money〕 // 값을 치르다 pay the price ; pay for an article // 진 빚을 치르다 pay off one's debts 《to》 // 감기를 치르다 suffer a cold // 시험을 치르다 take〔sit for〕 an examination // 형기를 치르다 serve one's term in prison // 손님을 치르다 entertain guests

치를 떨다 grind〔gnash〕 one's teeth ; [인색] be awfully stingy ; be very sparing ¶ 치를 떨고 분해하다 grind one's teeth with vexation 《at》

***치마** a skirt ¶ 치마끈 a girdle of a skirt // 치마의 주름 a pleat〔gather〕 on a skirt // 치마를 두르다〔입다〕 put on〔wear〕 a skirt // 치마를 벗다 remove〔take off, step out of〕 one's skirt // 그 녀석은 치마만 둘렀으면 다 좋아한다 He likes anything with skirts on. **—머리** a false hair used in making a full topknot **—상투** a topknot tied with false hair **—폭** the width of joined parts in a skirt ¶ 치마폭이 스물네 폭이다 be nosy ; be meddlesome

치마분 齒磨粉 tooth powder

치맛바람 ① [서슬] the swish of a skirt ② [차림새] informal dress ¶ 치맛바람으로 in informal attire ③ [여성의 힘] female influence〔power〕

치맛자락 the hem of a skirt ; the dress hem ; the train ; the skirt ¶ 치맛자락을 질질 끌며 걷다 walk with a trailing skirt

치매 癡呆 〚의학〛 imbecility ; dementia **—증** schizophrenia **마비성 —증** dementia paralytica **조발성(早發性) —증** dementia praecox

치매기다 number in ascending order ; start from the bottom in assigning numbers ¶ 번지를 치매기다 number the houses in ascending order

치먹다 ① [번호 등이] be numbered upward ¶ 번지가 치먹다 the houses are numbered upward ; the house numbers run upward ② [시골 물건이] get sold in the city

치먹이다 sell 《local products》 at the center of commerce ; supply a city〔town〕 with 《local products》

치먹히다 ① [번호 등이] be numbered upward ¶ 번지가 치먹히다 the houses are numbered upward
② [팔리다] be sold to the center of commerce ¶ 시골 물건이 서울로 치먹힌다 Local products are sold to *Seoul*. /Local products are in demand in *Seoul*.

치면하다 [액체가] be almost full to the brim ; fill 《a vessel》 almost full

‡**치명 致命** ¶ 치명적인 fatal ; mortal ; deadly ; killing ; lethal // 치명적으로 fatally ; mortally // 치명적인 과실 a fatal blunder // 치명적인 타격을 주다 deal 《a person》 a fatal blow ; strike 《a person》 a mortal blow // 한국의 해외 무역에 있어서 치명적인 타격 a deathblow to Korea's foreign trade // 그는 치명적인 타격을 받았다 He suffered a fatal blow. // 그것은 그 산업에 치명적인 타격이다 It is a deathblow to the industry.
—률 lethality **—상** a fatal〔mortal, death〕 wound ¶ 치명상을 받다 be mortally 〔fatally〕 wounded ; receive a fatal blow // 치명상을 주다 give 《a person》 a mortal wound // 그 상처가 치명상이 되었다 The wound proved fatal.

치목 治木 trimming timber (for building purposes) **— 하다** trim 《timber》

치목 穉木, 稚木 a young plant〔tree〕 ; a sapling ; a set

치민 治民 governing the people ; rule ; reign **— 하다** reign〔rule〕 over ; govern ¶ 치민의 도를 깨닫다 learn〔be awake to〕 the ways of governing the people of one's country

⁑치밀 緻密 minuteness ; elaborateness ; precision ; fineness ; delicacy ; accuracy **—하다** (be) minute ; fine ; nice ; close ; [정교] delicate ; elaborate ; [면밀] cautious ; accurate ; exact ¶ 치밀하게 closely ; minutely ; precisely // 치밀한 관찰 a close〔careful〕 observation // 치밀한 두뇌 a fine brain // 치밀한 계획 a careful〔an elaborate〕 plan // 치밀하게 조사하다 investigate minutely〔closely〕 // 그는 치밀한 사람이다 He is minute and particular.

치밀다 push〔shove, force〕 up ; raise up ; surge ; rage ; swell ; well up ¶ 치미는 분노 flaring anger // 치밀어 오르는 슬픔 the sorrow welling up within《one》// 분노가 치밀다 have a fit of anger ; get into a rage ; feel a lump rise in one's throat // 조수가 치민다 The tide rises. // 눈물이 치밀어 오른다 Tears spring〔well〕 in one's eyes. /Tears come to one's eyes.

치받다 butt up ; push up counter《to》; push up against ¶ (배가) 바람을 치받아 올라가다《a ship》sail against the wind

치받이 an upward slope ; an uphill road ; an incline ; an ascent ; a climb ; an upgrade ; 〖건축〗 mud plastered on the ceiling ¶ 길이 치받이다 The road is uphill〔rising〕. // 거기서부터 치받이다 There the road is running uphill.

치받치다 [불길·연기 따위가] rise ; belch ; soar ; flare ; [감정이] rise ; well ; flare ; [받치다] support ; prop ; bolster〔shore〕 up ¶ 연기가 치받치다 smoke rises // 불길이 치받치다 a flame flares〔blazes〕 up // 분노가 치받치다 flare up in anger ; feel a lump rise in one's throat // 기둥으로 치받치다 support《a wall》with a post // 지붕을 치받치다 give support to a roof

치병 治病 —하다 cure《a person of a disease》; remedy

치부 致富 acquisition of wealth ; making money **—하다** become rich ; amass a fortune

—자 one who makes money ; a money-maker

치부 恥部 the private〔privy〕 parts ; the intimate parts of the body ¶ 할렘 지구는 뉴욕의 치부다 The city of New York ought to be ashamed to have such a place as Harlem.

치부 置簿 bookkeeping ; writing down ; [책] an account book **—하다** keep books〔accounts〕 ; register ; write down ; enter in an account book ¶ 빌려 준 것을 치부하다 enter the loan

—책 a ledger ; an account book

치분 齒粉 tooth powder ⇨ 치마분

치사 致死 ¶ 치사의 causing death ; fatal ; lethal

—량 a fatal〔lethal〕 dose (약의) **과실 —** 〖법〗 homicide〔death〕 by misadventure **상해 —** bodily injury resulting in death **과실 —죄** accidental homicide

치사 致謝 appreciation ; gratitude ; extending thanks **—하다** thank《a person》 for ; appreciate ; extend thanks ; express《one's》gratitude《for》¶ …의 호의를 치사하다 appreciate《a person's》kindness ; thank《a person》 for his kindness

치사 恥事 —하다 (be) shameful ; dishonorable ; disgraceful ; ignominious ; [비열] mean ; dirty ¶ 치사스러운 꼴을 당하다 be put to shame ; humiliate〔disgrace〕 oneself // 치사스러운 꼴을 보이다 expose oneself to shame ; lay oneself open to scorn // 치사스러운 줄을 모르다 be shameless ; be brazen-faced ; be lost 〔dead〕 to all sense of shame // 치사스럽게 굴다 behave meanly〔shamelessly〕 // 소녀를 속이다니 참 치사하구나 What a shame to deceive a girl ! // 치사해요 놔주세요 For shame, let me go.

치사 致仕 [사직] resignation《on account of old age》 **—하다** resign (one's office) ; give up one's post〔appointment〕 ; step out

치산 治山 ① [산소(山所)를 보호함] keeping ancestral graves in order ② forest conservation〔protection〕 ; antiflood〔flood control〕 afforestation **—하다** keep ancestral graves in good shape ; take good care of the forests ; protect the forests ; afforest《a mountain》

— 치수(治水) antiflood〔flood control〕 afforestation

치산 治産 management of household affairs ; management of property **—하다** manage household affairs〔one's property〕

금(禁)— incompetency **준금(準禁)—** quasi-incompetency **금— 선고** ¶ 정신병에 의한 금치산 선고 interdiction of lunacy // 금치산 선고를 받다 be declared incompetent **금—자** 〖법〗 a person adjudged incompetent ; an interdict **준금—자** a quasi-incompetent person

치살리다 praise〔extol〕《a person》to the skies ; speak highly of ; sing the praises of ; flatter

치상 治喪 —하다 take charge of funeral rites ; perform a funeral service

치상 齒狀 dentiform ; tooth-shape

치석 齒石 〖의학〗 tartar ¶ 치석이 붙다 a tooth is coated with tartar // 치석을 없애다 remove the tartar《from teeth》

— 제거 scaling ¶ 치석 제거기 a scaler

치석 治石 trimming stone (for building purposes) ; stonecutting **—하다** cut 〔dress〕 stone ; trim stone

치성 致誠 devotion ; loyal〔faithful〕 service ; sacrificial service (to spirits) ¶ 치성을 드리다 render loyal service ; devote oneself《to》; offer a sacrifice (to spirits)

치세 治世 peaceful times〔ruling〕; a reign ; a regime ¶ …의 치세에〔하에〕 under〔in〕 the reign《of》// 왕의 치세 10년째에 in the tenth year of the king

치소 嗤笑 a despising〔scornful〕 laugh ; a sneer ; derision **—하다** deride ; laugh〔jeer, mock〕 at ; sneer at

치소 癡笑 idiotic laughter

‡**치솟다** ① [솟아오르다] rise suddenly (and swiftly) ; skyrocket ; shoot up ; zoom
② [감정 따위가] ⇨ 치밀다
¶ 불타고 있는 집에서 불길이 치솟았다 Flames shot up from the burning house. // 물가가 천정부지로 치솟고 있다 Prices are skyrocketing. /Prices are being boosted to the sky. /Prices go on soaring〔zooming〕.

†**치수 一數** measure ; measurement ; size ; dimensions ¶ 치수에 맞추어 지은 옷 clothes made to《a person's》 measure // 치수를 재어 by measure // 치수대로 to measure ; according to the measurements // 치수를 재다 measure《a thing》; take the measurements《of》// 치수를 잘못 재다 take wrong measurements // 옷의 치수를 재다 take《a person's》 measurements for new clothes // 치수를 말씀해 주시오 Give me your measurements, please.
—금 measurement by ruler〔yardstick〕; the ruler measure **—서** measurements

치수 治水 flood control ; river improvement **—하다** control floods ; improve water communications ; embank a river ; execute levee works ¶ 남강의 치수 flood control of the *Namgang*
— 계획 a water control project **— 공사** embankment〔levee〕 works ; water conservation works **— 공학** hydraulic engineering **한강 —** flood control of the river *Hangang*

치수 齒髓 the dental pulp ; the pulp (of a tooth)
—강(腔) the pulp cavity **—염(炎)** pulpitis ; endodontitis

치수 稚樹 a young tree

치수 내다 一數— measure《the length of》 ⇨ 치수

치수 대다 一數— take the measurements of ; measure (the length of) ¶ 광목을 치수대다 measure the length of a piece of cotton

치술 治術 administrative ability〔skill, capacity〕

치승 差勝 a slight betterment〔superiority〕 **—하다** be a little better ; be slightly superior ; surpass by a little

치신경 齒神經 〖해부〗 dental nerves

치신사납다 (be) slovenly ; indecent ; be deadly ashamed〔mortified〕; (be) shameful ; disreputable ; scandalous

치신없다 (be) undignified ; degraded ; unbecoming ; ungentlemanly ; ungentlemanlike ¶ 치신없는 짓 an undignified act〔behavior〕// 치신없는 사람 a person with no dignity

치심 侈心 a hankering for luxury ; a "champagne appetite"

치아 齒牙 a tooth
—학 odontology **—학자** an odontologist **비교 —** comparative odontology

치안 治安 (the) public peace〔order〕 ¶ 치안을 문란케 하는 자 a seditionary ; a peace breaker // 치안을 유지하다 maintain〔keep〕 public peace // 치안을 교란하다 break〔disturb〕 the peace // 치안 유지상 for security reasons
—감 Senior Superintendent General《Sr. Supt. Gen.》 **— 경찰** the security police **— 당국** law enforcement authorities **— 방해** breach of public order **— 방해 연설** a speech detrimental to〔subversive of〕 public peace and order ; a seditious speech **— 방해자** a peacebreaker **— 본부** the Headquarters of National Police **— 유지** maintenance of (the) public order **— 유지법** 〖법〗 the Maintenance of the Public Order Act **— 재판** a summary trial **— 조례** the Peace Regulations **— 판사** a justice of the peace《J. P.》

***치약 齒藥** dentifrice ; tooth paste ; tooth powder ; dental cream

치어 稚魚 a fry ; a fingerling ; [집합적] fry ; the young of fishes

치열 齒列 a set〔row〕 of teeth ¶ 치열이 고르다〔고르지 않다〕 have a regular〔an irregular〕 set of teeth
— 교정 correction of irregularities of the teeth ; straightening of irregular teeth ; orthodontia **— 교정궁(矯正弓)** a dental arch **— 교정술** orthodontics **— 교정의(醫)** an orthodontist

치열 熾烈 —하다 (be) intense ; keen ; severe ; fierce ¶ 치열한 전투 a fierce battle ; a sharp fighting // 치열한 경쟁 keen〔cutthroat〕 competition ; a bitter contest

치열 治熱 controlling a fever
이열 — Set a thief to catch a thief.

치염 齒炎 〖의학〗 odontitis

치오르다 rise《up》; ascend ; go up ; climb ¶ 하늘로 치오르다 soar〔go up〕 in the air // 동쪽 하늘로 치오르는 태양 the sun climbing the eastern sky

치올리다 lift up ; push up ¶ 공을 하늘로 치올리다 throw a ball up in the air // 머리를 치올리다 trim《a person's hair》 up ; shingle ; puff《a woman's hair》 high over the forehead

치외 법권 治外法權 extraterritoriality ; extraterritorial rights ¶ 치외 법권을 행사하다 exercise《one's》 extraterritoriality // 치외 법권을 철폐하다 abolish〔relinquish〕 extraterritoriality

†**치욕 恥辱** (a) disgrace ; (a) shame ; dishonor ; humiliation ; (an) insult ¶ 일가의 치욕 a disgrace to the family // 국가의 치욕 a disgrace to the nation ; a national disgrace ; a stain upon the national honor // 치욕을 주다 humiliate 《a person》 ; put 《a person》 to shame ; insult // 치욕을 받다 be disgraced ; be dishonored ; be subject to humiliation // 치욕을 견디다 pocket an insult〔affront〕 ; eat the leek ; eat crow 《미》 ; eat humble pie 《영》 // …을 치욕으로 생각하다 be ashamed of 《a person, doing》 ; feel〔think〕 it disgraceful 《to do》 ; feel shame 《to do》

치우다 [정리] put〔set〕 《things》 in order ; straighten up ; tidy up ; [없애다] clear away ; take away ; remove ; get out of the way ; [몰아 놓다] put〔store〕 away ; lay aside〔away〕 ; [시집보내다] marry off 《one's daughter》 ; give 《one's daughter》 in marriage to 《a person》 ¶ 길의 돌을 치우다 remove stones from the road // 식탁을 치우다 clear the table // 방을 치우다 tidy〔straighten〕 up a room ; put〔set〕 a room in order // 책을 책장에 치우다 replace a book in the bookcase // 물건을 광에 치우다 store things in a go-down // 집어치우다 get rid of ; do away with // 책 한 권을 읽어치우다 finish a book ; read through a book // 일을 해치우다 finish〔get through〕 the work ; be through with the work // 이 접시들을 치워도 될까요 May I clear away these dishes ?

***치우치다** [기울다] lean ; incline 《to, toward》 ; slant 《toward》 ; [편파적] be biased ; be partial 《to》 ; have a partiality 《for》 ; be prejudiced ; be unfair ¶ 치우친 생각 a biased〔one-sided, lopsided〕 view ; prejudice // 한쪽으로 치우친 무역 lopsided trade // 사치에 치우치다 be inclined to luxury ; be prone to extravagance // 판단이 이해 관계에 치우칠 때가 있다 Judgment is often biased by interest.

치유 治癒 recovering (from illness) ; cure ; healing **—하다** [고치다] cure ; heal ; [낫다] recover ; be recovered from ; get over ; recuperate ¶ 치유되지 않는 병 a stubborn disease which will yield to no remedy // 그 여자는 병원에 입원해서 곧 치유되었다 She recovered herself quickly in the hospital.

치음 齒音 〖음성〗 a sibilant ; a dental sound〔consonant〕

치이다[1] get hit ; be crushed ; be squeezed ; get run over ; get trapped〔entrapped〕 ¶ 기차에 치여 죽다 be run over and killed by a train // 곰이 덫에 치이다 a bear is trapped

치이다[2] [피륙의 올이] wear out ; wear〔be worn〕 through ; become seedy ; lose its weave

치이다[3] [값이] take ; cost ; be priced ; be valued ¶ 그가 산 집은 비싸게 치였다 The house he bought cost him dear. // 돈이 얼마 치입니까 What〔How much〕 will it cost ? // 자동차를 가진다면 얼마나 치입니까 How much does it cost you to keep an automobile ?

치인 癡人 an idiot ; a simpleton ; a fool ; a dunce ; a silly ; a nincompoop ¶ 치인의 꿈 a fool's dream

치자 治者 a ruler ; a sovereign ; a person in power ¶ 치자와 피치자 the ruler and the ruled

치자 癡子 ⇨ 치인(癡人)

치자 梔子 gardenia seeds

—나무 a gardenia ; a cape jasmine ; Gardenia jasminoides (학명) **—색** gamboge ; orange yellow

치잡다 take〔grab, snatch〕 up

치장 治粧 embellishment ; decoration ; adornment ; [얼굴의] make-up **—하다** embellish ; decorate ; adorn ; smarten〔spruce〕 up ; dress〔deck, doll〕 up ; beautify ; ornament〔adorn〕 oneself 《with》 ¶ 집을 치장하다 decorate〔pretty up〕 one's house // 가게 진열창을 치장하다 dress a shopwindow // 몸을 치장하다 adorn oneself ; pretty oneself up // 옷을 치장하다 dress〔roll〕 up ; be in gala dress // 얼굴을 치장하다 paint〔powder〕 one's face ; make one's toilet

치장 治裝 preparations for a journey ; arrangements of a traveling outfit **—하다** prepare for a journey ; be equipped for travel ; pack one's bags for a journey

치적 治績 results〔merits〕 of administration ; administrative record(s)〔achievements〕 ¶ 치적의 기념비 a monument in commemoration of 《a person's》 remarkable executive services // 그의 치적은 훌륭했다 His administration was a great success.

치전 致奠 performing a sacrifice to the dead **—하다** perform a sacrifice to the dead

치정 癡情 blind love ; foolish passion ; illicit love ; infatuation ¶ 치정에 끌려 carried away by a blind〔an amorous〕 passion // 둘 사이에 치정 관계가 있는 것 같다 It is suspected that there was a liaison〔an amorous relationship〕 between the two.

— 관계 connection with a love affair **— 범죄** a crime of (blind) passion **— 살인** a sex murder **— 살인 사건** a scandalous murder〔homicide〕 case

치조 齒槽 〖해부〗 an alveolus ; a socket for a tooth ¶ 치조의 alveolar

— 골막(骨膜) alveolar periosteum 《*pl.* ~s, -tea》 **— 농루** 〖의학〗 pyorrhoea alveolaris **— 돌기(突起)** an alveolar process **—염** alveolitis

치졸 稚拙 —하다 (be) childish ; crude ¶ 치졸의 미 beauty of artless simplicity // 치졸한 필치로 with uncertain childish strokes

치죄 治罪 punishment of crime ; penalty ; retribution —하다 punish 《a criminal》 ; bring 《a person》 to punishment ; penalize

치주 齒周 ¶ 치주의 periodontal ; peridental ; paradental

—염 paradentitis — 조직 periodontal tissue

치중 置重 attaching weight〔importance〕 to ; emphasis ; stress —하다 lay stress 《upon》 ; attach weight〔importance〕 《to》 ; give prominence 《to》 ; put〔set〕 value 《on》 ; make much 《of》 ¶ 너무 치중하다 give undue value〔stress〕 《to》 // 영어에 치중하다 put special stress on〔give weight to〕 English // 이 학교에서는 수학에 치중하고 있다 Special importance〔emphasis〕 is attached to the teaching of mathematics in this school.

치중 輜重 [병참] military supplies ; [짐] a pack〔load〕 on a horse

치즈 cheese ¶ 치즈 덩어리 a chunk of cheese // 치즈를 바른 빵 bread and cheese

— 크래커 cheese cracker

치지 도외 置之度外 setting aside〔apart〕 —하다 ignore ; slight ; take no account of ; leave out of account〔one's calculations〕 ; set aside〔apart〕 ¶ 그것은 치지도외하고 apart from that ; leaving〔setting〕 aside this

치질 痔疾 〖의학〗 hemorrhoids ; piles ¶ 치질이 있다 suffer from piles // 치질을 절개하다 excise a hemorrhoid tumor

— 수술 hemorrhoidectomy ; an operation for removing piles — 환자 a sufferer from piles ; a victim of piles

치천하 治天下 —하다 rule over the whole nation ; govern a country ; dictate to the world

치치다 [획을] stroke〔draw a line〕 upwards ; make an upward stroke ; [치올리다] raise ; lift ; toss〔throw〕 up ¶ 꼬리를 치치다 lift its tail

치켜들다 raise ; lift (up) ; give 《a stone》 a lift ; heave ; elevate ; hold〔put, boost〕 up ¶ 머리를 치켜들다 raise〔hold up〕 one's head ; toss the head // 칼을 치켜들고 with a sword raised overhead

치켜세우다 extol〔praise〕 to the skies ; speak highly of ; pay a tribute to ; sing the praises of 《a person》 ; boost ¶ 치켜세워 격려하다 encourage 《a person》 with high praise

치키다 raise ; lift ; heave ; pull up ; draw up ¶ 눈썹을 치키다 raise one's eyebrows // 바지를 치키다 pull up one's trousers

치킨 chicken

— 라이스 chicken and rice — 수프 chicken soup

치태 癡態 foolery ; silliness ; idiotic behavior ; tomfoolery ¶ 치태 부리다 make a fool of oneself 《over a woman》 ; cut a ridiculous figure

*치통 齒痛 (a) toothache ; dentalgia ¶ 치통용 약 a remedy for toothache // 치통이 나다 have (a) toothache ; suffer from a toothache

치평 治平 governing so as to secure peace —하다 govern so as to secure peace

치하 治下 under the rule 《of》 ; under the regime〔reign〕 《of》 ¶ 입헌 치하의 국민 a nation under a constitutional government

치하 致賀 congratulations ; compliments ; felicitations —하다 congratulate〔felicitate〕 《a person on something》 ; celebrate ¶ 치하하는 글 a congratulatory address ; a congratulation // …을 치하하여 in celebration〔honor〕 《of》 // 수고를 치하하다 thank 《a person》 for his services // 성공을 치하하다 congratulate 《a person》 on his success // 득남을 치하하다 congratulate 《a person》 on the birth of a son

치한 癡漢 [호색한] an amorous fool ; an erotomania ; a sex maniac ; [못난이] a fool ; an idiot

치핵 痔核 〖의학〗 hemorrhoids ; haemorrhoids ; piles

— 탈출(脫出) hemorrhoidal protrusion

치행 治行 ⇨치장(治裝)

치행 癡行 folly ; silliness ; a foolish move〔act〕 ; an idiotic thing to do

치환 置換 replacement ; substitution ; transposition ; 〖화학〗 metathesis —하다 substitute for (대용) ; replace ; displace ; transpose ; rearrange ; interchange the position ; metathesize ¶ A를 B로 치환하다 replace A with B ; substitute B for A

칙령 勅令 ⇨ 칙명

칙명 勅命 a royal order〔command, commission, mandate〕 ¶ 칙명으로 by Imperial order // 칙명을 따라 in accordance to an Imperial command

칙사 勅使 a royal envoy〔messenger〕 ¶ 칙사 대접을 하다 treat 《a person》 very courteously ; extend every courtesy 《to a person》 ; give 《a person》 a red carpet treatment 《미》

칙살스럽다 (be) miserly ; stingy ; be low〔base〕 ; be niggardly〔petty〕 《of》 ¶ 칙살스러운 생각 a narrow-minded idea // 칙살스럽게 살면서 돈을 모으다 save up money by living close〔stingy〕

칙서 勅書 a Royal letter〔message, writ, rescript〕

칙선 勅選 a nomination by the King〔Emperor〕

칙어 勅語 an Imperial message〔rescript〕 ; a message from the Throne

칙유 勅諭 Imperial instructions ; an Imperial mandate

칙임 勅任 a royal appointment

칙재 勅裁 royal decision〔sanction〕

칙지 勅旨 Imperial order〔will〕 ⇨ 칙명

칙칙폭폭 [증기 기관차 소리] chug-chug ; puff-puff ¶ 칙칙폭폭 소리를 내다 give off chugs-puffs

칙칙하다 [빛깔이] (be) dark ; gaudy ; loud ; [무성] thick ; dense ¶ 칙칙한 숲 a thick wood // 속이 칙칙하다 be black-hearted

칙필 勅筆 a royal autograph ; the king's own handwriting

칙허 勅許 royal permission〔sanction, consent〕

친- 親 ① [친족] true ; real ; by blood ; german ② [몸소] (for) oneself ; in person ; personal(ly) ③ [친근한] favoring ; pro- ¶ 친미(親美)의 pro-American // 친서방의 pro-Western // 친정부의 pro-government
 —사촌 a cousin-german

친가 親家 one's maiden home ⇨ 친정

친경 親耕 royal plowing〔ploughing〕 in person **—하다** 《the king》 plow in person

친고 親告 a personal accusation〔complaint〕 **—하다** accuse〔complain〕 personally

친고 親故 relatives and friends

***친교 親交** (close) friendship ; friendly relation〔terms〕; intimacy ¶ 친교가 있는 사람 a close〔an intimate〕 friend // 친교를 맺다 form a close friendship 《with》 // …와 친교가 있다 be on good〔intimate〕 terms with 《a person》; be friends 《with》; be hand in glove with 《a person》 // 친교를 꾀하다 promote friendly relations 《between, with》

****친구 親舊** a friend ; a companion ; company ; a comrade ; a pal ; a chum ; a fellow ¶ 나의 친구 a friend of mine ; one of my friends // 아버지의 친구 a friend of my father's ; one of my father's friends // 나의 친구 스미드 my friend Mr. Smith // 오랜 친구 an old friend ; a friend of long standing // 절친한 친구 a close friend ; a great friend // 막역한 친구 sworn〔bosom〕 friends // 진짜 친구 a true friend // 일생의 친구 a lifelong friend // 술친구 a drinking pal ; a boon companion // 학교 친구 a schoolmate // 장사 친구 a business friend〔associate〕 // 친구와 절교하다 be through with a friend // 친구가 되다 make friends 《with a person》; make a friend of 《a person》 // 좋은 친구와 사귀다 keep good company // 친구로 지내다 be friends with 《a person》; be on friendly terms with 《a person》; associate as a friend with 《a person》 // 사람은 그가 사귀는 친구로 알아 볼 수 있다 You can judge a man by the company he keeps. // 곤궁할 때의 친구가 참된 친구다 A friend in need is a friend indeed. // 친구 좋다는게 뭔가 What are friends for? // 나는 그저 당신과 친구가 되고 싶을 뿐이다 I just want to be friends with you.

친권 親權 〖법〗 parental rights〔authority〕; parental prerogatives ¶ 친권을 행사하다 exercise parental rights
 —자 a person in parental authority

친근 親近 intimacy ; familiarity ; friendship ; cordiality ; close intercourse **—하다** be intimate 《with》; be familiar 《with》 ¶ 친근한 사이 intimate relationship // …와 친근한 사이이다 be on terms of familiarity 《with》; be friends 《with》
 —감 the feeling of closeness ; affection ; a feeling of intimacy〔familiarity〕; affinity ¶ 친근감을 느끼다 feel friendly towards 《a person》; one's heart goes toward 《another》; take kindly to

친기 親忌 a sacrifice〔religious service〕 on the anniversary of the death of a parent

친남매 親男妹 one's real〔blood〕 brothers and sisters

친누이 親— one's real〔blood〕 sister

친독 親獨 ¶ 친독의 pro-German
 —주의 pro-Germanism **—주의자** a pro-German ; a Germanophil(e)

친동기 親同氣 one's real〔blood〕 brother〔sister〕

친로 親露 ¶ 친로적인 pro-Russian
 —주의 Russophilism **—주의자** a Russophil ; a pro-Russian ; a sympathizer of Russia

친명 親命 the order〔instruction, command〕 of one's parents

친모 親母 one's real〔blood〕 mother ⇨ 친어머니

친목 親睦 friendship ; friendliness ; friendly relations ; amity ; goodwill ; fraternization ¶ 회원의 친목을 도모하다 promote〔cultivate, foster〕 friendship〔fraternity〕 among the members
 — 관계 ¶ 친목 관계에 있다 be in〔on〕 rapport 《with》 **—회** a social meeting〔gathering〕; a get-together ; a reunion
 상호 — ¶ 상호 친목을 증진 시키다 cultivate〔promote, enhance〕 mutual friendship

친미 親美 pro-America ; pro-American
 — 정책 pro-American policies **—주의** pro-Americanism **—주의자** a pro-American **—파** the pro-Americans ; the sympathizers of America

***친밀 親密** intimacy ; close friendship〔relationship〕; amity **—하다** (be) intimate ; friendly ; close ; chummy ¶ 친밀한 벗 a close friend // 친밀하게 되다 become intimate 《with a person》; make friends 《with》 // 친밀하게 사귀다 associate with each other intimately // 친밀한 사이이다 be on intimate terms 《with》

친부 親父 one's real〔own〕 father

친부모 親父母 one's real〔own〕 parents ¶ 어린애는 낳아준 친부모보다 길러준 양부모를 더 따른다 A child is more attached to its foster parents than to its real parents.

친분 親分 friendship ; intimacy ; acquaintance ; closeness of friendship ¶ 친분이 있다 be acquainted 《with》; be familiar 《with》// 친분이 없다 be not acquainted 〔intimate〕《with》// 친분을 끊다 cut〔drop〕 one's acquaintance 《with》// 옛 친분을 새로이 하다 renew one's acquaintance 《with》// 친분을 맺다 become intimate 《with》; get acquainted 《with》

친불 親佛 (being) pro-French

친불친 親不親 whether intimate or not ; friends or not friends ¶ 친불친을 불구하고 regardless of the terms one is with 《a person》; regardless of relationship

친사돈 親査頓 the parents of one's son〔daughter〕-in-law

친산 親山 a parent's grave

친상 親喪 mourning for a parent ; bereavement of a parent ¶ 친상을 당하다 be bereaved of one's parents ; have a parent die ; be bereaved of a parent

친생자 親生子 one's (real) child ; a child of one's own

친서 親書 an autograph letter ¶ 대통령의 친서 an autograph letter from the President

친서 親署 a sign manual of the King 〔President〕; a Royal〔Presidential〕 signature **—하다** write one's signature in person ; autograph〔sign〕 personally

*__친선 親善__ goodwill ; friendship ; amity ; friendly relations ¶ 국제 친선을 도모하다 cultivate〔promote〕 international friendship // 친선 시합을 하다 have a friendly game

— 경기 a goodwill match **— 관계** friendly〔amicable〕 relations **— 방문** a 《three-day》 goodwill visit 《to a country》 **— 비행** a goodwill〔friendship〕 flight **— 사절** a goodwill mission〔envoy〕 **— 시합** a friendship game **— 여행** ¶ 유럽 7개국 방문 친선 여행에 출발하다 take off for a goodwill tour of seven European countries **— 조약** a treaty of amity **한미간(韓美間) —** ¶ 한미간 친선을 강화〔촉진〕하다 strengthen the ties of friendship between Korea and America ; promote 〔cultivate〕 friendly relations between Korea and America

친소 親疏 the relative degree of intimacy〔familiarity〕 ¶ 친소간에 whether intimate or not ; regardless of relationship // 친소를 가리지 않고 사귀다 associate〔mix〕 with people whether they are intimate with one or not ; mix with anybody without discrimination

친속 親屬 kinsfolk ; relatives ⇨ 친족

친손자 親孫子 one's own grandchildren

친솔 親率 the members of a family

친수 親受 receiving 《a thing》 in person **—하다** receive 《a thing》 in person

친수 親授 giving〔bestowing〕《a thing》 in person **—하다** give〔bestow〕《a thing》 in person

친수성 親水性 〖물리〗 hydrophile property

친숙 親熟 familiarity ; being familiar 《with》; being well acquainted 《with》 **—하다** be familiar 《with》; be well acquainted 《with》 ¶ 그와는 친숙한 사이다 He is my close acquaintance. / I am well acquainted with him. // 그는 사회문제에 친숙하다 He is familiar with〔is well versed in〕 social problems.

친심 親審 investigation in person **—하다** investigate in person

친아들 親— one's true〔real〕 son ; one's son by blood (as opposed to stepson)

친아버지 親— one's real〔own〕 father

친아우 親— one's real〔own〕 younger brother〔sister〕

†__친애 親愛__ love ; affection **—하다** love ; feel affection for ¶ 친애하는 (my) dear ; beloved // 친애하는 신사 숙녀 여러분 Ladies and gentlemen. // 친애하는 김선생님 My dear Mr. *Kim* (서신의 두서) // 친애하는 벗 one's dear friend

친어머니 親— one's real〔own〕 mother

친언니 親— one's real〔own〕 elder brother〔sister〕

친영 親英 pro-British

— 정책 a pro-British policy **—주의** Anglophilism **—주의자** a pro-British ; an Anglophil(e) **—파** the pro-British ; sympathizers of Britain

친우 親友 an intimate〔a close, a bosom, a fast〕 friend ; a chum ; a crony ; a pal ¶ 친우가 되다 become great friends ; become the best of friends // 그는 나의 친우다 He is one of my best friends.

친위대 親衛隊 the bodyguards ; the Royal guards ; the body guards

친위병 親衛兵 a bodyguard

친의 親誼 intimacy ⇨ 친분

친일 親日 pro-Japanese ; Japanophilism

—분자 a Japanophile ; a sympathizer for Japan **—파** the pro-Japanese group 〔party〕

친임 親任 a personal Royal appointment **—하다** appoint personally

—관 an official personally appointed by the King **—식** a ceremony of installation by His Majesty

친자 親炙 a close contact with one's teacher **—하다** have a close contact 《with one's teacher》; be under the personal influence 《of one's master》

친자식 親子息 one's real〔own〕 children

친재 親裁 royal decision **—하다** 《the king》 decide in person

친전 親展 "Personal" ; "Confidential"

†__친절 親切__ kindness ; goodness ; goodwill ; helpfulness ; friendliness **—하다** (be) kind ; good ; friendly ; kindly ; kindhearted ; obliging ; sweet ¶ 친절한 사람 a warmhearted〔kind〕 person // 친절한 행위 a kind act ; an act〔a piece〕 of kindness ; a kindness // 친절하게 kindly ;

kindheartedly ; with kindness ; obligingly // 친절심에서 out of kindness // 친절을 가장하고 with pretended kindness ; under the pretense of kindness // 친절하게 보이는 kindly-looking // 남의 친절을 이용하다 take advantage of another's kindness ; abuse 《a person's》 kindness // 친절을 베풀다 do 《a person》 a kindness ; do 《a person》 a good turn ; treat 《a person》 with kindness // 친절을 무시〔거절〕하다 ignore〔reject〕 kindness // 나는 감사한 마음으로 그의 친절을 받아들였다 I accepted his kindness with due gratitude. // 그는 친절하게도 그것을 조사해 주었다 He was kind〔good〕 enough to examine it. / He had the goodness〔kindness〕 to examine it for me. // 친절히 안내해 주셔서 고맙습니다 It was very kind of you to show me around, thank you. / I am very much obliged to you for your kindness in showing me around.

—심 kindliness ; kindheartedness ¶ 그에게는 친절심이라고는 없다 He has no warmth of heart.

친정 親政 direct royal rule ; royal governing in person

친정 親征 an expedition〔a campaign〕 《against the rebels》 conducted〔led〕 in person by the King〔Emperor〕

친정 親庭 the parent's home〔family〕 of a married woman ; the old home of one's wife ; one's maiden home ¶ 처를 친정에 보내다 send one's wife back to the home of her birth

친족 親族 a relative〔relation〕 ; a kinsman ; kinsfolk 《총칭》 ; kindred ; one's family circle ¶ 가까운 친족 a near relative // 먼 친족 a distant〔remote〕 relative // 친족이라고는 씨도 없다 have no relatives or in-laws 《in this town》

— 결혼 intermarriage ; consanguineous marriage **— 관계** kinship ; relationship **—법** the Domestic Relations Law **— 회사** a family firm **— 회의** a family council〔conference〕 **직계〔방계〕 —** lineal〔collateral〕 relatives

친지 親知 a close acquaintance ; an intimate friend ¶ 친지간에 among〔between〕 friends // 친지간에 싸우다 quarrel among〔between〕 friends

†친척 親戚 a relation ; a relative ; a connection ; a kinsman〔kinswoman〕 ; kinsfolk 《총칭》 ; kindred ; one's family circle ¶ 먼 친척 a distant relation // 가까운 친척 an intimate〔a near〕 relation // 그와는 친척이다 He is related to me. // 두 분은 친척되십니까 Are you two related ? // 당신은 대통령의 친척입니까 Are you related to the president ?

— 관계 relationship ; kinship **— 연고자** friends and relatives ; kith and kin **부〔모〕계 —** one's relative on the paternal〔maternal〕 side **일가 —** kith and kin ; relatives in blood and law ; all the relatives

친친 round and round tight ; winding tight ; coil upon coil ¶ 친친 감다 tie〔wind〕 many times round 《a thing》 ; wind 《a thing》 round and round tight

친친하다 be〔feel〕 stickily moist ; (be) clammy ¶ 친친한 손 clammy hands

친칠라 〖동물〗 a chinchilla

친탁 親— —하다 take after〔resemble〕 one's father's side (용모나 성격이)

친필 親筆 one's own handwriting ; an autograph ; a personal note ¶ 친필의 autographic // 그의 친필로 서명한 서류 a document signed in his own handwriting

— 유언 a holograph will **— 편지** an autograph letter ; a holograph letter

†친하다 親— (be) intimate ; familiar ; close ; friendly ; chummy 《구》 ; thick 《구》 ; be on good〔intimate〕 terms 《with》 ; be (good) friends 《with》 ; get on (very) well 《with》 ¶ 친한 친구 an intimate friend ; a fast〔great, close, bosom〕 friend ; a chum ; a crony (옛 친구) // 친하기 쉬운〔어려운〕 easy〔hard〕 to get acquainted with ; sociable〔unsociable〕 // 아주 친하다 be thick 《with》 ; be hand in glove 《구》 // 친해지다 be intimate〔familiar〕 《with》 ; become intimately acquainted 《with》 // 그는 친한 친구가 적다 He has few familiar friends. // 친한 사이에도 예절이 있어야 한다 Even among close friends courtesy should be maintained. /A hedge between keeps friendship green.

친할머니 親— one's own〔real〕 grandmother

친할아버지 親— one's own〔real〕 grandfather

친형 親兄 a man's own〔real〕 elder brother ; a woman's own〔real〕 elder sister

친형제 親兄弟 one's own brothers

친화 親和 friendship ; fellowship ; harmony ; 〖화학〗 affinity ; fraternity **—하다** (be) friendly ; intimate

—력 〖화학〗 chemical attraction ; affinity ; appetence

친환 親患 one's parent's illness

친히 親— ① [친하게] intimately ; familiarly ¶ 친히 사귀다 be in close association with ; be intimate with ; fraternize with ② [몸소] personally ; in (one's own) person ¶ 친히 관찰하다 observe personally ; make a personal observation // 친히 보다 see 《a thing》 with one's own eyes ; see 《a thing》 for oneself // 친히 방문하다 pay a personal visit 《to》 ; make a personal call 《on a person, at a person's house》 ; give a visit personally

†칠 七 seven ¶ 제 7의 the seventh

***칠 漆** ① [옻] lacquer ; japan **—하다** lacquer ; varnish〔cover〕 with lacquer
② [도료·바르는 것] paint(-ing) ; varnish(-

ing); daub(-ing); [얼룩] a stain; a blot; a smear —하다 paint (페인트를); varnish (바니시를); plaster; daub; coat; smear (얼룩) ¶ 물감칠 daubing colors on 《a thing》 // 잉크칠 an ink stain; a spot of ink // 페인트칠 painting; applying paint // 퍼렁칠 blue paint; blue color // 풀칠 pasting // 흙칠 a mud stain; a smear of mud // 흰칠을 한 벽 white-plastered wall

칠각 七角 seven angles
—형 a heptagon ¶ 칠각형의 heptangular

칠거지악 七去之惡 the seven valid causes for divorce

칠공 漆工 a lacquerer

칠기 漆器 lacquer ware; lacquered ware; lacquer

칠대양 七大洋 the Seven Seas

칠독 漆毒 lacquer poison(-ing)

칠떡거리다 drag; draggle; trail ¶ 칠떡칠떡 dragging; draggling; trailing // 치마가 칠떡거리다 one's skirt drags on the ground // 치마를 칠떡거리며 걷다 walk with a trailing skirt

칠떡칠떡 ⇨ 칠떡거리다

칠뜨기 七— ① [칠삭둥이] a person born prematurely at the 7th month of pregnancy ② [바보] a fool; a dunce; a moron; an idiot

칠락팔락 七落八落 ⇨ 칠령 팔락

칠렁거리다 overflow; run over; brim over; slop over〔out〕 ¶ 칠렁칠렁 overflowing; running over; brimming over

칠렁칠렁 (full) to the brim; to the full; brimfully; overflowingly; affluently
—하다 be full to the brim; be overflowing; keep splashing over ¶ 물이 칠렁칠렁 괴다 be splashing full of water

칠레 Chile ¶ 칠레의 Chilean; Chilian
— 사람 a Chilean; a Chilian — 초석(硝石) Chile saltpeter; cubic niter

칠령팔락 七零八落 unevenness; unsortedness; irregularity; lack of uniformity
—하다 (be) uneven; irregular; unsorted; be in scattered confusion; be at sixes and sevens; be all messed up

***칠면조 七面鳥** ① 〖새〗 a turkey; a turkey cock (수컷); a turkey hen (암컷) ② [줏대 없는 사람] a temperamental〔an unpredictable〕 person; a whimsical〔capricious〕 person; a timeserver

칠목기 漆木器 wooden lacquer ware

칠박 漆— a large lacquered wooden bowl

칠배 七倍 seven times; septuple —하다 multiply by seven; septuple ¶ 칠배성의 〖생물〗 heptaploid

칠변형 七邊形 a heptagon; a septangle

칠보 七寶 the Seven Treasures (gold, silver, lapis, crystal, coral, agate, pearl)

칠보재 七步才 outstanding literary talent

칠분도미 七分搗米 70-percent polished rice ¶ 칠분도미로 할 것 subject rice to a 70-percent refinement (상업 통신)

칠붓 漆— a lacquering brush; a paintbrush

칠삭둥이 七朔— ① 《a person》 born prematurely at the 7th month of pregnancy ② [바보] a fool; a dunce; a moron; an idiot

칠산화 七酸化 〖화학〗 ¶ 칠산화 유황〔망간〕 sulfur〔manganese〕 heptoxide

칠색 七色 seven colors; prismatic colors; the primary colors

칠생 七生 〖불교〗 the seven lives ¶ 칠생까지 even to the seventh life; through eternity

칠서 七書 [사서 삼경] the Seven Books (of Ancient China)

칠석 七夕 the seventh of July〔the 7th month〕 of the lunar calendar
—제(祭) the Star Festival; the Festival of the Weaver〔Star Vega〕

칠성 七星 [북두칠성] the Great Bear 《미》; the Plough 《영》; the Plow 《미》; the Great〔Big〕 Dipper 《미》; the seven stars (of the Big Dipper)
—각〔당〕 a Taoist shrine consecrated to the Big Dipper —판(板) the bottom lining board of a coffin

칠소반 漆小盤 a small lacquered dining table

칠순 七旬 ① [날] seventy days ② [연령] seventy years of age ¶ 칠순 노인 a person of seventy years old; a seventy years old man〔woman〕; an old man〔woman〕 at the age of seventy〔seventies〕

칠실 漆室 a dark room

†**칠십 七十** seventy ¶ 제70의 the seventieth

칠야 漆夜 a pitch-dark〔-black〕 night

칠언 七言 〖문학〗 a composition in classical Chinese verse which has seven characters〔syllables〕 to the line

칠언 절구 七言絶句 a quatrain with seven Chinese characters in each line〔with seven-word lines〕

칠엽수 七葉樹 〖식물〗 a horse chestnut; a buckeye ¶ 칠엽수의 열매 a conker; a horse chestnut

칠오조 七五調 〖문학〗 the seven-and-five-syllable meter ¶ 칠오조의 시 a poem〔verse〕 in seven-and-five-syllable meter

칠요일 七曜日 the seven days of the week

칠원성군 七元星君 ⇨ 칠성(七星) the Big Dipper

칠월 七月 July 《Jul., Jy.》
— 칠석 the seventh day of the seventh month of the lunar calendar — 혁명 the July Revolution (프랑스의)

칠일 漆— lacquering; painting; varnishing; daubing —하다 lacquer; paint; daub; varnish; do lacquering〔lacquer work〕; do painting〔paint work〕

칠장이 漆匠— a lacquerer; a painter

칠전팔기 七顚八起 an indefatigable struggle with adversity ; standing firm in difficulties **—하다** struggle with adversity indefatigably ; stand firm in difficulties ; be not giving in to adversity ¶ 칠전팔기의 노력 an undaunted struggle with adverse circumstances // 칠전팔기하라 If, at first, you don't succeed, try, try again.

칠전팔도 七顚八倒 —하다 undergo various difficulties〔hardships〕; writhe in agony ; toss oneself about in excessive pain ; be schooled in adversity ; go through many hardships

칠정 七情 the seven passions (of joy, anger, sorrow, fear, love, hate and lust)

칠창 漆瘡 inflammation of skin caused by lacquer poison ; boils caused by lacquer poison

칠칠치 못하다 (be) slovenly 《appearance, work》; lax 《discipline》; untidy〔dowdy〕《dress》; slack ; sloppy〔slipshod〕《work》 negligent 《in work》; unkempt 《hair》; loose 《style》 ¶ 칠칠치 못한 꼴로 in disheveled appearance // 그는 무엇을 시켜도 칠칠치 못하다 He does everything in a slovenly way〔slipshod manner〕. // 옷차림이 칠칠치 못한 사람은 일도 칠칠치 못하다 Anyone who's sloppy about his appearance is going to be sloppy in his work.

칠칠하다 ① [길차다] (be) well-grown ; exuberant ; fresh and crisp ¶ 칠칠한 배추 fresh and crisp cabbages ② [청결] (be) neat ; clean ③ [민첩] (be) smart ; deft ; bright ; quick ; nimble ¶ 칠칠한 솜씨다 be a spry old hand

†**칠판 漆板** a blackboard (흑판) ¶ 칠판을 지우다 wipe the blackboard

— 지우개 an eraser ; a wiper

칠팔월 七八月 July and〔or〕 August ¶ 칠팔월 수숫잎 a person who is weak-minded and changes his mind often // 칠팔월 은어 곯듯 한다 One has a hard time to make a living because of a sudden decrease of income.

칠포 漆布 ① lacquered hemp cloth ② [관에 씌우는] a piece of lacquered cloth pasted over a coffin to be lacquered

칠하다 漆— [옻을] lacquer ; [페인트를] paint ; coat ; [바니시를] varnish ; [에나멜을] enamel ; [얼룩지게] smear ; stain ; [분을] powder 《one's face》; [입술 연지를] rouge ¶ 갓 칠한 freshly-painted 〔-lacquered, -varnished〕 // 기름을 칠하다 oil ; lubricate ; plaster 《a thing》 with oil // 문을 희게 칠하다 paint the door white // (페인트로) 칠하여 지우다 paint out ; efface with paint // 페인트를 고르게 칠하다 spread the paint evenly // 지도에 색을 칠하다 color a map // 얼굴에 잉크를 칠하다 smear one's face with ink ; have one's face smeared with ink // 에나멜을 두번 칠하다 give two coats of enamel // 얼굴에 분을 두덕두덕 칠하다 powder one's face thick ; put on thick make-up // 전에 한 것처럼 프라이팬에 기름 칠하는 것을 잊지 마라 Don't forget to put oil in the frying pan the way you did last time.

칠함 漆函 a lacquered box〔case, chest〕

칠현 七賢 the Seven Sages (of ancient China)

칠현금 七絃琴 a heptachord ; a seven-stringed harp

칠흑 漆黑 pitch-black ; coal-black ; jet-black ¶ 칠흑 같은 검은 머리 jet-black hair ; raven hair

칡 〖식물〗 an arrowroot ; Pueraria hirsuta (학명)

—가루〔전분〕 arrowroot starch **—덩굴** the vines of arrowroots ¶ 칡덩굴에 엉키다 get entangled in arrowroot vines **—떡** a pudding-like arrowroot-starch cake **—탕(湯)** arrowroot starch gruel

칡범 a tiger ; a tigress (암컷)

칡소 a striped ox〔cow〕

***침** spittle ; saliva ; sputum ; spit ¶ 침을 흘리다 run saliva 침을 뱉다 spit ; eject saliva ; salivate // 사람에게 침을 뱉다 spit at 《a person》 // 마루〔길〕에 침을 뱉다 spit on the floor〔pavement〕 // 침을 바르다〔칠하다〕 moisten 《a thing》 at one's lips ; lubricate 《a thing》 with spittle // 손에 침칠을 하다 spit on one's hand ; get prepared (비유) // 마루에 침을 뱉지 말 것 No spitting on the floor.

침을 삼키다 관용 swallow one's saliva ; become tense (긴장) ; have an appetite for (먹고 싶어서)

침 針 [가시] a thorn ; a spine ; a prickle ; [바늘] a needle ; a stylus ; a hand (시계의) ; a sting (곤충의)

침 鍼 a needle (for acupuncture) ¶ 침을 놓다 acupuncture ; apply acupuncture

—술(術) acupuncture **—술사〔쟁이〕** an acupuncturist

침감 沈— a persimmon sweetened in salt water

침강 沈降 sedimentation ; precipitation ; sinking **—하다** precipitate ; sink

—소(素) 〖의학〗 [혈액 중의] precipitin **—수갱(竪坑)** a dropshaft **— 시험〔속도〕** [적혈구의] a sedimentation test〔rate〕 **—장치** a sinking set **적혈구 — 속도** blood sedimentation rate **적혈구 — 시험** a blood sedimentation test

침골 枕骨 the rear part of a skull

침공 侵攻 attack ; assault ; invade ; onset ; onslaught **—하다** attack ; assault ; assail ; set upon

침공 針孔 the eye of a needle ; a pinhole

— 사진기 a pinhole camera **— 사진(술)** pinhole photography

침구 侵寇 (an) invasion **—하다** invade

침구 鍼灸 acupuncture and moxibustion

—술(術) the practice of acupuncture and moxibustion —술사 a practitioner in acupuncture and moxibustion ; an acupuncturist

침구 寢具 bedclothes ; bedding ¶ 침구를 펴다 prepare a bed ; make the bed ; make up a bed

침낭 寢囊 a sleeping bag

침노하다 invade ; encroach on〔upon〕 ; conquer ; plunder ¶ 이웃나라를 침노하다 invade a neighboring country // 남의 권리를 침노하다 encroach upon another's right

침담그다 沈— cure 《a persimmon》 in salt water ; sweeten 《an astringent persimmon》 in salt water

†침대 寢臺 a bed ; a bedstead ; a couch (휴식용) ; a berth (기차의) ; a bunk (기선의) ; a cot (간이 침대) ¶ 접는 침대 a folding bed // 침대겸용 의자 a berthable seat ; a day bed ; a studio couch

—권 a berth ticket —료 a berth charge —보 a bedspread ; a bedcover —자동차 an ambulance —차 a sleeping car〔carriage〕 ; a sleeper 《미》 간이 — a cot 상〔하〕단 — [침대차의] an upper〔a lower〕 berth 소파 겸용 — a sofa〔day〕 bed 휴식용 — a couch

침독 poison caused from acupuncture

침략 侵掠 plunder ; pillage ; despoilment —하다 plunder ; pillage ; despoil ¶ 사람의 재물을 침략하다 despoil 《a person》 of his goods

⁑침략 侵略 aggression ; invasion ; raid ; encroachment ; inroad —하다 invade ; encroach on ; raid ¶ 침략적 행위 an aggressive act // 경제적 침략 an economic invasion // 공산군의 침략을 격퇴하다 repel Communist〔Red〕 aggression

—국 an aggressor (nation) —군 an invading army —자 an aggressor ; an invader ; a raider — 전쟁 an aggressive war —주의 a policy of aggression ; an aggressive policy —주의자 a systematic aggressor ; an advocate of aggressive policies — 행위 an act of aggression 경제적 — an economic invasion 무력 — an armed aggression 직접〔간접〕 — a direct 〔an indirect〕 aggression

침례 浸禮 〖기독교〗 immersion ; baptism by immersion ¶ 침례를 받다 receive baptism by immersion

—교파 the Baptist ; [개인] a Baptist —교회 the Baptist Church —주의 immersionism 전신(全身) — total immersion

침로 針路 a ship's course ¶ 침로에서 이탈하다 deviate〔swerve〕 from the course ; be driven out of one's course // 침로를 변경하다 alter〔shift, change〕 one's course // 침로를 잘못잡다 take a wrong course // 침로를 북으로 돌리다 steer one's course northward

침륜 沈淪 ruin ; fall ; collapse ; downfall ; wreck —하다 sink into obscurity ; be ruined ; go under ; go to ruin ¶ 침륜한 귀족 a ruined noble ; an aristocratic pauper ; the wreck of a noble

침마취 鍼痲醉 anesthesia by acupuncture ¶ 침마취를 시키다 anesthetize by acupuncture

침맞다 鍼— [침구] be treated with acupuncture ; get acupunctured ; [도난] get 《a thing》 pilfered ; be filched

침모 針母 a seamstress ; a needlewoman

침목 枕木 a sleeper 《영》 ; a tie 《미》 ; a cross-tie 《미》 ; a block ; a rail tie ¶ 침목을 괴다 support with a block

장(長)— a long tie〔sleeper 《영》〕 철도 — a sleeper ; a railroad tie 횡(橫)— a transverse sleeper

*침몰 沈沒 sinking ; foundering (침수에 따른) ; submersion —하다 sink ; founder ; go down ; be submerged ¶ 침몰시키다 sink 《a boat》 ; send 《a ship》 to the bottom // 배는 승무원을 태운 채 침몰했다 The ship went down with her crew.

—선 a sunken〔submerged〕 vessel ¶ 침몰선 구조 작업 salvage // 침몰선을 인양하다 salve a sunken vessel

†침묵 沈默 silence ; reticence ; taciturnity ¶ 침묵을 지키다 keep silent ; remain silent ; hold one's tongue ; save one's breath // 침묵을 깨다 break (the) silence // 침묵시키다 silence 《a person》 ; put 〔reduce〕 《a person》 to silence // 적의 포화를 침묵시키다 silence the enemy's guns // 침묵은 동의를 뜻한다 Silence gives consent. // 웅변은 은이고 침묵은 금이다 Speech is silver, silence is gold.

침방 寢房 a bedroom ⇨ 침실

침뱉다 spit ; salivate ; expectorate ¶ 얼굴에 침을 뱉다 spit on 《a person's》 face ; insult 《a person》 // 자기 얼굴에 침을 뱉다 disgrace oneself

침범 侵犯 invasion ; intrusion ; encroachment ; violation ; infringement —하다 invade ; intrude ; encroach ; violate ; infringe ; trespass ; make an inroad upon〔into〕 ¶ 직권을 침범하다 encroach upon 《a person's》 functions // 인권을 침범하다 violate personal rights // 국적 불명의 항공기가 아국 영공을 침범하였다 An unidentified aircraft violated our territorial air.

국경 — a border〔frontier〕 violation 영공(領空) — ¶ 영공을 침범하다 invade 《a country's》 territorial sky ; commit a violation of 《a country's》 territorial air space 타국 영토 — the invasion of another country 조약 — 행위 a violation of a treaty

침봉 針峰 [꽃꽂이의] a frog

침불안석 寢不安席 —하다 cannot sleep well due to anxiety

침사 沈思 contemplation ; meditation ; deep thought ; profound reflection ;

rumination —하다 be lost in thought ; be occupied with one's own thoughts ; contemplate ; meditate ; ponder ; muse 《on, upon, over, of》 ¶ 침사 묵고(默考)하다 be sunk deep in thought ; be lost in meditation

침삼키다 [침을] swallow saliva ; gulp down ; [부러워하다] one's mouth waters 《at the sight of》 ; be envious 《of》 ; covet 《for》 ; lust 《after, for》 (욕정으로)

침상 針狀 ¶ 침상의 needle-shaped ; pointed
— 결정체 a needle crystal ; 〖식물〗 a raphis 《*pl.* raphides》 —엽(葉) a needle leaf —체 a spicule ; 〖동물〗 a spiculum 《*pl.* -la》

*침상 寢牀 a bed ; a bedstead ; a couch

침소 寢所 a sleeping place ; a bed ; a bedchamber ; a bedroom ¶ 침소를 정하다 reserve a place to sleep

침소봉대 針小棒大 exaggeration ; overstatement ; grandiloquence ; magnification —하다 exaggerate ; magnify ; overstate ; overdraw ; make a mountain out of a molehill ¶ 침소봉대하여 말하다 exaggerate a story ; make one's story tall〔high〕 ; talk big ; turn geese into swans

침수 浸水 inundation ; flooding ; submersion 《under water》 ; [물] the flood water ; [잠김] soaking ; steeping —하다 be flooded ; be inundated ; be submerged ; be under water ; be deluged ; [배에] spring a leak ; leak ; make water ¶ 침수된 화물 wet〔sea-damaged〕 goods // (배가) 침수해서 침몰하다 founder // 침수를 헝겊으로 막다 stop the leak with rags // 침수 가옥은 2,000도 넘었다 Over 2,000 houses were flooded〔submerged〕. // 강물이 넘쳐 밭에 침수했다 The river overflowed its banks and inundated the fields.
— 가옥 a flooded house ; houses under water — 지구 flooded〔submerged, inundated〕 districts ; districts under water

침술 鍼術 acupuncture

침식 寢食 food and sleep ; eating and sleeping ¶ 침식을 잊다 forget one's food and sleep ; do not spare oneself // 침식을 잊고 공부하다 be absorbed in one's studies // 침식을 잊고 간호하다 nurse a sick person denying oneself all comforts // 침식을 같이하다 share board and room with ; live under the same roof ; eat off the same trencher

침식 浸蝕 corrosion ; erosion —하다 erode ; sculpture ; wear out ; eat into 〔away〕 ; bite 《on》 (부식) ; wash 《away, out》 (물로 인해서) ¶ 비바람의 침식 corrosion of the elements // 강이 바위를 침식해서 깊은 곳을 이루고 있다 The river has won deep channels through the soft rock.
— 대지 an eroded plateau — 분지 an eroded basin — 생물 an infestant — 작용 erosion ; erosive action 토양 — soil erosion

침식불안 寢食不安 no rest〔comfort〕 either in sleeping or in eating ; having constant anxiety —하다 be unable to eat and sleep comfortably ; be under constant anxiety

*침실 寢室 a bedroom ; a bedchamber ; a sleeping room

침염 浸染 dying〔taking dye〕 slowly ; a gradual addiction ; being infected little by little —하다 dye〔be dyed〕 gradually〔little by little〕 ; be addicted ; be infected with (병·악습에)

침엽 針葉 a needle (leaf) ; a needle-shaped leaf
—수 a needle-leaf tree ; an acicular tree

†침울 沈鬱 melancholy ; dejection ; depression ; gloominess ; low spirits —하다 (be) melancholy ; dismal ; gloomy ; saturnine ; depressed ¶ 침울한 얼굴 a dismal look ; a gloomy face

침윤 浸潤 permeation ; infiltration ; soakage ; saturation ; seepage —하다 permeate ; infiltrate into ; soak into ¶ 공산주의의 침윤을 방지하다 prevent the infiltration of communism
—법(法) 〖식물〗 the infiltration method —소(巢) 〖의학〗 an infiltrate —제(劑) 〖화학〗 a wetting(-out) agent 폐— 〖의학〗 amyloid infiltration of the lungs

침음 沈吟 [웅얼거림] murmuring to oneself ; [심사 숙고] meditation —하다 [웅얼거리다] murmur to oneself ; hum ; [숙고하다] meditate ; ponder 《over》 ; ruminate ; muse ; remain in deep thought

침의 寢衣 night dress ⇨ 자리옷

침의 鍼醫 a needle-doctor ; an acupuncturist

*침입 侵入 an invasion ; a raid ; an irruption ; an inroad ; an incursion ; an aggression ; trespass ; intrusion —하다 enter into (forcibly) ; invade ; make an invasion upon ; raid into ; make an inroad into ; march into ; encroach on ; penetrate into ; [인가 따위에] force one's way into ; force an entrance into ; trespass on ; burgle (구) ; break into 《a person's》 house ¶ 적국에 침입하다 invade the enemy's territory
—군 an invading army —자 an invader ; a trespasser ; an intruder 가택 — trespass on another's premises 주거 —죄 unlawful entry

침재 針才 skill〔talent〕 in needlework 〔sewing〕

침쟁이 鍼— a needle doctor ; an acupuncturist ; [아편 중독자] an opium 〔a dope〕 addict〔fiend〕

침적 沈積 deposition ; sedimentation —

하다 deposit ; be deposited ; settle
—물 deposits ; sludge
*침전 沈澱 precipitation ; deposition ; sedimentation ; settlement ; subsidence —하다 precipitate ; settle ; be deposited ¶ 바닥에 무엇인가 침전되어 있다 Something is deposited at the bottom.
—기(器) 〖물리·화학〗 a precipitator —농도 precipitation density —물(物) a deposit ; a precipitate ; a sediment ; lees —반응 precipitation reaction —분석 precipitation analysis —제(劑) a precipitator ; a precipitant —조(槽) a settling〔precipitation〕 tank —지(池) a settling pond ; a settling〔depositing〕 basin 〔reservoir〕 —지시약(指示藥) a precipitation indicator
침전 寢殿 ① 〖정자각〗 a T-shaped building in front of a tomb ② [임금의] the king's bedroom
침점 侵占 capturing〔occupying〕 by invasion ; capture ; encroaching —하다 encroach on ; occupy (after invasion) ; capture
침중 沈重 composure ; serenity ; gravity ; calmness ; seriousness —하다 (be) grave ; calm ; serious ; self-possessed ; very〔seriously, critically〕 ill (병이)
침질 鍼— acupuncture ; acupuncturation —하다 acupuncture ; acupuncturate ; apply〔treat with〕 acupuncture
*침착 沈着 self-possession ; composure ; presence of mind ; calmness ; coolness ; imperturbability —하다 (be) composed ; self-possessed ; calm ; cool ; collected ; sedate ; serene ; imperturbable ¶ 침착하게 calmly ; coolly ; composedly ; with composure〔presence of mind〕 // 침착한 태도 a calm〔quiet〕 attitude // 침착한 얼굴 a collected look // 침착한 성격 a staid character // 침착하게 행동하다 act with coolness // 침착을 잃다 be disconcerted ; lose one's presence of mind // 위급한 때에 침착하기란 쉬운 일이 아니다 A man can hardly sit tight in time of emergency. // 침착하게 입학 시험을 치렀다 He took the entrance exam with presence of mind.
침체 沈滯 stagnation ; dullness ; slackness ; inactivity —하다 (be) dull ; stagnant ; slack ; depressed ; inactive ¶ 침체 상태에 있다 be dull ; be stagnant ; be depressed // 경제계는 요즘 침체 상태에 있다 The latest economical status shows a downward trend. /Business is stagnant〔depressed, slack〕 recently. // 저 육상 선수는 최근에 침체 상태에 빠져 있는 것 같다 That track athlete's performance seems to have leveled off recently.
침침하다 沈沈— (be) dark ; gloomy ; cloudy ; dim ; blurred ; obscure ¶ 침침한 방 a dim-lit room // 나이와 더불어 눈이 침침해진다 Our sight grows dim with age. // 전등이 침침하다 The electric lamp gives a bad light.
침탈 侵奪 pillage ; plunder ; spoliation ; despoliation ; loot ; despoilment ; depredation ; 〖법〗 disseizin ; disseisin —하다 plunder ; pillage ; depredate ; despoil ; sack ; strip 《a person of something》 ; ravage 《a land》 ; disseize ; disseise ¶ 재산을 침탈하다 dispossess 《a person》 of property
—자 a disseizor 피—자 a disseizee
침통 鍼筒 a case〔box〕 for acupuncture needles
침통 沈痛 —하다 (be) grave ; touching ; pathetic ; sad ; mournful ¶ 침통한 말투로 in a sad〔dismal, mournful〕 tone // 침통한 얼굴을 하다 look grave〔sorrowful〕
침투 浸透 infiltration ; penetration ; permeation ; saturation ; osmosis —하다 infiltrate ; permeate ; penetrate ; saturate ; pass into ¶ 물이 모래에 침투하다 water percolates sand // 적군이 아군 진지에 침투했다 The enemy troops have infiltrated our front line.
—계수(係數) an osmotic coefficient —공작 infiltration (conspiracy) —분석 osmotic analysis ; dialysis —성 osmosis —압(壓) osmotic pressure —압계(壓計) an osmometer —압 측정 ¶ 침투압 측정을 하다 measure the osmotic pressure 《of》 —요법 osmotic treatment —작용 osmotic action —작전 infiltration operation 경제 — economic penetration 공산주의 — infiltration of communism 《into a country》
*침팬지 〖동물〗 a chimpanzee
침하 沈下 subsidence ; sinking ; settlement —하다 subside ; sink ; dip
*침해 侵害 infringement ; violation ; encroachment ; trespass ; disturbance (권리를) —하다 infringe〔encroach, trespass〕 on 《another's right》 ; violate ; damnify ; disturb ¶ 기본적 인권의 침해 an invasion of constitutional rights // A의 소가 B의 토지를 침해하는 경우 B는 소를 가둘 수 있다 If A's cattle trespass on B's land, B can impound them.
—자 a trespasser ; an invader 권리 — infringement〔violation〕 of one's rights ¶ 남의 권리를 침해하다 violate another's right ; disturb 특허권 — an infringement of the patent 판권〔저작권〕 — infringement of copyright
침향 沈香 〖식물〗 an aloeswood ; an agilawood ; Aquilaria agallocha (학명)
침형 針形 ⇨ 침상(針狀)
—엽(葉) 〖식물〗 an aciculate leaf
침흘리개 a slobberer ; a slaverer ; a driveler
침흘리다 drivel ; slaver ; drool ; run〔dribble〕 at the mouth ; [부러워하다] lust 《for》 ; gloat 《on, over》 ; be envious 《of》

¶ 침흘리며 바라보다 look on with one's mouth watering ; gloat over // 개가 먹이를 보고 침흘리다 The dog slavered over his food. // 그는 이런 적은 재산에 침흘리며 탐내고 있다 He's slavering after this small fortune.

칩거 蟄居 keeping the house ; domiciliary confinement ; seclusion ; sticking (close) to home **—하다** keep〔stay〕 indoors ; keep the house ; confine〔be cooped up〕 oneself in one's house ; shut oneself up 《in a room》 ¶ 누거에 칩거하다 shut oneself up in one's humble house // 나는 시골에 칩거하면서 한가로이 살고 싶다 I'd like to retire to the country and lead a leisurely life.
— 생활 living in seclusion ; a secluded life

칩떠보다 cast an upward glance ; lift 《up》〔raise〕 one's eyes ; cast up one's eyes 《to》 ; turn up the eyes

칩룡 蟄龍 a hidden dragon ; a dragon in concealment ; [사 람] a hidden hero〔great man〕

칩수 蟄獸 hibernating animals ; hibernants

칩충 蟄蟲 hibernating insects

칫솔 齒— a toothbrush ¶ 칫솔로 이를 닦다 brush one's teeth ; use a toothbrush

칭 稱 ① [이름] a name ; a title ; an appellation ; a designation ¶ …의 칭이 있다 be called ; be known as ; be known by the name of
② [문법의] person ¶ 3인칭 단수 the third person singular (number)

칭량 稱量 weighing ; estimation
—관〔병〕 a weighing tube〔bottle〕 **— 화폐** currency by weight

칭병 稱病 malingery ; counterfeit illness **—하다** malinger ; pretend to be ill ; sham illness ¶ 칭병하여 일에 나오지 아니하다 excuse oneself〔absent oneself〕 from work under the pretext of illness

칭사 稱辭 a eulogy ; a compliment ; praise ; laudation

칭송 稱頌 eulogy ; praise ; admiration ; applause **—하다** praise highly ; laud ; applaud ; admire ; eulogize ; pay a tribute to ¶ 덕을 칭송하다 extol 《a person's》 virtue // 모든 사람의 칭송을 받다 command universal admiration ; win general applause

칭양 稱揚 ⇨ 칭찬(稱讚)

칭얼거리다 whimper ; whine ; fret ; be peevish ¶ 어린애가 칭얼거리다 a baby cries peevishly // 칭얼거리는 아이를 달래다 soothe a hurt〔fretful〕 child

칭얼칭얼 ⇨ 칭얼거리다

칭원하다 稱寃— confess one's grudge ; state one's wrongs ; reproach ; complain ; blame ¶ 나를 칭원하지 마라 나는 잘못한 것 없다 Don't blame me, I have done nothing wrong to you.

†**칭찬 稱讚** praise ; applause ; admiration ; commendation ; laudation **—하다** praise ; applaud ; admire ; commend ; extol ; eulogize ; bestow praise on ; speak in high terms of ¶ 칭찬할 만한 laudable ; commendable ; praiseworthy ; admirable // 극구 칭찬하다 extol 《a person》 to the skies ; praise 《a person》 sky-high ; sing〔chant〕 another's praise // 칭찬받다 win〔receive, enjoy〕 praise ; gain the good word 《of》 ; get praised // 칭찬받을 가치가 있다 deserve admiration ; merit praise ; be worthy of praise

칭탁 稱託 a pretext ; an excuse ; a pretense ¶ …을 칭탁하여 under〔on〕 the pretext of ; under cover of **—하다** make a pretext〔pretense〕 of ; make an excuse of ; pretend 《to be ill》 ; use 《a thing》 as pretext ; feign ¶ 병을 칭탁하다 feign〔pretend〕 illness // 그는 병을 칭탁하고 면회를 사절했다 He declined to see me under pretense〔color〕 of illness.

칭탄 稱歎 admiration ; praise ; applause ; laudation **—하다** admire ; praise ; applaud ; laud ; extol

칭하다 稱— call ; name ; style ; denominate ; designate ; entitle ¶ 김이라고 칭하는 사람 a man named *Kim* ; a man by〔of〕 the name of *Kim* // 스스로 교육가라 칭하다 style oneself as a great educator // 소위 심리 소설이라 칭하는 것 what are called psychological novels // 인구 100만이라고 칭한다 The population is said to be one million. /The population is given〔put at〕 a million.

‡**칭호 稱號** a title ; an appellation ; a designation ; [명칭] a name ; a style ; [학위] a degree ¶ …의 칭호를 수여하다 confer the title〔degree〕 of... 《on a person》
박사 — the degree of doctor ; a doctorate **회사 —** the name of a company

ㅋ

카 [맛·냄새 따위가 독할 때] Phew ! ; Wow ! ; Ouch ! (매울때)
카 a car
—스테레오 a car stereo —페리 a car ferry 오픈 — a convertible
‡카나리아 〖새〗 a canary ; a canary bird
카나마이신 [항생 물질] kanamycin
카네이션 〖식물〗 a carnation ; a clove pink ¶ 빨간 카네이션을 가슴에 달고 있다 wear a red carnation on the breast
카네킨 canequine 《포》; calico 《영》; unbleached muslin 《미》
*카논 〖음악〗 a canon
카누 a canoe ¶ 카누 젓는 사람 a canoeist // 카누를 젓다 paddle a canoe
— 경조(競漕) a canoe race
카니발 a carnival
카다베린 〖생화〗 cadaverine
카덴차 〖음악〗 a cadenza 《이》
카드 ① a card ¶ 카드에 적어 두다 note down 《a matter》 on a card // 카드로 정리하다 arrange 《the data》 on a card system ② [트럼프] cards ; a card game ¶ 카드를 도르다 deal cards // 카드를 섞어 떼다 shuffle cards // 카드를 떼다 cut the cards // 카드를 젖히다 turn over a card // 카드로 점치다 tell one's fortune from cards // 분실된 신용 카드를 신고하려고 합니다 I'd like to report a lost card. // 현금으로 하시겠습니까 카드로 하시겠습니까 Cash or charge ?
— 놀이 card playing ¶ 카드 놀이를 하다 play (at) cards // 카드 놀이에서 부정을 하다 cheat at card — 목록 a card file —식 the card system ¶ 카드식 부기 bookkeeping on the card system — 한 벌 a pack〔deck〕 of cards —함〔색인〕 a card cabinet〔index〕
카드리유 quadrille 《프》
카드뮴 〖화학〗 cadmium 《Cd》
카디건 [스웨터] a cardigan
카랑카랑하다 《a voice》 be clear ; 《the weather》 crisp
*카레 curry ; [카레라이스] curry and rice ; curried rice
— 가루 curry powder — 소스 sauce 〔paste〕 — 요리 curried food ; a curry
카로틴 〖화학〗 carotin
카르타고 Carthago
카르테 Karte 《도》; 〖의학〗 a (clinical) chart 《for a patient》; a patient's chart
카르텔 〖경제〗 a cartel ; a kartell ; a trust ¶ 카르텔을 만들다 form a cartel ; cartelize
불황(不況) — a (business) recession cartel 수출 — an export cartel
카르툼 Khartoum
카리브 해 —海 the Caribbean Sea ¶ 카리브 해의 Caribbean
카리스마 〖종교〗 (a) charisma 《*pl.* -mata》; (a) charism 《*pl.* ~s》 ¶ 카리스마적 charismatic
카리에스 〖의학〗 caries ¶ 카리에스에 걸린 아이 a carious child
척추 — caries〔tuberculous osteitis〕 of the vertebrae ; spinal caries ; Pott's disease
‡카메라 a camera ¶ 카메라를 잘 받는 photogenic // 카메라에 익숙한 camera-wise // 카메라에 익숙하지 않은 camera-conscious // 카메라에 담다 photograph ; take a photograph〔picture〕 of ; film ; [스냅 사진] take a snapshot of ; snap // 카메라를 대다 aim one's camera // 카메라의 플래시를 받다 be subjected to camera flashes
—광 a photograph enthusiast ; a camera fiend ; a camera bug ; a shuttle bug 《미·속》 — 아이 camera eye — 앵글 a camera angle
카메라맨 a cameraman ; 〖영화〗 a cinematographer ¶ 신문사의 카메라맨 a press photographer
카메룬 Cameroun ; Cameroon
카멜레온 〖동물〗 a chameleon
카무플라주 camouflage —하다 camouflage
카바레 a cabaret
카바이드 〖화학〗 (calcium) carbide
카보이 a carboy ; a wicker box or basket to keep large bottles in
카복실 〖화학〗 carboxyl
—기(基) carboxyl radical
카본 〖화학〗 carbon
— 복사 a carbon copy — 원자로 carbon reactor〔pile〕 — 인화법 carbon process〔printing〕 —지 carbon (paper)
카불 Kabul (아프가니스탄의 수도)
카뷰레터 [자동차의] a carburetor
카비네판 —判 〖사진〗 a "cabinet" size plate ; a cabinet photograph
카빈총 —銃 a carbine (rifle)
카세인 〖화학〗 casein
*카세트 a cassette
— 테이프 a cassette tape — 테이프 리코더〔녹음기〕 a cassette tape recorder
카스텔라 castella 《포》; sponge cake
카스피 해 —海 the Caspian Sea
카시오페이아자리 〖천문〗 Cassiopeia
‡카우보이 a cowboy ; a bull puncher 《미·

속)
— 영화 a western (movie)
카운셀러 a counselor
카운셀링 counseling
카운터 [은행·상점 등의] a (service) counter ; [호텔의] an office ; a front desk ; [바의] a bar ¶ 카운터에 앉다 sit behind the counter
카운터블로 a counterblow
카운트 a count ; counting ; the score — 하다 take the count ; count ¶ 카운트 아웃이 되다 be counted out // 카운트는 원 앤드 원이다 The count is one ball, one strike. /The count is one and one. // (권투 선수가) 카운트 9에서 겨우 일어났다 He took a count of nine before getting up.
풀— a full count ((of three and two))
카운트다운 countdown (로켓 발사 따위에서)
카이로 Cairo
— 선언 the Cairo Declaration
카이저 수염 a Kaiser〔an upturned〕 mustache
카지노 a casino ((*pl.* ~s))
카카오 cacao
— 나무 a cacao tree —유(油) cacao oil
카키색 —色 khaki color
카타르 〖의학〗 catarrh
—성 폐렴 catarrhal pneumonia
카타스트로프 a catastrophe
카탈로그 a catalog(ue) ; a brochure ¶ 카탈로그에 올리다 catalog ; place〔put〕 ((an item)) on〔in〕
카테고리 〖철학〗 a category ¶ 카테고리로 나누다 categorize
‡카톨릭 [천주교] Catholicism ; the (Roman) Catholic church ((교회))
카투사 KATUSA ((Korean Augmentation Troops to the United States Army)) ¶ 카투사는 미군과 합동 근무를 한다 Katusas are on a joint duty with U. S. soldiers.
카틀렛 a cutlet
닭고기 — a chicken cutlet 포크 — a pork cutlet
카페 a café ; a coffee house〔shop〕 ; [우리 나라의] a bar ; a cabaret
카페인 〖화학〗 caffein(e)
‡카페테리아 a cafeteria ((미))
카펫 a carpet
카피 a copy
칵칵 with repeated cough (to clear one's throat)
칵칵거리다 keep coughing (to clear one's throat)
*칵테일 a cocktail ¶ 칵테일 파티를 열다 cocktail
— 글라스 a cocktail glass — 드레스 a cocktail dress — 파티 a cocktail party
칸 Cannes
칸나 〖식물〗 a canna (flower)
칸델라 ① [광도의 단위] 〖전기〗 candela ((cd)) ② [등] a metal hand lamp ; a lantern ; candelaar ((포))
‡칸막이 間— [막음] partitioning ; screening off ; [막는 것] a screen ; a partition — 하다 partition ; screen off ¶ 방 하나를 셋으로 칸막이하다 partition a room into three compartments
—벽(壁) a partition wall
칸수 —數 the number of *kan* ; the floor space of a house
칸초네 canzone ; conzonet
칸칸이 [방마다] (in) each〔every〕 room ; from room to room ; room by room
칸타빌레 〖음악〗 cantabile
칸타타 〖음악〗 cantata
칸트 Kant ¶ 칸트의 Kantian
— 철학 Kantism〔Kantianism〕 — 학파 the Kantists〔Kantians〕
†칼[1] a knife ; a sword (검) ; a saber (군도) ; a blade ¶ 칼을 갈다 sharpen a knife ; edge a knife // 칼을 차다 wear 〔carry〕 a sword (at one's side) // 칼을 빼다 draw a sword // 칼을 휘두르다 wield a sword // 칼로 찌르다 stab with a knife〔sword〕 // 칼이 잘 들다 a knife cuts well // 칼을 칼집에 넣다 put up a sword // 칼로 목을 찌르다 put a knife to ((a person's)) throat // 펜은 칼보다 강하다 The pen is mightier than the sword. // 악한이 칼을 빼들고 들어왔다 A ruffian broke in with a drawn sword.
—끝 the point of a sword〔a knife〕 —등 the back of a sword 면도— a razor (blade) 부엌— a kitchen knife 주머니— a pocket knife〔penknife〕 톱— a bandsaw

칼
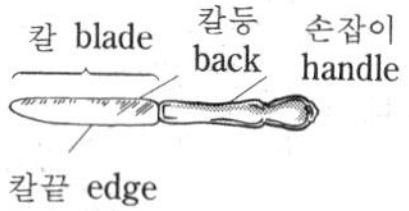

칼[2] [형구] a cangue ; a pillory ¶ 칼을 씌우다 put ((a person)) in pillory
칼을 쓰다 관용 wear a cangue ; be put in pillory
칼감 a roughneck ; a rowdy ; a hooligan ; a ruffian
칼국수 knife-cut noodles
칼깃 a plume ; long and stiff feathers of a bird
칼끝 the point of a knife〔sword〕
‡칼날 the blade of a knife〔sword〕 ¶ 칼날을 세우다 sharpen〔put an edge on〕 a knife // 칼날이 서다 the edge of a knife is sharp ; a knife takes an edge // 칼날이 무디다 The edge of a knife is dull

〔blunt〕.
칼날 쥔 놈이 자루 쥔 놈을 당할까 속담 It is better to be the hammer than the anvil.
칼데라 〖지질〗 a caldera
—호(수) a caldera lake
칼등 the back of a knife〔sword〕; the false edge
*칼라 [옷깃] a (shirt) collar
— 단추 a collar button 《미》; a collar stud 《영》 소프트〔더블〕 — a soft〔double〕 collar
칼라하리 사막 —沙漠 the Kalahari Desert
칼럼 [신문의] a column
칼럼니스트 a (newspaper) columnist
*칼로리 a calorie ; a calory 《cal.》 ¶ 칼로리가 많은 음식 calorific food // 칼로리가 적은 low-caloric // 칼로리가 많다〔적다〕 be high〔low〕 in caloric value ; have a high〔low〕 caloric value // 하루 1,800 칼로리를 유지하다 maintain an average of 1,800 calories〔maintain as much as 1,800 caloric diet〕 per day
—가(價) calorific value — 계산 calorie counting — 섭취량 caloric〔calorie〕 intake 《of 1,800 units》 —식(食) a multipurpose meal — 함유량 caloric content
*칼륨 〖화학〗 potassium 《K》
칼리 〖화학〗 kali ; kalium ; potassium
— 명반 potassium〔potash〕 alum — 비누 soft〔potash〕 soap — 비료 kali〔potash〕 fertilizer
칼립소 〖음악〗 calipso
칼맞다 get stabbed ; be cut ¶ 칼맞아 죽다 fall a victim to the dagger 《of an assassin》
칼모틴 〖화학〗 calmotin
칼부림 wielding a sword ; bloodshed (유혈극) —하다 wield a sword ; stab〔cut〕 at 《a person》 ¶ 칼부림에 이르다 develop into bloodshed
— 사태 an affair of bloodshed ¶ 칼부림 사태로 번지다 develop into bloodshed
칼붙이 an edged tool ; an edge tool ; a cutting instrument ; cutlery 《총칭》
칼새 〖새〗 (chimney) swift ; salangane
*칼슘 〖화학〗 calcium 《Ca》
— 주사 an injection of calcium
칼싸움 crossing swords ; fighting with swords —하다 fight with swords ; cross〔measure〕 swords 《with》
칼자국 a scar from a knife〔sword〕 ¶ 칼자국이 나다 get a blade scar // 칼자국을 내다 incise
칼자루 a handle ; a grip ; [단도] a haft ; [검] a hilt
칼잡이 a butcher
칼제비 ⇨ 칼국수
칼질 cutting ; [칼부림] wielding a knife —하다 cut ; wield a knife

*칼집 a scabbard ; a sheath ¶ 칼을 칼집에 넣다 scabbard a knife ; sheath a sword
칼춤 a sword dance ¶ 칼춤을 추다 perform a sword dance
칼침 —鍼 the thrust of a knife〔sword〕
칼칼하다 [목이] (be) thirsty ; dry 《미·속》
칼코등이 a sword-guard
칼크 Kalk 《도》; bleaching powder
칼판 a kitchen board ; a chopping board ; a block ; a trencher
칼피스 [음료] calpis
캄보디아 Cambodia ¶ 캄보디아의 Cambodian
— 사람 a Cambodian
캄브리아기 —紀 the Cambrian period
캄차카 Kamchatka
캄캄하다 (be) dark ; pitch-black ; somber ; murky ; gloomy ¶ 바깥은 캄캄했다 It was pitch-dark out of doors.
캄파(니아) Kampanya 《러》; a campaign
자금 — a fund-raising campaign
캄플라지 ⇨ 카무플라즈
캅셀 ⇨ 캡슐
캉캉 [춤의 일종] cancan 《프》
캐나다 Canada ¶ 캐나다의 Canadian
— 사람 a Canadian
*캐내다 dig ⇨ 캐다
*캐다 ① dig (up) ; unearth ; [식물을] gather ; pick ¶ 금을 캐다 dig gold // 나물을 캐다 dig up〔gather〕 edible plants // 캐 들어가다 dig one's way into
② [규명하다] dig〔pry, delve〕 into ; poke and pry ; inquire into ; probe 《a matter》 to the bottom (철저히) ¶ 글뜻을 캐다 explore the meaning of a sentence
캐디 〖골프〗 a caddie ; a caddy ¶ 캐디로 일하다 work as a caddie // 나는 지금껏 캐디로서 일하였다 I have caddied.
캐딜락 [자동차] a Cadillac (automobile) ; a Caddy 《미·속》
캐라코람 산맥 —山脈 the Karakoram Mountains
*캐러멜 a caramel
캐러밴 a caravan
— 슈즈 light mountain-climbing shoes 《with rubber soles》
캐럿 a carat ¶ 18캐럿의 금 gold 18 carats fine ; 18 carat gold
캐롤라인 제도 —諸島 the Caroline Islands
캐묻다 ask inquisitively ; be inquisitive 《about》; make a searching inquiry
캐비닛 a cabinet ; a chest of drawers
캐비지 [양배추] a cabbage
캐빈 a cabin
캐스터네츠 〖악기〗 (a pair of) castanets
캐스트 [배역] the cast 《of characters》 ¶ 미스 캐스트 miscasting // 올스타 캐스트 an all-star cast
캐스팅 보트 the casting vote ¶ 캐스팅

보트를 쥐다 hold the casting vote
캐시 cash
캐시미어 Kashmir ; cashmere
캐어묻다 ⇨ 캐묻다
캐처 〖야구〗 a catcher
캐치 catch ¶ 볼을 캐치하다 catch a ball // 정보를 캐치하다 obtain information
—볼 playing catch ¶ 캐치볼하다 play 〔have a〕 catch
캐치프레이즈 a catch phrase
캐터펄트 〖군사〗 a catapult ¶ 캐터펄트로 발사하다 catapult 《a deck plane》
캐피털리즘 capitalism
캑 coughing
캑캑 with repeated coughs or splutters ; hacking —하다 cough (and cough)
†캔디 a candy
캔버라 Canberra
‡캔버스 〖미술〗 a canvas
—틀 a stretcher
캔자스 Kansas 《Kan., Kans., Kas.》
캘리코 [흰 무명] calico
캘리퍼스 (a pair of) cal(l)ipers
캘리포니아 California 《Calif., Cal.》
캘린더 a calendar ¶ 캘린더를 넘기다 turn over a calendar // 캘린더를 한장 찢다 tear a sheet off the calendar
탁상〔벽걸이〕 — a desk〔wall〕 calendar
캘커타 Calcutta
캠퍼 〖약〗 camphor
— 주사 a camphor injection
캠퍼스 a campus
캠페인 a campaign
캠프 a camp ¶ 캠프를 치다 camp ; build 〔make, pitch, set up〕 (one's) camp // 캠프를 걷다 break up a camp
— 생활 camping —장 a campground ; a camp site —촌 a camping village
캠프파이어 a campfire ¶ 캠프파이어를 둘러싸고 앉다 sit around a campfire
*캠핑 camping ¶ 캠핑 가다 go camping ; leave for camping 《in》
— 용구 camping outfit — 의자 a campstool — 지역 a camping area ; a caravan park
†캡 a cap
*캡슐 a capsule ¶ 캡슐을 회수하다 recover a capsule
캡틴 a captain ⇨ 주장
*캥거루 〖동물〗 a kangaroo ¶ 새끼 캥거루 a joey // 작은 캥거루 a wallaby // 큰 캥거루 a wallaroo 《*pl.* ～s》
캉캉 with yelp after yelp ¶ 캉캉거리다 《a fox》 keep yelping
캉캉하다 (be) thin ; lean ; emaciated ¶ 캉캉한 얼굴 a haggard〔skinny, thin〕 face
*커녕 on the contrary ; far from ; anything but ; in no wise ; not at all ; instead of ¶ 칭찬은 커녕 꾸지람을 들었다 In place of praise, we heard scoldings. // 이 책은 이롭기는 커녕 아주 해롭다 So far from doing any good, this book does a good deal of harm. // 그 녀석 불어는 커녕 영어도 못한다 He knows no English, to say nothing of French. // 저금은 커녕 생활도 제대로 못할 지경이다 Far from saving money, I can hardly make my living. // 대학교는 커녕 고등학교도 졸업 못했다 Far from being a college graduate, he didn't even finish a high school.
‡커다랗다 (be) very big ; very large ; huge ; gigantic ¶ 커다란 손실 a great 〔terrific〕 loss // 집을 커다랗게 짓다 build an enormous house
커다래지다 become bigger〔larger〕 ; grow up ; gain size ; be expanded 〔extended〕 ; [키] become taller ; [사건] grow serious ¶ 키가 커다래지다 become taller ; acquire height // 사건이 커다래지다 a matter grows serious // 눈이 커다래지다 one's eyes dilate ; [놀라다] be surprised
커리큘럼 [전 교과 과정] a curriculum 《*pl.* ～s, -la》 ; [한 과목의] a course of study
커뮤니케이션 communication
매스 — mass communication
커미션 a commission〔rake-off〕 ¶ 1할의 커미션 《take》 a 10% commission 《on the sale》 // 커미션 브로커 a commission broker // 커미션을 받다 receive a commission 《on the sale of》 // 커미션을 먹다 take one's percentage
커버 [뚜껑] a cover ; a covering ; [책의] a jacket ; a (paper) wrapper ; a just cover〔wrapper, jacket〕 —하다 [보상] cover up 《a loss》 ; make up for 《a loss》 ; [경기에서] cover 《the second base》 ; back up ¶ 의자의 커버 a cover(ing)〔dust sheet〕 for a chair ; a chair cover // 커버를 씌우다 lay a cover ; cover 《a chair》 ; [책에] jacket // 커버를 벗기다〔떼다〕 take off the cover 《from》
커브 ① a curve ; a curve line ¶ 커브를 짓다 curve ; describe a curve ② [도로·선로 따위의 굽이] a curve ; a bend ¶ 급커브 a steep〔sharp〕 curve ; a sharp bend〔turn〕 // 내리막〔오르막〕 커브 a falling〔rising〕 curve // 커브를 틀다 bend 《to the right》 ; [자동차가] turn ; make a turn // 커브를 돌다 round a curve // (자동차가) 급커브를 틀다 turn ; turn sharply ; make a sharp turn 《at the intersection》 ③ [야구·테니스의] a curve ; a curve ball ; a hook ¶ 커브를 던지다 hurl〔throw〕 a curve
아웃— 〖야구〗 an outcurve 인— 〖야구〗 an incurve 슬로— 〖야구〗 a slow curve
커스터드 [과자] custard
커지다 grow big〔large〕 ; grow up (성장) ; expand (확장) ; become serious (중대화) ¶ 마음이 커지다 become emboldened // 화재가 커지다 a fire

spreads // 점점 커진다 It is getting bigger.

커터 a cutter
— **셔츠** a collared shirt

커트 〚영화〛 cutting ; a cut ; [판화·목판화] a woodcut ; a (pictorial) cut ; [절단] a cut ; cutting ; [정구·탁구] a cut
— **하다** cut 《a speech》; cross out ; strike off ; [공을] cut

†**커튼** a curtain ¶ 창의 커튼 a window curtain // 커튼을 내리다〔올리다〕 set up 〔take down〕 a curtain // 커튼을 치다 draw a curtain // 커튼을 제치다 draw a curtain back〔apart, aside〕

*__커프스__ cuffs
— **버튼** [꿰매인] cuff〔sleeve 《영》〕 buttons ; [뗄 수 있는] cuff〔sleeve〕 links

커피 coffee ¶ 밀크를 탄 커피 café au lait 《프》// 커피를 끓이다 make coffee ; brew coffee ; heat up 《some》 coffee ; have a coffee 《구》// 커피를 마시러 가다 go and have a cup of coffee ; go to coffee // 커피에 밀크를 타 마시다 drink 〔have〕 coffee with cream and sugar 《이때 milk라고 하지 않음》// 커피를 어떻게 드시겠습니까 How do you like your coffee ? /How would you like your coffee ? // 커피에 밀크와 설탕을 넣을까요 Will you have〔take〕 cream and sugar in your coffee ? // 커피를 마시고 싶다 I feel like a coffee. 《구》/ I'd like a coffee. 《구》
— **거르개** a coffee strainer — **끓이개** a coffee-maker — **나무** a coffee tree 〔bush〕 — **세트** a coffee set — **숍** a coffee shop — **열매** a coffee berry — **용구** coffee things — **원두** coffee beans — **잔** a coffee cup — **포트** a coffee pot

컨닝 cheating〔cribbing〕 in an examination ¶ 컨닝을 하다 cheat〔crib〕 in an examination
— **페이퍼** a crib ; a pony

-컨대 ¶ 요컨대 in short // 생각컨대 come to think of it // 원컨대 I wish〔want, desire〕 to 《do》

컨덕터 a conductor

컨디션 condition ¶ 컨디션이 좋다〔나쁘다〕 [운동에서] be in good〔bad〕 shape ; be in〔out of〕 condition // 몸 컨디션을 조절하다 adjust〔fix 《미·구》〕 one's physical condition // 몸의 컨디션이 더할 나위없이 좋다 I am in the best of my physical condition. // 그 타자는 올 시즌 컨디션이 정말 좋은 것 같다 It seems the batter is really in top form this season.

컨베이어 〚기계〛 a conveyor ; a conveyer
— **벨트** a conveyer belt — **시스템** a conveyer system

컨테이너 a container
— **선** a container〔containerized〕 ship 〔vessel〕 — **화** containerization ¶ 컨테이너화하다 containerize

컨트리 클럽 a country club

컬 a curl (of hair) ¶ 머리를 컬로 하다 curl one's hair // 컬이 풀리다 go out of curl

컬러 (a) colo(u)r
— **사진** a color photo — **텔레비전** 《a set of》 color television — **필름** a color film

컬컬하다 [목이] (be) thirsty ; dry 《미·속》

컴백 a comeback — **하다** come back 《to one's former work》; make a comeback

*__컴컴하다__ (be) dark ; black ; somber ; dim ; [마음] dark ; secretive ; black-hearted ; insidious ¶ 속이 컴컴한 사람 an insidious person ; a secretive person // 날이 컴컴해진다 It is getting dark.

컴퍼스 [양각기] 《a pair of》 compasses ; [나침의] the mariner's compass ; [다리] legs ; locomotives 《속》 ¶ 콤파스가 짧다〔길다〕 have short〔long〕 legs ; be short-〔long-〕legged

컴퓨터 an electric computer ¶ 컴퓨터화(化)하다, 컴퓨터로 처리하다 computerize ; process 《information》 with〔in〕 a computer ; feed 《data》 for a computer
— **시대** the computer age **아날로그〔디지털〕** — an analog(ue)〔digital〕 computer ☞ ❰p. 2157❱

†**컵** [우승배] a cup ; a trophy ; [잔] a drinking cup ¶ 유리컵 a drinking glass

컹컹거리다 《a dog》 keep barking

케냐 Kenya

케송병 —病 〚의학〛 caisson disease

케이맥 KMAG 《Korean Military Advisory Group》

*__케이블__ a cable ; cable
— **부설** cable laying〔placing〕 — **접속** cable splicing — **접속기** 〚군사〛 a cable connector — **철도** a funicular〔cable〕 railway **해저** — a submarine cable

케이블 카 a cable car ; a funicular railway coach ¶ 케이블 카의 선 a cable 〔funicular〕 railway ; [특히 매다는 식의] a suspension cable railway ; a cable railway ; an aerial cable ¶ 케이블 카로 by cable

케이스 ① [용기] a case ¶ 담배 케이스 a cigarette case // 케이스에 담다 pack 《wine bottles》 into a case ; pack a case with 《wine bottles》 ② [경우·사례] a case ¶ 케이스 바이 케이스로 case by case ; on a case-by-case basis // 이 문제들은 각각 케이스 바이 케이스로 처리한다 We'll deal with these questions separately, case by case〔on a case-by-case basis〕.

케이에스 KS 《Korean Standards》
— **상품** KS goods

케이오 K. O. 《knock-out》 ¶ 케이오시키

컴 퓨 터

① 개인용 컴퓨터(personal computer)

키보드 keyboard / 본체 main unit / 디스플레이장치(모니터) display unit; CRT(cathode-ray tube) display / 마우스 mouse / 커서 cursor / 액정 디스플레이 liquid-crystal display / 플로피 디스크장치 floppy disk unit / 하드 디스크장치 hard disk unit / 프린터 printer / 플로터 plotter (★데이터를 도면화하는 장치)

② 범용 컴퓨터(general purpose computer)

중앙처리 장치 CPU(central processing unit) / 자기(磁氣)테이프장치 magnetic tape unit [handler, storage] / 자기(磁氣) 디스크장치 magnetic disk unit [handler] / 카드 판독기 card reader / 단말기 terminal equipment / 라인프린터 line printer / 광학식(光學式) 문자판독기 OCR(optical character reader) / 광학식 마크판독기 OMR(optical mark reader) / 이미지스캐너 image scanner(★도형 입력장치) / 제어(制御)장치 control unit / 콘솔 console(★컴퓨터의 제어 탁자(대))

③ 컴퓨터의 종류

마이크로[초소형] 컴퓨터 micro-computer / 휴대용 컴퓨터 hand-held computer; portable computer / 슈퍼컴퓨터 super computer / 제5세대 컴퓨터 the fifth-generation computer / 미니컴퓨터 mini-computer / 슈퍼미니 컴퓨터 super mini-computer / 워드프로세서 word processor / 호환기 compatible machine / 호스트컴퓨터 host computer (★단말기·마이크로 컴퓨터를 거느린 대용량 컴퓨터) / 랩탑 컴퓨터 laptop pc (★무릎에 올려 놓을 수 있을 정도 크기의 휴대용 퍼스널 컴퓨터) / 탁상용 컴퓨터 desktop pc / 범용(汎用) 컴퓨터 general purpose computer

④ 컴퓨터의 구조

집적회로 IC(integrated circuit) / 대규모 집적회로 LSI(large-scale-integrated circuit) / 초대규모집적회로 VLSI(very large-scale integrated circuit) / 마이크로프로세서 micro-processor / 램 RAM (random access memory) (★random access 기억장치) / 롬 ROM(read only memory)(★읽기전용 기억장치) / 바이트 byte (★1 byte는 8 bit) / 비트 bit(★정보의 기본단위) / 워크스테이션 work station(★정보처리 시스템에 연결, 독립하여 단독으로도 처리 가능) / 하드웨어 hardware / 소프트웨어 software

⑤ 관련용어

▶운영체제 OS(operating system) (★컴퓨터의 관리를 위한 프로그램) / 제어프로그램 control program / 처리프로그램 processing program / 온라인 데이터처리 on-line data processing / 온라인 처리 on-line processing / (데이터의) 일괄처리 batch processing / 실시간[즉시처리] 시스템 real time system / 시분할(時分割) 방식 TSS (time-sharing system) (★하나의 컴퓨터를 멀리 있는 많은 사용자가 동시에 사용하기) / 분산(分散)처리 distributed processing / 네트워크 시스템 network system / 기업내 정보통신망 LAN(local area network) / 부가가치 통신망 VAN(value-added network) / 도스 DOS (disk operating system) / 데이터베이스 data base, database / 파일 file / (작업) 순서도 flow chart / 프로그래머 programmer / 컴퓨터 출판 DTP (desktop publishing)(★편집·조판·도표 등을 컴퓨터로 하는 것)

▶캐드 CAD(computer aided design) / 캠 CAM(computer aided manufactury) / 씨에이아이 CAI(computer aided instruction) / 씨엠아이 CMI(computer managed instruction) / 인공지능 AI (artificial intelligence) / 전문가 시스템 expert system / 음성응답시스템 ARS (audio response system)

▶프로그래밍 programming / 어셈블리언어 assembly language / 기계어 machine language[code] / 코볼 COBOL (common business oriented language (★사무용 공통 프로그램 언어) / 포트란 FORTRAN(formula translation)(★과학·기술·계산용 프로그램 언어) / 피엘 원 PL 1(programming language 1) / 프롤로그 PROLOG(programming in logic) / 베이직 BASIC(Beginner's All-Purpose Symbolic Instruction Code) / 컴파일러 compiler (★프로그램을 다른 기계어로 번역하는 것) / 서브루틴 subroutine (★특정 또는 다수 프로그램에서 되풀이 사용되는 독립된 명령군) / 디벅 debug / 명령(어) command / 아스키 ASCII(American Standard Cord for Information Interchange) / 인터페이스 interface (★CPU와 단말 장치와의 연결 부분을 이루는 회로) / 저장 save / 소팅 sorting / 정보 검색 IR(information retrieval)

ㅋ

다 knock out 《a boxer》
†케이크 a cake
케이폭 〖식물〗 Kapok
케이프타운 Capetown ; Cape Town
케이피 K.P. 《kitchen police》
케임브리지 ① [지명] Cambridge ② [학교 이름] Cambridge University
*케첩 ketchup ; catchup ; catsup
토마토 — tomato ketchup
*케케묵다 (be) old and stale ; old-fashioned ; outdated ; outmoded ; time-worn ; trite ¶ 케케묵은 쌀 stale rice // 케케묵은 빚 debt of long standing // 케케묵은 이야기 an old story // 케케묵은 표현 a trite expression ; an old cliche // 케케묵은 관습 an old-fashioned〔antiquated〕custom // 「눈보다 희다」는 다소 케케묵은 표현이다 "Whiter than snow" is an expression that sounds rather hackneyed.
켄터키 Kentucky 《Ky., Ken.》
켄트지 —紙 kent paper
켈로이드 〖의학〗 keloid ¶ 켈로이드상(狀)의 keloidal // 켈로이드상의 화상 a keloid burn
켈트
— 사람 a Celt ; [민족] the Celts —어(語) Celtic
켕기다 ① [줄 따위가] be stretched tightly ; be tensed ; be strained ¶ 줄이 켕기다 a rope is stretched tautly // 배가 켕기다 feel stiff in the belly // 힘줄이 켕기다 have a strain on the sinew ; feel a sinew taut
② [마음이] feel a strain ; feel ill at ease ; have something on one's conscience ¶ 왜 켕기느냐 대답을 못하게 Why don't you answer—something on your conscience〔mind〕? // 나는 조금도 켕기는 바가 없다 I have a clear conscience. /I have nothing to be ashamed of.
③ [잡아당겨서] stretch ; draw tight ; make taut ; [버티다] stand against each other
켜 a layer ; a ply ¶ 여러 켜로 쌓다 heap up in several layers
*켜다 ① [불을] light ; kindle ; turn〔switch〕on ¶ 촛불을 켜다 light a candle // 성냥을 켜다 strike a match // 가스등을 켜다 burn a gas ; light a gas lamp // 전등불을 켜다 turn〔switch〕on a light ② [톱으로] saw ; saw 《timber》 into 《boards》 ; [바이올린을] play 《a violin》 ; [물을] drink 《down, up》 ; [기지개를] (yawn and) stretch oneself ; [실을] spin 《thread》 off 《a cocoon》 ; [암컷을 부르다] give a mating call
켤레 a pair ¶ 구두〔양말〕 한 켤레 a pair of shoes〔socks, stockings〕 // 신 한 켤레가 외짝이 나다 shoes become an odd pair ; have one mate missing ; one of the pair loses its mate // 내 양말 두 켤레가 다 구멍이 났다 Two pairs of my socks are full of holes.
켯속 the situation ; the insides 《of a situation》 ; the secret 《of a matter》 ; the inside story 《of a matter》 ¶ 일의 켯속을 모르다 be not in the know ; be ignorant about things // 켯속을 알아야 손을 대지 I don't know where to start out.
코[1] [뜨게옷 따위의] a stitch
†코[2] ① a nose ; [코끼리의] a trunk ; [개·말의] a muzzle ; [돼지의] a snout ¶ 코가 막히다 one's nose is stopped up // 코가 열리다 one's nose opens up〔clears up〕 // 바로 코 앞에 있다 be〔lie〕 under one's very nose // 코를 맞대고 앉다 sit face to face // 코를 꺾다 humble 《a person's》 pride ; take 《a person》 down a peg or two
② nasal mucus ; snivel (콧물) ¶ 코 묻은 돈 a child's pocket money // 코를 흘리다 snivel ; one's nose runs // 코를 풀다 blow one's nose // 코를 씻다 wipe one's nose
—감기 a cold in the head ; coryza —기름 grease about the nostrils —끈 [신발의] a clog〔sandal〕 thong ; straps 《of》 ; a fore strap —끝 the tip of the nose ; a muffle —닦이 a (pocket) handkerchief ; a snot rag —딱지 nose dirt ; nose wax —안경 《a pair of》 eyeglasses ; a pince-nez ; a lorgnon ; nippers ¶ 안경이 미끄러져 내려 코안경이 되어 있다 His glasses have fallen low on his nose. —카타르 〖의학〗 nasal catarrh —피 nosebleed(ing) ; nasal hemorrhage ; 〖병리〗 epistaxis ¶ 코피가 나다 bleed at the nose —휴지 a paper handkerchief ; paper for wiping the nose 콧구멍 the nostrils 콧(구멍)털 the hairs of〔in〕 the nostrils ; a vibrissa 《*pl.* vibrissae》 콧날 the line of the nose 콧노래 humming ; crooning (가수의) 콧마루 the bridge〔line〕 of the nose 콧소리 a nasal voice〔tone, accent〕 ; a twang 콧숨 breathing through the nose ; snorting 갈퀴— a hooked nose 개발— a short, flat nose 납작— ¶ 납작코의 flat-nosed 들창— a turned-up nose 매부리— a Roman〔an aquiline〕 nose 뾰족— a pointed nose 사자 — a snub〔pug〕 nose 인공— an artificial nose 주먹— a ball-shaped nose 주부— a bulbous red nose ; a whisky nose 쇠—뚜레 a nose-block
코웃음 치다 관용 laugh sardonically〔ironically〕
코걸이 a nose pendant
*코골다 snore ¶ 코골며 시간을 보내다 snore the hours away〔out〕 // 코고는 바람에 스스로 깨다 snore oneself awake
코끝 the tip〔end〕 of one's nose
†코끼리 an elephant

— 사냥 elephant-hunting —코 the trunk〔proboscis〕 of an elephant 수— a bull elephant 아프리카 — an African〔a bush〕 elephant 암— a cow elephant 인도〔난장이〕 — an Indian〔a pygmy〕 elephant

코나크리 Conakry (키니의 수도)

코납작이 ① a person with a flat nose ② [기가 꺾인 사람] a person frustrated by shame

코냑 [브랜디] cognac

코너 ① [구석] a corner ② 〖야구·축구〗 a corner ¶ 코너로 공을 던지다 hurl〔throw, toss〕 a corner ball ; throw a ball cornerwise ③ [판매장의 한 구석] a special counter〔section〕《for children's wear》

—볼 a corner ball — 워크 throwing strikes at the corners of the plate —킥 a corner kick

코네티컷 Connecticut《Conn.》

코넷 [악기] a cornet

코노래 humming ; crooning ; a hum ⇨ 콧노래

코높다 (be) proud ; conceited ; snooty《미·속》; disdainful ; have one's nose in the air

코닥 [상표명] a Kodak (camera)

코담배 snuff

코대답 —對答 an indifferent〔a nonchalant〕 answer —하다 answer indifferently〔nonchalantly〕

코데인 〖화학〗 codein(e)

코드 [줄] a cord ; [전기줄] an electric cord

오산 검출(誤算檢出) — [컴퓨터] an error-detecting code 자동 검사 — [컴퓨터] a self-checking code

코딱지 dried mucus from the nose ; snot ; nose wax ¶ 코딱지를 후비다 pick one's nose

코떼다 get snubbed〔humbled, spurned, rejected〕; be rebuffed ¶ 돈 꾸어 달랬다가 코떼다 get turned down cold when one tries to borrow money

코뚜레 a nose-ring ; a cow's nose-ring

코란 the Koran

코러스 〖음악〗 a chorus

코레스폰던스 correspondence

코로나 〖천문〗 the corona (of the sun)

코르덴 corduroy

— 양복 a corduroy suit — 제품 corduroys

코르셋 a corset ; corsets stays《영》 ¶ 올인원 코르셋 an all-in-one corselet ; corselette // 코르셋 한 벌 a pair of corsets // 코르셋을 입다 adjust《a figure》 with corsets // 코르셋을 입은 corseted

코르시카 Corsica Island

코르크 a cork ¶ 코르크 마개를 하다〔뽑다〕 cork〔uncork〕《a bottle》

— 나무 a cork tree ; a cork oak — 따개 a cork screw — 마개 a cork

코린트식 —式 〖건축〗 [기둥의] the Corinthian order

— 기둥 a Corinthian column — 사원 a Corinthian temple

코맹맹이 a person who twangs ; a person who speaks through the nose

— 소리 a twang ¶ 코맹맹이 소리하다 twang ; speak through the nose

코머거리 a person with a congested nose

코메콘 COMECON ; the Council for Mutual Economic Assistance〔Aid〕 (동유럽 경제 상호 원조 회의)

코멘트 (a) comment《on》

노— No comment.

코뮈니케 a communiqué

공동 — a joint communiqué《프》 ¶ 한미 공동 코뮈니케를 발표하다 issue a joint ROK-U. S. communiqué《on》

코뮤니스트 a communist

코뮤니즘 communism

코미디 a comedy

코미디언 a comedian ; a comic actor

코믹 a comic ; [신문의] comics

코민테른 the Comintern《Communist International》

코민포름 the Cominform《Communist Information Bureau》

코밑수염 —鬚髯 a mustache《미》; a moustache《영》; tickler《속》

코바늘 a crochet hook

코발트 〖화학〗 cobalt《Co》 ¶ 코발트 빛의 cobaltic // 코발트 60 cobalt 60

— 폭탄 a cobalt bomb

코방귀 a pooh-pooh ; a snort ; pooh-poohing ; snorting

코방귀 뀌다 관용 poohpooh ; snort at ; sniff at

코방아 찧다 fall flat on one's face

코브라 〖동물〗 a cobra

코뿔소 ⇨ 무소

코세다 (be) headstrong ; stubborn ; self-assertive ¶ 코센 사람 a self-assertive fellow ; a stubborn person

코스 ① [경주·여행 따위의] a course ; [경기장·풀 따위의] a lane ; a track ; a route ; [골프의] a fairway ; [일부] a lap ; a leg ¶ 제1코스 Lane No. 1 // 하이킹 코스 a hiking trail // 하루 코스 a one-day course of trip // 첫〔마지막〕 코스 the first〔last〕 stage (of a course) ; the first〔last〕 lap (수영·여행 따위의) // 코스를 취하다 take a course // 코스를 바꾸지 않다 hold〔keep on〕 one's course // 전 코스를 완주〔주파〕하다 stay the course ② [방침] a course ; a policy ¶ (외교 따위의) 코스〔노선〕를 정하다 orientate《a diplomatic policy》 ③ [양식의] a course ¶ 5코스의 양식 a five-course dinner ④ [학과 과정] a course of study ¶ 프랑스어 코스를 밟다 take a course in French

코스모스 〖식물〗 a cosmos (flower)

코스모트론 〖물리〗 cosmotron
코스모폴리탄 a cosmopolitan
코스타리카 Costa Rica
코스트 (a) cost ¶ 코스트를 낮추다 reduce〔cut into〕 the cost // 코스트를 낮출 여지가 없다 There is no room for reducing the cost. // 코스트 다운이 되었다 The cost (per unit) went down.
— **업** an increase in cost — **인플레이션** cost-push inflation
코싸쥐다 cover one's face for shame ; hang one's head in shame ; be overwhelmed with shame
코안경 a pince-nez 《프》
코앞 under one's nose ; in front of one's nose ¶ 코앞에 있는 것을 못 보다 fail to see what is right under one's nose
코웃음 a sneer ; sneering ¶ 코웃음 치다 sneer
코일 a coil
코작
—**병(兵)** a Cossack
코즈메틱 cosmetics ¶ 코즈메틱을 바르다 apply cosmetics 《to》
코찡찡이 a habitual sniffer〔sniffler〕 ; a snuffer〔snuffler〕
코처 [운동의] a (sports) coach(er)
코청 the septum dividing the two nostrils
코치 [행위] coaching ; training ; [사람] a coach —**하다** coach ; train ; pupil(l)ize ¶ 야구팀을 코치하다 coach a baseball team // 배팅의 코치를 받다 be coached on batting
— **박스** 〖야구〗 a coach's box
코침 tickling one's nose —**주다** tickle one's nose
코카서스 Caucasia ; Caucasus ¶ 코카서스 인종 the Caucasian race
— **산맥** the Caucasus Mountains
코카인 〖화학〗 cocaine
— **중독** cocainism ; cocaine poisoning
코카콜라 Coca-Cola ; a coke 《속》
코 카타르 〖의학〗 nasal catarrh
코코아 cocoa ¶ 코코아를 마시다〔홀짝거리다〕 drink〔sip〕 cocoa
코콤 COCOM 《the Coordinating Committee for Export to Communist Area》
코크스 cokes
코탄젠트 〖수학〗 the cotangent
코털 the hairs of the nostril ; vibrissa ¶ 코털을 뽑다 pull out the hairs of the nostril
코트 [옷] a coat ; an overcoat
코트 a 《tennis》 court
코트디브와르 Côte d'Ivoire ; Ivory Coast
코튼 cotton
—**사(絲)** machine cotton ; cotton thread
코팅 [천·렌즈 따위의] coating
코펜하겐 Copenhagen
코프라 copra
—**유(油)** copra oil
코피 nosebleed(ing) ; nasal hemorrhage ; 〖병리〗 epistaxis ¶ 코피가 나다〔를 흘리다〕 bleed at the nose ; have a bloody nose ; one's nose bleeds
코허리 the narrow part of the nose (at the base)
코흘리개 a snotty-nosed kid ; a sniveler
콕 stinging〔pricking, poking, thrusting〕 hard〔fast, abruptly〕 ¶ 바늘로 콕 찌르다 pinprick with a needle // 벌이 콕 쏘다 a bee stings sharply // 닭이 콕 쪼다 a hen pecks at 《a thing》
콕콕 ① [찌름·쏨] repeatedly stinging 〔piercing, poking〕 ¶ 고추가 매워 콕콕 쏘다 red pepper keeps one's tongue stinging // 바늘로 콕콕 찌르다 keep pinpricking with a needle ② [쪼다] repeatedly pecking ; picking ¶ 닭이 병아리를 쪼다 a hen keeps pecking away at a chicken
콘덴서 〖물리〗 a condenser ; a capacitor
고정〔공기〕 — a fixed〔an air〕 condenser **유리〔가변, 결합〕** — a glass 〔variable, coupling〕 condenser
콘덴스트 밀크 condensed milk
콘돔 a condom ; a (contraceptive) sheath ; a rubber ; a French letter 《영·속》
콘사이스 concise ¶ 콘사이스형의 사전 a pocket(-sized) dictionary
콘서트 a concert ¶ 콘서트를 열다 give a concert
— **홀** a concert hall **레코드** — a record concert ; a gramophone
콘센트 〖전기〗 an〔a wall〕 outlet
콘스타치 cornstarch
콘스탄티노플 Constantinople
콘체르토 〖음악〗 a concerto
콘크리트 concrete ¶ 콘크리트의 concrete 《bridges》 // 덜 굳은 콘크리트 fresh concrete // 콘크리트로 굳히다〔를 바르다〕 concrete 《the pavement》 ; cover 《something》 with concrete
— **건물** a concrete building — **기초 공사** ground concrete work —**믹서** a concrete mixer —**차** a concrete mixer on wheels — **포장** concrete pavement **무근(無筋)** — plain concrete **철근** — **건물** a ferroconcrete〔reinforced concrete〕 building **현장 배합** — cast-in-place concrete
콘택트 렌즈 a contact lens ¶ 콘택트 렌즈를 끼우다 wear contact lenses
콘테스트 a contest
미인 — a beauty contest
콘트라베이스 〖악기〗 a double bass ; a contrabass
콘트라스트 a contrast ¶ 콘트라스트를 이루다 form〔make〕 a contrast 《with》
콘트랄토 〖음악〗 contralto
콘트롤 [제구력] control ¶ 콘트롤 하다 control // 콘트롤이 좋다〔나쁘다〕 〖야구〗 have a good〔poor〕 pitching control

콘티넨탈 continental
— 탱고 continental tango
콘티뉴어티 〖영화〗 a continuity
콘페토 a confetto 《pl. -tti》
콜 걸 a call girl 《미·속》
콜드 게임 〖야구〗 a called game ¶ 큰비 때문에 콜드 게임이 되었다 The game was called (off) because of a heavy rain.
콜드 크림 cold cream
콜라 cola ; kola
콜럼비아 [미국 South Carolina의 주도·미국의 대학 이름] Columbia
콜레라 〖의학〗 cholera ¶ 콜레라가 발생〔만연, 유행〕하다 cholera breaks out〔spreads, prevails〕∥콜레라에 걸리다 be infected with cholera
—균 a cholera germ〔bacillus 《pl. -cilli》〕
— 방역 본부 Anti-cholera Headquarters
— 예방 주사 the anti-cholera serum ¶ 콜레라 예방 주사를 놓다 inoculate 《a person》 against cholera — 환자 a cholera patient〔case〕 유사 — suspected cholera ; quasi-cholera 진성 — a genuine case of cholera ; Asiatic 〔malignant〕 cholera
콜로라도 Colorado 《Colo., Col.》
콜로라투라 소프라노 〖음악〗 coloratura soprano
콜로이드 〖화학〗 colloid ¶ 콜로이드의 colloidal
콜로타이프 〖인쇄〗 (a) collotype ¶ 콜로타이프로 하다 collotype
— 제판법(製版法) the collotype〔phototype〕 process —판(版) a collotype plate
콜록거리다 cough ; have a fit of coughing
콜록쟁이 a person with a hacking cough ; an asthmatic patient
콜록콜록 ¶ 콜록콜록 기침을 하다 keep coughing〔hacking〕
콜 론 〖경제〗 a call loan
콜론 a colon
콜롬보 Colombo
콜롬비아 Colombia ¶ 콜롬비아의 Colombian
— 사람 a Colombian
콜 머니 call money ; money on call
콜 사인 [전파 호출 부호] a call sign ; call letters
콜콜 snoring ; [물이] gurgling ¶ 콜콜거리다 snore ; keep snoring∥콜콜 자다 sleep snoring∥물이 콜콜 흘러 나오다 flow out steadily
콜타르 〖화학〗 coal tar
콜호즈 a kolkhoz 《러》 ; a collective farm
콤마 ① [구두점의] a comma ¶ 콤마로 끊다 put〔insert, use〕 a comma ; punctuate with a comma
② 〖수학〗 a decimal point ¶ 콤마 이하의 (below) the decimal ; [비유적] below 〔beneath〕 the mark ; below〔under〕 the par∥콤마 이하의 인간 a man of no account〔below the average〕 ; a nobody ∥그 녀석은 콤마 이하의 인간이다 He counts for practically nothing. /He is beneath our notice.
콤보 [재즈] a combo 《pl. ~s》
콤비 a combination ¶ 명콤비 a happy 〔good〕 combination∥…과 콤비로 ~하다 join force with ; tie up with...∥…과 콤비로 in combination 《with》∥그와는 좋은 콤비가 된다 I make a good combination with him.
명— a good〔an ideal〕 combination
콤비나트 an industrial complex
석유 화학 — a petro-chemical complex
콤팩트 a (powder) compact
콤퍼지션 a composition
콤프레서 〖기계〗 a compressor
콤플렉스 〖정신 분석〗 《have, develop》 a complex ¶ 열등 콤플렉스를 제거하다 rid 《a person》 of his inferiority complex ; dismiss a sense of inferiority (out of one's mind)∥콤플렉스를 가지고는 해낼 수가 없다 You can't work out with an obsessing notion.
*콧구멍 the nostrils
*콧김 the breath from the nose
콧날 the bridge〔line〕 of the nose ¶ 콧날이 선 미인 a beautiful woman with a shapely nose
콧노래 humming ; a hum —하다 hum ; croon
콧대 the bridge〔ridge〕 of the nose ¶ 콧대 센 사람 a self-assertive person ; a stiff-necked person∥내가 그의 콧대를 꺾어 놨지 I cut him down to size. /I put him in his place. ∥너는 콧대가 너무 높아서 혼기가 지나도록 독신으로 있는 거야 If you set your sights too high, you'll end up sitting on the shelf, you know.
콧대가 세다 [관용] be haughty〔stubborn, self-assertive〕
콧등 the ridge of the nose
콧마루 the ridge〔the bridge〕 of the nose ¶ 콧마루가 높다 have a high-bridged nose
콧물 watery discharge from the nose ; snivel ; nose drippings ; nasal mucus ¶ 콧물 흘리다 snivel ; drivel ; run at the nose∥콧물을 훌쩍거리다 snuffle∥열이 나고 콧물이 많이 나옵니다 I have a fever and a runny nose.
콧방울 the rounded sides of the nose
콧병 —病 nose trouble
콧살 wrinkles〔lines, furrows〕 around the nose
*콧소리 a nasal voice〔tone〕 ; a twang ¶ 콧소리로 말하다 speak through the nose ; nasalize the words ; twang
콧수건 —手巾 a (pocket) handkerchief ; a snot rag콧수염 a moustache ; a mustache 《미》
콧숨 breathing through the nose
콧잔등이 ⇨ 코허리
*콩¹ 〖식물〗 a bean ; a pea (완두) ; a soy-

ㅋ

bean (대두)
—과 〖식물〗 the pulse family ; Leguminosae —과 식물 a leguminous〔podded〕 plant ; a legume ; a legumen 《*pl.* -mina》 —깻묵 a bean cake —류 pulse 땅— kidney beans ; French beans 호— peanuts
콩밭에 가서 두부 찾는다 〖속담〗 To seek hot water under cold ice.
콩을 팥이라 해도 곧이 듣는다 〖속담〗 To say the crow is white.
콩² with a bang〔bump, thud〕
콩가루 (soy) bean flour
콩강정 a fried glutinous rice cake coated with soybean flour
콩고 the Congo (Brazzaville) ; the People's Republic of Congo ¶ 콩고의 Congo(l)ese
콩고물 soybean flour
콩과 —科 〖식물〗 leguminous plants
콩국 bean soup〔gruel〕
콩기 fettle ; spiritfulness ; mettlesomeness 《of person or horse》 ; being full of beans ¶ 콩기 있는 말 a horse in fine〔good〕 fettle // 콩기 있는 사람 a person of mettle // 그는 콩기 있는 사람이다 He is tough and quick fellow〔person〕.
콩기름 bean oil
콩깍지 bean chaff ; a hull ; a shuck
콩깻묵 a bean cake
콩꼬투리 a bean pod ; a legume
콩나물 bean sprouts
— 교실 overcrowded classrooms —국 bean sprouts soup — 대가리 〖음표〗 a musical note —밥 rice cooked with bean sprouts — 버스 an overloaded〔a jam-packed〕 bus — 시루 a jar for growing bean sprouts
콩노굿 bean flowers〔blossoms〕
콩댐 —하다 wax the floor paper with ground beans
콩독나방 —毒— 〖곤충〗 a yellow "bean" moth
콩밥 bean-mixed rice ¶ 콩밥먹다 eat bean-mixed rice ; 〖징역 살다〗 serve a penal servitude ; be put to prison
콩버무리 a bean-mixed rice cake
콩볶듯하다 crack ; crackle ; rattle ; snap ¶ 콩볶듯하는 기관총 소리 the crackling〔rattle〕 of machine guns
콩새 〖새〗 a Korean hawfinch ; Coccothraustes coccothraustes (학명)
콩설기 a rice cake with thin layers of beans in it
콩엿 bean candy ; bean-mixed rice taffy
콩잎 bean leaves
콩잎가뢰 〖곤충〗 a bean-leaf bug
콩자반 —佐飯 beans cooked in soy sauce
콩장 —醬 parched, seasoned beans
콩죽 —粥 mixed gruel of rice and beans
콩짜개 split beans〔peas〕
콩짜개덩굴 〖식물〗 a vine
콩찰떡 a rice cake made of glutinous rice with beans in it
콩켸팥켸 mess ; great disorder ; utter confusion ; a jumble ; pell-mell ; helter-skelter ¶ 모든 것이 콩켸팥켸가 되다 everything is at sixes and sevens // 비때문에 운동회도 콩켸팥켸가 됐다 The rain utterly spoiled the field day. // 회사의 재정은 콩켸팥켸가 됐다 The finances of the company went to rack and ruin.
콩콩 bowwow
콩쿠르 concours 《프》 ; a contest ; a competition ; a concurrence ¶ 노래 자랑 콩쿠르 an amateur singers' contest ; a talent show // 콩쿠르에 참가하다 take part in〔enter〕 a contest
— 우승 작품 a prizewinning film ; a prizewinner — 참가 작품 〖영화〗 a competitive film ; a film for concours 사진〔영화〕 — a camera〔movie〕 concours ; a photo〔movie〕 contest 음악 — a musical contest〔competition〕
콩탕 —湯 "bean broth" ; a soup made from bean flour
콩튀듯팥튀듯 —하다 be hopping mad ; jump up with anger
콩트 〖문학〗 a short-short〔brief〕 story ; a tale ; conte 《프》
콩팔칠팔 gibbering ; jabbering ; chattering —하다 gibber ; jabber ; chatter
콩팥 〖해부〗 ① 〖신장〗 the kidney ② 〖콩과 팥〗 soybeans and red beans
콩풀 a blister on pasted paper〔cloth〕
콰르텟 〖음악〗 a quartet(te)
콱 with a thrust ; thrusting〔poking, sticking〕 hard〔fast, abruptly〕 ¶ 칼로 콱 찌르다 thrust a dagger home // 화살이 나무에 콱 박히다 an arrow is stuck fast in a tree // 말문이 콱 막혔다 He was put to a nonplus. / Words failed him.
콴툼 〖물리〗 a quantum ; quanta
콸콸 gushing(ly) ; copiously ; in spout ; in a steady stream ¶ 콸콸 흘러나오다 flow out steadily ; gush out 《of》 // 코피가 콸콸 쏟아지다 one's nose bleeds badly // 상처에서 피가 콸콸 흘렀다 Blood came out from the wound in a copious flow.
‡광 with a boom ; with a thud〔bump, bang, thump〕 ¶ 광하고 떨어지다 fall heavily〔with a thump〕 ; plump // 짐을 광 내려 놓다 thump a bundle down // 광하고 소리가 나며 파열하다 go off with a bang // 광 넘어지다 fall with a thump // 광하고 부딪치다 bump against 《a wall》 // 지붕이 광하고 내려 앉다 a roof collapses with a thud // 그는 문을 광 닫았다 He shut the door with a bang. // 광하고 대포 소리가 났다 Bang went the gun.
광광거리다 〖터질 때〗 keep booming〔roaring〕 ; 〖떨어질 때〗 keep bumping〔thumping, thudding〕 ; reverberate ; resound
쾌 a string 《of 20 dried pollacks》
쾌감 快感 a pleasant sensation ; an agree-

ㅋ

able feeling ; physical comfort 〔satisfaction〕 ¶ 쾌감을 느끼다 feel comfortable〔agreeable, fine, nice〕
쾌거 快擧 an inspiring deed ; a brilliant 〔splendid〕 achievement ; a gallant deed ¶ 근래의 쾌거이다 be one of the most inspiring deeds in these days
쾌남아 快男兒 a fine〔spirited, good〕 fellow ; a good jolly fellow ; a nice guy ; a cheerful fellow ; a frank and hearty man ; a regular guy〔fellow〕《미》
쾌남자 快男子 ⇨ 쾌남아
쾌담 快談 a pleasant〔lively〕 talk ; a hearty chat **—하다** have a pleasant talk 《with》; enjoy a pleasant chat 《with》
쾌도 快刀 a sharp blade〔sword〕 ¶ 쾌도난마하다 cut the Gordian knot ; take a drastic〔radical〕 measure
쾌도난마 快刀亂麻 cutting the Gordian knot ¶ 쾌도난마의 솜씨를 보이다 cut the Gordian knot ; solve a knotty problem readily
쾌락 快諾 a ready consent〔assent〕; a willing consent **—하다** give a ready 〔prompt, willing〕 consent ; consent 〔agree, accept〕 readily ; accept 《an offer》 readily
*__쾌락 快樂__ pleasure ; enjoyment ; amenities **—하다** (be) pleasant ; delightful ¶ 육체적 쾌락 carnal〔sensual〕 pleasure // 인생의 쾌락 pleasure of life // 쾌락에 빠지다 be given to pleasure // 쾌락을 추구하다 seek〔pursue〕 pleasure ; gather (life's) roses // 인생의 쾌락을 다하다 drain the cup of pleasure to the dregs // 인생의 물질적 쾌락 the material amenities of life **—설〔주의〕** 〖윤리〗 hedonism ; hedonics ; epicureanism **—주의자** an epicurean ; a hedonist **감각적 —** the pleasures of senses ; sensual〔carnal〕 pleasures
쾌론 快論 a pleasant talk ⇨ 쾌담
쾌마 快馬 a swift horse ; a fleet steed
쾌미 快味 an agreeable sensation ; a pleasant taste ; delight ; pleasure
쾌변 快辯 fluency of speech ; eloquence ; oratory ¶ 쾌변을 토하다 make an eloquent address〔speech〕; display eloquence ; have a flower of words
쾌보 快報 good〔cheerful, encouraging, welcome〕 news ; glad tidings ; a joyful report
쾌복 快復 complete recovery ⇨ 쾌차
쾌사 快事 a pleasant matter〔event〕; a joyful event ; a delight ; a pleasure
쾌설 快雪 clearing oneself of disgrace ; vindication of one's honor **—하다** clear oneself of disgrace ; vindicate one's honor ; wipe out a shame ; exonerate
쾌속 快速 high〔great〕 speed ; celerity **—하다** (be) very fast ; swift ; speedy **—기** a fast-flying machine ; a clipper **—부대** a mobile unit **—선** an ocean greyhound ; a fast-sailing ship〔boat, liner〕; a clipper (ship) **— 열차** a fast train **—전차** a fast electric train ; a rapid service car **—정** a speedboat **—조(調)** 〖음악〗 allegro
쾌승 快勝 a signal〔decisive〕 victory **—하다** win an easy〔a signal, a decisive〕 victory
쾌유 快癒 complete recovery
쾌재 快哉 ¶ 쾌재를 외치다 utter yells of delight
쾌적 快適 agreeableness ; pleasantness ; delightfulness **—하다** (be) agreeable ; delightful ; pleasant
쾌조 快調 a good〔best, perfect, favorable, an excellent〕 condition ¶ 쾌조이다 be in the best condition // 쾌조를 보이다 go on smoothly ; progress favorably // 지금까지 일이 쾌조로 진행되고 있다. Up to now〔So far〕 things are working out all right.
쾌주 快走 fast sailing **—하다** sail〔run〕 fast〔at an exhilarating speed〕; scud ; clip 《미》
쾌차 快差 complete recovery ; restoration to health **—하다** be completely cured ; recover completely ; be restored to health ; regain one's health ; be well again ; be oneself again ¶ 병이 쾌차하다 get over an illness ; recover from illness
쾌척 快擲 —하다 generously throw out ; make a generous contribution ; give 《a fund》 willingly
쾌청 快晴 fine weather ; fair〔bright〕 and clear weather **—하다** (be) fine ; fair 〔bright〕 and clear ¶ 일기가 쾌청하다 The weather〔day〕 is as fine as can be.
쾌쾌하다 快快— (be) pleasant ; refreshing ; dashing and daring ; brisk ; [관대하다] generous ; big-hearted
*__쾌하다 快—__ [병이] be well again ; be recovered ; [유쾌] (be) delightful ; delighted ; happy ¶ 몸이 아주 쾌하다 I am perfectly well again.
쾌한 快漢 a jolly fellow〔dog〕; a nice man ; a brick ; a regular guy 《미》
⁑__쾌활 快活__ (be) cheerful ; cheery ; merry ; jolly ; gay ; jovial ; lively ; vivacious ; sprightly ; light-hearted ¶ 쾌활한 정신 a cheerful spirit // 쾌활하게 cheerfully ; gaily ; merrily ; lively ; vivaciously ; light-heartedly ; in light vein 〔humor〕
쾌히 快— [유쾌히] pleasantly ; agreeably ; cheerfully ; [기꺼이] gladly ; readily ; willingly ; with (good) grace ¶ 쾌히 승낙하다 willingly〔readily〕 consent 《to it》 // 시간을 쾌히 보내다 pass pleasant hours // 돈을 쾌히 빌려주다 lend money with a good grace // 쾌히 안내하다 readily show 《a person》 in // 쾌히 요구에 응하다 willingly comply with〔consent willingly to〕 another's request
쾨쾨하다 (be) stinking ; fetid ; foul-

ㅋ

smelling ¶ 생선이 썩어 쾨쾨하다 The fish is rotten and stinking. // 이 달걀은 쾨쾨하다 This egg smells bad. /This egg has a bad smell.
쿠냥 a Chinese girl
쿠데타 〖정치〗 a coup d'état 《프》 ¶ 쿠데타를 모의하다 plot a coup d'état 《to overthrow the government》 // 쿠데타를 일으키다 carry out〔execute〕 a coup d'état
군부 — a military coup **무혈 —** a bloodless coup
쿠렁쿠렁하다 (be) slack-filled ¶ 쿠렁쿠렁하게 채우다 slack-fill 《cereal boxes》
쿠릴 열도 —列島 the Kuril Islands ; the Kurils
쿠바 Cuba ¶ 쿠바의 Cuban
— 사람 a Cuban
***쿠션** a cushion ¶ 쿠션이 좋은 의자 a soft, comfortable chair // 스리 쿠션 〖당구〗 three-cushion billiards〔carom〕 ; three cushions
쿠알라룸푸르 Kuala Lumpur
쿠웨이트 [중동의] Kuwait ; Kuweit ¶ 쿠웨이트의 Kuwaiti
— 사람 a Kuwaiti
***쿠키** cookies ; biscuits
쿠폰 a coupon
—권 a coupon ticket **— 제도** a coupon system **주문용 —** an order coupon **호텔 —** a hotel coupon
쿡¹ [숙수] a cook
—장 a head cook ; a chef 《프》
쿡² stinging hard
쿨룩거리다 cough ; hack
쿨리 [노동자] a coolie ; a cooly
쿨쿨 snoring **—하다** snore ; keep snoring
†**쿵** with a bang〔bump, thud〕 ¶ 짐을 쿵 내려 놓다 bump a bundle down // 쿵 넘어지다 fall with a bump // 상자가 마루위에 쿵 떨어지다 a box falls on the floor with a bang
쿵쾅거리다 make din ; raise〔kick up〕 a racket ; romp about ; [포성 따위가] bang ; boom ¶ 쿵쾅거리며 걷다 bounce〔thump〕 along 《the passage- way》 ; walk heavily〔with heavy steps〕 ; tramp ; lumber ; stamp
쿵쿵 with bangs〔thuds, bumps〕 ¶ 마루위를 쿵쿵 달리다 《a child》 scamper around on the floor noisily // 방아를 쿵쿵 찧다 pound with a pestle // 상자를 땅위에 쿵쿵 던지다 bump boxes down on the ground
퀀셋 〖건축〗 a quonset hut ; a semicircular prefab
퀄퀄 gurgling ; spouting ¶ 퀄퀄거리다 gurgle ; spout // 병에서 물이 퀄퀄 쏟아지다 water gurgles out of a bottle // 샘물이 퀄퀄 쏟아지다 a spring spouts
퀘스천 마크 a question mark
퀘이커 교도 a Quaker
퀭하다 (be) big and hollow ; have big and lackluster eyes

퀴라소 [술] curaçao
퀴리 a curie
마이크로 — a microcurie
퀴벡 Quebec
***퀴즈** a quiz ; a quiz game ; a brain teaser 《속》
— 프로 a quiz show〔program〕 ; a panel shows ¶ 퀴즈 프로 사회자 a quizmaster // 퀴즈 프로 응답자 a panelist
퀴퀴하다 (be) fetid ; stinking ; foul-smelling ¶ 생선이 썩어서 냄새가 퀴퀴하다 The fish is rotten and stinking.
퀸 a queen
큐 〖당구〗 a (billiard) cue
큐비즘 〖미술〗 cubism
†**크기** size ; dimensions ; magnitude ; bulk (덩치) ; volume (용적) ¶ 상당한 크기의 of fairly large size ; of some size // 같은 크기의 of the same size ; equal in size // 휴대하기 편리한 크기다 be of (conveniently) portable size // 크기가 같다〔다르다〕 be〔be not〕 equal in size ; be of the same〔a different〕 size // 그 집은 어느 정도의 크기입니까 How large is the house? // 수컷과 암컷은 크기가 다르다 The male and female differ in size.
크나큰 ever so big〔large, great〕 ; as big〔large, great〕 as can be ; enormous ; huge ; colossal ; gigantic
크낙새 〖새〗 a Korean woodpecker
†**크다¹** [형상이] (be) big ; large ; great ; grand ; [거대] large ; gigantic ; immense ; colossal ; [광대] spacious ; extensive ; broad ; vast ; [덩치가] bulky ; massive ; voluminous ; [마음이] broad- minded ; [소리가] loud ; [수량이] large

> **참고** **big, large, great**는 다같이 크기를 나타내는 데 쓰이지만 **big**이 가장 구어적이고 널리 사용된다 **large**는 감정이 포함되지 않은 다소 딱딱한 표현 **great**는 「위대함」을 암시한다

¶ 큰 나라 a large country (면적이) ; a great country (위대한) ; a powerful country // 큰 실수 a gross〔big, great〕 mistake // 큰 재산 a large fortune // 큰형 one's eldest〔oldest〕 brother // 크게 big ; large ; [대규모로] on a large〔grand〕 scale ; in a large way // 크게 하다 enlarge ; extend ; magnify ; expand // 가게를 크게 하다 enlarge one's shop ; extend one's business // 눈을 크게 뜨다 open one's eyes wide // 수입에 크게 영향을 미치다 affect one's income // 큰 기대를 걸다 expect great things from 《a person》 // 그는 나이에 비해 크다 He is big for his age. // 그 사람은 마음이 크다 He is broad-minded. /He has a big heart. // 다음엔 크게 한번 내십시오 I'll let you be a big spender next time.
크다² [자라다] grow big ; grow (up) ; be

ㅋ

brought up ; be bred ¶ 다 큰 아이 a grown-up child // 도시〔시골〕에서 큰 아이 a city〔country〕-bred child // 모유〔인공 영양으〕로 큰 아이 a breast-bred〔bottle-fed〕 child // 나는 서울에서 나서 서울에서 컸다 I was born and bred 〔raised〕 in *Seoul*. // 나는 작년에 비해 10센티 키가 컸다 I have grown ten centimeters taller than last year.

크라운 [왕관] a crown

크라이슬러 [자동차의 상표명] a Chrysler ¶ 77년도형 크라이슬러 a '77 Chrysler ; the '77 model of the Chrysler

***크래커** a cracker ; a biscuit 《영》

***크랭크** a crank
—인 (하다) 〖영화〗 (start) filming **—축** a crankshaft

크레디트 a credit
— 카드 a credit card **장기〔단기〕 —** a long-〔short-〕term credit

크레믈린 the Kremlin

크레오소트 creosote

****크레용** (a) crayon ¶ 크레용으로 그리다 draw with crayons〔in crayon(s)〕
—화(畫) a picture in crayon ; a crayon drawing

크레인 a crane ; a derrick (배의) ¶ 크레인으로 들어올리다 lift〔hoist〕 《a thing》 with〔by means of〕 a crane 〔hoist〕

크레졸 cresol ¶ 크레졸의 cresylic // 크레졸 비눗물 saponated solution of cresol
— 비누 cresol soap

크레파스 crayon pastel

크로마뇽인 —人 〖인류〗 Cromagnon〔Cro-Magnon〕 man

크로스 레이트 〖경제〗 cross rates
영미 — the Anglo-American crossrates

크로스 카운터 〖권투〗 a cross counter

크로스컨트리 경주 —競走 a cross-country race〔run〕 ¶ 4천미터 크로스컨트리 경주를 하다 run 4,000 meters cross-country

크로켓 a croquette

크롤 〖수영〗 the crawl (stroke) ¶ 크롤로 헤엄치다 swim a crawl 《across the pool》

크롬 〖화학〗 chrome ; chromium 《Cr》
—강 chrome steel **— 도금** chromium plating **— 철광** chromic iron ore ; chromite **염화〔산화〕—** chrome chloride〔oxide〕 **제2—염** chrome salt

크루프 〖의학〗 croup ¶ 크루프성의 croupous // 크루프성 폐렴〔기관지염〕 croupous pneumonia〔bronchitis〕

크리미아 the Crimea

†**크리스마스** Christmas ; Xmas ; Yuletide ; Noel ; Christmas Day (당일) ¶ 크리스마스다운 (기분의) Christmas(s)y // 크리스마스에 at Christmas // 크리스마스를 경축하다〔지키다〕 keep〔observe〕 Christmas // 크리스마스 축하 인사를 하다 extend 〔offer〕 Christmas greetings 《to》 // 크리스마를 축하합니다 I wish you a merry Christmas! /A merry Christmas to you! // 크리스마스가 월요일이었으면 좋겠다 I wish Christmas fell on Monday.
— 선물 a Christmas present〔gift〕 ; a Christmas box (하인 등에게 주는) **— 케이크** a cake especially decorated for Christmas ; a Christmas cake 《영》 **— 트리** a Christmas tree ¶ 크리스마스 트리를 장식하다 dress a Christmas tree **— 휴가** the Christmas vacation **— 휴전** a Yuletide truce

크리스마스 이브 Christmas Eve ¶ 크리스마스 이브에 on Christmas Eve

크리스천 a Christian ¶ 크리스천답잖은 unchristian
— 네임 a Christian name

크리스털 crystal (glass)
— 제품 a crystal **— 정류기(整流器)** [증폭기] a crystal rectifier〔multiplier〕

****크리켓** 〖경기〗 cricket
— 선수 a cricketer ; a cricket player **— 팀** a cricket team ; an eleven

크리티시즘 criticism

크림 ① [식품] cream ¶ 크림상(狀)의 creamy ; creamlike // 크림을 떠내다 skim the cream 《from》 // 우유를 휘저어 크림을 만들다 churn cream ② [화장품] (skin) cream ¶ 크림을 바르다 cream 《one's face》 ; apply cream to 《one's hand》
— 그릇 a cream jug ; a cream pitcher 《미》 ; a creamer 《미》 **— 분리기** a cream separator ; a creamer **—빵** a cream bun **면도용 —** shaving cream **선탠 —** suntan cream **생—** fresh cream **아이스—** ice cream **콜드〔배니싱〕 —** cold〔vanishing〕 cream **핸드〔헤어, 립〕—** hand〔hair, lip〕 cream **화장용 —** cosmetic〔facial, face〕 cream

크림색 —色 cream (color) ¶ 크림색의, 크림색을 한 cream-colored ; creamy // 크림색으로 칠하다 paint 《a car》 cream

크메르 Khmer
—말 Khmer **— 사람** a Khmer

큰계집 one's wife (첩에 대해서)

큰고래 〖동물〗 a razorback (whale) ; a finback ; a rorqual

큰골 〖해부〗 the cerebrum

큰곰자리 〖천문〗 the Great Bear ; the Big Dipper ; Major

큰기침 a big 'ahem' ; clearing the throat loudly **—하다** clear one's throat loudly ; hem

큰길 a main〔principal〕 road〔street〕 ; a highway ; a thoroughfare ; a principal avenue

큰누이 the eldest sister

큰달 an odd month ; a long month

큰댁 —宅 the house of one's eldest brother ; the head family〔house〕 ; the main stock

큰돈 a large sum of money ; big money ; a lot of money ¶ 큰돈 들다 cost a great deal of money // 큰돈을 벌다 realize a large profit ; make a lot of money // 큰돈을 들여 만들다 build at great 〔huge〕 cost

//주식에서 큰돈을 벌었다 I made a killing in the stock market.

큰딸 one's eldest〔oldest《미》〕daughter

큰마누라 one's wedded wife ; a legal〔lawful〕wife

큰마음 [포부] great ambitions〔hopes〕; [관대] liberality ; generosity ¶ 큰마음 먹고 100 만원 기부하다 generously donate a million *won* //큰마음 쓰다 act generously //큰마음 먹고 미국 유학하다 go off to America to study with great ambitions

큰말 ① [큰소리] big talk ; bragging ② 〖언어〗 a heavy isotope of a word

큰머리 a woman's formal hairdo

큰문잡다 —門— usher《a distinguished guest》in or out the gate

큰물 an inundation ; a heavy flood ; a deluge ; an overflow ¶ 큰물 나다 be flooded ; be in flood ; have a flood ; be under water ; be inundated //큰물로 수천명이 집을 잃었다 Thousands of people were rendered houseless by the flood.

큰바늘 [시계의] the long〔minute〕hand

큰부리고지새 〖새〗 the large-billed grosbeak

큰북 〖악기〗 a large drum

큰불 [화재] a conflagration ; a big fire ; [총알] game-hunting gunfire ¶ 큰불 놓다 set a big fire ; [총알] fire a hunting gun

*큰비 a heavy rain ; a downpour ; a big rainfall ¶ 큰비가 온다 It rains heavily. /A heavy shower occurs. /We have a downpour.

큰사람 a great man ; an eminent person

큰사랑 —舍廊 the main guest room ; the living room of the elders of a family

큰사위 the husband of one's eldest daughter

큰살림 a luxurious household ; high living **—하다** live high

큰상 —床 a big dinner table ; a reception table presented to the guest of honor

큰상 받다 관용 《the guest of honor》 be presented with a formal table

†큰소리 ① a loud〔stentorian〕voice ; a yell ; a shout ¶ 큰소리로 부르다 call in a loud voice //큰소리 지르다 cry in a loud voice ; shout at the top of one's voice

② [야단치는 소리] a shout ; a growl ; a snarl ; a roar ; a brawl ¶ 큰소리쳐서 협박하다 shout threats at 《a person》

③ [과장] tall〔big〕talk ; loud boasting ; bragging ; high-sounding words ; exaggeration **—하다** talk big ; boast ; brag ; bluster ; swagger ¶ 큰소리 치는 사람 a brag ; a boaster ; a braggart

큰손녀 —孫女 the eldest granddaughter

큰손님 a distinguished〔an important〕guest ; a guest of honor

큰손자 —孫子 the eldest grandson

큰솥 a cauldron ; the biggest kettle in a kitchen

큰아기 a grown-up girl ; a big girl ; [맏딸] one's eldest daughter

큰아들 the eldest son

큰아버지 an uncle ; the elder brother of one's father

큰어머니 an aunt ; the wife of the elder brother of one's father

큰언니 a boy's eldest brother ; a girl's eldest sister

큰오빠 a girl's eldest brother

큰옷 an outer robe worn on ceremonial occasions

큰이 ① [남의 형제의 맏이] the eldest of another's children

② [본처] another's legal〔wedded〕wife

큰일 ① [중대사] an important affair ; a serious matter ; a serious〔difficult〕situation ; a great trouble ; a disaster ; a crisis (위기)

② [대업] a big enterprise〔plan, business〕

③ [예식·잔치] a big ceremony〔banquet〕; a wedding ; a funeral ¶ 큰일나다 become〔grow〕serious ; assume serious proportions ; a serious thing happens ; a serious problem pops up ; get into trouble ; be in a fix〔difficulty〕; be in hot water //큰일을 계획하다 plan a big enterprise // 큰일 났다 A terrible accident〔thing〕has happened. //정말 큰일 났구나 Good heavens, we really are in trouble ! //비가 곧 안 오면 큰일이다 If it doesn't rain soon, we're in for trouble.

큰일을 치르다 관용 go through〔carry out〕a wedding〔funeral〕

큰절¹ a deep bow (made by a woman with her hands put together before her forehead) **—하다** make a deep bow ; make an obeisance ; bow low ¶ 차례가 끝나면 어린이들은 부모에게 큰절을 한다 After the ceremony, children make deep bows to their parents.

큰절² [사찰] the main temple

큰집 ① a large house ② [종가] the house of one's eldest brother ; the house of the head family ; the main stock

큰처남 —妻男 the eldest of one's wife's brothers

큰체하다 be proud ; hold one's head high ; wear a high hat ; assume an air of importance

큰춤 dancing in a full dress ; a full-dress dance

큰치마 a long trailing skirt

큰칼 [형구] a big cangue ; a large pillory ; [칼] a large sword〔knife〕

큰코다치다 have a bitter experience ; have a hard time of it ; have a mishap ; pay dearly 《for》 ¶ 그것 때문에 큰코다쳤다 I paid dearly for it. /It cost me dear. //믿지 못할 사람을 믿었다가 큰코다쳤다 I made the bitter mistake of putting my faith in someone who could not be trust-

ㅋ

ed.
큰톱 a 2-man ripsaw
큰판 [도박의] a high play 《at cards》
큰할아버지 one's grandfather's elder brother ; a great-uncle ; a granduncle
큰형 ―兄 a man's eldest brother ; a woman's eldest sister
―수(嫂) the wife of a man's eldest brother
*클라리넷 〖악기〗 a clarinet ¶ 클라리넷을 불다 play on the clarinet
― 주자(奏者) a clarinet(t)ist ; a clarinet player
*클라이맥스 a climax ¶ 클라이맥스에 이르다 reach〔come to〕 the climax 《of a story》 ; culminate 《in》 // 이야기는 클라이맥스에 이르렀다 The story reached the most interesting part.
클라이밍 [등산] climbing
클래스 a class ¶ 클래스메이트 a classmate〔classfellow〕 // 클래스회 a class meeting
클래식 a classic ; classics 《총칭》
― 음악 classical music
클랙슨 a klaxon ; a horn ¶ 클랙슨을 울리다 sound〔toot, blow〕 a klaxon〔horn, honk〕
클러치 〖기계〗 a clutch
†클럽 ① [구락부] a club ; a society ; a fraternity (미국 남대생의) ; a sorority (여대생의) ; a clubhouse (건물) ¶ 클럽에 입회하다 join a club ; become a member of club // 클럽을 조직하다 organize a club
② [골프채] a club ; a playclub
③ [트럼프] clubs ¶ 클럽의 the ace of clubs
― 활동 〖교육〗 clubs〔extracurricular〕 activities ― 회비 club dues ― 회원 a member of a club ; a clubman ― 회원증 a membership card〔badge〕 국제 ― an international society 연극 ― a dramatic society 핵― 〖정치〗 the Nuclear club
클레이 사격 ―射擊 clay pigeon shooting
클레임 〖경제〗 a claim (for damages) ¶ 클레임에 응하다 meet a claim for damages // 클레임을 요구하다 make〔institute, bring forward, put in〕 a claim for compensation
클로렐라 〖식물〗 a chlorella
클로로다인 [마취제] chlorodyne
클로로마이세틴 〖약〗 chloromycetin
클로로키니네 [말라리아의 특효약]chloroquin(e)
클로로포름 [마취제] chloroform
클로로필 [엽록소] chlorophyll
클로르 〖화학〗 chloride
―산(酸) chloric acid ― 석회 chlorinated lime
*클로버 〖식물〗 a clover ¶ 네 잎 클로버 a four-leaf(ed) clover
클로즈 게임 a close game
클로즈업 〖영화〗 a close-up 《CU》 ; a close shot ; a close-up view 《of the moon》 ¶ 중(中) 정도의 클로즈업 a medium close-up // 클로즈업시킨 사진 a close-up picture // 클로즈업시키다 take a close-up 《of》 // 클로즈업되다 [비유적으로] be highlighted ; be in the limelight ; be brought to the fore // (텔레비전에서) 그녀의 얼굴을 클로즈업시키기 위해 카메라가 접근했다 The camera went in for a close-up〔close shot〕 of her face.
클리닝 cleaning ¶ 클리닝하러 보내다 send 《one's shirt》 to the cleaner's ; send 《one's suit》 to the laundry
드라이 ― dry cleaning
클린업트리오 〖야구〗 a cleanup trio
클린 히트 〖야구〗 a clean hit〔single〕 ¶ 클린 히트를 치다 smash out a clean hit
클린싱 크림 cleansing cream
클린치 〖권투〗 a clinch ; clinching ―하다 clinch ¶ 클린치하고 있다 be in a clinch
클립 ① [종이를 끼우는 것] a (paper) clip ¶ 서류를 클립으로 채우다 fasten papers with a clip ; clip papers
② [머리에 사용하는 것] a hairpin ; a hair slide ; [컬용] a curling pin ; a curler ¶ 그녀는 머리에 클립을 끼운 채 부엌일을 하고 있었다 She was doing kitchen work with curling pins in her hair〔with her hair (up) in curlers〕.
큼직이 big ; large ; greatly ; on a large〔grand〕 scale (대규모로) ¶ 마음을 큼직이 먹다 assume a generous attitude // 집을 큼직이 짓다 build a house big // 글자를 큼직이 쓰다 write in large characters〔letters〕 // 큼직이 100만원을 기부하다 generously donate a million *won*.
큼직하다 (be) quite〔fairly〕 big〔generous〕
*킁킁 "Sniff, sniff!" ¶ 코를 킁킁거리다 snuffle ; sniffle // 킁킁 냄새를 맡다 sniff 《at》 ; give a sniff 《at》
키¹ [까부는] a winnow ; a winnowing-fan ¶ 키질하다 winnow
키² [배의] a rudder ; a helm ; a (steering) wheel ¶ 키를 잡다 steer ; be at the helm // 키를 돌리다 turn the helm
―손잡이 a tiller ; a helm ―잡이 [조타(操舵)] steering ; [조타수] a helmsman ; a steersman ; a man at the helm〔wheel〕 ; [보트의] a cox(swain) ―잡이 기둥 a steering column〔pillar, post〕 ―잡이 대 a steering stand〔pedestal〕 ―잡이 바퀴(핸들) a steering wheel ―장치 a steering gear〔apparatus〕 ―축 a steering shaft ―판(板) a rudder plate 〔blade〕
*키³ [신장] stature ; height ¶ 키가 큰〔작은〕 사람 a man of great〔small, low, short〕 stature〔height〕 // 중키의 사람 a person of mean〔medium〕 stature 〔height〕 // 키가 작아서 on account of one's small stature // 키가 크다 [성장] grow〔increase〕 in stature // 키가 5피트 5인치이다 be five feet five inches in stature // 그는 나보다 3인치가량 키가 크다〔작다〕 He is three inches taller 〔shorter〕 than I. // 당신은 키가 얼

마나 됩니까 How tall are you?/What's your height?//나는 키에 비해서 체중이 모자란다 I'm underweight for my height.

키⁴ a key ¶ 키로 잠근〔유건(有鍵)의〕 keyed//키를 누르다 press down a key//타이프라이터의 키를 두드리다 pound〔strike, tap〕 the keys of a typewriter//전신의 키를 두드리다 operate a telegraph key; key

키장이 집에 헌 키 (속담) None more bare〔worse, shod〕 than to shoemaker's wife and the smith's mare./The shoemaker's son always goes barefoot.

키갈리 Kigali

키꼴 a large frame〔build〕; (being) large-built

키내림 pouring grain for winnowing —하다 pour out grain in the winnowing process

키네마 〖영화〗 a kinema; a cinema; a movie

키니네, 키닌 〖약〗 quinine

키다리 a tall man〔fellow〕; a gangling fellow 《미》

키드 [가죽] kid

—구두 kid shoes —장갑 kid gloves; kids

키부츠 [이스라엘 집단 농장] a kibbutz 《*pl.* -zim》

키순 —順 the order of height〔stature〕

†키스 a kiss 《on the cheek》; osculation; a smack (쪽 소리내는) 《속》 —하다 kiss 《a girl on the mouth》; give 《a person》 a kiss; give 《a person》 goodbye〔good night〕; kiss off//키스 않고 헤어지다 part with dry lips//입술에 키스하다 kiss 《a person》 on the lips; press a kiss upon one's lips//…에게 몰래 슬쩍 키스하다 steal a kiss from 《her》

키 스테이션 a key station

키스트 KIST 《the Korea Institute of Science and Technology》

키에프 Kiev

*키우다 bring up; rear; raise; foster; nurse; [동·식물을] breed; raise; [양성] cultivate; foster ¶ 애를 우유로 키우다 bring up a child on cow's milk//어린 나무를 키우다 nurse young plants//음악의 재능을 키우다 foster musical ability

키장다리 a very tall person; a longlegs

키질하다 winnow ¶ 쌀을 키질하다 winnow rice

키퍼 a keeper

골— a goalkeeper

키펀처 [키펀치의 조작자] a key puncher; a key-punch operator

키펀치 [전자 계산기용 카드의 천공기(穿孔機)] a key punch

키 포인트 a key point

키프로스 Cyprus

킥 〖축구〗 a kick —하다 kick 《the ball》

코너— 〖축구〗 a corner kick 페널티— 〖축구·럭비〗 a penalty kick

킥복싱 kick〔Siamese〕 boxing

킥오프 〖축구〗 a kickoff

킥킥 ⇨ 킥킥거리다

킥킥거리다 giggle; titter; keep giggling

킨샤사 Kinshasa

킬 ① Kiel ② Kiel Canal

*킬로 kilo-

—그램 kilogram —리터 kiloliter —미터 kilometer —볼트 kilovolt —사이클 kilocycle —와트 kilowatt

킬리만자로 Mt. Kilimanjaro

‡킬킬거리다 giggle; cackle; keep giggling

킷값하다 do it well; be up to par

킹사이즈 ¶ 킹사이즈의 king-size(d)

킹키나나무 〖식물〗 a quinquina

킹킹 ⇨ 킹킹거리다

킹킹거리다 groan; moan; whimper; keep whining; whimpering

ㅋ

타 打 a dozen ¶ 여러 타의 (many) dozens of // 타로 팔다 sell by the dozen // 그것을 두 타 주십시오 I will take two dozens of them.

타 他 the rest ; the other ; others ¶ 타의 추종을 불허하다 be peerless〔unrivalled, without a peer, matchless〕; have no equal〔parallel〕; be second to none

타가 他家 another family〔house〕

타개 打開 a break ; a breakthrough ; a new turn ; a solution **—하다** break 《a deadlock》; break through ; effect a breakthrough ¶ 정국의 타개 a development〔new turn〕of the political situation // 난국을 타개하다 find a way out of〔overcome, get out of〕the difficulties ; tide over a difficult situation // 애로를 타개하다 break〔uncork〕the bottleneck 《in production》

—책 a way out ; a countermeasure ; a remedy ; a plan for breaking a deadlock ; a solution to an impasse ; a plan for the way out ¶ 불황의 타개책을 강구하다 try to find a way out of depression

타건(법) 打鍵(法) 〔피아노의〕 a touch ; finger attack

†**타격 打擊** ① 〔때려 침〕 a blow ; a hit ; a crusher ; a stinger ; 〔충격〕 a shock ; 〔손해〕 damage ¶ 치명적 타격 a fatal〔mortal, smashing〕blow // 타격을 주다 strike〔deal〕a blow 《at》; give a blow 《to》 // 타격을 받다 get a blow 《on the head》; be hit 《by》; suffer a blow // 그 사건으로 그의 명성은 큰 타격을 받았다 The trouble caused severe damage to his reputation. // 그 화재는 그의 사업에 큰 타격을 주었다 The fire was a heavy〔serious〕blow to his business. // 내 사업체가 불경기로 인해 큰 타격을 받았다 My business has been hit hard by the recession.

② 『야구』 batting ; hitting ; a clout

—력 『야구』 hitting〔batting〕power ; 〔핵전략〕 striking power〔capability〕; the force de flappe 《프》 **—률** batting〔hitting〕average **— 부진** shortage of hits ; poor batting **—상(賞)** the batting award **—순** 『야구』 the batting order **— 십걸** ten top hitters **—왕** 『야구』 a champion batter ; the king of swat ; leading〔top〕hitter **—전** 『야구』 a game with many hits ; a batting〔slugging〕match〔contest〕《미·속》; a slugfest 《미·속》 **기동 —대** strike force

타견 他見 ① 〔남이 보는 바〕 showing to others ; exposure ¶ 타견을 불허한다 This must be kept strictly secret.

② 〔남의 의견〕 another person's opinion ; other's ideas〔views, suggestions〕 ¶ 타견을 들어보다 ask〔invite, seek, solicit〕another's opinion

타결 《seek》 a compromise〔settlement〕; 〔협정〕 an agreement **—하다** reach an agreement 《with》; make a compromise agreement 《with》; come to terms ¶ 원만하게 타결되다 come to a peaceful and satisfactory settlement

—점 a point of agreement **— 조건** terms of agreement

타계 他界 ① 〔다른 세계〕 another world ; the other world ② 〔죽음〕 death ; decease ; demise **—하다** depart (from) this life ; pass away ; die ; decease

†**타고나다** be born 《with》; be gifted〔endowed〕《with》 ¶ 타고난 born ; inborn ; natural ; native ; innate ; constitutional // 타고난 허약 체질 a constitutional weakness // 타고난 시인 a born poet // 타고난 예술적 재능 an inborn talent of art // 재간을 타고나다 be gifted with a talent // 재물을 타고나다 be born rich〔to wealth〕// 복을 타고나다 be born under a lucky star ; be born with a silver spoon in one's mouth // 사람은 이성을 타고 난다 Man is endowed with reason.

타고을 他— an alien〔a strange〕county ; another county〔province〕; another part of the country

타고장 他— another place ; a strange〔an alien〕place ¶ 타고장으로 이사가다 move to a strange place

타곳 他— a foreign〔an alien〕land ; a strange place ; another place ¶ 타곳으로 이사가다 move to a strange〔an unfamiliar〕place

타관 他關 a strange land ; a foreign country ⇨ 타향

타구 唾具 a spittoon ; a cuspidor

타구 打毬 a kind of polo

타구 打球 『야구』 batting ; 〔친 공〕 a batted ball

타국 他國 a foreign country ; a strange〔an alien〕land ; another country ¶ 타국의 foreign ; alien

—어 a foreign language ; a strange tongue **—인** a foreigner ; a stranger ;

an alien ; an outlander

타기 唾棄 casting away with contempt 〔hate〕; throwing away in disgust ; rejection **—하다** throw away in disgust ; detest ; hate ; abominate ; abhor ; reject ¶ 타기할 detestable ; disgusting ; abominable ; revolting

타기 舵機 a rudder ; a helm ; a steering gear ¶ 타기를 조종하다 steer 《the ship》

—실 the steering room

타끈하다 (be) stingy ; moneygrubbing ; penny-pinching ; niggardly ; miserly ; grudging

타내다 get 《from one's elders》; obtain ; receive ¶ 그는 어머니한테 용돈을 타냈다 He got pocket money from his mother. // 그들은 정부에서 보조금을 타냈다 They got a subsidy from the government.

타념 他念 different〔other〕 intention ; other thoughts ¶ 타념 없이 with undivided attention ; whole-heartedly ; earnestly // 타념 없이 공부하다 study with one's whole heart ; devote oneself to one's studies // 독서에 타념이 없다 be absorbed in reading

타누르기 〖씨름〗 pressing down 《a person》 with one's body

타닌 〖화학〗 tannin

—산 tannic acid **— 산염** tannate

****타다[1]** ① [불이] burn ; blaze ¶ 타고 있는 석탄 live coals ; blazing coals // 타고 있다 be burning〔blazing〕; be on fire ; be in flames ; be in a blaze // 잘 타다 burn well ; be easy to burn ; be quick to catch fire ; be combustible ; be inflammable // 잘 타지 않다 burn poorly〔ill, badly〕; be slow to catch fire ; be incombustible ; be uninflammable // 몽땅 타버리다 burn itself out ; be burned〔burnt〕 out // 확 타오르다 burst into flames ; flare up into flames // (집이) 홀딱 타다 《a house》 burn〔be burned〕 down ; be reduced to ashes ; be destroyed by fire // 타 죽다 be burned to death ; lose one's life in flames // 타다 남다 escape a fire (건물이)

② [눋다] burn ; scorch ; be scorched 〔burned, charred, singed〕 ¶ 새까맣게 타다 be〔get〕 burned〔scorched〕 black ; be charred ; be blackened with fire // 밥이 타다 the rice is scorched // 비가 오지 않아 밀이 탄다 The wheat is parched from lack of rain.

③ [볕에] be sunburned〔sunburnt〕; be tanned ; burn in the sun ¶ 볕에 탄 얼굴 a sunburned〔sunburnt〕 face // 볕에 타지 않게 하다 keep oneself from getting sunburnt // 그의 피부는 볕에 까맣게 탔다 His skin is deeply sunburned 〔tanned〕. // 너 햇볕에 탔구나 You've got a tan. // 너 새까맣게 탔구나 You're so brown.

④ [걱정으로] burn ; blaze ; glow ¶ 타오르는 정열 burning passion〔love〕 // 가슴이 타다 have heartburn // 애가 타다 be anxious〔worried〕; be agonized // 애국심이 타오르다 one's heart glows with patriotism // 분노가 타올랐다 Indignation glowed in my heart.

⑤ [바짝 마르다] dry up ; be dried up ; parch ; be parched 《up》; dry as a brick ¶ 목이 타다 have a dry throat ; be parched with thirst // 탄 입술 parched lips // 바짝 마른 논 a dried up 〔parched〕 rice paddy

⑥ [빛깔이] ¶ 타는 듯한 주홍빛 blazing scarlet // 타는 듯한 색채를 그리다 paint in glowing colors

타다[2] [섞다] put in ; mix ; blend ; mingle ; [불순물을] adulterate 《with》; dissolve ¶ 아무것도 타지 않은 pure ; straight // 물을 타다 add water ; dilute 〔adulterate〕 《something》 with water // 물감을 타다 dissolve dye (in water) // 술에 독을 타다 drop poison in the wine ; mix poison with wine ; poison the liquor // 술에 물을 타다 water the liquor // 물에 소금을 타다 dissolve salt in water ; salt the water // 빨간색에 흰색을 타다 blend red with some white // 물을 타지 않고 마시다 drink 《brandy》 neat〔straight〕 // 홍차에 위스키를 좀 타 주시오 Give me tea with a dash of whisky in it.

†타다[3] ① [탈것에] take ; get on〔in, into〕; ride in〔on〕; mount 《a horse》; (go on) board 《a ship》; step into 《a boat》 ¶ 버스(기차)를 타다 get on〔in, into〕 a bus〔train〕 // 택시를 타다 take a taxi // 자전거를 타다 ride (on) a bicycle // 비행기를 타다 fly in a plane // 기차(배, 비행기)를 타고 가다 go by train 〔ship, plane〕 // 1등차를 타고 가다 go 〔travel〕 first-class train // 택시를 타고 집으로 가다 taxi home // 부산에서 배를 타다 take a ship at *Pusan* ; sail from *Pusan* // 걸어갈까요 타고 갈까요 Shall we walk or drive ? // 62번 버스를 타는 것이 좋습니다 You had better take bus No. 62. // 여러분 곧 타 주십시오 All aboard ! // 우리가 매주 적어도 하루나 이틀 만이라도 차를 같이 타고 다니면 교통 체증이 훨씬 덜할 것이다 If we carpool at least one or two days a week, we would have far less traffic congestion. // 차를 같이 타고 다니는 것을 진지하게 생각할 때가 됐다 It's about time we gave serious thought to ridesharing.

② [얼음을] slide 《on the ice》; skate (스케이트를) ; ski (스키를) ¶ 얼음을 타고 놀다 have a slide on the ice

③ [산·나무 따위를] climb ¶ 산을 타다 climb (up) a mountain // 줄을 타다 walk

E

on a rope // 나무를 잘 타다 be a good climber ; be good at climbing (trees) ④ [틈을] seize ; take ; get ; take advantage of ; avail oneself of ¶ 기회를 타다 get〔seize〕 an opportunity // 틈을 타다 avail oneself of some free time // 약점을 타다 take advantage of 《a person's》 weakness // 그들은 어둠을 타고 도망쳤다 They made their good escape under cover of darkness.

타다⁴ [받다] get ; receive ; take ; gain ; be given ; be awarded ; win ¶ 월급을 타다 get〔receive〕 one's salary // 졸업장을 타다 receive a graduation certificate 〔diploma〕 // 상을 타다 win a prize // 박사 학위를 타다 take a doctorate

타다⁵ ① [쪼다] split ; grind ¶ 탄 보리 ground〔cracked〕 barley // 맷돌에 콩을 타다 split〔grind〕 peas on a grindstone ② [가르다] part ; divide ¶ 골을 타다 part one's hair in the middle // 박을 타다 halve a gourd

타다⁶ ① [느끼다] be apt to feel ; be sensitive to ¶ 부끄럼을 타다 be bashful〔shy, abashed〕 // 노염을 타다 be testy〔touchy, irascible〕 // 간지럼을 타다 be〔feel〕 ticklish ② [영향을 받다] be susceptible〔sensitive〕 to ; be allergic to ; suffer (easily) from ; affect ¶ 추위를 타다 be sensitive to cold // 여름을 타다 be affected by summer heat

타다⁷ ① [악기를] play (on) ; perform on ¶ 풍금을 타다 play (on) the organ ② [솜을] beat cotton out ; willow 〔whip〕 《cotton》 ¶ 탄 솜 rewhipped 〔renovated〕 old cotton

타닥거리다 ① [걸음을] plod〔trudge〕 along ; walk wearily ¶ 타닥타닥 ploddingly ; trudgingly // 타닥타닥 길을 걷다 plod one's way ② [살림을] barely manage to get along ; make a bare living ③ [두드리는 모양] beat pat-pat ¶ 책상위의 먼지를 타닥타닥 털다 dust a table pat-pat-pat

타달거리다 ① [걸음이] plod 〔trudge〕 ; walk very wearily ② [수레 따위가] clatter ; rattle ; clink dully

†**타당 妥當** propriety ; reasonableness ―하다 (be) proper ; reasonable ; right ; appropriate ; adequate ; valid ; fit ; opportune ; apposite ; pertinent ; be in place ¶ 타당하지 않은 inappropriate ; unsuitable ; unreasonable ; out of place // 타당한 발언 an opportune〔apposite〕 remark // 타당하다고 생각하다 regard 《it》 as appropriate // 네가 그렇게 하는 것은 타당하다 It is proper that you should do so.

―성 propriety ; appropriateness ; adequacy ; validity ; soundness ; pertinence 보편 ―성 universal validity

*****타도 打倒** knocking〔breaking〕 down ; overthrow ―하다 knock〔strike〕 down ; overthrow ; overturn ; topple down ; bring down ; throw〔kick〕 out ; defeat ¶ 공산주의를 타도하라 Down with communism !

타도 他道 another province ; other provinces

타동 他洞 another village〔community, block〕 ; other villages

*****타동 他動** 〖문법〗 a transitivity ¶ 타동의 transitive

―사 〖문법〗 a transitive verb

*****타락 墮落** depravity ; corruption ; degradation ; delinquency ―하다 go wrong ; go to the bad〔devil〕 ; go astray ; fall low ; become degraded 〔depraved〕 ; backslide ; be corrupted 〔ruined〕 ; degenerate ¶ 예술의 타락 decadence of art // 인격의 타락 degradation of character // 타락한 여자 a fallen 〔ruined〕 woman // 타락한 정치가 a corrupt politician // 타락한 학생 a depraved student // 타락시키다 degrade ; lead 《a person》 astray ; drag down // 그가 그처럼 타락할 줄은 몰랐다 I never thought he would fall so low.

―자 a degenerate (wretch) ; a backslider ; a castaway ; the fallen (총칭)

타락 駝酪 cow's milk

타락줄 a rope made of human hair

타란텔라 〖음악〗 (a) tarantella

타래 a bunch ; a skein ; a spiral ; a coil ¶ 마늘 한 타래 a bunch of garlic // 새끼 두 타래 two bunches〔coils〕 of rope // 실 세 타래 three skeins of thread

타래과 ―菓 a kind of honey-cake

타래박 a kind of long-handled well-dipper ; a dipper

타래버선 children's quilted socks with decorations on them

타래송곳 ① [마개뽑이] a corkscrew ② [뚫는 기구] a gimlet ; a drill

타래쇠 a kind of metal coil ; a spiral ; a volute

타래타래 in coil ; in spiral ; round and round ―하다 be in coil〔spiral〕 ¶ 새끼를 타래타래 감다〔사리다〕 coil the straw rope up

타력 他力 the power of another ; help from without ; outside help ; salvation from without (종교의) ¶ 타력에 의존하지 말라 Don't rely upon others.

― 구제 salvation〔justification〕 by faith

― 의존 reliance upon others

타력 打力 〖야구〗 batting〔hitting〕 power

타력 惰力 inertia ; momentum ; force of habit ¶ 타력으로 달리다 run by inertia

― 운전 coasting ; a coast 자기(磁氣) ― magnetic inertia 전기 ― electric inertia

타령 打令 [곡조의 하나] a kind of tune ; [민요] a ballad

타륜 舵輪 the helm ; the steering wheel ; the wheel

E

‡타르 tar
광물 — mineral tar
타마유 —油 coal tar
타매 唾罵 slander ; calumniation ; insult ; backbiting —하다 slander ; calumniate ; insult ; backbite ; call 《a person》 names ; abuse
타맥 打麥 barley harvest —하다 thresh〔harvest〕 the barley
타면 打綿 cotton beating
—기 a cotton gin ; a scutcher
타면 他面 the other side〔hand, phase, aspect〕 ; (on) the other hand
타목 a thick voice
타문 他聞 others' hearing ; outside rumors ; publicity ; reaching others' ears ¶ 타문을 꺼리는 일 a confidential matter // 타문을 꺼리다 fear publicity ; be anxious to keep 《a matter》 secret
타바스코 [상표명] Tabasco (소스의 일종)
타박 disparagement ; faultfinding 《with》 ; grumbling ; rebuke ; reprimand —하다 disparage ; find fault 《with》 ; grumble 《at》 ; object 《to》 ¶ 음식을 타박하다 grumble at〔about, over〕 the food // 옷이 맞지 않는다고 타박하다 complain about the fit of a garment // 도대체 칭찬하시는 겁니까 타박하시는 겁니까 Do you mean to speak well or evil of me?
—쟁이 a grumbler 음식 — grumbling at〔about, over〕 the food
‡타박 打撲 a blow ; a stroke ; a contusion ; knocking —하다 knock ; beat ; give a blow
—상 a bruise ; a contusion ¶ 타박상을 입다 be bruised ; get〔sustain〕 a bruise 《on one's leg》 // 타박상을 입히다 bruise ; contuse
타박거리다 plod ; walk with difficulty ¶ 타박타박 ploddingly ; walking with difficulty // 타박타박 걸어가다 plod along ; plod one's way
타박타박 [음식이] being dry ; not moist —하다 (be) dry ; be not moist ; be hard to chew ¶ 떡이 타박타박해서 먹기 힘들다 The rice cake is so dry it is hard to eat.
타방 他方 another side〔place, quarter〕 ; a different direction ¶ 타방에 있어서는 on the other hand ; while
타봉 打棒 〖야구〗 batting ¶ 타봉에 불이 붙다 pump out hits ; pound (a pitcher) // 타봉을 봉쇄하다 throttle the bats 《of the opposing team》
타분하다 (be) stale ; moldy ; musty ¶ 타분한 생선 stale fish // 타분한 생각 a musty idea
타블레트 a tablet
타블로이드 a tabloid ¶ 타블로이드판의 신문 a tabloid (newspaper)
타사 他事 other matters ¶ 타사를 돌볼 겨를이 없다 have no time to think about other things
타산 打算 calculation ; money-mindedness ; self-interest ; selfishness —하다 calculate ; reckon ; count ¶ 타산적인 calculating ; money-minded ; selfish ; mercenary // 타산적인 생각 a selfish idea ; a mercenary spirit // 타산적인 사람 a self-centered man // 그는 항상 타산적이다 He is always consulting his own interests.
타산지석 他山之石 an object lesson ; an example one may profit by ; food for thought ¶ 이것을 타산지석으로 삼아라 Let this be〔serve as〕 a good lesson to you. / This will afford an excellent lesson to you.
타산지석 (속담) Let another's shipwreck be your sea-mark. / It is good to learn at another men's cost.
타살 他殺 murder ; foul play ¶ 아무래도 타살 같다 There is every reason to believe that it is a murder.
타살 打殺 beating〔clubbing, knocking, striking〕 《a person》 to death ; striking 《a person》 dead —하다 beat〔club, knock, strike〕 《a person》 to death
타석 打席 〖야구〗 《times》 at bat 《a. b》 ¶ 타석에 서다 take one's turn at the bat // 그는 5타석 3안타였다 He made three hits in five at bats.
규정 —수 the required minimum number of times at bat 《for qualifying to be included in the batting record》
타선 打線 〖야구〗 the batting lineup ¶ 강력한 타선 a power-packed lineup of hitters ; a powerful batting lineup // 타선이 작렬하다 make many hits ; pump out hits // 상대 팀의 타선을 봉쇄하다 keep the opposing team's bats silent
타선 唾腺 〖해부〗 the salivary glands
타성 惰性 inertia ; momentum ; force of habit ; the course of least resistance ¶ 타성으로 담배를 피우다 smoke from force of habit
타성 他姓 another〔a different〕 surname
타성 他性 〖철학〗 differentness ; otherness
타소 他所 another place ; a different part of the country
타수 舵手 a helmsman ; a steersman ; a cox ; a coxswain
타수 打手 a hitter ; 〖야구〗 a batter ; 〖크리켓〗 a bowler
타수 打數 〖야구〗 ¶ 5타수 five at bats 《5 ab》 // 5타수 3안타를 치다 make three hits in five at bat
타순 打順 〖야구〗 the batting order
타스 Tass (소련의 통신사)
타악기 打樂器 a percussion instrument
타액 唾液 saliva ; sputum (가래) ; spittle (뱉은 침) ¶ 타액을 분비하다 salivate ; secrete saliva

—관〔구〕 the salivary duct〔corpuscle〕 —분비 salivation ; a flow of saliva —선 the salivary glands —소 ptyalin —폐지 retention of saliva

†타오르다 blaze〔light〕 up ; burn up ; burst into flame ¶ 타오르게 하다 set afire〔aflame, ablaze, alight〕

타울거리다 strive ; struggle ; be overeager

타원 楕圓 oval ; elliptical ¶ 타원의 elliptic(al) ; oval

— 궤도 elliptical orbit —규(規) an ellipsograph —운동 elliptic motion —율 ellipticity —주 〖수학〗 a cylindroid ; an elliptic cylinder —체 an oval figure ; 〖기하〗 an ellipsoid —형 an oval

*타월 a towel ⇨ 수건

타율 他律 another〔a different〕 order〔rule, discipline〕; heteronomy ¶ 타율의 heteronomous

타율 打率 〖야구〗 one's batting average 《bat. avg.》 ¶ 3할 6푼 7리의 타율을 올리다 compile a .367 (batting) average // 그의 타율은 3할 2푼 5리이다 He has a hitting〔batting〕 average of .325. 《three hundred twenty-five 라고 읽음》

타의 他意 another intention ; an ulterior motive ; a secret purpose ; malice ; ill will ¶ 타의 없다 bear no hard feelings ; have no desire but to // 별로 타의가 있어 한 것은 아니다 I have done it meaning no harm whatever.

타이¹ [태국] Thailand ¶ 타이의 Thai —말 Thai — 사람 a Thai ; a Thailander

타이² ① [동점] a tie ¶ 타이로 끝나다 end in a 《2-2》 tie // 타이를 이루다 tie the score ② ⇨ 넥타이

— 스코어 a tie score

타이곤 a tigon (수펌과 암사자 사이의 튀기)

타이르다 admonish ; remonstrate 《with》; reason 《with》; advise ; counsel ; talk to ; tell ; explain ; give 《a person》 instruction ¶ 타일러서 …시키다 persuade 《a person》 to 《do》 // 공부 잘 하라고 타이르다 advise 《a person》 to study hard // 타일러서 납득시키다 reason 《a person》 into compliance // 타일러서 그만두게 하다 reason 《a person》 out of 《doing》 // 잘못을 타이르다 reason with 《a person》 on his mistake // 잘 타이르다 give a good talking to 《on》; admonish 《a person》 earnestly 《on》

타이밍 timing ¶ 타이밍 감각 a 《good》 sense of timing // 타이밍이 좋다〔나쁘다〕 be timely〔untimely〕; be well〔not well〕 timed // 타이밍을 그르치다 mistime 《an action》 // 그 발언은 타이밍이 좋았다 The remark was well timed.

*타이어 a tire ; a tyre 《영》 ¶ 바람 빠진 타이어 a flat tire ; a flat // 바람이 덜 들어간〔너무 들어간〕 타이어 an under〔over〕-inflated tire // 닳은 타이어 a bald tire // 타이어가 없는 tireless // 타이어 자국 tire tracks ; the imprint of a tire tread // 타이어가 펑크 나다 a tire punctures ; have a puncture〔blowout〕 in a tire // 타이어에 바람을 넣다 inflate〔pump up〕 a tire ; get air into a tire // 타이어를 달다 tire ; put a tire 《on a wheel》 // 타이어를 바꿔 끼다 fix a new tire 《on a wheel》 // 펑크 난 타이어를 갈다 change a flat tire

— 공장 a tire plant — 펌프 a bicycle〔pneumatic〕 pump 고무 — a rubber tire 공기 — a pneumatic (tire) 통〔솔리드〕 — a solid tire

타이츠 tights ; leotards ¶ 타이츠를 입은 소녀 a girl in tights

타이트 스커트 a tight skirt

타이틀 ① [선수권] a title ; a championship ¶ 타이틀을 겨루다 play for the title // 타이틀을 방어하다 defend a title // 타이틀을 잃다 lose〔forfeit〕 a title // 타이틀을 빼앗다 gain a title ; win a championship // 그는 타이틀 방어에 성공했다 He made good his title defense. // 그는 알리에게 져서 타이틀을 잃었다 He lost his title to Ali. ② [표제] a title

— 롤 〖연극·영화〗 a title role ; a title〔name〕 part — 매치 〖권투〗 a title match — 페이지 a title page 논— 매치 a non-title match

*타이프라이터 a typewriter ; a machine 《미·속》 ¶ 타이프라이터를 치다 typewrite ; type ; do typing // 타이프라이터로 찍은 typewritten // 이것을 타이프라이터로 쳐주시오 I want to have〔get〕 it typed up.

— 인쇄물 typescript ; typewritten matter 휴대용 — a portable typewriter

*타이피스트 a typist ¶ 타이피스트로 취직하다 find〔get〕 a job as typist

— 학원 a typing school 영문〔국문〕 — a typist in English〔Korean〕

타인 他人 [다른 사람] another person ; others ; [미지의 사람] a stranger ; [국외자] an outsider ¶ 타인에게 친절히 하다 be kind to others // 타인의 욕을 하다 speak ill of another // 타인 취급을 하다 treat 《a person》 like a stranger ; make a stranger of 《a person》 // 타인은 참견 말라 A third party should not thrust his nose into these matters.

타일 他日 some day ; some other time〔day〕; another day〔time〕; some day or other ; in the future ; on some future occasion ; at some future date

*타일 a tile ¶ 타일을 깔다 tile ; lay〔set〕 tiles 《on》; face 《a thing》 with tiles // 타일을 깐 tiled 《bathroom》

— 공사 tiling ; tiler's work ; tilesetting

— 공장 a tilery

타일란드 ⇨ 타이

타임 time ¶ 타임을 재다 time ; clock ;

time the speed ¶ 타임업 The time is up.
— 레코더 a time clock〔recorder〕 — 머신 a time machine — 스위치 a time switch — 스터디 〖노동〗 time (and motion) study ; (motion and) time study —아웃 time out — 카드 a time card — 캡슐 a time capsule —키퍼 a timekeeper — 테이블 a timetable

타임스 [런던 타임즈] the Times

타입 ① [형·유형] (a) type ; (a) kind ; (a) sort ¶ 같은 타입의 사람 a person of the same type∥구식 타입의 사람 a person of old pattern〔an old fashioned type〕∥저런 타입의 사람 a man of that type〔kind, stripe〕∥마릴린 몬로 타입의 여자 women of the Marilyn Monroe type

*타자 打者 〖야구〗 a batter ; a batman ; a hitter ¶ 강타자 a slugger ; a heavy 〔hard〕 batter〔hitter〕∥1번 타자 the first hitter ; a lead-off man∥다음 타자 the next batter

타자 打字 typing ; typewriting
— 경기 a typewriting contest

타자기 打字機 a typewriter ¶ 타자기로 친 편지 a typewritten〔typed〕 letter∥타자기를 치다 typewrite ; type ; do typing
국문〔영문〕 — a Korean〔an English〕 character typewriter 휴대용 — a portable typewriter

타자수 打字手 a typist
— 양성소 a typing school 국문 — a typist in Korean ; an operator of the Korean typewriter 영문 — a typist in English

타작 打作 [마당질] threshing ; [추수] a harvest ; a crop ; a yield —하다 thresh (out) ; beat out ; harvest ¶ 보리를 타작하다 thresh barley∥벼 100석을 타작하다 harvest 100 bushels of rice ; have a hundred-bushel harvest
— 마당 a threshing ground

타전 打電 sending a telegram〔wire〕 ; telegraphing ; wiring —하다 send〔dispatch〕 a telegram〔wire〕 《to》 ; telegraph ; wire ; cable (해외로) ; wireless 《영》 ; radio 《미》 ¶ 즉시 오라고 그에게 타전하라 Cable him to come at once.

타점 打點 ① [붓으로] dotting ; marking with a dot ② [마음으로] singling out ; marking a choice in one's heart ③ 〖야구〗 a run batted in 《RBI》

*타조 駝鳥 〖새〗 an ostrich

타종 他宗 another〔a different〕 sect (종파) ; another religion (종교)

타종 打鐘 striking〔tolling〕 a bell —하다 strike〔toll, ring〕 a bell ; sound 〔ring〕 a gong

타죄 他罪 another crime〔offence〕 ; other crimes〔offences〕

타죽다 be burnt to death ; perish in the flames〔by fire〕

타진 打診 ① 〖의학〗 percussion ; tapping ② [떠 봄] sounding ; tapping —하다 percuss ; tap ; sound ; sound out ; put 〔throw〕 out a feeler ; tap ; fathom ¶ 의견을 타진하다 tap 《a person's》 opinion∥정세를 타진하다 float a trial balloon∥여론의 추세를 타진하다 gauge the trend of public opinion∥그 제안에 관해서 그녀의 생각을 타진해 보자 Let me sound her on the proposal.
—기 a plexor ; a plessor —음 percussion sound —판 a pleximeter

타짜(꾼) a dishonest gambler ; a card cheat ; a cardsharp(er) ; a slicker ; a trickster

타처 他處 another place ; other places ¶ 타처에(서) in〔at〕 another place ; elsewhere∥타처에서 온 사람들 people from other places ; out-of-town〔-village〕 people
— 지불 어음 a domiciled bill

타천 他薦 recommendation 《of other people》

타촌 他村 another village

타칭 他稱 〖문법〗 the third person

타코미터 〖기계〗 a tachometer

타타르 Tartary ; Tatary
—말 Ta(r)tar — 사람 a Ta(r)tar

타태 墮胎 ⇨ 낙태

타파 打破 breaking ; destruction ; defeat ; conquest ; overthrow —하다 break down 《evil customs》 ; overthrow 《bureaucracy》 ; explode 《a fallacy》 ; conquer 《a habit》 ; do away with ; destroy ; frustrate ; defeat ; abolish ¶ 군국주의 타파의 외침 a cry of "Down with militarism!"∥악습을 타파하다 do away with evil practice∥전쟁은 많은 인습을 타파했다 The war broke down many conventions.
계급 — abolition of class distinction

†타합 打合 a previous〔preliminary〕 arrangement ; preliminaries —하다 make (previous) arrangements ; arrange 《matters with a person, that》 ; prearrange ¶ 그 건에 관해서는 미리 타합이 돼 있다 Arrangements have been made on that matter. ∥미리 그들과 타합해 놓지 않으면 안된다 We must arrange with them beforehand.

타향 他鄕 another countryside ; a place away from home ; a foreign land ; foreign parts ¶ 타향에서 away from home ; in a strange land∥타향에서 떠돌아다니다 wander in a strange land ; be an exile from home∥10년이나 타향살이를 하다 be absent from home for 10 years

*타협 妥協 compromise ; an amicable agreement ; mutual concession ; give-and-take ; understanding —하다 compromise ; make 〔reach〕 a compromise ; come to terms 《with》 ; come to

E

an understanding 《with》; reach an agreement ; meet 《a person》 halfway ; split the difference ; give and take ¶ 타협적인 태도를 취하다 take a compromising〔conciliatory〕 attitude // 타협을 보다 reach an understanding // 타협의 여지가 없다 There is no room for compromise.
—안 a compromise (plan, proposal, measure) —자 a compromiser —점 common ground ; a point of compromise〔agreement〕 ¶ 타협점을 발견하다 find out a meeting point〔a point of compromise〕; come to an agreement

탁 [소리] with a bang〔snap, thud, pop〕; [풀림] less tense ; with relief ; [트임] widely ; unobstructedly ¶ 뚜껑을 탁 닫다 snap down the lid // 마음이 탁 놓이다 be〔feel〕 quite relieved // 숲을 나서자 시야가 탁 트였다 A wide prospect burst upon my view as I came out of the forest.

탁견 卓見 [의견] a fine idea ; distinguished〔excellent〕 views ; [식견] lofty outlook ; foresight ; farsightedness ; clear-sightedness ; penetration ¶ 탁견 있는 clear-sighted ; longheaded〔-sighted〕; farseeing // 탁견지사(之士) a man of far sight // 탁견이 있다 have a long head〔view〕; have a broad vision

*__탁구 卓球__ ping-pong ; table tennis ¶ 탁구를 치다 play ping-pong
—공 a ping-pong ball —대 a ping-pong table — 시합 a table-tennis tournament

탁랑 濁浪 turbid waves ; muddy waves

탁론 卓論 a lofty〔sound〕 argument ; an exalted view

탁류 濁流 a muddy stream ; a turbid current ¶ 탁류가 휩쓸고 있다 The muddy water rushes on in a vast expanse.

탁마 琢磨 [옥석을] polishing ; [학덕을] cultivating ; close application of oneself 《to》 —하다 polish 《a gem》; cultivate 《oneself》; apply oneself to 《one's study》 ¶ 탁마의 공에 의하여 by dint of one's hard〔indefatigable〕 work

탁목조 啄木造 〖새〗 a woodpecker

*__탁발 托鉢__ 〖불교〗 religious mendicancy ; friarhood —하다 《a Buddhist priest》 beg around ; go about as a begging priest
—승 a mendicant priest〔friar〕; a begging priest — 승단 a mendicant order

탁본 拓本 a rubbed copy ; a rubbing —하다 take a rubbing 《of》

탁상 卓上 (on) the table〔desk〕
— 계획 a desk plan — 공론 a desk theory ; an armchair argument ; an academic discussion — 선풍기 a desk fan — 시계 a table clock — 연설 an after-dinner speech ; a speech (made) at a dinner〔luncheon〕 — 전화 a desk〔table, cradle〕 telephone ¶ 탁상 전화대 the cradle

탁선 託宣 an oracle ; a divine message ; a revelation 《from a god》; pythonism

탁설 卓說 an excellent opinion ; distinguished〔excellent〕 views
명론 — sound arguments and excellent views ; an original worth listening to ; a feast of reason

탁성 濁聲 a thick〔hoarse〕 voice

탁송 託送 consignment —하다 consign ; send 《by, through, under the care of》
—품 a consignment 직송 —품 a direct consignment

탁수 濁水 muddy〔turbid〕 water

탁아소 託兒所 a day〔public〕 nursery ; a nursery school ; a pre-kindergarten

탁엽 托葉 〖식물〗 a stipule ⇨ 턱잎

탁용 擢用 selection (of men for employment) ⇨ 발탁 —하다 select ; employ

*__탁월 卓越__ excellence ; superiority ; eminence ; prominence ; preeminence —하다 (be) excellent ; eminent ; prominent ; distinguished ¶ 탁월한 학자 a prominent scholar // 탁월한 능력 superior ability // 인물 재질이 모두 탁월하다 surpass others both in character and ability

탁월풍 卓越風 〖기상〗 the prevailing wind

탁음 濁音 a voiced sound ; a sonant ¶ 탁음의 sonant
— 자음 a flat〔voiced〕 consonant

*__탁자 卓子__ a table ; a desk ¶ 둥근 탁자 a round table // 탁자에 둘러앉다 sit round the table // 탁자에 놓다 put 《a thing》 on the desk

탁잣손 卓子— a support under a shelf or table

탁절 卓絶 excellence ⇨ 탁월

탁절 卓節 lofty virtues ; noble character

탁주 濁酒 coarse liquor ; unrefined〔raw〕 *sul* ⇨ 막걸리

탁지 度地 land surveying ; a geodetic survey —하다 survey the land

탁출 卓出 excellence ⇨ 탁월

탁탁 ① [소리] with cracks〔pops, blows, snaps, bangs〕 ¶ 숯이 탁탁 튀다 pieces of charcoal pops and crackles
② [연이어] one after another ; in rapid succession ¶ 탁탁 쓰러지다 fall one after another
③ [일을] speedily ; rapidly ; one right after another ¶ 탁탁 처리하다 dispose of matters bang-bang-bang just like that ; do one's work in a brisk way
④ [침을] spit-spit ¶ 침을 탁탁 뱉다 spit and spit again ; go spit-spit-spit
⑤ [숨이] with gasping ; stiflingly ;

short of〔out of〕 breath ¶ 숨이 탁탁 막히다 be stifled ; be gasping for breath ; lose one's breath
탁탁거리다 keep cracking〔popping, snapping, banging〕 ¶ 장작이 타느라고 탁탁거리다 firewood crackles as it burns
탁탁하다 ① [올차다] (be) close-woven ; thick and strong ¶ 탁탁한 피륙 a fabric with close〔fine〕 texture ② [윤택하다] (be) abundant ; plentiful ¶ 살림이 탁탁하다 be well〔comfortably〕 off
탁하다 濁— ① [물 따위가] (be) muddy ; turbid ; dull ; thick ; impure ; cloudy ¶ 탁한 물 muddy water // 탁한 색 turbid color // 탁한 목소리 a thick voice // 탁한 공기 impure air // 탁한 세상 the corrupt world // 마음이 탁한 사람 a person with dark designs ; an inscrutable 〔untrustworthy〕 person // 가스는 방 안의 공기를 탁하게 한다 Gas spoils〔poisons〕 the air of a room. ② [안색이] (be) dark ; swarthy
탄 歎 grief ; lamentation
탄 炭 ⇨ 연탄
탄갱 炭坑 a coal mine ; a colliery ; [작업장] a coal pit
—부 a coal miner ; a collier **— 침수** a mine flood
탄고 炭庫 a coal cellar ; a coal bin〔bunker〕
탄공 彈孔 a shot hole
탄광 炭鑛 a coal mine ; a colliery
—부 a collier ; a coal miner ; a coal (mine) worker **—업** the coal mining industry **—주** a coal mine owner〔operator〕 ; a colliery proprietor **— 지대** a mining region〔area〕 ; the black country 《영》 **— 폭발** a mine〔colliery〕 explosion **— 회사** a coal mine company
탄금 彈琴 —하다 play (on) the *kayagŭm*〔*kŏmungo*〕
탄내 a scorched smell ¶ 탄내가 나다 smell scorched〔burned〕 // 그 과자는 탄내가 난다 The cake tastes scorched.
탄내 炭— (char) coal fumes
탄대 彈帶 a cartridge belt ; a cartridge bag
탄도 彈道 the trajectory〔path〕 of a missile〔bullet, projectile〕 ; the ballistics
— 계수 the coefficient of a trajectory **— 곡선** a ballistic curve **— 비행** a trajectory〔suborbital〕 flight **—탄** a ballistic missile **—학** ballistics **곡사〔직사, 저사(低射)〕 —** a curved〔flat, low〕 trajectory **단거리〔공중 발사〕 —** a short range〔an air-launched〕 ballistic missile ; an S. R. B. M. 〔A. L. B. M.〕 **정중 —** a bull's eye trajectory **대륙간〔중거리〕 —탄** an intercontinental〔intermediate-range〕 ballistic missile ; an I. C. B. M. 〔an I. R. B. M〕

탄두 彈頭 a warhead ; a head
미사일 — a missile warhead **수폭 —** an H-bomb〔hydrogen bomb〕 warhead **핵〔열핵〕—** a nuclear〔thermonuclear〕 warhead **핵— 미사일** a nuclear-tipped missile
탄띠 彈— a cartridge belt ⇨ 탄대
***탄력 彈力** elasticity ; elastic force ; flexibility ; resilience ; spring ; give ¶ 탄력 있는 elastic ; flexible ; buoyant ; resilient ; springy // 탄력 없는 nonelastic ; inelastic // 어린 나무의 탄력 있는 가지 the resilient bough of a young tree // 이 낡은 고무줄은 탄력이 없다 There is no spring left in these old rubber bands.
—계 an elastometer **— 고성능 폭약** cyclonite ; RDX **—률** the modulus〔coefficient〕 of elasticity **—성[탄성]** elasticity ; resilience ; spring ; give ; [융통성] flexibility ; adaptability ¶ 정신적 탄력성 resilience of mind **—소(素)** 〖생화학〗 elastin **— 시험** an elasticity test
탄로 坦路 a broad and level highway
탄로 綻露 disclosure ; detection ; exposure ; divulgence ¶ 탄로나다 be〔get〕 found out〔detected, divulged, exposed, revealed, laid bare〕 ; come to light ; come out // 비밀 결사의 조직이 탄로났다 The system of the secret society was disclosed. // 그의 구악이 탄로났다 His old crime〔secret〕 has come into light. // 그 음모는 탄로나고 말았다 The plot has been laid bare.
탄막 彈幕 a barrage
— 포화 covering fire ; curtain fire ; a curtain of fire **고정 —** a standing barrage **엄호 —** a covering barrage
탄말 炭末 charcoal dust
탄망 誕妄 falsehood ; absurdity **—하다** (be) false ; absurd
탄맥 炭脈 a coal seam〔vein〕
탄명스럽다 (be) fuzzy-minded ; vague ; ambiguous ; equivocal ; obscure
탄미 歎美 admiration ; adoration ; appreciation **—하다** admire ; appreciate ; adore ; praise ; laud ; extol ¶ 한국의 경치를 탄미하다 admire the beautiful scenery of Korea
—자 an admirer ; an adorer
†탄복 歎服 —하다 admire ; have〔feel〕 a great admiration for ¶ 탄복할 만한 admirable ; estimable
탄산 炭山 a coal mine
탄산 炭酸 〖화학〗 carbonic acid
—가리 potassium carbonate ; carbonate of potash ; pearl ash (조제(粗製)의) **— 가스** carbonic acid gas ; carbon dioxide (이산화탄소) **— 결핍증** 〖의학〗 acapnia **—기(基)** 〖화학〗 carboxyl ; the carboxyl radical〔group〕 **—석회〔칼슘〕** calcium carbonate ; carbonate of lime **—소다〔나트륨〕** sodium carbonate ; carbonate of

E

soda —수 carbonated water ; soda (water) ; mineral water 《영》 ; mineral(s) 《영·구》 ; (soda) pop 《미·구》 ; fizzwater —암모니아수 salt of hartshorn ; sal volatile 《라》 —암모늄 hartshorn ; ammonium carbonate ; sal volatile 《라》 —연 lead carbonate —염 a carbonate —지 carbon paper ; manifold paper —천(泉) a carburetted spring — 탈실〔제거〕 decarbonization

탄상 歎賞 admiration ; praise ; applause ; laudation —하다 admire ; praise ; extol ; speak highly of ; marvel at ¶ 보는 사람 모두가 탄상해 마지 않았다 All those who saw it were filled with〔lost in〕 admiration. // 그의 용기에 적도 탄상하지 않을 수 없었다 His bravery compelled applause even from his enemy.

†탄생 誕生 birth —하다 be〔get〕 born ; come into the world ; first see the light of day ¶ 어린아이의 탄생 a child's birth // 새로운 클럽의 탄생 the birth of a new club // 민주주의가 탄생했다 Democracy came into being〔existence〕.
—석 a birthstone —일 a birthday ; a natal day ¶ 탄생일을 축하하다 celebrate 《a person's》 birthday —지 one's birth〔native, natal〕 place ; one's place of birth 예수 —일 Christmas Day

탄성 歎聲 [탄식] a sigh ; a groan ; lamentation ; [감탄] admiration 《at, for》 ; an exclamation ¶ 탄성을 발하다 sigh ; heave〔breathe, utter〕 a sigh of despair〔grief〕 ; draw a long breath

탄성 彈性 elasticity ¶ 탄성이 있는 elastic ; springy
—계 an elastometer — 고무 elastic gum ; gum elastic ; India〔natural〕 rubber ; rubber ; caoutchouc — 곡선 elastics — 공학 elasticity engineering —률〔계수〕 the modulus〔coefficient〕 of elasticity — 설계 〖건축〗 an elastic design —소(素) 〖생화학〗 elastin — 역청 elaterite —체 an elastic body — 한계 〖물리〗 an elastic limit

‡탄소 炭素 〖화학〗 carbon 《C》
—강 carbon steel —봉 a carbon rod〔point〕 —선〔전구〕 a carbon filament〔lamp〕 — 제거〔탈실〕 decarbonization —지 carbon paper — 환식(環式) 화합물 carbocyclic compounds 방사성 — radio carbon ; radioactive carbon 《C_{14}》 ¶ 방사성 탄소에 의한 연대 측정 radiocarbon dating

탄수 炭水 coal and water ; 〖화학〗 carbon and hydrogen
—차 a (locomotive) tender

*탄수화물 炭水化物 〖화학〗 a carbohydrate

*탄식 歎息 a sigh ; lamentation ; deploring ; grief —하다 sigh ; heave〔draw, fetch〕 a sigh ; lament 《for》 ; deplore ; grieve ¶ 탄식하며 말하다 sigh out 《something》 // 자신의 불운을 탄식하다 lament (over) one's misfortune // 하늘을 쳐다보고 탄식하다 heave a sigh of despair looking heavenward // 그 비보에 접하여 일동은 깊이 탄식했다 The sad news drew deep sighs from all present. // 이 사회의 부패상을 보고 탄식하지 않을 수 없다 We cannot but deplore the corrupt conditions of this society.

탄신 誕辰 a royal birthday ; the king's birthday ; the birthday of sage〔saint〕 ¶ 제 85회 탄신일 the 85th birthday

탄알 彈— a shot ; a bullet ; a ball ; a shell (포탄) ¶ 탄알을 재다 load〔charge〕 《a gun》 // 탄알이 비 오듯 하다 bullets fall thick and fast

탄압 彈壓 suppression ; oppression ; pressure ; coercion ; crushing —하다 suppress ; oppress ; coerce ; crush ; clamp down on ; bring pressure upon 《a person》 ; use an iron hand ¶ 탄압적인 oppressive ; suppressive ; coercive ; highhanded // 탄압을 받다 be pressed ; be subjected to great pressure // 그들의 운동은 치안 방해로서 탄압받았다 Their movement was suppressed as a breach of the public peace.
— 정책 an oppressive〔a repressive〕 measure 무력 — military pressure 언론 — suppression of〔gag on〕 the press

*탄약 彈藥 ammunition
—고 a powder magazine ; a powder dump (임시의) ; a shot locker —대 a bandoleer〔bandolier〕 ; an ammunition〔a cartridge ; 〖군사〗 an ammo 《속》〕 belt — 상자 an ammunition box〔chest〕 ; a cartridge box ; 〖군사〗 a caisson — 제조소 an ammunition factory ; ammunition works — 집적소 an ammunition〔a munitions ; 〖군사〗 an ammo 《속》〕 dump —차 an ammunition car〔cart, wagon〕 ; a caisson ; a fourgon —창(廠) an ammunition depot〔park〕 —통 a cartridge ; rounds of ammunition ; a cartouche —합 an ammunition〔a cartridge〕 pouch

탄우 彈雨 a shower〔rain, hail〕 of bullets〔shells〕 ¶ 탄우 속에서 under a rain of shells ; in the thick of the battle

‡탄원 歎願 entreaty ; supplication ; appeal ; solicitation ; petition ; suit —하다 entreat〔supplicate, implore, beseech, solicit, sue〕 《a person》 for ; make suit ; petition 《the government》 ; appeal to 《a person》 for ¶ 탄원하는 표정으로 with an imploring look // 탄원을 받아들이다 listen to entreaty ; grant a petition // 국민은 그의 구명을 탄원했다 The people sent in a petition for his life.

E

—서 a (written) petition ¶ 탄원서를 제출하다 present〔send in〕 a (written) petition to —자 a supplicant ; a supplicator ; petitioner ; a suitor 《for some favor》
탄일 誕日 as royal birthday ⇨ 탄신
탄자 a blanket ; a rug
양— a carpet
탄저병 炭疽病 〖식물〗 anthracnose
탄전 炭田 coalfield
탄젠트 〖수학〗 a tangent 《ten》
탄주 彈奏 play ; performance —하다 play (on) 《the piano》; perform on ; pluck
—법 touch —자 a player ; a performer
탄지 burnt tobacco left over in a pipe
탄진 炭塵 coal dust
탄질 炭質 the quality of coal
탄차 炭車 a coal waggon ; a coal truck 《영》
탄착 彈着 hit ; graze ; impact
— 거리 range ; gunshot ; shooting distance — 관측 spotting ; rangefinding — 관측기 a spotter plane —점 a shooting objective ; the point of impact
탄창 彈倉 a magazine
탄층 炭層 a coal seam ; a coal bed
탄탄 坦坦 —하다 (be) level ; even ; flat ; smooth
— 대로 a broad and level highway
탄탄하다 (be) solid ; compact ; strong ; hard ; adamant ; stable ⇨ 튼튼하다
탄평 坦平 evenness ; flatness —하다 (be) even ; flat ; level ; smooth
탄피 彈皮 an empty cartridge
탄하 呑下 swallowing —하다 swallow ; down ; gulp down
탄하다 cavil〔rail〕 at ; find fault with 《a remark》; find fault with 《another's business》; criticize ; pick at ¶ 남의 말을 탄하다 cavil at what one has said // 남의 일을 탄하다 criticize another's affairs
*탄핵 彈劾 impeachment ; denunciation ; accusation ; censure ; arraignment
—하다 impeach 《a person of a crime》; denounce ; accuse 《a person of misdemeanor》; censure ; arraign ; call 《a thing》 in question
—안 an impeachment motion〔resolution〕; a censure vote ; a vote of censure ¶ 야당은 정부 탄핵안을 제출했다 The opposition introduced a motion of impeachment against the government.
— 연설 an impeachment address ; a denunciatory speech —자 an impeacher ; a denunciator — 재판소 the Impeachment Court ; a Court of Impeachment 《of Judges》
탄화 炭化 〖화학〗 carbonization —하다 carbonize ; char
—강(鋼) carbonic steel —규소 silundum —물 a carbide —법 (means of) carbonization — 불소 fluorocarbon — 수소 hydrocarbon ; carburetted hydrogen —철 cementite —칼슘 calcium carbide ; carbide of calcium
†탄환 彈丸 a projectile ; a shot ; a bullet ; a ball ; a cannon ball ; a shell (파열탄) ¶ 탄환이 통하지 않는 bulletproof ; shellproof // 탄환이 떨어지다 fire away all one's shots // 빗발치는 탄환 속을 나아가다 advance under a hail 〔shower, rain, storm〕 of bullets // 적에게 탄환을 퍼붓다 rain〔shower〕 shells upon the enemy
— 열차 a bullet-express〔very fast〕 train ; a flier — 저장실 a magazine ; a depot ; a storeroom for projectiles — 충격 〖의학〗 shell shock 고속도 — a high-speed shell〔ball〕
탄회 坦懷 open-heartedness ; candidness ; frankness —하다 (be) openhearted ; candid ; frank ; lack reservations
허심 — frankness ; candidness ; openmindedness
탄흔 彈痕 a bullet mark
†탈 a mask ; a disguise ¶ …의 탈을 쓰고 under the mask〔cloak〕 of ; under color of
탈을 쓰다 관용 wear a mask ; mask one's face ; dissemble ; play the hypocrite
탈을 벗다 관용 unmask ; throw off a mask 《of》; show one's true colors
탈 ① [변고] a hitch ; a trouble ; a snag ; a mishap ; something wrong ; breakdown ¶ 전차가 탈이 났다 The streetcar broke down. // 브레이크가 탈났다 Something is wrong〔the matter〕 with the brake. /The brake is out of order. // 기차가 탈이 나서 연착하였다 The train was delayed owing to some trouble. // 그 교섭은 아무 탈 없이 잘 진행되었다 There was no hitch in the negotiations. /The negotiations went well〔all right〕. // 이거 큰 탈났구나 Good heavens, we're in real trouble ! /What a fine fix we're in !
② [병] sickness ; illness ¶ 몸에 탈이 나다 get ill〔sick〕 // 그것은 배탈이 난 증거다 It bespeaks a disordered stomach.
③ [흠] a fault ; a defect ; a flaw ; [핑계] an excuse ; a pretext ; a plea ¶ 탈잡을 데가 없다 He has no fault to find with.
탈각 脫却 riddance ; cleaning out —하다 rid oneself of ; get rid of ; extricate oneself from ; shake oneself free from ; emerge form ¶ 우리는 봉건주의의 질곡에서 탈각하지 않으면 안 된다 We must free ourselves from the fetters of feudalism.
탈각 脫殼 —하다 cast off (the

E

shell) ; shed ; exuviate
**탈것 a vehicle ; a conveyance
☞ 《p. 2180》
탈격 脫格 『문법』 the ablative case
탈고 脫稿 completion of a manuscript —하다 finish writing ; complete the manuscript ¶ 그가 집필 중인 소설은 곧 탈고된다 The novel he is writing is near completion. // 그 저작은 벌써 탈고됐다 The work is already complete in manuscript.
탈곡 脫穀 threshing grain —하다 thresh the grain ; do the threshing
—기 a threshing〔thrashing〕 machine ; a thresher ; a thrasher —장 a threshing〔thrashing〕 floor
*탈구 脫臼 dislocation of a joint ; luxation —하다 get dislocated ; be put out of joint ¶ 왼팔이 탈구했다 He has had his left arm dislocated. /His left arm is out of joint.
— 교정 extension — 부전(不全) incomplete dislocation
탈놀음 a masque ; a masquerade —하다 put on a masque play
탈당 脫黨 withdrawal〔defection〕 from a political party ; breaking with a party ; bolting ; renegading ; secession —하다 withdraw〔resign, defect, bolt〕 from a party ; desert〔leave, abandon〕 a party ; break with a party ¶ 그는 민주당을 탈당했다 He resigned his membership of the Democratic party. // 그 당에서 탈당자가 속출했다 One member after another left the party.
— 성명(서) a (written) statement of one's secession from a party — 신고서 a written report of one's secession from the party —자 a party defector 〔deserter〕 ; a seceder ; a renegade ; a rat 《속》 ; a bolter 《미》
탈락 脫落 omission ; leaving out ; exclusion ; missing ; falling off —하다 be omitted ; be left out ; be excluded ; be missing ; fall off ¶ 공천에서 탈락되다 be left out of the public nomination
—자 a dropout 《속》 ¶ 고교 탈락자 a high school dropout
탈락거리다 keep slapping〔slipping, jogging, jerking, jolting, clattering〕 ¶ 마차가 탈락거리다 a wagon is jolting // 탈락거리며 걷다 clatter along
탈루 脫漏 omission ; being left out ; missing —하다 get omitted ; be left out ; be missing
탈리 脫離 drop off ⇨ 이탈
탈모 脫毛 falling out〔loss〕 of hair ; depilation ; fallen hair —하다 lose hair ; 《one's》 hair fall out ; 《a bird》 molt ¶ 이 세척제는 탈모를 방지한다 This lotion stops the hair from falling out.
—기 a depilator ; a grainer — 로션 depilatory lotion —제 a depilatory ; a hair remover —증 『의학』 alopecia ; depilation (agent) ; depilatory disease ; baldness ¶ 원형 탈모증 alopecia areata
탈모 脫帽 doffing one's hat〔cap〕 —하다 take off〔remove, doff〕 one's hat ; uncover ; expose one's head ; raise〔tip〕 one's hat
탈무드 『역사』 Talmud
탈문 脫文 a missing passage ; a lacuna
탈바가지 a mask made of calabash 〔gourd〕
탈바꿈 transformation ; metamorphosis —하다 change (the shape of) ; assume another〔a different〕 shape ; metamorphose ; transform
탈바닥 splashing ; slopping ; spattering ¶ 탈바닥거리다 splash ; bespatter
탈박 ⇨ 탈방
탈발 脫髮 loss of hair ⇨ 탈모
탈방 plop ; splashing ; slopping ¶ 탈방거리다 plop
탈법 행위 脫法行爲 an evasion of the law ; a slip from the grip of the law
탈분 脫糞 evacuation ; defecation —하다 empty〔open, evacuate〕 one's bowels ; go to stool ; void excreta
탈산 脫酸 『화학』 deoxidation —하다 deoxidize
탈상 脫喪 expiration of the period of mourning —하다 come out of〔finish〕 mourning ; leave off〔get over〕 mourning
탈색 脫色 decoloration ; decolorization ; decolorizing ; bleaching —하다 decolor ; decolorize ; bleach
—제 a decolorant ; a decolorizer ; a decolorizing agent ; a bleaching agent ; a bleach ; a discharge
탈선 脫線 ① 〔기차 따위가〕 derailment —하다 get〔be〕 derailed ; derail ; run off the line〔rails〕 ; leave the rails ; leave the metals 《영》 ; jump〔leave〕 the track 《미》 ; be ditched ¶ 폭설로 호남선 열차가 탈선했다 On account of the heavy snowfall, a train on the *Ho-Nam* line was derailed.
② 〔언행의〕 deviation ; aberration ; departure ; divergence ; digression ; side tracking —하다 〔행동이〕 deviate〔go away〕 from the right path ; get on the loose ; go astray〔wild〕 ; be eccentric ; 〔말·논의 따위가〕 digress〔wander〕 《from the subject》 ; get away from the main subject ; make a digression ; be off the (main) track ; get sidetracked ; be off the subject ¶ 탈선적인 연설 an irrelevant speech ; a speech full of deviation〔rambling remarks〕 // 논의가 탈선하다 argue beside the point ; the argument goes sidetracked ; stray too far from one's subject // (사상·방침 따위가) 갑작스레 탈선하다 fly off at a tan-

E

탈 것

1 종류

① 육상

▶차 car (★ 승용차만을 지칭한다.) / 버스 bus (★ 《미》에서는 시내버스·장거리버스에 모두 쓰지만 《영》에서는 장거리 버스를 coach라고 한다.) / 이층버스 double-decker (bus) / 미니버스 minibus / 트럭 truck; lorry 《영》 / 택시 taxi; cab / 밴 van / 소형트럭 pickup (truck) / (중형의) 경주용 차 sprint car / 리무진 limousine / 지프 jeep

▶전차 train / 노면전차 streetcar 《미》; tram 《영》 / 지하철 subway 《미》; underground; tube 《영》 / 모노레일 monorail

▶오토바이 motorcycle / 자전거 bicycle (★ bike라고도 한다.) / 스쿠터 scooter

▶마차 cart (★ 2륜마차는 cart, 4륜마차는 waggon 《영》, wagon 《미》) / 화물용 마차 dray / (차로 끄는) 이동주택 trailer ; mobile home 《미》; caravan 《영》

② 수상

▶배 boat (★ 크기에 관계없이 모든 배에 대한 총칭. 노젓는 배는 rowboat, 대형 선박은 ship.) / 기선 steamship / 나룻배, 연락선 ferryboat / 유람선 pleasure boat; sightseeing boat / 모터보트 motorboat / 수중익선 hydrofoil / 요트 yacht (★ 서양의 요트는 유람 또는 경주용으로 엔진이 달린 대형 쾌속선. 범선은 sailing yacht. 특히 외항 요트는 cruising yacht, cruiser라고 함. 2인승의 작은 요트는 dinghy.) / 여객선 passenger ship / 상선 merchant ship / 수송선 transport ship / 화물선 cargo ship / 어선 fishing boat / 순시선 patrol ship / 쇄빙선(碎氷船) icebreaker / 군함 warship / 전함 battleship / 구축함 destroyal / 순양함 cruiser / 잠수함 submarine / 원양 정기항로 ocean liner

③ 공중

▶비행기 airplane; plane; aeroplane 《영》 / 제트기 jet / 대형 여객기 airliner (★ 보통 정기항공편) / 점보제트기 jumbo jet / 수상비행기 hydroplane / 헬리콥터 helicopter; chopper 《미》 / 비행선 airship / 글라이더 glider

2 표현

버스·전차 등 공공 교통수단을 이용할 경우 동사는 대개 take를 사용한다. ¶ take the bus [train, subway]

교통수단을 표현할 경우에는 go [come] by 「…로 가다 [오다]」를 쓴다. 이 경우 교통수단은 무관사임에 유의. 또한 「차를 운전하며 가다」 drive, 「비행기로 가다」 fly 등 하나의 단어로 표현할 수도 있다.

¶ 버스 타고 갑시다. Let's take the bus. (★ Let's go by bus. 라고 할 수도 있다.) // 나는 차로 출근합니다. I go to work by car. / I drive to work.

▶버스와 전차는 get on [off].... / 승용차는 get in, get into [out of].... / 배, 비행기, 열차 등은 get on board[aboard]로 표현한다. 특히 비행기의 경우 「내리다」는 deplane, 「타다」는 emplane도 쓰인다. 「타(고 가)다」는 ride.

¶ 나는 버스를 탔다[내렸다] I got on [off] the bus. // 그는 배를 탔다[내렸다]. He went aboard [got off] the ship. (★ got on, went aboard 대신에 boarded를 쓸 수도 있다.) // 나는 버스를 타고 있었다. I was riding on a bus. (★ 《영》에서는 on 대신에 in을 씀.)

3 택시

▶개인택시 owner-driven cab[taxi]; individually-owned cab [taxi] / 회사 택시 fleet cab [taxi]

▶택시 강도 taxi holdup / 무선 호출택시 radio [radio-dispatched] cab[taxi] / 운전석 칸막이 mugger shield (★ 운전석과 객석을 투명한 플라스틱판으로 막아 강도를 예방하는 역할을 함.) / 택시 정류장 taxi terminal / 택시미터기 taxi meter, faremeter / 택시미터기를 꺾다 flag down the meter / 택시 기본요금 starting fare; flag-down ¶ 최초 기본 요금은 1000원이고 매 500미터마다 100원씩 가산된다. The fare is 1000 won for the first and 100 won for each additional 500 meters. / 10% 심야 할증 10% late night[hour] premium (over the daytime fare)

▶승차거부 (driver's) refusal to take a fare[customer] ¶ 택시 기사들은 종종 장거리 손님에게 승차 거부를 한다. Taxi drivers often refuse to take long-haul customers. / 손님을 골라태우는 운전수 choosy cabbie[cabby] ¶ 비오는 날에는 택시 운전기사들이 손님을 골라태운다. Taxi drivers become very choosy on rainy days. / 택시를 잡다 grab[pick up] a taxi / 신호해서 택시를 세우다 flag (down) a taxi

▶음주 측정 검사 balloon test / 음주 운전 drunken driving; driving while intoxicated (★ D.W.I로 약칭함.) / 음주

E

운전자 drunken driver
▶충돌 collision; crash; ramming／정면 충돌 frontal crash; head-on collision／추돌(追突) rear-end collision／다중추돌 multiple smashup[pileup] (★5중 추돌 5-car smashup)／전복사고(顚覆事故) rollover accident／사람을 치다 run down (a person); run over; hit／뺑소니 사고 hit-and-run accident／급발진 jack rabbit start／펑크 flat tire／자동 안전벨트 passive belt; automatic seat-belt

gent∥저 선생은 수업중 잘 탈선한다 The teacher is apt to get sidetracked in class. ∥그의 연설은 때때로 탈선한다 His speech is apt to ramble.
— 학생 an erratic student
탈선 脫船 running away from a ship; desertion from a ship **—하다** desert from a ship; run away from a ship
—자 a (ship-) deserter; a run-away sailor〔seaman〕
탈세 脫稅 evasion of taxes; tax evasion〔avoidance〕; tax dodging **—하다** evade〔dodge〕 a tax; defraud the revenue (수입을 속여서) ¶ 저 회사는 탈세의 혐의가 있다 That firm has fallen under suspicion of tax dodging. ∥저 상점은 지금까지 탈세해 왔다고 하더라 I hear that shop was found to have been evading taxes.
—액 the amount of the tax evasion **—자** a tax dodger〔evader, cheat〕; an evader of taxes **—품** smuggled goods; undeclared goods
탈속 脫俗 unworldliness; unconventionality; freedom (from social conventions); absence of vulgarity **—하다** be above worldly things; die to the world; rise above the world; be free from conventionality〔vulgarity〕; stand superior to worldliness
탈수 脫水 〖화학〗 dehydration **—하다** dehydrate
—기 a hydroextractor; a dehydrator; a desiccator; a drying machine; a drier〔dryer〕 **—소(素)** 〖화학〗 dehydrogenation; dehydrogenization **— 작용** dehydration **— 장치 전기 세탁기** a washer-dryer **—제** a dehydrating agent; a desiccant
탈습 脫濕 dehumidification **—하다** dehumidify
—기 a dehumidifier
탈싹 with a plop〔thud〕 ⇨ 털썩
탈싹거리다 keep plopping; thudding; keep bobbing; jolting
탈쓰다 ① [얼굴에] wear a mask; mask one's face; play the hypocrite
② [닮다] be the very image 《of》; be an exact likeness〔replica〕 《of》 ¶ 생김새가 어머니를 탈썼다 She is the spit and image of her mother. /She just looks like her mom.
탈염 脫鹽 desalinization; desalination; 〖화학〗 desalting; demineralization **—하다** desalt
—수 desalted〔demineralized〕 water **—소(素)** dechlorination
탈영 脫營 desertion from the barracks〔encampment〕; being AWOL
—하다 desert; go over the hill; go AWOL; break out of barrack; give leg-bail
—병 a deserter; a runaway soldier; a soldier who is AWOL
탈옥 脫獄 prison-breaking; a jail break; escaping from prison
—하다 break out of jail〔prison〕; escape from prison ¶ 탈옥을 기도하다 plan an escape from jail; try to break prison
—수 a prison-〔jail-〕breaker; an escaped prisoner〔convict〕
탈의 脫衣 disrobing; undressing; getting out of one's clothes **—하다** disrobe; get undressed; undress oneself; take off one's clothes
—실 a dressing〔changing〕 room; a locker room (체육장의); a bathhouse; a bathing booth (해수욕장의)
탈자 脫字 an omitted word〔letter〕; a missing word〔letter〕; an omission **—하다** omit〔leave out〕 a word ¶ 탈자가 많다 Many words are left out.
탈잡다 find fault with; blame; charge; pick at; accuse; make a pretext of ¶ 너는 왜 나를 탈잡으려고 하지 How come you nag at me all the time?
탈장 脫腸 〖의학〗 a rupture; a hernia
—대 a hernia support belt; a truss **—문(門)** a hernial orifice **— 수술** herniotomy **— 정복술(整腹術)** taxis **—증** a hernia
탈저 脫疽 gangrene; sphacelus
탈적 脫籍 cancellation of one's name in the register ⇨ 제적
탈주 脫走 escape; flight; desertion; abscondence; decampment; leg-bail
—하다 escape; flee; desert; abscond; decamp; run away; break loose; bolt ¶ 탈주를 기도하다 plan〔attempt〕 an escape
— 계획 an escape plan **—병** a deserter; a fugitive〔runaway〕 soldier **—자** an absconder; a runaway; a refugee; an escapee; a deserter; a fugitive; a defector
탈지 脫脂 removal of fat〔grease〕; fat-removed; non-fat **—하다** remove the fat〔grease〕
— 대두〔콩〕 defatted soybeans **—면**

E

absorbent cotton ; sanitary cotton ; cotton wool 《영》 ― 우유 skim milk ; non-fat milk
탈진 脫盡 exhaustion ―하다 get exhausted〔worn out, utterly fatigued〕; get pooped 《미·속》
탈질 脫窒 〖화학〗 denitrification ―하다 denitrify
†탈출 脫出 ① [도망함] escape ; extrication ; bailing out (of a plane) ② [빠짐] 〖의학〗 prolapse (직장 따위의) ; proptosis (눈 따위) ―하다 escape 《from》; get away from ; get out of ; extricate oneself from ; free〔liberate〕 oneself ; flee ; bail out ; fall down ; prolapse ¶ 적국을 탈출하다 escape from the enemy land // 그는 서울을 탈출했으나 체포되었다 He absconded from *Seoul*, but was arrested.
탈춤 a masque〔masked〕 dance
*탈취 脫臭 deodorizaton ―하다 deodorize
―제 a deodorant ; a deodorizer ; a deodorizing agent
탈취 奪取 capture ; seizure ; wresting ―하다 capture ; carry off ; seize ; wrest 《a thing》 《from》 ¶ 남의 소유물을 탈취하다 take another's property // 왕위를 탈취하다 usurp the throne // 요새를 탈취하다 carry a fortress
탈타리 a penniless ⇨ 빈털터리
탈탈 plodding ; with dull clink ; with clatter ¶ 탈탈 걷다 plod along // 달구지가 탈탈 굴러가다 a cart clatters along
탈토 脫兎 [몹시 빨리] ¶ 탈토같이 with the speed of a hare ; like a scared rabbit
탈퇴 脫退 secession ; withdrawal ―하다 secede〔withdraw, break away〕 《from》; leave ; disconnect oneself ¶ 그는 그 회에서 탈퇴하기로 작정했다 He has decided to secede〔withdraw〕 from the association.
―자 a seceder ; a bolter 《미》; a defector ; the kicker 《속》
탈피 脫皮 ① 〖동물〗 ecdysis 《*pl.* -ses》; shedding〔casting, peeling〕 off ; slough (off)
② [벗어남] emergence ―하다 shed 〔cast, peel〕 off the skin ; slough ; exuviate ; [벗어나다] emerge from ¶ 구태를 탈피하다 break from the convention ; outgrow one's former self // 뱀은 가을이 되면 탈피한다 A snake casts its skin in autumn.
탈하다 plead ; make a pretext of ; make an excuse of ; make a plea of ¶ 집안일을 탈하고 under the pretext of family affairs // 할 일이 있다고 탈하다 plead that one has business to attend to // 아프다고 탈하고 학교에 오지 않았다 He was absent from school with the excuse that he was ill.
탈함 脫艦 desertion from a warship ―하다 desert a warship
―자 a naval deserter ; a runaway marine
탈항 脫肛 〖의학〗 proctocele ; prolapse of the anus ―하다 suffer from prolapse of the anus
탈혈 脫血 ⇨ 실혈(失血)
*탈환 奪還 recapture ; retaking ; recovery ; forcible recovery ―하다 take back by force ; win back ; retake ; recapture ; recover ; regain ; reconquer
탈회 脫會 secession〔withdrawal〕 from a society ―하다 secede〔withdraw, resign〕 from a society ; break away from an association ; leave a society ; drop out (of an organization) ; drop 〔give up〕 one's membership ; cease to be a member
― 신고서〔계〕 a report of secession ―자 a seceder
탐 貪 avarice ; greed ; covetousness ―하다 covet ; be covetous 《of》; be greedy 《for》; devour ¶ 탐이 나는 물건 a want ; a thing desired ; an object of desire // 명리를 탐하다 covet fame and gain // 폭리를 탐하다 make an excessive〔undue〕 profit // 음식을 탐하다 devour〔eat〕 greedily // 누구든지 돈에는 탐을 내는 법이다 Love of money is common to all.
탐검 探檢 investigation ; probe ; examination ; inquiry ―하다 investigate ; probe ; examine ; make inquiry
― 기구 weather〔meteorological〕 balloons ― 비행 an exploratory flight 《over the Antarctic Continent》 ―선 a research ship ― 여행 an exploration ; an expedition ―자〔가〕 an explorer ; an expeditionary ; an expeditionist
탐관오리 貪官汚吏 a covetous〔corrupt〕 official
탐광 探鑛 prospecting ―하다 prospect 《a region for gold》
―자 a prospector
탐구 探求 a quest ; pursuit ; search ―하다 search for ; pursue 《truth》 ¶ 진리의 탐구 pursuit of truth
‡탐구 探究 search ; research ; investigation ; inquiry ; quest ; study ―하다 investigate ; make researches in〔on〕; inquire into ; search for ; explore ; delve into ¶ 과학적 탐구 scientific investigation // 학리의 탐구 a study of science // 진리를 탐구하다 investigate truth ; search for truth ; inquire into the truth
―물 a quest ―심 the spirit of inquiry ―자 an investigator ; an inquirer ; a searcher ¶ 그는 진지한 진리의 탐구자이다 He is an earnest seeker after truth.

E

탐나다 貪― be desirable ; be appetizing ; want ; desire ; wish〔care, long〕 for ; be covetous〔envious〕 of ; lust 《for, after》 ¶ 탐나는 여자 a desirable woman ; a woman after one's heart // 탐나는 음식 appetizing〔mouth-watering〕 food // 권력이 탐나다 I am covetous of power. /I lust for power. // 나는 저 책이 탐난다 I want〔wish to have〕 that book. // 그런 것은 조금도 탐나지 않는다 I don't care a bit for it.

*탐내다 貪― want ; desire ; covet ; lust 《for, after》 ; have a desire〔lust, yen〕 for ; be greedy for ; be covetous〔envious〕 of ; be mad after ; be dying for ¶ 돈을 탐내다 be greedy for money ; be moneymad // 음식을 탐내다 be ravenous (for food) // 남의 물건을 탐내다 covet what belongs to others // 그는 명예를 탐내지 않는다 He has no desire for fame.

**탐닉 耽溺 [빠짐] indulgence ; addiction ; [방탕] dissipation ; prodigality ; debauchery ―하다 be indulged ; abandon oneself to ; be addicted to ; be immersed in ; dissipate ; take to loose living ; be dissipated ¶ 쾌락에 탐닉하다 indulge in〔give oneself up to〕 pleasure // 주색에 탐닉하다 abandon oneself to liquor and sex ; be addicted to sensual pleasures ; indulge in woman and wine
― 생활 a fast〔riotous〕 life ; a life given to riotous pleasures ; a life of debauchery〔follies〕 ―자 an addict

탐독 耽讀 indulgence in reading ; avid reading ―하다 read with avidity〔avidly〕 ; be absorbed〔engrossed〕 in reading ; steep oneself 《in》 ; pore over 《a book》 ; devour ¶ 소설을 탐독하다 pore over a novel ; devour a novel ; be fond of〔have a passion for〕 novels ; be a great novel reader // 그는 탐정 소설을 탐독한다 He has a passion for detective stories.
―자 an inveterate reader

탐리 貪吏 a greedy〔grasping〕 official ; a covetous〔corrupt〕 official

탐리 貪利 greed ; avarice ; covetousness ; cupidity ; love of gain ―하다 be greedy〔avaricious, covetous, grasping〕

탐매 探梅 an excursion〔a visit〕 to places noted for apricot blossoms ; apricot-blossom viewing

탐문 探問 indirect inquiry ; roundabout investigation ; detection ―하다 inquire about indirectly ; find out indirectly ; pick up information ; detect ; search out ; trace out ; smell out ¶ 탐문한 바에 의하면 according to what we have learned

탐문 探聞 obtaining information (by inquiry) ―하다 obtain information (by inquiry) ; learn ; hear ; [형사 등이] snoop for information ; reach one's ears〔knowledge〕 《일이 주어》

탐미 耽美 love of beauty ¶ 탐미적인 aesthetic
―주의 (a)estheticism ―주의자 an (a)esthete ―파 the (a)esthetic school ; [단체] the (a)esthetes

탐방 with a splash〔plop〕 ⇨ 텀벙 ¶ 탐방거리다 keep plopping〔splashing〕 ; splash about

탐방 探訪 (private) inquiry ―하다 inquire 《into》 ; make inquiry of ; have an interview 《with》 ¶ 사회 탐방 private inquiry into social life // 탐방 기사를 쓰다 report 《for a newspaper》 ; write by the leg 《미》
―기 a report of inquiries ― 기사 a report ; a reportorial piece ― 기자 a (newspaper) reporter ; an interviewer ; a legman ; an assignment man

탐사 探査 exploration ; inquiry ; investigation ―하다 explore ; make inquiry 《about》 ; investigate ; inquire〔look〕 into ; pry into ; spy out

탐상 探賞 sightseeing ; exploration of beauties ; excursion ―하다 sightsee ; see〔do〕 the sights ; explore the sight

탐상기 探傷機 〖토목〗 a defectoscope ; 〖조선〗 a flaw detector

†탐색 探索 search ; inquiry ; investigation ; quest ; hunt ―하다 search ; look for ; research 《after, for》 ; inquire〔investigate〕 into ; hunt〔dig〕 up〔out〕 ¶ 엄중한 탐색을 명하다 order a rigid search 《of》 // 행방을 탐색하다 inquire into 《a person's》 whereabout
―자 an investigator ―전 an engagement in reconnaissance ― 행동 〖군사〗 a probing action 달―용 로켓 a lunar probe

탐스럽다 (be) desirable ; appetizing ; attractive ; very nice ; charming ; beautiful ; lovely ¶ 탐스러운 사과 an appetizing apple // 탐스러운 여인 a charming woman // 이게 제일 탐스럽다 This suits my taste best.

탐승 探勝 sightseeing ; a sightseeing excursion〔trip〕 ―하다 see〔do〕 the sights ; explore the scenery ; visit scenic spots ; go sightseeing
―객 sightseers ; excursionists ; trippers

탐식 貪食 gluttony ; voracity ; ravenousness ; edacity ―하다 eat greedily ; wolf one's food ; be gluttonous ; make a pig of oneself

탐심 貪心 avarice ; greed ; cupidity ; [부당한] an undue desire

*탐욕 貪慾 greed ; avarice ; rapacity ; covetousness ; cupidity ¶ 그는 탐욕의 덩어리다 He is avarice itself. /He is the incarnation of avarice.

탐장 貪贓 graft ; bribes **—하다** indulge in graft ; get by graft
—질 graft ; corrupt practice ; jobbery

탐재 貪財 love of money ; avarice ; greed ; coveting for property **—하다** lust after (property) ; be avaricious 〔greedy, money-mad〕 ; covet for property

⁑탐정 探偵 [일] detective service 〔work〕 ; secret investigation ; detection ; [군사상의] espionage ; [사람] a detective ; a criminal〔detective〕 agent ; a spy ; a sleuth 《미》 **—하다** investigate〔inquire into〕 《a matter》 secretly ; do detective work ; detect ; spy 《on a person, into a secret》 ; trace〔track〕 《a crime, criminal》 ; search for 《a culprit》 ; gumshoe 《미·속》 ¶ 탐정이 뒤를 밟다 be shadowed by a detective // 그들은 나의 행동을 탐정하고 있는 것 같다 They seem to be spying on my movements.
—견(犬) a police dog **—물** detective 〔crime〕 story ; a whodunit 《who done it》 (추리 소설) 《미·속》 ; a mystery story 《미》 **— 소설** a detective story 〔novel〕 ; detective fiction (장르의 명칭으로서) **—업** the man-hunting business
군사 — [일] espionage ; [사람] a (military) spy **비밀 —** a secret agent ; an undercover man〔investigator〕 ; a secret (-service) detective ; a private detective
사립 — a private detective〔investigator〕 ; a private eye 《속》 **사설 —소** a private detective agency〔firm〕

탐조 探照 throwing〔beaming〕 a searchlight **—하다** throw〔beam, turn〕 a searchlight 《on》
—등 a searchlight **이동〔고정〕 —등** a mobile〔stationary〕 searchlight

***탐지 探知** detection **—하다** find out ; detect ; search〔smell〕 out ; trace 《a crime》 ; learn 《a fact》 ¶ 비밀을 탐지하다 smell out a secret // 우리가 탐지한 바에 의하면 we have learned 《that》 // 경찰은 그들의 음모를 탐지했다 The police got wind of their plot.
—기 a detector ; a locator ; a 《people》 sniffer **— 기지** detection station **— 장치** detection equipment ; a monitoring device ; a detection〔detecting〕 device **—소(所)** [핵실험의] a monitoring station **전파 —기** a radar ; a radar set ; a radiolocator 《영》 ; a locator 《미》 ¶ 수중 전파 탐지기 a sonar ; an asdic

탐측 探測 sounding ; probing
—기 a probe ; a prober **— 기구** a pilot balloon **— 로켓** a sounding rocket

탐침 探針 〖의학〗 a probe ; a stylet ; an explorer

***탐탁하다** (be) satisfactory ; pleasing ; reliable ; be to one's satisfaction ; be in 《a person's》 favor ; suit〔catch, take〕 《a person's》 fancy ¶ 탐탁한 물건 an article to one's taste // 탐탁한 사람 a reliable person // 탐탁한 여자 a woman after one's heart // 탐탁하지 않은 인상 an unfavorable〔unpleasant〕 impression // 탐탁하지 않은 손님 an unlooked-for guest ; an unwelcome visitor // 탐탁스럽다 be satisfied〔pleased〕 《with》 ; find satisfactory with ; find favor with // 그와 동행하는 것은 별로 탐탁스럽지 않다 I am rather disinclined to go with him.

탐탐히 耽耽— covetously ; gloatingly ; with vigilant hostility ¶ 탐탐히 기다리다 be prepared for ; look forward to

탐폰 〖의학〗 a tampon

탐하다 貪— ⇨ 탐내다

탐해구 探海鉤 a creeper

탐해등 探海燈 a searchlight (that sweeps the sea) ; a flashlight ¶ 탐해등으로 해면을 살피다 sweep the sea with a searchlight // 탐해등을 비추다 turn 〔play〕 searchlight upon 《a thing》

탐해법 探海法 creeping

⁑탐험 探險 exploration ; expedition **—하다** explore ; make an exploration 《of》 ¶ 미탐험 지방 unexplored regions // 아프리카 탐험 기행 an account of an expedition to〔explorations in〕 Africa // 탐험하러 가다 go on an expedition 《to the Antarctic》 // 그는 아프리카 탐험으로 유명하다 He is famous as an explorer of Africa. // 그는 젊었을 때 내몽고 탐험을 시도했다 When young he undertook an expedition to Inner Mongolia.
—가〔자〕 an explorer ; an expeditionary ; an expeditionist **—대** an expedition〔expeditionary〕 party ; a party of explorers ¶ 탐험대를 조직〔지휘〕하다 organize〔lead, command〕 an expedition // 탐험대를 파견하다 dispatch an expeditionary force〔party〕 **— 대장** the leader〔chief〕 of an expedition **— 비행** an exploratory flight 《over the Antarctic Continent》 **—선** a research ship ; an expedition ship **— 여행** an expedition ; an exploration **남〔북〕극 —대** an Antarctic〔Arctic〕 expedition **아프리카 —기** an account of an expedition to〔explorations in〕 Africa

탐호 貪好 fanatic love ; devotion ; indulgence **—하다** indulge in ; be fond of ; be a fanatic lover of ; be devoted to ; take much delight in

탐혹 耽惑 addiction ; infatuation ; immersion ; spooniness **—하다** get addicted to ; get infatuated with ; immerse oneself in ¶ 여자에게 탐혹하다 be infatuated with a woman

†탑 搭 a tower ; a pagoda ; a steeple 《of a church》 ¶ 탑을 세우다 build〔put up〕 a tower
기념— a monument **방첨(方尖)—** an obelisk **뾰족—** a steeple **석—** a stone

E

monument 5층— a five-storied pagoda
탑꽃 塔— 〖식물〗 wild basil ; savory
탑본 榻本 a rubbed copy ; a rubbing
—하다 take a rubbing of
탑비 塔碑 a tower and a monument (at a tomb)
탑삭나룻 a shaggy beard ; a short bristly beard
탑삭부리 a man with a short bristly beard
탑새기주다 interfere with〔in〕; obstruct ; disturb ; get in way of ; hinder ¶ 남의 일에 탑새기주다 throw a monkey wrench into someone else's project ; upset 《a person's》 applecart
탑소록하다 (be) thick ; shaggy ⇨ 텁수룩하다
탑승 搭乘 boarding ; riding —하다 ride ; get into〔on〕; board ; get aboard ; embark ⇨ 타다 ¶ 비행기에 탑승하다 ride in an airplane
—객〔자〕 a passenger ; an occupant —석 〖항공〗 a cockpit —원 〖항공기 따위의〗 a crewman ; a crew member ; a flight crew (전원)
탑재 搭載 loading ; embarkation ; entrainment —하다 load ; embark ; entrain ; take in ¶ (기차에) 군인들을 탑재하다 entrain troops // (배에) 화물을 탑재하다 load a ship with goods ; get goods on board
—량 burden ; carrying capacity ; load ; burthen — 중량 weight on board —표 a load table
탑파 塔婆 a stupa 《범》 ¶ 탑파를 세우다 set up a stupa
탑형 塔型 tower〔steeple〕 type
— 크레인 a tower crane — 터빈 a steeple type turbine
†탓 ① [잘못] fault ; failure ; blame ; responsibility ¶ 남의 탓으로 돌리다 lay 《a fault》 at another's door // 그는 제 탓이라고 한다 He takes the blame upon himself. // 그것은 당신 탓이다 You are responsible for it. /The guilt is at your door.
② [까닭] reason ; ground ¶ 나이 탓으로 because of〔owing to〕 one's age // 아무 탓 없이 without any reason ; groundlessly // 몸이 아픈 탓으로 오지 못했다 Illness kept me from coming.
잘 되면 제 탓 못되면 조상 탓 ㊀속담 A bad workman always blames his tools.
탓하다 put〔lay〕 blame upon ; lay the fault to ; attach blame to ; blame ; impugn ; charge ; accuse ¶ 세상의 무정을 탓하다 accuse the hardness of the world // 왜 나를 탓하는 거야 Why do you try to shift the blame on me?
*탕[1] [소리] bang ; boom ¶ 문을 탕 닫다 bang the door ; slam the door shut // 대포를 탕 쏘다 boom a gun
탕[2] ① [국] soup ; broth ; soup offered at ancestor memorial service (제사용)
② [한약] medicine in draught (as opposed to pills or powder)
탕 湯 [목욕탕] a hot bath ; a public bath ¶ 탕에 가다 go to the bathhouse ; go to take a bath
남— a bath for men 여— the ladies section
탕감 蕩減 writing off 《debts》; remission ; cancellation —하다 write off 《a debt》; remit ; cancel ; forgive ¶ 빚을 탕감해 주다 write off a debt ; forgive 《a person》 a debt
탕개 a clamp ; a fastener ¶ 탕개를 먹이다 clamp ; tighten up
—목 a piece of wood used for tightening up a fastening rope —붙임 fastening (to) a block of wood with a guy (line) —줄 a guy ; a fastening rope
탕거리 湯— soup makings ; materials to prepare soup with ; ingredients for soup ; soup stock〔base〕
탕건 宕巾 a horsehair skullcap formerly worn by officials under their hats
*탕관 湯罐 a kettle ; a pot (used for preparing soup or a medical decoction)
탕기 湯器 a soup bowl〔dish〕
탕메 湯— soup and rice (offered at ancestor-memorial services)
탕면 湯麵 noodle soup ; noodles in broth
탕반 湯飯 boiled rice served in soup ; rice in broth ; rice soup
탕방 —房 〖건축〗 a room floored with large slabs of stone
탕부 蕩婦 a woman of loose morals ; a woman of easy virtue ; a lewd〔wanton〕 woman ; a libertine ; a demimondaine ; a slut
탕산 蕩産 —하다 squander one's fortune ; run〔go〕 through one's fortune
탕상 湯傷 a scald ¶ 탕상을 입다 scald oneself ; be〔get〕 scalded
탕솥 湯— a soup kettle
탕수 湯水 hot water ; hot-spring water
—통 a hot-water tank
탕수육 糖水肉 sweet and sour pork
탕심 蕩心 lewd thoughts ; salacious thinking ; a dissipated〔prodigal, profligate, riotous〕 mind
탕아 蕩兒 a debauchee ; a libertine ; a man of pleasure
탕약 湯藥 a medicinal decoction ; an infusion
탕일 蕩逸 dissipation ; profligacy ; prodigality ; debauchery
탕자 蕩子 a prodigal ; a libertine ; a debauchee
탕전 帑錢 the privy purse
탕진 蕩盡 waste ; squandering ; dissipation ; dilapidation —하다 squander ; run through ; dissipate ; waste ; exhaust ; dilapidate ¶ 가산을 탕진하다 squan-

E

der〔dissipate, exhaust, run through〕 one's fortune // 돈을 탕진하다 run through all one's money

탕치 湯治 a hot-spring cure ; treating an illness with hot baths **—하다** cure by hot baths ; take a hot-spring cure ¶ 온양에 탕치하러 가다 go to *Onyang* for baths
—객 visitors at hot springs **— 요양** spa treatment ; hot spring cure **—장** a spa ; hot springs ; a watering place

탕치다 蕩— ① [재산을] run through ; squander ; dissipate ¶ 노름으로 탕치다 gamble away one's fortune // 가산을 탕치다 squander one's fortune
② [빚을] write off ; let off 《a debtor》 ¶ 빚을 탕치다 write off a debt ; let 《a person》 off his debt

탕탕 ① [소리가] bang-bang ¶ 대포 소리가 탕탕 나다 a cannon is heard booming away ② [호언을] big ; with big words ; with hot air ¶ 거짓말을 탕탕 하다 lie through one's teeth ; tell big lies〔tall tales〕 // 탕탕 큰 소리하다 talk big ; brag ; be full of hot air ; talk through one's hat

탕탕거리다 keep banging〔booming〕

탕탕평평 蕩蕩平平 impartiality ; fairness ; equity **—하다** (be) impartial ; fair ; equitable ; unbiased

탕파 湯婆 a foot warmer ; a hot-water bottle〔bag〕 ; a foot pan

태¹ [깨진 금] a crack ; a fissure ¶ 태간 그릇 cracked ware ; crackle // 찻잔이 태가다 a teacup is cracked
태가다 관용 be cracked ; have a crack

태² [새 쫓는] a cracking whip (to scare birds away from crops)

태 胎 the amnion〔caul〕 and the placenta ; the womb
태를 가르다 관용 cut the umbilical cord

태 態 ① a form ; a figure ⇨ 맵시
② behavior ; bearing ; attitude ⇨ 행실
③ grammatical voice ⇨ 문법

태가 駄價 portage ; carriage ; freight ; freightage

태가다 be cracked ; be crackled ; have a crack

태고 太古 ancient times ; remote antiquity〔ages〕 ; prehistoric days ¶ 태고의 ancient ; primitive ; of immemorial antiquity // 태고적 사람들 ancient people // 태고부터 from time immemorial
—사 ancient history **— 시대〔계〕** the Archaean Era〔Group〕 ; ancient times ; antiquity

태공 太公 a grand duke ; a prince
—국 a grand duchy ; an archduchy **—비** a grand duchess

태공망 太公望 an angler ; a Waltonian

태과하다 太過— (be) excessive ; too much

태교 胎教 prenatal care of an unborn child through attention of a pregnant woman to her own mental health ; antenatal training

태권도 跆拳道 the Korean art of (empty-handed) self-defense ; *Taekwondo*

태그 매치 a tag-team match

태극 太極 the Great Absolute (in Chinese philosophy) 《the source of the dual principle of Yŭn and Yang》
—선(扇) a fan with the Yŭn-Yang symbol ; a *Taegŭk* fan

태극기 太極旗 the national flag of Korea ; the *Taegŭk* flag

태기 胎氣 signs〔indications〕 of pregnancy ; a feeling that one is pregnant

태깔 態— ① [태와 빛깔] figure〔form〕 and color ② [거만한 태도] a haughty attitude

태깔스럽다 態— (be) haughty ; arrogant

태껸 [각희] kicking and tripping (as a sport)

태나다 ① [모습] look nice ② ⇨ 태어나다

태낭 胎囊 〖동물〗 the embryonic sac ; the chorion

태내 胎內 the interior of the womb ; in the womb ¶ 태내의 아이 a child in the mother's womb
— 전염 〖의학〗 prenatal〔antenatal〕 infection

태내다 態— strike an attitude ; give oneself airs ; put on〔assume〕 airs

태다수 太多數 a great number ; a redundant number ; a multitude ; a multiplicity

†**태도 態度** an attitude ; manner ; behavior ; an air ; bearing ; a posture ; carriage ; deportment ; demeanor ¶ 신사적 태도 a gentlemanly attitude // 위엄 있는 태도 a dignified attitude // 의기 양양한 태도 a triumphant air // 애매한 태도를 취하다 sit on the fence // 태도를 변경하다 sing another song ; whistle a different tune // 태도가 얌전하다 be well-mannered ; be well-behaved ; have good manners // 태도를 고치다 improve one's behavior ; mend one's way // 그는 태도가 거만하다 He has a haughty bearings. // 윗 사람에게는 항상 겸손한 태도를 취해야 한다 You should always bear yourself modestly toward(s) your superiors. // 그의 모욕적인 태도를 더 이상 못 참겠다 I can no longer stomach his insulting manners.

태독 胎毒 〖의학〗 congenital boils 〔syphilis〕

태동 胎動 [태아의] quickening (of the womb) ; the movements of the fetus ; [징후] signs of forthcoming activity ; indication ; fomentation **—하다** quick-

E

en ; show sign of life ; indicate ¶ 조합의 민주화 태동이 보인다 There is a quickening of democratization of the union.
—기 the quickening period
태두 泰斗 an〔a great〕 authority ; a leading light ; an expert (전문가) ; a luminary ; a star ; a savant ¶ 경제학의 태두 a great authority on economics // 한국 의학계의 태두 a luminary in the medical profession of Korea
태람 台覽 inspection by a high official 〔dignitary〕
태령 太嶺, 泰嶺 a steep〔precipitous〕 and high pass ; a sharp divide
태마노 笞瑪瑙 a moss agate ; a Mocha stone
태막 殆膜 a fetal〔foetal〕 membrane ; an embryonic membrane
*태만 怠慢 negligence ; neglect ; [의무·직무의] default ; delinquency ; [부주의] inattention ; carelessness ; remissness ——하다 (be) negligent ; delinquent ; inattentive ; careless ; inadvertent ; remiss ¶ 당국의 태만을 공격하다 attack the authorities concerned for neglect of duty // 직무에 태만하다 be negligent 〔remiss〕 in one's duties ; neglect one's duties // 이 재해는 지사의 태만에서 일어났다 This evil has happened through the governor's default. // 근무를 태만히 하면 조만간에 해고당할 것이다 If you lie down on your job, you will be fired sooner or later.
직무 — neglect〔dereliction〕 of duty ; culpable neglect〔negligence〕 ; delinquency 직무 —자 a defaulter ; a delinquent
태먹다 ⇨ 태가다
태모 胎母 a pregnant woman
태몽 胎夢 a dream of conception
태무 殆無 ——하다 (be) very scarce ; virtually nonexistent ; very few ¶ 성공의 가능성이 태무하다 There is not the remotest chance of success. // 교통 사고가 없는 날이 태무하다 Scarcely a day passes without a traffic accident.
태반 太半 most ; the greater〔best, most〕 part 《of》 ; the great〔large〕 portion ; the majority 《of》 ¶ 태반은 mostly ; for the most part ; nearly all // 학생의 태반 most students ; most of the students // 투표자의 태반 the majority of the voters // 인생의 태반을 외국에서 보내다 spend the greater part of one's life abroad // 일은 태반 끝났다 We have broken the back of the work.
태반 胎盤 〖해부〗 the placenta ; the afterbirth
—염 placentitis 《*pl.* -titides》 —음 a placental souffle — 형성 placentation 미만성〔균등, 산재〕 — a placenta diffusa 반상 — a discoplacenta ; a discoid(al) placenta 유— 포유 동물 placental animals〔mammals〕 ; placentalia (유태 반류)
태백성 太白星 Venus ; the evening star
태벌 笞罰 flogging ⇨ 태형
태변 胎便 [배내똥] a meconium
태부리다 態— ⇨ 태내다
태부족 太不足 a great shortage〔want, dearth, lack〕 ——하다 be in great shortage ; be greatly wanted ; be much lacking
태산 泰山 a high mountain ; a tremendous thing ¶ 태산같이 믿다 place great reliance ; put one's utmost confidence // 태산같이 동하지 않다 be firm 〔be as steady〕 as a rock // 할 일이 태산같다 have ever so many things to do
태산중악 만장봉이 모진 광풍에 쓰러지거든 (속담) If the sky falls we shall catch larks. /If my aunt had been a man, she'd have been my uncle.
태산준령 泰山峻嶺 high and steep mountains
태상왕 太上王 the abdicated king
태상황 太上皇 an abdicated Emperor ; an ex-Emperor
†태생 胎生 ① 〖생물〗 viviparity ; viviparousness
② [출신] birth ; origin ; one's birth place ¶ 미국 태생의 한국인 an America-born Korean // 서울 태생 a person born in *Seoul* // 어디 태생이오 Where were you born ? /What is your birthplace ? // 그는 제주 태생이다 He comes 〔hails〕 from *Cheju*.
— 동물 a vivipara ; viviparous animals — 종자 a viviparous seed —학 embryology ; ontogenesis —학자 an embryologist
태서 泰西 the Occident ; the West ; the Western countries ¶ 태서의 Western ; Occidental
— 제국 the Western countries — 문명 Western civilization
태선 苔癬 〖의학〗 lichen
태세 態勢 an attitude ; setup ; preparations ; arrangements ¶ 태세를 갖추다 complete arrangements 《for, to do》 ; get fully prepared 《for, against, to do》 // 전투 태세를 취하다 held battle position
태수 太守 a governor general ; a viceroy
태심하다 太甚— (be) exceedingly severe ; extreme
*태아 胎兒 an embryo ; a fetus ; an unborn child ¶ 태아의 embryonic ; fetal
— 교육 antenatal training —기 the fetal〔prenatal〕 life — 절개술 embryotomy
*태양 太陽 the sun ¶ 태양의 solar ; the sun's ; of the sun ; heliacal // 태양은 열을 방사한다 The sun radiates heat. // 태

E

양이 뜬다〔진다〕 The sun rises〔sets〕. /The sun is coming up〔declines〕.
—경 a solar eyepiece —계 solar system ; a star system — 관측 solar observation ¶ 태양 관측기 a helioscope // 태양 관측 위성 an orbiting solar observatory 《OSO》 — 광선 the sun's ray ; the sunlight ; the rays of the sun ; sunbeams —년 the solar year —등 an artificial sunlight ; a sun〔sunray, heat〕 lamp ; a mercury(-vapor) lamp ; a sun —력 the solar calendar ; Julian calendar —로 solar furnace — 복사 solar radiation — 순환기 〖천문〗 the solar cycle — 숭배 the sun worship 〔cult〕 ; heliolatry —시 solar time —신 the sun god〔goddess〕 ; [희랍 신화] Helios —열 solar heat ; the heat of the sun rays — 열량계 a heliothermometer —월(月) a solar month —의(儀) 〖천문〗 a heliometer —일 a solar day — 전파 a solar noise ; solar radio-frequency radiation — 중심설 the Copernican system〔theory〕 ; heliocentricism — 흑점 a sunspot ; a solar spot

*태어나다 be born ; see the light (of day) ; come into the world ; come into being〔existence〕 ¶ 태어난 집 the house where one was born ; the home of one's birth // 부자로 태어나다 be born rich ; be born with a silver spoon in one's mouth // 가난한 집에 태어나다 be born of a poor family // 불구자로 태어나다 be born deformed // 그녀는 1969년 10월 24일에 태어났다 She was born on October 24, 1969〔the twenty-fourth of October, 1969〕. // 그들에게 사내 아이가 태어났다 A boy baby was born to them.

태업 怠業 a slowdown strike 《미》 ; sabotage ; deliberate idleness ; work stoppage ; a go-slow (strike) ; a ca'canny strike ; loafing on the job —하다 go on a slowdown strike ; go on sabotage ; start a work slowdown ; sabotage ; loaf on the job ¶ 태업 전술을 취하다 appeal to〔take up〕 slowdown tactics // 태업 기분으로 일하고 있다 be half on the loaf

태없다 (be) modest ; unassuming ; unaffected ¶ 그는 침착하고도 태없다 His manner is quiet and unassuming. // 그는 정말 태없는 사람이다 He never puts on〔assumes〕 airs.

*태연 泰然 coolness ; calmness ; composure —하다 (be) cool ; calm ; composed ; self-possessed ; unshaken ; collected ¶ 태연히 coolly ; calmly ; with composure ; in a self-possessed manner // 태연한 태도 a calm attitude // 아무 일 없는 듯이 태연히 앉아 있다 be sitting calmly as if nothing had happened // 그는 그 소식을 듣고도 태연하였다 He did not turn a hair at the news. /He kept his countenance at the sad news.

태연 자약 泰然自若 imperturbability ; composure ; self-possession ; presence of mind —하다 (be) perfectly calm ; cool and collected ; calm and self-possessed ; composed ; retain one's equanimity

태열 胎熱 〖의학〗 congenital fever

*태엽 a (mechanical) spring ; a mainspring ¶ 태엽을 감다 wind a spring // 태엽이 풀리다 a spring unwinds ; a spring runs down
— 장치 clockwork 시계 — a watch spring 실— a hair spring

†태우다[1] ① [연소] burn ; commit to the flames ; put in the fire ; incinerate ; lay in ashes ¶ 향을 태우다 burn incense // 집을 태우다 have one's house burnt down // 담배를 태우다 smoke a cigarette
② [그슬리다] scorch ; burn ; singe ; char ¶ 옷을 태우다 scorch one's clothes // 눈썹을 태우다 singe one's eyebrows // 밥을 태우다 burn the rice
③ [가슴·속을] burn (one's soul) ; agonize ; worry ¶ 속을 태우다 be worried〔anxious, agonized, anguished〕 ; burn with anguish // 사람의 속을 태우다 make 《a person》 worry ; make 《a person》 awfully anxious // 사랑으로 속을 태우다 burn with love

†태우다[2] [탈것에] carry ; accommodate ; let ride ; take 《a person on board》 ; give a ride ; pick up 《a person on foot》 ¶ (차가) 손님을 태우다 take on 〔pick up, load〕 passengers // 버스가 도중에서 손님을 태우다 a bus picks up passengers on the way // 말을 태우다 set 《a person》 on a horse // 자동차에 나를 좀 태워주시오 Give me a ride〔lift〕 in your car, please. // 이 기선은 여객 1,000명을 태울 수 있다 This steamer can accommodate a thousand passengers. // 차를 태워 주셔서 대단히 감사합니다 Thank you very much for the ride. // 집까지 차로 태워다 주실 수 있습니까 Can you give me a ride home?

태우다[3] ① [골을] have (one's hair) parted in the middle
② [쪼개게 하다] have something divided ¶ 콩을 태우다 have 《a person》 split peas on the grindstone
③ [갈라 주다] divide it 《among》 ; portion out ; apportion ¶ 재산을 아들들에게 태우다 divide one's property among one's sons

태우다[4] [연줄·그네를] pull〔let〕 in and out ¶ 연줄을 태우다 let the string of a kite in and out // 그네를 태우다 let the swing go back and forth

태위 胎位 〖의학〗 presentation (of the fetus)

태음 太陰 the moon

E

— 관측〔거리〕 lunar observation〔distance〕 —력 the lunar calendar — 순환기 the lunar cycle — 숭배 moon worship —시 lunar time — 시차 the parallax of the moon —일〔월, 년〕 a lunar day〔month, year〕 —조(潮) a lunar tide —학자 a selenologist ; a lunarian

태의 胎衣 ⇨ 태반(胎盤)

태자 太子 the Crown Prince ; the Prince Imperial ; the Heir Apparent
—궁 the Crown Prince's palace —기(旗) the Crown Prince's flag —비 the Crown Prince's wife ; the Princess

태작 駄作 a poor piece of writing ; an inferior work ; poor stuff ; trash ; rubbish ¶ 이 시는 태작이다 This poem is rubbish.∥저 사람이 쓰는 글은 모두가 태작이다 All that comes out of his pen is poor stuff.

태장 笞杖 [대막대] a bamboo paddle (used for punishment) ; [볼기침] beating (on the buttocks) ; flogging ; flagellation

태점 胎占 predicting the sex of an unborn child by divination

태조 太祖 the first Emperor〔King〕《of the dynasty》

태주 the spirit〔ghost〕 of a little girl who died of smallpox
—할미 a woman possessed by a *taeju*

태중 胎中 (in) pregnancy ; the period of maternity ¶ 그 여자는 태중이다 She is pregnant〔with child〕.

태질 [벼타작] threshing《grain》; flailing ; [메어침] thrashing ; beating hard ; throwing down —하다 thresh ; beat out《grain》; thrash ; beat hard ¶ 벼를 태질하다 beat the rice grains out∥아무를 태질하듯 하다 keep thrashing a person ; beat〔flail〕 a person hard

태질치다 ① [벼타작] thresh《grain》 ② [메어침] throw〔fling〕 down ¶ 사람을 태질치다 throw《a person》 down∥책을 마루 위에 태질치다 fling a book down on the floor∥태질치듯하다 hurry ; hurry《a person》

태초 太初 the beginning of the world

태치다 ⇨ 태질치다

‡**태클** [구기] a tackle —하다 tackle

태타 怠惰 ⇨ 나태

***태평 泰平, 太平** peace ; perfect〔profound〕 peace ; tranquility ; quiet —하다 (be) peaceful ; quiet ; tranquil ; easy(-going) ; carefree ¶ 태평한 peaceful ; tranquil ; quiet∥태평한 사람 an easy-going person ; a happy-go-lucky person∥태평한 세상에 in time of peace ; in the piping times of peace∥태평을 구가하다 enjoy the blessing of peace ; sing the praises of profound peace∥그는 매사에 태평이다 He takes things easy.
—가 a song of peace — 성대 a peaceful reign ; a reign of peace — 성사 happy events〔splendid enterprises〕 of a peaceful reign — 세계 a peaceful world ; a world at peace

†**태평양 太平洋** the Pacific (Ocean)
— 동맹 the Pacific Alliance — 문제 the Pacific question〔issues〕 ; the problems of Pacific relations — 방위 동맹 the Pacific Defense Alliance — 연안 the Pacific coast〔board〕 — 전쟁 the Pacific War — 지역 the Pacific area — 함대 the Pacific fleet — 항로 service on the Pacific — 회의 the Pan-Pacific Conference ; the Conference on Pacific Relations — 횡단 비행 a transpacific flight

***태풍 颱風** a typhoon
— 경보 a typhoon warning ¶ 태풍 경보를 발하다 issue〔give〕 a typhoon warning —권 the typhoon area — 주의보 a typhoon alert
태풍의 눈 관용 the typhonic center ; the eye of a typhoon

태형 笞刑 whipping ; flogging ; the lash ¶ 태형을 가하다 flog ; lash《a person》 on the buttocks

태환 兌換 conversion —하다 convert
—권 a convertible note — 은행 a bank of issue — 정지 suspension of specie payment — 제도 the conversion system — 준비금 convertible reserve

태후 太后 the Empress Dowager ; the Queen Mother

‡**택시** a taxi ; a taxicab ¶ 빈차로 손님을 찾아다니는 택시 a cruising taxi∥택시를 부르다 [소리를 질러] hail a taxi ; [전화로] call a taxi∥택시를 세우다 [손을 들어] halt a taxi∥택시를 잡다 get a taxi∥택시를 타다 take a taxi∥돈을 치르고 택시에서 내리다 pay off a taxi∥택시 영업을 하다 operate a taxi service∥어이 택시 Hey, taxi!
— 승차장 a taxi stand 《미》; a cabstand 《미》; a cab zone〔line〕《미》; a taxi rank 《영》

‡**택일 擇日** choice of〔choosing〕 an auspicious day —하다 choose an auspicious day ; fix upon the day ; fix a date

택지 擇地 selecting land ; the selection of site —하다 select as good land ; select a site《for》

택지 宅地 building land ; a building site ; home lots ; a curtilage
— 정리 laying out of a site〔of grounds〕

택출 擇出 selection ; choice ; option —하다 select ; choose ; opt ; pick out

‡**택하다 擇—** [선택하다] choose ; select ; make choice of ; prefer《to do this rather than that》; [선발하다] select ; pick out ; single out ¶ 친구를 택하다 choose one's friends∥사위를

E

택하다 pick out a son-in-law // 길일을 택하다 fix upon an auspicious day // 치욕보다 차라리 죽음을 택하다 prefer death to dishonor ; would rather die than live in disgrace // 너는 어느것을 택하느냐 What is your choice? // 부보다 학문을 택했다 I preferred learning to wealth. // 나는 맵시보다 마음을 택한다 I put heart before features.

탤런트 a talented person ; [집합적] 《young》 talent
— **스카웃** a talent scout **텔레비전** — a television personality ; [집합적] TV talent

탬버린 〖악기〗 a tambourine

탭 댄서 a tap dancer ; a soft-shoe shuffler 《속》

탭 댄스 a tap dance ¶ 탭 댄스를 추다 tap-dance

탯덩이 胎— a blockhead ; a fathead ; a dumbbell ; a simpleton

탯자리개 ropes for binding sheaves of grain

탯줄 胎— the umbilical cord ; the navel-string

탱 twang ; [금속의 날카로운 소리] tang ¶ 거문고 현의 탱하는 소리 the twang of a *kŏmungo* string // 탱하고 울리다 twang ; tang

탱고 〖음악〗 a tango ¶ 탱고를 추다 dance a tango

탱알 〖식물〗 a Tatarian aster

탱자 〖식물〗 a hardy (trifoliate) orange
—**나무** a hardy-orange tree

탱커 a tanker ; a tank ship
슈퍼〔매머드〕 — a supertanker **오일** — an oil tanker

†**탱크** ① 〖군사〗 a tank ; an armored motorcar ② [통] a (container) tank
— **로리** a tank lorry〔truck〕 —**병** a tank man ; a tanker —**선** ⇨ 탱커 —**용량** tankage ; the capacity of a tank **가스** — a gas tank **경**— a light tank **석유** — an oil tank **중**— a heavy tank

탱탱 —**하다** (be) taut ; tight ; tightly stretched ; distended ¶ 종기가 부어 탱탱하다 A boil is swollen up taut. // 줄이 탱탱하다 A line is tight.

탱화 **幀畫** 〖불교〗 a picture of Buddha to hang on the wall

터[1] ① [땅] a site ; a place ; building land ; a building lot〔site〕 ¶ 터를 돋우다 build up〔fill in, raise〕 the land for a building lot
② [기초] the foundation ; the ground ; footing ; foothold ; groundwork ; spadework ¶ 터가 잡히다 have a firm foothold ; be well-grounded // 이제 장사터가 잡혔다 He has his business well on its way.
장— a market place **절**— a temple site **집**— a building lot
터를 닦다 관용 prepare the ground for ; pave the way for

터[2] ① [처지] one's status〔lot, livelihood, social standing〕 ; family circumstances ¶ 나는 그렇게 사치할 터가 못된다 Circumstanced as I am, I can't afford such luxury.
② [관계] relationship ; friendship ; terms ¶ 그와는 아주 친한 터이다 I'm on very close terms with him.

터[3] [예정] intention ; expectation ¶ …할 터이다 intend ; have the intention of 《doing》 ; expect ; think of 《doing》 // 내가 직접 갈 터이다 I intend to go in person. // 지금쯤 도착했을 터인데 He should have arrived by this time 〔now〕.

터거리 ⇨ 턱[1]

*****터널** a tunnel ; an excavation ¶ 남산 터널 the *Namsan* Tunnel // 터널을 뚫다 build〔bore, drive, cut, excavate〕 a tunnel ; tunnel 《through》 // 터널을 지나가다 go〔pass〕 through a tunnel // 터널로 들어가다〔에서 나오다〕 go into 〔come out of〕 a tunnel
— **개통** the opening of a tunnel — **공사** tunneling work — **인부** a tunneler — **효과** 〖물리〗 a tunnel effect

†**터놓다** release ; unstop ; undam ; clear ; open 《it》 up ; let 《it》 go〔out〕 ; cut open ¶ 터놓고 without reserve ; frankly ; freely // 거래를 터놓다 open dealing // 터놓고 이야기하다 open one's heart 《to》 // 서로 가슴을 터놓고 이야기했다 We bared our bosoms to each other. // 그에게 술을 조금이라도 먹이면 그는 터놓고 이야기를 하는 경향이 있다 He tends to loosen up once you get a little liquor into him. // 요즈음은 터놓고 이야기하는 선생님들이 있다 Some teachers nowadays are really willing to let their hair down.

터다지다 consolidate (the foundation of a building) ; roll〔level〕 the ground 《for》 ¶ 집터를 터다지다 consolidate the foundation of a building

터닦다 ① [땅을] build up〔prepare〕 a site for a building ; clear the foundation of a building ; bulldoze ② [기초를] consolidate a foundation ; prepare the ground 《for》 ; pave the way 《for one's success》

터닺다 ⇨ 터다지다

터덜거리다 ① [걸음을] walk wearily ; plod ; trudge
② [소리를] sound cracked ; clink dully

터덜터덜 ① [걸음을] ploddingly ; trudgingly ¶ 터덜터덜 걷다 ⇨ 터덜거리다
② [소리나는 모양] rattling

터득 **攄得** understanding ; comprehension ; apprehension ; realization ; grasping —**하다** understand ; grasp ; apprehend ; realize ; get the knack 〔hang〕 of ; learn the rope ¶ 진리를

E

터득하다 understand〔perceive〕 a truth // 독서의 요령을 터득하다 get the knack of reading // 장사의 비결을 터득하다 master the tricks of a trade

터뜨리다 break ; burst ; tear ; blast ; explode ; detonate ; blow up ¶ 종기를 터뜨리다 break one's boil ; have one's boil break // 옷을 터뜨리다 get a rip in a garment // 주머니를 터뜨리다 tear open a bag // 타이어를 터뜨리다 have a blowout in a tire // 다이너마이트를 터뜨리다 set a dynamite off ; touch off a dynamite // 폭탄을 터뜨리다 explode a bomb // 울분을 터뜨리다 let loose one's indignation // 샴페인을 너무 일찍 터뜨리다 pop champagne too soon

터럭 hair ; feathers ¶ 센 터럭 gray hair ; white hairs // 터럭을 댄 외투 an overcoat lined with fur // 터럭이 빠지다 hair falls out〔comes off〕 ; lose one's hair // 닭의 터럭을 뽑다 pluck (the feathers of) a chicken // 인정이라고 터럭 끝 만큼도 없다 He has not a particle of tender feeling.

터리풀 〚식물〛 meadow-sweet ; dropwort

터릿선반 —旋盤 a turret lathe

터무니 a base ; a foundation ; a source ⇨ 터무니없다

***터무니없다** (be) unfounded ; groundless ; unreasonable ; absurd ; preposterous ; exorbitant ; excessive ; wild ; fabulous ; have no foundation ¶ 터무니없는 거짓말 a whopping lie // 터무니없는 요구 preposterous demand // 터무니없는 생각 the wild〔fabulous〕 idea // 터무니없는 값 an exorbitant price // 터무니없이 without any foundation ; without rime〔reason〕 ; extremely ; extraordinarily ; excessively ; absurdly ; fabulously // 터무니없이 사람을 욕하다 abuse 《a person》 for no reason at all // 터무니없이 되다 go to utter ruin ; go to wrack and ruin // 터무니없이 굴지 마라 Don't be absurd.

터미널 [종착역] a terminal (station) ; a terminus 《*pl.* ~es, -ni》 《영》 ; 〚전기〛 a terminal

터벅거리다 plod ; trudge ; totter ¶ 빗속을 터벅거리며 걷다 plod on〔along〕 in the rain

****터벅터벅** ploddingly ; walking with difficulty ; trudgingly ; totteringly ¶ 터벅터벅 걸어가다 plod〔trudge〕 along ; plod one's way

터번 [인도인이 쓰는] a turban ; a pugree ¶ 터반을 감은 turbaned

터보제트 엔진 〚항공〛 a turbo-jet engine

터보프롭 엔진 〚항공〛 a turbo-prop engine

터부 a taboo ; a tabu (금제·금기·금물) ¶ 터부로 하다 taboo ; put the taboo on 《something》 ; put 《something》 under taboo // 터부로 되어 있다 be taboo ; be under taboo

터분하다 ① [맛·냄새가] (be) unpleasant-tasting ; muddy-tasting ¶ 터분한 음식 untasty food ; dull fare // 입이 터분하다 have a muddy〔brown〕 taste in one's mouth
② [차림이] (be) sloppy ; untidy ; messy ¶ 터분한 사람 an untidy person
③ [흐린] (be) dim ; bleary ; bleared ¶ 눈이 터분하다 have bleary eyes ; one's eyes are bleary

***터빈** a 《gas, steam》 turbine

터세다 《a site》 (be) ill-omened ; unlucky ; ill-fated ; haunted ; jinxed ; ill-boding ; have an unfortunate site

터수 status ; relationship

터앝 the field〔vegetable garden〕 adjoining one's house ; a kitchen garden

터울 the age gap (among one's children) ; the disparity〔difference〕 of ages between siblings ¶ 터울이 잦다 be frequent in conceiving a baby // 그 집 아이들은 모두 두 살 터울이다 The children in that family are spaced two years apart.

터울거리다 make desperate〔frantic〕 efforts ; struggle hard 《with》

터울터울 hard ; eagerly ; desperately ; frantically

터잡다 pick out a site〔location, spot〕 ; locate

터전 a site ; a lot ; the grounds ¶ 넓은 터전 a large lot // 터전을 잡다 occupy〔pick up〕 a lot

터주 —主 the tutelary spirit of a house site ; a house guardian deity

터주다 permit ; allow ; leave 《it》 open ; give leave ; lift〔remove〕 the ban ¶ 길을 터주다 open a road 《for a person》 ; leave a road open // 외상을 터주다 give a charge account ; open a charge account for 《a person》 // 입학할 길을 터주다 leave a way open for entering a school // 후진들을 위해 길을 터주다 give the youngmen a chance

터지다 ① [금가다] break (down, away, loose) ; get broken ; be torn ; give way ; rip ; be cracked ; get chapped ; be roughened ¶ 터진 손 chapped hands // 종기가 터지다 a boil breaks // 입술이 터지다 one's lips crack // 옷이 터지다 (the seam of) a garment rips〔gives way〕 // 둑이 터지다 a dike collapses〔gives way〕 // 주머니가 터질 것 같다 The bag is ready to burst. // 가슴이 터질 것 같다 My heart is breaking.
② [폭발] explode ; burst ; break out ; occur〔happen〕 suddenly ; blow up ¶ 화약이 터지다 gun powder explodes // 중대 사건이 터지다 a serious matter pops up // 굉장한 소리를 내며 터지다

E

blow up with a terrific explosion // 전쟁이 터졌다 A war burst〔broke〕 out. // 그들의 쌓인 분노가 터졌다 Their smoldering resentment flared up〔burst into flame〕.
③ [폭로] get exposed ; be disclosed ; be brought〔come〕 to light ; be divulged

터치 (a) touch **—하다** touch ¶ 경묘한 터치 [연주법·화법] a light touch
—다운 〖축구〗 touchdown ¶ 터치다운하다 make a touchdown **—라인** touch-line **—아웃** 〖야구〗 touch out ¶ 터치아웃시키다〔되다〕 touch〔be touched〕 out

터키 ① [칠면조] a turkey ② Turkey ¶ 터키의 Turkish
—말 Turkish **— 모자** a Turkish cap ; a fez 《*pl.* fez(z)es》 **— 사람** a Turk **—탕** a Turkish bath ; a steam bath ; a hot house 《속》 **— 황제** the Sultan

터프 tough ¶ 터프한 tough ; hardy ; firm ; stubborn
—가이 a tough guy

***턱**[1] a jaw ; a chin ¶ 짐승의 턱 the chops of an animal // 턱을 쓰다듬다 rub one's chin // 턱으로 사람을 부리다 have 《a person》 at one's beck (and call) // 손으로 턱을 받치다 rest one's chin on one's hand(s)
—뼈 a jawbone ; a maxillary bone **—수염** a beard **—줄** [모자의] a chin-strap **아래—** the lower jaw ; the mandible ; the chin **위—** the upper jaw ; the maxilla **이중—** a double chin **주걱—** a lantern-jawed person ; a lantern jaw

턱[2] [불쑥 나온 곳] a projection ; a prominence ; an elevated place ; a raised spot ; a rise ; a hump ; a hummock ; a knoll ; a sill ¶ 턱지다 rise ; swell
고개— the top of a pass〔slope〕 **문—** a door〔window〕 sill ; the threshold

턱[3] [대접] a treat ; a feast ; a good meal ; an entertainment ¶ 한 턱을 내다 give a treat ; stand treat 《for a person》 ; stand 《somebody to something》 // 술을 한 턱 내다 treat〔stand〕 《a person》 to a drink ; buy 《a person》 a drink // 돌려 가며 한턱내다 treat 《friends》 by turns

턱[4] ① [안심하는 모양] ¶ 마음을 턱 놓다 put one's mind at complete ease // 마음이 턱 놓이다 be relieved ; feel reassured
② [잡는 모양] ¶ 손을 턱 잡다 hold 《a person's》 hand passionately // 손을 턱 내밀다 ask for 《it》 with no hesitation
③ [태연한 모양] ¶ 무대에 턱 나오다 take the stage with complete composure // 그 사람이 턱 우리 앞에 나타났다 He composedly appeared in front of us.

턱[5] ① [까닭] reason ; grounds ¶ 무슨 턱에 한 잔 사라는 거요 Why〔What for, For what reason〕 do you want me to buy you a drink? // 그럴 턱이 없다 There is no reason for that. // It is unreasonable. /It cannot be so.
② [정도] extent ; degree ¶ 아직 그 턱이다 That's all the further we've gotten. /It's still much the same. /No progress has been made.

턱걸이 ① [철봉의] chinning ; a chin-up ② [씨름의] hitting〔catching a person by〕 the chin ; a chin blow〔catch〕 ③ [의존] parasitism ; sponging off others 《미·구》 **—하다** chin oneself ; do a chin-up ; hit on〔catch by〕 the chin ; topple with a chin blow〔catch〕 ; sponge 《off, on a person for》 ; be a parasite ; lead a parasitic〔dependent〕 existence

턱까불다 ① [임종] give a death rattle ; breathe one's last ; expire ② [지껄임] chatter ; wag one's tongue

턱끈 [모자의] a chin strap

턱밀이 [씨름] a kind of hand-to-jaw wrestling **—하다** wrestle hand-to-jaw

턱밑 ① [턱의 밑] the tip of the chin ② [가까운] beneath one's chin ; right under one's nose ¶ 턱밑에 straight before one ; under one's nose ; before one's eyes // 턱밑에 두고도 보지 못한다 can't see〔fail to find〕 what is right under one's nose

턱받이 a pinafore ; a bib ; a feeder

턱살 the lower jaw ; the chin

턱솔 〖건축〗 the overlap where two pieces of wood are joined

턱시도 a tuxedo 《*pl.* ~s, ~es》 ; a dinner coat 《미》

***턱없다** (be) unreasonable ; exorbitant ; immoderate ¶ 턱없이 immoderately ; unreasonably ; exorbitantly // 턱없는 거짓말 a whopping lie ; an out-and-out lie // 턱없이 비싸다 be exorbitantly dear // 턱없이 탐내다 cry for the moon // 턱없이 돈을 쓰다 fool one's money away // 사람을 턱없이 칭찬하다 lavish praise on 《a person》 without rime〔reason〕

턱잎 〖식물〗 a stipule

턱자가미 the joint of the upper and lower jaws

턱주가리 the lower jaw ; the tip of the chin

턱지다 swell ; form a rise ; be hilly ¶ 턱진 길 a hilly road

턱짓 moving one's chin as a gesture ; pointing with one's chin **—하다** make a gesture by moving one's chin ; point with one's chin ¶ 턱짓으로 부리다 have 《a person》 at one's beck ; order 《a person》 about

턱찌끼 the remnants of a meal ; the

E

leftover ; leavings (at the table)
턱촌목 〖건축〗 a marking gauge
턱턱 ① [일을] ¶ 일을 턱턱 처리하다 do one's work in a brisk〔businesslike〕 way ; be quick in one's way ; finish one's work with dispatch
② [침을] ¶ 침을 아무데나 턱턱 뱉다 spit on everywhere
③ [연이어] ¶ 턱턱 쓰러지다 fall down one after another
④ [숨이] ¶ 이 방은 숨이 턱턱 막힌다 This room is very stuffy.
턴 [수영 따위의] a turn **—하다** turn ; make〔execute〕 a turn ; tip off the wall (풀에서) ¶ 그는 턴을 잘한다 He makes a beautiful turn.
턴테이블 [철도·레코드 플레이어의] a turntable
†**털** ① [사람의] hair ¶ 털이 없는 bald ; smooth ; hairless // 털 많은 손 hairy hands // 털이 많다 be thickly haired
② [짐승·새의] fur ; feather ; wool (양모) ¶ 닭의 털을 뽑다 pluck a chicken
③ [물건의] nap ; shag ; fuzz ; fluff ¶ 털이 일다 get fuzzy〔fluffy〕
—모자 a fur hat ; a woolen cap **—목도리** a comforter (털실로 짠) ; a boa (모피제) ; a tippet (모피제 어깨걸이) **—셔츠** (knitted) woolen underwear **—양말** woolen socks **—외투** a fur overcoat **겨드랑—** hair under the arm ; armpit hair **새—** bird feathers ; down **센—** gray hair **솜—** downy hair
털가죽 ⇨ 모피(毛皮)
털갈다 moult ; shed feathers〔hair〕 ¶ 털 가는 시절 the moulting season ; the moult
털갈이 [새의] molting ; [짐승의] coat-shedding ; shedding hair **—하다** [새가] molt ; [짐승이] shed 《its》 hair
털게 〖동물〗 a hairy crab
털구멍 pores (of the skin)
털끝 the end of a hair ; the tips of hair ; hair tips ; [근소] a bit ; a jot ; a whit ¶ 털끝만큼도 not in the least ; not at all ; not one bit ; not a whit ; not in the slightest degree // 털끝만큼도 개의치않다 don't care at all ; don't care a straw ; don't give a damn // 털끝만큼도 의심할 여지가 없다 There isn't the faintest shadow of a doubt about it. // 그렇게 할 생각은 털끝만큼도 없다 I haven't the slightest intention to do so. // 그에게는 양심이라곤 털끝만큼도 없다 He has not an atom〔ounce〕 of conscience in him.
털내의 —內衣 (knitted) woolen underwear
*__털다__ ① [떼다] shake off ; knock〔beat〕 off ; throw off ; dust ; brush up ¶ 모자의 먼지를 털다 shake the dust off one's hat ; brush up the dust // 담뱃재를 털다 flick the ashes from cigar〔cigarette〕 ; knock the ashes from a pipe
② [비우다] empty ; clear ¶ 주머니를 털다 empty one's purse〔pocket〕 // 그는 재산을 다 털어 먹었다 He ran through his fortunes.
③ [빼앗다] rob〔strip〕 《a person》 of ; make off with ¶ 도둑이 사람의 주머니를 털다 pick 《a person's》 pocket 《of》 ; a thief robs 《a person》 of his money // 도둑은 집안의 귀중품을 다 털어 갔다 The thief made off with all the valuables in the house.
털어서 먼지 안나는 사람 없다 속담 Every man has his faults. /No man is infallible.
털럭거리다 keep slapping〔jogging, jerking, jolting, clattering〕
털럭털럭 swingingly ; with slaps〔jolt〕 ; clatteringly
털리다[1] ① [떨어지다] get shaken〔knocked, beaten〕 off ; [먼지가] get dusted〔brushed off〕 ¶ 옷의 먼지가 잘 털리다 dust brushed off one's clothes readily ; one's clothes are easily dusted
② [몽땅 없어지다] get emptied ¶ 자루가 다 털리다 a bag is completely emptied
③ [도둑한테] get robbed 《of》
털리다[2] [털게 하다] have 《a person》 shake〔knock, beat, dust, brush〕 《it》 off
털메기 a roughly made straw sandal
털모자 —帽子 a fur hat ; a woolen cap
털목 —木 coarsely woven cotton
털방석 —方席 a fur cushion
털배자 —褙子 a fur waistcoat〔vest〕 ; a fur-lined Korean vest〔waistcoat〕
털버덕거리다 keep splashing〔slopping〕
털버덕털버덕 with a splash
털버선 woolen (Korean) socks
털벙 with a plop ; with a splash ⇨ 철벙
털보 a hairy〔shaggy, hirsute〕 person
털복숭아 〖식물〗 a downy peach
털북숭이 a hairy〔shaggy, hirsute〕 person〔thing〕
털붓 a writing〔painting〕 brush ; a hair pencil ; a brush
털붙이 ① [모피] furs ; fur pieces ; fur goods ; a skin
② [털옷] fur clothes ; woolen goods〔stuff〕
털빛 the color of hair ; the color of the fur
털수세 a thick bristling beard
†**털실** woolen yarn ; worsted ; knitting wool ¶ 털실로 뜨다 knit // 털실로 스웨터를 짜다 knit a sweater with wool
— 가게 a wool shop **— 뭉치** a knitting ball **— 장수** a woolman ; a dealer in wool
털썩 with a plop ; with a thud ; flop ¶

E

털썩거리다 keep plopping〔thudding, bobbing, jolting〕// 그릇을 털썩 떨어뜨리다 drop a plate with a thud // 털썩 주저앉다 plop (oneself) down ; sit flop ; flop into 《an armchair》 // 털썩 떨어지다 fall with a thud

털썩이잡다 ruin ; spoil ; fail ; blast ; wreck

털어놓다 ① [물건을] empty (out) ; shake out ; spill ; throw out ¶ 호주머니를 털어놓다 empty one's pocket
② [마음을] open one's heart ; unbosom oneself ; tell frankly ¶ 털어놓고 말하면 to be quite frank (with you) ; frankly speaking // 계획을 털어놓게 Come out with your plan. // 그는 뭐든지 다 나한테 털어놓는다 He keeps nothing from me. // 그는 어찌나 수다스러운 녀석인지 아무 비밀도 믿고 털어놓을 수가 없다 He is such a loud mouth that you can't trust him with any secrets. // 당신이 교묘하게 말꼬리를 돌리지만 않는다면 나도 솔직히 털어 놓겠소 If you cut that fancy footwork out, I'll let it all hang out, too.

털어먹다 spend the last cent ⇨ 떨어먹다

털옷 a fur〔woolen〕 garment

털외투 a fur〔woolen〕 (over)coat

털장갑 —掌甲 fur〔woolen〕 gloves

털집 a waster ; a squanderer ; a libertine ; a prodigal ; a dissipater ; a debauchee

털총이 a horse checkered with blue and black spots

털터리 ① [빈털터리] a man who is broke ; a man without ready money ; a man with empty pockets ; a penniless person
② [낡은 차] a rattling thing ; a rattletrap
③ [오토바이] a motorcycle

털털 ploddingly ; clinkingly ; clatteringly

털털하다 [사람이] (be) free and easy ; unaffected ; [맛이] somewhat puckery ¶ 시금 털털하다 be sourish

털토시 fur-lined wristlets

텀벙 with a plump〔splash, plop, flop〕 ¶ 목욕탕에 텀벙 들어가다 plump into the bath // 텀벙 물로 뛰어들어가다 jump〔plunge〕 into the water with a splash ; plop into the water

텀벙거리다 keep splashing〔plopping〕 ; splash about ¶ 물 속에서 텀벙거리다 splash about in the water

텁석 with a snatch〔snap〕 ; greedily ; all of a sudden ; suddenly ; firmly ¶ 텁석 덤비다 jump at ; make a sudden spring at // 텁석 쥐다 take sudden hold of ; snatch ; grasp greedily // 텁석 물다 snap at the bait

텁석나룻 bushy whiskers ; shaggy whiskers

텁석부리 a man with bushy whiskers

텁석텁석 with snatches ; with snaps ; greedily ¶ 텁석텁석 그러쥐다 keep snatching // 텁석텁석 받아 먹다 keep snapping at 《it》

텁수룩하다 (be) unkempt ; untrimmed ; shaggy ; bushy ¶ 텁수룩한 머리 long unkempt hair // 구레나룻이 텁수룩하게 나다 have a shaggy growth of whiskers

텁텁이 a sloppy person ; an easy person

텁텁하다 ① [입맛이] (be) unpleasant ; thick and tasteless ¶ 입속이 텁텁하다 have some unpleasant taste in one's mouth
② [눈이] (be) dim ; vague ; obscure
③ [성미가] (be) sloppy ; broad-minded ¶ 성미가 텁텁해서 누구하고도 잘 사귀다 be so broad-minded as to associate with men of all shades

텃고사 —告祀 offering a sacrifice to the tutelary spirit of a house site

텃구실 taxes on a house site ; a duty on site

텃도지 —賭地 rent for a house site ; the site tax

텃마당 the threshing ground of a community

텃밭 a field attached to a home site ; a kitchen garden

텃세 —貰 rent for a house site ; the site tax

텃세 —勢 **—하다** take advantage of being on one's own ground to act highhandedly ; lord (it) over a newcomer

텅 hollow ¶ 텅 빈 empty ; vacant ; bare // 가구가 없어 방안이 텅 빈 것 같다 The room looks bare without furniture.

텅스텐 〖화학〗 tungsten 《W》
— 전구 a tungsten light bulb

텅텅 ① [빈 모양] all hollow ¶ 방이 텅텅 비어 있다 A room is all empty. ② [총소리] bang, bang

테 ① [돌린 줄] a hoop ; a band ; a stripe ¶ 모자테 a hatband // 모자에 금테를 두르다 band a cap with gold stripes // 통에 테를 메우다 hoop a barrel ; put a hoop on a barrel
② [언저리] a rim ; a brim ; a frame ; a frill ¶ 안경테 the rim of spectacles ; a glass frame // 금테 안경 gold-rimmed spectacles // 무테 안경 rimless〔brimless〕 glasses // 테가 넓은 모자 a broad-brimmed hat
③ [타래] reel ¶ 실 여섯 테 six reels of coiled thread

***테너** 〖음악〗 ① [음역(音域)] tenor ② [사람] a tenor (singer)

†테니스 ⇨ 정구(庭球)

테니스

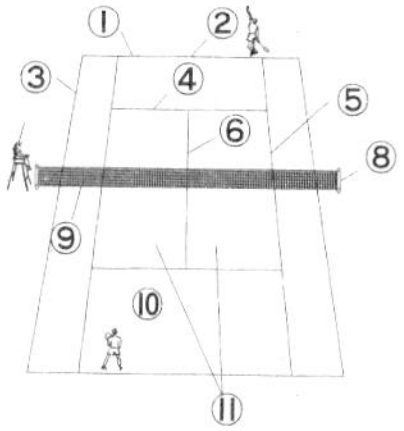

① 베이스 라인 base line
② 센터마크 center mark
③ 더블용 사이드라인 doubles sideline
④ 서비스 라인 service line
⑤ 싱글용 사이드라인 singles sideline
⑥ 센터 라인 center line
⑦ 심판 umpire
⑧ 포스트 post
⑨ 네트 net
⑩ 백 코트 back court
⑪ 포어 코트 fore court

*테두리 ① [둘레] girth ; circumference ; caliber ¶ 나무의 테두리 the girth of a tree ② [테] a hoop ; a rim ; a frame ③ [윤곽] an outline ; [범위] a limit ; a framework ¶ 테두리 안에서 within the limit 《of》// 예산의 테두리 안에서 within the framework of the budget // 법률의 테두리 안에서 within the legal limit // 사건의 테두리를 간단히 설명하다 give a brief outline of a case

테디 [여자용 속옷] teddies

테라마이신 『약』 terramycin

*테라스 a terrace ¶ 테라스에(서) on the terrace

테러 [행위] terrorism ; [사람] a terrorist ━하다 terrorize ¶ 테러의 희생이 되다 fall a victim to terrorism // 테러 작전을 개시하다 open a terror campaign 《against》
─단 a terrorist〔terror〕 organization ; terrorist ─리스트 a terrorist ─리즘 terrorism ─ 사건 a case of terrorism ; a terrorist outrage ─ 전술 terroristic tactics

테르밋 『화학』 thermite ; thermit
─법 aluminothermy ─ 용접 thermit welding

테르븀 『화학』 terbium
─ 금속류 terbium metals 산화 ─ terbia

테르펜 『화학』 terpene
─유 terpene oil ─틴 terpentine

테리어 『동물』 a terrier

테마 a theme ; a subject ; subject matter ¶ 음악의 테마 the theme of a music
─ 뮤직 theme music 연구 ─ the subject of study

테메(우)다 hoop ; bind with hoops ; put a hoop on ¶ 통에〔을〕 테메다 hoop a barrel ; put a hoop on a barrel

테밀이 rimming lattice strips (with rounded edges) ━하다 rim (lattice strips)

테밖 being outside the circle〔sphere〕 ¶ 정치의 테밖 outside the sphere of politics ; away from politics

테받다 copy ; imitate ; mimic ; model 《after, on》 ¶ 글씨를 테받다 write after a copy ; imitate a style of calligraphy // (남의) 수를 테받다 model one's embroidery 《after another's》

테베 『의학』 T. B. ; tuberculosis

테석테석 ━하다 (be) rough ; coarse ; unrefined

테세우스 [신화] Theseus

†테스트 a test ; testing ; workout 《미》 ; a quiz 《미》 ; [배우·가수의] a tryout ━하다 test (out) ; try (out) ; check out ¶ 테스트를 받다 take〔undergo〕 a test ; [가수 등이] get an audition // 테스트에 합격했다 pass the test
─ 케이스 a test case ─ 파일럿 a test pilot ─ 패턴 [텔레비전] a test pattern 객관식 ─ an objective test 실력 ─ an ability test 체력 ─ a physical test 학력〔상식〕 ─ an achievement〔a general knowledge〕 test

테실 reeled thread ; (a) thread reeled

테안 within the limit 《of》 ; within the circle〔bound, sphere〕 ¶ 성적이 입학자 테안에 들다 one's record (of grades) meets the standard for admission to the school

†테이블 a table ¶ 4인용의 테이블 a table for four // 곁 테이블 an end table // 테이블에 가득한 a tableful 《of dishes》 // 테이블에 앉다 sit down at〔to〕 a table // 테이블에 차린 것을 먹다 eat off a table // 테이블을 사이에 두고 앉다 [두사람이 주어] sit across a table ; [한 쪽이 주어] sit across from 《a person》 at a table // 테이블에 둘러 앉다 sit around a table
─ 매너 table manners ─보 a table cover ; [식탁의] a tablecloth ; a table spread 《미》 ─ 센터 a centerpiece ─ 스피치 an after-dinner speech

†테이프 [종이·천 따위의] (a) tape ; [녹음용] (magnetic) recording tape ; [환송·장식용의] a paper streamer ; a colored paper ribbon ¶ 골의 테이프 [육상 경기] the finish tape // 테이프 1릴 a reel〔spool〕 of tape // (녹음용) 30분용 테이프 a thirty-minute spool of tape // 테이프를 끊다 [육상 경기] breast the tape ; [개통식 따위에서] cut the tape 《for the new subway's first outbound train》 ; cut a ribbon 《on a new office

building》// 테이프에 녹음하다 record on a tape ; put 《the conversation》 on tape ; take a tape-recording of ; tape-record ; tape // 테이프에 취입하다 speak into a tape recorder // 테이프를 던지다 fling〔throw〕 paper streamers
— 녹음 tape recording — 리코더 a tape recorder — 송신기 a tape transmitter — 수신기 a tape receiver 스테레오 — a stereo tape 자기 — a magnetic tape

테일라이트 a taillight
테일러 a tailor
테제 These 《도》; 〖철학〗 a thesis
테크노크러시 technocracy
테크니션 a technician
테크니컬러 《in》 technicolor
테크닉 (a) technique ; technic
텍사스 Texas 《Tex.》 ¶ 텍사스의 Texan
— 사람 a Texan — 히트 〖야구〗 a Texas leaguer
텍스트 [교재] a text(book) ¶ 영어의 텍스트 an English textbook // 텍스트 24페이지를 펴시오 Open the text at〔Turn to 《미》〕 p. 24
—북 a textbook
텐서 〖수학·해부〗 a tensor
텐스 〖문법〗 the tense
†**텐트** a tent ; [대형의] a pavilion ; [소형의] a dog-tent ¶ 텐트를 치다〔걷다〕 pitch〔strike〕 a tent
— 생활 camping ; camping-out ; tent life ¶ 텐트 생활을 하다 camp out ; lodge in a tent 원형 — a bell tent
텔레그래프 telegraph
텔레마크 〖스키〗 a telemark
텔레미터 a telemeter ¶ 텔레미터로 전송(電送)하다 telemeter // 텔레미터로 반송하다 telemeter back
— 장치 a telemetering system
†**텔레비전** television 《TV》; the telly 《영·속》; [수상기] a television〔TV〕 (set) ; a teleset ; a telly 《영·속》; video (화면) ; audio (소리 부분) ¶ 텔레비전의 televisionary ; televisional // 20인치 텔레비전 a TV set with a 20-in. wide screen // 아동 취향의 텔레비전 프로 a kid program on TV ; a kidvid // 텔레비전 방송을 하다 telecast ; televise ; make a telecast // 텔레비전을 보다 watch〔look at, see, view〕 television // 텔레비전을 켜다〔끄다〕 turn on〔off〕 television〔a TV set〕 // 텔레비전으로〔에서〕 보다 teleview ; see 《a person》 on television ; watch 《the baseball game》 on TV // 텔레비전에 나오다 make a television appearance ; appear〔go〕 on television // 텔레비전에 달라붙어 있다 glue oneself to a television set ; be planted in front of a TV set
— 관계자 television people —광(狂) a television fanatic ; a vidiot 《미·속》 — 기사 a television technician — 뉴스 telenews — 드라마 a teleplay ; a television play — 방송 a television〔TV, video〕 broadcast ; a telecast ; a videocast — 방송국 a television〔TV〕 station — 방송자 a telecaster — 송신기 a television transmitter ; a televisor — 수상기 a television (set) ; a TV set ; a television receiver — 시청자 a televiewer ; a viewer — 영화 a telefilm ; a vidfilm — 전화 a television telephone ; a TV phone — 카메라 a telecamera ; a television〔TV〕 camera —탑 a television pylon〔mast〕 — 프로 a television program ; a TV show 컬러 — color television 흑백 — black-and-white television 연속 — 방송극 a television serial drama ; a soap opera 《미》 장시간의 — 프로 a telethon
텔레타이프 a teletype (writer) ; a teletype printing system ; a teleprinter ¶ 텔레타이프로 치다〔보내다〕 teletype ; send 《a message》 by teletype // 텔레타이프로 송신된 통신 a teletype (message)
텔레파시 [정신 감응] telepathy ¶ 텔레파시의 telepathic // 텔레파시를 행하는 사람 a telepathist // 텔레파시로 전하다 communicate by telepathy ; telepath
텔렉스 [상표명] Telex
템 as much as ; as long as ¶ 쌀 한 섬 템이나 먹다 eat a whole bag of rice // 두달 템이나 걸리다니 How come it takes as long as two months? // 100만 원 템이나 빚이 있다 He is in debt to the extent of a million *won*.
템스강 —江 [영국] the Thames River
템페라 [화법] a tempera (painting) : [그림] a tempera...
템포 tempo ; speed ¶ 눈이 팽팽 도는 시대의 템포 the dizzy tempo at which society now moves ; the bewildering quick changes of the time // 이 템포가 빠른 시대 this fast-moving age // 템포가 빠른 fast-moving〔-paced〕 (이야기 따위의) // 빠른〔느린〕 템포로 at quick〔slow〕 tempo // 템포가 빠르〔느리〕다 be quick〔slow〕 of moving ; be speedy〔tardy〕 // 템포에 맞추다 keep pace with the tempo 《of the day》 // 템포를 빨리하다 pick up in tempo // 템포가 맞지않다 be out of tempo // 이 소설은 템포가 빠르다 The plot develops rapidly in this novel.
텡쇠 ① [허약자] a person who looks strong but is actually quite weak ; a hollow shell of a person
② [바보] an empty-headed〔ignorant〕 person ; an ignoramus
토¹ a grammatical particle ; a postposition
토² [간장의] the scum〔sediment, dregs〕 of soy sauce

E

토건업 土建業 civil engineering and construction ; construction work
—자 a civil engineering and building contractor
토관 土管 a clay pipe〔tube〕; an earthen〔a drain〕pipe
토구 討究 study ; research ; investigation **—하다** study ; research ; investigate
토굴 〖조개〗 mud oysters
토굴 土窟 a cavern ; a cave ; a den ¶ 토굴에서 사는 사람 a cave dweller
토기 土器 earthenware ; crockery ; an earthen vessel
—장이 an earthenware maker ; a potter ; a ceramist **—점** a potter's shop ; a pottery shop ; an earthenwareshop
토끝 the end piece of a roll of fabric ; a fag-end
*__토끼__ a rabbit (집토끼) ; a hare (들토끼)
— 고기 hare meat **—굴** a rabbit burrow **— 사냥** 《go》 hare hunting **— 사육장** a rabbit warren ; a rabbitry **—장** a rabbit hutch
토끼 둘을 잡으려다 하나도 못 잡는다 속담 If you run after two hares, you will catch neither.
토끼다 run away ; flee ; escape ; decamp ; jump 《a town》 《미》; beat〔hook, hightail〕it 《미·속》
토끼뜀 (a) leapfrog ; leapfrogging **—하다** leapfrog 《over》; play leapfrog
토끼풀 〖식물〗 a clover ¶ 네잎의 토끼풀 a four-leaf(ed) clover
토농 土農 a native farmer ; an indigenous farmer
토너먼트 a tournament ; a tourney ¶ 토너먼트에서 1위가 되다 take first place in a tournament
토닉 [강장제] a tonic
토닥거리다 keep patting〔tapping, rapping〕
토닥토닥 ¶ 문을 토닥토닥 두드리다 be rapping at the door ⇨ 토닥거리다
토단 土壇 an earthen platform ; a terrace
토담 土— an earthen wall ; a mud-wall ; a dirt-wall
—장이 a mud-wall builder **—집** a mud-walled hut ; a dirt-walled house
토대 土臺 ① [건축의] a foundation ; a stereobate ; a ground sill ¶ 토대를 굳히다 solidify the foundation // 이 집은 토대가 튼튼하다 This house is built on a firm foundation.
② [일의] a foundation ; a base ; ground work ; a cornerstone ¶ 성공의 토대를 쌓다 pave the way for one's success // 초등 교육은 인간의 토대를 쌓는 교육이다 Primary education forms the groundwork for building up a man's character. // 이 소설은 경험을 토대로 쓴 것이다 This story is based on personal experience.

*__토라지다__ pout ; sulk ; get sulky〔cross〕 ¶ 돈을 빌려 주지 않는다고 토라지다 sulk over a rebuff on borrowing money // 그는 왜 토라졌나 What makes him (so) sulky ?
토란 土卵 〖식물〗 a taro ; an elephant's ear ; Colocasia antiquorum (학명)
—국 taro soup
토렴 pouring hot broth over rice a little at a time to heat them up **—하다** warm up 《boiled rice, noodles》 by applying hot water or soup repeatedly
토로 吐露 exposing〔revealing〕 one's thoughts **—하다** express 《one's views》; speak out 《one's mind》; set forth 《one's opinion》; lay bare 《one's heart》 ¶ 진정을 토로하다 reveal one's true heart ; lay bare one's heart
-토록 ① [하도록] to the point where it does〔say, is〕 ② [쯤] as much as ; to the extent of ¶ 그토록 많은가 Is there that much ? // 종일토록 노시오 Enjoy yourself all day long.
⁑__토론 討論__ a debate ; a discussion ; an oratorical contest ; a contention ; argumentation **—하다** debate ; discuss ; dispute ; argue ; deliberate ; contend

> 참고 **discuss**는 흔히 협력적 건설적으로 토론하는 것 **argue**는 어떤 주장을 지지 또는 반박하기 위하여 이유나 증거를 늘어놓고 논하는 것 **debate**는 흔히 큼직한 문제에 대해서 형식적인 토론을 하는 것 **dispute**는 때때로 감정적 대립적으로 의견을 주고 받는 것을 의미한다

¶ 활발한 토론 a living〔hot〕 discussion // 어떤 문제를 토론하다 debate on〔about〕 a subject // 토론을 종결짓다 close〔wind up〕 a discussion // 그 사실은 토론의 여지가 없다 The fact is beyond〔past〕 dispute.
—술 dialectic **—자** a debater ; a disputant **—회** a debate ; a forum ; a debating society ; an oratorical contest **자유〔집단〕—** free〔group〕 discussion
토론 종결 討論終結 [미국 의회] cloture of debate ; [영국 의회] closure of debate ; gag ; a guillotine ¶ 토론 종결을 동의하다 move the closure〔cloture〕
토륨 〖화학〗 thorium
토르소 a torso
토리[1] a spool of thread
—실 balled string〔thread〕
토리[2] [쇠고리] an iron ring fixed on the end of the shaft of an arrow
토리 土理 fertility of soil ; the nature of soil
토마루 土— a mud floor
⁑__토마토__ 〖식물〗 a tomato 《*pl.* ~es》; a love apple
— 소스 tomato sauce **— 케첩** tomato

E

ketchup〔catchup, catsup〕

*토막 a piece ; a bit ; a cut ; a block ¶ 토막나다 be broken into pieces // 토막내다 cut〔chop〕 into pieces
— 고기 chops〔cuts, slices〕 of meat — 나무 blocks of wood ; wood in blocks 생선 — a cut of fish

토막 土幕 a mud hut ; a cellar-hovel ; an underground shack

토막토막 into pieces ; piece by piece ¶ 생선을 토막토막 자르다 chop fish into pieces // 나무를 토막토막 베다 saw wood into pieces

토멸 討滅 conquest ; annihilation ; extermination — 하다 conquer ; annihilate ; exterminate

토목 土木 engineering works ; public works
— 건축 the engineering and construction industry — 공사 public works — 공학 civil engineering — 기계 civil engineering machinery 《총칭》 — 기사 a civil engineer — 사업 public〔engineering〕 works

토목공이 土木— a fool ; an ass ; a boor ; a dunce

토민 土民 the natives ; aborigines

토박이 natives ; aborigines
서울 — a Seoulite to the backbone ; a truebred Seoulite

토박하다 土薄— [땅이] (be) sterile ; barren ; infertile ; meager ; impoverished ; unproductive ¶ 토박한 땅 unproductive land // 이 밭은 토박해서 아무것도 할 수 없다 The field is too sterile to yield anything.

토벌 討伐 subjugation ; suppression — 하다 subjugate ; suppress ; put down ; subdue ¶ 공비를 토벌하다 liquidate 〔subdue〕 red guerrillas
—군 a punitive force —전 punitive expedition

토벽 土壁 a mud wall ; a dirt wall ; an earthen wall

토병 土兵 the native〔local〕 troops

토비 土匪 native insurgents ; rebellious natives ; local rebels

토비 討匪 suppression of rebels〔insurgents〕 — 하다 suppress〔put down〕 rebels

토사 土砂 earth and sand
— 붕괴 a washout ; a landslide ¶ 세 채의 가옥이 토사 붕괴로 무너지고 흙에 묻혔다 Three houses collapsed and were buried under a landslide.

토사 吐瀉 vomiting and diarrhea — 하다 vomit and run off at the bowels
—물 the matter vomited ; (a) discharge

토사곽란 吐瀉癨亂 acute gastroenteritis ; vomiting and diarrhea

토산 土山 an earthy mountain

토산물 土産物 local products ; native produce

토산불알 【한의】 a testicle swollen with elephantiasis

토색 土色 earth color

토색 討索 extortion ; exaction ; blackmail — 하다 extort (money) ; blackmail 《a person》 for ; practice extortion

토석류 土石流 an avalanche of earth and rocks

토설 吐說 ⇨ 실토(實吐)

*토성 土星 【천문】 Saturn

토성 土城 a mud〔an earthen〕 castle ; mud fortification

토속 土俗 local customs ; folkways

토스 a toss — 하다 toss 《a ball》

토스트 toast ¶ 토스트 한 조각 a slice of toast // 버터 바른 토스트 toast spread with butter ; buttered toast // 토스트 샌드위치 a club sandwich // 토스트를 굽다 toast bread ; make toast // 토스트에 버터를 바르다 spread toast with butter ; spread butter on toast
프렌치 — French toast

토시 wristlets (to protect against the cold)

토시살 beef attached to the spleen

토신 土神 a deity of earth ; an earth god

토실 吐實 — 하다 tell the truth ; own up to ; confess

토실토실 — 하다 (be) plump ; chubby ¶ 토실토실한 볼 chubby cheeks // 토실토실한 소녀 a plump girl

토심스럽다 吐心— (be) disgusting ; unpleasant ; feel bad

토악질 吐— vomiting (음식을) ; disgorgement (부정 이득을) — 하다 vomit ; disgorge ; throw up

토양 土壤 soil ; earth ¶ 비옥한〔메마른〕 토양 fertile〔sterile〕 soil
— 개량약 a soil conditioner — 조사 agronomical survey —학 soil science

토어 土語 the native〔local〕 language ; the vernacular tongue〔language〕

토역 土役 mud work ; earthwork — 하다 do mud work〔earthwork〕
—꾼 a navvy ; a construction laborer

토옥 土屋 a mud hut

토옥 土沃 the fertility〔richness〕 of soil — 하다 (be) rich ; fertile ; productive

†토요일 土曜日 Saturday

토욕 土浴 wallowing in mud〔dirt〕 — 하다 wallow in mud〔dirt〕

토용 土俑 a burial mound figure〔figurine〕 ; a clay image 《of a man, of an animal》

토우 土雨 a dust storm ; a rain of dust

토우 土偶 a clay doll〔icon〕

토의 討議 discussion ; debate ; deliberation — 하다 discuss ; debate〔deliberate〕 《upon》 ¶ 토의중의 문제 questions yet in debate // 토의에 붙이다 submit 《a subject》 to debate ; bring up

《a matter》 for discussion // 토의에 들어가다 open a debate ; enter into a discussion // 토의중이다 be under discussion
— 사항 items on the agenda —안 a subject for debate〔discussion〕 긴급 — an urgent consultation

토이기 土耳其 ⇨ 터키

토인 土人 a native ; an aboriginal ; aborigines 《총칭》

토일렛 a toilet ; a toilet room 《미》 ; toilet facilities
— 페이퍼 toilet paper〔tissue〕 ; bathroom tissue

토장 土葬 inhumation ; interment ; burial —하다 inhume ; bury ; inter

토장 土醬 bean paste ⇨ 된장

토적 土賊 local bandits ; local rebels〔insurgents〕

토적 討賊 suppression of a rebellion —하다 subdue a rebellion

토정 吐精 seminal emission ⇨ 사정

토정 吐情 —하다 speak one's mind ; open〔unlock〕 one's heart ; unbosom oneself

토제 土製 earthen ¶ 그 그릇은 토제다 That vessel is earthen〔made of earth〕.

토제 吐劑 an emetic

토족 土族 (relatives of) native gentry

토족 土足 muddy〔miry〕 feet ; [신을 신은] feet with shoes on ; shod feet ¶ 토족으로 올라가다 enter with one's shoes on

토주자 土鑄字 〖인쇄〗 a clay printing type

†**토지** 土地 ① [땅·흙] land ; a piece〔tract〕 of land ; a lot〔plot〕 ; soil ¶ 광대한 토지 a big tract of land // 메마른 토지 poor〔barren〕 soil // 토지를 경작하다 cultivate land ; till the soil
② [소유지] an estate ; real estate ¶ 토지에 투자하다 invest in real estate
③ [영지] territory
— 가옥 land and buildings — 개량 land improvement — 개발 estate〔land〕 development — 개혁 land reform — 구획 정리 land adjustment — 대장 a land-book ; a terrier — 등기부 a land register ; a terrier ; a cadastre — 매매 dealing in real estate ¶ 토지 매매 브로커 a real estate agent〔agency〕 ; a realtor 《미》 — 몰수 〖법〗 escheat — 법안 a land bill — 불법 점거자 a squatter — 사용세 a land use tax — 소유권 land ownership — 소유자 a landowner ; a landholder — 수용권 〖법〗 (right of) eminent domain — 제도 land system — 측량 land surveying

토질 土質 the nature of the soil ; the soil

토질 土疾 an endemic disease ; a local disease

토찌끼 dregs of soy sauce

토착 土着 aboriginality ; settling —하다 settle (in a new territory) ; become native ; become indigenous ¶ 토착의 aboriginal ; native(-born) ; indigenous
— 동물 the endemic animals —민 aborigines ; natives ; original settlers ¶ 경주에는 토착민들이 많다 *Kyŏngju* has a large number of families settled there for generations.

토치카 tochka 《러》 ; 〖군사〗 a pillbox
— 진지 a tochka position ; a cluster of pillboxes

토코페롤 〖생화학〗 tocopherol

토큰 [대용 화폐] a token (coin)
버스 — a bus token

토키 〖영화〗 a talkie ; a talking picture (film) ; a sound film ; talkies 《총칭》
— 대본 a talkie script — 만화 an animated cartoon

토탄 土炭 peat ; turf
—층 peat deposits

토털 total
— 스코어 total score

토테미즘 〖역사〗 totemism

토템 〖역사〗 a totem
— 숭배 totemism —폴 a totem pole

토파 吐破 speaking one's mind freely ; talking frankly —하다 tell〔say〕 frankly ; disclose freely ; talk without reserve

토플리스 a topless suit

토픽 a topic ; a subject 《of conversation》 ¶ 오늘의 토픽 current topics

***토하다** 吐— ① [게우다] vomit ; throw〔fetch〕 up ; [뱉다] spew ; spit ; [뿜다] emit ; eject ; belch ; send forth〔out, up〕 ¶ 먹은 것을 토하다 throw up what one has eaten ; vomit what one ate // 토할 것 같다 feel sick〔nausea〕 // 피를 토하다 spit〔cough up〕 blood // 화산이 연기와 재를 토해낸다 A volcano belches out smoke and ash. // 공장의 굴뚝이 뭉게뭉게 연기를 토해내고 있다 The factory chimney is sending up clouds of smoke.
② [토로] speak 《one's mind》 ; disclose ; confess 《the truth》 ; express ¶ 진심을 토하다 tell the truth ; tell what one has in mind ; disclose one's true intentions // 의견을 토하다 express〔give〕 one's opinion

토현삼 土玄蔘 〖식물〗 a figwort ; *Scrophularia koraiensis* (학명)

토혈 吐血 spitting〔vomiting〕 blood ; hemoptysis —하다 spit〔vomit〕 blood

토호 土豪 a landed proprietor ; a wealthy local farmer ; landed gentry
—질(하다) (practice) tyranny ; oppression

***톡** ① [소리] with a pat〔rap, thud, snap〕 ¶ 어깨를 톡 치다 give 《a person》 a pat on the shoulder // 돌에 톡 걸려 넘어지다 stumble over a stone

unexpectedly // 시계가 마루에 톡 떨어졌다 A watch has fallen on the floor with a thud.
② [모양] protrudingly ; bulgingly ¶ 배가 톡 나오다 have a bulging belly ; have a potbelly
③ [비어짐] popping out ¶ 밤알이 송이에서 톡 비어지다 a chestnut pops out of its burr

톡배다 (be) close-woven

톡탁 with a tap〔rap〕 ⇨ 툭탁

톡탁거리다 beat each other up ; exchange blow after blow ; fight each other

톡탁톡탁 beating each other repeatedly ; exchanging blows ; fighting

톡톡 with a pat ⇨ 톡

톡톡하다 ① [액체가] (be) thick ; rich ; heavy ② [피륙이] (be) thick ; close ; close-woven

톡톡히 ① [많이] much ; a lot ; a great deal ¶ 돈을 톡톡히 벌다 make quite a lot of money ② [심하게] severely ; hard ; heavily ; soundly ¶ 톡톡히 책망을 듣다 get severely scolded // 톡톡히 얻어맞다 be beaten soundly ; get a good beating ③ [치밀하게] close ; thick ¶ 베를 톡톡히 짜다 weave cloth thick

⁑**톤** a ton ; tonnage ¶ 미터톤 a metric ton ; a ton of 1,000 kilos // 미(美)톤 an American〔short〕 ton ; a ton of 2,000 lbs // 영(英)톤 a British〔long〕 ton ; a ton of 2,240 lbs // 톤당(當) per ton // 석탄 5톤 five ton(s) of coal // 10톤을 실은 배 a ten tonner // 5천톤짜리 기선 a steamer of 5,000 tons (burden〔burthen〕) // 5톤 적재 화차 a five-ton freight car 《미》; a five- ton waggon 《영》 // 이 배는 몇 톤입니까 What is the tonnage of this ship?
―세 tonnage dues **배수〔순〕―** a displacement〔net〕 ton **용적―** a measurement〔volume, freight〕 ton **적재―** a shipping ton **중량―** a deadweight ton 《DWT》 **총―** a gross ton

톤수 ―數 tonnage ¶ 이 배의 톤수는 3,000톤이다 This steamer is 3,000 tons burden. /This ship displaces 3,000 tons. (배수량)
― 증서 [조선] a tonnage certificate **등록 ―** registered tonnage **만재(滿載) 배수 ―** load displacement **배수〔순〕 ―** displacement〔net〕 tonnage **재화(載貨) 중량 ―** deadweight capacity〔tonnage〕 **적재 ―** capacity tonnage **총―** gross tonnage ; the total tonnage 《of a company's fleet》 (회사 전 선박의)

톨 a grain ; a nut ¶ 쌀 한 톨 a grain of rice

⁑**톱**¹ a saw ¶ 톱으로 켜다 cut with a saw ; saw 《of》
―날 a saw blade ; a saw tooth **―니** the teeth of a saw ; a saw tooth **―밥** sawdust **―손** the handle(s) of a saw **―양** a saw blade **―장이** a sawyer **―질** sawing

톱² the top ¶ 한 반의 톱 the top student of a class ; the head of the class // 톱뉴스로서 다루다 take 《an article》 as top news
―기사 the top article in a newspaper **―타자** 〖야구〗 a lead-off (man) ; the first batter

†**톱니바퀴** a saw-toothed〔serrated〕 wheel ; a toothed wheel ; a cogwheel ; a pitch〔gear〕 wheel ¶ 톱니바퀴의 이 a tooth ; a cog // 톱니바퀴 장치 a gear ; toothed gearing

톱상어 〖물고기〗 a saw-shark ; Pristiophorus japonicus (학명)

톱칼 a handsaw

톱클래스 ¶ 톱클래스의 leading ; foremost // 이 업종에서는 톱클래스인 상사의 하나 one of the leading〔top〕 firms in this line

톱톱하다 (be) thick ; heavy ; coarse

톱풀 〖식물〗 yarrow

톳 a bundle 《of layer》

톳나무 a large〔big〕 tree ; a gigantic 〔towering〕 tree

통¹ ① [배추 따위] the bulk ; the body ¶ 박 한 통 a gourd // 배추 두 통 two heads of cabbage // 배추 통이 크다 The cabbage has a large head.
② [광목 따위] a roll ¶ 광목 세 통 three rolls of cotton cloth // 필름 한 통 주십시오 Give me a roll of film. /I need a roll of film.

통² ① [사이에·때문에] consequence ; result ; influence (of something disturbing) ¶ 난리 통에 죽었다 He died in the ravage of war. // 그 통에 출발이 늦었다 The consequence was that my departure was delayed.
② [무리] a gang ; a group ; a party ; a junto ; cahoots ¶ 한 통이 되다 be in cahoots with ; be in collusion〔league〕 with ; collude with ; act in concert with

통³ [전혀] all ; the whole ; entirely ; utterly ; wholly ; in all ; collectively ¶ 요즈음 그는 통 오지 않는다 He doesn't come here at all these days. // 그는 동정심이라고는 통 없다 He has not a particle of sympathy.

⁑**통** 桶 a tub ; a kit ; a cask ; a barrel ; a pail ; a bucket ; a keg ; a can ; a canister ; a box ; a bowl ¶ 물 한 통 a pail of water // 성냥 한 통 a box of matches // 통 만드는 사람 a hooper ; a cooper // 통을 메우다 hoop a tube
―조림 canned food **물―** a water bucket **술―** a wine-barrel〔-cask〕

통 筒 a tube ; a pipe ; a gun barrel ; a tin ; a can ; caliber (역량) ¶ 소매통이 좁다 a sleeve is tight // 그는 통이 큰

E

사람이다 He is a man of big caliber.

통 統 [동리의] a neighborhood unit ; a small section of a city ; a *tong*
—장 the head of a *tong*

통 通 ① [사람] an authority ; an expert 《on》 ; a well-informed person ; a person in the know ¶ 그는 재정통이다 He is conversant with financial affairs. ② [서류의] a copy ; letters ; documents ¶ 서류 두 통 two copies of a document ; two documents // 편지 세 통 three letters
소식— informed sources

통가 Tonga (남태평양의 공화국)
—말 Tongan — 군도 the Tonga Islands ; the Friendly Islands — 사람 a Tongan — 왕국 the Kingdom of Tonga

통가리 a heap of grain put in a straw rain-shelter ; a rick〔stack〕 of corn

통가죽 ① [가죽] the whole skin 《of an animal》 ② [옷] a garment made so it can be laundered without the usual removal of seams ¶ 옷을 통가죽으로 빨다 wash〔launder〕 clothes whole ; launder clothes without removing the seams

통각 痛覺 sense〔sensation〕 of pain
—계(計) an algometer — 공포증 algophobia — 과민증 hyperalgesia — 탈실증(脫失症) analgesia

통각 洞角 a hollow horn

통각 統覺 『심리·철학』 apperception — 하다 apperceive

통감 統監 supervision ; superintendence command ; (Resident) General — 하다 supervise ; take supreme command 《of》

통감 痛感 — 하다 feel keenly〔acutely〕 ; fully realize ; be brought home to 《a person》 ¶ 상호 협조의 필요성을 통감하다 feel〔realize〕 keenly the necessity of mutual cooperation

통거리 all ; entirely ; completely ; wholly ¶ 땅을 통거리로 사다 buy up the whole lot of land // 그는 보석을 통거리로 팔았다 He sold jewels by the heap.

통겨주다 disclose ; reveal ; let out 《a secret》 ; tip off ; expose

통겨지다 ① [드러나다] get〔be〕 disclosed ; come to light ; be brought to light ; be exposed ; come out ¶ 비밀이 통겨지다 a secret is disclosed
② [어긋나다] come apart〔off〕 ; get dislocated ; be put out of joint ; be disjointed ; slip out ; miss (기회가) ¶ 뼈마디가 통겨지다 a joint becomes dislocated

통격 通格 『문법』 the common case

통격 痛擊 severe〔savage〕 attack ; a severe〔hard〕 blow — 하다 attack 《a person》 bitterly ; make a bitter〔heavy〕 attack 《on a person》 ; strike〔deal〕 a hard blow 《at》

통견 洞見 insight ; penetration ; divination ; acumen ; discernment — 하다 have insight into ; see through ; discern ; penetrate〔see〕 into

통경 痛徑 『수학』 the latus rectum (타원의)

통경제 痛經濟 an emmenagogue

통계 通計 ⇨ 통산(通算)

**통계 統計 statistics ; statistical data ; a numerical statement ; figures — 하다 take〔collect〕 statistics 《on》 ; gather statistics 《of》 ¶ 통계적〔의〕 statistical // 통계적〔상〕으로 statistically // 신뢰할 만한 자료에 의한 통계 statistics compiled from authentic sources // 통계에 의하면 statistics show〔teach us, disclose〕 《that》 ; according to statistics
—과〔관〕 a statistics section〔officer〕 —국 The Bureau of Statistics — 도표 a statistical graph ; a graph chart — 보고 returns ; a statistical report — 역학 statistical dynamics — 연감 a statistical yearbook — 조사〔분석, 자료〕 statistical research〔analysis, data〕 — 천문학 statistical astronomy —치(値) 『수』 statistics —표 a statistical table〔chart〕 ; (statistical) returns —학 (the science of) statistics ; statistology —학자 a statistician ; a statist ; a man of figures 범죄 — statistics of crimes 사망〔출산〕 — statistics of mortality〔birth〕 인구 — a census ; statistics of population ; vital statistics

통고 通告 notice ; notification ; announcement — 하다 notify 《a person》 of ; give notice of ; communicate 《a matter》 to 《a person》 ¶ 사전에 통고하다 give 《a person》 previous notice // 3일 전에 통고하다 give three days' notice // 통고없이 불참하다 absent oneself without notice // 통고를 내다 issue a notification // 그렇게 갑자기 통고하면 어떻게 이사합니까 How can we move on such short notice?
—서 a notice ; a written notice — 처분 noticed disposition

통고 痛苦 pain ; anguish ; a pang ; throes

통곡 痛哭 wailing ; lamentation ; keening ; loud weeping — 하다 weep loudly ; wail ; keen ; lament ; bemoan ; mourn〔weep〕 bitterly

†통과 通過 passage ; transit ; carriage ; passing — 하다 pass 《by, through, over, off》 ; get〔go〕 through ; carry 《a resolution》 ; be carried ; pass ¶ 세관을 통과하다 pass a custom house // 영국을 통과하다 pass through〔go by way of〕 England // 화물을 통과시키다 pass goods // 의안을 통과시키다 carry a bill ; pass a bill 《through》 ; put a measure through ; rush〔get〕 a bill through the House // 시내를 통과하다 clear

through a city // 시험을 무사히 통과하다 successfully pass an examination // 이럭저럭 시험에 통과하다 scrape through〔manage to pass〕 an examination // 그 의안은 만장 일치로 국회를 통과했다 The bill passed〔got through〕 the National Assembly by an unanimous vote. // 이 열차는 다음 역을 그대로 통과합니다 This train passes the next station without stopping. // 저기압 전선이 통과하기 때문에 내일은 반드시 날씨가 좋아질 것이다 A low-pressure front is passing through, so I'm sure it'll be nice tomorrow. // 이 견적은 회의에서 통과되지 않을 거라고 생각한다 I don't think this estimate will make it through conference.
—국 the territory of transit (이민의) —무역(품) transit trade (goods) —세 transit duty〔dues〕; tolls — 여객 a through〔transit〕 passenger〔traveler〕 —역 a nonstop station — 화물 [포장 표기] "Transit."; transit goods

통관 通款 secret communication with the enemy; treachery —하다 communicate secretly with the enemy

통관 通關 entry; clearance; customs clearance —하다 enter〔clear〕《a ship》; pass《through the customs inspection》 ¶ 통관 수속 때문에 for customs procedure // 통관 수속을 하다 clear; pass customs entry; go through customs formalities
—세 a clearance〔customs〕 fee — 수속 customs entry; customs formalities; clearance — 신고서 a bill of entry — 절차 customs formalities〔red-tape〕; customs entry; [출항의] clearance ¶ 통관 절차 때문에 for customs procedure // 통관 절차를 밟다 clear; pass customs entry; go through customs formalities —항 a port of entry — 허가서 a goods-clearance permit

통관 通觀 a general survey〔view〕 —하다 survey; take a general view〔survey〕《of》

통괄 統括 generalization; summarization; recapitulation; synthesis —하다 summarize; generalize; synthesize; epitomize

통교 通交 friendly relations —하다 enter into friendly relations《with》

통권 通卷 the consecutive number of volumes ¶ 제5권 제2호 (통권 10호) Vol. 5 No. 2 (Serial Number 10)

통규 通規 general〔common〕 principles; general rules〔provisions〕

통근 通勤 attending office; going to work; commuting; commutation —하다 attend〔go to〕 office; go to work; commute; go〔come〕 to work from outside; live out ¶ 그는 통근하고 있다 He comes to work from outside. // 그는 수원에서 통근하고 있다 He commutes from *Suwon*.
— 가능 구역 the commutable area —비 transit expenses to and from one's place of work —선(線) a commuter railroad — 수당 a commutation allowance — 시간 time to attend office; rush hour — 시설 commuting facilities — 열차 a commuters' train —자 a commuter; a living-out employee; a commutation passenger — 제도 living-out system — 정기 승차권 a commuter ticket — 지옥 a commuter-stampede

통금 ① [몰아친 값] the total price ② [도맷값] a wholesale price

통금 通禁 ⇨ 통행 금지
— 사이렌 a curfew siren — 시간 curfew hour — 위반 curfew violation ¶ 통금 위반자 a curfew violator — 해제 the removal〔lifting〕 of curfew

통기 通寄 notification ⇨ 통지

통기 通氣 ⇨ 통풍

통기공 通氣孔 a vent; a spilehole; an air pit (광산의)

통기다 loosen ⇨ 퉁기다

통김치 pickles made of whole cabbages

†통나무 a log; unsplit wood; a pole
— 다리 a log bridge

통념 通念 a common idea; a generally〔commonly〕 accepted idea ¶ 그것이 사회의 통념이다 The idea is universally accepted. /That is the idea generally accepted〔the received view〕.

통뇨 通尿 —하다 draw off the urine
—기(器) a catheter

통단 a large sheaf

통달 通達 mastery; conversance; expertise —하다 be conversant《with》; be well versed《in》; have a thorough knowledge《of》; be well posted《on》; be at home《in》 ¶ 고고학에 통달하다 be well versed in archeology // 영어에 통달하다 be versed〔well up〕 in English

통닭 the whole chicken

통대구 a dried whole codfish

통대자 通帶子 a double-woven band

통독 通讀 reading (a book) from beginning to end —하다 peruse; read through; read (a book) from cover to cover ¶ 그 책은 통독할 가치가 있다 The book is worth (while) reading through.

통돌다 [알려짐] be generally known〔informed, announced〕; be generally agreed upon; be widely circulated

통람 通覽 a general survey〔view〕; a perusal —하다 survey; look over; glance over; take a general〔cursory〕 view of; read through

통렬 痛烈 severity; fierceness; sharpness —하다 (be) severe; fierce;

E

sharp ; bitter ; scathing ; cutting ¶ 통렬히 severely ; fiercely ; sharply ; bitterly ; scathingly // 통렬히 비판하다 bitterly〔severely, scathingly〕 criticize // 그는 나를 통렬히 비난하였다 He called me down like anything.

통례 通例 a common〔an ordinary〕 practice ; the custom ; the rule ¶ 통례로 as an ordinary practice ; as a rule ; ordinarily ; customarily ; usually ; commonly ; generally ; on the whole // 통례의 usual ; customary ; common ; ordinary ; general // 그렇게 하는 것이 통례로 되어 있다 It is the custom to do so.

⁑**통로 通路** a passage ; a passageway ; a way ; a pathway ; a path ; a thoroughfare ; a roadway ; a road for passage ; an approach ; an aisle ; an avenue ¶ 통로측의 좌석 an aisle seat // 통로를 트다 clear a passage for 《a person》 // 통로에 있다〔서다〕 be〔stand〕 in the path of // 통로를 막다 obstruct〔block〕 the passage

통론 通論 an outline ; an introduction
문학 — an introduction to literature 법학 — an outline of law

통론 痛論 a heated discussion ; a vehement argument **—하다** argue〔discuss〕 vehemently〔earnestly〕 ; criticize severely

통리 通利 catharsis
—제 a cathartic

통마늘 a whole bulb of garlic

통말 桶— a bucket-shaped〔round〕 measure

통매 痛罵 condemnation ; denunciation ; an invective ; a diatribe ; harsh criticism **—하다** condemn ; denounce ; vituperate ; inveigh against ; criticize severely ; abuse grossly ; make a scathing denunciation 《of》

통메다 桶— ① hoop a tub ② be closely packed ; be crowded ; be packed like sardines ; be jammed

통메장이 桶— a hooper ; a cooper

통명 通名 a given name ; a popular〔common〕 name ; an alias

통모 通謀 —하다 conspire with ; work〔act〕 in concert〔collusion, league〕

통밀다 average ; regard all as the same ¶ 통밀어 사다 purchase en bloc // 손님은 통밀어 하루에 20명 꼴이다 The number of guests is 20 on an average a day.

통발[1] a weir made of willow or bamboo ; a fish trap

통발[2] 『식물』 a bladderwort

통방이 a rattrap

통법 通法 ① 『법』 general〔common〕 rules〔provisions〕 ② 『수학』 a principle〔rate〕 of conversion〔exchange〕 《of measures》

통변 通辯 interpretation ⇨ 통역

⁑**통보 通報** a report ; information ; a bulletin ; a dispatch **—하다** report ; inform 《a person of》 ; send information 《to》
기상 — a weather news ; a weather forecast 《미》

통보 通寶 currency ; coin
삼한(三韓)— a coin of the *Samhan* period

통부 通訃 information of one's death **—하다** send a letter announcing a death ; announce〔inform of〕 the death

통분 通分 『수학』 reduction of fractions to a common denominator **—하다** reduce 《fractions》 to a common denominator

통분 痛憤 great indignation **—하다** be greatly indignant

통사 通士 a man of the world

통사정하다 通事情— ① [사정함] disclose〔communicate〕 one's situation ; take 《a person》 into one's confidence ; tell frankly 《about》 ; confide to 《a person》
② [헤아려줌] sympathize with 《a person's sorrow》 ; get sympathetic understanding 《of》 ; enter into 《a person's》 feeling
③ [애원] beg 《for》 ; appeal 《to a person for mercy》 ; solicit earnestly

통산 通算 summing up ; the sum total **—하다** sum up ; add up ; aggregate ; total ; include ¶ 미결 일수를 통산하다 include the number of the days in the detention house // 통산하면 to sum up ; taken altogether // 통산해서 20년 the total period of 20 years // 통산하면 …이 되다 amount to ; add up to ; in all ; total to

통상 通常 ordinarily ; normally ; usually ; generally ; commonly ¶ 통상의 ordinary ; common ; usual ; regular
—복 everyday dress ; morning dress ; a business suit — 우편 ordinary mail ; ordinary post — 회원 an ordinary member

⁑**통상 通商** commerce ; trade ; commercial relations〔intercourse〕 **—하다** trade 《with a country》 ¶ 미국과 통상을 시작하다 open trade with America // 통상이 중지되어 있다 be under embargo
— 관계 trade relations —국 the Board of Trade — 금융 협정 a trade and commercial agreement —량 trade volume — 무역 trade and commerce — 사절단 a trade delegation — 위원 a trade commissioner — 장벽 trade barriers — 조약 a commercial treaty ; a trade agreement — 항해 조약 a treaty of commerce and navigation

통상 筒狀 cylinder-shape ¶ 통상의 cylindrical ; tubiform ; tubular

—화(花) a tubular flower
통상 대표부 通商代表部 the Trade Representation
통석 痛惜 lamentation ; deep regret ; great sorrow —하다 regret deeply ; lament ; be deeply grieved ¶ 통석해 마지 않다 It is much to be lamented. /I cannot but feel the deepest regret.
통설 通說 a common〔prevalent, widely held〕 view ; a popular〔prevailing〕 opinion ; an accepted theory
통성 洞性 ① 〖문법〗 the common gender ② ⇨ 통유(通有) (—성)
통성명 通姓名 exchanging names —하다 exchange names ; introduce themselves to each other
통소 洞簫 a bamboo flute ⇨ 통소
통속 [무리] a gang ; a cabal ; confederates ; [밀약] a secret agreement ; a cabal ¶ 음모를 꾸미는 통속 a gang of conspirators // 그는 그들과 한 통속이 되어 반란을 꾀했다 He attempted a rebellion with his fellow-conspirators. // 무슨 통속인지 짐작할 수 없다 I can't guess what secret agreement they've made.
통속 通俗 popularity ; conventionality ¶ 통속적인 common ; popular ; conventional // 통속적으로 popularly ; in popular style // 통속적인 기사 an unscientific account // 이 문제는 통속적으로 다루어지고 있다 The subject is treated in a popular vein. // 이 책은 통속적으로 재미있게 쓰여 있다 This book is written in an interesting, non-technical way. // 통속적으로 말하다 speak in plain language
— 문고 a popular〔a people's, an everyman's〕 library — 문학 a popular literature — 소설 a popular novel —어 popular language ; colloquialism — 음악 popular music —체 colloquial〔familiar〕 style —화 popularization ¶ 과학을 통속화하다 popularize science
*통솔 統率 command ; leadership ; control ; generalship —하다 command ; control ; lead ; assume the leadership 《of》 ¶ 통솔하에 있다 be under the command of // 통솔자가 되다 take the lead of ; stand at the head of ; be in command of 《an army》
—권 (right of) commandership ; leadership —력 (power of) command ; leadership —자 a leader ; a commander
통송곳 an awl ; a drill with a crescent blade
통수 統帥 supreme〔high〕 command ; leadership —하다 lead ; take command
—권 the prerogative of supreme command —자 a leader ; a supreme commander
*통신 通信 correspondence ; communication ; news ; intelligence ; information ; a dispatch ; a letter ; a report —하다 correspond with 《a person》 ; communicate 《a matter》 to 《a person》 ; keep up a correspondence 《with》 ; report 《for a paper》 ¶ 파리로부터의 통신에 의하면 according to news from Paris // 소식을 정부에 통신하다 communicate (the) information to the government // 신문에 통신하다 write〔report〕 for a newspaper // 양국간의 통신은 두절되었다 Communication between the countries has been interrupted. // 탐험대는 본국과 무전으로 통신을 계속했다 The expedition kept in touch〔communication〕 with home by wireless.
— 강의 a correspondence course — 강좌 instruction by correspondence ; a correspondence course ; lessons by mail ; special home study course ¶ 통신 강좌가 많은 상급 학교에 설치되어 있다 Correspondence courses are established in many higher learning institutions. —계(係) [회사의] a correspondence clerk — 공학 communication engineering — 교육 a correspondence course of education ; instruction by correspondence ; lessons by mail — 기관 an organ〔medium, channel〕 of communication — 기구〔기재〕 communications apparatus〔equipment, gear〕 — 기술 the technology of communications —대 a signal corps — 대학 a home study college ⇨ 방송 통신 대학 —란 the correspondence columns —망 a communications network ; communication facilities ; news gathering facilities —문 correspondence ; a communication ; a written message — 방해 communication jamming ; blanketing —병 a signal man 《미》 ; a signal corpsman ; a telegraphist — 보도 기관 vehicles of news —비 postage ; communication expense —사(士) a communications man ; a telegraph operator ; a wireless telegraph operator ; a radioman —사(社) a news agency — 사무 a post and telegraph service ; correspondence business — 사업 a communications service — 속도 〖전신〗 transmission speed ; telegraph〔signaling〕 speed — 시설 the communication facilities〔system, setup〕 —실 〖전신〗 an operating〔a communications〕 room —원 a correspondent ; a reporter — 위성 a communication satellite —탄 a communication bullet —통 a message tube ; a communication cylinder — 판매 mail-order business〔sales〕
통심정 通心情 rapport ; cordial understanding ; shared sympathy —하다 open one's heart ; have a cordial understanding 《with》 ; have a rapport ;

E

be in sympathy 《with》; confide in
통약 通約 reduction to a common measure; commensuration **—하다** reduce to a common measure; commensurate
—수 commensurate number
통양 痛痒 [아픔] pain and itch; [영향] concern; interest ¶ 조금도 통양을 느끼지 않다 be quite indifferent to; have no interest in; have no concern with; not to be affected
통어 統御 rule (통치); control (통제); management (관리) **—하다** rule; govern; control; manage; administrate; assume control of ¶ 통어하기 어려운 unmanageable; uncontrollable; ungovernable; unruly // 통어의 권한을 장악하다 have the whip hand of // 학생을 잘 통어하다 have the students well in hand
통언 痛言 cutting〔scathing〕 remarks; a bitter criticism
⁑**통역 通譯** interpreting; oral translation; interpretation; an interpreter (사람) **—하다** interpret; translate orally
—관 an (official) interpreter; a secretary interpreter **— 안내업** guide business ¶ 통역 안내업자 a guide (interpreter) **— 업무** interpretation service
동시 — (a) simultaneous interpretation
†**통용 通用** popular〔common〕 use; circulation; currency **—하다** be in common use; be current; pass; circulate; be good; be honored〔recognized〕; be available (차표 따위); hold good〔true〕 (규칙 따위) ¶ 이 화폐는 어디서나 통용됩니다 This coin passes freely〔goes〕 everywhere. // 이 차표는 며칠 동안 통용 되오 How long is this ticket available? // 영어는 세계 어디서나 통용된다 English is spoken all over the world. // 통용 기한은 당일 한 Good〔Valid〕 for the day of issue only.
— 기간 the valid period (of a ticket)
—문 a side gate; a gate for the general public **—어** a current word〔language〕; a popular usage; a word in current use **— 화폐** currency; a current coin
통운¹ 通運 a good luck; the better fortune; a stroke of good luck; a break **—하다** get lucky; come into luck; be in luck's way; fortune turns in one's favor; fortune smiles on one
대— a splendid stroke of luck
통운² 通運 transportation; forwarding; shipping; express **—하다** transport; forward; ship; carry; convey
— 기관 transportation facilities; means of transportation **— 회사** a transport company; an express company〔agency〕 《미》; a forwarding agent〔agency〕; shippers
통유 通有 commonness; a common trait **—하다** be common 《to》; be a common characteristic 《of》
—성 a common trait (성격); common properties of matter; a property common to all kinds of matter
통으로 wholly; all; collectively; in the lump; in the gross ¶ 통으로 삼키다 swallow 《a thing》 whole // 통으로 팔다 sell by the lump; sell wholesale
통음 痛飮 hard〔heavy〕 drinking; a carousal **—하다** imbibe〔drink〕 heavily; carouse; go on a binge
통인정 通人情 ⇨ 통사정
⁑**통일 統一** unity; unification; coordination; consolidation; uniformity; coherence; standardization (평준화); concentration **—하다** unify; coordinate; consolidate; standardize; concentrate ¶ 통일된 unified; uniform; systematic; homogeneous // 통일적인 unificative // 통일이 없다 lack unity; be without coordination // 나라를 통일하다 unify a nation; bring a country under a single authority // 철자법을 통일하다 standardize spelling rule // 가격을 통일하다 standardize the prices
—성 unity **— 전선** the united front; a common front **— 정부** a unified government **— 주체 국민회의** the National Conference for Unification **— 천하** unification〔domination〕 of the whole world **—체** a unified organization〔body〕 **남북 —** unification of North and South (Korea) **승공 —** unification through a victory over communism **정신 —** psychic〔mental〕 concentration **평화 —** peaceful unification **국토 —원** the Board of National Unification
통일 천하 統一天下 unification (of a country); domination of the whole world **—하다** unify a country; bring the whole country under one's rule; domineer over the land
통장 通帳 [은행의] a passbook; a bankbook; [외상 거래의] a chit-book ¶ 통장에 치부하다 enter into a chit-book
예금 — a bankbook; a deposit passbook **저금 —** a savings passbook
통장 統長 the head of a *tong*, subdivision of a city
통장수 桶— ① a tub〔pail〕 seller; a cooper ② a peddler of pickled seafood carried in a tub
통장이 桶— a hooper; a cooper
통장작 —長斫 log firewood; unsplit firewood
통전 通電 [전류를 통함] applying〔sending〕 an electric current 《to》; [알리는 전보] circular telegram〔cable〕 **—하다** [전류를] apply〔send〕 an electric current; turn on an electric current; [전보를] issue〔send〕 a circular telegram; circularize

E

통절 痛切 **—하다** (be) poignant ; keen ; acute ; severe ¶ 통절히 keenly ; severely ; acutely ; earnestly ; poignantly // 통절히 느끼다 feel keenly〔vividly〕; be brought home《to a person》// 결함을 통절히 느끼다 feel the shortcomings severely // 그 일은 통절히 느끼고 있습니다 It has been brought home to me. // 그 필요는 통절히 느껴졌다 The necessity was keenly felt.

통점 痛點 a pain spot

통정 通情 ① having frank talk ⇨ 통사정 ② rapport ⇨ 통심정 ③ adultery ⇨ 간통 ④ the way of the world (세상 인정)

통젖 the handles of a tub ; the bail of a pail

통제 統制 control ; regulation ; management **—하다** control ; exercise control over ; regulate ; hold under control ; govern ¶ 통제가 없는 unsystematic ; disorganized // 통제를 강화하다 tighten the control of // 그것은 정부가 통제하고 있다 It is under government control.

— 가격 controlled prices **— 경제** controlled〔managed, planned〕economy ; controlled economics **— 기관** a control agency〔organ, instrument〕; an organ for control **— 무역** controlled trade **— 폐지** decontrol **—품** controlled goods〔articles〕 **— 화폐** managed currency **국가 —(주의)** statism

통제부 統制府 a naval yard ; a naval station ; an admiralty port

*__통조림 桶—__ canned goods ; tinned provisions **—하다** can ; tin

— 공업 the packing〔canning《미》, tinning《영》〕industry **— 공장** a packing house ; a cannery ; a packing plant〔factory〕 **— 식품** canned provision〔goods〕 **—업자** a canner〔packer〕《미》; a tinner《영》 **— 제조법** canning **고기 —** canned〔tinned〕meat **쇠고기 —** tinned〔canned〕beef ; [조미한] corned beef

통줄 [연줄] the string let out by turning the kite-reel endways

통줄 주다 관용 let the string out fast by turning the kite-reel endways

통줄 筒— [쓰는] a round〔cylindrical〕rasp

통증 痛症 (an) ache ; a pain ; a pang ¶ (심한) 통증을 느끼다 feel a (sharp) pain // 요즈음 팔을 들 때마다 어깨에 통증이 온다 Lately my shoulders ache whenever I raise my arms. // 날이 차가워지면 허리에 통증이 온다 When it gets cold, my lower back aches.

†**통지 通知** notice ; notification ; advice (상업상의) ; communication ; information ; report **—하다** notify《a person》of ; give《a person》notice ; inform ; let《a person》know ; communicate《news to a person》; advise ¶ 추후 통지가 있을 때까지 till further notice // 미리 통지하다 give《a person》previous notice // 통지를 받다 receive〔have〕notice《of》// 사건을 본국 정부에 통지하다 communicate the matter to one's government // 서울에 도착하면 곧 통지해 주시오 Please let me know when you have arrived in *Seoul*.

—서 a notice ; a notification in writing ; 〖상업〗 an advice note ; a letter of advice **— 예금** deposit at call〔notice〕 **—(전)표** an advice slip **계약 만기〔지불 거절, 집회, 어음 부도〕 —** a notice of expiration of contract〔dishonor, meeting, protest〕 **해약〔이전〕 —** a notice of cancellation〔removal〕

통짜 the whole mass〔lump〕《of》; the whole (lot) ¶ 통짜로 ⇨ 통째

통짜다 ① [맞추다] put〔fit, piece〕together ; frame ; assemble ② [무리 짓다] form a gang〔group〕; pledge oneself to become a member of a gang ¶ 통짜고 음모하다 form a gang to plot // 서로 통짜다 form a group ; make secret pact

통짜로 all ; wholly ⇨ 통째

통째 all ; wholly ¶ 통째로 삼키다 swallow《a thing》whole ; gulp down // 닭을 통째로 먹다 eat up the whole chicken

통찰 洞察 discernment ; penetration ; insight **—하다** discern ; penetrate into ; see through ; fathom《one's heart》

—력 an insight ; penetration ; vision ¶ 통찰력 있는 discerning ; penetrative ; penetrating ; perceptive ; perspicacious // …의 통찰력이 있다 have an insight into… // 날카로운 통찰력을 지닌 사람 a man of keen insight // 그는 인간성에 대한 통찰력이 없었다 He had no insight into human nature. // 그는 놀랄 만한 통찰력을 갖고 있다 He can see through a brick wall.

통책 痛責 ⇨ 엄책(嚴責)

통처 通處 a sore〔tender〕spot〔point〕; a painful place in the body

통천하 通天下 all the earth ; (throughout) the world ; the whole world **—하다** prevail〔pervade〕all over the world ; reach every part of the world

통철 洞徹 mastery ⇨ 통달

통철 通徹 penetration ; permeation ; interpenetration **—하다** penetrate ; permeate ; interpenetrate

통첩 通牒 a note ; a notification ; a circular ; an instruction **—하다** notify《a person》of ; give notice to ; circularize ; instruct ; communicate ¶ 통첩을 발하다 send〔issue〕a notification

동문 — [외교상] a circular note **외교 —** a diplomatic note **최후 —** an ultimatum ¶ 최후 통첩을 보내다 send an

E

ultimatum
통촉 洞燭 seeing ; (sympathetic) understanding ; judgment ; discernment ── 하다 see ; realize ; understand ; judge ; discern
*통치 統治 rule ; reign ; government ── 하다 rule over 《a country, a people》 ; govern 《a country, a people》 ; hold sway over ; administer ¶ 국가의 통치 the administration of the state // 국가를 통치하다 rule〔reign〕 (over) a country ; govern a country ; exercise sovereign power // 영국의 통치하에 있다 be under British rule
─권 the supreme〔sovereign〕 power ; sovereignty ; majesty ¶ 통치권을 행사하다 exercise sovereign power ─ 기관 government organs〔machinery〕 ─자 a ruler ; the sovereign ─ 제도 a ruling system ─ 행위 an act of state 신탁 ─ trusteeship 위임 ─ mandatory rule〔administration〕
통치 通治 ── 하다 cure all kinds of diseases ; be (medically) effective on a broad spectrum
만병 ─약 a cure-all ; a panacea
통치마 a seamless one-piece skirt
통칙 通則 general principles ; general rules〔provisions〕
통칭 通稱 a popular name ; an alias ; a common designation
통쾌 痛快 a great〔keen〕 pleasure ; a thrill ── 하다 (be) most〔awfully〕 pleasant ; extremely delightful ; incisive ; very gratifying ; merciless ¶ 통쾌하게 to one's great satisfaction ; incisively ; trenchantly // 통쾌한 남자 a jolly fellow ; a man of spirits // 통쾌한 연설 a stunning speech // 통쾌한 논의 an incisive argument // 통쾌하게 느끼다 be highly delighted // 그의 약점을 통쾌하게 폭로했다 His weakness has been mercilessly disclosed. // 그의 이야기를 듣고 있으면 통쾌하다 It does my heart good to hear him speak.
통킹 Tonkin ; Tongking
─만 the gulf of Tonkin
통타 痛打 a crushing〔stinging, telling, punishing〕 blow ; a shrewd knock ; a crusher ; a crasher ; a stinger ── 하다 give a crushing blow 《to, on》 ¶ 통타 당하다 get a crushing blow 《from a person》
*통탄 痛歎 bitter lamentation ; deep regret ; bitter grief ── 하다 lament bitterly ; regret deeply ; grieve ; deplore ¶ 통탄할 deplorable ; lamentable // 정계에 의혹 사건이 빈발하는 것은 통탄할 일이다 It is deplorable〔much to be regretted〕 that scandals should occur so frequently in political circles.
통탕 with stamps ; with repeated poundings ; bang-bang ¶ 통탕거리다 keep stamping〔pounding, banging〕 ; go bang // 통탕거리며 마루 위를 돌아다니다 be scampering around on the floor // 총소리가 통탕거리다 a gun is〔guns are〕 banging away
통터지다 burst out ; explode ; pour out ¶ 울음이 통터지다 burst into tears ; burst out crying
통통 with a stamp ; poundingly ; resoundingly ; rub-a-dub ¶ 통통거리다 pound ; resound ; stamp // 마루를 통통 구르다 pound on the floor // 마루가 통통거리다 a floor resounds // 통통거리며 계단을 오르다 stamp upstairs
통통배 a motorboat ; a motor-powered boat
통통하다 (be) plump ; chubby ; full ; portly ; corpulent ¶ 통통한 볼 chubby cheeks // 통통하게 살찐 여자 a plump woman // 통통한 젖가슴 a full breast // 눈이 통통 붓다 one's eyes are all swollen 〔puffed up〕
통틀다 take 《it》 all and put 《it》 together (in one lump)
통틀어 in all ; all told ; altogether ; in total ; in the aggregate ¶ 통틀어 열 ten in all ; ten all told // 책은 통틀어 열 권입니다 There are ten books altogether. // 통틀어 얼맙니까 How much is it altogether? // What do you charge for them all? // 모인 돈은 통틀어 100만원에 이를 것이다 The money will total 〔aggregate, amount to〕 one million *won*.
통팥 whole〔unsplit〕 red beans
통폐 通弊 a common abuse〔evil〕 ¶ 이것들은 현대 사회의 통폐이다 These are evils common to all the classes in society.
*통풍 通風 ventilation ; airing ── 하다 let air in ; circulate air ¶ 통풍이 잘 되다 be well ventilated
─공(孔) a draft〔ventilating〕 hole ; a ventilation opening〔hole, square (사각의)〕 ; a funnel ; a vent ─관 an air pipe〔line〕 ; a vent pipe ; a ventilator ─구 a ventilating opening ; a fresh air inlet (여객기의 좌석 위의) ─기 a ventilator ; an aerator ; a fanner ─ 장치 the ventilation arrangement〔device, apparatus〕 ; a register (스토브·난로 따위) ─창 a ventilating window ─통 a ventilator ; an air duct
통풍 痛風 gout ; arthritis ¶ 통풍에 걸리다 be afflicted with gout
†통하다 通─ ① [길이] run ; be open for traffic ; lead to ¶ 이 문은 마당으로 통한다 This door leads〔opens〕 to the garden. // 그 길은 숲 속으로 통하고 있다 The road runs through the forest. // 이 읍에서 그 마을까지 철도가 통하고 있다 A railway runs from this town to that village. /A railway connects this town

E

with that village. // 모든 길은 로마로 통한다 All roads lead to Rome.
② [전류가] flow ; be charged ; be on ¶ 전기가 통한 쇠줄 a live wire ; an electrified wire // 이 선에는 전류가 통하고 있다 This line is charged with electric current.
③ [전화기] go through ; be put through ; 《a line》 be on ; be on the line ; 《the phone》 be working ¶ 전화가 통하지 않다 the line〔telephone service〕 is interrupted ; a call fails to go 〔get〕 through // 두 마을 사이에는 전화가 통하고 있다 Telephone service〔communication〕 is established between the two towns.
④ [혈액·공기가] go〔pass〕 through ; be circulated ¶ 공기가 잘 통하다 have good ventilation // 피가 잘 안 통하다 have a poor circulation of the blood // 피가 체내를 통하다 Blood goes through the body.
⑤ [언어가] be understood ; be spoken ; be the medium of communication ¶ 영어가 통하다 be able to speak English ; make oneself understood in English // 서로 말이 통하지 않다 be unable to communicate with each other because of the language barrier
⑥ [의사가] enjoy understanding ; understand (each other) ; be congenial 《to, with》 ¶ 서로 의사가 통하다 understand each other's sentiments // 서로 기맥을 통하다 have a tacit understanding with each other // 민정이 정부에 통하다 the conditions of the people are appreciated by the government // 자기의 의사를 통하다 make one's desire known
⑦ [뜻이] make sense ¶ 이 글은 뜻이 통하지 않는다 This sentence doesn't make sense.
⑧ [통달하다] be well versed 《in》 ; be an expert 《in, on》 ; be a master 《of》 ; be familiar 《with》 ; be well informed 《on》 ; be well up 《on》 ; be conversant 《with》 ; be well acquainted 《with》 ; be at home 《in》 ¶ 천문에 통하다 know a lot about astronomy // 불어에 통하다 be proficient in French ; know one's French // 내막에 통하다 be well up on the inside story // 사정에 통한 사람 a well-informed person // 그는 5개 국어에 통하고 있다 He has a good command of five languages.
⑨ [인정받다] pass 《for, as》 ; be known 《as》 ; go by the name of ¶ A란 이름으로 통하다 pass under the name of A ; go by the name of A // 권위자로 통하다 be acknowledged as an authority // 그는 부자로 통했다 He passed for a rich man.
⑩ [통용하다] pass ; circulate ; hold good ; be good ; be valid ¶ 규칙이 통하다 A regulation holds (good). // 그 증명서는 이미 통하지 않는다 The certification is no longer valid.
⑪ [용납하다] pass ; get by ; be admitted ; serve its purpose ¶ 네 의견은 통하지 않는다 Your opinion is not acceptable. // 그런 구실은 통하지 않는다 That sort of excuse won't go down〔get by〕. /Such excuses will not do any good.
⑫ [통과·경유] go〔pass〕 through ; get through ; via ¶ 마당을 통해서 through the garden // 라디오를 통해서 via radio // 사람을 통해서 through 《a person》 // 1년을 통하여 through the year ; all the year round // 전국을 통하여 throughout〔all over〕 the country
⑬ [내통하다] communicate secretly with ; betray ¶ 적에게 비밀을 통하다 betray a secret to the enemy ; let the enemy in on a secret // 누구와 통하고 있다 be in secret communication with somebody
⑭ [정을] become intimate with ; share intimacy with ; form a liaison with ; misconduct oneself with ; commit adultery with ; have illicit intercourse with ¶ 그 여자는 어떤 정치가와 정을 통했다 She had immoral relations with a statesman.

통학 通學 attending school **—하다** go to〔attend〕 school ¶ 도보로 통학하다 attend school on foot // 그는 소년 시절에 1년간 통학했을 뿐이었다 He had only a year's schooling in his boyhood.
— 구역 a school district ; [학생 모집 구역] a recruitment〔catchment〕 area ; an attendance unit **—생** a day scholar ; a day student ; a day boy ; an extern **—차** a school bus〔car, train〕

통한 痛恨 bitter grief〔sorrow, woe〕 ; deep regret ; mortification **—하다** grieve bitterly ; regret deeply ¶ 통한지사 a matter of great regret // …은 실로 통한할 일이다 It is to be greatly regretted 《that》

통할 統轄 supervision ; control ; superintendence **—하다** supervise ; control ; superintend ; preside over
— 구역 the area under the direct control **—자** one in charge ; one who assumes control 《of》

*__통합 統合__ unity ; unification ; synthesis ; combination ; coordination **—하다** unify ; synthesize ; unite ; combine ; coordinate ¶ 야당 통합 unification of parties out of power

통항 通航 navigation ; passage ; sailing ; communication by sea **—하다** navigate ; sail ; communicate by sea ¶ 이 강은 어디까지 배가 통항할 수 있습니까 How far is this river navigable ?

E

†**통행 通行** passing ; passage ; transit ; traffic **—하다** pass ; go (through, along) ¶ 통행할 수 있는 passable // 통행이 금지된 impassable // 통행을 금하다 close a road ; close the street to traffic // 통행을 방해하다 obstruct traffic ; obstruct the passage // 통행이 막혀 있다 Traffic is blocked. /Traffic is held〔tied〕 up.
—권 right-of-way〔passing〕; wayleave ; passage **—권(券)** a pass ; [적국·피점령지의] a safe-conduct (pass) ; a safeguard **— 금지** suspension of traffic ; [게시] Blocked. /Closed to traffic. /No thoroughfare. ¶ 통행 금지 구역 a "no passing" zone // 통행 금지 시간 curfew hour **—료** a toll ; passage money ¶ 통행료 징수소 a tollhouse ; a toll station **—세** transit duty ; a travel tax **—인** a passer-by ; a pedestrian (보행자) ; foot passenger ; a wayfarer ; a passer **—증** a pass ; a safeconduct **— 허가** wayleave **일방 —** [게시] One way only. **좌측 —** [게시] Keep to the left.

통혈 通穴 a ventilation opening ; a vent ; a funnel ; an air-shaft (광산의) ; an air-pit (터널의) **—하다** open ventilation

통호 通好 friendship ; friendly relationship〔intercourse〕 **—하다** contract intimacy《with》; hold intercourse《with》; enter into friendly relations《with》

통혼 通婚 marriage ; intermarriage **—하다**marry (with) ; intermarry《with》

통화 通貨 currency ; the medium of circulation ; current coins
—량 the amount of currency in circulation **— 수축** deflation〔contraction〕 of currency **— 안정** stabilization of currency **— 위조** counterfeiting of currency **— 유출〔유입〕** the efflux〔influx〕 of currency **— 저락** depreciation in currency **— 정책** fiscal〔currency〕 policy ; a monetary policy **— 제도** a currency〔monetary〕 system **—주의** currency principle **— 통제** currency control(s) **— 팽창** inflation ¶ 통화 팽창 정책 inflationism **감각〔비상, 보조, 자동, 십진〕 —** depreciated〔emergency, fractional, automatic, decimal〕 currency **금속〔교환, 혼합, 강제〕 —** metallic〔exchange, mixed, forced〕 currency

통화 通話 conversation by telephone ; a telephone call **—하다** talk over the telephone《with》; speak by telephone ¶ 통화 중에 while talking over the telephone // 통화 중입니다 The line is busy. // 통화가 될 겁니다 You'll get through. // 900-1234에 전화를 걸려고 하는데 통화중 신호만 들려요 I'm trying to reach 900-1234, but all I get is a busy signal.
—관 a speaking tube ; a voice pipe〔tube〕 **—구** the mouthpiece of a telephone ; the telephone **—도수계** a message-〔service-〕register ; a phonemeter **— 도수 제도** the message-rate 〔call〕 system **—량** telephone traffic **—로** a channel **—료** the call charge ; the fee〔charge〕 for a telephone call **—수** the number of telephone calls **—실** a booth

통환 通患 [걱정] a universal apprehension ; a common misgiving ; [폐해] a universal trouble ; a common evil

통회 痛悔 [기독교] contrition **—하다** be contrite

통효 通曉 mastery ; conversance ; thorough knowledge **—하다** be conversant《with》; be versed《in》; be posted《on》; be at home《in》; be well acquainted《with》 ¶ 불문학에 통효하다 be well read in French literature // 중국 역사에 통효하다 be conversant with Chinese history // 세계 사정에 통효하다 keep in touch with the whole world // 그는 그 일에 통효했다 He has the business at his finger tips.

톺다 ① [샅샅이] search everywhere for ; leave no stone unturned ② [삼을] soften and spread hemp tufts

⁑**퇴각 退却** ① [후퇴] retreat ; withdrawal ; retirement ; falling back **—하다** retreat ; beat〔make〕 a retreat ; withdraw ; retire ; fall back ; abandon ; give up ; evacuate ¶ 퇴각시키다 withdraw ; retire《troops》; order《troops》 to retire ; back // 총퇴각하고 있다 be in full retreat // 평양으로 퇴각하다 retreat 〔fall back〕 on *Pyŏngyang* // 퇴각을 엄호하다 cover a retreating army
② [거절] rejection ; refusal to accept **—하다** reject ; refuse to accept
—군 a retreating army ; an army in retreat **—로** a route of retreat ; a withdrawal route **— 명령** an order〔a signal〕 to retreat ; the retire (나팔에 의한) **—선** a line of retreat **총—** a full 〔general〕 retreat ¶ 총퇴각하다 be in full retreat

⁑**퇴거 退去** leaving ; quitting ; withdrawal ; evacuation ; going away ; exodus **—하다** leave ; withdraw ; evacuate ; go away ; retire ; depart ; quit ¶ 동양인의 아프리카 퇴거 an Oriental exodus from Africa // 퇴거를 명하다 order《a person》 out of a place ; deport (추방) // 퇴거시키다 expel《a person》 from
— 명령 an expulsion order ; a deportation order ; an order for departure ¶ 퇴거 명령을 받다 be ordered to quit《a place》 **본국 —** expatriation ; [추방] deportation

퇴경 退京 leaving the capital〔*Seoul*〕 **—하다** leave the capital〔*Seoul*〕

퇴고 堆敲 polish〔improvement〕 (of writing) ; elaboration (of writing) ; choice of diction **—하다** polish ; improve ¶ 퇴고에 퇴고를 거듭하다 work hard to polish out 《the composition》 // 퇴고의 여지가 있다 admit of further polish
퇴골 腿骨 the thigh bone ; a leg bone
퇴관 退官 retirement from office〔the government service〕 ; resignation of one's post〔commission (군인)〕 **—하다** retire from office〔the government service〕 ; resign
퇴교 退校 leaving school ; expulsion〔dismissal〕 from school ; withdrawal from school **—하다** leave〔give up〕 school ¶ 퇴교 처분을 받다 be dismissed〔expelled〕 from the school
퇴군 退軍 retreat ⇨ 퇴각
퇴근 退勤 leaving one's office〔one's desk, one's work〕 ; coming〔going〕 home from work **—하다** leave the office ; finish one's work (for the day) and leave ; get off and go home from work
— 시간 the closing hour〔time〕 ; the close of the office hours
퇴기 退妓 a retired *kisaeng* ; an ex-*kisaeng*
퇴기다 ① flip ; snap ; fillip ¶ 옷의 먼지를 퇴기다 flip a little dust from one's coat
② repel ; reject ; turn down ; splash ¶ 기름 종이가 물방울을 퇴기다 oil paper repels water
③ spring ; let off ⇨ 튀기다
퇴기둥 退— pillars of a verandah
퇴김 jerking (a kite string) ¶ 연줄을 퇴김 주다 give a jerk on the kite string
퇴김 주다 관용 jerk (a kite string)
퇴내다 退— be cloyed 《with》 ; be satiated 《with》 ; be glutted 《with》 ; be surfeited 《with》 ; be fed up 《with》 《미》 ; be up to one's ears 《in it》
퇴락 頹落 dilapidation ; ruin ; decay ; downfall **—하다** dilapidate ; go to ruin ; fall into decay ; decay ; decline
퇴로 退路 a path of retreat ; a withdrawal route ¶ 퇴로를 차단하다 cut off〔intercept〕 the retreat
퇴맞다 ⇨ 퇴박맞다
퇴물 退物 ① [남은 음식] a reception table after it has been removed ; leftover food ; leavings
② [써서 낡은] a hand-me-down ; a used thing ; a retired person ¶ 기생 퇴물 a retired *kisaeng* // 아버지의 퇴물을 입었다 He wore a hand-me-down from his father.
③ [거절당한] a reject ; a thing rejected〔refused, declined, sent back〕
퇴물림 退— a hand-me-down ⇨ 퇴물
퇴박맞다 get rejected ; be refused〔repelled, rebuffed〕 ; be sent back ; be turned down ¶ 그의 면회 신청은 퇴박맞았다 His request for an interview was refused.
퇴박하다 reject ; decline ; refuse ; turn down
***퇴보 退步** retrogression ; retrocession ; retrogradation ; a setback ; a backward step ; a step backward ; degeneration ; deterioration **—하다** go〔fall〕 backward ; suffer a relapse〔setback〕 ; retrograde ; retrocede ; take a backward step ; slide back〔backslide〕 ; be set back ; degenerate ; deteriorate ¶ 퇴보적인 retrograde ; retrogressive ; backward // 문명의 퇴보 the retrogression of civilization ; backward step in civilization // 퇴보한 국민 a degenerate people // 모든 일이 퇴보하고 있다 Things are going backward. // 병으로 쉬었더니 학력이 퇴보했다 My absence from school owing to illness has set me back in my studies.
퇴비 堆肥 a compost ; barnyard〔farmyard〕 manure
퇴사 退社 ① [퇴직] retirement from a company **—하다** retire〔withdraw〕 from a company ; leave a company
② [퇴근] leaving the office (for the day) **—하다** go home from〔leave〕 the office
퇴산 退散 dispersal ; dismissal ; discharge ; breaking up **—하다** disperse ; break up ; be dismissed〔discharged〕 ; be routed ; flee ; leave ¶ 퇴산시키다 disperse ; rout ; put 《a person》 to flight ; break // 적을 퇴산시키다 put the enemy to flight // 퇴산을 명하다 order 《the crowd》 away〔to disperse〕
퇴색 退色, 褪色 discoloration ; fading ; decolorization **—하다** get discolored ; discolor ; fade ; lose color ; 《color》 run ¶ 퇴색한 faded // 퇴색하지 않는 색 a fast〔a lasting, an unfading〕 color
—법 a bleach(ing)-out process
퇴석 退席 leaving one's seat **—하다** leave one's seat ; retire from ; withdraw (from one's presence)
퇴석 堆石 ① a pile of stones ② 〖지리〗 moraine ; an apron
퇴세 頹勢 a deteriorating situation ; an unfavorable situation ; a decline ; the downward tendency ; a decay ¶ 퇴세를 만회하다 mend〔improve, save〕 a deteriorating situation ; retrieve one's fortunes ; check one's decline ; restore the falling fortunes ; turn the tide of war
퇴속 退俗 —하다 retire from the Buddhist priesthood ; return to the laity
퇴속 頹俗 corrupt customs〔manners〕 ; degenerate morals ; decadence
퇴송 退送 sending back **—하다** send

back ; reject ; decline〔refuse〕 to accept
퇴수 退守 standing on the defensive **—하다** stand〔be, act, keep〕 on the defensive ; maintain existing conditions
퇴역 退役 retirement from service ; a (military) discharge **—하다** retire from service ; be discharged from military service ; resign one's commission
— 군인 an exservice man ; a veteran 《미》 **— 연금** a retiring pension **— 연령** the age limit **— 장교** a retired officer ; an (army) officer on the retired list **—함(艦)** a warship out of commission
퇴염 退染 ① [탈색] bleaching ② ⇨ 토렴
퇴영 retrogression ; conservatism **—하다** retrograde ; retrogress ¶ 퇴영적인 conservative ; retrogressive
— 정책 a conservative〔retrogressive〕 policy **—주의** conservatism
퇴운 退運 ⇨ 쇠운
퇴원 退院 leaving the hospital ; discharge from a hospital **—하다** leave the hospital ; be discharged〔released〕 from the hospital ¶ 퇴원이 허가되다 be given permission to leave the hospital // 방금 퇴원했다 be just out of hospital ; have just come out of hospital // 그는 곧 퇴원할 것입니다 He will soon be out of hospital.
퇴위 退位 abdication **—하다** abdicate (the throne) ¶ 퇴위시키다 depose ; dethrone
퇴일보하다(退一步—) take a step backward ; shrink back ; flinch
퇴임 退任 retirement from office ; vacation (of an office) **—하다** retire from office ; resign (from) one's post ; vacate an office ¶ 대사직에서 퇴임하다 relinquish one's appointment as Ambassador
퇴장 退場 leaving ; going away ; withdrawal **—하다** exit ; make one's exit ; walk out 《of the chamber》 ; leave 《the ground》 ; go away ; withdraw ¶ 퇴장을 명하다 order 《a person》 out of 《a room》 ; order to retire from 《a room》 // 아이들을 퇴장시키다 send the children out of the room // 배우가 퇴장한다 The actor makes his exit.
총— a general walk-out
퇴장 退藏 hoard(ing) **—하다** hoard 《goods》
— 물자 hoarded goods
퇴적 堆積 accumulation ; a heap ; a pile **—하다** accumulate ; be piled ; be〔get〕 heaped (up) ¶ 화물의 퇴적 the heaps of freight ; the accumulation of freights // 기차 불통 때문에 정거장에는 화물이 퇴적해 있다 Owing to the interruption of railway traffic, there are mountains of freight piled up at the station. // 책상에는 보고서가 퇴적해 있었다 I found the table heaped with bulletins.
—물 a deposit **—암** sedimentary rock ; [성층암] stratified rock **하안 —층** a river drift
퇴정 退廷 leaving the court **—하다** leave the court〔the courtroom〕 ; leave the royal court
퇴조 退潮 the ebb〔low〕 tide ; the ebbing〔falling〕 tide ; reflux ¶ 퇴조 시(時)에 at low water // 퇴조를 보이다 be on the ebb
—기(期) a period of ebb
퇴주 退酒 sacrificial wine emptied from the cup (in order to refill it with fresh wine)
—기(器) [그릇] a vessel for emptied wine
***퇴직 退職** retirement ; resignation **—하다** retire〔withdraw〕 from office ; go out of office ; go on the retired list ; resign an office ¶ 퇴직시키다 retire ; discharge ; dismiss 《a person》 // 퇴직을 명하다 place 《a person》 on the retired list ; retire 《a person》 // 연금〔일시금〕을 받고 퇴직하다 retire on pension〔a single sum〕 // 연금을 주어 퇴직시키다 pension off 《a person》 // 그는 무능하다는 이유로 강제 퇴직당했다 He was compulsorily retired as incompetent.
— 관리 a retired official **—금** retirement grants〔allowance, pay, emoluments, benefits〕 ; [정리의] a discharge allowance **— 수당** a retiring〔retirement, separation〕 allowance ; retirement〔dismissal, severance〕 pay ; [노후자의] a superannuation **— 연금** a retirement annuity〔pension〕 **— 연령** the retirement age ; [연한] the age limit **—자** a retired employee **— 적립금** a reserve for retirement allowance ; the accumulated fund for retirement
퇴진 退陣 decampment ; disengagement ; withdrawal **—하다** decamp ; break camp ; withdraw troop 《from》 ; disengage oneself〔withdraw〕 《from》 ; break encampment ¶ 야당은 내각의 퇴진을 요구했다 The Opposition requested the Cabinet to resign en bloc. // 그는 이미 제일선에서 퇴진해 있다 He is now relieved of a responsible position.
퇴짜 退— turning down ; rejection ; refusal ; rebuff ; a reject ; a thing refused ¶ 퇴짜 놓다 refuse ; reject ; turn down ; turn away ; send back // 퇴짜 맞다 get rejected ; meet with refusal ; meet a rebuff ; be turned down ; be sent back // 그녀는 결국 두 사람 다 퇴짜를 놓았다 She ended up dumping both of them.
퇴청 退廳 leaving a government office (for the day) **—하다** leave the (government) office for the day ¶ 퇴청 시

간 closing time ; the closing hour (of a government office) // 퇴청 시간은 몇 시입니까 What time does the office close? // 퇴청 시간은 5시입니다 The office closes at 5.

퇴출 退出 ① [관청·회사 따위에서] leaving ; [예배 후 목사·성가대의] recession ② [높은 사람 앞에서] withdrawal ━하다 leave 《the presence of》; retire

퇴치 退治 [정벌] conquest ; subjugation ; [박멸] wiping out ; elimination ; clean-up ; extermination ━하다 conquer ; subdue ; subjugate ; wipe out ; root out ; clean up ; eliminate ; exterminate ; destroy ¶ 모기의 퇴치 mosquito control // 쥐를 퇴치하다 rid 《a house》 of rats // 괴물을 퇴치하다 slay [kill] a monster // 해적을 퇴치하다 clear the sea of pirates // 산적을 퇴치하다 subjugate bandits // 말라리아를 퇴치하다 eliminate [stamp out] malaria
문맹 ─ a crusade against illiteracy

퇴침 退枕 a wooden pillow

퇴폐 頹廢 corruption ; degeneration ; demoralization ; decay ; decline ; decadence ; deterioration ━하다 get corrupted ; be demoralized ; degenerate ; decay ; decline ¶ 퇴폐한 degenerated ; corrupted ; decayed ; tumble-down ; ruined // 도의의 퇴폐 moral decadence ; the corruption of morals // 도의의 퇴폐가 오늘날과 같이 심한 적이 없었다 Never have public morals been more deplorably corrupt.
─기 a period of decadence ─주의 decadence ─파 the decadent school ─풍조 decadent (and degenerating) trend ¶ 퇴폐 풍조 퇴치 운동 antidecadence drive

퇴하다 退─ ① [무르다] return a thing and get a refund ; cancel a purchase ② [거절] reject ; turn down ; turn away ; send back ; refuse to accept [receive] ¶ 선물을 퇴하다 refuse to accept [turn down] a present // 뇌물을 퇴하다 reject the bribe // 혼담을 퇴하다 turn down a proposal of marriage ③ [더한 것을 덜다] take away [off] the excess

퇴학 退學 withdrawal from the school ; leaving school ━하다 leave [give up, quit] school [college] ; withdraw from school ; drop out ¶ 퇴학시키다 [부형이] withdraw 《one's son》 from school ; take 《one's son》 out of school ; [학교가] expel 《a student》 from school ; have 《a student》 leave school // 퇴학을 당하다 be expelled from school ; be dismissed [sent down] from school // 중도에 퇴학하다 leave school half-way // 가정 형편으로 퇴학하다 leave school for some family reasons [owing to some family circumstances]
─계[신고] a notice of withdrawal [quitting school, leaving school] ─생 a dropout ; an expelled student ─처분 expulsion of a student from a school

퇴행 退行 degradation ; [정신 분석] regression ━하다 degrade ; regress ¶ 퇴행성의 병 a degenerative disease

퇴혼 退婚 a breach of promise of marriage ━하다 decline a proposal of marriage ; break off an engagement

퇴화 退化 degeneration ; devolution ; involution ; degradation ; obsolescence ; retrogression ; atrophy ━하다 degenerate ; degrade ; retrograde ; atrophy ; be atrophied ¶ 퇴화한 degraded ; degenerated // 퇴화시키다 degrade ; degenerate // 사용하지 않는 기관은 퇴화한다 An unused organ will atrophy.
─ 기관 a rudiment ; a degenerated [rudimentary] organ ─ 동물 a degenerate (animal) ─ 작용 the process of degeneration

퇴회 退會 withdrawal (from a party, association) ; withdrawal from membership ; secession ━하다 withdraw 《from》; drop out ; secede ; resign one's membership
─ 신고[계] a notice of withdrawal ─자 a seceder ; a withdrawing [seceding] member

툇도리 退─ 『건축』 the beams of a verandah

툇마루 the floor of a Korean verandah

툇보 退─ the crossbeam of the floor of a verandah

투 套 ① [법식] a (set) form ; a style ¶ 편지 투 the forms of letter writing ; how to write letters ; letter writing ② [버릇] a way ; a habitual way ; a habit ; a manner ¶ 상투 a stereotyped way ; conventionality ; a platitude // 말투 one's way of talking // 그는 말투가 이상하다 He has a quaint way of speaking.

투강 投江 throwing 《a thing》 into the river ; [투신] drowning oneself ━하다 throw 《a thing》 into a river ; throw oneself into the river ; drown oneself

투견 鬪犬 a dogfight ; a fighting dog

투계 鬪鷄 a fighting cock ; a gamecock ; a game fowl ; cockfighting ; a cockfight ━하다 have [stage] a cockfight
─ 시합 a cock [cockfighting] match ─장 a cockpit ; a pit

투고 投稿 a contribution ━하다 contribute 《to》; write 《for》 ¶ 투고 환영 All contributions are welcome. // 그는 자주 이 잡지에 투고한다 He is a frequent contributor to this magazine.
─ 규정 contribution rules [regulations] ─란 the readers' column ─자 a contributor

투과 透過 『전기』 transmission ━하다

transmit ; [유리 따위를] permeate
—광 transmitted light —성 permeability
광선 — 〖의학〗 transillumination

투광기 投光器 a light projector ; a footlight ; a floodlight

투광 조명 投光照明 floodlighting ¶ 투광 조명을 받다 be floodlit

투구 a helmet ; a headpiece ¶ 투구를 쓰다 wear a helmet
—끈 a helmet cord

투구 投球 throwing a ball ; pitching —하다 throw a ball ; pitch
—기 [타격 연습용] a pitching machine ; a mechanical pitcher — 모션 a windup — 반칙 〖크리켓〗 no-ball —법 pitching —판 [연습용] a pitching board

투구벌레 〖곤충〗 a kind of beetle

투구풍뎅이 〖곤충〗 a beetle ; Allomyrina dichotomus (학명)

투그리다 snarl ready to fight

투기 妬忌 ⇨ 질투

*__투기 投機__ (a) speculation ; a venture ; an adventure ; spec 《속》 ; [증권] stockjobbery ; stockjobbing —하다 speculate 《on》 ; gamble ; engage〔dabble〕 in speculation ¶ 투기적인 speculative // 투기에 손을 대다 dabble in speculation ; go in for speculation // 값이 오를〔내릴〕 줄 알고 투기하다 speculate for a rise〔fall〕 // 투기적으로 하다 risk // 투기가 들어맞다 make a hit (in a speculation) // 투기에 손을 대어 큰 손해를 입다 lose heavily in speculation // 투기적으로 사다 buy on speculation
— 매입 a speculative buying —사 a speculator ; a stockjobber ; an adventurer — 사업 a speculative enterprise 〔venture〕 ; a speculative business — 시장 a speculative market —심 speculative spirit —열 a craze〔mania〕 for speculation ; speculative enthusiasm 〔craze〕 —주 a speculative stock

투기 投棄 abandonment —하다 abandon ; give up ; throw〔cast〕 away

투기 鬪技 a contest ; a match ; a competition
—자 a competitor ; a contestant —장 an arena ; a ring ; a ground ; a field

투깔스럽다 (be) coarse ; crude

투덕투덕하다 (be) plump ; plump-cheeked

*__투덜거리다__ grumble ; complain ; nag (잔소리를 하다) ; mutter〔mumble〕 《something》 to oneself ; murmur 《with discontent》 ¶ 투덜거리는 사람 a grumbler // 대우에 대해 투덜거리다 complain of one's treatment // 그는 무엇인가 혼자 투덜거리며 가 버렸다 He went away muttering something to himself.

투레질 《a suckling child》 blowing from the mouth —하다 blow from the mouth

투망 投網 a casting net ; a cast net ¶ 투망을 던지다 cast a net ; throw a castnet

투매 投賣 a bargain sale ; a sacrifice sale ; a less-than-cost bargain ; a slaughter sale ; dumping —하다 dump ; sell 《goods》 at a sacrifice 〔loss〕 ; sacrifice 《goods》
— 상품 distress merchandise 고급품 — High quality goods at lowest prices. (게시) 출혈 — a distress 〔slaughter〕 sale

*__투명 透明__ transparency ; pellucidity ; limpidness ; clearness ; clarity —하다 (be) transparent ; pellucid ; limpid ; clear ; diaphanous ; clear ¶ 투명하지 않다 be opaque ; be milky // 무색 투명한 colorless and transparent // 반 투명의 semitransparent ; translucent ; translucid // 투명하게 되다 become transparent ; clarify
—도 transparency ; the degree of clearness — 석고 selenite —지 tracing paper —질 〖생물〗 hyaloplasm —체 a transparent body —화 a transparency

투묘 投錨 anchoring ; mooring ; anchorage —하다 anchor ; moor ; cast〔drop, let fall〕 anchor
—등 an anchor light —지 an anchorage (ground)

투미하다 (be) dull ; stupid ; stolid ; silly ; heavy〔thick〕-headed ; dumb 《미》

투밀이 〖건축〗 rounding off the edges of lattice strips —하다 round off the edges of (lattice strips)

투박하다 (be) crude ; coarse ; uncouth ; ungainly ; unshapely ; dull and stout ¶ 투박한 그릇 crudely made dishes ; crockery // 투박한 옷감 thick coarse fabric ; muslin ; gunny ; gunnysack cloth

투베르쿨린 tuberculin ¶ 투베르쿨린 검사를 한 tuberculin-tested 《T. T.》 // 투베르쿨린 검사를 받다 be tuberculin-tested // 나의 투베르쿨린 반응은 양성〔음성〕이었다 My tuberculin reaction was positive〔negative〕.
— 반응 a tuberculin reaction — 반응 검사 a tuberculin test — 요법 tuberculin treatment — 양성〔음성〕 — 반응 a positive〔negative〕 reaction of a tuberculin test

투병 鬪病 a fight〔struggle〕 against a disease ¶ 투병 생활 5년 five years' struggle against a disease ; life under medical treatment for five years

*__투사 投射__ 〖수학〗 projection ; projecting ; 〖물리〗 incidence —하다 project 《on》
—각 an angle of incidence〔projection〕 —광 transmitted light —면 a plane of incidence —물 a projectile —법 〖심리〗 projective technique —선 an incident

ray

투사 鬪士 a fighter ; a combatant ; a champion ¶ 자유의 투사 a fighter for freedom // 진리의 투사 a champion of truth // 그는 투사형의 인간이다 He is a man of the athletic type.

—형(型) 〖심리〗 the athletic (type) 독립 — a leader of national independence movement 혁명 — a champion of revolution

투사 透寫 tracing —하다 trace (out) 《a writing, drawing》

—지 tracing paper —포(布) tracing cloth〔linen〕

투사 透射 ¶ 화학선 투사 성능이 있는 diactinic

—광 transmitted light〔rays〕 화학선 — transmitting of actinic rays

투상스럽다 (be) uncouth ⇨ 툽상스럽다

투서 投書 ① an anonymous note 〔notice〕 ; an anonymous communication〔letter〕 —하다 send 《a note》 anonymously ② 〔투고〕 contribution ; correspondence —하다 contribute 《an article to》 ; write a letter to ; send a contribution 《to a magazine, newspaper》

—제 suggestive system —함 a suggestion box ; a complaint box — 환영 Contributions are cordially invited.

***투석 投石** stone-throwing〔-hurling〕 —하다 throw〔cast, hurl〕 a stone 《at》

—기(器) a catapult

-투성이 covered〔smeared〕 with ; full of ; filled with ¶ 땀투성이의 full of sweat // 옷이 진흙투성이다 Your clothes are bespattered (all over) with mud. // 이 책은 먼지투성이다 This book is covered with dust. // 그는 결점투성이다 He is all fault〔a mass of fault〕.

****투수 投手** 〔야구의〕 a pitcher ; a hurler ; a twirler ; a moundsman ; 〔크리켓의〕 a bowler ¶ 투수를 교체하다 change 〔shift〕 a pitcher // 그는 투수로서 잘 싸웠다 He did well on the box.

—력 pitching strength 《of a team》 —전 a pitching〔mound〕 duel ; a pitchers' battle —진 the pitching staff 《of a team》 —판 the mound ; a pitcher's plate〔box〕 ; the rubber 《미·속》 구원 — a relief pitcher 선발 — the starting pitcher 승리〔패전〕 — a winning〔losing〕 pitcher 완투 — a thoroughgoing pitcher 왼손잡이 — a left-handed pitcher ; a left-hander ; a southpaw (pitcher) ; a lefty 《미·구》 ; a portsider 《미·구》

투수성 透水性 〖화학〗 water permeability

투숙 投宿 staying〔stopping〕 at 《a hotel》 —하다 stay〔stop〕 at 《a hotel》 ; put up at 《a hotel》 ; lodge 《in》 ; stop for the night 《at》 ; register〔check in〕 at a hotel

—자 a guest (registered at a hotel) ; a lodger

투승 投繩 〔올가미 밧줄〕 a lasso ; a lariat 《미》 ; 〔올가미 던지기〕 lassoing ; roping

투시 透視 ① 〔뚫어 봄〕 seeing through ② 〔알아차림〕 clairvoyance ; second sight —하다 see through ; divine ; sense ; see

—경 a fluoroscope —도 a perspective drawing〔view〕 ; an opened-up view 《of a factory》 showing the interior —력 〔천리안의〕 clairvoyant〔psychic〕 power ; 〔광학 기계의〕 penetration —자 a clairvoyant ; a clairvoyante (여자) — 촬영 fluoroscopy —화 a perspective drawing — 화법 perspective 형광 — 검사 〔x선의〕 fluoroscopy

투신 投身 ① 〔자살〕 suicide by drowning ; death by drowning —하다 drown oneself 《in a rivers》 ; commit suicide by drowning ; throw〔precipitate〕 oneself 《into the water》 ⇨ 투신자살

② 〔종사〕 —하다 be engaged 《in》 ; take part 《in》 ; involve oneself 《with》 ; attend to ; carry on ¶ 그는 정계에 투신하고 있다 He is engaged in the politics.

투신자살 投身自殺 a death leap 《from》 ; committing suicide by jumping (on the track) in front of a〔an onrushing〕 train ; suicide by drowning —하다 〔물에〕 drown oneself 《in a river》 ; commit suicide by drowning ; 〔건물 따위에서〕 leap〔plunge〕 to one's death ; kill oneself〔commit suicide〕 by plunging 《from》 ¶ 그녀는 다리에서 투신 자살했다 She took her own life by leaping from a bridge (into the river). // 그 남자는 달리는 열차에 투신 자살했다 The man rushed on to the track〔jumped in front of a train〕 and was run over.

투실투실 chubby ⇨ 토실토실

투심 妬心 jealousy ; envy

투안 偸安 snatching a moment of ease —하다 snatch a moment of ease ; try to gain ease

투약 投藥 medication ; (medical) prescription ; dosage ; administration (of medicine) —하다 prescribe medicine ; give〔administer, compound〕 a medicine ; medicate ¶ 환자에게 투약하다 prescribe for a patient ; dose a patient

투어 套語 a hackneyed expression 〔phrase〕 ; a cliche ; an old-cliche

투어리스트 a tourist

— 걸 a girl tourist guide

투여 投與 ⇨ 투약(投藥)

투열 透熱 〖물리〗 diathermancy

—계 a diathermometer —성(性) diathermancy — 요법 diathermic treat-

ment ; diathermy —체 a diathermanous substance
*투영 投影 ① [그림자] a cast shadow —하다 reflect ; cast a reflection ; throw an image on
② 〖수학〗 projection —하다 project
—도 a projection chart〔drawing〕; a raised plane ; 〖기하〗 a projected figure —면 a projected plane ; a plane〔surface〕 of projection —법 〖심리〗 projective technique —심 the center of projection — 화법 the method of projections
*투옥 投獄 imprisonment ; confinement —하다 cast 《a person》 into prison ; put 《a person》 in jail〔prison〕; imprison ; commit 《a person》 to prison ; throw 《a person》 into prison ¶ 투옥당하다 be put in prison〔jail〕; be sent〔taken〕 to jail ; be consigned to prison
투우 鬪牛 a fighting bull ; a bullfight —하다 fight a bull ; have a bullfight —사 a bullfighter ; a matador ; a toreador (마상의) —장 a bullring
투원반 投圓盤 the discus throw ; discus throwing
— 선수 a discus thrower
투입 投入 throwing〔putting〕 in ; input ; investment ; 〖심리〗 introjection —하다 throw〔put〕 《a thing》 in ; invest ; project 《a thing》 into ¶ 우편물 투입구 a letter drop
—물〔량〕 an input — 병력 commitment — 산출표 an input-output table — 자본 investment 대량 — a massive commitment 《of manpower》
*투자 投資 investment —하다 invest 《in》; put〔sink〕 《money》 in ; lay out 《one's money》 ¶ 확실한 투자 a sound investment // 광산에 투자하다 invest in a mine // 다행히 투자를 잘 해서 돈을 벌었다 Fortunately it proved a good investment.
— 계획 an investment plan ; an investment program — 시장 an investment market — 신탁 investment trust —액 an amount invested — 은행 an investment bank —인〔가〕 an investor ; capitalist (자본가) —주(株) investment stocks — 증권 an investment bond — 회사 an investment company 공공 — public investment 민간 — private investment 자본 — capital investment 해외 — investment in foreign country 한국 — 개발 공사 the Korea Investment Development Corporation
투자율 透磁率 (magnetic) permeability
투장 鬪將 ① [용장] a heroic〔brave〕 combatant
② [싸우는 지도자] a brave leader ; a champion 《of a principle》
*투쟁 鬪爭 fighting ; a fight ; a combat ; a struggle ; a conflict ; strife ; a campaign —하다 fight ; combat ; struggle ; strive 《with》
— 방침 struggle policy — 본부 the strikers' headquarters — 선언 the declaration of a struggle〔strike〕; a strike declaration ; a struggle manifesto —심 a combative spirit — 위원회 a struggle committee — 의식 strike〔struggle〕 consciousness — 자금 a strike〔struggle〕 fund — 전술 struggle tactics — 태세 a struggle setup〔formula〕 계급 — class strife〔struggle, war〕 권력 — power struggle ; struggle for power 무력 — an armed struggle 본능 — fighting〔competitive〕 instinct
투적거리다 ⇨ 토닥거리다
투전 投錢 a kind of money-throwing 〔coin-tossing〕 game ⇨ 돈치기
투전 鬪牋 Korean playing cards ; a game of cards ; gambling card —하다 play cards ; gamble with cards
—꾼 a card player ; a gambler
투정 grumbling ; growling —하다 grumble 《for》; growl ; fret ; be cross ; be peevish ¶ 어린애들은 이가 날 때 투정을 한다 Babies are fretful when cutting their teeth
밥— grumbling over〔at〕 one's food 잠— growling when one wakes up
투조 透彫 open work 《in sculpture》
투지 鬪志 a fighting〔combative, militant〕 spirit ; fight ¶ 투지에 불타다 be full of fight〔vitality〕; burn with combativeness ; be highly combative // 투지가 없다 have cold feet // 그는 젊었을 때는 투지가 만만했다 He was so〔pretty〕 much of a fighter in his younger days.
투창 投槍 javelin throw(ing) ; a dart —하다 throw the javelin
— 선수 a javelin thrower
†투척 投擲 throwing ; a throw —하다 throw ¶ 투척 경기 throwing event ; weight throwing ; shot-putting
투철 透徹 penetration ; thoroughness ; transparency ; clearness —하다 (be) penetrating ; lucid ; clear ; pure ; thorough ; thoroughgoing ; coherent ¶ 투철한 이론 intelligible theory // 투철한 두뇌 clear brains
투탄 投彈 dropping a bomb —하다 drop a bomb ; drop an explosive
투포환 投砲丸 the shotput —하다 put the shot
— 선수 a shot-putter
†투표 投票 vote ; voting ; suffrage ; poll ; ballot ; a vote ; a ballot ; a ticket —하다 vote 《for, against》; cast a vote ; record one's vote ; cast a ballot ¶ 다수의 투표를 얻어 by a majority of votes // 출석 회원의 3분의 2의 투표에 의해 by a vote of two-thirds of the

members present // 압도적 다수의 투표를 얻어 당선되다 be returned〔elected〕 by a majority of votes // 투표에 붙이다 put it to the vote // 투표로 결정하다 decide〔settle〕 by vote // 투표로 부결하다 vote down // 투표하러 가다 go to the poll // 투표를 매수하다 buy votes // A씨에게 투표하다 vote for〔in favor of〕 Mr. A // A씨에게 반대 투표하다 vote against〔in opposition to〕 Mr. A // 투표의 상황은 어떤가 How stands the poll? // 투표의 결과 찬성 80 반대 22였다 The vote stood at 80 ayes and 22 noes.

— 검사 scrutiny —구 a voting district; a polling area —권 voting right; the (right to) vote; the right of voting〔casting the ballot〕; suffrage; a voice; the voting power ¶ 투표권이 없는 사람 a voteless person — 기권자 a nonvoter — 마감 closing of the poll〔vote〕 — 방법 a method of voting; a voting method —소〔장〕 a polling place〔station〕; a polling〔voting〕 booth; the polls 《미》 —수 number of votes; vote; poll — 연령 voting age — 용지 ballot paper; a ballot; a voting card〔slip, paper〕; a (ballot) ticket — 율 a turnout (of voters) —일 a voting day — 입회인〔참관인〕 a scrutineer; a voting witness; a referee of voting — 자 a voter —함 a ballot box 거수〔발성, 기립〕 — vote by a show of hands〔acclamation, rising〕 결선 — a decisive〔final〕 ballot; a showdown vote 결정 — a casting vote 국민 — a plebiscite; a referendum 기명 — an open vote 단기〔연기〕 — a vote with single〔plural〕 entry 대리 — voting by proxy 무기명 — a secret vote; an unsigned ballot 무효 — a spoilt vote 미인 — a beauty competition ¶ 미인 투표 당선자 a beauty prize-winner 복식〔단식〕 — plural〔single〕 vote 부재 — absentee voting; voting by mail 불신임 — a vote of no confidence; a vote of censure 신임 — a vote of confidence 일반 — a popular vote 재— revoting 지명 — a roll-call vote 직접 — 《put it to》 a direct (popular) vote; 《elected by》 direct vote of the people 부정 —자 a ballot stuffer

투피스 a two-piece dress〔suit〕

*__투하 投下__ throwing down; dropping —하다 throw down; drop; airdrop ¶ 역에 폭탄을 투하하다 drop〔release〕 bombs upon a station

— 자본 invested capital; an investment; 〚경제〛 investment〔venture〕 capital —탄 a dropped bomb — 폭탄 an aerial bomb

투하 投荷 jettison; jetsam —하다 jettison

투함 投函 mailing; posting —하다 mail 《a letter》; put 《a letter》 in a (mail) box; post 《a letter》; drop 《a letter》 in to the letter box

투항 投降 surrender; capitulation (투항 조건) —하다 surrender; capitulate; give up〔lay down〕 one's arms

—자 a surrenderer — 조약 a treaty of surrender〔capitulation〕

투해머 投— 〚체육〛 a throw of the hammer

투혼 鬪魂 a fighting〔combative〕 spirit

투화 透化 vitrification —하다 vitrify

*__툭__ ① [소리] with a bang〔thud, pop〕; with a pat〔rap, snap〕 ⇨ 탁, 톡[1] ② [모양] protrudingly ⇨ 톡[2]

툭박지다 (be) coarse〔crude, rough〕 and simple

툭수리 차다 be reduced to beggary; be brought to begging

툭탁 with a tap〔rap〕; rat-tat —하다 beat each other; exchange blow after blow; fight each other; give a rat-tat ¶ 툭탁거리기 시작하다 come to blow; take to one's fists

툭툭 with bangs〔pats, snaps〕; protrudingly ⇨ 탁, 톡

툭툭하다 ① [국물이] (be) thick; rich; heavy

② [천이] (be) thick; close; close-woven

툭하면 at the slightest provocation; at the drop of a hat; without any reason; always; be apt to; be ready to ¶ 툭하면 싸우다 pick a fight at the slightest provocation〔at the drop of a hat〕 // 툭하면 치다 be ready to punch; punch 《a person》 at the slightest provocation // 그녀는 툭하면 운다 She is apt〔liable〕 to cry.

툰드라 tundra

— 지대 a tundra area

툴툴거리다 complain; grumble; growl; mutter ¶ 봉급이 적다고 툴툴거리다 complain about the salary; complain that one is not paid well // 그는 아버지가 자전거를 사 주지 않는다고 툴툴거렸다 He grumbled at his father for not buying him a bicycle.

툼벙 with a plump ⇨ 텀벙

툽상스럽다 (be) clumsy; uncouth; vulgar; boorish; crude; coarse ¶ 툽상스러운 구두 heavy〔unshapely〕 shoes // 툽상스러운 그릇 crudely made dishes; crockery // 툽상스럽게 대답하다 answer bluntly〔brusquely〕

툽툽하다 (be) thick; rich

퉁 ① [저질의 놋쇠] brass of inferior quality

② [소리] with a boom; booming ¶ 북을 퉁 울리다 boom a drum; beat a drum // 대포를 퉁 쏘다 fire a gun with a boom; boom a gun

퉁가리 〚물고기〛 a kind of freshwater cat-

fish
퉁겨지다 come apart ⇨ 퉁겨지다
퉁구스 a Tungus 《*pl.* ~(es)》; a Tunguz 《*pl.* ~(es)》
—어 Tungus ; Tunguz ; Tunguse
퉁기다 ① [받친 것을] spring ; snap ; slip ¶ 기둥 받침을 퉁기다 slip a pillar stay ② [뼈를] put out of joint ; dislocate ③ [기회를] miss〔lose, fling away〕 chance ; let a chance slip
퉁노구 a small pot made of cheap brass
퉁딴 an ex-convict police agent
퉁맞다 ⇨ 퉁바리맞다
퉁명스럽다 (be) blunt ; curt ; brusque ; bluff ; gruff ; abrupt ; unaffable ; impolite ; rude ; impudent ¶ 퉁명스럽게 bluntly ; curtly ; brusquely // 퉁명스러운 사람 a blunt person // 퉁명스러운 대답 a blunt〔brusque〕 answer // 퉁명스럽게 말하다 talk bluntly ; be blunt of speech ; speak stiffly
퉁바리 a woman's brass rice-bowl
퉁바리맞다 get rudely rebuffed ; get spurned point-blank
퉁방울 brass bell
퉁방울이 a pop-eyed〔goggle-eyed〕 person ; a popeye ¶ 퉁방울이 금붕어 a pop-eyed goldfish
퉁부처 a brass statue of Buddha
퉁소 a bamboo flute〔clarinet〕 ⇨ 퉁소
퉁어리적다 (be) senseless ; reckless (in behavior) ; indiscreet ; impudent ; thoughtless ; rash
퉁탕 beating ; pounding ; pattering ; stamping ; with a bang
퉁탕거리다 keep beating〔pounding, pattering〕 ¶ 어린애가 퉁탕거리며 마루 위를 돌아다닌다 A child is scampering around on the floor. // 총소리가 퉁탕거린다 A gun is〔Guns are〕 banging away.
퉁탕퉁탕 ① [구르는 소리] beating〔pounding, pattering〕 repeatedly ② [총소리] banging repeatedly〔confusedly〕
퉁퉁 with a stamp ; stamping ⇨ 통통
퉁퉁걸음 a stamp ; walking with pounding〔quick〕 steps
퉁퉁하다 (be) plump ⇨ 통통하다
퉤 spitting ¶ 퉤퉤 spit-spit !
튀각 fried kelp ; flake of kelp oiled and toasted
튀기 ① [혼혈·잡종] a half-breed ; a half-blood ; a hybrid ; a cross ; a crossbreed ¶ 한국인과 일본인과의 튀기 a person of mixed Korean and Japanese parentage ; a person of Korean and Japanese extraction // 백인과 흑인과의 튀기 a mulatto // 백인과 황색인과의 튀기 a Eurasian
② a hybrid between a male donkey and a cow
튀기다¹ ① flip ; fillip ; snap ; reject ; jerk ; repulse
② send 《a thing》 flying ; send 《a thing》 off ; splash ; spatter ; dabble ¶ 손가락으로 물을 튀기다 splash the water with one's finger
③ start ; scare away ¶ 꿩을 튀기다 start a pheasant // 토끼를 굴에서 튀기다 start a hare from its burrow
†**튀기다²** fry ; pop ¶ 쌀을 튀기다 pop rice // 생선을 기름에 튀기다 fry fish in oil
⁑**튀김** jerking ; [기름에] batter-fried food ; fritters
튀니스 Tunis (튀니지의 수도)
튀니지 Tunisia ¶ 튀니지의 Tunisian
— 사람 a Tunisian
†**튀다** ① [오르다] spring ; bound ; jump ; hop ; rebound ; leap ; bounce ; crack ; crackle ; sputter ; spatter ; spark ; splash ; splatter ; get spattered ; be splashed ¶ 공이 튀다 a ball bounces // 나무가 말라 튀다 a piece of board dries up and cracks // 불꽃이 튀다 sparks fly up // 숯불이 튀다 the burning charcoal sputters // 침이 튀다 saliva spatters // 흙물이 튀다 muddy water splashes
② [달아나다] fly (away) ; run away ; take to flight ; flee ¶ 사슴이 튀다 a deer starts // 도둑이 튀다 a robber takes to flight // 튀는 적 fleeing enemy // 그는 옥을 뚫고 튀었다 He broke jail and ran away.
튀밥 popped rice
†**튀어나다** bound ; bounce off ; rebound ; resile ; recoil ; spring back ¶ 공이 잘 튀어난다 The rubber ball bounds well.
튀어나오다 ① [숨은 것 따위가] jump〔leap, bounce〕 out ; spring out ; [뛰쳐나오다] rush〔burst〕 out ; [말 따위가] rush ¶ 말이 입 밖으로 튀어나왔다 Words rose to〔poured from〕 his lips. /He poured out words in a steady flow.
② [돌출하다] project ; protrude ; beetle ; shoot out ¶ 그의 눈은 튀어나와 있다 His eyes are starting out of their sockets.
튀하다 scald 《an animal or a bird to remove the hair or the feather》
튜너 [라디오·텔레비전의] a tuner
튜바 〖음악〗 a tuba
⁑**튜브** a tube ; [자전거·자동차의] an inner tube ¶ 튜브에 든 물감 tube colors // 튜브에 든 치약 a tube of tooth paste // 튜브에서 그림 물감을 짜내다 squeeze paint from a tube
튜턴 Teuton ¶ 튜튼의 Teutonic
— 인종 the Teutonic race〔peoples〕
***튤립** 〖식물〗 a tulip
트다¹ ① [싹이] sprout ; bud out ; spring〔come〕 up ; peep from the ground ¶ 싹이 트다 come into bud ; bud out
② [피부가] crack ; open up ; be〔get〕

chapped ¶ 손이 트다 one's hands get chapped ; have a chapped hand ③ [먼동이] 《the east》 break ; break open ; dawn ; grow light ; turn gray ¶ 동이 트다 it dawns ; the day breaks ; the eastern sky turns gray // 먼동이 터 온다 The eastern sky is gradually turning gray.

트다[2] [통하다] open ; clear 《the way》 ; make way 《for a person》 ; begin ; initiate ¶ 길을 트다 build〔open〕 a road ; make way 《for a person》 // 젊은이에게 길을 트다 give younger people a chance ; open the way of promotion for one's juniors // 성공에의 길을 트다 pave the way for success // 외상을 트다 open a charge account // 거래를 트다 enter into a business relation 《with》 ; open dealings // 은행과 거래를 트다 open an account with a bank

트더지다 be unsewn ; be rent ; be ripped ¶ 봉투가 트더지다 an envelope gets ripped // 옷이 트더지다 one's clothes are unsewn

트라이 [럭비] a try ¶ 트라이를 올리다 score a try ; make a successful try // 트라이로 득점하다 score on a try

트라이앵글 〖악기〗 a triangle

트라코마, 트라홈 〖의학〗 trachoma ¶ 트라코마에 걸린 trachomatous // 트라코마에 걸리다 suffer from〔be afflicted with〕 trachoma
급성 — acute trachoma

트라팔가르 Trafalgar

트래지코미디 〖연극〗 a tragicomedy

트래피스트 〖카톨릭〗 a Trappist
— **수도원** a Trappist monastery〔convent (여자의)〕

트랙 a track ¶ 트랙과 필드 track and field // 트랙 경기의 주자(走者) a track runner // 트랙 경기의 인기 선수 a track 〔cinder〕 star
— **경기** track events〔athletics〕 ; running events — **경기 대회** a track meet 〔meeting〕

*__트랙터__ a tractor ; a horse 《속》
경작용 — a farm〔an agricultural〕 tractor ; an agrimotor **대형** — a heavy-duty tractor **무한 궤도** — a caterpillar tractor

트랜스 〖전기〗 a transformer

트랜스발 Transvaal (남아프리카의 지방)

*__트랜지스터__ 〖물리〗 a transistor ¶ 트랜지스터화(化)하다 transistorize
— **라디오〔텔레비전〕** a transistor radio〔television〕 **광—** a phototransistor

트랩 [배의] a gangway (ladder) ; [비행기의] a ramp ; traps ¶ 트랩을 오르다 〔내리다〕 go up〔down〕 the gangway ladder〔the ramp〕

트랭퀼라이저 〖약〗 a tranquilizer

트러블 trouble ; scandal ; hard run 《속》 ¶ 가정의 트러블 a family trouble // 트러블을 일으키다 make〔stir up〕 trouble ; raise hell 《속》 // …와의 사이에 트러블을 일으키다 get into trouble with 《the police》 // 트러블을 일으키는 사람 a trouble-maker

트러스 〖건축·토목〗 a truss
—**교** a truss bridge

트러스트 〖경제〗 a (business) trust
— **금지법** an antitrust law

*__트럭__ a (motor) truck 《미》 ; an autotruck 《미》 ; a (motor-) lorry 《영》 ¶ 장거리를 운행하는 트럭 운전사 a long-distance truck driver // 트럭 3대의 짐 three truckloads〔lorryloads 《영》〕 of goods // 트럭으로 나르다 carry in a truck ; haul by truck〔by lorry truck 《영》〕 《goods》 // 이 가도는 언제나 트럭의 왕래가 빈번하다 This highway is always busy with trucks.
— **운송** trucking ; truck transport — **운송업계** the truck industry — **운송업자** a trucker — **운전사** a truck driver **군용** — a military truck ; a camion **무개(無蓋)** **소형** — a pickup (truck) (집배용(集配用))

⁑**트럼펫** 〖악기〗 a trumpet
— **연주자** a trumpeter

트럼프 ¶ 한 벌의 트럼프 a pack of cards ; a deck of cards 《미》 // 트럼프 사기꾼 a card sharper // 트럼프의 으뜸패 a trump (card) // 트럼프를 하는 사람 a cardplayer // (재수 보기 위해) 트럼프의 패를 떼어보다 lay cards《on the table》 // 트럼프의 패를 돌리다〔떼어내다〕 deal 〔cut〕 the cards // 트럼프로 도박을 하다 gamble at cards // 트럼프로 점을 치다 tell one's fortune from cards // 트럼프를 치다 play cards // 트럼프를 치고있다 be at cards

⁑**트렁크** ① [가방] a (cabin) trunk ; [손에 드는] a portmanteau 《*pl.* ~s, -x》 ; a suitcase 《미》 ; a valise ¶ 옷이 가득 든 트렁크 a trunkful of dress ② [자동차 뒤에 짐 싣는 곳] the trunk (compartment) ; the luggage compartment ; the boot ¶ 트렁크의 뚜껑 the trunk lid

트렁크

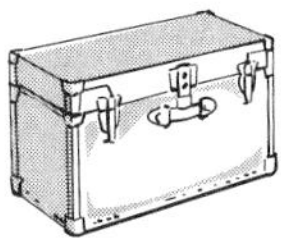

트레머리 a chignon ; hairdo in coil — **하다** do one's hair into a chignon ; wear a chignon

트레몰로 〖음악〗 tremolo 《이》

트레바리 a perverse person ; a cross-patch

*트레이너 a trainer
트레이닝 training ¶ 트레이닝을 받고 있다 be under〔in〕 training 《for the coming season》
— 셔츠 a training jacket —용 영화 a training film (운동 선수를 위한) — 캠프 a training camp — 팬츠 sweat pants ; a training trousers 하드 — hard training
트레이드 trade
트레이드마크 a trademark
트레이드 유니온 a trade union
*트레이싱 페이퍼 tracing paper
트레일러 a trailer ¶ 트레일러 캠프 a trailer camp
트레트레 ⇨ 타래타래
트롤 a trawl ; trawling
— 그물〔망(網)〕 a trawl ; a trawlnet ; a ground net —선 a trawl-boat ; a trawler — 어업 trawl fishery 오터 — an otter trawl
트로이 Troy ¶ 트로이의 Trojan ∥ 트로이의 목마 the Trojan Horse
— 전쟁 the Trojan War
트로이카 a troika
*트로피 a trophy ¶ 트로피를 획득하다 win a trophy
트롤리 ¶ 트롤리 버스 a trolley bus
트롬본 〖악기〗 a trombone
— 주자 a trombonist
트리밍 〖사진〗 trimming —하다 trim ; fringe ¶ 여성복의 트리밍 〖양재〗 the trimmings of lady's dress (주름 장식) ; lady's trimmings (장신구)
트리에스테 Trieste (이탈리아 북동부의 항구)
트리오 a trio 《*pl.* ~s》
보컬 — a vocal trio
트리코마이신 〖약〗 trichomycine
트리콧 〔옷감〕 tricot 《프》
트리폴리 Tripoli (리비아의 수도)
트릭 a trick ; a catch ; a shenanigan ; bunko 《미·속》 ¶ 영화의 트릭 제작 the fabrication of faked pictures ∥ 트릭에 사용하는 인형 a dummy ∥ 트릭을 쓰다 resort to tricks ∥ 트릭에 걸리다 be taken ; be tricked ; be a victim of somebody's shenanigans ∥ 트릭을 써서 …하게 하다 trick a person into doing
— 사진 a trick picture — 사진술(術) fake photography — 영화 a trick picture〔film〕 — 촬영 trick work — 플레이 a trick play
트릴(로) 〖음악〗 a trill ; a trillo 《*pl.* ~es, -li》
*트림 belching ; eructation ; a belch ; a burp —하다 belch ; burp ; eruct
트릿하다 ① 〔가슴·배가〕 (be) dyspeptic ; have an indigestion ; feel heavy on the stomach ; feel oppressed in the breast ¶ 속이 트릿하다 feel belchy
② 〔흐릿하다〕 (be) shady ; underhand ; indistinct ¶ 트릿한 사나이 a fellow of shady character
트위스트 a twist ¶ 트위스트를 추다 (dance a) twist
트이다 ① 〔길·장래가〕 get cleared ; be opened ; open ; spread (out) ¶ 트인 장소 an open place ∥ 터널이 트이다 a tunnel is opened ∥ 골짜기가 우리의 눈앞에 트이었다 The valley lies spread out before us.
② 〔생각이〕 be liberal〔open-hearted〕 ; become sensible ¶ 트인 사람 a sensible person ; a sophisticated person ; a man of the world ∥ 속이 트이다 be liberal〔openhearted, bighearted〕 ; have a liberal〔generous〕 mind ; have an understanding heart
③ 〔운이〕 become better ¶ 운이 트이는 것을 바라고 살다 live in hopes of better fortune
④ 〔구멍이〕 be pierced with a hole ; a hole is made
트적지근하다 feel〔be〕 uncomfortable in the stomach ; (be) belchy ¶ 너무 많이 먹어서 속이 트적지근하다 I have eaten too much and feel uncomfortable in the stomach.
트집 ① 〔틈〕 a split ; a gap ; an opening ; a difference ; an estrangement ; a crack ; a fissure ; a trouble ¶ 찻잔에 트집이 생겼다 The teacup cracked. / There is a crack in this teacup. ∥ 그 때문에 두 사람의 우정에는 트집이 갔다 That has caused a crack in their (bond of) friendship.
② 〔결점〕 a fault ; a blemish
트집나다 have a split ; have a hitch ; get warped〔bent, twisted, strained〕 ; get cracked
트집잡다 pick on ; pick a hole ; find fault with ¶ 사람의 말을 트집잡다 find fault with 《a person's》 remark ∥ 물건을 트집잡다 pick a hole in an article
트집쟁이 a faultfinder ; a nit-picker ; a nag(ger)
특가 特價 a special price〔offer〕 ; a bargain price ; a specially reduced price
— 제공 a special offer ¶ 한영 사전 특가 제공 Korean-English Dictionaries (offered) at a special price. — 판매 a bargain sale ; sale at special〔reduced〕 price ; 〔…의〕 a special (introduction) offer on… —품 articles offered at a special〔bargain〕 price ; a bargain ; a bargain-priced article ; 〔게시〕 Bargain Special ¶ 특가품 판매장 a bargain counter
특공 特功 special merit ; a great achievement ; distinguished service
특공대 特攻隊 a special attack corps ; a suicide squad ; a commando 《영》 ; a ranger corps 《미》 ¶ 인질들을 구출하기 위해 특공대를 파견하다 send the commandos to rescue the hostages 《held

by pro-Palestinian highjackers》
특과 特科 a special course ; 〖군사〗 an arm (of the army) other than infantry —병 a technical soldier —생 a student of a special course
**특권 特權 a privilege ; a special〔an exclusive〕 right ; a prerogative ¶ 외교관의 특권 diplomatic immunity // 특권이 있는 privileged ; prerogative // 특권을 부여하다 give a privilege ; confer privileges 《on a person》 // 특권을 향유하다 enjoy privileges 《of》 // 특권을 행사하다 exercise the privilege〔prerogative〕 《of》 // 특권을 잃다 be deprived of privileges
— 계급 the privileged class(es) ¶ 소수 특권 계급 a privileged minority ; the privileged few — 상실 lapse〔loss〕 of privileges — 침해 breach of privilege 단순〔복〕 — 〔주식〕 single〔compound〕 option
특근 特勤 special service ; special duty ; extra work ; overtime work —하다 do extra work ; work overtime ; be on special duty
— 수당 an allowance for extra work ; overtime allowance
특급 特急 a special〔limited〕 express (train) ; a superexpress
—권 a limited express ticket — 열차 a special express (train) ; a limited express (train) 《미》 ; a super-express ; a cannon ball 《속》 ; ball of fire 《속》 ; fireball ; highball
특급 特給 a special allowance〔grant, distribution〕 —하다 give a special grant of ; allow (as a special grant)
특급 特級 special grade ; 〔특등〕 superior quality
—주 a special class wine —품 a special grade article ; an extra fine 〔superfine〕 brand ; an article of superior quality
특기 特技 special ability〔skill, talent〕 ; speciality ; one's special〔distinctive〕 art ; one's special flairs
군사 — military occupational speciality 《MOS》
특기하다 特記— mention specially ; make special mention of ; write in large characters ⇨ 특필 ¶ 특기할 만한 것 what is specially noteworthy // 특기할 만하다 be worth〔deserve〕 special mention
특대 特待 special treatment〔courtesy〕 ; distinction —하다 give special treatment ; show special courtesy 《toward》 ; treat 《a person》 with distinction ¶ 특대받다 be treated with distinction
—권 a complimentary ticket —생 a scholarship student ; a foundationer 《영》 ; an exhibitioner 《영》 ¶ 특대생이 되다 get〔gain, obtain〕 a scholarship

특대 特大 outsize(d) ; extra-large ; oversize(d) ; king-size(d)
— 반절판〔사절판, 팔절판〕 a royal folio 《*pl.* ~s》〔quarto 《*pl.* ~s》, octavo 《*pl.* ~s》〕 —판〔양지〕 extra foolscap —품 〖상업〗 an imperial —호 〔잡지〕 an enlarged special edition ; a special enlarged issue〔number〕
특등 特等 special class〔grade〕 ; top〔premium〕 grade
—석 a special〔reserved〕 seat ; a box (극장의) —실 a special (class) room ; 〔기선의〕 a cabin deluxe —품 an A-1 (grade) article ; merchandise〔an article〕 of special quality ; premium goods ; an extra-fine〔super-fine〕 article 〔brand〕 ; 〖상업〗 a super
특례 特例 a special case〔example〕 ; a particular instance〔case〕 ; an exception ¶ 특례를 만들다 make an exception
전시 — a wartime exception
특매 特賣 a special〔bargain〕 sale ; a sale at a special price —하다 sell at a special price ; offer as a bargain ¶ 연2회의 서적 특매가 행해진다 Special sale of books is conducted twice a year.
— 기간 the period of special sale — 시장〔상가〕 a bazaar —일 a special bargain day ; 〔간판〕 Bargain (Sale) Day. —장 the Bargain Department ; "Bargains" ; a bargain counter ; 〔지하실의〕 a bargain basement —품 articles for special sale ; articles sold at special prices ; an article offered at a bargain (price) ; 〔표시〕 Bargains. /Bargain Items.
특면 特免 special exemption ; a special pardon ; a free pardon ; dispensation —하다 exempt specially ; give a special pardon ; grant a dispensation to ; dispense
특명 特命 special command〔order〕 ; special appointment —하다 order 〔appoint〕 specially ¶ 특명의 extraordinary // 특명을 띠고 on a special mission
— 검열관 a special inspector — 전권 공사 an Envoy Extraordinary and Minister Plenipotentiary ; a Minister Extraordinary and Plenipotentiary — 전권 대사 an Envoy Extraordinary and Ambassador Plenipotentiary ; an Ambassador Extraordinary and Plenipotentiary
특무 特務 special duty〔service〕
— 기관 the Special Service Agency 〔Organization〕 ; the secret (military) agency〔service〕 ; special service facilities —대 the Counter Intelligence Corps 《C. I. C.》 —병〔함〕 a special service〔an auxiliary〕 man〔vessel〕
특발 特發 〖의학〗 spontaneous origination ; idiogenesis —하다 arise〔origi-

nate〕 spontaneously〔idiopathically〕 ¶ 특발성의 idiopathic ; sporadic
—병 an idiopathy ; an idiopathic〔a sporadic, a primary〕 (case of) disease

특배 特配 special delivery ; special distribution ; a bonus **—하다** distribute 〔ration〕 exceptionally〔specially〕

†**특별 特別** being special ; exception ; speciality **—하다** (be) special ; extraordinary ; especial ; particular ; extra ; uncommon ; exceptional ; peculiar ¶ 특별히 specially ; especially ; particularly ; in particular ; exceptionally ; peculiarly ; extraordinarily ; uncommonly // 특별히 주의하다 pay special attention 《to》 // 특별한 취급을 하다 give 《a person》 special treatment ; make an exception 《of a person》 ; make discrimination in one's favor // 그 사람만은 특별이다 He is an exception〔a special case〕./He is different. // 나는 특별히 할 말이 없다 I have nothing particular to say.
— 공채〔세, 전보, 회계, 지출, 수당, 가봉〕 a special loan〔tax, telegram, account, grant, allowance, additional salary〕 — 국회 a special session of the Assembly — 규정 an express provision — 급행 a special〔limited〕 express ; a superexpress — 기획 a special project — 당좌 예금 a special current account — 명령 〖군사〗 special order — 배달 special delivery — 배당 an extra dividend —법 a special law — 변호인 a special counsel — 보조금 a special grant — 보좌관 [대통령의] the President's Special Adviser ; the Special Assistant 《for the Foreign Affairs》 to the President — 보호 건축물 specially preserved building — 상여 a special bonus —석 a reserved〔special〕 seat — 수당 a special〔an extra〕 allowance ; a bonus ; an allotment (미군) —시 a special city〔municipality〕 — 열차 a special train — 예산 a special budget — 요금 [초과의] an extra fee 〔charge〕 ; [할인의] a specially reduced fee — 위원 an extraordinary member of a committee〔commission〕 — 의회 a special session of the Assembly — 인출권 [IMF의] Special Drawing Rights 《SDR》 (잡지의) — 읽을 거리 a (magazine) feature — 임무 a special mission ; special duty〔service〕 — 임용 special appointment — 입장권 a complimentary〔special〕 ticket — 재판소 an extraordinary tribunal — 조처 special measures —직 the special Government service — 취급 special〔preferential〕 treatment〔handling〕 — 행위세 the special service tax —호 a special number ; an extra number〔issue〕 — 회계 the special account — 회원 a special member

특별기 特別機 a special plane ¶ 특별기편으로 미국에 가다 go to the United States by special plane

특별 훈련 特別訓練 special training ; intensive training ; crash course ¶ 그는 해외 근무를 위해서 영어의 특별 훈련을 받았다 He took special training in English for his overseas assignment.

특보 特報 a flash ; special news ; a special report **—하다** flash ; give a special report 《on》 ¶ 뉴스 특보 news flash // 전과를 특보하다 flash the military achievements

특사 特赦 an amnesty ; a special pardon ; a free pardon ; dispensation ; an act of grace **—하다** give as a special grant ; grant specially ¶ 정치범에 대하여 특사하다 grant a general amnesty to political prisoners // 특사에 의해 출옥하다 be released from prison on a general amnesty // 그들은 특사의 은전을 입었다 They were favored with special amnesty.
—권 the prerogative of mercy —령 an act of grace〔amnesty〕

특사 特使 a special envoy ; a special〔an express〕 messenger ; an ambassador at large ¶ 대통령의 특사 a presidential personal envoy // 특사를 파견하다 dispatch a special envoy ; send an express messenger

특사 特賜 a special grant 《from King》 **—하다** give as a special grant ; grant specially

특산물 特産物 a special product ; an indigenous product ; a (local) speciality ¶ 제주도의 주요 특산물 the principal products of *Chejudo* // 인삼은 개성의 특산물이다 Ginseng is a speciality〔indigenous to the soil〕 of *Kaesŭng*.
— 산지 special production localities

특상 特上 ¶ 특상의 the finest ; the choicest ; the best
—품 choice goods〔articles〕 ; an extra fine brand

특상 特賞 a special prize ; a special reward

†**특색 特色** a (specific) feature ; a specific character ; a characteristic ; a distinction ; a peculiarity ; a color ¶ 특색 있는 characteristic ; peculiar ; distinctive // 특색이 없는 featureless ; common // 특색을 나타내다 characterize ; mark ; color // 특색을 발휘하다 display one's characteristic (feature) // 이것이 현대의 특색이다 This is a unique feature of our time. // 그것은 한국의 특색을 잘 나타내고 있다 It is so characteristic of Korean./It is so characteristically Korean.

특선 特選 special selection〔choice, approval〕 ¶ 특선이 되다 be specially

selected
—품 choice goods
특설 特設 special establishment〔installation, accommodation〕 —하다 set up〔establish, organize〕 specially
— 도로 an accommodation road —링 a specially prepared ring — 전화 a specially installed telephone ; an unlisted telephone
†특성 特性 a special〔distinctive〕 quality ; a specific〔peculiar〕 character ; a characteristic ; a peculiarity ; a property ; a trait ; an attribute ; an individuality ; an idiosyncrasy ; a feature ; diagnosis (생물) ; genius (국어·법률의) ¶ 국민적 특성 a national trait // 인간의 특성 a characteristic of man // 특성을 발휘하다 show〔exhibit〕 a special quality
⁑특수 特殊 speciality ; peculiarity ; particularity ; characteristic —하다 (be) special ; specific ; peculiar ; particular ; characteristic ; distinct ; unique ¶ 특수한 예 a special example // 특수한 원인 a specific cause // 특수한 방법으로 in a particular way
—강(鋼) special steel — 교육 education for the handicapped〔retarded〕 — 무기 super weapons — 법인 a corporation〔juridical person〕 having a special status — 병기 a super weapon — 사정 special circumstances —성 particularity ; distinctiveness ; characteristics — 학교 a special school — 학급 a special class —화 specialization ; specification — 회사 a chartered company
특수 特需 special procurements ; emergency〔special procurement〕 demands〔orders〕《due to the outbreak of a war》
— 경기 a special procurement boom — 공장 a special procurement order plant — 수출품 special demand exports
특수 창조설 特殊創造說 〖생물〗 creationism ; the doctrine of special creation
—론자 a creationist
특약 特約 a special contract ; a special agreement〔arrangement〕
—하다 make〔enter into〕 a special contract 《with》; contract specially ¶ A. P. 특약 under a special contract with the A. P.
— 임금 special rates —점 a special agent ; an agency — 주점(酒店) a tied house
특용 特用 special use —하다 use specially ; have the special use of
†특유 特有 special quality —하다 (be) peculiar ; characteristic 《of》; proper ; particular ; specific ¶ 한국 특유의 풍습 a custom peculiar to Korea // 한국 특유의 미술 Korea's characteristic arts // 각자 특유한 방법으로 일하다 each works in his own particular way // 청결은 한국인 특유의 성질이다 Cleanliness is proper to the Koreans.
—성 peculiarity
특은 特恩 a special favor〔grace〕
특이 特異 —하다 (be) peculiar ; particular ; special ; unique ; unusual ; singular ¶ 그의 겉모양이 특이해서 눈에 띄었다 The singularity of his appearance attracted our attention. // 그는 특이한 사람이다 He's just not with it, is he?
—성 peculiarity ; particularity ; specialness ; uniqueness ; singularity — 세포 〖식물〗 an idioblast — 체질 idiosyncrasy ; allergy ; diathesis
특작 特作 a special production〔make〕
—품 a feature 《film》; a special film (영화의) 초— a super-production
특장 特長 a strong point ; a special feature ; a forte ; a merit
특전 特典 a privilege ; a special favor ; an advantage ¶ 본회 회원의 특전 advantages of membership in this society // 세금 면제의 특전 the privilege of exemption from taxation // 특전을 취소하다 revoke the privilege 《of》
특전 特電 a special telegram〔dispatch〕
로이터 — Reuter's special (service)
특점 特點 a distinctive〔distinguishing, characteristic〕 mark ; a characteristic ; a special feature ; peculiarity
†특정 特定 specification —하다 specify ¶ 특정의 specially fixed ; specified ; specific // 특정죄에 대한 감형 individually specified commutation of punishment
— 계약 a specified contract —물 a specific thing — 승계인 a singular successor — 업종 specially designated industries — 외래품 banned〔prohibited〕 import goods ; contrabands — 요금 a specified fare — 운임 special freight rates —인 a specific person ; a designated person
특제 特製 special make〔manufacture〕
—하다 make〔manufacture〕 specially ¶ 특제의 specially-made ; of special make ; specially bound
—본 a book in a special〔an extra〕 binding ; a deluxe edition (호화판) —품 a specially-made article ; specially made goods ; goods of special make ; specialities
특종 特種 ① [종류] a special kind ② [기사] exclusive news ; a scoop ; a news beat ¶ 특종을 잡다 get a scoop // 본지 독점의 특종 our clear scoop // 특종을 내다〔싣다〕 publish the exclusive news ; scoop
특지 特旨 a special Royal order ; special consideration〔order, grace〕 ; a special directive from the Throne
특지 特志 ① [뜻] special intention ; special interest ② [사람] a volunteer ;

a person interested

특진 特進 special promotion (of rank) ¶ 2계급 특진 a double promotion of rank

†특질 特質 a characteristic ; a property ; a special quality ; a specific character (특성)

특집 特輯 a special edition —하다 prepare as a special edition ; make up a special edition ¶ 뉴스 특집 a special — 기사 feature articles —호 a special number〔issue〕 ¶ 신년 특집호 a January number with New Year features ; a special January issue 일요 —판 Sunday features

†특징 特徵 a special〔distinctive〕 feature ; a distinguishing mark ; a characteristic ; a peculiarity ; a trait of character 〔personality〕 ; a stamp ; an idiosyncrasy ; identifying marks (인상의) ; individuality (개인의) ; diagnosis (생물의) ¶ 특징이 있는 characteristic ; peculiar ; remarkable ; striking // 서울의 특징 the keynote of *Seoul* // 특징 있는 얼굴 a face with a noticeable feature // 특징 있는 목소리 a distinguished voice // 특징이 없는 featureless ; common // 특징 있게 하다 mark ; characterize // 복장이 그 시대의 특징을 나타내고 있다 The costume is (specially) characteristic of the age. // 그 행동이 그의 특징을 나타내고 있다 The conduct characterizes 〔marks〕 him. // 그는 어딘가 특징이 있다 There is something about him which distinguishes him from others. // 그의 얼굴에 어떤 특징이 있습니까 Is there anything peculiar〔striking〕 about his face?

특채 特採 special appointment〔engagement, employment〕 —하다 employ specially ; take 《a person》 into service〔a company〕 specially

특청 特請 a special request —하다 request specially ; make special request ¶ 한 가지 특청이 있습니다 I would like to make a special request to you.

특출 特出 distinction ; prominence ; pre-eminence —하다 stand out ; find prominence ; attain distinction ; (be) distinguished ; prominent ; superior ; especially outstanding

특칭 特稱 special designation ; a special name ; 〖논리〗 a particular —하다 give a special name 《to》 ; designate in particular ; particularize
— 명제 a particular〔subaltern〕 proposition

특특하다 (be) closely〔rather finely〕 woven ; coarse and strong

‡특파 特派 dispatch ; special assignment —하다 dispatch specially ; send on special assignment ¶ 사원을 런던에 특파하다 dispatch〔send〕 an employee to London for special purposes
— 대사 an ambassador extraordinary — 사절 a special envoy ¶ 워싱턴 특파 사절로서 on special mission to Washington —원 a special correspondent ; a mission ; a delegate ; a special representative ¶ 뉴욕 타임즈 한국 특파원 a (special) correspondent of the New York Times to Korea

특품 特品 premium goods ; top(-grade) merchandise ; an article of special quality ; an extra fine brand

특필 特筆 special writing ; a special article ; special mention ; a feature —하다 write〔mention〕 specially ; single out for mention ; make a feature 《of》 ; feature ; give prominence 《to》 ¶ 특필할 만한 remarkable ; capital ; striking ; worthy of special mention // 특필할 만한 대사건 a big〔capital〕 event // 특필대서하다 write in golden〔red, large〕 letters

‡특허 特許 ① special permission ; a license ; a permit
② a charter
③ a patent —하다 give a special permission for ; license 《a person》 to do ; charter ; patent ¶ 특허를 출원〔신청〕하다 apply for a patent // 특허를 얻다 get a patent〔special permit〕 // 특허를 갖고 있다〔주다〕 hold〔give〕 a patent // 특허를 신청중이다 Patent pending. / Patent applied for.
— 계약 a licensing deal — 관리 patent administration —국 the Patent Bureau —권 a patent right ; the right to patent ; patent — 기한 a term of license — 대리인 a patent attorney —료 a patent fee — 명세서〔목록〕 a patent specification〔roll〕 —법 the patent law — 사무소 a patent attorney's office — 사용료 a patent royalty — 소유자 a patentee — 심사 patent examination — 은행 a chartered bank —장 a charter ; a special license 〔permit〕 ; a muniment — 출원인 an applicant for a patent — 출원중 Patent applied for. /Patent pending. — 침해 infringement of patent —품 a patented article 전매 —증 letters patent〔overt〕

특혜 特惠 a special favor〔benefit〕 ; a privilege ¶ 특혜의 preferential // 특혜를 받다 receive preferential treatment
— 관세 preferential tariff〔duties〕 — 대우 preferential treatment — 융자 a privileged〔preferential〕 loan —주의 preferentialism

특효 特效 special efficacy〔virtue, power〕 ¶ 그것은 신경통 치료에 특효가 있다 It is of sovereign remedy in curing neuralgia.
—약 a wonder〔miracle〕 drug

†특히 特— specially ; especially ; express-

ly ; particularly ; in particular ; in special measure ¶ 특히 주의하다 pay special attention // 특히 지적하다 expressly point out // 오늘 아침은 특히 춥다 It is especially cold this morning. // 특히 이렇다 할 일도 없다 I have nothing particular to do. // 특히 그 사건의 중요성을 강조한 신문도 있었다 Some newspapers emphasized in particular the importance of the accident. // 특히 불조심해라 Be extra careful about fire.

튼실하다 [사물이] (be) strong and firm ; solid ; substantial ; [사람이] strong and healthy ; sturdy ; stout

†**튼튼하다** (be) solid ; compact ; firm ; strong ; sturdy ; substantial ; healthy ; hardy ¶ 튼튼한 사람 a strong person // 튼튼한 집 a solid house // 튼튼히 만든 strongly〔solidly〕 built // 몸이 튼튼하다 have a strong body // 문 단속을 튼튼히 하다 fasten the door tightly〔securely〕

†**틀** ① [테] a frame ; framework
② [모형] a mold ; a matrix ¶ 틀에 넣고 붓다 cast into a mold
③ [공식] formality ¶ 틀에 박힌 stereotyped ; conventional // 틀에 박힌 문자 a set phrase ; a verbal formula ; an old cliche // 틀에 박힌 보고서들 중에서도 자네의 것은 유독 흥미가 있었다 After all the other cut-and-dried reports, yours was very interesting. // 틀에 박힌 방법으로는 경쟁에 이길 수 없다 We'll never beat the competition with conventional methods.
④ [기계] a machine ; a device ; a gadget
⑤ [도량] caliber ; capacity ; degree of ability ; [풍모] presence ; stateliness ¶ 사람의 틀이 크다 be 《a person》 of large caliber // 그 애는 틀이 장군틀이다 The child has the dignified presence of a future general.
사진— the frame of a picture **솜—** a gin ; a cotton gin ; a saw gin ; a willow **자수—** a tambour ; an embroidery frame **재봉—** a sewing machine

틀거지 dignity ; stateliness ; an imposing manner〔attitude〕 ¶ 틀거지가 있다 be dignified // 틀거지가 없다 lack dignity

틀국수 machine-made noodles

틀누비 machine-quilting ; quilting by a sewing machine

틀니 an artificial tooth 《*pl.* teeth》 ; a denture ¶ 틀니를 해 박다 have a false tooth put in

틀다 ① wind ; turn (on) ; twist ; wrench ¶ 오른쪽으로 틀다 turn to the right // 라디오를 틀다 turn on the radio // 전축을 틀다 play a phonograph ; set a gramophone going // 나사못을 틀다 turn a screw // 팔을 틀다 twist〔wrench〕 《a person's》 arm
② counteract ; thwart ; cross ; oppose ¶ 일을 틀다 counteract〔cross, thwart〕 《a person's》 business〔plan〕
③ tie up ; do up ¶ 상투를 틀다 tie up a topknot // 머리를 틀다 do〔put〕 one's hair up
④ gin ; willow ¶ 솜을 틀다 whip〔willow〕 cotton

*****틀리다** ① [꼬이다] get〔be〕 turned〔wound〕 ; get〔be〕 twisted〔wrenched, warped〕 ; get〔be〕 distorted ¶ 태엽이 틀리다 a spring is wound up // 창문이 틀리다 a window warps // 넥타이가 틀리다 one's tie gets twisted
② [잘못되다] go wrong〔amiss, awry〕 ; become wrong ; be mistaken〔erroneous, incorrect, different〕 ¶ 틀린 생각 a mistaken〔an erroneous〕 idea ; a wrong opinion // 틀린 판단 misjudgment ; miscalculation // 틀리지 않고 하다 go through without stumbling // 내 기억이 틀리지 않다면 if I remember right〔correctly〕 ; if my memory does not fail me // 그것은 분명히 틀린다 It is glaringly erroneous. // 내 선택은 틀리지 않았다 I made no mistake in selection. /I was right in my choice. // 그의 판단은 틀리지 않는다 He is infallible〔unerring〕 in his judgment. // 계산이 틀렸다 This has been added wrong. // 내 계산은 틀려 있었다 I was out in my calculations. // 어떻게 내가 이렇게 쉬운 문제를 틀렸을까 How could I have slipped up on such an easy question ?

*****틀림** ① [잘못] an error ; being wrong ; a mistake ; a fault ; a discrepancy ; slip
② [같지 않음] being not the same ; being different

†**틀림없다** ¶ 그럼에 틀림없다 There's no doubt about it. // 그는 틀림없이 성공할 것이다 He will certainly succeed. // 저쪽 쯤임에 틀림없다 It should be about there. // 그것은 좋은 방법임에는 틀림없지만 실행이 어렵다 It is a good method, to be sure, but it is hard to practice. // 틀림없는 계산 a correct calculation // 틀림없이 correctly ; exactly ; without fail ; beyond mistake ; certainly ; surely // 틀림없이 계획하다 make a sure plan // 그의 말은 틀림없다 What he says is right. // 틀림없이 전하겠습니다 I will make sure he gets the message.

틀살 〖건축〗 lagging

틀수하다 (be) calm ; unperturbed ; imperturbable ; dignified ; deliberate

틀스럽다 (be) dignified ; stately ; imposing

틀어넣다 push〔thrust〕 《in》 ; squeeze 《into》 ; stuff〔crowd, jam, tuck〕 《into》 ¶ 가방에 책을 틀어넣다 pack books into one's bag // 옷을 장에 틀어넣다 jam one's clothes into a chest

틀어막다 ① [구멍을] stop (up) ; stuff ; fill ; plug ¶ 쥐구멍을 틀어막다 stop up

a rathole // 솜으로 귀를 틀어막다 stuff cottons in one's ears
② [행동·말을] curb ; put a stop to ; restrain ; contain ¶ 입을 틀어막다 stop 《a person's》 mouth ; put a gag on ; bind 《a person》 to secrecy ; gag

틀어박다 cram ; stuff ; fill ; pack 《in》 ; stop 《up》 ; charge ; plug ⇨ 틀어넣다

틀어박히다 be isolated (from society) ; be confined in 《one's house》 ; shut oneself up 《in》 ; confine oneself to ; remain indoors ¶ 집에만 틀어박혀 있는 사람 a stay-at-home // 집에 틀어박히다 hold up at home // 서재에 틀어박히다 shut oneself up in one's study // 종일 방에 틀어박히다 keep one's room all day long // 이렇게 좋은 날 집 안에 틀어박혀 있어 Cooped up in the house on a nice day like this? // 집에만 늘 틀어박혀 있으면 친구를 못사귄다 If you shut yourself up in the house all the time, you won't be able to make any friends. // 그는 원고를 쓰기 위하여 호텔에 틀어박혔다 He's holed up in a hotel working on getting his manuscript finished.

틀어지다 ① [빗나가다] swerve ; sheer ; turn aside ; deviate ; go astray ¶ 이야기가 옆으로 틀어지다 wander from the subject
② [꼬이다] get〔be〕 twisted ; be distorted ; go〔be〕 awry ; kink ¶ 넥타이가 틀어져 있다 have one's tie twisted
③ [사이가] be alienated from ; be 〔become〕 estranged from 《each other》 ; fall out with ; dissent ¶ 저 두 형제는 요새 사이가 틀어져 있다 The two brothers have lately become estranged.
④ [일이] go wrong ; break down ; end in failure ; end in fiasco ; fizzle out ; go amiss ; prove abortive ¶ 그 사업은 원조가 부족해서 틀어졌다 The venture died for want of support.

틀자 an angle rule(r)

틀지다 (be) dignified ; have dignity ¶ 사람이 틀지어 믿을 만하다 be dignified and reliable

틀톱 a pit saw

*‡***틈** ① [벌어진 사이] a crevice ; a crack ; a gap ; an opening ; an aperture ; a rift ; a chink ¶ 문 틈 a chink〔crack〕 in the window〔door〕 // 틈이 나다 have a crevice〔crack〕 ; be cracked
② [겨를] spare〔leisure〕 time ; time to spare ; leisure ¶ 틈이 있다 have time to spare ; be free ; be at leisure〔liberty〕 // 틈이 없다 have no time ; be busy // 틈을 내다 find time ; make time
③ [간격] room ; spare ; interval ; time ¶ 빈틈없이 들어차다 be packed full ; be filled to capacity // 한 사람도 들어갈 틈이 없다 There is no room left for even a single person.
④ [기회] an opportunity ; a chance ¶ 틈을 타다 make the most of a chance ; seize an opportunity
⑤ [불화] friction ; estrangement ; alienation ¶ 둘 사이에 틈이 생기다 grow friction between the two

틈나다 ① [겨를이 생기다] have a spare 〔leisure〕 time ; become〔be〕 free ; be disengaged ; be not busy
② [틈이 생기다] be cracked ; be creviced ; be gapped
③ [서로 사이가 벌어지다] be〔become〕 estranged

틈내다 [겨를을 내다] find time 《to do》 ; make time ¶ 틈낼 수 있다면 if you can find time to spare

틈바구니 a crevice ⇨ 틈

틈바귀 ⇨ 틈바구니

틈새기 gap ; narrow space

틈입 闖入 trespassing ; intrusion ; forced entry **—하다** trespass on ; intrude into ; break in〔into〕 ; force into ; rush in ; burst into
—자 an intruder ; a trespasser

틈타다 seize an opportunity ; take advantage of ; avail oneself of ; make the most of a chance ¶ 적은 어둠을 틈타 밀어닥쳤다 The enemy advanced under cover of night.

틈틈이 ① [틈마다] at each gap ; in every opening ② [기회마다] at each moment of leisure ; at odd moments ; in one's spare moments ¶ 틈틈이 돼지를 기르다 raise pigs in one's spare moments // 틈틈이 공부하다 turn every odd moment to account for one's studies

티[1] [먼지] a mote ; dust ; a grit ; a particle ; a foreign element ¶ 눈에 티가 들다 have a mote in one's eye

티[2] [결점] a flaw ; a speck ; a spot ; a defect ; a blemish ¶ 옥에 티 a fly in the ointment ; a flaw in a gem

티[3] [모양] a style〔a touch, a smack, an air〕 《of》 ; manner ; way ¶ 시골티가 나다 have a bit of the country about one ; be countrified ; have hayseed in one's hair // 부자 티를 내다 give oneself the air of a millionaire ; act the lord // 걸음걸이가 선원티가 난다 His gait smacks of the sea.

티[4] ① [글자] the letter "T" ② [차] tea ③ [골프의] a (golf) tee
—세트 a tea set〔service〕 **—포트** a teapot **—형(型)** T-shape

티격나다 break up with ; fall out with ; split ; quarrel with ; be alienated 〔estranged〕 from ¶ …와 티격나다 be at odds〔at (a) jar〕 《with》

티격태격 [시비] disputing ; wrangling ; quarrelling **—하다** dispute ; quarrel

티그리스강 —江 the Tigris River

*티끌 dust ; a mote ¶ 티끌이 앉다 be covered with dust // 티끌만큼도 없다 have not a particle〔a bit, an atom, a fig, an ounce, a button, a hair〕// 티끌을 털다 shake off the dust // 티끌만큼의 가치도 없다 It is not worth a snap (of one's fingers). // 그 여자는 티끌만큼의 상식도 없다 She has not a bit of common sense. // 그에게는 양심이라곤 티끌만큼도 없다 He hasn't an ounce〔an atom〕 of conscience in him.
— 세상 this filthy world ; this world full of woes and cares
티끌 모아 태산 된다 〔속담〕 Many a mickle makes a muckle. /Many drops make a shower. /Little and often fills the purse. /Penny and penny laid up will be many. /A pin a day is a groat a year. /Many a little makes mickle.

티눈 a corn ¶ 발에 티눈이 박히다 have a corn on the sole of one's foot
—박이 a person who has a white blind speck on the pupil of his eye —약 a corn plaster

티뜯다 ① [흠을 찾다] find fault with ; pick a hole〔flaw〕 in ; cavil〔carp〕 at ; pick on ; nag ¶ 글을 티뜯다 pick a hole in what one has written // 사람을 티뜯다 pick on 《a person》
② [티를 뜯다] scrape off dirt ; clean

티라나 Tirana

티롤 the Tirol〔Tyrol〕

티룸 a tearoom

티밀이 rounded strips of window lattice

티벳 Tibet ¶ 티벳의 Tibetan
—말 Tibetan — 사람 a Tibetan

티보다 pick on ⇨ 티뜯다

티비 〖의학〗 T. B. ; TB ; t. b. ; tb 《tubercle bacillus》

티석티석 unevenly ; roughly ; irregularly ; coarsely ——하다 (be) uneven ; rough ; irregular ; coarse ¶ 표면이 티석티석하다 The surface touches rough.

티셔츠 a T-shirt ; a tee shirt 《미》

티스푼 [찻숟갈] a teaspoon

티엔티 T. N. T. ; TNT 《trinitrotoluene ; trinitrotoluol》

티오 [인원 편성표] T. O. ; TO 《table of organization》

티자 a T〔tee〕 square

티자 —字 T ¶ 티자형(形)의 T-shaped
—길 a T-junction —형 십자가 a tau cross

티적거리다 keep provoking ; keep picking on〔"riding"〕; keep carping at ; keep teasing〔needling〕; pick a quarrel

티적티적 ⇨ 티적거리다

티지르다 feed (a falcon) feed mixed with cotton

티처 a teacher

티케이오 〖권투〗 T. K. O. ; TKO 《technical knockout》

티켓 a ticket

티크 [나무] a teak ; [목재] teak (wood)
—재(材) teakwood ; teak

티타늄 〖화학〗 titanium 《Ti》

티토주의〔이즘〕 Titoism

티티새 〖새〗 a dusky thrush ; Turdus fuscada (학명)

티 파티 [다과회] a tea party

티푸스 〖의학〗 typhus

티피컬 typical ——하다 (be) typical ¶ 티피컬한 영국 신사 a typical English gentleman

티하다 show a spot〔a touch, a taste, an air〕 of... ; have something of... ⇨ 티[3]

틴에이저 teenager ; a teener ; a teenster ; bobby soxer〔socker〕

†팀 a team ¶ 원정 온 팀 a visiting team // 같은 팀의 동료 a teammate // 팀을 만들다 organize〔make up, get up〕 a team // 팀의 일원이다〔팀에 들어 있다〕 be a member of the team ; be on the 《football》 team
야구— a baseball team ; the nine 축구— a football〔soccer〕 team ; the eleven

팀워크 teamwork ¶ 팀워크가 짜여져 있다〔있지 않다〕 have fine〔be poor in〕 teamwork

팀파니 〖악기〗 the timpani (of an orchestra)

팁 ① [사례금] a tip ; a gratuity ; perquisite 《영》 ¶ 적은〔많은〕 팁 a small〔good, large〕 tip // 팁제도 the 《ten percent》 tipping system // 팁을 5,000원 주다 tip 《a waitress》 5,000 *won* // 팁을 듬뿍〔많이〕 주다 give a generous tip ; tip generously〔freely〕; tip well // 팁을 내다〔받다〕 offer〔accept〕 a tip // 팁을 아끼지 않다 be liberal with tips // 팁 일체 사절 No tips accepted. // 예를 들어 택시 운전 기사한테는 팁을 얼마나 줍니까 How much do you tip a taxi driver, for instance? // 유럽에서는 팁을 어떻게 주는지 말씀해 주십시오 Tell me about tipping in Europe.
② 〖야구〗 a tip ¶ 팁하다 tip 《a bat》

팅크 a tincture
요오드〔캠퍼〕— iodine〔camphor〕 tincture

팅팅 ⇨ 탱탱

ㅍ

파¹ 〖식물〗 a stone-leek ; a Welsh onion ; Allium fistulosum (학명) ; [양파] an onion ; [골파] a shallot
—밭 an onion patch
파² 〖음악〗 fa
†**파 派** [당파] a party ; a faction ; [학파·유파] a school ; [종파] a sect ; a denomination ; [파벌] a clique ; [단체] a group ¶ 관학파와 사학파의 싸움 a strife between the government and the private school factions // 두 파로 갈라지다 be divided into two parties〔schools, factions〕
고전(古典)〔낭만(浪漫)〕— [문학·예술·사상의] the classical〔romantic〕 school **광신—** a fanatical sect **급진—** the radicals **보수—** the conservatives **사학(私學)—** the private school faction **소장—** a young group **우—** the right wing **장로교—** the Presbyterian denomination **전전(戰前)〔후(後)〕—** the prewar〔postwar〕 generation **좌—** the left wing faction **주류—** the main stream faction ; the helming faction **헤겔학—** the Hegelian school **혁신—** the reformists
파 破 ① [물건의] damage ; breakage ; a flaw ; a tear ¶ 파한 [종이] torn ; tattered ; ripped ; rent ; [의류] ragged ; [물건] broken〔damaged〕 《goods》 ; defective 《articles》 // 파난 그릇 a broken dish ; a dish with a flaw in it // 파나다 break ; be broken ; get broken〔damaged〕 // 파내다 have 《it》 broken〔damaged〕
② [사람의] a defect ; a fault ; a weak point
파격 破格 an exception ; breaking rules ; irregularity ; 〖문법〗 a solecism ; a grammatical error ¶ 파격적인 special ; exceptional ; unprecedented ; unexampled ; unconventional ; [변칙의] abnormal ; broken // 파격적인 승진 an unprecedented promotion // 파격적인 염가 대매출 a great bargain sale ; "Bargain Special" // 파격적인 대우를 받다 enjoy exceptionally good treatment // 파격적인 혜택을 입다 be granted special favor // 파격 문구가 많다 be full of solecism
— 구문 〖문법〗 an anacoluthon 《*pl.* -tha》
파견 派遣 dispatch ; despatch ; detachment (분견)
—하다 dispatch ; despatch ; send (out) ; detach (분견하다) ¶ 군대를 파견하다 dispatch an army ; furnish a troop〔quota〕 // 사절을 파견하다 dispatch an envoy // 대사를 파견하다 accredit an ambassador 《to》
—군(軍) an expeditionary army〔force〕 ; troops furnished **—대** a detachment ; a contingent **— 대표** a delegate ; a deputy ; a delegation ; a mission 《총칭》
파경 破鏡 [거울] a broken mirror ② [달] a waning moon ; a crescent moon ③ [이혼] divorce
파계 破戒 offense against the Buddhist commandments ; transgression〔violation〕 of a commandment **—하다** violate a Buddhist commandment ; transgress ; apostatize
—승 a sinful〔corrupt〕 priest ; an apostate bonze ; a depraved monk **—자** a transgressor
파고 波高 the height of the wave
파고다 [불탑] a pagoda
— 공원 Pagoda Park
파고들다 ① [구명(究明)하다] inquire into ; investigate ; get to the bottom of 《a matter》 ; [규명하다] examine 《a matter》 closely ; look〔inquire〕 into 《a matter》 minutely ¶ 파고들며 연구하다 dig into 《a matter》
② [뚫고 들다] penetrate ; eat〔strike〕 into ¶ 가슴을 파고들다 penetrate one's mind ; be impressed on one's mind
파곡 波谷 the trough of the sea
파과 破瓜 puberty (of a girl) ; pubescence
—기(期) 《arrive at》 (the age of) puberty **—병** [정신병] hebephrenia
†**파괴 破壞** destruction ; demolition ; breakdown ; ruin ; havoc ; dilapidation

> 참고 **ruin** 일부 또는 전체의 붕괴, 도괴에 의한 손상 (이 손상은 보통 시간, 천후 따위 자연의 작용에 의한 것) **destruction** 화재, 폭발, 홍수 따위에 의한 전멸, 파괴 **havoc** 지진, 폭풍 따위에 의한 전면적 파괴, 황폐 **dilapidation** 자연의 힘에 의한 황폐 또는 방치에 의한 파손

—하다 destroy ; break ; ruin ; demolish ; wreck ; work〔wreak〕 havoc 《on》 ¶ 파괴적인 destructive ; subversive // 파괴하기 힘든 indestructive // 파괴적 사상 destructive ideas // 대량 파괴 무기 weapons of mass destruction // 폭격으로

파괴된 자리 a bomb ruin // 완전히 파괴되다 be totally destroyed // 제방이 파괴되었다 The embankments collapsed 〔gave way〕. // 홍수로 철도가 파괴되었다 The flood has destroyed the railroad track.
— 계수(係數) a modulus of rupture — 력 destructive power — 무기 destructive weapons — 분자 a subversive element ; a subversive ; a disrupter — 시험 a breaking〔rupture〕 test — 응력(應力) breaking stress —자 a destroyer ; a disrupter ; a wrecker ; a desolator ; a devastator — 작용 [세포의] destructive metabolism —주의 destructionism ; vandalism — 행위〔활동〕 subversive activities ; sabotage ¶ 공산 파괴 활동 Communist subversion

파국 破局 ① [판국의] catastrophe ; collapse ; cataclysm ¶ 파국적인 catastrophic ; disastrous // 파국에 직면하다 be confronted by catastrophe ; be faced with ruin // 파국으로 몰고 가다 drive into catastrophe ② [약국의] closing up one's drug store — 하다 close up one's drug store

파급 波及 spreading ; extending ; reaching — 하다 spread ; extend 《to》 ; reach ; affect ; influence ; propagate itself ¶ 전국에 파급하다 spread 〔extend〕 all over the country // 정계에 파급하다 affect the political world

*__파기__ 破棄 [파괴] destruction ; breaking off ; [무효] annulment ; [약속의] breach ; [법률 계약의] reversal ; recall ; revocation ; cancellation ; [조약의] abrogation ; denunciation — 하다 destroy ; break (off) ; annul ; reverse ; recall ; cancel ; abrogate ; denounce ¶ 공문서의 파기 the destruction of official documents // 외채(外債)의 파기 repudiation of foreign loans // 조약의 파기 the abrogation of a treaty // 원심을 파기하다 annul the original decision

파김치 [김치] stone-leek pickles
파김치가 되다 관용 be utterly exhausted ; get dead tired ; be ready to drop

파나다 破— get broken〔cracked, damaged〕 ; become defective ; have a flaw ¶ 파난 물건 a broken〔damaged〕 article ; defective goods

파나마 Panama
— 모자 a panama hat — 분쟁 the Panamanian dispute — 운하 the Panama Canal

파나물 green onion〔scallion〕 salad

파내다 dig out ; unearth ; disinter ; exhume (시체를) ; excavate ; extricate ¶ 땅에서 파내다 dig 《a thing》 from 〔out of〕 the ground // 금을 파내다 dig gold 《from a mine》 // 시체를 파내다 dig out〔disinter, exhume〕 a corpse // 감자를 파내다 dig up potatoes

파내다 破— have 《a thing》 broken 〔damaged〕 ; make 《it》 defective ; break down

⁑**파노라마** a panorama ¶ 파노라마 같은 풍경 a panoramic view

파니 idly ; lazily

†**파다** ① [구멍·구덩이를] dig ; excavate ; [굴을 수평으로] drive 《a tunnel》 ; dig out 《a tunnel》 ; bore (뚫다) ; [우물을] drill ; sink ; [동물이 구멍을] burrow ¶ 구멍〔무덤〕을 파다 dig a hole〔grave〕 // 땅을 파다 dig in the ground // 석탄을 파다 dig (for) coal ② [새기다] carve 《in, on》 ; engrave 《a wood with designs》 ; cut ; chisel (끌로) ¶ 도장을 파다 engrave a seal ③ [문제·학리를] probe 《a matter》 to the bottom ; investigate ; look〔inquire〕 into 《a matter》 ; [공부를] study hard ; hit the books ; bone up ¶ 원인을 파다 inquire into the reason // 학리를 파다 explore an abstruse theory // 탐정은 그 사건의 진상을 팠다 A detective went to the root of the matter.

파다하다 播多— (be) widely rumored ; wide-spread ¶ 그가 횡재했다는 소문이 파다하다 The news is wide-spread that he has made a fortune.

파다하다 頗多— (be) numerous ; abundant ; have a good many ; (be) quite frequent ; have quite often ¶ 그러한 예가 파다하다 We have a good many such examples. /That sort of thing happens quite often.

⁑**파닥거리다** [새가] flap ; flutter ; [물고기가] flop ; flounder ; leap ¶ 파닥파닥 [새가] flapping ; fluttering ; [물고기가] floundering // 새가 날개를 파닥거린다 A bird flaps its wings. // 돛이 바람에 파닥거린다 A sail flutters in the wind. // 물고기가 파닥거린다 A fish beats the water. /A fish shakes its tail.

파담 破談 breaking off ; rupture — 하다 break off 《an engagement》 ; be cancelled

†**파도** 波濤 waves ; billows ; a surge ; a swell ; [부서지는] a breaker ; [작은] a ripple ¶ 파도 소리 the sound〔roar〕 of sea ; the sea runs high // 파도를 헤치고 나가다 cut through high seas // 파도가 가라앉다 The sea goes down. /Waves subside. // 15 피트의 파도가 선체에 부딪쳐 부서졌다 Fifteen foot seas battered against the hull. // 파도가 물가로 밀려온다 The waves beat upon the seashore.
— 타기 surfboard-〔surf-〕riding ; surfing

*__파동__ 波動 a wave (motion) ; (an) undulation ; fluctuation — 하다 wave ; undulate ; fluctuate
—계(計) a cymometer ; [자기(自記)의] a kymograph — 역학〔광학〕 undulate 〔wave〕 mechanics〔optics〕 —설 the

ㅍ

wave〔undulatory〕 theory (of light) 경제 — an economic crisis 정치 — political upheaval 증권 — violent fluctuations (in shares)
파두 巴豆 a croton (plant)
파두츠 Vaduz
파드닥거리다 ⇨ 파닥거리다
파뜩 ⇨ 퍼뜩
파라과이 Paraguay ¶ 파라과이의 Paraguayan
— 사람 a Paraguayan
파라솔 a parasol ¶ 파라솔을 받쳐 들다 carry parasol over one's head
비치— a beach umbrella
파라슈트 a parachute ; a chute ⇨ 낙하산
파라오 Pharaoh《옛 이집트의 왕》
파라티온 [농약] parathion (insecticide)
— 중독 parathion poisoning
파라티푸스 〖의학〗 paratyphus ; paratyphoid fever
파라핀 〖화학〗 paraffin
— 연고 paraffin ointment —유 paraffinoid oil ; coal oil —지 paraffin paper
— 합성물 paraffinoid
파란 [법랑] enamel ¶ 파란을 입히다 enamel ; cover with enamel
파란 波瀾 ① [파도] waves ; surges ; billows ② [소란] troubles ; disturbance ; commotion ; a storm ; [성쇠] ups and downs ¶ 가정 파란 family trouble ; domestic troubles∥파란 많은 생애 a checkered〔an eventful, a stormy〕 career ; a life full of ups and downs 〔vicissitudes〕∥파란중첩한 국회 a stormy session of the National Assembly∥평지파란을 일으키는 사람 a trouble-maker ; a mischief-maker∥파란을 일으키다 create〔raise〕 a disturbance ; cause troubles ; stir up strife ; kick up a row∥그 발견은 과학계에 커다란 파란을 일으켰다 The discovery caused a tremendous commotion in the scientific world.
파랑 bule (color) ; green (초록)
—새 a bluebird ; [마테를링크의 동화극] The Blue Bird — 물감 (a) blue color 〔dye〕
파랑 波浪 [파도] waves ; [큰 파도] a billow ; a surge
— 주의보 a high sea warning
파랑이 a blue one ; a blue thing ; blue stuff
†파랗다 (be) blue ; green (초록) ; [안색이] pale ; pallid ¶ 파란 얼굴 a pale face∥파란 잎 green leaves∥파란 하늘 a blue sky∥파란 눈의 blue-eyed∥파란 옷을 입다 be dressed in blue∥그 여자는 파랗게 질렸다 She turned pale (in the face)./She lost her color.
파래 〖식물〗 a green layer ; a sea lettuce
파래박 a gourd-shell used for scooping water out of a boat
파래지다 turn〔become〕 blue〔green〕 ; [안색이] turn pale〔pallid〕 ¶ 나뭇잎이 파래지다 leaves turn〔become〕 green∥하늘이 개어 파래진다 The sky clears up and turns blue.∥그 여자의 얼굴이 파래졌다 Her face turned pale./She lost her color.
파렴치 破廉恥 shamelessness ; infamy ; ignominy ; impudence ; effrontery —하다 (be) shameless ; infamous ; ignominious ; disgraceful ; be dead to shame
—죄 an infamous offense〔crime〕 —한(漢) a shameless fellow〔dog〕 ; a knave ; a rogue
파륜 破倫 immorality ; incest《근친 상간》
파르대대하다, 파르스름하다 [청색·녹색] (be) bluish ; greenish ; [창백] (be) rather pale〔pallid〕
파르르 ① [떠는] shiveringly ; tremblingly ¶ 입술이 파르르 떨렸다 Her lips shivered.∥생각만 해도 전신이 파르르 떨린다 I tremble to think of it.
② [끓는] hissing ; sizzling ¶ 파르르 끓다 be hissing hot
③ [화내는] in a huff ; in a burst of flame ¶ 파르르 화를 내다 get into a huff
파르스름하다 (be) bluish ; greenish ; somewhat blue ; [창백하다] rather pale
파릇파릇 —하다 (be) freshly green ; fresh and green ; verdant ¶ 파릇파릇한 잔디밭 verdant lawns∥나뭇잎이 파릇파릇 돋아난다 The leaves come out on the trees all fresh and green.
†파리[1] 〖곤충〗 a fly ¶ 파리채로 파리를 잡다 swat〔flap〕 flies∥부채로 파리를 쫓다 fan the flies away∥파리가 쉬를 슬다 a fly blows∥파리가 한 마리 천장에 앉아 있다 There is a fly on the ceiling.∥파리가 쓰레기 더미에 까맣게 끓고 있다 Flies are swarming in clouds on the heap of garbage.
—똥 a flyspeck —약 flypoison ; insecticide (살충제) —잡이 a fly-catcher (그릇) ; fly paper (종이) —채 a flyflap ; a fly swatter —통 a flytrap ; a fly bottle 금— a blowfly 쉬— a fleshfly 집— a housefly
파리[2] Paris ¶ 파리의 Parisian
— 사람 a Parisian ; [여자] a Parisienne
—제(祭) the Fourteenth of July ; Le quatorze juillet《프》
파리모 a lump of hot〔molten〕 glass
파리 목숨 an ephemeral life ; a cheap life ; insignificant existence
파리하다 (be) thin ; lean ; haggard ; skinny ; gaunt ; emaciated ¶ 파리한 얼굴 a thin〔drawn〕 face∥파리한 얼굴을 한 사람 a thin-faced〔haggard〕 person∥파리해지다 become〔grow〕 thin ; get lean ; lose one's weight ; fall off∥전보

다 좀 파리해졌습니다 You have got a bit thinner than you were. /You appear to have lost flesh a bit.

파립 破笠 a worn-out〔torn〕 bamboo〔horsehair〕 hat ; a tattered〔crushed〕 hat

파먹다 ① [음식을] dig 《it》 out and eat 《it》; eat into ; bore into (벌레가) ¶ 땅을 파먹다 live by farming // 감자를 파먹다 dig up potatoes and eat them // 까치가 사과를 속까지 파먹었다 The magpie ate into an apple to the core.
② [도식] eat the bread of idleness ; live without working ; [기식] feed〔live, sponge〕 on 《a person》; eat 《a person's》 salt ; [재산 따위] eat away what one has ; eat 《a person》 up ¶ 일을 하지 않고 파먹다 vegetate without working ; lead an idle life

파면 罷免 dismissal〔removal〕 from office ; discharge **—하다** dismiss〔discharge, remove〕 《a person》 from office ; relieve 《a person》 of his post ; fire (미) ; give 《a person》 the sack ¶ 파면되다 be〔get〕 dismissed〔discharged〕; be relieved of one's post ; be fired ; get the sack // 직무 태만으로 파면되다 be dismissed for neglect of duty // 사장은 당장 그를 파면 했다 Boss fired him out in no time.

†**파멸 破滅** ruin ; destruction ; wreck ; downfall ; collapse ; undoing **—하다** ruin ; be ruined ; be wrecked ; go〔fall〕 to ruin ; be done for ; go to the devil〔dogs〕 ¶ 파멸을 자초하다 court〔invite〕 ruin ; bring ruin upon 《oneself》; ruin oneself // 도박으로〔술로〕 파멸을 자초했다 Gambling〔Drink〕 was his ruin〔undoing, destruction〕.

‡**파문 波紋** ① [수면의] a ripple ; a water ring ; a ripplet (작은 파문) ¶ 파문을 일으키다〔그리다〕 start a water ring ② [영향] a stir ; a sensation ¶ 파문을 일으키다 create a stir // 경제계에 파문을 던지다 cause a sensation〔create a stir〕 in the economic world ; agitate〔stir up〕 the economic world ③ [무늬] wave ¶ 파문 있는 비단 waved silk

파문 破門 [종교상의] excommunication ; [일반적] expulsion **—하다** excommunicate ; curse ; expel ; strike 《a person》 out of 《a list of students》 ¶ 파문되다 be excommunicated ; be expelled // 제자를 파문하다 expel one's student〔follower〕 // 그는 이단을 믿었기 때문에 교회에서 파문당했다 He was excommunicated from the church, because he believed in heresy.

†**파묻다**[1] bury ; [매장] lay 《a person》 to rest ; inter ; bury 《in a grave, under the ground》; inhume ¶ 파묻히다 get buried ; be interred ; be hidden ; be covered // 시체를 파묻다 bury a dead body // 보물을 땅속에 파묻다 bury〔hide〕 treasure under the ground // 두 손에 얼굴을 파묻다 bury one's face in one's hands // 산 채로 파묻다 bury 《a person》 alive // 눈에 파묻히다 be buried under snow // 그는 시골에 파묻혀 살았다 He buried himself〔lived a secluded life〕 in the country.

파묻다[2] [되풀이하여 묻다] inquire searchingly ; question inquisitively ; dig for information ; grill (미) ¶ 면직의 이유를 파묻다 demand 《of a person》 an explanation for one's dismissal

파묻히다 get〔be〕 buried ; be interred ; be hidden ¶ 눈에 파묻히다 be buried under snow // 시골에 파묻혀 살다 live oneself〔live an obscure life〕 in the country

파물 破物 a damaged〔defective〕 article ; damaged goods ; a broken stuff

파미 派美 ¶ 파미의 sent to America
— 사절단 the Korean mission (dispatched) to America **— 특사** a special envoy to Washington

파미르 고원 —高原 the Pamirs ; the Pamir Plateau

파발 擺撥 a post station〔house〕; a stage
—꾼 an express messenger ; a courier
—마 a post horse

파방치다 罷榜— break up 《one's home》; pack up ¶ 장사가 잘 되지 않아 파방쳤다 His business ran down, so he wound〔packed〕 up.

파방판 罷榜— (an) end ; (a) close ; the final scene ; the breaking-up time ; a termination ¶ 노름의 파방판 the final game 《of a gambling》 // 파방판이 되다 come to an end〔a close〕 // 파방판이 가까워지다 draw to an end〔a close〕

파벌 派閥 a clique ; a faction ¶ 파벌을 없애다 eliminate the factionalism // 여러 파벌로 갈라지다 split into petty factions
—심 a sectarian mind **— 싸움** a factional〔an interfactional〕 strife〔dispute〕; rivalry between factions ; interfactional rivalry 《over》 **—주의** factionalism

파별 派別 division 《by parties〔schools〕》

파병 派兵 dispatch of forces〔troops〕 **—하다** send an army 《against》; dispatch troops〔forces〕

파삭거리다, 파삭하다 (be) crisp ; crumbly ; dry and brittle

‡**파삭파삭 —하다** (be) crisp ; crumbly ; brittle ¶ 파삭파삭한 토스트 a crisp toast // 파삭파삭한 흙 crumbly soil

†**파산 破産** bankruptcy ; insolvency ; financial failure **—하다** go bankrupt ; go into bankruptcy ; fail ; be ruined ; come to a smash ¶ 파산 선고를 하다 adjudicate 《a person》 insolvent // 파산 선고를 받다 be declared bankrupt // 파산

ㅍ

정리를 하다 go into liquidation // 파산 직전에 있다 be on the verge〔brink〕 of bankruptcy〔ruin〕; face bankruptcy // 그는 투기에 실패하여 파산했다 He failed in speculation and went under. // 파산하지 않으려고 안간힘을 쓰고 있습니다 I'm doing my best to keep my head above the water.

— 관리인 a bankruptcy administrator — 관재인(管財人) a trustee in bankruptcy; a receiver —법 the Bankruptcy Law〔Act〕; the law of insolvency — 사건 a bankruptcy case — 선고 an adjudication of bankruptcy — 수속(手續) bankruptcy procedure〔proceedings〕 — 신청 a petition for bankruptcy —자 a bankrupt; an insolvent; a lame duck 《구》; a goner 《구》 — 채권 claims provable in bankruptcy — 채무 debts provable in bankruptcy — 청산인 an assignee〔a liquidator〕 in bankruptcy

파산적 —散炙 beef-and-onion shish kebab

파상 波狀 wave; undulation ¶ 파상의 wavy; wavelike; undulating; sinuated; 〖식물〗 gyrose

— 공격 a repeated attack; an attack in waves ¶ 파상 공격을 가하다 launch a series of attacks 《on》 —모(毛) 〖인류〗 wavy hair — 산지(山地) 〖지리〗 rolling mountains —열(熱) 〖병리〗 undulant fever — 파업〔스트라이크〕 a piston strike; a strike in waves

파상풍 破傷風 〖의학〗 tetanus; lockjaw

파생 派生 derivation —하다 derive 《from》; be derived 《from》; [사건] give rise to; develop ¶ 파생적인 derivative; secondary (2차적) // 영어의 수천 단어가 라틴어에서 파생되었다 Thousands of English words are derived from Latin.

—물(物) a derivative; an outgrowth; an offshoot — 소득 a derivative income —어 a derivative (word)

파선 破船 shipwreck; wreck; [난파선] a wrecked ship; a wreck; a shipwreck —하다 be wrecked; get shipwrecked; 《a ship》 wreck ¶ 배는 암초에 걸려 파선했다 The ship wrecked on a sunken rock.

파선 波線 a wave-line; a wavy line; a wave; an undulating line

***파손 破損** damage; injury; breakage; breakdown —하다 damage; give damage to; break ¶ 파손된 damaged; broken // 파손되기 쉬운 fragile; easy to break; apt to cause breakage // 기계의 파손 a breakdown of machine; a mechanical breakdown // 파손되다 be damaged〔injured〕; be broken (down); be destroyed; be impaired // 파손된 곳을 수리하다 repair the damage // 파손을 면하다 be〔remain〕 intact // 파손이 크다〔적다〕 suffer a heavy〔slight〕 damage

—물〔품〕 damaged goods — 부분 a damaged〔broken〕 part〔section〕; [제방 따위의] a breach; a crevasse 《미》

파송 派送 dispatch ⇨ 파견

***파쇄 破碎** smash; crush(ing); cracking (to pieces); fragmentation; 〖물리〗 spallation —하다 smash; crush; shatter; crack〔break〕 to pieces; break up; [광석을] spall

—기 a crusher; a disintegrator; [광석의] a spaller —력(力) 〖기계〗 crushing strength —성 폭탄 a fragmentation bomb —편(片) a splinter

파쇠 破— scrap iron; an iron splinter〔fragment〕

파쇼 fascio 《이》; [주의] fascism; [사람] fascist

— 사상 Fascism; fascistic ideas —화(化) fascistization

****파수 把守** [일] watch; guard; sentry; lookout; vigilance; [사람] a watchman; a guard; a sentry; 〖군사〗 a picket (전초) —하다 [보다] watch; stand watch〔guard, sentry, sentinel〕 《over》; keep a watch〔sentry, lookout〕 《over, for》; be on the lookout〔sentry〕; sentinel; 〖군사〗 picket ¶ 파수를 두다 set a watch 《on a house》; place a guard 《at the door》; keep a guard 《over the house》 // 엄중히 파수하다 keep a strict watch 《over》; guard 《the entrance》 strictly

—꾼 a watchman; a guard; a guardsman; a keeper; a lookout; [수영장의] a lifeguard 《미》 —막 a lookout; a watchhouse; a sentry box; [배의 마스트의] a crow's nest —병 a sentry; a sentinel

파스 〖약〗 PAS 《Para-Amino-Saycylic Acid》

파스텔 a pastel

— 화가 a pastelist

파슬리 〖식물〗 parsley

파슬파슬 crumbling —하다 (be) crumbly ¶ 떡이 파슬파슬 부스러지다 the rice cake crumbles

파시 波市 a seasonal fish market

파시스트 a fascist

파시즘 fascism

파악 把握 grasp(ing); grip; seizing; [이해] understanding —하다 grasp; grip; catch hold of; seize; understand ¶ 요점을 파악하다 grasp the point // 사태를 파악하다 grasp the situation // 의미를 파악하다 grasp〔catch〕 the meaning // 문제를 철저히 파악하고 있다 have a thorough grasp〔grip〕 of the problem // 그는 내 뜻을 거의 파악하지 못하고 있다 He has a feeble grip of my idea.

파안대소 破顔大笑 a broad smile (on

one's face) ── 하다 give〔show〕 a broad smile ; smile broadly ; break into a smile ; burst into laughter ¶ 파안대소하며 with a broad smile

파약 破約 a breach of contract〔promise〕 ── 하다 break an agreement ; infringe〔break〕 a promise〔contract〕 ¶ 그 계약은 파약되어 버렸다 The contract was broken off.

파업 罷業 giving〔closing〕 up one's business ; [동맹] a strike ; a walkout 《미》 ── 하다 go on (a) strike ; strike ; have a strike ; walk out ¶ 버스 운전사들의 파업 a strike of bus drivers // 파업 중이다 be on strike // 파업을 중지하다 call off a strike // 제강 직공들은 임금 인상을 요구하며 1주일간 파업했다 The steelworkers walked out on a week strike for higher wages. // 탄광에서 수차에 걸친 파업이 있었다 There were numerous strikes in the coal mines.
 ─권 the right to strike ─ 기금 a strike fund ─자 a striker ─ 지령 a strike order〔call〕 ─ 파괴자 a strike-breaker ; a scab ; a blackleg 《영·구》 ; a rat 《속》 ─ 활동 strike activities 농성 ─ a sit-down (strike) 동정 ─ a sympathetic strike 유〔무〕기한 ─ a strike for a definite〔indefinite〕 period 총─ a general strike

†**파열 破裂** explosion ; breakage ; bursting ; rupture (교섭·혈관 따위의) ── 하다 explode ; burst ; break up ; be disrupted ¶ 증기 기관의 파열 bursting of a boiler // 심장〔혈관〕의 파열 rupture of the heart〔a blood vessel〕 // 타이어의 파열 blowout of a tire // 거리의 수도관이 파열되었다 There was a burst in the water main on the street.
 ─ 방전(放電)〔전압〕 disruptive discharge〔voltage〕 ─음 〖음성〗 a plosive ; an explosive ; [폭탄 따위의] the crump (-ing) 《of a bomb》 ─점 the bursting〔breaking〕 point ─탄 an explosive ; a bomb ; a shell

파옥 破獄 prison〔jail〕 breaking ; jail break ; jail delivery ── 하다 break (from a) prison ; break (out of) jail ; escape from prison ; give legbail 《속》 ¶ 파옥을 꾀하다 attempt〔plan〕 an escape from jail ; try to break prison
 ─ 도주 breaking out of jail ; escaping from prison ─자 a prison〔jail〕 breaker ; an escaped prisoner〔convict〕

파운데이션 [여자의 속옷] foundation (garments) ; [밑화장용의] foundation

†**파운드** [화폐 단위] a pound 《£》 ; [무게] a pound 《lb ; *pl.* lbs》 ¶ 5파운드 지폐 a five pound note // 몸무게가 몇 파운드입니까 How many pounds do you weigh ?
 ─ 지역 the sterling area ─환 the pound exchange

파울 〖야구〗 foul 《f., f》 ¶ 파울의 foul // 파울을 치다 foul 《to the left stand》 // 파울을 주장하다 claim a foul // 파울(볼)을 받아 아웃시키다 foul out // 주심이 파울을 선언했다 The chief umpire called ; "Foul ball !"
 ─ 그라운드 《in》 foul ground ─ 볼〔팁, 플라이, 라인〕 a foul ball〔tip, fly, line〕

파이 a pie ; a potpie (주로 육류의) 《미》 ¶ 작은 파이 a patty ; a small pie // 고기를 넣은 파이 a meat pie ; a pâté 《프》 // 과일을 넣은 파이 a fruit pie ; a cobbler 《미》 ; a tart 《영》 // 파이의 껍질 (a) piecrust ; the shell of a pie

파이다 ⇨ 패다[2]

파이렉스 유리 [상표명·내열(耐熱) 유리] Pyrex

파이버 (vulcanized) fiber
 ─관 a fiber pipe ─ 글라스 fiber〔fibrous, spun〕 glass ; [상표명] Fiberglass ─ 보드 fiber board

파이트 ⇨ 투지(鬪志)

파이프 ① [관] a pipe ; a tube ¶ 파이프로 물을 끌다 lead water through a pipe // 파이프를 잇다 relay a pipe ② [흡연용] a (tobacco) pipe ; a cigarette holder (궐련용) ; a cigar holder (시가용) ¶ 파이프용 담배 pipe〔smoking〕 tobacco // 파이프에 담배를 담다 fill one's pipe (with tobacco) // 파이프를 물고 있다 be with a pipe in one's mouth // 파이프에 불을 당기다 light one's pipe
 ─ 오르간 a pipe organ 우물 ─ a well casing

파인더 〖사진〗 a (view) finder

‡**파인애플** a pineapple

파인 플레이 〖경기〗 a fine play〔performance〕 ¶ 파인 플레이를 하다 make a fine play ; give a fine performance

파일 八日 Buddha's birthday〔festival〕 ; the eighth of April of the lunar calendar
 ─등(燈) lanterns burned on Buddha's birthday

파일 [서류철] a file

파일럿 a pilot

파임내다 break an agreement ; spoil a plan ; make a plan worthless

*__파자마__ pajamas 《미》 ; pyjamas 《영》

파장 波長 wave length ¶ 파장이 같다 be equal in wave length ; be of the same wave length // 파장을 맞추다 tune in
 ─계(計) a cymometer ; a wavemeter ─대(帶) a wavelength range ─ 분광계(分光計) a wavelength spectrometer ─ 정조기(整調器) a tuner 고유 ─ a natural wavelength 장〔중, 단〕─ a long〔medium, short〕 wavelength

파장 罷場 [과거의] the conclusion of state examinations ; [시장의] close of a

ㅍ

marketplace ¶ 파장이 되다 come to a close ; a marketplace closes (up)

파재목 破材木 damaged〔defective〕 lumber

파쟁 派爭 a factional strife ; an interfactional strife〔dispute〕 ; rivalry between factions

파적 破寂 beguiling (the) time ; breaking the tedium ; diversion **—하다** break the tedium〔silence〕 ; beguile 〔kill〕 time ; divert oneself

파종 播種 sowing ; seeding **—하다** sow ; seed ¶ 밭에 파종을 하다 sow seed(s) in a field ; sow a field with seed(s) ∥보리를 파종하다 seed a field with〔to〕 barley∥봄에 옥수수를 파종하다 sow corn in (the) spring

—기(機) a sower ; a sowing〔seeding〕 machine ; a planter ; a seeder ; a seed drill **—량(量)** the quantity of sowed seeds **— 시기** the seedtime ; the sowing season ; the seeding season

파죽지세 破竹之勢 violent〔irresistible, crushing〕 force ¶ 파죽지세로 나아가다 carry〔sweep〕 all before 《one》 ; sweep away everything in one's way ; gather a cumulative force as it goes

파지 破紙 waste paper ; useless paper ; a defective〔tattered〕 sheet of paper ; remnants of paper

파직 罷職 dismissal〔removal〕 from office ; discharge **—하다** dismiss 〔remove〕 《a person》 from office ; discharge 《a person》 from his duties ; fire 《미》 ¶ 파직되다 be dismissed 〔removed〕 from office ; be discharged from office ; be fired 《미》

파찰음 破擦音 an affricate

파천 播遷 royal refuge ; royal flight from the palace ; an evacuation of the capital **—하다** the king flee from his palace ; evacuate the capital

파천황 破天荒 unprecedentedness ¶ 파천황의 record-breaking ; unprecedented ; unheard-of∥파천황의 사건 a most sensational event

파초 芭蕉 〖식물〗 a plantain ; a banana tree ; Musa basjoo (학명)

—꽃 a plantain flower **— 열매** a banana ; a plantain

파출 派出 dispatch ; [파생] derivation ; [군대 따위의] detachment ; sending out **—하다** send out ; dispatch ; detach ¶ 간호원을 파출하다 send out a nurse

— 간호원 a visiting nurse ; a nurse sent out **—부** a visiting housekeeper 〔maid〕 ; a charwoman **—소** a branch office ; [경찰] a police box ¶ 파출소에 신고하다 report to a policeman at the police stand ; [습득물 따위] take〔carry〕 《a thing found》 to a police box

***파충 爬蟲** 〖동물〗 a reptile ; a crawler

—류 the (order of) reptiles ; creeping things ; Reptilia (학명) **—류 시대** the reptilian age **—류학(學)** herpetology

파치 破— a waster ; broken〔damaged〕 articles ; defective goods ; [못 팔게 된] unsalable goods

파키스탄 Pakistan ¶ 파키스탄의 Pakistani

— 사람 a Pakistani

파킨슨 ¶ 파킨슨의 법칙 Parkinson's law **—병** 〖의학〗 Parkinsonism ; Parkinson's disease

파탄 破綻 ① [실패] failure ; ruin ; [결렬] rupture ; a breakoff ; disagreement ; [파산] bankruptcy **—하다** fail ; be ruined ; go bankrupt ; go to the wall ¶ 인격의 파탄을 가져오다 break up one's personality ; lead to the bankruptcy of one's character∥계획에 파탄이 생겼다 The plan fell through 〔failed〕. /The plan (has) miscarried 〔proved abortive〕. ∥사업이 파탄났다 He failed in business. /He has become bankrupt. ② [파열] breaking ; a rent ; a rip **—하다** be rent〔ripped〕 ; tear ; break 《up, down》

파트너 a partner

†**파티** a party ; a meeting ; a do 《*pl.* do's》 《영·구》 ; a shindig 《미·속》 ¶ 파티를 열다 give〔have, hold, throw 《미·속》〕 a party ; party∥파티에 나가다 attend〔take part in〕 a party∥그저 오늘은 파티를 하고 싶지 않다 I just don't feel like partying today.

— 기분 a party mood **남성〔여성〕(만의) —** a stag〔hen〕 party **축하 —** a celebration party

파파노인 a very old person ; a gray-haired old person

파파야 〖식물〗 a papaya

****파편 破片** a broken piece ; a fragment ; a splinter ; a scrap ; debris ¶ 포탄의 파편 splinters of a shell∥유리 파편 pieces of broken glass ; fragments of glass

파푸아 (the Island of) Papua

—말 Papuan **— 사람** a Papuan

***파피루스** 〖식물〗 a papyrus

파하다 破— [격파] beat ; defeat ; smash ; rout ; put to rout ; [파괴] crush ; destroy ¶ 적을 파하다 smash the enemy∥적진을 파하다 break through the enemy line

파하다 罷— end ; stop ; finish ; be over 〔out〕 ; [그만두다] give up ; quit ; put an end〔a period〕 《to》 ; make an end 《of》 ; [해산되다] break up ¶ 일을 파하다 stop work ; leave off work∥공부를 중도에서 파하다 give up studying halfway through ; leave school in midterm∥혼담을 파하다 break off marriage talks∥학교〔직장〕가 파한 후 after school〔office hours〕∥회사는 5시 반에 파한다 The office closes at five thirty.

파행 爬行 creeping ; crawling **—하다** creep ; crawl
— **동물** a reptile — **동작** crawling movement

파행 跛行 limping **—하다** limp
— **경기(景氣)** spotty prosperity ; a limping boom **—증** stringhalt (말의)

*__파헤치다__ ① [폭로하다] disclose〔reveal, let out〕《a secret》; expose 《another's crime》; unmask 《a deception》 ¶ 진상을 파헤치다 disclose〔reveal〕 the truth 《of》
② [발굴하다] open〔violate〕《a grave》; dig〔lay〕《a grave》 open

파혼 破婚 breaking off a betrothal〔an engagement〕 **—하다** break off the match ; break〔call〕 off a betrothal〔an engagement〕《with》

파훼 破毁 ① [파괴] destruction ; demolition **—하다** destroy ; break ; demolish ② [무효] annulment ; breach (약속의) ; [법률·계약 따위의] reversal ; recall ; revocation ; [조약 따위의] abrogation ; denunciation **—하다** annul ; reverse ; recall ; abrogate ; denounce ; quash ¶ 조약의 파훼 the denunciation〔abrogation〕 of a treaty // 판결을 파훼하다 annul〔quash〕 the decision

팍 violently ; hard ; flop ; [힘없이] weakly ; all at once ¶ 힘없이 팍 쓰러지다 drop down 《dead》; collapse // 팍 치다 hit 《a person》 hard ; punch 《a person》 violently // 칼로 팍 찌르다 thrust 《a person》 with a dagger // 팍 쓰러지다 fall flop ; flop down

팍삭 flopping〔plopping〕 down ; sinking **—하다** (be) crumbly ; friable ; fragile ¶ 팍삭 무너지다 crumble down // 팍삭 주저앉다 flop down // 팍삭 깨지다 break into smithereens

팍팍 with thrusts ⇨ 퍽퍽

팍팍하다 (be) dry and cloggy

판 ① [장소] a place ; a spot
② [판국] (the) state of affairs ; (the aspect of, the phase of) the situation ¶ 이러한 판에 at this juncture ; in the present juncture of things
③ [때] the moment ; [경우] the occasion ; the case ¶ 막판에 at the last moment // 위급한 판에 in the moment of danger ; at a critical moment // 막판에는 싸움이 되었다 It ended in a quarrel. // 화재로 그 근방은 난장판이 되었다 The fire occasioned terrible confusion in that neighborhood.
④ [승부] a match ; a game ; a contest ; a bout ; a round ¶ 세 판을 이기다〔지다〕 win〔lose〕 three games // 한 판 겨루다 have a match〔game, bout, tournament〕; have a turn 《at wrestling》 // 씨름을 한 판 겨루다 try a fall 《with》; have a wrestling bout 《with》 // 장기 한 판 둘까요 How about a game of chess ?
노름— a gambling table〔house〕 **싸움—** a battle field **씨름—** a Korean wrestling ring〔place〕

판 板 [판자] a board ; a plank (두꺼운)
—유리 plate glass **금속—** a plate ; a sheet (얇은) **레코드—** a phonograph record〔disk〕 **목—** a wooden board **얼음—** ice-covered ground〔river〕 **엘피〔에스피〕—** an LP〔SP〕 record ; a long-playing〔standard-playing〕 record **원(圓)—** a disk〔disc〕 **장기—** a chessboard **철—** an iron board **칠—** a blackboard

⁑**판 版** 〖인쇄〗 print ; printing ; [인쇄판] a plate ; a block (목판) ; [출판] an edition (증보·개정의) ; an impression (구판의) ¶ 판에 박은 conventional ; stereotype ; manneristic // 판을 짜다 compose ; set the types 《for》; do typesetting // 판을 새기다 engrave a block // 판을 거듭하다 go through〔run into〕 several editions // 신판을 내다 publish a new edition
개정— a revised edition **시내—** the city〔metropolitan〕 edition **신(新)—** a new edition **제2—** the second edition〔impression, printing〕 **증보—** a revised and enlarged edition **지방—** the local〔provincial〕 edition
판에 박은 말 관용 a set phrase

판 判 size ; [서적의] format ¶ 대판의 large-sized // 2절판의 책 a book in folio
국— small octavo **사륙—** crown octavo ; duodecimo **2〔4, 8〕절—** folio〔quarto, octavo〕

판 瓣 ① [화판] a petal ② [기계의] a valve ; [악기의] a ventil ; [피리의] a reed ③ [판막] a valve ¶ 반월판 a semilunar valve

판가름 [시비의] judging 《between right and wrong》; judgment ; [결전] a decisive battle〔match〕 **—하다** judge 《between right and wrong》; fight to a finish ; fight a decisive battle ¶ 판가름할 단계에 이르다 reach a decisive stage // 우리 둘 중에 누가 옳은지 판가름해 주시오 Judge between us. // 너의 아버지께 가서 판가름을 내고 말겠다 I'll go to your father and call for a showdown.

판각 板刻 wood engraving ; wood cutting ; engraving on wood **—하다** engrave 《a print》 on wood ; make a print from a wood-block
—본(本) a woodblock-printed book **—사(師)** a wood-engraver ; a wood-cutter ; a block-cutter **—술(術)** the art of engraving on wood ; xylography **—자(字)** a block letter **—화(畫)** a woodcut ; a wood-block print

판검사 判檢事 judges and prosecuting attorneys〔public prosecutors〕 ¶ (그 지역의) 판검사가 모두 참석했다 All the

ㅍ

judges and the public prosecutors (in that district) were present at the court.
— (채용) 시험 a judicial service examination

†**판결 判決** ① [시비의] (a) judgment ② [법] decision 《of a court》; adjudication; finding; sentence (선고) **—하다** decide; give (a) decision 《on a case》; pass judgment on a person; adjudicate; adjudge; sentence 《a person》 to 《death》 (선고하다) ¶ 사건의 판결 a decision about〔on〕 a case // 판결에 불복하다 protest against a decision; demur to a judgment // 판결을 지지하다 sustain the decision // 판결에 복종하다 accept the decision // 판결을 언도하다 deliver〔give, render〕 judgment; make a judgment; render a decision 《upon a prisoner》 // 판결을 재심하다 revise a judgment // 판결을 파기하다 quash a judgment // 판결을 취소하다 set aside〔reverse〕 a decision // 유죄〔무죄〕의 판결을 받다 receive〔be given〕 a verdict of guilty〔not guilty〕 // 내일 판결이 선고될 것이다 The decision (of the court) will be given tomorrow. // 판결은 원고의 승소〔패소〕로 되었다 The case was decided in favor of〔against〕 the plaintiff. // 재판관은 피고에게 유죄〔무죄〕 판결을 내렸다 The judge found the defendant guilty〔not guilty〕. // 그는 음주 운전으로 유죄 판결을 받았다 He was convicted of drunk driving.
—례 a judicial precedent; a leading case **—문** the ruling; the decision **—서(書)** a written judgment; a judgment paper **— 유예** reserving〔suspending〕 judgment **— 이유** reasons for judgment **— 주문(主文)** the text of a decision; formal adjudication **무죄 —** a judgment of a acquittal **유죄 —** a judgment of conviction **중간(中間) —** an interlocutory judgment **최종 —** the final decree 〔decision〕

판관 判官 [재판관] a judge; a justice

판관사령 判官使令 a henpecked husband; a man tied to his wife's apron strings

판공비 辦公費 expedience-fund; [접대비] expense account; [예비비] extra-expenses; [기밀비] confidential expenses

판국 版局 a situation; the state〔position〕 of affairs; the face〔phase〕 of the situation ¶ 위험한 판국에 in the perilous〔tricky, touchy〕 situation // 이런 판국에 under these circumstances; in this situation // 판국을 보다 observe 〔watch〕 the situation; watch how things develop; see which way the cat will jump

***판권 版權** copyright ⇨ 저작권 ¶ 판권을 얻다 obtain〔secure〕 the copyright 《on a book》; have 《a book》 copyrighted // 판권을 소유하다 hold〔own〕 the copyright // 판권을 침해하다 infringe a copyright; pirate
— 소유 ownership of copyright; [표기(表記)] Copyright〔All rights〕 reserved.; Copyrighted 《©》 **— 소유자** a copyright holder; a copyrighter **— 양도** transfer of a copyright **—장(張)** the copyright page **— 침해** an infringement of copyright; a copyright infringement; literary piracy

판금 板金 a metal plate; sheet metal
— 가공기 a sheet metal machine **—공(工)** a sheet metal worker

판나다 ① [끝나다] be〔get〕 finished; come to an end〔a close〕; end; close; be over ¶ 씨름이 판나다 a wrestling match is over〔up〕; the winner is decided // 싸움이 판나다 a fight is over; the winner is decided ② [없어지다] be all gone; run out; be exhausted ¶ 떡이 판나다 the rice cake is all gone ③ [파산] be ruined; go bankrupt ¶ 회사가 판나다 a company is bankrupt // 살림이 판나다 a family is ruined

판다르다 (be) entirely different 《from》; be quite another thing; be poles apart ¶ 판다르게 in a quite different way // 그의 성격은 나와는 판다르다 His character is diametrically opposed to mine. ⇨ 판이하다

***판단 判斷** judgment; adjudication; decision (단정); conclusion (결론); estimation (추단) **—하다** judge; form a judgment; decide; conclude; estimate; understand (이해); make out (이해); foretell (예언); interpret 《a dream》 (해석) ¶ 나의 판단으로는 in my (own) judgment // 잘못 판단하다 misjudge; make an error in judgment; judge erroneously // 신중한〔옳은〕 판단을 내리다 pass careful〔fair〕 judgment // 판단력을 잃다 lose one's judgment // 피상적인 판단을 내리다 bring superficial judgment 《to》 // 독자적인 판단을 내리다 form an independent judgment 《on a matter》 // 외관상으로 판단하다 judge by appearances // 그것은 자네 판단에 맡기겠다 I leave the matter entirely to your judgment. // 이것은 네가 판단할 일이다 It is up to you to judge. // 자기 자신이 판단하지 않으면 안 된다 You must judge for yourself. // 우리는 그를 미치광이로 판단했다 We concluded him to be mad. // 과연 그가 그렇게 했는지 안 했는지 나로서는 판단할 수 없다 I cannot tell whether he did so or not. // 그의 판단력은 훌륭하다 He has good judgment. // 남을 경솔히 판단하지 말라 Do not judge others hastily.

— 기준 a yardstick for judgment ; a standard of judgment —력(力) judgment ; discernment ; sense — 중지(中止) 〖철학〗 suspension of judgment ; epoche 《그》

판도 版圖 territory ; dominion ; domain ¶ 영국과 그 해외 판도 Great Britain and her overseas dominions // 판도를 넓히다 extend the territory 《of a country》

판독 判讀 interpretation ; reading ; decipherment (암호의) —하다 decipher ; read ; make out 《an old manuscript》 ; figure 《a thing》 out ¶ 판독하기 어려운 illegible ; indecipherable // 흘린 글씨이기 때문에 판독하기 어렵다 I find it hard to read the hurried writing.

판돈 money set upon the gambling table ; stakes ; a bet ; a wager ; all the money the gamblers have ¶ 판돈을 그러 당기다 rake in the stakes // 판돈을 쓸다 sweep the board ; take the pool

판돈을 떼다 관용 divide up stakes〔the money on the board〕

판둥거리다 loaf around ; idle away ; drone ; live in idleness ¶ 판둥판둥 idly ; sluggishly ; lazily

판들다 run out of〔run through〕 (one's fortune) ; get broke ; go bankrupt ; be ruined ¶ 가산을 판들다 run through one's fortune

판례 判例 〖법〗 a (judicial) precedent ; a leading case ¶ 판례를 인용하다 cite a precedent

—법 case law ; judicial precedents ; judiciary law ; judge-made law — 위반 contravention to judicial precedents — 집 law reports ; a lawbook

판로 販路 a market 《for goods》 ; an outlet ; a débouché 《프》 ¶ 국내 산업의 판로 an outlet for internal industry // 판로를 개척하다 find〔open, exploit〕 a market 《for》 // 판로를 잃다 lose one's market // 판로를 넓히다 extend〔enlarge〕 the market 《for》 // 뉴욕에 판로를 개척하다 cultivate a New York market // 세계 시장에 판로를 개척하다 find one's way into world market // 그 상품의 판로는 넓다〔좁다〕 There is a good market〔a small demand〕 for these articles.

수출 — an export outlet

판막 瓣膜 〖해부〗 a valve

—염(炎) valvulitis — 절개(술) valvulotomy —증 valvular disease 소(小)— a valvula 《*pl.* -lae》 심장 — heart valves ; valves of the heart 혈관 — valves of the veins 호흡 — pulmonary valves 심장 —증 mitral〔valvular〕 disease

판막음 bringing a game to an end by winning it ; coming out the winner of a game —하다 bring a game to an end by winning it ; come out the winner of a game

†**판매 販賣** sale ; selling ; marketing (시장에 냄) —하다 sell ; deal 《in》 ; market ¶ 현금 판매 a sale for cash〔money〕 ; a cash sale // 외상 판매 a sale on credit // 판매하고 있다 be on sale ; be on the market // 국산품의 판매를 장려하다 promote the sale of home manufactures // 판매고가 매월 100만원 이상 오르다 reach a sale over one million *won* every month // 판매 가격의 1할 할인으로 사다 buy 《goods》 at 10 per cent discount off the price

— 가격 the sale〔selling〕 price — 기점 a selling point — 대리점 a selling agency — 루트 a marketing route ; a distribution channel —망 a sales network ; a sales chart —부(과) a sales department ; a marketing section — 부장 a sales manager〔chief〕 ; [신문·잡지의] a circulation manager —비(費) the distribution cost —세 the sales 〔turnover〕 tax —소 a shop 《영》 ; a store 《미》 — 수단 sales tactics — 수익 the margin —술 salesmanship —업자 a distributor —원(員) a sales clerk ; a salesman ; a saleswoman ; a vendor (행상) —인 a seller ; a merchandiser ; a marketer ; an agent —전 sales war — 점(店) a shop 《영》 ; a store 《미》 — 정책 a sales policy — 조건 the condition of sale — 조합(組合) a marketing cooperative ; a marketing〔selling〕 cooperative association ; a sales guild — 촉진(促進) sales promotion 국채 — the public offer of government bonds 위탁 — consignment 특가 — a bargain sale ; sale at a special reduction 독점 — 계약 an exclusive sales contract 일수(一手) —권 the sole selling right 《for a product》 ; the franchise 《미》 자동 —기 a vending machine ; a slot machine 자동 — 식당 an automat 《미》 총—점 a selling agent

판명 判明 becoming clear —하다 become clear〔plain〕 ; be ascertained 〔confirmed〕 ; be known ; prove〔turn out〕 to be ; be identified as ¶ 자살자의 신분이 아직 판명되지 않았다 The suicide is not yet identified. // 그 보도가 허위임이 판명되었다 The report turned out false. // 정확한 원인은 끝내 판명되지 않을는지 모른다 The exact cause may never be cleared up. // 그의 거처가 확실히 판명되었다 The location of his residence is confirmed.

판목 版木 a printing〔an engraving〕 block ; a woodcut

판몰이 sweepstakes ; winning all the money (that there is around a gambling place) ; walking off with the stakes —하다 sweep the board〔deck, table〕 ; take the pool ; win all 《the

ㅍ

money⟫ ; walk off with the stakes

판무 辦務 management ; handling ⟪of business⟫ **—하다** manage ; handle ⟪business⟫
—관 a (diplomatic) commissioner 고등—관 a high commissioner 총—관 a commissioner-general

판무식 判無識 utter ignorance ; dense〔sheer〕illiteracy
—쟁이 an utterly ignorant person ; a densely illiterate person ; a total ignoramus ; a know-nothing

판박이 ① [책의] a printed book ② [모양의] a stereotyped ⟪form⟫ ; a conventional〔fixed〕thing ¶ 그는 아버지의 판박이다 He has a strong resemblance to his father. /He is a perfect counterpart of his father.
— 문구(文句) a set〔conventional〕phrase — 소리 a cliché ; a stock comment ; a trite remark ; a hackneyed〔stereotyped〕expression — 인사 conventional greeting ; a conventionally worded address

판벽 板壁 a wood siding wall
—널 a wainscot ; a clapboard ⟪미⟫ ; wainscotting ⟪총칭⟫

판별 判別 distinction ; discernment ; discrimination **—하다** distinguish ⟪between A and B⟫ ; tell ⟪A⟫ from ⟪B⟫ ; discriminate ⟪between, one from another⟫ ; judge ; mark〔notice〕the difference ⟪between⟫ ; tell ⟪things⟫ apart ¶ 판별할 수 있는〔없는〕distinguishable〔indistinguishable〕// 옳고 그름을 판별하다 discriminate between right and wrong // 진짜와 가짜를 판별하다 distinguish the imitations from the originals // 언뜻 봐서는 판별하기 힘들 것이다 You will not notice the difference at first sight. // 나로서는 양자를 판별하기 힘들다 I cannot tell one from the other.
—력 discrimination ; power of discernment ; judgment —식 〖수학〗 a discriminant

판본 板本 a woodblock-printed book

†**판사 判事** a judge ; a justice ; the judiciary ; the bench ⟪총칭⟫ ¶ (교수형을 즐기는) 가혹한 판사 a hanging judge // 판사의 경질 a change of the judges // 판사와 변호사 bench and bar ⟪총칭⟫
—석 a judgment seat ; a judge's bench ; the bench —직 judgeship ; the bench 대법원 — a Supreme Court judge 배석 — an associate〔a puisne〕judge ; an assessor 부장 — a presiding judge 수석〔차석〕 — a presiding〔side〕judge

판상 —上 the best〔finest〕thing of all ; A-one〔A-1〕; the ace ; the cream

판상 辦償 compensation ; indemnification ; reimbursement ; reparation ⇨ 변상

판상놈 —常— a lowly fellow ; a humble person ; a real trash〔scum〕

판서 判書 [옛 제도] a minister (of any one of the Six Boards of the Government)

판서 板書 a blackboard demonstration **—하다** write on the blackboard

판설다 (be) unfamiliar ⟪with the scene, ring, situation⟫

판세 版勢 ① [도박] the drift of a game ; the chances of a game
② [형세] the situation ; the state of affairs〔the things〕
③ [전망] the prospect ; outlook ; [징조] signs ; indications ; appearances ¶ 판세가 좋다〔나쁘다〕 prospects are bright〔gloomy〕; things look hopeful〔hopeless〕// 판세를 관망하다 see how the wind blows ; watch the situation ; wait for a turn of events // 판세를 뒤엎다 turn the tables ⟪against⟫

판셈 dividing the pooled assets of a debtor among the creditors ; distribution〔apportionment〕of a debtor's property among the creditors **—하다** divide up the pooled assets ⟪of a debtor⟫ ; distribute a debtor's property ⟪among the creditors⟫

판소리 the song〔reciting〕of a drama by the *chang* reciter **—하다** recite a dramatic song

판수 ① [점쟁이] a blind fortune-teller ② a blind song

판시세 版時勢 ① the drift of a game ; the situation ⇨ 판세 ② [시장의] current market price

판연 判然 —하다 (be) certain ; definite ; clear ; distinct ; evident ; explicit ; plain ¶ 판연히 distinctly ; distinctively ; clearly ; plainly ; palpably ; certainly ; definitely // 판연하게 되다 be ascertained ; be made sure

판유리 板琉璃 plate glass ; sheet glass (엷은) ; pane (창의)

판윤 判尹 [옛제도] the mayor of *Seoul*

판이 判異 —하다 (be) entirely different ⟪from⟫ ; diametrically opposed ¶ 판이한 의견 entirely different opinion〔view〕; diametrically opposed view

†**판자 板子** a board ; a plank (두꺼운) ; [총칭] boarding ; planking ¶ 얇은 판자 a thin board // 판자로 막다 board up // 켜서 판자로 만들다 saw into planks // 판자를 대다 board ; lay boards ⟪on⟫
— 울타리 a board fence〔wall〕⇨ 판장 — 지붕 a shingle roof 판잣집 a board shack ; a make-shift hut ; a shanty ¶ 판잣집이라도 좋으니 내집을 갖고 싶다 I wish to have a house of my own, however humble it may be.

판장 板墻 a board fence〔wall〕¶ 판장이 되다 get old and infirm

판장원 —壯元 the most outstanding〔tal-

ented〕 person present
판재 板材 boards for a coffin ⇨ 관재
판정 判定 judgment ; decision ; adjudication ; finding ; verdict (배심원의) **—하다** judge ; decide ; adjudicate《upon》 find ; give a verdict ¶ 심판의 판정 the umpire's decision // 판정으로 이기다 win on decision ; win a decision《over》
— 기준 a criterion (for judging)
판정승 判定勝 a decision ; a win〔victory〕 on decision **—하다** win〔score〕 a decision《over》; win by〔on〕 points《over》 ¶ 그는 심판 전원 일치의 판정승을 거두었다 He scored a unanimous decision (over his opponent). /He won the match in unanimous decision.
판정패 判定敗 **—하다** be defeated〔beaten〕 by a decision ; lose《a match》 on points
판중 —中 among the persons present
*판지 板紙 pasteboard ; cardboard
판차리다 get a place ready for《wrestling, gambling》; open《wrestling matches, gambling games》
판치다 excel all others present ; be the master of the situation ; be the cynosure ; come out the winner in a contest〔game〕 ¶ 그는 언제나 수학 시간에 판친다 He always excels in the mathematic class.
판탈롱 pantaloons
— 바지 a pants suit ; a pantaloon suit ; a pantsuit
판판이 every time ; every game ; all the time ; at every round ; on all occasions ¶ 판판이 지다 get defeated every time // 판판이 거짓말만 하다 lie all the time
판판하다 (be) flat ; even ; level ; smooth ¶ 판판한 길 a smooth road // 판판한 지붕 a flat roof // 길을 판판하게 닦다 level a road ⇨ 반반하다
판판히 smoothly
판하다 (be) wide ; broad ; vast ; boundless
판화 版畫 a print ; a woodcut ; an engraving
—가(家) a woodblock artist **—상** a printseller (사람) ; a printshop (가게) **—술** the art of engraving (on wood) ; xylograph ; woodblock printing ; a (pictorial) wood printing
판히 判— clearly ; distinctly ; plainly ; obviously ; patently ¶ 판히 보이다 be clearly〔distinctly〕 seen // 판히 들여다 보이다 be seen through clearly ; be patently transparent
*팔 an arm ¶ 팔을 끼고 with one's arms folded ; with folded arms ;《walk》 arm in arm《with》// 팔에 안장을 두르고 with a band round one's arm // 팔에 매달려 걷다 walk (along) on《a person's》 arm // 팔을 벌리다 extend〔stretch〕 one's arms // 팔을 쭉 뻗다 make a long arm // 팔을 걷다 bare one's arms // 팔에 안다 hug〔hold, embrace, have, take〕 in one's arms
팔은 안으로 굽는다. 〔속담〕 Men are blind in their own causes.
†팔 八 eight ¶ 제 8의 the eighth // 이마에 팔자를 짓다 knit〔contract〕 one's brows ; frown
팔각 八角 eight angles ¶ 팔각의 octagonal
—당 an octagonal building〔temple〕 **—정** an octagonal pavilion **—형** an octagon
팔걸이 an arm ; an armrest ; an elbowrest
— 의자 an armchair
팔괘 八卦 the Eight Trigrams for divination
*팔꿈치 an elbow ; 〖해부〗 a cubitus ¶ 팔꿈치의 관절 an elbow joint // 팔꿈치로 꾹 지르다 jog〔jostle, nudge〕《a person》 with one's elbow
팔난봉 a libertine ; a rake ; a debauchee ; a roué (프) ; all kinds of debauchery ¶ 팔난봉 다 부리다 indulge in all kinds of debauchery
†팔다 ① [판매] sell ; offer〔put〕《a thing》 for sale ; deal in《goods》 ¶ 팔 수 있는 salable // 팔 수 없는 unsalable // 팔 물건 an article for sale // 팔고 다니다 carry《vegetables》 about for sale ; hawk ; peddle // 싸게〔비싸게〕 팔다 sell《a thing》 cheap〔dear〕; sell《a thing》 at a low〔high〕 price // 이익을 보고 팔다 sell《a thing》 at a profit〔to good advantage〕// 손해를 보고〔밑지고〕 팔다 sell at a loss〔sacrifice〕; sell under cost ; sacrifice // 외상으로 팔다 sell on credit〔tick〕// 정가로〔할인해서〕 팔다 sell《a thing》 at fixed price〔a discount〕// 700원에 팔다 sell《a thing》 for 700 *won* // 한 개에 100원에 팔다 sell《a thing》 at 100 *won* a piece // 야드당 얼마에 팔다 sell by the yard // 몸을 팔다 prostitute oneself // 절개를 팔다 sell〔prostitute〕 one's chastity〔honor〕// 1원도 싸게 팔 수 없다 I won't sell it for a *won* less. // 이것은 얼마에 팝니까 How much do you charge for it? // 저 가게에서는 쌀을 판다 That store sells rice. /That store handles〔deals in〕 rice. /They sell rice at that store. /Rice is sold at that store. // 그것은 신세계에서 팔고 있다 You can buy it at〔It is procurable from〕 *Shinsegye*.
② [배반] sell ; betray《one's country》 ¶ 조국을 팔다 sell〔betray, be a traitor to〕 one's country
③ [정신·눈을] turn away〔aside〕; divert ; avert ¶ 눈을 팔다 look away〔aside〕; turn one's eyes away ; avert one's eyes // 정신을 팔다 divert one's attention《from work》

ㅍ

④ [이름을] take advantage of 《one's name》; trade on 《one's name》 ¶ 이름을 팔아서 under the pretext 《of》; trading 《on》// 이름을 팔다 take advantage of〔trade on〕 one's name〔reputation, prestige〕// 그런 일에 내 이름을 팔지 말아 주게 I don't want my name to be given〔mentioned〕 in such a connection.
⑤ [곡식을] buy〔purchase〕 《grain》 ¶ 쌀을 팔다 buy rice

*팔다리 leg(s) and arm(s); the limbs ¶ 팔다리가 쑤신다 I have a smarting pain in the limbs.
— 운동 an exercise for the limbs

팔도 八道 the Eight Provinces of Korea; all Korea
—강산 the scenery of all parts of Korea

팔등신 八等身 a well-proportioned figure ¶ 팔등신의 미인 a beautiful well-proportioned woman// 그 여자는 팔등신이다 She has a well-proportioned figure.

팔딱거리다 ① [가슴이] go pitapat; palpitate; throb; pulsate ¶ 가슴이 팔딱거리다 one's heart throbs〔palpitates, beats〕 (quick)// 맥이 팔딱거리다 the pulse beats〔pulsates〕 (quick)
② [물고기·개구리가] struggle; leap; jump; hop ¶ 물고기가 낚시에 걸려 팔딱거리다 a fish struggles caught on the hook

팔딱팔딱 ① [가슴이] pitapat; palpitating; throbbing; pulsating —하다 go pitapat ⇨ 팔딱거리다 ¶ 가슴이 팔딱팔딱 뛰다 one's heart throbs〔palpitates, beats〕 (quick)// 맥이 팔딱팔딱 뛰다 the pulse beats〔pulsates〕 (quick)
② [물고기·개구리가] struggling; leaping; jumping; hopping —하다 struggle ⇨ 팔딱거리다 ¶ 물고기가 팔딱팔딱 뛰다 a fish leaps〔jumps, struggles〕

팔뚝 the forearm; the wrist area

팔라듐 『화학』 palladium 《Pd》

팔락팔락 ⇨ 펄럭펄럭 ⇨ 펄럭거리다 (팔랑거리다)

팔랑개비 a paper windmill; a pinwheel

팔랑거리다 flap; flutter; wave ¶ 깃발이 바람에 팔랑거리다 A flag flaps〔flutters, waves〕 in the wind.// 나뭇잎이 바람에 팔랑거린다 The leaves flutter in the wind.

팔레스티나 Palestine

†팔리다 ① sell; be sold; be in demand; be salable (팔 수 있다) ¶ 잘 팔리는 물건 a good〔quick〕 seller// 잘 안 팔리는 물건 a poor seller// 가장 잘 팔리는 책 the best〔top〕 seller// 잘 팔리다 sell well; be in great demand〔request〕; have a good sale〔demand〕; be salable// 잘 팔리지 않다 do not sell; be in poor demand; have a poor sale; be unsalable// 즉시 팔리다 sell right away; meet a ready sale; obtain an immediate sale// 좋은 가격에 팔리다 fetch〔bring, command〕 a good price// 1,000원에 팔리다 be sold〔sell〕 for 1,000 *won*; fetch〔bring〕 1,000 *won*// 날개가 돋친 듯이 팔리다 sell like hot cakes〔wildfire, fun〕// 이 책이 가장 잘 팔렸다 This book was the best seller 《of the month》.// 그들이 내놓은 레코드는 지금 한국에서 잘 팔리고 있다 Their records are a hot mumber in Korea now.// 죄송합니다만 다 팔리고 없습니다 I'm sorry but they're all sold out.
② [눈·정신이] get turned away; be diverted; be attracted 《by》; be absorbed 《in》; lose one's head 《over》 ¶ 눈이 딴 데 팔리다 one's eyes go stray; look at something else// 정신이 딴 데 팔리다 one's attention wanders〔is distracted, is diverted〕// 이야기에 정신이 팔리다 be absorbed in conversation

†팔림새 sale; demand ¶ 팔림새가 좋은 물건 a good〔quick〕 seller// 팔림새가 나쁜 물건 a poor seller// 팔림새가 좋다 sell well; be in great demand; have〔enjoy〕 a good sale〔demand〕; be salable// 팔림새가 나쁘다 be in poor demand; have a poor sale; be unsalable

팔만 대장경 八萬大藏經 the Tripitaka Koreana (consisting over eighty thousand blocks)

팔매질 throwing; hurling —하다 throw; hurl
돌— stone throwing

팔면 八面 [면] eight sides〔faces〕; [팔방] all sides; [형용사적] 8-sided
—체 『기하』 an octahedron 《*pl.* -dra》
— 육비(六臂) [불상 따위의] eight faces and six arms; [재주의] being manysided〔all-round〕 정(正)—체 a regular octahedron

팔면부지 八面不知 an utter stranger

팔모 八— eight angles ⇨ 팔각 ¶ 팔모의 octagonal
—꼴 an octagon —살 octagonal lattice (work)

*팔목 the wrist; 『해부』 carpus ¶ 팔목을 잡다 grasp〔grab, grip〕 《a person》 by the wrist
—시계 ⇨ 손목(시계)

팔방 八方 the eight points of the compass; all directions〔sides〕; every side ¶ 팔방에〔으로〕 in all directions; in every direction〔quarter〕; on all sides〔quarters〕; on every side// 팔방을 살피다 keep an eye on all quarters

팔방미인 八方美人 a person who is affable〔speaks fair words〕 to everybody; everybody's friend; Jack of all trades (만물 박사) ¶ 팔방미인은 뛰어

난 재주는 없다 Jack of all trades, and master of none. // 팔방미인은 믿을 수 없다 A friend to everybody is a friend of nobody. // 저 정치인은 팔방미인이다 That politician speaks fair words to everybody. /That politician is everybody's friend. // 그녀는 팔방미인이다 She has a smile for everybody. /She tries to please everybody.

팔배태 the strip of cloth along the sleeve seam

팔베개 ¶ 팔베개를 베다 rest one's head on one's elbow

팔변형 八邊形 an octagon ¶ 팔변형의 octagonal

팔분 쉼표 八分—標 a quaver rest

팔분 음표 八分音標 a quaver ; an eighth note

팔분의 八分儀 an octant

팔불용 八不用 a good-for-nothing (fellow)

팔불출 八不出 a dull〔stupid〕 fellow ; a fool ; an ass ; a donkey ¶ 이 팔불출아 You stupid donkey !

팔삭둥이 八朔童— ① a baby born prematurely in the eighth month of pregnancy ② [모자라는 사람] a half〔dull〕-witted person ; a mentally deficient fellow ; an idiot

팔시간 八時間 eight hours

— 노동 eight-hour labor **—제** the eighthour day (system)

팔심 the strength of one's arm ; brawn ¶ 팔심이 세다 have strong〔brawny〕 arms

팔십 八十 eighty ; a fourscore ¶ 제 80 the eightieth

— 노인 an octogenarian ; an 80-year-old man〔woman〕; an old man〔woman〕 of eighty

팔싹 ① [연기·먼지가] suddenly ; lightly ¶ 먼지가 팔싹 나다 A cloud of dust rises lightly〔suddenly〕. ② [갑자기 앉는 모양] suddenly ¶ 땅에 팔싹 주저앉다 flop down on the ground // 집이 팔싹 주저앉다 a house collapses completely

팔씨름 wrestling with one's arms ; hand wrestling **—하다** have a hand wrestling

팔아내다 [잘팖] sell 《it》 well ; [팔아서 돈으로] pay in cash by selling

팔아먹다 [매각] sell ; sell off ; dispose of ; [명예 따위를] sell out ; sell one's honor ; [정신을] absorb (one's attention) ; engross one's mind

팔아치우다 sell off〔out〕; trade away ; dispose of ; clear out〔off〕 ¶ 헐값에 팔아치우다 sell 《an article》 for a mere song

팔오금 the crook of the arm

†팔월 八月 August

팔월 한가위 八月— August 15th of the lunar calendar ; the midautumn〔harvestmoon〕 festival

팔이 a peddler

신문— a newsboy

팔인교 八人轎 a palanquin〔sedan-chair〕 carried by eight bearers

팔일오 八一五 the Liberation Day 《August 15, 1945》 ¶ 팔일오 50주년 (기념식) (the ceremony of) the 50nd anniversary of the (1945) Liberation

팔자 八字 destiny ; fate ; one's lot ; one's doom ; one's star ; fortune ; luck ¶ 팔자 좋게 fortunately ; luckily ; as good luck would have it ; happily // 팔자 좋은 사람 a lucky man〔fellow〕// 팔자가 좋다 be fortunate ; be lucky ; have〔be blessed with〕 a good luck // 팔자가 사납다 be unfortunate ; be ill-fated // 팔자를 잘〔못〕 타고 나다 be born under a lucky〔an unlucky〕 star // 불행을 팔자로 돌리다 ascribe one's ill luck to fate // 일찍 죽을 팔자다 be fated to die young // 불행은 그 여자의 팔자였다 It was her destiny to be unfortunate. // 모두가 내 팔자야 It is all due to the stars I was born under.

팔자를 고치다 [관용] 《a woman》 marry again

팔자걸음 八字— an out-toed gait ; a swaggering gait (뽐내는) **—하다** turn one's toes out ; swagger ; strut 《about》

팔자땜 a compensation for one's doom 〔evil destiny〕; hardships undergone to ward off one's evil fate **—하다** undergo〔go through〕 hardship to ward off one's evil fate ; go through hell

팔재간 —才幹 skill with one's arms (씨름의)

팔절판 八切判 octavo (size)

팔죽지 the upper arm

팔짓 swinging one's arms ; gesturing with one's arms **—하다** swing〔gesture with〕 one's arms

팔짝 jumping up suddenly ⇨ 펄쩍

팔짱 folding one's arms ¶ 팔짱을 끼고 with one's arms folded ; with folded arms // 팔짱을 끼다 fold one's arms ; lock arms with 《a person》// 팔짱을 끼고 방관하다 look on with folded arms // (서로) 팔짱을 끼고 걷다 walk arm in arm with 《a person》

팔짱을 지르다 [관용] bring one's sleeves together with arms overlapping within

팔찌 ① [팔가락지] a bracelet ; a wristlet ; an armlet (영) ② [활 쏠 때의] an armband to hold one's sleeves

팔척장신 八尺長身 an eight-footer ; a very tall man

팔초하다 《a face》 be narrow and pointed

팔촌 八寸 ① [촌수] third cousin ; first cousin twice removed

사돈의 팔촌 [관용] one's cousin 40 times removed ; a stranger ② [치수] 8

ㅍ

chon〔inches〕

팔팔 ① [끓는 모양] boiling ; seething ¶ 물이 팔팔 끓다 water boils hard // 주전자가 팔팔 끓는다 The kettle sings. ② [체온이] burning ; feverish ¶ 몸이 팔팔 끓다 have a high〔violent〕 fever ; burn with fever ③ [날거나 뛰는 모양] fluttering ; flapping ¶ 새가 팔팔 날다 a bird flies fluttering〔flapping〕 its wings

팔팔 뛰다 관용 leap with surprise ; jump in a rage〔in protest〕

*팔팔하다 ① [성질이] (be) short〔quick〕-tempered ② [날듯이 생기 있다] (be) active ; quick ; agile ; spry ; look sharp ¶ 나이는 많으나 아직 팔팔하다 He may be old but he is still quite spry.

팔풍 八風 winds blown from every direction ; "the four winds"

―받이 a place exposed to the four winds ; a windy〔wind-swept〕 place

팔현금 八絃琴 an octachord

팔회목 the small of the arm ; a wrist

팜파스 [남미의 대초원] a pampa

―그라스(풀) a pampas grass

팝 pop (music)

― 싱어 a pop singer ― 아트 〖미술〗 pop art

팟국 scallion soup

팟종 s scallion stalk

팡 ⇨ 빵[2]

팡파르 a fanfare ; a flourish

팡파지다 (be) well-developed〔-rounded〕 ⇨ 펑퍼지다

팡파짐하다 (be) well-developed〔-rounded〕; pudgy ; stocky ⇨ 펑퍼짐하다

팡팡 [물이] copiously ; [눈이] heavily ; [소리가] pop pop ⇨ 펑펑

*팥 a red-bean ; an Indian bean ; Phaseolus angularis (학명)

팥고물 mashed red-bean (used to coat rice cake)

팥꼬투리 a red-bean pod

팥꽃 the red-bean blossom

팥꽃나무 〖식물〗 the lilac daphne

팥눈 the hilum of a red-bean

팥단자 ―團子 a red-bean dumpling

팥닭 〖새〗 a water-rail ; Rallus aquaticus (학명)

팥떡 rice cake coated with mashed red-beans

팥물 water in which red-beans were boiled

팥밥 rice cooked together with red-beans

팥배 a kind of wild pear

― 나무 a wild pear tree

팥비누 red-bean flour (used as a face soap)

팥소 bean-paste (jam)

팥죽 rice gruel boiled together with red-beans

*패 牌 ① [명패 따위] a tag ; a ticket ; a label ; a tablet ; a plate (평판·간판) ¶ 패를 내걸다 put up one's plate // 패를 차다 carry a permit

② [무리] a group ; a party ; a company ; a band ; a gang ; a team ¶ 우리 패 our group ; our team // 젊은 패 young folks // 패를 짓다 form a gang // 패를 갈라 놀다 play sides // 세패로 나누다 divide 《persons》 into three teams

③ [마작의] a (mah-jong) piece

명― a nameplate 문― a door-plate 상― a prize medal〔medallion〕 위― an ancestral tablet (조상의) ; a mortuary〔memorial〕 tablet (신위)

패 霸 supremacy ; leadership ; domination ; hegemony ¶ 패를 다투다 contend〔vie〕 for mastery〔supremacy〕《in》

패가 敗家 ruining one's family ; bankruptcy of a family ; squandering one's fortune ―하다 ruin one's family ; a family goes bankrupt ; squander〔dissipate〕 one's fortune

― 망신 ruining both oneself and one's family

패각 貝殼 a shell ¶ 패각상의 conchoidal

―대(帶) a shell zone ― 석회(石灰) shell lime ― 세공(細工) shellwork ― 접시〔남비〕 a scallop shell ― 추방 ostracism

패거리 牌― ⇨ 패(牌) ②

패검 佩劍 [차는 칼] side arms ; a sword worn ; [칼을 참] carrying〔wearing〕 a sword ―하다 carry〔wear〕 a sword ; gird on one's sword ¶ 패검하고 있다 be girt with a sword

패군 敗軍 a defeated army ¶ 패군지장은 병법을 논할 수 없다 A defeated〔vanquished〕 general should not talk of battles. /It is not for the vanquished to talk of war.

패권 霸權 supremacy ; mastery ; hegemony ; domination ; leadership ; supreme power ¶ 패권을 다투다 strive〔fight〕 for supremacy〔mastery〕; compete for dominance ; [경기에서] fight for a championship ; contend 《with others》 for a championship // 패권을 쥐다 hold sway 《over》; have〔assume〕 the hegemony 《of the land》; dominate ; secure mastery〔supreme power〕; hold supremacy // 해상의 패권을 쥐다 dominate〔rule〕 the seas ; be the mistress of the sea // 세계 시장에서 상업상의 패권을 다투다 struggle for commercial supremacy in the markets of the world

패기 霸氣 an ambitious spirit ; ambition ; aspiration ¶ 패기 있는 ambitious ; aspiring ; adventurous // 패기 없는 inert ; spiritless ; apathetic // 패기 있는 사람 a man of spirit ; an ambitious person // 패기 없는 사람 a dull〔an apathetic〕 person // 그는 패기가 있다 He is full of go. /He is full of pep. 《미·구》//

그는 패기가 없다 He lacks spirit.

*패다¹ ① [장작을] chop ; split ¶ 장작을 패다 chop〔split〕 firewood ② [때리다] beat ; strike ; hit 《a dog》 ; batter ; thrash ; [몽둥이로] drub ; club ¶ 늘씬 패다 beat 《a person》 to a jelly〔to a mummy〕// 패 주어야 해 He wants sticks. ③ [이삭이] be in the ear ; come into ears ¶ 2, 3일만 있으면 벼이삭이 모두 팰 것이다 The rice plants will all come into ears in a few days.

패다² ① [파게 하다] have〔let〕 《a person》 dig 《the ground》 ② [패이다] be〔get〕 dug ; be hollowed ¶ 낙숫물에 땅이 팼다 The raindrops have hollowed out the ground. // 비에 땅이 패서 도랑이 생겼다 The rain has worn a channel in the ground.

패담 悖談 an unreasonable remark ; indecent〔improper, immoral〕 talk ── 하다 say unreasonable thing ; talk unreasonably ; talk indecency〔immorality〕

패덕 悖德 immorality ; demoralization ; corruption
—자〔한〕 an immoral〔a corrupt, a depraved〕 man ; a scoundrel ; a ruffian ; a blackguard — 행위 immoral conduct ; an immoral act

패도 覇道 ruling by force ; military government〔rule〕
— 정책 the plans for world aggression 세계 — world domination

패드 [양재의] a pad ; [브래지어 속에 넣는] falsies 《미》 ¶ 패드를 약간 넣은 slightly padded 《shoulders》// 패드를 넣지 않은 padless 《shoulders》

패랭이 a rough hat of bamboo braid worn by mourners〔lowly persons〕

패랭이꽃 〖식물〗 a China〔Indian〕 pink ; a pink ; Dianthus sinensis (학명)

패러그래프 a paragraph

패러다이스 Paradise ; a paradise 《패러다이스 같은 낙원》

⁑패러독스 a paradox

패러림픽 [신체 장애자 경기 대회] the Paralympics (정식명 : the International Stoke Mandeville Games for the Paralysed)

패류 貝類 shellfish
—학 conchology —학자 a conchologist

패륜 悖倫 immorality ; depravity ¶ 패륜의 immoral ; depraved ; sinful
—아 an immoral〔a depraved〕 person

패리 悖理 irrationality ; absurdity ; illogicalness ; paralogism ── 하다 (be) irrational ; illogical ; absurd

패리티 〖경제〗 parity
— 가격 a parity price — 계산 a parity account

패망 敗亡 defeat ; ruin ── 하다 be defeated〔ruined, annihilated〕

패멸 敗滅 destruction ; ruin ; annihilation ; demolition ── 하다 be〔get〕 destroyed〔ruined, annihilated, demolished〕

패모 貝母 〖식물〗 a crown imperial ; a checkered lily ; Fritillaria verticillata (학명)

패물 貝物 shell goods ; shellware ; things made of coral〔amber, crystal, tortoiseshell〕

패물 佩物 personal ornaments ; a trinket ; trinketry 《총칭》 ; fixings

†패배 敗北 defeat ; reversal ; rout (궤주) ; discomfiture ── 하다 be defeated〔beaten, routed〕 ; suffer a reversal ; sustain a defeat ; lose a battle〔the day〕 ; be put to rout ; [경기에서] lose a game ; be out ¶ 완전히 패배하다 be completely defeated ; suffer a severe defeat // 적을 패배시키다 defeat the enemy ; put the enemy to rout // 패배를 인정하다 admit〔acknowledge〕 one's defeat ; throw〔toss〕 in the towel // 그는 패배를 자인하였다 He threw up his sponge.
—주의 defeatism —주의자 a defeatist

패병 敗兵 routed soldiers〔troops〕 ; a defeated army

패보 敗報 the news〔a report〕 of defeat

패사 稗史 an unofficial history ; a narrative history ; a legend

패산 敗散 rout ; a crushing defeat ── 하다 be routed ; be broken up ¶ 적을 패산시키다 disperse the enemy

패색 敗色 signs of defeat ; unfavorable signs in battle
패색이 짙다 관용 Defeat seems certain.

패석 貝石 a fossil shell ; a shelly stone

패설 悖說 an unreasonable remark ⇨ 패담

패설 稗說 ① [항담] talk〔gossip〕 of the town ; hearsay ② [설화] a romantic story ; a folktale

패세 敗勢 the reverse tide of a war ; signs of defeat ; a losing situation ; a backing situation ; unfavorable signs in battle

패션 (a) fashion
— 모델〔디자이너〕 a fashion model〔designer〕 — 쇼 a fashion show — 잡지 a fashion journal

패소 敗訴 a lost case ; losing a〔one's〕 suit ── 하다 lose a suit〔case〕 ; fail in an action ; 《the case》 go against 《the plaintiff》 ¶ 패소의 당사자 party defeated // 원고의 패소로 됐다 The verdict was〔Judgment was given〕 against the complainant. /The case went against the plaintiff.

패스 ① [무료 입장〔승차〕권] a pass ; a free ticket〔pass〕 ; [정기 승차권] a commutation ticket 《미》 ; a season ticket ② [합격] passing ── 하다 pass

ㅍ

¶ 시험에 패스하다 pass〔succeed in〕 an examination〔a test〕 // (물품이) 검사를 패스하다 pass muster ; stand the test ③ [통과] passing ―하다 pass ¶ (의안이) 국회를 패스하다 pass the House ④ [구기] a pass ; passwork ¶ 리턴 패스 a return pass ―하다 pass 《a ball to another》 // 패스에 의한 공격 a passing〔an aerial〕 attack

― 볼 〖야구〗 a passed ball ¶ 패스 볼로 득점하다 score on a passed ball ―포트 a passport (여권) 정기 ― a season ticket ; a commutation ticket 통근 ― a season ticket for workers

패습 悖習 a bad〔an evil〕 habit〔custom〕 ; a vicious〔pernicious〕 habit ; evil ways ; [악폐] an abuse ; a vice ¶ 패습을 없애다 break oneself of a bad habit (개인의) ; get rid of a bad custom (사회의)

패쌈 牌― a gang fight ―하다 have a gang fight

패쓰다 覇― [위기 모면] use a trick〔ruse〕 ; [바둑에서] make a no-man's point

패악 悖惡 wickedness ; depravity ; perverseness ―하다 (be) wicked ; depraved ; vicious ; perverse

패업 覇業 achievements〔exploits〕 of a conqueror ; domination ; hegemony

패역 悖逆 rebelliousness ; rebellion ; treason ―하다 (be) rebellious ; traitorous

패연 沛然 torrents (of rain) ; a violent downpour (of rain) ―하다 (be) heavy ; torrential ¶ 패연히 in torrents〔cataract〕 ; heavily

패용 佩用 wearing ―하다 wear 《one's medal, tag》 ; bear

패운 敗運 a declining〔losing〕 fortune ; being fated to lose ; one's waning star ; ill luck

패이다 be dug ; be split ⇨ 패다²

패인 敗因 a cause of defeat ; factors contributing to defeat ¶ 탄약의 부족이 패인이 되었다 The shortage of munitions resulted in the defeat.

패자 敗者 a loser ; [복수] the defeated〔conquered, vanquished〕

―전 a consolation match〔game〕 (경기의) ― 부활전 a repechage (프)

패자 覇者 a supreme ruler ; a champion

패잔 敗殘 survival after defeat ¶ 패잔의 defeated ; vanquished

―군 remnants of a defeated army〔troops〕 ; stragglers ; runaway troops ―병 remnants (of a defeated troop) ; stragglers ; runaway troops ¶ 패잔병을 규합하다 rally scattered troops〔remnants of the defeated troops〕 ―병 소탕 a mopping-up〔clean-up〕 operation

패잡다 get the deal ; lead trumps ; become the banker

패장 敗將 a defeated〔vanquished〕 general

패적 敗敵 a defeated〔vanquished〕 enemy ; a fleeing enemy

패전 敗戰 a defeat ; a lost battle ; a reverse ―하다 lose a battle〔war〕 ; be〔get〕 defeated ; be vanquished ; suffer〔sustain〕 a defeat

―국 a defeated〔vanquished〕 nation ―주의 defeatism ―주의자 a defeatist ―투수 〖야구〗 a losing pitcher

패전트 a pageant ; a show ; pageantry 《총칭》 ¶ 패전트를 하다 hold〔give, display〕 a pageant

패주 敗走 rout ; débâcle (프) ; flight ―하다 be routed ; be put to rout ; take to flight ; flee ¶ 적을 패주케 하다 rout the enemy ; put the enemy to rout〔flight〕 ; set an enemy flying

패총 貝塚 a shell mound〔heap〕 ; a kitchen midden

패퇴 敗退 defeat ⇨ 패배 ―하다 be defeated ; retreat ; be beaten ; lose a battle

패트런 a patron

패하다 敗― ① [싸움에] be defeated ; be beaten ; suffer a defeat ; lose 《a game, a battle, the day》 ; come off a loser ¶ 전쟁에 패하다 be defeated in a war ; lose (a) war // 장기에 패하다 be beaten in a game of chess // 소송에 패하다 lose a lawsuit // 1대 5로 패하다 be defeated〔lose the game〕 by a score of 1 to 5 // 그는 800표 차이로 패했다 He lost by 800 votes.

② [살림이] go to ruin ; get ruined ; go to the dogs ¶ 집안이 패하다 a family goes to ruin // 동네가 패하다 a village gets ruined

③ [몸이] get run-down ; waste away ; fail ; fall off ¶ 그의 몸은 요즘 몹시 패했다 His health has failed sadly of late.

패혈증 敗血症 〖의학〗 septic(a)emia ; blood poisoning

팩 weakly ⇨ 픽

***팬** 스포츠〔댄스, 야구, 음악, 영화〕 팬 a sports〔dance, ball, music, movie〕 fan〔enthusiast〕 // …의 대단한 팬 an enthusiastic〔a fanatical〕 admirer of ... // 팬이 많은 여배우 an actress with a large number of admirers

― 레터 fan mail ; a fan letter

팬더 〖동물〗 [작은 것] a (lesser) panda ; a bear cat ; a cat bear ; [큰 것] a giant〔great〕 panda

팬둥거리다 drone ; loaf around ; lead an idle life ⇨ 빈둥거리다

팬들거리다 lead an idle life ; idle〔loaf〕 one's time away ¶ 팬들팬들 idly ; indolently ⇨ 빈둥거리다

팬지 〖식물〗 a pansy ; a heartsease

팬츠 ① [속바지] underpants ; drawers ;

[운동 선수의] trunks ; tights ② [즈봉] pants 《미·속》 ; [승마용의] breeches ; [쇼트 팬츠] shorts
*팬케이크 a pancake
— 화장(품) pancake makeup
*팬터마임 a pantomime ; a dumb show ¶ 팬터마임을 하다 do one's pantomime 《of》 // 팬터마임을 하는 사람 a pantomimist
팬터지 [환상] a fantasy ; a phantasy ; [환상곡] a fantasia ; a fantasy
팬티 panties
— 스타킹 panty stockings ; a panty hose
팸플릿 a pamphlet ; a leaflet ; a brochure ¶ 팸플릿을 내다 pamphleteer // 팸플릿으로 나오다 be published in pamphlet form
팻말 牌— a notice〔bulletin〕 board
팽 ① [도는 모양] round ; around ; circling ; quickly ¶ 팽 돌다 go clear round // 운동장을 한바퀴 팽 돌아 run all round the ground ② [머리가] reelingly ¶ 머리가 팽 돌다 reel ; swim // 눈이 팽 돈다 My eyes swim. /I feel dizzy.
팽개치다 ① throw away〔aside〕 ; fling away ; cast away ¶ 창밖으로 팽개치다 throw〔fling〕 《a thing》 out of the window // 길가에 쓰레기를 팽개치다 throw away refuse along the road
② [내버려 두다] neglect ; lay aside ; leave〔let〕 《anything》 alone ¶ 일〔공부〕을 팽개치다 neglect one's work〔lessons〕 ; leave one's work〔lessons〕 undone // 그런 문제를 그냥 팽개쳐 두어서는 안된다 You must not leave the matter unsettled.
팽그르르 《spinning, whirling, revolving, turning》 around rapidly ¶ 팽그르르 돌다 turn (round) ; revolve // 팽이가 팽그르르 돈다 A top spins.
팽글팽글 《turning, spinning, revolving》 round and round rapidly ¶ 팽이가 팽글팽글 돈다 A top spins round and round.
팽나무 〖식물〗 a hackberry ; a (Chinese) nettle tree ; Celtis sinensis (학명)
팽대 膨大 swelling ; expansion —하다 swell ; expand
팽만 膨滿 inflation —하다 inflate ; be inflated
팽배 澎湃 the roaring of breakers ; surging —하다 surge ; roar ; churn ¶ 팽배하는 민주 사상 the flood-tide of democracy // 팽배하는 파도 surging waves
팽압 膨壓 〖식물〗 turgor pressure
*팽이 a (toy) top ¶ 팽이를 돌리다 spin a top // 팽이를 쳐서 돌리다 whip a top to make it spin
—치기 top spinning
†팽창 膨脹 swelling ; inflation ; expansion ; distension ; dilation ; increase (증가) ; growth (발전) —하다 swell ; expand ; inflate ; increase ; distend ; grow ¶ 도시의 팽창 the growth of a city // 통화의 팽창 inflation of currency // 비용의 팽창 an increase in expenses // 기체의 팽창 expansion of gases // 수은은 열을 가하면 팽창한다 Mercury expands by heat. // 열은 대개의 금속을 팽창시킨다 Heat expands most metals. // 서울시는 교외로 급속히 팽창해 간다 The city of *Seoul* is growing rapidly into the country. // 국고의 세출은 해마다 팽창한다 The State expenditure goes on increasing year by year.
—계(計) a dilatometer — 계수 the coefficient of expansion —력 expansive force〔power〕 ; tension —성 expansibility ; extensibility — 예산(豫算) an inflated budget ; swollen estimates —율 the rate of expansion — 정책 an expansionist policy ; a policy of expansion —제(劑) an inflating〔a blowing〕 agent —주의 expansionism —축(軸) a thermal axis —판(瓣) an expansion valve
팽패롭다 (be) cranky ; crotchety ; particular ; fastidious ¶ 팽패로운 사람 a cranky person ; a crosspatch
팽패리 a crank ; a crosspatch ; on irritable person ; a fuss-budget 《미·구》
팽팽 round and round ; rapidly ¶ 머리가 팽팽 돌다 feel dizzy // 팽이가 팽팽 돈다 A top spins round and round.
†팽팽하다 ① [밧줄 따위가] (be) tight ; taut ¶ 바지가 팽팽하다 one's trousers are tight // 줄이 팽팽하다 a rope is taut // 로프를 팽팽히 당기지 않으면 텐트가 처진다 If you don't pull the rope taut, the tent will sag.
② [성질이] (be) narrow-minded ; touchy ; testy ; peevish ¶ 팽팽한 사람 a narrow-minded〔testy〕 person
③ [세력이] (be) equal ; even ; equally-matched ¶ 세력이 팽팽하다 be well matched in strength〔power〕
팽팽하다 膨膨— (be) bursting 《with》 ; be filled to breaking point
팽하다 (be) moderate ; temperate ; just right
퍅퍅 unyieldingly ; firmly ; impetuously ¶ 퍅퍅 쏘다 make cutting remarks // 사람에게 퍅퍅 대들다 stand up to 《a person》 firmly
퍅하다 愎— (be) testy ; quick-tempered ; peppery ; waspish ; snappish ; peevish
퍼내다 bail〔dip, scoop, ladle〕 out 《water》 ; pump out ¶ 두손으로 퍼내다 scoop up 《water》 in one's hands // 독의 쌀을 퍼내다 take dry rice out of a jar // 솥에서 국을 퍼내다 ladle soup out of a kettle // 배의 물을 퍼내다 bail out a boat ⇨ 푸다

퍼니 idly ; lazily ; indolently ¶ 퍼니 놀다 lead an idle life ; loaf away one's days
퍼덕거리다 flap〔beat〕 the wings ; flutter ⇨ 파닥거리다 ¶ 새가 퍼덕거리다 The bird beats its wings.
퍼덕퍼덕 [새·돛 따위] flapping ; fluttering ; [물고기가] flopping ; leaping ; splashing
퍼드덕거리다 ⇨ 퍼덕거리다
*__퍼뜨리다__ spread ; diffuse ; circulate ; disseminate ; make popular ; advertise (광고) ; propagate (종교 따위를) ¶ 소문을 퍼뜨리다 spread a rumor∥공산 사상을 퍼뜨리다 propagate communism ; spread communist idea∥세상에 퍼뜨리다 spread abroad∥소문을 퍼뜨리다 circulate a false rumor∥그는 그 얘기를 퍼뜨렸다 He spread the story.
퍼뜩 suddenly ; in a flash ¶ 좋은 생각이 퍼뜩 떠올랐다 A good idea suddenly struck me. /A happy idea flashed across my mind. ∥시렁에 자루를 놓고 온 것을 퍼뜩 생각했다 It struck to me that I had left my bag on the rack.
퍼뜩퍼뜩 ⇨ 푸뜩푸뜩
퍼렁 blue ; blue color〔pigment〕
퍼렇다 (be) deep〔fresh〕 blue〔green〕 ⇨ 파랗다
퍼레이드 a parade
퍼르르 bubbling ; seething ; in a burst of flame ; in a huff ; trembling ⇨ 파르르
퍼머 a permanent (wave) ; a perm 《구》 **―하다** have one's hair permed〔permanently waved〕 ; set a wave 《into the hair》 ; have〔get〕 a perm(anent) ¶ 네 머리는 퍼머할 필요가 없는 곱슬머리라서 좋겠다 You're lucky to have naturally curly hair that doesn't have to be permed.
퍼먹다 ① [퍼서] scoop〔dip, ladle〕 and eat ¶ 밥을 숟가락으로 퍼먹다 scoop rice with a spoon and eat it ② [많이] shovel down〔up〕 ; eat greedily ; devour ¶ 음식을 퍼먹다 shovel up〔down〕 food ; shovel food into one's mouth
퍼벌하다 neglect one's appearance ; be careless about one's appearance
퍼붓다 ① [물 따위를] pour〔shower〕 《water》 upon ; [욕설을] heap ; hurl ; [포탄을] rain 《shells》 upon ¶ 욕설을 퍼붓다 rain abuses 《upon》 ; launch into abuses against 《a person》∥질문을 퍼붓다 shower 《a person》 with questions
② [비가] pour down ; rain in torrents ¶ 비가 억수같이 퍼붓는다 It rains cats and dogs. /It pours down.
퍼석퍼석 crumbly ; being fragile ⇨ 파삭파삭 **―하다** (be) fragile ; crumbly ; frail ; crisp
†**퍼센트** percent ; per cent 《%, p.c., per ct.》 ¶ 100퍼센트의 성공 a one-hundred percent success∥효과가 그야말로 100퍼센트다 It is certainly one-hundred percent efficiency. ∥율이 1퍼센트 올랐다 The ratio went up one percent. /The percentage was raised one point. ∥백퍼센트의 능률을 올리다 secure one-hundred percent efficiency∥5퍼센트의 이익을 남기다 get 5% interest∥취직률은 100퍼센트였다 The employment rate was 100 percent.
퍼센티지 (a) percentage
퍼스트 〖야구〗 [일루] first base ; [일루수] a first baseman
― 베이스 〖야구〗 ⇨ 퍼스트
퍼스트 레이디 [대통령·원수의 부인] the First Lady
퍼올리다 draw up ; scoop〔dip〕 up ; pump up (펌프로) ¶ 우물물을 퍼올리다 draw water from a well
*__퍼지다__ ① [넓어지다] spread out ; get broader ¶ 퍼진 가지 spreading branches∥뿌리가 퍼지다 roots spread∥끝이 퍼지다 the tip spreads out∥강은 강어귀에서 퍼지고 있다 The river broadens (out) at its mouth.
② [보급되다] spread (abroad) ; be diffused〔circulated, propagated〕 ¶ 널리 퍼진 미신 wide-spread superstition∥소문이 퍼지다 a rumor spreads (abroad) ∥그의 명성은 전국에 퍼졌다 His fame spread all over the country.
③ [퍼지다] ¶ 다림살이 잘 퍼진다 The cloth irons well.
④ [번영하다] ¶ 자손이 퍼지다 have numerous descendants
⑤ [병이] prevail (퍼지다)
퍼펙트 perfect
― 게임 〖야구〗 a perfect game
퍽[1] ① [힘있게] hard ; firmly ¶ 칼로 퍽 찌르다 thrust〔stab〕 with a knife
② [넘어지는 모양] with a thud〔flop〕 ¶ 퍽 쓰러지다 fall with a thud ; fall down all of heap
†**퍽**[2] [매우] very ; very much ; so ; quite 《구》 ; awfully ; greatly ; highly ; exceedingly ¶ 퍽 어려운 일 a task of great difficulty∥퍽 기쁘다 be very glad ; be much pleased∥퍽 덥다 be so hot∥퍽 인상적이다 be deeply impressive 〔impressed〕∥퍽 중병이다 be quite ill∥퍽 취하다 be quite drunk∥퍽 기쁘시겠습니다 How glad you must be ! ∥퍽 컸구나 What a big boy you've grown ! ∥퍽 재미 있었다 We had a mighty good time. /We were highly delighted.
퍽[3] a puck (아이스하키에서 쓰는)
퍽석 ① [맥없이] limply ; heavily ; with a flump ② [깨지는 모양] 《break》 easily ; fragilely
퍽퍽 ① [찌르는 모양] thrusting repeatedly ; hard ¶ 칼로 퍽퍽 찌르다 thrust the knife in again and again ② [쓰러지는 모양] with flop after flop ; thudding and thudding ¶ 퍽퍽 쓰러지다 fall

down on after another ③ [쏟아지는 모양] thick and fast ; in torrents ¶ 눈이 펑펑 쏟아지고 있다 The snow is falling thick and fast. ④ [깎이는 모양] yielding ; easily ¶ 이 연필은 펵펵 깎인다 This pencil sharpens easily.

펵펵하다 (be) dry and crumbling ; crisp ; brittle

편둥거리다 ⇨ 빈둥거리다

편들거리다 ⇨ 빈둥거리다

편뜻 in an instant ; instantly ; in a flash ; quickly ; immediately ⇨ 언뜻 ¶ 편뜻 좋은 생각이 났다 A good idea flashed across my mind. // 그의 이름이 편뜻 생각나지 않는다 His name does not occur to me instantly.

*펀치 〖권투〗 a punch ¶ 턱에 펀치를 먹이다 punch 《a person》 on the jaw 〔chin〕 ; land a punch on 《a person's》 jaw〔chin〕 // 펀치를 얻어맞다 get a punch 《on the nose》

편편하다 (be) even ; flat ⇨ 판판하다

편하다 (be) vast ; wide ; broad ; boundless ¶ 편한 바다 a vast sea

펄 a wide expanse of land ; a vast plain ; a prairie ⇨ 개펄

펄떡거리다 pitapat ; [심장이] palpitate ; flutter ; throb ; keep hopping〔jumping〕

*펄럭거리다 flutter ; flap ; wave ¶ 자락이 펄럭거리는 긴 치마 a long skirt flapping about the feet // 기가 바람에 펄럭거린다 A flag flutters〔flaps〕 in the wind.

펄럭펄럭 with a flutter〔flap, wave〕 ; fluttering ; flapping ; waving ¶ 깃발이 바람에 펄럭펄럭 나부끼다 a flag flaps in the wind

펄렁거리다 flutter ; flap ; wave ; fly ; stream (깃발 따위가) ⇨ 펄럭거리다

펄썩 [연기나 먼지가] puffily ; [주저앉는 모양] plump ; suddenly ¶ 바람이 불 때마다 먼지가 펄썩 났다 Every gust of wind stirred up the dust. // 그는 펄썩 주저앉았다 He sat down plump.

펄쩍 suddenly ; lightly ; fast ¶ 펄쩍 뛰다 jump ; leap ; start // 펄쩍 뛰며 좋아하다 jump for joy // 성이 나서 펄쩍 뛰다 start up with anger // 펄쩍 달리다 run fast

펄쩍펄쩍 jumping〔leaping, springing〕 up and down ¶ 펄쩍펄쩍 뛰다 jump up and down // 성나서 펄쩍펄쩍 뛰다 bounce with anger

펄펄 ① [끓는 모양] boiling ; seething ¶ 물이 펄펄 끓고 있다 The water is boiling. ② [뜨거운 모양] feverish (체온이) ; burning hot (온돌방이) ¶ 그는 몸이 펄펄 끓는다 He has a very high fever. ③ [새·깃발이] fluttering ; flapping ¶ 기가 바람에 펄펄 나부낀다 The flag flutters〔flaps〕 in the wind.

펄펄하다 ① [성질이] (be) short-tempered ; quick-tempered ; hot-tempered ; fiery
② [생기가] lively ; vigorous ; energetic ; quick ¶ 나이에도 불구하고 그는 아직 펄펄하다 In spite of his age, he is in the pink of health. ⇨ 팔팔하다

*펄프 pulp ¶ 펄프로 하다 (reduce to) pulp
— 목재 wood pulp 인견 — rayon pulp
—재 pulpwood

펌블 〖야구〗 a fumble —하다 fumble 《a grounder》

*펌프 a pump ¶ 펌프를 틀다 work a pump // 펌프로 물을 퍼내다 pump out water ; pump the water out
공기 — an air pump 밀— a force pump 빨— a suction pump 배수 — a drainage pump 증기 — a steam pump 진공 — a vacuum pump

펑 pop —하다 pop ¶ 펑하고 with a pop ; with an explosion // 펑하고 마개가 빠졌다 The cork came out with a pop. // 나는 펑하는 소리를 들었다 I heard it go pop !

펑퍼지다 get well-developed ; get well-rounded ¶ 펑퍼진 엉덩이 well-rounded hips // 펑퍼진 어깨 well-developed 〔broad〕 shoulders

펑퍼짐하다 (be) gently curved ; be spacious ¶ 펑퍼짐한 언덕 a gently sloping hill // 펑퍼짐한 엉덩이 well-rounded hips

펑펑 ① [물이] with a rush ; with force ; violently ¶ (물이) 펑펑 나오다 《water》 gush〔stream〕 out ; spout with force〔violently〕
② [눈·비가] heavily ¶ 비가 펑펑 쏟아진다 It rains heavily〔hard, in torrents, in showers, cats and dogs〕. // 눈이 펑펑 내린다 It snows heavily. /The snow falls thick and fast.
③ [총소리] pop pop ; bang bang ; keep popping〔banging〕 ¶ 총소리가 펑펑 울렸다 Bang ! bang ! went the gun.

페넌트 a pennant ¶ 페넌트를 다투다 compete for pennant
— 레이스 a pennant race

페널티 〖경기〗 a penalty
—골 [럭비] a penalty goal — 에어리어 〖축구〗 a penalty area —킥 〖축구·럭비〗 a penalty kick

페놀 phenol
— 수지 phenolic rosins

페놀프탈레인 phenolphthalein

*페니 a penny 《*pl.* -nies, pence》

> 참고 **pence**는 금액 **pennies**는 화폐의 개수를 말할 때에 쓰임

⇨ 펜스 ¶ 반 페니 a half-penny [héipni] // 1페니 반 three halfpence [héipəns]

페니실린 〖약〗 penicillin ¶ 10만 단위의 페니실린 100,000 units penicillin
— 분말 penicillin dust — 쇼크 a penicillin shock — 연고 a penicillin ointment — 주사 a penicillin shot 유랍(油

蠟) — oil wax penicillin 혼합 — mixed penicillin
*페달 a pedal ¶ 페달을 밟다 pedal 《a bicycle》
페더급 —級 [권투의] featherweight class
— 선수 a featherweight
페루 Peru ¶ 페루의 Peruvian
— 사람 a Peruvian
페르시아 Persia ¶ 페르시아의 Persian
— 말 Persian — 사람 a Persian
페르시아 만 —灣 the Persian Gulf
페미니스트 a feminist
페미니즘 feminism
페소 [화폐 단위] a peso 《*pl.* ~s》《P》
*페스트 『의학』 (a) pest ; the bubonic 〔black〕 plague
—균 pest bacilli
페스티벌 a festival
페시미스트 a pessimist
페시미즘 pessimism
페어 플레이 fair play ¶ 페어 플레이를 하자 Let's play fair 《cricket》. /Play the game !
페이 pay
페이스 (a) pace ¶ 자기의 페이스로 at one's own pace // 페이스가 빠르다 be quickly paced // 남의 페이스를 흐트러뜨리다 throw one's rival out of his stride ; force the pace of one's rival // 자기 페이스를 지키다 proceed at one's own pace ; do not overpace〔outpace〕 oneself ; keep within one's speed
†페이지 a page ; a leaf ¶ 오른쪽 페이지 the right-hand page ; the recto 《*pl.* -s》// 왼쪽 페이지 the left-hand page ; the verso 《*pl.* -s》// 반대 페이지 the opposite page // 여백(의) 페이지 a blank page // 신문의 마지막 페이지 《on》 the back page of a newspaper // 1 페이지 크기의 full page 《frontispiece》// 페이지가 달리지 않은 unpaged ; pageless ; without pagination // 500페이지의 책 a book of 500 pages // 페이지의 위〔중간, 아래〕에 at the top〔middle, bottom〕 of a page // (제) 3 페이지에 on the third page ; on page 3 // 5 내지 10 페이지에 on pages〔p. p〕 5-10 // 페이지를 달다 page ; paginate // 90 페이지를 열다 open 《the book》 at〔to〕 page 90 ; find page 90 // 페이지를 넘기다 turn (over) the leaves〔pages〕 of a book ; thumb〔leaf〕 through the pages
페이퍼 [종이] paper ; [사포] sandpaper ¶ 페이퍼로 문지르다 sandpaper ; polish with sandpaper
— 플랜 a plan on paper ; a paper formula
†페인트 [뼁끼] paint ¶ 페인트를 칠하다 paint // 페인트가 벗겨지다 the paint comes off // 페인트 주의 [게시] Wet paint 《미》; Fresh paint 《영》
—장이 a painter 수성 — water-paint
페치카 pechka 《러》; a Russian brick stove
페티코트 a petticoat ; an undershirt
페팅 petting ¶ 가벼운 페팅 soft petting ; necking // 뜨거운 페팅 heavy petting
페퍼민트 peppermint
†펜 a pen ¶ …라는 펜네임으로 under the pen name of ... // 펜을 들다 take up one's pen ; take pen in hand // 펜을 놓다 put down one's pen
—글씨 pen writing —네임 a pen name —대 a penholder ; a pen-handle —접시 a pen tray —촉 a pen point ; a nib 《영》
펜더 [자동차의 흙받기] a fender
펜맨십 [펜 습자] penmanship ; [공책] a copybook
펜스 pence ⇨ 페니 ¶ 2 펜스 [금액] twopence [tʌ́pəns] ; [동화] a twopenny [tʌ́pni]
펜습자 —習字 penmanship
펜실베이니아 Pennsylvania 《Pa., Penn., Penna.》
‡펜싱 fencing
— 선수 a fencer ; a foilsman
펜클럽 the P. E. N. Club 《the International Association of Poets, Playwrights, Editors, Essayists, and Novelists》
펜타곤 [미국 국방성] the Pentagon
‡펜팔 a pen pal ; a pen-friend
펜화 —畫 line drawing ; [그림] a pen (-and-ink) sketch ; a drawing in pen and ink
펠리컨 『새』 a pelican
*펠트 felt
— 모자 a (soft) felt hat
펩신 pepsin
펩톤 peptone
펫서리 [피임구] a pessary
*펭귄 a penguin
펴내다 [발행하다] publish ; issue ; bring out
펴낸이 a publisher
펴놓다 ① [동작] unfold ; spread ; [상태] lay 《a thing》 spread〔open〕; keep 〔leave〕 《a book》 open ¶ 이부자리를 펴놓다 make〔prepare〕 a bed ; keep bedding〔a bed〕 spread ② [마음을] open 《one's heart》 《to》; lay 《one's heart》 bare ; unbosom 《oneself》
†펴다 ① [벌리다] spread (out) ; open ; [접힌 것을] unfold ; [오무라진 것을] stretch (out) ; [구김살을] smooth out ; [굽은 것을] straighten ; [말린 것을] unroll ; uncoil ¶ 구김살을 펴다 smooth out wrinkles ; iron out wrinkles (다리미로) // 날개를 펴다 spread its wings // 몸을 펴다 straighten oneself ; pull oneself up // 손가락을 펴다 spread out one's fingers // 신문을 펴다 unfold a newspaper // 이부자리를 펴다 spread bedding ; make a bed // 철사를 펴다 stretch

ㅍ

〔uncoil〕 wire // 허리를 펴다 stretch one's back // 책의 10 페이지를 펴라 Open your book at page ten. /Turn your book to page 10.

② [마음을] ease ; be〔feel〕 at ease ; relieve ; feel relieved ¶ 기를 펴다 relieve one's mind ; be animated // 선생이 엄해서 학생들이 기를 못 편다 The teacher is so strict that the students are ill at ease.

③ [옹색함을] relieve ; ease ; alleviate ; improve ¶ 그는 나의 옹색함을 펴주었다 He helped me out of (financial) difficulty.

④ [공포하다] spread ; promulgate ; propagate ¶ 지식을 펴다 promulgate knowledge // 새 종교를 펴다 spread〔promulgate〕 a new form of religion

⑤ [세력을] extend ; establish (부식하다) ¶ 세력을 펴다 extend one's power〔influence〕

펴이다 ① [펴지다] get unfolded〔straightened, smoothed〕 ② [형편이] get better ; mend ; improve ; be eased ③ [일 따위가] get straightened out ; be smoothed 《down, over》

***펴지다** ① [펼쳐지다] get unfolded〔unrolled, spread, laid spread〕; unfold ; unroll ; spread ② [주름이] get smoothed ; be flattened ; smooth 《out》; flatten 《down》 ③ [굽은 것이] get straightened ; straighten (out, up) ④ [닫힌 것이] open ; be laid open

편 [떡] rice cake

†**편 便** ① [한쪽] a side ; a part ; [방향] a direction ; a way ¶ 양편에 on both sides ; on either〔each〕 side // 왼편에 on the left hand〔side〕 // 한편으로는 on the one hand // 그는 게으른 편이다 He is rather idle.

② [한패] a party ; a side ; a team (경기에서) ¶ 우리 편 our side〔party, team〕 // 상대 편 the other side ; the opposite party〔side〕

③ [기회·인편] chance ; opportunity ¶ 인편에 by means of someone ; under the favor of 《a person》 // 편이 있는 대로 on the first opportunity // 철도〔배〕 편에 by rail〔sea, ship〕

편 編 compilation ; editing ¶ 김박사 편 compiled〔edited〕 by Dr. *Kim*

***편 篇** [권] a volume ; a book ; [장·절] a chapter ; a section ; a part ; a canto (시의) ¶ 상〔중, 하〕 편 the first〔second, third〕 volume // 제1편 chapter〔part〕 one ; the first chapter〔part〕 // 한편의 시 a piece of poetry ; a poem

편가르다 便— divide into (two) teams〔parties〕 ¶ 편갈라 놓다 play sides // 편갈라 일하다 work in teams〔groups〕

편각 偏角 〖지리〗 declination ; angle of deviation ; 〖수학〗 amplitude

—계(計) a declinometer **자기(磁氣) —** magnetic declination

편강 片薑 sliced dried ginger

⁑**편견 偏見** (a) prejudice ; a bias ; a distorted〔prejudiced, biased〕 view ; a prejudiced opinion ¶ 편견이 있는 partial ; prejudiced // 편견이 없는 unbiased ; impartial ; without prejudice // 인종적〔종교적〕 편견 racial〔religious〕 prejudice // 편견을 가지다 hold a biased view ; have a prejudice against 《a person, a thing》; be biased〔prejudiced〕 against 《a person, a thing》 // 편견을 버리다 cast〔put〕 away a prejudice ; get over one's prejudice

편곡 編曲 arrangement **—하다** arrange ¶ A씨 편곡의 곡 a piece arranged by Mr. A // 악곡을 바이올린〔4부합창〕 곡으로 편곡하다 arrange a piece for the violin〔four voices〕 // 이 바이올린 곡은 피아노로도 편곡되어 있다 This music for the violin also arranged for the piano.

편광 偏光 polarized light ; polarization (of light)

—각(角) a polarizing angle ; an angle of polarization **—경(鏡)** a polarimeter ; a polariscope **—계** a polarimeter **—기(器)** a polarizer ; a polariscope **—면(面)** a plane of polarization **— 측정(測定)** polarimetry **— 탄성(彈性)**(학) photoelasticity **—판(板)** a polarizing plate **— 프리즘** a polarizer **— 현미경** a polarization microscope **인조(人造) —판(板)** a polaroid

편년 編年 recording chronologically

—사 a chronicle ; annals **—체** chronological form〔order〕

편뇌 片腦 camphor

편달 鞭撻 [격려] encouragement ; urging ; whipping ; [채찍질] lashing ; whipping **—하다** urge ; encourage ; spur on ; whip ; lash ¶ 자기를 편달하다 spur oneself // 가일층 편달해 주십시오 I must seek your further advice and encouragement.

편답 遍踏 travel ⇨ 편력

편당 偏黨 [한편의 당파] a faction ; a wing ; a clique ; a group ; [당파에 쏠림] partiality for a party **—하다** be partial to a party ; side with a party ¶ 편당을 짓다 form a faction

편대 編隊 a formation ; forming ranks ; forming a column (종대) ; getting in line (횡대) ¶ 5대 편대로 in a five-plane formation // 편대를 짓다 form ranks ; get in line ; make a formation

— 비행 formation flying ; a formation flight ; flying in formation ¶ 편대 비행을 하다 fly in formation ; make a formation flight **—장** a flight leader

편도 片道 one way ; each way ¶ 편도 500원 five hundred *won* one way // 편도는 기차로 가고 돌아올 때는 걷다 take

the train one way〔go by train〕 and walk back // 로마까지 2등 편도 한장 주시오 One second-class one-way ticket to Rome, please. 《미》/Give me a second-class single to Rome. 《영》 // 편도입니까 왕복입니까 Do you want a one-way ticket or a round-trip?
— 승차권 a one-way ticket 《미》; a single (ticket) 《영》 — 요금 a one-way fare 《미》; a single fare 《영》 — 항해 a one-way〔single〕 voyage
편도 扁桃 『식물』 an almond; the almond tree; Prunus amygdalus (학명)
—루 almond oil
편도선 扁桃腺 a tonsil; an amygdala 《*pl.* -lae》 ¶ 편도선이 붓다 get〔have〕 a swollen tonsil
— 비대 tonsillar hypertrophy; an enlarged tonsil; swollen tonsils — 수술 tonsillectomy —염 tonsillitis; quinsy
편두통 偏頭痛 『의학』 (a) megrim; (a) migraine; (a) hemicrania; a sick headache ¶ 편두통이 나다 have〔suffer from〕 a migraine
†편들다 便— side with; take 《a person's》 part; take side with; stand in with; stand by; support; back ⇨ 편 ¶ 아들을 편들다 side with one's son // 너는 어느 쪽에 편드니 Which side are you on? // 그는 민주당을 편들었다 He supported the Democratic Party. // 여론은 그에게 편들었다 Public opinion was in his favor. // 그는 언제나 우리에게 편든다 He is always on our side. // 신은 정의에 편들어 주신다 God is on the side of justice.
*편람 便覽 a handbook; a manual; a guide
영어 — a handbook of English
편람표 便覽表 a chart; a table
계산 — a ready reckoner
편력 遍歷 travels; travelling about; a tour; roaming; pilgrimage; itinerancy —하다 travel〔tour〕 about; roam; rove over; itinerate ¶ 전국을 편력하다 make a tour of the country; wander〔roam〕 about the country
—자 a pilgrim; an itinerant; a rover
독서 — wanderings through the world of books 연애 — love life ¶ 그의 연애 편력은 매우 다채로운 것이었다 His love life was very colorful.
편류 偏流 『항공』 (a) drift; (a) deflection; [포술] windage
—각 a drift angle —계 a drift meter
*편리 便利 convenience; expediency; handiness (간편함); facilities (설비의); advantage (이익) —하다 (be) convenient; handy; expedient; serviceable; useful ¶ 편리한 장소 a convenient place // 편리하게 만든 집 a commodious house // 편리하지 않은 inconvenient // 편리상 for the sake of convenience // 사용하기에 편리하다 be convenient for use; be easy to use // 편리를 제공하다 give〔afford〕 every facility 《for》 // 편리를 도모하다 accommodate 《a person》; serve〔suit〕 《a person's》 convenience // 편리하게 하다 facilitate // 교통이 편리하다 be convenient for transportation // 공중의 편리를 도모하다 promote the benefit of the public // 이 사전은 포켓에 넣기에 편리하다 This dictionary is handy for the pocket. // 되도록이면 좀더 편리한 곳으로 이사가고 싶다 If possible, we would like to move to a more convenient place. // 이 기계는 아주 편리하게 되어 있다 The machine is skilfully devised for convenient use. // 요즈음은 버스 덕택으로 이 마을도 드디어 편리하게 됐다 Thanks to the bus service, this village has become convenient at last. // 모두 교통이 편리한 곳들인가요 Are they all easily accessible?
편린 片鱗 a part; a portion; a glimpse ¶ 그것으로 그의 성격의 편린을 알아볼 수 있다 It enables us to get a glimpse of his personality.
편마암 片麻岩 gneiss
편만 遍滿 pervasiveness; diffuseness; omnipresence; ubiquity —하다 (be) diffuse; pervasive; permeate; omnipresent; extend all round; spread about
편면 片面 [한쪽면] one side
편모 偏母 one's lone mother; one's widowed mother ¶ 편모 시하에 있다 be under one's lone mother's roof
— 슬하 having only one's mother to serve
편모 鞭毛 a flagellum
—충 a flagellate —충류 Flagellata
편무 片務 a unilateral duty〔obligation, responsibility〕 ¶ 편무적 unilateral
— 계약 a unilateral〔an independent, a one-sided〕 contract
편무역 片貿易 one-side〔one-way〕 trade
편물 編物 [뜨개질] knitting; (a) knitwork; crochet (갈고리 바늘의); [뜬것] knitted goods —하다 knit; crochet; do knitting
—기 a knitting machine — 바늘 a knitting needle; a knitting pin
*편법 便法 an easy〔a handy〕 method; a short cut〔way〕; an expedient; an expediency; a convenient mode; an expedient means; an expediential policy ¶ 일시적 편법 a temporary expedient // 편법을 쓰다 adopt〔resort to〕 an expedient
편벽 偏僻 one-sidedness; partiality; bias; eccentricity —하다 (be) partial; biased; one-sided; eccentric
편복 便服 plain clothes; everyday clothes〔wear〕; weekday clothes; home

wear
편상화 編上靴 lace boots ; laced boots〔shoes〕
편서풍 偏西風 〖기상〗 the prevailing westerlies
편성 偏性 one-sidedness ; partiality ; a particular inclination ; an eccentricity ¶ 편성의 biased ; partial ; one-sided ; eccentric
편성 編成 organization ; formation ; composition ; footing **—하다** organize ; form ; compose ; comply ; draw up (예산 따위를) ; frame ; embody ¶ 예산을 편성하다 draw up an estimate ; make up a budget // 학급을 편성하다 organize a class // 편성되다 it consists 《of》 ; it is composed 《of》 // 함대를 편성하다 organize a squadron // 혼성 여단을 편성하다 form a mixed brigade // 2개 중대로 편성하다 organize into two companies // 군대는 전시 편성을 하고 있다 The army is on a war footing. // 한 학급은 60명으로 편성되어 있다 A class consists of sixty pupils.
예산 — the compilation of a budget **전시 —** a war footing〔organization〕 **프로 —** [라디오·TV의] the drawing〔getting〕 up of a (radio, TV) program(me) ; program(m)ing
편수 a head artisan〔craftsman〕 ; a master carpenter (대목의)
편수 編修 editing ; compilation **—하다** edit ; compile ; cut
—관 an editorial officer ; an (official) editor **—국** the Text Book Compilation Bureau **—원** the (editorial) staff member
편술 編述 editing ; compilation ; writing **—하다** edit ; compile ; write
편승 便乘 a ride in a passing automobile〔boat〕 **—하다** get〔take〕 a ride in 《a passing automobile, boat》 ; [기회에] take advantage of ; avail oneself of ; [시류에] climb〔hop, jump〕 on the bandwagon ¶ 그는 대통령 전세기에 편승하여 미국으로 갔다 Being given a ride in the chartered plane for President, he left for America. // 그 회사는 환경 문제라는 시류에 편승하는 것처럼 보인다 The company seems to be jumping on the environmental bandwagon.
편식 偏食 an unbalanced〔a one-sided〕 diet **—하다** have an unbalanced diet
편심 偏心 a one-sided mind ; a partial disposition ; 〖기계〗 eccentricity
—기(器) an eccentric **—력(力)** eccentric force **—륜(輪)** an eccentric (wheel) **—률(率)** eccentricity **— 반경(半徑)〔거리〕** an eccentric radius 《*pl.* -dii, ～es》 **—봉(棒)** an eccentric rod
편쌈 便— a gang fight ; a fight between two groups **—하다** have a gang fight
—꾼 a gang fighter
편안 便安 being well ; peace ; tranquility ; ease ; comfort ; coziness **—하다** (be) peaceful ; tranquil ; calm ; well ; quiet ; restful ; [안이] easy ; comfortable ; free from anxiety ; cozy ¶ 편안히 peacefully ; quietly ; calmly ; tranquilly ; in peace ; at rest // 편안한 생활 a quiet〔peaceful〕 life ; an easy〔a carefree〕 life (안락한) // 마음이 편안하다 feel at ease ; have one's mind at rest ; have a clear conscience // 편안한 생활을 하다 lead a quiet life ; live in peace ; live in comfort〔easy circumstances〕 // 편안한 잠을 자다 get to a calm〔peaceful〕 sleep // 마음이 편안치 않다 be uneasy in mind ; be ill at ease
편암 片岩 schist
결정 — crystalline schist
편애 偏愛 partiality 《for》 ; favoritism **—하다** love with partiality ; be partial to ; show favoritism
편액 扁額 a tablet ; a framed picture ; a plaque
편언 片言 ① [한마디말] a word ; a few words
② [한쪽말] one side 《of an argument〔a story〕》
편영 片影 a shadow ; a sign ; a speck 《of cloud, of sail》 ¶ 적의 편영도 볼 수가 없었다 Not a sign of the enemy was to be found. /There was no sign of the enemy.
편육 片肉 slices of boiled meat
‡편의 便宜 convenience ; accommodation ; facility ; benefit ; advantage ; expediency **—하다** (be) convenient ; handy ; advantageous ; expedient ; accommodating ¶ 편의한 방법 an expedient measure // 편의상 for convenience'(s) sake ; for convenience ; from personal convenience ; as a matter of convenience // 편의를 도모하다 consult 《a person's》 convenience ; accommodate 《a person》 ; consider 《a person's》 advantage ; give accommodation 《to》 // 교통의 편의를 도모하다 facilitate communication // 공중의 편의를 도모하다 contribute to the convenience of the public // 편의를 얻다 obtain facilities 《for》 ; get many advantages // 편의를 보아주다 accommodate 《a person》
—주의 opportunism ; expediency ; timeserving **—주의자** an opportunist ; a timeserver
편의대 便衣隊 plain-clothes soldiers (who infiltrate enemy-held territory)
편이 便易 facility ; handiness ; convenience **—하다** (be) convenient ; handy ; easy
편익 便益 benefit ; facility ; advantage ; convenience **—하다** (be) convenient ; beneficial ; advantageous ; helpful

ㅍ

¶ 상호 편익을 위해서 for mutual benefit // 편익을 얻다 be benefited ; benefit

편입 編入 ① entry ; admission ; incorporation 《in》; 〖군사〗 enlistment ; enrollment 《in》 ② [짜넣기] weaving 《in》 **—하다** [부류에] class 《with》; include 《in》; [예산에] insert ; [학급에] put〔admit, enroll〕《in》; [군에] assign 《to the infantry》; [합병] incorporate 〔enroll〕《into》; [전입] transfer 《to the reserve》 ¶ 시에 편입되다 be incorporated into a city // 그는 시험을 쳐서 4학년에 편입 되었다 He has been admitted through examination into the fourth year class. // 그는 신체검사에 합격하여 보병에 편입됐다 He passed the physical examination and was assigned to the infantry.

—생 an enrol(l)ee ; an enrolled student **— 시험** an examination for special admission 《into a certain class》

*__편자__ a horseshoe ¶ 편자 박는 사람 a horseshoer ; a farrier 《영》 // 말에 편자를 박다 shoe a horse

편자 編者 an editor ; a compiler ; an author

편재 遍在 omnipresence ; ubiquity ; immanence **—하다** (be) omnipresent ; ubiquitous ; immanent ; widespread ¶ 편재하는 신 the omnipresent God

편재 偏在 maldistribution **—하다** be maldistributed ¶ 물자가 편재하고 있다 Materials are maldistributed.

편재 騙財 swindle ; defraudation **—하다** swindle ; defraud ; get by swindling ; cheat 《a person》 out of 《property》

편저 編著 compilation ; redaction **—하다** compile ; redact

—자 a compiler ; a redactor

편전 便殿 a royal palace 《to live in》; a side room of a palace

‡**편제 編制** formation ; organization ; footing ; compilation ⇨ 편성 **—하다** form ; organize ; compose ¶ 2개 중대로 편제하다 organize into two companies

평시〔전시〕 — a peace〔war〕 footing 〔organization〕

편주 扁舟 a small boat ; a skiff

일엽— a tiny〔little〕 boat ; a skiff

편죽 片竹 a piece〔chip〕 of bamboo

편중 偏重 preponderance **—하다** [무게] preponderate ; [중점] attach〔give〕 too much importance 《to》; make too much of ; lean upon ¶ 지능 교육의 편중 too much intellectual training

†**편지 片紙, 便紙** a letter ; a note ; an epistle ; a communication ; a billet (단신) ; a favor (상업문에서) ¶ 5일부의 편지 the letter dated (of) the 5th // 편지를 잘〔못〕 쓰는 사람 a good〔poor〕 correspondent // 편지의 취지 the effect 〔purport, text〕 of a letter // 편지를 쓰다 write a letter ; write 《a person》 a letter ; write to 《a person》 // 편지를 주고 받다 correspond with each other ; exchange letters // 편지를 부치다 mail a letter // 편지를 써 놓고 가다 leave a letter for 《a person》 // 편지 쓰기를 싫어하다 hate letter-writing // 편지의 답장을 하다 answer a letter // 편지로 신청하다 apply by letter // 편지를 부치다 post a letter // 편지를 받다 get〔receive〕 a letter // 편지를 봉하다〔펴보다〕 seal〔open, unseal〕 a letter // 편지로 주문하다 write for // 편지를 아직 못받았습니다 Your letter has not yet reached me. // 그에게서 매주 편지가 옵니다 We hear from him every week. // 나에게 편지가 오지 않았어요 Is there any mail for me ? // 도착하시면 편지를 해주십시오 Please write me a letter when you arrive there.

— 내왕 correspondence ; communication ; exchange of letters **— 사연** the contents of a letter **—지** letter〔writing〕 paper **—철** a letter file〔rack, clip〕 **—통** a mailbox 《미》; a letter box 《영》; a postbox **—투〔틀〕** letter writing conventions ; a letter-writing model **사례〔감사〕 —** a letter of thanks ; a thank-you letter ; an appreciative letter **안부 —** a letter inquiring after someone's health **연애 —** a love letter **영문 —** a letter in English **인사 —** (a letter of) greetings

편지질 便紙— exchange of letters ; correspondence ; communication **—하다** exchange letters ; correspond 《with each other》

편집 偏執 bias ; obstinacy **—하다** stick to 《one's prejudice》; show bias

—광 [병] monomania ; [광인] a monomaniac **—병(病)** paranoia ; paranoea **—병 환자** a paranoi(a)c ; a paranoeac

‡**편집 編輯** editing ; compilation **—하다** edit ; compile ; prepare for the press ¶ 편집 회의를 열다 hold an editorial conference // 잡지를 편집하다 edit a magazine

— 고문 an associate〔advisory〕 editor **— 마감** the editorial deadline ; the time for going to (the) press **— 방침** an editorial policy **—부** an editorial department **—실** the editorial room ; [신문의] the desk **—원** (a member of) the editorial staff ; a〔an editorial〕 staff member **—자** an editor ; a compiler ; a redactor ; [필름의] a (film) cutter **—장** the managing editor ; the chief editor ; the editor in chief ; [신문사의] the copy chief 《미》; [간행물의] the general editor **— 차장(次長)** [신문의] a subeditor ; a copyreader 《미》; a deskman 《속》 **— 회의** an editorial conference **— 후기(後記)** the editor's

〔editorial〕 comments
편집국 編輯局 an editorial office〔board, bureau, section 《미》〕; a news office
— 부국장 the deputy managing editor
—장 the managing〔chief〕 editor
편짓다 片— [목재를] sort 《lumber》 according to use; arrange 《ginseng》 to make a fixed number of pound lots
편짜다 便— form a team〔party〕; make up parties; separate into groups ¶ 편 짜서 화투하다 play cards in teams // 셋이 편짜다 three band together to form a team
편짝 便— a side; one side ¶ 이〔저〕편짝 this〔the other〕 side // 우리 편짝 our side〔party〕// 길 한편짝 one side of the road // 양편짝에 on both sides; on each side // 건너편짝에 across; on the other side // 반대편짝에 opposite; on the opposite side // 한편짝으로 기울다 lean to one side // 한편짝 말만 듣고는 송사를 못한다 You can't give a fair judgment hearing only one party.
편차 偏差 declination; deflection; variation; drift (항로의)
—계(計) 〖측량〗 a declinometer **—치(値)** the deviation (value) **자기 —** magnetic declination **평방(平方) —** 〖통계〗 variance **표준 —** 〖통계〗 the standard〔root mean square〕 deviation
편찬 編纂 compilation; editing **—하다** compile; edit ¶ 이 책은 잘 편찬되어 있다 This book is excellently got up. // 그 한영사전은 지금 편찬중이다 The Korean-English dictionary is in preparation〔the course of compilation〕.
—물(物) a compilation **—소(所)〔부(部)〕** the editorial office〔department〕 **—원(員)** the editorial staff **— 위원** a compilation committee **—자** a compiler; an editor
편찮다 [불편하다] (be) inconvenient; uncomfortable; [병으로] unwell; upset; distressed; indisposed ¶ 몸이 편찮아서 on account of illness // 몸이 편찮다 feel〔be〕 unwell // 감기로 편찮다 be indisposed with a cold // 어디 편찮으십니까 Is anything the matter〔wrong〕 with you? / 어머님께선 언제부터 편찮으십니까 How long〔Since when〕 has your mother been ill? // 그 분은 몸이 편찮아서 오늘 결근하셨습니다 He is out sick today. /He called in sick today.
편청 —淸 honey for dipping rice cakes in
편충 鞭蟲 〖동물〗 a (human) whipworm
편취 騙取 defraudation; swindle **—하다** obtain by fraud; defraud 《a person》 of 《a thing》; cheat 《a person》 out of 《a thing》 ¶ 재산을 편취하다 defraud 《a person》 of his property // 금전을 편취하다 swindle 《a person》 out of money; swindle money out of 《a person》
—자 a swindler; a defrauder
편친 偏親 a parent; an only parent; a single parent
— 시하 having only one parent to serve
편토 片土 a small piece of land; a small plot of ground
편파 偏頗 partiality; favoritism; discrimination; one-sidedness; unfairness **—하다** (be) partial; one-sided; unfair; biased ¶ 편파 없는 impartial; fair // 편파됨이 없이 without partiality; impartially; fairly // 편파적으로 partially; unfairly; discriminatingly // 사람을 편파적으로 냉대〔후대〕하다 discriminate against〔in favor of〕 《a person》
편편이 片片— [조각조각으로] in pieces〔fragments〕 ¶ 편편이 깨지다 come to pieces
편편이 便便— by each messenger; with each mail
†편편하다 便便— ① [아무 일 없다] (be) free; have nothing to do ② [편안하다] be free from care; (be) comfortable; peaceful ¶ 편편히 놀다 idle about; idle away; be at an idle end // 편편히 지내다 lead a comfortable life; live in peace
편평 扁平 —하다 (be) flat; even; level; horizontal ¶ 편평한 지붕 a flat roof // 편평한 길 a level road // 도로 표면을 편평하게 고르다 make the surface of a road level
—족(足) 〖병리〗 flat foot; splayfoot; [발] a flatfoot 《*pl.* -feet》; a splayfoot 《*pl.* -feet》 ¶ 편평족이다 be flat-footed; have flatfeet
편포 片脯 dried slices of beef
†편하다 便— ① [편안] (be) comfortable; easy; untroubled; be free from cares ¶ 편한 살림 an easy life; a comfortable living // 발이 편한 신 comfortable shoes to wear // 편하게 comfortably; in comfort; easily; at ease; at home // 편하게 살다 live in comfort〔easy circumstances〕; lead an easy life // 편하게 쉬다 take a good rest; have a good night's rest (자다) // 마음을 편하게 하다 ease〔relieve〕 one's mind; relax // 몸을 편하게 하다 take a rest; rest from work; make oneself comfortable〔at home〕; relax // 마음이 편하다 be free from care; have a clear conscience; have nothing to worry about // 양친을 편하게 해드리다 let one's parents lead a comfortable life // 그것으로 마음이 편해졌다 It is a load off my mind. /I was quite relieved by that. // 편안하게 앉으십시오 Please make yourself comfortable〔at home〕. /Please relax. // 나이 더 들어서 돈 걱정없이 편히 살고 싶으면 열심히 일해라 Work hard if you want to get on Easy Street when you get

older.

② [편리] (be) convenient ; handy ; expedient ⇨ 편리

③ [용이] (be) easy ; light ; simple ¶ 편하게 easily ; with ease〔facility〕; without difficulty〔trouble〕// 편한 일 an easy task ; a soft job ; light work // 편하게 돈벌이 하다 make an easy gain ; make easy money

편향 偏向 propensity ; tendency ; inclination ; 〖물리〗 deflection **—하다** lean 《to, toward》; incline 《toward》

— 교육 education influenced by ideological prejudices ; ideologically prejudiced education —판(板)〔코일〕 [브라운관의] a deflecting plate〔coil〕 우익(右翼) — [공산당의] right-wing deviationism

편협 偏狹, 褊狹 narrow-mindedness ; illiberality **—하다** (be) narrow-minded ; illiberal ; intolerant ; hidebound

편형 동물 扁形動物 the platyhelminthes

***펼치다** open ; spread ; outstretch ; extend ; expand ; unfold ; unroll ¶ 우산을 펼치다 unfurl〔open〕 one's umbrella // 책을 펼치다 open a book // 편지를 펼치다 unfold a letter // 지도를 펼치다 spread a map // 꾸러미를 펼치다 unfold a package // 자리를 펼치다 spread a mat // 손을 펼치다 open one's hand // 두팔을 펼쳐 진심으로 환영하다 give 《a person》 a warm welcome with open arms // 새가 날개를 펼쳤다 The bird expanded its wings. // 넓은 평야가 눈앞에 펼쳐 있다 A broad plain spreads before us.

폄 貶 —하다 disparage ; depreciate ; belittle ; speak ill of

폄강 貶降 downgrading ; degrading ; demotion **—하다** downgrade ; degrade ; demote ; reduce to a lower rank

폄론 貶論 adverse criticism ; disparagement **—하다** disparage ; censure

폄척 貶斥 ① downgrading ; demotion ② censure ; disparagement **—하다** downgrade ; demote ; censure ; disparage ⇨ 폄강

평 平 ① [평평한] flat ; even ; plain ② [보통의] common ; ordinary ; plain

—교사 a common teacher —사원 a mere clerk —의원 an ordinary Assemblyman

평 評 criticism ; a comment ; a review **—하다** comment 《on》; criticize ; review 《a book》; speak of 《a person》 ¶ 평평이 좋다〔나쁘다〕 be favorably〔unfavorably〕 received ; be popular〔unpopular〕 with〔among〕 // 시사(時事)를 평하다 comment on current events // 평이 나빠지다 get a bad character ; become unpopular // 그것은 평할 가치가 없다 It is beneath criticism. // 그것에 대해 아무런 평도 가하지 않았다 He made no comment on it.

신문— a newspaper comment〔press comments〕 《on》 영화— a review of movies

평 坪 a *pyŏng* 《a unit of area》; a land measure of six square *chuck* ¶ 50평이다 cover 50 *pyŏng* // 평당 2천원이다 cost〔be valued at〕 2,000 *won* per *pyŏng*

—당(當) per *pyŏng* —수 the number of *pyŏng* ; an area ; acreage ; floor space (건평) ; space (넓이) ¶ 평수가 넓다 be spacious

평가 平價 〖경제〗 par ; parity ¶ 평가로 at par // 평가 이상으로〔이하로〕 above〔below〕 par // 파운드의 평가를 5퍼센트 절하하다 evaluate〔devalue〕 the pound by 5 per cent

— 이상(以上)〔이하(以下)〕 (be) above〔below〕 par — 절상 revaluation〔upward (re)valuation, upvaluation〕 《of》 ¶ 평가 절상하다 revaluate〔revalue, upvalue, revalue upward〕 《the currency, the *won*》 — 절하 devaluation ¶ 평가 절하하다 devaluate〔devalue〕 《the currency》 — 환시세 exchange rate at par 법정 — mint par ; par of exchange

†평가 評價 valuation ; appraisal ; appraisement ; rating ; assessment (과세 따위를 위한) ; estimation (인물의) ; evaluation (교육의) **—하다** value ; appraise ; estimate ; judge ; assess ; rate ; evaluate ¶ 평가하는 사람 an appraiser ; an assessor ; a valuer // 사람을 평가하다 judge〔estimate〕 《a person》; size〔sum, weigh〕 up // 손해를 평가하다 estimate the damages // 높이〔낮게〕 평가하다 rate 《a thing》 high〔low〕; set a high〔low〕 value on 《a person's talent》 // 과대〔과소〕 평가하다 overestimate〔underestimate〕 // 집을 600만원으로 평가하다 value〔appraise〕 the house at six million *won* // 그 보석은 5천불로 평가된다 The jewel is rated as worth 5,000 dollars. // 외모로 사람을 평가해서는 안 된다 We should not judge a man by his appearance.

—액 appraised〔estimated〕 value ; an appraisement —익(益)〔손(損)〕 an appraisal profit〔loss〕 —자(者)〔인(人)〕 an appraiser ; an assessor ; a valuer 과대 — overestimation 과소 — underestimation 재— revaluation ; reappraisal 토지(土地) — valuation of land

평각 平角 〖기하〗 a straight angle

평견 平絹 plain silk

***평결 評決** a decision ; a verdict **—하다** decide ; render a verdict 《on》 ¶ 원고에 유리한 평결 a verdict for the plaintiff

평경 平鏡 clear glasses (with unrefracted lenses) ⇨ 맞보기

평고대 平高臺 〖건축〗 a bar along the

edge of eaves
평골 平— a kind of flat-soled leather shoe last
평교 平交 friends of about the same age
—간 friendship among people of comparable age
평교자 平轎子 a sedan chair
†**평균** 平均 an average ; the mean **—하다** average ; take〔strike〕 an average ; take the mean 《of》 ¶ 평균의 average ; mean // 평균하여 on an〔the〕 average // 일인 평균 a〔per〕 head ; per capita // 평균 이상〔이하〕이다 be above〔below〕 the average // 그는 월수입이 평균 백만원이 된다 His income averages 1,000,000 *won* a month. // 그는 하루 평균 7시간을 일한다 He works seven hours a day on the average. // 평균해서 35라는 수가 나온다 We get 35 as average. // 본교에서는 평균 60점 이하는 낙제로 친다 A student who fails to get an average mark of 60 is rejected〔not promoted〕 at this school. // 그 나라에 있어서의 평균 수명은 72세이다 The average length of life in that country is seventy-two.
— 거리(距離) the mean distance **— 기온(氣溫)** the mean air〔atmospheric〕 temperature **—량(量)〔가(價)〕** 〖물리〗 the normal **— 분점(分點)** 〖천문〗 a mean equinox **—수〔율〕** the mean number〔ratio〕 **— 수명** the average life (-span) 《of the Koreans》 **—시** the mean time **— 여명** 〖보험〗 average future lifetime ; life expectancy ; expectation of life **— 연령** the average age **— 오차** the mean error **— 온도** the mean temperature **— 운동** the mean motion **—점** the average mark **— 정오(正午)** the mean noon **—치** the mean〔average〕 value **— 태양시〔일〕** mean (solar) time〔day〕 **산술〔기하〕 —** the arithmetical〔geometric〕 mean **연〔월〕 —** yearly〔monthly〕 mean **조화 —** the harmonic average
평균대 平均臺 〖체조〗 a balance beam ¶ 그녀는 평균대 체조로 금메달을 땄다 She won the gold medal in the beam event.
평균화 平均化 leveling (off) ; equalization ; standardization **—하다** level 《the various classes》 ; make equal ; even off ; standardize 《the mode of living》
평나막신 平— flat wooden shoes
평년 平年 a common〔non-leap〕 year (윤년 아닌) ; a normal〔an average〕 year (예년) ¶ 평년작 이상이다 be above the normal〔average〕 crop〔harvest〕 // 기온은 평년과 같다 We have the average temperature.
—작 a normal crop〔harvest〕 ; an average crop ¶ 평년작 이상〔이하〕 above〔below〕 the average
평다리치다 sit at one's ease with legs stretched out
평단 評壇 the republic of literary〔art〕 critics ¶ 평단의 제1인자 the greatest literary〔art〕 critic 《in Korea》
⁑**평등** 平等 equality ; equability ; parity **—하다** (be) equal ; even ; equable ; impartial (차별 없는) ¶ 평등한 권리 an equal right // 평등하게 equally ; evenly ; impartially ; without discrimination // 평등하게 하다 equalize ; even ; make equal // 평등하게 분배하다 divide equally // 평등하게 대하다 treat 《persons》 impartially // 죽음은 만인을 평등하게 한다 Death levels all men. // 사람은 모두 평등하게 태어났다 All men are created equal. // 만인은 법 앞에 평등하다 All men are equal under〔in the eye of〕 the law.
—론자(論者) a leveler ; an equalitarian ; an egalitarian **—주의** the principle of equality ; equalitarianism ; egalitarianism **—화(化)** equalization ; equaling out ; 〖언어〗 level(l)ing **기회 —** equality of opportunity **민족 —** racial equality **인권 —** the equality of human rights
평란 平亂 suppression of rebellion ; repression of uprising **—하다** suppress a rebellion ; repress〔quell〕 an uprising
평로 平爐 an open-hearth furnace
—강(鋼) open-hearth steel
평론 評論 criticism ; a comment ; a commentary ; a critique ; a review (저작물의) ; an editorial comment (신문·잡지의) **—하다** criticize ; review ; comment 《on》 ¶ 평론의 평론 the review of reviews // 시국을 평론하다 comment on the current situation
—가 a critic ; a reviewer (신간 비평 따위의) ; a commentator (시사의) ; a columnist (신문·시사·문예의) **—문** a critical essay **— 잡지** a review **—집(集)** "Essays in Criticism" (책 이름) **문예 —** literary criticism ; a book review ¶ 문예 평론가 a literary critic ; a book reviewer **시사 —** a comment on current topics ; a contemporary review **영문학 —** a critique〔criticism〕 of English literature
평말 平— an even measure (of grain)
평맥 平脈 normal pulse
†**평면** 平面 a plane ; a level ¶ 평면의 plane ; level ; flat
—각 a plane angle **—경(鏡)** a plane mirror **— 교차** grade crossing 《미》 ; crossing at grade ; level crossing 《영》 ¶ 평면 교차점 a grade crossing 《미》 ; a level crossing 《영》 **— 기하** plane geometry **—도(圖)** a plane figure ; a ground plan (건축의) **— 도법** ichnography **— 묘사(描寫)** a plane delineation

ㅍ

; an objective description — 삼각법 plane trigonometry — 좌표 plane coordinates — 지도 a map on Mercator's〔mercator〕 projection ; a Mercator 〔mercator〕 chart — 천체도(天體圖) a planisphere — 항법(航法) plane sailing —형 a plane figure 투영(投影) — a plane of projection

평미레 a grain leveler ; a kind of strickle

평미리치다 level 《grain》 ; measure by an even measure ; level off ; even ; equalize ; make even〔uniform〕 ¶ 밭 이랑을 평미리치다 level down the ridges of a field

***평민 平民** the common people ; a commoner ; a plebeian ¶ 평민적인 democratic ; plebeian // 평민적인 사람 a democratic person // 평민 태생이다 be a commoner by birth

— 재상 a commoner premier —주의 democratism ; democracy —주의자 a democrat

평반자 平— a level ceiling (made of a wooden frame pasted across with paper)

평방 平方 the square (of a number) ; a square (평방형) ¶ 평방의 square // 1마일 평방 one mile square // 1평방 마일 one square mile // 평방을 전개하다 extract the square root 《of》 ; find the square 《of》

—근 a square root (of a number) ¶ 3은 9의 평방근이다 Three is the square root of nine. // 4의 평방근은 2이다 The (square〔second〕) root of 4 is 2. /Root 4 is 2. // 평방근을 구하다 extract〔find〕 the square root 《of》 —근비(根比) (a) subduplicate ratio —수(數) a square number —적(積) square measure —형 a square

†**평범 平凡** commonplaceness ; commonness ; mediocrity ; banality ; platitude —하다 (be) common ; ordinary ; commonplace ; humdrum ; banal ; mediocre ; featureless ; homely ¶ 평범한 사람 a mediocrity ; a humdrum // 평범한 얼굴 a featureless〔plain〕 face // 평범한 문장 an ordinary〔indifferent〕 composition // 평범한 말 a trite saying ; a platitude // 평범한 경치 tame〔mediocre, monotonous〕 scenery // 그는 평범하게 살았다 He lived a humdrum life. // 그 이야기는 평범했다 The story fell flat. // 그녀의 얼굴은 평범하다 Her face lacks distinction. // 그날도 평범하게 지났다 The day passed uneventfully. // 그는 평범한 운명을 타고났다 He is doomed to mediocrity. // 그 소설은 평범한 이야기였는데 왜 그 작품이 뽑혔는지 의문이다 The novel was such a run-of-the-mill story it's a wonder to me why it was ever selected. // 너의 계획은 너무 평범하다 Your plan is just too run-of-the-mill.

평복 平服 an ordinary〔everyday〕 dress ; plain clothes ; civilian clothes (사복) ; an undress ; mufti —하다 wear plain clothes ¶ 평복을 입은 (dressed) in plain clothes ; in mufti

평분 平分 equal〔even〕 division —하다 divide evenly〔equally〕 ; divide into two equal parts

—선 a bisecting line

평사원 平社員 a mere clerk

평삭 平削 facing ; planing —하다 face ; plane

—반(盤) 〖기계〗 a planer ; a planing machine

평상 平床 a wooden bed

평상 平常 normal (times) ¶ 강물은 평상보다 5피트 불었다 The river rose five feet high above normal. // 철도는 평상 상태로 복구됐다 The railroad service has been restored to normal〔normalcy〕.

평상시 平常時 normal times ; [부사적] normally ; usually ; as a usual thing ; commonly ; ordinarily ; customarily ¶ 평상시의 normal ; ordinary ; usual ; everyday ; common

평생 平生 one's (whole) life ; a lifetime ¶ 평생의 한 a lifelong regret // 평생에 단 한번 once in a lifetime // 평생을 두고 (for) all one's life ; throughout one's life ; through life ; during one's whole life // 평생을 편안하게 살다 spend one's life in easy circumstances ; live comfortably to the end // 연구에 한평생을 바치다 devote a lifetime to the study 《of》 // 그는 평생을 독신으로 지냈다 He remained single〔a bachelor, unmarried〕 all his life. // 자네는 평생에 한번 있을까 말까 하는 기회를 놓쳤어 You've just missed a once-in-a-lifetime chance.

— 소원 one's lifelong desire ; a desire cherished for life

평석 評釋 critical notes ; annotation ; commentary —하다 annotate

평소 平素 ordinary times ¶ 평소에 usually ; ordinarily ; at ordinary〔normal〕 times ; always (늘) // 평소와 같이 as usual // 평소의 소원 one's long-cherished wish // 그에게는 평소와 다른 점이 없었다 There was nothing unusual 〔strange〕 about him. // 그는 평소보다 빨리 일어났다 He got up earlier than usual.

평수 坪數 ① the number of *pyeong* ; acreage ; area ② [건평] floor space 〔area〕 ; [넓이] space ¶ 평수가 넓은 집 a spacious house // 평수가 꽤 넓다 be pretty spacious

평시 平時 ① [평화시] time of peace ; peacetime ② [평상시] ordinary〔normal〕

times ¶ 평시의 in peace time ; peacetime ; in time of peace ; in normal
— 국제법 international law in time of peace — 봉쇄(封鎖) 『국제법』 pacific blockade — 산업 peacetime industry — 정원(定員) peace establishment — 편제 peace organization〔footing〕
*평신도 平信徒 a lay believer ; a layman
평안 平安 well-being ; peace ; tranquility ; calmness ; quietness —하다 be well ; be in peace ; (be) peaceful ; quiet ; calm ; tranquil ¶ 평안히 in peace ; peacefully // 평안히 앉으십시오 Please sit comfortably. // 항해의 평안함을 기원합니다 I wish you a happy voyage〔bon voyage〕.
평야 平野 a plain ; a champaign ; an open field ¶ 그 산은 평야 가운데 있다 The mountain rises above the plain.
평어 評語 [비평의 말] a comment ; a critical remark ; [성적을 나타내는 말] a grade ; grading
평언 評言 a (critical) remark ; a comment
평열 平熱 the normal temperature ¶ 열이 내리고 아주 평열이 되었다 The fever has left me, and I'm quite cool.
평영 平泳 the breaststroke
평온 平溫 ① an average temperature ② a normal temperature ¶ 인체의 평온은 36.9도이다 The normal temperature of the human body is 36.9 degrees.
†평온 平穩 calmness ; quiet(ness) ; tranquility ; serenity —하다 (be) calm ; quiet ; tranquil ; serene ; peaceful

> 참고 **calm** 혼란이나 흥분이 없는 상태 **tranquil** calm보다 본질적이고 영구적인 평온 상태 **serene** 맑고 흐리지 않고 조용한 상태 **peaceful** 혼란이 없는 상태

¶ 평온 무사히 in peace and quiet // 평온해지다 become quiet ; quiet down // 동부 전선은 극히 평온하다 Everything is quiet on the eastern front.
평원 平原 a plain ; a champaign ; a prairie 《미》
— 광야 a wide plain ; a vast moorland
평유 平癒 recovery 《from illness》 ; restoration to health —하다 recover 《from》 ; recover health ; regain one's health ; get well
평의 平議 conference ; consultation ; deliberation ; discussion (토의) —하다 confer ; discuss ; take counsel ; hold a conference〔council〕 ; consult together 《with》 ¶ 문제를 평의에 부치다 submit a matter to discussion // 평의는 결정되었다 The conference has come to a decision.
—원 a councilor ; [재단의] a trustee (일원) ; a board of trustees (단체) —회 a council ; [회의] a conference ; a meeting of the board of trustees
평이 平易 easiness (용이) ; plainness (평명) ; simplicity (단순) —하다 (be) easy ; plain ; simple ¶ 평이하게 easily ; plainly ; simply // 평이한 문체 a simple〔plain〕 style // 평이하게 말하면 in plain words ; to put it simply〔plainly〕 ; to use simple〔plain〕 language // 평이하게 설명하다 explain simply // 평이하게 하다 simplify
평일 平日 ① [일요일에 대한] a weekday ¶ 평일에 on weekdays ② [평소] ordinary days〔time〕 ¶ 평일의 normal ; ordinary ; usual ; everyday // 평일에는 on ordinary days ; usually
평작 a medium-sized〔an ordinary〕 arrow
평작 平作 a normal〔an average〕 crop 〔harvest〕 ¶ 벼는 평작이 예상된다 The rice is expected to be an average crop.
평저 平底 a flat bottom
—선 a flat-bottomed boat ; a flatboat
평전 評傳 a critical biography
평점 評點 examination〔grade〕 marks ; grades ; evaluation marks (물건의)
평정 平靜 calm ; composure ; serenity ; tranquility ; equability —하다 (be) calm ; serene ; composed ; tranquil ; peaceful ; equable ¶ 마음의 평정 presence〔peace, serenity〕 of mind // 평정을 가장하다 feign calmness // 평정을 되찾다 recover composure ; quiet down // 마음의 평정을 지키다〔잃다〕 keep〔lose〕 one's composure
평정 平定 suppression ; repression ; subdual —하다 suppress ; quell ; subdue ; subjugate ; put down ¶ 반란을 평정하다 put down rebels // 천하를 평정하다 subjugate the whole country ; establish〔restore〕 peace in the country
— 계획 pacification program
평정 評定 rating ; valuation ; evaluation —하다 rate 《a person's merit》 ; evaluate
근무 — the efficiency rating system
평좌 平坐 sitting comfortably ; sitting at one's ease —하다 sit comfortably ; sit at one's ease
평주 評註 a commentary ; glosses ; notes and comments —하다 comment 〔gloss〕 upon 《the text》 ; annotate
—자 a commentator ; an annotator
평준 平準 ① [수준] level ② [평균] equality
—점 a level point —화 equalization ¶ 평준화하다 equalize
평지 『식물』 a rape ; a coleseed
평지 平地 level land〔ground〕 ; a flat ; a plain (평원) ; a flat country ¶ 평지 낙상하다 fall down and get hurt on the level ground ; have an accident

ㅍ

— 풍파 an unexpected disturbance〔trouble〕; a storm in a teacup ¶ 평지 풍파를 일으키다 raise a disturbance where everything is in peace ; raise troubles unnecessarily〔where there is no cause〕; flutter〔cause a flutter in〕 the dovecot(e)s ; make waves

평직 平織 plain fabrics

평집 平— 〖건물〗 a small house (with but three or four crossbeams)

평찌 an arrow flying low and level

평치 平治 peaceful rule〔governing〕 —하다 rule〔govern〕《a country》 peacefully

*평탄 平坦 evenness ; flatness ; [마음·일의] calmness ; composure ; tranquility ; peace of mind ; smoothness —하다 (be) even ; flat ; level ; [마음·일이] calm ; composed ; tranquil ; smooth ¶ 길을 평탄케 하다 level a road // 그의 일생은 평탄했다 His life ran in a groove.

평토 平土 leveling ground after burial —하다 level off《a grave》

—장(葬) burying without making a mound on the grave

평판 平板 a flat board ; a slat ; a lath

평판 平版 lithograph ; offset

— 인쇄(술) lithography ; offset printing — 인쇄공 a lithographer ; an offset printer — 인쇄소 a lithographer ; a lithoprinter

⁑평판 評判 [명성] reputation ; fame ; popularity (인기) ; notoriety (악명) ; repute ; a name ; the world opinion ; a report ; a rumor ; a gossip —하다 talk (much) of ; talk about ; rumor ¶ 평판이 난 reputed ; famed ; notorious // 평판이 좋다〔나쁘다〕 be well〔ill〕 spoken of ; have a good〔bad〕 reputation〔character〕; be popular〔unpopular〕// 평판을 얻다 get〔win〕 a reputation ; win popularity // 평판이 떨어지다 lose one's good reputation // 그 지역은 깡패 때문에 평판이 좋지 않다 The quarter is notorious for hoodlums. // 그는 여성들 사이에 평판이 좋다 He is popular among ladies. // 그는 정직하다는 평판이 있다 He has a name for honesty. // 그는 아주 도량이 크다는 평판이다 He is reputed to be very generous.

†평평하다 平平— ① [평탄] (be) flat ; level ; even ; horizontal ② [평범] (be) ordinary ; commonplace

평풍 屛風 a folding screen ⇨ 병풍

평하다 評— criticize ; comment《on》 ⇨ 비평하다 ¶ 시사 문제를 평하다 comment on the news of the day // 남을 사기꾼이라 평하다 speak of a person as an impostor

⁑평행 平行 parallel ; parallelism —하다 (be) paralleled《to, with》; run parallel to〔with〕; go side by side ¶ 선과 평행하여 parallel to a line ; in parallel with a line // 가로가 철도와 평행하여 있다 The street parallels the railroad.

—권(圈) a parallel circle —력(力) 〖물리〗 parallel forces —봉(棒) 〖체조〗 parallel bars — 사변형 a parallelogram — 선 parallel lines — 육면체 a parallelepiped —자 a parallel rule(r) — 좌표 Cartesian coordinates

*평형 平衡 equilibrium ; balance ; counterbalance ; counterpoise ; equipoise —하다 be balanced ; be poised ; be in equilibrium ¶ 평형을 유지하다 balance ; equilibrate ; poise // 평형을 잃다 lose the balance ; overbalance // 신체의 평형을 유지하다 keep〔preserve〕 one's balance

— 가격(價格) 〖경제〗 parity — 감각 the sense of equilibrium — 교부금 an equalization grant《to a local government》 —력(力) 〖물리〗 a counterbalance ; an equilibrant —륜(輪) a balance wheel (시계의) — 부하(負荷) a balanced load — 상태 (a state of) equilibrium — 수준기 a balance level —추(錘) 〖기계〗 a counterbalance ; a counterweight — 코일 〖전기〗 a balance coil 안정〔불안정〕 — stable〔unstable〕 equilibrium 화학(化學) — chemical equilibrium

†평화 平和 peace ; harmony (화합) ¶ 평화롭다, 평화스럽다 (be) peaceful ; harmonious // 평화적인 peaceful ; pacific ; amicable // 마음의 평화 peace of mind // 평화적으로 peacefully ; in peace ; harmoniously // 영구적 평화 a lasting〔a permanent, an everlasting〕 peace // 평화를 유지하다〔깨뜨리다〕 keep〔break〕 peace // 세계 평화를 교란하다 disturb the peace of the world // 평화적으로 해결하다 settle《a matter》 amicably // 평화를 회복하다 restore peace // 평화를 확립하다 establish〔secure〕 peace // 국제 평화를 촉진함이 우리의 사명이다 Our mission is to promote peace among the nations. // 우리들은 전쟁이냐 평화냐의 기로에 직면하고 있다 We are faced with the choice between war and peace. // 세계 평화를 위협하는 문제들이 많이 있다 There are many issues which threaten the peace of the world.

— 공세 a peace offensive — 공존 peaceful coexistence ¶ 평화 공존 노선(路線) the "peaceful coexistence" line — 교섭 peace negotiations〔talks〕 — 기념일 [제1차 대전의] Armistice Day — 단체 a pacifist organization —론자 a pacifist ; [경멸적] a peacemonger《미》 — 문제 a peace issue — 봉사단 the Peace Corps (Volunteers)《미》 ¶ 평화 봉사단원 a Peace Corpsman — 사절 a peace envoy — 산업 (a) peaceful〔peacetime〕 industry — 애호 국민 a peace-loving nation — 운동 a peace

ㅍ

(pacifist) movement(campaign) — 유지군 [UN의] a peace(peacekeeping) force — 이용 peaceful uses 《of atomic energy》 — 정책 policy of universal peace — 조약 a peace treaty — 조항 〖노동〗 a peace clause —주의 pacifism ¶ 평화주의자 a pacifist — 행진 a peace march — 혁명 a bloodless revolution — 회담 peace talks — 회복(극복) restoration(return) of peace — 회의 a peace conference ¶ 국제 평화 회의 an international peace conference 가정 — domestic peace(harmony) 세계 — world peace ; the peace of the world 집단 — collective peace

평활 平— an archery practice bow

평활 平滑 evenness ; smoothness —하다 (be) smooth ; level ; flat ; even ¶ 평활하게 하다 smooth ; make smooth

—근(筋) 〖해부〗 a smooth muscle ¶ 평활근 종(腫) a leiomyoma 《*pl.* -mata》

평활 平闊 —하다 (be) level and broad ; flat and wide

*폐 肺 〖해부〗 the lungs ¶ 폐의 pulmonary ; pneumonic // 약한 폐 a weak chest // 그는 오른쪽 폐가 나쁘다 His right lung is affected.

—경변(硬變) 〖의학〗 pulmonary cirrhosis ; pneumonocirrhosis —경화(硬化) 〖의학〗 induration of the lung —동(정)맥 the pulmonary artery(vein) —디스토마 pulmonary distomiasis —병 환자 a consumptive (patient) — 절제(切除) pneumonectomy ; pneumectomy —호흡(呼吸) pulmonary respiration 우(좌)— the right(left) lung

*폐 幣 ① [폐단] an evil ; a vice ; abuses ; a bad custom ; evil practices ¶ 음주의 폐 the evil of drink ; the bad habit of drinking ; the evil of intemperance // 관습의 폐 the evil of convention

② [괴로움] trouble ; bother ¶ 사람에게 폐를 끼치다 trouble another ; cause (give) 《a person》 trouble ; put 《a person》 to trouble // 폐를 끼쳐 미안합니다 I am sorry to have caused you so much trouble. // 큰 폐가 안된다면 그러지 It's not too much bother, I will. // 자네 호의는 고맙지만 난 자네에게 폐를 끼치고 싶지 않네 Thank you for your generosity, but I don't want to be an imposition upon you.

폐- 幣 my ; our

—사(점) our company(store)

폐가 幣家 my (humble) house

폐가 廢家 ① [집] a ruined house ; a deserted house ② an extinct family —하다 the house comes to an end ¶ 그 집안은 폐가가 되었다 The family has become extinct(has died out).

폐간 廢刊 discontinuance 《of a publication》 —하다 cease to publish ; discontinue issuing 《a newspaper, magazine》 ; stop publishing ¶ 폐간이 되다 be discontinued ; go out of print (절판)

폐갱 廢坑 ⇨ 폐광(廢鑛)

폐결핵 肺結核 〖의학〗 phthisis ; (pulmonary) tuberculosis ; consumption ¶ 폐결핵에 걸리다 suffer from pulmonary tuberculosis

— 환자 a consumptive (patient)

폐경 肺經 the lungs ; the pulmonary system

폐경기 閉經期 the (time of) menopause

폐관 閉管 a closed pipe (악기의) ; a matrass (취관 분석용의)

폐관 閉館 closing 《its doors》 —하다 close 《its doors》 ; be closed

폐광 廢鑛 an abandoned(unworked) mine ; a dead pit ; a disused mine —하다 abandon a mine ; disuse a mine ¶ 폐광되다 be abandoned(disused)

폐교 廢校 abolition(closing) of a school —하다 abolish(close) a school ¶ 폐교되다 be abolished(closed, discontinued)

*폐기 廢棄 [풍속·제도의] disuse ; abolition ; abandonment ; [법의] repeal ; denunciation ; abrogation ; defeasance —하다 disuse ; abolish ; abandon ; renounce ; discard (습관을) ; [법을] abrogate ; repeal ; dissolve ; denounce (조약을) ¶ 폐기되다 fall(come) into disuse // 조약을 폐기하다 abrogate a treaty

—물 scrapped material ; waste (matter) ¶ 폐기물 처리 [원자로의] disposal of (radioactive) waste matter // 미처리 폐기물 untreated waste (matter) // 방사성(放射性) 폐기물 radioactive waste matter(products) ; atomic waste // 산업 폐기물 industrial waste (products)

폐기 廢氣 used steam ; exhaust (steam)

— 청소 scaveng(er)ing

폐기종 肺氣腫 〖의학〗 emphysema of the lungs ; vesicular emphysema

폐끼치다 弊— cause(give) 《a person》 trouble ; put 《a person》 to trouble ; trouble 《a person》 ⇨ 폐(弊) ②

폐낭 肺囊 a lung sac

폐농 廢農 giving up farming ; failure in farming —하다 give up(stop) farming ; fail in farming

폐단 弊端 an evil ; an abuse ; a vice ; evil practices ¶ 폐단을 고치다 remedy (correct) an abuse // 거기에는 여러 가지 폐단이 따른다 It is attended by many evils.

폐동맥 肺動脈 the pulmonary artery

폐디스토마 肺— pulmonary distoma ; distoma pulmona ; [병명] pulmonary distomatosis(distomiasis)

*폐렴 pneumonia ⇨ 폐염

폐롭다 弊— ① [귀찮다] (be) bother-

ㅍ

some ; troublesome ¶ 폐롭게 굴다 cause trouble // 손님이 폐롭다 A guest is bothersome. ② [성질이] (be) particular ; fussy ; fastidious ; queer ¶ 폐로운 사람 a fussy〔queer〕 person ; a fussbudget ; an odd fish〔duck〕

폐륜 廢倫 failing to marry ; remaining single ―하다 remain single ; do not marry

폐리 弊履 worn-out sandals

폐립 廢立 dethronement and enthronement ―하다 depose a king and enthrone 《another》 ; change 《king》

폐막 閉幕 closing the curtain ; the falling of the curtain ―하다 end ; close ; come to a close ; close the curtain on ; bring to an end

폐문 肺門 the hilum of a lung ; the pulmonary hilum

― 임파선염 tuberculous adenitis of the hilum (of a lung)

폐문 閉門 closing a gate ―하다 close a gate ; shut a door ; close up

― 시간 the closing time

폐문 廢門 closing ―하다 close〔shut up〕 ; keep 《a door》 shut〔closed〕 ¶ 폐문해 두다 keep the door shut〔closed〕

†폐물 廢物 a useless article〔thing〕 ; waste (material) ; refuse (찌끼) ; trash ¶ 공장에서 나오는 폐물 the waste from a factory // 폐물이 되다 become useless ; go〔run〕 to waste

― 이용 the utilization of waste material〔products〕 ; wealth from waste ― 처리 waste disposal 인간 ― the scum of the community〔earth〕 ; the social scum

폐방 廢房 a deserted room ; a disused room ―하다 stop using a room ; shut off a room ; desert a room

폐백 幣帛 ① [신부의] gifts offered to the parents of the bridegroom by the bride ② [신랑의] silks offered to the bride by the bridegroom

폐병 廢兵 a disabled〔crippled〕 soldier

폐병 肺病 consumption ; a lung〔pulmonary〕 disease〔complaints〕 ; a lung 〔chest〕 trouble ¶ 폐병으로 죽다 die of consumption // 그는 폐병을 앓고 있다 He is suffering from consumption.

―약 a pneumonic ; a pulmonic ― 환자 a consumptive (patient) ; a lunger 《미·속》

폐부 肺腑 ① [폐] the lungs ② [마음속] the bottom〔depths〕 of one's heart ; one's inmost heart ③ [급소] a vital point ; a critical area ¶ 그의 말은 폐부에서 우러 나온 것이다 His speech was a true expression of his heart.

폐부를 찌르다 관용 give a home〔deep〕 thrust ; cut to the quick ; drive〔thrust〕 home ; go to the heart

폐비 廢妃 deposal of a queen ; a deposed queen ―하다 depose a queen ; depose as queen

폐사 弊社 our company〔firm〕

폐사 廢寺 a ruined temple

폐사 斃死 ―하다 fall dead ; perish ; die

폐색 閉塞 blockade ; blocking ; stoppage ―하다 blockade ; block (up) ; bottle up ¶ 항구를 폐색하다 block up〔blockade, bottle up〕 a port ; block the entrance to a harbor

― 구간 〖철도〗 a (block) section ―대(隊) a blockading squadron〔expedition〕 ―선 a blockader ― 신호 〖철도〗 a block signal ―음 occlusive ― 전선 〖기상〗 an occluded front 장(腸)― 〖의학〗 obstruction of the intestines ; ileus

폐선 廢船 a scrapped〔retired〕 ship ; an abandoned ship ―하다 scrap a vessel

†폐쇄 閉鎖 closing ; closure ; a lockout (공장 폐쇄) ―하다 close ; shut ; lock ; wind up ; lock out ¶ 자동 폐쇄의 self-closing // 우리는 내일로 이 사업을 폐쇄한다 We will wind up this business tomorrow.

―기 breech mechanism ― 기관(機關) closed institutions〔organizations〕 ― 사회 the closed society ―음 implosive ― 회사 a close〔closed〕 corporation 공장 ― a (factory) lockout (노동 쟁의 때의) ; a closedown 《미》

폐수 廢水 〖기계〗 wastewater

― 처리 wastewater treatment ― 처리 장치 a wastewater disposal plant 공장 ― factory wastes

폐수종 肺水腫 edema of the lungs

폐습 弊習 evil customs〔practices〕 ; evils ; a bad habit ; abuses ¶ 폐습을 없애다 break down〔do away with〕 evil customs // …의 폐습에 젖어 있다 be tainted with a bad habit 《of》 // 폐습을 시정하다 remedy〔correct〕 abuses

폐시키다 弊― annoy ; bother ; cause trouble to 《a person》 ; trouble 《a person》

폐식 閉式 closing of a ceremony ―하다 close〔break up〕 a ceremony

폐안 廢案 a rejected measure〔bill, project〕 ; a draft withdrawn〔discarded〕 ¶ 폐안으로 하다 withdraw〔discard〕 a draft ; let a proposal drop

폐암 肺癌 cancer of the lung

폐어 廢語 an obsolete〔a disused〕 word

폐어 肺魚 〖물고기〗 a lungfish ; a dipnoan (fish)

―류 Dipnoi (학명)

폐업 廢業 quitting〔closing〕 of one's business ―하다 give up〔close, quit〕 one's business ; shut up one's shop ; give up one's practice (의사·변호사가) ¶ 폐업하게 되다 be driven out of business

― 신고 a report of cessation of business ¶ 폐업 신고를 내다 report the

cessation of business
폐염 肺炎 〖의학〗 pneumonia ; inflammation of the lungs
— 간균(桿菌) a pneumobacillus 《pl. -cilli》 — 구균(球菌) a pneumococcus 《pl. -cocci》 급성 — acute pneumonia 기관지 — bronchial pneumonia ; bronchopneumonia 양쪽〔한쪽〕 — double〔single〕 pneumonia 엽성(葉性) — lobar pneumonia
폐엽 肺葉 〖해부〗 a lobe of the lung ; a lunglobe
폐옥 廢屋 a dilapidated house ; a house left in ruin
폐왕 廢王 a dethroned〔deposed〕 king ; an ex-king ; a former king
폐용 廢用 disuse —하다 disuse ¶ 폐용되다 go out of use
폐원 閉院 the closing〔recess〕 of the Assembly〔Parliament〕 —하다 close ; recess (the Assembly, the Parliament)
—식 the closing ceremony of the Assembly
폐위 廢位 dethronement —하다 dethrone ; depose 《a sovereign》 ; take the crown from 《a king》
폐유 廢油 waste〔rejected, defective〕 oil
폐읍 弊邑 ① a corrupt〔an evil〕 town ② my (our) town
폐인 廢人 a disabled person ; a crippled person (불구자) ; an invalid (병자)
폐일언하고 蔽一言— in a word ; in short ; to sum up
폐장 肺臟 〖해부〗 the lungs ⇨ 폐
폐장 閉場 closing 《of a place》 —하다 close ; be closed
—식 a closing ceremony
폐적 廢嫡 disinheritance —하다 disinherit
폐절 廢絶 extinction —하다 become extinct ; go into extinction ; be discontinued
—가 an extinct family
폐절제 肺切除 〖의학〗 pneumonectomy ; pneumectomy
폐점 弊店 our shop ; we
폐점 閉店 [파함] closing a store ; [폐함] closing down a store ; closing of operations —하다 [파하다] close a store ; close one's doors ; [폐하다] closedown〔wind up〕 business ; give up one's business ; go out of business
— 방매 a closing sale — 세일 a going-out-of-business sale — 시간 the closing time
폐정 閉廷 dismissing the court —하다 dismiss the court ¶ 폐정되다 the court adjourns
폐정 弊政 maladministration ; misgovernment ; misrule
폐정맥 肺靜脈 a pulmonary vein
폐제 弊帝 a deposed〔dethroned〕 emperor ; an exemperor
폐제 弊制 a monetary system
*폐지 廢止 abolition ; disuse ; discontinuance ; [법 따위의] abrogation ; annulment ; nullification —하다 abolish ; disuse ; do away with ; discontinue ; [법 따위를] abrogate ; annul ; rescind ; repeal ; quash ; fall into disuse ¶ 이 법률은 2년 전에 폐지되었다 The law was repealed two years ago.
폐지 閉止 stoppage —하다 stop ; cease ; close
월경 — menopause
폐진증 肺塵症 〖의학〗 pneumonoconiosis
폐질 廢疾 an incurable〔a fatal〕 disease
— 보험 disability insurance —자 a disabled person ; a cripple for life
폐차 廢車 a scrapped car〔train〕 ; a car〔train〕 out of commission ; a car〔train〕 retired from service
폐창 廢娼 abolition of licensed prostitution ; abolition of white slavery —하다 abolish licensed prostitution〔white slavery〕
— 운동 a purification campaign
폐첨 肺尖 〖해부〗 the apex of a lung
— 카타르 the catarrh of the apex (of the lungs) ; capillary bronchitis ; pulmonary apicitis
폐출혈 肺出血 a lung hemorrhage ; hemorrhage from the lungs
폐충혈 肺充血 〖의학〗 hyperemia〔congestion〕 of lungs
폐침윤 肺浸潤 (amyloid) infiltration of the lungs
폐포 肺胞 a germinal cell ; a blastosphere
폐품 廢品 waste articles〔materials〕 ; useless〔castaway〕 articles
— 이용 the utilization of waste material〔products〕 — 회수 collection〔reclamation〕 of waste articles〔materials〕 ; recovery of scrap ¶ 폐품 회수업자 a rag-and-bone merchant ; a ragman ; a junkman 《미》
폐풍 弊風 evil customs ; bad habits ⇨ 폐습
*폐하 陛下 [3인칭] His〔Her〕 Majesty 《H. M.》 ; [2인칭] Your Majesty
황제 — His Majesty ; H. M. the Emperor ¶ 영국 여왕 폐하 H. M. the Queen of England ; Her Britannic Majesty 《H. B. M》 황후 — Her Majesty ; H. M. the Empress
*폐하다 廢— ① [제도 따위를] abolish ; abandon ; discard ; cast aside ; give over ; do away with ② [법률 따위를] repeal ; annul ; abrogate ③ [군주를] dethrone ; depose ; discrown ④ [일 따위를] discontinue ; quit ; give up ¶ 학업을 폐하다 give up one's studies ; lay aside one's books // 허례를 폐하다 do away with formalities ; dispense with formalities

ㅍ

폐학 廢學 giving up one's studies ―하다 discontinue〔give up, abandon〕 one's studies ; leave school

폐함 廢艦 a scrapped warship ; a ship placed out of commission ; a decommissioned warship ¶ 폐함 처분하다 put《a warship》out of commission ; decommission ; scrap《a warship》

폐합 廢合 abolition and amalgamation ―하다 abolish and amalgamate ¶ 국과(局課)의 폐합 rearrangement of bureaus and sections

― 정리 reorganization ; rearrangement

폐해 弊害 an evil ; evil practices ; abuses ; an ill〔a bad〕 effect ; an evil influence ¶ 폐해가 따르다 be attended by evils // 폐해를 끼치다 exert an evil influence《upon》

†폐허 廢墟 the ruins ¶ 폐허가 된 성 a castle in ruins // 그 도시는 폐허가 되어 있다 The city is now in ruins.

폐화 閉花 『식물』 a cleistogamic〔cleistogamous〕 flower

― 수정(受精) cleistogamy

폐환 肺患 lung trouble ⇨ 폐병

폐활량 肺活量 the capacity of the lungs ; breathing capacity

―계 a pneumatometer ; a spirometer

― 측정법 spirometry ; pulmometry

폐회 閉會 closing of a meeting ; a close ; adjournment ―하다 close《a meeting》; adjourn ¶ 폐회중이다 be out of session (의회가) // 폐회되다 be closed // 폐회를 선언하다 declare the meeting closed

―사 a closing address ¶ 폐회사를 하다 give a closing address ―식 a closing ceremony

폐회로 閉回路 a closed circuit

폐흉막 肺胸膜 『해부』 the pulmonary pleura

-포 period ¶ 달〔해〕포 a period of about a month〔year〕

포 脯 slices of dried meat seasoned with spices ¶ 포를 뜨다 slice meat

육― slices of dried beef

*포 砲 ① [대포] a gun ; a cannon ; a piece ; a battery ; gunnery《총칭》; ordnance ; artillery ② a bombard (옛 무기의) ¶ 포를 쏘다 fire a gun

8인치 ― an 8-inch gun

포 苞架 『식물』 a bract ¶ 포가 없는 ebracteate

포가 砲架 a gun carriage ; a gun mount ¶ 포가를 설치하다 set a gun carriage

포개다 pile up ; heap up ; put one upon another ; lay one on top of the other ; stack ¶ 장작을 포개다 stack firewood // 포개지다 lie one upon〔on top of〕 another ; overlap ; be laid over

포갬포갬 one upon〔over〕 another ; in piles〔heaps, stacks, layers〕 ¶ 이부자리를 포갬포갬 쌓다 pile bedclothes one upon another

*포격 砲擊 bombardment ; cannonade ; an artillery attack ; gunnery ; gunshot ―하다 bombard ; cannonade ; shell ; fire on《a ship, fort》 ¶ 포격을 개시하다 open fire《on》// 포격을 받다 be bombarded ; be attacked with artillery

포경 捕鯨 whaling ; whale fishing

― 기지 a whaling station ― 모선 a whaling mother ship ―선 a whaler ; a whaleboat ; a whaling vessel ― 선단 a fleet of whalers ― 선원〔선장〕 a whaling man〔master〕 ―업 whale fishing〔fishery〕; the whaling industry ―장 a whaling ground ―포 a harpoon gun ― 회사 a whaling company 국제 ― 협정 International Whaling Convention

포경 包莖 『의학』 phimosis

― 수술 an operation for phimosis

포고 布告 proclamation ; promulgation ; announcement ; notification ; declaration ; a decree (포고문) ―하다 proclaim ; announce ; declare ; decree ; promulgate ; notify ¶ 포고를 발하다 issue〔make〕 a proclamation // 선전 포고하다 declare war against〔upon〕

―령 a decree ; an edict ―문 a declaration ; a decree

포괄 包括 inclusion ; comprehension ―하다 include ; comprehend ; comprise ; contain ; embrace ; cover ¶ 포괄적(으로) inclusive(ly) ; comprehensive(-ly) ; general(ly)

― 범위 the coverage《of an agreement》 ― 보험 증권 a blanket policy ― 승계인 a general successor ― 유증 a universal legacy ― 허가 a blanket permission ― 허가제 the open general license system (수입의)

포교 布敎 propagation《of religion》; missionary work ; mission ; propagandism ―하다 propagate ; evangelize ; propagandize ¶ 포교에 종사하다 be engaged in missionary work

―단 a mission ; a propaganda ― 사업 missionary work ―자 a missionary worker ; a propagator ; an evangelist ― 지구 a mission (field)

포구 浦口 an inlet ; a port ; a boat landing

포구 砲口 the muzzle《of a gun》; the caliber (구경)

― 장전식 포 a muzzle loading gun

포군 砲軍 [포병대] artillery ; [병사] an artilleryman

포근포근 all soft and comfortable ―하다 be all soft and comfortable

포근하다 ① (be) soft and comfortable ; downy ; fluffy ② (be) mild ; warm ¶ 포근한 이부자리 a soft and comfortable bed // 겨울 날씨가 포근하다 It is mild for the winter.

포근히 comfortably ; softly ; sound(ly)

포금 砲金 gun metal
포기 a root ; a plant ; a head ¶ 카네이션 한 포기 one carnation plant // 알이 찬 배추 포기 a cabbage with a good head
— 가름 a division ; multiplication of a plant by separating the roots
*포기 抛棄 abandonment ; resignation ; [권리의] surrender ; renunciation ; waiving ; disclaimer ; waiver ; [요구의] relinquishment —하다 abandon ; give up ; throw up ; resign 《one's right》 ; forsake ; renounce 《war》 ; surrender ; waive ; forfeit ¶ 지위를 포기하다 throw up one's position // 계획을 포기하다 abandon〔give up〕 one's attempt〔plan〕 // 권리를 포기하다 renounce〔resign〕 the right // 그 방면의 권위자라도 포기를 했다 Even an authority in the field has thrown up his hands.
— 확인증 a release
포닥포닥 ⇨ 퍼덕퍼덕
포달 abusive〔offensive, foul〕 language ; insulting remarks ; abuse ; an insult ¶ 포달부리다 call all sorts of names ; curse and swear ; abuse 《a person》 soundly // 포달스럽다 be willful ; be wayward ; be naughty ; be perverse // 포달지다 be spiteful ; be wicked
포대 布袋 a burlap bag
포대 包袋 ⇨ 부대(負袋)
포대 砲臺 a battery ; [요새] a fort ; a fortress ; a casemate ¶ 포대를 구축하다 construct〔erect〕 a battery ; build a fort
포대기 a quilt for little children ; baby's bedding
*포도 葡萄 grapes ; [나무] a grape vine
—나무 a grapevine ; a grapevine plant
—당 grape sugar ; dextrose ; glucose
— 덩굴 a grape vine —밭 a vineyard ; a grapery ; a grape plantation —산 〖화학〗 racemic acid —상구균 a staphylococcus 《*pl.* -cocci》 —색 dark purple —석(石) 〖광석〗 prehnite —송이 a bunch of grapes —원 a vineyard ; a vinery ; a grapery ; a grape plantation — 재배 vine culture ; viticulture ; vine〔grape〕 growing — 재배자 a grape grower ; a viniculturist ; an oenologist —주 (grape) wine ; port (wine) ; vinous liquor —즙 grape juice 건— raisins
*포도 鋪道, 舖道 a paved street ; a pavement
포도 暴徒 a mob ⇨ 폭도
포도 대장 捕盜大將 a police chief 《in ancient times》
포도동 with a flitter ; fluttering —하다 flutter ; flap rapidly 《the wings》
포도동거리다 flitter and flitter ; fluter and flutter ; keep flapping
포도청 捕盜廳 [옛 제도의] the police bureau

*포동포동 —하다 (be) chubby ; plump ; buxom (여자가) ¶ 얼굴이 포동포동한 full-cheeked // 포동포동한 얼굴 a chubby face // 살이 포동포동 찌다 be plump
포란 抱卵 brooding over eggs for hatching ; sitting ; incubation (of eggs)
포렴 布簾 a shop-curtain ; a sign-curtain
†포로 捕虜 a prisoner (of war) 《P. O. W.》 ; a war prisoner ; a captive ¶ 포로로 하다 take 《a person》 prisoner〔captive〕 // 포로가 되다 be taken prisoner(s)
— 교환 an exchange of prisoners — 교환 협정 the Prisoners of War Exchange Pact — 송환 the repatriation of prisoners of war — 수용소 a prisoners' camp ; a concentration camp ; an internment camp — 학대 POW atrocities
포르말린 〖약〗 formalin
포르토노보 Porto-Novo
포르토프랭스 Port-au-Prince
포르투갈 Portugal ¶ 포르투갈의 Portuguese
— 말 Portuguese — 사람 a Portuguese ; the Portuese 《총칭》
*포마드 pomade ; hair grease ¶ 포마드를 바르다 pomade〔apply pomade to〕 the hair
포만 飽滿 satiety ; satiation —하다 be sated 《with》 ; be satiated 《with》 ; be full 《of》
포말 泡沫 a bubble ; a foam ; a froth
— 회사 a bubble company
포목 布木 linen and cotton ; dry goods 《미》 ; drapery 《영》
—전 a linen shop ; a dry goods store 《미》 ; a draper's 《영》
포문 砲門 [군함의] a gunport ; a porthole ; an embrasure (성채의) ; a muzzle (포구) ¶ 일제히 포문을 열었다 All the guns opened fire simultaneously.
포물선 抛物線 〖수학〗 a parabola ¶ 포물선을 그리다 describe a parabola
—경(鏡) a parabolic reflector — 궤도 a parabolic orbit〔track〕 — 안테나 a parabola antenna — 운동 a parabolic motion —체 a paraboloid 반(半)— a semiparabola 보통〔3차〕 — a common〔cubic〕 parabola
포미 砲尾 the gun breech ; the breech (of a cannon)
포박 捕縛 arrest ; apprehension ; capture —하다 arrest ; apprehend ; catch ; seize ; nab 《속》 ; take ; place under arrest ¶ 그들은 일제히 포박되었다 Sweeping〔Wholesale〕 arrests were made of them. /They ware rounded up.
포배기 doubling ; folding ; laying one upon another

포백 布帛 line and silk ; hemp and silk
포백 曝白 bleaching ⇨ 표백
*포병 砲兵 artillery ; an artilleryman ; a gunner
—과 the artillery branch — 기지 an artillery base —대 an artillery outfit ; the artillery — 대대 an artillery battalion — 사령관 an artillery commander — 연대 an artillery regiment —전 an artillery duel〔engagement〕 — 중대 a battery — 진지 《talk up》 an artillery〔a gun〕 position
포복 匍匐 creeping —하다 creep ; crawl ; grovel ; walk on one's hands and knees ; go on all fours ¶ 포복성의 prostrate (식물의) // 적의 참호에 포복으로 접근하다 approach to the enemy trench by crawling and creeping
— 식물 a groundling — 척후 a sneaking〔crawling〕 patrol
포복 절도 抱服絶倒 —하다 hold〔shake, split〕 one's sides with laughter ; laugh oneself into convulsions ; be convulsed with laughter ¶ 포복 절도시키다 throw 《a person》 into convulsions
포볼 『야구』 four balls ; a base on balls ; a walk ; a pass ¶ 포볼로 1루에 나가다 get a base〔walk to first〕 on balls ; get a walk〔free ticket〕
*포부 抱負 aspiration ; ambition ¶ 포부가 큰 ambitious ; aspirant ; aspiring // 포부를 말하다 express one's hopes〔wishes〕 ; speak of one's aspiration // 큰 포부를 가지다 have a great ambition ; entertain a high aspiration ; aspire after greatness
포삭포삭 —하다 (be) brittle ; fragile ; crumbly
포살 砲殺 shooting to death ; execution by shooting —하다 shoot 《a person》 to death ; execute by shooting ¶ 포살되다 be shot dead〔to death〕
포살 捕殺 [잡아서 죽임] catching and killing —하다 catch and kill
포상 砲床 a gun platform ; a gun emplacement
포상 褒賞 a prize ; a reward —하다 give a prize 《to》 ; praise and reward ¶ 포상을 주다〔받다〕 award〔receive, win〕 a prize
— 수령자 a prize winner ; a prizeman — 수여 prize giving —장 a testimonial
*포석 布石 strategic arrangement of *badook* stones —하다 arrange stones in strategic position (in the game of *badook*)
포석 鋪石 a paving stone ¶ 포석이 깔린 도로 a road paved with stones // 포석을 깔다 pave 《a street》 with stones
포섭 包攝 winning 《a person》 over to one's side ; bringing round ; 『논리』 subsumption ; connotation —하다 win 《a person》 over to one's side ; bring 《a person》 round〔over〕 to one's side ; draw〔pull〕 《a person》 into one's side ¶ 포섭책을 강구하다 contrive to win 《a person》 over
포성 砲聲 the sound of firing ; the boom〔roaring〕 of a gun〔cannon〕 ; cannonade ¶ 포성이 천지를 진동했다 The roar of guns shook heaven and earth. / The cannon's roar rent the air.
포수 砲手 a hunter (사냥꾼) ; an artillery man (대포수) ; an artillerist ; a gunner (해군의)
포수 捕手 『야구』 a catcher
포술 砲術 gunnery ; artillery
—가 a gunner ; an artillerist — 교관 a gunnery instructor — 연습 gunnery practice —장(長) a chief gunner
포스 아웃 『야구』 a force-out ¶ 포스 아웃 시키다 force 《a runner》 out
*포스터 a poster ; a placard ; a bill ; [그림이 있는 것] a pictorial poster ; [글자만의 것] a plain poster ; [활자로 인쇄한 것] a letter-press poster ¶ 포스터를 붙이다 put up a poster ; post a bill ; placard 《a fence》 // 포스터를 떼어내다 tear off a poster
— 광고 billing — 선전 publicity〔advertizement〕 with posters 광고 — an ad-poster
포슬포슬 ⇨ 파슬파슬
포승 捕繩 a rope to bind a criminal with
포식 捕食 『생태』 predation ; predatism —하다 prey upon 《birds》
— 동물 a predator ; a predatory animal
포식 飽食 gluttony ; satiation —하다 satiate〔glut〕 oneself ; be fed up 《with》 ; eat one's fill ; eat to one's heart's content ; sate one's appetite ¶ 포식 난의하다 be well-fed and well-clad ; be rich and indolent
포신 砲身 a gun barrel ; the barrel of a gun〔cannon〕
포실하다 (be) well-off ; rich ; wealthy ¶ 포실한 생활을 하다 live comfortably
*포악 暴惡 atrocity ; violence ; outrageousness ; tyranny ; savagery —하다 (be) atrocious ; outrageous ; heinous ; brutal ; fiendish ; diabolical ¶ 인도에 어긋난 포악 행위 an outrage against humanity
포안 砲眼 an embrasure ; a gun hole
포연 砲煙 cannon smoke ; powder smoke ; the smoke of cannon ¶ 포연 탄우 아래 under a rain〔shower〕 of shells (and amidst powder smoke) ; in the thick of the battle
포열 砲列 a train of artillery ; a battery ¶ 포열을 치다 arrange〔lay〕 a field battery ; place guns in position
포영 泡影 foam and shadow ; [덧없음] uncertainty ; transiency
*포옹 抱擁 an embrace ; a hug —하다

embrace; hug; cuddle; hold 《a person》 to one's breast〔in one's arms〕 ¶ 포옹해 줘요 Give me a hug, darling.

포용 包容 [포괄] comprehension; implication; inclusion; [관용] tolerance; catholicity (아량) ━하다 [뜻을] comprehend; imply; include; embrace; [사람을] tolerate
━력 capacity; tolerance; [아량] catholicity; broad-mindedness ¶ 포용력이 큰 사람 a magnanimous〔catholic, broad-minded〕 person; a tolerant person ━성 catholicity; magnanimity; capacity

포워드 〖구기〗 a forward 《F. W.》

*포위 包圍 a siege; an investment; envelopment; encirclement ━하다 [둘러싸다] surround; encircle; hem 〔close〕 in; [군대가] invest; envelop; beleaguer; besiege; lay siege to 《a fort》; [경관이] throw a cordon round ¶ 포위를 풀다 raise the siege 《of》; withdraw // 적의 포위를 돌파하다 break through the besieging enemy forces 〔lines〕
━ 공격 an enveloping attack; a siege ━군 an investing〔a besieging〕 army ━망 an encircling net; an iron ring ━부대 encircling〔enveloping〕 forces 〔troops〕; a flanking party ━ 사격 an enveloping〔a converging〕 fire ━ 작전 an encircling〔enveloping, outflanking〕 operation ━전 a siege warfare; a battle of encirclement

포유 包有 containing; holding 《a thing in》 ━하다 contain; hold; have 《in》

포유 哺乳 lactation; suckling; nursing ━하다 suckle; give suck to; nurse
━ 기관 a mamma 《*pl.* -mae》 ━ 동물 a mammal ━ 동물학 mammalogy; therology ━류 Mammalia (학명)

포육 脯肉 slices of dried meat

포의 布衣 a scholar without a government office
━ 한사(寒士) a poor scholar without a government office

포의 胞衣 〖해부〗 the placenta; the afterbirth
━ 불하증(不下症) failure of the placenta to descend ━수 the amniotic fluid

포인터 [개] a pointer

포인트 ① [요점] the point 《of story》 ② [소수점] a (decimal) point ③ [전철기] a (railway) switch; points; a point switch ④ [활자] point ¶ 9포인트 활자 (a) 9-point type ⑤ [경기의 득점] a point; a score ¶ 포인트로 이기다 outpoint 《a person》 // 포인트를 얻다 win 〔get, score〕 a point ⑥ [시세] a point ⑦ 〖항해〗 [나침반의] a course; a point

포자 胞子 〖식물〗 a spore; 〖동물〗 a cyst ¶ 포자가 생기는 sporiferous
━ 생식 spore〔sporic〕 reproduction; sporation; sporogenesis; sporogony ━세포 a sporoblast ━엽 a sporophyl(l) ━체 a sporophyte ━충류 Sporozoa (학명) 무━ 생식 apospory

포장 布帳 a linen awning; a curtain; a fall
━마차 a covered carriage; a calash; a covered wagon 《미》

*포장 包裝 packing ━하다 pack; wrap 《a thing》 up ¶ 포장이 좋다〔나쁘다〕 be properly〔defectively〕 packed // 포장을 풀다 undo a package // 종이로 포장하다 wrap 《it》 up in paper
━물 a package ━비 the packing charge (과일 따위의) ━ 작업장 a packhouse ━ 재료 packing materials ━지(紙) packing〔wrapping〕 paper; a (paper) wrapper; brown paper

포장 包藏 wrapping and putting away; storing up; concealment (of a thing); packing well ━하다 wrap up; wrap away; wrap and put away; store up

포장 褒章 a medal (of merit)

*포장 鋪裝 pavement; paving ━하다 pave; surface ¶ 도로를 아스팔트로 포장하다 pave a street with asphalt
━ 공사 pavement works; paving ━ 도로 a paved〔surfaced〕 road; pavement ━ 벽돌 paving brick ━ 재료 paving materials; road metal

포장 褒奬 incitement; encouragement ━하다 praise and encourage; laud; incite

포전 砲戰 an artillery duel〔engagement〕; a mutual bombardment〔cannonade〕

포전 圃田 a vegetable garden〔yard〕; a kitchen garden

포졸 捕卒 a policeman; a detective; a raiding constable

포좌 砲座 〖군사〗 a gun platform; a barbette (성의); [포가] a gun carriage; a gun mount; a cage

포주 抱主 the master〔mistress〕 of a brothel; a pimp

포즈 a pose ¶ 포즈를 취하다 pose (oneself) 《as a mode》; strike〔get into〕 pose; take one's pose; posture; arrange oneself

포지션 a position ¶ 자기 포지션을 지키다 stand〔guard〕 one's position

포진 布陣 the lineup ━하다 line up; take one's position

포집다 pile up; heap up; lay upon another ¶ 그릇을 포집다 pile up dishes

포차 砲車 a gun carriage

포착 捕捉 [붙잡음] capture; [뜻의] catching; grasping; understanding ━하다 capture; catch; grasp; seize; apprehend ¶ 포착하기 어려운 elusive; evasive; intangle; hard to understand

〔catch〕// 뜻을 포착하다 grasp the meaning
포척 布尺 a tape-measure
포촌 浦村 a seaside village
포충망 捕蟲網 an insect net
포츠담 Potsdam
— 선언 the Potsdam Declaration〔Conference〕 (of 1945) — 협정 the Potsdam Agreement
포커 poker
— 페이스 a poker face ; a dead pan 《미·속》 ; a deadpan face 《미·속》
포켓 a pocket ; a kick 《속》 ¶ 안〔옆〕 포켓 an inside〔a side〕 pocket // 상의의〔바지의〕 포켓 a coat〔trouser(s)〕 pocket // 바지의 뒷포켓 a hip〔back〕 pocket // 포켓 속을 뒤지다 search one's pocket ; feel in one's pocket for 《a thing》 // 포켓에 넣다 pocket ; put 《a thing》 in〔into〕 a pocket ; drop 《a volume》 into one's pocket
—북 a pocket(-sized) book —판 a pocket edition ¶ 포켓판 사전 a pocket dictionary
*포크[1] ¶ 식탁〔디저트, 샐러드〕용 포크 a table〔dessert, salad〕 fork
포크[2] pork
— 소테 pork sauté
포크 댄스 a folk dance ; folk dancing
포크 볼 〚야구〛 a fork ball
포크송 a folk song
— 가수 a folk singer
포타슘 〚화학〛 potassium
포타즈 [진한 수프] potage 《프》
†포탄 砲彈 a cannon ball ; a shell ; a shot ¶ 적에게 포탄을 퍼붓다 rain shells upon the enemy // 포탄이 소리를 내며 머리 위를 지나갔다 A shell passed overhead with a screech.
포탈 逋脫 evasion of taxes ; tax evasion 〔avoidance〕 —하다 evade〔dodge〕 a tax ; defraud the revenue
세금 —자 a tax evader
포탑 砲塔 a (gun) turret ; a cupola (군함의)
포태 胞胎 conception ; pregnancy —하다 conceive ; get〔become〕 pregnant ; go with child ; be in the family way
포터 a (beggage) porter ; a redcap 《미》
포터블 portable 《radio》
포트사이드 Port Said
포폄 褒貶 praise and censure ; criticism —하다 criticize
*포플러 a poplar
포플린 poplin ; broadcloth 《미》
포피 包皮 the foreskin ; the prepuce
— 결석(結石) 〚의학〛 a preputial concretion ; a postholith —염(炎) posthitis ; acroposthitis — 절단(切斷) circumcision
포학 暴虐 tyranny ; outrage ; atrocity —하다 (be) tyrannical ; outrageous ; atrocious ¶ 포학한 군주 a tyrant
— 무도 tyranny and injustice
포함 〚민속〛 the inspired utterances of a shaman —하다 《a shaman》 yell (out) inspired words
†포함 包含 inclusion ; comprehension ; implication —하다 include ; contain ; comprise ; hold ; comprehend ; embrace ; cover ; implicate ; [뜻을] imply ; connotate

> 참고 **contain** 알맹이 또는 부분으로서 그 안에 갖고 있다 **hold** 수용 능력이 있다 물론 때에 따라서는 contain과 같은 뜻으로도 쓰인다 **include** 구성분자로서 그 안에 포함한다 **comprise** 범위가 확실한 것에 대해서 그것이 그 범위 안에 포함되다의 뜻

¶ 모든 요금을 포함하여 all charges included // 그 소녀를 포함해서 6명이 초대되었다 Six were invited, including the girl.
—량 the (amount of) content —률 the percentage of content
포함 砲艦 a gunboat
포합 抱合 ① [화합] combination —하다 combine ② [껴안음] an embrace —하다 embrace
— 기관 claspers —물 a compound
포합어 抱合語 〚언어〛 an incorporating language
포항 浦港 harbor and port
포호 咆號 ⇨ 포효(咆哮)
포화 布靴 cloth shoes ; canvas shoes ; tennis shoes
포화 砲火 gunfire ; shellfire ; artillery fire ; fire ¶ 치열한 포화 a heavy fire // 포화를 열다 open fire // 포화를 퍼붓다 rain fire on 《an enemy》 // 포화를 집중하다 concentrate the fire // 적의 포화에 응하다 answer the fire of the enemy
십자 — cross fire
포화 飽和 〚화학〛 saturation —하다 be〔become〕 saturated
—기 a saturator — 기관차 a saturative locomotive —도 a degree of saturation
— 상태 saturation ¶ 지금 교원의 수요는 포화 상태에 있다 There is no demand for teachers now. — 용액〔화합물〕 a saturated solution〔compound〕
— 전류〔곡선〕 a saturation current 〔curve〕 —점 a saturated point ; the saturation point — 증기 saturated vapor
포환 砲丸 a cannonball ; a slug ; 〚경기〛 a shot
포환 던지기 砲丸— shot-put(ting) —하다 put the shot
— 선수 a shot-putter ; a weight putter
†포획 捕獲 capture ; seizure —하다 capture ; seize ; catch ; make a prize of 《a thing》
—고 catch —량 a catch 《of whales》 —

물 a prize ; a booty —선〔군함〕 a captured ship〔warship〕 —자 a captor

*포효 咆哮 [짐승의] a roar ; a howl ; howling ; a bellow ; yelling (고함) —하다 roar ; howl ; bellow ; yell ¶ 포효하는 파도 소리를 듣다 hear the roar of the sea

폭¹ ① [깊게] deeply ; soundly ; completely ¶ 폭 잠들었다 fall asleep soundly ② [힘있게] thrusting hard ③ [꼭 덮거나 싸다] wrapping carefully 〔tightly〕 ¶ 담요로 몸을 폭 싸다 wrap oneself in a blanket ④ [함빡 곯다] boil ¶ 폭 삶다 boil to pulp ⑤ [남김 없이] with nothing left ; exhaustively ⑥ [꺼지다] sink ; hollow ¶ 발 밑의 땅이 폭 꺼졌다 The ground under his feet sank all of a sudden. ⑦ [폭삭] wholly ⇨ 폭삭

폭² ① [정도] ¶ 그녀는 나의 누이동생 폭밖에 안된다 She must be of same age as my younger sister. // 두 시간 폭은 된다 It's about two hours. ② [셈] ¶ 잘된 폭이야 It turned out all right, I guess.

†폭 幅 ① [넓이] width ; breadth ¶ 폭이 넓은 wide ; broad // 폭을 넓히다 widen ; broaden // 그것은 폭이 1미터이다 It has a width of one meter. /It is one meter wide. ② [세력·영향력] range ; influence ; power ¶ 폭이 있는 influential ; powerful ③ [도량] magnanimity ; generosity ¶ 폭이 넓은 사람 a large 〔broad〕-minded person ④ [족자·조각의] a scroll ; a strip ; a picture ; a piece ¶ 무명 한 폭 a strip of calico

폭거 暴擧 [난폭] outrage ; violence ; [폭동] a riot ; an insurrection ; a disturbance ; [무모한 기도] a reckless attempt ; a leap in the dark ¶ 폭거를 경고하다 warn 《a person》 against recklessness

폭격 爆擊 bombing ; bombardment ; a bombing attack〔raid〕 —하다 bomb ; bombard ; make a bombing raid ; drop a bomb 《on》 ¶ 폭격으로 집을 잃은 사람들 people bombed out ; bombed-out people

—기 a bombing plane ; a bomber —기대 a squadron of bombers —대 a bombing squad ; an air-strike force —수 a bombardier ¶ B-52의 폭격수 a B-52 bombardier — 조준기 a bomb sight 융단 — blanket bombing 전략 — strategic bombing 정밀 — precision bombing 전투 —기 a fighter-bomber 중〔경〕—기 a heavy〔light〕 bomber

*폭군 暴君 a tyrant ; a despot (전제 군주) ; an autocrat

‡폭도 暴徒 rioters ; a mob ; mobsters ; insurgents ; mutineers (군대의) ¶ 폭도의 한 무리 a mob of rioters // 폭도에게 습격 당하다 be mobbed // 폭도를 진압하다 put down〔suppress, pacify〕 a mob

‡폭동 暴動 a riot ; a disturbance ; rioting ; an uprising ; a seditious act of violence ; [반란] an insurrection ; a rebellion ; a mutiny (군대의) ¶ 폭동을 일으키다 raise〔start, get up〕 a riot ; rise in riot〔rebellion〕 ; create a disturbance // 폭동을 선동하다 instigate a riot // 폭동을 진압하다 suppress〔put down, quell〕 a riot ; repress a disturbance // 폭동을 무력으로 진압하다 put down a riot by force // 폭동이 일어나다 a riot arises〔breaks out〕

—자 a rioter ; a rebel ; an insurgent ; a mutineer (군대의) —죄 a charge of sedition〔rioting〕 무장 — armed revolt

폭등 暴騰 a sudden〔great, sharp〕 rise ; a (big) jump ; a boom ; skyrocketing —하다 jump ; soar ; rise suddenly ; boom ; shoot skyward ; skyrocket ¶ 폭등하는 물가 soaring prices ; boom prices // 건축 재료비의 폭등 a great rise in the price of building materials // 500원에서 1,000원으로 폭등하다 jump from 500 *won* to 1,000 *won* // 물가가 폭등하다 Prices take a jump.

*폭락 暴落 a slump ; a (sharp) break ; a crash ; a smash ; a heavy fall〔decline〕 —하다 decline heavily〔sharply〕 ; slump ; fall suddenly ; toboggan (미) ¶ 생사의 폭락 a heavy fall of the silk market // 주식의 폭락 a slump in stocks // 500원 대로 폭락하다 slump to the 500 *won* level

폭려 暴戾 tyranny ; atrocity —하다 (be) tyrannical ; tyrannous ; outrageous ; brutal ; atrocious

†폭력 暴力 violence ; force ¶ 폭력으로 by (main) force // 폭력을 행사하다 use 〔employ, resort to〕 violence〔force〕 ; use one's fist // 폭력을 가하다 cause violence 《to》 ; commit violence 《towards》 ; commit an outrage 《on》

—단 a terrorist organization ; a touch gang ; a gang of racketeers〔ruffians, bulldozers〕 —단 검거 an antigangster drive ; the round up of racketeers —배 hooligans ; streettoughs ¶ 폭력배 단속을 강화하다 tighten control on hooligans — 범죄 a crime of violence — 정치 Bolshevik terrorism in politics — 행사 use of violence〔force〕 ; strong arm — 행위 an act of violence — 혁명 a Bolshevik revolution 조직 — violence committed by criminal organization 집단 — organized violence

폭렬 爆裂 explosion ⇨ 폭발

‡폭로 暴露 exposure ; disclosure ; divulgence ; discovery ; exposal ; detection —하다 [드러내다] disclose ; reveal ; show ; divulge 《a secret》 ; expose 《another's crime》 ; betray 《another's plot》 ; lay bare ; bring 《a matter》 to

light ; [드러나다] be discovered ; be detected ; be found out ; be revealed [disclosed, exposed] ; be laid bare ; come[be brought] to light ¶ 비밀을 폭로하다 lay bare 《a person's》 secret // 사기꾼의 정체를 폭로하다 expose an impostor // 그는 무식을 폭로했다 He betrayed his ignorance.

— 기사 a telltale story ¶ 폭로 기사 전문의 신문 a scandal sheet — 문학 debunking literature — 소설 a telltale story — 전술 exposure[mudslinging] tactics

폭론 暴論 an irrational argument[contention] ; a wild argument ; an unfair opinion ¶ 폭론을 토하다 make absurd remarks

폭뢰 爆雷 a depth bomb[charge]

폭리 暴利 excessive profits ; profiteering (부당한) ; [고리] exorbitant interest ; usury ¶ 폭리를 취하다 profiteer ; make undue[unreasonable] profits 《on》 ; derive excessive interests // 폭리를 단속하다 control profiteering

(전시) —자 a (war) profiteer — 취체령 an anti-profiteering ordinance

폭명 爆鳴 detonation

— 가스 detonating gas

폭민 暴民 a mob ; rioters ; insurgents

— 정치 mobocracy ; ochlocracy ; mob rule ; mass rule

†**폭발 爆發** explosion ; detonation ; blow-up ; blasting ; bursting ; blowing up ; eruption (화산의) **—하다** explode ; burst (up) ; blow up ; detonate ; [화산이] erupt ; go into eruption ¶ 가스[분노, 불만]의 폭발 of gas explosion [anger, discontent] // 분노가 폭발하다 《a person》 fly into a passion ; burst into a rage ; explode with anger[rage] // 분노를 폭발시키다 let loose one's indignation // 무시무시한 소리를 내며 폭발하다 blow up with a terrific explosion // 가스 폭발로 파괴되다 be wrecked by a gas explosion // 화약통이 폭발했다 The barrel of gunpowder blew up. // 화산이 폭발했다 A volcano burst[went] into eruption. // 혁명이 폭발했다 A revolution burst[broke] out. // 그들의 평소의 울분이 폭발했다 Their smoldering resentment burst into flame.

— 가스 explosive gas ; [광산의] fire damp —관 a detonator —력 explosive power —력학 pyrodynamics —물 an explosive — 방지 장치 [기관의] a hydrostat —성 explosiveness — 신관 a detonating fuse —약 blasting[detonating] powder ; an explosive compound ; Hercules powder (광산용) —점 the point of explosion ; the site of an explosion —탄 an explosive shell ; a bomb 원자[핵] — atomic[nuclear] explosion

폭발적 爆發的 explosive ; tremendous ¶ 폭발적 인기 tremendous popularity // 인구의 폭발적 증가 a population explosion

폭분 爆粉 fulminating powder

폭사 暴死 a tragically sudden death ; a violent death **—하다** die a tragically sudden death ; die[meet with] a violent death

폭사 爆死 death resulting from bombing ; death by explosion **—하다** be killed by a bomb ; be bombed to death ; be killed in an explosion

폭삭 ① entirely ; wholly ; completely ; all ¶ 그 건물이 폭삭 주저앉았다 The building collapsed completely. ② crumbly ; fragilely ; frailly ; to a crisp

폭서 暴暑 intense[severe, torrid] heat

⁑**폭설 暴雪** a heavy snow ; a storm of snow

폭성 爆聲 explosion ; detonation

폭소 爆笑 a burst[roar] of laughter ; an explosive laugh[laughter] **—하다** burst out laughing ; burst into laughter [a laugh] ¶ 폭소를 터뜨렸다 There was a burst into laughter. // 청중은 그의 재담에 폭소했다 The audience burst out laughing at his joke. /His joke was greeted with bursts of laughter.

폭스 트롯 《dance》 a fox trot

***폭식 暴食** intemperance in eating ; gluttony ; voracity ; voracious eating ; gorging **—하다** overeat ; eat too much ; eat to[in] excess ; be intemperate in eating ; gorge ; be voracious[ravenous]

—가 a heavy[an excessive] eater ; a voracious eater ; a glutton ; a gourmand

폭신폭신 ⇨ 푹신푹신

폭신하다 (be) soft ; cushiony ⇨ 푹신하다

폭심 爆心 an epicenter

—지 the center of a bombed area

폭압 暴壓 oppression ; coercion ; repression ; curbin[checking, holding down] by force **—하다** oppress ; coerce ; repress ; curb[check] by force

폭약 爆藥 an explosive (compound) ; blasting powder ; detonator ¶ 폭약을 장치하다 lay an explosive // 폭약에 점화하다 set off the blasting powder

고성능 — a high explosive

폭양 曝陽 the blazing sunlight ; the burning sun

폭언 暴言 violent[abusive] language ; harsh[wild] words ; intemperate speech **—하다** use violent[strong] language ; speak vehemently ; utter wild words

폭우 暴雨 a pouring[heavy, violent] rain ; a downpour (of rain) ; a torrential rain

폭원 幅員, 幅圓 the width (of a land lot) ; breadth ¶ (선박의) 최대 폭원

the breadth extreme
폭위 暴威 tyranny ; abuse of power ; great violence ¶ 폭위를 떨치다 be rampant ; be furious ; be violent ; tyrannize over 《the people》 ; play the tyrant ; act with violence ; [폭풍이] rage (with violence)
폭음 暴飮 heavy〔deep〕 drinking ; excessive drinking ; intemperance ━하다 drink hard〔heavily, deep〕 ; drink to excess ; overdrink ; drink too much ¶ 폭음 폭식하다 eat and drink immoderately ; commit excesses
—가 a hard drinker ; a wine bibber ; a soaker
폭음 爆音 [폭발의] an explosion ; a detonation ; an explosive〔a bursting〕 sound ; crump (폭탄의) 《속》 ; [엔진의] teufteuf ; [비행기의] buzzing ; burring ; drumming〔whir(r)〕 (of a propeller) ¶ 폭음을 내며 날다 fly with a whir ; thunder overhead
폭정 暴政 tyranny ; despotism ; despotic government ; tyrannical rule〔government〕 ¶ 폭정을 펴다 tyrannize over a country ; rule a nation with a high hand
폭주 暴走 〖야구〗 a reckless run ━하다 run recklessly
— 열차 a runaway train
폭주 暴酒 heavy〔excessive〕 drinking ; toping (상습적) ━하다 drink heavily ; drink too much ; overdrink ; tope
폭주 輻輳 overcrowding ; congestion 《of goods, traffic》 ; pressure 《of order》 ; influx 《of people》 ; concourse ━하다 congest ; be congested 《with》 ; be (over)crowded ; gather ¶ 교통량의 폭주 a traffic congestion〔jam〕 // 주문의 폭주 pressure of orders // 화물〔우편물, 기사〕의 폭주 a congestion of goods〔mail-matter, news〕 // 폭주를 완화하다 relieve the congestion 《of goods》
*폭죽 爆竹 a firecracker ; a petard ; a squib ¶ 폭죽을 터뜨리다 set off firecrackers
폭취 暴醉 ━하다 be〔get〕 beastly〔dead〕 drunk
폭침 爆沈 sinking by explosion ; blowing up ━하다 blow up 《a ship》 ; sink by explosion
*폭탄 爆彈 a bomb ; a bomb shell ¶ 폭탄적 요구 a bombshell demand // 1만톤의 폭탄을 적재하고 with a 10,000 ton bomb load // 폭탄을 투하하다 drop〔deliver, release, throw〕 a bomb 《on》
— 선언 a bombshell declaration — 적재량 bomb-carrying capacity (비행기의) — 적재실 a bomb chamber — 조준기 a bomb(ing) sight — 투하 bomb-dropping ; bombing — 투하기 a bomb release 고성능 — a TNT bomb 방향 가변 — an azon bomb 수소 — a hydrogen bomb ; an H-bomb 시한 — a time bomb 심해 — a depth bomb 원자 — an atomic bomb ; an A-bomb 음향 — a scream bomb ; a buzz bomb 초대형 — a blockbuster 플라스틱 — a plastic bomb
폭투 暴投 [야구] a wild pitch〔throw〕 ; wild pitching ━하다 pitch wild 《to a batter》 ; throw a wild ball 《to a fielder》
†폭파 爆破 blasting ; blowing ; explosion ━하다 blast ; blow up ; explode ; demolish ¶ 철도를 폭파하다 pound rail lines 《with bombs》 // 암석을 폭파하다 blast a rock 《with dynamite》
—약 blasting powder〔charge〕 — 작업 blasting operations —전(栓) a blasting needle
*폭포 瀑布 ⇨ 폭포수(瀑布水)
나이아가라 — (The) Niagara Falls
폭포수 瀑布水 a waterfall ; a falls ; a cascade (작은) ; a cataract (큰) ¶ 폭포수가 되어 떨어지다 fall in a cascade〔in torrents〕 ; cascade down // 폭포수처럼 쏟아지다 fall〔come down〕 in cataracts〔torrents〕
폭폭 ① [찌르다] piercing repeatedly ② [썩다] rotting rapidly ③ [삶다] boiling completely〔well〕 ④ [욕] abusing roundly ⑤ [쏟다] pouring violently ⇨ 푹푹
*폭풍 暴風 a storm ; a windstorm ; a stormwind ; a wild〔violent, stormy〕 wind ; a tempest ; a gale (강풍) ; a typhoon (태풍) ; a hurricane (구풍)

> 참고 **storm**은 가장 일반적인 말 **tempest**는 storm보다 더욱 격렬한 것으로서 「큰 폭풍우」라는 뜻의 점잖은 말 **typhoon**은 동남아시아의 「태풍」 **hurricane**은 서인도 제도의 폭풍

¶ 폭풍의 중심 a storm center ; the eye of a storm // 폭풍의 진로 〖기상〗 a storm lane // 폭풍을 무릅쓰고 braving〔daring〕 a storm // 폭풍을 만나다 encounter a storm // 폭풍이 일어난다 A storm arises〔comes on〕. // 폭풍이 분다 It blows a gale〔storm〕. // 폭풍이 오려고 한다 A storm is approaching〔coming up〕. // 그 배는 심한 폭풍으로 난파했다 The ship was wrecked in a terrible storm.
— 경보(신호) a storm warning〔signal〕 —권 a storm zone〔area〕 —설 a snowstorm ; a blizzard — 진로 a storm lane 대— a tempestuous wind ; a furious storm
폭풍 爆風 a bombshell〔detonation〕 blast
†폭풍우 暴風雨 a rainstorm ; a storm ; a tempest ; a typhoon ; a hurricane
폭한 暴寒 severe〔intense〕 cold
폭한 暴漢 a ruffian ; a rowdy ; a rough ; a hooligan ; a desperado ; a

tough 《미·속》; a bully 《미·속》 ¶ 폭한에게 습격당하다 be assaulted by a ruffian

폭행 暴行 (an act of) violence; an outrage; violation; riotous conduct; an attack; an assault **—하다** behave violently; act outrageously; assault; attack ¶ 주정뱅이들의 폭행 outrages committed by a drunken mob // 여자에 대한 폭행 an outrage on a woman // 폭행을 가하다 do violence 《to》; commit an outrage〔act of violence〕《against》
—자 an outrager; a rioter **가중(加重)—** 〖법〗 an aggravated assault

폰 〖물리〗 phon ¶ 비행기의 폭음은 120폰이었다 The airplane engine registered 120 phons.

폴라로이드 [인조 편광판] a polaroid
— 카메라 a polaroid camera

폴란드 Poland ¶ 폴란드의 Polish
— 말 Polish **— 사람** a Pole; the Poles 《총칭》

폴로 〖경기〗 polo
— 경기자 a poloist; a polo player

폴로네즈 〖음악·무용〗 Polonaise

폴로늄〖화학〗 polonium 《Po》

폴로 셔츠 a polo shirt

폴리네시아 Polynesia ¶ 폴리네시아의 Polynesian

폴리에스테르 〖화학〗 polyester
—계 섬유 a polyester (fiber)

폴리에틸렌 〖화학〗 Polyethylene

폴카 [춤] Polka

폼 [운동가의] form ¶ 폼이 좋다 have a well-balanced〔proportioned〕 form // 그의 수영 폼은 훌륭하다 His swimming form is excellent.

폼페이 Pompeii

폿소리 砲— ⇨ 포성

퐁당 with a plop; with a splash ¶ 퐁당 물에 빠지다 fall plop into the water // 퐁당 물에 뛰어들다 jump〔plunge〕 into the water with a splash // 퐁당퐁당 헤엄치다 swim splashing the water

퐁당거리다 keep splashing〔plunging〕 ¶ 물속에서 퐁당거리다 splash〔spatter〕 about in the water

퐁당퐁당 with splashes; with splash after splash ⇨ 퐁당

퐁퐁 ① [구멍이 터지는] breaking open repeatedly ② [샘솟는] bubbling; gurgling

표 表 [일람표 따위] a table; a tabular statement〔exhibit〕; [예정표] a schedule; [도표] a diagram; a chart; [목록] a list ¶ 표에 나타난 것과 같이 as shown in the table // 표를 작성하다 compile〔draw up, make up〕 a table // 표로 작성하다 tabulate 《a thing》; list; make a list of; make 《a thing》 into a table // 상세한 것은 다음 표와 같다 Details are tabulated as follows.
성적— a school record; a transcript **시간—** a time table; a schedule (학교의) **어형 변화—** 〖문법〗 a paradigm **예정—** a schedule **정가—** a price list; a tariff (of charge) **통계—** a statistical table

†표 票 ① a ticket; a coupon ¶ 2일간 유효표 a ticket with a 2-day time limit // 표파는 곳 a booking office 《영》; a ticket window〔office〕 《미》; a box office (극장의) // 서울까지의 표 한 장 a ticket to *Seoul*; a one-way〔single〕 ticket to *Seoul* // 표를 사다 get〔buy〕 a ticket; book 《for *Pusan*》 // 표를 찍다 punch〔clip〕 a ticket // 부산까지의 2등표를 한 장 주십시오 (Please give me) a second-class (ticket) to *Pusan*.
② [투표의] a vote ¶ 깨끗한 한 표 a clean〔an honest〕 vote // 1만표를 얻다 poll 10,000 votes
—수 (the number of) votes **꼬리—** a tag **반액—** a half-fare ticket **배—** a boat ticket **부동—** a floating vote **왕복—** a return ticket; a round-trip ticket 《미》 **찬부동(贊否同)—** a tie vote

†표 標 ① [증거] a written statement; a proof; an evidence; a testimony; a deed ② [부호] a mark; a sign **—하다** mark 《a thing》; put a mark 《on》 ¶ 표를 한 marked // 표가 없는 unmarked // 별표를 하다 mark with an asterisk〔stars〕; asterisk ③ [휘장] a badge; a mark; an emblem ¶ 모표 a badge on one's cap // 회원표 a membership badge ④ [상표] a brand; a trademark ¶ 말표 the Horse Brand (상표) ⑤ [표시] a token; a sign; a manifestation ¶ 감사하다는 표로 as a small token of one's appreciation; in token of one's gratitude

표결 表決 vote; voting; decision by vote **—하다** vote〔take a vote〕 《on》; divide〔take division〕 《on》; call the roll 《on》 《미》; call for a roll call 《on》; put〔submit〕 《a bill》 to a vote〔ballot〕 ¶ 아슬아슬한 표결 a close vote // 감사의 표결 a vote of thanks // 결의를 표결에 붙이다 put a resolution to the vote
—권 a vote

표결 票決 a vote; voting; a decision by vote **—하다** take a vote 《on》 ¶ 표결에 붙이다 put〔submit〕 《a bill》 to a vote〔ballot〕
—권 a vote

표고 〖식물〗 a shiitake (mushroom); Cortinellus shiitake (학명)

표고 標高 ⇨ 해발(海拔)

표구 表具 mounting; papering **—하다** mount 《a picture》; paper
—사 a paper hanger; a mounter; a paperer

표기 表記 ① [겉에 쓰기] inscription on the face ¶ 표기의 mentioned〔inscribed〕 on the face〔outside〕 // 표기의 주소 the address mentioned on the

outside ; the above address
② [내용 표시] declaration ¶ 표기의 declared ; insured
— 가격 declared〔insured〕 value — 금액 the sum inscribed on the face 가격 — 우편물 mail matter with value declared

표기 標記 a mark ; a sign **—하다** mark 《a thing》; put a mark on 《a thing》

표나다 表— be characteristic 《of》; be conspicuous ; stand out ; [흔적] make a mark ; show signs ; give evidence 《of》; leave traces ¶ 표나게 conspicuously ; strikingly ; remarkably ; markedly // 표나는 색 a gay〔loud〕 color // 표나지 않는 색 a neutral tint ; a quiet color // 표나게 굴다 act conspicuous // 진보의 표가 안나다 show no sign〔mark〕 of progress // (흠친) 표가 안 나게 하다 leave no trace behind // 회색은 먼지 묻은 표가 안 난다 Gray does not show the dust.

표독 慓毒 ferocity ; brutality ; fierceness **—하다** (be) fierce ; ferocious ; brutal ¶ 표독스러운 얼굴로 with a look of venom // 표독하게 말하다 speak daggers to 《a person》

표등 標燈 a target lamp ; a signal lamp〔light〕

****표류 漂流** drifting **—하다** drift 《about》; be adrift ¶ 그 배는 6일간 표류했다 The vessel drifted about〔was adrift〕 six days.
—물 floatage ; a drift ; driftage ; flotsam (표류 화물) —선 a drifting ship ; a castaway (ship) ; a derelict (난파한) —자 a castaway ; a person adrift on the sea

표리 表裏 inside and outside ; a right and wrong side ; ins and outs ; obverse and reverse ; [양면] two〔both〕 sides ; [언동이] double-dealing ; duplicity ¶ 인생의 표리 the ins and outs of life // 표리 없는 single-hearted ; single-minded // 표리가 있는 double-dealing ; two-faced ; treacherous // 표리가 있는 근무 eyeservice // 표리가 있다 carry two faces under one hood ; play a double game // 그는 표리가 있는 사람이다 He has two faces. /He plays a double game.
— 일체 inside and outside together ; both sides (as one)

표리 부동 表裏不同 treacherousness ; deceptiveness **—하다** (be) treacherous ; deceptive ; doublefaced ¶ 저 하녀는 표리 부동하다 That maid works hard only when her mistress is watching.

†표면 表面 [윗면] the surface ; the face ; [외부] the exterior ; the outside ; [외관] appearance ; superficies ; show ¶ 표면의 external ; outside ; outward ; superficial ; apparent ; seeming ; ostensible // 표면의 이유 an ostensible reason ; a plausible excuse // 표면에 on the surface〔face〕 // 표면으로는 outwardly ; externally ; ostensibly ; professedly // 표면에 나타나다 get shown on the face〔surface〕 ; appear〔be〕 in the public eye ; appear above〔come to〕 the surface // 사건의 진상은 결코 표면만 보고는 모르는 것이다 The true condition of affairs is not to be known by external appearances.
— 경화(硬化) [철강의] case hardening ; surface hardening — 마취 〖의학〗 surface〔permeation〕 anesthesia —압(壓) surface pressure — 장력 〖물리〗 surface tension —파 a surface wave

***표면적 表面的** surface area

표면화 表面化 **—하다** disclose ; reveal bring to the fore〔to the surface, to light〕 ; come to the surface〔front, a head〕 ; be disclosed〔revealed〕 ; come into the open ; break cover ; take the wraps off ; make public ; be made public ; become an issue ¶ 그 사건으로 그들의 의도가 표면화되었다 The events have disclosed their designs.

***표명 表明** expression ; demonstration ; manifestation **—하다** express ; make an expression 《of》; demonstrate ; show ; manifest ¶ 입후보의 표명 announcement of one's candidacy // 감사의 뜻을 표명하다 express〔show〕 one's gratitude ; give expression to one's gratitude // 반대 의사를 표명하다 express oneself against 《a matter》; declare against

표목 標木 ⇨ 푯말

표박 漂泊 [방랑] wandering ; roaming ; vagabondage ; tramp ; [표류] drifting **—하다** wander about ; tramp ; vagabond ; roam ; drift
— 인종 a nomadic race〔tribe〕

표방 標榜 ① [내세움] advocacy ; espousal ; standing **—하다** profess 《oneself for》; stand for ; adapt a platform〔slogan, motto〕 《of》 ¶ 정의를 표방하다 claim to stand for justice ; champion the cause of justice ; be clothed with righteousness ② [알림] publishing **—하다** publish ¶ 선행을 표방하다 publish 《a person's》 good deed

표밭 票— a favorable voting constituency 《for the Democrat》

표백 表白 expression ; manifestation ; exhibition ; confession (자백) **—하다** express ; manifest ; confess

***표백 漂白** bleaching **—하다** bleach
—분 bleaching powder ; chloride of lime —액 a bleaching solution —제 bleaching agent ; a bleach ; a decolorant

***표범 豹—** 〖동물〗 a leopard ; a panther

—나비 a fritillary 미국— an American leopard ; a jaguar 암— a leopardess ; a pantheress 흑— a black leopard
표변 豹變 sudden change ; volte-face —하다 change suddenly ; change front ; switch ; [변절] turn one's coat ; turn round ; rat
*표본 標本 [박물의] a specimen ; [견본] a sample ; [전형] a type ; an example ¶ 알코올에 절인 표본 a specimen in spirits
— 조사 a sample survey — 조사법 sampling method — 진열실 a specimen room〔gallery〕 — 추출 (random) sampling —용 바늘 a setting needle 동물〔식물〕 — a zoological〔a botanical〕 specimen 박제 — a stuffed specimen 진열용 — a museum specimen
표상 表象 ① [상징] a symbol ; an emblem —하다 symbolize ; emblematize ; be symbolic(al) 《of》 ; be emblematic(al) 《of》 ¶ 평화의 표상 an emblem of peace ② 〖철학〗 an idea ; 〖심리〗 a (re)presentation 《of》 ¶ 표상의 중심 the center of ideas
—설 representation —주의 presentationism 부분 — a partial idea
표석 表石 a grave marker ; a tombstone ⇨ 묘표
표석 漂石 〖지질〗 an erratic block〔boulder〕
표석 標石 a stone post〔landmark〕 ; a boundary stone ; a milestone
†표시 表示 indication ; expression ; manifestation ; demonstration ; [마음의] a token ; a mark ; a sign —하다 indicate ; show ; manifest ; express ; give expression 《to》 ; be indicative 《of》 ; [기호 따위] represent ; mark ; put a mark 《on》 ¶ 감사의 표시로 in token〔as a token〕 of one's gratitude〔appreciation〕 // 사랑의 표시로 in sign of love // 의사를 표시하다 indicate one's intention ; express one's will // 기호로 표시하다 represent by signs // 열십자로 표시되어 있다 It is marked by a cross. // 빨간 등불은 위험을 표시한다 A red light indicates〔denotes〕 "Danger".
—기(器) a telltale ; an indicator ; an annunciator ¶ 방향 표시기 a direction indicator (한란계 따위의) — 도수 a reading —약 〖화학〗 an indicator 의사 — a gesture ; expression of one's intention
표식 標識 a mark ⇨ 표지
표실 漂失 —하다 drift away ⇨ 유실(流失)
표어 標語 a slogan ; a motto ; a catchword ; a catchphrase ; a watchword ; a rallying word ; a cant ; a cry ¶ 적절한 표어 a fitting motto 《for》 // 선거의 표어 an election slogan // 표어를 모집하다 offer a prize for the best motto
표연 飄然 —하다 (be) airy ; aimless ¶ 표연히 abruptly ; casually ; unexpectedly ; [목적 없이] aimlessly // 그는 표연히 집을 나갔다 He left home aimlessly.
표음 表音 phonetic representation —하다 represent〔write〕 phonetically
— 문자 phonetic symbols ; phonetics —주의 phoneticism
표의 表意 semantic〔ideographic〕 representation —하다 represent〔write〕 the meanings ; write in ideographs
— 문자 ideographs ; hieroglyph ; pictographs ; semantic symbols
표일 飄逸 —하다 (be) buoyant ; light ; free ; unconventional ; Bohemian ; aloof ¶ 표일한 사람 a queer fish ; a Bohemian
표장 標章 an emblem ; a sign ; a mark ; a badge
†표적 表迹 [부호] a sign ; a mark ; [흔적] traces ; marks ; [표시] a token ; a sign ; a manifestation ; [증거] a certificate ; a proof 《of》 ; evidence 《of》 ; a testimony 《to》 ; [기념품] a memento ; a souvenir ¶ 감사의 표적으로 in token of one's gratitude // 사랑의 표적으로 in sign of love // 표적으로 그 페이지를 접어두다 double over a leaf to mark the page // 표적을 안 남기다 leave no trace behind
*표적 標的 a target ; a mark ¶ 표적을 벗어나다 miss〔fall beside〕 the mark
— 사격 a target practice (미사일 실험의) — 지역 a target area —함 a target ship
표절 剽竊 plagiarism ; (literary) piracy ; crib ; abstraction —하다 pirate ; plagiarize ; crib ; abstract
—물 a plagiarism ; a crib —자 a (literary) pirate ; a plagiarizer ; a plagiarist
표절따 驃— a brown horse with white mane and tail
표점 標點 ⇨ 표적(標的)
†표정 表情 (facial) expression ; a look ; a countenance ¶ 표정이 있는〔풍부한〕 expressive ; significant // 표정이 없는 expressionless ; inexpressive ; immobile ; blank ; wooden ; flat // 슬픈 표정 a sad expression〔countenance〕 // 의혹의 표정 an expression of doubt // 표정있는 얼굴 an expressive face // 무표정한 얼굴 a blank look // 천연스런 표정을 하고 있다 keep one's countenance // 표정이 굳어지다 harden one's face
†표제 表題, 標題 [책의] a title ; [신문의] a heading ; a head (line) ; a caption 《미》 ; [문장의] a superscription ¶ 그 책의 표제는 「인간과 자연」이다 The book is entitled〔bears the title〕 "Man and Nature".
—어 an entry ; a lemma 《*pl.* -ta》 — 음악 program music —지(紙) a title paper 《of a book》 ; a title piece 부

(副)— a subtitle ; a subhead(ing)

표주 標柱 a signpost ; a marking post

표주 標註 a marginal note ; a top note **—하다** note in the margin ; add a note《to》

표주박 瓢— a gourd dipper ; a calabash

†**표준 標準** a standard ; a level (사회적·정신적) ; a norm ; a criterion (비판의) ; a canon ; a measure

> 참고 **standard** 물건의 품질·가치·양·정도 따위를 결정하는 공인의 기준 **criterion** 사람·물건·업적 따위의 본질·가치 따위를 시험하기 위하여 사용되는 표준

¶ 표준의 standard ; standardized ; normal ; regular ; average (평균의) // 표준 이하의 substandard ; below standard // 일정한 표준 a fixed standard // 표준에 달하다 come up to the standard〔mark〕// 표준을 정하다 fix〔set, set up, settle〕the standard

— 가격 a standard price **— 감각** standard〔normal〕sensation **— 궤간(軌間)** 『철도』 the standard gauge **— 기록** the standard record ; [예선 통과의] the qualifying time〔distance〕 **— 기압** the standard atmospheric〔barometric〕 pressure **— 상태** 『물리』 a normal state **—생활비** the standard〔average〕 cost of living **—시** standard time ; Greenwich (Mean) Time《G. M. T.》 **— 시계** a chronometer **—액(液)** a standard solution **—어〔말〕** the standard language **—영어** standard English **— 항성** 『천문』 a standard star **—형** a standard type **—화** standardization ¶ 표준화하다 standardize **국제 —화 기구** the International Standards Organization

표지 表紙 a cover ; binding ¶ 표지를 씌우다 cover《a book》

— 의장 a cover design **— 커버** a (book) jacket **앞〔뒤〕—** a front〔back〕 cover **종이〔가죽, 클로스〕—** a paper〔leather, cloth〕 cover

표지 標紙 a mark ; a note ; a certificate ; a check ; a bill ; a receipt

*__표지 標識__ a mark ; a sign ; a signal ; a beacon (항로의)

—등 a beacon light **—물** a signal **도로〔교통〕 —** a signpost **지상 —** ground mark **항공 —** an air beacon **항로 —** channel marks **조류 —법** birdbanding 《미》; bird-ringing《영》

표징 表徵 a sign ; a mark ; a symbol ; an indication

표차롭다 表— stand out ; (be) striking ; conspicuous ; prominent

표착 漂着 drifting ashore **—하다** be cast〔thrown〕 ashore ; be washed ashore ; drift〔float〕 ashore ¶ 어선 한 척이 부산 해안에 표착했다 A fishing boat was cast away on the coast of *Pusan*.

—물 a drift ; driftage ; a wreckage (난파선의)

표찰 標札 a label ; a bill ; a tally (나무·쇠 따위) ; a sticker (풀로 붙이는) ¶ 표찰을 붙이다 paste a bill

표창 表彰 commendation ; awarding ; honoring ; public acknowledgment of one's meritorious services ; citation **—하다** commend (officially) ; honor〔do honor to〕《a person》; give recognition 《for》; reward ; make public recognition 《of a person's service》; cite ¶ 표창받다 win official commendation

—대(臺) an honor platform ; a victory 〔winners'〕 rostrum《*pl.* ~s, -ra》 **—식** a commendation ceremony ; a ceremony of awarding an honor **—장** a letter of commendation ; a citation (군대의)

표출 表出 ⇨ 표현

표층 表層 the outer (most) layer〔stratum〕

표토 表土 top〔surface〕 soil ; 『지질』 regolith

표표하다 表表— (be) conspicuous ; distinguished ; famous ; renowned ; noted

표표(히) 飄飄(—) [가볍게] buoyantly ; airily ; [경쾌하게] with a light heart ; [정처없이] wandering ; roaming ; [초연히] aloof from the world

표피 表皮 『해부』 the cuticle ; the epidermis ; the outer skin ; hypodermis ; [나무의] the bark ¶ 표피의 epidermal ; epidermic

— 세포 an epidermal cell **— 조직** the epidermal tissue **— 탈락** desquamation

†**표하다 表—** express ; show ; manifest ; demonstrate ; offer ¶ 감사의 뜻을 표하다 express〔show〕 one's gratitude // 경의를 표하다 pay respects《to》; do《a person》 honor // 축의를 표하다 offer one's congratulations

표하다 標— mark ; put a mark《on》¶ 연필로 표하다 mark in pencil // 읽은 곳을 표하다 mark the place that one has read

표한 剽悍 fierceness ; ferocity ; savageness **—하다** (be) fierce ; ferocious ; savage

†**표현 表現** expression ; presentation ; representation ; manifestation **—하다** express ; represent ; manifest ¶ 표현적인 expressive ; expressional // 예술적 표현 artistic presentation // 그는 적절한 표현을 사용했다 He used an apt〔appropriate〕 expression. // 그 감동은 도저히 말로 표현할 수 없다 I can't find the words to describe how moving it was.

—력 power of expression **—법** expression ; how to express oneself **—주의** expressionism **—파** the expressionists **— 형식** forms of expression

푯대 標— a sign〔mark, signal〕post
푯돌 標— a stone marker ; a marker stone ; a landmark stone ; a milestone ¶ 푯돌을 세우다 set up a landmark stone
푯말 標— a signpost ¶ 푯말을 세우다 set up a signpost
푸 ① [내뿜는 소리] with a "whew" ; with a light whistle ② [힘없는 방귀 소리] with a light "poop"
푸가 〖음악〗 a (musical) fugue
푸근푸근 —하다 be all soft and comfortable ⇨ 포근포근
푸근하다 ① [자리 따위] (be) soft ; comfortable ; downy ¶ 푸근한 이부자리 downy bedding ② [날씨가] (be) mild ; soft ; warm ; [성질이] gentle ; [마음이] feel good〔comfortable〕; be in an expansive mood ; be relaxed ¶ 푸근한 성질 a gentle disposition // 푸근한 겨울 날씨 mild winter weather
푸나무 plants and trees ; vegetation
푸나무서리 a place luxuriant〔overgrown〕with vegetation ; a thicket
푸네기 one's near relatives ; one's flesh and blood
푸념 ① [무당의] the ravings of a shaman ② [불평] a complaint ; a grievance —하다 rave ; [불평] complain ; grumble ¶ 음식에 대해 푸념하다 make a complaint about one's food ; grumble at〔about, over〕one's food
푸다 ① [물을] dip out ; bail out ; draw ; pump ¶ 우물물을 푸다 draw water from a well // 배에서 괸 물을 푸다 bail water out of a boat ② [곡식·밥을] scoop out ; take out ¶ 솥에서 밥을 푸다 scoop rice out of a pot // 뒤주에서 쌀을 푸다 take rice out of a bin
푸닥거리 an exorcism ; an exorcising service with prayers and offerings —하다 perform an exorcism ; charm
푸닥지다 (be) abundant ; profuse
푸대접 —待接 cold〔unkind〕treatment ; cold reception ; inhospitality —하다 treat〔receive〕《a person》coldly〔unkindly, in a cold way, with coldness〕; receive 《a person》 with indifference ; give 《a person》 a cold reception ; be inhospitable to ¶ 푸대접을 참다 submit to cold treatment // 그는 푸대접을 받았다 He was given cold reception. /He was treated in a cold way.
푸두둥 fluttering
푸두둥거리다 flitter and flitter ; flutter and flutter
푸둥푸둥 ⇨ 포동포동
푸드덕 with a flap
푸(드)덕거리다 ⇨ 퍼덕거리다
푸드득 with gush
푸들 a poodle
*****푸딩** pudding
푸뜩푸뜩 often ; frequently ; from time to time —하다 (be) intermittent ¶ 생각이 푸뜩푸뜩나다 ideas pop up ; an idea occurs to on now and then
푸르께하다 (be) bluish ; greenish
†**푸르다** ① [색] (be) blue ; azure ; green ¶ 푸른 대나무 green bamboo // 푸른 바다 the blue sea // 푸른 하늘 the blue sky ; the blue heavens
② [서슬이] (be) sharp ¶ 서슬이 푸르다 have a sharp edge ; be high and mighty
푸르데데하다 (be) bluish ; greenish ; rather pale〔pallid〕
푸르디푸르다 be blue as blue can be ; be green as green can be ; (be) deeply blue〔green〕
푸르락붉으락 —하다 turn alternately pale and red
푸르르 bubbling ; seething ; in a burst of flame ; in a huff ; trembling ; flapping
*****푸르스름하다** (be) bluish ; greenish ; viridescent ; [서술적] be tinged with blue ; have a bluish〔greenish〕tint
푸르죽죽하다 ⇨ 푸르데데하다
푸릇푸릇 all spotted green or blue ; green〔blue〕here and there —하다 be all spotted green or blue ; be green〔blue〕here and there ¶ 풀이 푸릇푸릇 돋아나다 grass sprouts out-all green here and there
푸만하다 feel stuffy from overeating
푸새[1] starching —하다 starch 《clothes》 ¶ 옷을 푸새하다 starch clothes
푸새[2] grasses ; plants
푸서 a ravel ; a frayed end
푸서기 a crumbly〔brittle〕thing ; a frail〔delicate〕person
푸석돌 a crumbly stone ; a soft stone
푸석푸석 all crisp ; crumbly —하다 (be) crisp ; crumbly ; brittle ; fragile ¶ 푸석푸석한 흙 crumbly soil
푸석하다 (be) crisp ; crumbly ; friable
푸성귀 vegetables ; greens ; greenstuff
푸성귀는 떡잎부터 알고 사람은 어렸을 때부터 안다 속담 First impressions are the most lasting. /The first blow is halfly the battle.
푸솜 raw cotton
푸슬푸슬 ⇨ 파슬파슬
푸접없다 (be) unfriendly ; cold and distant ; cool ¶ 푸접없는 대답을 하다 reply snappishy
푸주 —廚 a butcher's shop ; a meat store
—한 a butcher ; a meatman
푸지다 (be) abundant ; plentiful ; rich ; liberal ; profuse ¶ 푸진 음식 abundant food // 푸진 대접 liberal treatment // 푸지게 먹다 eat plenty〔freely〕
푸짐하다 (be) abundant ; profuse ; generous
푸집개 a cover for weapons

푸하다 (be) bulged ; swollen ; inflated ; untidy ¶ 푸한 머리 untidy hair // 푸한 짐 a loose bundle

푹 ① [빈틈 없이] 《wrapping》 carefully ; with no gaps ¶ 푹 싸다 wrap 《it》 all up carefully // 이불을 푹 덮다 tuck the bedding up snug ② [느긋하게] fast ; sound(ly) ¶ 잠이 푹 들다 fall sound asleep // 잠을 푹 자다 sleep soundly // 하루 푹 쉬고 나면 내일은 다시 일하러 나올 수 있을 겁니다 A good day's rest should bring him back to work tomorrow. ③ [흠뻑] completely ; entirely ¶ 푹 삶다 boil hard〔well〕 ④ [죄다] exhaustively ; with nothing left over ; completely ¶ 병의 물을 푹 쏟다 pour all water out of a bottle

푹석푹석 — **하다** (be) crisp ; crumbly ; friable ; brittle

푹신푹신 all soft〔pliant, resilient, yielding, elastic, bouncy, springy〕 — **하다** (be) all soft etc.

푹신하다 (be) soft ; cushiony ; spongy ; elastic ; bouncy ; springy ; soft and fluffy ; downy ¶ 푹신한 침대 a comfortable bed

푹푹 ① [힘있게] with repeated force ¶ 바늘로 푹푹 쑤시다 prick 《one's body》 with a needle repeatedly ② [따끔따끔하게] prickly ; prickingly ; tinglingly ¶ 손가락이 푹푹 쑤신다 My finger is pricking〔tingling〕. ③ [아낌없이] freely ; carelessly ; lavishly ; unsparingly ¶ 돈을 푹푹 쓰다 spend money freely〔carelessly〕 ; be lavish〔liberal〕 of one's money ④ [썩는 모양] completely ; perfectly ¶ 푹푹 썩다 grow rotten fast ⑤ [흠뻑] hard ; well ¶ 푹푹 삶다 boil hard〔well〕 ⑥ [찌는 듯이] sultry ; muggy ¶ 푹푹 찌는 날씨 sultry weather // 날씨가 푹푹 찐다 It is steaming hot. ⑦ [깊이] deeply ¶ 발이 푹푹 빠지다 one's feet sink deep 《in the mud, in the snow》

푹하다 (be) warm ⇨ 푸근하다

*__푼__ ① [화폐] a *pun* ; a penny ¶ 한 푼의 가치도 없다 It isn't worth a farthing. // 한 푼을 절약하면 한 푼을 번다 A penny saved is a penny gained〔earned〕. ② [무게] a *pun* ; one tenth of a *don* ; a Korean pennyweight ③ [길이] a *pun* ; one tenth of a *chi* 《Korean inch》

푼거리 buying〔selling〕 firewood by the bundle ; dealing in a small way — **하다** buy〔sell〕 firewood by the bundle ; deal in a small way

— **나무** firewood sold by bunches

푼거리질 buying firewood by the bundle — **하다** buy firewood by the bundle ¶ 가난해서 나무를 푼거리질하다 be so poor that one buys the firewood a bunch at a time

푼끌 a small chisel

푼나무 firewood sold by the bundle ⇨ 푼거리(—나무)

푼내기 ① [도박] penny gambling ; penny ante ② ⇨ 푼거리

— **흥정** small-time business ; business on a small scale ; small dealings

푼더분하다 ① [얼굴이] (be) plump ; well-rounded ; full ¶ 푼더분한 얼굴 a full face ② [후하다] (be) ample ; plentiful ¶ 푼더분한 보수 rich payment // 푼더분한 대접 a liberal reception

푼돈 loose cash〔coins〕 ; petty cash ; pennies ; broken money ; a small amount of money ¶ 푼돈을 모으다 save a petty penny ; save pocket money // 푼돈을 아끼다 be penny-wise // 푼돈을 아끼려다 큰돈을 잃는다 Penny-wise and pound-foolish.

푼사 ...and some *pun* ¶ 두 돈 푼사 two *don* and some *pun*

푼사 floss (silk) ; filoselle

푼수 ① [정도·비율] rate ; ratio ; percentage ¶ …의 푼수로 at a rate of... ② [신분] ⇨ 분수 ①

푼어치 a pennyworth ; a penny's worth ; penny merchandise

푼주 a rather shallow porcelain bowl

푼치 a little difference ; a small gap ¶ 푼치도 양보하지 않다 do not recede〔yield〕 an inch

푼푼이 penny by penny ; little by little ¶ 푼푼이 모은 돈 money saved penny by penny ; a pretty money saved little by little

푼푼하다 ① [넉넉하다] (be) enough ; sufficient ; abundant ; plentiful ② [활달하다] (be) liberal ; generous ; magnanimous

푼푼히 [넉넉히] amply ; abundantly ; sufficiently ; [활달히] liberally ; generously

풀소 cattle fed on nothing but grass during the summer

— **가죽** the poor-quality hide of such cattle — **고기** the tasteless beef from such cattle

†**풀**¹ grass(es) ; a plant ; a weed (잡초) ; a herb (약초) ; herbage 《총칭》 ; pasture (목초) ¶ 한 포기의 풀 a root of grass // 풀이 난 땅 grass-grown land ; weedy〔grassy〕 ground // 풀이 나지 않은 땅 barren〔arid〕 ground // 풀을 뜯어 먹다 feed on grass ; graze (마소가) // 정원의 풀을 뽑다 weed a garden ; pull up weed in the garden // 봄이 되면 풀이 돋아 난다 In spring the grass comes out.

풀베기 싫어하는 놈이 단수만 센다. 속담 Idle folks lack no excuses.

‡**풀**² ① paste (밀가루의) ; starch (녹말의) ; glue (갖풀) ; size (공업용) ¶ 빳빳하게 풀을 먹인 셔츠 a stiffly starched shirt // 풀을 먹이다 starch 《one's shirt》

//풀을 바르다 paste ; stick 《a thing》 with paste ; apply paste to 《a thing》// 풀을 쑤다 make paste〔starch〕
② [기운] one's spirits ¶ 그는 사장에게 꾸중을 듣고 풀이 죽어 있었다 He was reprimanded by the president and was feeling down.
고무— gum (arabic) ; mucilage
풀³ [수영장] a swim(ming) pool ; a swimming bath 《영》 ; [(공동 이익을 위한) 출자·계산 등] a pool ¶ 자금을 풀해 두다 put money into a pool
— 강의제(講義制) a faculty pool system — 계산 a pool account 실내 — an indoor swimming pool
풀가사리 〚식물〛 a glue plant ; Gloiopeltis furcata (학명)
풀갓 a pasture preserve
풀기 ① [옷의] starch(iness) ¶ 풀기가 있는 starchy ; starched//풀기가 센 셔츠 a stiffly starched shirt
② [활기] liveliness ; animation ; activity ; vigor ; vitality ¶ 풀기가 있다 be full of spirit〔life〕; be vigorous〔animated〕//풀기가 없다 be spiritless〔dull, inert〕; be downcast ; be in low spirits
풀끝 a touch of starch ; a dash of paste
풀내 the smell of grass ; [숨막힐 듯한] fumes〔a sickening smell〕 of grass〔hay〕
풀다 ① [짐·끈 따위를] untie 《a string》; undo 《a bundle》; unbind 《a bandage》; loosen 《one's hair》; unloosen ; unpack 《a package》; unfasten 《a rope》; unravel 《a thread》; disentangle 《a knot》; unsew 《a garment》; unlace 《one's shoes》; fray (천의 가장자리를) ; [짠 것을] unweave ; ravel ; untwist (꼰 것을) ¶ 머리를 풀다 let down one's hair ; loosen one's hair ; 《a woman》 goes into mourning
② [문제를] solve 《a question》; work out 《a difficult problem》; answer 《a question》; unravel ¶ 뜻을 풀다 clear up〔interpret, explain〕 the meaning//수수께끼를 풀다 solve〔interpret, guess〕 a riddle ; answer〔solve, make out〕 a puzzle//암호를 풀다 decipher a code//학생들이 산수 문제를 풀고 있다 The pupils are doing〔working〕 the sums on their papers.
③ [의심을] resolve ; dispel ; satisfy ; clear away〔up〕 《one's doubts》; [오해를] remove 《a misunderstanding》 ¶ 모든 의혹이 풀렸다 All doubts were resolved.
④ [원한을] vent ; satisfy ; wreak ; revenge ; pay off 《old scores》; [울적함을] dispel ; dissipate 《gloom》; relieve 《dullness》; [노여움을] appease ; disarm 《one's anger》; [소원을] realize 《one's desire》; gratify 《one's wishes》; satisfy 《one's desire》; have 《one's wish》 fulfilled ¶ 기분을 풀다 divert oneself ; recreate〔refresh〕 oneself//원한을 풀다 vent one's spite ; satisfy〔wreak〕 one's grudge ; revenge oneself ; pay〔wipe〕 off old scores//시장기를 풀다 appease one's hunger//힘든 하루 일과를 마치고 나서 기분을 풀기 위해 무엇을 합니까 What do you do for relaxation after a hard day's work?/What do you do to unwind after a hard day's work?
⑤ [타다] dissolve 《salt in water》; melt ¶ 물감을 풀다 dissolve dye〔color〕
⑥ [해제하다] remove 《a prohibition, the embargo》; lift 《the ban》; dissolve ; release ; disengage ; absolve ; free ; acquit ¶ 금령을 풀다 lift the ban ; remove a prohibition//봉쇄를 풀다 remove〔raise, lift〕 a blockade//포위를 풀다 raise a siege
⑦ [꿈 따위를] read ; interpret ; expound 《one's dream》 ¶ 성명을 풀다 interpret〔expound〕 divination by the letters〔characters〕 of a name//점괘를 풀다 interpret〔expound〕 one's divination sign
⑧ [코를] blow 《one's nose》
⑨ [몸을] warm up (경기에 앞서) ; [해산하다] deliver 《a baby》; give birth to a child
⑩ [논으로 만들다] turn〔convert〕 land into 《a paddy》
풀대님 wearing one's breeches without tying their ends up at the ankle ¶ 풀대님하고 sloppily dressed ; in untidy attire
풀둥 a grassy sandbank
풀떡 lightly ; nimbly ; quickly ⇨ 풀떡거리다
풀떡거리다 [심장이] throb ; palpitate ; [뛰다] jump〔leap〕 repeatedly
풀떼기 a thick cereal gruel
풀또기 〚식물〛 the flowering plum
풀려나다 get free 《of, from》; free oneself 《of, from》 ¶ 개가 사슬에서 풀려났다 The dog freed itself of its chain.
†**풀리다** ① [맨 것이] come〔get〕 loose〔untied, undone, unfasten〕; [얽힌 것이] come〔get〕 disentangled〔unravelled〕; [뭉친 것이] come〔get〕 dissolved ; [구두끈이] become unlaced ; get loose ; [짠 것이] come〔get〕 unweaved〔raveled〕; [꼰 것이] become untwisted ; [천의 가장자리가] fray ; become frayed ¶ 머리가 풀리다 one's hair gets loose//엉킨 매듭이 풀리다 a knot comes disentangled〔untied, undone〕
② [추위가] become warm ; abate ¶ 추위가 풀리다 cold weather turns〔becomes〕 warm//(얼었던 몸이) 차차 풀린다 I am thawing.
③ [문제가] be〔get〕 solved〔unrav-

elled〕; be worked out; meet with solution ¶ 풀리지 않는 문제 an unsoluble〔unsolved〕 problem // 수수께끼가 풀렸다 A puzzle was solved. // 이 문제는 어쨌든 잘 풀릴 것이다 This problem will work itself out somehow.
④ [의심·오해가] be resolved〔dispelled, dissipated〕; disappear; vanish; be removed ¶ 의혹이 풀리다 a doubt is resolved〔cleared away〕// 오해가 풀리다 a misunderstanding is removed // 혐의가 풀리다 be cleared of a charge
⑤ [원한이] get vented; be satisfied; be revenged; [기분이] be〔feel〕 refreshed; be enlivened; cheer up; haw; [노여움이] be appeased〔pacified, disarmed〕; relent《toward》; thaw; [소원이]《one's desire》 be realized;《one's wishes》 be gratified;《one's wish》 be fulfilled ¶ 노여움이 풀리다 one's anger is gone〔appeased〕; one's anger has melted away // 마음이 풀리다 become cordial〔genial〕; thaw《toward a person》// 원한이 풀리다 one's grudge is satisfied〔wreaked〕// 산보를 하면 기분이 풀릴 것이다 A walk will cheer you up.
⑥ [해제되다] be removed; be lifted; be dissolved; be disengaged; be absolved; be released; be freed ¶ 금령이 풀리다 a ban is lifted; a prohibition is removed // 봉쇄가 풀리다 a blockade is lifted〔raised, removed〕// 포위가 풀리다 a siege is raised
⑦ [타지다] dissolve; melt ¶ 밀가루가 잘 풀리다 flour dissolves well
⑧ [돈이] be〔get〕 circulated; be released; go into circulation ¶ 새 화폐가 풀리다 the new currency goes into circulation // 은행 돈이 풀리다 money in the bank is released
⑨ [피로가] recover from《one's fatigue》; [힘이]《one's strength》 be gone

풀막 一幕 a grass-roofed shed; a thatched hut

풀매 a small handmill〔quern〕

풀매듭 a knot that is easily untied; a knot that unties itself

풀머리 loosened〔let-down〕 hair **—하다** let〔wear〕 one's hair down

풀먹이다 starch《clothes》

풀멤버 [정회원] a full〔regular〕 member ¶ 풀멤버의 자격 full membership

***풀무** (a pair of) bellows; a forge (야로)

풀무질 blowing with the bellows **—하다** blow with the bellows; work〔blow〕 the bellows

풀밭 a grass field; a meadow; a lawn (잔디밭); a grass (plot) ¶ 풀밭에서 놀다 play on the grass

풀백 〖축구〗 a fullback《f. b., fb》

풀베이스 〖야구〗 full base ¶ 풀베이스로 하다 fill the bases

풀보기 the first after-marriage visit of a bride to her parents-in-law

풀빛 (dark) green

풀세트 〖정구〗 a full set
— 게임 a full-set game〔match〕

풀솜 floss (silk)
—나물 cottonweed; Gnaphalium japonicum (학명) **—할머니** a maternal grandmother

풀숲 a cluster of grass; a bush; a thicket

풀스피드 full speed ¶ 풀스피드로 달리다 run (at) full speed

풀쌀 rice for making rice-paste

풀썩 《a cloud of dust, smoke》 rising suddenly ¶ 연기가 풀썩 났다 A cloud of smoke rose suddenly. // 자동차가 지날 때 먼지가 풀썩 났다 A motorcar raised a cloud of dust as it passed.

풀썩풀썩 《dust, smoke》 lightly rising ⇨ 풀썩

풀쐐기 〖곤충〗 a caterpillar

풀쑤다 ① [풀을] make paste; make〔prepare〕 starch ② [재산을] squander〔dissipate〕《a fortune》

풀어내다 ① [얽힌 것을] unravel; disentangle《tangled thread》 ② [문제를] solve〔work out, unravel〕《a difficult problem》 ¶ 수수께끼를 풀어내다 solve〔interpret, find out, guess〕 a riddle; answer〔solve, figure out〕 a puzzle ③ [오해를] remove《a misunderstanding》

****풀어 놓다** ① [맨 것을] undo; untie; unpack; unfasten; loose; loosen; unloose; unlace (끈을) ¶ 꾸러미를 풀어 놓다 undo〔untie〕 a bundle; unpack a package
② [놓아주다] release; unloose; free; set free; liberate; cast〔let〕 loose; loose (hold of) ¶ 소를 목장에 풀어 놓다 turn out cattle to graze; put cattle to grass // 비밀을 탐지하기 위해 사람을 풀어 놓다 set〔put〕 men on a secret investigation; turn out men to spy on《a matter》

풀어먹이다 ① [사람에게] distribute《food》 among the people
② [귀신에게] perform an exorcism with sacrificial food to drive out evil spirits

풀어주다 set《a person》 free; liberate《a person》; release《a person》

풀어지다 ① [국수가]《noodle》 turn soft ② [눈이]《one's eyes》 become bleared; go〔get〕 bleary ⇨ 풀리다

풀이 ① [설명] explanation; interpretation; clarification; clearing up ⇨ 해석(解釋) **—하다** explain; clarify; clear up ② [접미사] removing; dispelling; [무당의] exorcism; a shamanistic rite **—하다** remove《a misunderstanding》; dispel《one's doubts》; exorcise

풀잎 a leaf of grass ; a blade
— **피리** a reed (pipe)
풀죽다 ① [옷이] lose its starch ; come unstarched ¶ 옷이 풀죽다 clothes lose their starch
② [기세가 죽다] lose one's starch ; be dejected〔disheartened, discouraged〕; feel blue〔gloomy, depressed〕; be in low spirit ; be in the dumps〔blues, mopes〕 ¶ 풀이 죽어서 다니다 go around down in〔at〕 the mouth // 여자 친구에게 차인 것 정도로 그렇게 풀죽지 말아라 Don't get so down just because your girlfriend ditched you.
풀질 pasting ; applying paste — **하다** paste ; apply paste《to》
풀집 a paste-seller's shop
풀쩍 [문을] opening〔closing〕 the door suddenly ; [몸 따위를] lightly leaping〔jumping〕 — **하다** open〔close〕《the door》 suddenly ; lightly leap〔jump〕
풀쩍거리다 keep opening and closing《the door》; come in and go out all the time ; keep coming in and going out
풀쳐생각 unburdening one's mind ; putting one's mind at ease ; relaxing ; taking it easy — **하다** unburden one's mind《of》; put one's mind at ease《about》; relax ; take it easy
풀치 〖물고기〗 a young hairtail〔scabbard fish〕
풀치다 pardon〔forgive〕 generously ¶ 생각을 풀치다 put one's mind at ease
풀칠 ① [종이 따위에] applying paste《to》 ② [생계] bare livelihood ; a hand-to-mouth existence — **하다** paste ; apply paste ; [입에] gain a bare livelihood ; live from hand to mouth ; maitain a hand-to-mouth existence ¶ 뼈 빠지게 일해서 겨우 입에 풀칠하다 work hard merely to keep the wolf from the door
풀카운트 〖야구〗 a full count《of three two》
풀칼 a wooden paper-knife used to spread paste
풀포수 —泡水 starching《paper》 before oiling — **하다** starch《cloth》 before oiling
풀풀 ① [새가] flapping ; fluttering ¶ 새가 풀풀 날다 a bird flies flapping its wings ② [끓는 모양] boiling hard ; seething ¶ 물이 풀풀 끓는다 Water is boiling up.
풀풀하다 (be) easily angry ; short-tempered ; irascible ; petulant
풀피리 a reed (pipe)
품[1] ① [옷의] width《of a coat》 ¶ 품이 넓다〔좁다〕 be of broad〔narrow〕 width
② [가슴] the bosom ; the breast ¶ 손을 품에 끼고 with one's hands in one's bosom // 품 속에 넣다 put〔tuck〕《a thing》 in one's bosom // 품에 안다 hold〔carry〕《a baby》 in one's bosom ; embrace ; hug ; embosom
뒷— the width between armpits **앞—** the breast width
품[2] labor ; work ¶ 하루 품 a day's work〔labor〕 // 품이 들다 require labor〔work〕 // 품을 덜다 save labor〔work〕 // 품을 팔다 work〔labor〕 for wages ; work as a day laborer // 품을 갚다 work〔labor〕 in return ; return work for work
품[3] [됨됨이] appearance ; looks ; shape (모양) ; the way《one looks, behaves》 ¶ 사람된 품 one's character〔nature〕 // 사람이 생긴 품 one's appearance〔looks, shape〕 // 걷는 품 the way one walks // 몸가지는 품이 신사답다 He bears〔behaves〕 himself like a gentleman. ¶ 품이 높다〔낮다〕 be high〔low〕 in official rank
품값 wages ; pay ; cost of labor
품갚음 — **하다** return work for work ; work in return ; exchange labor
품격 品格 grace ; elegance ; refinement ; dignity ; character ; nobility ¶ 품격이 있다 be elegant〔refined, dignified〕 // 품격을 높이다 ennoble《a person》; dignify〔elevate〕 one's character // 품격을 떨어뜨리다 lose one's dignity ; degrade oneself
품계 品階 grade ; rank ; degree of official rank ¶ 품계가 높은 사람 a person of high rank
품고 稟告 a report〔statement〕《to a superior》 — **하다** report〔tell, inform, state〕《a superior》《of》
품귀 品貴 a shortage〔scarcity〕 of goods ¶ 품귀 상태이다 be scarce ; The stock is small〔low〕./The stocks are in short supply.
품꾼 a day laborer ; a wageworker
†**품다**[1] ① [안다] hold〔carry, take〕 in one's bosom ; embrace ; hug ; embosom ¶ 비수를 가슴에 품다 carry〔put, conceal〕 a dagger in one's bosom // 애기를 품에 품다 hold a baby in one's bosom
② [알을] sit ; brood《on eggs》
③ [마음에] entertain《hope, a view》 cherish《a desire》; harbor《suspicion》; bear《malice》; hold ; have ¶ …할 마음을 품다 have a mind to《do》 // 원한을 품다 harbor〔bear〕 a grudge
품다[2] ① [벗기다] skin (the *mosi-pul*) with a *pum-kal* ② [물을] pump (water)
품달 稟達 a report《to a superior》 ⇨ 품고
품돈 wages ; pay for one's labor
품등 品等 quality and grade
품명 品名 names of goods
품목 品目 the name of an article ; a list of articles ; an item (한 품목) ¶ 품목

별로 by item // 주요 수출 품목 the chief items of export // 품목별로 나누다 itemize ; divide by〔in〕 items
품별 品別 assortment ; classification **—하다** assort ; classify
품사 品詞 〖문법〗 a part of speech
—론 accidence **팔—** the eight parts of speech
품삯 wages ; hire ; pay
품성 品性 character ¶ 품성이 훌륭한〔천한〕 사람 man of fine〔low〕 character // 품성을 도야하다 form〔build〕 character
품성 稟性 nature ; natural gift〔disposition〕
품속 the bosom ¶ 품속에 in one's bosom // 품속에 간직하다 keep in one's bosom // 품속에 껴안다 hold〔carry, press〕 《a person》 in one's bosom
품안 ⇨ 품속
품앗다 exchange work ; work in turn for one another
품앗이 exchange of work ; working in turn for one another **—하다** exchange work ; work in turn for one another
*__품위 品位__ ① [품격] elegance ; grace ; dignity ; refinement ¶ 품위 있는 refined ; elegant ; dignified ; graceful ; high-toned // 품위 없는 사람 a man of coarse character // 품위 없는 언사 vulgar language // 품위를 높이다 ennoble 《a person》 ; dignify〔elevate〕 one's character // 품위를 떨어뜨리다 lose one's dignity ; degrade oneself // 품위를 지키다 keep〔maintain〕 one's dignity
② [품직·직위] rank ; position
③ [품등] grade ; [품질] quality ; fineness (순도) ; standard (금속의) ; carat (금의) ¶ 품위가 낮은 광석 low-grade ore // 품위가 낮다 be low in quality〔grade〕
품의 稟議 consultation 《with a superior》 **—하다** consult 《with a superior》 ; confer 《with a superior》
품절 品切 absence〔out〕 of stock ¶ 품절이 되다 run out of stock
품종 品種 [종류] a kind ; a description ; a grade (상품 따위) ; a variety (변종) ; breed (가축의)
— 개량 improvement of breed (가축의) ; plant breeding (식물의)
†**품질 品質** quality ¶ 품질이 좋다〔나쁘다〕 be of good〔inferior〕 quality // 품질을 개량하다 improve 《a thing》 in quality // …에 비해 품질이 낮다 be inferior to 《a thing》 in quality
— 관리 quality control **— 보증** [게시] Quality guaranteed. **— 본위** [게시] Quality first. **— 저하** deterioration
품팔다 work〔labor〕 for wages ; hire oneself out as a day laborer
품팔이 hiring oneself out as a day laborer ; doing day labor ; being a wageworker **—하다** work for wages ; hire oneself out as a day laborer
—꾼 a day laborer ; a wageworker ; a farm hand〔laborer〕
품평 品評 criticism ; evaluation ; comment **—하다** criticize ; evaluate ; comment 《on》
품평회 品評會 a competitive show〔exhibition〕 ; a fair
개 — a dog show **농산물 —** an agricultural show〔fair〕
품하다 稟— tell〔report to〕 《one's superior》 ; propose ; request ¶ …할 것을 품하나이다 I beg to propose〔request〕 you 《that》
†**품행 品行** conduct ; behavior ; deportment (학생의) ; demeanor ; moral character ; morals ¶ 품행이 단정한〔나쁜〕 사람 a man of good〔loose〕 conduct // 품행이 단정하다 be well-conducted〔-behaved〕 ; be of good conduct // 품행이 나쁘다 be illconducted 〔behaved〕 ; be of bad conduct // 그는 품행이 단정하다 His conduct is perfect〔good〕. /He conducts himself well. /He has a clean character.
풋- [덜 익은] green ; unripe ; [새로운] new ; fresh ; young ; early ; unexperienced
풋감 a green〔an unripe〕 persimmon
풋거름 ⇨ 녹비 (綠肥)
풋것 freshly harvested fruit〔vegetables, grain〕 of the year
풋게 early-autumn crab
풋고추 unripe〔green〕 red pepper
풋곡식 —穀— new grain〔cereals〕 ; unripe grain〔cereals〕
풋과실 —果實 green〔unripe〕 fruits
풋김치 *Kimchi* prepared with young vegetables
풋나무 ⇨ 풋장
풋나물 seasoned vegetables prepared with the first of the season
풋내 the smell of greens ¶ 풋내나다 have a smell of fresh young greens ; sound like a greenhorn
풋내기 ① a raw inexperienced person ; a greenhorn ; a green hand ; a novice ; a fledgling ¶ 그러한 기계를 다루는 데는 풋내기를 쓰면 안된다 I don't think you should have a novice use a machine. ② a restless〔fidgety〕 person (들뜬 사람)
풋담배 green tobacco
풋대추 [덜익은] green jujubes ; [말리지 않은] fresh jujubes
풋돈냥 a small amount of money which has casually come into one's hand ; a petty fortune
풋머리 [무렵] the season when things are just ripening or coming to market ; [처음 무렵] early in the season
풋바심 —하다 harvest grain before it

is ripe
풋밤 unripe chestnuts
풋배 green〔unripe〕 pears
풋벼 green〔unripe〕 rice
—바심 harvesting unripe rice
풋볼 football ; footer 《영·구》 ; [사커] soccer ; socker ; association football ; [럭비] rugger ; rugby football
풋사랑 calf love ; puppy love
풋솜씨 lack of skill ; undeveloped 〔imperfect〕 skill ; poor hand
풋워크 〖구기·권투〗 footwork ¶ 풋워크가 어지러워지다 lose ones footwork // 그의 풋워크는 좋다〔나쁘다〕 His footwork is good〔poor〕.
풋잠 a light sleep just begun
풋장 branch fuel cut and dried in autumn
풋장기 —將棋 unskilled chess ; a green hand at chess
풋콩 unripe beans〔peas〕
풍 with poop ⇨ 붕 ¶ 방귀를 풍 뀌다 break wind "poop"
풍[1] 風 [바람] wind ¶ 동풍 the east wind
풍[2] 風 [허풍] a boast ; a brag ; exaggeration ; tall〔big〕 talk ; gas 《구》 ; hot air 《구》 ¶ 풍을 떨다〔치다〕 brag ; exaggerate ; gas 《구》 ; talk big〔tall, gas〕 ; blow one's own trumpet ; draw a long bow ; be full of hot air // 그의 이야기에는 좀 풍이 섞였다 His statement is rather exaggerated.
풍[3] 風 palsy ⇨ 풍병
-풍 風 ① [양식] a style ; a mode ; a fashion ; a type ¶ 프랑스풍 a French style〔fashion〕 // 미국풍의 건물 an American style building ② [풍습] manners (and customs) ; a custom ; way ¶ 영국풍을 따라 according to English manners ; after the fashion of England // 옛 풍을 지키다 keep to the good old ways
도회— town〔urbane〕 manners ; urbanity 시골— rural manners ; rurality
풍각쟁이 風角— a street〔strolling〕 singer〔musician〕 (who takes his music from door to door)
풍간 諷諫 exhortation by innuendo 〔insinuation〕 —하다 exhort by innuendo〔insinuation〕
풍격 風格 [성격·인격] character ; personality ; idiosyncrasy ; [풍채] appearance [문예상의] style ; gusto ; race ¶ 풍격이 있는 사람 a man of distinctive 〔remarkable〕 character
*풍경 風景 [경치] a landscape ; scenery ; a scene ; [전망] a view ; a sight ¶ 바다의 풍경 a seascape // 진해의 풍경 the scenery of *Chinhae* // 풍경이 수려한 곳 a beauty spot ; a place of scenic beauty // 풍경이 수려하여 유명하다 be famous for its scenic beauty
—미 scenic beauty —화 a landscape (painting, picture) —화가 a landscape painter 가두 — a street scene ; a scene on the street 전원 — a rural landscape ; a scene of the countryside
풍경 風磬 a wind-bell with a "fish" clapper
풍경치다 風磬— keep going in and out busily
풍계묻이 [어린이 놀이] searching out what has been hidden under the ground by the other party ; "hidden treasure" —하다 play "hidden treasure"
풍광 風光 scenery ; view ¶ 풍광이 명미하다 have beautiful scenery ; have great scenic〔natural〕 beauty
풍교 風敎 education of public morals
풍구 風— ① a winnower ; a winnowing machine ② bellows (풀무)
*풍금 風琴 an organ ¶ 풍금을 치다 play (on) the organ // 풍금을 배우다 take lessons in playing the organ〔organ lessons〕 ; learn on the organ // 풍금을 잘 치다 be a skillful performer on the organ
—관(管) an organ pipe — 연주가 an organist ; an organ grinder 손— an accordion 전기 — an electric organ
풍기 風紀 discipline (기율) ; public morals〔decency〕 (사회의) ; manners (풍속) ¶ 풍기를 단속하다 enforce discipline ; control public morals // (사회의) 풍기에 해롭다 be injurious to public morals〔decency〕 ; be an offense against public decency
— 문란 demoralization ; the corruption〔decay, relaxation〕 of public morals ¶ 풍기 문란케 하다 corrupt public morals ; commit an indecency ; practice prostitution (매춘하다)
풍기다 ① [냄새를] give out 《an odor》 ; send forth ; scent ; shed ; stink (악취를) ¶ 좋은 냄새를 풍기다 shed〔give out, send forth〕 a sweet scent〔fragrance〕 // 술 냄새가 풍기다 smell〔stink〕 of wine // 하수가 악취를 풍긴다 The ditch stinks〔makes smell〕.
② [겨 검불을] winnow〔fan〕 《grain》 ¶ 겨를 풍기다 winnow〔fan〕 away chaff
③ [새를] scatter 《birds》 ; start 《birds》
*풍년 豊年 a year of abundance ; a fruitful〔an abundant, a rich, a bumper〕 year ; a good harvest (풍작) ¶ 금년은 풍년이 될 것 같다 We shall probably have a good harvest this year. /A bumper harvest is anticipated here this year.
— 거지 one who gets nothing at a time when everyone else gains —우(雨) seasonable rain which harbingers a good harvest — 축제 the celebration of a good harvest ; a harvest festival
풍덩 with a splash ; with a plop ⇨ 퐁당

풍덩거리다 keep splashing〔plunging〕
풍덩풍덩 with splashes ; with splash after splash ¶ 물에 풍덩풍덩 뛰어들다 jump into the water splash-splash-splash ; plunge into the water
풍뎅이 a gold bug ; a May beetle ; a May bug
풍도 風度 one's appearance and attitude ¶ 대인의 풍도 the attitude〔bearing〕 of a gentleman
풍동 風洞 a wind tunnel ; an air〔a wind〕 channel
— 시험 a wind tunnel test
풍떨다 ⇨ 풍²(風)
풍랑 風浪 wind and waves ; heavy seas ¶ 풍랑과 싸우다 battle with〔struggle against〕 the wind and waves // 풍랑이 심하다 The waves are high. /The sea is running high.
풍량계 風量計 an airflow meter
풍력 風力 the velocity〔force〕 of the wind ; wind force ¶ 풍력은 한 시간에 50마일에 달했다 The wind attained a velocity of fifty miles an hour.
—계 an anemometer〔anemograph〕 **—계급** a wind scale **— 계수** 〖건축〗 a coefficient of wind force **—도** 〖토목〗 a wind force diagram **— 발전소** 〖전기〗 a wind power plant〔station〕 **— 측정법** anemometry
풍로 風爐 a portable cooking furnace ; a small kitchen range
풍로 風露 wind and dew
풍류 風流 elegance ; taste ; refinement ¶ 풍류를 아는 tasteful ; elegant ; refined ; graceful ; romantic // 풍류를 모르는 사람 a prosaic person ; a matter-of fact man // 풍류적인 생활을 하다 live a poetical〔an idyllic〕 life // 풍류를 알다 have an eye for the picturesque ; have a love of the poetical
—가 a man of refined taste ; a person of a romantic turn of mind **—랑(郎)** an elegant young man ; a gay blade ; a young dandy ; a man-about-town **—인(人)** a man of taste **—장** elegant society
풍만 豊滿 ① [풍부] abundance ; plenty ② [비만] plumpness ; corpulence **— 하다** (be) abundant ; plentiful ; [비만] plump ; buxom ; corpulent ¶ 육체가 풍만한 미인 a plump and voluptuous beauty
풍매 風媒 wind-fertilization ; anemophily **— 식물** an anemophile **—화** an anemophilous flower
풍모 風貌 features ; mien ; looks ; appearance ¶ 풍모가 당당한 사람 a grand〔stately〕-looking person
풍문 風聞 a rumor ; a report ; hearsay ; a (town) talk ¶ 풍문에 의하면 Rumor has it 《that》〔says 《that》〕 ; It is rumored 《that》 // 풍문을 퍼뜨리다 spread〔start, circulate〕 a rumor ; set a rumor afloat
풍물 風物 ① [경치] scenery ; natural features ; nature ; landscape ② [풍속·사물] scenes and manners ¶ 한국의 풍물 things Korean ; the country and the people of Korea ③ [농악기] instruments for folk music
—시 a poem concerning a landscape ; natural poetry
*__풍미 風味__ flavor ; savor ; taste ; relish ¶ 풍미 있는 delicious ; dainty ; savory ; tasty ; spicy ; of fine flavor // 독특한 풍미 a racy flavor
풍미 風靡 —하다 overwhelm ; dominate ; sway ; predominate ; sweep ; make a clean sweep 《of》 ¶ 인심을 풍미하다 sway the minds of men // 천하를 풍미하다 take the world by storm ; rule the time (사상 따위가) // 그의 세력은 전국을 풍미했다 His influence was overwhelming throughout the country.
풍범선 風帆船 a sailing ship〔boat, vessel〕 ; a sailer
풍병 風病 ① nervous disorders ; paralysis ; palsy ② leprosy (문둥병)
†**풍부 豊富** abundance ; affluence ; plenty ; wealth ; richness ; opulence ; plentitude **—하다** (be) abundant ; plentiful ; plenteous ; copious ; ample ; rich ; opulent ; affluent ; exuberant ¶ 풍부한 자원 abundant resources // 풍부한 음식 abundance of food // 풍부한 물자 an abundance of material supplies // 풍부한 지식 a great store〔stock, wealth〕 of knowledge ; a mine of information // 내용이 풍부한 책 a work of rich contents // 내용을 풍부히 하다 enrich the contents // 이 지방은 사과가 풍부하다 This region abounds in apples. / Apples are abundant in this district. // 그는 학문이 풍부하다 He has a great store of learning. // 미국은 천연자원이 풍부하다 The United States is rich in natural resources. // 그 여자는 이야깃거리가 풍부하다 She has such an ample store of topics.
풍비박산 風飛雹散 —하다 scatter in all directions ; be all scattered
풍산종자 風散種子 〖식물〗 a parachute (seed)
풍상 風霜 wind and frost ; [고생] hardships ¶ 풍상을 겪다 suffer hardships
풍서란 風—欄 〖건축〗 weather stripping ; a strip of wood fixed along a windowsill〔doorsill〕 to keep out the wind
풍선 風扇 ① [선풍기] a punka(h) ; a fan ; an electric fan ② [농기구] a winnower
풍선 風船 a balloon ¶ 풍선을 날리다 fly〔send up〕 a balloon

—껌 bubble gum ; a piece of bubble gum (낱개) — 폭탄 a balloon bomb 고무 — a toy balloon 광고 — an advertising〔ad〕 balloon

풍설 風雪 wind and snow ; a snowstorm ; a blizzard ¶ 풍설을 무릅쓰고 in defiance〔the face, the teeth〕 of the wind and snow

대— a heavy〔blinding〕 snowstorm

풍설 風說 a rumor ; an unfounded report ; hearsay ; a talk ¶ 가지가지 풍설 various rumors // 풍설이 유포되다 a rumor gets afloat〔abroad〕

⁑풍성 豊盛 abundance ; plentitude ; affluence ; opulence ; richness —하다 (be) abundant ; plenteous ; affluent ; opulent ; rich ; exuberant

풍성 風聲 ① [바람 소리] the sound of wind ② [명성] fame ; repute ¶ 풍성으로 알다 know 《a person》 by repute

풍세 風勢 the force〔velocity〕 of the wind ¶ 풍세를 이용하다 take advantage of the wind

*풍속 風俗 manners ; customs ; popular 〔public〕 morals ¶ 풍속을 괴란하다 corrupt public morals ; deprave good manners // 풍속을 해하다 be injurious to public morals

—도〔화〕 a genre picture〔painting〕 — 문학 genre literature — 사범 [행위] a violation of public morals ; an indecent offense ; [사람] violaters of public morals — 소설 a novel of manners — 습관 manners and customs

풍속 風速 the velocity of the wind ; wind velocity ¶ 한 시간 15 킬로의 풍속으로 at a speed of 15 kilometers an hour

—계 an anemometer ; a wind gauge — 측정법 anemometry 순간 최대 — the maximum instantaneous wind speed

풍수 風水 ① divination by configuration of the ground ② a geomancer

—설 the theory of configuration of the ground —학 geomancy ; geomantic studies

풍수지리설 風水地理說 〖민속〗 The theory of divison based on topography

풍수해 風水害 damage from〔by〕 storm and flood ¶ 이번 풍수해는 극심하다 Serious〔Great〕 damage has been caused by the storms and floods.

— 대책 measures against natural disasters

†풍습 風習 customs ; manners ; practices ¶ 풍습에 따르다 observe a custom // 이 지방에는 아직 옛날 풍습이 남아 있다 Some old customs still obtain〔prevail〕 in this part of the country.

풍식 風蝕 wind erosion ; weathering

풍신 風神 ① [풍백] the god of wind ② [풍채] appearance ; presence ; mien ¶ 풍신 좋은 사람 a man of noble〔fine〕 presence // 풍신이 좋다 have a fine appearance〔presence〕

풍신기 風信器 an anemoscope ; a weathercock ; a vane

풍아 風雅 elegance ; grace ; refinement ; daintiness —하다 (be) elegant ; graceful ; refined ; tasteful ¶ 풍아한 마음 poetical turn of mind

풍악 風樂 classic music

풍압 風壓 wind pressure

—계 a pressure anemometer

풍어 豊漁 a big〔heavy〕 catch ; a big haul ¶ 정어리의 풍어 a big catch of sardine

풍염 豊艶 voluptuousness ; voluptuous beauty —하다 (be) voluptuous ; plump and beautiful

풍요 豊饒 richness ; wealth ; abundance —하다 (be) rich ; abundant ; plentiful ; bountiful ; opulent

풍우 風雨 wind and rain ; a storm ; a rainstorm ¶ 풍우에 시달린 weather beaten // 풍우를 무릅쓰고 in spite〔the teeth〕 of the storm

풍운 風雲 ① wind and cloud ② [형세] the state of affairs ; the situation ¶ 풍운의 뜻 a great ambition ; an aspiration after fame // 풍운을 불러일으키다 bring about a crisis

—아 a lucky adventurer ; a soldier of fortune — 조화 mysteries of wind and cloud ; exercise of supernatural power

풍월 風月 ① wind and moon ; beauties of nature ¶ 풍월을 즐기다 enjoy (the beauties of) nature // 풍월을 벗 삼다 converse〔commune〕 with nature ② [시가] poetry (dealing with the wind and the moon) —하다 dabble in poetry ; write poetry ¶ 풍월을 짓다 compose a poem

—객 a person who dabbles in poetry ; a poet

풍위 風位 the direction of the wind ¶ 풍위가 바뀌다 the wind shifts // 풍위를 측정하다〔나타내다〕 define〔indicate〕 the direction of the wind

*풍유 諷諭 exhortation by insinuation ; 〖수사〗 an allegory —하다 exhort by insinuation ; use an allegory

⁑풍자 諷刺 a satire ; a sarcasm ; an innuendo ; an irony —하다 satirize ; lampoon ¶ 사회에 대한 풍자 a satire on society // 악정에 대한 풍자 a satire against misgovernment

—가 a satirist ; a lampooner —문 a lampoon — 문학 satirical literature — 소설 a satirical novel —시 a satirical poem —화 a caricature 사회 — a satire on society

⁑풍작 豊作 a good〔a rich, an abundant〕 harvest ; a bumper〔heavy〕 crop ¶ 풍작의 해 a bumper crop year // 벼의 대풍작 an extremely bountiful rice harvest

//금년은 일반적으로 풍작이었다 This year the crop was generally abundant〔plentiful〕.
풍장 風葬 aerial sepulture〔burial〕
풍재 風災 damage from wind ; a disaster caused by wind
풍적토 風積土 〚지질〛 aeolian soil
풍전 風前 before〔facing〕 the wind
풍전등화 風前燈火 a light before the wind ; a candle flickering in the wind ¶ 풍전등화 같이 위태롭다 be as dangerous as sitting on a barrel of gunpowder ; be in an extremely precarious position//그의 운명은 풍전등화와 같다 His fate hangs in the balance. /His life hangs by a thread〔hair〕.
풍정 風情 elegance ; refinement ; tasteful appearance ; an artistic air
풍조 風鳥 a bird of paradise
*****풍조 風潮** ① [바닷물] the lee tide ② [추세] a tendency ; a trend ; a drift ; the tide ; fashion ; stream ¶ 풍조를 따르다 go with the stream of the times//풍조를 역행하다 swim〔go〕 against the stream of the times ; run counter to the fashion of the world
세상 — the trend〔drift〕 of the world ; the tone of society ; the fashion of the world
*****풍족 豊足** abundance ; plenty ; ampleness ; opulence **— 하다** (be) abundant ; pentiful ; ample ; opulent ¶ 풍족한 자원 abundant resources//풍족하게 살다 live in plenty〔abundance〕//재정이 풍족하다 be financially well-off//수산물이 풍족하다 be rich in marine products
풍증 風症 ⇨ 풍병(風病) ①
풍지 風紙 paper flaps to cover window chinks
풍진 風疹 〚의학〛 rubella ; German measles
풍진 風塵 ① [티끌] wind-blown dust ② [속세] worldly affairs ; cares of life ¶ 풍진을 피하다 live in seclusion ; lead a sequestered life
— 세상 this world of woe and tumult
세상 — troubles of life〔of the world〕
*****풍차 風車** ① a windmill ② ⇨ 풍구(風—) ③ ⇨ 팔랑개비
—간 a windmill shed **— 발전기** a fan-driven generator
풍차 風遮 ① [두건] a fur hood ② [바지의] a cloth belt attached to children's trousers
풍채 風采 appearance ; air ; mien ; presence ; bearing ¶ 풍채가 당당한 사람 a man of commanding presence〔appearance〕//풍채가 좋다 have a fine presence
풍취 風趣 taste ; flavor ; elegance ¶ 풍취 있는 tasteful ; tasty ; elegant//풍취 없는 tasteless ; dry ; dull ; insipid
풍치 風致 taste ; elegance ; scenic beauty ¶ 풍치 있는〔좋은〕 tasteful ; elegant ; charming//풍치 없는 tame 《scenery》//정원은 풍치가 있다 This garden is tastefully arranged.
—림 an ornamental plantation〔forest〕 **— 지구** a scenic area〔zone〕
풍치다 ⇨ 풍²(風)
풍침 風枕 an air cushion ; a pneumatic pillow
풍토 風土 natural features 《of a region ; climate ¶ 풍토의 climatic ; endemic (지방적)//풍토에 순화하다 acclimatize ; acclimate oneself 《to》 《미》
—기(記) topography **—병** an endemic disease ; a vernacular〔local〕 disease **— 순화** acclimatization ; acclimation **—학** climatology
풍파 風波 ① wind and waves ; a storm ; a tempest ; rough seas ¶ 풍파를 무릅쓰고 in the face〔teeth〕 of wind and waves ; battling against the raging billows//풍파를 만나다 be caught by a storm//해상은 풍파가 거칠다 The sea is rough. /The wind and waves are high.
② [불화] a trouble ; a disturbance ; a quarrel
③ [고생] hardships ; a storm ¶ 인생의 풍파 the storms of life//풍파를 겪다 suffer hardships
가정 — family troubles ; domestic discord ¶ 가정 풍파가 끊이지 않았다 There were constant troubles in that family. /His home was never free from family troubles. **세상 —** the storms〔rough and tumble〕 of life
풍편 風便 rumor ; hearsay ¶ 풍편에 듣다 know by hearsay
풍하중 風荷重 a wind load
풍해 風害 damage from wind ⇨ 풍재
풍향 風向 the direction of the wind ; the wind ¶ 풍향이 바뀌다 shift〔veer〕 《round to the east》
—기(器) an anemoscope
풍혹 楓— an outgrown gnarl of a maple tree
풍화 風化 〚지질〛 weathering ; 〚화학〛 efflorescence **— 하다** weather ; effloresce ¶ 풍화하는 efflorescent//바위가 풍화하여 기이한 형태로 되어 있다 The rocks are weathered into fantastic forms.
—물 efflorescence **— 석회** airslaked lime **— 작용** weathering ; the action of the elements
풍흉 豊凶 a good and bad harvest ; a rich or poor harvest
퓨리처상 —賞 the Pulitzer Prize 《for drama》 ¶ 퓨리처상 수상작(품) a Pulitzer Prize work
퓨리턴 [청교도] a Puritan ; [엄격한 사람] a puritan ; [주의] Puritanism
퓨마 〚동물〛 a puma

퓨즈 〖물리〗 a fuse ¶ 퓨즈로 잇다〔를 넣다〕 fit〔put〕 a fuse《to》∥퓨즈가 끊어지다 a fuse is burnt out

퓽 whizzing ; ping (금속음) ¶ 퓽소리가 나다 whiz(z) ; swish

프라우다 Pravda (소련 공산당 기관지)

*프라이 [요리] a fry ; something fried ¶ 프라이로 한 fried∥프라이로 하다 fry
— 남비 a fryer — 에그 fried eggs ; a sunny-side up (미) —팬 a frying pan ; a skillet 새우 — fried prawns ; a fried lobster

프라이드 pride ¶ 프라이드가 높은 proud ; self-respecting

프라이버시 privacy ¶ 프라이버시 침해 an invasion of privacy∥프라이버시를 침해하다 disturb〔invade, violate〕《a person's》 privacy

프라임레이트 〖경제〗 the prime rate

프락치 a fraction
— 활동 fraction activities

*프랑 [프랑스의 화폐] a franc (기호 fr.)

*프랑스 France ¶ 프랑스의 French∥프랑스제의 Franch-made
— 국기 the national flag of France ; the Tricolor —말〔어〕 French ; the French language ¶ 제2외국어로 프랑스어를 배우다 minor in French (미) — 사람〔인〕 a Frenchman ; a Frenchwoman (여) ; [총칭] the French — 요리 French cuisine〔cookery〕 ; dishes à la Francaise — 혁명 the French Rovolution

프래그머티즘 〖철학〗 pragmatism

프랜차이즈 〖야구〗 franchise

프런트 [호텔의] the front〔reception〕 desk (미) ¶ 프런트를 부르다 call the front desk

프런티어 정신 —精神 the frontier spirit

프레스 ① [누르기] press ¶ 프레스가 잘된 바지 [다림질이] well〔sharply〕 pressed trousers ② [신문] the press ③ 〖역도〗 [중량 들어올리기] press ¶ 프레스에서 125킬로 들어올리다 lift 125 kilos in press
— 박스 [신문 기자석] the press box — 캠페인 a press campaign — 코드 the press code

프레스코 fresco ; wall painting ¶ 프레스코화를 그리다 paint in fresco ; fresco
—화(畫) a fresco《*pl.* -(e)》; a mural (painting) in fresco — 화가 a frescoer ; a fresco painter

프레시 fresh ¶ 프레시하게 느껴지다 feel fresh ; find something fresh《in a picture》

프레 올림픽 the Pre-Olympics ; the Pre-Olympic Games

프레젠트 a present ; a gift ──하다 give〔make〕 a present《to a person》; make《a person》 a present of

프레파라트 [현미경의] a slide

프렐류드 〖음악〗 a prelude

‡프로 ① [직업적인] pro ; professional ; [직업 선수] a professional player ; a pro《*pl.* ~s》(구) ¶ 프로급의《a player》 on a professional level∥프로로 돌다 turn professional〔pro〕 ② ⇨ 프롤레타리아 ③ ⇨ 프로그램 ④ 프로덕션 ⑤ ⇨ 퍼센트
— 레슬링 pro(fessional) wrestling — 야구〔축구〕 a pro baseball〔football〕 대북(對北) 방송 — a pogram beamed at North Korea 라디오〔텔레비전〕 — a radio〔T. V.〕 program 특별 — a special〔feature〕 program ; [인기 프로] an attraction

프로그래머 [전자 계산기의] a (computer) programmer

†프로그램 a program(me) ; a card (미·구) ¶ 프로그램에 들어 있다 be on the program∥프로그램에 올리다 put on〔in〕 the program ; bill《an actor》∥프로그램을 진행시키다 run off the events∥프로그램을 짜다 make〔arrange, draw up, prepare, map out〕 a program《of》
— 학습 program(m)ed learning

프로덕션 〖영화〗 a production ; a (movie) studio《*pl.* ~s》

프로듀서 a producer
공동 — a coproducer

프로메테우스 Prometheus

프로세스 (a) process
— 건판(乾板) 〖사진〗 a process plate
— 치즈 process(ed) cheese

프로이트 Freud, Sigmund (오스트리아 1856-1939)
— 학설, —주의 Freudianism

프로젝트 a project
— 메더드 〖교육〗 the project method

프로카인 [마취제의 일종] procain

프로테스탄트 〖기독교〗 Protestant ; [주의] Protestantism ; [신자] a Protestant

프로텍터 [방호구] a《chest》 protector ; a《shin》 guard

프로토악티늄 〖화학〗 protoactinium

프로톤 〖물리·화학〗 a proton

프로판가스 propane〔liquefied, petroleum〕 gas ; LP gas ; propane

프로퍼갠더 propaganda (work) ; publicity

‡프로펠러 a propeller ; an airscrew (영) ; a prop (항공·속) ¶ 프로펠러를 돌리다 spin the propeller
—기(機) a propeller(-driven) plane ; a prop(-driven) plane — 소리 the burr〔roar〕 of a propeller

프로포즈 a proposal of marriage《to a girl》 ──하다 propose《to a girl》

프로필 a profile ; [인물 단평] a brief character sketch ¶ 김선생의 프로필 a sketch of Mr. Kim's career and personality

프록 코트 a frock (coat) ; a Prince Albert (미·속)

프론트 데스크 [호텔의] the front〔reception〕 desk ¶ 수화기를 들고 프론트 데스크를 부르다 pick up the telephone and call the front desk

*__프롤레타리아__ [사람] a proletarian ; [계급] the proletariat(e)
— **독재** dictatorship of the proletariat ; proletarian dictatorship — **문학〔예술〕** proletarian literature〔art〕 — **혁명** a proletarian revolution

프롤로그 a prolog(ue)

프롬프터 a (theater) prompter

프리깃 a frigate (ship)

프리드로우 〖농구〗 a free throw

프리랜서 a free lance ; a free-lancer (특히 문필업 관계의) ¶ 프리랜서의 저널리스트 a free-lance journalist

프리마 돈나 [가극의] a prima donna 《*pl.* ~s, prime donne》《이》 ¶ 가극의 프리마 돈나 the prima donna in an opera

프리미엄 a premium 《*pl.* ~s》 ¶ 프리미엄부(附)로 at a premium 《of 20 percent》// 프리미엄이 붙다 command a premium // 프리미엄을 붙이다 place〔put〕 a premium 《on》

프리 배팅 〖야구〗 free batting ; batting practice

*__프리즘__ 〖물리〗 a prism ¶ 프리즘의 굴절〔반사〕 prismatic refraction〔reflection〕
— **쌍안경** prismatic binoculars **직각** — a right-angled prism

프리지어 〖식물〗 a freesia

프리킥 〖축구〗 a free kick

프리타운 Freetown

프리토리아 Pretoria (남아프리카 공화국 수도)

프리 패스 a free ticket ; a pass admitting a person free

프린세스 a princess

프린스 a prince

프린트 a print ; [등사한 것] a mimeographed copy ; [옷감] print ; calico 《미》
— **배선** 〖전기〗 a printed circuit〔wire〕
— **업자** a (mimeograph) printer

프토마인 〖화학〗 ptomaine
— **중독** ptomaine poisoning

프티 부르주아 [사람] a petty〔petit〕 bourgeois ; [계급] petty〔petite〕 bourgeoisie

플라네타륨 〖천문〗 a planetarium

플라멩코 [집시의 춤 또는 그 음악] flamenco

플라스마 〖물리〗 plasma ; 〖생리〗 (blood) plasma
— **물리학** plasma physics — **이론** plasma theory

*__플라스크__ a flask

*__플라스틱__ (a) plastic ; plastics 《단·복수를 다 같이 씀》
— **모델** a plastics model — **제품** a plastic ; plastic goods

플라워 디자이너 a flower designer

플라이 〖야구〗 a fly (ball) ¶ 플라이를 치다 fly (a ball) ; pop (up, out) ; hit a fly ball
내야〔외야〕 — an infield〔outfield〕 fly **센터〔레프트, 라이트〕** — a center〔left, right〕 fly **희생** — a sacrifice fly

플라이급 —級 〖경기〗 the fly weight ¶ 플라이급의 flyweight
— **선수** a flyweight **세계** — **선수권** the world flyweight championship

플라이어 〖기계〗 [방적기·인쇄기] a flyer ; a flier

플라이잉 [경주] a breakaway ; a premature start —**하다** break away ; make a premature start ; jump the gun

플라즈마 plasma ⇨ 플라스마

*__플라타너스, 플라탄(나무)__ 〖식물〗 platanus ; a plane tree

플라토닉 Platonic ; spiritual
— **러브** Platonic love

플라티나 〖화학〗 platinum 《Pt》

*__플란넬__ flannel
— **제품** flannels

플랑드르 Flanders

플랑크톤 〖생물〗 plankton

플래시 a flash ; [회중 전등] an electric torch ; a flashlight 《미》 ¶ 플래시를 켜다〔비추다〕 flash one's torch // 플래시를 터뜨리다 light a flash bulb ; snap a flashlight // 플래시 세례를 받다 be in a flood of flashlights

플래시백 〖영화〗 flashback —**하다** flash back ; backlash 《to》

플래카드 a placard

†__플랜__ a plan ¶ 플랜을 세우다 make〔form, map out〕 a plan 《for》 ; lay a plan

플랜지 a flange
—**관** a flange(d) pipe

플랜트 plant
— **수출** the export of industrial plants ; plant export

*__플랫__ 〖음악〗 a flat ; 《b》 ; 〖경주〗 《12 seconds》 flat

‡__플랫폼__ [승강장] a 《train》 platform ; a track ¶ 제2 플랫폼 Track Two // 플랫폼에 들어가다 enter the platform

‡__플러스__ plus ; a plus ; addition ; adding —**하다** add 《two》 to 《six》 ; [기여하다] contribute 《to》 ¶ 조금이라도 플러스가 된다면 if there is any gain // 그건 플러스 마이너스 제로다 That would mean no gain 《for you》. // 플러스는 커녕 도리어 마이너스가 되었다 It was nothing more than a loss. // 3 플러스 4는 7 Three plus four is〔makes, equalse〕 seven. /Three and four are seven.
— **알파** plus something

플럭 a plug ¶ 플럭을 꽂다 plug in

플레밍 Fleming, Alexander (영 1881-1955)
— **진공관** a Fleming('s) valve

플레어 스커트 a flared skirt
플레이 a play
 파인 — a fine play
플레이 볼 〖체육〗 play ball
플레이어 [사람] a player ; [축음기] a record player
플레이트 a plate ; 〖야구〗 a pitcher's plate ; the home plate ¶ 플레이트를 밟다 take the plate〔mound〕
 — **전류** plate current **홈** — the home plate
플로렌스 Florence ⇨ 피렌체
플로리다 Florida 《Fla., Flor.》
플롯 a plot ¶ 소설의 플롯 the plot of a story
플루토늄 〖화학〗 Plutonium 《Pu》
*__플루트__ 〖악기〗 a flute
플리머드 Plymouth (영국의 항구·미국의 도시)
 —**록** [닭] Plymouth Rock
플리츠 a pleat ¶ 스커트의 플리츠 pleats on〔in〕 the skirt
플리퍼 a flapper 《미》
†**피**¹ ① [혈액] blood ; gore (핏덩이) ¶ 피의 바다 a sea of blood // 피의 순환 the circulation of the blood // 피 묻은 손수건 a bloodstained〔blood-smeared〕 handkerchief // 피 끓는 청년 a young blood // 피도 눈물도 없는 사람 a bloodless 〔cold-blood, stone-hearted〕 fellow // 피비린내 나는 bloody // 피에 굶주린 bloodthirsty // 피가 나다 《one's arms》 bleed ; blood runs out ; blood starts // 피가 마르다 blood becomes thin〔thins down〕 // 피가 배다 become permeated with blood // 피가 나도록 때리다 whip 《a person》 till he sheds blood // 피를 멈추다 stop bleeding ; stanch blood // 피를 빨다 suck up blood // 피를 빼다 draw blood 《from》 ; deplete one's blood (방혈) // 피를 토하다 vomit blood (토혈) ; spit〔eject〕 blood (각혈) // 피를 흘리다 spill〔shed〕 blood // 피투성이가 되다 be covered with blood all over ; be soaked with blood // 싸움터는 피바다가 되었다 The battlefield was flooded with blood. // 아직도 상처에서 피가 흐르고 있었다 Blood is still oozing from the wound. // 사건은 피를 안 보고 원만히 해결됐다 The affair was settled amicably without bloodshed. // 그 여자는 병들어 얼굴에 핏기가 없다 Her cheeks are pale with sickness.
 ② [혈연] blood ; blood relation ; consanguinity (혈족) ¶ 피를 나눈 형제 a blood brother ; brothers of the same blood // 피가 섞이다 have mixed blood ; be halfblooded // 외국인의 피가 섞여 있다 be of alien blood // 피는 물보다 진하다 Blood is thicker than water. // 핏줄은 어찌할 수 없다 Blood will tell.
피로 피를 씻는다 [속담] Blood will have blood.
 피가 끓다 [관용] one's blood stirs 〔boils, turns〕
 피를 나누다 [관용] be of the same blood ; be blood-related
피² 〖식물〗 barnyard millet ; Echinochloa frumentacea (학명)
피³ [경멸] pshaw ; with a sneer **—하다** sneer
피검 被檢 being arrested ¶ 피검되다 be arrested ; be rounded up
 —**자** the arrested ; a person in custody
피겨 스케이팅 figure skating **—하다** skate〔cut〕 figures (on the ice)
피격 被擊 being fired at ; suffering attack ¶ 피격 당하다 be attacked 《by》 ; be assaulted〔raided〕
*__피고 被告__ [민사의] a defendant ; [형사의] the accused
 — **대리인** a defendant's representative
 — **변호인** the counsel for the defense 〔accused〕 —**석** the dock ; the bar **공동** — a codefendant
피고름 bloody pus
피고용자 被雇傭者 an employee ; an employe
†**피곤 疲困** fatigue ; weariness ; tiredness ; exhaustion **—하다** (be) tired ; fatigued ; wearied ; exhausted
피골 皮骨 skin and bones ¶ 피골이 상접하다 be reduced to a skeleton ; be all skin and bones // 피골이 상접한 사람 a man of skin and bones ; an anatomy
피그미족 —族 a Pygmy ; a Pigmy
피근피근 refusing to listen ; stubbornly ; obstinately **—하다** (be) stubborn ; obstinate ; perverse
피나무 〖식물〗 a linden tree ; a lime tree ; a bass (wood) ; Tilid amurensis japonica (학명)
*__피난 避難__ refuge ; shelter ; harborage ; evacuation **—하다** take〔seek〕 refuge ; take〔find〕 shelter ; retire to a safe place ; get under cover ; escape ; evacuate
 — **명령** an evacuation order ¶ 홍수의 위험이 있어 읍민에게 피난 명령이 내렸다 In view of the threatening flood, the people of the town were ordered to evacuate their homes. —**민** refugees —**살이** refugee life —**자** a refugee ; an evacuee —**처** a place of refuge〔safety〕 ; a shelter ; a refuge ; an asylum —**항** a harbor of refuge ; a port of shelter〔refuge〕
피날레 a finale
피납 被拉 ⇨ 납치(拉致) ¶ 피납되다 be taken away〔captive〕
피낭 被囊 〖동·식물〗 a cyst
피닉스 the phoenix〔phenix〕 ⇨ 불사조
피눈물 tears of blood ; bitter tears ¶ 피눈물을 흘리다 weep tears of blood ; shed bitter tears
피넛 a peanut

— 버터 peanut butter

*피다 ① [꽃이] come〔be〕 out ; 《trees》 blossom ; flower ; 《flowers》 bloom ; open ¶ 막 핀 장미 a new-blown rose // 오랑캐 꽃〔복숭아꽃〕이 필 무렵에 in the violet〔peach-blossom〕 time // 피어 있다 be in bloom〔flower〕 ; be out ; be open // 아름답게 피어 있다 be in beautiful bloom // 활짝 피어 있다 be in full bloom ; be at its best // 활짝 피어 나다 burst into bloom // 사과꽃이 피기 시작했다 The apple trees began to put forth their blossoms.
② [불을] burn ; make〔build, light〕 《a fire》 ¶ 난로를 피우다 make a fire in the stove ; light the fire // 향을 피우다 burn incense
③ [기타] ¶ 얼굴빛이 피다 one's complexion blooms ; look better // 그들은 지나간 일로 이야기의 꽃을 피우고 있었다 They talked eagerly about the past.

피담보인 被擔保人 a warrantee

피대 皮帶 a conveyor belt

피더 a feeder

피동 被動 passivity ; passiveness ¶ 피동적(으로) passive(ly)
—사(詞) a passive verb

피둥피둥 ① [몸이] fat ; plump ; corpulent ② [말을] refusing to listen ; stubborn ―하다 (be) fat ; plump ; corpulent ; stubborn ; heedless ¶ 피둥피둥 살찌다 be fat〔corpulent〕 // 아직도 피둥피둥하다 be hale and hearty

*피드백 〖전기〗 feedback — 시스템 the feedback system — 장치 a feedback mechanism

피딱지[1] a clot of blood ; a blood clot ¶ 말라서 피딱지가 되었다 The blood had dried and formed a crust.

피딱지[2] [종이] poor-quality paper made of mulberry bark

피땀 greasy sweat ¶ 피땀을 흘리며 일하다 toil and moil

피똥 bloody stools ; excrement mixed with blood

피뜩 suddenly ; quickly ¶ 피뜩 지나가다 pass quickly

피뜩피뜩 [종종] at times〔intervals〕 ; by fits (and starts)

피라미 〖물고기〗 a dace ; Zacco platypus (학명)

⁑피라미드 a pyramid ¶ 피라미드 모양의 pyramidal

피레네 산맥 — 山脈 the Pyrenees

피렌체 Firenze ; Florence

피력 披瀝 stating frankly〔openly〕 ―하다 state 《one's view》 frankly ; express ; open ; confess ; reveal ; set forth 《one's views, one's heart》 ¶ 의견을 피력하다 express one's view ; voice one's opinion // 흉중을 피력하다 open one's heart〔bosom〕 《to》 ; unbosom oneself

⁑피로 披露 [발표] announcement ; [소개] introduction ; [광고] advertisement ―하다 announce ; introduce ; advertise
—연 a dinner for making an announcement ¶ 피로연을 베풀다 give a dinner in announcement of 《one's marriage》 결혼 —연 a wedding reception〔feast〕 ; a wedding dinner 《미》

*피로 疲勞 fatigue ; weariness ; exhaustion ―하다 (be) tired ; fatigued ; exhausted ¶ 피로한 기색 a tired look ; signs of fatigue // 피로를 느끼다 feel fatigued〔tired〕 // 피로가 풀리다 be relieved of one's fatigue // 녹초가 되도록 피로하다 be dog-tired ; be tired to death // 당신은 피로가 쌓여 있다 You've just let your fatigue build up.

피뢰기 避雷器 a lightning arrester ; an arrester

피뢰침 避雷針 a lightning rod〔conductor〕

⁑피륙 piece goods ; dress goods (여자·어린이용) ; drapery 《영》 ; dry goods 《미》 ; textiles
— 장수 a draper

†피리 a pipe ; a flute ; a recorder ; a fife (군용) ¶ 피리를 불다 play a flute ; play 《a tune》 on the flute ; pipe
— 구멍 a stop〔finger hole〕 of a flute
— 소리 the sound of a flute ; piping (sound) — 연주자 a flute player ; a flutist ; a piper ; a fifer —혀 a reed 풀 — a reed

피리어드 [종지부] a period ; a full stop ¶ 피리어드를 찍다 put a period〔an end〕 《to》

피마 —馬 〖동물〗 a (grown-up) mare
—유 castor oil

피막 皮膜 a film ; 〖해부〗 a tapetum
— 조직 〖식물〗 epithelium

피막 被膜 〖해부·동물〗 a tunic ¶ 피막이 있는 tunicate ; tunicated

피막이풀 〖식물〗 a marsh pennywort ; Hydrocotyle sibthorpioides (학명)

피망 〖식물〗 a pimento 《*pl.* ～s》 ; a green pepper

피맺히다 be bruised

피명 被命 ―하다 be ordered〔appointed〕 ; receive an (official) order〔appointment〕

피밥 cooked barnyard millet

피배서인 被背書人 an endorsee ; an indorsee

피병원 避病院 an isolation hospital

피보증인 被保證人 the principal debtor ; a warrantee

피보험물 被保險物 an insured article ; insured property

피보험자 被保險者 an insured person ; the insured 《총칭》

피보호국 被保護國 a dependency ; a dependent state

피보호자 被保護者 a ward ; a protégé

(남자) 《프》; a protégée (여자) 《프》
피복 被服 clothing
—대〔비〕 clothing allowance〔expense〕 —상 a clothier —재(材) clothing material
피복 被覆 covering; a mantle —하다 cover
—선(線) covered〔coated〕 wire —재료 covering material
피봉 皮封 an envelope ⇨ 겉봉
†피부 皮膚 〖해부〗 the skin ¶ 피부가 거칠다 have a rough skin // 피부가 곱다〔약하다〕 have a fair〔delicate〕 skin
— 감각〔호흡〕 skin〔cutaneous〕 sensation〔respiration〕 — 건조증 xeroderma — 경화증 scleroma; scleroderma —과 dermatology —과 의사 a dermatologist; a skin specialist — 기생 진균(眞菌) a dermatophyte — 미백제 a skin beautifier; cold cream —병 a skin〔cutaneous〕 disease —병학 dermatology — 봉합 skin suture — 색소 결핍증 alphodermia — 성형술 dermatoplasty —암 cutaneous cancer; cancer of the skin —염 dermatitis; cutitis — 위축 atrophy of the skin — 이식술 skin grafting
피브리노겐 fibrinogen
피브린 fibrin
피비린내 bloody stink; bloodiness ¶ 피비린내 나는 싸움 a bloody fight〔battle〕
피사 Pisa ¶ 피사의 사탑 the Leaning Tower of Pisa
피사리 weeding ¶ 피사리하다 pick out〔pluck〕 weeds; weed 《a rice field》
피사체 被寫體 a subject
피살 被殺 being killed〔murdered〕 ¶ 피살되다 get killed
피상 皮相 [외관] an outward look; [천박] superficiality ¶ 피상적인 superficial; shallow; surface // 피상적 견해 a superficial〔surface〕 view // 자네 관찰은 피상적이다 You take a superficial view of the matter.
피상고인 被上告人 an appellee
피상속인 被相續人 〖법〗 an ancestor; a predecessor; an inheritee
피새 a quick temper ¶ 피새 내다 lose one's temper easily // 피새 놓다 slander; vilify
피서 避暑 summering —하다 summer; pass〔spend〕 the summer 《at, in》 ¶ 피서를 가다 go to a summer resort // 지리산으로 피서를 가다 go to Mt. *Jiri* to avoid the heat of the town (for the summer)
—객 a summer visitor〔resident〕; a summer colony 《총칭》 — 계절 the season of summer exodus —지 a summer resort —(지) 안내 a guide-book to summer resorts
피선 被選 —하다 be〔get〕 elected; be chosen
피선거권 被選擧權 eligibility for election; qualification for election; electoral eligibility ¶ 피선거권이 있다 be eligible for 《an M.P.》; be qualified to run for 《an M.P.》
피선거인 被選擧人 an eligible person; the elect
*피스톤 a piston
피스톨 [권총] a pistol; a revolver
피습 被襲 —하다 be〔get〕 attacked; be assaulted
피승수 被乘數 〖수학〗 a multiplicand
피신 避身 (secret) escape; refuge; shelter; concealing oneself —하다 escape secretly; take refuge〔shelter〕; conceal〔hide〕 oneself; beat a safe retreat ¶ 안전한 곳으로 피신하다 take refuge〔sanctuary〕 in 《a place》
피아 彼我 self and others; both sides; he and I; they and we; this and that ¶ 피아의 mutual // 피아 국정이 다르다 The conditions of the two countries are different each other.
†피아노 a piano ¶ 피아노를 치다 play (on) the piano // 피아노를 배우다 take piano lessons 《from a person》
— 독주 a piano solo 《by Mr. *Son*》 —용 의자 a piano stool — 조율사 a piano-tuner 그랜드 — a (concert) grand piano 수형(竪型) — an upright piano 자동 — a player piano; a pianola

피아노

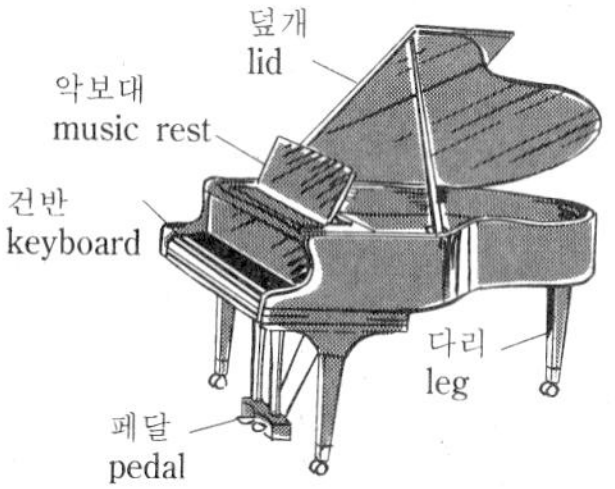

*피아니스트 a pianist
피아르 P.R. 《public relations》 —하다 publicize; advertise
— 영화 a PR film —카 a public relations car — 활동 public relations (activities)
피안 彼岸 ① 〖불교〗 Paramita (바라밀다) 《범》; Nirvana (열반) 《범》
② [맞은편] the other side〔shore〕 ¶ 태평양의 피안 《on》 the other shore〔side〕 of the Pacific
피압박 민족 被壓迫民族 the oppressed〔downtrodden〕 people〔nation〕
— 해방(운동) (the campaign for) lib-

eration of the oppressed people〔nation〕
피앙세 [남자] a fiancé 《프》; [여자] a fiancée 《프》
†**피어나다** ① [불이] burn up again; rekindle (itself) ¶ 숯불이 피어나다 the charcoal fire glows again ② [소생] come back to life; come to oneself; be brought to life; come to one's senses; revive; recover oneself ③ [생활이] 《it》 ease up; recover ④ [꽃이] 《a flower》 come out; come into bloom; bloom
피어오르다 go up; rise; ascend ⇨ 피다 ¶ 뭉게뭉게 피어오르다 curl〔roll〕 up
피에로 〖연극〗 a pierrot; a clown
피에조 전기 —電氣 piezoelectricity
피엑스 〖미육군〗 a post exchange; a PX
피엘오 P. L. O. 《Palestine Liberation Organization》
***피우다** ① [불을] make〔build〕 《a fire》; burn; kindle ¶ 난로에 불을 피우다 make〔start〕 a fire in a stove // 장작을 피우다 burn firewood ② [담배를] smoke 《tobacco, a pipe》; have a smoke ¶ 담배를 뻐끔뻐끔 피우다 puff at one's pipe〔cigar, cigarette〕 // 여송연을 피우며 이야기하다 talk over cigars ③ [냄새를] give off〔send out〕 《an odor》; emit 《a scent》; scent ¶ 꽃이 좋은 냄새를 피웠다 The flowers scented〔perfumed〕 the air. ④ [먼지를] raise〔make, kick up〕 《dust》 ⑤[재주를] do; play; display; perform ¶ 익살을 피우다 play the fool; jest // 재주를 피우다 play〔do〕 tricks ⑥ [꽃을] make 《flowers》 open〔bloom〕
피육 皮肉 skin and flesh
피의자 被疑者 a suspect; a suspected person ¶ 살인 사건의 피의자 a suspect in a murder; a suspected murderer // 피의자의 사진 photographs of criminal suspects
피임 被任 appointment to an office —하다 be appointed; be named ¶ 그는 외무부 장관으로 피임되었다 He was appointed Minister of Foreign Affairs.
피임 避姙 contraception; prevention of conception〔maternity〕 —하다 prevent conception
— 기구 a contraceptive appliance —법 a contraceptive measure〔method, device〕; a preventive method of conception — 수술 a contraceptive operation〔treatment〕 —약〔제〕 a contraceptive —용 젤리 contraceptive jelly 경구—약 an oral contraceptive (pill); the pill
피자식물 被子植物 an angiosperm ⇨ 속씨 식물
피장파장 (both) the same; no difference between 《us》; equal; a draw; quits ¶ 피장파장이다 They are practically the same. /That makes us no difference.
피점령국 被占領國 an occupied country
피제수 被除數 〖수학〗 a dividend
피조물 被造物 a created thing; a creature; creation 《총칭》
피죽 —粥 gruel made of barnyard millet
피죽 皮竹 bamboo sheath
피죽새 〖새〗 a bulbul
피지 皮紙 ⇨ 피딱지[2]
피지 皮脂 sebum; smegma
—선(腺) 〖해부〗 sebaceous glands
피지급 被支給 receiving payment
—인 a payee
피지샘 皮脂— 〖해부〗 a sebaceous gland; Glandula sebadcea (학명)
피진 皮疹 〖의학〗 efflorescence; exanthema
피질 皮質 〖생물〗 cortex
피차 彼此 this and that; you and I; both sides; each other ¶ 피차 돕다 help each other // 피차 사랑하다 love each other // 피차 다를 것이 없다 There's no need for quarrelling back and forth.
피차간 彼此間 between you and me; between both sides〔parties〕; both of us ¶ 피차간에 사이가 좋지 않다 The two do not get on well each other.
피차일반 彼此一般 both the same; no difference between them〔us, him and me〕 ¶ 피차일반이다 be mutually equal 〔the same〕 // 가난하기는 피차일반이다 I am as poor as you. /When it comes to being poor, we're in the same boat.
피처 〖야구〗 a (baseball) pitcher ¶ 피처를 맡다 pitch; play as a pitcher
— 플레이트 a pitcher's plate; the mound
피천 petty money
피천 한 닢 없다 관용 be penniless
피천 被薦 —하다 be recommended
피청구인 被請求人 a claimee
피체 被逮 —하다 be arrested; get caught
피초청국 被招請國 an invited country
— 대표 a visiting delegate
피츠버그 Pittsburgh (미국의 도시)
피층 皮層 〖식물〗 cortex
***피치** [아스팔트] pitch; 〖야구〗 a pitch; 〖음악〗 a pitch; [배의] pitching; [고조] peak; top ¶ 급 피치로 at high speed // 피치를 올리다〔떨어뜨리다〕 quicken 〔slacken〕 the pace; get up〔slow down〕 the speed
피치자 被治者 the governed; the ruled ¶ 치자와 피치자 (the) ruler and (the) ruled
피치카토 〖음악〗 pizzicato
피침 被侵 suffering invasion; being raided; being violated —하다 be invaded; be raided〔violated〕
피칭 pitching ¶ 피칭 연습을 하다 practice pitching

— 머신 a pitching machine
피켈 [등산용] a pickel
피켓 a picket ; picketing ¶ 피켓을 치다 keep a picket 《at a factory》; picket 《a place》
피콜로 〖악기〗 a piccolo
피크 [절정] a peak ¶ 피크때에 at peak hours
피크닉 a picnic —가다 picnic ; go on a picnic ; have a picnic
피크르산 —酸 〖화학〗 picric acid
피클 [절인 것] pickles
— 라인 a picket line
피탈 被奪 suffering robbery ; having 《something》 taken away —하다 be robbed of 《a thing》; have 《something》 taken away
피통치 被統治 being subject 《to》; being governed〔ruled〕 《by》
—국 a subject state
피투성이 ¶ 피투성이의 bloody ; blood-stained ; blood-soaked // 피투성이가 되다 be smeared〔covered〕 with blood ; be spattered all over with blood ; be bloodied // 피투성이가 되어 bathed with 〔in〕 blood // 그는 얼굴이 피투성이가 되어 병원에 실려갔다 He was carried into the hospital, his face a mass of bleeding flesh.
피트 feet 《ft.》《*sing.* a foot》 ¶ 6피트 3인치 six feet three inches ; 6 ft. 3 in. ; 6'3" // 그는 키가 5피트 6인치다 He stands five feet six inches high.
피티에이 Parent Teacher Association 《PTA》
피펫 〖화학〗 a pipette
피폐 疲弊 impoverishment ; exhaustion ; poverty —하다 become impoverished 〔exhausted〕; become poor ¶ 농촌의 피폐 the impoverished conditions of the rural communities // 재정의 피폐 financial exhaustion // 피폐해 있다 be in an exhausted condition ; be in poverty // 피폐시키다 impoverish
피폭 被爆 being bombed —되다 be bombed ; suffer from bombing ¶ 원폭의 피폭자 a victim of an atomic air raid
— 도시 an air-raided city ; a city which has suffered from bombing — 지구 a bombed block〔area〕
피피엠 [백만분율〔비〕] ppm (parts per million의 약어)
피하 皮下 under the skin ¶ 피하의 hypodermic ; hypoderma ; subcutaneous // 피하 주사를 놓다 inject 《medicine》 under the skin ; inject hypodermically
—선(腺) a hypodermal gland — 주사 hypodermic〔subcutaneous〕 injection — 주사기 a hypodermic injector〔syringe〕 — 주입〔이식〕 implantation — 지방 subcutaneous fat — 출혈 hypodermal bleeding —층 〖식물〗 the hypoderm ; the hypoderma — 투약 hypodermic medication
†피하다 避— ① [비키다·멀리하다] avoid 《the heat》; avert〔ward off〕 《danger》; keep〔stand〕 away from 《danger》; keep out of 《harm's way》; keep off 《evil》; shun (싫어서) ; dodge 《a car》; duck 《a blow》; escape 《danger, death, disaster》 ¶ 피할 수 없는 unavoidable ; inevitable // 길을 피하다 get out of the way // 나쁜 친구를 피하다 avoid〔keep aloof from〕 bad company // 날아오는 돌을 피하다 duck a stone thrown at one // 더위를 피하다 avoid the summer heat // 사람의 눈을 피하다 avoid〔avert〕 people's eyes ; avoid〔elude〕 observation 〔public notice〕 // 암초를 피하다 steer clear of a rock // 자동차를 피하다 dodge a car ; step aside from a car ; get out of the way of a car // 재난을 피하다 escape disaster〔mishap〕 // 죽음을 피하다 escape death ; be saved from death // 충돌을 피하다 head off the collision // 폭풍우를 피하다 take shelter〔get away〕 from a storm // 차는 길에 있는 동물을 피해서 갔다 The car sheered away from the animal in the road. // 한적한 뒷골목을 피하십시오 Stay away from lonely back streets.
② [피신] take refuge ⇨ 피신하다
③ [책임·의무를] shirk ; evade ; sidestep ; dodge 《a responsibility》; duck ¶ 답변을 피하다 evade an answer // 징병을 피하다 evade military service // 책임을 피하다 shirk one's responsibility
피한 避寒 wintering ; hibernation —하다 winter 《at, in》; pass〔spend〕 the winter 《at, in》; go to 《a place》 during〔for〕 the winter ; hibernate
—지 a winter resort ; winter quarters
피할 데 避— a refuge 《from danger》; a shelter 《from rain》; an escape (도망갈 구멍) ¶ 피할 데를 마련하다 leave room for retreat
*피해 被害 damage ; injury ; harm ; casualties ¶ 인축의 피해 casualties to men and beasts // 피해를 입다 be damaged 《by》; be injured 《by》 // 피해를 주다 damage ; do damage 《to》 // 피해를 면하다 be undamaged ; [물건이] be intact ; [사람이] escape injury // 피해가 심하다 be badly damaged ; be hard hit 《by》; much damage is inflicted 《on》 // 태풍의 피해는 광범위했다 The typhoon caused extensive〔widespread〕 damage.
— 망상 persecution mania ; a delusion of persecution — 범위 the extent of damage —액 the (amount of) damage —자 [재난의] a sufferer ; [도난 따위의] a victim ; the injured (party) (부상자)
피험자 被驗者 [실험의] a subject ; a testee

피혁 皮革 hides (and skins); leather (무두질한)
—공 a tanner — 공업 the leather industry —상 a dealer in hides and skins; a pelterer 인공 — artificial 〔man-made〕 leather 합성 — synthetic leather
피화 避禍 —하다 escape disaster 〔calamity〕; keep out of harm's way
피회하다 避廻— run about trying to escape; roam around escaping from the pursuer
피후견자 被後見者 a ward
픽 ① [쓰러지는 모양] ¶ 픽 쓰러지다 fall down feebly〔weakly〕 ② [웃는 모양] ¶ 픽 웃다 smile aimlessly ③ [새는 모양] ¶ 픽 소리내며 타이어의 바람이 빠졌다 Air hissed to escape from the tire.
픽션 (a) fiction
*픽업 a pickup
픽픽 ① [쓰러짐] all weakly; feebly ¶ 픽픽 쓰러지다 several fall down feebly ② [웃음] all smiling aimlessly ¶ 픽픽 웃다 several laugh listlessly
†핀 a pin ¶ (옷에) 핀을 지르다〔꽂다〕 pin up (a garment); fasten with a pin; pin 《a thing》 on〔to〕... ; get 《a thing》 fixed with a pin
넥타이— a tiepin; a scarf pin 머리— a hairpin 안전— a safety pin 압— a thumbtack 옷— a safety pin
핀둥거리다 ⇨ 빈둥거리다
핀들거리다 ⇨ 빈들거리다
핀란드 Finland ¶ 핀란드의 Finnish
— 말 Finnish — 사람 a Finn
핀볼 pinball
핀셋 a pincette (프); 《a pair of》 tweezers ¶ 핀셋으로 집다 hold〔pick up〕 《a thing》 with tweezers; tweeze
핀잔 a rebuke; chiding; a reprimand; scolding; snubbing; upbraiding; personal reproof〔remarks〕 —하다 rebuke; reprimand; scold; snub; chide; rate; upbraid; reprove 《a person》 to his face ¶ 핀잔을 맞다 be rebuked〔reprimanded, scolded, snubbed, chided, rated, upbraided〕
핀치 a pinch ¶ 핀치를 벗어나다 tide over a crisis // 핀치를 맞이하다 be thrown into a pinch〔fix〕
— 히터〔러너〕 〖야구〗 a pinch hitter 〔runner〕
핀트 ① [초점] a focus 《*pl.* ~es, -ci》 ¶ 핀트를 맞추다 focus one's camera on 《an object》; bring 《an object》 into focus; adjust the focus 《of a lens》 // 핀트가 맞다〔안맞다〕 be in〔out of〕 focus ② [요점] the point ¶ 핀트가 맞다 be to the point
필 匹 [마소의] a head ¶ 소 두 필 two head of cows
필 疋 a roll 《of cloth》 ¶ 무명 두 필 two rolls of cotton cloth // 필로 사다 buy 《it》 by the roll
필 畢 finished; done; completed —하다 finish; end; complete ¶ 학업을 필하다 complete〔finish〕 a school course; complete one's schooling // 지불필 "Paid."
필가 筆架 a writing-brush rack; a pen rack
필가 筆家 a calligrapher; a calligraphist; a penman
필갑 筆匣 a writing-brush case; a pen case
필견 必見 ¶ 필견의 명화다 The film is a 'must'.
필경 筆耕 copying; stencil-paper writing (등사판의) —하다 copy; stencil (등사)
—료(料) a copying fee —자 a copyist; a stenciler (등사판의) ⇨ 붓끝
필경 畢竟 after all; finally; in the end; in the long run ¶ 필경에 가서는 실력이 이긴다 Real ability will win in the end. // 필경에 가서는 그 여자와 결혼할 것이다 He will marry her after all.
필공 筆工 a writing-brush maker
필관 筆管 the stem of a writing brush
필기 筆記 taking notes; notes (필기한 것) —하다 take notes 《of》; write 〔note, put, jot〕 down ¶ 연설을 필기하다 take down a speech
— 시험 a written examination — 용지 writing paper —자 a copyist; a stenographer (속기사) —장 a notebook
필낭 筆囊 a bag for writing brushes
필누비 匹— quilting cloth
필단 筆端 ① [붓끝] the tip of the pen〔brush〕 ② [필세] a stroke of the pen〔brush〕
필담 筆談 conversation by writing —하다 talk by means of writing ¶ 말은 필담으로 하였다 The conversation was carried on in writing.
필답 筆答 a written answer〔reply〕; answering in writing —하다 answer in writing
— 시험 a written examination
필독 必讀 required reading; indispensable〔must〕 reading ¶ 필독의 책 a must book
—서 a must book ¶ 이것은 학생들의 필독서이다 This is a book every student must read.
필두 筆頭 ① [붓끝] the tip of a writing brush ② [연명의 첫째] the first on the list〔in a roll〕 ¶ 그의 이름이 필두에 올라 있다 His name heads〔tops〕 the list. / His name stands first on the list. ③ [우두머리] the head; senior
필드 〖경기〗 the field
— 경기 field sports — 종목 a field event
필딩 〖야구〗 fielding
필라델피아 Philadelphia

필라리아 〖동물〗 the filaria ⦅*pl.* ~e⦆
—병 〖의학〗 filarial disease
*필라멘트 〖전기〗 a filament
필력 筆力 the power of the pen 〔brush〕; a stroke〔dash〕 of the pen
필름 film ¶ 한 권의 필름 a reel〔spool〕 of film // 필름에 담다 film ⦅a scene⦆
필리핀 the Philippines ¶ 필리핀의 Philippine ; Filipino
— 공화국 the Republic of Commonwealth of the Philippines — 군도 the Philippine Islands ; the Philippines — 사람 a Filipino ⦅*pl.* ~s, *fem.* -na⦆
필마 匹馬 a single horse
— 단기 a solitary ride without servant — 단창 fighting alone
필멸 必滅 being doomed to perish ; 〖종교〗 annihilation ¶ 필멸의 perishable ; mortal ; doomed to decay
생자— All living things must die. /No birth without death.
필명 筆名 [명예] a name〔fame〕 as a calligrapher ; [이름] a pen name ; a nom de plume ⦅프⦆ ¶ 필명이 높다 be a famous calligrapher〔writer〕
필묵 筆墨 brush and Chinese ink ; pen and ink
필반자 匹— ① [평반자] a level ceiling ② [반지(紙)] ceiling paper in rolls
필법 筆法 [운필법] a style of penmanship ; the technique of calligraphy ; how to use the brush ; [문체] a style of writing ¶ 힘찬 필법 a powerful stroke of the brush // 춘추의 필법 the style of the Confucian Annals, the *Chunchu*
필봉 筆鋒 ① [붓끝] the tip of a writing brush ② [필력] the power〔force〕 of the pen ¶ 필봉이 날카롭다 be forcible〔sharp〕 in one's argument 〔style〕; the force of one's pen is sharp
필부 匹夫 [한 남자] a man ; an individual man ; [신분이 낮은 남자] an ordinary〔a common〕 man ; a man of lowly birth ¶ 필부 필부 humble men and women ; the populace ; common people ; Jack and Jill
—지용 foolhardiness
필부 匹婦 [한 여자] a woman ; an individual woman ; [신분이 낮은 여자] an ordinary〔a common〕 woman ; a woman of lowly birth
‡필사 必死 [꼭 죽음] inevitable death ; [목숨을 겲] desperation ¶ 필사적인 desperate ; frantic // 필사적으로 desperately ; in desperation ; frantically ; for one's life // 필사적 각오 preparedness for death // 필사 필중의 무기 the sure-death and sure-hitting arms // 필사적으로 노력하다 make desperate efforts // 필사적으로 헤엄치다〔달리다〕 swim〔run〕 for one's life
‡필사 筆寫 copying ; transcription —하다 copy ; transcribe
—자 the calligrapher
필산 筆算 calculation with figures ; ciphering —하다 calculate with figures ; cipher ; figure with pen〔pencil〕
필살 必殺 ¶ 필살의 일격 ⦅deal, deliver⦆ a deathblow ; a mortal blow ; a home thrust // 필살의 각오로 determined to bring sure death ⦅to⦆
필생 畢生 coexistence with life ¶ 필생의 lifelong // 필생의 노력 one's lifelong efforts // 필생의 사업 one's lifework // 필생의 역작〔걸작〕 one's magnum opus 〔masterpiece〕 // 필생의 힘을 다하다 do one's utmost ; make a supreme effort ⦅for⦆
필생 筆生 a stenciler (등사판의) ; a copyist
필석 筆石 〖고생물〗 a graptolite
필설 筆舌 brush and tongue ; writing and speech ¶ 필설로 다할 수 없다 be beyond words〔expression, description〕 // 그 참상〔경치의 장관〕은 필설로 다할 수 없다 The miserableness〔The grandeur of the spectacle〕 beggars 〔baffles〕 all description.
필세 筆勢 a stroke of the brush〔pen〕; the style of penmanship (필법) ; the power of the pen (필력)
필수 必須 essentiality ¶ 필수의 indispensable ; essential ; requisite ; necessary
— 과목 a required subject ; a compulsory course〔subject〕 — 조건 an indispensable〔essential〕 condition — 조항 a mandatory clause
†필수품 必需品 a necessary ; a necessity ; a requisite ; an essential
생활 — the necessaries〔necessities〕 of life ; living necessaries
필승 必勝 certain〔sure, unfailing〕 victory ¶ 필승의 신념 faith in certain victory ; the conviction of sure victory // 필승을 기하고 with a firm conviction of ultimate victory // 필승을 기하다 be sure 〔certain〕 of victory (자신) ; resolve to secure〔win, gain〕 a victory at any cost (각오)
필시 必是 certainly ; surely ; decidedly ; inevitably ; without doubt ¶ 필시 …이다 be certain〔sure〕 to ⦅do⦆ ⇨ 필연
필역 畢役 completion of construction work —하다 finish〔complete〕 a construction work
†필연 必然 ① necessity ; inevitability ② [필시·꼭] certainly ; surely ; decidedly ; inevitably ; without doubt ¶ 필연적인 necessary ; inevitable ; certain ; sure ; natural ; 〖논리〗 apodictic // 필연적인 결과로서 as a necessary〔an inevitable〕 consequence // 그것은 필연적인 결과이다 It follows as a logical〔nat-

ural〕 consequence. /It must of necessity be so.
—성 inevitability ; necessity 논리적〔물리적〕 — logical〔physical〕 necessity
필연 筆硯 pen and ink(-stone) ; [문필] literary work ¶ 필연을 벗삼다 be engaged in literary work
†필요 必要 necessity ; need ; requirement ; indispensability **—하다** (be) necessary ; needed ; needful ; requisite ; essential ; indispensable ¶ 필요 없는 unnecessary ; needless ; uncalled-for // 필요에 따라 as occasion demands〔arises, calls〕// 필요에 의해서 under the necessity《of》; from〔out of〕 necessity // 필요할 경우 in case of need〔necessity〕; if〔when〕 necessary ; if need be 《시》// …가〔이〕 필요하다 need ; be in need of ; require ; 《a thing》 be needed〔required〕// …에 필요하다 be necessary for〔to〕; be essential to〔for〕; be requisite to〔for〕// …할 필요가 있다 have got to 《do》《구》; have to 《do》《구》; must 《do》; need 《to do》// …할 필요가 없다 need not 《do》; do not have to 《do》; there is no need〔necessity〕 for〔of〕《something, doing》; it is unnecessary〔needless〕 to 《do》// 그는 그 지시를 따르는 것이 필요하다 It is necessary that he (should) follow the directions. /It is necessary for him to follow the directions. /He must follow the directions. // 그에게 두 번 말할 필요가 없었다 It was not necessary to tell him twice. / He didn't need to be told twice. // 필요하면 또 오겠다 I will come again if necessary. // 서두를 필요가 있습니까 Is there any need to hurry ? // 그는 불평을 할 필요가 없다 There is no necessity〔need〕 for him to complain. // 내가 그렇게 해야 할 필요가 어디 있습니까 What need have I to do so ? // 너는 좀 쉴 필요가 있다 You have need of〔to take〕 a rest. // 내가 오늘 올 필요가 있습니까 Need I come today ? // 내 시계는 수리할 필요가 있다 My watch needs〔wants〕 mending. // 그 일을 완성하는 데는 돈이 얼마나 필요한가 How much (money) is it necessary〔required〕 to complete the work ? // 그에게 필요 이상의 돈을 주지 마십시오 Don't give him more money than is necessary〔he needs〕. // 그는 조언이 필요하다 He is〔stands〕 in need of advice. /Someone should give him advice. // 어린이에게는 충분한 수면이 필요하다 Children must have plenty of sleep. // 어린이에게는 하루 9시간의 수면이 필요하다 A child requires nine hours' sleep a day. // 저 나무는 물이 필요하다 That tree wants water. // 가르치는 데는 인내가 필요하다 Patience is a requirement in teaching. // 책을 빌리려면 열람 카드가 필요하다 A library card is a requisite for taking out a book. // 이 병은 즉시 수술할 필요가 있다 This disease demands〔calls for〕 an immediate operation. // 이 집은 수리가 필요하다 This house is in want of repair. // 필요는 발명의 어머니 Necessity is the mother of invention. // 필요 앞에 법 없다 Necessity knows〔has〕 no law. // 우리는 그때그때 필요할 때마다 임시 직원을 채용한다 From time to time as the need arises, we take on part-time help.
—성 necessity —악 a necessary evil —조건 a necessary〔indispensable〕 condition ; a requirement ; a sine qua non 《라》 —품 an indispensable〔a necessary〕 article ; a necessity ; a requisite
필유곡절 必有曲折 There's a reason for everything.
†필자 筆者 the writer ; the author ¶ 이 글의 필자 the present writer
†필적 筆跡 [형적] a holograph ; a calligraphic specimen ; [솜씨] handwriting ; penmanship ; one's hand ¶ 여자의 필적 a feminine handwriting // 읽기 힘든 필적 an illegible hand (writing) // 필적이 좋다〔나쁘다〕 write a good〔poor, bad〕 hand // 필적을 모방하다 copy 《a person's》 hand // 필적을 감정하다 give an expert opinion on handwriting
— 감정 an analysis of a person's handwriting ; graphoanalysis
‡필적 匹敵 a rival ; a match ; an equal **—하다** equal ; rival ; be as good as ; be a match for ; can match ; be equal to ; compare with ; stand comparison with ¶ 필적할 자가 없다 have no equal〔match〕; be without a match〔peer〕; be unrivaled ; be peerless 〔matchless〕
필전 筆戰 paper warfare ; a paper battle ; a war of the pen **—하다** fight with one's pen
필주 筆誅 denunciation in writing ¶ 필주를 가하다 denounce 《a person》 in writing ; openly attack in a paper ; impeach with the pen
필중 必中 making certain to hit the target ¶ 일발 필중을 기하다 aim carefully so as to hit the target with the first shot
필지 必至 inevitability **—하다** be inevitable〔unavoidable〕; be sure to come
필지 必知 a must to know ; indispensable information
필진 筆陣 [포진] a maneuver in a battle by pen ; [진용] the writing staff ; a line up of the writers ¶ 필진을 펴다 set forth one's argument 《for, against》
필첩 筆帖 ① [필적집] specimens of handwriting
② [공책] a notebook

필촉 筆觸 a touch of a brush
필치 筆致 ① [필력] a stroke of the brush〔pen〕; a touch ¶ 그의 필치는 훌륭하다 The strokes of his brushes are fine. ② [문체] style ¶ 그의 필치는 경묘하고 원숙하다 His style is easy and well mellowed.
필터 [카메라의] a (color) filter ; [담배의] a filter tip ¶ 필터 달린 담배 a cigarette with a filter tip ; a filter-tip cigarette ; a tipped cigarette
자외선 — an ultraviolet filter
*필통 筆筒 a writing-brush case (붓갑) ; a pencil case (연필통) ; a writing-brush stand (붓통)
필하다 畢— finish ; complete ; end ; be 〔get〕 through ; make an end of ¶ 일을 필하다 finish〔complete〕 one's work
필하모닉 〖음악〗 philharmonic
필화 筆禍 a serious slip of the pen ¶ 필화를 입다 be indicted for one's writings
필휴 必携 indispensableness ; [안내서] a handbook ; a manual ¶ 학생 필휴의 책 a book indispensable to students
필히 必— [반드시] certainly ; surely ; [꼭] by all (manner of) means ; at any cost ¶ 필히 …하다 be sure〔certain〕 to 《do》; be bound to 《do》; never fail to 《do》
핌프 [뚜쟁이] a pimp ; a pander
핍근 逼近 approach —하다 approach ; draw near〔up, on〕; near ; gain upon ; be near〔close〕 at hand ; be imminent
핍박 逼迫 [궁핍] pressure 《for money》; stringency 《of money market》; tightness ; [급박] urgency ; [박해] persecution ; molestation —하다 become tight ; get stringent ; be urgent ; persecute ; molest ¶ 재정의 핍박 stiffened〔tight, difficult〕 financial conditions ; financial stringency〔pressure〕// 금융계가 핍박하다 The money market is stringent. /Money is close. /Money is tight.
핍쌀 hulled barnyard millet
핍재 乏材 a shortage of (men of) talent
핍진 逼眞 verisimilitude ; truthfulness to life —하다 (be) verisimilar ; be true to life ⇨ 박진(迫眞)
핏겨 the inner and outer husk of barnyard millet
핏골집 a kind of sausage
*핏기 —氣 the color of the skin〔face〕; complexion ¶ 핏기가 없다 have a bad complexion ; look pale〔sallow, unwell〕
핏대 a blood vessel ; a vein
핏대를 올리다 관용 have one's blood up ; be furious with anger ; get red-hot with anger
*핏덩어리 ① a clot of blood ; a blood clot ② [갓난아이] a newborn baby
핏발 congestion ; a bloodshot condition ¶ 핏발 선 눈 bloodshot eyes
핏발이 서다 관용 be bloodshot ; be congested
핏빛 blood red ¶ 핏빛으로 물들다 be dyed in blood red
핏자국 a blood stain ; a mark of blood ¶ 핏자국이 묻은 bloodstained
핏줄 ① [혈관] a vein ; a blood vessel ② [혈통] blood ; blood relation ; stock ; lineage ; a family line ¶ 핏줄을 받다 be related by blood ; be of the same blood // 핏줄이 끊어졌다 The line has died out. // 핏줄은 속일 수 없다 Heredity will out. /Blood is thicker than water.
핑 ① [도는 모양] round ; circling ¶ 핑 돌다 turn round ; circle ② [둘러싸는 모양] around ; surrounding ¶ 핑 둘러서다 《people》 stand around in a circle ③ [현기증] dizzy ; giddy ¶ 머리가 핑 돌다 get dizzy〔giddy〕
핑거 볼 a finger bowl ¶ 핑거 볼에 손을 씻다 rinse one's finger tips in a finger bowl
*핑계 excuse ; apology ; [구실] a pretext ; a plea —하다 make an excuse 《of》; offer as a pretext ; offer an apology ¶ 핑계로 by way of excuse // 아프다는 핑계로 on the pretext〔under the pretense, with a plea〕 of illness // 자선을 핑계삼아 under the cloak of charity // 몰랐다고〔아프다고〕 핑계하다 plead ignorance〔illness〕// 그것은 핑계에 불과하다 That is only pretext. // 또 그 핑계인가 The same old excuse ! // 그는 병을 핑계삼아 일을 쉬고 싶어한다 He wants excused from his work under the pretext of ill health.
게으른 여편네 아이 핑계 대듯 속담 Idle folks lack no excuses.
핑구 a toy top with a small knob at the top
핑그르르 around smoothly ¶ 팽이가 핑그르르 돌다 a top spins
핑글핑글 round and round smoothly ¶ 핑글핑글 돌다 turn round and round ; circle ; spin // 방이 핑글핑글 도는 것 같았다 The room seemed to spin round.
핑크 pink
— 무드 an amorous mood
핑퐁 ping-pong ; table tennis ¶ 핑퐁을 치다 play ping-pong
—대 a ping-pong table
핑핑 round and round ; quickly ¶ 핑핑 돌다 [몸이] turn〔revolve〕 rapidly ; spin ; twirl ; whirl ; spin oneself round and round ; [눈이] feel dizzy〔giddy〕
핑핑하다 ① [꽉 켕기다] (be) tight ; taut ; tense ¶ 핑핑하게 tightly ; tautly // 줄을 핑핑히 당기다 stretch a rope tight 〔taut〕 ② [우열이 없다] (be) even

《with》; equal 《to》; evenly〔equally〕 matched ¶ 핑핑한 경주 a close contest; a level race // 둘은 힘이 서로 핑핑하다 The two are evenly matched in strength〔force〕. ③ [팽창하다] be swollen hard; (be) bloated; bulging (out); baggy; big ¶ 핑핑하게 to the full; hard // 너무 먹어서 핑핑해진 소 a cow bloated with overeating

핑핑히 ① [팽팽히] tautly; tightly ¶ 줄을 핑핑히 당기다 stretch a rope taut〔tight〕 ② [딴딴히] hard; powerfully ¶ 핑핑히 붓다 swell up hard

ㅎ

하¹ [하도] very ; much ; extremely ; hard ; awfully ¶ 하 비싸다 be very expensive // 하 졸라대다 tease hard for 《a thing》 // 하 피곤하다 be very tired

하² [입김] with a hot wet breath ¶ 하 하다 breathe on 《a thing》 to dampen〔wet〕 it

하³ [감탄·웃음] Ha ! /Aha !

하 下 ① [하등] the low class〔grade〕 ¶ 하의 하 the lowest〔worst〕 of its kind ; the lowest of the low ; the poorest 〔worst〕 of all // 상하의 구별 없이 both high and low // 평균보다 하다 be below the average

② [아래] below ; under ; underneath ¶ 일격하에 at a blow // 감독〔지휘〕 하에 under the supervision〔baton, direction〕 《of》 // 하와 같다 be as follows // 일언지하에 거절하다 refuse flatly

③ [하권] the last volume

하가 何暇 ¶ 하가에 in what spare 〔leisure〕 time // 어느 하가에 책을 읽나 When would I find time for reading ?

하가 下嫁 the marriage of a princess to someone of lower rank

하감 下疳 a chancre

경성 — a hard chancre 연성 — a soft chancre

하감 下瞰 —하다 look down 《upon》 ; take a bird's-eye view 《of》 ; command a view 《of》

—도 a bird's-eye view ; an air view

하감하다 下鑑— read an inferior's letter ; read a letter submitted (by an inferior) ; kindly peruse

하갑개골 下甲介骨 〖해부〗 the turbinate 〔turbinal〕 (bone) ; the nasal concha

하강 下降 descent ; a fall ; a drop ; a decline (경기의) ; subsidence (함몰)

—하다 descend ; fall ; drop ; go〔come〕 down ; subside ; sink ¶ 기온의 하강 a drop in temperature // 선녀가 하강하다 a fairy descends into the world // 기온이 화씨 30°로 하강했다 The thermometer dropped to 30° F.

하객 賀客 a well-wisher ; a congratulator

†-하게하다 ① [원인이 되다] cause it to be ; cause 《a person to do》 ② [시키다] have 《a person do》 ; get 《a person to do》 ; have〔get〕 《a thing done by a person》

하계 夏季 the summer season ; summer

하계 下界 [현세] the lower world ; this world ; [지상] the earth ¶ 하계의 sublunary ; mundane ; earthly ; temporal // 하계의 일 mundane〔worldly〕 affairs // 이 하계에서는 here below // 하계를 내려다보다 look down upon the earth

하계 下計 the worst〔poorest〕 plan

하고 [및] and ; [함께] with ; along with ; [대해서] against ¶ 아버지하고 나 father and I // 적하고 싸우다 fight against the enemy // 그녀는 그 사람하고 결혼했다 She married him. /She was married to him.

하고많다 (be) plenty ; plentiful ; abundant ; innumerable ; numerous ¶ 이것은 하고많은 것 중에서 그 일례에 불과하다 This is merely an instance among the many. // 하고많은 사람들이 대통령을 전송하러 공항으로 갔다 So large crowds of people went to the airport to see the president off.

하곡 夏穀 summer crops ; wheat and barley

— 수매가(收買價) the barley purchasing price

-하곤 하다 make a habit〔practice〕 of 《doing》 ; do from time to time ; sometimes do ; used to do ; would do

하관 下官 a lower〔subordinate〕 official ; a junior〔petty, minor〕 official

하관 下棺 —하다 lower a coffin into the grave

하관 下觀 the lower part of the face ; the jaw (area)

하관(이) 빨다 관용 have a pointed jaw

하교 下敎 ① [전교] an order from the king ; a royal command ② [교시] an instruction〔order〕 from a superior

하구 河口 the mouth of a river ; a river-mouth ; an estuary

—항 an estuary harbor

하국 夏菊 〖식물〗 an elecampane ; Inula britanica (학명)

하권 下卷 the last volume ; the second volume (두 권 중의) ; the third volume (세 권 중의)

하극상 下剋上 the lower dominating the upper ; overpowering of seniors by juniors ; The tail wags the dog.

*하급 下級 a low(er) class〔grade〕 ¶ 하급의 low-class ; lower ; junior ; inferior // 하급으로 격하시키다 reduce to a lower grade ; degrade ; demote 《미》

— 관리 a low-grade government clerk ; a petty〔minor, subordinate, low-ranking〕 official — 관청 a subordinate office — 노동자 a low-class laborer —반 a lower class ; an under class — 법원 a lower〔lesser, an inferior〕 court — 사원 the lower grade personnel of a company — 산화물 〖화학〗 suboxide —생 a lower-class student 〔boy, girl〕 ; an underclassman 《미》 — 선원 petty crewmen ; sailors and stokers —자 a subordinate ; a lower-grade personnel — 장교 a junior officer — 재판소 a lower〔an inferior〕 court — 직원 the lower-grade personnel of a government〔public〕 office —품 lower-grade goods

하기 下記 ¶ 하기의 the following ; what is mentioned below ; stated below // 하기와 같이 as follows ; as in the following // 하기 상품을 보내주십시오 Please send us the undermentioned articles.
— 사항 the following items — 상품〔예문〕 articles〔examples〕 enumerated hereunder

하기 夏期 summer ; summer time ; the summer season
— 강습회 a summer school — 강좌 a summer lecture course — 방학 the summer vacation (from school) — 연습장 a workbook for the summer vacation ; a summer drill〔exercise〕 book — 학기 a summer session — 휴가 a summer vacation ; the summer holidays

하기는 in fact ; in truth ; indeed ¶ 하기는 그것이 틀림없다 Really it must be so. // 하기는 그래 It's a fact. /Yes, you are quite right.

하기식 下旗式 a flag-lowering ceremony ; 〖군사〗 a retreat
— 나팔 a retreat

하기야 indeed ; definitely ¶ 하기야 내가 잘못일지도 모르지 I may, in fact, be wrong.

†하나[1] ① 〔한 개〕 one ; one thing ; a unit ¶ 하나의 one ; single (단일의) ; only ; sole ; unique (유일의) // 단 하나 a single ; only one // 하나 하나 one by one ; one at a time ; piece by piece ; separately // 사과 하나 an apple // 비누 하나 a cake〔bar〕 of soap // 하나로 되어 in a body ; in perfect harmony ; in efficient teamwork // 하나도 남김 없이 without exception ; to the very last // 하나에서 열까지 from beginning to end ; everything // 하나로 만들다 unite〔make〕 into one // 하나로 되다 become one ; be united ; unite (together) // 그것은 하나에 100원입니다 It is a hundred *won* each〔a piece〕. // 그는 제 이름 하나 쓸 줄 모른다 He can't even〔so much as〕 write his own name. // 하늘에는 구름 하나 없었다 There was not a single (speck of) cloud in the sky. // 하나는 녹색이고 또 하나는 빨강이다 One is green and the other (is) red. // 그것을 할 수 있는 방법은 하나밖에 없다 There is only one way to do〔doing〕 it. // 사업의 성공 여부는 너의 노력 하나에 달려 있다 Your success in your undertaking depends solely upon your efforts. // 실수를 하나만 덜했어도 되는 건데 I made one too many mistakes.
② 〔동일한〕 the same ; one and the same ¶ 한 하숙에 in the same boarding house // 우리 생각은 하나다 Our ideas are the same.
③ 〔한번〕 once ; just ¶ 하나 부탁할게 있소 I want to ask you just a little favor.

하나[2] however ; but ; yet

하나님 God ⇨ 하느님

하나하나 one by one ; one at a time ; piece by piece ; 〔개별적으로〕 individually ; separately

하녀 下女 a main(-servant) ; a domestic(-servant)

하념 下念 gracious consideration ; care ; concern —하다 give gracious consideration to ; care for ; be concerned for

†하느님 God ; the Lord ; Providence ; the Almighty ; the Supreme Being ; the Creator ; the Divinity ; Allah (회교의) ¶ 하느님의 은혜 the grace of God ; divine blessing // 하느님을 믿다 believe in God // 하느님께 빌다 pray to God 《for》 // 하느님께 맹세하다 swear by god // 하느님 맙소사 Heaven forbid !

하느작거리다 flutter ; quiver ; tremble

하는 수 없이 unavoidably ; inevitably ; for lack of anything better ; reluctantly ; unwillingly ¶ 하는 수 없이 …하다 be obliged〔compelled, forced〕 to 《do》

†하늘 ① the sky ; the heavens ; the air ¶ 맑은 하늘 a clear〔bright, serene〕 sky // 흐린 하늘 a cloudy sky // 비가 올 듯한 하늘 a watery sky // 하늘을 나는 새 birds of the air ; birds on the wing // 하늘 높이 high up in the sky ; aloft in the air // 하늘의 용사 an air hero ; a hero〔an ace〕 of the air // 하늘의 요새 a flying fortress // 변화가 심한 가을 하늘 the fickle weather of autumn // 하늘을 날다 fly through the sky // 하늘로 날아오르다 soar up to the sky ; soar skyward // 하늘은 구름으로 덮여 있었다 The sky was blotted out by clouds. /The sky was overspread with clouds. // 환성이 하늘을 찔렀다 Shouts of joy rent the sky. /The sky resounded with rejoicing. // 하늘을 보니 당장이라도 소나기가 올 것 같다 From the look of the sky, I'd say we're due for a shower in any minute.
② 〔천당〕 Heaven ¶ 하늘에 계신 아버지 our Father which art in Heaven
③ 〔섭리〕 Heaven ; Providence ; 〔하느님〕 God ¶ 하늘이 주신 god-given // 하

ㅎ

늘을 원망하다 quarrel with Providence // 하늘을 두려워 하다 fear god // 하늘의 도움을 빌다 call upon Heaven for help
—나라 (the kingdom of) Heaven ; Paradise ; Elysium (천당) **—빛** sky blue ; sky-blue color ; azure ¶ 하늘빛의 sky-blue ; azure
하늘이 무너져도 솟아날 구멍이 있다 속담 There is a way out of every situation, however bad. /If it were not for hope the heart would break.
하늘은 스스로 돕는 자를 돕는다 속담 Heaven helps those who help themselves.
하늘보고 침 뱉기 속담 Who spits against the heaven〔the wind〕, it falls in his face.
하늘에 돌 던지는 격 속담 An arrow shot upright falls on the shooter's head.

하늘가재 〖곤충〗 a (kind of) beetle

하늘거리다 sway ; swing ; tremble ; waver ; quiver ; flicker ; flare

하늘나리 〖식물〗 a morningstar lily

하늘다람쥐 〖동물〗 a flying squirrel ; Petaurista leucogenys hintoni (학명)

하늘박쥐 〖동물〗 a (kind of) bat

하늘밥도둑 〖곤충〗 a mole-cricket ; Gryllotalpa africana (학명)

하늘소 〖곤충〗 a long-horned beetle ; a cerambysid ; a long-corn (beetle)

하늘지기 〖식물〗 a (kind of) sedge

하늘하늘 ① [가볍게] lightly ; buoyantly ; in a light〔an airy〕 manner
② [촉감] **—하다** (be) soft ; spongy ; fluffy

하늬(바람) a west wind

†**하다**[1] ① [행하다] do ; act ; make practice ; try ¶ 일을 하다 work ; do a job // 공부를 하다 study ; work // 가려고 하다 try to go // 영어를 하다 speak English // 어리석은 짓을 하다 do a silly thing // 만날 약속을 하다 make an appointment // 동창회를 하다 hold an alumni meeting // 경솔한 짓을 하다 act rashly // 나쁜 짓을 하다 commit a crime // 자살을 하다 commit suicide // 할 수 있다 be able to do ; be feasible // 할 수 없다 be unable to do ; be infeasible // 운동을 하다 take exercises // 야구를 하다 play baseball // 그 돈을 어떻게 할 작정이오 What are you going to do with the money ? // 무엇이든 할 바에는 훌륭히 하라 Whatever you do, do it well. // 하라는 대로 해라 안 그러면 좋지 않다 Do what I say, or else. // 나는 한번 한다 하면 반드시 하는 사람이다 When I say I will do it, I mean business.
② [삼다] make ¶ 양자로 하다 adopt a child // 부하로 하다 place 《a person》 under one's orders // 그 여자를 아내로 하다 make the woman one's wife
③ [종사하다] be engaged in ; [노릇하다] act〔serve〕 as ¶ 무역업을 하다 be engaged in foreign trade // 종노릇 하다 serve as a slave // 안내역을 하다 act as guide // 중매를 하다 act as go-between // 의사 노릇을 하다 practice medicine // 책방을 하다 keep〔run〕 a bookstore // 공무원 노릇을 하다 work as an official // 경관〔선생〕을 하다 be a policeman〔teacher〕 // 식모를 하다 serve as (a) maid // 놀부역을 하다 play (the role of) *Nolbu*
④ [경험하다] experience ; go〔come〕 through ; undergo ¶ 고생을 하다 undergo hardship // 우리 가족은 모두 해외 생활을 한 바 있다 My family have all lived abroad.
⑤ [비용이 들다] cost ; be worth ; be valued ¶ 10만원 하는 시계 a watch (which is) worth 100,000 *won* // 사과 한 개에 500원 한다 The apples are 500 *won* each. // 그것은 얼마 합니까 How much did it cost (you) ? /How much did you pay〔give〕 for it ?
⑥ [음식을] eat ; take ; have ; drink (마시다) ; smoke (피우다) ¶ 점심을 하다 have lunch // 그는 술도 담배도 하지 않는다 He neither drinks nor smokes.
⑦ [착용하다] wear ; be wearing ; have on ; be dressed ¶ 귀걸이를 하다 wear earmuffs // 거지 같은 차림을 하고 있다 be dressed like a beggar
⑧ [말하다] say ; talk ; speak ; remark ¶ 지금 뭐라고 했니 What did you say just now ?
⑨ [부르다] call ; name ¶ 그 개는 존이라고 한다 The dog is called John. // 하와이는 흔히 태평양의 낙원이라고 한다 Hawaii is often referred to as the Paradise of the Pacific.

하다[2] [매우] be quite ; be indeed ¶ 많기도 하다 be numerous indeed

†**-하다** [접미사] ¶ 사랑하다 love ; like ; be fond of // 공부하다 study // 결혼하다 get married // 분주하다 be busy (with one's work) // 기뻐하다 be glad ; be pleased 《with》

하다못해 go so far as to (do) ; be driven by dire necessity to (do) ; unavoidably ; inevitably ; from necessity ; at one's wit's end ; at the least ; at the extreme〔end, limit〕 ; finally ; at last ; it ended in ¶ 좋아서 한 노릇이 아니라 하다못해 한 짓이다 I did it of necessity, not of choice. // 하다못해 그만두고 말았다 It ended in my giving it up. // 하다못해 그에게 1,000원을 주었다 Finally I gave him 1,000 *won*. // 입씨름을 하다못해 나중에는 서로 치고 받고 했다 The quarrel ended in their coming to blow.

하단 下段 ① [글의] a lower column〔line〕 ② [하층] a lower step〔tier〕 ; a lower berth

ㅎ

하단 下端 the lower end 《of a pole》; [페이지·서적의] the tail
하단 下壇 **—하다** leave〔go down, descend from〕 the platform〔pulpit〕
하달 下達 a command; orders; a mandate **—하다** command; order; give〔deliver〕 orders; convey to the people ¶ 상의 하달 conveying the will and ideas of those governing to those who are governed
하답 下答 **—하다** answer〔reply〕 《to one's inferior》; give an answer〔a reply〕 《to one's inferior》
하대 下待 contemptuous〔scornful〕 treatment; disrespectful〔icy〕 treatment; inhospitable〔cold〕 reception; frigid reception **—하다** treat contemptuously; give a cold reception; receive 《a person》 with indifference; be inhospitable to ¶ 하대받다 be treated contemptuously; meet with harsh usage; get a cold reception
하도 too much; excessively; very much; so hard; remarkably; greatly; immensely; terribly ¶ 이 책은 하도 어려워서 못 읽겠다 This book is too difficult for me to read.
하도롱지 —紙 brown wrapping-paper
하돈 河豚 『물고기』 a swellfish; a globe fish; a puffer
하동거리다 ⇨ 허둥거리다
하등 下等 [열등] inferiority; [하급] a lower class〔grade〕; [질이] coarseness; [상스럼] bad form〔taste〕; vulgarity ¶ 하등의 low; inferior; coarse; vulgar; in bad taste // 하등 석탄 low class coal; coal of inferior quality // 하등 취미 a plebeian〔bad〕 taste
— 동물 the lower animals **— 사회** the lower classes; the lower order of society **— 선객** a steerage passenger **— 식물** the plants of a lower order **—품** an article of inferior quality; an inferior article
하등 何等 (not) in the slightest degree; (not) in any way; (not) at all; (nothing) whatever ¶ 하등의 이유도 없이 without any reason; for naught // 하등의 관계가 없다 have no connection whatever; have nothing to do with it // 하등의 수입이 안된다 bring nothing in // 그에게 하등 도움이 되는 것이 없다 It will get him nowhere.
†**하락** 下落 [가격의] a fall〔drop, decline〕 《in price》; depreciation; a slump (폭락); [품질의] deterioration; degradation; sag; sink; degrade **—하다** fall (off); decline; drop; come down ¶ 달러의 하락 the fall〔depreciation〕 of the dollar // 물가는 하락의 경향이 있다 Prices are coming down〔showing a downward tendency〕. /Things are dropping in prices. // 주가가 하락하고 있다 The stocks are quoted low.
— 경향〔세〕 a downward movement; a falling tendency
하략 下略 the rest omitted; omitted below; omission from here on; the concluding part omitted **—하다** omit the rest
하량 下諒 **—하다** condescend to take note of; consider; look upon; take into consideration ¶ 사정이 이러하오니 하량하소서 Such being the case, I beg you will kindly excuse me〔sympathize with my situation〕.
-하러 to 《do》; in order to 《do》; for the purpose of ¶ 나는 일하러 간다 I am going to work.
하렘 [회교의] a harem; [처첩] concubines; [규중] women's quarters
하려 下慮 gracious consideration ⇨ 하념
하령회 夏令會 『기독교』 a summer church conference; a summer religious retreat
하례 下隷 a male slave〔servant〕
하례 賀禮 a congratulatory ceremony; a celebration **—하다** hold a congratulatory ceremony; celebrate; congratulate
하로동선 夏爐冬扇 useless things (as the fireplace in summer and the fan in winter)
하롱거리다 act〔behave〕 rashly〔carelessly〕; be flippant; be frivolous; be light; take a rash step; act on impulse
하롱하롱 rashly; carelessly; flippantly ¶ 하롱하롱 까불다 behave flippantly〔lightly〕
하료 下僚 [부하] one's subordinates; [하급 관리] a petty official
†**하루** ① a〔one〕 day; the daytime (밤에 대해) ¶ 하루 세 번 three times a day // 하루에 per diem 《라》; per day; a day // 하루 이틀에 in a day or two; in a few days // 하루 걸러 every other〔second〕 day; on alternate days // 하루 종일 all day (long); all through the day; the whole day; from morning to〔till〕 night // 단 하루 one〔a single〕 day // 하루 일 a day's work // 하루 여덟 시간 eight hours a day // 하루하루 day after〔by〕 day // 하루 세 끼 먹는다 We usually take three meals a day. // 하루 종일 비가 왔다 It rained all day long. // 어제는 하루 종일 너를 기다렸다 I waited for you the whole of〔all day long〕 yesterday. // 로마는 하루 사이에 이루어지지 않았다 Rome was not built in a day. // 하루 종일 질질 끌 셈이냐 We haven't got all day.
② [어느날] ¶ 하루는 one day; someday
하루갈이 the size of field or paddy that takes a day's plowing
하루거리 tertian malarial fever
하루바삐 as soon as possible ¶ 하루바

ㅎ

빼 하다 lose no time in doing 《a thing》// 하루바삐 회복되시기를 빕니다 I pray for your earliest possible recovery.

하루살이 『곤충』 a day-fly ; a May-fly ; a shad-fly ; an ephemera ¶ 하루살이 같은 인생 this ephemeral life〔existence〕

하루아침 one morning ¶ 하루아침에 one morning all of a sudden ; overnight ; suddenly ; in a (single) day ; in a brief interval〔space of time〕// 하루아침에 부자가 되다 wake up to find oneself suddenly rich // 그것은 하루아침에 되지 않는다 It is not to be done in a day. // 대사업은 하루아침에 이루어지는 것이 아니다 Rome was not built in a day.

하루치 one day's portion ; rations ¶ 하루치의 배급량 a day's ration

***하루하루** day after day ; day by day ; one day after another ¶ 하루하루 추워진다 It is getting colder day by day. // 일을 하루하루 끌었다 He kept on putting off the task from day to day.

하룻강아지 a (one-day-old) puppy
하룻강아지 범 무서운 줄 모른다 속담 An ignorant person doesn't stand in awe of the great. /Fools rush in where angels fear to tread.

하룻날 [초하루] the first day 《of a month》; [어느 날] one day ; a certain day

하룻밤 one〔a〕 night ; [밤새] all night ; all the night through ; overnight ¶ 하룻밤 사이에 in a single night // 하룻밤을 자다 stop overnight ; put up for the night // 하룻밤을 보내다 pass a night 《in, at》; sit up all night

하류 下流 ① [하천의] the downstream ; the lower courses〔reaches, part〕 of a stream ; the lower ¶ 한강 하류에 on the lower *Han* river // 3마일 하류에 한 마을이 있다 There is a village three miles downstream.
② [사회의] a lower social stratum
— **계급** the lower classes — **사회** the lower classes ; the lower order〔stratum〕 of society — **생활** (a) low life

하류 河流 a stream

하륙 下陸 landing ; unloading ; disembarkment — **하다** land 《cargo》; disembark (군대 따위가) ; discharge ; unload 《a ship》

하르르 — **하다** (be) flimsy ⇨ 흐르르

하릅 a one-year-old horse〔ox〕; a yearling
— **송아지** a year-old calf

하리놀다 calumniate ; slander ; libel ; defame ; abuse ; speak ill of 《a person》

하리다[1] (be) stupid ; silly ⇨ 흐리다

하리다[2] [사치하다] indulge in luxury ; luxuriate ; be extravagant ¶ 옷에 하리다 be extravagant in one's clothes // 음식에 하리다 luxuriate〔wallow〕 in food

하리들다 be crossed ; suffer from a cross ; get thwarted ; get interfered ¶ 계획에 하리들다 be crossed〔suffer from a cross〕 in one's plan

하리망당하다 (be) vague 《in memory》 ⇨ 흐리멍덩하다

하리타분하다 ⇨ 흐리터분하다

하릴없다 ① [불가피하다] (be) unavoidable ; inevitable ; helpless ; cannot be helped ; there is no help for it ; nothing can be done about it ¶ 하릴없이 unavoidably ; inevitably ; without choice ; helplessly ; with no other course // 달리 하릴없다 There is no other way〔alternative〕 left to me.
② [틀림없다] (be) correct ; perfect ; precise ¶ 하릴없이 precisely ; correctly ; unmistakably

하릴없이 unavoidably ; inevitably ; inescapably ; without choice〔alternative〕; helplessly ; against one's will ¶ 하릴없이 …하다 be obliged〔compelled〕 to 《do》

하림하다 下臨— ① [귀인 내방] condescend to come ; come ; visit ② [강림] a deity descends 《upon》

하마 下馬 dismounting 《from a horse》; getting off a horse — **하다** dismount 《from a horse》; get off a horse ; alight from a horse
—**비** a stone tablet indicating that one should dismount from a horse ; a notice requiring riders to dismount —**석** a stepping stone used in mounting or dismounting —**평** an outsider's irresponsible talk ; rumor ; hearsay

하마 河馬 『동물』 a hippopotamus 《*pl.* ~es, -mi》; a hippo 《속》; a riverhorse

***하마터면** [거의] nearly ; almost ; [간신히] barely ; narrowly ; by a hair's breadth ¶ 하마터면 물에 빠질 뻔했다 I was nearly drowned. /I came very near being drowned. // 하마터면 죽을 것을 살았다 I was saved from death by a hair's breadth. // 하마터면 차에 칠 뻔했다 I narrowly missed being run over.

하마평 下馬評 an outsider's irresponsible talk ; gossip ; an advance rumor

하마하마 《opportunities, perils》 impending one after another

하면 夏眠 (a) estivation — **하다** (a) estivate

하명 下命 [명령] an order from above ; a command ; [주문] an order — **하다** order ; give〔deliver〕 an order ; command ¶ 하명을 바랍니다 We solicit your orders.

하모니 harmony

하모니카 『악기』 a harmonica ¶ 하모니카를 불다 play the harmonica

하묘 下錨 anchoring ; mooring ; dropping anchor — **하다** drop〔cast〕

anchor ; anchor ; moor ¶ 하묘중이다 be at anchor
—지 an anchorage
하문 下門 the vulva ; the vagina
하문하다 下問— ask ; inquire ; consult ; seek counsel of 《one's underling》 ¶ 불치(不恥) 하문하다 be not ashamed to seek counsel of an inferior
하물 荷物 luggage 《영》; baggage 《미》; freight ; cargo ; merchandise
—간 a cargo compartment —선 a cargo ship ; a freighter —차 a freight car
*하물며 [긍정] much〔still〕 more ; [부정] much〔still〕 less ; not to speak of ; to say nothing of ¶ 그는 영작을 잘 한다 하물며 읽는데 있어서야 He can write English well, much more can he read it. // 그는 경제학도 잘 모른다 하물며 케인즈에 있어서야 He knows little economics, much less Keynes. // 대수나 기하도 잘 모른다 하물며 미적분에 있어서야 He does not know algebra or geometry, to say nothing of calculus.
하미 下米 low-grade rice ; rice of inferior quality
하민 下民 the common people ; lower class people ; the masses
하바네라 〖음악〗 (a) habanera
하바로프스크 Khabarovsk
하박 下膊 〖해부〗 the forearm ; the antebrachium
—골 forearm bones ; the radius and the ulna
하박하박하다 ⇨ 허벅허벅하다
하반 河畔 the banks of a river ; the riverbank ¶ 하반의 《a hotel, a villa》 by the riverside
하반 下半 the latter half ; the lower half
—기 the second〔latter〕 half of the year —신 the lower half of one's body
하백 河伯 the God of water
하번 下番 relief from〔going off〕 duty 〔guard〕; one who comes off duty —하다 be relieved from duty ; go〔be〕 off duty
하복 下腹 the lower part of the belly ; the abdomen ¶ 하복의 abdominal // 하복이 아프다 have〔feel〕 pain in the abdomen
—부 abdominal region
하복 夏服 summer clothes〔uniform〕; (clothes for) summer wear
하부 下付 granting ; a grant ; issue —하다 grant ; give ; issue ¶ 면허를 하부하다 issue a license〔permit〕
—금 a grant ; a subsidy ; a bounty
하부 下部 the lower part ; the lower part of the body (아랫동이)
— 기관 a subordinate office〔agency〕
— 조직 a substructure ; a lower branch of an organization ; a subordinate〔subsidiary〕 organization

하분하분하다 (be) soft and juicy
하비 下婢 a maidservant ⇨ 하녀
하비다 ① [할퀴다] scratch ; claw ; maul ② [헐뜯다] find fault 《with》; speak ill of ③ ⇨ 후비다
하뿔사 O my ! ⇨ 아뿔싸
*하사 下賜 a Royal〔an Imperial〕 gift 〔grant〕 —하다 give ; grant ; bestow ; donate ¶ 폐하께서 금일봉을 하사하셨다 The Emperor granted a monetary gift.
—금 an Imperial grant〔bounty〕 —품 an Imperial gift
하사 何事 anything ; everything ; something ; what matter ¶ 하사를 막론하고 in all matters ; in everything // 정신일도 하사 불성 Where there is a will, there is a way.
하사 下司 a lower post ; a subordinate office〔agency〕
하사 下士 a staff sergeant ; [해군] a petty officer second class
하사 賀詞, 賀辭 ⇨ 축사(祝辭)
*하사관 下士官 [육군] a noncommissioned officer ; a non-com 《미·구》; [해군] a petty officer
하산 下山 a descent from a mountain
—하다 descend〔go down, climb down〕 a mountain ; go〔come〕 downhill
하상 河床 a river bed
하서 下書 a letter (from a superior)
하선 下船 leaving (a) ship ; getting off a ship —하다 leave〔get off〕 a ship ; disembark ; go ashore
하선 下線 an underline ¶ 하선 친 부분 the underlined part // 하선을 긋다 underline
하선 荷船 a cargo boat ; a lighter ; a freighter ; a barge ; a tramp-boat
하세 下世 passing away ; death ; demise ; seclusion from society —하다 (an esteemed person) pass away ; die ; retire from society ; go to live in seclusion
*하소연 an appeal ; a petition ; a complaint —하다 appeal to 《a person》; supplicate ; complain of ; confide in ¶ 고통을 하소연하다 complain of pain // 억울함을 하소연하다 complain of an injustice // 서러운 사정을 하소연하다 plead one's grievous situation // 동정해 달라고 하소연하다 appeal to 《a person》 for his sympathy
*하수 下水 foul water ; sewage
—관 a drain pipe ; a sewer pipe —구(口) a sink-hole ; an outfall ; a gully hole —구(溝) a drain ; a sewer ; a ditch ; a gutter —도 a drainage〔sewerage〕 system ; a drain ¶ 하수도를 치다 clean〔scour〕 a drain // 하수도를 만들다 lay out a drain —도 공사 drainage 〔sewerage〕 works — 정화 sewage purification — 처리장 a sewage disposal〔treatment〕 plant

ㅎ

하수 下手 ① [솜씨가 못함] unskillfulness ; awkwardness ; being clumsy ; lack of talent ; a poor hand
② [살인] **—하다** murder ; lay 《murderous》 hands on
③ [착수] **—하다** start〔set〕 to work ; launch ; lay hold of
—인 the perpetrator of 《a crime》 ; a culprit ; a murderer ; the slayer ¶ 폭행의 하수인을 찾다 trace the outrage home to its perpetrator
하수 下垂 drooping ; nutation (눈꺼풀의) **—증(症)** [눈꺼풀의] ptosis **뇌—체** the pituitary body **위—증** gastroptosis
하수 河水 river water
***하숙 下宿** boarding ; lodging ; board and lodging ; board and room 《미》 **—하다** lodge ; board ; take up one's quarters 〔lodgings〕 ¶ 하숙 생활을 하다 live in lodgings〔a lodging house〕// 하숙을 옮기다 change one's lodgings // 하숙을 치다 run〔operate, keep〕 a lodging house // 나는 김씨집에 하숙하고 있다 I board with Mr. *Kim*〔at Mr. *Kim's* house〕.
—방 a rented room ; a room for rent **—비** the charge for board and lodging ; board charge **—생** a student boarder **—인** a lodger ; a boarder ; a paying guest ; a board resident ; a roomer 《미》 **—집** (one's) lodgings ; a lodging〔boarding〕 house ; a rooming house 《미》
하순 下旬 the last〔the closing〕 ten days 《of a month》 ; the latter part 《of a month》 ¶ 3월 하순에 toward the end of March ; late in March ; in the latter part of March // 7월 하순 중에 during the last ten days of July
하순 下脣 the lower lip ; the (lower) labium
하시 下視 ① [아래를] looking down **—하다** look down ; overlook ; take〔command〕 a bird's-eye view of ; see 《a place》 below one's eyes
② [경멸] contempt ; scorn ; disdain ; slight **—하다** despise ; scorn ; disdain ; look down (up) on ; make〔set〕 light of ; hold 《a person》 in contempt
하악골 下顎骨 the lower jaw-bone
하안 河岸 a riverside ; a riverbank ; a waterfront
하야 下野 —하다 go out of office ; retire〔go back〕 to private life ; retire from public life ; resign one's public 〔government〕 post
하야말갛다 《one's complexion》 be clean and fair
하야말쑥하다 《one's complexion》 be clean and fair
하양 white ; whiteness ; a white tint 〔tinge〕
하얗다 pure white ; snow white ; as white as snow ; immaculately white ¶ 저 노인의 머리는 하얗다 The old man has a white head of hair.
하얘지다 turn〔become〕 (snow-) white ; whiten ; turn gray
하얼삔 Harbin
***하여간 何如間** anyhow ; anyway ; at any rate ; in any case ; at all events ; somehow or other ; in any circumstances ; generally speaking ¶ 그것은 하여간 be that as it may // 하여간 해 보겠습니다 I will do so, anyway. // 하여간 오는 거지 You are coming anyway. // 하여간 해 보는 것이 좋다 At all events you had better try. // 하여간 이 세상은 돈이 제일 필요한 것이다 It is often the case that money is the first thing needed in this society.
하여금 letting ; making ; forcing ¶ 그로 하여금 편지를 쓰게 하다 make him write a letter // 나로 하여금 그것을 하게 하라 Let me do it.
하여튼 何如— anyhow ; anyway ⇨ 하여간
하역 荷役 loading and unloading ; stevedoring ; cargo-working **—하다** load and unload ; do the cargo-working ¶ 석탄의 하역을 하다 load coal
— 인부 a stevedore ; a longshoreman 《미》 **—일** lay days **— 장치** a cargo handling gear
하연 賀宴 a banquet〔feast〕 in celebration ; festivities ¶ 하연을 베풀다 give 〔hold〕 a banquet 《in honor of the occasion》
하열 下劣 baseness ; meanness ; vulgarity **—하다** (be) base ; mean ; sordid ; low ; vulgar
하염없다 be lost〔absorbed〕 in thought ; (be) absent-minded ; blank ; dispirited ; bored ; have a dull time ¶ 하염없이 vacantly ; blankly ; abstractedly ; absent-mindedly ; in a daze // 하염없는 날 idle days // 하염없이 걸어가다 stroll absent-mindedly
하염직하다 be worth ; be worthy of ; deserve (of) ; merit ; be entitled to ¶ 칭찬하염직하다 merit〔deserve, rate〕 praise // 그의 업적은 감탄하염직하다 His achievement entitles him to our admiration.
하오 下午 afternoon ; post meridiem 《P. M.》 ¶ 하오 2시에 at two o'clock in the afternoon ; at two P. M. ; at fourteen hundred hours
하옥 下獄 imprisonment ; confinement **—하다** send to prison〔jail〕 ; throw into〔put in, cast into〕 prison ; imprison
하원 下院 the Lower House〔Chamber〕 ; the House ; the House of Commons 《영》 ; the House of Representatives 《미·일》 ; the Chamber of

Deputies 《프·이》
— 의원 a member of the House of Commons 《영》; a Representative 《미》
‡하위 下位 a low(er) rank; a subordinate position; a low grade ¶ 하위의 subordinate; low-ranking
— 타자 low-ranking batters (야구에서)
— 팀 low-ranking teams
하의 夏衣 summer clothes〔wear〕
하의 下衣 (a pair of) trousers; breeches; pantaloons; pants ¶ 하의를 입다 wear〔put on〕 trousers
하의 下意 the will and ideas of the lower-grade personnel; the will of the people; the popular opinion ¶ 하의를 상달(上達)하다 convey the will of those who are governed to those who govern
하이 high
하이드라짓 ⇨ 히드라짓
하이라이트 a highlight ¶ (텔레비전 프로) 금주의 하이라이트 this week's TV highlights
하이어 a hired car; a taxi ¶ 하이어를 잡다 hire a taxi
하이에나 〖동물〗 a hyena
하이웨이 a highway
하이잭 [항공기 탈취] highjacking of an airplane; skyjacking
하이칼라 ① [칼라] a high collar ② [유행을 따름] stylishness; dandyism; smartness; chic; [멋쟁이] a smartly dressed person; a person of fashion; a dandy; a swell; a fop; a Beau Brummell ¶ 하이칼라 옷 a smart dress ③ [이발] one's hair in foreign style ¶ 하이칼라(머리)를 하다 cut〔wear〕 one's hair in foreign style
하이커 a hiker
하이 클래스 high class ⇨ 고급(高級)
‡하이킹 hiking; a hike —가다, —하다 go on a hike; go hiking; hike
— 코스 a hiking course
하이틴 one's late teens ¶ 하이틴의 소녀 a girl in her late teens // 그녀는 하이틴이다 She is late in her teens.
하이파이 high fidelity ¶ 하이파이의 high-fidelity; hi-fi 《속》
— 재생 장치 a high fidelity sound reproduction system
하이픈 a hyphen ¶ 두 낱말을 하이픈으로 잇다 hyphen〔hyphenate〕 two words
하이힐 high-heeled shoes; 《wear》 high heels
†하인 下人 a servant; a maidservant; a menial ¶ 하인을 두다 keep a servant
하인 何人 who; what〔whatever〕 person; anyone; anybody ¶ 하인을 막론하고 들여서는 아니 된다 You shouldn't let anybody in, whoever it may be. // 하인을 막론하고 이 법률을 어긴 자는 처벌받는다 Whoever breaks this law shall be punished.

하인방 下引枋 a sill; the baseboard (of a room)
하인배 下人輩 servants; menials
하일 夏日 summer days
하자 瑕疵 〖법〗 defect ¶ 하자있는 권원(權原) a defective title
— 담보 a warranty — 담보 증서 a warranty deed
*하자마자 as soon as; no sooner than; hardly〔scarcely〕 ... when〔before〕; soon〔shortly〕 after; the moment; the instant; immediately ¶ 우리가 착석하자마자 막이 올랐다 We had no sooner sat down than the curtain rose. // 그가 외출을 하자마자 눈이 내리기 시작했다 Scarcely had he gone out when it began to snow. // 거기에 도착하자마자 비가 오기 시작했다 I had hardly reached there when it began to rain.
하잘것없다 (be) insignificant; negligible; trifling; trivial; petty; small; be of little importance; be of no account〔consequence〕; (be) worthless; valueless ¶ 하잘것 없는 일로 다투었다 We quarreled〔We had a quarrel〕 over a trifle. // 하잘것없는 일로 시간을 낭비했다 I have spent time (in) doing a trivial task〔poor job〕.
하장 賀狀 a complimentary〔congratulatory〕 letter〔card〕; a greeting card; greetings
연— a New Year's card; New Year's greetings
하저 河底 the bottom of a river; a river bed
하적호 河跡湖 a river-bad lake
하전 荷電 electric charge; being charged with electricity
— 입자 a charged particle
하절 夏節 the summer season; summer
하정 下情 ① [심정] my humble mind〔intention〕; my situation ② [민정] the condition〔thoughts, ways〕 of the people ¶ 하정에 통하다 be familiar with the ways of the lower classes
하정 賀正 New Year's greetings; a Happy New Year!
*하제 下劑 a purgative (medicine); an evacuant; a scourer; a laxative; cathartic
하주 荷主 the owner of baggage; a goods-holder; a shipper; a consignor
하중 荷重 load
안전 — safety load 제한 — proof load
*하지 夏至 the summer solstice
—선 the Tropic of Cancer (북회귀선)
하지 下肢 the lower limbs
†하지만 but; however; though; notwithstanding; nevertheless; none the less ¶ 그가 옳을는지 모른다 하지만 나는 그렇게 생각하지 않는다 He may be right, but I don't think so. // 하지만 나중에 그

는 그것을 포기하기로 정했다 Later, however, he decided to give it up. // 그가 그렇게 말했다고는 하지만 믿을 필요는 없다 Even though he said so, you need not believe him. // 반대는 강하지만 그는 그것을 실시하겠다고 고집하였다 He insisted on putting it in force notwithstanding (that) the resistance was strong.

-하지 않도록 last... ; for fear (that) ... ; so as not to... ; so that... may not...

-하지 않을 수 없다 cannot help 《it》; 《it》 cannot be helped ; cannot choose but 《do》; have no choice〔option, recourse〕 but 《to do》; be inevitable ¶ 나는 동의하지 않을 수 없었다 I could not withhold consent. // 나는 그를 탓하지 않을 수 없었다 I was unable to stop blaming him.

하지하 下之下 the lowest of its kind 〔the low〕; the poorest〔worst〕 of all ¶ 하지하의 lowest ; the worst

하직 下直 leave-taking ; saying good-bye ; leaving **―하다** take leave 《of》; say good-bye 《to》; bid farewell 《to》; make one's adiéu 《to》; leave ¶ 웃어른에게 하직하다 take leave of one's elders // 고향을 하직하다 leave one's native place // 이 세상을 하직하다 leave this world ; die

하차 下車 getting off 《a train, a bus》 **―하다** alight ; get down 《from》; get off ; get out 《of》; leave ¶ 그는 대구에서 하차했다 있을까요 He alighted (from the train) at *Taegu.* // 이 표로 도중에 하차를 할 수 있습니까 With this ticket, can we make a stop or two along the way? // 나는 대전에서 도중 하차합니다 I shall break my journey〔stop off, stop over〕 at *Taejon.* // 이 표는 도중 하차가 안됩니다 No stopover is allowed on this ticket.

―구(口) the way out **―역** the station where one gets off (the train) ; a departing point **도중 ―** stopover ; stop off

†**하찮다** (be) worthless ⇨ 하치않다

하책 下策 the worst policy〔plan〕

하처 何處 what place ; where ; wherever ⇨ 어디

하천 下賤 the lowest people ; (people of) the lowest classes

하천 河川 rivers ; waterways

― 개수 river-improvement (work) **― 공사** river conservation work **― 공학** riparian〔river〕 engineering **― 부지** the (dry) riverbed **― 어업** river fishery **― 오염** the river contamination **― 측량** river surveying **―학** potamology

하청 下請 a subcontract **―하다** subcontract ¶ 하청을 주다 sublet ; underlet

― 공장 a subcontract factory〔plant〕 **―인** a subcontractor

하청 河淸 ¶ 백년하청을 기다린다 "One might as well wait a hundred years for the Yellow River to flow clear."/ When the sky falls, we shall catch the lark.

하체 下體 the lower part of the body ; 〔음부〕 privy parts ; privates

하초 下焦 the lower belly above the bladder

***하층 下層** a lower layer ; a substratum 《*pl.* -ta》; the lower class (사회의) ; downstairs (아래층)

― 계급 the lower classes **―민** the people of the lower classes ; the (great) unwashed ; 〔경멸적〕 the rabble ; the ragtag〔tagrag〕 (and bobtail) **― 사회** the lower classes ; lower class society ; the proletariat ; the lower social strata ; the masses **― 생활** (a) low life

하치 下― an article of inferior quality ; low-grade goods ; the poorest 〔worst〕 stuff ; the most inferior stuff ¶ 이것은 하치다 This article is of inferior quality.

***하치않다** (be) worthless ; valueless ; good-for-nothing ; poor ; trashy ; trivial ; petty ; insignificant ; be of no account ; be of little importance ¶ 하치않은 일 a matter of no importance 〔weight〕; a trifling thing ; a trivial affair ; a trifle // 하치않은 자식 a worthless fellow ; a small fry ; a nobody // 하치않게 여기다 belittle ; make〔think〕 nothing of // 하치않은 일로 떠들어 대다 make a fuss about trifles // 그는 하치않은 일로 성을 냈다 He lost his temper on a slight provocation.

하치장 荷置場 a yard ; a storage space ; a depository ; a repository

***하키** 〖경기〗 hockey

― 스틱 a hockey stick **아이스〔필드〕 ―** ice〔field〕 hockey

하퇴 下腿 the lower leg

― 골 the leg bones ; the fibula and the tibia **― 동맥** the crural artery **― 절단** the amputation of lower leg

하트 〔심장〕 the heart ; 〔마음〕 heart ; 〔트럼프〕 a heart ¶ 하트의 퀸〔에이스, 잭〕 the queen〔ace, knave〕 of hearts

―형 a heart shape ; a heart ¶ 하트형의 heart-shaped

하편 下篇 the last〔second, third〕 volume of a book ⇨ 하권

하표 賀表 《present》 a congratulatory address ; an address of loyalty

‡**하품** yawning ; a yawn〔gape〕 **―하다** (give a) yawn ; gape ¶ 하품을 참다 stifle〔suppress〕 a yawn ; choke down a yawn // 하품하며 기지개하다 stretch 《oneself》 with a yawn // 하품하며 중얼거

리다 yawn something out // 하품을 손으로 가리다 hide a yawn behind one's hand // 그 선생의 강의는 하품이 나온다 That teacher gives us dull lectures. /The teacher bores us with his lecture. // 하품을 자주 하시는군요 You have the gapes. // 남이 하품하는 것을 보면 자기도 하품난다 Yawning is catching.

하품 下品 ① [상스러움] vulgarity ; coarseness ; grossness ; bad taste ② [하치] poor quality ; low grade

***하프** 〖악기〗 a harp ¶ 하프를 연주하다 play the harp
— **연주자** a harpist

하프늄 〖화학〗 hafnium

하프시코드 〖악기〗 a harpsichord

하프 타임 half time

하필 何必 Why necessarily ? /Why of all things ? ¶ 하필이면 of all occasion 〔places, persons〕 // 하필 그가 올 줄은 몰랐다 He was the last person of all that I expected to come. /I little expected that he, of all persons should come. // 하필 왜 시기가 나쁠 때만 그가 오는지 모르겠다 I don't know why he always chooses to come at the wrong moment. // 하필 시험 당일에 열병에 걸리다니 Imagine coming down with a fever on the day of his entrance exams, of all times.

하하 ha ha ; laugh (with joy)

하학 下學 dismissal of a class ; ending of the school day **— 하다** school is over ; school gets〔lets〕 out ; school ends for the day ; leave school ¶ 하학 후에 after school (hours) ; out of school hours
— **시간** dismissal time **— 종** the dismissal bell

하한 下限 the lowest limit ; the greatest lower bound ; the inferior limit

하항 河港 a river port

하해 河海 rivers and seas ¶ 하해 같은 은혜 great favor ; unlimited grace

하행 下行 going away from the capital 〔*Seoul*〕 ; going down **— 하다** go down ; go away from *Seoul*
— **열차** a down-train

하향 下向 looking〔facing, bending〕 downward ¶ 하향 기미다 begin to decline〔fall〕 ; show a downward tendency
— **세〔경향〕** a downward〔declining〕 tendency ; downtrend

하향 下鄕 going to one's country home

하현 下弦 the last phase〔quarter〕 of the moon ¶ 하현의 달 the waning moon

하혈 下血 discharging blood ; a bloody flux **— 하다** discharge〔pass〕 blood ; bleed ; flux

하환 어음 荷換— a documentary bill ¶ 하환 어음을 작성하다 draw a documentary bill 《on》
— **신용장** a documentary (letter of) credit

하회 下廻 falling short **— 하다** fall short of ; be below ; be lower〔less〕 than ¶ 어제 시세를 100원 하회하다 be a hundred *won* lower than the previous day's closing quotation // 금년 수출액은 작년의 그것을 하회한다 This year's exports fall short of last year's.

하회 下回 the next time ; the next chapter 《of a novel》 ; the reply 《to a letter》 ¶ 하회를 기다리다 await 《a person's》 reply

학 學 learning (학문) ; study (연구) ; studies (학업) ; science (학술) ; scholarly attainments ; scholarship ; erudition (학식) ; knowledge (지식)

학 鶴 a crane ; a stork ⇨ 두루미

학감 學監 a school superintendent ; a dean

학개서 —書 〖성경〗 the Book of Haggai ; Haggai 《Hag.》

학계 學界 learned circles ; the academic〔learned〕 world ¶ 학계의 권위 an authority of the academic world // 영문학계 learned circles of English literature // 학계에 공헌하다 do much for the cause of learning // 그는 학계에 연구를 발표했다 He laid his studies before the academic world.

†학과 學科 [과목] a school subject ; a subject of study ; [과정] a course of study ; a curriculum ; a school course
— **시험** an examination in academic subjects — **증설** establishment of new departments **정규 —** regular academic work

†학과 學課 a lesson ; school work ; class work ¶ 학과를 복습〔예습〕하다 review 〔prepare〕 one's lesson
— **명(名)** names of studies — **시간표** a teaching schedule ; a schedule (of lesson hours)

학관 學館 an academy ; an institute ; an educational institution
영어 — an English-language institute

†학교 學校 a school ; an educational establishment〔institution〕 《총칭》 ¶ 학교에서 in〔at〕 school // 학교가 파한 후 after school (is over) // 학교에 다녔을 때 in one's school days // 학교에 다니다 go to school ; attend school // 학교에 들어가다 enter〔be admitted into〕 a school // 학교에 보내다 send〔put〕 《a person》 to school // 학교를 졸업하다 graduate from school ; complete the school course // 학교를 그만두다 leave school ; quit school // 학교를 설립하다 found〔establish〕 a school // 학교가 시작되다〔끝나다〕 school begins〔closes〕 // 학교를 쉬다 stay away // 어느 학교를 나왔습니까 Where did you go to school ?
— **경영자** a school proprietor ; a

ㅎ

school operator 《미》 — 교육 school education ; schooling — 급식 school feeding ; school lunch〔meal〕 — 방송 [텔레비전·라디오의] the school hour — 법인 an educational foundation — 생활 school〔college〕 life — 선생 a school teacher — 성적 one's school record — 신문 a school paper — 용품 school things〔requisites〕 —장(長) a headmaster ; a principal ; a superintendent —장(葬) a school funeral —차(差) scholastic disparity among schools — 친구 a schoolmate ; a schoolfellow 중— a middle school 고등 — a high school 대— a college ; a university 음악 — a school〔an academy〕 of music 초등— a primary〔an elementary〕 school

*학구 學究 study ; learning ; [사람] a village-school teacher ; a student ; a scholar ¶ 학구적 scholastic ; academic // 학구적 생활 a scholastic〔an academic〕 life // 학구적 정신 a scholastic spirit

학구 學區 a school district
—제 the school district system

학군 學群 a school group
—제 the school group〔district〕 system
제2 — the second school group

학군단 學軍團 ⇨ 학도 군사 훈련단

†학급 學級 a (school) class ; a grade 《미》; a form 《영》 ¶ 학급을 편성하다 organize a class
— 문고 a classroom library —회 a class meeting

†학기 學期 a (school) term ; a semester 《미》; a session 《미》 ¶ 제1학기 the first term〔semester〕
—말 the close〔end〕 of a school term —말 시험 a term〔terminal〕 examination —말 휴가 term-end holidays 신— the new〔fresh〕 term 제1— the first term ; [2학기제의] the first semester

학내 學內 ¶ 학내의〔에〕 in the university ; within the campus ; on campus ; intramural 《game, team》 // 학내신문 a school newspaper

*학년 學年 an academic〔a school〕 year ; a scholastic year ; a grade 《미》 ; a form 《영》 ¶ 그는 6학년이다 He is in the sixth form〔grade〕. // 너는 몇 학년이냐 —1학년입니다 What grade are you in ? I'm in the first grade.
—말 the end of a school year —말 시험 a final〔an annual〕 examination 신— a new school year

학당 學堂 a school ; a village school

*학대 虐待 ill-treatment ; maltreatment 《영》; mistreatment 《미》 —하다 ill-treat ; maltreat ; mistreat ; treat with cruelty ; abuse ; be hard upon ; give 《a person》 hard measure ; be cruel to ¶ 아내를 학대하다 abuse one's wife // 가난한 자를 학대하다 oppress the poor // 당신이 학대받는 것을 내버려 둘 수 없다 I can't allow you to be ill-treated.
동물 — 방지회 the Society for the Prevention of Cruelty to Animals 《S. P. C. A.》

학덕 學德 learning and virtue ¶ 학덕을 겸비한 사람 a man with both learning and virtue

학도 學徒 a student ; a scholar ; a pupil ¶ 플라톤 학도 followers of Plato // 사회과학 학도 a student of social science
—대 a students' corps — 동원령 the Student Mobilization Law —병 a student soldier — 호국단 the Student National Defense Corps

학도 군사 훈련단 學徒軍事訓練團 Reserve Officers' Training Corps 《R. O. T. C.》

학동 學童 a school child ; a schoolboy 〔schoolgirl〕

학력 學力 scholarship ; scholarly (scholastic) attainments ; scholastic ability ¶ 학력이 우수하다 be excellent in scholarship ; be an excellent scholar // 대학 졸업자와 동등한 학력이 있다 be equipped with attainments equal to the college graduate
— 고사 a scholastic ability〔an achievement〕 test ; an examination in academic subjects

학력 學歷 an academic background ; a school〔an academic〕 career ; (formal) schooling ¶ 학력을 불문하고 irrespective of the academic background 〔educational preparations〕 // 그는 학력이 없다 He has no formal schooling. // 그는 학력도 별로 없이 박사가 되었다 He has been made a Doctor, though he has pursued no regular course of studies.

학령 學齡 school age ¶ 학령 미달의 아이 children under school age ; a preschool child // 학령에 달하다 reach school age
— 아동 children of school age ; school-aged children ; schoolable children

학리 學理 a theory ; a scientific principle ¶ 학리적 theoretical // 학리의 응용 application of scientific principles // 학리를 연구하다 study the principles of science

학명 學名 〖생물〗 a scientific name ; a technical term
동물 — a zoological name 식물 — a botanical name

학모 學帽 a school cap

학무 學務 educational〔school〕 affairs
—과 a section of educational affairs — 위원 a member of a school board

*학문 學問 [학업] learning ; study ; [학식] scholarship ; knowledge ; [학교 교육] schooling ; [면학] studies ; scholas-

tic pursuit ; [학술] a science ¶ 학문적(으로) scientific(ally) // 학문을 위한 학문 learning for learning's sake // 학문을 하다 study ; pursue learning ; engage in studies // 학문을 좋아하다 be fond of study〔learning〕// 학문에 전념하다 devote oneself to one's studies // 학문에는 왕도가 없다 There is no royal road to learning.

학벌 學閥 an academic clique ; academical cliquism〔sectarianism〕; school fraternity ¶ 학벌의 폐해 the evils of academic clique // 학벌을 짓다 form an academic clique
— **싸움** rivalry between school factions

학병 學兵 a student soldier

학보 學報 a gazette

학부 學府 a seat of learning ; an academic center ; an educational institution ¶ 최고 학부 the highest institution of learning ; a university

†**학부 學部** a faculty ; a department ; a college (종합 대학의)
—**장** the dean of a university faculty **공**— a college〔school〕of engineering ; an engineering department **문**〔**교양, 이, 의, 농, 경제, 정치, 법**〕— the Faculty of Literature〔Liberal Arts, Physical Science, Medicine, Agriculture, Economics, Political Science, Law〕

학부형 學父兄 parents of students
—**회** a parents' association

*__학비 學費__ school expenses ; an educational expenses ; the cost of schooling ¶ 학비를 대다 pay 《a person's》 school expenses ; supply a student with his school expenses // 학비에 곤란을 받다 be hard up for school expenses // 고학으로 학비를 벌다 earn one's school expenses by working.

‡**학사 學士** a university〔college〕graduate ; a bachelor of arts〔science〕
— **등록제** the bachelor registration system ; the college graduate registry system — **학위** a bachelor's degree — **회** the old boys' association of a university ; the alumni association of a university **경제**— Bachelor of Economics **문**— Bachelor of Arts **의**— Bachelor of Medicine

학사 學事 school affairs ; education (al) matters
— **보고** a report on education matters
— **시찰** (an) educational inspection

학사 學舍 a school (building) ; an institute

*__학살 虐殺__ slaughter ; massacre ; butchery ; carnage ; holocaust ; genocide — **하다** slaughter ; massacre ; butcher
—**자** a slaughterer ; a slayer **대량** — a large-scale massacre ; a holocaust

†**학생 學生** a student ; a pupil ; a schoolboy ; a schoolgirl ; a scholar

> 참고 **student**는 주로 고교생 이상 특히 「대학생」을 말한다 **pupil**은 「초 중 고교생」 또는 개인적 교수를 받는 생도를 말한다 **schoolboy schoolgirl**은 「초 중 고교생」의 뜻 단순히 boy girl 이라고 생략하는 수가 많다 **scholar**는 원래 「학자」라고 하는 뜻이지만 「pupil 보다 연소한 생도」의 뜻으로도 쓰인다

¶ 학생용 intended for the use of students // 학생의 날 Student's Day // 학생수 5,000명의 대학 a university with a student enrollment of 5,000
—**가(街)** the students' quarter — **기질** the spirit of the student — **보도** student guidance —**복** a school uniform — **부장** a dean of students — **생활** student life ; college life — **시대** one's student〔school〕days — **신문** a school paper — **운동** a student movement — **증** a student's (identification) card — **친구** a schoolmate —**회** a students' association — **회관** the students' hall ; a student union

학생감 學生監 the dean of students ; a censor ; a proctor

†**학설 學說** a theory ; a doctrine ¶ 신 학설을 세우다 set up〔formulate, advance〕a new theory

학수 鶴壽 a long life〔longevity〕

학수고대 鶴首苦待 — **하다** look forward to ; await with impatience ¶ 당신과의 상봉을 학수고대하고 있다 I am eagerly looking forward to seeing you.

학술 學術 [과학] science ; [학문] learning ; scholarship ; [학문과 예술] art(s) and science(s) ¶ 학술적 연구 scientific research // 학술상의 scientific ; academic // 학술상 scientifically // 학술 연구를 위하여 해외로 가다 go abroad for the prosecution of one's study
— **강연** a scientific lecture — **논문** a scientific treatise ; an academic essay〔dissertation, thesis〕; a paper —**서** a scientific〔learned〕book〔work〕 — **잡지** a scientific〔learned〕journal

학술원 學術院 the (Korean) Academy of Arts and Sciences ¶ 학술원 회원 a member of the (Korean) Academy ; an Academician
미국 — the American Council of Learned Societies

학습 學習 studying ; learning — **하다** study ; learn ¶ 학습을 지도하다 coach one's study
—**서** a study book ; a handbook for students —**자** a learner —**장** a workbook ; a drill book — **지도 요령** a course of study

학승 學僧 a learned priest

†**학식 學識** scholarship ; learning ; schol-

ㅎ

arly attainments ; knowledge ¶ 심오한 학식 profound knowledge〔learning〕; erudition // 학식이 있는 learned ; erudite // 학식이 없다 lack scholarship ; be uneducated ; be ignorant ; be unlettered

학업 學業 studies ; school work ; scholarship ; scholastic achievement ¶ 학업을 끝마치다 complete one's study // 학업을 부지런히 하다 study one's lessons with diligence // 학업을 중단하다 give up one's studies ; leave school // 학업 성적이 우수하다 be a good scholar ; do well at school // 학업에 태만하다 neglect one's school work

학예 學藝 art(s) and science(s) ; liberal arts ; literary accomplishments ; culture (문화·교양)

—난〔면〕 the literary column(s)〔page〕
—부 a department of art and science
—회 a literary exhibition ; literary exercises ; a class day

학용품 學用品 school things〔supplies〕

학우 學友 a schoolmate ; a fellow student ; a classmate

—회 a students' society〔association〕; an old boys' association ; an alumni association (졸업생의)

****학원 學園** a school ; an educational institution ; a campus ¶ 학원의 자유 academic freedom

— 난입(亂入) intrusion into campus — 분쟁 a campus dispute — 사찰 inspection on campus activities — 생활 school life ; student life ; campus life — 제(祭) a campus〔school〕 festival

학원 學院 an (educational) institute ; an academy ; a school ; a seminary

자동차 — a driver's school

학위 學位 an academic degree ; a doctorate ¶ 학위를 주다 grant a degree 《to a person》; confer a degree on 《a person》; award 《a person》 a degree // 학위를 받다 be granted a degree ; have a degree conferred on 《one》 // 학위를 획득하다 take〔secure, obtain, win〕 a degree (from a university)

— 논문 a thesis for a degree ; a doctoral dissertation〔thesis〕 — 수여식 the (ceremony of) conferment of a degree ; the presentation day — 제도 the system of university degrees 명예 — an honorary degree 박사 — a doctor's degree ; a doctorate

****학자 學者** a scholar ; a learned man ; a man of learning ; an erudite ; a savant ; an academical person (학구) ¶ 학자인 체 하는 사람 a pedant // 학자적 scholarly ; academic // 학자인 체하다 assume the air of scholar ; be pedantic // 그는 학자다운 데가 있다 He has something of the scholar in him. // 그는 세계적으로 유명한 학자이다 He is a scholar of world-wide fame.

— 고문단 [대통령의] a brain trust 《미》

학자 學資 school expenses ; educational cost

— 보험 educational endowment insurance

학자금 學資金 ⇨ 학비

***학장 學長** a dean ; a president ; a rector

학재 學才 scholastic talent〔capacity, ability〕

학적 學籍 a school register ; a college register ¶ 학적에 올리다 put one's name on the school register // 학적에서 빼버리다 strike 《a person's》 name off the school register // 학적부에 기명하다 enter 《a person's》 name in school register

—부 a school〔college〕 register ¶

학점 學點 a unit ; a point ; a credit ¶ 30학점을 따다 take 30 units // 4학점의 불어 강의를 수강하다 take a French course for 4 credits〔points〕

— 교환제 cross registration system

학정 虐政 oppressive〔tyrannical〕 government ; (grinding) tyranny ; despotism ¶ 학정에 신음하다 groan under tyranny

학제 學制 an educational system ; a school system ¶ 학제를 개혁하다 reform〔reorganize〕 the school system

— 개혁〔개편〕 a reform〔reorganization〕 of the school system — 개혁안 the proposed educational system reform

학질 瘧疾 〖의학〗 malaria ; malarial 〔miasmatic〕 fever ¶ 학질에 걸리다 be sick with malaria // 학질은 모기가 매개한다 Malaria is carried by the mosquito.

— 모기 〖곤충〗 an anopheles (mosquito) — 예방제 an anti-malarial

학창 學窓 a school ; a campus ; an educational institute ¶ 학창을 떠나다 leave school ; graduate from school

— 생활 school〔student〕 life

학춤 鶴— ① [학의 춤] the dance of a crane ② [사람이 추는] a dance in the costume of a crane

학칙 學則 school regulations ¶ 학칙을 정하다 frame school regulations // 학칙을 어기다 break〔violate, go against〕 school regulations

학통 學統 a scholastic mantle

학파 學派 a school ; a sect ; a doctrinal faction ¶ 학파를 이루다 found a school // 두 학파로 갈라지다 be divided into two different schools

에피쿠로스 — the school of Epicurus
헤겔 — the Hegelian school

학풍 學風 academic traditions〔features〕 (특징) ; a method of study (연구법) ; a school (학파) ; school character (학교의 기풍) ¶ 학풍을 세우다 establish a school tradition // 둘은 같은 철학자이지만 학풍이 다르다 Philosophers as they both are, they belong to different schools.

학해 學海 the world of knowledge〔literature and science〕; the vast field of learning ; the academic world ¶ 학해의 지침 a guiding star of the world of knowledge

학행 學行 learning〔scholarship〕 and virtue

학형 學兄 Mr. ... ; you

학회 學會 a learned society ; an institute ; an academy
물리 — a physical society **영문** — (the) English Literary Society《of Korea》 **한글** — the Korean Language (Research) Society

†한 ① [하나의] one ; a ¶ 한 해 a〔one〕 year // 한 노인을 만났다 I met an old man. // 그들은 우리를 멋지게 한 방 먹였어 They did a beautiful number on us. ② [같은] the same ¶ 한 집에 in the same house ③ [온] whole ; entire ¶ 한 고을을 차지하다 possess whole county // 한 겨울을 스케이트로 보내다 spend all the winter in skating ④ [한창] the peak ; the extreme ; the most ; the very ¶ 한겨울 midwinter // 한가운데 the very middle ⑤ [약] about ; approximately ¶ 한 열흘 about 10 days ⑥ [큰] large ; big ; great ¶ 한길 a main〔high, broad〕 street // 한시름 a big worry ; a great anxiety
한 부모는 열 자식을 거느려도 열 자식은 한 부모를 못 거느린다 속담 One father can support ten children, ten children cannot support one father. /One father is enough to govern one hundred sons, but not a hundred sons one father.
한 갯물이 열 갯물 흐린다 속담 One drop of poison infects the whole tun of wine.

한 恨 [원한] a grudge ; a heartburning ; rancor ; spite ; hatred ; [한탄] a lamentation ; a regret ; grief ; deploring ¶ 천추의 한 a lasting regret // 한이 되는 일 a grudge ; grievances // 한 많은 regrettable ; hateful // 한이 없다 have nothing to regret // 한을 품다 bear〔cherish, nurse〕 a grudge ; have a grudge against ; harbor enmity toward // 한을 풀다 vent one's spite ; satisfy one's grudge ; revenge oneself on《the offender》

한 限 ① [한계] a limit ; limits ; bounds ¶ 한있는 limited ; finite // 한 없는 limitless ; boundless ; endless ; eternal ; unlimited // 한 없이 unlimitedly ; without limit ; endlessly ; eternally // 한 없는 기쁨 a never-failing〔an everlasting, an eternal〕 joy // 한 없이 넓은 바다 a boundless sea // 인간의 힘에는 한이 있다 There is a limit to man's power〔strength〕. // 인간의 진보에는 한이 없다 Human progress knows no bounds. ② [기한] a time limit ; a term ; a period ¶ 이달 25일 한 not later than the 25th inst.〔this month〕// 열흘을 한하고 돈을 꾸어 주다 lend money on the condition that it be returned within ten days ③ [범위] as〔so〕 far as ¶ 살아 있는 한 as long as one lives // 금회 한 for this once ; for this time only // 할 수 있는 한 as much〔far〕 as possible〔one can〕// 학생에 한해서 입장 허가 Admission to students only. // 이번에 한해서 용서하겠다 I will forgive you for this once〔time only〕. // 100미터 경주에서 그 소년은 힘있는 한 달렸으나 꼴찌였다 In the 100 meter race, the boy ran to the limit of his strength〔as far as he could〕, but he came in last. // 가격에 대해서는 될 수 있는 한 싸게 드리겠습니다 As for the price, we will do everything we can to please you. // 내가 알고 있는 한에서는 그는 악인이 아니다 As〔So〕 far as I know, he is not a wicked man.

한가 恨— resentment ; umbrage **—하다** resent ; take umbrage at ; blame

†한가 閑暇 **—하다** (be) free ; leisure(d) ; not busy ; unoccupied (한산) ; dull ; slack ; inactive ¶ 한가로이 in a leisurely way ; with leisure // 한가할 때 when《one》 have time to spare ; at leisure ; in one's spare time // 돈 있고 한가한 사람들 wealthy leisured people ; the idle-rich // 한가하다 I am free〔not engaged〕. // 이것은 한가할 때 할 일이다 This is for leisure hours. // 저희들 장사는 이제 차차 한가해집니다 Our business is entering the off season.

한가닥 ¶ 한가닥의 희망 a ray〔flush, shadow〕 of hope // 한가닥 희망을 안다 cling to the last hope // 그가 죽어서 한 가닥 희망마저 잃었다 His death deprived me of the last hope〔the sole remaining hope〕.

†한가운데 the very middle ; the center ; the midst ; the heart ¶ 한가운데의 middle ; central // 길 한가운데 the center of the street // 대도시의 한가운데 in the heart of a big city // 과녁 한가운데를 맞히다 hit the target right in the center

한가위 August 15th of the lunar calendar ; the Harvest Moon festival ⇨ 추석

한가을 ① [수확기] the busy harvesting season ; the busy harvest time ② [가을] the whole autumn〔fall〕; all autumn long ¶ 한가을 아무 것도 않고 놀다 idle away the whole fall〔autumn〕

한가지 ① [일종] a kind ; a sort ; a variety ; one thing (한가지 일) ; another kind ¶ 그것도 한가지 방법이다 It is a kind of way to do it. /It is another way to do it.

ㅎ

② [동일] the same ¶ 한가지의 [동일] the same ; one and the same ; [비슷한] similar ; like ; common (공통) // 오늘 가나 내일 가나 한가지다 It makes little difference whether I go today or tomorrow. // 이 사람들은 국적은 다르지만 이해 관계는 한가지다 These men differ in nationality, but their interests are identical〔common〕. // 삶을 아끼고 죽음을 두려워하는 것은 사람이나 하등 동물이나 한가지다 Love of life and fear of death are common to man and lower animals.

한각 閑却 negligence ; neglect ; oversight **—하다** neglect ; ignore ; disregard ; overlook

한간 一間 a〔one〕 *kan* ¶ 한간방 a room one *kan* in area

한갓 simply ; merely ; only ; alone ¶ 한갓 …이란 이유로 simply because... // 한갓 시간의 문제 merely a question of time // 그것은 한갓 핑계에 불과하다 That is simply an excuse, and nothing more.

한갓지다 (be) quiet ; tranquil ; retired ; unhurried and quiet ; peaceful and leisurely ; secluded ¶ 한갓진 곳 a quiet〔secluded〕 place ; an out-of-the-way place

한개 一箇 one ; a unit (단위) ¶ 사과 한개 an apple // 비누 한개 a cake〔bar〕 of soap // 한개씩 one by one

한거 閒居 a quiet〔secluded, retired〕 life ; a leisurely life ; an idle life **—하다** lead a retired life ; lead an idle life ; live a leisurely life ¶ 소인이 한거하면 나쁜 짓을 한다 The devil makes work for idle hands.

한걱정 a big worry〔trouble〕 ; a great anxiety ; a great headache ¶ 한걱정 생기다 have a great headache // 한걱정 놓다 be relieved of a great anxiety

†**한걸음** a step ; a pace ¶ 한걸음에 at a stride // 한걸음 한걸음 step by step // 한걸음 앞서 가다 go a step ahead 《of a person》 // 피로하여 한걸음도 더 못 걷겠다 I am too tired to walk another step.

천리길도 한걸음부터 〔속담〕 A journey of a thousand miles begins with one step.

***한겨울** midwinter ; the dead〔depth〕 of winter

한결 [눈에 띄게] conspicuously ; remarkably ; [한층] much more ; still more ; especially (특히) ¶ 한결 눈에 띄다 stand out conspicuously // 고치니까 한결 보기가 낫다 The change makes it look nicer. // 막내이니만큼 한결 더 귀엽다 I love him all the more because he is my youngest child. // 비를 맞은 단풍은 한결 아름답다 Rain adds a special charm to the red-tinted autumnal leaves. // 고독감이 한결 더해진다 My sense of isolation becomes doubly acute.

†**한결같다** (be) constant ; never changing ; consistent ; uniform ¶ 한결같은 사랑 constant love // 한결같은 집착 unfailing〔unwavering〕 perseverance // 한결같은 태도 a consistent attitude

한결같이 constantly ; consistently ; invariably ; as ever ¶ 한결같이 사랑하다 love 《a person》 as ever // 차별 철폐를 한결같이 주장하다 consistently advocate abolishing discrimination

한겻 a quarter of a day ¶ 한겻 일 a job that will take several hours ; a quarter-day's work

†**한계** 限界 a boundary ; a limit ; bounds ; limitations ; a margin ; circumscription ; compass ¶ 인간 능력의 한계 the limitation of human faculty〔power〕 // 한계를 짓다 define the boundary ; place a limit 《on》 ; set limits〔bounds〕 《to》 ; limit // 한계를 넘다 pass〔exceed, overstep〕 the limit ; get out of bounds // 자유의 한계를 지어주다 show to what lengths "freedom" is permitted to go

— 가격 a ceiling〔maximum〕 price ; a price ceiling **— 각도** 〖항공〗 a critical angle **— 개념** a concept of limitation **— 능률** marginal efficiency **— 생산** marginal productivity **— 생산비** marginal cost of production **—선** a boundary〔limiting〕 line **— 속도** critical speed **— 온도** critical temperature **— 원가** marginal cost **— 효용(설)** (the theory of) marginal utility

한계 韓系 of Korean ancestry

— 미국인 a Korean-American

한계점 限界点 the critical point ; the uppermost〔superior〕 limit ; the maximum ¶ 한계점에 도달하다 reach〔be at〕 the top〔uppermost limit〕

한고비 the most serious moment ; the most painful hour〔moment〕 ; climax ; crucial〔critical〕 moment ; acme ; high tide ; zenith ; peak ¶ 한고비를 넘다 pass the crisis ; pass out of danger ; turn the corner (병 따위가) ; the worst is over // 물가 등귀도 이젠 한고비를 넘었겠지 We have doubtlessly passed the crest of the prices. // 병세가 한고비를 넘었다 The worst symptom have subsided. // 그 외교 문제도 이제는 한고비를 넘었다 The diplomatic question has now passed its critical point. // 꽃이 한고비 지났다 The flowers are past their prime.

한교 韓僑 Koreans abroad ; overseas Koreans

한구 漢口 Hankow

한구석 a corner ; a nook ; a secluded place ¶ 한구석에 in a corner〔nook〕 //

교실 한구석에 놓다 put 《a thing》 in a corner of a classroom // 시골 한구석에 박히다 be stuck in a secluded village
한국 寒國 a cold country〔region〕
한국 寒菊 a winter chrysanthemum
†**한국 韓國** Korea ; the Republic of Korea 《R. O. K.》 ¶ 한국 사정에 밝다 be well-informed on Korean affairs // 한국화하다 Koreanize
—계(系) of Korean descent〔parentage〕 **— 국민** the Korean (people) **— 동란〔전쟁〕** the Korean War **—말〔어〕** Korean ; the Korean language **— 사람** a Korean **—식** Korean style **— 요리** Korean dishes **— 육군** the Republic of Korea Army 《R. O. K. A.》 **— 은행** the Bank of Korea **— 정부** the Korean Government **—제** Korean make ; a Korean-made 《camera》 **—화** Koreanization **—학** Koreanology
한국 개발 금융 공사 韓國開發金融公社 the Korea Development Finance Corp 《K. D. F. C.》
한국 개발 연구원 韓國開發硏究院 the Korea Development Institute
한국 과학 기술 연구소 韓國科學技術硏究所 ⇨ 키스트
한군데 one place ; the same place ¶ 그 시계를 파는 가게가 한군데 있다 There is one store where the watch is sold.
한극 寒極 the coldest region in the world
한근심 a big worry ; a great anxiety ¶ 한근심 놓다 be relieved of a great anxiety
한글 the Korean alphabet ; the Korean language ; Korean literature
—날 *Hangeul* Proclamation Day **— 맞춤법** the rules〔system〕 of spelling of *Hangeul* **— 전용** exclusive use of *Hangeul* **—학자** a *Hangeul* scholar
한기 寒氣 the cold ; a cold wave ; the cold weather ; a cold snap (급격한 온도 저하) 《미》 ; chill ; chilliness ¶ 한기를 느끼다 feel cold // 한기가 나다 feel a chill ; feel chilly ; have a chill〔a cold fit〕
한길[1] a main street〔road〕 ; a highway ; a thoroughfare ¶ 한길을 막다 block the road
한길[2] [깊이의] one fathom ¶ 깊이가 한 길이다 be a fathom deep
***한꺼번에** ① at a time ; at a stretch 〔breath, sitting, stroke〕 ¶ 과자를 한꺼번에 다 먹어 버리다 eat all the cakes up at one sitting // 책을 한꺼번에 다 읽다 read straight through the book
② [동시에] at the same time ; all together ; simultaneously ¶ 하나 하나 가지 않고 모두 한꺼번에 가다 instead of going one by one, they all go together // 사람이 한꺼번에 밀어닥쳤다 People crowed in all at the same time.
***한껏** as far〔much〕 as possible ; as much as one can ; to the best of one's ability ; to the utmost ; to one's heart's content ¶ 한껏 잡아 당기다 pull with all one's strength // 한껏 즐기다 enjoy oneself to one's heart's content // 한껏 먹다 eat one's fill // 한껏 울다 cry〔weep〕 one's fill ; have a good cry // 한껏 일하다 work to the best of one's ability ; work as hard as one can
한끝 one〔an〕 end ; an edge ; a side ; the tail end ; the extremity ¶ 끈의 한 끝을 잡다 hold one end of a rope // 줄 한끝에 돌을 달다 tie a stone to the end of a rope
한끼 a〔one〕 meal ¶ 한끼에 세그릇 먹다 eat three bowls at a meal // 하루에 한끼만 먹다 have only one meal a day
한나절 half a day ¶ 한나절 일 half-a-day's work
한낮 high noon ; noonday ; noontide ; midday ; broad daylight
한낱 ① [하나] one (item) ② [하잘것 없는] only ; mere(ly) ; nothing but
한내 限內 ① [기한 안] within a time limit ; within a definite period of time ② [경계 안쪽] within a boundary ③ [규정 안] within a limitation〔rule, proviso〕
한눈 ① [한쪽 눈] one eye ¶ 한눈으로 보다 look with one eye
② [한번 보기] a look ; a (single) glance ; a glimpse ¶ 한눈에 at a look ; at a glance // 매출 상황을 한눈에 알 수 있는 리스트를 만들어 줄 수 있겠나 I wonder if you couldn't make a list that would give the sales situation at a glance. // 그 빌딩은 근사한 수족관이 있고 스카이 라운지에서는 서울 시내를 한눈에 내려다 볼 수가 있지요 The building has a nice aquarium and from its sky lounge you can have a bird's-eye view of Seoul.
한눈팔다 look away〔off, aside〕 ; see off ; take one's eyes off ; look at something else ¶ 한눈 팔면서 걷다 walk along gazing around
한다하는 prominent ; influential ¶ 한다하는 학자 an eminent scholar
한닥거리다 sway ; move ; shake ; wobble
한닥이다 ⇨ 한닥거리다
한닥한닥 moving〔swaying, shaking, wobbling〕 repeatedly ¶ 한닥한닥하는 의자 a rickety〔an unsteady, shaky〕 chair
한달 a〔one〕 month
한달음에 straight through ; without a pause for breath ; at a run ¶ 나는 여기까지 한달음에 달려왔다 I ran all the way down to here.
‡**한담 閑談** a leisurely conversation ; a chat ; chit-chat ; idle talk ; a gossip
— 하다 chat 《with》 ; have a chat

ㅎ

《with》 ¶ 한담으로 시간을 보내다 chat the time away ; pass one's time in a quiet talk
— 설화 a chat ; a leisurely conversation

한대 寒帶 〖지리〗 the Frigid Zone ; the arctic regions
— 동물〔식물〕 a polar animal〔plant〕 — 지방 the cold latitudes 북〔남〕— the Arctic〔Antarctic〕 zone

한댕거리다 oscillate〔swing, shake〕 slightly

한댕한댕 dangling ; dangle-dangle —하다 ⇨ 한댕거리다

한더위 intense〔extreme〕 heat ; severe〔torrid〕 heat ; the hot season ; the hottest weather

한데[1] a place ⇨ 한군데

한데[2] the open (air) ; out of doors ; outdoors ; the wrong place ¶ 한데서 자다 sleep under the open sky // 씨를 한데 심다 sow seeds outside
— 우물 a well outside the house enclosure 한뎃부엌 an outdoors kitchen 한뎃뒷간 an outside privy〔latrine〕

한뎃솥 an outdoor oven ; an oven set up outside the kitchen

한도 限度 a limit ; bounds ¶ 최대 한도 the maximum〔uppermost〕 limit // 최소 한도 the minimum〔bottommost〕 // 최저 한도의 생활 the minimum standard of living // 최대 한도까지 to the utmost limit // 한도를 정하다 fix the limit ; set a limit // 한도를 넘다 pass〔exceed, overstep〕 the limit ; go beyond the limit ; go too far // 한도 내에서 그치다 keep within bounds〔the limits〕 // 인내에도 한도가 있다 Human patience has its limits. // 나는 신용카드를 융자 한도액까지 이미 다 써 버렸다 I've already used them all up to the limit.

한독 悍毒 ferocity ; fierceness ; cruelty ; savagery —하다 (be) fierce ; ferocious ; cruel ; savage ; truculent

한독 韓獨 Korea and Germany ¶ 한독의 Korean and German

한돌림 one〔a〕 round ; one circumference ¶ 술이 한돌림 돌다 have a round of drinks

한동기 一同氣 ⇨ 한동생

한동생 a brother〔sister〕-german ; full brothers and sisters

한동안 (for) quite a time〔while〕 ¶ 한동안 머물다 stay quite a while

한동자 cooking rice again soon after a meal 《for an unexpected guest》

한되다 恨— be regrettable ; be deplorable ; be lamentable ; be pitiable〔pitiful〕 ¶ 자식의 무지함이 한되다 regret one's child's ignorance // 젊어서 공부 못한 것이 한된다 I regret that I could not study while young.

한두 one or two ; a couple ¶ 한두 사람 one or two persons // 한두 번 once or twice // 한두 해 a year or two

한둘 one or two

한드랑거리다 swing ⇨ 한들거리다

한드랑한드랑 moving to and fro ; swaying

한드작거리다 swing ⇨ 한들거리다

한드작한드작 ⇨ 한드랑한드랑

한들거리다 dangle ; sway ; swing ; shake ; tremble ; vibrate ; waver ; flicker ¶ 한들거리는 등불 a flickering light

한들고사리 〖식물〗 the mountain bladderfern

한들한들 shaking ; trembling ; swaying

한때 a time ; once ; (at) one time ; for a time〔while〕 ; temporarily ; provisionally ¶ 한때 번창하다 flourish for a while // 고생하는 것도 한때다 Your suffering is only momentary. // 그의 인기도 한때에 지나지 않았다 He enjoyed a mere mushroom〔transient〕 popularity.

한란 寒暖 heat and cold ; temperature

***한란계 寒暖計** a thermometer ; the mercury ¶ 최고〔최저〕 한란계 a maximum〔minimum〕 thermometer // 한란계는 실내에서 30도를 나타내고 있다 The thermometer reads〔stands at, indicates, registers, records〕 30°C in the room.
섭씨〔화씨〕 — a centigrade〔Fahrenheit〕 thermometer

한랭 寒冷 cold ; coldness ; chill ; chilliness —하다 be cold ; chilly
— 전선 〖기상〗 a cold front

한랭사 寒冷紗 (victoria) lawn ; cheesecloth ; 〖제본〗 crash

한량 閑良 a prodigal ; a profligate ; a debauchee

한량 限量 a limited quantity ; a limit ; a limits ; bounds ¶ 한량 없는 unlimited ; unmeasurable ; limitless ; boundless ; infinite ; endless // 위를 보면 한량이 없다 Do not compare yourself with those above you. /You can not keep up with Joneses. // 욕심에는 한량이 없다 Desire〔avarice〕 knows no bounds〔limits〕.

한량하다 寒涼— 〔몰골〕 (be) thin and languid ; pale and wan ; desolate ; 〔날씨가〕 cold ; chilly

한련 旱蓮 a kind of small-leafed lotus ; a tropaeolum
—과 〖식물〗 Tropaeolaceae —초(草) a kind of aster

한류 寒流 a cold current

한림 翰林 the Royal Academy ; 〔벼슬〕 a Royal archivist〔chronicler, historian〕

한마 悍馬 an unruly〔a restive〕 horse ; a fierce〔vicious〕 horse

한마디 a (single) word —하다 speak a word about ; make a remark〔comment〕 on ¶ 한마디도 없이 without a single word // 한마디도 들리지 않는다 fail to catch a word // 한마디 말씀드리겠

습니다 I should like to say a word〔make a remark〕. // 한마디의 사과도 없이 가버렸다 He went away without a word of apology. // 그들이 처음 미국에 왔을 때는 영어를 한마디도 못했다 They didn't speak a word of English when they first came to the states. // 한마디로 말하면 네가 당장 여기에 왔으면 한다 To make a long story〔To make short of a long story〕, I'd like you to get over here right away.

한마음 one mind ; like-mindedness ; unanimity ; accord ; concord ¶ 한마음으로 with one accord // 한마음으로 협력하다 cooperate in harmony ; work with one mind

한마지로 汗馬之勞 meritorious services in war ; distinguished war services

한만 韓滿 Korea and Manchuria
— **국경** the frontier of Korea and Manchuria ; the Korean-Manchurian border

한매 寒梅 an early plum blossom

한명 限命 the appointed limit of life ; the destined duration of life ; the span of life

한모금 a draft ; a draught ; a drop (극소량) ¶ 한모금에 at a draft // 한모금의 물 a draught of water

한목 all together ; all at one time ¶ 일년치 봉급을 한목타다 receive a year's pay in a lump

한몫 a share ; a portion ; a quota ; a whack 《속》; a rake-off ; a split ; a divvy ¶ 단단히〔크게〕 한몫 보다 take the lion's share // 이익을 한몫 단단히 보다 get a good share of the profit
한몫 보다 (관용) have a share in ; take one's share in ; share〔participate〕 in (the profits) ; get one's whack 《속》 //

한무릎공부 —工夫 concentrated study for a fairly long time

한묵 翰墨 [필묵] writing brush and indian ink ; pen and ink ; [문한(文翰)] writing ; drawing

한문 漢文 Chinese composition ; Chinese writing
—자 Chinese characters **—학** Chinese literatures ; Chinese classics

한문자 閑文字 idle〔useless〕 words ; idle literature

한물 the best season ; the peak ; the height ¶ 한물이다 be at 《their》 best ; be in (the best) season // 한물이 지나다 be past 《their》 season // 딸기는 지금 한물이다 Strawberries are in season. // 창경궁에 벚꽃이 한물이다 The cherry blossoms at *Changkyŏng* Palace are at their best〔in full bloom〕. // 그 가수는 한물갔다 The singer is over the hill. /The singer is washed up. /The singer is finished. // 내 나이 오십이 되었으니 나도 한물갔어 I turned fifty, so I'm over the hill now. // 그 연예인은 한물갔지만 완전히 끝난 것은 아니다 The entertainer is over the hill, but he is not a has-been〔goner〕 yet // 그는 이제 한물갔다 He is history. /He is a goner. /He is has-been.

한미 韓美 Korea and America ¶ 한미의 Korean-American
— **경제 협력 위원회** the Korea-U. S. Economic Cooperation Committee 《ECC》 — **관계** Korean-American relations — **문제** a Korean-American question — **상호 방위 협정** the ROK-U. S. Mutual Defense Agreement — **원자력 협정** the ROK-U. S. Atomic Energy Agreement — **재단** the American-Korean Foundation 《A. K. F.》 — **행정 협정** the ROK-U. S. Agreement on Status-of-Forces in Korea ; the ROK-U. S. Status-of-Forces Agreement — **협회** the Korean-American Association — **환율** *won*-dollar exchange rate

한미 寒微 —하다 (be) poor and lowly ¶ 출신이 한미하다 be of lowly origin

한밑천 a sizable amount of capital ¶ 한밑천 잘 장만하다 amass a sizable fortune // 주식에서 한밑천 벌었다 I made a killing in the stock market.

한바닥 [중심지] the center ; the heart ; the main point ¶ 시장 한바닥 the center〔heart〕 of a market (place)

한바퀴 a round ; a turn ¶ 한바퀴 돌다 take a turn ; go round // 공원을 한바퀴 돌다 take a turn in the park // 집을 한바퀴 돌다 go round a house

한바탕 a scene ; a round ; a bout ; an event ; a fall (씨름) ¶ 한바탕 울다 cry for a spell // 씨름을 한바탕하다 have a bout of wrestling // 한바탕 싸움 소동을 벌이다 have a nice scene with 《a person》 // 한바탕 야단을 치다 give 《a person》 a good scolding

한 발 a〔one〕 step ¶ 한 발 한 발 step by step ; slowly ; gradually ¶ 한 발 앞으로 나아가다 take〔make〕 a step forward // 한 발 뒤로 물러서다 take a step backward // 한 발 늦어 그를 만나지 못했다 I missed him by a second.

한발 旱魃 a drought〔drouth〕 ; a spell of dry weather ; lack of rain ¶ 한발의 계속 a long drought ; a long spell of dry weather // 한발의 피해 damage from a drought // 한발로 인해 곡물이 흉작이 되었다 The drought has ruined the crops.
— **대책** measures against drought ; counter-drought measures — **피해** drought damage ; damage from a drought

한 발짝 ⇨ 한 발 ¶ 한 발짝도 밖에 안 나가다 keep indoors ; keep the house // 나는 지쳐서 한 발짝도 움직일 수가 없었다 I was so fatigued that I was unable to take another step.

‡한밤중 midnight ; the middle〔dead〕 of the night ¶ 한밤중에 in the middle of (the) night ; at midnight ; at (the) dead of night // 한밤중까지 far〔half way〕 into the night ; until the middle of the night // 한밤중에 피아노를 치다니 당신 정신이 나갔소 what's the (big) idea of playing the piano in the middle of night ?

한밥 ① [먹이] a feed(ing) ② [누에의] the last round of feed for silkworms

한방 一房 one room ; the same room ; [온방] the whole room

한방 漢方 Chinese (herb) medicine
—약 a Chinese (herb) medicine —의 a herb doctor ; a doctor〔physician〕 of the Chinese school

한 방울 a drop 《of water》 ¶ 한 방울씩 drop by drop

*한배¹ ① [사람의] a womb ; a venter ; a belly ¶ 한배의 형제 brothers of the same venter ② [동물의] a litter ¶ 돼지 새끼 한배 a litter of pigs // 한배의 강아지 puppies of the same litter

한배² ① 〖음악〗 (a) tempo ② [화살의] a bowshot

*한번 once ; one time ; one round ¶ 단 한번 only once ; once for all // 한번에 at once ; at a time ; at the same time // 한번 더 once more // 1년에 한번 once a year // 한번 보다 take a look 《at》 // 한번 가볼만한 곳이다 The place is worth a visit. // 한번에 두가지 일을 하지 마라 Do not attend to two things at a time. // 나는 한번에 손님을 한 사람 밖에 상대할 수 없다 I can only take one customer at a time. // 한번에 책을 몇 권이나 빌려 가지고 나갈 수 있습니까 ? How many books can I check out at a time ?
한번 실수는 병가의 상사(商事)다 〔속담〕 A stumble may prevent fall.
한번 엎지른 물은 주워 담지 못한다 〔속담〕 It is no use crying over spilt milk. / Grieve when the chance is past, it is too late. /what's done cannot be undone.
한번 한 말은 어디든지 날아간다 〔속담〕 Words have wings, and cannot be recalled. /Words and feathers the wind carries away. /Words are but wind.

한 벌 a suit ; a set ¶ 여름옷 한 벌 a summer suit ; a suit for summer wear // 의복 한벌 a suit of clothes // 화장품 한 벌 a toilet set // 찻잔 한 벌 a set of tea cups

한벽처 閑僻處 a secluded〔remote〕 place ; an isolated place

한복 韓服 Korean clothes〔costume, attire〕 ¶ 한복을 입은 in Korean dress〔clothes〕 // 한복을 입고 있다 be in Korean clothes ; have Korean clothes on

한복판 the very middle ; the center ; the heart ¶ 길 한복판 the middle of the road // 서울 한복판 the heart of *Seoul* // 과녁 한복판을 맞히다 hit the target right in the center

한부 悍婦 a tomboy ; a virago ; a shrew ; a vixen ; a termagant

한불 韓佛 Korea and France ¶ 한불의 Korean-French

한사 限死 desperation —하다 risk〔venture〕 one's life 《for》 ; stake one's life 《on》 ; be desperate〔frantic〕

한사 恨事 a pity ; a matter for regret ; a deplorable〔regrettable〕 matter

한사 寒士 a penniless〔poor〕 scholar

한 사람 ¶ 한 사람 한 사람〔한 사람씩〕 one at a time ; one by one ; [잇따라] one after another ; [개별적으로] individually ; in turn (교대로) // 나는 한 사람 한 사람씩 물어보았다 I asked them one after another.

한사리 the flood〔spring〕 tide

한사업 閑事業 an idle project ; a matter of minor importance

한사코 限死— at the risk of one's life ; with〔for〕 all one's life ; to the last ; desperately ; doggedly ; persistently ; relentlessly ¶ 한사코 달려들다 go at desperately // 한사코 싸우다 fight at the risk of one's life ; fight desperately // 한사코 조르다 tease 《a person for a thing》 persistently // 한사코 반대하다 persist in one's opposition

한산 閑散 ① [한가] leisure —하다 be at leisure ; be off work ; have time to spare ; (be) disengaged ¶ 한산한 사람 a leisured〔leisurely〕 person ; a man of leisure // 거리가 이 시간에는 한산하다 The traffic is light about this time.
② [불경기] dullness ; inactivity ; slackness ; flatness —하다 (be) stagnant ; inactive ; dull ; slack ¶ 한산한 시장 a dull〔flat〕 market // 상거래가 한산하다 Trade is stagnant.
—기 a slack season ; an off season

한살 ¶ 한살의 (one-)year old 《child》

한삼덩굴 Japanese hop ; Humulus japonicus (학명)

한색 寒色 a cold color

한생전 限生前 one's whole life ; a lifetime ; all one's life

한서 寒暑 cold and heat ; temperature ; winter and summer ¶ 한서의 차가 적다 The climate is moderate. /The weather is agreeable. // 한서의 차가 심하다 The climate is extreme both in summer and winter. /The heat and cold are extreme.

한서 漢書 [중국 서적] Chinese books〔classics〕 ; Chinese literature

한선 汗腺 〖해부〗 a sweat-gland ; Glandula sudorifera (학명)

한세상 一世上 ① [일평생] a lifetime ;

one's (whole) life ¶ 한세상을 통해서 from the cradle to the grave ; from birth to death // 독신으로 한세상을 보내다 remain single all one's life〔to the end of one's life〕
② [한창때] heyday ; the golden age ; one's best day ; the best time in one's life ; the heyday of one's life ¶ 그 사람도 한세상 지났다 He has seen his best days. /His sun is set. /He is a has-been now. 《미》 // 누구나 다 한세상은 있는 법이다 Every dog has his day and every man has his hour.

한센씨병 一氏病 Hansen's disease ⇨ 나병

한소 閑所 a quiet place

한소 韓蘇 Korea and Soviet Union
— 관계 the relations between Korea and Soviet Russia ; Korean-Russian relations **— 국경** the Korean-Russian border

한속 [같은 뜻] the same mind〔intention〕; [공모] conspiracy ; confederacy ¶ 한속이 되다 conspire with ; be in league with ; plot together ; go cahoots with 《미·속》 // 한속이 되어서 속이다 conspire together to cheat 《a person》 // 그들은 한속이다 They are an associate〔a confederate〕. // 둘이 한속이다 The two are of one mind. /They are in cahoots.

한 손 one hand ; each hand ¶ 그 일은 한 손으로는 힘들었다 It was hard work one-handed.
—잡이 a one-handed person

한손놓다 be finished ; end ; come〔be brought〕 to an end ¶ 겨우 한손놓았다 I have got the work off my hands. // 일은 한손놓았다 The work is by and large finished.

한수 一手 a trick ; a move ; a skill ; a game ; a means ¶ 한수 높다 be a cut above // 러시아가 다른 공화국들보다 한수 위에 서게 될 것 같습니다 I think Russia will be more equal than other republics.

한순 一巡 one round of shooting five arrows ¶ 활을 한순 쏘다 have a round of shooting five arrows

한순배 一巡杯 one round of drink ¶ 한순배 돌리다 pass (the liquor) around once

한술 a spoonful〔bite, morsel of food〕; [적은 음식] a small quantity 《of food》 ¶ 한술 뜨다 take a spoonful of food ; have a bite

한술 더 뜨다 be superior in wisdom ; outwit ; outsmart

†**한숨** ① [탄식] a (deep) sigh ; a deep〔heavy〕 breath ; an amorous sigh (연인들의) ; a sigh of relief (안심의) ¶ 한숨 쉬며 with a sigh // 한숨 쉬다 (heave a) sigh ; draw a long breath // 모두들 안도의 한숨을 쉬었다 Every one gave a sigh of relief.
② [호흡·휴식] a breath ; a rest ; pause ; relief ; a wink of sleep ; a nap ; a snatch of sleep ; a doze ¶ 한숨에 at a stroke ; at a breath ; at a stretch ; without stopping // 한숨 쉬고 after a pause // 한숨 쉬다〔들이다〕 take breath〔a rest〕; pause for breath // 한숨 자다 have a nap〔sleep, siesta〕; get a sleep ; sleep a wink // 이 근처에서 한숨 돌립시다 Why don't we take a short breather about here ?

한습 a one-year-old 《horse, ox》
—말 a pony one year old ; a yearling (pony)

한습 寒濕 ① cold and moisture ② 『한의』 rheumatism in the lower part of the body

한시 限時 time limit
—법 a law in force only for a limited period of time

한시 漢詩 a Chinese poem ; Chinese poetry 《총칭》

한시도 一時— even for a moment ¶ 한시도 잊지 않다 keep〔bear〕 《a thing》 in mind all the time ; never forget even for a moment // 한시도 몸에서 떼지 않다 always carry 《a thing》 about〔on〕 one

한시름 a big worry ; a great anxiety ; a great headache ¶ 자네 말을 듣고 한시름 놓았네 I worried a lot before you told me.
한시름 놓다 관용 be relieved of a great anxiety

한식 寒食 『민속』 the 105th day after the winter solstice (on which sacrificial food is offered at the ancestral tombs)

한식 韓式 Korean (style) ¶ 한식의 Korean-style
—집 a Korean-style house

한식 韓食 Korean-style food ¶ 한식을 드시겠습니까 양식을 드시겠습니까 Will you have Korean-style food or Western-style food ?

한심 寒心 **—하다** (be) pitiful ; pitiable ; regretful ; wretched ; miserable ; sorrowful ; lamentable ; grievous ¶ 한심한 일 a matter of regret ; a source〔cause〕 of disappointment ; a disheartening〔discouraging〕 thing // 한심한 사람 a hopeless fellow // 한심한 살림 a miserable〔wretched〕 life ; a scanty livelihood // 한심하기 짝이 없다 be extremely deplorable // 애가 저렇게 지각이 없으니 장차 무엇이 될는지 한심하다 Since the boy hasn't any sense at all, I am deeply concerned over his future.

한 쌍 一雙 a pair ; a couple ; a brace ¶ 좋은 한 쌍을 이루다 make〔form〕 a good pair ; be a good match 《for》

한아 閒雅 elegance ; gracefulness ; dain-

ㅎ

tiness 《of a scene》 —하다 (be) graceful ; elegant ; dainty ; refined

한아름 an armful ¶ 한아름의 책 an armful of books

한악 悍惡 ferocity ; fierceness ; cruelty ; savagery ; barbarity —하다 (be) ferocious ; fierce ; cruel ; savage ; barbarous

한야 寒夜 a cold night ; a winter night

한약 漢藥 a Chinese medicine ; a herb remedy ; herbs

—국 a dispensary of Chinese medicine ; a herb shop

한양 韓洋 [형용사적] Korean and European〔foreign〕

—식 절충 a compromise between Korean and European styles

한어 韓語 Korean (language) ; a Korean word

한어 漢語 Chinese (language) ; a Chinese word (어귀)

*한없다 限— (be) unlimited ; boundless ; endless ; limitless ; infinite ; unmeasurable ; eternal (영원) ¶ 한없이 endlessly ; unlimitedly ; boundlessly ; without end〔limit〕 ; extremely ; exceedingly ; greatly ; immensely // 한없는 일 endless work // 한없는 생명 eternal life // 한없는 바다 the boundless sea // 한없는 천지 the boundless universe // 아들을 한없이 사랑하다 love one's son no end 〔ever so much〕

한없다 恨— be gratified ; have nothing to be regretted〔desired〕 ; be perfectly happy

*한여름 ① [한창] midsummer ; the middle of summer ¶ 한여름 더위 the midsummer heat ② [한철] the whole summer ; all summer long ¶ 한여름도 잠깐 가다 the summer passes away quickly // 한여름 낚시질만 하다 do nothing but fish all summer long

한역 韓譯 translation into Korean ; a Korean translation —하다 translate into Korean ; put into Korean

영문 — translation from English into Korean ; English-(to)-Korean translation

한역 漢譯 translation into Chinese ; a Chinese translation —하다 translate 〔put〕 into Chinese

한열 寒熱 heat and cold ; chillness and fever

한염 旱炎 tropical〔torrid, intense〕 heat

한영 韓英 Korean-English

— 사전 a Korean-English dictionary

한옆 one side〔flank〕 ¶ 한옆으로 비키다 step aside

한오금 [활의] the large crook of an archer bow

한옥 韓屋 a Korean-style house

한외 限外 out of bounds ; beyond the limit ¶ 지폐의 한외 발행 excess〔extra〕 issue of paper currency

— 발행 excess issue ; overissue ; an extra issue — 원심기 an ultracentrifuge — 현미경 an ultramicroscope

한용 悍勇 dauntlessness ; intrepidity ; audacity ; boldness ; daring ; fearlessness ; valor —하다 (be) dauntless ; intrepid ; audacious ; bold ; daring

한우 寒雨 winter rain ; a cold rain (찬비)

한우충동 汗牛充棟 innumerable books

한운 閒雲 floating〔drifting〕 clouds ; wandering clouds ; a drift of cloud

—야학(野鶴) wandering clouds and wild cranes ¶ 한운야학을 벗삼다 lead a leisurely life

한움큼 a handful ; a grasp ; a grip ¶ 한움큼의 소금 a handful of salt // 한움큼에 (움켜) 쥐다 make one grip of

한월 寒月 a winter〔wintry〕 moon

한위 寒威 severe cold

한유 閒遊 idling ; loafing —하다 amuse oneself ; idle away the time ; loaf ; spend time idly

한은 韓銀 ⇨ 한국(—은행)

한음 漢音 the classical Chinese pronunciation of Chinese characters ; the original pronunciation of Chinese characters

한음식 —飮食 a snack (meal) ; a meal taken at an irregular time

한의 漢醫 a physician of the Chinese 〔the old〕 school ; a herb doctor

—사 ⇨ 한의(漢醫) —학 Chinese medicine〔medical science〕

한이 韓伊 Korea and Italy ¶ 한이의 Korean-Italian

한인 韓印 Korea and India ¶ 한인의 Korean-Indian

한인 閒人 a leisured person ; an idle person ; a man of leisure ; a loafer

—물입(勿入) No admittance except on business. (게시)

한인 韓人 a Korean ; a Coréen 《프》

한인 漢人 a Chinese

한일 韓日 Korea and Japan ¶ 한일의 Korean-Japanese

— 각료 회담 the Korea-Japan Ministerial Conference — 사전 a Korean-Japanese dictionary — 회담 the Korean-Japanese Conference

한일 경제 협의회 韓日經濟協議會 the Korea-Japan Economic Association

한일월 閑日月 leisure ; spare time ; an idle life ¶ 한일월을 보내다 live a quiet〔retired〕 life

한일자 —一字 ¶ 한일자로 in a straight line〔beeline〕 ; straight ; in an air line ; as the crow flies // 입을 한일자로 다물다 close one's lips firmly

*한입 a mouthful ; a bite ; a morsel of food ¶ 한입에 at a mouthful // 한입 가득 먹다 cram 《a thing》 in one's mouth

한자 漢字 a Chinese character〔ideo-

ㅎ

graph〕 ¶ 한자로 쓰다 write in Chinese characters

—어 a word written in Chinese characters — 제한 limitation in〔restriction on〕 the use of Chinese characters — 철폐 abolition of Chinese characters 상용(常用) — the Chinese characters for common use

*한잔 ① a cup《of tea》; a glass《of wine》; a glassful ; a cupful ¶ 한잔의 물 a glass of water // 커피〔차〕 한잔 a cup of coffee〔tea〕// 우유 한잔 a bowl of milk // 차를 한잔 더 드시겠습니까 Will you have another cup of tea?

② [술] a glass of wine ; a drink ; a shot ; slug《of whiskey》 ¶ 한잔 하다 have a drink〔glass of wine〕// 한잔 들이킨 기분으로 under the influence of wine ; be slightly intoxicated // 모두 한잔 하고 싶어했다 They were all dying for a drink. // 한잔 했다 I had a little drink. /I'm a little bit high. // 한잔 더 하겠습니까? Would you care for a refill? // 오늘밤 어디가서 한잔하세 Let's go someplace and have a drink tonight. // 내가 술 한잔 사겠다 Have a drink on me. // 술 한잔 더 주시오 Give me a refill please. /Give one more, Please. // 맥주 한잔 정도는 해가 전혀 없을 거야 One little beer isn't going to hurt anything.

한잠 a sleep ; a nap ; a deep〔sound〕 sleep ¶ 한잠 자다 take〔have〕 a sleep〔nap〕; sleep well〔soundly〕; fall into a deep sleep (숙면) // 어젯밤은 한잠도 못 잤다 I could not get a wink of sleep last night. /I could not sleep a wink last night.

한재 旱災 damage〔calamity〕 from a drought ; a drought disaster ¶ 한재를 입다 suffer from a drought

— 지구 the drought-stricken district

한저녁 a late supper

†한적 閒寂 quiet(ness) ; tranquility —하다 (be) quiet ; secluded ; sequestered ; restful ¶ 한적한 마을 a sequestered〔secluded〕 village // 한적하게 살다 live a retired life

한적 漢籍 Chinese literature ; Chinese classics

한절 寒節 the cold season ; midwinter

한 점 一點 a dot ; a speck ; a spot ; a point ; a mark ¶ 하늘에는 구름 한 점 없다 There is not a speck of cloud in the sky.

한점 寒點 [피부의] a cold point〔spot〕

†한정 限定 limitation ; qualification ; 〖논리〗 determination ; definition (뜻의) —하다 limit ; define (뜻을) ; restrict ; place limit upon ; set limits to ; qualify ¶ 한정된 limited ; defined // 한정된 지면 limited space // 회원을 100명으로 한정하다 limit membership to 100

— 가격 the ceiling price ; the (price) ceiling — 번호 a copy number —사(詞) 〖문법〗 a definitive (word) ; a determinative ; a determiner ; a qualifier — 상속 qualified acceptance of heritage — 승인 limited recognition — 치산(治產) quasi-incompetence — 치산자 a quasi-incompetent (person) —판 a limited edition〔publication〕; a numbered copy

한제 韓製 (of) Korean make〔manufacture〕; made in Korea ¶ 한제의 Korean made ; of Korean make ; home-made (국산의)

한제 寒劑 a freezing mixture ; a cryogen

한조각 a piece《of》; a bit ; a fragment ¶ 빵 한조각 a piece of bread // 한조각의 양심 a bit of conscience

한족 韓族 the Korean race

한족 漢族 the Han〔Chinese〕 race

한종신 限終身 all life long ; for life ; throughout one's life ; till death

한종일 限終日 all day (long) ; until sunset

한줄기 ① [한가닥] a streak ; a ray ¶ 한줄기의 희망 a ray〔gleam〕 of hope ② [한바탕] a spell ¶ 소나기가 한줄기 오다 have a (spell of) shower

한줌 a handful《of rice》; a lock《of wool》 ¶ 한줌의 토지 a small lot《of land》

한중 韓中 Korea and China ¶ 한중의 Korean-Chinese

— 무역 Korean-Chinese trade ; Sino-Korean trade — 사전 a Korean-Chinese dictionary — 합작 영화 a Korean-and-Chinese-made film ; a film jointly made by Koreans and Chinese

한중 寒中 midwinter ; the cold season ; the depth of winter ¶ 한중에 during the cold season ; in (the depth of) winter

— 훈련 midwinter training ; winter exercise

한즉 if so ; then ¶ 한즉 인제 어떻게 하는 것이 좋을까 Then, what should we do now?

한증 汗蒸 a sudatorium ; a sudatory ; a sweating bath ; a steam〔vapor〕 bath

—하다 take a sweating〔steam〕 bath

—막 a sweating bathroom

한지 韓紙 Korean paper

한지 寒地 a cold region

— 식물 a psychrophyte

한지 閑地 a quiet place ; a retired〔secluded〕 place

한직 閑職 a sinecure (office) ; an easy post〔position, office〕 ¶ 한직이 아니다 be hardly a sinecure ; be not a〔no〕 sinecure

한집안 a family ; one's folk ; members of a family ; one's family people ; [친척] relatives ; a clan ; one's kinsfolk ¶ 한

집안 같이 취급하다 treat 《a person》 as a member of one's family ; give 《a person》 family comforts // 한집안이나 다름 없다 be in close relation with each other

한짝 one odd ; one〔a〕 direction ; one side

한쪽 a quarter ; one side ; one hand ; one way ¶ 한쪽으로 기울다 lean to one side // 한쪽으로 비키다 step aside // 한쪽 귀가 안들리다 be deaf in one ear

†**한차례** one round ; a turn ; once ; a time ¶ 씨름을 한차례 하다 have a round of wrestling

한찬 漢讚 Buddhist hymns of praise translated in Chinese character

*__한참__ ① [한동안] for some time ; for a time〔while〕; for a spell ¶ 한참만에 after a good while // 소나기가 한참 퍼부었다 There was a shower for some time.
② [휴식] a rest ; a break ; a spell ; a period 《between breaks》; one time ; one stretch ; one sitting ¶ 한참의 일 a spell of work

한창 ① [절정] the height ; the summit ; the zenith ; the peak ; the climax ; [꽃의] 《in》 full bloom ; 《at it's》 best ; [인생의] prime ; flower ; bloom ¶ 여자〔남자〕의 한창 때 《in》 the prime of womanhood〔manhood〕// 젊은 한창 때에 in the prime of youth ; in one's days // 한창 더위에 in the heat of the day // 꽃이 한창이다 Flowers are at their best〔in full bloom〕. // 요사이는 딸기가 한창이다 Strawberries are in (season) now. // 지금이 한창 여름이다 It is the height of summer now. // 그 아가씨는 지금이 한창 때이다 She is in the prime 〔flower bloom〕 of youth. // 그는 한창 때가 지났다 He is past the prime of his life. // 꽃은 이제 한창 때가 지났다 The flowers are past their best.
② [부사적] ¶ 한창일 때 in the midst 《of》; at the height 《of》; in full swing // 폭풍이 한창일 때 in the midst of a storm // 낮이 한창 더울 때에 in the heat of the day // 영국은 당시 한창 전쟁중이었다 England was then at the height 〔thick〕 of the war. // 경기가 한창이다 The game is in full swing〔blast〕. // 그는 지금 한창 일할 나이다 He is just at the prime of life.

한천 旱天 dry weather ; a (spell of) drought ; [염천] hot〔broiling〕 weather ¶ 한천의 자우(慈雨) a rainfall eagerly longed for

한천 寒天 ① [추운 철] cold〔freezing〕 weather ; a bleak〔cold〕 wintry sky ② [식품] Bengal isinglass ; (vegetable) gelatin ; gelidium jelly
— 배양기(培養基) gelatin culture medium

한철 one season

한촌 寒村 a poor〔humble〕 village ; a remote〔a forlorn, an out-of-the-way〕 hamlet ; a deserted village

한추위 severe〔intense〕 cold ; a spell of cold weather ; a cold snap

*__한층 一層__ ① [더욱] more ; still more ; all the more ¶ 한층 더 책임을 무겁게 하다 make the responsibility heavier // 한층 더 공부하다 work harder // 한층 더 노력하다 make greater efforts // 8월이 되면 한층 더 더워진다 It gets hotter in August // 막내 아들이 돼서 한층 더 귀엽다 I love him more because he is my youngest son. ② [층계] a step ; the first step〔flight, story, level, floor〕

한치 an inch ¶ 한치도 《not》 at all ; 《not》 a bit // 한치의 땅도 양보하지 않다 cede not an inch of ground // 나는 그 문제에 관한 한 한치도 양보하지 않겠다 I will not yield an inch on that matter.

한카래꾼 a team of three plowmen

한칼 ① a single〔one〕 stroke 《of a sword》 ¶ 한칼로 베다 cut down with a single stroke of a sword ② [고기] a slice of meat

*__한탄 恨歎__ sigh ; lamentation ; grief ; deploring ; woe ; affliction **—하다** sigh 《for grief》; heave〔fetch〕 a sigh ; lament ; have a heavy〔broken〕 heart ; moan ; be grieved 〔sad〕; grieve ; deplore ¶ 한탄할 deplorable ; regrettable ; lamentable // 자식이 없음을 한탄하다 regret that one is childless // 죽음을 한탄하다 lament for the death // 한탄할 노릇이다 It is to be regretted 《that》

한턱 a treat ; an entertainment ; a feast ; hospitability **—하다** stand treat for 《one's friend》; give 《a person》 a treat ; treat 《another》 to 《something》; blow 《another》 to 《a drink》; stand 《something》 ¶ 저녁을 한턱 내다 give a dinner 《for a person》; entertain 《a person》 with a dinner // 그는 우리에게 술을 한턱 냈다 He treated us to a drink. // 이번엔 내가 한턱할 차례다 This is my treat now. / This is on me. // 신세를 진 대가로 한턱 내겠다 Let me treat you to a meal in return for the help you've given me. // 그는 한턱을 낸 후에 나에게 이 일을 부탁했다 After treating me to a meal, he asked me to do this job.

한테 to ; at ; for ; by 《a person》 ¶ 개한테 돌을 던지다 throw a stone at a dog // 그것은 누구한테 온 편지냐 Who 〔Whom〕 is the letter for ? // 누구한테 들었냐 By whom were you told ? /Who told you ?

한테서 from ; of ; through ¶ 멀리 친구한테서 온 편지 a letter from a friend far away // 자네 이야기는 김군한테서 들었네 I heard of you through Mr.

Kim.

한통 ① [활의] the middle (part) of an archery bow ; the grip of a bow ② ⇨ 한통속

한통속 one and the same group ; partisans ; fellow adherents〔conspirators〕; a party ¶ 음모의 한통속 a party to a plot // 한통속이 되어 in conspiracy〔collusion, cahoots〕《with》

한통치다 group together ; put〔add, join〕together ¶ 한통쳐서 (lumping) all together ; as a group ; in the gross ; in one lot ; including ; inclusive of // 모두 한통쳐서 도둑놈으로 생각하다 regard all of them as robbers // 차비 기타를 한통쳐서 여비가 얼마나 들까 How much will the traveling expenses be including the railroad fares and all other items?

한파 寒波 a cold wave ¶ 한파가 전국을 엄습했다 A cold wave swept〔hit〕(over) the country. /Freezing weather gripped〔seized〕(over) the country.

*__한판__ a game ; a round ; a bout (씨름 따위의) ¶ 씨름을 한판하다 have a round of wrestling // 장기를 한판 두다 play 〔have〕a bout〔game〕of chess

— 승부 a contest of single round

한 팔 [한쪽의 팔] one arm ; [신뢰하는 조력자] a right-hand man ; one's right hand ¶ 그는 다급할 때 당신의 한 팔 노릇을 할거요 He will be a good help〔of much service〕to you in case of need.

한패 —牌 one of the (same) party 〔group, set〕; fellows ; a confederate ¶ 그도 한패임에 틀림없다 He must be one of the party.

†**한편 —便** [한쪽] one side ; one hand ; the other side ; one way ; in the mean time ; meanwhile ; in addition to ¶ 한편에 on one side // 한편에는… 또 한편에는 on the one hand... and on the other (hand) // 길의 한편을 걷다 keep to one side of the road // 한편에 치우치다 be one-sided ; lean to one side // 그에게 사실을 말해주고 싶지만 한편으로는 그의 감정을 상해주고 싶지 않다 I feel like telling him the truth, but on the other hand I'd hate to hurt his feelings. // 소녀들은 도시락을 꺼내는 한편 소년들은 불을 피웠다 The girls laid out the picnic lunch, while the boys built a fire.

한평생 —平生 a lifetime ; one's (whole) life ; all one's life ; throughout one's life ; as long as one lives ; to the end of one's life ¶ 한평생을 통하여 from birth to death ; from the cradle to the grave // 한평생 한번의 기회 the chance of a lifetime // 한평생의 일 one's lifework // 그는 물리학의 연구에 한평생을 바쳤다 He devoted〔dedicated〕his life to the study of physics. // 그는 한평생을 망쳤다 He made a failure of his life. // 그는 한평생 행복하게 지냈다 He was happy all his life.

한푼 a penny ; a coin ; a copper ; a farthing ¶ 한푼 없는 penniless // 한푼 없이 되다 be reduced to beggary // 한푼도 받지 않고 without a cent of remuneration // 한푼의 가치도 없다 be not worth a (brass) farthing

한풀꺾이다 flinch 《from difficulties》; falter ; be broken in spirits ; wince 《under the blow》; be discouraged ; be disheartened ; be demoralized〔daunted〕 ¶ 밀려오는 대 병력을 보고 그들은 한풀 꺾였다 They flinched before the great force marching against them. // 첫번에 실패하자 그의 열의는 한풀 꺾였다 The initial failure daunted〔chilled〕his ardor.

한풀다 恨— attain〔carry out, gratify, fulfil, realize〕one's (cherished) desire ¶ 드디어 한을 풀었다 I have had my desire〔wish〕fulfilled at last. // 그는 오랫동안 맺힌 한을 풀었다 What he had long hoped for came true.

한풀이 恨— —하다 vent one's spite ; satisfy one's grudge ; revenge oneself 《on》; pay off old scores ; take revenge 《on a person for something》; satisfy one's resentment ; get even with 《a person》

한풍 寒風 a cold〔an icy, a chilly〕wind ¶ 살을 에이는 듯한 한풍 a cutting〔biting, piercing, bleak〕wind

한하다 限— limit ; restrict ¶ 성인에 한한 영화 film for adults only // 사원에 한하여 입장을 허가함 Admission to employees only. // 이 표는 1인 1매에 한한다 This ticket admits〔is good for〕one person only.

한학 漢學 Chinese literature ; Chinese classics ; sinology

—자 a scholar of Chinese classics

한한사전 漢韓辭典 a Chinese-Korean dictionary

한해 旱害 damage〔calamity〕from drought ; drought disaster ¶ 한해를 입다 suffer from a drought

— 지구 a drought-stricken area

한해 寒害 damage from cold weather ¶ 동북 지방에 한해가 있었다 In the North-eastern districts the crops suffered damage due to cold weather.

한해살이 〖식물〗 an annual plant ; annuals

한호 韓濠 Korea and Australia ¶ 한호의 Korean-Australian

한화 閑話 idle〔small, leisurely〕talk ; gossip ; a chat ; chitchat **—하다** talk idly ; chat ; have chitchat ; gossip

—휴제 Now let's come to the point.

한화 韓貨 [화폐] Korean money〔currency〕; [화물] Korean goods

한화 韓華 [형용사적] Korean-Chinese

ㅎ

할 割 percentage ; percent ; rate ; proportion ¶ 1할 ten percent // 3할 할인해서 팔다 sell at 30 percent discount

할갑다 (be) loose ⇨ 헐겁다

할거 割據 — 하다 hold one's own ground ; maintain one's independence (of the central government) ; hold each one's own sphere of influence ; jealously defend sectional authority
군웅— rivalry of local barons 군웅—시대 the age of rival chiefs〔warlords〕

할근거리다 gasp (for breath) ; pant ; wheeze ; puff (and blow) ; breathe hard〔heavily〕 ¶ 숨을 할근거리면서 말하다 gasp out ; puff out ; speak while panting

할근할근 gasping〔ly〕 ; wheezingly — 하다 breathe in a gasping way

할기족족 with a displeased〔reproachful〕 look from the corner of one's eyes — 하다 look displeased〔discontented〕

할깃거리다, 할낏거리다 ⇨ 흘깃거리다

할날 one day ; a day

‡**할당 割當** allotment ; quota ; rationing ; assignment ; allocation ; apportionment ; division ; distribution — 하다 assign ; allot ; allocate ; apportion ; divide 《between》 ; distribute 《among》 ; prorate (안분) ; assess (부과) ¶ 일을 할당하다 assign 《a person》 for a task // 각각 할당하다 allot a share to each // 100만원이 우리과에 할당됐다 One million *won* was allotted to our section.
—금 allotment ; assessment —량〔액〕 a quota ; an allotment ; a stint ¶ 전력의 할당량 an allocated amount of power // 오늘 할당량은 다했다 We've made our quota for the day ! — 배급 quota delivery ; rationing —제 the quota system —표 an allotment chart 수출 —제 the export quota system

할듯할듯 be ready to do ; be about 〔going〕 to do ; nearly — 하다 look as if one is going to do

할딱거리다 pant ; puff ; breathe heavily ; be out of breath ¶ 숨이 차서 할딱거리다 be panting for breath

할딱할딱 panting ; puffing ; breathing heavily ¶ 할딱할딱 달리다 run along panting

할똥말똥 hesitantly ; half-heartedly — 하다 hesitate to 《do》 ; be half-hearted

할랑거리다 ① 〔물건이〕 be loose ; be loose-fitting ② 〔행동이〕 be rash ; be hasty ; be precipitate ; be careless ; be heedless ; be thoughtless

할랑하다 (be) loose ; loose-fitting

할래발딱 ⇨ 헐레벌떡

할렐루야 halleluiah ; hallelujah

할례 割禮 〖종교〗 circumcision — 하다 circumcise ; perform the circumcision

할로겐 〖화학〗 halogen
— 화합물 halide

할말 what one wants〔has〕 to say ; one's say ¶ 네게 할말이 있다 I have something to tell you. // 너는 아무 것도 할말이 없을 텐데 I don't think you have anything to complain of.

†**할머니** a grandmother ; a grandma ; an old woman〔lady〕 (노파) ; a granny (구)

할멈 〔노파〕 an old woman ; a granny ; a goody (지체가 낮음) ; 〔하녀 따위〕 an old housekeeper

할미 〔조모〕 a grandmother ; a grandma ; 〔노파〕 an old〔aged〕 woman

할미꽃 〖식물〗 a pasqueflower ; Pulsatilla koreana (학명)

할미새 〖새〗 a wagtail ; Motacillidae (학명)

할복 割腹 self-disembowelment ; suicide by disembowelment — 하다 disembowel oneself ; rip up one's own abdomen〔belly〕
— 자살 suicide by disembowelment

할부 割賦 allotment ; quota — 하다 allot ; set〔put〕 quota 《on, to》
— 구매 installment purchase —금 an allotment — 상환 amortization — 지불 payment by installment — 판매 selling on an installment basis

할선 割線 〖기하〗 a secant

할쑥하다 (be) thin ; haggard ; gaunt ; emaciated ; worn out ; careworn ; wearied ; exhausted ¶ 할쑥한 얼굴 a haggard〔worn〕 face // 병으로 할쑥해지다 become worn out from illness ; be pulled down by one's illness // 그녀는 비탄에 젖어 할쑥해졌다 Sorrow has left its traces on her face.

†**할아버지** a grandfather ; a grandpa ; an old man (노인)

할아범 an old〔aged〕 man

†**할애 割愛** — 하다 part with 《a thing》 ; share 《a thing with a person》 ; spare 《a thing》 ; give up reluctantly ¶ 식량을 할애하다 spare part of provisions 《for another》

할양 割讓 cession ; alienation — 하다 cede 《territory》 ; alienate 《a piece of land》 ¶ 토지의 할양 the cession of territory

‡**할인 割引** discount ; reduction ; an allowance ; price-cutting — 하다 discount ; reduce ; cut off ¶ 할인하여 at a reduced price ; at a discount ; at a cut rate // 수표를 은행에서 할인하다 get a bill discounted at a bank // 1할 할인하다 give 10 percent discount
— 가격 a reduced price —권 a discount ticket〔coupon〕 — 기간 the term of discount — 소매점 a discount house — 수표 a discounted bill — 승차권 a reduced rate〔fare〕 ticket ; a cheap ticket — 시간 reduced fare hours — 어음 a discount(ed) bill — 요금 a dis-

count (charge, commission) —율 a discount rate 단체 — a group(-trip) reduction 어음 — bill discounting 은행 — bank〔bankers'〕 discount 재— rediscount 현금 — cash discount 수표 — 중매인 a discount broker

할인 割印 a tally impression ¶ 할인을 찍은 서류 documents with a tally impression // 할인을 찍다 imprint a seal ; affix a seal over two edges〔at the joining of two papers〕

할일 things to do ¶ 할일이 많다 have lots to do ; be busy // 할일(이) 없다 have nothing to do // 너를 위해 할일이 없는지 Is there anything I can do for you?

할주 割註 an inserted note

*__할증 割增__ an extra (fare, charge) ; a premium ; a bonus —하다 increase proportionally ; pay〔give〕 an extra〔a premium〕

—금 a premium ¶ 할증금부 채권 a premium bond ; a premium-bearing debenture — 발행 issuance of bonds at a premium — 배당금 an extra dividend ; a bonus — 비율 a premium rate — 요금 an extra charge ; a surcharge — 임금 extra〔premium, increased〕 wages ; progressive wages ; extra〔premium〕 pay

할짝거리다 lick〔lap〕 lightly ; keep licking

할쭉거리다 lick lightly ⇨ 할짝거리다

할쭉하다 (be) haggard

‡**할퀴다** scratch ; claw ; maul ¶ 사람의 얼굴을 (손톱으로) 할퀴다 scratch《a person's》 face (with one's fingernails) // 싸움을 해서 크게 할퀴었다 be badly mauled in a fight

‡**핥다** lick ; lap ¶ 깨끗이 핥다 lick clean // 우유를 깨끗이 핥다 lap up milk

핥아먹다 ① [혓바닥으로] lick up ; lap up ② [남의 물건을] swindle ; defraud ; cheat ; wheedle ; fleece ¶ 남의 물건을 핥아먹다 acquire《a person's》 things by fraud

핥아세다 acquire by fraud ⇨ 핥아먹다

핥이다 be〔get〕 licked ; [핥게 하다] have 《a thing》 licked ¶ 개에게 손을 핥이다 have one's hand licked by a dog

함 函 a box ; a chest ; a case ¶ 함진아비 a box bearer〔carrier〕

사서— a post-office box《P. O. B.》 옷— a clothes chest 우편— a mailbox

함거 檻車 a cage-cart

함교 艦橋 the bridge (of a warship) ; the navigating platform

— 갑판 the bridge deck 전〔후〕— the fore〔after〕 bridge

함구 緘口 —하다 hold one's tongue ; keep one's mouth shut ; keep one's lips tight ; keep〔be〕 silent ¶ 함구불언하다 refuse to talk ; say nothing

—령 a gag law〔rule〕

함기 艦旗 an ensign

†**함께** together《with, along》; in company with ; in unison ¶ 영문 이력서 및 최근 사진 2매와 함께 along with a personal history statement in English and two recent photographs // 함께 가다 go together〔with〕; accompany《a person》 // 함께 일하다 work together

함닉 陷溺 —하다 ① [물에] drown ; fall into ; sink ② [주색에] indulge 《in》; be addicted ; give oneself up

함당 含糖 ¶ 함당의 〖화학〗 saccharated

—량 the amount of contained sugar

함대 艦隊 a fleet (대함대) ; a squadron (소함대) ¶ 함대를 파견하다 dispatch a squadron // 태평양에 함대를 배치하다 station a squadron in the Pacific

— 기지 a fleet base — 사령관 the commander of a fleet 무적 — the Invincible Armada 분견〔상비〕 — a detached〔standing〕 squadron 연습 — a training squadron 연합 — a combined fleet 유격 — a flying squadron ; a task force 의용 — a volunteer fleet 주력 — the main fleet 현존 — a fleet in being

‡**함락 陷落** ① [토지의] fall ; subsidence ; sinking ; caving in ; collapse ② [적진의] fall ; reduction —하다 fall in ; subside ; sink ; collapse ; cave in ; be reduced

— 지진 〖지질〗 a fallen earthquake —호 a depression lake ; a cave-in lake

함량 含量 content ; contained quantity

알코올 — the alcohol content

함령 艦齡 the age〔life〕 of a warship

함루 含淚 —하다《tears》 stand〔come to, gather in〕 one's eyes ; be moved to tears ;《one's eyes》 swim〔dim, glisten〕 with tears ; be going to shed tears

함몰 陷沒 depression ; subsidence ; a cave-in ; sinking —하다 sink ; subside ; be depressed ; cave in ; collapse

— 지진 a fallen earthquake —해 an ingression sea —호 a depression lake

함묵 含默 silence ; dumbness ; reticence —하다 keep silent〔quiet〕; hold one's tongue ; keep one's mouth shut

함미 艦尾 the stern of a warship

—묘(錨) a stern anchor —포 a stern chaser

함바기 〖식물〗 Stephania japonica (학명)

함박 ① [함지박] a scooped wooden dish ② ⇨ 함박꽃

함박꽃 〖식물〗 a peony (flower)

함박꽃나무 〖식물〗 a magnolia ; Magnolia parviflora (학명)

함박눈 large flakes of snow ¶ 함박눈이 오다 it snows in large flakes

함박조개 〖조개〗 a surf〔hen, sea〕 clam ; Spisula Sachalinensis (학명)

함봉 緘封 seal ; sealing ⇨ 봉함

ㅎ

*함부로 indiscriminately ; at random ; thoughtlessly ; disorderly ; recklessly ; without permission〔good reason〕; rudely ; as one pleases〔likes, chooses〕; at will ; on one's own authority ¶ 사람을 함부로 치다 hit 《a person》 without reason ; beat 《a person》 mercilessly // 나무를 함부로 자르다 cut trees without permission〔at random〕// 돈을 함부로 쓰다 spend money recklessly // 말을 함부로 하다 talk without thinking ; have a careless manner of speaking // 함부로 침을 뱉는 사람은 100달러의 벌금을 물어야 한다 A reckless spitter will be fined one hundred dollars.

함부르크 Hamburg (독일의 도시)

함분 含憤 bearing anger ; harboring resentment ―하다 bear resentment 《towards》; hold a grudge 《against》

함빡 all (in all) ; thoroughly ; completely ¶ 함빡 젖은 옷 dripping-wet clothes // 비에 함빡 젖다 one's clothes are all wet with rain ; be drenched with rain to the skin

함상 艦上 ¶ 함상의〔에서〕 aboard 《a war vessel》

함석 zinc ; galvanized iron sheet ; sheet-zinc ¶ 함석으로 지붕을 덮다 roof with galvanized iron sheets

― 지붕 a zinc roof ― 집 a house with a zinc roof〔with galvanized iron roofing〕 ― 판 sheet zinc ; a galvanized iron sheet

함선 艦船 warships and other vessels 〔craft〕

*함성 喊聲 a war cry ; a battle cry ; a great outcry ¶ 함성을 올리다 raise 〔give〕 a battle cry

함소 含笑 ―하다 hold a laugh in one's mouth ; have〔wear〕 a smile about one's mouth

함수 含水 ¶ 함수의 〖화학〗 hydrous ; hydrated

―량 the amount of contained water ― 탄소 a carbohydrate ― 화합물 a hydrated compound ; a hydrate

함수 函數 〖수학〗 a (mathematical) function

― 관계 functional relation ―론 the theory of function ―식 a functional formula 대수〔미분, 삼각〕 ― an algebraic〔a differential, trigonometric〕 function

함수 鹹水 salt water ; sea water ; brine

―어 a saltwater fish ―호 a salt lake ; a lagoon

함수 艦首 the bow (of a warship)

―포 a bow gun〔chaser〕

함수초 含羞草 〖식물〗 a sensitive plant ; Mimosa pudica (학명)

함실 a smooth-bottom fireplace

―방 a room with a hypocaust heated by a smooth-bottom fireplace ― 아궁이 ⇨ 함실

함실함실 ⇨ 흠실흠실

함씨 咸氏 your nephew

함양 涵養 cultivation ; culture ; fostering ―하다 cultivate ; foster ; develop ; build (up) ; train ; promote ¶ 국력을 함양하다 build〔promote〕 national power // 덕성을 함양하다 build〔cultivate〕 moral character

함열 艦列 a column ; a line ahead

함원 含怨 ―하다 bear 《a person》 a grudge ; have a grudge〔rancor, grievance〕 《against》; bear〔harbor, cherish, nurse〕 ill will 《against》

함유 含有 ―하다 contain ; have 《in》; hold ; include

―량 content ― 성분 a component 알코올 ―량 alcohol content ¶ 위스키는 알코올 함유량이 많다 Whisky contains a large percentage of alcohol. 지방 ―량 fat content

함유 수지 含油樹脂 oleoresin

함입 陷入 depression ; subsidence ―하다 depress ; subside ; sink

함자 銜字 your〔his〕 name ¶ 선생님의 함자가 어떻게 되십니까 Could you tell me your name, sir ?

함장 艦長 the captain of a warship

―실 the captain's cabin

함재 艦載 carrying aboard a warship ; loading on a warship ―하다 carry 〔load〕 aboard a warship

―기 a deck plane ; a ship plane ― 수뢰정 a torpedo launch

함적 艦籍 the Navy list ¶ 함적에서 빼다 strike 《a ship》 off the Navy list

*함정 陷穽 a pitfall ; a pit ; a trap ; a snare ¶ 함정을 놓다 lay〔set〕 a trap 《for》// 함정에 빠지다 fall into a pit〔trap, snare〕; be trapped ; be caught in a trap ; fall a victim to 《a person's》 plot // 함정에 빠뜨리다 pit ; trap ; entrap ; snare // 자신이 만든 함정에 빠지다 be caught in one's own snare ; be hoist with one's own petard

함정 艦艇 war vessels ; naval vessels

함지 a large scooped wooden vessel 〔bowl〕

―박 a scooped wooden dish

함지 陷地 sunken land ; a hollow

함체 艦體 the hull of a warship

*함축 含蓄 implication ; significance ; comprehension ; suggestiveness ―하다 imply ; signify ; suggest ; comprehend ¶ 함축성 있는 significant ; pregnant ; implicit ; implicative ; suggestive (암시적) // 그가 말하는 것은 함축성이 있다 What he says is full of suggestions.

함치르르 ―하다 (be) sleek ; slick ; glossy ; bright ⇨ 흠치르르

함포 艦砲 the guns of a warship

― 사격 bombardment from a warship 〔by naval guns〕; naval bombardment

함함하다 (be) soft and glossy
함혐 含嫌 harboring suspicion〔enmity〕 ―하다 be suspicious of ; feel enmity toward
함호 鹹湖 a salt lake
함흥차사 咸興差使 a lost〔truant〕 messenger ¶ 그는 미국에 가더니 함흥차사가 되어버렸다 He has gone to America never to return〔for good (and all)〕.
합 合 ① the sum total ; grand total ¶ 합이 100만원이다 the sum total is one million *won* ; amount up to a million *won* ② ⇨ 홉 (용량의 단위) ③ 〖철학〗 (a) synthesis ④ [싸움] a bout ; a pass
합 盒 a brass bowl with a lid
합각 合閣 gable
― 지붕 a gable roof ― 처마 gable eaves
†합격 合格 success in an examination ; passing an examination ; eligibility ⟪for an office⟫ ―하다 [시험에] pass〔succeed in, be successful in, go through, get through, make it through〕 an examination ; [심사에] be accepted ; be selected ; be chosen ; be found eligible ; [물건 따위가] come up to the standard〔mark〕 ; stand the test ; pass muster ; pass inspection ¶ 서울대학교 입학 시험에 합격하다 succeed in〔pass〕 the entrance examination to *Seoul* National University // 합격 발표는 3월 1일이다 The result of the examination will be announced on March 1.
―률 the ratio of successful applicants ― 여부 success or failure ―자 a successful candidate ―점 a passing mark ―증 a certificate ― 통지 a notice of ⟪a person's⟫ success in examination ―품 goods found acceptable ; tested goods
†합계 合計 the sum total ; the total (amount, sum) ; the aggregate ―하다 add〔sum〕 up ; total ; foot up ⟪미⟫ ¶ 합계하여 in total ; in the aggregate ; altogether ; put together ; in all ; all told // 합계 100권의 책 a total of 100 books ; 100 books all told // 합계액 2,000원 2,000 *won* in total // 합계를 내다 figure out a sum // 합계 5,000원이 되다 amount to 5,000 *won* in all // 합계가 얼마입니까? What does it ring〔add〕 up to?
*합금 合金 an alloy ; a compound metal ―하다 alloy ⟪metals⟫ ; make an alloy ⟪of⟫
―강(鋼) alloy(ed) steel
합기도 合氣道 *hapkido*, an art of self-defense
합내 閤內 your family
― 제절 all (members of) your family
합당 合當 fitness ; suitability ; appropriateness ―하다 (be) fit ; suitable ; proper ; adequate ; apt ; appropriate ; right ¶ 합당한 예 a proper example
합당 合黨 a party merger ―하다 ⟪parties⟫ merge ; merge ⟪parties⟫
*합동 合同 combination ; union ; amalgamation ; incorporation ; merger ; fusion ; coalition ; 〖수학〗 congruence 〔congruity〕 ―하다 combine ; unite ; effect a union ; amalgamate ; merge ; enter into combination ; incorporate ¶ 합동해서 unitedly ; jointly ; in combination ; in partnership
― 결혼(식) a mass〔group, joint〕 wedding (ceremony) ― 관리〔경영〕 joint control〔management〕 ― 사업 a joint undertaking〔venture〕 ; a combine ― 선거 연설〔정견 발표회〕 the joint election speech〔campaign〕 rally ― 신문 syndicated〔chain〕 papers ― 위령제 a joint service for the (war) dead ― 위원회 a joint committee ―장 a joint funeral ― 재판 a common trial ― 참모 회의 의장 the Chairman of the Joint Chiefs of Staff ; the JCS Chairman ― 회의 a joint session〔convention〕 기업 ― a trust ; a cartel
합뜨리다 ⇨ 합치다
합력 合力 ① 〖물리〗 a resultant (force) ② [협력] joint efforts ; combined strength ; cooperation ―하다 join ⟪with⟫ ; cooperate ⟪with⟫ ; pull〔work〕 together
합류 合流 ① [냇물] confluence ; conflux ―하다 join ; flow together ¶ 그 강은 한강과 합류한다 That river joins the *Han* river. ② [합동] joining ; linking ; union ―하다 join ; unite〔link up〕 ⟪with⟫ ; be merged ⟪into⟫ ; incorporate ⟪with⟫ ¶ 두 정당이 합류하다 two political parties get together
―점 the confluence ⟪of rivers⟫
합리 合理 rationality ; reasonableness ―하다 (be) rational ; reasonable ; logical ¶ 합리적으로 rationally ; reasonably // 산업의 합리화 the rationalization of industry // 합리화하다 rationalize
―성 rationality ―주의 rationalism ―주의자 a rationalist ―화 rationalization ¶ 합리화하다 rationalize 산업 ―화 the industrial rationalization ; the rationalization of industry
합명 合名 merger ; partnership ―하다 merge ; form a partnership
― 회사 an unlimited partnership ; a general partnership
합반 合班 a combined class ―하다 combine ⟪two⟫ classes
― 교실 a combined classroom ― 수업 combined classwork
합방 合邦 unification of two countries ; annexation ―하다 annex ; get unified
한일 ― the Japanese annexation of Korea

*합법 合法 lawfulness ; legality ; legitimacy ¶ 합법적 lawful ; legal ; legitimate

참고 **lawful** 국법과 교회의 규율 도덕률 따위에 합치하다 **legal** 국법 또는 그 실시 수속에 문자 그대로 합치하다 **legitimate** 법률 습관 당국자 따위로부터 정당하다고 인정받다

¶ 합법적 수단으로 by lawful〔legal, legitimate〕 means // 합법적 정부 a legitimate government
—성 lawfulness —주의 legitimacy ; legalism —화 legalization

*합병 合倂 combination ; union ; amalgamation ; consolidation ; merger ; coalition ; fusion (정당의) ; [병합] annexation (영토의) ; affiliation (회사의) ; incorporation (편입) —하다 combine ; unite ; amalgamate ; merge ; annex ; affiliate ; be incorporated 《with》 ¶ 두 회사를 합병하다 merge〔amalgamate〕 two companies // 갑과 을을 합병하다 combine〔consolidate, unite〕 one thing with another // 합병 상담은 어느 정도 진행되고 있습니까? Has there been any progress in the merger talk?
— 선거 a combined election — 수업 combined classwork〔teaching〕 ; teaching (to) a combined class —증 a complication ¶ 합병증이 생기다 develop a complication ; a complication arises〔sets in〕 —호(號) a combined number

합보시기 a cup with a lid

합본 合本 ① joint stock ⇨ 합자 ② [책] binding several copies into one volume —하다 bind together in one volume ¶ 5월호는 6월호와 합본되어 있다 The May number is bound with the June number.

합부인 閤夫人 your〔his〕 wife

합사 合祀 enshrining together —하다 dedicate to several deities ; enshrine together

합사 合絲 a braid ; a plaited thread ; twisting threads together —하다 plait threads ; twist threads together

합삭 合朔 the conjunction of moon and sun

합산 合算 adding up ; footing —하다 add up ; add〔put〕 together ; sum up ; aggregate ; total ; foot up
—액 total (amount)

합살머리 honeycomb tripe

합석 合席 sitting〔meeting, consulting〕 together —하다 sit〔meet, consult〕 together ¶ 식당에서 다른 사람과 합석하다 share a table with another at a restaurant

합선 合線 〖전기〗 (a) short (circuit) —하다 make a short circuit

*합성 合成 〖물리〗 composition ; 〖화학〗 synthesis —하다 compose ; compound ; synthesize ¶ 힘〔파동〕의 합성 및 분해 composition and resolution of forces〔waves〕 // 원료를 합성 형태로 공급하다 supply raw materials in compound form
— 가속도 a resultant acceleration — 고무〔연료, 염료, 석유, 섬유, 수지〕 synthetic rubber〔fuel, dyestuff, oil, fiber, resin〕 —금 an alloy ; synthetic gold —력 a resultant force —물 a compound ; a complex ; a composite ; a synthetic〔synthesized〕 product —분 a component (part) — 비료 compound fertilizer — 세제(洗劑) a synthetic detergent —어 a compound word — 운동 〖물리〗 resultant motion —음 a complex sound —주 compound〔synthetic〕 liquor

합세 合勢 joining forces ; forming an alliance —하다 join forces ; form an alliance

합수 合水 confluence〔junction, joining, meeting〕 of two streams —하다 flow together ; join ; meet

합숙 合宿 joint billet ; lodging together —하다 lodge〔board〕 together ; be billeted together〔with〕 (군대)
—소 a boarding house ; a dormitory ; a training camp (스포츠의) ; a joint billet — 훈련 camp training ¶ 합숙 훈련을 하다 stay in a camp for training

합승 合乘 riding together ; sharing a vehicle —하다 ride together ¶ 택시에 합승하다 share a cab 《with》
—객 a fellow passenger —차 a jitney (cab) ; an omnibus

합심 合心 unison ; accord ; concert —하다 be united ; act in concert 《with》 ¶ 합심하여 with one accord

*합의 合意 mutual agreement ; mutual 〔common〕 consent ; concurrence —하다 come to an agreement ; be agreed ; agree with each other ¶ 쌍방 합의하에 by mutual consent〔agreement〕 // 일동 합의하에 by common consent // 합의에 도달하다 reach an agreement
— 결혼 a consensual marriage — 문서 the text of minute — 이혼 a divorce by mutual agreement — 정사 a double suicide by pact

합의 合議 consultation ; conference ; counsel —하다 consult〔counsel〕 together ; confer 《with》 ; hold the conference ; take〔go into〕 counsel ¶ 합의하에 after consultation ; by mutual 〔common〕 consent
— 사항 items of understanding — 재판 collegial〔collegiate〕 judgment — 재판소 a collegiate court —제 a representative〔council〕 system ; a parliamentary system ; a collegiate system

ㅎ

합일 合— union ; unity ; oneness —하다 unite ; be united ; consolidate
합자 合資 joint stock ; partnership —하다 join stocks ; enter〔go〕 into partnership
— 회사 a limited partnership ; a joint stock company
합작 合作 coauthorship (저작) ; collaboration (협동) ; a joint〔composite〕 work 〔production〕 (합작물) ; cooperation (협력) —하다 collaborate 《with a person in a task》 ; produce conjointly ; write jointly ; work together ; cooperate 《with a person, in a work, for a purpose》 ¶ 화가 수명의 합작 the joint performance of several artists
—자 a collaborator ; a joint author ; a coauthor — 투자 joint venture — 회사 a joint-venture company 국공(國共) — Kuomintang-Communist cooperation 한미 — 영화 a Korean-American joint-product film 한중 — 영화 a joint Korean-Chinese production
합장 合掌 —하다 clasp〔hold〕 one's hands (손을 접어서) ; put〔press〕 one's open hands together (손을 펴서) ; join the hands〔palms〕 ¶ 합장하고 with one's hands pressed〔clasped〕 in prayer
— 배례 worshipping with the palms of the hands together
합장 合葬 burying together —하다 bury〔inter〕 together ¶ 처를 남편과 합장하다 bury the wife together with her husband
합재떨이 an ashtray with a lid
합저 合著 [저술] joint authorship ; [저서] a joint work —하다 work jointly ; make a joint work
—자 a joint author ; a collaborator
합주 合酒 home-brewed alcoholic beverage (made from glutinous rice for summertime drink)
*합주 合奏 (a) concert ; (an) ensemble —하다 play in concert ; perform as a group
—곡 an ensemble —단(團) a musical ensemble (group) ; a concert group 2부 — a duet(te) 3부 — a trio 4부 — a quartet(te) 5부 — a quintet(te)
합죽거리다 mumble with a toothless mouth
합죽선 合竹扇 a fan with spokes made of double slips of bamboo
합죽이 a person who looks toothless ; a toothless person with pursed lips
합죽하다 《a toothless mouth》 (be) puckered ; pursed ; look toothless
합죽할미 a toothless old hag
합죽합죽 mumbling ; toothlessly mouthing
합중국 合衆國 a federation ; united states
미— the United States of America
*합창 合唱 chorus ; concerted singing ; ensemble —하다 sing together ; sing in chorus ; chant in unison ¶ 다 같이 크리스마스 캐롤을 합창했다 We all joined in singing the Christmas carols.
—곡 a chorus ; a choral ; a part song —대 a chorus ; a choir (교회의) — 대원 a chorus〔choir〕 girl〔boy〕 ; a chorister —자 a chorist ; a chorister 남성 — a chorus for men's voices 2〔3, 4, 5〕부 — a duet(te)〔trio, quartet(te), quintet(te)〕 혼성〔남녀〕 — a mixed chorus
합창 合瘡 healing up —하다 heal up
합체 合體 union ; combination ; incorporation ; amalgamation ; merger ; consolidation —하다 unite ; be united ; incorporate ; combine ; be combined ; consolidate ; amalgamate ; merge
합치 合致 agreement ; accord ; concurrence ; [부합] coincidence ; tally —하다 agree 《with》 ; accord 《with》 ; be in accord 《with》 ; concur ; coincide 《with》 ; tally 《with》 ¶ 당신의 말은 사실과 합치하지 않는다 Your statement does not square〔check, tally〕 with the facts.
†합치다 合— ① [하나로] put together ; unite ; combine ; connect ; join together ; [병합하다] amalgamate ; merge ; annex ¶ 손을 합치다 join〔clasp〕 one's hands ; place one's hands together // 종이 두 장을 합치다 put two sheets of paper together // 힘을 합치다 join efforts // 두 반을 한 반으로 합치다 combine two classes // 각 파를 합쳐서 한 당으로 만들다 combine the factions into a party
② [합계하다] sum up ; add up ; total ¶ 10에 5를 합치다 add five to ten
③ [혼합하다] mix ; admix ; compound ; combine ¶ 물과 술을 합치다 mix liquor with water // 나는 그것을 모두 합쳐버렸다 I mixed all of them up.
합판 合版 joint publication —하다 publish jointly
합판 合板 a veneer board ; plywood
프린트 — printed plywood
합판 合辦 joint management ⇨ 합작(合作) —하다 manage jointly
합판화 合瓣花 『식물』 a compound 〔gamopetalous〕 flower
합평 合評 a joint review〔criticism〕 —하다 jointly criticize
—회 a meeting for a joint review ; a panel discussion
*합하다 合— ① [여럿이] unite ⇨ 합치다
② [마음에] fit ; suit ; agree ; harmonize with ; be in accord with ; be in tune with ¶ 마음에 합하다 be after one's heart ; agree with 《a person》 ; be

ㅎ

pleased with // 취미에 합하다 suit one's taste // 의견이 합하다 opinions agree ; see eye to eye

합헌 合憲 ¶ 합헌의 constitutional
—성 constitutionality

합환주 合歡酒 nuptial cups ; the wedding drink ¶ 합환주를 주고 받다 exchange nuptial cups

핫- ① [솜옷] padded with cotton wool ② [배우자 있는] having a spouse
—아비 a man with a wife ; a married man ; a husband —어미 a woman with a husband ; a married woman ; a wife

핫것 cotton-padded clothes〔bedding〕

핫길 the lowest grade ; the most inferior stuff ; a low grade article ; inferior quality

핫도그 [빵] a hot dog 《미》

핫두루마기 a men's outercoat padded〔wadded〕with cotton

핫바지 cotton-padded trousers

핫반 doubled sheets of cotton wool

핫옷 cotton-padded clothes

핫이불 cotton-padded bedclothes

핫저고리 a cotton-padded〔-wadded〕jacket

핫케이크 a hot cake ; a griddle cake ; a wheat cake ; a pancake

핫퉁이 ① [솜많이 둔 옷] clothes padded thick with cotton wool ② [철 지난 옷] cotton-padded clothes worn out of season

***항 項** a clause (조항) ; a paragraph (문장의) ; an item (항목) ; a term (수학의) ¶ 제3조 제2항 Article Ⅲ, clause 2 // 방정식의 1항 a term〔member〕of an equation // 재정의 항을 참고하시오 See under "Finance."

항 港 a harbor ; a port ⇨ 항구
부산— *Pusan* harbor 자유— a free port

항간 巷間 the world ; the street ; the town ¶ 항간에 떠도는 이야기 a topic widely talked about ; the talk of the town // 항간에서 들리는 바에 의하면 a rumor has it 《that》 ; it is said〔rumored〕《that》 ; people〔they〕say 《that》

항거 抗拒 resistance ; disobedience ; rebellion ―하다 resist ; oppose ; disobey
—죄 an offense of resisting lawful order

항고 抗告 〖법〗 a complaint ; an appeal ; a protest ―하다 complain 《against a decision》 ; appeal 《from a decision》 ; file a protest 《against》 ¶ 즉시 항고하다 lodge an immediate complaint 《with》 ; make an immediate appeal 《against》
— 기간 the term for complaint —심 hearing of a complaint —인 a complainant ; a complainer —장 a bill〔memorandum〕of complaint 준(準)— a quasi-complaint 즉시 — an immediate complaint ¶ 즉시 항고하다 lodge an immediate complaint ; make an immediate appeal 《against》 특별 — a special complaint

***항공 航空** aviation ; flight ; aerial navigation ; air voyage〔travel〕
—계 the aerial world ; aviation circles — 교통 관제 air traffic control 《A. T. C.》 — 기 aircraft ; a flying machine ; an airplane — 기록기 a flight recorder — 기사 an aeronautical engineer — 기상 기록기 an aerometeorograph — 기상학 aeronautical meteorology ; aerology — 기지 an air base —대 the air force ; a flying〔an air, an aviation〕corps — 등기 registered airmail — 등대 an aerial beacon〔light-house〕; a route beacon —로 an air〔aerial〕route〔line〕; an airway ; an air lane ; a skyway — 모함 an aircraft carrier ; a flattop ; a carrier ; a seaplane tender — 물리학 aerophysics —법 〖법〗 the Aviation Act —병(兵) an airman ; a flier ; an aircraft(s)man 《영》 — 병력(조약) an air force (treaty) — 보험 flight〔aviation〕insurance —복 aviation garment — 부대 an air force〔corps〕— 사 an airman ; a flier ; an aviator — 사업 air transportation business ; air service — 사진 an aerial photograph — 수송 air transportation ; air service — 술 aeronautics ; aviation ; airmanship ; the art of flying — 시대 the air age — 시설 air service ; airline facilities — 심리학 aviation psychology — 연구소 an aeronautical research institute — 요금 an air fare — 우편 air mail ; airpost 《영》 ¶ 항공 우편으로 by air mail — 우표 an airmail stamp — 의학 aeromedicine — 지도 an air map ; an aerial chart — 측량 an aerial survey —편 《send a letter by》 airmail — 표지 an air(way) beacon —학 aeronautics — 학교 an aviation school — 학회 a society for aeronautical and space science — 회사 an airline (company) 국제 — 협회 the International Air Transportation Association 《IATA》 내(耐)—성 airworthiness 대한 —사 Korean Air Lines 《KAL》 민간 — 규제 the Civil Air Regulations

항구 恒久 permanency ; perpetuity ; eternity ―하다 (be) permanent ; perpetual ; lasting ; eternal ¶ 항구적 permanent ; lasting ; perpetual ; everlasting ; eternal // 항구적 평화를 확립하다 establish permanent peace
— 기관 permanent machinery — 대책 permanent measures —성 permanency

†항구 港口 a port ; a harbor

참고 **port**는 주로 상업 항구를 가리키고 도시를 포함시킨 기분으로 사용한다 **harbor**는 「정박소」이며 도시를 포함하지 않는 경우가 많다

— 도시 a port city〔town〕 —세(稅) port〔harbor〕 dues

항구화 恒久化 perpetuation —하다 perpetuate 《the world peace》

항균성 抗菌性 antibiosis ¶ 항균성의 antibiotic

— 물질 antibiotic (substance)

항내 港內 the inside of a harbor

— 시설 harbor facilities

항다반사 恒茶飯事 a matter of common〔everyday〕 occurrence

항담 巷談 a town talk ; a talk of the town ⇨ 항설

항도 港都 a port city

항독소 抗毒素 an anti-venom ; an antitoxin(e)

— 치료법 an antitoxin treatment

항등식 恒等式 〖수학〗 an identical equation ; an identity

항라 亢羅 a kind of silk gauze ; sheer silk

저(紵)— sheer cambric

항렬 行列 degree of relationship〔kindred〕 ¶ 항렬로 아저씨뻘이다 be one's uncle by descent

항례 恒例 usage ; convention ⇨ 상례

항로 航路 a route ; a course ; a fairway ; a steamer lane ; a line ; a service ; a run ¶ 항로를 정하다 lay a course ; shape one's course // 항로를 바꾸다 change course // 항로를 남으로 잡다 steer south

—도 a track chart — 목표 a seamark — 변경 a deviation (of route) — 부표 a fairway buoy — 신호 a marine signal — 표지 a nautical mark ; a navigation(al) aid ; a beacon 구주 — the European (steamship) line〔service〕 규정〔자유〕 — special〔free〕 service 부정기 — an irregular service〔line〕 비행 — an air line ; an air route ; an airway 외국 — an ocean lane〔route, service〕 정기 — a regular service〔line〕

항론 抗論 refutation ; repudiation ; controversy ; contradiction ; confutation —하다 refute ; repudiate ; controvert ; contradict

항만 港灣 harbors ; harbors and bays

— 개량 harbor improvement — 공사 harbor construction work —과 the harbor works section — 노동자 a port laborer ; a longshoreman — 시설 harbor facilities — 운송 transportation service in harbors —청 the Korea Maritime and Port Authority — 하역(荷役) harbor loading and unloading

항명 抗命 disobedience〔insubordination〕

—하다 disobey 《a person's》 order

—죄 mutiny

*항목 項目 an item ; a head ; [조항] a clause ; a provision ¶ 항목별로 나누다 itemize // 그것은 이 항목에 들어 있다 It is included under this head. /It belongs in〔to〕 this category.

—별 표 an itemized list

항목화 項目化 itemization ; specification —하다 itemize ; specify ; set down by items

항무 港務 harbor affairs ; port business

항문 肛門 〖해부〗 the anus ¶ 항문의 anal

—경(鏡) a proctoscope ; a rectal speculum —공 the anal orifice —과 proctology —과 의사 a proctologist — 괄약근 the anal sphincters —병 an anal〔a rectal〕 ailment ; [치질] piles ; hemorrhoids — 병원 an anal diseases hospital — 부 the anal region

항법 航法 navigation

극지(極地) — 〖항공〗 polar navigation 무선〔천문〕 — radio〔celestial〕 navigation 추측 — dead reckoning

항변 抗辯 [피고의] a plea ; defense ; [항론] a protest ; refutation ; confutation ; contradiction ; an answer —하다 make a plea ; demur ; refute ; confute ; contradict ; argue 《with》 ; file a protest ¶ 사실 부인의 항변 a plea of the general issue // 의문 소멸의 항변 a plea in discharge // 상관에게 항변하다 remonstrate with one's superior // 소추에 항변하지 않다 file no answer to the suit

(소송) 각하 — a plea in abatement 방소(妨訴) — a plea in abatement

항병 降兵 a surrendered soldier〔army〕

항병력 抗病力 resisting power〔immunity〕 against disease

*항복 降伏, 降服 surrender ; submission (복종) ; capitulation (조건부의) —하다 surrender 《to》 ; capitulate 《to》 ; hang the white flag ; lay down one's arms ; submit 《to》 ; yield 《to》 ; bow 《to》 ; give in 《to》 ¶ 항복시키다 cause 《the enemy》 to surrender ; bring 《the enemy》 under〔to his knees〕 // 그들은 항복을 거부하고 최후의 1인까지 싸웠다 They disdained laying down their arms and fought to the last man.

— 권고(서) a summons to surrender

— 기 a white flag ; a flag of surrender

— 문서 the surrender documents ; an instrument of surrender — 조건 terms of capitulation 무조건〔조건부〕 — unconditional〔conditional〕 surrender

항산 恒産 fixed property ; a fixed〔constant〕 livelihood ¶ 항산을 가진 사람 a person of fixed property ; a person who has a stable income

항산균 抗酸菌 an acid-fast bacterium

ㅎ

*항상 恒常 always ; at all times ; constantly ; habitually ; as a rule ; customarily ; ordinarily ; incessantly ¶ 그는 항상 나에게 친절히 대해 왔다 He has always been kind to me.
항상 주거 杭上住居 a pile〔stilt〕dwelling 〔house〕; a house on piles ; a lake dwelling
항생 물질 抗生物質 〖의학〗 an antibiotic —학 antibiotics
항서 降書 a capitulatory letter ; a written surrender
항설 巷說 gossip〔rumor〕in the streets ; town talk ¶ 항설이 분분하다 Wild rumors are abroad.
항성 恒星 a fixed〔permanent〕star ; a sun ¶ 항성의 sidereal
—시〔일, 년〕sidereal time〔day, year〕— 주기 a sidereal revolution
항성 恒性 constancy ; permanency ¶ 항성의 constant
항세 港稅 port duty ; harbor dues
†항소 抗訴 〖법〗 the appeal suit ; an appeal 《to a higher court》 —하다 appeal ; enter〔lodge〕 an appeal 《against》 ¶ 항소를 기각하다 dismiss 〔turn down〕an appeal // 항소를 철회하다 withdraw an appeal
—권 the right of appeal — 법원 an appellate court —심 a trial on an appeal case — 이유 the grounds of an appeal —인 an appellant —장 a petition of appeal — (제기)기간 the term allowed for appeal
항속 航續 cruising ; flight ; flying
— 거리 a cruising〔flying〕 radius 〔range〕— 력 a cruising〔flying〕power 〔capacity〕— 시간 the duration of cruise〔flight〕
항쇄 족쇄 項鎖足鎖 a pillory and shackles
항습 恒習 a usual〔regular, steady, customary〕habit
항시 恒時 the usual (time) ; always ⇨ 항상
항시 港市 a port town〔city〕
항심 恒心 a constant〔steady〕 mind ; constancy ; steadiness ¶ 항산 없는 사람은 항심이 없다 A real property, a real purpose. /Competency is for constancy of mind. /Property makes for steadiness〔stability〕.
*항아리 缸— a jar ; a pot
꿀— a honey jar 물— a water jar
항아리손님 缸— 〖의학〗 parotitis ; mumps ⇨ 이하선염
항암제 抗癌劑 an anti-cancer medicine
항언 抗言 protestation ; a protest ; a rejoinder ; a retort —하다 protest ; make a protest ; retort ; rejoin ; oppose
항오 行伍 ranks ; files ; an array ; a formation ¶ 항오 정연하다 be in regular rank ; be in perfect order

항온 恒溫 constant temperature
—기(器) a pyrostat —조(槽) a thermostat — 항습기(恒濕器) a thermohygrostat
항외 港外 outside the port〔harbor〕 ¶ 항외에 정박하다 lie at anchor off the harbor // 배가 항외로 나가다 sail out of a harbor
— 정박지 a roadstead
항용 恒用 ordinariness ; a commonplace ; [부사적] always ; at all times
항원 抗原 〖생리〗 an antigen
—균 an antigenic germ
*항의 抗議 a protest ; a remonstrance ; an objection ; an exception —하다 protest ; make a protest ; offer〔raise〕 an objection 《to》; object 《to》; take an exception 《to》 ¶ 항의를 제출하다 enter 〔file〕a protest 《against》
— 데모 a protest demonstration 〔parade〕— 서〔문〕a written protest —자 a challenger — 집회 a protest meeting 엄중 — a strong protest ¶ 엄중 항의를 제출하다 lodge a strong protest 《with the Japanese government against...》
항의 巷議 street talk ; discussion along the byways
항일 抗日 anti-Japan ; resistance to Japan ; anti-Japanese
— 사상 anti-Japanese sentiments — 운동 an anti-Japanese movement — 투쟁 an anti-Japanese struggle〔fight〕
항쟁 抗爭 contention ; opposition ; dispute ; wrangle ; struggle ; resistance —하다 contend ; dispute ; wrangle ; struggle 《against》; resist ; offer resistance ; oppose ¶ 내부의 항쟁 an internal strife ; a storm in a tea cup
항적 抗敵 resistance ; hostility
항적 航跡 a wake (behind a sailing ship) ; a furrow ; a track
항전 抗戰 (armed) resistance ; fighting 《against》 —하다 resist ; offer (armed) resistance ; fight 《against》 ¶ 철저한 항전 do-or-die resistance
—력 power of resistance 대일 — resistance to Japan
항정[1] [목덜미] the back neck of a dog〔pig〕
항정[2] [쇠고기] chuck beef
항정 航程 ① [배의] the run〔passage〕of a ship ; the distance covered by a ship ; a sailing distance ¶ 1일간의 항정 a day's sail
② [비행기의] a lap ; a leg ¶ 최초〔최후〕의 항정 the first〔last〕lap ; the first 〔last〕leg of a flying course // 전항정을 날다 fly〔cover〕the whole distance // 그 비행기의 항정은 3,000킬로미터이다 The plane covers a distance of 3,000 kilometers.
—선 a log line — 지시기 a distance

recorder —표 a logbook
항존 恒存 〖물리〗 conservation
에너지 — conservation of energy 〔force〕
항주 航走 sailing ; run —하다 sail ; run
—력 cruising speed — 마력 break horse power 《B. H. P.》
항진 亢進 rise ; acceleration ; exasperation ; exacerbation (병세 따위의) —하다 rise ; accelerate ; grow worse
심계(心悸) — heart acceleration ; palpitation (of the heart)
항진 航進 —하다 sail ; proceed ; steam ; fetch ¶ 매시 10해리를 항진하다 steam ten miles an hour
항차 much〔still〕 more of less ⇨ 하물며
항체 抗體 〖생리〗 an antibody
항풍 恒風 a constant wind
†항해 航海 voyage ; a navigation ; a crossing ; a passage (over the sea) ; a (sea) trip ; a cruise —하다 sail ; make a voyage 《to》 ; navigate ; make a crossing 《over the ocean》 ; take a passage 《for》 ; cruise ¶ 다음 항해에 on the next trip〔voyage〕 // 항해중이다 [사람이] be on a voyage ; [사람·배가] be at sea ; [배가] be under canvas ; be afloat // 태평양을 항해하다 sail the Pacific // 항해중 무사하기를 빌다 wish 《a person》 bon voyage // 유쾌한 항해를 하다 enjoy a pleasant sea trip〔voyage〕 // 그 배는 부산 하와이 간을 항해한다 The ship plies between *Pusan* and Hawaii.
— 계기 a nautical instrument —권 the right of navigation — 당직 a mariner on watch duty —도 a navigator's chart —사 a (first) mate ; a navigation officer ¶ 1등 항해사 the chief〔first〕 mate // 2등〔3등〕 항해사 the second〔third〕 mate — 생활 seafaring (life) —선 a service ship — 성능 sea-going qualities — 속력 sea〔service〕 speed — 수당 a sea (service) allowance — 술 (the art of) navigation ; seamanship — 시간 hours under way — 실습생 an apprentice officer —업 shipping〔carrying〕 trade — 일지 a voyage log ; a logbook ¶ 항해 일지에 기입하다 log —자 a mariner ; a seaman ; a navigator —장 a navigating officer —표 nautical tables 연안 — coastwise sailings 원양 — an ocean voyage ; a long cruise 처녀 — a maiden voyage
*항행 航行 navigation ; sailing ; a cruise —하다 navigate ; sail ; steam ; cruise ¶ 항행중 at sea ; on sail ; on a voyage // 항행중의 배 a steamer now under way〔on a run〕
— 구역 a navigation area — 구역 제한 plying limit —권 the right of navigation
항혈청 抗血清 〖의학〗 an antiserum 《*pl.* ~s, -ra》
항효소 抗酵素 an antiferment
항히스타민제 抗—劑 an antihistaminic agent〔medicine〕 ; an antihistamine
*해[1] the sun ¶ 해가 뜨다 the sun rises 〔comes up〕 // 해가 지다 the sun sets 〔goes down, sinks〕 // 해가 저물다 it gets dark // 해가 기울다 the sun declines // 해가 흐리다 the sun is clouded over // 방에 해가 비친다 The sun shines into the room. // 해가 들지 않은 곳에 두어라 Put it in the shade.
†해[2] ① [일년] a year ¶ 해마다 every year ; year after year // 해가 다 가다 be at the end of the year // 해가 바뀌다 the year changes ; the New Year comes round // 새해를 맞다 ring in the New Year ; greet〔hail〕 the New Year ; welcome the New Year ② [낮] the daytime ¶ 해가 길다〔짧다〕 have long 〔short〕 day // 해가 점점 짧아진다 The days are getting shorter. // 봄이 되면 해가 길어진다 In spring the day gains on the night.
해[3] with a light giggle ¶ 해 웃다 give a light giggle
해[4] [것] a possession ¶ 내해 mine // 이것은 뉘해냐 Whose is this ?
해 亥 the Sign of the Boar ; the last of the twelve horary signs
—년 the year of the Boar —시 the hour of the Boar 《the hours from 10 o'clock to 12 in the evening》
†해 害 [위해] injury ; damage ; harm ; mischief ; hurt ; [손상] detriment ; [해독] evil ; an evil influence ; evil〔harmful, injurious〕 effects ; a baneful influence

> 참고 **injury**는 사람에 대해서나 물건에 대해서나 일반적으로 쓰이는 말 **damage**는 물건의 가치·신용 따위 무생물에게 주어지는 해를 말한다

—하다 injure ; damage ; harm ; hurt ; spoil ; impair ; mar ¶ 해로운 injurious ; harmful ; noxious ; baneful // 음주의 해 the ill〔bad〕 effects of drinking ; the curse of drink // 해를 입다 suffer damage ; be damaged ; suffer from evil effects // 해가 되다 be injurious ; be harmful ; be destructive // 해를 가하다 do injury 《to》 ; inflict injury 《upon》 ; cause damage〔loss〕 ; do damage 《to》 // 건강을 해치다 injure one's health // 사람의 감정을 해치다 hurt 《a person's》 feelings // 작물에는 거의 해가 없었다 The crops suffered little harm. // 너무 강한 광선은 눈에 해롭다 Too much light is bad for the eyes. // 과도한 음주는 건강에 해가 된다 Excessive drinking is injurious to〔bad for〕 (the) health.
해- [그해에 새로난] (of) the current year ;

ㅎ

new ¶ 햇콩 the first crop of soybeans for the year
해- 該 that ; the said ; the 《person, matter》 in question ¶ 해교 that school ; the said school // 해인물 the man in question ; the said person
해각 海角 a promontory ; a headland ; a point ; a cape
해갈하다 解渴— appease〔quench, slake〕 one's thirst
해감 water sediment ; fur ¶ 해감내가 나다 smell of mud // 해감이 끼다 fur forms
해거름 sunset ; sundown ; dusk ; nightfall ¶ 해거름에 at sunset〔nightfall〕
†해결 解決 solution ; settlement ; fixing (up) —하다 solve 《a question》; settle 《a problem》; effect a settlement ; bring 《a matter》 to a settlement ; fix (up) 《a problem》 ¶ 원만〔만족〕한 해결 an amicable〔a satisfactory〕 settlement // 해결할 수 있는 문제 a solvable problem // 문제를 평화적으로 해결하다 bring a matter to a peaceful settlement // 나는 그 문제의 해결에 고심하고 있다 I am racking my brains to find a solution to the problem. // 원만히 해결되었다 A settlement has been reached without friction. // 그들은 서로 양보하여 분쟁을 해결했다 They settled the dispute by mutual concession. // 이 문제는 어쨌든 잘 해결될 것이다. This problem will work itself out somehow.
— 조건 terms of settlement —책 a means of settling 《the trouble》; a solution
해경 海景 a (sea-)coast landscape ; a seascape ; a marine〔sea〕 view
—화 a seapiece
‡해고 解雇 discharge ; dismissal ; lay-off —하다 discharge ; dismiss ; fire (out) ; lay off ; turn off ¶ 해고되다 be dismissed〔discharged〕; be fired ; be dropped from the pay-roll ; get fired 〔sacked〕 《속》 // 해고 당하지 않도록 노력하다 make effort to retain〔preserve, remain in〕 one's employment
— 기준 criteria for personnel dismissal — 수당 a discharge allowance ; dismissal pay —자 a discharged person ; a laid-off worker —장 a certificate of discharge from employment ; one's service clearance (paper) — 통지 a dismissal notice ; a notice of dismissal ; a warning 지명 — discharge by naming specific individuals 집단 — a mass dismissal
‡해골 骸骨 a skeleton ; bones ; a skull ; a cranium ¶ 해골같은 얼굴의 skull-faced
해공전 海空戰 air-sea operations ; a battle between aircraft and warships
해관 海關 the maritime customs
—세 customs duties ; import duties — 세율 customs tariff
해괴 駭怪 strangeness ; eccentricity ; oddity ; scandalousness ; monstrousness —하다 (be) strange ; eccentric ; scandalous ; monstrous ; odd ; extraordinary ¶ 해괴한 처사 an extraordinary 〔odd, outrageous〕 measure // 해괴 망측하다 be extremely scandalous〔disgraceful〕 // 해괴하게 굴다 behave outrageously
해교 解膠 〖화학〗 peptization —하다 peptize
해구 海區 a section of the sea ; a marine zone
해구 海口 the entrance to a harbor ; the mouth of a harbor ; the approach to a bay
해구 海狗 a seal ; a sea bear ; a sea cat ; an eared seal
—신 the penis of a sea bear
해구 海寇 pirates ; sea marauders
해구 海溝 a〔an ocean〕 deep ; a (sea) trench
민다나오 — the Mindanao Trench
해국 海國 an island country ; a maritime country ; a seagirt country
—민 a maritime nation —주의 navalism
‡해군 海軍 the navy ; the naval service ; the fleet ; naval forces ¶ 해군의 naval ; navy // 해군을 확장하다 expand 〔increase〕 the Navy
—국 a sea〔naval〕 power — 군악대 the Marine band — 기지 a naval base — 기(旗) the navy flag —기(機) a navy plane — 기념일 Navy Day — 대학 the naval staff college —력 naval power 〔strength〕; sea power — 무관 a naval attache — 병원 a naval hospital — 본부 the Navy Headquarters — 부대 naval circles — 사관〔장교〕 a naval officer — 사관 학교 the Naval Academy —성 the Navy Department ; the Admiralty 《영》 — 장관 the Minister of Navy — 재판소 the Court of Admiralty — 조병창 a naval arsenal — 참모 총장 the Chief of Naval Operations 《C. N. O.》 — 함선 naval vessels
해굽성 —性 〖식물〗 positive heliotropism
해금 奚琴 a Korean fiddle
해금 解禁 removal of the embargo ; lifting of the ban —하다 remove the embargo ; lift the ban ; cancel a ban ¶ 금지 기사의 해금 the lifting of the press ban
—기 the open season ; the opening of the shooting season 금— the lifting of the gold embargo ; the lifting of the embargo on gold
해기 海氣 sea air ; a smell of the sea ; a sea breeze ; the oceanic atmosphere
—욕 sea-air bathing
해기 海技 seamanship
해껏 all day long ; until sunset ; till dark

ㅎ

¶ 해껏 일하다 work till dark
해끄무레하다 (be) fair and whitish ¶ 해끄무레한 얼굴 a fair and whitish face
해끄스름하다 (be) whitish
해끔하다 (be) whitish and clean
해낙낙하다 (be) satisfied ; content(ed) ; pleased ; settle 《for》 ; find satisfaction
*해난 海難 a disaster at sea ; a shipwreck ; perils of the sea ; a shipping casualty ¶ 해난을 당하다 meet with a disaster at sea ; be shipwrecked
— 구조 sea-rescue work ; lifesaving — 구조선 a salvage boat — 구조소 a lifesaving station — 구조원 a life saver — 구호 salvage — 신호 an SOS ; a distress signal — 심판법 the Marine Accidents Inquiry Act — 심판소 the Maritime Distress Inquiry Agency — 심판 위원회 the Maritime Accident Inquiry Committee — 작업 salvage work〔operation〕 — 증명서 a wreck certificate ; an extended protest
해납작하다 be white and broad
해내 海內 the whole country ¶ 해내에 in the whole country〔land〕 ; within the four seas
†해내다 ① [완수하다] accomplish ; achieve ; carry through ; perform ; fulfil ; succeed 《in》 ¶ 맡은 일을 해내다 perform the work assigned to one // 계획한 바를 해내다 carry through an undertaking // 너는 큰 일을 해냈다 You have achieved a great work. // 나는 그것을 끝까지 해내겠다 I will go through with it.
② [이겨내다] go at ; beat ; lick ; put down ; get the better of ¶ 씨름에서 세 사람을 해내다 beat three persons in wrestling // 그는 주인을 말로 해냈다 He argued his master down.
‡해넘이 (the) sunset ; sundown 《미》 ¶ 해넘이에 at sunset
해녀 海女 a woman diver ¶ 진주잡이 해녀 a woman diver for pearls
해년 亥年 〖민속〗 the Year of the Boar
해님 the sun ¶ 해님과 달님 the sun and the moon
해단 解團 disbandment —하다 disband 《an athletic team》
—식 the ceremony of disbandment
해달 海獺 〖동물〗 a sea otter
*해답 解答 a solution 《to a problem》 ; an answer 《to a question》 —하다 solve 《a problem》 ; answer 《a question》 ¶ 해답할 수 있는〔없는〕 문제 an answerable〔unanswerable〕 question ; a solvable〔an insolvable〕 problem // 바른 해답을 하다 give a correct answer ; answer correctly // 나는 그 문제의 해답을 못 냈다 I failed to answer the question.
—자 a solver ; an answerer 시험 문제 — answers to examination questions
해당 解黨 dissolution (of a party) ; dismissal —하다 dissolve (a party)
해당 該當 —하다 come〔fall〕 under ; come〔fall〕 within the purview of ; correspond to ; be applicable to ¶ 제2조에 해당하다 conform to Article 2 // 해당 항목을 보다 turn to the appropriate heading // 그것은 형법 제 2조에 해당한다 It comes under Article 2 of the Criminal Code.
— 사항 pertinent〔relevant〕 data 추방 명령 —자 those affected by the purge directives
해당 작용 解糖作用 glycolysis
해당화 海棠花 〖식물〗 a wild rose ; a sweet brier〔briar〕 ; Rosa rugosa (학명)
해대 解隊 disbanding ; disbandment —하다 disband ; disembody
해대다 attack ; go at ; lick ; abuse ; beat ¶ 사람을 해대다 go at 《a person》 // 그는 싸움에서 두 사람을 해댈 수 있다 He can lick two persons in a fight.
-해도 if ; even if ; even though ; although ¶ 가령 네가 옳다고 해도 even if you are in the right // 아무리 운다 해도 소용없다 It's no use crying over it.
해도 海圖 a hydrographic chart ; a (maritime) chart ¶ 해도에 실려 있는 섬 an charted island
해도 海濤 sea waves ; billow
—실 a chartroom —학 chartology
해도 海島 an island in the sea
해독 害毒 evil ; harm ; mischief ; virus ; poison ; an evil〔a baneful〕 influence ; taint ; canker ¶ 문명의 해독 the canker of civilization // 해독을 끼치다 cause damage 《to》 ; exert a baneful influence // 이런 종류의 책은 사회에 해독을 끼친다 Books of this kind work mischief to society.
해독 解毒 counteracting〔neutralizing〕 poison —하다 counteract〔neutralize〕 the poisonous effects ; mithridatize
—제 an antidote ; a counterpoison ; a mithridate ; a toxicide
해독 解讀 decoding ; deciphering —하다 decipher ; decode ¶ 부호를 해독하다 interpret the signs〔marks〕
해돈 海豚 a porpoise ; a dolphin ⇨ 돌고래
‡해돋이 (the) sunrise ; (the) sunup 《미》 ¶ 해돋이에 at sunrise
해동 解凍 thawing ; a thaw —하다 thaw
해동갑 —同甲 coinciding with the sunset ; until sunset ; all day long —하다 coincide with the sunset ¶ 해동갑해서 일을 하다 work till sunset
해동청 海東靑 a duck hawk ⇨ 송골매
해득 解得 understanding ; comprehension ; apprehension ; grasp —하다 understand ; comprehend ; grasp ; apprehend ¶ 해득력이 있다 have understanding // 해득할 수 없다 be above

ㅎ

one's apprehension // 해득력이 둔한 사람 a man of feeble apprehension
해뜨리다 wear away〔out, down〕 ⇨ 해어뜨리다
해뜩거리다 ⇨ 희뜩거리다
해뜩해뜩 ―하다 be spotted with white
해라하다 use the plain style of speech
해란초 海蘭草 〖식물〗 a kind of toadflax
해람 解纜 unmooring ; sailing off ; leaving ―하다 weigh anchor ; unmoor ; sail 《from》 ; set sail ; leave 《a port》
해로 海路 a sea route ; a seaway ¶ 해로로 by sea // 해로로 가다 go by sea〔water〕
해로 偕老 growing old together in wedded life ―하다 grow old together in wedded life ¶ 100년 해로를 맹세하다 promise to live together till they shall become Darby and Joan // 100년 해로하다 《husband and wife》 share the happily married years together
해로 동혈 偕老同穴 ① [부부의] growing old together and sharing a common grave ―하다 grow old together and are buried in the same grave ⇨ 해로(偕老)
② 〖동물〗 Venus's-flower-basket
†해롭다 害― (be) harmful ; injurious ; detrimental ; be bad 《for》 ; have an injurious effect 《on》 ¶ 심신에 해롭다 affect both mind and body // 술은 건강에 해롭다 Drinking is injurious to one's health. // 담배가 해롭다는 것은 주지의 사실이다 Everyone knows the harm of tobacco. // 간접 흡연은 건강에 매우 해롭다 Second-hand smoking is a big health hazard.
해롱거리다 behave like a spoilt child ⇨ 희롱거리다
해류 海流 an ocean current ; a current
―도 a current chart ―병 an ocean current bottle
해륙 海陸 land and sea
― 양서 동물 an amphibious animal ; an amphibian ― 양용 비행기〔전차〕 an amphibious plane〔tank〕 ― 양면 작전 amphibious operations
해리 海里 a nautical mile ; a knot
해리 海狸 〖동물〗 a beaver
―향(香) castor (the secretion from a beaver's groin)
해리 解離 〖화학〗 dissociation ―하다 dissociate
*해마 海馬 [물고기] a sea horse ; [하마] a hippocampus ; [해상] a walrus
해마다 every year ; each year ; year after year ; annually
해만 海灣 ① a bay ; a gulf ② sea and bay
해말갛다 (be) fair ; fair-skinned
해말쑥하다 (be) clear and fair ; fair-skinned
해맑다 be white and clean
해망적다 (be) dull ; stupid ; silly
해머 a hammer
― 던지기 hammer throwing ¶ 해머 던지기 선수 a hammer thrower
*해먹 a hammock ; a hanging bed ; a swinging couch ¶ 해먹을 치다 sling a hammock // 해먹에서 자다 sleep in a hammock
해먹다 do something bad〔bothersome〕 ; "do the damn thing" ; take unjust possession of something ; "latch on to" ; earn a living by ; live by ¶ 은행의 돈을 해먹다 embezzle money from a bank // 일이 하도 힘들어서 도저히 해먹을 수 없다 The job is really too hard for me to do.
해면 海面 the surface of the sea ; the sea level ¶ 해면에 떠오르다 float up to the surface of the sea // 해면은 거울과 같았다 The sea was as smooth as glass.
⁑해면 海綿 a sponge
― 고무 sponge rubber ― 동물 the Porifera ―상 조직 spongy parenchyma ― 조직 spongy tissue ―질 spongy matter ; sponginess ―철 sponge iron ―체 spongy body 목욕용 ― a bath sponge
해면 解免 release ; exoneration (from duty, obligation) ; acquittal ; discharge ; firing (from a job) ―하다 release ; exonerate ; acquit ; discharge
해명 解明 elucidation ; explanation ―하다 elucidate ; explain ; make clear ¶ 해명을 요구하다 demand〔call for〕 an explanation 《from》
―서 a letter of explanation
해명 海鳴 rumbling〔calling〕 of the sea ; oceanic noise ; sea noise
해몽 解夢 interpretation of a dream ―하다 interpret a dream
―가 a dream reader ; an oneirocritic
해묘 海錨 a drag〔sea, floating〕 anchor ; a drogue
해무 海務 maritime〔marine, sea〕 affairs
해무 海霧 a sea fog ; a fog on the sea ¶ 해무는 오후에야 갰다 The sea fog lifted in the afternoon.
해묵다 [물건이] get a year old ; age a year ; [일이] drag on for a year old
해묵히다 [일을] let work drag on for a year without getting finished ; [물건을] let 《a thing》 get to be year
해물 海物 marine products
―상 a dealer in marine products
해미 a thick sea fog ; a heavy fog on the sea
해미 海味 sea food
해바라기 〖식물〗 a sunflower ; Helianthus annuns(학명)
해바라지다 ⇨ 헤벌어지다
해박 該博 erudition ; profundity ―하다 (be) erudite ; profound ; extensive ¶

해박한 지식 profound (and extensive) learning // 그는 해박한 학식의 소유자다 He is a man of great learning〔erudition〕.

해반닥거리다 goggle ; turn one's eyes up and down ¶ 눈을 해반닥거리며 괴로와하다 turn one's eyes up and down in agony

해반드르르하다 (be) fair and charming

해반주그레하다 (be) fair-complexioned

해반지르르하다 (be) fair-complexioned ; neat and fair

해발 海拔 above the sea ; above (the) sea level ¶ 그 산은 해발 3,000미터이다 The mountain is〔rises〕 3,000 meters above the sea level.

해발쭉하다 ⇨ 헤벌쭉하다

†해방 解放 liberation ; deliverance ; disengagement ; release ; emancipation ; disenthralment —하다 liberate ; disengage ; emancipate ; release ; set free ; deliver ; extricate ¶ 노예를 해방하다 emancipate slaves ; set slaves —자 a liberator ; an emancipator — 전쟁〔운동〕 a liberation war〔campaign〕 — 지구 a liberated area 노예 — emancipation of slaves ; manumission 노예 —령 the Emancipation Act (미국 남북 전쟁시의) 여성 — 운동 a movement for the emancipation of women

해방 海防 coast〔coastal〕 defense ; maritime defense

—함 a coast guard ship ; a coastal defense ship

해방 亥方 〖민속〗 the Direction of the Boar (⇨ northwest-by-north)

해법 海法 maritime law ; sea laws

해법 解法 a solution ; a key to solution

*해변 海邊 the beach ; the seashore ; the seaside ; the coast ¶ 해변을 소요하다 ramble〔stroll〕 about the beach

— 평지 a coastal plain

해병 海兵 a marine

—대 the marine corps —대원 a marine ; a leatherneck 《미·속》

해보 海堡 [해안 포대] a coast battery ; [방파제] a breakwater

†해보다 ① [시험해보다] try ; have a try 《at》 ; attempt ; make an attempt〔a trial〕 《at》 ; try one's hand 《at》 ¶ 일을 해보다 try a job ; try work // 할 수 있는 데까지 해보다 try what could be done ; try one's best // 한잔 해볼래 Won't you try a cup? // 누가 제일 빠른가 해보자 Let's try and see who can run the fastest. // 그렇게 하도록 한번 해보겠습니다 I'll try. /I'll have a try at it. /I'll have a crack at it. /I'll give it a shot. /I'll have〔take〕 a shot at it.

② [경험해보다] experience ; know ; try ¶ 고생을 해보다 know hardship // 사랑을 해보다 experience love

③ [끝까지] pit one's strength ; fight ; stand against ¶ 그 놈과는 끝까지 해보겠다 I will fight him to the bitter end.

*해부 解剖 ① [의학상의] dissection ; postmortem ; autopsy ② [분석] an analysis —하다 dissect ; anatomize ; hold a postmortem ; hold an autopsy ; analyze ¶ 해부상의 anatomical // 해부의 결과 on dissection // 해부의 결과 타살로 판명됐다 The postmortem examination showed that it was a case of murder.

—대 a dissecting table —도(刀) a dissecting knife ; a scalpel —도(圖) an anatomical chart —론 analytics —실 a dissecting room —자 a dissector ; a prosector —체 an anatomy (모형의) —학 anatomy —학자 an anatomist 생체 — vivisection 시체 — autopsy ; a postmortem 인체 — dissection of a human body

해빙 解氷 thawing (of ice) ; a thaw —하다 thaw ¶ 한강이 해빙되었다 The *Han* river is now free from ice.

—기 the thawing season

해빙 海氷 sea ice

해사 海事 maritime affairs〔matters〕

— 감정인 a marine surveyor — 금융 shipping finance —법 the law of admiralty — 법규 sea laws —부 the Maritime Department — 심판소 the Marine〔Admiralty〕 Court — 협회 the Marine Association

해사 海蛇 a sea snake

—좌 〖천문〗 Hydra ; the Water Snake

해사하다 (be) fair-complexioned ; fair

해산 解産 marine products

— 동물 marine animals —업 the marine products industry —업자 a dealer in marine products〔sea foods〕

*해산 解散 ① [흩어짐] break-up ; dispersion ② [해체] dissolution ; disorganization ; liquidation ; disbandment —하다 break up ; disperse ; dissolve ; disorganize ; disband ; liquidate ; wind up ¶ 회의를 해산하다 break up a meeting // 해산을 명하다 order 《a meeting》 to break up ; order 《a crowd》 to disperse // 군중을 해산시키다 disperse a crowd // 회의는 9시에 해산했다 The meeting rose at nine o'clock. // 수학 여행에서 돌아온 학생들은 역 앞에서 해산했다 The students back from their excursion broke up in front of the station.

—식 a disbandment ceremony 강제 — compulsory winding-up 임의 — voluntary winding-up

해산 解産 childbirth ; delivery ; parturition ; confinement ; accouchement 《프》 —하다 give birth to ; be delivered of ¶ 해산기의 임박 approaching maternity // 남아를 해산하다 give birth to a boy ; be delivered of a boy // 그녀는 어젯밤에 해산했다 She had a baby last night. /She became a mother last night. //그녀는 내달에 해산할 예정이다 She is expected to give birth to a child next month.

—기 period〔term〕 of delivery ; one's time — 미역 seaweed fed to a woman just out of childbirth —비 childbirth 〔delivery〕 expenses —실 a delivery 〔labor〕 room — 어미 a woman just out of childbirth — 촉진제 an oxytocic 첫— one's first confinement

해산물 海産物 marine products ¶ 해산물이 풍부하다 be rich in marine products

— 가공품 processed marine products —상(인) a dealer in marine products

해삼 海蔘 a sea slug ; a trepang ; a sea cucumber

*해상 海上 on the sea ; sea ; maritime ; marine ¶ 해상에서 on the sea ; afloat ; at sea//해상의 자유 freedom of the seas//해상의 패자 the mistress of the seas

— 경비대 coast guards —권 maritime power ; sea power ¶ 해상권을 장악하다 rule the sea — 근무 sea service ; sea duty ; service afloat — 무역 seaborne 〔floating〕 trade ; overseas trade —법 maritime law — 보급로 a seaborne supply route — 보안 maritime〔marine〕 safety — 보험 marine insurance — 봉쇄 naval〔sea〕 blockade — 비행〔교통〕 oversea flight〔communications〕 — 생활 seafaring〔a sailor's〕 life ; an ocean life — 수송 marine transportation — 자위대 [일본의] the Maritime Self-defense Force

해상 海床 the bottom〔bed〕 of the sea ; the ocean〔sea〕 floor

해상 海商 ① [해상업] marine commerce ② [업자] a sea treader

해상 海象 『동물』 a morse ; a walrus

해상 解喪 ⇨ 탈상(脫喪) —하다 come out of〔finish〕 mourning ; leave off〔get over〕 mourning

해생 동물 海生動物 a maritime animal

해생 식물 海生植物 a marine plant

해서 楷書 the square style of Chinese handwriting ; the printed style of writing

해석 解析 analysis ; analytical research —하다 analyze

— 기하학 『수학』 analytical geometry —학 analytics — 함수 an analytic function

*해석 解釋 [판단] interpretation ; [추정] construction ; [번역] translation ; [정의] definition ; [설명] explanation ; [해설] exposition ; [주석] comment ; an explanatory note ; a commentary —하다 interpret ; construe ; put a construction 《on》 ; translate ; define ; explain ; expound ; comment ¶ 법의 해석 the construction of law〔ordinance〕//선의〔악의〕로 해석하다 interpret favorably〔unfavorably〕 ; put a good〔bad〕 construction 《upon》//여러 가지로 해석하다 interpret variously//그의 연설은 정부에 대한 공격으로 해석되었다 His speech was construed as an attack on the government. //좋을대로 해석해라 Put your own construction on it. //침묵은 반드시 동의를 뜻한다고만 해석될 수는 없다 Silence is not always to be read as consent.

문법적 — a grammatical interpretation 영문 —법 English translation techniques

해설 解說 explanation ; elucidation ; commentary ; interpretation ; exposition —하다 explain ; comment on 《the text》 ; expound 《a doctrine》 ; interpret ; elucidate

—자 a commentator ; an expounder ; an exponent (of science) 뉴스 — news comment(ary)

해성 단계 海成段階 a sea terrace

해성층 海成層 the sea layer

해소 咳嗽 a cough ⇨ 해수

해소 海嘯 ① the sound of ebbing waves —하다 《ebbing waves》 resound ② [해일] tidal waves ; a sea-quake ; a seismic wave

해소 解消 ① [해산] dissolution ; disorganization ; liquidation —하다 be dissolved ; be disorganized ; be liquidated ② [해약] annulment ; cancellation —하다 cancel 《a contract》 ; annul ; break off ¶ 약혼의 해소 annulment〔cancellation〕 of an engagement ③ [해결] solution ; settlement —하다 be solved ; be settled ¶ 정계의 불안은 해소 되었다 The political unrest died down.

해소 解訴 withdrawal〔discontinuance〕 of a case —하다 withdraw a case

해소수 a little over〔more than〕 a year

해소일 —消日 idling away one's time ; leading an idle life —하다 idle〔loaf〕 away one's day ; waste the time

해손 海損 sea damage ; average (loss)

— 공탁금 an average deposit — 정산(精算)〔정산서, 정산인〕 an average adjustment〔statement, adjuster〕 — 조항〔계약, 계약 증서〕 an average clause〔agreement, bond〕 — 화물 sea-damaged goods 공동〔단독〕 — general〔particular〕 average

해송 海松 [곰솔] a species of pine ; Pinus Thunbergii (학명) ; [잣나무] Big Cone Pine

해수 咳嗽 a cough ; a tussis ; a coughing

—병〔증〕 consumption —약 cough medicine ; a cough remedy ; cough drops ; cough syrup

해수 海水 sea water ; salt water ; brine ¶ 해수에서 자란 풀 salt grasses
—욕 sea-bathing ; a sea bath ¶ 해수욕을 하다 bathe in the sea ; enjoy a bath in the sea **—욕복** a bathing suit〔dress, costume〕; a swim suit **—욕장** a swimming〔bathing〕 beach ; a bathing resort 〔place〕; a watering place 《영》
해수 海獸 a sea〔marine〕 animal
해수침(해) 海水侵(害) 〖보험〗 damage by seawater ¶ 해수침을 입다 be damaged by seawater
해시 亥時 〖민속〗 the watch of the Boar ① the last of the 12 double-hours (⇨ the period between 9 and 11 p.m.) ② the 23d of the 24 hours(⇨ 9 : 30~10 : 30 p.m.)
해시계 —時計 a sundial ; a dial
해시라이스 rice with hashed meat (and potatoes)
해식 海蝕 erosion of the sea
해식 解式 〖수학〗 a solution 《of, to》; a key 《to》
해신 海神 the sea god ; the god of the sea ; Neptune (로마의) ; Poseidon (희랍의)
해심 海深 the depth of the sea ¶ 해심을 재다 sound〔plumb〕 the sea // 해심 30 피트이다 The water is 30 feet deep. / There is a thirty feet depth of water.
해쓱하다 (be) pale ; pallid ; wan ¶ 흙빛처럼 해쓱하다 be ashy pale // 그 여자의 얼굴은 해쓱해보였다 She looked pale.
해씨 該氏 the said gentleman ; the man himself
⁑**해악 害惡** evil ; harm ; mischief ¶ 사회의 해악을 바로 잡다 cure the ills of society
⁑**해안 海岸** the seashore ; the coast ; the seaside ; the seaboard ; the waterfront ; the beach ; the strand

> 참고 **coast**는 지도 따위의 「해안선」「연안」 **seashore**는 「해안의 토지」 **seaside**는 정양지로서의 「해안」 **beach**는 「물가」 그리고 **stand**는 시어로서 「나루터」

¶ 해안의 seaside ; coastal ; seashore // 해안에서 on〔by〕 the seashore ; by〔at〕 the seaside // 해안을 산보하다 take a walk along the beach // 해안을 따라 항해하다 sail coastwise〔along the coast〕 // 그는 해안에 별장을 가지고 있다 He has a villa at the seaside.
— 거리〔통〕 the (sea, water) front **— 경비** coast(al) defense **— 경비대** the coast guard **—도(島)** a coastal island **—선** the shoreline ; the coastline **— 지방** a seaside〔coast〕 district **— 평야** a coastal plain **— 포대** a coast-battery〔-fort〕
해안메꽃 海岸— 〖식물〗 a kind of convolvulus
해야 하다 have to 《do》; must 《do》; should 《do》; ought to 《do》 ¶ 곧 출발해야 한다 I must set out at once. // 자식은 부모님께 순종해야 한다 Children should obey their parents.
해약 解約 cancellation〔annulment〕 of a contract **— 하다** cancel〔rescind, annul〕 a contract ; call off
— 반환금 surrender value
⁑**해양 海洋** the sea(s) ; the ocean ¶ 해양의 자유 the freedom of the sea
— 경찰대 the National Maritime Police **— 국가** a maritime power **— 기상대** a marine meteorological observatory **— 대학** a mercantile marine college **— 문학** sea literature **— 물리학** oceanophysics **— 생물** oceanic life **—성 기후** oceanic climate **— 소설** a sea-story **— 식물** an oceanophyte **— 지리학** ocean geography **—학** oceanography
해어 海魚 sea fish
해어 海語 nautical terms ; sea-terms
— 사전 a dictionary of nautical terms
해어뜨리다 wear away〔down〕 ¶ 옷을 해어뜨리다 wear out one's clothes
해어지다 get〔be〕 worn out〔away, down〕; get tattered ¶ 옷이 누덕누덕 해어지다 One's clothes are worn to rags. // 바지의 엉덩이 부위가 해어져 버렸다 The seat of my pants has worn through.
해엄 解嚴 — 하다 call off the guard ; [계엄령을] lift〔repeal〕 martial law
해역 海域 a sea area
해연 海燕 ① 〖동물〗 a kind of sea urchin ; Clypeaster japonicus (학명) ② [바다제비] 〖새〗 a (stormy) petrel
해연 海淵 the lowest depth of an ocean ; the deep ; the abyss
해연풍 海軟風 a sea breeze
해열 解熱 removal〔alleviation〕 of fever **— 하다** alleviate a fever
—제 a fever remedy ; an antifebrile ; a febrifuge ; an antipyretic
해오라기 〖새〗 the white〔snowy〕 heron
해오라기난초 〖식물〗 a (kind of) orchis
해왕성 海王星 〖천문〗 Neptune
*__해외 海外__ foreign countries ; overseas ¶ 해외로 abroad ; overseas ; beyond the seas ; across the ocean // 해외로부터 from abroad // 해외로 가다 go abroad // 해외로 진출하다 advance abroad // 해외로 수출하다 export // 해외 여행을 하다 travel abroad // 그는 해외 사정에 정통하다 He has a thorough knowledge of foreign affairs. // 그는 해외 시찰 여행에서 돌아왔다 He returned from a tour of inspection abroad. // 토요일 오후에 해외에 나갑니다 I'm going overseas saturday afternoon.
— 공관 a diplomatic office in the foreign country **— 근무** overseas ser-

ㅎ

vice ; detached service — 근무 수당 overseas service allowance — 만유 a foreign tour — 무역 foreign〔overseas〕 trade — 문학 foreign literature — 발전 overseas expansion — 방송 overseas 〔international〕 broadcasting — 사정 foreign affairs — 시장 overseas markets — 시찰 a tour of inspection abroad — 여행 a trip abroad — 유학 a study abroad — 이주 emigration — 전보 overseas cable(gram) — 진출 overseas expansion — 통신 news from abroad — 투자 an overseas〔foreign〕 investment — 파병 overseas dispatch 〔deployment〕 of armed forces —판 an overseas edition — 홍보 활동 an overseas information activity 한국 — 개발 공사 the Korea Overseas Development Corporation

해우 海牛 a sea cow ; a manatee ; a dugong
—류 Sirenian

*해운 海運 marine〔sea, ocean〕 transportation ; shipping ; maritime〔seaborn〕 traffic
—계 the shipping world〔circles〕 — 관리 control of marine transportation — 국(國) a maritime power —국(局) the Maritime Transportation Bureau — 동맹 a shipping conference — 보호 정책 a protective shipping policy —업 the shipping industry ; marine transportation business —업자 a shipping agent ; shipping interests 《총칭》 — 정책 a shipping policy 대한 — 공사 the Korea Shipping Corporation 《KSC》

해웃값 a charge for a prostitute 〔*kisaeng*〕 ; a prostitute's fee

해원 海員 a seaman ; a mariner ; a sailor ; a crew 《총칭》
— 생활 a seafaring life ; a sailor's life — 양성소 a seamen's training school — 용어 a nautical term — 조합〔협회〕 a seamen's association

해읍스름하다 (be) whitish ; not quite white enough

해의 海衣 [김] laver ; sloke

해의 害意 malicious intent ; malice ; ill will ¶ 해의를 품다 bear 《a person》 malice

해이 解弛 relaxation ; slackening ; looseness —하다 relax ; get〔become〕 loose ; slacken ; flag ; become remiss ; be off one's guard ¶ 해이한 기강 slackened discipline // 마음이 해이하다 one's attention relaxes

해인초 海人草 〖식물〗 Corsican weed (맥닌의 원료)

해일 亥日 〖민속〗 the Day of the Boar

해일 海溢 tidal〔storm〕 waves ; overflowing of the sea ; a sea-quake ; a seismic wave —하다 《the sea》 overflow ; have tidal wave ¶ 해일에 휩쓸리다 be washed〔swept〕 away by a tidal wave
— 경보 a tidal wave warning

해임 解任 release from office ; dismissal ; discharge ; displacement —하다 release 《a person》 from office ; dismiss ; relieve 《a person》 of his post ; discharge ; recall ; displace 《a person》 from his position
—장 a letter of dismissal〔discharge〕 —제 the recall system

*해자 垓子 a moat

해자 楷字 the square style of Chinese handwriting

해작질 toying with one's food〔drink〕 —하다 toy〔trifle〕 with one's food 〔drink〕

해장 drinking to relieve a hangover —하다 chase a hangover with a drink before breakfast
—국 a broth to chase a hangover —술 alcohol used as a hangover-chaser

해장 海葬 a burial at sea〔in the sea〕 —하다 bury at sea〔in the sea〕 ; consign 《a person's body》 to a watery grave ; commit 《a person's body》 to the waves

*해저 海低 the bottom〔bed〕 of the sea ; the sea-bottom ; the sea-bed ; the floor of the ocean
— 동식물 sea-floor plants and animals ; submarine organisms ; the benthos — 여행자 an aquanaut — 유전 a submarine oil field — 전보 a cablegram ; a submarine telegram — 전선 a submarine cable ; the cable — 전신 cable (service) ; cabling ; submarine telegraphy ¶ 해저 전신으로 by cable — 지진 a submarine earthquake — 탄전 a submarine coal field — 터널 an undersea tunnel ; a submarine tunnel — 화산 a submarine volcano
☞ ⦅ p. 2336 ⦆

*해적 海賊 a pirate ; a sea robber ¶ 해적이 출몰하는 바다 pirate-infested waters // 해적질을 하다 commit piracy ; pirate ; make a piratical raid 《on a ship》 ; rob at sea
—기 a black flag ; the Jolly Roger —선 a pirate ship ; a sea rover —판 a pirated edition〔version〕 — 행위 piracy

해적호 海賊湖 an island sea-lake

해전 before sunset

해전 海戰 a naval battle〔engagement, action〕 ; a sea fight ¶ 해전 중이다 A naval battle is underway〔going on〕.
트라팔가 — the Battle of Trafalgar

해정 海程 distance by sea

*해제 解除 ① [취소] cancellation ; removal ; revocation ; dissolution ; rescission
② [해방] release ; absolution ; discharge ; acquittal ; exoneration —하다 cancel ; revoke ; dissolve ; rescind ;

해저 · 해양 개발

1 해양과 해저

▶해양개발 ocean development / 해양자원 resources of the sea; marine resources / 해양과학 ocean science; oceanography / 해양생물 marine organism / 해양생물학 marine biology / 해양생물학자 marine biologist / 해양공학 oceanics; offshore technology / 해양국 maritime country[nation] / 해양법 the law of the sea; the sea laws / UN해양법회의(海洋法會議) the United Nations Conference on the Law of the Sea; the U.N. Law of the Sea Conference / 해양오염 sea contamination; contamination of sea water / 엘리뇨 El Nino

▶해저자원 seabed [undersea, offshore] resources; sea [ocean] bottom resources / 해저광물자원 mineral resources at the sea bottom; submarine[offshore] minerals / 해저유전 submarine[offshore] oilfield / 해저탐사기 underwater detection machinery

▶공해(公海) high [open] sea / 공해상의 선박 ships on the high seas / 영해(領海) territorial waters [sea] / 영해침범 the violation of territorial waters; the intrusion into territorial waters / 경제수역(水域) (exclusive) economic zone [waters] / 대륙붕 continental shelf / 해류 ocean current / 계절해류 seasonal current / 조류(潮流) tidal current

2 어업과 수산자원

▶어업 fishing industry / 어업자원 fishing resources / 연안(沿岸)어업 coastal[offshore] fishing / 원양어업 deep-sea fishing; ocean [pelagic] fishing / 조업구역할당 assignment[allotment] of fishing areas / 어업수역 fishing ground [zone, area] / 어업전관수역 exclusive fishing zone / 어업권 fishing rights / 밀어획 poaching / 밀어획자 poacher / 저인망(底引網)어업 trawl fishing; trawling / 주낙(어업) long-line fishing; long-lining / 흘림걸그물 drift net fishing / 어선 fishing vessel[boat, ship] / 어선단 fishing fleet / 어획량 fish catch; haul / 풍어년 bumper (fish crop) year / 흉어년 lean (fish crop) year

▶포경(捕鯨) whaling; whale fishing / 포경선 whaler / 포경선단 whaling fleet / 감시관 inspector / 감시선 patrol boat / 금어(령) fishing ban [moratorium] / 남획 overfishing

▶양식(養殖) sea farming; marine culture / 양어장 fish farm; breeding pond / 인공부화 artificial hatching (of fish eggs) / 산란장 spawning ground / 회유어(回遊魚) wide-ranging [ocean-ranging] fish / 소강성(溯江性)어 anadromous fish / 강하성(降下性)어 catadromous fish / 해양목장 marine ranch / 수산시험장 marine laboratory

3 표현

¶ 오염물질의 유출은 어장을 파괴한다. The flow of pollutants into the sea causes the fishing ground to be spoiled. // 난류와 한류가 교차되는 곳은 해저에 쌓인 영양분이 수면으로 올라오기 때문에 풍부한 어장이 된다. A junction between a warm current and a cold current is a rich fishing ground, for the nutritive substances accumulated on the bottom flood up to the surface. / 그 배는 영해를 2마일이나 들어와 있다. The ship was two miles inside [into] the territorial waters. / 외국어선단이 한국의 전관어업수역을 침범했다. A foreign fishing fleet intruded into Korean exclusive fishing zone. / 양식은 한국 어업의 중요한 부분을 차지할 것이다. Aquaculture is going to be an important part of the Korean fishing industry. / 적조(赤潮)현상으로 양식장의 약 150만 치어들이 죽었다. Red tide killed about one million five hundred-thousand fry in the aquafarm.

---

remove ; lift ; release ; free ; absolve ; exonerate 《a person from an obligation》; relieve ; acquit 《a person of his responsibility》 ¶ 계약을 해제하다 cancel〔rescind〕 a contract ; dissolve ; rescind
— 조항〔조건〕 a resolutive clause〔condition〕 계약 — revocation〔rescission, cancellation〕 of a contract 무장 — disarming ; disarmament ; demilitarization 폭풍 경보 — lifting of a storm warning ; all clear

해제 解題 a bibliographical introduction
—하다 give a bibliographical explanation 《of》
—자 a bibliographer 한서(漢書) — bibliographical notes on Chinese literature

해조 諧調 melody ; harmony
해조 害鳥 an injurious bird ; vermin
해조 海鳥 a seabird ; a seafowl 《총칭》
—분 guano
해조 海潮 the tide ; a current
해조 海藻 seaweeds ; marine plants ; algae ; seaware (비료용)
해주다 do 《a thing》 for 《a person》 ; help with ; do as a favor ¶ 심부름을 해주다 run an errand 《for a person》 // 편지 번역을 해주다 translate a letter for 《a person》
해죽 smiling sweetly ; beamingly ¶ 해죽 웃다 smile sweetly 《at a person》 ; smile a sweet smile
해죽거리다[1] [걷다] ⇨ 헤죽거리다
해죽거리다[2] [웃다] ⇨ 히죽거리다
해중 海中 the middle〔bottom〕 of the sea ¶ 해중에 in the sea ; undersea(s) ; overboard // 해중에 뛰어들다 jump 〔plunge〕 into the sea ; jump overboard (배에서)
— 핵실험 an undersea nuclear test — 화산 ⇨ 해저 화산
해지 解止 〖법〗 termination —하다 abandon ; terminate ; close ¶ 파산 절차의 해지 the termination of bankrupt procedure
해지다[1] be worn out ⇨ 해어지다
해지다[2] [저물다] the sun sets
해직 解職 release from office ; dismissal —하다 release 《a person》 from his office〔position〕 ; relieve 《a person》 of his post ; dismiss ; discharge
— 수당 a discharge allowance ; dismissal〔severance〕 pay — 통고 a dismissal notice
해질녘 ¶ 해질녘에 at sunset ; toward sundown
해질때, 해질무렵 ⇨ 해질녘
해질성 —性 〖식물〗 negative heliotropism ; apheliotropism ¶ 해질성의 apheliotropic
해찰궂다 ⇨ 해찰스럽다
해찰스럽다 (be) brash ; rash ; rough ; fresh ; rude ; imprudent ; careless ; inconsiderate ; flippant ; frivolous ; unserious
해찰하다 ① [집적거려 해침] meddle with and spoil things ② [다른 짓을 함] do〔give one's attention to〕 something else while one is at work ¶ 해찰이 심한 사람 a scatterbrain
해척 解尺 selling 《cloth》 by the measure ; retailing cloth —하다 sell by the measure ; retail cloth
‡해체 解體 ① [분해] taking to pieces ; dismantling ; dismantlement ② [해산] dissolution ; disorganization ; liquidation ③ [해부] dissection —하다 disjoint 《a machine》 ; take〔pull〕 《a machine》 to pieces ; dismantle 《an engine》 ; demount ; dissolve ; disorganize ; liquidate ; disband ; dissect ¶ 기계를 해체하다 take a machine to pieces ; disjoint a machine // 정당을 해체하다 disband〔dissolve〕 a factory
선박 —업자 a ship breaker
*해초 海草 seaweeds ; sea plants ; algae ⇨ 해조(海藻)
식용 — edible seaweeds
해초류 海鞘類 〖동물〗 Ascidiacea
해춘 解春 thawing ; the beginning of spring ; the spring thaw —하다 it thaws ; spring begins ; the spring thaw sets in
*해충 害蟲 a noxious〔harmful〕 insect ; a blight ; vermin 《총칭》 ¶ 해충을 박멸하다 exterminate vermin〔noxious insects〕
— 구제 extermination of vermin ¶ 해충 구제 인부 an (insect) exterminator
해치 a hatch ¶ 해치의 뚜껑 a hatch cover
*해치다 害— injure ; harm ; hurt ; impair ; do 《a person》 harm ; spoil ; mar ; damage

> 참고 **injure** 가장 널리 쓰이는 말 특히 외부나 건강 따위를 해치다 **harm** injure보다 고통·고뇌가 더 강하다 **damage** 손해에 의한 가치의 소실을 강조한다 **hurt** 사람이나 물건에 물질적·정신적 손해를 주다 **impair** 물건의 가치나 능력을 감소시키다 **spoil** 손해의 정도가 impair 보다 훨씬 크다

¶ 건강을 해치다 injure one's health // 감정을 해치다 hurt 《a person's》 feelings // 사람을 해치다 do harm to〔injure, kill〕 《a person》 // 미관을 해치다 mar 〔injure〕 the beauty 《of》
‡해치우다 finish up ; do completely ; get 《it》 done ¶ 일을 해치우다 get through with one's work // 일은 분명히 그때까지 해치울게요 I'll be sure to get it into shape by then.
해타 懈惰 laziness ⇨ 해태
해탈 解脫 deliverance (of one's soul) ; (Buddhistic) emancipation ; salvation —하다 be delivered from 《sin, passions, attachments》 ¶ 사파를 해탈하다 be delivered from worldly existence ; be cut loose from the ties of the earth
해태 a mythical unicorn-lion (as the guardian of palace against fire)
해태 海苔 laver ; sloke
해태 懈怠 idleness ; laziness ; indolence ; sloth ; sluggishness —하다 (be) lazy ; idle ; indolent ; slothful ; sluggish
해토 解土 thawing of the ground —하다 《the ground》 thaw
— 머리 the beginning of the thaw
해퇴 海退 〖지리〗 regression
*해파리 〖동물〗 a jellyfish ; a medusa
해판 解版 distribution of printing type —하다 distribute type

—공 a type distributor
해포 a year or so ; about a year
해포석 海泡石 meerschaum ; sepiolite
해표 海豹 〖동물〗 a sea leopard ; a seal
해풍 海風 a sea wind〔breeze〕
해필 奚必 ⇨ 하필
해하다 害— ⇨ 해치다
*해학 諧謔 a jest ; humor ; a joke ; good-humored banter ; pleasantry ; fun ; a wisecrack 《미》 ¶ 해학적인 humorous ; witty
—가 a humorist ; a wit ; a joker —곡 a scherzo — 소설 a humorous story
해항 海港 a seaport
해해거리다 giggle ; cackle ; titter
†해협 海峽 straits ; a channel ; a sound 대한 — the Straits of Korea 영국 — the English Channel
해화석 海花石 〖동물〗 star coral
해후 邂逅 a chance〔casual〕 meeting ; a fortuitous meeting ; an encounter —하다 meet by chance ; happen〔chance〕 to meet ; come〔fall〕 across 《a person》 ; encounter
— 상봉 ⇨ 해후
‡핵 核 [세포의] a nucleus 《*pl.* -lei》 ; [과실의] a kernel ; a core
—가족 a nuclear family —개발 nuclear development —공격 a nuclear attack 〔strike〕 —군비 nuclear armament(s) —농축 pycnosis ; pyknosis —물리학 nuclear physics —붕괴 disintegration of a cell nucleus ; karyoclasis —시대 the atomic〔nuclear〕 age —연료 nuclear fuel —융합 fusion of cell nuclei ; nuclear fusion —전쟁 a nuclear war —탄두 a nuclear warhead 원자— the nucleus of an atom ; an atomic nucleus
핵과 核果 a stone-fruit ; a drupe ; a putamen
핵막 核膜 nuclear membrane
핵무기 核武器 nuclear weapons
— 보유국 a nuclear power 전술〔전략〕 — a tactical〔strategic〕 nuclear weapon
핵무장 核武裝 nuclear〔atomic〕 armament(s) —하다 be armed with nuclear weapons
—국 a nuclear-armed country — 금지 지역 a denuclearized zone
핵물질 核物質 nuclear materials
핵반응 核反應 nuclear reaction
핵분열 核分裂 (nuclear) fission ; division of a cell nucleus —하다 fission ; undergo fission
— 물질 fissionable materials — 연쇄 반응 fission chain reaction — 폭탄 a (nuclear) fission bomb
핵산 核酸 nucleic acid
리보 — ribonucleic acid 《RNA》
핵실험 核實驗 a nuclear test〔experiment〕 ; nuclear testing
— 경쟁 nuclear testing competition — 금지 협정 a nuclear test ban agreement —장 a nuclear testing ground 고공(高空) — a high altitude nuclear test 대기권 — an atmospheric nuclear test 지하 — an underground nuclear test
핵심 核心 a kernel ; the core ¶ 문제의 핵심 the kernel〔heart〕 of a question // 핵심을 찌르다 touch the core ; penetrate to the pith ; get at the kernel 〔heart〕 of a subject // 오늘날과 같은 경제 전쟁 시대에는 국익이 문제의 핵심이다 In this era of economic wars, national interest is the name of the game. // 최소의 비용을 들여 최대의 이익을 남기는 것 그것이 문제의 핵심이다 Making the most profit at the lowest cost, that's the name of the game.
핵우산 核雨傘 the 《U. S》 nuclear umbrella ¶ 핵우산의 보호하에 두다 put 《a nation》 under the protection of 《American》 nuclear umbrellas
핵인 核仁 〖생물〗 a nucleolus 《*pl.* -li》
핵자 核子 〖물리〗 a nucleon
중(重)— a hyperon
핵질 核質 〖생물〗 karyoplasm ; nucleoplasm
핵폭발 核爆發 a nuclear explosion 〔blast〕 ¶ 핵폭발을 행하다 set off a nuclear explosion
— 장치〔실험〕 a nuclear device〔test〕
핵폭탄 核爆彈 a nuclear bomb
핸드백 a handbag ; a pocketbook 《미》
†핸들 [자전거의] a handle bar ; a pull ; [자동차의] a (steering) wheel ; [도어의] a knob ¶ 핸들을 잡다 sit at the wheel // 핸들을 우〔좌〕로 꺾다 wheel right〔left〕 // 내가 핸들을 잡을게 Let me take the wheel.
핸들링 〖축구〗 a hand touch
‡핸디캡 a handicap ¶ …에게 핸디캡을 주다 give a person a handicap // 약한 것이 핸디캡이 되다 be handicapped by one's weakness // 핸디캡 없이 달리다 start from scratch
†핸섬 handsome ¶ 핸섬한 남자 a handsome〔good-looking〕 man
핼쑥하다 look thin〔haggard, gaunt, emaciated〕 《from》 ; look worn out ¶ 얼굴이 핼쑥해진 사람 a haggard-faced 〔drawing- looking〕 person // 열병으로 핼쑥하다 look consumed by fever
‡햄[1] ham
—샌드위치 ham-sandwiches —샐러드 ham and salad —에그 ham and eggs
햄[2] [아마추어 무선가] a (radio) ham
햄버그스테이크 a hamburger 《미》 ; a Hamburg steak
햅쌀 new rice ; the year's crop of rice
—밥 rice cooked from the new crop
햇- new ; the first product of the year ¶ 햇것 a new crop ; the year's crop // 햇곡식 a new crop of grain ; the year's harvest

햇귀 early morning sunshine ; the first rays of the sun ; the sun's rays ; a sunny spot
햇덧 a short autumn〔fall〕 day
햇무리 a halo ; a ring around the sun **—하다** the sun has a ring around it
햇무리구름 〖기상〗 a cirrostratus cloud
햇물 ① ⇨ 햇무리 ② [샘물] a spring that gushes forth only after the year's rainy season
햇발 sunbeams ⇨ 햇살
*햇볕 sunbeams ; sunlight ¶ 햇볕을 쬐다 bask in the sun ; sunbathe // 이 방은 햇볕이 잘 들지 않는구나 This room doesn't get much sunshine, doesn't it? // 내 작품이 햇볕을 보기 전에 내가 죽게 될지도 모르겠다 I wonder if I'll die before my work sees the light of day.
†햇빛 sunshine ; sunlight ¶ 햇빛에 쬐다 sun ; expose to the sun // 햇빛에 말리다 dry in the sun // 햇빛이 방 안에 들어오다 the sun streams into the room // 그곳은 햇빛이 많이 비치지 않는 곳이야 That place doesn't get very much sun.
햇살 sunbeams ; sunlight ; the rays of the sun ¶ 햇살을 쬐다 bask〔bathe〕 in the sun // 햇살을 받다 be in the sun
햇수 —數 the number of years
햇콩 new beans ; the year's crop of beans
햇팥 new red beans ; the year's crop of red beans
†행 行 ① a line ; a row ¶ 12페이지 위에서 다섯 행째에 in the fifth line of the twelfth page from the beginning〔top〕 ② [시의] a line (of verse) ; a verse
행 幸 happiness ; good luck ; fortune ¶ 행인지 불행인지 for good or for evil ; luckily or unluckily
—행 行 [가는 곳] bound for ; for 《*Seoul*》 ¶ 서울행 열차 a train for *Seoul* ; a *Seoul*-bound train
행각 行脚 ① [수행의] a pilgrimage **—하다** go on (a) pilgrimage ; make a pilgrimage ② [도보 여행] traveling on foot ; a walking tour **—하다** travel on foot ; go on a walking tour ¶ 사기 행각에 나서다 go on a fraud〔pilferage〕 tour
—승(僧) an itinerant monk ; a priest on a pilgrimage
행간 行姦 committing adultery **—하다** commit adultery〔fornication〕 ; have illicit intercourse 《with》 ; fornicate 《with》 ⇨ 간음(姦淫)
행간 行間 space between lines ¶ 행간을 띄다 leave space between lines ; space out // 행간을 띄지 않고 짜다 [인쇄] compose solid // 행간을 좁히다 tighten up the line spacing
행객 行客 a traveler ; a tourist ; a wayfarer ; a stranger
†행군 行軍 a march ; marching **—하다** march ¶ 4열 종대로 시내를 행군하다 parade a street in four columns // 행군 명령을 내리다 give the route
— 대형 march formation **—로** a route ; a line of march **— 명령** a march〔marching〕 order **— 속도** 〖군사〗 time **— 종대** a marching column ; a column of route **강—** a forced march **설중 —** a march in the snow
행궁 行宮 a temporary palace
행낭 行囊 a mail-bag〔-sack〕 ; a pouch
행내기 an ordinary person ; a mediocrity ; a common being ¶ 그는 행내기가 아니다 He is no ordinary type.
행년 行年 one's age〔years〕
†행동 行動 (an) action ; (an) act ; (a) movement ; conduct ; behavior ; doings **—하다** act ; behave (oneself) ; conduct oneself ; move ¶ 행동에 옮기다 put into action ; carry out // 행동의 자유 the freedom of action〔movement〕 // 행동을 일으키다 start action ; make a move // 행동으로 나타내다 show in one's manner // 행동을 같이하다 act 《with a person》 ; sail in the same boat 《with》 ; act in concert 《with》 ; act together ; cooperate 《with a person》 // 행동을 감시하다 watch 《a person's》 movements // 행동이 대담하다 be bold in action ; act boldly // 행동이 기민하다 be prompt in action // 행동의 자유를 속박하다 restrain 《a person's》 freedom of action ; tie 《a person's》 hands // 그의 행동은 신사적이었다 He behaved (himself) like a gentleman. // 앞으로는 좀더 행동을 신중히 하지 않으면 안된다 You must be more prudent in future about what you do. // 자네가 행동으로 보여 주기 전에는 자네 말을 믿지 않겠어 I won't believe you until you put your money where your mouth is. // 행동을 조심해라 Clean up your act. /Behave yourself. // 그러한 행동은 때때로 그 아이가 귀여워서 그러는 것으로 간주되기도 한다 Such an act is sometimes considered a gesture of affection for the child. // 그녀에게는 행동으로 보여 주어라 You've got to show her where you stand. // 우선 그들의 반응을 보고 나서 행동하자 For the moment, let's wait and see how they respond before we make our next move.
— 과학 behavioral sciences **—대** an action group〔corps〕 **—력** acting power **— 반경** 〖군사〗 a radius of action〔operation〕 ; a cruising〔an action〕 radius **— 방향** a line of action **— 범위** a sphere of action **—주의** 〖심리〗 behaviorism **군사 —** military action ; military movements ; hostile action **단독 —** separate action **단체 —** group〔united〕 action **자유 —** free〔independent〕 action ; a free

hand 적대 — hostile operations 직접 — direct action

행동 개시 行動開始 〚군사〛 deployment —하다 deploy《an army, a troop》
— 시간 (the) H-hour ; (the) zero hour ¶ 행동 개시 시간 30분전 H-hour minus thirty

행동 거지 行動擧止 bearing ; manners ; all one's actions ¶ 행동 거지에 조심하다 behave oneself with discretion

행동 미술 行動美術 action painting
—가 an action painter ; an actionist

행동 통일 行動統一 action in concert 《with》; united action —하다 act in concert 《with》 ¶ 파업자들끼리 행동 통일이 안되고 있다 There is lack of unity among the strikers.

행락 行樂 enjoyment ; amusement ; pleasure ; a good time —하다 have a good time ; enjoy〔amuse〕 oneself
—객 a holiday-maker ; a hiker —지 a pleasure〔holiday〕 resort

행랑 行廊 rooms on both sides of the main gate where servants live ; servants' quarters
—것 a servant ; a menial —살이 the life of a (resident) servant — 아범 a man servant

행려 行旅 travel
— 병사자 a person who died unidentified on the road — 병자 an ill wayfarer ; a charity patient

⁑행렬 行列 [행진] a procession ; a parade ; [물건을 살 때의] a queue ; 〚수학〛 matrix ¶ 행렬의 선두〔후미〕 the head〔tail〕 of a procession〔queue〕// 행렬을 짓다 stand in line ; form a queue // 행렬에 뛰어들다 break into〔crash〕 a line ; jump the queue 《영》
—식 〚수학〛 a determinant 가장〔등〕 — costume〔lantern〕 procession

행로 行路 a path ; a road ; a course ; a career ¶ 행로지인(之人) a (mere) stranger〔passerby〕; an outsider
인생 — the path of life ; life's journey ; stages of a man's career

행리 行李 a baggage 《미》; a luggage 《영》

행림 杏林 physicians ; medical men
—계 medical circles

행망적다 (be) careless ; negligent ; inattentive

행매 行賣 ① [팔기 시작함] —하다 begin to sell ; start selling ② [행상] —하다 peddle ; hawk

행방 行方 one's whereabouts ; one's traces ; the place (where) one has gone ¶ 행방이 묘연한 missing ; lost // 행방을 감추다 cover one's traces ; disappear ; conceal one's whereabouts // 행방을 찾다 trace ; search〔hunt, look〕 for // 행방을 알아내다 locate 《a person》; discover the trace of 《a missing man》; track down // 그는 행방 불명이다 He is missing. /His whereabouts is unknown. // 탐정은 그 여자의 행방을 알아냈다 The detective located her.
— 불명자 a missing person ; the missing 《집합적》

행보 行步 walking ; going on foot —하다 walk ; go on foot

†행복 幸福 happiness ; felicity ; well-being ; bliss ; blessedness ; good fortune (행운) —하다 (be) happy ; blessed ; blissful ; fortunate ; lucky ; felicitous ¶ 행복의 절정 the seventh heaven // 행복의 추구 the pursuit〔quest〕 of happiness // 인생의 행복 human happiness ; happiness and comforts of life // 행복을 누리다 enjoy happiness // 행복을 빌다 wish 《a person》 every happiness // 행복하게 살다 live a happy life ; live happily // 나는 참으로 행복하다 I'm as happy as a king〔skylark〕.
—감 euphoria ; a feeling of well-being —론 eud(a)emonics —설 eud(a)emonism

행불행 幸不幸 happiness or misery ; good or bad luck ; weal or woe ; good or ill fortune ; lights and shadows ¶ 인생의 행불행 the lights and shadows of life

행사 行使 use ; exercise —하다 use ; employ ; exercise ¶ 권리를 행사하다 exercise one's rights // 무력을 행사하다 appeal〔resort〕 to firearms // 투표권을 행사하다 cast one's vote // 특권을 행사하다 employ one's privilege

행사 行事 an event ; a function ; an observance
— 예정 the schedule 연중 — annual functions〔events, observances〕; the year's regular events

행상 行商 [일] peddling ; hawking ; [행상인] a peddler 《미》; a hawker —하다 peddle ; hawk
—업 pedlary —인 a peddler ; a pedlar ; a hawker ; an itinerant vendor

행상 行賞 awarding 《a person》 a prize ; bestowal of rewards —하다 award a prize to 《a person》; give a reward ; reward 《a person for his services》

행색 行色 ① [차림새] appearance ; externals ② [행동] demeanor ; attitude ; behavior ¶ 행색이 초라하다 look shabby

행서 行書 the semi-cursive style of writing

행선 行船 sailing —하다 sail

⁑행선지 行先地 one's destination ; the end of one's journey ; the place where one is going

⁑행성 行星 a planet ⇨ 유성

행세 行世 ① conduct ; behavior ; manners —하다 conduct oneself ; behave

well ¶ 행세를 잘못하다 misconduct oneself ; misbehave
② [가장] (false) show ; make-believe ; pretense **—하다** pass oneself off 《as》; pretend ; affect ¶ 백만 장자로 행세하다 pose as a millionaire
행세 行勢 **—하다** wield〔exercise, exert〕 power〔authority〕 《over》; hold〔bear〕 sway ; have a hold 《on, over》
행수 行首 the head〔leader〕 of a group ; a boss
행수 行數 the number of lines
행습 行習 a habit ; a practice **—하다** make it a habit to 《do》; be in the habit of 《doing》
행신 行身 behavior ; deportment ; manners ⇨ 처신
행실 行實 behavior ; conduct ; deportment ; demeanor ; manners ¶ 행실이 나쁜 사람 a man of loose conduct〔morals〕// 행실이 좋다 be well-behaved ; show good deportment〔conduct〕
행악 行惡 violence ; wickedness **—하다** do violence〔evil, wrong〕; practice wickedness
행여 幸— by chance ; possibly ¶ 행여 올까 하여 기다렸다 I have waited in case you might drop by.
행여나 幸— by chance ⇨ 행여
†**행운 幸運** good luck ; good fortune ; a lucky〔good〕 break 《미》 ¶ 행운의 fortunate ; lucky // 행운을 빌다 wish 《a person》 good luck // 행운을 빕니다 Good luck ! /I wish you the best of luck. /I'll keep my fingers crossed for you. // 나에게 행운이 찾아올 날을 기다리겠다 I will wait for the day my ship comes in.
—아 a lucky person ; a child of fortune ; a Fortune's favorite〔pet, minion〕
행운 유수 行雲流水 smooth ; going smoothly ; being free and easy
행원 行員 a bank employee ; a bank clerk
†**행위 行爲** an act ; an action ; a deed ; behavior ; conduct ; a work ; doings

> 참고 **act**와 **action**은 혼동되는 일이 있거니와 **act**가 단순·일시적·개인적인데 반하여 **action**은 복잡·계속적·집합적이니, 말하자면 act의 집약임

¶ 도덕적 행위 a moral act // 영웅적 행위 a heroic deed
— 능력 (legal) capacity **— 무능력** (legal) incompetence **—세** the service tax **—자** a doer ; a transactor ; a performer **—지** the place of an act **도덕(적) —** a moral act **법률 —** a juristic act **부정 —** irregularities ; irregular practices **불법 —** an illegal〔unlawful〕 act ; a wrong **상—** a commercial transaction **영웅적 —** a heroic deed **자선 —** an act of charity **정당 —** a justifiable〔legitimate〕 act
행음 行淫 committing adultery ⇨ 행간
행인 行人 a passer-by ; a foot passenger ; a wayfarer ; a pedestrian
행인 杏仁 an apricot stone
행자 行者 an ascetic ; a pilgrim
행장 行狀 ① [품행] behavior ; deportment ; conduct ; demeanor ; doings ; manners
② [사후 기록] records of a deceased person's life ; a necrology ; a history of the deceased
행장 行裝 travel gear ; a traveler's equipment ; a traveling outfit〔suit〕 ¶ 행장을 차리다〔갖추다〕 prepare〔equip, outfit〕 oneself for a journey // 행장을 풀다 take a rest after a travel ; change one's traveling suit for everyday dress
행재소 行在所 the King's temporary quarters
행적 行蹟 the achievements of one's lifetime ; one's work〔contributions〕
행전 行纏 leggings ; putties〔puttees〕 ¶ 행전을 치다 wrap one's legs with putties
*‡***행정 行政** administration ¶ 행정적〔상의〕 executive ; administrative // 행정 기구의 간소화 simplification of administration system // 행정적 수완이 있다 have administrative ability〔capacity〕
— 각부 administrative branches **— 감독〔관리〕** administrative control〔management〕 **— 개혁** a reform of the administrative structure ; an administrative reform **—관** an executive〔administrative〕 official ; an administrator ; an executive **— 관청** a government〔an administrative〕 office **— 구획** an administrative district〔division, section〕; jurisdiction **—권** administrative〔executive〕 power〔authority〕 **— 기관** an administrative organ〔body, machinery〕; an executive agency **— 기구** administrative organization **— 명령** an administrative order **—법** the Administrative Law **— 법령** an administrative decree **—부** the Executive ; the Administration **— 사무** administrative affairs **— 서사** an administrative scrivener **— 소송** administrative litigation **— 수완** administrative ability〔capacity〕 **—원** [중국의] the Executive Council **— 재판소** the Court of Administrative Litigation **— 조치** administrative measure〔action〕 **— 처벌** the administrative punishment **— 처분** administrative measure〔disposition〕 **—학** political science **— 협정** an administrative agreement ☞ ◀ p2342▶
행정 行程 ① road distance ; a distance to cover ; a journey ② 〖기계〗 a stroke ; a throw (of a switch) ; an

행 정

▶행정 administration; government; the executive / 행정 기관 administrative [governmental] organ [office, agency]; executive branch of government structure; executive machinery / 행정 지도 administrative guidance / 행정 감사 administrative inspection[audit] / 행정 개혁 administrative reform / 행정권 administrative rights [authority]

▶정부 government; administration (주로 미) / 중앙 정부 central[national, Federal (미)] government / 지방 정부 local government / 임시 정부 provisional government

▶내각 cabinet ¶ 내각을 개조하다 reshuffle a cabinet // 내각이 총사퇴했다. The cabinet resigned en bloc.; The entire cabinet resigned. // 조각(組閣)하다 form a cabinet / 각의(閣議) cabinet meeting / 정례 각의 regular cabinet meeting / 임시 각의 extraordinary cabinet meeting

▶각료(閣僚) cabinet minister [member] / 수상[국무 총리] prime minister; premier(★ 국무 총리의 각료 파면권 the right of dismissal) / 부수상[부총리] deputy prime minister / 수상 대리 acting prime minister

▶장관 minister (미·영); secretary (미) / 관료 bureaucrat; bureaucracy (★관료 전체, 또는 관료 제도의 뜻도 있음) / 관료 정치 government of bureaucracy

▶공무원 public worker [servant] / 국가 공무원 (national) government worker / 지방 공무원 local government worker / 공직 public office / 임명직 appointive office / 엽관 제도(獵官制度) spoils system

▶관저(官邸) official residence (★ 미국 대통령 관저 1600 Pennsylvania Avenue; 영국 수상 관저 10 Downing Street; 총리 관저 Prime Minister's Official Residence)

▶정책 결정 policy decision / 백서(白書) white paper (★ 외교 백서는 Diplomatic Blue Book으로 외교 청서라고 번역하기도 한다.)

▶지방 행정 local administration [government] / 광역(廣域) 행정 local government on a broader unit area; broader-based local government / 지방 자치체(地方自治體) local self-government [autonomy]

excursion

행주 a dish cloth〔towel〕 ¶ 행주질하다 wipe with a dish cloth
—치마 an apron

행중 行中 a company ; a party ¶ 행중에 끼다 join the company〔group〕

†**행진 行進** a march ; a parade **—하다** march ; proceed ; parade ¶ 죽음의 행진 a death march // 행진중이다 be on the march ; be marching // 의기 양양하게 행진하다 march off in triumph
—가 a marching song **—곡** a march ; field music **결혼 —곡** a wedding march **군대 —곡** a military march **장송 —곡** a funeral march

행짜 ⇨ 행티

행차 行次 an honored going〔coming〕; a visit ; a trip ; traveling **—하다** go ; come ; visit ; go on a trip

행커치프 a handkerchief 《*pl.* ~s, -chieves》

행티 ill-willed behavio(u)r ; injury ; mischief ¶ 행티 사납다 be peevish〔mean, malicious, ill-disposed〕// 행티 부리다 show an ill will ; do mean things

행패 行悖 —하다 do violence ; misbehave 《oneself》 ¶ 행패를 부리다 behave badly ; commit an outrage

행포 行暴 violence ; lawless acts **—하다** do violence ; commit lawless acts ; perpetrate an outrage

행하 行下 ① a gift of money from a master to his servant ; a tip ; a gratuity ② [놀음차] a tip ; a gratuity ; a consideration ¶ 행하를 주다 give 《a person》 a tip

행하다 行— ① do ; act ; behave ; conduct oneself ; [실행하다] carry out ; perform ; practice ; execute ; fulfill ; commit ; enforce ¶ 나쁜 짓을 행하다 do wrong ; do an evil thing // 선을 행하다 do good ; do what is good // 기적을 행하다 work a miracle // 의무를 행하다 perform〔do〕 one's duties // 말은 쉽고 행하기는 어렵다 It is easier to preach than to practice. /Easier said than done.
② [거행하다] hold ; celebrate ; observe ; keep ¶ 시험을 행하다 hold〔give〕 an examination // 의식을 행하다 hold a ceremony // 장례를 행하다 hold a funeral // 결혼식을 행하다 have a wedding ceremony

행형 行刑 ① [사형을] execution ; decap-

itation ② [형벌을] the execution of a sentence —하다 execute ; decapitate
행화 杏花 『식물』 an apricot blossom
행흉 行凶 murder ; assassination —하다 commit murder
향 向 [방향] a direction ; a quarter ; [방위] situation ; [집의] exposure ; aspect ¶ 남향집 a house facing south // 서향이다 [집이] look to the west ; [창이] open to the west // 의자의 방향을 바꾸다 rearrange the set of chairs // 우주선의 방향을 바꾸다 reorient the spacecraft
*향 香 perfume ; incense ¶ 향을 피우다 burn incense
—갑 an incense case
향가 鄕歌 native songs
향곡 鄕曲 the country ; country districts
향관 鄕貫 the birthplace of one's first ancestor ⇨ 관향
향관 鄕關 one's (ancestral) home ; one's native place
향교 鄕校 a Confucian temple and a school belonging to it
향국 鄕國 one's native place ; one's home (land) ; one's home province
향군 鄕軍 [재향 군인] a veteran ; an ex-serviceman ; an ex-soldier ; reservists ; [부대] veterans troops ¶ 백만 향군을 무장시키다 provide〔furnish, supply〕 one million veterans with arms
향긋하다 (be) fragrant ; have a faint sweet scent
*향기 香氣 fragrance ; perfume ; aroma ; a sweet smell〔odor〕 ; a scent ¶ 향기로운 fragrant ; aromatic ; sweet-smelling ; (sweet) scented ; odoriferous // 사향의 향기 the perfume of musk // 향기를 발하다 emit〔send forth〕 a sweet fragrance〔smell〕 ; smell sweet // 향기가 떠돌다 be fragrant with the scent
—학 osmics 꽃— the scent of a flower 과일 — the aroma of fruit
‡향기롭다 香氣— (be) fragrant ; aromatic ; sweet-smelling ; sweet-scented ; odoriferous ¶ 향기로운 꽃 a fragrant flower // 향기로운 냄새 a sweet〔fragrant〕 smell // 향기로운 향수 an aromatic perfume // 장미와 라일락은 향기롭다 Roses and lilacs smell sweet〔have fine scents〕.
향꽂이 香— an incense dish (with a stickholder)
향나무 香— 『식물』 aromatic trees 〔plants〕 ; a Chinese juniper
향내, 향냄새 香— ⇨ 향기(香氣)
향년 享年 one's age at death ¶ 향년 60 He died at the age of 60. /He died at sixty.
향당 鄕黨 a village community ; villagers ; townspeople
향도 嚮導 a guide ; a fugleman (군대의) ; guidance ; conduct ; leading ; leadership —하다 guide ; conduct ; lead ; fugle ¶ …의 향도로 led〔guided, headed〕 《by》 ; under the guidance 《of》
—기(機) a leader plane — 구축함 a destroyer〔flotilla〕 leader —자 a guide ; a leader ; a fugleman (군대의) —함 a leader〔guide〕 ship
향동 向東 facing east —하다 face (the) east ; look toward (the) east
*향락 享樂 enjoyment ; pleasure —하다 enjoy ¶ 향락적(인) pleasure-seeking〔-loving〕 ; given to pleasure // 향락하는 사람 a merrymaker ; a pleasure seeker
— 생활 a gay life ; dissipation —아 a pleasure seeker ; a playboy —주의 epicurism (미식주의) ; epicureanism ; hedonism ; dilettantism —주의자 an epicurean ; a hedonist
향랑각시 香娘閣氏 ⇨ 노래기
향랑자 香娘子 ⇨ 바퀴[2]
향로 香爐 an incense-burner ; a bronze censer
—석(石) the stone before a tomb that the incense burner is put on
‡향료 香料 ① [식품의] spices ; spicery ② [화장품의] materials for making perfume〔incense〕 ; perfume ; perfumery ; a romatic essence〔oils〕
—류 perfumery — 식물 aromatic plants
향리 鄕里 one's home town〔native village〕
향목 香木 aromatic trees ⇨ 향나무
향미 香味 flavor ; smack
—료 flavorings ; seasonings ; spices
향방 向方 [방위] a direction ; an aspect (집의) ; bearings (위치) ; [목적지] a course ; a destination ¶ 향방을 모르다 do not know direction ; have no sense // 사태〔배〕의 향방을 확인하다 take the bearings
향배 向背 for or against ; submission or disobedience ; pro or con ¶ 향배를 결정하다〔분명히 하다〕 define〔clarify〕 one's attitude 《toward》
향복 享福 enjoying happiness ; receiving bliss —하다 enjoy happiness ; receive blessings
향북 向北 facing (the) north —하다 face (the) north ; look toward (the) north
향불 香— an incense fire ; burning incense ¶ 향불을 피우다 burn incense
향사 鄕士 a country gentleman ; a squire
향사 向斜 『지질』 a syncline
†향상 向上 elevation ; rise ; [개선] improvement ; betterment ; [진보] advancement ; progress —하다 rise ; be elevated ; become higher ; improve ; advance ; progress ¶ 지위의 향상 a rise in position // 질의 향상 improvement in quality // 체위의 향상 improvement in physique // 취미의 향상 elevation of taste // 생활 수준을 향상시키다 elevate the

standard of living // 여자의 사회적 지위를 향상시키다 raise〔elevate〕 the social status of women // 사회 복지를 향상시키다 promote social welfare // 노동자의 생활을 향상시키다 improve the conditions of laborers
—심 a desire to improve oneself ; aspiration ; ambition
향속 鄕俗 country〔rural〕 ways〔manners, customs〕
향수 享受 enjoyment ; fruition —하다 enjoy
향수 享壽 enjoying the longevity —하다 enjoy old age ; live to a ripe old age ¶ 100세를 향수하다 be blessed with a longevity of a hundred (years)
향수 香水 a perfume ; a scent ; perfumed〔scented〕 water ; liquid scents ; a synthetic〔an artificial〕 perfume (인공의) ; a floral perfume (꽃에서 딴) ; perfumery 《총칭》 ¶ 향수를 바르다〔뿌리다〕 use〔wear, put on〕 perfume ; perfume // 손수건에 향수를 바르다 perfume〔scent〕 a handkerchief // 지금 뿌린 향수는 뭐죠 What's that perfume you're wearing ?
—병 a perfume bottle — 분무기 a scent-sprayer〔-atomizer〕
‡향수 鄕愁 homesickness ; nostalgia ; thoughts of home ; nostomania (병적인) ¶ 향수를 느끼다 feel homesick ; long very much for one's home // 향수를 느끼게 하다 make 《a person》 homesick〔sick for home〕 ; excite nostalgia
향습성 向濕性 positive hydrotropism
‡향신료 香辛料 spice
향악 鄕樂 Korean music
향연 香煙 ① [향의] the smoke of incense burning ② [담배] fragrant tobacco〔cigarettes〕
향연 饗宴 a banquet ; a dinner ; a feast ; an entertainment ¶ 향연을 베풀다 hold〔give〕 a banquet〔dinner〕 // 향연에 초청하다 invite 《a person》 to a dinner
†향유 享有 enjoyment ; possession —하다 enjoy ; possess ; participate in 《benefit》 ¶ 인권의 향유 및 행사 the enjoyment and exercise of human rights
향유 香油 ① [참기름] sesame oil ② [머리기름] perfumed hair-oil
향유고래 〖동물〗 a sperm whale ; a cachalot
향응 饗應 an entertainment ; a treat ; a dainty repast ; a banquet ; a dinner ; a feast —하다 entertain 《a person at dinner》 ; treat ; give 《a person》 a treat ; feast 《a person》 ; give a party ; hold a banquet ¶ 향응을 받다 be treated 《to a dinner》
—장 a banqueting hall
향응 響應 ① [메아리] resonance ; consonance ; response —하다 resonate ; respond 《to》 ; echo ② [호응] acting in concert —하다 act in concert〔unison〕 《with》 ; follow suit
향의 向意 intention ; inclination ; thought —하다 intend to ; be inclined to ; have a mind to 《do》
향일 向日 turning toward the sunlight
향일성 向日性 (positive) heliotropism
향자 向者 the other day ; some〔a few〕 days ago
향전 香奠 ⇨ 부의(賻儀)
향점 向點 〖천문〗 the apex
태양 — the solar apex
향지성 向地性 〖식물〗 (positive) geotropism
향초 香草 ① [풀] fragrant grass ② [담배] fragrant tobacco
향촉 香燭 incense and candles (used in sacrifices)
향촌 鄕村 the country ; a country village ; country districts
향취 香臭 fragrance ⇨ 향기
향탕 香湯 perfumed water for laving a corpse
향토 鄕土 one's native place〔province, land〕 ; one's home ; one's birthplace ; the country ¶ 향토의 자랑 a pride of a locality
— 문학 folk literature — 민요〔무용〕 a folk song〔dance〕 —색 local color —애 love for one's native place ; local patriotism — 예비군 the local defense force ; the local reserved army corps ; a reservist — 예술 local crafts ; provincial art — 음악 folk〔local〕 music —지 (誌) a local history
향포 香蒲 a bulrush ⇨ 부들
†향하다 向— ① [대하다] face ; front ; look out on ; turn towards ¶ 벽을 향하여 facing the wall // 바다를 향하다 look out on the sea // 서로 향해서 앉다 sit face to face with each other // 바람을 향하여 서다 stand breasting the wind
② [가다] proceed to ; go to〔towards〕 ; start for ; leave for ; make〔head〕 for ; be bound〔headed〕 for ; be off to ¶ 미국을 향하다 [배가] leave〔start, head〕 for America ; [비행기가] head on to America // 육지를 향해 항해하다 sail towards the land // 배는 남쪽을 향해 달렸다 The ship sailed south 〔towards the south〕.
③ [쏠리다] lean towards ; tend towards ¶ 마음이 고향을 향하다 one's mind go off to one's home ; yearn for home
향학심 向學心 desire〔love〕 for learning ; intellectual appetite ; a scholarly bent ¶ 향학심에 불타는 사람 an ardent lover of learning // 향학심에 불타다 burn with the desire for learning ; aspire after further knowledge ; be ardent 〔very eager〕 to seek knowledge

향학열 向學熱 enthusiasm for〔a zest for, an ardent love of〕 learning
향합 香盒 an incense box〔jar〕
향화 香火 ① [향불] incense fire ; burning incense ② [제사] an ancestor-memorial service
향후 向後 hereafter ; henceforth ; from now on
허 虛 an unguarded position ; unpreparedness ; a weak point ; a weakness ; one's blind side ¶ 법의 허를 찌르다 defeat the ends of justice // 허를 찌르다 make a surprise attack 《on the enemy》 ; catch a person off his guard // 허를 찔리다 be thrown off one's guard ; be caught napping
†**허가 許可** permission ; leave ; [승인] approval ; sanction ; grant ; [면허] (a) license ; a permit ; a certificate ; [입학·입장] admission ; [인정] authorization ; authority ; [특허] concession **―하다** permit ; allow ; give leave 《to》 ; sanction ; approve 《of》 ; grant ; license ; give admittance ; admit ; authorize ; concede

> [참고] **permit**가 **allow**보다 격식을 차린 말이고 단정적 **allow**는 특히 부주의·태만으로 인하여「…하도록 버려두다」의 뜻으로 사용되는 수가 많다

¶ 허가를 얻어 with 《a person's》 permission // 허가 없이 without permission 〔leave〕 // 정부의 허가 government clearance // 허가의 실효 loss of validity of permission // 허가를 신청하다 apply for a license ; file an application // 건축 허가가 아직 안 나오다 be not yet given a construction permit // 정부는 두 대학교 신설을 허가했다 The government has sanctioned the establishment of two new universities.
―서 a warrant ; a written permission
―제 a licence system **―증** a permit ; a license ; a charter ; a permit card **건축 ―** permission to build **상륙 ―** shore leave **입학 ―** admission to a school
☞ ◀ p. 2346 ▶
허겁 虛怯 faintheartedness ; funk ; cowardice
―쟁이 a pudding heart ; a coward ; a funk
허겁지겁 hurry-scurry ; flustered ; in a flurry ; confusedly ⇨ 허둥지둥 **―하다** be flustered ; fluster ; scurry ; be all in a fluster
허공 虛空 the empty sky〔air〕 ; the empty space ; an empty void ; [공중] the air ; the sky ¶ 허공에 뜬 hanging in the air // 허공을 잡다 grasp at the air // 허공에 사라지다 vanish into thin air // 허공을 바라보다 stare into space
허구 虛構 a fabrication ; a fiction ; a lie ; a falsehood ; a concoction ; an invention ; a made-up thing ; a fake ; a misrepresentation ¶ 허구의 made-up ; fabricated ; fictitious ; false ; invented ; unfounded ; concocted ; misrepresented
허구렁 虛- an empty hole ; a pit ¶ 허구렁에 빠지다 fall into a pit
허구리 the sides of one's waist ; the flank ⇨ 옆구리
허구하다 許久― be a very〔pretty〕 long time ; (be) very long ¶ 허구한 세월을 덧없이 보내다 spend many long years in vain
허근 虛根 〖수학〗 an imaginary root
허기 虛飢 hunger ¶ 허기지다 be famished ; be〔go〕 hungry ; be exhausted with hunger ; [욕망이] hunger 《for》 ; thirst 《after, for》 ; hanker after ; be hungry for
―증 a hungry feeling ; a gnawing hunger ¶ 허기증이 나다 be〔feel〕 hungry
허기지다 虛飢― ① [마음이] be composing ② [배고파] feel hungry
허깨비 [환영] a phantom ; a hallucination ; [유령] a spook ; a goblin ; a ghost ¶ 허깨비를 보다 see a phantom // 허깨비에 홀리다 be lured by an illusion // 허깨비가 나온다 The ghost walks.
허니문 a honeymoon ; a wedding trip 〔tour, journey〕 ; a bridal journey
허다 許多 many ; much ; great〔vast〕 numbers **―하다** (be) numerous ; innumerable ; frequent ; common ; many ¶ 그런 예가 허다하다 We have a number of examples of that sort.
허닥하다 begin to take out what is stored away ; get〔eat〕 into the stores ; nibble on what has been set aside
허덕거리다 [숨이 차서] pant ; gasp for breath ; be exhausted ; be tired out ; [애쓰다] struggle ; make frantic efforts ; strive wildly ; work madly ¶ 허덕허덕 panting ; gasping ; between gasps ; out of breath // 숨이 차서 허덕거리다 gasp for breath ; be short of breath // 무거운 짐을 지고 허덕거리다 pant under a heavy load // 피로해서 허덕거리다 be dog-tired ; walk one's legs off // 매일의 학과에 허덕거리다 be overtasked〔too busy〕 with one's daily lessons // 기일까지 일을 끝내려고 허덕거리다 work madly to get the job done by the deadline date
허덕이다 languish ; be tormented〔tortured〕 《by》 ¶ 빈곤에 허덕이는 사람 a poverty-stricken person // 생활에 허덕이다 languish in poverty ; be tormented by poverty ; be poverty-stricken ; struggle with the poverty // 고갈에 허덕이다 suffer from thirst

허 가

「~ 해도 좋습니까?」 등과 같이 상대방의 허가를 구할 경우 「Can I[we]..., please?나 May I[we]...?」 등을 쓰는 것이 일반적이다. 그러나 상황에 따라 Would it be possible...?/I wonder [was wondering] if I could...?/Do you mind if...?/Mind if...?/All right...?/Let me..., would you?/Have I got the go-ahead...?/With your permission I should like to.... 등과 같이 여러 가지 표현을 쓸 수 있다.

이에 대한 응답은 긍정적일 때는 Yes, certainly./Of course (you can).... /By all means (do)..../Yes, that's fine[all right]./Go ahead (and)....등을 쓸 수 있고 부정적일 때는 I'm afraid you can't..../I'm afraid not./I'm afraid I can't let you..../I'd like to, but..../(Sorry,) no way. 등의 표현이 있다.

① Can I[we]...?/May I[we]...?

¶ 친구와 오늘 밤 영화보러 가도 돼요? — 안돼. Can I go and see a movie with my friends tonight? — No, you may not.[No, you can't.]// 잠깐 개인적으로 말씀 좀 드려도 될까요? — 좋습니다. May I speak to you for a moment in private, please? — Yes, you may. [Yes, certainly[please]./Certainly./Sure.] (★ 허가를 구할 때는 May I...?를 많이 쓰고 허물없는 사이에는 Can I...?를 쓴다.)// 참고 서적은 열람실 밖으로 가져갈 수 없습니다. Reference books must not be removed from the reading room. // 당신 이름을 물어도 될까요?— 상관없습니다. Might I ask your name? — Sure, go ahead. (★ might는 정중한 표현으로서 초면일 경우에 자주 사용한다.)

② Do[Would] you mind if...?/Is it all right (if)...?

mind 뒤에는 동명사나 if절이 붙는다. mind는 「마음에 걸리다」라는 뜻이므로 Yes.로 대답하면 안되고 Not at all. 또는 Of course not.로 하여야 한다.

¶ 오늘 오후 일찍 집에 가도 되겠습니까?— 네, 물론 좋습니다. Do you mind if I go home early this afternoon? — No, not at all. [Of course not.] //여기 앉아도 되겠습니까? — 그러시지요. Do you mind if I sit here? — Be my guest. //길을 안내해 주시겠습니까? — 미안합니다. 저도 초행입니다. Would you mind showing me the way? — I'm sorry, but I'm a stranger here. // 이곳에서 담배를 피워도 괜찮겠습니까? — 아니오, 피울 수 없습니다. Is it all right if I smoke here? — No, you can't. // 이 편지 복사해도 괜찮겠습니까? — 네, 물론이죠. Is it all right for me to make a copy of this letter? — That's all right by me. [Yes, of course. /Certainly.]// 그를 초대해도 좋겠습니까? — 안될 이유가 없지요. Would it be all right if we invite him? — No reason why not.

③ I wonder (if)....

「…하면 어떨지」의 뜻으로 간접적으로 허가를 구하는 정중한 표현.

¶ 질문 하나 해도 괜찮겠습니까? I wonder if I might ask you a question. // 문을 여는게 어떨까요? — 네, 좋습니다. I wonder whether I might trouble you to open the door? — Yes, of course. // 이 짐 나르는 것 도와주면 어때요? — 좋구말구요. I'm just wondering if you could help me carry these parcels. — Certainly. (★감정을 넣어서 말할 때는 진행형을 사용.)

④ permit... to do..../permission/be allowed to do..../let..../feel free to do....

어떤 사안에 대해 적극적으로 분명하게 허가를 내릴 때는 permit, 소극적인 태도로 허가를 내릴 때는 allow, 보다 구어적인 표현으로는 let를 쓴다. 또 「언제라도 (~ 하겠다고) 말씀하시지요.」와 같이 상대방의 의사를 간접적으로 청할 경우 feel free to do.... 를 쓴다.

¶ 누가 너에게 저 컴퓨터를 써도 좋다고 그랬니? Who gave you permission to use that computer? // 집을 짓기 전에 시 건축 당국의 허가를 받아야 된다. Before you build a house you have to get permission from the city planning authorities. // 흡연은 홀에서만 허용된다. Smoking is permitted only in the hall. // 시험에 계산기를 써도 좋대? Are we allowed to use calculators in the exam? // 우리는 TV를 하루에 두 시간밖에 볼 수 없다. We are only allowed to watch television for two hours a day. // 네 전화 좀 써도 되겠니? — 물론이지. Will you let me use your phone? — Yes, please do. // 질문이 있으시면 중간에 언제라도 하시기 바랍니다. Please feel free to stop me and ask questions whenever you like.

허덕지덕, 허덕허덕 panting ; gasping for breath ; dog-tired ; striving madly ; frantically

허두 虛頭 opening words〔remarks〕 ¶ 허두를 꺼내다 open words〔remarks〕 ; begin to say

허둥거리다 be flurried〔fluttered, flustered〕 ; be thrown into confusion ; rush about madly ¶ 어쩔 줄 몰라 허둥거리다 be so flustered that one doesn't know what to do

허둥지둥 all flustered ; in a hurry ; hurriedly ━하다 get〔be〕 all flustered ¶ 허둥지둥 도망치다 flee helter-skelter ; run away with bare life // 허둥지둥 밖으로 뛰어나가다 hurry〔rush, dash〕 out ; go out hurriedly

허드레 odds and ends ; trash
 ─꾼 an odd-job man ; an odd-jobber 허드렛물 water for sundry uses 허드렛일 odd jobs ; a trifling job

허드재비 an object of no importance ; a trash ; odd bits〔jobs〕 ⇨ 허드레

허든거리다 flounder ; reel 《about》 ; have trouble with one's legs

허든허든 reelingly ; staggeringly ; falteringly ; unsteadily

허들 [장애물] a hurdle ; [허들 레이스] a hurdle race
 ─ 선수 a hurdler ; a hurdle skipper

†허락 許諾 [승인] consent ; assent ; approval ; sanction ; [허가] permission ; permit ; leave ; grant ━하다 consent to ; assent to ; give consent to ; approve 《of》 ; permit ; allow ; grant ; give 《a person》 leave ; admit (입학을) ; afford (자력이) ¶ 허락을 얻어 with 《a person's》 permission // 허락 없이 without permission〔leave〕 // 사정이 허락하는 한 so far as circumstances permit // 허락을 요청하다 ask permission of 《a person》 // 여자가 몸을 허락하다 surrender one's chastity〔body〕 to a man ; give oneself to a man's embrace // 그는 딸의 결혼을 허락하지 않았다 He forbade his daughter to marry. // 그 여자는 외출하고 싶었지만 어머니가 허락하지 않았다 She wanted to go out but her mother disapproved. // 퇴장을 허락받았다 He was permitted to leave. // 사정이 허락하면 가겠다 I will go if circumstances permit.

허랑 방탕 虛浪放蕩 looseness ; (self-) indulgence ; loose morals ; dissoluteness ; profligacy ━하다 (be) loose ; dissolute ; profligate ; dissipated ¶ 허랑 방탕한 사람 a profligate ; a man of loose conduct ; a fast liver // 허랑 방탕한 생활을 하다 lead a dissolute〔loose, dissipate, fast〕 life ; live fast ; be given to self-indulgence〔dissolution〕

허례 虛禮 empty forms ; formalities ; formal courtesy ; artificial manners ¶ 허례적인 언사 just complimentary words ; vain〔empty〕 words // 허례에 흐르다 lapse into an empty custom // 허례를 폐하다 dispense with empty forms ; do away with mere formalities
 ─ 허식 vanity

허룩하다 (be) more or less empty ; almost empty ¶ 쌀자루가 허룩하다 a rice bag is almost empty

허름하다 (be) shabby ; mean ; seedy ; poor-looking ; [싸다] cheap ; low ¶ 허름한 옷 shabby clothes // 허름한 집 a shabby house // 허름한 물건 a cheap article ; trumpery // 그는 주제가 허름했다 He looked seedy. /He was poorly dressed.

허릅숭이 an unreliable person ; a careless〔reckless〕 fellow

⁑허리 ① [신체의] the waist ; the small of the back ; the loin ; the haunch (짐승의) ; the pelvic region ¶ 허리가 가는 slim〔slender〕-waisted ; narrow-hipped // 허리가 굵은 full-hipped ; full in the hips // 허리가 구부러진 노인 an old man bent〔bowed, stooping〕 with age // 허리를 굽히다 bend the body ; bend oneself ; stoop down ; bow // 허리가 구부러졌다 one's body has become bent // 허리에 칼을 차다 wear〔carry〕 a sword at one's side // 요즈음 어쩐지 허리가 아프다 My lower back has been giving me some trouble lately.
 ② [옷의] the waist (of clothes) ¶ 치마 허리를 달다 attach the waist part of a skirt
 ─ 둘레 a waist measure ¶ 허리 둘레가 32인치 a waist measure of 32 inches ─뼈 the hucklebone 허릿심 [허리의] the stamina of one's waist ¶ 허릿심이 세다 have a strong back ; [화살의] the resilience of the middle of an arrow 바지─ the waist of trousers
 허리를 펴다 관용 straighten〔stretch〕 oneself

허리끈 ⇨ 허리띠

*허리띠 a belt ; a sash (여자용의) ; a girdle ; a band ; belting 《총칭》 ¶ 허리띠를 매다 tie a belt〔sash〕 // 허리띠를 풀다 untie〔undo〕 a belt ; ungirdle oneself
 허리띠에 상고장 들었다 속담 None can guess the jewel by the casket〔cabinet〕.

허리세장 the waist strut of an A-frame

허리질러 across the middle

허리춤 inside the waist of one's trousers ¶ 허리춤에 손을 넣다 put one's hand into the waist of one's trousers

허리치기 〖유도〗 a hip throw ; waist techniques ; 〖레슬링〗 a cross-buttock

허리케인 a hurricane

허리통 the measure of one's waist ; waist measure ¶허리통이 굵다 have a big waist // 허리통을 재다 measure one's waist

허릿매 the shape of one's waist ; the waistline ¶ 허릿매가 곱다 have a shapely waist

허망 虛妄 falsehood ; falsity ; untruth **— 하다** (be) vain ; untrue ; false ; unreliable ; groundless ¶ 허망지설 a groundless〔an unreliable〕 view

허명 虛名 an empty name ; a false reputation ; notoriety ; publicity ¶ 허명을 떨치다 win a false reputation ; gain notoriety〔unenviable publicity〕// 허명무실하다 be vain ; be false ; be empty ; be unsubstantial ; be nominal

‡**허무 虛無** nothingness ; nihility ; nihil **— 하다** (be) nonexistent ; nil ; null ; futile ; vain ; empty ; nihilistic ¶ 허무맹랑하다 be empty ; be chimerical ; be false ; be groundless ; be unreliable ; be irresponsible

—감 a sense of futility **— 사상** nihilistic thoughts〔ideas〕 **—주의** nihilism **—주의자** a nihilist

허문 虛聞 a false〔groundless〕 rumor ; a canard ⇨ 데마

허물[1] a skin ; a shell ; a covering ; a scar (흉터) ¶ 허물이 있다 have〔bear〕 a scar // 허물이 생기다 《one's hand》 be scarred // 뱀이 허물을 벗다 a snake casts off its skin

허물[2] [과실] a fault ; an error ; a mistake ; a misdeed ; a blame ; [결점] a fault ; a defect ; a shortcoming ; a flaw ; a weak point ¶ 허물 있는 defective ; faulty // 허물 없는 faultless ; blameless ; flawless ; perfect // 허물을 들추다 find fault 《with》 ; look for a fault // 허물을 감추다 conceal a defect // 허물을 용서하다 forgive 《a person》 for his fault // 허물을 눈감아 주다 overlook〔pass over〕 《a person's》 mistake ; wink〔connive〕 at 《a person's》 misdeed // 허물을 고치다 correct a fault ; remedy〔amend〕 a fault // 그는 허물이 없다 He is free from faults. /He is above criticism. // 허물 없는 사람은 없다 Every man is liable to error.

허물다 pull〔tear, break, take〕 down ; destroy ; demolish ¶ 건물을 허물다 demolish〔tear down, pull down, destroy〕 a building // 벽을 허물다 take〔break〕 down a wall ; flatten out a wall

허물벗다[1] ① [뱀 따위가] cast off the skin ; slough ; exuviate ¶ 뱀이 허물벗다 a snake casts off its skin
② [피부] 《the skin》 peel off ; be scraped

허물벗다[2] clear oneself of a false charge ; exculpate oneself

허물어지다 crumble down ; collapse ; fall down ; be destroyed ; give way (다리 따위가) ¶ 집이 허물어지다 a house collapses // 지진으로 둑이 허물어졌다 The earthquake destroyed the embankment. // 건물이 요란한 소리를 내며 허물어졌다 The building fell down with a crash.

허물없다 be on familiar〔friendly〕 terms ; (be) unceremonious ; frank ¶ 허물없는 교제 friendly intercourse // 허물없는 사이이다 be on familiar terms with each other

허밍 humming **— 하다** hum 《a tune》

허박 虛薄 ⇨ 허약(虛弱)

허발 voracity **— 하다** (be) voracious ; gluttonous ; ravenous

허방 a hollow ; a sunken〔hollow〕 place ; a depression ¶ 허방을 디디다 step in a hollow // 허방에 빠지다 fall into a sunken

—다리 ⇨ 함정(陷穽)

허방짚다 miscalculate ; fall because of a miscalculation ; be frustrated ; miss

허방치다 miscalculate ⇨ 허방짚다

허벅다리 the thigh

허벅살 the flesh of the thigh

허벅지 the fleshy inside of the thigh

허벅허벅 very soft ; all flabby **— 하다** be very soft ; be all flabby

허병 虛病 ⇨ 꾀병

허보 虛報 a false report ; false news ¶ 허보를 전하다 circulate a false report

허분허분 soft and juicy **— 하다** (be) soft and juicy

†**허비 虛費** waste ; useless expenses **— 하다** waste 《money》 ; cast〔throw〕 away ¶ 시간〔돈〕의 허비 a waste of time〔money〕 // 쓸데 없는 일에 돈을 허비하다 waste one's money on useless things

허비다 scratch ; maul (맹수가) ; pick (귀를) ¶ 손톱으로 귀를 허비다 pick one's ears with one's fingernail ⇨ 후비다

허비적거리다 keep picking〔digging out〕 《with a fingernail》 ; scratch ¶ 귀를 허비적거리다 pick one's ears with fingernail ⇨ 후비적거리다

허사 虛辭 〖문법〗 ① an expletive ② ⇨ 허언(虛言)

허사 虛事 a vain attempt ; a failure ¶ 허사로 돌아가다 come to naught〔nothing〕 ; end in failure ; be in vain ; prove futile // 엉뚱한 단서를 좇다가 1주일간의 수사가 허사가 되었다 We've followed a wrong clue and a whole week's investigation is down the tubes.

허사비 ⇨ 허수아비

허상 虛像 〖물리〗 a virtual image

허설 虛設 a false〔groundless〕 report 〔story〕

허섭쓰레기 odd ends ; odd bits ; rubbish ; trash ; waste ; offal

허세 虛勢 a bluff ; a bluster ; a fanfaronade ; a false show of power〔influence, strength, courage〕; a bold front ¶ 허세를 부리다 bluff; make a show of power; show off 《one's ability》; bark from a distance; four-flush 《미·속》// 선생께서는 정말 허세를 부리시는군요 I bet you're putting up a bare front.

허송 虛送 wasting time ⇨ 허송 세월

허송 세월 虛送歲月 wasting〔killing〕 time; passing time aimlessly〔idly〕 —하다 waste〔kill〕 time; pass time aimlessly〔idly〕; idle one's time away

허수 虛數 an imaginary quantity〔number〕

⁑허수아비 a scarecrow; [무능자] a dummy; [괴뢰] a puppet; a figurehead ¶ 허수아비를 세우다 set up scarecrows 《in a paddy field》// 허수아비 노릇을 하다 be puppet

— 사장 a dummy boss; a nominal boss

허수하다 feel a certain emptiness ⇨ 허전하다

허술하다 ① (be) shabby; worn-out; humble; poor ¶ 허술한 옷 shabby clothes // 허술한 집 a shabby〔humble〕 cottage

② [부주의하다] (be) careless; negligent; inattentive; rude ¶ 허술한 방비 a loose defense // 허술한 틈을 노리다 watch for an unguarded moment // 그는 허술한 점이 없지 He really touches all the bases, doesn't he?

허스키 《in》 a husky voice

허식 虛飾 affectation; ostentation; false〔glittering〕 display; show; foppery; coxcombry; dandism —하다 affect; show off ¶ 허식적 ostentatious; showy // 허식없는 unaffected; plain // 허식을 좋아하다 be fond of〔care for〕 demonstration〔display〕 // 모든 허식을 폐하다 get rid of all vain ornamentations

—가 a fop; a dandy; a dude; a showman — 허영 pomps and vanities

허실 虛實 truth and falsehood; fact and fiction ¶ 허실을 확인하다 ascertain the truth

허심 虛心 disinterestedness; dispassionateness; freedom from prejudice; an open mind

허심 탄회 虛心坦懷 frankness; candidness; open-mindedness —하다 be open-minded; frank; candid ¶ 허심 탄회하게 이야기하다 speak frankly; have a heart-to-heart talk 《with》

허심하다 許心- confide 《in》; trust; admit〔take〕 《a person》 into one's confidence; make a confident 《of a person》

*허약 虛弱 weakness; infirmity; feebleness; debility; imbecility (정신의); 〖의학〗 adynamia; asthenia —하다 (be) weak; feeble; infirm; frail; decrepit; delicate

> 참고 **weak** 일반어 **infirm** 병과 노령 때문에 허약해지다 **feeble** infirm과 같은 뜻이지만 일반적으로 불쌍하다는 느낌이 따른다 **decrepit** 노령으로 약해지다 **frail** 나면서부터 허약하다

¶ 허약한 사람 a weakling // 신체가 허약하다 have a weak〔delicate〕 constitution; be in delicate health // 그는 날 때부터 몸이 허약하다 He is born weak.

—아(兒) a weak〔frail, delicate〕 child

허언 虛言 a lie; a falsehood; an untruth; a fabrication (날조) —하다 tell a lie〔falsehood〕; lie

허여 許與 ⇨ 허락(許諾)

허여멀겋다 (be) nice and fair; have a fair complexion

허여멀쑥하다 (be) nice and fair

허열 虛熱 consumptive fever

⁑허영 虛榮 vanity; vainglory; empty fame ¶ 여자의 허영 feminine vanity // 허영에 찬 여자 a woman full of〔with〕 vanity

—심 (a sense of) vanity ¶ 허영심을 불러일으키다〔만족시키다〕 excite〔satisfy〕 《a person's》 vanity

허영거리다 totter; falter; be shaky; stagger ¶ 허영거리는 걸음 faltering 〔tottering〕 steps // 앓고나서 허영거리다 be shaky after one's illness

허영허영 totteringly; falteringly; staggeringly

허옇다 (be) very white; snow-white; pure white; quite pale

허예지다 get〔become〕 pure white

허욕 虛慾 vain ambitions; avarice; greed ¶ 허욕 많은 사람 a grasping person

⁑허용 許容 permission; allowance; approval; sanction; admission; [용서] pardon; forgiveness; toleration —하다 permit; approve; sanction; grant; allow; admit; tolerate; pardon; forgive ¶ 관용상 허용되어 있다 It is sanctioned by usage.

— 범위 a permitted limit — 시간 allowed time — 오차 an allowable〔a permissible〕 error — 온도〔응력〕 allowable〔permissible〕 temperature 〔stress〕 — 한도 a tolerance limit; the maximum permissible limit ¶ 방사능 허용 한도 the maximum permissible exposure to radiation

허우룩하다 feel a certain emptiness; be lonely; feel the miss 《of》 ¶ 자네가 없어 퍽 허우룩했네 We missed you badly.

허울 appearance; show; look ¶ 허울이 좋다 have a good-looking appearance // 허울이 좋은 하늘타리 a thing not so good as it looks // 집이 허울은 좋은데 안은 보잘것이 없다 The house looks nice from the outside but the inside is nothing much to look at.

*허위 虛僞 falsehood ; fiction ; 〖논리〗 fallacy ¶ 허위 진술을 하다 make a false statement ; [증인이] commit perjury
— 고발 a false accusation — 신고〔보고〕 a false〔mendacious〕 return〔report〕 — 진술 misrepresentation — 행위 a fraud act

허위넘다 struggle up〔over〕 ; cross〔go over〕 《a mountain》 pantingly

허위단심 struggling with all one's might ; laboriously ¶ 아들을 보려고 허위단심 먼 곳을 찾아가다 struggle a long distance to see one's son

허위대 a (fine) tall figure〔build〕 ¶ 허위대가 좋다 have a fine figure∥허위대가 좋은 사람 a man of portly presence

허위적거리다 struggle ; paw 《the air》 ; flounder ¶ 팔을 허위적거리며 걷다 walk swinging one's arms∥물 밖으로 헤어나오려고 허위적거리다 paw the air to get out of the water

허위적허위적 struggling ; pawing the air ¶ 허위적허위적 걷다 walk swinging one's arms

허장성세 虛張聲勢 an empty boast ; bluff ; boaster ; bravado —하다 bluff ; bluster ; swagger

허적거리다 ransack ; rummage ; scatter ¶ 서랍속을 허적거리다 rummage in drawer ; ransack a drawer∥(닭들이) 건초 더미를 허적거리다 《chickens》 scatter a bunch of hay

허적이다 ⇨ 허적거리다

허전거리다 totter ; falter ; stagger ¶ 허전거리며 걸어가다 totter along

*허전하다 feel empty ; miss 《a thing》 ; feel lonesome ¶ 호주머니가 허전하다 I have a light purse.∥네가 없어서 허전하다 We miss you very much.∥혼자 집에 돌아가는 것은 어쩐지 허전하다 I feel so lonely going home alone.

허전허전 tottering ; faltering ; staggering ; teetering ; shambling

허점 虛點 a blind point〔spot〕 ¶ 법의 허점을 찌르다 make an illicit use of law∥허점을 노리다 watch for an unguarded point∥허점을 보이다 lay oneself open to attack ; be off one's guard

허정 —하다 (be) empty ; hollow ; vacant ; vacuous

허정거리다 lose one's legs ; stagger ; walk stumblingly

허족 虛足 〖동물〗 a pseudopodium 《*pl.* -dia》 ⇨ 위족(僞足)

허줏굿 a shaman's initiatory dance to invoke the spirit

허청대고 blindly ; plunging right in ; recklessly ; at random ; happy-go-lucky ¶ 일을 허청대고 시작하다 plunge into a deal recklessly∥허청대고 아무를 찾아가다 go to visit a person without making sure whether he will be home ; give a person a reckless visit

허초점 虛焦點 〖물리〗 a virtual focus

허출하다 (be) hungry ; feel hungry ¶ 배가 허출하다 be hungry ; have an empty stomach

허탄 虛誕 untruth ⇨ 허망

허탈 虛脫 〖의학〗 collapse ; prostration ; atrophy ; marasmus ; blankness of (mind) ; despondency —하다 collapse ; atrophy ; be prostrated ; be despondent
— 상태 a state of despondency〔collapse〕 ¶ 허탈 상태에 있다 be thoroughly absent-minded ; show an abstracted air ; be utterly discouraged

허탕 lost〔fruitless〕 labor ; vain effort ¶ 허탕치다 labor in vain ; come to nothing ; make vain efforts∥만나러 갔다 허탕치다 make a fruitless call∥모든 노력이 허탕이 되었다 All our efforts were in vain.∥그의 일은 결국 허탕으로 끝났다 His work has been for nothing after all.

허투 虛套 feigning ; sham ; pretense ; simulation ¶ 그것은 허투로 하는 동정이다 It is only mock sympathy.

허투루 carelessly ; negligently ; in a slovenly way ; roughly ¶ 허투루 다루다 handle roughly〔carelessly〕∥허투루 쓰다 write carelessly∥일을 허투루 하다 do a rough job

허튼계집 a loose〔an unchaste〕 woman ; a slut ; a slattern ; a woman of loose morals ; a wanton

허튼고래 a hypocaust supported by scattered columns (as opposed to flues)

허튼맹세 —盟誓 an irresponsible〔an reliable〕 oath

허튼모 rice seedlings planted in random fashion (not in even rows)

허튼소리 irresponsible utterance ; an unreliable〔a baseless〕 talk ; idle talk ¶ 허튼 소리가 아니다 be no joke∥허튼 소리 좀 작작해라 Away with your lies!

허튼수작 —酬酌 an unreliable talk ; idle talk ⇨ 허튼소리

허튼톱 a saw that can be used as either a crosscut saw or a ripsaw

허파 the lungs ; lights (소·양·돼지의)
허파에 바람이 들다 관용 be easily tempted to laugh ; be giggly

허풍 虛風 boasting ; bragging ; a big talk ; exaggeration ; a fanfaronade ¶ 허풍 떨다〔치다〕 boast ; brag ; talk big ; exaggerate ; swagger ; make a mountain out of a molehill ; blow one's own trumpet∥그 사람 말에는 좀 허풍이 있다 His statement is rather exaggerated.
—선이 a boaster ; a braggart ; a gasbag

허풍선 虛風扇 a bellows ; a blower

허하다 虛— [속이] (be) hollow ; empty ; vacant ; void ; [기력이] weak ; feeble ; delicate ; frail

허하다 許— [허가하다] permit ; allow ; give permission for ; [허락하다] grant ; approve ; accept

허한 虛汗 (a) cold sweat〔perspiration〕

허행 虛行 a trip in vain ; a fruitless journey ; a disappointing trip **—하다** make a trip in vain ; make a fruitless trip

허허[1] ha-ha ; with a laugh ¶ 허허 웃다 laugh loudly

허허[2] [놀람·칭찬] Oh ! ; Well ! ; Why ! ; Heavens ! ¶ 허허 김군 아닌가 Well, well, well. If it is not Mr. *Kim.* // 허허 또 졌는 걸 Gosh, I've lost again.

허허바다 a vast expanse of ocean ; the vast expanse of water ; a vast empty sea

허허벌판 a vast expanse of plain ; a prairie

허허실실 虛虛實實 taking things as they come ; leaving a matter to take its course ¶ 허허실실의 전술 diamond cut diamond

허혼 許婚 approval of marriage〔engagement〕; consent to a marriage ; accepting one's hand in marriage **—하다** approve of〔consent to〕one's marriage

허화 虛華 empty〔outward〕show ; ostentation

허황 虛荒 —하다 (be) false ; ungrounded ; unbelievable ; unreliable

헌 old ; shabby ; worn-out ; second-hand **—옷** old〔worn-out〕clothes **—신문** an old newspaper **—책** a secondhand〔used〕book

헌 고리도 제 짝이 있다 ⟨속담⟩ Every Jack has his Jill.

헌 짚신도 짝이 있다 ⟨속담⟩ Every Jack has his Jill.

헌거 軒擧 elation ; high spirits ; exuberance ; euphoria ¶ 헌거롭다 [의기가] be high-spirited ; be triumphant ; be elated ; [풍채가] be imposing ; be portly

헌걸스럽다 (be) elated ; high-spirited ; [풍채] stately ; imposing《appearance》

헌걸차다 be full of elation ; (be) elated

헌것 old〔worn-out, second-hand, used〕things

헌계집 a once married woman ; a woman who has lost her man

헌금 獻金 a gift of money ; a contribution ; a donation ; a subscription ; [교회에서] a collection ; [불전에서] an offering **—하다** contribute ; donate ; subscribe ¶ 헌금을 모으다 take up a collection (교회에서) // 10만원을 헌금하다 make a contribution of 100,000 *won*《to the funds》

—자 a contributor ; a donor **—함** a collection box **정치 —** contribution of political funds

헌납 獻納 presentation ; offer ; contribution ; donation **—하다** present ; offer ; contribute ; donate ¶ 군자금을 헌납하다 make contributions to〔toward〕war funds

—식 a dedication〔presentation〕ceremony **—자** a contributor ; a donor **—품** an offering ; a present ; a gift

헌당 獻堂 the dedication of a church〔temple〕; consecration **—하다** consecrate a church

—식 a dedication ceremony

헌데 an abscess ; a tumor ; a swelling ¶ 헌데가 도지다 A tumor gets bad again.

헌등 獻燈 a votive lantern ; the dedication〔presentation〕of a lantern to temple **—하다** dedicate〔present〕a lantern to a temple

헌배 獻盃 —하다 offer《a person》a cup of wine ; drink to《another's》health

*헌법 憲法** a constitution ; constitutional law ; organic law ¶ 헌법상의 constitutional // 헌법상의 권리 one's constitutional rights // 민주주의에 입각한 헌법 a constitution based on democracy ; a democratic nation's constitution // 헌법을 제정하다 establish〔frame〕a constitution // 헌법을 개정하다 revise the constitution

— 개정 amendment of a constitution **— 기관** a constitutional institution **— 기념일** [제헌절] Constitutional Day **— 발포(發布)** the promulgation of the constitution **— 옹호자** a constitutionalist ; a constitutionist **— 옹호 운동** a movement for protection of the constitution **— 위반** an unconstitutional act ¶ 그것은 헌법 위반이다 That is against the Constitution. /That is a violation of the Constitution. /That is unconstitutional. **— 재판소** the Constitutional Court **— 정신** the spirit of the constitution ; constitutional principles **— 정치** constitutional government ; constitutionalism **— 제도** a constitutional regime **— 제정** enactment of a constitution **— 제정권** constituent power **—학자** a constitutionalist **대한민국 —** the Constitution of Korea **성문〔불문〕 —** a written〔an unwritten〕constitution

헌병 憲兵 a gendarme ; gendarmerie《총칭》; a military policeman《M. P.》

—대 the military police《M. P.》(미육군) ; the shore patrol《S. P.》(미해군) ; the gendarmerie ; the gendarmes ; the provost guard **— 사령관** a provost marshal **— 사령부** the provost marshal headquarters **— 장교** a provost officer《미》; a gendarmerie officer **—**

파견대 a detachment of the military police ; a provost guard
헌사 獻辭 (a) dedication ; a dedicatory letter
헌상 獻上 an offering to a superior ; presentation —하다 present 《a thing to a superior》
—품 an offering ; a present
헌쇠 scrap-iron ; ferrous scraps
헌수 獻壽 a toast to a person's longevity —하다 offer a toast to a person's longevity
헌시 獻詩 a dedicated poem —하다 present〔dedicate〕 a poem 《to》
헌신 獻身 self-sacrifice ; devotion —하다 devote〔dedicate〕 oneself 《to》; sacrifice oneself 《to》 ¶ 헌신적인 devotional ; devoted // 헌신적으로 일을 하다 work devotedly ; work in dead earnest // 그는 과학을 위해서 헌신적으로 노력했다 He served the cause of science at the sacrifice of his life.
헌신짝 a worn-out shoe ; an old shoe
헌신짝같이 버리다 관용 throw it away like an old shoe
헌작 獻酌 offering a cup of drink (to one's superior in a ceremony or to spirits in a sacrificial ceremony) —하다 offer a cup of drink
‡헌장 憲章 a constitution ; a charter of constitution
국민 교육 — The National Charter of Education 대— [영국의] the Magna Carta ; the Great Charter 대서양 — the Atlantic Charter 어린이 — the Children's Charter 어머니 — the Mother's Charter 유엔 — the United Nation's Charter
헌정 憲政 constitutional government ; constitutionalism ¶ 헌정을 실시하다 adopt constitutional government
— 옹호 운동 a movement for safeguarding〔defending〕 constitutionalism — 위기 a constitutional crisis — 질서 constitutional order
헌정 獻呈 offering ; presentation —하다 offer ; present
—본 a presentation copy —판 an author's copy
헌짚신 worn-out straw sandals
헌짚신도 짝이 있다 속담 Every jack has his gill.
헌책 —册 a secondhand〔used〕 book
—사 a secondhand bookstore —장수 a secondhand bookseller
헌책 獻策 suggestion ; recommendation ; advice ; counsel —하다 suggest a plan ; advance〔make〕 suggestions ; lay one's program 《before》; offer〔propose〕 a plan 《on a problem》; make recommendations
헌칠민틋하다 be svelte 《프》; have a dashing figure
헌칠하다 have a well-proportioned figure
헌털뱅이 ⇨ 헌것
헌팅캡 a hunting cap (경마 기수용) ; a sporting cap (일반적인 것)
헌혈 獻血 donation of blood —하다 donate blood
—자 a blood donor
헐값 歇— a low price ; a dirt-cheap price ¶ 헐값으로 사다 buy 《a thing》 cheap as dirt // 헐값으로 팔다 sell 《a thing》 for its scrap value // 헐값으로 팔리다 be sold at a giveaway price
헐객 歇客 a loose man ; a libertine ; a dissolute person
헐겁다 (be) loose ; loose-fitting
헐근거리다 gasp ; pant ; wheeze ; breathe hard
헐다[1] ① [피부가] get〔have〕 a tumor on it ; be sore ¶ 얼굴이 헐다 have a swelling on one's face ② [옷이] get old ; become shabby ; wear out ¶ 옷이 헐다 one's clothes wear out
헐다[2] ① [쌓은 것을] destroy ; demolish ; pull〔break, take, tear〕 down ¶ 벽을 헐다 take〔break〕 down a wall // 집을 헐다 pull down a house
② [험담하다] slander ; speak ill of 《a person》; censure ; libel ; defame ¶ 본인없는 데서 헐어 말하는 사람 a backbiter // 사람을 헐어 말하다 speak ill of 《a person》 ③ [돈을] break ; change ¶ 500원 짜리를 헐다 break〔change〕 a 500 *won* bill〔note〕
헐떡거리다 gasp ; pant ; breathe hard 〔heavily〕; puff ¶ 그 여자는 헐떡거리며 두서너마디 말했다 She gasped a few words.
헐떡이다 gasp ⇨ 헐떡거리다
‡헐떡하다 [얼굴이] (be) pale ; wan ; worn ; [눈이] hollow ; sunken
헐떡헐떡 gasping and panting ; puffing and blowing —하다 puff and pant 〔blow〕
*헐뜯다 slander ; defame ; disparage ; speak ill of ; pick on ¶ 사람을 헐뜯다 pick on 《a person》; speak ill of 《a person》 // 그 여자를 헐뜯을 생각이 아니라면 그런 말은 하지 말아라 Don't say that unless you want to do her dirt.
헐렁거리다 ① [물건이] be loose ; fit loose ¶ 신이 헐렁거리다 one's shoes fit loose ② [행동이] act〔behave〕 rashly〔imprudently〕; be light〔frivolous〕
헐렁이 a frivolous person ; an imprudent person
헐렁하다 (be〔fit〕) loose ; loose-fitting ¶ 올의 코가 성긴 것 중에서 크고 헐렁한 것으로 주십시오 I want something big and baggy, with a loose knit.
헐렁헐렁 ① [헐거워] loose ; too big ; [바지가] baggy —하다 be baggy ; be loose ¶ 나에겐 헐렁헐렁하다 This is

too large for me. ∥바지의 무릎 부분이 헐렁헐렁하다 The trousers are baggy at the knees.
② [행동이] frivolously ; imprudently ━하다 (be) all unstable ; terribly unstable ¶ 사람이 헐렁헐렁하다 He is very unstable〔pretty shaky〕.

헐레벌떡 panting and puffing ; helter-skelter ¶ 헐레벌떡 달려가다 run along panting and puffing

헐리다 get pulled〔torn, taken〕 down ; be destroyed〔demolished〕 ; be torn to pieces ¶ 집이 헐리다 A house is demolished.

헐리우드 Hollywood ¶ 헐리우드 같은 Hollywoodish∥헐리우드의 스타 a Hollywood star

헐벗다 be poorly〔shabbily〕 clothed ; be in rags ¶ 헐벗은 사람 a person in rags∥헐벗은 산 a bare〔bald〕 mountain

헐수할수없다 be quite hopeless〔impossible〕 ; be at one's wit's end ; be at the end of one's tether

헐쑥하다 (be) thin and pale ; drawn ; lean ; emaciated ⇨ 핼쑥하다

헐어지다 ① [낡아지다] get old ; become shabby ; wear out ② [무너지다] collapse ; crumble ; fall down

헐하다 歇— ① [값이] (be) cheap ; inexpensive ; low (in price) ¶ 헐하게 사다 buy cheap ② [쉽다] (be) easy ; light ; simple ¶ 헐한 일 light work ③ [벌이] (be) light ; lenient ¶ 헐한 벌 light〔lenient〕 punishment

헐후하다 歇後— ⇨ 허름하다, 허술하다

험객 險客 ① [성질이 험악한] a roughneck ; a tough〔sinister, dangerous〕 character ② [험구가] a foul-mouthed person ; a slanderer

험구 險口 slander ; abuse ; [사람] a foul-mouthed person ; a slanderous person ━하다 slander ; abuse ; defame ; speak ill of 《a person》

험난 險難 danger ; difficulty ; roughness ; toughness ━하다 (be) rough and difficult ; perilous ; be full of danger

험담 險談 slander ; abuse ; calumny ; backbiting ━하다 slander ; speak ill of 《a person》 ; talk scandal about ; backbite ¶ 일초만 빨랐어도 그는 우리가 험담하는 소리를 들었을거야 One second earlier and he would have heard us bad-mouthing him.

험로 險路 a steep path ; a rough〔rugged〕 road ; a breakneck road

험산 險山 a rugged〔steep〕 mountain

***험상 險狀** ruggedness ; roughness ; grimness ; sinisterness ¶ 험상궂다 be sinister ; be savage-looking ; be rugged ; be rough ; be grim∥험상스러운 길 a rugged road∥험상스러운 얼굴 a grim face ; a sinister look

험상 險相 an uncanny〔a weird〕 look〔countenance〕 ; black looks

***험악 險惡** ━하다 [위험하다] (be) dangerous ; [날씨가] threatening ; rough ; [길이] rugged ; [사태가] grave ; critical ; [악독하다] foul ; malicious ¶ 험악한 날씨 stormy〔rough〕 weather∥험악한 길 a rugged〔bad〕 road∥사태가 험악해졌다 Matters have taken a bad turn.

험조 險阻 ruggedness

험준 險峻 steepness ; precipitousness ━하다 (be) steep ; precipitous ; rugged ¶ 험준한 산길 a steep mountain pass∥험준한 산 a rugged mountain

험하다 險— ① [험준] (be) steep ; precipitous ; rugged ¶ 험한 길 a rugged road ② [날씨가] (be) foul ; stormy ; rough ¶ 험한 날씨 foul〔rough〕 weather ③ [험상] (be) sinister ; grim ; savage-looking ¶ 험한 얼굴 a grim〔sinister〕 face ④ [험악] (be) serious ; critical ; grave ¶ 험한 형세 a critical situation

헙수룩하다 [머리털이] (be) shaggy ; unkempt ; dishevelled ; [차림새가] shabby ; poor-looking ; seedy ¶ 헙수룩한 옷 shabby clothes

헙헙하다 (be) lavish ; liberal ; easygoing

헛가게 a booth ; a stall

***헛간** a barn ; an open shed

헛걸음 a trip〔call〕 in vain ; a fruitless〔disappointing〕 journey ━하다 make a trip in vain ; go in vain ; make a fruitless call ¶ 집에 없을지 모르나 헛걸음하는 셈치고 가 보시오 He may not be at home, but you might go just on chance.

헛구역 —嘔逆 queasiness ; a queasy feeling ¶ 헛구역나다 be queasy

헛글 fruitless learning

헛기운 a show of courage ; [술취한 때의] Dutch courage

헛기침 clearing one's throat ; ahem ━하다 clear one's throat

헛김 an air leak ; a leak ━나다 get a leak ; spring a leak ; leak ; [맥빠짐] be dispirited ; be discouraged〔dejected〕 ; be cast down ; be in low spirits

헛노릇 a fruitless〔vain〕 effort ; lost labor ━하다 labor in vain ; do useless work

헛다리짚다 fail ; fall through ; flub 《미》 ; [비유적] miscalculate ; miss ; make a wrong guess ; be wide of the mark ; fall〔come〕 short of one's expectation

헛돈 money thrown away ; wasted money ¶ 헛돈 쓰다 waste one's money 《on》

헛돌다 [바퀴가] skid ; [기계가] run idle

†**헛되다** (be) vain ; futile ; fruitless ;

empty ; unavailing ; unreliable ; untrue ; false ; groundless ¶ 헛된 노력 vain efforts // 헛된 세상 the futile world // 시간을 헛되이 보내다 pass one's time idly

*헛되이 [무익하게] in vain ; vainly ; uselessly ; [보람없이] fruitlessly ; futilely ; [목적도 없이] aimlessly ; [한가히] idly

헛된말 idle words ; empty talk ; unbelievable words

헛듣다 mishear ; hear amiss ¶ 사람의 말을 헛듣다 mishear 《a person's》 remark ; misunderstand

†헛디디다 miss one's step ; lose one's footing ; take a false step ¶ 계단을 헛디디다 miss one's footing on the stairs

헛맹세 an idle〔a false, an empty〕 pledge〔vow〕 ━하다 make an idle〔a false, an empty〕 pledge〔vow〕

헛물켜다 make vain〔fruitless〕 efforts ; labor in vain

헛발 ¶ 헛발디디다 take〔make〕 a false step

헛방 ―放 a miss ; a wrong hit ; a blank shot ; empty talk

헛방 놓다 관용 miss one's aim ; fail to hit

헛방 ―房 a lumber room〔closet〕 ; a storeroom

헛방귀 a gentle fart

헛배부르다 have gas in the stomach ; be troubled with flatulence〔tympanites〕 ; have a false sense of satiety

헛보다 get the wrong view 《of》 ; fail to see (properly) ; mistake

헛보이다 get improperly seen ; be misviewed ; get〔be〕 mistaken

헛불 a random shot ; a poor shot

헛불 놓다 관용 misshoot ; miss a shot

헛소동 ―騷動 much ado about nothing ; (a case of) much cry and little wool ━하다 make a fuss about nothing

헛소리 [정신 없는 말] talking in delirium ; [헛말] gibberish ; empty talk ; nonsense ; silly talk ━하다 talk in delirium ; talk nonsense

헛소문 ―所聞 a groundless〔false〕 rumor

헛손질 pawing the air ━하다 paw the air

헛수 a useless〔wrong〕 move ¶ 헛수를 두다 make a useless〔wrong〕 move

헛수고 vain effort ; lost〔fruitless〕 labor ━하다 make vain efforts ; work in vain ; lose one's labor ¶ 헛수고로 돌아가다 one's labor comes to nothing

헛심 wasted strength ; fruitless effort

헛애 ⇨ 헛수고 ¶ 헛애를 쓰다 make vain effort ; waste one's time and labor ; beat the air

헛웃음 a feigned〔forced〕 smile ; a simper ; a smirk ¶ 헛웃음을 웃다 smirk ; simper ; force〔affect〕 a laugh

헛일 vain effort ; lost〔fruitless〕 labor ━하다 make vain efforts ; one's labor is lost ; exert oneself to no avail

헛잠 a feigned sleep ; playing possum ¶ 헛잠을 자다 feign to be asleep ; sham sleep

헛잡다 fail to grip〔clutch, grasp〕 ; miss catching ; miss one's hold ; let slip ; [잘못 고르다] pick up wrongly ; [도둑을] arrest by mistake

헛장 a brag ; big〔tall〕 talk ; a bluff

헛짚다 ⇨ 헛다리짚다

헛청 ―廳 a building turned into an open shed

헛청 기둥이 칙간 기둥 흉본다 속담 The kettle calls the pot black-brows.

헛총 ―銃 a blank cartridge ; a blank shot

―질 blank firing

헛총을 놓다 관용 fire blank shots

헛치다 fail to hit ; miss 《one's aim》 ; [잘못 휘두르다] swing side ; strike at the air ; [권투에서] swish the air

헛코 골다 pretend to snore ; feign sleep by snoring

헛턱 [빈 턱] an unrealized entertainment ; a Barmecide's feast

헛헛증 ―症 hungriness ; a chronic hunger ¶ 헛헛증이 있다 suffer from chronic hunger

헛헛하다 be (very) hungry ; feel hungry

헝가리 Hungary ¶ 헝가리의 Hungarian

―말 Hungarian ― 사람 a Hungarian

헝거 스트라이크 a hunger strike

헝겁지겁 leaping with joy ; in raptures ; transported with joy

†헝겊 a piece〔scrap〕 of cloth ; a rag

―신 cloth〔canvas〕 shoes ; duck shoes

― 조각 a small piece of cloth ; a scrap of cloth

헝클다 tangle ; entangle ; kink ; dishevel ¶ 머리를 헝클다 dishevel one's hair // 실을 헝클다 tangle thread

†헝클어지다 be〔get〕 tangled ; be entangled ; be in a tangle ¶ 헝클어진 머리 dishevelled hair // 헝클어진 실 tangled thread

헤 ¶ 헤하고 웃다 laugh with one's mouth wide open

헤게모니 hegemony ¶ 헤게모니를 잡다 hold hegemony

헤근거리다 be shaky〔unsteady〕 ; be rickety

헤근헤근 in a tottering〔shaking〕 manner ; unstably ¶ 사개가 헤근헤근 놀다 dovetails wobble // 책상 다리가 헤근헤근거리다 The legs of the table are groggy.

헤다¹ swim

헤다² act〔behave〕 as one likes ; have one's own way

헤다³ count ⇨ 세다

헤다⁴ rinse away ; wash out ⇨ 헹구다

헤대다 move about busily ; bustle about
헤덤비다 rush about ; busy oneself about
*헤드라이트 a headlight ¶ 헤드라이트를 켜다〔끄다〕 turn on〔off〕 the headlight
헤드폰 a headphone ; a headset
헤딩 heading 《a soccer ball》 ━하다 head 《the ball》
헤뜨러지다 be〔get〕 scattered (about) ; be dispersed ; be littered (up) ¶ 사방으로 헤뜨러지다 disperse in all directions
헤뜨리다 scatter 《about》; strew ; disperse ¶ 군중을 헤뜨리다 disperse a crowd // 방에 종이 조각을 헤뜨리다 litter a room with scraps of paper
헤라클레스 『신화』 Heracles ; Hercules
헤로인 『약』 heroin(e)
헤로인 [여주인공] a heroine
헤르니아 『의학』 hernia
헤르츠 『물리』 a hertz 《Hz》
 ─파(波) a hertzian〔an electric wave〕
†헤매다 ① [돌아다니다] wander〔roam〕 about ; rove ; walk around ; search around 《for》 ¶ 이리저리 헤매다 wander from place to place // 거리를 헤매다 wander about in the street // 산중에서 길을 잃고 헤매다 lose one's way in the woods // 사람을 찾아 거리를 헤매다 comb the road for a person
 ② [불안] be at a loss ; be perplexed ; have a hard time ¶ 어쩔 줄 몰라 헤매다 be at a loss what to do
헤먹다 (be) loose(-fitting) ; 《a hole》 get loose
헤모글로빈 『생리』 hemoglobin
헤무르다 feeble ; flaccid ; unstrung ; falling apart ; be brittle and limp ¶ 헤무른 사람 a feeble〔sapless〕 person // 헤무른 살 flaccid〔flabby〕 flesh
헤묽다 weak and watery ; fragile and thin ; flabby and pale
헤번드르르 glossily ; smoothly ⇨ 번드르르
헤벌어지다 be very wide ; get shallow ¶ 헤벌어진 그릇 an open shallow dish
헤벌쭉 wide open ━하다 (be) wide open ¶ 헤벌쭉 웃다 smile a broad smile
헤브라이 『역사』 the Hebrews ⇨ 히브리, 헤브루
 ─즘 Judaism
헤브루 Hebrew
 ─ 문학 Hebrew literature ─ 사람 a Hebrew ─ 사상 Hebrewism
헤비급 ─級 the heavyweight (division)
 ─ 권투 선수 a heavyweight (boxer)
헤살 slander ; an obstacle ¶ 헤살놓다 obstruct ; hinder 《a person》 《in his work, from working》; slander ; disparage // 나의 일에 헤살놓지 마라 Don't intrude where you are not wanted.
 ─꾼 a slanderer ; an obstructionist

헤식다 (be) brittle ; fragile ; frail ; soft ; flabby ; infirm ¶ 헤식은 쌀 soft rice
헤실바실 frittering away ; inadvertently running out of ¶ 돈을 헤실바실 다 써버리다 fritter away all the money one has // 헤실바실 쌀이 다 없어지다 the rice runs out before one is aware of it // 헤실바실한 지지는 거절한다 I refuse a half-hearted support.
헤싱헤싱하다 (be) loose ; slack
*헤아리다 ① [고려하다] consider ; weigh ; ponder ; deliberate ¶ 일을 잘 헤아려서 하다 undertake a plan with due consideration ② [추측하다] fathom ; sound ; conjecture ; surmise ¶ 사람의 마음을 헤아리다 fathom a person ③ [수를] count ; calculate ; compute ; estimate ¶ 헤아릴 수 없다 be incalculable〔innumerable〕
헤어나다 get out of ; get over ; find one's way out of ; extricate oneself from ¶ 곤경에서 헤어나다 extricate oneself from difficulties ; get out of trouble // 헤어나갈 길이 없다 have no way out
헤어네트 a hairnet
헤어리베치 『식물』 a hairy vetch
헤어브러시 a hairbrush
헤어스타일 a hair style
†헤어지다 ① [이별] part from ; part company 《with》; separate ; divorce oneself 《from》; bid farewell (고별) ; break up (분산) ¶ 친구와 헤어지다 part from a friend // 헤어져서 살다 live separately ; live apart from each other // 아내와 헤어지다 divorce one's wife // 그들은 헤어진대 They are splitting up. // 제인은 또 남자 친구하고 헤어졌다 Jane broke up with her boyfriend again. // 금년 들어 그는 벌써 5명의 여자 친구와 헤어졌다 So far this year, he has split up with five girl friends.
 ② [흩어지다] get scattered〔strewn, dispersed〕 ¶ 졸업생이 각처로 헤어지다 The graduates are scattered in all directions. ③ [갈라지다] become chapped
헤어토닉 hair tonic
헤어핀 a hairpin
†헤엄 swimming ; a swim ¶ 헤엄치다 swim ; have a swim // 헤엄치는 사람 a swimmer // 헤엄 잘 치는 사람 an expert〔a good〕 swimmer // 헤엄쳐 건너다 swim across // 강으로 헤엄치러 가다 go swimming in the river // 나는 헤엄을 조금도 못친다 I can't swim a stroke.
 개─ the dog paddle
헤이그 The Hague
헤적이다 rummage ; ransack
헤죽거리다 walk briskly swinging one's arms
헤죽헤죽 walking briskly swinging one's arms

헤집다 tear up ; dig up ; turn up
헤치다 ① [파다] dig up ; turn up ¶ 흙을 파헤치다 dig up earth
② [흩뜨리다] scatter ; disperse ; break up ¶ 군중을 헤치다 disperse a crowd
③ [좌우로] push aside ; make one's way through ; pull apart ; plow one's way through ¶ 군중을 헤치고 나가다 elbow one's way through a crowd // 배가 물결을 헤치고 나갔다 A boat plowed through the waves.
헤프다 ① [몸가짐이나 물건이] be not durable ; be easy to wear out ; be soon used up ; be loose ; be dissolute ¶ 이 비누는 헤프다 This soap doesn't last long. // 저 여자는 몸가짐이 헤프다고 한다 I hear she sleeps around.
② [돈이] (be) wasteful ; uneconomical ; extravagant ¶ 돈을 헤프게 쓰다 be wasteful of money ; spend money lavishly // 너는 돈 씀씀이가 너무 헤프다 You're too much of a spendthrift.
③ [입이] (be) verbose ; voluble ; talkative ; wordy ¶ 그는 입이 헤프다 He talks too much. /He is a verbose speaker.
헤피 wastefully ; extravagantly ; lavishly ¶ 돈을 헤피 쓰다 waste money ; squander money
헤하다 beam with joy ; grin
헥타르 a hectare
헥토- [미터법의] hecto-
—그램 a hectogram —리터 hectoliter —미터 a hectometer
헬레니즘 〖역사〗 Hellenism
*헬륨 〖화학〗 helium 《기호 He》
헬리오트로프 〖식물〗 a heliotrope
†헬리콥터 a helicopter ; a chopper 《미·속》 ; a copter 《구》 ¶ 헬리콥터로 가다 helicopter (off) 《to》 // 헬리콥터로 운반되다 be transported by helicopter
구급용 — an ambulance helicopter 전투용 — a helicopter gunship
헬리포트 a heliport ; a copterport
헬멧 a helmet ; a hard hat ¶ 헬멧을 쓴 경찰대 a squad of helmeted police
헬싱키 Helshinki
헷갈리다 ① [마음이] be confused〔in confusion〕 ; one's attention is distracted ; one's thoughts are scattered ¶ 아이들이 떠들어서 정신이 헷갈리다 The children are too noisy for one to concentrate.
② [뜻이] be confused〔tangled〕 ; be hard to find〔see, make out〕 ¶ 두 글자의 뜻이 헷갈리다 the two words are confused in meaning
헹가래 tossing ; hoisting 《one》 shoulder-high
헹가래 치다 관용 toss〔hoist〕 《a person》 shoulder-high
헹구다 rinse away ; wash out ¶ 빨래를 헹구다 rinse laundry in fresh water after washing
헹글헹글 loose(-bodied) 《coat》 ; baggy ; too large ; loose-fitting 《trousers》 —하다 (be) baggy ; loose ; flabby ; flaccid
†혀 [사람의] a tongue ; [동물의] a lingua ¶ 혀가 잘 돌아가다 have a glib tongue ; be oily-tongued // 혀가 돌지 않는다 be tongue-tied ; have a thick voice // 혀를 깨물다 bite one's tongue
혀를 내밀다 관용 put out one's tongue ; stick out one's tongue ; loll out the tongue (개가)
혀를 차다 관용 click one's tongue ; be wonder-struck
혀꼬부랑이 lisper ; a person with a speech impediment
혀끝 the tip of the tongue
혀짜래기 ⇨ 혀짤배기
혀짤배기 a tongue-tied person ¶ 혀짤배기의 lisping 《child》 // 혀짤배기 말을 하다 lisp (out) ; speak with a lisp
혀차다 click one's tongue ; tut ; be wonder-struck
혁대 革帶 a leather belt
— 장식 a buckle
†혁명 革命 a revolution ; a revolutionary upheaval ¶ 혁명을 일으키다 start〔raise〕 a revolution // IBM은 제조업에 혁명을 가져왔다 The IBM system has brought about a revolution in the manufacturing industry.
—가 a revolutionist ; a revolutionary —가(歌) a revolutionary song —군 a revolutionary army —기 a red flag —기념일 Bastille Day 《프》 —당〔사상, 전쟁, 정부〕 a revolutionary party〔idea, war, government〕 —아 a man of revolutionary temperament — 사상 revolutionary ideas — 운동 revolutionary government 무력 — an armed revolution 무혈 — a bloodless revolution 사회 — a social revolution 산업 — an industrial revolution 평화 — a peaceful revolution 폭력 — a revolution by force〔violence〕 프랑스 — the French Revolution
*혁신 革新 reform ; renovation ; innovation —하다 reform ; renovate ; innovate ¶ 정계의 혁신 a political reform // 혁신의 기운이 움직이고 있다 The leaven of reform is working.
— 운동 a reform movement — 정당 a reformist group —파 a reformist group 사상 — a revolution in thought
혁정 革正 reform —하다 reform
혁제 革製 ¶ 혁제의 leather 《gloves》
—품 leather products〔goods〕 ; leathercraft
혁혁 赫赫 —하다 (be) bright ; brilliant ; radiant ; glorious ; distinguished ¶ 혁혁한 무훈 distinguished services // 명성이 혁혁하다 have a brilliant reputa-

tion
현 弦 ① [활의 시위] a bowstring ② [악기의] a string ; a chord ; (cat) gut ③ 〖기하〗 a chord (호의) ; a subtense (사선) ; a hypotenuse (직각삼각형의 사변) ④ [달의] a quarter
현 現 the present ; the existence ; the actuality
—내각 the present Cabinet —대통령 the President in office
*현 絃 a string ; a chord ; catgut ; gut (바이올린의)
현 舷 ⇨ 뱃전
현가 現價 the present〔current〕 price
현격 懸隔 a difference ; a disparity ; a discrepancy ; an inequality ; a gap ; a gulf ; a chasm —하다 (be) different ; wide apart ; unequal ¶ 현격한 차이 a wide difference〔gap〕 // 연령의 현격 a difference〔disparity〕 of age 《between the two》 // 빈부의 현격 the gulf〔cleavage〕 between the poor and the rich ; difference in wealth
†현관 玄關 the porch ; the entrance ; the front door
현관 顯官 a high official ; a (government) dignitary
현교 懸橋 a suspended〔suspension〕 bridge
현군 賢君 a wise〔good〕 king
현금 現今 the present day〔time〕 ; today ; now ; at present ; nowadays ; in these days ; in modern days ⇨ 현재, 오늘날
‡현금 現金 cash ; actual〔ready〕 money ; cash down ; prompt〔spot〕 cash ; ready funds ¶ 현금으로 사다〔팔다〕 buy〔sell〕 《a thing》 for cash ; purchase〔sell〕 《a thing》 outright // 현금으로 지불하다 pay in cash ; present ready money ; pay down 《미》 // 수표를 현금으로 바꾸다 cash a check ; cash in ; get〔have〕 a check cashed // 현금으로 하시겠습니까 카드로 하시겠습니까 Cash or charge ?
— 가격 a cash〔spot〕 price — 거래〔매매〕 a cash transaction ; cash business — 교환 cash on delivery 《c. o. d》 — 급여액 cash wages — 등록기 a cash register — 보유고 cash in〔on 《미》〕 hand —불 cash payment — 상환 cash redemption — 수입 a cash income — 자산 cash assets — 지불 cash payment ; down payment 《미》 — 지불 주문 cash with order 《C. W. O., c. w. o.》 — 지불 할인 cash discount —주의 pay-as-you-go policy ; mercenariness ; no-credit policy — 출납부 a cash book — 출납원 a cashier — 판매주의 cash and carry 《미》 —화 encashment ¶ 현금화하다 encash ; cash 《a check》 ; cash in 《수표 따위》
*현기 眩氣 dizziness ; giddiness ; vertigo
—증 vertigo ; dizziness ; giddiness ; scotoma ¶ 너무 바빠서 현기증이 날 정도다 I'm so busy it almost makes my head swim.
현녀 賢女 a wise woman
현달 顯達 —하다 attain eminence and acquire fame ; win fame and eminence ; become famous and successful
‡현대 現代 the present age〔day, generation〕 ; our time ; modern times ; today ¶ 현대 present-day ; modern ; current ; of our time ; of today ; contemporary ; present // 현대식의 up-to-date ; modern // 현대의 한국 present-day Korea ; modern〔contemporary〕 Korea // 현대화하다 modernize ; be modernized
— 교육 modern education —극 a modern play ; a drama of present-day life —문 current style — 문학 current literature — 사상 modern thought 〔ideas〕 ; modernism —사 contemporary history — 사조 current thought ; [시대정신] the spirit of the times — 생활 present-day life —식 modern style ¶ 현대식 건물 a building in modern style —어 a living language — 영어 present-day English —인 a modern (person) ; the moderners — 작가 modern〔contemporary〕 writers —전 modern war (fare) —(어)판 a modern edition〔version〕 —풍 a modern style 〔fashion〕 ; modernism ; modernness
*현대화 現代化 modernization ; updating —하다 modernize ; update ¶ 완전히 현대화되다 be completely modernized
현등 舷燈 [선박의] a side light ; [항공기의] a position light
현란 眩亂 dizziness ; the whirl of the brain —하다 (be) dizzy ; dazed ; confused
현란 絢亂 gorgeousness ; brilliancy ; floweriness ; gaudiness ; splendor —하다 (be) gorgeous ; brilliant ; splendid ; florid
현량 賢良 wisdom and virtue —하다 (be) wise and good〔virtuous〕
현리 玄理 an esoteric principle
†현명 賢明 wisdom ; intelligence ; sagacity ; prudence ; good sense ; advisability (득책) —하다 (be) wise ; sage ; perspicacious ; sapient ; judicious ; prudent ; discreet ; well-advised ; advisable

> 참고 **wise** 넓은 지식 경험 이해를 기저로 하여 올바르게 판단 또는 대처하는 능력이 있다 **sage** 노년 경험 철학적 경험에서 오는 지혜가 깊다 **sapient** 현명 또는 학식을 의미하는 문어로서 때때로 반어적으로 사용된다 **judicious** 올바른 판단에 의하여 현명한 결정을 하는 능력이 있다 **prudent** 실제적인 일에 있어 적절한 방침을 발견하는 능력이 있다

¶ 현명한 사람 a wise man ; an intelligent person ; a long-headed person // 현명한 판단 sound judgment // 현명한 조처를 취하다 adopt〔take up〕 a wise policy ; act wisely ; show wisdom 《in handling a matter》
현명 顯名 ─하다 win a name ; gain fame ; become famous〔prominent〕
현모 賢母 a wise mother
─양처 a wise mother (to children) and a good wife (to her husband)
현목 玄木 unbleached cotton cloth
현몽 現夢 ─하다 appear〔come to 《a person》〕 in a dream
현묘 玄妙 abstruseness ; occultness ; mysteriousness ; miraculousness ; mystery ─하다 (be) abstruse ; occult ; recondite ; deep ; mysterious ¶ 현묘한 사상 profound ideas
현무암 玄武岩 〖광물〗 basalt ; whinstone
현물 現物 the actual thing〔article〕 ; [주식의] spot goods ; spots ; actual shares 《영》 ; stocks 《미》 ¶ 현물로 지불하다 pay 《taxes》 in kind
─ 가격 spot prices〔quotation〕 ─ 거래 [물건의] spot trading ; spot transaction ; [증권의] over-the-counter business ─ 급여 an allowance in kind ─ 배상 reparation in kind ─ 소득 income in kind ─ 시장 the spot market ; the spots ; the over-the-counter market ─ 인도 delivery of the goods ─점 a spot firm ─ 중매인 a spot broker ─ 출자 investment in kind
현미 玄米 uncleaned〔unhulled, unpolished〕 rice ; brown rice
─기(機) a (rice) huller ; a husker
*현미경 顯微鏡 a microscope ¶ 백배의 현미경 a microscope of 100 magnifications // 현미경으로 보다 look at 《a thing》 through a microscope ; see 《a thing》 under a microscope // 현미경의 초점을 맞추다 focus a microscope 《on, upon》
─ 검사 a microscopic examination ─ 관찰 fractography ─ 분석 a microscopic analysis ─ 사진 a microphotograph ─ 사진기 a photomicroscope 금속 ─ a metallographic microscope 복합 ─ compound microscope 수술용 ─ an operating microscope 쌍안 ─ a binocular microscope 전자 ─ an electron microscope 한외(초) ─ an ultramicroscope 형광 ─ a fluorescence microscope ; an ultraviolet microscope
현미 화학 顯微化學 microchemistry
현부 賢婦 a virtuous daughter-in-law ; a wise〔virtuous〕 woman
현부인 賢夫人 a wise woman ; a lady of wisdom〔high intelligence〕 ; your (hono(u)red) wife
현사 賢士 a wise scholar ; a sage
현삼 玄參 a kind of figwort ; Scrophularia buergeriana (학명)
현상 現狀 the present situation〔state〕 ; the actual state〔condition〕 ; the existing state of things〔affairs〕 ; the existing condition〔circumstances〕 ; the status quo ¶ 한국의 현상 the present state of affairs in Korea // 경제계의 현상 the present〔prevailing〕 economic situation〔condition〕 // 현상을 유지하다 maintain the status quo // 현상에 만족하다 be content with a matter as it is // 현상을 타파하다 burst〔break〕 the situation ; do away with the present state of things
─ 유지 maintenance of the status quo
─ 타파 destruction of the status quo
*현상 現象 a phenomenon 《*pl.* -mena》 ; an appearance ; a happening ¶ 일시적 현상 a passing phase
─계 〖철학〗 the phenomenal world ─ 과학 a phenomenal science ─론〔학〕 phenomenology 물리 ─ physical development 사회 ─ a social phenomenon 언어 ─ phenomena of language 자연 ─ a natural phenomenon
현상 現像 developing ; development ─하다 develop 《a film》
─ 과도 overdevelopment ─ 부족 underdevelopment ─실〔소〕 a processing laboratory ─액 a developer ; a developing solution ─지 a developing-out paper 《D. O. P.》 ─ 처리기 a processor ─ 촉진제 an accelerator
현상 賢相 a wise minister of state ; a wise premier
현상 懸賞 offer of a prize〔reward〕 ; a prize ; a reward ─하다 offer a prize〔reward〕 ; set a price on 《an offender's head》
─ 광고 a prize ad ; an advertisement for prize contest ─금 a prize (money) ─ 논문 a prize essay ─ 당선 소설 a prize-winning novel ─ 당선자 a prize winner ─ 모집 a prize contest ─ 문제〔과제〕 a subject〔problem〕 for a prize contest
현상태 現狀態 the present state of things ; the present circumstances ¶ 현상태로는 as matters stand (now)
현성 賢聖 sages〔wise men〕 and saints
현세 現世 this world ; this life ; the present age
─고(苦) one's "troubled lot below" ─ 주의 secularism
현세기 現世紀 this century ; the present century
현손 玄孫 descendants of the fourth generation ; a great-great-grandson
현송 現送 specie shipment ; cash sending ; shipment of gold ─하다 send in cash ; ship ; make a shipment of gold ¶ 금을 현송하다 ship gold 《to》 ; make a gold shipment 《to》
현수 現數 [현재의 수] the actual num-

ber 《of》; effective strength ; effectives (군대의)

‡현수 懸垂 suspension
— 운동 exercising on a horizontal bar —막 a hanging〔suspended〕 banner 〔placard〕

현수교 懸垂橋 ⇨ 적교(吊橋)

현수선 懸垂線 『수학』 a catenary

현숙 賢淑 womanly〔feminine〕 wisdom and virtue ; fidelity — 하다 (be) wise and virtuous ; graceful ; fidel

현시 現時 the present time ; today ; now

현시 顯示 revelation ; show ; display — 하다 show ; display ; unfold ; reveal ; uncover

현시대 現時代 the present age ⇨ 현대

현신 賢臣 a wise retainer ; a loyal vassal

현신하다 現身- present oneself before a superior ; put in one's appearance ; appear

†현실 現實 actuality ; the actual ; reality ; the realities of life ; a hard fact (공론에 대한) ¶ 현실적 realistic ; materialistic ; matter-of-fact ; pragmatic (실익주의) // 우리국가의 경제 현실 the reality of our national economy // 현실을 무시하다 ignore realities // 그는 현실에 묻혀서 이상을 잊었다 Absorbed in the actual, he has lost sight of the ideal.
—감 the sense of the real —계 the real world — 도피 escapism —론 a bread-and-butter theory ; realism —성 actuality ; reality —주의 actualism ; realism ; secularism —주의자 an actualist ; a realist —파 the actualists ; the realists — 폭로 disillusionment ; disillusion ¶ 현실 폭로의 비애 the sorrow 〔anguish〕 of disillusion

현실화 現實化 actualization ; realization ; materialization — 하다 actualize ; realize ; materialize ; translate 《ideas》 into reality ; [금리·환율 따위의] readjust to a realistic level ¶ 환율(換率)을 현실화하다 readjust the *won*-dollar exchange rate to a realistic level

현악 絃樂 string music
—기 a string(ed) instrument ; the strings —단 a string band — 사중주 a string quartet(te) — 합주 a string orchestra ; a string ensemble

현안 懸案 a pending question〔problem〕; an outstanding question ¶ 다년간의 현안 a long-pending question ; a question long under consideration // 한미간의 현안 a question pending between Korea and America // 현안으로 남겨두다 leave 《a matter》 in abeyance ; leave 《a question》 for future settlement ; leave 《a question》 undecided ; table 《a bill, a resolution》 for further discussion 《미》

현애 懸崖 an overhanging cliff ; a precipice ; an escarp

현양 顯揚 exaltation ; extolment — 하다 gain fame ; become famous ; extol ; exalt

현업 現業 《actual》 work-site operations
—원 an outdoor〔a field〕 worker ; a blue-collar worker

현역 現役 active service ; service on full pay (휴직에 대한) ¶ 현역에 복무중이다 be in active service ; be on service // 현역에서 퇴역하다 retire from active service
— 군인 a soldier on service ; a serviceman on active duty — 명부 the active list — 선수 a player on the playing list〔active membership〕 — 장교 an officer on the active list —함(艦) a vessel in commission ; a commissioned vessel

현옹수 懸壅垂 ⇨ 목젖

현요 顯要 — 하다 (be) prominent ; preeminent ; distinguished ; [중요하다] responsible ; important

현우 賢友 a wise〔an intelligent〕 friend

현우 賢愚 wisdom or folly ; cleverness or foolishness ; the wise and the foolish

현월 玄月 September of the lunar month

현유 現有 actuality ; the actual〔existing〕 being ¶ 현유의 existent ; in being ; on hand
— 세력 effective strength

현인 賢人 a wise man ; a sage

현임 現任 the present office〔post〕
—자 the present holder of the office

현자 賢者 a wise man ; a sage ; a man of high intelligence

†현장 現場 the (actual) spot ; the scene (of action) ; the scene of labor (작업의) ; a job-site ¶ 현장에서 on the spot〔ground〕 // 사건이 발생한 현장 the very spot where the accident took place // 현장을 목격하다 be an eyewitness of the disaster〔accident〕 // 범인은 현장에서 잡혔다 The offender〔criminal〕 was arrested〔caught〕 red-handed. // 살인 현장에서 피 묻은 손수건이 발견되었다 A blood-stained towel was found on the scene of murder. // 그분은 지금 현장에 나가 있습니다 He is out in the field right now.
— 감독 a site〔field〕 overseer ; an on-the-job superintendent — 검증 an on-the-spot inspection 《of the scene of a murder》; a spot investigation — 보고 a field report — 부재 증명 an alibi — 시찰 a spot inspection — 조사 an on-the-spot survey ; a field study

†현재 現在 ① the present (time) ; now ; at present ¶ 현재의 present ; existing ; current // 현재까지 up to now ; up 〔down〕 to date // 현재의 상태 the pre-

sent〔existing〕 state of things // 현재의 주소 one's present address // 나는 현재의 지위에 만족한다 I am contented where I am.
② [문법] the present tense ¶ 그 동사는 현재이다 The verb is in the present.
③ [실제] actuality ¶ 현재의 회원수 the actual membership
— 시제〔완료〕 『문법』 the present tense〔perfect〕 —(인)원 the present members on the list〔roll〕

현재 賢才 distinguished ability〔talent〕; a man of talent〔ability〕; a wise man

현재 顯在 —하다 be actualized
— 실업(失業) actual〔revealed〕 unemployment

‡현저 顯著 —하다 (be) notable; remarkable; marked; conspicuous; salient; striking; distinguished; considerable; noticeable; evident; obvious; eminent; prominent; outstanding; manifest

> 참고 **eminent** 동류보다 우수하다 **prominent** 다수의 사람 속에서 뛰어나 적어도 지방적으로는 유명하다 **distinguished** 동류보다 훨씬 뛰어난 어떤 현저한 장점을 가지고 있어 유명하다

¶ 현저한 공적 distinguished services // 현저한 차 a sharp〔striking〕 difference // 효과가 현저하다 have a marvelous effect〔efficacy〕

현저히 顯著— remarkably; markedly; considerably ¶ 현저히 다른 substantially different // …과는 현저히 다르다 be a far cry from...

현절 懸絶 —하다 be widely〔diametrically〕 different 《from》; be wide apart 《in》; be far removed 《from》

현정부 現政府 the present Government; the present Administration

현제 舷梯 an accommodation ladder; a gangway ladder 《of a vessel》; gangway

*현존 現存 existing; extant; living —하다 exist; be in existence; be extant; subsist; remain subsisting ¶ 현존의 existing; living; actual; extant
— 작가 a living writers

현주 現住 actual residence —하다 dwell〔reside, live〕 at present
—민 a native; natives —소 one's present address〔domicile, abode, residence〕; where one is living at present
—자 a current occupant

현주 懸註 adding notes〔comments〕; annotations —하다 add notes〔comments〕; annotate

현지 現地 the actual place; the (very) spot; the field
— 기관 a field organization — 로케이션 on-the-spot location — 방송 an on-the-spot broadcast — 보고 a spot〔fresh-hand〕 report — 본부 the field headquarters — 시간 local time — 시찰 여행 a fact-finding tour — 연구 research in the field; a field trip —인 the natives — 제대 the discharge in one's service area — 조달 self-subsistence〔-sufficiency〕 on the spot — 조사 a spot〔field〕 survey〔study, investigation, inquiry〕 ¶ 현지 조사를 하다 study the question on the spot〔scene〕
— 조사반 a field investigation party — 지도원 a field supervisor — 특파원 a correspondent on the scene〔in the field〕

현직 現職 the present office〔post〕; the office now occupied〔held〕
— 경찰관 a policeman on the active list〔in active service〕 — 대통령 the incumbent president

현직 顯職 a high office; an eminent〔a prominent〕 post ¶ 현직에 있는 사람 dignitaries; men of high office

현찰 現札 cash; actual〔ready〕 money; good〔hard〕 coin

현창 舷窓 a porthole

현책 賢策 a wise policy ¶ …하는 것이 현책이다 it is well-advised〔advisable〕 to do 《a thing》

현처 賢妻 a wise〔virtuous〕 wife; an intelligent wife; a good housewife

현철 賢哲 a sage; the wise 《총칭》; sagacity; wisdom —하다 (be) wise; sagacious; intelligent

현출 現出 ⇨ 노출(露出)

현충일 顯忠日 the Memorial Day

현충탑 顯忠塔 a memorial monument

현측 舷側 a (ship's) side ¶ 현측에 《bring a boat》 alongside a ship
— 인도 free alongside (ship) 《f. a. s.》

현칭 現稱 the present name

현탁액 懸濁液 『물리·화학』 suspension

현판 懸板 a hanging board (with a picture or some calligraphy on it); a tablet

현품 現品 the actual article〔goods〕; stock in hand; goods in stock; stocks
— 급여 wages〔an allowance〕 in kind
— 상환불(相換拂) cash〔collect 《미》〕 on delivery 《C. O. D.》 — 선도(先渡) goods promptly delivered

현하 現下 the present time ⇨ 현금

현하구변 懸河口辯 fluency in speech; eloquence; an eloquent speech ¶ 현하구변(지변)을 토하다 display one's oratorical prowess; speak with great eloquence

현학 衒學 pedantry; display〔parading〕 of one's (book-)learning ¶ 현학적 pedantic
—자 a pedant; a gerundgrinder

†현행 現行 existing; current; prevailing ¶ 현행의 existing; present; current;

(actually) in force ; in operation // 현행대로 same as at present // 현행 제도하에서는 under the present system
— 교과서 the text books now in use — 규정 the regulations in force ; the standing rules — 맞춤법 the current spelling system —범〔죄〕 a flagrant offense〔delict〕; [사람] a criminal taken in an act of crime ¶ 현행범으로 붙들리다 caught red-handed (흉행의) ; be apprehended while committing a crime —법 existing〔operative〕 law ; the law in force — 제도 the present system ; the system in force〔existence〕 — 조약 the existing treaty — 화폐 the current coinage ; the currency now in circulation

현현 顯現 a manifestation ; an expression ; evidence —하다 manifest ; express ; evidence

*현혹 眩惑 dazzlement ; bewilderment ; a daze —하다 dazzle ; daze ; blind ¶ 현혹당하다 be dazzled《by the splendor》

현화 現化 realization ; actualization ; incarnation —하다 be realized ; actualize ; become incarnate

현화식물 顯花植物 a phanerogamous plant ; a phanerogam ⇨ 꽃식물

현황 現況 the present condition〔status, situation〕; the present position

현훈 眩暈 dizziness ; giddiness ; vertigo (현훈증)

혈 穴 [구멍] a hole ; an aperture ; an opening ; a perforation ; [풍수 지리의] a spot where influences to one's fortune converge ; [침의] a region for acupuncture

혈거 穴居 cave dwelling ; troglodytism —하다 live〔dwell〕 in a cave
— 생활 cave dwelling — 시대 the cave〔troglodytic〕 period〔age〕 —인 a caveman ; a cave-dweller ; a troglodyte —학 angiology

혈관 血管 『해부』 a blood vessel ; an artery ; a vein
— 경련 an angiospasm ; a vascular spasm — 경화 hardening〔sclerosis〕 of the walls of the blood vessel — 수축인자 a vasoexiter material《V. E. M.》 — 신경 vasomotor nerves — 신경 마비 vasomotor paralysis — 압축기 a compressor — 절개(술) angiotomy —종(腫) an angioma《*pl.* ~s, -meta》 — 파열 rupture〔bursting, laceration〕 of the blood vessels — 협착〔폐색〕 angiostenosis — 확장 인자 a vasodepressor material《V. D. M.》 — 확장제 a vasodilator

혈괴 血塊 clotted blood ; a clot of blood ; gore ¶ 옷에 혈괴가 붙어 있었다 The clothing was stained with clots of blood.

혈구 血球 a blood-corpuscle ; a globule
— 계수 the blood count — 세포 결핍 the deficiency of red corpuscles ; oligocythemia ; aglobulism —소 hemoglobin — 응집 agglutination of (red) blood cells 백— a leucocyte ; a migratory cell ; a white blood corpuscle〔cell〕 적— a red blood corpuscle ; a hematocyte 적— 감소증 the deficiency of red corpuscles ; oligocythemia ; aglobulism

혈기 血氣 ① [체력] vitality ; strength ; stamina ② [의기] animal spirits ; hot blood ; youthful vigor〔ardor〕 ¶ 젊은 혈기 youthful follies〔indiscretion〕// 혈기 왕성한 젊은이 a sanguine〔vigorous〕 youth ; a young man in full vigor // 혈기가 왕성하다 be full of youthful vigor ; be in the prime of health ; be in one's hot〔raw, vigorous〕 youth

혈농 血膿 bloody pus〔matter〕

혈뇨 血尿 『의학』 h(a)ematuria

혈담 血痰 blood(y) phlegm

혈로 血路 ¶ 혈로를 열다 find a perilous way out ; cut〔carve out〕 a way through《the enemy》

혈루 血淚 tears of blood ; bitter tears ¶ 혈루를 흘리다 shed〔cry〕 bitter tears

혈맥 血脈 [혈관] a blood vessel ; a vein (정맥) ; an artery (동맥) ; [혈연] blood relationship ; consanguinity
— 상통(相通) consanguinity ; blood relationship

혈맹 血盟 a blood pledge

혈반 血班 a blood spot

혈변 血便 bloody excrement

혈병 血餠 a blood clot ; a cruor

혈상 血相 the color of one's face ; a threatening〔menacing〕 look ⇨ 혈색(血色)

혈색 血色 color of the face ; complexion ¶ 혈색이 좋다〔나쁘다〕 look well〔pale〕; have a ruddy〔bad〕 complexion // 혈색이 좋아지다〔나빠지다〕 gain〔lose〕 color // 혈색이 좋지 않다 look pale ; have a bad complexion ; look sallow

혈색소 血色素 hemoglobin

혈서 血書 writing in blood ; something written in blood —하다 write in blood ¶ 혈서로 맹세하다 write a pledge with〔in〕 one's blood

혈석 血石 『광물』 bloodstone

혈성 血誠 devotion ; sincerity ; loyalty

혈세 血稅 ① [병역·의무] compulsory〔obligatory〕 military service ② [가혹한 세금] a tax paid by the sweat of one's brow ¶ 혈세를 과하다 tax《people》 to the bone

혈속 血屬 a blood-relation ; a relative〔connection〕 by blood ; a kinsman (남자) ; a kinswoman ; kinsfolk ; kinship

혈손 血孫 descendants related by blood

혈안 血眼 a bloodshot eye ¶ 혈안이 되

어서 madly ; desperately ; frantically // 혈안이 되어서 찾다 look for 《a thing》 with eager〔feverish〕 eyes ; make a frantic search for

혈압 血壓 blood pressure ¶ 혈압을 재다 measure one's blood pressure
—계 a sphygmomanometer (팔에 감는) —계 밴드 a blood pressure cuff — 저하제 a depressant 고〔저〕— high〔low〕 blood pressure 정상 — normal blood pressure 최저〔최고〕 — minimum〔maximum〕 blood pressure

*혈액 血液 blood
— 강장제 a blood tonic — 검사 a blood test — 결핍 a deficiency of blood ; anaemia — 과다 an excess of blood — 금고〔은행〕 a blood bank — 기생충 a blood parasite —병 a blood trouble〔disorder〕 — 색소 hemochrom ; hemochromorgen — 성분 constituent parts of the blood — 순환 circulation (of blood) ¶ 혈액 순환을 잘 되게 하다 promote〔quicken, stimulate〕 the circulation of blood ; make the blood circulate more freely — 응고 the coagulation〔clotting〕 of blood ; blood coagulation — 정화 purification of the blood — 제공자 a blood donor —학 h(a)ematology —형 a type of blood ; a blood type

혈연 血緣 blood relation ; kin ; kith and kin ; one's flesh and blood
— 관계 blood relationship ; kinship ; blood ties ; consanguinity — 단체 a kinship society

혈온 血溫 blood heat ; the temperature of blood

혈우병 血友病 h(a)emophilia ; bleeder's disease
— 환자 a h(a)emophiliac ; a bleeder

혈육 血肉 ① [피와 살] blood and flesh ② one's own children (자녀) ; kinsmen ; blood relations ¶ 슬하에 혈육이 없다 be childless
— 상쟁 domestic discord〔trouble〕

*혈장 血漿 〖해부〗 blood plasma ; serum
— 공장 plasma plant

혈전 血栓 〖의학〗 a thrombus ¶ 혈전증의 thrombotic
— 생성 thrombosis 뇌—증 cerebral 〔coronary〕 thrombosis

혈전 血戰 a bloody〔sanguinary〕 battle ; a desperate〔bloody〕 fight ; a murderous battle ; a desperate〔bloody〕 fight ; a murderous battle ; a war to the knife 〔death〕 —하다 fight a bloody battle ; fight desperately

*혈족 血族 [관계] kinship ; blood-relationship ; ties of blood ; [사람] one's flesh and blood ; a blood-relation ; a relative〔connection〕 by blood ; kinsfolk ; kith and kin
— 결혼 marriage within the blood ; a consanguineous marriage — 관계 blood relationship ; kinship

혈청 血清 〖의학〗 serum 《*pl.* sera》 ; lymph
— 반응 (a) serum reaction ; a seroreaction —병 a serum disease — 요법 serum treatment〔therapy〕 ; serotherapy — 주사 a serum injection — 진단 serum diagnosis ; serodiagnosis —학 serology 예방 — a preventive serum 항— antiserum

혈충 血忠 the utmost loyalty

혈침 血沈 precipitation of blood ¶ 혈침을 재다 measure the precipitation of 《a person's》 blood

*혈통 血統 bloodlineage ; pedigree ; stock ; a family line ; descent ¶ 혈통이 좋다〔나쁘다〕 come of a good〔bad〕 stock // 혈통이 끊어지다 The line has died out.
— 배양 〖동물〗 pedigree culture —서 a hard book (소·양 따위의) —주의 jus sanguinis (국적 취득의)

혈투 血鬪 a bloody fight ⇨ 혈전(血戰)

혈판 血判 a sealing of blood —하다 seal〔sign〕 with one's blood ¶ 연판장에 혈판하다 seal a compact with blood
—장 a petition〔pledge〕 sealed with blood

혈한 血汗 ① 〖의학〗 a blood sweat ② [피와 땀] blood and sweat

혈행 血行 blood circulation ¶ 혈행을 좋게 하다 quicken〔facilitate〕 the circulation〔flow〕 of the blood
—계 a tachometer — 기관 circulatory organs — 장애 interruption in blood circulation

혈혈 孑孑 solitary ; alone —하다 be all alone
— 단신 all alone in the world ; have neither friends nor relatives

혈흔 血痕 a blood stain ; a mark〔spot〕 of blood ¶ 혈흔이 묻은 blood-stained

혐기 嫌忌 aversion ; abhorrence ; dislike —하다 feel aversion to〔toward〕 ; abhor ; dislike

혐염 嫌厭 dislike ; loathing ; disgust ; hate ; detestation —하다 dislike ; loathe ; hate ; be disgusted 《with》

*혐오 嫌惡 hatred ; dislike ; disgust ; aversion ; repugnance ; abomination ; abhorrence ; antipathy —하다 hate ; dislike ; detest ; be averse to ; abominate ; loathe ¶ 혐오의 정을 품다 feel hatred 《toward》 ; feel repugnance to revolt at ; nurse hatred 《against》 ; feel like vomiting〔sickening〕 at

‡혐의 嫌疑 ① [의심] suspicion ; charge ; accusation —하다 suspect 《of a crime》 ; throw〔cast〕 suspicion 《on》 ; suspect 《a person》 ¶ 살인 혐의로 on suspicion〔on a charge, under accusation〕 of murder // 혐의를 받다 fall

〔come〕 under suspicion ; be placed in a false position ; be suspected 《of》; be charged 《with》∥혐의를 씻다 clean oneself of suspicion (자신의) ; [타인의] clean 《a person》 of suspicion ; give 《a person》 a clean bill of health 《구》∥간첩 혐의로 체포되다 be arrested on (the) suspicion of espionage〔being a spy〕∥그의 덕택으로 나도 엉뚱하게 혐의를 받고 있다 Thanks to him, I've come under suspicion too. ∥독직 혐의를 받아오던 장관이 마침내 사임했다 That government minister who was under a cloud of suspicion finally resigned. ② [미움] dislike ; aversion ━하다 dislike ; feel an aversion to

―자 a suspected person ; a suspect ; a criminal suspect (범죄의)

혐점 嫌點 a cause of suspicion ; a suspicious aspect ; a questionable point

협 峽 a gorge ; a ravine ; a defile

협각 夾角 『수학』 an included angle

협객 俠客 a man of chivalrous spirit ; a chivalrous person ; a self-styled humanitarian ; a street knight

협격 挾擊 attack on both sides 〔flanks〕; pincer attack ⇨ 협공(挾攻) ━하다 catch 《the enemy》 in a crossfire ; attack 《the enemy》 from both sides

*협곡 峽谷 a gorge ; a ravine ; a glen ; a canyon ; a gullet ; a gulch 《미》

협골 頰骨 the cheekbone ; the zygomatic bone

협공 挾攻 an attack on both sides 〔flanks〕; a double attack ; pincers 《미》; a pincer attack ━하다 attack from both sides ; pincer ¶ 적을 협공하다 attack the enemy from both sides ; double upon the enemy∥협공을 받다 be attacked on the both sides ; find oneself between two fires

― 작전 a pincer operation

협궤 狹軌 a narrow gauge

― 철도 a narrow gauge railway

협기 俠氣 a chivalrous spirit ; chivalry ¶ 협기가 있는 사람 a gallant〔chivalrous〕 man

*협동 協同 cooperation ; collaboration ; association ; union ; partnership ; joint endeavor ━하다 cooperate ; collaborate ; work together ; unite ; act in concert〔union〕; join forces with

― 기업 a cooperative〔joint〕 enterprise ― 농장 a collective farm ; [옛소련의] a kolkhoz ; [이스라엘의] a kibbutz ― 작전 concerted〔united, combined〕 operations ― 정신 cooperative spirit ; esprit de corps ; the spirit of teamwork ― 조합 a cooperative society〔association, union〕 ―체 a community ; a communal society

협량 狹量 narrow-〔small-〕mindedness ━하다 (be) narrow-minded ; ungenerous ; intolerant ; illiberal

⁑협력 協力 cooperation ; conjunction ; common action ; concert ; joint efforts ; pulling〔working〕 together ; combined strength ; solidarity ━하다 cooperate with ; work together ; pull〔hang〕 together ; unite one's efforts 《with》; coact ; join forces 《with》; get together ; tie up ; make a united effort ¶ 협력하여 in cooperation〔concert〕 《with》∥긴밀한 협력 close cooperation ; a tie-up 《with》 《미》∥정신적〔물질적〕 협력 spiritual〔material〕 cooperation

―자 a collaborator ; a co-worker 경제 ― economic co-operation 상호 ― mutual co-operation

협로 夾路 a branch road

협로 峽路 a mountain road ; a defile

협로 狹路 a marrow road ; a branch road (큰 길의) ; a mountain road (산속의)

협만 峽灣 a fjord

협문 夾門 a small side gate〔door〕

†협박 脅迫 a threat ; a menace ; terrorism ; coercion ; 『법』 intimidation ━하다 threaten ; intimidate ; menace ; bulldoze 《미》; coerce ; compel ; force ¶ 협박적인 threatening ; menacing ; intimidatory∥협박하여 5천원을 빼앗다 blackmail 《a person》 of 5,000 *won*∥협박하여 서명시키다 coerce 《a person》 into signing a document∥권총으로 협박하다 threaten 《a person》 with a revolver∥협박적인 태도를 취하다 assume a threatening attitude 《toward》

―자 an intimidator ―장 a threatening〔an intimidation〕 letter ― 전화 《get》 a threatening (telephone) call ―죄 (a crime of) intimidation 폭행 ― actual compulsion

협사 俠士 a chivalrous person ⇨ 협객

협살 挾殺 『야구』 run-down ━하다 run down

*협상 協商 negotiation ; conversations ; an understanding ; an agreement ; a convention ; an entente (cordiale) ━하다 negotiate ¶ 협상을 맺다 conclude an entente 《with》

―국 the Entente Powers ; the Allies ― 조약 an entent (cordiale) 《프》; an agreement ; an understanding ; a convention 삼국 ― the Triple Entente 화친 ― an entente cordiale

협성 協成 collaboration ━하다 collaborate ; work out together ; accomplish in concert〔cooperation〕

협소 狹小 narrowness ; smallness ━하다 (be) small and narrow ; confined ; cramped ; limited ; small-sized ¶ 협소한 장소 a limited space∥협소한 방 a small room∥지역이 협소하다 be small in area

협실 夾室 a side room

협심 協心 cooperation ; unison ; accord ; concert —하다 unite ; be united ; act in unison ¶ 협심하여 in unison 〔union〕; unitedly ; with one accord

협심증 狹心症 angina pectoris ; stenocardia ; stricture of the heart ; heart attack

협애 狹隘 narrowness ; tightness ; limitedness —하다 (be) narrow ; small ; limited ; confined ; tight ; cramped

†협약 協約 an agreement ; a convention ; a pact ; an entente (cordiale) —하다 enter into〔conclude〕 an agreement ; agree on

—국 a party to an agreement〔entente〕 노동 — a labor agreement〔pact〕 단체 — a collective agreement 통상 — a commercial entente

협업 協業 cooperation ; cooperative work —하다 cooperate ; work together

‡협의 協議 conference ; council ; consultation ; deliberation ; discussion —하다 confer 《with》; consult 《with》; deliberate 《on a matter》; discuss 《a matter》; talk over ; hold conference ¶ 협의하에 upon deliberation ; after consultation 《with》; by mutual consent 〔agreement〕// 협의가 이루어지다 reach 〔arrive at〕 an agreement ; reach〔come to〕 a decision

— 단체 a conference group — 사항 subjects〔topics〕 of discussion ; the (conference) agenda ; the program ; a matter for consultation — 이혼 a divorce by agreement —회 a conference ; a council

협의 狹義 a narrow sense ; a restricted meaning ¶ 협의의 교육 education in a narrow sense // 협의로 해석하다 construe in a limited〔restricted〕 sense of the term

협잡 挾雜 fraudulence ; trickery ; juggling ; cheating ; swindle ; imposture ; deception —하다 cheat ; swindle ; embezzle ; commit fraud ; impose ¶ 도박에서 협잡하다 cheat in gambling // 5천원을 협잡당하다 be cheated〔gulled〕 of 5,000 *won* 《by》

—군〔배〕 an imposter ; a fraud ; a fake ; a trickster —물 an adulteration ; a fake — 투표 fraudulent voting

*협장 脇杖 crutches ¶ 협장을 짚고 걷다 walk on crutches ⇨ 목다리

‡협정 協定 agreement ; arrangement ; convention ; pact —하다 agree upon 《the price》; arrange 《with》; stipulate 《with》; make〔conclude, enter into〕 an agreement ; make arrangements 《for》 ¶ 협정을 맺다 conclude a convention // 협정을 이행하다 fulfil〔carry out, act up to〕 one's agreement // 협정에 실패하다 fail to reach an agreement ; reach no agreement // 한미간에 협정이 이루어졌다 An agreement was reached between Korea and America.

— 가격 a price agreed (upon) ; an agreed price ; a specified〔stipulated〕 price —서 a protocol ; a written agreement ; an agreement — 세율 a conventional tariff —안 an agreement proposal — 임금 wages agreed (upon) ; agreed wages — 조항 agreed terms ; stipulations 관세 — a customs agreement 국제 — an international agreement ; an accord 상호 — a bilateral agreement 신사 — a gentlemen's agreement 운임 — a freight convention 잠정 — a modus vivendi 《라》; a temporary agreement 정책 — a policy agreement 정전 — a cease-fire agreement ; a truce accord 편무(片務) — a unilateral agreement 평화 — a peace accord 포로 교환 — an agreement for exchange of war prisoners 행정 — an administrative agreement 휴전 — an armistice agreement

‡협조 協助 help ; aid ; assistance ; support (후원) ; cooperation (협력) —하다 help 《a person in his work》; aid 〔assist〕 《in a person's work》 ¶ K씨의 협조로 with the help of Mr. K ; through Mr. K's aid // 협조를 바라다 ask for help

—자 a helper ; an assistant ; a supporter 상호 — mutual help〔aid〕; cooperation

협조 協調 cooperation ; concerted action ; concord ; harmony (조화) ; conciliation (타협) —하다 cooperate ; act in concert 《with》; act harmoniously 《with》 ¶ 협조적 태도 a conciliatory attitude // 자유 국가간의 협조 close cooperation between free nations // 협조적 정신으로 in a spirit of cooperation〔conciliation〕

—성 cooperativeness ; cooperation ¶ 협조성을 결한 lacking in cooperation ; incooperative —심 a spirit of harmony —적 cooperative ; conciliatory ; harmonious 노사 — harmony between labor and capital〔management〕

협주곡 協奏曲 a concerto

협죽도 夾竹桃 『식물』 a sweet oleander ; a rosebay ; a garden phlox

협착 狹窄 [좁음] narrowness ; 『의학』 stricture ; constriction ; strangulation ; stenosis ; contraction —하다 (be) narrow ; small ; limited ; strangulated ; constricted

— 골반 a contracted pelvis — 사격 miniature cartridge practice ; morris-tube practice —탄 a miniature cartridge ; miniature munition 요도〔직장〕 — 『의학』 stricture of the urethra〔rectum〕

협찬 協贊 consent ; agreement ; ap-

proval ; sanction ; authorization —하다 approve ; sanction ; consent 《to》; authorize
협촌 峽村 a mountain〔an isolated〕 village ; a remote hamlet
협하다 狹— (be) narrow-minded ; illiberal ; ungenerous ; chicken-minded
협화 協和 harmony ; concord ; concert ; 〖음악〗 consonance —하다 be in harmony〔concord〕 with ; act in concert ; be consonant 《with》
—음 〖음악〗 a consonance ; a concord ; euphony — 음정 consonant intervals
협회 協會 a society ; an association ; a league
농구 — the Basketball League 아시아 — the Asiatic Society 저작가 — the Authors' League
혓바늘 an eruption on the tongue ¶ 혓바늘이 돋다 have a rough tongue
혓바닥 the flat of the tongue ¶ 혓바닥으로 핥다 lap with the tongue
혓소리 〖문법〗 a lingual (sound)
*형 兄 an elder brother ; [선배] a senior ¶ 형으로 섬기다 regard 《a person》 as one's senior
맏〔막내〕— one's eldest〔youngest elder〕 brother 매〔자〕— a brother-in-law 처— a sister-in-law 친— a full 〔whole〕 brother
*형 刑 a punishment ; a penalty ; a sentence (선고) ¶ 형의 적용 the application of a punishment // 형을 받다 be sentenced to ; be convicted // 형에 처하다 condemn 《a person》 to a penalty ; sentence 《a person》 to // 형을 언도하다 pass〔pronounce〕 a sentence on // 형의 집행을 유예하다 suspend〔stay〕 the execution of a sentence ; pass a suspended sentence on
재산— a pecuniary punishment 종신— a life sentence ; imprisonment for life
형 形 shape ; form ; format
대〔중, 소〕— large〔medium, small〕 size
†형 型 [원형] a model ; a mold ; a matrix ; [양식] style ; type ; pattern ¶ 포드의 최신형 자동차 the latest models of Ford cars
형강 形鋼 section〔shape〕 steel
— 기둥 a rolled steel column — 압연기(壓延機) a rolling mill for section steel
형관 荊冠 a crown〔garland〕 of thorns
형광 螢光 fluorescent light
— 도료 a fluorescent paint —등 a fluorescent lamp — 물질 a fluorescent material —성 fluorescence ; fluorescent — 안료 a fluorescent pigment — 엑스선 fluorescence X-rays — 조명 fluorescent lighting —체 a fluorescent substance — 투시경 a fluoroscope — 표백 fluorescent bleaching
형구 刑具 an implement of punishment 〔torture〕
형국 形局 aspect ; appearance ; phase ; a situation
형극 荊棘 brambles ; thorns ¶ 형극의 길 a thorny path ; a brambly way ; the way of the Cross (수난의 길)
형기 刑期 the term of imprisonment ; a prison term ; the term of penal servitude ; one's time ¶ 형기가 만료되어 출옥하다 leave prison〔be set free〕 at the expiration of one's term
형륙 刑戮 —하다 condemn 《a person》 to capital punishment ; send to the scaffold
형률 刑律 penal code ; criminal law
형명 刑名 the name of a penalty 〔crime〕; charge
형무소 刑務所 a prison ; a jail ; a penitentiary ⇨ 교도소(矯導所)
‡형벌 刑罰 a punishment ; a penalty —하다 punish ; inflict〔impose〕 a punishment〔penalty〕 on ; bring 《a person》 to justice ¶ 형벌을 받다 receive a punishment ; get punished // 형벌을 면하다 escape punishment〔justice〕 // 형벌을 엄하게 하다 administer justice rigidly ; deal strictly with 《a person》
형법 刑法 〖법〗 criminal law ; jus criminale ; crown law 《영》 ¶ 형법상의 criminal ; penal // 형법상의 범죄 a penal 〔an indictable〕 offense // 형법상의 죄인 a penal offender ; a criminal in the eye of the law
— 위반 a penal offense —전 the penal code —학 criminal jurisprudence — 학자 an authority on〔an expert in, a scholar of〕 the criminal code 국제 — international criminal law
형부 兄夫 a brother-in-law ; the husband of a girl's elder sister
*형사 刑事 ① [사건] a criminal〔penal〕 case ¶ 형사상의 criminal ; penal // 형사상의 책임 penal responsibility // 침입자는 형사 고발될 것임 Trespassers will be prosecuted. (게시) ② [사람] a (police) detective ; a police investigator ; a hound of the law
— 문제 a criminal case ; a penal offense —범 a criminal〔penal〕 offense ; an indictable offense — 법원 a criminal court — 보상 criminal compensation — 사건 a criminal case ; a penal offence — 소송 criminal action 〔prosecution〕 ¶ 형사 소송법 the Criminal Procedure Code — 재판 a criminal trial — 정책 a criminal policy — 피고인 a prisoner at the bar ; the accused —학 〖법〗 criminology ; penology 사복 — a plainclothesman
형상 形狀 shape ; form ; configuration
형상 形象 ① [물건의] shape ; form ② [상상의] a shape ; a figure ; an appear-

ance ; a phenomenon 《*pl.* -mena》

형색 形色 form and color ; general looks ; appearance

형석 螢石 〖광물〗 fluorspar ; fluorite

형설 螢雪 diligent study ¶ 형설의 공 (the fruits of) diligent study // 형설의 공을 쌓다 prosecute one's studies for years ; apply oneself closely to one's studies

†**형성 形成** formation **—하다** form ; make ; constitute ; mold ; take shape ; come into being ; build up

—기(期) a formative period ¶ 인격 형성기 the formative period in the life of a man **—물질** 〖동물〗 a formative substance **— 부전** hypoplasia **— 세포** a formative cell **—소** formative stuff ; plastic element **—질** 〖동물〗 formative substance **—층** 〖식물〗 cambium **인간—** character building

형세 形勢 ① [사물의] the situation ; the position〔state〕 of affairs ; the state of things ; [전망] the prospects ; the outlook ; [징후] signs ; indications ; appearances ; symptoms ¶ 형세를 관망하다 watch the situation ; watch the development of affairs ; wait for a turn of events // 형세가 불리하다 The situation is unfavorable. // 형세가 일변했다 The situation has taken on a new aspect.

② [살림의] circumstances ¶ 형세가 어렵다〔넉넉하다〕 be in difficult〔easy〕 circumstances // 형세가 말이 아니다 be extremely〔unspeakably, indescribably, deplorably〕 poor ; be badly off

형소법 刑訴法 the Criminal Procedure Code

***형수 兄嫂** the wife of one's elder brother

***형식 形式** a form ; a formality ; a mode (철학) ¶ 형식상 for form's sake // 형식적 formal ; conventional // 형식적으로 formally ; for the sake of formality // 형식 불변의 원리 the principle of permanence of formal laws // 형식적 관념론 formal idealism // 형식적인 인사 a greeting for form's sake // 형식을 차리지 않고 informally ; without ceremony // 형식에 맞추다 conform to forms // 정당한 형식을 밟다 go through due formalities // 형식을 차리다 observe forms ; be ceremonious ; be formal ; be〔stand〕 on ceremony

— 논리 formal logic **— 도야** formal building of character **—론** formalism **—미** the beauty of form **— 분류** form classification **— 세목** form subdivisions **—주의** 〖예술〗 formalism **—주의자** a formalist **— 표목(標目)** 〖도서〗 a form heading

형안 炯眼 a quick〔sharp, keen〕 eye ; a piercing〔penetration〕 eye ; penetration ; perspicacity ; acuteness ; keen insight ; far-sightedness ¶ 형안의 keen-sighted ; sharp-eyed ; perspicacious ; penetrative

***형언 形言** description ; expression **—하다** describe ; express ¶ 형언할 수 없는 indescribable ; inexpressible ; unspeakable ; unutterable // 형언할 수 없다 It is beyond description. /It beggars〔baffles〕 description. /It is indescribable.

형옥 形獄 ① [형] a penalty ; a punishment ; imprisonment ② [감옥] a prison

⁑**형용 形容** ① [형상] form ; figure ; appearance ② [수식] qualification ; modification ; [서술] description ; [비유] a metaphor ; a figure of speech ; a figurative expression **—하다** qualify ; modify ; describe ; put into words ; use a figure〔metaphor〕 ; express figuratively ¶ 형용해서 말하면 figuratively speaking // 형용할 수 없다 be beyond expression ; beggar〔baffle〕 description ; be indescribable // 그 경치는 형용할 수 없을 만큼 아름답다 The scenery is beautiful beyond all description.

—사 an adjective **—어** an epithet

***형이상 形而上** ¶ 형이상의 metaphysical ; abstract ; immaterial ; incorporeal

—학 metaphysics ; metaphysical philosophy **—학자** a metaphysician **—학적 유심론〔결정론〕** metaphysical idealism 〔determinism〕

형이하 形而下 ¶ 형이하의 physical ; concrete ; corporeal ; material

—학 a concrete〔physical〕 science

형장 刑場 an execution-ground ; a place of execution ¶ 형장의 이슬로 사라지다 die on the execution-ground〔scaffold (교수대)〕

형장 兄丈 you

형적 形迹 [흔적] traces ; vestiges ; marks ; signs ; indications ; evidence ¶ 눈물의 형적 traces of tears // 고대 문명의 형적 vestiges of ancient civilization // 형적이 있다〔없다〕 There is an indication〔no indication〕 《that》. // 형적을 남기지 않다 leave no trace behind 《a person》 // 형적을 없애다 remove all traces ; cover up one's traces

형정 刑政 penal administration

—국 Bureau of Penal Administration

†**형제 兄弟** brothers (남) ; sisters (여) ; brethren (동포) ¶ 형제의 brotherly ; sisterly ; fraternal // 피를 나눈 형제 a brother by blood // 형제의 의를 맺다 make a blood brother compact ; form brotherly ties

— 싸움 a guarrel〔trouble〕 between brothers **—애** brotherly affection **사촌—** cousins **이복 —** half brothers **젖—** milk brothers〔sisters〕 ; fosterbrothers **친—** full brothers〔sisters〕

형제 자매 兄弟姉妹 brothers and sisters ; brethren

형조 刑曹 [옛제도] the Ministry of Justice

— 판서 the Minister of Justice

형지 型紙 a paper pattern 《for a dress》

형질 形質 ① form and nature〔quality〕 ② 〖생물〗 characteristics

— 세포 a plasma cell — 인류학 physical anthropology 유전(遺傳) — an inherited character

형처 荊妻 my wife

†형체 形體 form ; shape ; the body ¶ 형체를 갖추다 be given a form ; be embodied

형태 形態 form ; shape ; 〖심리〗 configuration ; Gestalt 《도》 ¶ 형태를 취하다 assume the form 《of》// 형태를 바꾸다 transform ; transfigure // 얼음, 눈, 수증기는 모두 물의 다른 형태다 Ice, snow, and steam are different forms of water.

—론(論) 〖언어〗 morphology ¶ 형태론적 구조 morphologic construction —미 physical beauty ; the beauty of form — 변화 〖언어〗 modification — 분류 form class ; classification of size —소 a morpheme — 심리학 Gestalt psychology — 음운론 morphophonemics —학 morphology

형통 亨通 —하다 go well ; turn out well ; prove successful ¶ 만사가 형통하다 everything goes well

형틀 刑— a chair in which a criminal is fastened to be interrogated

형판 型板 a die plate ; a template ; a mold

—금 set iron — 유리 figured glass

⁑형편 形便 ① [일의 경로·결과] the situation ; the state 《of things》; the aspect 《of affairs》; the development 《of an affairs》 ¶ 형편에 따라 according to the development of the situation // 지금 형편으로는 as things are〔stand〕 now // 일을 형편에 맡기다 allow the situation to develop in its own way // 형편을 보아 결정하자 Let us see how things turn out before we decide. // 그는 술을 너무 마셔서 말도 제대로 못하는 형편이었다 He drank so much that he wound up barely able to talk. // 이번 기간의 매상은 형편없다 Sales this term have been a washout.

② [살림의] one's family circumstances 〔fortune〕; one's family situation ¶ 형편이 넉넉하다 be well off ; be amply provided for // 형편이 어렵다 be badly off

③ [형세] a condition ; a state ; convenience ; circumstances ¶ 형편상 for convenience's sake ; in view of circumstances // 적의 형편을 살피다 watch the movements of the enemy // 시내 형편은 어떤가 How is it in the city ? // 나는 이 곳의 형편을 모른다 I am a stranger here〔in this place〕.

재정 — financial conditions

형편없다 ¶ 형편없이 undescribably ; terribly ; mercilessly ; extremely ; completely ; utterly // 형편없이 고생하다 suffer terribly〔miserably〕 《from》// 형편없이 지다 be beaten all hollow

형평 衡平 balance ; equilibrium ; equipoise

— 운동 the social equality movement ; the leveling movement — 원칙 the principle of equity

형해 形骸 [뼈대] the body ; a frame ; a skeleton ; framework ; [잔해] a ruin ; a wreck ¶ 그 절은 형해마저 남기지 않았다 Nothing remains of the temple now. / No traces of the temple are now visible.

형형 炯炯 glaring ; piercing ; penetrating

—하다 (be) glaring ; piercing ; penetrating ; gleaming ; sharp ¶ 안광이 형형하다 be eagle-eyed ; have glittering eyes

형형색색 形形色色 all sorts and kinds ; various ; diverse ; sundry ¶ 형형색색의 의견 diverse views ; various opinions // 형형색색으로 variously ; in various 〔many〕 ways

혜고 惠顧 [왕림] a gracious 《your, his》 visit ; [돌봐줌] 《your, his》 kind regards〔attention〕 —하다 kindly visit ; regard with kindness ; treat with benevolence

혜람 惠覽 gracious perusal 《of a letter》 —하다 deign to read ; kindly read

혜림 惠臨 《your, his》 gracious visit —하다 graciously visit ; kindly come

혜민 慧敏 —하다 (be) clever ; sagacious ; shrewd ; astute

혜사 惠賜 —하다 bestow ; graciously give ; kindly grant

혜서 惠書 your kind〔gracious〕 letter ¶ 6월 10일부의 혜서 your favor of the 10th of June

⁑혜성 彗星 a comet ¶ 혜성과 같은 meteoric ; meteor-like ; comet-like // 정계의 혜성 a dark horse in politics ; a political meteor // 혜성과 같이 나타나 혜성과 같이 사라지다 disappear as suddenly as one appears

—년 comet year

혜시 惠示 your kind instruction〔information〕 —하다 kindly show〔instruct, inform〕

혜시 惠施 —하다 kindly give ; bestow ; give 《money》 in charity〔alms〕

혜안 慧眼 a piercing〔penetrating〕 eye ; a keen insight ; a quick〔sharp〕 eye ; penetration ; perspicacity

혜여 惠與 —하다 bestow ; graciously give ; kindly grant

혜존 惠存 [증정본에] with the compli-

ments (of the author) ; To〔Presented to〕 Mr. . . . with best wishes from. . .
혜증 惠贈 ―하다 bestow
혜찰 惠札 your kind〔gracious〕 letter
*혜택 惠澤 a favor ; benefaction ; kindness ; benefit ; benevolence ¶ 문명의 혜택 the benefits of civilization // 혜택을 입다 be benefited ; receive favors ; enjoy benevolent influence ; be indebted《to》
혜한 惠翰 your kind〔gracious〕 letter ⇨ 혜서
혜함 惠函 your kind〔gracious〕 letter
호 with a blow〔puff〕 ―하다 blow
호 戶 a house ; a door ; family ¶ 50호 fifty housed〔families〕 // 가가 호호 from door to door
호 壕 [참호] a trench ; [방공호] an underground air-raid shelter ; a dugout
호 湖 a lake ⇨ 호수(湖水)
미시간― Lake Michigan
호 號 ① [아호] a pen name ; a title (명칭) ② [번호] a number ; an issue ¶ 호를 다산이라고 부르는 작가 a writer with the pen name of *Dasan* // 제 14 호실 Room No. 14
일― number one 차― the next number〔issue〕
호― 好 good
―기회 a fine opportunity
호가 呼價 the price asked〔offered〕; a bid ―하다 ask〔bid, offer〕 a price《for》 ¶ 20원 비싸게 호가되다 be quoted twenty *won* higher
호가호위 狐假虎威 an ass in lion's skin
†호각 號角 a whistle ¶ 호각을 불다 blow a whistle
호각 互角 equality ; evenness ; par ; a good match ¶ 호각을 이루다 get even《with》// 호각의 형세이다 be well matched〔balanced〕 in strength〔power〕
호감 好感 good feeling ; goodwill ; a favorable〔good〕 impression ¶ 호감을 사다 win《a person's》 favor〔goodwill〕 // 호감을 주다 give〔make〕 a good impression ; impress《a person》 favorably // 그는 인간적이고 호감이 간다 He is human and likable.
호강 comfort ; luxury ; pomp ; pomposity ―하다 live in luxury〔comfort, clover〕; enjoy luxury ¶ 호강스러운 살림 a luxurious life ; a soft life
호객 呼客 [행위] touting ; [매춘의] a pander ―하다 tout ; solicit patronage
―군 a tout(er) ; a (hotel) runner《미》
호걸 豪傑 a hero ; a great〔gallant〕 man ; an extraordinary man ¶ 호걸스럽다 be heroic ; be gallant ; be brave ; be intrepid
― 남자 a heroic〔gallant〕 man ― 웃음 a broad〔a hearty, an open〕 laugh ―풍 a heroic〔gallant〕 air
호격 呼格 〖문법〗 the vocative case
호경기 好景氣 prosperous conditions ; good times ; a boom
― 시대 prosperous days ; good times ; a boom period 전쟁 ― a war boom
호곡 號哭 wailing ; weeping aloud ―하다 wail ; weep aloud ; bewail ; lament aloud ; cry bitterly
호과 胡瓜 a cucumber
호광 弧光 an arc light
―등 an arc lamp ―로(爐) an arc furnace ― 전압 arcing voltage
호구 好球 〖야구〗 a nice ball ¶ 호구를 놓치다 miss a nice ball
호구 戶口 the number of houses and families ; population
― 조사 census taking ; a census ¶ 호구 조사하다 take a census
호구 虎口 ① a tiger's mouth ; [비유적] the jaws of death ; danger ¶ 호구에 들어가다 get into a perilous place // 호구에서 벗어나다 escape from the jaws of death ; get out of danger ; escape with bare life ② [바둑의] a cross surrounded by three white〔black〕 stones
호구 糊口 [겨우 먹고 삶] bare livelihood ; [생활] living ; livelihood ; subsistence ―하다 make one's living ; gain a bare livelihood ; live from hand to mouth ; eke out a living ; keep the pot boiling ¶ 호구지책 a means of livelihood〔living〕; a way to make ends meet ; pot-boiling // 호구지책이 막연하다 have no means of livelihood ; find it difficult to make a living
호국 護國 defense of the fatherland ¶ 호국의 꽃으로 산화하다 die fighting gloriously for the country ; die a heroic death in action
호궁 胡弓 a Chinese fiddle
호기 好期 a good〔favorable〕 season ; a good〔right〕 time《of one's life》
호기 好機 a good〔golden, favorable〕 opportunity ; a favorable chance ; a good time〔occasion〕; a psychological moment ¶ 호기를 이용하다 take a advantage of an opportunity〔occasion〕; avail oneself of a good opportunity // 호기를 기다리다 wait and see ; gain time // 호기를 포착하다 seize〔take〕 an opportunity ; take the tide at the flood // 호기를 놓치다 miss〔loss, pass up, let slip, overlook, throw away〕 a golden opportunity ; miss〔let go, lose〕 a chance // 오랜 숙망을 달성하는 데 천재일우의 호기다 This is the time of all times to attain our long-cherished desire.
호기 豪氣 a heroic〔gallant〕 temper〔air〕; a sturdy〔an intrepid〕 spirit ; a stout heart ; bravery ; heroism ¶ 호기롭다 be heroic ; be brave ; be gallant ; be intrepid ; be plucky ; be stout-hearted

호기 부리다 (관용) display bravery ; swagger ; play the hero ; pose as a hero
호기 呼氣 expiration ; exhalation
— 검사 a breath test
호기성 好氣性 〖식물〗 aerotropism ¶ 호기성의 aerotropic ; aerobic
*호기심 好奇心 curiosity ; inquisitiveness ¶ 호기심에서 out of curiosity ; prompted〔impelled〕 by curiosity // 호기심이 강하다 be curious ; be full of curiosity ; be inquisitive // 호기심이 생기다 become curious ; feel curious // 호기심을 일으키다 arouse〔stimulate〕 one's curiosity // 호기심을 끌다 excite〔arouse〕 one's curiosity // 호기심을 만족시키다 gratify 〔satisfy〕 one's curiosity
호깨나무 a raisin tree ; Hovenia dulcis (학명)
호남 湖南 [지방] the *Honam* district 〔area〕 ; the *Cholla-do* provinces ; the southwestern part〔section〕 of Korea
— 고속도로 *Honam*〔*Taejon-Sunchon*〕 expressway —선 the *Honam*〔*Taejon-Mokpo*〕 (Railroad〔Railway〕) Line — 평야 the *Honam* plains
호남아 好男兒 [미남자] a handsome man ; a good-〔fine-〕looking man ; a man of great personal beauty ; [훌륭한 인물] a fine fellow
호녀 胡女 a Manchurian〔Chinese〕 woman ; a barbarian woman
호농 豪農 a wealthy farmer ; a rich farmer
호다 broad-stitch ; sew〔stitch〕 together
호담 豪膽 boldness ; dauntlessness ; a stout heart ; intrepidity ; fearlessness — 하다 (be) intrepid ; fearless ; dauntless ; daring ; plucky
호도 胡桃 a walnut ⇨ 호두
호도 糊塗 temporizing ; makeshift — 하다 patch up ; shuffle ; gloss over ; varnish ; temporize ¶ 호도지책 an expedient // 그는 결코 사실을 호도하지 않았다 He never glossed over the matter.
호도깝스럽다 (be) rash ; reckless ; unstable ; shaky
호도애 〖새〗 an eastern turtledove
호되다 (be) severe ; hard ; harsh ; violent ; cruel ; intense ; furious ¶ 호되게 severely ; violently ; furiously ; hard // 호된 일 hard〔heavy〕 work // 호된 추위 severe〔intense〕 cold // 호된 통증 an acute pain // 호된 경쟁 a cutthroat competition // 호된 형벌 a severe punishment // 호된 일을 겪다 have a bitter experience ; have a hard time of it // 호되게 꾸짖다 scold severely
*호두 a walnut ¶ 호두 까는 집게 nutcrackers // 호두를 까다 crack a walnut
—나무 a walnut tree —속 the kernel of a walnut ; very complicated stuff ; a maze —잠(簪) a jade hairpin with a walnut-shaped top
호두속 the kernel of a walnut ; [미궁(迷宮)] a maze ; a labyrinth
호드기 a reed pipe
호드득거리다 ① [튀는 소리] crackle ; pop ; snap ¶ 콩이 호드득거린다 Beans keep popping. // 숯불이 호드득거린다 The burning charcoal keeps snapping ② [사람이] act rashly ; be imprudent ; be frivolous
호드득호드득 ① [소리] popping ; crackling ; snapping ¶ 옥수수가 호드득호드득 튀다 corn keeps popping ② [방정] rashly ; imprudently
호들갑 떨다 be extravagant〔over excited〕 in speech ; be bubbling over ; be exuberant
호들갑스럽다 (be) abrupt and frivolous ; flippant ; rash ; imprudent ⇨ 호들갑 떨다 ¶ 호들갑스런 수작 flippant remarks // 호들갑스럽게 굴다 act hastily ; take a rash step ; act with no deliberation
호등 弧燈 an arc lamp〔light〕
호떡 胡— a Chinese stuffed pancake
호라지좆 〖식물〗 asparagus
호락질 single-handed farming —하다 farm single-handed
호락호락 easily ; readily ; yielding —하다 (be) ready ; easily manageable ; tractable ¶ 나는 호락호락 넘어가지 않는다 I won't let〔allow〕 myself to be taken in.
호란 胡亂 〖역사〗 a Manchu war
병자(丙子)— the Manchu war of 1636
호랑 虎狼 tigers and wolves ; wild beasts ; [사람] a brute ; a cruel person ¶ 호랑지심 a cruel mind〔heart〕
호랑나비 a large spotted butterfly
†호랑이 ① 〖동물〗 a tiger ; a tigress (암컷) ; the king of the jungle (별명) ¶ 호랑이 새끼 a cub // 호랑이 꼬리 밟는 심정으로 in fear and trembling
② [사람] a formidable〔fierce〕 person ; a tiger
—굴 a tiger's den
호랑이 굴에 가야 호랑이 새끼를 잡는다 (속담) Nothing venture, nothing have 〔win〕. /Nought venture, nought have.
호랑이가 굶으면 환관도 먹는다 (속담) Hungry dogs will eat dirty pudding.
호랑이도 제 말하면 온다 (속담) Talk of the devil, and he is bound to appear. / Talk of the devil, and he'll either come or send. /Talk of the devil, and he will appear.
호래아들 a boor ; a barbarian ; a rude 〔an ill-natured〕 person
호렴 胡— crude salt ; [천일염] bag salt ; sun-dried salt
호령 號令 a (word of) command ; an order ; a yell ; a shout —하다 command ; order ; give an order〔a com-

mand〕; dictate ; [호통하다] yell ; shout ; storm at ; call down ; scold vehemently ¶ 호령을 내리다 give a (word of) command // 천하에 호령하다 dictate to the whole world ; hold sway over the whole country // 부하를 호령하다 yell at one's subordinates

호례 好例 a good〔fine〕 example ; a good instance

호로딸기 葫蘆— 〖식물〗 a kind of berry

호로병 葫蘆瓶 a calabash ⇨ 호리병

호로파 葫蘆巴 〖식물〗 Trigonella

호롱 a kerosene lamp

호루라기 a whistle

호르르 [타는 소리] rapidly ; lightly ; [새가] flapping ; fluttering ; [호루라기의] whistling ; piping ¶ 호르르 타버리다 burn rapidly // 호르르 날아가다 fly with a flap of the wings // 호르르 불다 whistle ; pipe

*__호르몬__ hormone

남성〔여성〕 — the male〔female〕 sex hormone

호른 [악기] a horn

호리 a one-ox plow

—질 one-ox plowing ¶ 호리질하다 plow with a one-ox plow

호리 毫釐 the slightest degree ¶ 호리지차 the slightest difference〔deviation〕

—불차(不差) exactness ; lacking any difference

‡__호리다__ ① [홀리다] fascinate ; charm ; bewitch ; captivate ② [빼앗다] seduce ⇨ 후리다 ¶ 여자를 잘 호리는 남자 a woman-killer ; a Don Juan // 남자를 잘 호리는 여자 a vamp

호리병 葫—瓶 a calabash ; a gourd bottle

—박 〖식물〗 a bottle gourd

‡__호리호리하다__ (be) (tall and) willowy ; slender ; slim ⇨ 후리후리하다

호마 胡馬 a Manchurian horse

—유 sesame oil ; gingili

호마 胡麻 〖식물〗 sesame ; a gingili (plant) ; Sesamum orientale (학명) ; [씨] a sesame seed

호말 毫末 a minute particle ; the least thing ; [부사적] 《not》 in the least ; 《not》 a bit〔jot, whit〕 ; 《not》 in the slightest degree ; in no degree

호매 豪邁 dauntlessness ; valor ; intrepidity ; indomitableness **—하다** (be) undaunted ; dauntless ; indomitable ; intrepid ; brave ; valiant ; valorous ¶ 호매한 기상 an indomitable〔intrepid〕 spirit

호면 胡麵 Chinese noodles ⇨ 당면

호명 呼名 calling 《a person》 by name ; (a) roll call ; (a) call-over **—하다** call (over) the names

—자 a caller

호모 homo ; homosexual

호모 사피엔스 〖인류〗 Homo sapiens

호모초 護謨草 〖식물〗 a kind of goosefoot

호무 毫無 —하다 be not in the least ; be not at all ; be not a bit ¶ 그것에는 의심할 여지가 호무하다 There is not the faintest shadow of doubt about it.

호미 a weeding hoe

호미씻이 a feast〔break〕 in the middle of the agricultural season **—하다** have a hoe-washing break

호미자락 the lower part of a hoe blade ¶ 비가 호미자락만큼 오다 have a rain that soaks the soil an inch deep

*__호밀 胡—__ 〖식물〗 rye

호바늘꽃 胡— 〖식물〗 the Manchurian willowweed

*__호박__ 〖식물〗 a pumpkin ; a squash ¶ 호박 같은 여자 a plain〔an ill-favored〕 woman // 호박 같은 얼굴 a fat pumpkin face

—고지 dried slices of young pumpkin

—밭 a pumpkin plantation **—씨** a pumpkin seed

호박 琥珀 〖광물〗 amber ; succinite ¶ 호박의 amber-colored 《hair, skin》

—산 succinic acid **—색** amber (color) ; lime **—유** amber oil **—잠(簪)** an amber hairpin ; amberoid

호박개 〖동물〗 a stout hairy dog

호박벌 〖곤충〗 a carpenter bee

호반 虎班 the military nobility

호반 湖畔 a lake side ; the shores of a lake ¶ 호반의 lakeside ; by the lake // 호반의 호텔 a hotel on〔by〕 the lake ; a lakeside hotel // 호반을 소요하다 ramble along the shores of a lake

— 도시 a lake city **— 시인** (one of) the Lake Poets **—파** the Lake school

호반새 〖새〗 a kingfisher

호발 毫髮 the tiniest〔most minute〕 hair ; [비유적] a single iota ; [부사적] 《not》 a bit〔jot, whit〕 ; 《not》 in the slightest degree ¶ 호발부동(不動)하다 do not budge an inch ; don't move at all

호방 豪放 —하다 (be) large-〔broad-〕minded ; free〔open〕-hearted ; unaffected ; Bohemian

호배추 胡— a Chinese cabbage

호범꼬리 胡— 〖식물〗 the Manchurian bistort

호법 護法 [국법의] the defense of the constitution ; [종교의] the defense of a religion

호변 好辯 eloquence ; oratory ; fluency (달변)

—가 an eloquent speaker

호별 戶別 each house ; house-by-house ; house-to-house ; door-by-door ¶ 호별로 from house to house ; from door to door // 호별 방문을 하다 call 〔visit〕 from door to door ; make house-to-house call〔visit〕

— 방문 a house-to-house〔door-to-door〕 visit ; [선거의] a house-to-house

canvass —세 a house rate〔tax〕 — 조사 a house-to-house investigation〔census〕
호복 胡服 a Chinese garment〔gown〕
호봉 號俸 serial step ; salary step ¶ 10 호봉 the tenth-class salary
호봉 胡蜂 a (ground) wasp ⇨ 말벌
호부 豪富 a rich〔wealthy〕 person
호부 好否 likes and〔or〕 dislikes ; good and〔or〕 bad ¶ 호부간에 whether one likes it or not
호불호 好不好 likes and〔or〕 dislikes ⇨ 호부(好否)
호비수리 胡— 〖식물〗 the Manchurian bushclover
호비칼 a gouge ; a router
호사 好事 a happy event ; a good occasion ¶ 호사다마 Lights are usually followed by shadows. /There's always a slip between the cup and the lip.
—가 a busybody ; a go-getter ; a hustler
호사 豪奢 extravagance ; luxury ; sumptuousness ; magnificence —하다 live in clover ; luxuriate in ¶ 호사스럽다 be extravagant〔luxurious, sumptuous, magnificent, grand〕∥호사스러운 생활을 하다 live in great splendor
—바치 a fancy-pants ; a fancy dresser ; a dandy ; a fop
호산 呼算 [주판의] addition (and subtraction) of figures read (out) aloud
호상 互相 mutual ⇨ 상호
호상 豪商 a wealthy merchant〔businessman〕
호상 護喪 ① [사람] the funeral director ②[일] taking charge of〔directing〕 a funeral —하다 take charge of〔direct〕 a funeral
—소 the funeral-director's (office) —차지 the funeral director
호상 湖上 ¶ 호상의 on〔in〕 the lake
— 가옥 a lake dwelling — 생활자 a lake dweller
호상 好喪 a propitious mourning (of a person dying old and rich)
호색 好色 sensuality ; amorousness ; lewdness ; lasciviousness ; licentiousness ; lust ; eroticism —하다 be fond of sex ; (be) sensual ; lustful ; wanton ; lascivious ; lewd
—가〔한〕 a lewd〔lascivious〕 man ; a sensualist ; a lecher ; a Don Juan ; a satyr — 문학 pornographic〔obscene〕 literature ; pornography —증 〖병리〗 erotomania
호생 互生 〖식물〗 growing in alternation ¶ 호생의 alternate
—엽 alternate leaves
호생지덕 好生之德 the grace of sparing a life by pardoning a condemned person
호선 互先 ¶ 호선으로 두다 〖바둑〗 have the first move in alternate games
— 바둑 an unhandicapped match of *badook*
호선 互選 mutual election —하다 elect by mutual vote ; elect from among themselves ; elect upon a mutual basis ¶ 의장은 의원 중에서 호선되었다 The chairman was elected by the committee from among its members
— 의원 a member elected by mutual vote — 자격 qualification for mutual election — 투표 mutual vote
호선 弧線 an arc ; a crescent-shaped line
호성적 好成績 good grades 《in one's studies》 ; good 《business》 results 〔showing〕 ¶ 호성적을 올리다 obtain〔gain〕 good〔excellent〕 results
†**호소 呼訴** an appeal ; a petition ; a complaint (불평) —하다 appeal 《to》 ¶ 이성에 호소하다 appeal to one's reason ∥국민에게 호소하다 appeal to the people〔nation〕
호소 湖沼 lakes and marshes ¶ 호소의 lacustrine
—학 limnology
호송 護送 escort ; convoy —하다 escort ; convoy ; remove 《a person》 under due escort ; [수인을] send 《a person》 under guard 《to a prison》 ¶ 호송하에 under escort of 《a warship》∥수송선을 호송하다 convoy transports
—선 a convoy ship —차 a prison van ; a patrol wagon ; a Black Maria
†**호수 湖水** a lake ¶ 호숫가에 있는 호텔 a hotel on the lake ; a lakeside hotel
호수 戶數 the number of houses〔families〕
호수 好手 [바둑·장기의] a good move
호수 號數 number ; a register〔serial〕 number ¶ 호수를 거듭하다 go through 〔run into〕 several editions
집— the number of a house
호스 a hose ; a hosepipe
소방 — a fire hose
⁑**호스텔** a hostel
유스— a youth hostel
호스트 a host
호스티스 a hostess ; [여급] a barmaid
호승지벽 好勝之癖 love of beating others ; a competitive spirit
호시절 好時節 a nice〔good〕 season 〔time〕 ; a favorable season ; the prime of 《youth》
호시탐탐 虎視眈眈 —하다 glare at ; be vigilantly hostile ; keep a vigilant eye 《on a person》 ; watch for an opportunity〔chance〕 ; seek eagerly for 《a position》 ¶ 호시탐탐히 with vigilant hostility ; gloatingly
호신 護身 self-protection ; self-defense ; self-preservation —하다 protect oneself ; defend oneself ; preserve oneself ¶ 호신용으로 for self-protection ; for

use in self-defense
—도 a sword for self-protection〔for one's own protection〕 —부(符) an amulet《carried on oneself》; a talisman《*pl.* ~s》《against traffic accidents》 —술 the art of self-defense
호심 湖心 the heart〔center〕 of a lake
호심경 護心鏡 a breast-plate
호안 好顔 a happy face ; a bright look
호안 護岸 protecting the banks ; an embankment ; [해안의] a sea wall 〔bank〕
— 공사 shore〔bank〕 protection works ; embankment ; bank revetment
호양 互讓 mutual concession〔conciliation〕; compromise ; give and take —하다 make a mutual concession ; compromise ¶ 호양 정신에 입각하여 based on the spirit of compromise // 호양적 정신을 가지고 in a conciliatory〔compromising〕 spirit ; in a give-and-take spirit
호언 豪言 big〔tall〕 talk ; boasting ; a rant ; a bombast ; fancy〔high-flown〕 words —하다 talk big ; talk bombastically〔boastfully〕; brag ; rant ; boast ; vaunt
—장담 big talk ; boasting
호언 好言 kind words ; nice words
호역 虎疫 ⇨ 콜레라
호연 好演 a good acting ; an excellent performance《of a play》 —하다 put up a good show
호연 皓然 ① [흰모양] pure〔snow〕 white —하다 (be) clear ; patent ② [명백한 모양] clearly ; patently —하다 (be) clear ; patent
호연 浩然 vastness ; magnanimity —하다 (be) vast ; magnanimous ¶ 호연지기를 기르다 revive one's exhausted 〔spent〕 energy ; refresh〔recreate〕 oneself《with》; enliven one's spirits
호열자 虎列剌 cholera ¶ 호열자가 발생〔만연, 유행〕하다 an epidemic of cholera breaks out〔spreads, prevails〕
—균 a cholera germ〔bacterium, bacillus〕 —예방주사 the anticholera serum ¶ 호열자 예방주사를 맞다 have a shot 《in the arm》 against cholera ; inoculate 《a person》 against cholera — 환자 a cholera patient ; a case of cholera 의사 — suspected〔quasi-〕 cholera 진성 — malignant〔epidemic〕 cholera ; a genuine case of cholera
호오 好惡 one's likes and dislikes ; fancy ¶ 호오를 몹시 가리다 be very partial〔unjust〕《to》
호외 戶外 the open air ; the open ¶ 호외의 open-air ; outdoor ; outside // 호외에서 in the open air ; out of doors ; outdoors ; under the open sky ; outside
— 생활〔운동〕 outdoor life〔sports〕
호외 號外 an extra (edition)《of a newspaper》; a special ¶ 호외로 보도하다 announce《an event》 in an extra // 「호외요」라고 외치다 shout extras
호우 豪雨 a heavy rain〔rainfall〕; a torrential rain ; a downpour ; a cloudburst ; cataracts of rain ; a drencher 《속》
— 주의보 torrential〔heavy〕 rain warning 집중 — a local downpour
호운 好運 good fortune ; (good) luck ; propitious fate ; a lucky〔good〕 break 《미》 ⇨ 행운
†호위 護衛 guard ; escort ; [군함·군대가] convoy (집단적) —하다 guard ; escort ; convoy《a ship, supplies》 ¶ 경관의 호위하에 under police escort // 호위를 두다 place《a person》 under escort 〔guard〕
—병 a guard ; a military escort ; a bodyguard — 순경 a policeman on guard ; a police escort —함〔선〕 a convoy
호유 豪遊 extravagant merrymaking ; an orgy —하다 take to〔indulge in〕 extravagant merrymaking ; have〔go on〕 a great spree
호음 豪飮 heavy〔deep〕 drinking ; a carouse ; a drinking orgy〔spree〕 —하다 drink heavily〔deep, hard〕; carouse ; swill ; soak《미·구》
호읍 號泣 wailing ; lamentation ; moaning —하다 wail ; weep〔cry〕 aloud ; lament ; moan
호응 呼應 ① [서로 부름] hailing (to) each other —하다 hail (to) each other ② [기맥 상통] acting in concert ; response ; unison —하다 act in concert〔unison〕《with》; respond《to》; in cooperation《with》; in collusion 《with》 (공모) // 육해공군이 서로 호응하여 적을 공격했다 Land, sea and air forces attacked the enemy in concert. ③ 〖문법〗 concord ; agreement ¶ 시제의 호응 sequence of tenses
†호의 好意 [선의] goodwill ; good wishes ; [우의] friendliness ; [친절] kindness ; favor ; [알선] good offices ; courtesy ¶ 호의적 friendly ; well-meaning ; warm-hearted ; benevolent ; kind ; kindly // 호의의 충고 well-meant advice // 호의적 해결 an amicable settlement // 호의로 by〔through〕 the kindness〔courtesy, good offices〕《of》// 호의를 가지고 with good intentions // 호의에 감사하다 thank《a person》 for his kindness ; extend〔offer〕 one's thanks for《another's》 kindness ; appreciate the good offices done by another // 호의에 보답하다 return《a person's》 favor 《by》// 호의를 가지다 feel〔entertain〕 goodwill《toward》; be friendly《to》; be favorably disposed《to, toward》;

mean well〔kindly〕《to, by》// 호의를 보이다 show a friendly feeling 《for》; show a feeling of amity 《toward》// 호의를 거절하다 reject 《a person's》 kind intentions ; decline 《a person's》 kind offer // 호의를 무시하다 disregard〔ignore〕《a person's》 goodwill〔kind offer〕

호의 好誼 good〔close, warm, fast〕friendship

호의호식 好衣好食 dressing well and faring richly ; living in clover **—하다** dress well and fare richly ; live well

호인 好人 a good(-natured) person ; a good〔nice〕 fellow ; a nice chap ; a good and honest fellow

호인 胡人 a Manchurian ; a barbarian (야만인)

호장 虎杖 〖식물〗 a Korean knotweed ; a polygonaceous plant

호장 豪壯 ① [호화] splendor ; grandeur ; magnificence ② [호담] vigorousness ; boldness ; bravery **—하다** (be) grand ; splendid ; magnificent ; vigorous ; bold ; brave

호재료 好材料 good material ; excellent data ; 〖증권〗 favorable〔strong〕 indications

호저 豪豬 〖동물〗 a porcupine

호적 戶籍 [등록] census registration ; [호적부] a census register ; a family register ¶ 호적에 싣다 have one's name entered〔listed〕 in the census register〔record〕// 호적을 조사하다 check up one's family register // 호적에는 양자로 되어 있다 He is registered as an adopted son.

—계 a registrar **— 등(초)본** a copy〔an abstract〕 of one's family register **—리(吏)** an official in charge of family registration ; a census official **—법** the Family Register Law **—부** a family register **— 수수료** the family registration fee ; a fee for family registration **— 증명서** a family-register certificate ; one's identity paper〔card〕

호적 胡笛 a kind of clarinet ⇨ 날라리

호적 號笛 a whistle ; a hooter ; a horn ; a siren ¶ 호적을 불다 hoot ; whistle

호적 好適 **—하다** (be) suitable ; fit ; good ; best ; ideal ¶ 스키의 호적지 an ideal〔the best〕 place for skiing // 주말을 보내기에는 호적지이다 It is a good place to stay in for the weekend〔stay over the weekend〕.

—지(地) an ideal place 《for》

호적수 好敵手 a good rival〔match〕; a good〔worthy〕 opponent ; one's closest rival ¶ 호적수를 만나다 meet one's match // 호적수가 나타났다 A noticeable rival came up. /We found a good rival 《in our trade》. /We found our match.

***호전 好戰** warmongering ; militarism ; bellicosity ; belligerence ; a pro-war inclination ¶ 호전적 belligerent ; bellicose ; warlike ; pro-war ; militaristic // 호전적 민족 a warlike race // 호전적 언사를 쓰다 employ〔use〕 warlike language

—가 a warlover **—국** a warlike country

호전 好轉 a favorable turn〔move〕; a turn〔change〕 for the better ; improvement ; a rally ; pickup **—하다** improve ; take a favorable turn ; change〔take a turn〕 for the better ¶ 식량 사정의 호전 improvement in the food situation // 국면이 호전하고 있다 The tables are turning in our favor. // 경기가 호전하고 있다 Business is looking up〔picking up〕. // 경제가 호전되고 있다 보십니까 Do you think the economy is picking up?

호접 蝴蝶 〖곤충〗 a butterfly

호젓하다 [쓸쓸하다] (be) lonely ; desolate ; solitary ; lonesome ; [고요하다] quiet ; still ; silent ; hushed ; deserted ¶ 호젓한 거리 a deserted〔hushed, still〕 street // 호젓한 산길 a lonely mountain path

호정 戶庭 a front yard ; a courtyard

— 출입 [노인·환자] moving around in the yard ¶ 호정 출입을 못하다 be confined to bed

호정 糊精 〖화학〗 dextrin(e)

호조 戶曹 〖옛제도〗 the Ministry of Finance

호조 好調 being in good condition〔shape〕; a favorable tone〔tendency, trend〕; favorableness ; satisfactoriness ¶ 호조의 good ; favorable ; satisfactory ; improved ; promising // 호조이다 be in good condition〔form, shape〕; be in the pink 《of health》// 호조를 보이다 take a favorable turn ; turn for the better ; show a favorable tendency

호족 豪族 a powerful family〔clan〕

호졸근하다 [옷 따위가] (be) limp ; be wet enough to lose starch ; (be) droop ; [몸이] (be) limp with exhaustion ; (be) tired ; droop ¶ 옷이 이슬에 젖어 호졸근하다 one's clothes get wet with dew and lose their starch // 피로해서 몸이 호졸근하다 be tired out ; droop with fatigue ⇨ 후줄근하다

호종 胡種 a person of a thing from Manchuria ; the Manchurian origin

호종 扈從 attendance **—하다** attend on 《a dignitary》; be in attendance on 《the king》

—자 [한명] an attendant ; a follower ; [전체] a train of attendants ; a suite

호주 戶主 the head of a family ; the master of a house ; a householder ¶ 호주와의 관계 relation to the head of a family

—권 the right to be the head of a family ; the birthright **— 상속권** the right of succeeding (to) 《a person》 as the head of a family ─ 상속인 the heir(ess)

호주 濠洲 (the Commonwealth of) Australia ¶ 호주(산)의 Australian
─ 사람 an Australian

호주 豪酒 heavy drinking ; [사람] a heavy drinker

호주 好酒 love of liquor ─하다 be fond of liquor ; like to drink
─객 a 《heavy》 drinker

†호주머니 a pocket ¶ 호주머니에 손을 넣고 with one's hands (buried) in the pockets // 호주머니가 두둑하다 have a long〔heavy〕 purse // 호주머니가 비다 have a cold purse // 호주머니 사정이 좋다 have a heavy purse ; be in cash 〔funds〕 // 호주머니 사정이 나쁘다 be short of money ; have a light purse
조끼 ─ a vest pocket

호지 胡地 Manchuria ; a savage land

호지 護持 [보호] defense ; protection ; [부지] retention ─하다 [지키다] defend ; protect ; [부지하다] uphold ; retain

호초 胡椒 black pepper ⇨ 후추

호출 呼出 a call ; a calling out ; a summons ; a subpoena (법원의) ─하다 call ; call out ; summon(s) ; 〖법〗 cite ; summon ¶ 급하시면 무선 호출기로 불러 보시지요 If it's urgent, you may wish to call him through his beeper.
─료 the fee for a summons ─ 부호 a call sign ─장 a (writ of) summons 〔subpoena〕 자동 ─ an automatic calling

호치 皓齒 clean-white〔pearly〕 teeth

호치키스 a stapler ; a Hotchikiss (paper-fastener)

호칭 互稱 the name〔title〕 that each calls the other ; mutual designations
─ 도수 〖전화〗 (the number of) calls
─료 the fee for summons ; [전화의] a call fee ; the fee for a call ─ 부호 〖무전〗 a call sign ; call letters ─장 a (writ of) summons 《*pl.* ~es》 ; a subpoena 자동 ─ an automatic calling 즉시 ─ [전자계산기의] random〔rapid〕 access

호칭 呼稱 a name ; a title ; a designation ; an appellation ─하다 call ; name ; designate

호콩 胡─ a peanut ⇨ 땅콩

호쾌 豪快 ─하다 (be) exciting ; stirring ; animating ; heroic 《attempt》 ¶ 호쾌한 인물 a large-hearted man

호크 a hook ; a snap hook ¶ 호크로 채우다 hook up 《a dress》

호타 好打 〖야구〗 a good〔nice〕 hit ─하다 make a good〔nice〕 hit ; swat
─자 a good〔nice〕 hitter

호타순 好打順 the best part of the batting order

호탕 豪宕 grandeur ; magnanimity ─하다 (be) magnanimous ; large-minded

호탕 浩蕩 being vast〔boundless, broad-minded〕

†호텔 a hotel ¶ 호텔 생활을 하다 make one's home in a hotel // 호텔에 묵다 stay at a hotel ; check in 《미》 (숙박비를 물고 호텔을 나오는 것을 check out이라 함) // 호텔을 경영하다 run a hotel
─ 보이 a bellboy 《미》 ; a page boy 《영》 ─업자 a hotelman ─ 경영자 a hotelkeeper ☞ ◖ p. 2375 ◗

호통 hurling words of thunder ─하다 hurl words of thunder at ; rage〔rave〕 at ; call down ; scold vehemently ; storm at ; bawl 《a person》 out
─바람 《at the instigation of》 the yell or shout ¶ 주인 호통바람에 혼이 나다 be startled at the yell of one's master

호투 好投 〖야구〗 clean〔fine〕 pitching 〔delivery〕 ─하다 pitch well〔a good pitch〕

호패 號牌 [옛제도] an identity tag

호평 好評 favorable criticism ; a favorable comment〔reception, opinion〕 ; public favor ─하다 criticize〔comment on〕 favorably ; give a favorable reception to ; receive well〔favorably〕 ¶ 호평이다 be popular 《with students》 ; be highly〔favorably〕 spoken of ; enjoy 〔gain, win〕 popularity // 호평을 받다 be favorably commented upon ; meet with public approval ; gain public favor ; be given a favorable reception // 그 영화는 호평을 받았다 The film is being well received by its audiences.
대─ great public favor

호포 號砲 a signal gun ¶ 호포를 쏘다 fire a signal gun

호풍 胡風 ① [풍속] Manchurian〔barbarous〕 customs ② [바람] the north wind

호프 (a) hope ; a youth of promise ¶ 우리 학교의 호프 the hope of our school

호피 虎皮 a tiger skin〔fur〕
─ 방석 a tiger-skin cushion〔rug〕

호학 好學 love of learning ; intellectual thirst ; philomathy ─하다 be fond of〔love〕 learning

호한 好漢 a fine〔nice〕 fellow ; a jolly fellow ; a nice guy

호한 浩瀚 voluminousness ; bulkiness ─하다 (be) extensive ; voluminous ; bulky

호항 湖港 a lake harbor

호헌 운동 護憲運動 a Constitution protection movement ; a movement for safeguarding constitutional government〔for the defense of the Constitution〕

호혈 虎穴 a tiger's den ¶ 호혈에 들어가

호 텔

① 종류

▶비즈니스맨용 호텔 (traveling) businessman's hotel; (low-)budget hotel/일류 호텔 first(-rate, -class) hotel; top notch hotel/호화 호텔 deluxe hotel/최고급 호텔 five-star hotel/단기 체류 관광객용 호텔 transient hotel/관광과 휴양용 호텔 resort hotel/장기 체류자용 호텔 residential hotel/휴양지의 호텔 apartment hotel

▶모텔 motel (★자동차 여행객용)/유스호스텔 (youth) hostel/(유럽의) 장기 체류자용 하숙풍 호텔 pension/(영국의) 민박풍 호텔 guesthouse/간이 숙박소 B & B(a Bed and Breakfast)《영》; flop house 《미》 (★주로 남자 전용의 불결한 시설의)/여인숙 inn

② 객실·내부

▶1인실 single(-bedded) room/(더블 베드의) 2인실 double room (★싱글 베드가 두 개 있는 것은 twin(-bedded) room)

▶목욕실 bath/수세식 변소 flush toilet/샤워 shower/욕조 bathtub/수하물 보관소 suitcase rack/임시 침대 extra bed; rollaway bed

▶호화 객실 suite (★침실, 거실 등 2개 이상의 방으로 구성되어 있다. 방 개수에 따라서 three-room suite, four-room suite로 쓴다. 호텔 바깥쪽에 면하여 전망 좋은 방은 outside room, 안쪽에 있는 방은 inside room. 보통 outside room이 더 상등급에 속한다.)

▶로비 lobby/식당 restaurant/경식당 coffee shop/연회실 banquet hall/나이트클럽 nightclub

③ 예약

▶예약 reservation/예약 재확인 reconfirmation/예약 취소 cancel; cancellation/예약계 reservation clerk/회계 cashier/객실계 room clerk

▶프론트 front desk; reception/프론트계 front desk clerk/숙박 수속 registration/체크인 check-in (★등록을 하고 키를 받아서 방을 사용하기까지의 전 과정을 가리킴.)/체크아웃 check-out (★계산을 하고 호텔을 나가는 것.)

④ 요금

▶숙박 요금 hotel rate[charge] (★영국에서는 EP(European Plan)이라고 하여 숙박료에 식대는 포함시키지 않는다. 미국의 1박 3식 포함의 AP(American Plan)는 관광지의 호텔(resort hotel)을 제외하고는 거의 없다. 간단한 아침 식사 요금을 포함시키는 것은 CP(Continental Plan)이라고 한다.)/1박 2식 숙박 요금 MAP(Modified American Plan)/2식 포함 숙박 요금 hotel rate[charge] with breakfast and dinner included/숙박료 청구서 bill/팁 tip

⑤ 서비스

▶보이 bellboy; bellhop 《미》; page boy《영》; buttons/포터 porter

▶서비스료 service charge/잡요금 miscellaneous[incidental] charge/서비스부 the valet service (★세탁·구두닦이 등 투숙객의 편의를 돌보아 주는 부서)/룸서비스 room service/웨이터 waiter/웨이트리스 waitress/메이드 chambermaid; maid (★청소나 침대 정리를 하는 여성)/교환원 operator

⑥ 표현

¶ 호텔 예약을 하여 주시겠습니까? Will you arrange[make] (for) my hotel reservations? (★여행사에 의뢰시) // 호텔 예약을 하고 싶습니다. — 예, 알겠습니다. 어느 호텔로 해드릴까요? I'd like to make my hotel reservations. — Certainly, sir. Which hotel would you like? // 1인실로 할까요, 2인실로 할까요? — 1인실로 하겠습니다. Would you like a single (room) or a twin [double]? — I'd like a single. // 요금은 얼마입니까? 1박에 3만원입니다. What's (room) rate? — Thirty thousand won per night. // 그 방에 목욕실도 있습니까? Does the room have a bath? // 좋습니다. 1인실로 예약해 주십시오. That's fine. Will you reserve a single there? // 며칠 동안 묵으실 겁니까? How long [How many nights] are you going to stay (there)? // 내가 예약을 확인할 필요가 있겠습니까? Do I have to confirm my reservation?

¶ 체크아웃 시간은 언제입니까? When [What] is the check-out time? (★보통 오전 10부터 오후 2시 사이이며 그때를 초과하면 추가 요금을 지불하여야 한다.) // 오늘밤 [4월 20일 수요일] 1박 하고 싶은데 빈방 있습니까? I'd like a room for tonight [Wednesday, April 20]. Is there a vacancy[vacant room]? / I'd like to stay at your hotel tonight [on Wednesday, April 20]. Do you have a vacancy [vacant room; room available]? // 1인실은 모두 차있지만 2인실이라면 비어있습니다. All our singles[single rooms] are filled up [taken, occupied] now, but we could let you have a twin. // 이 방은 얼마에 묵을 수 있습니까? — 목욕탕이 딸리지 않은 2인실은 2만원이고, 딸린 방은 3만원입니다. How much is the room? — A double room with no [without a] bath is 20,000 won. With bath, 30,000 won. // 10퍼센트의 서비스료가 청구서에 포함되어 있습니다. A ten percent service charge will be added to your bill. // 내 이름은 존 스미스라고 합니다. 방을 예약해 두었습니다. — 이 숙박계 좀 작성해 주십시오. 3일동안 묵으실 겁니까? My name is John Smith. I have a reservation. — Will you please fill out this registration card? You're going to stay for three nights? // 좋습니다. 이렇게 하면 되겠습니까? — 감사합니다. That's right. Will this do? [Here you are.] — Thank you, sir. // 식사 시간은 언제입니까? — 아침 식사는 7시부터 9시, 점심은 11시부터 2시, 저녁 식사는 5시부터 9시까지입니다. What [When] are the mealtimes? — Breakfast is from seven to nine, lunch from eleven to two, and dinner from five to nine. // 방은 517호실입니다. 보이가 방까지 안내하여 드릴 것입니다. Your room is No. 517. The bellboy here will show you to your room. // 이 호텔에서는 팁이 필요없습니다. Tipping is unnecessary in[at] this hotel. // 보이에게 5,000원의 팁을 주었다. I tipped the bellboy 5,000 won.

다 put one's head into the lion's mouth ; tread on the tail of a lion // 호혈에서 벗어나다 escape from the jaws of death // 호혈에 들어가야 범을 잡는다 Nothing ventures, nothing has〔gets, wins, gains〕. /He who would search for pearls must dive deep.

호협 豪俠 chivalrousness ; gallantry ; bravery **—하다** (be) chivalrous ; gallant ; brave ; valiant

호형 弧形 an arc (form, shape)

호형호제 呼兄呼弟 close friendship **—하다** call each other brother ; be intimate with each other ; be good friends

호혜 互惠 reciprocity ; mutual benefits **— 관세율** a reciprocal〔bargaining〕 tariff **— 무역 협정** a fair〔reciprocal〕 trade agreement **— 조약** a reciprocal treaty ; a treaty of reciprocity **—주의** reciprocity (principle) ; a principle of reciprocity **— 통상〔무역〕** reciprocal trading〔trade〕

호호¹ blowing and blowing ; puff-puff **—하다** blow and blow ; puff and puff ¶ 추워서 손을 호호 불다 blow on one's hands to keep them warm

호호² ho ! ho ! ¶ 호호 웃다 smile ; giggle

호호 戶戶 house after house ; door-to-door ; every house〔door, family〕

호호 浩浩 (being) vast ; boundless **—하다** (be) vast ; boundless ¶ 호호탕탕 vast

호호 皓皓 white ; bright ; clean **—하다** (be) white ; bright ; clean

호호백발 皓皓白髮 hoary hair

호호탕탕하다 浩浩蕩蕩— (be) vast boundless ; endless ; immense

‡**호화 豪華** splendor ; pomp ; gorgeousness ; magnificence ; extravagance ¶ 호화롭다 be splendid ; be deluxe ; be pompous ; be gorgeous ; be most luxurious ; be sumptuous《volumes》// 호화찬란하다 be gorgeous ; be brilliant ; be dazzling ; be sumptuous // 호화로운 저택 a palatial mansion // 거참 호화판이로군 This is really wonderful. **—선** a de luxe〔luxury, palatial〕 liner ; a luxury ship **— 제본** luxury binding **—판** an edition de luxe ; a de luxe edition《미》; a sumptuous volume

호환 虎患 a disaster caused by tigers ; the ravages of tigers

호황 好況 a prosperous condition ; a favorable aspect ; prosperity ; a boom ; a brisk market (시황) ¶ 호황이다 be prosperous ; be in a prosperous condition ; boom《미》; be in good demand (매매가) // 호황을 보이다 show signs of prosperity ; present a favorable aspect **— 시대** prosperous days〔times〕 ; boom days《미》; flush times

†**호흡 呼吸** ① [숨] breath ; breathing ; respiration **—하다** breathe ; respire ; draw one's breath ¶ 호흡이 곤란하다 have difficulty in breathing ; breathe with difficulty ; breathe hard ; labor for breath // 호흡을 세다 count the respirations // 심호흡을 하다 draw a deep breath ; take deep breaths ; breathe deep // 코로 호흡을 하다 breathe through the nose ② [장단] tune ; time ; rhythm ¶ 호흡을 맞추다 keep time《with》; beat time **— 곤란(困難)** difficulty in breathing ; difficult breathing ; laboring breath ; dyspn(o)ea **—기** a respiratory organ **—기능** respiratory function **—력** inhaling capacity **— 색소〔열〕**〖식물〗 a respiration pigment〔heat〕 **무—〔— 정지〕**〖의학〗 apn(o)ea **심—** deep breathing **복식 —** abdominal breathing **인공 —** artificial respiration **— 중추** the respiratory center

‡**혹¹** a wen ; a lump (타박으로) ; a swell-

ing ; a tumor ; a bump ; an excrescence ; a protuberance ; an outgrowth ; a hump (낙타의) ; [나무의] a knot 《on a tree》; a knob ; a node ¶ 혹을 떼다 cut away a wen // 혹이 가라앉다 a bump subsides

혹 떼러 갔다가 혹 붙여 온다 속담 Many go out for Wool and come home shorn.

혹² ① [마시는 모양] with a breath〔gulp〕 **—하다** gulp ¶ 한숨에 혹 들이마시다 drink 《it》 down in one gulp ② [입김소리] with a puff **—하다** puff ¶ 혹 불어 끄다 puff out

혹 或 ① [혹시] maybe ; perhaps ; possibly ; probably ; by chance ¶ 혹 그럴는지 모른다 It may be so. /It is not impossible. // 혹 오늘 안올지 모른다 He may possibly not come today. ② [혹간] sometimes ; at times ; rarely ¶ 혹 틈이 있으면 책을 읽는다 I read books once in a while when I have time. ③ [또는] or ; or else ; either... or ¶ 편지를 내든 혹은 전보를 치든 해야 한다 You must either cable or write to him. ④ [혹자] some (people) ¶ 혹은 붉고 혹은 검다 Some are red, others black. // 혹은 그렇게 말한다 Some people say so.

혹간 或間 sometimes ⇨ 간혹

혹닉 惑溺 indulgence ; addiction **—하다** indulge in ; be addicted〔given〕 to 《drinking》 ¶ 주색에 혹닉하다 be addicted to sensual pleasures

혹독 酷毒 severity ; harshness **—하다** (be) severe ; harsh ; rigorous ¶ 혹독한 추위 severely cold weather // 이번 부장은 부하를 혹독하게 다루는 것으로 유명한 것 같다 It seems our new boss has a reputation for coming down hard on the people under him.

혹란 惑亂 bewilderment ; confusion **—하다** (be) bewildered ; confused ¶ 혹란케하다 bewilder ; confuse ; turn 《a person's》 brain

혹렬 酷烈 severity ; intensity ; extremity **—하다** (be) severe ; intense ; harsh ; rigorous

혹부리 a wenny man

혹사 酷使 driving hard ; abuse ; exploitation **—하다** work 《a person》 hard ; drive 《a person》 hard ; overdrive 《oneself》; keep〔hold, put〕 《a person's》 nose to the grindstone ; order about〔around〕 ¶ 혹사하는 사람 a hard master // 혹사 당하는 노동자 downtrodden workers // 두뇌를 혹사하다 overtax one's brain // 하인을 혹사하다 drive one's servants too hard ; sweat one's servants // 어린애들을 혹사해서는 안된다 Children shall not be exploited. // 부장은 그녀를 혹사한다 The boss orders her around. /The boss has her wrapped around his little finger. /The boss got her under his thumb.

혹사 酷似 a striking resemblance ; close affinity ; a close likeness **—하다** resemble closely ; bear a close resemblance〔a strong likeness〕 《to》; be the counterpart of 《the original》; be the very picture of 《one's father》; be a copy of

혹살 [쇠고기의] beef round ; round of beef

혹서 酷暑 intense〔severe, torrid〕 heat ¶ 혹서의 계절 the hot season ; the hottest weather // 혹서에 견디다 stand the heat of summer

혹설 或說 one opinion ; a certain view〔theory〕

혹성 惑星 〖천문〗 a planet ; a primary (위성을 가진) ⇨ 유성

— 로켓 an interplanetary rocket **—상성운** a planetary nebula **— 운동〔환류〕** planetary motion〔circulation〕 **대〔소〕—** a major〔minor〕 planet **외〔내〕—** a superior〔an inferior〕 planet

혹세 무민 惑世誣民 —하다 seduce the public ; delude〔deceive〕 the people

혹시 或是 ① [때로는] sometimes ; once in a while ; rarely ¶ 4월에도 혹시 눈이 오는 수가 있다 It sometimes snows in April. ② [아마] maybe ; perhaps ; possibly ; probably ¶ 혹시 김군을 아십니까 Do you happen to know *Mr. Kim*?

혹신 惑信 misguided〔fatuous〕 belief **—하다** misguidedly〔fatuously〕 believe

혹심 酷甚 being extreme〔severe〕 **—하다** (be) extreme ; severe ¶ 혹심한 벌 a cruel〔severe〕 punishment // 혹심한 피해를 입다 suffer heavy losses

혹애 惑愛 dotage ; infatuation **—하다** dote upon ; be infatuated with ; love 《a person》 to idolatry

혹야 或也 ⇨ 혹시(或是)

혹열 酷熱 brutal heat ⇨ 혹서

혹염 酷炎 intense heat ⇨ 혹서

혹왈 或曰 some say ; ... others say ; it is said

혹위 —胃 [소 따위의] a paunch ; a rumen

혹자 或者 ① [사람] someone ; a certain person ② [혹시] maybe ; perhaps

혹평 酷評 severe〔harsh, bitter, sharp〕 criticism ; a cruel remark ; scathing〔slashing, vitriolic〕 criticism ; strictures ; hypercriticism **—하다** sharply〔bitterly, severely〕 criticize ; speak bitterly of 《a person》; pass strictures 《on》; say harsh things about 《an opposition party》 to pieces ; hypercriticize ; pound〔beat, score〕 《a person》 like anything 《미》 ¶ 저서가 혹평을 받다 be subjected to severe criticism

—가 a severe〔bitter, sharp〕 critic ; a hypercritic

혹하다 惑— ① [반하다] be infatuated with 《a woman》; be captivated〔fascinated〕 by 《a woman's beauty》; be gone on 《a girl》; be charmed ¶ 아름다움에 혹하다 be smitten with 《a person's》 charms; fall a victim to 《a person's》 charms ② [환락에] indulge 《in》; be addicted 《to》; abandon oneself 《to》 ③ [사도에] be deluded; be misled; be led into error; be trapped ¶ 무당의 말에 혹하다 be deluded by a shaman's predictions

혹한 酷寒 severe〔intense, bitter〕 cold; the depth of winter; a hard〔severe〕 winter ¶ 혹한지절에 when we are in the coldest season; in these days of midwinter // 혹한에 견디다 endure〔stand〕 the intense cold

혹형 酷刑 a severe punishment〔penalty〕 **—하다** punish severely; inflict a severe punishment 《on》

혹혹 [마심] with gulp after gulp; [불다] puffing and puffing

혹화 酷禍 a dire〔terrible, horrible, cruel〕 disaster〔calamity〕

혼 魂 a soul (넋); a spirit (정신); a ghost (혼령) ¶ 아버지의 혼 the ghost of one's father // 혼나간 몸 a body without a soul; an absent-minded person // 혼이 떠나다 the spirit〔soul〕 departs the body

혼가 婚家 a family that has a wedding reception

혼가 婚嫁 marriage ⇨ 혼인

혼겁 魂怯 extreme astonishment **—하다** be scared〔terrified〕 out of one's wits

혼곤 昏困 —하다 (be) languid; faint; drowsy

혼구 婚具 a wedding outfit

혼기 婚期 marriageable age ¶ 혼기에 달한 딸 a marriageable daughter〔girl〕 // 혼기가 되다 be of marriageable age // 혼기가 넘다 be past the marriageable age; become an old maid // 혼기를 잃다 lose〔miss〕 a chance of marriage

혼나다 ① [놀라다] get frightened out of one's wits; become startled; [무서워하다] be horrified〔appalled〕; be scared ¶ 도적은 개가 짖어 혼나서 달아났다 The burglar was frightened away by the barking of the dog. ② [곤란을 겪다] have a bitter experience; have a hard time of it; have an awful time; have a hell of a time; pay dearly 《for》 ¶ 아버지한테 혼나다 be severely scolded by one's father // 시험치르느라고 혼나다 sweat out an exam // 배고파서 혼나다 be perished with hunger // 그것 때문에 혼났다 I paid dearly for it. /It cost me dear. // 태국에 갔다가 영어가 통하지 않아 혼났다〔난처했다〕 When I went to Thailand, I had trouble because no one understood English. // 택시 잡느라고 혼났다 I had a heck of a time flagging down a cab.

혼내다 ① [놀래다] frighten 《a person》 out of his wits; startle; [겁주다] horrify; appal; scare ② give 《a person》 a good scolding〔severe punishment〕; make 《a person》 hard time; teach 《a person》 a lesson ¶ 이런 짓을 했으니 혼내줄테다 I'll make you smart for this. /You shall have to pay for this. // 오늘은 정말 그 녀석을 혼내줄 거다 Today I'm really going to give him what-for.

혼담 婚談 marriage talk(s) ¶ 혼담이 있다 have a proposal of marriage // 혼담을 성립시키다 arrange a marriage

혼담 魂膽 soul; mind

혼도 昏倒 swoon; faint **—하다** swoon; fall into a swoon; faint (away); have a fainting fit; be stunned; fall〔drop〕 unconscious; be knocked senseless

혼돈 混沌 chaos; nebulosity; disorder; confusion **—하다** (be) chaotic; nebulous; confused; disorderly ¶ 혼돈 상태에 있다 be in a chaotic state; be in (a state of) chaos // 혼돈한 상태에 빠지다 be reduced to a chaotic state; be thrown into confusion〔disorder〕
 — 세계〔천지〕 chaos

⁑혼동 混同 confusion; mixing; 〖법〗 merger **—하다** confuse〔confound, mix up〕 《one thing with another》; mistake 《one thing》 for 《the other》; run into each other ¶ 혼동해서 indiscriminately; confusedly // 공사를 혼동하다 mix up public and private matters // 자유와 방종을 혼동하다 confound liberty with license // 나는 그를 다른 사람과 혼동했다 I got him mixed up with someone else.

혼뜨다 魂— be frightened ⇨ 혼나다

⁑혼란 昏亂 (mental) derangement; confusion; perplexity; disconcertment; muddle; bewilderment **—하다** (be) deranged; confused; perplexed; muddled; bewildered ¶ 그의 머리는 혼란하다 His head is in a whirl. /He is confused.

***혼란 混亂** confusion; disorder; disorganization; chaos; pell-mell; a jumble **—하다** (be) confused; disordered; chaotic; be thrown into confusion〔disorder〕; be in confusion ¶ 내부의 혼란 internal disorder // 혼란 상태에 있다 be in a state of disorder; be in utter confusion // 형세를 혼란시키다 confuse the situation // 혼란을 초래하다 lead to〔give rise to, result in〕 confusion // 혼란에 빠져 있다 fall into utter confusion // 전 시내가 혼란에 빠져 있다 The whole city is plunged in confusion. // 일시 대혼란을 야기했다 Great confusion

prevailed for a time.
혼령 魂靈 a spirit ; a soul ⇨ 영혼
*혼례 婚禮 a marriage ceremony ; a wedding ; nuptials ¶ 혼례에 참석하다 attend〔be present at〕 a wedding
혼류 混流 cross currents
— 송풍기〔터빈〕 a mixed flow fan〔turbine〕
혼매 昏昧 ignorance ; stupidity —하다 (be) ignorant ; stupid
혼미 昏迷 stupidity ; derangement ; confusion —하다 (be) stupid ; confused ¶ 혼미한 상태에 빠지다 be thrown into confusion
혼방 混紡 mixed〔blended〕 spinning ¶ 3할 혼방 30 per cent staple cotton yarn
—사 mixed〔blended〕 yarn
혼백 魂帛 a temporary spirit tablet
— 상자 a spirit box
혼백 魂魄 the soul ; the spirit ; the ghost
혼비백산 魂飛魄散 —하다 get frightened out of one's senses ; be scared out of one's wits
혼사 婚事 marriage ; nuptials
혼상 婚喪 marriage(s) and funeral(s)
혼색 混色 a compound color ; color mixing —하다 mix colors
혼서 婚書 a marriage letter sent to the bride's family from the bridegroom's ; horoscopes of a betrothal couple
혼선 混線 ① [전신 전화의] cross-wires ; entanglement of wires —하다 get entangled ; be mixed ; be crossed ¶ 전화가 혼선되어 있다 The wires〔lines〕 are mixed./The lines are crossed. ② [혼란] confusion —하다 confuse ¶ 말에 혼선이 있다 His ideas are confused.
— 방어〖전기〗 cross protection — 상태 confusion ; a mess 간헐 — intermittent contact
혼성 混成 mixture ; composition —하다 mix ; mingle ; compound
— 가스 mixed gas —물 a mixture ; a compound ; a medley —어 a hybrid (word) ; a blend ; a portmanteau word — 여단 a mixed〔composite〕 brigade — 열차 a composite train — 음성 효과 a montage —주 a mixed drink ; a cocktail —팀 a combined team
혼성 混聲 mixed voices
— 사부 합창 a mixed quartette ; a mixed chorus in four voices〔voice parts〕
혼솔 broad-stitched seams ; bastings
혼솔 渾率 whole family
혼수 昏睡 ① [깊이 잠듦] a deep sleep ② [무의식] coma ; trance ; stupor ; sinking ;〖의학〗 lethargy —하다 become comatose ; fall〔lapse〕 into a coma
— 상태 a comatose state ; a lethargic condition ¶ 혼수 상태에 빠지다 become comatose ; fall〔lapse〕 into a coma〔trance〕 // 혼수 상태에 있다 be in a state of coma 개안성 —〖의학〗 coma vigil
혼수 婚需 articles essential to a marriage ceremony ; marriage expenses
혼식 混食 mixed〔compound〕 food —하다 eat mixed〔compound〕 food
혼신 混信〖통신〗 jamming ; (an) interference ; a cross tone ; crosstalk
혼신 渾身 the whole body ; all the body ¶ 혼신의 힘을 내다 put forth every ounce of one's energies ; put one's energy into one's work
혼야 昏夜 a dark midnight
혼약 婚約 engagement ; betrothal ; a (marriage) contract ; a promise of marriage〔to marry〕 ; a marriage promise ; affiance —하다 make an engagement ; engage oneself to ; be engaged〔betroth ed, affianced〕 to ; give one's hand to ⇨ 약혼
혼연 渾然 wholly ; in perfect harmony ; entirely ¶ 혼연 일체가 되다 be united〔joined〕 together ; form a complete〔harmonious〕 whole
혼외 婚外 ¶ 혼외의 extramarital ; extramatrimonial // 혼외정사의 경험 extramarital experiences
혼욕 混浴 promiscuous〔mixed〕 bathing —하다 bathe promiscuously
혼용하다 混用— use 《a thing》 together with 《another》 ; mix ¶ 한글과 한자를 혼용하다 mingle *Hangeul* with Chinese characters
†혼인 婚姻 marriage ; intermarriage ; matrimony ; wedlock —하다 marry ; be〔get〕 married to ; enter into matrimony ¶ 혼인을 취소하다 annul one's marriage // 혼인 신고를 하다 register one's marriage
—계〔신고〕 a report of marriage ; a marriage registration — 관계 marital relations ; [사람] in-laws — 능력 puberty ; marriageability —집 a house〔family〕 with a wedding occurring
혼일 混一 unification ; consolidation ; amalgamation —하다 unify ; consolidate ; amalgamate
혼일 婚日 wedding day
혼입 混入 mixing ; mingling ; adulteration —하다 mix ; mingle ; intermix ; adulterate (불순물을)
†혼자 alone ; single ; by oneself ; for oneself ; single-handed ¶ 혼자 여행하다 travel alone // 혼자 살다 live alone ; remain single ; be unmarried ; remain a bachelor〔spinster〕 // 혼자 남다 be left alone ; be left to oneself // 혼자 식사하다 eat by oneself // 혼자 웃다 smile to oneself // 방을 혼자 쓰다 have a room to oneself // 일을 혼자 하다 work alone ; do

all the work by oneself // 어린애가 혼자 깼다 The child awoke of itself. // 그는 그것을 혼자 했다 He did it by himself. // 낡은 오막살이집에서 혼자 산다 He lives by himself in an old cottage. // 나는 이 세상에서 나 혼자이다 I am all alone in the world. // 나 혼자 집에 있어요 I'm home alone. // 차를 혼자 타고 다니는 사람들이 너무 많다 There are too many solo drivers.

혼자 사는 동네 면장(面長)이 구장(區長) 속담 When the cat's away, the mice will play. /Well kens the mouse when the cat's out of mouse.

혼자말 soliloquy ; a monolog ; talking to oneself **—하다** talk to oneself ; soliloquize ; think aloud

혼작 混作 growing mixed crops ; mixed cultivation ; crop-mixing **—하다** grow〔cultivate〕 as mixed crops

*__혼잡 混雜__ confusion ; disorder ; congestion ; bustling **—하다** be in confusion 〔disorder〕 ; be crowded ; be congested ¶ 아침〔저녁〕의 혼잡한 시간 the morning〔evening〕 rush hours // 혼잡 속에서 in the confusion // 교통의 혼잡을 완화하다 relieve traffic congestion // 혼잡속을 헤치고 가다 push one's way through a crowd // 도시의 거리는 혼잡하다 The streets of cities are congested.

교통 — a traffic congestion〔jam〕

혼잣손 single-handedness ; a single hand ¶ 혼잣손으로 일하다 work single-handed

혼재 婚材 a marriageable person

혼재 混載 mixed loading **—하다** load various〔miscellaneous〕 goods together

— 화물 a mixed cargo

혼전 婚前 ¶ 혼전의 premarital ; before marriage

— 관계 one's premarital relations ; [육체 관계] premarital sex

혼전 混戰 a confused〔mixed〕 fight ; a free fight ; a free-for-all (fight) ; a mêlée **—하다** fight in confusion ; get into a free fight

혼절 昏絶 fainting ; a swoon **—하다** faint ; swoon ; lose one's senses〔consciousness〕 ; fall into a swoon

혼쭐나다 魂— [혼나다] be frightened ; be startled ; be appalled ; have a hard time (of it) ; have a terrible experience ; have bitter experiences ; [황홀] be transported〔enraptured〕 with delight ¶ 아무를 혼쭐나게 하다 strike a person dumb

혼처 婚處 a marriageable family〔person〕

혼천의 渾天儀 〖천문〗 a celestial globe

혼취 昏醉 dead-drunkenness ; intoxication ; inebriation **—하다** be dead drunk ; be inebriated ; be intoxicated

혼취 婚娶 ⇨ 혼인(婚姻)

혼탁 混濁 muddiness ; turbidity **—하다** (be) muddy ; thick ; turbid ¶ 혼탁한 세상 the corrupt world

‡**혼합 混合** mixing ; mingling ; admixture ; intermixture **—하다** mix ; mingle ; blend ; compound ; intermix ; commingle

— 경기 a mixed competition〔race〕 ; medley **— 교육** a mixed education ; coeducation **—기(機)** a mixer ; a mixing machine **—물** a mixture ; a blend ; a medley ; a compound (혼합물) ; an amalgam ; alloy ; an admixture **—법** 〖수학〗 alligation **— 비례** a mixed proportion ; the mixture ratio ; the air-fuel ratio **— 비료** compound manure ; mixed fertilizer ; compost 《for fertilizing land》 **—세** mixed (tax-)duties **—주** blended liquor ; mixed spirits ; a mixed drink ; a cocktail (칵테일)

혼행 婚行 a trip to marry ; a marriage procession **—하다** go to the house of one's bride〔bridegroom〕 to perform the wedding

혼혈 混血 mixed blood〔breed〕 ¶ 혼혈의 half-blood ; half-caste

—아 a half-blood〔-breed〕 ; a mixed blood child ; a mulatto 《*pl.* ~(e)s》 (흑백의) ; a Eurasian (서양과 동양의) ¶ 혼혈아의 문제 the problem of mixed blood〔half-breeds〕

혼혼하다 昏昏— (be) confused ; muddled ; unconscious ; dark ; be in a stupor ; unreasonable ; irrational

혼화 混化 compound ; blend **—하다** be made into a compound ; compound 《with》 ; blend into

혼화 混和 mixture ; blend ; mingling **—하다** mix ; blend ; mingle 《with》

—기 a mixer ; crutcher (비누의) **—물** intimate mixture ; an admixture ; an infusion ; [고무] a compound **—성** miscibility **—제** a compound

혼효 混淆 confusion ; mixture ; a jumble ; a mess ; a tangle **—하다** mix up ; (be) confused ; jumbled ; tangled ; be messed up

옥석 — a medley of chaff and corn 〔grain〕 ; a mixture of jewels and stones ; a jumble of wheat and tares 〔thread and thrum〕

홀- [짝 없음] single ; sole ; solo ; lone

—몸 a single man〔woman〕 **—아비** a widower

홀 笏 a mace ; a baton

—나무 a wood out of which official tablets are made

홀 a hall

댄스 — a dance〔dancing〕 hall **뮤직 —** a music hall

홀가분하다 ① (be) light ; nimble ; free and easy ; unencumbered ¶ 홀가분한 행장 a light traveling outfit // 홀가분한 동작 nimble movement // 홀가분한 기분

으로 with a light heart // 몸이 홀가분하다 be unencumbered ; feel free and easy ② [다루기가] (be) easy 《to deal with》; simple ; light ¶ 홀가분한 문제 a simple〔an easy〕question

홀꽃노루발 〖식물〗 singleblossom pyrola

홀대 忽待 inhospitable〔unkind〕 treatment ; neglecting ; slighting **— 하다** treat 《a person》 unkindly〔inhospitably〕; neglect〔slight〕《a person》

홀딩 〖배구·농구〗 holding

홀딱 ① [벗는 모양] (removing it) completely ; quickly ; [뒤집는 모양] (turning it) inside out ; [뛰어 넘는 모양] with a jump ; in a bound ; easily ¶ 옷을 홀딱 벗다 take one's clothes off completely〔quickly〕; strip down ; slip off one's clothes // 머리가 홀딱 벗어지다 one's head is as bald as an egg // 저고리를 홀딱 뒤집다 turn one's coat inside out ② [반하는 모양] deeply (in love with) ; madly ③ [속는 모양] (be) nicely (taken in) ; fall an easy victim to another's trick

홀딱거리다 slip all the time ; be apt to slip out ¶ 홀딱홀딱 loosely ; slipperily ⇨ 훌떡거리다

홀라들이다 ⇨ 훌라들이다

홀랑 all naked ¶ 옷을 홀랑 벗다 strip oneself all naked // 젖이 홀랑 들어나다 one's breasts are exposed naked

홀랑거리다 ⇨ 훌렁거리다

†**홀로** alone ; single-handed ¶ 홀로 살다 live alone ; remain single // 홀로 싸우다 fight alone〔single-handed〕// 홀로 되다 be widowed ; lose one's husband

***홀리다** [현혹] get possessed ; be bewitched ; [매혹] be fascinated ; get infatuated ; get captivated ; get enchanted ; [유혹] get tempted ; be deluded ; be tricked ¶ 귀신한테 홀리다 be possessed by〔with〕 a devil // 여자한테 홀리다 get infatuated with a woman ; be gone on a woman // 돈에 홀려 나쁜 짓을 하다 be tempted by money to do wrong

홀림길 a maze ; a labyrinth ¶ 홀림길에 빠지다 be lost in a maze ; beat a loss

홀맺다 tie〔knot〕《a thing》 securely〔tightly〕

홀몸 a single〔an unmarried〕 person ; a person without a spouse ¶ 평생을 홀몸으로 지내다 remain single all one's life

홀보드르르하다 (be) nice and soft

홀소리 a vowel ⇨ 모음

***홀수** 一數 an odd〔uneven〕 number ; a cardinal number

홀스타인 [젖소 품종] a Holstein (cow)

홀시 忽視 contempt ; neglect ; disregard **— 하다** despise ; hold 《a person》 in contempt ; look down on ; make light of ; neglect ; slight

홀씨 〖생물〗 a spore

홀아비 a widower
— 살림 the life of a widower ; a single life ; a bachelor life

홀아비김치 *kimchi* prepared with radish〔*bae-chu*〕 alone

홀아비꽃대 〖식물〗 a piperaceous plant

홀알 an unfertilized egg ; a wind egg

홀앗이살림 living alone ; being unmarried ; remaining single ; a household with no encumbrances

홀어미 a widow

홀연 忽然 suddenly ; all of a sudden ; on a sudden ; abruptly ; unexpectedly ; in an instant ; in a flash ¶ 홀연히 사라지다 vanish as if by magic // 홀연히 나타나다 appear suddenly // 그는 홀연히 안개속으로 사라졌다 He faded in a flash into the fog.

홀짝 ① with a jump〔bound〕; suddenly ; swiftly ; nimbly ¶ 새가 홀짝 날아가다 a bird suddenly takes off and flies away // 개천을 홀짝 건너뛰다 leap over a ditch with a jump ② [콧물을] sniffling ; snivelling ; [액체를] sipping ; supping ; slurping ; sucking at a gulp ¶ 국을 홀짝 들이마시다 slurp up〔gulp down〕 soup

홀짝거리다 [액체를] keep sipping〔slurping, sucking〕; [콧물을] keep sniffling〔snivelling〕; [울다] weep〔cry〕 with sniffling ¶ 국을 홀짝 거리다 slip〔slurp up〕 soup // 어린애가 홀짝거린다 A child cries and sniffles.

홀짝이다 ⇨ 홀짝거리다

홀짝홀짝 ① [코를] sniffling〔snivelling〕 repeatedly ② [울다] weeping and sniffling away ¶ 홀짝홀짝 울다 weep and sniffle away ③ [국물을] with sip after sip〔slurp after slurp〕; sucking away ¶ 국을 홀짝홀짝 들이마시다 keep sipping〔slurping up〕 soup

홀쭉이 a lanky person ; a man tall as a church steeple

홀쭉하다 (be) thin ; slim ; slender ; be pinched ; [뾰족하다] (be) pointed ; tapering ¶ 허리가 홀쭉하다 have a slim waist // 볼이 홀쭉하다 have hollow cheeks ; have a pinched look // 꼬리가 홀쭉하다 have a pointed〔slim〕 tail // 나무 끝이 홀쭉하다 A tree has a tapering top.

홀쳐매다 tie up ¶ 자루를 홀쳐매다 tie up the top of a bag

홀치기 [염색] variegation ; dapple ; [천] variegated cloth ¶ 홀치기 염색의 variegated

홀태[1] a threshing machine ; a thresher ⇨벼훑이

홀태[2] [생선] a slim fish without spawn ; [물건] a slim thing

홀태바지 skin-tight trousers

홀태버선 a tight sock

홀태부리 the nose〔front end〕 of a

pointed object

홀태질 threshing〔stripping〕 grain from the ear on a threshing machine ─하다 thresh

홀하다 忽─ ① [경솔·소홀] (be) careless ; heedless ; inadvertent ; inconsiderate ; negligent ; hasty ; rash ; thoughtless ¶ 대접이 홀하다 be careless 〔inhospitable〕 in treating 《a person》// 행동이 홀하다 act〔behave〕 rashly ② [대수롭지 않다] be of little importance ; be of no account〔value〕 ; (be) frivolous〔insignificant〕

홀홀 in flames (불이) ; with leaps and bounds (뛰는 모양) ; flying (나는 모양) ; with slurps (들어마시는 모양) ; tossing and tossing (던지는 모양) ⇨ 훌훌

홀홀하다 ⇨ 훌훌하다

*홈 a groove ¶ 홈을 파다 hollow out 〔cut〕 a groove ; groove

홈 ① [가정] one's home ② 〖야구〗 the home base〔plate〕

─룸 〖교육〗 a home room ─워크 a homework

‡홈런 〖야구〗 a home run ; a homer ; a circuit clout〔blow, drive〕 ; a round-tripper ; a four-bagger 《미·속》 ¶ 홈런을 치다 hit〔clout, slam〕 a home run 《over the left field fence》

─ 더비 a home-run derby ─왕 a homerun king〔leader〕 만루 ─ a grand slam homer

홈스트레치 〖경마〗 the homestretch ¶ 홈스트레치에 들어오다 get on the homestretch

홈스펀 homespun ¶ 홈스펀의 homespun 《cloth》

홈식 homesickness ; nostalgia ¶ 홈식에 걸린 사람 a homesick person // 홈식에 걸리다 get〔become〕 homesick

홈인하다 get〔reach, go〕 home ; cross the (home) plate ; score

홈질 broad stitching ─하다 broadstitch

홈착거리다 [더듬다] search ; fumble ; [눈물을] wipe away ¶ 주머니를 홈착거리다 search〔fumble around in〕 one's pocket // 눈물을 홈착거리다 keep wiping tears from one's eyes

홈치작거리다 search〔fumble〕 leisurely ¶ 주머니를 홈치작거리다 search〔fumble around in〕 one's pocket leisurely

홈타기 a diverging point ; a fork ; a crossroads ; the parting of the ways ; a crotch 《미》 ¶ 홈타기진 forked // 나무 홈타기 the crotch of a tree // 나무 홈타기에 앉다 sit on the fork of a tree

*홈통 ─桶 an eaves trough ; a gutter ; a spout ; [문지방의] a groove on a window frame〔doorsill〕

홈통은 썩지 않는다 속담 Standing pools gather filth. /The used key is always bright.

홈파다 cut〔hollow out〕 a groove ; groove ¶ 설겆이 대에 홈파다 groove a sink shelf

홈패다 get grooved ; be dug out ¶ 길이 비에 홈패다 a road is dug out by the rain

홈홈하다 wear〔display〕 a satisfied look

홉[1] a unit of weight

홉[2] 〖식물〗 a hop ; hops 《열매》 ¶ 홉으로 맛을 내다 hop ; flavor with hops

홉뜨다 roll one's eyes back till the white shows

홋홋이 without encumbrances ; with no ties〔dependents〕 ¶ 딸린 식구없이 둘이서 홋홋이 살다 the couple leads a carefree life with no one else to worry about except themselves

홋홋하다 (be) unencumbered ; carefree ; have no encumbrances〔dependents, ties〕 ¶ 홋홋한 살림 a carefree household with few dependents to worry about ; a household with no encumbrances

홍 紅 red ; crimson

홍꼭지 紅─ a kite with a round piece of red paper at its top

홍당무 a red radish ; a carrot ¶ 부끄러워 얼굴이 홍당무가 되다 be flushed with shame

홍대 鴻大, 洪大 ─하다 (be) huge ; enormous ; gigantic ; colossal ; immense ; tremendous

홍도 紅桃 [나무] a peach tree which puts out red blossoms ; [꽃] a red peach blossom

홍두 紅荳 〖식물〗 the rosary-pea

홍두깨 ① a wooden roller used in smoothing cloth (by wrapping and beating it on it) ¶ 어두운 데 홍두깨 a sudden and unexpected mention of something ; a wooden roller thrust out in the dark ② [쇠고기] a kind of beef jowl

─ 다듬이질 roller-smoothing ; pressing (cloth) ─질 roller smoothing ; pressing (cloth) ─틀 a block for a frame to roll cloth on

홍등가 紅燈街 a red-light district ; a brothel area ; gay quarters ¶ 홍등가에 다니다 visit〔frequent〕 the gay quarters // 남몰래 홍등가에 다니는 사람 a surreptitious frequenter of the gay quarters ; a sly dog

홍련 紅蓮 a red lotus

홍로점설 紅爐點雪 a drop in the bucket

홍루 紅淚 [미인의 눈물] tears of a fair ; [피눈물] tears of blood ; bitter tears ¶ 홍루를 흘리다 shed bitter tears

홍매 紅梅 red plum blossoms ¶ 홍매색 light pink

홍모 鴻毛 wild-goose down ¶ 목숨을 홍모같이 가볍게 여기다 make nothing of one's life ; hold one's life as nothing

홍문 紅門 ① [정문(旌門)] a red gate erected in hono(u)r of a loyal retainer, a filial son or a virtuous woman ② ⇨ 홍살문
홍방울새 紅— 〖새〗 a mealy red-poll
홍백 紅白 red and white
—전 a contest between red and white teams ; a contest〔tourney〕 between two groups
홍보 弘報 public information ; publicity ; public relations
—과(課) the Public Information Section **—지(誌)** a public relations magazine **— 활동** publicity〔information〕 work 〔activities〕 ☞ ◖ p. 2384 ◗
홍보석 紅寶石 a ruby
홍분 紅粉 paint〔rouge〕 and powder ; paint ; [화장] makeup ; dressing ; toilet
홍살문 紅—門 a red gate with spiked top
홍삼 紅蔘 ginseng steamed red
홍색 紅色 red ; a red color ; [홍색짜리] a new bride (dressed in her red skirt)
홍소 哄笑 a roar of laughter ; loud laughter ; [천한] a guffaw ; a horse laugh **—하다** roar with laughter ; laugh loud(ly) ; burst out laughing ; guffaw
홍송 紅松 a red pine
†**홍수 洪水** a flood ; an inundation ; a deluge

> 참고 **flood** 냇물 따위가 범람하여 육지 전면을 덮는 경우 **deluge** 흘러가는 도중 모든 물건을 휩쓸어 파괴하며 지나가는 대홍수 **inundation** 딱딱한 말 부근 일면을 덮는 큰 물

¶ 노아의 홍수 Noah's flood ; the Deluge ; the Flood // 책의 홍수 a flood of books // 편지의 홍수 a deluge of letters // 홍수가 나다 have a flood ; get flooded ; be inundated
— 예보〔경보〕 flood forecast〔warnings〕 **— 조절** flood control **— 지대〔구역〕** a flooded〔an inundated〕 area〔district〕 **대—** a great〔disastrous, heavy, big〕 flood ; a deluge ; a cataclysm
홍수 紅樹 a mangrove tree
—림 a mangrove forest
홍수막이 〖민속〗 an exorcism held at the beginning of the year to dispel evils for the year
홍수막이 洪水— damming against **—하다** dam《up》
홍순 紅脣 red lips ; a woman's lips ; [꽃] a half-open flower
홍시 紅柿 a red-ripe persimmon
홍실 紅— red thread(s)
홍안 紅顔 rosy cheeks ; a ruddy〔rosy〕 face ¶ 홍안의 미소년 a handsome〔fair〕 youth ; a rosy-cheeked youth
홍어 洪魚 〖어류〗 a skate ; a thorn back
홍업 鴻業 a great undertaking〔enterprise〕
*__홍역 紅疫__ the measles ¶ 홍역에 걸리다 catch〔have, get〕 the measles
홍연대소 哄然大笑 —하다 laugh broadly〔loudly〕 ; burst out laughing ; burst into〔roar with〕 laughter
홍염 紅焰 red flame ; 〖천문〗 a solar prominence
홍엽 紅葉 red leaves ; autumn colors 〔tints〕 ; [단풍잎] red maple foliage
홍예 a rainbow ; an arch
홍예 틀다 관용 build as an arch ; arch《a gate》
—다리 an arched bridge **—대** a pier **—문** the arch of a gate ; an arched gate
홍옥 紅玉 ruby ; carbuncle ; [사과] a Jonathan
홍위병 紅衛兵 [중국의] the Red Guards ; [한 사람] a Red Guard
홍은 鴻恩 great favor〔benevolence〕
홍익 弘益 public benefit ; a boon to mankind ; promotion of public welfare **—하다** promote public welfare
— 인간 devotion to the welfare of mankind ; humanitarianism ¶ 홍익 인간의 이념 the humanitarian ideal
홍인종 紅人種 the red race ; American Indian
홍일점 紅一點 the only woman among those present
홍적세 洪積世 〖지질〗 a diluvial〔diluvian〕 epoch
홍적층 洪積層 〖지질〗 a diluvium《*pl.* ~s, -via》; a diluvial formation ¶ 홍적층토 diluvium ; diluvial soil〔deposits〕
홍조 紅潮 ① flushing ¶ 얼굴에 홍조를 띠다《one's face》 be flushed ; blush ② [바다] reflections of the morning sun on the see ③ [월경] menses ; menstruation periods ; monthlies
홍진 紅塵 red dust ; thick dust
— 만장 a cloud of dust **— 세계** the dusty world
홍차 紅茶 tea ; black tea ¶ 설탕과 크림을 넣은 홍차 tea with sugar and cream
*__홍채 虹彩__ the iris (of the eye)
—염(炎) iritis **— 절제(술)** 〖의학〗 iridectomy
홍초 紅— [초] a red candle ; [연] a paper kite that is all red except for the tail
홍치마 紅— a red skirt
홍콩 〖지리〗 Hongkong
홍하 紅蝦 〖물고기〗 a (spiny) lobster
홍학 紅鶴 〖새〗 a flamingo《*pl.* ~(e)s》
홍합 紅蛤 〖조개〗 a sea mussel ; Mytilus orassitesta (학명)
홍해 紅海 〖지리〗 the Red Sea
홑- single ; one-ply ; single layer ¶ 홑이다 be single-layered ; be one sheet ; be one-ply
홑겹 a single layer

홍보·광고

① 홍보

▶퍼블릭 릴레이션 PR(public relations) / 퍼블릭 어페어즈 PA(public affairs) / 코퍼레이트 커뮤니케이션 CC (corporate communication) / 재무홍보 IR(investor relations) / 연차보고서 annual report / 매스컴 대책 press relations / 뉴스 릴리즈 news release / 기업 시민, 코퍼레이트 시티즌 CC(corporate citizens)
▶기자 회견 press conference / 고객 대책 customer relations / 지역(커뮤니티) 대책 community relations
▶기업 이미지 통합 전략 CI(corporate identity) / 사업 영역 corporate domain / 기업 이념 corporate philosophy / 기업 문화, 사풍 corporate culture
▶로빙 lobbying / 로비 lobby / 로비스트 lobbyist / 외국 대리인 등록법 FARA; Foreign Agent Registration Act / 공청회 public hearing

② 광고

▶광고 advertisement; ad / (~에) 광고를 내다 advertise in....; buy (a) space [ad] in....; take (out) an ad in.... / 광고를 신청하다 apply for an ad space / 광고맨 adperson / 상업광고 business[commercial] advertisement / 기업광고 corporate advertisement; institutional advertising / 상품광고 product advertisement / 공익광고 public service advertisement; public interest advertisement; social advertisement / 산업광고 trade advertising / 프로세스 광고 process ad (★상품의 기능을 알기 쉽게 자세히 설명하여 상품의 이해도에 중점을 둔 것) / 의견광고 opinion[advocacy] ad; issue-oriented ad / (타사제품과의) 비교광고 comparative advertising; knocking copy 《영》 / 안내 광고 classified[want] ad / 옥외 광고 outdoor advertising
▶전면 광고 full-page ad / 게재(揭載)횟수 insertion ¶ 1회 게재마다 5만원 50,000 won per insertion / 광고 크기 ad size; size of an ad / 광고의 양 volume of ads; ad volume
▶광고 대리점 advertising agency [agent] / 광고주 advertiser / 광고비 ad rates / 광고 수수료 agency commission / 광고 문안 작성자[카피라이터] copy writer / 광고 디자이너 (ad) layout man

③ 표현

¶ 그 광고는 한국의 중산층에 성공적으로 파고 들었다. The ad successfully penetrated[pervaded, permeated] the Korean middle class. // 귀사의 광고는 50만의 구매력이 있는 젊은층이 읽게 될 것이다. Your ad carries to five hundred thousand youths with money to spend. // 광고 요금은 발행 부수에 따라 결정되므로 각 신문에 따라 다르다. Ad rates differ from one newspaper to another because they are set according to the size of circulation. // 5인치 3단의 광고를 내고 싶다. I want the ad to be 5 inches by 3 columns. // 신제품 광고를 위해 회사는 5개지(紙)에 광고를 예약했다. The company reserved spaces in five newspapers to promote its new product. // 회사는 신제품 선전을 위해 신문에 대광고를 냈다. The company took out big ads in newspapers to advertise their new product.

홑눈 〖동물〗 a stemma 《*pl.* -mata, ~s》; an ocellus 《*pl.* -lli》
홑담 a single-layered wall
홑대패 a single-edged plane
홑몸 ① [배우자 없는] a single〔an unmarried〕 person; a bachelor; a spinster (여자); bachelorhood; spinsterhood ¶ 홑몸이 되다 be left alone; be left to oneself // 홑몸으로 살다 live single; lead a bachelor's〔spinster's〕 life ② [임신하지 않은] a woman who is not pregnant
홑바지 (Korean women's) undergarment
홑반 a single layer of cotton wool
—뿌리 a garment with a single layer of cotton padding
홑벌 [단벌] a single one; the only one; [한겹] single-ply; a single-ply〔one-layer〕 one
— 문서 a single copy of a document
— 바지 unlined trousers **—옷** the only clothes one has
홑벌사람 a shallow-minded person
홑벽 —壁 a single partition; a thin wall
홑소리 a single sound; a monosyllabic sound
홑실 a single-ply thread; singles
홑옷 unlined clothes
홑으로 ① [한겹으로] with〔in〕 one layer; singly ¶ 홑으로 된 single; one-fold ② [적은 수효로] in low〔small〕 numbers; [단순히] simply; easily ¶ 그의 법률지식은 홑으로 볼 수 없다 He has no small knowledge of the law.

홑이불 a single-layer quilt ; a (bed) sheet
홑지다 become simple ; be simplified
홑집 a single-wing house ; a shack
홑창 —窓 〖건축〗 a sliding window without an inner window
홑치마 [한겹의] an unlined skirt ; [속에 입은 것이 없는] a skirt worn without an underskirt
*화 火 ① [성] anger ; ire ; wrath ; pent-up resentment ¶ 화를 내다 get angry〔indignant, enraged, infuriated〕; flare up ; fly into a rage ; fly off the handle ; blow one's top∥좀체로 화를 안낸다 be slow to anger∥걸핏하면 화를 낸다 He gets angry on the slightest provocation. /He easily takes offense. ∥나는 그의 행동에 화가 난다 I am vexed at his behavior. ② a stifling sensation in the chest ; a feeling of a pressure in the chest
화 禍 a disaster ; a calamity ; a misfortune ; an evil ; a woe ¶ 화를 당하다 meet with a disaster∥화를 자초하다 invite〔court〕 disaster ; bring calamity upon oneself∥화를 면하다 be saved from disaster∥화를 피하다 keep off a misfortune∥험구가 화되다 one's evil tongue brings down〔leads to〕 ruin∥화불 단행이다 Misfortunes never come single. /It never rains but it pours.
화 和 the total (amount) ; the sum ¶ 대수적 화 an algebraical sum∥삼각형의 내각의 화는 2직각이다 The internal angles of a triangle added together make two right angles.
-화 化 ¶ 기화(氣化)하다 evaporate ; gasify∥액화하다 liquefy∥ 영화화하다 make into a film ; film ; filmize ; make a motion picture of
기계— mechanization 도시— urbanization 미국— Americanization 합리— rationalization
‡화가 畫家 a painter ; an artist
동양— an Oriental painter 서양— an artist of Western painting 인물— a portrait painter 풍경— a landscape painter
화가 畫架 an easel
화간 和姦 fornication ; collusion in adultery ; adultery with consent —하다 fornicate 《with》
화강석 花崗石 granite
*화강암 花崗岩 granite ¶ 화강암의 granitic
화객선 貨客船 a cargo-passenger ship〔boat, steamer〕; a mixed boat ; an intermediate ship
화격 畫格 [화법] art of drawing ; [화품] artistic merit ; style
화경 火耕 〖농업〗 cultivation of a burnt field
화경 火鏡 a burning glass ; a sunglass
화경 花莖 〖식물〗 a flower stalk ; a scape
화경 花梗 a flower stalk ; a footstalk ; a peduncle
화고 畫稿 a study ; a sketch ; a dessin 《프》
화공 火功 attacking with fire —하다 attack with fire
화공 畫工 a painter ; an artist
화공 靴工 a shoemaker
화공품 火工品 an article processed with heat
‡화관 花冠 [관] a woman's ceremonial coronet ; [꽃의] the corolla
화광 火光 the light of fire ¶ 화광 충천하다 flame lights up the sky
화광동진 和光同塵 ① [현자의] 《the life of a wise man》 mingling with the world by hiding the light of his wisdom and virtue ② 〖불교〗 the state of Buddhas and bodhisattvas concealing their glory and mingling among the living beings on earth for the purpose of saving the souls of the latter
화교 華僑 Chinese merchants residing abroad ; Chinese emigrants ; Chinese residents abroad
화구 火口 [아궁이] a fuel intake〔mouth〕; [분화구] the mouth of a volcano ; a crater
—곡(谷) a crater valley —구(丘) a volcanic cone —벽(壁) a crater wall —원(原) a crater basin —호(湖) a crater lake 부— a secondary crater
화근 禍根 the root〔cause〕 of evil〔calamity〕; the source of misfortune ¶ 화근을 없애다 eliminate the root of evil ; lay the axe to the root of evil∥화근을 남기다 contain the seeds of trouble ; be fraught with evil∥ 화근이 뿌리 깊다 The cause of the trouble is deep-rooted〔lies deep-seated〕.
—거리 a source of future misfortune ; something that will make trouble
화급 火急 urgency ; exigency ; emergency —하다 (be) urgent ; pressing ; crying ; demanding ; exigent
화기 火氣 [답답한 기운] a stifling sensation in the chest ; [노기] anger ; ire ; [불기] heat of fire ¶ 화기 없는 방에서 in an unheated room∥화기 엄금 Inflammable. / No Fire.
화기 火器 [무기] firearms ; [화로] a fire
경— light firearms ; small arms 공용(共用) — a crew-served weapon 소— a rifle ; small arms 자동 — automatic weapons 중— heavy weapons
화기 和氣 harmony ; peacefulness ; concord ; [날씨] beautiful warm weather ¶ 화기 애애한 가정 a home in peace and harmony ; a harmonious household ∥화기 애애하다 be peaceful ; be harmonious∥그 여자는 옆에 있을 때마다

화기 애애한 기운이 감돈다 The atmosphere mellows whenever she's around.

화기 花期 the flower season ; a flowering season

화끈거리다 burn ; glow ; flush ; feel hot ; throb with heat ¶ 술을 먹어 얼굴이 화끈거리다 one's face is flushed with drink // 추워서 뺨이 화끈거리다 one's cheeks glow with the cold air // 온 몸이 화끈거리다 one's body is all aglow

화끈달다 get enraged ; be infuriated ; be maddened ¶ 화끈 달아 excitedly ; in a passion ; in hot blood // 화끈 달아 말도 안 나왔다 I got too excited for words.

화끈화끈 glowing ; burning ; flushing ; throbbing with heat ¶ 추워서 뺨이 화끈화끈하다 one's cheeks glow with the cold air

‡화나다 火— get angry〔enraged, indignant, infuriated〕; get mad ¶ 화나게 하다 enrage ; provoke ; offend ; exasperate ; make 《a person》 angry ; drive 《a person》 crazy〔mad, nuts, insane〕; drive〔push, thrust〕 《a person》 to the wall ; stir 《a person's》 wrath // 나 화났어 I'm seeing red ! // 그건 정말 화나는 일이군 That really ticks me off. // 그녀는 나를 화나게 한다 She drives me crazy〔nuts, mad, to the wall, out of my mind〕.

화난 火難 a fire (disaster) ; the scourge of fire ¶ 화난을 만나다 [사람이] suffer from a fire ; be rendered〔made〕 homeless by fire ; [집이] be burnt down〔up〕; be destroyed by fire

화난 禍難 disaster ; a misfortune ; a mishap ; a calamity

화내다 火— give vent to one's anger ; get angry ; flare up ; fly into a rage ; blow one's top ¶ 아무 것도 아닌 일에 화내다 lose one's temper for nothing // 걸핏하면 화내다 get angry on the slightest provocation // 그렇게 화내지 마라 Don't lose your temper so quickly. // 화내지 마라 Don't be angry. /Don't be mad. /Don't steam. /Don't get all steamed up.

화냥년 loose woman ; a wanton〔dissolute〕 woman

화냥질 ⇨ 서방질

화농 化膿 suppuration ; maturation ; festering ; purulence ; pyosis ; gathering **—하다** suppurate ; mature ; fester ; come to a head ; gather ¶ 화농성의 suppurative ; festering

—균 a suppurative germ ; pyogenic bacteria **—성 염증** purulent inflammation **—열** a maturative〔suppurative〕 fever **— 작용** pyogenesis **—제** a maturative

화닥닥 hurry-scurry ; with a start ; madly ¶ 화닥닥거리다 start ; fluster

화단 花壇 a flower-bed ; a flower garden

화단 畫壇 the world of artists ; painting circles ; [진열장] an art gallery

화답 和答 a response **—하다** respond 《in singing, reciting》

화대 花代 a charge for a *kisaeng*

화대 花臺 a flowerpot stand

화덕 火— a cooking stove ; a stove ; [화로] a live charcoal pot

화도 畫道 (the art of) painting

화도 畫圖 pictures ; paintings

화독 火毒 inflammation caused by a burn

—내 the smell of burnt food

화동 和同 unison ; harmony ; concord **—하다** get in unison ; be in harmony

화두 話頭 topic〔subject〕 of conversation ¶ 화두를 바꾸다 change the topic ; shift the conversation

화드득 [소리] with a single great slush〔slosh〕; with a bang〔crackle, whiz〕

화드득거리다 keep going slosh ; keep banging〔crackling, whizzing〕 ¶ 화드득화드득 with slosh after slosh ; banging〔crackling, whizzing〕 away

화라지 a long spread-out branch ; a bough ; a limb

화락 和樂 harmony ; unity ; peace **—하다** get along amicably ; be at peace with each other ; live in unity〔harmony〕 ¶ 그 집은 온 집안이 화락하다 Perfect peace reigns in his family. / They live in perfect harmony.

화란 和蘭 ⇨ 네덜란드

화랑 花郞 the flower of youth in *Silla* dynasty (who excelled in beauty, bravery and military arts)

—도(徒) ⇨ 화랑 **—이** 〖민속〗 a kind of theatrical performer

화랑 畫廊 a picture〔an art〕 gallery

†화려 華麗 splendor ; magnificence ; gorgeousness ; brilliance ; sumptuousness **—하다** (be) splendid ; magnificent ; gorgeous ; brilliant ; sumptuous ¶ 화려한 옷 gay costume〔attire〕 // 화려한 생활 gay life

화력 火力 heating〔caloric〕 power ; the force of the fire ; [군대의] fire power

— 발전 a steam〔thermal〕 power generation **— 발전소** a steam〔thermoelectric〕 power plant〔station〕 **— 전기** a steam〔thermal〕 power electricity ; steam-generated electricity **— 증강** 〖군사〗 increase in〔of〕 fire power **— 지원** 〖군사〗 fire support

화로 火爐 a (charcoal) brazier ; a fire pot〔box〕 ¶ 화로에 불을 쪼이다 warm oneself at a brazier ; warm one's hands over a brazier // 화로를 둘러싸고 앉다 sit around a brazier

화로수 花露水 a floral perfume

화룡점정 畫龍點睛 the finishing touch 《on a thing》; final achievement ; ultimate accomplishment

화류 花柳 flowers and willows ; [계집] prostitutes ; a woman of the gay world ¶ 화류계에 드나들다 frequent the gay quarters

—계 gay quarters〔world〕; pleasure quarters ; the demimonde ; the red-light districts 《미》 —병 a social disease ; a venereal disease 《VD, V. D.》; [매독] syphilis ; pox 《속》; [임질] gonorrhea ; clap 《속》 —항(巷) a resort for pleasure and dissipation

화류 樺榴 red sandalwood

—장 a chest made of red sandalwood

화면 畫面 [영사막의] a screen ; [그림의] a canvas ; 『기하』 a picture plane

— 구성 the composition of a picture —비(比) picture ratio

화목 火木 firewood

화목 花木 a flower plant ; a flowering plant ; a flowering tree

*화목 和睦 harmony ; intimacy ; peace ; concord —하다 be friendly with ; be on intimate terms with ¶ 화목하게 지내다 be friendly with ; get along amicably // 그들은 아주 화목하게 지낸다 They are on very friendly terms. /They live very happily together.

화무십일홍 花無十日紅 [속담] Pride will have a fall. /Every flood〔tide〕 hath its ebb.

화문 火門 a vent ; a touchhole ¶ 화문을 막은 대포 spiked gun

— 마개 a ventplug ; [대포의] a spike

화문 花紋 flower patterns ; figures of flowers

—석 a mat woven with flower patterns

*화물 貨物 goods ; freight 《미》; cargo (뱃짐) ; commodities ; merchandise

—계 a freight section〔clerk〕; a freight man — 보관증 a warrant ; a warehouse receipt —선 a cargo boat〔steamer, liner (정기선)〕; a freight boat〔vessel〕; a freighter 《미》; a transport (수송선) ; a tramp (부정기) ; an ocean tramp (외양 부정기) — 수송 freight traffic〔transportation〕 — 수송기 a cargo〔goods〕 plane ; an air freighter — 송장(送狀)〔통지서〕 a manifest ; a waybill — 양륙 cargo unloading — 운송 goods transport 《영》; shipment 《미》; shipping ; freight — 운임 goods rates 《영》; freight (rates) 《미》; freightage ; [철도의] railway freight charges — 인환증 [선하증권] a consignment sheet ; a bill of lading 《미》; receipt note 《영》 — 자동차 a truck ; a (motor-) lorry 《영》; a freight car 《미》; a goods van 《영》 — 증권 a bill of lading〔parcels〕 —차 a freight car — 취급소 a goods〔freight〕 office (역의) ; a forwarding agency ; an express (company) (통운회사) — 취급인 a freighter ; a freight〔goods, forwarding〕 agent ; an expressman 《미》; a shipping clerk (계원) — 폭주 congestion of freight traffic — 환(換)어음 《draw》 a documentary draft〔bill〕 ¶ 화물 환어음 신용장 a documentary (letter of) credit 공수 — airborne goods 중량 — hard goods 철도 — rail freight 표류 — [해상 보험] flotsam

화미 華美 splendor ; pomp ; gorgeousness ; gaiety ; gaudiness ; showiness —하다 (be) splendid ; gorgeous ; gay ; gaudy ; showy

화밀 花蜜 (floral) nectar

화반 火斑 『의학』 cutis marmorata ; livedo calorica ; a marbled skin

화반 花盤 ① 『건축』 a board put on top of the first cornice on a pillar to hold the beam support ② [꽃 담는] a kind of flowerpot shaped like a flower

화반석 花斑石 red marble

화반자 花— ⇨ 소란 반자

화방 火防 『건축』 a wall with wainscot of mud and stone

화방 花房 a flower shop

화방 畫房 [화실] a studio ; an atelier 《프》; [화랑] a gallery

화방 畫舫 a decorated pleasure boat

화방수 —水 a whirl (pool) ; an eddy

화백 畫伯 an artist ; a (noted, master) painter

화벌 華閥 a distinguished family ; a titled family

*화법 畫法 the art of drawing ; the canons of painting ¶ 화법에 맞다〔맞지 않다〕 be in〔out of〕 drawing

산수 — landscape painting

화법 話法 『문법』 narration

직접〔간접〕 — direct〔indirect〕 narration ; the direct〔indirect〕 speech

화변 禍變 a disaster ; a calamity ; a misfortune

화병 火病 an ailment supposedly caused by one's pent-up〔stored〕 resentment〔animosity, grudge〕 and mental depression

화병 花甁 a (flower) vase ¶ 화병에 꽃을 꽂다 put a flower in a vase

화보 a plump-faced woman

화보 花譜 a catalog of flowers ; a horticultural guide

화보 畫報 a pictorial ; an illustrated magazine ; a graphic ; a picture report

시사 — news in pictures ; a pictorial record〔survey〕 of current events

화보 畫譜 a picture album

화복 禍福 fortune and misfortune ; weal and woe ; good and evil ; happiness and misery ¶ 인생의 화복 the ups and downs〔vicissitudes〕 of life ; the happiness and misery of life

화본 畫本 a canvas ; a drawing paper
화본과 禾本科 〖식물〗 Graminaceae (학명)
— 식물 grasses
화부 火夫 a stoker ; a fireman
화분 花盆 a flowerpot
*화분 花粉 pollen ; another dust
— 모세포 a pollen mother cell —열 hay fever
화사 花詞 flower〔floral〕 language ; the language of flowers
화사 畫師 a painter ; an artist
화사 花蛇 a striped snake
†화사 華奢 luxury ; pomp ; splendor —하다 (be) luxurious ; pompous ; splendid
화사첨족 畫蛇添足 a superfluity ; a redundancy ; a fifth wheel
‡화산 火山 a volcano
—국 a volcanic country —군(群) a volcanic group —대〔지대〕 a volcanic zone 〔region〕 —맥 a volcanic chain〔range〕 — 분출물 ejecta —사(砂) volcanic sand —암(岩) volcanic〔igneous〕 rocks ; lava (용담) — 암맥 a volcanic dike — 열도(列島) a chain of volcanic 〔volcano〕 islands — 작용 volcanism ; volcanic action — 지진 a volcanic earthquake —탄(彈) a volcanic bomb —토 trass —학 volcanology —학자 a volcanologist — 현상 a volcanic phenomenon ; volcanism — 활동 volcanic activity —회 volcanic ashes ; puzzolana 해저 — a submarine volcano 활〔휴, 사〕— an active〔a dormant, an extinct〕 volcano
‡화살 an arrow ¶ 빗발 같은 화살 a shower of arrows // 화살처럼 빠르다 be as swift as an arrow ; shoot like an arrow // 활에 화살을 먹이다 fix an arrow in a bow ; put an arrow to the string // 화살을 쏘다 shoot〔send〕 an arrow // 화살이 과녁에 들어가 맞다 an arrow hits the mark〔target〕 // 세월은 화살과 같이 흐른다 Time flies like an arrow.
—대 the shaft of an arrow —촉 an arrowhead —표 an arrow
화살나무 〖식물〗 a winged euonymus
화상 火床 a (fire) grate
화상 火傷 a burn ; a scald ¶ 화상을 입다 get burned〔scalded〕 ; suffer a burn ; scald oneself // 손에 화상을 입었다 I got burnt in the hand.
화상 和尙 a Buddhist priest ; a bonze
화상 畫像 a portrait ; a picture
— 면적 [텔레비전] a picture area
화상 華商 a Chinese merchant
화색 和色 a genial expression ; a ruddy complexion ; a peaceful countenance
화생 化生 metamorphosis ; transformation —하다 transform
화생방전 化生放戰 〖군사〗 chemical, biological and radiological warfare ; CBR warfare
화서 花序 inflorescence ; anthotaxy
유한〔원심〕 — definite〔centrifugal〕 inflorescence
화서지몽 華胥之夢 a (midday) nap ; a siesta
화석 火石 a flint ⇨ 부싯돌
*화석 化石 a fossil ; fossilization ; petrifaction —하다 fossilize ; petrify ¶ 동물〔식물〕의 화석 a fossil animal 〔plant〕 ; a zoolite
— 수지 fossil resin — 인류 fossil men —층(層) a fossil bed〔stratum〕 —학 paleontology ; fossilology —학자 a paleontologist ; a fossilologist ; a fossilist
화선지 畫宣紙 Chinese drawing paper
화섬 化纖 a chemical〔synthetic〕 fiber
화성 火星 Mars
—인 a Martian ; an inhabitant of Mars
화성 化成 transformation ; change ; metamorphosis —하다 transform ; change ; metamorphose
— 공업 the chemical (and synthetic) industry — 비료 chemical〔synthetic〕 fertilizer ; a compound〔complex〕 fertilizer
화성 火成 ¶ 화성의 igneous
— 광상 igneous deposits —설 the vulcanian theory
화성 和聲 〖음악〗 harmony ; concord ; consonance ¶ 화성적 harmonic
—법 the law of harmony —학 harmonics ; the science of harmony 개리(開離)〔밀집〕 — open〔close〕 harmony
화성 畫聖 a great artist ; a master painter
화성암 火成岩 igneous rocks
화세 火勢 the force of fire
화솥 a hat-shaped〔wide-brimmed〕 kettle
화수 花樹 a flowering tree
화수 花穗 〖식물〗 a spike ; [옥수수 따위] an ear ¶ 억새의 화수 the ears of a euralia // 화수가 나온 억새 a euralia in the ear
화수분 a mythical tray which keeps multiplying whatever is put on it ; an inexhaustible fountain of wealth
화수회 花樹會 a convivial party of the members of a clan ; a family reunion
화순 花脣 a petal ; a flower leaf ; [미인의 입술] the lips of a beautiful woman
화순 和順 obedience ; docility ; gentleness ; submissiveness ; compliance ; meekness —하다 (be) obedient ; docile ; gentle ; submissive ; complaisant ; pliant ; meek ; yielding
화술 話術 the art of conversation ¶ 화술에 능한 사람 a good conversationalist
화승 火繩 a fuse ; a match-cord
—총 a matchlock (gun) ; a firelock ; a hackbut ; a harquebus
화시 花時 the flower season

화식 火食 cooked food ; eating of cooked food —하다 eat cooked food ; eat cooked
화식 和食 Japanese-style food ; [요리] Japanese dishes ⇨ 왜식
화식 貨殖 moneymaking —하다 make money ¶ 화식에 급급하다 be bent on 〔engrossed in〕 moneymaking
—론 chrematistics
화식도 花式圖 a (botanical) diagram of a flower
화식조 火食鳥 〖새〗 a cassowary
화신 化身 incarnation ; impersonation ; an avatar ¶ 악마의 화신 a devil incarnate〔in the flesh〕; an incarnate fiend // 욕심의 화신 the incarnation of avarice ; avarice itself // 사탄은 악의 화신이다 Satan is evil personified. // 그 악한은 악마의 화신이었다 The villain was a fiend incarnate.
화신 花信 tidings of flowers ; news about flowers in bloom
—풍 spring breezes〔presaging blossoms〕
화실 火室 [기관차 따위의] a fire box
화실 畫室 an atelier ; an artist's studio
화심 花心 [꽃의] the heart〔central part〕 of a flower ; [미인의] the heart of a beautiful woman
화심 禍心 evil intention ; treacherous designs ; perfidious mind
*화씨 華氏 Fahrenheit ¶ 화씨 50도 50°F
— 한란계 a Fahrenheit thermometer
화압 花押 a signature
†화약 火藥 gunpowder ; powder ¶ 대포에 화약을 재다 load a gun // 화약을 지고 불로 들어가다 invite danger ; enter the fire carrying gunpowder ; be playing with fire
—고 a powder magazine ; an explosive warehouse —류 explosives —선 a powder vessel — 제조소〔공장〕 a powder plant〔mill〕 — 취급법 the gunpowder law〔act〕 — 취급인 a dealer in〔handler of〕 gunpowder 무백〔백색〕 — smokeless〔white〕 gunpowder 혼합〔화합〕 — an explosive mixture〔compound〕
화연 花宴 a banquet celebrating one's sixtieth birthday
화염 火焰 a flame ; a blaze ¶ 화염에 싸이다 be enveloped〔wrapped〕 in flames
— 방사기 a flame thrower〔projector〕 — 방사 전차 a flame-throwing tank — 병 an (incendiary) bottle grenade ; a fire-bottle〔bomb〕; a gasoline bomb ; a Molotov cocktail ; a frangible grenade — 용접 flame welding
화엽 花葉 a petal ; [꽃과 잎] blossoms and leaves
화예 a stamen ; a pistil ⇨ 꽃술
†화요일 火曜日 Tuesday
화용 花容 a lovely face
—월태 a lovely face and graceful carriage
화운 和韻 composing a verse in response (following the rhymes〔rimes〕 used by another)
화원 花園 a flower garden
화월 花月 flowers and the moon ; the moon shining on flowers
화음 和音 〖음악〗 a chord ; an accord ¶ 화음의 chordal
—계 a harmonometer 기초 — the primitive chord 변화 — an altered chord 5도 — the fifth 주〔부〕 — a tonic〔secondary〕 chord
화음 華音 the modern Chinese readings of Chinese characters ; Chinese pronunciation
화응 和應 response ; agreement —하다 respond to ; agree with
화의 和議 negotiations for peace ; a peace conference ; reconciliation ; 〖법〗 composition (채권자와) —하다 negotiate for peace ; make reconciliations 《with》 ¶ 화의를 맺다 conclude peace 《with》; make a reconciliation 《with》 // 화의를 제안하다 make overtures of〔for〕 peace // 화의를 간청하다 sue for peace
—법 〖법〗 the Composition Law — 사건 a composition matter ; a case of composition — 신청 application〔petition〕 for composition — 절차 composition proceeding (상법) ; procedures of composition — 채권〔채권자〕 a composition obligation〔creditor〕
화이트 소스 white sauce
화이트 칼라 an office worker ; a white-collar worker ¶ 화이트 칼라의 white-collar
화이트 하우스 the White House
화인 火印 [낙인] a brand (mark) ; [되] a stamped grain measure ¶ 화인을 찍다 brand
화인 火因 the origin〔cause〕 of a fire ¶ 화인 불명의 화재 a fire of unknown origin
화인 禍因 the cause〔root〕 of evil ; the cause of trouble ¶ 화인을 남기다 sow the seeds of evil
화잠 花簪 a bridal hairpin (inlaid with jewels)
화장 火葬 cremation —하다 cremate ; burn to ashes
— 인부 a cremator ; a burner at a crematory —터 a crematorium 《*pl.* ~s, -ria》; a crematory ; a cremation ground 전기 — electric cremation
*화장 化粧 toilet ; make-up ; dressing ; beauty care —하다 make one's toilet ; paint〔powder〕 one's face (배우가) ; apply make-up ¶ 화장용의 for toilet (use, purpose) ; cosmetic // 엷은〔짙은〕 화장 light〔heavy〕 toilet // 눈물로 화장이 지워졌다 Her tears washed away the paint from her face.

—값〔료〕 beauty expenses ; a (lady's) pocket money ; pin money ¶ 월급 몽땅 받아 봐야 화장값 밖에 안돼요 My whole income goes out to cover my beauty expenses. —대 a dressing table ; a toilet stand ; a toilet table ; a dresser 《미》 — 도구 a toilet set ; a dressing equipage (케이스에 넣은 세트) —복 a dressing gown ; a camisole ; a wrapper ; a negligee (부인용의) ; a robe-de-chambre 《프》 ; a peignoir 《프》 — 비누 a toilet soap — 상자 a vanity (case〔box〕) ; a dressing case〔bag〕 ; [장식한 상자] a fancy box —수 toilet water〔lotion〕 ; face lotion ; eau de Cologne ; beauty wash —실 the ladies powder room ; a rest room ; a toilet (room) ; a lavatory — 크림 facial cream —품 toilet articles ; cosmetics ; a beautifier ; beauty aids ; makeup ; a beauty product —품류 toiletries —품점 a cosmetic shop〔store〕 밑— make-up base ; a foundation ¶ 크림으로 밑화장하다 use some cream as a make-up base 짙은〔엷은〕 — heavy 〔light〕 makeup

화장걸음 —長— leisurely steps ; a gentlemanly gait

†화재 火災 a fire ; a conflagration (큰 화재) ; a blaze ¶ 화재가 나다 a fire breaks out ; there is a fire // 극장에 화재가 났다 The theater is on fire. // 화재 위문차 방문하다 make a call to express one's sympathy after a fire

— 경보기 a fire alarm — 경보 장치 fire-warning facilities — 방지 운동 an anti-fire campaign — 보험 fire insurance — 예방 주간 Fire Prevention Week — 원인 the cause of a fire — 탐지기 a fire detector — 통계〔통보〕 fire statistics〔information〕

화재 畫才 an artistic talent

화적 火賊 ⇨ 불한당

화전 火田 ground burnt off for cultivation ; fields cleared for cultivation by burning

—민 fire-field farmers ; brand-tillers

화전 火箭 an incendiary arrow ; a fiery dart ; a flare ; a rocket (signal)

화전 和戰 peace and war〔war and peace〕 ¶ 화전의 결정 a decision of the question of peace or war // 화전 양방으로 대비하다 be prepared for both war and peace

— 조약 a peace treaty

화전 花煎 ① [꽃전] a cake made in the shape of a flower ② [부꾸미] fried-flower cookies

화전 火戰 a shooting battle ; a fire fight

화전지 花箋紙 paper for writing letters〔poems〕

화젓가락 火— fire tongs ⇨ 부젓가락

*화제 話題 a subject〔topic, theme〕 of conversation ¶ 화제가 풍부한 사람 a person of ample stock of topics // 화제에 오르다 become a topic of conversation ; be brought into conversation ; be talked about // 화제를 바꾸다 change the topic of conversation // 항간의 화제에 오르고 있다 be the talk of the town // 화제를 바꾸지 마라 Don't change the subject. // 그녀는 요즘 화제에 자주 오른다 She's in the news a lot these days.

화제 畫題 [그림 제목] the subject〔title〕 of a painting ; a subject for a picture ; [그림 위의] a composition written on a picture to explain it

화조 花鳥 flowers and birds ; birds that visit flowers ¶ 화조풍월을 벗삼다 enjoy (the beauties of) nature

—월석 flowery mornings and moonlit nights ; the most beautiful time of the year — 화첩 an album of flowers and birds

화족 華族 [사람] a peer ; a noble (man) ; [총칭] the nobility ; the peerage ; the aristocracy

화주 火酒 [주정] alcohol ; [독한 술] strong liquor ; firewater 《미·속》

화주 花柱 the style (of a flower)

화주 貨主 a property owner ; a goods holder

화중군자 花中君子 the lotus flower

화중왕 花中王 the peony

화중지병 畫中之餠 pie in the sky ; a desirable but unobtainable object

화증 火症 anger ; fury ; ire ; passion ¶ 화증이 나다 get angry〔mad〕 ; fly into temper〔a rage〕 ; flare up ; blow one's top

화지 畫紙 drawing paper

화집 畫集 a book of paintings

세잔 — [서명] (A Collection of) Cézanne Paintings

화차 火車 a train ⇨ 기차

화차 貨車 a freight car ; a goods wagon〔van〕

— 인도 free on rail 《f. o. r.》 《영》 ; free on board 《f. o. b.》 《미》 — 인도 가격 an f. o. b. price 《미》 ; an f. o. r. price 《영》 — 항송선(航送船) a freight-car ferryboat 무개 — an open〔a flat〕 wagon ; a goods truck ; a flat car 《미》 ; a gondola car (측면이 없는) 유개 — a covered wagon ; a freight car 《미》

*화창 和暢 balminess ; brightness (of weather) ; placidity —하다 [날씨가] (be) balmy ; bright ; sunny ; genial ; [마음이] (be) content(ed) and peaceful ; placid and happy ¶ 화창한 날씨 genial〔serene〕 weather // 화창한 봄날 a genial day in spring ; a balmy spring day

화채 花菜 juice mixed with fruits as a punch

화채 花債 ⇨ 해웃값
화첩 畫帖 a picture book ; a picture album
화초 花草 flowers ; flowering plants
—밭 flower garden —장이 a florist ; a floriculturist ; a flower man — 재배 floriculture —집 a flower〔florist's〕 shop — 품평회 a flower show
화촉 華燭 [초] painted candles ; [결혼식] a wedding ceremony
— 동방(洞房) the bridal room for the wedding night — 지전(之典) a wedding〔nuptials, marriage〕 ceremony
화촉을 밝히다 관용 celebrate a wedding ; solemnize a marriage
화축 花軸 ⇨ 꽃대
화충 협동 花沖協同 harmonious cooperation —하다 cooperate harmoniously〔in harmony〕
화치다 《a ship》 roll ; 《a boat》 rock
화친 和親 amity ; friendly relations —하다 make peace 《with》 ¶ 화친을 맺다 enter into friendly relations 《with》
화침 火針 a red-hot needle (used in breaking a boil) ¶ 화침질하다 break〔open, lance〕 a boil with a red-hot needle
화탁 花托 〖식물〗 the receptacle of a flower ; the torus ; the thalamus
화톳불 a bonfire ; a split-log fire ; a fire in the open air ¶ 화톳불을 놓다 make a bonfire
화통 〖건축〗 a cross groove at the top of a pillar
화통 火筒 a smokestack ; a funnel
화투 花鬪 Korean playing cards ; flower cards ¶ 화투치다 play〔shuffle〕 flower cards
화판 花瓣 〖식물〗 a (flower) petal
화판 畫板 a drawing board
화편 花片 flower petals
화평 和平 peace ; harmony ; placidity —하다 (be) peaceful ; harmonious ; placid ¶ 화평을 제창하다 make an overture of peace
†화폐 貨幣 money ; currency (통화) ; coin (경화) ¶ 화폐의 구매력 purchasing power of money // 화폐를 주조하다 mint coins
— 가치 currency value ; value of currency ; value in money ; valuta — 개혁 currency reform ; [평가 절하] devaluation — 경제 monetary economy — 교환 가치 the exchange value of a currency — 교환소 a money change booth — 동맹 a monetary union —법 〖법〗 the Coinage Act — 본위〔단위〕 a monetary standard〔unit〕 —석 〖고생물〗 a nummulite — 석회암 nummulitic limestone — 소득 monetary〔money〕 income — 위조 counterfeiting ; coining — 위조자 a counterfeiter ; a coiner — 유통액 the amount〔volume〕 of coins in circulation ; the amount of currency — 제도 the coinage〔currency, monetary〕 system — 주조 coinage ; mintage 법정 — legal tender 보조 — a subsidiary〔an auxiliary〕 currency〔coin〕 본위 — standard money 위조 — a counterfeit coin〔piece of currency, money〕 ; an imitation coin ☞ ◖ p. 2392 ◗
화포 花苞 the bract of a flower
화포 花布 dark blue cloth with white flower patterns which is used for making the cover of a sleeping mat ; figured cotton cloth
화포 花砲 fireworks ; pyrotechnics
화포 火砲 a gun ; a firearm
— 공격 gunfire
화포 畫布 a canvas
화폭 畫幅 a picture ; a drawing
화풀이 satisfying resentment ; letting off steam ; venting one's wrath —하다 satisfy one's resentment ; let off steam ; vent one's wrath 《on》 ; wreak one's anger 《on》 ¶ 나한테 화풀이 할 것 없다 You shouldn't take your anger out on me. // 그는 화풀이거리를 찾아냈다 He found vent for his anger. // 나한테 화풀이하지 마라 Don't take it out on me.
화품 畫品 artistic merit of a picture ; a style of a picture
화풍 和風 a gentle breeze ; a balmy wind
화풍 畫風 a style of painting ¶ 터너의 화풍 the brush of Turner
화피 花被 the perianth of a flower ; the floral envelope
화필 畫筆 a painting brush ; a painter's〔an artist's〕 brush
화하다 和— ① [섞다·타다] mix ; admix ; mingle ; blend ② [온화하다] (be) mild ; gentle ; genial ; pacific
화하다 化— ① [자동사] change ; turn ; be transformed ; metamorphose ; [타동사] change〔transform〕 ; turn into 《something else》 ¶ 타서 재로 화하다 burn to ashes // 죽어서 흙으로 화하다 die and decompose into earth // 한국화하다 be Koreanized ② [통달하다] be well versed 《in》 ; be a past master 《at》 ; be well posted 《on》 ; be at home 《in, on》 ¶ 그림에 화하다 be a master of painting // 장사에 화하다 be very good at business
‡화학 化學 chemistry ¶ 화학적(으로) chemical(ly)
— 결합 chemical combination ; chemical bond — 공업 chemical industry — 공학 chemical instruments〔appliances, implements〕 — 기호 chemical signs〔symbols〕 — 기호법 chemical notation — 반응 a chemical reaction — 방정식 a chemical equation — 변화 a chemical change — 병기 chemical

화 폐

① 지폐(紙幣)와 경화(硬貨)의 종류

▶지폐는 미국에서는 보통 bill, 또는 구어(口語)로서 paper money, 지폐 한 장을 가리킬 때는 greenback으로 쓴다. 영국에서는 보통 note(★정식은 bank note), 총칭은 paper money로 쓴다.

▶경화는 《영》·《미》 모두 coin을 쓴다. 미국에서는 1센트(penny), 5센트(nickel), 10센트(dime), 25센트(quarter), 50센트(half dollar).(★( )안은 통칭명) 영국에서는 1/2페니(half penny), 1페니(penny), 2펜스(two pence), 5펜스(five pence), 10펜스(ten pence), 20펜스(twenty pence), 50펜스(fifty pence), 1파운드(one pound)가 있다.

② 단위

미국 센트 cent(¢)
달러 1 dollar($)=100¢
영국 페니 penny(p) 《복수 pence》
파운드 1 pound(£)=100p
(★ $, £는 숫자 앞에 붙이고, ¢, p는 숫자 뒤에 붙인다.)

¶ $15 fifteen dollars // $10.15 ten dollars and fifteen cents // $9.98. nine ninety-eight; nine dollars (and) ninety-eight cents // 10¢ ten cents // £5 five pounds // £7.30 seven pounds thirty // £12.50 twelve fifty (pound); twelve pounds (and) fifty pence // 10p ten pence

③ 거스름돈 (change)

미국이나 영국에서는 가게에서 거스름돈을 건넬 때 우리식으로 1000원을 내고 950원짜리를 사면 1000-950=50원을 거슬러 주는 것이 아니라 이와 반대로 물건값에 거스름돈을 더하는 방식으로 계산한다.

예를 들어 10달러로 9달러 15센트의 물건을 샀다면 우선 10센트(dime)를 건네고 "Nine twenty-five."라고 말한 다음 다시 25센트를 건네고 "Nine fifty."라고 말하고, 다시 50센트를 건네면서 "Ten dollars."라고 한다. 즉, 물건 값 9달러 15센트에서 지불한 돈 ten dollars가 될 때까지 단위별로 더해가는 계산 방법을 쓴다.

weapons ― 분석 chemical analysis ― 비료 a chemical〔artificial〕 fertilizer〔manure〕 ―선 actinic rays ― 섬유 a synthetic〔chemical〕 fiber ―식 a chemical formula〔equation symbol〕 ― 실험실 a chemical laboratory ― 약품 (raw) chemicals ; chemotherapeutant ― 연구소 the Institute for Chemical Research ― 요법 〖의학〗 chemotherapy ― 원소 a chemical hydrator ―자 a chemist ― 작용 chemical action ―전 chemical warfare ―제 chemicals ― 제품 chemical goods〔products〕 ― 조미료 a chemical seasoning (stuff) ― 친화력 chemical affinity ― 펄프 chemical pulp ― 합성 chemical synthesis ; 〖식물〗 chemosynthesis 농예 ― agricultural chemistry 물리 ― physical chemistry 분석 ― analytical chemistry 실용〔응용〕 ― practical〔applied〕 chemistry 실험 ― experimental chemistry 열〔의〕 ― thermal〔medical〕 chemistry 유기〔무기〕 ― organic〔inorganic〕 chemistry 이론〔순정(純正)〕 ― theoretical〔pure〕 chemistry 정밀〔종합〕 ― fine〔synthetic〕 chemistry

화합 化合 chemical combination ―하다 combine 《with》 ¶ 수소와 산소는 화합해서 물이 된다 Hydrogen combines with oxygen to form water.
―량 combining weight ―력 chemical affinity ; combining power ―물 a (chemical) compound ―수 water of hydration ; combined water ―열 heat of combination

화합 和合 harmony ; concord ; unity ; union ―하다 harmonize 《with》 ; be in harmony ; be in accord 《with》 ; agree 《with》 ¶ 일가의 화합 a harmonious family life // 화합하여 살다 live in perfect harmony
―성 〖식물〗 compatibility ― 일치 unity ; unanimity

***화해 和解** reconciliation ; peacemaking ; an amicable settlement ; accommodation compromise ; composition ―하다 be reconciled 《with》 ; make up 《with》 ; make peace 《with》 ; compromise 《with》 ; arrive at a compromise ; heal an old feud ; come to〔reach〕 an amicable settlement ; settle 《things》 amicably ¶ 양자간의 화해 a reconciliation between the two // 화해할 수 없는 irreconcilable // 아내와 화해하다 effect a reconciliation with one's wife // 서로 화해해서 다시 친구가 되자 Let us become reconciled and friends again.

화향 花香 ① [꽃향기] the smell〔scent, fragrance〕 of flowers ¶ 방에는 화향이 그득하였다 Flowers perfumed the room. ② 〖불교〗 flowers and incense

(offered before the tablet of the deceased)

화현 和絃 〖음악〗 a chord ; a concord

화협 和協 harmony ; harmonious cooperation —하다 be in harmony ; cooperate 《with》 ¶ 화협하여 in harmony ; in close cooperation

화형 火刑 the stake ; burning at the stake

화호불성 畫虎不成 failing to succeed in imitating another person

*화환 花環 a garland ; a wreath ; a lei ¶ 화환을 바치다 place a wreath 《on the grave》

화환(어음) 貨換(—) a documentary draft〔bill〕 ; a document bill ; a value bill ¶ 화환 어음을 발행하다 draw a documentary bill 《on a person》

화훼 花卉 flowering grass〔plants〕
— 재배〔원예〕 floriculture ; cultivation of flowers — 재배〔원예〕가 a floriculturist — 품평회 a flower-show ; a floricultural show

확¹ [세게] with a great puff ; blowing hard ; with a gust ; [불이] flaring up ; with a burst ¶ 촛불을 확 불어 끄다 blow out a candlelight // 확 타오르다 flare up // 바람이 확 분다 A gust of wind blows. // 불이 확 종이에 당긴다 Paper catches fire. // 불이 별안간에 확 타올랐다 The fire sprang into a blaze.

확² [절구의] the hollow of a grain mortar ¶ 절구 확이 넓다 a mortar has a large bowl

확견 確見 a definite opinion〔view, idea〕

†확고 確固 firmness ; fixedness —하다 (be) firm ; fixed ; determined ; resolute ¶ 확고한 결심 a firm determination〔resolution〕 // 확고한 신념 a firm belief // 확고한 증거 positive proof

확답 確答 a definite〔decisive〕 answer —하다 answer〔reply〕 definitely ; give 《a person》 a definite answer ¶ 확답을 주지 않다 give no definite answer

‡확대 擴大 magnification ; enlargement —하다 magnify ; enlarge ; spread ; expand ¶ 전쟁의 확대 the spread of war // 2배로 확대된 사진 a twice enlarged photo // 사진을 확대하다 enlarge a photograph // 문제가 확대되다 a problem spreads〔grows〕 // 20배로 확대하다 magnify an object 20 times // 이 현미경은 물체를 800배로 확대한다 This microscope magnifies objects eight hundred times. // 이 사진을 확대하고 싶다 I want this picture enlarged〔blown up〕.
—경 a magnifying glass〔lens〕 ; a magnifier ; [현미경의] an amplifier —기(器) an enlarger — 시험 an expansion test — (투쟁) 위원회 a (fighting) committee with enlarged membership — 유전자 an extension gene —율 magnification〔magnifying〕 power ; the degree〔scale〕 of enlargement ; 〖사진〗 an enlargement ratio ; lens power —자 an enlarged scale — 재생산 expansive reproduction ; reproduction on an enlarged scale

확론 確論 an infallible〔irrefutable〕 argument ; a self-evident proposition ; an established theory —하다 discuss〔argue〕 definitely

확률 確率 probability ; likelihood ¶ 확률이 크다 it is quite probable that ; it is likely that // 성공할 확률은 3분지 1이다 The probability of success is one to three.
— 곡선 〖통계〗 a probability curve — 오차 〖통계〗 a probable error — 표본 a probability〔random〕 sample — 함수 〖수학〗 a probability function

†확립 確立 establishment —하다 establish ; settle ; fix ¶ 확립된 definite ; established ; settled // 평화의 확립 the establishment of peace // 지위를 확립하다 establish one's position

확문 確聞 —하다 learn from reliable sources ; learn reliably ¶ 확문한 바에 의하면 according to a reliable source ; according to an authentic report

†확보 確報 a confirmed〔definite, sure〕 report ; definite〔authentic〕 news ; a reliable〔an authentic〕 communication —하다 give a definite report

확보 確保 security ; insurance ; guarantee —하다 secure ; ensure〔insure〕 ; assure ; guarantee ¶ 식량을 확보하다 secure foodstuffs // 그런 상품 지식으로는 고객을 확보할 수 없다 You'll never win over customers unless you know more about the products.

확산 擴散 〖물리〗 diffusion —하다 diffuse ¶ 빛의 확산 diffusion of light
—체 a diffuser ; 〖원자물리〗 a diffusate — 투과 diffuse transmission 핵 — spread of nuclear arms ; nuclear proliferation ¶ 핵 확산 금지〔방지〕 조약〔협정〕 non-〔anti-〕proliferation treaty〔agreement〕 ; nuclear ban treaty

확설 確說 an established theory ⇨ 확론

*확성기 擴聲器 a loud speaker ; a (sound) magnifier ; a megaphone ; a speech trumpet

확성장치 擴聲裝置 《on》 a public-address system 《PA, P. A., p. a. system》

확쇠 〖건축〗 an iron saucer on which a door pivots

확수 確守 ⇨ 고수(固守)

†확신 確信 conviction ; a firm belief ; confidence (자신) ; assurance —하다 be〔feel〕 convinced 《of》 ; believe firmly ; be〔feel〕 confident 《of》 ; be sure 《of》 ; feel certain 《of》 ; hold (a firm belief) ; be assured 《of》 ¶ 그는 자기가

옳다고 확신하고 있다 He is convinced that he is right. // 너의 성공을 확신한다 I am confident of your success. // 지식은 힘이라고 확신한다 It is my firm belief that knowledge is power. // 변호사는 그 죄수의 무죄를 확신하고 있다 The lawyer is convinced of the innocence of the prisoner. // 그는 신의 존재를 확신하고 있다 He is positive as to the existence of God. // 날이 갈수록 더욱 확신이 굳어졌다 I was confirmed in my belief with the lapse of time.

†**확실 確實** certainty ; reliability ; trustworthiness ; authenticity **—하다** (be) certain ; sure ; secure ; [신뢰할 수 있는] reliable ; trustworthy ; true ; [정확한] authentic ; valid ; [견실한] sound ; solid ¶ 확실한 투자 a sound investment // 확실한 방법 a sure〔safe〕 method // 확실한 증거 positive proof ; conclusive evidence // 확실한 대답 a definite answer // 확실한 보증인 a reliable surety // 확실한 것은 모르겠지만 if I am correctly informed // 확실성이 있다 wear an aspect of certainty // 그가 성공할 것은 확실하다 He is sure to succeed. // 그가 임명되는 것은 확실하다 He is sure to be appointed. / His appointment is certain. // 비가 올 것만은 확실하다 I can assure you of one thing. It is going to rain. // 저 사람의 판단은 확실하다 His judgment is infallible. // 내가 승진을 하게 될지 못하게 될지는 아직 확실하지 않다 It's up in the air whether I'll get a promotion or not.

—성 reliability ; certainty ; soundness **절대 —** infallibility

확실히 確實— certainly ; surely ; for certain ; to be sure ; for sure ; definitely ; [의심할 여지없이] beyond (a) doubt ; doubtless ; indubitably ; [견실하게] steadily ; [틀림없이] without fail ; [맹세코] upon one's honor〔word〕; in all conscience ¶ 내가 확실히 아는 바로는 to my certain knowledge // 확실히 하다 ensure ; make sure 《of》 // 그것은 확실히 틀린다 It is certainly wrong. // 확실히는 모른다 I don't know it for certain.

확약 確約 a definite promise **—하다** promise definitely〔faithfully〕; give one's word 《to》; commit oneself 《to》; give〔make〕 a definite promise ¶ 확약은 할 수 없다 I cannot make a definite promise〔appointment〕.

*__확언 確言__ a definite〔positive〕 statement ; assurance ; assertion ; affirmation **—하다** tell for certain ; speak positively ; state〔say〕 definitely ; assert ; assure ; affirm ¶ 그 점은 확언하기 어렵다 I am not positive about the point.

확연 確然 definitely ; positively ; certainly ; surely **—하다** (be) definite ; positive ; certain ; sure

확인 確因 a definite cause〔reason〕

‡**확인 確認** confirmation ; affirmation ; certification ; validation **—하다** confirm ; corroborate ; verify ; affirm ; put one's seal 《to》; validate ; certify ¶ 미확인의 unconfirmed // 무효 확인을 청구하다 call for the affirmation of the nullity of a resolution // 사생아의 아버지를 확인하다 affiliate a child to a parent // 이 보고는 아직 확인되지 않았다 This report is not yet confirmed. /This is an unconfirmed report. // 수표 한 장이 있는데 부도 수표가 아닌지 확인해 주시겠습니까 Could you verify a check please? /Could you check and see if this is good?

— 반응 〖화학〗 confirmatory reaction **— 사항** items confirmed〔verified〕 **—서** a (written) confirmation ; a confirmation document **— 신용장** confirmed letter of credit〔L. C.〕 **—자** 〖법〗 a confirmor ; an identifier **—장** a confirmation sheet **— 통지서** a confirmation note **— 판결** a declaratory judgment

> [참고] **confirm** 의심스러운 일의 진부를 확실한 것에 비추어 확인하다 **corroborate** 어떤 사람의 진술이나 증언을 다른 사람의 진술이나 새로운 사실에 비추어 확인하다 **verify** 조사 비교 참조 따위를 해서 사실의 정확함을 증명하다 **authenticate** 알고 있는 사람의 증언에 의해서 일의 진실함을 증명하다

‡**확장 擴張** expansion ; extension ; enlargement ; aggrandizement ; increment ; dilation **—하다** expand ; extend ; enlarge ; aggrandize ; increase (증가) ; widen (도로 따위) ¶ 판로를 확장하다 extend the market // 업무를 확장하다 expand〔extend〕 the business // 점포를 확장하다 enlarge the store

— 공사 extension work **—론자** an expansionist **— 명제** 〖논리〗 an ampliative proposition **— 정책** a policy of expansion **군비 —** the expansion of armaments ; an armaments boost **영토 —** territorial expansion **도로 — 계획** a street-widening project **영토 —론** (territorial) expansionism ; imperialism **영토 —론자** an expansionist

확전 擴戰 (war) escalation

*__확정 確定__ decision ; settlement ; conclusion ; [확인] confirmation **—하다** decide ; settle ; fix ; confirm ¶ 확정된 settled ; fixed ; decided ; certain ; definite // 확정적으로 definitely ; conclusively ; once and for all // 확정되다 get decided ; be settled ; be fixed ; be confirmed ; come to a definite decision // 이것은 확정된 사실이다 This is an estab-

lished fact. // 그것은 아직 확정되지 않았다 The matter is not yet definitely settled. // 그의 해외 파견이 확정되었다 It is decided that he shall be sent abroad.
— 금액 a definite amount — 매매〔신청, 주문〕 a firm bargain〔offer, order〕 — 부채〔신용장〕 a fixed charge〔letter of credit〕 — 사항 a definitely settled matter — 신고 [소득세의] a final (income tax) return〔declaration〕 ¶ 확정 신고를 하다 turn in a final return 《of one's income tax》 —안 a final draft — 의무〔채무〕 a determinate obligation — 일자 a fixed date ; an inconvertible date — 판결 an irrevocable〔a final and conclusive〕 judgment

확증 確證 positive proof ; proof positive ; conclusive evidence —하다 prove〔show〕 positively ; prove beyond doubt ; give positive proof 《of》; corroborate ¶ 확증적 corroborative ; confirmatory // 확증을 얻다 have positive evidence

확집 確執 adherence to one's own opinion ; [불화] discord ; differences ; antagonism ; strife ; feud —하다 adhere〔stick, cling〕 to (one's own opinion)

확청 廓淸 purification ; (thorough) cleaning ; a cleanup ; a shake-up ; purge ; expurgation —하다 purify ; clean (up) ; purge ; cleanse

확충 擴充 expansion ; amplification (부연) ; 〖논리〗 distribution —하다 expand ; amplify ; distribute ¶ 생산력 확충 an expansion of productive capacity // 사업을 확충하다 expand business
—성 expansibility

확호 確乎 firmly ; resolutely ; determinedly —하다 (be) firm ; adamant

확확 ① [세게] with great puffs ; with gusts ; huffing and puffing ¶ 바람이 확확 불다 have gust after gust of wind ② [불이] with flame after flame ; with burst after burst ¶ 불이 솜에 확확 당기다 cotton flames up

환[1] [줄] a kind of file〔rasp〕 ; a serrated iron piece or a wooden stick with shark skin on its edge ¶ 환 쓸다 file ; rasp

환[2] [그림] a rough drawing ; a cheap painting ; a sketch ; a painting
환을 치다 (관용) draw〔make〕 a sketch

환 丸 a pill ⇨ 환약

환 換 a note of exchange ; a check ; [환전] a money order ¶ 환을 발행하다 draw a bill of exchange // 환으로 송금하다 send by money order // 1,000원짜리 환을 한 장 주시오 Give me a postal money order for one thousand *won*. // 이 환을 현금으로 바꾸어야겠다 I shall have this money order cashed.
—거래〔조작〕 exchange transactions 〔operation〕 —관리 〖상업〗 exchange control ; restrictions on exchange —발행인 a drawer —시세 the (foreign) exchange rates ; the rate of exchange ; an exchange quotation —시장〔은행, 환산표〕 an exchange market 〔bank, table〕 —어음 ⇨ 환어음(換—) 《프》 내국— domestic exchange 외국— foreign exchange 우편— a postal money order 전보— a telegraphic remittance

환 環 〖화학〗 [원자의] a ring
—검류계(檢流計) a loop galvanometer

환가 換價 conversion (into money) ; realization —하다 convert into money ; cash ; sell ; realize ¶ 재산을 환가하다 realize property
— 불능 자산 unrealizable assets —성 marketability ; market value —율 a conversion rate

⁑**환각 幻覺** a hallucination ; an illusion ¶ 환각을 일으키다 hallucinate ; have hallucinations
—병〔증〕 hallucinosis — 예술〔음악〕 psychedelic art〔music〕 —제 a hallucinogen ; a hallucinogenic drug ¶ 환각제 상용자 a psychedelic — 파괴 dishallucination

환갑 還甲 one's 60th birthday anniversary
— 노인 a sexagenarian — 잔치 a banquet on one's 60th birthday ¶ 환갑 잔치를 베풀다 give a banquet on one's 60th birthday

†**환경 環境** environment ; surroundings ; circumstances ¶ 환경에 좌우되다 be influenced by one's environment // 새로운 환경에 순응해야 한다 You have to adapt yourself to your new circumstances. // 사람은 환경의 동물이다 Man is the creature of circumstances. // 나는 환경에 순응하려고 애썼다 I tried to accommodate myself to the circumstances.
— 공학〔파괴〕 environmental engineering〔disruption〕 — 교육 education from one's environment — 기준 an environmental standard 《for sulphurous acid gas》 — 보호 the protection of environment — 보호법 the environmental protection law — 위생(학) environmental hygiene〔hygienics〕 — 의학 geomedicine — 제어 장치 environmental control system 가정 — home environment〔surroundings〕 생활 — life〔living〕 environment ; living conditions ; 〖생물〗 habitat ☞ ◀ p. 2396 ▶

환곡 換穀 exchanging grain —하다 exchange grain

환골탈태 換骨奪胎 adaptation ; modification ; recast 《writing》

환공 環攻 besiegement —하다 besiege ; attack on all sides

환 경

① 환경

환경 environment / 환경 보전 environmental preservation; preservation of the environment / 환경 보전주의자 environmentalist; (environmental) preservationist / 환경 의학 environmental medicine / 환경 위생학 environmental hygienics / 환경처 the Ministry of Environment / 환경 백서 White Paper on the Environment / 환경 기준 environmental (quality) standard / 환경권 the right to protect[preserve] one's environment; the right of entitlement to a good environment; the environment right

② 공해

공해 environmental pollution [destruction] / 공해병 disease caused by environment pollution[contamination]; pollution-triggered disease / 공해병 인정 환자 officially certified patient[victim] of a pollution disease / 공해 방지 prevention of (environment) pollution[disruption] / 공해 방지 조례 pollution control ordinance / 2차 공해 secondary pollution; pollution suffered as the consequence of another pollution / 풍해 wind damage[hazard] / 연해(煙害) smoke damage[hazard] / 배연탈류(排煙脫硫) desulfurization of flue[stack] gas; flue gas desulfurization / 배연 세정 장치 flue [stack] gas scrubber / 스모그 smog / 광화학 스모그 photochemical smog; white smog / 배기 가스 (auto) exhaust [emission] / 배기 가스 규제 emission control / 소음 공해 noise pollution / 산성비 acid rain; acid precipitation / 산성진(塵) acid dust / 산성 안개 acid mist / 적조(赤潮) red tide / 부(富)영양화 eutrophication / 산업 폐기물 industrial waste / 고형 산업 폐기물 solid (industrial) waste / 폐산 used acid / 방사성 폐기물 radioactive waste; nuclear waste / 침전물 sludge / 수질 오염 water pollution / 수질 기준 water quality standards / 해양[상] 투기 oceandumping; dumping at sea / 오염 pollution; contamination / 환경 오염 environmental pollution[contamination] / 오염도 (오염당하는 측의) degree of contamination / 오염도 (오염하는 측의) polluting potential / 오염 행위 act of pollution / 오염자 polluter / 오염자 부담의 원칙 polluter-pay(s)-principle; p.p.p. / 폐기물 처리장 garbage[refuse] dump / 오존층 ozone layer; ozonosphere / 생물 화학적산소 요구량 biochemical oxygen demand; BOD / 화학적 산소 요구량 chemical oxygen demand; COD / 피피엠 parts per million (PPM, ppm) / 수내한도(受耐限度) sufferable limit; limit of sufferance [tolerance] / 감시 측정소 monitoring post [station] / 생태학 ecology 생태계 ecosystem / 기름의 유출, 유출유 oil spill[slick]; spilled oil / 유출유 제거(작업) oil-spill cleanup / 유출유 제거업 oil-spill cleanup business / 유출유 제거업자 oil-spill cleanupper / 떠내는 작업 (유출유의) skimming / (유출유의) 떠내는 장치 skimmer; skimming equipment[device] / 유흡착제 sorbent / 폐유 오일 blob of waste oil (that forms in the sea); gooey lump that waste oil forms into after being dumped at sea; waste oil clot / 오일 팬스 oil fence; floating barrier[booms] to contain oil spill

환과고독 **鰥寡孤獨** widowers and widows, orphans and childless persons; helpless persons

환관 **宦官** a eunuch

환국 **還國** return to one's country ⇨ 귀국

환군 **還軍** the withdrawal of troops; a troop withdrawal **—하다** withdraw (an army)

환궁 **還宮** **—하다** return to the palace

환권 **換券** changing old deeds〔documents〕 for new ones **—하다** change《deeds, documents》

환금 **換金** an exchange (of money) **—하다** exchange **— 수수료** a commission〔charge〕 for exchange **—업자** an exchange broker; a money changer **— 작물** a cash crop **— 판매** realization sales

환급 **還給** return; restoration **—하다** return; restore

환기 **喚起** rousing; awakening **—하다** rouse; arouse; awaken; call《a person's attention》; excite; stir up ¶ 주의를 환기시키다 call《a person's》 attention to《a fact》// 여론을 환기시키다 rouse〔arouse, stir up〕 public opinion

***환기** **換氣** a change of air; ventilation **—하다** change air; ventilate ¶ 환기가 잘 되다 be well ventilated

—공〔관〕 a ventilating hole〔pipe〕 —구 a ventilating opening —선(풍기) a ventilation〔ventilating〕 fan ; an extractor fan — 작용 〖심리〗 ventilation — 장치 ventilation facilities〔equipment, arrangement〕 ; a ventilator ; a ventilating device ¶ 이 영화관은 완전한 환기 장치가 되어 있다 This movie house has the most thorough ventilation. —창 a vent ; a window for ventilation —탑 a ventilating tower

환난 患難 misfortune ; trouble ; distress

환납 還納 —하다 return (public goods)

환담 歡談 a pleasant conversation —하다 have a pleasant chat〔talk〕 ; hobnob with ⟪a person⟫

*환대 歡待 a warm〔cordial〕 reception ; hospitality ; welcome —하다 receive hospitably〔warmly〕 ; make ⟪a person⟫ welcome ; accord a hospitable〔cordial〕 reception ; treat〔entertain〕 hospitably ¶ 환대를 받다 be cordially received ; be kindly and hospitably treated

환도 環刀 a saber ; a sword
—뼈 the hipbone — 상어 a thresher shark

환도 還都 returning to the capital ; returning of an evacuated government —하다 return to the capital ; return

환등 幻燈 a film slide ; a magic lantern ; a stereopticon views〔slides〕
—기(계) a magic lantern apparatus ; a stereopticon ; a slide projector — 필름 a film strip —화 a slide

환락 歡樂 pleasure ; enjoyment ; merriment ; mirth ; merrymaking —하다 enjoy oneself ; have fun ¶ 환락 생활 the primrose path // 인생의 환락 the pleasure of life // 도시의 환락 the city delights // 환락을 추구하다 seek pleasure ; gather (life's) roses
—가 the entertainment sections (of a town) ; an amusement center〔quarter〕 ; gay quarters ; a pleasure hunt ; a red-light district ⟪미⟫ —경(境) a pleasure resort ; an abode of pleasure ; a place with many amenities

환롱 幻弄 cheating ⟪a person⟫ by switching objects —하다 cheat ⟪a person⟫ by switching ⟪objects⟫ ; switch ⟪objects⟫ while one is unaware ¶ 내가 없는 동안에 물건을 환롱쳐 놓았다 He switched the thing while I was away.

환류 還流 a reflux ; 〖전기〗 a return current — 하다 flow back to ; return to ; have a reflux ¶ 자금의 환류 the reflux of capital

환매 還買 〖상업〗 redemption ; repurchase ; 〖증권〗 covering —하다 buy back ; repurchase ; redeem ; 〖증권〗 cover short
— 계약 a repurchase agreement —권 the right of repurchase —인 a redeemer

환매 換買 barter ; bartering truck —하다 barter ; trade ; truck ; dicker ; swap

환멸 幻滅 disillusion ; disillusionment ¶ 환멸의 비애를 느끼다 be disillusioned ; feel the bitterness of disillusionment

환몽 幻夢 an empty dream

환문 喚問 summons —하다 summon ⟪a person⟫ for examination

환물 換物 conversion of money into goods —하다 convert money into goods

환부 患部 the affected part ¶ 환부를 치료하다 dress an affected part

환부 還付 return ; restoration ; restitution ; retrocession —하다 return ; give back ; restore ; restitute ; retrocede
— 가산금 an additional amount to a refundment —금(金) refund —세 the refund tax

환부 鰥夫 a widower

환불 還拂 (a) refundment ; (a) refund ; (a) rebate ; (a) drawback ; (a) repayment ; (a) reimbursement —하다 pay back ; repay ; make repayment of ; refund ; reimburse ; allow a drawback ; rebate ; kickback ¶ 대금을 환불하다 return the price paid // 관세를 환불하다 draw back the duties paid
—금 a refund ; a repayment ; a rebate ; a kickback ; a drawback 전액 — (a) repayment in full ; a full refund

환산 換算 change ; conversion ; exchange —하다 change〔convert〕 ⟪into⟫ ; exchange ¶ 달러를 원으로 환산하다 convert dollars into *won*
— 계수〔식〕 a conversion factor〔formula〕 — 온도〔질량〕 reduced temperature 〔mass〕 —율 the exchange rates —표 a conversion〔an exchange〕 table ; a stock conversion formula

*환상 幻想 an illusion ; a vision ; a fantasy ; a phantasm ; a dream ; a reverie ¶ 환상적인 fantastical ; phantasmal ; dreamy ; visionary
—가 a visionary ; a dreamer ; a fantast ; an illusionist —곡 a fantasia ; a fantasy —주의 illusionism

환상 幻像 a phantom ; an illusion ; a vision ; a phantasm ; an apparition

환상 環狀 a ring shape ; annulation ¶ 환상의 ring-shaped ; circular ; loop
— 가로 a circumferential〔ring〕 street — 노선〔녹지〕 a ring route〔green〕 — 도로 a circular〔loop, ring〕 road ; a loop 〔belt〕 highway ; a beltline avenue (도시의) —선 a loop line ; a belt line (도시 전차의) ⟪미⟫ — 성운 〖천문〗 the Ring Nebula — 연골 ring〔cricoid〕 cartilage — 열석(列石) 〖고고〗 a stone circle — 전류 ring current

환생 還生 rebirth ; revival ; reincarnation

—하다 be born again ; come back to life ; revive ; be reincarnated
환성 歡聲 a shout of joy〔jubilation〕; a hurrah ; a cheer ¶ 환성을 올리다 set up a shout of joy ; give cheers ; shout 〔cry, yell, whoop〕 for joy
환세 換歲 change of the year
환속 還俗 —하다 leave the priesthood ; return to secular life
환송 還送 sending back ; returning —하다 send back ; return
환송 歡送 a farewell ; a send-off ; —하다 give 《a person》 a send-off ; send〔see〕《a person》 off
—식 farewell〔send-off〕 ceremonies —회 a farewell party ; a send-off party
환수 還收 redemption
—권 the right of redemption ¶ 환수권 상실 foreclosure
환술 幻術 the black art ; magic arts ; sorcery ; witchcraft ; magic tricks
환시 環視 looking on ; watching —하다 look on ; watch ¶ 중인 환시에 in the full view of the public ; in public // 중인 환시의 대상이 되다 become the object of public attention
환심 歡心 favor ; good graces ¶ 그는 상사의 환심을 얻기에 노력하고 있다 He is doing his best to win the favor of his superiors.
환심 사다 관용 curry favor with 《a person》; court 《a person's》 good graces ; win 《a person's》 favor ; ingratiate oneself 《with a person》
‡환약 丸藥 a pill ; a globule ; a bolus ; pellet ; a pilule
환어음 換— a bill of exchange ; a draft ; a draught ¶ 5백달러의 환어음을 발행하다 draw a bill of exchange 《on a person》 for 500 dollars // 환어음을 할인하다 discount a bill of exchange〔draft〕
— 기입장 a draft book — 지불인 drawee 기명식 — a special bill 단기〔장기〕 — a sort〔long〕 dated bill〔paper〕 보통 — a clean bill 부도〔거절〕 — dishonored〔protested〕 draft 일람불 — a bill at sight 정기불 — a time bill 〔draft〕
환언 換言 —하다 say〔put〕 in other words ¶ 환언하면 in other words ; that is to say ; to wit ; namely
*환영 幻影 a phantom ; a vision ; a phantasm
†환영 歡迎 welcome ; reception —하다 welcome ; give 《a person》 a welcome ; receive warmly〔well〕; bid 《a person》 welcome ; give a reception〔an ovation〕 to ¶ 환영을 받다 be warmly welcomed ; be given a welcome ; be given a warm reception ; be liked // 환영을 받지 못하다 be not welcomed ; be disliked // 쌍수를 들어 환영하다 welcome with open arms // 박수로 환영하다 give an ovation (with clapping of hands) // 그런 책은 환영받을 것이다 Such books will meet with a favorable reception. // 그의 글은 독자들이 그다지 환영하지 않는다 His writing isn't well received by the reading public. // 당신은 언제든지 환영하겠습니다 You are always welcome. // 독자의 투고를 환영합니다 Contributions from readers are cordially invited. // 운임 인하는 일반 시민으로부터 환영받았다 The fare reduction was well received by the public.
— 만찬회 a reception dinner ¶ 귀국〔귀향〕 환영 만찬회 a welcome-home dinner 《in honor of》 —사 an address〔a speech〕 of welcome 《in honor of》; a welcoming speech ; a welcome address — 아치〔문〕 a welcome arch ; a gate of honor — 위원회 a reception committee —자 a welcomer —회 a welcome party ; a reception ¶ 우리 학교는 신임 교장의 환영회를 열었다 Our school gave a reception to our new principal. 대— a hearty welcome〔reception〕; an enthusiastic ovation
환우기 換羽期 the molting season
환원 還元 restoration ; 〖화학〗 reduction ; resolution (분해) ; deoxidation (산화물의) —하다 restore ; be restored ; reduce ; be reduced 《to》; resolve (itself into elements) ; deoxidate ; deoxidize ¶ 환원시키다 vivify // 화합물은 그 원소로 환원된다 The compound resolves itself into its elements.
—당 reducing sugar —법〔설〕 reductionism ¶ 간접 환원법 〖논리〗 indirect reduction —염 reducing flames — 작용 a reducing process — 장치 a reductor —제 a reducing〔deoxidating〕 agent ; a reducer ; a reductant —철 reduced iron — 효소 reductase ; reducing enzyme
환월 幻月 a paraselene ; a mock moon ; a moon dog
환위 換位 transposition ; 〖논리〗 conversion ; 〖문법〗 inversion —하다 transpose ; convert ; invert ¶ 환위적인 conversive // 환위할 수 있는 convertible
— 명제 〖논리〗 a converse proposition
환유 換喩 metonymy ¶ 환유어(語) a metonym
환율 換率 an exchange rate ¶ 1달러 대 86펜스의 환율로 at the exchange of 86 pence to the dollar
— 변경 exchange rate fluctuation — 인상 a raise in exchange rates 대미(對美)— the (exchange) rate on America ; the U.S. dollar rate 고정 —제 a fixed〔pegged〕 exchange rate system 변동 —제 a fluctuating〔floating〕 exchange rate system
환일 幻日 〖기상〗 a parhelion 《*pl.* -lia》; a mock sun ; parheliacal ring〔circle〕; a sun dog

†환자 患者 a patient ; a sufferer ; a case 《of cholera》 ¶ 새 환자가 자꾸 생긴다 New cases are reported one after another. // 적리 환자가 2명 발생했다 Two cases of dysentery occurred. // 저 의사는 이 근방에 환자를 많이 가지고 있다 The doctor has a great many patients in this part of the city. // 저 병원은 환자를 100명 가량 수용할 수 있다 The hospital can accommodate 100 patients or so.
— 명부 a sick list — 운반차 an ambulance 내과〔외과〕 — a medical〔surgical〕 subject 무료 — a free patient ; a charity patient 수술 — a surgical patient ; a surgery case 신— a new 〔fresh〕 case 외래 — an outpatient 입원 — an inpatient 진성〔의사〕 — a genuine〔suspected〕 case 《of cholera》
환장 換腸 —하다 become a changed man ; go crazy ; be out of one's mind ¶ 그 여자는 환장했다 Her mind is in a welter of confusion. // 그는 비탄의 나머지 환장했다 Grief drove him to distraction.
환장이 a dauber ; a hack painter
환전 換錢 a money order
환절 換節 a change of seasons
—기 a change of season
환절 環節 〖동물〗 a (ring-like body) segment ; a somite ; a metamere ; an annulation〔annulated segment〕 ; a ring
— 동물 the Annelida
환지 —紙 sketching paper
환지 換地 replotting ; land substitution ; [토지] a substitute lot ; the land substituted for
— 설계〔지정, 처분〕 the design〔designation, disposal〕 of replotting — 예정지 the reserved land for replotting
환짓다 丸— make a pill
환천희지 歡天喜地 ecstasy ; rapture ; a transport of joy
환초 環礁 an atoll ; a lagoon island
환치다 sketch ; paint ; draw a rough sketch 《of》 ; daub
환태평양 環太平洋 ¶ 환태평양 지진대 the circum-pan-Pacific earthquake belt
환택 還宅 returning to one's honored home ; going home —하다 return home ; come home ; get home
환퇴 還退 having a sold article returned ; refunding a purchase ; returning a purchase 《for refund》 —하다 have a sold article returned ; return a purchase 《for refund》 ; get a purchase refunded ; cancel〔repeal〕 a purchase (해약하다)
환표 換票 ① bill of exchange ② [선거의] ballot switching ; voting irregularities —하다 switch ballots ; commit voting irregularities
환품 換品 exchange of goods〔articles〕 —하다 exchange 《goods》
환풍기 換風機 a ventilation〔ventilating〕 fan ; an extractor fan
*환하다 ① [앞이] (be) clear ; open ; unobstructed ; [밝다] bright ; [얼굴이] big and open ; fine-looking ¶ 길이 환하다 a road is clear ; a road is wide open // 환히 보이다 get an unobstructed view // 방〔불〕이 환하다 a room〔light〕 is bright // 얼굴이 환하다 have a big open face ② [명백] (be) clear ; plain ; evident ; obvious ; [통달] be well versed 《in》 ; be well acquainted 《with》 ; be familiar 《with》 ¶ 시장 시세에 환하다 be conversant with the market prices // 지방 지리에 환하다 be familiar with the lay of the land // 정국에 환하다 be up on the political situation // 네 속은 내가 환하게 알고 있다 I can see through your mind〔intention〕 clearly.
환향 還鄕 —하다 return to one's native soil〔hometown〕 ; go back home
금의— returning home in glory ; returning home loaded with honors
환형 環形 a ring shape ¶ 환형의 ring-shaped ; looped
— 동물 〖동물〗 an annelid ; a round 〔segmented〕 worm — 동물류 Annelida
†환호 歡呼 cheers ; a shout of joy ; a hurrah ; an ovation ; an acclamation —하다 cheer ; give cheers ; shout for joy ; acclaim ; hurrah ¶ 환호리에 amidst hearty cheers // 환호성을 울리다 shout for joy ; set up a shout of joy // 환호성으로 맞이하다〔보내다〕 greet〔send off〕 《a person》 with hearty cheers
환혹 幻惑 fascination ; bewitching ; glamor —하다 fascinate ; bewitch ; glamor ¶ 환혹적인 fascinating ; bewitching ; glamorous
환후 患候 the sickness〔illness〕 of a person honored
‡환희 歡喜 joy ; rejoicing ; delight ; gladness ; glee —하다 rejoice 《at, in》 ; be very glad ; be gleeful
†활 a bow ¶ 활의 명수 an expert archer // 활을 메우다 make a bow // 활을 쏘다 shoot an arrow ; shoot with a bow (and arrow) // 활을 당기다 draw〔bend〕 a bow // 활에 살을 메우다 fix〔put, fit〕 an arrow to the bow // 활에 줄을 달다 string a bow
활강 滑降 descent
— 경기 a downhill race ; downhill competition 사(斜)— 〖스키〗 traversing 직— 〖스키〗 straight descent ; schussing ; a schuss
활개 [팔] one's arms ; one's limbs ; [날개] the wings of bird ¶ 활개치다 [팔] swing one's arms ; [날개] flap the wings ; flutter // 활개치며 걷다 walk swinging one's arms // 네 활개치다 walk with a swaggering gait ; strut ; swagger

about ; swing one's arms and legs
활개똥 a runny discharge from diarrhea
활갯짓 strutting ; swaggering ; swinging one's arms **—하다** strut ; swagger 《about》 ; swing one's arms
활계 活計 the means of subsistence ; a livelihood ; a living
활고자 the tips of a bow (to which the string is attached)
활공 滑空 gliding ; a glide ; volplane **—하다** glide ; volplane
— 거리 gliding distance **—기** a glider
활극 活劇 a realistic scene (실제의) ; a stormy〔riotous〕 scene (소동) ; an action film (영화) ; an action-packed drama (연극) ¶ 활극을 연출하다 make a scene ; have a nice scene
서부 — a Western (film) ; a horse opera 《미·속》
‡**활기 活氣** vigor ; life ; vitality ; energy ; liveliness ; activity ; sprightliness ; animation ; vivacity ¶ 활기 있다 be full of life〔vigor〕 ; be vigorous〔lively, energetic, spirited〕// 활기 없다 be lifeless 〔inactive, dull, weak〕// 활기를 띠다 become active ; be animated ; begin to show life ; become lively ; be spurred // 이 마을에는 별로 활기가 없다 There is not much life in this country village. // 장내는 이야기 소리와 웃음 소리로 활기를 띠고 있다 The hall is alive with chatter and laughter. // 경제계가 활기를 띠었다 The economic world showed signs of life. // 한국의 여러 산업 활동이 매우 활기를 띠게 되었다 Various industrial activities in Korea were greatly animated. // 그는 평상시의 활기가 사라졌다 His usual energy deserted him. // 오늘은 평상시의 활기찬 네가 아닌 것 같다 You don't seem your usual energetic self today.
활달 豁達 magnanimity ; broad-mindedness ; frankness ; liberality ; generosity **—하다** (be) magnanimous ; broad-minded ; frank ; liberal ; generous
활대 the cross-stick at the top of a sail
†**활동 活動** activity ; action ; motion ; operation ; working ; service ; strenuous exertion **—하다** be active ; lead an active life ; take an active part 《in》 ; lead a stirring life ; display 〔show〕 activity ¶ 활동적인 active ; energetic ; dynamic // 활동시키다 bring into play ; call into activity // 그의 활동 범위는 크다 He has a wide sphere of action. // 경찰이 활동을 개시했다 The police got into action. // 수영은 전신의 근육을 활동시키므로 당신에게는 가장 좋은 운동이라고 생각한다 I think swimming is best for you as it brings all the muscles of the body into active play. // 그 여자는 연예계에서 아직도 활동을 하고 있지 She's still active in the showbiz.
—가 a man of action〔active habits〕 ; an active〔energetic〕 person ; a go-getter 《속》 ; a (real) pusher ; a man who is (thoroughly) alive ; a live wire ; a man of (restless) energy ; an activist ; a rustler 《미·구》 ; a hustler **—력** energy ; vitality ; activity **— 무대** one's field 〔stage〕 of action〔activity〕 **— 범위** a sphere〔scope〕 of activity〔action〕 **— 사진** motion pictures **— 전류** an action current **—주의** activism ; energism **과외 —** extracurricular〔extracurriculum〕 activities **교내〔연구〕 —** school〔learned〕 activities **정신 —** mental activity ; the activity of one's mind **정치 —** political activities
활동 滑動 〖기계〗 sliding **—하다** slide
활등 the back of a bow
—코 a high-bridged nose
활딱 ① [벗어짐] swept clear〔bright〕 ¶ 머리가 활딱 벗겨지다 get all bald // 구름이 활딱 벗겨지다 clouds get all swept away ② [뒤집힘] turning over suddenly〔completely〕 ; topsy-turvy ¶ 배가 활딱 뒤집히다 a boat capsizes all at once // 집안이 활딱 뒤집히다 a house is all upset
활량 an idler ; a drone ⇨ 한량
활력 活力 vital power〔energy〕 ; life forces ; vitality ; pep 《속》 ; energy
—설 〖철학〗 vitalism **—소** a tonic ; a vitamin **— 위축** 〖의학〗 abiotrophy **— 회복** revitalization **과도 —** 〖의학〗 sthenia
활로 活路 a way out (of a difficulty) ; a means of escape ; ways〔means〕 of living ¶ 활로를 개척하다 find a way out of a difficulty ; cut one's way through the enemy (적의 포위에서) ; find a way of living
활머리 the top plait of false hair formerly worn by a bride at her wedding ceremony
활무대 活舞臺 the sphere〔field〕 of activity ; an arena ; stage ; field ; theater ; a living stage ¶ 세계의 활무대 the international arena
활물 活物 a living creature
— 기생 a parasitism on living things
†**활발 活潑** liveliness ; briskness ; activity ; vivacity ; sprightliness ; vigor ; animation **—하다** (be) lively ; brisk ; active ; quick ; open ; free ; vivacious ; vigorous ; sprightly ; full of life〔animation〕 ¶ 활발한 사람 an active person // 활발한 기상 a vigorous spirit // 무역의 활발성 activity of trade // 활발히 briskly ; actively ; lively // 동작이 활발하다 be quick in action // 활발히 대답하다 answer without reserve // 시장이 활발하다 The market is active〔buoyant〕. // 사내아이가 계집아이보다 활발하다 A boy

is more active than a girl. // 시황은 오전 중 활발했다 The tone of the market was buoyant in the morning.

활변 滑便 loose bowels ; a loose passage (of fecal matter) ; lax stools

활보 闊步 —하다 stride ; strut ; swagger ⟪about⟫ ; walk with great strides ¶ 거리를 활보하다 strut along a street

활불 活佛 a living Buddha (생불) ; a benevolent person (자비로운 사람) ; an incarnation of Buddha

활비비 a bowstring drill

활빈당 活貧黨 (a band of) Robin-Hoods ; outlaws who rob in order to help the poor

활빙 滑氷 (ice-) skating **—하다** (ice-) skate

활사 活寫 a vivid description **—하다** make a vivid description ⟪of⟫ ; describe vividly ; make ⟪a historical character⟫ live ; paint quite a lively picture ⟪of⟫

활살 活殺 life and death ¶ 활살 자재하다 have the power of life and death over ⟪a person⟫ ; have ⟪a person⟫ at one's mercy ; have another's life in one's hands ; have ⟪a person⟫ in one's power〔grasp, clutches〕

활상 滑翔 soaring **—하다** soar
—기 a soaring plane ; a soarer ; a sailplane

활새머리 a short crop

활색 活塞 〖공학〗 a piston

활석 滑石 talc ; steatite
—분 talcum powder **— 편암(片岩)** talc schist

활선 活線 〖전기〗 a live wire
— 작업 operations〔work〕 on a live wire ; live-wire operations〔work〕 ; a hot-line job

활성 活性 (being) active ; activated ¶ 활성화하다 activate
— 산소〔수소, 질소〕 active oxygen 〔hydrogen, nitrogen〕 **—선** actinic rays **— 인자** an active factor **—제** an activator **— 탄소** activated carbon **—화(化)** activation

활수 滑手 liberality ; generosity **—하다** (be) liberal (in giving) ; generous ; openhanded

활시위 a bowstring ¶ 활시위를 메우다〔풀다〕 string〔unstring〕 a bow

활안 活眼 penetrating eyes ; penetration ; insight

활액 滑液 〖해부〗 synovia

⁑**활약 活躍** activity ; action **—하다** be active ⟪in⟫ ; take〔play〕 an active part ⟪in⟫ ; get into〔be in〕 action ; display 〔show〕 activity ¶ 정계에서 활약하다 play an active part in politics // 간첩이 활약하고 있다 A spy is active.

활어 活魚 live fish
— 무역 trade of live fish **—선** a live-fish transport (ship)

활연 豁然 all of a sudden ; in a sudden flash ; [환하게] extensively ¶ 활연 큰들이 열리다 a wide plain suddenly spreads out before one's eyes // 활연 깨닫다 be awakened with〔come to〕 a sudden flash (of realization) ; a truth bursts upon one

활엽수 闊葉樹 a broad-leaved tree ; a latifoliate tree

⁑**활용 活用** practical use〔application〕 ; 〖문법〗 inflection ; conjugation ; declension **—하다** apply ; utilize ; make the most of ; put to practical use ; make practical application of ; 〖문법〗 inflect (어미가) ; conjugate (동사가) ; decline (격이) ¶ 지식을 활용하다 put knowledge to practical use // 사실을 활용하다 take advantage of a fact // 진리를 실생활에 활용하다 apply a truth to one's life // 그는 인재를 잘 활용했다 He made the best use of talent.
—례 a paradigm ; an inflectional paradigm ; a paradigmatic set (of examples) **—어** inflected words **—형** an inflectional form ; an inflected form

활인화 活人畫 a living picture ; a tableau vivant (프)

†**활자 活字** a printing type ; type ⟪총칭⟫ ¶ 활자체로 쓰다 write in print // 활자를 짜다 set (up) type // 이름은 활자체로 쓰시오 Print your name. /Write your name in block letters. // 이것은 몇호 활자인가 What size is this type ?
—(합)금 type metal **—면** type face **—본** a printed book **—봉** a type bar **—인쇄** typeprinting ; typography **— 주조** type founding ; type casting **— 주조기** a type-caster ; a type-casting machine **— 주조소** a type-foundry **—체** print ¶ 활자체로 쓰다 write ⟪one's name⟫ in block letters **— 케이스** a case ; typesetter's stand (미) ; a compositor's frame **—판** a printed edition **—화** printing ; putting (a manuscript) into print ; typesetting **루비 —** ruby type (영) ; agate type (미) **악보 —** a font of music type **연자(連字) —** a ligature **포인트체 —** point type **표음 —** a phonotype ; 〖음성〗 a phonetic sign **합자〔성어〕 —** a logotype **5호 —** No. 5 type ; small pica (4호와 5호의 사이) **6호 —** No. 6 type ; brevier **7호 —** No. 7 type ; ruby type (미) ; brilliant type (영) **8포인트 —** 8-point type

활주 —柱 〖건축〗 an arched support

⁑**활주 滑走** gliding ; skating ; sliding ; planing **—하다** glide ; skate ; slide ; [비행기의] taxi (지상에서) ; volplane (공중에서) ¶ 비행기가 활주한다 A plane taxis along the runway〔over the water〕.
—각 a gliding angle **—기** a glider **—대** a glide **—로** a runway ; an airstrip ; a

landing strip ; a taxiway —륜 a landing 〔an alighting〕 gear〔wheel〕 —정 a gliding boat ; a glider —주(奏) 〖음악〗 glissando 공중 — volplaning ; gliding 빙상 — (ice-) skating ; sliding ; glissading 선회 — a spiral glide 이륙 — 〖항공〗 a taking-off run 착륙 — 〖항공〗 a landing run
활죽 the propstick of a sail
활줌통 the handle of a bow
활집 a bow case
*활짝 [넓게] extensively ; widely ; [완전히] entirely ; completely ¶ 활짝 갠 하늘 a cloudless sky // 창문을 활짝 열다 throw open the window // 나무에 꽃이 활짝 피어 있었다 The tree was in full bloom. // 날씨가 활짝 갰다 The weather has cleared up.
활짱 the body of a bow
— 묶음 braces ; pointed parentheses
활차 滑車 a pulley ; a block ; a tackle
— 관절 〖해부〗 the pivot joint ; the trochoid — 장치 (a) tackle ; a whip ; a pulley block 가동 — a movable pulley ; a running block 고정 — a fixed pulley 신축 — an expanding pulley 유동〔정지〕 — a running〔standing〕 pulley
활착 活着 taking〔striking〕 root ; rooting ; rootage —하다 take〔strike〕 root
활촉 —鏃 an arrowhead ; the barb (point) of an arrow
활터 an archery field
활판 活版 (movable) type printing ; printing ; typography
— 기계 a printing press — 기술 typography —본 a printed book —소 a printing house〔office, establishment〕; a print shop 《미》 —업자 a typographer — 인쇄 type printing ; typography — 인쇄물 printed matter ; letterpress
활하다 滑— (be) smooth ; [헐겁다] loose ; [변이] soft ; easy ¶ 활한 뒤 soft easy stool
활화 活畫 a picturesque scene (ry)
활화산 活火山 an active volcano
활활 [불길이] in great flames ; vigorously ; [부채질] briskly ; vigorously ¶ 장작이 활활 타다 firewood burns vigorously // 활활 부채질하다 fan oneself briskly
활황 活況 activity ; an active state of things ¶ 활황을 띠다 show activity ; be active〔lively, brisk〕
홧김 火— (under) the influence of anger ¶ 홧김에 in a fit of anger ; in the heat of passion
홧술 火— liquor drunk in anger
홧홧 hot ; fiery ; feverish
홧홧하다 (be) 〔feel〕 hot ; fiery ; feverish ¶ 얼굴이 홧홧달다 feel one's face burning // 몸이 홧홧달다 be feverish // 숯불이 홧홧하다 charcoal burns hot // 몸이 홧홧하다 be hot 《with a fever》

황 黃 yellow ; a yellow color
황 簧 a reed
황갈색 黃褐色 a yellowish brown color ; a tawny color ¶ 황갈색의 yellowish brown
황감 黃柑 a mandarin orange ; Citrus nobilis (학명)
황감 惶感 deep gratitude —하다 (be) exceedingly〔deeply, reverently〕 grateful ¶ 황감하게도 graciously
황겁 惶怯 fear ; awe —하다 (be) afraid ; awed ; awe-stricken ; fearful
황경나무 黃— 〖식물〗 an Amur cork tree
황계 黃鷄 a yellow hen
황고 皇考 one's deceased father
황고랑 黃— a yellow horse
황고사리 黃— 〖식물〗 a kind of hypolepidaceous fern
황고집 —固執 a bull-headed〔pig-headed〕 person
황공 惶恐 —하다 (be) awe-stricken ; be afraid ; (be) fearful ¶ 황공 무지하다 be extremely awe-stricken
황구 黃口 a fledgling
황구 黃狗 a yellow dog
황구렁이 黃— a kind of yellow serpent
황국 黃菊 a yellow chrysanthemum
황금 黃金 gold ¶ 황금의 gold ; golden // 황금은 만능이다 A golden key will open most locks. /Money makes the mare (to) go.
—국 an El Dorado (이상향) —률 the golden rule — 만능(주의) mammonism ; the almighty dollar principle ¶ 황금 만능주의자 a mammonist ; a mammonite — 만능 시대 a mammonish age — 분할(分割) the golden section —색 a gold (-en) color ; golden yellow — 숭배 money〔mammon-〕worship ; mammonism ; plutolatry ; idolizing the golden calf — 시대 the golden age〔era, period〕; the age of gold ; the millennium ; [전성기] the palmy days —열 gold fever ; the gold rush — 정략 dollar diplomacy ; a policy of bribing (one's way)
황금 黃芩 〖식물〗 a kind of skullcap plant
황급 惶急 extreme haste ; urgency —하다 (be) urgent ; pressed and agitated ¶ 황급히 hastily ; in haste
황기 黃旗 a yellow flag
황기 黃耆 〖식물〗 a kind of milk vetch ; [그 뿌리] milk vetch root
황기끼다 —氣— be intimidated〔cowed, awe-struck〕
황녀 皇女 an Imperial〔a Royal〕 princess ; a princess ; a princess of the blood
황달 黃疸 jaundice
황답 荒畓 a barren paddy-field
황당 荒唐 absurdity ; nonsense —하다

(be) absurd ; fabulous ; preposterous ; wild ; nonsensical
—객 a wild talker ; a windbag ; a braggart

황당 무계 荒唐無稽 absurdity ; nonsense ; claptrap —하다 (be) absurd ; wild ; nonsensical ; incoherent ; fantastic ; fabulous ; preposterous ¶ 황당 무계한 이야기 an absurd story ; sheer nonsense ; a cock-and-bull story // 황당 무계한 풍설을 퍼뜨리다 set wild rumors afloat

황대구 黃大口 a dried codfish with its belly cut open

황도 皇都 the capital of an empire ; the Imperial metropolis

*황도 黃道 the ecliptic
—광 zodiacal light —대 the zodiac —면 the plane of the ecliptic

황동 黃銅 brass
—색 brass yellow —전 brass coins

황등롱 黃燈籠 ⇨ 황사 등롱

황락 荒落 —하다 (be) desolate ; deserted ; bleak

황랍 黃蠟 yellow beeswax
—촉 a yellow-beeswax candle

†황량 荒涼 —하다 (be) desolate ; dreary ; deserted ; wild ; ruined ¶ 황량한 원야 a desolate plane ; a wilderness

황련 黃連 [깽깽이 뿌리] barberry root

황례포 皇禮砲 an Imperial salute ¶ 21 발의 황례포를 쏘다 fire an Imperial salute of 21 guns

황로 荒路 a rough〔rugged〕 road

황록색 黃綠色 a yellowish green

황룡 黃龍 a yellow dragon
—수(鬚) a variety of chrysanthemum

황릉 皇陵 an Imperial sepulchre ; an Emperor's tomb

황린 黃燐 yellow phosphor
— 성냥 locofoco

황림 荒林 a neglected〔overgrown〕 woods

황마 黃麻 yellow hemp
— 부대 a jute〔gunny〕 bag

황막 荒漠 —하다 (be) wild ; vast ; boundless ¶ 황막한 평야 a vast wilderness ; a vast wasteland

황망 惶忙 —하다 (be) very busy

황망 慌忙 —하다 (be) hurried ; flurried ; agitated ¶ 황망히 in a flurry ; helter-skelter

황매 黃梅 a yellow plum (tree)

황명 皇命 an Imperial order〔command, mandate〕

황모 黃毛 hair from a weasel's tail ; fur of the weasel
—필 a writing brush made of weasel-tail hair

†황무 荒蕪 wilderness ; barrenness ; desolation —하다 (be) wild ; waste ; barren
—지 a waste land ; a wilderness ; a waste ¶ 그 토지의 대부분은 아직도 황무지이다 The greater part of the land still lies waste.

황민 荒民 famine sufferers ; famine-stricken people

황바리 〖동물〗 a kind of crab with two long feelers

황밤 黃— dried shelled chestnuts

황봉 黃蜂 ⇨ 참벌

황부루 黃— a yellow-whitish horse

황비 皇妃 the Queen ; the Empress

황사 皇嗣 the Crown Prince ; the Imperial heir

황사 黃砂 yellow〔sandy〕 sand ¶ 고비 사막으로부터 불어온 황사 sandy dust which blew here from the Gobi Desert
— 현상 sandy dust phenomena ; yellow dust cloud that often blows over 《Korea》

황사 등롱 黃紗燈籠 [옛 제도] a yellow-gauze lantern (carried by low-ranking officials)

황산 黃酸 sulphuric acid ; oil of vitriol
—동 copper sulphate —아연 sulfate of zinc —암모늄 ammonium sulfate —염 a sulphate —지 parchment paper —칼리〔마그네슘〕 potassium〔magnesium〕 sulfate

황상 皇上 the present Emperor ; His Majesty

*황새 〖새〗 a stork

황새걸음 long strides ; the gait of a stork —하다 walk in large strides ¶ 참새가 황새걸음하려 한다 try to do what is beyond one's capacity ; a sparrow tries to walk like a stork

황새풀 cotton grass ; a kind of sedge

황색 黃色 yellow ; a yellow color
— 신문 a yellow paper〔journal〕 ; the yellow press 《총칭》 ; yellow journalism (경영) — 인종 the yellow race ; the Asiatics〔Asians〕

황석 黃石 〖광물〗 yellow calcite

황석어 黃石魚 ⇨ 참조기

황설 荒說 an absurd story ; tommyrot ; nonsense ; balderdash

황성 皇城 the Imperial city ; the Capital

황성 荒城 a ruined castle

⁑황소 〖동물〗 a bull
황소 뒷걸음 치다가 쥐 잡는다 (속담) The net of the sleeper catches fish.

황소걸음 a slow step ; a leisurely pace —하다 walk slowly〔leisurely〕

황소바람 a heavy draft (of air) ; a big blow
바늘 구멍으로 황소바람 들어온다 (속담) The small hole made with a needle lets in a big blow.

황손 皇孫 an Imperial grandson ; the grandson of an Emperor

황송 惶悚 [황공] awe ; being awe-stricken ; [죄송] being indebted〔grateful〕 (for bother) —하다 [황공] (be)

awe-stricken ; [죄송] indebted ; obliged ; grateful ¶ 말씀드리기 황송합니다만 May I humbly inform you《that》// 그런 말씀을 하시니 황송합니다 Please don't mention it.
황숙하다 黃熟— ripen yellow ; fully ripen
황술레 黃— a kind of large yellow pear
황실 皇室 the Imperial Household〔House, Family〕
—비 the Imperial Household expenses〔allowances〕; the civil list《영》— 재산 the Imperial estate〔property〕; the property of the Imperial Household
황아 荒— sundries ; variety goods
—장수 a peddler of sundries —전 a variety〔notions〕store ; a dime store
*황야 荒野 a wilderness ; a waste ; desert land ; the wilds
황어 黃魚 〖물고기〗 a dace
황연 黃鉛 chrome yellow
—광 wulfenite
황연 晃然 —하다 (be) bright ; clear ¶ 황연 대각하다 see through clearly ; understand perfectly
황열(병) 黃熱(病) 〖의학〗 yellow fever〔jack〕
황오리 黃— 〖새〗 a sheldrake
황옥 黃玉 topaz ; yellow jade
황운 皇運 the fortunes of an Emperor
황원 荒原 ⇨ 황야
황위 皇位 the Imperial Throne ¶ 황위를 잇다〔에 오르다〕 succeed to〔ascend〕the throne
— 계승 (순서〔서열〕) (the order of) succession to the Imperial throne〔influence〕
황위 皇威 imperial prestige
황육 黃肉 beef
황은 皇恩 Imperial grace〔benevolence〕
황음 荒淫 sexual indulgence ; carnal excesses ; dissipation ¶ 황음무도하다 be dissipated and depraved
황의 黃衣 ① [옷] yellow clothes ② ⇨ 황자(黃子)
황인종 黃人種 the yellow race
황자 皇子 an Imperial prince ; a prince of the Blood
황자 黃子 wheat malt
황작 黃雀 ① [꾀꼬리] a golden oriole ② [참새] a sparrow
황잡 荒雜 —하다 (be) incoherent ; desultory ; slipshod ; loose ; unsystematic ¶ 황잡한 논의 an incoherent argument // 황잡한 생각 loose ideas // 황잡한 지식 unsystematic knowledge
황적색 黃赤色 yellowish red ; poppy red
황전 荒田 deserted〔neglected, overgrown〕field ; overgrown land ; uncultivated〔unopened〕fields
*황제 皇帝 an Emperor ¶ 황제의 Imperial // 황제의 자리에 앉다 ascend〔accede to〕the Imperial throne
—기(旗) the Imperial〔Royal〕standard
— 폐하 His Majesty the Emperor 독일 — the Kaiser 러시아 — the Czar〔Tsar〕 신성 로마 — the Roman Emperor
황조 皇祖 Imperial ancestors
황조 皇祚 the Imperial Throne ¶ 황조를 잇다 ascend the Throne
황조 黃鳥 〖새〗 a golden oriole
황조롱이 〖새〗 a kestrel
황족 皇族 the Imperial family ; royalty
— 회의 the Imperial Family Council
황지 荒地 waste〔barren〕 land ; a desolation ; a desert ; badlands ; a wilderness
황지 黃紙 yellow paper
황진 黃塵 ① dust in the air ; airborne dust ② [속진] mundane affairs ¶ 만장의 황진 a cloud of dust // 황진 만장의 도시 a dustswept city
황차 況且 much more ; much less ⇨ 하물며
황채 黃菜 a dish of sliced ripe cucumber
황천 皇天 ① [하늘] High Heaven ; Heaven on High ; God's Heaven ② [하느님] God ¶ 황천은 굽어 살피소서 God is my very witness. /So help me heaven.
— 후토 the gods of heaven and earth
황천 荒天 stormy weather
황천 黃泉 Hades ; the land of the dead
—객 a dead person ¶ 황천객이 되다 turn up one's toes ; die ; kick the bucket ; drop off the hooks —길 the way to Hades ; death ¶ 황천길을 떠나다 go to one's last home
황철광 黃鐵鑛 iron pyrites
황청 黃淸 yellow honey
황체 黃體 〖해부〗 [난소의] a corpus luteum《*pl.* corpora lutea》
— 호르몬 progesterone ; progestin(e)
황초 黃— ⇨ 황촉
황촉 荒燭 [밀초] a beeswax candle
황촉규 黃蜀葵 〖식물〗 a kind of hibiscus
황촌 荒村 a deserted〔desolate〕 village ; a ghost town
황치마 黃— a kite which is white in the upper half and yellow in the lower half
황칠 黃漆 a yellow dye from *Cheju* Island ; yellow lacquer
— 나무 Textoria morbifera (학명)
황탄 荒誕 —하다 (be) absurd ; fantastic ; nonsensical ; utter nonsense ; fallacious ; sophistical
황태손 皇太孫 the eldest grandson of the Emperor
*황태자 皇太子 the Crown Prince ; the Prince Imperial ; the Heir Apparent to the Throne ¶ 황태자를 책봉하다 proclaim the Heir Apparent to the Throne
—기 the Crown Prince's flag —비 the

Crown Princess — 전하 His Imperial Highness the Crown Prince 영국 — the Prince of Wales
황태후 皇太后 the Empress Dowager ; the Queen Mother
황토 黃土 yellow earth ; loess
—색 ocher (yellow) ; mud yellow
황토 荒土 barren land ; wasteland ; a waste ; [전쟁으로 인한] war-devastated 〔-battered〕 land ; a bombed area ¶ 황토가 되어 있다 lie waste
황통 皇統 the Imperial line(age) ¶ 황통을 잇다 accede to the Throne
황파 黃— scallions〔green onions〕 grown in an underground cellar
황파 荒波 rough seas ; heavy seas ; high waves ; raging waves ¶ 황파가 일다 be rough ; be high
황평 양서 黃平兩西 〖지리〗 the two western provinces of *Hwanghae* and *Pyeongan*
†황폐 荒廢 ruin ; waste ; devastation ; desolation ; dilapidation —하다 (be) ruined ; be〔lie〕 in ruins ; (be) devastated ; desolate ¶ 황폐케 하다 devastate ; lay waste〔in ruins〕
—지 waste land ; a devastated region
— 지구 〖건축·토목〗 a blighted area 삼림 — forest denudation
황포 黃袍 the royal robe
황하 黃河 the Yellow River ; the Hwang Ho
황하다 荒— (be) rough ; careless ; sloppy ; slipshod ¶ 황한 사람 a slipshod person
황해 黃海 the Yellow Sea
황해쑥 黃海— 〖식물〗 a kind of wormwood
*황혼 黃昏 dusk ; twilight ; gloaming ; crepuscule ¶ 황혼에 at dusk〔sundown〕 ; in the gathering darkness // 황혼이 되다 Dusk falls.
*황홀 恍惚 rapture ; ecstasy ; trance —하다 be in raptures〔ecstasies〕 ; (be) enraptured ; raptured ; charmed ; entranced ; ecstatic ¶ 황홀한 광경 a charming spectacle // 황홀하여 in raptures ; in ecstasies // 황홀하게 하다 enrapture ; fascinate ; charm ; hold 《a person》 spellbound // 황홀하여 바라보다 look at 《a thing》 enraptured〔lost in delight〕 // 음악에 황홀해지다 be carried away by the music // 그 여자는 황홀해졌다 She was thrown into ecstasy.
—경 an ecstatic state ; a trance ; an ecstasy
황화 荒貨 ⇨ 황아
황화 黃化 〖화학〗 sulfuration〔sulphuration 《영》〕 ; sulfurization —하다 sulfurate ; sulfurize
— 고무 vulcanized India rubber —물 a sulfide〔sulphide 《영》〕 — 암모늄〔은, 수소, 철, 동〕 ammonium〔silver, hydrogen, iron, copper〕 sulfide
황화 黃花 a yellow chrysanthemum
황화 黃禍 the yellow peril〔disaster〕
‡황후 皇后 the Empress ; the Queen
— 폐하 Her (Imperial) Majesty〔H. (I.) M.〕 the Empress
*홰[1] a perch ; a roost ; [닭이 우는 횟수] cockcrow ¶ 닭이 홰에 오르다 a hen goes to roost // 닭이 두홰 울다 the cock crows twice
홰[2] a torch ; a firebrand ; a flambeau ; a link ¶ 홰를 켜다 light〔kindle〕 a torch // 홰를 들다 carry a torch in one's hands
홰[3] [옷걸이] ⇨ 횃대
홰나무 〖식물〗 a kind of locust tree
홰치다 flap the wings ; flutter ¶ 닭이 홰치다 a hen flaps its wings
홰홰 round and round ¶ 단장을 홰홰 휘두르다 brandish a stick // 횃불을 홰홰 휘두르다 swing a torch round and round
*홱 [재빠르게] with a bang〔snap〕 ; with dispatch ; quickly ; [차가] with a swish ; speedily ; fast ; [힘차게] flinging ; with a bang ; [뿌리치는 모양] with a shove〔jerk〕 ; [채찍으로] with a whack ¶ 일을 홱 해치우다 finish a job with a bang // 책을 홱 던지다 fling a book away with a bang // 팔을 홱 뿌리치다 jerk one's arm loose ; shove 《a person》 away with one's arm // 홱 뿌리치고 도망가다 tear oneself away from 《another's grasp》 // 채찍으로 홱 갈기다 whack〔give a whack〕 with a whip // 자동차가 홱 지나가다 A car zooms by.
홱홱 [재빠르게] bang-bang(-bang) ; whambang ; snap-snap ; with dispatch ; quickly ; [차가] swish-swish ; whoosh-whoosh ; speedily ; fast ; [힘차게] flinging repeatedly ; bang-bang(-bang) ; [뿌리치는 모양] with shove after shove ; with jerk after jerk ; [채찍으로] with whack after whack ¶ 일을 홱홱 해치우다 finish one's job quickly // 책을 홱홱 던지다 bang books away // 홱홱 팔을 뿌리치다 keep jerking one's arm loose ; keep shoving 《a person》 away with one's arm // 채찍으로 홱홱 갈기다 keep whacking with a whip ; keep whipping 《a person》
횃군 a linkman ; a linkboy
‡횃대 a clothes rack〔hanger〕 ; a clotheshorse
횃댓보 a clothes protector put over a clothes rack
‡횃불 a torchlight ; a torch ; a flambeau ¶ 횃불빛으로 by torchlight // 횃불을 들다 carry a torch in one's hand // 횃불을 켜다 light〔kindle〕 a torch
— 행렬 a torchlight procession
횃줄 a clothesline
횅댕그렁하다 be〔feel〕 hollow ; empty ¶ 횅댕그렁한 방 an empty room // 손님이

다 가서 방이 횅댕그렁하다 The room feels empty now that all the guests have left.

횅하다 ① [정통하다] be well versed 《in》; be familiar 《with》; be well acquainted 《with》; be well posted; be at home 《in》 ¶ 이곳 지리에 횅하다 know the lay of the land around here // 글에 횅하다 be well versed in literature // 길을 횅하게 알다 know the road well // 그는 자기 일에 횅하다 He has the business at his finger's tips.
② [텅 비어 있다] (be) vacant; deserted; empty ¶ 집이 횅하다 A house is empty. // 거리가 횅하다 A street is deserted.

회 ⇨ 회두리

회 灰 lime ⇨ 석회; [벽토] mortar; plaster; stucco ¶ 회를 바르다 plaster; stucco
—반죽(을 바르다) plaster; mortar

회 蛔 a roundworm; an intestinal worm; a mawworm; an ascarid

†**회** 會 [집회] a meeting; a gathering; an assembly; [사교적인] a party; a get-together; [회의] a conference; [단체] a society; a club; an association —하다 hold a meeting; get together; have a conference; hold〔give〕a party ¶ 회를 열다 hold〔open〕a meeting; give a party // 회를 조직하다 form〔organize〕a society // 회에 가입하다 join a society; associate oneself with a society // 회에서 나오다 leave〔resign from〕a society // 그는 그를 위해서 열린 회에 참석하였다 He attended a party given in his honor. // 우리는 무주회(無酒會)를 열었다 We held a teetotal meeting. // 회는 4시에 해산되었다 The meeting broke up at four o'clock. // 회가 유예되었다 The meeting fell through. // 회는 연 2회 회장에 의하여 소집된다 The meeting shall be called by the president twice a year.
동창— alumni association (조직); an alumni reunion (모임) 변호사— a lawyers' association

회 膾 sliced raw fish〔meat〕; a raw fish〔meat〕dish ¶ 회를 치다 prepare a raw fish〔meat〕dish // 회를 먹다 eat it raw
다랑어— slices of raw tuna; sliced raw tuna 육— seasoned raw meat

***회** 回 [횟수] a time; [경기의] a round; a game; a bout; [야구의] an inning〔innings 《영》〕; [연재물의] an installment ¶ 1회 once; one time // 3회 three times // 야구의 제9회전 the ninth inning; the pay-off // 권투의 제2회전 the second round of boxing // 3회 승부의 씨름 a three-round〔-bout, -game〕wrestling match〔contest〕// 회를 거듭하다 do〔hold〕it several times // 그것을 5회 해보시오 Do it five times. // 경기의 첫회가 열렸다 The first bout is taking place.

회갑 回甲 one's 61th birthday anniversary ¶ 회갑 잔치(를 베풀다) (give) a banquet on one's 61th birthday // 회갑을 축하하다 celebrate 《a person's》 61th birthday ⇨ 환갑
— 노인 a sexagenarian

***회개** 悔改 repentance; penitence —하다 repent 《of》; be penitent 《of, over》; turn over a new leaf; mend one's ways

회검 懷劍 a dirk; a dagger; a poniard

‡**회견** 會見 an interview; a meeting —하다 have an interview〔a talk〕《with》; interview; meet ¶ 회견을 청하다 ask for an interview 《with》 // 회견을 허락하다 grant 《a person》 an interview
—담 an interview —자 an interviewer; a visitor 기자 — a news〔press〕conference (기자단과의); a press interview ¶ TV 기자 회견 a televised news〔press〕conference 단독 — a single interview; an exclusive interview 《with》 비공식 — an informal interview

회계 會計 accounts; accounting (출납); [계산서] a bill; an account —하다 keep accounts; account; count; reckon; [지불] pay a bill
— 감사 audit; auditing — 감사관 an auditor; a commissioner of audit —과 the accounting section; treasury; an accounts section —관 an accountant; a treasurer; 『군사』 a fiscal officer — 단위 the unit of accounting —법 the financial law — 보고 a financial〔an accounts〕report; a treasurer's report —부 an account book; books; a book of account (원부); a financial book —사 a treasurer; an accountant ¶ 공인 회계사 a certified public accountant 《C. P. A., CPA》 《미》; a chartered accountant 《C. A.》 《영》 — 서류 financial documents —실 a counting-house; a counting room 《미》 — 연도 a fiscal〔financial〕year —원 an accountant; a treasurer; a paymaster; [출납계] a cashier — 주임 a chief accountant —학 accounting; accountancy 일반 — general accounts 특별 — special accounts

***회고** 回顧 reflection; recollection; retrospect —하다 look back 《on, over》; reflect 《upon》; recall; recollect; retrospect ¶ 회고와 전망 retrospect and prospect // 과거를 회고하면 looking back upon the past
—록 reminiscences; memoirs — 장면 [영화의] a retrospective shot —전(展) the retrospective(s) 《of a person's art works》

회고 懷古 reminiscence; recollection;

retrospection ; cherishing thoughts of the past —하다 reminisce ¶ 회고적인 retrospective // 그 광경을 보니 회고의 정이 일었다 The sight carried us back to the good old days.
—담 reminiscences ¶ 회고담을 하다 talk about good old days ; reminisce —시 a reminiscent poem
회공 —하다 become hollow〔empty〕
회과 悔過 repentance ; penitence —하다 repent 《of》; be penitent 《of》 ¶ 회과 자책하다 repent one's sins and reproach oneself
회관 會館 a hall ; an assembly hall 기독교 청년 — the Y. M. C. A. (Hall)
회교 回敎 〖종교〗 Mohammedanism ; Islamism ; Islam
—국 a Mohammedan country —도 a Mohammedan ; a Moslem — 사원 a mosque — 연맹 the Moslem League
회구 懷舊 recollection ⇨ 회고(懷古)
회국 回國 ① ⇨ 귀국(歸國) ② traveling about the country ; making a pilgrimage —하다 travel about the country ; make a pilgrimage
회군 回軍 a troop withdrawal ; the withdrawal of army troops —하다 withdraw (an army)
*회귀 回歸 recurrence (주기) ; a revolution ; 〖수학〗regression
—하다 revolve ; recur ; make one full revolution ; come round ; double back 《to》
— 계수 a regression coefficient — 곡선 a regression curve —년 a tropical year —대 the tropical zone — 무풍대 the calm zone of the tropics —선 the tropic ; 〖수학〗 a regression line —열 recurrent fever ; relapsing fever ; typhinia — 전격〔궤조, 전락〕 a return shock〔rail, circuit〕 남—선 the tropic of Capricorn 북—선 the tropic of Cancer
회규 會規 the rules〔regulations〕 of a society ; the bylaw of an assembly
회기 回忌 an anniversary of 《a person's》 death
회기 回期 date of return
회기 會期 a session ; a sitting ; a term (기간) ¶ 국회 회기중 during the Assembly Session // 회기 연장 the extension of a session // 박람회의 회기는 4월 1일부터 5월 15일까지이다 The exhibition is open from April 1 to May 15.
회나무 〖식물〗 a Korean spindle tree
*회담 會談 a talk ; a conversation ; a parley (담판) ; a conference (회의) ; an interview (회견) —하다 talk together ; have a talk 《with》; confer 《with》; have a conference 《with》; have an interview 《with》 ¶ 결말 없는 긴 회담 an inconclusive〔a protracted〕 conference ; an endless discussion ; a conference leading to no result〔end〕
본— full-dress〔main〕 talks 비공식 — an off-the-record conference ; an informal get-together 3국〔자〕 — a tripartite〔3-nation〕 conference 실무 — the working-level talks 여야(중진) — bipartisan conference (of key leaders) 예비 — preliminary talks 전화 — a telephone interview 정상(급)〔영수(급)〕 — a summit(-level) meeting 한일 — the Korean-Japanese Conference
†회답 回答 a reply ; an answer ; a response
—하다 answer ; reply ; give an answer〔a reply〕 ; respond to ¶ 회답으로 in answer〔reply〕 《to》 // 회답을 하지 않다 make no reply〔answer〕 ; answer 《a person》 nothing // 나의 전갈에 대해서 그에게서는 한 마디의 회답도 없었다 No word came from him in answer to my message. // 속히 회답 바랍니다 Please answer me〔my letter〕 as soon as possible.
회당 會堂 [예배당] a church ; a chapel ; [공회당] a hall ; an assembly hall
회독 回讀 —하다 read 《a book》 in turn ; circulate reading material
—료 a fee for the circulating library —회 a circulating library ¶ 잡지 회독회 a circulating association of magazines ; a circulating magazine library
회독 會讀 —하다 have a meeting for reading and discussing a book together
회동 會同 —하다 gather together ; have a meeting ; assemble ; get together
회동그라지다 [눈이] open wide ; [놀라다] get surprised ; be startled
회동그랗다 ① [일이 끝나다] be completely finished ; be completed
② [눈이] be wide-eyed with surprise
회두 回頭 —하다 [머리를 돌리다] turn one's head around ; turn one's face〔head〕 ; 〖카톨릭〗 turn back to the fold ¶ 회두시키다 convert 《an apostate》
회두 會頭 the president 《of a society, a chamber of commerce and industry》 ⇨ 회장
회두리 the end〔finish〕 ; the last round
— 씨름 the last round of a wrestling match —판 the last round
회람 回覽 circulation ; reading in turn ¶ 회람판을 돌리다 pass on a circular notice
— 문고 a circulating library — 잡지 a circulating magazine ; a magazine for circulating 《among》 —판 《pass on》 a circular notice ; a circulating bulletin ; a notification board ; 《send round》 a cir-

cular
*회랑 回廊 a corridor ; a passage ; a gallery ; a veranda ; a cloister
공중 — an air corridor 《to》
회례 回禮 —하다 return a courtesy ; return 《a person's》 visit ; make 《a person》 a present in return ¶ 회례로 in acknowledgment 《of》 ; on return for
회례 廻禮 —하다 pay social visit ; go around making calls ¶ 신년의 회례를 하다 make the New Year's calls
회로 回路 ① 〖전기〗 a circuit ② the way back ; the return way ¶ 회로에 on one's way back
— 시험기 a circuit tester — 접속기 [전자 계산기의] a circuit closer — 제어기 a circuit controller — 차단기 a circuit breaker 고정〔근접, 근속(近續), 재생, 집적, 그리드〕 — a stationary〔an adjoining, an adjacent, a regenerative, an integrated, a grid〕 circuit 직렬〔병렬〕 — a series〔parallel〕 circuit 진공관 — a vacuum tube circuit
회로 懷爐 a pocket heater ; a portable body warmer ; a hand-warmer
회록 會錄 ⇨ 회의(—록)
회뢰 賄賂 bribery ; a bribe (물건) ¶ 회뢰를 주다 bribe 《a person》 ; offer a bribe ; grease the palm // 회뢰를 받다 take〔accept, receive〕 a bribe 《from》 ; be bribed ; graft 《미·구》
— 사건 a graft case 《미》 ; a bribery case
회류 回流 flowing round ; [흐름] a round current ; a circular stream —하다 flow round
회류 會流 confluence ; conflux ; a confluent —하다 flow〔run〕 together ; merge 《into》 ; join
—점 a junction ; a (point of) confluence
회리바람 a whirlwind ; a cyclone ; a twister ; an eddywind ; a tornado
—꽃 a kind of anemone ; Anemone reflexa (학명)
회리밤 a full single chestnut within a burr
회마 回馬 a return horse ; turning a person's horse round
회매하다 feel neat and tidy〔light〕 ; (be) neat and tidy ; light
회맹 會盟 a league ; a covenant〔compact〕
—하다 league〔band〕 together ; form a league ; enter into a covenant
회명 會名 the name of a society〔an association〕
회명 晦冥 darkness
—하다 (be) dark
회모 懷慕 longing ; yearning —하다 long〔yearn〕 for ¶ 돌아가신 어머님을 회모하여 울다 cry for one's deceased mother
회목 the wrist or the ankle
회목 檜木 a kind of cypress ; the Chinese juniper
회무 會務 affairs〔business〕 of a society〔an association〕
회문 回文 [회장] a circular (letter) ; a round-robin ¶ 회문을 돌리다 send a circular letter ; circulate a letter
회백색 灰白色 light gray ; light ash color
회백수염 灰白髓炎 poliomyelitis
회백질 灰白質 〖해부〗 gray〔grey 《영》〕 matter
회벽 灰壁 a lime-plastered wall ; a plastered wall
회보 回報 a report ; a reply ; an answer
—하다 send an answer ; bring back a report
회보 會報 a bulletin ; society〔association〕 reports ; the transactions of a society ¶ 협회는 연 2회 회보를 내기로 되어 있다 The society is to issue a bulletin twice a year.
동창회 — an alumni bulletin ; an alumnae bulletin (여학교의)
*회복 回復 recovery ; recuperation (건강) ; restoration (복구) ; retrieval (명예 따위) ; rehabilitation (재건) ; revival (부활)
—하다 recover ; get better ; be well again ; regain ; restore ; get〔win〕 back ; retrieve ; rehabilitate ¶ 경기의 회복 the revival of business // 명예를 회복하다 regain one's good reputation // 재산을 회복하다 retrieve〔regain〕 one's fortune // 건강을 회복하다 regain 〔recover〕 one's health ; be restored to health // 신용을 회복하다 win back the confidence 《of》 // 원기를 회복하다 recover strength ; be refreshed ; revive one's spirit // 의식을 회복하다 recover consciousness // 그는 회복의 가망이 전혀 없다 There is not the ghost of a chance of his recovery. // 그는 거의 회복되고 있다 He has almost recovered his health. // 조만간 경기가 회복될 것이다 The economy will turn around sooner or later. // 당신은 그가 미국 경제를 회복시키리라고 생각하십니까 Do you think he will turn around the U.S. economy? // 곧 의식이 회복될 테니까 걱정마세요 He will come to soon. Don't worry. // 다행히 아버지께서는 회복하셨다. Fortunately, my father's taken a turn for the better.
—기 (period of) convalescence ; catabasis 《*pl.* -bases》 ¶ 회복기 환자 병실〔병동〕 a convalescent ward —력 recuperative powers 권리 — recovery of rights 물권 — 소송 〖법〗 replevin 원기 — recruitment
*회복 恢復 restoration ; rehabilitation ;

회신 灰燼 ashes ; embers ¶ 회신으로 화하다 be reduced to ashes ; be burnt to the ground (건물 따위) ; be razed to the ground (도시·건물 따위)

회심 悔心 remorse ; repentance ; penitence

회심 回心 a change of heart ; conversion ; regeneration **—하다** change one's heart ; convert ; repent ; turn over a new leaf

회심 會心 congeniality ; complacency ¶ 회심지우 a congenial friend // 회심의 작품 a work after one's heart // 회심의 미소를 짓다 smile a complacent〔self-satisfied〕 smile

—처 what one is happy about ; the source of one's complacency〔satisfaction〕

회약 蛔藥 an anthelmintic ; santonic ; a vermifuge

회양목 〚식물〛 the boxwood tree

회연 會宴 a banquet ⇨ 연회

회오 悔悟 repentance ; remorse ; penitence ; regret **—하다** repent 《of》 ; be〔grow〕 penitent 《of》 ; feel remorse 《for, over》 ; be sorry 《for, about》 ¶ 회오의 눈물 tears of remorse

—자 a penitent ; a contrite sinner

회오리바람 a whirlwind ; a cyclone ; a twister

회오리밤 ⇨ 회리밤

회오리봉 —峰 a conical peak

회우 會友 a fellow member

⁑회원 會員 a member (of a society, an association) ; membership 《총칭》 ¶ 회원의 자격 qualifications for membership // 회원의 특전 privileges of membership // 회원이 아닌 사람 nonmembers // 회원을 모집하다 collect〔raise, seek〕 members // 회원이 되다 become a member 《of》 ; join 《a society, a club》 // 회원이 200명이다 have a membership of 200

—국 a member nation **— 기장** a membership badge **— 명부** a membership list **— 배지** a membership badge **—제〔조직〕** the membership system **—증** a membership card **명예 —** an honorary member **유지 —** a supporting member **정—** a regular〔full〕 member ; a member in full and regular standing **종신 —** a life member **준—** an associate member **찬조 —** a patron (member) **통상〔특별〕 —** an ordinary〔a special〕 member

회유 懷柔 conciliation ; pacification ; appeasement **—하다** conciliate ; pacify ; appease ; placate ; win 《a person》 over (끌어들이다) ¶ 그들은 우리를 회유하려고 갖은 술책을 다 썼다 They took every measure to win us over.

—책 an appeasement measure〔policy〕 ; a conciliatory〔pacification〕 measure〔policy〕

회유 回遊 migration **—하다** migrate

—어(魚) a migratory〔wandering〕 fish

회유 回遊 an excursion ; a tour ; a cruise **—하다** make〔go on〕 an excursion ; make a cruise〔tour〕 ; make a round〔circular〕 trip

—객 an excursionist ; a tripper 《영》 **—선** an excursion boat **— 승차권** a tourist〔circular〕 ticket ; a round-trip ticket 《영》 **— 여행** a circular tour〔trip〕

회음 會飮 compotation ; carousing **—하다** drink together ; have a drinking party ; carouse

—자 a compotator

회음 會陰 〚해부〛 the perineum

—부 the perineal region

⁑회의 會議 a meeting ; a conference ; an assembly ; a convention ; a congress ; a council ; a session (회기중의)

> 참고 **meeting**은 일반어 **council**은 「평의회」「종교회의」 따위의 뜻 **conference**는 meeting보다 좀 딱딱한 말 **convention**은 「평의회」「연차 대회」 따위의 뜻 **assembly**는 조직성 통일성이 있는 회합이며 정치 종교 따위의 회의에 자주 쓰인다 그리고 **rally**는 미국에서 사용되는 구어이며 「정치 대회」 따위의 뜻으로 많이 쓰인다 **institute, institution, society**는 「학회」「협회」 따위의 뜻이며 「조직」에 중점을 둔다

—하다 meet ; confer ; sit (in conference) ; hold a meeting〔conference〕 ¶ 회의에 참석하다 attend a meeting〔conference〕 // 그는 지금 회의 중이다 He is in conference now. // 그들은 지방 조합 대표와 연일 회의를 열었다 They held daily conferences with the local union representatives. // 그들은 그 문제에 관해서 회의 중이다 They are now sitting on the question.

—록 assembly〔conference〕 records ; minutes ; proceedings **—소** a meeting〔an assembly〕 hall **—실** a conference〔council, board, an assembly〕 room **—장** a meeting hall ; an assembly hall ; a conference place〔hall〕 ; council house **국무 —** the Cabinet council **국제 —** an international convention〔conference〕 **긴급 —** 《hold, convoke》 an urgent conference〔meeting〕 **당무 —** an executive committee (meeting) **본—** a plenary session (국회의) **비밀 —** a closed-door〔secret〕 conference〔session〕 ; a meeting behind closed doors **평화〔군축, 친족, 원탁〕 —** a peace〔disarmament, family, round-table〕 conference ☞ ◖p. 2412◗

∗회의 懷疑 doubt ; skepticism ; incredulity ; unbelief ; disbelief **—하다** doubt ;

회 의

회의영어는 일반적인 대화체보다는 통상 General English, 즉 speaking and writing of educated people in their private or public affairs (공식·비공식적인 장소에서의 교양인의 구어·문어)를 기준으로 하며 개인의 의견보다는 다수의 의견을 수렴하여 회의 결과를 정책에 반영할 수 있도록 진행해야 한다.

▶회의를 열다
¶ 이것으로 회의를 열겠습니다 Well, ladies and gentlemen, I think we should begin. / Perhaps we'd better get started. / Shall we start? // 나는 김입니다. 이 회의의 사회를 맡게 되었습니다. My name is Kim, and I will serve as the chairperson of this meeting.

▶의사진행
¶ 우선 당신 과(課)의 간단한 현상설명부터 해주십시오. Would you like to open the discussion by briefly explaining the present situation of your section? // 이 견해를 어떻게 생각하십니까 What do you think about the idea? // 자, 계속해 주십시오. Let's move on.

▶의견을 구한다
¶ 당신의 의견은 어떻습니까 What about you? // 연공서열에 대해서 김선생 당신의 의견은 어떻습니까 What about your views on the seniority system, Mr. Kim? // 산업 로보트의 구입에 대해 어느 분이 의견을 말씀하시겠습니까 (출석자 전원에게) Has anybody any comments on the introduction of industrial robots? // 여기에 의견이 어떻습니까 Would you like to comment here?

▶의견을 말한다
¶ 전적으로 찬성입니다. I'm completely in favor of that. / I've absolutely no objections. // 전적으로 반대합니다. I really can't accept that. / I'm completely against that. // 찬성입니다. I'm in favor of that. // 유감이지만 반대입니다. I'm sorry, but I can't accept that. // 이것에 대해서는 회사가 비용부담을 해야 한다고 확신합니다. I'm sure that the company should pay for it. / It's perfectly clear to me that the company should pay for it. // 연구개발부문을 강화해야 한다고 생각합니다. I think that we should strengthen our R&D efforts. // 해결책은 단하나 이윤을 극대화하는 것입니다. The only solution is to sell products at a large profit. // 종업원에게 문화적·교육적 기회를 만들어 주어야만 한다고 생각합니다. I would suggest that we offer educational opportunities to employees. // 반대입니다. I don't agree. // 전면 반대합니다. I disagree completely. / That's out of the question. // 동의합니다. I agree. // I think you are right. // 전면적으로 동의합니다. I quite agree. / I'm in complete agreement. / Exactly!

▶의견의 유보
¶ 말씀하신 것은 알겠지만 사정은 조금씩 바뀌고 있습니다. I see your point but things are slowly changing.

▶제안·아이디어를 구한다
¶ 김선생님, 당신의 의견은 어떻습니까 What's your opinion, Mr. Kim? // 제안을 몇 가지 내십시오. (출석자 전원에게) I'd like to hear some of your suggestions.

▶기타
¶ 말씀 중에 미안하지만 한마디 하겠습니다. I'm sorry to interrupt you, but let me say a word. // 지금 그 문제를 끄집어내야만 한다고는 생각하지 않습니다. I don't think we should discuss it further now. // 더이상 없으면 이것으로 끝마치겠습니다. If that's everything, we can stop[finish] here.

---

have 《one's》 doubts 《about》; be skeptical 《about》 ¶ 회의적인 skeptic(al); incredulous // 그는 10대에 인생에 대한 회의에 시달렸다 He was tormented by his doubts about life in his teen age.
ㅡ론자 a skeptic; a Pyrrhonian; a Pyrrhonist **ㅡ설〔론〕** (the argument of) skepticism **ㅡ주의** (the principle of) skepticism **ㅡ파** the skeptic school; the skeptics **순수 ㅡ론** absolute〔Pyrrhonic〕 skepticism; Pyrrhonism

회의 문자 會意文字 an ideograph

회의안 回議案 a circular bill

회임 懷妊 pregnancy; conception ⇨ 임신

회잉 懷孕 pregnancy; conception **ㅡ하다** become pregnant; conceive

회자 膾炙 [회와 구운 고기] raw meat

and roast meat ; [인구에] (what is found) in everyone's mouth **—하다** be in everyone's mouth ; be on everybody's mouth ; become the talk of all ; be a household word ; be well known to everybody

회자정리 會者定離 Those who meet must part. /We never meet but we part.

회장 回腸 the ileum
—염 ileitis **— 절개(술)** ileostomy

회장 回裝 ① [저고리의] colorful strips of cloth for trimmings (on a woman's coat) ② [병풍 따위의] the border edging 《of a screen〔scroll, map〕》

회장 會長 the president (of a society) ; the chairman (of a committee, an assembly) ¶ 회장이 되다 take the chair ; preside over (at) a meeting // 언어 학회는 C박사를 회장으로 추대하고 있다 The philological society has Dr. C for president〔elects Dr. C as its chairman〕.
— 대리 the acting chairman **—석** the chair **—직** [지위] presidency ; chairmanship **이사회 —** [회사의] the chairman of the board of directors

회장 會場 a place of meeting〔assembly〕; a hall ; a meeting place ; [터] the grounds ; a site ¶ 회장은 어디입니까 Where is the meeting to be held?
박람— the exposition ground

회장 會葬 attending a funeral **—하다** attend〔go to〕a funeral ; be (present) at a funeral
—자 attendants at a funeral ; persons who attend a funeral ; mourners ¶ 장례식에는 다수의 회장자가 있었다 There was a large attendance at the funeral. /The funeral was largely attended.

회장 回章 a circular (letter) ¶ 회장을 돌리다 send a circular (letter)

회저 壞疽 〖의학〗 gangrene ; necrosis ¶ 회저가 생기다 gangrene sets in

회전 回電 a reply telegram ; a return wire ; a wired reply **—하다** answer a telegram ; wire back

†**회전 回轉** revolution ; rotation ; gyration ; 〖경제〗 turnover **—하다** revolve 《round, about》; rotate ; go〔move〕round ; gyrate ; turn ; spin

> 참고 **turn** 「원형으로 돌다」라는 뜻의 일반어 **revolve** 다른 물체를 중심으로 해서 뱅뱅 회전하다 **rotate** 자신의 축을 중심으로 해서 회전하다

¶ 1분간에 2,000번 회전하다 make 2,000 revolutions a minute // 지구는 태양의 주위를 회전한다 The earth moves〔revolves〕around the sun. // 스크류가 굉장한 속력으로 회전했다 The screw went round at a very great speed.
— 거울 a rotating mirror **— 경기** 〖스키〗 a slalom **—계(計)** a revolution-indicator〔-counter〕; a trochometer (차의 회전에 의하여 주행거리를 재는) ; a hodometer ; a speed counter **— 기계** a rotary machine **— 기관** a rotary engine **— 기금〔자금〕** 《employ》 a revolving fund **—등** a revolving light ; a flashlight (등대용) **—력** turning force ; rotatory power **—로** a revolving furnace〔kiln〕; a rotary oven **—면** the surface of revolution **— 목마** a merry-go-round ; a giddy-go-round ; a whirligig ; a carousel 《미》; a roundabout 《영》 **— 무대** a revolving stage **—문** a turnstile ; a revolving door **— 반경** a radius of rotation〔gyration〕; a turning radius **— 서가〔책꽂이〕** a revolving bookstand〔bookcase〕 **— 속도** revolutions per minute 《RPM》; speed of revolution **— 속도계** a revolution〔rev〕counter ¶ 자동 회전기록 속도계 a tachograph **—수** the number of rotations〔revolutions〕; rotational frequency ; [엔진의] rev count ; the rate of rotation **— 스위치** a rotary switch **— 운동** a rotary〔rotatory〕motion ; a rotation ; (a) revolution ; a slewing motion (크레인의) **—율** a turnover (rate) (자금의) **—의** a gyroscope ; a gyrostat **— 의자** a swivel〔pivot, revolving〕chair **—익(翼)** [헬리콥터의] a rotor (blade) ; a rotating airfoil ; [송〔선〕풍기 따위의] a wafter **—자(子)** a rotor ; a rotator **—창** a pivoted window **—체** a body of revolution〔rotation〕 **—축** the axis of rotation〔gyration〕; a pivot ; a shaft **— 테이블** a rotary table **— 포탑** a revolving turret **대—** 〖스키〗 a giant slalom

회전 會戰 a battle ; a fight ; an engagement ; an encounter **—하다** fight 《a battle》; encounter ; meet ; engage 《the enemy》

회절 廻折 〖물리〗 diffraction **—하다** diffract
—각 the angle of diffraction **— 격자(格子)** a diffraction grid〔screen〕 **—상〔대(帶)〕** a diffraction figure〔zone〕 **—파〔선, 음〕** a diffracted wave〔ray, sound〕

회정 回程 a return trip ; the return way ; the way back **—하다** return ; retrace 《one's step》; start on one's way back ¶ 회정에 오르다 start on one's way back ; begin one's return trip

회조 回漕 sea〔marine〕transportation ; shipping **—하다** forward〔transport〕by sea ; ship
—업 shipping business〔trade〕; marine transportation business **—업자** a shipping agent〔agency〕

회죄 悔罪 penitence ; repenting one's

sin

회주 會主 the promoter〔manager, sponsor〕 of a meeting ; the host of a party

*회중 會衆 an audience ; (the) assembled people ; an attendance ; attendants ; a congregation (교회의) ; a gathering ¶ 많은 회중 a large attendance // 회중은 그의 웅변에 깊이 감동했다 The audience were deeply moved by his eloquence.

회중 懷中 one's pocket ; [마음 속] the bosom ; one's mind〔heart〕 ¶ 회중물에 조심하시라 Beware of pickpockets.
—경 a pocket mirror — 시계 a (pocket) watch ; a ticker 《속》 — 일기 a pocket(-sized) diary — 전등 a flashlight 《미》 ; an electric torch ; a torch (lamp) ; a flashlamp

회지 會誌 a bulletin ; the transactions (학회의)
동창회 — an alumni bulletin ; an alumnae bulletin (여학교의)

회진 灰塵 ashes ⇨ 회신(灰燼)

회진 回診 (a doctor's) round of visits —하다 visit〔go the round of〕 one's patients ; make sick calls ¶ 의사 선생님께서 곧 회진하실 것입니다 The doctor will soon come round to see you.

회집 會集 (a) gathering ; an assemblage ; a crowd —하다 gather together ; get together ; assemble

회천 回天 restoration of the national prestige —하다 rehabilitate 《a nation》 ¶ 회천지업 a great undertaking to restore the national prestige ; a Herculean〔tremendous〕 task ; an epoch-making deed〔feat, exploit〕

회청 回靑 ⇨ 회회청

회청색 灰靑色 grayish blue

회초간 晦初間 about〔toward〕 the end of the month and the beginning of the next

‡회초리 a switch ; a rod ¶ 버들 회초리 a switch from a willow tree // 회초리로 때리다 whip 《a person》 with a switch

회춘 回春 recovery ; restoration to health ; rejuvenation —하다 recover ; regain one's health ; be rejuvenated
—기 Indian summer (노년의) —제 a rejuvenator (tonic) ; an aphrodisiac ; an erogenous drug

회충 蛔蟲 a roundworm ; a belly-worm ¶ 회충이 생기다 get roundworms
—병 ascari(di)asis —증 stomach trouble from roundworms

회치다 膾— slice raw fish〔meat〕 and season it ¶ 생선을 회치다 prepare a raw fish dish

회칙 回勅 [로마 교황의] an encyclical (letter) ; an encyclic

회칙 會則 the regulations〔rules〕 of a society〔an association〕 ¶ 우리 클럽에는 회칙과 부칙이 있다 Our club has a constitution and bylaws.

회태 懷胎 pregnancy
— 기간 a gestation period — 연령 〚심리〛 conception age

회판 the end ; the finish ; the last round

회편 回便 a return courier ; a return messenger ; return post〔mail〕

회포 懷抱 one's inmost thoughts ¶ 슬픈 회포 sad thoughts

회피 回避 evasion ; avoidance ; shirking —하다 evade ; shirk ; avoid ; elude ; keep out of 《war》 ; shun ; dodge ¶ 책임을 회피하다 evade〔shirk〕 one's responsibility // 납세를 회피하다 elude taxation // 내가 무어라고 말해도 그는 문제를 회피했다 Whatever I might say, he dodged the issue.
— 전술 dodging〔evasive〕 tactics

회한 悔恨 remorse ; repentance ; regret ; contrition —하다 regret ; repent ; be penitent of ¶ 회한의 눈물 penitent tears ; tears of repentance 〔remorse〕

*회합 會合 a meeting ; a gathering ; an assembly ; a congregation

> 참고 **meeting** 일단의 사람들이 일을 결정한다든가 토론을 하기 위하여 어떤 한 장소에 모이는 것 **assembly** 전자보다 다소 딱딱한 말로서 공통의 목적에 대하여 상의하기 위하여 모이는 또는 소집하는 회 **gathering** 비공식적인 또는 비조직적인 사람들의 모임

—하다 meet ; gather together ; assemble ; congregate ¶ 회합일 a meeting day // 회합의 약속을 하다 make an appointment
— 약속 an appointment ; a date 《미》 ; tryst — 장소 a place of meeting ; an assembling place ; a rendezvous ; a venue 《속》

회항 回航 [순항] cruising ; sailing about ; a cruise ; [귀항] a return cruise ; sailing back —하다 sail about ; [귀항] bring〔take〕 a ship home ; bring a ship to 《*Pusan*》

회향 回向 [얼굴] the turn of a face ; [불교에서] a Buddhist memorial (for the dead) ; a mass (for the response of a soul) —하다 turn one's face ; [불교에서] hold a memorial service

회향 懷鄕 longing〔yearning〕 for home ; homesickness —하다 long〔yearn〕 for home ; be homesick ; be nostalgic
—병 homesickness ; nostalgia ¶ 회향병에 걸리다 feel〔get〕 homesick〔nostalgic〕

회향 茴香 fennel
—풀 the fennel plant

회혼 回婚 the 60th wedding anniversary

†회화 會話 conversation ; talk ; chat ; a dialogue (대화) —하다 converse〔talk〕 《with》 ; have a conversation〔talk〕 《with》 ¶ 회화체로 in a colloquial style

//회화체의 영어 the colloquial〔spoken〕 English//영어 회화 연습을 하다 practice speaking English//영어로 회화하다 talk〔converse〕 in English 《with》//그녀는 영어 회화를 잘한다 She speaks English well./She is a good speaker of English./She is good at English conversation.
—문 colloquial literature — 실력 one's speaking ability —책 a conversation book —체 colloquialism ; colloquial style 영어 — a conversation in English
회화 繪畫 pictures ; paintings (유화) ; drawings (선화) ¶ 회화적인 pictorial ; picturesque ; graphic
—(진열)관 an art gallery ; a picture gallery — 문자 a hieroglyph(ic) ; picture writing (집합적) — 전람회 an art 〔a painting〕 exhibition ; an exhibition〔a showing〕 of pictures ; a picture show
회화나무 ⇨ 홰나무
회환 回還 return ; coming back —하다 return ; come〔get〕 back
회회 ⇨ 휘휘
회회교 回回教 Mohammedanism ; Islam ; Islamism
—국 a Mohammedan country ; a Moslem land — 기원 the Mohammedan〔Muhammadan〕 Era —도 a Mohammedan ; a Moslem〔Muslim, Muslem〕 《*pl.* ～(s)》; an Islamite — 사원 a mosque
회회청 回回青 blue dye used for glazing porcelain
회회하다 恢恢— (be) vast ; immense ; roomy
회훈 回訓 government instructions (sent in response to request) —하다 give 〔send〕 return instructions ; reply with instructions
회흘 回紇 〖역사〗 the Uigurs
획 ⇨ 휙
획 畫 a stroke ; a dash ¶ 세 획으로 된 글자 a character made in three strokes ; a 3-stroke character//획을 내려〔가로〕 긋다 make a vertical〔horizontal〕 stroke//획을 비끼치다 make a slant stroke
***획기적 劃期的** epoch-making 《events》; epochal ¶ 획기적 사건〔발견〕 an epoch-making event〔discovery〕//획기적 기록 an epoch-making record//그것은 한국 역사에 획기적인 일이다 It marks an epoch in Korean history.
†**획득 獲得** acquisition ; acquirement

> 참고 **acquirement**는 정신적인 것에 대하여 **acquisition**은 물질적인 것에 대하여 사용하는 일이 많다

—하다 get ; acquire ; win ; obtain ; get possession of ¶ 권리를 획득하다 acquire rights
— 면역성 acquired immunity —물 an acquisition ; gainings — 형질 〖생물〗 an acquired character
획력 畫力 the power of a stroke (in painting or calligraphy)
획법 畫法 the canons of brushing strokes ; a style of penmanship
획수 畫數 the number of strokes (in a Chinese character) ; the stroke count
획순 畫順 the order of making strokes in writing a Chinese character ¶ 획순을 틀리게 쓰다 write 《a character》 making strokes in a wrong order
획시대 劃時代 ¶ 획시대적인 epoch-making
획연 劃然 —하다 (be) distinct ; clear-cut ; sharp ¶ 획연히 distinctly ; clearly ; sharply//확연히 구별하다 draw a sharp〔hard and fast〕 line (of demarcation) 《between》; make a clear distinction 《between》
획인 畫引 an index arranged according to the total number of strokes in each Chinese character
획일 畫一 uniformity ; standardization ¶ 획일의 uniform ; standardized//획일적 교육 uniform education//획일화하다 unify ; standardize
—주의 (the principle of) standardization
획정 劃定 demarcation ; delimitation —하다 demarcate 《the boundary line》; delimit ; define
획책 畫策 planning ; scheming ; a plan ; a scheme ; a stratagem ; a project —하다 plan ; scheme ; lay〔make〕 plans ; maneuver (책동하다)
획획 ① [도는 모양] round and round ; whirling ; fast ¶ 획획 돌다 turn〔go〕 round and round ; spin ; twirl ; whirl ; wheel
② [바람이 부는 모양] whistling ; with a whistle〔whiz(z)〕 ¶ 바람이 하루 종일 획획 불었다 The wind whistled all day long.
횟가루 powdered lime ; lime powder
횟감 膾— ingredients for making a dish of raw fish and vegetables seasoned in vinegar
횟돌 limestone
횟반 a lump of solidified lime ; a hardened〔condensed〕 mass of lime
횟수 回數 the number of times ; the frequency〔oftenness〕 ¶ 횟수를 거듭하다 repeat//그의 이번 학기의 결석 횟수를 조사해 주시오 Please examine how many times he was absent this term.
횟잎나무 〖식물〗 a small spindle tree
횡 橫 width ; crossways ⇨ 가로
횡갱 橫坑 〖광산〗 a drift ; a driftway ; an adit ; a tunnel
횡격막 橫隔膜 the diaphragm
횡관 橫貫 running〔cutting〕 across —

하다 run〔cut〕 across
*횡단 橫斷 crossing ; crosscutting ; intersection ; traversing ; traversal —하다 cross ; get〔go〕 across ; traverse ; intersect ; divide crosswise ¶ 대서양을 횡단하다 cross the Atlantic Ocean // 선로를 횡단하다 go across a track // 한 줄기 길이 들판을 횡단하고 있다 A single path intersects the field. // 그는 무단 도로 횡단으로 받은 교통 위반 딱지를 교통 경찰관 앞에서 찢어 버렸다 He tore up a traffic citation for jaywalking in front of the police officer who'd ticketed him.
—로 a crosscut (road) ; a shortcut ; a 《park》 transverse —면 a cross〔transverse〕 section ; a transection — 보도 a street〔pedestrian〕 crossing ; a crosswalk ; a walkway ; pedestrians' crossing ¶ 이 횡단 보도를 건너자 Let's take this crosswalk. —선 a transversal line — 자료 〚경제〛 cross-section data 대륙 — 철도 a transcontinental railroad〔railway〕 대서양 — 비행〔케이블〕 a transatlantic flight〔cable〕 북극 — 비행 a transpolar flight ; a flight across the pole 태평양 — 비행 a transpacific flight ; a flight across the Pacific
횡대 橫隊 a rank ; a line ; a line abreast ¶ 횡대로 in line〔flank〕 // 횡대가 되다 form in line ; be drawn up in〔into〕 line
— 비행 flying in line abreast — 사격 line firing — 행진 march(ing) in a line 2열 — a double line
횡도 橫道 [부정] unrighteous ways ; injustice ; wickedness ; iniquity ; [옆길] a side road ; a by-road ; a byway
횡득 橫得 an unexpected gain ; a windfall ; a godsend —하다 have a windfall ; gain an unexpected profit
횡듣다 hear amiss ; mishear ; misunderstand ¶ 사람의 말을 횡듣다 mishear 《a person》
횡렬 橫列 a line ; a line abreast
횡령 橫領 seizure ; usurpation ; unlawful possession ; embezzlement (금전의) ; misappropriation —하다 usurp ; seize (upon) ; jump 《a claim》 ; dispossess 《a person of his property》 ; embezzle ; misappropriate ¶ 재산을 횡령하다 seize 《a person's》 property // 그는 회사 기금을 횡령하였다 He helped himself to company funds.
—자 an embezzler ; a usurper ; a dispossessor ; an embezzler —죄 embezzlement ; disseizin〔disseisin〕 권리〔선취 특권〕 — claim jumping (불하된 토지·광물 따위의)
횡류 橫流 overflow ; flowing sideways ② [비유적] sale through illegal channels —하다 sell 《goods》 through illegal channels〔on the black market〕 —되다 《goods》 flow into illicit channels ; flow into the black market ; smuggle in
횡문근 橫紋筋 a striated muscle
횡보 橫步 —하다 walk sideways ; sidle 《through the door》 ; edge along
횡보다 see wrongly ; misjudge ; be deceived ¶ 사람을 횡보다 make a wrong estimation of a person
횡사 橫死 a violent〔tragic〕 death ; an accidental death —하다 meet (with) a violent death ; die a violent〔tragic〕 death ; die by violence ; come to a tragic death ; die in one's boots
횡서 橫書 horizontal writing ; writing horizontally〔in a lateral line, sideways〕 —하다 write horizontally〔in a lateral line, sideways〕 ; write from left to right
횡선 橫線 a horizontal〔cross〕 line ; 〚수학〛 an abscissa (횡좌표) ¶ 횡선을 긋다 cross
— 수표 a crossed check
횡설수설 橫說竪說 (a) random〔wild〕 talk ; contradictory〔absurd, outlandish〕 remarks ; a gibberish ; a jargon ; nonsense —하다 talk at random ; talk wild(ly) ; speak contradictorily ¶ 횡설수설하는 대답 a roaming reply // 네 말은 횡설수설이라 이해할 수 없다 What you say is all Greek to me.
횡수 橫數 unexpected〔unlooked-for〕 fortune〔misfortune〕 ; a chance〔an accidental〕 hit ; a fluke ¶ 횡수로 돈을 모으다 make money by sheer good luck // 횡수로 이기다 win by chance〔a fluke〕
횡수막이 橫數— an exorcism held at the beginning of the year to get rid of evil spirits
횡액 橫厄 unexpected bad luck ; unexpected〔unforeseen〕 disaster〔calamity〕 ; a misfortune ; a mishap
횡와 橫臥 —하다 lie on one's side
횡의 橫議 irrelevant discussions ; a digression ; a sidetracked argument
횡일 橫溢 —하다 overflow ; be filled 〔full〕 to overflowing ; be replete with ; be saturated with ; be overflowing with
횡재 橫財 a windfall ; unexpected fortune〔gains〕 —하다 come into unexpected fortune ; have a windfall ¶ 자네는 언제나 횡재하기만 바라는군 You're always looking to making a big killing.
횡적 橫笛 a (cross〔transverse〕) flute ; a fife
횡전 橫轉 a lateral turning ; a (barrel) roll (비행기의) —하다 turn sideways〔laterally〕 ; make a barrel roll
횡절 橫截 —하다 cut across
횡철 橫綴 spelling sideways ; sidewise spelling
횡탈 橫奪 usurpation ; unlawful seizure ; embezzlement —하다 usurp ; seize upon 《a person's property》 ; seize by

force ; embezzle 《money》
횡파 橫波 〚물리〛 transverse wave
횡포 橫暴 oppression (압제) ; violence ; tyranny (포학) ; high-handedness (고압) **—하다** (be) arbitrary ; tyrannical ; oppressive ; violent ; high-handed ; unreasonable ¶ 횡포한 방법으로 in a high-handed manner // 경찰의 횡포 the arrogance of the police // 군부의 횡포 the despotism of the militarists
*횡행 橫行 rampancy ; prevalence ; prevalency **—하다** (be) rampant ; prevalent ; overrun ¶ 해적이 횡행하는 바다 a pirate-ridden sea ; a sea infested with pirates // 밤거리에 도적이 횡행한다 The streets are infested with robbers at night.
효 孝 filial piety〔duty, devotion〕; obedience to parents ¶ 부모에게 효를 다하다 tend one's parents with filial piety ; be dutiful〔obedient, devoted〕 to one's parents // 효는 백행의 근본이다 Filial piety is the source of all virtues.
효 效 efficacy ⇨ 효능, 효과
효경 孝經 the Book of Filial Duty
†효과 效果 effect ; effectiveness ; avail ; (the) good of 《something》; efficacy (약의) ; efficiency (능률) ; [결과] result ; fruit ¶ 효과 있는 effective ; fruitful ; [약이] efficacious ; potent // 효과 없는 ineffective ; fruitless ; to no purpose ; of no good // 효과가 있다 be effective〔effectual, fruitful〕; take effect ; do 《a person》 good ; prove fruitful ; bear fruit // 효과가 없다 be ineffective〔ineffectual, fruitless〕; have no effect ; prove fruitless ; be not so hot 《미·구》// 소기의 효과를 거두다 obtain the desired results ; reap the desired fruits // 우리가 한 모든 광고가 아무런 효과도 거두지 못한 것 같다 All that advertising we did seems to have had no effect whatsoever.
극적 — a dramatic effect 무대 — a stage effect 배색 — color effects 선전 — propaganda effect 음향 — sound effects ; acoustics
‡효과적 效果的 effective ; effectual ; efficient ; efficacious (약 따위) ¶ 비효과적인 ineffective ; ineffectual // 효과적으로 effectively ; with effect
효녀 孝女 a filial〔dutiful〕 daughter
*효능 效能 efficacy ; virtue ; properties 《of a medicine》; benefit ; good ; use ¶ 약의 효능 the virtue〔effect〕 of medicine ; the efficacy of a remedy // 효능이 있다 be effective ; be good 《for》; be efficacious // 효능 없다 be ineffective ; be inefficacious ; be no good 《for》; be useless ; be of no avail // (약의) 효능이 나타나다 take effect // 이 약은 무엇에 효능이 있습니까 What is this medicine good for? // 이것은 그 병에 틀림 없이 효능이 있다 This is a sure remedy for the disease. // 이 약은 나에게는 조금도 효능이 없었다 The medicine had no effect on me.
—률 efficiency —서 a statement of virtues ; a puff (과대(誇大)한) ; a puffing advertisement
효도 孝道 filial piety〔duty〕 ¶ 효도를 다하다 be dutiful〔obedient〕 to one's parents ; practice filial piety toward one's parents ; discharge one's filial duties
효득 曉得 [이해] understanding ; comprehension ; [파악] grasp ; hold **—하다** understand ; comprehend ; grasp ; seize
†효력 效力 effect ; virtue ; efficacy ; [법적] validity ; effect ; force ¶ 효력이 있다 be effective〔efficacious, valid〕 // 효력이 없다 be ineffective〔inefficacious, null and noid (법적으로)〕 // 효력 있는 계약 a valid contract // 효력을 발생하다 become effective ; come into effect〔force, operation, validity〕; take effect ; become operative // 효력을 잃다 lose effect〔validity〕; become invalid ; go out of force // 법적 효력을 갖다 have legal force // 동일한 효력을 갖다 have the same force 《as》
— 검정 assay (약물의) — 발생 effectivation ; effectuation ; effect
*효모 酵母 yeast ; leaven ; barm
—균 yeast fungus 《*pl.* ~es, -gi》; organized ferment
효복 孝服 ⇨ 상복(喪服)
효부 孝婦 a filial〔dutiful, obedient, devoted〕 daughter-in-law
효성 孝誠 filial piety ¶ 효성스럽다 be dutiful // 효성이 지극하다 be devoted to one's parents // 부모에게 효성을 다하다 discharge one's duties to one's parents ; show great devotion to one's parents
효성 曉星 Venus (금성) ; the morning star (샛별) ¶ 문단의 효성 a star〔luminary〕 in the literary world ; a literary star ; a star writer
효소 酵素 enzym(e) ; ferment
—원(原) 〚생화학〛 zymogen(e) 당화〔소화〕 — diastasic〔digestive〕 enzyme 자당(蔗糖)〔전화(轉化)〕 — invertase 항— antienzyme 황색(산화) — flavoprotein
효소학 酵素學 〚생화학〛 enzymology
—자 an enzymologist
효수 梟首 **—하다** hang up the head of a decapitated criminal ¶ 효수 경중하다 display the criminals' heads as a warning to the people
—대 a gibbet ; a stock
효순 孝順 dutifulness ; obedience ; filial piety **—하다** (be) filial〔dutiful, obedient〕 《to one's parents》
효시 嚆矢 [최초] the beginning ; the first ; the first person 《to do》; the

pioneer ⟪in⟫ ; [선례] the first instance ⟪of⟫ ¶ 그가 …의 효시였다 He was the first to ⟪do⟫. ∥미국 유학은 그를 효시로 한다 He was the first one to go to America for study.

효신세 曉新世 〚지질〛 the Paleocene (epoch)

효심 孝心 filial devotion〔duty, piety〕 ¶ 효심이 있는 dutiful ; filial ; devoted ; pious ; faithful ⟪to one's parents⟫

효양 孝養 dutiful service to one's parents ; the discharge of filial duties 〔piety, devotion〕 ¶ 부모에게 효양을 다하다 take good care of one's parents ; be dutiful〔obedient, faithful〕 to one's parents ; discharge one's duties to one's parents ; attend on one's parents with devotion

효열 孝烈 filial piety and chastity ; a filial〔dutiful, devoted〕 son and a chaste daughter

효용 效用 [용도] use ; [유용성] utility ; usefulness ; [효험] effect ; good ; virtue ¶ 돈의 효용 the utility of money ∥효용이 있다 be useful〔effective, good〕 ∥효용이 없다 be of no use ; avail nothing ∥무슨 효용이 있는가 What is the good ⟪of education⟫?

— 가치 effective value — 극대 원칙 the principle of maximum utility — 체감 법칙 〚경제〛 the law of diminishing utility〔returns〕 자연〔최종, 전부, 잉여〕 — 〚경제〛 gratuitous〔final, total, surplus〕 utility 한계 — marginal utility

효용 驍勇 bravery ; valiancy ; valor ; prowess —하다 (be) valiant ; valorous ; brave

효웅 梟雄 a villain-type hero ; a cruel and clever warrior who uses any means to attain his end

효유 曉諭 instruction ; inculcation ; admonition ; persuasion —하다 instruct ; inculcate ; instill ; admonish ; reason with ; persuade

효율 效率 the utility factor ; 〚기계〛 efficiency ; [기관의] duty

— 곡선 an efficiency curve — 시험 an efficiency test — 인자 an efficiency factor — 평가 merit rating 기계 — the modulus of a machine 열— thermal efficiency 종합〔전〕 — overall efficiency

효자 孝子 a dutiful〔faithful, devoted, good, an obedient〕 son

효장 驍將 a valiant〔veteran〕 general ; a leader

효제 孝悌 filial piety and brotherly love

— 충신(忠信) filial piety and brotherly love together with loyalty and sincerity

효종 曉鐘 the morning bell

효천 曉天 dawn ; the morning sky

효행 孝行 filial piety〔devotion〕 ; filial duty ; obedience to parents ¶ 부모에게 효행하다 be dutiful〔devoted, obedient〕 to one's parents ; practice filial piety toward one's parents ; discharge one's filial duties

효험 效驗 efficacy ; effect ; virtue ⟪of a medicine⟫ ¶ 효험이 있다 be efficacious 〔effective〕 ; do ⟪a person⟫ good ; take effect ∥효험이 없다 be ineffective〔inefficacious〕 ; do ⟪a person⟫ no good ; have no effect ∥이 약은 위장에 아주 효험이 있다 This is a good remedy for stomach trouble. /This medicine works wonders on dyspepsia.

후 blowing ; with a puff ¶ 후 불다 whiff ; puff ∥촛불을 후 불어 끄다 blow out a candlelight with a puff

†후 後 ① [시간·순서] after ; afterward (s) ; later ; […이래] since ; hence ; […다음] next to ; following ; [위치] behind ¶ 그후 after that ; then ; afterward ; subsequently ∥2, 3일 후에 [지금부터] in a few days ; a few days from now ; [과거 어느때 부터] after a few days ; a few days after ∥그후 내내 ever since ∥2년 후 after two years ; two years after〔later〕 ∥지금으로부터 10년 후 ten years hence ; ten years from now〔this time〕 ∥1970년 후의 after〔posterior to〕 the year 1970 ∥조반 후 after breakfast ∥임명후 following〔subsequent to〕 the appointment ⟪of⟫ ∥50년 후의 세계 the world fifty years hence ∥후에 전화하겠다 I'll call you up〔give a ring, telephone you〕 later (on). ∥후에 후회할 것이다 You'll be sorry afterwards. ∥후에 또 뵙겠습니다 See you later. /So long. ∥그 후로는 그를 만나지 못했다 I haven't seen him since. ∥이 일은 후에 해도 된다 This work can wait. ② [추후] later ; after ; farther〔further〕

—고구려 later *Koguryŏ* —더침 complications from childbirth

후 后 an empress ; a queen

후 侯 [후작] a marquis

후가 後嫁 a woman's second marriage

†후각 嗅覺 the sense of smell ; the smell ; the olfactory sensation ¶ 후각이 예민하다 have a keen nose〔sense of smell〕

—계 an olfactometer — 과민〔감퇴〕 hypersmia〔hyposmia〕 — 기관 the organ of smell ; an olfactory organ — 동물 an osmatic animal — 신경 the olfactory nerve — 작용 olfaction

후각 後覺 coming to understand behind 〔later than〕 others ; a late-comer ; a follower —하다 come to understand after others ; attain enlightenment behind others

후감 嗅感 the olfactory sensation ⇨ 후각

후갑판 後甲板 the quarterdeck

후거리 後— a saddle breeching

후견 後見 guardianship ; wardship ; tute-

lage ; tutorage ── 하다 act as guardian 《for》 ; look after 《children》 ; guard ; have the wardship of 《a person》 ¶ 후견을 받다 be placed under the guardianship 《of》 ; be under〔in〕 ward
─인 〖법〗 a guardian ; a tutor ; a curator ; a committee ; [연기자의] a prompter ; an assistant (마술사 따위의) ; [권투 선수의] a (personal) manager 피─인 a ward

후계 後繼 succession ── 하다 succeed to 《another's office, estate》 ; succeed 《a person》 in his office
─ 내각 the succeeding〔incoming〕 Cabinet ─자 a successor ; an inheritor ; [보충 교대자] a replacement ; [후사] an heir (남자) ; an heiress (여자) ¶ 김씨의 후계자로 선출되다 be elected〔chosen, picked out〕 as successor to Mr. *Kim*

후고 後顧 [뒤를 돌봄] looking back ; [후환] future troubles ; [후일의 은고] future favors ── 하다 look back ; worry over the future ; worry about one's family left behind ¶ 후고의 염려 [장래의] anxiety〔solicitude〕 about one's future ; [가정의] anxiety about one's home ; family care // 후고를 염려하다 be anxious about one's home〔one's family〕 // 후고의 염려를 없애다 free 《a person》 from family cares ; free 《a person》 from anxiety about one's home ; free 《a person》 from solicitude (anxiety) about the future

후골 喉骨 the Adam's apple

후관 嗅官 the organ of smell ; the olfactory organ

후광 後光 [윤광] a halo ; a nimbus (원광) ; an aureola〔aureole〕 ; a glory ; a corona (태양의) ¶ 후광이 비치다 a halo appears〔develops〕 round 《a person's》 head ; one's head is surmounted by an aureole

후군 後軍 the rearguard ; the rear of an army ¶ 후군이 되다 close〔bring up〕 the rear

후굴 後屈 〖의학〗 retroflexion
자궁 ─증 the retroflexion of the uterus

후궁 後宮 [궁] a royal harem ; [사람] a royal concubine〔harem〕

후기 後期 the latter term〔period〕 ; the last〔second〕 half year ; the final term ¶ 전쟁의 후기 the late period〔stage〕 of a war
─ 결산 settlement of accounts for the second half ─ 대학 the second group of universities〔colleges〕 ─ 배당 a dividend for the second half ─ 시험 the second-term〔final〕 examination ─ 인상파 the later impressionists ; the post-impressionists ─ 환자 a late case

후기 後記 a postscript 《P. S.》 ; an afternote
편집 ─ a postscript by the editor

후끈 ── 하다 (be) hot ; flushed ; be in a glow ; be all of a glow

후끈거리다 feel hot〔warm〕 ; burn ; flush ; glow ¶ 후끈후끈 hotly ; warmly // 술을 마시니 얼굴이 후끈거린다 My cheeks are flushed with wine. // 몸이 후끈거렸다 My body was all of a glow.

후난 後難 ⇨ 후환(後患)

후년 後年 [내내년] year after next ; [훗날에] later years ; later ¶ 후년에 가서 in future years ; in later〔after〕 years ; in years to come ; in one's later years 〔days〕
내─ three years from now

후념 後念 a musical refrain ⇨ 후렴

후뇌 後腦 〖해부〗 the hindbrain

후닥닥 with a start ; with a jump ; suddenly ; [급히] in a hurry ; in a flurry ; hurrying ; rushing ¶ 후닥닥 놀라다 be suddenly startled // 후닥닥 계단을 뛰어내리다〔오르다〕 hurry downstairs〔upstairs〕 // …을 후닥닥 해치우다 work in a hasty manner ; scamp

후닥닥거리다 scamper ; keep jumping ; get startled repeatedly ; [급히 서두르다] hurry ; rush ; make haste ¶ 일을 빨리 끝내려고 후닥닥거리다 rush to get a job done in a hurry // 닭이 기적 소리에 놀라서 후닥닥거리다 Chickens scamper at the sound of a train whistle.

후단 後段 [이야기 따위의] the latter part 《of a tale》 ; [연극 따위의] the latter scene〔act〕 ¶ 전조 후단의 규정 the provisions of the latter part of the preceding article // 후단에 설명하는 바와 같이 as stated〔described〕 farther on ; as referred to later〔hereinafter〕 ; as is touched upon in a later chapter

후당 後堂 a separate house in the rear

후대 後代 future〔coming〕 generations ; after〔later〕 ages ¶ 후대에 이름을 전하다 hand one's name down to posterity ; immortalize one's name

후대 厚待 a warm〔cordial, hearty〕 reception ; hospitable treatment ; hospitality ; entertainment ; welcome ── 하다 give a warm〔cordial〕 reception ; entertain warmly ; receive warmly ; treat hospitably〔liberally〕 ¶ 후대를 받다 be received cordially ; be accorded a warm welcome ; receive a hospitable treatment

후대 後隊 [대열] the rear ranks ; [부대] troops in rear

후더침 後─ complications arising from childbirth〔illness〕 ; afterpains

후덕 厚德 liberality ; generosity ; liberal favor ; great virtue
─ 군자 a liberal gentleman ; a virtuous gentleman

후두 喉頭 〖해부〗 the larynx ¶ 후두의

laryngeal ; faucal
—개(蓋) 〖해부〗 the epiglottis — 결핵 tuberculosis of the larynx —경 a laryngoscope — 구멍 the ventricle of the larynx —낭 a laryngeal pouch〔sac〕 —부 the laryngeal region —암 cancer of the larynx —염 laryngitis —음 laryngeal voice〔sound〕 — 절개술 laryngotomy — 카타르 laryngeal catarrh

후두 後頭 〖의학〗 the occiput ; the back of the head
— 결절 the occipital protuber —골 the occipital (bone) —부 the occipital region —엽 the occipital lobe

후두두 with a patter ¶ 후두두 쏟아지는 비 a pelting rain〔shower〕∥비가 후두두 내리고 있다 The rain is falling in drops.

후둥이 後— the later born of two twins ; the younger twin

후드 a hood ¶ 후드가 달린 with a hood

후드득거리다 [방정떨다] act frivolously ; behave in a giddy way ; [툭툭 튀는 소리] keep crackling〔popping〕 ¶ 후드득후드득 crackling ; popping

후들거리다 tremble ; shake ; shiver ¶ 다리가 후들거리다 one's legs are trembling∥무서워 후들거리다 tremble with〔for〕 fear

후들후들 trembling ; shivering ¶ 후들후들 떨리는 손으로 with trembling hands

후등 後燈 a rear-light ; a tail light

후딱 quickly ; speedily ; at once ; promptly ; immediately ; in an instant〔a moment, a jiffy〕 ¶ 일을 후딱 해치우다 get a job done in a jiffy∥후딱 자리에서 일어나다 leave one's seat promptly ∥후딱 해라 Make it snappy !

후딱후딱 all quickly〔rapidly, with dispatch, with alacrity〕 ¶ 일을 후딱후딱 해치우다 finish one's work one right after another

후락 朽落 —하다 [노후하다] be worn out ; decay ; [퇴색하다] fade ; discolor

후래 삼배 後來三杯 the latecomer has to drink three glasses in a row ; making up for lost time ; catching up with the drinking

후래 선배 後來先杯 latecomers should be treated first

후략 後略 omission of what follows ; the rest omitted

후레아들 a boor ; a lout ; an ill-bred〔ill-mannered〕 fellow

후려 後慮 anxiety〔solicitude〕 about one's future ¶ 후려를 없애다 free《a person》 from solicitude〔anxiety〕 about the future

후려치다 lash ; thrash ; whip ¶ 채찍으로 사람을 후려치다 lash《a person》 with a whip ; whip《a person》

후련하다 feel relieved〔better, easier〕 ; feel unburdened ¶ 토하고 나니 속이 후련하다 feel better after throwing up∥할 말을 다 하니 속이 후련하다 I feel easier now that I have got what I had to say off my chest. ∥빚을 갚고 나니 후련하다 The load is off my mind now that I have cleared off my debts. ∥하고 싶은 말을 하고 나니 이제 속이 후련하다 I've said what I wanted to say, and now I feel like a load's been taken off my chest.

*후렴 後斂 a (musical) refrain

후록 厚祿 a generous stipend ; a liberal salary ; rich emoluments

후루루 [불다] whistling ; blowing ; [타는 모양] flickeringly ; in a flame

후루룩 [날다] with a flutter ; [마시다] with a slurp〔gulp, gurgle〕 ¶ 새가 후루룩 날아가다 a bird flutters away∥죽을 후루룩 들이마시다 slurp down one's porridge

후루룩거리다 [새가] keep fluttering ; fly ; [마시다] keep slurping

후리 ⇨ 후릿그물

후리다 ① beat at ; pummel ; flail ; shave 〔plain〕 off ; mow〔cut〕 down ¶ 낫으로 풀을 후리다 mow〔cut〕 down grass with a sickle ② [혹하다] captivate ; charm ; bewitch ; seduce ③ [그물로] round up ; net ; bag ; catch (with a net) ¶ 그물로 새〔고기〕를 후리다 chase〔catch〕 birds〔fish〕 with a net ④ [채가다] snatch ; carry off ; run away with ; steal ¶ 도둑이 부인의 손에서 지갑을 후려갔다 The thief snatched away the purse in a lady's hand.

후리질 fishing with a net ; seining —하다 fish with a (large) net ; seine

후리후리하다 (be) tall and slender ; lank ; willowy ¶ 후리후리한 몸매 a willowy〔slender, graceful〕 figure

후림 seduction ; a seductive trick ; a wile ¶ 후림에 넘어가다 be caught by a trick
— 비둘기 a decoy pigeon

후림대 the poles at both ends of a fishing net ; [후림] seduction ; conquest ; trick ; wile
— 수작 seductive words

후림불 a by-blow ; entanglement ; involvement ¶ 후림불에 걸려들다 suffer a by-blow ; get entangled〔involved〕 in

후릿고삐 lashing rein〔halter〕

후릿그물 a large fishing net ; a dragnet ; a seine

후면 後面 the back side ; the reverse side ; the rear ¶ 학교의 후면에 in the rear〔at the back〕 of the school

후무리다 take possession of《a thing》 surreptitiously ; embezzle ; appropriate dishonestly ; pocket

후문 後門 a back〔rear〕 gate ⇨ 뒷문

후문 後聞 an after-talk〔rumor〕

후물거리다 mumble ; gum ; chew〔mouth〕 with toothless gums

후물림 後— handing down ; a hand-me-down (물건) ¶ 형의 후물림 옷 clothes handed down from one's brother

후물후물 mumbling ; gumming ; chewing 〔mouthing〕 with toothless gums **—하다** mumble ⇨ 후물거리다

*__후미__ a cove ; an inlet ; a creek ; an arm of the sea ; an embayment

후미 後尾 the tail end ; the rear ; [배의 고물] the stern ¶ 후미에 at the rear 〔back〕《of》

— 경호 the rear guard **—등(燈)** a tail light

후미지다 [강·해변이] form an inlet〔a cove〕;《the water》get a bend《in it》; bend in ; [장소가] get deep ; be retired〔secluded〕 ¶ 후미진 곳 a deep spot (in the water) ; an inlet ; a cove ; a secluded spot ; a recess ; a nook

후박 厚薄 thick and〔or〕 thin ; (being) liberal and〔or〕 stingy ; much and〔or〕 little ; [불공평] partiality ¶ 후박이 없이 without partiality ; impartially // 상여에 후박이 있다 be partial in giving rewards〔bonus〕

후박나무 厚朴— the silver magnolia ; Magnolia hypoleuca (학명)

후반 後半 the latter〔second〕 half ¶ 후반 생략 the last part omitted // 19세기의 후반에 in the latter half of the 19th century ; late in the 19th century

—기 the latter〔second〕 half of the year **—생(生)** the latter half〔part〕 of one's life **—전** the second half of the game ; 〚야구〛 the latter half of the ninth innings

후방 後方 the rear ¶ 후방의 rear ; back ; backward // 후방에 in〔at〕 the rear ; at the back ; behind // 후방으로 rearward ; backward // 적의 후방을 습격하다 attack〔take〕 the enemy in the rear ; make a raid behind the enemy's line // 후방을 교란하다 harass the rear (guards) // 후방에 배속되다 be assigned to the base

— 근무 rear service (at the base) ; service〔duties〕 in the rear〔behind the battle line, on the home front (본국의)〕 **— 기지** a rear base **— 부대** troops in rear **— 제대(梯隊)** rear echelon **— 지역** the communications zone

후배 後輩 one's junior ; [젊은이들] younger men ; the younger generation ¶ 학교의 후배 one's junior in school // 후배를 돌봐주다 patronize one's juniors // 나의 3년 후배다 He is three years behind me《in school》. // 그는 우리보다 훨씬 후배다 He is many years our junior《in service, in graduation》. // 그녀는 나의 3년 후배다 She is three years my junior.

후배주 後配株 〚증권〛 a deferred stock〔share〕

후벼내기 a tool used for digging out chisel dust

후보 後報 the succeeding report ; further information ; additional news ¶ 후보를 기다리고 있다 The report remains to be confirmed. /We are in expectation of further details.

후보 厚報 a generous〔rich〕 remuneration〔compensation, reward, pay〕

⁑**후보 候補** [입후보] candidature ; candidacy《미》; [후보자] a candidate ¶ 유력한 후보 a strong candidate // 의외로 유력한 신진 후보 a dark horse // 공화당 공천 후보로 on the Republican ticket // 후보로 나서다 be a candidate for ; run for《Congress》《미》; stand for《Parliament》《영》// 후보로 세우다 put forward〔put up〕《a person》as a candidate ; lay in《a person》for a vacant position (빈 자리에) // 후보를 사퇴하다 withdraw《a person's》candidacy // 후보자를 지원하다 support〔back up, boost〕 a candidate // 후보자의 난립을 방지하다 check random candidacy

—생 a cadet **— 선수** a substitute (player) **—자** a candidate ; an applicant ¶ 후보자 경력 공보 the candidates' career bulletin **—자 명부** an eligible list ; an elective list ; a slate《미》; a ticket **—자 지명** nomination of a candidate **—지** proposed site ; a most suitable place《for》《미》; a first choice《for》 **— 희망자** a prospective candidate **공천 —** an official〔adopted, authorized〕 candidate ; a party candidate **낙선 —** a defeated candidate **당선 —** a successful candidate **사관 —생** [간부 후보생] an officer's candidate ; [사관생도] a cadet ; a midshipman《해군의》

후보름 後— the latter half of a month

후부 後夫 one's second husband ; one's remarried man

*__후부 後部__ the rear ; the back〔hind〕 part ; the rear end《of a train》; [배의] the stern ¶ 후부의 back ; rear ; hind // 후부에 at the rear〔the back〕

후분 後分 one's luck〔fortune〕 in one's later years〔life〕 ¶ 후분이 좋다 be lucky in one's later years

후불 後拂 deferred〔post〕 payment ; future payment ¶ 후불로 사다 buy《a thing》on time

후비 后妃 an empress ; a queen

후비 後備 the second reserve

—역 the second reserve

후비다 scoop〔scrape, dig〕 out ; gouge ; [귀·코를] pick ¶ 귀〔코〕를 후비다 pick one's ears〔nose〕

후비적거리다 keep scooping〔scraping〕

out ; keep gouging ; [귀·코를] keep picking ¶ 귀〔코〕를 후비적거리다 keep picking one's ears〔nose〕
후비적후비적 gouging ; scooping〔scraping, digging〕 out ; [코 따위를] picking
후사 後事 affairs after one's death (죽은 뒤의) ; future〔later〕 affairs (장래의) ¶ 후사를 부탁하다 entrust 《a person》 with future affairs ; ask 《a person》 to take care of things after one's death ; give 《a person》 the charge of one's affairs
후사 後嗣 an heir (남자) ; an heiress (여자) ; [후계자] a successor
후사 厚謝 a generous〔handsome〕 reward ; a handsome remuneration〔recompense〕 **—하다** reward 《a person》 generously〔handsomely〕 ; remunerate 〔recompense〕 handsomely
후산 後産 (bearing) the afterbirth **—하다** bear the afterbirth
후살이 後— remarriage ; a second marriage (for a woman) ; [사람] a woman who marries again
후생 後生 [후진] juniors ; younger students〔scholars〕 ; [내세] the life〔world〕 after death ; the future life〔existence〕 ; [후세대] future generations
후생 厚生 the welfare〔well-being〕 of people ; public〔social〕 welfare ; [건강의 증진] promotion of health
— 경제학 welfare economics ; the economics of welfare **— 사업** public welfare enterprises ; social work **— 시설** welfare facilities **— 연금** a welfare annuity〔pension〕
후성 後成 〖지질〗 epigenesis
—설 〖생물〗 (the theory of) epigenesis
후세 後世 the future ; coming age ; [사람] future generations ; posterity ¶ 후세에 이름을 전하다 hand one's name down to posterity ; be remembered for ages to come // 후세에 이름을 남기다 retain one's name in history ; earn one's place in history // 후세의 판단에 맡기다 let posterity judge for itself
후속 後續 succession ; succeeding ; following ¶ 후속의 succeeding ; following
— 부대 reinforcements
후손 朽損 decay ; rot **—하다** decay ; fall into〔go to〕 decay ; rot (away) ; be dilapidated
후손 後孫 descendants ; an offspring ; a scion ; posterity 《총칭》 ¶ …의 후손이다 be descended from ; be a descendant of
후송 後送 evacuation ; sending back 《to the rear》 **—하다** send 《a person》 back 《to the rear》 ; evacuate
— 병원 an evacuation hospital **— 환자** an evacuated casualty
후수 厚酬 a generous pay ; a big〔handsome〕 compensation〔reward〕
후술 後述 —하다 say〔mention, describe, touch upon〕 later
후신 後身 one's future being ; one's later self ; [후계자] the successor
후신경 嗅神經 olfactory nerves
후실 後室 one's second wife
후안 厚顔 impudence ; effrontery ; shamelessness ; cheek ¶ 후안 무치한 사람 a shameless〔brazen-faced〕 fellow ; a saucy〔cheeky〕 person // 후안 무치하다 be brazen-faced ; be impudent ; be shameless
후열 後列 the back〔rear〕 row〔rank〕
후예 後裔 descendants ⇨ 후손
후원 後苑, 後園 a rear〔back〕 garden ; a back yard 《미》
†**후원 後援** support ; backing ; patronage ; help ; assistance ; aid **—하다** support ; give〔lend〕 support to ; back up ; give backing to ; stand by ; second ; stick up for 《a person》 ¶ 여론의 후원 the backing of public opinion // …의 후원하에 under the auspices of ; through the sponsorship of ; with the support of ; sponsored〔backed up〕 by // 재정적으로 후원하다 support 《a person》 financially ; back 《a person》 up financially // 당신의 후원을 부탁합니다 I hope to have your support.
—군 a reinforcement ; a support **—단체** a supporters' organization **—자** a supporter ; a sponsor ; a patron **—회** an aid association ; a backers'〔supporters'〕 association
후위 後衛 [군] the rear guard ; the rear (of an army) ; [정구] a back player ; [축구] a back ¶ 후위가 되다 bring up the rear
후유 [소리] with a sigh ; whew ! ; Lord bless me ! ¶ 피로해서 후유 한숨을 쉬다 sigh with fatigue〔exhaustion〕 // 후유하고 짐을 내려놓다 let one's burden down with a "whew !"
후유증 後遺症 ① 〖의학〗 a sequela 《*pl.* ~e》 ② [비유적] aftermath ¶ 선거의 후유증 the aftermath of elections
후은 厚恩 great favor ; great obligations ; indebtedness ; deep kindness ¶ 후은을 입다 receive great kindness ; owe 《a person》 great obligations ; be deeply indebted 《to》 // 후은을 잊지 않겠습니다 I shall always consider myself indebted to you. /I shall never forget your great favor.
후음 喉音 a guttural sound ; gutturals
후의 厚意 great kindness ; kind intentions ; favor ¶ 후의에 감사하다 thank 《a person》 for his kindness ; appreciate the good offices done by another // 후의를 거절하다 decline 《a person's》 kind offer
후의 厚誼 close〔warm, fast〕 friendship ; kindness ¶ 후의에 보답하다

repay 《a person》 for his kindness ; do something for 《a person's》 favor // 후의에 감격하다 be deeply affected by 《a person's》 generous act // 재직중의 후의를 감사합니다 Thank you for your kindness during my years of service here. // 저에게 배풀어 주신 후의에 감사드립니다 I'm very grateful for everything you do for me.

후인 後人 future generations ; posterity

후일 後日 some (other) day ; later days ; the future ¶ 후일에 in (the) future ; one of these days ; later ; some other day // 후일에 대비하여 as a warning for the future // 화를 후일에 남기다 sow seeds of trouble for the future // 후일을 생각하다 be mindful of the future // 후일 또 만나자 I'll see you again.

—담(譚) reminiscences ; remembrance ; recollections ; subsequent events ; a sequel〔sequence〕《to a story》

‡**후임 後任** [사람] a successor (to a post) ; a person to take one's place ¶ …의 후임으로 in succession to ; as a successor to // …의 후임이 되다 succeed 《a person》 in his post ; take 《a person's》 place // 그는 A씨의 후임으로 장관에 임명되었다. He was appointed the chief in succession〔as successor〕 to Mr. A.

—난 the difficulty of finding a successor **— 시장** the incoming mayor **—자** a successor

†**후자 後者** the latter ; the other ¶ 전자와 후자 the former and the other // 전자가 후자보다 낫다 The one is better than the other.

***후작 侯爵** a marquis ; a marquess

— 부인 a marchioness

후작 後作 the second crop

후장 後裝 breechloading

—총 a breechloading rifle〔gun〕

후장 後場 〚증권〛 the afternoon session

후정 厚情 kindness ; good wishes ; hospitality ; kind intentions ; favor

후정 後庭 a back〔rear〕 garden ; a backyard (미) ; a rear yard

후제 後— 《at》 some later time

후조 候鳥 a migratory bird ; a bird of passage ; migrants 《총칭》

후주 後酒 weak liquor ; liquor made from brewer's grains

후주곡 後奏曲 〚음악〛 a postlude

후줄근하다 (be) limp ; wilted ; droopy ; flaggy ; be a little soggy ; be wet enough to lose starch

후중 a quality coffin made of pine board

후중 後重 being constipated〔costive〕

— 하다 (be) constipated ; costive

후즈후 a Who's Who 《명사록(名士錄)》

후지 厚志 kind intention〔thought〕 ; kindness(es) ; favor ; good wishes ¶ 후지에 깊이 감사드립니다 Many thanks for your kindness.

후진 後陣 a rear guard

후진 後進 [후배] a junior ; a younger man ; the rising〔younger〕 generation 《총칭》 ; [후진성] underdevelopment ; backwardness ; lack〔slowness〕 of progress ; lagging behind ¶ 후진을 돌보다 look after〔be helpful to〕 one's juniors // 후진에게 길을 열어주다 make room for the younger generation ; give young men a chance // 후진을 위해 용퇴하다 resign in favor of one's juniors ; resign to open the way for the promotion of one's juniors

—국 a backward〔less advanced〕 nation ; an underdeveloped country **—력** 〚조선〛 astern〔backing〕 power **—성** backwardness ; laggardliness **— 장치** 〚기계〛 backward gear **— 지역** underdeveloped areas **— 지역 개발 계획** Backward Countries Development Plan **— 터빈** an astern turbine **—파(波)** a retrograding〔retrogressing〕 wave

후처 後妻 a second wife ¶ 후처를 얻다 take a second wife

후천 後天 a posterior ; postnatal nature ¶ 후천적 a posterior ; postnatal ; acquired // 성격은 후천적으로 형성된다 You can form your own personal character in the course of your lifetime.

— (획득) 형질 acquired characteristics

‡**후추** pepper ; black pepper ¶ 후추를 치다 sprinkle pepper 《on》 ; pepper // 작아도 후추가 맵다 be small but peppery

—과 piperaceae **— 나무** the black pepper plant

후춧가루 ground pepper ; pepper grounds

후충 候蟲 seasonal insects ; insects of the season

후취 後娶 taking a second wife ; a second marriage ; [사람] one's second wife **— 하다** take a second wife ; marry for the second time ; remarry

후치사 後置詞 〚문법〛 a postposition

후탈 [병후·산후의] later complications of a disease ; a post-convalescence trouble ; complications from childbirth ; an afterbirth trouble ; [사건 처리 후의] (troublesome) aftermath〔aftereffect〕 ; repercussions ¶ 후탈 없게 잘 처리하다 handle things so that there will be no trouble later on

후터분하다 (be) a bit sultry〔muggy〕 ; stuffy ¶ 후터분한 날씨 rather sultry weather // 후터분한 더위다 The heat is rather oppressive.

후텁지근하다 (be) sultry ; sticky ; stuffy

***후퇴 後退** retreat ; retrocession ; recession ; retrogression **— 하다** retreat ; go〔move〕 back ; back ; recede ; retrocede ; retrograde ; [배가] drop〔move, go〕 astern ¶ 전략적 후퇴 a strategic retreat // 차를 후퇴시키다 back a car **— 명령** an order to retreat **— 이동** retrograde movement **—익(翼)** a swept-back wing **경기 —** a business recession

후파문하다 (be) ample ; sizable ; plentiful

후편 後便 a later messenger ; a later mail ; a later opportunity ; [뒤쪽] the back side

후편 後篇 [후반] the latter part ; the concluding part ; the second〔last〕 volume (전편에 대하여) ; [속편] a sequel

후폐 朽廢 decay **—하다** decay ; be 〔become〕 dilapidated ; be ruined

후피 동물 厚皮動物 Pachydermata《총칭》; a pachyderm《단칭》

후하다 厚— ① [두껍다] (be) thick ② [인심이] (be) kind ; kind-hearted ; warm ; hospitable ; [인색하지 않다] generous ; liberal ; free〔open〕-handed ¶ 후한 대접 a cordial reception ; liberal entertainment // 후한 보수 a generous reward // 시골은 도시보다 인심이 후하다 People are friendlier in the country than in the city. // 하루에 2달러면 후한 편이다 Two dollars a day will be generous.

후학 後學 younger students〔scholars〕; one's junior(s)

후항 後項 the succeeding〔following〕 clause ; a later item ; 〖수학〗 the consequent ; the latter term

후행 後行 escorting a bride〔bridegroom〕; [사람] an escort of a bride 〔bridegroom〕 **—하다** escort〔accompany〕 (a bride, a bridegroom)

후형질 後形質 〖생물〗 metaplasm

후형체 後形體 〖생물〗 a metaplasmic body ; a metaplast

후환 後患 later〔future〕 trouble ; later complication ; an evil consequence ¶ 후환을 남기다 sow seeds of the source of evils

⁑후회 後悔 repentance ; regret ; remorse ; penitence ; contrition ; compunction

> 참고 **regret** 이미 행해진 행위에 대한 불만·아쉬움 **remorse** 자기가 범한 돌이킬 수 없는 부당 행위에 대한 양심의 가책과 슬픔 **compunction** 자기가 범한 부당 행위에 대해 느끼는 강렬한 일시적 양심의 가책

—하다 regret ; repent《of》; be sorry 〔penitent〕《for》; suffer remorse《over》 ¶ 그런 짓을 한 것을 후회한다 I regret to have done〔having done〕 such a thing. // 그는 죄를 후회한다 He is penitent for his sin. // 젊었을 때의 어리석은 짓을 후회한다 I am sorry for follies of my youth. // 게을렀던 것을 후회한다 I repent of having been idle. // 내가 한 짓을 몹시 후회한다 I feel awfully sorry for what I have done. // 후회 막급이다 There is no use repenting later. / Regret will not mend matters. /There is no use in crying over spilt milk. // 내가 한 일을 후회하고 있어요 I'm sorry about what I did. // 자네 말을 듣지 않고 그 여자와 결혼한 것을 후회하네 I'm sorry I didn't listen to you and married her.

후후 with puff after puff ; blowing and blowing ¶ 후후 불다 keep puffing // 촛불을 후후 불어 끄다 blow out the candles one after another

후후년 後後年 three years from now

⁑훅¹ with a sip〔slurp〕; quickly ; with a gulp ¶ 국을 훅 들이마시다 slurp up soup ; gulp soup down

훅² 〖권투〗 a hook ; [갈고리단추] a hook and eye ¶ 훅을 채우다 hook (up)《a dress》// 훅을 넣다 (deliver a) hook

훅하다 go at eagerly ; jump at ; be eager to ¶ 과자라면 훅한다 He always jumps at cakes. // 돈이라면 훅한다 He is eager to make money.

훅훅 with sip after sip〔slurp after slurp〕; sucking away ¶ 국을 훅훅 들이마시다 slurp away at the soup

훈 暈 [햇무리·달무리] a halo ; a ring ; a corona ; a burr ; [번진 자리] blurs ; blurred fringes

훈 訓 the Korean translation of a Chinese character ¶ 훈을 달다 add the Korean equivalent to a Chinese character ; show the meaning of a Chinese character by adding a Korean renderings

훈 [훈족] the Huns

훈감하다 (be) rich and savo(u)ry〔flavo(u)rful〕; tasteful ; delicious ; tasty 《구》

***훈계 訓戒** admonition ; exhortation ; a lecture ; [경고] caution ; warning **—하다** admonish ; exhort ; instruct ; lecture ; caution《against》; warn《a person against》 ¶ 과도의 흡연을 훈계하다 caution《a person》 against excessive smoking

훈고 exposition ; exegesis (성경의) ; interpretation ; annotation ; a commentary ; scholia (of a Chinese classic) **—학** exegetics ; exegetical studies **—학자** a scholiast

훈고 訓告 admonition ; exhortation ; a lecture **—하다** admonish《a person for his fault》; exhort《a person to work harder》; read《a person》 a homily〔lesson〕

훈공 勳功 distinguished services ; meritorious deeds ; merits ; exploits ¶ 훈공에 비추어 in recognition of one's (distinguished) services // 훈공을 세우다 distinguish oneself ; render distinguished services ; serve with distinction

훈기 勳記 a patent of decoration ; a diploma (of merit, of decoration)

훈기 薰氣 warm air ; warmth ; heat ¶ 몸의 훈기 the body heat ; human warmth

훈김 薰— [훈기] warm air ; [세력] influence ; power ¶ 아버지 훈김으로 출세하다 rise in the world through one's father's influence

훈도 薰陶 discipline ; training ; education ; instruction ; tuition **—하다** discipline ; drill ; train ; instruct ; educate ¶ A 선생의 훈도를 받다 study under 〔receive instruction from〕 Mr. A

훈독 訓讀 the Korean reading〔rendering, translation〕 of a Chinese character ; rendering Chinese writings into Korean

훈등 勳等 an order of merit

†훈련 訓練 training ; drill ; discipline ; practice ; exercise ; schooling **—하다** train 《in》 ; drill 《in》 ; practice ; discipline ; exercise

> 참고 **drill**은 끊임 없이 되풀이 하여 무엇인가를 가르치고 규율 있는 단체훈련을 시킨다는 뜻이고 **train**은 가르쳐서 익숙하게 만든다든가 자격을 얻게 한다는 뜻 그리고 **practice**는 학습을 하기도 하고 익숙하게 되기 위하여 되풀이 실천하는 것을 의미한다

¶ 잘 훈련된 well-trained〔disciplined〕 // 훈련받다 be trained ; undergo training // 군대가 훈련을 받고 있다 The troops are in training〔being drilled〕. // 신입 사원들을 훈련시켜야 한다 You have to break in the new employees.

— 교관 a drill-master **— 비행** a training flight **—사** [개의] a dog trainer ; a handler **—장** a training camp ; a drill field **자기 —** self-discipline

훈련 교본 訓練敎本 a drill book ; a training manual ; drill regulations

보병 — drill regulations for the infantry

훈련소 訓練所 a training school〔station, institute〕 ¶ 육군 신병 훈련소 an army training camp for recruits

***훈령 訓令** instruction ; an official order ; a directive **—하다** instruct ; order ; give〔issue〕 orders〔instructions〕 ; direct ¶ 정부 훈령에 의하여 by instructions from the government // 다음 훈령을 기다리다 await〔wait for〕 further instructions

— 전보 a telegraphic instruction **—집** a directory

훈륜 暈輪 a halo ; a ring ; a corona ; a burr

훈민정음 訓民正音 [한글] the Korean script

훈방 訓放 —하다 dismiss 《a person》 with a caution ¶ 경찰은 그를 훈방했다 The police dismissed him with a caution.

훈사 訓辭 an admonitory speech ; instructions ¶ 졸업식에서의 교장 선생님의 훈사 the principal's address on a commencement day

훈수 訓手書 [장기·바둑의] help from an outsider ; a hint ; a tip **—하다** help from the side 《with》 ; give a hint〔tip〕 《on》 ¶ 장기 훈수하다 help 《a person》 with a move in chess // 훈수 없기다 No help from the outsiders !

훈시 訓示 instruction ; admonition ; an address ; [훈령·게시] official instruction ; official announcements ; a directive **—하다** instruct ; admonish ; address ; [훈령·게시] give〔issue〕 instructions ; give a directive ; give out official announcements

훈신 勳臣 a meritorious subject ; a statesman of merit

훈약 薰藥 〖한의〗 errhine ; a medicinal snuff ¶ 훈약을 쐬다 apply errhine

훈연 燻煙 〖화학〗 smoking

— 건조 smoke seasoning **—실** a smoking chamber

훈영 暈影 〖사진〗 a halation

훈위 勳位 an order of merit ; court rank and honors

훈유 訓諭 admonition ; exhortation **—하다** admonish ; exhort

훈육 訓育 instruction ; training ; discipline ; education **—하다** instruct ; train ; discipline ; educate ¶ 훈육상의 educational ; disciplinary

— 주임 a teacher in charge of discipline〔moral training〕

훈작 勳爵 order of merit and peerage

훈장 訓長 a (village) schoolmaster ; a teacher

***훈장 勳章** a medal ; a decoration ; an order ; a mark of honor ¶ 훈장을 달다 wear a decoration // 훈장을 타다 be conferred a decoration // 훈장을 수여하다 decorate ; confer a decoration〔an order〕 《upon》 ; [친히] pin a decoration upon the breast 《of》 // 대통령께서 몸소 그 장군에게 훈장을 달아 주었다 President decorated the general personally 〔in person〕.

훈전 訓電 telegraphic instructions **—하다** send〔give〕 instructions by wire ; send telegraphic instructions ¶ 정부의 훈전을 바라다 ask for telegraphic instructions from the government

훈제 燻製, 薰製 smoking (of meat) ; smoke-drying ¶ 훈제의 smoked ; smoke-dried // 훈제로 하다 smoke ; smoke-dry

— 연어 smoked salmon

훈족 一族 the Huns ; the Hun tribes
훈증 薰蒸 [더위] mugginess ; sultriness ; [소독] fumigation **—하다** (be) sultry ; muggy ; fumigate
— 소독기 a fumigator **—제** a fumigant
훈풍 薰風 a balmy wind ; a warm breeze
훈학 訓學 instruction (in a village school) ; teaching
훈화 訓話 admonition ; precepts ; an admonitory speech ; an apologue ¶ 오늘 아침에 교장 선생님의 훈화가 있었다 The principal spoke to us this morning.
훈훈하다 薰薰— (be) (comfortably) warm ¶ 몸이 훈훈해지다 get warm // 방이 훈훈하다 A room is comfortably warm.
훌근번쩍 goggling ; bulging〔popping〕 one's eyes **—하다** goggle ; bulge〔pop〕 one's eyes
훌닦다 give a whipping ; nag ; pick on ; fuss at ; berate ¶ 훌닦아 세우다 give《a person》snuff // 그녀는 사소한 것까지 그를 훌닦아서 불행케 하고 있다 // She makes his life miserable nagging him to death.
훌닦이다 get nagged〔picked on, berated, fussed at〕
훌떡 ① [벗는 모양] quickly ; nimbly ; absolutely ; completely (죄다) ¶ 훌떡 벗고 stark-naked ; with nothing on // 훌떡 벗다 strip oneself of one's clothes ; strip oneself bare
② [뒤집히는 모양] entirely ; perfectly ¶ 저고리를 훌떡 뒤집다 turn a coat inside out (entirely)
③ [뛰어넘는 모양] quickly ; nimbly ¶ 담을 훌떡 뛰어넘다 jump〔leap〕 over a fence nimbly
④ [덮는 모양] ¶ 머리부터 훌떡 이불을 뒤집어 쓰다 pull one's bedclothes over one's head
⑤ [벗어지는 모양] ¶ 가죽이 훌떡 벗어졌다 The skin peeled off.
훌떡거리다 be apt to slip out ;《one's shoes》slip all the time
훌떡훌떡 loosely ; slipperily ¶ 신이 훌떡훌떡 벗어지다 one's shoes keep slipping《all the time》
훌라댄서 a hula dancer
훌라댄스 hula (hula) ¶ 훌라댄스를 추다 dance hula
훌라들이다 [쑤셔댐] hand-thresh back and forth ; [훑음] shuck back and forth ; [문지름] scrub the inside of an object clean ; scrub out ; [드나듦] let《someone, a thing》in and out
훌라후프 a hula hoop ; hula-hooping ¶ 훌라후프를 돌리다 hula-hoop
훌렁 quickly ; nimbly ⇨ 훌떡
훌렁거리다 (be) loose ¶ 훌렁훌렁 loosely // 옷이 훌렁거린다 The clothes hang loose on me.
훌렁이질 [쑤셔댐] hand-threshing back and forth ; [훑음] shucking back and forth ; [문지름] scrubbing the inside of an object clean ; [드나듦] letting in and out **—하다** ⇨ 훌라들이다
훌렁하다 (be) loose ¶ 바지의 무릎이 훌렁하다 The trousers are baggy at the knee. // 이 옷은 너무 훌렁하다 This suit is too loose for me.
†**훌륭하다** ① [좋다] (be) nice ; fine ; handsome ; excellent ; splendid ; superb ; magnificent ¶ 훌륭한 선물 a handsome〔nice〕 present // 훌륭한 저택 a magnificent mansion // 훌륭한 풍채를 가진 사람 a man of respectable appearance // 그는 영어를 훌륭하게 한다 He speaks very good English. // 이 번역은 훌륭하다 This translation is superbly done. // 멀리서 보니 훌륭하다 It looks fine at a distance.
② [존경할 만하다] (be) respectable ; honorable ; decent ; commendable ; worthy (가치 있는) ¶ 훌륭한 인물 a respectable person // 훌륭한 직업 a respectable occupation // 훌륭한 목적 a worthy end // 그를 훌륭한 사람이라 본다 I have a high opinion of him.
③ [감탄] (be) admirable ; praiseworthy ; creditable ; commendable ; exemplary ¶ 훌륭한 저작 an admirable writing // 훌륭한 행동 a commendable act // 훌륭한 효자 an exemplary son // 훌륭한 업적 a creditable achievement
④ [고상] (be) noble ; lofty ; high ¶ 훌륭한 인격자 a person of character // 훌륭한 정신 a noble spirit // 당신의 동기는 훌륭했다 You have acted from noble〔high〕 motives. // 그 생각은 훌륭하다 The idea is (a) noble (one).
⑤ [위대] (be) great ; prominent ; eminent ¶ 훌륭한 학자 an eminent scholar // 훌륭한 사람이 되다 become a great man ; become great〔prominent〕 ; get on in life (출세하다) // 그는 훌륭한 사람이 되어 고향에 돌아왔다 He returned home loaded with honors.
⑥ [공정] (be) fair ; square ; honest ¶ 훌륭한 승부 fair play // 훌륭한 처치 a square deal
⑦ [충분] (be) sufficient ; good enough ; justifiable ; worthy ¶ 훌륭한 이유 a good reason ; a justifiable reason // 훌륭한 증거 sufficient evidence
훌부드르르하다 ⇨ 훌부들하다
훌부들하다 (be) nice and soft
훌부시다 ① [깨끗이] rinse out ; wash clean ¶ 병을 훌부시다 rinse out a bottle ② [음식을] eat up ; dispose of ; dispatch ; finish ; make short work of ¶ 떡 한 그릇을 잠깐 동안에 훌부시다 dispose of a dish of rice cakes in no time at all

훌뿌리다 shake off 《a person》 with contempt ; shake oneself free from 《the grasp》; [요구 따위를] refuse 《a person's request》 point-blank ; give a flat denial

훌쩍 [날쌔게] quickly ; with a jump ; nimbly ; [마시는 모양] at a gulp ; at a draught ¶ 훌쩍 말에 올라타다〔말에서 내리다〕 swing in〔from〕 the saddle ; spring on〔off〕 the horse // 훌쩍 들이마시다 gulp down a drink // 훌쩍 날아가다 fly off

훌쩍거리다 [액체를] sip ; sup ; suck (up) ; [콧물을] keep sniffing〔snuffing〕; [울다] sob ; snivel ; blubber ¶ 훌쩍훌쩍 sipping ; [울다] sobbingly ; blubberingly // 훌쩍거리며 말하다 sob out ; say between sobs // 훌쩍거리며 마시다 sip a cup of tea

훌쭉하다 [몸이] (be) slender ; slim ; lanky ; [끝이] long and sharp〔pointed〕

훌훌 ① [나는 모양] flying ; fluttering ; [뛰는 모양] with leaps and bounds ; lightly ; nimbly ¶ 새가 훌훌 날아가다 A bird flutters away. // 사슴이 훌훌 재를 넘어가다 A deer leaps and bounds over a hill. ② [타는 모양] in flames ¶ 장작이 훌훌 타다 Firewood goes up in flames. ③ [던지는 모양] hurling〔throwing〕 with ease ; [벗는 모양] slipping off 《one's clothes》 ¶ 짐짝을 훌훌 던지다 hurl baggage with ease // 옷을 훌훌 벗다 slip off one's clothes

훌훌하다 (be) watery ; soft ¶ 풀을 훌훌하게 쑤다 prepare starch soft

훑다 thrash ; hackle ; strip ; [제거하다] remove ; scrub out ¶ 벼를 훑다 thrash rice // 버들잎을 훑다 strip off the leaves of a willow // 버들가지의 껍질을 훑다 scrub away the bark of a willow twig // 오징어 속을 훑어내다 clean〔remove the entrails of〕 a squid

‡**훑어보다** give a searching glance at ; look carefully at ; scrutinize ¶ 사람을 위 아래로 훑어보다 look a person up and down ; take a careful look at a person ; survey a person from top to bottom // 경찰은 여자를 한 번 훑어보았다 The cop gave the woman the once-over.

훑이 a tool for threshing〔stripping, shucking〕

훑이다 get〔be〕 threshed〔hackled, stripped, shucked〕; [제거되다] get〔be〕 removed〔scrubbed off〕; [빠지다] contract ; shrink ; shrivel ¶ 벼가 잘 훑이지 않다 the rice is hard to thresh // 설사하고 나니 몸이 훑이다 get thin after a siege of diarrhea

훔척거리다 ① [더듬어 뒤지다] grope〔fumble, feel〕 《for the matches》; feel about〔around〕 《for》 ¶ 호주머니 속의 동전을 훔척거리다 feel〔fumble〕 in one's pocket for a coin ② [눈물을 씻다] wipe〔dash〕 one's tears away 《with the back of one's hand》; wipe one's wet eyes

훔쳐내다 wipe out〔up, off〕; mop ; swab ; [절도] swipe ; steal ; pilfer ¶ 먼지를 훔쳐내다 wipe off the dust // 걸레로 물을 훔쳐내다 wipe up the water with a cloth

훔쳐때리다 beat up ; thrash ; wallop ; slug〔slog〕

훔쳐먹다 embezzle ; steal ; swipe ¶ 회사 돈을 훔쳐먹다 embezzle the money of a firm // 훔쳐먹는 맛이 그만이다 Stolen fruit tastes sweet. /Stolen kisses are sweet.

훔쳐보다 steal a glance〔look〕 《at》; look〔glance〕 furtively 《at》; watch 《a person》 with a furtive eye ¶ 얼굴을 살짝 훔쳐보다 steal a look at 《a person's》 face // 다른 사람의 일기를 훔쳐보는 것은 터무니 없는 일이다 That's terrible, sneaking a look into someone else's diary.

훔치개질 [후무르기] swiping ; stealing ; [닦기] wiping out〔up, off〕; mopping ; swabbing **—하다** swipe ; steal ; wipe out〔up, off〕; mop ; swab

†**훔치다** ① [절도] swipe ; steal ; pilfer ; filch ; purloin ; take ; walk〔make〕 off with

> 참고 **steal** 일반어 **pilfer** 다소 딱딱한 말 소량의 물건을 훔치다 **filch** 값싼 물건을 몰래 훔치다 **purloin** 위의 세 말 어느 것에도 해당되는 문어

¶ 훔친 물건 stolen goods // 훔쳐 도망가다 run away〔make off〕 《with》 // 훔친 것이 맛이 좋다 Stolen kisses are sweetest. // 그 치는 가게에서 돈을 훔치다 잡혔다 That guy got caught with his hand in the till.
② [닦다] wipe (off) ; mop ¶ 훔쳐내다 wipe off〔out〕 // 걸레로 책상을 훔치다 wipe a desk with a cloth

훔켜잡다 grasp〔grab, seize, catch, snatch〕 quickly〔firmly〕; clutch ; hold on to ¶ 새를 훔켜잡다 catch a bird quickly // 멱살을 훔켜잡다 grab 《a person》 by the neck firmly

훔켜쥐다 ⇨ 훔켜잡다

훔파다 groove

훔패다 ⇨ 홈패다

훔훔하다 wear〔display〕 a look of satisfaction

***훗날** 後— later days ; some (other) day ¶ 훗날에 some (other) day ; later on ; in (the) future ; one of these days // 훗날을 위해 for future reference (참고) ; as a future proof (증거)

훗달 後— next month

훗배앓이 後— afterpains ; complications

following childbirth
훗번 後— next time ; next round ; next game
훗사람 ⇨ 후인(後人)
훗서방 後書房 a second husband ¶ 훗서방을 얻다 marry again ; remarry
훗일 ⇨ 뒷일
훗훗하다 (be) uncomfortably warm ; very warm〔hot〕
훙거 薨去 ⇨ 훙서(薨逝)
훙서 薨逝 (a royal) death ; demise ; decease **—하다** die ; pass away
훤당 萱堂 your (honored) mother
훤소 喧騷 noise ; din ; uproar ; tumult ; clamor **—하다** (be) noisy ; tumultuous ; boisterous
훤칠하다 have a full well-developed figure ; (be) strapping ¶ 훤칠한 여자 a strapping girl
훤하다 ① [흐릿하게 밝다] (be) dimly white ; gray ; light ¶ 훤한 하늘 a light sky ; a dawning sky ; a clearing sky // 훤하기도 전에 출발하다 start in the gray of the morning // 하늘 한쪽이 훤하게 트이다 part of the sky is clearing up // 훤하게 동이 튼다 The dawn begins to whiten the sky. // 아직 훤해지지도 않았다 There is yet time before daybreak. ② [앞이] (be) open ; unobstructed ; [얼굴이] bright ; sunny ; [통달] familiar 《with》 ¶ 신수가 훤하십니다 You look like a million. // 그는 이 업계에 관해 훤하다 He's quite an expert when it comes to what goes on in this business.
훨떡 quickly ⇨ 훌떡
훨썩 by far ; far (out) and away ; a good deal ¶ 훨썩 물러서다 stand way back // 예상보다 훨썩 낫다 be better than (was) expected ; be good beyond expectation
*__훨씬__ ① [정도] by far ; by a long way ; far and away ; by long〔all〕 odds ; out and away ¶ 이것이 훨씬 낫다 This is far〔much〕 better. /This is far and away〔out and away〕 the best. // 둘 중에서 그가 학력이 훨씬 낫다 He is (by) far the better scholar of the two. // 병세가 지난 주보다 훨씬 낫다 He is miles better than he was last week.
② [공간적으로] far (away, off) ; in the distance ; a long way off ¶ 훨씬 저편에 far away ; far-off ; in the distance ; far ahead // 훨씬 뒤떨어져 있다 be a long way behind
③ [시간적으로] ¶ 훨씬 이전에 a long time ago
훨쩍 wide ; broad ; [정도] very ; exceedingly ⇨ 활짝
훨찐 very wide ; far apart ; open wide ; extensively
훨훨 ① [나는 모양] with a flapping ; lightly ; gently ¶ 훨훨 날아가버리다 flutter away // 바람에 훨훨 날리다 fall fluttering in the wind ② [불이] in great flames ; vigorously ③ [부채질] briskly ; vigorously
훼기 毁棄 demolition ; damage ; destruction ; 〖법〗 a wilful injury **—하다** demolish ; destroy ; damage ; wilfully injure
*__훼방 毁謗__ [비방] slander ; calumny ; defamation ; vilification ; [방해] interference ; interruption **—하다** slander ; defame ; vilify ; traduce ; backbite ; speak ill of ; [방해] interfere with ; interrupt ; thwart ; get in the way of ¶ 남의 계획을 훼방하다 counteract〔cross, thwart〕 a person's plan〔design〕 // 남의 출세를 훼방하다 stand in the way of a person's promotion // 훼방하지 마라 Don't put a spoke in my wheel !
—자 a slanderer ; a calumniator
훼살 hindrance ; interruption ; interference ; obstruction **—하다** thwart ; hinder ; interrupt ; interfere with ; disturb ; stand in 《another's》 way ; throw〔place〕 an obstacle in 《another's》 path ; put a spoke in 《another's》 wheel
훼상 毁傷 injury ; wound ; bodily harm ; damage **—하다** injure ; wound ; inflict an injury 《upon》
훼손 毁損 damage ; injury ; [체면·명예를] defamation ; libel **—하다** damage ; injure ; impair ; spoil ; [체면·명예를] defame ; injure 《a person's》 reputation ¶ (일이) …의 명예를 훼손하다 affect〔defame〕 《a person's》 reputation // 공공물을 훼손하다 destroy public property
—본(本) a damaged book **명예 —** defamation ; libel
훼언 毁言 (a) slander ; a libel ; calumny ; defamation **—하다** slander ; libel ; calumniate ; defame ; speak ill of
훼예 毁譽 censure or praise ; (public) criticism ; public opinion **—하다** censure or praise ; criticize ¶ 훼예포폄을 개의치 않다 care for neither praise nor blame ; be indifferent to public criticism ; be deaf to the caprice of public opinion // 그에 대한 훼예는 반반이다 Public opinion of him is evenly divided between praise and censure.
훼예 포폄 毁譽褒貶 ⇨ 훼예(毁譽)
훼절 毁節 forgoing〔throwing away, surrendering〕 one's integrity ; selling out **—하다** forgo one's integrity ; sell out
휑뎅그렁하다 (be) hollow ; empty ⇨ 휑하다
휑하다 (be) hollow ; empty ; vacant ; deserted ; [통달] be familiar with ¶ 그 집은 휑했다 The house looked very bare.
휘 [한숨소리] sighing ; with a sigh ; [바람소리] whistling ; with a puff〔whiff〕 ;

with a whistle ; swishing (채찍소리) ¶ 휘 한숨 쉬며 with a sigh // 한숨을 휘 쉬다 heave a sigh // 바람이 휘휘 불다 The wind whistles. /The wind blows and puffs. // 바람이 솔밭을 휘휘 불고간다 The wind whistles through a pine forest.

휘 諱 ① [이름] the name of a king 〔one's ancestor〕 ② [죽은 뒤의] a posthumous designation〔name, title〕

휘감기다 ① get wound (round) ¶ 담쟁이가 휘감긴 나무 a tree entwined with an ivy // 몸을 뱀한테 휘감기다 have a snake wind round one's body // 기계의 피대에 휘감겨 들어가다 be caught by 〔entangled in〕 the conveyer belt of a machine

② [산란해지다] get distracted ; get confused ¶ 사람들이 외치는 소리에 정신이 휘감기다 be confused by the shouts of people

휘감다 wind〔twine, twist〕 around ; coil ; tie〔fasten〕 around ¶ 밧줄을 둘둘 휘감다 round a rope in a coil // 부러진 다리에 붕대를 휘감다 bandage up〔bind up〕 a broken leg

휘갑치다 ① [일을] settle ; clear up ; adjust ; dispose of 《a matter》 ¶ 일을 휘갑치다 settle a matter ; get a matter settled // 집안일을 휘갑치다 clear up one's household affairs

② [가장자리를] hem 《up》 ; stitch up ¶ 멍석 가장자리를 휘갑치다 hem the edges of a straw mat

휘갑하다 ⇨ 휘갑치다 ①

휘기 諱忌 ―하다 conceal ; keep 《a matter》 secret ; hush (up)

휘날리다 [바람에] flap ; fly ; wave (in the wind) ; flutter ; [명성을] make 《one's name》 resound ¶ 기폭이 바람에 휘날린다 The flag flaps〔waves〕 in the wind.

휘늘어지다 hang down ; droop ¶ 휘늘어진 버들 a drooping〔weeping〕 willow // 허리까지 휘늘어진 검은 머리 black hair that comes down to one's waist

***휘다** ① [휘어지다] get bent ; get curved ; get crooked

② bend ; curve ; crook ¶ 쇠줄을 휘다 bend〔curve〕 a wire // 사과나무가 열매로 휘어졌다 The boughs of the apple tree are weighed down with fruit. /The boughs of the apple tree are drooping under the weight of the fruit.

③ [휘어잡다] bend to one's will ; hold 《another》 in one's hand ; command ¶ 완고한 마음을 휘다 bend 《a person's》 stubborn heart

휘달리다 ① [분주하게 지내다] be always in a whirl ; live a very busy life ② [달아나다] rush away ; run at full speed ¶ 자동차가 휘달린다 A car tears along.

휘도 輝度 〖물리〗 brightness

휘돌다 whirl ; turn ; spin ; rotate ; revolve ; go round ¶ 갑(岬)을 휘돌아가다 go round a cape // 사람을 끌고 시내를 휘돌아 다니다 take 《a person》 all over the city

휘돌리다 whirl ; rotate ; turn ; spin ; revolve ¶ 팽이를 휘돌리다 whirl a top ; spin a top // 손으로 바퀴를 휘돌리다 spin a wheel by hand // 프로펠러를 휘돌리다 rotate a propeller

휘동광 輝銅鑛 〖광물〗 chalcocite

휘두들기다 beat hard〔to a jelly〕 ; batter ; pommel

†휘두르다 ① [칼 따위] brandish ; flourish ; wield ¶ 칼〔팔〕을 휘두르다 flourish a sword〔one's arms〕 // 저 선수가 야구 방망이 휘두르는 방법을 어떻게 생각하십니까 What do you think of the way that player swings the bat ?

② [정신을] confuse ; bewilder ¶ 마음을 휘둘리다 be〔get〕 confused

③ [사람을] make a puppet of 《a person》 ; twist 《a person》 round one's little finger ¶ 휘둘리다 be under 《a person's》 control〔thumb〕 // 그녀는 남편을 휘두른다 She keeps her husband under her thumb.

휘둥그러지다 become wide-eyed ; get surprised ; be startled ¶ 눈이 휘둥그러져서 with one's eyes wide open (in astonishment) ; with wide wondering eyes // 놀라서 눈이 휘둥그러지다 stare 〔open one's eyes〕 in wonder〔astonishment〕

휘둥그렇다 (be) wide-eyed (with surprise)

휘뚜루 pantologically ; variously ; diversely ; severally ; in many〔various, different〕 ways ; in every way ; manifoldly ¶ 휘뚜루 쓰이다 have various 〔many〕 uses

휘뚝거리다 ① totter ; wobble ; be unsteady ¶ 굽높은 구두를 신고 휘뚝거리다 totter on high heels // 책상 다리가 휘뚝거린다 The legs of a table are wobbling〔wobbly〕.

② [조바심] feel nervous〔jittery〕 ; be worried ; upset ¶ 마음이 휘뚝거리다 feel nervous 《about》 ; be much worried 《about》

휘뚝휘뚝 tottering ; wobbling ; unsteadily ¶ 휘뚝휘뚝한 발디딤 an insecure footing

휘뚤휘뚤 winding ; meandering **―하다** (be) winding ; meandering ; sinuous ; serpentine ¶ 길이 휘뚤휘뚤하다 A road is winding.

휘말다 ① [적셔서 더럽히다] make wet and dirty ; spoil ¶ 옷을 휘말다 get ones clothes wet and dirty ② [마구 휘감다] wind around carelessly ; treat carelessly

휘말리다 be rolled〔wrapped, engulfed〕《in》; be dragged 《into》; be caught 《in a machine》; be involved〔entangled〕《in a war》; get mixed up 《in a trouble》 ¶ 남을 계책에 휘말리게 하다 make a person tangled in the meshes of a plot

휘몰다 drive hard ; urge on ; hasten ; speed up ; hurry ¶ 차를 휘몰다 drive a car fast ; step on the gas // 가축을 휘몰아 들이다 drive in the cattle // 말을 휘몰다 urge on a horse // 노동자들을 휘몰아 일을 마치게 하다 drive workmen to finish a job // 자동차를 휘몰아 현장으로 급행하다 rush〔hasten〕 to the scene in a car

*****휘몰아치다** [바람이] blow violently〔boisterously〕; blow hard ; blow great guns ; storm boisterously ; [눈이] fall in whirls ; fall thick and fast ¶ 휘몰아치는 바람 a raging〔roaring〕 wind // 휘몰아치는 눈 a swirling snow/whirls of snow

휘몰이 chasing 《into a place》; rounding up ; corralling ; driving **—하다** chase 《into a place》; round up ; corral

휘묻이 —하다 lay ; layer 《a tree》

*****휘발 揮發** volatilization **—하다** volatilize ¶ 휘발성의 volatile // 가솔린은 휘발성이다 Gasoline is volatile. // 휘발성이 매우 강함 Highly Volatile〔Flammable〕. (경고문)
—기(器) a carburettor ; a vaporizer **—물** a volatile matter **—성** volatility **—유** benzine ; volatile oil ; gasoline ; naphtha ¶ 이 차는 휘발유를 참 많이 소비합니다 This car is a gas guzzler.

휘보 彙報 an itemized collection of reports ; a bulletin ; a magazine (잡지)

휘석 輝石 〖광물〗 pyroxene

휘선 輝線 〖물리〗 the bright line
— 스펙트럼 a bright-line spectrum

휘슬 a whistle

휘양 a kind of cold-weather headgear

휘어넘어가다 fall for another's wiles〔words〕; be deceived

휘어대다 force〔squeeze, push〕 in

휘어들다 get〔be〕 forced〔squeezed, pushed〕 in

휘어박다 bring down ; throw down ; [굴복시키다] bring 《a person》 to his knee ; break 《a person's》 will ; force 《a person》 to give in

휘어박히다 get brought down ; be thrown down ; [굴복하다] yield ; give in ; submit ; surrender ; succumb to

휘어잡다 ① hold something supple〔bent, doubled up〕 in one's hand ; grasp ; clutch ; grab ¶ 버들 가지를 휘어잡다 hold willow branches in one's hand // 섬섬옥수를 휘어잡다 grab a girl's nice soft hands
② [사람을] control ; have 《a person》 under one's control〔in one's grasp〕; lead 《a person》 by the nose ; keep 《a person》 under one's thumb ¶ 휘어잡히다 be under 《a person's》 control〔thumb〕; be domineered over〔managed〕 by

휘어지다 get bent ; be curved〔crooked〕; curve ; warp ¶ 쇠줄이 휘어지다 a wire gets bent // 판자가 휘어지다 a board warps

휘영청 《shine》 bright(ly)〔broadly〕 ¶ 휘영청 밝은 달 a glorious silvery moon // 달이 휘영청 밝다 The moon beams down.

휘우뚱 —하다 totter ; shake ; reel ; (be) rickety ; unsteady ; unstable ¶ 한쪽으로 휘우뚱하다 be leaning to one side ; be out of the perpendicular

휘우듬하다 (be) slightly crooked ; somewhat bent〔curved〕

휘은광 輝銀鑛 〖광물〗 argentite ; silver glance

휠체어 a wheel chair ; an invalid chair

휘장 揮帳 a curtain ; a curtain screen ; a hanging ; a bunting ¶ 휘장을 치다 draw〔stretch〕 a curtain

휘장 徽章 an insignia ; a badge ; an emblem ; an ensign (군인들의) ¶ 휘장을 달다 put on〔wear〕 a badge

휘적거리다 swing (one's arms) ¶ 팔을 휘적거리며 걷다 walk with a swagger

휘적휘적 swinging one's arms ¶ 휘적휘적 걷다 swagger

†**휘젓다** ① stir (round and round) ; whip ; beat ; churn ; [팔을] swing (one's arms) ¶ 우유를 휘젓다 churn milk // 커피를 휘젓다 stir the coffee // 팔을 휘저으며 걷다 walk swinging one's arms // 달걀을 잘 휘저어야 한다 You must beat〔whip〕 up an egg.
② [어지럽게] upset ; disarrange ; disturb ; ruffle ¶ 서랍 속을 휘젓다 disarrange (what is in) a drawer // 사람의 마음을 휘젓다 disturb 《a person's》 mind ; upset 《a person》

휘정거리다 stir up (the sediments in water) ; muddle

휘주근하다 ① [늘어지다] (be) limp ; flabby ; flaccid ¶ 휘주근해지다 become limp〔floppy〕 ② [지쳐서] (be) languid ; dull ¶ 휘주근해지다 be dead tired ; be dog-tired ; be fagged out // 휘주근해서 땅바닥에 철퍽 앉다 sink exhausted on the ground // 더워서 몸이 휘주근하다 The heat makes me feel languid. // 다리가 휘주근하다 My legs feel heavy. // 팔다리가 휘주근하다 My limbs feel like lead.

휘지다 get worn out ; be exhausted ; be fagged out

휘지르다 soil〔spoil〕 《clothes》; make dirty ; stain ¶ 바지를 온통 휘질렀다 I have got my pants all dirty. // 차가 내

바지를 온통 휘질러 놓았다 A motorcar spattered filth on the trousers.

휘지비지 諱之秘之 **—하다** hush up《a matter》; smother〔suppress〕《a matter》; keep《a matter》secret〔dark〕 ¶ 결과를 휘지비지해 버리다 obscure the issue // 휘지비지해 두다 leave《a question》undecided // 휘지비지되다 be dropped; become hazy; end in smoke

휘집 彙集 collection; assortment **—하다** collect; assort

휘철광 輝鐵鑛〖광물〗specular iron ore

휘청거리다 yield; (be) flexible; pliant; supple; stagger; totter ¶ 휘청휘청 yielding; flexibly; pliantly; shakily; totteringly

휘추리 a switch; a spray; a rod

휘탄 輝炭 bright coal

†**휘파람** a whistle ¶ 휘파람으로 신호하다 whistle by way of a signal

휘파람을 불다 관용 whistle; give a whistle

휘필 揮筆 writing ⇨ 휘호

휘하 麾下 (troops) under the banner〔command〕《of》 ¶ 휘하에 모이다 rally round《a person》; join〔follow〕the banner《of》; enlist in the banner《of》

휘하다 諱— avoid mentioning〔using〕; shun; put a taboo on ¶ 임금의 이름을 휘하다 avoid using〔mentioning〕a king's name

휘호 揮毫 wielding a brush; [서] writing; [화] painting; drawing **—하다** wield a brush; write; draw; paint

—료 a fee〔an honorarium〕for a painting

*****휘황찬란하다** 輝煌燦爛— (be) resplendent; brilliant; iridescent; [부절조] chameleonic; unreliable; fickle ¶ 불빛이 휘황찬란한 거리 a bright-lit street // 불빛이 휘황찬란한 무대 a high-lighted stage

휘황하다 ⇨ 휘황찬란하다

휘휘 round and round ¶ 휘휘 감다 wind《a rope》round《a thing》// 단장을 휘휘 휘두르다 flourish one's stick

휘휘하다 (be) dreary; desolate; forlorn ¶ 휘휘한 촌락 a deserted village // 휘휘한 황야 a desolate wilderness

*****휙** [돌아가는 모양] with a swerve〔jerk, whirl〕; with a gust; [바람이] with a sweep; with a whistle; whizzing; [던지는 꼴] lightly and nimbly ¶ 휙 열리다 fling〔throw〕open // 문이 휙 열렸다 The door flew open. // 화살이 휙하고 날아갔다 An arrow whizzed past. // 바람이 휙 불었다 There was a gust of wind. // 야만인들이 사자를 향해 창을 휙휙 던졌다 The savages darted spears at the lion.

휩싸다 wrap up; surround; [비호] protect; shield; take《a person》under one's wings ¶ 애기를 담요로 휩싸다 wrap a baby in a blanket // 머리를 붕대로 휩싸다 bind round one's head

휩싸이다 get wrapped up; [비호] get protected; be shielded; be kept under one's wings ¶ 불길에 휩싸이다 be enveloped in flames // 비밀에 휩싸이다 be shrouded in mystery; be wrapped in a shroud of mystery

*****휩쓸다** sweep《away, up, off》 ¶ 경기를 휩쓸다 sweep〔win〕all the games〔matches, bouts〕; win a sweeping victory // 전 유럽을 휩쓸다 sweep over the whole of Europe // 유행병이 나라 안을 휩쓸었다 A pestilence swept over〔through〕the country.

휩쓸리다 ① [모조리] (be) swept《away, up, off, over》 ¶ 물결에 휩쓸리다 be swept away by the waves; be swallowed up by the waves // 군중 속에 휩쓸리다 be swept along in the crowd // 공황에 휩쓸리다 be seized with a panic ② [설치는 힘에] be overrun; suffer a rampage

휫손 managing〔controlling〕ability; having the upper hand; having things well in hand ¶ 휫손이 다 be able〔shifty, tactful〕

†**휴가** 休暇 holidays; a vacation; leave of absence (사가); furlough (장기 휴가)

> 참고 **holiday**는 어떤 휴가에도 널리 쓰인다 영국에서는 **vacation**은 주로 대학과 법정의 긴 휴가에 쓰이지만 미국에서는 vacation과 holiday의 구별이 없다

¶ 일주일 간의 휴가 a week's holiday // 휴가중에 during the holidays〔vacation〕 // 휴가를 얻다 take a holiday〔vacation〕; vacation (미) // 휴가를 주다 grant《a person》leave of absence // 언제 여름 휴가가 시작됩니까 When are you to break up for the summer? // 그는 휴가중이다 He is away on leave. /He is away on〔for the〕vacation. // 그는 휴가로 귀국해 있다 He is home on leave〔furlough〕. // 휴가 중 신문 배달을 중지시켜 주십시오 I'd like to put our newspaper on vacation hold.

—원 a leave application **동계 —** the winter〔Christmas〕vacation〔holidays〕 **병—** sick leave **생리 —** a special holiday for woman workers **여름 —** the summer holidays〔vacation〕 **유급 —** a paid holiday〔vacation〕

휴간 休刊 suspension of publication; discontinuation **—하다** suspend〔discontinue〕publication; stop issue ¶ 연중 무휴간이다 be issued all the year round // 내일은 휴간입니다 There will be no issue of the paper tomorrow.

—일 [신문의] a 'no-issue' day

휴강 休講 (a professor's) skipping a

lecture ; no lecture (for the day) —하다 skip lecture ; give no lecture (for the day) ; absent oneself from school ¶ 김교수 금일 휴강 Prof. *Kim* is absent today. /No lecture given today by prof. *Kim*.

*휴게 休憩 a rest ; a recess ; a break ; an interval〔intermission〕 (막간의) ; a respite —하다 rest ; take a rest 〔break, recess, time-out〕 ; take breath ¶ 10분간 휴게 ten minutes' recess ; ten minutes' interval (막간)
—소 a resting place — 시간 a recess ; a rest-period —실 a rest room ; a lounge ; an anteroom ; a lobby (호텔의) ; a foyer (극장의) ; a pavilion (경기장의) 도중 — a layover (여객기의)

휴관 休館 —하다 close 《a theater》 ¶ 금일 휴관 Closed for today. (게시)

휴교 休校 (temporary) closure of a school ; temporary cessation of study —하다 close (school) temporarily ; cease study temporarily ¶ 당분간 휴교다 School is closed for some while ahead〔for the time being〕.
동맹 — students' strike

†휴대 携帶 carrying along 《with one》 —하다 carry 《a thing》 with one ; take with one ; bring〔take〕 《a thing》 with one ¶ 휴대용의 portable ; handy (to carry) // 휴대용 라디오 a portable radio // 최신식 무기를 휴대하다 be equipped with the latest weapons // 큰 돈을 휴대하다 have a large sum of money on〔with one〕 // 총기는 휴대 금지이다 The carrying of firearms is prohibited.
— 식량 〚군사〛 field〔combat〕 ration — 연료 canned fuel —용 라디오〔무선 전화기〕 a portable radio〔radiophone〕 — 전화기 a pocket〔portable〕 telephone — 카메라 a hand camera —품 personal effects ; one's belongings ; hand luggage ; hand baggage 《미》 —품 보관소 a cloakroom ; a checkroom 《미》 — 흉기 carried weapons

휴등 休燈 giving up the use of a lamp 〔an electric light〕 —하다 cease to use a lamp〔an electric light〕 ; suspend the use of an electric light

휴머니스트 a humanist ; a humanitarian

휴머니즘 humanism ; humanitarianism

휴머니티 humanity ; humaneness

휴먼릴레이션 〚노동〛 human relations (H. R.)

휴면 休眠 dormancy ; [누에의] quiescence ; quiescency ¶ 휴면중인 dormant ; resting ; diapausing 《larvae》
—기 a period of dormancy ; a resting stage ; diapause

휴박 休泊 —하다 [쉬다] rest ; take 〔have〕 a rest ; [자다] have〔take〕 a nap

†휴식 休息 rest ; a respite ; repose ; recess ; relaxation ; relief —하다 rest ; take a rest ; repose ; take breath 〔break〕 ¶ 잠깐 휴식하다 rest a while ; take a little〔short〕 rest // 학교에서는 정오에 한 시간 휴식한다 Our school has an hour's recess at noon.
—소 a rest place ; a lounge — 시간 a recess ; a breathing time ; a break — 자본 idle capital〔money〕

†휴양 休養 (a) rest ; repose ; relaxation ; recreation ; recuperation (병후의) —하다 rest ; take a rest ; relax ; enjoy oneself ; repose ; recuperate ¶ 하루 휴양하다 take〔have〕 a day off for recreation // 휴양하러 온천에 가다 go to hot springs for relaxation〔recuperation〕 // 그는 휴양이 필요하다 He is〔stands〕 in need of rest. // 당신은 휴양하는게 좋겠다 You'd better have a rest (for some days).
— 생활 one's recreation life — 시설 recreation facilities — 여행 a trip of recreation —지 a recreation center ; a rest area

휴업 休業 closing ; suspension of business〔trading〕 (영업의) ; a shutdown (공장의) ; holidays〔vacation〕 (학교의) ; no performance (극장의) —하다 [상점 따위가] close one's doors ; be closed ; suspend business〔operation〕 ; [노동자가] rest from labor ; take one's day off〔take a holiday〕 《미》 ¶ 휴업 중의 공장 an idle factory // 휴업 중의 은행 a closed bank // 당일 은행은 휴업이다 Banks are closed for the day. // 저 공장은 아직도 휴업 중이다 The factory still remains idle. // 금일 휴업 Closed today. /Closed for the day.
— 보상금 a compensation for business suspension —일 a holiday ; a business holiday (고용자에 대한) 강제 — a lay-off 《미》 임시 — a special holiday

휴연 休演 canceling a performance 〔appearance〕 ; suspension of performance —하다 cancel a performance 〔appearance〕 ; suspend the performance (극장이) ; absent oneself from the stage (사람이) ¶ 금일 휴연함 "Today's performance canceled."

*휴일 休日 a holiday ; an off-day ; a rest day ¶ 한달에 두번 휴일을 주다 give 《a person》 two off-days each month ; give 《a person》 two days off per month // 휴일을 이용하여 여행하다 go away for the vacation ; go on a weekend trip // 바닷가에서 휴일을 보내다 spend a seaside holiday // 그 가게는 일요일은 휴일이다 The shop does't open on Sunday.
— 근무 holiday work — 수당 non-duty allowance — 여행 a holiday trip ; a weekend trip ; a vacation trip 《미》 —

법정 a legal holiday — 은행 a bank holiday 《영》 임시 — a special holiday

휴장 休場 ① [극장 따위의] closure 《of a theater》 —하다 be closed 《for a month》 ② [배우 따위의] absence 《from the stage》; nonappearance —하다 absent oneself〔be absent〕 from 《the stage》

휴전 休電 suspension of power supply ¶ 오늘은 휴전일이다 We have no power supply today.

—일 a no-power day

휴전 休戰 an armistice; a truce; a cease-fire; a suspension of hostilities —하다 make a truce; suspend hostilities; cease fire; conclude an armistice ¶ 휴전 중이다 be under suspension of fire // 휴전을 요구하다 ask for a truce // 휴전 협정을 맺다 conclude a treaty of truce 《with》

— 교섭 truce〔cease-fire〕 negotiations 〔talks, conferences〕 —기 a flag of truce — 기념일 Armistice Day; Veterans' Day 《미》 — 명령 orders to suspend hostilities; a ceasefire —선 a truce line; the ceasefire line — 조약 an agreement〔a treaty〕 of truce 〔armistice〕 — 협정 a ceasefire agreement; the Armistice Agreement — 회담 truce〔armistice〕 talks 중립국 — 감시단 the Neutral Nations' Supervisory Commission for Armistice

휴정 休廷 recess〔adjournment〕 of court; holding no court —하다 court is recessed〔adjourned〕; hold no court ¶ 토요일은 휴정이다 No court will be held on Saturday. // 월요일까지 휴정했다 The court was adjourned till Monday.

—일 a non-judicial day; a day when the court is in adjournment〔recess〕

휴지 休止 pause; cessation; suspension; stoppage; standstill; discontinuance; a deadlock ¶ 휴지부를 찍다 put a period to; stop // 업무가 휴지 상태에 있다 Business is at a standstill.

— 부호 『음악』 a rest; a pause; 『문법』 a period — 상태 a standstill; a deadlock 운전 — a halt in the operation; a tie-up of operation

***휴지 休紙** toilet paper; waste paper; paper scraps ¶ 이렇게 되면 조약은 휴지나 마찬가지다 The treaty is now a mere scrap of paper.

—통 a waste(-paper) basket

휴직 休職 suspension from office〔service〕; temporary rest〔retirement〕from office —하다 temporarily rest〔retire〕 from one's office; be suspended from office〔duty〕; get placed〔be put〕 on the reserve list; be temporarily laid off ¶ 휴직한 retired; on the retired〔half-pay〕 list

—급 half pay — 장교 a suspended officer; an officer on the half-pay list

휴진 休診 suspension of medical examination —하다 do not accept patients; suspend diagnosis ¶ 금일 휴진 Office is closed today. / No consultations 〔appointments〕 today〔to be held〕. / Closed for today.

—일 a non-consultation day

휴학 休學 temporary absence from school; temporary rest from study —하다 absent oneself from school; temporarily stay away from school for a time ¶ 오랫동안 휴학하고 있다 be long absent from school // 휴학 허가를 얻다 obtain leave of absence 《for a term》 // 3개월간의 휴학원을 내다 ask leave of absence for three months

—생 a student on leave of absence 〔who stays out of school temporarily〕 동맹 — a students' strike

휴한 休閑 fallow

—지 idle〔fallow〕 land; land in fallow

휴항 休航 suspension of sailing —하다 suspend sailing; be laid up (배가)

휴행 携行 —하다 take〔carry〕with one; take along

휴화산 休火山 a dormant〔an inactive, a sleeping〕 volcano ¶ 그것은 휴화산이다 The volcano lies dormant〔asleep〕.

‡**휴회 休會** adjournment; recess —하다 adjourn; recess; take a recess; suspend the session ¶ 휴회 중이다 be in recess; be not in session // 휴회를 선언하다 declare adjournment; call a recess // …까지 휴회하다 adjourn until〔till〕...

자연 — automatic adjournment

휼계 譎計 a trick; an evil〔a wicked, a crafty〕 design; an artifice; a vicious plan; a nasty piece〔bit〕 of work; skulduggery 《미·속》 ¶ 휼계를 쓰다 make crafty designs; resort to skulduggery // 휼계에 넘어가다 fall a prey to an iniquitous plot; fall for a scheme

휼금 恤金 a relief fund; relief money

휼미 恤米 the relief grain〔rice〕

휼민 恤民 the relief〔aid〕 of the sufferers〔the indigent〕 —하다 relieve〔aid〕 the sufferers〔the indigent〕; give relief〔aid〕 to the sufferers〔the indigent〕

휼병 恤兵 the relief〔aid〕 of the soldiers 〔troops〕 —하다 give relief〔aid, comfort〕 to the soldiers〔troops〕

휼전 恤典 the government's special grace〔favor〕 to relieve the sufferers; charity relief from the government for the victims 《of》

흉 ① a scar ¶ 흉 있는 얼굴 a scarred face; a face with a scar // 이마에 흉이 있다 have a scar on the forehead; one's forehead bears a scar〔is scarred〕 // 흉이 없어지다 the scar dies away; the scar leaves no trace

② [결점] a defect ; a fault ; a drawback ; a flaw ; a blemish ¶ 흉잡다 find fault with ; pick out another's defects // 흉 없는 사람 없다 Nobody is perfect.
흉가 凶家 a house of ill omen ; a haunted house
흉간 胸間 one's breast ; one's chest
— 근통(筋痛) [신경통] pleurodynia
흉갑 胸甲 〖동물〗 a breastplate ; a plastron ; a steel corset
—류 〖동물〗 [갑각류(甲殼類) 중의] Thoracostraca
흉강 胸腔 the thoracic〔chest〕 cavity
흉격 胸膈 the lower chest
흉계 凶計 a wicked plan〔scheme〕 ; an evil〔a sinister〕 plot ; a reprehensive project ¶ 흉계를 꾸미다 devise wicked designs
흉골 胸骨 〖해부〗 the sternum 《*pl.* ~s, -na》 ; the breastbone ¶ 흉골의 sternal
—통 sternalgia
흉곽 胸廓 〖해부〗 the thorax 《*pl.* ~es, -races》 ; the chest ¶ 흉곽이 넓다〔좁다〕 have a broad〔narrow〕 chest
— 성형술 〖의학〗 thoracoplasty
흉금 胸襟 the bosom ; the heart ; the inner mind ¶ 흉금을 털어놓고 이야기하다 have a heart-to-heart talk 《with》 ; talk frank chat 《with》 ; talk without reserve
흉금을 털어놓다 관용 unbosom oneself 《to》 ; open〔lay bare〕 one's heart 《to》 ; admit 《a person》 into one's confidence
흉기 凶器 a deadly weapon ; a murderous〔lethal, destructive〕 weapon ; arms ; weapons ¶ 흉기를 든 강도 an armed burglar〔robber〕 // 흉기를 휴대하다 carry a (deadly) weapon
*흉내 imitation ; mimicry ; mock ¶ 흉내내다 imitate ; mimic ; copy ; ape ; monkey // 남의 말을 흉내내다 mimic 《a person's》 way of talking // 내 흉내 좀 그만 낼 수 없니 Will you stop being a copycat, please?
—말 an onomatopoeia〔onomatope, onomatopoetic word〕 ; an echo-word
—쟁이 a (clever) mimic ; a copycat ; an imitator
*흉년 凶年 a bad year ; a lean year ; a year of a bad harvest ; a year of famine ¶ 흉년지다 have a bad harvest
— 거지 a beggar in a lean year ; much work with little result
흉년에 윤달 속담 Ill comes often on the back of worse.
흉노 匈奴 〖역사〗 the Huns
흉당 凶黨 [악당들] rioters ; outlaws ; ruffians ; [역적들] rebels ; traitors ; insurgents
흉도 凶徒 [악당] a gang of scoundrels ; rascals ; villains ; rogues ; blackguards ; [폭도] rioters ; outlaws ; rebels ; insurgents
흉막 胸膜 〖해부〗 the pleura 《*pl.* -rae》
—염 〖의학〗 pleurisy
흉몽 凶夢 a bad dream ; an evil dream ; a nightmare ¶ 흉몽을 꾸다 have (a) nightmare // 흉몽에서 깨다 start (up) from a nightmare
흉문 凶聞 bad news ; news of death ; tragic news
흉물 凶物 an evil person ; a villain ; a snake
흉배 胸背 ① [가슴과 등] breast and back ② [관복의] embroidered patches on the breast and on the back of official uniforms
흉벽 胸壁 ① [가슴의 외벽] walls of the chest ② 〖군사〗 a breastwork ; a parapet
흉변 凶變 a disaster ; a calamity ; a catastrophe ; [암살] assassination ; murder ¶ 흉변을 당하다 suffer a calamity ; get assassinated〔murdered〕
흉보 凶報 bad news ; news of 《a person's》 death ; a death notice ¶ 유족에게 흉보를 전하다 inform〔break〕 the sad news to the family of the deceased
흉보다 speak ill〔unfavorably〕 of ; disparage ; speak against ; talk scandal about ¶ 안 듣는 데서 흉보다 backbite ; speak ill of 《a person》 behind his back
흉복 胸腹 ① [가슴과 배] the chest〔breast〕 and the abdomen〔belly〕 ② [횡격막 부분] the midriff area
—통 a pain in the midriff
흉부 胸部 the breast ; the chest ; the thorax ; the corselet (곤충의) ¶ 흉부에 관통상을 입다 be shot through the breast // 흉부에 심한 통증을 느낀다 feel a sharp pain in the chest
— 질환 a chest trouble〔disease〕
흉사 凶事 an event of ill omen ; a disaster ; an evil ; a misfortune ; an untoward incident
흉상 凶狀 [태도] a vile〔malicious, wicked, crafty〕 attitude ; [모양] (an) ugly〔unsightly, unseemly〕 appearance ; a vicious〔sinister〕 look
흉상 凶相 ① [상격] an evil physiognomy ② [외모] an ugly face ; an unseemly appearance ; a vicious look ¶ 흉상이다 be evil-favored〔-faced〕 ; be ferocious-looking ; be sinister-looking ; be evil-looking
*흉상 胸像 a bust ¶ 흉상을 만들다 set up〔erect〕 the bust 《of a person》
흉수 凶手, 兇手 the hands〔clutches, fangs〕 of an outlaw〔assailant, assassin〕 ; [사람] a villain ; a ruffian ; a scoundrel ; an outlaw ; an assailant ; a murderer〔a killer, an assassin〕 (살인자)
흉악 凶惡 —하다 [성질이] (be) atrocious ; heinous ; brutal ; felon ; villain-

ous ; wicked ; cruel ; [용모가] (be) ugly ; bad ¶ 흉악한 짓 a felon deed // 흉악성을 띠다 have a touch of brutality ; be something of a villain // 흉악 망측하다 be extremely wicked〔malignant, ugly〕
—범 a brutal criminal **—범죄** a heinous〔dreadful〕 crime **—성** brutality ; atrocity ; heinousness
흉어 凶漁 a poor catch of fish ¶ 잇따른 흉어로 어부들이 죽을 지경이다 Fishermen are hard hit by the prolonged scarcity of fish.
흉위 胸圍 the circumference〔girth〕 of the chest ¶ 넓은〔좁은〕 흉위 a broad〔narrow〕 chest // 흉위를 재다 measure the chest ; take 《a person's》 chest measurement // 흉위가 90센티이다 I measure 90 centimeters round the chest.
흉음 凶音 bad〔unfortunate〕 news (of one's death)
흉인 凶刃 an assassin's dagger〔blade〕 ¶ 흉인에 쓰러지다 fall a victim to an assassin's dagger
흉일 凶日 a bad day ; a black〔black-letter〕 day ; an ill-starred day ; an unlucky day
흉작 凶作 a bad〔poor, lean〕 crop〔harvest〕 ; a failure of crops ¶ 흉작의 해 a bad year ; a lean year 《for the rice crop》 // 흉작으로 owing to failure of crops // 금년은 벼가 흉작이다 The rice crop is short〔has failed〕 this year. /There is a short crop of rice this year.
흉잡다 find fault with 《a person》 ; carp〔cavil〕 at 《faults》 ; pick at ; criticize
흉잡히다 be found fault with ; be disparaged ; get criticized
흉장 胸墻 a breast-high wall ; a breastwork ; a parapet
흉적 凶賊, 兇賊 a bloody robber〔bandit〕 ; a rowdy
흉조 凶兆 an ill〔evil〕 omen ; a portent ; a sign of evil ¶ 흉조의 portentous ; ill-boding〔-omened〕 ; ominous
흉중 胸中 one's bosom〔heart, mind, feelings, thoughts, intentions〕 ; one's inmost heart ¶ 흉중에 in one's heart ; inwardly // 흉중을 터놓다 unbosom oneself ; open〔lay bare〕 one's heart ; unburden one's mind ; lay one's card on the table (교섭에서) // 흉중에 깊이 간직하다 keep 《a secret》 in the inmost recess of one's heart ; hug 《a secret》 to one's bosom // 그의 흉중을 짐작할 수 없었다 It was impossible to fathom his real intention. /I could not make out what was passing in his mind〔what he really means〕.
흉증 凶證 ① an ill〔evil〕 omen ⇨ 흉조
② [음흉함] slyness ; snakiness ; insidiousness ¶ 흉증스러운 사람 an insidious man ; a deep one ; a snake // 흉증스러운 수단 underhand measures
흉추 胸椎 〖해부〗 the thoracic vertebrae
흉측 凶測 —하다 (be) terribly wicked〔evil, villainous〕
흉탄 兇彈 a shot by a villain ; an assassin's bullet ¶ 흉탄에 쓰러지다 fall a victim to an assassin's bullet ; be shot to death by a villain ; be killed by an assassin's bullet
‡흉터 a scar〔cicatrice〕 ¶ 아물어서 흉터만 남다 heal to a scar // 흉터가 아직 남아 있다 The scar remains.
흉통 胸痛 a pain in the chest ; pleurodynia ¶ 흉통을 앓다 have a chest pain ; have a pain in the chest
‡흉포 凶暴 ferocity ; atrocity ; brutality ; barbarity ; outrage ; heinousness **—하다** (be) ferocious ; atrocious ; brutal ; outrageous ; heinous
흉풍 凶豊 famine and plenty ; rich and poor harvest ; the ups and downs of the crops ¶ 흉풍이 없다 usually have a good steady harvest
***흉하다 凶—** ① [불길] (be) ominous ; ill-omened ; portentous ; inauspicious ; sinister ; unlucky ; evil ; bad ¶ 흉한 예감 ominous presentiment // 흉한 꿈 an unlucky dream
② [보기에] (be) ugly ; bad-〔ugly-〕 looking ; plain ; unseemly ; unsightly ; indecent ; terrible ¶ 흉한 짓 a bad〔wicked〕 act // 흉한 복장 shabby dress // 흉한 여자 an ugly-woman // 보기 흉하다 make an ill appearance // 흉하지 않다 be presentable // 그 여자의 얼굴은 흉하다 She is an ugly looking woman. // 노상에서 그런 짓을 하면 보기 흉하다 It doesn't look well to do such a thing in the street.
흉하적 faultfinding ; carping ; picking flaws **—하다** find fault with ; look for defects ; pick flaws ; carp〔cavil〕 at 《a person's faults》
흉한 凶漢 [악한] a villain ; a ruffian ; a rascal ; a miscreant ; [암살자] an assassin ; an assailant ; a murderer ¶ 흉한의 손에 쓰러지다 fall a victim to an assassin ; be killed by an assassin ; be murdered // 흉한을 체포하다 arrest〔nab〕 a murderer
흉해 凶害 assassination ; murder
흉행 兇行 violence ; outrage ; a crime (범죄) ; murder (살인) ; assassination (암살) ¶ 흉행을 저지르다 commit〔perpetrate〕 a crime // 그는 질투로 말미암아 이런 흉행을 저질렀다 Jealousy drove him to commit the crime.
—자 an assailant ; a perpetrator ; a murderer ; an assassin **—현장** a scene of crime〔murder, assassination〕

흉허물 faults ; defects ; flaws
흉허물 없다 be intimate enough to overlook each other's faults ; be confidential with 《a person》
흉험 凶險 slyness ; wiliness ; snakiness —하다 (be) sly ; wily ; snaky ; underhand ¶ 흉험한 수단을 쓰다 use subtle tricks〔underhand measures〕
흉헙다 凶— (be) ugly ; awful ; terrible ¶ 보기 흉헙다 be awful to look at // 빛이 흉헙다 The color is dreadful.
흉화 凶禍 an evil〔a terrible〕disaster 〔calamity〕 ¶ 흉화를 입다 get murdered〔assassinated〕; meet with evil
흉흉하다 洶洶— ① [민심이] (be) panic-stricken ; be filled with alarm ; be in consternation ¶ 전쟁으로 인심이 흉흉하다 People are panic-stricken with the outbreak of war.
② [물결이] 《the waves》 (be) high ; 《the sea》 (be) rough ; furious, running high
흐너뜨리다 pull〔take〕 down ; demolish ; destroy
흐너지다 fall down ; give way ; collapse
흐놀다 long for ; yearn after ; sigh for ¶ 고향을 흐놀다 long for home
*흐느끼다 sob ; be choked with 《the cold》 ¶ 흐느껴 울다 sob ; be choked with tears ; be drowned in tears // 흐느끼며 말하다 speak with sobs ; say 《a thing》 between sobs
흐느적거리다 flutter ; sway gently ; wave
흐느적흐느적 —하다 get loose ; get shaky ; get wobbly ; become rickety
흐늑거리다 ⇨ 흐느적거리다
흐늘거리다 ① [놀고 지내다] loiter ; idle ; loaf ; dawdle ; trifle ¶ 흐늘거리고 놀다 dawdle about ; loaf around
② [흔들거리다] dangle ; hang loosely ; swing ; sway gently ¶ 바람에 흐늘거리다 tremble in the breeze ; sway in〔to〕 the wind
흐늘어지다 dangle ⇨ 휘늘어지다
흐늘쩍거리다 move around idly〔sluggishly〕 ¶ 흐늘쩍거리며 걷다 poke along ; walk slowly
흐늘쩍흐늘쩍 slowly ; sluggishly ; idly ¶ 흐늘쩍흐늘쩍 걷다 loiter ; stroll ; poke along
흐늘흐늘 ① dangling ; swaying gently 〔easily〕 ② flimsily —하다 dangle ; sway gently ; (be) flimsy ; squashy ; pulpy ; soft ¶ 버들가지가 바람에 흐늘흐늘 움직인다 The willow branches are swaying gently in the wind.
흐드러지다 ① [썩 탐스럽다] become splendid ; (be) splendid ; fetching ; attracting ¶ 흐드러진 여자 a fetching girl // 꽃이 흐드러지게 피다 flowers come out splendidly ② [무르익어서] get overripe〔too soft〕
흐들갑스럽다 be extravagant〔overexcited〕 in speech
흐려지다 ① [날이] get cloudy〔overcast〕; cloud 《up, over》; become covered with clouds ② [눈이] get bleary ; grow dim ¶ 나이 먹는 데 따라 눈이 흐려지다 one's eyes grow dim as one gets old // 눈물로 눈이 흐려지다 be blurred with tears ; tears blur one's eyes
†흐르다¹ ① [유동] flow ; stream ; run ; trickle (졸졸) ; ooze (스며 나오다) ; run down (흘러 내리다) ; gutter ¶ 흐르는 시내 a running stream // (강이) 바다로 흐르다 find (its) way to the sea // 물은 항상 낮은 곳으로 흐른다 Water always flows downward. /Water always finds its own level. // 강이 숲 사이로 흐른다 The river flows through the forests. // 물이 흐르지 않다 The water stands still〔is stagnant〕. // 눈물이 그녀의 뺨을 흘러내렸다 Tears streamed 〔ran, rolled〕 down her cheeks. // 작은 시냇물이 골짜기를 속삭이며 조용히 흐른다 A small brook glides through the valley with a murmur.
② [부동하다] float ; drift ¶ 꽃잎이 냇물 위로 흐른다 Petals float down the stream.
③ [넘치다] overflow ; run over ; brim over ; drop ¶ 사발의 물이 흐른다 The water in a bowl spills out. // 너무 많이 부으면 흐릅니다 Never fill the cup too full, or it will brim over.
④ [쏠리다] lapse〔fall〕 into ; run 〔incline〕 to ; be carried away by ; be swayed by ¶ 사치에 흐르다 become extravagant ; lapse into luxury // 감정에 흐르다 be swayed by sentiment // 극단에 흐르다 run to extremes ; go to excess
⑤ [세월이] elapse ; pass (away) ; flow by ; slip by (어느 새) ¶ 세월이 흐르다 time passes〔goes by, rolls on〕 // 세월이 자꾸 흘렀다 The years flowed〔went〕 on. // 몇 해가 흘렀다 Several years elapsed〔passed away, flowed away〕.
⑥ [새다] leak ¶ 파이프에서 물이 흐른다 Water is leaking from the pipe.
⑦ [퍼지다] prevail ¶ 얼마 동안 무거운 침묵이 흘렀다 An awkward silence hung between them for a time.
흐르다² [흘레하다] 《animals》 copulate 《with》; couple ; mate ; [새가] tread 《a hen》; pair ; [짐승이] cover
흐르르 —하다 (be) flimsy ; flabby ; squashy ¶ 이 풀먹인 칼라는 더운 날에는 흐르르해진다 This starched collar soon gets limp in hot weather.
흐름 [흐르는 것] flowing ; [물줄기] a flow ; a stream ; a current ; [페인트 따위] run ; running ¶ 물의 흐름 the flow of (flowing) water
*흐리다¹ ① [혼탁] (be) muddy ; turbid ; impure ; thick ; cloudy (술 따위가) ¶

흐린 물 muddy water // 비가 와서 강물이 흐리다 The rain has made the river muddy. /The river looks thick after the rain.
② [날씨가] (be) cloudy ; overcast ¶ 흐린 날씨〔하늘〕 a cloudy weather〔sky〕 // 날이 흐리다 It is cloudy. // 하늘이 아주 흐리다 The sky is overcast. /The sky has clouded up〔has thickly clouded over〕.
③ [희미하다] (be) vague ; dim ; faint ; obscure ; indistinct ; hazy ; misty ; blurred 《image》; watery 《color》; dreamy 《scene》 ¶ 흐린 램프 밑에서 독서하다 read in the dim light of lamp // 불빛이 흐리다 A light is dim.
④ [시력이] (be) dim ; dull ; bleary ; bleared ; blurry ; blurred ; turbid ¶ 눈이 흐리다 have dim eyes ; have bleary eyes // 눈물 때문에 눈이 흐리다 be blurred with tears ; tears blur one's eyes〔vision〕 // 나이를 먹으면 눈이 흐려진다 Our sight grows dim〔misty〕 with age. /One's eyes are dimmed with age.
⑤ [기억 따위가] (be) vague ; hazy ; fuzzy ; obscure ; blurry ; blurred ¶ 흐린 사람 a fuzzy-minded people // 기억이 흐리다 have a vague memory // 셈이 흐리다 be hazy about the accounts

†**흐리다²** ① [날씨가] become〔get〕 cloudy〔overcast〕; cloud 《up, over》; become covered with clouds
② [말끝을] equivocate ; prevaricate ; quibble ¶ 말끝을 흐리다 say an ambiguous thing ; make an equivocal reply ; leave one's statement vague ; give a noncommittal answer
③ [혼탁하게 하다] make 《water》 muddy〔turbid〕; muddy ; make 《wine》 cloudy ¶ 물을 흐리다 muddy water ; make 《water》 muddy〔cloudy〕
④ [명예 따위를] stain ; blemish ; defile ; sully ¶ 집안의 명예를 흐리다 bring〔invite〕 disgrace on one's family ; stain the good name of one's family

흐리마리 ―하다 (be) vague ; indefinite ; ambiguous ; obscure ; doubtful ¶ 태도가 흐리마리하다 maintain an uncertain〔ambiguous〕 attitude ; sit on the fence // 대답이 흐리마리하다 give an evasive reply ; be vague in one's answer ; answer ambiguously〔vaguely〕

‡**흐리멍덩하다** (be) dim ; vague ; faint ; confused ; muddled ; dubious ; hazy ¶ 기억이 흐리멍덩하다 have a dim〔hazy〕 recollection 《of》; remember dimly // 흐리멍덩한 태도 an ambiguous attitude // 사태가 흐리멍덩하다 A situation is confused. // 머리가 흐리멍덩하다 I feel my brains muddled. // 너의 이야기는 흐리멍덩하다 Your statement is too hazy.

흐리터분하다 ① [사물이] (be) cloudy ; hazy ; indistinct ; obscure ¶ 흐리터분한 날씨 cloudy〔gloomy〕 weather // 셈이 흐리터분하다 be hazy about the accounts
② [마음이] (be) dark-minded ; be not open ; (be) shady ; underhand ¶ 흐리터분한 짓 underhand dealing // 그의 행동에는 흐리터분한 점이 있다 His action will not bear the light of public criticism.

‡**흐릿하다** (be) rather cloudy〔dim, blurred, dull, indistinct, vague, hazy〕 ¶ 눈이 흐릿해진다 The eyes grow dim. // 안개 속에 등불 빛이 흐릿하다 Lights are burning dimly in the fog.

흐무러지다 ① [너무 익다] get overripe
② [물에 불어서] get very soft〔too soft〕 ¶ 쌀이 물에 불어 흐무러지다 rice gets very soft soaking up water

흐무뭇하다 (be) quite pleasing〔gratifying, satisfactory〕; (be) greatly pleased〔gratified, satisfied〕; be quite content 《with》

흐물흐물 ―하다 (be) overripe ; very soft ¶ 흐물흐물해지다 be reduced to jelly〔pulp〕 // 흐물흐물하도록 삶다 boil to pulp

흐뭇이 contentedly ; satisfactorily ; sufficiently

흐뭇하다 (be) pleasing ; gratifying ; satisfying ; (be) pleased ; gratified ; satisfied ¶ 흐뭇해서 웃다 smile with satisfaction ; chuckle with delight // 그는 성공해서 흐뭇해 했다 He hugged himself on his success.

흐벅지다 (be) plump ; full

흐슬부슬 ―하다 (be) crumbling ; be not viscous ; be not sticky ; be not adhesive ; (be) unglutinous ¶ 과자가 흐슬부슬하다 cakes crumble // 이 밥은 흐슬부슬하다 The boiled rice is poor in gluten.

흐지부지 ① [흐리멍덩] hushing up ; in secret ¶ 결말이 흐지부지 되다 an issue ends in smoke // 독직 사건을 흐지부지 해버리다 hush up a case of bribery ; put the lid on a corruption scandal
② wasting ; to no purpose ¶ 돈을 흐지부지 써 버리다 waste〔throw away〕all the money // 쌀이 흐지부지 다 없어지다 Rice is used up wastefully.

***흐트러뜨리다** ① [흩다] scatter ; disperse ; dispel ¶ 닭이 모이를 흐트러뜨리다 a hen scatters its feed ② [산란] dishevel ; mess up ¶ 머리를 흐트러뜨리다 get one's hair disheveled // 방을 흐트러뜨리다 have the room in disorder
③ [정신을] distract ¶ 정신을 흐트러뜨리다 distract one's attention

흐트러지다 scatter ; disperse ; get scattered〔dispersed〕; [산란] get disheveled〔messed up〕; [정신이] be distracted ¶ 쌀이 흐트러지다 rice is scattered // 사방으로 흐트러지다 scatter about in all

directions // 머리가 흐트러지다 one's hair gets disheveled // 불꽃이 사방으로 흐트러져 튀었다 Sparks flew in all directions. // 그의 정신이 흐트러지지 않도록 조용히 해라 Don't make a noise, or his attention will be distracted.
흐흐 pshaw ; pooh ; humph
흑 [흐느낌] with a sob ¶ 흑 울다 sob ; weep
흑 黑 black ; a black color ⇨ 흑색 ; [바둑돌] a black *paduk* stone〔piece〕
흑갈색 黑褐色 dark brown
흑고래 黑― a black whale
흑광 黑鑛 〖광물〗 a black ore
흑내장 黑內障 〖의학〗 black cataract ; amaurosis
흑노 黑奴 a negro slave
흑니토 黑泥土 〖지질〗 muck soil ; mull
흑다이아 黑― a black diamond ; coal
*흑단 黑檀 ebony
흑당 黑糖 ① ⇨ 흑설탕 ② [엿] black rice candy
흑대두 黑大豆 black soybeans
흑도 黑陶 [중국 고대의] black pottery
흑두 黑豆 black beans
흑두루미 黑― 〖새〗 hooded crane
흑두 재상 黑頭宰相 a young minister
흑룡강 黑龍江 the Heilung River
흑막 黑幕 a black curtain ; [내막] concealed circumstances ; the inside ¶ 흑막에 숨어 있다 be behind the scenes // 흑막에서 움직이다 pull the wires 《from behind》 // 틀림없이 무슨 흑막이 있을게다 Someone is certainly pulling the wire. /There must be someone at the bottom of this affair.
흑맥주 黑麥酒 black〔dark〕 beer ; porter ; bock beer
흑반 黑斑 a black spot ; melasma
흑발 黑髮 black hair ¶ 흑발의 여자 a black-haired woman // 윤이 흐르는 흑발 glossy black hair
흑백 黑白 black and white ; [시비] right and wrong ; good and bad ¶ 금명간에 흑백을 가려달라 I must have justice done in a day or so.
― 사진〔영화〕 a black and white picture〔film〕
흑백을 가리다 관용 tell good from bad ; discriminate between right and wrong
흑보기 a cross-eyed person ; a squint eye ; a squinter
흑빵 黑― brown bread ; dark bread
흑사병 黑死病 the black plague ; pest ; the black death
흑사탕 黑砂糖 muscovado ; crude sugar
흑삼릉 黑三稜 〖식물〗 a plant similar to a cattail
흑색 黑色 black ; a black color
― 도료 blacking ― 인종 the black〔colored〕 race ―증 〖의학〗 melanosis 《*pl.* -noses》 ― 화약 black (gun-) powder ; blasting powder
흑설탕 黑雪糖 muscovado〔unrefined, raw〕 sugar ⇨ 흑사탕(黑砂糖)
흑셔츠 黑― [셔츠] a black shirt ; [역사] the Black Shirts ; the Fascists
흑수 黑手 an evil design ; a sinister scheme
흑수 黑穗 a blighted ear of grain (깜부기)
―단 the Black Hand ―병 smut
흑수정 黑水晶 morion ; dark cairngorm
흑심 黑心 a black heart ; evil intentions ; dark designs ¶ 흑심이 있는 evil-disposed〔-minded〕 ; black-hearted
흑싸리 黑― [화투의] a black-bush-clover card 《of *hwatu,* or flower-card game》
흑암 黑暗 dead〔total〕 darkness ―하다 (be) pitch-dark ; be (as) dark〔black〕 as pitch
흑야 黑夜 a dark night ; a pitch-dark night ; the black of night
흑연 黑鉛 black lead ; graphite ; plumbago
―광 a graphite deposit
흑연 黑煙 black〔dense, murky〕 smoke ¶ 자욱한 흑연 a dense cloud of black smoke
흑요석 黑曜石 〖광물〗 obsidian
흑운 黑雲 dark〔black〕 clouds
흑운모 黑雲母 〖광물〗 biotite
흑의 黑衣 black clothes ; a black dress ¶ 흑의를 입은 사람 a person in black // 흑의를 입다 be dressed in black
**흑인 黑人 a Negro ; a colored person ; a darky ; a nigger ¶ 흑인 여자 a negress ; a negro〔colored〕 woman
― 거주 지구 a black ghetto ―극 a blackface show ― 문제 the Negro problem〔question〕 ― 분리 반대자 an antisegregationist ― 분리 정책 the segregation policy ― 여자 a Negress ; a Negro〔colored〕 woman ― 영가 a Negro spiritual ― 옹호 negrophilism ¶ 흑인 옹호자 a negrophil(e) ― 음악 Negro music ―종 the black〔colored〕 race ; the Negro ― 지대 the Black Belt ― 차별 대우 segregation 《미》 ; [남아프리카] apartheid ¶ 흑인 차별 대우 폐지론자 a nigger lover ― 학교 a colored school
흑자 黑子 black checkers ⇨ 흑지 ; [사마귀] a mole
흑자 黑字 black letters ; black figures ¶ (재정이) 흑자이다 be in the black
흑적 黑滴 〖천문〗 the black drop
흑적색 黑赤色 dark-red color
흑점 黑點 a black spot ; a macula ¶ 태양의 흑점 a sunspot ; a spot on the sun
흑조 黑潮 the Black〔Japan〕 Current ; the Black Stream
흑죽학죽 ① [어름어름 넘김] settling 《a

matter》 in the dark ; cursorily ; hurriedly ② [엉터리로] desultorily ; perfunctorily ; hit-or-miss ¶ 일을 흑죽학죽 해치우다 do a hit-or-miss job of it
흑지 黑— black checkers ; black stones used in *paduk*
흑책질 **—하다** thwart ; frustrate ; baffle ; interrupt ; throw an obstacle in another's path
흑체 黑體 〚물리〛 a black body
— 방사(放射) black body radiation
흑칠 黑漆 black lacquer
흑탄 黑炭 black coal
흑토 黑土 black soil〔earth〕
—대 the black earth zone〔district〕
*****흑판** 黑板 a blackboard ¶ 흑판을 닦다 wipe the blackboard
— 지우개 an eraser ; a chalk eraser ; a wiper
흑해 黑海 the Black Sea
흑흑 sobbing ; with sobs ¶ 흑흑 느껴울다 sob ; weep convulsively
흔감 欣感 joy ; rejoicing **—하다** rejoice 《over》 ; feel great joy
흔덕거리다 sway ; swing ; rock ; be shaky
흔덕이다 be loose ; be unsteady ; be shaky ; totter
흔드렁거리다 swing ; sway
흔드적거리다 swing ; sway
흔들거리다 swing ; sway ; be swayed ; shake
†**흔들다** shake ; wave ; swing ; sway ; wag ; rock ¶ 손을 흔들어 작별하다 wave a farewell // 머리를 흔들다 shake one's head // 기를 흔들다 wave a flag // 단장을 흔들다 swing one's stick // 흔들어 떨어뜨리다 shake 《leaves》 down // 손수건을 흔들다 wave〔flutter〕 one's handkerchief // 약병을 흔들다 shake a medicine bottle // 개가 꼬리를 흔든다 The dog wags his tail. // 바람이 창을 흔든다 The wind rattles a window. // 사람의 마음을 흔들어 놓다 disturb 《a person》
†**흔들리다** shake ; sway ; rock ; tremble ; joggle ; jolt (차가) ; swing (매달린 것이) ; waver (마음이) ¶ 좌우로 흔들리다 rock from side to side // 집이 흔들린다 A house sways〔shakes〕. // 책상다리가 흔들린다 The leg of a table shakes. // 나뭇가지가 바람에 흔들린다 Branches sway in the wind. // 배가 몹시 흔들린다 The ship rolls〔pitches〕 heavily. // 버스가 흔들린다 A bus joggles. // 창이 바람에 흔들린다 A window is rattled by the wind. // 나뭇잎이 바람에 흔들린다 The leaves stir in the wind. // 이가 흔들린다 A tooth is loose. // 시계추가 흔들리고 있다 The pendulum is in motion. // 그의 결심은 흔들리지 않았다 He remained firm in his resolution.
흔들 목마 —木馬 a rocking horse ; a cockhorse ; a hobbyhorse
흔들비쭉이 a pouter ; a person who is given to sulking ; a peevish fellow
흔들의자 —椅子 a rocking chair ; a rocker
흔들흔들 swingingly ; wavingly ; swayingly ; rockingly ; shakily **—하다** sway ; swing ; rock
흔연하다 欣然— (be) happy ; cheerful ; joyful ¶ 흔연히 gladly ; with pleasure ; cheerfully ; readily ; willingly ; with good grace // 흔연히 승낙하다 consent readily ; accept willingly ; be glad to accept
†**흔적** 痕迹 marks ; traces ; vestiges ; track ; signs ; indications ; evidences

> 참고 **trace** 존재했던 것 또는 발생했던 것에 의하여 남겨진 표적 **vestige** 지금은 이미 존재하지 않는 것의 유물 **track** trace와 동의어이지만 특히 오랫동안 남는 것

¶ 이로 문 흔적 an impression of teeth // 사람 몸에 있는 꼬리의 흔적 the vestige of a tail in the human body // 고대 문명의 흔적 vestiges of ancient civilization // 흔적이 있다 bear the marks 《of》 // 흔적을 남기다 leave traces 《of》 // 흔적을 남기지 않다 leave no trace behind 《one》 // 흔적을 발견하다 find traces〔marks〕 《of》 // 흔적없이 사라지다 disappear ; cover one's trail ; vanish into thin air // 도둑이 창으로 들어온 흔적이 있다 There are evidences of the burglar having entered by the window. // 그가 있었다는 흔적은 전혀 보이지 않았다 I found no vestiges of his presence.
— 기관 〚생물〛 a vestigial〔rudimentary〕 organ
흔전거리다 live in easy circumstances ; be well off ; live in luxury
흔전만전 in plenty ; in profusion ; copiously ¶ 흔전만전 쓸 돈이 있다 have money enough and to spare // 돈을 흔전만전 쓰다 spend money freely〔in profusion〕
흔전하다 (be) plentiful ; abundant ; profuse ; copious
흔쾌 欣快 **—하다** (be) pleasant ; happy ; delightful ; joyful
*****흔하다** (be) plentiful ; rife ; common ; commonplace ; be met with everywhere ¶ 흔한 일 a commonplace affair // 흔해빠진 이야기 an old story // 흔한 책 a book that can easily be had // 흔하지 않은 uncommon ; extraordinary // 돈이 흔하다 money is in plentiful supply // 흔한 것이 여자다 If there's one thing we have enough of, it's woman. // 그런 물건은 흔하지 않다 Such things are by no means common.

흔흔히 欣欣— gladly ; joyously ⇨ 흔연
흔희 欣喜 joy ; delight ; gladness ; exultation ; rejoicing —하다 rejoice ; be glad ; be delighted 《with》¶ 흔희 작약하다 jump〔dance〕 for joy ; leap with joy ; exult ; be in raptures
흔히 [풍부히] profusely ; plentifully ; [보통·종종] usually ; commonly ; frequently ; often ; [주로] mostly ; [대개] generally ¶ 흔히 쓰이는 말 a frequently used word // 흔히 있는 일 a common〔an everyday〕 affair ; not an uncommon case 《with》; a matter of common occurrence // 젊은이들이 흔히 저지르는 과오 a blunder (that) young men are apt to make // 학생들에게 흔히 있는 일이지만 as is usual with students // 흔히 …하다 be apt to ; be liable 《to》; be susceptible ; be natural // 흔히 있다 be (all too) common ; be met with everywhere // 흔히 있는 일이다 They are common enough. // 그런 사람은 흔하지 않다 You will have to seek far and wide to find such a man. /A man of his kind is rarely to be met with. // 돈이 흔히 돌아다닌다 There is plenty of money around. // 이런 일은 흔히 있는 일이다 Such things are apt to happen. // 이 병은 흔히 어린이들이 잘 걸린다 This disease prevails much among children. // 그는 흔히 그런 말을 한다 He has the way of talking like that.
흘게늦다 (be) loose ; loose-jointed ; loose-hinged ¶ 저 친구는 흘게늦다 He wants screwing up.
흘겨보다 leer at 《a person》; glance sidewise 《at》; look at sideways ; look out of the corner of one's eye(s) ; cast a sidelong glance at 《a person》; look askance 《at》
흘근거리다 walk slowly〔lazily〕; proceed at reduced speed
흘근흘근 slowly ; lazily ; sluggishly ; tardily ; dawdlingly ; lingeringly —하다 ⇨ 흘근거리다
흘금거리다 keep looking sideways ; keep leering〔eyeing〕; look askance at 《a person》 frequently
흘금흘금 looking sideways over and over again ; leering and leering ; ogling and ogling ¶ 흘금흘금 보다 keep eyeing
흘긋거리다 keep looking sideways
흘기다 give a sharp sidelong glance 〔glare, scowl〕 《at》; look askance 《at》 ¶ 무섭게 흘겨보다 give a fierce sidelong scowl
흘기죽죽 with a displeased look from the corner of one's eyes —하다 look displeased〔discontented〕
흘깃 with a glance ¶ 흘깃 보다 cast a glance at 《a person》; cast 《a person》 a searching glance
흘깃거리다 keep glaring〔scowling〕 《at》
흘끔하다 [눈이] (be) sunken ; be hollow 《with tiredness, etc.》 ¶ 앓고 나서 눈이 흘끔하다 one's eyes are sunken after an illness
*흘끗 at a glance ¶ 흘끗 보다 catch a glimpse of ; steal a glance at // 자동차 지나가는 것이 흘끗 눈에 띄다 catch a glimpse of a car passing by
흘끗흘끗 glancing sideways over and over again ¶ 흘끗흘끗 보다 keep glancing to one side
흘낏거리다 ⇨ 흘깃거리다
흘떼기 the sinewy〔membranous〕 parts of meat ; a tough piece〔part〕
흘러가다 flow ; run ; float〔drift〕 along ; fly (시간이) ¶ (강이) 바다로 흘러가다 find its way to the sea // 덧없이 흘러가는 청춘 시대 the flying years of youth // 세월은 흘러간다 Time flies.
흘러나오다 [유출하다] flow out ; run out ; effuse ; stream〔pour〕 out ; spring forth〔out〕; gush forth (분출하다) ; ooze out (고름 따위가) ; [배수되다] drain out ; [수문에서] sluice ¶ 호수에서 흘러나오는 강 a river which proceeds from the lake // 졸졸 흘러나오다 drain through // 상처에서 피가 흘러나왔다 The blood flowed out from the wound.
†흘러내리다 ① [떨어지다] fall ; drop ; run 〔stream, pour〕 down ¶ 눈물이 그녀의 볼을 줄줄 흘러내렸다 Tears ran 〔streamed, coursed, rolled, trickled〕 down her cheeks. ② [미끄러져] slip 〔slide, glide〕 down ; work down ¶ 흘러내리는 바지를 치켜올리다 pull〔hitch〕 up one's trousers
흘러들다 flow in〔into〕; pour〔run, stream〕 in〔into〕; find one's way into ; empty〔drain, discharge〕 (itself) into ¶ 그 강은 만으로 흘러들어 간다 The river pours〔falls〕 into the bay.
흘러보다 sound 《out》; tap ; feel 《a person's》 pulse ¶ 사람의 속을 흘러보다 sound 《a person's》 mind ; sound 《a person》 out // 사람의 의견을 흘러보다 sound 《a peron's》 views ; seek 《a person's》 opinion
흘레 copulation ; coupling ; coition —하다 mate ; copulate ; couple ; pair ¶ 흘레붙이다 couple ; mate ; make a match // 말을 흘레붙이다 serve a horse
†흘리다 ① spill ; drop ; shed ¶ 눈물을〔피를〕 흘리다 shed tears〔blood〕 // 물을 흘리다 spill water 《on》 // 땀을 흘리다 sweat // 콧물을 흘리다 run at the nose
② [잃다] drop ; lose ¶ 돈을 흘리다 lose one's money // 지갑을 흘렸다 I have dropped my purse.
③ [조금씩] give 《it》 out piecemeal ; give 《it》 in driblets
④ [글씨를] scribble ; write in a cursive

hand ¶ 편지를 흘려쓰다 scribble a letter
⑤ [귓전으로] take no notice 《of》
흘림 the cursive〔running〕 style of penmanship ; writing in a cursive hand ¶ 흘림으로 쓰다 write in a cursive hand ; scribble busily
흘림흘림 by〔in〕 driblets ; little by little ; by piecemeal ¶ 돈을 흘림흘림 갚다 return money in driblets
흘립 屹立 **—하다** tower 《above the clouds》 ; rise 《into the air》 ¶ (바위가) 수면에 흘립하다 rocks rise sheer from the water
흘미죽죽 cursorily ; all fouled up ; snafu 《미·군속》 **—하다** be all fouled up ; (be) snafu
흘수 吃水 draft ; water drawn (by a vessel) ; sea gauge ¶ 흘수가 깊은〔얕은〕배 a deep〔light, shallow〕-draft vessel ; a ship of deep〔light〕 draft
—선 the draft (line) ; the water line —표 the draft mark 만재 —선 the load-line
흘쩍거리다 dawdle〔loaf〕 at ; idle along ; delay ; slow up ¶ 일을 흘쩍거리다 dawdle at one's work ; loaf on the job
흘쩍흘쩍 dawdlingly ; idly ; indolently ; lazily ; sluggishly **—하다** ⇨ 흘쩍거리다
†**흙** earth ; soil ; the ground (지면) ; clay (질흙) ¶ 흙으로 덮다 cover 《a thing》 with earth ; heap up earth ; earth up // 흙을 파다 dig up earth ; dig in the ground ; [농사짓다] till the soil ; do farming // 흙으로 돌아가다 return to dust
흙감태기 being covered all over with mud ¶ 흙감태기가 되다 be covered all over with mud
흙구덩이 a hole〔hollow, cavity〕 in the ground
흙내 the smell of the soil ; the smell of earth
흙내 맡다 관용 (나무가) take〔strike〕 root
흙다리 a mud bridge
흙담 a mud wall
흙더미 a heap of earth
흙더버기 《covered with》 caked mud splashes ; all mud-splashed〔-splattered〕
흙덩어리 ⇨ 흙덩이
흙덩이 a clod ; a lump of earth
흙뒤 〖해부〗 Achilles' tendon
흙막이 〖토목〗 retaining of earth ; sheeting ; sheathing ; timbering
—널 a sheathing board ; a poling board — 버팀대 a bridge strut —벽 a retaining wall
흙먼지 dust ; a cloud of dust ; a dust storm ¶ 흙먼지를 일으키다〔날리다〕 raise〔kick up〕 a cloud of dust // 흙먼지를 일으키며 달리다 run with clouds of dust behind
흙무더기 a heap〔pile〕 of earth
흙뭉치 a ball〔lump〕 of earth
흙뭉텅이 a large ball of earth〔mud, clay〕
흙받기 [미장이의] a (plasterer's) mortarboard ; [자동차의] a splashboard ; a mudguard
흙밥 a spadeful〔hoeful〕 of earth
흙방 —房 a mud-plastered room
흙벽 —壁 a mud-plastered wall
흙벽돌 —甓— a block of dried mud ; adobe ; a sun-dried brick
—집 an adobe house ; an adobe
흙비 a dust storm ; a sandstorm
흙빛 earth color ; brown ¶ 흙빛의 ashy ; pale // 얼굴이 흙빛이 되다 turn pale as ashes ; turn ghastly〔deadly〕pale
흙빨래 **—하다** soil (one's clothes) with muddy water
흙손 a plasterer's trowel ; a float
—끌 a trowel-shaped chisel used for finishing gutters
흙손질 troweling ; plastering with a trowel **—하다** trowel ; plaster with a trowel ; level with a float
흙일 earthwork(s) ; plastering **—하다** do earthwork ; do the plastering ¶ 흙일하는 사람 a coolie ; a navvy (토역꾼)
흙장난 playing with earth **—하다** play with earth
흙질 mud-plastering **—하다** mud-plaster ; do the mud〔plastering〕 work ; stucco ; trowel
흙창 —窓 a double-papered window
흙칠 **—하다** soil〔smear〕 with mud ; be stained with mud
흙탕 ① [질퍽한 곳] mud ; a muddy place〔spot〕 《in a road》 ; a mire ¶ 흙탕길 a muddy road // 흙탕속에 빠지다 get stuck in the mud ② ⇨ 흙탕물
흙탕물 muddy water
흙투성이 (being) covered all over with mud〔earth〕 ¶ 네 저고리는 흙투성이다 Your coat is covered with mud.
***흠** 欠 ① [상처 자국] a scar ; a cicatrice ¶ 그는 얼굴에 흠이 있다 He has〔bears〕 a scar on his face.
② [물건의] a flaw ; a scratch〔crack, speck〕 ; a bruise (과일의) ¶ 흠이 있는 flawed ; cracked ; disfigured ; bruised // 흠이 없다 be flawless ; be perfect // 흠이 있다 be scratched〔cracked, disfigured〕 ; have a flaw in // 그 금강석에는 흠이 있다 There is a flaw in the diamond.
③ [결점] a defect ; a flaw ; a blemish ; a drawback ¶ 게으른 것이 흠이다 The bad thing about him is his laziness. // 흠없는 사람은 없다 Nobody is perfect. // 그의 흠이라면 단지 술마시는 것뿐이다 Drinking is one flaw in his otherwise perfect character.
흠 Hum ! /Hm ! /Hmph !

흠결 欠缺 shortage ; deficiency ; want ; deficit
흠구덕 欠― backbiting ; malicious gossip **―하다** backbite ; disparage to excess ; overcriticize ; slander
흠나다 欠― ⇨ 흠지다
흠내다 欠― scar ; make a scar ; make a flaw〔crack, scratch〕 ¶ 얼굴에 흠내다 scar one's face
흠뜯다 欠― disparage ; belittle ; speak ill (of) ; run 《a person》 down ¶ 남이 해놓은 일을 흠뜯다 disparage〔belittle〕《a person's》 achievement // 남을 흠뜯어서는 안된다 You must not speak ill of others.
흠모 欽慕 admiration ; adoration **―하다** admire ; adore ; make an idol of ¶ 그는 여전히 동향인의 흠모를 받고 있다 He is still the idol of his countrymen.
흠빨다 suck hard
흠빨며 감빨다 관용 suck in〔up〕 greedily
*__흠뻑__ very much ; all ; completely ¶ 흠뻑 젖은 옷 dripping clothes // 비가 흠뻑 오다 have much rain // 흠뻑 젖다 be dripping wet ; be wet through (and through) ; be drenched〔soaked, wet〕 to the skin // 흠뻑 기뻐하다 be greatly pleased ; be much delighted // 땀에 흠뻑 젖다 be all in sweat (사람이) ; be wringing wet with sweat (옷이)
흠신 欠身 ―하다 bow low ; make a bow
흠실흠실 (boiled) soft ; tender ; yielding to the touch **―하다** be boiled soft ¶ 흠실흠실하게 삶다 reduce to jelly〔pulp〕 // 고기를 흠실흠실 삶다 boil meat tender
흠씬 enough ; sufficiently ; to the fullest measure ; thoroughly ; utterly ; completely ¶ 고기를 흠씬 삶다 boil meat to pulp〔soft enough〕 // 흠씬 먹다 eat one's fill // 비가 흠씬 오다 have sufficient rain
흠앙 欽仰 adoration ; reverence ; high esteem **―하다** adore ; revere ; look up to with reverence ; esteem highly
흠잡다 欠― find fault with ; pick flaws ; look for defects ; carp〔cavil〕 at ¶ 흠잡을 데가 없다 be faultless ; be free from fault ; be above criticism ; leave nothing to be desired ; be perfect // 게으른 것을 흠잡다 criticize 《a person's》 laziness // 그는 남의 흠잡기를 좋아한다 He is fond of finding fault with others. // 흠잡을 데라고는 저것밖에 없다 That's the only fly in the ointment.
흠점 欠點 ⇨ 결점
흠정 欽定 ―하다 authorize ; establish ¶ 흠정의 authorized〔established〕 by the king ; compiled by royal order
― 시인 a poet laureate **―역 성서** the Authorized Version (of the Bible) ; the King James Bible **― 헌법** a constitution granted by the king
흠지다 欠― get scarred ; get marred〔cracked〕 ; be scratched ; have a flaw〔scratch, crack, speck〕
흠지러기 stringy ends of meat
흠집 欠― a scar ; a cicatrice ¶ 이마에 흠집이 있다 have a scar on one's forehead
흠축 欠縮 shortage ; deficiency ; want ; deficit ; lack ¶ 흠축 가다〔나다〕 be〔fall, run〕 short ; be insufficient ; be shy 《of》 ; make a deficit 《of》
흠치르르 sleek ; glossy **―하다** (be) sleek ; glossy ¶ 흠치르르 윤이 흐르다 be sleek ; be smooth and glossy
흠칫 recoiling〔shrinking〕 with a fright〔surprise〕 **―하다** recoil ; shrink ; pull back 《one's head, neck, shoulders》 in surprise〔fright〕
흡각 吸角 〖의학〗 a cupping glass
―법 〖의학〗 cupping
흡광 吸光 〖물리〗 extinction
흡기 吸氣 inhalation **―하다** inhale ; breathe in
―기 an aspirator
흡력 吸力 absorptivity ; absorption power
흡반 吸盤 a sucker ; a sucking disk ; an acetabulum
흡사 恰似 [명사적] close resemblance ; [부사적] just as ; as if〔though〕 ; as it were **―하다** (be) alike ; be just as ; be much (about) the same ; closely resemble ¶ 아주 흡사하다 be as like as two peas〔eggs〕 ; be exactly alike ; be a replica ; be a copy 《of》 // 흡사 죽은 것 같다 look as if dead ; be more dead than alive // 흡사 미친 사람 같다 look as if one were mad // 흡사 달이 뜬 것 같이 훤하다 It is as bright as if the moon had risen.
흡상 吸上 suction ; sucking **―하다** suck〔draw, pump〕 up
‡**흡수 吸收** absorption ; assimilation ; suction ; decalescence (열의) ; extinction (빛의) **―하다** absorb ; assimilate ; suck in

> 참고 **absorb** 무엇인가를 흡수하였을 때 흡수된 것이 그 개성을 잃고 녹아 버린다 **assimilate** 무엇인가를 흡수하였을 때 흡수된 것을 중요한 요소로 한다

¶ 흡수성의 absorbent ; absorptive // 미국의 인구 흡수력 American capacity for absorbing new population // 혈액 내에 흡수 되다 be absorbed into blood // 실업자를 흡수하다 absorb the jobless into work ; mobilize labor (for public work) // 서양 문명을 흡수하다 assimilate Western civilization // 해면은 물을 흡수한

다 A sponge absorbs water.
—관 an absorption tube —기(器) an absorber —력 absorption force —성 absorptiveness ¶ 흡수성의 absorbent ; absorptive —열 heat absorption — 작용 absorption —제 an absorbent — 조직 an absorptive tissue — 코일 an absorbing coil

흡수 吸水 suction (of water) ; water suction
—관 a siphon — 펌프 a suction pump 적재 —량 load draught

흡습 吸濕 moisture absorption
—성 hygroscopic property ; hygroscopicity ¶ 흡습성이 강하다 be highly 〔very〕 hygroscopic — 시험 a moisture absorption test —체 a moisture absorbent — 팽창 hygroscopic swelling

⁑흡연 吸煙 smoking (tobacco) —하다 smoke (tobacco, a cigarette, a pipe) ; have a smoke ; have a pipe ¶ 흡연 금지 No smoking (is allowed here). // 과도한 흡연은 몸에 해롭다 It is bad for the health to smoke like a chimney. // 과도한 흡연은 성대를 해치기 쉽다 Much smoking tends to injure the voice. // 간접 흡연은 건강에 매우 해롭다 Second-hand smoking is a big health hazard.
—실 a smoking room —자 a smoker —차 a smoking car ; a smoker ; a smoking carriage

흡연 洽然 —하다 (be) satisfying ; gratifying ¶ 흡연히 to one's satisfaction ; gratifyingly

흡연히 翕然— spontaneously ; with one accord ¶ 세상 사람들의 동정이 흡연히 그에게로 집중되었다 The sympathy of the whole community was centered upon him. /He captured the sympathy of the world 《by it》.

흡열 吸熱 heat absorption
— 반응(反應) 〖화학〗 (an) endothermic 〔endoergic〕 reaction — 화합물 an endothermic compound

흡음 吸音 sound absorption
—력〔제〕 sound-absorbing power〔materials〕 —율 acoustic absorptivity

흡인 吸引 absorption ; suction ; attraction —하다 absorb ; suck up ; attract
—기 an aspirator —력 absorption force — 작용 absorption ; attraction

흡입 吸入 inhalation ; inspiration —하다 inhale ; inspire ; suck in
—관 an induction pipe —기 an inhaler ; an inspirator ; a nebulizer —판(瓣) an inlet valve

흡장 吸藏 〖화학〗 occlusion —하다 occlude

흡족 洽足 —하다 (be) sufficient ; ample ; enough ; satisfactory ¶ 흡족히 to one's heart's content ; sufficiently ; enough ; fully // 흡족히 먹다 eat one's fill ; do full justice to 《the dinner》 // 흡족히 먹었습니다 I've had enough, thank you. // 그만하면 그에게 흡족하게 해준 거다 You have done enough for him.

흡착 吸着 absorption
—기 an absorber —제 an absorbent

흡출 吸出 sucking out ; drawing out —하다 suck out ; draw out

흡혈 吸血 blood-sucking
—귀 a vampire ; a bloodsucker — 동물 a bloodsucker

흣대 a potter's (shaping) stick

흥 Hum ! /Hm ! /Hmph ! /Pish !

*흥 興 fun ; pleasure ; mirth ; merriment ; joy ; excitement ¶ 흥에 겨워 in the excess of mirth // 흥이 나다 get merry〔excited〕 《over something》 ; become interested 《in》 ; warm up 《to one's work》 // 흥을 깨치다 spoil pleasure〔fun〕 ; kill joy ; put〔throw〕 a wet blanket on // 흥을 돋구다 add to the amusement // 흥에 못이기다 be overwhelmed with mirth // 흥이 깨져버렸다 The spell is broken. // 너의 어색한 농담으로 흥이 깨져버렸다 That crummy joke you told went over like a lead balloon.

흥감 exaggeration ; grandiosity ; bombast ; a tall〔big〕 talk —하다 be given to exaggeration ; (be) bombastic ; high-flown ; pompous ¶ 흥감스럽게 exaggeratedly ; pompously ; with much ado // 흥감스럽게 떠들어대다 make a fuss too much
흥감 부리다 〔관용〕 exaggerate ; stretch ; blow one's own trumpet〔horn〕 ; talk big〔tall〕

흥건하다 be full of water ; have too much liquid in (음식이) ¶ 웅덩이에 빗물이 흥건히 괴었다 A puddle is full of rainwater. // 김치가 흥건하다 The *kimch'i* has too much juice. // 국이 흥건하다 Soup is watery.

*흥겹다 興— be full of fun ; (be) delightful ; exciting ¶ 흥겹게 gaily ; delightfully ; merrily // 한참 흥겨운 판에 in the midst of one's merriment // 흥겨운 하루 a day full of fun ; a fun-packed day ; an exciting day // 흥겹게 놀다 make merry ; have fun ; be absorbed in play // 흥겨워하다 amuse 〔disport〕 oneself ; have fun ; be amused

흥글방망이놀다 interfere with ; meddle in ; thwart ; frustrate ; disturb

흥기 興起 rise ; ascendancy —하다 rise ; ascend

흥김 興— (in) the midst of merriment ; (under) the influence of excitement ¶ 흥김에 큰 소리로 노래부르다 have such a good time that one sings in a loud voice

흥나다 興— get merry ; grow excited ;

have fun ¶ 흥나서 노래부르다 sing with much mirth // 흥나면 시를 읊는다 When I am in the mood I recite poems.

흥덩흥덩 being full of water ; having too much water in it **—하다** have too much water in it

흥뚱새 〖새〗 a tree pipit ; Anthus hodgsoni (학명)

흥뚱항뚱 carelessly ; heedlessly ; recklessly ; half-heartedly ¶ 흥뚱항뚱 듣다 pay little〔no〕 attention to ; listen to 《a person》 in an absent sort of way // 일을 흥뚱항뚱하다 do a job carelessly

흥망 興亡 rise and fall ; ups and downs ; vicissitudes ¶ 로마의 흥망 the rise and fall of Rome ; the destinies of Rome // 민족의 흥망 the varied fortunes of races // 국가의 흥망에 관한 문제 a problem affecting the destinies of the nation // 나는 흥망을 걸고 이 사업을 해보겠다 I will try my luck with this business.

— 성쇠 rise and〔or〕 fall together with prosperity and〔or〕 decay ¶ 로마 제국의 흥망 성쇠 the rise and fall of the Roman Empire

†**흥미 興味** interest ; zest ; taste ; gusto ¶ 흥미 있다 be interesting ; be amusing ; be entertaining // 흥미 없다 be uninteresting ; be dull ; be of no interest // 깊은 흥미를 가지고 with keen〔deep〕 interest // 흥미 위주로 for the sake of arousing the interest 《of》 // 흥미를 가지다 take〔have〕 an interest in ; be〔become〕 interested in // 흥미를 일으키다 arouse〔awaken, stimulate〕 interest in 《a thing》 ; get 《a person》 interested in // 흥미를 깨뜨리다 spoil 《a person's》 pleasure ; kill joy // 흥미를 잃다 lose interest in // 흥미 진진하다 be full of interest // 문학에 비상한 흥미를 가지다 take a great interest in literature // 그런 일에는 흥미 없다 Such things have no interest for me. // 그 영화는 매우 흥미 있었다 I've got a lot of fun out of〔from〕 the picture. /The picture thrilled me a great deal. // 작가가 노력한 흔적은 보이지만 독자의 흥미를 끌 만한 무엇인가가 없다 I can see signs of the writer's effort, but it just doesn't have that something to grab the reader's interest.

흥미 본위 興味本位 ¶ 흥미 본위의 읽을거리 amusing〔light〕 reading // 흥미 본위의 문학 popular literature // 나는 그 일을 흥미 본위로 하고 있다 I am doing the job for the fun of it.

†**흥분 興奮** excitement ; excitation ; agitation ; stimulation **—하다** be〔grow, get〕 excited ; excite oneself ; be aroused ; be stimulated ; get wrought up ; work oneself up ; take on 《구》 ; get a kick〔thrill〕 《속》 ¶ 흥분하여 excitedly ; in excitement ; in a dither ; in a sweat // 흥분시키다 excite ; work 《a person》 up ; stimulate ; stir up ; arouse 《a person's》 feelings // 매우 흥분하고 있다 be on a tiptoe of excitement // 흥분이 가라앉다 calm down ; cool down // 흥분을 가라앉히다 cool down 《a person's hot temper》 ; calm down 《the agitation》 // 흥분하지 말라 Don't get excited. /Don't be upset. /Calm down. /Take it easy. // 흥분하여 심장 마비로 죽었다 Excited, he collapsed with a heart attack. // 환자를 흥분시키면 안된다 The patient must not be excited. // 그 소식을 듣고 모두가 흥분했다 The news excited everybody. // 무얼 그리 흥분하고 있나 What are you so nervous about? // 흥분하지 말고 내 말 좀 끝까지 들어봐 Don't steam. Hear me out. // 흥분을 가라 앉힌 연후에 곰곰히 생각해 보니 나 역시 잘못을 했다는 것을 깨달을 수 있었다 After I cooled off and thought it over, I could see that I was in the wrong, too. // 네가 십대들의 우상때문에 흥분할 나이는 지났다고 생각했다 I thought you were past the age of getting worked up over teen idols.

— 상태 excited condition〔state〕 **—성** excitability ; irritability **— 음료** an exhilarating drink ; a pick-me-up **—제** a stimulant ; an excitant ; an exciter ; a cordial ; an invigorator **신경성 —** 〖생리〗 erethism **이상 —성** hyperirritability

흥성흥성 興盛興盛 flourishing ; thriving ; roaring ; booming **—하다** (be) prosperous ; thriving ; flourishing ; roaring ; booming ¶ 장사가 흥성흥성하다 one's business is booming〔thriving〕

흥신소 興信所 an inquiry agency〔office〕 ; a credit bureau

상업 — a commercial inquiry agency

흥야항야 ⇨ 흥이야항이야

흥얼거리다 hum ; croon ; sing to oneself

흥얼흥얼 humming ; crooning ¶ 흥얼흥얼 혼자 노래하다 hum (a song) to oneself ; croon to oneself

흥업 興業 promotion of industries ; an industrial enterprise **—하다** promote industries ; undertake an industrial enterprise

흥에띄다 興— be all wrapped up in one's enjoyment ; be seized with mirth ; be in the excess of mirth

흥이야항이야 meddling ; interfering **—하다** thrust〔poke〕 one's nose into ; intermeddle ; obtrude oneself to ¶ 남의 일에 흥이야항이야하다 thrust〔poke, stick〕 one's nose into another person's business

***흥정** ① a bargain ② [매매] buying and selling ; purchase and sale ; marketing **—하다** strike a bargain ; haggle over

terms ; [거래] do business ; deal ; [매매] buy and sell ¶ 흥정붙이다 act as (a) broker ; help strike a bargain // 흥정을 맺다 strike a bargain // 흥정은 붙이고 싸움은 말리란다 One should help bargaining and stop quarrels.
— 거리 merchandise —꾼 a broker (거간꾼) ; a dealer ; a trader ; parties to a bargain

흥진비래 興盡悲來 After fun comes sorrow. /After joy come tears.

흥청거리다 exult ; be highly elated ; crow ; indulge in revelry ¶ 요릿집을 돌아다니며 흥청거리다 paint the town red // 그는 성공해서 흥청거리고 있다 He is transported with his success.

흥청망청 with elation ⇨ 흥청흥청

흥청흥청 with elation ; exultantly ; merrily ; gaily ¶ 흥청흥청 놀고 마시다 go on the racket ; hold high junks ; drink the cup of pleasure to the dregs

흥취 興趣 interest ; gusto ; taste ⇨ 흥미 ¶ 흥취가 있다 be interesting ; be fun

흥치 興致 fun ; pleasure ; delight ; interest ; [운치] taste ; elegance (아치)

흥타령 —打令 a kind of folksong with a "hum" at the end of each line

흥패 興敗 rise and fall ; fate ; destiny ¶ 국가의 흥패에 관한 중대한 문제 a great question affecting the destinies of the nation // 일국의 흥패가 달려 있는 싸움 a battle on which the fate of a country depends ; a battle which decides the fate of a country

흥하다 興— rise ; [번영하다] prosper ; thrive ; flourish ; boom ; be prosperous 〔flourishing, thriving〕 ¶ 흥하는 집안 a prosperous〔thriving〕 family // 장사가 흥하다 business prospers〔flourishes, thrives, booms〕 ; do good〔prosperous〕 business // 흥하든 망하든 해보겠다 I will try, sink or swim. /I will make a spoon or spoil a horn.

†**흥행 興行** [사업] the entertainment industry ; a show enterprise ; [연예] a performance ; a show ; a run **—하다** give a performance ; perform ; show ; run 《a show》 ; produce 《a play》 ; exhibit ¶ 흥행 가치 있는 영화 a picture of proven box-office power ; a film with audience appeal // 흥행 가치 있는 배우 a box-office star // 지방 순회 흥행 길을 떠나다 be on the road 《미》 // 1일 2회 흥행이 있다 There are two performances given a day. /They give two shows a day.
— 가치 box-office value ; audience value —계 the entertainment world〔circle〕 — 계통 circuit ; a chain —권 right of performance〔production〕 ; producing rights ; dramatic〔stage〕 rights (연극의) —단 a (theatrical) company ; a troupe —물 a performance ; a show ; a production ; an exhibition —사 a showman — 성적 a box-office record —세 an entertainment tax — 수익 box-office profits —장 a show place ; a circus (서커스의) —주 a promoter 순회 — a roadshow 야간 — a night performance 장〔단〕기 — a long〔short〕 run 주간 — a matinée

흥흥 hum hum ; hmph hmph

흥흥거리다 ① [콧노래] hum ; croon ; sing to oneself ② [울다] whine ; whimper

흩날리다 scatter ; blow off〔away〕 ¶ 낙엽이 바람에 흩날리고 없다 The dead leaves have blown away.

흩다 scatter ; disperse ; strew ; dishevel (머리털을) ¶ 머리털을 흩뜨리고 with one's disheveled hair // 휴지 조각을 흩다 scatter bits of waste paper

‡**흩뜨리다** scatter about ; disperse ; [머리 따위를] dishevel ⇨ 흩다

†**흩뿌리다** scatter〔strew〕 about ; sprinkle

***흩어지다** scatter 《about》 ; get scattered 《about》 ; disperse ; break up ¶ 소문이 흩어지다 a rumor gets abroad // 꽃이 바람에 흩어지다 Blossoms are scattered in the wind. // 열 두 가족이 사방으로 흩어졌다 The family of twelve scattered far and wide. // 공원에는 쓰레기가 흩어져 있다 The parks are scattered with rubbish.

흩이다 be scattered ; be dispersed ¶ 꽃이 바람에 흩인다 Blossoms are scattered by the wind.

희가 戲歌 a limerick ; a comic〔funny〕 song

희가극 喜歌劇 a comic opera

희가스 稀— 〖화학〗 noble gas
—류 원소 rare gas

‡**희곡 戲曲** a drama ; a play ¶ 희곡적 dramatic(al) // 희곡화하다 dramatize
— 작가 a dramatist ; a playwright ; a playwriter — 작법 dramaturgy —집 a collection of plays —화 dramatization ¶ 희곡화하다 dramatize

희구 希求 desire ; want ; aspiration **—하다** desire 《to do》 ; aspire 《after》 ; seek ; demand ; call〔ask〕 for 《a thing》

희귀 稀貴 rareness ; rarity **—하다** (be) rare ; curious ; uncommon ; unusual ; phenomenal ¶ 희귀한 물건 a rarity ; a curiosity ; rare articles // 희귀한 일 a rarity // 희귀한 사건 a rare〔an uncommon〕 occurrence〔event〕 // 희귀한 책 a rare book // 극히 희귀한 물건 a black swan ; a white crow ; a blue dahlia

‡**희극 喜劇** a comedy ; a farce (광대극) ; a funny show 《미》 ¶ 희극적 comic ; farcical // 희극을 상연하다 play a comedy // 한바탕 희극이 벌어졌다 A comic scene was enacted on the spot.
— 문학 comic literature — 배우 a

comic actor (남자)〔actress (여자)〕; a comedian (남자) ; a comedienne (여자) — 영화 a comic film — 작가 a comic dramatist ; a comedy writer ; a comedian 음악 — a musical comedy

희극 戲劇 ① 〖연극〗 a farce ② [행동] a farcical〔ludicrous〕 act ; a frivolous conduct

희금속 稀金屬 rare metals

희기 喜氣 merriness ; gleefulness ; gay spirits ; a mood of cheerfulness ; a happy feeling

희끄무레하다 (be) whitish ; rather fair ¶ 희끄무레한 얼굴 a rather fair face

희끄스름하다 whitish

희끈거리다 get〔feel〕 dizzy〔giddy〕 ; one's head turns〔swims〕

희끈희끈 dizzily ; giddily ; shakily ; reelingly

희끔하다 (be) whitish

희끗거리다 get dizzy ⇨ 희끈거리다

희끗희끗 spotted〔speckled〕 with white ; grizzled ; grizzly — 하다 (be) grizzled ; grizzly ¶ 머리가 희끗희끗한 사람 a grizzle-haired man

희나리 green firewood ; wet firewood

희넓적하다 (be) white and broad〔flat〕

*희년 稀年 seventy years of age

†희다 (be) white ; fair (피부가) ; [머리가] gray ; hoary ¶ 얼굴이 희다 have a fair〔white〕 face // 머리가 희다 have gray hair // 눈같이 희다 be snow-white // 살결이 희다 have a fair complexion ; be of light complexion

흰 개 꼬리 굴뚝에 3년 두어도 흰 개 꼬리다 (속담) A crow is never the white for washing herself.

희담 戲談 a joke ; a jest ; a pleasantry ; a banter

희대 稀代 uncommonness ; rarity ¶ 희대의 uncommon ; rare ; extraordinary ; unique ; unheard-of // 희대의 악한 a notorious〔double-dyed〕 villain // 희대의 영웅 a unique hero

희디희다 (be) snow-white ; pure white ; as white as snow

희떱다 [허영] (be) showy ; vain ; vainglorious ; snobbish ; conceited ; pretentious

희뜩거리다 get very dizzy〔giddy, shaky〕 ; reel

희뜩머룩이 a free〔lavish〕 spender ; a spendthrift ; a scattergood ; a high roller 《미·속》

희뜩희뜩 — 하다 (be) dotted with white ; grizzly (머리가) ¶ 머리가 희뜩희뜩한 gray-haired ; grizzled ; grizzle-haired

희락 喜樂 joy and pleasure ; felicity ; happiness

희랍 希臘 Greece ⇨ 그리스
— 정교회 the Greek〔Orthodox〕 Church

희로 喜怒 joy and anger ; emotion ; feelings
—애락 joy and anger together with sorrow and pleasure ; feelings ; emotions ¶ 희로애락을 드러내다 betray〔show, give vent to〕 one's feelings // 희로애락의 감정을 드러내지 않다 disguise one's feelings

희롱 戲弄 ridiculing ; jesting ; a joke — 하다 joke with ; poke fun at ; make fun〔sport〕 of ; kid ; ridicule ; tease ; toy〔sport〕 with ; flirt with (남녀가) ¶ 희롱조로 in mocking tone // 운명의 희롱 a trick of fate // 희롱조로 말하다 say a thing in〔for〕 sport

희룽거리다 jest ; play pranks ; frolic ; make fun〔sport〕 of

희룽희룽 playing pranks ; frolicking ; joking ; kidding〔horsing〕 around ; cavorting ; cutting capers

희맑다 (be) white and clean

†희망 希望 [소망] hope ; wish ; desire ; [포부] aspiration ; ambition ; [기대] prospect ; anticipation — 하다 hope for ; be hopeful of ; wish ; be desirous of ; aspire to〔after〕 ; anticipate ¶ 오래 품어온 희망 one's long-cherished desire ; one's dearest ambition // 일루의 희망 a ray of hope // 간절한 희망 an ardent desire ; an earnest wish // 희망을 가지고 in hopes of ; in the hope that ; with the hope〔desire〕 of // 희망에 찬 청년들 young hopefuls // 희망이 충만해 있다 be full of hope ; be hopeful // 희망이 없다 be hopeless ; there is no hope of // 희망을 가지다 cherish a hope〔desire〕 // 희망을 걸다 anchor one's hope in〔on〕 ; pin one's hope to // 희망을 성취하다 realize one's wish ; attain one's desire // 희망을 가지게 하다 encourage 《a person's》 hope // 희망을 잃다 lose one's hope ; despair // 희망에 살다 live in hope
— 음악회 a request concert —자 a candidate ; an aspirant —적 관측 one's wishful thinking ¶ 희망적 관측과 냉엄한 현실을 혼동하다 confuse wishful thinking with grim reality — 조건 terms〔conditions〕 desired

희망봉 希望峯 the Cape of Good Hope

희멀겋다 (be) white and glossy ; nice and fair

희멀쑥하다 (be) white and clean ; clean and fair

희묵 戲墨 my (humble) writing ; my (unworthy) drawing

희문 戲文 nonsense literature ; a burlesque ; a literary parody ; humorous writing
— 작가 a humorist

희묽다 (be) white and flabby ; wan

†희미 稀微 dimness ; faintness ; vagueness ; mistiness — 하다 (be) faint ; dim ; vague ; indistinct ; misty ; hazy ¶

희미하게 faintly ; dimly ; vaguely // 희미한 빛 a glimmer // 희미해지다 become faint〔dim〕// 희미하게 기억하다 have a dim recollection 《of》// 날이 밝아지면서 별빛이 차차 희미해졌다 The stars faded before the encroaching day. // 먼 곳에 빛이 희미하게 보인다 A light glimmers in the distance.

*희박 稀薄 thinness ; rarity ; rarefaction **—하다** (be) thin ; weak ; dilute ; rare ; rarefied ; sparse ¶ 희박한 공기 rarefied〔thin〕air // 희박하게 하다 rarefy 《air》; weaken ; thin ; dilute (액체를) // 인구가 희박한 지역 a sparsely〔thinly〕-populated district // 그건 네가 벼락 맞을 가능성 보다 가능성이 더 희박해 That's even slimmer than your chance of being struck by a lightning. // 그건 가능성이 희박한 일이다 It's going to be a long shot.

희번덕거리다 keep goggling one's eyes ; turn one's eyes up and down ¶ 눈을 희번덕거리며 괴로와하다 turn one's eyes up and down in agony

희번덕희번덕 goggling〔bulging, popping〕one's eyes

희번드르르하다 (be) fair and radiant

희번들하다 ⇨ 희번드르르하다

희번주그레하다 (be) neat and fair

희번지르르하다 (be) neat and fair

희번하다 (be) dimly white ; dawn gray ; faintly light ¶ 동녘 하늘이 희번해졌다 The dawn whitened the eastern sky.

희보 喜報 good news ; glad tidings

희불그레하다 (be) pinkish

희붐하다 (be) faintly light ; white ¶ 희붐해지다 grow light ; turn gray

희비 喜悲 joy and sorrow ¶ 희비가 교차하다 have mingled feelings of joy and sorrow

—극 a tragicomedy **— 쌍곡선** mingled feelings of joy and sorrow

희사 喜事 a matter for joy〔congratulation〕; a joy ; a happy event ; rejoicings

희사 喜捨 almsgiving ; alms ; charity ; donation ; oblation **—하다** give alms ; give in charity 《to》; give a donation of ; donate ; offer

—금 alms ; a gift of money ; money given in charity ; offerings ; donations **—함** an offertory chest〔box〕

희색 喜色 a joyful look ; a glad countenance ; a happy〔pleased〕look ¶ 희색만면하다 look joyful〔happy〕; be all smiles ; beam // 그의 얼굴에 희색이 떠올랐다 A look of pleasure came to his face.

†**희생 犧牲** a sacrifice ; a self-sacrifice ; a scapegoat ; a prey **—하다** sacrifice ; victimize ; make a scapegoat〔victim〕of ¶ 희생적 정신 a self-sacrificing spirit // …을 희생하여 at the sacrifice〔expense〕《of》// 어떤 희생을 치르더라도 at all costs〔any cost〕// 희생되다 be sacrificed ; fall a victim〔prey〕《to》// 자기를 희생하다 sacrifice oneself ; make a martyr of oneself

—물 an object of sacrifice ; a victim **—자** a victim ; a prey ; a scapegoat **— 정신** a spirit of (self-)sacrifice **—타** 〖야구〗 a sacrifice (hit)

희서 稀書 a rare book

— 도서관 a rare〔treasure〕book library

희석 稀釋 〖화학〗 dilution **—하다** dilute **—도** dilution **—액** diluted〔weak〕solution **—제** a diluent

희세 稀世 uncommonness ; rarity ; uniqueness ¶ 희세의 uncommon ; rare ; extraordinary ; unique ; phenomenal // 희세의 영웅 a hero for the century ; an extraordinary hero

희소 稀少 scarcity ; rarity **—하다** (be) scarce ; rare

— 가치 scarcity value **— 물자** scarce materials **—성** scarcity

희소 喜笑 **—하다** laugh with joy

희소식 喜消息 good news ; glad tidings ¶ 무소식이 희소식이다 No news is good news. // 희소식을 듣고 그는 좋아 날뛰었다 At the glad tidings he was beside himself with joy.

희수 稀壽 one's seventieth birthday

희수 喜壽 seventy seven years of age

희아리 dried red pepper spoiled with white spots

희언 戲言 ⇨ 희담(戲談)

희열 喜悅 joy ; delight ; gladness ; glee ; rapture

희염산 〖화학〗 diluted hydrochloric acid

희우 喜雨 a welcome rain ; a beneficial rain ; a rain after drought

희원 希願 (a) hope ; (a) wish ; (a) desire **—하다** hope ; wish ; desire ¶ 그것은 본인이 가장 희원하는 바이다 That is what I desire most. ⇨ 희망(希望)

희유 稀有 rareness ; uncommon **—하다** (be) rare ; uncommon ; phenomenal ¶ 희유한 물건 a black swan ; a blue dahlia ; a white crow // 이런 일은 희유하다 Such a thing rarely happens.

희유 嬉遊 **—하다** play merrily ; have a good time ; have fun ; make merry

—곡 〖음악〗 a divertimento 《*pl.* -ti》《이》

희읍스름하다 (be) whitish ; be not white〔clean〕enough

희작 戲作 writing for amusement ; light literature

희종 稀種 a rare kind ; a rare variety

희질산 稀窒酸 〖화학〗 dilute nitric acid

희짓다 戲— interfere ; obstruct ; set up a block

희치희치 〔피륙·종이가〕 worn out here and there ; out of shape here and

there ; [벗어지다] peeling〔coming〕 off here and there **—하다** be worn〔out of shape, peeling off〕 here and there
희타 犧打 〖야구〗 a sacrifice (hit) ; sacrifice batting ⇨ 희생(—타)
희토류 원소 稀土類元素 the rare-earth elements
희필 戲筆 my (humble) writing ; my (unworthy) drawing
희학 戲謔 joking ; jesting ; kidding ; a sport ; a prank ; a banter **—하다** joke ; jest ; make fun 《of》 ; play 《with》 ; kid ¶ 그는 희학을 잘한다 He is a man of wit and humor.
— **백출** frequent flashes of humor **—질** joking ; jesting ; kidding
희한 稀罕 rarity ; scarcity **—하다** (be) rare ; curious ; scarce ; uncommon ¶ 희한한 물건 a rarity // 희한한 사람 a rare person
희화 戲畫 a caricature ; a comic picture
희황산 稀黃酸 〖화학〗 dilute sulphuric acid
희희 laughing idiotically ; simpering ¶ 희희 웃다 simper ; laugh like an idiot
희희낙락 喜喜樂樂 rejoicing ; jubilation **—하다** rejoice ; jubilate ; have a jubilee ; be in delight
흰개미 〖곤충〗 a white ant ; a termite
흰골무떡 finger-sized rice cakes without spice covering
흰곰 a white〔polar〕 bear
흰곰팡이 mildew ¶ 흰곰팡이 투성이의 mildewed ; mildewy
흰나비 a cabbage butterfly ; a cabbage white
흰누룩 malt made of barley flour and glutinous rice
흰눈썹뜸부기 〖새〗 an eastern water rail
흰담비 〖동물〗 an ermine
흰둥이 [병적인] an albino 《*pl.* ~s》 ; an albiness (여성형) ; [백인] a white man ; a white 《속》
흰떡 a white〔bar-shaped〕 rice cake
흰머리 white〔gray〕 hair 《머리털》 ; a gray head 《머리》
흰무리 rice cakes steamed without shaping
흰바곳 〖식물〗 a kind of aconite or wolfsbane plant
흰밥 plain white rice (cooked with nothing mixed in) ; boiled rice
흰소리 a snobbish〔pretentious〕 remark ; a loud boast ; bluffing ; bragging
흰신 white shoes
흰쌀 polished rice ; white rice
흰쑥 〖식물〗 a kind of wormwood
흰여우 〖동물〗 a white〔silver〕 fox ; a blue〔an arctic〕 fox
흰엿 white rice candy
†**흰옷** white clothes
흰잎엉겅퀴 〖식물〗 a kind of thistle
흰자 ⇨ 흰자위
— **가루** powdered eggs **—질** ⇨ 단백질
흰자위 [눈의] the white of the eye ; [달걀의] the white of an egg ; glair ; albumen
흰죽 rice gruel ¶ 흰죽을 끓이다 boil rice down into gruel // 어린애에게 흰죽을 먹이다 feed gruel to a little child (with a spoon)
흰줄 a white stripe〔line〕
흰쥐 a white rat ; an albino rat
흰털 white hair〔fur, wool〕
흰털바늘꽃 a kind of willowweed
흰털제비꽃 a kind of violet
흰토끼 a white rabbit
흰팥 small white beans
흰포도주 —葡萄酒 white wine ; Rhine wine
흰표범 —豹— 〖동물〗 an ounce ; a snow leopard〔panther〕 ; Felis uncia (학명)
힁하다 (be) dazed ; stupefied ; stunned ; feel one's head turning 〔whirling, swimming〕 // 머리가 힁하다 one's head turns〔whirls〕 // 정신이 힁하다 be stupefied〔stunned〕
힁허케 fast ; swiftly ; speedily ¶ 힁허케 걷다 walk fast
히드라짓 〖약〗 hydrazide
이소니코틴산 — hydrazide of isonicotinic acid
***히말라야** Himalaya(s) ¶ 히말라야의 Himalayan
— **산맥** the Himalayas ; the Himalayan Mountains
히브리 ¶ 히브리의 Hebrew
—말 Hebrew **— 사람** a Hebrew
히브리서 —書 〖성경〗 The Epistle of St. Paul (the Apostle) to the Hebrews ; Hebrews 《Heb.》
히스타민 〖화학〗 histamine
항(抗) —제 an antihistaminic (agent)
***히스테리** 〖의학〗 hysteria ; hysterics ¶ 히스테리의 hysteric(al) // 히스테리를 일으키다 go into hysterics ; get hysterics ; get a conniption fit
***히아신드** 〖식물〗 a hyacinth
히어로 a hero
히어링 hearing
히터 a heater ¶ 히터를 켜다〔끄다〕 turn on〔off〕 the heater
히죽거리다 give one sweet smile after another ; keep smiling sweetly
‡**히죽이** with a sweet〔happy, contented〕 smile ¶ 히죽이 웃다 smile sweetly ; beam with a smile ; smile a sweet smile
히죽히죽 with sweet smile after sweet smile
히치하이커 a hitchhiker
히치하이크 a hitchhike ; 《go on》 hitchhiking **—하다** hitchhike〔hitch〕 (one's way) 《to》 ; make one's way 《to a place》 by thumbing rides
히트 ① 〖야구〗 a (single) hit ¶ 히트를

치다 (make a) hit ② [성공] a hit ; a success ¶ 히트 치다 [일이] make〔be〕 a (great) hit ; [사람이] win a success //지금 히트하고 있는 노래로는 어떤 것이 있니 What hit songs are out right now? //우리 회사는 최근 히트 상품이 없어 Our company hasn't had a hit product recently.
—송 a hit song —앤런 hit-and-run play 클린 — a clean hit 텍사스 — 〖야구〗 a Texas leaguer ; blooper
히포콘드리 〖의학〗 hypochondria
히피족 —族 a hippie ; hippies 《총칭》
히히 he, he !
히히거리다 ⇨ 해해거리다
*__힌두__ ¶ 힌두 (사람)의 Hindu ; Hindoo
—교 Hinduism ; Hindooism — 교도 a Hindu —말 Hindustani ; Hindostani — 사람 a Hindu ; a Hindoo
힌트 a hint ¶ 힌트를 주다 give〔drop, provide, furnish〕 a hint //힌트를 얻다 get〔receive〕 a hint ; take a hint
힐끗 ⇨ 흘끗
힐기죽거리다 sway one's body〔hips〕 (in walking)
힐기죽힐기죽 swaying one's body〔hips〕
힐난 詰難 criticism ; censure ; reproach —하다 criticize ; censure ; denounce ¶ 실패를 힐난하다 needle 《a person》 over the failure of 《미》
힐문 詰問 close questioning ; cross-questioning ; cross-examination ; rigid inquiry —하다 question〔examine〕 closely ; cross-question ; cross-examine ; put 《a person》 through close examination ; grill ; press 《a person》 hard with questions
힐책 詰責 rebuke ; reprimand ; reproof ; reproach ; blame ; censure —하다 rebuke ; reprimand ; reprove ; reproach ; blame ; censure ¶ 부주의를 힐책하다 reproach〔reprove〕 《a person》 for his carelessness ; take 《a person》 to task for his carelessness
†**힘** ① [체력] (physical) strength ; (main) force ; might ; vigor ; energy

> 참고 **strength**는 내부에 감추어진 능력이고 그것이 외부로 활동하여 **force**가 된다 **power**는 어느 쪽의 의미에도 사용된다 **might**는 특히 강력한 힘을 의미한다

¶ 힘이 센 strong ; mighty ; powerful // 힘 없는 weak ; feeble ; powerless // 힘 없이 feebly ; dejectedly ; disappointedly // 힘이 있는 한 while one's strength lasts //힘을 겨루다 have a strength contest ; try〔measure, match〕 one's strength against another's //힘을 내다 put forth〔out〕 one's strength //힘이 빠지다 one's strength is gone ; weaken ; be enervated //힘을 쓰다 put forth one's strength //힘껏 당기다 pull with all one's strength
② [물리적] force ; power ; energy ¶ 증기의 힘 the power of steam //열의 힘 the energy of heat //전기의 힘 electric power〔energy〕 //자연의 힘 natural forces
③ [능력] ability ; prowess ; power ; capacity ; capability ; faculty ¶ 힘이 있는 able ; capable ; competent //힘이 모자라는 incapable ; incompetent //힘이 자라는 한 as far as one can ; to the best〔utmost〕 of one's ability ; for all one is worth
④ [노력] effort(s) ; endeavor ; exertion ; labor ¶ 자기힘으로 by one's own efforts ; for oneself ; on one's own //힘을 다하다 make every effort〔endeavor〕 ; exert oneself for 《a thing》 //힘을 들이다 devote one's energies to ; put labor〔work, effort〕 into ; put one's back to ; put one's shoulder to the wheel ; devote oneself 《to》 ; put one's heart and soul 《into》 //힘이 모자라다 be beyond one's power ; be more than one can do
⑤ [효력] efficacy ; power ; influence ¶ 약의 힘 the efficacy〔virtue〕 of a drug // …의 힘으로 by force of ; by dint of ; by〔in〕 virtue of ; on the strength of ; through //그는 인내와 근면의 힘으로 오늘날의 그를 이룩하였다 By dint of perseverance and industry he has made what he is.
⑥ [조력] help ; assistance ; support ; good offices ; aid ; service ; contribution ¶ …의 힘으로 by the aid〔help〕 of ; by dint〔virtue〕 of //힘을 빌다 enlist the help 《of》 //힘을 빌리다 help ; aid ; give assistance〔aid〕 to ; lend a helping hand to ; extend help //힘이 되다 help ; be helpful ; stand by
⑦ [강조] emphasis ; stress ; power ; force ¶ 힘을 준 emphatic //힘을 주어 emphatically ; forcibly //힘 있는 문장 forceful〔powerful〕 sentences //힘 있는 연설 a powerful〔an effective〕 speech
⑧ [위력] influence ; sway ; power ; authority ; might ; weight ¶ 힘 있는 powerful ; mighty //돈의 힘 the power of money //경찰의 힘 the power〔authority〕 of the police //전통의 힘 the weight of tradition //힘을 내다 pluck〔muster〕 up one's courage〔spirits〕 //정부의 힘으로 by the authority of the government
⑨ [정신적인] courage ; spirit ; heart ; nerve ; pep ; ginger ¶ 힘을 얻다 be encouraged ; gain courage ; be cheered up ; be emboldened //힘을 내다 pluck〔muster〕 up one's courage〔spirits〕 //힘내 Cheer up ! /Be of good cheer ! /Perk up ! /Snap out of it.

힘겨룸 strength contest ; measuring one's strength with another's **—하다** try〔measure〕 one's strength〔ability〕 against 《another》; have a strength contest ; break a lance with

†힘겹다 ⇨ 힘부치다

힘껏 with all one's might ; with might and main ; as hard as one can ; to the best of one's ability ¶ 힘껏 일하다 work hard as one can ; work with all one's might ; work up to capacity // 힘껏 돕다 do one's best〔utmost〕 to help

힘꼴 muscle ; brawn ¶ 힘꼴이나 쓰는 남자 a strong man ; a man of great strength

*힘들다 (be) exacting ; arduous ; strenuous ; toilsome ; tough ; painful ; [어렵다] hard ; difficult ; stiff ¶ 힘드는 일 an arduous〔a strenuous〕 job // 힘드는 문제 a difficult problem // 몸을 굽히기가 힘들다 have trouble in bending // 더워서 일하기가 힘들다 be so hot that it is hard to work // 이 일이 상당히 힘들지 않니 This is pretty tricky, isn't it?

힘들이다 make an effort ; exert oneself ; take pains〔trouble〕; elaborate 《on》 ¶ 일에 힘들이다 put in one's strength into one's work // 힘들여 운반하다 carry the load laboriously

힘부치다 be not strong〔capable〕 enough to ; be beyond one's power〔ability〕; be beyond one ; be too much for one ¶ 내게는 힘부치는 일이다 The task is beyond〔out of〕 my ability. /The task exceeds my strength.

힘빼물다 boast of one's prowess ; pretend to strength ; act mighty

†힘세다 (be) strong ; powerful ¶ 그는 아주 힘세다 He is of Herculean strength. /He is as strong as a horse.

⁑힘쓰다 ① put forth one's strength 《to lift a stone》 ② [애쓰다] exert oneself ; make an effort ; endeavor ; do one's best ; strive ; labor ; toil ¶ 힘써 공부하다 study hard ③ [도와주다] help ; give a hand ; lend one's help ¶ 김군이 힘써주어서 through the efforts〔good offices〕 of Mr. *Kim* ; by the kind assistance of Mr. *Kim* // 친구의 취직을 위해서 힘쓰다 help a friend land a job

힘없이 feebly ; droopingly ; dejectedly ¶ 힘없는 목소리로 in a feeble voice

*힘입다 owe ; be indebted to 《a person》 for 《a matter》; enjoy 《a person's》 favor ¶ 아버지의 교육에 힘입어 성공하다 owe one's success to one's father's education // 그는 부친에게 힘입은 바 크다 He owes much to his father. /He is much indebted to his father.

힘있다 ① [힘세다] (be) strong ; have strength ② [문장·어조가] (be) forceful ; powerful ; heavy ③ [지위·권력으로 보아] (be) influential ; carry weight ; have power ¶ 힘있는 사람 an influential person ; a person who carries some weight

힘자랑 boast of〔pride in〕 one's strength **—하다** boast〔be proud〕 of one's strength

힘주다 devote one's strength 《to》; concentrate 《upon》; put〔lay, place〕 《on》; emphasize ¶ 이 단계에서는 너무 많은 힘을 주지 마라 Don't get too worked up at this stage.

힘줄 [근육] a tendon ; a sinew ; a muscle ; [혈관] a vein ; [섬유] a fiber ; a string ¶ 힘줄이 당기다 have a strain in a muscle

고기 — strings in the meat ; stringy meat

힘줌말 an intensive〔emphatic〕 word

†힘차다 (be) forcible ; powerful ; (be) full of strength ; (be) energetic ; [벅차다] hard ; difficult ; laborious ; tough ¶ 힘차게 forcibly ; strongly ; powerfully ; vigorously // 힘찬 표현 a forcible expression // 힘찬 연설 a powerful speech

힙 the hip

힝 clearing one's nose

힝그럭 an arrowhead in the shape of a willow leaf

힝힝 clearing one's nose repeatedly

부 록

1. 시추에이션 생활영어

1 전화

◆ 전화 걸 때

(이름 대기)
① 여보세요. 저는 민수인데요.
Hello. This is Min-su.
② 저는 동아출판사에서 일하고 있는 민수예요.
I'm Min-su of Dong-A Publishing company.
③ 여보세요. 존 박사 사무실입니다.
Hello. Dr. John's office.
④ 고려호텔입니다. 뭘 도와드릴까요?
The Korea Hotel. Can I help you?

(상대방을 확인하기)
① 캐시니?
Is this Cathy?
② 캐시하고 통화할 수 있을까요?
May I speak to Cathy?
③ 링컨씨 계십니까?
Is Mr. Lincoln in, please?
④ 브라운 선생 댁입니까?
Is this Mr. Brown's residence〔home〕?
⑤ 퍼시픽 무역입니까?
Is this Pacific Trading Company?

(잘못 걸었을 때)
① 234-4567번이 아니에요?
Isn't this 234-4567?
② 잘못 걸었군요. 죄송합니다.
My mistake. I'm sorry.
③ 혼선이 된 것 같군요.
The lines seem to be mixed up.

(연결이 잘 안됐을 때)
① 일단 끊었다가 다시 걸어 보시죠.
Please hang up and try your call again.
② 끊었다가 다시 걸겠습니다.
I'll hang up and call again.
③ 전화 연결 상태가 좋지 않은가 봅니다. 나중에 다시 걸겠습니다.
The connection seems to be very bad. I'll call back later.

(자리에 없을 때)
① 그 분이 어디 있는지 아시겠어요?
Do you have any idea where he is right now?
② 전할 말을 부탁드려도 될까요?
Can I leave a message?
③ 그 분은 언제쯤 돌아오실까요?
When do you expect him back?

◆ 전화 받을 때

(이름 대기)
① 캐시인데요.
This is Cathy.
② 본인인데요〔말씀하세요〕.
Speaking.

(상대방을 확인하기)
① 누구시지요?
Who's calling, please?
② 한 번 더 이름과 전화번호를 말씀해 주시겠어요?
Your name and phone number again, please.

(잘 안들릴 때)
① 말씀이 잘 안들리는 데요.
I can barely hear you./ I can't hear you very well.
② 좀 크게 말씀해 주시겠습니까?
Speak louder, please!/ Could you speak up?

(잘못 걸린 전화)
① 잘못 거셨는 데요.
You have (got) the wrong number.
② 그런 분 없는 데요. 몇 번에 거셨죠?
There's no one by that name. What number are you dialing?

(자리에 없을 때)
① 지금 출타 중이십니다.
Sorry, he is out〔not here〕 now./ I'm sorry, but I think he's stepped out.
② 지금 자리에 안 계십니다.
He's not at his desk right now.
③ 그런 분은 없는데요.
There's no one here by that name.
④ 754-3265로 전화를 해보시죠. 그 여자는 지금 거기 있어요.
Please call 754-3265. She is there right now.
⑤ 4시 경에는 돌아올 겁니다.
He will be back around four.
⑥ 집으로 연락해 보시지요.

Why don't you try calling him at home?
⑦ 754-4765번의 테리 존스가 전화해 달라고 한다고 전해 주시겠습니까?
Would you ask him to call Terry Jones at 754-4765?
⑧ 그가 돌아오면 톰에게 전화해 달라고 전해 주시겠습니까? 그가 제 번호를 알고 있습니다.
Could you tell him to give Tom a call when he gets back? He has my number.
⑨ 그러면 저에게 전화 좀 걸어달라고 할 수 있습니까?
In that case, could you have him call me back?

◆ 시외 전화

① 워싱턴에 장거리전화를 하고 싶은 데요.
I'd like to make a long-distance call to Washington, D.C.
② 시카고에 전화를 하고 싶은 데요.
I want to place a call to Chicago, please.
③ 샌프란시스코에 수신인 부담 장거리 전화를 하고 싶은데요.
I need to place a long-distance collect call to San Francisco.
④ 몇 번에 거시려고 하는 데요?
What number are you calling?
⑤ 직접 다이얼을 돌리시죠. 시카고의 지역 번호는 312번입니다.
You can dial it yourself. The area code for Chicago is 312.
⑥ 끊고 기다리세요. 잠시 후에 다시 전화 드리겠습니다.
Hang up please and I'll call you back.

◆ 기타

① 선생님과 통화를 해서 즐거웠습니다.
Nice talking to you.
② 받아 적어 주시겠어요?
Could you write it down?
③ 전화해 주셔서 감사합니다.
Thank you for your call. / Thanks for calling.
④ 전화 받으세요.
You have a call. / There's a call for you. / It's for you. / You're wanted on the phone.
⑤ 말씀하시지요.
Please go ahead.
⑥ 번호는 맞는 데요.
You have the right number.
⑦ 죄송하지만 그분은 지금 다른 전화를 받고 계신 데요. 어느 분이 전화하셨다고 전해드릴까요?
I'm sorry, but he's on another line. May I ask who's calling, please?
⑧ 죄송하지만 그는 잠깐 동안은 이 전화를 받을 수 없을 것 같군요.
I'm sorry, but it looks like he won't be through with this call for quite a while.
⑨ 이렇게 늦은〔이른〕 시각에 전화해서 미안합니다.
I'm sorry I'm calling at this early〔late〕 hour.
⑩ 직장으로 전화하지 말고 집으로 전화하세요.
Don't call me at work. Call me at home.

○ 대화 1 ○

A: 교환입니다.
Operator.
B: 교환, 시카고에 전화하려고 하는 데요. 전화 번호는 905-2754입니다.
Operator, I'd like to place a call to Chicago. The number is 905-2754.
A: 상대방 분의 성함이 어떻게 됩니까?
What's the name of the party you're calling?
B: 로저 윌슨입니다.
Roger Wilson.

○ 대화 2 ○

A: 교환입니다.
Operator.
B: 교환, 워싱턴에 지명 통화를 하고 싶은데요. 전화 번호는 917-7564인데 지역 국번은 잘 모릅니다.
Operator. I'd like to place a person-to-person call to Washington. The number is 917-7564, but I don't know the area code.
A: 통화하시고자 하는 분이 누구십니까?
Who do you want to speak to?
B: 내선 245번으로 연결되는 사람이면 아무든 상관 없습니다.
I'll speak to anyone at extension 245.

○ 대화 3 ○

A: 고려 호텔입니다. 뭘 도와드릴까요?
The Korea Hotel. Can I help you?
B: 네. 245호실 좀 연결해 주세요.
Yes, please. Could you give me room 245?

A:잠깐만 기다리세요. (잠시 후에) 죄송합니다만 통화 중이네요.
Just a moment, please. (After a while) I'm sorry, but the line is busy.
B:그러면 메시지 좀 남겨 주시겠습니까?
In that case, could you leave a message for me?
A:물론이죠. 말씀하십시오.
Of course. Go ahead, please.
B:저는 존 스미스라고 하는데 내일 아침 다시 전화하겠다고 전해 주십시오.
This is John Smith, and I'll call back later tomorrow morning.
A:알겠습니다. 스미스 씨. 말씀 전해 드리겠습니다.
All right, Mr. Smith. I'll pass on the message.
B : 감사합니다.
Thank you very much.
A : 천만에요.
You're welcome.

◌ 대화 4 ◌

A:여보세요.
Hello.
B:존슨씨 계십니까?
May I speak to Mr. Johnson?
A:그런 분은 여기 안 계신데요.
There's no one here by that name.
B:그래요? 거기 832-6439입니까?
Really? Isn't this 832-6349?
A:아닌 데요.
No, it isn't.
B:폐를 끼쳐 죄송합니다.
I'm sorry to disturb you.
A:천만에요.
That's all right.

☞ 시내〔시외〕 통화는···

▶ 시내 통화에 해당하는 영어는 local call. 한 지역의 국번(area code)을 사용하는 통화를 말한다. 시외 통화는 Long Distance Call이라고 하는데, area code가 다른 지역 사이에 이루어지는 통화를 말한다. 시외 전화를 걸 때에는, area code 앞에 1을 덧붙인다. (*ex.*1-213-000-0000) 202-456-1422라는 전화 번호는 202가 지역국번 (area code), 456이 시내 국번이다.

▶ 읽을 때는 two-oh-two, four-five-six, one-four-double-two〔one-four-two-two, fourteen twenty-two〕라고 읽는다. 5000, 5500 같은 번호의 경우에는, oh를 되풀이하는 대신, 5000은 five thousand, 5500은 five five hundred, fifty five hundred, fifty-five double-oh라고 읽는다.

▶ area code와 전화 번호를 알고 있는 경우에는, 교환수를 통하지 않고, 통화(direct-dial call/do-it-yourself call/dialing call)를 할 수 있다. 특히 교환수(operator)를 필요로 한 전화 (operator-assisted call)는 대개, person-to-person call, collect call, 크레디트 카드 통화 (credit call:크레디트 카드를 사용하는 통화), 공중 전화에서의 장거리 통화 등이다. 크레디트 카드로 통화를 할 때에는, 교환수에게 통화하고자 하는 사람의 이름을 알려주면서, 크레디트 카드로 "Charge, please."라는 의사표시를 한 다음에 본인이 소지하고 있는 크레디트 카드의 번호를 알려 준다. 미국에서는 전화 가입자(telephone subscriber)에게는, 통화 시간과 통화 요금 (telephone charges) 등이 기재된 전화명세서(phone〔telephone〕 bill)가 빠짐 없이 우송되어 온다.

☞ 대부분의 나라에는···

직통으로 전화를 걸 수 있는 국제 다이얼 통화 ISD(international subscriber dialing call)가 있는데, 교환수를 통하는 것보다도 비용이 싸게 먹힌다. 직통 전화를 할 수 없을 때에는 전화번호 0을 선택하고, 교환수에게 의뢰를 한다. 요즈음은 Home Country Direct라는 전화 서비스가 있어서, 외국에서도 모국의 교환수를 불러낼 수 있다.

▶ 전화가 도중에 끊기거나, 잡음이 심한 경우에는 즉시 교환수를 불러내서, I was cut off while talking. (도중에 전화가 끊겼다)라고 하거나 Something is wrong with this connection. (혼선입니다) 등으로 이야기할 수 있다.

2 쇼핑

(구경만 할 때)
I'm just looking around, thank you.

(물건을 찾을 때)
I am looking for..../Do you have..../I'd like to see..../ Please show me....

(취급장소를 물을 때)
Where could I get〔find〕 the .... ?

(물건을 고를 때)
① (아내 생일 선물로는) 어떤 것이 좋을까요?